Complete Guide to Colleges

2003

THOMSON ™
PETERSON'S

Australia • Canada • Mexico • Singapore • Spain • United Kingdom • United States

THOMSON
PETERSON'S™

About The Thomson Corporation and Peterson's

With revenues of US$7.2 billion, The Thomson Corporation (www.thomson.com) is a leading global provider of integrated information solutions for business, education, and professional customers. Its Learning businesses and brands (www.thomsonlearning.com) serve the needs of individuals, learning institutions, and corporations with products and services for both traditional and distributed learning.

Peterson's, part of The Thomson Corporation, is one of the nation's most respected providers of lifelong learning online resources, software, reference guides, and books. The Education Supersite℠ at www.petersons.com—the Internet's most heavily traveled education resource—has searchable databases and interactive tools for contacting U.S.-accredited institutions and programs. In addition, Peterson's serves more than 105 million education consumers annually.

For more information, contact Peterson's, 2000 Lenox Drive, Lawrenceville, NJ 08648; 800-338-3282; or find us on the World Wide Web at www.petersons.com/about.

ISBN 0-7689-1114-1

Printed in the United States of America

10 9 8 7 6 5 4 3 2 1 04 03 02

Contents

FOUR-YEAR COLLEGES

TWO-YEAR COLLEGES

A Note from the Peterson's Editors

For more than 35 years, Peterson's has given students and parents the most comprehensive, up-to-date information on undergraduate institutions in the United States and Canada. Peterson's researches the data published in *Peterson's Complete Guide to Colleges*, with information furnished by the colleges, and ensures the data is accurate at the time of publishing.

This guide also features advice and tips on the college search and selection process, such as how to consider the factors that truly make a difference in your college search process, how to understand the application process, how to file for financial aid, how to decide if a two-year college is right for you, how to approach transferring between colleges, and what's in store for adults returning to college. If you seem to be getting more, not less, anxious about choosing and getting into the right college, *Peterson's Complete Guide to Colleges* provides just the right help, giving you the information you need to make important college decisions and ace the admissions process.

Opportunities abound for students, and this guide can help you find what you want in a number of ways.

For advice and guidance in the college search and selection process, just turn the page. Providing a quick overview of the college application process, our *College Countdown Calendar* outlines the pertinent month-by-month milestones. *Surviving Standardized Tests* describes the most frequently used tests and lists test dates for 2002–03. Of course, part of the college selection process involves visiting the schools themselves, and *The Whys and Whats of College Visits* is just the planner you need to make those trips well worth your while. Next, *Applying 101* provides advice on how best to approach the application phase of the process. *Who's Paying for This? Financial Aid Basics, Middle Income Families: Making the Financial Aid Process Work,* and our *Financial Aid Countdown Calendar* all provide you with the essential information on how to meet your educational expenses. *What International Students Need to Know About Admission to U.S. Colleges and Universities* is a basic guide with helpful tips on college admissions for non–U.S. citizens and can also be useful to U.S. citizens. *Visa Requirements and Regulations for Students in Nonimmigrant Status* is an article designed particularly for students overseas who are considering a U.S. college education. In *What You Need to Know About Two-Year Colleges,* the basic features and advantages of two-year colleges are outlined. *Frequently Asked Questions About Transferring* takes a look at the two-year college scene from the perspective of a student who is looking toward the day when he or she may pursue additional education at a four-year institution. *Returning to School: Advice for Adult Students* is an analysis of the pros and cons (mostly pros) of returning to college after already having begun a professional career.

Our **OPTIONS, OPTIONS, OPTIONS** section gives you some sneak peeks into specific institutions and programs that may be just right for you, including information on honors programs and colleges, career colleges, historically black colleges and universities, and opportunities through the military.

Both the **Four-Year Colleges** and the **Two-Year Colleges** sections contain *How to Use This Section,* explaining some of the key factors you need to consider in the college search process and how to locate this information in the individual college profiles presented in the guide.

For information about particular colleges, turn to the **College Profiles and Special Announcements** sections. Here you'll find our unparalleled and newly expanded college descriptions, arranged alphabetically by state. They provide a complete picture of need-to-know information about accredited four-year and two-year colleges—including admission rates, majors, current expenses, financial aid, student life, and campus safety. All the information you need to apply is placed together at the conclusion of each college profile.

Peterson's publishes a full line of resources to help you and your family with any information you need to guide you through the admissions process. Peterson's publications can be found at your local bookstore, library, and high school guidance office—or visit us on the Web at Petersons.com. Colleges will be pleased to know that Peterson's helped you in your selection. Admissions staff members are more than happy to answer questions, address specific problems, and help in any way they can. The editors at Peterson's wish you great success in your college search.

The College Admissions Process:

AN OVERVIEW

College Countdown Calendar

This practical month-by-month calendar is designed to help you stay on top of the process of applying to college. For most students, the process begins in September of the junior year of high school and ends in June of the senior year. You may want to begin considering financial aid options, reviewing your academic schedule, and attending college fairs before your junior year.

JUNIOR YEAR

September

- ❒ Check with your counselor to make sure your course credits will meet college requirements.
- ❒ Be sure you are involved in one or two extracurricular activities.
- ❒ Begin building your personal list of colleges on the undergraduate channel of petersons.com.

October

- ❒ Register for and take the PSAT.

November

- ❒ Strive to get the best grades you can. A serious effort will provide you with the most options during the application process.

December

- ❒ Get involved in a community service activity.
- ❒ Begin to read newspapers and a weekly news magazine.
- ❒ Buy *SAT Success, ACT Success,* or *TOEFL CBT Success* and begin to study for the tests.

January

- ❒ With your school counselor, decide when to take the ACT, SAT I, and SAT II Subject Tests (and which Subject Tests to take). If English is not your primary language and you are planning on attending a college in North America, decide when to take the TOEFL test.
- ❒ Keep your grades up!

February

- ❒ Plan a challenging schedule of classes for your senior year.
- ❒ Think about which teachers you will ask to write recommendations.
- ❒ Check www.nacac.com/fairs.html for schedules and locations of college fairs.

March

- ❒ Register for the tests you will take this spring (ACT, SAT I, SAT II, and the TOEFL test).
- ❒ Meet with your school counselor to discuss college choices.
- ❒ Review your transcript and test scores with your counselor to determine how competitive your range of choices should be.
- ❒ Use petersons.com on the Web to do initial college research.
- ❒ Develop a preliminary list of 15 to 20 colleges and universities and search for information on them.
- ❒ Start scheduling campus visits. When school is in session (but never during final exams) is the best time. Summers are OK, but will not show you what the college is really like. If possible, save your top college choices for the fall. Be aware, however, that fall is the busiest visit season, and you will need advance planning. Don't forget to write thank-you letters to your interviewers.

April

- ❒ Take any standardized tests you have registered for.
- ❒ Create a list of your potential college choices and begin to record personal and academic information that can be later transferred to your college applications.

May

- ❒ Plan college visits and make appointments.
- ❒ Structure your summer plans to include advanced academic work, travel, volunteer work, or a job.
- ❒ Confirm your academic schedule for the fall.

Summer

- ❒ Begin working on your application essays.
- ❒ Write to any colleges on your list that do not accept the Common Application to request application forms.

SENIOR YEAR

September

- ❒ Register for the ACT, SAT I, SAT II, and TOEFL test, as necessary.
- ❒ Check with your school counselor for the fall visiting schedule of college reps.
- ❒ Ask appropriate teachers if they would write recommendations for you (don't forget to write thank-you letters when they accept).
- ❒ Meet with your counselor to compile your final list of colleges.

October

- ❒ Mail or send early applications electronically after carefully checking them to be sure they are neat and completely filled out.
- ❒ Photocopy or print extra copies of your applications to use as a backup.
- ❒ Take the tests you have registered for.
- ❒ Don't be late! Keep track of all deadlines for transcripts, recommendations, etc.

November

- ❒ Be sure that you have requested your ACT and SAT scores be sent to your colleges of choice.
- ❒ Complete and submit all applications. Print or photocopy an extra copy for your records.

December

- ❒ Take any necessary ACT, SAT I, SAT II, or TOEFL tests.
- ❒ Meet with your counselor to verify that all is in order and that transcripts are out to colleges.

January

- ❒ Prepare the Free Application for Federal Student Aid (FAFSA), available at www.fafsa.ed.gov or through your school counseling office. An estimated income tax statement (which can be corrected later) can be used. The sooner you apply for financial aid, the better your chances.

February

- ❒ Send in your FAFSA via the Web or U.S. mail.
- ❒ Be sure your midyear report has gone out to the colleges
to which you've applied.
- ❒ Let your colleges know of any new honors or accomplishments that were not in your original application.

March

- ❒ Register for any Advanced Placement (AP) tests you might take.
- ❒ Be sure you have received a FAFSA acknowledgment.

April

- ❒ Review the acceptances and financial aid offers you receive.
- ❒ Go back to visit one or two of your top-choice colleges.
- ❒ Notify your college of choice that you have accepted its offer (and send in a deposit by May 1).
- ❒ Notify the colleges you have chosen not to attend of your decision.

May

- ❒ Take AP tests.

June

- ❒ Graduate! Congratulations and best of luck.

Adapted from *Get Organized* by Edward B. Fiske and Phyllis Steinbrecher (Peterson's).

Surviving Standardized Tests

WHAT ARE STANDARDIZED TESTS?

Colleges and universities in the United States use tests to help evaluate applicants' readiness for admission or to place them in appropriate courses. The tests that are most frequently used by colleges are the ACT Assessment of American College Testing, Inc., and the College Board's SAT. In addition, the Educational Testing Service (ETS) offers the TOEFL test, which evaluates the English-language proficiency of nonnative speakers. The tests are offered at designated testing centers located at high schools and colleges throughout the United States and U.S. territories and at testing centers in various countries throughout the world. The ACT Assessment test and the SAT tests are each taken by more than a million students each year. The TOEFL test is taken by more than 300,000 students each year.

Upon request, special accommodations for students with documented visual, hearing, physical, or learning disabilities are available. Examples of special accommodations include tests in Braille or large print and such aids as a reader, recorder, magnifying glass, or sign language interpreter. Additional testing time may be allowed in some instances. Contact the appropriate testing program or your guidance counselor for details on how to request special accommodations. Here is a brief description of each testing program.

College Board SAT Program

The SAT Program consists of the SAT I Reasoning Test and the SAT II Subject Tests. The SAT I is a 3-hour test made up of seven sections, primarily multiple-choice, that measures verbal and mathematical abilities. The three verbal sections test vocabulary, verbal reasoning, and critical reading skills. Emphasis is placed on reading passages, which are 400–850 words in length. Some reading passages are paired; the second opposes, supports, or in some way complements the point of view expressed in the first. The three mathematics sections test a student's ability to solve problems involving arithmetic, algebra, and geometry. They include questions that require students to produce their own responses, in addition to questions that students can choose from four or five answer choices. Calculators may be used on the SAT I mathematics sections.

The SAT II Subject Tests are 1-hour tests, primarily multiple-choice, in specific subjects that measure students' knowledge of these subjects and their ability to apply that knowledge. Some colleges may require or recommend these tests for placement, or even admission. The Subject Tests measure a student's academic achievement in high school and may indicate readiness for certain college programs. Tests offered include Writing, Literature, U.S. History, World History, Mathematics Level IC, Mathematics Level IIC, Biology E/M (Ecological/Molecular), Chemistry, Physics, French, German, Modern Hebrew, Italian, Latin, and Spanish, as well as Foreign Language Tests with Listening in Chinese, French, German, Japanese, Korean, Spanish, and English Language Proficiency (ELPT). The Mathematics Level IC and IIC tests require the use of a scientific calculator.

SAT scores are automatically sent to each student who has taken the test. On average, they are mailed about three weeks after the test. Students may request that the scores be reported to their high schools or to the colleges to which they are applying.

ACT Assessment Program

The ACT Assessment Program is a comprehensive data collection, processing, and reporting service designed to assist in educational and career planning. The ACT Assessment instrument consists of four academic tests, taken under timed conditions, and a Student Profile Section and Interest Inventory, completed when students register for the ACT.

The academic tests cover four areas—English, mathematics, reading, and science reasoning. The ACT consists of 215 multiple-choice questions and takes approximately 3 hours and 30 minutes to complete with breaks (testing time is actually 2 hours and 55 minutes). They are designed to assess the student's educational development and readiness to handle college-level work. The minimum standard score is 1, the maximum is 36, and the national average is 21.

The Student Profile Section requests information about each student's admission and enrollment plans, academic and out-of-class high school achievements and aspirations, and high school course work. The student is also asked to supply biographical data and self-reported high school grades in the four subject-matter areas covered by the academic tests.

ACT has a number of career planning services, including the ACT Interest Inventory, which is designed to measure six major dimensions of student interests–business contact, business operations, technical, science, arts, and social service. Results are used to compare the student's interests with those of college-bound students who later majored in each of

DON'T FORGET TO . . .

- Take the SAT or ACT before application deadlines
- Note that test registration deadlines precede test dates by about six weeks
- Register to take the TOEFL test, if English is not your native language and you are planning on studying at a North American college
- Practice your test-taking skills with *Peterson's SAT Success*, *Peterson's ACT Success*, and *Peterson's TOEFL CBT Success* (all available with software)
- Contact the College Board or American College Testing, Inc., in advance if you need special accommodations when taking tests

a wide variety of areas. Inventory results are also used to help students compare their work-activity preferences with work activities that characterize twenty-three "job families."

Because the information resulting from the ACT Assessment Program is used in a variety of educational settings, American College Testing, Inc., prepares three reports for each student: the Student Report, the High School Report, and the College Report. The Student Report normally is sent to the student's high school, except after the June test date, when it is sent directly to the student's home address. The College Report is sent to the colleges the student designates.

Early in the school year, American College Testing, Inc., sends registration packets to high schools across the country that contain all the information a student needs to register for the ACT Assessment. High school guidance offices also receive a supply of *Preparing for the ACT Assessment,* a booklet that contains a complete practice test, an answer key, and general information about preparing for the test. You may also be interested in *Peterson's ACT Success.*

Test of English as a Foreign Language (TOEFL)

The TOEFL test is used by various organizations, such as colleges and universities, to determine English proficiency. The test is mainly offered in a computer-based format (TOEFL CBT), although the paper-based test is still offered in some areas. Eventually, the TOEFL will be completely computer-based.

The TOEFL tests students in the areas of listening, structure, reading comprehension, and writing. Score requirements are set by individual institutions. For more information on TOEFL, and to obtain a copy of the Information Bulletin, contact the Educational Testing Service.

Peterson's TOEFL CBT Success can help you prepare for the exam. The CD version of the book includes a launch to Peterson's online practice test. The test can also be taken for a small fee at www.petersons.com.

Contact your secondary school counselor for full information about the SAT and ACT programs and the TOEFL test.

2002–03 ACT AND SAT TEST DATES

ACT

September 28, 2002*
October 26, 2002
December 14, 2002
February 8, 2003**
April 12, 2003
June 14, 2003

All test dates fall on a Saturday. Tests are also given on the Sundays following the Saturday test dates for students who cannot take the test on Saturday because of religious reasons. The basic ACT registration fee for 2000–01 was $23 ($26 in Florida and $38 outside of the U.S.).

*The September test is available only in Arizona, California, Florida, Georgia, Illinois, Indiana, Maryland, Nevada, North Carolina, Pennsylvania, South Carolina, Texas, and Washington.

**The February test date is not available in New York.

SAT

October 12, 2002 (SAT I and SAT II)
November 2, 2002 (SAT I, SAT II, and Language Tests with Listening, including ELPT*)
December 7, 2002 (SAT I and SAT II)
January 25, 2003 (SAT I, SAT II, and ELPT)
April 5, 2003 (SAT I only)**
May 3, 2003 (SAT I and SAT II)
June 7, 2003 (SAT I and SAT II)

For the 2001–02 academic year, the basic fee for the SAT I Reasoning Test was $25, which included the $14 basic registration and reporting fee. The basic fee for the SAT II Subject Tests was $11 for the Writing Test, $8 for the Language Tests with Listening, and $6 each for all other Subject Tests. Students can take up to three SAT II Subject Tests on a single date, and a $14 basic registration and reporting fee should be added for each test date. Tests are also given on the Sundays following the Saturday test dates for students who cannot take the test on Saturday because of religious reasons. Fee waivers are available to juniors and seniors who cannot afford test fees.

*Language Tests with Listening (including the English Language Proficiency Test, or ELPT) are only offered on November 3; the ELPT is offered on November 3 and January 26 at some test centers. See the Registration Bulletin for details.

**The April 5 test date is only available in the U.S. and its territories.

The Whys and Whats of College Visits

Dawn B. Sova, Ph.D.

The campus visit should not be a passive activity for you and your parents, and you will have to take the initiative and use all of your senses to gather information beyond that provided in the official tour. You will see many important indicators during your visit that will tell you more about the true character of a college and its students than the tour guide will reveal. Know what to look for and how to assess the importance of such indicators.

What Should You Ask and What Should You Look For?

Your first stop on a campus visit is the visitor center or admissions office, where you will probably have to wait to meet with a counselor and undergo the interview. Colleges usually plan to greet visitors later than the appointed time in order to give them the opportunity to review some of the campus information that is liberally scattered throughout the visitor waiting room. Take advantage of the time to become even more familiar with the college by arriving 15 to 30 minutes before your appointment to observe the behavior of staff members and to browse through the yearbooks and student newspapers that will be available.

If you prepare in advance, you will have already reviewed the college catalog and map of the campus. These materials familiarize you with the academic offerings and the physical layout of the campus, but the true character of the college and its students emerges in other ways.

Begin your investigation with the visitor center staff members. As a student's first official contact with the college, they should make every effort to welcome prospective students and to project a friendly image.

- How do they treat you and other prospective students who are waiting? Are they friendly and willing to speak with you, or do they try their hardest to avoid eye contact and conversation?
- Are they friendly with each other and with students who enter the office, or are they curt and unwilling to help?
- Does the waiting room have a friendly feeling or is it cold and sterile?

If the visitor center staff members seem indifferent to *prospective* students, there is little reason to believe that they will be warm and welcoming to current students. View such behavior as a warning to watch very carefully the interaction of others with you during the tour. An indifferent or unfriendly reception in the admissions office may be simply the first of many signs that attending this college will not be a pleasant experience.

Look through several yearbooks and see the types of activities that are actually photographed, as opposed to the activities that colleges promise in their promotional literature. Some questions are impossible to answer if the college is very large, but for small and moderately sized colleges the yearbook is a good indicator of campus activity.

- Has the number of clubs and organizations increased or decreased in the past five years?
- Do the same students appear repeatedly in activities?
- Do sororities and fraternities dominate campus activities?
- Are participants limited to one sex or one ethnic group or are the participants diverse?
- Are all activities limited to the campus, or are students involved in activities in the community?

Use what you observe in the yearbooks as a means of forming a more complete understanding of the college, but don't base your entire impression on just one facet. If time permits, look through several copies of the school newspaper, which should reflect the major concerns and interests of the students. The paper is also a good way to learn about the campus social life.

- Does the paper contain a mix of national and local news?
- What products or services are advertised?
- How assertive are the editorials?
- With what topics are the columnists concerned?
- Are movies and concerts that meet your tastes advertised or reviewed?
- What types of ads appear in the classified section?

The newspaper should be a public forum for students, and, as such, should reflect the character of the campus and of the student body. A paper that deals only with seemingly safe and well-edited topics on the editorial page and in regular feature columns might indicate administrative censorship. A lack of ads for restaurants might indicate either a lack of good places to eat or that area restaurants do not welcome student business. A limited mention of movies, concerts, or other entertainment might reveal a severely limited campus social life. Even if ads and reviews are included, you can also learn a lot about how such activities reflect your tastes.

You will have only a limited amount of time to ask questions during your initial meeting with the admissions counselor, for very few schools include a formal interview in the initial campus visit or tour. Instead, this brief meeting is often just a social nicety that allows the admissions office to begin a file for the student and to record some initial impressions. Save your questions for the tour guide and for campus members that you meet along the way.

How Can You Assess the True Character of a College and Its Students?

Colleges do not train their tour guides to deceive prospective students, but they do caution guides to avoid unflattering topics and campus sites. Does this mean that you are condemned to see only a sugarcoated version of life on a particular college campus? Not at all, especially not if you are observant.

Most organized campus visits include such campus facilities as dormitories, dining halls, libraries, student activity and recreation centers, and the health and student services centers. Some may only be pointed out, while you will walk through others. Either way, you will find that many signs of the true character of the college emerge if you are observant.

Bulletin boards in dormitories and student centers contain a wealth of information about campus activities, student concerns, and campus groups. Read the posters, notices, and messages to learn what *really* interests students. Unlike ads in the school newspaper, posters put up by students advertise both on- and off-campus events, so they will give you an idea of what is also available in the surrounding community.

Review the notices, which may cover either campus-wide events or events that concern only small groups of students. The catalog may not mention a performance group, but an individual dormitory with its own small theater may offer regular productions. Poetry readings, jam sessions, writers' groups, and other activities may be announced and show diversity of student interests on that campus.

Even the brief bulletin board messages offering objects for sale and noting objects that people want to purchase reveal a lot about a campus. Are most of the items computer related? Or do the messages specify compact discs, audio equipment, or musical instruments? Are offers to barter goods or services posted? Don't ignore the "ride wanted" messages. Students who want to share rides home during a break may specify widely diverse geographical locations. If so, then you know that the student body is not limited to only the immediate area or one locale. Other messages can also enhance your knowledge of the true character of the campus and its students.

As you walk through various buildings, examine their condition carefully.

- Is the paint peeling, and do the exteriors look worn?
- Are the exteriors and interiors of the building clean?
- Do they look well maintained?
- Is the equipment in the classrooms up-to-date or outdated?

Pay particular attention to the dormitories, especially to factors that might affect your safety. Observe the appearance of the structure, and ask about the security measures in and around the dormitories.

- Are the dormitories noisy or quiet?
- Do they seem crowded?
- How good is the lighting around each dormitory?
- Are the dormitories spread throughout the campus or are they clustered in one main area?
- Who has access to the dormitories in addition to students?
- How secure are the means by which students enter and leave the dormitory?

While you are on the subject of dormitory safety, you should also ask about campus safety. Don't expect that the guide will rattle off a list of crimes that have been committed in the past year. To obtain that information, access the recent year of issues of the *Chronicle of Higher Education* and locate its yearly report on campus crime. Also ask the guide about safety measures that the campus police take and those that students have initiated.

- Can students request escorts to their residences late at night?
- Do campus shuttle buses run at frequent intervals all night?
- Are "blue-light" telephones liberally placed throughout the campus for students to use to call for help?
- Do the campus police patrol the campus regularly?

If the guide does not answer your questions satisfactorily, wait until after the tour to contact the campus police or traffic office for answers.

Campus tours usually just point out the health services center without taking the time to walk through. Even if you don't see the inside of the building, you should take a close look at the location of the health services center and ask the guide questions about services.

- How far is the health center from the dormitories?
- Is a doctor always on call?
- Does the campus transport sick students from their dormitories or must they walk?
- What are the operating hours of the health center?
- Does the health center refer students to the town hospital?

If the guide can't answer your questions, visit the health center later and ask someone there.

Most campus tours seem to take pride in showing students their activities centers, which may contain snack bars, game rooms, workout facilities, and other means of entertainment. Should you scrutinize this building as carefully as the rest? Of course. Outdated and poorly maintained activity equipment contributes to your total impression of the college. You should also ask about the hours, availability, and cost (no, the activities are usually *not* free) of using the bowling alleys, pool tables, air hockey tables, and other items.

As you walk through campus with the tour, also look carefully at the appearance of the students who pass. The way in which both men and women groom themselves, the way they dress, and even their physical bearing communicate a lot more than any guidebook can. If everyone seems to conform to the same look, you might feel that you would be uncomfortable at the college, however nonconformist that look might be. On the other hand, you might not feel comfortable on a campus that stresses diversity of dress and behavior, and your observations now can save you discomfort later.

- Does every student seem to wear a sorority or fraternity t-shirt or jacket?
- Is everyone of your sex sporting the latest fad haircut?
- Do all of the men or the women seem to be wearing expensive name-brand clothes?
- Do most of the students seem to be working hard to look outrageous in regard to clothing, hair color, and body art?
- Would you feel uncomfortable in a room full of these students?

Is appearance important to you? If it is, then you should consider very seriously if you answer *yes* to any of the above questions. You don't have to be the same as everyone else on campus, but standing out too rigorously may make you unhappy.

As you observe the physical appearance of the students, also listen to their conversations as you pass them? What are they talking about? How are they speaking? Are their voices and accents all the same, or do you hear diversity in their speech? Are you offended by their language? Think how you will feel if surrounded by the same speech habits and patterns for four years.

Where Should You Visit on Your Own?

Your campus visit is not over when the tour ends because you will probably have many questions yet to be answered and many places to still be seen. Where you go depends upon the extent to which the organized tour covers the campus. Your tour should take you to view residential halls, health and student services centers, the gymnasium or field house, dining halls, the library, and recreational centers. If any of the facilities on this list have been omitted, visit them on your own and ask questions of the students and staff members you meet. In addition, you should step off campus and gain an impression of the surrounding community. You will probably become bored with life on campus and spend at least some time off campus. Make certain that you know what the surrounding area is like.

The campus tour leaves little time to ask impromptu questions of current students, but you can do so after the tour. Eat lunch in one of the dining halls. Most will allow visitors to pay cash to experience a typical student meal. Food may not be important to you now while you are living at home and can simply take anything you want from the refrigerator at any time, but it will be when you are away at college with a meal ticket to feed you.

- How clean is the dining hall? Consider serving tables, floors, and seating.
- What is the quality of the food?
- How big are the portions?
- How much variety do students have at each meal?
- How healthy are the food choices?

While you are eating, try to strike up a conversation with students and tell them that you are considering attending their college. Their reactions and advice can be eye-opening. Ask them questions about the academic atmosphere and the professors.

- Are the classes large or small?
- Do the majority of the professors only lecture or are tutorials and seminars common?
- Is the emphasis of the faculty career oriented or abstract?
- Do they find the teaching methods innovative and stimulating or boring and dull?
- Is the academic atmosphere pressured, lax, or somewhere in between?
- Which are the strong majors? the weak majors?
- Is the emphasis on grades or social life or a mix of both at the college?
- How hard do students have to work to receive high grades?

Current students can also give you the inside line on the true nature of the college social life. You may gain some idea through looking in the yearbook, in the newspaper, and on the bulletin boards, but students will reveal the true highs and lows of campus life. Ask them about drug use, partying, dating rituals, drinking, and anything else that may affect your life as a student.

- Which are the most popular club activities?
- What do students do on weekends? Do most go home?
- How frequently do concerts occur on campus? Ask them to name groups that have recently performed.
- How can you become involved in specific activities (name them)?
- How strictly are campus rules enforced and how severe are penalties?
- What counseling services are available?
- Are academic tutoring services available?
- Do they feel that the faculty really cares about students, especially freshmen?

You will receive the most valuable information from current students, but you will only be able to speak with them after the tour is over. And you might have to risk rejection as you try to initiate conversations with students who might not want to reveal how they feel about the campus. Still, the value of this information in making the right decision is worth the chance.

If you have the time, you should also visit the library to see just how accessible research materials are and to observe the physical layout. The catalog usually specifies the days and hours of operation, as well as the number of volumes contained in the library and the number of periodicals to which it subscribes. A library also requires accessibility, good lighting, an adequate number of study carrels, and lounge areas for students. Many colleges have created 24-hour study lounges for students who find the residence halls too noisy for studying, although most colleges claim that they designate areas of the residences as "quiet study" areas. You may not be interested in any of this information, but when you are a student you will have to make frequent use of the campus library so you should know what is available. You should at least ask how extensive their holdings are in your proposed major area. If they have virtually nothing, you will have to spend a lot of time ordering items via interlibrary loan or making copies, which can become expensive. The ready answer of students that they will obtain their information from the Internet is unpleasantly countered by professors who demand journal articles with documentation.

Make a point of at least driving through the community surrounding the college, because you will be spending time there shopping, dining, working in a part-time job, or attending events. Even the largest and best-stocked campus will not meet all of your social and personal needs. If you can spare the time, stop in several stores to see if they welcome college students.

- Is the surrounding community suburban, urban, or rural?
- Does the community offer stores of interest, such as bookstores, craft shops, boutiques?
- Do the businesses employ college students?
- Does the community have a movie or stage theater?
- Are there several types of interesting restaurants?
- Do there seem to be any clubs that court a college clientele?
- Is the center of activity easy to walk to, or do you need a car or other transportation?

You might feel that a day is not enough to answer all of your questions, but even answering some questions will provide you with a stronger basis for choosing a college. Many students visit a college campus several times before making their decision, as you also should. Keep in mind that for the rest of your life you will be associated with the college that you attend. You will spend four years of your life at this college. The effort of spending several days to obtain the information to make your decision is worthwhile.

Dawn B. Sova, Ph.D., is a former newspaper reporter and columnist, as well as the author of more than eight books and numerous magazine articles.

Applying 101

The words "applying yourself" have several important meanings in the college application process. One meaning refers to the fact that you need to keep focused during this important time in your life, keep your priorities straight, and know the dates that your applications are due so you can apply on time. The phrase might also refer to the person who is really responsible for your application--you.

You are the only person who should compile your college application. You need to take ownership of this process. The intervention of others should be for advisement only. The guidance counselor is not responsible for completing your applications, and your parents shouldn't be typing them. College applications must be completed in addition to your normal workload at school, college visits, and SAT, ACT, or possibly, TOEFL testing.

FOLLOW THESE TIPS WHEN FILLING OUT YOUR APPLICATION:

1. **Follow the directions to the letter.** You don't want to be in a position to ask an admissions officer for exceptions due to your inattentiveness.
2. **Make a photocopy** of the application and work through a rough draft before you actually fill out the application copy to be submitted.
3. **Proofread all parts of your application,** including your essay. Again, the final product indicates to the admissions staff how meticulous and careful you are in your work.
4. **Submit your application as early as possible,** provided all of the pieces are available. If there is a problem with your application, this will allow you to work through it with the admissions staff in plenty of time. If you wait until the last minute, it not only takes away that cushion but also reflects poorly on your sense of priorities.

STANDARDIZED TESTS

In all likelihood, you will take the SAT I, the ACT, or both tests sometime during your junior year of high school and, perhaps, again in your senior year if you are trying to improve your scores. If your native language is not English, you may also have to take the TOEFL test.

THE APPLICATION

The application is your way of introducing yourself to a college admissions office. As with any introduction, you should try to make a good first impression. The first thing you should do in presenting your application is to find out what the college or university needs from you. Read the application carefully to find out the application fee and deadline, required standardized tests, number of essays, interview requirements, and anything else you can do or submit to help improve your chances for acceptance.

Completing college applications yourself helps you learn more about the schools to which you are applying. The information a college asks for in its application can tell you much about the school. State university applications often tell you how they are going to view their applicants. Usually, they select students based on GPAs and test scores. Colleges that request an interview, ask you to respond to a few open-ended questions, or require an essay are interested in a more personal approach to the application process and may be looking for different types of students than those sought by a state school.

In addition to submitting the actual application, there are several other items that are commonly required. You will be responsible for ensuring that your standardized test scores and your high school transcript arrive at the colleges you apply to. Most colleges will ask that you submit teacher recommendations as well. Select teachers who know you and your abilities well and allow them plenty of time to complete the recommendations. When all portions of the application have been completed and sent in, whether electronically or by mail, make sure you follow up with the college to ensure their receipt.

THE APPLICATION ESSAY

Some colleges may request one essay or a combination of essays and short-answer topics to learn more about who you are and how well you can communicate your thoughts. Common essay topics cover such simple themes as writing about yourself and your experiences or why you want to attend that particular school. Other colleges will ask that you show your imaginative or creative side by writing about a favorite author, for instance, or commenting on a hypothetical situation. In such cases, they will be looking at your thought processes and your level of creativity.

Whereas the other portions of your application—your transcript, test scores, and involvement in extracurricular activities—are a reflection of what you've accomplished up to this point, your application essay is an opportunity to present yourself in the here and now. The essay shows your originality and verbal skills and is very important. Test scores and grades may represent your academic results, but your essay shows how you approach a topic or problem and express your opinion.

Admissions officers, particularly those at small or mid-size colleges, use the essay to determine how you, as a student, will fit into life at that college. The essay, therefore, is a critical component of the application process. Here are some tips for writing a winning essay:

- Colleges are looking for an honest representation of who you are and what you think. Make sure that the tone of the essay reflects enthusiasm, maturity, creativity, the ability to communicate, talent, and your leadership skills.
- Be sure you set aside enough time to write the essay, revise it, and revise it *again*. Running the "spell check" feature on your computer will only detect a fraction of the errors you probably made on your first pass at writing it. Take a break and then come back to it and reread it. You will probably notice other style, content, and grammar problems—and ways that you can improve the essay overall.
- Always answer the question that is being asked, making sure that you are specific, clear, and true to your personality.
- Enlist the help of reviewers who know you well—friends, parents, teachers—since they are likely to be the most honest and will keep you on track in the presentation of your true self.

THE PERSONAL INTERVIEW

Although it is relatively rare that a personal interview is actually required, many colleges recommend that you take this opportunity for a face-to-face discussion with a member of the admissions staff. Read through the application materials to determine whether or not a college places great emphasis on the interview. If they strongly recommend that you have one, it may work against you to forego it.

In contrast to a group interview and some alumni interviews, which are intended to provide information about a college, the personal interview is viewed both as an information session and as further evaluation of your skills and strengths. You will meet with a member of the admissions staff who will be assessing your personal qualities, high school preparation, and your capacity to contribute to undergraduate life at the institution. On average, these meetings last about 45 minutes—a relatively short amount of time in which to gather information and leave the desired impression—so here are some suggestions on how to make the most of it.

1. **Scheduling Your Visit.** Generally, students choose to visit campuses in the summer or fall of their senior year. Both times have their advantages. A summer visit, when the campus is not in session, generally allows for a less hectic visit and interview. Visiting in the fall, on the other hand, provides the opportunity to see what campus life is like in full swing. If you choose the fall, consider arranging an overnight trip so that you can stay in one of the college dormitories. At the very least, you should make your way around campus to take part in classes, athletic events, and social activities. Always make an appointment and avoid scheduling more than two college interviews on any given day. Multiple interviews in a single day hinder your chances of making a good impression, and your impressions of the colleges will blur into each other as you hurriedly make your way from place to place.
2. **Preparation.** Know the basics about the college before going for your interview. Read the college viewbook or catalog in addition to this guide. You will be better prepared to ask questions that are not answered in the literature and that will give you a better understanding of what the college has to offer. You should also spend some time thinking about your strengths and weaknesses and, in particular, what you are looking for in a college education. You will find that as you get a few interviews under your belt, they will get easier. You might consider starting with a college that is not a top contender on your list, where the stakes are not as high.
3. **Asking Questions.** Inevitably, your interviewer will ask you, "Do you have any questions?" Not having one may suggest that you're unprepared or, even worse, not interested. When you do ask questions, make sure that they are ones that matter to you and that have a bearing on your decision about whether or not to attend. The questions that you ask will give the interviewer some insight into your personality and priorities. Avoid asking questions that can be answered in the college literature—again, a sign of unpreparedness. Although the interviewer will undoubtedly pose questions to you, the interview should not be viewed merely as a question-and-answer session. If a conversation evolves out of a particular question, so much the better. Your interviewer can learn a great deal about you from how you sustain a conversation. Similarly, you will be able to learn a great deal about the college in a conversational format.
4. **Separate the Interview from the Interviewer.** Many students base their feelings about a college solely on their impressions of the interviewer. Try not to characterize a college based only on your personal reaction, however, since your impressions can be skewed by whether you and your interviewer hit it off. Pay lots of attention to everything else that you see, hear, and learn about a college. Once on campus, you may never see your interviewer again.

In the end, remember to relax and be yourself. Don't drink jitters-producing caffeinated beverages prior to the interview, and suppress nervous fidgets like leg-wagging, finger-drumming, or bracelet-jangling. Your interviewer will expect you to be somewhat nervous, which will relieve some of the pressure. Consider this an opportunity to put forth your best effort and to enhance everything that the college knows about you up to this point.

THE FINAL DECISION

Once you have received your acceptance letters, it is time to go back and look at the whole picture. Provided you received more than one acceptance, you are now in a position to compare your options. The best way to do this is to compare your original list of important college-ranking criteria with what you've discovered about each college along the way. In addition, you and your family will need to factor in the financial aid component, which is discussed in detail on the following pages. You will need to look beyond these cost issues and the quantifiable pros and cons of each college, however, and know that you have a good feeling about your final choice. Before sending off your acceptance letter, you need to feel confident that the college will feel like home for the next four years. Once the choice is made, the only hard part will be waiting for an entire summer before heading off to college!

Who's Paying for This? Financial Aid Basics

A college education can be expensive—costing more than $100,000 for four years at some of the higher priced private colleges and universities. Even at the lower cost state colleges and universities, the cost of a four-year education can approach $50,000. Figuring out how you and your family will come up with the necessary funds to pay for your education requires planning, perseverance, and learning as much as you can about the options that are available to you.

Paying for college cannot be looked on as a four-year financial commitment. For most families, paying the total cost of a student's college education out of a current savings account is simply not possible. For families that have planned ahead and have financial savings established for higher education, the burden is a lot easier. But for most, coming up with the funds takes the pooling of current income and assets and investing in longer-term loan options. These family resources, together with possible financial assistance from the state and federal government, institutional resources, and private donors, enable millions of students each year to attend the institution of their choice.

HOW FINANCIAL AID IS AWARDED

When you apply for aid, your family's financial situation is analyzed using a government-approved formula called the Federal Methodology. This formula looks at five items:

1. Particular make-up of the family.
2. Income of the parents.
3. Assets of the parents.
4. Income of the student.
5. Assets of the student.

This analysis determines the amount you and your family are expected to contribute toward your college expenses, called your Expected Family Contribution or EFC. (The chart at the end of this article will give you an approximate idea of your family's EFC.) If the EFC is equal to or more than the cost at a particular college, then you do not demonstrate financial need. However, even if you don't have financial need, you may still qualify for aid, as there are grants, scholarships, and loan programs that are not need-based.

If the cost of your education is greater than your EFC, then you do demonstrate financial need and will qualify for assistance. The amount of your financial need that can be met varies from school to school. Some are able to meet your full need, while others can only cover a certain percentage. Here's the formula:

Cost of Attendance
– Expected Family Contribution

= Financial Need

The EFC remains constant, but your need will vary according to the costs of attending a given college. In general, the higher the tuition and fees at a particular college, the higher their cost of attendance will be. It is important to remember that you do not have to be "needy" to qualify for financial aid. Many middle and upper-middle income families qualify for need-based financial aid.

SOURCES OF FINANCIAL AID

The largest single source of aid is the federal government, which awards almost $74 billion to more than 8½ million students each year.

The next largest source of financial aid is found in the college and university community. Institutions award an estimated $8 billion to students each year. Most of this aid is awarded to students who have a demonstrated need based on the Federal Methodology. Some institutions use a different formula, the Institutional Methodology, to award their own funds in conjunction with other forms of aid. Institutional aid may be either need-based or non-need-based. Aid that is not based on need is usually awarded for a student's academic performance (merit awards), specific talents or abilities, or to attract the type of students a college most wants to enroll.

Another large source of financial aid is state government. All states offer grant and/or scholarship aid, most of which is need-based. However, more and more states are offering substantial merit-based aid programs. Most state programs award aid only to students attending college in that state.

Other sources of financial aid include:

- Private agencies
- Foundations
- Corporations
- Clubs
- Fraternal and service organizations
- Civic associations
- Unions

- Religious groups that award grants, scholarships, and low-interest loans
- Employers that provide tuition reimbursement benefits for employees and their children

More information about these different sources of aid is available from high school guidance offices, public libraries, college financial aid offices, and directly from the sponsoring organizations.

APPLYING FOR FINANCIAL AID

Every student must complete the Free Application for Federal Student Aid (FAFSA) to be considered for financial aid. The FAFSA is available in your high school guidance office, many public libraries, colleges in your area, or directly from the U.S. Department of Education.

Students also can apply for federal student aid over the Internet using the interactive FAFSA on the Web. FAFSA on the Web can be accessed at http://www.fafsa.ed.gov. It can be used with any computer, including Macintosh, UNIX, and Windows-based systems. Also, both the student and at least one parent should apply for a federal pin number at http://www.pin.ed.gov. The pin number serves as your electronic signature when applying for aid on the Web.

To award their own funds, some colleges require an additional application, the Financial Aid PROFILE form. The PROFILE asks additional questions that some colleges and awarding agencies feel provide a more accurate assessment of the family's ability to pay for college. It is up to the college to decide whether it will use only the FAFSA or both the FAFSA and the Financial Aid PROFILE. PROFILE applications are available from the high school guidance office and on the Web. Both the paper application and the Web site list those colleges and programs that use the PROFILE form.

If Every College You're Applying to for Fall 2003 Requires Just the FAFSA

. . . then it's pretty simple: Complete the FAFSA after January 1, 2003, being certain to send it in before any college-imposed deadlines. (You are not permitted to send in the 2003-04 FAFSA before January 1, 2003.) Most college FAFSA application deadlines are in February or early March. It is easier if you have all your financial records for the previous year available, but if that is not possible, you are strongly encouraged to use estimated numbers.

After you send in your FAFSA, either with the paper application or electronically, you'll receive a Student Aid Report (SAR) in the mail that includes all of the information you reported and shows your EFC. Be sure to review the SAR, checking to see if the information you reported is accurate. If you used estimated numbers to complete the FAFSA, you may have to resubmit the SAR with any corrections to the data. The college(s) you have designated on the FAFSA will receive the information you reported and will use that data to make their decision. In many instances, the colleges you've applied to will ask you to send copies of your and your parents' income tax returns for 2002, plus any other documents needed to verify the information you reported.

If a College Requires the PROFILE

Step 1: Register for the Financial Aid PROFILE in the fall of your senior year in high school.

Registering for the Financial Aid PROFILE begins the financial aid process. You register by calling the College Scholarship Service at 1-800-778-6888 and providing basic demographic information, a list of colleges to which you are applying, and your credit card number to pay for the service. Petersons.com is a great starting place for finding help with registration and other financial aid assistance.

Registration packets with a list of the colleges that require the PROFILE are available in most high school guidance offices.

There is a fee for using the Financial Aid PROFILE application ($22 for the first college and $16 for each additional college). You must pay for the service by credit card when you register. If you do not have a credit card, you will be billed.

Step 2: Fill out your customized Financial Aid PROFILE.

A few weeks after you register, you'll receive in the mail a customized financial aid application that you can use to apply for institutional aid at the colleges you've designated as well as from some private scholarship programs, like the National Merit Scholarship. (Note: if you've waited until winter and a college's financial aid application deadline is approaching, you can get overnight delivery by paying an extra fee.) The PROFILE contains all the questions necessary to calculate your "institutional" EFC, plus the questions that the colleges and organizations you've designated require you to answer. Your individualized packet will also contain a customized cover letter instructing you what to do and informing you about deadlines and requirements for the colleges and programs you designated when you registered for the PROFILE, codes that indicate which colleges wanted which additional questions, and supplemental forms (if any of the colleges to which you are applying require them—e.g. the Business/Farm Supplement for students whose parents own a business or farm or the Divorced/Separated Parents' Statement).

Make sure you submit your PROFILE by the earliest deadline listed. Two to four weeks after you do so, you will receive an acknowledgment and a report estimating your "institutional" EFC based on the data elements you provided in your PROFILE. Remember, this is a different formula from the federal system that uses the FAFSA.

FINANCIAL AID PROGRAMS

There are three types of financial aid:

1. Gift-aid (including scholarships and grants)—Scholarships and grants are funds that do not have to be repaid.
2. Loans—Loans must be repaid, usually after graduation; the amount you have to pay back is the total you've borrowed plus any accrued interest. This is considered a source of self-help aid.

3. Student employment—Student employment is a job arranged for you by the financial aid office. This is a second source of self-help aid.

The federal government has two large grant programs—the Federal Pell Grant and the Federal Supplemental Educational Opportunity Grant. These grants are targeted to low-to-moderate income families with significant financial need. The federal government has a student employment program called Federal Work-Study, which offers jobs both on and off campus; and several loan programs, including those for students and for parents of undergraduate students.

There are two types of student loan programs, subsidized and unsubsidized. The Subsidized Stafford Loan and the Federal Perkins Loan are need-based, government-subsidized loans. Students who borrow through these programs do not have to pay interest on the loan until after they graduate or leave school. The Unsubsidized Stafford Loan and the parent loan programs are not awarded based on need, and borrowers are responsible for interest while the student is in school. There are different methods on how these loans are administered. Once you choose your college, the financial aid office will guide you through this process.

After you've submitted your financial aid application and you've been accepted for admission, each college will send you a letter describing your financial aid award. Most award letters show estimated college costs, how much you and your family are expected to contribute, and the amount and types of aid you have been awarded. Most students are awarded aid from a combination of sources and programs. Hence, your award is often called a financial aid "package."

IF YOU DON'T QUALIFY FOR NEED-BASED AID

If you are not eligible for need-based aid, you can still find ways to lessen the burden on your parents.

Here are some suggestions:

- Search for merit scholarships. You can start at the initial stages of your application process. College merit awards are becoming increasingly important as more and more colleges award these grants to students they especially want to attract. As a result, applying to a college at which your qualifications put you at the top of the entering class may give you a larger merit award. Another source of aid to look for is private scholarships that are given for special skills and talents.
- Seek employment during the summer and the academic year. The student employment office at your college can help you locate a school-year job. Many colleges and local businesses have vacancies remaining after they have hired students who are receiving federal work-study financial aid.
- Borrow through the Unsubsidized Stafford Loan programs. These are open to all students. The terms and conditions are similar to the subsidized loans. The biggest difference is that the borrower is responsible for the interest while still in college, although most lenders permit students to delay paying the interest right away and add the accrued interest to the total amount owed. You must file the FAFSA to be considered.
- After you've contributed what you can through scholarships, working, and borrowing, your parents will be expected to meet their share of the college bill (the Expected Family Contribution). Many colleges offer monthly payment plans that spread the cost over the academic year. If the monthly payments are too high, parents can borrow through the Federal Parent Loan for Undergraduate Students (PLUS), through one of the many private education loan programs available, or through home equity loans and lines of credit. Families seeking assistance in financing college expenses should inquire at the financial aid office about what programs are available at the college. Some families seek the advice of professional financial advisers and tax consultants.

HOW IS YOUR FAMILY CONTRIBUTION CALCULATED?

Approximate Expected Family Contribution

ASSETS		INCOME BEFORE TAXES								
		$ 20,000	30,000	40,000	50,000	60,000	70,000	80,000	90,000	100,000
$ 20,000										
FAMILY SIZE	3	$ 220	2,100	3,200	5,400	8,700	11,800	14,800	17,600	20,400
	4	0	1,400	2,000	4,000	7,400	10,500	13,400	15,900	19,300
	5	0	300	1,300	3,000	6,200	9,300	12,200	15,100	18,100
	6	0	0	600	2,100	5,000	7,800	10,800	13,700	16,600
$ 30,000										
FAMILY SIZE	3	$ 220	2,100	3,200	5,400	8,700	11,800	14,800	17,600	20,400
	4	0	1,400	2,000	4,000	7,400	10,500	13,400	15,900	19,300
	5	0	300	1,300	3,000	6,200	9,300	12,200	15,100	18,100
	6	0	0	600	2,100	5,000	7,800	10,800	13,700	16,600
$ 40,000										
FAMILY SIZE	3	$ 220	2,200	3,300	5,600	8,900	11,900	14,900	14,700	21,700
	4	0	1,500	2,100	4,100	7,500	10,700	13,600	16,000	20,400
	5	0	400	1,400	3,100	6,300	9,400	12,300	15,200	18,100
	6	0	0	600	2,200	5,100	8,000	11,000	13,900	16,700
$ 50,000										
FAMILY SIZE	3	$ 600	2,500	3,800	6,200	9,500	12,500	15,500	18,300	21,200
	4	0	1,800	2,400	4,600	8,200	11,300	14,200	16,700	20,000
	5	0	600	1,600	3,500	6,900	10,000	12,900	15,700	18,700
	6	0	0	900	2,500	5,700	8,600	11,600	14,500	17,300
$ 60,000										
FAMILY SIZE	3	$ 800	2,900	4,200	6,700	10,100	13,100	16,000	18,900	21,800
	4	140	2,000	2,700	5,100	8,700	11,900	14,800	17,600	20,600
	5	0	900	1,900	3,900	7,500	10,600	13,500	16,300	19,300
	6	0	0	1,200	2,900	6,300	9,200	12,200	15,100	17,900
$ 80,000										
FAMILY SIE	3	$ 1,400	3,500	5,100	7,800	11,000	14,200	17,100	20,000	22,900
	4	600	2,600	3,400	6,100	9,800	12,900	15,700	18,300	21,600
	5	0	1,400	2,500	4,800	8,600	11,700	14,600	17,400	20,400
	6	0	300	1,700	3,600	7,300	10,200	13,200	16,000	19,100
$100,000										
FAMILY SIZE	3	$ 1,800	4,400	6,100	8,900	12,300	15,300	18,200	21,100	24,000
	4	1,200	3,300	4,200	7,200	10,900	14,000	16,800	15,400	22,700
	5	100	1,900	3,200	5,800	9,700	12,800	15,600	18,500	21,500
	6	0	900	2,300	4,400	8,400	11,400	14,400	17,200	20,100
$120,000										
FAMILY SIZE	3	$ 2,500	5,300	7,300	10,100	13,400	16,300	19,300	22,300	25,100
	4	1,700	4,100	5,100	8,400	12,100	15,200	18,000	20,600	23,900
	5	600	2,500	4,000	6,900	10,800	13,900	16,600	19,600	22,600
	6	250	1,400	2,900	5,400	9,600	12,500	15,500	18,300	21,200
$140,000										
FAMILY SIZE	3	$ 3,200	6,500	8,400	11,200	14,500	17,400	20,400	23,300	26,200
	4	2,300	5,100	6,200	9,500	13,200	16,200	19,100	21,700	25,000
	5	1,200	3,200	4,900	8,100	11,900	15,100	17,900	20,800	23,800
	6	800	1,900	3,700	6,500	10,700	13,600	16,500	19,400	22,400

Middle-Income Families: Making the Financial Aid Process Work

Richard Woodland

A recent report from the U.S. Department of Education's National Center for Education Statistics (August 2001) took a close look at how middle-income families finance a college education. The report, Middle Income Undergraduates: Where They Enroll and How They Pay for Their Education, was one of the first detailed studies of these families. Even though 31 percent of middle-income families have the entire cost of attendance covered by financial aid, there is widespread angst among middle-income families that, while they earn too much to qualify for grant assistance, they are too financially strapped to pay the spiraling costs of higher education.

First, we have to agree on what constitutes a "middle-income" family. For the purposes of the federal study, middle income is defined as those families with incomes between $35,000 and $70,000. The good news is that 52 percent of these families received grants, while the balance received loans. Other sources of aid, including work-study, also helped close the gap.

So how do these families do it? Is there a magic bullet that will open the door to significant amounts of grants and scholarships?

The report found some interesting trends. One way a family can make college more affordable is by choosing less expensive colleges. In fact, in this income group, 29 percent choose to enroll in low- to moderate-cost schools. These include schools where the total cost is less than $8500 per year. In this sector, we find the community colleges and lower-priced state colleges and universities. But almost half of these middle-income families choose schools in the upper-level tier, with costs ranging from $8500 to $16,000. The remaining 23 percent enrolled at the highest-tier schools, with costs above $16,000. Clearly, while cost is a factor, middle-income families are not limiting their choices based on costs alone.

The report shows that families pay these higher costs with a combination of family assets, current income, and long-term borrowing. This is often referred to as the "past-present-future" model of financing. In fact, just by looking at the Expected Family Contributions, it is clear that there is a significant gap in what families need and what the financial aid process can provide. Families are closing this gap by making the financial sacrifices necessary to pay the current price at higher-cost schools, especially if they think their child is academically strong. The report concludes that parents are more likely to pay for a higher-priced education if their child scores above 1200 on the SATs.

The best place for middle-income families to start is with their high school guidance office. This office has a lot of good information on financial aid and valuable leads on local scholarships. Most guidance officers report that there are far fewer applicants for these locally based scholarships than one would expect. So read the literature that they send home, and be sure that there is follow-up on the application process. A few of those $500-$1000 scholarships can add up!

Second, be sure to attend a financial aid awareness program. If your school does not offer one, contact your local college financial aid office and see when and where they will be speaking. You can get a lot of "inside" information on how the process works.

Next, be sure to file the correct applications for aid. Remember, each school will have a different set of requirements. For example, many higher-cost private colleges will require the PROFILE application to be filed. Other schools will have their own institutional aid application. All schools will require the Free Application for Federal Student Aid (FAFSA). Watch the deadlines! It is imperative that you meet the school's published application deadline. Generally, schools are not very flexible about this, so be sure to double-check the due date of your application.

Finally, become a smart educational consumer. Peterson's has a wide range of resources available to help you understand the process. Be sure to check your local library, bookstore, and of course, the Internet. Two great Web sites to check are http://www.petersons.com and http://www.finaid.org.

Once admitted to the various colleges and universities, you will receive an award notice outlining the aid you are eligible to receive. If you feel the offer is not sufficient, or if you have some unique financial problems, call the school's financial aid office to see if you can have your case reviewed again. The financial aid office is the best source for putting the pieces together and making it work.

The financial aid office will help you determine what the "net price" is. This is the actual out-of-pocket expenses that you will need to cover. Through a combination of student and parent loans, most families are able to cover these expenses.

Many students help close the gap by working while in school. While this works for many students, research shows that too many hours spent away from your studies will negatively impact on your academic success. Most experts feel that working 10 to 15 hours a week is optimal.

An overlooked source of aid is the recent tax credits given to middle-income families. Rather than extending eligibility for traditional sources of grant assistance to middle-income families, congress and the president have built into the federal tax system significant tax credits for middle-income families. While it may be seven or eight months before you see the credit, families in this income group can safely count on this benefit, usually about $1500 per student. This is real money in your pocket. You do not need to itemize your deductions to get this tax credit.

Millions of middle-income families send their children to colleges and universities every year. Only 8 percent attend the lowest-priced schools. By using the concept of past-present-future financing, institutional assistance, meaningful targeted tax relief, and student earnings, you can afford even the highest-cost schools.

Richard Woodland is Director of Financial Aid at Rutgers University–Camden.

Financial Aid Countdown

CALENDAR

Richard Woodland

JUNIOR YEAR

Fall

Now is the time to get serious about the colleges in which you are interested. Meet with the guidance office to help you narrow down your. Hopefully by the spring, your list will have about five to ten solid choices. College visits are always a great idea-remember this will be the place you spend the next four years, so check out the campus early.

- ❒ Register for the Preliminary SAT (PSAT).
- ❒ Check out local financial aid nights in the area. Be sure to attend these invaluable sessions, especially if this is the first time the family is sending someone off to college. Try to learn the financial aid lingo. Get some of the literature available and start to familiarize yourself with the various programs.
- ❒ Take the PSAT and the National Merit Scholarship Qualifying Test in October.
- ❒ Do some Web browsing! There are many great, free scholarship search engines available. Now is the time to see if you might qualify for scholarships.
- ❒ Have your parents check with their employers and church and fraternal organizations for possible scholarship opportunities.
- ❒ Check with your guidance office for the qualifications and deadlines of local awards.

Winter

- ❒ Keep checking for scholarships! Remember that this is the one area over which you have control. The harder you work the better your chances for success.
- ❒ Register and study for the SAT (I and II). Most college-controlled scholarship programs count the SATs heavily in their decision process. Signing up for a prep course is usually money well spent. If you decide not to take a course, then your next best resource is the bookstore. The SAT is definitely not a test that you can cram for the night before. Invest in a comprehensive test-prep guide. Using a study guide will help you get an idea of your math and verbal strengths and weaknesses. Start to schedule a little extra time to study the areas that give you problems.

Spring

- ❒ Spring Break—a great time to visit colleges. Do you have a top ten list? Start narrowing your list down now.
- ❒ Review the requirements for the local scholarships. What do you need to do now and this summer to improve your chances? Take the SATs.
- ❒ Look for a summer job, especially one that might tie in with your college plans.

Summer

- ❒ It's college visit time, so load up the van! Begin to ask yourself some questions: Is this where I see myself getting my undergraduate degree? Can I adjust to the seasons, the town surrounding the campus, the distance from home, the college size?

SENIOR YEAR

Fall

- ❒ Can you get your list down to five choices? Once you get focused on your five choices, make a list of what each college requires for admission and financial aid. Be sure your list prominently shows all deadlines.
- ❒ Which colleges require the Profile application? Many private colleges use this form for institutional aid. You need to file this comprehensive form in late September or early October.
- ❒ Get your scholarship applications filed by the published deadline. Remember, you have three sources: parent sources (employer, religious, fraternal), high school (local awards from PTA, Kiwanas, Lions Club, etc.), and Web-based search engines.
- ❒ If planning to retake the SAT, be sure to register now.
- ❒ You and your parents must attend a financial aid night presentation. Some of these sessions offer help in completing forms, while others offer a broader view of the process. Contact the presenter (usually a local college professional) to be sure you are getting the information you need.

Winter

- ❒ Get the Free Application for Federal Student Aid (FAFSA). This is the key form for financial aid for all schools across the country. Remember, watch your deadlines, but do not file before January 1. Be sure to keep a copy of the form, whether you file electronically or with the paper form. Got some questions? Call the local financial aid office. Also, many states have special call-in programs in January and February, Financial Aid Awareness Month.
- ❒ As the letters of admission start to arrive, the financial aid award letter should be right behind. The important question for parents: What is the bottom line? Remember, aid at a lower-cost state school will be less than a higher-cost private college. But what will you be required to pay? This can be confusing, so watch for gift aid (scholarships and grants), student loans, and parent loans. The school with the lowest sticker price (tuition, fees, room, and board) might not be the cheapest when you factor in the aid package.

Spring

- ❒ Still not sure where to go? The financial aid package at your top choice just not enough? Call the financial aid office and the admissions office. Talk it over. While schools don't like to bargain, they are usually willing to take a second look, especially for the high achievers. By May 1, you must make your final decision. Notify the college and find out what you need to do next. Tell the other colleges you are not accepting their offers of admission and financial aid.

Summer

- ❒ Time to crunch the numbers. Parents, get information from the college on the estimated charges. Deduct the aid package, and then plan for how you will pay the out-of-pocket expenses. Contact the college financial aid office for the best parental loan program.

Congratulations! Remember that you need to reapply for aid every year!

What International Students Need to Know About Admission to U.S. Colleges and Universities

Kitty M. Villa

Selecting an institution and securing admission require a significant investment of time and effort.

There are two principles to remember about admission to a university in the United States. First, applying is almost never a one-time request for admission but an ongoing process that may involve several exchanges of information between applicant and institution. "Admission process" or "application process" means that a "yes" or "no" is usually not immediate, and requests for additional information are to be expected. To successfully manage this process, you must be prepared to send additional information when requested and then wait for replies. You need a thoughtful balance of persistence to communicate regularly and effectively with your selected universities and patience to endure what can be a very long process.

The second principle involves a marketplace analogy. The most successful applicants are alert to opportunities to create a positive impression that sets them apart from other applicants. They are able to market themselves to their target institution. Institutions are also trying to attract the highest-quality student that they can. The admissions process presents you with the opportunity to analyze your strengths and weaknesses as a student and to look for ways to present yourself in the most marketable manner.

BEGINNING THE APPLICATION PROCESS: SELECTING INSTITUTIONS

With more than 3,000 institutions of higher education in the U.S., how do you begin to narrow your choices down to the institutions that are best for you? There are many factors to consider, and you must ultimately decide which factors are most important to you.

Location

You may spend several years studying in the U.S. Do you prefer an urban or rural campus? Large or small metropolitan area? If you need to live on campus, will you be unhappy at a university where most students commute from off-campus housing? How do you feel about extremely hot summers or cold winters? Eliminating institutions that do not match your preferences in terms of location will narrow your choices.

Recommendations from Friends, Professors, or Others

There are valid academic reasons to consider the recommendations of people who know you well and have firsthand knowledge about particular institutions. Friends and contacts may be able to provide you with "inside information" about the campus or its academic programs to which published sources have no access. You should carefully balance anecdotal information with your own research and your own impressions. However, current and former students, professors, and others may provide excellent information during the application process.

Your Own Academic and Career Goals

Consideration of your academic goals is more complex than it may seem at first glance. All institutions do not offer the same academic programs. This guide identifies those institutions that offer your desired field of study. The application form usually provides a definitive listing of the academic programs offered by an institution. A course catalog describes the degree program and all the courses offered. In addition to printed sources, there is a tremendous amount of institutional information available through the Internet. Program descriptions, even course descriptions and course syllabi, are often available to peruse via computer.

You may be interested in the rankings of either the university or of a program of study. Keep in mind, however, that rankings usually assume that quality is quantifiable. Rankings are usually based on presumptions about how data relate to quality that are likely to be unproven. It is important to carefully consider the source and the criteria of any ranking information before believing and acting upon it.

Your Own Educational Background

You may be concerned about the interpretation of your educational credentials, since your country's degree nomenclature and the grading scale may differ from those in the U.S. Universities use reference books about the educational systems of other countries to help them understand specific educational credentials. Generally, these credentials are interpreted by each institution; there is not a single interpretation that applies to every institution. The lack of uniformity is good news for most students, since it means that students from a wide variety of educational backgrounds can find a U.S. university that is appropriate to their needs.

To choose an appropriate institution, you can and should do an informal self-evaluation of your educational background. This self-analysis involves three important questions:

How Many Years of Study Have You Completed?

Completion of secondary school with at least twelve total years of education usually qualifies students to apply for undergraduate (bachelor's) degree programs. Completion of a university degree program that involves at least sixteen years of total education qualifies one to apply for admission to graduate (master's) degree programs in the U.S.

Does the Education That You Have Completed in Your Country Provide Access to Further Study in the U.S.?

Consider the kind of institution where you completed your previous studies. If educational opportunities in your country are limited, it may be necessary to investigate many U.S. institutions and programs in order to find a match.

Are Your Previous Marks or Grades Excellent, Average, or Poor?

Your educational record influences your choice of U.S. institutions. If your grades are average or poor, it may be advisable to apply to several institutions with minimally difficult or noncompetitive entrance levels.

YOU are one of the best sources of information about the level and quality of your previous studies. Awareness of your educational assets and liabilities will serve you well throughout the application process.

SECOND STEP—PLANNING AND ASSEMBLING THE APPLICATION

Planning and assembling a university application can be compared to the construction of a building. First, you must start with a solid foundation, which is the application form itself. The application form usually contains a wealth of useful information, such as deadlines, fees, and degree programs available at that institution. To build a solid application, it is best to obtain the form well in advance of the application deadline.

How to Obtain the Application Form

Traditionally, a request for an application form is made in writing. Some institutions still follow this style. Many institutions now accept requests for application forms by e-mail, fax, or telephone. Increasingly, universities use and accept one application form that needs to be completed only once and then can be sent to several institutions.

Application forms may also be available at a U.S. educational advising center associated with the American Embassy or Consulate in your country. These centers are excellent resources for international students and provide information about standardized test administration, scholarships, and other matters to students who are interested in studying in the U.S. Your local U.S. Embassy or Consulate can guide you to the nearest educational advising center.

Completing the Application Form

Whether sent by mail or electronically, the application form must be neat and thoroughly filled out. Parts of the application may not seem to apply to you or your situation. If you are unsure, do your best to answer the question. If you must leave it blank or have questions, write notes on the form indicating where you have questions or concerns.

Remember that this is a process. You provide information, and your proposed university then requests clarification and further information. If you have questions, it is better to initiate the entire process by submitting the application form rather than asking questions before you apply. The university will be better able to respond to you after it has your application. Always complete as much as you can. Do not permit uncertainty about the completion of the application form to cause unnecessary delays.

What Are the Key Components of a Complete Application?

Institutional requirements vary, but the standard components of a complete application include:

- Transcript
- Required standardized examination scores
- Letters of recommendation
- Letter of financial support
- Application fee

Transcript

A complete academic record or transcript includes all courses completed, grades earned, and degrees awarded. Most universities require an official transcript to be sent directly from the school or university. In many other countries, however, the practice is to issue official transcripts and degree certificates directly to the student. If you have only one official copy of your transcript, it may be a challenge to get additional certified copies that are acceptable to U.S. universities. Some institutions will issue additional official copies for application purposes.

If your institution does not provide this service, you may have to seek an alternate source of certification. As a last resort, you may send a photocopy of your official transcript, explain that you have only one original, and ask the university for advice on how to deal with this situation.

Standardized Examinations

Arranging to take the examinations and earning the required scores seem to cause the most anxiety for international students.

The university application form usually indicates which examinations are required. The standardized examination required most often for undergraduate admission is the Test of English as a Foreign Language (TOEFL). In most countries, TOEFL has changed from a paper-and-pencil test to a computer-based test. Institutions may also require the SAT I of undergraduate applicants. Some institutions also require the Test of Spoken English (TSE). These standardized examinations are administered by the Educational Testing Service (ETS).

These examinations are offered in almost every country of the world. It is advisable to begin planning for standardized examinations at least six months prior to the application deadline of your desired institutions. Test centers fill up quickly, so it is important to register as soon as possible. Information about the examinations is available at U.S. educational advising centers associated with embassies or consulates.

Questions about test formats, locations, dates, and registration may be addressed to:

TOEFL/TSE Services–Princeton
P.O. Box 6151
Princeton, New Jersey 08541-6151
Web sites: http://www.ets.org
http://www.toefl.org
Telephone: 609-771-7100
Fax: 609-771-7500

Most universities require that the original test scores, not a student copy, be sent directly by the testing service. When you register for the test, be sure to indicate that the testing service should send the test scores directly to your proposed universities.

Minimum Score Requirements

You should usually begin your application process before you receive your test scores. Delaying submission of your application until the test scores arrive may cause you to miss deadlines and negatively effect the outcome of your application. If you want to know your scores in order to assess your chances of admission to an institution with rigorous admission standards, you should take the tests early.

Many universities in the U.S. set minimum required scores on the TOEFL or on other standardized examinations. Test scores are an important factor, but most institutions also look at a number of other factors in their consideration of a candidate for admission.

Evidence of Financial Support

Evidence of financial support is required to issue immigration documents to admitted students. This is part of a complete application package but usually plays no role in determining admission. Most institutions make admissions decisions without regard to the source and amount of financial support.

Letters of Recommendation

Most institutions require one or more letters of recommendation. The best letters are written by former professors, employers, or others who can comment on your academic achievements or professional potential.

Some universities provide a special form for the letters of recommendation. If possible, use the forms provided. If you are applying to a large number of universities, however, or if your recommenders are not available to complete several forms, it may be necessary for you to duplicate a general recommendation letter.

Application Fee

Most universities also require an application fee, ranging from $25 to $100, which must be paid to initiate consideration of the application.

THIRD STEP—DISTINGUISH YOUR APPLICATION

To distinguish your application—to market yourself successfully—is ultimately the most important part of the application process. As you select your prospective universities, you begin to analyze your strengths and weaknesses as a prospective student. As you complete your application, you should strive to create a positive impression and set yourself apart from other applicants, to highlight your assets and bring these qualities to the attention of the appropriate university administrators and professors. Applying early is a very easy way to distinguish your application.

Deadline or Guideline?

The application deadline is the last date that an application for a given semester will be accepted. Often, the application will specify that all required documents and information be submitted before the deadline date. To meet the deadlines, start the application process early. This also gives you more time to take—and perhaps retake and improve—the required standardized tests.

Admissions deliberations may take several weeks or months. In the meantime, most institutions accept additional information, including improved test scores, after the posted deadline.

Even if your application is initially rejected, you may be able to provide additional information to change the decision. You can request reconsideration based on additional information, such as improved test scores, strong letters of recommendation, or information about your rank in class. Applying early allows more time to improve your application. Also, some students may decide not to accept their offers of admission, leaving room for offers to students on a waiting list. Reconsideration of the admission decisions can occur well beyond the application deadline.

Think of the deadline as a guideline rather than an impermeable barrier. Many factors—the strength of the application, the student's research interests, the number of spaces available at the proposed institution—can override the enforcement of an application deadline. So, if you lack a test score or transcript by the official deadline, you may still be able to apply and be accepted.

Statement of Purpose

The statement of purpose is your first and perhaps best opportunity to present yourself as an excellent candidate for admission. Whether or not a personal history essay or statement of purpose is required, always include a carefully written statement of purpose with your applications. A compelling statement of purpose does not have to be lengthy, but it should include some basic components:

- Part One—Introduce yourself and describe your previous educational background. This is your opportunity to describe any facet of your educational experience that you wish to emphasize. Perhaps you attended a highly ranked secondary school or university in your home country. Mention the name and any noteworthy characteristics of the secondary school or university from which you graduated. Explain the grading scale used at your university. Do not forget to mention your rank in your graduating class and any honors you may have received. This is not the time to be modest.
- Part Two—Describe your current academic interests and goals. It is very important to describe in some detail your specific study or career interests. Think about how these will fit into those of the institution to which you are applying, and mention the reasons why you have selected that institution.
- Part Three—Describe your long-term goals. When you finish your program of study, what do you plan to do next? If you already have a job offer or a career plan, describe it. Give some thought to how you'll demonstrate that studying in the U.S. will ultimately benefit others.

Use Personal Contacts When Possible

Appropriate and judicious use of your own network of contacts can be very helpful. Friends, former professors, former students of your selected institutions, and others may be willing to advise you during the application process and provide you with introductions to key administrators or professors. If suggested, you may wish to contact certain professors or administrators by mail, telephone, or e-mail. A personal visit to discuss your interest in the institution may be appropriate. Whatever your choice of communication, try to make the encounter pleasant and personal. Your goal is to make a positive impression, not to rush the admission decision.

There is no single right way to be admitted to U.S. universities. The same characteristics that make the educational choice in the U.S. so difficult—the number of institutions and the variety of programs of study—are the same attributes that allow so many international students to find the institution that's right for them.

Kitty M. Villa is the Assistant Director of the International Office at the University of Texas at Austin.

Visa Requirements and Regulations for Students in Nonimmigrant Status

Deane Atkinson

Attending a college or university in the United States brings exciting challenges to an international student. Once you are admitted to a college or university in the U.S., you will face the task of sorting through all the visa and entry requirements and understanding the immigration regulations. The best source of information is the student immigration adviser at the college or university you will be attending.

Since more than 450,000 international students attend U.S. colleges each year, most colleges and universities routinely provide the appropriate documents and instructions for visa applications to accepted students once sufficient personal information and funding verification have been provided. Schools also frequently provide orientation, immigration advising, and student handbooks to help international students understand immigration regulations and to introduce them to advisers who will assist them throughout their stay. In fact, upon arrival in the U.S., international students are presented with so many informational sessions and packets that it may be difficult to sort through all of the material. However, maintaining legal nonimmigrant status is critical, and it is important to understand the basic regulations from the beginning.

THE FIRST HURDLE—OBTAINING A VISA

To attend a U.S. college or university, you must obtain a visa. A visa is a stamp for your passport, issued by a U.S. embassy or consulate, that constitutes permission to enter the country. The stamp indicates the visa type, the time period in which entry is allowed, and the number of entries permitted. The stamp may only be obtained outside the U.S. Most international students are issued an F-1 visa; sponsored and exchange students are usually issued a J-1 visa. Procedures for obtaining a visa are as follows:

- Upon receipt of the appropriate document (I-20 for F-1 students, IAP-66 for J-1 students), contact the closest U.S. embassy or consulate for information concerning procedures for visa applications. Many consulates and embassies issue visas on a mail-in or appointment basis, so it saves time and frustration to contact them in advance for specific policies and procedures. Check with the embassy or consulate concerning processing times and fees, which may vary depending on reciprocity with your country.
- Carry plenty of documentation but present only what is requested. Visa applicants must provide a valid passport, an I-20 or IAP-66, and verification of funding. Extra documentation might include anything that establishes ties to the home country (such as future job offers, proof of property ownership, or involvement in family business).

If an interview is required, here are some tips from the NAFSA Association of International Educators:

- Anticipate that the interview will be in English; if it is possible, practice English conversation with a native speaker.
- Keep your answers to the officer's questions short and to the point. Consular officers are under considerable pressure to conduct a quick and efficient interview.
- If your spouse is applying for an accompanying F-2 or J-2 visa, be aware that F-2 dependents cannot be employed in the U.S. Be prepared to show an ability to support your family, and address how your spouse intends to spend his or her time in the U.S. Some activities, such as volunteer work and attending school part-time, are permitted.
- Maintain a positive attitude. Focus on your educational objective and express your desire to return home to use that education.

If you are denied a student visa, try to get the reason for the denial in writing. Ask the officer for a list of documents he or she would suggest you bring in order to overcome the refusal.

If you plan to enter the U.S. on a B-1/B-2 visa, you must enter as a "prospective student," or you may be required to return to your home country. Most important, do not enter the U.S. on a visa waiver that only allows a 90-day stay for tourism or business and will not permit a change of status or an extension.

Once your visa has been issued, think of it as a permit to enter, not a permit to stay in, the U.S. It must be valid at the time of entry and for any later periods of re-entry. The length of stay is determined by the dates of the I-20 and IAP-66 documents and continued enrollment, not by the length of your visa.

VISA'S BEEN ISSUED—TIME TO TRAVEL

Now that your visa has been issued, you are on your way. At the port of entry in the U.S., present your I-20 or IAP-66 with your passport and valid visa to the Immigration and Naturalization Service (INS) official. Once again, you may be questioned about your funding and educational objectives and the school you will attend. Feel comfortable giving the same information that you gave at the visa interview.

Once this process is complete, the INS inspector issues an I-94, indicating your status and duration of stay, and returns a stamped portion of your I-20 or IAP-66. The I-94 is a small, white, square card that is usually stapled to your passport across from the visa stamp. This document is important to keep during your stay in the U.S. and must be relinquished upon departure.

WELCOME TO THE U.S.—SCHOOL BEGINS

You have arrived on campus. School officials will provide you with information about your housing assignment, class registration, orientation, and other information for new students. Included in this documentation you will find information on maintaining your status as an international student. Do not lose this paperwork. Typically, an international student adviser will be assigned to help you deal with all of these matters. International student advisers work for the university, not the INS. If an adviser is not assigned to you, be sure to contact your college or university's international student office immediately.

The easiest way to understand how to maintain valid F-1 or J-1 status is to remember your purpose for coming to the U.S.—to be a student. As long as an international student registers as a full-time student, maintains valid documents that reflect academic objectives, observes employment restrictions, and works toward an academic goal, he or she should have no problem complying with student immigration regulations. Here are some specific regulations:

- At first, a student may only attend the school that originally issued his or her documents to enter the country. Once a student has been enrolled for one semester, it is easy to transfer to other schools in the U.S.
- Full-time enrollment is required during fall and spring semesters: 12 hours for undergraduates, 9 hours for graduates. It is not necessary to enroll in summer sessions for continuing students. Students initially admitted during the summer must enroll in the first summer session. INS does not allow enrollment exceptions for some academic or medical problems; therefore, it is best to consult the student immigration adviser before dropping a class or enrolling for less than a full course of study.
- You may seek employment incidental to student status only on campus, and you are limited to 20 hours per week during fall and spring sessions and 40 hours per week during summer and vacation periods. Any off-campus employment must be authorized by INS or, in limited cases (for example, curricular practical training), by the student immigration adviser. An authorization for a twelve-month period of employment is available and is frequently granted after graduation to help a student gain experience in a degree field.
- Documents must be maintained to reflect the correct school, degree program, and expected length of stay. A new I-20 or IAP-66 must be processed for extensions, changes to major or degree level, or school transfers. Timing is important, and the new documents must be processed within a limited period. Passports must be valid at all times.

A bill was passed by the U.S. Congress in September 1996, called the "Illegal Immigration Reform and Immigrant Responsibility Act of 1996." The bill created considerable ramifications for "overstaying" and "unlawful presence." Of primary significance is the fact that the bill does not change any regulations for international students who maintain their status. It does, however, affect any student who terminates his or her study and does not leave the U.S. within the grace period appropriate for that status (as it also affects any nonimmigrant in the U.S. who stays beyond his or her authorized period). Again, the bill does not place any new restrictions or limitations on students who maintain their status.

The best way to maintain your status is to be informed. Here are some tips:

- Always contact the student immigration adviser with questions about status, travel, and visa requirements. Academic advisers are not aware of INS regulations, so double-check with your immigration adviser if enrollment or academic problems might affect your student status.
- Do not work off campus without employment authorization.
- Do not travel outside the U.S. without the immigration adviser's endorsement on your I-20 or IAP-66.
- Make sure you understand the purpose and validity requirement of each immigration document.
- Do not rely on the advice of international or American student friends. Their circumstances may be different from yours, or regulations may have changed. Ask your student immigration adviser.

Immigration regulations are not in place to restrict your studies. Instead, they enhance your experience by allowing continued enrollment. This student status helps you meet all of your educational objectives and gain authorized employment in your field.

Deane Atkinson is Assistant Director, International Office, of the University of Texas at Austin.

What You Need to Know About Two-Year Colleges

David R. Pierce

Two-year colleges—better known as community colleges—are often called "the people's colleges." With their open-door policies (admission is open to individuals with a high school diploma or its equivalent), community colleges provide access to higher education for millions of Americans who might otherwise be excluded from higher education. Community college students are diverse, of all ages, races, and economic backgrounds. While many community college students enroll full-time, an equally large number attend on a part-time basis so they can fulfill employment and family commitments as they advance their education.

Today, there are more than 1,100 community colleges in the United States. They enroll more than 5.6 million students, who represent 45 percent of all undergraduates in the United States. Nearly 55 percent of all first-time freshmen begin their higher education in a community college.

Community colleges can also be referred to as either technical or junior colleges, and they may either be under public or independent control. What unites these two-year colleges is that they are regionally accredited, postsecondary institutions, whose highest credential awarded is the associate degree. With few exceptions, community colleges offer a comprehensive curriculum, which includes transfer, technical, and continuing education programs.

IMPORTANT FACTORS IN A COMMUNITY COLLEGE EDUCATION

The student who attends a community college can count on receiving quality instruction in a supportive learning community. This setting frees the student to pursue his or her own goals, nurture special talents, explore new fields of learning, and develop the capacity for lifelong learning.

From the student's perspective, four characteristics capture the essence of community colleges:

- They are community-based institutions that work in close partnership with high schools, community groups, and employers in extending high-quality programs at convenient times and places.
- Community colleges are cost effective. Annual tuition and fees at public community colleges average approximately half those at public four-year colleges and less than 15 percent of private four-year institutions. In addition, since most community colleges are generally close to their students' homes, these students can also save a significant amount of money on the room, board, and transportation expenses traditionally associated with a college education.
- They provide a caring environment, with faculty members who are expert instructors, known for excellent teaching and for meeting students at the point of their individual needs, regardless of age, sex, race, current job status, or previous academic preparation. Community colleges join a strong curriculum with a broad range of counseling and career services that are intended to assist students in making the most of their educational opportunities.
- Many offer comprehensive programs, including transfer curricula in such liberal arts programs as chemistry, psychology, and business management, that lead directly to a baccalaureate degree and career programs that prepare students for employment or assist those already employed to upgrade their skills. For those students who need to strengthen their academic skills, community colleges also offer a wide range of developmental programs in mathematics, languages, and learning skills, designed to prepare the student for success in college studies.

GETTING TO KNOW YOUR TWO-YEAR COLLEGE

The first step in determining the quality of a community college is to check the status of its accreditation. Once you have established that a community college is appropriately accredited, find out as much as you can about the programs and services it has to offer. Much of that information can be found in materials the college provides. However, the best way to learn about your college is to visit in person.

During a campus visit, be prepared to ask a lot of questions. Talk to students, faculty members, administrators, and counselors about the college and its programs, particularly those in which you have a special interest. Ask about available certificates and associate degrees. Don't be shy. Do what you can to dig below the surface. Ask college officials about the transfer rate to four-year colleges. If a college emphasizes student services, find out what particular assistance is offered, such as educational or career guidance. Colleges are eager to provide you with the information you need to make informed decisions.

COMMUNITY COLLEGES CAN SAVE YOU MONEY

If you are able to live at home while you attend college, you will certainly save money on room and board, but it does cost something to commute. Many two-year colleges can now offer you instruction in your own home through cable television or public broadcast stations or through home study courses that can save both time and money. Look into all your options, and be sure to add up all the costs of attending various colleges before deciding which is best for you.

FINANCIAL AID

Many students who attend community colleges are eligible for a range of financial aid programs, including Federal Pell Grants, Perkins and Stafford Loans, state aid, and on-campus jobs. Your high school counselor or the financial aid officer at a community college will also be able to help you. It is in your interest to apply for financial aid months in advance of the date you intend to start your college program, so find out early what assistance is available to you. While many community colleges are able to help students who make a last-minute decision to attend college, either through short-term loans or emergency grants, if you are considering entering college and think you might need financial aid, it is best to find out as much as you can as early as you can.

WORKING AND GOING TO SCHOOL

Many two-year college students maintain full-time or part-time employment while they earn their degrees. Over the years, a steadily growing number of students have chosen to attend community colleges while they fulfill family and employment responsibilities. To enable these students to balance the demands of home, work, and school, most community colleges offer classes at night and on weekends.

For the full-time student, the usual length of time it takes to obtain an associate degree is two years. However, your length of study will depend on the course load you take: the fewer credits you earn each term, the longer it will take you to earn a degree. To assist you in moving more quickly to your degree, many community colleges now award credit through examination or for equivalent knowledge gained through relevant life experiences. Be certain to find out the credit options that are available to you at the college in which you are interested. You may discover that it will take less time to earn a degree than you first thought.

PREPARATION FOR TRANSFER

Studies have repeatedly shown that students who first attend a community college and then transfer to a four-year college or university do at least as well academically as the students who entered the four-year institutions as freshmen. Most community colleges have agreements with nearby four-year institutions to make transfer of credits easier. If you are thinking of transferring, be sure to meet with a counselor or faculty adviser before choosing your courses. You will want to map out a course of study with transfer in mind. Make sure you also find out the credit-transfer requirements of the four-year institution you might want to attend.

ATTENDING A TWO-YEAR COLLEGE IN ANOTHER REGION

Although many community colleges serve a specific county or district, they are committed (to the extent of their ability) to the goal of equal educational opportunity without regard to economic status, race, creed, color, sex, or national origin. Independent two-year colleges recruit from a much broader geographical area—throughout the United States and, increasingly, around the world.

Although some community colleges do provide on-campus housing for their students, most do not. However, even if on-campus housing is not available, most colleges do have housing referral services.

NEW CAREER OPPORTUNITIES

Community colleges realize that many entering students are not sure about the field in which they want to focus their studies or the career they would like to pursue. Often, students discover fields and careers they never knew existed. Community colleges have the resources to help students identify areas of career interest and to set challenging occupational goals.

Once a career goal is set, you can be confident that a community college will provide job-relevant, technical education. About half of the students who take courses for credit at community colleges do so to prepare for employment or to acquire or upgrade skills for their current job. Especially helpful in charting a career path is the assistance of a counselor or a faculty adviser, who can discuss job opportunities in your chosen field and help you map out your course of study.

In addition, since community colleges have close ties to their communities, they are in constant contact with leaders in business, industry, organized labor, and public life. Community colleges work with these individuals and their organizations to prepare students for direct entry into the world of work. For example, some community colleges have established partnerships with local businesses and industries to provide specialized training programs. Some also provide the academic portion of apprenticeship training, while others offer extensive job-shadowing and cooperative education opportunities. Be sure to examine all of the career-preparation opportunities offered by the community colleges in which you are interested.

David R. Pierce is President of the American Association of Community Colleges.

Frequently Asked Questions About Transferring

Muriel M. Shishkoff

Among the students attending two-year colleges are a large number who began their higher education knowing they would eventually transfer to a four-year school to obtain their bachelor's degree. There are many reasons why students are going this route. Upon graduating from high school, some simply do not have definite career goals. Although they don't want to put their education on hold, they prefer not to pay exorbitant amounts in tuition while trying to "find themselves." As the cost of a university education escalates—even in public institutions—the option of spending the freshman and sophomore years at a two-year college looks attractive to many students. Others attend a two-year college because they are unable to meet the initial entrance standards—a specified grade point average (GPA), standardized test scores, or knowledge of specific academic subjects—required by the four-year school of their choice. Many such students praise the community college system for giving them the chance to be, academically speaking, "born again." In addition, students from other countries often find that they can adapt more easily to language and cultural changes at a two-year school before transferring to a larger, more diverse four-year college.

If your plan is to attend a two-year college with the ultimate goal of transferring to a four-year school, you will be pleased to know that the increased importance of the community college route to a bachelor's degree is recognized by all segments of higher education. As a result, many two-year schools have revised their course outlines and established new courses in order to comply with the programs and curricular offerings of the universities. Institutional improvements to make transferring easier have also proliferated at both the two- and four-year levels. The generous transfer policies of the Pennsylvania, New York, and Florida state university systems, among others, reflect this attitude; these systems accept *all* credits from students who have graduated from accredited community colleges.

If you are interested in moving from a two-year college to a four-year school, the sooner you make up your mind that you are going to make the switch, the better position you will be in to transfer successfully (that is, without having wasted valuable time and credits). The ideal point at which to make such a decision is *before* you register for classes at your two-year school; a counselor can help you plan your course work with an eye toward fulfilling the requirements needed for your major course of study.

Naturally, it is not always possible to plan your transferring strategy that far in advance, but keep in mind that the key to a successful transfer is *preparation,* and preparation takes time—time to think through your objectives and time to plan the right classes to begin work at that school.

As students face the prospect of transferring from a two-year to a four-year school, many thoughts and concerns about this complicated and often frustrating process race through their minds. Here are answers to the questions that are most frequently asked by transferring students.

Q Does every college and university accept transfer students?

A Most four-year institutions accept transfer students, but some do so more enthusiastically than others. Graduating from a community college is an advantage at, for example, Arizona State University and the University of Massachusetts Boston; both accept more community college transfer students than traditional freshmen. At the State University of New York at Albany, graduates of two-year transfer programs within the State University of New York System are given priority for upper-division (i.e., junior- and senior-level) vacancies.

Schools offering undergraduate work at the upper division only, such as Metropolitan State University in St. Paul, Minnesota, are especially receptive to transfer applications. On the other hand, some schools accept only a few transfer students; others refuse entrance to sophomores or those in their final year. Princeton University requires an "excellent academic record and particularly compelling reasons to transfer." Check the catalogs of several colleges for their transfer requirements before you make your final choice.

Q Do students who go directly from high school to a four-year college do better academically than transfer students from community colleges?

A On the contrary: some institutions report that transfers from two-year schools who persevere until graduation do *better* than those who started as freshmen.

Q Why is it so important that my two-year college be accredited?

A Four-year colleges and universities accept transfer credit only from schools formally recognized by a regional, national, or professional educational agency. This accreditation signifies that an institution or program of study meets or exceeds a minimum level of educational quality necessary for meeting stated educational objectives.

Q After enrolling at a four-year school, may I still make up necessary courses at a community college?

A Some institutions restrict credit after transfer to their own facilities. Others allow students to take a limited number of transfer courses after matriculation, depending on the subject matter. A few provide opportunities for cross-registration or dual enrollment, which means taking classes on more than one campus.

Q What do I need to do to transfer?

A First, send for your high school and college transcripts. Having chosen the school you wish to transfer to, check its admission requirements against your transcripts. If you find that you are admissible, file an application as early as possible before the deadline. Part of the process will be asking your former schools to send *official transcripts* to the admission office, i.e., not the copies you used in determining your admissibility.

Plan your transfer program with the head of your new department as soon as you have decided to transfer. Determine the recommended general education pattern and necessary preparation for your major. At your present school, take the courses you will need to meet transfer requirements for the new one.

Q What qualifies me for admission as a transfer student?

A Admission requirements for most four-year institutions vary. Depending on the reputation or popularity of the school and program you wish to enter, requirements may be quite selective and competitive. Usually, you will need to show satisfactory test scores, an academic record up to a certain standard, and completion of specific subject matter.

Transfer students can be eligible to enter a four-year school in a number of ways: by having been eligible for admission directly upon graduation from high school, by making up shortcomings in grades (or in subject matter not covered in high school) at a community college, or by satisfactory completion of necessary courses or credit hours at another postsecondary institution. Ordinarily, students coming from a community college or from another four-year institution must meet or exceed the receiving institution's standards for freshmen and show appropriate college-level course work taken since high school. Students who did not graduate from high school can present proof of proficiency through results on the General Educational Development (GED) test.

Q Are exceptions ever made for students who don't meet all the requirements for transfer?

A Extenuating circumstances, such as disability, low family income, refugee or veteran status, or athletic talent, may permit the special enrollment of students who would not otherwise be eligible but who demonstrate the potential for academic success. Consult the appropriate office—the Educational Opportunity Program, the disabled students' office, the athletic department, or the academic dean—to see whether an exception can be made in your case.

Q How far in advance do I need to apply for transfer?

A Some schools have a rolling admission policy, which means that they process transfer applications as they are received, all year long. With other schools, you must apply during the priority filing period, which can be up to a year before you wish to enter. Check the date with the admission office at your prospective campus.

Q Is it possible to transfer courses from several different institutions?

A Institutions ordinarily accept the courses that they consider transferable, regardless of the number of accredited schools involved. However, there is the danger of exceeding the maximum number of credit hours that can be transferred from all other schools or earned through credit by examination, extension courses, or correspondence courses. The limit placed on transfer credits varies from school to school, so read the catalog carefully to avoid taking courses you won't be able to use. To avoid duplicating courses, keep attendance at different campuses to a minimum.

Q What is involved in transferring from a semester system to a quarter or trimester system?

A In the semester system, the academic calendar is divided into two equal parts. The quarter system is more aptly named trimester, since the academic calendar is divided into three equal terms (not counting a summer session). To convert semester units into quarter units or credit hours, simply multiply the semester units by one and a half. Conversely, multiply quarter units by two thirds to come up with semester units. If you are used to a semester system of fifteen- to sixteen-week courses, the ten-week courses of the quarter system may seem to fly by.

Q Why might a course be approved for transfer credit by one four-year school but not by another?

A The beauty of postsecondary education in the United States lies in its variety. Entrance policies and graduation requirements are designed to reflect and serve each institution's mission. Because institutional policies vary so widely, schools may interpret the subject matter of a course from quite different points of view. Given that the granting of transfer credit indicates that a course is viewed as being, in effect, parallel to one offered by the receiving institution, it is easy to see how this might be the case at one university and not another.

Q Must I take a foreign language to transfer?

A Foreign language proficiency is often required for admission to a four-year institution; such proficiency also often figures in certain majors or in the general education pattern. At Princeton University, for example, where foreign language proficiency is a graduation requirement, all students must demonstrate it by the end of their junior year.

However, at the University of Southern California and other schools, the foreign language competence necessary for admission can be certified before entrance. Often, two or three years of a single language in high school will do the trick. Find out if scores received on Advanced Placement examinations, placement examinations given by the foreign language department, or SAT II Subject Tests will be accepted in lieu of college course work.

Q Will the school to which I'm transferring accept pass/no pass, pass/fail, or credit/no credit grades in lieu of letter grades?

A Usually, a limit is placed on the number of these courses you can transfer, and there may be other restrictions as well. If you want to use other-than-letter grades for the fulfillment of general education requirements or lower-division (freshman and sophomore) preparation for the major, check with the receiving institution.

Q Which is more important for transfer—my grade point average or my course completion pattern?

A Some schools believe that your past grades indicate academic potential and overshadow prior preparation for a specific degree program. Others require completion of certain introductory courses before transfer to prepare you for upper-division work in your major. In any case, appropriate course selection will cut down the time to graduation and increase your chances of making a successful transfer.

Q What happens to my credits if I change majors?

A If you change majors after admission, your transferable course credit should remain fairly intact. However, because you may need extra or different preparation for your new major, some of the courses you've taken may now be useful only as electives. The need for additional lower-level preparation may mean you're staying longer at your new school than you originally planned. On the other hand, you may already have taken courses that count toward your new major as part of the university's general education pattern.

Returning to School: Advice for Adult Students

Sandra Cook, Ph.D.

Many adults think about returning to school for a long time without taking any action. One purpose of this article is to help the "thinkers" finally make some decisions by examining what is keeping them from action. Another purpose is to describe not only some of the difficulties and obstacles that adult students may face when returning to school but also tactics for coping with them.

If you have been thinking about going back to college, and believing that you are the only person your age contemplating college, you should know that approximately 7 million adult students are currently enrolled in higher education institutions. This number represents 50 percent of total higher education enrollments. The majority of adult students are enrolled at two-year colleges.

There are many reasons why adult students choose to attend a two-year college. Studies have shown that the three most important criteria that adult students consider when choosing a college are location, cost, and availability of the major or program desired. Most two-year colleges are public institutions that serve a geographic district, making them readily accessible to the community. Costs at most two-year colleges are far less than at other types of higher education institutions. For many students who plan to pursue a bachelor's degree, completing their first two years of college at a community college is an affordable means to that end. If you are interested in an academic program that will transfer to a four-year institution, most two-year colleges offer the "general education" courses that comprise most freshman and sophomore years. If you are interested in a vocational or technical program, two-year colleges excel in providing this type of training.

UNCERTAINTY, CHOICE, AND SUPPORT

There are three different "stages" in the process of adults returning to school. The first stage is uncertainty. Do I really want to go back to school? What will my friends or family think? Can I compete with those 18-year-old whiz kids? Am I too old? The second stage is choice. Once the decision to return has been made, you must choose where you will attend. There are many criteria to use in making this decision. The third stage is support. You have just added another role to your already-too-busy life. There are, however, strategies that will help you accomplish your goals—perhaps not without struggle, but with grace and humor. Let's look at each of these stages.

Uncertainty

Why are you thinking about returning to school? Is it to:

- fulfill a dream that had to be delayed?
- become more educationally well-rounded?
- fill an intellectual void in your life?

These reasons focus on *personal growth*.

If you are returning to school to:

- meet people and make friends
- attain and enjoy higher social status and prestige among friends, relatives, and associates
- understand/study a cultural heritage, or
- have a medium in which to exchange ideas,

you are interested in *social and cultural opportunities*.

If you are like most adult students, you want to:

- qualify for a new occupation
- enter or reenter the job market
- increase earnings potential, or
- qualify for a more challenging position in the same field of work.

You are seeking *career growth*.

Understanding the reasons why you want to go back to school is an important step in setting your educational goals and will help you to establish some criteria for selecting a college. However, don't delay your decision because you have not been able to clearly define your motives. Many times, these aren't clear until you have already begun the process, and they may change as you move through your college experience.

Assuming that you agree that additional education will be of benefit to you, what is it that keeps you from returning to school? You may have a litany of excuses running through your mind:

- I don't have time.

- I can't afford it.
- I'm too old to learn.
- My friends will think I'm crazy.
- The teachers will be younger than me.
- My family can't survive without me to take care of them every minute.
- I'll be X years old when I finish.
- I'm afraid.
- I don't know what to expect.

And that is just what these are—excuses. You can make school, like anything else in your life, a priority or not. If you really want to return, you can. The more you understand your motivation for returning to school and the more you understand what excuses are keeping you from taking action, the easier your task will be.

If you think you don't have time: The best way to decide how attending class and studying can fit into your schedule is to keep track of what you do with your time each day for several weeks. Completing a standard time-management grid (each day is plotted out by the half hour) is helpful for visualizing how your time is spent. For each 3-credit-hour class you take, you will need to find 3 hours for class plus 6 to 9 hours for reading-studying-library time. This study time should be spaced evenly throughout the week, not loaded up on one day. It is not possible to learn or retain the material that way. When you examine your grid, see where there are activities that could be replaced with school and study time. You may decide to give up your bowling league or some time in front of the TV. Try not to give up sleeping, and don't cut out every moment of free time. There are also a number of smaller ways to divert time to school. Here are some suggestions that have come from adults who have returned to school:

- Enroll in a time-management workshop. It helps you rethink how you use your time.
- Don't think you have to take more than one course at a time. You may eventually want to work up to taking more, but consider starting with one. (It is more than you are taking now!)
- If you have a family, start assigning those household chores that you usually do to them—and don't redo what they do.
- Use your lunch hour or commuting time for reading.

If you think you cannot afford it: As mentioned earlier, two-year colleges are extremely affordable. If you cannot afford the tuition, look into the various financial aid options. Most federal and state funds are available to full- and part-time students. Loans are also available. While many people prefer not to accumulate a debt for school, these same people will think nothing of taking out a loan to buy a car. After five or six years, which is the better investment? Adult students who work should look into whether their company has a tuition-reimbursement policy. There are also an increasing number of private scholarships, available through foundations, service organizations, and clubs, that are focused on adult learners. Your public library and a college financial aid adviser are two excellent sources for reference materials regarding financial aid.

If you think you are too old to learn: This is pure myth. A number of studies have shown that adult learners perform as well as or better than traditional-age students.

If you are afraid your friends will think you're crazy: Who cares? Maybe they will, maybe they won't. Usually, they will admire your courage and be just a little jealous of your ambition (although they'll never tell you that). Follow your dreams, not theirs.

If you are concerned because the teachers or students will be younger than you: Don't be. The age differences that may be apparent in other settings evaporate in the classroom. If anything, an adult in the classroom strikes fear into the hearts of some 18-year-olds because adults have been known to be prepared, ask questions, be truly motivated, and be there to learn!

If you think your family will have a difficult time surviving while you are in school: If you have done everything for them up to now, they might struggle. Consider this an opportunity to help them become independent and self-sufficient. Your family can only make you feel guilty if you let them. You are not abandoning them; you are becoming an educational role model. When you are happy and working toward your goals, everyone benefits. Admittedly, it sometimes takes time for them to realize this. For single parents, there are schools that have begun to offer support groups, child care, and cooperative babysitting.

If you're appalled at the thought of being X years old when you graduate in Y years: How old will you be in Y years if you don't go back to school?

If you are afraid or don't know what to expect: Know that these are natural feelings when one encounters any new situation. Adult students find that their fears usually dissipate once they begin classes. Fear of trying is usually the biggest roadblock to the reentry process.

No doubt you have dreamed up a few more reasons for not making the decision to return to school. Keep in mind that what you are doing is making up excuses, and you are using these excuses to release you from the obligation to make a decision about your life. The thought of returning to college can be scary. Anytime anyone ventures into unknown territory, there is a risk, but taking risks is a necessary component of personal and professional growth. It is your life, and you alone are responsible for making the decisions that determine its course. Education is an investment in your future.

Choice

Once you have decided to go back to school, your next task is to decide where to go. If your educational goals are well defined (e.g., you want to pursue a degree in order to change careers), then your task is a bit easier. But even if your educational goals are still evolving, do not deter your return. Many students who enter higher education with a specific major in mind change that major at least once.

Most students who attend a public two-year college choose the community college in the district in which they live. This is generally the closest and least expensive option if the school offers the programs you want. If you are planning to begin your education at a two-year college and then transfer to a four-year school, there are distinct advantages to choosing your four-year school early. Many community and four-year colleges have "articulation" agreements that designate what credits from the two-year school will transfer to the four-year college and how. Some four-year institutions accept an associate degree as equivalent to the freshman and sophomore years, regardless of the courses you have taken. Some four-year schools accept two-year college work only on a course-by-course basis. If you can identify which school you will transfer to, you can know in advance exactly how your two-year credits will apply, preventing an unexpected loss of credit or time.

Each institution of higher education is distinctive. Your goal in choosing a college is to come up with the best student-institution fit—matching your needs with the offerings and characteristics of the school. The first step in choosing a college is to determine what criteria are most important to you in attaining your educational goals. Location, cost, and program availability are the three main factors that influence an adult student's college choice. In considering location, don't forget that some colleges have conveniently located branch campuses. In considering cost, remember to explore your financial aid options before ruling out an institution because of its tuition. Program availability should include not only the major in which you are interested, but also whether or not classes in that major are available when you can take them.

Some additional considerations beyond location, cost, and programs are:

- Does the school have a commitment to adult students and offer appropriate services, such as child care, tutoring, and advising?
- Are classes offered at times when you can take them?
- Are there academic options for adults, such as credit for life or work experience, credit by examination (including CLEP and PEP), credit for military service, or accelerated programs?
- Is the faculty sensitive to the needs of adult learners?

Once you determine which criteria are vital in your choice of an institution, you can begin to narrow your choices. There are myriad ways for you to locate the information you desire. Many urban newspapers publish a "School Guide" several times a year in which colleges and universities advertise to an adult student market. In addition, schools themselves publish catalogs, class schedules, and promotional materials that contain much of the information you need, and they are yours for the asking. Many colleges sponsor information sessions and open houses that allow you to visit the campus and ask questions. An appointment with an adviser is a good way to assess the fit between you and the institution. Be sure to bring your questions with you to your interview.

Support

Once you have made the decision to return to school and have chosen the institution that best meets your needs, take some additional steps to ensure your success during your crucial first semester. Take advantage of institutional support and build some social support systems of your own. Here are some ways of doing just that:

- Plan to participate in any orientation programs. These serve the threefold purpose of providing you with a great deal of important information, familiarizing you with the campus and its facilities, and giving you the opportunity to meet and begin networking with other students.
- Take steps to deal with any academic weaknesses. Take mathematics and writing placement tests if you have reason to believe you may need some extra help in these areas. It is not uncommon for adult students to need a math refresher course or a program to help alleviate math anxiety. Ignoring a weakness won't make it go away.
- Look into adult reentry programs. Many institutions offer adults workshops focusing on ways to improve study skills, textbook reading, test-taking, and time-management skills.
- Build new support networks by joining an adult student organization, making a point of meeting other adult students through workshops, or actively seeking out a "study buddy" in each class—that invaluable friend who shares and understands your experience.
- You can incorporate your new status as "student" into your family life. Doing your homework with your children at a designated "homework time" is a valuable family activity and reinforces the importance of education.
- Make sure you take a reasonable course load in your first semester. It is far better to have some extra time on your hands and to succeed magnificently than to spend the entire semester on the brink of a breakdown. Also, whenever possible, try to focus your first courses not only on requirements, but also in areas of personal interest.
- Faculty members, advisers, and student affairs personnel are there to help you during difficult times—let them assist you as often as necessary.

After completing your first semester, you will probably look back in wonder at why you thought going back to school was so imposing. Certainly, it's not without its occasional exasperations. But, as with life, keeping things in perspective and maintaining your sense of humor make the difference between just coping and succeeding brilliantly.

Sandra Cook, Ph.D., is Director of the University Advising Center at San Diego State University.

Honors: An A+ Education

Dr. Joan Digby

WHO ARE HONORS STUDENTS?

If you are a strong student filled with ideas, longing for creative expression, and ready to take on career-shaping challenges, then an honors education is just for you. Honors programs and colleges offer some of the finest undergraduate degrees available in American colleges and do it with students in mind. The essence of honors is personal attention, top faculty members, enlightening seminars, illuminating study-travel experiences, research options, career-building internships-all designed to enhance a classic education and prepare you for life achievements. And here's an eye-opening bonus: honors programs and colleges may reward your past academic performance by giving you scholarships that will help you pay for your higher education.

Take your choice of institutions: community college, state or private four-year college, or large research university. There are honors opportunities in each. What they share in common is an unqualified commitment to academic excellence. Honors education teaches students to think and write clearly, to be excited by ideas, and to become independent, creative, self-confident learners. It prepares exceptional students for professional choices in every imaginable sphere of life: arts and sciences, engineering, business, health, education, medicine, theater, music, film, journalism, media, law, politics—invent your own professional goal, and honors will guide you to it! There are hundreds of honors programs and honors colleges around the country. Whichever one you choose, you can be sure to enjoy an extraordinarily fulfilling undergraduate education.

Who are you? Perhaps a high school junior making out your first college applications, a community college student seeking to transfer to a four-year college, or possibly a four-year college student doing better than you had expected. You might be an international student, a varsity athlete, captain of the debate team, or second violin in the campus orchestra. Whether you are the first person in your family to attend college or an adult with a grown family seeking a new career, honors might well be right for you. Honors programs admit students with every imaginable background and educational goal.

How does honors satisfy them and give them something special? Read what students in some of our member programs say. Although they refer to particular colleges, their experiences are typical of what students find exciting about honors education on hundreds of campuses around the country.

"Honors is not just a class or a degree but rather a family that you can count on. I was an out-of-state student, not knowing anyone, and honors helped me [make] the drastic change from high school student to college scholar. Through its educators as well as its students, honors has changed my life for the better."

Chris Whitford
Business major
University of Maine, Orono

"Having interested people who remember my name and monitor my progress made a big difference to me. . .. The crossover of disciplines is amazing. I use notes from philosophy class in botany and ecology. The text in ecology uses terms I studied in botany, and they all refer to Aristotle and algebra. Finishing this program has made it a part of me, and it will alter the outcome of my life."

Andre Chenault
Tulsa Community College

"Although the structure of my engineering courses makes involvement in the Honors Program difficult, my honors classes have been the perfect break from my major. Rather than sitting in yet another classroom with 20+ students being told how things are, through honors I get to sit in a classroom with 16 or fewer students and actually discuss the material. Discussion and paper assignments in my honors courses have kept me on my toes."

Colin Smith
Villanova University

"Through engaging discussions and readings in seminars like African Literature and Politics and Literature of the Apocalypse, Christ College has challenged me to examine my view of the world by introducing me to different ideas, cultures, beliefs, and lifestyles."

Gretchen Eelkema
Chemistry and French major
Valparaiso University, Christ College

"I went to an arts high school that allowed me to participate in . . music, theater, and the visual arts. . . I had trouble finding a college that would allow me to create a specialized major (and that would be within my budget!). I gave up and settled on Cal State Fullerton as a temporary solution . . . I was also accepted into their Honors Program and I soon discovered that it was the best thing I could have done. . . . To my surprise [my honors director] was an art professor and was excited to create a major specialized to my interests. Unexpectedly Cal State Fullerton became the perfect school for me, but it could not have come about without the special attention I received in the Honors Program."

Joy Shannon
College of the Arts, California State University, Fullerton

These portraits don't tell the whole story, but they should give you a sense of what it means to be part of an honors program or honors college. Outside of class, honors students often run track, run the student government, and write the college newspaper. They are everywhere on campus: in plays and concerts, in laboratories and libraries, in sororities and fraternities. Some are clear about their majors and professions; others need direction and advice. One of the great strengths of honors programs is that they are nurturing environments that encourage students to be well-rounded and help students make life choices.

WHAT IS AN HONORS PROGRAM?

An honors program is a sequence of courses designed specifically to encourage independent and creative learning. Whether you want to attend a large state university or a private one, a small or large four-year college, or your local community college, you can make the decision to join an honors program. For more than half a century, honors education, given definition by the National Collegiate Honors Council, has been an institution on American campuses. Although honors programs have many different designs, there are typical components. In two-year colleges, the programs often concentrate on special versions of general education courses and may have individual capstone projects that come out of the students' special interest. In four-year colleges and universities, honors programs are generally designed for students of almost every major in every college on campus. In some cases, they are given additional prominence as honors colleges. Whether a program or a college, honors is most often structured as a general education or core component followed by advanced courses (often called colloquia or seminars) and a thesis or creative project, which may or may not be in the departmental major. Almost always, honors curriculum is incorporated within whatever number of credits is required of every student for graduation. Honors very rarely requires students to take additional credits. Students who complete an honors program or honors college curriculum frequently receive transcript and diploma notations as well as certificates, medallions, or other citations at graduation ceremonies.

While researching honors programs and colleges, you will begin to see typical patterns of academic programming, and that is where you must choose the program or college best suited to your own needs. In every case, catering to the student as an individual plays a central role in honors course design. Most honors classes are small (under 20 students); most are discussion-oriented, giving students a chance to present their own interpretations of ideas and even teach a part of the course. Many classes are interdisciplinary, which means they are taught by faculty members from two or more departments, providing different perspectives on a subject. All honors classes help students develop and articulate their own perspectives by cultivating both verbal and written style. They help students mature intellectually, preparing them to engage in their own explorations and research. Some programs even extend the options for self-growth to study abroad and internships in science, government, the arts, or business related to the major. Other programs encourage or require community service as part of the honors experience. In every case, honors is an experiential education that deepens classroom learning and extends far beyond.

Despite their individual differences, all honors programs and honors colleges rely on faculty members who enjoy working with bright, independent students. The ideal honors faculty members are open-minded and encouraging master teachers. They want to see their students achieve at their highest capacity, and they are glad to spend time with students in discussions and laboratories, on field trips and at conferences, or online in e-mail. They often influence career decisions, provide inspiring models, and remain friends long after they have served as thesis advisers.

WHERE ARE HONORS PROGRAMS AND HONORS COLLEGES LOCATED?

Because honors programs and honors colleges include students from many different departments or colleges, they usually have their own offices and space on campus. Some have their own buildings. Most programs have honors centers or lounges where students gather together for informal conversations, luncheons, discussions, lectures, and special projects.

Many honors students have cultivated strong personal interests that have nothing to do with classes; they may be experts at using the Internet; they may be fine artists or poets, musicians or racing car enthusiasts. Some volunteer in hospitals or do landscape gardening to pay for college. Many work in retail stores and catering. Some inline skate and others collect antique watches. When they get together in honors lounges, there is always an interesting mixture of ideas.

In general, honors provides an environment in which students feel free to talk about their passionate interests and ideas, knowing they will find good listeners and sometimes arguers. There is no end to conversations among honors students. Like many students in honors, you may feel a great relief in finding a sympathetic group that respects your intelligence and creativity. In honors, you can be eccentric, you can be yourself! Some lifelong friendships, even marriages, are the result of social relationships developed in honors programs. Of course you will make other friends in classes, clubs, and elsewhere on campus, even through e-mail! But the honors program will build strong bonds too.

In the honors center, whether program or college, you will also find the honors director or dean. The honors director often serves as a personal adviser to all of the students in the program. Many programs also have peer counselors and mentors who are upperclass honors students and know the ropes from a student's perspective and experience. Some have specially assigned honors advisers who guide honors students through their degrees, assist in registration, and answer every imaginable question. The honors office area usually is a good place to meet people, ask questions, and solve problems.

ARE YOU READY FOR HONORS?

Admission to honors programs and honors colleges is generally based on a combination of several factors: high school or previous college grades, SAT or ACT scores, personal essay, and extracurricular achievements. To stay in honors, students need to maintain a certain GPA (grade point average) and show progress toward the completion of the specific honors program or college requirements. Since you have probably exceeded admissions standards all along, maintaining your GPA will not be as big a problem as it sounds. Your faculty members and your honors director are there to help you succeed in the program. Most honors programs have very low attrition rates, because students enjoy classes and do well. You have every reason to believe that you can make the grade.

Of course, you must be careful about how you budget your time for studying. Honors encourages well-rounded, diversified students, and you should play a sport if you want to, work at the radio station, join the clubs that interest you, or pledge a sorority or fraternity. You might find a job in the food service or library that will help you pay for your car expenses, and that also is reasonable. But remember, each activity takes time, and you must strike a balance that will leave you enough time to do your homework, prepare for seminar discussions, do your research, and do well on exams. Choose the extracurricular activities and work opportunities on campus that attract you, but never let them overshadow your primary purpose-to be a student.

Sometimes even the very best students who apply for honors admissions are frightened by the thought of speaking in front of a group, giving seminar papers, or writing a thesis. But if you understand how the programs work, you will see that there is nothing to be frightened about. The basis of honors is confidence in the student and building the student's self-confidence. Once you are admitted to an honors program, you have already demonstrated your academic achievement in high school or college classes. Once in an honors program, you will learn how to formulate and structure ideas so that you can apply critical judgment to sets of facts and opinions. In small seminar classes, you practice discussion and arguments, so by the time you come to the senior thesis or project, the method is second nature. For most honors students, the senior thesis, performance, or portfolio presentation is the project that gives them the greatest fulfillment and pride. In many honors programs and colleges, students present their work either to other students or to faculty members in their major departments. Students often present their work at regional and national honors conferences. Some students even publish their work jointly with their faculty mentors. These are great achievements, and they come naturally with the training. There is nothing to be afraid of. Just do it! Honors will make you ready for life.

Dr. Joan Digby is Director of the Honors Program at Long Island University, C.W. Post Campus.

The Expanding Role of America's Career Colleges

Most of us have been told all of our lives, "If you don't go to college, you'll never get a good job." Many of us have been conditioned to equate a traditional four-year college degree with a guarantee of professional success. This is not necessarily the case. While we are currently enjoying a time of unprecedented prosperity, it was only a few years ago that a college degree meant little, if anything, in and of itself. During the downsizing of years past, degree holders were standing in the same unemployment lines as the less educated.

Most employers look upon a person with a college degree as a person with persistence and stamina. With a degree as a credential, the newly graduated enter the workforce with a reasonably proven ability to learn but often without a marketable skill. To overcome that pitfall, many college graduates attend career colleges to expand their experience and learn skills that will get them a job. In fact, on many career college campuses, more than 40 percent of the students already have their baccalaureate degrees. This is a trend that should continue.

Recent statistics indicate that nearly 65 percent of the workforce in this country is made up of skilled laborers. Only 20 percent of that same workforce are considered professionals. These figures show that the majority of this nation's new jobs in the next decade will require strong technical skills—the exact type of skills taught in this country's career colleges.

If you lack the time and financial resources to spend four years beyond high school in a traditional college or university, a career college is an excellent alternative. Whether this choice is made directly out of high school or after spending a few years in the workforce, successful completion of the program is not likely to be affected.

In good economic times or bad, you will always have a distinct advantage if you have a demonstrable skill and can be immediately productive while continuing to learn and improve. If you know how to use technology, work collaboratively, and find creative solutions, you will always be in demand. Fewer than half of the students who start at a traditional college will ever obtain their degree. One half or two thirds of a degree is of little value; all the time and financial resources invested in this situation produce no dividend because they do not develop marketable skills.

Like most of us, you will spend more of your waking hours in the workplace than anywhere else. If you don't like what you are doing—the financial, emotional, and spiritual rewards are not there—it is likely that you will be unhappy and not do well. As you begin to decide on how to prepare for the future, consider the following guidelines:

- Identify what interests you, and consider careers that relate to these interests
- Seek the counsel of individuals working in the jobs in which you are interested
- Try to combine school and real-world work experience during your training
- Understand that skills are transferable, and your initial job choice may prepare you for other opportunities

Career colleges offer scores of opportunities to learn the technical skills required by many of today's and tomorrow's top jobs. This is especially true in the areas of computer and information technology, health care, and hospitality (culinary arts, travel and tourism, and hotel and motel management). Career colleges range in size from those with a handful of students to universities with thousands enrolled. They are located in every state in the nation and share one common objective—to prepare students for a successful career in the world of work through a focused, intensive curriculum. America's career colleges are privately owned and operated for-profit companies. Instead of using tax support to operate, career colleges pay taxes. Because career colleges are businesses, they must be responsive to the workforce needs of their communities or they will cease to exist.

When choosing an institution of higher education, you should consider the following:

- What percentage of the students who begin programs actually graduate?
- Of those who graduate, how many get jobs in their chosen career, and how long does it take to be hired?
- Is there full-service placement assistance available at the school?

Today's jobs demand skills that are ever changing. In the future , this demand will be even greater. The education system necessary to provide you with the skills you need exists; it is made up of this country's career and technical colleges.

Historically Black Colleges and Universities: An Academic Evolution

Levirn Hill

Years ago, African Americans attended black colleges and universities because they had no choice. Students today attend black colleges and universities for very different reasons. Inexpensive and academically rigorous, they keep alive the history and traditions of the African-American experience while at the same time welcoming an increasing number of students of other races and backgrounds into their community. From highly competitive universities offering undergraduate and graduate programs to noncompetitive two-year colleges with open admissions, historically or predominantly black colleges and universities remain the best-kept secret in higher education.

DIVERSE STUDENT POPULATIONS

While the original mission of Historically Black Colleges and Universities (HBCUs) was the education of African Americans, these institutions of higher education have expanded their mission to recruit and educate other-race students as well. Several of these institutions offer other-race scholarships.

RIGOROUS ACADEMIC PROGRAMS

HBCUs, in their variety, can meet the needs of every student whatever their previous level of academic preparation. Black colleges and universities range from highly competitive comprehensive universities with Phi Beta Kappa Chapters to noncompetitive institutions with open admissions. Forty percent of black graduate students who earn doctorates received their undergraduate training from an HBCU. The vast majority of black students admitted to American medical schools are graduates of black colleges.

MORE THAN AN EDUCATION

Many of the students considered to be the cream of high school students choose "Ebony League" or black institutions of higher education for their rigorous academic programs and their caring environments. Other students choose these schools for the positive black role models, while still others want to experience the rich black culture and social life while getting their college degrees.

SECOND CHANCE PROGRAMS

Many HBCUs have open admissions policies, which give students a second chance at a college education. Students who have completed their high school education or received the GED but do not meet college admission requirements can be accepted at these schools. I received a second chance through the remedial program, which Virginia Union University offered to a limited number of students. Because I showed promise as a student, I was accepted at the University as a nonmatriculated student. I took remedial courses during my first semester to meet entrance requirements needed to matriculate. I went on to receive my undergraduate and graduate degrees at a majority university that had previously denied my application.

LOWER COSTS

Tuition, room, and board are often two to three times less expensive than Ivy League or Big Ten schools with comparative academic or athletic programs. For these and many other reasons, students choose black colleges and universities to get their college education.

Levirn Hill is the author of Black American Colleges and Universities.

OPTIONS OPTIONS OPTIONS

The Military and Higher Education

The first part of this section offers an overview of the opportunities that exist today for students who wish to explore the possibility of financing their higher education by participating in ROTC or attending a service academy. This information is provided in order to help students and families make well-informed decisions about this important investment. The second part of this section presents, in the Army's own words and photos, a detailed description of one military financial aid option—the Army ROTC Program.

The Military as a Source of Financial Aid

One of the major problems facing families today is how to come up with the money to meet college expenses. Many people are unaware that the military is a source of financial aid. Its focus, however, is quite different from that of other sources: military financial aid programs do not consider need but are either a payment for training or a reward for service. This large source of money (about $1 billion each year) can prove quite helpful in assisting a wide range of students. The military financial aid programs are by far the largest source of college money that is not based on need.

HOW THE MILITARY PROVIDES FINANCIAL AID

One form of military financial aid is college money for officer candidates: tuition assistance and monthly pay in return for the student's promise to serve as an officer in the Army, Navy, Air Force, Marine Corps, Coast Guard, or Merchant Marine. Most of this money is awarded to high school seniors who go directly to college. The main benefits are reduced or free tuition and $100 to $150 per month if the student is enrolled in the Reserve Officers' Training Corps (ROTC) Scholarship Program or free tuition, room and board, and $500 per month if the student is enrolled at one of the service academies. ROTC units are located on college campuses and provide military training for a few hours a week. The five service academies (West Point, Annapolis, the Air Force Academy, the Coast Guard Academy, and the Merchant Marine Academy) are military establishments that combine education and training for the armed forces. For those already in college, financial aid is obtainable through ROTC scholarships for enrolled students or special commissioning programs.

By participating in ROTC, attending a service academy, or enrolling in a special program for military commissioning, a student not only can become an officer but also can become eligible for financial aid, thus turning the dream of an affordable college education into a reality. The military trains students to become officers and pays them to learn at the same time. (A detailed look at one such program, that of the Army ROTC, appears following this article.)

IS OFFICER TRAINING RIGHT FOR YOU?

Military scholarship programs exist largely to provide money to college students as they go through officer training, and, in return, the military receives from the students a commitment to serve in the armed forces. The military's goal is to produce, through this method of attracting outstanding young men and women, "entry-level" officers who are well educated both academically and in the workings of the military itself. Obviously, you would not be the ideal candidate for one of these programs if you had moral or religious reservations about serving your country as a military officer. You also should not apply if the program's main appeal for you is the money. The financial benefits may be very important, but their attraction should be balanced by genuine feelings on your part that you will seriously consider becoming an officer, you will undertake military training with a positive attitude, and you will be flexible and open-minded about your plans. Applicants are typically young men or women who are willing to serve at least four or five years as officers in exchange for four years of a good education at little or no cost.

First: Are You the Military Type?

At the outset, it is essential that you determine whether or not you are cut out to be in the military. Take a personal inventory: What are you like? How do you relate to others? What kind of organization do you want to be part of?

- Do you consider yourself intelligent, well-rounded, energetic, organized, and somewhat athletic? Are you a serious student with good grades in precollege courses and an aptitude for science and math?
- Are you outgoing? Does leadership appeal to you? Do you work well with others, both in groups and in one-on-one situations? Can you willingly take direction from others?
- Can you exist in a structured and disciplined environment? Do you have strong feelings of patriotism? Are you willing to defend your country in a time of war?
- If "yes" is your answer to most of these questions, you are the type of individual the military services are interested in. Even more important, you may be the type of person who can be comfortable with the military's lifestyle. Although there are many different types of military officers—from the quiet intellectual to the extroverted athlete—the average officer usually conforms to a set of general characteristics: a mixture of certain personal traits and a willingness to be part of and contribute to a large and very structured organization.

Second: What Kind of Military Training Might Be Appropriate for You?

If your personal inventory revealed you to be at least somewhat the "military type," your next step is to see which of the programs offered by the different services is best for you. Now ask yourself which of the following most closely describes your feelings at present.

1. I have firsthand knowledge of military service. I can picture myself as an officer, perhaps even a career officer. I have experience with discipline, both in taking and in

giving orders. I plan to major in science or engineering while I'm in college. Obtaining a top-quality education at very low cost is very important to me.

2. Service in the military is of interest to me. I don't have much direct experience, but I'm willing to learn more. I'm not sure whether I'm ready to immerse myself completely in a military environment as a college student. I've done well in math and science, but I may decide to major in another field. I can look forward to the prospect of four years of service as an officer before deciding whether to stay on. A tuition scholarship is appealing, and it would widen the range of colleges that are within my reach.
3. I don't have a negative attitude toward the military, but it's not something I know much about. I might be interested in giving it a look. Studying math and science may not be for me; my interests are probably in other areas. I'm concerned about paying for college, but my parents could help me for at least one or two years.
4. I don't think I'm the military type, but actually I haven't thought that much about it. I doubt if I would go for the discipline. Certainly, I wouldn't want to commit to anything until I've been in college for a few years and can see my choices more clearly. I might be able to see myself serving in the military—if I could get duty that matches my academic interests. I could use a scholarship, but I plan to seek financial aid through other sources.

When you've determined which of the foregoing paragraphs mostly closely describes your attitude toward military service, review the following items, the numbers of which generally relate to the numbers above.

1. Think seriously about competing for an appointment to a service academy. (You must be nominated by an official source, usually your congressional representative. Each member of Congress has a set number of nominees he or she can recommend for admission. Neither political influence nor a personal relationship with the member of Congress is necessary.)
2. Plan to enter the national ROTC four-year scholarship competition.
3. Join an ROTC unit in college and see what the military is like. Scholarship opportunities are available if you decide to stay on.
4. Don't get involved with a military program yet, but keep the service in mind for possible entrance after two years of college.
5. It should go without saying that it's best to avoid extreme discrepancies between the two lists. For example, if description number 4 applies, a military academy or even the four-year scholarship is probably not right for you. It would be far wiser to choose item three or four. Later on, after you are enrolled in college, you might find that certain aspects of the military complement your academic interests and that the military lifestyle is something you can adapt to. If, on the other hand, description number 1 suits you, it will be worth your while to pursue either the ROTC scholarship or service academy option when you graduate from high school. If you are this far along in your thinking about a possible future in the military, you can take advantage of both the financial benefits the services offer and the head start you will get toward a possible military career by trying for an officer training program.

Preparation While in High School

Enrolling in a precollege program while you're attending high school will improve your chances of winning a four-year ROTC scholarship or receiving an appointment to a service academy. For the most part, the services don't require that you take specific subjects (the exceptions are the Coast Guard Academy and the Merchant Marine Academy). Nonetheless, the Army, Navy, Air Force, and Marine Corps all stress the importance of a good high school curriculum. They suggest the following: 4 years of English, 4 years of math (through calculus), 2 years of a foreign language, 2 years of laboratory science, and 1 year of American history.

Being an active member of your school and community is also important, as is holding leadership positions in sports and/or other extracurricular activities. If your high school has a Junior ROTC unit, join the detachment; doing so could improve your chances of being selected for an ROTC scholarship or admitted to a service academy.

Standardized Tests

For entrance into the academies and most other colleges, be prepared to take the SAT I or ACT, used by college admission offices as one of the measures of a prospective college student's academic potential. For more details, see Surviving Standardized Tests.

Who Is a Successful Candidate?

A fictional though typical winner of a four-year ROTC scholarship or an appointment to a service academy exhibits certain kinds of characteristics. That person (whom we will call John Doe):

- Follows a curriculum that includes 4 years of English, 4 years of math, 3 or 4 years of a foreign language, 2 years of laboratory science, and 2 years of history—with some of the courses at the honors level. John maintains a B+ average and ranks in the top 15 percent of his class. On the SAT I, he received scores of 610 verbal and 640 math (based on original, rather than recentered, scores). (Had he taken the ACT, his composite score would have been 28.)
- Is a member of the National Honor Society. He holds an office in student government and is a candidate for Boys State. John has a leadership position on the student newspaper and is a member of both the debate panel and math club. He is active in varsity athletics and is cocaptain of the basketball team.
- Is one of the top all-around students in his class and makes a positive contribution to both his school and community. He is described as intelligent, industrious, well-organized, self-confident, concerned, and emotionally mature.
- The services believe and expect that a person with John Doe's abilities and traits will do well in college—in both academic and military training—and will also have great potential to become a productive officer after graduation.

Facts About the Officer Training Programs

Officer Pay and Benefits. As a military officer, you will be paid the standard rate for all members of the armed forces of your rank and length of service. In addition to your salary, significant fringe benefits include free medical care and a generous retirement plan.

The Difference Between a Regular and a Reserve Officer. Officer training programs offer Regular and Reserve commissions. However, all initial commissions after September 30, 1996, have been Reserve only. You should be aware of the difference between the two designations.

When commissioned as a Regular officer, you are on a career path in the military. In the event that you choose not to serve at least twenty years, you must write a letter asking if you can resign your commission. Such requests are normally accepted once you have completed your minimum service obligation. If you plan to make the military your career, it is a definite advantage to be a Regular officer.

As a Reserve officer, you contract for a specific term, for example, four years of active duty in the case of an ROTC scholarship. Nearly all Air Force ROTC second lieutenants are in this category, along with about 85 percent of Army ROTC graduates. If you want to remain on active duty after your initial obligation, you must request to sign on for a second term.

There is another category of Reserve officer—those who are assigned to the Reserve Forces rather than to active duty. About 50 percent of the officers who are commissioned through the Army ROTC are given orders to the National Guard or Army Reserve. After attending the Basic Course for six months, these officers join the Reserve Forces to finish their obligated service as "weekend warriors." In this case, the time commitment is 7½ years in the Reserve, the first 5½ years involving drills one weekend per month and two weeks of active duty per year. During the last two years of obligated service, these officers are transferred to inactive Reserve status, in which drills are not required.

Women Officers. Virtually all of the officer training programs are open to women. With the exception of differences in height and weight standards and lower minimums on the physical fitness test, the eligibility rules, benefits, and obligations are the same for both genders. When it comes to duty assignments, however, there is a notable difference between men and women. Depending on the branch of the service, this law restricts the types of jobs women can choose. Other than the limits imposed by certain combat restrictions for women, the position of women within the military has improved considerably in the past ten years. There are variations among the services, but overall, women make up between 8 and 20 percent of the officers, and they are gradually but steadily moving into the higher-ranking positions.

Medical Requirements. Candidates for an ROTC scholarship must pass a medical examination. You need take only one physical, even if you apply for more than one type of scholarship. Medical standards vary considerably and can be quite complicated. Nevertheless, it is worth having an idea of the general medical requirements at the outset, particularly the eyesight and height and weight rules. Keep in mind, too, that medical standards change periodically, and some of them may be waived under certain conditions. (Service academy medical requirements for the Army and Navy/Marine Corps are the same as the ROTC requirements; the Air Force requirements are also the same except that flight training has its own height and vision standards; and the Coast Guard and Merchant Marine medical requirements are similar to Naval ROTC, except that eyesight standards for the Merchant Marine are more lenient.)

THE ROTC PROGRAMS

The predominant way for a college student to become a military officer is through the Reserve Officers' Training Corps program. ROTC is offered by the Army, Navy, and Air Force, while students taking the Marine Corps option participate in Naval ROTC. (The Coast Guard and Merchant Marine do not sponsor ROTC programs.)

Each service that has an ROTC program signs an agreement with a number of colleges to host a unit on their campuses. Each of these units has a commanding officer supervising a staff of active-duty officers and enlisted servicemembers who conduct the military training of cadets and midshipmen. This instruction includes regular class periods in which military science is taught as well as longer drill sessions in which students concentrate on developing leadership qualities through participation in military formations, physical fitness routines, and field exercises.

It is not necessary for you to attend a college that hosts a unit to participate in ROTC. You may attend any of the approved colleges that have a cross-enrollment contract and participate in ROTC at the host institution, provided you are accepted into the unit and you are able to arrange your schedule so that you have time to commute to the ROTC classes and drill sessions.

As a member of an ROTC unit, you are a part-time cadet or midshipman. You are required to wear a uniform and adhere to military discipline when you attend an ROTC class or drill, but not at other times. Since this involvement averages only about 4 hours per week, most of the time you will enjoy the same lifestyle as a typical college student. You must realize, however, that while you are an undergraduate, you are being trained to become an officer when you graduate. You therefore will have a number of obligations and responsibilities your classmates do not face. Nevertheless, the part-time nature of your military training is the major difference between participating in ROTC and enrolling at a service academy, where you are in a military environment 24 hours a day.

In each ROTC unit there are two types of student—scholarship and nonscholarship. Although the focus of this section is on military programs that provide tuition aid, it should be pointed out that you may join an ROTC unit after you get to college even if you don't receive a scholarship. You take the same ROTC courses as a scholarship student, and you may major in nearly any subject. You can drop out at any time prior to the start of your junior year. If you continue, you will be paid a monthly stipend for your last two years of college and be required to attend a summer training session between your junior and senior years. Upon graduation, you will be commissioned as a second lieutenant or ensign. For the Army, your minimum active-duty obligation is six months; four years if you are in the Air Force or Navy.

The major source of scholarships is the four-year tuition scholarship program. Four-year scholarships are awarded to high school seniors on the basis of a national competition. Each year, more than 4,000 winners are selected (roughly 2,000 Army, 1,300 Navy, and 1,300 Air Force) from about 25,000 applicants. Recipients of four-year Army, Air Force, and Naval ROTC scholarships may attend either a host college or approved cross-enrollment college. In return for an Army ROTC scholarship, you must serve eight years in the Active Army, Army Reserve, or Army National Guard or a combination thereof. For scholarships from other services, four years' active duty service is required. After you accept the scholarship, you have a one-year grace period before you incur a military obligation. Prior to beginning your sophomore year, you may simply withdraw from the program. If you drop out after that time, you may be permitted to leave without penalty, ordered to active duty as an enlisted servicemember, or required to repay the financial aid you have received. The military will choose one of these three options, depending on the circumstances of your withdrawal.

Should you decide to try for a four-year ROTC scholarship, it is important that you apply to a college to which you can bring an ROTC scholarship. Because there is always the possibility you may not be accepted at your first choice, it is a good idea to apply to more than one college with an ROTC affiliation. In the case of Army and Air Force ROTC scholarships, both of which may require you to major in a specified area, you also need to be admitted to the particular program for which the scholarship is offered. For example, if you win an Air Force ROTC scholarship designated for an engineering major, you must be accepted into the engineering program as well as to the college as a whole.

While the majority of new ROTC scholarships are four-year awards given to high school seniors, each service sets aside scholarships for students who are already enrolled in college and want to try for this kind of military financial aid for their last two or three years. These in-college scholarships are a rapidly growing area within the ROTC program, since the services are finding they can do a better job of selecting officer candidates after observing one or two years of college performance. Of further interest to applicants is the fact that for some of the services, the selection rate is quite a bit higher for the two- and three-year awards than it is for the four-year scholarship. For example, in a recent year, Air Force ROTC accepted 37 percent of its candidates for four-year awards and 63 percent of its candidates for two- and three-year awards. Most of these in-college scholarships are given to students who join an ROTC unit without a scholarship and then decide to try for a tuition grant. Since a cadet or midshipman takes the same ROTC courses whether on scholarship or not, it makes good sense for those who are not receiving aid to apply for an in-college award.

Even if you have not been a member of an ROTC unit during your first two years in college, it is possible to receive a two-year scholarship, provided you apply by the spring of your sophomore year. If you win a two-year scholarship, you will go to a military summer camp where you will receive training equivalent to the first two years of ROTC courses. You then join the ROTC unit for your junior and senior years. (There are also limited opportunities for non-ROTC members to try for a three-year in-college scholarship; interested students should check with an ROTC unit.)

If you receive a two- or three-year scholarship, your active-duty obligation is two to eight years. You will not have the one-year grace period four-year scholarship winners have in which to decide whether they want to remain in ROTC. You must make up your mind whether or not you want to stay when you attend your first military science class as a scholarship student.

You may be married and still receive an ROTC scholarship (you may not be married in the service academies). The benefits are the same regardless of whether you are married or single.

In summary, there are four ways to participate in ROTC: as a winner of a four-year scholarship (or, in some cases, a three-year award) for high school seniors; as a recipient of a two- or three-year scholarship for ROTC members who are not initially on scholarship; by receiving an in-college scholarship (usually for two years) designated for students who have not yet joined an ROTC unit; or as a nonscholarship student.

This section, adapted from *How the Military Will Help You Pay for College: The High School Student's Guide to ROTC, the Academies, and Special Programs,* second edition, by Don M. Betterton (Peterson's), has provided an overview of the options available if you choose to turn to the military as a source of financial aid. One such option, Army ROTC, is discussed in detail in the following pages.

The Army ROTC Program

Through Army ROTC, a student can become an officer while pursuing a regular college degree.

WHAT IS ROTC?

Army ROTC is a college program that enables students not only to graduate with a degree in their chosen college majors but also to receive officers' commissions in the U.S. Army, the Army National Guard, or the Army Reserve.

ROTC courses are like any other college elective. And most college students can try ROTC for a year without incurring any military service obligation.

ROTC cadets are eligible for numerous financial benefits, including scholarships worth in some cases more than $60,000.

ROTC graduates have the opportunity to serve full time as officers in the active Army or serve part time in the Army National Guard or Reserve while pursuing regular civilian careers or continuing their education.

Students at hundreds of colleges and universities nationwide have access to Army ROTC programs, and about 40,000 students participate each year.

WHAT ARE THE BENEFITS OF ARMY ROTC?

Army ROTC helps ensure a young person's success in college and in life. It builds confidence and teaches the planning and time-management skills needed to succeed in college and the leadership, management, and motivational skills critical to success in life. These skills are not just taught in class. ROTC cadets can practice them in special ROTC activities and summer training. ROTC classes last just a few hours a week and at most colleges fulfill elective requirements.

Army ROTC provides a competitive edge that will be of value in either a military or a civilian career. In fact, many civilian employers place a premium on the skills and experience gained through ROTC.

According to its headquarters at Fort Monroe, Virginia, Army ROTC describes the type of cadets it is seeking as, "scholars, athletes, and leaders." In other words, Army ROTC wants students who are:

- athletically inclined (even if they have not played team sports);
- attracted to physical challenge;
- at least a B student;
- have served in leadership positions in community or student organizations; and
- motivated by serving and doing for others.

Such young people, according to Army ROTC, are most likely to exhibit the personal and professional integrity and the ability to work as a team that are so critical to today's Army officer.

Army ROTC provides the leadership and management training that will help make students a success in college and in life.

WHAT TYPES OF FINANCIAL BENEFITS ARE AVAILABLE?

In the face of today's growing college costs, Army ROTC offers merit-based scholarships that can help pay tuition and on-campus educational expenses.

Juniors and seniors in ROTC, plus certain other ROTC cadets, receive allowances ranging from $2000 to $4000 each school year and are paid to attend a special summer camp.

Students who enroll in Army ROTC at college and who also join the National Guard or Army Reserve are eligible for other financial benefits. For more information, students should contact the Professor of Military Science at the college they plan to attend.

WHAT IS THE COMMITMENT?

College freshmen can try Army ROTC without making any commitment to join the Army. That commitment does not usually come until the junior year.

When students graduate with officers' commissions, they can serve in the active Army, the Army National Guard, the Army Reserve, or a combination for a total of eight years.

In the active Army, they serve full time as Army officers. In the Guard or Reserve, they serve part time, generally one weekend a month and two weeks during the summer, while pursuing their chosen civilian careers.

THE FOUR-YEAR PROGRAM

Army ROTC is traditionally a four-year college program consisting of a two-year Basic Course and a two-year Advanced Course.

The Basic Course is usually taken during a college student's freshman and sophomore years. The subjects taught cover such areas as management principles, military history and tactics, leadership development, communication skills, first aid, land navigation, and rappelling.

Most students incur no military obligation by participating in the Basic Course, and all necessary ROTC textbooks, materials, and uniforms are furnished without cost.

After completing the Basic Course, only students who have demonstrated leadership potential and who meet scholastic, physical, and moral standards are eligible to enroll in the Advanced Course.

The Advanced Course is normally taken during a college student's junior and senior years. Instruction includes further training in leadership, organization theory, management, military tactics, strategic thinking, and professional ethics.

ROTC cadets in the Advanced Course attend a paid Advanced Camp during the summer between their junior and senior years. This camp further permits cadets to put into practice the principles and theories they have learned in the classroom. It also exposes them to Army life in a tactical and field environment.

All ROTC cadets in the Advanced Course receive an allowance of $3000 or $4000 each school year and are paid to attend Advanced Camp. They are also furnished, without cost, all necessary ROTC textbooks, materials, and uniforms.

Before entering the Advanced Course, ROTC cadets must sign contracts that certify an understanding of their future Army service obligation, which is for eight years. This obligation may be fulfilled through various combinations of full-time active duty and part-time reserve forces duty depend-

More than 20 percent of all current ROTC cadets are women.

ing upon a cadet's personal preference and the needs of the Army at the time of commissioning.

ROTC cadets selected for reserve forces duty actually serve on active duty for three to six months before they join a National Guard or Army Reserve unit. This is so that they can attend an Officer Basic Course to receive additional Army training. Reserve officers generally serve part time in the National Guard or Army Reserve while they pursue regular full-time civilian careers.

THE TWO-YEAR PROGRAM

Students can also be commissioned after only two years of ROTC instruction.

This program is open to students who did not take Army ROTC during their first two years of college. Two-year program cadets include community and junior college graduates who have transferred to a four-year institution, graduate students, high school students planning to attend a Military Junior College, veterans, and members of the National Guard or the Army Reserve.

Students can take advantage of the two-year program by successfully completing a paid Basic Camp (usually attended between the sophomore and junior years of college) and entering the Advanced Course.

Veterans and members of the National Guard and Army Reserve do not have to attend Basic Camp since their prior military service serves as the prerequisite for entering the Advanced Course.

Students interested in the two-year ROTC program should contact the nearest on-campus Army ROTC office for information before the end of the sophomore year of college.

EXTRACURRICULAR ACTIVITIES

Like regular college students, ROTC cadets participate in a wide variety of social, educational, professional, and athletic activities. Most of these activities are sponsored by the colleges hosting Army ROTC, but some are sponsored by ROTC itself.

Ranger Challenge is sponsored by Army ROTC and includes competition in patrolling, marksmanship, rope-bridge building, and a 10-kilometer run. Each ROTC unit fields a Ranger Challenge team that competes against teams from ROTC units at other colleges and universities.

These and other challenging activities offer leadership opportunities that increase self-confidence.

THE SCHOLARSHIP PROGRAM

Army ROTC offers valuable four-year scholarships to students entering college as freshmen and two- or three-year scholarships to students with two or three years remaining toward their bachelor's degrees.

These scholarships may pay thousands of dollars toward college tuition and required educational fees. In addition, they provide a specified amount for textbooks, supplies, and equipment. Each scholarship recipient also receives a personal allowance of $2000 to $4000 for each school year the scholarship is in effect.

Army ROTC scholarships are merit scholarships awarded on a competitive basis. Selection is based on high school or college grades, SAT or ACT scores, personal recommendations, physical fitness, athletic and extracurricular activities, leadership potential, a personal interview, and other criteria as prescribed by regulation.

All ROTC units offer instruction in some type of adventure training, including rappelling, orienteering, mountaineering, or white-water rafting.

OPTIONS OPTIONS OPTIONS

Many of these scholarships are specifically targeted to students pursuing degrees in engineering, nursing, the physical sciences, or other technical programs.

Army ROTC scholarship winners who fail to complete the ROTC program or do not accept commissions as Army officers will be required to pay back the amount of their scholarships or serve as enlisted soldiers in the Army. This provision is binding for three- and four-year scholarship winners when they enter the sophomore year and for two-year scholarship winners when they enter the junior year.

Completed applications for four-year Army ROTC scholarships must be postmarked by November 15 of a high school student's senior year. Applications for two- and three-year scholarships are usually due by March of a college student's freshman and sophomore years. Since special application forms and procedures are required, interested students should contact Army ROTC for information well before these deadlines.

ARMY NURSE CORPS

Army ROTC offers two-, three-, and four-year scholarships to qualified students who are seeking bachelor's degrees in nursing. Most of these scholarships must be used at certain nursing programs affiliated with ROTC. These programs are called Partnership in Nursing Education (PNE) programs. Army ROTC nurse candidates join the Army Nurse Corps upon graduation from an accredited nursing program, successful completion of a state board examination, and commissioning as Army officers.

Eligible students who desire to attend one of the historically black colleges or universities (HBCU) that host Army ROTC may apply for an ROTC four-year HBCU Scholarship.

Students seeking a bachelor's degree in nursing are especially encouraged to enroll in Army ROTC.

The management training provided through Army ROTC is just as important to a nursing career as it is to any other career, and nursing students enrolled in Army ROTC can receive special nursing leadership experiences.

In lieu of attending the regular ROTC Advanced Camp, ROTC nursing cadets attend the ROTC Nurse Summer Training Program (NSTP). NSTP allows ROTC nurse cadets to develop both leadership and nursing skills. It introduces the cadets to the Army Medical Department and the roles and responsibilities of an Army Nurse Corps officer. NSTP cadets report to Army hospitals for clinical training under the supervision of Army Nurse Corps office "preceptors." These professionals work one-on-one with the cadets throughout the training, which concentrates on "hands-on" experiences in areas like medical-surgical wards and intensive care units.

The Army also provides Army nurses specialty training. Army nurses can apply for clinical specialty courses in such areas as obstetrics/gynecology, critical care, perioperative, and psychiatric health nursing. They can also become nurse anesthetists.

In addition to training, the Army offers nurses many unique benefits. Army nurses serve around the world, get thirty days paid vacation from the start of their career, and don't lose seniority when changing geographical areas or specialties.

OPPORTUNITIES FOR SCIENCE OR ENGINEERING STUDENTS

Army scientists designed America's first earth satellite, developed the first operational computer, and devised innovative production methods for transistors and titanium, among other scientific discoveries. All this was accomplished by giving priority to scientific knowledge and investing in students who put their scientific skills to work while serving the nation.

As Army officers, students have exciting opportunities to be a part of world-class science from the very beginning of their careers. The Army also provides many students fully funded graduate tuition programs for approved courses of study. No matter which scientific or technical course of college study students choose, the Army offers them a chance to gain technical skills and leadership experience sooner and in more fields than any other employer.

THE SIMULTANEOUS MEMBERSHIP PROGRAM

The Simultaneous Membership Program (SMP) allows students to attend college, participate in Army ROTC, serve part time in the Army National Guard or Army Reserve, and receive generous Army benefits.

SMP cadets receive their Guard or Reserve pay; G.I. Bill benefits, if eligible; and a monthly ROTC allowance. In many states, Guard and Reserve members are eligible for additional state benefits. In some states, this includes free tuition at state-supported colleges and universities.

OPPORTUNITIES FOR VETERANS

Veterans who attend college can enroll in Army ROTC and participate in the two-year program. Their prior military service could fulfill the requirements for the Basic Course, so they could start ROTC in the Advanced Course.

In addition to the Veterans Administration benefits to which they are already entitled, veterans in ROTC receive the annual ROTC allowance each school year and may apply for ROTC scholarships.

Soldiers who have two years of active duty may be eligible for an Army ROTC scholarship. These "Green-to-Gold" scholarships allow selected soldiers to be released from the Army in order to attend college. Interested soldiers should contact the nearest on-campus Army ROTC office or their installation Education Offices for details.

Army ROTC—Leadership Excellence Starts Here.

WHAT DOES BECOMING AN ARMY OFFICER MEAN?

Army officers are leaders, thinkers, doers, and decision makers, proudly serving their country in a role that is vital to the national defense. They are required to have traits such as courage, confidence, integrity, and self-discipline.

In the Army, ROTC graduates start out as Second Lieutenants. Most become eligible for promotion and new job assignments at regular intervals.

In addition to their pay, they qualify for excellent medical, educational, and retirement benefits as well as other entitlements.

In the active Army, ROTC graduates have the opportunity to serve on Army posts located across the nation as well as abroad. In the Army National Guard or Army Reserve, they are able to serve close to where they live and work.

ADDITIONAL INFORMATION

To get more information about Army ROTC and any of the specific programs described above, students should call 800-USA-ROTC (toll-free) or contact the Professor of Military Science at a college hosting Army ROTC. Students can also write: College Army ROTC, QUEST Center, Attn: Department PG99, P.O. Box 3279, Warminster, Pennsylvania 18974-9872. Information about Army ROTC is also available on the World Wide Web at www.armyrotc.com.

OPTIONS OPTIONS OPTIONS OPTIONS

Army ROTC Colleges and Universities

Army ROTC is offered at the colleges and universities listed below. Students at other institutions can often take ROTC at a nearby college campus; note that affiliated schools may cross state boundaries. The four-digit code that follows each institution name should be used to identify the college when seeking further information.

ALABAMA

- †• Alabama Agricultural and Mechanical University, Normal (1002)
- ■ Auburn University, Auburn (1009)
- ‡ Auburn University at Montgomery, Montgomery (8310)
- ‡ Jacksonville State University, Jacksonville (1020)
- ○ Marion Military Institute, Marion (1026)
- ■• Tuskegee University, Tuskegee (1050)
- ■ University of Alabama, Tuscaloosa (1051)
- ■ University of Alabama at Birmingham, Birmingham (1052)
- ‡ University of North Alabama, Florence (1016)
- ■ University of South Alabama, Mobile (1057)

ALASKA

- † University of Alaska Fairbanks, Fairbanks (1063)

ARIZONA

- ■ Arizona State University, Tempe (1081)
- ■ Northern Arizona University, Flagstaff (1082)
- ■ University of Arizona, Tucson (1083)

ARKANSAS

- ■ Arkansas State University, State University (1090)
- ■ University of Arkansas, Fayetteville (1108)
- ‡• University of Arkansas at Pine Bluff, Pine Bluff (1086)
- ‡ University of Central Arkansas, Conway (1092)

CALIFORNIA

- † California Polytechnic State University, San Luis Obispo (1143)
- ■ California State University, Fresno (1147)
- California State University, Fullerton (1137)
- † Claremont-McKenna College, Claremont (1168)
- ■ San Diego State University, San Diego (1151)
- † Santa Clara University, Santa Clara (1326)
- † University of California, Berkeley (1312)
- † University of California, Davis (1313)
- ■ University of California, Los Angeles (1315)
- † University of California, Santa Barbara (1320)
- ‡ University of San Francisco, San Francisco (1325)
- ■ University of Southern California, Los Angeles (1328)

COLORADO

- † Colorado State University, Fort Collins (1350)
- † University of Colorado at Boulder, Boulder (1370)
- † University of Colorado at Colorado Springs, Colorado Springs (4509)

CONNECTICUT

- ■ University of Connecticut, Storrs (29013)

DELAWARE

- ■ University of Delaware, Newark (1431)

DISTRICT OF COLUMBIA

- ‡ Georgetown University, Washington (1445)
- ■• Howard University, Washington (1448)

FLORIDA

- † Embry-Riddle Aeronautical University, Daytona (1479)
- ■• Florida Agricultural and Mechanical University, Tallahassee (1480)
- Florida International University, Miami (9635)
- † Florida Institute of Technology, Melbourne (1469)
- Florida Southern College, Lakeland (1488)
- ‡ Florida State University, Tallahassee (1489)
- ■ University of Central Florida, Orlando (3954)
- ■ University of Florida, Gainesville (1535)
- ■ University of South Florida, Tampa (1537)
- University of Tampa, Tampa (1538)
- University of West Florida, Pensacola (3955)

GEORGIA

- Augusta State University, Augusta (1552)
- ‡ Columbus State University, Columbus (1561)
- †• Fort Valley State University, Fort Valley (1566)
- † Georgia Institute of Technology, Atlanta (1569)
- ○ Georgia Military College, Milledgeville (1571)
- ■ Georgia Southern University, Statesboro (1572)
- ‡ Georgia State University, Atlanta (1574)
- ‡* North Georgia College, Dahlonega (1585)
- † University of Georgia, Athens (1598)

GUAM

- University of Guam, Mangilao (3935)

HAWAII

- ■ University of Hawaii, Honolulu (1610)

IDAHO

- ‡ Boise State University, Boise (1616)
- † University of Idaho, Moscow (1626)

ILLINOIS

- Eastern Illinois University, Charleston (1674)
- Illinois State University, Normal (1692)
- ■ Northern Illinois University, DeKalb (1737)
- † Southern Illinois University Carbondale, Carbondale (1758)
- Southern Illinois University Edwardsville, Edwardsville (1759)
- ■ University of Illinois at Chicago, Chicago (1776)
- ‡ University of Illinois at Urbana-Champaign, Champaign (1775)
- Western Illinois University, Macomb (1780)
- Wheaton College, Wheaton (1781)

INDIANA

- ‡ Ball State University, Muncie (1786)
- ‡ Indiana University Bloomington, Bloomington (1809)
- ■ Indiana University-Purdue University Indianapolis, Indianapolis (1813)
- ■ Purdue University, West Lafayette (1825)
- † Rose-Hulman Institute of Technology, Terre Haute (1830)
- † University of Notre Dame, Notre Dame (1840)

IOWA

- † Iowa State University of Science and Technology, Ames (1869)
- ■ University of Iowa, Iowa City (1892)
- University of Northern Iowa, Cedar Falls (1890)

KANSAS

- † Kansas State University, Manhattan (1928)
- ■ Pittsburgh State University, Pittsburg (1926)
- ■ University of Kansas, Lawrence (1948)

KENTUCKY

- ‡ Eastern Kentucky University, Richmond (1963)
- Morehead State University, Morehead (1976)
- ■ University of Kentucky, Lexington (1989)
- ■ University of Louisville, Louisville (1999)
- ■ Western Kentucky University, Bowling Green (2002)

LOUISIANA

- ‡• Grambling State University, Grambling (2006)

† Louisiana State University and Agricultural and Mechanical College, Baton Rouge (2010)
‡ Northwestern State University of Louisiana, Natchitoches (2021)
‡• Southern University and Agricultural and Mechanical College, Baton Rouge (9636)
† Tulane University, New Orleans (2029)

MAINE

■ University of Maine, Orono (2053)

MARYLAND

Bowie State College, Bowie (2062)
■ Johns Hopkins University, Baltimore (2077)
† Loyola College in Maryland, Baltimore (2078)
• Morgan State University, Baltimore (2083)
Western Maryland College, Westminster (2109)

MASSACHUSETTS

† Boston University, Boston (2130)
† Massachusetts Institute of Technology, Cambridge (2178)
■ Northeastern University, Boston (2199)
■ University of Massachusetts, Amherst (2221)
† Worcester Polytechnic Institute, Worcester (2233)

MICHIGAN

Central Michigan University, Mount Pleasant (2243)
‡ Eastern Michigan University, Ypsilanti (2259)
■ Michigan State University, East Lansing (2290)
† Michigan Technological University, Houghton (2292)
‡ Northern Michigan University, Marquette (2301)
■ University of Michigan, Ann Arbor (9092)
† Western Michigan University, Kalamazoo (2330)

MINNESOTA

■ Minnesota State University, Mankato, Mankato (2360)
St. John's University, Collegeville (2379)
■ University of Minnesota, Minneapolis (3969)

MISSISSIPPI

‡• Alcorn State University, Lorman (2396)
• Jackson State University, Jackson (2410)
† Mississippi State University, Mississippi State (2423)
† University of Mississippi, University (2440)
■ University of Southern Mississippi, Hattiesburg (2441)

MISSOURI

‡ Central Missouri State University, Warrensburg (2454)
• Lincoln University, Jefferson City (2479)
Missouri Western State College, St. Joseph (2490)
Southwest Missouri State University, Springfield (2503)
‡ Truman State University, Kirksville (2495)
■ University of Missouri-Columbia, Columbia (2516)
† University of Missouri-Rolla, Rolla (2517)
† Washington University in St. Louis, St. Louis (2520)
○ Wentworth Military Academy and Junior College, Lexington (2522)

MONTANA

■ Montana State University, Bozeman (2532)
University of Montana, Missoula (2536)

NEBRASKA

‡ Creighton University, Omaha (2542)
■ University of Nebraska, Lincoln (2565)

NEVADA

■ University of Nevada, Reno (2568)

NEW HAMPSHIRE

■ University of New Hampshire, Durham (2589)

NEW JERSEY

■ Princeton University, Princeton (2627)
† Rutgers, The State University of New Jersey, New Brunswick (6964)
‡ Seton Hall University, South Orange (2632)

NEW MEXICO

○ New Mexico Military Institute, Roswell (2656)
■ New Mexico State University, Las Cruces (2657)

NEW YORK

Canisius College, Buffalo (2681)
† Clarkson University, Potsdam (2699)
† Cornell University, Ithaca (2711)
Fordham University, Bronx (2722)
† Hofstra University, Hempstead (2732)
‡ Niagara University, Niagara (2788)
† Rochester Institute of Technology, Rochester (2806)
St. Bonaventure University, St. Bonaventure (2817)
St. John's University, Jamaica (2823)
Siena College, Loudonville (2816)
State University of New York College at Brockport, Brockport (2841)
■ Syracuse University, Syracuse (2882)

NORTH CAROLINA

Appalachian State University, Boone (2906)
Campbell University, Buies Creek (2913)
■ Duke University, Durham (2920)
‡ East Carolina University, Greenville (2923)
Elizabeth City State University, Elizabeth City (2926)
■• North Carolina Agricultural and Technical State University, Greensboro (2905)
† North Carolina State University at Raleigh, Raleigh (2972)
• St. Augustine's College, Raleigh (2968)
■ University of North Carolina at Chapel Hill (2974)
■ University of North Carolina at Charlotte, Charlotte (2975)
Wake Forest University, Winston-Salem (2978)

NORTH DAKOTA

† North Dakota State University, Fargo (9265)
■ University of North Dakota, Grand Forks (3005)

OHIO

‡ Bowling Green State University, Bowling Green (3018)
‡ Capital University, Columbus (3023)
• Central State University, Wilberforce (3026)
John Carroll University, Cleveland (3050)
‡ Kent University, Kent (3051)
■ Ohio State University, Columbus (6883)
† Ohio University, Athens (3100)
■ University of Akron, Akron (3123)
■ University of Cincinnati, Cincinnati (3125)
† University of Dayton, Dayton (3127)
■ University of Toledo, Toledo (3131)
‡ Wright State University, Dayton (9168)
Xavier University, Cincinnati (3144)

OKLAHOMA

Cameron University, Lawton (3150)
† Oklahoma State University, Stillwater (3170)
‡ University of Central Oklahoma, Edmond (3152)
■ University of Oklahoma, Norman (3184)

OREGON

† Oregon State University, Corvallis (3210)
University of Oregon, Eugene (3223)
■ University of Portland, Portland (3224)

PENNSYLVANIA

† Bucknell University, Lewisburg (3238)
Dickinson College, Carlisle (3253)
† Drexel University, Philadelphia (3256)
Edinboro University of Pennsylvania, Edinboro (3321)
■ Gannon University, Erie (3266)
‡ Indiana University of Pennsylvania, Indiana (8810)
† Lehigh University, Bethlehem (3289)
Lock Haven University of Pennsylvania, Lock Haven (3323)
■ Pennsylvania State University, University Park Campus, University Park (6965)
Shippensburg University of Pennsylvania, Shippensburg (3326)
‡ Slippery Rock University of Pennsylvania, Slippery Rock (3327)
‡ Temple University, Pennsylvania (3371)
■ University of Pennsylvania, Philadelphia (3378)
■ University of Pittsburgh, Pittsburgh (3379)
‡ University of Scranton, Scranton (3384)
○ Valley Forge Military Academy and Junior College, Wayne (3386)
■ Widener University, Chester (3313)

PUERTO RICO

■ University of Puerto Rico, Mayaguez (3944)
University of Puerto Rico, Rio Piedras Campus, Rio Piedras (7108)

RHODE ISLAND

Providence College, Providence (3406)
■ University of Rhode Island, Kingston (3414)

SOUTH CAROLINA

†* The Citadel, Charleston (3423)
■ Clemson University, Clemson (3425)
Furman University, Greenville (3434)
Presbyterian College, Clinton (3445)
• South Carolina State University, Orangeburg (3446)

■ University of South Carolina, Columbia (3448)
Wofford College, Spartanburg (3457)

SOUTH DAKOTA

† South Dakota School of Mines and Technology, Rapid City (3470)
■ South Dakota State University, Brookings (3471)
University of South Dakota, Vermillion (10300)

TENNESSEE

‡ Austin Peay State University, Clarksville (3478)
‡ Carson-Newman College, Jefferson City (3481)
■ East Tennessee State University, Johnson City (3487)
‡ Middle Tennessee State University, Murfreesboro (3510)
■ Tennessee Technological University, Cookeville (3523)
■ The University of Memphis, Memphis (3509)
■ University of Tennessee, Knoxville, Knoxville (3530)
† University of Tennessee at Martin, Martin (3531)
■ Vanderbilt University, Nashville (3535)

TEXAS

■• Prairie View Agricultural and Mechanical University, Prairie View (3630)
† St. Mary's University of San Antonio, San Antonio (3623)
Sam Houston State University, Huntsville (3606)
Southwest Texas State University, Canyon (3615)
‡ Stephen F. Austin State University, Nacogdoches (3624)
Tarleton State University, Stephenville (3631)
† Texas Agricultural and Mechanical University, College Station (10366)
† Texas Agricultural and Mechanical University, Kingsville (3639)
‡ Texas Christian University, Fort Worth (3636)
■ Texas Tech University, Lubbock (3644)
† University of Houston, Houston (3652)
■ University of Texas at Arlington, Arlington (3656)
■ University of Texas at Austin, Austin (3658)
■ University of Texas at El Paso, El Paso (3661)
‡ University of Texas-Pan American, Edinburg (3599)
■ University of Texas at San Antonio, San Antonio (10115)

UTAH

■ Brigham Young University, Provo (3670)
■ University of Utah, Salt Lake City (3675)
‡ Weber State University, Ogden (3680)

VERMONT

■* Norwich University, Northfield (3692)
■ University of Vermont, Burlington (3696)

VIRGINIA

College of William and Mary, Williamsburg (3705)
George Mason University, Fairfax (3749)
‡• Hampton University, Hampton (3714)
‡ James Madison University, Harrisonburg (3721)
‡• Norfolk State University, Norfolk (3765)
■ Old Dominion University, Norfolk (3728)
University of Richmond, Richmond (3744)
■ University of Virginia, Charlottesville (6968)
†* Virginia Military Institute, Lexington (3753)
† Virginia Polytechnic Institute and State University, Blacksburg (3754)
• Virginia State University, Petersburg (3764)

WASHINGTON

Central Washington University, Ellensburg (3771)
■ Eastern Washington University, Cheney (3775)
■ Gonzaga University, Spokane (3778)
Pacific Lutheran University, Tacoma (3785)
■ Seattle University, Seattle (3790)
■ University of Washington, Seattle (3798)
■ Washington State University, Pullman (3800)

WEST VIRGINIA

‡ Marshall University, Huntington (3815)
• West Virginia State College, Institute (3826)
■ West Virginia University, Morgantown (3827)

WISCONSIN

■ Marquette University, Milwaukee (3863)
University of Wisconsin-LaCrosse, LaCrosse (3919)
■ University of Wisconsin-Madison, Madison (3895)
‡ University of Wisconsin-Oshkosh, Oshkosh (9630)
University of Wisconsin-Stevens Point, Stevens Point (3924)

WYOMING

■ University of Wyoming, Laramie (3932)

Becoming an Army officer is an exciting opportunity. And the best part is that, through Army ROTC, a student can become an officer while pursuing a regular college degree.

There are many ways to obtain a scholarship application or simply more information about Army ROTC:

1. Contact the Professor of Military Science at one of the colleges or universities listed on the previous pages.
2. Write to: College Army ROTC
   QUEST Center
   Attn: Department PG99
   P.O. Box 3279
   Warminster, PA 18974-9872
3. Call 800-USA-ROTC (toll-free).
4. Call the Army ROTC Advisor nearest you

New York/New England	978-796-2243/2547
Delaware Valley	609-562-3275
Mid-Atlantic	703-805-4040
Southeastern	910-396-8408
Florida/Georgia	912-692-8544
Midwest	847-266-3105
Bluegrass	502-624-4475
Ohio Valley	573-596-6680
Southern Central	256-955-7577
Northwest	253-967-6025
North Central	719-526-9261
Southwest	831-242-7726
Southwest Central	210-221-2055

5. Check out Army ROTC on the World Wide Web: http://www.armyrotc.com

Four-Year COLLEGES

How to Use This Section

By using all the information in this section of the guide, you will find the colleges worthy of the most important top ten list on the planet—yours.

The first thing you will need to do is decide what type of institution of higher learning you want to attend. Each of the more than 2,100 four-year colleges and universities in the United States is as unique as the people applying to it. Although listening to the voices and media hype around you can make it sound as though there are only a few elite schools worth attending, this simply is not true. By considering some of the following criteria, you will soon find that the large pool of interesting colleges has been narrowed to a more reasonable number.

1. Size and Category. Schools come in all shapes and sizes, from tiny rural colleges of 400 students to massive state university systems serving 100,000 students or more. If you are coming from a small high school, a college with 3,500 students may seem large to you. If you are currently attending a high school with 3,000 students, selecting a college of a similar size may not feel like a new enough experience. Some students coming from very large impersonal high schools are looking for a place where they will be recognized from the beginning and offered a more personal approach. If you don't have a clue about what size might feel right to you, try visiting a couple of nearby colleges of varying sizes. You do not have to be seriously interested in them; just feel what impact the number of students on campus has on you.

Large Universities. Large universities offer a wide range of educational, athletic, and social experiences. Universities offer a full scope of undergraduate majors and award master's and doctoral degrees as well. Universities are usually composed of several smaller colleges. Depending on your interest in a major field or area of study, you would likely apply to a specific college within the university. Each college has the flexibility to set its own standards for admission, which may differ from the overall average of the university. For example, a student applying to a university's College of Arts and Sciences might need a minimum GPA of 3.2 and a minimum SAT I score of 1200. Another, applying to the College of Engineering, may find that a minimum GPA of 3.8 and SAT I score of 1280 are the standards. The colleges within a university system also set their own course requirements for earning a degree.

Universities may be public or private. Some large private universities, such as Harvard, Yale, Princeton, University of Pennsylvania, New York University, Northwestern, and Stanford, are well-known for their high entrance standards, the excellence of their education, and the success rates of their graduates. These institutions place a great deal of emphasis on research and compete aggressively for grants from the federal government to fund these projects. Large public universities, such as the State University of New York (SUNY) System, University of Michigan, University of Texas, University of Illinois, University of Washington, and University of North Carolina, also support excellent educational programs, compete for and win research funding, and have successful graduates. Public universities usually offer substantially lower tuition rates to in-state students, although their tuitions to out-of-state residents are often comparable to private institutions.

At many large universities, sports play a major role on campus. Athletics can dominate the calendar and set the tone year-round at some schools. Alumni travel from far and wide to attend their alma mater's football or basketball games, and the campus, and frequently the entire town, grinds to a halt when there is a home game. Athletes are heroes and dominate campus social life.

What are some other features of life on a university campus? Every kind of club imaginable, from literature to bioengineering and chorus to politics, can be found on most college campuses. You will be able to play the intramural version of almost every sport in which the university fields interscholastic teams and join fraternities, sororities, and groups dedicated to social action. You can become a member of a band, an orchestra, or perhaps a chamber music group or work on the newspaper, the literary magazine, and the Web site. The list can go on and on. You may want to try out a new interest or two or pursue what you have always been interested in and make like-minded friends along the way.

Take a look at the size of the classrooms in the larger universities and envision yourself sitting in that atmosphere. Would this offer a learning environment that would benefit you?

Liberal Arts Colleges. If you have considered large universities and come to the conclusion that all that action could be a distraction, a small liberal arts college might be right for you. Ideally tucked away on a picture-perfect campus, a liberal arts college generally has fewer than 5,000 students. The mission of most liberal arts schools is learning for the sake of learning, with a strong emphasis on creating lifelong learners who will be able to apply their education to any number of careers. This contrasts with objectives of the profession-based preparation of specialized colleges.

Liberal arts colleges cannot offer the breadth of courses provided by the large universities. As a result, liberal arts colleges try to create a niche for themselves. For instance, a college may place its emphasis on its humanities departments, whose professors are all well-known published authors and international presenters in their areas of expertise. A college may highlight its science departments by providing state-of-the-art facilities where undergraduates conduct research side by side with top-notch professors and copublish their findings in the most prestigious scientific journals in the country. The personal approach is very important at liberal arts colleges. Whether in advisement, course selection, athletic programs tailored to students' interests, or dinner with the department head at her home, liberal arts colleges emphasize that they get to know their students.

If they are so perfect, why doesn't everyone choose a liberal arts college? Well, the small size limits options. Fewer people may mean less diversity. The fact that many of these colleges encourage a study-abroad option (a student elects to spend a semester or a year studying in another country) reduces the number of students on campus even further. Some liberal arts colleges have a certain reputation that does not appeal to some students. You should ask yourself questions about the campus life that most appeals to you. Will you fit in with the campus culture? Will the small size mean that you go through your social options quickly? Check out the activities listed on the Student Center bulletin board. Does the student body look diverse enough for you? Will what is happening keep you busy and interested? Do the students have input into decision making? Do they create the social climate of the school?

Small Universities. Smaller universities, often combine stringent admissions policies, handpicked faculty members, and attractive scholarship packages. These institutions generally have undergraduate enrollments of about 4,000 students. Some are more famous for their graduate and professional schools, but have established strong undergraduate colleges. Smaller universities balance the great majors options of large universities with a smaller campus community. They offer choices but not to the same extent as large universities. On the other hand, by limiting admissions and enrollment, they manage to cultivate some of the characteristics of a liberal arts college. Like a liberal arts college, a small university may emphasize a particular program and go out of its way to draw strong candidates in a specific area, such as premed, to its campus. Universities such as Johns Hopkins University, University of Notre Dame, Vanderbilt University, Washington University in St. Louis, and Wesleyan University in Connecticut are a few examples of this category.

Specialized Colleges. Another alternative to the liberal arts college or to the large university is the technical or otherwise specialized college. Their goal is to offer a specialized and saturated experience in a particular field of study. Such an institution might limit its course offerings to engineering and science, the performing or fine arts, or business. Schools such as the California Institute of Technology, Carnegie Mellon University, Massachusetts Institute of Technology, and Rensselaer Polytechnic Institute concentrate on attracting the finest math and science students in the country. At other schools, like Bentley College in Massachusetts or Bryant College in Rhode Island, students eat, sleep, and breathe business. These institutions are purists at heart and strong believers in the necessity of focused, specialized study to produce excellence in their graduates' achievements. If you are certain about your chosen path in life and want to immerse yourself in subjects such as math, music, or business to be best prepared for a particular kind of career, you will fit right in.

Religious Colleges. Many private colleges have religious origins, and many of these have become secular institutions with virtually no trace of their religious roots. Others remain dedicated to a religious way of education. What sets religious colleges apart is the way they combine faith, learning, and student life. Faculty members and administrators are hired with faith as a criterion as much as their academic credentials.

Single-Gender Colleges. There are strong arguments that being able to pursue one's education without the distraction, competition, and stress caused by the presence of the opposite sex helps a student evolve a stronger sense of her or his self-worth; achieve more academically; have a more fulfilling, less pressured social life; and achieve more later in life. For various historic, social, and psychological reasons, there are many more all-women than all-men colleges. A strict single-sex environment is rare. Even though the undergraduate day college adheres to an all-female or all-male admissions policy, coeducational evening classes or graduate programs and coordinate facilities and classes shared with nearby coed or opposite-sex institutions can result in a good number of students of the opposite sex being found on campus. Women's colleges, such as Scripps College, Smith College, Sweet Briar College, and Wellesley College, pride themselves on turning out leaders. If you want to concentrate on your studies and hone your leadership qualities, a single-gender school might be an option.

2. Location. Location and distance from home are two other important considerations. If you have always lived in the suburbs, choosing an urban campus can be an adventure, but after a week of the urban experience, will you long for a grassy campus and open space? On the other hand, if you choose a college in a rural area, will you run screaming into the Student Center some night looking for noise, lights, and people? The location—urban, rural, or suburban—can directly affect how easy or how difficult adjusting to college life will be for you.

Don't forget to factor in distance from home. Everyone going off to college wants to think he or she won't be homesick, but sometimes it's nice to get a home-cooked meal or to do the laundry in a place that does not require quarters. Even your kid sister may seem like less of a nuisance after a couple of months away.

Here are some questions you might ask yourself as you go through the selection process: In what part of the country do I want to be? How far away from home do I want to be? What is the cost of returning home? Do I need to be close to a city? How close? How large of a city? Would city life distract me? Would I concentrate better in a setting that is more rural or more suburban?

3. Entrance Difficulty. Many students will look at a college's entrance difficulty as an indicator of whether or not they will be admitted. For instance, if you have an excellent academic record, you might wish to *primarily* consider those colleges that are highly competitive. Although entrance difficulty does not translate directly to quality of education, it indicates which colleges are attracting large numbers of high-achieving students. A high-achieving student body usually translates into prestige for the college and its graduates. Prestige has some advantages but should definitely be viewed as a secondary factor that might tip the scales when all the other important factors are equal. Never base your decision on prestige alone!

The other principle to keep in mind when considering this factor is to not sell yourself short. If everything else tells you that a college might be right for you, but your numbers just miss that college's average range, apply there anyway. Your numbers—grades and test scores—are undeniably important in the admissions decision, but there are other considerations. First, lower grades in honors or AP courses will impress colleges more than top grades in regular-track courses because they demonstrate that you are the kind of student willing to accept challenges. Second, admissions directors are looking for different qualities in students that can be combined to create a multifaceted class. For example, if you did poorly in your freshman and sophomore years but made a great improvement in your grades in later years, this usually will impress a college. If you are likely to contribute to your class because of your special personal qualities, a strong sense of commitment and purpose, unusual and valuable experiences, or special interests and talents, these factors can outweigh numbers that are weaker than average. Nevertheless, be practical. Overreach yourself in a few applications, but put the bulk of your effort into gaining admission to colleges where you have a realistic chance for admission.

4. The Price of an Education. The price tag for higher education continues to rise, and it has become an increasingly important factor for people. While it is necessary to consider your family's resources when choosing a list of colleges to which you might apply, never eliminate a college solely because of cost. There are many ways to pay for college, including loans, and a college education will never depreciate in value like other purchases. It is an investment in yourself and will pay back the expense many times over in your lifetime. You may be able to obtain the necessary financial aid to allow you to enroll in your higher-priced college of choice.

CRITERIA FOR INCLUSION IN THIS BOOK

The term "four-year college" is the commonly used designation for institutions that grant the baccalaureate degree. Four years is the average amount of time required to earn this degree, although some bachelor's degree programs may be completed in three years, others require five years, and part-time programs may take considerably longer. Upper-level institutions offer only the junior and senior years and accept only students with two years of college-level credit. Therefore, "four-year college" is a conventional term that accurately describes most of the institutions included in this section, but should not be taken literally in all cases.

To be included in this section, an institution must have full accreditation or be a candidate for accreditation (preaccreditation) status by an institutional or specialized accrediting body recognized by the U.S. Department of Education or the Council for Higher Education Accreditation (CHEA). Institutional accrediting bodies, which review each institution as a whole, are as follows: the six regional associations of schools and colleges (Middle States, New England, North Central, Northwest, Southern, and Western), each of which is responsible for a specified portion of the United States and its territories; the Accrediting Association of Bible Colleges (AABC); the Accrediting Council for Independent Colleges and Schools (ACICS); the Accrediting Commission for Career Schools and Colleges of Technology (ACCSCT); the Distance Education and Training Council (DETC); the American Academy for Liberal Education; the Council on Occupational Education; and the Transnational Association of Christian Colleges and Schools (TRACS). Program registration by the New York State Board of Regents is considered to be the equivalent of institutional accreditation, since the board requires that all programs offered by an institution meet its standards before recognition is granted. A Canadian institution must be chartered and authorized to grant degrees by the provincial government, affiliated with a chartered institution, or accredited by a recognized U.S. accrediting body. This section also includes institutions outside the United States that are accredited by these U.S. accrediting bodies. There are recognized specialized accrediting bodies in more than forty different fields, each of which is authorized to accredit specific programs in its particular field. For specialized institutions that offer programs in one field only, we designate this to be the equivalent of institutional accreditation. A full explanation of the accrediting process and complete information on recognized accrediting bodies can be found online at http://www.chea.org.

RESEARCH PROCEDURES

The data contained in the college indexes and college profiles were researched between fall 2001 and spring 2002 through *Peterson's Annual Survey of Undergraduate Institutions.* Questionnaires were sent to the more than 2,000 colleges and universities that met the inclusion criteria outlined above. All data included in this edition have been submitted by officials (usually admissions and financial aid officers, registrars, or institutional research personnel) at the colleges. In addition, many of the institutions that submitted data were contacted directly by the Peterson's research staff to verify unusual figures, resolve discrepancies, or obtain additional data. All usable information received in time for publication has been included. The omission of any particular item from an index or profile listing signifies that the information is either not applicable to that institution or not available. Because of Peterson's comprehensive editorial review and because all material comes directly from college officials, we believe that the information presented in this section is accurate. You should check with a specific college or university at the time of application to verify such figures as tuition and fees, which may have changed since publication.

MAJORS INDEX

This index presents hundreds of undergraduate fields of study that are currently offered most widely, according to the colleges' responses on *Peterson's Annual Survey of Undergraduate Institutions.* The majors appear in alphabetical order, each followed by an alphabetical list of the schools that offer a bachelor's-level program in that field. Liberal Arts and Studies indicates a general program with no specified major.

The terms used for the majors are those of the U.S. Department of Education Classification of Instructional Programs (CIPs). Many institutions, however, use different terms. In addition, although the term "major" is used in this section, some colleges may use other terms, such as "concentration," "program of study," or "field."

COLLEGE PROFILES AND SPECIAL ANNOUNCEMENTS

The college profiles contain basic data in capsule form for quick review and comparison. The following outline of the profile format shows the section headings and the items that each section covers. Any item that does not apply to a particular college or for which no information was supplied is omitted from that college's profile. **Special Announcements,** which appear in the profiles just below the bulleted highlights, have been written by those colleges that wished to supplement the profile data with additional information.

Bulleted Highlights

The bulleted highlights feature important information for quick reference and comparison. The number of *possible* bulleted highlights that an ideal profile would have if all questions were answered in a timely manner are represented below. However, not every institution provides all of the information necessary to fill out every bulleted line. In such instances, the line will not appear.

First bullet

Institutional control: Private institutions are designated as independent (nonprofit), proprietary (profit-making), or independent, with a specific religious denomination or affiliation. Nondenominational or interdenominational religious orientation is possible and would be indicated.

Public institutions are designated by the source of funding. Designations include federal, state, province, commonwealth (Puerto Rico), territory (U.S. territories), county, district (an educational administrative unit often having boundaries different from units of local government), city, state and local (local may refer to county, district, or city), or state-related (funded primarily by the state but administratively autonomous).

Religious affiliation is also noted here.

Institutional type: Each institution is classified as one of the following:

Primarily two-year college: Awards baccalaureate degrees, but the vast majority of students are enrolled in two-year programs.

Four-year college: Awards baccalaureate degrees; may also award associate degrees; does not award graduate (postbaccalaureate) degrees.

Five-year college: Awards a five-year baccalaureate in a professional field such as architecture or pharmacy; does not award graduate degrees.

Upper-level institution: Awards baccalaureate degrees, but entering students must have at least two years of previous college-level credit; may also offer graduate degrees.

Comprehensive institution: Awards baccalaureate degrees; may also award associate degrees; offers graduate degree programs, primarily at the master's, specialist's, or professional level, although one or two doctoral programs may be offered.

University: Offers four years of undergraduate work plus graduate degrees through the doctorate in more than two academic or professional fields.

Founding date: If the year an institution was chartered differs from the year when instruction actually began, the earlier date is given.

System or administrative affiliation: Any coordinate institutions or system affiliations are indicated. An institution that has separate colleges or campuses for men and women but shares facilities and courses it is termed a coordinate institution. A formal administrative grouping of institutions, either private or public, of which the college is a part, or the name of a single institution with which the college is administratively affiliated is a system.

Second bullet

Calendar: Most colleges indicate one of the following: *4-1-4, 4-4-1,* or a similar arrangement (two terms of equal length plus an abbreviated winter or spring term, with the numbers referring to months); *semesters; trimesters; quarters; 3-3* (three courses for each of three terms); *modular* (the academic year is divided into small blocks of time; course of varying lengths are assembled according to individual programs); or *standard year* (for most Canadian institutions).

Third bullet

Degree: This names the full range of levels of certificates, diplomas, and degrees, including prebaccalaureate, graduate, and professional, that are offered by this institution.

Associate degree: Normally requires at least two but fewer than four years of full-time college work or its equivalent.

Bachelor's degree (baccalaureate): Requires at least four years but not more than five years of full-time college-level work or its equivalent. This includes all bachelor's degrees in which the normal four years of work are completed in three years and bachelor's degrees conferred in a five-year cooperative (work-study plan) program. A cooperative plan provides for alternate class attendance and employment in business, industry, or government. This allows students to combine actual work experience with their college studies.

Master's degree: Requires the successful completion of a program of study of at least the full-time equivalent of one but not more than two years of work beyond the bachelor's degree.

Doctoral degree (doctorate): The highest degree in graduate study. The doctoral degree classification includes Doctor of Education, Doctor of Juridical Science, Doctor of Public Health, and the Doctor of Philosophy in any nonprofessional field.

First professional degree: The first postbaccalaureate degree in one of the following fields: chiropractic (DC, DCM), dentistry (DDS, DMD), medicine (MD), optometry (OD), osteopathic medicine (DO), rabbinical and Talmudic studies (MHL, Rav), pharmacy (BPharm, PharmD), podiatry (PodD, DP, DPM), veterinary medicine (DVM), law (JD), or divinity/ministry (BD, MDiv).

First professional certificate (postdegree): Requires completion of an organized program of study after completion of the first professional degree. Examples are refresher courses or additional units of study in a specialty or subspecialty.

Post-master's certificate: Requires completion of an organized program of study of 24 credit hours beyond the master's degree but does not meet the requirements of academic degrees at the doctoral level.

Fourth bullet

Setting: Schools are designated as *urban* (located within a major city), *suburban* (a residential area within commuting distance of a major city), *small-town* (a small but compactly settled area not within commuting distance of a major city), or *rural* (a remote and sparsely populated area). The phrase *easy access to . . .* indicates that the campus is within an hour's drive of the nearest major metropolitan area that has a population greater than 500,000.

Fifth bullet

Endowment: The total dollar value of donations to the institution or the multicampus educational system of which the institution is a part.

Sixth bullet

Student body: An institution is coed (coeducational—admits men and women), primarily (80 percent or more) women, primarily men, women only, or men only.

Undergraduate students: Represents the number of full-time and part-time students enrolled in undergraduate degree programs as of fall 2001. The percentage of full-time undergraduates and the percentages of men and women are given.

Seventh bullet

Entrance level: See guidelines in "The Five Levels of Entrance Difficulty" explanation box.

Percent of applicants admitted: The percentage of applicants who were granted admission.

Special Announcements

These messages have been written by those colleges that wished to supplement the profile data with additional, timely, important information.

COLLEGE PROFILE

Undergraduates

For fall 2001, the number of full- and part-time undergraduate students is listed. This list provides the number of states and U.S. territories, including the District of Columbia and Puerto Rico (or, for Canadian institutions, provinces and territories), and other countries from which undergraduates come. Percentages are given of undergraduates who are from out of state; Native American, African American, and Asian American or Pacific Islander; international students; transfer students; and living on campus

THE FIVE LEVELS OF ENTRANCE DIFFICULTY

1. **Most difficult:** More than 75 percent of the current freshmen were in the top 10 percent of their high school class and scored above 1310 on the SAT I (verbal and mathematical combined) or above 29 on the ACT (composite); about 30 percent or fewer of the applicants to this class were accepted.
2. **Very difficult:** More than 50 percent of the current freshmen were in the top 10 percent of their high school class and scored above 1230 on the SAT I or above 26 on the ACT; about 60 percent or fewer of the applicants were accepted.
3. **Moderately difficult:** More than 75 percent of the current freshmen were in the top half of their high school class and scored above 1010 on the SAT I or above 18 on the ACT; about 85 percent or fewer of the applicants were accepted.
4. **Minimally difficult:** Most current freshmen were not in the top half of their high school class and scored somewhat below 1010 on the SAT I or below 18 on the ACT; up to 95 percent of the applicants were accepted.
5. **Noncompetitive:** Virtually all applicants were accepted regardless of high school rank or test scores. Many public institutions are required to admit all state residents.

Retention: The percentage of 2000 freshmen (or, for upper-level institutions, entering students) who returned for the fall 2001 term.

Freshmen

Admission: Figures are given for the number of students who applied for fall 2001 admission, the number of those who were admitted, and the number who enrolled. Freshman statistics include the average high school GPA; the percentage of freshmen who took the SAT I and received verbal and math scores above 500, above 600, and above 700, as well as the percentage of freshmen taking the ACT who received a composite score of 18 or higher.

Faculty

Total: The total number of faculty members; the percentage of full-time faculty members as of fall 2001; and the percentage of full-time faculty members who hold doctoral/first professional/terminal degrees.

Student-faculty ratio: The school's estimate of the ratio of matriculated undergraduate students to faculty members teaching undergraduate courses.

Majors

This section lists the major fields of study offered by the college.

Academic Programs

Details are given here on study options available at each college.

Accelerated degree program: Students may earn a bachelor's degree in three academic years.

Academic remediation for entering students: Instructional courses designed for students deficient in the general competencies necessary for a regular postsecondary curriculum and educational setting.

Adult/continuing education programs: Courses offered for nontraditional students who are currently working or are returning to formal education.

Advanced placement: Credit toward a degree awarded for acceptable scores on College Board Advanced Placement tests.

Cooperative (co-op) education programs: Formal arrangements with off-campus employers allowing students to combine work and study in order to gain degree-related experience, usually extending the time required to complete a degree.

Distance learning: For-credit courses that can be accessed off campus via cable television, the Internet, satellite, videotapes, correspondence course, or other media.

Double major: A program of study in which a student concurrently completes the requirements of two majors.

English as a second language (ESL): A course of study designed specifically for students whose native language is not English.

External degree programs: A program of study in which students earn credits toward a degree through a combination of independent study, college courses, proficiency examinations, and personal experience. External degree programs require minimal or no classroom attendance.

Freshmen honors college: A separate academic program for talented freshmen.

Honors programs: Any special program for very able students offering the opportunity for educational enrichment, independent study, acceleration, or some combination of these.

Independent study: Academic work, usually undertaken outside the regular classroom structure, chosen or designed by the student with the departmental approval and instructor supervision.

Internships: Any short-term, supervised work experience usually related to a student's major field, for which the student earns academic credit. The work can be full- or part-time, on or off campus, paid or unpaid.

Off-campus study: A formal arrangement with one or more domestic institutions under which students may take courses at the other institution(s) for credit.

Part-time degree program: Students may earn a degree through part-time enrollment in regular session (daytime) classes or evening, weekend, or summer classes.

Self-designed major: Program of study based on individual interests, designed by the student with the assistance of an adviser.

Services for LD students: Special help for learning-disabled students with resolvable difficulties, such as dyslexia.

Study abroad: An arrangement by which a student completes part of the academic program studying in another country. A college may operate a campus abroad or it may have a cooperative agreement with other U.S. institutions or institutions in other countries.

Summer session for credit: Summer courses through which students may make up degree work or accelerate their program.

Tutorials: Undergraduates can arrange for special in-depth academic assignments (not for remediation) working with faculty one-on-one or in small groups..

ROTC: Army, Naval, or Air Force Reserve Officers' Training Corps programs offered either on campus or at a cooperating host institution [designated by (C)].

Unusual degree programs: Nontraditional programs such as a 3-2 degree program, in which 3 years of liberal arts study is followed by two years of study in a professional field at another institution (or in a professional division of the same institution), resulting in two bachelor's degrees or a bachelor's and a master's degree.

Library

This section lists the name of the main library; the number of other libraries on campus; numbers of books, microform titles, serials, commercial online services, and audiovisual materials.

Computers on Campus

This paragraph includes the number of on-campus computer terminals and PCs available for general student use and their locations; computer purchase or lease plans; PC requirements for entering students; and campuswide computer network, e-mail, and access to computer labs, the Internet, and software.

Student Life

Housing options: The institution's policy about whether students are permitted to live off campus or are required to live on campus for a specified period; whether freshmen-only, coed, single-sex, cooperative, and disabled student housing options are available. The phrase *college housing not available* indicates that no college-owned or -operated housing facilities are provided for undergraduates and that noncommuting students must arrange for their own accommodations.

Activities and organizations: Lists information on drama-theater groups, choral groups, marching bands, student-run campus newspapers, student-run radio stations and social organizations (sororities, fraternities, eating clubs, etc.) and how many are represented on campus.

Campus security: Campus safety measures including 24-hour emergency response devices (telephones and alarms) and patrols by trained security personnel, student patrols, late-night transport-escort service, and controlled dormitory access (key, security card, etc.).

Student services:
Information provided indicates services offered to students by the college, such as legal services, health clinics, personal-psychological counseling and women's centers.

Athletics

Membership in one or more of the following athletic associations is indicated by initials.

NCAA: National Collegiate Athletic Association

NAIA: National Association of Intercollegiate Athletics

NCCAA: National Christian College Athletic Association

NSCAA: National Small College Athletic Association

NJCAA: National Junior College Athletic Association

CIAU: Canadian Interuniversity Athletic Union

The overall NCAA division in which all or most intercollegiate teams compete is designated by a roman numeral I, II, or III. All teams that do not compete in this division are listed as exceptions.

Sports offered by the college are divided into two groups: intercollegiate (**M** or **W** following the name of each sport indicates that it is offered for men or women) and intramural. An **s** in parentheses following an **M** or **W** for an intercollegiate sport indicates that athletic scholarships (or grants-in-aid) are offered for men or women in that sport, and a **c** indicates a club team as opposed to a varsity team.

Standardized Tests

The most commonly required standardized tests are ACT, SAT I, and SAT II Subject Tests, including the SAT II: Writing. These and other standardized tests may be used for selective admission, as a basis for counseling or course placement, or for both purposes. This section notes if a test is used for admission or placement and whether it is required, required for some, or recommended.

In addition to the ACT and SAT I, the following standardized entrance and placement examinations are referred to by their initials:

ABLE: Adult Basic Learning Examination

ACT ASSET: ACT Assessment of Skills for Successful Entry and Transfer

ACT PEP: ACT Proficiency Examination Program

CAT: California Achievement Tests

CELT: Comprehensive English Language Test

CPAt: Career Programs Assessment

CPT: Computerized Placement Test

DAT: Differential Aptitude Test

LSAT: Law School Admission Test

MAPS: Multiple Assessment Program Service

MCAT: Medical College Admission Test

MMPI: Minnesota Multiphasic Personality Inventory

OAT: Optometry Admission Test

PAA: Prueba de Aptitude Académica (Spanish-language version of the SAT I)

PCAT: Pharmacy College Admission Test

PSAT: Preliminary SAT

SCAT: Scholastic College Aptitude Test

SRA: Scientific Research Association (administers verbal, arithmetical, and achievement tests)

TABE: Test of Adult Basic Education

TASP: Texas Academic Skills Program

TOEFL: Test of English as a Foreign Language (for international students whose native language is not English)

WPCT: Washington Pre-College Test

Costs

Costs are given for the 2002–03 academic year or for the 2001–02 academic year if 2002–03 figures were not yet available. Annual expenses may be expressed as a comprehensive fee (including full-time tuition, mandatory fees, and college room and board) or as separate figures for full-time tuition, fees, room and board, or room only. For public institutions where tuition differs according to residence, separate figures are given for area or state residents and for nonresidents. Part-time tuition is expressed in terms of a per-unit rate (per credit, per semester hour, etc.) as specified by the institution.

The tuition structure at some institutions is complex in that freshmen and sophomores may be charged a different rate from that for juniors and seniors, a professional or vocational division may have a different fee structure from the liberal arts division of the same institution, or part-time tuition may be prorated on a sliding scale according to the number of credit hours taken. Tuition and fees may vary according to academic program, campus/location, class time (day, evening, weekend), course/credit load, course level, degree level, reciprocity agreements, and student level. Room and board charges are reported as an average for one academic year and may vary according to the board plan selected, campus/location, type of housing facility, or student level. If no college-owned or -operated housing facilities are offered, the phrase *college housing not available* will appear in the Housing section of the Student Life paragraph.

Tuition payment plans that may be offered to undergraduates include tuition prepayment, installment payments, and deferred payment. A tuition prepayment plan gives a student the option of locking in the current tuition rate for the entire term of enrollment by paying the full amount in advance rather than year by year. Colleges that offer such a prepayment plan may also help the student to arrange financing.

The availability of full or partial undergraduate tuition waivers to minority students, children of alumni, employees or their children, adult students, and senior citizens may be listed.

Financial Aid

Financial aid information presented represents aid awarded to undergraduates for the 2001–02 academic year. Figures are given for the number of undergraduates who applied for aid, the number who were judged to have need, and the number who had their need met. The number of Federal Work-Study and/or part-time jobs and average earnings are listed, as well as the number of non-need based awards that were made. Non-need based awards are college-administered scholarships for which the college determines the recipient and amount of each award. These scholarships are awarded to full-time undergraduates on the basis of merit or personal attributes without regard to need, although they many certainly be given to students who also happen to need aid. The average percent of need met, the average financial aid package awarded to undergraduates (the amount of scholarships, grants, work-study payments, or loans in the institutionally administered financial aid package divided by the number of students who received any financial aid—amounts used to pay the officially designated Expected Family Contribution (EFC), such as PLUS or other alternative loans, are excluded from the amounts reported), the average amount of need-based gift aid, and the average amount of non-need based aid are given. Average indebtedness, which is the average per-borrower indebtedness of the last graduating undergraduate class from amounts borrowed at this institution through any loan programs, excluding parent loans, is listed last.

Applying

Application and admission options include the following:

Early admission: Highly qualified students may matriculate before graduating from high school.

Early action plan: An admission plan that allows students to apply and be notified of an admission decision well in advance of the regular notification dates. If accepted, the candidate is not committed to enroll; students may reply to the offer under the college's regular reply policy.

Early decision plan: A plan that permits students to apply and be notified of an admission decision (and financial aid offer, if applicable) well in advance of the regular notification date. Applicants agree to accept an offer of admission and to withdraw their applications from other colleges. Candidates who are not accepted under early decision are automatically considered with the regular applicant pool, without prejudice.

Deferred entrance: The practice of permitting accepted students to postpone enrollment, usually for a period of one academic term or year.

Application fee: The fee required with an application is noted. This is typically nonrefundable, although under certain specified conditions it may be waived or returned.

Requirements: Other application requirements are grouped into three categories: required for all, required for some, and recommended. They may include an essay, standardized test scores, a high school transcript, a minimum high school grade point average (expressed as a number on a scale of 0 to 4.0, where 4.0 equals A, 3.0 equals B, etc.), letters of recommendation, an interview on campus or with local alumni, and, for certain types of schools or programs, special requirements such as a musical audition or an art portfolio.

Application deadlines and notification dates: Admission application deadlines and dates for notification of acceptance or rejection are given either as specific dates or as *rolling* and *continuous.* Rolling means that applications are processed as they are received, and qualified students are accepted as long as there are openings. Continuous means that applicants are notified of acceptance or rejection as applications are processed up until the date indicated or the actual beginning of classes. The application deadline and the notification date for transfers are given if they differ from the dates for freshmen. Early decision and early action application deadlines and notification dates are also indicated when relevant.

Freshmen Application Contact

The name, title, and telephone number of the person to contact for application information are given at the end of the profile. The admission office address is listed. Toll-free telephone numbers may also be included. The admission office fax number and e-mail address, if available, are listed, provided the school wanted them printed for use by prospective students.

College Profiles and Special Announcements

This section contains detailed factual profiles of colleges, covering such items as background facts, enrollment figures, faculty size, admission requirements, expenses, financing, housing, student life, campus security, undergraduate majors and degrees, and whom to contact for more information. In addition, there are **Special Announcements** from college administrators about new programs or special events. The data in each of these profiles, collected from fall 2001 to spring 2002, come solely from *Peterson's Annual Survey of Undergraduate Institutions,* which was sent to deans or admission officers at each institution. The profiles are organized state by state and arranged alphabetically within those sections by the official names of the institutions.

ALABAMA

ALABAMA AGRICULTURAL AND MECHANICAL UNIVERSITY
Normal, Alabama

- **State-supported** university, founded 1875
- **Calendar** semesters
- **Degrees** bachelor's, master's, doctoral, and post-master's certificates
- **Suburban** 2001-acre campus
- **Endowment** $31.0 million
- **Coed**
- **Minimally difficult** entrance level

AAMU is a dynamic and progressive multicultural institution with a strong commitment to academic excellence. Some 100 programs are offered through 6 schools. The School of Graduate Studies offers the MS, MBA, MSW, MEd, MURP, EdS, and PhD degrees. Serving approximately 6,000 students, the research institution ably meets the challenges launched by the nation's 2nd-largest research park in Huntsville, Alabama, and the world beyond. Moreover, AAMU students placed on *USA Today*'s Academic Teams in 1997, 1998, 1999, and 2000. Scholarships are available in academics, athletics, music, and theater.

Faculty *Student/faculty ratio:* 21:1.
Student Life *Campus security:* 24-hour patrols, late-night transport/escort service, controlled dormitory access.
Athletics Member NCAA. All Division I except football (Division I-AA).
Standardized Tests *Recommended:* ACT (for admission).
Financial Aid Of all full-time matriculated undergraduates who enrolled in 2001, 3866 applied for aid, 3734 were judged to have need, 1709 had their need fully met. 439 State and other part-time jobs. *Average percent of need met:* 53. *Average financial aid package:* $5086. *Average need-based loan:* $5649. *Average need-based gift aid:* $2980. *Average indebtedness upon graduation:* $17,125.
Applying *Options:* common application, electronic application, deferred entrance. *Application fee:* $10. *Required:* high school transcript, minimum 2.0 GPA. *Recommended:* 1 letter of recommendation.
Admissions Contact Mr. Antonio Boyle, Director of Admissions, Alabama Agricultural and Mechanical University, PO Box 908, Normal, AL 35762. *Phone:* 256-851-5245. *Toll-free phone:* 800-553-0816. *Fax:* 256-851-9747. *E-mail:* aboyle@asnaam.aamu.edu.

ALABAMA STATE UNIVERSITY
Montgomery, Alabama

- **State-supported** comprehensive, founded 1867, part of Alabama Commission on Higher Education
- **Calendar** semesters
- **Degrees** associate, bachelor's, and master's
- **Urban** 114-acre campus
- **Endowment** $15.1 million
- **Coed,** 4,711 undergraduate students, 88% full-time, 58% women, 42% men
- **Minimally difficult** entrance level, 64% of applicants were admitted

Undergraduates 4,135 full-time, 576 part-time. Students come from 39 states and territories, 6 other countries, 30% are from out of state, 93% African American, 0.2% Asian American or Pacific Islander, 0.2% Hispanic American, 0.0% Native American, 0.3% international, 4% transferred in, 43% live on campus.
Freshmen *Admission:* 6,798 applied, 4,322 admitted, 1,280 enrolled. *Average high school GPA:* 2.65. *Test scores:* SAT verbal scores over 500: 15%; SAT math scores over 500: 17%; ACT scores over 18: 39%; SAT verbal scores over 600: 3%; SAT math scores over 600: 2%; ACT scores over 24: 4%.
Faculty *Total:* 356, 61% full-time, 43% with terminal degrees. *Student/faculty ratio:* 18:1.
Majors Accounting; art; art education; biology; business administration; business education; business marketing and marketing management; chemistry; child care/development; community services; computer science; criminal justice/law enforcement administration; early childhood education; economics; education; elementary education; English; finance; French; history; information sciences/systems; journalism; liberal arts and sciences/liberal studies; marine biology; mass communications; mathematics; medical laboratory technician; medical records administration; music; music teacher education; occupational therapy; physical education; political science; pre-medicine; psychology; public relations; radio/television broadcasting; recreation/leisure studies; science education; secondary education; secretarial science; social sciences; social work; sociology; Spanish; special education; speech/rhetorical studies; teacher assistant/aide; theater arts/drama.
Academic Programs *Special study options:* academic remediation for entering students, adult/continuing education programs, advanced placement credit, cooperative education, double majors, honors programs, internships, off-campus study, part-time degree program, study abroad, summer session for credit. *ROTC:* Army (c), Navy (b). *Unusual degree programs:* 3-2 engineering with Auburn University at Montgomery, Tuskegee University.
Library Levi Watkins Learning Center with 395,321 titles, 1,299 serial subscriptions, 42,304 audiovisual materials, an OPAC, a Web page.
Computers on Campus 380 computers available on campus for general student use. A campuswide network can be accessed from off campus that provide access to e-mail. Internet access, online (class) registration, at least one staffed computer lab available.
Student Life *Housing Options:* men-only, women-only. *Activities and Organizations:* drama/theater group, student-run newspaper, choral group, marching band, Student Orientation Services Leaders, Voices of Praise Gospel Choir, Student Government Association, university bands, Commuter Student Association, national fraternities, national sororities. *Campus security:* 24-hour emergency response devices and patrols, late-night transport/escort service, self-defense education, well-lit campus. *Student Services:* health clinic, personal/psychological counseling.
Athletics Member NCAA. All Division I except football (Division I-AA). *Intercollegiate sports:* baseball M(s), basketball M(s)/W(s), bowling W, cross-country running M(s)/W(s), golf M(s), softball W(s), tennis M(s)/W(s), track and field M(s)/W(s), volleyball W(s). *Intramural sports:* baseball M, basketball M/W, field hockey M, softball M/W, swimming M/W, tennis M/W, track and field M/W, volleyball M/W.
Standardized Tests *Recommended:* SAT I or ACT (for admission).
Costs (2001–02) *One-time required fee:* $150. *Tuition:* area resident $2904 full-time; state resident $121 per credit part-time; nonresident $5808 full-time, $2242 per credit part-time. Full-time tuition and fees vary according to course load, degree level, and student level. Part-time tuition and fees vary according to course load, degree level, and student level. *Room and board:* $3500. Room and board charges vary according to housing facility. *Payment plans:* installment, deferred payment. *Waivers:* employees or children of employees.
Financial Aid Of all full-time matriculated undergraduates who enrolled in 2001, 3516 applied for aid, 3268 were judged to have need, 198 had their need fully met. 815 Federal Work-Study jobs (averaging $1846). 175 State and other part-time jobs (averaging $857). In 2001, 459 non-need-based awards were made. *Average percent of need met:* 75%. *Average financial aid package:* $10,158. *Average need-based loan:* $3411. *Average need-based gift aid:* $3793. *Average non-need based aid:* $1863. *Average indebtedness upon graduation:* $25,125.
Applying *Options:* common application, early admission, deferred entrance. *Required:* high school transcript, minimum 2.0 GPA. *Application deadlines:* 7/30 (freshmen), 7/30 (transfers). *Notification:* continuous (freshmen).
Admissions Contact Mrs. Danielle Kennedy-Lamar, Director of Admissions and Recruitment, Alabama State University, PO Box 271, Montgomery, AL 36101-0271. *Phone:* 334-229-4291. *Toll-free phone:* 800-253-5037. *Fax:* 334-229-4984. *E-mail:* dlamar@asunet.alasu.edu.

AMERICAN COLLEGE OF COMPUTER & INFORMATION SCIENCES
Birmingham, Alabama

- **Proprietary** comprehensive, founded 1988
- **Calendar** continuous
- **Degrees** bachelor's and master's (offers only distance learning degree programs)
- **Coed,** 1,400 undergraduate students
- **Moderately difficult** entrance level

Undergraduates Students come from 120 other countries.
Faculty *Total:* 26, 23% full-time, 35% with terminal degrees.
Majors Computer science; information sciences/systems; system administration.
Academic Programs *Special study options:* academic remediation for entering students, accelerated degree program, adult/continuing education programs, advanced placement credit, double majors, external degree program, honors programs, part-time degree program.

Costs (2001–02) *Tuition:* Full-time tuition and fees vary according to program. Part-time tuition and fees vary according to program. No tuition increase for student's term of enrollment. *Payment plans:* tuition prepayment, installment, deferred payment.

Applying *Options:* common application, electronic application. *Application fee:* $20. *Required:* high school transcript. *Application deadline:* rolling (freshmen), rolling (transfers).

Admissions Contact Ms. Natalie Nixon, Director of Admissions, American College of Computer & Information Sciences, 2101 Magnolia Avenue, Birmingham, AL 35205. *Phone:* 205-323-6191. *Toll-free phone:* 800-767-AICS. *Fax:* 205-328-2229. *E-mail:* admiss@accis.edu.

ANDREW JACKSON UNIVERSITY
Birmingham, Alabama

- **Private** comprehensive, founded 1994
- **Degrees** bachelor's and master's (offers primarily external degree programs)
- **Coed,** 134 undergraduate students, 49% women, 51% men

Undergraduates 16% African American, 3% Asian American or Pacific Islander, 3% Hispanic American, 3% Native American.

Faculty *Total:* 25, 48% with terminal degrees. *Student/faculty ratio:* 6:1.

Majors Business; communications; criminal justice studies.

Costs (2001–02) *Tuition:* $375 per course part-time.

Admissions Contact Ms. Bell Woods, Director of Admissions, Andrew Jackson University, 10 Old Montgomery Highway, Birmingham, AL 35209. *Phone:* 205-871-9288.

ATHENS STATE UNIVERSITY
Athens, Alabama

- **State-supported** upper-level, founded 1822, part of The Alabama College System
- **Calendar** semesters
- **Degree** bachelor's
- **Small-town** 45-acre campus
- **Coed,** 2,573 undergraduate students, 42% full-time, 66% women, 34% men
- **Noncompetitive** entrance level, 80% of applicants were admitted

Undergraduates 1,069 full-time, 1,504 part-time. Students come from 5 states and territories, 9 other countries, 5% are from out of state, 11% African American, 0.5% Asian American or Pacific Islander, 0.4% Hispanic American, 2% Native American, 21% transferred in.

Freshmen *Admission:* 530 applied, 425 admitted.

Faculty *Total:* 117, 55% full-time, 39% with terminal degrees. *Student/faculty ratio:* 22:1.

Majors Accounting; art; behavioral sciences; biology; business administration; business management/administrative services related; chemistry; computer science; criminal justice/law enforcement administration; early childhood education; elementary education; English; health science; history; humanities; human resources management; information sciences/systems; mathematics; physical education; physics; political science; psychology; religious studies; science education; science technologies related; secondary education; sociology; special education; trade/industrial education.

Academic Programs *Special study options:* adult/continuing education programs, advanced placement credit, cooperative education, distance learning, double majors, independent study, internships, off-campus study, part-time degree program, summer session for credit. *ROTC:* Army (c).

Library Athens State University Library with 102,475 titles, 317 serial subscriptions, an OPAC, a Web page.

Computers on Campus 200 computers available on campus for general student use. A campuswide network can be accessed from off campus. Internet access, at least one staffed computer lab available.

Student Life *Housing Options:* coed. *Activities and Organizations:* drama/theater group, student-run newspaper, national sororities. *Campus security:* 24-hour emergency response devices, controlled dormitory access. *Student Services:* personal/psychological counseling.

Athletics Member NAIA. *Intercollegiate sports:* basketball M(s), softball W(s). *Intramural sports:* table tennis M/W, volleyball M/W.

Costs (2001–02) *Tuition:* state resident $2550 full-time, $85 per semester hour part-time; nonresident $5100 full-time, $170 per semester hour part-time. Full-time tuition and fees vary according to course load. Part-time tuition and fees vary according to course load. *Required fees:* $180 full-time, $6 per semester hour. *Room and board:* room only: $900. *Waivers:* employees or children of employees.

Financial Aid Of all full-time matriculated undergraduates who enrolled in 2001, 2442 applied for aid, 1942 were judged to have need.

Applying *Options:* deferred entrance. *Application fee:* $30. *Application deadline:* rolling (transfers). *Notification:* continuous (transfers).

Admissions Contact Ms. Necedah Henderson, Coordinator of Admissions, Athens State University, 300 North Beaty Street, Athens, AL 35611-1902. *Phone:* 256-233-8217. *Toll-free phone:* 800-522-0272. *Fax:* 256-233-6565. *E-mail:* henden@athens.edu.

AUBURN UNIVERSITY
Auburn University, Alabama

- **State-supported** university, founded 1856
- **Calendar** quarters
- **Degrees** bachelor's, master's, doctoral, first professional, and post-master's certificates
- **Small-town** 1875-acre campus
- **Endowment** $216.4 million
- **Coed,** 18,922 undergraduate students, 90% full-time, 48% women, 52% men
- **Moderately difficult** entrance level, 76% of applicants were admitted

Undergraduates 17,096 full-time, 1,826 part-time. Students come from 54 states and territories, 61 other countries, 30% are from out of state, 7% African American, 1% Asian American or Pacific Islander, 0.9% Hispanic American, 0.5% Native American, 0.8% international, 7% transferred in, 17% live on campus. *Retention:* 81% of 2001 full-time freshmen returned.

Freshmen *Admission:* 13,645 applied, 10,362 admitted, 3,755 enrolled. *Average high school GPA:* 3.34. *Test scores:* SAT verbal scores over 500: 74%; SAT math scores over 500: 80%; ACT scores over 18: 96%; SAT verbal scores over 600: 25%; SAT math scores over 600: 32%; ACT scores over 24: 47%; SAT verbal scores over 700: 4%; SAT math scores over 700: 5%; ACT scores over 30: 7%.

Faculty *Total:* 1,230, 91% full-time, 89% with terminal degrees. *Student/faculty ratio:* 16:1.

Majors Accounting; adult/continuing education; aerospace engineering; agricultural economics; agricultural education; agricultural engineering; agricultural sciences; animal sciences; anthropology; applied mathematics; architectural engineering; architectural environmental design; architecture; art; biochemistry; bioengineering; biology; broadcast journalism; business administration; business economics; business education; business marketing and marketing management; chemical engineering; chemistry; child care/development; civil engineering; clothing/apparel/textile studies; computer engineering; criminology; developmental/child psychology; early childhood education; economics; education of the visually handicapped; electrical engineering; elementary education; engineering; English; environmental science; finance; fine/studio arts; food sciences; forestry sciences; French; geography; geological engineering; geology; German; graphic design/commercial art/illustration; health education; health services administration; history; home economics; home economics education; horticulture science; hotel and restaurant management; housing studies; human resources management; individual/family development; industrial design; industrial/manufacturing engineering; interior architecture; international business; journalism; landscape architecture; logistics/materials management; management information systems/business data processing; marine biology; mass communications; materials engineering; mathematics; mechanical engineering; medical laboratory technician; medical laboratory technology; medical technology; microbiology/bacteriology; molecular biology; music (piano and organ performance); music teacher education; nursing; nutrition studies; operations management; ornamental horticulture; philosophy; physical education; physics; political science; poultry science; predentistry; pre-law; pre-medicine; pre-veterinary studies; psychology; public administration; public relations; radio/television broadcasting; recreation/leisure studies; science education; secondary education; social work; sociology; Spanish; speech-language pathology/audiology; speech/rhetorical studies; speech therapy; textile sciences/engineering; theater arts/drama; trade/industrial education; transportation technology; wildlife management; zoology.

Academic Programs *Special study options:* accelerated degree program, adult/continuing education programs, advanced placement credit, cooperative education, distance learning, double majors, English as a second language, honors programs, independent study, internships, part-time degree program, services for LD students, study abroad, summer session for credit. *ROTC:* Army (b), Navy (b), Air Force (b).

Library R. B. Draughon Library plus 2 others with 2.5 million titles, 18,919 serial subscriptions, 629,038 audiovisual materials, an OPAC, a Web page.

Auburn University (continued)

Computers on Campus 600 computers available on campus for general student use. A campuswide network can be accessed from student residence rooms and from off campus. Online (class) registration, at least one staffed computer lab available.

Student Life *Housing Options:* coed, men-only, women-only, disabled students. *Activities and Organizations:* drama/theater group, student-run newspaper, radio and television station, choral group, marching band, Student Government Association, University Program Council, IMPACT, Panhellenic Council, Interfraternity Council, national fraternities, national sororities. *Campus security:* 24-hour emergency response devices and patrols, late-night transport/escort service, controlled dormitory access. *Student Services:* health clinic, personal/psychological counseling.

Athletics Member NCAA. All Division I except football (Division I-A). *Intercollegiate sports:* baseball M(s), basketball M(s)/W(s), cross-country running M(s)/W(s), golf M(s)/W(s), gymnastics W(s), soccer W(s), softball W(s), swimming M(s)/W(s), tennis M(s)/W(s), track and field M(s)/W(s), volleyball W(s). *Intramural sports:* badminton M(c)/W(c), basketball M/W, bowling M/W, equestrian sports W, fencing M/W, football M/W, golf M/W, gymnastics M(c)/W(c), lacrosse M(c)/W(c), racquetball M/W, rugby M(c), sailing M/W, soccer M(c)/W(c), softball M/W, swimming M(c)/W(c), table tennis M/W, tennis M/W, track and field M/W, volleyball M(c)/W(c), weight lifting M(c)/W(c), wrestling M(c).

Standardized Tests *Required:* SAT I or ACT (for admission).

Costs (2001–02) *Tuition:* state resident $3260 full-time, $135 per credit hour part-time; nonresident $9780 full-time, $405 per credit hour part-time. Full-time tuition and fees vary according to program. Part-time tuition and fees vary according to program. *Required fees:* $120 full-time. *Room and board:* room only: $2130. Room and board charges vary according to housing facility. *Waivers:* children of alumni and employees or children of employees.

Financial Aid Of all full-time matriculated undergraduates who enrolled in 2001, 6799 applied for aid, 4413 were judged to have need. In 2001, 770 non-need-based awards were made. *Average percent of need met:* 60%. *Average financial aid package:* $5752. *Average need-based loan:* $3763. *Average need-based gift aid:* $2473. *Average indebtedness upon graduation:* $18,069.

Applying *Options:* early admission, early action, deferred entrance. *Application fee:* $25. *Required:* high school transcript, minimum 2.0 GPA. *Required for some:* minimum 3.0 GPA. *Application deadline:* 8/1 (freshmen), rolling (transfers). *Notification:* continuous (freshmen).

Admissions Contact Dr. John Fletcher, Acting Assistant Vice President of Enrollment Management, Auburn University, 202 Mary Martin Hall, Auburn University, AL 36849-0001. *Phone:* 334-844-4080. *Toll-free phone:* 800-AUBURN9. *E-mail:* admissions@mail.auburn.edu.

AUBURN UNIVERSITY MONTGOMERY
Montgomery, Alabama

- **State-supported** comprehensive, founded 1967, part of Auburn University
- **Calendar** quarters
- **Degrees** bachelor's, master's, and doctoral
- **Suburban** 500-acre campus
- **Endowment** $17.2 million
- **Coed,** 4,166 undergraduate students, 61% full-time, 64% women, 36% men
- **Moderately difficult** entrance level

Undergraduates 2,541 full-time, 1,625 part-time. Students come from 34 states and territories, 18 other countries, 3% are from out of state, 34% African American, 2% Asian American or Pacific Islander, 1% Hispanic American, 0.6% Native American, 1% international, 9% transferred in, 16% live on campus.

Freshmen *Admission:* 613 enrolled. *Test scores:* ACT scores over 18: 87%; ACT scores over 24: 22%; ACT scores over 30: 1%.

Faculty *Total:* 318, 57% full-time, 48% with terminal degrees. *Student/faculty ratio:* 18:1.

Majors Accounting; art; biology; business; business administration; business economics; business marketing and marketing management; communications; criminal justice studies; elementary education; English; finance; foreign languages/literatures; history; human resources management; liberal arts and sciences/liberal studies; management information systems/business data processing; mathematics; nursing; physical sciences; political science; psychology; secondary education; sociology.

Academic Programs *Special study options:* academic remediation for entering students, accelerated degree program, adult/continuing education programs, advanced placement credit, cooperative education, distance learning, double majors, English as a second language, honors programs, independent study, internships, off-campus study, part-time degree program, services for LD students, student-designed majors, study abroad, summer session for credit. *ROTC:* Army (b), Air Force (c).

Library Auburn University Montgomery Library with 292,586 titles, 5,820 serial subscriptions, 24,158 audiovisual materials, an OPAC, a Web page.

Computers on Campus 300 computers available on campus for general student use. A campuswide network can be accessed from student residence rooms and from off campus. Internet access, online (class) registration, at least one staffed computer lab available.

Student Life *Housing Options:* coed, disabled students. *Activities and Organizations:* drama/theater group, student-run newspaper, choral group, Student Government Association, Baptist Campus Ministries, International Student Association, African-American Student Alliance, national fraternities, national sororities. *Campus security:* 24-hour emergency response devices and patrols, student patrols, late-night transport/escort service. *Student Services:* health clinic, personal/psychological counseling.

Athletics Member NAIA. *Intercollegiate sports:* baseball M(s), basketball M(s)/W(s), soccer M(s)/W(s), tennis M(s)/W(s). *Intramural sports:* basketball M/W, bowling M/W, football M/W, soccer M/W, softball M/W, tennis M/W, volleyball M/W.

Standardized Tests *Required:* SAT I or ACT (for admission).

Costs (2001–02) *One-time required fee:* $25. *Tuition:* state resident $3210 full-time, $107 per semester hour part-time; nonresident $9630 full-time, $321 per semester hour part-time. Full-time tuition and fees vary according to course load. *Required fees:* $230 full-time, $5 per credit, $40 per term part-time. *Room and board:* $4770; room only: $1890. *Payment plan:* deferred payment. *Waivers:* employees or children of employees.

Financial Aid Of all full-time matriculated undergraduates who enrolled in 2001, 55 Federal Work-Study jobs (averaging $4000).

Applying *Options:* electronic application, deferred entrance. *Application fee:* $25. *Required:* high school transcript. *Application deadline:* rolling (freshmen), rolling (transfers). *Notification:* continuous (freshmen).

Admissions Contact Ms. Valerie Samuel, Assistant Director, Admissions, Auburn University Montgomery, PO Box 244023, Montgomery, AL 36124-4023. *Phone:* 334-244-3667. *Toll-free phone:* 800-227-2649. *Fax:* 334-244-3795. *E-mail:* auminfo@mickey.aum.edu.

BIRMINGHAM-SOUTHERN COLLEGE
Birmingham, Alabama

- **Independent Methodist** comprehensive, founded 1856
- **Calendar** 4-1-4
- **Degrees** bachelor's, master's, and postbachelor's certificates
- **Urban** 196-acre campus
- **Endowment** $131.9 million
- **Coed,** 1,347 undergraduate students, 95% full-time, 60% women, 40% men
- **Moderately difficult** entrance level, 92% of applicants were admitted

Birmingham-Southern is a nationally ranked institution noted for an outstanding record of job placement and graduate admission to medical, law, and professional schools. In addition, the Mentor Program, service learning, leadership development, and international programs are also excellent opportunities. *U.S. News & World Report, Money* magazine, and *National Review* have also recognized Southern, which has one of three Phi Beta Kappa chapters in Alabama.

Undergraduates 1,279 full-time, 68 part-time. Students come from 28 states and territories, 23% are from out of state, 7% African American, 3% Asian American or Pacific Islander, 0.5% Hispanic American, 0.5% Native American, 0.1% international, 3% transferred in, 84% live on campus. *Retention:* 84% of 2001 full-time freshmen returned.

Freshmen *Admission:* 1,047 applied, 961 admitted, 388 enrolled. *Average high school GPA:* 3.35. *Test scores:* SAT verbal scores over 500: 93%; SAT math scores over 500: 87%; ACT scores over 18: 100%; SAT verbal scores over 600: 53%; SAT math scores over 600: 44%; ACT scores over 24: 81%; SAT verbal scores over 700: 12%; SAT math scores over 700: 6%; ACT scores over 30: 21%.

Faculty *Total:* 131, 75% full-time, 80% with terminal degrees. *Student/faculty ratio:* 12:1.

Majors Accounting; art; art education; art history; Asian studies; biology; business administration; chemistry; computer science; dance; drawing; early childhood education; economics; education; elementary education; English; fine/studio arts; French; German; history; human resources management; interdisciplinary studies; international business; mathematics; music; music history; music (piano and organ performance); music teacher education; music (voice and choral/opera performance); painting; philosophy; physics; political science; pre-dentistry; pre-law; pre-medicine; printmaking; psychology; religious studies; sculpture; secondary education; sociology; Spanish; theater arts/drama.

Academic Programs *Special study options:* accelerated degree program, adult/continuing education programs, advanced placement credit, double majors, honors programs, independent study, internships, off-campus study, part-time degree program, student-designed majors, study abroad, summer session for credit. *ROTC:* Army (c), Air Force (c). *Unusual degree programs:* 3-2 engineering with Auburn University, Columbia University, Washington University in St. Louis, University of Alabama at Birmingham; nursing with Vanderbilt University; environmental studies with Duke University.

Library Charles Andrew Rush Learning Center/N. E. Miles Library with 170,103 titles, 1,155 serial subscriptions, 23,801 audiovisual materials, an OPAC, a Web page.

Computers on Campus 156 computers available on campus for general student use. A campuswide network can be accessed from student residence rooms and from off campus. At least one staffed computer lab available.

Student Life *Housing:* on-campus residence required through senior year. *Options:* men-only, women-only, disabled students. *Activities and Organizations:* drama/theater group, student-run newspaper, radio station, choral group, Southern Volunteer Services, Student Conservancy, Residence Hall Association, national fraternities, national sororities. *Campus security:* 24-hour emergency response devices and patrols, late-night transport/escort service, controlled dormitory access, vehicle safety inspection. *Student Services:* health clinic, personal/psychological counseling.

Athletics Member NCAA. All Division I. *Intercollegiate sports:* baseball M(s), basketball M(s)/W(s), cross-country running M(s)/W(s), golf M(s)/W(s), riflery W(s), soccer M(s)/W(s), softball W(s), tennis M(s)/W(s), volleyball W(s). *Intramural sports:* basketball M/W, fencing M, football M/W, golf M/W, racquetball M, soccer M/W, softball M/W, tennis M/W, volleyball M/W.

Standardized Tests *Required:* SAT I or ACT (for admission).

Costs (2001–02) *Comprehensive fee:* $23,165 includes full-time tuition ($16,810), mandatory fees ($375), and room and board ($5980). Full-time tuition and fees vary according to class time and course load. Part-time tuition: $700 per credit. Part-time tuition and fees vary according to class time and course load. *Room and board:* College room only: $3320. Room and board charges vary according to board plan and housing facility. *Payment plan:* installment. *Waivers:* children of alumni and employees or children of employees.

Financial Aid Of all full-time matriculated undergraduates who enrolled in 2001, 648 applied for aid, 502 were judged to have need, 171 had their need fully met. 142 Federal Work-Study jobs (averaging $1818). 157 State and other part-time jobs (averaging $1371). In 2001, 654 non-need-based awards were made. *Average percent of need met:* 82%. *Average financial aid package:* $14,189. *Average need-based loan:* $4261. *Average need-based gift aid:* $10,805. *Average non-need based aid:* $8483. *Average indebtedness upon graduation:* $13,000.

Applying *Options:* common application, electronic application, early admission, early action, deferred entrance. *Application fee:* $25. *Required:* essay or personal statement, high school transcript, minimum 2.0 GPA, 1 letter of recommendation. *Required for some:* interview. *Recommended:* interview. *Application deadline:* rolling (freshmen), rolling (transfers). *Notification:* continuous (freshmen), 12/15 (early action).

Admissions Contact Ms. DeeDee Barnes Bruns, Vice President for Admission and Financial Aid, Birmingham-Southern College, Box 549008, Birmingham, AL 35254. *Phone:* 205-226-4696. *Toll-free phone:* 800-523-5793. *Fax:* 205-226-3074. *E-mail:* admissions@bsc.edu.

COLUMBIA SOUTHERN UNIVERSITY

Orange Beach, Alabama

- **Proprietary** comprehensive
- **Calendar** modular
- **Degrees** certificates, bachelor's, and master's (offers only distance learning degree programs)
- **Coed,** 1,600 undergraduate students
- **Noncompetitive** entrance level

Undergraduates Students come from 54 states and territories, 42 other countries.

Freshmen *Admission:* 3,709 admitted.

Faculty *Total:* 45, 2% full-time, 76% with terminal degrees. *Student/faculty ratio:* 135:1.

Majors Business administration; business information/data processing related; business marketing and marketing management; computer management; criminal justice studies; environmental science; fire protection/safety technology; fire services administration; health services administration; human resources management related; international business; occupational safety/health technology; sport/fitness administration.

Academic Programs *Special study options:* academic remediation for entering students, adult/continuing education programs, distance learning, external degree program.

Costs (2001–02) *Tuition:* $125 per credit hour part-time. No tuition increase for student's term of enrollment. *Payment plans:* tuition prepayment, installment. *Waivers:* employees or children of employees.

Applying *Options:* common application, electronic application. *Application fee:* $25. *Required for some:* high school transcript. *Application deadline:* rolling (freshmen), rolling (transfers).

Admissions Contact Mr. Poche Waguespack, Dean of Students, Columbia Southern University, 24847 Commercial Avenue, Orange Beach, AL 36561. *Phone:* 334-981-3771 Ext. 110. *Toll-free phone:* 800-977-8449. *E-mail:* tommy@columbiasouthern.edu.

CONCORDIA COLLEGE

Selma, Alabama

Admissions Contact Ms. Gwendolyn Moore, Director of Admissions, Concordia College, 1804 Green Street, PO Box 1329, Selma, AL 36701. *Phone:* 334-874-7143. *Fax:* 334-874-3728.

EDUCATION AMERICA, SOUTHEAST COLLEGE OF TECHNOLOGY, MOBILE CAMPUS

Mobile, Alabama

- **Independent** 4-year, part of Education America
- **Degrees** associate and bachelor's
- 631 undergraduate students, 100% full-time
- 100% of applicants were admitted

Undergraduates Students come from 3 states and territories, 7% are from out of state, 38% African American, 3% Asian American or Pacific Islander, 0.8% Hispanic American, 0.3% Native American. *Retention:* 90% of 2001 full-time freshmen returned.

Freshmen *Admission:* 135 applied, 135 admitted. *Average high school GPA:* 2.65.

Faculty *Total:* 41, 76% full-time, 10% with terminal degrees. *Student/faculty ratio:* 16:1.

Majors Computer engineering technology; computer/information sciences; computer systems networking/telecommunications; drafting; information sciences/systems; operations management; Web/multimedia management/webmaster.

Student Life *Housing:* college housing not available. *Activities and Organizations:* Association of Information Technology Professionals, Instrumentation Technology Association.

Costs (2001–02) *Tuition:* $21,285 full-time, $221 per credit hour part-time. No tuition increase for student's term of enrollment. *Required fees:* $3600 full-time. *Waivers:* employees or children of employees.

Financial Aid Of all full-time matriculated undergraduates who enrolled in 2001, 1076 applied for aid. 8 Federal Work-Study jobs (averaging $4500). *Average indebtedness upon graduation:* $16,000.

Applying *Application fee:* $50. *Required:* high school transcript.

Admissions Contact Mr. Randall Olson, Director of Recruitment, Education America, Southeast College of Technology, Mobile Campus, 828 Downtowner Loop West, Mobile, AL 36609. *Phone:* 251-343-8200 Ext. 221. *Toll-free phone:* 251-343-8200 Ext. 201 (in-state); 800-866-0850 Ext. 201 (out-of-state). *Fax:* 251-343-0577.

FAULKNER UNIVERSITY

Montgomery, Alabama

- **Independent** comprehensive, founded 1942, affiliated with Church of Christ
- **Calendar** semesters
- **Degrees** associate, bachelor's, master's, and first professional
- **Urban** 75-acre campus
- **Endowment** $9.7 million
- **Coed,** 2,338 undergraduate students, 73% full-time, 61% women, 39% men
- **Minimally difficult** entrance level, 71% of applicants were admitted

Faulkner University (continued)

Undergraduates 1,698 full-time, 640 part-time. Students come from 11 states and territories, 4 other countries, 11% are from out of state, 39% African American, 0.6% Asian American or Pacific Islander, 0.7% Hispanic American, 0.7% Native American, 0.5% international, 45% transferred in, 59% live on campus. *Retention:* 48% of 2001 full-time freshmen returned.

Freshmen *Admission:* 604 applied, 428 admitted, 390 enrolled. *Test scores:* ACT scores over 18: 70%; ACT scores over 24: 23%; ACT scores over 30: 4%.

Faculty *Total:* 62, 94% full-time, 63% with terminal degrees. *Student/faculty ratio:* 19:1.

Majors Accounting; athletic training/sports medicine; biblical studies; biology; biomedical technology; business administration; business education; business machine repair; business marketing and marketing management; computer management; computer typography/composition; criminal justice/law enforcement administration; criminology; dietetics; divinity/ministry; early childhood education; education; elementary education; emergency medical technology; engineering; English; history; humanities; human resources management; industrial radiologic technology; information sciences/systems; liberal arts and sciences/liberal studies; medical assistant; medical laboratory technician; medical records administration; medical technology; occupational therapy; paralegal/legal assistant; pastoral counseling; physical education; physical sciences; physical therapy; political science; pre-engineering; pre-law; psychology; religious education; religious studies; respiratory therapy; secondary education; secretarial science; social sciences; sport/fitness administration; theology.

Academic Programs *Special study options:* academic remediation for entering students, accelerated degree program, adult/continuing education programs, advanced placement credit, double majors, independent study, internships, off-campus study, part-time degree program, services for LD students, summer session for credit.

Library Gus Nichols Library plus 2 others with 118,039 titles, 1,183 serial subscriptions, 730 audiovisual materials, an OPAC, a Web page.

Computers on Campus 85 computers available on campus for general student use. Internet access, at least one staffed computer lab available.

Student Life *Housing:* on-campus residence required through junior year. *Options:* coed, men-only, women-only. *Activities and Organizations:* drama/theater group, student-run newspaper, choral group, social clubs, student government, Ambassadors, Thespians, Acappella Chorus. *Campus security:* 24-hour patrols, late-night transport/escort service. *Student Services:* women's center.

Athletics Member NAIA, NCCAA. *Intercollegiate sports:* baseball M(s), basketball M(s), cross-country running M/W, softball W(s), volleyball W(s). *Intramural sports:* basketball M/W, football M/W, softball M/W, volleyball M/W.

Standardized Tests *Required:* SAT I or ACT (for admission).

Costs (2001–02) *Comprehensive fee:* $13,000 includes full-time tuition ($8700) and room and board ($4300). Full-time tuition and fees vary according to program. Part-time tuition: $290 per semester hour. Part-time tuition and fees vary according to program. *Room and board:* College room only: $2050. Room and board charges vary according to board plan and student level. *Payment plans:* installment, deferred payment. *Waivers:* adult students and employees or children of employees.

Financial Aid Of all full-time matriculated undergraduates who enrolled in 2001, 1613 applied for aid, 1371 were judged to have need, 151 had their need fully met. 135 Federal Work-Study jobs (averaging $1250). 5 State and other part-time jobs (averaging $550). In 2001, 57 non-need-based awards were made. *Average percent of need met:* 62%. *Average financial aid package:* $7000. *Average need-based loan:* $4700. *Average need-based gift aid:* $2600. *Average non-need based aid:* $1850. *Average indebtedness upon graduation:* $18,000.

Applying *Options:* common application, electronic application, early admission, deferred entrance. *Application fee:* $10. *Required:* high school transcript, minimum 2.0 GPA, 2 letters of recommendation. *Recommended:* essay or personal statement, interview. *Application deadline:* rolling (freshmen), rolling (transfers).

Admissions Contact Mr. Keith Mock, Director of Admissions, Faulkner University, 5345 Atlanta Highway, Montgomery, AL 36109. *Phone:* 334-386-7200. *Toll-free phone:* 800-879-9816. *Fax:* 334-386-7137. *E-mail:* admissions@faulkner.edu.

HERITAGE CHRISTIAN UNIVERSITY
Florence, Alabama

- **Independent** comprehensive, founded 1971, affiliated with Church of Christ
- **Calendar** semesters
- **Degrees** associate, bachelor's, and master's
- **Small-town** 43-acre campus
- **Endowment** $3.5 million
- **Coed,** 149 undergraduate students, 40% full-time, 21% women, 79% men
- **Noncompetitive** entrance level, 100% of applicants were admitted

Undergraduates Students come from 25 states and territories, 10 other countries, 57% are from out of state, 10% African American, 0.7% Hispanic American, 11% international.

Freshmen *Admission:* 17 applied, 17 admitted.

Faculty *Total:* 22, 18% full-time, 18% with terminal degrees. *Student/faculty ratio:* 9:1.

Majors Biblical studies.

Academic Programs *Special study options:* accelerated degree program, adult/continuing education programs, distance learning, external degree program, independent study, internships, part-time degree program, summer session for credit.

Library Overton Memorial Library with 50,000 titles, 260 serial subscriptions.

Computers on Campus 12 computers available on campus for general student use.

Student Life *Activities and Organizations:* Missions Club, Preachers Club, Student Government Association, Christian Ladies Organization. *Student Services:* personal/psychological counseling.

Athletics *Intramural sports:* softball M/W.

Standardized Tests *Required:* English proficiency test.

Costs (2002–03) *Tuition:* $5824 full-time, $208 per hour part-time. *Required fees:* $480 full-time, $20 per hour. *Room only:* $1300. *Payment plans:* installment, deferred payment. *Waivers:* employees or children of employees.

Financial Aid Of all full-time matriculated undergraduates who enrolled in 2001, 58 applied for aid, 58 were judged to have need, 58 had their need fully met. In 2001, 15 non-need-based awards were made. *Average percent of need met:* 38%. *Average financial aid package:* $4650. *Average need-based loan:* $2550. *Average need-based gift aid:* $2262.

Applying *Options:* early admission, deferred entrance. *Application fee:* $25. *Required:* high school transcript, 3 letters of recommendation. *Recommended:* interview. *Application deadline:* rolling (freshmen), rolling (transfers). *Notification:* continuous until 7/1 (freshmen).

Admissions Contact Mr. Jim Collins, Director of Enrollment Services, Heritage Christian University, PO Box HCU, Florence, AL 35630-0050. *Phone:* 256-766-6610 Ext. 48. *Toll-free phone:* 800-367-3565.

HERZING COLLEGE
Birmingham, Alabama

- **Proprietary** primarily 2-year, founded 1965, part of Herzing Institutes, Inc
- **Calendar** semesters
- **Degrees** diplomas, associate, and bachelor's
- **Urban** campus
- **Coed,** 600 undergraduate students, 66% full-time, 29% women, 72% men
- **Minimally difficult** entrance level

Undergraduates 398 full-time, 202 part-time. Students come from 3 states and territories, 7 other countries, 1% are from out of state, 43% African American, 0.2% Asian American or Pacific Islander, 0.5% Hispanic American, 8% transferred in. *Retention:* 6% of 2001 full-time freshmen returned.

Freshmen *Admission:* 55 enrolled. *Average high school GPA:* 3.00.

Faculty *Total:* 27, 33% full-time, 78% with terminal degrees. *Student/faculty ratio:* 20:1.

Majors Business machine repair; business management/administrative services related; computer/information sciences; computer programming; computer science; data processing technology; electrical/electronic engineering technology; information sciences/systems; secretarial science.

Academic Programs *Special study options:* adult/continuing education programs, advanced placement credit, cooperative education, external degree program, internships, student-designed majors, summer session for credit.

Computers on Campus 125 computers available on campus for general student use. Internet access, at least one staffed computer lab available.

Student Life *Housing:* college housing not available. *Campus security:* 24-hour emergency response devices, late-night transport/escort service, security guard. *Student Services:* personal/psychological counseling, women's center.

Costs (2001–02) *Tuition:* $23,520 full-time, $250 per credit hour part-time. Full-time tuition and fees vary according to location and program. Part-time tuition and fees vary according to location and program. *Payment plan:* installment. *Waivers:* employees or children of employees.

Applying *Options:* early admission, deferred entrance. *Application deadline:* rolling (freshmen), rolling (transfers). *Notification:* continuous (freshmen).

Admissions Contact Mr. Michael A. Cates, Admissions Coordinator, Herzing College, 280 West Valley Avenue, Birmingham, AL 35209. *Phone:* 205-916-2800. *Fax:* 205-916-2807.

HUNTINGDON COLLEGE
Montgomery, Alabama

- **Independent United Methodist** 4-year, founded 1854
- **Calendar** 4-1-4
- **Degrees** certificates, associate, and bachelor's
- **Suburban** 58-acre campus with easy access to Birmingham
- **Endowment** $35.7 million
- **Coed,** 615 undergraduate students, 94% full-time, 65% women, 35% men
- **Moderately difficult** entrance level, 82% of applicants were admitted

Undergraduates 577 full-time, 38 part-time. Students come from 21 states and territories, 12 other countries, 19% are from out of state, 7% African American, 1% Asian American or Pacific Islander, 0.3% Hispanic American, 0.8% Native American, 4% international, 5% transferred in, 65% live on campus. *Retention:* 80% of 2001 full-time freshmen returned.

Freshmen *Admission:* 579 applied, 473 admitted, 152 enrolled. *Average high school GPA:* 3.38. *Test scores:* SAT verbal scores over 500: 93%; SAT math scores over 500: 70%; ACT scores over 18: 96%; SAT verbal scores over 600: 47%; SAT math scores over 600: 39%; ACT scores over 24: 48%; SAT verbal scores over 700: 8%; ACT scores over 30: 4%.

Faculty *Total:* 66, 62% full-time, 59% with terminal degrees. *Student/faculty ratio:* 12:1.

Majors Accounting; American studies; applied art; art; art education; athletic training/sports medicine; biology; business administration; business economics; business marketing and marketing management; cell and molecular biology related; chemistry; chemistry education; communications; computer graphics; computer science; creative writing; dance; drama/dance education; ecology; education; English; English education; environmental science; European studies; exercise sciences; history; history education; interdisciplinary studies; international business; international relations; liberal arts and sciences/liberal studies; mathematics; mathematics education; multi/interdisciplinary studies related; music; music (piano and organ performance); music teacher education; music (voice and choral/opera performance); paralegal/legal assistant; physical education; physical therapy; political science; pre-dentistry; pre-law; pre-medicine; pre-veterinary studies; psychology; public administration; recreation/leisure facilities management; recreation/leisure studies; religious education; religious studies; secondary education; Spanish; speech/rhetorical studies; sport/fitness administration; theater arts/drama.

Academic Programs *Special study options:* accelerated degree program, adult/continuing education programs, advanced placement credit, cooperative education, double majors, honors programs, independent study, internships, off-campus study, part-time degree program, student-designed majors, study abroad, summer session for credit. *ROTC:* Army (c), Air Force (c). *Unusual degree programs:* 3-2 engineering with Auburn University, The University of Alabama at Birmingham.

Library Houghton Memorial Library with 97,436 titles, 443 serial subscriptions, 1,811 audiovisual materials, a Web page.

Computers on Campus 75 computers available on campus for general student use. A campuswide network can be accessed from student residence rooms and from off campus that provide access to personal computer given to each entering student. Internet access, at least one staffed computer lab available.

Student Life *Housing:* on-campus residence required through junior year. *Options:* coed. *Activities and Organizations:* drama/theater group, student-run newspaper, choral group, Circle K, SGA, Civitan, International Student Association, BACCHUS, national fraternities, national sororities. *Campus security:* 24-hour emergency response devices and patrols, late-night transport/escort service, controlled dormitory access, electronic video surveillance. *Student Services:* health clinic, personal/psychological counseling.

Athletics Member NCAA. All Division III. *Intercollegiate sports:* baseball M, basketball M/W, crew M(c)/W(c), cross-country running M/W, golf M, sailing M(c)/W(c), soccer M/W, softball W, tennis M/W, volleyball W. *Intramural sports:* basketball M/W, crew M/W, fencing M/W, football M/W, golf M/W, rugby M/W, soccer M/W, softball M/W, table tennis M/W, tennis M/W, volleyball M/W, weight lifting M/W.

Standardized Tests *Required:* SAT I or ACT (for admission).

Costs (2001–02) *Comprehensive fee:* $18,170 includes full-time tuition ($11,500), mandatory fees ($920), and room and board ($5750). Full-time tuition and fees vary according to class time, reciprocity agreements, and student level. Part-time tuition: $450 per semester hour. Part-time tuition and fees vary according to class time and course load. *Room and board:* Room and board charges vary according to housing facility. *Payment plan:* deferred payment. *Waivers:* employees or children of employees.

Financial Aid Of all full-time matriculated undergraduates who enrolled in 2001, 464 applied for aid, 371 were judged to have need, 197 had their need fully met. In 2001, 151 non-need-based awards were made. *Average percent of need met:* 91%. *Average financial aid package:* $10,654. *Average need-based loan:* $3127. *Average need-based gift aid:* $6561. *Average non-need based aid:* $5691. *Average indebtedness upon graduation:* $15,324.

Applying *Options:* common application, electronic application, early admission, deferred entrance. *Application fee:* $25. *Required:* high school transcript, minimum 2.25 GPA. *Required for some:* essay or personal statement, 2 letters of recommendation, interview. *Recommended:* 3 letters of recommendation. *Application deadline:* rolling (freshmen), rolling (transfers).

Admissions Contact Mrs. Laura Huncan, Director of Admissions, Huntingdon College, 1500 East Fairview Avenue, Montgomery, AL 36106. *Phone:* 334-833-4496. *Toll-free phone:* 800-763-0313. *Fax:* 334-833-4347. *E-mail:* admiss@huntingdon.edu.

ITT TECHNICAL INSTITUTE
Birmingham, Alabama

- **Proprietary** primarily 2-year, founded 1994, part of ITT Educational Services, Inc
- **Calendar** quarters
- **Degrees** associate and bachelor's
- **Suburban** campus
- **Coed,** 443 undergraduate students
- **Minimally difficult** entrance level

Majors Computer/information sciences related; computer programming; drafting; electrical/electronic engineering technologies related; information technology.

Student Life *Housing:* college housing not available. *Activities and Organizations:* student-run newspaper. *Campus security:* 24-hour emergency response devices.

Costs (2001–02) *Tuition:* Full-time tuition and fees vary according to program. Part-time tuition and fees vary according to program. $260—$330 per credit hour.

Applying *Options:* deferred entrance. *Application fee:* $100. *Required:* high school transcript, interview. *Recommended:* letters of recommendation. *Application deadline:* rolling (freshmen), rolling (transfers). *Notification:* continuous (freshmen).

Admissions Contact Mr. Jerome Ruffin, Director of Recruitment, ITT Technical Institute, 500 Riverhills Business Park, Birmingham, AL 35242. *Phone:* 205-991-5410. *Toll-free phone:* 800-488-7033. *Fax:* 205-991-5025.

JACKSONVILLE STATE UNIVERSITY
Jacksonville, Alabama

- **State-supported** comprehensive, founded 1883
- **Calendar** 4-1-4
- **Degrees** bachelor's and master's
- **Small-town** 345-acre campus with easy access to Birmingham
- **Endowment** $25.7 million
- **Coed,** 7,011 undergraduate students, 80% full-time, 58% women, 42% men
- **Minimally difficult** entrance level, 47% of applicants were admitted

Undergraduates 5,593 full-time, 1,418 part-time. Students come from 35 states and territories, 75 other countries, 10% are from out of state, 10% transferred in, 20% live on campus. *Retention:* 60% of 2001 full-time freshmen returned.

Freshmen *Admission:* 2,300 applied, 1,077 admitted, 1,205 enrolled. *Average high school GPA:* 3.11.

Faculty *Total:* 386, 69% full-time, 41% with terminal degrees. *Student/faculty ratio:* 22:1.

Majors Accounting; anthropology; Army R.O.T.C./military science; art; biology; business administration; business marketing and marketing management; chemistry; clothing/textiles; communications; computer/information sciences; corrections; criminal justice/law enforcement administration; dietetics; early childhood education; ecology; economics; education; educational media design; educational psychology; electrical/electronic engineering technology; elementary education; English; environmental biology; exercise sciences; finance; forensic technology; French; genetics; geography; geology; German; health education; health/physical education; history; home economics; home economics education;

Jacksonville State University (continued)
industrial technology; law enforcement/police science; marine biology; mathematics; middle school education; music; music teacher education; nursing; nutrition science; occupational safety/health technology; physical education; physics; political science; psychology; recreation/leisure studies; secondary education; social work; sociology; Spanish; special education; theater arts/drama.

Academic Programs *Special study options:* academic remediation for entering students, accelerated degree program, adult/continuing education programs, advanced placement credit, cooperative education, English as a second language, honors programs, internships, part-time degree program, services for LD students, summer session for credit. *ROTC:* Army (b).

Library Houston Cole Library with 420,583 titles, 4,791 serial subscriptions, 32,875 audiovisual materials, an OPAC, a Web page.

Computers on Campus 330 computers available on campus for general student use. A campuswide network can be accessed from off campus. Internet access, at least one staffed computer lab available.

Student Life *Housing Options:* coed, men-only, women-only, disabled students. *Activities and Organizations:* drama/theater group, student-run newspaper, radio station, choral group, marching band, Student Government Association, Archaeology Club, Campus Fellowship Clubs, Computer Science Club, Biology Club, national fraternities, national sororities. *Campus security:* 24-hour emergency response devices and patrols, student patrols, late-night transport/escort service, night security officer in female residence halls. *Student Services:* health clinic, personal/psychological counseling.

Athletics Member NCAA. All Division I except football (Division I-AA). *Intercollegiate sports:* baseball M(s), basketball M(s)/W(s), cross-country running M(s)/W(s), golf M(s)/W(s), riflery M(s)/W(s), softball W(s), tennis M(s)/W(s), volleyball W(s). *Intramural sports:* badminton M(c)/W(c), basketball M(c)/W(c), bowling M(c)/W(c), football M(c), golf M(c)/W(c), racquetball M(c)/W(c), soccer M(c)/W(c), softball M(c)/W(c), table tennis M(c)/W(c), tennis M(c)/W(c), volleyball M(c)/W(c).

Standardized Tests *Required:* SAT I or ACT (for admission).

Costs (2001–02) *One-time required fee:* $10. *Tuition:* state resident $2940 full-time, $123 per hour part-time; nonresident $5880 full-time, $246 per hour part-time. Full-time tuition and fees vary according to course load and reciprocity agreements. Part-time tuition and fees vary according to course load and reciprocity agreements. *Room and board:* $3080; room only: $1150. Room and board charges vary according to board plan and housing facility. *Waivers:* senior citizens and employees or children of employees.

Financial Aid Of all full-time matriculated undergraduates who enrolled in 2001, 350 Federal Work-Study jobs, 420 State and other part-time jobs. *Average indebtedness upon graduation:* $13,500.

Applying *Options:* early admission, deferred entrance. *Application fee:* $20. *Required:* high school transcript. *Application deadline:* rolling (freshmen), rolling (transfers). *Notification:* continuous (freshmen).

Admissions Contact Ms. Martha Mitchell, Freshman Admission and Recruiting, Jacksonville State University, 700 Pelham Road North, Jacksonville, AL 36265. *Phone:* 256-782-5363. *Toll-free phone:* 800-231-5291. *Fax:* 256-782-5291. *E-mail:* kcambron@jsucc.edu.

JUDSON COLLEGE
Marion, Alabama

- **Independent Baptist** 4-year, founded 1838
- **Calendar** semesters
- **Degree** bachelor's
- **Rural** 80-acre campus with easy access to Birmingham
- **Endowment** $14.0 million
- **Women only,** 345 undergraduate students, 84% full-time
- **Moderately difficult** entrance level, 81% of applicants were admitted

Undergraduates 289 full-time, 56 part-time. Students come from 21 states and territories, 2 other countries, 17% are from out of state, 11% African American, 1% Asian American or Pacific Islander, 1% Native American, 0.6% international, 2% transferred in, 63% live on campus. *Retention:* 58% of 2001 full-time freshmen returned.

Freshmen *Admission:* 99 enrolled. *Average high school GPA:* 3.11. *Test scores:* SAT verbal scores over 500: 75%; SAT math scores over 500: 25%; ACT scores over 18: 88%; SAT verbal scores over 600: 25%; ACT scores over 24: 36%; ACT scores over 30: 7%.

Faculty *Total:* 34, 91% full-time, 68% with terminal degrees. *Student/faculty ratio:* 10:1.

Majors Art; biology; business; chemistry; criminal justice studies; education; elementary education; English; English education; exercise sciences; fashion merchandising; history; information sciences/systems; interdisciplinary studies; mathematics; mathematics education; middle school education; modern languages; music; music teacher education; psychology; religious studies; science education; secondary education; social science education.

Academic Programs *Special study options:* academic remediation for entering students, accelerated degree program, adult/continuing education programs, advanced placement credit, distance learning, double majors, external degree program, honors programs, independent study, internships, off-campus study, part-time degree program, student-designed majors, study abroad, summer session for credit. *ROTC:* Army (c). *Unusual degree programs:* 3-2 engineering with University of Alabama.

Library Bowling Library with 68,474 titles, 197 serial subscriptions, 6,874 audiovisual materials, an OPAC, a Web page.

Computers on Campus 40 computers available on campus for general student use. Internet access, at least one staffed computer lab available.

Student Life *Housing:* on-campus residence required through senior year. *Options:* women-only. *Activities and Organizations:* drama/theater group, student-run newspaper, choral group, marching band, Student Government Association, Campus Ministries, College Republicans, Social Committee, A-Board. *Campus security:* 24-hour emergency response devices and patrols, late-night transport/escort service, controlled dormitory access. *Student Services:* personal/psychological counseling.

Athletics Member NCCAA. *Intercollegiate sports:* basketball W(s), equestrian sports W, softball W(s), tennis W(s), volleyball W(s). *Intramural sports:* basketball W, equestrian sports W, field hockey W, soccer W, softball W, swimming W, table tennis W, tennis W, volleyball W, weight lifting W.

Standardized Tests *Required:* SAT I or ACT (for admission).

Costs (2001–02) *Comprehensive fee:* $13,790 includes full-time tuition ($8150), mandatory fees ($340), and room and board ($5300). Full-time tuition and fees vary according to course load. Part-time tuition: $235 per semester hour. Part-time tuition and fees vary according to course load. *Payment plan:* installment. *Waivers:* employees or children of employees.

Financial Aid Of all full-time matriculated undergraduates who enrolled in 2001, 262 applied for aid, 211 were judged to have need, 59 had their need fully met. 60 Federal Work-Study jobs (averaging $1000). 72 State and other part-time jobs (averaging $1100). In 2001, 51 non-need-based awards were made. *Average percent of need met:* 85%. *Average financial aid package:* $9212. *Average need-based gift aid:* $6049. *Average non-need based aid:* $5168. *Average indebtedness upon graduation:* $11,398.

Applying *Options:* common application, electronic application, early admission, deferred entrance. *Application fee:* $25. *Required:* high school transcript, minimum 2.0 GPA, 2 letters of recommendation, interview. *Recommended:* essay or personal statement. *Application deadline:* rolling (freshmen), rolling (transfers). *Notification:* continuous (freshmen).

Admissions Contact Mrs. Charlotte Clements, Director of Admissions, Judson College, PO Box 120, Marion, AL 36756. *Phone:* 334-683-5110 Ext. 110. *Toll-free phone:* 800-447-9472. *Fax:* 334-683-5158. *E-mail:* admissions@future.judson.edu.

MILES COLLEGE
Birmingham, Alabama

Admissions Contact Mr. Cornell Howard, Interim Director of Admissions and Recruitment, Miles College, PO Box 3800, Birmingham, AL 35208. *Phone:* 205-929-1657.

OAKWOOD COLLEGE
Huntsville, Alabama

- **Independent Seventh-day Adventist** 4-year, founded 1896
- **Calendar** semesters
- **Degrees** associate and bachelor's
- 1200-acre campus
- **Coed,** 1,778 undergraduate students, 89% full-time, 57% women, 43% men
- **Minimally difficult** entrance level, 55% of applicants were admitted

Undergraduates 1,582 full-time, 196 part-time. Students come from 39 states and territories, 22 other countries, 68% are from out of state, 85% African American, 0.3% Asian American or Pacific Islander, 0.4% Hispanic American, 0.3% Native American, 11% international, 5% transferred in, 68% live on campus. *Retention:* 70% of 2001 full-time freshmen returned.

Freshmen *Admission:* 847 applied, 464 admitted, 399 enrolled. *Average high school GPA:* 2.97. *Test scores:* SAT verbal scores over 500: 43%; SAT math scores

over 500: 35%; ACT scores over 18: 55%; SAT verbal scores over 600: 12%; SAT math scores over 600: 7%; ACT scores over 24: 13%; SAT verbal scores over 700: 1%; SAT math scores over 700: 1%.

Faculty *Total:* 161, 63% full-time, 47% with terminal degrees. *Student/faculty ratio:* 14:1.

Majors Accounting; applied mathematics; biblical studies; biochemistry; biology; business administration; business education; chemistry; computer science; dietetics; economics; elementary education; engineering; English; French; graphic design/commercial art/illustration; history; home economics; home economics education; information sciences/systems; interdisciplinary studies; mass communications; mathematics; medical technology; music; music teacher education; natural sciences; nursing; occupational therapy; pastoral counseling; physical education; physical therapy; psychology; religious education; religious studies; science education; secretarial science; social sciences; social work; Spanish; theology.

Academic Programs *Special study options:* academic remediation for entering students, advanced placement credit, double majors, honors programs, internships, off-campus study, part-time degree program, study abroad. *Unusual degree programs:* 3-2 engineering with Alabama Agricultural and Mechanical University, The University of Alabama in Huntsville.

Library Eva B. Dykes Library with 128,000 titles, 610 serial subscriptions, 5,135 audiovisual materials.

Computers on Campus 300 computers available on campus for general student use. A campuswide network can be accessed from student residence rooms and from off campus. At least one staffed computer lab available.

Student Life *Housing:* on-campus residence required for freshman year. *Options:* men-only, women-only. *Activities and Organizations:* student-run newspaper, radio station, choral group, United Student Movement. *Campus security:* 24-hour patrols, student patrols, late-night transport/escort service. *Student Services:* health clinic, personal/psychological counseling.

Athletics *Intramural sports:* basketball M/W, football M, golf M, gymnastics M/W, racquetball M/W, soccer M, softball M/W, swimming M/W, table tennis M/W, tennis M/W, track and field M/W, volleyball M/W.

Standardized Tests *Required:* SAT I or ACT (for admission).

Costs (2001–02) *Comprehensive fee:* $14,904 includes full-time tuition ($9172), mandatory fees ($248), and room and board ($5484). Part-time tuition: $395 per credit hour. Part-time tuition and fees vary according to course load. *Required fees:* $124 per term part-time. *Room and board:* College room only: $2370. Room and board charges vary according to board plan. *Payment plan:* installment. *Waivers:* employees or children of employees.

Financial Aid Of all full-time matriculated undergraduates who enrolled in 2001, 1422 applied for aid, 1422 were judged to have need, 131 had their need fully met. *Average percent of need met:* 77%. *Average financial aid package:* $6500. *Average need-based loan:* $4500. *Average need-based gift aid:* $2500. *Average non-need based aid:* $2000. *Average indebtedness upon graduation:* $15,000.

Applying *Options:* common application, early action, deferred entrance. *Application fee:* $20. *Required:* high school transcript, letters of recommendation. *Application deadline:* rolling (freshmen), rolling (transfers). *Notification:* 4/15 (early action).

Admissions Contact Mr. Fred Pullins, Director of Enrollment Management, Oakwood College, 7000 Adventist Boulevard, NW, Huntsville, AL 35896. *Phone:* 256-726-7354. *Toll-free phone:* 800-358-3978. *Fax:* 256-726-7154. *E-mail:* admission@oakwood.edu.

SAMFORD UNIVERSITY
Birmingham, Alabama

- **Independent Baptist** university, founded 1841
- **Calendar** 4-1-4
- **Degrees** certificates, associate, bachelor's, master's, doctoral, first professional, post-master's, and postbachelor's certificates
- **Suburban** 180-acre campus
- **Endowment** $261.1 million
- **Coed,** 2,890 undergraduate students, 93% full-time, 63% women, 37% men
- **Moderately difficult** entrance level, 88% of applicants were admitted

A Samford education is carefully crafted to provide personal empowerment, academic and career competency, social and civic responsibility, and ethical and spiritual strength. It is built around broadening international awareness and the development of transferable skills, such as computer familiarity in every academic major, to keep Samford graduates on the leading edge in a constantly changing career environment.

Undergraduates 2,679 full-time, 211 part-time. Students come from 42 states and territories, 22 other countries, 53% are from out of state, 6% African American, 0.7% Asian American or Pacific Islander, 0.8% Hispanic American, 0.5% Native American, 0.5% international, 4% transferred in, 65% live on campus. *Retention:* 84% of 2001 full-time freshmen returned.

Freshmen *Admission:* 1,903 applied, 1,675 admitted, 663 enrolled. *Average high school GPA:* 3.60. *Test scores:* SAT verbal scores over 500: 81%; SAT math scores over 500: 79%; ACT scores over 18: 99%; SAT verbal scores over 600: 39%; SAT math scores over 600: 34%; ACT scores over 24: 61%; SAT verbal scores over 700: 11%; SAT math scores over 700: 7%; ACT scores over 30: 14%.

Faculty *Total:* 409, 62% full-time, 63% with terminal degrees. *Student/faculty ratio:* 13:1.

Majors Accounting; art; Asian studies; athletic training/sports medicine; biblical studies; biochemistry; biology; business administration; cartography; chemistry; classics; community services; computer science; counseling psychology; criminal justice/law enforcement administration; dietetics; early childhood education; elementary education; engineering physics; English; environmental science; exercise sciences; foreign languages/literatures; French; general studies; geography; German; graphic design/commercial art/illustration; Greek (ancient and medieval); health/physical education; history; humanities; human resources management; individual/family development; interior design; international business; international relations; journalism; Latin American studies; Latin (ancient and medieval); marine biology; mathematics; music (general performance); music (piano and organ performance); music teacher education; music theory and composition; music (voice and choral/opera performance); nursing; philosophy; physical education; physics; political science; psychology; public administration; religious music; religious studies; science education; science/technology and society; social science education; social sciences; sociology; Spanish; speech education; speech/rhetorical studies; theater arts/drama; visual/performing arts.

Academic Programs *Special study options:* accelerated degree program, adult/continuing education programs, advanced placement credit, cooperative education, double majors, honors programs, internships, off-campus study, part-time degree program, services for LD students, student-designed majors, study abroad, summer session for credit. *ROTC:* Army (c), Air Force (b). *Unusual degree programs:* 3-2 engineering with The University of Alabama at Birmingham, Auburn University, Washington University in St. Louis, University of Southern California, Mercer University.

Library Samford University Library plus 3 others with 428,432 titles, 11,117 serial subscriptions, 12,857 audiovisual materials, an OPAC, a Web page.

Computers on Campus 350 computers available on campus for general student use. A campuswide network can be accessed from student residence rooms. At least one staffed computer lab available.

Student Life *Housing:* on-campus residence required through sophomore year. *Options:* men-only, women-only, disabled students. *Activities and Organizations:* drama/theater group, student-run newspaper, radio and television station, choral group, marching band, student ministries, student government, student bar, national fraternities, national sororities. *Campus security:* 24-hour emergency response devices and patrols, student patrols, late-night transport/escort service. *Student Services:* health clinic, personal/psychological counseling.

Athletics Member NCAA. All Division I except football (Division I-AA). *Intercollegiate sports:* baseball M(s), basketball M(s)/W(s), cross-country running M(s)/W(s), golf M(s)/W(s), soccer W(s), softball W(s), tennis M(s)/W(s), track and field M(s)/W(s), volleyball W(s). *Intramural sports:* basketball M/W, bowling M/W, football M/W, soccer M(c), softball M/W, table tennis M/W, volleyball M/W.

Standardized Tests *Required:* SAT I or ACT (for admission).

Costs (2001–02) *Comprehensive fee:* $16,340 includes full-time tuition ($11,490) and room and board ($4850). Full-time tuition and fees vary according to course load. Part-time tuition: $381 per semester hour. Part-time tuition and fees vary according to course load. *Room and board:* College room only: $2362. Room and board charges vary according to board plan and housing facility. *Waivers:* employees or children of employees.

Financial Aid Of all full-time matriculated undergraduates who enrolled in 2001, 1419 applied for aid, 1030 were judged to have need, 287 had their need fully met. 380 Federal Work-Study jobs (averaging $1511). 535 State and other part-time jobs (averaging $689). In 2001, 1068 non-need-based awards were made. *Average percent of need met:* 76%. *Average financial aid package:* $9442. *Average need-based loan:* $3370. *Average need-based gift aid:* $5743. *Average indebtedness upon graduation:* $14,958.

Applying *Options:* common application, early admission, deferred entrance. *Application fee:* $25. *Required:* essay or personal statement, high school transcript, 1 letter of recommendation. *Recommended:* interview. *Application deadline:* 8/1 (freshmen), rolling (transfers).

Admissions Contact Dr. Phil Kimrey, Dean of Admissions and Financial Aid, Samford University, 800 Lakeshore Drive, Samford Hall, Birmingham, AL 35229-0002. *Phone:* 205-726-3673. *Toll-free phone:* 800-888-7218. *Fax:* 205-726-2171. *E-mail:* seberry@samford.edu.

SOUTHEASTERN BIBLE COLLEGE
Birmingham, Alabama

- **Independent nondenominational** 4-year, founded 1935
- **Calendar** semesters
- **Degrees** associate and bachelor's
- **Suburban** 10-acre campus
- **Endowment** $1.4 million
- **Coed,** 202 undergraduate students, 76% full-time, 35% women, 65% men
- **Moderately difficult** entrance level, 53% of applicants were admitted

Undergraduates 154 full-time, 48 part-time. Students come from 15 states and territories, 9% African American, 1.0% Hispanic American, 1.0% international, 41% live on campus. *Retention:* 62% of 2001 full-time freshmen returned.

Freshmen *Admission:* 80 applied, 42 admitted, 62 enrolled.

Faculty *Total:* 22, 55% full-time, 55% with terminal degrees. *Student/faculty ratio:* 13:1.

Majors Biblical languages/literatures; biblical studies; divinity/ministry; education; elementary education; liberal arts and sciences/liberal studies; music; pastoral counseling; physical education; religious education; religious music; religious studies; secondary education; theology.

Academic Programs *Special study options:* academic remediation for entering students, adult/continuing education programs, advanced placement credit, external degree program, internships, part-time degree program, summer session for credit.

Library Gannett-Estes Library with 38,510 titles, 114 serial subscriptions, 1,862 audiovisual materials, an OPAC.

Computers on Campus 10 computers available on campus for general student use. Internet access, at least one staffed computer lab available.

Student Life *Housing:* on-campus residence required through senior year. *Options:* coed. *Activities and Organizations:* choral group, Student Council, Student Missions Fellowship, chorale. *Campus security:* 24-hour emergency response devices, student patrols. *Student Services:* health clinic, personal/psychological counseling.

Athletics *Intercollegiate sports:* basketball M/W. *Intramural sports:* basketball M/W, table tennis M/W, volleyball M/W.

Standardized Tests *Required:* SAT I or ACT (for admission).

Costs (2002–03) *Comprehensive fee:* $10,140 includes full-time tuition ($6500), mandatory fees ($100), and room and board ($3540). Part-time tuition: $225 per semester hour. *Required fees:* $25 per term part-time. *Payment plan:* installment. *Waivers:* children of alumni and employees or children of employees.

Financial Aid Of all full-time matriculated undergraduates who enrolled in 2001, 153 applied for aid, 88 were judged to have need, 6 had their need fully met. 10 Federal Work-Study jobs (averaging $1200). 10 State and other part-time jobs (averaging $2000). *Average percent of need met:* 60%. *Average financial aid package:* $6457. *Average need-based loan:* $1720. *Average need-based gift aid:* $2870. *Average indebtedness upon graduation:* $20,000.

Applying *Options:* common application, deferred entrance. *Application fee:* $20. *Required:* essay or personal statement, high school transcript, minimum 2.0 GPA, 3 letters of recommendation. *Required for some:* interview. *Application deadline:* rolling (freshmen), rolling (transfers). *Notification:* continuous (freshmen).

Admissions Contact Mr. Adam McClendon, Admissions Director, Southeastern Bible College, 3001 Highway 280 East, Birmingham, AL 35243. *Phone:* 205-970-9209. *Toll-free phone:* 800-749-8878. *Fax:* 205-970-9207. *E-mail:* amcclendon@sebc.edu.

SOUTHERN CHRISTIAN UNIVERSITY
Montgomery, Alabama

- **Independent** comprehensive, founded 1967, affiliated with Church of Christ
- **Calendar** semesters
- **Degrees** certificates, bachelor's, master's, doctoral, and first professional
- **Urban** 9-acre campus
- **Endowment** $162,287
- **Coed,** 195 undergraduate students, 95% full-time, 32% women, 68% men
- **Minimally difficult** entrance level

Undergraduates 186 full-time, 9 part-time. Students come from 48 states and territories, 2 other countries, 73% are from out of state, 29% African American, 7% Hispanic American, 0.5% Native American. *Retention:* 85% of 2001 full-time freshmen returned.

Faculty *Total:* 24, 75% full-time, 100% with terminal degrees. *Student/faculty ratio:* 14:1.

Majors Biblical languages/literatures; biblical studies; counselor education/guidance; theology.

Academic Programs *Special study options:* accelerated degree program, adult/continuing education programs, advanced placement credit, distance learning, external degree program, internships, part-time degree program, summer session for credit.

Library Southern Christian University Library with 73,000 titles, 500 serial subscriptions, an OPAC, a Web page.

Computers on Campus 5 computers available on campus for general student use. A campuswide network can be accessed from off campus. Internet access, online (class) registration available.

Student Life *Housing:* college housing not available. *Student Services:* personal/psychological counseling.

Standardized Tests *Required:* SAT I or ACT (for admission).

Costs (2001–02) *Tuition:* $7680 full-time, $320 per semester hour part-time. Part-time tuition and fees vary according to course load. *Required fees:* $800 full-time, $400 per term part-time. *Payment plan:* tuition prepayment. *Waivers:* senior citizens and employees or children of employees.

Financial Aid Of all full-time matriculated undergraduates who enrolled in 2001, 96 applied for aid, 80 were judged to have need, 60 had their need fully met. 6 Federal Work-Study jobs (averaging $1500). In 2001, 8 non-need-based awards were made. *Average percent of need met:* 50%. *Average financial aid package:* $5400. *Average need-based gift aid:* $1800. *Average non-need based aid:* $3200. *Average indebtedness upon graduation:* $16,500.

Applying *Options:* common application. *Application fee:* $50. *Required:* high school transcript, minimum 2.0 GPA. *Application deadline:* rolling (freshmen), rolling (transfers).

Admissions Contact Mr. Rick Johnson, Director of Enrollment Management, Southern Christian University, 1200 Taylor Road, Montgomery, AL 36117. *Phone:* 334-387-3877 Ext. 213. *Toll-free phone:* 800-351-4040 Ext. 213. *E-mail:* admissions@southernchristian.edu.

SOUTH UNIVERSITY
Montgomery, Alabama

- **Proprietary** primarily 2-year, founded 1887
- **Calendar** quarters
- **Degrees** associate and bachelor's
- **Urban** 1-acre campus
- **Coed, primarily women,** 240 undergraduate students, 62% full-time, 81% women, 19% men
- **Minimally difficult** entrance level, 100% of applicants were admitted

Undergraduates 148 full-time, 92 part-time. Students come from 1 other state, 0% are from out of state, 66% African American, 0.4% Asian American or Pacific Islander, 0.4% Hispanic American, 20% transferred in.

Freshmen *Admission:* 36 applied, 36 admitted, 36 enrolled.

Faculty *Total:* 28, 32% full-time, 14% with terminal degrees. *Student/faculty ratio:* 11:1.

Majors Accounting; business administration; health science; information sciences/systems; medical assistant; paralegal/legal assistant.

Academic Programs *Special study options:* academic remediation for entering students, double majors, internships, part-time degree program, summer session for credit.

Library South College Library with 5,000 titles, 43 serial subscriptions.

Computers on Campus 37 computers available on campus for general student use. Internet access, at least one staffed computer lab available.

Student Life *Housing:* college housing not available. *Campus security:* evening security guard.

Standardized Tests *Required for some:* SAT I or ACT (for admission).

Costs (2001–02) *Tuition:* $8685 full-time, $2195 per term part-time. Full-time tuition and fees vary according to course load and program. Part-time tuition and fees vary according to course load and program. *Payment plans:* installment, deferred payment. *Waivers:* employees or children of employees.

Financial Aid Of all full-time matriculated undergraduates who enrolled in 2001, 36 Federal Work-Study jobs (averaging $816).

Applying *Application fee:* $25. *Required:* high school transcript, interview. *Required for some:* 3 letters of recommendation. *Application deadline:* rolling (transfers). *Notification:* continuous (freshmen).

Admissions Contact Ms. Anna Pearson, Director of Admissions, South University, 122 Commerce Street, Montgomery, AL 36104-2538. *Phone:* 334-263-1013. *Fax:* 334-834-9559. *E-mail:* mtgfd@southuniversity.edu.

SPRING HILL COLLEGE
Mobile, Alabama

- **Independent Roman Catholic (Jesuit)** comprehensive, founded 1830
- **Calendar** semesters
- **Degrees** certificates, associate, bachelor's, master's, and postbachelor's certificates
- **Suburban** 500-acre campus
- **Endowment** $35.5 million
- **Coed,** 1,244 undergraduate students, 82% full-time, 62% women, 38% men
- **Moderately difficult** entrance level, 77% of applicants were admitted

Undergraduates 1,022 full-time, 222 part-time. Students come from 33 states and territories, 9 other countries, 49% are from out of state, 14% African American, 1% Asian American or Pacific Islander, 4% Hispanic American, 0.7% Native American, 2% international, 7% transferred in, 58% live on campus. *Retention:* 82% of 2001 full-time freshmen returned.

Freshmen *Admission:* 1,000 applied, 774 admitted, 253 enrolled. *Average high school GPA:* 3.37. *Test scores:* SAT verbal scores over 500: 64%; SAT math scores over 500: 58%; ACT scores over 18: 96%; SAT verbal scores over 600: 28%; SAT math scores over 600: 23%; ACT scores over 24: 50%; SAT verbal scores over 700: 6%; SAT math scores over 700: 4%; ACT scores over 30: 10%.

Faculty *Total:* 126, 55% full-time, 66% with terminal degrees. *Student/faculty ratio:* 14:1.

Majors Accounting; advertising; arts management; art therapy; biology; business administration; business marketing and marketing management; chemistry; chemistry related; computer/information sciences; early childhood education; elementary education; engineering science; English; English related; environmental science; finance; fine/studio arts; general studies; graphic design/commercial art/illustration; history; humanities; international business; international relations; journalism; marine biology; mathematics; nursing; philosophy; political science; pre-dentistry; pre-medicine; pre-veterinary studies; psychology; public relations; radio/television broadcasting; secondary education; social sciences; Spanish; theater arts/drama; theology.

Academic Programs *Special study options:* academic remediation for entering students, accelerated degree program, adult/continuing education programs, advanced placement credit, distance learning, double majors, English as a second language, honors programs, independent study, internships, off-campus study, part-time degree program, services for LD students, student-designed majors, study abroad, summer session for credit. *ROTC:* Army (c), Air Force (c). *Unusual degree programs:* 3-2 engineering with Marquette University, University of Alabama at Birmingham, University of Florida; accounting.

Library Thomas Byrne Memorial Library with 88,100 titles, 1,324 serial subscriptions, 336 audiovisual materials, an OPAC, a Web page.

Computers on Campus 141 computers available on campus for general student use. A campuswide network can be accessed from student residence rooms and from off campus. Internet access, at least one staffed computer lab available.

Student Life *Housing:* on-campus residence required through junior year. *Options:* coed, men-only, women-only. *Activities and Organizations:* drama/theater group, student-run newspaper, choral group, Student Government Association, Multicultural Student Union, Circle K, Campus Programming Board, SHORES (Spring Hill Ocean Research and Exploration Society), national fraternities, national sororities. *Campus security:* 24-hour emergency response devices and patrols, late-night transport/escort service, controlled dormitory access. *Student Services:* health clinic, personal/psychological counseling.

Athletics Member NAIA. *Intercollegiate sports:* baseball M(s), basketball M(s)/W(s), cross-country running M(s)/W(s), golf M(s)/W(s), soccer M(s)/W(s), softball W(s), swimming M(s)/W(s), tennis M(s)/W(s), volleyball W(s). *Intramural sports:* basketball M/W, football M, golf M/W, lacrosse M(c), racquetball M/W, rugby M(c), softball M/W, swimming M/W, volleyball M/W.

Standardized Tests *Required:* SAT I or ACT (for admission).

Costs (2002–03) *Comprehensive fee:* $24,632 includes full-time tuition ($16,980), mandatory fees ($1112), and room and board ($6540). Part-time tuition: $636 per semester hour. *Required fees:* $36 per semester hour. *Room and board:* College room only: $3300. Room and board charges vary according to board plan and housing facility. *Payment plan:* deferred payment. *Waivers:* employees or children of employees.

Financial Aid Of all full-time matriculated undergraduates who enrolled in 2001, 941 applied for aid, 659 were judged to have need, 129 had their need fully met. 193 Federal Work-Study jobs (averaging $1154). 99 State and other part-time jobs (averaging $1621). In 2001, 259 non-need-based awards were made. *Average percent of need met:* 82%. *Average financial aid package:* $14,751. *Average need-based loan:* $3998. *Average need-based gift aid:* $11,305. *Average indebtedness upon graduation:* $17,050.

Applying *Options:* common application, electronic application, early admission, deferred entrance. *Application fee:* $25. *Required:* essay or personal statement, high school transcript, 1 letter of recommendation. *Recommended:* minimum 2.5 GPA, interview. *Application deadlines:* 7/1 (freshmen), 8/10 (transfers). *Notification:* continuous (freshmen).

Admissions Contact Ms. Florence W. Hines, Dean of Enrollment Management, Spring Hill College, 4000 Dauphin Street, Mobile, AL 36608-1791. *Phone:* 251-380-3030. *Toll-free phone:* 800-SHC-6704. *Fax:* 251-460-2186. *E-mail:* admit@shc.edu.

STILLMAN COLLEGE
Tuscaloosa, Alabama

Admissions Contact Mr. Mason Bonner, Director of Admissions, Stillman College, P.O. Box 1430, 3600 Stillman Boulevard, Tuscaloosa, AL 35403. *Phone:* 205-366-8817. *Toll-free phone:* 800-841-5722.

TALLADEGA COLLEGE
Talladega, Alabama

- **Independent** 4-year, founded 1867
- **Calendar** semesters
- **Degree** bachelor's
- **Small-town** 130-acre campus with easy access to Birmingham
- **Endowment** $5.7 million
- **Coed,** 540 undergraduate students, 94% full-time, 64% women, 36% men
- **Minimally difficult** entrance level, 70% of applicants were admitted

Undergraduates 510 full-time, 30 part-time. Students come from 26 states and territories, 43% are from out of state, 98% African American, 0.2% Hispanic American, 1% transferred in, 77% live on campus. *Retention:* 72% of 2001 full-time freshmen returned.

Freshmen *Admission:* 1,655 applied, 1,151 admitted, 191 enrolled. *Average high school GPA:* 3.00. *Test scores:* ACT scores over 18: 47%; ACT scores over 24: 5%.

Faculty *Total:* 51, 78% full-time, 51% with terminal degrees. *Student/faculty ratio:* 10:1.

Majors Accounting; African-American studies; biology; biology education; business administration; chemistry; chemistry education; computer science; economics; education; English; English education; finance; French; French language education; history; history education; marketing research; mathematics; mathematics education; music; music teacher education; music (voice and choral/opera performance); physics; pre-dentistry; pre-law; pre-medicine; psychology; public administration; science education; social work; sociology; Spanish.

Academic Programs *Special study options:* academic remediation for entering students, adult/continuing education programs, cooperative education, double majors, independent study, internships, off-campus study, part-time degree program. *ROTC:* Army (c). *Unusual degree programs:* 3-2 engineering with Tuskegee University, Georgia Institute of Technology, Florida Agricultural and Mechanical University; nursing with Jacksonville State University; veterinary medicine, allied health with Tuskegee University.

Library Savery Library with 117,000 titles, 88 serial subscriptions, 300 audiovisual materials, an OPAC.

Computers on Campus 105 computers available on campus for general student use. A campuswide network can be accessed from off campus. Internet access, at least one staffed computer lab available.

Student Life *Housing Options:* men-only, women-only. *Activities and Organizations:* drama/theater group, student-run newspaper, choral group, Student Government Association, Crimson Ambassadors, Greek letter organizations, academic major clubs, religious based organizations, national fraternities, national sororities. *Campus security:* 24-hour patrols, late-night transport/escort service, campus police. *Student Services:* health clinic, personal/psychological counseling.

Athletics Member NAIA. *Intercollegiate sports:* baseball M(s), basketball M(s)/W(s), cross-country running M/W, golf M/W, volleyball W(s).

Standardized Tests *Required:* SAT I or ACT (for admission).

Costs (2002–03) *Comprehensive fee:* $10,147 includes full-time tuition ($6232), mandatory fees ($520), and room and board ($3395). Full-time tuition and fees vary according to course load. Part-time tuition: $260 per credit hour. Part-time tuition and fees vary according to course load. *Required fees:* $143 per term part-time. *Room and board:* College room only: $1566. *Payment plan:* deferred payment. *Waivers:* employees or children of employees.

Talladega College (continued)

Financial Aid Of all full-time matriculated undergraduates who enrolled in 2001, 457 applied for aid, 408 were judged to have need, 18 had their need fully met. 227 Federal Work-Study jobs. *Average need-based loan:* $3587. *Financial aid deadline:* 6/30.

Applying *Options:* common application, electronic application, deferred entrance. *Application fee:* $25. *Required:* essay or personal statement, high school transcript, minimum 2.0 GPA, 1 letter of recommendation. *Application deadline:* 4/1 (freshmen), rolling (transfers).

Admissions Contact Mr. Johnny Byrd, Enrollment Manager, Talladega College, 627 West Battle Street, Talladega, AL 35160. *Phone:* 256-761-6235. *Toll-free phone:* 800-762-2168 (in-state); 800-633-2440 (out-of-state). *Fax:* 256-362-2268. *E-mail:* be21long@talladega.edu.

TROY STATE UNIVERSITY
Troy, Alabama

- **State-supported** comprehensive, founded 1887, part of Troy State University System
- **Calendar** semesters
- **Degrees** associate, bachelor's, master's, and post-master's certificates
- **Small-town** 577-acre campus
- **Coed,** 4,607 undergraduate students, 78% full-time, 60% women, 40% men
- **Moderately difficult** entrance level, 72% of applicants were admitted

Undergraduates 3,580 full-time, 1,027 part-time. Students come from 49 states and territories, 55 other countries, 23% African American, 0.6% Asian American or Pacific Islander, 1% Hispanic American, 0.8% Native American, 6% international, 8% transferred in, 28% live on campus. *Retention:* 74% of 2001 full-time freshmen returned.

Freshmen *Admission:* 2,438 applied, 1,766 admitted, 857 enrolled.

Faculty *Total:* 380, 55% full-time, 29% with terminal degrees. *Student/faculty ratio:* 19:1.

Majors Accounting; art; art education; art history; athletic training/sports medicine; biology; broadcast journalism; business administration; business education; chemistry; computer/information sciences; corrections; early childhood education; education; elementary education; English; finance; fine/studio arts; health education; history; journalism; marine biology; mathematics; music teacher education; nursing; physical education; physical sciences; political science; pre-dentistry; pre-medicine; pre-veterinary studies; psychology; recreation/leisure studies; science education; secondary education; social sciences; social work; sociology; special education; speech/rhetorical studies; theater arts/drama.

Academic Programs *Special study options:* academic remediation for entering students, accelerated degree program, adult/continuing education programs, advanced placement credit, distance learning, double majors, English as a second language, honors programs, independent study, internships, part-time degree program, services for LD students, student-designed majors, summer session for credit. *ROTC:* Army (b), Air Force (b).

Library Wallace Library with 389,524 titles, 2,692 serial subscriptions, an OPAC, a Web page.

Computers on Campus 487 computers available on campus for general student use. A campuswide network can be accessed from student residence rooms and from off campus. Internet access, at least one staffed computer lab available.

Student Life *Housing:* on-campus residence required for freshman year. *Options:* coed, men-only, women-only. *Activities and Organizations:* drama/theater group, student-run newspaper, television station, choral group, marching band, University Band, University Choir, yearbook, Union Board, national fraternities, national sororities. *Campus security:* 24-hour patrols, student patrols, late-night transport/escort service, controlled dormitory access. *Student Services:* health clinic, personal/psychological counseling, women's center.

Athletics Member NCAA. All Division I except football (Division I-AA). *Intercollegiate sports:* baseball M(s), basketball M(s)/W(s), cross-country running M(s)/W(s), golf M(s)/W(s), soccer W(s), softball W(s), tennis M(s)/W(s), track and field M(s)/W(s), volleyball W(s). *Intramural sports:* basketball M/W, bowling M/W, cross-country running M, football M/W, golf M/W, soccer M, softball M/W, swimming M/W, tennis M/W, track and field M, volleyball M/W.

Standardized Tests *Required:* SAT I or ACT (for admission).

Costs (2001–02) *Tuition:* state resident $3020 full-time, $127 per credit hour part-time; nonresident $6040 full-time, $254 per credit hour part-time. *Required fees:* $276 full-time, $13 per credit hour. *Room and board:* $4400; room only: $2130. Room and board charges vary according to board plan and housing facility. *Payment plan:* installment. *Waivers:* employees or children of employees.

Financial Aid Of all full-time matriculated undergraduates who enrolled in 2001, 3026 applied for aid, 2532 were judged to have need, 280 had their need fully met. 306 Federal Work-Study jobs (averaging $1815). In 2001, 71 non-need-based awards were made. *Average percent of need met:* 80%. *Average financial aid package:* $3743. *Average need-based loan:* $4281. *Average need-based gift aid:* $2015. *Average non-need based aid:* $2862. *Average indebtedness upon graduation:* $17,125.

Applying *Options:* deferred entrance. *Application fee:* $20. *Required:* high school transcript. *Recommended:* interview. *Application deadline:* rolling (freshmen), rolling (transfers).

Admissions Contact Mr. Buddy Starling, Dean of Enrollment Services, Troy State University, Adams Administration Building, Room 134, Troy, AL 36082. *Phone:* 334-670-3179. *Toll-free phone:* 800-551-9716. *Fax:* 334-670-3733. *E-mail:* bstar@trojan.troyst.edu.

TROY STATE UNIVERSITY DOTHAN
Dothan, Alabama

- **State-supported** comprehensive, founded 1961, part of Troy State University System
- **Calendar** semesters
- **Degrees** associate, bachelor's, master's, and post-master's certificates
- **Small-town** 250-acre campus
- **Coed,** 1,499 undergraduate students, 45% full-time, 64% women, 36% men
- **Minimally difficult** entrance level, 58% of applicants were admitted

Undergraduates 668 full-time, 831 part-time. Students come from 9 states and territories, 1 other country, 11% are from out of state, 20% African American, 2% Asian American or Pacific Islander, 2% Hispanic American, 1% Native American, 0.1% international, 18% transferred in. *Retention:* 46% of 2001 full-time freshmen returned.

Freshmen *Admission:* 106 applied, 62 admitted, 50 enrolled. *Average high school GPA:* 3.10. *Test scores:* ACT scores over 18: 100%; ACT scores over 24: 31%; ACT scores over 30: 1%.

Faculty *Total:* 110, 47% full-time, 47% with terminal degrees. *Student/faculty ratio:* 21:1.

Majors Biology; business administration; business management/administrative services related; computer/information sciences; criminal justice studies; early childhood education; elementary education; English; history; liberal arts and studies related; mathematics; physical sciences; psychology; science education; secondary education; social sciences; sociology.

Academic Programs *Special study options:* academic remediation for entering students, accelerated degree program, advanced placement credit, distance learning, double majors, independent study, internships, part-time degree program, services for LD students, summer session for credit.

Library Troy State University Dotham Library with 100,223 titles, 609 serial subscriptions, 13,879 audiovisual materials, an OPAC, a Web page.

Computers on Campus 150 computers available on campus for general student use. Internet access, at least one staffed computer lab available.

Student Life *Housing:* college housing not available. *Activities and Organizations:* Creative Writing Club, American Marketing Association, Alpha Upsilon Alpha, Gamma Beta Phi, Delta Mu Delta. *Campus security:* 24-hour patrols. *Student Services:* personal/psychological counseling.

Standardized Tests *Required for some:* SAT I or ACT (for admission).

Costs (2001–02) *Tuition:* state resident $3020 full-time, $127 per credit hour part-time; nonresident $6040 full-time, $254 per credit hour part-time. *Required fees:* $276 full-time, $275 per year part-time. *Payment plan:* installment. *Waivers:* senior citizens and employees or children of employees.

Financial Aid Of all full-time matriculated undergraduates who enrolled in 2001, 570 applied for aid, 537 were judged to have need, 250 had their need fully met. 156 Federal Work-Study jobs (averaging $2037). *Average percent of need met:* 40%. *Average need-based loan:* $4791. *Average need-based gift aid:* $2840.

Applying *Options:* common application, electronic application, deferred entrance. *Application fee:* $20. *Required:* high school transcript, minimum 2.0 GPA. *Recommended:* minimum 3.0 GPA. *Application deadline:* rolling (freshmen), rolling (transfers).

Admissions Contact Mr. Bob Willis, Director of Enrollment Services, Troy State University Dothan, PO Box 8368, Dothan, AL 36304-0368. *Phone:* 334-983-6556 Ext. 205. *Fax:* 334-983-6322. *E-mail:* bwillis@tsud.edu.

TROY STATE UNIVERSITY MONTGOMERY
Montgomery, Alabama

- **State-supported** comprehensive, founded 1965, part of Troy State University System

- **Calendar** quarters
- **Degrees** associate, bachelor's, master's, and post-master's certificates
- **Urban** 6-acre campus
- **Coed**
- **Noncompetitive** entrance level

Undergraduates 1% are from out of state.
Faculty *Total:* 222, 16% full-time, 57% with terminal degrees. *Student/faculty ratio:* 20:1.
Majors Accounting; business; business administration; computer/information sciences; English; finance; history; human resources management; liberal arts and studies related; marketing research; mathematics; political science; psychology; social sciences.
Academic Programs *Special study options:* academic remediation for entering students, accelerated degree program, adult/continuing education programs, advanced placement credit, distance learning, double majors, external degree program, honors programs, independent study, part-time degree program, services for LD students, student-designed majors, summer session for credit. *ROTC:* Army (c), Air Force (c).
Library Troy State University Montgomery Library with 34,864 titles, 476 serial subscriptions, 9,194 audiovisual materials, an OPAC, a Web page.
Computers on Campus 190 computers available on campus for general student use. A campuswide network can be accessed from off campus. Internet access, online (class) registration, at least one staffed computer lab available.
Student Life *Housing:* college housing not available. *Campus security:* 24-hour emergency response devices, late-night transport/escort service, evening patrols by security. *Student Services:* personal/psychological counseling.
Standardized Tests *Required:* SAT I (for placement). *Recommended:* ACT (for placement).
Costs (2001–02) *Tuition:* state resident $3020 full-time, $117 per semester hour part-time; nonresident $6040 full-time, $234 per semester hour part-time. *Required fees:* $60 full-time, $30 per term part-time. *Payment plan:* deferred payment. *Waivers:* employees or children of employees.
Financial Aid Of all full-time matriculated undergraduates who enrolled in 2001, 746 applied for aid, 746 were judged to have need, 215 had their need fully met. 23 Federal Work-Study jobs (averaging $1583). In 2001, 142 non-need-based awards were made. *Average percent of need met:* 39%. *Average need-based loan:* $4282. *Average need-based gift aid:* $3125.
Applying *Options:* electronic application, early admission, deferred entrance. *Application fee:* $20. *Required:* high school transcript, minimum 2.0 GPA. *Application deadline:* rolling (freshmen), rolling (transfers).
Admissions Contact Mr. Frank Hrabe, Director of Enrollment Management, Troy State University Montgomery, PO Drawer 4419, Montgomery, AL 36103-4419. *Phone:* 334-241-9506. *Toll-free phone:* 800-355-TSUM. *E-mail:* admit@tsum.edu.

TUSKEGEE UNIVERSITY
Tuskegee, Alabama

- **Independent** comprehensive, founded 1881
- **Calendar** semesters
- **Degrees** bachelor's, master's, doctoral, and first professional
- **Small-town** 4390-acre campus
- **Coed,** 2,510 undergraduate students, 94% full-time, 58% women, 42% men
- **Moderately difficult** entrance level, 67% of applicants were admitted

Undergraduates 2,354 full-time, 156 part-time. Students come from 44 states and territories, 23 other countries, 64% are from out of state, 98% African American, 0.0% Asian American or Pacific Islander, 0.1% Hispanic American, 1% international, 3% transferred in, 63% live on campus. *Retention:* 74% of 2001 full-time freshmen returned.
Freshmen *Admission:* 2,319 applied, 1,550 admitted, 662 enrolled. *Average high school GPA:* 3.00. *Test scores:* SAT verbal scores over 500: 22%; SAT math scores over 500: 21%; ACT scores over 18: 42%; SAT verbal scores over 600: 3%; SAT math scores over 600: 3%; ACT scores over 24: 4%.
Faculty *Total:* 256, 87% full-time, 71% with terminal degrees. *Student/faculty ratio:* 12:1.
Majors Accounting; aerospace engineering; agricultural business; agricultural sciences; agronomy/crop science; animal sciences; architecture; biology; business administration; business marketing and marketing management; chemical engineering; chemistry; computer science; construction/building inspection; construction technology; dietetics; economics; electrical engineering; elementary education; engineering-related technology; English; environmental science; finance; food sciences; history; hospitality management; hospitality/recreation marketing operations; management science; marketing operations; mathematics; mechanical engineering; medical technology; natural resources management; nursing; nutrition science; occupational therapy; physics; plant sciences; political science; poultry science; psychology; social work; sociology.
Academic Programs *Special study options:* academic remediation for entering students, cooperative education, English as a second language, honors programs, internships, off-campus study, part-time degree program, summer session for credit. *ROTC:* Army (b), Air Force (b). *Unusual degree programs:* 3-2 forestry with Auburn University, Iowa State University of Science and Technology, University of Michigan, Idaho State University.
Library Hollis B. Frissell Library plus 3 others with 623,824 titles, 81,157 serial subscriptions, an OPAC.
Computers on Campus 1000 computers available on campus for general student use. A campuswide network can be accessed from student residence rooms and from off campus. Internet access, online (class) registration, at least one staffed computer lab available.
Student Life *Housing:* on-campus residence required through sophomore year. *Activities and Organizations:* drama/theater group, student-run newspaper, choral group, marching band, national fraternities, national sororities. *Campus security:* 24-hour emergency response devices and patrols, late-night transport/escort service. *Student Services:* health clinic, personal/psychological counseling.
Athletics Member NCAA. All Division II. *Intercollegiate sports:* baseball M(s), basketball M(s)/W(s), cross-country running M/W, football M(s), golf M(s), riflery M/W, soccer M, tennis M(s)/W(s), track and field M(s)/W(s), volleyball W(s). *Intramural sports:* badminton M/W, basketball M/W, football M, golf M, gymnastics M/W, riflery M/W, soccer M, swimming M/W, tennis M/W, track and field M/W, volleyball M/W.
Standardized Tests *Required:* SAT I or ACT (for admission).
Costs (2002–03) *Comprehensive fee:* $16,464 includes full-time tuition ($10,584), mandatory fees ($200), and room and board ($5680). Full-time tuition and fees vary according to course load and program. Part-time tuition: $427 per credit. Part-time tuition and fees vary according to course load and program. *Room and board:* Room and board charges vary according to housing facility. *Payment plan:* installment. *Waivers:* employees or children of employees.
Financial Aid Of all full-time matriculated undergraduates who enrolled in 2001, 2476 applied for aid, 2104 were judged to have need, 774 had their need fully met. 372 Federal Work-Study jobs (averaging $2425). In 2001, 245 non-need-based awards were made. *Average percent of need met:* 81%. *Average financial aid package:* $11,161. *Average need-based loan:* $4682. *Average need-based gift aid:* $3950. *Average non-need based aid:* $3000. *Average indebtedness upon graduation:* $17,125.
Applying *Options:* electronic application, early admission. *Application fee:* $25. *Required:* high school transcript, minimum 2.0 GPA. *Application deadlines:* 4/15 (freshmen), 4/15 (transfers).
Admissions Contact Ms. Iolantha E. Spencer, Admissions, Tuskegee University, 102 Old Administration Building, Tuskegee, AL 36088. *Phone:* 334-727-8500. *Toll-free phone:* 800-622-6531.

THE UNIVERSITY OF ALABAMA
Tuscaloosa, Alabama

- **State-supported** university, founded 1831, part of University of Alabama System
- **Calendar** semesters
- **Degrees** bachelor's, master's, doctoral, first professional, and post-master's certificates
- **Suburban** 1000-acre campus with easy access to Birmingham
- **Coed,** 15,201 undergraduate students, 89% full-time, 53% women, 47% men
- **Moderately difficult** entrance level, 79% of applicants were admitted

Undergraduates 13,515 full-time, 1,686 part-time. Students come from 51 states and territories, 70 other countries, 21% are from out of state, 15% African American, 1% Asian American or Pacific Islander, 1.0% Hispanic American, 0.6% Native American, 2% international, 8% transferred in, 25% live on campus. *Retention:* 82% of 2001 full-time freshmen returned.
Freshmen *Admission:* 7,864 applied, 6,250 admitted, 2,420 enrolled. *Average high school GPA:* 3.39. *Test scores:* SAT verbal scores over 500: 74%; SAT math scores over 500: 72%; ACT scores over 18: 99%; SAT verbal scores over 600: 29%; SAT math scores over 600: 30%; ACT scores over 24: 46%; SAT verbal scores over 700: 5%; SAT math scores over 700: 6%; ACT scores over 30: 8%.
Faculty *Total:* 1,044, 83% full-time, 84% with terminal degrees. *Student/faculty ratio:* 19:1.
Majors Accounting; advertising; aerospace engineering; American studies; anthropology; art history; Asian studies; athletic training/sports medicine;

The University of Alabama (continued)
biological/physical sciences; biology; business administration; business economics; business marketing and marketing management; chemical engineering; chemistry; civil engineering; classics; clothing/apparel/textile studies; computer/information sciences; consumer economics; criminal justice studies; dance; early childhood education; electrical engineering; elementary education; English; finance; fine/studio arts; French; geography; geology; German; health facilities administration; health professions and related sciences; history; home economics; home economics related; hotel and restaurant management; individual/family development; industrial/manufacturing engineering; interdisciplinary studies; interior design; international relations; journalism; Latin American studies; management information systems/business data processing; management science; marine biology; mathematics; mechanical engineering; metallurgical engineering; microbiology/bacteriology; music; music teacher education; nursing; nutrition studies; philosophy; physical education; physics; political science; psychology; public relations; radio/television broadcasting; religious studies; Russian; secondary education; social work; sociology; Spanish; special education; speech-language pathology/audiology; speech/rhetorical studies; theater arts/drama.

Academic Programs *Special study options:* academic remediation for entering students, accelerated degree program, adult/continuing education programs, advanced placement credit, cooperative education, distance learning, double majors, English as a second language, external degree program, freshman honors college, honors programs, independent study, internships, off-campus study, part-time degree program, services for LD students, student-designed majors, study abroad, summer session for credit. *ROTC:* Army (b), Air Force (b).

Library Amelia Gayle Gorgas Library plus 8 others with 3.4 million titles, 17,788 serial subscriptions, 480,498 audiovisual materials, an OPAC, a Web page.

Computers on Campus 1450 computers available on campus for general student use. A campuswide network can be accessed from student residence rooms and from off campus. Internet access, at least one staffed computer lab available.

Student Life *Housing Options:* coed, men-only, women-only, disabled students. *Activities and Organizations:* drama/theater group, student-run newspaper, radio and television station, choral group, marching band, Coordinating Council of Student Organizations, Residence Hall Association, International Student Association, Student Government Association, African-American Association, national fraternities, national sororities. *Campus security:* 24-hour emergency response devices and patrols, student patrols, late-night transport/escort service, controlled dormitory access, crime prevention programs, community police protection. *Student Services:* health clinic, personal/psychological counseling, women's center, legal services.

Athletics Member NCAA. All Division I except football (Division I-A). *Intercollegiate sports:* baseball M(s), basketball M(s)/W(s), cross-country running M(s)/W(s), golf M(s)/W(s), gymnastics W(s), soccer W(s), softball W(s), swimming M(s)/W(s), tennis M(s)/W(s), track and field M(s)/W(s), volleyball W(s). *Intramural sports:* badminton M/W, basketball M/W, bowling M/W, crew M(c)/W(c), equestrian sports M(c)/W(c), football M/W, golf M/W, lacrosse M(c), racquetball M/W, rugby M, soccer M(c)/W(c), softball M/W, table tennis M/W, tennis M/W, track and field M/W, volleyball M/W, water polo M/W, wrestling M.

Standardized Tests *Required:* SAT I or ACT (for admission).

Costs (2001–02) *Tuition:* $137 per credit hour part-time; state resident $3292 full-time, $137 per credit hour part-time; nonresident $8912 full-time, $340 per credit hour part-time. Full-time tuition and fees vary according to course load. Part-time tuition and fees vary according to course load. *Room and board:* $4110; room only: $2560. Room and board charges vary according to board plan and housing facility. *Payment plans:* installment, deferred payment. *Waivers:* employees or children of employees.

Financial Aid Of all full-time matriculated undergraduates who enrolled in 2001, 10276 applied for aid, 6346 were judged to have need, 1342 had their need fully met. 1000 Federal Work-Study jobs (averaging $2630). In 2001, 2922 non-need-based awards were made. *Average percent of need met:* 71%. *Average financial aid package:* $7313. *Average need-based loan:* $4450. *Average need-based gift aid:* $2736. *Average non-need based aid:* $3531. *Average indebtedness upon graduation:* $19,386.

Applying *Options:* common application, electronic application, early admission, deferred entrance. *Application fee:* $25. *Required:* high school transcript, minimum 2.0 GPA. *Required for some:* interview. *Application deadline:* 7/1 (freshmen), rolling (transfers). *Notification:* 9/1 (freshmen).

Admissions Contact Dr. Lisa B. Harris, Assistant Vice President for Undergraduate Admissions and Financial Aid, The University of Alabama, Box 870132, Tuscaloosa, AL 35487-0132. *Phone:* 205-348-5666. *Toll-free phone:* 800-933-BAMA. *Fax:* 205-348-9046. *E-mail:* admissions@ua.edu.

THE UNIVERSITY OF ALABAMA AT BIRMINGHAM

Birmingham, Alabama

- **State-supported** university, founded 1969, part of University of Alabama System
- **Calendar** quarters
- **Degrees** certificates, bachelor's, master's, doctoral, first professional, post-master's, and postbachelor's certificates
- **Urban** 265-acre campus
- **Endowment** $233.6 million
- **Coed,** 9,945 undergraduate students, 68% full-time, 59% women, 41% men
- **Moderately difficult** entrance level, 91% of applicants were admitted

Undergraduates 6,769 full-time, 3,176 part-time. Students come from 40 states and territories, 77 other countries, 5% are from out of state, 30% African American, 3% Asian American or Pacific Islander, 0.9% Hispanic American, 0.3% Native American, 3% international, 8% transferred in, 13% live on campus. *Retention:* 72% of 2001 full-time freshmen returned.

Freshmen *Admission:* 3,172 applied, 2,886 admitted, 1,292 enrolled. *Average high school GPA:* 3.12. *Test scores:* ACT scores over 18: 84%; ACT scores over 24: 30%; ACT scores over 30: 6%.

Faculty *Total:* 796, 91% full-time, 86% with terminal degrees. *Student/faculty ratio:* 18:1.

Majors Accounting; African-American studies; anthropology; bioengineering; biological/physical sciences; biology; business administration; business economics; business marketing and marketing management; chemistry; civil engineering; communications; computer/information sciences; criminal justice/corrections related; cytotechnology; early childhood education; electrical engineering; elementary education; English; finance; fine/studio arts; French; health education; history; materials engineering; mathematics; mechanical engineering; medical radiologic technology; medical records administration; medical technology; music; nuclear medical technology; nursing; philosophy; physical education; physician assistant; physics; political science; psychology; respiratory therapy; secondary education; social sciences and history related; social work; sociology; Spanish; special education; visual/performing arts.

Academic Programs *Special study options:* academic remediation for entering students, adult/continuing education programs, advanced placement credit, cooperative education, double majors, honors programs, independent study, internships, off-campus study, part-time degree program, services for LD students, student-designed majors, study abroad, summer session for credit. *ROTC:* Army (b), Air Force (c). *Unusual degree programs:* 3-2 accounting.

Library Mervyn Sterne Library plus 1 other with 5,288 serial subscriptions, 37,366 audiovisual materials, an OPAC, a Web page.

Computers on Campus 400 computers available on campus for general student use. A campuswide network can be accessed from off campus. Internet access, online (class) registration, at least one staffed computer lab available.

Student Life *Housing Options:* coed, women-only. *Activities and Organizations:* drama/theater group, student-run newspaper, radio station, choral group, marching band, Campus Ministries, service-oriented groups, sports affiliated groups, national fraternities, national sororities. *Campus security:* 24-hour emergency response devices and patrols, late-night transport/escort service, controlled dormitory access. *Student Services:* health clinic, personal/psychological counseling, women's center.

Athletics Member NCAA. All Division I except football (Division I-A), softball (Division II). *Intercollegiate sports:* baseball M(s), basketball M(s)/W(s), cross-country running W(s), golf M(s)/W(s), riflery M/W, soccer M(s)/W(s), softball W(s), swimming W(s), tennis M(s)/W(s), track and field W(s), volleyball W(s). *Intramural sports:* badminton M/W, baseball M, basketball M/W, bowling M/W, football M/W, golf M/W, racquetball M/W, soccer M/W, softball M/W, swimming M/W, table tennis M/W, tennis M/W, track and field M/W, volleyball M/W, wrestling M.

Standardized Tests *Required:* SAT I or ACT (for admission).

Costs (2001–02) *Tuition:* state resident $2970 full-time, $99 per hour part-time; nonresident $5940 full-time, $198 per hour part-time. Full-time tuition and fees vary according to course load and program. Part-time tuition and fees vary according to course load and program. *Required fees:* $670 full-time. *Room and board:* $6471; room only: $2588. Room and board charges vary according to housing facility. *Waivers:* employees or children of employees.

Financial Aid Of all full-time matriculated undergraduates who enrolled in 2001, 4626 applied for aid, 3433 were judged to have need, 582 had their need

fully met. In 2001, 929 non-need-based awards were made. *Average percent of need met:* 38%. *Average financial aid package:* $8890. *Average need-based loan:* $4244. *Average need-based gift aid:* $2691. *Average non-need based aid:* $2490. *Average indebtedness upon graduation:* $17,485.

Applying *Options:* early admission, deferred entrance. *Application fee:* $25. *Required:* high school transcript, minimum 2.0 GPA. *Application deadlines:* 7/1 (freshmen), 7/15 (transfers).

Admissions Contact Ms. Chenise Ryan, Director of Undergraduate Admissions, The University of Alabama at Birmingham, Office of Undergraduate Admissions, 260 HUC, 1530 3rd Avenue south, Birmingham, AL 35294-1150. *Phone:* 205-934-8221. *Toll-free phone:* 800-421-8743. *Fax:* 205-975-7114. *E-mail:* UndergradAdmit@uab.edu.

THE UNIVERSITY OF ALABAMA IN HUNTSVILLE

Huntsville, Alabama

- **State-supported** university, founded 1950, part of University of Alabama System
- **Calendar** semesters
- **Degrees** bachelor's, master's, doctoral, post-master's, and postbachelor's certificates
- **Suburban** 376-acre campus
- **Endowment** $21.7 million
- **Coed,** 5,466 undergraduate students, 62% full-time, 50% women, 50% men
- **Moderately difficult** entrance level, 84% of applicants were admitted

Undergraduates 3,397 full-time, 2,069 part-time. Students come from 45 states and territories, 66 other countries, 11% are from out of state, 14% African American, 4% Asian American or Pacific Islander, 2% Hispanic American, 2% Native American, 4% international, 11% transferred in, 12% live on campus. *Retention:* 71% of 2001 full-time freshmen returned.

Freshmen *Admission:* 1,198 applied, 1,004 admitted, 628 enrolled. *Average high school GPA:* 3.36. *Test scores:* SAT verbal scores over 500: 74%; SAT math scores over 500: 75%; ACT scores over 18: 98%; SAT verbal scores over 600: 32%; SAT math scores over 600: 39%; ACT scores over 24: 57%; SAT verbal scores over 700: 7%; SAT math scores over 700: 10%; ACT scores over 30: 9%.

Faculty *Total:* 446, 62% full-time. *Student/faculty ratio:* 14:1.

Majors Accounting; art; biology; business administration; business marketing and marketing management; chemical engineering; chemistry; civil engineering; computer engineering; computer/information sciences; electrical engineering; elementary education; English; finance; foreign languages/literatures; history; industrial/manufacturing engineering; management information systems/business data processing; mathematics; mechanical engineering; music; nursing; philosophy; physics; political science; psychology; sociology; speech/rhetorical studies.

Academic Programs *Special study options:* academic remediation for entering students, accelerated degree program, adult/continuing education programs, advanced placement credit, cooperative education, distance learning, double majors, English as a second language, honors programs, independent study, internships, off-campus study, part-time degree program, services for LD students, summer session for credit. *ROTC:* Army (c). *Unusual degree programs:* 3-2 engineering with Morris Brown College, Oakwood College, Moorehouse College, Clark Atlanta University, Fisk University.

Library University of Alabama in Huntsville Library with 627,132 titles, 1,668 serial subscriptions, 2,677 audiovisual materials, an OPAC, a Web page.

Computers on Campus 520 computers available on campus for general student use. A campuswide network can be accessed from student residence rooms and from off campus. Internet access, online (class) registration, at least one staffed computer lab available.

Student Life *Housing Options:* coed. *Activities and Organizations:* drama/theater group, student-run newspaper, choral group, Student Government Association, Association for Campus Entertainment, Circle K International, Anointed Voices, Institute of Electrical and Electronic Engineers, national fraternities, national sororities. *Campus security:* 24-hour emergency response devices and patrols, late-night transport/escort service, controlled dormitory access. *Student Services:* health clinic, personal/psychological counseling.

Athletics Member NCAA. All Division II. *Intercollegiate sports:* baseball M(s), basketball M(s)/W(s), cross-country running M(s)/W(s), ice hockey M(s), soccer M(s)/W(s), softball W, tennis M(s)/W(s), volleyball W(s). *Intramural sports:* badminton M/W, basketball M/W, crew M(c)/W(c), football M/W, racquetball M/W, soccer M/W, softball M/W, tennis M/W, volleyball M/W.

Standardized Tests *Required:* SAT I or ACT (for admission).

Costs (2001–02) *Tuition:* state resident $3536 full-time, $793 per term part-time; nonresident $7430 full-time, $1660 per term part-time. Full-time tuition and fees vary according to course load. Part-time tuition and fees vary according to course load. *Room and board:* $4380; room only: $3080. Room and board charges vary according to board plan and housing facility. *Payment plan:* deferred payment. *Waivers:* employees or children of employees.

Financial Aid Of all full-time matriculated undergraduates who enrolled in 2001, 2618 applied for aid, 1333 were judged to have need, 464 had their need fully met. 82 Federal Work-Study jobs (averaging $3614). In 2001, 881 non-need-based awards were made. *Average percent of need met:* 70%. *Average financial aid package:* $6612. *Average need-based loan:* $4706. *Average need-based gift aid:* $3065. *Average non-need based aid:* $1786. *Average indebtedness upon graduation:* $16,900.

Applying *Options:* common application, electronic application, early admission, deferred entrance. *Application fee:* $20. *Required:* high school transcript. *Application deadlines:* 8/15 (freshmen), 8/15 (transfers). *Notification:* continuous until 8/15 (freshmen).

Admissions Contact Ms. Sabrina Williams, Associate Director of Admissions, The University of Alabama in Huntsville, 301 Sparkman Drive, Huntsville, AL 35899. *Phone:* 256-824-6070. *Toll-free phone:* 800-UAH-CALL. *Fax:* 256-824-6073. *E-mail:* admitme@email.uah.edu.

UNIVERSITY OF MOBILE

Mobile, Alabama

- **Independent Southern Baptist** comprehensive, founded 1961
- **Calendar** semesters
- **Degrees** associate, bachelor's, and master's
- **Suburban** 830-acre campus
- **Endowment** $8.6 million
- **Coed,** 1,803 undergraduate students, 77% full-time, 68% women, 32% men
- **Moderately difficult** entrance level, 98% of applicants were admitted

Undergraduates 1,380 full-time, 423 part-time. Students come from 23 states and territories, 14 other countries, 25% African American, 0.6% Asian American or Pacific Islander, 0.8% Hispanic American, 2% Native American, 1% international, 12% transferred in, 20% live on campus.

Freshmen *Admission:* 450 applied, 440 admitted, 302 enrolled. *Test scores:* ACT scores over 18: 90%; ACT scores over 24: 36%; ACT scores over 30: 6%.

Faculty *Total:* 154, 56% full-time, 44% with terminal degrees. *Student/faculty ratio:* 17:1.

Majors Accounting; art; athletic training/sports medicine; behavioral sciences; biological/physical sciences; biology; business administration; chemistry; computer science; early childhood education; economics; elementary education; English; environmental science; general studies; history; humanities; information sciences/systems; mass communications; mathematics; music; nursing; physical education; political science; psychology; religious education; religious studies; secondary education; social sciences; sociology; theater arts/drama.

Academic Programs *Special study options:* academic remediation for entering students, accelerated degree program, adult/continuing education programs, advanced placement credit, double majors, English as a second language, honors programs, independent study, internships, part-time degree program, summer session for credit. *ROTC:* Army (c), Air Force (c). *Unusual degree programs:* 3-2 engineering with Auburn University and University of South Alabama; cytotechnology, medical technology, medical record administration, nuclear medical technology, occupational therapy with University of Alabama at Birmingham, law with Tulane University.

Library J. L. Bedsole Library plus 2 others with 100,250 titles, 1,043 serial subscriptions, 2,222 audiovisual materials, an OPAC.

Computers on Campus 100 computers available on campus for general student use. A campuswide network can be accessed from off campus. Internet access, at least one staffed computer lab available.

Student Life *Housing:* on-campus residence required for freshman year. *Options:* men-only, women-only. *Activities and Organizations:* drama/theater group, student-run newspaper, choral group, Campus Activity Board, Baptist Campus Ministry, Student Government Association, Fellowship of Christian Athletes. *Campus security:* 24-hour emergency response devices and patrols. *Student Services:* health clinic, personal/psychological counseling.

Athletics Member NAIA. *Intercollegiate sports:* baseball M(s), basketball M(s)/W(s), cross-country running M(s)/W(s), golf M(s)/W(s), soccer M(s)/W(s), softball W(s), tennis W(s), track and field M(s)/W(s). *Intramural sports:* badminton M/W, baseball M, basketball M/W, cross-country running M/W, football M/W, golf M/W, soccer M/W, softball M/W, swimming M/W, table tennis M/W, tennis M/W, track and field M/W, volleyball M/W, weight lifting M/W.

Standardized Tests *Required:* SAT I or ACT (for admission).

Costs (2001–02) *Comprehensive fee:* $13,620 includes full-time tuition ($8670), mandatory fees ($100), and room and board ($4850). Full-time tuition and fees

University of Mobile (continued)
vary according to course load. Part-time tuition: $289 per semester hour. Part-time tuition and fees vary according to course load. *Required fees:* $20 per term. *Room and board:* Room and board charges vary according to board plan. *Payment plan:* installment. *Waivers:* employees or children of employees.

Financial Aid Of all full-time matriculated undergraduates who enrolled in 2001, 1272 applied for aid, 821 were judged to have need. 96 Federal Work-Study jobs (averaging $1545). In 2001, 179 non-need-based awards were made. *Average percent of need met:* 53%. *Average financial aid package:* $7242. *Average need-based loan:* $4290. *Average need-based gift aid:* $3350. *Average indebtedness upon graduation:* $18,000.

Applying *Options:* common application, early admission, deferred entrance. *Application fee:* $30. *Required:* high school transcript, minimum 2.0 GPA. *Required for some:* interview. *Application deadline:* rolling (freshmen), rolling (transfers). *Notification:* continuous (freshmen), 11/15 (early action).

Admissions Contact Mr. Brian Boyle, Director of Admissions, University of Mobile, PO Box 13220, Mobile, AL 36663-0220. *Phone:* 251-442-2287. *Toll-free phone:* 800-946-7267. *Fax:* 251-442-2498. *E-mail:* adminfo@umobile.edu.

UNIVERSITY OF MONTEVALLO
Montevallo, Alabama

- **State-supported** comprehensive, founded 1896
- **Calendar** semesters
- **Degrees** bachelor's, master's, and post-master's certificates
- **Small-town** 106-acre campus with easy access to Birmingham
- **Endowment** $2.0 million
- **Coed,** 2,559 undergraduate students, 90% full-time, 68% women, 32% men
- **Moderately difficult** entrance level, 73% of applicants were admitted

Undergraduates 2,296 full-time, 263 part-time. Students come from 18 states and territories, 21 other countries, 2% are from out of state, 14% African American, 0.5% Asian American or Pacific Islander, 1.0% Hispanic American, 0.7% Native American, 2% international, 10% transferred in, 37% live on campus. *Retention:* 71% of 2001 full-time freshmen returned.

Freshmen *Admission:* 1,342 applied, 973 admitted, 533 enrolled. *Average high school GPA:* 3.24. *Test scores:* ACT scores over 18: 91%; ACT scores over 24: 33%; ACT scores over 30: 3%.

Faculty *Total:* 199, 66% full-time, 62% with terminal degrees. *Student/faculty ratio:* 16:1.

Majors Accounting; art; art education; biology; broadcast journalism; business administration; business marketing and marketing management; ceramic arts; chemistry; dietetics; drawing; early childhood education; elementary education; English; family/consumer studies; fashion merchandising; fine/studio arts; French; graphic design/commercial art/illustration; health/physical education; history; home economics; home economics education; interior design; international relations; management information systems/business data processing; mass communications; mathematics; music; music (piano and organ performance); music teacher education; music (voice and choral/opera performance); photography; political science; pre-dentistry; pre-law; pre-medicine; pre-veterinary studies; printmaking; psychology; radio/television broadcasting; retail management; sculpture; social sciences; social work; sociology; Spanish; speech-language pathology/audiology; speech/rhetorical studies; theater arts/drama.

Academic Programs *Special study options:* academic remediation for entering students, accelerated degree program, advanced placement credit, double majors, honors programs, independent study, internships, part-time degree program, services for LD students, study abroad, summer session for credit. *ROTC:* Army (c), Air Force (c). *Unusual degree programs:* 3-2 engineering with Auburn University, University of Alabama at Birmingham.

Library Carmichael Library with 153,409 titles, 868 serial subscriptions, 2,523 audiovisual materials, an OPAC, a Web page.

Computers on Campus 250 computers available on campus for general student use. A campuswide network can be accessed from student residence rooms and from off campus. At least one staffed computer lab available.

Student Life *Housing:* on-campus residence required for freshman year. *Options:* coed, men-only, women-only. *Activities and Organizations:* drama/theater group, student-run newspaper, television station, choral group, Golden Key, Student Government Association, University Programming Council, Campus Ministries, African-American Association, national fraternities, national sororities. *Campus security:* 24-hour emergency response devices and patrols, late-night transport/escort service, controlled dormitory access. *Student Services:* health clinic, personal/psychological counseling.

Athletics Member NCAA. All Division II. *Intercollegiate sports:* baseball M(s), basketball M(s)/W(s), golf M(s)/W(s), soccer M(s)/W(s), tennis W(s), volleyball W(s). *Intramural sports:* basketball M/W, bowling M, football M, golf M, tennis M/W, volleyball M/W.

Standardized Tests *Required:* SAT I or ACT (for admission).

Costs (2001–02) *Tuition:* state resident $3690 full-time, $123 per credit hour part-time; nonresident $7380 full-time, $246 per credit hour part-time. Full-time tuition and fees vary according to course load. Part-time tuition and fees vary according to course load. *Required fees:* $284 full-time, $40 per term part-time. *Room and board:* $3576; room only: $2296. Room and board charges vary according to board plan and housing facility. *Payment plan:* deferred payment. *Waivers:* senior citizens and employees or children of employees.

Financial Aid Of all full-time matriculated undergraduates who enrolled in 2001, 1756 applied for aid, 897 were judged to have need, 300 had their need fully met. 136 Federal Work-Study jobs (averaging $1410). 368 State and other part-time jobs (averaging $1545). In 2001, 438 non-need-based awards were made. *Average percent of need met:* 68%. *Average financial aid package:* $3288. *Average need-based loan:* $1548. *Average need-based gift aid:* $2184. *Average non-need based aid:* $1947. *Average indebtedness upon graduation:* $16,481.

Applying *Options:* common application, electronic application, early admission, deferred entrance. *Application fee:* $25. *Required:* high school transcript, minimum 2.0 GPA. *Recommended:* interview. *Application deadline:* 8/1 (freshmen), rolling (transfers).

Admissions Contact Mr. William C. Cannon, Director of Admissions, University of Montevallo, Station 66030, Montevallo, AL 35115-6030. *Phone:* 205-665-6030. *Toll-free phone:* 800-292-4349. *Fax:* 205-665-6032. *E-mail:* admissions@montevallo.edu.

UNIVERSITY OF NORTH ALABAMA
Florence, Alabama

- **State-supported** comprehensive, founded 1830, part of Alabama Commission on Higher Education
- **Calendar** semesters
- **Degrees** bachelor's and master's
- **Urban** 125-acre campus
- **Endowment** $4.8 million
- **Coed,** 4,852 undergraduate students, 84% full-time, 59% women, 41% men
- **Minimally difficult** entrance level, 82% of applicants were admitted

Undergraduates 4,079 full-time, 773 part-time. Students come from 31 states and territories, 31 other countries, 17% are from out of state, 11% African American, 0.6% Asian American or Pacific Islander, 0.7% Hispanic American, 2% Native American, 2% international, 11% transferred in, 19% live on campus. *Retention:* 65% of 2001 full-time freshmen returned.

Freshmen *Admission:* 1,675 applied, 1,374 admitted, 829 enrolled. *Average high school GPA:* 2.94. *Test scores:* SAT verbal scores over 500: 38%; SAT math scores over 500: 69%; ACT scores over 18: 81%; SAT math scores over 600: 15%; ACT scores over 24: 28%; ACT scores over 30: 3%.

Faculty *Total:* 196. *Student/faculty ratio:* 21:1.

Majors Accounting; biological sciences/life sciences related; biology; business administration; business economics; business marketing and marketing management; chemistry; computer/information sciences; counseling psychology; criminal justice/law enforcement administration; early childhood education; education (multiple levels); elementary education; English; finance; fine arts and art studies related; fine/studio arts; foreign languages/literatures; general studies; geography; geology; history; home economics; management information systems/business data processing; marine biology; mathematics; music; nursing; parks, recreation, leisure and fitness studies related; physical sciences; physics; political science; psychology; secondary education; social work; sociology; special education; speech/rhetorical studies.

Academic Programs *Special study options:* academic remediation for entering students, accelerated degree program, adult/continuing education programs, advanced placement credit, cooperative education, distance learning, double majors, English as a second language, independent study, internships, part-time degree program, services for LD students, summer session for credit. *ROTC:* Army (b).

Library Collier Library with 343,468 titles, 1,792 serial subscriptions, 8,945 audiovisual materials, an OPAC, a Web page.

Computers on Campus 500 computers available on campus for general student use. A campuswide network can be accessed from student residence rooms and from off campus. Internet access, at least one staffed computer lab available.

Student Life *Housing Options:* coed, men-only, women-only. *Activities and Organizations:* drama/theater group, student-run newspaper, radio station, choral group, marching band, Student Government Association, University Program Council, Baptist Campus Ministries, Physical Education Majors Club, Residence Hall Association, national fraternities, national sororities. *Campus security:* 24-hour emergency response devices and patrols, student patrols, late-night transport/escort service, controlled dormitory access. *Student Services:* health clinic, personal/psychological counseling.

Athletics Member NCAA. All Division II. *Intercollegiate sports:* baseball M(s), basketball M(s)/W(s), cross-country running M(s)/W(s), football M(s), golf M(s), soccer W(s), softball W(s), tennis M(s)/W(s), volleyball W(s). *Intramural sports:* badminton M/W, baseball M, basketball M/W, bowling M/W, cross-country running M/W, football M/W, golf M, racquetball M/W, softball W, swimming M/W, table tennis M/W, tennis M/W, volleyball M/W, weight lifting M/W.

Standardized Tests *Required:* SAT I or ACT (for admission).

Costs (2001–02) *Tuition:* state resident $2848 full-time, $106 per credit hour part-time; nonresident $5392 full-time, $212 per credit hour part-time. Part-time tuition and fees vary according to course load. *Required fees:* $830 full-time, $14 per credit hour, $24 per credit hour part-time. *Room and board:* $3662. Room and board charges vary according to board plan. *Payment plan:* installment. *Waivers:* employees or children of employees.

Financial Aid Of all full-time matriculated undergraduates who enrolled in 2001, 2898 applied for aid, 2312 were judged to have need, 1021 had their need fully met. 215 Federal Work-Study jobs (averaging $1242). 430 State and other part-time jobs (averaging $1227). *Average percent of need met:* 57%. *Average financial aid package:* $3774. *Average need-based loan:* $6396. *Average need-based gift aid:* $2287. *Average indebtedness upon graduation:* $16,529.

Applying *Options:* early admission, deferred entrance. *Application fee:* $25. *Required:* high school transcript. *Application deadline:* rolling (freshmen), rolling (transfers).

Admissions Contact Mrs. Kim O. Mauldin, Director of Admissions, University of North Alabama, Office of Admissions, Box 5011, Florence, AL 35632-0001. *Phone:* 256-765-4680. *Toll-free phone:* 800-TALKUNA. *Fax:* 256-765-4329. *E-mail:* admis1@unanov.una.edu.

UNIVERSITY OF SOUTH ALABAMA
Mobile, Alabama

- **State-supported** university, founded 1963
- **Calendar** semesters
- **Degrees** certificates, bachelor's, master's, doctoral, first professional, and postbachelor's certificates
- **Suburban** 1215-acre campus
- **Endowment** $306.0 million
- **Coed,** 9,572 undergraduate students, 62% full-time, 58% women, 42% men
- **Moderately difficult** entrance level, 93% of applicants were admitted

Undergraduates 5,979 full-time, 3,593 part-time. Students come from 40 states and territories, 100 other countries, 22% are from out of state, 17% African American, 3% Asian American or Pacific Islander, 1% Hispanic American, 0.7% Native American, 6% international, 10% transferred in, 19% live on campus. *Retention:* 71% of 2001 full-time freshmen returned.

Freshmen *Admission:* 2,444 applied, 2,282 admitted, 1,457 enrolled. *Average high school GPA:* 3.10. *Test scores:* ACT scores over 18: 97%; ACT scores over 24: 38%; ACT scores over 30: 4%.

Faculty *Total:* 917, 75% full-time, 60% with terminal degrees. *Student/faculty ratio:* 22:1.

Majors Accounting; anthropology; art; art history; atmospheric sciences; biology; biomedical science; business; business administration; business economics; business marketing and marketing management; chemical engineering; chemistry; civil engineering; communications; computer engineering; computer/information sciences; criminal justice/law enforcement administration; early childhood education; electrical engineering; elementary education; English; finance; foreign languages/literatures; geography; geology; health/medical preparatory programs related; history; liberal arts and studies related; mathematical statistics; mathematics; mechanical engineering; medical technology; music; music (general performance); music theory and composition; nursing; philosophy; physical education; physical therapy; physics; political science; psychology; radiological science; respiratory therapy; secondary education; sociology; special education; speech-language pathology/audiology; theater arts/drama.

Academic Programs *Special study options:* academic remediation for entering students, accelerated degree program, adult/continuing education programs, advanced placement credit, cooperative education, English as a second language, internships, part-time degree program, services for LD students, student-designed majors, study abroad, summer session for credit. *ROTC:* Army (b), Air Force (b).

Library University Library plus 1 other with 578,615 titles, 3,981 serial subscriptions, 13,349 audiovisual materials, an OPAC.

Computers on Campus 325 computers available on campus for general student use. A campuswide network can be accessed from student residence rooms and from off campus. Internet access, at least one staffed computer lab available.

Student Life *Housing Options:* coed. *Activities and Organizations:* drama/theater group, student-run newspaper, radio and television station, choral group, Student Government Association, Black Student Union, Nontraditional Student Committee, national fraternities, national sororities. *Campus security:* 24-hour emergency response devices and patrols, late-night transport/escort service. *Student Services:* health clinic, personal/psychological counseling, legal services.

Athletics Member NCAA. All Division I. *Intercollegiate sports:* baseball M(s), basketball M(s)/W(s), cross-country running M(s)/W(s), fencing M(c)/W(c), football M(c), golf M/W, sailing M(c)/W(c), soccer W(s), tennis M(s)/W(s), track and field M(s)/W(s), volleyball W(s). *Intramural sports:* badminton M/W, basketball M/W, bowling M/W, golf M/W, racquetball M/W, soccer M/W, softball M/W, table tennis M/W, tennis M/W, volleyball M/W, water polo M/W.

Standardized Tests *Required:* SAT I or ACT (for admission).

Costs (2001–02) *Tuition:* state resident $2910 full-time, $99 per semester hour part-time; nonresident $5820 full-time, $198 per semester hour part-time. Full-time tuition and fees vary according to class time, course load, and program. Part-time tuition and fees vary according to class time, course load, and program. *Required fees:* $160 full-time, $121 per term part-time. *Room and board:* $3746; room only: $2028. Room and board charges vary according to board plan and student level. *Payment plan:* installment. *Waivers:* employees or children of employees.

Financial Aid Of all full-time matriculated undergraduates who enrolled in 2001, 4077 applied for aid, 4043 were judged to have need, 100 had their need fully met. 120 Federal Work-Study jobs, 400 State and other part-time jobs. *Average percent of need met:* 45%. *Average financial aid package:* $5702.

Applying *Options:* early admission. *Application fee:* $25. *Required:* high school transcript. *Recommended:* minimum 2.0 GPA. *Application deadlines:* 8/10 (freshmen), 8/10 (transfers). *Notification:* continuous until 8/10 (freshmen).

Admissions Contact Ms. Melissa Jones, Director, University of South Alabama, 307 University Boulevard, Mobile, AL 36688-0002. *Phone:* 251-460-6141. *Toll-free phone:* 800-872-5247. *E-mail:* admiss@jaguarl.usouthal.edu.

THE UNIVERSITY OF WEST ALABAMA
Livingston, Alabama

- **State-supported** comprehensive, founded 1835
- **Calendar** semesters
- **Degrees** associate, bachelor's, and master's
- **Small-town** 595-acre campus
- **Endowment** $1.6 million
- **Coed,** 1,625 undergraduate students, 92% full-time, 54% women, 46% men
- **Minimally difficult** entrance level, 69% of applicants were admitted

Undergraduates 1,503 full-time, 122 part-time. Students come from 23 states and territories, 6 other countries, 15% are from out of state, 41% African American, 0.1% Asian American or Pacific Islander, 0.4% Hispanic American, 0.5% Native American, 0.9% international, 12% transferred in, 35% live on campus. *Retention:* 80% of 2001 full-time freshmen returned.

Freshmen *Admission:* 844 applied, 582 admitted, 332 enrolled. *Test scores:* ACT scores over 18: 64%; ACT scores over 24: 17%.

Faculty *Total:* 97, 88% full-time, 60% with terminal degrees. *Student/faculty ratio:* 18:1.

Majors Accounting; athletic training/sports medicine; biology; business administration; chemistry; early childhood education; elementary education; engineering technology; English; history; industrial technology; management information systems/business data processing; marine biology; mathematics; nursing; physical education; psychology; sociology; special education.

Academic Programs *Special study options:* academic remediation for entering students, accelerated degree program, advanced placement credit, double majors, honors programs, internships, off-campus study, part-time degree program, services for LD students, summer session for credit. *ROTC:* Army (c), Air Force (c). *Unusual degree programs:* 3-2 engineering with Auburn University; forestry with Auburn University.

Library Julia Tutwiler Library with 141,755 titles, 5,000 serial subscriptions, 6,900 audiovisual materials, an OPAC, a Web page.

Computers on Campus 250 computers available on campus for general student use. A campuswide network can be accessed from student residence rooms and from off campus. Internet access, at least one staffed computer lab available.

Student Life *Housing:* on-campus residence required through sophomore year. *Options:* coed, men-only, women-only. *Activities and Organizations:* drama/theater group, student-run newspaper, choral group, Campus Outreach, national

The University of West Alabama (continued)
fraternities, national sororities. *Campus security:* 24-hour patrols. *Student Services:* health clinic, personal/psychological counseling.

Athletics Member NCAA. All Division II. *Intercollegiate sports:* baseball M(s), basketball M(s)/W(s), cross-country running M(s)/W(s), football M(s), softball W(s), volleyball W(s). *Intramural sports:* basketball M/W, football M/W, golf M/W, softball M/W, table tennis M/W, tennis M/W, volleyball M/W.

Standardized Tests *Required:* SAT I or ACT (for admission).

Costs (2001–02) *Tuition:* state resident $2784 full-time, $116 per semester hour part-time; nonresident $5568 full-time, $232 per semester hour part-time. Part-time tuition and fees vary according to class time. *Required fees:* $390 full-time. *Room and board:* $2874; room only: $1110. Room and board charges vary according to board plan and housing facility. *Payment plan:* deferred payment. *Waivers:* employees or children of employees.

Financial Aid Of all full-time matriculated undergraduates who enrolled in 2001, 1325 applied for aid, 1038 were judged to have need. In 2001, 219 non-need-based awards were made. *Average financial aid package:* $7753. *Average need-based loan:* $3526. *Average need-based gift aid:* $3308. *Average non-need based aid:* $2272. *Average indebtedness upon graduation:* $15,000.

Applying *Options:* common application, electronic application, early admission, deferred entrance. *Application fee:* $20. *Required:* high school transcript, minimum 2.0 GPA. *Application deadline:* rolling (freshmen), rolling (transfers). *Notification:* continuous (freshmen).

Admissions Contact Mr. Richard Hester, Vice President for Student Affairs, The University of West Alabama, Station 4, Livingston, AL 35470. *Phone:* 205-652-3400 Ext. 3578. *Toll-free phone:* 800-621-7742 (in-state); 800-621-8044 (out-of-state). *Fax:* 205-652-3522. *E-mail:* rhester@uwa.edu.

Virginia College at Birmingham
Birmingham, Alabama

- **Proprietary** 4-year, founded 1989
- **Calendar** quarters
- **Degrees** diplomas, associate, and bachelor's
- **Urban** 1-acre campus
- **Coed,** 1,641 undergraduate students, 100% full-time, 64% women, 36% men
- **Moderately difficult** entrance level, 77% of applicants were admitted

Undergraduates 1,641 full-time. Students come from 7 states and territories, 6 other countries, 0% are from out of state, 53% African American, 0.8% Asian American or Pacific Islander, 0.7% Hispanic American, 0.2% Native American. *Retention:* 73% of 2001 full-time freshmen returned.

Freshmen *Admission:* 550 applied, 425 admitted, 491 enrolled. *Average high school GPA:* 2.5.

Faculty *Total:* 159, 69% full-time. *Student/faculty ratio:* 10:1.

Majors Business administration; computer/information sciences; drafting; electrical/electronic engineering technology; health services administration; information technology; interior design; medical assistant; paralegal/legal assistant; secretarial science.

Library Elma Bell Library plus 2 others with 3,900 titles, 120 serial subscriptions, 40 audiovisual materials, an OPAC.

Computers on Campus 80 computers available on campus for general student use.

Student Life *Housing:* college housing not available.

Costs (2002–03) *Tuition:* $8000 full-time, $185 per credit hour part-time. Full-time tuition and fees vary according to program. Part-time tuition and fees vary according to program. No tuition increase for student's term of enrollment. *Required fees:* $100 full-time. *Payment plan:* installment. *Waivers:* employees or children of employees.

Applying *Required:* high school transcript. *Application deadline:* rolling (freshmen). *Notification:* continuous (freshmen).

Admissions Contact Ms. Bibbie J. McLaughlin, Director of Admissions, Virginia College at Birmingham, 65 Bagby Drive, PO Box 19249, Birmingham, AL 35209. *Phone:* 205-802-1200 Ext. 207. *Fax:* 205-802-7045. *E-mail:* bibbie@vc.edu.

ALASKA

Alaska Bible College
Glennallen, Alaska

- **Independent nondenominational** 4-year, founded 1966
- **Calendar** semesters
- **Degrees** certificates, associate, and bachelor's
- **Rural** 80-acre campus
- **Endowment** $20,600
- **Coed,** 44 undergraduate students, 77% full-time, 34% women, 66% men
- **Minimally difficult** entrance level, 77% of applicants were admitted

Undergraduates 34 full-time, 10 part-time. Students come from 17 states and territories, 68% are from out of state, 3% Asian American or Pacific Islander, 11% Native American, 41% transferred in, 90% live on campus. *Retention:* 50% of 2001 full-time freshmen returned.

Freshmen *Admission:* 13 applied, 10 admitted, 9 enrolled. *Average high school GPA:* 3.19. *Test scores:* SAT verbal scores over 500: 100%; SAT math scores over 500: 50%; ACT scores over 18: 50%; SAT verbal scores over 600: 100%; ACT scores over 24: 25%; ACT scores over 30: 25%.

Faculty *Total:* 12, 25% full-time, 17% with terminal degrees. *Student/faculty ratio:* 6:1.

Majors Biblical studies; interdisciplinary studies; missionary studies; pastoral counseling; religious education; teaching English as a second language; theology.

Academic Programs *Special study options:* academic remediation for entering students, advanced placement credit, double majors, internships, part-time degree program, student-designed majors.

Library Alaska Bible College Library Center with 27,911 titles, 130 serial subscriptions, 252 audiovisual materials.

Computers on Campus 10 computers available on campus for general student use. A campuswide network can be accessed from that provide access to e-mail. Internet access, at least one staffed computer lab available.

Student Life *Housing:* on-campus residence required through sophomore year. *Options:* men-only, women-only. *Activities and Organizations:* student-run radio station. *Campus security:* 24-hour emergency response devices, campus curfew enforced. *Student Services:* personal/psychological counseling.

Athletics *Intramural sports:* basketball M(c)/W(c), volleyball M(c)/W(c).

Standardized Tests *Required:* SAT I or ACT (for admission).

Costs (2002–03) *Comprehensive fee:* $9275 includes full-time tuition ($5175) and room and board ($4100). Part-time tuition: $210 per credit. *Room and board:* Room and board charges vary according to board plan. *Payment plan:* installment.

Financial Aid Of all full-time matriculated undergraduates who enrolled in 2001, 16 applied for aid, 14 were judged to have need, 12 had their need fully met. 10 State and other part-time jobs (averaging $1800). *Financial aid deadline:* 7/5.

Applying *Options:* deferred entrance. *Application fee:* $25. *Required:* essay or personal statement, high school transcript, minimum 2.0 GPA, 2 letters of recommendation, interview, health form. *Application deadlines:* 7/1 (freshmen), 7/1 (transfers). *Notification:* 7/15 (freshmen).

Admissions Contact Ms. Jackie Colwell, Admissions Officer, Alaska Bible College, Box 289, Glennallen, AK 99588-0289. *Phone:* 907-822-3201. *Toll-free phone:* 800-478-7884. *Fax:* 907-822-5027. *E-mail:* info@akbible.edu.

Alaska Pacific University
Anchorage, Alaska

- **Independent** comprehensive, founded 1959
- **Calendar** semesters
- **Degrees** certificates, associate, bachelor's, and master's
- **Suburban** 170-acre campus
- **Endowment** $31.9 million
- **Coed,** 433 undergraduate students, 65% full-time, 72% women, 28% men
- **Moderately difficult** entrance level, 96% of applicants were admitted

Undergraduates 281 full-time, 152 part-time. Students come from 29 states and territories, 5 other countries, 18% are from out of state, 4% African American, 3% Asian American or Pacific Islander, 4% Hispanic American, 17% Native American, 2% international, 19% transferred in, 22% live on campus. *Retention:* 56% of 2001 full-time freshmen returned.

Freshmen *Admission:* 54 applied, 52 admitted, 43 enrolled. *Average high school GPA:* 3.12. *Test scores:* SAT verbal scores over 500: 70%; SAT math scores over 500: 37%; ACT scores over 18: 80%; SAT verbal scores over 600: 15%; SAT math scores over 600: 4%; ACT scores over 24: 30%; ACT scores over 30: 5%.

Faculty *Total:* 75, 41% full-time. *Student/faculty ratio:* 7:1.

Majors Accounting; business administration; elementary education; environmental science; human services; liberal arts and sciences/liberal studies; natural resources management; psychology; recreation/leisure studies.

Academic Programs *Special study options:* academic remediation for entering students, accelerated degree program, adult/continuing education programs, advanced placement credit, distance learning, double majors, independent study, internships, part-time degree program, services for LD students, student-designed majors, study abroad, summer session for credit.

Library Consortium Library with 676,745 titles, 3,842 serial subscriptions, an OPAC, a Web page.
Computers on Campus 35 computers available on campus for general student use. Internet access, at least one staffed computer lab available.
Student Life *Housing:* on-campus residence required for freshman year. *Options:* coed. *Activities and Organizations:* drama/theater group, student-run newspaper, choral group, Environmental Club, Student Government Association, Nordic Ski Club, Student Organization of Native Americans, Drama Club. *Campus security:* 24-hour emergency response devices. *Student Services:* personal/psychological counseling.
Athletics *Intramural sports:* basketball M/W, skiing (cross-country) M/W, soccer M/W.
Standardized Tests *Required:* SAT I or ACT (for admission).
Costs (2001–02) *Comprehensive fee:* $20,127 includes full-time tuition ($14,400), mandatory fees ($80), and room and board ($5647). Full-time tuition and fees vary according to program. Part-time tuition: $600 per semester hour. Part-time tuition and fees vary according to program. No tuition increase for student's term of enrollment. *Required fees:* $40 per term part-time. *Room and board:* Room and board charges vary according to board plan and housing facility. *Payment plan:* deferred payment. *Waivers:* adult students, senior citizens, and employees or children of employees.
Financial Aid Of all full-time matriculated undergraduates who enrolled in 2001, 407 applied for aid. *Average percent of need met:* 80%. *Average financial aid package:* $13,500.
Applying *Options:* electronic application, early decision, deferred entrance. *Application fee:* $25. *Required:* essay or personal statement, high school transcript, minimum 2.0 GPA, 2 letters of recommendation. *Required for some:* interview. *Application deadlines:* 2/1 (freshmen), 2/1 (transfers). *Early decision:* 1/1. *Notification:* 3/15 (freshmen), 1/15 (early decision).
Admissions Contact Mr. Ernie Norton, Director of Admissions, Alaska Pacific University, 4101 University Drive, Anchorage, AK 99508-4672. *Phone:* 907-564-8248. *Toll-free phone:* 800-252-7528. *Fax:* 907-564-8317. *E-mail:* admissions@alaskapacific.edu.

SHELDON JACKSON COLLEGE
Sitka, Alaska

- **Independent** 4-year, founded 1878, affiliated with Presbyterian Church (U.S.A.)
- **Calendar** semesters
- **Degrees** certificates, associate, and bachelor's
- **Small-town** 320-acre campus
- **Endowment** $1.4 million
- **Coed,** 251 undergraduate students, 53% full-time, 55% women, 45% men
- **Noncompetitive** entrance level, 66% of applicants were admitted

Undergraduates 133 full-time, 118 part-time. Students come from 26 states and territories, 66% are from out of state, 16% transferred in, 80% live on campus. *Retention:* 60% of 2001 full-time freshmen returned.
Freshmen *Admission:* 154 applied, 101 admitted, 98 enrolled. *Average high school GPA:* 2.71.
Faculty *Total:* 47, 47% full-time. *Student/faculty ratio:* 14:1.
Majors Alcohol/drug abuse counseling; business administration; education; elementary education; humanities; interdisciplinary studies; liberal arts and sciences/liberal studies; marine biology; oceanography; secondary education; social sciences.
Academic Programs *Special study options:* academic remediation for entering students, advanced placement credit, double majors, independent study, internships, part-time degree program, services for LD students, student-designed majors.
Library Stratton Library with 100,000 titles, 300 serial subscriptions, an OPAC, a Web page.
Computers on Campus 50 computers available on campus for general student use. A campuswide network can be accessed from student residence rooms and from off campus. Internet access, at least one staffed computer lab available.
Student Life *Housing:* on-campus residence required through sophomore year. *Options:* coed. *Activities and Organizations:* drama/theater group, choral group, Boxing Club, Culture Club, Social Justice Club, Bible Study. *Campus security:* 24-hour patrols, controlled dormitory access. *Student Services:* personal/psychological counseling.
Athletics *Intramural sports:* badminton M/W, basketball M/W, bowling M/W, field hockey M/W, football M/W, lacrosse M/W, racquetball M/W, riflery M/W, soccer M/W, softball M/W, swimming M/W, table tennis M/W, volleyball M/W, water polo M/W, weight lifting M/W.
Costs (2001–02) *Comprehensive fee:* $14,940 includes full-time tuition ($7650), mandatory fees ($370), and room and board ($6920). Part-time tuition: $360 per credit. Part-time tuition and fees vary according to degree level. *Required fees:* $65 per term part-time. *Room and board:* College room only: $3520. Room and board charges vary according to board plan and housing facility. *Payment plan:* installment. *Waivers:* children of alumni and employees or children of employees.
Financial Aid Of all full-time matriculated undergraduates who enrolled in 2001, 156 applied for aid, 130 were judged to have need, 130 had their need fully met. 90 Federal Work-Study jobs (averaging $1400). 20 State and other part-time jobs (averaging $1250). In 2001, 2 non-need-based awards were made. *Average percent of need met:* 60%. *Average financial aid package:* $7300. *Average need-based loan:* $2300. *Average need-based gift aid:* $600. *Average non-need based aid:* $2500. *Average indebtedness upon graduation:* $30,000. *Financial aid deadline:* 5/1.
Applying *Options:* common application, electronic application, deferred entrance. *Application fee:* $25. *Required:* high school transcript. *Recommended:* essay or personal statement, minimum 2.0 GPA. *Application deadlines:* 7/15 (freshmen), 7/15 (transfers). *Notification:* continuous (freshmen).
Admissions Contact Ms. Elizabeth Lower, Director of Admissions, Sheldon Jackson College, 801 Lincoln Street, Sitka, AK 99835. *Phone:* 907-747-5208. *Toll-free phone:* 800-478-4556. *Fax:* 907-747-6366. *E-mail:* elower@sj-alaska.edu.

UNIVERSITY OF ALASKA ANCHORAGE
Anchorage, Alaska

- **State-supported** comprehensive, founded 1954, part of University of Alaska System
- **Calendar** semesters
- **Degrees** certificates, associate, bachelor's, and master's
- **Urban** 428-acre campus
- **Endowment** $7.3 million
- **Coed,** 14,404 undergraduate students, 41% full-time, 61% women, 39% men
- **Noncompetitive** entrance level, 75% of applicants were admitted

Undergraduates 5,929 full-time, 8,475 part-time. Students come from 50 states and territories, 41 other countries, 4% African American, 5% Asian American or Pacific Islander, 4% Hispanic American, 10% Native American, 3% international, 7% live on campus. *Retention:* 68% of 2001 full-time freshmen returned.
Freshmen *Admission:* 3,898 applied, 2,918 admitted, 1,249 enrolled. *Average high school GPA:* 2.90.
Faculty *Total:* 1,240, 37% full-time. *Student/faculty ratio:* 13:1.
Majors Accounting; aircraft mechanic/airframe; aircraft pilot (professional); air traffic control; anthropology; architectural engineering technology; art; auto mechanic/technician; aviation management; aviation technology; biological/physical sciences; business administration; business economics; business machine repair; business marketing and marketing management; chemistry; civil engineering; computer/information sciences; computer science; criminal justice/law enforcement administration; culinary arts; dental assistant; dental hygiene; diesel engine mechanic; drafting; early childhood education; economics; education; electrical/electronic engineering technology; elementary education; emergency medical technology; engineering technology; English; finance; fire science; foreign languages/literatures; health science; heating/air conditioning/refrigeration; heavy equipment maintenance; history; home economics; human services; information sciences/systems; interdisciplinary studies; journalism; management information systems/business data processing; mass communications; mathematics; medical assistant; medical laboratory technician; music; music (general performance); music teacher education; natural sciences; nursing; paralegal/legal assistant; petroleum technology; physical education; political science; psychology; science/technology and society; secondary education; social work; sociology; surveying; theater arts/drama; welding technology.
Academic Programs *Special study options:* academic remediation for entering students, adult/continuing education programs, advanced placement credit, cooperative education, internships, off-campus study, part-time degree program, services for LD students, student-designed majors, study abroad, summer session for credit.
Library Consortium Library with 522,495 titles, 3,479 serial subscriptions.
Computers on Campus 500 computers available on campus for general student use. A campuswide network can be accessed from student residence rooms and from off campus. Internet access, at least one staffed computer lab available.
Student Life *Housing Options:* coed. *Activities and Organizations:* drama/theater group, student-run newspaper, radio station, Accounting Club, African-American Students Association, Association of Latin-American Spanish Students, Inter-Varsity Christian Fellowship, Student Nurses Association. *Campus security:*

University of Alaska Anchorage (continued)
24-hour emergency response devices and patrols, student patrols, late-night transport/escort service, controlled dormitory access. *Student Services:* health clinic, personal/psychological counseling, women's center.

Athletics Member NCAA. All Division II. *Intercollegiate sports:* basketball M(s)/W(s), cross-country running M(s), gymnastics W(s), ice hockey M(s), skiing (cross-country) M(s)/W(s), skiing (downhill) M(s)/W(s), swimming M(s), volleyball W(s). *Intramural sports:* basketball M/W, field hockey M/W, ice hockey M/W, racquetball M/W, soccer M/W, volleyball M/W, weight lifting M/W.

Standardized Tests *Required for some:* SAT I or ACT (for placement), ACT ASSET.

Costs (2001–02) *Tuition:* state resident $2398 full-time; nonresident $6354 full-time. Full-time tuition and fees vary according to class time, class time, and course load. Part-time tuition and fees vary according to class time, class time, and course load. *Required fees:* $350 full-time. *Room and board:* $5780; room only: $3380. Room and board charges vary according to board plan and housing facility. *Payment plan:* deferred payment. *Waivers:* minority students, children of alumni, adult students, senior citizens, and employees or children of employees.

Financial Aid Of all full-time matriculated undergraduates who enrolled in 2001, 3382 applied for aid, 1686 were judged to have need, 295 had their need fully met. 129 Federal Work-Study jobs (averaging $2557). In 2001, 575 non-need-based awards were made. *Average percent of need met:* 92%. *Average financial aid package:* $6933. *Average need-based loan:* $4720. *Average need-based gift aid:* $3016. *Average non-need based aid:* $2824.

Applying *Options:* common application, early admission, deferred entrance. *Application fee:* $35. *Required:* minimum 2.0 GPA. *Required for some:* high school transcript. *Application deadline:* rolling (freshmen), rolling (transfers).

Admissions Contact Ms. Cecile Mitchell, Director of Enrollment Services, University of Alaska Anchorage, Administration Building, Room 176, Anchorage, AK 99508-8060. *Phone:* 907-786-1558. *Fax:* 907-786-4888.

UNIVERSITY OF ALASKA FAIRBANKS

Fairbanks, Alaska

- **State-supported** university, founded 1917, part of University of Alaska System
- **Calendar** semesters
- **Degrees** certificates, associate, bachelor's, master's, and doctoral
- **Small-town** 2250-acre campus
- **Coed,** 6,309 undergraduate students, 51% full-time, 59% women, 41% men
- **Moderately difficult** entrance level, 81% of applicants were admitted

UAF is America's premier institution of northern scholarship, discovery, and adventure. Located in Interior Alaska, a land of rivers, forests, mountains, wildlife, and the Northern Lights, the University is known for research in arctic phenomena, including global climate change. The 2,250-acre campus boasts state-of-the-art classrooms, laboratories, recreational facilities, and residence halls.

Undergraduates 3,193 full-time, 3,116 part-time. Students come from 52 states and territories, 28 other countries, 15% are from out of state, 4% African American, 3% Asian American or Pacific Islander, 3% Hispanic American, 16% Native American, 2% international, 7% transferred in, 26% live on campus. *Retention:* 62% of 2001 full-time freshmen returned.

Freshmen *Admission:* 1,626 applied, 1,320 admitted, 889 enrolled. *Average high school GPA:* 3.07. *Test scores:* SAT verbal scores over 500: 60%; SAT math scores over 500: 56%; ACT scores over 18: 75%; SAT verbal scores over 600: 24%; SAT math scores over 600: 21%; ACT scores over 24: 33%; SAT verbal scores over 700: 5%; SAT math scores over 700: 3%; ACT scores over 30: 7%.

Faculty *Total:* 592, 60% full-time. *Student/faculty ratio:* 9:1.

Majors Accounting; accounting technician; aircraft mechanic/airframe; aircraft pilot (professional); anthropology; area studies related; art; aviation technology; biological/physical sciences; biology; business administration; chemistry; child care provider; civil engineering; communications; community services; computer installation/repair; computer science; conservation and renewable natural resources related; criminal justice/corrections related; culinary arts; drafting; early childhood education; earth sciences; economics; education; electrical engineering; elementary education; English; fire science; fishing sciences; foreign languages/literatures; foreign languages/literatures related; geography; geological engineering; geology; history; industrial technology; Japanese; journalism; liberal arts and sciences/liberal studies; linguistics; mathematical statistics; mathematics; mechanical engineering; medical assistant; mental health services related; mining/petroleum technologies related; multi/interdisciplinary studies related; music; Native American studies; natural resources management; paralegal/legal assistant; petroleum engineering; philosophy; physics; physics related; political science; psychology; public health; Russian/Slavic studies; secretarial science; social work; sociology; theater arts/drama; vehicle/mobile equipment mechanics and repair related; wildlife management.

Academic Programs *Special study options:* academic remediation for entering students, accelerated degree program, adult/continuing education programs, advanced placement credit, cooperative education, distance learning, double majors, honors programs, independent study, internships, off-campus study, part-time degree program, services for LD students, student-designed majors, study abroad, summer session for credit. *ROTC:* Army (b).

Library Rasmuson Library plus 8 others with 586,421 titles, 6,825 serial subscriptions, 662,500 audiovisual materials, an OPAC, a Web page.

Computers on Campus 500 computers available on campus for general student use. A campuswide network can be accessed from student residence rooms and from off campus. Internet access, at least one staffed computer lab available.

Student Life *Housing Options:* coed, disabled students. *Activities and Organizations:* drama/theater group, student-run newspaper, radio and television station, choral group, United Campus Ministry, Northern Chinese Student Association, Golden Key National Honor Society, UAF Good Time Swing Dance Club, University Women's Association, national fraternities, national sororities. *Campus security:* 24-hour emergency response devices and patrols, student patrols, late-night transport/escort service, controlled dormitory access, ID check at door of residence halls, crime prevention and safety workshops. *Student Services:* health clinic, personal/psychological counseling, women's center, legal services.

Athletics Member NCAA. All Division II except ice hockey (Division I). *Intercollegiate sports:* basketball M(s)/W(s), cross-country running M(s)/W(s), ice hockey M(s), riflery M(s)/W(s), skiing (cross-country) M(s)/W(s), volleyball W(s). *Intramural sports:* badminton M/W, basketball M/W, bowling M/W, cross-country running M/W, fencing M/W, gymnastics M/W, ice hockey M/W, racquetball M/W, riflery M/W, skiing (cross-country) M/W, skiing (downhill) M/W, soccer M/W, softball M/W, swimming M/W, table tennis M/W, tennis M/W, volleyball M/W, water polo M/W, wrestling M.

Standardized Tests *Required:* SAT I or ACT (for admission).

Costs (2001–02) *Tuition:* state resident $2535 full-time, $85 per credit part-time; nonresident $7605 full-time, $254 per credit part-time. Full-time tuition and fees vary according to class time, course load, program, reciprocity agreements, and student level. Part-time tuition and fees vary according to class time, course load, program, and reciprocity agreements. *Required fees:* $960 full-time, $5 per credit, $30 per term part-time. *Room and board:* $4770; room only: $2510. Room and board charges vary according to board plan, housing facility, and location. *Payment plan:* deferred payment. *Waivers:* children of alumni, senior citizens, and employees or children of employees.

Applying *Options:* electronic application, early admission, deferred entrance. *Application fee:* $35. *Required:* high school transcript, minimum 2.0 GPA. *Application deadlines:* 8/1 (freshmen), 8/1 (transfers).

Admissions Contact Ms. Nancy Dix, Interim Director of Admissions and Enrollment Management, University of Alaska Fairbanks, PO Box 757480, Fairbanks, AK 99775-7480. *Phone:* 907-474-7500. *Toll-free phone:* 800-478-1823. *Fax:* 907-474-5379. *E-mail:* fyapply@uaf.edu.

UNIVERSITY OF ALASKA SOUTHEAST

Juneau, Alaska

- **State-supported** comprehensive, founded 1972, part of University of Alaska System
- **Calendar** semesters
- **Degrees** certificates, associate, bachelor's, and master's
- **Small-town** 198-acre campus
- **Coed,** 2,799 undergraduate students
- **Noncompetitive** entrance level

Undergraduates Students come from 39 states and territories, 6 other countries. *Retention:* 62% of 2001 full-time freshmen returned.

Majors Accounting; auto mechanic/technician; biology; business administration; construction technology; early childhood education; education; elementary education; environmental science; hospitality management; liberal arts and sciences/liberal studies; marine biology; marine technology; paralegal/legal assistant; political science; secretarial science; travel/tourism management.

Academic Programs *Special study options:* academic remediation for entering students, adult/continuing education programs, advanced placement credit, cooperative education, internships, off-campus study, part-time degree program, services for LD students, student-designed majors, summer session for credit.

Library Egan Memorial Library with 102,171 titles, 1,500 serial subscriptions, an OPAC, a Web page.

Computers on Campus 75 computers available on campus for general student use. A campuswide network can be accessed from student residence rooms and from off campus. Internet access, at least one staffed computer lab available.
Student Life *Housing Options:* coed. *Activities and Organizations:* student-run newspaper, choral group, Native Student Club. *Campus security:* 24-hour emergency response devices and patrols, late-night transport/escort service, controlled dormitory access. *Student Services:* health clinic, personal/psychological counseling.
Athletics *Intercollegiate sports:* riflery M(c)/W(c). *Intramural sports:* basketball M/W, racquetball M/W, riflery M/W, skiing (cross-country) M/W, skiing (downhill) M/W, softball M/W, tennis M/W, volleyball M/W.
Standardized Tests *Recommended:* SAT I or ACT (for placement).
Costs (2001–02) *Tuition:* state resident $1896 full-time; nonresident $5952 full-time. Full-time tuition and fees vary according to class time and course load. Part-time tuition and fees vary according to class time and course load. *Required fees:* $166 full-time. *Payment plans:* installment, deferred payment. *Waivers:* senior citizens and employees or children of employees.
Financial Aid Of all full-time matriculated undergraduates who enrolled in 2001, 21 Federal Work-Study jobs (averaging $2594).
Applying *Options:* common application, early admission, deferred entrance. *Application fee:* $35. *Required:* high school transcript, minimum 2.0 GPA. *Required for some:* essay or personal statement. *Application deadline:* rolling (freshmen), rolling (transfers).
Admissions Contact Mr. Greg Wagner, Director of Admissions, University of Alaska Southeast, 11120 Glacier Highway, Juneau, AK 99801. *Phone:* 907-465-6239. *Fax:* 907-465-6365. *E-mail:* jyuas@acadi.alaska.edu.

ARIZONA

AIBT International Institute of the Americas
Phoenix, Arizona

- **Independent** primarily 2-year
- **Calendar** semesters
- **Degrees** certificates, diplomas, associate, and bachelor's
- **Coed,** 1,036 undergraduate students, 100% full-time, 72% women, 28% men
- **Noncompetitive** entrance level, 100% of applicants were admitted

Undergraduates 1,036 full-time. Students come from 7 states and territories, 2% are from out of state, 11% African American, 5% Asian American or Pacific Islander, 36% Hispanic American, 12% Native American, 2% transferred in.
Freshmen *Admission:* 1,617 applied, 1,617 admitted, 350 enrolled.
Faculty *Total:* 95, 58% full-time, 25% with terminal degrees. *Student/faculty ratio:* 11:1.
Majors Accounting related; business administration; business information/data processing related; computer/information technology services administration and management related; criminal justice/law enforcement administration; health professions and related sciences; information technology; medical assistant; medical transcription.
Academic Programs *Special study options:* accelerated degree program, adult/continuing education programs, cooperative education, distance learning, internships, summer session for credit.
Library Learning Resrouce Center with 1,974 titles, 1,750 serial subscriptions, 120 audiovisual materials, an OPAC, a Web page.
Computers on Campus 421 computers available on campus for general student use. Internet access, online (class) registration, at least one staffed computer lab available.
Student Life *Housing:* college housing not available. *Campus security:* 24-hour emergency response devices.
Costs (2002–03) *Tuition:* $7800 full-time, $260 per credit part-time. Full-time tuition and fees vary according to program. No tuition increase for student's term of enrollment. *Required fees:* $350 full-time. *Payment plan:* tuition prepayment. *Waivers:* employees or children of employees.
Applying *Options:* electronic application, early admission, deferred entrance. *Required:* interview, High School Diploma or GED. *Application deadline:* rolling (freshmen). *Notification:* continuous (freshmen).
Admissions Contact Mark Wright, Admission Representative, AIBT International Institute of the Americas, 6049 North 43 Avenue, Phoenix, AZ 85019. *Phone:* 888-884-2428. *Toll-free phone:* 888-884-2428 Ext. 218 (in-state); 800-793-2428 (out-of-state). *Fax:* 602-973-2572. *E-mail:* info@aibt.edu.

American Indian College of the Assemblies of God, Inc.
Phoenix, Arizona

- **Independent** 4-year, founded 1957, affiliated with Assemblies of God
- **Calendar** semesters
- **Degrees** associate and bachelor's
- **Urban** 10-acre campus
- **Coed,** 72 undergraduate students, 82% full-time, 58% women, 42% men
- **Minimally difficult** entrance level, 46% of applicants were admitted

Undergraduates Students come from 8 states and territories, 32% are from out of state, 3% African American, 1% Asian American or Pacific Islander, 6% Hispanic American, 74% Native American. *Retention:* 88% of 2001 full-time freshmen returned.
Freshmen *Admission:* 35 applied, 16 admitted. *Average high school GPA:* 3.30.
Faculty *Total:* 25, 32% full-time, 4% with terminal degrees. *Student/faculty ratio:* 6:1.
Majors Business administration; elementary education; pastoral counseling.
Academic Programs *Special study options:* academic remediation for entering students, distance learning, double majors, independent study, internships.
Library Cummings Memorial Library with 13,000 titles, 120 serial subscriptions.
Computers on Campus 20 computers available on campus for general student use. Internet access, at least one staffed computer lab available.
Student Life *Housing:* on-campus residence required through senior year. *Activities and Organizations:* drama/theater group, Missions Fellowship, Associated Student Body, yearbook. *Campus security:* student patrols. *Student Services:* personal/psychological counseling.
Athletics *Intercollegiate sports:* basketball M. *Intramural sports:* basketball M/W, bowling M/W, table tennis M/W, volleyball M/W.
Standardized Tests *Required:* SAT I or ACT (for admission).
Costs (2002–03) *Comprehensive fee:* $7810 includes full-time tuition ($3930), mandatory fees ($400), and room and board ($3480). Full-time tuition and fees vary according to course load. Part-time tuition: $131 per credit hour. Part-time tuition and fees vary according to course load.
Applying *Required:* high school transcript, 1 letter of recommendation. *Recommended:* essay or personal statement. *Application deadlines:* 8/15 (freshmen), 8/15 (transfers).
Admissions Contact Ms. Sandy Ticeahkie, Admissions Coordinator, American Indian College of the Assemblies of God, Inc., 10020 North 15th Avenue, Phoenix, AZ 85021. *Phone:* 602-944-3335 Ext. 234. *Toll-free phone:* 800-933-3828. *Fax:* 602-943-8299. *E-mail:* aicadm@juno.com.

Arizona State University
Tempe, Arizona

- **State-supported** university, founded 1885, part of Arizona State University
- **Calendar** semesters
- **Degrees** bachelor's, master's, doctoral, first professional, post-master's, and postbachelor's certificates
- **Suburban** 814-acre campus with easy access to Phoenix
- **Endowment** $207.1 million
- **Coed,** 35,191 undergraduate students, 79% full-time, 52% women, 48% men
- **Moderately difficult** entrance level, 87% of applicants were admitted

Undergraduates 27,967 full-time, 7,224 part-time. Students come from 52 states and territories, 104 other countries, 23% are from out of state, 3% African American, 5% Asian American or Pacific Islander, 11% Hispanic American, 2% Native American, 4% international, 10% transferred in, 18% live on campus. *Retention:* 76% of 2001 full-time freshmen returned.
Freshmen *Admission:* 18,129 applied, 15,702 admitted, 6,203 enrolled. *Average high school GPA:* 3.34. *Test scores:* SAT verbal scores over 500: 70%; SAT math scores over 500: 76%; ACT scores over 18: 92%; SAT verbal scores over 600: 26%; SAT math scores over 600: 33%; ACT scores over 24: 46%; SAT verbal scores over 700: 5%; SAT math scores over 700: 6%; ACT scores over 30: 7%.
Faculty *Total:* 1,814, 94% full-time, 83% with terminal degrees. *Student/faculty ratio:* 20:1.
Majors Accounting; aerospace engineering; African-American studies; anthropology; architecture; art; art history; biochemistry; bioengineering; biological sciences/life sciences related; biological specializations related; biology; botany; business administration; business marketing and marketing management; ceramic arts; chemical engineering; chemistry; Chinese; city/community/regional planning; civil engineering; communications; computer engineering; computer sci-

Arizona State University (continued)

ence; construction technology; criminal justice studies; dance; drawing; early childhood education; economics; electrical engineering; elementary education; English; exercise sciences; family resource management studies; finance; fine/studio arts; French; geography; geology; German; graphic design/commercial art/illustration; hearing sciences; Hispanic-American studies; history; humanities; industrial design; industrial/manufacturing engineering; interdisciplinary studies; interior architecture; Italian; Japanese; journalism; landscape architecture; management information systems/business data processing; materials engineering; mathematics; mechanical engineering; medical technology; metal/jewelry arts; microbiology/bacteriology; molecular biology; music; music (general performance); music teacher education; music theory and composition; music therapy; Native American studies; nursing; philosophy; photography; physics; political science; pre-law; printmaking; psychology; purchasing/contracts management; radio/television broadcasting; real estate; recreation/leisure studies; religious studies; Russian; sculpture; secondary education; social work; sociology; Spanish; special education; theater arts/drama; women's studies.

Academic Programs *Special study options:* academic remediation for entering students, accelerated degree program, adult/continuing education programs, advanced placement credit, cooperative education, distance learning, double majors, honors programs, independent study, internships, off-campus study, part-time degree program, services for LD students, study abroad, summer session for credit. *ROTC:* Army (b), Air Force (b).

Library Hayden Library plus 4 others with 2.4 million titles, 28,159 serial subscriptions, 1.3 million audiovisual materials, an OPAC, a Web page.

Computers on Campus A campuswide network can be accessed from student residence rooms and from off campus. Internet access, at least one staffed computer lab available.

Student Life *Housing Options:* coed, men-only, women-only, disabled students. *Activities and Organizations:* drama/theater group, student-run newspaper, radio and television station, choral group, marching band, Ski Club, Outing Club, Students Against Discrimination (SAD), national fraternities, national sororities. *Campus security:* 24-hour emergency response devices and patrols, late-night transport/escort service. *Student Services:* health clinic, personal/psychological counseling, women's center, legal services.

Athletics Member NCAA. All Division I except football (Division I-A). *Intercollegiate sports:* baseball M(s), basketball M(s)/W(s), cross-country running M(s)/W(s), golf M(s)/W(s), gymnastics W(s), soccer W(s), softball W(s), swimming M(s)/W(s), tennis M(s)/W(s), track and field M(s)/W(s), volleyball W(s), wrestling M(s). *Intramural sports:* badminton M(c)/W(c), basketball M/W, bowling M/W, cross-country running M/W, equestrian sports M(c)/W(c), fencing M(c)/W(c), field hockey M(c), football M, golf M/W, gymnastics M(c)/W(c), ice hockey M(c)/W(c), lacrosse M(c)/W(c), racquetball M/W, rugby M(c)/W(c), soccer M/W, softball M/W, swimming M/W, table tennis M/W, tennis M/W, track and field M/W, volleyball M/W, water polo W(c), weight lifting M/W, wrestling M.

Standardized Tests *Required:* SAT I or ACT (for admission).

Costs (2001–02) *Tuition:* state resident $2412 full-time, $126 per credit part-time; nonresident $10,278 full-time, $428 per credit part-time. *Required fees:* $76 full-time, $19 per term part-time. *Room and board:* $5416; room only: $3138. Room and board charges vary according to board plan and housing facility. *Waivers:* employees or children of employees.

Financial Aid Of all full-time matriculated undergraduates who enrolled in 2001, 17001 applied for aid, 10173 were judged to have need, 1932 had their need fully met. In 2001, 6495 non-need-based awards were made. *Average percent of need met:* 69%. *Average financial aid package:* $6958. *Average need-based loan:* $3939. *Average need-based gift aid:* $3864. *Average indebtedness upon graduation:* $17,662.

Applying *Options:* early action. *Application fee:* $40 (non-residents). *Required:* high school transcript, minimum 3.0 GPA. *Application deadline:* rolling (freshmen), rolling (transfers). *Notification:* continuous (freshmen), 12/1 (early action).

Admissions Contact Mr. Timothy J. Desch, Director of Undergraduate Admissions, Arizona State University, Box 870112, Tempe, AZ 85287-0112. *Phone:* 480-965-7788. *Fax:* 480-965-3610. *E-mail:* ugradinq@asu.edu.

ARIZONA STATE UNIVERSITY EAST
Mesa, Arizona

- **State-supported** comprehensive, founded 1995, part of Arizona State University
- **Calendar** semesters
- **Degrees** bachelor's and master's
- **Suburban** 600-acre campus with easy access to Phoenix
- **Endowment** $4.3 million
- **Coed,** 1,862 undergraduate students, 34% full-time, 50% women, 50% men
- **Moderately difficult** entrance level, 38% of applicants were admitted

Undergraduates 642 full-time, 1,220 part-time. Students come from 38 states and territories, 11% are from out of state, 2% African American, 5% Asian American or Pacific Islander, 11% Hispanic American, 2% Native American, 2% international, 14% transferred in, 7% live on campus. *Retention:* 0% of 2001 full-time freshmen returned.

Freshmen *Admission:* 472 applied, 181 admitted, 128 enrolled. *Average high school GPA:* 3.30. *Test scores:* SAT math scores over 500: 73%; ACT scores over 18: 88%; SAT math scores over 600: 21%; ACT scores over 24: 45%; SAT math scores over 700: 1%; ACT scores over 30: 2%.

Faculty *Total:* 84, 89% full-time, 82% with terminal degrees. *Student/faculty ratio:* 16:1.

Majors Aerospace engineering technology; agricultural business; business; communications related; computer engineering technology; dietetics; electrical/electronic engineering technology; elementary education; environmental technology; food sciences; health/physical education/fitness related; industrial technology; interdisciplinary studies; international agriculture; mechanical engineering technology; natural resources management; nutrition studies; pre-veterinary studies; psychology; science technologies related.

Academic Programs *Special study options:* accelerated degree program, advanced placement credit, distance learning, double majors, honors programs, independent study, internships, part-time degree program, services for LD students, student-designed majors, study abroad, summer session for credit. *ROTC:* Army (c), Air Force (c).

Library ASU East Library with 4.3 million titles, 144 serial subscriptions, 57 audiovisual materials, an OPAC, a Web page.

Computers on Campus 216 computers available on campus for general student use. A campuswide network can be accessed from off campus that provide access to specialized software applications. Internet access, online (class) registration, at least one staffed computer lab available.

Student Life *Housing Options:* coed, disabled students. *Activities and Organizations:* Professional Golf Management Club, Aero Management Tech—Student Advisory Committee, Graphic Information Technology Club, National Agri-Marketing Association, One Nation Club, national fraternities, national sororities. *Campus security:* 24-hour emergency response devices and patrols, late-night transport/escort service. *Student Services:* health clinic, personal/psychological counseling.

Standardized Tests *Recommended:* SAT I or ACT (for admission).

Costs (2001–02) *One-time required fee:* $26. *Tuition:* state resident $2412 full-time, $126 per semester hour part-time; nonresident $10,278 full-time, $428 per semester hour part-time. Full-time tuition and fees vary according to location. Part-time tuition and fees vary according to course load and location. *Required fees:* $13 per term part-time. *Room and board:* $4740; room only: $2440. Room and board charges vary according to board plan and housing facility. *Waivers:* employees or children of employees.

Financial Aid Of all full-time matriculated undergraduates who enrolled in 2001, 250 applied for aid, 168 were judged to have need, 25 had their need fully met. 7 Federal Work-Study jobs (averaging $1940). 103 State and other part-time jobs (averaging $3485). In 2001, 46 non-need-based awards were made. *Average percent of need met:* 68%. *Average financial aid package:* $7555. *Average need-based loan:* $4693. *Average need-based gift aid:* $3884. *Average non-need based aid:* $3772.

Applying *Options:* common application, electronic application, early action. *Application fee:* $40. *Required:* high school transcript. *Recommended:* minimum 3.0 GPA. *Application deadline:* rolling (freshmen), rolling (transfers). *Notification:* 12/1 (early action).

Admissions Contact Ms. Carmen Newland, Program Coordinator (Enrollment), Arizona State University East, 7001 East Williams Field Road #20, Mesa, AZ 85212. *Phone:* 480-727-1165. *Toll-free phone:* 480-965-7788. *Fax:* 480-727-1008. *E-mail:* carmen.newland@asu.edu.

ARIZONA STATE UNIVERSITY WEST
Phoenix, Arizona

- **State-supported** upper-level, founded 1984, part of Arizona State University
- **Calendar** semesters
- **Degrees** bachelor's, master's, and postbachelor's certificates
- **Urban** 300-acre campus
- **Coed,** 4,226 undergraduate students, 55% full-time, 71% women, 29% men
- **Moderately difficult** entrance level, 98% of applicants were admitted

Undergraduates 2,329 full-time, 1,897 part-time. Students come from 17 states and territories, 20 other countries, 2% are from out of state, 4% African

American, 4% Asian American or Pacific Islander, 16% Hispanic American, 2% Native American, 2% international, 24% transferred in.

Freshmen *Admission:* 327 applied, 322 admitted.

Faculty *Total:* 311, 60% full-time, 51% with terminal degrees. *Student/faculty ratio:* 17:1.

Majors Accounting; American studies; biology; business administration; communications; criminal justice/law enforcement administration; elementary education; English; history; interdisciplinary studies; international business; political science; psychology; recreation/leisure studies; secondary education; social sciences; social work; sociology; Spanish; special education; visual/performing arts; women's studies.

Academic Programs *Special study options:* adult/continuing education programs, distance learning, double majors, honors programs, independent study, internships, part-time degree program, services for LD students, student-designed majors, summer session for credit.

Library ASU West Library with 314,760 titles, 3,429 serial subscriptions, 25,534 audiovisual materials, an OPAC, a Web page.

Computers on Campus 391 computers available on campus for general student use. A campuswide network can be accessed from off campus. Internet access, at least one staffed computer lab available.

Student Life *Housing:* college housing not available. *Activities and Organizations:* student-run newspaper, Justice Studies Club, American Marketing Association West, Beta Alpha Psi Accounting Honor Society, Communication Club of ASU West, Outdoor Recreation Club. *Campus security:* 24-hour emergency response devices and patrols, student patrols, late-night transport/escort service. *Student Services:* health clinic, personal/psychological counseling, women's center.

Standardized Tests *Required:* SAT I or ACT (for admission).

Costs (2001–02) *Tuition:* state resident $2412 full-time, $126 per credit hour part-time; nonresident $10,278 full-time, $428 per credit hour part-time. Part-time tuition and fees vary according to course load. *Required fees:* $76 full-time, $19 per term part-time. *Waivers:* employees or children of employees.

Financial Aid Of all full-time matriculated undergraduates who enrolled in 2001, 1142 applied for aid, 946 were judged to have need, 946 had their need fully met. 88 Federal Work-Study jobs (averaging $2510). 217 State and other part-time jobs (averaging $2592). In 2001, 196 non-need-based awards were made. *Average percent of need met:* 100%. *Average financial aid package:* $7237. *Average need-based loan:* $4352. *Average need-based gift aid:* $3775.

Applying *Options:* common application, electronic application, deferred entrance. *Application fee:* $40. *Application deadline:* rolling (transfers).

Admissions Contact Ms. B.J. Hart, Manager, Admission Services, Arizona State University West, 4701 West Thunderbird Road, PO Box 37100, Phoenix, AZ 85069-7100. *Phone:* 602-543-8093. *Fax:* 602-543-8312.

THE ART INSTITUTE OF PHOENIX

Phoenix, Arizona

- **Proprietary** 4-year, founded 1995, part of The Art Institutes
- **Calendar** quarters
- **Degrees** diplomas, associate, and bachelor's
- **Suburban** campus
- **Coed, primarily men,** 1,122 undergraduate students, 90% full-time, 36% women, 64% men
- **Minimally difficult** entrance level

The Art Institute of Phoenix offers programs in creative and applied arts year-round, allowing students to continue to work uninterrupted toward their degrees. The faculty, many of whom are working professionals, strives to strengthen students' skills, cultivate their talents, stimulate minds, and nurture creative spirits through well-designed curricula.

Undergraduates 1,010 full-time, 112 part-time. Students come from 36 states and territories, 34% are from out of state, 2% African American, 1% Asian American or Pacific Islander, 9% Hispanic American, 2% Native American, 0.4% international, 26% transferred in, 20% live on campus.

Freshmen *Admission:* 412 admitted, 412 enrolled. *Average high school GPA:* 2.75.

Faculty *Total:* 71, 46% full-time. *Student/faculty ratio:* 20:1.

Majors Culinary arts; design/visual communications; film/video production; graphic design/commercial art/illustration.

Academic Programs *Special study options:* academic remediation for entering students, advanced placement credit, cooperative education, honors programs, internships, services for LD students.

Library Resource Center with 1,900 titles, 110 serial subscriptions.

Computers on Campus 120 computers available on campus for general student use. Internet access, at least one staffed computer lab available.

Student Life *Housing Options:* men-only, women-only. *Activities and Organizations:* student-run newspaper, Computer Arts and Animation Club, Student Activities Council, Gay and Straight Student Alliance, A.I.G.A. (AmericalnInstitute of Graphic Arts), International Student Club. *Campus security:* 24-hour emergency response devices, controlled dormitory access, security guard during open hours. *Student Services:* personal/psychological counseling.

Standardized Tests *Recommended:* SAT I or ACT (for placement).

Costs (2001–02) *One-time required fee:* $150. *Tuition:* $14,304 full-time, $298 per credit part-time. Full-time tuition and fees vary according to course load, degree level, and program. Part-time tuition and fees vary according to degree level and program. No tuition increase for student's term of enrollment. *Room only:* $5324. Room and board charges vary according to housing facility. *Payment plans:* installment, deferred payment. *Waivers:* employees or children of employees.

Applying *Options:* common application. *Application fee:* $50. *Required:* essay or personal statement, high school transcript, interview. *Recommended:* minimum 2.0 GPA. *Application deadline:* rolling (freshmen), rolling (transfers).

Admissions Contact Director of Admissions, The Art Institute of Phoenix, 2233 West Dunlap Avenue, Phoenix, AZ 85021-2859. *Phone:* 602-678-4300 Ext. 102. *Toll-free phone:* 800-474-2479. *Fax:* 602-216-0439. *E-mail:* udyavar@aii.edu.

CHAPARRAL COLLEGE

Tucson, Arizona

- **Proprietary** primarily 2-year, founded 1972
- **Calendar** 5 five-week modules
- **Degrees** certificates, diplomas, associate, and bachelor's (bachelor's degree in business administration only)
- **Suburban** campus with easy access to Phoenix
- **Coed,** 343 undergraduate students, 100% full-time, 59% women, 41% men
- **Noncompetitive** entrance level, 54% of applicants were admitted

Undergraduates 343 full-time. Students come from 1 other state, 3 other countries, 0% are from out of state, 5% African American, 1% Asian American or Pacific Islander, 38% Hispanic American, 14% Native American.

Freshmen *Admission:* 145 applied, 79 admitted, 125 enrolled.

Faculty *Total:* 29, 38% full-time, 21% with terminal degrees. *Student/faculty ratio:* 25:1.

Majors Accounting; business administration; computer installation/repair; computer systems networking/telecommunications; criminal justice studies; legal administrative assistant; secretarial science.

Academic Programs *Special study options:* academic remediation for entering students, internships, summer session for credit.

Library 6,000 titles, 65 serial subscriptions, 500 audiovisual materials, a Web page.

Computers on Campus 150 computers available on campus for general student use. Internet access, at least one staffed computer lab available.

Student Life *Housing:* college housing not available. *Activities and Organizations:* student-run newspaper. *Campus security:* 24-hour emergency response devices. *Student Services:* personal/psychological counseling.

Costs (2002–03) *Tuition:* $7590 full-time.

Applying *Options:* common application. *Application fee:* $25. *Required:* high school transcript, interview. *Required for some:* letters of recommendation. *Application deadline:* rolling (freshmen), rolling (transfers).

Admissions Contact Becki Rossini, Lead Representative, Chaparral College, 4585 E. Speedway No. 204, Tucson, AZ 85712. *Phone:* 520-327-6866. *Fax:* 520-325-0108.

COLLINS COLLEGE: A SCHOOL OF DESIGN AND TECHNOLOGY

Tempe, Arizona

- **Proprietary** 4-year, founded 1978, part of Career Education Corporation
- **Calendar** trimesters
- **Degrees** certificates, associate, and bachelor's
- **Urban** 3-acre campus with easy access to Phoenix
- **Coed,** 1,804 undergraduate students, 100% full-time, 32% women, 68% men
- 65% of applicants were admitted

Collins College: A School of Design and Technology (continued)

Undergraduates Students come from 49 states and territories, 8% African American, 4% Asian American or Pacific Islander, 19% Hispanic American, 5% Native American.

Freshmen *Admission:* 2,553 applied, 1,651 admitted.

Faculty *Total:* 70, 86% full-time, 11% with terminal degrees.

Majors Computer maintenance technology; design/visual communications; film/video production; graphic design/commercial art/illustration.

Library Al Collins Graphic Design School Library with 1,000 titles, a Web page.

Computers on Campus 402 computers available on campus for general student use. Internet access available.

Student Life *Housing Options:* coed, cooperative, disabled students. *Student Services:* personal/psychological counseling.

Standardized Tests *Recommended:* SAT I or ACT (for admission).

Costs (2001–02) *Tuition:* $10,082 full-time.

Applying *Options:* common application, early admission, deferred entrance. *Required:* essay or personal statement, high school transcript, interview. *Application deadline:* rolling (freshmen), rolling (transfers). *Notification:* continuous (freshmen).

Admissions Contact Ms. Patti Drace, Director of Admissions and Marketing, Collins College: A School of Design and Technology, 1140 South Priest, Tempe, AZ 85281. *Phone:* 480-966-3000 Ext. 147. *Toll-free phone:* 800-876-7070. *Fax:* 480-966-2599. *E-mail:* jen@alcollins.com.

DeVry University
Phoenix, Arizona

- **Proprietary** 4-year, founded 1967, part of DeVry, Inc
- **Calendar** semesters
- **Degrees** associate and bachelor's
- **Urban** 18-acre campus
- **Coed,** 3,050 undergraduate students, 77% full-time, 24% women, 76% men
- **Minimally difficult** entrance level, 90% of applicants were admitted

Undergraduates 2,347 full-time, 703 part-time. Students come from 38 states and territories, 4 other countries, 32% are from out of state, 6% African American, 6% Asian American or Pacific Islander, 15% Hispanic American, 5% Native American, 0.9% international, 8% transferred in. *Retention:* 41% of 2001 full-time freshmen returned.

Freshmen *Admission:* 1,196 applied, 1,078 admitted, 636 enrolled.

Faculty *Total:* 112, 33% full-time. *Student/faculty ratio:* 27:1.

Majors Business administration/management related; business computer programming; business systems networking/ telecommunications; computer engineering technology; electrical/electronic engineering technology; information sciences/systems; operations management.

Academic Programs *Special study options:* academic remediation for entering students, accelerated degree program, adult/continuing education programs, advanced placement credit, cooperative education, part-time degree program, services for LD students, summer session for credit. *ROTC:* Air Force (b).

Library Learning Resource Center with 20,100 titles, 125 serial subscriptions, 1,563 audiovisual materials, an OPAC.

Computers on Campus 371 computers available on campus for general student use. A campuswide network can be accessed from off campus. At least one staffed computer lab available.

Student Life *Housing:* college housing not available. *Activities and Organizations:* student-run newspaper, radio station, Telecommunications Club, Board and Ski Club, Travel Club, SIFE, Institute of Electronic and Electrical Engineers. *Campus security:* 24-hour emergency response devices, student patrols, late-night transport/escort service, trained security personnel on duty, lighted pathways/ sidewalks.

Athletics *Intramural sports:* softball M/W.

Standardized Tests *Recommended:* SAT I or ACT (for admission).

Costs (2001–02) *Tuition:* $8740 full-time, $310 per credit hour part-time. Full-time tuition and fees vary according to course load. Part-time tuition and fees vary according to course load. *Required fees:* $65 full-time. *Payment plans:* installment, deferred payment. *Waivers:* employees or children of employees.

Financial Aid Of all full-time matriculated undergraduates who enrolled in 2001, 2575 applied for aid, 2412 were judged to have need, 149 had their need fully met. In 2001, 167 non-need-based awards were made. *Average percent of need met:* 50%. *Average financial aid package:* $8537. *Average need-based loan:* $6272. *Average need-based gift aid:* $3873. *Average indebtedness upon graduation:* $13,147.

Applying *Options:* electronic application, deferred entrance. *Application fee:* $50. *Required:* high school transcript, interview. *Application deadline:* rolling (freshmen), rolling (transfers). *Notification:* continuous (freshmen).

Admissions Contact DeVry University, 2149 West Dunlap, Phoenix, AZ 85021-2995. *Phone:* 602-870-9201 Ext. 451. *Toll-free phone:* 800-528-0250. *Fax:* 602-331-1494. *E-mail:* webadmin@devry-phx.edu.

Education America, Tempe Campus
Tempe, Arizona

Admissions Contact 875 West Elliot Road, Suite 216, Tempe, AZ 85284. *Toll-free phone:* 800-395-4322.

Embry-Riddle Aeronautical University
Prescott, Arizona

- **Independent** comprehensive, founded 1978
- **Calendar** semesters
- **Degrees** bachelor's and master's
- **Small-town** 547-acre campus
- **Endowment** $34.8 million
- **Coed, primarily men,** 1,724 undergraduate students, 91% full-time, 16% women, 84% men
- **Moderately difficult** entrance level, 79% of applicants were admitted

Undergraduates 1,568 full-time, 156 part-time. Students come from 53 states and territories, 33 other countries, 78% are from out of state, 1% African American, 6% Asian American or Pacific Islander, 5% Hispanic American, 1% Native American, 9% international, 6% transferred in, 49% live on campus. *Retention:* 77% of 2001 full-time freshmen returned.

Freshmen *Admission:* 1,330 applied, 1,045 admitted, 375 enrolled. *Average high school GPA:* 3.38. *Test scores:* SAT verbal scores over 500: 74%; SAT math scores over 500: 81%; ACT scores over 18: 96%; SAT verbal scores over 600: 25%; SAT math scores over 600: 35%; ACT scores over 24: 55%; SAT verbal scores over 700: 2%; SAT math scores over 700: 5%; ACT scores over 30: 8%.

Faculty *Total:* 113, 67% full-time, 48% with terminal degrees. *Student/faculty ratio:* 18:1.

Majors Aerospace engineering; aircraft pilot (professional); aviation/airway science; aviation management; business administration; computer engineering; computer/information sciences; electrical engineering; engineering; engineering technology.

Academic Programs *Special study options:* academic remediation for entering students, adult/continuing education programs, advanced placement credit, cooperative education, distance learning, double majors, English as a second language, independent study, internships, part-time degree program, services for LD students, study abroad, summer session for credit. *ROTC:* Army (b), Air Force (b).

Library ERAU—Prescott Campus Library with 26,130 titles, 575 serial subscriptions, 2,194 audiovisual materials, an OPAC, a Web page.

Computers on Campus 200 computers available on campus for general student use. A campuswide network can be accessed from student residence rooms and from off campus. At least one staffed computer lab available.

Student Life *Housing:* on-campus residence required for freshman year. *Options:* coed, men-only, disabled students. *Activities and Organizations:* student-run newspaper, radio station, Hawaii Club, Strike Eagles, Theta XI, American Institute of Aeronautics and Astronautics (AIAA), Arnold Air Society, national fraternities, national sororities. *Campus security:* 24-hour emergency response devices and patrols, student patrols, late-night transport/escort service. *Student Services:* health clinic, personal/psychological counseling.

Athletics Member NAIA. *Intercollegiate sports:* volleyball W(s), wrestling M(s). *Intramural sports:* archery M/W, badminton M/W, basketball M/W, bowling M/W, cross-country running M/W, fencing M(c)/W(c), lacrosse M(c)/W(c), racquetball M/W, rugby M(c)/W(c), skiing (cross-country) M(c)/W(c), skiing (downhill) M(c)/W(c), soccer M(c)/W(c), softball M/W, swimming M/W, table tennis M/W, tennis M/W, track and field M/W, volleyball M/W, weight lifting M/W.

Standardized Tests *Required:* SAT I or ACT (for admission).

Costs (2001–02) *Comprehensive fee:* $23,250 includes full-time tuition ($17,850), mandatory fees ($360), and room and board ($5040). Full-time tuition and fees vary according to course load and program. Part-time tuition: $745 per credit hour. Part-time tuition and fees vary according to course load and program. *Room and board:* College room only: $2340. Room and board charges vary according to board plan, housing facility, and location. *Waivers:* employees or children of employees.

Financial Aid Of all full-time matriculated undergraduates who enrolled in 2001, 1156 applied for aid, 983 were judged to have need. 133 Federal Work-Study jobs (averaging $466). 597 State and other part-time jobs. *Average financial aid package:* $9736. *Average need-based loan:* $3569. *Average need-based gift aid:* $6161. *Average indebtedness upon graduation:* $21,421. *Financial aid deadline:* 6/30.
Applying *Options:* common application, electronic application, early admission, early decision, deferred entrance. *Application fee:* $30. *Required:* high school transcript, minimum 2.0 GPA. *Required for some:* minimum 3.0 GPA, medical examination for flight students. *Recommended:* essay or personal statement, letters of recommendation, interview. *Application deadline:* rolling (freshmen), rolling (transfers). *Early decision:* 12/1. *Notification:* continuous (freshmen), 12/15 (early decision).
Admissions Contact Bill Thompson, Director of Admissions, Embry-Riddle Aeronautical University, 3200 Willow Creek Road, Prescott, AZ 86301. *Phone:* 928-777-6692. *Toll-free phone:* 800-888-3728. *Fax:* 928-777-6606. *E-mail:* admit@pc.erau.edu.

GRAND CANYON UNIVERSITY
Phoenix, Arizona

- **Independent Southern Baptist** comprehensive, founded 1949
- **Calendar** semesters
- **Degrees** certificates, diplomas, bachelor's, and master's
- **Suburban** 90-acre campus
- **Endowment** $5.4 million
- **Coed,** 1,609 undergraduate students, 82% full-time, 64% women, 36% men
- **Moderately difficult** entrance level, 69% of applicants were admitted

Grand Canyon University represents a well-rounded Christian education. True to the founding mission "to train young men and women in an environment that makes for high scholarship and Christian character," the University provides both traditional and innovative programs that enable students to think critically and creatively, solve problems through open-minded analysis, and communicate effectively.

Undergraduates 1,327 full-time, 282 part-time. Students come from 40 states and territories, 14 other countries, 19% are from out of state, 3% African American, 2% Asian American or Pacific Islander, 7% Hispanic American, 1% Native American, 3% international, 19% transferred in, 30% live on campus. *Retention:* 76% of 2001 full-time freshmen returned.
Freshmen *Admission:* 823 applied, 567 admitted, 371 enrolled. *Average high school GPA:* 3.44. *Test scores:* ACT scores over 18: 82%; ACT scores over 24: 29%; ACT scores over 30: 7%.
Faculty *Total:* 274, 35% full-time, 22% with terminal degrees. *Student/faculty ratio:* 16:1.
Majors Accounting; art; art education; athletic training/sports medicine; biblical studies; biology; business administration; business economics; business education; business marketing and marketing management; chemistry; criminal justice/law enforcement administration; divinity/ministry; economics; elementary education; English; environmental biology; exercise sciences; finance; fine/studio arts; graphic design/commercial art/illustration; history; human resources management; international business; international relations; liberal arts and sciences/liberal studies; literature; mass communications; mathematics; music; music business management/merchandising; music (piano and organ performance); music teacher education; music (voice and choral/opera performance); nursing; physical education; physical sciences; political science; pre-dentistry; pre-law; pre-medicine; pre-veterinary studies; psychology; religious music; religious studies; science education; secondary education; social sciences; sociology; special education; speech/rhetorical studies; theater arts/drama; theology; wildlife biology; wind/percussion instruments.
Academic Programs *Special study options:* academic remediation for entering students, accelerated degree program, adult/continuing education programs, advanced placement credit, cooperative education, distance learning, double majors, English as a second language, freshman honors college, honors programs, independent study, internships, off-campus study, part-time degree program, study abroad, summer session for credit. *ROTC:* Army (b), Air Force (c). *Unusual degree programs:* 3-2 engineering with Arizona State University.
Library Fleming Library with 75,905 titles, 1,174 serial subscriptions, 404 audiovisual materials, an OPAC.
Computers on Campus 119 computers available on campus for general student use. Internet access, at least one staffed computer lab available.
Student Life *Housing:* on-campus residence required through sophomore year. *Options:* men-only, women-only. *Activities and Organizations:* drama/theater group, student-run newspaper, choral group. *Campus security:* 24-hour emergency response devices and patrols, student patrols, late-night transport/escort service, controlled dormitory access. *Student Services:* health clinic.
Athletics Member NCAA. All Division II. *Intercollegiate sports:* baseball M(s), basketball M(s)/W(s), golf M(s), soccer M(s)/W(s), tennis W(s), volleyball W(s). *Intramural sports:* basketball M/W, football M/W, softball M/W, volleyball M/W.
Standardized Tests *Required:* SAT I or ACT (for admission).
Costs (2001–02) *Comprehensive fee:* $15,000 includes full-time tuition ($9500), mandatory fees ($1000), and room and board ($4500). Full-time tuition and fees vary according to course load. Part-time tuition: $438 per semester hour. Part-time tuition and fees vary according to course load. *Required fees:* $10 per semester hour. *Room and board:* Room and board charges vary according to board plan and housing facility. *Payment plan:* installment. *Waivers:* employees or children of employees.
Financial Aid Of all full-time matriculated undergraduates who enrolled in 2001, 993 applied for aid, 855 were judged to have need, 120 had their need fully met. In 2001, 241 non-need-based awards were made. *Average percent of need met:* 41%. *Average financial aid package:* $8405. *Average need-based gift aid:* $2918. *Average non-need based aid:* $3958. *Average indebtedness upon graduation:* $46,640.
Applying *Application fee:* $50. *Required:* high school transcript, minimum 3.0 GPA. *Required for some:* essay or personal statement, 3 letters of recommendation, interview. *Recommended:* minimum 3.0 GPA. *Application deadline:* rolling (freshmen), rolling (transfers). *Notification:* continuous until 9/1 (freshmen).
Admissions Contact Mrs. April Chapman, Director of Admissions, Grand Canyon University, 3300 West Camelback Road, PO Box 11097, Phoenix, AZ 86017-3030. *Phone:* 602-589-2855 Ext. 2811. *Toll-free phone:* 800-800-9776. *Fax:* 602-589-2580. *E-mail:* admiss@grand-canyon.edu.

INTERNATIONAL BAPTIST COLLEGE
Tempe, Arizona

- **Independent Baptist** comprehensive, founded 1980
- **Calendar** 4-1-4
- **Degrees** certificates, associate, bachelor's, master's, and doctoral
- **Suburban** 12-acre campus with easy access to Phoenix
- **Coed**
- **Minimally difficult** entrance level

Standardized Tests *Recommended:* SAT I and SAT II or ACT (for admission).
Applying *Options:* common application, early admission. *Application fee:* $25. *Required:* essay or personal statement, 3 letters of recommendation. *Recommended:* high school transcript.
Admissions Contact Dr. Stanley Bushey, Administrative Services Director, International Baptist College, 2150 East Southern Avenue, Tempe, AZ 85282. *Phone:* 480-838-7070. *Toll-free phone:* 800-422-4858. *Fax:* 480-838-1533.

ITT TECHNICAL INSTITUTE
Phoenix, Arizona

- **Proprietary** primarily 2-year, founded 1972, part of ITT Educational Services, Inc
- **Calendar** quarters
- **Degrees** associate and bachelor's
- **Urban** 2-acre campus
- **Coed,** 417 undergraduate students
- **Minimally difficult** entrance level

Majors Computer programming; data processing technology; design/applied arts related; drafting; electrical/electronic engineering technologies related.
Academic Programs *Special study options:* academic remediation for entering students.
Library 450 titles, 6 serial subscriptions.
Computers on Campus 100 computers available on campus for general student use. Internet access available.
Student Life *Housing:* college housing not available. *Activities and Organizations:* Student Activities Council. *Student Services:* personal/psychological counseling.
Costs (2001–02) *Tuition:* Full-time tuition and fees vary according to program. Part-time tuition and fees vary according to program. $260—$330 per credit hour.
Financial Aid Of all full-time matriculated undergraduates who enrolled in 2001, 10 Federal Work-Study jobs (averaging $4000).
Applying *Options:* deferred entrance. *Application fee:* $100. *Application deadline:* rolling (freshmen).

ITT Technical Institute (continued)

Admissions Contact Mr. Gene McWhorter, Director of Recruitment, ITT Technical Institute, 4837 East McDowell Road, Phoenix, AZ 85008-4292. *Phone:* 602-252-2331. *Toll-free phone:* 800-879-4881.

METROPOLITAN COLLEGE OF COURT REPORTING

Phoenix, Arizona

- **Proprietary** 4-year, founded 1991
- **Calendar** trimesters
- **Degrees** certificates, associate, and bachelor's
- **Suburban** 1-acre campus
- **Coed, primarily women**
- 100% of applicants were admitted

Faculty *Student/faculty ratio:* 12:1.

Applying *Options:* common application, electronic application, early admission, deferred entrance. *Application fee:* $50. *Required:* high school transcript, interview, typing test.

Admissions Contact Ms. Shannon Buchanan, Admissions, Metropolitan College of Court Reporting, 4640 East Elwood Street, Suite 12, Phoenix, AZ 85040. *Phone:* 480-955-5900. *Fax:* 480-894-8999.

NORTHCENTRAL UNIVERSITY

Prescott, Arizona

Admissions Contact 600 East Gurley Street #E, Prescott, AZ 86301. *Toll-free phone:* 800-903-9381.

NORTHERN ARIZONA UNIVERSITY

Flagstaff, Arizona

- **State-supported** university, founded 1899
- **Calendar** semesters
- **Degrees** bachelor's, master's, and doctoral
- **Small-town** 730-acre campus
- **Coed,** 13,740 undergraduate students, 84% full-time, 60% women, 40% men
- **Moderately difficult** entrance level, 80% of applicants were admitted

Undergraduates 11,502 full-time, 2,238 part-time. Students come from 55 states and territories, 66 other countries, 15% are from out of state, 2% African American, 2% Asian American or Pacific Islander, 10% Hispanic American, 7% Native American, 1% international, 12% transferred in, 53% live on campus. *Retention:* 64% of 2001 full-time freshmen returned.

Freshmen *Admission:* 8,094 applied, 6,439 admitted, 2,238 enrolled. *Average high school GPA:* 3.42. *Test scores:* SAT verbal scores over 500: 67%; SAT math scores over 500: 67%; SAT verbal scores over 600: 22%; SAT math scores over 600: 24%; SAT verbal scores over 700: 3%; SAT math scores over 700: 3%.

Faculty *Total:* 1,389, 51% full-time, 64% with terminal degrees. *Student/faculty ratio:* 17:1.

Majors Accounting; advertising; American government; anthropology; art; art education; art history; arts management; astronomy; biology; biology education; botany; business; business administration; business economics; business marketing and marketing management; cell and molecular biology related; chemistry; chemistry related; civil engineering; communications; communications related; computer/information sciences; construction technology; counselor education/guidance; criminal justice/law enforcement administration; dental hygiene; drama/dance education; ecology; economics; education; education administration; education of the speech impaired; electrical engineering; elementary education; engineering; engineering physics; English; English education; environmental engineering; environmental science; exercise sciences; finance; forestry sciences; French; general studies; geochemistry; geography; geology; German; health education; history; history education; hotel and restaurant management; humanities; industrial arts education; interior design; international relations; journalism; liberal arts and sciences/liberal studies; liberal arts and studies related; management information systems/business data processing; marine biology; mathematics; mathematics education; mechanical engineering; microbiology/bacteriology; music; music (general performance); music teacher education; Native American studies; nursing; philosophy; photography; physical education; physical sciences; physics; physics education; physics related; political science; pre-law; pre-medicine; pre-veterinary studies; psychology; public policy analysis; public relations; radio/television broadcasting; recreation/leisure studies; religious studies; science education; science technologies related; social science education; social sciences; social work; sociology; Spanish; Spanish language education; special education; speech/rhetorical studies; teacher education, specific programs related; teaching English as a second language; theater arts/drama; wildlife management; women's studies; zoology.

Academic Programs *Special study options:* academic remediation for entering students, accelerated degree program, advanced placement credit, cooperative education, distance learning, double majors, English as a second language, external degree program, freshman honors college, honors programs, independent study, internships, off-campus study, part-time degree program, services for LD students, study abroad, summer session for credit. *ROTC:* Army (b), Air Force (b).

Library Cline Library with 523,860 titles, 6,253 serial subscriptions, 28,535 audiovisual materials, an OPAC, a Web page.

Computers on Campus 620 computers available on campus for general student use. A campuswide network can be accessed from student residence rooms and from off campus. Internet access, online (class) registration, at least one staffed computer lab available.

Student Life *Housing Options:* coed, men-only, women-only, disabled students. *Activities and Organizations:* drama/theater group, student-run newspaper, radio and television station, choral group, marching band, ASNAU, Black Student Union, New Student Organization, Cardinal Key, Blue Key, national fraternities, national sororities. *Campus security:* 24-hour emergency response devices and patrols, late-night transport/escort service, controlled dormitory access. *Student Services:* health clinic, personal/psychological counseling, women's center, legal services.

Athletics Member NCAA. All Division I except football (Division I-AA). *Intercollegiate sports:* basketball M(s)/W(s), cross-country running M(s)/W(s), golf W(s), soccer W(s), swimming W(s), tennis M(s)/W(s), track and field M(s)/W(s), volleyball W(s). *Intramural sports:* archery M/W, badminton M/W, baseball M, basketball M/W, bowling M/W, cross-country running M/W, football M/W, ice hockey M, lacrosse W, racquetball M/W, rugby M, skiing (cross-country) M/W, skiing (downhill) M/W, soccer M(c), softball M/W, swimming W, table tennis M/W, volleyball M/W, water polo M/W, weight lifting M/W.

Standardized Tests *Required:* SAT I or ACT (for admission).

Costs (2001–02) *Tuition:* state resident $2412 full-time, $126 per semester hour part-time; nonresident $7790 full-time, $428 per semester hour part-time. Full-time tuition and fees vary according to program. Part-time tuition and fees vary according to course load and program. *Required fees:* $76 full-time, $38 per term part-time. *Room and board:* $4910; room only: $2440. Room and board charges vary according to board plan and housing facility. *Waivers:* employees or children of employees.

Financial Aid Of all full-time matriculated undergraduates who enrolled in 2001, 10724 applied for aid, 6221 were judged to have need, 2496 had their need fully met. 561 Federal Work-Study jobs (averaging $1447). In 2001, 992 non-need-based awards were made. *Average percent of need met:* 81%. *Average financial aid package:* $7006. *Average need-based loan:* $5264. *Average need-based gift aid:* $3936. *Average non-need based aid:* $2630. *Average indebtedness upon graduation:* $16,202.

Applying *Options:* electronic application, deferred entrance. *Application fee:* $40. *Required:* high school transcript. *Required for some:* essay or personal statement, letters of recommendation, interview. *Recommended:* minimum 3.0 GPA. *Application deadline:* rolling (freshmen), rolling (transfers). *Notification:* continuous (freshmen).

Admissions Contact Ms. Pamela Van Wyck, Assistant Director, Northern Arizona University, PO Box 4084, Flagstaff, AZ 86011. *Phone:* 928-523-6008. *Toll-free phone:* 888-MORE-NAU. *Fax:* 928-523-6023. *E-mail:* undergraduate.admissions@nau.edu.

PRESCOTT COLLEGE

Prescott, Arizona

- **Independent** comprehensive, founded 1966
- **Calendar** quarters
- **Degrees** bachelor's and master's
- **Small-town** campus
- **Endowment** $150,000
- **Coed,** 827 undergraduate students, 89% full-time, 59% women, 41% men
- **Moderately difficult** entrance level

Undergraduates 736 full-time, 91 part-time. Students come from 44 states and territories, 1 other country, 83% are from out of state, 1% African American, 0.7% Asian American or Pacific Islander, 3% Hispanic American, 5% Native American, 0.4% international, 21% transferred in. *Retention:* 55% of 2001 full-time freshmen returned.

Freshmen *Admission:* 85 enrolled. *Test scores:* SAT math scores over 500: 86%; SAT math scores over 600: 37%; SAT math scores over 700: 4%.
Faculty *Total:* 83, 59% full-time, 29% with terminal degrees. *Student/faculty ratio:* 12:1.
Majors Accounting; anthropology; architectural environmental design; art; art therapy; bilingual/bicultural education; biology; communications; computer/information sciences; criminal justice studies; dance; early childhood education; ecology; education; elementary education; English education; environmental education; environmental science; film studies; history; human ecology; humanities; individual/family development; interdisciplinary studies; Latin American studies; liberal arts and sciences/liberal studies; literature; management science; marine science; mathematics education; mental health/rehabilitation; middle school education; music teacher education; natural resources conservation; natural resources management; philosophy; photography; physical education; political science; psychology; recreation/leisure studies; science education; secondary education; social science education; sociology; Spanish; special education; theater arts/drama; wildlife management.
Academic Programs *Special study options:* accelerated degree program, adult/continuing education programs, advanced placement credit, cooperative education, double majors, external degree program, independent study, internships, off-campus study, services for LD students, student-designed majors, summer session for credit.
Library Prescott College Library with 20,000 titles, 250 serial subscriptions, 1,000 audiovisual materials, an OPAC, a Web page.
Computers on Campus 30 computers available on campus for general student use. At least one staffed computer lab available.
Student Life *Housing:* college housing not available. *Activities and Organizations:* student-run newspaper, Student Union, Amnesty International, Student Environmental Network. *Student Services:* personal/psychological counseling.
Costs (2001–02) *Tuition:* $13,300 full-time, $398 per credit hour part-time. Full-time tuition and fees vary according to course load and program. Part-time tuition and fees vary according to course load and program. *Required fees:* $755 full-time, $130 per year part-time. *Payment plan:* installment. *Waivers:* employees or children of employees.
Financial Aid Of all full-time matriculated undergraduates who enrolled in 2001, 541 applied for aid, 507 were judged to have need. 125 Federal Work-Study jobs (averaging $818). 8 State and other part-time jobs (averaging $931). *Average percent of need met:* 53%. *Average financial aid package:* $5297. *Average need-based gift aid:* $2779. *Average indebtedness upon graduation:* $15,891.
Applying *Options:* deferred entrance. *Application fee:* $25. *Required:* essay or personal statement, high school transcript, 2 letters of recommendation. *Required for some:* interview. *Application deadlines:* 2/1 (freshmen), 2/1 (transfers). *Notification:* 3/15 (freshmen).
Admissions Contact Ms. Shari Sterling, Director of Admissions, Prescott College, 220 Grove Avenue, Prescott, AZ 86301-2990. *Phone:* 928-778-2090 Ext. 2101. *Toll-free phone:* 800-628-6364. *Fax:* 928-776-5137. *E-mail:* rdpadmissions@prescott.edu.

SOUTHWESTERN COLLEGE
Phoenix, Arizona

- **Independent Conservative Baptist** 4-year, founded 1960
- **Calendar** 4-4-1
- **Degrees** associate and bachelor's
- **Urban** 19-acre campus
- **Coed,** 309 undergraduate students, 89% full-time, 55% women, 45% men
- **Minimally difficult** entrance level, 66% of applicants were admitted

Undergraduates 276 full-time, 33 part-time. Students come from 15 states and territories, 1 other country, 17% are from out of state, 4% African American, 2% Asian American or Pacific Islander, 5% Hispanic American, 1% Native American, 0.3% international, 18% transferred in, 49% live on campus. *Retention:* 67% of 2001 full-time freshmen returned.
Freshmen *Admission:* 111 applied, 73 admitted, 71 enrolled. *Average high school GPA:* 3.30.
Faculty *Total:* 32, 34% full-time, 19% with terminal degrees. *Student/faculty ratio:* 24:1.
Majors Biblical studies; business administration; counseling psychology; divinity/ministry; elementary education; pastoral counseling; religious education; religious music; religious studies; secondary education; theology.
Academic Programs *Special study options:* academic remediation for entering students, accelerated degree program, adult/continuing education programs, advanced placement credit, internships, summer session for credit. *ROTC:* Air Force (c).
Library R. S. Beal Library with 32,000 titles, 293 serial subscriptions, 2,567 audiovisual materials.
Computers on Campus 27 computers available on campus for general student use. At least one staffed computer lab available.
Student Life *Housing:* on-campus residence required through senior year. *Options:* men-only, women-only. *Activities and Organizations:* student-run newspaper, choral group. *Campus security:* controlled dormitory access.
Athletics Member NSCAA. *Intercollegiate sports:* basketball M/W, volleyball W. *Intramural sports:* basketball M/W, softball M/W, table tennis M/W, volleyball M/W.
Costs (2002–03) *Comprehensive fee:* $13,380 includes full-time tuition ($9300), mandatory fees ($260), and room and board ($3820). Full-time tuition and fees vary according to program. Part-time tuition: $385 per credit. Part-time tuition and fees vary according to program. *Required fees:* $225 per term part-time. *Room and board:* College room only: $2870.
Financial Aid Of all full-time matriculated undergraduates who enrolled in 2001, 235 applied for aid, 207 were judged to have need, 23 had their need fully met. 26 Federal Work-Study jobs (averaging $1300). In 2001, 46 non-need-based awards were made. *Average percent of need met:* 90%. *Average financial aid package:* $4500. *Average need-based loan:* $1200. *Average need-based gift aid:* $1400. *Average non-need based aid:* $750. *Average indebtedness upon graduation:* $16,125.
Applying *Options:* deferred entrance. *Application fee:* $25. *Required:* essay or personal statement, high school transcript, minimum 2.0 GPA, 1 letter of recommendation. *Application deadlines:* 8/15 (freshmen), 8/15 (transfers). *Notification:* continuous until 8/27 (freshmen).
Admissions Contact Mrs. Karen Lokken, Admissions Coordinator, Southwestern College, 2625 East Cactus Road, Phoenix, AZ 85032-7042. *Phone:* 602-992-6101 Ext. 108. *Toll-free phone:* 800-247-2697. *Fax:* 602-404-2159. *E-mail:* admissions@southwesterncollege.edu.

UNIVERSITY OF ADVANCING COMPUTER TECHNOLOGY
Tempe, Arizona

- **Proprietary** comprehensive, founded 1983
- **Calendar** semesters
- **Degrees** certificates, diplomas, associate, bachelor's, and master's
- **Urban** campus
- **Coed,** 717 undergraduate students, 100% full-time, 18% women, 82% men

Undergraduates 6% African American, 3% Asian American or Pacific Islander, 11% Hispanic American, 1% Native American, 2% international.
Freshmen *Admission:* 459 admitted.
Faculty *Total:* 50, 82% full-time. *Student/faculty ratio:* 15:1.
Majors Computer graphics; computer programming; computer systems analysis; data processing technology; design/visual communications; film/video production; graphic design/commercial art/illustration.
Academic Programs *Special study options:* accelerated degree program.
Library University of Advancing Computer Technology Library with a Web page.
Computers on Campus 190 computers available on campus for general student use. A campuswide network can be accessed from off campus. Internet access, online (class) registration, at least one staffed computer lab available.
Student Life *Housing:* college housing not available. *Activities and Organizations:* student-run newspaper, television station, Web Club, Gaming Club, Animation Club, Video Club, student government. *Campus security:* 24-hour patrols. *Student Services:* personal/psychological counseling.
Standardized Tests *Required:* SAT I or ACT (for admission).
Costs (2001–02) *One-time required fee:* $100. *Comprehensive fee:* $16,790 includes full-time tuition ($11,844) and room and board ($4946). Part-time tuition: $329 per credit hour. *Room and board:* College room only: $2630.
Applying *Required:* high school transcript, interview. *Required for some:* minimum 2.5 GPA. *Recommended:* essay or personal statement. *Application deadline:* rolling (freshmen).
Admissions Contact Mr. Dominic Pistillo, President, University of Advancing Computer Technology, 2625 West Baseline Road, Tempe, AZ 85283-1042. *Phone:* 602-383-8228. *Toll-free phone:* 602-383-8228 (in-state); 800-658-5744 (out-of-state). *Fax:* 602-383-8222. *E-mail:* admissions@uact.edu.

THE UNIVERSITY OF ARIZONA
Tucson, Arizona

- **State-supported** university, founded 1885, part of Arizona Board of Regents
- **Calendar** semesters

The University of Arizona (continued)

- **Degrees** bachelor's, master's, doctoral, first professional, and post-master's certificates
- **Urban** 351-acre campus
- **Endowment** $282.5 million
- **Coed,** 27,532 undergraduate students, 85% full-time, 53% women, 47% men
- **Moderately difficult** entrance level, 84% of applicants were admitted

Undergraduates 23,325 full-time, 4,207 part-time. Students come from 55 states and territories, 130 other countries, 27% are from out of state, 3% African American, 6% Asian American or Pacific Islander, 14% Hispanic American, 2% Native American, 4% international, 20% live on campus.

Freshmen *Admission:* 19,719 applied, 16,613 admitted, 5,949 enrolled. *Average high school GPA:* 3.35. *Test scores:* SAT verbal scores over 500: 73%; SAT math scores over 500: 77%; ACT scores over 18: 93%; SAT verbal scores over 600: 29%; SAT math scores over 600: 35%; ACT scores over 24: 51%; SAT verbal scores over 700: 5%; SAT math scores over 700: 6%; ACT scores over 30: 9%.

Faculty *Total:* 1,413, 98% full-time, 97% with terminal degrees. *Student/faculty ratio:* 18:1.

Majors Accounting; aerospace engineering; agricultural economics; agricultural education; agricultural engineering; agricultural sciences; animal sciences; anthropology; architecture; art education; art history; astronomy; atmospheric sciences; biochemistry; biology; biology education; business; business economics; business marketing and marketing management; cell biology; chemical engineering; chemistry; chemistry education; city/community/regional planning; civil engineering; classics; communication disorders; communications; computer engineering; computer/information sciences; consumer economics; creative writing; criminal justice/law enforcement administration; dance; drama/dance education; early childhood education; earth sciences; East Asian studies; ecology; economics; electrical engineering; elementary education; engineering; engineering physics; engineering related; English; English education; enterprise management; environmental science; evolutionary biology; finance; fine/studio arts; foreign languages education; French; French language education; geography; geological engineering; geology; German; German language education; health education; health services administration; Hispanic-American studies; history; history education; home economics education; humanities; human resources management; individual/family development; industrial/manufacturing engineering; Italian; journalism; Judaic studies; landscape architecture; Latin American studies; liberal arts and sciences/liberal studies; linguistics; management information systems/business data processing; materials science; mathematics; mathematics education; mechanical engineering; medical technology; microbiology/bacteriology; Middle Eastern studies; mining/mineral engineering; multi/interdisciplinary studies related; music; music (general performance); music related; music teacher education; nuclear engineering; nursing; nutritional sciences; operations management; optics; philosophy; physical education; physics; physics education; physiology; plant sciences; political science; pre-veterinary studies; psychology; public administration; radio/television broadcasting; religious studies; Russian; science education; secondary education; social science education; social studies education; sociology; soil sciences; Spanish; Spanish language education; special education; speech education; systems engineering; teacher education, specific programs related; theater arts/drama; theater design; visual/performing arts; water resources engineering; wildlife management; women's studies.

Academic Programs *Special study options:* adult/continuing education programs, advanced placement credit, distance learning, double majors, English as a second language, freshman honors college, honors programs, independent study, internships, part-time degree program, services for LD students, study abroad, summer session for credit. *ROTC:* Army (b), Air Force (b). *Unusual degree programs:* 3-2 business administration with American Graduate School of International Management.

Library University of Arizona Main Library plus 5 others with 4.7 million titles, 26,908 serial subscriptions, 49,171 audiovisual materials, an OPAC, a Web page.

Computers on Campus 1750 computers available on campus for general student use. A campuswide network can be accessed from student residence rooms and from off campus. Internet access, at least one staffed computer lab available.

Student Life *Housing Options:* coed, men-only, women-only. *Activities and Organizations:* drama/theater group, student-run newspaper, radio and television station, choral group, marching band, Student Government Association, national fraternities, national sororities. *Campus security:* 24-hour patrols, student patrols, late-night transport/escort service, emergency telephones. *Student Services:* health clinic, personal/psychological counseling, women's center, legal services.

Athletics Member NCAA. All Division I except football (Division I-A). *Intercollegiate sports:* baseball M(s), basketball M(s)/W(s), cross-country running M(s)/W(s), golf M(s)/W(s), gymnastics W(s), ice hockey M(c), lacrosse M(c)/W(c), rugby M(c)/W(c), soccer M(c)/W(s), softball W(s), swimming M(s)/W(s), tennis M(s)/W(s), track and field M(s)/W(s), volleyball M(c)/W(s), wrestling M(c). *Intramural sports:* badminton M/W, basketball M/W, bowling M/W, cross-country running M/W, football M/W, golf M/W, racquetball M/W, soccer M/W, softball M/W, swimming M/W, table tennis M/W, tennis M/W, track and field M/W, volleyball M/W, water polo M/W, weight lifting M/W, wrestling M.

Standardized Tests *Required:* SAT I or ACT (for admission).

Costs (2001–02) *One-time required fee:* $720. *Tuition:* state resident $2412 full-time, $134 per unit part-time; nonresident $10,278 full-time, $436 per unit part-time. Part-time tuition and fees vary according to course load. *Required fees:* $78 full-time, $78 per year. *Room and board:* $6124; room only: $3100. Room and board charges vary according to board plan and housing facility. *Waivers:* minority students and employees or children of employees.

Financial Aid Of all full-time matriculated undergraduates who enrolled in 2001, 18203 applied for aid, 10274 were judged to have need. *Average financial aid package:* $9228. *Average need-based gift aid:* $2657. *Average indebtedness upon graduation:* $17,772.

Applying *Options:* electronic application, early admission. *Application fee:* $45 (non-residents). *Required:* high school transcript. *Required for some:* minimum 3.0 GPA, letters of recommendation, interview. *Application deadlines:* 4/1 (freshmen), 5/1 (transfers). *Notification:* continuous until 8/1 (freshmen).

Admissions Contact Ms. Lori Goldman, Director of Admissions, The University of Arizona, PO Box 210040, Tucson, AZ 85721-0040. *Phone:* 520-621-3237. *Fax:* 520-621-9799. *E-mail:* appinfo@arizona.edu.

UNIVERSITY OF PHOENIX-PHOENIX CAMPUS
Phoenix, Arizona

- **Proprietary** comprehensive, founded 1976
- **Calendar** continuous
- **Degrees** certificates, associate, bachelor's, master's, doctoral, post-master's, and postbachelor's certificates (courses conducted at 54 campuses and learning centers in 13 states)
- **Urban** campus
- **Coed,** 4,683 undergraduate students, 100% full-time, 54% women, 46% men
- **Noncompetitive** entrance level

Undergraduates Students come from 36 states and territories, 3% are from out of state.

Freshmen *Admission:* 42 admitted.

Faculty *Total:* 1,019, 3% full-time, 23% with terminal degrees. *Student/faculty ratio:* 14:1.

Majors Accounting; business administration; business marketing and marketing management; counseling psychology; criminal justice/law enforcement administration; enterprise management; information technology; management information systems/business data processing; management science; nursing science; public administration and services related.

Academic Programs *Special study options:* accelerated degree program, adult/continuing education programs, advanced placement credit, distance learning, external degree program, independent study.

Library University Library with 17.5 million titles, 9,000 serial subscriptions, an OPAC, a Web page.

Computers on Campus A campuswide network can be accessed from off campus. Internet access, at least one staffed computer lab available.

Student Life *Housing:* college housing not available. *Campus security:* 24-hour patrols, late-night transport/escort service.

Costs (2001–02) *Tuition:* $8100 full-time. Full-time tuition and fees vary according to location and program. *Payment plan:* deferred payment. *Waivers:* employees or children of employees.

Applying *Options:* deferred entrance. *Application fee:* $85. *Required:* 2 years of work experience. *Required for some:* high school transcript. *Application deadline:* rolling (freshmen), rolling (transfers).

Admissions Contact Ms. Beth Barilla, Director of Admissions, University of Phoenix-Phoenix Campus, 4615 East Elwood Street, Phoenix, AZ 85040-1958. *Phone:* 480-927-0099 Ext. 1216. *Toll-free phone:* 800-776-4867 (in-state); 800-228-7240 (out-of-state). *Fax:* 480-894-1758. *E-mail:* beth.barilla@apollogrp.edu.

UNIVERSITY OF PHOENIX-SOUTHERN ARIZONA CAMPUS
Tucson, Arizona

- **Proprietary** comprehensive
- **Calendar** continuous

- **Degrees** certificates, associate, bachelor's, master's, doctoral, post-master's, and postbachelor's certificates (courses conducted at 54 campuses and learning centers in 13 states)
- **Coed,** 2,130 undergraduate students, 105% full-time, 57% women, 48% men
- **Noncompetitive** entrance level

Undergraduates Students come from 30 states and territories, 3% are from out of state.
Freshmen *Admission:* 35 admitted.
Faculty *Total:* 381, 3% full-time, 22% with terminal degrees. *Student/faculty ratio:* 14:1.
Majors Accounting; business administration; business marketing and marketing management; enterprise management; information technology; management information systems/business data processing; nursing; nursing science; public administration and services related.
Academic Programs *Special study options:* accelerated degree program, adult/continuing education programs, advanced placement credit, distance learning, external degree program, independent study.
Library University Library with 17.5 million titles, 9,000 serial subscriptions, an OPAC, a Web page.
Computers on Campus A campuswide network can be accessed from off campus. Internet access, at least one staffed computer lab available.
Student Life *Housing:* college housing not available.
Costs (2001–02) *Tuition:* $7800 full-time. Full-time tuition and fees vary according to location and program. *Payment plan:* deferred payment. *Waivers:* employees or children of employees.
Applying *Options:* deferred entrance. *Application fee:* $85. *Required:* 2 years of work experience. *Required for some:* high school transcript. *Application deadline:* rolling (freshmen), rolling (transfers).
Admissions Contact Ms. Beth Barilla, Director of Admissions, University of Phoenix-Southern Arizona Campus, 4615 East Elwood Street, Phoenix, AZ 85040-1958. *Phone:* 480-927-0099 Ext. 1218. *Toll-free phone:* 800-228-7240. *Fax:* 480-594-1758. *E-mail:* beth.barilla@apollogrp.edu.

WESTERN INTERNATIONAL UNIVERSITY
Phoenix, Arizona

- **Proprietary** comprehensive, founded 1978
- **Calendar** continuous
- **Degrees** certificates, associate, bachelor's, and master's
- **Urban** 4-acre campus
- **Endowment** $20,000
- **Coed,** 2,627 undergraduate students, 100% full-time, 53% women, 47% men
- **Moderately difficult** entrance level

Undergraduates 2,627 full-time. Students come from 38 other countries, 3% African American, 2% Asian American or Pacific Islander, 5% Hispanic American, 0.5% Native American, 2% international.
Freshmen *Admission:* 113 enrolled.
Faculty *Total:* 230. *Student/faculty ratio:* 10:1.
Majors Accounting; behavioral sciences; business administration; business marketing and marketing management; computer management; criminal justice/law enforcement administration; finance; health services administration; information sciences/systems; international business; international relations; liberal arts and sciences/liberal studies.
Academic Programs *Special study options:* accelerated degree program, adult/continuing education programs, advanced placement credit, double majors, English as a second language, external degree program, honors programs, independent study, part-time degree program, study abroad, summer session for credit.
Library Learning Resource Center with 7,500 titles, 125 serial subscriptions, a Web page.
Computers on Campus 30 computers available on campus for general student use. Internet access, at least one staffed computer lab available.
Student Life *Housing:* college housing not available. *Activities and Organizations:* Delta Mu Delta, Student Association, International Student Organization. *Campus security:* 24-hour emergency response devices and patrols, late-night transport/escort service.
Costs (2002–03) *Tuition:* $8320 full-time, $260 per credit hour part-time.
Applying *Options:* deferred entrance. *Application fee:* $85. *Required:* high school transcript, minimum 2.5 GPA, interview. *Required for some:* 3 letters of recommendation. *Recommended:* 3 letters of recommendation. *Application deadline:* rolling (freshmen), rolling (transfers).
Admissions Contact Ms. Jo Arney, Director of Student Services, Western International University, 9215 North Black Canyon Highway, Phoenix, AZ 85021-2718. *Phone:* 602-943-2311 Ext. 139.

ARKANSAS

ARKANSAS BAPTIST COLLEGE
Little Rock, Arkansas

- **Independent Baptist** 4-year, founded 1884
- **Calendar** semesters
- **Degrees** associate and bachelor's
- **Urban** campus
- **Coed,** 225 undergraduate students
- **Noncompetitive** entrance level, 100% of applicants were admitted

Undergraduates 98% African American.
Freshmen *Admission:* 68 applied, 68 admitted. *Average high school GPA:* 2.00.
Faculty *Total:* 31, 55% full-time. *Student/faculty ratio:* 9:1.
Majors Adult/continuing education; business administration; computer science; elementary education; liberal arts and sciences/liberal studies; religious studies; secondary education; social work.
Academic Programs *Special study options:* academic remediation for entering students, accelerated degree program, adult/continuing education programs, part-time degree program, summer session for credit.
Computers on Campus 25 computers available on campus for general student use.
Athletics Member NAIA. *Intercollegiate sports:* basketball M/W, volleyball M/W.
Costs (2001–02) *Comprehensive fee:* $6120 includes full-time tuition ($2400), mandatory fees ($120), and room and board ($3600). Part-time tuition: $100 per semester hour. *Required fees:* $30 per term part-time.
Applying *Options:* deferred entrance. *Required:* high school transcript. *Application deadline:* rolling (freshmen).
Admissions Contact Mrs. Annie A. Hightower, Registrar, Arkansas Baptist College, 1600 Bishop Street, Little Rock, AR 72202-6067. *Phone:* 501-374-7856 Ext. 19.

ARKANSAS STATE UNIVERSITY
Jonesboro, Arkansas

- **State-supported** comprehensive, founded 1909, part of Arkansas State University System
- **Calendar** semesters
- **Degrees** certificates, associate, bachelor's, master's, doctoral, post-master's, and postbachelor's certificates
- **Small-town** 900-acre campus with easy access to Memphis
- **Endowment** $10.1 million
- **Coed,** 9,426 undergraduate students, 80% full-time, 58% women, 42% men
- **Moderately difficult** entrance level, 82% of applicants were admitted

Undergraduates 7,513 full-time, 1,913 part-time. Students come from 37 states and territories, 38 other countries, 10% are from out of state, 13% African American, 0.7% Asian American or Pacific Islander, 0.8% Hispanic American, 0.2% Native American, 1% international, 9% transferred in, 22% live on campus. *Retention:* 71% of 2001 full-time freshmen returned.
Freshmen *Admission:* 2,757 applied, 2,255 admitted, 1,704 enrolled. *Average high school GPA:* 3.22. *Test scores:* ACT scores over 18: 82%; ACT scores over 24: 37%; ACT scores over 30: 3%.
Faculty *Total:* 543, 79% full-time, 54% with terminal degrees. *Student/faculty ratio:* 19:1.
Majors Accounting; agribusiness; agricultural education; agricultural sciences; animal sciences; art; art education; athletic training/sports medicine; auto mechanic/technician; biology; biology education; business administration; business economics; business education; business marketing and marketing management; chemistry; chemistry education; computer/information sciences; criminology; data processing technology; development economics; early childhood education; economics; education related; electrical/electronic engineering technology; emergency medical technology; engineering; engineering-related technology; English; English education; exercise sciences; finance; French; French language education; general studies; geography; graphic design/commercial art/illustration; graphic/printing equipment; health education; health/physical education; history;

Arkansas State University (continued)

industrial arts education; international business; journalism; law enforcement/police science; management information systems/business data processing; mathematics; mathematics education; medical radiologic technology; medical technology; middle school education; music; music (general performance); music teacher education; nursing; philosophy; physical education; physical therapy assistant; physics; physics education; plant sciences; political science; psychology; radio/television broadcasting; secretarial science; social science education; social work; sociology; Spanish; Spanish language education; special education; speech-language pathology/audiology; speech/rhetorical studies; theater arts/drama; travel/tourism management; wildlife management.

Academic Programs *Special study options:* academic remediation for entering students, accelerated degree program, advanced placement credit, cooperative education, distance learning, double majors, English as a second language, honors programs, independent study, internships, off-campus study, part-time degree program, services for LD students, study abroad, summer session for credit. *ROTC:* Army (b).

Library Dean B. Ellis Library with 557,643 titles, 1,773 serial subscriptions, 8,377 audiovisual materials, an OPAC, a Web page.

Computers on Campus 556 computers available on campus for general student use. A campuswide network can be accessed from student residence rooms and from off campus. Internet access, online (class) registration, at least one staffed computer lab available.

Student Life *Housing:* on-campus residence required for freshman year. *Options:* men-only, women-only. *Activities and Organizations:* drama/theater group, student-run newspaper, radio and television station, choral group, marching band, Student Government Association, Greek organizations, intramurals, academic clubs, minority/international organizations, national fraternities, national sororities. *Campus security:* 24-hour emergency response devices and patrols. *Student Services:* health clinic, personal/psychological counseling.

Athletics Member NCAA. All Division I except football (Division I-A). *Intercollegiate sports:* baseball M(s), basketball M(s)/W(s), cross-country running M(s)/W(s), golf M(s)/W(s), soccer W(s), tennis W(s), track and field M(s)/W(s), volleyball W(s). *Intramural sports:* archery M/W, badminton M/W, basketball M/W, bowling M/W, football M/W, golf M/W, racquetball M/W, soccer M/W, softball M/W, table tennis M/W, tennis M/W, volleyball M/W.

Costs (2001–02) *Tuition:* state resident $3360 full-time, $112 per credit hour part-time; nonresident $8580 full-time, $286 per credit hour part-time. Full-time tuition and fees vary according to course load and location. Part-time tuition and fees vary according to course load and location. *Required fees:* $910 full-time, $28 per credit hour, $35 per term part-time. *Room and board:* $3210. Room and board charges vary according to board plan and housing facility. *Payment plan:* installment. *Waivers:* children of alumni, senior citizens, and employees or children of employees.

Financial Aid Of all full-time matriculated undergraduates who enrolled in 2001, 5958 applied for aid, 5656 were judged to have need, 2895 had their need fully met. 350 Federal Work-Study jobs (averaging $1400). *Average percent of need met:* 65%. *Average financial aid package:* $2400. *Average need-based loan:* $2000. *Average need-based gift aid:* $2200. *Average indebtedness upon graduation:* $13,800.

Applying *Options:* early admission, deferred entrance. *Application fee:* $15. *Required:* high school transcript, minimum 2.0 GPA, proof of immunization, proof of enrollment in selective service for men over 18. *Application deadline:* rolling (freshmen), rolling (transfers). *Notification:* continuous (freshmen).

Admissions Contact Ms. Paula James Lynn, Director of Admissions, Arkansas State University, PO Box 1630, State University, AR 72467. *Phone:* 870-972-3024. *Toll-free phone:* 800-382-3030. *Fax:* 870-910-8094. *E-mail:* admissions@astate.edu.

ARKANSAS TECH UNIVERSITY
Russellville, Arkansas

- **State-supported** comprehensive, founded 1909
- **Calendar** semesters
- **Degrees** certificates, associate, bachelor's, and master's
- **Small-town** 517-acre campus
- **Endowment** $6.7 million
- **Coed,** 5,205 undergraduate students, 84% full-time, 52% women, 48% men
- **Minimally difficult** entrance level, 52% of applicants were admitted

Undergraduates 4,378 full-time, 827 part-time. Students come from 30 states and territories, 35 other countries, 6% are from out of state, 4% African American, 1% Asian American or Pacific Islander, 1% Hispanic American, 1% Native American, 1% international, 6% transferred in, 24% live on campus. *Retention:* 64% of 2001 full-time freshmen returned.

Freshmen *Admission:* 2,685 applied, 1,408 admitted, 1,239 enrolled. *Average high school GPA:* 3.22. *Test scores:* ACT scores over 18: 82%; ACT scores over 24: 34%; ACT scores over 30: 3%.

Faculty *Total:* 300, 70% full-time, 50% with terminal degrees. *Student/faculty ratio:* 20:1.

Majors Accounting; agricultural business; art; art education; biology; biology education; business administration; business education; chemistry; chemistry education; computer science; creative writing; early childhood education; economics; electrical/electronic engineering technology; electrical engineering; elementary education; engineering; engineering physics; English; English education; foreign languages education; foreign languages/literatures; French; general studies; geology; German; history; hospitality management; information technology; international relations; journalism; management science; mathematics; mathematics education; mechanical engineering; medical assistant; medical records administration; medical technology; middle school education; music; music teacher education; natural resources protective services; natural sciences; nuclear engineering; nursing; office management; physical education; physical sciences; psychology; recreation/leisure facilities management; rehabilitation therapy; social studies education; sociology; Spanish; speech education; speech/rhetorical studies; sport/fitness administration; wildlife biology.

Academic Programs *Special study options:* academic remediation for entering students, accelerated degree program, adult/continuing education programs, advanced placement credit, distance learning, double majors, English as a second language, honors programs, independent study, internships, off-campus study, part-time degree program, services for LD students, study abroad, summer session for credit. *ROTC:* Army (b).

Library Ross Pendergraft Library and Technology Center with 229,450 titles, 1,245 serial subscriptions, 3,991 audiovisual materials, an OPAC, a Web page.

Computers on Campus 258 computers available on campus for general student use. A campuswide network can be accessed from student residence rooms and from off campus. Internet access, online (class) registration, at least one staffed computer lab available.

Student Life *Housing:* on-campus residence required through sophomore year. *Options:* coed, men-only, women-only, disabled students. *Activities and Organizations:* drama/theater group, student-run newspaper, radio and television station, choral group, marching band, Student Government Association, Student Activities Board, Wesley Foundation, Chi Alpha, Baptist Student Union, national fraternities, national sororities. *Campus security:* 24-hour patrols, late-night transport/escort service, controlled dormitory access. *Student Services:* health clinic.

Athletics Member NCAA. All Division II. *Intercollegiate sports:* baseball M(s), basketball M(s)/W(s), cross-country running W(s), football M(s), golf M(s), tennis W(s), volleyball W(s). *Intramural sports:* basketball M/W, football M, golf M/W, racquetball M/W, soccer M/W, softball M/W, swimming M/W, table tennis M/W, tennis M/W, volleyball M/W.

Standardized Tests *Required:* SAT I or ACT (for admission), SAT II: Writing Test (for admission).

Costs (2001–02) *Tuition:* state resident $2796 full-time, $123 per semester hour part-time; nonresident $5952 full-time, $246 per semester hour part-time. Full-time tuition and fees vary according to location. Part-time tuition and fees vary according to location. *Required fees:* $180 full-time, $65 per term part-time. *Room and board:* $3280. Room and board charges vary according to board plan and housing facility. *Payment plan:* deferred payment. *Waivers:* senior citizens and employees or children of employees.

Financial Aid Of all full-time matriculated undergraduates who enrolled in 2001, 2607 applied for aid, 2155 were judged to have need, 623 had their need fully met. 175 Federal Work-Study jobs (averaging $1038). 433 State and other part-time jobs (averaging $1097). In 2001, 1046 non-need-based awards were made. *Average percent of need met:* 54%. *Average financial aid package:* $4389. *Average need-based loan:* $1980. *Average need-based gift aid:* $2344. *Average non-need based aid:* $3287. *Average indebtedness upon graduation:* $14,762.

Applying *Options:* electronic application, early admission, deferred entrance. *Required:* high school transcript, minimum 2.0 GPA. *Required for some:* 2 letters of recommendation, interview. *Notification:* continuous (freshmen).

Admissions Contact Ms. Shauna Donnell, Director of Enrollment Management, Arkansas Tech University, L.L. "DOC" Bryan Student Services Building, Suite 141, Russellville, AR 72801-2222. *Phone:* 501-968-0404. *Toll-free phone:* 800-582-6953. *Fax:* 501-964-0522. *E-mail:* tech.enroll@mail.atu.edu.

CENTRAL BAPTIST COLLEGE
Conway, Arkansas

- **Independent Baptist** 4-year, founded 1952
- **Calendar** semesters

- **Degrees** associate and bachelor's
- **Small-town** 11-acre campus
- **Endowment** $774,274
- **Coed,** 358 undergraduate students, 89% full-time, 46% women, 54% men
- **Minimally difficult** entrance level, 86% of applicants were admitted

Undergraduates 318 full-time, 40 part-time. Students come from 13 states and territories, 4 other countries, 12% are from out of state, 8% African American, 1% Asian American or Pacific Islander, 1% Hispanic American, 0.6% Native American, 1% international, 8% transferred in, 40% live on campus.

Freshmen *Admission:* 201 applied, 172 admitted, 101 enrolled. *Average high school GPA:* 3.14. *Test scores:* ACT scores over 18: 70%; ACT scores over 24: 25%; ACT scores over 30: 1%.

Faculty *Total:* 35, 49% full-time, 20% with terminal degrees. *Student/faculty ratio:* 16:1.

Majors Biblical studies; business administration; counseling psychology; data processing technology; education; general studies; human resources management; mathematics; music; music business management/merchandising; music related; religious education; religious music; theological studies/religious vocations related; theology/ministry related.

Academic Programs *Special study options:* academic remediation for entering students, adult/continuing education programs, advanced placement credit, internships, part-time degree program, summer session for credit. *ROTC:* Army (c).

Library J. E. Cobb Library with 47,222 titles, 311 serial subscriptions, 898 audiovisual materials.

Computers on Campus 25 computers available on campus for general student use. Internet access, at least one staffed computer lab available.

Student Life *Housing:* on-campus residence required through senior year. *Activities and Organizations:* drama/theater group, student-run newspaper, choral group. *Student Services:* personal/psychological counseling.

Athletics Member NJCAA. *Intercollegiate sports:* baseball M, basketball M/W, volleyball W. *Intramural sports:* badminton M/W, basketball M, bowling M/W, football M, golf M, softball M/W, table tennis M/W, tennis M/W, volleyball M/W.

Standardized Tests *Required:* ACT (for admission).

Costs (2001–02) *One-time required fee:* $20. *Comprehensive fee:* $10,272 includes full-time tuition ($5904), mandatory fees ($480), and room and board ($3888). Part-time tuition: $246 per credit hour. *Required fees:* $440 per term part-time. *Room and board:* College room only: $1100. Room and board charges vary according to board plan. *Payment plans:* installment, deferred payment. *Waivers:* employees or children of employees.

Applying *Options:* common application, electronic application, early admission. *Application fee:* $25. *Required:* essay or personal statement, high school transcript, minimum 2.0 GPA, 2 letters of recommendation. *Application deadlines:* 8/15 (freshmen), 8/15 (transfers).

Admissions Contact Mr. Cory Calhoun, Admissions Counselor, Central Baptist College, 1501 College Avenue, Conway, AR 72034. *Phone:* 501-329-6872 Ext. 167. *Toll-free phone:* 800-205-6872. *Fax:* 501-329-2941. *E-mail:* cjackson@cbc.edu.

HARDING UNIVERSITY
Searcy, Arkansas

- **Independent** comprehensive, founded 1924, affiliated with Church of Christ
- **Calendar** semesters
- **Degrees** bachelor's and master's
- **Small-town** 200-acre campus with easy access to Little Rock
- **Endowment** $95.0 million
- **Coed,** 4,078 undergraduate students, 94% full-time, 54% women, 46% men
- **Moderately difficult** entrance level, 70% of applicants were admitted

Located in the beautiful foothills of the Ozark Mountains, Harding is one of America's more highly regarded private universities. At Harding, students build lifetime friendships and, upon graduation, are highly recruited. Harding's Christian environment and challenging academic program develop students who can compete and succeed.

Undergraduates 3,818 full-time, 260 part-time. Students come from 50 states and territories, 48 other countries, 69% are from out of state, 4% African American, 0.5% Asian American or Pacific Islander, 1% Hispanic American, 1% Native American, 6% international, 6% transferred in, 84% live on campus. *Retention:* 77% of 2001 full-time freshmen returned.

Freshmen *Admission:* 1,967 applied, 1,384 admitted, 1,017 enrolled. *Average high school GPA:* 3.30. *Test scores:* SAT verbal scores over 500: 85%; SAT math scores over 500: 76%; ACT scores over 18: 91%; SAT verbal scores over 600: 42%; SAT math scores over 600: 36%; ACT scores over 24: 49%; SAT verbal scores over 700: 6%; SAT math scores over 700: 6%; ACT scores over 30: 12%.

Faculty *Total:* 301, 69% full-time, 51% with terminal degrees. *Student/faculty ratio:* 16:1.

Majors Accounting; advertising; American studies; art; art education; art therapy; biblical languages/literatures; biblical studies; biochemistry; biological/physical sciences; biology; business administration; business marketing and marketing management; chemistry; child care/development; communication disorders; communications; computer engineering; computer/information sciences; computer science; criminal justice studies; data processing technology; dietetics; early childhood education; economics; education of the specific learning disabled; elementary education; English; exercise sciences; family/consumer studies; fashion merchandising; finance; French; general studies; graphic design/commercial art/illustration; health services administration; history; humanities; human resources management; interior design; international business; international relations; journalism; mass communications; mathematics; mathematics education; medical technology; missionary studies; music; music (piano and organ performance); music teacher education; music (voice and choral/opera performance); nursing; painting; pastoral counseling; physical education; physics; political science; pre-dentistry; pre-law; pre-medicine; pre-veterinary studies; psychology; public administration; public relations; radio/television broadcasting; religious studies; sales operations; science education; social sciences; social work; Spanish; sport/fitness administration; stringed instruments; theater arts/drama.

Academic Programs *Special study options:* academic remediation for entering students, accelerated degree program, adult/continuing education programs, advanced placement credit, cooperative education, double majors, English as a second language, freshman honors college, honors programs, internships, part-time degree program, services for LD students, student-designed majors, study abroad, summer session for credit. *ROTC:* Army (c). *Unusual degree programs:* 3-2 engineering with University of Arkansas, Georgia Institute of Technology, University of Missouri-Rolla, Louisiana Tech University, University of Southern California.

Library Brackett Library plus 1 other with 321,928 titles, 1,368 serial subscriptions, 7,481 audiovisual materials, an OPAC, a Web page.

Computers on Campus 150 computers available on campus for general student use. A campuswide network can be accessed from student residence rooms and from off campus. Internet access, online (class) registration, at least one staffed computer lab available.

Student Life *Housing:* on-campus residence required through senior year. *Options:* men-only, women-only. *Activities and Organizations:* drama/theater group, student-run newspaper, radio station, choral group, marching band, University Singers, RENEW (environmental group), JOY, concert choir, Omicron Delta Kappa. *Campus security:* 24-hour emergency response devices and patrols. *Student Services:* health clinic, personal/psychological counseling.

Athletics Member NCAA. All Division II. *Intercollegiate sports:* baseball M, basketball M(s)/W(s), cross-country running M(s)/W(s), football M(s), golf M, soccer M/W, tennis M(s)/W(s), track and field M(s)/W(s), volleyball W(s). *Intramural sports:* baseball M, basketball M/W, bowling M/W, cross-country running M/W, football M/W, golf M/W, gymnastics W, racquetball M/W, soccer M/W, softball M/W, swimming M/W, table tennis M/W, tennis M/W, track and field M/W, volleyball M/W, weight lifting M/W.

Standardized Tests *Required:* SAT I or ACT (for admission).

Costs (2001–02) *Comprehensive fee:* $13,528 includes full-time tuition ($8730), mandatory fees ($300), and room and board ($4498). Full-time tuition and fees vary according to course load. Part-time tuition: $291 per semester hour. Part-time tuition and fees vary according to course load. *Required fees:* $13 per semester hour. *Room and board:* College room only: $2100. Room and board charges vary according to board plan and housing facility. *Payment plans:* tuition prepayment, installment. *Waivers:* senior citizens and employees or children of employees.

Financial Aid Of all full-time matriculated undergraduates who enrolled in 2001, 2854 applied for aid, 2219 were judged to have need, 472 had their need fully met. 538 Federal Work-Study jobs (averaging $337). 1289 State and other part-time jobs (averaging $763). In 2001, 1330 non-need-based awards were made. *Average percent of need met:* 73%. *Average financial aid package:* $9086. *Average need-based loan:* $4210. *Average need-based gift aid:* $5073. *Average indebtedness upon graduation:* $20,998.

Applying *Options:* common application, electronic application, early admission, deferred entrance. *Application fee:* $25. *Required:* high school transcript, 2 letters of recommendation, interview. *Application deadlines:* 7/1 (freshmen), 7/1 (transfers).

Admissions Contact Mr. Mike Williams, Assistant Vice President of Admissions, Harding University, Box 11255, Searcy, AR 72149-0001. *Phone:* 501-279-4407. *Toll-free phone:* 800-477-4407. *Fax:* 501-279-4865. *E-mail:* admissions@harding.edu.

HENDERSON STATE UNIVERSITY
Arkadelphia, Arkansas

- **State-supported** comprehensive, founded 1890
- **Calendar** semesters
- **Degrees** associate, bachelor's, and master's
- **Small-town** 135-acre campus with easy access to Little Rock
- **Coed,** 3,115 undergraduate students, 89% full-time, 57% women, 43% men
- **Moderately difficult** entrance level, 69% of applicants were admitted

Undergraduates 2,779 full-time, 336 part-time. Students come from 25 states and territories, 28 other countries, 10% are from out of state, 15% African American, 0.4% Asian American or Pacific Islander, 1% Hispanic American, 0.8% Native American, 3% international, 9% transferred in, 33% live on campus. *Retention:* 64% of 2001 full-time freshmen returned.

Freshmen *Admission:* 1,697 applied, 1,166 admitted, 490 enrolled. *Average high school GPA:* 3.26. *Test scores:* SAT verbal scores over 500: 56%; SAT math scores over 500: 67%; ACT scores over 18: 92%; SAT verbal scores over 600: 19%; SAT math scores over 600: 33%; ACT scores over 24: 35%; SAT verbal scores over 700: 4%; SAT math scores over 700: 4%; ACT scores over 30: 2%.

Faculty *Total:* 217, 75% full-time, 67% with terminal degrees. *Student/faculty ratio:* 16:1.

Majors Accounting; aircraft pilot (professional); art; art education; athletic training/sports medicine; biology; biology education; business; business education; chemistry; chemistry education; child care/guidance; computer/information sciences; early childhood education; elementary education; English; English education; history; home economics; home economics education; journalism; management information systems/business data processing; mathematics; mathematics education; medical technology; middle school education; music; music (general performance); music teacher education; nursing; painting; physical education; physics; physics education; political science; psychology; public administration; recreation/leisure facilities management; science education; secretarial science; social work; sociology; Spanish; Spanish language education; speech education; speech/rhetorical studies; teacher education, specific programs related; theater arts/drama.

Academic Programs *Special study options:* academic remediation for entering students, advanced placement credit, distance learning, honors programs, internships, off-campus study, part-time degree program, services for LD students, summer session for credit.

Library Huie Library with 274,639 titles, 11,500 serial subscriptions, 18,254 audiovisual materials, an OPAC, a Web page.

Computers on Campus 125 computers available on campus for general student use. A campuswide network can be accessed from student residence rooms and from off campus. At least one staffed computer lab available.

Student Life *Housing:* on-campus residence required for freshman year. *Options:* coed, men-only, women-only. *Activities and Organizations:* drama/theater group, student-run newspaper, radio and television station, choral group, marching band, Heart and Key, Student Government Association, Residence Hall Association, national fraternities, national sororities. *Campus security:* 24-hour patrols, controlled dormitory access. *Student Services:* health clinic, personal/psychological counseling.

Athletics Member NCAA. All Division II. *Intercollegiate sports:* baseball M(s), basketball M(s)/W(s), cross-country running W(s), football M(s), golf M, softball W(s), swimming M(s)/W(s), tennis M(s)/W(s), volleyball W(s). *Intramural sports:* basketball M/W, football M, golf M/W, soccer M, swimming M/W, tennis M/W, volleyball W.

Standardized Tests *Required:* SAT I or ACT (for admission). *Recommended:* ACT (for admission).

Costs (2001–02) *One-time required fee:* $20. *Tuition:* state resident $2736 full-time, $114 per semester hour part-time; nonresident $5472 full-time, $228 per semester hour part-time. Full-time tuition and fees vary according to course load. Part-time tuition and fees vary according to course load. *Room and board:* Room and board charges vary according to board plan and housing facility. *Waivers:* senior citizens and employees or children of employees.

Financial Aid Of all full-time matriculated undergraduates who enrolled in 2001, 2337 applied for aid, 1423 were judged to have need, 408 had their need fully met. 107 State and other part-time jobs (averaging $1648). In 2001, 411 non-need-based awards were made. *Average percent of need met:* 72%. *Average financial aid package:* $5482. *Average need-based loan:* $3610. *Average need-based gift aid:* $4200. *Average non-need based aid:* $5535. *Average indebtedness upon graduation:* $13,000.

Applying *Options:* electronic application, deferred entrance. *Required:* high school transcript. *Required for some:* essay or personal statement, 3 letters of recommendation. *Recommended:* minimum 2.5 GPA. *Application deadline:* 7/15 (freshmen), rolling (transfers). *Notification:* continuous (freshmen).

Admissions Contact Ms. Vikita Hardwrick, Director of University Relations/Admissions, Henderson State University, 1100 Henderson Street, PO Box 7560, Arkadelphia, AR 71999-0001. *Phone:* 870-230-5028. *Toll-free phone:* 800-228-7333. *Fax:* 870-230-5066. *E-mail:* hardwrv@hsu.edu.

HENDRIX COLLEGE
Conway, Arkansas

- **Independent United Methodist** comprehensive, founded 1876
- **Calendar** three courses for each of three terms
- **Degrees** bachelor's and master's
- **Suburban** 158-acre campus
- **Endowment** $120.2 million
- **Coed,** 1,079 undergraduate students, 99% full-time, 54% women, 46% men
- **Very difficult** entrance level, 82% of applicants were admitted

Undergraduates 1,067 full-time, 12 part-time. Students come from 32 states and territories, 13 other countries, 31% are from out of state, 5% African American, 2% Asian American or Pacific Islander, 2% Hispanic American, 1% Native American, 3% transferred in, 80% live on campus. *Retention:* 84% of 2001 full-time freshmen returned.

Freshmen *Admission:* 1,056 applied, 871 admitted, 279 enrolled. *Average high school GPA:* 3.70. *Test scores:* SAT verbal scores over 500: 94%; SAT math scores over 500: 89%; ACT scores over 18: 100%; SAT verbal scores over 600: 66%; SAT math scores over 600: 55%; ACT scores over 24: 87%; SAT verbal scores over 700: 20%; SAT math scores over 700: 10%; ACT scores over 30: 33%.

Faculty *Total:* 91, 87% full-time, 87% with terminal degrees. *Student/faculty ratio:* 13:1.

Majors Accounting; anthropology; art; biology; business economics; chemistry; computer science; economics; elementary education; English; French; German; history; interdisciplinary studies; international relations; mathematics; music; philosophy; physical education; physics; political science; psychology; religious studies; sociology; Spanish; theater arts/drama.

Academic Programs *Special study options:* advanced placement credit, double majors, independent study, internships, off-campus study, student-designed majors, study abroad. *ROTC:* Army (c). *Unusual degree programs:* 3-2 engineering with Columbia University, Vanderbilt University, Washington University in St. Louis.

Library Olin C. and Marjorie H. Bailey Library with 232,663 titles, 731 serial subscriptions, 4,965 audiovisual materials, an OPAC, a Web page.

Computers on Campus 75 computers available on campus for general student use. A campuswide network can be accessed from student residence rooms and from off campus. At least one staffed computer lab available.

Student Life *Housing:* on-campus residence required through senior year. *Options:* coed, men-only, women-only. *Activities and Organizations:* drama/theater group, student-run newspaper, radio station, choral group, Volunteer Action Center, Sophomore Council, Young Democrats, Big Buddy, Social Committee. *Campus security:* 24-hour emergency response devices and patrols, late-night transport/escort service, controlled dormitory access. *Student Services:* health clinic, personal/psychological counseling.

Athletics Member NCAA. All Division III. *Intercollegiate sports:* baseball M, basketball M/W, cross-country running M/W, golf M/W, rugby M(c), soccer M/W, softball W, swimming M/W, tennis M/W, track and field M/W, volleyball W. *Intramural sports:* badminton M/W, basketball M/W, football M/W, racquetball M/W, soccer M/W, softball M/W, tennis M/W, volleyball M/W.

Standardized Tests *Required:* SAT I or ACT (for admission).

Costs (2001–02) *Comprehensive fee:* $18,463 includes full-time tuition ($13,071), mandatory fees ($640), and room and board ($4752). Part-time tuition: $1452 per course. *Required fees:* $230 per term part-time. *Room and board:* College room only: $1992. Room and board charges vary according to housing facility. *Payment plan:* installment. *Waivers:* employees or children of employees.

Financial Aid Of all full-time matriculated undergraduates who enrolled in 2001, 683 applied for aid, 524 were judged to have need, 184 had their need fully met. 244 Federal Work-Study jobs (averaging $1441). 183 State and other part-time jobs (averaging $1173). *Average percent of need met:* 87%. *Average financial aid package:* $12,451. *Average need-based loan:* $4268. *Average need-based gift aid:* $8862. *Average indebtedness upon graduation:* $9048.

Applying *Options:* common application, electronic application, deferred entrance. *Application fee:* $40. *Required:* essay or personal statement, high school transcript. *Required for some:* interview. *Recommended:* 2 letters of recommendation. *Application deadline:* rolling (freshmen), rolling (transfers). *Notification:* continuous (freshmen).

Admissions Contact Mr. Art Weeden, Vice President for Enrollment, Hendrix College, 1600 Washington Avenue, Conway, AR 72032. *Phone:* 501-450-1362. *Toll-free phone:* 800-277-9017. *Fax:* 501-450-3843. *E-mail:* adm@hendrix.edu.

JOHN BROWN UNIVERSITY
Siloam Springs, Arkansas

- **Independent interdenominational** comprehensive, founded 1919
- **Calendar** semesters
- **Degrees** associate, bachelor's, and master's
- **Small-town** 200-acre campus
- **Endowment** $37.3 million
- **Coed,** 1,537 undergraduate students, 94% full-time, 55% women, 45% men
- **Moderately difficult** entrance level, 84% of applicants were admitted

Undergraduates 1,442 full-time, 95 part-time. Students come from 43 states and territories, 33 other countries, 68% are from out of state, 2% African American, 1.0% Asian American or Pacific Islander, 2% Hispanic American, 1% Native American, 8% international, 5% transferred in, 69% live on campus. *Retention:* 80% of 2001 full-time freshmen returned.

Freshmen *Admission:* 677 applied, 571 admitted, 242 enrolled. *Average high school GPA:* 3.51. *Test scores:* SAT verbal scores over 500: 76%; SAT math scores over 500: 80%; ACT scores over 18: 93%; SAT verbal scores over 600: 32%; SAT math scores over 600: 36%; ACT scores over 24: 51%; SAT verbal scores over 700: 9%; SAT math scores over 700: 8%; ACT scores over 30: 9%.

Faculty *Total:* 120, 78% full-time, 66% with terminal degrees. *Student/faculty ratio:* 16:1.

Majors Accounting; art; athletic training/sports medicine; biblical studies; biochemistry; biology; broadcast journalism; business administration; business education; chemistry; computer graphics; construction engineering; construction management; divinity/ministry; early childhood education; education; electrical engineering; elementary education; engineering; engineering/industrial management; engineering technology; English; environmental science; exercise sciences; graphic design/commercial art/illustration; health education; health services administration; history; interdisciplinary studies; international business; international relations; journalism; liberal arts and sciences/liberal studies; mass communications; mathematics; mechanical engineering; medical technology; middle school education; missionary studies; music; music (piano and organ performance); music teacher education; music (voice and choral/opera performance); pastoral counseling; physical education; pre-law; pre-medicine; pre-veterinary studies; psychology; public relations; radio/television broadcasting; recreation/leisure facilities management; religious education; religious studies; secondary education; social sciences; special education; teaching English as a second language; theology.

Academic Programs *Special study options:* academic remediation for entering students, adult/continuing education programs, advanced placement credit, double majors, English as a second language, external degree program, freshman honors college, honors programs, independent study, internships, services for LD students, study abroad. *ROTC:* Army (c), Air Force (c).

Library Arutunoff Learning Resource Center plus 4 others with 93,190 titles, 1,580 serial subscriptions, 8,310 audiovisual materials, an OPAC, a Web page.

Computers on Campus 75 computers available on campus for general student use. A campuswide network can be accessed from student residence rooms and from off campus. Internet access, at least one staffed computer lab available.

Student Life *Housing:* on-campus residence required through junior year. *Options:* coed, men-only, women-only. *Activities and Organizations:* drama/theater group, student-run newspaper, radio and television station, choral group, Student Government Association, Student Ministries Organization, Student Missionary Fellowship, African Heritage Fellowship. *Campus security:* 24-hour emergency response devices and patrols, late-night transport/escort service. *Student Services:* health clinic, personal/psychological counseling.

Athletics Member NAIA. *Intercollegiate sports:* basketball M(s)/W(s), soccer M(s), swimming M(s)/W(s), tennis M(s)/W(s), volleyball W(s). *Intramural sports:* baseball M, basketball M/W, football M/W, racquetball M/W, rugby M, soccer M/W, softball M/W, tennis M/W, volleyball M/W.

Standardized Tests *Required:* SAT I or ACT (for admission).

Costs (2002–03) *Comprehensive fee:* $17,822 includes full-time tuition ($12,464), mandatory fees ($560), and room and board ($4798). Part-time tuition: $450 per credit hour. Part-time tuition and fees vary according to course load and program. *Room and board:* Room and board charges vary according to board plan and housing facility. *Waivers:* minority students, adult students, senior citizens, and employees or children of employees.

Financial Aid Of all full-time matriculated undergraduates who enrolled in 2001, 873 applied for aid, 767 were judged to have need, 156 had their need fully met. 243 Federal Work-Study jobs (averaging $1540). In 2001, 258 non-need-based awards were made. *Average percent of need met:* 56%. *Average financial aid package:* $10,439. *Average need-based loan:* $4866. *Average need-based gift aid:* $6858.

Applying *Options:* common application, deferred entrance. *Application fee:* $25. *Required:* essay or personal statement, high school transcript, minimum 2.5 GPA, 2 letters of recommendation. *Recommended:* interview. *Application deadlines:* 3/1 (freshmen), 3/1 (transfers). *Notification:* 5/1 (freshmen).

Admissions Contact Ms. Karyn Byrne, Application Coordinator, John Brown University, 200 West University Street, Siloam Springs, AR 72761-2121. *Phone:* 501-524-7454. *Toll-free phone:* 877-JBU-INFO. *Fax:* 501-524-4196. *E-mail:* jbuinfo@acc.jbu.edu.

LYON COLLEGE
Batesville, Arkansas

- **Independent Presbyterian** 4-year, founded 1872
- **Calendar** semesters
- **Degree** bachelor's
- **Small-town** 136-acre campus
- **Endowment** $48.6 million
- **Coed,** 526 undergraduate students, 92% full-time, 57% women, 43% men
- **Very difficult** entrance level, 78% of applicants were admitted

Challenging yet supportive, selective yet affordable, Lyon has won recognition as one of the South's finest liberal arts colleges. The College's acclaimed faculty members, residential house system, student-run honor system, and international study opportunities all help prepare Lyon graduates for success. Students will succeed in graduate and professional school, in their careers, and in their lives.

Undergraduates 486 full-time, 40 part-time. Students come from 21 states and territories, 15 other countries, 17% are from out of state, 3% African American, 1% Asian American or Pacific Islander, 2% Hispanic American, 1% Native American, 5% international, 6% transferred in, 76% live on campus. *Retention:* 87% of 2001 full-time freshmen returned.

Freshmen *Admission:* 439 applied, 344 admitted, 127 enrolled. *Average high school GPA:* 3.56. *Test scores:* SAT verbal scores over 500: 74%; SAT math scores over 500: 74%; ACT scores over 18: 98%; SAT verbal scores over 600: 29%; SAT math scores over 600: 33%; ACT scores over 24: 66%; SAT math scores over 700: 4%; ACT scores over 30: 8%.

Faculty *Total:* 56, 73% full-time, 66% with terminal degrees. *Student/faculty ratio:* 11:1.

Majors Accounting; art; biology; business administration; chemistry; computer science; economics; English; environmental science; history; mathematics; music; philosophy and religion related; political science; psychology; Spanish; theater arts/drama.

Academic Programs *Special study options:* academic remediation for entering students, advanced placement credit, double majors, independent study, internships, part-time degree program, student-designed majors, study abroad, summer session for credit. *Unusual degree programs:* 3-2 engineering with University of Missouri-Rolla.

Library Mabee-Simpson Library with 147,893 titles, 1,160 serial subscriptions, 5,250 audiovisual materials, an OPAC, a Web page.

Computers on Campus 60 computers available on campus for general student use. A campuswide network can be accessed from student residence rooms and from off campus. Internet access, at least one staffed computer lab available.

Student Life *Housing:* on-campus residence required through senior year. *Options:* men-only, women-only. *Activities and Organizations:* drama/theater group, student-run newspaper, choral group, Baptist Christian Ministry, Ambassadors, Student Activities Council, Black Students' Association, concert choir, national fraternities, national sororities. *Campus security:* 24-hour patrols, late-night transport/escort service. *Student Services:* health clinic, personal/psychological counseling.

Athletics Member NAIA. *Intercollegiate sports:* baseball M(s), basketball M(s)/W(s), cross-country running M(s)/W(s), golf M(s)/W(s), soccer M, tennis M(s)/W(s), volleyball W(s). *Intramural sports:* archery M/W, badminton M/W, basketball M/W, football M/W, racquetball M/W, soccer M/W, softball M/W, table tennis M/W, tennis M/W, volleyball M/W.

Standardized Tests *Required:* SAT I or ACT (for admission).

Costs (2002–03) *One-time required fee:* $200. *Comprehensive fee:* $17,320 includes full-time tuition ($11,540), mandatory fees ($400), and room and board ($5380). Part-time tuition: $480 per credit hour. Part-time tuition and fees vary according to course load. *Room and board:* College room only: $2215. *Payment plan:* installment. *Waivers:* employees or children of employees.

Financial Aid Of all full-time matriculated undergraduates who enrolled in 2001, 341 applied for aid, 304 were judged to have need, 101 had their need fully met. 120 Federal Work-Study jobs (averaging $986). 57 State and other part-time jobs (averaging $1221). In 2001, 143 non-need-based awards were made. *Average*

Lyon College (continued)
percent of need met: 75%. *Average financial aid package:* $12,558. *Average need-based loan:* $3459. *Average need-based gift aid:* $9516. *Average indebtedness upon graduation:* $13,104.

Applying *Options:* common application, electronic application, deferred entrance. *Application fee:* $25. *Required:* essay or personal statement, high school transcript, 1 letter of recommendation. *Recommended:* minimum 2.5 GPA, interview. *Application deadline:* rolling (freshmen), rolling (transfers). *Notification:* continuous (freshmen).

Admissions Contact Lyon College, PO Box 2317, Batesville, AR 72503-2317. *Phone:* 870-698-4250. *Toll-free phone:* 800-423-2542. *Fax:* 870-793-1791. *E-mail:* admissions@lyon.edu.

OUACHITA BAPTIST UNIVERSITY
Arkadelphia, Arkansas

- **Independent Baptist** 4-year, founded 1886
- **Calendar** semesters
- **Degrees** associate and bachelor's
- **Small-town** 84-acre campus with easy access to Little Rock
- **Endowment** $45.2 million
- **Coed,** 1,657 undergraduate students, 96% full-time, 53% women, 47% men
- **Moderately difficult** entrance level, 84% of applicants were admitted

Undergraduates 1,584 full-time, 73 part-time. Students come from 32 states and territories, 62 other countries, 47% are from out of state, 4% African American, 0.4% Asian American or Pacific Islander, 0.7% Hispanic American, 0.2% Native American, 4% international, 3% transferred in, 83% live on campus. *Retention:* 74% of 2001 full-time freshmen returned.

Freshmen *Admission:* 863 applied, 724 admitted, 401 enrolled. *Average high school GPA:* 3.45. *Test scores:* SAT verbal scores over 500: 77%; SAT math scores over 500: 70%; ACT scores over 18: 95%; SAT verbal scores over 600: 36%; SAT math scores over 600: 31%; ACT scores over 24: 50%; SAT verbal scores over 700: 7%; SAT math scores over 700: 4%; ACT scores over 30: 15%.

Faculty *Total:* 147, 76% full-time, 57% with terminal degrees. *Student/faculty ratio:* 13:1.

Majors Accounting; art; art education; biblical studies; biology; business administration; business education; business marketing and marketing management; chemistry; computer science; dietetics; early childhood education; education; English; finance; French; history; home economics; home economics education; mass communications; mathematics; middle school education; music; music (piano and organ performance); music teacher education; music theory and composition; music (voice and choral/opera performance); pastoral counseling; philosophy; physical education; physics; political science; pre-dentistry; psychology; religious music; religious studies; Russian; science education; secondary education; social sciences; sociology; Spanish; special education; speech-language pathology/audiology; speech/rhetorical studies; theater arts/drama; theology.

Academic Programs *Special study options:* academic remediation for entering students, accelerated degree program, advanced placement credit, cooperative education, double majors, English as a second language, honors programs, internships, off-campus study, part-time degree program, study abroad, summer session for credit. *ROTC:* Army (c).

Library Riley-Hickinbotham Library plus 1 other with 139,278 titles, 1,931 serial subscriptions, 8,306 audiovisual materials, an OPAC.

Computers on Campus 164 computers available on campus for general student use. A campuswide network can be accessed from student residence rooms and from off campus. Internet access, at least one staffed computer lab available.

Student Life *Housing:* on-campus residence required through senior year. *Options:* men-only, women-only. *Activities and Organizations:* drama/theater group, student-run newspaper, television station, choral group, marching band, Phi Beta Lambda, SELF, Student Education Association, Student Foundation, International Club. *Campus security:* 24-hour emergency response devices and patrols, controlled dormitory access. *Student Services:* health clinic, personal/psychological counseling.

Athletics Member NCAA. All Division II. *Intercollegiate sports:* baseball M(s), basketball M(s)/W(s), cross-country running M/W, football M(s), golf M(s), soccer M/W, swimming M(s)/W(s), tennis M(s)/W(s), volleyball W(s). *Intramural sports:* basketball M/W, football M/W, soccer M, softball M/W.

Standardized Tests *Required:* SAT I or ACT (for admission).

Costs (2001–02) *Comprehensive fee:* $16,460 includes full-time tuition ($11,800), mandatory fees ($210), and room and board ($4450). Full-time tuition and fees vary according to course load. Part-time tuition: $347 per semester hour. Part-time tuition and fees vary according to course load. No tuition increase for student's term of enrollment. *Room and board:* Room and board charges vary according to board plan and housing facility. *Payment plans:* tuition prepayment, installment. *Waivers:* employees or children of employees.

Financial Aid Of all full-time matriculated undergraduates who enrolled in 2001, 1263 applied for aid, 811 were judged to have need, 200 had their need fully met. 410 Federal Work-Study jobs (averaging $1500). 296 State and other part-time jobs (averaging $1560). In 2001, 450 non-need-based awards were made. *Average percent of need met:* 75%. *Average financial aid package:* $12,500. *Average need-based loan:* $3669. *Average need-based gift aid:* $6689. *Average indebtedness upon graduation:* $11,660. *Financial aid deadline:* 6/1.

Applying *Options:* early admission, deferred entrance. *Application fee:* $25. *Required:* high school transcript, minimum 2.5 GPA. *Recommended:* interview. *Application deadlines:* 8/15 (freshmen), 8/15 (transfers). *Notification:* continuous (freshmen).

Admissions Contact Mrs. Rebecca Jones, Director of Admissions Counseling, Ouachita Baptist University, 410 Ouachita Street, Arkadelphia, AR 71998-0001. *Phone:* 870-245-5110. *Toll-free phone:* 800-342-5628. *Fax:* 870-245-5500. *E-mail:* jonesj@sigma.obu.edu.

PHILANDER SMITH COLLEGE
Little Rock, Arkansas

- **Independent United Methodist** 4-year, founded 1877
- **Calendar** semesters
- **Degree** bachelor's
- **Urban** 25-acre campus
- **Endowment** $9.6 million
- **Coed,** 859 undergraduate students, 77% full-time, 64% women, 36% men
- **Noncompetitive** entrance level, 73% of applicants were admitted

Undergraduates 662 full-time, 197 part-time. Students come from 14 states and territories, 19 other countries, 9% are from out of state, 97% African American, 0.7% Hispanic American, 2% international, 9% transferred in, 17% live on campus. *Retention:* 60% of 2001 full-time freshmen returned.

Freshmen *Admission:* 264 applied, 194 admitted, 171 enrolled. *Average high school GPA:* 2.44. *Test scores:* ACT scores over 18: 24%; ACT scores over 24: 1%.

Faculty *Total:* 82, 57% full-time, 48% with terminal degrees. *Student/faculty ratio:* 12:1.

Majors Biological/physical sciences; biology; business administration; chemistry; computer science; early childhood education; education administration/supervision related; elementary/middle/secondary education administration; English; health/physical education; hospitality management; mathematics; music; organizational behavior; political science; psychology; religious studies; social work; sociology.

Academic Programs *Special study options:* academic remediation for entering students, adult/continuing education programs, cooperative education, independent study, internships, services for LD students, summer session for credit. *ROTC:* Army (c).

Library M. L. Harris Library with 60,000 titles, 280 serial subscriptions, 196 audiovisual materials, an OPAC, a Web page.

Computers on Campus 95 computers available on campus for general student use. A campuswide network can be accessed from off campus. Internet access, at least one staffed computer lab available.

Student Life *Housing:* on-campus residence required for freshman year. *Options:* men-only, women-only. *Activities and Organizations:* drama/theater group, student-run newspaper, choral group, Student Government Association, Pre-Alumni Council, Student Christian, Delta Sigma Theta Sorority, Inc., national fraternities, national sororities. *Campus security:* 24-hour patrols. *Student Services:* health clinic, personal/psychological counseling.

Athletics Member NSCAA. *Intercollegiate sports:* basketball M/W, volleyball W.

Standardized Tests *Required:* SAT I or ACT (for placement).

Costs (2001–02) *Comprehensive fee:* $7366 includes full-time tuition ($4056), mandatory fees ($264), and room and board ($3046). Part-time tuition: $169 per credit hour. *Required fees:* $11 per credit hour. *Room and board:* College room only: $1484.

Applying *Options:* common application, electronic application, deferred entrance. *Application fee:* $10. *Required:* high school transcript. *Application deadline:* rolling (freshmen), rolling (transfers). *Notification:* continuous (freshmen).

Admissions Contact Mrs. Arnella Hayes, Admission Officer, Philander Smith College, 812 West 13th Street, Little Rock, AR 72202-3718. *Phone:* 501-370-5310. *Toll-free phone:* 800-446-6772. *Fax:* 501-370-5225. *E-mail:* admissions@philander.edu.

SOUTHERN ARKANSAS UNIVERSITY-MAGNOLIA
Magnolia, Arkansas

- **State-supported** comprehensive, founded 1909, part of Southern Arkansas University System
- **Calendar** semesters
- **Degrees** associate, bachelor's, and master's
- **Small-town** 781-acre campus
- **Endowment** $15.6 million
- **Coed,** 2,863 undergraduate students, 86% full-time, 56% women, 44% men
- **Moderately difficult** entrance level, 82% of applicants were admitted

Undergraduates 2,473 full-time, 390 part-time. Students come from 24 states and territories, 33 other countries, 22% are from out of state, 24% African American, 0.2% Asian American or Pacific Islander, 2% Hispanic American, 0.4% Native American, 4% international, 8% transferred in, 37% live on campus. *Retention:* 67% of 2001 full-time freshmen returned.

Freshmen *Admission:* 1,142 applied, 938 admitted, 581 enrolled. *Test scores:* ACT scores over 18: 77%; ACT scores over 24: 22%; ACT scores over 30: 1%.

Faculty *Total:* 168, 73% full-time, 56% with terminal degrees. *Student/faculty ratio:* 20:1.

Majors Accounting; agricultural business; agricultural education; agricultural sciences; art; art education; biological/physical sciences; biology; biology education; broadcast journalism; business; business education; chemistry; chemistry education; community services; computer/information sciences; criminal justice studies; early childhood education; elementary education; engineering physics; English; English education; exercise sciences; general studies; history; industrial technology; journalism; mass communications; mathematics; mathematics education; medical technology; music teacher education; nursing; physical education; physics education; political science; psychology; science education; secretarial science; social studies education; social work; sociology; Spanish; Spanish language education; theater arts/drama.

Academic Programs *Special study options:* academic remediation for entering students, accelerated degree program, adult/continuing education programs, advanced placement credit, distance learning, double majors, independent study, internships, part-time degree program, services for LD students, study abroad, summer session for credit.

Library Magale Library with 1.1 million titles, 965 serial subscriptions, 9,877 audiovisual materials, an OPAC, a Web page.

Computers on Campus 150 computers available on campus for general student use. A campuswide network can be accessed from off campus. Internet access, at least one staffed computer lab available.

Student Life *Housing:* on-campus residence required through sophomore year. *Options:* men-only, women-only. *Activities and Organizations:* drama/theater group, student-run newspaper, radio station, choral group, marching band, Student Government Association, IMPACT, national fraternities, national sororities. *Campus security:* 24-hour emergency response devices, student patrols, late-night transport/escort service, controlled dormitory access. *Student Services:* health clinic, personal/psychological counseling.

Athletics Member NCAA. All Division II. *Intercollegiate sports:* baseball M(s), basketball M(s)/W(s), cross-country running M/W(s), football M(s), golf M, softball W(s), tennis W(s), track and field M/W, volleyball W(s). *Intramural sports:* badminton M/W, basketball M/W, football M, golf M, softball M/W, swimming M/W, table tennis M/W, tennis M/W, volleyball M/W.

Standardized Tests *Required:* ACT (for admission).

Costs (2001–02) *Tuition:* state resident $2496 full-time, $104 per credit hour part-time; nonresident $3840 full-time, $160 per credit hour part-time. Full-time tuition and fees vary according to course load. Part-time tuition and fees vary according to course load. *Required fees:* $220 full-time, $6 per credit hour. *Room and board:* $3082. *Payment plans:* installment, deferred payment. *Waivers:* children of alumni, senior citizens, and employees or children of employees.

Financial Aid Of all full-time matriculated undergraduates who enrolled in 2001, 1964 applied for aid, 1300 were judged to have need, 1184 had their need fully met. 857 Federal Work-Study jobs (averaging $2468). In 2001, 388 non-need-based awards were made. *Average percent of need met:* 100%. *Average financial aid package:* $6059. *Average need-based loan:* $2912. *Average need-based gift aid:* $3498. *Average non-need based aid:* $2604. *Average indebtedness upon graduation:* $15,075.

Applying *Options:* early admission, deferred entrance. *Required:* high school transcript. *Application deadlines:* 8/15 (freshmen), 8/15 (transfers).

Admissions Contact Ms. Sarah Jennings, Dean of Enrollment Services, Southern Arkansas University-Magnolia, PO Box 9382, 100 East University, Magnolia, AR 71754-9382. *Phone:* 870-235-4040. *Fax:* 870-235-5005. *E-mail:* addanne@saumag.edu.

UNIVERSITY OF ARKANSAS
Fayetteville, Arkansas

- **State-supported** university, founded 1871, part of University of Arkansas System
- **Calendar** semesters
- **Degrees** bachelor's, master's, doctoral, and first professional
- **Suburban** 445-acre campus
- **Endowment** $234.0 million
- **Coed,** 12,818 undergraduate students, 84% full-time, 48% women, 52% men
- **Moderately difficult** entrance level, 89% of applicants were admitted

Undergraduates 10,825 full-time, 1,993 part-time. Students come from 49 states and territories, 109 other countries, 9% are from out of state, 6% African American, 3% Asian American or Pacific Islander, 1% Hispanic American, 2% Native American, 3% international, 9% transferred in, 23% live on campus. *Retention:* 82% of 2001 full-time freshmen returned.

Freshmen *Admission:* 4,470 applied, 3,994 admitted, 2,330 enrolled. *Average high school GPA:* 3.52. *Test scores:* SAT verbal scores over 500: 76%; SAT math scores over 500: 81%; ACT scores over 18: 99%; SAT verbal scores over 600: 37%; SAT math scores over 600: 42%; ACT scores over 24: 58%; SAT verbal scores over 700: 8%; SAT math scores over 700: 9%; ACT scores over 30: 16%.

Faculty *Total:* 866, 92% full-time. *Student/faculty ratio:* 16:1.

Majors Accounting; agribusiness; agricultural education; agricultural engineering; agronomy/crop science; American studies; animal sciences; anthropology; architecture; art; biology; botany; business; business administration; business economics; business marketing and marketing management; chemical engineering; chemistry; civil engineering; classics; clothing/apparel/textile studies; communications; computer engineering; computer/information sciences; criminal justice studies; data processing technology; earth sciences; economics; electrical engineering; elementary education; English; finance; food sciences; French; geography; geology; German; health/physical education; health professions and related sciences; history; home economics; horticulture science; housing studies; individual/family development; industrial/manufacturing engineering; international business; international relations; journalism; landscape architecture; logistics/materials management; mathematics; mechanical engineering; microbiology/bacteriology; Middle Eastern studies; middle school education; multi/interdisciplinary studies related; music (general performance); nursing; nutrition studies; ornamental horticulture; philosophy; physics; plant protection; political science; poultry science; pre-medicine; psychology; public administration; recreation/leisure studies; social work; sociology; Spanish; special education; speech-language pathology/audiology; theater arts/drama; trade/industrial education; zoology.

Academic Programs *Special study options:* advanced placement credit, cooperative education, distance learning, double majors, English as a second language, honors programs, independent study, internships, off-campus study, part-time degree program, services for LD students, study abroad, summer session for credit. *ROTC:* Army (b), Air Force (b).

Library David W. Mullins Library plus 5 others with 643,468 titles, 15,431 serial subscriptions, 26,673 audiovisual materials, an OPAC, a Web page.

Computers on Campus 1415 computers available on campus for general student use. A campuswide network can be accessed from student residence rooms and from off campus. Internet access, at least one staffed computer lab available.

Student Life *Housing:* on-campus residence required for freshman year. *Options:* coed, men-only, women-only. *Activities and Organizations:* drama/theater group, student-run newspaper, radio and television station, choral group, marching band, University Programs, Booster Club, Associated Student Government, Black Students Association, Alpha Phi Omega, national fraternities, national sororities. *Campus security:* 24-hour emergency response devices and patrols, student patrols, late-night transport/escort service, controlled dormitory access, RAD (Rape Aggression Defense program). *Student Services:* health clinic, personal/psychological counseling, women's center, legal services.

Athletics Member NCAA. All Division I except football (Division I-A). *Intercollegiate sports:* baseball M(s), basketball M(s)/W(s), cross-country running M(s)/W(s), golf M(s)/W(s), gymnastics W(s), soccer W(s), softball W(s), swimming W(s), tennis M(s)/W(s), track and field M(s)/W(s), volleyball W(s). *Intramural sports:* badminton M/W, basketball M/W, bowling M(c)/W(c), football M/W, golf M/W, racquetball M/W, rugby M(c)/W(c), soccer M/W, softball M/W, swimming M/W, table tennis M/W, tennis M/W, volleyball M(c)/W(c), water polo M/W.

Standardized Tests *Required:* SAT I or ACT (for admission).

Costs (2001–02) *Tuition:* state resident $3116 full-time, $113 per credit hour part-time; nonresident $8674 full-time, $309 per credit hour part-time. Full-time tuition and fees vary according to course load, degree level, program, and student level. Part-time tuition and fees vary according to course load, degree level,

University of Arkansas (continued)
program, and student level. *Required fees:* $764 full-time. *Room and board:* $4454. Room and board charges vary according to board plan and housing facility. *Payment plan:* installment. *Waivers:* senior citizens and employees or children of employees.

Financial Aid Of all full-time matriculated undergraduates who enrolled in 2001, 6505 applied for aid, 4856 were judged to have need, 1704 had their need fully met. 933 Federal Work-Study jobs (averaging $1941). In 2001, 2724 non-need-based awards were made. *Average percent of need met:* 74%. *Average financial aid package:* $8028. *Average need-based loan:* $3848. *Average need-based gift aid:* $3377. *Average non-need based aid:* $5771. *Average indebtedness upon graduation:* $19,383.

Applying *Options:* common application, electronic application, early admission, early action, deferred entrance. *Application fee:* $30. *Required:* high school transcript. *Required for some:* letters of recommendation. *Recommended:* essay or personal statement, minimum 3.0 GPA, 1 letter of recommendation. *Application deadlines:* 8/15 (freshmen), 8/15 (transfers). *Notification:* 11/15 (freshmen), 12/15 (early action).

Admissions Contact Ms. Maxine Jones, Interim Director, University of Arkansas, 200 Silas H. Hunt Hall, Fayetteville, AR 72701-1201. *Phone:* 479-575-5346. *Toll-free phone:* 800-377-8632. *Fax:* 479-575-7515. *E-mail:* uafadmis@uark.edu.

UNIVERSITY OF ARKANSAS AT FORT SMITH
Fort Smith, Arkansas

- **State and locally supported** primarily 2-year, founded 1928, part of University of Arkansas System
- **Calendar** semesters
- **Degrees** certificates, associate, and bachelor's
- **Suburban** 108-acre campus
- **Endowment** $27.4 million
- **Coed,** 5,746 undergraduate students, 44% full-time, 57% women, 43% men
- **Noncompetitive** entrance level, 100% of applicants were admitted

Undergraduates 2,541 full-time, 3,205 part-time. Students come from 22 states and territories, 3 other countries, 11% are from out of state, 4% African American, 4% Asian American or Pacific Islander, 2% Hispanic American, 3% Native American, 0.3% international, 6% transferred in. *Retention:* 55% of 2001 full-time freshmen returned.

Freshmen *Admission:* 1,921 applied, 1,921 admitted, 1,153 enrolled. *Average high school GPA:* 3.05. *Test scores:* SAT verbal scores over 500: 25%; ACT scores over 18: 72%; ACT scores over 24: 18%.

Faculty *Total:* 293, 48% full-time. *Student/faculty ratio:* 19:1.

Majors Auto mechanic/technician; business administration; cartography; dental hygiene; drafting; electrical/electronic engineering technology; emergency medical technology; environmental technology; general studies; gerontological services; graphic design/commercial art/illustration; industrial technology; liberal arts and sciences/liberal studies; machine technology; management information systems/business data processing; medical radiologic technology; multi/interdisciplinary studies related; nursing; operating room technician; paralegal/legal assistant; respiratory therapy; secretarial science; welding technology.

Academic Programs *Special study options:* academic remediation for entering students, accelerated degree program, adult/continuing education programs, advanced placement credit, cooperative education, distance learning, English as a second language, honors programs, internships, off-campus study, part-time degree program, services for LD students, summer session for credit.

Library Boreham Library with 59,101 titles, 647 serial subscriptions, 1,266 audiovisual materials, an OPAC, a Web page.

Computers on Campus 919 computers available on campus for general student use. A campuswide network can be accessed from off campus that provide access to online grade reports, online subscription databases. Internet access, online (class) registration, at least one staffed computer lab available.

Student Life *Housing:* college housing not available. *Activities and Organizations:* student-run newspaper, choral group, Student Activities Council, Phi Beta Lambda, Phi Theta Kappa, student publications, Baptist Student Union. *Campus security:* 24-hour emergency response devices and patrols, late-night transport/escort service.

Athletics Member NJCAA. *Intercollegiate sports:* baseball M(s), basketball M(s)/W(s), volleyball W(s). *Intramural sports:* basketball M/W, football M, table tennis M/W.

Standardized Tests *Required for some:* ACT ASSET, ACT COMPASS. *Recommended:* ACT (for placement).

Costs (2001–02) *Tuition:* area resident $1260 full-time, $41 per credit part-time; state resident $1590 full-time, $52 per credit part-time; nonresident $3090 full-time, $102 per credit part-time. Full-time tuition and fees vary according to class time and degree level. Part-time tuition and fees vary according to class time and degree level. *Required fees:* $30 full-time, $15 per term part-time. *Payment plan:* installment. *Waivers:* senior citizens and employees or children of employees.

Financial Aid Of all full-time matriculated undergraduates who enrolled in 2001, 110 Federal Work-Study jobs (averaging $3000). 94 State and other part-time jobs (averaging $3000).

Applying *Options:* early admission, deferred entrance. *Required:* high school transcript. *Application deadline:* rolling (freshmen), rolling (transfers).

Admissions Contact Mr. Scott McDonald, Director of Admissions and School Relations, University of Arkansas at Fort Smith, 5210 Grand Avenue, PO Box 3649, Fort Smith, AR 72913-3649. *Phone:* 501-788-7125. *Toll-free phone:* 888-512-5466. *Fax:* 501-788-7016. *E-mail:* westark@systema.westark.edu.

UNIVERSITY OF ARKANSAS AT LITTLE ROCK
Little Rock, Arkansas

- **State-supported** university, founded 1927, part of University of Arkansas System
- **Calendar** semesters
- **Degrees** certificates, associate, bachelor's, master's, doctoral, first professional, and post-master's certificates
- **Urban** 150-acre campus
- **Endowment** $7.6 million
- **Coed,** 9,184 undergraduate students, 59% full-time, 62% women, 38% men
- **Minimally difficult** entrance level, 97% of applicants were admitted

Undergraduates 5,447 full-time, 3,737 part-time. Students come from 45 states and territories, 43 other countries, 4% are from out of state, 32% African American, 2% Asian American or Pacific Islander, 2% Hispanic American, 0.6% Native American, 3% international, 8% transferred in, 3% live on campus. *Retention:* 64% of 2001 full-time freshmen returned.

Freshmen *Admission:* 960 applied, 933 admitted, 795 enrolled.

Faculty *Total:* 793, 60% full-time. *Student/faculty ratio:* 11:1.

Majors Accounting; advertising; anthropology; art; art history; biology; business; business administration; business marketing and marketing management; chemistry; computer engineering technology; computer programming; computer science; construction technology; criminal justice/law enforcement administration; early childhood education; economics; education; education of the hearing impaired; electrical/electronic engineering technology; elementary education; English; environmental health; finance; French; general studies; geology; health education; health science; history; information sciences/systems; international business; international relations; journalism; landscape architecture; law enforcement/police science; liberal arts and sciences/liberal studies; mathematics; mechanical engineering technology; music; nursing; philosophy; physics; political science; psychology; radio/television broadcasting; sign language interpretation; social work; sociology; Spanish; speech-language pathology/audiology; speech/rhetorical studies; surveying; technical/business writing; theater arts/drama.

Academic Programs *Special study options:* academic remediation for entering students, accelerated degree program, adult/continuing education programs, advanced placement credit, cooperative education, English as a second language, freshman honors college, honors programs, independent study, internships, off-campus study, part-time degree program, services for LD students, student-designed majors, study abroad, summer session for credit. *ROTC:* Army (b).

Library Ottenheimer Library plus 1 other with 3,998 serial subscriptions, an OPAC.

Computers on Campus 500 computers available on campus for general student use. A campuswide network can be accessed from off campus. Internet access, at least one staffed computer lab available.

Student Life *Housing Options:* coed. *Activities and Organizations:* student-run newspaper, choral group, national fraternities, national sororities. *Campus security:* 24-hour emergency response devices, student patrols, late-night transport/escort service. *Student Services:* health clinic, personal/psychological counseling, women's center.

Athletics Member NCAA. All Division I. *Intercollegiate sports:* baseball M(s), basketball M(s), cross-country running M(s)/W(s), golf M(s)/W(s), soccer W(s), swimming W, tennis M(s)/W(s), track and field M/W(s), volleyball W(s). *Intramural sports:* archery M/W, badminton M/W, basketball M, bowling M/W, football M/W, golf M/W, swimming M/W, table tennis M/W, tennis M/W, volleyball M/W.

Standardized Tests *Required:* SAT I or ACT (for placement).

Costs (2001–02) *Tuition:* state resident $2664 full-time, $111 per credit hour part-time; nonresident $6894 full-time, $286 per credit hour part-time. *Required fees:* $474 full-time, $20 per credit hour. *Room and board:* room only: $2600.

Applying *Options:* early admission, deferred entrance. *Required:* high school transcript, minimum 2.5 GPA, proof of immunization. *Application deadline:* rolling (freshmen), rolling (transfers). *Notification:* continuous (freshmen).

Admissions Contact John Noah, Director of Admissions, University of Arkansas at Little Rock, 2801 South University Avenue, Little Rock, AR 72204-1099. *Phone:* 501-569-3127. *Toll-free phone:* 800-482-8892. *Fax:* 501-569-8915.

UNIVERSITY OF ARKANSAS AT MONTICELLO
Monticello, Arkansas

- **State-supported** comprehensive, founded 1909, part of University of Arkansas System
- **Calendar** semesters
- **Degrees** associate, bachelor's, and master's
- **Small-town** 400-acre campus
- **Coed**
- **Noncompetitive** entrance level

Faculty *Student/faculty ratio:* 17:1.

Student Life *Campus security:* 24-hour emergency response devices and patrols.

Athletics Member NCAA. All Division II.

Standardized Tests *Required:* SAT I or ACT (for placement). *Recommended:* ACT (for placement).

Costs (2001–02) *Tuition:* state resident $2250 full-time, $75 per hour part-time; nonresident $5190 full-time, $173 per hour part-time. *Required fees:* $420 full-time, $14 per hour, $5 per hour part-time. *Room and board:* $2780. Room and board charges vary according to board plan and housing facility.

Financial Aid Of all full-time matriculated undergraduates who enrolled in 2001, 189 Federal Work-Study jobs (averaging $929). 296 State and other part-time jobs (averaging $1163). *Average indebtedness upon graduation:* $13,599.

Applying *Options:* early admission, deferred entrance. *Required:* high school transcript, proof of immunization.

Admissions Contact Mary Whiting, Director of Admissions, University of Arkansas at Monticello, PO Box 3600, Monticello, AR 71656. *Phone:* 870-460-1026. *Toll-free phone:* 800-844-1826. *Fax:* 870-460-1321. *E-mail:* admissions@uamont.edu.

UNIVERSITY OF ARKANSAS AT PINE BLUFF
Pine Bluff, Arkansas

- **State-supported** comprehensive, founded 1873, part of University of Arkansas System
- **Calendar** semesters
- **Degrees** associate, bachelor's, and master's
- **Urban** 327-acre campus
- **Coed,** 3,052 undergraduate students, 89% full-time, 56% women, 44% men
- **Minimally difficult** entrance level, 72% of applicants were admitted

Undergraduates 2,729 full-time, 323 part-time. Students come from 30 states and territories, 17 other countries, 18% are from out of state, 96% African American, 0.1% Asian American or Pacific Islander, 0.2% Hispanic American, 0.0% Native American, 0.9% international, 5% transferred in. *Retention:* 70% of 2001 full-time freshmen returned.

Freshmen *Admission:* 1,631 applied, 1,173 admitted, 709 enrolled. *Test scores:* SAT verbal scores over 500: 13%; SAT math scores over 500: 16%; ACT scores over 18: 31%; ACT scores over 24: 2%.

Faculty *Total:* 217, 79% full-time, 45% with terminal degrees. *Student/faculty ratio:* 16:1.

Majors Accounting; agricultural economics; agricultural education; agricultural sciences; agronomy/crop science; animal sciences; art; art education; auto mechanic/technician; biology; business administration; business economics; business education; chemistry; clothing/textiles; computer science; corrections; criminal justice/law enforcement administration; dietetics; early childhood education; economics; elementary education; English; environmental biology; fashion merchandising; fish/game management; gerontology; history; home economics; home economics education; hotel and restaurant management; industrial arts; industrial technology; law enforcement/police science; mathematics; music; music teacher education; nursing; physical education; physics; political science; pre-medicine; psychology; recreation/leisure studies; secondary education; social sciences; social work; sociology; special education; speech/rhetorical studies; theater arts/drama; trade/industrial education.

Academic Programs *Special study options:* academic remediation for entering students, accelerated degree program, adult/continuing education programs, advanced placement credit, cooperative education, distance learning, double majors, external degree program, honors programs, independent study, internships, off-campus study, part-time degree program, services for LD students, summer session for credit. *ROTC:* Army (b). *Unusual degree programs:* 3-2 engineering with University of Arkansas (Fayetteville).

Library Watson Memorial Library with 287,857 titles, 3,041 serial subscriptions, an OPAC.

Computers on Campus 1000 computers available on campus for general student use. A campuswide network can be accessed from student residence rooms. Internet access, at least one staffed computer lab available.

Student Life *Housing Options:* coed. *Activities and Organizations:* drama/theater group, student-run newspaper, choral group, marching band, Pre-Alumni, Honors College, Alpha Kappa Alpha Sorority, national fraternities, national sororities. *Campus security:* 24-hour emergency response devices. *Student Services:* health clinic, personal/psychological counseling.

Athletics Member NCAA, NAIA. All NCAA Division I except football (Division I-AA), golf (Division I-AA). *Intercollegiate sports:* baseball M, basketball M(s)/W(s), cross-country running M/W, track and field M/W, volleyball W(s). *Intramural sports:* baseball M, basketball M, bowling M/W, cross-country running M, football M/W, golf M/W, gymnastics M/W, racquetball M/W, softball M/W, swimming M/W, table tennis M/W, tennis M/W, track and field M/W, volleyball M/W, weight lifting M/W.

Standardized Tests *Required:* ACT (for placement), SAT I or ACT (for placement).

Costs (2001–02) *Tuition:* state resident $2490 full-time, $83 per credit hour part-time; nonresident $5790 full-time, $193 per credit hour part-time. Full-time tuition and fees vary according to course load. Part-time tuition and fees vary according to course load. *Required fees:* $719 full-time. *Room and board:* $4716; room only: $2560. Room and board charges vary according to board plan and housing facility. *Payment plan:* installment. *Waivers:* senior citizens and employees or children of employees.

Applying *Options:* early admission, deferred entrance. *Required:* high school transcript, minimum 2.0 GPA. *Application deadline:* 8/1 (freshmen). *Notification:* 8/10 (freshmen).

Admissions Contact Mrs. Erica W. Fulton, Director of Admissions and Academic Records, University of Arkansas at Pine Bluff, UAPB Box 17, 1200 University Drive, Pine Bluff, AR 71601-2799. *Phone:* 870-575-8487. *Toll-free phone:* 800-264-6585. *Fax:* 870-543-2021.

UNIVERSITY OF ARKANSAS FOR MEDICAL SCIENCES
Little Rock, Arkansas

- **State-supported** upper-level, founded 1879, part of University of Arkansas System
- **Calendar** semesters
- **Degrees** certificates, associate, bachelor's, master's, doctoral, and first professional (bachelor's degree is upper-level)
- **Urban** 5-acre campus
- **Endowment** $22.1 million
- **Coed,** 673 undergraduate students
- **Very difficult** entrance level

Undergraduates 15% African American, 2% Asian American or Pacific Islander, 2% Hispanic American, 0.6% Native American.

Majors Biomedical technology; cytotechnology; dental hygiene; emergency medical technology; industrial radiologic technology; medical technology; nuclear medical technology; nursing; operating room technician; respiratory therapy.

Academic Programs *Special study options:* part-time degree program, services for LD students. *ROTC:* Army (c).

Library Medical Sciences Library with 183,975 titles, 1,567 serial subscriptions, an OPAC, a Web page.

Computers on Campus A campuswide network can be accessed from student residence rooms and from off campus. Internet access, at least one staffed computer lab available.

Student Life *Housing Options:* coed. *Campus security:* 24-hour emergency response devices and patrols, late-night transport/escort service, controlled dormitory access.

Athletics *Intramural sports:* basketball M/W, football M, golf M.

Costs (2002–03) *Tuition:* state resident $3144 full-time; nonresident $3144 full-time. Full-time tuition and fees vary according to program. Part-time tuition and fees vary according to program. *Room and board:* room only: $1530.

University of Arkansas for Medical Sciences (continued)

Financial Aid Of all full-time matriculated undergraduates who enrolled in 2001, 477 applied for aid, 357 were judged to have need. *Average percent of need met:* 65%. *Average financial aid package:* $3000. *Average need-based loan:* $4000. *Average need-based gift aid:* $500. *Average indebtedness upon graduation:* $7000.

Admissions Contact University of Arkansas for Medical Sciences, 4301 West Markham-Slot 601, Little Rock, AR 72205-7199.

UNIVERSITY OF CENTRAL ARKANSAS

Conway, Arkansas

- **State-supported** comprehensive, founded 1907
- **Calendar** semesters
- **Degrees** associate, bachelor's, master's, doctoral, post-master's, and postbachelor's certificates
- **Small-town** 365-acre campus
- **Endowment** $10.1 million
- **Coed,** 7,540 undergraduate students, 93% full-time, 60% women, 40% men
- **Moderately difficult** entrance level, 73% of applicants were admitted

UCA is a comprehensive university with Colleges of Business Administration, Education, Liberal Arts, Health and Applied Sciences, Fine Arts and Communication, and Natural Sciences and Mathematics. More than $100 million in construction, diversification of faculty, and a developing international program are major recent advancements. On-campus housing is available for 2,000 students.

Undergraduates 6,987 full-time, 553 part-time. Students come from 36 states and territories, 53 other countries, 7% are from out of state, 15% African American, 1.0% Asian American or Pacific Islander, 1% Hispanic American, 0.8% Native American, 2% international, 7% transferred in, 22% live on campus. *Retention:* 66% of 2001 full-time freshmen returned.

Freshmen *Admission:* 3,459 applied, 2,520 admitted, 1,698 enrolled. *Average high school GPA:* 3.40. *Test scores:* ACT scores over 18: 89%; ACT scores over 24: 45%; ACT scores over 30: 7%.

Faculty *Total:* 516, 79% full-time, 55% with terminal degrees. *Student/faculty ratio:* 18:1.

Majors Accounting; art; athletic training/sports medicine; biological/physical sciences; biology; business; business administration; business education; business marketing and marketing management; chemistry; child care/guidance; community health liaison; computer/information sciences; early childhood education; economics; elementary education; elementary/middle/secondary education administration; English; English composition; English education; environmental science; exercise sciences; finance; French; general studies; geography; health education; history; home economics; home economics education; industrial arts education; insurance/risk management; international economics; journalism; management information systems/business data processing; mathematics; mathematics education; medical radiologic technology; medical technology; middle school education; music; music (general performance); music teacher education; nuclear medical technology; nursing; occupational therapy; philosophy; physical education; physical sciences; physical therapy; physical therapy assistant; physics; political science; psychology; public administration; reading education; religious studies; respiratory therapy; science education; social studies education; sociology; Spanish; special education; speech education; speech-language pathology/audiology; speech/rhetorical studies.

Academic Programs *Special study options:* academic remediation for entering students, accelerated degree program, advanced placement credit, cooperative education, distance learning, double majors, English as a second language, freshman honors college, honors programs, internships, part-time degree program, study abroad, summer session for credit. *ROTC:* Army (b). *Unusual degree programs:* 3-2 engineering with Arkansas State University.

Library Torreyson Library with 414,709 titles, 2,561 serial subscriptions, an OPAC, a Web page.

Computers on Campus 500 computers available on campus for general student use. A campuswide network can be accessed from student residence rooms and from off campus. Internet access, at least one staffed computer lab available.

Student Life *Housing:* on-campus residence required for freshman year. *Options:* coed, men-only, women-only. *Activities and Organizations:* drama/theater group, student-run newspaper, radio and television station, choral group, marching band, Student Government Association, Royal Rooters, student orientation staff, Ambassadors, national fraternities, national sororities. *Campus security:* 24-hour emergency response devices and patrols, student patrols, late-night transport/escort service, controlled dormitory access, security personnel at entrances during evening hours. *Student Services:* health clinic, personal/psychological counseling.

Athletics Member NCAA. All Division II. *Intercollegiate sports:* baseball M, basketball M(s)/W(s), cross-country running W, football M(s), soccer M/W, softball W, tennis W, volleyball W(s). *Intramural sports:* badminton M/W, basketball M/W, bowling M/W, cross-country running W, football M/W, racquetball M/W, soccer M(c), softball M/W, swimming M/W, table tennis M/W, tennis M/W, track and field M/W, volleyball M/W.

Standardized Tests *Required:* SAT I or ACT (for admission).

Costs (2001–02) *Tuition:* state resident $3060 full-time, $128 per credit hour part-time; nonresident $6120 full-time, $255 per credit hour part-time. Part-time tuition and fees vary according to course load. *Required fees:* $678 full-time, $25 per credit hour, $29 per term part-time. *Room and board:* $3490; room only: $1990. Room and board charges vary according to board plan and housing facility. *Payment plan:* installment. *Waivers:* senior citizens and employees or children of employees.

Financial Aid Of all full-time matriculated undergraduates who enrolled in 2001, 509 Federal Work-Study jobs (averaging $1382). 706 State and other part-time jobs (averaging $1631).

Applying *Options:* electronic application, early admission, deferred entrance. *Required:* high school transcript. *Required for some:* minimum 2.75 GPA. *Application deadline:* rolling (freshmen), rolling (transfers). *Notification:* continuous (freshmen).

Admissions Contact Ms. Penny Hatfield, Director of Admissions, University of Central Arkansas, 201 Donaghey Avenue. *Phone:* 501-450-5145. *Toll-free phone:* 800-243-8245. *Fax:* 501-450-5228. *E-mail:* admisson@ecom.uca.edu.

UNIVERSITY OF THE OZARKS

Clarksville, Arkansas

- **Independent Presbyterian** 4-year, founded 1834
- **Calendar** semesters
- **Degree** bachelor's
- **Small-town** 56-acre campus with easy access to Little Rock
- **Endowment** $64.2 million
- **Coed,** 654 undergraduate students, 96% full-time, 55% women, 45% men
- **Moderately difficult** entrance level, 82% of applicants were admitted

Undergraduates 627 full-time, 27 part-time. Students come from 21 states and territories, 15 other countries, 26% are from out of state, 3% African American, 0.6% Asian American or Pacific Islander, 3% Hispanic American, 2% Native American, 16% international, 5% transferred in, 64% live on campus. *Retention:* 65% of 2001 full-time freshmen returned.

Freshmen *Admission:* 446 applied, 367 admitted, 194 enrolled. *Average high school GPA:* 3.41. *Test scores:* SAT verbal scores over 500: 50%; SAT math scores over 500: 38%; ACT scores over 18: 90%; SAT verbal scores over 600: 24%; SAT math scores over 600: 9%; ACT scores over 24: 37%; ACT scores over 30: 4%.

Faculty *Total:* 56, 73% full-time, 54% with terminal degrees. *Student/faculty ratio:* 11:1.

Majors Accounting; art; art education; biology; business administration; business education; business marketing and marketing management; chemistry; communications; early childhood education; English; environmental science; history; mathematics; middle school education; music; music teacher education; physical education; physics; political science; pre-dentistry; pre-medicine; preveterinary studies; psychology; religious education; respiratory therapy; science education; social sciences; sociology; theater arts/drama.

Academic Programs *Special study options:* academic remediation for entering students, advanced placement credit, cooperative education, double majors, English as a second language, internships, part-time degree program, services for LD students, study abroad, summer session for credit. *Unusual degree programs:* 3-2 engineering with University of Arkansas; theology with University of Dubuque.

Library Robson Library plus 1 other with 106,000 titles, 589 serial subscriptions, 3,797 audiovisual materials, an OPAC, a Web page.

Computers on Campus 125 computers available on campus for general student use. A campuswide network can be accessed from student residence rooms and from off campus. At least one staffed computer lab available.

Student Life *Housing:* on-campus residence required through sophomore year. *Options:* coed, men-only, women-only. *Activities and Organizations:* drama/theater group, student-run television station, choral group, Phi Beta Lambda, Planet Club, SGA, Student Foundation Board, Baptist Campus Ministries. *Campus security:* 24-hour emergency response devices, late-night transport/escort service. *Student Services:* health clinic.

Athletics Member NCAA. All Division III. *Intercollegiate sports:* baseball M, basketball M/W, cross-country running M/W, golf M, soccer M/W, softball W, tennis M/W. *Intramural sports:* badminton M/W, basketball M/W, bowling M/W, football M/W, racquetball M/W, soccer M, softball M/W, table tennis M/W, tennis M/W, volleyball M/W, weight lifting M/W.

Standardized Tests *Required:* SAT I or ACT (for admission).
Costs (2001–02) *Comprehensive fee:* $13,904 includes full-time tuition ($9348), mandatory fees ($276), and room and board ($4280). Part-time tuition and fees vary according to course load. *Room and board:* Room and board charges vary according to board plan. *Payment plan:* installment. *Waivers:* employees or children of employees.
Financial Aid Of all full-time matriculated undergraduates who enrolled in 2001, 591 applied for aid, 328 were judged to have need, 110 had their need fully met. 109 Federal Work-Study jobs (averaging $1300). In 2001, 203 non-need-based awards were made. *Average percent of need met:* 68%. *Average financial aid package:* $11,919. *Average need-based loan:* $3145. *Average need-based gift aid:* $11,301. *Average non-need based aid:* $8060. *Average indebtedness upon graduation:* $13,200.
Applying *Options:* electronic application, deferred entrance. *Application fee:* $10. *Required:* minimum 2.0 GPA. *Required for some:* essay or personal statement, letters of recommendation, interview. *Application deadlines:* rolling (freshmen), 8/15 (transfers). *Notification:* continuous (freshmen).
Admissions Contact Mr. James D. Decker, Director of Admissions, University of the Ozarks, 415 North College Avenue, Clarksville, AR 72830-2880. *Phone:* 501-979-1209. *Toll-free phone:* 800-264-8636. *Fax:* 501-979-1355. *E-mail:* admiss@ozarks.edu.

WILLIAMS BAPTIST COLLEGE
Walnut Ridge, Arkansas

- **Independent Southern Baptist** 4-year, founded 1941
- **Calendar** semesters
- **Degrees** associate and bachelor's
- **Rural** 186-acre campus
- **Endowment** $4.0 million
- **Coed,** 683 undergraduate students, 74% full-time, 58% women, 42% men
- **Minimally difficult** entrance level, 75% of applicants were admitted

Williams Baptist College is a 4-year, liberal arts college affiliated with the Arkansas Baptist State Convention located in Walnut Ridge, Arkansas. The College offers more than 22 academic programs with an average class size of 17 and is one of the least expensive private colleges in the US. Williams, a member of the NAIA, fields varsity teams in 6 sports. Telephone: 800-722-4434 (toll-free); World Wide Web: http://www.wbcoll.edu

Undergraduates 503 full-time, 180 part-time. Students come from 14 states and territories, 6 other countries, 21% are from out of state, 3% African American, 0.2% Asian American or Pacific Islander, 1% Hispanic American, 0.6% Native American, 2% international, 6% transferred in, 62% live on campus. *Retention:* 61% of 2001 full-time freshmen returned.
Freshmen *Admission:* 499 applied, 372 admitted, 149 enrolled. *Average high school GPA:* 3.20. *Test scores:* ACT scores over 18: 81%; ACT scores over 24: 29%.
Faculty *Total:* 43, 67% full-time, 35% with terminal degrees. *Student/faculty ratio:* 16:1.
Majors Art; art education; biology; business administration; computer/information sciences; divinity/ministry; early childhood education; education; elementary education; English; fine/studio arts; history; liberal arts and sciences/liberal studies; music; music teacher education; pastoral counseling; physical education; pre-dentistry; pre-law; pre-medicine; psychology; religious education; religious music; religious studies; secretarial science; theology.
Academic Programs *Special study options:* academic remediation for entering students, adult/continuing education programs, advanced placement credit, double majors, honors programs, independent study, internships, off-campus study, part-time degree program, student-designed majors, study abroad, summer session for credit. *ROTC:* Army (c).
Library Felix Goodson Library with 57,321 titles, 284 serial subscriptions, an OPAC.
Computers on Campus 71 computers available on campus for general student use. Internet access, at least one staffed computer lab available.
Student Life *Housing:* on-campus residence required through senior year. *Options:* men-only, women-only. *Activities and Organizations:* drama/theater group, choral group, Campus Ministries, Fellowship of Christian Athletes, international club, Alpha Psi Omega. *Campus security:* 24-hour emergency response devices, student patrols. *Student Services:* personal/psychological counseling.
Athletics Member NAIA, NCCAA. *Intercollegiate sports:* baseball M(s), basketball M(s)/W(s), golf M(s), soccer M(s), softball W(s), volleyball W(s). *Intramural sports:* basketball M/W, football M, golf M/W, racquetball M/W, softball M/W, table tennis M/W, tennis M/W, volleyball M/W.
Standardized Tests *Required:* SAT I or ACT (for admission).
Costs (2002–03) *Comprehensive fee:* $11,250 includes full-time tuition ($7300), mandatory fees ($350), and room and board ($3600). Part-time tuition: $305 per hour. Part-time tuition and fees vary according to course load. *Required fees:* $175 per term part-time. *Room and board:* Room and board charges vary according to housing facility. *Payment plan:* installment. *Waivers:* senior citizens and employees or children of employees.
Financial Aid Of all full-time matriculated undergraduates who enrolled in 2001, 422 applied for aid, 312 were judged to have need. 176 Federal Work-Study jobs (averaging $939). 51 State and other part-time jobs (averaging $920). In 2001, 95 non-need-based awards were made. *Average financial aid package:* $7462. *Average need-based loan:* $3078. *Average need-based gift aid:* $2328. *Average non-need based aid:* $3092. *Average indebtedness upon graduation:* $15,818.
Applying *Options:* electronic application. *Application fee:* $20. *Required:* high school transcript, minimum 2.5 GPA. *Recommended:* essay or personal statement, interview. *Application deadline:* rolling (freshmen), rolling (transfers).
Admissions Contact Ms. Angela Flippo, Director of Admissions, Williams Baptist College, PO Box 3665, Walnut Ridge, AR 72476. *Phone:* 870-886-6741 Ext. 4117. *Toll-free phone:* 800-722-4434. *Fax:* 870-886-3924. *E-mail:* admissions@wbcoll.edu.

CALIFORNIA

ACADEMY OF ART COLLEGE
San Francisco, California

- **Proprietary** comprehensive, founded 1929
- **Calendar** semesters
- **Degrees** certificates, associate, bachelor's, and master's
- **Urban** 3-acre campus
- **Coed,** 5,535 undergraduate students, 63% full-time, 43% women, 57% men
- **Noncompetitive** entrance level, 63% of applicants were admitted

Undergraduates 3,484 full-time, 2,051 part-time. Students come from 41 states and territories, 52 other countries, 39% are from out of state, 3% African American, 15% Asian American or Pacific Islander, 8% Hispanic American, 0.6% Native American, 29% international, 12% transferred in, 13% live on campus. *Retention:* 58% of 2001 full-time freshmen returned.
Freshmen *Admission:* 854 applied, 535 admitted, 460 enrolled. *Average high school GPA:* 2.60.
Faculty *Total:* 587, 17% full-time, 15% with terminal degrees. *Student/faculty ratio:* 15:1.
Majors Advertising; applied art; art; computer graphics; drawing; fashion design/illustration; fashion merchandising; film studies; film/video production; fine/studio arts; graphic design/commercial art/illustration; industrial design; interior design; photography; printmaking; sculpture; textile arts.
Academic Programs *Special study options:* academic remediation for entering students, adult/continuing education programs, English as a second language, independent study, internships, part-time degree program, summer session for credit.
Library Academy of Art College Library with 19,500 titles, 285 serial subscriptions, 90,000 audiovisual materials, an OPAC.
Computers on Campus 600 computers available on campus for general student use. Internet access, at least one staffed computer lab available.
Student Life *Housing Options:* coed. *Activities and Organizations:* Circle of Nations, Advertising Club, Western Art Directors Club, Pinoy and Pinay Artists Club, Taiwanese Student Association. *Campus security:* late-night transport/escort service, ID check at all buildings.
Athletics *Intramural sports:* soccer M/W.
Costs (2002–03) *Tuition:* $12,000 full-time, $500 per unit part-time. Full-time tuition and fees vary according to course load. Part-time tuition and fees vary according to course load. *Required fees:* $60 full-time, $30 per term part-time. *Room only:* $8400. Room and board charges vary according to housing facility. *Payment plan:* installment.
Financial Aid Of all full-time matriculated undergraduates who enrolled in 2001, 1580 applied for aid, 1345 were judged to have need, 58 had their need fully met. 37 Federal Work-Study jobs (averaging $3107). *Average percent of need met:* 36%. *Average financial aid package:* $6441. *Average need-based loan:* $3756. *Average need-based gift aid:* $5581. *Average indebtedness upon graduation:* $28,000.

Academy of Art College (continued)

Applying *Options:* common application, early admission, deferred entrance. *Application fee:* $100. *Required:* high school transcript. *Recommended:* minimum 2.0 GPA, interview, portfolio. *Application deadline:* rolling (freshmen), rolling (transfers).

Admissions Contact Ms. Eliza Alden, Vice President-Admissions, Academy of Art College, 79 New Montgomery Street, San Francisco, CA 94105. *Phone:* 415-263-7757 Ext. 7757. *Toll-free phone:* 800-544-ARTS. *Fax:* 415-263-4130. *E-mail:* info@academyart.edu.

ALLIANT INTERNATIONAL UNIVERSITY
San Diego, California

- **Independent** university, founded 1952, part of Alliant International University
- **Calendar** quarters
- **Degrees** certificates, bachelor's, master's, doctoral, and postbachelor's certificates
- **Suburban** 200-acre campus
- **Endowment** $286,726
- **Coed,** 535 undergraduate students, 94% full-time, 58% women, 42% men
- **Moderately difficult** entrance level, 51% of applicants were admitted

Undergraduates 502 full-time, 33 part-time. Students come from 30 states and territories, 61 other countries, 24% are from out of state, 12% African American, 9% Asian American or Pacific Islander, 19% Hispanic American, 1% Native American, 25% international, 38% transferred in, 48% live on campus. *Retention:* 58% of 2001 full-time freshmen returned.

Freshmen *Admission:* 569 applied, 291 admitted, 15 enrolled. *Average high school GPA:* 3.10.

Faculty *Total:* 118, 44% full-time. *Student/faculty ratio:* 16:1.

Majors Architecture; business administration; communications; elementary education; English; English education; environmental science; hotel and restaurant management; information sciences/systems; international business; international relations; journalism; liberal arts and sciences/liberal studies; political science; psychology; sociology; travel/tourism management.

Academic Programs *Special study options:* academic remediation for entering students, adult/continuing education programs, advanced placement credit, English as a second language, honors programs, independent study, internships, part-time degree program, services for LD students, study abroad, summer session for credit. *ROTC:* Army (c).

Library Walter Library with 130,000 titles, an OPAC, a Web page.

Computers on Campus 80 computers available on campus for general student use. A campuswide network can be accessed from student residence rooms. Internet access, online (class) registration, at least one staffed computer lab available.

Student Life *Housing:* on-campus residence required for freshman year. *Options:* coed. *Activities and Organizations:* student-run newspaper, Residence Hall Association, Pacific Islanders Club, Student Council, Rotaract, Sigma Iota Epsilon. *Campus security:* 24-hour emergency response devices and patrols, student patrols, late-night transport/escort service. *Student Services:* health clinic, personal/psychological counseling.

Athletics Member NAIA. *Intercollegiate sports:* cross-country running M(s)/W(s), soccer M(s)/W(s), tennis M(s)/W(s), track and field M/W, volleyball W(s). *Intramural sports:* basketball M/W, cross-country running M/W, football M/W, golf M/W, soccer M/W, softball M/W, table tennis M/W, tennis M/W, volleyball M/W.

Costs (2001–02) *Comprehensive fee:* $20,520 includes full-time tuition ($13,950), mandatory fees ($390), and room and board ($6180). Full-time tuition and fees vary according to course load. Part-time tuition: $340 per unit. Part-time tuition and fees vary according to course load. *Required fees:* $130 per term part-time. *Payment plan:* deferred payment. *Waivers:* employees or children of employees.

Financial Aid Of all full-time matriculated undergraduates who enrolled in 2001, 399 applied for aid, 252 were judged to have need, 79 had their need fully met. 214 Federal Work-Study jobs (averaging $3221). In 2001, 122 non-need-based awards were made. *Average percent of need met:* 84%. *Average financial aid package:* $17,331. *Average need-based loan:* $3378. *Average need-based gift aid:* $11,210. *Average non-need based aid:* $5638. *Average indebtedness upon graduation:* $21,780.

Applying *Options:* common application, deferred entrance. *Application fee:* $40. *Required:* high school transcript, minimum 2.0 GPA. *Recommended:* minimum 3.0 GPA. *Application deadline:* rolling (freshmen), rolling (transfers).

Admissions Contact Ms. Susan Topham, Director of Admissions, Alliant International University, 10455 Pomerado Road, San Diego, CA 92131-1799. *Phone:* 858-635-4772. *Fax:* 858-635-4739. *E-mail:* admissions@alliant.edu.

AMERICAN INTERCONTINENTAL UNIVERSITY
Los Angeles, California

- **Proprietary** comprehensive, founded 1982
- **Calendar** 5 10-week terms
- **Degrees** associate, bachelor's, and master's
- **Urban** campus
- **Coed,** 1,058 undergraduate students
- **Noncompetitive** entrance level

Undergraduates Students come from 42 other countries.

Faculty *Total:* 70, 37% full-time, 39% with terminal degrees. *Student/faculty ratio:* 24:1.

Majors Business administration; business marketing and marketing management; computer management; fashion design/illustration; fashion merchandising; film/video production; graphic design/commercial art/illustration; interior design; management information systems/business data processing; photography; travel/tourism management.

Academic Programs *Special study options:* academic remediation for entering students, accelerated degree program, English as a second language, internships, part-time degree program, study abroad, summer session for credit.

Library 20,000 titles, 228 serial subscriptions.

Computers on Campus 45 computers available on campus for general student use. Internet access, at least one staffed computer lab available.

Student Life *Housing Options:* coed, men-only, women-only. *Activities and Organizations:* drama/theater group, student-run newspaper. *Student Services:* personal/psychological counseling.

Applying *Options:* early admission, deferred entrance. *Application fee:* $35. *Required:* essay or personal statement, high school transcript, 2 letters of recommendation, interview. *Application deadline:* rolling (freshmen), rolling (transfers).

Admissions Contact Mr. Sam Hinojosa, Director of Admissions, American InterContinental University, 12655 West Jefferson Boulevard, Los Angeles, CA 90066. *Phone:* 310-302-2423. *Fax:* 310-302-2001.

ANTIOCH UNIVERSITY LOS ANGELES
Marina del Rey, California

- **Independent** upper-level, founded 1972, part of Antioch University
- **Calendar** quarters
- **Degrees** bachelor's, master's, post-master's, and postbachelor's certificates
- **Urban** 1-acre campus with easy access to Los Angeles
- **Endowment** $12,743
- **Coed**
- **Moderately difficult** entrance level

Faculty *Student/faculty ratio:* 21:1.

Student Life *Campus security:* 24-hour emergency response devices, late-night transport/escort service.

Costs (2001–02) *One-time required fee:* $350. *Tuition:* $13,600 full-time, $355 per unit part-time. Full-time tuition and fees vary according to course load and program. Part-time tuition and fees vary according to course load and program.

Applying *Options:* deferred entrance. *Application fee:* $60.

Admissions Contact Ms. Chloe Reid, Executive Dean, Antioch University Los Angeles, 13274 Fiji Way, Marina del Rey, CA 90292-7090. *Phone:* 310-578-1080 Ext. 244. *Toll-free phone:* 800-7ANTIOCH. *Fax:* 310-822-4824. *E-mail:* admissions@antiochla.edu.

ANTIOCH UNIVERSITY SANTA BARBARA
Santa Barbara, California

- **Independent** upper-level, founded 1977, part of Antioch University
- **Calendar** quarters
- **Degrees** bachelor's and master's
- **Small-town** campus with easy access to Los Angeles
- **Coed,** 130 undergraduate students, 51% full-time, 82% women, 18% men
- **Minimally difficult** entrance level

Undergraduates 66 full-time, 64 part-time. 4% African American, 5% Asian American or Pacific Islander, 11% Hispanic American, 0.8% Native American, 0.8% international.
Faculty *Total:* 57, 25% full-time. *Student/faculty ratio:* 15:1.
Majors General studies.
Academic Programs *Special study options:* academic remediation for entering students, accelerated degree program, adult/continuing education programs, independent study, internships, part-time degree program, student-designed majors, summer session for credit.
Computers on Campus 12 computers available on campus for general student use. A campuswide network can be accessed from off campus. At least one staffed computer lab available.
Student Life *Housing:* college housing not available. *Campus security:* late-night transport/escort service.
Costs (2001–02) *Tuition:* $10,800 full-time, $360 per credit hour part-time. Part-time tuition and fees vary according to course load. *Payment plan:* installment. *Waivers:* employees or children of employees.
Financial Aid Of all full-time matriculated undergraduates who enrolled in 2001, 12 Federal Work-Study jobs (averaging $3827).
Applying *Options:* common application, deferred entrance. *Application fee:* $60. *Application deadline:* rolling (transfers).
Admissions Contact Mrs. Carol Flores, Director of Admissions, Antioch University Santa Barbara, 801 Garden Street, Santa Barbara, CA 93101-1580. *Phone:* 805-962-8179 Ext. 113. *Fax:* 805-962-4786. *E-mail:* cflores@antiochsb.edu.

ARGOSY UNIVERSITY-ORANGE COUNTY
Orange, California

Admissions Contact 3745 Chapman Avenue, Suite 100, Orange, CA 92868. *Toll-free phone:* 800-716-9598.

ARMSTRONG UNIVERSITY
Oakland, California

- **Independent** comprehensive, founded 1918
- **Calendar** semesters
- **Degrees** associate, bachelor's, and master's
- **Urban** campus with easy access to San Francisco
- **Coed**
- **Moderately difficult** entrance level

Student Life *Campus security:* 24-hour emergency response devices, student patrols, patrols by trained security personnel during daytime hours.
Applying *Options:* common application, deferred entrance. *Application fee:* $50. *Required:* high school transcript, minimum 2.0 GPA. *Recommended:* essay or personal statement, letters of recommendation.
Admissions Contact Ms. Sarah Hofberg, Director of Admission, Armstrong University, 1608 Webster Street, Oakland, CA 94612. *Phone:* 510-835-7900 Ext. 10. *Fax:* 510-835-8935. *E-mail:* info@armstrong-u.edu.

ART CENTER COLLEGE OF DESIGN
Pasadena, California

- **Independent** comprehensive, founded 1930
- **Calendar** trimesters
- **Degrees** bachelor's and master's
- **Suburban** 175-acre campus with easy access to Los Angeles
- **Endowment** $20.0 million
- **Coed,** 1,377 undergraduate students, 100% full-time, 40% women, 60% men
- **Very difficult** entrance level, 65% of applicants were admitted

Undergraduates 1,377 full-time. Students come from 43 states and territories, 37 other countries, 19% are from out of state, 2% African American, 32% Asian American or Pacific Islander, 10% Hispanic American, 0.7% Native American, 17% international, 2% transferred in. *Retention:* 94% of 2001 full-time freshmen returned.
Freshmen *Admission:* 1,129 applied, 730 admitted, 43 enrolled. *Average high school GPA:* 3.10.
Faculty *Total:* 409, 16% full-time. *Student/faculty ratio:* 12:1.
Majors Advertising; architectural environmental design; art; film studies; graphic design/commercial art/illustration; industrial design; photography; visual/performing arts.
Academic Programs *Special study options:* accelerated degree program, adult/continuing education programs, advanced placement credit, independent study, internships, summer session for credit.
Library James LeMont Fogg Library with 73,595 titles, 385 serial subscriptions, 5,265 audiovisual materials, an OPAC.
Computers on Campus 225 computers available on campus for general student use. Internet access, at least one staffed computer lab available.
Student Life *Housing:* college housing not available. *Activities and Organizations:* Contraste, Chroma, Women's Alliance, Korean Student Alliance, Industrial Design Society Student Chapter. *Campus security:* 24-hour emergency response devices and patrols. *Student Services:* personal/psychological counseling.
Standardized Tests *Required for some:* SAT I or ACT (for admission).
Costs (2001–02) *Tuition:* $21,110 full-time. *Payment plan:* installment. *Waivers:* employees or children of employees.
Financial Aid Of all full-time matriculated undergraduates who enrolled in 2001, 936 applied for aid, 904 were judged to have need. 174 Federal Work-Study jobs (averaging $2300). *Average percent of need met:* 50%. *Average financial aid package:* $13,573. *Average need-based loan:* $5668. *Average need-based gift aid:* $7480. *Average indebtedness upon graduation:* $42,846.
Applying *Options:* deferred entrance. *Application fee:* $45. *Required:* essay or personal statement, high school transcript, portfolio. *Recommended:* minimum 3.0 GPA, interview. *Application deadline:* rolling (freshmen), rolling (transfers).
Admissions Contact Ms. Kit Baron, Vice President of Student Services, Art Center College of Design, 1700 Lida Street, Pasadena, CA 91103-1999. *Phone:* 626-396-2373. *Fax:* 626-795-0578. *E-mail:* admissions@artcenter.edu.

THE ART INSTITUTE OF CALIFORNIA
San Diego, California

- **Proprietary** 4-year, founded 1981, part of The Art Institutes/Argosy
- **Calendar** quarters
- **Degrees** associate and bachelor's
- **Urban** campus
- **Coed,** 490 undergraduate students, 100% full-time, 37% women, 63% men
- **Minimally difficult** entrance level, 85% of applicants were admitted

Undergraduates 490 full-time. Students come from 15 states and territories, 30% are from out of state, 2% African American, 8% Asian American or Pacific Islander, 12% Hispanic American, 5% international, 2% transferred in. *Retention:* 85% of 2001 full-time freshmen returned.
Freshmen *Admission:* 200 applied, 170 admitted, 83 enrolled. *Average high school GPA:* 2.6.
Faculty *Total:* 21, 14% full-time, 5% with terminal degrees. *Student/faculty ratio:* 28:1.
Majors Advertising; communications related; design/applied arts related; graphic design/commercial art/illustration.
Academic Programs *Special study options:* double majors, internships, summer session for credit.
Library The Art Institute of California Library with 1,100 titles, 17 serial subscriptions, an OPAC.
Computers on Campus 150 computers available on campus for general student use. Internet access, at least one staffed computer lab available.
Student Life *Housing:* college housing not available. *Activities and Organizations:* student-run newspaper, Advertising Club, Communicating Art Club. *Campus security:* 24-hour emergency response devices.
Costs (2001–02) *Tuition:* $14,600 full-time. Full-time tuition and fees vary according to program. *Payment plans:* tuition prepayment, installment.
Applying *Options:* common application, electronic application, deferred entrance. *Application fee:* $30. *Required:* essay or personal statement, high school transcript, interview. *Application deadline:* rolling (freshmen), rolling (transfers). *Notification:* continuous (freshmen).
Admissions Contact Ms. Sandy Park, Director of Admissions, The Art Institute of California, 10025 Mesa Rum Road, San Diego, CA 92122. *Phone:* 858-546-0602 Ext. 3117. *Toll-free phone:* 866-275-2422 Ext. 3117. *Fax:* 858-457-0903. *E-mail:* info@aii.edu.

THE ART INSTITUTE OF CALIFORNIA-SAN FRANCISCO
San Francisco, California

- **Independent** 4-year, founded 1939, part of Educational Management Corporation

The Art Institute of California-San Francisco (continued)

- **Calendar** quarters
- **Degrees** associate and bachelor's
- **Urban** campus
- **Coed,** 345 undergraduate students, 81% full-time, 43% women, 57% men
- **Moderately difficult** entrance level

Undergraduates 279 full-time, 66 part-time. 8% African American, 14% Asian American or Pacific Islander, 20% Hispanic American, 1% Native American, 5% international.
Freshmen *Admission:* 75 enrolled.
Faculty *Total:* 48, 17% full-time. *Student/faculty ratio:* 12:1.
Majors Business marketing and marketing management; computer graphics; fashion design/illustration; graphic design/commercial art/illustration.
Academic Programs *Special study options:* accelerated degree program, internships, part-time degree program, summer session for credit.
Computers on Campus 2 computers available on campus for general student use. At least one staffed computer lab available.
Student Life *Housing:* college housing not available. *Activities and Organizations:* student-run newspaper. *Campus security:* 24-hour emergency response devices.
Costs (2002–03) *Tuition:* $16,464 full-time, $343 per credit hour part-time. *Required fees:* $150 full-time.
Applying *Options:* common application, deferred entrance. *Application fee:* $50. *Required:* essay or personal statement, high school transcript. *Recommended:* minimum 2.0 GPA, 2 letters of recommendation, interview. *Application deadline:* rolling (freshmen), rolling (transfers).
Admissions Contact Mr. Doug Worsley, Director of Admissions, The Art Institute of California-San Francisco, 1170 Market Street, San Francisco, CA 94102-4908. *Phone:* 415-865-0198 Ext. 2536. *Toll-free phone:* 888-493-3261.

THE ART INSTITUTE OF LOS ANGELES
Santa Monica, California

- **Proprietary** primarily 2-year
- **Calendar** quarters
- **Degrees** associate and bachelor's
- 1,200 undergraduate students

Admissions Contact Bill Tsatsoulis, Director of Admissions, The Art Institute of Los Angeles, 2900 31st Street, Santa Monica, CA 90405-3035. *Phone:* 310-752-4700. *Toll-free phone:* 888-646-4610.

ART INSTITUTE OF SOUTHERN CALIFORNIA
Laguna Beach, California

- **Independent** 4-year, founded 1962
- **Calendar** semesters
- **Degree** certificates and bachelor's
- **Small-town** 9-acre campus with easy access to Los Angeles
- **Endowment** $625,000
- **Coed,** 280 undergraduate students, 100% full-time, 46% women, 54% men
- **Moderately difficult** entrance level, 93% of applicants were admitted

The Art Institute of Southern California (AISC) hosts an annual open house and portfolio review to introduce prospective students and their families to the school. Individuals may schedule personal tours and portfolio reviews by contacting Anthony Padilla, Dean of Admissions, or Susan DeRosa, Assistant Dean of Admissions. Campus hours are Monday-Friday, 9 a.m. to 5 p.m.

Undergraduates 280 full-time. Students come from 29 states and territories, 36% are from out of state. *Retention:* 88% of 2001 full-time freshmen returned.
Freshmen *Admission:* 220 applied, 204 admitted, 50 enrolled. *Average high school GPA:* 3.32. *Test scores:* SAT verbal scores over 500: 88%; SAT math scores over 500: 80%; ACT scores over 18: 100%; SAT verbal scores over 600: 66%; SAT math scores over 600: 32%; ACT scores over 24: 80%; SAT verbal scores over 700: 16%; SAT math scores over 700: 10%; ACT scores over 30: 10%.
Faculty *Total:* 62, 16% full-time. *Student/faculty ratio:* 10:1.
Majors Art; design/visual communications; drawing; graphic design/commercial art/illustration.
Academic Programs *Special study options:* academic remediation for entering students, adult/continuing education programs, advanced placement credit, English as a second language, independent study, internships, off-campus study, part-time degree program, summer session for credit.
Library Ruth Salyer Library plus 1 other with 16,000 titles, 100 serial subscriptions, 8 audiovisual materials, an OPAC.
Computers on Campus 70 computers available on campus for general student use. A campuswide network can be accessed from off campus. Internet access, at least one staffed computer lab available.
Student Life *Housing:* college housing not available. *Activities and Organizations:* student-run newspaper. *Campus security:* 24-hour emergency response devices. *Student Services:* personal/psychological counseling.
Standardized Tests *Required:* SAT I or ACT (for admission).
Costs (2001–02) *Tuition:* $14,285 full-time, $595 per unit part-time. *Payment plan:* installment. *Waivers:* employees or children of employees.
Applying *Options:* common application, electronic application, deferred entrance. *Application fee:* $35. *Required:* essay or personal statement, high school transcript, minimum 3.0 GPA, 1 letter of recommendation, interview, portfolio. *Recommended:* minimum 3.5 GPA. *Application deadlines:* 3/2 (freshmen), 4/2 (transfers). *Notification:* 5/1 (freshmen).
Admissions Contact Mr. Anthony Padilla, Dean of Admissions, Art Institute of Southern California, 2222 Laguna Canyon Road, Laguna Beach, CA 92651-1136. *Phone:* 949-376-6000 Ext. 232. *Toll-free phone:* 800-255-0762. *Fax:* 949-376-6009. *E-mail:* admissions@aisc.edu.

AZUSA PACIFIC UNIVERSITY
Azusa, California

- **Independent nondenominational** comprehensive, founded 1899
- **Calendar** semesters
- **Degrees** bachelor's, master's, doctoral, and first professional
- **Small-town** 60-acre campus with easy access to Los Angeles
- **Endowment** $21.5 million
- **Coed,** 3,654 undergraduate students, 98% full-time, 64% women, 36% men
- **Moderately difficult** entrance level, 70% of applicants were admitted

At Azusa Pacific, a Christian liberal arts university, students are challenged academically, participate in dynamic leadership experiences, and utilize the latest technology, gaining the skills needed to reach their goals. Located 26 miles northeast of Los Angeles, APU offers 40 undergraduate majors, 19 master's programs, 3 doctoral programs, and extensive credential and certificate programs.

Undergraduates 3,569 full-time, 85 part-time. Students come from 43 states and territories, 50 other countries, 18% are from out of state, 3% African American, 5% Asian American or Pacific Islander, 12% Hispanic American, 0.5% Native American, 2% international, 11% transferred in, 62% live on campus. *Retention:* 79% of 2001 full-time freshmen returned.
Freshmen *Admission:* 2,257 applied, 1,581 admitted, 763 enrolled. *Average high school GPA:* 3.59. *Test scores:* SAT verbal scores over 500: 77%; SAT math scores over 500: 76%; ACT scores over 18: 96%; SAT verbal scores over 600: 52%; SAT math scores over 600: 29%; ACT scores over 24: 45%; SAT verbal scores over 700: 7%; SAT math scores over 700: 4%; ACT scores over 30: 7%.
Faculty *Total:* 736, 29% full-time. *Student/faculty ratio:* 16:1.
Majors Accounting; applied art; art; athletic training/sports medicine; biblical studies; biochemistry; biology; business administration; business marketing and marketing management; chemistry; communications; computer science; cultural studies; divinity/ministry; English; health science; history; international relations; liberal arts and sciences/liberal studies; management information systems/business data processing; mathematics; music; natural sciences; nursing; philosophy; physical education; physics; political science; pre-engineering; pre-law; psychology; religious studies; social sciences; social work; sociology; Spanish; theology.
Academic Programs *Special study options:* academic remediation for entering students, accelerated degree program, adult/continuing education programs, advanced placement credit, cooperative education, distance learning, double majors, English as a second language, freshman honors college, honors programs, internships, off-campus study, part-time degree program, services for LD students, study abroad, summer session for credit. *ROTC:* Army (c).
Library Marshburn Memorial Library plus 2 others with 147,377 titles, 1,411 serial subscriptions, an OPAC, a Web page.
Computers on Campus 300 computers available on campus for general student use. A campuswide network can be accessed from off campus. Internet access, at least one staffed computer lab available.
Student Life *Activities and Organizations:* drama/theater group, student-run newspaper, choral group, marching band, community service groups, choir, outreach ministries groups, Habitat for Humanity. *Campus security:* 24-hour

emergency response devices and patrols, student patrols, late-night transport/escort service, controlled dormitory access. *Student Services:* health clinic, personal/psychological counseling.

Athletics Member NAIA. *Intercollegiate sports:* baseball M(s), basketball M(s)/W(s), cross-country running M(s)/W(s), football M(s), golf M(s), soccer M(s)/W(s), softball W(s), tennis M(s), track and field M(s)/W(s), volleyball M/W(s). *Intramural sports:* basketball M/W, football M/W, golf M/W, skiing (downhill) M/W, soccer W, volleyball M/W.

Standardized Tests *Required:* SAT I or ACT (for admission).

Costs (2001–02) *Comprehensive fee:* $23,725 includes full-time tuition ($16,840), mandatory fees ($655), and room and board ($6230). Part-time tuition: $655 per unit. Part-time tuition and fees vary according to course load. *Required fees:* $35 per term part-time. *Room and board:* College room only: $3600. Room and board charges vary according to board plan, housing facility, and student level. *Payment plan:* installment. *Waivers:* employees or children of employees.

Financial Aid Of all full-time matriculated undergraduates who enrolled in 2001, 2086 applied for aid, 1461 were judged to have need, 274 had their need fully met. 453 Federal Work-Study jobs (averaging $1500). In 2001, 528 non-need-based awards were made. *Average percent of need met:* 74%. *Average financial aid package:* $6859. *Average need-based loan:* $4151. *Average need-based gift aid:* $7413. *Financial aid deadline:* 8/1.

Applying *Options:* early admission, early action, deferred entrance. *Application fee:* $45. *Required:* essay or personal statement, high school transcript, minimum 2.5 GPA, 2 letters of recommendation. *Required for some:* interview. *Application deadlines:* 7/1 (freshmen), 7/1 (transfers). *Notification:* continuous (freshmen), 2/15 (early action).

Admissions Contact Mrs. Deana Porterfield, Dean of Enrollment, Azusa Pacific University, 901 East Alosta Avenue, PO Box 7000, Azusa, CA 91720-7000. *Phone:* 626-812-3016. *Toll-free phone:* 800-TALK-APU. *E-mail:* admissions@apu.edu.

Bethany College of the Assemblies of God

Scotts Valley, California

- **Independent** comprehensive, founded 1919, affiliated with Assemblies of God
- **Calendar** semesters
- **Degrees** certificates, associate, bachelor's, and master's
- **Small-town** 40-acre campus with easy access to San Francisco and San Jose
- **Endowment** $500,000
- **Coed,** 504 undergraduate students, 74% full-time, 38% women, 62% men
- **Minimally difficult** entrance level, 74% of applicants were admitted

Undergraduates 374 full-time, 130 part-time. Students come from 21 states and territories, 10 other countries, 8% African American, 4% Asian American or Pacific Islander, 15% Hispanic American, 0.4% Native American, 0.6% international, 21% transferred in. *Retention:* 76% of 2001 full-time freshmen returned.

Freshmen *Admission:* 208 applied, 154 admitted, 84 enrolled. *Average high school GPA:* 3.21. *Test scores:* SAT verbal scores over 500: 53%; SAT math scores over 500: 50%; SAT verbal scores over 600: 24%; SAT math scores over 600: 21%; SAT verbal scores over 700: 5%; SAT math scores over 700: 5%.

Faculty *Total:* 72, 38% full-time, 26% with terminal degrees. *Student/faculty ratio:* 11:1.

Majors Alcohol/drug abuse counseling; biblical languages/literatures; biblical studies; divinity/ministry; early childhood education; education; elementary education; English; interdisciplinary studies; international relations; liberal arts and sciences/liberal studies; music teacher education; pastoral counseling; psychology; religious music; social sciences; theater arts/drama; theology.

Academic Programs *Special study options:* academic remediation for entering students, accelerated degree program, adult/continuing education programs, advanced placement credit, distance learning, external degree program, independent study, internships, part-time degree program, services for LD students, summer session for credit.

Library Wilson Library with 59,453 titles, 858 serial subscriptions.

Computers on Campus 17 computers available on campus for general student use. A campuswide network can be accessed from off campus. Internet access, at least one staffed computer lab available.

Student Life *Housing:* on-campus residence required through junior year. *Activities and Organizations:* drama/theater group, student-run newspaper, choral group. *Campus security:* 24-hour emergency response devices, student patrols, controlled dormitory access. *Student Services:* personal/psychological counseling.

Athletics Member NAIA. *Intercollegiate sports:* basketball M(s)/W(s), softball W(s), volleyball M(s)/W(s). *Intramural sports:* basketball M/W, volleyball M/W.

Standardized Tests *Required:* SAT I or ACT (for admission).

Costs (2002–03) *Comprehensive fee:* $17,122 includes full-time tuition ($11,360), mandatory fees ($600), and room and board ($5162). Full-time tuition and fees vary according to location. Part-time tuition: $450 per unit. Part-time tuition and fees vary according to location. *Required fees:* $85 per term part-time. *Room and board:* College room only: $2390. Room and board charges vary according to board plan. *Payment plan:* installment. *Waivers:* employees or children of employees.

Financial Aid Of all full-time matriculated undergraduates who enrolled in 2001, 336 applied for aid, 290 were judged to have need, 59 had their need fully met. 62 Federal Work-Study jobs (averaging $1659). In 2001, 19 non-need-based awards were made. *Average percent of need met:* 40%. *Average financial aid package:* $10,875. *Average need-based loan:* $4424. *Average need-based gift aid:* $7066. *Average non-need based aid:* $5545. *Average indebtedness upon graduation:* $18,931.

Applying *Options:* early admission, deferred entrance. *Application fee:* $35. *Required:* essay or personal statement, high school transcript, minimum 2.0 GPA, 2 letters of recommendation, Christian commitment. *Application deadlines:* 7/1 (freshmen), 7/1 (transfers). *Notification:* continuous until 7/31 (freshmen).

Admissions Contact Ms. Pam Smallwood, Director of Admissions, Bethany College of the Assemblies of God, 800 Bethany Drive, Scotts Valley, CA 95066-2820. *Phone:* 831-438-3800 Ext. 1400. *Toll-free phone:* 800-843-9410. *Fax:* 831-438-4517. *E-mail:* info@bethany.edu.

Bethesda Christian University

Anaheim, California

- **Independent** comprehensive, founded 1978, affiliated with Full Gospel World Mission
- **Calendar** semesters
- **Degrees** certificates, bachelor's, master's, and first professional
- **Endowment** $3.0 million
- 171 undergraduate students, 66% full-time
- **Moderately difficult** entrance level

Faculty *Student/faculty ratio:* 15:1.

Student Life *Campus security:* student patrols, late-night transport/escort service, 24-hour security monitor.

Financial Aid Of all full-time matriculated undergraduates who enrolled in 2001, 27 applied for aid, 27 were judged to have need. *Average percent of need met:* 60. *Average financial aid package:* $3337. *Average need-based loan:* $2277. *Average need-based gift aid:* $2409. *Average indebtedness upon graduation:* $2500.

Applying *Options:* common application. *Application fee:* $25. *Required:* essay or personal statement, high school transcript, minimum 2.0 GPA, 3 letters of recommendation, interview, 2 photographs.

Admissions Contact Ms. Haein Hong, Admissions & Registrar, Bethesda Christian University, 730 N. Euclid Street, Anaheim, CA 92801. *Phone:* 714-517-1945. *Fax:* 714-517-1948. *E-mail:* admin@bcu.edu.

Biola University

La Mirada, California

- **Independent interdenominational** university, founded 1908
- **Calendar** 4-1-4
- **Degrees** certificates, bachelor's, master's, doctoral, and first professional
- **Suburban** 95-acre campus with easy access to Los Angeles
- **Endowment** $16.7 million
- **Coed,** 2,949 undergraduate students, 91% full-time, 61% women, 39% men
- **Moderately difficult** entrance level, 55% of applicants were admitted

Undergraduates 2,676 full-time, 273 part-time. Students come from 43 states and territories, 40 other countries, 21% are from out of state, 4% African American, 8% Asian American or Pacific Islander, 8% Hispanic American, 0.4% Native American, 4% international, 8% transferred in, 69% live on campus. *Retention:* 83% of 2001 full-time freshmen returned.

Freshmen *Admission:* 2,351 applied, 1,304 admitted, 650 enrolled. *Average high school GPA:* 3.56. *Test scores:* SAT verbal scores over 500: 77%; SAT math scores over 500: 77%; ACT scores over 18: 99%; SAT verbal scores over 600: 39%; SAT math scores over 600: 36%; ACT scores over 24: 56%; SAT verbal scores over 700: 8%; SAT math scores over 700: 5%; ACT scores over 30: 10%.

Faculty *Total:* 315, 49% full-time, 64% with terminal degrees. *Student/faculty ratio:* 18:1.

Biola University (continued)

Majors Adult/continuing education; anthropology; art; biblical studies; bilingual/bicultural education; biochemistry; biology; business administration; clinical psychology; communication disorders; computer/information sciences; divinity/ministry; drawing; education; education (K-12); elementary education; English; exercise sciences; fine/studio arts; graphic design/commercial art/illustration; history; humanities; mathematics; missionary studies; music; nursing; pastoral counseling; philosophy; physical education; physical sciences; pre-law; psychology; radio/television broadcasting; religious education; religious studies; secondary education; social sciences; sociology; Spanish; theology.

Academic Programs *Special study options:* academic remediation for entering students, accelerated degree program, adult/continuing education programs, advanced placement credit, cooperative education, double majors, English as a second language, freshman honors college, honors programs, independent study, internships, off-campus study, part-time degree program, services for LD students, study abroad, summer session for credit. *ROTC:* Army (c), Air Force (c). *Unusual degree programs:* 3-2 engineering with University of Southern California; biblical and theological studies.

Library Rose Memorial Library with 259,285 titles, 1,188 serial subscriptions, 10,343 audiovisual materials, an OPAC, a Web page.

Computers on Campus 115 computers available on campus for general student use. A campuswide network can be accessed from student residence rooms and from off campus. Internet access, online (class) registration, at least one staffed computer lab available.

Student Life *Housing:* on-campus residence required through sophomore year. *Options:* men-only, women-only. *Activities and Organizations:* drama/theater group, student-run newspaper, radio and television station, choral group, Korean Student Association, Brothers and Sisters in Christ, Accounting Society, Maharlika (Filipino Club), SOUL (Seeking Out Unity and Love). *Campus security:* 24-hour emergency response devices and patrols, student patrols, late-night transport/escort service, controlled dormitory access, access gates to roads through the middle of campus. *Student Services:* health clinic, personal/psychological counseling, legal services.

Athletics Member NAIA. *Intercollegiate sports:* baseball M(s), basketball M(s)/W(s), cross-country running M(s)/W(s), soccer M(s)/W(s), softball W(s), swimming M(s)/W(s), tennis W(s), track and field M(s)/W(s), volleyball W(s). *Intramural sports:* basketball M/W, football M/W, softball M/W, volleyball M/W, water polo M/W.

Standardized Tests *Required:* SAT I or ACT (for admission).

Costs (2002–03) *Comprehensive fee:* $24,384 includes full-time tuition ($18,454) and room and board ($5930). Full-time tuition and fees vary according to program. Part-time tuition: $769 per unit. Part-time tuition and fees vary according to course load and program. *Room and board:* College room only: $3120. Room and board charges vary according to board plan and housing facility. *Payment plan:* installment. *Waivers:* employees or children of employees.

Financial Aid Of all full-time matriculated undergraduates who enrolled in 2001, 1748 applied for aid, 1471 were judged to have need, 300 had their need fully met. 79 Federal Work-Study jobs (averaging $2692). *Average percent of need met:* 78%. *Average financial aid package:* $13,651. *Average need-based loan:* $3061. *Average need-based gift aid:* $8457. *Average indebtedness upon graduation:* $23,952.

Applying *Options:* common application, electronic application, early admission, deferred entrance. *Application fee:* $45. *Required:* essay or personal statement, high school transcript, 2 letters of recommendation, interview. *Recommended:* minimum 3.0 GPA. *Application deadlines:* 6/1 (freshmen), 6/1 (transfers).

Admissions Contact Mr. Greg Vaughan, Director of Enrollment Management, Biola University, 13800 Biola Avenue, La Mirada, CA 90639. *Phone:* 562-903-4752. *Toll-free phone:* 800-652-4652. *Fax:* 562-903-4709. *E-mail:* admissions@biola.edu.

BROOKS INSTITUTE OF PHOTOGRAPHY
Santa Barbara, California

Admissions Contact Ms. Inge B. Kautzmann, Director of Admissions, Brooks Institute of Photography, 801 Alston Road, Santa Barbara, CA 93108. *Phone:* 805-966-3888 Ext. 4601. *Toll-free phone:* 888-304-3456. *Fax:* 805-564-1475. *E-mail:* admissions@brooks.edu.

CALIFORNIA BAPTIST UNIVERSITY
Riverside, California

- **Independent Southern Baptist** comprehensive, founded 1950
- **Calendar** 4-4-1-1
- **Degrees** bachelor's and master's
- **Suburban** 75-acre campus with easy access to Los Angeles
- **Endowment** $5.0 million
- **Coed,** 1,580 undergraduate students, 80% full-time, 65% women, 35% men
- **Minimally difficult** entrance level, 79% of applicants were admitted

Undergraduates 1,264 full-time, 316 part-time. Students come from 19 states and territories, 5% are from out of state, 6% African American, 3% Asian American or Pacific Islander, 12% Hispanic American, 0.6% Native American, 6% transferred in, 45% live on campus. *Retention:* 81% of 2001 full-time freshmen returned.

Freshmen *Admission:* 793 applied, 625 admitted, 216 enrolled. *Average high school GPA:* 3.26. *Test scores:* SAT verbal scores over 500: 53%; SAT math scores over 500: 48%; ACT scores over 18: 90%; SAT verbal scores over 600: 16%; SAT math scores over 600: 10%; ACT scores over 24: 20%; SAT verbal scores over 700: 1%; SAT math scores over 700: 2%; ACT scores over 30: 1%.

Faculty *Total:* 188, 42% full-time, 36% with terminal degrees. *Student/faculty ratio:* 19:1.

Majors Art; behavioral sciences; biology; business administration; communications; criminal justice studies; English; exercise sciences; fine/studio arts; history; information sciences/systems; liberal arts and sciences/liberal studies; mathematics; music; organizational behavior; philosophy; political science; psychology; religious studies; social sciences; theology/ministry related.

Academic Programs *Special study options:* accelerated degree program, adult/continuing education programs, advanced placement credit, cooperative education, double majors, independent study, internships, off-campus study, part-time degree program, study abroad, summer session for credit. *ROTC:* Army (c).

Library Annie Gabriel Library with 87,688 titles, 428 serial subscriptions, 4,242 audiovisual materials, an OPAC, a Web page.

Computers on Campus 132 computers available on campus for general student use. A campuswide network can be accessed from student residence rooms and from off campus that provide access to intranet. Internet access, at least one staffed computer lab available.

Student Life *Housing Options:* men-only, women-only. *Activities and Organizations:* drama/theater group, student-run newspaper, choral group, Student Senate, Fellowship of Christian Athletes, Blue Crew, Christian Student Organizations, Black Student Union. *Campus security:* 24-hour emergency response devices and patrols, student patrols, late-night transport/escort service, controlled dormitory access. *Student Services:* health clinic, personal/psychological counseling.

Athletics Member NAIA. *Intercollegiate sports:* baseball M(s), basketball M(s)/W(s), cross-country running M(s)/W(s), soccer M(s)/W(s), softball W(s), swimming M(s)/W(s), track and field M(s)/W(s), volleyball M(s)/W(s), water polo M(s)/W(s). *Intramural sports:* basketball M/W, bowling M/W, football M/W, golf M, softball M/W, table tennis M/W, tennis M/W, volleyball M/W.

Standardized Tests *Required:* SAT I or ACT (for admission).

Costs (2001–02) *Comprehensive fee:* $16,736 includes full-time tuition ($10,920), mandatory fees ($770), and room and board ($5046). Full-time tuition and fees vary according to course load and program. Part-time tuition: $420 per unit. Part-time tuition and fees vary according to course load and program. *Room and board:* College room only: $2250. Room and board charges vary according to board plan and housing facility. *Payment plans:* installment, deferred payment. *Waivers:* employees or children of employees.

Financial Aid Of all full-time matriculated undergraduates who enrolled in 2001, 1213 applied for aid, 1187 were judged to have need, 1079 had their need fully met. 80 Federal Work-Study jobs (averaging $1000). In 2001, 69 non-need-based awards were made. *Average percent of need met:* 91%. *Average financial aid package:* $9600. *Average need-based gift aid:* $5000. *Average indebtedness upon graduation:* $18,300.

Applying *Options:* common application, early admission, deferred entrance. *Application fee:* $30. *Required:* essay or personal statement, high school transcript, minimum 2.5 GPA, 2 letters of recommendation. *Recommended:* interview. *Application deadlines:* 8/18 (freshmen), 8/2 (transfers). *Notification:* continuous until 9/6 (freshmen).

Admissions Contact Mr. Allen Johnson, Director, Undergraduate Admissions, California Baptist University, 8432 Magnolia Avenue, Riverside, CA 92504-3297. *Phone:* 909-343-4212. *Toll-free phone:* 877-228-8866. *Fax:* 909-343-4525. *E-mail:* admissions@calbaptist.edu.

CALIFORNIA CHRISTIAN COLLEGE
Fresno, California

- **Independent religious** 4-year
- **Calendar** semesters

- **Degrees** associate and bachelor's
- **Endowment** $60,000
- **Coed,** 77 undergraduate students, 77% full-time, 31% women, 69% men
- **Noncompetitive** entrance level, 100% of applicants were admitted

Undergraduates 59 full-time, 18 part-time. Students come from 2 states and territories, 5 other countries, 1% are from out of state, 19% African American, 3% Asian American or Pacific Islander, 3% Hispanic American, 45% international, 17% transferred in, 10% live on campus. *Retention:* 23% of 2001 full-time freshmen returned.

Freshmen *Admission:* 32 applied, 32 admitted, 17 enrolled.

Faculty *Total:* 10, 10% with terminal degrees. *Student/faculty ratio:* 8:1.

Majors Biblical studies; pre-theology.

Academic Programs *Special study options:* academic remediation for entering students, accelerated degree program, cooperative education, independent study, part-time degree program, summer session for credit.

Library Cortese Library with 13,154 titles, 7 serial subscriptions, 430 audiovisual materials.

Computers on Campus 6 computers available on campus for general student use. Internet access, at least one staffed computer lab available.

Student Life *Housing:* on-campus residence required through sophomore year. *Options:* coed. *Activities and Organizations:* drama/theater group, student-run newspaper, choral group. *Student Services:* personal/psychological counseling.

Athletics Member NCCAA. *Intercollegiate sports:* basketball M, volleyball W.

Standardized Tests *Recommended:* SAT I or ACT (for admission).

Costs (2001–02) *Comprehensive fee:* $7575 includes full-time tuition ($4000), mandatory fees ($425), and room and board ($3150). Full-time tuition and fees vary according to course load. Part-time tuition: $165 per unit. Part-time tuition and fees vary according to course load. *Payment plan:* installment. *Waivers:* employees or children of employees.

Applying *Application fee:* $40. *Required:* essay or personal statement, high school transcript, minimum 2.0 GPA, 3 letters of recommendation, statement of faith, moral/ethical statement. *Recommended:* interview. *Application deadline:* rolling (freshmen), rolling (transfers). *Notification:* continuous (freshmen).

Admissions Contact Mrs. Marjorie James, Registrar, California Christian College, 4881 East University Avenue, Fresno, CA 93703. *Phone:* 559-251-4215 Ext. 5565. *Fax:* 559-251-4231. *E-mail:* cccfresno@aol.com.

CALIFORNIA COLLEGE FOR HEALTH SCIENCES
National City, California

- **Proprietary** comprehensive, founded 1978
- **Calendar** continuous
- **Degrees** certificates, diplomas, associate, bachelor's, and master's (offers primarily external degree programs)
- **Urban** 2-acre campus with easy access to San Diego
- **Coed,** 5,263 undergraduate students
- **Noncompetitive** entrance level

Undergraduates Students come from 52 states and territories, 15 other countries, 90% are from out of state, 0% live on campus. *Retention:* 85% of 2001 full-time freshmen returned.

Faculty *Total:* 19, 21% full-time, 21% with terminal degrees.

Majors Accounting; business; early childhood education; finance; health science; health services administration; medical records administration; respiratory therapy.

Academic Programs *Special study options:* distance learning, external degree program, part-time degree program.

Computers on Campus A campuswide network can be accessed from off campus.

Student Life *Housing:* college housing not available.

Costs (2001–02) *Tuition:* $399 per course part-time. Full-time tuition and fees vary according to course load and program. Part-time tuition and fees vary according to course load and program. *Payment plan:* installment.

Financial Aid Of all full-time matriculated undergraduates who enrolled in 2001, 96 applied for aid, 96 were judged to have need. In 2001, 1 non-need-based awards were made. *Average percent of need met:* 60%. *Average financial aid package:* $5082. *Average need-based loan:* $2366. *Average need-based gift aid:* $2057. *Average non-need based aid:* $4000. *Average indebtedness upon graduation:* $14,125.

Applying *Options:* deferred entrance. *Application fee:* $50. *Required:* high school transcript. *Required for some:* employment in a health science field. *Recommended:* employment in a health science field. *Application deadline:* rolling (freshmen), rolling (transfers).

Admissions Contact Ms. Marita Gubbe, Director of Student Affairs, California College for Health Sciences, 2423 Hoover Avenue, National City, CA 91950. *Phone:* 619-477-4800 Ext. 320. *Toll-free phone:* 800-221-7374. *Fax:* 619-477-4360. *E-mail:* admissions@cchs.edu.

CALIFORNIA COLLEGE OF ARTS AND CRAFTS
San Francisco, California

- **Independent** comprehensive, founded 1907
- **Calendar** semesters
- **Degrees** bachelor's and master's
- **Urban** 4-acre campus
- **Endowment** $18.2 million
- **Coed,** 1,164 undergraduate students, 88% full-time, 60% women, 40% men
- **Moderately difficult** entrance level, 71% of applicants were admitted

California College of Arts & Crafts (CCAC) is the only regionally accredited school of art, architecture, and design on the West Coast. The College is distinguished by the interdisciplinary nature and breadth of its programs in fine art, design, and architecture, which are taught by a faculty of practicing professionals. Current initiatives include a revitalized first-year program and the expansion of on- and off-campus student housing.

Undergraduates 1,020 full-time, 144 part-time. Students come from 37 states and territories, 25 other countries, 23% are from out of state, 2% African American, 12% Asian American or Pacific Islander, 6% Hispanic American, 0.8% Native American, 7% international, 16% transferred in, 12% live on campus. *Retention:* 80% of 2001 full-time freshmen returned.

Freshmen *Admission:* 451 applied, 321 admitted, 123 enrolled. *Average high school GPA:* 3.12. *Test scores:* SAT verbal scores over 500: 74%; SAT math scores over 500: 55%; ACT scores over 18: 86%; SAT verbal scores over 600: 24%; SAT math scores over 600: 18%; ACT scores over 24: 36%; SAT verbal scores over 700: 5%; ACT scores over 30: 9%.

Faculty *Total:* 326, 10% full-time, 56% with terminal degrees. *Student/faculty ratio:* 10:1.

Majors Applied art; architecture; art; ceramic arts; drawing; fashion design/illustration; film studies; fine/studio arts; graphic design/commercial art/illustration; industrial design; interior architecture; metal/jewelry arts; painting; photography; printmaking; sculpture; textile arts.

Academic Programs *Special study options:* academic remediation for entering students, advanced placement credit, double majors, independent study, internships, off-campus study, services for LD students, student-designed majors, study abroad, summer session for credit.

Library Meyer Library plus 1 other with 57,800 titles, 320 serial subscriptions, 800 audiovisual materials, an OPAC, a Web page.

Computers on Campus 160 computers available on campus for general student use. A campuswide network can be accessed from student residence rooms and from off campus. Internet access, at least one staffed computer lab available.

Student Life *Housing Options:* coed. *Activities and Organizations:* student-run newspaper, American Institute of Architecture—Student Chapter, American Institute of Graphic Arts—Student Chapter, Women's Caucus for the Arts, International Student Club, Artists That Are Queer. *Campus security:* 24-hour emergency response devices and patrols, late-night transport/escort service. *Student Services:* personal/psychological counseling.

Standardized Tests *Recommended:* SAT I or ACT (for admission).

Costs (2001–02) *Comprehensive fee:* $27,466 includes full-time tuition ($20,440), mandatory fees ($250), and room and board ($6776). Full-time tuition and fees vary according to course load. Part-time tuition: $852 per unit. Part-time tuition and fees vary according to course load. *Required fees:* $90 per term part-time. *Room and board:* College room only: $4400. Room and board charges vary according to housing facility. *Payment plans:* installment, deferred payment. *Waivers:* employees or children of employees.

Financial Aid Of all full-time matriculated undergraduates who enrolled in 2001, 601 applied for aid, 546 were judged to have need, 33 had their need fully met. 196 Federal Work-Study jobs (averaging $1200). 56 State and other part-time jobs (averaging $2500). In 2001, 15 non-need-based awards were made. *Average percent of need met:* 68%. *Average financial aid package:* $15,594. *Average need-based loan:* $4705. *Average need-based gift aid:* $9378. *Average non-need based aid:* $9055. *Average indebtedness upon graduation:* $25,400.

Applying *Options:* common application, electronic application, deferred entrance. *Application fee:* $40. *Required:* essay or personal statement, high school transcript, minimum 2.0 GPA, 2 letters of recommendation, portfolio. *Required for some:* interview. *Recommended:* interview. *Application deadline:* rolling (freshmen), rolling (transfers). *Notification:* continuous (freshmen).

Admissions Contact Molly Ryan, Director of Admissions, California College of Arts and Crafts, 1111 Eighth Street at 16th and Wisconsin, San Francisco, CA

California College of Arts and Crafts (continued)
94107. *Phone:* 415-703-9523 Ext. 9532. *Toll-free phone:* 800-447-1ART. *Fax:* 415-703-9539. *E-mail:* enroll@ccac-art.edu.

CALIFORNIA INSTITUTE OF INTEGRAL STUDIES
San Francisco, California

- **Independent** upper-level, founded 1968
- **Calendar** semesters
- **Degrees** certificates, bachelor's, master's, and doctoral
- **Coed**

Faculty *Student/faculty ratio:* 19:1.
Applying *Options:* deferred entrance. *Application fee:* $65.
Admissions Contact California Institute of Integral Studies, 1453 Mission Street, San Francisco, CA 94103. *Phone:* 415-575-6156. *Fax:* 415-575-1268. *E-mail:* info@ciis.edu.

CALIFORNIA INSTITUTE OF TECHNOLOGY
Pasadena, California

- **Independent** university, founded 1891
- **Calendar** 3 ten-week terms
- **Degrees** bachelor's, master's, and doctoral
- **Suburban** 124-acre campus with easy access to Los Angeles
- **Endowment** $1.2 billion
- **Coed,** 942 undergraduate students, 100% full-time, 33% women, 67% men
- **Most difficult** entrance level, 15% of applicants were admitted

Academics—with a focus on math, science, and engineering—in a research environment characterize Caltech. The core curriculum emphasizes the fundamentals of each of the sciences plus study in the humanities and social sciences. Caltech values and encourages study and research across disciplines. A renowned faculty and facilities, including the Jet Propulsion Laboratory, contribute to Caltech's reputation as one of the world's major research centers.

Undergraduates 942 full-time. Students come from 47 states and territories, 33 other countries, 58% are from out of state, 2% African American, 25% Asian American or Pacific Islander, 7% Hispanic American, 0.3% Native American, 10% international, 2% transferred in, 87% live on campus. *Retention:* 97% of 2001 full-time freshmen returned.
Freshmen *Admission:* 3,365 applied, 515 admitted, 214 enrolled. *Test scores:* SAT verbal scores over 500: 100%; SAT math scores over 500: 100%; SAT verbal scores over 600: 99%; SAT math scores over 600: 100%; SAT verbal scores over 700: 80%; SAT math scores over 700: 98%.
Faculty *Total:* 322, 91% full-time, 95% with terminal degrees. *Student/faculty ratio:* 3:1.
Majors Aerospace engineering; applied mathematics; astronomy; astrophysics; biochemistry; biology; business economics; cell biology; chemical engineering; chemistry; civil engineering; computer engineering; computer science; earth sciences; economics; electrical engineering; engineering; engineering physics; environmental engineering; geochemistry; geology; geophysics/seismology; history; literature; materials science; mathematics; mechanical engineering; molecular biology; neuroscience; nuclear physics; physical sciences; physics; social sciences.
Academic Programs *Special study options:* double majors, independent study, internships, off-campus study, services for LD students, student-designed majors, study abroad. *ROTC:* Army (c), Air Force (c).
Library Millikan Library plus 10 others with 2.9 million titles, 3,200 serial subscriptions, an OPAC, a Web page.
Computers on Campus 600 computers available on campus for general student use. A campuswide network can be accessed from student residence rooms and from off campus. Internet access, at least one staffed computer lab available.
Student Life *Housing:* on-campus residence required for freshman year. *Options:* coed. *Activities and Organizations:* drama/theater group, student-run newspaper, choral group, ASCIT, Entrepreneur's Club, instrumental music groups, Glee Club, Theater Arts. *Campus security:* 24-hour emergency response devices and patrols, late-night transport/escort service. *Student Services:* health clinic, personal/psychological counseling, women's center.
Athletics Member NCAA. All Division III. *Intercollegiate sports:* baseball M, basketball M/W, cross-country running M/W, fencing M/W, golf M/W, ice hockey M(c), rugby M(c), soccer M/W(c), swimming M/W, tennis M/W, track and field M/W, volleyball M(c)/W, water polo M/W(c). *Intramural sports:* badminton M/W, baseball M, basketball M/W, cross-country running M/W, football M/W, ice hockey M, racquetball M, soccer M/W, softball M/W, squash M/W, swimming M/W, table tennis M/W, tennis M/W, track and field M/W, volleyball M/W, water polo M/W.
Standardized Tests *Required:* SAT I (for admission), SAT II: Writing Test (for admission).
Costs (2002–03) *Comprehensive fee:* $29,118 includes full-time tuition ($21,903), mandatory fees ($216), and room and board ($6999). *Payment plans:* installment, deferred payment. *Waivers:* employees or children of employees.
Financial Aid Of all full-time matriculated undergraduates who enrolled in 2001, 585 applied for aid, 537 were judged to have need, 537 had their need fully met. 316 Federal Work-Study jobs (averaging $2082). 48 State and other part-time jobs (averaging $2316). In 2001, 374 non-need-based awards were made. *Average percent of need met:* 100%. *Average financial aid package:* $22,648. *Average need-based loan:* $1304. *Average need-based gift aid:* $19,132. *Average non-need based aid:* $8900. *Average indebtedness upon graduation:* $12,214.
Applying *Options:* electronic application, early admission, early action, deferred entrance. *Application fee:* $50. *Required:* essay or personal statement, high school transcript, 3 letters of recommendation. *Application deadlines:* 1/1 (freshmen), 3/1 (transfers). *Notification:* 4/1 (freshmen), 12/30 (early action).
Admissions Contact Ms. Charlene Liebau, Director of Admissions, California Institute of Technology, 1200 East California Boulevard, Pasadena, CA 91125-0001. *Phone:* 626-395-6341. *Toll-free phone:* 800-568-8324. *Fax:* 626-683-3026. *E-mail:* ugadmissions@caltech.edu.

CALIFORNIA INSTITUTE OF THE ARTS
Valencia, California

- **Independent** comprehensive, founded 1961
- **Calendar** semesters
- **Degrees** certificates, bachelor's, master's, and postbachelor's certificates
- **Suburban** 60-acre campus with easy access to Los Angeles
- **Endowment** $86.1 million
- **Coed,** 830 undergraduate students, 99% full-time, 42% women, 58% men
- **Very difficult** entrance level, 36% of applicants were admitted

Undergraduates 823 full-time, 7 part-time. Students come from 47 states and territories, 41 other countries, 55% are from out of state, 5% African American, 11% Asian American or Pacific Islander, 10% Hispanic American, 2% Native American, 11% international, 12% transferred in, 40% live on campus. *Retention:* 92% of 2001 full-time freshmen returned.
Freshmen *Admission:* 1,242 applied, 448 admitted, 135 enrolled.
Faculty *Total:* 267, 52% full-time. *Student/faculty ratio:* 6:1.
Majors Art; computer graphics; dance; film studies; fine/studio arts; graphic design/commercial art/illustration; jazz; music; music (piano and organ performance); music (voice and choral/opera performance); photography; sculpture; stringed instruments; theater arts/drama.
Academic Programs *Special study options:* advanced placement credit, independent study, internships, services for LD students, student-designed majors, study abroad.
Library Main Library plus 1 other with 95,973 titles, 613 serial subscriptions, 20,611 audiovisual materials, an OPAC, a Web page.
Computers on Campus 87 computers available on campus for general student use. A campuswide network can be accessed from student residence rooms and from off campus. Internet access, at least one staffed computer lab available.
Student Life *Housing Options:* coed, disabled students. *Activities and Organizations:* drama/theater group, student-run radio and television station, choral group. *Campus security:* 24-hour emergency response devices and patrols, late-night transport/escort service, controlled dormitory access. *Student Services:* health clinic, personal/psychological counseling.
Costs (2001–02) *Comprehensive fee:* $28,535 includes full-time tuition ($22,190), mandatory fees ($345), and room and board ($6000). *Room and board:* College room only: $3230. Room and board charges vary according to housing facility. *Waivers:* employees or children of employees.
Financial Aid Of all full-time matriculated undergraduates who enrolled in 2001, 651 applied for aid, 542 were judged to have need, 66 had their need fully met. 183 Federal Work-Study jobs (averaging $2624). 25 State and other part-time jobs (averaging $2400). In 2001, 70 non-need-based awards were made. *Average percent of need met:* 81%. *Average financial aid package:* $19,525. *Average need-based loan:* $5448. *Average need-based gift aid:* $10,434. *Average non-need based aid:* $4002. *Average indebtedness upon graduation:* $25,069.
Applying *Options:* deferred entrance. *Application fee:* $60. *Required:* essay or personal statement, high school transcript, portfolio or audition. *Required for some:* letters of recommendation, interview. *Application deadline:* rolling (freshmen), rolling (transfers). *Notification:* continuous (freshmen).

Admissions Contact Ms. Carol Kim, Director of Enrollment Services, California Institute of the Arts, 24700 McBean Parkway, Valencia, CA 91355. *Phone:* 661-255-1050. *E-mail:* admiss@calarts.edu.

CALIFORNIA LUTHERAN UNIVERSITY

Thousand Oaks, California

- **Independent Lutheran** comprehensive, founded 1959
- **Calendar** semesters
- **Degrees** bachelor's and master's
- **Suburban** 290-acre campus with easy access to Los Angeles
- **Endowment** $29.1 million
- **Coed,** 1,846 undergraduate students, 88% full-time, 57% women, 43% men
- **Moderately difficult** entrance level, 83% of applicants were admitted

A small, private university with 2,700 students, California Lutheran University is known for its supportive and challenging academic environment and for it's outstanding graduate placement. Biology, education, and business anchor a curriculum of 34 majors and 29 minors. CLU is located in the safe, neighborly city of Thousand Oaks and, on the World Wide Web, at http://www.CLUnet.edu.

Undergraduates 1,631 full-time, 215 part-time. Students come from 37 states and territories, 19 other countries, 22% are from out of state, 2% African American, 5% Asian American or Pacific Islander, 12% Hispanic American, 0.6% Native American, 3% international, 9% transferred in, 65% live on campus. *Retention:* 79% of 2001 full-time freshmen returned.

Freshmen *Admission:* 1,029 applied, 859 admitted, 392 enrolled. *Average high school GPA:* 3.40. *Test scores:* SAT verbal scores over 500: 63%; SAT math scores over 500: 65%; ACT scores over 18: 95%; SAT verbal scores over 600: 18%; SAT math scores over 600: 21%; ACT scores over 24: 39%; SAT verbal scores over 700: 2%; SAT math scores over 700: 2%; ACT scores over 30: 4%.

Faculty *Total:* 241, 46% full-time. *Student/faculty ratio:* 15:1.

Majors Accounting; art; athletic training/sports medicine; biochemistry; biology; business administration; business marketing and marketing management; chemistry; computer science; criminal justice/law enforcement administration; economics; English; French; geology; German; history; information sciences/systems; interdisciplinary studies; international relations; liberal arts and sciences/liberal studies; mass communications; mathematics; molecular biology; music; philosophy; physical education; physics; political science; psychology; religious studies; social sciences; sociology; Spanish; theater arts/drama.

Academic Programs *Special study options:* accelerated degree program, adult/continuing education programs, advanced placement credit, cooperative education, double majors, independent study, internships, off-campus study, part-time degree program, student-designed majors, study abroad, summer session for credit. *ROTC:* Army (c), Air Force (c).

Library Pearson Library with 125,032 titles, 586 serial subscriptions, 720 audiovisual materials, an OPAC, a Web page.

Computers on Campus 135 computers available on campus for general student use. A campuswide network can be accessed from student residence rooms and from off campus. Internet access, at least one staffed computer lab available.

Student Life *Housing:* on-campus residence required through junior year. *Options:* coed, disabled students. *Activities and Organizations:* drama/theater group, student-run newspaper, radio and television station, choral group, student government, Music and Drama Clubs, Service Organizations, Campus Ministry Organizations, Multicultural Organizations. *Campus security:* 24-hour emergency response devices and patrols, late-night transport/escort service, controlled dormitory access, escort service; shuttle service. *Student Services:* health clinic, personal/psychological counseling, women's center.

Athletics Member NCAA. All Division III. *Intercollegiate sports:* baseball M, basketball M/W, cross-country running M/W, football M, golf M, soccer M/W, softball W, tennis M/W, track and field M/W, volleyball W. *Intramural sports:* basketball M/W, football M/W, rugby M(c), soccer M/W, softball M/W, tennis M/W, volleyball M(c)/W.

Standardized Tests *Required:* SAT I or ACT (for admission).

Costs (2001–02) *Comprehensive fee:* $25,456 includes full-time tuition ($18,600), mandatory fees ($200), and room and board ($6656). Part-time tuition: $600 per unit. *Room and board:* College room only: $3246. Room and board charges vary according to board plan. *Payment plan:* installment. *Waivers:* employees or children of employees.

Financial Aid Of all full-time matriculated undergraduates who enrolled in 2001, 1186 applied for aid, 996 were judged to have need, 270 had their need fully met. 415 Federal Work-Study jobs (averaging $1797). 21 State and other part-time jobs (averaging $2723). *Average percent of need met:* 85%. *Average financial aid package:* $15,280. *Average need-based loan:* $3464. *Average need-based gift aid:* $11,350. *Average indebtedness upon graduation:* $15,795.

Applying *Options:* electronic application, deferred entrance. *Application fee:* $50. *Required:* essay or personal statement, high school transcript, minimum 2.75 GPA, 1 letter of recommendation. *Recommended:* minimum 3.0 GPA, interview. *Application deadlines:* 6/1 (freshmen), 6/1 (transfers). *Notification:* continuous until 6/15 (freshmen).

Admissions Contact Mr. Darryl Calkins, Dean of Undergraduate Enrollment, California Lutheran University, Office of Admission, #1350, Thousand Oaks, CA 91360. *Phone:* 805-493-3135. *Toll-free phone:* 877-258-3678. *Fax:* 805-493-3114. *E-mail:* cluadm@clunet.edu.

CALIFORNIA MARITIME ACADEMY

Vallejo, California

- **State-supported** 4-year, founded 1929, part of California State University System
- **Calendar** semesters
- **Degree** bachelor's
- **Suburban** 67-acre campus with easy access to San Francisco
- **Coed, primarily men,** 653 undergraduate students, 94% full-time, 20% women, 80% men
- **Moderately difficult** entrance level, 58% of applicants were admitted

Undergraduates 612 full-time, 41 part-time. Students come from 20 states and territories, 14 other countries, 13% are from out of state, 3% African American, 11% Asian American or Pacific Islander, 6% Hispanic American, 1% Native American, 6% international, 10% transferred in, 65% live on campus. *Retention:* 93% of 2001 full-time freshmen returned.

Freshmen *Admission:* 352 applied, 204 admitted, 191 enrolled. *Average high school GPA:* 3.05.

Faculty *Total:* 75, 65% full-time, 35% with terminal degrees. *Student/faculty ratio:* 15:1.

Majors Business administration; engineering technologies related; marine technology; mechanical engineering.

Academic Programs *Special study options:* academic remediation for entering students, advanced placement credit, distance learning, internships, summer session for credit. *ROTC:* Navy (c).

Library Hugh Gallagher Library plus 1 other with 28,377 titles, 273 serial subscriptions, 241 audiovisual materials, an OPAC, a Web page.

Computers on Campus 50 computers available on campus for general student use. A campuswide network can be accessed from student residence rooms and from off campus. Internet access, at least one staffed computer lab available.

Student Life *Housing:* on-campus residence required through junior year. *Options:* coed. *Activities and Organizations:* student-run newspaper, Sailing Club, Dive Club, Drill Team. *Campus security:* 24-hour patrols, student patrols. *Student Services:* health clinic, personal/psychological counseling.

Athletics Member NAIA. *Intercollegiate sports:* basketball M, crew M/W, golf M/W, rugby M, sailing M/W, soccer M/W, volleyball W, water polo M/W. *Intramural sports:* baseball M, basketball M/W, football M/W, golf M/W, racquetball M/W, rugby M, sailing M/W, softball M/W, tennis M/W, volleyball M/W.

Standardized Tests *Required:* SAT I or ACT (for admission).

Costs (2002–03) *One-time required fee:* $1450. *Tuition:* state resident $0 full-time; nonresident $7380 full-time. Full-time tuition and fees vary according to program and student level. *Required fees:* $2386 full-time. *Room and board:* $6180; room only: $2730. Room and board charges vary according to board plan and housing facility. *Payment plan:* installment.

Financial Aid Of all full-time matriculated undergraduates who enrolled in 2001, 335 applied for aid, 263 were judged to have need, 99 had their need fully met. 18 Federal Work-Study jobs (averaging $1500). *Average percent of need met:* 78%. *Average financial aid package:* $7899. *Average need-based loan:* $4499. *Average need-based gift aid:* $4719. *Average indebtedness upon graduation:* $6999.

Applying *Options:* electronic application. *Application fee:* $55. *Required:* high school transcript, minimum 2.0 GPA, health form. *Application deadlines:* 4/1 (freshmen), 4/1 (transfers). *Notification:* continuous (freshmen).

Admissions Contact California Maritime Academy, PO Box 1392, Vallejo, CA 94590-0644. *Phone:* 707-654-1331. *Toll-free phone:* 800-561-1945. *Fax:* 707-654-1336. *E-mail:* admission@csum.edu.

CALIFORNIA NATIONAL UNIVERSITY FOR ADVANCED STUDIES

North Hills, California

Admissions Contact 16909 Parthenia Street, North Hills, CA 91343.

California Polytechnic State University, San Luis Obispo

San Luis Obispo, California

- **State-supported** comprehensive, founded 1901, part of California State University System
- **Calendar** quarters
- **Degrees** bachelor's and master's
- **Small-town** 6000-acre campus
- **Endowment** $2.7 million
- **Coed,** 17,066 undergraduate students, 94% full-time, 45% women, 55% men
- **Moderately difficult** entrance level, 47% of applicants were admitted

Undergraduates 16,095 full-time, 971 part-time. Students come from 48 states and territories, 41 other countries, 4% are from out of state, 0.9% African American, 11% Asian American or Pacific Islander, 10% Hispanic American, 0.9% Native American, 0.7% international, 6% transferred in, 17% live on campus. *Retention:* 89% of 2001 full-time freshmen returned.

Freshmen *Admission:* 18,755 applied, 8,760 admitted, 3,003 enrolled. *Average high school GPA:* 3.63. *Test scores:* SAT verbal scores over 500: 82%; SAT math scores over 500: 91%; ACT scores over 18: 96%; SAT verbal scores over 600: 34%; SAT math scores over 600: 56%; ACT scores over 24: 62%; SAT verbal scores over 700: 4%; SAT math scores over 700: 11%; ACT scores over 30: 8%.

Faculty *Total:* 1,161, 56% full-time, 55% with terminal degrees. *Student/faculty ratio:* 20:1.

Majors Aerospace engineering; agricultural business; agricultural engineering; agricultural sciences; agronomy/crop science; animal sciences; applied art; architectural engineering; architecture; art; biochemistry; biology; business administration; chemistry; city/community/regional planning; civil engineering; computer engineering; computer science; dairy science; developmental/child psychology; early childhood education; economics; electrical engineering; engineering science; English; environmental biology; environmental engineering; farm/ranch management; food sciences; forestry; graphic design/commercial art/illustration; graphic/printing equipment; history; horticulture science; human resources management; industrial/manufacturing engineering; industrial technology; journalism; landscape architecture; liberal arts and sciences/liberal studies; management information systems/business data processing; materials engineering; mathematical statistics; mathematics; mechanical engineering; mechanical engineering technology; microbiology/bacteriology; music; nutrition science; ornamental horticulture; philosophy; physical education; physical sciences; physics; political science; pre-medicine; psychology; recreation/leisure studies; social sciences; speech/rhetorical studies; trade/industrial education.

Academic Programs *Special study options:* academic remediation for entering students, advanced placement credit, cooperative education, distance learning, double majors, English as a second language, external degree program, honors programs, independent study, internships, off-campus study, part-time degree program, services for LD students, study abroad, summer session for credit. *ROTC:* Army (b).

Library Kennedy Library with 1.2 million titles, 2,617 serial subscriptions, 48,300 audiovisual materials, an OPAC, a Web page.

Computers on Campus 1880 computers available on campus for general student use. A campuswide network can be accessed from student residence rooms and from off campus. At least one staffed computer lab available.

Student Life *Housing Options:* coed, men-only, women-only. *Activities and Organizations:* drama/theater group, student-run newspaper, radio station, choral group, marching band, Ski Club, American Marketing Association, Rose Float Club, MECHA, Society of Women Engineers, national fraternities, national sororities. *Campus security:* 24-hour emergency response devices and patrols, student patrols, late-night transport/escort service, controlled dormitory access. *Student Services:* health clinic, personal/psychological counseling, women's center, legal services.

Athletics Member NCAA. All Division I except football (Division I-AA). *Intercollegiate sports:* baseball M(s), basketball M(s)/W(s), cross-country running M(s)/W(s), equestrian sports M/W, golf M(s), gymnastics W(s), soccer M/W, softball W(s), swimming M/W, tennis M/W, track and field M(s)/W(s), volleyball W(s), wrestling M(s). *Intramural sports:* baseball M, basketball M, bowling M/W, crew M, fencing M/W, football M, golf M, gymnastics M, lacrosse M, racquetball M/W, rugby M, skiing (cross-country) M/W, skiing (downhill) M/W, soccer M/W, softball W, volleyball M/W, water polo M/W.

Standardized Tests *Required:* SAT I or ACT (for admission).

Costs (2001–02) *Tuition:* state resident $0 full-time; nonresident $5904 full-time, $164 per unit part-time. Full-time tuition and fees vary according to course load. Part-time tuition and fees vary according to course load. *Required fees:* $2153 full-time. *Room and board:* $6594; room only: $3690. Room and board charges vary according to board plan. *Payment plan:* installment. *Waivers:* senior citizens and employees or children of employees.

Financial Aid Of all full-time matriculated undergraduates who enrolled in 2001, 8657 applied for aid, 5691 were judged to have need, 554 had their need fully met. *Average percent of need met:* 80%. *Average financial aid package:* $6765. *Average need-based loan:* $3493. *Average need-based gift aid:* $1410. *Average indebtedness upon graduation:* $12,908.

Applying *Options:* electronic application, early admission, early decision. *Application fee:* $55. *Required:* high school transcript. *Application deadlines:* 11/30 (freshmen), 11/30 (transfers). *Early decision:* 10/31. *Notification:* 3/1 (freshmen), 12/15 (early decision).

Admissions Contact Mr. James Maraviglia, Director of Admissions and Evaluations, California Polytechnic State University, San Luis Obispo, San Luis Obispo, CA 93407. *Phone:* 805-756-2311. *Fax:* 805-756-5400. *E-mail:* admprosp@calpoly.edu.

California State Polytechnic University, Pomona

Pomona, California

- **State-supported** comprehensive, founded 1938, part of California State University System
- **Calendar** quarters
- **Degrees** bachelor's and master's
- **Urban** 1400-acre campus with easy access to Los Angeles
- **Endowment** $12.5 million
- **Coed,** 17,005 undergraduate students, 81% full-time, 43% women, 57% men
- **Moderately difficult** entrance level, 67% of applicants were admitted

Undergraduates 13,773 full-time, 3,232 part-time. Students come from 52 states and territories, 116 other countries, 2% are from out of state, 3% African American, 34% Asian American or Pacific Islander, 23% Hispanic American, 0.5% Native American, 5% international, 8% transferred in, 8% live on campus. *Retention:* 78% of 2001 full-time freshmen returned.

Freshmen *Admission:* 11,003 applied, 7,389 admitted, 2,170 enrolled. *Average high school GPA:* 3.25. *Test scores:* SAT verbal scores over 500: 42%; SAT math scores over 500: 64%; ACT scores over 18: 75%; SAT verbal scores over 600: 9%; SAT math scores over 600: 24%; ACT scores over 24: 18%; SAT verbal scores over 700: 1%; SAT math scores over 700: 3%; ACT scores over 30: 2%.

Faculty *Total:* 1,205, 55% full-time, 46% with terminal degrees. *Student/faculty ratio:* 20:1.

Majors Accounting; aerospace engineering; agricultural business; agricultural education; agricultural engineering; agricultural sciences; agronomy/crop science; animal sciences; anthropology; applied mathematics; architecture; art; behavioral sciences; bilingual/bicultural education; biological technology; biology; botany; business administration; business marketing and marketing management; chemical engineering; chemistry; city/community/regional planning; civil engineering; computer engineering; computer/information sciences; computer science; construction technology; counselor education/guidance; cultural studies; dietetics; earth sciences; economics; electrical/electronic engineering technology; electrical engineering; engineering technology; English; farm/ranch management; finance; geography; geology; graphic design/commercial art/illustration; history; home economics; horticulture science; hotel and restaurant management; humanities; human resources management; industrial/manufacturing engineering; information sciences/systems; insurance/risk management; international business; journalism; landscape architecture; liberal arts and sciences/liberal studies; mass communications; materials engineering; mathematical statistics; mathematics; mechanical engineering; mechanical engineering technology; microbiology/bacteriology; music; nutrition science; ornamental horticulture; petroleum engineering; philosophy; physical education; physics; plant protection; political science; pre-law; pre-medicine; pre-veterinary studies; psychology; public administration; public relations; real estate; social sciences; sociology; soil conservation; Spanish; surveying; telecommunications; theater arts/drama; urban studies; zoology.

Academic Programs *Special study options:* academic remediation for entering students, adult/continuing education programs, advanced placement credit, cooperative education, double majors, English as a second language, internships, off-campus study, part-time degree program, services for LD students, study abroad, summer session for credit. *ROTC:* Army (b), Air Force (c).

Library University Library with 433,342 titles, 5,863 serial subscriptions, 10,799 audiovisual materials, an OPAC, a Web page.

Computers on Campus 1864 computers available on campus for general student use. A campuswide network can be accessed from student residence rooms and from off campus. Internet access, at least one staffed computer lab available.

Student Life *Housing Options:* coed. *Activities and Organizations:* drama/theater group, student-run newspaper, choral group, Rose Float Club, Ridge Runners Ski Club, Barkada (Asian Club), American Marketing Association, Cal Poly Society of Accountants, national fraternities, national sororities. *Campus security:* 24-hour emergency response devices and patrols, student patrols, late-night transport/escort service, video camera surveillance. *Student Services:* health clinic, personal/psychological counseling, women's center.

Athletics Member NCAA. All Division II. *Intercollegiate sports:* baseball M(s), basketball M(s)/W(s), cross-country running M(s)/W(s), soccer M(s)/W(s), tennis M(s)/W(s), track and field M(s)/W(s), volleyball W(s). *Intramural sports:* basketball M/W, bowling M/W, football M/W, softball M/W, tennis M/W, volleyball M/W.

Standardized Tests *Required:* SAT I or ACT (for admission).

Costs (2001–02) *Tuition:* state resident $0 full-time; nonresident $7380 full-time, $164 per unit part-time. Part-time tuition and fees vary according to course load. *Required fees:* $1772 full-time, $443 per term part-time. *Room and board:* $6843. Room and board charges vary according to board plan and housing facility. *Payment plan:* installment. *Waivers:* senior citizens and employees or children of employees.

Financial Aid Of all full-time matriculated undergraduates who enrolled in 2001, 8206 applied for aid, 6739 were judged to have need, 2740 had their need fully met. 911 Federal Work-Study jobs (averaging $2037). In 2001, 51 non-need-based awards were made. *Average percent of need met:* 87%. *Average financial aid package:* $7173. *Average need-based loan:* $2769. *Average need-based gift aid:* $4788. *Average non-need based aid:* $1258. *Average indebtedness upon graduation:* $10,165.

Applying *Options:* electronic application. *Application fee:* $55. *Required:* high school transcript, minimum 2.0 GPA. *Application deadlines:* 4/1 (freshmen), 5/1 (transfers). *Notification:* 11/1 (freshmen).

Admissions Contact Ms. Dena Bennett, Assistant Director of Admissions, California State Polytechnic University, Pomona, Pomona, CA 91768. *Phone:* 909-869-2991. *Fax:* 909-869-4529. *E-mail:* cppadmit@csupomona.edu.

CALIFORNIA STATE UNIVERSITY, BAKERSFIELD
Bakersfield, California

- **State-supported** comprehensive, founded 1970, part of California State University System
- **Calendar** quarters
- **Degrees** bachelor's and master's
- **Urban** 575-acre campus
- **Coed,** 5,228 undergraduate students, 79% full-time, 65% women, 35% men
- **Moderately difficult** entrance level

Undergraduates Students come from 16 states and territories, 48 other countries, 7% African American, 6% Asian American or Pacific Islander, 31% Hispanic American, 1% Native American, 2% international, 4% live on campus.

Freshmen *Test scores:* ACT scores over 18: 50%; ACT scores over 24: 14%; ACT scores over 30: 1%.

Faculty *Total:* 484, 60% full-time.

Majors Anthropology; art; biology; business administration; chemistry; computer science; criminal justice/law enforcement administration; developmental/child psychology; economics; English; finance; geology; history; interdisciplinary studies; land use management; liberal arts and sciences/liberal studies; mass communications; mathematics; music; nursing; philosophy; physical education; physics; political science; psychology; public administration; religious studies; sociology; Spanish; theater arts/drama.

Academic Programs *Special study options:* academic remediation for entering students, accelerated degree program, adult/continuing education programs, advanced placement credit, cooperative education, distance learning, double majors, English as a second language, external degree program, freshman honors college, honors programs, independent study, internships, off-campus study, part-time degree program, services for LD students, student-designed majors, study abroad, summer session for credit.

Library Walter W. Stiern Library with 354,016 titles, 2,260 serial subscriptions, a Web page.

Computers on Campus 600 computers available on campus for general student use. A campuswide network can be accessed from student residence rooms and from off campus. Internet access, at least one staffed computer lab available.

Student Life *Housing Options:* coed. *Activities and Organizations:* drama/theater group, student-run newspaper, choral group, MECHA, LUPE, STAAR, Psi Chi, Art Club, national fraternities, national sororities. *Campus security:* 24-hour emergency response devices and patrols, late-night transport/escort service. *Student Services:* health clinic, personal/psychological counseling, women's center.

Athletics Member NCAA. All Division II except wrestling (Division I). *Intercollegiate sports:* basketball M(s), golf M(s), soccer M(s), softball W(s), swimming M(s)/W(s), tennis W(s), track and field M(s)/W(s), volleyball W(s), water polo W(s), wrestling M(s). *Intramural sports:* archery M/W, badminton M/W, baseball M/W, basketball M/W, fencing M/W, football M/W, golf M/W, gymnastics M/W, racquetball M/W, riflery M/W, soccer M, softball M/W, swimming M/W, tennis W, volleyball M/W, weight lifting M/W, wrestling M/W.

Standardized Tests *Required:* SAT I or ACT (for admission). *Recommended:* SAT II: Subject Tests (for admission).

Costs (2001–02) *Tuition:* state resident $0 full-time; nonresident $4920 full-time, $164 per unit part-time. *Required fees:* $1797 full-time, $399 per term part-time. *Room and board:* $5400.

Financial Aid Of all full-time matriculated undergraduates who enrolled in 2001, 3110 applied for aid, 2688 were judged to have need, 740 had their need fully met. 165 Federal Work-Study jobs (averaging $1506). 24 State and other part-time jobs (averaging $2648). In 2001, 127 non-need-based awards were made. *Average percent of need met:* 86%. *Average financial aid package:* $5889. *Average need-based loan:* $3118. *Average need-based gift aid:* $3815. *Average non-need based aid:* $1690. *Average indebtedness upon graduation:* $3632.

Applying *Options:* electronic application, early admission, deferred entrance. *Application fee:* $55. *Required:* high school transcript. *Application deadlines:* 9/23 (freshmen), 9/23 (transfers). *Notification:* continuous (freshmen).

Admissions Contact Dr. Homer S. Montalvo, Associate Dean of Admissions and Records, California State University, Bakersfield, 9001 Stockdale Highway, Bakersfield, CA 93311-1099. *Phone:* 805-664-2160. *Toll-free phone:* 800-788-2782.

CALIFORNIA STATE UNIVERSITY, CHICO
Chico, California

- **State-supported** comprehensive, founded 1887, part of California State University System
- **Calendar** semesters
- **Degrees** certificates, bachelor's, master's, post-master's, and postbachelor's certificates
- **Small-town** 119-acre campus
- **Endowment** $18.1 million
- **Coed,** 14,634 undergraduate students, 90% full-time, 53% women, 47% men
- **Moderately difficult** entrance level, 90% of applicants were admitted

Undergraduates 13,174 full-time, 1,460 part-time. Students come from 44 states and territories, 48 other countries, 1% are from out of state, 2% African American, 5% Asian American or Pacific Islander, 10% Hispanic American, 1% Native American, 2% international, 11% transferred in, 12% live on campus. *Retention:* 81% of 2001 full-time freshmen returned.

Freshmen *Admission:* 7,899 applied, 7,139 admitted, 2,128 enrolled. *Average high school GPA:* 3.16. *Test scores:* SAT verbal scores over 500: 53%; SAT math scores over 500: 57%; ACT scores over 18: 80%; SAT verbal scores over 600: 13%; SAT math scores over 600: 16%; ACT scores over 24: 23%; SAT verbal scores over 700: 1%; SAT math scores over 700: 1%; ACT scores over 30: 2%.

Faculty *Total:* 1,014, 61% full-time, 62% with terminal degrees. *Student/faculty ratio:* 20:1.

Majors Agricultural business; agricultural education; agricultural sciences related; agronomy/crop science; American studies; animal sciences; anthropology; applied mathematics; architectural engineering technology; art; art education; art history; Asian studies; atmospheric sciences; biochemistry; biology; business; business administration; business marketing and marketing management; chemistry; city/community/regional planning; civil engineering; communication disorders; communications; community health liaison; computer engineering; computer/information sciences; computer/information sciences related; criminal justice/law enforcement administration; cultural studies; design/visual communications; early childhood education; earth sciences; economics; educational media design; electrical engineering; engineering related; English; English education; environmental science; exercise sciences; finance; fine/studio arts; French; geography; geology; German; health education; health science; health services administration; history; humanities; human resources management; industrial technology; information sciences/systems; interdisciplinary studies; interior design; international relations; journalism; Latin American studies; legal studies; liberal arts and sciences/liberal studies; management information systems/business data processing; mathematical statistics; mathematics; mathematics education; mechanical engineering; medical laboratory assistant; microbiology/bacteriology; music; music (general performance); music teacher education; natural resources management; nursing; nutrition studies; operations management; philosophy; physical education; physical sciences; physics; political science; pre-dentistry; pre-medicine; pre-veterinary studies; psychology; public

California State University, Chico (continued)
administration; public relations; radio/television broadcasting; range management; recreational therapy; recreation/leisure facilities management; recreation/leisure studies; religious studies; science education; social science education; social sciences; social work; sociology; Spanish; speech/rhetorical studies; theater arts/drama; theater arts/drama and stagecraft related.

Academic Programs *Special study options:* academic remediation for entering students, adult/continuing education programs, advanced placement credit, cooperative education, distance learning, double majors, English as a second language, honors programs, independent study, internships, off-campus study, part-time degree program, services for LD students, student-designed majors, study abroad, summer session for credit.

Library Meriam Library with 928,450 titles, 13,390 serial subscriptions, 20,215 audiovisual materials, an OPAC, a Web page.

Computers on Campus 1000 computers available on campus for general student use. A campuswide network can be accessed from student residence rooms and from off campus that provide access to student account information. Internet access, at least one staffed computer lab available.

Student Life *Housing Options:* coed, disabled students. *Activities and Organizations:* drama/theater group, student-run newspaper, radio station, choral group, The Edge, Newman Center, Audio Engineering Society, Snowboard Club, Hillel/Jewish Student Union, national fraternities, national sororities. *Campus security:* 24-hour emergency response devices and patrols, student patrols, late-night transport/escort service, controlled dormitory access, crime prevention workshops, RAD self-defense Program, Chico Safe Rides, blue light emergency phones. *Student Services:* health clinic, personal/psychological counseling, women's center, legal services.

Athletics Member NCAA. All Division II. *Intercollegiate sports:* baseball M, basketball M/W, bowling M(c)/W(c), cross-country running M/W, golf M/W, lacrosse M(c)/W(c), rugby M(c)/W(c), skiing (downhill) M(c)/W(c), soccer M/W, softball W, track and field M/W, volleyball M(c)/W, water polo M(c)/W(c). *Intramural sports:* badminton M/W, basketball M/W, bowling M/W, fencing M(c)/W(c), football M/W, golf M/W, soccer M/W, softball M/W, swimming M/W, tennis M/W, volleyball M/W, weight lifting M/W, wrestling M(c).

Standardized Tests *Required:* SAT I or ACT (for admission).

Costs (2002–03) *Tuition:* state resident $0 full-time; nonresident $7380 full-time, $246 per term part-time. Part-time tuition and fees vary according to course load. *Required fees:* $2086 full-time, $1043 per term part-time. *Room and board:* $6973; room only: $4729. Room and board charges vary according to board plan and housing facility. *Payment plans:* installment, deferred payment. *Waivers:* senior citizens and employees or children of employees.

Financial Aid Of all full-time matriculated undergraduates who enrolled in 2001, 355 Federal Work-Study jobs, 92 State and other part-time jobs (averaging $1661).

Applying *Options:* common application, electronic application, deferred entrance. *Application fee:* $55. *Required:* high school transcript. *Application deadline:* 11/30 (freshmen). *Notification:* 3/1 (freshmen).

Admissions Contact Mr. John F. Swiney, Director of Admissions, California State University, Chico, Chico, CA 95929-0722. *Phone:* 530-898-4879. *Toll-free phone:* 800-542-4426. *Fax:* 530-898-6456. *E-mail:* info@csuchico.edu.

CALIFORNIA STATE UNIVERSITY, DOMINGUEZ HILLS

Carson, California

- **State-supported** comprehensive, founded 1960, part of California State University System
- **Calendar** semesters
- **Degrees** bachelor's and master's
- **Urban** 350-acre campus with easy access to Los Angeles
- **Coed,** 7,764 undergraduate students, 59% full-time, 70% women, 30% men
- **Moderately difficult** entrance level, 76% of applicants were admitted

Undergraduates 4,603 full-time, 3,161 part-time. Students come from 29 states and territories, 42 other countries, 2% are from out of state, 30% African American, 10% Asian American or Pacific Islander, 34% Hispanic American, 0.6% Native American, 1% international, 16% transferred in. *Retention:* 73% of 2001 full-time freshmen returned.

Freshmen *Admission:* 2,722 applied, 2,081 admitted, 598 enrolled.

Faculty *Total:* 762, 42% full-time, 48% with terminal degrees. *Student/faculty ratio:* 21:1.

Majors Accounting; African-American studies; anthropology; applied art; art; art history; behavioral sciences; bilingual/bicultural education; biochemistry; biology; business administration; business marketing and marketing management; chemistry; child care/development; computer science; criminal justice/law enforcement administration; cytotechnology; earth sciences; economics; English; finance; fine/studio arts; French; geography; geology; gerontology; graphic design/commercial art/illustration; health science; health services administration; history; humanities; human resources management; human services; information sciences/systems; interdisciplinary studies; international business; labor/personnel relations; liberal arts and sciences/liberal studies; linguistics; literature; management information systems/business data processing; mass communications; mathematics; medical assistant; medical laboratory technician; medical technology; Mexican-American studies; microbiology/bacteriology; music; music teacher education; nuclear medical technology; nursing; philosophy; physical education; physician assistant; physics; political science; pre-dentistry; pre-law; pre-medicine; pre-veterinary studies; psychology; public administration; public health; public relations; real estate; recreation/leisure studies; religious studies; sociology; Spanish; theater arts/drama.

Academic Programs *Special study options:* academic remediation for entering students, adult/continuing education programs, advanced placement credit, cooperative education, English as a second language, external degree program, honors programs, internships, off-campus study, part-time degree program, student-designed majors, study abroad, summer session for credit. *ROTC:* Army (c), Air Force (c).

Library Leo F. Cain Educational Resource Center with 440,181 titles, an OPAC, a Web page.

Computers on Campus 200 computers available on campus for general student use. At least one staffed computer lab available.

Student Life *Housing Options:* coed. *Activities and Organizations:* drama/theater group, student-run newspaper, television station, choral group, national fraternities, national sororities. *Campus security:* student patrols, late-night transport/escort service. *Student Services:* health clinic, personal/psychological counseling, women's center, legal services.

Athletics Member NCAA. All Division II. *Intercollegiate sports:* badminton M(c)/W(c), basketball M(s)/W(s), soccer M(s)/W(s), volleyball W(s). *Intramural sports:* basketball M/W, soccer M/W, volleyball W.

Standardized Tests *Required for some:* SAT I or ACT (for admission).

Costs (2001–02) *One-time required fee:* $5. *Tuition:* state resident $0 full-time; nonresident $7380 full-time, $246 per unit part-time. Part-time tuition and fees vary according to course load. *Required fees:* $1800 full-time, $570 per term part-time. *Room and board:* $6156; room only: $4032. Room and board charges vary according to housing facility. *Payment plan:* installment. *Waivers:* employees or children of employees.

Financial Aid Of all full-time matriculated undergraduates who enrolled in 2001, 4019 applied for aid, 3987 were judged to have need, 2231 had their need fully met. 274 Federal Work-Study jobs (averaging $2084). In 2001, 20 non-need-based awards were made. *Average financial aid package:* $6546. *Average need-based loan:* $3912. *Average need-based gift aid:* $3683. *Average indebtedness upon graduation:* $14,868.

Applying *Options:* electronic application, early admission. *Application fee:* $55. *Required:* high school transcript. *Application deadline:* rolling (freshmen), rolling (transfers). *Notification:* continuous (freshmen).

Admissions Contact Information Center, California State University, Dominguez Hills, 1000 East Victoria Street, Carson, CA 90747-0001. *Phone:* 310-243-3696.

CALIFORNIA STATE UNIVERSITY, FRESNO

Fresno, California

- **State-supported** comprehensive, founded 1911, part of California State University System
- **Calendar** semesters
- **Degrees** certificates, bachelor's, master's, and doctoral
- **Urban** 1410-acre campus
- **Endowment** $56.6 million
- **Coed,** 16,086 undergraduate students, 80% full-time, 58% women, 42% men
- **Moderately difficult** entrance level, 66% of applicants were admitted

Undergraduates 12,796 full-time, 3,290 part-time. Students come from 43 states and territories, 67 other countries, 1% are from out of state, 5% African American, 12% Asian American or Pacific Islander, 28% Hispanic American, 1% Native American, 3% international, 11% transferred in, 5% live on campus. *Retention:* 64% of 2001 full-time freshmen returned.

Freshmen *Admission:* 9,013 applied, 5,941 admitted, 2,005 enrolled. *Average high school GPA:* 3.29. *Test scores:* SAT verbal scores over 500: 35%; SAT math scores over 500: 41%; ACT scores over 18: 56%; SAT verbal scores over 600: 8%; SAT math scores over 600: 11%; ACT scores over 24: 14%; SAT verbal scores over 700: 1%; SAT math scores over 700: 1%; ACT scores over 30: 1%.

Faculty *Total:* 1,190, 56% full-time. *Student/faculty ratio:* 13:1.

Majors Accounting; African-American studies; agricultural business; agricultural education; agronomy/crop science; animal sciences; anthropology; art; biological/physical sciences; biology; business administration; business education; business marketing and marketing management; cell biology; chemistry; child care/development; civil engineering; communication disorders; computer engineering; computer science; construction technology; criminology; dance; dietetics; ecology; economics; electrical engineering; elementary education; English; family/consumer studies; finance; French; geography; geology; graphic design/commercial art/illustration; health science; history; human resources management; industrial arts; industrial/manufacturing engineering; industrial technology; interior design; international business; journalism; liberal arts and sciences/liberal studies; linguistics; management information systems/business data processing; mass communications; mathematics; mechanical engineering; Mexican-American studies; microbiology/bacteriology; molecular biology; music; music history; music teacher education; natural sciences; nursing; nutrition science; occupational health/industrial hygiene; occupational safety/health technology; ornamental horticulture; philosophy; physical education; physical therapy; physics; physiology; plant sciences; political science; pre-law; psychology; public administration; public relations; radio/television broadcasting; real estate; recreation/leisure studies; religious studies; social work; sociology; Spanish; speech-language pathology/audiology; speech/rhetorical studies; surveying; theater arts/drama; trade/industrial education; women's studies; zoology.

Academic Programs *Special study options:* academic remediation for entering students, accelerated degree program, adult/continuing education programs, advanced placement credit, cooperative education, distance learning, double majors, English as a second language, freshman honors college, honors programs, independent study, internships, off-campus study, part-time degree program, services for LD students, student-designed majors, study abroad, summer session for credit. *ROTC:* Army (b), Air Force (b).

Library Henry Madden Library with 977,198 titles, 2,500 serial subscriptions, 71,482 audiovisual materials, an OPAC, a Web page.

Computers on Campus 853 computers available on campus for general student use. A campuswide network can be accessed from off campus that provide access to common applications. Internet access, at least one staffed computer lab available.

Student Life *Housing Options:* coed. *Activities and Organizations:* drama/theater group, student-run newspaper, radio station, choral group, marching band, national fraternities, national sororities. *Campus security:* 24-hour emergency response devices and patrols, late-night transport/escort service, controlled dormitory access. *Student Services:* health clinic, personal/psychological counseling, women's center.

Athletics Member NCAA. All Division I except football (Division I-A). *Intercollegiate sports:* baseball M(s), basketball M(s)/W(s), cross-country running M(s)/W(s), equestrian sports W(s), golf M(s), soccer M(s)/W(s), softball W(s), swimming W(s), tennis M(s)/W(s), track and field M(s)/W(s), volleyball W(s), wrestling M(s). *Intramural sports:* archery M/W, badminton M/W, baseball M, basketball M/W, bowling M/W, cross-country running M/W, equestrian sports W, fencing M/W, golf M/W, gymnastics M/W, racquetball M/W, skiing (cross-country) M/W, softball W, swimming W, tennis M/W, volleyball M/W, water polo M, wrestling M.

Standardized Tests *Required:* SAT I or ACT (for admission).

Costs (2001–02) *Tuition:* state resident $0 full-time; nonresident $7666 full-time, $246 per unit part-time. Full-time tuition and fees vary according to course load. Part-time tuition and fees vary according to course load. *Required fees:* $1762 full-time, $581 per term part-time. *Room and board:* $6000. Room and board charges vary according to board plan and housing facility. *Waivers:* senior citizens and employees or children of employees.

Financial Aid Of all full-time matriculated undergraduates who enrolled in 2001, 9082 applied for aid, 8205 were judged to have need, 4348 had their need fully met. 490 Federal Work-Study jobs (averaging $1913). In 2001, 589 non-need-based awards were made. *Average percent of need met:* 54%. *Average financial aid package:* $6184. *Average need-based loan:* $3620. *Average need-based gift aid:* $4145. *Average non-need based aid:* $2705. *Average indebtedness upon graduation:* $14,006.

Applying *Options:* common application, electronic application. *Application fee:* $55. *Required:* high school transcript. *Application deadlines:* 7/28 (freshmen), 7/28 (transfers). *Notification:* 8/1 (freshmen).

Admissions Contact Ms. Vivian Franco, Director, California State University, Fresno, 5150 North Maple Avenue, M/S JA 57, Fresno, CA 93740-8026. *Phone:* 559-278-2261. *Fax:* 559-278-4812. *E-mail:* donna_mills@csufresno.edu.

CALIFORNIA STATE UNIVERSITY, FULLERTON
Fullerton, California

- **State-supported** comprehensive, founded 1957, part of California State University System
- **Calendar** semesters
- **Degrees** bachelor's and master's
- **Suburban** 225-acre campus with easy access to Los Angeles
- **Endowment** $7.1 million
- **Coed,** 25,071 undergraduate students, 70% full-time, 60% women, 40% men
- **Moderately difficult** entrance level, 69% of applicants were admitted

Undergraduates 17,509 full-time, 7,562 part-time. Students come from 45 states and territories, 81 other countries, 1% are from out of state, 3% African American, 24% Asian American or Pacific Islander, 25% Hispanic American, 0.6% Native American, 4% international, 13% transferred in, 2% live on campus. *Retention:* 79% of 2001 full-time freshmen returned.

Freshmen *Admission:* 13,721 applied, 9,474 admitted, 2,882 enrolled. *Average high school GPA:* 3.20. *Test scores:* SAT verbal scores over 500: 40%; SAT math scores over 500: 52%; ACT scores over 18: 74%; SAT verbal scores over 600: 8%; SAT math scores over 600: 14%; ACT scores over 24: 19%; SAT verbal scores over 700: 1%; SAT math scores over 700: 1%; ACT scores over 30: 2%.

Faculty *Total:* 1,822, 39% full-time. *Student/faculty ratio:* 21:1.

Majors Accounting; advertising; African-American studies; American studies; anthropology; applied mathematics; art; art education; art history; Asian-American studies; biochemistry; biology; business administration; business economics; business marketing and marketing management; ceramic arts; chemistry; civil engineering; clinical psychology; communication disorders; communications; comparative literature; computer science; criminal justice/law enforcement administration; cultural studies; dance; drawing; economics; electrical engineering; engineering; engineering science; English; finance; fine/studio arts; French; geography; geology; German; graphic design/commercial art/illustration; health/physical education; health professions and related sciences; Hispanic-American studies; history; information sciences/systems; international business; Japanese; journalism; Latin American studies; liberal arts and sciences/liberal studies; linguistics; mathematical statistics; mathematics; mechanical engineering; music; music (general performance); music history; music (piano and organ performance); music teacher education; music (voice and choral/opera performance); nursing; nursing related; operations research; philosophy; photography; physical education; physics; political science; pre-dentistry; pre-medicine; pre-veterinary studies; printmaking; psychology; public administration; public relations; radio/television broadcasting; religious studies; Russian/Slavic studies; sculpture; sociology; Spanish; speech-language pathology/audiology; speech/rhetorical studies; stringed instruments; taxation; theater arts/drama; wind/percussion instruments; women's studies.

Academic Programs *Special study options:* academic remediation for entering students, adult/continuing education programs, advanced placement credit, cooperative education, double majors, English as a second language, honors programs, independent study, internships, off-campus study, part-time degree program, services for LD students, student-designed majors, study abroad, summer session for credit. *ROTC:* Army (b).

Library California State University, Fullerton Library with 654,790 titles, 2,455 serial subscriptions, an OPAC.

Computers on Campus 1000 computers available on campus for general student use. A campuswide network can be accessed from student residence rooms and from off campus. Internet access, at least one staffed computer lab available.

Student Life *Housing Options:* coed. *Activities and Organizations:* drama/theater group, student-run newspaper, radio station, choral group, national fraternities, national sororities. *Campus security:* 24-hour emergency response devices and patrols, student patrols, late-night transport/escort service. *Student Services:* health clinic, personal/psychological counseling, women's center, legal services.

Athletics Member NCAA. All Division I. *Intercollegiate sports:* baseball M(s), basketball M(s)/W(s), bowling M(c)/W(c), cross-country running M(s)/W(s), fencing M(s)/W(s), gymnastics W(s), rugby M(c), soccer M(s)/W(s), softball W(s), tennis W(s), track and field M(s)/W(s), volleyball W(s), wrestling M(s). *Intramural sports:* archery M/W, badminton M/W, basketball M/W, bowling M/W, cross-country running M/W, fencing M/W, football M/W, gymnastics M/W, racquetball M/W, skiing (cross-country) M/W, skiing (downhill) M/W, soccer M/W, softball M/W, table tennis M/W, tennis M/W, volleyball M/W, wrestling M.

Standardized Tests *Required:* SAT I or ACT (for admission).

California State University, Fullerton (continued)

Costs (2001–02) *Tuition:* state resident $0 full-time; nonresident $7380 full-time, $246 per unit part-time. *Required fees:* $1849 full-time, $625 per term part-time. *Room and board:* room only: $3993. *Payment plan:* installment. *Waivers:* minority students and employees or children of employees.

Financial Aid Of all full-time matriculated undergraduates who enrolled in 2001, 9765 applied for aid, 7703 were judged to have need, 296 had their need fully met. 1142 Federal Work-Study jobs (averaging $2179). In 2001, 1385 non-need-based awards were made. *Average percent of need met:* 71%. *Average financial aid package:* $5871. *Average need-based loan:* $3498. *Average need-based gift aid:* $4602. *Average indebtedness upon graduation:* $12,001.

Applying *Options:* electronic application. *Application fee:* $55. *Required:* high school transcript, minimum 2.0 GPA. *Application deadline:* rolling (freshmen), rolling (transfers). *Notification:* continuous (freshmen).

Admissions Contact Ms. Nancy J. Dority, Admissions Director, California State University, Fullerton, Office of Admissions and Records, PO Box 6900, Fullerton, CA 92834-6900. *Phone:* 714-278-2370.

CALIFORNIA STATE UNIVERSITY, HAYWARD

Hayward, California

- **State-supported** comprehensive, founded 1957, part of California State University System
- **Calendar** quarters
- **Degrees** certificates, bachelor's, master's, post-master's, and postbachelor's certificates
- **Suburban** 343-acre campus with easy access to San Francisco and San Jose
- **Endowment** $5.4 million
- **Coed,** 9,528 undergraduate students, 75% full-time, 64% women, 36% men
- **Moderately difficult** entrance level, 89% of applicants were admitted

California State University, Hayward, is the San Francisco Bay Area's metropolitan university. Located in the hills overlooking the heart of the Bay, CSUH offers the unique advantages of small classes, acclaimed instructors, and low cost, combined with easy access to the opportunities and attractions of the Silicon Valley and San Francisco.

Undergraduates 7,105 full-time, 2,423 part-time. Students come from 50 states and territories, 86 other countries, 11% African American, 25% Asian American or Pacific Islander, 11% Hispanic American, 0.7% Native American, 5% international, 13% transferred in, 4% live on campus. *Retention:* 80% of 2001 full-time freshmen returned.

Freshmen *Admission:* 3,628 applied, 3,225 admitted, 716 enrolled. *Average high school GPA:* 3.14.

Faculty *Total:* 761, 47% full-time, 57% with terminal degrees. *Student/faculty ratio:* 21:1.

Majors Accounting; advertising; African-American studies; anthropology; applied mathematics; art history; arts management; Asian-American studies; athletic training/sports medicine; biochemistry; biology; biomedical technology; broadcast journalism; business administration; business economics; business marketing and marketing management; business systems networking/ telecommunications; ceramic arts; chemistry; child care/development; computer graphics; computer science; corrections; creative writing; criminal justice/law enforcement administration; cultural studies; dance; developmental/child psychology; drawing; ecology; economics; English; environmental science; exercise sciences; finance; fine/studio arts; French; geography; geology; gerontology; graphic design/commercial art/illustration; health science; history; human ecology; human resources management; individual/family development; industrial/manufacturing engineering; information sciences/systems; interdisciplinary studies; international relations; journalism; Latin American studies; law enforcement/police science; liberal arts and sciences/liberal studies; management information systems/ business data processing; mass communications; mathematical statistics; mathematics; medical laboratory technician; Mexican-American studies; music; Native American studies; nursing; organizational psychology; painting; philosophy; photography; physical education; physical sciences; physics; political science; pre-dentistry; pre-medicine; pre-veterinary studies; printmaking; psychology; public administration; public relations; purchasing/contracts management; real estate; recreational therapy; recreation/leisure studies; religious studies; sculpture; social work; sociology; Spanish; speech-language pathology/audiology; speech/rhetorical studies; telecommunications; theater arts/drama.

Academic Programs *Special study options:* academic remediation for entering students, accelerated degree program, adult/continuing education programs, advanced placement credit, cooperative education, distance learning, double majors, English as a second language, honors programs, independent study, internships, off-campus study, part-time degree program, services for LD students, student-designed majors, study abroad, summer session for credit.

Library California State University, Hayward Library plus 1 other with 908,577 titles, 2,210 serial subscriptions, 28,416 audiovisual materials, an OPAC, a Web page.

Computers on Campus 700 computers available on campus for general student use. A campuswide network can be accessed from student residence rooms and from off campus. Internet access, online (class) registration, at least one staffed computer lab available.

Student Life *Housing Options:* coed. *Activities and Organizations:* drama/ theater group, student-run newspaper, radio and television station, choral group, Vietnamese Student Association, Accounting Association, Philipino-American Students Association, Movimiento Estudiantil Chicano, Hayward Orientation Team, national fraternities, national sororities. *Campus security:* 24-hour emergency response devices and patrols, late-night transport/escort service. *Student Services:* health clinic, personal/psychological counseling, legal services.

Athletics Member NCAA, NAIA. All NCAA Division III. *Intercollegiate sports:* baseball M, basketball M/W, cross-country running M/W, soccer M/W, softball W, swimming W, volleyball W, water polo W. *Intramural sports:* badminton M/W, basketball M/W, golf M/W, gymnastics M, racquetball M/W, soccer M/W, softball M/W, swimming M/W, tennis M/W, volleyball M/W, weight lifting M/W.

Standardized Tests *Required for some:* SAT I or ACT (for admission).

Costs (2001–02) *Tuition:* state resident $0 full-time; nonresident $7380 full-time, $164 per unit part-time. Full-time tuition and fees vary according to course load. Part-time tuition and fees vary according to course load. *Required fees:* $1767 full-time, $376 per term part-time. *Room and board:* room only: $3200. *Payment plan:* installment. *Waivers:* senior citizens and employees or children of employees.

Financial Aid Of all full-time matriculated undergraduates who enrolled in 2001, 2927 applied for aid, 2670 were judged to have need, 403 had their need fully met. *Average percent of need met:* 67%. *Average financial aid package:* $6932. *Average need-based loan:* $4930. *Average need-based gift aid:* $5215. *Average indebtedness upon graduation:* $10,951.

Applying *Options:* electronic application, deferred entrance. *Application fee:* $55. *Required:* high school transcript. *Application deadlines:* 9/7 (freshmen), 9/7 (transfers). *Notification:* continuous (freshmen).

Admissions Contact Ms. Susan Lakis, Associate Director of Admissions, California State University, Hayward, 25800 Carlos Bee Boulevard, Hayward, CA 94542-3035. *Phone:* 510-885-3248. *Fax:* 510-885-3816. *E-mail:* adminfo@csuhayward.edu.

CALIFORNIA STATE UNIVERSITY, LONG BEACH

Long Beach, California

- **State-supported** comprehensive, founded 1949, part of California State University System
- **Calendar** semesters
- **Degrees** bachelor's and master's
- **Suburban** 320-acre campus with easy access to Los Angeles
- **Coed,** 27,305 undergraduate students, 77% full-time, 59% women, 41% men
- **Moderately difficult** entrance level, 85% of applicants were admitted

Undergraduates 21,151 full-time, 6,154 part-time. Students come from 44 states and territories, 101 other countries, 3% are from out of state, 7% African American, 21% Asian American or Pacific Islander, 23% Hispanic American, 0.6% Native American, 5% international, 12% transferred in, 7% live on campus. *Retention:* 81% of 2001 full-time freshmen returned.

Freshmen *Admission:* 19,567 applied, 16,566 admitted, 4,517 enrolled. *Average high school GPA:* 3.17. *Test scores:* SAT verbal scores over 500: 40%; SAT math scores over 500: 52%; ACT scores over 18: 68%; SAT verbal scores over 600: 9%; SAT math scores over 600: 14%; ACT scores over 24: 18%; SAT verbal scores over 700: 1%; SAT math scores over 700: 1%; ACT scores over 30: 1%.

Faculty *Total:* 1,924, 53% full-time, 50% with terminal degrees. *Student/faculty ratio:* 20:1.

Majors Accounting; aerospace engineering; African-American studies; anthropology; applied mathematics; art; art education; art history; Asian studies; athletic training/sports medicine; biochemistry; bioengineering; biology; broadcast journalism; business administration; business economics; business marketing and marketing management; cell biology; ceramic arts; chemical engineering; chemistry; child care/development; Chinese; civil engineering; clothing/textiles; comparative literature; computer engineering; computer engineering technology; computer science; construction management; construction technology; creative writing; criminal justice/law enforcement administration; dance; dietetics; drawing; earth sciences; economics; electrical/electronic engineering technology; electrical engineering; engineering; engineering/industrial management; engineering technology; English; entomology; environmental technology; exercise sciences; fashion merchandising; film studies; film/video production; finance; fine/studio arts; French; geography; geology; German; graphic design/commercial art/illustration; health science; health services administration; history; home economics; human resources management; individual/family development; industrial design; industrial technology; interdisciplinary studies; interior design; international business; international relations; Japanese; journalism; liberal arts and sciences/liberal studies; literature; marine biology; mass communications; materials engineering; mathematical statistics; mathematics; mechanical engineering; metal/jewelry arts; Mexican-American studies; microbiology/bacteriology; music; music history; music (voice and choral/opera performance); nursing; ocean engineering; philosophy; photography; physical education; physics; physiology; political science; printmaking; psychology; public health; public relations; quality control technology; radio/television broadcasting; recreation/leisure studies; religious studies; sculpture; social work; sociology; Spanish; speech-language pathology/audiology; speech/rhetorical studies; textile arts; theater arts/drama; trade/industrial education; women's studies; zoology.

Academic Programs *Special study options:* academic remediation for entering students, accelerated degree program, adult/continuing education programs, advanced placement credit, distance learning, double majors, English as a second language, honors programs, independent study, internships, off-campus study, part-time degree program, services for LD students, student-designed majors, study abroad, summer session for credit. *ROTC:* Army (b).

Library University Library with 781,111 titles, 5,424 serial subscriptions, 68,354 audiovisual materials, an OPAC, a Web page.

Computers on Campus 2000 computers available on campus for general student use. A campuswide network can be accessed from off campus. Internet access, at least one staffed computer lab available.

Student Life *Housing Options:* coed. *Activities and Organizations:* drama/theater group, student-run newspaper, radio and television station, choral group, national fraternities, national sororities. *Campus security:* 24-hour emergency response devices and patrols, student patrols, late-night transport/escort service. *Student Services:* health clinic, personal/psychological counseling, women's center, legal services.

Athletics Member NCAA. All Division I. *Intercollegiate sports:* archery M(c)/W(c), badminton M(c)/W(c), basketball M(s)/W(s), bowling M(c)/W(c), crew M(c)/W(c), cross-country running M(s)/W(s), fencing M(c)/W(c), rugby M(c), sailing M(c)/W(c), skiing (downhill) M(c)/W(c), soccer M(c)/W(c), softball W(s), swimming M(s)/W(s), table tennis M(c), tennis W(s), track and field M(s)/W(s), volleyball M(s)/W(s), water polo M(s)/W(c). *Intramural sports:* basketball M/W, gymnastics M/W, racquetball M/W, softball W, swimming M/W, table tennis W(c), tennis W, track and field M(c)/W(c), volleyball M/W.

Standardized Tests *Required:* SAT I or ACT (for admission).

Costs (2001–02) *Tuition:* state resident $0 full-time; nonresident $7380 full-time, $246 per unit part-time. Full-time tuition and fees vary according to program. Part-time tuition and fees vary according to course load and program. *Required fees:* $1744 full-time, $572 per term part-time. *Room and board:* $5800. Room and board charges vary according to board plan. *Payment plan:* installment. *Waivers:* senior citizens and employees or children of employees.

Financial Aid Of all full-time matriculated undergraduates who enrolled in 2001, 11030 applied for aid, 10459 were judged to have need, 3954 had their need fully met. In 2001, 1540 non-need-based awards were made. *Average percent of need met:* 76%. *Average financial aid package:* $7200. *Average need-based loan:* $3387. *Average need-based gift aid:* $3532. *Average indebtedness upon graduation:* $6190.

Applying *Options:* electronic application. *Application fee:* $55. *Required:* high school transcript. *Application deadline:* 11/30 (freshmen). *Notification:* continuous (freshmen).

Admissions Contact Mr. Thomas Enders, Director of Enrollment Services, California State University, Long Beach, Brotman Hall, 1250 Bellflower Boulevard, Long Beach, CA 90840. *Phone:* 562-985-4641.

CALIFORNIA STATE UNIVERSITY, LOS ANGELES

Los Angeles, California

- **State-supported** comprehensive, founded 1947, part of California State University System
- **Calendar** quarters
- **Degrees** bachelor's, master's, and doctoral
- **Urban** 173-acre campus
- **Endowment** $17.5 million
- **Coed,** 13,898 undergraduate students, 72% full-time, 61% women, 39% men
- **Moderately difficult** entrance level, 53% of applicants were admitted

Undergraduates 4% are from out of state, 8% African American, 20% Asian American or Pacific Islander, 49% Hispanic American, 0.4% Native American, 4% international, 4% live on campus.

Freshmen *Admission:* 9,201 applied, 4,856 admitted.

Faculty *Total:* 1,155, 52% full-time. *Student/faculty ratio:* 21:1.

Majors African-American studies; anthropology; art; biochemistry; biology; business administration; chemistry; civil engineering; communication disorders; computer science; criminal justice/law enforcement administration; dance; earth sciences; economics; electrical engineering; engineering; English; fire protection/safety technology; French; geography; geology; health science; history; industrial arts education; industrial technology; interdisciplinary studies; Japanese; Latin American studies; liberal arts and sciences/liberal studies; mathematics; mechanical engineering; Mexican-American studies; microbiology/bacteriology; music; music (general performance); natural sciences; nursing; nutritional sciences; nutrition studies; philosophy; physical education; physics; political science; psychology; radio/television broadcasting; rehabilitation therapy; social sciences; social work; sociology; Spanish; speech/rhetorical studies; theater arts/drama; trade/industrial education.

Academic Programs *Special study options:* academic remediation for entering students, accelerated degree program, adult/continuing education programs, advanced placement credit, cooperative education, English as a second language, honors programs, internships, off-campus study, part-time degree program, services for LD students, student-designed majors, study abroad, summer session for credit. *ROTC:* Army (c), Air Force (c).

Library John K. Kennedy Memorial Library with 1.7 million titles, 2,438 serial subscriptions, 4,309 audiovisual materials, an OPAC, a Web page.

Computers on Campus 1500 computers available on campus for general student use. A campuswide network can be accessed from off campus. Internet access, at least one staffed computer lab available.

Student Life *Housing Options:* coed. *Activities and Organizations:* drama/theater group, student-run newspaper, television station, choral group, Amnesty International, Institute of Electrical and Electronics Engineer, Hispanic Business Society, Asian Unified, ABACUS Computer Society, national fraternities, national sororities. *Campus security:* 24-hour emergency response devices, student patrols, late-night transport/escort service. *Student Services:* health clinic, personal/psychological counseling, women's center, legal services.

Athletics Member NCAA. All Division II. *Intercollegiate sports:* baseball M(s), basketball M(s)/W(s), cross-country running M(s)/W(s), soccer M(s)/W(s), tennis M(s)/W(s), track and field M(s)/W(s), volleyball W(s). *Intramural sports:* basketball M/W, bowling M/W, gymnastics M/W, racquetball M/W, soccer M/W, softball M/W, swimming M/W, tennis M/W, track and field M/W, volleyball M/W, water polo M/W, wrestling M.

Standardized Tests *Required:* SAT I or ACT (for admission).

Costs (2001–02) *Tuition:* state resident $0 full-time; nonresident $7686 full-time, $164 per unit part-time. Part-time tuition and fees vary according to course load. *Required fees:* $1782 full-time, $393 per term part-time. *Room and board:* $6399. *Payment plan:* installment. *Waivers:* employees or children of employees.

Financial Aid Of all full-time matriculated undergraduates who enrolled in 2001, 7035 applied for aid, 6670 were judged to have need. 355 Federal Work-Study jobs (averaging $3563). 11 State and other part-time jobs (averaging $3761). *Average percent of need met:* 73%. *Average financial aid package:* $6612. *Average need-based loan:* $3663. *Average need-based gift aid:* $5676.

Applying *Options:* common application, electronic application, early admission. *Application fee:* $55. *Required:* high school transcript. *Application deadlines:* 6/15 (freshmen), 6/15 (transfers).

Admissions Contact Mr. Vince Lopez, Assistant Director of Outreach and Recruitment, California State University, Los Angeles, 5151 State University Drive, Los Angeles, CA 90032-8530. *Phone:* 323-343-3839. *E-mail:* admission@calstatela.edu.

CALIFORNIA STATE UNIVERSITY, MONTEREY BAY

Seaside, California

- **State-supported** comprehensive, founded 1994, part of California State University
- **Calendar** semesters
- **Degrees** diplomas, bachelor's, master's, and postbachelor's certificates
- 1500-acre campus with easy access to San Jose
- **Endowment** $520,445
- **Coed,** 2,753 undergraduate students, 97% full-time, 58% women, 42% men
- **Minimally difficult** entrance level, 83% of applicants were admitted

California State University, Monterey Bay (continued)

Undergraduates 2,673 full-time, 80 part-time. Students come from 34 states and territories, 5% are from out of state, 4% African American, 6% Asian American or Pacific Islander, 27% Hispanic American, 0.9% Native American, 52% transferred in, 65% live on campus. *Retention:* 76% of 2001 full-time freshmen returned.

Freshmen *Admission:* 3,023 applied, 2,508 admitted, 565 enrolled. *Average high school GPA:* 3.08.

Faculty *Total:* 280, 41% full-time. *Student/faculty ratio:* 20:1.

Majors Art; behavioral sciences; business administration; communications; earth sciences; environmental biology; environmental science; foreign languages/literatures; humanities; human services; interdisciplinary studies; international business; international relations; liberal arts and sciences/liberal studies; telecommunications; theater arts/drama.

Academic Programs *Special study options:* academic remediation for entering students, cooperative education, distance learning, double majors, external degree program, independent study, internships, part-time degree program, services for LD students, student-designed majors.

Student Life *Housing:* on-campus residence required through sophomore year. *Options:* men-only, women-only, disabled students. *Activities and Organizations:* drama/theater group, student-run newspaper, radio station, choral group, MECHA. *Campus security:* 24-hour emergency response devices and patrols, student patrols, late-night transport/escort service, controlled dormitory access. *Student Services:* health clinic, personal/psychological counseling.

Athletics Member NAIA. *Intercollegiate sports:* basketball M/W, cross-country running M/W, golf M/W, soccer M/W, volleyball W. *Intramural sports:* rugby M/W, sailing M/W.

Standardized Tests *Required:* SAT I or ACT (for admission).

Costs (2002–03) *Tuition:* state resident $0 full-time, $246 per unit part-time; nonresident $7872 full-time, $246 per unit part-time. Full-time tuition and fees vary according to course load and student level. Part-time tuition and fees vary according to course load and student level. *Required fees:* $928 full-time, $628 per term part-time. *Room and board:* $5220; room only: $3000. Room and board charges vary according to housing facility. *Payment plans:* installment, deferred payment. *Waivers:* senior citizens and employees or children of employees.

Applying *Options:* deferred entrance. *Application fee:* $55. *Required:* high school transcript, minimum 2.0 GPA. *Application deadline:* rolling (freshmen), rolling (transfers). *Notification:* continuous (freshmen).

Admissions Contact Ms. Valarie E. Brown, Director of Admissions and Records, California State University, Monterey Bay, 100 Campus Center, Building 47, Seaside, CA 93955. *Phone:* 831-582-4093. *Fax:* 831-582-3087. *E-mail:* moreinfo-prospective@csumb.edu.

California State University, Northridge

Northridge, California

- **State-supported** comprehensive, founded 1958, part of California State University System
- **Calendar** semesters
- **Degrees** bachelor's and master's
- **Urban** 353-acre campus with easy access to Los Angeles
- **Endowment** $25.6 million
- **Coed,** 24,462 undergraduate students, 75% full-time, 59% women, 41% men
- **Moderately difficult** entrance level, 83% of applicants were admitted

Undergraduates 18,321 full-time, 6,141 part-time. Students come from 40 states and territories, 7 other countries, 1% are from out of state, 8% African American, 13% Asian American or Pacific Islander, 26% Hispanic American, 0.6% Native American, 4% international, 14% transferred in. *Retention:* 73% of 2001 full-time freshmen returned.

Freshmen *Admission:* 10,600 applied, 8,788 admitted, 3,298 enrolled.

Faculty *Total:* 1,746, 48% full-time.

Majors Accounting; aerospace engineering; African-American studies; African studies; anthropology; applied art; applied mathematics; art; art education; art history; astrophysics; athletic training/sports medicine; biochemistry; biology; broadcast journalism; business administration; business education; business marketing and marketing management; cartography; cell biology; ceramic arts; chemical engineering; chemistry; child care/development; civil engineering; classics; clothing/textiles; computer engineering; computer science; creative writing; cultural studies; dance; developmental/child psychology; dietetics; drawing; earth sciences; economics; electrical engineering; engineering; engineering physics; English; environmental biology; environmental engineering; environmental health; family/consumer studies; fashion merchandising; film studies; film/video production; finance; fine/studio arts; food products retailing; food sciences; food services technology; French; geography; geology; geophysics/seismology; German; gerontology; graphic design/commercial art/illustration; health education; health science; health services administration; Hispanic-American studies; history; home economics; home economics education; humanities; industrial design; industrial/manufacturing engineering; industrial radiologic technology; information sciences/systems; interior design; international business; Italian; journalism; liberal arts and sciences/liberal studies; linguistics; literature; management information systems/business data processing; materials engineering; mathematical statistics; mathematics; mechanical engineering; medical laboratory technician; medical technology; Mexican-American studies; microbiology/bacteriology; molecular biology; music; music history; music (piano and organ performance); music teacher education; music (voice and choral/opera performance); nuclear engineering; nursing; nutrition science; occupational safety/health technology; operations research; philosophy; photography; physical education; physical therapy; physics; political science; pre-dentistry; pre-law; pre-medicine; pre-veterinary studies; psychology; radio/television broadcasting; real estate; recreational therapy; recreation/leisure studies; religious studies; retail management; Russian; sculpture; secretarial science; sign language interpretation; social work; sociology; Spanish; special education; speech-language pathology/audiology; speech/rhetorical studies; stringed instruments; systems engineering; teaching English as a second language; textile arts; theater arts/drama; urban studies; wind/percussion instruments; women's studies.

Academic Programs *Special study options:* academic remediation for entering students, accelerated degree program, adult/continuing education programs, advanced placement credit, English as a second language, honors programs, off-campus study, part-time degree program, services for LD students, student-designed majors, study abroad, summer session for credit. *ROTC:* Army (c), Air Force (c).

Library Oviatt Library with 1.2 million titles, 2,754 serial subscriptions, an OPAC.

Computers on Campus A campuswide network can be accessed from off campus. Internet access, online (class) registration available.

Student Life *Housing Options:* coed. *Activities and Organizations:* drama/theater group, student-run newspaper, radio station, choral group, marching band, national fraternities, national sororities. *Campus security:* 24-hour emergency response devices, late-night transport/escort service. *Student Services:* health clinic, personal/psychological counseling, women's center.

Athletics Member NCAA. All Division I except football (Division II). *Intercollegiate sports:* baseball M(s), basketball M(s)/W(s), cross-country running M(s)/W(s), football M(s), golf M(s), soccer M(s), softball W(s), swimming M(s)/W(s), tennis W(s), track and field M(s)/W(s), volleyball M(s)/W(s). *Intramural sports:* baseball M, basketball M/W, bowling M(c)/W(c), cross-country running M/W, football M/W, golf M, ice hockey M(c), racquetball M/W, rugby M(c), sailing M(c)/W(c), skiing (downhill) M(c)/W(c), soccer M/W, softball W, swimming M/W, table tennis M(c)/W(c), tennis W, track and field M/W, volleyball M/W.

Standardized Tests *Recommended:* SAT I or ACT (for admission).

Costs (2002–03) *Tuition:* nonresident $7718 full-time, $248 per unit part-time. *Required fees:* $1814 full-time, $607 per term part-time. *Room and board:* $6400. Room and board charges vary according to housing facility. *Waivers:* senior citizens and employees or children of employees.

Financial Aid Of all full-time matriculated undergraduates who enrolled in 2001, 15075 applied for aid, 14150 were judged to have need, 4389 had their need fully met. 841 Federal Work-Study jobs (averaging $1593). *Average percent of need met:* 89%. *Average financial aid package:* $7830. *Average need-based loan:* $3532. *Average need-based gift aid:* $4270. *Average indebtedness upon graduation:* $13,170.

Applying *Options:* electronic application, early admission, early action. *Application fee:* $55. *Required:* high school transcript. *Application deadline:* 11/30 (freshmen), rolling (transfers). *Notification:* continuous (freshmen), 9/30 (early action).

Admissions Contact Ms. Mary Baxton, Associate Director of Admissions and Records, California State University, Northridge, 18111 Nordhoff Street, Northridge, CA 91330-8207. *Phone:* 818-677-3777. *Fax:* 818-677-3766. *E-mail:* admissions.records@csun.edu.

California State University, Sacramento

Sacramento, California

- **State-supported** comprehensive, founded 1947, part of California State University System
- **Calendar** semesters
- **Degrees** bachelor's, master's, and doctoral
- **Urban** 288-acre campus
- **Coed,** 21,506 undergraduate students, 75% full-time, 57% women, 43% men

■ **Moderately difficult** entrance level, 52% of applicants were admitted

Undergraduates 16,050 full-time, 5,456 part-time. Students come from 45 states and territories, 53 other countries, 2% are from out of state, 6% African American, 19% Asian American or Pacific Islander, 13% Hispanic American, 1% Native American, 2% international, 15% transferred in, 5% live on campus. *Retention:* 75% of 2001 full-time freshmen returned.

Freshmen *Admission:* 9,733 applied, 5,020 admitted, 2,413 enrolled. *Average high school GPA:* 3.18. *Test scores:* SAT verbal scores over 500: 42%; SAT math scores over 500: 50%; ACT scores over 18: 65%; SAT verbal scores over 600: 9%; SAT math scores over 600: 14%; ACT scores over 24: 18%; SAT verbal scores over 700: 1%; SAT math scores over 700: 1%; ACT scores over 30: 1%.

Faculty *Total:* 1,473, 55% full-time, 52% with terminal degrees. *Student/faculty ratio:* 21:1.

Majors Accounting; anthropology; art; Asian studies; bilingual/bicultural education; biology; business administration; business education; chemistry; communication equipment technology; computer engineering; computer/information sciences; construction technology; criminal justice/law enforcement administration; cultural studies; early childhood education; ecology; economics; education; education (multiple levels); electrical engineering; engineering; English; environmental health; family/consumer studies; French; geography; geology; German; gerontology; health/physical education; history; humanities; interior design; journalism; liberal arts and sciences/liberal studies; mass communications; mathematics; mechanical engineering; mechanical engineering technology; music; nursing; philosophy; physical sciences; physics; political science; psychology; public administration; recreation/leisure facilities management; recreation/leisure studies; social sciences; social work; sociology; Spanish; speech-language pathology/audiology; theater arts/drama; theology; women's studies.

Academic Programs *Special study options:* academic remediation for entering students, advanced placement credit, cooperative education, distance learning, double majors, English as a second language, internships, off-campus study, part-time degree program, services for LD students, student-designed majors, study abroad, summer session for credit. *ROTC:* Army (c), Air Force (b).

Library California State University, Sacramento Library with 770,779 titles, 4,040 serial subscriptions, 152,128 audiovisual materials, an OPAC, a Web page.

Computers on Campus 700 computers available on campus for general student use. A campuswide network can be accessed from student residence rooms and from off campus. Internet access, online (class) registration, at least one staffed computer lab available.

Student Life *Housing Options:* coed. *Activities and Organizations:* drama/theater group, student-run newspaper, radio station, choral group, marching band, Ski Club, American Marketing Association, Society for Advancement of Management, Accounting Society, Human Resources Management Association, national fraternities, national sororities. *Campus security:* 24-hour emergency response devices and patrols, student patrols, late-night transport/escort service, controlled dormitory access. *Student Services:* health clinic, personal/psychological counseling, women's center, legal services.

Athletics Member NCAA. All Division I except football (Division I-AA). *Intercollegiate sports:* baseball M(s), basketball M(s)/W(s), bowling M(c)/W(c), crew M(s)/W(s), cross-country running M(s)/W(s), golf M(s), gymnastics W(s), lacrosse M(c)/W(c), racquetball M(c)/W(c), rugby M(c), skiing (downhill) M(c)/W(c), soccer M(s)/W(s), softball W(s), tennis M(s)/W(s), track and field M(s)/W(s), volleyball M(c)/W(s). *Intramural sports:* badminton M/W, basketball M/W, bowling W, crew M/W, football M/W, golf M/W, racquetball M/W, skiing (downhill) M/W, soccer M/W, softball M/W, table tennis M/W, tennis M/W, volleyball M/W, weight lifting M/W.

Standardized Tests *Required for some:* SAT I or ACT (for admission).

Costs (2001–02) *Tuition:* state resident $0 full-time; nonresident $8808 full-time, $246 per unit part-time. *Required fees:* $1887 full-time, $644 per term part-time. *Room and board:* $5601; room only: $3462. Room and board charges vary according to board plan. *Payment plan:* installment. *Waivers:* senior citizens.

Financial Aid Of all full-time matriculated undergraduates who enrolled in 2001, 8252 applied for aid, 7104 were judged to have need, 1015 had their need fully met. 652 Federal Work-Study jobs, 130 State and other part-time jobs. *Average percent of need met:* 75%. *Average financial aid package:* $6779. *Average need-based loan:* $3647. *Average need-based gift aid:* $1633.

Applying *Options:* electronic application, deferred entrance. *Application fee:* $55. *Required:* high school transcript, minimum 2.0 GPA. *Application deadlines:* rolling (freshmen), 8/1 (transfers). *Notification:* continuous (freshmen).

Admissions Contact Mr. Emiliano Diaz, Director of University Outreach Services, California State University, Sacramento, 6000 J Street, Lassen Hall, Sacramento, CA 95819-6048. *Phone:* 916-278-7362. *Fax:* 916-278-5603. *E-mail:* admissions@csus.edu.

CALIFORNIA STATE UNIVERSITY, SAN BERNARDINO

San Bernardino, California

■ **State-supported** comprehensive, founded 1965, part of California State University System
■ **Calendar** quarters
■ **Degrees** bachelor's and master's
■ **Suburban** 430-acre campus with easy access to Los Angeles
■ **Coed,** 11,019 undergraduate students, 83% full-time, 63% women, 37% men
■ **Moderately difficult** entrance level, 100% of applicants were admitted

Undergraduates 9,110 full-time, 1,909 part-time. Students come from 31 states and territories, 84 other countries, 1% are from out of state, 11% African American, 7% Asian American or Pacific Islander, 29% Hispanic American, 1% Native American, 3% international, 14% transferred in, 4% live on campus. *Retention:* 44% of 2001 full-time freshmen returned.

Freshmen *Admission:* 3,250 applied, 3,239 admitted, 1,315 enrolled. *Average high school GPA:* 3.11. *Test scores:* SAT verbal scores over 500: 26%; SAT math scores over 500: 31%; ACT scores over 18: 60%; SAT verbal scores over 600: 4%; SAT math scores over 600: 6%; ACT scores over 24: 7%; SAT math scores over 700: 1%.

Faculty *Total:* 588, 74% full-time. *Student/faculty ratio:* 19:1.

Majors Accounting; African-American studies; American studies; anthropology; art; art history; biochemistry; biology; business administration; business economics; business marketing and marketing management; chemistry; computer/information sciences; computer science; creative writing; criminal justice/law enforcement administration; developmental/child psychology; dietetics; economics; English; environmental science; finance; French; geography; geology; graphic design/commercial art/illustration; health education; health science; health services administration; history; humanities; human services; individual/family development; interdisciplinary studies; liberal arts and sciences/liberal studies; management information systems/business data processing; mass communications; mathematics; Mexican-American studies; music; natural sciences; nursing; nutrition science; philosophy; physical education; physics; political science; psychology; public administration; social sciences; social work; sociology; Spanish; theater arts/drama; trade/industrial education.

Academic Programs *Special study options:* academic remediation for entering students, adult/continuing education programs, advanced placement credit, cooperative education, English as a second language, external degree program, honors programs, off-campus study, part-time degree program, services for LD students, student-designed majors, study abroad, summer session for credit. *ROTC:* Army (b), Air Force (b).

Library Pfau Library with 466,000 titles, 2,350 serial subscriptions.

Computers on Campus 1300 computers available on campus for general student use. A campuswide network can be accessed from student residence rooms and from off campus. Internet access, at least one staffed computer lab available.

Student Life *Housing Options:* coed, women-only. *Activities and Organizations:* drama/theater group, student-run newspaper, radio station, choral group, national fraternities, national sororities. *Campus security:* 24-hour emergency response devices and patrols, student patrols, late-night transport/escort service, residence staff on call 24-hours. *Student Services:* health clinic, personal/psychological counseling, women's center.

Athletics Member NCAA. All Division II. *Intercollegiate sports:* baseball M(s), basketball M(s)/W(s), golf M(s), soccer M(s)/W(s), softball W(s), swimming M(s)/W(s), volleyball W(s). *Intramural sports:* basketball M/W, field hockey M/W, football M/W, soccer M/W, softball M, volleyball M/W.

Standardized Tests *Required for some:* SAT I or ACT (for admission).

Costs (2001–02) *Tuition:* nonresident $7511 full-time, $164 per credit part-time. Part-time tuition and fees vary according to course load. *Required fees:* $1733 full-time. *Room and board:* $4783; room only: $3555. Room and board charges vary according to housing facility.

Financial Aid Of all full-time matriculated undergraduates who enrolled in 2001, 8291 applied for aid, 8291 were judged to have need, 8291 had their need fully met. 441 Federal Work-Study jobs; 185 State and other part-time jobs. *Average percent of need met:* 73%. *Average financial aid package:* $8851. *Average need-based loan:* $4100.

Applying *Options:* early admission. *Application fee:* $55. *Required:* high school transcript, minimum 2.0 GPA. *Application deadline:* rolling (freshmen), rolling (transfers). *Notification:* continuous (freshmen).

Admissions Contact Ms. Cynthia Shum, Admissions Counselor, California State University, San Bernardino, 5500 University Parkway, San Bernardino, CA 92407-2397. *Phone:* 909-880-5212. *Toll-free phone:* 909-880-5188. *Fax:* 909-880-7034. *E-mail:* moreinfo@mail.csusb.edu.

CALIFORNIA STATE UNIVERSITY, SAN MARCOS
San Marcos, California

- **State-supported** comprehensive, founded 1990, part of California State University System
- **Calendar** semesters
- **Degrees** bachelor's and master's
- **Suburban** 302-acre campus with easy access to San Diego
- **Endowment** $5.9 million
- **Coed,** 5,217 undergraduate students, 65% full-time, 60% women, 40% men
- **Moderately difficult** entrance level, 62% of applicants were admitted

Undergraduates 3,403 full-time, 1,814 part-time. 1% are from out of state, 3% African American, 9% Asian American or Pacific Islander, 18% Hispanic American, 0.9% Native American, 2% international, 21% transferred in, 2% live on campus. *Retention:* 60% of 2001 full-time freshmen returned.

Freshmen *Admission:* 3,540 applied, 2,201 admitted, 545 enrolled. *Average high school GPA:* 3.17. *Test scores:* SAT verbal scores over 500: 48%; SAT math scores over 500: 50%; SAT verbal scores over 600: 10%; SAT math scores over 600: 13%; SAT verbal scores over 700: 1%.

Faculty *Total:* 398, 49% full-time, 60% with terminal degrees. *Student/faculty ratio:* 18:1.

Majors Accounting; biochemistry; biology; business administration; cell biology; chemistry; communications; computer science; ecology; economics; English; history; liberal arts and sciences/liberal studies; mathematics; molecular biology; political science; psychology; science education; social sciences; sociology; Spanish; visual/performing arts; women's studies.

Academic Programs *Special study options:* academic remediation for entering students, adult/continuing education programs, advanced placement credit, distance learning, double majors, English as a second language, independent study, internships, off-campus study, part-time degree program, services for LD students, student-designed majors, study abroad, summer session for credit. *ROTC:* Air Force (c).

Library Library and Information Services with 147,784 titles, 2,138 serial subscriptions, 7,888 audiovisual materials, an OPAC, a Web page.

Computers on Campus 487 computers available on campus for general student use. A campuswide network can be accessed from student residence rooms and from off campus. Internet access, online (class) registration, at least one staffed computer lab available.

Student Life *Housing Options:* men-only, women-only, disabled students. *Activities and Organizations:* student-run newspaper, Accounting Club, Liberal Studies Club, MECHA, Sigma IOTA Epsilon, national fraternities, national sororities. *Campus security:* 24-hour patrols, student patrols, late-night transport/escort service. *Student Services:* health clinic, personal/psychological counseling, women's center.

Athletics Member NAIA. *Intercollegiate sports:* golf M(s). *Intramural sports:* basketball M/W, football M/W, soccer M/W, volleyball M/W.

Standardized Tests *Required:* SAT I or ACT (for admission).

Costs (2001–02) *One-time required fee:* $5. *Tuition:* state resident $0 full-time; nonresident $5904 full-time, $246 per credit hour part-time. Part-time tuition and fees vary according to course load. *Required fees:* $1706 full-time. *Room and board:* Room and board charges vary according to housing facility. *Waivers:* senior citizens and employees or children of employees.

Financial Aid Of all full-time matriculated undergraduates who enrolled in 2001, 1994 applied for aid, 1663 were judged to have need. 33 State and other part-time jobs (averaging $1115). In 2001, 59 non-need-based awards were made. *Average financial aid package:* $5638. *Average need-based loan:* $3917. *Average need-based gift aid:* $3849. *Average non-need based aid:* $360. *Average indebtedness upon graduation:* $13,009.

Applying *Options:* electronic application. *Application fee:* $55. *Required:* high school transcript, minimum 3.0 GPA. *Application deadline:* rolling (freshmen), rolling (transfers).

Admissions Contact Ms. Cherine Heckman, Director of Admissions, California State University, San Marcos, San Marcos, CA 92096-0001. *Phone:* 760-750-4848. *Fax:* 760-750-3285. *E-mail:* apply@csusm.edu.

CALIFORNIA STATE UNIVERSITY, STANISLAUS
Turlock, California

- **State-supported** comprehensive, founded 1957, part of California State University System
- **Calendar** 4-1-4
- **Degrees** bachelor's and master's
- **Small-town** 220-acre campus
- **Coed,** 5,624 undergraduate students, 68% full-time, 67% women, 33% men
- **Moderately difficult** entrance level, 68% of applicants were admitted

Undergraduates 3,847 full-time, 1,777 part-time. Students come from 31 states and territories, 62 other countries, 1% are from out of state, 3% African American, 9% Asian American or Pacific Islander, 25% Hispanic American, 1% Native American, 1% international, 17% transferred in, 5% live on campus. *Retention:* 81% of 2001 full-time freshmen returned.

Freshmen *Admission:* 1,875 applied, 1,281 admitted, 587 enrolled. *Average high school GPA:* 3.30. *Test scores:* SAT verbal scores over 500: 57%; SAT math scores over 500: 59%; ACT scores over 18: 63%; SAT verbal scores over 600: 9%; SAT math scores over 600: 10%; ACT scores over 24: 13%; SAT verbal scores over 700: 1%; SAT math scores over 700: 1%.

Faculty *Total:* 463, 57% full-time, 56% with terminal degrees. *Student/faculty ratio:* 18:1.

Majors Accounting; anthropology; art; biology; business; business administration; business marketing and marketing management; chemistry; child guidance; cognitive psychology/psycholinguistics; communications; computer/information sciences; computer science; criminal justice/law enforcement administration; economics; English; finance; French; geography; geology; history; industrial arts education; liberal arts and sciences/liberal studies; mathematics; music; nursing; operations management; painting; philosophy; physical education; physical sciences; physics; political science; printmaking; psychology; sculpture; social sciences; sociology; Spanish; theater arts/drama.

Academic Programs *Special study options:* academic remediation for entering students, adult/continuing education programs, advanced placement credit, cooperative education, distance learning, double majors, English as a second language, honors programs, independent study, internships, off-campus study, part-time degree program, services for LD students, student-designed majors, study abroad, summer session for credit.

Library Vasche Library with 338,736 titles, 1,984 serial subscriptions, 4,077 audiovisual materials, an OPAC, a Web page.

Computers on Campus 150 computers available on campus for general student use. A campuswide network can be accessed from student residence rooms and from off campus. Internet access, at least one staffed computer lab available.

Student Life *Housing Options:* coed. *Activities and Organizations:* drama/theater group, student-run newspaper, radio station, choral group, marching band, Phi Sigma Sigma sorority, Alpha Xi Delta sorority, SnoBord-em Club, Theta Chi fraternity, MECHA, national fraternities, national sororities. *Campus security:* 24-hour emergency response devices and patrols, student patrols, late-night transport/escort service, controlled dormitory access. *Student Services:* health clinic, personal/psychological counseling, women's center.

Athletics Member NCAA. All Division II. *Intercollegiate sports:* baseball M, basketball M/W, cross-country running M/W, golf M, soccer M/W, softball W, tennis M/W, track and field M/W, volleyball W. *Intramural sports:* basketball M/W, football M, soccer M, softball M/W, swimming M/W, volleyball M/W, weight lifting M/W.

Standardized Tests *Required:* SAT I or ACT (for admission).

Costs (2001–02) *Tuition:* state resident $0 full-time; nonresident $7380 full-time. *Required fees:* $1875 full-time, $556 per term part-time. *Room and board:* $7020; room only: $4635. Room and board charges vary according to board plan and housing facility. *Waivers:* senior citizens.

Financial Aid Of all full-time matriculated undergraduates who enrolled in 2001, 2796 applied for aid, 2468 were judged to have need, 325 had their need fully met. 189 Federal Work-Study jobs (averaging $1913). In 2001, 93 non-need-based awards were made. *Average percent of need met:* 63%. *Average financial aid package:* $6354. *Average need-based loan:* $3947. *Average need-based gift aid:* $4668. *Average non-need based aid:* $1892. *Average indebtedness upon graduation:* $13,000.

Applying *Options:* electronic application, deferred entrance. *Application fee:* $55. *Required:* high school transcript. *Application deadlines:* 5/31 (freshmen), 5/31 (transfers).

Admissions Contact Admissions Office, California State University, Stanislaus, Enrollment Services, 801 West Monte Vista Avenue, Mary Stuart Rogers Gateway Center, Room 120, Turlock, CA 95382. *Phone:* 209-667-3070. *Toll-free phone:* 800-300-7420. *Fax:* 209-667-3788. *E-mail:* outreach_help_desk@stan.csustan.edu.

CHAPMAN UNIVERSITY
Orange, California

- **Independent** comprehensive, founded 1861, affiliated with Christian Church (Disciples of Christ)
- **Calendar** 4-1-4
- **Degrees** certificates, bachelor's, master's, and first professional

- **Suburban** 42-acre campus with easy access to Los Angeles
- **Endowment** $192.9 million
- **Coed,** 3,127 undergraduate students, 92% full-time, 56% women, 44% men
- **Moderately difficult** entrance level, 77% of applicants were admitted

Undergraduates 2,881 full-time, 246 part-time. Students come from 40 states and territories, 35 other countries, 33% are from out of state, 10% transferred in, 45% live on campus. *Retention:* 86% of 2001 full-time freshmen returned.

Freshmen *Admission:* 2,195 applied, 1,690 admitted, 744 enrolled. *Average high school GPA:* 3.55. *Test scores:* SAT verbal scores over 500: 88%; SAT math scores over 500: 91%; ACT scores over 18: 97%; SAT verbal scores over 600: 39%; SAT math scores over 600: 43%; ACT scores over 24: 50%; SAT verbal scores over 700: 6%; SAT math scores over 700: 5%; ACT scores over 30: 5%.

Faculty *Total:* 465, 47% full-time. *Student/faculty ratio:* 13:1.

Majors Accounting; advertising; American studies; applied mathematics; art; art history; athletic training/sports medicine; biochemistry; biology; broadcast journalism; business administration; business economics; business marketing and marketing management; chemistry; comparative literature; computer science; creative writing; criminal justice/law enforcement administration; dance; economics; English; environmental science; European studies; exercise sciences; film studies; film/video production; finance; fine/studio arts; food sciences; French; graphic design/commercial art/illustration; health science; history; information sciences/systems; international business; journalism; Latin American studies; legal studies; liberal arts and sciences/liberal studies; literature; mass communications; music; music (piano and organ performance); music teacher education; music therapy; music (voice and choral/opera performance); peace/conflict studies; philosophy; physical education; political science; pre-dentistry; pre-law; pre-medicine; pre-veterinary studies; psychology; public relations; religious studies; social sciences; social work; sociology; Spanish; speech/rhetorical studies; stringed instruments; theater arts/drama; wind/percussion instruments; women's studies.

Academic Programs *Special study options:* academic remediation for entering students, accelerated degree program, adult/continuing education programs, advanced placement credit, cooperative education, double majors, English as a second language, honors programs, independent study, internships, part-time degree program, services for LD students, study abroad, summer session for credit. *ROTC:* Army (c), Air Force (c).

Library Thurmond Clarke Memorial Library plus 1 other with 203,915 titles, 2,121 serial subscriptions, 3,350 audiovisual materials, an OPAC, a Web page.

Computers on Campus 278 computers available on campus for general student use. A campuswide network can be accessed from off campus. Internet access, at least one staffed computer lab available.

Student Life *Housing Options:* coed. *Activities and Organizations:* drama/theater group, student-run newspaper, radio station, choral group, Associated Students, Disciples on Campus, Gamma Beta Phi honor society, national fraternities, national sororities. *Campus security:* 24-hour emergency response devices and patrols, late-night transport/escort service, full safety education program. *Student Services:* health clinic, personal/psychological counseling.

Athletics Member NCAA. All Division III. *Intercollegiate sports:* baseball M, basketball M/W, crew M/W, cross-country running M/W, football M, golf M/W, lacrosse M(c)/W(c), soccer M/W, softball W, swimming W, tennis M/W, track and field W, volleyball W, water polo M/W. *Intramural sports:* badminton M/W, basketball M/W, bowling M/W, football M, golf M/W, soccer M/W, softball M/W, table tennis M/W, tennis M/W, volleyball M/W.

Standardized Tests *Required:* SAT I or ACT (for admission). *Recommended:* SAT II: Subject Tests (for admission).

Costs (2002–03) *Comprehensive fee:* $31,398 includes full-time tuition ($22,700), mandatory fees ($616), and room and board ($8082). Part-time tuition: $705 per credit. Part-time tuition and fees vary according to course load. *Room and board:* College room only: $4506. Room and board charges vary according to board plan and housing facility. *Payment plans:* tuition prepayment, installment, deferred payment. *Waivers:* children of alumni and employees or children of employees.

Financial Aid Of all full-time matriculated undergraduates who enrolled in 2001, 1932 applied for aid, 1896 were judged to have need, 1896 had their need fully met. 467 Federal Work-Study jobs (averaging $1614). *Average percent of need met:* 100%. *Average financial aid package:* $17,767. *Average need-based loan:* $5729. *Average need-based gift aid:* $12,107. *Average indebtedness upon graduation:* $19,242.

Applying *Options:* common application, electronic application, early admission, early action, deferred entrance. *Application fee:* $40. *Required:* essay or personal statement, high school transcript, minimum 2.75 GPA, 1 letter of recommendation. *Recommended:* minimum 3.5 GPA, interview. *Application deadlines:* 1/31 (freshmen), 3/15 (transfers). *Notification:* continuous (freshmen), 1/15 (early action).

Admissions Contact Mr. Michael O. Drummy, Associate Dean for Enrollment Services and Chief Admission Officer, Chapman University, One University Drive, Orange, CA 92866. *Phone:* 714-997-6711. *Toll-free phone:* 888-CUAPPLY. *Fax:* 714-997-6713. *E-mail:* admit@chapman.edu.

Charles R. Drew University of Medicine and Science
Los Angeles, California

- **Independent** comprehensive, founded 1966
- **Calendar** trimesters
- **Degrees** associate, bachelor's, master's, and doctoral
- **Coed**
- **Moderately difficult** entrance level

Standardized Tests *Required:* SAT I or ACT (for admission).

Financial Aid *Financial aid deadline:* 7/31.

Applying *Application fee:* $35. *Required:* essay or personal statement, high school transcript, minimum 2.0 GPA, 3 letters of recommendation, interview.

Admissions Contact Ms. Mala Sharma, Director of Enrollment Services, Charles R. Drew University of Medicine and Science, 1731 East 120th Street, Los Angeles, CA 90059. *Phone:* 323-563-4832.

Christian Heritage College
El Cajon, California

- **Independent nondenominational** 4-year, founded 1970
- **Calendar** semesters
- **Degree** certificates and bachelor's
- **Suburban** 32-acre campus with easy access to San Diego
- **Endowment** $236,310
- **Coed,** 636 undergraduate students, 87% full-time, 58% women, 42% men
- **Moderately difficult** entrance level, 46% of applicants were admitted

Undergraduates 551 full-time, 85 part-time. Students come from 28 states and territories, 6 other countries, 7% are from out of state, 7% African American, 4% Asian American or Pacific Islander, 10% Hispanic American, 0.6% Native American, 2% international, 17% transferred in, 50% live on campus. *Retention:* 61% of 2001 full-time freshmen returned.

Freshmen *Admission:* 200 applied, 92 admitted, 95 enrolled. *Average high school GPA:* 3.30. *Test scores:* SAT verbal scores over 500: 58%; SAT math scores over 500; 49%; ACT scores over 18: 85%; SAT verbal scores over 600: 10%; SAT math scores over 600: 9%; ACT scores over 24: 37%; SAT verbal scores over 700: 1%; ACT scores over 30: 11%.

Faculty *Total:* 78, 46% full-time, 27% with terminal degrees. *Student/faculty ratio:* 11:1.

Majors Adult/continuing education; athletic training/sports medicine; aviation technology; biblical studies; biology; business administration; communications; divinity/ministry; education; education (K-12); elementary education; English; history; individual/family development; interdisciplinary studies; liberal arts and sciences/liberal studies; mathematics; music; music teacher education; music (voice and choral/opera performance); pastoral counseling; physical education; psychology; religious music; secondary education; social sciences; theology.

Academic Programs *Special study options:* academic remediation for entering students, adult/continuing education programs, advanced placement credit, double majors, English as a second language, independent study, internships, part-time degree program, student-designed majors, study abroad, summer session for credit. *ROTC:* Army (c), Air Force (c).

Library Christian Heritage College Library plus 1 other with 75,000 titles, 1,215 serial subscriptions.

Computers on Campus 32 computers available on campus for general student use. Internet access, at least one staffed computer lab available.

Student Life *Housing:* on-campus residence required through senior year. *Options:* men-only, women-only. *Activities and Organizations:* choral group, Senate, Missions Club, Aviators Club, Women of Influence, Hope Ministries. *Campus security:* 24-hour emergency response devices and patrols. *Student Services:* health clinic, personal/psychological counseling.

Athletics Member NAIA, NCCAA. *Intercollegiate sports:* basketball M(s)/W(s), cross-country running M(s)/W(s), soccer M(s)/W(s), volleyball W(s). *Intramural sports:* basketball M/W, football M, soccer M/W, softball M/W, swimming M/W, tennis M/W, volleyball M/W.

Standardized Tests *Required:* SAT I or ACT (for admission).

Christian Heritage College (continued)

Costs (2001–02) *One-time required fee:* $70. *Comprehensive fee:* $17,880 includes full-time tuition ($12,156), mandatory fees ($394), and room and board ($5330). Full-time tuition and fees vary according to class time, course load, and program. Part-time tuition: $415 per credit. Part-time tuition and fees vary according to class time, course load, and program. *Room and board:* Room and board charges vary according to housing facility. *Payment plan:* installment. *Waivers:* employees or children of employees.

Financial Aid Of all full-time matriculated undergraduates who enrolled in 2001, 698 applied for aid, 419 were judged to have need, 109 had their need fully met. 38 Federal Work-Study jobs (averaging $1461). 44 State and other part-time jobs (averaging $1130). In 2001, 58 non-need-based awards were made. *Average percent of need met:* 48%. *Average financial aid package:* $9194. *Average need-based loan:* $3693. *Average need-based gift aid:* $3500. *Average non-need based aid:* $1500. *Average indebtedness upon graduation:* $15,124.

Applying *Options:* electronic application, early decision, deferred entrance. *Application fee:* $25. *Required:* essay or personal statement, high school transcript, 2 letters of recommendation. *Recommended:* minimum 2.75 GPA, interview. *Application deadlines:* 8/1 (freshmen), 8/1 (transfers). *Early decision:* 12/31. *Notification:* continuous (freshmen).

Admissions Contact Ms. Jennifer Wiersma, Director of Admissions, Christian Heritage College, 2100 Greenfield Drive, El Cajon, CA 92019-1157. *Phone:* 619-588-7747. *Toll-free phone:* 800-676-2242. *Fax:* 619-440-0209. *E-mail:* chcadm@adm.christianheritage.edu.

CLAREMONT MCKENNA COLLEGE
Claremont, California

- **Independent** 4-year, founded 1946, part of The Claremont Colleges Consortium
- **Calendar** semesters
- **Degree** bachelor's
- **Small-town** 50-acre campus with easy access to Los Angeles
- **Endowment** $367.2 million
- **Coed,** 1,044 undergraduate students, 100% full-time, 47% women, 53% men
- **Very difficult** entrance level, 29% of applicants were admitted

Claremont McKenna College (CMC) offers a traditional liberal arts education with a twist: within the context of a liberal arts curriculum, CMC focuses on educating students for leadership in public policy and public affairs. CMC's enrollment of 1,000 students ensures that students receive a personalized educational experience. However, as one of the Claremont Colleges, CMC provides its students with the academic, intellectual, social, and athletic resources typical of a medium-sized university.

Undergraduates 1,044 full-time. Students come from 47 states and territories, 22 other countries, 41% are from out of state, 4% African American, 15% Asian American or Pacific Islander, 9% Hispanic American, 0.4% Native American, 3% international, 7% transferred in, 97% live on campus. *Retention:* 94% of 2001 full-time freshmen returned.

Freshmen *Admission:* 2,898 applied, 831 admitted, 262 enrolled. *Test scores:* SAT verbal scores over 500: 100%; SAT math scores over 500: 100%; SAT verbal scores over 600: 92%; SAT math scores over 600: 93%; SAT verbal scores over 700: 45%; SAT math scores over 700: 51%.

Faculty *Total:* 160, 87% full-time, 100% with terminal degrees. *Student/faculty ratio:* 7:1.

Majors Accounting; African-American studies; American studies; art; Asian studies; biochemistry; biology; biophysics; chemistry; Chinese; classics; computer science; economics; engineering/industrial management; English; environmental science; European studies; film studies; French; German; Greek (modern); history; international business; international economics; international relations; Italian; Japanese; Latin American studies; Latin (ancient and medieval); legal studies; literature; mathematics; Mexican-American studies; modern languages; music; philosophy; physics; physiological psychology/psychobiology; political science; pre-dentistry; pre-law; pre-medicine; psychology; religious studies; Russian; Spanish; theater arts/drama; women's studies.

Academic Programs *Special study options:* accelerated degree program, advanced placement credit, double majors, honors programs, independent study, internships, off-campus study, student-designed majors, study abroad. *ROTC:* Army (b), Navy (c), Air Force (c). *Unusual degree programs:* 3-2 business administration with Claremont Graduate School, University of Chicago; engineering with Stanford University, Harvey Mudd College, Columbia University, Washington University in St. Louis, University of California System schools, University of Southern California; education, management information systems, computer information systems with Claremont Graduate School.

Library Honnold Library plus 3 others with 2.0 million titles, 6,028 serial subscriptions, 606 audiovisual materials, an OPAC, a Web page.

Computers on Campus 120 computers available on campus for general student use. A campuswide network can be accessed from student residence rooms and from off campus. At least one staffed computer lab available.

Student Life *Housing:* on-campus residence required for freshman year. *Options:* coed. *Activities and Organizations:* drama/theater group, student-run newspaper, radio station, choral group, student government, Debate/Forensics Club, newspaper, Volunteer Student Admission Committee, Civitas (community service club). *Campus security:* 24-hour emergency response devices and patrols, student patrols, late-night transport/escort service, controlled dormitory access. *Student Services:* health clinic, personal/psychological counseling, women's center.

Athletics Member NCAA. All Division III. *Intercollegiate sports:* badminton M(c)/W(c), baseball M, basketball M/W, cross-country running M/W, football M, golf M, lacrosse M(c)/W(c), rugby M(c)/W(c), skiing (downhill) M(c)/W(c), soccer M/W, softball W, swimming M/W, tennis M/W, track and field M/W, volleyball M(c)/W, water polo M/W. *Intramural sports:* archery M/W, badminton M/W, basketball M/W, bowling M/W, fencing M/W, football M/W, golf W, racquetball M/W, sailing M/W, soccer M/W, softball M/W, squash M/W, swimming M/W, table tennis M/W, tennis M/W, volleyball M/W, water polo M/W, weight lifting M/W.

Standardized Tests *Required:* SAT I or ACT (for admission). *Recommended:* SAT II: Subject Tests (for admission).

Costs (2001–02) *Comprehensive fee:* $32,700 includes full-time tuition ($24,540) and room and board ($8160). Part-time tuition: $4060 per course. *Room and board:* College room only: $4080. Room and board charges vary according to board plan and housing facility. *Payment plans:* tuition prepayment, installment. *Waivers:* employees or children of employees.

Financial Aid Of all full-time matriculated undergraduates who enrolled in 2001, 671 applied for aid, 607 were judged to have need, 607 had their need fully met. 386 Federal Work-Study jobs (averaging $1286). 430 State and other part-time jobs (averaging $1566). In 2001, 101 non-need-based awards were made. *Average percent of need met:* 100%. *Average financial aid package:* $21,769. *Average need-based loan:* $2935. *Average need-based gift aid:* $17,505. *Average non-need based aid:* $7121. *Average indebtedness upon graduation:* $15,944. *Financial aid deadline:* 2/1.

Applying *Options:* common application, electronic application, early admission, early decision, deferred entrance. *Application fee:* $50. *Required:* essay or personal statement, high school transcript, minimum 3.0 GPA, 2 letters of recommendation. *Recommended:* interview. *Application deadlines:* 1/1 (freshmen), 4/1 (transfers). *Early decision:* 11/15 (for plan 1), 1/1 (for plan 2). *Notification:* 4/1 (freshmen), 12/15 (early decision plan 1), 2/15 (early decision plan 2).

Admissions Contact Mr. Richard C. Vos, Vice President/Dean of Admission and Financial Aid, Claremont McKenna College, 890 Columbia Avenue, Claremont, CA 91711. *Phone:* 909-621-8088. *E-mail:* admission@mckenna.edu.

CLEVELAND CHIROPRACTIC COLLEGE-LOS ANGELES CAMPUS
Los Angeles, California

Admissions Contact 590 North Vermont Avenue, Los Angeles, CA 90004-2196. *Toll-free phone:* 800-446-CCLA.

COGSWELL POLYTECHNICAL COLLEGE
Sunnyvale, California

- **Independent** 4-year, founded 1887
- **Calendar** trimesters
- **Degree** bachelor's
- **Suburban** 2-acre campus with easy access to San Francisco and San Jose
- **Endowment** $6.8 million
- **Coed, primarily men,** 413 undergraduate students, 48% full-time, 12% women, 88% men
- **Moderately difficult** entrance level, 100% of applicants were admitted

Cogswell Polytechnical College is dedicated to providing students with superior education in engineering and the visual arts. Students learn the theory and gain the practical skills to begin work immediately in their chosen areas of engineering and the visual arts.

Undergraduates 197 full-time, 216 part-time. Students come from 20 states and territories, 9% are from out of state, 2% African American, 15% Asian

American or Pacific Islander, 7% Hispanic American, 0.2% Native American, 2% international, 16% transferred in, 9% live on campus. *Retention:* 87% of 2001 full-time freshmen returned.

Freshmen *Admission:* 32 applied, 32 admitted, 25 enrolled.

Faculty *Total:* 48, 29% full-time, 31% with terminal degrees. *Student/faculty ratio:* 15:1.

Majors Audio engineering; computer graphics; electrical/electronic engineering technology; electrical engineering; engineering; fire science; graphic design/commercial art/illustration.

Academic Programs *Special study options:* adult/continuing education programs, advanced placement credit, distance learning, external degree program, part-time degree program, summer session for credit.

Library Cogswell College Library with 11,257 titles, 102 serial subscriptions, 359 audiovisual materials, an OPAC.

Computers on Campus 125 computers available on campus for general student use. A campuswide network can be accessed from off campus. Internet access, at least one staffed computer lab available.

Student Life *Housing Options:* men-only, women-only. *Activities and Organizations:* student-run newspaper, ASB. *Campus security:* 24-hour emergency response devices.

Standardized Tests *Recommended:* SAT I and SAT II or ACT (for admission).

Costs (2002–03) *Tuition:* $9600 full-time, $400 per credit part-time. Full-time tuition and fees vary according to course load. Part-time tuition and fees vary according to course load. *Room only:* $6300. *Payment plan:* deferred payment. *Waivers:* employees or children of employees.

Financial Aid Of all full-time matriculated undergraduates who enrolled in 2001, 160 applied for aid, 128 were judged to have need. 6 Federal Work-Study jobs (averaging $750). *Average percent of need met:* 42%. *Average financial aid package:* $5410. *Average need-based loan:* $3510. *Average need-based gift aid:* $4358. *Average indebtedness upon graduation:* $19,118.

Applying *Options:* common application, deferred entrance. *Application fee:* $50. *Required:* essay or personal statement, high school transcript, minimum 2.5 GPA. *Required for some:* letters of recommendation, interview, portfolio. *Application deadlines:* 6/1 (freshmen), 6/1 (transfers). *Notification:* continuous (freshmen).

Admissions Contact Mr. Paul A. Schreivogel, Dean of Recruitment and Marketing, Cogswell Polytechnical College, 1175 Bordeaux Drive, Sunnyvale, CA 94089. *Phone:* 408-541-0100 Ext. 112. *Toll-free phone:* 800-264-7955. *Fax:* 408-747-0764. *E-mail:* admin@cogswell.edu.

COLEMAN COLLEGE
La Mesa, California

- **Independent** comprehensive, founded 1963
- **Calendar** quarters
- **Degrees** certificates, associate, bachelor's, and master's
- **Suburban** campus with easy access to San Diego
- **Coed,** 1,003 undergraduate students
- **Moderately difficult** entrance level

Undergraduates Students come from 19 states and territories, 1% are from out of state, 5% African American, 15% Asian American or Pacific Islander, 12% Hispanic American, 0.7% international.

Faculty *Total:* 101.

Majors Business administration; computer engineering technology; computer/information sciences; industrial technology; secretarial science.

Academic Programs *Special study options:* accelerated degree program, part-time degree program, services for LD students, summer session for credit.

Library Coleman College LaMesa Library with 66,800 titles, 69 serial subscriptions, an OPAC, a Web page.

Computers on Campus 420 computers available on campus for general student use. Internet access, at least one staffed computer lab available.

Student Life *Housing:* college housing not available. *Campus security:* 24-hour emergency response devices and patrols, late-night transport/escort service. *Student Services:* personal/psychological counseling.

Costs (2001–02) *Tuition:* $6000 full-time, $150 per unit part-time.

Applying *Options:* common application, deferred entrance. *Required:* high school transcript, interview. *Application deadline:* rolling (freshmen), rolling (transfers). *Notification:* continuous (freshmen).

Admissions Contact Admissions Department, Coleman College, 7380 Parkway Drive, La Mesa, CA 91942-1532. *Phone:* 619-465-3990. *Fax:* 619-465-0162. *E-mail:* jschafer@cts.com.

COLUMBIA COLLEGE-HOLLYWOOD
Tarzana, California

- **Independent** 4-year, founded 1952
- **Calendar** quarters
- **Degrees** associate and bachelor's
- **Urban** 1-acre campus
- **Coed,** 109 undergraduate students, 100% full-time, 21% women, 79% men
- **Minimally difficult** entrance level, 85% of applicants were admitted

Undergraduates 109 full-time. Students come from 23 states and territories, 10 other countries, 47% are from out of state, 4% African American, 5% Asian American or Pacific Islander, 7% Hispanic American, 16% international, 32% transferred in. *Retention:* 83% of 2001 full-time freshmen returned.

Freshmen *Admission:* 48 applied, 41 admitted, 10 enrolled. *Average high school GPA:* 3.3.

Faculty *Total:* 27. *Student/faculty ratio:* 5:1.

Majors Broadcast journalism; film studies; film/video production; radio/television broadcasting; telecommunications.

Academic Programs *Special study options:* accelerated degree program, adult/continuing education programs, part-time degree program, summer session for credit.

Library Joseph E. Blath Memorial Library with 5,500 titles, 23 serial subscriptions, 220 audiovisual materials, an OPAC.

Computers on Campus 12 computers available on campus for general student use. Internet access, at least one staffed computer lab available.

Student Life *Housing:* college housing not available. *Campus security:* late-night transport/escort service. *Student Services:* personal/psychological counseling.

Standardized Tests *Recommended:* SAT I (for admission).

Costs (2001–02) *Tuition:* $10,500 full-time, $3000 per term part-time. Full-time tuition and fees vary according to class time, course load, and program. *Required fees:* $225 full-time, $75 per term part-time. *Payment plans:* installment, deferred payment.

Financial Aid Of all full-time matriculated undergraduates who enrolled in 2001, 79 applied for aid, 79 were judged to have need. 3 Federal Work-Study jobs (averaging $2023). *Average financial aid package:* $3827. *Average need-based gift aid:* $3745. *Average indebtedness upon graduation:* $35,125.

Applying *Options:* deferred entrance. *Application fee:* $50. *Required:* essay or personal statement, high school transcript, minimum 2.0 GPA, 2 letters of recommendation, interview. *Application deadline:* rolling (freshmen). *Notification:* continuous until 9/1 (freshmen).

Admissions Contact Amanda Kraus, Admissions Director, Columbia College-Hollywood, 18618 Oxnard Street, Tarzana, CA 91356. *Phone:* 818-345-8414. *Fax:* 818-345-9053. *E-mail:* cchadfin@columbiacollege.edu.

CONCORDIA UNIVERSITY
Irvine, California

- **Independent** comprehensive, founded 1972, affiliated with Lutheran Church-Missouri Synod
- **Calendar** semesters
- **Degrees** bachelor's, master's, and postbachelor's certificates
- **Suburban** 70-acre campus with easy access to Los Angeles
- **Endowment** $5.8 million
- **Coed,** 1,112 undergraduate students, 91% full-time, 67% women, 33% men
- **Moderately difficult** entrance level, 28% of applicants were admitted

Undergraduates Students come from 25 states and territories, 17 other countries, 17% are from out of state, 3% African American, 7% Asian American or Pacific Islander, 9% Hispanic American, 0.9% Native American, 1% international, 68% live on campus. *Retention:* 80% of 2001 full-time freshmen returned.

Freshmen *Admission:* 939 applied, 266 admitted. *Average high school GPA:* 3.41. *Test scores:* SAT verbal scores over 500: 55%; SAT math scores over 500: 55%; ACT scores over 18: 81%; SAT verbal scores over 600: 14%; SAT math scores over 600: 14%; ACT scores over 24: 25%; SAT verbal scores over 700: 2%; SAT math scores over 700: 1%; ACT scores over 30: 5%.

Faculty *Total:* 115, 36% full-time, 26% with terminal degrees. *Student/faculty ratio:* 16:1.

Majors Art; behavioral sciences; biology; business administration; communications; divinity/ministry; early childhood education; elementary education; English; exercise sciences; history; humanities; liberal arts and sciences/liberal studies; mathematics; music; physical therapy; political science; pre-law; premedicine; psychology; religious education; secondary education; social work; theater arts/drama; theology.

Concordia University (continued)

Academic Programs *Special study options:* adult/continuing education programs, advanced placement credit, cooperative education, distance learning, double majors, English as a second language, freshman honors college, honors programs, independent study, internships, off-campus study, part-time degree program, student-designed majors, summer session for credit.

Library Concordia University Library with 93,899 titles, 3,679 audiovisual materials, an OPAC, a Web page.

Computers on Campus 42 computers available on campus for general student use. A campuswide network can be accessed from student residence rooms. At least one staffed computer lab available.

Student Life *Housing:* on-campus residence required through junior year. *Options:* men-only, women-only. *Activities and Organizations:* drama/theater group, student-run newspaper, radio station, choral group, Student Senate, Fellowship of Christian Athletes, Student Life Board, Intramurals, Outreach. *Campus security:* 24-hour patrols, student patrols, late-night transport/escort service, lighted walkways. *Student Services:* health clinic, personal/psychological counseling.

Athletics Member NAIA. *Intercollegiate sports:* baseball M(s), basketball M(s)/W(s), cross-country running M(s)/W(s), soccer M(s), softball W(s), track and field M(s)/W(s), volleyball W(s). *Intramural sports:* badminton M/W, baseball M, basketball M/W, bowling M/W, football M/W, golf M/W, soccer M/W, softball M/W, table tennis M/W, tennis M/W, volleyball M/W.

Standardized Tests *Required:* SAT I or ACT (for admission).

Costs (2001–02) *Comprehensive fee:* $22,290 includes full-time tuition ($16,480) and room and board ($5810). Part-time tuition: $500 per unit. *Room and board:* College room only: $3460. Room and board charges vary according to board plan. *Payment plan:* installment. *Waivers:* employees or children of employees.

Financial Aid Of all full-time matriculated undergraduates who enrolled in 2001, 796 applied for aid, 592 were judged to have need, 173 had their need fully met. 50 Federal Work-Study jobs (averaging $2000). 275 State and other part-time jobs (averaging $2000). In 2001, 204 non-need-based awards were made. *Average percent of need met:* 30%. *Average financial aid package:* $8600. *Average need-based loan:* $3500. *Average need-based gift aid:* $6200. *Average non-need based aid:* $2200. *Average indebtedness upon graduation:* $15,500. *Financial aid deadline:* 6/30.

Applying *Options:* common application, electronic application, deferred entrance. *Application fee:* $40. *Required:* high school transcript, 2 letters of recommendation. *Recommended:* minimum 2.8 GPA, interview. *Application deadline:* rolling (freshmen), rolling (transfers). *Notification:* continuous until 4/1 (freshmen).

Admissions Contact Ms. Lori McDonald, Director of Enrollment Services, Concordia University, 1530 Concordia West, Irvine, CA 92612-3299. *Phone:* 949-854-8002 Ext. 1170. *Toll-free phone:* 800-229-1200. *Fax:* 949-854-6894. *E-mail:* admission@cui.edu.

DESIGN INSTITUTE OF SAN DIEGO

San Diego, California

- **Proprietary** 4-year, founded 1977
- **Calendar** semesters
- **Degree** bachelor's
- **Urban** campus
- **Coed,** 350 undergraduate students
- **Noncompetitive** entrance level

Undergraduates Students come from 10 states and territories, 15 other countries. *Retention:* 87% of 2001 full-time freshmen returned.

Freshmen *Average high school GPA:* 2.5.

Faculty *Total:* 50.

Majors Interior design.

Academic Programs *Special study options:* internships, part-time degree program.

Library 5,000 titles, 90 serial subscriptions, an OPAC.

Computers on Campus 50 computers available on campus for general student use. At least one staffed computer lab available.

Student Life *Housing:* college housing not available. *Activities and Organizations:* American Society of Interior Designers, International Interior Designers Association, Illuminating Electrical Society.

Costs (2002–03) *Tuition:* $10,800 full-time.

Applying *Application fee:* $25. *Required:* high school transcript, minimum 2.0 GPA. *Recommended:* interview. *Application deadline:* rolling (freshmen), rolling (transfers).

Admissions Contact Ms. Paula Parrish, Director of Admissions, Design Institute of San Diego, 8555 Commerce Avenue, San Diego, CA 92121-2685. *Phone:* 619-566-1200. *Toll-free phone:* 800-619-4DESIGN. *Fax:* 619-566-2711. *E-mail:* admissions@disd.edu.

DEVRY UNIVERSITY

West Hills, California

- **Proprietary** 4-year, founded 1999, part of DeVry, Inc
- **Calendar** semesters
- **Degrees** associate and bachelor's
- **Coed,** 1,351 undergraduate students, 63% full-time, 24% women, 76% men
- **Minimally difficult** entrance level, 78% of applicants were admitted

Undergraduates 854 full-time, 497 part-time. Students come from 9 states and territories, 7 other countries, 1% are from out of state, 6% African American, 31% Asian American or Pacific Islander, 26% Hispanic American, 0.7% Native American, 0.7% international, 0.1% transferred in. *Retention:* 56% of 2001 full-time freshmen returned.

Freshmen *Admission:* 612 applied, 477 admitted, 501 enrolled.

Faculty *Total:* 84, 23% full-time. *Student/faculty ratio:* 16:1.

Majors Business administration/management related; business systems analysis/design; business systems networking/ telecommunications; computer engineering technology; electrical/electronic engineering technology; information sciences/systems; operations management.

Academic Programs *Special study options:* academic remediation for entering students, adult/continuing education programs, advanced placement credit, cooperative education, part-time degree program, services for LD students, summer session for credit.

Library Learning Resource Center with 4,647 titles, 75 serial subscriptions, 91 audiovisual materials, an OPAC.

Computers on Campus 155 computers available on campus for general student use. A campuswide network can be accessed from off campus.

Student Life *Housing:* college housing not available. *Activities and Organizations:* Associated Student Body, Computer Information Systems/Telecommunication Association, Womens Caucus, United Island Student Association, Institute of Electronics and Electrical Engineers. *Campus security:* 24-hour emergency response devices, late-night transport/escort service, lighted pathways/sidewalks.

Athletics *Intramural sports:* archery M, basketball M, football M, softball M.

Standardized Tests *Recommended:* SAT I or ACT (for admission).

Costs (2001–02) *Tuition:* $9140 full-time, $320 per credit hour part-time. Full-time tuition and fees vary according to course load. Part-time tuition and fees vary according to course load. *Required fees:* $65 full-time. *Payment plans:* installment, deferred payment. *Waivers:* employees or children of employees.

Financial Aid Of all full-time matriculated undergraduates who enrolled in 2001, 952 applied for aid, 903 were judged to have need, 25 had their need fully met. *Average percent of need met:* 44%. *Average financial aid package:* $8702. *Average need-based gift aid:* $4697.

Applying *Options:* electronic application, deferred entrance. *Application fee:* $50. *Required:* high school transcript, interview. *Application deadline:* rolling (freshmen), rolling (transfers). *Notification:* continuous (freshmen).

Admissions Contact DeVry University, 22801 Roscoe Boulevard, West Hills, CA 91304. *Phone:* 818-932-3001. *Fax:* 818-713-8118.

DEVRY UNIVERSITY

Fremont, California

- **Proprietary** 4-year, founded 1998, part of DeVry, Inc
- **Calendar** semesters
- **Degrees** associate and bachelor's
- **Suburban** 17-acre campus with easy access to San Francisco
- **Coed,** 2,278 undergraduate students, 82% full-time, 22% women, 78% men
- **Minimally difficult** entrance level, 84% of applicants were admitted

Undergraduates 1,873 full-time, 405 part-time. Students come from 22 states and territories, 15 other countries, 3% are from out of state, 6% African American, 40% Asian American or Pacific Islander, 17% Hispanic American, 6% Native American, 2% international, 1% transferred in. *Retention:* 60% of 2001 full-time freshmen returned.

Freshmen *Admission:* 810 applied, 680 admitted, 640 enrolled.

Faculty *Total:* 88, 61% full-time. *Student/faculty ratio:* 26:1.

Majors Business administration/management related; business systems analysis/design; business systems networking/ telecommunications; computer engineering technology; electrical/electronic engineering technology; information sciences/systems; operations management.

Academic Programs *Special study options:* academic remediation for entering students, accelerated degree program, adult/continuing education programs, advanced placement credit, cooperative education, part-time degree program, services for LD students, summer session for credit.

Library Learning Resource Center with 11,000 titles, 50 serial subscriptions, 206 audiovisual materials, an OPAC.

Computers on Campus 325 computers available on campus for general student use. A campuswide network can be accessed from off campus. Internet access, at least one staffed computer lab available.

Student Life *Housing:* college housing not available. *Activities and Organizations:* student-run newspaper, Latino-American Student Organization, Telecommunications Club, Chess Club. *Campus security:* 24-hour emergency response devices and patrols, late-night transport/escort service, lighted pathways/sidewalks.

Athletics *Intramural sports:* baseball M, basketball M, soccer M.

Standardized Tests *Recommended:* SAT I or ACT (for admission).

Costs (2001–02) *Tuition:* $9800 full-time, $345 per credit hour part-time. Full-time tuition and fees vary according to course load. Part-time tuition and fees vary according to course load. *Payment plans:* installment, deferred payment. *Waivers:* employees or children of employees.

Financial Aid Of all full-time matriculated undergraduates who enrolled in 2001, 1983 applied for aid, 1819 were judged to have need, 102 had their need fully met. In 2001, 164 non-need-based awards were made. *Average percent of need met:* 50%. *Average financial aid package:* $9593. *Average need-based loan:* $6699. *Average need-based gift aid:* $6036.

Applying *Options:* electronic application, deferred entrance. *Application fee:* $50. *Required:* high school transcript, interview. *Application deadline:* rolling (freshmen), rolling (transfers). *Notification:* continuous (freshmen).

Admissions Contact Mr. Bruce Williams, New Student Coordinator, DeVry University, 6600 Dumbarton Circle, Fremont, CA 94555. *Phone:* 510-574-1111. *Toll-free phone:* 888-393-3879.

DeVry University
Pomona, California

- **Proprietary** 4-year, founded 1983, part of DeVry, Inc
- **Calendar** semesters
- **Degrees** associate and bachelor's
- **Urban** 15-acre campus with easy access to Los Angeles
- **Coed,** 3,669 undergraduate students, 70% full-time, 26% women, 74% men
- **Minimally difficult** entrance level, 85% of applicants were admitted

Undergraduates 2,583 full-time, 1,086 part-time. Students come from 21 states and territories, 24 other countries, 2% are from out of state, 8% African American, 34% Asian American or Pacific Islander, 31% Hispanic American, 0.5% Native American, 2% international, 0.0% transferred in. *Retention:* 49% of 2001 full-time freshmen returned.

Freshmen *Admission:* 1,178 applied, 1,003 admitted, 1,056 enrolled.

Faculty *Total:* 144, 33% full-time. *Student/faculty ratio:* 25:1.

Majors Business administration/management related; business systems analysis/design; business systems networking/ telecommunications; computer engineering technology; electrical/electronic engineering technology; information sciences/systems; operations management.

Academic Programs *Special study options:* academic remediation for entering students, accelerated degree program, adult/continuing education programs, advanced placement credit, cooperative education, part-time degree program, services for LD students, summer session for credit.

Library Learning Resource Center with 9,149 titles, 79 serial subscriptions, 875 audiovisual materials, an OPAC.

Computers on Campus 492 computers available on campus for general student use. A campuswide network can be accessed from off campus. Internet access, online (class) registration, at least one staffed computer lab available.

Student Life *Housing:* college housing not available. *Activities and Organizations:* student-run newspaper, Phi Beta Lambda, Society of Hispanic Professional Engineers, National Society of Black Engineers, International Telecommunications Management Association, United Islands Student Association. *Campus security:* 24-hour emergency response devices, late-night transport/escort service.

Athletics *Intramural sports:* basketball M/W, softball M/W.

Standardized Tests *Recommended:* SAT I or ACT (for admission).

Costs (2001–02) *Tuition:* $9140 full-time, $320 per credit hour part-time. Full-time tuition and fees vary according to course load. Part-time tuition and fees vary according to course load. *Required fees:* $65 full-time. *Payment plans:* installment, deferred payment. *Waivers:* employees or children of employees.

Financial Aid Of all full-time matriculated undergraduates who enrolled in 2001, 2961 applied for aid, 2799 were judged to have need, 98 had their need fully met. In 2001, 161 non-need-based awards were made. *Average percent of need met:* 46%. *Average financial aid package:* $8655. *Average need-based loan:* $5819. *Average need-based gift aid:* $4957. *Average indebtedness upon graduation:* $16,431.

Applying *Options:* electronic application, deferred entrance. *Application fee:* $50. *Required:* high school transcript, interview. *Application deadline:* rolling (freshmen), rolling (transfers). *Notification:* continuous (freshmen).

Admissions Contact Ms. Melanie Guerra, New Student Coordinator, DeVry University, 901 Corporate Center Drive, Pomona, CA 91768-2642. *Phone:* 909-622-8866. *Toll-free phone:* 800-243-3660. *Fax:* 909-868-4165.

DeVry University
Long Beach, California

- **Proprietary** 4-year, founded 1984, part of DeVry, Inc
- **Calendar** semesters
- **Degrees** associate and bachelor's
- **Urban** 23-acre campus with easy access to Los Angeles
- **Coed,** 2,853 undergraduate students, 71% full-time, 28% women, 72% men
- **Minimally difficult** entrance level, 81% of applicants were admitted

Undergraduates 2,021 full-time, 832 part-time. Students come from 23 states and territories, 13 other countries, 3% are from out of state, 13% African American, 32% Asian American or Pacific Islander, 26% Hispanic American, 0.8% Native American, 2% international, 0.0% transferred in. *Retention:* 45% of 2001 full-time freshmen returned.

Freshmen *Admission:* 829 applied, 675 admitted, 800 enrolled.

Faculty *Total:* 129, 32% full-time. *Student/faculty ratio:* 22:1.

Majors Business administration/management related; business systems analysis/design; business systems networking/ telecommunications; computer engineering technology; electrical/electronic engineering technology; information sciences/systems; operations management.

Academic Programs *Special study options:* academic remediation for entering students, adult/continuing education programs, advanced placement credit, cooperative education, part-time degree program, services for LD students, summer session for credit.

Library Learning Resource Center with 8,973 titles, 80 serial subscriptions, 741 audiovisual materials, an OPAC.

Computers on Campus 385 computers available on campus for general student use. A campuswide network can be accessed from off campus. At least one staffed computer lab available.

Student Life *Housing:* college housing not available. *Activities and Organizations:* Teamnet, Society of Hispanic Professional Engineers, National Society of Black Engineers, Institute of Electronics and Electrical Engineers, United Islands. *Campus security:* 24-hour emergency response devices and patrols, late-night transport/escort service, motion detectors, closed hours.

Athletics *Intramural sports:* basketball M/W, soccer M/W, softball M/W, volleyball M/W.

Standardized Tests *Recommended:* SAT I or ACT (for admission).

Costs (2001–02) *Tuition:* $9140 full-time, $320 per credit hour part-time. Full-time tuition and fees vary according to course load. Part-time tuition and fees vary according to course load. *Required fees:* $65 full-time. *Payment plans:* installment, deferred payment. *Waivers:* employees or children of employees.

Financial Aid Of all full-time matriculated undergraduates who enrolled in 2001, 2275 applied for aid, 2184 were judged to have need, 56 had their need fully met. In 2001, 88 non-need-based awards were made. *Average percent of need met:* 45%. *Average financial aid package:* $8465. *Average need-based loan:* $5849. *Average need-based gift aid:* $4897. *Average indebtedness upon graduation:* $15,493.

Applying *Options:* electronic application, deferred entrance. *Application fee:* $50. *Required:* high school transcript, interview. *Application deadline:* rolling (freshmen), rolling (transfers). *Notification:* continuous (freshmen).

Admissions Contact Ms. Lisa Flores, New Student Coordinator, DeVry University, 3880 Kilroy Airport, Long Beach, CA 90806. *Phone:* 562-427-0861. *Toll-free phone:* 800-597-0444. *Fax:* 562-997-5371.

Dominican School of Philosophy and Theology
Berkeley, California

- **Independent Roman Catholic** upper-level, founded 1932
- **Calendar** semesters

Dominican School of Philosophy and Theology (continued)

- **Degrees** bachelor's, master's, and first professional
- **Urban** campus with easy access to San Francisco
- **Endowment** $2.0 million
- **Coed,** 17 undergraduate students, 100% full-time, 12% women, 88% men
- **Moderately difficult** entrance level

Undergraduates 17 full-time. Students come from 8 states and territories, 50% are from out of state, 6% African American, 12% Asian American or Pacific Islander, 12% Hispanic American, 100% transferred in, 17% live on campus.

Faculty *Total:* 24, 58% full-time, 92% with terminal degrees. *Student/faculty ratio:* 6:1.

Majors Philosophy.

Academic Programs *Special study options:* double majors, independent study, off-campus study, part-time degree program, study abroad.

Library Flora Lamson Hewlett Library plus 1 other with 401,086 titles, 1,526 serial subscriptions, 8,143 audiovisual materials, an OPAC, a Web page.

Computers on Campus 4 computers available on campus for general student use. Internet access available.

Student Life *Housing Options:* coed, cooperative. *Activities and Organizations:* DSPT Associated Students. *Campus security:* late night transport/escort service. *Student Services:* personal/psychological counseling, women's center.

Costs (2002–03) *Tuition:* $9000 full-time, $375 per credit part-time. *Required fees:* $50 full-time, $50 per year part-time. *Room only:* Room and board charges vary according to housing facility. *Payment plan:* installment.

Applying *Options:* early admission, deferred entrance. *Application fee:* $30. *Application deadline:* rolling (transfers). *Notification:* continuous (transfers).

Admissions Contact Ms. Susan McGinnis Hardie, Admissions Director, Dominican School of Philosophy and Theology, 2401 Ridge Road, Berkeley, CA 94709-1295. *Phone:* 510-883-2073. *Fax:* 510-849-1372. *E-mail:* smcginnishardie@dspt.edu.

DOMINICAN UNIVERSITY OF CALIFORNIA
San Rafael, California

- **Independent** comprehensive, founded 1890, affiliated with Roman Catholic Church
- **Calendar** semesters
- **Degrees** bachelor's, master's, and postbachelor's certificates
- **Suburban** 80-acre campus with easy access to San Francisco
- **Endowment** $10.1 million
- **Coed,** 946 undergraduate students, 71% full-time, 77% women, 23% men
- **Moderately difficult** entrance level, 50% of applicants were admitted

Undergraduates 672 full-time, 274 part-time. Students come from 17 states and territories, 18 other countries, 5% are from out of state, 7% African American, 12% Asian American or Pacific Islander, 10% Hispanic American, 0.6% Native American, 4% international, 10% transferred in, 20% live on campus. *Retention:* 78% of 2001 full-time freshmen returned.

Freshmen *Admission:* 713 applied, 354 admitted, 130 enrolled. *Average high school GPA:* 3.34. *Test scores:* SAT verbal scores over 500: 57%; SAT math scores over 500: 54%; SAT verbal scores over 600: 22%; SAT math scores over 600: 13%; SAT verbal scores over 700: 2%.

Faculty *Total:* 228, 24% full-time, 41% with terminal degrees. *Student/faculty ratio:* 12:1.

Majors Art; art history; biology; communications; computer graphics; creative writing; English; environmental science; history; humanities; human resources management; interdisciplinary studies; international business; international relations; liberal arts and sciences/liberal studies; music; nursing; occupational therapy; political science; psychology; religious studies.

Academic Programs *Special study options:* academic remediation for entering students, adult/continuing education programs, advanced placement credit, double majors, English as a second language, honors programs, independent study, internships, off-campus study, part-time degree program, services for LD students, student-designed majors, study abroad, summer session for credit. *ROTC:* Army (c), Air Force (c).

Library Archbishop Alemany Library plus 1 other with 102,813 titles, 389 serial subscriptions, 1,107 audiovisual materials, an OPAC, a Web page.

Computers on Campus 52 computers available on campus for general student use. A campuswide network can be accessed from student residence rooms and from off campus. Internet access, at least one staffed computer lab available.

Student Life *Housing Options:* coed. *Activities and Organizations:* drama/theater group, student-run newspaper, radio station, choral group, Humans Interested in Psychology Club, science club, art club, multicultural club. *Campus security:* 24-hour patrols, late-night transport/escort service, controlled dormitory access. *Student Services:* health clinic, personal/psychological counseling.

Athletics Member NAIA. *Intercollegiate sports:* basketball M(s)/W(s), soccer M(s)/W(s), softball W(s), tennis M/W, volleyball W(s). *Intramural sports:* volleyball M.

Standardized Tests *Required:* SAT I or ACT (for admission). *Recommended:* SAT II: Subject Tests (for admission).

Costs (2002–03) *Comprehensive fee:* $30,070 includes full-time tuition ($20,320), mandatory fees ($350), and room and board ($9400). Full-time tuition and fees vary according to program. Part-time tuition: $847 per unit. Part-time tuition and fees vary according to program. *Required fees:* $175 per term part-time. *Room and board:* Room and board charges vary according to board plan. *Payment plan:* installment. *Waivers:* employees or children of employees.

Financial Aid Of all full-time matriculated undergraduates who enrolled in 2001, 549 applied for aid, 413 were judged to have need, 101 had their need fully met. 249 Federal Work-Study jobs (averaging $851). 68 State and other part-time jobs (averaging $3764). *Average percent of need met:* 81%. *Average financial aid package:* $15,289. *Average need-based loan:* $4056. *Average need-based gift aid:* $9458.

Applying *Options:* common application, electronic application, early admission, deferred entrance. *Application fee:* $40. *Required:* essay or personal statement, high school transcript, minimum 2.5 GPA, 1 letter of recommendation. *Required for some:* interview. *Application deadline:* rolling (freshmen), rolling (transfers). *Notification:* continuous until 8/15 (freshmen).

Admissions Contact Mr. Art Criss, Director of Admissions, Dominican University of California, 50 Acacia Avenue, San Rafael, CA 94901-2298. *Phone:* 415-257-1376. *Toll-free phone:* 888-323-6763. *Fax:* 415-385-3214. *E-mail:* enroll@dominican.edu.

EDUCATION AMERICA UNIVERSITY
San Diego, California

Admissions Contact 123 Camino de la Reina, North Building, Suite 100, San Diego, CA 92108. *Toll-free phone:* 800-214-7001.

EMMANUEL BIBLE COLLEGE
Pasadena, California

- **Independent** 4-year, affiliated with Church of the Nazarene
- **Calendar** quarters
- **Degrees** associate and bachelor's
- **Endowment** $51,000
- 20 undergraduate students, 30% full-time
- 100% of applicants were admitted

Faculty *Student/faculty ratio:* 10:1.

Student Life *Campus security:* 24-hour emergency response devices and patrols.

Applying *Options:* common application, early admission. *Application fee:* $25. *Required:* essay or personal statement, high school transcript, interview, Christian commitment. *Required for some:* letters of recommendation. *Recommended:* letters of recommendation.

Admissions Contact Mr. Yeghia Babikian, President, Emmanuel Bible College, 1605 East Elizabeth Street, 1536 East Howard Street, Pasadena, CA 91104. *Phone:* 626-791-2575. *Fax:* 626-398-2424.

FRESNO PACIFIC UNIVERSITY
Fresno, California

- **Independent** comprehensive, founded 1944, affiliated with Mennonite Brethren Church
- **Calendar** semesters
- **Degrees** associate, bachelor's, and master's
- **Suburban** 42-acre campus
- **Endowment** $4.9 million
- **Coed,** 909 undergraduate students, 91% full-time, 68% women, 32% men
- **Moderately difficult** entrance level, 73% of applicants were admitted

Undergraduates 824 full-time, 85 part-time. Students come from 16 states and territories, 10 other countries, 3% are from out of state, 2% African American, 3% Asian American or Pacific Islander, 22% Hispanic American, 0.8% Native American, 5% international, 38% transferred in, 52% live on campus. *Retention:* 82% of 2001 full-time freshmen returned.

Freshmen *Admission:* 551 applied, 404 admitted, 201 enrolled. *Average high school GPA:* 3.54. *Test scores:* SAT verbal scores over 500: 51%; SAT math scores over 500: 51%; ACT scores over 18: 85%; SAT verbal scores over 600: 16%; SAT math scores over 600: 15%; ACT scores over 24: 35%; SAT verbal scores over 700: 1%; ACT scores over 30: 5%.

Faculty *Total:* 181, 42% full-time. *Student/faculty ratio:* 16:1.

Majors Accounting; applied mathematics; athletic training/sports medicine; biblical studies; bilingual/bicultural education; biology; business administration; business marketing and marketing management; chemistry; computer/information sciences; developmental/child psychology; divinity/ministry; education; elementary education; English; finance; history; humanities; international business; liberal arts and sciences/liberal studies; literature; mass communications; mathematics; music; music teacher education; natural sciences; nonprofit/public management; pastoral counseling; physical education; political science; pre-law; pre-medicine; psychology; religious music; religious studies; science education; secondary education; social sciences; social work; sociology; Spanish; sport/fitness administration.

Academic Programs *Special study options:* accelerated degree program, adult/continuing education programs, advanced placement credit, cooperative education, distance learning, double majors, English as a second language, independent study, internships, off-campus study, part-time degree program, services for LD students, student-designed majors, study abroad, summer session for credit.

Library Hiebert Library with 148,000 titles, 2,000 serial subscriptions, 6,000 audiovisual materials, an OPAC, a Web page.

Computers on Campus 68 computers available on campus for general student use. A campuswide network can be accessed from student residence rooms and from off campus.

Student Life *Housing:* on-campus residence required through sophomore year. *Options:* men-only, women-only. *Activities and Organizations:* drama/theater group, student-run newspaper, choral group, International Club, Kid's Klub, Amigos Unidos, Slavic club, women's soccer club. *Campus security:* 24-hour emergency response devices and patrols, student patrols, late-night transport/escort service, controlled dormitory access. *Student Services:* health clinic, personal/psychological counseling.

Athletics Member NAIA. *Intercollegiate sports:* basketball M(s)/W(s), cross-country running M(s)/W(s), soccer M(s)/W, track and field M(s)/W(s), volleyball W(s). *Intramural sports:* basketball M/W, bowling M/W, football M/W, soccer M/W, volleyball M/W.

Standardized Tests *Required:* SAT I or ACT (for admission).

Costs (2002–03) *Comprehensive fee:* $21,046 includes full-time tuition ($16,200), mandatory fees ($216), and room and board ($4630). Part-time tuition: $575 per unit. *Room and board:* College room only: $2000. Room and board charges vary according to board plan and housing facility. *Payment plan:* installment. *Waivers:* senior citizens and employees or children of employees.

Financial Aid Of all full-time matriculated undergraduates who enrolled in 2001, 727 applied for aid, 670 were judged to have need, 114 had their need fully met. 415 Federal Work-Study jobs (averaging $1590). In 2001, 98 non-need-based awards were made. *Average percent of need met:* 80%. *Average financial aid package:* $14,241. *Average need-based loan:* $2325. *Average need-based gift aid:* $9864. *Average indebtedness upon graduation:* $16,909.

Applying *Options:* electronic application, early admission, deferred entrance. *Application fee:* $40. *Required:* essay or personal statement, high school transcript, 1 letter of recommendation. *Required for some:* interview. *Application deadline:* rolling (freshmen), rolling (transfers). *Notification:* continuous until 7/31 (freshmen).

Admissions Contact Cary Templeton, Assistant Dean of Enrollment Services, Fresno Pacific University, Fresno, CA 93702. *Phone:* 559-453-2039. *Toll-free phone:* 800-660-6089. *Fax:* 559-453-2007. *E-mail:* ugadmis@fresno.edu.

GOLDEN GATE UNIVERSITY
San Francisco, California

- **Independent** university, founded 1853
- **Calendar** trimesters
- **Degrees** certificates, associate, bachelor's, master's, doctoral, and first professional
- **Urban** campus
- **Endowment** $17.3 million
- **Coed,** 1,015 undergraduate students, 27% full-time, 60% women, 40% men
- **Moderately difficult** entrance level, 100% of applicants were admitted

Undergraduates 277 full-time, 738 part-time. Students come from 61 other countries, 5% are from out of state, 9% African American, 13% Asian American or Pacific Islander, 8% Hispanic American, 0.4% Native American, 19% international, 12% transferred in. *Retention:* 80% of 2001 full-time freshmen returned.

Freshmen *Admission:* 26 applied, 26 admitted, 26 enrolled.

Faculty *Total:* 662, 5% full-time, 19% with terminal degrees. *Student/faculty ratio:* 17:1.

Majors Accounting; business administration; business marketing and marketing management; computer/information technology services administration and management related; finance; human resources management; information sciences/systems; international business; operations management; telecommunications.

Academic Programs *Special study options:* academic remediation for entering students, accelerated degree program, adult/continuing education programs, advanced placement credit, cooperative education, distance learning, English as a second language, internships, off-campus study, part-time degree program, summer session for credit.

Library Golden Gate University Library plus 1 other with 79,204 titles, 3,335 serial subscriptions, an OPAC.

Computers on Campus 52 computers available on campus for general student use. Internet access, at least one staffed computer lab available.

Student Life *Housing:* college housing not available. *Activities and Organizations:* student-run newspaper, American Marketing Association, Korean Student Association, Japanese Student Association, Thai Student Association, Computing Society. *Campus security:* late-night transport/escort service. *Student Services:* personal/psychological counseling.

Athletics *Intramural sports:* cross-country running M(c)/W(c), racquetball M(c)/W(c), tennis M(c)/W(c).

Costs (2001–02) *Tuition:* $9192 full-time, $1149 per course part-time. *Payment plan:* installment. *Waivers:* employees or children of employees.

Applying *Options:* common application, electronic application, deferred entrance. *Application fee:* $55. *Required:* high school transcript, minimum 2.0 GPA. *Required for some:* minimum 3.2 GPA, interview. *Recommended:* essay or personal statement, minimum 3.0 GPA. *Application deadlines:* 6/1 (freshmen), 6/1 (out-of-state freshmen), 6/1 (transfers). *Notification:* continuous (freshmen), continuous (out-of-state freshmen).

Admissions Contact Golden Gate University, 536 Mission Street, San Francisco, CA 94105-2968. *Phone:* 415-442-7800. *Toll-free phone:* 800-448-4968. *Fax:* 415-442-7807. *E-mail:* info@ggu.edu.

HARVEY MUDD COLLEGE
Claremont, California

- **Independent** comprehensive, founded 1955, part of The Claremont Colleges Consortium
- **Calendar** semesters
- **Degrees** bachelor's and master's
- **Suburban** 33-acre campus with easy access to Los Angeles
- **Endowment** $168.2 million
- **Coed,** 706 undergraduate students, 100% full-time, 32% women, 68% men
- **Most difficult** entrance level, 34% of applicants were admitted

Undergraduates 706 full-time. Students come from 43 states and territories, 15 other countries, 54% are from out of state, 0.7% African American, 22% Asian American or Pacific Islander, 4% Hispanic American, 0.6% Native American, 3% international, 1% transferred in, 96% live on campus. *Retention:* 94% of 2001 full-time freshmen returned.

Freshmen *Admission:* 1,524 applied, 516 admitted, 176 enrolled. *Test scores:* SAT verbal scores over 500: 100%; SAT math scores over 500: 100%; SAT verbal scores over 600: 96%; SAT math scores over 600: 100%; SAT verbal scores over 700: 62%; SAT math scores over 700: 90%.

Faculty *Total:* 85, 93% full-time, 99% with terminal degrees. *Student/faculty ratio:* 9:1.

Majors Biology; chemistry; computer science; engineering; mathematics; physics.

Academic Programs *Special study options:* advanced placement credit, double majors, internships, off-campus study, services for LD students, student-designed majors, study abroad. *ROTC:* Army (c), Air Force (b). *Unusual degree programs:* 3-2 management/engineering with Claremont McKenna College.

Library Honnold Library plus 1 other with 1.4 million titles, 4,321 serial subscriptions, 606 audiovisual materials, an OPAC, a Web page.

Computers on Campus 200 computers available on campus for general student use. A campuswide network can be accessed from student residence rooms and from off campus. At least one staffed computer lab available.

Student Life *Housing:* on-campus residence required for freshman year. *Options:* coed. *Activities and Organizations:* drama/theater group, student-run newspaper, radio station, choral group, Delta "H" Outdoor Club, Etc. Players—

Harvey Mudd College (continued)
Drama Club, club sports, Jazz Orchestra, Society of Women Engineers. *Campus security:* 24-hour emergency response devices and patrols, late-night transport/escort service. *Student Services:* health clinic, personal/psychological counseling, women's center.

Athletics Member NCAA. All Division III. *Intercollegiate sports:* baseball M, basketball M/W, cross-country running M/W, football M, golf M, soccer M/W, softball W, swimming M/W, tennis M/W, track and field M/W, volleyball W, water polo M/W. *Intramural sports:* badminton M(c)/W(c), basketball M/W, fencing M(c)/W(c), football M/W, ice hockey M(c), lacrosse M(c)/W(c), rugby M(c)/W(c), sailing M(c)/W(c), soccer M/W, swimming M/W, table tennis M(c)/W(c), tennis M/W, volleyball M/W, water polo M.

Standardized Tests *Required:* SAT I (for admission), SAT II: Writing Test (for admission).

Costs (2001–02) *Comprehensive fee:* $34,050 includes full-time tuition ($24,929), mandatory fees ($577), and room and board ($8544). *Room and board:* College room only: $4345. Room and board charges vary according to board plan. *Payment plan:* installment. *Waivers:* employees or children of employees.

Financial Aid Of all full-time matriculated undergraduates who enrolled in 2001, 485 applied for aid, 409 were judged to have need, 408 had their need fully met. 252 Federal Work-Study jobs (averaging $1840). 7 State and other part-time jobs (averaging $1959). In 2001, 155 non-need-based awards were made. *Average percent of need met:* 100%. *Average financial aid package:* $19,256. *Average need-based loan:* $4647. *Average need-based gift aid:* $15,080. *Average non-need based aid:* $5044. *Average indebtedness upon graduation:* $17,968. *Financial aid deadline:* 2/1.

Applying *Options:* common application, electronic application, early decision, deferred entrance. *Application fee:* $50. *Required:* essay or personal statement, high school transcript, 3 letters of recommendation. *Recommended:* interview. *Application deadlines:* 1/15 (freshmen), 4/1 (transfers). *Early decision:* 11/15. *Notification:* 4/1 (freshmen), 12/15 (early decision).

Admissions Contact Mr. Deren Finks, Vice President and Dean of Admissions and Financial Aid, Harvey Mudd College, 301 East 12th Street, Claremont, CA 91711. *Phone:* 909-621-8011. *Fax:* 909-607-7046. *E-mail:* admission@hmc.edu.

HOLY NAMES COLLEGE
Oakland, California

- **Independent Roman Catholic** comprehensive, founded 1868
- **Calendar** semesters
- **Degrees** bachelor's, master's, and postbachelor's certificates
- **Urban** 60-acre campus with easy access to San Francisco
- **Endowment** $7.8 million
- **Coed, primarily women,** 506 undergraduate students, 59% full-time, 78% women, 22% men
- **Moderately difficult** entrance level, 71% of applicants were admitted

Undergraduates 300 full-time, 206 part-time. Students come from 11 states and territories, 11 other countries, 3% are from out of state, 33% African American, 8% Asian American or Pacific Islander, 14% Hispanic American, 0.4% Native American, 6% international, 23% transferred in, 45% live on campus. *Retention:* 69% of 2001 full-time freshmen returned.

Freshmen *Admission:* 167 applied, 119 admitted, 46 enrolled. *Average high school GPA:* 3.12. *Test scores:* SAT verbal scores over 500: 31%; SAT math scores over 500: 26%; SAT verbal scores over 600: 5%; SAT math scores over 600: 8%.

Faculty *Total:* 124, 31% full-time. *Student/faculty ratio:* 11:1.

Majors Area studies related; biological sciences/life sciences related; business administration; computer science related; English; history; humanities; human resources management; human services; international relations; liberal arts and sciences/liberal studies; music; nursing science; philosophy; pre-medicine; psychology; religious studies; sociology.

Academic Programs *Special study options:* academic remediation for entering students, accelerated degree program, adult/continuing education programs, advanced placement credit, distance learning, double majors, English as a second language, honors programs, independent study, internships, off-campus study, part-time degree program, services for LD students, student-designed majors, study abroad, summer session for credit. *ROTC:* Army (c), Air Force (c).

Library Cushing Library with 111,062 titles, 376 serial subscriptions, 4,350 audiovisual materials, a Web page.

Computers on Campus 69 computers available on campus for general student use. A campuswide network can be accessed from student residence rooms and from off campus. Internet access, at least one staffed computer lab available.

Student Life *Housing Options:* coed, women-only. *Activities and Organizations:* drama/theater group, choral group, Phi Kappa Delta Speech Club, AASU, Global Outlook, The Drama Club, Asian Pacific Club. *Campus security:* 24-hour emergency response devices, late-night transport/escort service, controlled dormitory access, electronically operated main gate. *Student Services:* personal/psychological counseling.

Athletics Member NAIA. *Intercollegiate sports:* basketball M(s)/W(s), cross-country running M(s)/W(s), golf M(s), soccer M(s)/W(s), volleyball W(s). *Intramural sports:* badminton M/W, basketball M/W, soccer M/W, softball M/W, swimming M/W, table tennis M/W, volleyball M/W, weight lifting M/W.

Standardized Tests *Required:* SAT I or ACT (for admission).

Costs (2002–03) *Comprehensive fee:* $25,870 includes full-time tuition ($18,150), mandatory fees ($120), and room and board ($7600). Full-time tuition and fees vary according to course load. Part-time tuition: $360 per unit. Part-time tuition and fees vary according to class time and location. *Required fees:* $60 per term part-time. *Room and board:* College room only: $3800. Room and board charges vary according to housing facility. *Payment plan:* installment. *Waivers:* employees or children of employees.

Financial Aid Of all full-time matriculated undergraduates who enrolled in 2001, 262 applied for aid, 262 were judged to have need, 48 had their need fully met. 68 Federal Work-Study jobs (averaging $2000). *Average percent of need met:* 75%. *Average financial aid package:* $21,225. *Average indebtedness upon graduation:* $17,000.

Applying *Options:* common application, electronic application, deferred entrance. *Application fee:* $35. *Required:* essay or personal statement, high school transcript, 1 letter of recommendation. *Required for some:* interview. *Application deadlines:* 8/1 (freshmen), 8/1 (transfers). *Notification:* continuous (freshmen).

Admissions Contact Mr. Jeffrey D. Miller, Vice President for Enrollment Management, Holy Names College, Admission Office, Oakland, CA 94619. *Phone:* 510-436-1351. *Toll-free phone:* 800-430-1321. *Fax:* 510-436-1325. *E-mail:* admissions@admin.hnc.edu.

HOPE INTERNATIONAL UNIVERSITY
Fullerton, California

- **Independent** comprehensive, founded 1928, affiliated with Christian Churches and Churches of Christ
- **Calendar** 4-1-4
- **Degrees** certificates, associate, bachelor's, and master's
- **Suburban** 16-acre campus with easy access to Los Angeles
- **Endowment** $2.1 million
- **Coed,** 703 undergraduate students, 82% full-time, 53% women, 47% men
- **Moderately difficult** entrance level, 42% of applicants were admitted

Undergraduates 576 full-time, 127 part-time. Students come from 22 states and territories, 20 other countries, 34% are from out of state, 4% African American, 4% Asian American or Pacific Islander, 14% Hispanic American, 0.2% Native American, 11% international, 6% transferred in. *Retention:* 63% of 2001 full-time freshmen returned.

Freshmen *Admission:* 368 applied, 156 admitted, 96 enrolled. *Average high school GPA:* 3.07.

Faculty *Total:* 62, 44% full-time, 45% with terminal degrees. *Student/faculty ratio:* 15:1.

Majors Athletic training/sports medicine; biblical studies; business administration; child care/development; early childhood education; elementary education; English education; general studies; individual/family development; interdisciplinary studies; missionary studies; music teacher education; physical therapy; physiological psychology/psychobiology; psychology; religious music; social science education; social sciences; social work.

Academic Programs *Special study options:* academic remediation for entering students, accelerated degree program, adult/continuing education programs, advanced placement credit, distance learning, double majors, English as a second language, honors programs, independent study, internships, off-campus study, part-time degree program, student-designed majors, summer session for credit.

Library Hurst Memorial Library with 72,000 titles, 468 serial subscriptions, 600 audiovisual materials, an OPAC.

Computers on Campus 32 computers available on campus for general student use. A campuswide network can be accessed from off campus. Internet access, at least one staffed computer lab available.

Student Life *Housing:* on-campus residence required through sophomore year. *Options:* men-only, women-only. *Activities and Organizations:* drama/theater group, student-run newspaper, choral group. *Campus security:* 24-hour emergency response devices, student patrols. *Student Services:* health clinic, personal/psychological counseling.

Athletics *Intercollegiate sports:* basketball M(s)/W(s), soccer M(s)/W(s), softball W(s), tennis M(s)/W(s), volleyball M(s)/W(s). *Intramural sports:* golf M, tennis M(c)/W(c).

Standardized Tests *Required:* SAT I or ACT (for admission).
Costs (2002–03) *Comprehensive fee:* $19,192 includes full-time tuition ($14,100) and room and board ($5092). Part-time tuition and fees vary according to course load. *Room and board:* College room only: $2422. Room and board charges vary according to board plan and housing facility. *Payment plan:* installment. *Waivers:* senior citizens and employees or children of employees.
Financial Aid Of all full-time matriculated undergraduates who enrolled in 2001, 585 applied for aid, 520 were judged to have need, 99 had their need fully met. 94 Federal Work-Study jobs (averaging $2000). In 2001, 85 non-need-based awards were made. *Average percent of need met:* 62%. *Average financial aid package:* $9610. *Average need-based loan:* $3896. *Average need-based gift aid:* $7372. *Average non-need based aid:* $8649. *Average indebtedness upon graduation:* $17,125.
Applying *Options:* early admission, deferred entrance. *Application fee:* $20. *Required:* essay or personal statement, high school transcript, minimum 2.5 GPA, 2 letters of recommendation. *Required for some:* interview. *Application deadlines:* 6/1 (freshmen), 5/1 (transfers). *Notification:* continuous until 7/1 (freshmen).
Admissions Contact Ms. Midge Madden, Office Manager, Hope International University, 2500 East Nutwood Avenue, Fullerton, CA 92831-3138. *Phone:* 714-879-3901 Ext. 2235. *Toll-free phone:* 800-762-1294 Ext. 2235. *Fax:* 714-526-0231 Ext. 2235. *E-mail:* mfmadden@hiu.edu.

HUMBOLDT STATE UNIVERSITY
Arcata, California

- **State-supported** comprehensive, founded 1913, part of California State University System
- **Calendar** semesters
- **Degrees** certificates, diplomas, bachelor's, and master's
- **Rural** 161-acre campus
- **Endowment** $11.8 million
- **Coed,** 6,418 undergraduate students, 89% full-time, 55% women, 45% men
- **Moderately difficult** entrance level, 74% of applicants were admitted

Undergraduates 5,722 full-time, 696 part-time. Students come from 48 states and territories, 16 other countries, 4% are from out of state, 3% African American, 3% Asian American or Pacific Islander, 8% Hispanic American, 3% Native American, 0.5% international, 12% transferred in, 18% live on campus. *Retention:* 76% of 2001 full-time freshmen returned.
Freshmen *Admission:* 3,833 applied, 2,829 admitted, 722 enrolled. *Average high school GPA:* 3.20. *Test scores:* SAT verbal scores over 500: 65%; SAT math scores over 500: 62%; ACT scores over 18: 83%; SAT verbal scores over 600: 24%; SAT math scores over 600: 21%; ACT scores over 24: 40%; SAT verbal scores over 700: 4%; SAT math scores over 700: 1%; ACT scores over 30: 3%.
Faculty *Total:* 565, 55% full-time, 63% with terminal degrees. *Student/faculty ratio:* 16:1.
Majors Accounting; anthropology; applied mathematics; art; art education; art history; biochemistry; biology; botany; broadcast journalism; business administration; business marketing and marketing management; cell biology; chemistry; child care/development; developmental/child psychology; early childhood education; economics; education; elementary education; English; environmental biology; environmental engineering; environmental science; exercise sciences; fine/studio arts; fish/game management; forestry; French; geography; geology; German; history; industrial arts; information sciences/systems; journalism; liberal arts and sciences/liberal studies; marine biology; mathematics; medical technology; microbiology/bacteriology; molecular biology; music; music teacher education; Native American studies; natural resources conservation; natural resources management; natural sciences; nursing; oceanography; philosophy; physical education; physical sciences; physics; political science; pre-dentistry; pre-law; pre-medicine; pre-veterinary studies; psychology; range management; recreation/leisure facilities management; recreation/leisure studies; religious studies; secondary education; social sciences; social work; sociology; Spanish; speech/rhetorical studies; theater arts/drama; toxicology; water resources; wildlife management; zoology.
Academic Programs *Special study options:* academic remediation for entering students, adult/continuing education programs, advanced placement credit, cooperative education, distance learning, double majors, English as a second language, honors programs, independent study, internships, off-campus study, part-time degree program, services for LD students, student-designed majors, study abroad, summer session for credit.
Library 528,680 titles, 3,169 serial subscriptions, 46,391 audiovisual materials, an OPAC, a Web page.
Computers on Campus 600 computers available on campus for general student use. A campuswide network can be accessed from student residence rooms and from off campus. Internet access, online (class) registration, at least one staffed computer lab available.
Student Life *Housing Options:* coed. *Activities and Organizations:* drama/theater group, student-run newspaper, radio station, choral group, marching band, student radio station, Student Environmental Action Coalition, Youth Educational Services, Ballet Folklorico, International Student Union, national fraternities, national sororities. *Campus security:* 24-hour emergency response devices and patrols, late-night transport/escort service, controlled dormitory access. *Student Services:* health clinic, personal/psychological counseling, women's center, legal services.
Athletics Member NCAA. All Division II. *Intercollegiate sports:* basketball M(s)/W(s), crew M(c)/W, cross-country running M(s)/W(s), football M(s), lacrosse M(c)/W(c), rugby M(c)/W(c), soccer M(s)/W(s), softball W(s), track and field M(s)/W(s), volleyball M(c)/W(s). *Intramural sports:* baseball M(c), basketball M/W, football M, golf M, racquetball M/W, soccer M/W, softball M/W, swimming M/W, volleyball M/W, water polo M/W.
Standardized Tests *Required for some:* SAT I or ACT (for admission).
Costs (2002–03) *Tuition:* state resident $1892 full-time, $246 per unit part-time; nonresident $5904 full-time. *Required fees:* $1892 full-time, $629 per term part-time. *Room and board:* $6690; room only: $3825. Room and board charges vary according to board plan and housing facility. *Payment plan:* installment. *Waivers:* senior citizens and employees or children of employees.
Financial Aid Of all full-time matriculated undergraduates who enrolled in 2001, 3933 applied for aid, 3139 were judged to have need, 954 had their need fully met. *Average percent of need met:* 77%. *Average financial aid package:* $7384. *Average need-based loan:* $3770. *Average need-based gift aid:* $4360. *Average indebtedness upon graduation:* $14,500.
Applying *Options:* electronic application. *Application fee:* $55. *Required:* high school transcript, minimum 2.0 GPA. *Application deadlines:* rolling (freshmen), 11/30 (transfers). *Notification:* continuous (freshmen).
Admissions Contact Ms. Rebecca Kalal, Assistant Director of Admissions, Humboldt State University, 1 Harpst Street, Arcata, CA 95521-8299. *Phone:* 707-826-4402. *Fax:* 707-826-6194. *E-mail:* hsuinfo@humboldt.edu.

HUMPHREYS COLLEGE
Stockton, California

Admissions Contact Ms. Wilma Okamoto Vaughn, Dean of Administration, Humphreys College, 6650 Inglewood Avenue, Stockton, CA 95207-3896. *Phone:* 209-478-0800. *Fax:* 209-478-8721.

INSTITUTE OF COMPUTER TECHNOLOGY
Los Angeles, California

- **Proprietary** 4-year, founded 1981
- **Calendar** quarters
- **Degrees** certificates, diplomas, associate, and bachelor's
- **Urban** campus
- **Coed,** 286 undergraduate students, 100% full-time, 27% women, 73% men
- **Noncompetitive** entrance level, 30% of applicants were admitted

Undergraduates 286 full-time. Students come from 1 other state, 4 other countries, 0% are from out of state, 11% African American, 36% Asian American or Pacific Islander, 23% Hispanic American, 15% international, 2% transferred in.
Freshmen *Admission:* 121 applied, 36 admitted.
Faculty *Total:* 25. *Student/faculty ratio:* 21:1.
Majors Business administration; computer science.
Academic Programs *Special study options:* advanced placement credit, independent study, internships.
Library Main Library plus 1 other with 2,000 titles.
Computers on Campus 100 computers available on campus for general student use. Internet access, at least one staffed computer lab available.
Student Life *Housing:* college housing not available. *Campus security:* 24-hour patrols.
Costs (2002–03) *Tuition:* $20,495 full-time. No tuition increase for student's term of enrollment. *Payment plans:* tuition prepayment, installment. *Waivers:* employees or children of employees.
Applying *Options:* common application. *Application fee:* $75. *Required:* high school transcript, interview.
Admissions Contact Mr. Phil Singer, Director of Admissions, Institute of Computer Technology, 3200 Wilshire Boulevard 4th Floor, Los Angeles, CA 90010. *Phone:* 213-383-8300 Ext. 112. *E-mail:* psinger@ictcollege.edu.

Interior Designers Institute
Newport Beach, California

Admissions Contact 1061 Camelback Road, Newport Beach, CA 92660.

International Technological University
Santa Clara, California

Admissions Contact 1650 Warburton Avenue, Santa Clara, CA 95050.

ITT Technical Institute
Rancho Cordova, California

- **Proprietary** primarily 2-year, founded 1954, part of ITT Educational Services, Inc
- **Calendar** quarters
- **Degrees** associate and bachelor's
- **Urban** 5-acre campus
- **Coed,** 533 undergraduate students
- **Minimally difficult** entrance level

Majors Computer/information sciences related; computer programming; design/visual communications; drafting; electrical/electronic engineering technologies related; electromechanical instrumentation and maintenance technologies related; information technology.

Student Life *Housing:* college housing not available.

Costs (2001–02) *Tuition:* Full-time tuition and fees vary according to program. Part-time tuition and fees vary according to program. $260—$330 per credit hour.

Applying *Options:* deferred entrance. *Application fee:* $100. *Required:* high school transcript, interview. *Recommended:* letters of recommendation. *Application deadline:* rolling (freshmen), rolling (transfers). *Notification:* continuous (freshmen).

Admissions Contact Mr. Bob Menszer, Director of Recruitment, ITT Technical Institute, 10863 Gold Center Drive, Rancho Cordova, CA 95670-6034. *Phone:* 916-851-3900. *Toll-free phone:* 800-488-8466.

ITT Technical Institute
Oxnard, California

- **Proprietary** primarily 2-year, founded 1993, part of ITT Educational Services, Inc
- **Calendar** quarters
- **Degrees** associate and bachelor's
- **Urban** campus with easy access to Los Angeles
- **Coed,** 549 undergraduate students
- **Minimally difficult** entrance level

Faculty *Total:* 22, 73% full-time.

Majors Computer programming; drafting; electrical/electronic engineering technologies related; electrical/electronic engineering technology; information technology.

Library Learning Resource Center plus 1 other with 877 titles, 71 serial subscriptions.

Computers on Campus 12 computers available on campus for general student use. Internet access, at least one staffed computer lab available.

Student Life *Housing:* college housing not available. *Campus security:* 24-hour emergency response devices and patrols.

Costs (2001–02) *Tuition:* Full-time tuition and fees vary according to program. Part-time tuition and fees vary according to program. $260—$330 per credit hour.

Applying *Options:* deferred entrance. *Application fee:* $100. *Required:* high school transcript, letters of recommendation, interview. *Recommended:* minimum 2.0 GPA. *Application deadline:* rolling (freshmen), rolling (transfers).

Admissions Contact Ms. Lorraine Bunt, Director of Recruitment, ITT Technical Institute, 2051 Solar Drive, Suite 150, Oxnard, CA 93030. *Phone:* 805-988-0143 Ext. 112. *Toll-free phone:* 800-530-1582. *Fax:* 805-988-1813.

ITT Technical Institute
San Bernardino, California

- **Proprietary** primarily 2-year, founded 1987, part of ITT Educational Services, Inc
- **Calendar** quarters
- **Degrees** associate and bachelor's
- **Urban** campus with easy access to Los Angeles
- **Coed,** 862 undergraduate students
- **Minimally difficult** entrance level

Majors Computer/information sciences related; computer programming; drafting; electrical/electronic engineering technologies related; industrial design; information technology.

Student Life *Housing:* college housing not available.

Costs (2001–02) *Tuition:* Full-time tuition and fees vary according to program. Part-time tuition and fees vary according to program. $260—$330 per credit hour.

Applying *Options:* deferred entrance. *Application fee:* $100. *Required:* high school transcript, interview. *Recommended:* letters of recommendation. *Application deadline:* rolling (freshmen), rolling (transfers). *Notification:* continuous (freshmen).

Admissions Contact Ms. Maria Alamat, Director of Recruitment, ITT Technical Institute, 630 E Brier Drive, San Bernardino, CA 92408. *Phone:* 909-889-3800 Ext. 11. *Toll-free phone:* 800-888-3801. *Fax:* 909-888-6970.

ITT Technical Institute
Anaheim, California

- **Proprietary** primarily 2-year, founded 1982, part of ITT Educational Services, Inc
- **Calendar** quarters
- **Degrees** associate and bachelor's
- **Suburban** 5-acre campus with easy access to Los Angeles
- **Coed,** 691 undergraduate students
- **Minimally difficult** entrance level

Majors Computer/information sciences related; computer programming; drafting; electrical/electronic engineering technologies related; information technology.

Student Life *Housing:* college housing not available. *Activities and Organizations:* student-run newspaper.

Costs (2001–02) *Tuition:* Full-time tuition and fees vary according to program. Part-time tuition and fees vary according to program. $260—$330 per credit hour.

Applying *Options:* deferred entrance. *Application fee:* $100. *Required:* high school transcript, interview. *Recommended:* letters of recommendation. *Application deadline:* rolling (freshmen), rolling (transfers). *Notification:* continuous (freshmen).

Admissions Contact Mr. Ramon Abreu, Director of Recruitment, ITT Technical Institute, 525 North Muller Avenue, Anaheim, CA 92801. *Phone:* 714-535-3700.

ITT Technical Institute
San Diego, California

- **Proprietary** primarily 2-year, founded 1981, part of ITT Educational Services, Inc
- **Calendar** quarters
- **Degrees** associate and bachelor's
- **Suburban** campus
- **Coed,** 885 undergraduate students
- **Minimally difficult** entrance level

Majors Computer/information sciences related; computer programming; data processing technology; drafting; electrical/electronic engineering technologies related.

Student Life *Housing:* college housing not available.

Costs (2001–02) *Tuition:* Full-time tuition and fees vary according to program. Part-time tuition and fees vary according to program. $260—$330 per credit hour.

Applying *Options:* deferred entrance. *Application fee:* $100. *Required:* high school transcript, interview. *Recommended:* letters of recommendation. *Application deadline:* rolling (freshmen), rolling (transfers). *Notification:* continuous (freshmen).

Admissions Contact Ms. Sheryl Schulgen, Director of Recruitment, ITT Technical Institute, 9680 Granite Ridge Drive, Suite 100, San Diego, CA 92123. *Phone:* 858-571-8500.

ITT Technical Institute
Sylmar, California

- **Proprietary** primarily 2-year, founded 1982, part of ITT Educational Services, Inc

■ **Calendar** quarters
■ **Degrees** associate and bachelor's
■ **Urban** campus with easy access to Los Angeles
■ **Coed,** 715 undergraduate students
■ **Minimally difficult** entrance level

Majors Computer/information sciences related; computer programming; design/applied arts related; drafting; electrical/electronic engineering technologies related; information technology.

Student Life *Housing:* college housing not available.

Costs (2001–02) *Tuition:* Full-time tuition and fees vary according to program. Part-time tuition and fees vary according to program. $260—$330 per credit hour.

Applying *Options:* deferred entrance. *Application fee:* $100. *Required:* high school transcript, interview. *Recommended:* letters of recommendation. *Application deadline:* rolling (freshmen), rolling (transfers). *Notification:* continuous (freshmen).

Admissions Contact Mr. Albert Naranjo, Director of Recruitment, ITT Technical Institute, 12669 Encinitas Avenue, Sylmar, CA 91342-3664. *Phone:* 818-364-5151. *Toll-free phone:* 800-363-2086.

ITT Technical Institute
West Covina, California

■ **Proprietary** primarily 2-year, founded 1982, part of ITT Educational Services, Inc
■ **Calendar** quarters
■ **Degrees** associate and bachelor's
■ **Suburban** 4-acre campus with easy access to Los Angeles
■ **Coed**
■ **Minimally difficult** entrance level

Majors Computer/information sciences related; computer programming; drafting; electrical/electronic engineering technologies related; information technology; robotics technology.

Student Life *Housing:* college housing not available.

Costs (2001–02) *Tuition:* Full-time tuition and fees vary according to program. Part-time tuition and fees vary according to program. $260—$330 per credit hour.

Financial Aid Of all full-time matriculated undergraduates who enrolled in 2001, 20 Federal Work-Study jobs (averaging $4500).

Applying *Options:* deferred entrance. *Application fee:* $100. *Required:* high school transcript, interview. *Recommended:* letters of recommendation. *Application deadline:* rolling (freshmen), rolling (transfers). *Notification:* continuous (freshmen).

Admissions Contact Mr. John Drinkall, Director of Recruitment, ITT Technical Institute, 1530 West Cameron Avenue, West Covina, CA 91790-2711. *Phone:* 626-960-8681. *Toll-free phone:* 800-414-6522. *Fax:* 626-330-5271.

ITT Technical Institute
Hayward, California

■ **Proprietary** primarily 2-year, founded 1994, part of ITT Educational Services, Inc
■ **Calendar** quarters
■ **Degrees** associate and bachelor's
■ 286 undergraduate students
■ **Minimally difficult** entrance level

Majors Computer/information sciences related; computer programming; electrical/electronic engineering technologies related; electrical/electronic engineering technology; information technology.

Student Life *Housing:* college housing not available.

Costs (2001–02) *Tuition:* Full-time tuition and fees vary according to program. Part-time tuition and fees vary according to program. $260—$330 per credit hour.

Financial Aid Of all full-time matriculated undergraduates who enrolled in 2001, 20 Federal Work-Study jobs.

Applying *Options:* deferred entrance. *Application fee:* $100. *Required:* high school transcript, interview. *Recommended:* letters of recommendation. *Application deadline:* rolling (freshmen), rolling (transfers).

Admissions Contact Ms. Kathleen Paradis, Director of Recruitment, ITT Technical Institute, 3979 Trust Way, Hayward, CA 94545. *Phone:* 510-785-8522.

John F. Kennedy University
Orinda, California

■ **Independent** comprehensive, founded 1964
■ **Calendar** quarters
■ **Degrees** bachelor's, master's, doctoral, first professional, post-master's, and postbachelor's certificates
■ **Suburban** 14-acre campus with easy access to San Francisco
■ **Coed,** 210 undergraduate students, 10% full-time, 80% women, 20% men
■ **Noncompetitive** entrance level

Undergraduates 20 full-time, 190 part-time. 0% are from out of state, 17% transferred in.

Faculty *Total:* 715, 5% full-time, 67% with terminal degrees. *Student/faculty ratio:* 12:1.

Majors Accounting; business administration; humanities; liberal arts and sciences/liberal studies; psychology; retail management.

Academic Programs *Special study options:* adult/continuing education programs, advanced placement credit, independent study, off-campus study, part-time degree program, services for LD students, student-designed majors, summer session for credit.

Library Robert M. Fisher Library with 91,170 titles, 811 serial subscriptions, 1,854 audiovisual materials, an OPAC, a Web page.

Computers on Campus 50 computers available on campus for general student use. At least one staffed computer lab available.

Student Life *Housing:* college housing not available. *Activities and Organizations:* student-run newspaper. *Campus security:* late-night transport/escort service. *Student Services:* personal/psychological counseling.

Costs (2001–02) *Tuition:* $11,610 full-time, $258 per quarter hour part-time. Full-time tuition and fees vary according to course load and program. Part-time tuition and fees vary according to course load and program. *Required fees:* $36 full-time, $9 per term part-time. *Payment plan:* deferred payment. *Waivers:* employees or children of employees.

Financial Aid Of all full-time matriculated undergraduates who enrolled in 2001, 11 applied for aid, 11 were judged to have need, 11 had their need fully met. *Average percent of need met:* 80%. *Average financial aid package:* $7000. *Average need-based loan:* $6000. *Average need-based gift aid:* $1000. *Average indebtedness upon graduation:* $23,000.

Applying *Options:* common application, deferred entrance. *Application fee:* $50. *Application deadline:* rolling (transfers).

Admissions Contact Ms. Ellena Bloedorn, Director of Admissions and Records, John F. Kennedy University, 12 Altarinda Road, Orinda, CA 94563-2603. *Phone:* 925-258-2213. *Toll-free phone:* 800-696-JFKU. *Fax:* 925-254-6964. *E-mail:* proginfo@jfku.edu.

La Sierra University
Riverside, California

Admissions Contact Dr. Tom Smith, Vice President for Enrollment Services, La Sierra University, 4700 Pierce Street, Riverside, CA 92515-8247. *Phone:* 909-785-2432. *Toll-free phone:* 800-874-5587. *Fax:* 909-785-2901. *E-mail:* ivy@polaris.lasierra.edu.

LIFE Bible College
San Dimas, California

■ **Independent** 4-year, founded 1923, affiliated with International Church of the Foursquare Gospel
■ **Calendar** semesters
■ **Degrees** associate and bachelor's
■ **Suburban** 9-acre campus with easy access to Los Angeles
■ **Endowment** $2.1 million
■ **Coed,** 480 undergraduate students, 74% full-time, 48% women, 52% men
■ **Moderately difficult** entrance level, 96% of applicants were admitted

Undergraduates 357 full-time, 123 part-time. Students come from 32 states and territories, 47% are from out of state, 4% African American, 5% Asian American or Pacific Islander, 14% Hispanic American, 2% Native American, 0.6% international, 16% transferred in, 54% live on campus. *Retention:* 67% of 2001 full-time freshmen returned.

Freshmen *Admission:* 72 applied, 69 admitted, 58 enrolled. *Average high school GPA:* 3.18. *Test scores:* SAT verbal scores over 500: 56%; SAT math scores over 500: 44%; ACT scores over 18: 89%; SAT verbal scores over 600: 19%; SAT math scores over 600: 7%; SAT math scores over 700: 2%.

LIFE Bible College (continued)

Faculty *Total:* 35, 46% full-time, 26% with terminal degrees. *Student/faculty ratio:* 18:1.

Majors Biblical studies; pastoral counseling; theology.

Academic Programs *Special study options:* adult/continuing education programs, advanced placement credit, cooperative education, distance learning, external degree program, independent study, internships, part-time degree program, services for LD students, study abroad, summer session for credit.

Library LIFE Alumni Library with 29,824 titles, 253 serial subscriptions, 1,445 audiovisual materials, an OPAC.

Computers on Campus 25 computers available on campus for general student use. Internet access, at least one staffed computer lab available.

Student Life *Housing:* on-campus residence required for freshman year. *Options:* men-only, women-only. *Activities and Organizations:* drama/theater group, student-run newspaper, choral group, tutoring, chorale. *Campus security:* 24-hour emergency response devices, part-time security personnel. *Student Services:* personal/psychological counseling.

Athletics Member NCCAA. *Intercollegiate sports:* basketball M/W, volleyball W. *Intramural sports:* cross-country running M/W, soccer M.

Standardized Tests *Required:* SAT I or ACT (for admission). *Recommended:* SAT II: Writing Test (for admission).

Costs (2002–03) *Comprehensive fee:* $10,300 includes full-time tuition ($6450), mandatory fees ($250), and room and board ($3600). Part-time tuition: $215 per credit hour. Part-time tuition and fees vary according to course load. *Payment plan:* installment. *Waivers:* children of alumni and employees or children of employees.

Financial Aid Of all full-time matriculated undergraduates who enrolled in 2001, 320 applied for aid, 278 were judged to have need. 17 Federal Work-Study jobs (averaging $1335). *Average percent of need met:* 42%. *Average financial aid package:* $4999. *Average need-based gift aid:* $3297. *Average indebtedness upon graduation:* $10,441.

Applying *Options:* common application, electronic application, deferred entrance. *Application fee:* $35. *Required:* essay or personal statement, high school transcript, minimum 2.0 GPA, 3 letters of recommendation, Christian testimony. *Application deadlines:* 7/1 (freshmen), 7/1 (transfers). *Notification:* continuous (freshmen).

Admissions Contact Mrs. Linda Hibdon, Admissions Director, LIFE Bible College, 1100 Covina Boulevard, San Dimas, CA 91773-3298. *Phone:* 909-599-5433 Ext. 343. *Toll-free phone:* 877-886-5433. *Fax:* 909-599-6690. *E-mail:* adm@lifebible.edu.

LINCOLN UNIVERSITY

Oakland, California

- **Independent** comprehensive, founded 1919
- **Calendar** semesters
- **Degrees** certificates, bachelor's, and master's
- **Urban** 2-acre campus
- **Coed,** 129 undergraduate students, 100% full-time, 40% women, 60% men
- **Minimally difficult** entrance level

Undergraduates Students come from 1 other state, 37 other countries.

Faculty *Total:* 35, 23% full-time. *Student/faculty ratio:* 14:1.

Majors Accounting; business administration; computer science; economics; international business; management information systems/business data processing.

Academic Programs *Special study options:* advanced placement credit, English as a second language, internships, summer session for credit.

Library Lincoln Library with 17,532 titles, 642 serial subscriptions.

Computers on Campus 20 computers available on campus for general student use. Internet access, at least one staffed computer lab available.

Student Life *Housing:* college housing not available. *Activities and Organizations:* student-run newspaper. *Campus security:* 24-hour emergency response devices. *Student Services:* personal/psychological counseling.

Standardized Tests *Required:* Michigan English Language Assessment Battery.

Costs (2001–02) *Tuition:* $6360 full-time. *Required fees:* $761 full-time.

Applying *Options:* deferred entrance. *Application fee:* $50. *Required:* high school transcript, minimum 2.0 GPA. *Required for some:* essay or personal statement, letters of recommendation, interview. *Application deadlines:* 8/31 (freshmen), 8/31 (transfers).

Admissions Contact Ms. Vivian Xu, Admissions Officer, Lincoln University, 401 15th Street, Oakland, CA 94612. *Phone:* 415-221-1212 Ext. 115. *Fax:* 415-387-9730.

LOMA LINDA UNIVERSITY

Loma Linda, California

- **Independent Seventh-day Adventist** university, founded 1905
- **Calendar** quarters
- **Degrees** certificates, associate, bachelor's, master's, doctoral, first professional, post-master's, and postbachelor's certificates
- **Small-town** campus with easy access to Los Angeles
- **Endowment** $153.0 million
- **Coed,** 997 undergraduate students, 73% full-time, 75% women, 25% men

Undergraduates Students come from 29 states and territories, 28 other countries, 23% are from out of state, 7% African American, 21% Asian American or Pacific Islander, 18% Hispanic American, 0.9% Native American, 7% international, 25% live on campus.

Faculty *Total:* 2,330, 46% full-time. *Student/faculty ratio:* 2:1.

Majors Cytotechnology; dental hygiene; dietetics; emergency medical technology; medical radiologic technology; medical records administration; medical technology; nursing; occupational therapy; occupational therapy assistant; operating room technician; physical therapy assistant; respiratory therapy; speech-language pathology/audiology.

Academic Programs *Special study options:* distance learning, English as a second language, independent study, off-campus study.

Library Del E. Webb Memorial Library with 322,657 titles, 1,394 serial subscriptions, an OPAC, a Web page.

Computers on Campus A campuswide network can be accessed from student residence rooms and from off campus that provide access to on-line courses. Internet access, online (class) registration, at least one staffed computer lab available.

Student Life *Housing:* on-campus residence required through senior year. *Options:* men-only, women-only. *Activities and Organizations:* student-run newspaper, choral group, Students for International Mission Services, Students Computing Organization. *Campus security:* 24-hour emergency response devices and patrols, late-night transport/escort service. *Student Services:* health clinic, personal/psychological counseling.

Athletics *Intramural sports:* basketball M/W, football M, racquetball M/W, soccer M/W, softball M/W, tennis M/W, volleyball M/W.

Costs (2001–02) *Tuition:* $15,600 full-time, $420 per unit part-time. Full-time tuition and fees vary according to course load, degree level, and program. Part-time tuition and fees vary according to course load, degree level, and program. *Room only:* $2724. Room and board charges vary according to housing facility. *Payment plan:* installment.

Financial Aid Of all full-time matriculated undergraduates who enrolled in 2001, 596 applied for aid, 542 were judged to have need, 167 had their need fully met. 265 Federal Work-Study jobs (averaging $3705). *Average percent of need met:* 81%. *Average financial aid package:* $15,386. *Average need-based loan:* $4270. *Average need-based gift aid:* $3058. *Average indebtedness upon graduation:* $34,913.

Applying *Options:* common application. *Application fee:* $50.

Admissions Contact Loma Linda University, Loma Linda, CA 92350.

LOYOLA MARYMOUNT UNIVERSITY

Los Angeles, California

- **Independent Roman Catholic** comprehensive, founded 1911
- **Calendar** semesters
- **Degrees** bachelor's, master's, first professional, and postbachelor's certificates
- **Suburban** 128-acre campus
- **Coed,** 5,144 undergraduate students, 93% full-time, 57% women, 43% men
- **Very difficult** entrance level, 60% of applicants were admitted

Undergraduates 4,808 full-time, 336 part-time. Students come from 46 states and territories, 70 other countries, 20% are from out of state, 6% African American, 11% Asian American or Pacific Islander, 19% Hispanic American, 0.8% Native American, 2% international, 4% transferred in, 57% live on campus. *Retention:* 87% of 2001 full-time freshmen returned.

Freshmen *Admission:* 7,468 applied, 4,446 admitted, 1,258 enrolled. *Average high school GPA:* 3.35. *Test scores:* SAT verbal scores over 500: 86%; SAT math scores over 500: 87%; SAT verbal scores over 600: 35%; SAT math scores over 600: 40%; SAT verbal scores over 700: 4%; SAT math scores over 700: 4%.

Faculty *Total:* 802, 47% full-time, 64% with terminal degrees. *Student/faculty ratio:* 13:1.

Majors Accounting; African-American studies; art history; biochemistry; biology; business administration; chemistry; civil engineering; classics; computer science; dance; economics; electrical engineering; engineering physics; English; European studies; film/video production; fine/studio arts; French; Greek (modern); history; humanities; Latin (ancient and medieval); liberal arts and sciences/liberal studies; mass communications; mathematics; mechanical engineering; Mexican-American studies; music; natural sciences; philosophy; physics; political science; psychology; sociology; Spanish; theater arts/drama; theology; urban studies.

Academic Programs *Special study options:* accelerated degree program, adult/continuing education programs, advanced placement credit, cooperative education, double majors, honors programs, independent study, internships, part-time degree program, services for LD students, student-designed majors, study abroad, summer session for credit. *ROTC:* Army (c), Navy (c), Air Force (b).

Library Charles von der Ahe Library plus 1 other with 487,232 titles, 9,505 serial subscriptions.

Computers on Campus 200 computers available on campus for general student use. A campuswide network can be accessed from student residence rooms and from off campus. Internet access, at least one staffed computer lab available.

Student Life *Housing Options:* coed, men-only, women-only. *Activities and Organizations:* drama/theater group, student-run newspaper, radio station, choral group, service clubs, Student Government and Activity Board, Community Service Opportunities, Student Media Opportunities, Clubs and Organizations, national fraternities, national sororities. *Campus security:* 24-hour emergency response devices and patrols, late-night transport/escort service, controlled dormitory access. *Student Services:* health clinic, personal/psychological counseling.

Athletics Member NCAA. All Division I. *Intercollegiate sports:* baseball M(s), basketball M(s)/W(s), crew M/W(s), cross-country running M(s)/W(s), golf M(s), lacrosse M(c)/W(c), rugby M(c), soccer M(s)/W(s), softball W(s), swimming W(s), tennis M(s)/W(s), volleyball M(s)/W(s), water polo M(s)/W(s). *Intramural sports:* basketball M/W, football M/W, soccer M/W, softball M/W, tennis M/W, volleyball M/W.

Standardized Tests *Required:* SAT I or ACT (for admission).

Costs (2001–02) *Comprehensive fee:* $28,754 includes full-time tuition ($20,342), mandatory fees ($612), and room and board ($7800). Part-time tuition: $845 per unit. Part-time tuition and fees vary according to course load. *Required fees:* $4 per unit, $16 per term part-time. *Room and board:* Room and board charges vary according to board plan and housing facility. *Payment plan:* installment. *Waivers:* employees or children of employees.

Financial Aid Of all full-time matriculated undergraduates who enrolled in 2001, 3702 applied for aid, 2712 were judged to have need, 1121 had their need fully met. 1801 Federal Work-Study jobs (averaging $2484). 1785 State and other part-time jobs. In 2001, 340 non-need-based awards were made. *Average percent of need met:* 91%. *Average financial aid package:* $20,688. *Average need-based loan:* $4955. *Average need-based gift aid:* $11,858. *Average indebtedness upon graduation:* $18,775.

Applying *Options:* electronic application, early admission, deferred entrance. *Application fee:* $45. *Required:* essay or personal statement, high school transcript, 1 letter of recommendation. *Recommended:* interview. *Application deadlines:* 2/1 (freshmen), 6/1 (transfers). *Notification:* continuous (freshmen).

Admissions Contact Mr. Matthew X. Fissinger, Director of Admissions, Loyola Marymount University, One LMU Drive, Xavier Hall. *Phone:* 310-338-2750. *Toll-free phone:* 800-LMU-INFO. *E-mail:* admissions@lmu.edu.

THE MASTER'S COLLEGE AND SEMINARY

Santa Clarita, California

- **Independent nondenominational** comprehensive, founded 1927
- **Calendar** semesters
- **Degrees** certificates, bachelor's, master's, and first professional
- **Suburban** 110-acre campus with easy access to Los Angeles
- **Endowment** $2.8 million
- **Coed,** 1,174 undergraduate students, 94% full-time, 51% women, 49% men
- **Moderately difficult** entrance level, 80% of applicants were admitted

Undergraduates 1,106 full-time, 68 part-time. Students come from 43 states and territories, 29 other countries, 35% are from out of state, 2% African American, 3% Asian American or Pacific Islander, 5% Hispanic American, 0.9% Native American, 4% international, 11% transferred in, 69% live on campus. *Retention:* 81% of 2001 full-time freshmen returned.

Freshmen *Admission:* 526 applied, 420 admitted, 237 enrolled. *Average high school GPA:* 3.65. *Test scores:* SAT verbal scores over 500: 80%; SAT math scores over 500: 74%; ACT scores over 18: 95%; SAT verbal scores over 600: 41%; SAT math scores over 600: 33%; ACT scores over 24: 54%; SAT verbal scores over 700: 7%; SAT math scores over 700: 3%; ACT scores over 30: 6%.

Faculty *Total:* 113, 42% full-time. *Student/faculty ratio:* 23:1.

Majors Accounting; actuarial science; American government; applied mathematics; biblical languages/literatures; biblical studies; biological/physical sciences; biology; business administration; computer/information sciences; divinity/ministry; education; elementary education; English; environmental biology; finance; history; home economics; liberal arts and sciences/liberal studies; management information systems/business data processing; mass communications; mathematics; middle school education; music; music business management/merchandising; music (piano and organ performance); music teacher education; music (voice and choral/opera performance); natural sciences; nutrition science; pastoral counseling; physical education; physical sciences; political science; pre-medicine; public relations; radio/television broadcasting; religious education; religious music; religious studies; science education; secondary education; speech/rhetorical studies; theology.

Academic Programs *Special study options:* academic remediation for entering students, accelerated degree program, adult/continuing education programs, advanced placement credit, cooperative education, double majors, external degree program, independent study, internships, off-campus study, part-time degree program, services for LD students, study abroad, summer session for credit.

Library Powell Library plus 1 other with 106,701 titles, 1,450 serial subscriptions, 10,326 audiovisual materials, an OPAC, a Web page.

Computers on Campus 57 computers available on campus for general student use. A campuswide network can be accessed from student residence rooms. Internet access, at least one staffed computer lab available.

Student Life *Housing:* on-campus residence required through sophomore year. *Options:* men-only, women-only. *Activities and Organizations:* College Chorale, Summer Missions, Intramurals, Church Ministries, Drama Club. *Campus security:* 24-hour patrols. *Student Services:* health clinic, personal/psychological counseling.

Athletics Member NAIA, NCCAA. *Intercollegiate sports:* baseball M(s), basketball M(s)/W(s), cross-country running M(s)/W(s), golf M, soccer M(s)/W(s), softball W(s), volleyball W(s). *Intramural sports:* basketball M/W, football M/W, golf M/W, softball M/W, tennis M/W, volleyball M/W.

Standardized Tests *Required:* SAT I or ACT (for admission).

Costs (2001–02) *Comprehensive fee:* $22,400 includes full-time tuition ($16,420), mandatory fees ($200), and room and board ($5780). Full-time tuition and fees vary according to course load. Part-time tuition: $650 per credit hour. Part-time tuition and fees vary according to course load. *Required fees:* $100 per term part-time. *Room and board:* College room only: $3200. Room and board charges vary according to board plan. *Payment plan:* installment. *Waivers:* employees or children of employees.

Financial Aid Of all full-time matriculated undergraduates who enrolled in 2001, 807 applied for aid, 708 were judged to have need, 148 had their need fully met. 45 Federal Work-Study jobs (averaging $2666). 191 State and other part-time jobs (averaging $2501). In 2001, 240 non-need-based awards were made. *Average percent of need met:* 74%. *Average financial aid package:* $12,794. *Average need-based loan:* $3896. *Average need-based gift aid:* $9397. *Average indebtedness upon graduation:* $13,000.

Applying *Options:* electronic application, early admission, early action, deferred entrance. *Application fee:* $35. *Required:* essay or personal statement, high school transcript, minimum 2.75 GPA, 2 letters of recommendation, interview. *Application deadlines:* 3/2 (freshmen), 3/2 (transfers). *Notification:* 4/1 (freshmen), 12/22 (early action).

Admissions Contact Mr. Yaphet Peterson, Director of Enrollment, The Master's College and Seminary, Santa Clarita, CA 91321. *Phone:* 661-259-3540 Ext. 3365. *Toll-free phone:* 800-568-6248. *Fax:* 661-288-1037. *E-mail:* enrollment@masters.edu.

MENLO COLLEGE

Atherton, California

- **Independent** 4-year, founded 1927
- **Calendar** semesters
- **Degree** bachelor's
- **Small-town** 45-acre campus with easy access to San Francisco
- **Endowment** $4.0 million
- **Coed,** 668 undergraduate students, 84% full-time, 43% women, 57% men
- **Minimally difficult** entrance level, 70% of applicants were admitted

Undergraduates 561 full-time, 107 part-time. Students come from 18 states and territories, 17 other countries, 17% are from out of state, 7% African American, 15% Asian American or Pacific Islander, 10% Hispanic American, 0.3% Native American, 6% international, 15% transferred in, 66% live on campus. *Retention:* 48% of 2001 full-time freshmen returned.

Freshmen *Admission:* 845 applied, 590 admitted, 105 enrolled. *Average high school GPA:* 3.10.

Menlo College (continued)

Faculty *Total:* 58, 43% full-time, 40% with terminal degrees. *Student/faculty ratio:* 17:1.

Majors Business administration; liberal arts and sciences/liberal studies; mass communications.

Academic Programs *Special study options:* academic remediation for entering students, accelerated degree program, adult/continuing education programs, advanced placement credit, double majors, English as a second language, freshman honors college, honors programs, independent study, internships, part-time degree program, services for LD students, student-designed majors, study abroad, summer session for credit. *ROTC:* Army (c), Air Force (c).

Library Bowman Library with 55,000 titles, 350 serial subscriptions, an OPAC, a Web page.

Computers on Campus 80 computers available on campus for general student use. At least one staffed computer lab available.

Student Life *Housing:* on-campus residence required through sophomore year. *Options:* coed. *Activities and Organizations:* drama/theater group, student-run newspaper, radio and television station, International Club, Residence Hall Association, French Club, Media Network, Hawaiian Club. *Campus security:* 24-hour emergency response devices and patrols. *Student Services:* health clinic, personal/psychological counseling.

Athletics Member NCAA, NAIA. All NCAA Division III. *Intercollegiate sports:* baseball M, basketball M/W(c), cross-country running M/W, football M, golf M/W, soccer M/W, softball W, tennis M/W, track and field M/W, volleyball W. *Intramural sports:* basketball M, softball M/W.

Standardized Tests *Required:* SAT I or ACT (for admission).

Costs (2002–03) *Comprehensive fee:* $29,000 includes full-time tuition ($20,200), mandatory fees ($400), and room and board ($8400). Part-time tuition and fees vary according to course load. *Room and board:* Room and board charges vary according to housing facility. *Payment plan:* installment. *Waivers:* employees or children of employees.

Financial Aid Of all full-time matriculated undergraduates who enrolled in 2001, 407 applied for aid, 384 were judged to have need, 29 had their need fully met. 47 Federal Work-Study jobs (averaging $1577). In 2001, 168 non-need-based awards were made. *Average percent of need met:* 75%. *Average financial aid package:* $12,202. *Average need-based loan:* $4113. *Average need-based gift aid:* $4349. *Average non-need based aid:* $7054. *Average indebtedness upon graduation:* $7792.

Applying *Options:* electronic application, early action, deferred entrance. *Application fee:* $40. *Required:* essay or personal statement, high school transcript, 1 letter of recommendation. *Recommended:* minimum 3.0 GPA, interview. *Application deadline:* rolling (freshmen), rolling (transfers). *Notification:* continuous (freshmen), 1/30 (early action).

Admissions Contact Dr. Greg Smith, Dean of Admission and Financial Aid, Menlo College, 1000 El Camino Real, Atherton, CA 94027. *Phone:* 650-543-3910. *Toll-free phone:* 800-556-3656. *Fax:* 650-617-2395. *E-mail:* admissions@menlo.edu.

MILLS COLLEGE
Oakland, California

- **Independent** comprehensive, founded 1852
- **Calendar** semesters
- **Degrees** bachelor's, master's, and doctoral
- **Urban** 135-acre campus with easy access to San Francisco
- **Endowment** $157.5 million
- **Women only,** 742 undergraduate students, 94% full-time
- **Moderately difficult** entrance level, 74% of applicants were admitted

Why Mills? Why a women's college? Because half of the College's professors are women, which is not the case at coeducational institutions, students have successful role models in every field. All of Mills' excellent undergraduate resources are committed to women. When women graduate from Mills, they know they can succeed. That confidence makes all the difference.

Undergraduates 699 full-time, 43 part-time. Students come from 36 states and territories, 12 other countries, 25% are from out of state, 9% African American, 9% Asian American or Pacific Islander, 9% Hispanic American, 0.8% Native American, 13% transferred in, 56% live on campus. *Retention:* 80% of 2001 full-time freshmen returned.

Freshmen *Admission:* 113 enrolled. *Average high school GPA:* 3.47. *Test scores:* SAT verbal scores over 500: 82%; SAT math scores over 500: 71%; SAT verbal scores over 600: 43%; SAT math scores over 600: 29%; SAT verbal scores over 700: 16%; SAT math scores over 700: 2%.

Faculty *Total:* 158, 55% full-time, 77% with terminal degrees. *Student/faculty ratio:* 10:1.

Majors American studies; anthropology; art; art history; biochemistry; biology; business economics; chemistry; comparative literature; computer science; creative writing; cultural studies; dance; developmental/child psychology; early childhood education; economics; education; elementary education; English; environmental science; fine/studio arts; French; German; Hispanic-American studies; history; interdisciplinary studies; international relations; liberal arts and sciences/liberal studies; mathematical statistics; mathematics; music; philosophy; premedicine; psychology; public policy analysis; social sciences; sociology; theater arts/drama; women's studies.

Academic Programs *Special study options:* adult/continuing education programs, advanced placement credit, double majors, independent study, internships, off-campus study, part-time degree program, services for LD students, student-designed majors. *ROTC:* Army (c).

Library F. W. Olin Library plus 1 other with 189,814 titles, 2,029 serial subscriptions, 6,046 audiovisual materials, an OPAC, a Web page.

Computers on Campus 66 computers available on campus for general student use. A campuswide network can be accessed from student residence rooms and from off campus. At least one staffed computer lab available.

Student Life *Housing Options:* women-only, cooperative. *Activities and Organizations:* drama/theater group, student-run newspaper, choral group, class organizations, MECHA, ASA (Asian Sisterhood Alliance), Mills Environmental Organization, BWC (Black Women's Collective). *Campus security:* 24-hour emergency response devices and patrols, late-night transport/escort service, controlled dormitory access. *Student Services:* health clinic, personal/psychological counseling, women's center.

Athletics Member NCAA. All Division III. *Intercollegiate sports:* crew W, cross-country running W, soccer W, tennis W, volleyball W. *Intramural sports:* badminton W, basketball W, fencing W, soccer W, softball W, tennis W, volleyball W, weight lifting W.

Standardized Tests *Required:* SAT I or ACT (for admission). *Recommended:* SAT II: Subject Tests (for admission).

Costs (2001–02) *Comprehensive fee:* $28,622 includes full-time tuition ($19,500), mandatory fees ($1122), and room and board ($8000). Part-time tuition: $3250 per course. Part-time tuition and fees vary according to course load. *Room and board:* Room and board charges vary according to board plan and housing facility. *Payment plan:* installment. *Waivers:* employees or children of employees.

Financial Aid Of all full-time matriculated undergraduates who enrolled in 2001, 597 applied for aid, 531 were judged to have need, 169 had their need fully met. 216 Federal Work-Study jobs (averaging $1997). 178 State and other part-time jobs (averaging $2218). *Average percent of need met:* 86%. *Average financial aid package:* $20,391. *Average need-based loan:* $4456. *Average need-based gift aid:* $14,636. *Average indebtedness upon graduation:* $17,163.

Applying *Options:* common application, early action, deferred entrance. *Application fee:* $40. *Required:* high school transcript, 3 letters of recommendation, essay or graded paper. *Recommended:* interview. *Application deadlines:* 2/1 (freshmen), 3/2 (transfers). *Notification:* 3/30 (freshmen), 12/30 (early action).

Admissions Contact Avis Hinkson, Dean of Admission, Mills College, 5000 MacArthur Boulevard, Oakland, CA 94613-1000. *Phone:* 510-430-2135. *Toll-free phone:* 800-87-MILLS. *Fax:* 510-430-3314. *E-mail:* admission@mills.edu.

MOUNT ST. MARY'S COLLEGE
Los Angeles, California

- **Independent Roman Catholic** comprehensive, founded 1925
- **Calendar** semesters
- **Degrees** certificates, associate, bachelor's, master's, and postbachelor's certificates
- **Suburban** 71-acre campus
- **Endowment** $46.9 million
- **Coed, primarily women,** 1,694 undergraduate students, 77% full-time, 95% women, 5% men
- **Moderately difficult** entrance level

Undergraduates 1,308 full-time, 386 part-time. Students come from 21 states and territories, 3% are from out of state, 11% African American, 15% Asian American or Pacific Islander, 45% Hispanic American, 0.3% Native American, 0.1% international, 5% transferred in. *Retention:* 85% of 2001 full-time freshmen returned.

Freshmen *Admission:* 343 enrolled. *Average high school GPA:* 3.50. *Test scores:* SAT verbal scores over 500: 66%; SAT math scores over 500: 56%; SAT verbal scores over 600: 17%; SAT math scores over 600: 12%; SAT verbal scores over 700: 4%.

Faculty *Total:* 269, 30% full-time, 38% with terminal degrees. *Student/faculty ratio:* 16:1.

Majors Accounting; American studies; art; art education; biochemistry; biology; business administration; business education; business marketing and marketing management; chemistry; developmental/child psychology; early childhood education; education; elementary education; English; French; gerontology; health services administration; history; international business; liberal arts and sciences/liberal studies; mathematics; music; music teacher education; music (voice and choral/opera performance); nursing; occupational therapy assistant; philosophy; physical therapy assistant; political science; pre-dentistry; pre-law; pre-medicine; psychology; religious studies; secondary education; social sciences; sociology; Spanish; urban studies.

Academic Programs *Special study options:* academic remediation for entering students, accelerated degree program, adult/continuing education programs, advanced placement credit, double majors, freshman honors college, honors programs, independent study, internships, off-campus study, part-time degree program, services for LD students, student-designed majors, study abroad, summer session for credit. *ROTC:* Army (c), Navy (c), Air Force (c).

Library Charles Williard Coe Memorial Library with 140,000 titles, 750 serial subscriptions, an OPAC, a Web page.

Computers on Campus 85 computers available on campus for general student use. A campuswide network can be accessed from student residence rooms and from off campus. At least one staffed computer lab available.

Student Life *Activities and Organizations:* drama/theater group, student-run newspaper, choral group, Latinas Unidas, student government, Pi Theta Mu, Kappa Delta Chi, Student Ambassadors, national sororities. *Campus security:* 24-hour patrols, controlled dormitory access. *Student Services:* health clinic, personal/psychological counseling, women's center.

Athletics *Intramural sports:* basketball W, cross-country running W, swimming W, tennis W, track and field W, volleyball W.

Standardized Tests *Required:* SAT I or ACT (for admission). *Recommended:* SAT I (for admission).

Costs (2001–02) *Comprehensive fee:* $26,047 includes full-time tuition ($17,888), mandatory fees ($700), and room and board ($7459). Full-time tuition and fees vary according to program. Part-time tuition: $680 per unit. Part-time tuition and fees vary according to program. *Required fees:* $350 per term part-time. *Room and board:* Room and board charges vary according to housing facility. *Payment plan:* deferred payment. *Waivers:* employees or children of employees.

Applying *Options:* common application, electronic application, early action, deferred entrance. *Application fee:* $40. *Required:* essay or personal statement, high school transcript, minimum 2.0 GPA, 1 letter of recommendation. *Recommended:* minimum 3.0 GPA, interview. *Application deadlines:* rolling (freshmen), 3/15 (transfers). *Notification:* continuous (freshmen), 1/1 (early action).

Admissions Contact Ms. Katy Murphy, Executive Director of Admissions and Financial Aid, Mount St. Mary's College, 12001 Chalon Road, Los Angeles, CA 90049-1599. *Phone:* 310-954-4252. *Toll-free phone:* 800-999-9893. *E-mail:* admissions@msmc.la.edu.

MT. SIERRA COLLEGE
Monrovia, California

- **Proprietary** 4-year
- **Degree** bachelor's
- **Coed,** 1,100 undergraduate students, 99% full-time, 30% women, 70% men
- **Moderately difficult** entrance level, 73% of applicants were admitted

Undergraduates 1,085 full-time, 15 part-time. Students come from 7 states and territories, 3 other countries, 5% are from out of state, 5% African American, 26% Asian American or Pacific Islander, 26% Hispanic American, 4% Native American, 5% transferred in.

Freshmen *Admission:* 380 applied, 279 admitted, 279 enrolled. *Average high school GPA:* 2.79.

Faculty *Total:* 50, 44% full-time, 14% with terminal degrees. *Student/faculty ratio:* 20:1.

Academic Programs *Special study options:* accelerated degree program, adult/continuing education programs, distance learning, independent study, internships, summer session for credit.

Library Mt. Sierra College Learning Research Center.

Computers on Campus 300 computers available on campus for general student use. A campuswide network can be accessed from off campus. Internet access, online (class) registration, at least one staffed computer lab available.

Costs (2001–02) *Tuition:* $8559 full-time, $162 per unit part-time. Full-time tuition and fees vary according to course load and program. *Required fees:* $800 full-time, $192 per unit. *Payment plan:* installment.

Applying *Options:* electronic application. *Application fee:* $95. *Required:* high school transcript, interview. *Notification:* 10/1 (freshmen).

Admissions Contact Mr. Robert Gray, Director of Admissions, Mt. Sierra College, 101 E. Huntington Drive, Monrovia, CA 91016. *Phone:* 626-873-2100 Ext. 213. *Toll-free phone:* 888-MtSierra. *Fax:* 626-359-5528.

MUSICIANS INSTITUTE
Hollywood, California

Admissions Contact Mr. Steve Lunn, Admissions Representative, Musicians Institute, 1655 North McCadden Place, Hollywood, CA 90028. *Phone:* 323-462-1384 Ext. 156. *Toll-free phone:* 800-255-PLAY.

THE NATIONAL HISPANIC UNIVERSITY
San Jose, California

- **Independent** 4-year, founded 1981
- **Calendar** semesters
- **Degrees** certificates, associate, bachelor's, and postbachelor's certificates
- **Urban** 1-acre campus
- **Endowment** $1.0 million
- **Coed,** 350 undergraduate students
- **Minimally difficult** entrance level, 82% of applicants were admitted

Undergraduates Students come from 4 states and territories, 6 other countries. *Retention:* 86% of 2001 full-time freshmen returned.

Freshmen *Admission:* 179 applied, 146 admitted.

Faculty *Total:* 40, 28% full-time, 100% with terminal degrees. *Student/faculty ratio:* 14:1.

Majors Business administration; computer programming; education; information sciences/systems; liberal arts and sciences/liberal studies.

Academic Programs *Special study options:* academic remediation for entering students, accelerated degree program, adult/continuing education programs, advanced placement credit, cooperative education, English as a second language, internships, off-campus study, part-time degree program, study abroad, summer session for credit.

Library University Library with 10,000 titles, 40 serial subscriptions.

Computers on Campus 40 computers available on campus for general student use. Internet access, at least one staffed computer lab available.

Student Life *Housing:* college housing not available. *Activities and Organizations:* Teatro De Los Pobres, Student Government Association. *Campus security:* 24-hour emergency response devices and patrols. *Student Services:* personal/psychological counseling.

Standardized Tests *Recommended:* SAT I and SAT II or ACT (for admission), SAT II: Writing Test (for admission).

Costs (2002–03) *Tuition:* $3100 full-time, $125 per credit part-time. *Required fees:* $50 per term part-time. *Payment plan:* installment.

Applying *Options:* common application, electronic application. *Application fee:* $50. *Required:* essay or personal statement, high school transcript, minimum 2.0 GPA, letters of recommendation, interview. *Application deadlines:* 8/15 (freshmen), 8/15 (transfers). *Notification:* continuous (freshmen).

Admissions Contact Office of Admissions, The National Hispanic University, 14271 Story Road, San Jose, CA 95127-3823. *Phone:* 408-254-6900.

NATIONAL UNIVERSITY
La Jolla, California

- **Independent** comprehensive, founded 1971
- **Calendar** quarters
- **Degrees** certificates, diplomas, associate, bachelor's, master's, post-master's, and postbachelor's certificates
- **Urban** 15-acre campus
- **Endowment** $160.4 million
- **Coed,** 5,360 undergraduate students, 51% full-time, 57% women, 43% men
- **Noncompetitive** entrance level, 100% of applicants were admitted

Undergraduates 2,737 full-time, 2,623 part-time. Students come from 64 other countries, 0% are from out of state, 13% African American, 10% Asian American or Pacific Islander, 19% Hispanic American, 1% Native American, 2% international, 16% transferred in. *Retention:* 53% of 2001 full-time freshmen returned.

Freshmen *Admission:* 168 applied, 168 admitted, 63 enrolled.

National University (continued)

Faculty *Total:* 821, 14% full-time, 70% with terminal degrees. *Student/faculty ratio:* 16:1.

Majors Accounting; banking; behavioral sciences; biological sciences/life sciences related; business administration; business marketing and marketing management; communications; computer science; criminal justice/law enforcement administration; criminal justice studies; earth sciences; finance; health services administration; human resources management; information sciences/systems; interdisciplinary studies; journalism; legal studies; liberal arts and sciences/liberal studies; mathematics; nursing science; occupational safety/health technology; operations management; psychology; sport/fitness administration.

Academic Programs *Special study options:* accelerated degree program, adult/continuing education programs, advanced placement credit, distance learning, double majors, English as a second language, independent study, internships, off-campus study, part-time degree program, services for LD students, summer session for credit. *ROTC:* Army (c), Air Force (c).

Library Central Library with 195,783 titles, 19,851 serial subscriptions, 5,198 audiovisual materials, an OPAC, a Web page.

Computers on Campus 2152 computers available on campus for general student use. A campuswide network can be accessed from off campus. Internet access, online (class) registration, at least one staffed computer lab available.

Student Life *Housing:* college housing not available. *Campus security:* 24-hour emergency response devices and patrols, late-night transport/escort service.

Costs (2001–02) *Tuition:* $7965 full-time, $885 per course part-time. Full-time tuition and fees vary according to course load. Part-time tuition and fees vary according to course load. *Required fees:* $60 full-time. *Waivers:* employees or children of employees.

Applying *Options:* deferred entrance. *Application fee:* $60. *Required:* high school transcript, interview. *Required for some:* essay or personal statement. *Application deadline:* rolling (freshmen), rolling (transfers). *Notification:* continuous (freshmen).

Admissions Contact Ms. Nancy Rohland, Associate Regional Dean, San Diego, National University, 11255 North Torrey Pines Road, La Jolla, CA 92037. *Phone:* 858-541-7701. *Toll-free phone:* 800-628-8648. *Fax:* 858-642-8710. *E-mail:* nrohland@nu.edu.

NEW COLLEGE OF CALIFORNIA
San Francisco, California

- **Independent** comprehensive, founded 1971
- **Calendar** semesters
- **Degrees** certificates, bachelor's, master's, and first professional certificates
- **Urban** campus
- **Coed,** 234 undergraduate students
- **Noncompetitive** entrance level

Undergraduates Students come from 5 other countries. *Retention:* 87% of 2001 full-time freshmen returned.

Faculty *Total:* 90, 44% full-time. *Student/faculty ratio:* 15:1.

Majors Humanities.

Academic Programs *Special study options:* academic remediation for entering students, accelerated degree program, advanced placement credit, cooperative education, English as a second language, internships, part-time degree program, student-designed majors, study abroad.

Library New College Library with 24,000 titles, 50 serial subscriptions.

Computers on Campus 10 computers available on campus for general student use. At least one staffed computer lab available.

Student Life *Housing:* college housing not available. *Activities and Organizations:* drama/theater group, student-run newspaper. *Campus security:* trained security personnel. *Student Services:* personal/psychological counseling, legal services.

Costs (2001–02) *One-time required fee:* $35. *Tuition:* $9190 full-time, $395 per unit part-time. Full-time tuition and fees vary according to program. Part-time tuition and fees vary according to course load and program. *Required fees:* $50 full-time, $25 per term part-time.

Applying *Options:* deferred entrance. *Application fee:* $50. *Required:* essay or personal statement, high school transcript. *Required for some:* 2 letters of recommendation. *Recommended:* interview. *Application deadline:* rolling (freshmen), rolling (transfers). *Notification:* continuous (freshmen).

Admissions Contact Ms. Jean Lee, Admissions Inquiry Office, New College of California, 50 Fell Street, San Francisco, CA 94102-5206. *Phone:* 415-437-3429. *Toll-free phone:* 888-437-3460. *Fax:* 415-865-2636. *E-mail:* cmesposito@ncgate.newcollege.edu.

NEWSCHOOL OF ARCHITECTURE & DESIGN
San Diego, California

- **Proprietary** comprehensive, founded 1980
- **Calendar** quarters
- **Degrees** associate, bachelor's, master's, and first professional
- **Urban** campus
- **Coed, primarily men,** 8 undergraduate students, 88% full-time, 13% women, 88% men
- **Moderately difficult** entrance level, 100% of applicants were admitted

Undergraduates 7 full-time, 1 part-time. Students come from 4 states and territories, 15% are from out of state, 25% Hispanic American, 13% transferred in, 10% live on campus. *Retention:* 82% of 2001 full-time freshmen returned.

Freshmen *Admission:* 1 enrolled. *Average high school GPA:* 2.50.

Faculty *Total:* 56, 9% full-time, 7% with terminal degrees. *Student/faculty ratio:* 14:1.

Majors Applied art; architectural engineering technology; architecture; art; computer graphics; graphic design/commercial art/illustration.

Academic Programs *Special study options:* academic remediation for entering students, adult/continuing education programs, advanced placement credit, cooperative education, English as a second language, internships, off-campus study, part-time degree program, study abroad, summer session for credit.

Library Newschool of Arts Foundation Library with 7,500 titles, 50 serial subscriptions, 250 audiovisual materials.

Computers on Campus 14 computers available on campus for general student use. Internet access, at least one staffed computer lab available.

Student Life *Housing:* college housing not available. *Options:* coed. *Activities and Organizations:* student-run newspaper, American Institute of Architects—Student Chapter. *Campus security:* 24-hour emergency response devices, controlled dormitory access. *Student Services:* personal/psychological counseling.

Costs (2001–02) *One-time required fee:* $100. *Tuition:* $17,325 full-time, $385 per unit part-time. Full-time tuition and fees vary according to course load. *Required fees:* $189 full-time, $53 per quarter part-time. *Payment plans:* tuition prepayment, installment, deferred payment. *Waivers:* employees or children of employees.

Financial Aid Of all full-time matriculated undergraduates who enrolled in 2001, 71 applied for aid. 6 Federal Work-Study jobs (averaging $1544). In 2001, 6 non-need-based awards were made. *Average percent of need met:* 90%. *Average financial aid package:* $9700. *Average non-need based aid:* $5000. *Average indebtedness upon graduation:* $40,000.

Applying *Options:* early decision. *Application fee:* $75. *Required:* essay or personal statement, high school transcript, minimum 2.5 GPA, interview. *Required for some:* portfolio. *Recommended:* letters of recommendation. *Application deadlines:* 8/30 (freshmen), 8/30 (out-of-state freshmen), 8/30 (transfers). *Early decision:* 7/1. *Notification:* continuous (freshmen), continuous (out-of-state freshmen).

Admissions Contact Ms. Lexi Rogers, Director of Admissions, Newschool of Architecture & Design, 1249 F Street, San Diego, CA 92101-6634. *Phone:* 619-235-4100 Ext. 106. *Toll-free phone:* 619-235-4100 Ext. 106. *E-mail:* admissions@newschoolarch.edu.

NORTHWESTERN POLYTECHNIC UNIVERSITY
Fremont, California

- **Independent** comprehensive, founded 1984
- **Calendar** trimesters
- **Degrees** bachelor's, master's, and doctoral
- **Urban** 2-acre campus with easy access to San Francisco and San Jose
- **Coed,** 206 undergraduate students, 63% full-time, 37% women, 63% men
- 61% of applicants were admitted

Undergraduates 130 full-time, 76 part-time. Students come from 20 states and territories, 35 other countries, 50% are from out of state, 15% transferred in, 11% live on campus. *Retention:* 85% of 2001 full-time freshmen returned.

Freshmen *Admission:* 18 applied, 11 admitted, 5 enrolled.

Faculty *Total:* 78, 10% full-time, 58% with terminal degrees. *Student/faculty ratio:* 15:1.

Majors Business administration; computer engineering; computer science; electrical engineering.

Academic Programs *Special study options:* advanced placement credit, English as a second language, independent study, internships, part-time degree program, summer session for credit.

Library NPU Library plus 1 other with 12,000 titles, 200 serial subscriptions, 200 audiovisual materials.

Computers on Campus 150 computers available on campus for general student use. A campuswide network can be accessed from student residence rooms and from off campus. Internet access, at least one staffed computer lab available.
Student Life *Housing Options:* coed, men-only, women-only. *Activities and Organizations:* NPU Student Association, Table Tennis Club, IEEE Student Chapter, Softball Club. *Campus security:* late-night transport/escort service.
Standardized Tests *Required:* SAT I (for placement), SAT II: Subject Tests (for placement).
Costs (2002–03) *Tuition:* $9000 full-time, $250 per unit part-time. *Required fees:* $45 full-time, $15 per term part-time. *Room only:* $4800.
Applying *Application fee:* $50. *Required:* high school transcript, minimum 2.0 GPA. *Application deadlines:* 8/15 (freshmen), 8/15 (transfers). *Notification:* continuous (freshmen).
Admissions Contact Mr. Jack Xie, Director of Admission, Northwestern Polytechnic University, 117 Fourier Avenue, Fremont, CA 94539-7482. *Phone:* 510-657-5913. *Fax:* 510-657-8975. *E-mail:* npuadm@npu.edu.

NOTRE DAME DE NAMUR UNIVERSITY
Belmont, California

- **Independent Roman Catholic** comprehensive, founded 1851
- **Calendar** semesters
- **Degrees** bachelor's and master's
- **Suburban** 80-acre campus with easy access to San Francisco
- **Endowment** $5.9 million
- **Coed,** 967 undergraduate students, 61% full-time, 72% women, 28% men
- **Moderately difficult** entrance level, 84% of applicants were admitted

Undergraduates 592 full-time, 375 part-time. Students come from 24 states and territories, 17 other countries, 10% are from out of state, 7% African American, 12% Asian American or Pacific Islander, 16% Hispanic American, 0.8% Native American, 6% international, 57% transferred in, 36% live on campus. *Retention:* 74% of 2001 full-time freshmen returned.
Freshmen *Admission:* 429 applied, 359 admitted, 117 enrolled. *Average high school GPA:* 3.20. *Test scores:* SAT verbal scores over 500: 32%; SAT math scores over 500: 37%; ACT scores over 18: 71%; SAT verbal scores over 600: 8%; SAT math scores over 600: 10%; ACT scores over 24: 18%; SAT math scores over 700: 2%.
Faculty *Total:* 180, 33% full-time. *Student/faculty ratio:* 13:1.
Majors Accounting; advertising; art; behavioral sciences; biochemistry; biology; business administration; business economics; business marketing and marketing management; communications; communications related; computer science; computer software engineering; education; elementary education; English; finance; fine/studio arts; French; graphic design/commercial art/illustration; history; humanities; human services; international business; liberal arts and sciences/liberal studies; music; music (general performance); music (piano and organ performance); music (voice and choral/opera performance); philosophy; political science; pre-dentistry; pre-law; pre-medicine; psychology; religious studies; secondary education; social sciences; sociology; stringed instruments; theater arts/drama.
Academic Programs *Special study options:* academic remediation for entering students, accelerated degree program, adult/continuing education programs, advanced placement credit, cooperative education, double majors, English as a second language, independent study, internships, off-campus study, part-time degree program, services for LD students, study abroad, summer session for credit. *ROTC:* Air Force (c). *Unusual degree programs:* 3-2 engineering with Boston University.
Library College of Notre Dame Library with 726 serial subscriptions, 8,314 audiovisual materials, an OPAC.
Computers on Campus 50 computers available on campus for general student use. A campuswide network can be accessed from off campus. Internet access, at least one staffed computer lab available.
Student Life *Housing Options:* coed, men-only, women-only. *Activities and Organizations:* drama/theater group, student-run newspaper, choral group, Associated Students of Notre Dame de Namur University, BizCom, Social Action Club, Alianza Latina, Hawaiian Club. *Campus security:* 24-hour emergency response devices and patrols, late-night transport/escort service, controlled dormitory access. *Student Services:* health clinic, personal/psychological counseling.
Athletics Member NAIA. *Intercollegiate sports:* basketball M/W, soccer M/W, softball W, volleyball W.
Standardized Tests *Required:* SAT I or ACT (for admission).
Costs (2002–03) *Comprehensive fee:* $28,372 includes full-time tuition ($19,100), mandatory fees ($290), and room and board ($8982). Part-time tuition: $460 per credit. *Required fees:* $50 per term part-time. *Room and board:* Room and board charges vary according to board plan and housing facility. *Payment plan:* installment. *Waivers:* employees or children of employees.
Applying *Options:* early action, deferred entrance. *Application fee:* $40. *Required:* essay or personal statement, high school transcript, 1 letter of recommendation. *Required for some:* interview. *Application deadline:* rolling (freshmen), rolling (transfers). *Notification:* continuous (freshmen).
Admissions Contact Ms. Melissa Garcia, Assistant Director for Undergraduate Admission, Notre Dame de Namur University, 1500 Ralston Avenue, Belmont, CA 94002-1997. *Phone:* 650-508-3532. *Toll-free phone:* 800-263-0545. *Fax:* 650-508-3426. *E-mail:* admiss@ndnu.edu.

OCCIDENTAL COLLEGE
Los Angeles, California

- **Independent** comprehensive, founded 1887
- **Calendar** semesters
- **Degrees** bachelor's and master's
- **Urban** 120-acre campus
- **Endowment** $286.0 million
- **Coed,** 1,770 undergraduate students, 100% full-time, 58% women, 42% men
- **Very difficult** entrance level, 48% of applicants were admitted

Undergraduates Students come from 46 states and territories, 34 other countries, 32% are from out of state, 79% live on campus. *Retention:* 92% of 2001 full-time freshmen returned.
Freshmen *Admission:* 3,636 applied, 1,745 admitted. *Test scores:* SAT verbal scores over 500: 88%; SAT math scores over 500: 91%; SAT verbal scores over 600: 56%; SAT math scores over 600: 53%; SAT verbal scores over 700: 13%; SAT math scores over 700: 10%.
Faculty *Total:* 179, 74% full-time. *Student/faculty ratio:* 12:1.
Majors American studies; anthropology; art history; Asian studies; biochemistry; biology; business economics; chemistry; cognitive psychology/psycholinguistics; comparative literature; economics; environmental science; exercise sciences; fine/studio arts; French; geology; history; international relations; mathematics; music; philosophy; physics; physiological psychology/psychobiology; political science; psychology; public policy analysis; religious studies; sociology; Spanish; theater arts/drama; women's studies.
Academic Programs *Special study options:* accelerated degree program, advanced placement credit, double majors, honors programs, independent study, internships, off-campus study, services for LD students, student-designed majors, study abroad, summer session for credit. *ROTC:* Army (c), Navy (c), Air Force (c). *Unusual degree programs:* 3-2 engineering with California Institute of Technology, Columbia University.
Library Mary Norton Clapp Library plus 2 others with 481,822 titles, 1,135 serial subscriptions, an OPAC, a Web page.
Computers on Campus 131 computers available on campus for general student use. A campuswide network can be accessed from student residence rooms and from off campus. Internet access, online (class) registration, at least one staffed computer lab available.
Student Life *Housing:* on-campus residence required for freshman year. *Options:* coed, women-only. *Activities and Organizations:* drama/theater group, student-run newspaper, radio station, choral group, Asian-Pacific Islander Alliance, community service, Inter-faith Student Council, Black Student Alliance, MECHA/ALAS, national fraternities. *Campus security:* 24-hour emergency response devices and patrols, student patrols, late-night transport/escort service, controlled dormitory access, community police services. *Student Services:* health clinic, personal/psychological counseling, women's center, legal services.
Athletics Member NCAA. All Division III. *Intercollegiate sports:* badminton M(c)/W(c), baseball M, basketball M/W, cross-country running M/W, fencing M(c)/W(c), field hockey W(c), football M, golf M/W, lacrosse M(c)/W(c), rugby M(c)/W(c), skiing (downhill) M(c)/W(c), soccer M/W, softball W, swimming M/W, tennis M/W, track and field M/W, volleyball M(c)/W, water polo M/W. *Intramural sports:* badminton M/W, baseball M, basketball M/W, cross-country running M/W, fencing M/W, field hockey M/W, football M/W, golf M/W, ice hockey M(c), lacrosse M/W, rugby M/W, sailing M/W, skiing (cross-country) M/W, skiing (downhill) M/W, soccer M/W, swimming M/W, tennis M/W, volleyball M/W, water polo M/W.
Standardized Tests *Required:* SAT I or ACT (for admission). *Recommended:* SAT II: Subject Tests (for admission), SAT II: Writing Test (for admission).
Costs (2001–02) *Comprehensive fee:* $32,520 includes full-time tuition ($25,200), mandatory fees ($220), and room and board ($7100). *Room and board:* College room only: $3890. Room and board charges vary according to board plan and housing facility. *Payment plans:* tuition prepayment, installment. *Waivers:* employees or children of employees.
Financial Aid Of all full-time matriculated undergraduates who enrolled in 2001, 1203 applied for aid, 1005 were judged to have need, 327 had their need

Occidental College (continued)
fully met. In 2001, 266 non-need-based awards were made. *Average percent of need met:* 93%. *Average financial aid package:* $25,810. *Average need-based loan:* $4374. *Average need-based gift aid:* $20,495.

Applying *Options:* common application, early admission, early decision, deferred entrance. *Application fee:* $50. *Required:* essay or personal statement, high school transcript, 2 letters of recommendation. *Recommended:* interview. *Application deadlines:* 1/15 (freshmen), 3/15 (transfers). *Early decision:* 11/15. *Notification:* 4/1 (freshmen), 12/15 (early decision).

Admissions Contact Mr. Vince Cuseo, Director of Admission, Occidental College, 1600 Campus Road, Los Angeles, CA 90041-3314. *Phone:* 323-259-2700. *Toll-free phone:* 800-825-5262. *Fax:* 323-341-4875. *E-mail:* admission@oxy.edu.

OTIS COLLEGE OF ART AND DESIGN
Los Angeles, California

- **Independent** comprehensive, founded 1918
- **Calendar** semesters
- **Degrees** certificates, bachelor's, and master's
- **Urban** 5-acre campus
- **Coed,** 927 undergraduate students
- **Moderately difficult** entrance level, 64% of applicants were admitted

Undergraduates Students come from 25 other countries, 2% African American, 28% Asian American or Pacific Islander, 11% Hispanic American, 0.2% Native American, 11% international, 6% live on campus. *Retention:* 24% of 2001 full-time freshmen returned.

Freshmen *Admission:* 563 applied, 361 admitted. *Average high school GPA:* 3.09. *Test scores:* SAT verbal scores over 500: 44%; SAT math scores over 500: 59%; ACT scores over 18: 90%; SAT verbal scores over 600: 14%; SAT math scores over 600: 20%; ACT scores over 24: 37%; SAT verbal scores over 700: 1%; SAT math scores over 700: 2%; ACT scores over 30: 5%.

Faculty *Total:* 198, 14% full-time, 38% with terminal degrees. *Student/faculty ratio:* 11:1.

Majors Applied art; architectural environmental design; art; drawing; fashion design/illustration; fine/studio arts; graphic design/commercial art/illustration; interior design; photography; sculpture.

Academic Programs *Special study options:* academic remediation for entering students, adult/continuing education programs, advanced placement credit, cooperative education, English as a second language, freshman honors college, honors programs, independent study, internships, off-campus study, services for LD students, study abroad, summer session for credit.

Library Millard Sheets Library with 27,000 titles, 154 serial subscriptions, 2,000 audiovisual materials, an OPAC, a Web page.

Computers on Campus 220 computers available on campus for general student use. A campuswide network can be accessed from that provide access to library on-line catalog. Internet access, at least one staffed computer lab available.

Student Life *Housing:* college housing not available. *Options:* coed. *Activities and Organizations:* Student Government Association, international students organization, Otis Students in Service (OASIS), literary magazine (club), Campus Crusade. *Campus security:* 24-hour patrols. *Student Services:* personal/psychological counseling.

Standardized Tests *Required for some:* SAT I or ACT (for admission).

Costs (2001–02) *Tuition:* $19,840 full-time, $662 per credit part-time. *Required fees:* $400 full-time, $225 per term part-time. *Payment plan:* installment. *Waivers:* employees or children of employees.

Financial Aid Of all full-time matriculated undergraduates who enrolled in 2001, 655 applied for aid, 649 were judged to have need. 20 State and other part-time jobs (averaging $1000). In 2001, 52 non-need-based awards were made. *Average percent of need met:* 80%. *Average financial aid package:* $16,000. *Average need-based loan:* $5500. *Average need-based gift aid:* $5000. *Average indebtedness upon graduation:* $23,000.

Applying *Options:* common application, electronic application, early admission, deferred entrance. *Application fee:* $50. *Required:* essay or personal statement, high school transcript, minimum 2.5 GPA, portfolio. *Recommended:* 1 letter of recommendation, interview. *Application deadline:* rolling (freshmen), rolling (transfers). *Notification:* continuous (freshmen).

Admissions Contact Mr. Marc D. Meredith, Dean of Admissions, Otis College of Art and Design, 9045 Lincoln Boulevard, Los Angeles, CA 90045-9785. *Phone:* 310-665-6820. *Toll-free phone:* 800-527-OTIS. *Fax:* 310-665-6821. *E-mail:* otisart@otisart.edu.

PACIFIC OAKS COLLEGE
Pasadena, California

- **Independent** upper-level, founded 1945
- **Calendar** semesters
- **Degrees** bachelor's, master's, post-master's, and postbachelor's certificates
- **Small-town** 2-acre campus with easy access to Los Angeles
- **Endowment** $6.8 million
- **Coed, primarily women,** 258 undergraduate students, 7% full-time, 93% women, 7% men
- 86% of applicants were admitted

Undergraduates 17 full-time, 241 part-time. Students come from 34 states and territories, 30% are from out of state, 12% African American, 4% Asian American or Pacific Islander, 29% Hispanic American, 2% Native American, 21% transferred in.

Freshmen *Admission:* 185 applied, 159 admitted.

Faculty *Total:* 52, 54% full-time, 38% with terminal degrees. *Student/faculty ratio:* 9:1.

Majors Child care/development; early childhood education; elementary education; human services; individual/family development; special education.

Academic Programs *Special study options:* adult/continuing education programs, distance learning, internships, off-campus study, part-time degree program, summer session for credit.

Library Andrew Norman Library with 18,451 titles, 106 serial subscriptions, 161 audiovisual materials, an OPAC.

Computers on Campus 4 computers available on campus for general student use. A campuswide network can be accessed from off campus that provide access to on-line class listings. Internet access, at least one staffed computer lab available.

Student Life *Housing:* college housing not available. *Activities and Organizations:* Latina/o Support Group.

Costs (2001–02) *Tuition:* $13,260 full-time, $550 per unit part-time. Full-time tuition and fees vary according to program. Part-time tuition and fees vary according to program. *Required fees:* $60 full-time, $30 per term part-time. *Payment plan:* installment. *Waivers:* employees or children of employees.

Financial Aid Of all full-time matriculated undergraduates who enrolled in 2001, 61 applied for aid, 58 were judged to have need, 28 had their need fully met. *Average percent of need met:* 70%. *Average financial aid package:* $10,000. *Average need-based gift aid:* $2000. *Average indebtedness upon graduation:* $20,000.

Applying *Options:* deferred entrance. *Application fee:* $55. *Application deadline:* 6/1 (transfers). *Notification:* continuous until 9/1 (transfers).

Admissions Contact Ms. Marsha Franker, Director of Admissions, Pacific Oaks College, Admissions Office, Pacific Oaks College, 5 Westmoreland Place, Pasadena, CA 91103. *Phone:* 626-397-1349. *Toll-free phone:* 800-684-0900. *Fax:* 626-577-6144. *E-mail:* admissions@pacificoaks.edu.

PACIFIC STATES UNIVERSITY
Los Angeles, California

- **Independent** comprehensive, founded 1928
- **Calendar** quarters
- **Degrees** bachelor's and master's
- **Urban** 1-acre campus
- **Coed,** 86 undergraduate students, 100% full-time, 42% women, 58% men
- **Minimally difficult** entrance level

Undergraduates 86 full-time. 10% are from out of state, 100% Asian American or Pacific Islander. *Retention:* 76% of 2001 full-time freshmen returned.

Freshmen *Admission:* 60 enrolled.

Faculty *Total:* 16, 25% full-time, 63% with terminal degrees. *Student/faculty ratio:* 20:1.

Majors Business administration; computer science; electrical engineering.

Academic Programs *Special study options:* accelerated degree program, adult/continuing education programs, English as a second language, independent study, student-designed majors, study abroad, summer session for credit.

Library University Library plus 1 other with 15,000 titles, 108 serial subscriptions, an OPAC.

Computers on Campus 25 computers available on campus for general student use. At least one staffed computer lab available.

Student Life *Housing:* college housing not available. *Campus security:* patrols by trained security personnel during campus hours.

Costs (2001–02) *One-time required fee:* $280. *Tuition:* $8400 full-time, $195 per unit part-time. *Required fees:* $480 full-time.

Applying *Options:* common application, electronic application, early admission, deferred entrance. *Application fee:* $50. *Required:* essay or personal statement, high school transcript. *Application deadline:* 6/15 (freshmen). *Notification:* continuous (freshmen).

Admissions Contact Mr. Seth Ozen, Admissions Officer, Pacific States University, 1516 South Western Avenue, Los Angeles, CA 90006. *Phone:* 323-731-2383. *Toll-free phone:* 888-200-0383. *E-mail:* admission@psuca.edu.

PACIFIC UNION COLLEGE
Angwin, California

- **Independent Seventh-day Adventist** comprehensive, founded 1882
- **Calendar** quarters
- **Degrees** associate, bachelor's, and master's
- **Rural** 200-acre campus with easy access to San Francisco
- **Endowment** $14.2 million
- **Coed,** 1,417 undergraduate students, 92% full-time, 56% women, 44% men
- **Moderately difficult** entrance level, 59% of applicants were admitted

Undergraduates 1,309 full-time, 108 part-time. Students come from 41 states and territories, 24 other countries, 19% are from out of state, 6% African American, 19% Asian American or Pacific Islander, 10% Hispanic American, 0.4% Native American, 8% international, 17% transferred in, 70% live on campus.

Freshmen *Admission:* 1,126 applied, 664 admitted, 481 enrolled.

Faculty *Total:* 115, 90% full-time, 43% with terminal degrees. *Student/faculty ratio:* 12:1.

Majors Accounting; advertising; applied mathematics; art; art history; astrophysics; behavioral sciences; biblical studies; biochemistry; biology; biophysics; business administration; business education; business marketing and marketing management; chemistry; child care provider; child care services management; computer/information sciences; computer management; computer programming; computer science; consumer services; data processing technology; dietetics; dietician assistant; divinity/ministry; drafting; early childhood education; education; education (K-12); electrical/electronic engineering technology; elementary education; engineering; engineering design; engineering technology; English; exercise sciences; family/community studies; family/consumer studies; fashion merchandising; finance; fine/studio arts; French; graphic/printing equipment; history; home economics; home economics education; industrial arts; industrial technology; information sciences/systems; institutional food services; interdisciplinary studies; interior design; international business; journalism; land use management; laser/optical technology; legal administrative assistant; liberal arts and sciences/liberal studies; management information systems/business data processing; mass communications; mathematics; medical administrative assistant; medical technology; music; music (piano and organ performance); music teacher education; nursing; nutrition science; pastoral counseling; photography; physical education; physical sciences; physics; political science; pre-dentistry; pre-engineering; pre-law; pre-medicine; pre-veterinary studies; psychology; public relations; recreation/leisure studies; religious studies; robotics; secretarial science; social sciences; social work; sociology; Spanish; speech-language pathology/audiology; theology; transportation technology.

Academic Programs *Special study options:* academic remediation for entering students, accelerated degree program, adult/continuing education programs, advanced placement credit, cooperative education, distance learning, double majors, English as a second language, freshman honors college, honors programs, independent study, internships, off-campus study, part-time degree program, services for LD students, student-designed majors, study abroad, summer session for credit.

Library W. E. Nelson Memorial Library with 240,213 titles, 930 serial subscriptions, 54,114 audiovisual materials, an OPAC, a Web page.

Computers on Campus 134 computers available on campus for general student use. A campuswide network can be accessed from student residence rooms and from off campus. Internet access, at least one staffed computer lab available.

Student Life *Housing:* on-campus residence required through senior year. *Options:* men-only, women-only. *Activities and Organizations:* drama/theater group, student-run newspaper, choral group, Student Association, Business Club, Asian Student Association, Korean Adventist Student Association, Black Student Forum. *Campus security:* 24-hour emergency response devices and patrols, late-night transport/escort service. *Student Services:* health clinic, personal/psychological counseling.

Athletics Member NAIA. *Intercollegiate sports:* basketball M/W, cross-country running M/W, volleyball M/W. *Intramural sports:* baseball M/W, basketball M/W, cross-country running M/W, football M, golf M/W, gymnastics M/W, soccer M/W, softball M/W, tennis M/W, volleyball M/W.

Standardized Tests *Required:* SAT I and SAT II or ACT (for placement).

Costs (2002–03) *One-time required fee:* $30. *Comprehensive fee:* $21,381 includes full-time tuition ($16,455), mandatory fees ($120), and room and board ($4806). Part-time tuition: $470 per credit. No tuition increase for student's term of enrollment. *Required fees:* $40 per term part-time. *Room and board:* College room only: $2895. *Payment plans:* installment, deferred payment. *Waivers:* senior citizens and employees or children of employees.

Financial Aid Of all full-time matriculated undergraduates who enrolled in 2001, 1216 applied for aid, 1192 were judged to have need, 137 had their need fully met. 101 Federal Work-Study jobs (averaging $788). In 2001, 18 non-need-based awards were made. *Average percent of need met:* 72%. *Average financial aid package:* $11,162. *Average need-based loan:* $4958. *Average need-based gift aid:* $7437. *Average non-need based aid:* $5615. *Average indebtedness upon graduation:* $12,000.

Applying *Options:* electronic application, deferred entrance. *Application fee:* $30. *Required:* high school transcript, minimum 2.3 GPA, 3 letters of recommendation. *Application deadline:* rolling (freshmen), rolling (transfers).

Admissions Contact Pacific Union College, Enrollment Services. *Phone:* 707-965-6425. *Toll-free phone:* 800-862-7080. *Fax:* 707-965-6432. *E-mail:* enroll@puc.edu.

PATTEN COLLEGE
Oakland, California

- **Independent interdenominational** comprehensive, founded 1944
- **Calendar** semesters
- **Degrees** certificates, associate, bachelor's, master's, and postbachelor's certificates
- **Urban** 5-acre campus with easy access to San Francisco
- **Endowment** $274,588
- **Coed,** 446 undergraduate students, 46% full-time, 40% women, 60% men
- **Noncompetitive** entrance level, 58% of applicants were admitted

Undergraduates 207 full-time, 239 part-time. Students come from 12 states and territories, 5% are from out of state, 15% live on campus. *Retention:* 65% of 2001 full-time freshmen returned.

Freshmen *Admission:* 67 applied, 39 admitted, 10 enrolled. *Average high school GPA:* 2.80.

Faculty *Total:* 58, 28% full-time. *Student/faculty ratio:* 14:1.

Majors Biblical studies; business administration; divinity/ministry; early childhood education; liberal arts and sciences/liberal studies; pastoral counseling; religious music.

Academic Programs *Special study options:* accelerated degree program, adult/continuing education programs, advanced placement credit, distance learning, double majors, honors programs, internships, part-time degree program, services for LD students, summer session for credit.

Library Patten Library with 35,000 titles, 250 serial subscriptions, an OPAC.

Computers on Campus 25 computers available on campus for general student use. Internet access, at least one staffed computer lab available.

Student Life *Housing Options:* coed. *Activities and Organizations:* drama/theater group, student-run newspaper, choral group, Student Council, Patten College Chorus, Patten Symphonette. *Campus security:* 24-hour emergency response devices, student patrols, late-night transport/escort service. *Student Services:* personal/psychological counseling.

Athletics Member NAIA, NCCAA. *Intercollegiate sports:* basketball M(s)/W(s), cross-country running M(s)/W(s), golf M(s), soccer M(s)/W(s), softball W(s).

Standardized Tests *Required:* SAT I or ACT (for admission).

Costs (2002–03) *Comprehensive fee:* $15,040 includes full-time tuition ($9240) and room and board ($5800). Full-time tuition and fees vary according to course load. Part-time tuition: $385 per credit. *Payment plan:* installment. *Waivers:* employees or children of employees.

Applying *Options:* early admission, deferred entrance. *Application fee:* $30. *Required:* essay or personal statement, high school transcript, minimum 2.5 GPA, 2 letters of recommendation. *Recommended:* interview. *Application deadline:* 7/31 (freshmen), rolling (transfers). *Notification:* continuous (freshmen).

Admissions Contact Ms. Inez Bailey, Director of Admissions, Patten College, 2433 Coolidge Avenue, Oakland, CA 94601. *Phone:* 510-261-8500 Ext. 765. *Fax:* 510-534-4344.

PEPPERDINE UNIVERSITY
Malibu, California

- **Independent** university, founded 1937, affiliated with Church of Christ
- **Calendar** semesters

Pepperdine University (continued)

- **Degrees** bachelor's, master's, doctoral, and first professional (the university is organized into five colleges: Seaver, the School of Law, the School of Business and Management, the School of Public Policy, and the Graduate School of Education and Psychology. Seaver College is the undergraduate, residential, liberal arts school of the University and is committed to providing education of outstanding academic quality with particular attention to Christian values)
- **Small-town** 830-acre campus with easy access to Los Angeles
- **Coed,** 2,936 undergraduate students, 84% full-time, 57% women, 43% men
- **Very difficult** entrance level, 28% of applicants were admitted

Undergraduates 2,462 full-time, 474 part-time. Students come from 51 states and territories, 70 other countries, 52% are from out of state, 7% African American, 8% Asian American or Pacific Islander, 11% Hispanic American, 1% Native American, 8% international, 1% transferred in, 48% live on campus. *Retention:* 87% of 2001 full-time freshmen returned.

Freshmen *Admission:* 6,147 applied, 1,691 admitted, 607 enrolled. *Average high school GPA:* 3.63. *Test scores:* SAT verbal scores over 500: 90%; SAT math scores over 500: 94%; ACT scores over 18: 100%; SAT verbal scores over 600: 48%; SAT math scores over 600: 59%; ACT scores over 24: 81%; SAT verbal scores over 700: 9%; SAT math scores over 700: 14%; ACT scores over 30: 23%.

Faculty *Total:* 680, 53% full-time, 94% with terminal degrees. *Student/faculty ratio:* 12:1.

Majors Accounting; advertising; art; athletic training/sports medicine; biology; business administration; chemistry; communications; computer science; economics; education; elementary education; English; French; German; history; humanities; interdisciplinary studies; international business; international relations; journalism; liberal arts and sciences/liberal studies; mathematics; music; music teacher education; natural sciences; nutrition science; philosophy; physical education; political science; pre-dentistry; pre-law; pre-medicine; psychology; public relations; religious education; religious studies; secondary education; sociology; Spanish; speech/rhetorical studies; telecommunications; theater arts/drama.

Academic Programs *Special study options:* accelerated degree program, advanced placement credit, double majors, honors programs, independent study, internships, part-time degree program, student-designed majors, study abroad, summer session for credit. *ROTC:* Army (c), Navy (c), Air Force (c). *Unusual degree programs:* 3-2 engineering with University of Southern California, Washington University in St. Louis, Boston University.

Library Payson Library plus 2 others with 515,238 titles, 3,882 serial subscriptions.

Computers on Campus 292 computers available on campus for general student use. A campuswide network can be accessed from student residence rooms.

Student Life *Housing:* on-campus residence required through sophomore year. *Options:* men-only, women-only, disabled students. *Activities and Organizations:* drama/theater group, student-run newspaper, radio and television station, choral group, Student Government Association, Black Student Union, International Club, Alpha Chi Honor Society, Golden Key Honor Society, national fraternities, national sororities. *Campus security:* 24-hour emergency response devices and patrols, student patrols, late-night transport/escort service, front gate security, 24-hour security in residence halls, controlled access, crime prevention programs. *Student Services:* health clinic, personal/psychological counseling.

Athletics Member NCAA. All Division I. *Intercollegiate sports:* baseball M(s), basketball M(s)/W(s), cross-country running M(s)/W(s), golf M(s)/W(s), lacrosse M(c), rugby M(c), soccer M(c)/W(s), swimming W(s), tennis M(s)/W(s), volleyball M(s)/W(s), water polo M(s). *Intramural sports:* badminton M/W, basketball M/W, crew M/W, cross-country running M/W, field hockey W, football M/W, golf M/W, lacrosse M, sailing M/W, soccer M/W, softball M/W, swimming M/W, tennis M/W, volleyball M/W.

Standardized Tests *Required:* SAT I or ACT (for admission).

Costs (2002–03) *Comprehensive fee:* $34,300 includes full-time tuition ($26,280), mandatory fees ($90), and room and board ($7930). Part-time tuition: $820 per unit. *Room and board:* College room only: $5040. Room and board charges vary according to housing facility. *Payment plans:* tuition prepayment, installment, deferred payment. *Waivers:* employees or children of employees.

Financial Aid Of all full-time matriculated undergraduates who enrolled in 2001, 1765 applied for aid, 1210 were judged to have need, 309 had their need fully met. In 2001, 253 non-need-based awards were made. *Average percent of need met:* 91%. *Average financial aid package:* $26,610. *Average need-based loan:* $6064. *Average need-based gift aid:* $16,004. *Average non-need based aid:* $12,214. *Average indebtedness upon graduation:* $28,620.

Applying *Options:* common application, electronic application, early action. *Application fee:* $55. *Required:* essay or personal statement, high school transcript, 2 letters of recommendation. *Recommended:* interview. *Application deadlines:* 1/15 (freshmen), 1/15 (transfers). *Notification:* 4/1 (freshmen), 12/15 (early action).

Admissions Contact Mr. Paul A. Long, Dean of Admission and Enrollment Management, Pepperdine University, 24255 Pacific Coast Highway, Malibu, CA 90263-4392. *Phone:* 310-506-4392. *Fax:* 310-506-4861. *E-mail:* admission-seaver@pepperdine.edu.

PITZER COLLEGE
Claremont, California

- **Independent** 4-year, founded 1963, part of The Claremont Colleges Consortium
- **Calendar** semesters
- **Degree** bachelor's
- **Suburban** 35-acre campus with easy access to Los Angeles
- **Endowment** $47.1 million
- **Coed,** 921 undergraduate students, 94% full-time, 62% women, 38% men
- **Moderately difficult** entrance level, 54% of applicants were admitted

Undergraduates 869 full-time, 52 part-time. Students come from 44 states and territories, 14 other countries, 46% are from out of state, 6% African American, 10% Asian American or Pacific Islander, 14% Hispanic American, 0.9% Native American, 3% international, 4% transferred in, 92% live on campus. *Retention:* 82% of 2001 full-time freshmen returned.

Freshmen *Admission:* 2,282 applied, 1,228 admitted, 224 enrolled. *Average high school GPA:* 3.53. *Test scores:* SAT verbal scores over 500: 96%; SAT math scores over 500: 91%; ACT scores over 18: 99%; SAT verbal scores over 600: 64%; SAT math scores over 600: 53%; ACT scores over 24: 82%; SAT verbal scores over 700: 16%; SAT math scores over 700: 5%; ACT scores over 30: 23%.

Faculty *Total:* 75, 75% full-time, 97% with terminal degrees. *Student/faculty ratio:* 12:1.

Majors African-American studies; American history; American studies; anthropology; art; art history; Asian-American studies; Asian studies; biology; chemistry; classics; dance; economics; engineering; engineering/industrial management; English; environmental science; European history; European studies; film studies; fine/studio arts; French; German; history; interdisciplinary studies; international relations; Latin American studies; linguistics; literature; mathematics; Mexican-American studies; neuroscience; philosophy; physics; political science; pre-medicine; psychology; religious studies; romance languages; Russian; science/technology and society; sociology; Spanish; theater arts/drama; women's studies.

Academic Programs *Special study options:* adult/continuing education programs, advanced placement credit, cooperative education, double majors, English as a second language, honors programs, independent study, internships, off-campus study, part-time degree program, services for LD students, student-designed majors, study abroad. *Unusual degree programs:* 3-2 public administration, mathematics with Claremont Graduate University.

Library Honnold Library plus 3 others with 2.0 million titles, 6,000 serial subscriptions, 606 audiovisual materials, an OPAC, a Web page.

Computers on Campus 96 computers available on campus for general student use. A campuswide network can be accessed from student residence rooms and from off campus. Internet access, at least one staffed computer lab available.

Student Life *Housing:* on-campus residence required through junior year. *Options:* coed, women-only, cooperative, disabled students. *Activities and Organizations:* drama/theater group, student-run newspaper, radio station, choral group, Student Senate, The Other Side, Without A Box, Residence Hall Association. *Campus security:* 24-hour emergency response devices and patrols, late-night transport/escort service, controlled dormitory access. *Student Services:* health clinic, personal/psychological counseling, women's center.

Athletics Member NCAA. All Division III. *Intercollegiate sports:* baseball M, basketball M/W, cross-country running M/W, football M, golf M, soccer M/W, softball W, swimming M/W, tennis M/W, track and field M/W, volleyball W, water polo M/W, wrestling M. *Intramural sports:* badminton M/W, baseball M, basketball M/W, fencing M(c)/W(c), football M, lacrosse M(c)/W(c), rugby M(c), sailing M(c)/W(c), skiing (downhill) M(c)/W(c), soccer M/W, softball W, tennis M/W, track and field M/W, volleyball M(c)/W, water polo M(c)/W(c).

Standardized Tests *Required:* SAT I or ACT (for admission). *Recommended:* SAT II: Subject Tests (for admission), SAT II: Writing Test (for admission).

Costs (2001–02) *Comprehensive fee:* $33,930 includes full-time tuition ($24,160), mandatory fees ($2870), and room and board ($6900). Full-time tuition and fees vary according to course load. Part-time tuition: $3020 per course. Part-time tuition and fees vary according to course load. *Required fees:* $358 per course, $104 per term part-time. *Room and board:* College room only: $4470. Room and board charges vary according to board plan. *Payment plans:* installment, deferred payment. *Waivers:* employees or children of employees.

Financial Aid Of all full-time matriculated undergraduates who enrolled in 2001, 480 applied for aid, 460 were judged to have need, 460 had their need fully met. 337 Federal Work-Study jobs (averaging $2551). In 2001, 23 non-need-based awards were made. *Average percent of need met:* 100%. *Average financial aid package:* $25,375. *Average need-based loan:* $4682. *Average need-based gift aid:* $19,468. *Average non-need based aid:* $9783. *Average indebtedness upon graduation:* $20,900. *Financial aid deadline:* 2/1.

Applying *Options:* common application, electronic application, early admission, early action, deferred entrance. *Application fee:* $40. *Required:* essay or personal statement, high school transcript, 3 letters of recommendation. *Recommended:* interview. *Application deadlines:* 1/15 (freshmen), 4/15 (transfers). *Notification:* 4/1 (freshmen), 1/1 (early action).

Admissions Contact Dr. Arnaldo Rodriguez, Vice President for Admission and Financial Aid, Pitzer College, 1050 North Mills Avenue, Claremont, CA 91711-6101. *Phone:* 909-621-8129. *Toll-free phone:* 800-748-9371. *Fax:* 909-621-8770. *E-mail:* admission@pitzer.edu.

POINT LOMA NAZARENE UNIVERSITY

San Diego, California

- **Independent Nazarene** comprehensive, founded 1902
- **Calendar** semesters
- **Degrees** bachelor's, master's, post-master's, and postbachelor's certificates
- **Suburban** 88-acre campus
- **Endowment** $21.0 million
- **Coed,** 2,353 undergraduate students, 97% full-time, 60% women, 40% men
- **Moderately difficult** entrance level, 76% of applicants were admitted

Undergraduates 2,281 full-time, 72 part-time. Students come from 36 states and territories, 14 other countries, 22% are from out of state, 0.8% African American, 4% Asian American or Pacific Islander, 7% Hispanic American, 0.7% Native American, 1% international, 7% transferred in, 67% live on campus. *Retention:* 79% of 2001 full-time freshmen returned.

Freshmen *Admission:* 1,365 applied, 1,038 admitted, 474 enrolled. *Average high school GPA:* 3.62. *Test scores:* SAT verbal scores over 500: 75%; SAT math scores over 500: 77%; ACT scores over 18: 96%; SAT verbal scores over 600: 28%; SAT math scores over 600: 31%; ACT scores over 24: 45%; SAT verbal scores over 700: 4%; SAT math scores over 700: 3%; ACT scores over 30: 6%.

Faculty *Total:* 277, 49% full-time, 34% with terminal degrees. *Student/faculty ratio:* 16:1.

Majors Accounting; art; athletic training/sports medicine; biochemistry; biology; British literature; business administration; business communications; business home economics; chemistry; child care/development; communications; computer science; dietetics; economics; engineering physics; family studies; graphic design/commercial art/illustration; health/physical education; history; home economics; journalism; liberal arts and sciences/liberal studies; management information systems/business data processing; mass communications; mathematics; music; music business management/merchandising; nursing; organizational psychology; philosophy; philosophy and religion related; physics; political science; psychology; religious music; religious studies; romance languages; social sciences; social work; sociology; Spanish; speech/rhetorical studies; theater arts/drama.

Academic Programs *Special study options:* academic remediation for entering students, advanced placement credit, double majors, English as a second language, internships, off-campus study, part-time degree program, services for LD students, study abroad, summer session for credit. *ROTC:* Army (c), Navy (c), Air Force (c).

Library Ryan Library with 120,991 titles, 637 serial subscriptions, 7,449 audiovisual materials, an OPAC, a Web page.

Computers on Campus 125 computers available on campus for general student use. A campuswide network can be accessed from student residence rooms and from off campus. At least one staffed computer lab available.

Student Life *Housing:* on-campus residence required through junior year. *Options:* men-only, women-only. *Activities and Organizations:* drama/theater group, student-run newspaper, radio station, choral group, Cai Delta Psi, Psi Omega Theta, SNAPL (nurses association), Chi Beta Sigma, national sororities. *Campus security:* 24-hour patrols, student patrols, late-night transport/escort service. *Student Services:* health clinic, personal/psychological counseling, women's center.

Athletics Member NAIA. *Intercollegiate sports:* baseball M(s), basketball M(s)/W(s), cross-country running M(s)/W(s), golf M(s), soccer M(s), softball W(s), tennis M(s)/W(s), track and field M(s)/W(s), volleyball W(s). *Intramural sports:* badminton M/W, baseball M, basketball M/W, bowling M/W, cross-country running M/W, football M/W, golf M/W, racquetball M/W, sailing M/W, soccer M/W, softball M/W, swimming M/W, table tennis M/W, tennis M/W, track and field M/W, volleyball M/W, water polo M/W, weight lifting M/W.

Standardized Tests *Required:* SAT I or ACT (for admission). *Recommended:* SAT I (for admission).

Costs (2001–02) *Comprehensive fee:* $21,620 includes full-time tuition ($14,800), mandatory fees ($500), and room and board ($6320). Full-time tuition and fees vary according to course load. Part-time tuition: $617 per unit. Part-time tuition and fees vary according to course load and student level. *Required fees:* $20 per unit. *Room and board:* Room and board charges vary according to board plan. *Payment plan:* installment. *Waivers:* senior citizens and employees or children of employees.

Financial Aid Of all full-time matriculated undergraduates who enrolled in 2001, 1922 applied for aid, 1415 were judged to have need, 358 had their need fully met. 450 Federal Work-Study jobs (averaging $1590). In 2001, 461 non-need-based awards were made. *Average percent of need met:* 76%. *Average financial aid package:* $11,493. *Average need-based loan:* $4041. *Average need-based gift aid:* $7428. *Average non-need based aid:* $6616.

Applying *Options:* early action, deferred entrance. *Application fee:* $45. *Required:* essay or personal statement, high school transcript, minimum 2.8 GPA, 2 letters of recommendation. *Required for some:* interview. *Application deadline:* 3/1 (freshmen), rolling (transfers). *Notification:* continuous (freshmen), 1/15 (early action).

Admissions Contact Mr. Scott Shoemaker, Director of Admissions, Point Loma Nazarene University, 3900 Lomaland Drive, San Diego, CA 92106-2899. *Phone:* 619-849-2273. *Toll-free phone:* 800-733-7770. *Fax:* 619-849-2601. *E-mail:* admissions@ptloma.edu.

POMONA COLLEGE

Claremont, California

- **Independent** 4-year, founded 1887, part of The Claremont Colleges Consortium
- **Calendar** semesters
- **Degree** bachelor's
- **Suburban** 140-acre campus with easy access to Los Angeles
- **Endowment** $1.1 billion
- **Coed,** 1,577 undergraduate students, 98% full-time, 49% women, 51% men
- **Most difficult** entrance level, 29% of applicants were admitted

Pomona is one of the nation's premier liberal arts colleges. Its widely diverse student body enjoys a broad range of resources and opportunities backed by financial holdings that are among the strongest of any college of comparable size. Pomona is the founding member of the Claremont Colleges, offering the benefits of a university setting with the advantages of a small college.

Undergraduates 1,544 full-time, 33 part-time. Students come from 49 states and territories, 67% are from out of state, 6% African American, 16% Asian American or Pacific Islander, 9% Hispanic American, 0.3% Native American, 2% international, 1% transferred in, 95% live on campus. *Retention:* 98% of 2001 full-time freshmen returned.

Freshmen *Admission:* 3,712 applied, 1,078 admitted, 393 enrolled. *Average high school GPA:* 3.90. *Test scores:* SAT verbal scores over 500: 100%; SAT math scores over 500: 100%; ACT scores over 18: 100%; SAT verbal scores over 600: 96%; SAT math scores over 600: 95%; ACT scores over 24: 99%; SAT verbal scores over 700: 66%; SAT math scores over 700: 69%; ACT scores over 30: 67%.

Faculty *Total:* 227, 76% full-time, 90% with terminal degrees. *Student/faculty ratio:* 9:1.

Majors African-American studies; American studies; anthropology; art; art history; Asian studies; astronomy; biochemistry; biology; cell biology; chemistry; Chinese; classics; computer science; dance; East Asian studies; ecology; economics; English; environmental science; film studies; fine/studio arts; French; geochemistry; geology; German; Hispanic-American studies; history; humanities; interdisciplinary studies; international relations; Japanese; liberal arts and sciences/liberal studies; linguistics; mathematics; Mexican-American studies; microbiology/bacteriology; modern languages; molecular biology; music; neuroscience; philosophy; physics; political science; pre-medicine; psychology; public policy analysis; religious studies; romance languages; Russian; sociology; Spanish; theater arts/drama; women's studies.

Academic Programs *Special study options:* advanced placement credit, double majors, independent study, internships, off-campus study, student-designed majors, study abroad. *Unusual degree programs:* 3-2 engineering with California Institute of Technology, Washington University in St. Louis.

Library Honnold Library plus 3 others with 2.1 million titles, 5,733 serial subscriptions, 4,361 audiovisual materials, an OPAC, a Web page.

Computers on Campus 180 computers available on campus for general student use. A campuswide network can be accessed from student residence rooms and from off campus. Internet access, at least one staffed computer lab available.

Pomona College (continued)

Student Life *Housing:* on-campus residence required for freshman year. *Options:* coed. *Activities and Organizations:* drama/theater group, student-run newspaper, radio station, choral group, student government, music organizations, service organizations, intramural sports. *Campus security:* 24-hour emergency response devices and patrols, late-night transport/escort service, controlled dormitory access. *Student Services:* health clinic, personal/psychological counseling, women's center.

Athletics Member NCAA. All Division III. *Intercollegiate sports:* baseball M, basketball M/W, cross-country running M/W, football M, golf M/W, soccer M/W, softball W, swimming M/W, tennis M/W, track and field M/W, volleyball W, water polo M/W. *Intramural sports:* badminton M(c)/W(c), basketball M/W, cross-country running M/W, fencing M/W, field hockey W(c), football M, golf M/W, lacrosse M(c)/W(c), racquetball M/W, rugby M(c)/W(c), sailing M(c)/W(c), skiing (cross-country) M(c)/W(c), skiing (downhill) M(c)/W(c), soccer M/W, softball M/W, squash M/W, swimming M/W, tennis M/W, track and field M/W, volleyball M/W, water polo M/W.

Standardized Tests *Required:* SAT I or ACT (for admission).

Costs (2001–02) *Comprehensive fee:* $33,960 includes full-time tuition ($24,750), mandatory fees ($260), and room and board ($8950). Part-time tuition: $4125 per course. *Room and board:* College room only: $5830. Room and board charges vary according to board plan. *Payment plan:* installment. *Waivers:* employees or children of employees.

Financial Aid Of all full-time matriculated undergraduates who enrolled in 2001, 916 applied for aid, 800 were judged to have need, 800 had their need fully met. 242 Federal Work-Study jobs (averaging $1650). 491 State and other part-time jobs (averaging $1650). In 2001, 97 non-need-based awards were made. *Average percent of need met:* 100%. *Average financial aid package:* $24,200. *Average need-based loan:* $3000. *Average need-based gift aid:* $19,700. *Average non-need based aid:* $2407. *Average indebtedness upon graduation:* $15,600. *Financial aid deadline:* 2/1.

Applying *Options:* common application, electronic application, early admission, early decision, deferred entrance. *Application fee:* $55. *Required:* essay or personal statement, high school transcript, 2 letters of recommendation. *Recommended:* minimum 3.0 GPA, interview, portfolio or tapes for art and performing arts programs. *Application deadlines:* 1/2 (freshmen), 3/15 (transfers). *Early decision:* 11/15 (for plan 1), 12/28 (for plan 2). *Notification:* 4/10 (freshmen), 12/15 (early decision plan 1), 2/15 (early decision plan 2).

Admissions Contact Mr. Bruce Poch, Vice President and Dean of Admissions, Pomona College, 333 North College Way, Claremont, CA 91711. *Phone:* 909-621-8134. *Fax:* 909-621-8952. *E-mail:* admissions@pomona.edu.

ST. JOHN'S SEMINARY COLLEGE
Camarillo, California

- **Independent Roman Catholic** 4-year, founded 1939
- **Calendar** semesters
- **Degree** certificates, diplomas, and bachelor's
- **Suburban** 100-acre campus with easy access to Los Angeles
- **Men only,** 99 undergraduate students, 92% full-time
- **Moderately difficult** entrance level, 100% of applicants were admitted

Undergraduates 91 full-time, 8 part-time. Students come from 4 states and territories, 14% are from out of state, 18% transferred in, 95% live on campus. *Retention:* 94% of 2001 full-time freshmen returned.

Freshmen *Admission:* 13 enrolled. *Average high school GPA:* 3.10.

Faculty *Total:* 31, 58% full-time, 35% with terminal degrees. *Student/faculty ratio:* 5:1.

Majors English; philosophy; Spanish; theology.

Academic Programs *Special study options:* academic remediation for entering students, adult/continuing education programs, advanced placement credit, double majors, English as a second language, honors programs, independent study, off-campus study, part-time degree program, services for LD students.

Library Carrie Estelle Doheney Library plus 1 other with 68,000 titles, 142 serial subscriptions, 3,067 audiovisual materials, an OPAC, a Web page.

Computers on Campus 26 computers available on campus for general student use. A campuswide network can be accessed from off campus. Internet access, at least one staffed computer lab available.

Student Life *Housing:* on-campus residence required through senior year. *Options:* men-only. *Activities and Organizations:* drama/theater group, choral group, La Hermandad, Vietnamese Club, Forensics Club, Pacifica Club, choir. *Campus security:* late night and front gate security. *Student Services:* personal/psychological counseling.

Standardized Tests *Recommended:* SAT I or ACT (for admission).

Costs (2002–03) *Comprehensive fee:* $14,255 includes full-time tuition ($8000), mandatory fees ($255), and room and board ($6000). Part-time tuition: $200 per unit. *Payment plans:* installment, deferred payment.

Financial Aid Of all full-time matriculated undergraduates who enrolled in 2001, 47 applied for aid, 44 were judged to have need, 10 had their need fully met. In 2001, 3 non-need-based awards were made. *Average percent of need met:* 72%. *Average financial aid package:* $8581. *Average need-based loan:* $3309. *Average need-based gift aid:* $4959. *Average non-need based aid:* $3000. *Average indebtedness upon graduation:* $10,753.

Applying *Application fee:* $40. *Required:* essay or personal statement, high school transcript, 2 letters of recommendation, interview, intention of studying for Roman Catholic priesthood. *Application deadlines:* 6/21 (freshmen), 6/21 (transfers). *Notification:* continuous until 8/20 (freshmen).

Admissions Contact Ms. Kathryn Y. Musashi, Director of Admissions, St. John's Seminary College, Camarillo, CA 93012-2599. *Phone:* 805-482-2755 Ext. 2002. *Fax:* 805-987-5097.

SAINT MARY'S COLLEGE OF CALIFORNIA
Moraga, California

- **Independent Roman Catholic** comprehensive, founded 1863
- **Calendar** 4-1-4
- **Degrees** certificates, bachelor's, master's, and doctoral
- **Suburban** 420-acre campus with easy access to San Francisco
- **Endowment** $85.2 million
- **Coed,** 3,061 undergraduate students, 81% full-time, 62% women, 38% men
- **Moderately difficult** entrance level, 77% of applicants were admitted

Undergraduates 2,468 full-time, 593 part-time. Students come from 29 states and territories, 33 other countries, 11% are from out of state, 6% African American, 8% Asian American or Pacific Islander, 14% Hispanic American, 0.8% Native American, 2% international, 5% transferred in, 62% live on campus. *Retention:* 82% of 2001 full-time freshmen returned.

Freshmen *Admission:* 3,230 applied, 2,491 admitted, 609 enrolled. *Average high school GPA:* 3.38. *Test scores:* SAT verbal scores over 500: 74%; SAT math scores over 500: 76%; ACT scores over 18: 97%; SAT verbal scores over 600: 25%; SAT math scores over 600: 23%; ACT scores over 24: 36%; SAT verbal scores over 700: 2%; SAT math scores over 700: 3%; ACT scores over 30: 5%.

Faculty *Total:* 467, 39% full-time. *Student/faculty ratio:* 13:1.

Majors Accounting; anthropology; art; art education; art history; biology; business administration; chemistry; dance; economics; education; engineering; English; French; German; Greek (modern); health education; history; interdisciplinary studies; international business; international relations; Latin (ancient and medieval); liberal arts and sciences/liberal studies; literature; mass communications; mathematics; modern languages; music; nursing; philosophy; physical education; physics; political science; pre-dentistry; pre-law; pre-medicine; pre-veterinary studies; psychology; religious studies; secondary education; sociology; Spanish; theater arts/drama; theology; women's studies.

Academic Programs *Special study options:* adult/continuing education programs, advanced placement credit, double majors, external degree program, honors programs, independent study, internships, off-campus study, part-time degree program, student-designed majors, study abroad. *ROTC:* Army (c), Air Force (c). *Unusual degree programs:* 3-2 engineering with Washington University in St. Louis, University of Southern California, Boston University; nursing with Samuel Merritt College.

Library St. Albert Hall plus 1 other with 153,576 titles, 1,066 serial subscriptions, 6,925 audiovisual materials, an OPAC, a Web page.

Computers on Campus 250 computers available on campus for general student use. A campuswide network can be accessed from student residence rooms and from off campus. Internet access, at least one staffed computer lab available.

Student Life *Housing Options:* coed, women-only, disabled students. *Activities and Organizations:* drama/theater group, student-run newspaper, radio and television station, choral group, MECHA, Student Alumni Association, Black Student Union, Intervarsity Christian Fellowship, Asian Pacific America Student Association. *Campus security:* 24-hour emergency response devices and patrols, late-night transport/escort service. *Student Services:* health clinic, personal/psychological counseling, women's center.

Athletics Member NCAA. All Division I except football (Division I-AA). *Intercollegiate sports:* baseball M(s), basketball M(s)/W(s), crew W, cross-country running M(s)/W(s), golf M(s), lacrosse M(c)/W, rugby M(c), soccer M(s)/W(s), softball W(s), tennis M(s)/W(s), volleyball M(c)/W(s). *Intramural sports:* basketball M/W, bowling M/W, crew M/W, cross-country running M/W, football M/W, golf M/W, lacrosse M/W, rugby M, skiing (cross-country) M/W, skiing (downhill) M/W, soccer M/W, softball M/W, table tennis M/W, tennis M/W, volleyball M/W, water polo M/W.

Standardized Tests *Required:* SAT I or ACT (for admission).
Costs (2001–02) *Comprehensive fee:* $27,575 includes full-time tuition ($19,390), mandatory fees ($135), and room and board ($8050). Full-time tuition and fees vary according to program. Part-time tuition: $2425 per course. *Room and board:* College room only: $4450. Room and board charges vary according to board plan and housing facility. *Payment plans:* tuition prepayment, installment. *Waivers:* employees or children of employees.
Financial Aid Of all full-time matriculated undergraduates who enrolled in 2001, 1773 applied for aid, 1407 were judged to have need, 436 had their need fully met. In 2001, 275 non-need-based awards were made. *Average percent of need met:* 88%. *Average financial aid package:* $14,578. *Average need-based loan:* $4198. *Average need-based gift aid:* $14,487. *Average indebtedness upon graduation:* $17,465.
Applying *Options:* common application, electronic application, early action, deferred entrance. *Application fee:* $45. *Required:* essay or personal statement, high school transcript, minimum 2.0 GPA, 1 letter of recommendation. *Required for some:* minimum 3.0 GPA, interview. *Recommended:* minimum 3.0 GPA. *Application deadlines:* 2/1 (freshmen), 7/1 (transfers). *Notification:* continuous (freshmen), 1/15 (early action).
Admissions Contact Ms. Dorothy Benjamin, Dean of Admissions, Saint Mary's College of California, PO Box 4800, Moraga, CA 94556-4800. *Phone:* 925-631-4224. *Toll-free phone:* 800-800-4SMC. *Fax:* 925-376-7193. *E-mail:* smcadmit@stmarys-ca.edu.

SAMUEL MERRITT COLLEGE
Oakland, California

- **Independent** comprehensive, founded 1909
- **Calendar** 4-1-4
- **Degrees** bachelor's, master's, and post-master's certificates (bachelor's degree offered jointly with Saint Mary's College of California)
- **Urban** 1-acre campus with easy access to San Francisco
- **Endowment** $17.6 million
- **Coed, primarily women,** 257 undergraduate students
- **Moderately difficult** entrance level, 71% of applicants were admitted

Undergraduates Students come from 2 states and territories, 1 other country, 1% are from out of state, 11% live on campus. *Retention:* 100% of 2001 full-time freshmen returned.
Freshmen *Admission:* 38 applied, 27 admitted. *Average high school GPA:* 3.13. *Test scores:* SAT verbal scores over 500: 60%; SAT math scores over 500: 100%; ACT scores over 18: 80%; SAT verbal scores over 600: 40%; SAT math scores over 600: 20%; ACT scores over 24: 20%.
Faculty *Total:* 92, 45% full-time. *Student/faculty ratio:* 8:1.
Majors Health science; nursing.
Academic Programs *Special study options:* academic remediation for entering students, advanced placement credit, distance learning, double majors, independent study, internships, off-campus study, services for LD students, study abroad, summer session for credit. *ROTC:* Army (c), Navy (c), Air Force (c).
Library John A. Graziano Memorial Library plus 1 other with 11,000 titles, 540 serial subscriptions, 900 audiovisual materials.
Computers on Campus 48 computers available on campus for general student use. Internet access, at least one staffed computer lab available.
Student Life *Housing Options:* coed. *Activities and Organizations:* student-run newspaper, Multicultural Group, California Nursing Students Association, Student Body Association. *Campus security:* 24-hour emergency response devices and patrols, late-night transport/escort service, controlled dormitory access, 24-hour controlled access. *Student Services:* health clinic, personal/psychological counseling.
Athletics *Intercollegiate sports:* baseball M, basketball M/W, crew M/W, cross-country running M/W, football M, golf M, rugby M, soccer M/W, tennis M/W, volleyball M/W. *Intramural sports:* archery M/W, badminton M/W, bowling M/W, gymnastics M/W, racquetball M/W, soccer M/W, softball M/W, swimming M/W, tennis M/W, volleyball M/W, weight lifting M/W.
Standardized Tests *Required:* SAT I or ACT (for admission).
Costs (2001–02) *Tuition:* $18,300 full-time, $767 per unit part-time. *Required fees:* $50 full-time. *Room only:* $3780.
Applying *Options:* common application, deferred entrance. *Application fee:* $35. *Required:* essay or personal statement, high school transcript, minimum 2.5 GPA, 1 letter of recommendation. *Required for some:* interview. *Application deadlines:* 3/1 (freshmen), 3/1 (transfers). *Notification:* continuous (freshmen).
Admissions Contact Mr. John Garten-Shuman, Director of Admissions, Samuel Merritt College, 370 Hawthorne Avenue, Oakland, CA 94609-3108. *Phone:* 510-869-6727. *Toll-free phone:* 800-607-MERRITT. *Fax:* 510-869-6525. *E-mail:* admission@samuelmerritt.edu.

SAN DIEGO STATE UNIVERSITY
San Diego, California

- **State-supported** university, founded 1897, part of California State University System
- **Calendar** semesters
- **Degrees** certificates, bachelor's, master's, doctoral, post-master's, and postbachelor's certificates
- **Urban** 300-acre campus
- **Endowment** $65.8 million
- **Coed,** 27,871 undergraduate students, 77% full-time, 57% women, 43% men
- **Moderately difficult** entrance level, 63% of applicants were admitted

Undergraduates 21,523 full-time, 6,348 part-time. Students come from 48 states and territories, 83 other countries, 3% are from out of state, 4% African American, 15% Asian American or Pacific Islander, 21% Hispanic American, 0.7% Native American, 3% international, 10% transferred in, 48% live on campus. *Retention:* 75% of 2001 full-time freshmen returned.
Freshmen *Admission:* 25,226 applied, 15,946 admitted, 4,255 enrolled. *Average high school GPA:* 3.36. *Test scores:* SAT verbal scores over 500: 50%; SAT math scores over 500: 61%; ACT scores over 18: 82%; SAT verbal scores over 600: 10%; SAT math scores over 600: 16%; ACT scores over 24: 25%; SAT verbal scores over 700: 1%.
Faculty *Total:* 1,924, 54% full-time. *Student/faculty ratio:* 17:1.
Majors Accounting; aerospace engineering; African-American studies; agricultural business; American studies; anthropology; applied mathematics; art; art education; art history; Asian studies; astronomy; biology; biology education; business administration; business marketing and marketing management; chemical and atomic/molecular physics; chemical engineering; chemistry; chemistry education; chemistry related; child care/development; civil engineering; classics; communication disorders; communications related; comparative literature; computer education; computer engineering; computer/information sciences; creative writing; criminal justice/law enforcement administration; dance; design/visual communications; drama/dance education; ecology; economics; electrical engineering; engineering; English; English education; environmental science; European studies; evolutionary biology; finance; financial management and services related; fine arts and art studies related; foreign languages education; French; French language education; geochemistry; geography; geological sciences related; geology; German; German language education; gerontology; health professions and related sciences; Hispanic-American studies; history; hospitality services management related; hotel and restaurant management; humanities; industrial arts; information sciences/systems; interior design; international business; international economics; international relations; Japanese; journalism; journalism and mass communication related; Latin American studies; liberal arts and sciences/liberal studies; linguistics; marine biology; marketing/distribution education; mass communications; mathematical statistics; mathematics; mathematics/computer science; mathematics education; mechanical engineering; microbiology/bacteriology; multi/interdisciplinary studies related; music; music related; nursing; nutrition science; nutrition studies; painting; paleontology; philosophy; physical education; physical sciences; physics; political science; pre-law; psychology; public administration; public relations; quantitative economics; radio/television broadcasting; real estate; recreation/leisure studies; religious studies; Russian; Russian/Slavic studies; science education; sculpture; social science education; social sciences; social sciences and history related; social work; sociology; Spanish; Spanish language education; speech/rhetorical studies; teacher education, specific programs related; technical education; theater arts/drama; theoretical/mathematical physics; travel/tourism management; urban studies; women's studies; zoology.
Academic Programs *Special study options:* academic remediation for entering students, advanced placement credit, distance learning, double majors, English as a second language, honors programs, independent study, internships, off-campus study, part-time degree program, services for LD students, student-designed majors, study abroad, summer session for credit. *ROTC:* Army (b), Navy (b), Air Force (b).
Library Malcolm A. Love Library with 1.3 million titles, 5,092 serial subscriptions, 23,246 audiovisual materials, an OPAC, a Web page.
Computers on Campus 400 computers available on campus for general student use. A campuswide network can be accessed from student residence rooms and from off campus. Internet access, online (class) registration, at least one staffed computer lab available.
Student Life *Housing Options:* coed, disabled students. *Activities and Organizations:* drama/theater group, student-run newspaper, radio and television station, choral group, marching band, American Marketing Association, Associated Students, Student Accounting Society, Residence Hall Association, MECHA, national fraternities, national sororities. *Campus security:* 24-hour emergency

San Diego State University (continued)
response devices and patrols, student patrols, late-night transport/escort service. *Student Services:* health clinic, personal/psychological counseling, women's center.

Athletics Member NCAA. All Division I except football (Division I-A). *Intercollegiate sports:* baseball M(s), basketball M(s)/W(s), cross-country running W(s), golf M(s)/W(s), soccer M(s)/W(s), softball W(s), swimming W(s), tennis M(s)/W(s), track and field W(s), volleyball M(s)/W(s), water polo W(s). *Intramural sports:* basketball M/W, bowling M/W, crew M/W(c), football M/W, golf M/W, ice hockey M(c), lacrosse M(c), racquetball M/W, rugby M(c), sailing M(c)/W(c), skiing (downhill) M(c)/W(c), soccer M/W, softball M/W, table tennis M/W, volleyball M/W, wrestling M.

Standardized Tests *Required:* SAT I or ACT (for admission).

Costs (2001–02) *Tuition:* state resident $0 full-time; nonresident $5904 full-time, $246 per unit part-time. Full-time tuition and fees vary according to location. Part-time tuition and fees vary according to location. *Required fees:* $1776 full-time, $588 per term part-time. *Room and board:* $7970; room only: $4622. Room and board charges vary according to board plan and housing facility. *Payment plan:* installment. *Waivers:* senior citizens and employees or children of employees.

Financial Aid Of all full-time matriculated undergraduates who enrolled in 2001, 12900 applied for aid, 9800 were judged to have need, 3500 had their need fully met. In 2001, 260 non-need-based awards were made. *Average percent of need met:* 87%. *Average financial aid package:* $8000. *Average need-based loan:* $3700. *Average need-based gift aid:* $4200. *Average non-need based aid:* $2000. *Average indebtedness upon graduation:* $13,000.

Applying *Options:* electronic application, early action. *Application fee:* $55. *Required:* high school transcript, minimum 2.0 GPA. *Application deadline:* 11/30 (freshmen). *Notification:* 3/1 (freshmen), 1/15 (early action).

Admissions Contact Prospective Student Center, San Diego State University, 5500 Campanile Drive, San Diego, CA 92182-7455. *Phone:* 619-594-6886. *Fax:* 619-594-1250. *E-mail:* admissions@sdsu.edu.

SAN FRANCISCO ART INSTITUTE
San Francisco, California

- **Independent** comprehensive, founded 1871
- **Calendar** semesters
- **Degrees** certificates, bachelor's, master's, and postbachelor's certificates
- **Urban** 3-acre campus
- **Endowment** $8.3 million
- **Coed,** 488 undergraduate students, 83% full-time, 56% women, 44% men
- **Moderately difficult** entrance level, 82% of applicants were admitted

The Interdisciplinary Core Program offers students with no previous college experience an intensive introduction to the visual arts. A structured program of studio practice and academic study, the Core Program also provides sufficient flexibility for the individual creative freedom for which SFAI has long been known. Most important, the program allows young artists to share their experiences and ideas with their peers.

Undergraduates 407 full-time, 81 part-time. Students come from 24 states and territories, 18 other countries, 33% are from out of state, 2% African American, 6% Asian American or Pacific Islander, 8% Hispanic American, 2% Native American, 11% international, 24% transferred in. *Retention:* 62% of 2001 full-time freshmen returned.

Freshmen *Admission:* 220 applied, 181 admitted, 66 enrolled.

Faculty *Total:* 115, 30% full-time. *Student/faculty ratio:* 8:1.

Majors Art; ceramic arts; drawing; film studies; fine/studio arts; painting; photography; sculpture.

Academic Programs *Special study options:* academic remediation for entering students, accelerated degree program, adult/continuing education programs, advanced placement credit, double majors, English as a second language, external degree program, independent study, internships, off-campus study, part-time degree program, services for LD students, study abroad, summer session for credit.

Library Anne Bremer Memorial Library with 35,500 titles, 210 serial subscriptions, 121,000 audiovisual materials.

Computers on Campus 39 computers available on campus for general student use. Internet access, at least one staffed computer lab available.

Student Life *Housing:* college housing not available. *Activities and Organizations:* Student Senate. *Campus security:* 24-hour patrols, security cameras. *Student Services:* personal/psychological counseling.

Standardized Tests *Required:* SAT I or ACT (for admission).

Costs (2002–03) *Tuition:* $22,176 full-time, $924 per unit part-time. Part-time tuition and fees vary according to course load. *Payment plan:* installment. *Waivers:* employees or children of employees.

Financial Aid Of all full-time matriculated undergraduates who enrolled in 2001, 316 applied for aid, 291 were judged to have need, 19 had their need fully met. 282 Federal Work-Study jobs. In 2001, 70 non-need-based awards were made. *Average percent of need met:* 72%. *Average financial aid package:* $18,480. *Average need-based loan:* $4638. *Average need-based gift aid:* $11,821. *Average indebtedness upon graduation:* $23,936.

Applying *Options:* deferred entrance. *Application fee:* $50. *Required:* essay or personal statement, high school transcript, portfolio. *Recommended:* interview. *Application deadline:* 8/27 (freshmen), rolling (transfers). *Notification:* continuous until 4/15 (freshmen).

Admissions Contact Mark Takiguchi, Director of Admissions, San Francisco Art Institute, 800 Chestnut Street, San Francisco, CA 94133. *Phone:* 415-749-4500. *Toll-free phone:* 800-345-SFAI. *E-mail:* admissions@sfai.edu.

SAN FRANCISCO CONSERVATORY OF MUSIC
San Francisco, California

- **Independent** comprehensive, founded 1917
- **Calendar** semesters
- **Degrees** diplomas, bachelor's, master's, and post-master's certificates
- **Urban** 2-acre campus
- **Endowment** $30.3 million
- **Coed,** 146 undergraduate students, 94% full-time, 56% women, 44% men
- **Moderately difficult** entrance level, 63% of applicants were admitted

Undergraduates 137 full-time, 9 part-time. Students come from 28 states and territories, 16 other countries, 49% are from out of state, 3% African American, 12% Asian American or Pacific Islander, 7% Hispanic American, 1% Native American, 20% international, 13% transferred in. *Retention:* 86% of 2001 full-time freshmen returned.

Freshmen *Admission:* 116 applied, 73 admitted, 21 enrolled. *Average high school GPA:* 3.34. *Test scores:* SAT verbal scores over 500: 73%; SAT math scores over 500: 80%; SAT verbal scores over 600: 46%; SAT math scores over 600: 27%; SAT verbal scores over 700: 9%; SAT math scores over 700: 7%.

Faculty *Total:* 94, 26% full-time, 21% with terminal degrees. *Student/faculty ratio:* 6:1.

Majors Music; music (general performance); music (piano and organ performance); music theory and composition; music (voice and choral/opera performance); stringed instruments; wind/percussion instruments.

Academic Programs *Special study options:* academic remediation for entering students, advanced placement credit, independent study, part-time degree program.

Library Conservatory Library with 36,821 titles, 80 serial subscriptions, 14,614 audiovisual materials, an OPAC.

Computers on Campus 7 computers available on campus for general student use. Internet access available.

Student Life *Housing:* college housing not available. *Activities and Organizations:* choral group. *Campus security:* late-night transport/escort service. *Student Services:* health clinic, personal/psychological counseling.

Standardized Tests *Required:* SAT I or ACT (for admission). *Recommended:* SAT I (for admission).

Costs (2001–02) *Tuition:* $20,500 full-time, $905 per credit part-time. Part-time tuition and fees vary according to course load. *Required fees:* $280 full-time, $140 per term part-time. *Payment plan:* installment. *Waivers:* employees or children of employees.

Financial Aid Of all full-time matriculated undergraduates who enrolled in 2001, 105 applied for aid, 91 were judged to have need, 35 had their need fully met. In 2001, 4 non-need-based awards were made. *Average percent of need met:* 71%. *Average financial aid package:* $14,235. *Average need-based loan:* $5542. *Average need-based gift aid:* $10,254. *Average non-need based aid:* $4175. *Average indebtedness upon graduation:* $20,835.

Applying *Options:* early admission. *Application fee:* $70. *Required:* high school transcript, 2 letters of recommendation, audition. *Application deadlines:* 2/1 (freshmen), 2/1 (transfers). *Notification:* 4/1 (freshmen).

Admissions Contact Susan Dean, Director of Admissions, San Francisco Conservatory of Music, 1201 Ortega Street, San Francisco, CA 94122-4411. *Phone:* 415-759-3431. *Fax:* 415-759-3499. *E-mail:* admit@sfcm.edu.

SAN FRANCISCO STATE UNIVERSITY

San Francisco, California

- **State-supported** comprehensive, founded 1899, part of California State University System
- **Calendar** semesters
- **Degrees** certificates, bachelor's, master's, doctoral, and postbachelor's certificates
- **Urban** 90-acre campus
- **Endowment** $3.6 million
- **Coed,** 20,166 undergraduate students, 72% full-time, 59% women, 41% men
- **Moderately difficult** entrance level, 61% of applicants were admitted

Undergraduates 14,521 full-time, 5,645 part-time. Students come from 48 states and territories, 113 other countries, 1% are from out of state, 6% African American, 33% Asian American or Pacific Islander, 13% Hispanic American, 0.6% Native American, 7% international, 15% transferred in, 7% live on campus. *Retention:* 75% of 2001 full-time freshmen returned.

Freshmen *Admission:* 11,900 applied, 7,266 admitted, 1,987 enrolled. *Average high school GPA:* 3.02. *Test scores:* SAT verbal scores over 500: 46%; SAT math scores over 500: 49%; ACT scores over 18: 72%; SAT verbal scores over 600: 16%; SAT math scores over 600: 14%; ACT scores over 24: 26%; SAT verbal scores over 700: 1%; SAT math scores over 700: 2%; ACT scores over 30: 2%.

Faculty *Total:* 1,712, 44% full-time, 46% with terminal degrees. *Student/faculty ratio:* 20:1.

Majors Accounting; African-American studies; American studies; anthropology; applied mathematics; art; astronomy; astrophysics; atmospheric sciences; biochemistry; biological/physical sciences; biology; botany; business administration; business marketing and marketing management; cell biology; chemistry; Chinese; civil engineering; classics; clothing/textiles; comparative literature; computer science; creative writing; criminal justice/law enforcement administration; dance; dietetics; ecology; economics; electrical engineering; English; film studies; finance; food products retailing; French; geography; geology; German; health education; health science; history; home economics; hospitality management; humanities; industrial arts; industrial design; information sciences/systems; interior design; international business; international relations; Italian; Japanese; journalism; labor/personnel relations; liberal arts and sciences/liberal studies; literature; marine biology; mathematical statistics; mathematics; mechanical engineering; Mexican-American studies; microbiology/bacteriology; molecular biology; music; nursing; philosophy; physical education; physical sciences; physics; physiology; political science; psychology; radio/television broadcasting; real estate; recreation/leisure studies; religious studies; retail management; Russian; social sciences; social work; sociology; Spanish; speech-language pathology/audiology; speech/rhetorical studies; technical/business writing; theater arts/drama; trade/industrial education; transportation technology; urban studies; women's studies; zoology.

Academic Programs *Special study options:* academic remediation for entering students, accelerated degree program, adult/continuing education programs, advanced placement credit, cooperative education, double majors, English as a second language, honors programs, independent study, internships, off-campus study, part-time degree program, services for LD students, student-designed majors, study abroad, summer session for credit. *ROTC:* Navy (c), Air Force (c).

Library J. Paul Leonard Library plus 2 others with 761,760 titles, 5,186 serial subscriptions, 71,675 audiovisual materials, an OPAC, a Web page.

Computers on Campus 1474 computers available on campus for general student use. A campuswide network can be accessed from student residence rooms and from off campus. At least one staffed computer lab available.

Student Life *Housing Options:* coed, disabled students. *Activities and Organizations:* drama/theater group, student-run newspaper, radio and television station, choral group, African Student Union, Asian Student Union, Laraza Student Organization, Filipino Collegial Endeavor, Sigma Sigma Sigma, national fraternities, national sororities. *Campus security:* 24-hour emergency response devices and patrols, student patrols, late-night transport/escort service, controlled dormitory access. *Student Services:* health clinic, personal/psychological counseling, women's center, legal services.

Athletics Member NCAA. All Division II. *Intercollegiate sports:* baseball M(s)/W(s), basketball M(s)/W(s), cross-country running M(s)/W(s), soccer M(s)/W(s), softball W(s), swimming M(s)/W(s), track and field M(s)/W(s), volleyball W(s), wrestling M(s). *Intramural sports:* basketball M/W, swimming M/W, volleyball M/W, wrestling M.

Standardized Tests *Required for some:* SAT I or ACT (for admission).

Costs (2002–03) *Tuition:* state resident $1428 full-time; nonresident $5904 full-time. *Required fees:* $398 full-time. *Room and board:* $6930; room only: $4268.

Financial Aid Of all full-time matriculated undergraduates who enrolled in 2001, 8369 applied for aid, 7474 were judged to have need, 2366 had their need fully met. *Average percent of need met:* 76%. *Average financial aid package:* $8154. *Average need-based loan:* $5806. *Average need-based gift aid:* $4696. *Average indebtedness upon graduation:* $29,021.

Applying *Application fee:* $55. *Required:* high school transcript. *Application deadline:* rolling (freshmen). *Notification:* continuous (freshmen).

Admissions Contact Ms. Patricia Wade, Admissions Officer, San Francisco State University, 1600 Holloway Avenue, Administration 154, San Francisco, CA 94132. *Phone:* 415-338-2037. *Fax:* 415-338-7196. *E-mail:* ugadmit@sfsu.edu.

SAN JOSE CHRISTIAN COLLEGE

San Jose, California

- **Independent nondenominational** 4-year, founded 1939
- **Calendar** quarters
- **Degrees** certificates, associate, and bachelor's
- **Urban** 9-acre campus
- **Coed,** 312 undergraduate students
- **Noncompetitive** entrance level, 35% of applicants were admitted

Undergraduates Students come from 7 states and territories, 7 other countries, 7% African American, 14% Asian American or Pacific Islander, 9% Hispanic American, 0.4% Native American, 13% international, 25% live on campus. *Retention:* 62% of 2001 full-time freshmen returned.

Freshmen *Admission:* 79 applied, 28 admitted. *Average high school GPA:* 2.83. *Test scores:* SAT verbal scores over 500: 38%; SAT math scores over 500: 35%; ACT scores over 18: 35%; SAT verbal scores over 600: 10%; SAT math scores over 600: 8%.

Faculty *Total:* 66, 18% full-time, 30% with terminal degrees. *Student/faculty ratio:* 18:1.

Majors Biblical studies; divinity/ministry; education; music; pastoral counseling; religious studies; theology.

Academic Programs *Special study options:* academic remediation for entering students, accelerated degree program, advanced placement credit, cooperative education, double majors, English as a second language, internships, part-time degree program, services for LD students, summer session for credit.

Library San Jose Christian College Memorial Library with 31,689 titles, 157 serial subscriptions.

Computers on Campus 12 computers available on campus for general student use. A campuswide network can be accessed from off campus. Internet access, at least one staffed computer lab available.

Student Life *Housing:* on-campus residence required through sophomore year. *Options:* men-only, women-only. *Activities and Organizations:* drama/theater group, choral group, Missions Club, student leadership, Drama Team, music ensemble. *Campus security:* student patrols, late-night transport/escort service, day and evening patrols by trained security personnel. *Student Services:* personal/psychological counseling.

Athletics Member NSCAA. *Intercollegiate sports:* basketball M/W, soccer M, volleyball W. *Intramural sports:* basketball M/W, football M/W, softball M/W, tennis M/W, volleyball M/W.

Standardized Tests *Required:* SAT I or ACT (for admission).

Costs (2001–02) *Comprehensive fee:* $16,461 includes full-time tuition ($10,176), mandatory fees ($810), and room and board ($5475). Full-time tuition and fees vary according to program. Part-time tuition: $212 per quarter hour. Part-time tuition and fees vary according to program. *Required fees:* $175 per term part-time. *Room and board:* Room and board charges vary according to board plan. *Payment plan:* deferred payment. *Waivers:* employees or children of employees.

Financial Aid Of all full-time matriculated undergraduates who enrolled in 2001, 226 applied for aid, 226 were judged to have need. 18 Federal Work-Study jobs (averaging $1792). *Average financial aid package:* $6244. *Average need-based loan:* $1737. *Average need-based gift aid:* $1514.

Applying *Options:* deferred entrance. *Application fee:* $30. *Required:* essay or personal statement, high school transcript, minimum 2.0 GPA, 2 letters of recommendation, letter of introduction. *Application deadlines:* 8/1 (freshmen), 8/1 (transfers). *Notification:* continuous (freshmen).

Admissions Contact Ms. Stephany Haskins, Admissions Counselor, San Jose Christian College, San Jose, CA. *Phone:* 408-278-4333. *Toll-free phone:* 800-355-7522. *Fax:* 408-293-7352. *E-mail:* rjones@sjchristian.edu.

San Jose State University
San Jose, California

- **State-supported** comprehensive, founded 1857, part of California State University System
- **Calendar** semesters
- **Degrees** bachelor's and master's
- **Urban** 104-acre campus
- **Endowment** $2.4 million
- **Coed,** 22,241 undergraduate students, 70% full-time, 51% women, 49% men
- **Moderately difficult** entrance level, 66% of applicants were admitted

Undergraduates 15,477 full-time, 6,764 part-time. Students come from 43 states and territories, 104 other countries, 80% are from out of state, 4% African American, 40% Asian American or Pacific Islander, 15% Hispanic American, 0.6% Native American, 4% international, 12% transferred in, 10% live on campus.

Freshmen *Admission:* 13,522 applied, 8,867 admitted, 2,768 enrolled. *Average high school GPA:* 3.11. *Test scores:* SAT verbal scores over 500: 37%; SAT math scores over 500: 57%; SAT verbal scores over 600: 9%; SAT math scores over 600: 19%; SAT verbal scores over 700: 1%; SAT math scores over 700: 2%.

Faculty *Total:* 1,622, 48% full-time.

Majors Accounting; adapted physical education; advertising; aerospace engineering; African-American studies; American studies; anthropology; applied mathematics; art; art history; athletic training/sports medicine; atmospheric sciences; aviation/airway science; aviation management; aviation technology; behavioral sciences; biochemistry; biology; broadcast journalism; business administration; business marketing and marketing management; cartography; chemical engineering; chemistry; child care/development; Chinese; civil engineering; computer engineering; computer science; criminal justice/law enforcement administration; criminology; dance; developmental/child psychology; dietetics; East Asian studies; ecology; economics; electrical engineering; engineering; English; entomology; environmental health; environmental science; environmental technology; European studies; exercise sciences; film studies; finance; fine/studio arts; food sciences; food services technology; French; geography; geology; geophysics/seismology; German; graphic design/commercial art/illustration; health/physical education; health science; health services administration; history; hospitality management; humanities; human resources management; industrial design; industrial/manufacturing engineering; industrial technology; interior design; international business; Japanese; journalism; liberal arts and sciences/liberal studies; linguistics; management information systems/business data processing; marine biology; materials engineering; mathematical statistics; mathematics; mechanical engineering; microbiology/bacteriology; molecular biology; music; music (general performance); music teacher education; music theory and composition; music (voice and choral/opera performance); natural sciences; nuclear technology; nursing; nutrition science; occupational therapy; oceanography; operations management; philosophy; photography; physical education; physical sciences; physics; physiology; political science; psychology; public administration; public policy analysis; public relations; radio/television broadcasting; recreational therapy; recreation/leisure facilities management; recreation/leisure studies; religious studies; social sciences; social work; sociology; Spanish; speech-language pathology/audiology; speech/rhetorical studies; technical/business writing; theater arts/drama; visual/performing arts.

Academic Programs *Special study options:* academic remediation for entering students, accelerated degree program, adult/continuing education programs, advanced placement credit, cooperative education, distance learning, double majors, English as a second language, honors programs, independent study, internships, off-campus study, part-time degree program, services for LD students, student-designed majors, study abroad, summer session for credit. *ROTC:* Army (b), Air Force (b).

Library Robert D. Clark Library plus 1 other with 1.1 million titles, 2,504 serial subscriptions, 37,146 audiovisual materials, an OPAC, a Web page.

Computers on Campus 993 computers available on campus for general student use. A campuswide network can be accessed from student residence rooms and from off campus. Internet access, online (class) registration, at least one staffed computer lab available.

Student Life *Housing Options:* coed. *Activities and Organizations:* drama/theater group, student-run newspaper, radio station, choral group, marching band, national fraternities, national sororities. *Campus security:* 24-hour emergency response devices and patrols, student patrols, late-night transport/escort service. *Student Services:* health clinic, personal/psychological counseling, women's center.

Athletics Member NCAA. All Division I except football (Division I-A). *Intercollegiate sports:* baseball M(s), basketball M(s)/W(s), cross-country running M(s)/W(s), golf M(s)/W(s), gymnastics W(s), soccer M(s)/W(s), softball W, swimming W(s), tennis W(s), volleyball W(s), water polo W(s). *Intramural sports:* archery M/W, badminton M/W, baseball M, basketball M/W, bowling M/W, cross-country running M(c)/W(c), field hockey W(c), football M, ice hockey M(c), lacrosse M(c), racquetball M/W, rugby M(c), soccer M/W, softball M/W, tennis M/W, track and field M(c)/W(c), volleyball M(c)/W, water polo M/W.

Standardized Tests *Required for some:* SAT I or ACT (for admission).

Costs (2002–03) *Tuition:* state resident $0 full-time; nonresident $5904 full-time, $246 per unit part-time. Part-time tuition and fees vary according to course load. *Required fees:* $1912 full-time, $651 per term part-time. *Room and board:* $7220; room only: $4240. Room and board charges vary according to board plan. *Payment plan:* installment. *Waivers:* senior citizens and employees or children of employees.

Financial Aid Of all full-time matriculated undergraduates who enrolled in 2001, 7681 applied for aid, 6419 were judged to have need, 1718 had their need fully met. 660 Federal Work-Study jobs (averaging $2322). *Average percent of need met:* 77%. *Average financial aid package:* $7573. *Average need-based loan:* $3316. *Average need-based gift aid:* $4898. *Average non-need based aid:* $2081. *Average indebtedness upon graduation:* $10,428.

Applying *Options:* common application, electronic application. *Application fee:* $55. *Required:* high school transcript. *Application deadline:* rolling (freshmen), rolling (transfers). *Notification:* continuous (freshmen).

Admissions Contact Mr. John Bradbury, Interim Director of Admissions, San Jose State University, One Washington Square, San Jose, CA 95192-0001. *Phone:* 408-924-2000. *Fax:* 408-924-2050. *E-mail:* contact@sjsu.edu.

Santa Clara University
Santa Clara, California

- **Independent Roman Catholic (Jesuit)** university, founded 1851
- **Calendar** quarters
- **Degrees** bachelor's, master's, doctoral, first professional, post-master's, and postbachelor's certificates
- **Suburban** 104-acre campus with easy access to San Francisco and San Jose
- **Endowment** $448.9 million
- **Coed,** 4,279 undergraduate students, 97% full-time, 54% women, 46% men
- **Moderately difficult** entrance level, 63% of applicants were admitted

Undergraduates 4,151 full-time, 128 part-time. Students come from 48 states and territories, 54 other countries, 31% are from out of state, 2% African American, 19% Asian American or Pacific Islander, 14% Hispanic American, 0.4% Native American, 3% international, 4% transferred in, 47% live on campus. *Retention:* 92% of 2001 full-time freshmen returned.

Freshmen *Admission:* 6,048 applied, 3,824 admitted, 1,018 enrolled. *Average high school GPA:* 3.38. *Test scores:* SAT verbal scores over 500: 89%; SAT math scores over 500: 95%; ACT scores over 18: 100%; SAT verbal scores over 600: 47%; SAT math scores over 600: 62%; ACT scores over 24: 81%; SAT verbal scores over 700: 8%; SAT math scores over 700: 14%; ACT scores over 30: 15%.

Faculty *Total:* 623, 66% full-time. *Student/faculty ratio:* 12:1.

Majors Accounting; anthropology; art; art history; biological/physical sciences; biology; business administration; business economics; business marketing and marketing management; chemistry; civil engineering; classics; communications; computer engineering; computer science; economics; electrical engineering; engineering; engineering physics; English; finance; French; Greek (ancient and medieval); history; interdisciplinary studies; Italian; Latin (ancient and medieval); liberal arts and sciences/liberal studies; management information systems/business data processing; mathematics; mechanical engineering; music; philosophy; physics; political science; psychology; religious studies; sociology; Spanish; theater arts/drama.

Academic Programs *Special study options:* advanced placement credit, cooperative education, double majors, honors programs, independent study, internships, student-designed majors, study abroad, summer session for credit. *ROTC:* Army (b), Air Force (c).

Library Orradre Library plus 1 other with 454,470 titles, 8,919 serial subscriptions, 12,570 audiovisual materials, an OPAC, a Web page.

Computers on Campus 535 computers available on campus for general student use. A campuswide network can be accessed from student residence rooms and from off campus. At least one staffed computer lab available.

Student Life *Housing Options:* coed. *Activities and Organizations:* drama/theater group, student-run newspaper, radio and television station, choral group, Community Action Program, Associated Students, Activities Programming Board, Multicultural Programming Board, Residence Hall Association. *Campus security:* 24-hour emergency response devices and patrols, late-night transport/escort service, controlled dormitory access. *Student Services:* health clinic, personal/psychological counseling, legal services.

Athletics Member NCAA. All Division I. *Intercollegiate sports:* baseball M(s), basketball M(s)/W(s), crew M/W, cross-country running M(s)/W(s), field hockey W(c), golf M(s)/W(s), lacrosse M(c)/W(c), rugby M(c)/W(c), soccer M(s)/W(s), softball W(s), tennis M(s)/W(s), volleyball M(c)/W(s), water polo M(s). *Intramural sports:* basketball M/W, football M/W, racquetball M/W, soccer M/W, softball M/W, swimming M/W, tennis M/W, volleyball M/W, weight lifting M/W.

Standardized Tests *Required:* SAT I or ACT (for admission).

Costs (2001–02) *Comprehensive fee:* $31,008 includes full-time tuition ($22,572) and room and board ($8436). Full-time tuition and fees vary according to program and student level. Part-time tuition: $2380 per course. Part-time tuition and fees vary according to course load and student level. *Room and board:* College room only: $5301. Room and board charges vary according to board plan and housing facility. *Payment plans:* tuition prepayment, installment, deferred payment. *Waivers:* employees or children of employees.

Financial Aid Of all full-time matriculated undergraduates who enrolled in 2001, 3097 applied for aid, 2791 were judged to have need, 900 had their need fully met. 417 Federal Work-Study jobs (averaging $1314). 5 State and other part-time jobs (averaging $761). In 2001, 645 non-need-based awards were made. *Average percent of need met:* 79%. *Average financial aid package:* $16,715. *Average need-based loan:* $6100. *Average need-based gift aid:* $14,055. *Average non-need based aid:* $3854. *Average indebtedness upon graduation:* $24,810.

Applying *Options:* common application, electronic application, deferred entrance. *Application fee:* $50. *Required:* essay or personal statement, high school transcript, 1 letter of recommendation. *Recommended:* interview. *Application deadlines:* 1/15 (freshmen), 5/15 (transfers). *Notification:* continuous until 4/1 (freshmen).

Admissions Contact Ms. Sandra Hayes, Dean of Undergraduate Admissions, Santa Clara University, 500 El Camino Real, Santa Clara, CA 95053. *Phone:* 408-554-4700. *Fax:* 408-554-5255. *E-mail:* ugadmissions@scu.edu.

SCRIPPS COLLEGE
Claremont, California

- **Independent** 4-year, founded 1926, part of The Claremont Colleges Consortium
- **Calendar** semesters
- **Degrees** bachelor's and postbachelor's certificates
- **Suburban** 30-acre campus with easy access to Los Angeles
- **Endowment** $184.5 million
- **Women only,** 798 undergraduate students, 99% full-time
- **Very difficult** entrance level, 64% of applicants were admitted

Undergraduates 788 full-time, 10 part-time. Students come from 41 states and territories, 15 other countries, 52% are from out of state, 3% African American, 13% Asian American or Pacific Islander, 6% Hispanic American, 0.5% Native American, 2% international, 3% transferred in, 92% live on campus. *Retention:* 77% of 2001 full-time freshmen returned.

Freshmen *Admission:* 201 enrolled. *Average high school GPA:* 3.70. *Test scores:* SAT verbal scores over 500: 98%; SAT math scores over 500: 96%; ACT scores over 18: 100%; SAT verbal scores over 600: 80%; SAT math scores over 600: 64%; ACT scores over 24: 90%; SAT verbal scores over 700: 27%; SAT math scores over 700: 14%; ACT scores over 30: 30%.

Faculty *Total:* 90, 68% full-time, 84% with terminal degrees. *Student/faculty ratio:* 11:1.

Majors African-American studies; American studies; anthropology; art; art history; Asian-American studies; Asian studies; biochemistry; biology; chemistry; Chinese; classics; computer science; dance; East Asian studies; economics; English; environmental science; European studies; film/video and photographic arts related; fine/studio arts; foreign languages/literatures; French; geology; German; Hispanic-American studies; history; international relations; Italian; Japanese; Judaic studies; Latin American studies; Latin (ancient and medieval); legal studies; linguistics; mathematics; Mexican-American studies; modern languages; molecular biology; music; neuroscience; philosophy; physics; physiological psychology/psychobiology; political science; psychology; religious studies; Russian; science/technology and society; sociology; Spanish; theater arts/drama; visual and performing arts related; women's studies.

Academic Programs *Special study options:* accelerated degree program, advanced placement credit, double majors, honors programs, independent study, internships, off-campus study, part-time degree program, student-designed majors, study abroad. *ROTC:* Army (c), Air Force (c). *Unusual degree programs:* 3-2 business administration with Claremont Graduate School; engineering with Stanford University, University of Southern California, Harvey Mudd College, University of California, Berkeley, Washington University in St. Louis, Columbia University, Boston University; public policy, religion, government, international studies, economics, philosophy with Claremont Graduate University.

Library Honnold Library plus 4 others with 1.4 million titles, 4,321 serial subscriptions, 606 audiovisual materials, an OPAC, a Web page.

Computers on Campus 72 computers available on campus for general student use. A campuswide network can be accessed from student residence rooms and from off campus. Internet access, at least one staffed computer lab available.

Student Life *Housing:* on-campus residence required for freshman year. *Options:* women-only, disabled students. *Activities and Organizations:* drama/theater group, student-run newspaper, radio station, choral group, College Council, Asian/Black/Latina Clubs, National Organization for Women, Sexual Assault Task Force, Family. *Campus security:* 24-hour emergency response devices and patrols, late-night transport/escort service, controlled dormitory access. *Student Services:* health clinic, personal/psychological counseling, women's center.

Athletics Member NCAA. All Division III. *Intercollegiate sports:* basketball W, cross-country running W, fencing W(c), golf W, lacrosse W(c), rugby W(c), skiing (downhill) W(c), soccer W, softball W, swimming W, tennis W, track and field W, volleyball W, water polo W. *Intramural sports:* basketball W, football W, soccer W, softball W, volleyball W, water polo W.

Standardized Tests *Required:* SAT I or ACT (for admission).

Costs (2001–02) *Comprehensive fee:* $32,500 includes full-time tuition ($24,268), mandatory fees ($132), and room and board ($8100). Full-time tuition and fees vary according to program. Part-time tuition: $3050 per course. Part-time tuition and fees vary according to program. *Required fees:* $132 per year part-time. *Room and board:* College room only: $4400. Room and board charges vary according to board plan. *Payment plan:* installment. *Waivers:* employees or children of employees.

Financial Aid Of all full-time matriculated undergraduates who enrolled in 2001, 444 applied for aid, 366 were judged to have need, 366 had their need fully met. 306 Federal Work-Study jobs (averaging $1705). In 2001, 53 non-need-based awards were made. *Average percent of need met:* 100%. *Average financial aid package:* $21,731. *Average need-based loan:* $4141. *Average need-based gift aid:* $17,417. *Average non-need based aid:* $12,324. *Average indebtedness upon graduation:* $13,394.

Applying *Options:* common application, electronic application, early decision, deferred entrance. *Application fee:* $50. *Required:* essay or personal statement, high school transcript, 3 letters of recommendation, graded writing sample. *Recommended:* minimum 3.0 GPA, interview. *Application deadlines:* 2/1 (freshmen), 4/1 (transfers). *Early decision:* 11/1 (for plan 1), 1/1 (for plan 2). *Notification:* 4/1 (freshmen), 12/15 (early decision plan 1), 2/15 (early decision plan 2).

Admissions Contact Ms. Patricia F. Goldsmith, Dean of Admission and Financial Aid, Scripps College, Claremont, CA 91711-3948. *Phone:* 909-621-8149. *Toll-free phone:* 800-770-1333. *Fax:* 909-607-7508. *E-mail:* admission@scrippscol.edu.

SHASTA BIBLE COLLEGE
Redding, California

- **Independent nondenominational** 4-year, founded 1971
- **Calendar** semesters
- **Degrees** certificates, diplomas, associate, bachelor's, and master's
- **Small-town** 25-acre campus
- **Endowment** $1.1 million
- **Coed,** 91 undergraduate students, 64% full-time, 48% women, 52% men
- **Noncompetitive** entrance level, 100% of applicants were admitted

Undergraduates 58 full-time, 33 part-time. Students come from 5 states and territories, 1 other country, 3% are from out of state, 30% transferred in. *Retention:* 60% of 2001 full-time freshmen returned.

Freshmen *Admission:* 4 applied, 4 admitted, 4 enrolled. *Average high school GPA:* 3.00.

Faculty *Total:* 28, 21% full-time, 82% with terminal degrees. *Student/faculty ratio:* 11:1.

Majors Biblical studies; education; education administration.

Academic Programs *Special study options:* academic remediation for entering students, adult/continuing education programs, distance learning, double majors, independent study, part-time degree program.

Library The Library plus 1 other with 30,321 titles, 103 serial subscriptions.

Computers on Campus 6 computers available on campus for general student use.

Student Life *Housing Options:* men-only, women-only. *Activities and Organizations:* student-run newspaper. *Student Services:* personal/psychological counseling, women's center.

Costs (2002–03) *Tuition:* $5600 full-time, $175 per unit part-time. *Required fees:* $270 full-time, $220 per year part-time. *Room only:* $1575.

Financial Aid Of all full-time matriculated undergraduates who enrolled in 2001, 56 applied for aid, 20 were judged to have need. 8 Federal Work-Study jobs

Shasta Bible College (continued)
(averaging $1563). 12 State and other part-time jobs (averaging $1235). *Average percent of need met:* 67%. *Average financial aid package:* $2677. *Average need-based gift aid:* $1000.

Applying *Options:* common application. *Application fee:* $35. *Required:* essay or personal statement, high school transcript, 4 letters of recommendation.

Admissions Contact Ms. Dawn Rodriguez, Registrar, Shasta Bible College, 2980 Hartnell Avenue, Redding, CA 96002. *Phone:* 530-221-4275. *Toll-free phone:* 800-800-45BC (in-state); 800-800-6929 (out-of-state). *Fax:* 530-221-6929. *E-mail:* ggunn@shasta.edu.

SIMPSON COLLEGE AND GRADUATE SCHOOL
Redding, California

- **Independent** comprehensive, founded 1921, affiliated with The Christian and Missionary Alliance
- **Calendar** 4-4-1
- **Degrees** certificates, associate, bachelor's, and master's
- **Suburban** 60-acre campus
- **Endowment** $2.6 million
- **Coed,** 146 undergraduate students, 100% full-time, 67% women, 33% men
- **Moderately difficult** entrance level, 63% of applicants were admitted

Undergraduates 146 full-time. Students come from 28 states and territories, 7 other countries, 34% are from out of state, 0.5% African American, 5% Asian American or Pacific Islander, 5% Hispanic American, 1% Native American, 1% international, 60% transferred in, 88% live on campus. *Retention:* 72% of 2001 full-time freshmen returned.

Freshmen *Admission:* 663 applied, 419 admitted, 146 enrolled. *Average high school GPA:* 3.36. *Test scores:* SAT verbal scores over 500: 56%; SAT math scores over 500: 44%; ACT scores over 18: 86%; SAT verbal scores over 600: 16%; SAT math scores over 600: 14%; ACT scores over 24: 30%; SAT verbal scores over 700: 1%; SAT math scores over 700: 1%; ACT scores over 30: 4%.

Faculty *Total:* 75, 53% full-time, 41% with terminal degrees. *Student/faculty ratio:* 19:1.

Majors Biblical studies; business administration; communications; education; elementary education; English; English education; general studies; history; human resources management; liberal arts and sciences/liberal studies; mathematics; mathematics education; missionary studies; music; music teacher education; pastoral counseling; psychology; religious education; religious music; secondary education; social science education; social sciences.

Academic Programs *Special study options:* accelerated degree program, adult/continuing education programs, advanced placement credit, distance learning, double majors, English as a second language, independent study, internships, off-campus study, part-time degree program, services for LD students, student-designed majors, study abroad, summer session for credit.

Library Start-Kilgour Memorial Library with 66,103 titles, 316 serial subscriptions, 1,139 audiovisual materials, an OPAC, a Web page.

Computers on Campus 26 computers available on campus for general student use. A campuswide network can be accessed from student residence rooms and from off campus. Internet access, at least one staffed computer lab available.

Student Life *Housing:* on-campus residence required through junior year. *Options:* men-only, women-only, disabled students. *Activities and Organizations:* drama/theater group, student-run newspaper, choral group, Student Senate, Missions Committee, psychology club, drama club, Spiritual Action Committee. *Campus security:* 24-hour emergency response devices, student patrols, controlled dormitory access, late night security patrols by trained personnel. *Student Services:* health clinic, personal/psychological counseling.

Athletics Member NAIA, NCCAA. *Intercollegiate sports:* baseball M, basketball M/W, soccer M/W, softball W, volleyball W. *Intramural sports:* badminton M, baseball M(c), basketball M/W, cross-country running M(c)/W(c), football M/W, golf M(c), soccer M, table tennis M/W, tennis M(c)/W(c), volleyball M/W.

Standardized Tests *Required:* SAT I or ACT (for admission).

Costs (2001–02) *Comprehensive fee:* $17,880 includes full-time tuition ($11,840), mandatory fees ($630), and room and board ($5410). Part-time tuition: $505 per credit hour. *Room and board:* Room and board charges vary according to board plan. *Payment plan:* deferred payment. *Waivers:* employees or children of employees.

Financial Aid Of all full-time matriculated undergraduates who enrolled in 2001, 667 applied for aid, 615 were judged to have need, 117 had their need fully met. 210 Federal Work-Study jobs (averaging $550). In 2001, 48 non-need-based awards were made. *Average percent of need met:* 82%. *Average financial aid package:* $10,815. *Average need-based loan:* $3181. *Average need-based gift aid:* $6377. *Average non-need based aid:* $7507.

Applying *Options:* electronic application, deferred entrance. *Application fee:* $20. *Required:* essay or personal statement, high school transcript, minimum 2.0 GPA, 2.0 letters of recommendation, Christian commitment. *Required for some:* interview. *Application deadline:* rolling (freshmen), rolling (transfers). *Notification:* continuous (freshmen).

Admissions Contact Mrs. Beth Spencer, Director of Enrollment Support, Simpson College and Graduate School, 2211 College View Drive, Redding, CA 96003. *Phone:* 530-226-4606 Ext. 2602. *Toll-free phone:* 800-598-2493. *Fax:* 530-226-4861. *E-mail:* admissions@simpsonca.edu.

SONOMA STATE UNIVERSITY
Rohnert Park, California

- **State-supported** comprehensive, founded 1960, part of California State University System
- **Calendar** semesters
- **Degrees** bachelor's and master's
- **Small-town** 220-acre campus with easy access to San Francisco
- **Endowment** $27.1 million
- **Coed,** 6,278 undergraduate students, 85% full-time, 64% women, 36% men
- **Moderately difficult** entrance level, 92% of applicants were admitted

Undergraduates 5,341 full-time, 937 part-time. Students come from 39 states and territories, 38 other countries, 2% are from out of state, 2% African American, 5% Asian American or Pacific Islander, 10% Hispanic American, 1% Native American, 2% international, 14% transferred in, 21% live on campus. *Retention:* 78% of 2001 full-time freshmen returned.

Freshmen *Admission:* 5,029 applied, 4,638 admitted, 1,039 enrolled. *Average high school GPA:* 3.20. *Test scores:* SAT verbal scores over 500: 61%; SAT math scores over 500: 59%; SAT verbal scores over 600: 15%; SAT math scores over 600: 14%; SAT verbal scores over 700: 2%; SAT math scores over 700: 1%.

Faculty *Total:* 502, 51% full-time, 61% with terminal degrees. *Student/faculty ratio:* 21:1.

Majors African-American studies; American studies; anthropology; applied mathematics; art; art history; biology; botany; business administration; business economics; cell biology; chemistry; computer science; criminal justice/law enforcement administration; cultural studies; developmental/child psychology; drawing; earth sciences; ecology; economics; English; environmental education; environmental science; fine/studio arts; French; geography; geology; German; health science; Hispanic-American studies; history; interdisciplinary studies; liberal arts and sciences/liberal studies; literature; marine biology; mass communications; mathematical statistics; mathematics; medical laboratory technician; microbiology/bacteriology; multi/interdisciplinary studies related; music; music teacher education; Native American studies; nursing; philosophy; physical education; physics; physiology; political science; pre-dentistry; pre-law; pre-medicine; pre-veterinary studies; printmaking; psychology; sculpture; sociology; Spanish; theater arts/drama; women's studies; zoology.

Academic Programs *Special study options:* academic remediation for entering students, accelerated degree program, adult/continuing education programs, advanced placement credit, cooperative education, distance learning, double majors, English as a second language, honors programs, independent study, internships, off-campus study, part-time degree program, services for LD students, student-designed majors, study abroad, summer session for credit. *ROTC:* Army (c), Navy (c), Air Force (c).

Library Jean and Charles Schultz Information Center with 571,505 titles, 2,402 serial subscriptions, 7,951 audiovisual materials, an OPAC, a Web page.

Computers on Campus 300 computers available on campus for general student use. A campuswide network can be accessed from student residence rooms and from off campus. Internet access, at least one staffed computer lab available.

Student Life *Housing Options:* coed, women-only. *Activities and Organizations:* drama/theater group, student-run newspaper, radio station, choral group, Accounting Forum, Sonoma Earth Action, Re-Entry Student Association, La-Crosse Club, Intervarsity Christian Fellowship, national fraternities, national sororities. *Campus security:* 24-hour emergency response devices and patrols, student patrols, late-night transport/escort service. *Student Services:* health clinic, personal/psychological counseling, women's center, legal services.

Athletics Member NCAA. All Division II. *Intercollegiate sports:* baseball M, basketball M/W, cross-country running W, soccer M/W, softball W, tennis M/W, track and field W, volleyball W. *Intramural sports:* baseball M, basketball M/W, soccer M/W, softball M/W, track and field W, volleyball M/W.

Standardized Tests *Required:* SAT I or ACT (for admission).

Costs (2001–02) *Tuition:* state resident $0 full-time; nonresident $7380 full-time, $246 per unit part-time. Part-time tuition and fees vary according to course load. *Required fees:* $2032 full-time, $716 per term part-time. *Room and* *board:* $6921; room only: $4338. Room and board charges vary according to board plan and housing facility. *Payment plan:* deferred payment. *Waivers:* employees or children of employees.

Financial Aid Of all full-time matriculated undergraduates who enrolled in 2001, 3104 applied for aid, 1995 were judged to have need, 961 had their need fully met. 225 Federal Work-Study jobs (averaging $2300). In 2001, 123 non-need-based awards were made. *Average percent of need met:* 80%. *Average financial aid package:* $6575. *Average need-based loan:* $5000. *Average need-based gift aid:* $4487. *Average non-need based aid:* $1408. *Average indebtedness upon graduation:* $15,000.

Applying *Options:* electronic application, early admission. *Application fee:* $55. *Required:* high school transcript. *Application deadlines:* 12/31 (freshmen), 1/31 (transfers). *Notification:* continuous (freshmen).

Admissions Contact Sonoma State University, Rohnert Park, CA 94928. *Phone:* 707-664-2114. *Fax:* 707-664-2060. *E-mail:* csumentor@sonoma.edu.

SOUTHERN CALIFORNIA BIBLE COLLEGE & SEMINARY

El Cajon, California

Admissions Contact 2075 East Madison Avenue, El Cajon, CA 92019.

SOUTHERN CALIFORNIA INSTITUTE OF ARCHITECTURE

Los Angeles, California

- **Independent** comprehensive, founded 1972
- **Calendar** semesters
- **Degrees** bachelor's and master's
- **Urban** campus
- **Coed,** 218 undergraduate students
- **Moderately difficult** entrance level

Undergraduates Students come from 35 states and territories, 17 other countries. *Retention:* 41% of 2001 full-time freshmen returned.

Freshmen *Average high school GPA:* 3.0. *Test scores:* SAT verbal scores over 500: 85%; SAT math scores over 500: 95%; SAT verbal scores over 600: 35%; SAT math scores over 600: 50%.

Faculty *Total:* 89.

Majors Architecture.

Academic Programs *Special study options:* academic remediation for entering students, advanced placement credit, cooperative education, English as a second language, internships, study abroad, summer session for credit.

Library Kappe Library with 10,000 titles, 70 serial subscriptions.

Computers on Campus 30 computers available on campus for general student use. Internet access, at least one staffed computer lab available.

Student Life *Housing:* college housing not available. *Activities and Organizations:* student-run newspaper, Student Council, Academic Council. *Campus security:* 24-hour emergency response devices and patrols.

Standardized Tests *Required:* SAT I or ACT (for admission).

Costs (2002–03) *Tuition:* $17,406 full-time. *Required fees:* $70 full-time.

Applying *Options:* deferred entrance. *Application fee:* $60. *Required:* essay or personal statement, high school transcript, minimum 2.0 GPA, 3 letters of recommendation, portfolio. *Recommended:* interview. *Application deadline:* rolling (freshmen), rolling (transfers). *Notification:* continuous until 7/1 (freshmen).

Admissions Contact Ms. Debra Abel, Director of Admissions, Southern California Institute of Architecture, Freight Yard, 960 East 3rd Street, Los Angeles, CA 90013. *Phone:* 213-613-2200 Ext. 320. *Toll-free phone:* 800-774-7242. *Fax:* 213-613-2260. *E-mail:* admissions@sciarc.edu.

STANFORD UNIVERSITY

Stanford, California

- **Independent** university, founded 1891
- **Calendar** quarters
- **Degrees** bachelor's, master's, doctoral, and first professional
- **Suburban** 8180-acre campus with easy access to San Francisco
- **Endowment** $8.2 billion
- **Coed,** 7,279 undergraduate students, 89% full-time, 51% women, 49% men
- **Most difficult** entrance level, 13% of applicants were admitted

Undergraduates 6,452 full-time, 827 part-time. Students come from 52 states and territories, 58 other countries, 51% are from out of state, 9% African American, 25% Asian American or Pacific Islander, 11% Hispanic American, 2% Native American, 5% international, 1% transferred in, 94% live on campus. *Retention:* 98% of 2001 full-time freshmen returned.

Freshmen *Admission:* 19,052 applied, 2,406 admitted, 1,615 enrolled. *Average high school GPA:* 3.86. *Test scores:* SAT verbal scores over 500: 100%; SAT math scores over 500: 100%; ACT scores over 18: 100%; SAT verbal scores over 600: 94%; SAT math scores over 600: 96%; ACT scores over 24: 98%; SAT verbal scores over 700: 67%; SAT math scores over 700: 71%; ACT scores over 30: 67%.

Faculty *Total:* 1,701, 98% full-time, 98% with terminal degrees. *Student/faculty ratio:* 7:1.

Majors African studies; American studies; anthropology; archaeology; art; Asian studies; biology; chemical engineering; chemistry; Chinese; civil engineering; classics; communications; comparative literature; computer science; earth sciences; East Asian studies; economics; electrical engineering; engineering; English; environmental engineering; environmental science; French; geology; geophysics/seismology; German; history; industrial/manufacturing engineering; interdisciplinary studies; international relations; Italian; Japanese; linguistics; materials engineering; materials science; mathematics; mathematics/computer science; mechanical engineering; Mexican-American studies; music; Native American studies; petroleum engineering; philosophy; physics; political science; psychology; public policy analysis; religious studies; science/technology and society; Slavic languages; sociology; Spanish; systems science/theory; theater arts/drama; urban studies; women's studies.

Academic Programs *Special study options:* advanced placement credit, double majors, honors programs, independent study, internships, off-campus study, services for LD students, student-designed majors, study abroad, summer session for credit. *ROTC:* Army (c), Navy (c), Air Force (c).

Library Green Library plus 18 others with 7.0 million titles, 44,504 serial subscriptions, 1.3 million audiovisual materials, an OPAC, a Web page.

Computers on Campus 1000 computers available on campus for general student use. A campuswide network can be accessed from student residence rooms and from off campus. Internet access, online (class) registration, at least one staffed computer lab available.

Student Life *Housing:* on-campus residence required for freshman year. *Options:* coed, women-only, cooperative, disabled students. *Activities and Organizations:* drama/theater group, student-run newspaper, radio and television station, choral group, marching band, Ram's Head (theatre club), Axe Committee (athletic support), Business Association of Engineering Students, Asian American Student Association, Stanford Daily, national fraternities, national sororities. *Campus security:* 24-hour emergency response devices and patrols, late-night transport/escort service, controlled dormitory access. *Student Services:* health clinic, personal/psychological counseling, women's center, legal services.

Athletics Member NCAA, NAIA. All NCAA Division I except football (Division I-A). *Intercollegiate sports:* baseball M(s), basketball M(s)/W(s), crew M/W(s), cross-country running M(s)/W(s), equestrian sports M(c)/W(c), fencing M(s)/W(s), field hockey M(c)/W(s), golf M(s)/W(s), gymnastics M(s)/W(s), ice hockey M(c), lacrosse M(c)/W, racquetball M(c)/W(c), rugby M(c)/W(c), sailing M(c)/W, skiing (cross-country) M(c)/W(c), skiing (downhill) M(c)/W(c), soccer M(s)/W(s), softball W(s), squash M(c)/W(c), swimming M(s)/W(s), tennis M(s)/W(s), track and field M(s)/W(s), volleyball M(s)/W(s), water polo M(s)/W(s), wrestling M(s). *Intramural sports:* archery M/W, badminton M/W, baseball M, basketball M/W, bowling M/W, cross-country running M/W, field hockey W, football M/W, golf M/W, gymnastics M/W, soccer M/W, softball M/W, swimming M/W, table tennis M/W, tennis M/W, track and field M/W, volleyball M/W, water polo M/W, wrestling M.

Standardized Tests *Required:* SAT I or ACT (for admission). *Recommended:* SAT II: Subject Tests (for admission), SAT II: Writing Test (for admission).

Costs (2001–02) *Comprehensive fee:* $34,222 includes full-time tuition ($25,917) and room and board ($8305). *Room and board:* Room and board charges vary according to board plan and housing facility. *Payment plans:* installment, deferred payment.

Financial Aid Of all full-time matriculated undergraduates who enrolled in 2001, 3150 applied for aid, 2676 were judged to have need, 2420 had their need fully met. 516 Federal Work-Study jobs (averaging $1633). 816 State and other part-time jobs (averaging $1369). In 2001, 1323 non-need-based awards were made. *Average percent of need met:* 98%. *Average financial aid package:* $22,819. *Average need-based loan:* $3045. *Average need-based gift aid:* $20,199. *Average non-need based aid:* $4616. *Average indebtedness upon graduation:* $17,185.

Applying *Options:* early admission, early decision, deferred entrance. *Application fee:* $65. *Required:* essay or personal statement, high school transcript, 2 letters of recommendation. *Application deadlines:* 12/15 (freshmen), 3/15 (transfers). *Early decision:* 11/1. *Notification:* 4/1 (freshmen), 12/15 (early decision).

Stanford University (continued)

Admissions Contact Ms. Robin G. Mamlet, Dean of Undergraduate Admissions and Financial Aid, Stanford University, Old Union 232, Old Union, 520 Lasuen Mall, Stanford, CA 94305. *Phone:* 650-723-2091. *Fax:* 650-723-6050. *E-mail:* undergrad.admissions@forsythe.stanford.edu.

THOMAS AQUINAS COLLEGE
Santa Paula, California

- **Independent Roman Catholic** 4-year, founded 1971
- **Calendar** semesters
- **Degree** bachelor's
- **Rural** 170-acre campus with easy access to Los Angeles
- **Endowment** $8.8 million
- **Coed,** 301 undergraduate students, 100% full-time, 50% women, 50% men
- **Very difficult** entrance level, 87% of applicants were admitted

Undergraduates 301 full-time. Students come from 36 states and territories, 3 other countries, 51% are from out of state, 0.7% African American, 3% Asian American or Pacific Islander, 8% Hispanic American, 0.3% Native American, 7% international, 100% live on campus. *Retention:* 88% of 2001 full-time freshmen returned.

Freshmen *Admission:* 124 applied, 108 admitted, 64 enrolled. *Average high school GPA:* 3.70. *Test scores:* SAT verbal scores over 500: 100%; SAT math scores over 500: 98%; ACT scores over 18: 100%; SAT verbal scores over 600: 77%; SAT math scores over 600: 60%; ACT scores over 24: 90%; SAT verbal scores over 700: 26%; SAT math scores over 700: 6%; ACT scores over 30: 30%.

Faculty *Total:* 29, 93% full-time, 66% with terminal degrees. *Student/faculty ratio:* 11:1.

Majors Interdisciplinary studies; liberal arts and sciences/liberal studies; western civilization.

Library St. Bernardine Library with 45,000 titles, 130 serial subscriptions, 2,000 audiovisual materials.

Computers on Campus 10 computers available on campus for general student use. At least one staffed computer lab available.

Student Life *Housing:* on-campus residence required through senior year. *Options:* men-only, women-only. *Activities and Organizations:* drama/theater group, choral group, choir, drama club, Legion of Mary, language clubs, pro-life ministry. *Campus security:* 24-hour emergency response devices, student patrols, daily security daytime patrol. *Student Services:* health clinic, personal/psychological counseling.

Athletics *Intramural sports:* basketball M/W, football M, soccer M/W, softball M/W, table tennis M/W, tennis M/W, volleyball M/W, weight lifting M.

Standardized Tests *Required:* SAT I or ACT (for admission).

Costs (2001–02) *Comprehensive fee:* $20,500 includes full-time tuition ($15,900) and room and board ($4600). *Payment plan:* installment.

Financial Aid Of all full-time matriculated undergraduates who enrolled in 2001, 230 applied for aid, 218 were judged to have need, 218 had their need fully met. 1192 State and other part-time jobs (averaging $2974). In 2001, 6 non-need-based awards were made. *Average percent of need met:* 100%. *Average financial aid package:* $13,559. *Average need-based loan:* $3292. *Average need-based gift aid:* $8798. *Average non-need based aid:* $2083. *Average indebtedness upon graduation:* $15,295.

Applying *Options:* common application, early admission, deferred entrance. *Required:* essay or personal statement, high school transcript, 3 letters of recommendation. *Required for some:* interview. *Recommended:* minimum 2.0 GPA. *Application deadline:* rolling (freshmen). *Notification:* continuous (freshmen).

Admissions Contact Mr. Thomas J. Susanka Jr., Director of Admissions, Thomas Aquinas College, 10000 North Ojai Road, Santa Paula, CA 93060-9980. *Phone:* 805-525-4417 Ext. 361. *Toll-free phone:* 800-634-9797. *Fax:* 805-525-9342. *E-mail:* admissions@thomasaquinas.edu.

TOURO UNIVERSITY INTERNATIONAL
Los Alamitos, California

- **Independent** comprehensive
- **Degrees** certificates, bachelor's, master's, doctoral, and postbachelor's certificates
- **Coed,** 446 undergraduate students, 70% full-time, 35% women, 65% men
- **Minimally difficult** entrance level, 89% of applicants were admitted

Undergraduates 313 full-time, 133 part-time. Students come from 50 states and territories, 15 other countries, 90% are from out of state, 96% transferred in. *Retention:* 85% of 2001 full-time freshmen returned.

Freshmen *Admission:* 266 applied, 236 admitted, 17 enrolled. *Average high school GPA:* 3.10.

Faculty *Total:* 19, 63% full-time, 68% with terminal degrees. *Student/faculty ratio:* 7:1.

Majors Business; health education; health services administration; hospitality management; management information systems/business data processing; public health.

Academic Programs *Special study options:* adult/continuing education programs, distance learning, off-campus study, part-time degree program, summer session for credit.

Library Touro Cyber Library with 18,352 titles, 12,000 serial subscriptions, an OPAC, a Web page.

Computers on Campus A campuswide network can be accessed from off campus. Internet access, online (class) registration available.

Student Life *Housing:* college housing not available.

Standardized Tests *Required for some:* SAT I (for admission), ACT (for admission), SAT I or ACT (for admission), SAT I and SAT II or ACT (for admission), SAT II: Subject Tests (for admission), SAT II: Writing Test (for admission).

Costs (2002–03) *Tuition:* $6400 full-time, $200 per credit part-time. *Payment plan:* deferred payment. *Waivers:* employees or children of employees.

Applying *Options:* common application, electronic application. *Application fee:* $75. *Required:* high school transcript, minimum 3.0 GPA. *Required for some:* essay or personal statement. *Recommended:* interview. *Application deadline:* rolling (freshmen). *Notification:* continuous (freshmen).

Admissions Contact Wei Ren, Registrar, Touro University International, 10542 Calle Lee, Los Alamitos, CA 90720. *Phone:* 714-816-0366. *Toll-free phone:* 714-816-0366. *Fax:* 714-816-0367. *E-mail:* rkoester@tourou.edu.

UNIVERSITY OF CALIFORNIA, BERKELEY
Berkeley, California

- **State-supported** university, founded 1868, part of University of California System
- **Calendar** semesters
- **Degrees** certificates, bachelor's, master's, doctoral, and first professional
- **Urban** 1232-acre campus with easy access to San Francisco
- **Endowment** $1.7 billion
- **Coed,** 22,677 undergraduate students, 93% full-time, 52% women, 48% men
- **Very difficult** entrance level, 26% of applicants were admitted

Undergraduates 21,046 full-time, 1,631 part-time. Students come from 53 states and territories, 100 other countries, 14% are from out of state, 4% African American, 40% Asian American or Pacific Islander, 10% Hispanic American, 0.6% Native American, 4% international, 7% transferred in, 34% live on campus. *Retention:* 95% of 2001 full-time freshmen returned.

Freshmen *Admission:* 32,963 applied, 8,715 admitted, 3,748 enrolled. *Average high school GPA:* 3.76. *Test scores:* SAT verbal scores over 500: 91%; SAT math scores over 500: 95%; SAT verbal scores over 600: 68%; SAT math scores over 600: 82%; SAT verbal scores over 700: 30%; SAT math scores over 700: 46%.

Faculty *Total:* 1,804, 80% full-time, 98% with terminal degrees. *Student/faculty ratio:* 17:1.

Majors African-American studies; American studies; anthropology; applied mathematics; architecture; art; art history; Asian-American studies; Asian studies; astrophysics; bioengineering; business administration; chemical engineering; chemistry; Chinese; civil engineering; classics; comparative literature; computer/information sciences; cultural studies; earth sciences; economics; electrical engineering; engineering; engineering physics; English; environmental engineering; environmental science; film/video production; forestry sciences; French; genetics; geography; geology; geophysics/seismology; German; Greek (ancient and medieval); Hispanic-American studies; history; industrial/manufacturing engineering; interdisciplinary studies; Italian; Japanese; landscape architecture; Latin American studies; Latin (ancient and medieval); legal studies; linguistics; mass communications; materials engineering; mathematical statistics; mathematics; mechanical engineering; Middle Eastern studies; molecular biology; music; Native American studies; natural resources conservation; natural resources management; nuclear engineering; nutritional sciences; peace/conflict studies; petroleum engineering; philosophy; physical sciences; physics; political science; psychology; religious studies; Scandinavian languages; Slavic languages; social sciences; social work; sociology; Southeast Asian studies; Spanish; speech/rhetorical studies; theater arts/drama; women's studies.

Academic Programs *Special study options:* accelerated degree program, adult/continuing education programs, advanced placement credit, distance learning, double majors, English as a second language, honors programs, independent study, internships, off-campus study, services for LD students, student-designed majors, study abroad, summer session for credit. *ROTC:* Army (b).

Library Doe Library plus 30 others with 12.3 million titles, 139,455 serial subscriptions, 83,367 audiovisual materials, an OPAC, a Web page.

Computers on Campus 600 computers available on campus for general student use. A campuswide network can be accessed from student residence rooms and from off campus. Internet access, online (class) registration, at least one staffed computer lab available.

Student Life *Housing:* on-campus residence required for freshman year. *Options:* coed, men-only, women-only. *Activities and Organizations:* drama/theater group, student-run newspaper, radio and television station, choral group, marching band, national fraternities, national sororities. *Campus security:* 24-hour emergency response devices and patrols, late-night transport/escort service, controlled dormitory access, Office of Emergency Preparedness. *Student Services:* health clinic, personal/psychological counseling, women's center, legal services.

Athletics Member NCAA. All Division I except football (Division I-A). *Intercollegiate sports:* baseball M(s), basketball M(s)/W(s), crew M(s)/W(s), cross-country running M(s)/W(s), field hockey W(s), golf M(s)/W(s), gymnastics M(s)/W(s), lacrosse W(s), rugby M(s), soccer M(s)/W(s), softball W(s), swimming M(s)/W(s), tennis M(s)/W(s), track and field M(s)/W(s), volleyball W(s), water polo M(s)/W(s). *Intramural sports:* badminton M(c)/W(c), basketball M/W, crew M(c)/W(c), fencing M(c)/W(c), field hockey M(c), football M/W, gymnastics M(c)/W(c), ice hockey M(c)/W(c), lacrosse M(c), racquetball M(c)/W(c), rugby W(c), sailing M(c)/W(c), skiing (downhill) M(c)/W(c), soccer M/W(c), softball M/W, squash M(c)/W(c), tennis M(c)/W(c), volleyball M(c).

Standardized Tests *Required:* SAT I or ACT (for admission), SAT II: Subject Tests (for admission), SAT II: Writing Test (for admission).

Costs (2001–02) *Tuition:* state resident $0 full-time; nonresident $10,704 full-time. Full-time tuition and fees vary according to program. *Required fees:* $4122 full-time. *Room and board:* $10,047. Room and board charges vary according to board plan and housing facility. *Payment plan:* installment.

Financial Aid Of all full-time matriculated undergraduates who enrolled in 2001, 14432 applied for aid, 9832 were judged to have need, 5725 had their need fully met. In 2001, 2444 non-need-based awards were made. *Average percent of need met:* 92%. *Average financial aid package:* $11,441. *Average need-based loan:* $4312. *Average need-based gift aid:* $7991. *Average non-need based aid:* $2390. *Average indebtedness upon graduation:* $14,648.

Applying *Options:* electronic application. *Application fee:* $40. *Required:* essay or personal statement, high school transcript, minimum 2.8 GPA for California residents; 3.4 for all others. *Application deadlines:* 11/30 (freshmen), 11/30 (transfers). *Notification:* 3/31 (freshmen).

Admissions Contact Pre-Admission Advising, Office of Undergraduate Admission and Relations With Schools, University of California, Berkeley, Berkeley, CA 94720. *Phone:* 510-642-3175. *Fax:* 510-642-7333. *E-mail:* ouars@uclink.berkeley.edu.

UNIVERSITY OF CALIFORNIA, DAVIS

Davis, California

- **State-supported** university, founded 1905, part of University of California System
- **Calendar** quarters
- **Degrees** bachelor's, master's, doctoral, first professional, and postbachelor's certificates
- **Suburban** 5993-acre campus with easy access to San Francisco
- **Endowment** $354.0 million
- **Coed,** 21,294 undergraduate students, 88% full-time, 57% women, 43% men
- **Very difficult** entrance level, 63% of applicants were admitted

Undergraduates 18,692 full-time, 2,602 part-time. Students come from 49 states and territories, 113 other countries, 4% are from out of state, 3% African American, 35% Asian American or Pacific Islander, 10% Hispanic American, 0.8% Native American, 1% international, 9% transferred in, 25% live on campus. *Retention:* 99% of 2001 full-time freshmen returned.

Freshmen *Admission:* 27,937 applied, 17,569 admitted, 4,408 enrolled. *Average high school GPA:* 3.71. *Test scores:* SAT verbal scores over 500: 77%; SAT math scores over 500: 92%; ACT scores over 18: 94%; SAT verbal scores over 600: 36%; SAT math scores over 600: 58%; ACT scores over 24: 59%; SAT verbal scores over 700: 6%; SAT math scores over 700: 13%; ACT scores over 30: 9%.

Faculty *Total:* 1,950, 83% full-time, 98% with terminal degrees. *Student/faculty ratio:* 19:1.

Majors Aerospace engineering; African-American studies; African studies; agricultural business; agricultural economics; agricultural education; agricultural engineering; American studies; animal sciences; anthropology; art; art history; atmospheric sciences; biochemistry; bioengineering; biology; botany; cell biology; chemical engineering; chemistry; Chinese; civil engineering; clothing/apparel/textile studies; comparative literature; computer engineering; design/visual communications; East Asian studies; economics; electrical engineering; engineering; English; entomology; environmental biology; food sciences; French; genetics; geology; German; history; horticulture science; individual/family development; international agriculture; international relations; Italian; Japanese; landscape architecture; linguistics; materials engineering; mathematical statistics; mathematics; mechanical engineering; Mexican-American studies; microbiology/bacteriology; music; Native American studies; natural resources conservation; nutrition science; philosophy; physical education; physics; physiology; political science; poultry science; psychology; range management; religious studies; Russian; sociology; Spanish; speech/rhetorical studies; theater arts/drama; women's studies; zoology.

Academic Programs *Special study options:* academic remediation for entering students, adult/continuing education programs, advanced placement credit, double majors, English as a second language, freshman honors college, honors programs, independent study, internships, part-time degree program, services for LD students, student-designed majors, study abroad, summer session for credit. *ROTC:* Army (b), Air Force (c).

Library Peter J. Shields Library plus 5 others with 2.9 million titles, 45,665 serial subscriptions, an OPAC, a Web page.

Computers on Campus 600 computers available on campus for general student use. A campuswide network can be accessed from student residence rooms and from off campus that provide access to software packages. Internet access, at least one staffed computer lab available.

Student Life *Housing Options:* coed, men-only, women-only. *Activities and Organizations:* drama/theater group, student-run newspaper, radio station, choral group, marching band, Filipino Student Organization, Vietnamese Student Association, Jewish Student Union, Alpha Phi Omega, national fraternities, national sororities. *Campus security:* 24-hour emergency response devices and patrols, student patrols, late-night transport/escort service, controlled dormitory access, rape prevention programs. *Student Services:* health clinic, personal/psychological counseling, women's center, legal services.

Athletics Member NCAA. All Division II except gymnastics (Division I), wrestling (Division I). *Intercollegiate sports:* baseball M, basketball M/W, cross-country running M/W, football M, golf M, gymnastics W, soccer M/W, softball W, swimming M/W, tennis M/W, track and field M/W, volleyball W, water polo M, wrestling M. *Intramural sports:* archery M(c)/W(c), badminton M(c)/W(c), basketball M/W, crew M(c)/W(c), equestrian sports M(c)/W(c), fencing M(c)/W(c), football M/W, golf M/W, gymnastics M(c), ice hockey M(c)/W, lacrosse M(c)/W(c), racquetball M(c)/W(c), riflery M(c)/W(c), rugby M(c), sailing M(c)/W(c), skiing (cross-country) M(c)/W(c), skiing (downhill) M(c)/W(c), soccer M/W, softball M/W, swimming W(c), table tennis M/W, tennis M/W, volleyball M(c)/W, water polo W(c).

Standardized Tests *Required:* SAT II: Writing Test (for admission).

Costs (2001–02) *Tuition:* state resident $0 full-time; nonresident $10,704 full-time, $1784 per term part-time. *Required fees:* $4594 full-time, $1080 per term part-time. *Room and board:* $6982. Room and board charges vary according to board plan and housing facility. *Payment plan:* installment. *Waivers:* employees or children of employees.

Financial Aid Of all full-time matriculated undergraduates who enrolled in 2001, 11518 applied for aid, 8455 were judged to have need, 1193 had their need fully met. In 2001, 1487 non-need-based awards were made. *Average percent of need met:* 81%. *Average financial aid package:* $8807. *Average need-based loan:* $3682. *Average need-based gift aid:* $6509. *Average non-need based aid:* $1695.

Applying *Options:* electronic application. *Application fee:* $40. *Required:* essay or personal statement, high school transcript. *Application deadlines:* 11/30 (freshmen), 11/30 (transfers). *Notification:* continuous until 5/15 (freshmen).

Admissions Contact Dr. Gary Tudor, Director of Undergraduate Admissions, University of California, Davis, Undergraduate Admission and Outreach Services, 175 Mrak Hall, Davis, CA 95616. *Phone:* 530-752-2971. *Fax:* 530-752-1280. *E-mail:* thinkucd@ucdavis.edu.

UNIVERSITY OF CALIFORNIA, IRVINE

Irvine, California

- **State-supported** university, founded 1965, part of University of California System
- **Calendar** quarters
- **Degrees** bachelor's, master's, doctoral, and first professional
- **Suburban** 1489-acre campus with easy access to Los Angeles
- **Endowment** $126.3 million

University of California, Irvine (continued)
■ **Coed,** 17,723 undergraduate students, 96% full-time, 52% women, 48% men
■ **Moderately difficult** entrance level, 59% of applicants were admitted

Undergraduates 16,971 full-time, 752 part-time. Students come from 35 states and territories, 39 other countries, 2% are from out of state, 7% transferred in, 30% live on campus. *Retention:* 91% of 2001 full-time freshmen returned.
Freshmen *Admission:* 29,178 applied, 17,165 admitted, 4,042 enrolled. *Average high school GPA:* 3.66. *Test scores:* SAT verbal scores over 500: 84%; SAT math scores over 500: 92%; SAT verbal scores over 600: 33%; SAT math scores over 600: 56%; SAT verbal scores over 700: 5%; SAT math scores over 700: 13%.
Faculty *Total:* 989, 76% full-time, 95% with terminal degrees. *Student/faculty ratio:* 18:1.
Majors Anthropology; art; art history; biology; chemical engineering; chemistry; civil engineering; classics; cognitive psychology/psycholinguistics; comparative literature; computer engineering; computer/information sciences; computer science; criminology; cultural studies; dance; East Asian studies; ecology; economics; electrical engineering; engineering; English; environmental engineering; film studies; fine/studio arts; French; geography; German; history; human ecology; humanities; international relations; linguistics; literature; mathematics; mechanical engineering; music; philosophy; physics; political science; psychology; Russian; social sciences; sociology; Spanish; theater arts/drama; women's studies.
Academic Programs *Special study options:* academic remediation for entering students, adult/continuing education programs, advanced placement credit, cooperative education, double majors, English as a second language, honors programs, independent study, internships, off-campus study, services for LD students, study abroad, summer session for credit. *ROTC:* Army (c), Air Force (c).
Library Main Library plus 1 other with 2.4 million titles, 19,287 serial subscriptions, 88,308 audiovisual materials, an OPAC, a Web page.
Computers on Campus 500 computers available on campus for general student use. A campuswide network can be accessed from student residence rooms and from off campus. Internet access, online (class) registration, at least one staffed computer lab available.
Student Life *Housing Options:* coed, men-only, women-only, disabled students. *Activities and Organizations:* drama/theater group, student-run newspaper, radio station, choral group, ASUCI, Kababayan, national fraternities, national sororities. *Campus security:* 24-hour emergency response devices and patrols, late-night transport/escort service. *Student Services:* health clinic, personal/psychological counseling, women's center, legal services.
Athletics Member NCAA. All Division I. *Intercollegiate sports:* basketball M(s)/W(s), crew M/W, cross-country running M/W(s), golf M(s), sailing M/W, soccer M/W, swimming M(s)/W(s), tennis M(s)/W(s), track and field W(s), volleyball M/W(s), water polo M(s). *Intramural sports:* badminton M/W, baseball M, basketball M/W, bowling M(c)/W(c), crew W(c), cross-country running M/W, fencing M(c)/W(c), football M, golf M/W, ice hockey M(c)/W(c), lacrosse M(c)/W, racquetball M/W, rugby M(c), sailing M(c)/W(c), skiing (cross-country) M(c)/W(c), skiing (downhill) M(c)/W(c), soccer M/W, swimming M/W, table tennis M/W, tennis M/W, track and field M/W, volleyball M/W, water polo M/W, weight lifting M/W, wrestling M.
Standardized Tests *Required:* SAT I or ACT (for admission), SAT II: Subject Tests (for admission), SAT II: Writing Test (for admission).
Costs (2001–02) *Tuition:* state resident $0 full-time, $1067 per term part-time; nonresident $15,630 full-time, $2912 per term part-time. *Required fees:* $4556 full-time. *Room and board:* $7098. Room and board charges vary according to board plan and housing facility. *Payment plan:* installment.
Financial Aid Of all full-time matriculated undergraduates who enrolled in 2001, 10651 applied for aid, 8174 were judged to have need, 1367 had their need fully met. 1790 Federal Work-Study jobs (averaging $1653). 21 State and other part-time jobs (averaging $554). In 2001, 579 non-need-based awards were made. *Average percent of need met:* 86%. *Average financial aid package:* $9481. *Average need-based loan:* $4048. *Average need-based gift aid:* $6892. *Average non-need based aid:* $2958.
Applying *Application fee:* $40. *Required:* essay or personal statement, high school transcript, minimum 2.0 GPA. *Application deadlines:* 11/30 (freshmen), 11/30 (transfers). *Notification:* continuous until 3/1 (freshmen).
Admissions Contact Dr. Susan Wilbur, Director of Admissions, University of California, Irvine, 204 Administration, Irvine, CA 92697-1075. *Phone:* 949-824-6701.

UNIVERSITY OF CALIFORNIA, LOS ANGELES
Los Angeles, California

■ **State-supported** university, founded 1919, part of University of California System
■ **Calendar** quarters
■ **Degrees** bachelor's, master's, doctoral, and first professional
■ **Urban** 419-acre campus
■ **Endowment** $1.3 billion
■ **Coed,** 25,328 undergraduate students, 95% full-time, 55% women, 45% men
■ **Very difficult** entrance level, 27% of applicants were admitted

Undergraduates 24,108 full-time, 1,220 part-time. Students come from 50 states and territories, 100 other countries, 3% are from out of state, 4% African American, 37% Asian American or Pacific Islander, 14% Hispanic American, 0.5% Native American, 3% international, 10% transferred in, 31% live on campus. *Retention:* 97% of 2001 full-time freshmen returned.
Freshmen *Admission:* 40,739 applied, 10,953 admitted, 4,246 enrolled. *Test scores:* SAT verbal scores over 500: 91%; SAT math scores over 500: 96%; ACT scores over 18: 98%; SAT verbal scores over 600: 63%; SAT math scores over 600: 77%; ACT scores over 24: 72%; SAT verbal scores over 700: 19%; SAT math scores over 700: 36%; ACT scores over 30: 24%.
Faculty *Total:* 2,305, 76% full-time, 98% with terminal degrees. *Student/faculty ratio:* 17:1.
Majors Aerospace engineering; African-American studies; African languages; American literature; American studies; anthropology; applied art; applied mathematics; Arabic; art; art history; Asian-American studies; astrophysics; atmospheric sciences; biochemistry; biology; business economics; cell biology; chemical engineering; chemistry; Chinese; civil engineering; classics; cognitive psychology/psycholinguistics; communications; comparative literature; computer engineering; computer science; design/visual communications; earth sciences; East Asian studies; ecology; economics; electrical engineering; English; European studies; exercise sciences; film studies; French; geochemistry; geography; geological engineering; geology; geophysical engineering; geophysics/seismology; German; Greek (modern); Hebrew; history; international economics; international relations; Italian; Japanese; Judaic studies; Latin American studies; Latin (ancient and medieval); linguistics; marine biology; materials engineering; materials science; mathematics; mechanical engineering; Mexican-American studies; microbiology/bacteriology; Middle Eastern studies; molecular biology; music; musicology; neuroscience; nursing; philosophy; physics; physiological psychology/psychobiology; plant sciences; political science; Portuguese; psychology; radio/television broadcasting; religious studies; Russian; Russian/Slavic studies; Scandinavian languages; Slavic languages; sociology; Southeast Asian studies; Spanish; theater arts/drama; women's studies.
Academic Programs *Special study options:* academic remediation for entering students, adult/continuing education programs, advanced placement credit, distance learning, double majors, English as a second language, honors programs, independent study, internships, off-campus study, services for LD students, student-designed majors, study abroad, summer session for credit. *ROTC:* Army (b), Navy (b), Air Force (b).
Library University Research Library plus 13 others with 7.5 million titles, 93,854 serial subscriptions, 4.6 million audiovisual materials, an OPAC, a Web page.
Computers on Campus A campuswide network can be accessed from student residence rooms and from off campus. At least one staffed computer lab available.
Student Life *Housing Options:* coed, cooperative. *Activities and Organizations:* drama/theater group, student-run newspaper, radio station, choral group, marching band, Student Alumni Association, student government, Rally Committee, national fraternities, national sororities. *Campus security:* 24-hour emergency response devices, student patrols, late-night transport/escort service. *Student Services:* health clinic, personal/psychological counseling, women's center, legal services.
Athletics Member NCAA. All Division I except football (Division I-A). *Intercollegiate sports:* baseball M(s), basketball M(s)/W(s), cross-country running M(s)/W(s), golf M(s)/W(s), gymnastics W(s), soccer M(s)/W(s), softball W(s), swimming W(s), tennis M(s)/W(s), track and field M(s)/W(s), volleyball M(s)/W(s), water polo M(s)/W(s). *Intramural sports:* badminton M/W, basketball M/W, bowling M/W, crew M/W, cross-country running M/W, fencing M/W, football M/W, golf M/W, gymnastics M/W, ice hockey M/W, lacrosse M/W, racquetball M/W, rugby M/W, sailing M/W, skiing (cross-country) M/W, skiing (downhill) M/W, soccer M/W, squash M/W, swimming M/W, tennis M/W, track and field M/W, volleyball M/W, water polo M/W, weight lifting M, wrestling M.
Standardized Tests *Required:* SAT I or ACT (for admission), SAT II: Writing Test (for admission).
Costs (2001–02) *Tuition:* state resident $0 full-time; nonresident $11,074 full-time. *Required fees:* $4236 full-time. *Room and board:* $8991. Room and board charges vary according to board plan and housing facility.
Financial Aid Of all full-time matriculated undergraduates who enrolled in 2001, 14843 applied for aid, 11994 were judged to have need, 3200 had their need fully met. 2400 Federal Work-Study jobs (averaging $2152). 320 State and other part-time jobs (averaging $1500). In 2001, 1571 non-need-based awards were

made. *Average percent of need met:* 83%. *Average financial aid package:* $10,905. *Average need-based loan:* $4617. *Average need-based gift aid:* $8024. *Average non-need based aid:* $2357. *Average indebtedness upon graduation:* $16,825.

Applying *Options:* electronic application. *Application fee:* $40. *Required:* essay or personal statement, high school transcript. *Recommended:* minimum 3.5 GPA. *Application deadlines:* 11/30 (freshmen), 11/30 (transfers).

Admissions Contact Dr. Rae Lee Siporin, Director of Undergraduate Admissions, University of California, Los Angeles, 405 Hilgard Avenue, Los Angeles, CA 90095. *Phone:* 310-825-3101. *E-mail:* ugadm@saonet.ucla.edu.

UNIVERSITY OF CALIFORNIA, RIVERSIDE

Riverside, California

- **State-supported** university, founded 1954, part of University of California System
- **Calendar** quarters
- **Degrees** bachelor's, master's, and doctoral
- **Urban** 1200-acre campus with easy access to Los Angeles
- **Endowment** $62.7 million
- **Coed,** 12,714 undergraduate students, 96% full-time, 54% women, 46% men
- **Very difficult** entrance level, 85% of applicants were admitted

University of California, Riverside combines the comprehensive excellence of the nation's finest public university with the individual attention of a small campus. Accessible classes and faculty interaction contribute to an optimal learning environment and favorable graduation rates. Extensive support services and activities ensure students' academic success and personal fulfillment. Ample housing and financial aid are available.

Undergraduates 12,248 full-time, 466 part-time. Students come from 35 states and territories, 22 other countries, 1% are from out of state, 6% African American, 42% Asian American or Pacific Islander, 22% Hispanic American, 0.5% Native American, 2% international, 6% transferred in, 30% live on campus. *Retention:* 84% of 2001 full-time freshmen returned.

Freshmen *Admission:* 20,980 applied, 17,909 admitted, 3,273 enrolled. *Average high school GPA:* 3.47. *Test scores:* SAT verbal scores over 500: 53%; SAT math scores over 500: 74%; ACT scores over 18: 81%; SAT verbal scores over 600: 17%; SAT math scores over 600: 34%; ACT scores over 24: 27%; SAT verbal scores over 700: 2%; SAT math scores over 700: 7%; ACT scores over 30: 3%.

Faculty *Total:* 714, 83% full-time, 98% with terminal degrees. *Student/faculty ratio:* 19:1.

Majors African-American studies; anthropology; art history; Asian-American studies; Asian studies; biochemistry; biology; biomedical science; botany; business administration; business economics; chemical engineering; chemistry; Chinese; classics; comparative literature; computer science; creative writing; cultural studies; dance; economics; electrical engineering; English; entomology; environmental engineering; environmental science; fine/studio arts; French; geology; geophysics/seismology; German; history; humanities; individual/family development; Latin American studies; liberal arts and sciences/liberal studies; linguistics; mathematical statistics; mathematics; mechanical engineering; Mexican-American studies; music; Native American studies; neuroscience; philosophy; physical sciences; physics; physiological psychology/psychobiology; political science; pre-law; psychology; public administration; religious studies; Russian; Russian/Slavic studies; social sciences; sociology; Spanish; theater arts/drama; women's studies.

Academic Programs *Special study options:* academic remediation for entering students, accelerated degree program, adult/continuing education programs, advanced placement credit, cooperative education, distance learning, double majors, freshman honors college, honors programs, independent study, internships, off-campus study, part-time degree program, services for LD students, student-designed majors, study abroad, summer session for credit. *ROTC:* Army (c), Air Force (c).

Library Tomas Rivera Library plus 6 others with 2.0 million titles, 19,294 serial subscriptions, 48,489 audiovisual materials, an OPAC, a Web page.

Computers on Campus 600 computers available on campus for general student use. A campuswide network can be accessed from student residence rooms and from off campus. Internet access, online (class) registration, at least one staffed computer lab available.

Student Life *Housing Options:* coed. *Activities and Organizations:* drama/theater group, student-run newspaper, radio station, choral group, Associated Students, UCR Ambassadors, Community Service/Human Corps Program, BEAR FACTS Student Orientation, national fraternities, national sororities. *Campus security:* 24-hour emergency response devices and patrols, student patrols, late-night transport/escort service, controlled dormitory access. *Student Services:* health clinic, personal/psychological counseling, women's center, legal services.

Athletics Member NCAA. All Division II. *Intercollegiate sports:* baseball M(s), basketball M(s)/W(s), cross-country running M(s)/W(s), lacrosse M(c), softball W(s), tennis M(s)/W(s), track and field M(s)/W(s), volleyball W(s). *Intramural sports:* badminton M/W, basketball M/W, bowling M/W, fencing M/W, field hockey M(c)/W(c), football M/W, golf M/W, racquetball M/W, rugby M(c)/W(c), skiing (cross-country) M(c)/W(c), skiing (downhill) M(c)/W(c), soccer M(c)/W(c), softball M/W, tennis M/W, volleyball M/W, water polo M/W.

Standardized Tests *Required:* SAT I or ACT (for admission), SAT II: Writing Test (for admission).

Costs (2001–02) *Tuition:* state resident $0 full-time; nonresident $10,704 full-time. *Required fees:* $4379 full-time. *Room and board:* $7200. Room and board charges vary according to board plan and housing facility. *Payment plans:* installment, deferred payment.

Financial Aid Of all full-time matriculated undergraduates who enrolled in 2001, 9199 applied for aid, 7684 were judged to have need, 2376 had their need fully met. 1444 Federal Work-Study jobs (averaging $2775). 81 State and other part-time jobs (averaging $1514). *Average percent of need met:* 83%. *Average financial aid package:* $9536. *Average need-based loan:* $3543. *Average need-based gift aid:* $7037. *Average indebtedness upon graduation:* $11,283.

Applying *Options:* electronic application, early admission. *Application fee:* $40. *Required:* essay or personal statement, high school transcript, minimum 2.82 GPA. *Application deadline:* 11/30 (freshmen), rolling (transfers). *Notification:* continuous (freshmen).

Admissions Contact Ms. Laurie Nelson, Director of Undergraduate Admission, University of California, Riverside, 1138 Hinderaker Hall, Riverside, CA 92521. *Phone:* 909-787-3411. *Fax:* 909-787-6344. *E-mail:* discover@pop.ucr.edu.

UNIVERSITY OF CALIFORNIA, SAN DIEGO

La Jolla, California

- **State-supported** university, founded 1959, part of University of California System
- **Calendar** quarters
- **Degrees** bachelor's, master's, doctoral, and first professional
- **Suburban** 1976-acre campus with easy access to San Diego
- **Endowment** $1.2 billion
- **Coed,** 17,506 undergraduate students, 99% full-time, 52% women, 48% men
- **Very difficult** entrance level, 43% of applicants were admitted

Undergraduates 17,255 full-time, 251 part-time. 3% are from out of state, 1% African American, 35% Asian American or Pacific Islander, 10% Hispanic American, 0.5% Native American, 2% international, 6% transferred in, 34% live on campus. *Retention:* 93% of 2001 full-time freshmen returned.

Freshmen *Admission:* 38,051 applied, 16,458 admitted, 3,982 enrolled. *Average high school GPA:* 3.99. *Test scores:* SAT verbal scores over 500: 92%; SAT math scores over 500: 98%; ACT scores over 18: 100%; SAT verbal scores over 600: 59%; SAT math scores over 600: 81%; ACT scores over 24: 94%; SAT verbal scores over 700: 14%; SAT math scores over 700: 33%; ACT scores over 30: 40%.

Faculty *Total:* 1,045, 84% full-time, 98% with terminal degrees. *Student/faculty ratio:* 19:1.

Majors Aerospace engineering; anthropology; applied mathematics; archaeology; art; art history; biochemistry; bioengineering; biology; biophysics; biotechnology research; cell biology; chemical and atomic/molecular physics; chemical engineering; chemistry; chemistry education; Chinese; classics; cognitive psychology/psycholinguistics; computer engineering; computer science; creative writing; cultural studies; dance; earth sciences; ecology; economics; electrical engineering; engineering; engineering physics; engineering science; English; environmental science; film studies; fine/studio arts; foreign languages/literatures; French; German; history; human ecology; interdisciplinary studies; Italian; Japanese; Judaic studies; Latin American studies; linguistics; literature; management science; mass communications; mathematics; mathematics education; mechanical engineering; medicinal/pharmaceutical chemistry; microbiology/bacteriology; molecular biology; multimedia; music; music history; natural resources management; philosophy; physics; physics education; physiology; political science; psychology; quantitative economics; religious studies; Russian; Russian/Slavic studies; sociology; Spanish; structural engineering; systems engineering; theater arts/drama; urban studies; women's studies.

Academic Programs *Special study options:* accelerated degree program, cooperative education, double majors, English as a second language, freshman honors college, honors programs, independent study, internships, off-campus study, services for LD students, student-designed majors, study abroad, summer session for credit.

Library Geisel Library plus 7 others with 2.6 million titles, 25,000 serial subscriptions, 87,625 audiovisual materials, an OPAC, a Web page.

University of California, San Diego (continued)

Computers on Campus 1020 computers available on campus for general student use. A campuswide network can be accessed from student residence rooms and from off campus that provide access to e-mail. Internet access, online (class) registration, at least one staffed computer lab available.

Student Life *Housing Options:* coed, disabled students. *Activities and Organizations:* drama/theater group, student-run newspaper, radio and television station, choral group, Radically Inclined Snow Ski Club, MECHA (Movimiento Estudiantil Chicano de Aztlan), national fraternities, national sororities. *Campus security:* 24-hour emergency response devices and patrols, late-night transport/escort service, crime prevention programs. *Student Services:* health clinic, personal/psychological counseling, women's center, legal services.

Athletics Member NCAA. All Division II. *Intercollegiate sports:* baseball M, basketball M/W, crew M/W, cross-country running M/W, fencing M/W, golf M, soccer M/W, softball W, swimming M/W, tennis M/W, track and field M/W, volleyball M/W, water polo M/W. *Intramural sports:* archery M(c)/W(c), badminton M/W, basketball M/W, equestrian sports M/W, fencing M(c)/W(c), football M(c)/W(c), golf M/W, gymnastics M(c)/W(c), ice hockey M, lacrosse M(c)/W(c), racquetball M/W, rugby M(c), sailing M(c)/W(c), skiing (downhill) M(c)/W(c), soccer M(c)/W(c), table tennis M(c)/W(c), tennis M/W, track and field M/W, volleyball M(c)/W(c), wrestling M(c)/W(c).

Standardized Tests *Required:* SAT I or ACT (for admission).

Costs (2001–02) *One-time required fee:* $370. *Tuition:* state resident $0 full-time; nonresident $14,567 full-time. *Required fees:* $3863 full-time. *Room and board:* $7510. Room and board charges vary according to board plan. *Payment plan:* deferred payment.

Financial Aid Of all full-time matriculated undergraduates who enrolled in 2001, 10411 applied for aid, 8044 were judged to have need, 7683 had their need fully met. 3957 Federal Work-Study jobs (averaging $2241). 232 State and other part-time jobs (averaging $2107). In 2001, 1300 non-need-based awards were made. *Average percent of need met:* 97%. *Average financial aid package:* $10,407. *Average need-based loan:* $3850. *Average need-based gift aid:* $6957. *Average non-need based aid:* $2769. *Average indebtedness upon graduation:* $13,275.

Applying *Options:* electronic application. *Application fee:* $40. *Required:* essay or personal statement, high school transcript, minimum 2.8 GPA. *Required for some:* minimum 3.4 GPA. *Application deadlines:* 11/30 (freshmen), 11/30 (transfers). *Notification:* 3/31 (freshmen).

Admissions Contact Associate Director of Admissions and Relations with Schools, University of California, San Diego, 9500 Gilman Drive, 0021, La Jolla, CA 92093-0021. *Phone:* 858-534-4831. *E-mail:* admissionsinfo@ucsd.edu.

UNIVERSITY OF CALIFORNIA, SANTA BARBARA

Santa Barbara, California

- **State-supported** university, founded 1909, part of University of California System
- **Calendar** quarters
- **Degrees** bachelor's, master's, and doctoral
- **Suburban** 989-acre campus
- **Coed,** 17,724 undergraduate students, 96% full-time, 54% women, 46% men
- **Very difficult** entrance level, 50% of applicants were admitted

Undergraduates 16,990 full-time, 734 part-time. Students come from 48 states and territories, 35 other countries, 5% are from out of state, 3% African American, 14% Asian American or Pacific Islander, 15% Hispanic American, 0.9% Native American, 1% international, 7% transferred in, 21% live on campus. *Retention:* 91% of 2001 full-time freshmen returned.

Freshmen *Admission:* 33,986 applied, 17,011 admitted, 3,649 enrolled. *Average high school GPA:* 3.73. *Test scores:* SAT verbal scores over 500: 85%; SAT math scores over 500: 91%; SAT verbal scores over 600: 45%; SAT math scores over 600: 60%; SAT verbal scores over 700: 8%; SAT math scores over 700: 15%.

Faculty *Total:* 963, 82% full-time. *Student/faculty ratio:* 19:1.

Majors African-American studies; anthropology; applied history; art history; Asian-American studies; Asian studies; biochemistry; biology; biopsychology; business economics; cell biology; chemical engineering; chemical engineering technology; chemistry; Chinese; classics; communications; comparative literature; computer science; dance; ecology; economics; electrical/electronic engineering technology; electrical engineering; English; environmental science; film studies; fine/studio arts; French; geography; geology; geophysics/seismology; German; history; interdisciplinary studies; Islamic studies; Italian; Japanese; Latin American studies; legal studies; linguistics; marine biology; mathematical statistics; mathematics; mechanical engineering; medieval/renaissance studies; Mexican-American studies; microbiology/bacteriology; Middle Eastern studies; molecular biology; music; pharmacology; philosophy; physics; physiology; political science; Portuguese; psychology; religious studies; Slavic languages; sociology; Spanish; theater arts/drama; women's studies; zoology.

Academic Programs *Special study options:* academic remediation for entering students, accelerated degree program, advanced placement credit, freshman honors college, honors programs, independent study, internships, off-campus study, services for LD students, student-designed majors, summer session for credit. *ROTC:* Army (b).

Library Davidson Library with 2.6 million titles, 18,155 serial subscriptions, 101,100 audiovisual materials, an OPAC, a Web page.

Computers on Campus 3000 computers available on campus for general student use. A campuswide network can be accessed from off campus. At least one staffed computer lab available.

Student Life *Housing Options:* coed, cooperative. *Activities and Organizations:* drama/theater group, student-run newspaper, radio station, choral group, national fraternities, national sororities. *Campus security:* 24-hour emergency response devices, late-night transport/escort service. *Student Services:* health clinic, personal/psychological counseling, women's center, legal services.

Athletics Member NCAA. All Division I. *Intercollegiate sports:* baseball M(s), basketball M(s)/W(s), bowling M(c)/W(c), crew M(c)/W(c), cross-country running M(s)/W(s), fencing M(c)/W(c), field hockey W(c), golf M(s)/W(c), gymnastics M/W(s), lacrosse M(c)/W(c), rugby M(c), sailing M(c)/W(c), skiing (downhill) M(c)/W(c), soccer M(s)/W(s), softball W(s), swimming M(s)/W(s), tennis M(s)/W(s), track and field M(s)/W(s), volleyball M(s)/W(s), water polo M(s)/W. *Intramural sports:* badminton M/W, basketball M/W, bowling M/W, crew M/W, cross-country running M/W, football M/W, golf M/W, gymnastics M/W, racquetball M/W, soccer M/W, softball M/W, squash M/W, tennis M/W, volleyball M/W, water polo M/W.

Standardized Tests *Required:* SAT I or ACT (for admission), SAT II: Subject Tests (for admission).

Costs (2001–02) *Tuition:* state resident $0 full-time; nonresident $11,074 full-time. *Required fees:* $3841 full-time. *Room and board:* $7891; room only: $5655. Room and board charges vary according to housing facility. *Waivers:* employees or children of employees.

Financial Aid Of all full-time matriculated undergraduates who enrolled in 2001, 9276 applied for aid, 7303 were judged to have need, 2912 had their need fully met. In 2001, 1761 non-need-based awards were made. *Average percent of need met:* 87%. *Average financial aid package:* $8851. *Average need-based loan:* $3767. *Average need-based gift aid:* $5923. *Average non-need based aid:* $4236.

Applying *Options:* electronic application, early admission. *Application fee:* $40. *Required:* essay or personal statement, high school transcript. *Required for some:* interview. *Application deadlines:* 11/30 (freshmen), 11/30 (transfers). *Notification:* 3/15 (freshmen).

Admissions Contact Mr. William Villa, Director of Admissions/Relations with Schools, University of California, Santa Barbara, Santa Barbara, CA 93106. *Phone:* 805-893-2485. *Fax:* 805-893-2676. *E-mail:* appinfo@sa.ucsb.edu.

UNIVERSITY OF CALIFORNIA, SANTA CRUZ

Santa Cruz, California

- **State-supported** university, founded 1965, part of University of California System
- **Calendar** quarters
- **Degrees** certificates, bachelor's, master's, and doctoral
- **Small-town** 2000-acre campus with easy access to San Francisco and San Jose
- **Endowment** $85.3 million
- **Coed,** 12,034 undergraduate students, 95% full-time, 57% women, 43% men
- **Very difficult** entrance level, 81% of applicants were admitted

Undergraduates 11,382 full-time, 652 part-time. 6% are from out of state, 2% African American, 16% Asian American or Pacific Islander, 13% Hispanic American, 0.9% Native American, 1% international, 8% transferred in, 42% live on campus. *Retention:* 87% of 2001 full-time freshmen returned.

Freshmen *Admission:* 19,578 applied, 15,833 admitted, 3,023 enrolled. *Average high school GPA:* 3.47. *Test scores:* SAT verbal scores over 500: 77%; SAT math scores over 500: 80%; ACT scores over 18: 89%; SAT verbal scores over 600: 40%; SAT math scores over 600: 41%; ACT scores over 24: 53%; SAT verbal scores over 700: 8%; SAT math scores over 700: 7%; ACT scores over 30: 8%.

Faculty *Total:* 691, 70% full-time. *Student/faculty ratio:* 19:1.

Majors American studies; anthropology; applied mathematics; art; art history; Asian studies; astrophysics; biochemistry; biology; botany; business economics; cell biology; chemistry; Chinese; classics; cognitive psychology/psycholinguistics; comparative literature; computer engineering; computer science; creative writing; dance; developmental/child psychology; drawing; earth sciences; East Asian studies; ecology; economics; electrical engineering; English related; environmental science; European history; family/community studies; film studies; film/video production; foreign languages/literatures; French; geology; geophysics/seismology; German; Greek (ancient and medieval); Hispanic-American studies; history; information sciences/systems; international economics; Italian; Italian studies; Japanese; Latin American studies; Latin (ancient and medieval); legal studies; linguistics; literature; marine biology; mathematics; mathematics education; molecular biology; music; peace/conflict studies; philosophy; photography; physics; physiological psychology/psychobiology; plant sciences; political science; printmaking; psychology; religious studies; Russian/Slavic studies; sculpture; social psychology; sociology; South Asian studies; Southeast Asian studies; Spanish; theater arts/drama; theater design; women's studies.

Academic Programs *Special study options:* academic remediation for entering students, adult/continuing education programs, advanced placement credit, cooperative education, double majors, English as a second language, freshman honors college, honors programs, independent study, internships, off-campus study, part-time degree program, services for LD students, student-designed majors, study abroad, summer session for credit. *ROTC:* Army (c), Navy (c), Air Force (c). *Unusual degree programs:* 3-2 engineering with University of California, Berkeley.

Library McHenry Library plus 9 others with 1.2 million titles, 10,004 serial subscriptions, 500,000 audiovisual materials, an OPAC, a Web page.

Computers on Campus 200 computers available on campus for general student use. A campuswide network can be accessed from student residence rooms and from off campus. Internet access, at least one staffed computer lab available.

Student Life *Housing Options:* coed, men-only, women-only. *Activities and Organizations:* drama/theater group, student-run newspaper, radio station, choral group, Asian Pacific Islander Student Alliance, African/Black Student Alliance, Movimiento Estudiantil Chicano de Aztlan, Students Alliance of North American Indians, Estudiantes Para Salud del Pueblo, national fraternities, national sororities. *Campus security:* 24-hour emergency response devices and patrols, late-night transport/escort service, controlled dormitory access, evening main gate security, campus police force and fire station. *Student Services:* health clinic, personal/psychological counseling, women's center, legal services.

Athletics Member NCAA. All Division III. *Intercollegiate sports:* basketball M/W, fencing M(c)/W(c), lacrosse M(c)/W(c), rugby M, sailing M(c)/W(c), soccer M, swimming M/W, tennis M/W, volleyball M/W, water polo M/W. *Intramural sports:* badminton M/W, basketball M/W, cross-country running M/W, fencing M/W, racquetball M/W, rugby M(c), soccer M/W, softball M/W, tennis M/W, volleyball M/W.

Standardized Tests *Required:* SAT I or ACT (for admission).

Costs (2002–03) *Tuition:* state resident $0 full-time; nonresident $10,704 full-time. *Required fees:* $4300 full-time. *Room and board:* $9355; room only: $6825. Room and board charges vary according to board plan and housing facility. *Payment plans:* installment, deferred payment.

Financial Aid Of all full-time matriculated undergraduates who enrolled in 2001, 6540 applied for aid, 4906 were judged to have need, 2749 had their need fully met. In 2001, 293 non-need-based awards were made. *Average percent of need met:* 93%. *Average financial aid package:* $10,262. *Average need-based loan:* $4027. *Average need-based gift aid:* $6465. *Average non-need based aid:* $2781. *Average indebtedness upon graduation:* $13,133.

Applying *Options:* electronic application. *Application fee:* $40. *Required:* essay or personal statement, high school transcript. *Application deadlines:* 11/30 (freshmen), 11/30 (transfers). *Notification:* 3/1 (freshmen).

Admissions Contact Mr. Kevin M. Browne, Executive Director of Admissions and University Registrar, University of California, Santa Cruz, Admissions Office, Cook House, Santa Cruz, CA 95064. *Phone:* 831-459-5779. *Fax:* 831-459-4452. *E-mail:* admissions@cats.ucsc.edu.

UNIVERSITY OF JUDAISM
Bel Air, California

- **Independent Jewish** comprehensive, founded 1947
- **Calendar** semesters
- **Degrees** bachelor's and master's
- **Suburban** 28-acre campus with easy access to Los Angeles
- **Coed,** 106 undergraduate students, 92% full-time, 57% women, 43% men
- **Moderately difficult** entrance level, 87% of applicants were admitted

Undergraduates 98 full-time, 8 part-time. Students come from 22 states and territories, 2 other countries, 31% are from out of state, 3% African American, 10% Hispanic American, 6% international, 18% transferred in, 60% live on campus. *Retention:* 58% of 2001 full-time freshmen returned.

Freshmen *Admission:* 78 applied, 68 admitted, 26 enrolled. *Average high school GPA:* 3.4. *Test scores:* SAT verbal scores over 500: 62%; SAT math scores over 500: 62%; ACT scores over 18: 100%; SAT verbal scores over 600: 27%; SAT math scores over 600: 27%; ACT scores over 24: 25%; SAT verbal scores over 700: 5%; SAT math scores over 700: 5%.

Faculty *Total:* 91, 21% full-time, 42% with terminal degrees. *Student/faculty ratio:* 6:1.

Majors Business economics; interdisciplinary studies; Judaic studies; liberal arts and sciences/liberal studies; literature; political science; pre-medicine; psychology.

Academic Programs *Special study options:* academic remediation for entering students, accelerated degree program, adult/continuing education programs, advanced placement credit, honors programs, internships, off-campus study, part-time degree program, student-designed majors, study abroad. *Unusual degree programs:* 3-2 education.

Library Ostrow Library with 105,000 titles, 400 serial subscriptions, a Web page.

Computers on Campus 16 computers available on campus for general student use. At least one staffed computer lab available.

Student Life *Housing:* on-campus residence required through junior year. *Options:* coed. *Activities and Organizations:* drama/theater group, student-run newspaper, radio station, choral group, ASUJC, Graduate Student Association, Resident Life Council, College Urban Fellows, UJ Chorale. *Campus security:* 24-hour emergency response devices and patrols, controlled dormitory access. *Student Services:* health clinic, personal/psychological counseling.

Athletics *Intramural sports:* basketball M/W, football M/W, softball M/W.

Standardized Tests *Required:* SAT I or ACT (for admission).

Costs (2001–02) *Comprehensive fee:* $23,630 includes full-time tuition ($15,000), mandatory fees ($530), and room and board ($8100). Part-time tuition: $625 per unit. *Required fees:* $530 per year part-time. *Waivers:* employees or children of employees.

Financial Aid Of all full-time matriculated undergraduates who enrolled in 2001, 57 applied for aid, 52 were judged to have need. In 2001, 6 non-need-based awards were made. *Average percent of need met:* 99%. *Average financial aid package:* $17,683. *Average need-based loan:* $5508. *Average need-based gift aid:* $7042. *Average non-need based aid:* $7500. *Average indebtedness upon graduation:* $13,574.

Applying *Options:* early decision, deferred entrance. *Application fee:* $35. *Required:* essay or personal statement, high school transcript, 2 letters of recommendation. *Required for some:* interview. *Recommended:* minimum 3.2 GPA, interview. *Application deadlines:* 1/31 (freshmen), 4/15 (transfers). *Early decision:* 11/15. *Notification:* continuous (freshmen), 12/15 (early decision).

Admissions Contact Ms. Jillian Rothschild, Assistant Director of Undergraduate Admissions, University of Judaism, 15600 Mulholland Drive, Bel Air, CA 90077. *Phone:* 310-476-9777 Ext. 299. *Toll-free phone:* 888-853-6763. *Fax:* 310-471-3657. *E-mail:* admissions@uj.edu.

UNIVERSITY OF LA VERNE
La Verne, California

- **Independent** university, founded 1891
- **Calendar** 4-1-4
- **Degrees** certificates, associate, bachelor's, master's, doctoral, first professional, post-master's, and postbachelor's certificates (also offers continuing education program with significant enrollment not reflected in profile)
- **Suburban** 26-acre campus with easy access to Los Angeles
- **Coed,** 1,422 undergraduate students, 94% full-time, 60% women, 40% men
- **Moderately difficult** entrance level, 72% of applicants were admitted

The University of La Verne is an independent university located in southern California that emphasizes a liberal arts foundation in addition to career preparation. The 4-1-4 academic calendar and an enrollment of approximately 1,300 students translates into flexible scheduling, generous access to course work, and faculty focus on individual student success.

Undergraduates 1,343 full-time, 79 part-time. Students come from 21 states and territories, 14 other countries, 5% are from out of state, 9% African American, 7% Asian American or Pacific Islander, 36% Hispanic American, 0.8% Native American, 1% international, 9% transferred in, 35% live on campus. *Retention:* 82% of 2001 full-time freshmen returned.

Freshmen *Admission:* 1,164 applied, 838 admitted, 309 enrolled. *Average high school GPA:* 3.44. *Test scores:* SAT verbal scores over 500: 50%; SAT math scores over 500: 51%; ACT scores over 18: 81%; SAT verbal scores over 600: 10%; SAT math scores over 600: 12%; ACT scores over 24: 22%; SAT verbal scores over 700: 2%; SAT math scores over 700: 1%; ACT scores over 30: 2%.

Faculty *Total:* 232, 42% full-time, 53% with terminal degrees. *Student/faculty ratio:* 14:1.

University of La Verne (continued)

Majors Accounting; adult/continuing education; anthropology; art; behavioral sciences; biological/physical sciences; biology; broadcast journalism; business administration; business economics; business marketing and marketing management; chemistry; child care/development; communications; comparative literature; computer science; criminology; developmental/child psychology; early childhood education; education; elementary education; English; environmental biology; French; German; health services administration; history; international business; international relations; journalism; liberal arts and sciences/liberal studies; mathematics; music; music teacher education; natural resources management; natural sciences; organizational behavior; paralegal/legal assistant; philosophy; physical education; physics; political science; pre-dentistry; pre-law; premedicine; psychology; public administration; radio/television broadcasting; religious studies; secondary education; social sciences; sociology; Spanish; theater arts/drama.

Academic Programs *Special study options:* academic remediation for entering students, accelerated degree program, adult/continuing education programs, advanced placement credit, distance learning, double majors, English as a second language, freshman honors college, honors programs, independent study, internships, off-campus study, part-time degree program, services for LD students, student-designed majors, study abroad, summer session for credit.

Library Wilson Library plus 1 other with 215,000 titles, 3,600 serial subscriptions, an OPAC, a Web page.

Computers on Campus 150 computers available on campus for general student use. A campuswide network can be accessed from student residence rooms and from off campus that provide access to on-line grade information. Internet access, at least one staffed computer lab available.

Student Life *Housing Options:* coed, women-only. *Activities and Organizations:* drama/theater group, student-run newspaper, radio and television station, choral group, Latino Student Forum (LSF), Interfraternity/Sorority Council, African-American Student Association (AASA), ASF (Associated Students Federation), Alpha Kappa Psi, national fraternities, national sororities. *Campus security:* 24-hour emergency response devices and patrols, late-night transport/escort service, controlled dormitory access, whistle program. *Student Services:* health clinic, personal/psychological counseling.

Athletics Member NCAA. All Division III. *Intercollegiate sports:* baseball M, basketball M/W, cross-country running M/W, football M, golf M, soccer M/W, softball W, swimming M/W, tennis M/W, track and field M/W, volleyball M/W, water polo M/W. *Intramural sports:* basketball M/W, skiing (downhill) M/W, softball M/W, table tennis M/W, tennis M/W, volleyball M/W.

Standardized Tests *Required:* SAT I or ACT (for admission).

Costs (2001–02) *Comprehensive fee:* $24,280 includes full-time tuition ($18,000) and room and board ($6280). Full-time tuition and fees vary according to course load, degree level, location, and program. Part-time tuition: $555 per unit. Part-time tuition and fees vary according to course load, degree level, location, and program. *Required fees:* $30 per term part-time. *Room and board:* College room only: $3120. Room and board charges vary according to board plan, housing facility, and location. *Payment plans:* installment, deferred payment. *Waivers:* employees or children of employees.

Financial Aid Of all full-time matriculated undergraduates who enrolled in 2001, 1090 applied for aid, 1011 were judged to have need, 228 had their need fully met. 585 Federal Work-Study jobs (averaging $2018). In 2001, 15 non-need-based awards were made. *Average percent of need met:* 82%. *Average financial aid package:* $17,746. *Average need-based loan:* $4254. *Average need-based gift aid:* $12,815. *Average non-need based aid:* $2610.

Applying *Options:* common application, electronic application, deferred entrance. *Application fee:* $50. *Required:* essay or personal statement, high school transcript, 2 letters of recommendation. *Recommended:* interview. *Application deadline:* rolling (freshmen), rolling (transfers). *Notification:* continuous (freshmen).

Admissions Contact Ms. Lisa Meyer, Dean of Admissions, University of La Verne, 1950 Third Street, La Verne, CA 91750-4443. *Phone:* 800-876-4858. *Toll-free phone:* 800-876-4858. *Fax:* 909-392-2714. *E-mail:* admissions@ulv.edu.

UNIVERSITY OF PHOENIX-NORTHERN CALIFORNIA CAMPUS

Pleasanton, California

- **Proprietary** comprehensive
- **Calendar** continuous
- **Degrees** certificates, associate, bachelor's, master's, doctoral, post-master's, and postbachelor's certificates (courses conducted at 54 campuses and learning centers in 13 states)
- **Coed,** 5,231 undergraduate students, 100% full-time, 59% women, 41% men
- **Noncompetitive** entrance level

Undergraduates Students come from 27 states and territories, 2% are from out of state.

Freshmen *Admission:* 31 admitted.

Faculty *Total:* 791, 1% full-time, 21% with terminal degrees. *Student/faculty ratio:* 13:1.

Majors Accounting; business administration; business marketing and marketing management; information technology; management information systems/business data processing; management science; nursing science; public administration and services related.

Academic Programs *Special study options:* accelerated degree program, adult/continuing education programs, advanced placement credit, distance learning, external degree program, independent study.

Library University Library with 17.5 million titles, 9,000 serial subscriptions, an OPAC, a Web page.

Computers on Campus A campuswide network can be accessed from off campus. Internet access, at least one staffed computer lab available.

Student Life *Housing:* college housing not available.

Costs (2001–02) *Tuition:* $10,200 full-time. Full-time tuition and fees vary according to location and program. *Payment plan:* deferred payment. *Waivers:* employees or children of employees.

Applying *Options:* deferred entrance. *Application fee:* $85. *Required:* 2 years of work experience. *Required for some:* high school transcript. *Application deadline:* rolling (freshmen), rolling (transfers).

Admissions Contact Ms. Beth Barilla, Director of Admissions, University of Phoenix-Northern California Campus, 4615 East Elwood Street, Phoenix, AZ 85040-1958. *Phone:* 480-927-0099 Ext. 1218. *Toll-free phone:* 877-4-STUDENT. *Fax:* 480-594-1758. *E-mail:* beth.barilla@apollogrp.edu.

UNIVERSITY OF PHOENIX-SACRAMENTO CAMPUS

Sacramento, California

- **Proprietary** comprehensive
- **Calendar** continuous
- **Degrees** certificates, associate, bachelor's, master's, doctoral, post-master's, and postbachelor's certificates (courses conducted at 54 campuses and learning centers in 13 states)
- **Coed,** 2,865 undergraduate students, 100% full-time, 58% women, 42% men
- **Noncompetitive** entrance level

Undergraduates Students come from 23 states and territories, 2% are from out of state.

Freshmen *Admission:* 31 admitted.

Faculty *Total:* 302, 2% full-time, 19% with terminal degrees. *Student/faculty ratio:* 13:1.

Majors Accounting; business administration; human services; information technology; management information systems/business data processing; management science; nursing science.

Academic Programs *Special study options:* accelerated degree program, adult/continuing education programs, advanced placement credit, distance learning, external degree program, independent study.

Library University Library with 17.5 million titles, 9,000 serial subscriptions, an OPAC, a Web page.

Computers on Campus A campuswide network can be accessed from off campus. Internet access, at least one staffed computer lab available.

Student Life *Housing:* college housing not available.

Costs (2001–02) *Tuition:* $10,500 full-time. Full-time tuition and fees vary according to location and program. *Payment plan:* deferred payment. *Waivers:* employees or children of employees.

Applying *Options:* deferred entrance. *Application fee:* $85. *Required:* 2 years of work experience. *Required for some:* high school transcript. *Application deadline:* rolling (freshmen), rolling (transfers).

Admissions Contact Ms. Beth Barilla, Director of Admissions, University of Phoenix-Sacramento Campus, 4615 East Elwood Street, Phoenix, AZ 85040-1958. *Phone:* 480-927-0099 Ext. 1218. *Toll-free phone:* 800-266-2107. *Fax:* 480-594-1758. *E-mail:* beth.barilla@apollo.grp.edu.

UNIVERSITY OF PHOENIX-SAN DIEGO CAMPUS

San Diego, California

- **Proprietary** comprehensive
- **Calendar** continuous

■ **Degrees** certificates, associate, bachelor's, master's, doctoral, post-master's, and postbachelor's certificates (courses conducted at 54 campuses and learning centers in 13 states)
■ **Coed,** 2,879 undergraduate students, 100% full-time, 52% women, 48% men
■ **Noncompetitive** entrance level

Undergraduates Students come from 27 states and territories, 2% are from out of state.
Freshmen *Admission:* 13 admitted.
Faculty *Total:* 920, 1% full-time, 18% with terminal degrees. *Student/faculty ratio:* 13:1.
Majors Accounting; business administration; business marketing and marketing management; enterprise management; information technology; management information systems/business data processing; nursing science; public administration and services related.
Academic Programs *Special study options:* accelerated degree program, adult/continuing education programs, advanced placement credit, distance learning, external degree program, independent study.
Library University Library with 17.5 million titles, 9,000 serial subscriptions, an OPAC, a Web page.
Computers on Campus A campuswide network can be accessed from off campus. Internet access, at least one staffed computer lab available.
Student Life *Housing:* college housing not available.
Costs (2001–02) *Tuition:* $9750 full-time. *Payment plan:* deferred payment. *Waivers:* employees or children of employees.
Applying *Options:* deferred entrance. *Application fee:* $85. *Required:* 2 years of work experience. *Required for some:* high school transcript. *Application deadline:* rolling (freshmen), rolling (transfers).
Admissions Contact Ms. Beth Barilla, Director of Admissions, University of Phoenix-San Diego Campus, 4615 East Elwood Street, Phoenix, AZ 85040-1958. *Phone:* 480-927-0099 Ext. 1218. *Toll-free phone:* 888-UOP-INFO. *Fax:* 480-594-1758. *E-mail:* beth.barilla@apollogrp.edu.

University of Phoenix-Southern California Campus
Fountain Valley, California

■ **Proprietary** comprehensive
■ **Calendar** continuous
■ **Degrees** certificates, associate, bachelor's, master's, doctoral, post-master's, and postbachelor's certificates (courses conducted at 54 campuses and learning centers in 13 states)
■ **Coed,** 9,469 undergraduate students, 100% full-time, 41% women, 59% men
■ **Noncompetitive** entrance level

Undergraduates Students come from 35 states and territories, 1% are from out of state.
Freshmen *Admission:* 67 admitted.
Faculty *Total:* 1,267, 1% full-time, 21% with terminal degrees. *Student/faculty ratio:* 13:1.
Majors Accounting; business administration; information technology; nursing science; public administration and services related.
Academic Programs *Special study options:* accelerated degree program, adult/continuing education programs, advanced placement credit, distance learning, external degree program, independent study.
Library University Library with 17.5 million titles, 9,000 serial subscriptions, an OPAC, a Web page.
Computers on Campus A campuswide network can be accessed from off campus. Internet access, at least one staffed computer lab available.
Student Life *Housing:* college housing not available.
Costs (2001–02) *Tuition:* $10,470 full-time. Full-time tuition and fees vary according to location and program. *Payment plan:* deferred payment. *Waivers:* employees or children of employees.
Applying *Options:* deferred entrance. *Application fee:* $85. *Required:* 2 years of work experience. *Required for some:* high school transcript. *Application deadline:* rolling (freshmen), rolling (transfers).
Admissions Contact Ms. Beth B arilla, Director of Admissions, University of Phoenix-Southern California Campus, 4615 East Elwood Street, Phoenix, AZ 85040-1958. *Phone:* 480-927-0099 Ext. 1218. *Toll-free phone:* 800-228-7240. *E-mail:* beth.barilla@apollogrp.edu.

University of Redlands
Redlands, California

■ **Independent** comprehensive, founded 1907
■ **Calendar** 4-1-4
■ **Degrees** bachelor's, master's, post-master's, and postbachelor's certificates
■ **Small-town** 140-acre campus with easy access to Los Angeles
■ **Endowment** $59.8 million
■ **Coed,** 1,946 undergraduate students, 98% full-time, 58% women, 42% men
■ **Moderately difficult** entrance level, 77% of applicants were admitted

Undergraduates 1,905 full-time, 41 part-time. Students come from 42 states and territories, 18 other countries, 27% are from out of state, 3% African American, 6% Asian American or Pacific Islander, 11% Hispanic American, 0.7% Native American, 0.8% international, 4% transferred in, 74% live on campus. *Retention:* 81% of 2001 full-time freshmen returned.
Freshmen *Admission:* 2,478 applied, 1,909 admitted, 614 enrolled. *Average high school GPA:* 3.50. *Test scores:* SAT verbal scores over 500: 83%; SAT math scores over 500: 83%; ACT scores over 18: 96%; SAT verbal scores over 600: 31%; SAT math scores over 600: 32%; ACT scores over 24: 44%; SAT verbal scores over 700: 5%; SAT math scores over 700: 3%; ACT scores over 30: 4%.
Faculty *Total:* 233, 57% full-time, 61% with terminal degrees. *Student/faculty ratio:* 12:1.
Majors Accounting; anthropology; art history; Asian studies; biology; business; business administration; chemistry; computer science; creative writing; economics; education; elementary education; English; environmental science; fine/studio arts; French; German; history; interdisciplinary studies; international relations; liberal arts and sciences/liberal studies; literature; management information systems/business data processing; mathematics; music; music (general performance); music history; music (piano and organ performance); music teacher education; music theory and composition; music (voice and choral/opera performance); philosophy; physics; political science; psychology; religious studies; secondary education; sociology; Spanish; speech-language pathology/audiology; speech therapy.
Academic Programs *Special study options:* academic remediation for entering students, adult/continuing education programs, advanced placement credit, double majors, freshman honors college, honors programs, independent study, internships, off-campus study, services for LD students, student-designed majors, study abroad. *ROTC:* Army (c), Air Force (c).
Library Armacost Library with 246,725 titles, 1,876 serial subscriptions, 10,870 audiovisual materials, an OPAC, a Web page.
Computers on Campus 277 computers available on campus for general student use. A campuswide network can be accessed from student residence rooms and from off campus. Internet access, at least one staffed computer lab available.
Student Life *Housing:* on-campus residence required through senior year. *Options:* coed, men-only, women-only, cooperative, disabled students. *Activities and Organizations:* drama/theater group, student-run newspaper, choral group, Associated Students, service organizations, cultural organizations, social awareness groups. *Campus security:* 24-hour emergency response devices and patrols, student patrols, late-night transport/escort service, controlled dormitory access, safety whistles. *Student Services:* health clinic, personal/psychological counseling, women's center.
Athletics Member NCAA. All Division III. *Intercollegiate sports:* baseball M, basketball M/W, cross-country running M/W, football M, golf M, lacrosse W, soccer M/W, softball W, swimming M/W, tennis M/W, track and field M/W, volleyball W, water polo M/W. *Intramural sports:* badminton M/W, basketball M/W, bowling M/W, football M/W, racquetball M/W, soccer M/W, softball M/W, table tennis M/W, tennis M/W, volleyball M/W, water polo M/W.
Standardized Tests *Required:* SAT I or ACT (for admission).
Costs (2001–02) *Comprehensive fee:* $29,246 includes full-time tuition ($21,180), mandatory fees ($226), and room and board ($7840). Part-time tuition: $662 per credit. Part-time tuition and fees vary according to course load. *Required fees:* $40 per term part-time. *Room and board:* College room only: $4370. Room and board charges vary according to board plan and housing facility. *Payment plan:* installment. *Waivers:* employees or children of employees.
Financial Aid Of all full-time matriculated undergraduates who enrolled in 2001, 1572 applied for aid, 1325 were judged to have need, 790 had their need fully met. 686 Federal Work-Study jobs (averaging $2062). In 2001, 123 non-need-based awards were made. *Average percent of need met:* 74%. *Average financial aid package:* $21,440. *Average need-based loan:* $4491. *Average need-based gift aid:* $15,840. *Average non-need based aid:* $8569.
Applying *Options:* common application, electronic application, early admission, deferred entrance. *Application fee:* $40. *Required:* essay or personal state-

University of Redlands (continued)
ment, high school transcript, 2 letters of recommendation. *Recommended:* interview. *Application deadline:* 7/1 (freshmen), rolling (transfers). *Notification:* continuous (freshmen).

Admissions Contact Mr. Paul Driscoll, Dean of Admissions, University of Redlands, PO Box 3080, Redlands, CA 92373-0999. *Phone:* 909-335-4074. *Toll-free phone:* 800-455-5064. *Fax:* 909-335-4089. *E-mail:* admissions@uor.edu.

UNIVERSITY OF SAN DIEGO

San Diego, California

- **Independent Roman Catholic** university, founded 1949
- **Calendar** 4-1-4
- **Degrees** bachelor's, master's, doctoral, and first professional
- **Urban** 180-acre campus
- **Endowment** $97.9 million
- **Coed,** 4,809 undergraduate students, 96% full-time, 60% women, 40% men
- **Moderately difficult** entrance level, 50% of applicants were admitted

The University of San Diego (USD) is located in a beautiful setting overlooking Mission Bay and the Pacific ocean. USD is a Roman Catholic university that is committed to belief in the existence of God, the dignity of human beings, and service to the community.

Undergraduates 4,639 full-time, 170 part-time. Students come from 50 states and territories, 67 other countries, 45% are from out of state, 2% African American, 7% Asian American or Pacific Islander, 14% Hispanic American, 1% Native American, 3% international, 8% transferred in, 43% live on campus. *Retention:* 88% of 2001 full-time freshmen returned.

Freshmen *Admission:* 6,702 applied, 3,378 admitted, 1,004 enrolled. *Average high school GPA:* 3.75. *Test scores:* SAT verbal scores over 500: 87%; SAT math scores over 500: 89%; ACT scores over 18: 97%; SAT verbal scores over 600: 40%; SAT math scores over 600: 48%; ACT scores over 24: 64%; SAT verbal scores over 700: 5%; SAT math scores over 700: 5%; ACT scores over 30: 8%.

Faculty *Total:* 654, 48% full-time, 77% with terminal degrees. *Student/faculty ratio:* 16:1.

Majors Accounting; anthropology; art; biology; business administration; business economics; chemistry; computer science; economics; education; electrical engineering; English; French; Hispanic-American studies; history; humanities; industrial/manufacturing engineering; international relations; liberal arts and sciences/liberal studies; marine science; mass communications; mathematics; music; oceanography; philosophy; physics; political science; pre-medicine; psychology; religious studies; sociology; Spanish; urban studies.

Academic Programs *Special study options:* adult/continuing education programs, advanced placement credit, double majors, honors programs, independent study, internships, off-campus study, part-time degree program, study abroad, summer session for credit. *ROTC:* Army (c), Navy (b), Air Force (c).

Library Helen K. and James S. Copley Library plus 1 other with 500,000 titles, 2,600 serial subscriptions, 14,000 audiovisual materials, an OPAC.

Computers on Campus 260 computers available on campus for general student use. A campuswide network can be accessed from student residence rooms and from off campus. Internet access, online (class) registration, at least one staffed computer lab available.

Student Life *Housing:* on-campus residence required for freshman year. *Options:* coed, women-only, disabled students. *Activities and Organizations:* drama/theater group, student-run newspaper, television station, choral group, International Student Organization, Student Alumni Association, United Front/Multicultural Center, Associated Student Government, national fraternities, national sororities. *Campus security:* 24-hour emergency response devices and patrols, student patrols, late-night transport/escort service, controlled dormitory access, escort service. *Student Services:* health clinic, personal/psychological counseling, women's center, legal services.

Athletics Member NCAA. All Division I. *Intercollegiate sports:* baseball M(s), basketball M(s)/W(s), crew M/W, cross-country running M(s)/W(s), equestrian sports W(c), football M, golf M(s), ice hockey M(c), lacrosse M(c)/W(c), rugby M(c), soccer M(s)/W(s), softball W, swimming W(s), tennis M(s)/W(s), volleyball M(c)/W(s). *Intramural sports:* basketball M/W, football M/W, golf M/W, sailing M(c)/W(c), skiing (downhill) M(c)/W(c), soccer M/W, softball M/W, tennis M/W, volleyball M/W, water polo M/W, wrestling M(c).

Standardized Tests *Required:* SAT I or ACT (for admission). *Recommended:* SAT II: Writing Test (for admission).

Costs (2001–02) *Comprehensive fee:* $28,898 includes full-time tuition ($20,350), mandatory fees ($108), and room and board ($8440). Part-time tuition: $705 per unit. Part-time tuition and fees vary according to course load. *Room and board:* Room and board charges vary according to board plan and housing facility. *Payment plan:* installment. *Waivers:* employees or children of employees.

Financial Aid Of all full-time matriculated undergraduates who enrolled in 2001, 2991 applied for aid, 2151 were judged to have need, 1012 had their need fully met. 583 Federal Work-Study jobs (averaging $2119). 116 State and other part-time jobs (averaging $4285). In 2001, 568 non-need-based awards were made. *Average percent of need met:* 93%. *Average financial aid package:* $17,965. *Average need-based loan:* $4693. *Average need-based gift aid:* $13,746. *Average non-need based aid:* $10,237. *Average indebtedness upon graduation:* $23,800.

Applying *Options:* electronic application, early admission, early action, deferred entrance. *Application fee:* $55. *Required:* essay or personal statement, high school transcript, 1 letter of recommendation. *Application deadlines:* 1/5 (freshmen), 3/1 (transfers). *Notification:* 4/15 (freshmen), 1/31 (early action).

Admissions Contact Mr. Stephen Pultz, Director of Undergraduate Admissions, University of San Diego, 5998 Alcala Park, San Diego, CA 92110. *Phone:* 619-260-4506. *Toll-free phone:* 800-248-4873. *Fax:* 619-260-6836. *E-mail:* admissions@sandiego.edu.

UNIVERSITY OF SAN FRANCISCO

San Francisco, California

- **Independent Roman Catholic (Jesuit)** university, founded 1855
- **Calendar** 4-1-4
- **Degrees** certificates, bachelor's, master's, doctoral, first professional, and post-master's certificates
- **Urban** 55-acre campus
- **Endowment** $145.0 million
- **Coed,** 4,687 undergraduate students, 94% full-time, 62% women, 38% men
- **Moderately difficult** entrance level, 79% of applicants were admitted

Undergraduates 4,429 full-time, 258 part-time. Students come from 52 states and territories, 71 other countries, 22% are from out of state, 4% African American, 26% Asian American or Pacific Islander, 11% Hispanic American, 0.5% Native American, 9% international, 8% transferred in, 48% live on campus. *Retention:* 82% of 2001 full-time freshmen returned.

Freshmen *Admission:* 3,835 applied, 3,038 admitted, 844 enrolled. *Average high school GPA:* 3.33. *Test scores:* SAT verbal scores over 500: 68%; SAT math scores over 500: 68%; ACT scores over 18: 93%; SAT verbal scores over 600: 25%; SAT math scores over 600: 24%; ACT scores over 24: 36%; SAT verbal scores over 700: 5%; SAT math scores over 700: 3%; ACT scores over 30: 6%.

Faculty *Total:* 778, 37% full-time, 92% with terminal degrees. *Student/faculty ratio:* 13:1.

Majors Accounting; adult/continuing education; advertising; applied economics; architecture; athletic training/sports medicine; bilingual/bicultural education; biochemistry; biology; biophysics; broadcast journalism; business; business administration; business marketing and marketing management; chemistry; communications; computer/information sciences; computer science; drawing; economics; education; education administration; elementary education; English; environmental science; exercise sciences; fashion design/illustration; finance; fine/studio arts; French; graphic design/commercial art/illustration; health/physical education; history; hotel and restaurant management; industrial design; information sciences/systems; interdisciplinary studies; interior design; international business; journalism; liberal arts and sciences/liberal studies; management information systems/business data processing; mass communications; mathematics; nursing; nursing administration; nursing (public health); painting; philosophy; photography; physical education; physics; political science; pre-dentistry; pre-law; pre-medicine; pre-veterinary studies; printmaking; psychology; public administration; radio/television broadcasting; religious studies; secondary education; sociology; Spanish; sport/fitness administration; theology; visual/performing arts.

Academic Programs *Special study options:* academic remediation for entering students, accelerated degree program, adult/continuing education programs, advanced placement credit, cooperative education, distance learning, English as a second language, external degree program, honors programs, internships, off-campus study, part-time degree program, services for LD students, student-designed majors, study abroad, summer session for credit. *ROTC:* Army (b), Air Force (c). *Unusual degree programs:* 3-2 engineering with University of Southern California; physics.

Library Gleeson Library plus 2 others with 755,000 titles, 2,706 serial subscriptions, 1,730 audiovisual materials, an OPAC, a Web page.

Computers on Campus 250 computers available on campus for general student use. A campuswide network can be accessed from student residence rooms and from off campus. Internet access, online (class) registration, at least one staffed computer lab available.

Student Life *Housing:* on-campus residence required through sophomore year. *Options:* coed, women-only. *Activities and Organizations:* drama/theater group, student-run newspaper, radio station, choral group, Student Leadership, Student Media, College Players, national fraternities, national sororities. *Campus security:* 24-hour emergency response devices and patrols, late-night transport/escort service, controlled dormitory access. *Student Services:* health clinic, personal/psychological counseling.

Athletics Member NCAA. All Division I. *Intercollegiate sports:* baseball M(s), basketball M(s)/W(s), cross-country running M(s)/W(s), fencing M(c)/W(c), golf M(s)/W(s), riflery M(s)/W(s), soccer M(s)/W(s), tennis M(s)/W(s), volleyball M(c)/W(s). *Intramural sports:* badminton M/W, basketball M/W, bowling M/W, crew M, cross-country running M/W, fencing M/W, field hockey W, football M/W, racquetball M/W, rugby M, soccer M/W, softball M/W, swimming M/W, table tennis M/W, tennis M/W, volleyball M/W, water polo M.

Standardized Tests *Required:* SAT I or ACT (for admission).

Costs (2001–02) *Comprehensive fee:* $29,110 includes full-time tuition ($20,190), mandatory fees ($120), and room and board ($8800). Part-time tuition: $740 per credit. *Required fees:* $120 per year part-time. *Room and board:* College room only: $6300. Room and board charges vary according to board plan and housing facility. *Payment plan:* installment. *Waivers:* employees or children of employees.

Financial Aid Of all full-time matriculated undergraduates who enrolled in 2001, 2229 applied for aid, 2019 were judged to have need, 204 had their need fully met. *Average percent of need met:* 77%. *Average financial aid package:* $17,528. *Average need-based loan:* $5345. *Average need-based gift aid:* $9910.

Applying *Options:* common application, electronic application, early action, deferred entrance. *Application fee:* $55. *Required:* essay or personal statement, high school transcript, minimum 2.8 GPA, 1 letter of recommendation. *Required for some:* interview. *Recommended:* minimum 3.0 GPA. *Application deadline:* 2/1 (freshmen), rolling (transfers). *Notification:* continuous until 8/15 (freshmen), 1/15 (early action).

Admissions Contact Mr. William Henley, Director of Admissions, University of San Francisco, Office of Admissions, 2130 Fulton Street, San Francisco, CA 94117-1080. *Phone:* 415-422-6563. *Toll-free phone:* 800-CALL USF. *Fax:* 415-422-2217. *E-mail:* admissions@usfca.edu.

UNIVERSITY OF SOUTHERN CALIFORNIA

Los Angeles, California

- **Independent** university, founded 1880
- **Calendar** semesters
- **Degrees** bachelor's, master's, doctoral, first professional, post-master's, postbachelor's, and first professional certificates
- **Urban** 155-acre campus
- **Endowment** $2.1 billion
- **Coed,** 16,020 undergraduate students, 96% full-time, 50% women, 50% men
- **Very difficult** entrance level, 32% of applicants were admitted

Hailed for linking a powerful educational community with a diverse city and neighborhood, USC is the largest private university in the west. USC students benefit from a creative research and teaching menu. Majors and minors in demanding traditional liberal arts and science programs and 18 respected professional schools are offered. Living in Southern California gives students a comprehensive academic and hands-on experience.

Undergraduates 15,405 full-time, 615 part-time. Students come from 52 states and territories, 100 other countries, 31% are from out of state, 6% African American, 22% Asian American or Pacific Islander, 14% Hispanic American, 0.8% Native American, 7% international, 8% transferred in, 35% live on campus. *Retention:* 94% of 2001 full-time freshmen returned.

Freshmen *Admission:* 26,294 applied, 8,435 admitted, 2,780 enrolled. *Average high school GPA:* 3.93. *Test scores:* SAT verbal scores over 500: 99%; SAT math scores over 500: 99%; ACT scores over 18: 100%; SAT verbal scores over 600: 77%; SAT math scores over 600: 86%; ACT scores over 24: 99%; SAT verbal scores over 700: 25%; SAT math scores over 700: 36%; ACT scores over 30: 48%.

Faculty *Total:* 2,103, 64% full-time, 72% with terminal degrees. *Student/faculty ratio:* 11:1.

Majors Accounting; acting/directing; aerospace engineering; African-American studies; American literature; American studies; anthropology; architectural engineering; architecture; art; art history; Asian-American studies; astronomy; audio engineering; biochemistry; bioengineering; biology; biophysics; British literature; broadcast journalism; business administration; chemical engineering; chemistry; Chinese; city/community/regional planning; civil engineering; classics; comparative literature; computer engineering; computer science; creative writing; cultural studies; dental hygiene; East Asian studies; economics; education; education (K-12); electrical engineering; engineering/industrial management; engineering mechanics; English; environmental engineering; environmental science; exercise sciences; film studies; film/video production; fine/studio arts; French; geography; geology; German; gerontology; Greek (ancient and medieval); health science; Hispanic-American studies; history; history of philosophy; industrial/manufacturing engineering; interdisciplinary studies; international relations; Italian; Japanese; jazz; journalism; Judaic studies; landscape architecture; Latin (ancient and medieval); linguistics; marine biology; mass communications; mathematics; mechanical engineering; Mexican-American studies; molecular biology; music; music business management/merchandising; music (general performance); music (piano and organ performance); music theory and composition; music (voice and choral/opera performance); natural resources management; neuroscience; nursing; petroleum engineering; philosophy; physical sciences; physics; physiological psychology/psychobiology; play/screenwriting; political science; psychology; public administration; public relations; radio/television broadcasting; radio/television broadcasting technology; religious studies; Russian; sociology; Spanish; stringed instruments; structural engineering; systems engineering; theater arts/drama; theater design; urban studies; water resources; water resources engineering; wind/percussion instruments; women's studies.

Academic Programs *Special study options:* accelerated degree program, advanced placement credit, cooperative education, double majors, English as a second language, freshman honors college, honors programs, independent study, internships, off-campus study, part-time degree program, services for LD students, student-designed majors, study abroad, summer session for credit. *ROTC:* Army (b), Navy (b), Air Force (b). *Unusual degree programs:* 3-2 economics, mathematics, accounting.

Library Doheny Memorial Library plus 22 others with 3.5 million titles, 28,661 serial subscriptions, 3.2 million audiovisual materials, an OPAC, a Web page.

Computers on Campus 2300 computers available on campus for general student use. A campuswide network can be accessed from student residence rooms and from off campus that provide access to on-line degree progress, grades, financial aid summary. Internet access, at least one staffed computer lab available.

Student Life *Housing Options:* coed, cooperative, disabled students. *Activities and Organizations:* drama/theater group, student-run newspaper, radio and television station, choral group, marching band, Troy Camp, USC Helenes, Program Board, Student Senate, Alpha Phi Omega, national fraternities, national sororities. *Campus security:* 24-hour emergency response devices and patrols, student patrols, late-night transport/escort service, controlled dormitory access. *Student Services:* health clinic, personal/psychological counseling, women's center.

Athletics Member NCAA. All Division I except football (Division I-A). *Intercollegiate sports:* baseball M(s), basketball M(s)/W(s), crew W(s), cross-country running W(s), golf M(s)/W(s), sailing M/W, soccer W(s), swimming M(s)/W(s), tennis M(s)/W(s), track and field M(s)/W(s), volleyball M(s)/W(s), water polo M(s)/W(s). *Intramural sports:* badminton M(c)/W(c), basketball M/W, bowling M(c)/W(c), crew M(c), cross-country running M(c)/W(c), equestrian sports M(c)/W(c), fencing M(c)/W(c), field hockey M(c)/W(c), football M/W, golf M(c)/W(c), ice hockey M(c)/W(c), lacrosse M(c), racquetball M(c)/W(c), riflery M(c)/W(c), rugby M(c), sailing M(c)/W(c), skiing (cross-country) M(c)/W(c), skiing (downhill) M(c)/W(c), soccer M(c)/W(c), softball W(c), squash M(c)/W(c), swimming M/W, tennis M(c)/W(c), track and field M(c)/W(c), volleyball M(c)/W(c), water polo M(c)/W(c), wrestling M(c).

Standardized Tests *Required:* SAT I or ACT (for admission). *Required for some:* SAT II: Subject Tests (for admission).

Costs (2001–02) *Comprehensive fee:* $33,647 includes full-time tuition ($25,060), mandatory fees ($473), and room and board ($8114). Part-time tuition: $844 per credit hour. Part-time tuition and fees vary according to course load. *Required fees:* $473 per term part-time. *Room and board:* College room only: $4430. Room and board charges vary according to board plan and housing facility. *Payment plans:* tuition prepayment, installment, deferred payment. *Waivers:* employees or children of employees.

Financial Aid Of all full-time matriculated undergraduates who enrolled in 2001, 9417 applied for aid, 7920 were judged to have need, 7417 had their need fully met. 6285 Federal Work-Study jobs (averaging $2438). In 2001, 2044 non-need-based awards were made. *Average percent of need met:* 99%. *Average financial aid package:* $23,961. *Average need-based loan:* $5091. *Average need-based gift aid:* $16,362. *Average non-need based aid:* $12,308. *Average indebtedness upon graduation:* $20,619.

Applying *Options:* electronic application, early admission, deferred entrance. *Application fee:* $65. *Required:* essay or personal statement, high school transcript. *Required for some:* letters of recommendation. *Recommended:* letters of recommendation, interview. *Application deadlines:* 1/10 (freshmen), 3/1 (transfers). *Notification:* 4/1 (freshmen).

Admissions Contact Ms. Laurel Baker-Tew, Director of Admission, University of Southern California, University Park Campus, Los Angeles, CA 90089. *Phone:* 213-740-1111. *Fax:* 213-740-6364. *E-mail:* admapp@enroll1.usc.edu.

University of the Pacific
Stockton, California

- **Independent** university, founded 1851
- **Calendar** semesters
- **Degrees** bachelor's, master's, doctoral, and first professional
- **Suburban** 175-acre campus with easy access to Sacramento
- **Endowment** $130.9 million
- **Coed,** 3,185 undergraduate students, 97% full-time, 58% women, 42% men
- **Moderately difficult** entrance level, 78% of applicants were admitted

Comprehensive is the best word to describe the University of the Pacific. The integration of liberal arts and sciences with professional study provides undergraduate students with a wealth of academic opportunities in a personally supportive community. Located halfway between the San Francisco Bay and the Sierra Nevada mountains, Pacific offers its students a wide variety of educational, cultural, recreational, and social opportunities.

Undergraduates 3,096 full-time, 89 part-time. Students come from 37 states and territories, 14 other countries, 20% are from out of state, 3% African American, 26% Asian American or Pacific Islander, 10% Hispanic American, 0.9% Native American, 3% international, 7% transferred in, 55% live on campus. *Retention:* 87% of 2001 full-time freshmen returned.

Freshmen *Admission:* 3,162 applied, 2,475 admitted, 732 enrolled. *Average high school GPA:* 3.42. *Test scores:* SAT verbal scores over 500: 75%; SAT math scores over 500: 83%; ACT scores over 18: 98%; SAT verbal scores over 600: 28%; SAT math scores over 600: 41%; ACT scores over 24: 50%; SAT verbal scores over 700: 4%; SAT math scores over 700: 8%; ACT scores over 30: 6%.

Faculty *Total:* 622, 58% full-time, 87% with terminal degrees. *Student/faculty ratio:* 13:1.

Majors Art; art history; biochemistry; bioengineering; biology; business administration; chemistry; chemistry related; civil engineering; classics; communications; computer engineering; computer science; economics; education; electrical engineering; engineering/industrial management; engineering physics; English; environmental science; exercise sciences; fine/studio arts; French; geology; German; graphic design/commercial art/illustration; history; information sciences/systems; interdisciplinary studies; international relations; Japanese; mathematics; mechanical engineering; music; music business management/merchandising; music history; music (piano and organ performance); music teacher education; music theory and composition; music therapy; music (voice and choral/opera performance); pharmacy; philosophy; physical sciences; physics; political science; psychology; religious studies; social sciences; sociology; Spanish; special education; speech-language pathology/audiology; theater arts/drama.

Academic Programs *Special study options:* academic remediation for entering students, accelerated degree program, adult/continuing education programs, advanced placement credit, cooperative education, double majors, English as a second language, honors programs, independent study, internships, part-time degree program, services for LD students, student-designed majors, study abroad, summer session for credit. *ROTC:* Air Force (c).

Library Holt Memorial Library plus 1 other with 689,733 titles, 3,747 serial subscriptions, 8,377 audiovisual materials, an OPAC, a Web page.

Computers on Campus 274 computers available on campus for general student use. A campuswide network can be accessed from student residence rooms and from off campus. Internet access, online (class) registration, at least one staffed computer lab available.

Student Life *Housing:* on-campus residence required through sophomore year. *Options:* coed. *Activities and Organizations:* drama/theater group, student-run newspaper, radio station, choral group, student government, cultural organizations, marketing club, Model United Nations, national fraternities, national sororities. *Campus security:* 24-hour emergency response devices and patrols, late-night transport/escort service, controlled dormitory access. *Student Services:* health clinic, personal/psychological counseling, legal services.

Athletics Member NCAA. All Division I. *Intercollegiate sports:* baseball M(s), basketball M(s)/W(s), cross-country running W(s), field hockey W(s), golf M(s), soccer W(s), softball W(s), swimming M(s)/W(s), tennis M(s)/W(s), volleyball M(s)/W(s), water polo M(s)/W(s). *Intramural sports:* badminton M(c)/W(c), basketball M/W, bowling M/W, crew M(c)/W(c), equestrian sports M(c)/W(c), football M/W, golf M/W, lacrosse M(c)/W(c), racquetball M/W, rugby M(c), soccer M(c)/W(c), softball M/W, tennis M/W, volleyball M/W, water polo M/W.

Standardized Tests *Required:* SAT I or ACT (for admission).

Costs (2001–02) *Comprehensive fee:* $28,255 includes full-time tuition ($21,150), mandatory fees ($375), and room and board ($6730). Part-time tuition and fees vary according to course load. *Room and board:* College room only: $3230. Room and board charges vary according to board plan and housing facility. *Payment plan:* deferred payment. *Waivers:* employees or children of employees.

Financial Aid Of all full-time matriculated undergraduates who enrolled in 2001, 2403 applied for aid, 2108 were judged to have need, 737 had their need fully met. In 2001, 451 non-need-based awards were made. *Average financial aid package:* $23,877. *Average need-based loan:* $3777. *Average need-based gift aid:* $16,996.

Applying *Options:* common application, electronic application, early admission, early action, deferred entrance. *Application fee:* $50. *Required:* essay or personal statement, high school transcript, minimum 2.5 GPA, 1 letter of recommendation. *Required for some:* audition for music program. *Recommended:* minimum 3.0 GPA, interview. *Application deadlines:* 2/15 (freshmen), 2/15 (transfers). *Notification:* continuous (freshmen), 1/15 (early action).

Admissions Contact Mr. Marc McGee, Director of Admissions, University of the Pacific, Stockton, CA 95211-0197. *Phone:* 209-946-2211. *Toll-free phone:* 800-959-2867. *Fax:* 209-946-2413. *E-mail:* admissions@uop.edu.

University of West Los Angeles
Inglewood, California

- **Independent** upper-level, founded 1966
- **Calendar** trimesters
- **Degrees** certificates, bachelor's, and first professional
- **Suburban** 2-acre campus with easy access to Los Angeles
- **Coed,** 69 undergraduate students, 9% full-time, 72% women, 28% men
- **Minimally difficult** entrance level

Undergraduates 6 full-time, 63 part-time. Students come from 1 other state, 0% are from out of state, 45% African American, 7% Asian American or Pacific Islander, 23% Hispanic American, 10% transferred in.

Faculty *Total:* 21, 5% full-time, 95% with terminal degrees. *Student/faculty ratio:* 10:1.

Majors Legal administrative assistant; legal studies; paralegal/legal assistant; prelaw.

Academic Programs *Special study options:* academic remediation for entering students, adult/continuing education programs, independent study, internships, part-time degree program.

Library Kelton Library with 33,000 titles, 250 serial subscriptions.

Computers on Campus 20 computers available on campus for general student use. Internet access, at least one staffed computer lab available.

Student Life *Housing:* college housing not available. *Activities and Organizations:* student-run newspaper, Black Law Students Association, American Trial Lawyers Association, Asian Pacific American Law Students Association, Toastmasters. *Campus security:* late-night transport/escort service.

Costs (2001–02) *Tuition:* $6075 full-time, $225 per unit part-time. *Required fees:* $360 full-time, $120 per term part-time. *Payment plan:* installment. *Waivers:* employees or children of employees.

Applying *Options:* electronic application, deferred entrance. *Application fee:* $55. *Application deadline:* rolling (transfers).

Admissions Contact Ms. Yvonne Alwag, Admissions Counselor, University of West Los Angeles, School of Paralegal Studies, 1155 West Arbor Vitae Street, Inglewood, CA 90301-2902. *Phone:* 310-342-5287. *Fax:* 310-342-5296. *E-mail:* aalwag@uwla.edu.

Vanguard University of Southern California
Costa Mesa, California

- **Independent** comprehensive, founded 1920, affiliated with Assemblies of God
- **Calendar** semesters
- **Degrees** bachelor's and master's
- **Suburban** 38-acre campus with easy access to Los Angeles
- **Endowment** $4.5 million
- **Coed,** 1,578 undergraduate students, 76% full-time, 60% women, 40% men
- **Moderately difficult** entrance level, 87% of applicants were admitted

Vanguard University, a comprehensive Christian university of liberal arts and professional studies, is one of only five universities in the state of California to have national accreditation for athletic training education. Vanguard is the only private institution to have this certification for athletic trainers in California.

Undergraduates 1,196 full-time, 382 part-time. Students come from 41 states and territories, 18 other countries, 9% are from out of state, 4% African American,

3% Asian American or Pacific Islander, 12% Hispanic American, 1% Native American, 1% international, 16% transferred in, 75% live on campus. *Retention:* 74% of 2001 full-time freshmen returned.

Freshmen *Admission:* 667 applied, 583 admitted, 326 enrolled. *Average high school GPA:* 3.31. *Test scores:* SAT verbal scores over 500: 55%; SAT math scores over 500: 46%; SAT verbal scores over 600: 12%; SAT math scores over 600: 11%; SAT verbal scores over 700: 1%; SAT math scores over 700: 1%.

Faculty *Total:* 105, 41% full-time, 35% with terminal degrees. *Student/faculty ratio:* 17:1.

Majors Accounting; anthropology; athletic training/sports medicine; biblical studies; biological/physical sciences; biology; business administration; business marketing and marketing management; chemistry; education; English; exercise sciences; film/video production; finance; health/physical education; history; interdisciplinary studies; international business; management information systems/ business data processing; mass communications; mathematics; music; pastoral counseling; physical education; physical therapy; political science; pre-law; psychology; radio/television broadcasting; religious education; religious studies; secondary education; social sciences; sociology; Spanish; speech/rhetorical studies; theater arts/drama.

Academic Programs *Special study options:* academic remediation for entering students, accelerated degree program, adult/continuing education programs, advanced placement credit, double majors, independent study, internships, off-campus study, part-time degree program, study abroad, summer session for credit.

Library O. Cope Budge Library with 212,676 titles, 1,066 serial subscriptions, 2,241 audiovisual materials, an OPAC, a Web page.

Computers on Campus 140 computers available on campus for general student use. A campuswide network can be accessed from student residence rooms and from off campus. Internet access, at least one staffed computer lab available.

Student Life *Housing:* on-campus residence required through senior year. *Options:* men-only, women-only. *Activities and Organizations:* drama/theater group, student-run newspaper, choral group, student ministries. *Campus security:* 24-hour emergency response devices and patrols, late-night transport/escort service. *Student Services:* personal/psychological counseling.

Athletics Member NAIA. *Intercollegiate sports:* baseball M(s), basketball M(s)/W(s), cross-country running M(s)/W(s), soccer M(s)/W(s), softball W(s), tennis M(s)/W(s), track and field M(s)/W(s), volleyball W(s). *Intramural sports:* badminton M/W, basketball M/W, football M/W, golf M/W, racquetball M/W, softball M/W, table tennis M/W, tennis M/W, volleyball M/W, weight lifting M/W.

Standardized Tests *Required:* SAT I or ACT (for admission).

Costs (2001–02) *Comprehensive fee:* $20,212 includes full-time tuition ($14,224), mandatory fees ($720), and room and board ($5268). Part-time tuition: $593 per unit. *Room and board:* College room only: $3000. Room and board charges vary according to board plan and housing facility. *Payment plan:* installment. *Waivers:* employees or children of employees.

Financial Aid Of all full-time matriculated undergraduates who enrolled in 2001, 1048 applied for aid, 890 were judged to have need, 215 had their need fully met. 80 Federal Work-Study jobs (averaging $2000). In 2001, 105 non-need-based awards were made. *Average percent of need met:* 72%. *Average financial aid package:* $12,575. *Average need-based loan:* $3207. *Average need-based gift aid:* $10,115. *Average non-need based aid:* $4347. *Average indebtedness upon graduation:* $14,860. *Financial aid deadline:* 3/2.

Applying *Options:* common application, electronic application, deferred entrance. *Application fee:* $30. *Required:* essay or personal statement, high school transcript, minimum 2.5 GPA, 1 letter of recommendation. *Required for some:* interview. *Application deadline:* rolling (freshmen), rolling (transfers). *Notification:* continuous until 8/31 (freshmen).

Admissions Contact Vanguard University of Southern California, 55 Fair Drive, Costa Mesa, CA 92626. *Phone:* 714-556-3610 Ext. 327. *Toll-free phone:* 800-722-6279. *Fax:* 714-966-5471. *E-mail:* admissions@vanguard.edu.

WESTMONT COLLEGE

Santa Barbara, California

- **Independent nondenominational** 4-year, founded 1937
- **Calendar** semesters
- **Degrees** bachelor's and postbachelor's certificates
- **Suburban** 133-acre campus with easy access to Los Angeles
- **Endowment** $17.2 million
- **Coed,** 1,374 undergraduate students, 99% full-time, 63% women, 37% men
- **Moderately difficult** entrance level, 75% of applicants were admitted

Undergraduates 1,360 full-time, 14 part-time. Students come from 41 states and territories, 34% are from out of state, 0.6% African American, 5% Asian American or Pacific Islander, 7% Hispanic American, 2% Native American, 0.4% international, 4% transferred in, 88% live on campus. *Retention:* 85% of 2001 full-time freshmen returned.

Freshmen *Admission:* 1,335 applied, 1,001 admitted, 370 enrolled. *Average high school GPA:* 3.65. *Test scores:* SAT verbal scores over 500: 96%; SAT math scores over 500: 95%; ACT scores over 18: 100%; SAT verbal scores over 600: 53%; SAT math scores over 600: 56%; ACT scores over 24: 76%; SAT verbal scores over 700: 13%; SAT math scores over 700: 8%; ACT scores over 30: 7%.

Faculty *Total:* 142, 60% full-time. *Student/faculty ratio:* 13:1.

Majors Anthropology; art; art education; biology; business; business economics; chemistry; communications; computer science; dance; economics; education; elementary education; engineering physics; English; English education; exercise sciences; French; history; liberal arts and sciences/liberal studies; mathematics; mathematics education; modern languages; music; neuroscience; philosophy; physical education; physics; political science; pre-dentistry; pre-law; pre-medicine; pre-pharmacy studies; pre-theology; pre-veterinary studies; psychology; religious studies; secondary education; social science education; social sciences; sociology; Spanish; theater arts/drama.

Academic Programs *Special study options:* accelerated degree program, advanced placement credit, cooperative education, double majors, honors programs, independent study, internships, off-campus study, services for LD students, student-designed majors, study abroad, summer session for credit. *ROTC:* Army (c), Air Force (c). *Unusual degree programs:* 3-2 engineering with Washington University in St. Louis; Boston University; University of Southern California; University of California, Berkeley; Los Angeles; Santa Barbara; California Polytechnic State University; Stanford University.

Library Roger John Voskuyl Library with 156,348 titles, 3,211 serial subscriptions, 8,015 audiovisual materials, an OPAC.

Computers on Campus 100 computers available on campus for general student use. A campuswide network can be accessed from student residence rooms and from off campus. Internet access, at least one staffed computer lab available.

Student Life *Housing Options:* coed, disabled students. *Activities and Organizations:* drama/theater group, student-run newspaper, radio station, choral group, Christian Concerns, student government, Leadership Development, Music and Theater Ensembles, intramural athletics. *Campus security:* 24-hour emergency response devices and patrols, late-night transport/escort service, controlled dormitory access. *Student Services:* health clinic, personal/psychological counseling, women's center.

Athletics Member NAIA. *Intercollegiate sports:* baseball M(s), basketball M(s)/W(s), cross-country running M(s)/W(s), lacrosse W(c), rugby M(c), soccer M(s)/W(s), tennis M(s)/W(s), track and field M(s)/W(s), volleyball M(c)/W(s). *Intramural sports:* badminton M/W, basketball M/W, bowling M/W, cross-country running M/W, football M/W, golf M/W, racquetball M/W, soccer M(c)/W, softball M/W, swimming M/W, table tennis M/W, tennis M/W, volleyball M/W, water polo M/W.

Standardized Tests *Required:* SAT I or ACT (for admission).

Costs (2001–02) *Comprehensive fee:* $29,748 includes full-time tuition ($21,654), mandatory fees ($602), and room and board ($7492). *Room and board:* College room only: $4350. Room and board charges vary according to board plan. *Payment plans:* installment, deferred payment. *Waivers:* employees or children of employees.

Financial Aid Of all full-time matriculated undergraduates who enrolled in 2001, 898 applied for aid, 745 were judged to have need, 99 had their need fully met. In 2001, 426 non-need-based awards were made. *Average percent of need met:* 75%. *Average financial aid package:* $16,235. *Average need-based loan:* $5395. *Average need-based gift aid:* $11,307. *Average indebtedness upon graduation:* $17,558.

Applying *Options:* common application, electronic application, early action. *Application fee:* $50. *Required:* essay or personal statement, high school transcript. *Required for some:* letters of recommendation, interview. *Recommended:* minimum 3.0 GPA, letters of recommendation, interview. *Application deadlines:* 2/15 (freshmen), 3/1 (transfers). *Notification:* 4/1 (freshmen), 1/15 (early action).

Admissions Contact Mrs. Joyce Luy, Director of Admissions, Westmont College, 955 La Paz Road, Santa Barbara, CA 93108. *Phone:* 805-565-6200 Ext. 6005. *Toll-free phone:* 800-777-9011. *Fax:* 805-565-6234. *E-mail:* admissions@westmont.edu.

WESTWOOD COLLEGE OF AVIATION TECHNOLOGY-LOS ANGELES

Inglewood, California

- **Proprietary** primarily 2-year, founded 1942
- **Calendar** quarters
- **Degrees** associate, bachelor's

Westwood College of Aviation Technology-Los Angeles (continued)

- **Urban** campus
- **Coed, primarily men,** 560 undergraduate students
- **Noncompetitive** entrance level

Faculty *Total:* 31, 100% full-time.
Majors Aviation technology.
Academic Programs *Special study options:* part-time degree program.
Computers on Campus 24 computers available on campus for general student use.
Costs (2002–2003) *Tuition:* Standard program price $3355 per term, lab fees and books additional, 5 terms/year, program length: associate degree, 7 terms; bachelor's degree, 14 terms.
Applying *Application fee:* $75. *Application deadline:* rolling (freshmen). *Notification:* continuous (freshmen).
Admissions Contact Mr. Steve Sexton, Director of Admissions, Westwood College of Technology–Los Angeles, 8911 Aviation Boulevard, Inglewood, CA 90301-2904. *Phone:* 310-337-4444. *Toll-free phone:* 800-597-9680.

WESTWOOD COLLEGE OF TECHNOLOGY-ANAHEIM
Anaheim, California

- **Proprietary** primarily 2-year
- **Degrees** associate, bachelor's
- **Coed,** 650 undergraduate students

Faculty *Total:* 24, 79% full-time.
Majors Computer systems networking/telecommunications; design/visual communication; electrical/electronic engineering technology; graphic design/commercial art/illustration.
Costs (2002–2003) *Tuition:* Standard program price $3355 per term, lab fees and books additional, 5 terms/year, program length: associate degree, 7 terms; bachelor's degree, 14 terms.
Admissions Contact Mr. Ron Milman, Director of Admissions, Westwood College of Technology–Anaheim, 2461 West La Palma Avenue, Anaheim, CA 92801. *Phone:* 714-226-9990.

WESTWOOD COLLEGE OF TECHNOLOGY-INLAND EMPIRE
Upland, California

- **Proprietary** primarily 2-year
- **Degrees** associate, bachelor's
- **Coed**

Faculty *Total:* 4.
Majors Computer systems networking/telecommunications; design/visual communication; electrical/electronic engineering technology; graphic design/commercial art/illustration.
Costs (2002–2003) *Tuition:* Standard program price $3355 per term, lab fees and books additional, 5 terms/year, program length: associate degree, 7 terms; bachelor's degree, 14 terms.
Admissions Contact Renae Ferchert, Director of Admissions, Westwood College of Technology–Inland Empire, 20 West 7th Street, Upland, CA 91786. *Phone:* 909-931-7550.
Admissions Contact 20 West 7th Street, Upland, CA 91786.

WHITTIER COLLEGE
Whittier, California

- **Independent** comprehensive, founded 1887
- **Calendar** 4-1-4
- **Degrees** bachelor's, master's, and first professional
- **Suburban** 95-acre campus with easy access to Los Angeles
- **Endowment** $51.4 million
- **Coed,** 1,263 undergraduate students, 98% full-time, 58% women, 42% men
- **Moderately difficult** entrance level, 80% of applicants were admitted

Undergraduates 1,243 full-time, 20 part-time. Students come from 33 states and territories, 20 other countries, 27% are from out of state, 5% African American, 8% Asian American or Pacific Islander, 26% Hispanic American, 1% Native American, 4% international, 7% transferred in, 60% live on campus. *Retention:* 74% of 2001 full-time freshmen returned.
Freshmen *Admission:* 1,511 applied, 1,209 admitted, 348 enrolled. *Average high school GPA:* 3.13. *Test scores:* SAT verbal scores over 500: 69%; SAT math scores over 500: 67%; ACT scores over 18: 93%; SAT verbal scores over 600: 28%; SAT math scores over 600: 23%; ACT scores over 24: 32%; SAT verbal scores over 700: 6%; SAT math scores over 700: 4%; ACT scores over 30: 5%.
Faculty *Total:* 133, 72% full-time. *Student/faculty ratio:* 12:1.
Majors Art; biochemistry; biology; business administration; chemistry; developmental/child psychology; early childhood education; economics; English; French; history; international relations; liberal arts and sciences/liberal studies; mathematics; music; philosophy; physical education; physics; political science; psychology; religious studies; social work; sociology; Spanish; theater arts/drama.
Academic Programs *Special study options:* academic remediation for entering students, accelerated degree program, adult/continuing education programs, advanced placement credit, double majors, independent study, internships, off-campus study, services for LD students, student-designed majors, study abroad, summer session for credit. *ROTC:* Army (c), Air Force (c). *Unusual degree programs:* 3-2 engineering with University of Southern California, Dartmouth College, University of Minnesota, Columbia University, Washington University in St. Louis, Case Western Reserve University, Colorado State University.
Library Bonnie Bell Wardman Library plus 1 other with 225,337 titles, 1,357 serial subscriptions, an OPAC, a Web page.
Computers on Campus 150 computers available on campus for general student use. A campuswide network can be accessed from student residence rooms and from off campus. At least one staffed computer lab available.
Student Life *Housing:* on-campus residence required through junior year. *Options:* coed, women-only. *Activities and Organizations:* drama/theater group, student-run newspaper, radio station, choral group, Hispanic Students Association, Hawaiian Islander Club, choir, Asian Students Association, Students Organized for Multicultural Awareness. *Campus security:* 24-hour emergency response devices and patrols, late-night transport/escort service, controlled dormitory access. *Student Services:* health clinic, personal/psychological counseling.
Athletics Member NCAA. All Division III. *Intercollegiate sports:* baseball M, basketball M/W, cross-country running M/W, football M, golf M, lacrosse M/W, soccer M/W, softball W, swimming M/W, tennis M/W, track and field M/W, volleyball W, water polo M/W. *Intramural sports:* basketball M/W, bowling M/W, football M/W, racquetball M/W, skiing (downhill) M/W, softball M/W, table tennis M/W, tennis M/W, volleyball M/W, water polo M/W.
Standardized Tests *Required:* SAT I or ACT (for admission). *Recommended:* SAT II: Subject Tests (for admission).
Costs (2001–02) *Comprehensive fee:* $28,378 includes full-time tuition ($21,036), mandatory fees ($300), and room and board ($7042). *Room and board:* College room only: $3920. Room and board charges vary according to board plan and housing facility. *Payment plan:* installment. *Waivers:* children of alumni and employees or children of employees.
Financial Aid *Financial aid deadline:* 3/2.
Applying *Options:* common application, electronic application, early action, deferred entrance. *Application fee:* $35. *Required:* essay or personal statement, high school transcript, minimum 2.0 GPA, 2 letters of recommendation. *Required for some:* minimum 3.5 GPA. *Recommended:* minimum 2.5 GPA, interview. *Application deadline:* rolling (freshmen), rolling (transfers). *Notification:* continuous (freshmen), 12/31 (early action).
Admissions Contact Ms. Urmi Kar, Dean of Enrollment, Whittier College, 13406 E Philadelphia Street, PO Box 634, Whittier, CA 90608-0634. *Phone:* 562-907-4238. *Fax:* 562-907-4870. *E-mail:* admission@whittier.edu.

WOODBURY UNIVERSITY
Burbank, California

- **Independent** comprehensive, founded 1884
- **Calendar** semesters
- **Degrees** bachelor's and master's
- **Suburban** 23-acre campus with easy access to Los Angeles
- **Endowment** $7.1 million
- **Coed,** 1,189 undergraduate students, 72% full-time, 56% women, 44% men
- **Moderately difficult** entrance level, 79% of applicants were admitted

Undergraduates 855 full-time, 334 part-time. Students come from 27 other countries, 7% African American, 15% Asian American or Pacific Islander, 30% Hispanic American, 0.6% Native American, 7% international, 17% transferred in, 16% live on campus. *Retention:* 75% of 2001 full-time freshmen returned.
Freshmen *Admission:* 330 applied, 260 admitted, 118 enrolled. *Average high school GPA:* 3.26. *Test scores:* SAT verbal scores over 500: 41%; SAT math scores over 500: 45%; SAT verbal scores over 600: 6%; SAT math scores over 600: 10%.

Faculty *Total:* 206, 20% full-time, 44% with terminal degrees. *Student/faculty ratio:* 11:1.
Majors Accounting; architecture; business administration; business administration/management related; business marketing and marketing management; communications; fashion design/illustration; fashion merchandising; graphic design/commercial art/illustration; history; information sciences/systems; interdisciplinary studies; interior architecture; political science; psychology.
Academic Programs *Special study options:* academic remediation for entering students, accelerated degree program, adult/continuing education programs, advanced placement credit, double majors, independent study, internships, part-time degree program, services for LD students, study abroad, summer session for credit.
Library Los Angeles Times Library with 63,079 titles, 4,014 serial subscriptions, 16,420 audiovisual materials, an OPAC, a Web page.
Computers on Campus 116 computers available on campus for general student use. A campuswide network can be accessed from off campus. Internet access, at least one staffed computer lab available.
Student Life *Housing Options:* coed. *Activities and Organizations:* student-run newspaper, Associated Student Government, Fashion Guild, American Institute of Architecture Students, Delta Sigma Phi, Reliving Intercultural Experiences (RICE), national fraternities, national sororities. *Campus security:* 24-hour patrols, late-night transport/escort service, controlled dormitory access. *Student Services:* health clinic, personal/psychological counseling.
Athletics *Intramural sports:* basketball M/W, soccer M/W, volleyball M/W.
Standardized Tests *Required:* SAT I or ACT (for admission).
Costs (2001–02) *Comprehensive fee:* $24,798 includes full-time tuition ($18,204), mandatory fees ($140), and room and board ($6454). Full-time tuition and fees vary according to program. Part-time tuition: $584 per unit. Part-time tuition and fees vary according to class time and program. *Required fees:* $145 per term part-time. *Room and board:* College room only: $3660. Room and board charges vary according to board plan and housing facility. *Payment plans:* installment, deferred payment. *Waivers:* employees or children of employees.
Financial Aid Of all full-time matriculated undergraduates who enrolled in 2001, 1183 applied for aid, 1003 were judged to have need, 620 had their need fully met. 100 Federal Work-Study jobs (averaging $1500). In 2001, 26 non-need-based awards were made. *Average percent of need met:* 85%. *Average financial aid package:* $19,750. *Average need-based loan:* $4300. *Average need-based gift aid:* $10,000. *Average non-need based aid:* $5057.
Applying *Options:* deferred entrance. *Application fee:* $30. *Required:* essay or personal statement, high school transcript, minimum 2.0 GPA, 2 letters of recommendation. *Required for some:* portfolio. *Recommended:* minimum 3.0 GPA, interview. *Application deadline:* rolling (freshmen), rolling (transfers).
Admissions Contact Mr. Don St. Clair, Vice-President of Enrollment Planning, Woodbury University, 7500 Glenoaks Boulevard, Burbank, CA 91504-1099. *Phone:* 818-767-0888. *Toll-free phone:* 800-784-WOOD. *Fax:* 818-767-7520. *E-mail:* admissions@vaxb.woodbury.edu.

Yeshiva Ohr Elchonon Chabad/West Coast Talmudical Seminary
Los Angeles, California

- **Independent Jewish** 4-year, founded 1953
- **Calendar** semesters
- **Degree** bachelor's
- **Urban** 4-acre campus
- **Men only**
- **Moderately difficult** entrance level

Student Life *Campus security:* 24-hour emergency response devices, student patrols.
Applying *Options:* common application, early admission, deferred entrance. *Required:* high school transcript, minimum 2.0 GPA, interview, oral examination. *Required for some:* letters of recommendation. *Recommended:* letters of recommendation.
Admissions Contact Rabbi Ezra Binyomin Schochet, Dean, Yeshiva Ohr Elchonon Chabad/West Coast Talmudical Seminary, 7215 Waring Avenue, Los Angeles, CA 90046-7660. *Phone:* 213-937-3763.

COLORADO

Adams State College
Alamosa, Colorado

- **State-supported** comprehensive, founded 1921, part of State Colleges in Colorado
- **Calendar** semesters
- **Degrees** associate, bachelor's, and master's
- **Small-town** 90-acre campus
- **Endowment** $8.1 million
- **Coed,** 2,034 undergraduate students, 86% full-time, 54% women, 46% men
- **Moderately difficult** entrance level, 71% of applicants were admitted

Undergraduates 1,750 full-time, 284 part-time. Students come from 46 states and territories, 3 other countries, 19% are from out of state, 4% African American, 1% Asian American or Pacific Islander, 28% Hispanic American, 2% Native American, 0.4% international, 8% transferred in, 45% live on campus. *Retention:* 59% of 2001 full-time freshmen returned.
Freshmen *Admission:* 1,999 applied, 1,411 admitted, 568 enrolled. *Average high school GPA:* 3.06. *Test scores:* SAT verbal scores over 500: 44%; SAT math scores over 500: 50%; ACT scores over 18: 75%; SAT verbal scores over 600: 16%; SAT math scores over 600: 14%; ACT scores over 24: 16%; ACT scores over 30: 2%.
Faculty *Total:* 138, 71% full-time. *Student/faculty ratio:* 15:1.
Majors Accounting; advertising; art; art education; art history; athletic training/sports medicine; biological/physical sciences; biology; biology education; business administration; business education; business marketing and marketing management; ceramic arts; chemistry; chemistry education; communications; computer science; criminology; design/visual communications; drawing; earth sciences; economics; elementary education; English; English education; environmental science; exercise sciences; finance; fine/studio arts; geology; history; history education; international business; journalism; liberal arts and sciences/liberal studies; mathematics; mathematics education; medical technology; metal/jewelry arts; music; music (general performance); music teacher education; music (voice and choral/opera performance); painting; photography; physical education; physics; political science; pre-dentistry; pre-law; pre-medicine; pre-pharmacy studies; pre-veterinary studies; printmaking; psychology; science education; sculpture; secondary education; social sciences; social studies education; social work; sociology; Spanish; Spanish language education; speech/rhetorical studies; textile arts; theater arts/drama; wildlife biology.
Academic Programs *Special study options:* academic remediation for entering students, accelerated degree program, adult/continuing education programs, advanced placement credit, distance learning, double majors, independent study, internships, off-campus study, part-time degree program, services for LD students, student-designed majors, summer session for credit.
Library Nielsen Library with 472,594 titles, 1,646 serial subscriptions, 1,954 audiovisual materials, an OPAC, a Web page.
Computers on Campus 261 computers available on campus for general student use. A campuswide network can be accessed from student residence rooms and from off campus. Internet access, online (class) registration, at least one staffed computer lab available.
Student Life *Housing:* on-campus residence required through sophomore year. *Options:* coed, women-only. *Activities and Organizations:* drama/theater group, student-run newspaper, radio station, choral group, marching band, student government, Student Ambassadors, Program Council, Circle K, Tri Beta. *Campus security:* 24-hour emergency response devices and patrols, student patrols, late-night transport/escort service, controlled dormitory access. *Student Services:* health clinic, personal/psychological counseling.
Athletics Member NCAA. All Division II. *Intercollegiate sports:* basketball M(s)/W(s), cross-country running M(s)/W(s), football M(s), golf M(s), softball W(s), track and field M(s)/W(s), volleyball W(s), wrestling M(s). *Intramural sports:* basketball M/W, football M/W, golf M/W, racquetball M/W, soccer M/W, softball M/W, swimming M/W, tennis M/W, volleyball M/W, water polo M/W.
Standardized Tests *Required:* SAT I or ACT (for admission).
Costs (2002–03) *Tuition:* state resident $1700 full-time, $84 per semester hour part-time; nonresident $6518 full-time, $321 per semester hour part-time. Full-time tuition and fees vary according to reciprocity agreements. Part-time tuition

Adams State College (continued)

and fees vary according to course load. *Required fees:* $667 full-time, $24 per semester hour. *Room and board:* $5607; room only: $2751. Room and board charges vary according to board plan and housing facility. *Payment plans:* installment, deferred payment. *Waivers:* senior citizens and employees or children of employees.

Financial Aid Of all full-time matriculated undergraduates who enrolled in 2001, 1431 applied for aid, 1378 were judged to have need, 364 had their need fully met. In 2001, 8 non-need-based awards were made. *Average percent of need met:* 88%. *Average financial aid package:* $7184. *Average need-based loan:* $3064. *Average need-based gift aid:* $2897. *Average non-need based aid:* $164. *Average indebtedness upon graduation:* $15,234.

Applying *Options:* common application, electronic application, early admission, deferred entrance. *Application fee:* $25. *Required:* high school transcript, minimum 2.0 GPA. *Required for some:* essay or personal statement, letters of recommendation, interview. *Application deadlines:* 8/1 (freshmen), 8/1 (transfers).

Admissions Contact Mr. Matt Gallegas, Director of Admissions, Adams State College, 208 Edgemont Boulevard, Alamosa, CO 81102. *Phone:* 719-587-7712. *Toll-free phone:* 800-824-6494. *Fax:* 719-587-7522. *E-mail:* ascadmit@adams.edu.

THE ART INSTITUTE OF COLORADO
Denver, Colorado

- **Proprietary** 4-year, founded 1952, part of Education Management Corporation
- **Calendar** quarters
- **Degrees** diplomas, associate, and bachelor's
- **Urban** campus
- **Coed,** 2,253 undergraduate students, 78% full-time, 44% women, 56% men
- **Minimally difficult** entrance level, 74% of applicants were admitted

Undergraduates 1,760 full-time, 493 part-time. Students come from 49 states and territories, 50% are from out of state, 3% African American, 4% Asian American or Pacific Islander, 5% Hispanic American, 1% Native American, 3% international, 0.5% transferred in, 9% live on campus. *Retention:* 65% of 2001 full-time freshmen returned.

Freshmen *Admission:* 1,084 applied, 800 admitted, 1,163 enrolled.

Faculty *Total:* 167, 40% full-time, 14% with terminal degrees. *Student/faculty ratio:* 20:1.

Majors Advertising; art; computer graphics; culinary arts; film/video production; graphic design/commercial art/illustration; industrial design; interior design; multimedia; photography.

Academic Programs *Special study options:* academic remediation for entering students, adult/continuing education programs, advanced placement credit, distance learning, external degree program, independent study, internships, part-time degree program, services for LD students, study abroad.

Library Colorado Institute of Art Learning Resource Center with 13,100 titles, 200 serial subscriptions, an OPAC.

Computers on Campus 400 computers available on campus for general student use. Internet access, at least one staffed computer lab available.

Student Life *Housing Options:* coed. *Activities and Organizations:* Culinary Student Forum, Computer Animation Club, Student Chapter—American Society of Interior Designers. *Campus security:* 24-hour emergency response devices. *Student Services:* personal/psychological counseling.

Costs (2001–02) *Comprehensive fee:* $27,240 includes full-time tuition ($19,840) and room and board ($7400). Full-time tuition and fees vary according to course load and degree level. Part-time tuition: $310 per credit. Part-time tuition and fees vary according to course load and program. No tuition increase for student's term of enrollment. *Room and board:* Room and board charges vary according to board plan, housing facility, and location. *Payment plan:* installment. *Waivers:* employees or children of employees.

Financial Aid Of all full-time matriculated undergraduates who enrolled in 2001, 1621 applied for aid, 1621 were judged to have need. 34 State and other part-time jobs. *Average indebtedness upon graduation:* $30,000.

Applying *Options:* early admission, deferred entrance. *Application fee:* $50. *Required:* essay or personal statement, high school transcript, interview. *Application deadline:* rolling (freshmen), rolling (transfers).

Admissions Contact Barbara Browning, Vice President and Director of Admissions, The Art Institute of Colorado, 1200 Lincoln Street, Denver, CO 80203. *Phone:* 303-837-0825 Ext. 4729. *Toll-free phone:* 800-275-2420. *Fax:* 303-860-8520. *E-mail:* aicinfo@aii.edu.

COLORADO CHRISTIAN UNIVERSITY
Lakewood, Colorado

- **Independent interdenominational** comprehensive, founded 1914
- **Calendar** semesters
- **Degrees** associate, bachelor's, and master's
- **Suburban** 26-acre campus with easy access to Denver
- **Endowment** $2.9 million
- **Coed,** 1,763 undergraduate students, 72% full-time, 55% women, 45% men
- **Moderately difficult** entrance level, 75% of applicants were admitted

Undergraduates 1,278 full-time, 485 part-time. Students come from 45 states and territories, 15 other countries, 32% are from out of state, 6% African American, 1% Asian American or Pacific Islander, 5% Hispanic American, 0.7% Native American, 0.9% international, 7% transferred in, 40% live on campus. *Retention:* 68% of 2001 full-time freshmen returned.

Freshmen *Admission:* 906 applied, 675 admitted, 271 enrolled. *Average high school GPA:* 3.43. *Test scores:* SAT verbal scores over 500: 68%; SAT math scores over 500: 67%; ACT scores over 18: 93%; SAT verbal scores over 600: 30%; SAT math scores over 600: 25%; ACT scores over 24: 46%; SAT verbal scores over 700: 3%; SAT math scores over 700: 2%; ACT scores over 30: 6%.

Faculty *Total:* 119, 41% full-time, 34% with terminal degrees. *Student/faculty ratio:* 11:1.

Majors Accounting; art; biblical studies; biology; broadcast journalism; business; business administration; communications; computer/information sciences; divinity/ministry; English; health/physical education/fitness related; history; humanities; human resources management; information sciences/systems; liberal arts and sciences/liberal studies; management information systems/business data processing; mass communications; mathematics; music; music (general performance); music (voice and choral/opera performance); pastoral counseling; political science; psychology; recreation/leisure studies; religious music; theater arts/drama; theology.

Academic Programs *Special study options:* academic remediation for entering students, accelerated degree program, adult/continuing education programs, advanced placement credit, cooperative education, distance learning, double majors, honors programs, independent study, internships, off-campus study, part-time degree program, services for LD students, student-designed majors, study abroad, summer session for credit. *ROTC:* Army (c), Air Force (c).

Library Clifton Fowler Library plus 1 other with 71,565 titles, 1,192 serial subscriptions, 4,200 audiovisual materials, an OPAC, a Web page.

Computers on Campus 13 computers available on campus for general student use. A campuswide network can be accessed from student residence rooms and from off campus. Internet access, at least one staffed computer lab available.

Student Life *Housing:* on-campus residence required for freshman year. *Options:* coed. *Activities and Organizations:* drama/theater group, student-run newspaper, radio station, choral group, FAT Boys (inner city ministry to homeless), SALT (Snowboarding as a Living Testimony), Snappers (retirement homes ministry), Student Government, Trash Club. *Campus security:* 24-hour emergency response devices and patrols. *Student Services:* health clinic, personal/psychological counseling, women's center.

Athletics Member NCAA. All Division II. *Intercollegiate sports:* basketball M(s)/W(s), cross-country running M/W, golf M(s), soccer M(s)/W(s), tennis M(s)/W(s), volleyball W(s).

Standardized Tests *Required:* SAT I or ACT (for admission).

Costs (2001–02) *Comprehensive fee:* $17,714 includes full-time tuition ($12,244) and room and board ($5470). Full-time tuition and fees vary according to program. Part-time tuition: $510 per semester hour. Part-time tuition and fees vary according to program. *Room and board:* College room only: $3200. Room and board charges vary according to board plan and housing facility. *Payment plan:* installment. *Waivers:* employees or children of employees.

Financial Aid Of all full-time matriculated undergraduates who enrolled in 2001, 776 applied for aid, 637 were judged to have need, 99 had their need fully met. 138 Federal Work-Study jobs (averaging $1169). *Average percent of need met:* 56%. *Average financial aid package:* $8546. *Average need-based loan:* $3799. *Average need-based gift aid:* $5483.

Applying *Options:* common application, electronic application, deferred entrance. *Application fee:* $40. *Required:* essay or personal statement, high school transcript, 2 letters of recommendation. *Required for some:* 3 letters of recommendation, interview. *Application deadline:* 8/1 (freshmen).

Admissions Contact Ms. Kim Myrick, Director of Admissions, Colorado Christian University, 180 South Garrison Street, Lakewood, CO 80226-7499. *Phone:* 303-963-3403. *Toll-free phone:* 800-44-FAITH. *Fax:* 303-963-3201. *E-mail:* admission@ccu.edu.

THE COLORADO COLLEGE
Colorado Springs, Colorado

- **Independent** comprehensive, founded 1874
- **Calendar** modular
- **Degrees** bachelor's and master's (master's degree in education only)
- **Urban** 90-acre campus with easy access to Denver
- **Endowment** $380.0 million
- **Coed,** 1,934 undergraduate students, 99% full-time, 55% women, 45% men
- **Very difficult** entrance level, 69% of applicants were admitted

Founded in 1874, Colorado College is a private, 4-year, coeducational college. Its 90-acre campus is located in downtown Colorado Springs (metro population 508,870) on the front range of the Rocky Mountains, 70 miles south of Denver. It employs an innovative, one-course-at-a-time approach (the Block Plan) in structuring its traditional liberal arts and sciences curriculum.

Undergraduates 1,921 full-time, 13 part-time. Students come from 46 states and territories, 25 other countries, 69% are from out of state, 2% African American, 4% Asian American or Pacific Islander, 6% Hispanic American, 1% Native American, 2% international, 2% transferred in, 74% live on campus. *Retention:* 98% of 2001 full-time freshmen returned.

Freshmen *Admission:* 3,402 applied, 2,337 admitted, 479 enrolled. *Test scores:* SAT verbal scores over 500: 93%; SAT math scores over 500: 95%; ACT scores over 18: 99%; SAT verbal scores over 600: 67%; SAT math scores over 600: 67%; ACT scores over 24: 85%; SAT verbal scores over 700: 19%; SAT math scores over 700: 16%; ACT scores over 30: 23%.

Faculty *Total:* 206, 82% full-time. *Student/faculty ratio:* 9:1.

Majors Anthropology; art history; Asian studies; biochemistry; biology; chemistry; classics; comparative literature; creative writing; dance; economics; economics related; English; environmental science; ethnic/cultural studies related; film studies; fine/studio arts; French; geology; German; history; history related; liberal arts and studies related; mathematics; mathematics/computer science; music; neuroscience; philosophy; physics; political science; psychology; quantitative economics; religious studies; Romance languages related; Russian/Slavic studies; social sciences and history related; sociology; Spanish; theater arts/drama; women's studies.

Academic Programs *Special study options:* advanced placement credit, double majors, English as a second language, honors programs, independent study, off-campus study, services for LD students, student-designed majors, study abroad, summer session for credit. *ROTC:* Army (c). *Unusual degree programs:* 3-2 engineering with Rensselaer Polytechnic Institute, Washington University in St. Louis, University of Southern California, Columbia University.

Library Tutt Library plus 2 others with 481,050 titles, 4,010 serial subscriptions, 40,473 audiovisual materials, an OPAC, a Web page.

Computers on Campus 237 computers available on campus for general student use. A campuswide network can be accessed from student residence rooms and from off campus. Internet access, online (class) registration, at least one staffed computer lab available.

Student Life *Housing:* on-campus residence required through junior year. *Options:* coed, men-only, women-only. *Activities and Organizations:* drama/theater group, student-run newspaper, radio station, choral group, Community Service Center, student government, arts and crafts organizations, Outdoor Recreation Committee, Theater Workshop, national fraternities, national sororities. *Campus security:* 24-hour emergency response devices and patrols, late-night transport/escort service, controlled dormitory access, whistle program. *Student Services:* health clinic, personal/psychological counseling, women's center.

Athletics Member NCAA. All Division III except ice hockey (Division I), soccer (Division I). *Intercollegiate sports:* basketball M/W, cross-country running M/W, equestrian sports M(c)/W(c), field hockey M(c)/W(c), football M, ice hockey M(s)/W(c), lacrosse M/W, rugby M(c)/W(c), skiing (downhill) M(c)/W(c), soccer M/W(s), softball W, swimming M/W, tennis M/W, track and field M/W, volleyball M(c)/W, water polo M(c)/W(c). *Intramural sports:* basketball M/W, football M/W, ice hockey M/W, racquetball M/W, soccer M/W, softball M/W, volleyball M/W.

Standardized Tests *Required:* SAT I or ACT (for admission).

Costs (2001–02) *Comprehensive fee:* $31,525 includes full-time tuition ($24,528), mandatory fees ($365), and room and board ($6632). Part-time tuition: $767 per credit hour. *Room and board:* College room only: $3288. Room and board charges vary according to board plan. *Payment plan:* installment. *Waivers:* employees or children of employees.

Financial Aid Of all full-time matriculated undergraduates who enrolled in 2001, 924 applied for aid, 835 were judged to have need, 498 had their need fully met. 377 State and other part-time jobs (averaging $1450). *Average percent of need met:* 92%. *Average financial aid package:* $20,719. *Average need-based loan:* $3319. *Average need-based gift aid:* $17,980. *Average indebtedness upon graduation:* $14,076.

Applying *Options:* common application, electronic application, early action, deferred entrance. *Application fee:* $40. *Required:* essay or personal statement, high school transcript, 3 letters of recommendation. *Application deadlines:* 1/15 (freshmen), 4/1 (transfers). *Notification:* 4/1 (freshmen), 12/15 (early action).

Admissions Contact Mr. Mark Hatch, Dean of Admission and Financial Aid, The Colorado College, 900 Block North Cascade, West, Colorado Springs, CO 80903-3294. *Phone:* 719-389-6344. *Toll-free phone:* 800-542-7214. *Fax:* 719-389-6816. *E-mail:* admission@coloradocollege.edu.

COLORADO SCHOOL OF MINES
Golden, Colorado

- **State-supported** university, founded 1874
- **Calendar** semesters
- **Degrees** bachelor's, master's, doctoral, and first professional
- **Small-town** 373-acre campus with easy access to Denver
- **Endowment** $112.0 million
- **Coed,** 2,556 undergraduate students, 96% full-time, 25% women, 75% men
- **Very difficult** entrance level, 82% of applicants were admitted

Undergraduates 2,441 full-time, 115 part-time. Students come from 51 states and territories, 62 other countries, 21% are from out of state, 1% African American, 5% Asian American or Pacific Islander, 6% Hispanic American, 0.7% Native American, 4% international, 4% transferred in, 25% live on campus. *Retention:* 83% of 2001 full-time freshmen returned.

Freshmen *Admission:* 1,702 applied, 1,401 admitted, 600 enrolled. *Average high school GPA:* 3.70. *Test scores:* SAT verbal scores over 500: 87%; SAT math scores over 500: 98%; ACT scores over 18: 100%; SAT verbal scores over 600: 45%; SAT math scores over 600: 74%; ACT scores over 24: 84%; SAT verbal scores over 700: 9%; SAT math scores over 700: 18%; ACT scores over 30: 19%.

Faculty *Total:* 327, 62% full-time. *Student/faculty ratio:* 13:1.

Majors Chemical engineering; chemistry; civil engineering; computer science; economics; electrical engineering; engineering; engineering physics; engineering science; environmental engineering; geological engineering; geophysical engineering; mathematics; mechanical engineering; metallurgical engineering; mining/mineral engineering; petroleum engineering.

Academic Programs *Special study options:* academic remediation for entering students, accelerated degree program, advanced placement credit, cooperative education, double majors, English as a second language, honors programs, independent study, internships, services for LD students, study abroad, summer session for credit. *ROTC:* Army (b), Air Force (c).

Library Arthur Lakes Library with 102,533 titles, 1,840 serial subscriptions, 48 audiovisual materials, an OPAC, a Web page.

Computers on Campus A campuswide network can be accessed from student residence rooms and from off campus. At least one staffed computer lab available.

Student Life *Housing Options:* coed. *Activities and Organizations:* drama/theater group, student-run newspaper, choral group, marching band, Residence Hall Association, Society of Women Engineers, American Institute of Chemical Engineers, national fraternities, national sororities. *Campus security:* 24-hour emergency response devices and patrols. *Student Services:* health clinic, personal/psychological counseling.

Athletics Member NCAA. All Division II. *Intercollegiate sports:* baseball M(s), basketball M(s)/W(s), cross-country running M(s)/W(s), football M(s), golf M(s), skiing (downhill) M, soccer M, softball W(s), swimming M(s)/W(s), tennis M(s)/W(s), track and field M(s)/W(s), volleyball W(s), wrestling M(s). *Intramural sports:* badminton M/W, basketball M/W, cross-country running M/W, football M/W, racquetball M/W, soccer M/W, softball M/W, swimming M/W, tennis M/W, track and field M/W, volleyball M/W.

Standardized Tests *Required:* SAT I or ACT (for admission).

Costs (2001–02) *Tuition:* state resident $5190 full-time, $205 per semester hour part-time; nonresident $16,875 full-time, $669 per semester hour part-time. Part-time tuition and fees vary according to course load. *Required fees:* $708 full-time. *Room and board:* $5680; room only: $2400. Room and board charges vary according to board plan and housing facility. *Payment plan:* installment. *Waivers:* minority students.

Financial Aid Of all full-time matriculated undergraduates who enrolled in 2001, 1870 applied for aid, 1650 were judged to have need, 1650 had their need fully met. 282 Federal Work-Study jobs (averaging $850). 295 State and other part-time jobs. In 2001, 210 non-need-based awards were made. *Average percent of need met:* 100%. *Average financial aid package:* $12,100. *Average need-based loan:* $4000. *Average need-based gift aid:* $4800. *Average non-need based aid:* $4500. *Average indebtedness upon graduation:* $17,500.

Colorado School of Mines (continued)

Applying *Options:* electronic application, deferred entrance. *Application fee:* $45. *Required:* high school transcript. *Required for some:* essay or personal statement, letters of recommendation, interview. *Recommended:* rank in upper one-third of high school class. *Application deadlines:* 6/1 (freshmen), 6/1 (transfers). *Notification:* continuous (freshmen).

Admissions Contact Ms. Tricia Douthit, Assistant Director of Enrollment Management, Colorado School of Mines, 1600 Maple Street, Golden, CO 80401-1842. *Phone:* 303-273-3224. *Toll-free phone:* 800-446-9488. *Fax:* 303-273-3509. *E-mail:* admit@mines.edu.

COLORADO STATE UNIVERSITY

Fort Collins, Colorado

- **State-supported** university, founded 1870, part of Colorado State University System
- **Calendar** semesters
- **Degrees** bachelor's, master's, doctoral, and first professional
- **Urban** 666-acre campus with easy access to Denver
- **Endowment** $134.1 million
- **Coed,** 19,899 undergraduate students, 89% full-time, 52% women, 48% men
- **Moderately difficult** entrance level, 78% of applicants were admitted

Undergraduates 17,809 full-time, 2,090 part-time. Students come from 55 states and territories, 57 other countries, 20% are from out of state, 2% African American, 3% Asian American or Pacific Islander, 6% Hispanic American, 1% Native American, 1% international, 9% transferred in, 24% live on campus. *Retention:* 81% of 2001 full-time freshmen returned.

Freshmen *Admission:* 11,806 applied, 9,223 admitted, 3,720 enrolled. *Average high school GPA:* 3.50. *Test scores:* SAT verbal scores over 500: 75%; SAT math scores over 500: 78%; ACT scores over 18: 99%; SAT verbal scores over 600: 27%; SAT math scores over 600: 31%; ACT scores over 24: 53%; SAT verbal scores over 700: 4%; SAT math scores over 700: 4%; ACT scores over 30: 7%.

Faculty *Total:* 934, 100% full-time, 99% with terminal degrees. *Student/faculty ratio:* 18:1.

Majors Accounting; agribusiness; agricultural economics; agricultural education; agricultural engineering; agricultural extension; agricultural sciences; agronomy/crop science; American studies; animal sciences; anthropology; applied mathematics; art; art education; art history; Asian studies; athletic training/sports medicine; biochemistry; biology; biology education; botany; business administration; business education; business marketing and marketing management; ceramic arts; chemical engineering; chemistry; chemistry education; civil engineering; clothing/apparel/textile studies; computer engineering; computer science; construction technology; creative writing; criminal justice studies; dance; dietetics; drawing; economics; electrical engineering; engineering physics; engineering science; English; English education; entomology; environmental engineering; environmental health; equestrian studies; exercise sciences; farm/ranch management; finance; fine/studio arts; fishing sciences; forestry sciences; French; French language education; geology; German; German language education; graphic design/commercial art/illustration; history; home economics; home economics education; horticulture science; hotel and restaurant management; humanities; individual/family development; industrial arts; industrial technology; information sciences/systems; interior design; journalism; landscape architecture; landscaping management; Latin American studies; liberal arts and sciences/liberal studies; marketing/distribution education; mathematical statistics; mathematics; mathematics education; mechanical engineering; metal/jewelry arts; microbiology/bacteriology; music; music (general performance); music teacher education; music therapy; natural resources management; nursery management; nutrition science; painting; philosophy; photography; physical education; physical sciences; physics; physics education; plant protection; political science; pre-dentistry; pre-law; pre-medicine; pre-veterinary studies; printmaking; psychology; public relations; radio/television broadcasting; range management; real estate; recreation/leisure facilities management; science education; sculpture; social sciences; social studies education; social work; sociology; soil conservation; soil sciences; Spanish; Spanish language education; speech/rhetorical studies; technical education; textile arts; theater arts/drama; trade/industrial education; turf management; water resources; wildlife management; zoology.

Academic Programs *Special study options:* accelerated degree program, adult/continuing education programs, advanced placement credit, cooperative education, distance learning, double majors, English as a second language, honors programs, independent study, internships, off-campus study, part-time degree program, services for LD students, student-designed majors, study abroad, summer session for credit. *ROTC:* Army (b), Air Force (b).

Library William E. Morgan Library plus 3 others with 1.2 million titles, 21,208 serial subscriptions, 9,428 audiovisual materials, an OPAC, a Web page.

Computers on Campus A campuswide network can be accessed from student residence rooms and from off campus. Internet access, at least one staffed computer lab available.

Student Life *Housing:* on-campus residence required for freshman year. *Options:* coed. *Activities and Organizations:* drama/theater group, student-run newspaper, radio and television station, choral group, marching band, Club Sports Association, Associated Students (student government), Office of Community Services, Colorado Public Interest Research Group, national fraternities, national sororities. *Campus security:* 24-hour emergency response devices and patrols, student patrols, late-night transport/escort service, controlled dormitory access. *Student Services:* health clinic, personal/psychological counseling, women's center, legal services.

Athletics Member NCAA. All Division I except football (Division I-A). *Intercollegiate sports:* basketball M(s)/W(s), cross-country running M(s)/W(s), golf M/W, softball W, swimming W(s), tennis W, track and field M(s)/W(s), volleyball W(s). *Intramural sports:* badminton M(c)/W(c), baseball M(c)/W(c), basketball M/W, equestrian sports M/W, fencing M(c)/W(c), golf M/W, gymnastics M(c)/W(c), ice hockey M(c)/W(c), lacrosse M(c)/W(c), racquetball M(c)/W(c), riflery M(c)/W(c), rugby M(c)/W(c), skiing (downhill) M/W, soccer M/W, softball M/W, tennis M/W, volleyball M/W, water polo M/W, weight lifting M/W, wrestling M.

Standardized Tests *Required:* SAT I or ACT (for admission).

Costs (2001–02) *One-time required fee:* $150. *Tuition:* state resident $3502 full-time, $139 per credit part-time; nonresident $10,944 full-time, $608 per credit part-time. Full-time tuition and fees vary according to program. Part-time tuition and fees vary according to course load and program. *Required fees:* $750 full-time, $34 per credit. *Room and board:* $5670. Room and board charges vary according to board plan and housing facility. *Payment plan:* installment. *Waivers:* employees or children of employees.

Financial Aid Of all full-time matriculated undergraduates who enrolled in 2001, 9585 applied for aid, 6974 were judged to have need, 3048 had their need fully met. 1246 State and other part-time jobs (averaging $1699). In 2001, 2288 non-need-based awards were made. *Average percent of need met:* 82%. *Average financial aid package:* $7288. *Average need-based loan:* $5085. *Average need-based gift aid:* $3624. *Average indebtedness upon graduation:* $13,796.

Applying *Options:* electronic application, deferred entrance. *Application fee:* $30. *Required:* high school transcript. *Recommended:* essay or personal statement, letters of recommendation. *Application deadlines:* 7/1 (freshmen), 7/1 (transfers). *Notification:* continuous (freshmen).

Admissions Contact Ms. Mary Ontiveros, Director of Admissions, Colorado State University, Spruce Hall, Fort Collins, CO 80523-0015. *Phone:* 970-491-6909. *Fax:* 970-491-7799. *E-mail:* admissions@vines.colostate.edu.

COLORADO TECHNICAL UNIVERSITY

Colorado Springs, Colorado

- **Proprietary** comprehensive, founded 1965
- **Calendar** quarters
- **Degrees** certificates, associate, bachelor's, master's, and doctoral
- **Suburban** 14-acre campus with easy access to Denver
- **Coed,** 1,322 undergraduate students, 24% full-time, 24% women, 76% men
- **Minimally difficult** entrance level, 93% of applicants were admitted

Undergraduates 314 full-time, 1,008 part-time. Students come from 10 states and territories, 7 other countries, 2% are from out of state, 8% African American, 4% Asian American or Pacific Islander, 6% Hispanic American, 0.4% Native American, 1% international, 9% transferred in.

Freshmen *Admission:* 217 applied, 201 admitted, 201 enrolled.

Faculty *Total:* 136, 25% full-time, 35% with terminal degrees. *Student/faculty ratio:* 20:1.

Majors Business administration; computer engineering; computer science; electrical/electronic engineering technology; electrical engineering; human resources management; information sciences/systems; management information systems/business data processing; telecommunications.

Academic Programs *Special study options:* academic remediation for entering students, accelerated degree program, adult/continuing education programs, advanced placement credit, cooperative education, distance learning, double majors, independent study, internships, part-time degree program, services for LD students, summer session for credit. *ROTC:* Army (c).

Library Colorado Technical University Library with 22,245 titles, 4,389 serial subscriptions, 620 audiovisual materials, an OPAC, a Web page.

Computers on Campus 130 computers available on campus for general student use. A campuswide network can be accessed from off campus. Internet access, at least one staffed computer lab available.

Student Life *Housing:* college housing not available. *Activities and Organizations:* Institute of Electrical and Electronics Engineers, Society of Logistic Engineers, Association of Computing Machinery, Society of Women Engineers, Phi Beta Lambda. *Campus security:* 24-hour emergency response devices, late-night transport/escort service.
Standardized Tests *Recommended:* SAT I or ACT (for admission).
Costs (2002–03) *One-time required fee:* $100. *Tuition:* $8775 full-time, $195 per quarter hour part-time. Part-time tuition and fees vary according to course load. *Required fees:* $207 full-time, $56 per term part-time. *Payment plan:* installment. *Waivers:* employees or children of employees.
Financial Aid Of all full-time matriculated undergraduates who enrolled in 2001, 26 Federal Work-Study jobs (averaging $7761).
Applying *Options:* deferred entrance. *Application fee:* $50. *Required:* high school transcript. *Required for some:* essay or personal statement. *Recommended:* minimum 3.0 GPA, interview. *Application deadline:* rolling (freshmen), rolling (transfers). *Notification:* continuous (freshmen).
Admissions Contact Ms. Terri Johnson, Director of Admissions, Colorado Technical University, 4435 North Chestnut Street, Colorado Springs, CO 80907-3896. *Phone:* 719-598-0200. *Fax:* 719-598-3740. *E-mail:* tjohnson@cos.coloradotech.edu.

Colorado Technical University Denver Campus
Greenwood Village, Colorado

- **Proprietary** comprehensive, founded 1965, part of Whitman Education Group
- **Calendar** quarters
- **Degrees** certificates, associate, bachelor's, master's, doctoral, and postbachelor's certificates
- **Urban** 1-acre campus with easy access to Denver
- **Coed,** 214 undergraduate students, 20% full-time, 27% women, 73% men
- **Minimally difficult** entrance level, 67% of applicants were admitted

Undergraduates 43 full-time, 171 part-time. Students come from 12 states and territories, 7 other countries, 2% are from out of state, 8% African American, 6% Asian American or Pacific Islander, 6% Hispanic American, 1.0% Native American, 8% international, 7% transferred in.
Freshmen *Admission:* 61 applied, 41 admitted, 41 enrolled.
Faculty *Total:* 51, 10% full-time, 25% with terminal degrees. *Student/faculty ratio:* 14:1.
Majors Business administration; computer/information sciences; computer science; information sciences/systems.
Academic Programs *Special study options:* academic remediation for entering students, adult/continuing education programs, advanced placement credit, cooperative education, external degree program, honors programs, independent study, part-time degree program.
Library Colorado Technical University Resource Center with 2,262 serial subscriptions, 15 audiovisual materials.
Computers on Campus 25 computers available on campus for general student use. Internet access, at least one staffed computer lab available.
Student Life *Housing:* college housing not available. *Activities and Organizations:* Association of Information Technology Professionals. *Campus security:* 24-hour emergency response devices and patrols, late-night transport/escort service.
Standardized Tests *Recommended:* SAT I or ACT (for admission).
Costs (2002–03) *One-time required fee:* $100. *Tuition:* $8775 full-time, $195 per quarter hour part-time. Full-time tuition and fees vary according to course load. Part-time tuition and fees vary according to course load. *Required fees:* $207 full-time, $54 per term part-time. *Payment plan:* installment. *Waivers:* employees or children of employees.
Financial Aid Of all full-time matriculated undergraduates who enrolled in 2001, 2 Federal Work-Study jobs.
Applying *Options:* deferred entrance. *Application fee:* $50. *Required:* high school transcript. *Required for some:* essay or personal statement. *Recommended:* minimum 3.0 GPA, interview. *Application deadline:* rolling (freshmen), rolling (transfers). *Notification:* continuous (freshmen).
Admissions Contact Ms. Terri Johnson, Director of Admissions, Colorado Technical University Denver Campus, 5775 DTC Boulevard, Suite 100, Greenwood Village, CO 80111. *Phone:* 303-694-6600. *Fax:* 303-694-6673. *E-mail:* ctudenver@coloradotech.edu.

Denver Technical College
Denver, Colorado

- **Proprietary** 4-year, founded 1945, part of DeVry, Inc
- **Calendar** quarters
- **Degrees** associate and bachelor's
- **Urban** 1-acre campus
- **Coed, primarily men,** 269 undergraduate students, 64% full-time, 24% women, 76% men
- **Moderately difficult** entrance level, 89% of applicants were admitted

Undergraduates 171 full-time, 98 part-time. Students come from 9 states and territories, 3 other countries, 6% are from out of state, 14% African American, 4% Asian American or Pacific Islander, 10% Hispanic American, 0.7% Native American, 2% international.
Freshmen *Admission:* 307 applied, 273 admitted, 215 enrolled.
Faculty *Total:* 62, 31% full-time. *Student/faculty ratio:* 5:1.
Majors Business administration/management related; business systems analysis/design; computer engineering technology; electrical/electronic engineering technology; information sciences/systems; system administration.
Academic Programs *Special study options:* academic remediation for entering students, accelerated degree program, adult/continuing education programs, cooperative education, honors programs, part-time degree program, summer session for credit.
Library 5,037 titles, 46,172 serial subscriptions, 446 audiovisual materials, an OPAC.
Computers on Campus 435 computers available on campus for general student use. At least one staffed computer lab available.
Student Life *Housing:* college housing not available. *Activities and Organizations:* student-run newspaper, Student Activities Association, Institute of Electrical and Electronic Engineers (IEEE), Association of Information Technology Professionals (AITP). *Campus security:* 24-hour emergency response devices, late-night transport/escort service, lighted pathways/sidewalks.
Standardized Tests *Recommended:* SAT I or ACT (for admission).
Costs (2001–02) *Tuition:* $9400 full-time, $330 per credit hour part-time. Full-time tuition and fees vary according to course load. Part-time tuition and fees vary according to course load. *Payment plans:* installment, deferred payment. *Waivers:* employees or children of employees.
Applying *Options:* deferred entrance. *Application fee:* $50. *Required:* high school transcript, interview. *Application deadline:* rolling (freshmen), rolling (transfers). *Notification:* continuous (freshmen).
Admissions Contact Ms. Pam Smith, Directors of Admissions, Denver Technical College, 925 South Niagara Street, Denver, CO 80224. *Phone:* 303-329-3340. *Toll-free phone:* 303-329-3340. *Fax:* 303-329-0955.

Denver Technical College at Colorado Springs
Colorado Springs, Colorado

- **Proprietary** 4-year, founded 1945
- **Calendar** quarters
- **Degrees** certificates, associate, and bachelor's
- **Urban** 3-acre campus with easy access to Denver
- **Coed**
- **Noncompetitive** entrance level

Student Life *Campus security:* 24-hour patrols, late-night transport/escort service.
Standardized Tests *Recommended:* SAT I or ACT (for placement).
Applying *Application fee:* $75. *Required:* high school transcript. *Required for some:* essay or personal statement, interview.
Admissions Contact Mr. Rick Modman, Director of Admissions, Denver Technical College at Colorado Springs, 225 South Union Boulevard, Colorado Springs, CO 80910. *Phone:* 719-632-3000 Ext. 8133. *Fax:* 719-632-1909.

DeVry University
Colorado Springs, Colorado

- **Proprietary** 4-year, founded 2001, part of DeVry, Inc
- **Calendar** semesters
- **Degrees** associate and bachelor's
- **Coed,** 128 undergraduate students, 70% full-time, 29% women, 71% men

DeVry University (continued)
- 87% of applicants were admitted

Undergraduates 90 full-time, 38 part-time. Students come from 6 states and territories, 1 other country, 5% are from out of state, 14% African American, 5% Asian American or Pacific Islander, 12% Hispanic American, 2% Native American, 0.8% international.

Freshmen *Admission:* 163 applied, 141 admitted, 114 enrolled.

Faculty *Total:* 50, 22% full-time. *Student/faculty ratio:* 4:1.

Majors Business administration/management related; business systems analysis/design; electrical/electronic engineering technology; information sciences/systems; system administration.

Student Life *Housing:* college housing not available. *Activities and Organizations:* Association for Information Technology Professionals. *Campus security:* 24-hour emergency response devices and patrols, late-night transport/escort service, safety pamphlets, lighted sidewalks/pathways.

Standardized Tests *Recommended:* SAT I or ACT (for admission).

Costs (2001–02) *Tuition:* $9400 full-time, $330 per credit hour part-time. Full-time tuition and fees vary according to course load. Part-time tuition and fees vary according to course load. *Payment plans:* installment, deferred payment. *Waivers:* employees or children of employees.

Financial Aid Of all full-time matriculated undergraduates who enrolled in 2001, 104 applied for aid, 95 were judged to have need, 1 had their need fully met. *Average percent of need met:* 34%. *Average financial aid package:* $5217. *Average need-based loan:* $3319. *Average need-based gift aid:* $4172.

Applying *Application fee:* $50. *Required:* high school transcript, interview. *Application deadline:* rolling (freshmen), rolling (transfers). *Notification:* continuous (freshmen).

Admissions Contact Mr. Rick Rodman, Director of Admissions, DeVry University, 925 South Niagara Street, Denver, CO 80224. *Phone:* 303-329-3340 Ext. 7221.

DeVry University
Denver, Colorado

Admissions Contact 925 South Niagara Street, Denver, CO 80224.

Education America, Colorado Springs Campus
Colorado Springs, Colorado

Admissions Contact 6050 Erin Park Drive, #250, Colorado Springs, CO 80918. *Toll-free phone:* 719-264-1234.

Education America, Denver Campus
Lakewood, Colorado

Admissions Contact Admissions Office, Education America, Denver Campus, 11011 West 6th Avenue, Lakewood, CO 80215-0090. *Phone:* 303-426-1000. *Toll-free phone:* 800-999-5181.

Fort Lewis College
Durango, Colorado

- **State-supported** 4-year, founded 1911, part of Colorado State University System
- **Calendar** modified trimesters
- **Degree** bachelor's
- **Small-town** 350-acre campus
- **Endowment** $12.4 million
- **Coed,** 4,441 undergraduate students, 91% full-time, 47% women, 53% men
- **Moderately difficult** entrance level, 84% of applicants were admitted

Undergraduates 4,039 full-time, 402 part-time. Students come from 50 states and territories, 16 other countries, 34% are from out of state, 1% African American, 0.8% Asian American or Pacific Islander, 5% Hispanic American, 16% Native American, 1% international, 8% transferred in, 34% live on campus. *Retention:* 55% of 2001 full-time freshmen returned.

Freshmen *Admission:* 3,118 applied, 2,623 admitted, 1,110 enrolled. *Average high school GPA:* 2.91. *Test scores:* SAT verbal scores over 500: 50%; SAT math scores over 500: 46%; ACT scores over 18: 61%; SAT verbal scores over 600: 12%; SAT math scores over 600: 11%; ACT scores over 24: 15%; SAT verbal scores over 700: 1%; SAT math scores over 700: 1%; ACT scores over 30: 2%.

Faculty *Total:* 231, 69% full-time, 61% with terminal degrees. *Student/faculty ratio:* 19:1.

Majors Accounting; agricultural business; anthropology; archaeology; art; art education; Asian studies; biochemistry; biology; business administration; business marketing and marketing management; cell biology; chemistry; computer science; cultural studies; early childhood education; economics; education; elementary education; engineering/industrial management; English; environmental biology; European studies; finance; fine/studio arts; geology; history; humanities; information sciences/systems; international business; Latin American studies; liberal arts and sciences/liberal studies; literature; mass communications; mathematical statistics; mathematics; modern languages; molecular biology; music; music teacher education; philosophy; physical education; physics; political science; pre-dentistry; pre-law; pre-medicine; pre-veterinary studies; psychology; secondary education; sociology; Spanish; theater arts/drama; travel/tourism management.

Academic Programs *Special study options:* academic remediation for entering students, accelerated degree program, adult/continuing education programs, advanced placement credit, cooperative education, distance learning, double majors, English as a second language, honors programs, independent study, internships, off-campus study, part-time degree program, services for LD students, student-designed majors, study abroad, summer session for credit. *Unusual degree programs:* 3-2 engineering with Colorado State University, Colorado School of Mines, University of New Mexico, University of Colorado at Boulder; forestry with Colorado State University, Northern Arizona University.

Library John F. Reed Library with 167,723 titles, 2,742 serial subscriptions, 3,600 audiovisual materials, an OPAC, a Web page.

Computers on Campus 500 computers available on campus for general student use. A campuswide network can be accessed from student residence rooms and from off campus. Internet access, online (class) registration, at least one staffed computer lab available.

Student Life *Housing:* on-campus residence required for freshman year. *Options:* coed. *Activities and Organizations:* drama/theater group, student-run newspaper, radio station, choral group, marching band, Business Club, AISES (American Indian Science and Engineering Club), Circle K, cycling sport club, Dance Team. *Campus security:* 24-hour emergency response devices and patrols, late-night transport/escort service, controlled dormitory access. *Student Services:* health clinic, personal/psychological counseling, legal services.

Athletics Member NCAA. All Division II. *Intercollegiate sports:* baseball M(c), basketball M(s)/W(s), cross-country running M(s)/W(s), football M(s), golf M(s), lacrosse M(c), rugby M(c)/W(c), skiing (cross-country) M(c)/W(c), skiing (downhill) M(c)/W(c), soccer M(s)/W(s), softball W(s), track and field M(c)/W(c), volleyball M(c)/W(s). *Intramural sports:* badminton M/W, basketball M/W, cross-country running M/W, football M/W, lacrosse M/W, racquetball M/W, soccer M/W, softball M/W, track and field M/W, volleyball M/W, water polo M/W, wrestling M/W.

Standardized Tests *Required:* SAT I or ACT (for admission).

Costs (2001–02) *One-time required fee:* $55. *Tuition:* state resident $1792 full-time, $108 per credit hour part-time; nonresident $8874 full-time, $552 per credit hour part-time. Full-time tuition and fees vary according to reciprocity agreements. Part-time tuition and fees vary according to course load and reciprocity agreements. *Required fees:* $729 full-time, $79 per term part-time. *Room and board:* $5424; room only: $2996. Room and board charges vary according to board plan and housing facility. *Waivers:* minority students and employees or children of employees.

Financial Aid Of all full-time matriculated undergraduates who enrolled in 2001, 2603 applied for aid, 2170 were judged to have need, 436 had their need fully met. 175 Federal Work-Study jobs (averaging $1490). In 2001, 221 non-need-based awards were made. *Average percent of need met:* 80%. *Average financial aid package:* $7106. *Average need-based loan:* $3766. *Average need-based gift aid:* $3812. *Average non-need based aid:* $2025. *Average indebtedness upon graduation:* $14,102.

Applying *Options:* electronic application, deferred entrance. *Application fee:* $20. *Required:* high school transcript, minimum 2.0 GPA. *Recommended:* essay or personal statement, letters of recommendation, interview. *Application deadlines:* 8/1 (freshmen), 7/15 (transfers). *Notification:* continuous (freshmen).

Admissions Contact Ms. Sheri Rochford, Dean of Admissions and Development, Fort Lewis College, 1000 Rim Drive, Durango, CO 81301. *Phone:* 970-247-7184. *Fax:* 970-247-7179. *E-mail:* admission@fortlewis.edu.

ITT Technical Institute
Thornton, Colorado

- **Proprietary** primarily 2-year, founded 1984, part of ITT Educational Services, Inc
- **Calendar** quarters
- **Degrees** associate and bachelor's
- **Suburban** 2-acre campus with easy access to Denver
- **Coed,** 419 undergraduate students
- **Minimally difficult** entrance level

Majors Computer/information sciences related; computer programming; drafting; electrical/electronic engineering technologies related; information technology.

Student Life *Housing:* college housing not available. *Activities and Organizations:* student-run newspaper.

Costs (2001–02) *Tuition:* Full-time tuition and fees vary according to program. Part-time tuition and fees vary according to program. $260—$330 per credit hour.

Applying *Options:* deferred entrance. *Application fee:* $100. *Required:* high school transcript, interview. *Recommended:* letters of recommendation. *Application deadline:* rolling (freshmen), rolling (transfers). *Notification:* continuous (freshmen).

Admissions Contact Mr. Richard F. Hansen, Director, ITT Technical Institute, 500 East 84th Avenue, Suite B12, Thornton, CO 80229. *Phone:* 303-288-4488. *Toll-free phone:* 800-395-4488.

Johnson & Wales University
Denver, Colorado

- **Independent** 4-year, founded 1993
- **Calendar** modular
- **Degrees** associate and bachelor's
- **Small-town** campus
- **Endowment** $178.8 million
- **Coed,** 646 undergraduate students, 96% full-time, 43% women, 57% men
- **Minimally difficult** entrance level, 81% of applicants were admitted

Undergraduates 619 full-time, 27 part-time. Students come from 36 states and territories, 7% African American, 3% Asian American or Pacific Islander, 13% Hispanic American, 1% Native American.

Freshmen *Admission:* 894 applied, 726 admitted, 287 enrolled. *Average high school GPA:* 2.86. *Test scores:* SAT verbal scores over 500: 42%; SAT math scores over 500: 45%; SAT verbal scores over 600: 13%; SAT math scores over 600: 11%; SAT math scores over 700: 1%.

Faculty *Total:* 35, 57% full-time. *Student/faculty ratio:* 18:1.

Majors Business administration; business marketing and marketing management; culinary arts.

Academic Programs *Special study options:* adult/continuing education programs, cooperative education, internships, part-time degree program, services for LD students, summer session for credit.

Library Johnson & Wales University Library with 2,369 titles, 47 serial subscriptions, 320 audiovisual materials, an OPAC, a Web page.

Computers on Campus 20 computers available on campus for general student use. A campuswide network can be accessed from student residence rooms and from off campus. Internet access, at least one staffed computer lab available.

Student Life *Housing:* on-campus residence required for freshman year. *Options:* coed. *Campus security:* 24-hour emergency response devices and patrols, student patrols, late-night transport/escort service.

Standardized Tests *Required for some:* SAT I or ACT (for admission). *Recommended:* SAT I or ACT (for admission).

Costs (2002–03) *Comprehensive fee:* $26,163 includes full-time tuition ($17,652), mandatory fees ($630), and room and board ($7881). Full-time tuition and fees vary according to program. Part-time tuition and fees vary according to program. No tuition increase for student's term of enrollment. *Payment plans:* installment, deferred payment. *Waivers:* employees or children of employees.

Financial Aid Of all full-time matriculated undergraduates who enrolled in 2001, 518 applied for aid, 427 were judged to have need, 24 had their need fully met. In 2001, 43 non-need-based awards were made. *Average percent of need met:* 70%. *Average financial aid package:* $11,837. *Average need-based loan:* $5927. *Average need-based gift aid:* $4167. *Average non-need based aid:* $3861. *Average indebtedness upon graduation:* $6444.

Applying *Options:* common application, deferred entrance. *Required:* high school transcript. *Required for some:* minimum 3.0 GPA. *Recommended:* minimum 2.0 GPA, interview. *Application deadline:* rolling (freshmen), rolling (transfers). *Notification:* continuous (freshmen).

Admissions Contact Mr. Dave McKlveen, Director of Admissions, Johnson & Wales University, 7150 Montview Boulevard, Denver, CO 80220. *Phone:* 303-256-9300. *Toll-free phone:* 877-598-3368. *Fax:* 303-256-9333. *E-mail:* admissions@jwu.edu.

Jones International University
Englewood, Colorado

- **Independent** upper-level, founded 1995
- **Calendar** 6 8-week terms
- **Degrees** certificates, bachelor's, and master's
- **Endowment** $5.0 million
- **Coed**
- **Noncompetitive** entrance level

Undergraduates 90% are from out of state.

Faculty *Total:* 124, 5% full-time. *Student/faculty ratio:* 12:1.

Majors Business communications; computer/information technology services administration and management related.

Academic Programs *Special study options:* accelerated degree program, adult/continuing education programs, distance learning, external degree program, independent study, part-time degree program, summer session for credit.

Computers on Campus Online (class) registration available.

Student Life *Housing:* college housing not available.

Costs (2002–03) *Tuition:* $4500 full-time, $750 per course part-time. *Required fees:* $240 full-time, $40 per course. *Payment plan:* deferred payment. *Waivers:* employees or children of employees.

Applying *Options:* common application, electronic application, deferred entrance. *Application fee:* $75. *Application deadline:* rolling (transfers). *Notification:* continuous (transfers).

Admissions Contact Ms. Candice Morrissey, Associate Director of Admissions, Jones International University, 9697 East Mineral Avenue, Englewood, CO 80112. *Phone:* 303-784-8247. *Toll-free phone:* 800-811-5663 Ext. 8247. *Fax:* 303-784-8547. *E-mail:* admissions@international.edu.

Mesa State College
Grand Junction, Colorado

- **State-supported** comprehensive, founded 1925, part of State Colleges in Colorado
- **Calendar** semesters
- **Degrees** certificates, associate, bachelor's, and master's
- **Small-town** 42-acre campus
- **Coed,** 5,297 undergraduate students, 75% full-time, 58% women, 42% men
- **Minimally difficult** entrance level, 99% of applicants were admitted

Undergraduates 3,981 full-time, 1,316 part-time. Students come from 46 states and territories, 9% are from out of state, 9% transferred in, 18% live on campus. *Retention:* 60% of 2001 full-time freshmen returned.

Freshmen *Admission:* 1,104 applied, 1,096 admitted, 1,044 enrolled. *Average high school GPA:* 3.03. *Test scores:* SAT verbal scores over 500: 46%; SAT math scores over 500: 48%; ACT scores over 18: 74%; SAT verbal scores over 600: 12%; SAT math scores over 600: 12%; ACT scores over 24: 18%; SAT verbal scores over 700: 1%; SAT math scores over 700: 1%; ACT scores over 30: 1%.

Faculty *Total:* 321, 64% full-time, 45% with terminal degrees. *Student/faculty ratio:* 18:1.

Majors Accounting; anthropology; applied art; applied mathematics; art; auto mechanic/technician; behavioral sciences; biology; broadcast journalism; business administration; business economics; business marketing and marketing management; chemistry; computer science; counselor education/guidance; criminal justice/law enforcement administration; criminology; culinary arts; early childhood education; education; electrical/electronic engineering technology; elementary education; engineering; English; environmental technology; exercise sciences; finance; geology; graphic design/commercial art/illustration; heavy equipment maintenance; history; hotel and restaurant management; humanities; human resources management; human services; industrial radiologic technology; industrial technology; information sciences/systems; legal administrative assis-

Mesa State College (continued)

tant; liberal arts and sciences/liberal studies; machine technology; mass communications; mathematical statistics; mathematics; medical administrative assistant; middle school education; music; music teacher education; nursing; physical education; physical sciences; physics; political science; pre-engineering; preveterinary studies; psychology; public relations; radiological science; radio/television broadcasting; science education; secondary education; secretarial science; social sciences; sociology; theater arts/drama; travel/tourism management; welding technology.

Academic Programs *Special study options:* academic remediation for entering students, accelerated degree program, adult/continuing education programs, advanced placement credit, cooperative education, distance learning, double majors, honors programs, independent study, internships, off-campus study, part-time degree program, services for LD students, student-designed majors, study abroad, summer session for credit.

Library John U. Tomlinson Library with 329,681 titles, 1,010 serial subscriptions, 25,578 audiovisual materials, an OPAC, a Web page.

Computers on Campus 350 computers available on campus for general student use. A campuswide network can be accessed from off campus. Internet access, online (class) registration, at least one staffed computer lab available.

Student Life *Housing:* on-campus residence required through sophomore year. *Options:* coed. *Activities and Organizations:* drama/theater group, student-run newspaper, radio and television station, choral group, Environmental Club, Student Body Association, KMSA Radio Station, Rodeo Club, Campus Residents Association. *Campus security:* 24-hour emergency response devices and patrols, late-night transport/escort service, controlled dormitory access. *Student Services:* health clinic, personal/psychological counseling, legal services.

Athletics Member NCAA. All Division II. *Intercollegiate sports:* baseball M(s), basketball M(s)/W(s), cross-country running W(s), football M(s), golf W(s), soccer W(s), softball W(s), tennis M(s)/W(s), volleyball W(s). *Intramural sports:* basketball M/W, equestrian sports M/W, football M/W, golf M/W, lacrosse M, racquetball M/W, skiing (cross-country) M/W, skiing (downhill) M/W, soccer M/W, softball M/W, swimming M/W, tennis M/W, track and field M/W, volleyball M/W, water polo M/W, weight lifting M/W.

Standardized Tests *Required:* SAT I or ACT (for admission).

Costs (2001–02) *Tuition:* state resident $1688 full-time, $84 per credit hour part-time; nonresident $6515 full-time, $326 per credit hour part-time. *Required fees:* $600 full-time. *Room and board:* $5763; room only: $2877.

Financial Aid Of all full-time matriculated undergraduates who enrolled in 2001, 3190 applied for aid, 2890 were judged to have need. 144 Federal Work-Study jobs (averaging $1580). *Average percent of need met:* 54%. *Average financial aid package:* $5142. *Average need-based loan:* $3031. *Average need-based gift aid:* $2210. *Average indebtedness upon graduation:* $12,900.

Applying *Options:* common application, early admission, deferred entrance. *Application fee:* $30. *Required:* high school transcript, minimum 2.0 GPA. *Required for some:* 1 letter of recommendation, interview. *Application deadlines:* 8/15 (freshmen), 8/15 (transfers).

Admissions Contact Mr. Mike Poll, Associate Director, Admissions and Recruitment, Mesa State College, PO Box 2647, Grand Junction, CO 81502-2647. *Phone:* 970-248-1875. *Toll-free phone:* 800-982-MESA. *Fax:* 970-248-1973. *E-mail:* admissions@mesastate.edu.

METROPOLITAN STATE COLLEGE OF DENVER
Denver, Colorado

- **State-supported** 4-year, founded 1963, part of State Colleges in Colorado
- **Calendar** semesters
- **Degree** certificates and bachelor's
- **Urban** 175-acre campus
- **Endowment** $2.2 million
- **Coed,** 18,445 undergraduate students, 56% full-time, 57% women, 43% men
- **Minimally difficult** entrance level, 86% of applicants were admitted

Undergraduates 10,356 full-time, 8,089 part-time. Students come from 40 states and territories, 66 other countries, 1% are from out of state, 6% African American, 4% Asian American or Pacific Islander, 13% Hispanic American, 0.9% Native American, 1% international, 12% transferred in. *Retention:* 62% of 2001 full-time freshmen returned.

Freshmen *Admission:* 4,034 applied, 3,475 admitted, 2,230 enrolled. *Average high school GPA:* 2.84. *Test scores:* SAT verbal scores over 500: 43%; SAT math scores over 500: 35%; ACT scores over 18: 66%; SAT verbal scores over 600: 11%; SAT math scores over 600: 10%; ACT scores over 24: 14%; SAT verbal scores over 700: 1%; ACT scores over 30: 1%.

Faculty *Total:* 1,000, 45% full-time. *Student/faculty ratio:* 21:1.

Majors Accounting; African-American studies; anthropology; art; atmospheric sciences; aviation management; behavioral sciences; biology; chemistry; civil engineering technology; computer/information sciences; computer science; criminal justice/law enforcement administration; economics; education (K-12); electrical/electronic engineering technology; English; environmental science; exercise sciences; finance; foreign languages/literatures; health services administration; history; hospitality management; human services; industrial design; industrial technology; journalism; land use management; management science; marketing research; mathematics; mechanical engineering technology; Mexican-American studies; music (general performance); music teacher education; nursing; philosophy; physics; political science; psychology; public relations; recreation/leisure studies; social work; sociology; Spanish; speech/rhetorical studies; surveying; urban studies.

Academic Programs *Special study options:* accelerated degree program, adult/continuing education programs, advanced placement credit, cooperative education, distance learning, double majors, external degree program, honors programs, independent study, internships, off-campus study, part-time degree program, services for LD students, student-designed majors, study abroad, summer session for credit. *ROTC:* Air Force (c).

Library Auraria Library with 555,984 titles, 7,364 serial subscriptions, 15,750 audiovisual materials, an OPAC, a Web page.

Computers on Campus 700 computers available on campus for general student use. A campuswide network can be accessed from off campus. Internet access, online (class) registration, at least one staffed computer lab available.

Student Life *Housing:* college housing not available. *Activities and Organizations:* drama/theater group, student-run newspaper, choral group, Political Science Association, Accounting Students Organization, Christian Students Organization, LGBTA, Golden Key National Honor Society. *Campus security:* 24-hour emergency response devices and patrols, late-night transport/escort service. *Student Services:* health clinic, personal/psychological counseling, women's center, legal services.

Athletics Member NCAA. All Division II. *Intercollegiate sports:* baseball M(s), basketball M(s)/W(s), soccer M(s)/W(s), swimming M(s)/W(s), tennis M(s)/W(s), volleyball W(s). *Intramural sports:* badminton M(c)/W(c), baseball M/W, basketball M/W, football M/W, golf M/W, lacrosse M(c), racquetball M/W, rugby M(c), soccer M/W, softball M/W(c), swimming M/W, tennis M/W, volleyball M(c)/W(c), water polo M(c)/W(c).

Standardized Tests *Required for some:* SAT I or ACT (for admission).

Costs (2002–03) *Tuition:* state resident $1949 full-time, $80 per credit part-time; nonresident $8147 full-time, $335 per credit part-time. Full-time tuition and fees vary according to course load and location. Part-time tuition and fees vary according to course load and location. *Required fees:* $530 full-time, $33 per credit. *Payment plan:* deferred payment. *Waivers:* senior citizens.

Financial Aid Of all full-time matriculated undergraduates who enrolled in 2001, 5621 applied for aid, 5109 were judged to have need. 242 Federal Work-Study jobs (averaging $2788). 685 State and other part-time jobs (averaging $2872). In 2001, 494 non-need-based awards were made. *Average percent of need met:* 55%. *Average financial aid package:* $5809. *Average need-based loan:* $3794. *Average need-based gift aid:* $3427. *Average non-need based aid:* $1747. *Average indebtedness upon graduation:* $18,222.

Applying *Options:* common application, electronic application, deferred entrance. *Application fee:* $25. *Required:* high school transcript. *Required for some:* essay or personal statement, letters of recommendation. *Recommended:* minimum 2.0 GPA. *Application deadline:* 8/12 (freshmen), rolling (transfers). *Notification:* continuous (freshmen).

Admissions Contact Ms. Miriam Tapia, Associate Director, Metropolitan State College of Denver, PO Box 173362, Campus Box 16, Denver, CO 80217-3362. *Phone:* 303-556-2615. *Fax:* 303-556-6345.

NAROPA UNIVERSITY
Boulder, Colorado

- **Independent** comprehensive, founded 1974
- **Calendar** semesters
- **Degrees** bachelor's, master's, and post-master's certificates
- **Urban** 4-acre campus with easy access to Denver
- **Endowment** $3.0 million
- **Coed,** 463 undergraduate students, 76% full-time, 65% women, 35% men
- **Moderately difficult** entrance level, 97% of applicants were admitted

Undergraduates 350 full-time, 113 part-time. Students come from 39 states and territories, 9 other countries, 39% are from out of state, 1% African American, 1% Asian American or Pacific Islander, 3% Hispanic American, 0.9% Native American, 1% international, 24% transferred in, 6% live on campus. *Retention:* 60% of 2001 full-time freshmen returned.

Freshmen *Admission:* 113 applied, 110 admitted, 45 enrolled.
Faculty *Total:* 209, 16% full-time, 44% with terminal degrees. *Student/faculty ratio:* 12:1.
Majors Art; creative writing; dance; dance therapy; early childhood education; ecology; environmental science; horticulture science; interdisciplinary studies; literature; music; Native American studies; psychology; religious studies; theater arts/drama.
Academic Programs *Special study options:* adult/continuing education programs, advanced placement credit, cooperative education, distance learning, double majors, independent study, internships, part-time degree program, services for LD students, student-designed majors, study abroad, summer session for credit.
Library Allen Ginsberg Library with 30,000 titles, 111 serial subscriptions, 11,916 audiovisual materials, an OPAC, a Web page.
Computers on Campus 18 computers available on campus for general student use. Internet access, at least one staffed computer lab available.
Student Life *Housing Options:* coed. *Activities and Organizations:* drama/theater group, student-run newspaper, choral group, Student Union of Naropa (SUN), Garuda Theater, Student Union for Ethnic Inclusion, Diversity Awareness Working Group, Students for a Free Tibet. *Campus security:* controlled dormitory access. *Student Services:* personal/psychological counseling.
Costs (2001–02) *Comprehensive fee:* $20,866 includes full-time tuition ($14,490), mandatory fees ($566), and room and board ($5810). Full-time tuition and fees vary according to course load. Part-time tuition: $483 per semester hour. Part-time tuition and fees vary according to course load. *Required fees:* $283 per term part-time. *Room and board:* College room only: $4410. Room and board charges vary according to board plan and housing facility. *Payment plans:* tuition prepayment, installment, deferred payment. *Waivers:* employees or children of employees.
Financial Aid Of all full-time matriculated undergraduates who enrolled in 2001, 237 applied for aid, 220 were judged to have need, 13 had their need fully met. 194 Federal Work-Study jobs (averaging $4822). 8 State and other part-time jobs (averaging $4500). *Average percent of need met:* 80%. *Average financial aid package:* $18,120. *Average need-based gift aid:* $7580. *Average indebtedness upon graduation:* $18,921.
Applying *Options:* deferred entrance. *Application fee:* $35. *Required:* essay or personal statement, high school transcript, 2 letters of recommendation, interview. *Application deadline:* rolling (freshmen), rolling (transfers).
Admissions Contact Ms. Sally Forester, Admissions Counselor, Naropa University, 2130 Arapahoe Avenue, Boulder, CO 80302. *Phone:* 303-546-5285. *Toll-free phone:* 800-772-0410. *Fax:* 303-546-3583. *E-mail:* admissions@naropa.edu.

NATIONAL AMERICAN UNIVERSITY
Colorado Springs, Colorado

- **Proprietary** 4-year, founded 1941
- **Calendar** quarters
- **Degrees** certificates, diplomas, associate, bachelor's, and master's
- **Suburban** 1-acre campus with easy access to Denver
- **Coed,** 325 undergraduate students
- **Noncompetitive** entrance level

Undergraduates Students come from 3 states and territories, 5 other countries.
Faculty *Total:* 29, 7% full-time.
Majors Accounting; business administration; hotel and restaurant management; information sciences/systems; travel/tourism management.
Academic Programs *Special study options:* academic remediation for entering students, accelerated degree program, adult/continuing education programs, English as a second language, external degree program, internships, part-time degree program, summer session for credit.
Library National American University Library with 10,000 titles, 100 serial subscriptions.
Computers on Campus 40 computers available on campus for general student use. At least one staffed computer lab available.
Student Life *Housing:* college housing not available. *Campus security:* late-night transport/escort service.
Standardized Tests *Required for some:* ACT (for placement).
Costs (2001–02) *Tuition:* $9600 full-time, $200 per credit hour part-time.
Applying *Options:* deferred entrance. *Application fee:* $25. *Required:* high school transcript, interview. *Application deadline:* rolling (freshmen), rolling (transfers).
Admissions Contact Ms. Dawn Collins, Director of Admissions, National American University, 5125 North Academy Boulevard, Colorado Springs, CO 80918. *Phone:* 719-277-0588. *Toll-free phone:* 888-471-4781. *Fax:* 719-471-4751. *E-mail:* nau@clsp.uswest.net.

NATIONAL AMERICAN UNIVERSITY
Denver, Colorado

- **Proprietary** 4-year, founded 1974, part of National College
- **Calendar** quarters
- **Degrees** certificates, diplomas, associate, and bachelor's
- **Urban** campus
- **Coed**
- **Noncompetitive** entrance level

Standardized Tests *Recommended:* SAT I or ACT (for placement).
Applying *Options:* deferred entrance. *Application fee:* $25. *Required:* high school transcript.
Admissions Contact Mr. Tom De Felice, Director of Admissions, National American University, 1325 South Colorado Blvd, Suite 100, Denver, CO 80222. *Phone:* 303-758-6700. *Fax:* 303-758-6810.

NAZARENE BIBLE COLLEGE
Colorado Springs, Colorado

- **Independent** 4-year, founded 1967, affiliated with Church of the Nazarene
- **Calendar** quarters
- **Degrees** diplomas, associate, and bachelor's
- **Urban** 64-acre campus with easy access to Denver
- **Endowment** $1.4 million
- **Coed,** 473 undergraduate students, 41% full-time, 30% women, 70% men
- **Noncompetitive** entrance level, 60% of applicants were admitted

Undergraduates 195 full-time, 278 part-time. Students come from 49 states and territories, 86% are from out of state, 3% African American, 2% Asian American or Pacific Islander, 1% Hispanic American, 2% Native American, 0.8% international. *Retention:* 89% of 2001 full-time freshmen returned.
Freshmen *Admission:* 240 applied, 144 admitted, 32 enrolled.
Faculty *Total:* 23. *Student/faculty ratio:* 14:1.
Majors Biblical studies; pastoral counseling; pre-theology; religious education; religious music; women's studies.
Academic Programs *Special study options:* academic remediation for entering students, internships, part-time degree program, summer session for credit.
Library Trimble Library with 50,358 titles, 180 serial subscriptions, an OPAC.
Computers on Campus 6 computers available on campus for general student use. A campuswide network can be accessed from off campus. Internet access, at least one staffed computer lab available.
Student Life *Housing:* college housing not available. *Activities and Organizations:* student-run newspaper, choral group. *Campus security:* student patrols. *Student Services:* personal/psychological counseling.
Costs (2001–02) *Tuition:* $8976 full-time, $187 per semester hour part-time. *Required fees:* $270 full-time, $10 per term part-time.
Financial Aid Of all full-time matriculated undergraduates who enrolled in 2001, 199 applied for aid, 199 were judged to have need. 7 Federal Work-Study jobs (averaging $2600). *Average indebtedness upon graduation:* $15,498.
Applying *Options:* common application, deferred entrance. *Application fee:* $20. *Required:* essay or personal statement, high school transcript, 2 letters of recommendation. *Application deadlines:* 8/31 (freshmen), 8/31 (transfers).
Admissions Contact Dr. David Phillips, Director of Admissions/Public Relations, Nazarene Bible College, 1111 Academy Park Loop, Colorado Springs, CO 80910-3704. *Phone:* 719-884-5031. *Toll-free phone:* 800-873-3873. *Fax:* 719-884-5199.

PLATT COLLEGE
Aurora, Colorado

- **Proprietary** primarily 2-year, founded 1986
- **Calendar** quarters
- **Degrees** diplomas, associate, and bachelor's
- **Suburban** campus
- **Coed,** 215 undergraduate students, 100% full-time, 51% women, 49% men
- **Noncompetitive** entrance level, 100% of applicants were admitted

Platt College (continued)

Freshmen *Admission:* 47 applied, 47 admitted.

Faculty *Total:* 22, 64% full-time. *Student/faculty ratio:* 14:1.

Majors Advertising; computer graphics; computer/information technology services administration and management related; graphic design/commercial art/illustration; multimedia; Web page, digital/multimedia and information resources design.

Academic Programs *Special study options:* academic remediation for entering students, advanced placement credit.

Student Life *Housing:* college housing not available.

Costs (2001–02) *Tuition:* $7560 full-time. *Required fees:* $75 full-time.

Applying *Application fee:* $75. *Required:* high school transcript, interview. *Application deadline:* rolling (freshmen), rolling (transfers).

Admissions Contact Admissions Office, Platt College, 3100 South Parker Road, Suite 200, Aurora, CO 80014-3141. *Phone:* 303-369-5151. *E-mail:* admissions@plattcolo.com.

REGIS UNIVERSITY
Denver, Colorado

- **Independent Roman Catholic (Jesuit)** comprehensive, founded 1877
- **Calendar** semesters
- **Degrees** bachelor's and master's
- **Suburban** 90-acre campus
- **Endowment** $24.2 million
- **Coed,** 7,450 undergraduate students
- **Moderately difficult** entrance level, 86% of applicants were admitted

The Regis Guarantee ensures that entering freshmen will graduate in 4 years—or take the additional course work at no charge. The Learn and Earn Program offers every new freshman the opportunity to work on campus to gain valuable experience and money to help defray expenses. These programs, and its 125-year history of offering high-quality, value-oriented Jesuit education, make Regis a leader in the Rocky Mountain region.

Undergraduates Students come from 40 states and territories, 11 other countries, 39% are from out of state, 4% African American, 2% Asian American or Pacific Islander, 8% Hispanic American, 0.8% Native American, 0.6% international. *Retention:* 79% of 2001 full-time freshmen returned.

Freshmen *Admission:* 1,245 applied, 1,068 admitted. *Average high school GPA:* 3.24. *Test scores:* SAT verbal scores over 500: 73%; SAT math scores over 500: 66%; ACT scores over 18: 97%; SAT verbal scores over 600: 26%; SAT math scores over 600: 27%; ACT scores over 24: 46%; SAT verbal scores over 700: 6%; SAT math scores over 700: 5%; ACT scores over 30: 7%.

Faculty *Total:* 942, 16% full-time, 40% with terminal degrees. *Student/faculty ratio:* 14:1.

Majors Accounting; biochemistry; biology; business administration; chemistry; communications; computer science; criminal justice/law enforcement administration; economics; education; elementary education; English; environmental science; French; history; human ecology; humanities; liberal arts and sciences/liberal studies; mathematics; medical records administration; neuroscience; nursing; philosophy; political science; pre-dentistry; pre-law; pre-medicine; pre-veterinary studies; psychology; religious studies; sociology; Spanish; visual/performing arts.

Academic Programs *Special study options:* academic remediation for entering students, accelerated degree program, adult/continuing education programs, advanced placement credit, cooperative education, double majors, external degree program, freshman honors college, honors programs, independent study, internships, off-campus study, part-time degree program, services for LD students, student-designed majors, study abroad, summer session for credit. *ROTC:* Army (c), Navy (c), Air Force (c). *Unusual degree programs:* 3-2 engineering with Washington University in St. Louis.

Library Dayton Memorial Library with 430,514 titles, 7,850 serial subscriptions, 104,887 audiovisual materials, an OPAC, a Web page.

Computers on Campus 300 computers available on campus for general student use. A campuswide network can be accessed from student residence rooms and from off campus. At least one staffed computer lab available.

Student Life *Housing:* on-campus residence required for freshman year. *Options:* coed. *Activities and Organizations:* drama/theater group, student-run newspaper, radio station, choral group, Programming Activities Council, hall governing boards, Student Executive Board, Outdoor Club, Rugby Club. *Campus security:* 24-hour emergency response devices and patrols, student patrols, late-night transport/escort service, controlled dormitory access. *Student Services:* health clinic, personal/psychological counseling.

Athletics Member NCAA. All Division II. *Intercollegiate sports:* baseball M(s), basketball M(s)/W(s), golf M(s), lacrosse M(s)/W(s), rugby M(c), skiing (cross-country) M(c), skiing (downhill) M(c), soccer M(s)/W(s), softball W(s), volleyball W(s). *Intramural sports:* basketball M/W, bowling M/W, football M/W, ice hockey M(c), softball M/W, table tennis M/W, volleyball M/W.

Standardized Tests *Required:* SAT I or ACT (for admission). *Recommended:* SAT II: Subject Tests (for admission).

Costs (2001–02) *Comprehensive fee:* $25,720 includes full-time tuition ($18,400), mandatory fees ($170), and room and board ($7150). Part-time tuition: $570 per semester hour. *Required fees:* $60 per term part-time. *Room and board:* College room only: $4200. Room and board charges vary according to board plan and housing facility. *Payment plan:* deferred payment. *Waivers:* adult students, senior citizens, and employees or children of employees.

Financial Aid Of all full-time matriculated undergraduates who enrolled in 2001, 1052 applied for aid, 605 were judged to have need, 235 had their need fully met. 146 Federal Work-Study jobs (averaging $2200). 505 State and other part-time jobs (averaging $2000). In 2001, 356 non-need-based awards were made. *Average percent of need met:* 85%. *Average financial aid package:* $14,771. *Average need-based loan:* $4409. *Average need-based gift aid:* $10,322. *Average indebtedness upon graduation:* $22,000.

Applying *Options:* common application, deferred entrance. *Application fee:* $40. *Required:* essay or personal statement, high school transcript, minimum 2.2 GPA, 1 letter of recommendation. *Required for some:* 2 letters of recommendation, interview. *Application deadlines:* 8/15 (freshmen), 8/15 (transfers). *Notification:* continuous (freshmen).

Admissions Contact Mr. Vic Davolt, Director of Admissions, Regis University, 3333 Regis Boulevard, Denver, CO 80221-1099. *Phone:* 303-458-4905. *Toll-free phone:* 800-388-2366 Ext. 4900. *Fax:* 303-964-5534. *E-mail:* regisadm@regis.edu.

ROCKY MOUNTAIN COLLEGE OF ART & DESIGN
Denver, Colorado

- **Proprietary** 4-year, founded 1963
- **Calendar** trimesters
- **Degree** bachelor's
- **Urban** 1-acre campus
- **Coed,** 425 undergraduate students, 79% full-time, 54% women, 46% men
- **Moderately difficult** entrance level, 74% of applicants were admitted

Undergraduates 335 full-time, 90 part-time. Students come from 36 states and territories, 24% are from out of state, 1% African American, 2% Asian American or Pacific Islander, 9% Hispanic American, 0.2% Native American, 0.7% international, 18% transferred in, 18% live on campus.

Freshmen *Admission:* 106 applied, 78 admitted, 76 enrolled. *Average high school GPA:* 2.9.

Faculty *Total:* 61, 33% full-time, 90% with terminal degrees. *Student/faculty ratio:* 12:1.

Majors Art education; film/video and photographic arts related; graphic design/commercial art/illustration; interior design; painting; sculpture.

Academic Programs *Special study options:* academic remediation for entering students, accelerated degree program, advanced placement credit, cooperative education, double majors, independent study, internships, part-time degree program, summer session for credit.

Library Rocky Mountain College of Art and Design Library with 6,287 titles, 65 serial subscriptions.

Computers on Campus 47 computers available on campus for general student use. Internet access, at least one staffed computer lab available.

Student Life *Housing:* on-campus residence required for freshman year. *Activities and Organizations:* Artists Representative Team, The American Society of Interior Designers, The American Institute of Graphic Arts, Art Directors Club of Denver, International Animated Film Association. *Student Services:* personal/psychological counseling.

Athletics *Intramural sports:* softball M/W.

Standardized Tests *Required for some:* SAT I and SAT II or ACT (for admission).

Costs (2001–02) *Tuition:* $11,472 full-time, $478 per credit part-time. *Required fees:* $90 full-time, $15 per term part-time. *Room only:* $3000. *Payment plan:* installment. *Waivers:* employees or children of employees.

Financial Aid Of all full-time matriculated undergraduates who enrolled in 2001, 418 applied for aid, 390 were judged to have need, 17 had their need fully met. 19 Federal Work-Study jobs (averaging $1774). 3 State and other part-time jobs (averaging $1667). In 2001, 8 non-need-based awards were made. *Average*

percent of need met: 24%. *Average financial aid package:* $3725. *Average need-based loan:* $3708. *Average need-based gift aid:* $2262. *Average non-need based aid:* $1434.

Applying *Options:* common application, deferred entrance. *Application fee:* $35. *Required:* essay or personal statement, high school transcript, minimum 2.0 GPA, 1 letter of recommendation, interview, portfolio. *Application deadline:* rolling (freshmen), rolling (transfers).

Admissions Contact Rocky Mountain College of Art & Design, 6875 East Evans Avenue, Denver, CO 80224-2329. *Phone:* 303-753-6046. *Toll-free phone:* 800-888-ARTS. *Fax:* 303-759-4970. *E-mail:* admit@rmcad.edu.

TEIKYO LORETTO HEIGHTS UNIVERSITY
Denver, Colorado

Admissions Contact 3001 South Federal Boulevard, Denver, CO 80236-2711.

UNITED STATES AIR FORCE ACADEMY
Colorado Springs, Colorado

- **Federally supported** 4-year, founded 1954
- **Calendar** semesters
- **Degree** bachelor's
- **Suburban** 18,000-acre campus with easy access to Denver
- **Coed, primarily men,** 4,365 undergraduate students, 100% full-time, 16% women, 84% men
- **Most difficult** entrance level, 17% of applicants were admitted

Undergraduates 4,365 full-time. Students come from 54 states and territories, 22 other countries, 95% are from out of state, 6% African American, 4% Asian American or Pacific Islander, 6% Hispanic American, 1% Native American, 0.8% international, 100% live on campus. *Retention:* 90% of 2001 full-time freshmen returned.

Freshmen *Admission:* 9,552 applied, 1,619 admitted, 1,202 enrolled. *Average high school GPA:* 3.80. *Test scores:* SAT verbal scores over 500: 98%; SAT math scores over 500: 99%; SAT verbal scores over 600: 66%; SAT math scores over 600: 79%; SAT verbal scores over 700: 15%; SAT math scores over 700: 25%.

Faculty *Total:* 531, 100% full-time, 55% with terminal degrees. *Student/faculty ratio:* 8:1.

Majors Aerospace engineering; area studies; atmospheric sciences; behavioral sciences; biochemistry; biological/physical sciences; biology; business administration; chemistry; civil engineering; computer science; economics; electrical engineering; engineering; engineering mechanics; engineering science; English; environmental engineering; geography; history; humanities; interdisciplinary studies; legal studies; materials science; mathematics; mechanical engineering; military studies; operations research; physics; political science; social sciences.

Academic Programs *Special study options:* academic remediation for entering students, advanced placement credit, double majors, English as a second language, independent study, internships, off-campus study, student-designed majors, study abroad, summer session for credit.

Library United States Air Force Academy Library plus 2 others with 445,379 titles, 1,693 serial subscriptions, 4,458 audiovisual materials, an OPAC, a Web page.

Computers on Campus A campuswide network can be accessed from student residence rooms and from off campus.

Student Life *Housing:* on-campus residence required through senior year. *Options:* coed. *Activities and Organizations:* drama/theater group, student-run newspaper, radio station, choral group, marching band, Cadet Ski Club, choir, Scuba Club, Aviation Club, Drum and Bugle Corps. *Campus security:* 24-hour emergency response devices and patrols, late-night transport/escort service, self-defense education, well-lit campus. *Student Services:* health clinic, personal/psychological counseling, legal services.

Athletics Member NCAA. All Division I except football (Division I-A). *Intercollegiate sports:* baseball M, basketball M/W, cross-country running M/W, fencing M/W, golf M, gymnastics M/W, ice hockey M, lacrosse M, riflery M/W, rugby W(c), skiing (cross-country) M(c)/W(c), skiing (downhill) M(c)/W(c), soccer M/W, softball W(c), swimming M/W, tennis M/W, track and field M/W, volleyball W, water polo M, weight lifting M(c)/W(c), wrestling M. *Intramural sports:* archery M(c)/W(c), basketball M/W, bowling M(c)/W(c), cross-country running M/W, racquetball M/W, rugby M/W, soccer M/W, softball M/W, swimming M/W, tennis M/W, volleyball M/W, water polo M/W, wrestling M.

Standardized Tests *Required:* SAT I or ACT (for admission).

Costs (2001–02) *Tuition:* Tuition, room and board, and medical and dental care are provided by the U.S. government. Each cadet receives a salary from which to pay for uniforms, supplies, and personal expenses. Entering freshmen are required to deposit $2500 to defray the initial cost of uniforms and equipment.

Applying *Required:* essay or personal statement, high school transcript, minimum 2.0 GPA, interview, authorized nomination. *Application deadlines:* 1/31 (freshmen), 1/31 (transfers). *Notification:* continuous until 5/15 (freshmen).

Admissions Contact Mr. Rolland Stoneman, Associate Director of Admissions/Selections, United States Air Force Academy, HQ USAFA/RR 2304 Cadet Drive, Suite 200, USAF Academy, CO 80840-5025. *Phone:* 719-333-2520. *Toll-free phone:* 800-443-9266. *Fax:* 719-333-3012. *E-mail:* rr_webmail@usafa.af.mil.

UNIVERSITY OF COLORADO AT BOULDER
Boulder, Colorado

- **State-supported** university, founded 1876, part of University of Colorado System
- **Calendar** semesters
- **Degrees** bachelor's, master's, doctoral, and first professional
- **Suburban** 600-acre campus with easy access to Denver
- **Endowment** $204.0 million
- **Coed,** 23,998 undergraduate students, 89% full-time, 48% women, 52% men
- **Moderately difficult** entrance level, 79% of applicants were admitted

Undergraduates 21,382 full-time, 2,616 part-time. Students come from 53 states and territories, 113 other countries, 33% are from out of state, 2% African American, 6% Asian American or Pacific Islander, 6% Hispanic American, 0.7% Native American, 1% international, 6% transferred in, 25% live on campus. *Retention:* 82% of 2001 full-time freshmen returned.

Freshmen *Admission:* 18,486 applied, 14,637 admitted, 5,020 enrolled. *Average high school GPA:* 3.48. *Test scores:* SAT verbal scores over 500: 86%; SAT math scores over 500: 89%; ACT scores over 18: 99%; SAT verbal scores over 600: 37%; SAT math scores over 600: 47%; ACT scores over 24: 65%; SAT verbal scores over 700: 5%; SAT math scores over 700: 8%; ACT scores over 30: 10%.

Faculty *Total:* 2,121, 60% full-time, 50% with terminal degrees. *Student/faculty ratio:* 15:1.

Majors Accounting; advertising; aerospace engineering; American studies; anthropology; applied mathematics; architectural engineering; architectural environmental design; art; Asian studies; astronomy; biochemistry; biology; broadcast journalism; business administration; business marketing and marketing management; cell biology; chemical engineering; chemistry; Chinese; civil engineering; classics; communication disorders; communications; computer engineering; computer/information sciences; computer science; cultural studies; dance; economics; electrical engineering; engineering physics; English; environmental engineering; environmental science; exercise sciences; film studies; finance; fine/studio arts; French; geography; geology; German; history; humanities; international relations; Italian; Japanese; journalism; linguistics; management information systems/business data processing; mass communications; mathematics; mechanical engineering; molecular biology; multi/interdisciplinary studies related; music; music teacher education; philosophy; physics; political science; psychology; religious studies; Russian/Slavic studies; sociology; Spanish; theater arts/drama; visual and performing arts related; women's studies.

Academic Programs *Special study options:* accelerated degree program, adult/continuing education programs, advanced placement credit, cooperative education, distance learning, double majors, English as a second language, freshman honors college, honors programs, independent study, internships, off-campus study, part-time degree program, services for LD students, student-designed majors, study abroad, summer session for credit. *ROTC:* Army (b), Navy (b), Air Force (b). *Unusual degree programs:* 3-2 nursing with University of Colorado Health Sciences Center; child health associate, dental hygiene, medical technology, pharmacy at University of Colorado Health Sciences Center.

Library Norlin Library plus 5 others with 2.7 million titles, 14,772 serial subscriptions, 60,202 audiovisual materials, an OPAC, a Web page.

Computers on Campus 1700 computers available on campus for general student use. A campuswide network can be accessed from student residence rooms and from off campus that provide access to standard and academic software, student government voting. Internet access, online (class) registration, at least one staffed computer lab available.

Student Life *Housing:* on-campus residence required for freshman year. *Options:* coed, disabled students. *Activities and Organizations:* drama/theater group, student-run newspaper, radio and television station, choral group, marching band, student government, ski and snowboard club, Environmental Center, AIESEC, Program Council, national fraternities, national sororities. *Campus security:* 24-hour emergency response devices and patrols, student patrols, late-night transport/escort service, University police department. *Student Services:* health clinic, personal/psychological counseling, women's center, legal services.

University of Colorado at Boulder (continued)

Athletics Member NCAA. All Division I except football (Division I-A). *Intercollegiate sports:* baseball M(c), basketball M(s)/W(s), bowling M(c)/W(c), crew M(c)/W(c), cross-country running M(s)/W(s), equestrian sports M(c)/W(c), fencing M(c)/W(c), field hockey M(c)/W(c), golf M(s)/W(s), ice hockey M(c)/W(c), lacrosse M(c)/W(c), racquetball M(c)/W(c), rugby M(c)/W(c), skiing (cross-country) M(s)/W(s), skiing (downhill) M(s)/W(s), soccer M(c)/W(s), softball W(c), squash M(c)/W(c), swimming M(c)/W(c), tennis M(s)/W(s), track and field M(s)/W(s), volleyball M(c)/W(s), water polo M(c)/W(c). *Intramural sports:* badminton M/W, basketball M/W, cross-country running M(c)/W(c), football M/W(c), ice hockey M/W, racquetball M/W, skiing (cross-country) M(c)/W(c), skiing (downhill) M(c)/W(c), soccer M/W(c), softball M/W, squash M/W, table tennis M/W, tennis M/W, volleyball M/W(c), water polo M/W.

Standardized Tests *Required:* SAT I or ACT (for admission).

Costs (2001–02) *One-time required fee:* $35. *Tuition:* state resident $2614 full-time; nonresident $16,624 full-time. Full-time tuition and fees vary according to program. Part-time tuition and fees vary according to course load and program. *Required fees:* $743 full-time. *Room and board:* $5898; room only: $3066. Room and board charges vary according to board plan, housing facility, and location. *Payment plan:* deferred payment. *Waivers:* senior citizens.

Financial Aid Of all full-time matriculated undergraduates who enrolled in 2001, 11287 applied for aid, 5434 were judged to have need, 1885 had their need fully met. 611 Federal Work-Study jobs. In 2001, 4109 non-need-based awards were made. *Average percent of need met:* 75%. *Average financial aid package:* $9434. *Average need-based loan:* $3954. *Average need-based gift aid:* $4060. *Average indebtedness upon graduation:* $16,737.

Applying *Options:* electronic application, deferred entrance. *Application fee:* $40. *Required:* essay or personal statement, high school transcript, minimum 2.0 GPA. *Required for some:* audition for music program. *Recommended:* minimum 3.0 GPA, letters of recommendation. *Application deadlines:* 2/15 (freshmen), 4/1 (transfers). *Notification:* continuous until 5/1 (freshmen).

Admissions Contact Mr. Kevin MacLennan, Associate Director, University of Colorado at Boulder, 552 UCB, Boulder, CO 80309-0552. *Phone:* 303-492-1394. *Fax:* 303-492-7115. *E-mail:* apply@colorado.edu.

UNIVERSITY OF COLORADO AT COLORADO SPRINGS

Colorado Springs, Colorado

- **State-supported** comprehensive, founded 1965, part of University of Colorado System
- **Calendar** semesters
- **Degrees** certificates, bachelor's, master's, and doctoral
- **Suburban** 400-acre campus with easy access to Denver
- **Endowment** $16.0 million
- **Coed,** 5,244 undergraduate students, 74% full-time, 61% women, 39% men
- **Moderately difficult** entrance level, 74% of applicants were admitted

Undergraduates 3,872 full-time, 1,372 part-time. Students come from 44 states and territories, 26 other countries, 13% are from out of state, 4% African American, 6% Asian American or Pacific Islander, 9% Hispanic American, 1% Native American, 0.4% international, 12% live on campus. *Retention:* 63% of 2001 full-time freshmen returned.

Freshmen *Admission:* 2,288 applied, 1,683 admitted, 641 enrolled. *Average high school GPA:* 3.36. *Test scores:* SAT verbal scores over 500: 64%; SAT math scores over 500: 66%; ACT scores over 18: 91%; SAT verbal scores over 600: 18%; SAT math scores over 600: 25%; ACT scores over 24: 31%; SAT verbal scores over 700: 2%; SAT math scores over 700: 3%; ACT scores over 30: 2%.

Faculty *Total:* 437, 57% full-time, 54% with terminal degrees. *Student/faculty ratio:* 16:1.

Majors Accounting; anthropology; applied mathematics; art; biology; business administration; business marketing and marketing management; chemistry; communications; computer engineering; computer/information sciences; computer science; ecology; economics; electrical engineering; English; finance; fine/studio arts; geography; health science; history; mathematics; mechanical engineering; nursing; philosophy; physics; political science; pre-dentistry; pre-law; pre-medicine; pre-veterinary studies; psychology; sociology; Spanish.

Academic Programs *Special study options:* accelerated degree program, adult/continuing education programs, advanced placement credit, cooperative education, distance learning, double majors, independent study, internships, part-time degree program, services for LD students, summer session for credit. *ROTC:* Army (b).

Library University of Colorado at Colorado Springs Kraemer Family Library with 380,948 titles, 2,171 serial subscriptions, 5,055 audiovisual materials, an OPAC, a Web page.

Computers on Campus 350 computers available on campus for general student use. A campuswide network can be accessed from student residence rooms and from off campus. At least one staffed computer lab available.

Student Life *Housing Options:* coed, men-only, women-only. *Activities and Organizations:* drama/theater group, student-run newspaper, choral group, Business Club, Science Club, Ski Club, United Students of Color, psychology club. *Campus security:* 24-hour emergency response devices and patrols, student patrols, late-night transport/escort service, controlled dormitory access. *Student Services:* health clinic, personal/psychological counseling, women's center.

Athletics Member NCAA. All Division II. *Intercollegiate sports:* baseball M(c), basketball M(s)/W(s), cross-country running M(s)/W(s), golf M(s), soccer M(s)/W(c), softball W(s), tennis M(s)/W(s), track and field M/W, volleyball M(c)/W(s). *Intramural sports:* badminton M/W, basketball M/W, bowling M/W, cross-country running M/W, fencing M(c)/W(c), ice hockey M(c), racquetball M/W, skiing (cross-country) M/W, skiing (downhill) M(c)/W(c), soccer M/W, softball M/W, table tennis M/W, tennis M/W, volleyball M/W, weight lifting M/W.

Standardized Tests *Required:* SAT I or ACT (for admission).

Costs (2001–02) *Tuition:* state resident $3550 full-time, $119 per credit hour part-time; nonresident $14,014 full-time, $555 per credit hour part-time. Full-time tuition and fees vary according to program. Part-time tuition and fees vary according to program. *Required fees:* $700 full-time, $350 per term part-time. *Room and board:* $5893; room only: $3370. Room and board charges vary according to board plan and housing facility. *Payment plan:* deferred payment. *Waivers:* employees or children of employees.

Financial Aid Of all full-time matriculated undergraduates who enrolled in 2001, 2774 applied for aid, 2025 were judged to have need, 1105 had their need fully met. 228 Federal Work-Study jobs (averaging $3439). 213 State and other part-time jobs (averaging $3556). In 2001, 170 non-need-based awards were made. *Average percent of need met:* 70%. *Average financial aid package:* $6646. *Average need-based loan:* $3627. *Average need-based gift aid:* $3848. *Average indebtedness upon graduation:* $12,229.

Applying *Options:* electronic application, deferred entrance. *Application fee:* $45. *Required:* high school transcript. *Application deadlines:* 7/1 (freshmen), 7/1 (transfers). *Notification:* continuous (freshmen).

Admissions Contact Mr. James Tidwell, Assistant Admissions Director, University of Colorado at Colorado Springs, PO Box 7150, Colorado Springs, CO 80933-7150. *Phone:* 719-262-3383. *Toll-free phone:* 800-990-8227 Ext. 3383. *E-mail:* admrec@mail.uccs.edu.

UNIVERSITY OF COLORADO AT DENVER

Denver, Colorado

- **State-supported** university, founded 1912, part of University of Colorado System
- **Calendar** semesters
- **Degrees** bachelor's, master's, and doctoral
- **Urban** 171-acre campus
- **Endowment** $9.8 million
- **Coed,** 8,790 undergraduate students, 54% full-time, 57% women, 43% men
- **Moderately difficult** entrance level, 73% of applicants were admitted

Undergraduates 4,774 full-time, 4,016 part-time. Students come from 37 states and territories, 57 other countries, 2% are from out of state, 4% African American, 10% Asian American or Pacific Islander, 10% Hispanic American, 1% Native American, 10% international. *Retention:* 78% of 2001 full-time freshmen returned.

Freshmen *Admission:* 1,596 applied, 1,160 admitted, 559 enrolled. *Average high school GPA:* 3.30. *Test scores:* SAT verbal scores over 500: 62%; SAT math scores over 500: 61%; ACT scores over 18: 86%; SAT verbal scores over 600: 22%; SAT math scores over 600: 20%; ACT scores over 24: 34%; SAT verbal scores over 700: 3%; SAT math scores over 700: 3%; ACT scores over 30: 3%.

Faculty *Total:* 933. *Student/faculty ratio:* 14:1.

Majors Anthropology; applied mathematics; biology; business administration; chemistry; civil engineering; communications; computer science; economics; electrical engineering; English; English composition; fine/studio arts; French; geography; geology; German; history; mathematics; mechanical engineering; music; philosophy; physics; political science; psychology; sociology; Spanish; theater arts/drama.

Academic Programs *Special study options:* academic remediation for entering students, adult/continuing education programs, advanced placement credit, cooperative education, distance learning, double majors, honors programs, independent study, internships, off-campus study, part-time degree program, services for LD students, student-designed majors, study abroad, summer session for credit. *ROTC:* Army (b), Air Force (c).

Library Auraria Library with 555,794 titles, 4,364 serial subscriptions, 15,720 audiovisual materials, an OPAC, a Web page.
Computers on Campus 577 computers available on campus for general student use. A campuswide network can be accessed from off campus. Internet access, online (class) registration, at least one staffed computer lab available.
Student Life *Housing:* college housing not available. *Activities and Organizations:* drama/theater group, student-run newspaper, television station, choral group, American Marketing Club, Psi Chi Honor Society, Model United Nations, Pre-Health Careers Club, Snow Bashers. *Campus security:* 24-hour emergency response devices and patrols, student patrols, late-night transport/escort service. *Student Services:* health clinic, personal/psychological counseling, legal services.
Athletics *Intramural sports:* lacrosse M(c), rugby M(c), skiing (downhill) M(c)/W(c), water polo M(c)/W(c).
Standardized Tests *Required:* SAT I or ACT (for admission).
Costs (2001–02) *One-time required fee:* $25. *Tuition:* state resident $2490 full-time, $135 per semester hour part-time; nonresident $12,224 full-time, $734 per semester hour part-time. Full-time tuition and fees vary according to program. Part-time tuition and fees vary according to course load and program. *Required fees:* $444 full-time. *Payment plans:* installment, deferred payment. *Waivers:* senior citizens and employees or children of employees.
Financial Aid Of all full-time matriculated undergraduates who enrolled in 2001, 2150 applied for aid, 1950 were judged to have need, 299 had their need fully met. In 2001, 300 non-need-based awards were made. *Average percent of need met:* 59%. *Average financial aid package:* $5682. *Average need-based loan:* $3726. *Average need-based gift aid:* $3843. *Average non-need based aid:* $3166.
Applying *Options:* common application, electronic application, deferred entrance. *Application fee:* $40. *Required:* high school transcript, minimum 2.5 GPA. *Application deadlines:* 7/22 (freshmen), 7/22 (transfers). *Notification:* continuous (freshmen).
Admissions Contact University of Colorado at Denver, 1250 14th Street. *Phone:* 303-556-3287. *Fax:* 303-556-4838. *E-mail:* admissions@castle.cudenver.edu.

UNIVERSITY OF COLORADO HEALTH SCIENCES CENTER
Denver, Colorado

- **State-supported** upper-level, founded 1883, part of University of Colorado System
- **Calendar** semesters
- **Degrees** bachelor's, master's, doctoral, first professional, post-master's, and first professional certificates
- **Urban** 40-acre campus
- **Endowment** $393.5 million
- **Coed,** 369 undergraduate students, 100% full-time, 86% women, 14% men
- **Moderately difficult** entrance level, 55% of applicants were admitted

Undergraduates 10% are from out of state, 4% African American, 11% Asian American or Pacific Islander, 8% Hispanic American, 1% Native American.
Freshmen *Admission:* 275 applied, 152 admitted.
Faculty *Total:* 1,700.
Majors Dental hygiene; nursing.
Academic Programs *Special study options:* adult/continuing education programs, advanced placement credit, distance learning, internships, summer session for credit.
Library Denison Library plus 1 other with 250,000 titles, 1,650 serial subscriptions, an OPAC, a Web page.
Computers on Campus 36 computers available on campus for general student use. A campuswide network can be accessed from off campus. Internet access, online (class) registration, at least one staffed computer lab available.
Student Life *Housing:* college housing not available. *Campus security:* 24-hour patrols, late-night transport/escort service. *Student Services:* health clinic, personal/psychological counseling.
Athletics *Intramural sports:* basketball M/W, football M, softball M/W, volleyball M/W.
Costs (2001–02) *Tuition:* state resident $8790 full-time, $151 per credit hour part-time; nonresident $19,300 full-time, $514 per credit hour part-time. Full-time tuition and fees vary according to class time and program. Part-time tuition and fees vary according to class time and program. *Required fees:* $190 full-time. *Payment plans:* installment, deferred payment.
Applying *Options:* electronic application. *Application deadline:* 10/1 (transfers). *Notification:* continuous (transfers).
Admissions Contact Dr. David P. Sorenson, Director of Admissions, University of Colorado Health Sciences Center, 4200 East Ninth Avenue, Denver, CO 80262. *Phone:* 303-315-7676. *Fax:* 303-315-3358.

UNIVERSITY OF DENVER
Denver, Colorado

- **Independent** university, founded 1864
- **Calendar** quarters
- **Degrees** bachelor's, master's, doctoral, and first professional
- **Suburban** 125-acre campus
- **Endowment** $165.9 million
- **Coed,** 4,110 undergraduate students, 89% full-time, 57% women, 43% men
- **Moderately difficult** entrance level, 72% of applicants were admitted

Undergraduates 3,641 full-time, 469 part-time. Students come from 52 states and territories, 54 other countries, 50% are from out of state, 4% African American, 5% Asian American or Pacific Islander, 6% Hispanic American, 1% Native American, 5% international, 5% transferred in, 43% live on campus. *Retention:* 86% of 2001 full-time freshmen returned.
Freshmen *Admission:* 4,275 applied, 3,069 admitted, 964 enrolled. *Average high school GPA:* 3.40. *Test scores:* SAT verbal scores over 500: 79%; SAT math scores over 500: 84%; ACT scores over 18: 93%; SAT verbal scores over 600: 32%; SAT math scores over 600: 39%; ACT scores over 24: 61%; SAT verbal scores over 700: 6%; SAT math scores over 700: 5%; ACT scores over 30: 12%.
Faculty *Total:* 923, 46% full-time. *Student/faculty ratio:* 9:1.
Majors Accounting; animal sciences; anthropology; art; art education; art history; Asian-American studies; biochemistry; biological/physical sciences; biology; biopsychology; business; business administration; business economics; business marketing and marketing management; chemistry; communications; computer engineering; computer/information sciences; construction management; creative writing; economics; electrical engineering; engineering; English; environmental science; finance; fine/studio arts; French; geography; German; graphic design/commercial art/illustration; history; hospitality management; hotel and restaurant management; international business; international relations; Italian; journalism; Latin American studies; mathematical statistics; mathematics; mechanical engineering; molecular biology; music; music (general performance); musicology; operations research; philosophy; physics; political science; psychology; public administration; real estate; religious studies; Russian; social sciences; sociology; Spanish; theater arts/drama; women's studies.
Academic Programs *Special study options:* accelerated degree program, adult/continuing education programs, advanced placement credit, cooperative education, double majors, English as a second language, freshman honors college, honors programs, independent study, internships, part-time degree program, services for LD students, student-designed majors, study abroad, summer session for credit. *ROTC:* Army (c), Air Force (c). *Unusual degree programs:* 3-2 international studies.
Library Penrose Library with 1.3 million titles, 5,788 serial subscriptions, 1,736 audiovisual materials, an OPAC, a Web page.
Computers on Campus 750 computers available on campus for general student use. A campuswide network can be accessed from student residence rooms and from off campus. At least one staffed computer lab available.
Student Life *Housing:* on-campus residence required through sophomore year. *Options:* coed. *Activities and Organizations:* drama/theater group, student-run newspaper, choral group, student government, club sports council, Programming Board, International Student Organization, Residence Hall Association, national fraternities, national sororities. *Campus security:* 24-hour emergency response devices and patrols, late-night transport/escort service, controlled dormitory access, 24-hour locked residence hall entrances. *Student Services:* health clinic, personal/psychological counseling, women's center.
Athletics Member NCAA. All Division I. *Intercollegiate sports:* basketball M(s)/W(s), cross-country running M(s)/W(s), golf M(s)/W(s), gymnastics W(s), ice hockey M(s), lacrosse M(s)/W(s), skiing (cross-country) M(s)/W(s), skiing (downhill) M(s)/W(s), soccer M(s)/W(s), swimming M(s)/W(s), tennis M(s)/W(s), volleyball M(c)/W(s). *Intramural sports:* badminton M/W, baseball M(c)/W(c), basketball M/W, cross-country running M(c)/W(c), equestrian sports M(c)/W(c), football M/W, ice hockey M(c)/W(c), racquetball M/W, rugby M(c)/W(c), skiing (downhill) M(c)/W(c), soccer M(c)/W(c), softball M/W, squash M/W, tennis M(c)/W(c), volleyball M(c)/W(c), water polo M(c)/W(c).
Standardized Tests *Required:* SAT I or ACT (for admission).
Costs (2001–02) *Comprehensive fee:* $28,782 includes full-time tuition ($21,456), mandatory fees ($579), and room and board ($6747). Full-time tuition and fees vary according to class time, course load, and program. Part-time tuition: $596 per quarter hour. Part-time tuition and fees vary according to class time, course load, and program. *Room and board:* Room and board charges vary according to board plan and housing facility. *Payment plan:* deferred payment. *Waivers:* employees or children of employees.
Financial Aid Of all full-time matriculated undergraduates who enrolled in 2001, 2627 applied for aid, 1471 were judged to have need, 579 had their need

University of Denver (continued)
fully met. 355 Federal Work-Study jobs (averaging $1072). 352 State and other part-time jobs (averaging $1471). In 2001, 765 non-need-based awards were made. *Average percent of need met:* 90%. *Average financial aid package:* $18,247. *Average need-based loan:* $4798. *Average need-based gift aid:* $6912. *Average non-need based aid:* $6651. *Average indebtedness upon graduation:* $19,836.

Applying *Options:* common application, electronic application, early admission, early action, deferred entrance. *Application fee:* $50. *Required:* essay or personal statement, high school transcript, 2 letters of recommendation. *Required for some:* minimum 2.0 GPA. *Recommended:* minimum 2.7 GPA. *Application deadlines:* 2/1 (freshmen), 2/1 (transfers). *Notification:* 3/1 (freshmen), 1/15 (early action).

Admissions Contact Ms. Colleen Hillmeyer, Director of New Student Programs, University of Denver, University Park, Denver, CO 80208. *Phone:* 303-871-2782. *Toll-free phone:* 800-525-9495. *Fax:* 303-871-3301. *E-mail:* admission@du.edu.

UNIVERSITY OF NORTHERN COLORADO
Greeley, Colorado

- **State-supported** university, founded 1890
- **Calendar** semesters
- **Degrees** bachelor's, master's, and doctoral
- **Suburban** 240-acre campus with easy access to Denver
- **Endowment** $81.4 million
- **Coed,** 10,161 undergraduate students, 90% full-time, 61% women, 39% men
- **Moderately difficult** entrance level, 78% of applicants were admitted

Undergraduates 9,137 full-time, 1,024 part-time. Students come from 49 states and territories, 52 other countries, 5% are from out of state, 2% African American, 4% Asian American or Pacific Islander, 7% Hispanic American, 0.6% Native American, 0.7% international, 9% transferred in, 30% live on campus. *Retention:* 70% of 2001 full-time freshmen returned.

Freshmen *Admission:* 6,709 applied, 5,229 admitted, 2,140 enrolled. *Average high school GPA:* 3.23. *Test scores:* SAT verbal scores over 500: 61%; SAT math scores over 500: 62%; ACT scores over 18: 92%; SAT verbal scores over 600: 19%; SAT math scores over 600: 18%; ACT scores over 24: 34%; SAT verbal scores over 700: 2%; SAT math scores over 700: 2%; ACT scores over 30: 3%.

Faculty *Total:* 588, 73% full-time, 65% with terminal degrees. *Student/faculty ratio:* 21:1.

Majors African-American studies; art; biology; business administration; chemistry; communications; dietetics; earth sciences; economics; English; exercise sciences; French; geography; German; gerontological services; hearing sciences; Hispanic-American studies; history; interdisciplinary studies; journalism; mathematics; medical technology; music; music teacher education; nursing; philosophy; physics; political science; psychology; public health education/promotion; recreation/leisure facilities management; social sciences; sociology; Spanish; speech-language pathology; theater arts/drama.

Academic Programs *Special study options:* academic remediation for entering students, adult/continuing education programs, advanced placement credit, cooperative education, distance learning, double majors, English as a second language, external degree program, honors programs, independent study, internships, off-campus study, part-time degree program, services for LD students, student-designed majors, study abroad, summer session for credit. *ROTC:* Army (b), Air Force (b).

Library James A. Michener Library plus 2 others with 711,965 titles, 3,219 serial subscriptions, 40,224 audiovisual materials, an OPAC, a Web page.

Computers on Campus 1100 computers available on campus for general student use. A campuswide network can be accessed from student residence rooms and from off campus. Internet access, online (class) registration, at least one staffed computer lab available.

Student Life *Housing:* on-campus residence required for freshman year. *Options:* coed, women-only. *Activities and Organizations:* drama/theater group, student-run newspaper, radio station, choral group, marching band, national fraternities, national sororities. *Campus security:* 24-hour emergency response devices and patrols, student patrols, late-night transport/escort service, controlled dormitory access. *Student Services:* health clinic, personal/psychological counseling, women's center, legal services.

Athletics Member NCAA. All Division II. *Intercollegiate sports:* baseball M(s), basketball M(s)/W(s), cross-country running W(s), football M(s), golf M(s)/W(s), lacrosse M(c), rugby M(c)/W(c), soccer M(c)/W(s), softball W(s), swimming W(s), tennis M(s)/W(s), track and field M(s)/W(s), volleyball W(s), wrestling M(s). *Intramural sports:* basketball M/W, football M/W, soccer M/W, softball M/W, volleyball M/W, water polo M/W.

Standardized Tests *Required:* SAT I or ACT (for admission).

Costs (2001–02) *Tuition:* state resident $2155 full-time, $120 per hour part-time; nonresident $9825 full-time, $546 per hour part-time. Full-time tuition and fees vary according to course load. *Required fees:* $687 full-time, $35 per hour. *Room and board:* $5240; room only: $2450. Room and board charges vary according to board plan and housing facility. *Payment plan:* deferred payment.

Financial Aid Of all full-time matriculated undergraduates who enrolled in 2001, 7043 applied for aid, 4264 were judged to have need, 796 had their need fully met. 347 Federal Work-Study jobs (averaging $1435). 2271 State and other part-time jobs (averaging $1465). In 2001, 768 non-need-based awards were made. *Average percent of need met:* 76%. *Average financial aid package:* $6705. *Average need-based loan:* $3345. *Average need-based gift aid:* $2588. *Average non-need based aid:* $2033.

Applying *Options:* common application, electronic application, deferred entrance. *Application fee:* $30. *Required:* high school transcript, minimum 2.9 GPA. *Required for some:* interview. *Application deadline:* rolling (freshmen), rolling (transfers).

Admissions Contact Mr. Gary O. Gullickson, Director of Admissions, University of Northern Colorado, Greeley, CO 80639. *Phone:* 970-351-2881. *Toll-free phone:* 888-700-4UNC. *Fax:* 970-351-2984. *E-mail:* unc@mail.unco.edu.

UNIVERSITY OF PHOENIX-COLORADO CAMPUS
Lone Tree, Colorado

- **Proprietary** comprehensive
- **Calendar** continuous
- **Degrees** certificates, associate, bachelor's, master's, doctoral, post-master's, and postbachelor's certificates (courses conducted at 54 campuses and learning centers in 13 states)
- **Coed,** 2,016 undergraduate students, 100% full-time, 54% women, 46% men
- **Noncompetitive** entrance level

Undergraduates Students come from 35 states and territories, 39% are from out of state.

Freshmen *Admission:* 28 admitted.

Faculty *Total:* 363, 2% full-time, 24% with terminal degrees. *Student/faculty ratio:* 13:1.

Majors Accounting; business administration; criminal justice/law enforcement administration; information technology; management information systems/business data processing; management science; nursing science; public administration and services related.

Academic Programs *Special study options:* accelerated degree program, adult/continuing education programs, advanced placement credit, distance learning, external degree program, independent study.

Library University Library with 17.5 million titles, 9,000 serial subscriptions, an OPAC, a Web page.

Computers on Campus A campuswide network can be accessed from off campus. Internet access, at least one staffed computer lab available.

Student Life *Housing:* college housing not available.

Costs (2001–02) *Tuition:* $7950 full-time. Full-time tuition and fees vary according to location and program. *Payment plan:* deferred payment. *Waivers:* employees or children of employees.

Applying *Options:* deferred entrance. *Application fee:* $85. *Required:* 2 years of work experience. *Required for some:* high school transcript. *Application deadline:* rolling (freshmen), rolling (transfers).

Admissions Contact Ms. Beth Barilla, Director of Admissions, University of Phoenix-Colorado Campus, 4615 East Elwood Street, Phoenix, AZ 85040-1958. *Phone:* 480-927-0099 Ext. 1218. *Toll-free phone:* 800-228-7240. *Fax:* 480-594-1758. *E-mail:* beth.barilla@apollogrp.edu.

UNIVERSITY OF PHOENIX-SOUTHERN COLORADO CAMPUS
Colorado Springs, Colorado

- **Proprietary** comprehensive
- **Calendar** continuous
- **Degrees** certificates, associate, bachelor's, master's, doctoral, post-master's, and postbachelor's certificates (courses conducted at 54 campuses and learning centers in 13 states)
- **Coed,** 606 undergraduate students, 100% full-time, 55% women, 45% men
- **Noncompetitive** entrance level

Undergraduates Students come from 14 states and territories, 2% are from out of state.

Freshmen *Admission:* 18 admitted.

Faculty *Total:* 80, 6% full-time, 46% with terminal degrees. *Student/faculty ratio:* 12:1.

Majors Accounting; business administration; criminal justice/corrections related; information technology; management information systems/business data processing; management science; nursing science; public administration and services related.

Academic Programs *Special study options:* accelerated degree program, adult/continuing education programs, advanced placement credit, distance learning, external degree program, independent study.

Library University Library with 17.5 million titles, 9,000 serial subscriptions, an OPAC, a Web page.

Computers on Campus A campuswide network can be accessed from off campus. Internet access, at least one staffed computer lab available.

Student Life *Housing:* college housing not available.

Costs (2001–02) *Tuition:* $7950 full-time. Full-time tuition and fees vary according to location and program. *Payment plan:* deferred payment. *Waivers:* employees or children of employees.

Applying *Options:* deferred entrance. *Application fee:* $85. *Required:* 2 years of work experience. *Required for some:* high school transcript. *Application deadline:* rolling (freshmen), rolling (transfers).

Admissions Contact Ms. Beth Barilla, Director of Admissions, University of Phoenix-Southern Colorado Campus, 4615 East Elwood Street, Phoenix, AZ 85040-1958. *Phone:* 480-927-0099 Ext. 1218. *Toll-free phone:* 800-228-7240. *Fax:* 480-894-1758. *E-mail:* beth.barilla@apollogrp.edu.

UNIVERSITY OF SOUTHERN COLORADO
Pueblo, Colorado

- **State-supported** comprehensive, founded 1933, part of Colorado State University System
- **Calendar** semesters
- **Degrees** bachelor's and master's
- **Suburban** 275-acre campus with easy access to Colorado Springs
- **Endowment** $2.3 million
- **Coed,** 5,324 undergraduate students, 63% full-time, 57% women, 43% men
- **Moderately difficult** entrance level, 83% of applicants were admitted

Undergraduates 3,354 full-time, 1,970 part-time. Students come from 44 states and territories, 37 other countries, 8% are from out of state, 4% African American, 2% Asian American or Pacific Islander, 25% Hispanic American, 1% Native American, 4% international, 7% transferred in, 18% live on campus. *Retention:* 66% of 2001 full-time freshmen returned.

Freshmen *Admission:* 1,634 applied, 1,356 admitted, 667 enrolled. *Average high school GPA:* 3.08. *Test scores:* SAT verbal scores over 500: 34%; SAT math scores over 500: 33%; ACT scores over 18: 72%; SAT verbal scores over 600: 5%; SAT math scores over 600: 8%; ACT scores over 24: 17%; SAT verbal scores over 700: 3%; SAT math scores over 700: 1%; ACT scores over 30: 1%.

Faculty *Total:* 240, 66% full-time, 53% with terminal degrees. *Student/faculty ratio:* 17:1.

Majors Accounting; advertising; applied art; art; art education; athletic training/sports medicine; auto mechanic/technician; biology; biomedical technology; broadcast journalism; business administration; business marketing and marketing management; chemistry; civil engineering technology; clinical psychology; computer engineering technology; computer programming; computer science; construction technology; corrections; criminology; developmental/child psychology; education; electrical/electronic engineering technology; elementary education; engineering technology; English; environmental biology; environmental health; exercise sciences; experimental psychology; film/video production; finance; history; industrial arts; industrial/manufacturing engineering; information sciences/systems; instrumentation technology; journalism; mass communications; mathematics; mathematics education; mechanical engineering technology; middle school education; music; music teacher education; nursing; physical education; physics; political science; pre-dentistry; pre-law; pre-medicine; pre-veterinary studies; psychology; public relations; radio/television broadcasting; recreation/leisure studies; science education; secondary education; social sciences; social studies education; social work; sociology; Spanish; Spanish language education; speech/rhetorical studies; telecommunications.

Academic Programs *Special study options:* accelerated degree program, adult/continuing education programs, advanced placement credit, cooperative education, distance learning, double majors, English as a second language, external degree program, honors programs, independent study, internships, off-campus study, part-time degree program, services for LD students, study abroad, summer session for credit. *ROTC:* Army (c).

Library University of Southern Colorado Library with 270,761 titles, 1,327 serial subscriptions, 16,862 audiovisual materials, an OPAC, a Web page.

Computers on Campus 521 computers available on campus for general student use. A campuswide network can be accessed from student residence rooms and from off campus. Internet access, at least one staffed computer lab available.

Student Life *Housing:* on-campus residence required for freshman year. *Options:* coed. *Activities and Organizations:* student-run newspaper, radio and television station, choral group, Belmont Residence Hall Association, Associate Student Government, Hawaii Club, Medical Science Society, Student Social Worker's Association, national fraternities, national sororities. *Campus security:* 24-hour emergency response devices and patrols, late-night transport/escort service, controlled dormitory access. *Student Services:* health clinic, personal/psychological counseling.

Athletics Member NCAA. All Division II. *Intercollegiate sports:* baseball M, basketball M(s)/W(s), golf M(s), soccer M/W, softball W(s), tennis M(s)/W(s), volleyball W(s), wrestling M(s). *Intramural sports:* basketball M/W, soccer M, softball M/W, tennis M/W, volleyball M/W, weight lifting M/W, wrestling M.

Standardized Tests *Required:* SAT I or ACT (for admission).

Costs (2001–02) *One-time required fee:* $45. *Tuition:* state resident $1940 full-time, $122 per semester hour part-time; nonresident $9220 full-time, $486 per semester hour part-time. Full-time tuition and fees vary according to reciprocity agreements. Part-time tuition and fees vary according to reciprocity agreements. *Required fees:* $509 full-time, $25 per semester hour. *Room and board:* $5372; room only: $2612. Room and board charges vary according to board plan and housing facility. *Payment plans:* installment, deferred payment. *Waivers:* senior citizens and employees or children of employees.

Financial Aid Of all full-time matriculated undergraduates who enrolled in 2001, 1685 applied for aid, 1463 were judged to have need, 92 had their need fully met. In 2001, 423 non-need-based awards were made. *Average percent of need met:* 58%. *Average financial aid package:* $5640. *Average need-based loan:* $3012. *Average need-based gift aid:* $3111. *Average indebtedness upon graduation:* $5521.

Applying *Options:* common application, electronic application, deferred entrance. *Application fee:* $25. *Required:* high school transcript. *Required for some:* essay or personal statement, letters of recommendation. *Application deadline:* rolling (freshmen), rolling (transfers). *Notification:* continuous (freshmen).

Admissions Contact Ms. Pamela L. Anastassiou, Director of Admissions and Records, University of Southern Colorado, 2200 Bonforte Boulevard, Pueblo, CO 81001. *Phone:* 719-549-2461. *Toll-free phone:* 877-872-9653. *Fax:* 719-549-2419. *E-mail:* info@uscolo.edu.

WESTERN STATE COLLEGE OF COLORADO
Gunnison, Colorado

- **State-supported** 4-year, founded 1901, part of State Colleges in Colorado
- **Calendar** semesters
- **Degree** bachelor's
- **Small-town** 381-acre campus
- **Endowment** $7.2 million
- **Coed,** 2,302 undergraduate students, 91% full-time, 42% women, 58% men
- **Moderately difficult** entrance level, 85% of applicants were admitted

Western is home to more than 2,500 students pursuing undergraduate degrees in a range of liberal arts and science areas and compatible professional disciplines. Small classes afford students tremendous amounts of hands-on instruction from faculty members. The residential setting in the midst of the Rocky Mountains gives students ample opportunity for campus involvement and spectacular recreational activities. For more information, students may visit the Western Web site at http://www.western.edu/welcome.html.

Undergraduates 2,103 full-time, 199 part-time. Students come from 50 states and territories, 11 other countries, 28% are from out of state, 1% African American, 0.9% Asian American or Pacific Islander, 5% Hispanic American, 0.6% Native American, 9% transferred in, 41% live on campus. *Retention:* 53% of 2001 full-time freshmen returned.

Freshmen *Admission:* 1,811 applied, 1,540 admitted, 589 enrolled. *Average high school GPA:* 2.93. *Test scores:* SAT verbal scores over 500: 52%; SAT math scores over 500: 49%; ACT scores over 18: 81%; SAT verbal scores over 600: 12%; SAT math scores over 600: 11%; ACT scores over 24: 18%; SAT math scores over 700: 1%; ACT scores over 30: 1%.

Faculty *Total:* 137, 78% full-time, 66% with terminal degrees. *Student/faculty ratio:* 20:1.

Majors Accounting; American studies; anthropology; art; art education; athletic training/sports medicine; biology; business administration; business marketing

Western State College of Colorado (continued)
and marketing management; chemistry; clinical psychology; computer science; economics; education; elementary education; English; environmental science; exercise sciences; fine/studio arts; French; geology; graphic design/commercial art/illustration; history; human resources management; industrial arts; international business; journalism; law enforcement/police science; management information systems/business data processing; mass communications; mathematics; molecular biology; music; music teacher education; physical education; physics; political science; pre-dentistry; pre-law; pre-medicine; pre-veterinary studies; psychology; public policy analysis; radio/television broadcasting; recreation/leisure facilities management; recreation/leisure studies; science education; secondary education; social sciences; sociology; Spanish; special education; theater arts/drama.

Academic Programs *Special study options:* accelerated degree program, adult/continuing education programs, advanced placement credit, cooperative education, double majors, honors programs, internships, off-campus study, part-time degree program, services for LD students, student-designed majors, study abroad, summer session for credit.

Library Savage Library with 1.7 million titles, 875 serial subscriptions, 4,763 audiovisual materials, an OPAC, a Web page.

Computers on Campus 125 computers available on campus for general student use. A campuswide network can be accessed from student residence rooms and from off campus. Internet access, online (class) registration, at least one staffed computer lab available.

Student Life *Housing:* on-campus residence required for freshman year. *Options:* coed, men-only, women-only. *Activities and Organizations:* drama/theater group, student-run newspaper, radio and television station, choral group, Mountain Search and Rescue Team, student government association, Rodeo Club, Wilderness Pursuits, Peak Productions, national fraternities. *Campus security:* 24-hour emergency response devices and patrols, student patrols, late-night transport/escort service, controlled dormitory access. *Student Services:* health clinic, personal/psychological counseling.

Athletics Member NCAA. All Division II. *Intercollegiate sports:* baseball M(c), basketball M(s)/W(s), cross-country running M(s)/W(s), football M(s), ice hockey M(c), lacrosse M(c)/W(c), rugby M(c)/W(c), skiing (cross-country) M(s)/W(s), skiing (downhill) M(s)/W(s), soccer M(c)/W(c), track and field M(s)/W(s), volleyball M(c)/W(s), wrestling M(s)/W(c). *Intramural sports:* basketball M/W, football M/W, golf M/W, soccer M/W, softball M/W, tennis M/W, volleyball M/W, wrestling M.

Standardized Tests *Required:* SAT I or ACT (for admission).

Costs (2001–02) *Tuition:* state resident $1622 full-time, $81 per credit hour part-time; nonresident $7672 full-time, $384 per credit hour part-time. Full-time tuition and fees vary according to course load. Part-time tuition and fees vary according to course load. *Required fees:* $781 full-time, $100 per credit hour. *Room and board:* $5690; room only: $2784. Room and board charges vary according to board plan and housing facility. *Payment plans:* installment, deferred payment. *Waivers:* senior citizens and employees or children of employees.

Financial Aid Of all full-time matriculated undergraduates who enrolled in 2001, 1577 applied for aid, 946 were judged to have need, 212 had their need fully met. 220 Federal Work-Study jobs. In 2001, 420 non-need-based awards were made. *Average percent of need met:* 60%. *Average financial aid package:* $9880. *Average need-based loan:* $4880. *Average need-based gift aid:* $2500. *Average non-need based aid:* $1000. *Average indebtedness upon graduation:* $12,500.

Applying *Options:* common application, deferred entrance. *Application fee:* $25. *Required:* high school transcript. *Required for some:* essay or personal statement, 2 letters of recommendation, interview. *Recommended:* minimum 2.5 GPA. *Application deadline:* rolling (freshmen), rolling (transfers). *Notification:* continuous (freshmen).

Admissions Contact Mr. Timothy L. Albers, Director of Admissions, Western State College of Colorado, 600 North Adams Street, Gunnison, CO 81231. *Phone:* 970-943-2119. *Toll-free phone:* 800-876-5309. *Fax:* 970-943-2212. *E-mail:* talbers@western.edu.

Westwood College of Technology-Denver North

Denver, Colorado

- **Proprietary** primarily 2-year, founded 1953
- **Calendar** 5 terms
- **Degrees** diplomas, associate, bachelor's, and postbachelor's certificates
- **Suburban** 11-acre campus
- **Coed,** 969 undergraduate students, 68% full-time, 27% women, 73% men
- **Moderately difficult** entrance level, 45% of applicants were admitted

Undergraduates 656 full-time, 313 part-time. Students come from 21 states and territories, 10 other countries, 14% are from out of state, 4% African American, 5% Asian American or Pacific Islander, 13% Hispanic American, 0.4% Native American, 0.1% international. *Retention:* 22% of 2001 full-time freshmen returned.

Freshmen *Admission:* 2,198 applied, 996 admitted, 555 enrolled.

Faculty *Total:* 103, 41% full-time, 4% with terminal degrees. *Student/faculty ratio:* 11:1.

Majors Architectural drafting; auto mechanic/technician; business administration/management related; computer engineering technology; computer/information technology services administration and management related; computer programming; computer systems networking/telecommunications; design/visual communications; electrical/electronic engineering technology; graphic design/commercial art/illustration; heating/air conditioning/refrigeration; hotel and restaurant management; mechanical drafting; medical assistant; medical transcription; surveying.

Academic Programs *Special study options:* academic remediation for entering students, accelerated degree program, advanced placement credit, internships, summer session for credit.

Library DIT Library with 2,500 titles, 90 serial subscriptions.

Computers on Campus 150 computers available on campus for general student use. Internet access available.

Student Life *Housing:* college housing not available. *Activities and Organizations:* student government, Athletic Club, American Institute of Graphic Arts, Social Club. *Campus security:* 24-hour emergency response devices. *Student Services:* personal/psychological counseling.

Costs (2002–03) *Tuition:* $16,775 full-time, $2516 per term part-time. Full-time tuition and fees vary according to course load and program. Part-time tuition and fees vary according to course load and program. *Required fees:* $900 full-time, $382 per credit, $120 per term part-time. *Payment plan:* installment. *Waivers:* employees or children of employees.

Applying *Options:* deferred entrance. *Application fee:* $100. *Required for some:* high school transcript. *Recommended:* interview. *Application deadline:* rolling (freshmen), rolling (transfers). *Notification:* continuous (freshmen).

Admissions Contact Ms. Nicole Blaschko, New Student Coordinator, Westwood College of Technology-Denver North, 7350 North Broadway, Denver, CO 80221-3653. *Phone:* 303-650-5050 Ext. 329. *Toll-free phone:* 800-992-5050.

Westwood College of Technology-Denver South

Denver, Colorado

- **Proprietary** primarily 2-year
- **Degrees** associate, bachelor's
- **Coed,** 421 undergraduate students

Faculty *Total:* 38, 37% full-time.

Majors Business administration/management related; computer programming; computer systems networking/telecommunications; design/visual communication; electrical/electronic engineering technology; graphic design/commercial art/illustration.

Costs (2002–2003) *Tuition:* Standard program price $3355 per term, lab fees and books additional, 5 terms/year, program length: associate degree, 7 terms; bachelor's degree, 14 terms.

Admissions Contact Mr. Ron DeJong, Director of Admissions, Westwood College of Technology–Denver South, 3150 South Sheridan Boulevard, Denver, CO 80227. *Phone:* 303-934-1122.

Admissions Contact 3150 South Sheridan Boulevard, Denver, CO 80227.

Yeshiva Toras Chaim Talmudical Seminary

Denver, Colorado

Admissions Contact Rabbi Israel Kagan, Dean, Yeshiva Toras Chaim Talmudical Seminary, 1400 Quitman Street, Denver, CO 80204-1415. *Phone:* 303-629-8200.

CONNECTICUT

ALBERTUS MAGNUS COLLEGE
New Haven, Connecticut

- **Independent Roman Catholic** comprehensive, founded 1925
- **Calendar** semesters
- **Degrees** associate, bachelor's, and master's
- **Suburban** 55-acre campus with easy access to New York City and Hartford
- **Endowment** $8.0 million
- **Coed,** 1,881 undergraduate students, 92% full-time, 66% women, 34% men
- **Moderately difficult** entrance level, 98% of applicants were admitted

For more than 75 years, the individual learning experience has been the focus of Albertus Magnus College's extraordinary educational program. This straight-arrow mission allows faculty members to develop the academic, personal, and professional strengths of each individual student. Students can visit the Web site (http://www.albertus.edu) or call (800-578-9160) for details.

Undergraduates 1,736 full-time, 145 part-time. Students come from 11 states and territories, 4 other countries, 4% are from out of state, 19% African American, 1.0% Asian American or Pacific Islander, 7% Hispanic American, 0.6% Native American, 0.6% international, 2% transferred in, 60% live on campus. *Retention:* 84% of 2001 full-time freshmen returned.

Freshmen *Admission:* 361 applied, 355 admitted, 110 enrolled. *Average high school GPA:* 2.50. *Test scores:* SAT verbal scores over 500: 50%; SAT math scores over 500: 44%; SAT verbal scores over 600: 15%; SAT math scores over 600: 9%; SAT verbal scores over 700: 5%.

Faculty *Total:* 68, 53% full-time, 69% with terminal degrees. *Student/faculty ratio:* 15:1.

Majors Accounting; art; art history; art therapy; biology; business economics; business marketing and marketing management; chemistry; child care/development; classics; criminal justice/law enforcement administration; economics; English; finance; fine/studio arts; French; graphic design/commercial art/illustration; health services administration; history; humanities; human services; information sciences/systems; interdisciplinary studies; international business; international economics; Italian; liberal arts and sciences/liberal studies; mass communications; mathematics; photography; political science; pre-dentistry; pre-law; pre-medicine; pre-veterinary studies; psychology; religious studies; romance languages; social sciences; sociology; Spanish; theater arts/drama; urban studies.

Academic Programs *Special study options:* academic remediation for entering students, accelerated degree program, adult/continuing education programs, advanced placement credit, distance learning, double majors, English as a second language, freshman honors college, honors programs, independent study, internships, off-campus study, part-time degree program, services for LD students, student-designed majors, summer session for credit.

Library Rosary Hall with 538 serial subscriptions, 817 audiovisual materials, a Web page.

Computers on Campus 75 computers available on campus for general student use. A campuswide network can be accessed from student residence rooms and from off campus. Internet access, at least one staffed computer lab available.

Student Life *Housing Options:* coed, women-only. *Activities and Organizations:* drama/theater group, student-run newspaper, Student Government Association, College Drama, Minority Student Union. *Campus security:* 24-hour emergency response devices and patrols, late-night transport/escort service, controlled dormitory access. *Student Services:* health clinic, personal/psychological counseling.

Athletics Member NCAA. All Division III. *Intercollegiate sports:* baseball M, basketball M/W, cross-country running M/W, soccer M, softball W, tennis M/W, volleyball W. *Intramural sports:* basketball M/W, racquetball M/W, soccer M, squash M/W, table tennis M/W.

Standardized Tests *Required:* SAT I or ACT (for admission). *Recommended:* SAT II: Subject Tests (for admission), SAT II: Writing Test (for admission).

Costs (2001–02) *Comprehensive fee:* $22,154 includes full-time tuition ($14,760), mandatory fees ($486), and room and board ($6908). Full-time tuition and fees vary according to class time and program. Part-time tuition: $492 per credit. Part-time tuition and fees vary according to class time and program. *Payment plan:* installment. *Waivers:* senior citizens and employees or children of employees.

Financial Aid Of all full-time matriculated undergraduates who enrolled in 2001, 950 applied for aid, 520 were judged to have need, 400 had their need fully met. In 2001, 20 non-need-based awards were made. *Average percent of need met:* 85%. *Average financial aid package:* $8000. *Average need-based loan:* $4300. *Average need-based gift aid:* $7000. *Average non-need based aid:* $7000. *Average indebtedness upon graduation:* $15,625.

Applying *Options:* deferred entrance. *Application fee:* $35. *Required:* high school transcript, 1 letter of recommendation. *Required for some:* minimum 2.5 GPA. *Recommended:* minimum 2.5 GPA, interview. *Application deadline:* rolling (freshmen), rolling (transfers). *Notification:* continuous (freshmen).

Admissions Contact Ms. Rebecca George, Associate Dean of Admissions, Albertus Magnus College, New Haven, CT 06511-1189. *Phone:* 203-773-8501. *Toll-free phone:* 800-578-9160. *Fax:* 203-773-5248. *E-mail:* admissions@albertus.edu.

BETH BENJAMIN ACADEMY OF CONNECTICUT
Stamford, Connecticut

Admissions Contact Rabbi David Mayer, Director of Admissions, Beth Benjamin Academy of Connecticut, 132 Prospect Street, Stamford, CT 06901-1202. *Phone:* 203-325-4351.

CENTRAL CONNECTICUT STATE UNIVERSITY
New Britain, Connecticut

- **State-supported** comprehensive, founded 1849, part of Connecticut State University System
- **Calendar** semesters
- **Degrees** bachelor's and master's
- **Suburban** 294-acre campus
- **Endowment** $7.1 million
- **Coed,** 9,551 undergraduate students, 69% full-time, 52% women, 48% men
- **Moderately difficult** entrance level, 65% of applicants were admitted

Undergraduates 6,636 full-time, 2,915 part-time. Students come from 26 states and territories, 50 other countries, 11% are from out of state, 7% African American, 3% Asian American or Pacific Islander, 5% Hispanic American, 0.4% Native American, 0.9% international, 8% transferred in, 29% live on campus. *Retention:* 72% of 2001 full-time freshmen returned.

Freshmen *Admission:* 4,660 applied, 3,013 admitted, 1,296 enrolled. *Test scores:* SAT verbal scores over 500: 45%; SAT math scores over 500: 46%; SAT verbal scores over 600: 7%; SAT math scores over 600: 7%; SAT verbal scores over 700: 1%; SAT math scores over 700: 1%.

Faculty *Total:* 801, 49% full-time, 39% with terminal degrees. *Student/faculty ratio:* 17:1.

Majors Accounting; actuarial science; anthropology; art; art education; athletic training/sports medicine; biology; business administration; business marketing and marketing management; chemistry; civil engineering technology; communications; computer/information sciences; construction technology; criminology; design/visual communications; early childhood education; earth sciences; economics; elementary education; engineering technology; English; finance; French; geography; German; history; industrial arts education; industrial technology; interdisciplinary studies; international business; Italian; management information systems/business data processing; mathematics; mechanical engineering technology; medical technology; music; music teacher education; nursing; philosophy; physical education; physical sciences; physics; plastics technology; political science; psychology; social sciences; social work; sociology; Spanish; special education; theater arts/drama; tourism promotion operations; trade/industrial education.

Academic Programs *Special study options:* academic remediation for entering students, adult/continuing education programs, advanced placement credit, cooperative education, English as a second language, honors programs, internships, off-campus study, part-time degree program, services for LD students, student-designed majors, study abroad, summer session for credit. *ROTC:* Army (c), Air Force (c).

Library Burritt Library plus 1 other with 620,958 titles, 2,813 serial subscriptions, 5,224 audiovisual materials, an OPAC.

Computers on Campus 230 computers available on campus for general student use. A campuswide network can be accessed from student residence rooms and from off campus. Internet access, at least one staffed computer lab available.

Student Life *Housing Options:* coed. *Activities and Organizations:* drama/theater group, student-run newspaper, radio station, choral group, Inter-residence Council, student radio station, Program Council, Outing Club, NAACP, national fraternities, national sororities. *Campus security:* 24-hour emergency response devices and patrols, student patrols, late-night transport/escort service. *Student Services:* health clinic, personal/psychological counseling, women's center.

Athletics Member NCAA. All Division I except football (Division I-AA). *Intercollegiate sports:* baseball M(s), basketball M(s)/W(s), cross-country running M(s)/W(s), fencing M(c)/W(c), golf M(s)/W(s), lacrosse M(c)/W(s), soccer

Central Connecticut State University (continued)
M(s)/W(s), softball W(s), swimming M(s)/W(s), tennis M(s)/W(s), track and field M(s)/W(s), volleyball W(s). *Intramural sports:* badminton M/W, basketball M/W, equestrian sports M/W, field hockey W(c), football M, gymnastics W, rugby M(c)/W(c), soccer M/W, softball M/W, tennis M/W, volleyball M/W.
Standardized Tests *Required:* SAT I (for admission).
Costs (2001–02) *Tuition:* state resident $2226 full-time, $190 per credit hour part-time; nonresident $7204 full-time, $190 per credit hour part-time. Full-time tuition and fees vary according to class time, class time, and reciprocity agreements. Part-time tuition and fees vary according to class time and class time. *Required fees:* $2148 full-time, $48 per term part-time. *Room and board:* $6030; room only: $3500. Room and board charges vary according to board plan. *Payment plans:* installment, deferred payment. *Waivers:* senior citizens and employees or children of employees.
Financial Aid Of all full-time matriculated undergraduates who enrolled in 2001, 3356 applied for aid, 2507 were judged to have need, 714 had their need fully met. *Average percent of need met:* 68%. *Average financial aid package:* $5711. *Average need-based loan:* $2891. *Average need-based gift aid:* $2905. *Average indebtedness upon graduation:* $18,600.
Applying *Options:* common application, electronic application. *Application fee:* $40. *Required:* high school transcript, minimum 2.0 GPA. *Required for some:* interview. *Recommended:* minimum 3.0 GPA, 1 letter of recommendation. *Application deadlines:* 5/1 (freshmen), 5/1 (transfers). *Notification:* continuous until 7/1 (freshmen).
Admissions Contact Ms. Myrna Garcia-Bowen, Director of Admissions, Central Connecticut State University, 1615 Stanley Street, New Britain, CT 06050-4010. *Phone:* 860-832-2285. *Toll-free phone:* 800-755-2278. *Fax:* 860-832-2522. *E-mail:* admissions@ccsu.edu.

CHARTER OAK STATE COLLEGE
New Britain, Connecticut

- **State-supported** 4-year, founded 1973
- **Calendar** continuous
- **Degrees** associate and bachelor's (offers only external degree programs)
- **Small-town** campus
- **Endowment** $521,269
- **Coed,** 1,496 undergraduate students, 50% women, 50% men
- **Noncompetitive** entrance level

Undergraduates 1,496 part-time. Students come from 46 states and territories, 30% are from out of state, 8% African American, 1% Asian American or Pacific Islander, 4% Hispanic American, 0.9% Native American, 0.1% international, 7% transferred in.
Faculty *Total:* 69, 78% with terminal degrees.
Majors Liberal arts and sciences/liberal studies.
Academic Programs *Special study options:* accelerated degree program, adult/continuing education programs, advanced placement credit, distance learning, external degree program, independent study, part-time degree program, services for LD students, student-designed majors.
Student Life *Housing:* college housing not available.
Costs (2002–03) *Tuition:* state resident $125 per credit part-time; nonresident $175 per credit part-time. *Required fees:* $20 per term part-time. *Payment plan:* installment. *Waivers:* adult students.
Applying *Options:* electronic application, deferred entrance. *Application fee:* $45. *Application deadline:* rolling (transfers).
Admissions Contact Mr. Harry White, Dean of Enrollment Management, Charter Oak State College, 55 Paul Manafort Drive, New Britain, CT 06053-2142. *Phone:* 860-832-3855. *Fax:* 860-832-3855. *E-mail:* info@charteroak.edu.

CONNECTICUT COLLEGE
New London, Connecticut

- **Independent** comprehensive, founded 1911
- **Calendar** semesters
- **Degrees** bachelor's and master's
- **Suburban** 702-acre campus
- **Endowment** $150.3 million
- **Coed,** 1,835 undergraduate students, 96% full-time, 59% women, 41% men
- **Very difficult** entrance level, 34% of applicants were admitted

Undergraduates 1,755 full-time, 80 part-time. Students come from 42 states and territories, 69 other countries, 77% are from out of state, 3% African American, 3% Asian American or Pacific Islander, 3% Hispanic American, 0.5% Native American, 8% international, 2% transferred in, 98% live on campus. *Retention:* 93% of 2001 full-time freshmen returned.
Freshmen *Admission:* 4,318 applied, 1,482 admitted, 472 enrolled. *Test scores:* SAT verbal scores over 500: 100%; SAT math scores over 500: 100%; ACT scores over 18: 100%; SAT verbal scores over 600: 87%; SAT math scores over 600: 84%; ACT scores over 24: 93%; SAT verbal scores over 700: 32%; SAT math scores over 700: 18%; ACT scores over 30: 17%.
Faculty *Total:* 194, 80% full-time, 80% with terminal degrees. *Student/faculty ratio:* 11:1.
Majors African studies; American studies; anthropology; architecture; area studies related; art; art history; astrophysics; biochemistry; biology; botany; cell and molecular biology related; chemistry; chemistry related; Chinese; classics; computer/information sciences; dance; East Asian studies; Eastern European area studies; ecology; economics; engineering physics; English; ethnic/cultural studies related; film studies; French; German; history; human ecology; interdisciplinary studies; international relations; Italian; Japanese; Latin American studies; mathematics; medieval/renaissance studies; music; music related; music teacher education; neuroscience; philosophy; physics; physics education; political science; psychology; religious studies; Russian; sociology; Spanish; theater arts/drama; urban studies; women's studies; zoology.
Academic Programs *Special study options:* accelerated degree program, adult/continuing education programs, advanced placement credit, double majors, honors programs, independent study, internships, off-campus study, part-time degree program, student-designed majors, study abroad, summer session for credit. *Unusual degree programs:* 3-2 engineering with Washington University in St. Louis.
Library Charles Shain Library plus 1 other with 436,582 titles, 2,357 serial subscriptions, 142,303 audiovisual materials, an OPAC, a Web page.
Computers on Campus 461 computers available on campus for general student use. A campuswide network can be accessed from student residence rooms and from off campus. Internet access, at least one staffed computer lab available.
Student Life *Housing Options:* coed, cooperative, disabled students. *Activities and Organizations:* drama/theater group, student-run newspaper, radio station, choral group, Student Government Association, Student Activity Council, unity clubs, sports clubs, student radio station. *Campus security:* 24-hour emergency response devices and patrols, late-night transport/escort service, controlled dormitory access. *Student Services:* health clinic, personal/psychological counseling, women's center.
Athletics Member NCAA. All Division III. *Intercollegiate sports:* basketball M/W, crew M/W, cross-country running M/W, equestrian sports M(c)/W(c), field hockey W, ice hockey M/W, lacrosse M/W, sailing M/W, soccer M/W, squash M/W, swimming M/W, tennis M/W, track and field M/W, volleyball M/W, water polo M/W. *Intramural sports:* baseball M(c), basketball M/W, equestrian sports M/W, football M, golf M/W, ice hockey M/W, lacrosse M, rugby M/W, sailing M/W, skiing (cross-country) M/W, skiing (downhill) M/W, soccer M/W, softball M/W, tennis M/W, volleyball M/W.
Standardized Tests *Recommended:* SAT I (for admission).
Costs (2001–02) *Payment plan:* installment. *Waivers:* senior citizens and employees or children of employees.
Financial Aid Of all full-time matriculated undergraduates who enrolled in 2001, 860 applied for aid, 795 were judged to have need, 795 had their need fully met. 657 Federal Work-Study jobs (averaging $1046). *Average percent of need met:* 100%. *Average financial aid package:* $21,943. *Average need-based loan:* $4465. *Average need-based gift aid:* $18,737. *Average indebtedness upon graduation:* $18,602. *Financial aid deadline:* 1/15.
Applying *Options:* common application, early decision, deferred entrance. *Application fee:* $55. *Required:* essay or personal statement, high school transcript, minimum 2.0 GPA, 2 letters of recommendation. *Recommended:* interview. *Application deadlines:* 1/1 (freshmen), 4/1 (transfers). *Early decision:* 11/15 (for plan 1), 1/1 (for plan 2). *Notification:* 4/1 (freshmen), 12/15 (early decision plan 1), 2/15 (early decision plan 2).
Admissions Contact Ms. Martha Merrill, Dean of Admissions and Financial Aid, Connecticut College, 270 Mohegan Avenue, New London, CT 06320-4196. *Phone:* 860-439-2200. *Fax:* 860-439-4301. *E-mail:* admission@conncoll.edu.

EASTERN CONNECTICUT STATE UNIVERSITY
Willimantic, Connecticut

- **State-supported** comprehensive, founded 1889, part of Connecticut State University System
- **Calendar** semesters
- **Degrees** associate, bachelor's, and master's
- **Small-town** 178-acre campus
- **Endowment** $60,000

- **Coed,** 4,994 undergraduate students, 72% full-time, 58% women, 42% men
- **Moderately difficult** entrance level, 64% of applicants were admitted

Undergraduates 3,573 full-time, 1,421 part-time. Students come from 28 states and territories, 30 other countries, 8% are from out of state, 7% African American, 2% Asian American or Pacific Islander, 3% Hispanic American, 1% Native American, 2% international, 7% transferred in, 41% live on campus. *Retention:* 74% of 2001 full-time freshmen returned.

Freshmen *Admission:* 2,913 applied, 1,870 admitted, 862 enrolled. *Test scores:* SAT verbal scores over 500: 48%; SAT math scores over 500: 49%; SAT verbal scores over 600: 8%; SAT math scores over 600: 9%; SAT verbal scores over 700: 1%; SAT math scores over 700: 1%.

Faculty *Total:* 351, 50% full-time, 51% with terminal degrees. *Student/faculty ratio:* 16:1.

Majors Accounting; art; biology; business; business administration; communications; computer/information sciences; early childhood education; economics; elementary education; English; general studies; history; liberal arts and sciences/liberal studies; mathematics; physical education; political science; psychology; social work; sociology; Spanish; sport/fitness administration.

Academic Programs *Special study options:* academic remediation for entering students, adult/continuing education programs, advanced placement credit, cooperative education, distance learning, double majors, freshman honors college, honors programs, independent study, internships, off-campus study, part-time degree program, services for LD students, student-designed majors, study abroad, summer session for credit. *ROTC:* Army (c), Air Force (c).

Library J. Eugene Smith Library with 205,869 titles, 6,260 serial subscriptions, 2,514 audiovisual materials, an OPAC, a Web page.

Computers on Campus 518 computers available on campus for general student use. A campuswide network can be accessed from student residence rooms and from off campus. Internet access, at least one staffed computer lab available.

Student Life *Housing Options:* coed, women-only. *Activities and Organizations:* drama/theater group, student-run newspaper, radio and television station, choral group, Nubian Society, Organization of Latin American Students, International Student Organization, West Indian Student Society. *Campus security:* 24-hour emergency response devices and patrols, student patrols, late-night transport/escort service, controlled dormitory access. *Student Services:* health clinic, personal/psychological counseling, women's center.

Athletics Member NCAA. All Division III. *Intercollegiate sports:* baseball M, basketball M/W, cross-country running M/W, field hockey W, soccer M/W, softball W, track and field M/W, volleyball W. *Intramural sports:* badminton M/W, basketball M/W, bowling M/W, cross-country running M/W, football M, golf M, gymnastics W, lacrosse M/W, racquetball M/W, rugby M, skiing (cross-country) M/W, skiing (downhill) M/W, soccer M/W, squash M/W, swimming M/W, tennis M/W, track and field M/W, volleyball M/W, water polo M/W.

Standardized Tests *Required:* SAT I or ACT (for admission).

Costs (2002–03) *Tuition:* state resident $2313 full-time, $200 per credit hour part-time; nonresident $7485 full-time, $200 per credit hour part-time. Full-time tuition and fees vary according to degree level. Part-time tuition and fees vary according to course load, degree level, and reciprocity agreements. *Required fees:* $2400 full-time, $60 per term part-time. *Room and board:* Room and board charges vary according to board plan and housing facility. *Payment plans:* installment, deferred payment. *Waivers:* senior citizens and employees or children of employees.

Financial Aid Of all full-time matriculated undergraduates who enrolled in 2001, 3050 applied for aid, 2562 were judged to have need, 1518 had their need fully met. 168 Federal Work-Study jobs (averaging $771). 94 State and other part-time jobs (averaging $746). In 2001, 195 non-need-based awards were made. *Average percent of need met:* 90%. *Average financial aid package:* $5165. *Average need-based loan:* $3990. *Average need-based gift aid:* $4430. *Average non-need based aid:* $1410. *Average indebtedness upon graduation:* $10,200. *Financial aid deadline:* 3/15.

Applying *Options:* common application, electronic application, early admission, deferred entrance. *Application fee:* $40. *Required:* high school transcript. *Required for some:* interview. *Recommended:* essay or personal statement, letters of recommendation, rank in upper 50% of high school class. *Application deadline:* rolling (transfers). *Notification:* continuous (freshmen).

Admissions Contact Ms. Kimberly Crone, Director of Admissions and Enrollment Management, Eastern Connecticut State University, 83 Windham street, Willimantic, CT 06336. *Phone:* 860-465-5286. *Toll-free phone:* 877-353-3278. *Fax:* 860-465-5544. *E-mail:* admissions@easternct.edu.

FAIRFIELD UNIVERSITY
Fairfield, Connecticut

- **Independent Roman Catholic (Jesuit)** comprehensive, founded 1942
- **Calendar** semesters
- **Degrees** bachelor's, master's, and post-master's certificates
- **Suburban** 200-acre campus with easy access to New York City
- **Endowment** $126.4 million
- **Coed,** 4,164 undergraduate students, 82% full-time, 55% women, 45% men
- **Moderately difficult** entrance level, 49% of applicants were admitted

Undergraduates 3,399 full-time, 765 part-time. Students come from 33 states and territories, 43 other countries, 74% are from out of state, 3% African American, 3% Asian American or Pacific Islander, 5% Hispanic American, 0.2% Native American, 2% international, 1% transferred in, 80% live on campus. *Retention:* 90% of 2001 full-time freshmen returned.

Freshmen *Admission:* 7,128 applied, 3,504 admitted, 832 enrolled. *Average high school GPA:* 3.6. *Test scores:* SAT verbal scores over 500: 91%; SAT math scores over 500: 93%; SAT verbal scores over 600: 45%; SAT math scores over 600: 52%; SAT verbal scores over 700: 6%; SAT math scores over 700: 5%.

Faculty *Total:* 476, 47% full-time, 57% with terminal degrees. *Student/faculty ratio:* 13:1.

Majors Accounting; American studies; art; biology; business administration; business marketing and marketing management; chemistry; clinical psychology; computer science; computer software engineering; economics; electrical engineering; engineering related; English; finance; French; German; history; information sciences/systems; international relations; management information systems/business data processing; mass communications; mathematics; mechanical engineering; modern languages; music history; neuroscience; nursing; philosophy; physics; political science; psychology; religious studies; secondary education; sociology; Spanish.

Academic Programs *Special study options:* adult/continuing education programs, advanced placement credit, double majors, freshman honors college, honors programs, independent study, internships, part-time degree program, services for LD students, study abroad, summer session for credit. *ROTC:* Army (c). *Unusual degree programs:* 3-2 engineering with University of Connecticut, Rensselaer Polytechnic Institute, Columbia University, Stevens Institute of Technology.

Library Dimenna-Nyselius Library with 293,191 titles, 1,790 serial subscriptions, 9,924 audiovisual materials, an OPAC, a Web page.

Computers on Campus 150 computers available on campus for general student use. A campuswide network can be accessed from student residence rooms and from off campus. Internet access, online (class) registration, at least one staffed computer lab available.

Student Life *Housing:* on-campus residence required through senior year. *Options:* coed, disabled students. *Activities and Organizations:* drama/theater group, student-run newspaper, radio and television station, choral group, student government, Glee Club, Drama Club, multicultural organizations, Mission Volunteers. *Campus security:* 24-hour emergency response devices and patrols, late-night transport/escort service, controlled dormitory access, bicycle patrols. *Student Services:* health clinic, personal/psychological counseling, women's center.

Athletics Member NCAA. All Division I except football (Division I-AA). *Intercollegiate sports:* baseball M(s), basketball M(s)/W(s), crew M(c)/W, cross-country running M/W, equestrian sports M(c)/W(c), field hockey W(s), golf M/W, ice hockey M(s), lacrosse M(s)/W(s), soccer M(s)/W(s), softball W(s), swimming M(s)/W(s), tennis M(s)/W(s), volleyball W(s). *Intramural sports:* basketball M/W, fencing M(c)/W(c), football M, lacrosse M(c)/W(c), racquetball M/W, rugby M(c)/W(c), sailing M(c)/W(c), skiing (cross-country) M(c)/W(c), skiing (downhill) M/W, soccer W(c), table tennis M/W, tennis M/W, track and field M/W, volleyball M/W.

Standardized Tests *Required:* SAT I or ACT (for admission). *Recommended:* SAT II: Subject Tests (for admission).

Costs (2001–02) *Comprehensive fee:* $30,885 includes full-time tuition ($22,430), mandatory fees ($455), and room and board ($8000). Part-time tuition: $330 per credit. Part-time tuition and fees vary according to course load. *Required fees:* $50 per term part-time. *Room and board:* College room only: $4900. Room and board charges vary according to board plan and housing facility. *Payment plan:* installment. *Waivers:* employees or children of employees.

Financial Aid Of all full-time matriculated undergraduates who enrolled in 2001, 2098 applied for aid, 1724 were judged to have need, 496 had their need

Fairfield University (continued)
fully met. 400 Federal Work-Study jobs. In 2001, 301 non-need-based awards were made. *Average percent of need met:* 79%. *Average financial aid package:* $16,203. *Average need-based loan:* $3884. *Average need-based gift aid:* $9786. *Average non-need based aid:* $4895. *Average indebtedness upon graduation:* $19,873.

Applying *Options:* common application, early decision, deferred entrance. *Application fee:* $55. *Required:* high school transcript, minimum 3.0 GPA, 1 letter of recommendation, rank in upper 20% of high school class. *Recommended:* interview. *Application deadlines:* 2/1 (freshmen), 6/1 (transfers). *Early decision:* 11/15. *Notification:* 4/1 (freshmen), 1/1 (early decision).

Admissions Contact Ms. Judith M. Dobai, Director of Admission, Fairfield University, 1073 North Benson Road, Fairfield, CT 06430-5195. *Phone:* 203-254-4100. *Fax:* 203-254-4199. *E-mail:* admis@mail.fairfield.edu.

HARTFORD COLLEGE FOR WOMEN
Hartford, Connecticut

- **Independent** 4-year, founded 1933
- **Calendar** 6 7-week terms
- **Degrees** certificates, associate, and bachelor's (offers mainly evening and weekend programs)
- **Suburban** 13-acre campus
- **Women only,** 178 undergraduate students, 7% full-time
- **Moderately difficult** entrance level, 50% of applicants were admitted

Undergraduates Students come from 3 states and territories, 1 other country, 1% are from out of state, 18% African American, 1% Asian American or Pacific Islander, 6% Hispanic American, 0.6% Native American, 0.6% international.

Freshmen *Admission:* 101 applied, 50 admitted.

Faculty *Total:* 17, 41% full-time. *Student/faculty ratio:* 7:1.

Majors Legal studies; liberal arts and sciences/liberal studies; paralegal/legal assistant; women's studies.

Academic Programs *Special study options:* academic remediation for entering students, accelerated degree program, adult/continuing education programs, advanced placement credit, double majors, independent study, internships, off-campus study, part-time degree program, summer session for credit.

Library Bess Graham Library with 61,822 titles, 101 serial subscriptions.

Computers on Campus 40 computers available on campus for general student use. Internet access, at least one staffed computer lab available.

Student Life *Activities and Organizations:* drama/theater group, student-run newspaper, radio station, choral group, Student Paralegal Association, Women's Leadership Association. *Campus security:* 24-hour emergency response devices and patrols, late-night transport/escort service. *Student Services:* health clinic, personal/psychological counseling, women's center.

Standardized Tests *Required for some:* SAT I (for admission).

Costs (2001–02) *Tuition:* $365 per credit part-time. Part-time tuition and fees vary according to class time, course load, location, and program. No tuition increase for student's term of enrollment. room and board is available at the University of Hartford. *Required fees:* $55 per term part-time. *Payment plan:* installment. *Waivers:* employees or children of employees.

Applying *Options:* common application, deferred entrance. *Application fee:* $35. *Required:* essay or personal statement, interview. *Recommended:* letters of recommendation. *Application deadline:* rolling (freshmen), rolling (transfers). *Notification:* continuous until 9/1 (freshmen).

Admissions Contact Ms. Annette Rogers, Admissions Director, Hartford College for Women, 1265 Asylum Avenue, Hartford, CT 06105-2299. *Phone:* 860-768-5646. *Toll-free phone:* 888-GO-TO-HCW. *Fax:* 860-768-5693. *E-mail:* arogers@mail.hartford.edu.

HOLY APOSTLES COLLEGE AND SEMINARY
Cromwell, Connecticut

- **Independent Roman Catholic** comprehensive, founded 1956
- **Calendar** semesters
- **Degrees** associate, bachelor's, master's, first professional, and post-master's certificates
- **Small-town** campus
- **Coed,** 38 undergraduate students, 24% full-time, 45% women, 55% men
- **Noncompetitive** entrance level

Undergraduates 9 full-time, 29 part-time. Students come from 8 states and territories, 1 other country, 90% are from out of state, 13% Asian American or Pacific Islander, 13% transferred in, 80% live on campus. *Retention:* 100% of 2001 full-time freshmen returned.

Faculty *Total:* 29, 48% full-time, 72% with terminal degrees. *Student/faculty ratio:* 8:1.

Majors Biblical studies; humanities; philosophy; religious studies; social sciences; theology.

Academic Programs *Special study options:* academic remediation for entering students, accelerated degree program, adult/continuing education programs, English as a second language, internships, part-time degree program.

Library Holy Apostles College and Seminary Library with 84,584 titles, 250 serial subscriptions.

Computers on Campus 10 computers available on campus for general student use. Internet access available.

Student Life *Housing:* on-campus residence required through senior year. *Options:* men-only. *Activities and Organizations:* drama/theater group, student-run newspaper, choral group, Toastmasters. *Campus security:* 24-hour emergency response devices and patrols. *Student Services:* health clinic, personal/psychological counseling.

Costs (2001–02) *One-time required fee:* $75. *Comprehensive fee:* $14,320 includes full-time tuition ($7920) and room and board ($6400). Full-time tuition and fees vary according to program. Part-time tuition: $585 per course. Part-time tuition and fees vary according to program. *Required fees:* $195 per credit. *Payment plan:* installment. *Waivers:* employees or children of employees.

Financial Aid Of all full-time matriculated undergraduates who enrolled in 2001, 3 applied for aid, 3 were judged to have need. *Average percent of need met:* 50%. *Average financial aid package:* $9358. *Average need-based loan:* $3200. *Average need-based gift aid:* $6150.

Applying *Options:* common application, deferred entrance. *Application fee:* $50. *Required:* high school transcript, interview. *Required for some:* letters of recommendation. *Application deadline:* rolling (freshmen), rolling (transfers).

Admissions Contact Very Rev. Douglas Mosey CSB, Director of Admissions, Holy Apostles College and Seminary, 33 Prospect Hill Road, Cromwell, CT 06416-2005. *Phone:* 860-632-3010. *Toll-free phone:* 800-330-7272. *Fax:* 860-632-3075. *E-mail:* holy_apostles@msn.com.

LYME ACADEMY COLLEGE OF FINE ARTS
Old Lyme, Connecticut

- **Independent** 4-year, founded 1976
- **Calendar** semesters
- **Degree** certificates and bachelor's
- **Small-town** 3-acre campus
- **Endowment** $1.5 million
- **Coed,** 203 undergraduate students, 33% full-time, 66% women, 34% men
- **Moderately difficult** entrance level, 48% of applicants were admitted

Undergraduates 66 full-time, 137 part-time. Students come from 23 states and territories, 1 other country, 42% are from out of state, 1% African American, 2% Asian American or Pacific Islander, 8% Hispanic American, 1% Native American, 1% international, 11% transferred in. *Retention:* 48% of 2001 full-time freshmen returned.

Freshmen *Admission:* 29 applied, 14 admitted, 13 enrolled. *Average high school GPA:* 3.10. *Test scores:* SAT verbal scores over 500: 59%; SAT math scores over 500: 55%; SAT verbal scores over 600: 33%; SAT math scores over 600: 11%; SAT verbal scores over 700: 11%.

Faculty *Total:* 25, 44% full-time, 52% with terminal degrees. *Student/faculty ratio:* 7:1.

Majors Drawing; painting; sculpture.

Academic Programs *Special study options:* cooperative education, off-campus study, part-time degree program, summer session for credit.

Library Nancy Kriebly Library with 8,492 titles, 60 serial subscriptions, 120 audiovisual materials, an OPAC.

Computers on Campus 6 computers available on campus for general student use. Internet access available.

Student Life *Housing:* college housing not available. *Activities and Organizations:* student-run newspaper, Student Association. *Student Services:* personal/psychological counseling.

Standardized Tests *Recommended:* SAT I (for admission).

Costs (2001–02) *Tuition:* $12,200 full-time, $509 per credit part-time. Full-time tuition and fees vary according to class time and student level. Part-time tuition and fees vary according to class time and student level. *Required fees:* $570 full-time, $285 per term part-time. *Payment plan:* installment. *Waivers:* employees or children of employees.

Financial Aid Of all full-time matriculated undergraduates who enrolled in 2001, 45 applied for aid, 40 were judged to have need. 2 Federal Work-Study jobs (averaging $2833). 4 State and other part-time jobs (averaging $1070). *Average* *percent of need met:* 51%. *Average financial aid package:* $5996. *Average indebtedness upon graduation:* $12,248. *Financial aid deadline:* 3/15.

Applying *Options:* electronic application, deferred entrance. *Application fee:* $35. *Required:* essay or personal statement, high school transcript, 2 letters of recommendation, portfolio. *Required for some:* interview. *Recommended:* minimum 2.0 GPA, interview. *Application deadline:* rolling (freshmen), rolling (transfers).

Admissions Contact Christopher Rose, Associate Dean of Enrollment Management, Lyme Academy College of Fine Arts, 84 Lyme Street, Old Lyme, CT 06371. *Phone:* 860-434-5232 Ext: 122. *Fax:* 860-434-8725. *E-mail:* admissions@lymeacademy.edu.

MITCHELL COLLEGE

New London, Connecticut

- **Independent** primarily 2-year, founded 1938
- **Calendar** semesters
- **Degrees** associate and bachelor's
- **Suburban** 67-acre campus with easy access to Hartford and Providence
- **Endowment** $6.0 million
- **Coed,** 708 undergraduate students, 83% full-time, 51% women, 49% men
- **Minimally difficult** entrance level, 63% of applicants were admitted

Undergraduates 588 full-time, 120 part-time. Students come from 19 states and territories, 12 other countries, 42% are from out of state, 10% African American, 1% Asian American or Pacific Islander, 5% Hispanic American, 5% Native American, 3% international, 5% transferred in, 80% live on campus.

Freshmen *Admission:* 1,024 applied, 641 admitted, 288 enrolled. *Average high school GPA:* 2.65. *Test scores:* SAT verbal scores over 500: 15%; SAT math scores over 500: 13%; ACT scores over 18: 57%; SAT verbal scores over 600: 2%; SAT math scores over 600: 2%; ACT scores over 24: 14%.

Faculty *Total:* 60, 33% full-time, 23% with terminal degrees. *Student/faculty ratio:* 12:1.

Majors Accounting; athletic training/sports medicine; biological/physical sciences; business administration; child care/development; criminal justice/law enforcement administration; developmental/child psychology; early childhood education; engineering; graphic design/commercial art/illustration; human services; individual/family development; liberal arts and sciences/liberal studies; marine biology; physical education; physical sciences; psychology; recreational therapy; recreation/leisure studies; sport/fitness administration.

Academic Programs *Special study options:* adult/continuing education programs, advanced placement credit, double majors, English as a second language, internships, part-time degree program, services for LD students, summer session for credit.

Library Mitchell College Library plus 1 other with 42,000 titles, 90 serial subscriptions, 50 audiovisual materials, an OPAC.

Computers on Campus 155 computers available on campus for general student use. A campuswide network can be accessed from student residence rooms and from off campus. Internet access, at least one staffed computer lab available.

Student Life *Housing Options:* coed, men-only, women-only. *Activities and Organizations:* drama/theater group, student-run newspaper, choral group, Multicultural Club, Business Club, student government, student newspaper, Outdoor Adventure Club. *Campus security:* 24-hour emergency response devices and patrols, student patrols, late-night transport/escort service, controlled dormitory access. *Student Services:* health clinic, personal/psychological counseling.

Athletics Member NJCAA. *Intercollegiate sports:* baseball M(s), basketball M(s)/W(s), cross-country running M/W, golf M/W, lacrosse M(s), sailing M/W, soccer M(s)/W(s), softball W(s), tennis M/W, volleyball W(s). *Intramural sports:* badminton M/W, baseball M, basketball M/W, bowling M/W, cross-country running M/W, football M/W, golf M/W, ice hockey M, sailing M/W, soccer M/W, softball M/W, table tennis M/W, tennis M/W, volleyball M/W, weight lifting M/W.

Standardized Tests *Required:* SAT I or ACT (for admission).

Costs (2001–02) *Comprehensive fee:* $23,950 includes full-time tuition ($15,600), mandatory fees ($850), and room and board ($7500). Part-time tuition: $250 per credit hour. Part-time tuition and fees vary according to course load. *Required fees:* $35 per term part-time. *Payment plan:* installment. *Waivers:* employees or children of employees.

Financial Aid Of all full-time matriculated undergraduates who enrolled in 2001, 65 Federal Work-Study jobs (averaging $1000).

Applying *Options:* common application, electronic application, early admission, early action, deferred entrance. *Application fee:* $30. *Required:* essay or personal statement, high school transcript, minimum 2.0 GPA, letters of recommendation. *Recommended:* interview. *Application deadline:* rolling (freshmen), rolling (transfers). *Notification:* continuous until 8/30 (freshmen).

Admissions Contact Ms. Kathleen E. Neal, Director of Admissions, Mitchell College, 437 Pequot Avenue, New London, CT 06320. *Phone:* 860-701-5038. *Toll-free phone:* 800-443-2811. *Fax:* 860-444-1209. *E-mail:* admissions@mitchell.edu.

PAIER COLLEGE OF ART, INC.

Hamden, Connecticut

- **Proprietary** 4-year, founded 1946
- **Calendar** semesters
- **Degrees** certificates, diplomas, associate, and bachelor's
- **Suburban** 3-acre campus with easy access to New York City
- **Coed,** 284 undergraduate students, 56% full-time, 55% women, 45% men
- **Minimally difficult** entrance level, 73% of applicants were admitted

Undergraduates 160 full-time, 124 part-time. Students come from 4 states and territories, 1 other country, 1% are from out of state, 7% transferred in. *Retention:* 78% of 2001 full-time freshmen returned.

Freshmen *Admission:* 110 applied, 80 admitted, 69 enrolled. *Test scores:* SAT verbal scores over 500: 42%; SAT math scores over 500: 27%; SAT verbal scores over 600: 20%; SAT math scores over 600: 5%; SAT verbal scores over 700: 4%; SAT math scores over 700: 1%.

Faculty *Total:* 45, 22% full-time, 7% with terminal degrees. *Student/faculty ratio:* 6:1.

Majors Art; commercial photography; design/visual communications; fine/studio arts; graphic design/commercial art/illustration; interior design; painting; photography.

Academic Programs *Special study options:* academic remediation for entering students, advanced placement credit, independent study, part-time degree program, services for LD students, summer session for credit.

Library Adele K. Paier Memorial Library with 11,515 titles, 69 serial subscriptions, 66,136 audiovisual materials.

Computers on Campus 20 computers available on campus for general student use. At least one staffed computer lab available.

Student Life *Housing:* college housing not available. *Activities and Organizations:* Student Council. *Campus security:* evening patrols by security. *Student Services:* personal/psychological counseling.

Standardized Tests *Required:* SAT I or ACT (for admission).

Costs (2001–02) *Tuition:* $10,900 full-time, $350 per semester hour part-time. Full-time tuition and fees vary according to course load, degree level, and program. Part-time tuition and fees vary according to course load, degree level, and program. *Required fees:* $300 full-time, $33 per term part-time. *Payment plan:* installment. *Waivers:* senior citizens and employees or children of employees.

Financial Aid Of all full-time matriculated undergraduates who enrolled in 2001, 102 applied for aid, 92 were judged to have need, 1 had their need fully met. *Average percent of need met:* 62%. *Average financial aid package:* $6717. *Average need-based loan:* $3446. *Average need-based gift aid:* $3460. *Average indebtedness upon graduation:* $13,536.

Applying *Options:* deferred entrance. *Application fee:* $25. *Required:* high school transcript, minimum 2.0 GPA, 2 letters of recommendation, interview, portfolio. *Recommended:* essay or personal statement. *Application deadline:* rolling (freshmen), rolling (transfers). *Notification:* continuous (freshmen).

Admissions Contact Ms. Lynn Pascale, Secretary to Admissions, Paier College of Art, Inc., 20 Gorham Avenue, Hamden, CT 06514-3902. *Phone:* 203-287-3031. *Fax:* 203-287-3021. *E-mail:* info@paierart.com.

QUINNIPIAC UNIVERSITY

Hamden, Connecticut

- **Independent** comprehensive, founded 1929
- **Calendar** semesters
- **Degrees** bachelor's, master's, first professional, and postbachelor's certificates
- **Suburban** 300-acre campus with easy access to Hartford
- **Endowment** $79.8 million
- **Coed,** 5,056 undergraduate students, 91% full-time, 63% women, 37% men
- **Moderately difficult** entrance level, 74% of applicants were admitted

The $7-million Lender School of Business Center features local area network classrooms, satellite service, and the Ed McMahon Center for Mass Communications, one of the most advanced in higher education. The communications facilities include TV and radio studios, print journalism and desktop publishing laboratories, a news technology center, and audio and video equipment. The

Quinnipiac University (continued)
center establishes national recognition for the undergraduate and graduate mass communication and business programs.

Undergraduates 4,585 full-time, 471 part-time. Students come from 26 states and territories, 15 other countries, 72% are from out of state, 2% African American, 2% Asian American or Pacific Islander, 4% Hispanic American, 0.3% Native American, 0.3% international, 3% transferred in, 70% live on campus. *Retention:* 83% of 2001 full-time freshmen returned.

Freshmen *Admission:* 7,281 applied, 5,371 admitted, 1,187 enrolled. *Average high school GPA:* 3.20. *Test scores:* SAT verbal scores over 500: 71%; SAT math scores over 500: 77%; ACT scores over 18: 91%; SAT verbal scores over 600: 15%; SAT math scores over 600: 21%; ACT scores over 24: 50%; SAT verbal scores over 700: 2%; SAT math scores over 700: 2%; ACT scores over 30: 6%.

Faculty *Total:* 435, 61% full-time. *Student/faculty ratio:* 16:1.

Majors Accounting; actuarial science; advertising; applied mathematics; athletic training/sports medicine; biochemistry; biological/physical sciences; biology; broadcast journalism; business administration; business economics; business marketing and marketing management; chemistry; child care/development; communications related; computer science; criminal justice studies; developmental/child psychology; economics; education; English; entrepreneurship; film studies; film/video production; finance; gerontology; health products/services marketing; health services administration; history; human resources management; human services; information sciences/systems; international business; international relations; journalism; laboratory animal medicine; legal studies; liberal arts and sciences/liberal studies; literature; mass communications; mathematics; medical laboratory technology; microbiology/bacteriology; nursing; occupational therapy; paralegal/legal assistant; physical therapy; physician assistant; physiological psychology/psychobiology; political science; pre-dentistry; pre-law; pre-medicine; pre-veterinary studies; psychology; public relations; radiological science; respiratory therapy; social sciences; sociology; Spanish; veterinary technology; Web page, digital/multimedia and information resources design; zoology.

Academic Programs *Special study options:* adult/continuing education programs, advanced placement credit, double majors, honors programs, independent study, internships, part-time degree program, services for LD students, student-designed majors, study abroad, summer session for credit. *ROTC:* Army (c), Air Force (c).

Library Arnold Bernhard Library plus 1 other with 285,000 titles, 4,400 serial subscriptions, an OPAC, a Web page.

Computers on Campus 200 computers available on campus for general student use. A campuswide network can be accessed from student residence rooms and from off campus. Internet access, at least one staffed computer lab available.

Student Life *Housing Options:* coed. *Activities and Organizations:* drama/theater group, student-run newspaper, radio and television station, choral group, student government, Social Programming Board, drama club, student newspaper, national fraternities, national sororities. *Campus security:* 24-hour emergency response devices and patrols, late-night transport/escort service, controlled dormitory access. *Student Services:* health clinic, personal/psychological counseling, women's center.

Athletics Member NCAA. except baseball (Division I), men's and women's basketball (Division I), men's and women's cross-country running (Division I), field hockey (Division I), golf (Division I), men's and women's ice hockey (Division I), men's and women's lacrosse (Division I), men's and women's soccer (Division I), softball (Division I), men's and women's tennis (Division I), men's and women's track and field (Division I), volleyball (Division I) *Intercollegiate sports:* baseball M(s), basketball M(s)/W(s), cross-country running M(s)/W(s), field hockey W(s), golf M(s), ice hockey M(s)/W(s), lacrosse M(s)/W(s), soccer M(s)/W(s), softball W(s), tennis M(s)/W(s), track and field M(s)/W(s), volleyball W(s). *Intramural sports:* baseball M, basketball M/W, bowling M/W, field hockey M/W, soccer M/W, softball W, tennis M/W, volleyball M/W.

Standardized Tests *Required:* SAT I or ACT (for admission).

Costs (2001–02) *Comprehensive fee:* $27,370 includes full-time tuition ($18,000), mandatory fees ($840), and room and board ($8530). Part-time tuition: $450 per credit. Part-time tuition and fees vary according to course load. *Required fees:* $90 per course. *Room and board:* Room and board charges vary according to board plan and housing facility. *Payment plans:* installment, deferred payment. *Waivers:* employees or children of employees.

Financial Aid Of all full-time matriculated undergraduates who enrolled in 2001, 3289 applied for aid, 2648 were judged to have need, 383 had their need fully met. 1204 Federal Work-Study jobs (averaging $1800). 40 State and other part-time jobs (averaging $1605). In 2001, 313 non-need-based awards were made. *Average percent of need met:* 70%. *Average financial aid package:* $12,195. *Average need-based loan:* $4009. *Average need-based gift aid:* $6839. *Average non-need based aid:* $3225. *Average indebtedness upon graduation:* $17,170.

Applying *Options:* common application, electronic application, early admission, deferred entrance. *Application fee:* $45. *Required:* essay or personal statement, high school transcript, 1 letter of recommendation. *Required for some:* minimum 3.0 GPA. *Recommended:* minimum 2.5 GPA, interview. *Application deadlines:* 2/15 (freshmen), 6/1 (transfers). *Notification:* continuous until 3/1 (freshmen).

Admissions Contact Ms. Joan Isaac Mohr, Vice President and Dean of Admissions, Quinnipiac University, 275 Mount Carmel Avenue, Hamden, CT 06518-1940. *Phone:* 203-582-8600. *Toll-free phone:* 800-462-1944. *Fax:* 203-582-8906. *E-mail:* admissions@quinnipiac.edu.

SACRED HEART UNIVERSITY
Fairfield, Connecticut

- **Independent Roman Catholic** comprehensive, founded 1963
- **Calendar** semesters
- **Degrees** certificates, associate, bachelor's, master's, and post-master's certificates (also offers part-time program with significant enrollment not reflected in profile)
- **Suburban** 56-acre campus with easy access to New York City
- **Endowment** $23.3 million
- **Coed,** 4,137 undergraduate students, 69% full-time, 63% women, 37% men
- **Moderately difficult** entrance level, 73% of applicants were admitted

Undergraduates 2,837 full-time, 1,300 part-time. Students come from 28 states and territories, 34 other countries, 41% are from out of state, 7% African American, 2% Asian American or Pacific Islander, 6% Hispanic American, 0.2% Native American, 2% international, 8% transferred in, 68% live on campus. *Retention:* 81% of 2001 full-time freshmen returned.

Freshmen *Admission:* 4,300 applied, 3,118 admitted, 766 enrolled. *Average high school GPA:* 3.10. *Test scores:* SAT verbal scores over 500: 65%; SAT math scores over 500: 66%; SAT verbal scores over 600: 16%; SAT math scores over 600: 17%; SAT verbal scores over 700: 2%; SAT math scores over 700: 2%.

Faculty *Total:* 455, 34% full-time, 41% with terminal degrees. *Student/faculty ratio:* 12:1.

Majors Accounting; art; athletic training/sports medicine; biochemistry; biological/physical sciences; biology; business administration; business economics; business marketing and marketing management; chemistry; computer/information sciences; computer science; criminal justice/law enforcement administration; data processing technology; drawing; early childhood education; economics; education; elementary education; English; environmental biology; environmental science; film studies; film/video production; finance; graphic design/commercial art/illustration; history; international business; international relations; journalism; legal administrative assistant; liberal arts and sciences/liberal studies; literature; mass communications; mathematics; middle school education; modern languages; music; nursing; occupational therapy; paralegal/legal assistant; philosophy; physical therapy; political science; pre-dentistry; pre-medicine; pre-veterinary studies; psychology; radio/television broadcasting; religious studies; secondary education; social work; sociology; Spanish; sport/fitness administration; theater arts/drama; women's studies.

Academic Programs *Special study options:* academic remediation for entering students, accelerated degree program, adult/continuing education programs, advanced placement credit, cooperative education, distance learning, double majors, English as a second language, freshman honors college, honors programs, independent study, internships, part-time degree program, student-designed majors, study abroad, summer session for credit. *Unusual degree programs:* 3-2 physical therapy, occupational therapy, education, religious studies, chemistry, information technology, health systems management.

Library Ryan-Matura Library with 141,431 titles, 2,911 serial subscriptions, 11,594 audiovisual materials, an OPAC, a Web page.

Computers on Campus 110 computers available on campus for general student use. A campuswide network can be accessed from student residence rooms and from off campus that provide access to Intranet. Internet access, online (class) registration, at least one staffed computer lab available.

Student Life *Housing Options:* coed, disabled students. *Activities and Organizations:* drama/theater group, student-run newspaper, radio station, choral group, marching band, student government association, recreational clubs, Campus Ministry, multicultural clubs. *Campus security:* 24-hour emergency response devices and patrols, late-night transport/escort service, controlled dormitory access, campus housing has sprinklers and fire alarms. *Student Services:* health clinic, personal/psychological counseling, women's center.

Athletics Member NCAA. All Division I except football (Division I-AA). *Intercollegiate sports:* baseball M, basketball M(s)/W(s), bowling M/W, crew M/W, cross-country running M/W, equestrian sports W, fencing M/W, field hockey W, golf M/W, ice hockey M(s)/W, lacrosse M/W, rugby M(c)/W(c), skiing (downhill) M(c)/W(c), soccer M/W, softball W, swimming W, tennis M/W, track and field M/W, volleyball M/W, wrestling M. *Intramural sports:* basketball M/W, bowling M/W, football M/W, golf M/W, soccer M/W, softball M/W, tennis M/W, volleyball M/W.

Standardized Tests *Required:* SAT I or ACT (for admission).

Costs (2001–02) *Comprehensive fee:* $25,058 includes full-time tuition ($17,000), mandatory fees ($60), and room and board ($7998). Part-time tuition: $350 per credit. *Required fees:* $60 per term part-time. *Room and board:* College room only: $5738. Room and board charges vary according to board plan. *Payment plans:* installment, deferred payment. *Waivers:* senior citizens and employees or children of employees.

Financial Aid Of all full-time matriculated undergraduates who enrolled in 2001, 2354 applied for aid, 1931 were judged to have need, 516 had their need fully met. 500 Federal Work-Study jobs (averaging $971). 241 State and other part-time jobs (averaging $980). In 2001, 479 non-need-based awards were made. *Average percent of need met:* 73%. *Average financial aid package:* $11,735. *Average need-based loan:* $4576. *Average need-based gift aid:* $7809. *Average indebtedness upon graduation:* $16,500.

Applying *Options:* common application, electronic application, early admission, early decision, deferred entrance. *Application fee:* $45. *Required:* essay or personal statement, high school transcript, minimum 3.0 GPA, 1 letter of recommendation. *Recommended:* minimum 3.2 GPA, interview. *Application deadline:* rolling (freshmen), rolling (transfers). *Early decision:* 10/1 (for plan 1), 12/1 (for plan 2). *Notification:* continuous (freshmen), 10/15 (early decision plan 1), 12/15 (early decision plan 2).

Admissions Contact Ms. Karen N. Guastelle, Dean of Undergraduate Admissions, Sacred Heart University, 5151 Park Avenue, Fairfield, CT 06432-1000. *Phone:* 203-371-7880. *Fax:* 203-365-7607. *E-mail:* enroll@sacredheart.edu.

SAINT JOSEPH COLLEGE

West Hartford, Connecticut

- **Independent Roman Catholic** comprehensive, founded 1932
- **Calendar** semesters
- **Degrees** certificates, bachelor's, and master's
- **Suburban** 84-acre campus with easy access to Hartford
- **Endowment** $11.7 million
- **Women only,** 1,287 undergraduate students, 55% full-time
- **Moderately difficult** entrance level, 37% of applicants were admitted

Saint Joseph College provides outstanding academic, professional, and leadership opportunities for women. More than 25 majors are accompanied by internships locally or abroad. Success in every program springs from the liberal arts and sciences curriculum and active mentoring by faculty members, advisers, and alumnae. This mentoring guides students directly into postgraduate business, professional, and academic communities. Students serve on every College committee from strategic planning to Web site development, and, like the founding Sisters of Mercy, they perform community service around the world.

Undergraduates 705 full-time, 582 part-time. Students come from 10 states and territories, 15% are from out of state, 12% African American, 2% Asian American or Pacific Islander, 6% Hispanic American, 0.2% Native American, 6% transferred in, 45% live on campus. *Retention:* 72% of 2001 full-time freshmen returned.

Freshmen *Admission:* 208 enrolled. *Test scores:* SAT verbal scores over 500: 48%; SAT math scores over 500: 39%; SAT verbal scores over 600: 12%; SAT math scores over 600: 10%; SAT verbal scores over 700: 3%; SAT math scores over 700: 4%.

Faculty *Total:* 84, 86% full-time, 85% with terminal degrees. *Student/faculty ratio:* 11:1.

Majors Accounting; American studies; art education; art history; biochemistry; biology; business administration; chemistry; child care/development; computer science; dietetics; early childhood education; economics; education; elementary education; English; environmental science; family/consumer studies; French; history; home economics; home economics education; humanities; liberal arts and sciences/liberal studies; mathematics; medical technology; modern languages; music teacher education; natural sciences; nursing; nutrition science; philosophy; political science; pre-law; pre-medicine; psychology; religious studies; secondary education; social sciences; social work; sociology; Spanish; special education.

Academic Programs *Special study options:* academic remediation for entering students, accelerated degree program, adult/continuing education programs, advanced placement credit, distance learning, double majors, English as a second language, honors programs, internships, off-campus study, part-time degree program, services for LD students, student-designed majors, study abroad, summer session for credit.

Library Pope Pius XII Library plus 1 other with 164,283 titles, 605 serial subscriptions, 3,282 audiovisual materials, an OPAC.

Computers on Campus 150 computers available on campus for general student use. A campuswide network can be accessed from student residence rooms and from off campus. Internet access, at least one staffed computer lab available.

Student Life *Activities and Organizations:* drama/theater group, choral group, Student Government Association, Student Nurse Association, psychology club, SJC choir, business society. *Campus security:* 24-hour emergency response devices and patrols, late-night transport/escort service, controlled dormitory access. *Student Services:* health clinic, personal/psychological counseling, legal services.

Athletics Member NCAA. All Division III. *Intercollegiate sports:* basketball W, cross-country running W, soccer W, softball W, swimming W, tennis W, volleyball W. *Intramural sports:* basketball W, soccer W, softball W, swimming W, tennis W, volleyball W.

Standardized Tests *Required:* SAT I or ACT (for admission).

Costs (2001–02) *Comprehensive fee:* $25,960 includes full-time tuition ($17,860), mandatory fees ($500), and room and board ($7600). Part-time tuition: $455 per credit. *Required fees:* $50 per course. *Room and board:* College room only: $3580. Room and board charges vary according to board plan. *Payment plan:* installment. *Waivers:* senior citizens and employees or children of employees.

Financial Aid Of all full-time matriculated undergraduates who enrolled in 2001, 100 Federal Work-Study jobs (averaging $1000). 110 State and other part-time jobs (averaging $1500). *Average financial aid package:* $16,662. *Average indebtedness upon graduation:* $12,995.

Applying *Options:* electronic application, early admission, early decision, early action, deferred entrance. *Application fee:* $35. *Required:* minimum 2.5 GPA, 1 letter of recommendation. *Application deadlines:* 5/1 (freshmen), 7/1 (transfers). *Notification:* continuous until 6/14 (freshmen), 12/15 (early action).

Admissions Contact Ms. Mary Yuskis, Director of Admissions, Saint Joseph College, 1678 Asylum Avenue, West Hartford, CT 06117. *Phone:* 860-231-5216. *Toll-free phone:* 800-285-6565. *Fax:* 860-233-5695. *E-mail:* admissions@mercy.sjc.edu.

SOUTHERN CONNECTICUT STATE UNIVERSITY

New Haven, Connecticut

- **State-supported** comprehensive, founded 1893, part of Connecticut State University System
- **Calendar** semesters
- **Degrees** bachelor's, master's, and post-master's certificates
- **Urban** 168-acre campus with easy access to New York City
- **Endowment** $1.3 million
- **Coed,** 8,316 undergraduate students, 76% full-time, 64% women, 36% men
- **Moderately difficult** entrance level, 69% of applicants were admitted

Undergraduates 6,295 full-time, 2,021 part-time. Students come from 43 states and territories, 26 other countries, 7% are from out of state, 13% African American, 2% Asian American or Pacific Islander, 5% Hispanic American, 0.2% Native American, 1% international, 9% transferred in, 33% live on campus. *Retention:* 74% of 2001 full-time freshmen returned.

Freshmen *Admission:* 4,551 applied, 3,125 admitted, 1,584 enrolled. *Test scores:* SAT verbal scores over 500: 50%; SAT math scores over 500: 44%; SAT verbal scores over 600: 9%; SAT math scores over 600: 6%; SAT verbal scores over 700: 1%; SAT math scores over 700: 1%.

Faculty *Total:* 906, 45% full-time. *Student/faculty ratio:* 15:1.

Majors Accounting; art education; art history; athletic training/sports medicine; biochemistry; biology; botany; business administration; business economics; chemistry; communications; community services; computer science; creative writing; early childhood education; earth sciences; economics; education; elementary education; English; finance; fine/studio arts; French; geography; German; graphic design/commercial art/illustration; history; Italian; journalism; liberal arts and sciences/liberal studies; library science; literature; marine biology; mathematics; microbiology/bacteriology; nursing; philosophy; physical education; physics; political science; pre-dentistry; pre-law; pre-medicine; pre-veterinary studies; psychology; public health; recreation/leisure studies; science education; secondary education; social sciences; social work; sociology; Spanish; special education; theater arts/drama; zoology.

Academic Programs *Special study options:* academic remediation for entering students, accelerated degree program, adult/continuing education programs, advanced placement credit, cooperative education, distance learning, double majors, freshman honors college, honors programs, independent study, intern-

Southern Connecticut State University (continued)

ships, off-campus study, part-time degree program, services for LD students, student-designed majors, study abroad, summer session for credit. *ROTC:* Army (c), Air Force (c).

Library Hilton C. Buley Library with 495,660 titles, 3,549 serial subscriptions, an OPAC, a Web page.

Computers on Campus 300 computers available on campus for general student use. A campuswide network can be accessed from student residence rooms and from off campus. Internet access, at least one staffed computer lab available.

Student Life *Housing Options:* coed. *Activities and Organizations:* drama/theater group, student-run newspaper, radio station, choral group, marching band, People to People, Pre-Law Society, Accounting Society, Crescent Players, Black Student Union, national fraternities, national sororities. *Campus security:* 24-hour emergency response devices and patrols, late-night transport/escort service, controlled dormitory access. *Student Services:* health clinic, personal/psychological counseling, women's center.

Athletics Member NCAA. All Division II except gymnastics (Division I). *Intercollegiate sports:* baseball M, basketball M/W, cross-country running M/W, field hockey W, football M, golf M, gymnastics M/W, soccer M/W, softball W, swimming M/W, track and field M/W, volleyball W, wrestling M(s). *Intramural sports:* badminton M/W, basketball M/W, cross-country running M/W, football M, golf M/W, gymnastics M/W, ice hockey M(c), rugby M(c)/W(c), skiing (downhill) M/W, soccer M/W, softball W, volleyball M/W.

Standardized Tests *Required:* SAT I (for admission).

Costs (2001–02) *Tuition:* state resident $2226 full-time, $190 per credit part-time; nonresident $8199 full-time, $190 per credit part-time. Full-time tuition and fees vary according to reciprocity agreements. *Required fees:* $1800 full-time. *Room and board:* $6588. Room and board charges vary according to housing facility. *Payment plan:* installment. *Waivers:* senior citizens and employees or children of employees.

Financial Aid Of all full-time matriculated undergraduates who enrolled in 2001, 4599 applied for aid, 2463 were judged to have need, 886 had their need fully met. 109 Federal Work-Study jobs (averaging $1538). In 2001, 107 non-need-based awards were made. *Average percent of need met:* 79%. *Average financial aid package:* $6056. *Average need-based loan:* $2951. *Average need-based gift aid:* $3915. *Average non-need based aid:* $2284.

Applying *Options:* common application, electronic application, deferred entrance. *Application fee:* $40. *Required:* essay or personal statement, high school transcript. *Recommended:* letters of recommendation. *Application deadlines:* 7/1 (freshmen), 7/1 (transfers). *Notification:* continuous (freshmen).

Admissions Contact Ms. Paula Kennedy, Associate Director of Admissions, Southern Connecticut State University, Admissions House, New Haven, CT 06515-1202. *Phone:* 203-392-5651. *Fax:* 203-392-5727. *E-mail:* adminfo@scsu.ctstateu.edu.

TEIKYO POST UNIVERSITY
Waterbury, Connecticut

- **Independent** 4-year, founded 1890
- **Calendar** semesters
- **Degrees** certificates, associate, bachelor's, and postbachelor's certificates
- **Suburban** 70-acre campus with easy access to Hartford
- **Endowment** $6.1 million
- **Coed,** 1,350 undergraduate students, 45% full-time, 65% women, 35% men
- **Minimally difficult** entrance level, 78% of applicants were admitted

Western Connecticut's only 4-year, private, accredited, coeducational, international business and liberal arts university. This globally focused university is known for its comprehensive and affordable education, study-abroad programs, and ideal environment for learning and growth, where students experience large-university academics in a small, collegial atmosphere.

Undergraduates 614 full-time, 736 part-time. Students come from 15 states and territories, 22 other countries, 14% are from out of state, 17% African American, 2% Asian American or Pacific Islander, 10% Hispanic American, 0.3% Native American, 4% international, 5% transferred in, 52% live on campus. *Retention:* 78% of 2001 full-time freshmen returned.

Freshmen *Admission:* 836 applied, 653 admitted, 202 enrolled. *Average high school GPA:* 2.25. *Test scores:* SAT verbal scores over 500: 18%; SAT math scores over 500: 16%; SAT verbal scores over 600: 2%; SAT math scores over 600: 5%; SAT verbal scores over 700: 1%; SAT math scores over 700: 1%.

Faculty *Total:* 153, 20% full-time. *Student/faculty ratio:* 11:1.

Majors Accounting; biology; business administration; business administration/management related; business marketing and marketing management; criminal justice/law enforcement administration; early childhood education; English; environmental science; equestrian studies; finance; history; human services; international business; liberal arts and sciences/liberal studies; management information systems/business data processing; paralegal/legal assistant; psychology; sociology.

Academic Programs *Special study options:* academic remediation for entering students, accelerated degree program, adult/continuing education programs, advanced placement credit, cooperative education, distance learning, double majors, English as a second language, independent study, internships, part-time degree program, services for LD students, study abroad, summer session for credit. *ROTC:* Army (c).

Library Trauriq Library and Resource Center with 84,066 titles, 566 serial subscriptions, 600 audiovisual materials, an OPAC.

Computers on Campus 70 computers available on campus for general student use. A campuswide network can be accessed from student residence rooms and from off campus that provide access to software applications. At least one staffed computer lab available.

Student Life *Housing:* on-campus residence required for freshman year. *Options:* coed. *Activities and Organizations:* drama/theater group, student-run newspaper, choral group, Step Squad, Post Theatrical Players, Res. Hall Council, Student Government Association, Program Board. *Campus security:* 24-hour emergency response devices and patrols, late-night transport/escort service. *Student Services:* health clinic, personal/psychological counseling.

Athletics Member NCAA, NAIA. All NCAA Division II. *Intercollegiate sports:* baseball M(s), basketball M(s)/W(s), cross-country running M(s)/W(s), equestrian sports M(s)/W(s), soccer M(s)/W(s), softball W(s), volleyball W(s). *Intramural sports:* basketball M/W, racquetball M/W, soccer M/W, softball M/W, table tennis M/W, tennis M/W, volleyball M/W, water polo M/W.

Standardized Tests *Recommended:* SAT I or ACT (for admission).

Costs (2001–02) *One-time required fee:* $100. *Comprehensive fee:* $21,800 includes full-time tuition ($14,900), mandatory fees ($300), and room and board ($6600). Part-time tuition: $495 per credit. Part-time tuition and fees vary according to class time and course load. *Payment plans:* installment, deferred payment. *Waivers:* minority students, senior citizens, and employees or children of employees.

Financial Aid Of all full-time matriculated undergraduates who enrolled in 2001, 614 applied for aid, 505 were judged to have need. 241 Federal Work-Study jobs (averaging $1262). 18 State and other part-time jobs (averaging $2056). *Average percent of need met:* 75%. *Average financial aid package:* $12,000. *Average need-based gift aid:* $4500. *Average indebtedness upon graduation:* $17,500.

Applying *Options:* common application, electronic application, deferred entrance. *Application fee:* $40. *Required:* high school transcript, 1 letter of recommendation. *Recommended:* essay or personal statement, interview. *Application deadline:* rolling (freshmen), rolling (transfers). *Notification:* continuous until 9/1 (freshmen).

Admissions Contact Mr. William Johnson, Senior Assistant Director of Admissions, Teikyo Post University, PO Box 2540, Waterbury, CT 06723. *Phone:* 203-596-4520. *Toll-free phone:* 800-345-2562. *Fax:* 203-756-5810. *E-mail:* tpuadmiss@teikyopost.edu.

TRINITY COLLEGE
Hartford, Connecticut

- **Independent** comprehensive, founded 1823
- **Calendar** semesters
- **Degrees** bachelor's and master's
- **Urban** 100-acre campus
- **Endowment** $343.0 million
- **Coed,** 2,074 undergraduate students, 91% full-time, 51% women, 49% men
- **Very difficult** entrance level, 30% of applicants were admitted

Undergraduates 1,882 full-time, 192 part-time. Students come from 46 states and territories, 41 other countries, 79% are from out of state, 6% African American, 5% Asian American or Pacific Islander, 5% Hispanic American, 0.1% Native American, 4% international, 1% transferred in, 96% live on campus. *Retention:* 91% of 2001 full-time freshmen returned.

Freshmen *Admission:* 5,476 applied, 1,668 admitted, 493 enrolled. *Test scores:* SAT verbal scores over 500: 96%; SAT math scores over 500: 97%; ACT scores over 18: 98%; SAT verbal scores over 600: 73%; SAT math scores over 600: 76%; ACT scores over 24: 77%; SAT verbal scores over 700: 20%; SAT math scores over 700: 20%; ACT scores over 30: 23%.

Faculty *Total:* 249, 79% full-time, 82% with terminal degrees. *Student/faculty ratio:* 9:1.

Majors American studies; anthropology; art; art history; biochemistry; bioengineering; biology; chemistry; classics; comparative literature; computer science;

creative writing; dance; economics; education; electrical engineering; engineering; English; fine/studio arts; French; German; history; interdisciplinary studies; international relations; Italian; Judaic studies; mathematics; mechanical engineering; modern languages; music; neuroscience; philosophy; physics; political science; psychology; public policy analysis; religious studies; Russian; sociology; Spanish; theater arts/drama; women's studies.

Academic Programs *Special study options:* accelerated degree program, adult/continuing education programs, advanced placement credit, double majors, honors programs, independent study, internships, off-campus study, student-designed majors, study abroad, summer session for credit. *ROTC:* Army (c).

Library Trinity College Library plus 2 others with 962,703 titles, 3,492 serial subscriptions, 228,596 audiovisual materials, an OPAC, a Web page.

Computers on Campus 315 computers available on campus for general student use. A campuswide network can be accessed from student residence rooms and from off campus that provide access to e-mail, Web pages. Internet access, online (class) registration, at least one staffed computer lab available.

Student Life *Housing Options:* coed, disabled students. *Activities and Organizations:* drama/theater group, student-run newspaper, radio and television station, choral group, Community Outreach, Habitat for Humanity, Activities Council, student government, Multi-Cultural Affairs Committee. *Campus security:* 24-hour emergency response devices and patrols, late-night transport/escort service, controlled dormitory access. *Student Services:* health clinic, personal/psychological counseling, women's center.

Athletics Member NCAA. All Division III. *Intercollegiate sports:* baseball M, basketball M/W, crew M/W, cross-country running M/W, equestrian sports M(c)/W(c), fencing M(c)/W(c), field hockey W, football M, golf M, ice hockey M/W, lacrosse M/W, riflery M(c)/W(c), rugby M(c)/W(c), sailing M(c)/W(c), skiing (downhill) M(c)/W(c), soccer M/W, softball W, squash M/W, swimming M/W, tennis M/W, track and field M/W, volleyball M(c)/W, water polo M(c)/W(c), wrestling M. *Intramural sports:* basketball M/W, field hockey W, football M, soccer M/W, softball M/W, squash M/W, swimming M/W, tennis M/W, track and field M/W, weight lifting M/W.

Standardized Tests *Required:* SAT II: Writing Test (for admission).

Costs (2002–03) *One-time required fee:* $25. *Comprehensive fee:* $34,300 includes full-time tuition ($25,880), mandatory fees ($906), and room and board ($7514). Part-time tuition: $8630 per term. Part-time tuition and fees vary according to program. *Room and board:* College room only: $4524. Room and board charges vary according to board plan. *Payment plan:* installment. *Waivers:* adult students and employees or children of employees.

Financial Aid Of all full-time matriculated undergraduates who enrolled in 2001, 951 applied for aid, 850 were judged to have need, 850 had their need fully met. 610 Federal Work-Study jobs (averaging $1475). 10 State and other part-time jobs (averaging $1200). In 2001, 10 non-need-based awards were made. *Average percent of need met:* 100%. *Average financial aid package:* $22,860. *Average need-based loan:* $4100. *Average need-based gift aid:* $19,799. *Average non-need based aid:* $5300. *Average indebtedness upon graduation:* $17,800. *Financial aid deadline:* 3/1.

Applying *Options:* common application, electronic application, early admission, early decision, deferred entrance. *Application fee:* $50. *Required:* essay or personal statement, high school transcript, 3 letters of recommendation. *Recommended:* interview. *Application deadlines:* 1/15 (freshmen), 4/1 (transfers). *Early decision:* 11/15 (for plan 1), 2/1 (for plan 2). *Notification:* 4/1 (freshmen), 12/15 (early decision plan 1), 2/28 (early decision plan 2).

Admissions Contact Mr. Larry Dow, Dean of Admissions and Financial Aid, Trinity College, 300 Summit Street, Hartford, CT 06106-3100. *Phone:* 860-297-2180. *Fax:* 860-297-2287. *E-mail:* admissions.office@trincoll.edu.

UNITED STATES COAST GUARD ACADEMY

New London, Connecticut

- **Federally supported** 4-year, founded 1876
- **Calendar** semesters
- **Degree** bachelor's
- **Suburban** 110-acre campus
- **Coed,** 917 undergraduate students, 100% full-time, 28% women, 72% men
- **Very difficult** entrance level, 7% of applicants were admitted

Undergraduates 917 full-time. Students come from 50 states and territories, 8 other countries, 94% are from out of state, 5% African American, 5% Asian American or Pacific Islander, 6% Hispanic American, 0.9% Native American, 2% international, 100% live on campus. *Retention:* 84% of 2001 full-time freshmen returned.

Freshmen *Admission:* 5,621 applied, 404 admitted, 282 enrolled. *Test scores:* SAT verbal scores over 500: 98%; SAT math scores over 500: 100%; ACT scores over 18: 100%; SAT verbal scores over 600: 63%; SAT math scores over 600: 78%; ACT scores over 24: 91%; SAT verbal scores over 700: 12%; SAT math scores over 700: 21%; ACT scores over 30: 30%.

Faculty *Total:* 110, 100% full-time, 41% with terminal degrees. *Student/faculty ratio:* 8:1.

Majors Civil engineering; electrical engineering; management science; marine science; mechanical engineering; naval architecture/marine engineering; operations research; political science.

Academic Programs *Special study options:* double majors, English as a second language, independent study, internships, off-campus study, summer session for credit.

Library Waesche Hall Library with 150,000 titles, 1,690 serial subscriptions, an OPAC, a Web page.

Computers on Campus 120 computers available on campus for general student use. A campuswide network can be accessed from student residence rooms and from off campus that provide access to laptop for each student. Internet access, at least one staffed computer lab available.

Student Life *Housing:* on-campus residence required through senior year. *Options:* coed. *Activities and Organizations:* drama/theater group, choral group, marching band. *Campus security:* 24-hour patrols, student patrols. *Student Services:* health clinic, personal/psychological counseling, legal services.

Athletics Member NCAA. All Division III. *Intercollegiate sports:* baseball M, basketball M/W, bowling M(c)/W(c), crew M/W, cross-country running M/W, football M, golf M(c)/W(c), ice hockey M(c), lacrosse M(c)/W(c), riflery M/W, rugby M(c)/W(c), sailing M/W, soccer M/W, softball W, swimming M/W, tennis M/W(c), track and field M/W, volleyball W, water polo M(c), wrestling M. *Intramural sports:* basketball M/W, bowling M/W, football M, golf M/W, racquetball M/W, sailing M/W, skiing (downhill) M(c)/W(c), soccer M/W, softball M/W, table tennis M/W, track and field M/W, volleyball M/W, water polo M, wrestling M.

Standardized Tests *Required:* SAT I or ACT (for admission).

Costs (2001–02) *Tuition:* Tuition, room and board, and medical and dental care are provided by the U.S. government. Each cadet receives a salary from which to pay for uniforms, supplies, and personal expenses. Entering freshmen are required to deposit $3000 to defray the initial cost of uniforms and equipment.

Applying *Options:* early action. *Required:* essay or personal statement, high school transcript, 3 letters of recommendation. *Required for some:* interview. *Application deadline:* 12/15 (freshmen). *Notification:* continuous (freshmen), 12/15 (early action).

Admissions Contact Capt. Susan D. Bibeau, Director of Admissions, United States Coast Guard Academy, 31 Mohegan Avenue, New London, CT 06320-4195. *Phone:* 860-444-8500. *Toll-free phone:* 800-883-8724. *Fax:* 860-701-6700. *E-mail:* admissions@cga.uscg.mil.

UNIVERSITY OF BRIDGEPORT

Bridgeport, Connecticut

- **Independent** comprehensive, founded 1927
- **Calendar** semesters
- **Degrees** certificates, associate, bachelor's, master's, doctoral, first professional, and post-master's certificates
- **Urban** 86-acre campus with easy access to New York City
- **Coed,** 1,181 undergraduate students, 74% full-time, 56% women, 44% men
- **Moderately difficult** entrance level, 83% of applicants were admitted

The University of Bridgeport offers scholarships and grants to students, including the Challenge Grant, which funds up to $3000; the Academic Grant, up to $6000; the Academic Scholarship, up to $10,000; and the Academic Excellence and Leadership Scholarship, which provides full tuition and room and board. All awards are renewable for four years, based on satisfactory academic achievement and good standing. Students may also be eligible for financial aid in addition to a scholarship or grant. For more information, students may telephone 800-EXCEL-UB (toll-free) or visit the Web site at http://www.bridgeport.edu.

Undergraduates 870 full-time, 311 part-time. Students come from 37 states and territories, 65 other countries, 39% are from out of state, 21% African American, 5% Asian American or Pacific Islander, 10% Hispanic American, 0.3% Native American, 34% international, 7% transferred in, 47% live on campus. *Retention:* 75% of 2001 full-time freshmen returned.

Freshmen *Admission:* 1,355 applied, 1,131 admitted, 184 enrolled. *Average high school GPA:* 2.71. *Test scores:* SAT verbal scores over 500: 33%; SAT math scores over 500: 35%; SAT verbal scores over 600: 9%; SAT math scores over 600: 15%; SAT verbal scores over 700: 2%; SAT math scores over 700: 4%.

Faculty *Total:* 302, 28% full-time. *Student/faculty ratio:* 12:1.

University of Bridgeport (continued)

Majors Accounting; art; biology; business administration; business marketing and marketing management; computer engineering; computer science; dental hygiene; economics; English; fashion merchandising; finance; graphic design/commercial art/illustration; humanities; human services; industrial design; information sciences/systems; interdisciplinary studies; interior architecture; international business; international relations; journalism; liberal arts and sciences/liberal studies; mass communications; mathematics; medical technology; music; pre-dentistry; pre-law; pre-medicine; pre-veterinary studies; religious studies; respiratory therapy; social sciences.

Academic Programs *Special study options:* academic remediation for entering students, accelerated degree program, adult/continuing education programs, advanced placement credit, cooperative education, distance learning, double majors, English as a second language, honors programs, independent study, internships, off-campus study, part-time degree program, services for LD students, student-designed majors, summer session for credit. *ROTC:* Army (b).

Library Wahlstrom Library with 272,430 titles, 2,117 serial subscriptions, 5,485 audiovisual materials, an OPAC, a Web page.

Computers on Campus 350 computers available on campus for general student use. A campuswide network can be accessed from student residence rooms and from off campus. At least one staffed computer lab available.

Student Life *Housing:* on-campus residence required through sophomore year. *Options:* coed. *Activities and Organizations:* student-run newspaper, radio station, choral group, Student Congress, International Relations Club, Black Students Alliance, Scuba Club, Japanese Student Association, national sororities. *Campus security:* 24-hour emergency response devices and patrols, student patrols, late-night transport/escort service. *Student Services:* health clinic, personal/psychological counseling, women's center.

Athletics Member NCAA. All Division II. *Intercollegiate sports:* baseball M(s), basketball M(s)/W(s), cross-country running M/W, gymnastics W(s), soccer M(s)/W(s), softball W(s), volleyball M/W(s). *Intramural sports:* basketball M/W, football M/W, golf M/W, racquetball M/W, soccer M/W, softball M/W, tennis M/W.

Standardized Tests *Required:* SAT I or ACT (for admission). *Required for some:* SAT II: Subject Tests (for admission).

Costs (2001–02) *Comprehensive fee:* $23,082 includes full-time tuition ($14,720), mandatory fees ($862), and room and board ($7500). Full-time tuition and fees vary according to program. Part-time tuition: $400 per credit. Part-time tuition and fees vary according to program. *Required fees:* $50 per term part-time. *Room and board:* College room only: $3980. Room and board charges vary according to board plan. *Payment plans:* installment, deferred payment. *Waivers:* senior citizens and employees or children of employees.

Applying *Options:* electronic application, early admission, early action, deferred entrance. *Application fee:* $40. *Required:* essay or personal statement, high school transcript, minimum 2.0 GPA. *Required for some:* interview, portfolio, audition. *Recommended:* 1 letter of recommendation, interview. *Application deadline:* 4/1 (freshmen), rolling (transfers). *Notification:* continuous until 8/1 (freshmen), 1/15 (early action).

Admissions Contact Joseph Marrone, Director of Undergraduate Admissions, University of Bridgeport, 380 University Avenue, Bridgeport, CT 06601. *Phone:* 203-576-4552. *Toll-free phone:* 800-EXCEL-UB (in-state); 800-243-9496 (out-of-state). *Fax:* 203-576-4941. *E-mail:* admit@bridgeport.edu.

UNIVERSITY OF CONNECTICUT
Storrs, Connecticut

- **State-supported** university, founded 1881
- **Calendar** semesters
- **Degrees** associate, bachelor's, master's, doctoral, first professional, and post-master's certificates
- **Rural** 4178-acre campus
- **Coed,** 14,050 undergraduate students, 93% full-time, 52% women, 48% men
- **Moderately difficult** entrance level, 68% of applicants were admitted

Recognized for its excellent academic programs, knowledgeable professors, and top-notch athletics, the University of Connecticut (UConn) has also been called a "top value" and "best buy." A top-rated research university, UConn is currently in the midst of a historic building program called UCONN 2000, which is a nationally unprecedented ten-year, $1-billion program to renew, rebuild, and enhance UConn campuses for the next century.

Undergraduates 13,085 full-time, 965 part-time. Students come from 48 states and territories, 43 other countries, 23% are from out of state, 5% African American, 6% Asian American or Pacific Islander, 5% Hispanic American, 0.2% Native American, 0.9% international, 4% transferred in, 65% live on campus. *Retention:* 88% of 2001 full-time freshmen returned.

Freshmen *Admission:* 12,843 applied, 8,791 admitted, 3,149 enrolled.

Faculty *Total:* 1,075, 96% full-time, 93% with terminal degrees.

Majors Accounting; acting/directing; actuarial science; agricultural animal husbandry/production management; agricultural economics; agricultural education; agricultural sciences; agronomy/crop science; animal sciences; anthropology; applied mathematics; art history; bioengineering; biology; biophysics; business; business marketing and marketing management; cell and molecular biology related; chemical engineering; chemistry; civil engineering; classics; communications; computer engineering; computer science; cytotechnology; dietetics; drama/theater literature; Eastern European area studies; ecology; economics; electrical engineering; elementary education; engineering physics; engineering related; English; environmental engineering; environmental science; finance; fine/studio arts; French; general studies; geography; geology; German; health/medical diagnostic and treatment services related; health services administration; history; horticulture science; horticulture services; individual/family development; industrial/manufacturing engineering; insurance/risk management; Italian; journalism; landscape architecture; Latin American studies; linguistics; management information systems/business data processing; management science; marine biology; materials engineering; mathematical statistics; mathematics; mechanical engineering; medical technology; Middle Eastern studies; multi/interdisciplinary studies related; music; music teacher education; natural resources conservation; nursing; nutritional sciences; pathology; pharmacy; philosophy; physical education; physical therapy; physics; physiology; political science; Portuguese; pre-pharmacy studies; psychology; real estate; recreation/leisure facilities management; Russian/Slavic studies; sociology; Spanish; special education; theater arts/drama; theater arts/drama and stagecraft related; theater design; urban studies; women's studies.

Academic Programs *Special study options:* academic remediation for entering students, accelerated degree program, adult/continuing education programs, advanced placement credit, cooperative education, distance learning, double majors, English as a second language, honors programs, independent study, internships, off-campus study, part-time degree program, services for LD students, student-designed majors, study abroad, summer session for credit. *ROTC:* Army (b), Air Force (b). *Unusual degree programs:* 3-2 education, pharmacy.

Library Homer Babbidge Library plus 3 others with 2.5 million titles, 9,913 serial subscriptions, 31,149 audiovisual materials, an OPAC, a Web page.

Computers on Campus 1800 computers available on campus for general student use. A campuswide network can be accessed from student residence rooms and from off campus that provide access to e-mail. Internet access, online (class) registration, at least one staffed computer lab available.

Student Life *Housing Options:* coed, men-only, women-only, disabled students. *Activities and Organizations:* drama/theater group, student-run newspaper, radio and television station, choral group, marching band, national fraternities, national sororities. *Campus security:* 24-hour emergency response devices, late-night transport/escort service. *Student Services:* health clinic, personal/psychological counseling, women's center.

Athletics Member NCAA. All Division I except football (Division I-AA). *Intercollegiate sports:* baseball M(s), basketball M(s)/W(s), crew W, cross-country running M(s)/W(s), field hockey W(s), golf M, ice hockey M(s), lacrosse W, soccer M(s)/W(s), softball W(s), swimming M(s)/W(s), tennis M/W, track and field M(s)/W(s), volleyball W(s). *Intramural sports:* badminton M/W, baseball M, basketball M/W, bowling M(c)/W(c), crew M(c), cross-country running M/W, equestrian sports M(c)/W(c), fencing M(c)/W(c), football M, gymnastics W(c), ice hockey M(c)/W(c), lacrosse M(c)/W(c), racquetball M/W, rugby M(c)/W(c), sailing M(c)/W(c), skiing (downhill) M(c)/W(c), soccer M/W, softball M/W, squash M/W, swimming M/W, table tennis M/W, tennis M/W, track and field M/W, volleyball M/W, water polo W, weight lifting M(c), wrestling M(c).

Standardized Tests *Required:* SAT I or ACT (for admission).

Costs (2001–02) *Tuition:* state resident $4448 full-time, $185 per credit part-time; nonresident $13,566 full-time, $565 per credit part-time. Part-time tuition and fees vary according to course load. *Required fees:* $1376 full-time. *Room and board:* $6298; room only: $3348. Room and board charges vary according to board plan and housing facility. *Payment plans:* installment, deferred payment. *Waivers:* employees or children of employees.

Financial Aid Of all full-time matriculated undergraduates who enrolled in 2001, 8802 applied for aid, 6172 were judged to have need, 2104 had their need fully met. In 2001, 1698 non-need-based awards were made. *Average percent of need met:* 74%. *Average financial aid package:* $8163. *Average need-based loan:* $3422. *Average need-based gift aid:* $5070. *Average non-need based aid:* $4136. *Average indebtedness upon graduation:* $14,394.

Applying *Options:* common application, early admission, early action, deferred entrance. *Application fee:* $50. *Required:* essay or personal statement, high school transcript. *Recommended:* 1 letter of recommendation. *Application deadlines:* 3/1 (freshmen), 5/1 (transfers). *Notification:* 1/1 (early action).

Admissions Contact Mr. Brian Usher, Associate Director of Admissions, University of Connecticut, 2131 Hillside Road, Unit 3088, Storrs, CT 06269-3088. *Phone:* 860-486-3137. *Fax:* 860-486-1476. *E-mail:* beahusky@uconnvm.uconn.edu.

UNIVERSITY OF HARTFORD

West Hartford, Connecticut

- **Independent** comprehensive, founded 1877
- **Calendar** semesters
- **Degrees** associate, bachelor's, master's, and doctoral
- **Suburban** 320-acre campus with easy access to Hartford
- **Endowment** $79.5 million
- **Coed,** 5,425 undergraduate students, 79% full-time, 52% women, 48% men
- **Moderately difficult** entrance level, 72% of applicants were admitted

Undergraduates 4,284 full-time, 1,141 part-time. Students come from 45 states and territories, 74 other countries, 61% are from out of state, 9% African American, 2% Asian American or Pacific Islander, 4% Hispanic American, 0.2% Native American, 4% international, 4% transferred in, 64% live on campus. *Retention:* 71% of 2001 full-time freshmen returned.

Freshmen *Admission:* 9,051 applied, 6,495 admitted, 1,434 enrolled. *Test scores:* SAT verbal scores over 500: 62%; SAT math scores over 500: 66%; ACT scores over 18: 89%; SAT verbal scores over 600: 16%; SAT math scores over 600: 19%; ACT scores over 24: 35%; SAT verbal scores over 700: 2%; SAT math scores over 700: 2%; ACT scores over 30: 8%.

Faculty *Total:* 690, 44% full-time. *Student/faculty ratio:* 13:1.

Majors Accounting; actuarial science; architectural engineering technology; art history; audio engineering; bioengineering; biology; business administration; business economics; business marketing and marketing management; ceramic arts; chemical engineering technology; chemistry; civil engineering; communications; community services; computer engineering; computer engineering technology; computer/information sciences; criminal justice/law enforcement administration; dance; drawing; early childhood education; economics; electrical/electronic engineering technology; electrical engineering; elementary education; engineering; engineering technology; English; entrepreneurship; environmental engineering; film studies; film/video production; finance; foreign languages/literatures; graphic design/commercial art/illustration; health science; history; industrial/manufacturing engineering; information sciences/systems; insurance/risk management; interdisciplinary studies; international relations; jazz; Judaic studies; legal studies; liberal arts and sciences/liberal studies; management information systems/business data processing; mathematics; mechanical engineering; mechanical engineering technology; medical radiologic technology; medical technology; music; music business management/merchandising; music (general performance); music history; music teacher education; music theory and composition; nursing; occupational therapy; painting; paralegal/legal assistant; philosophy; photography; physical therapy; physics; political science; pre-dentistry; psychology; public administration; respiratory therapy; sculpture; secondary education; sociology; special education; technical/business writing; theater arts/drama; women's studies.

Academic Programs *Special study options:* academic remediation for entering students, adult/continuing education programs, advanced placement credit, cooperative education, English as a second language, honors programs, internships, off-campus study, part-time degree program, services for LD students, student-designed majors, study abroad, summer session for credit. *ROTC:* Army (c), Air Force (c). *Unusual degree programs:* 3-2 engineering with Stonehill College.

Library Mortenson Library with 522,640 titles, 3,131 serial subscriptions, 29,096 audiovisual materials, an OPAC, a Web page.

Computers on Campus 380 computers available on campus for general student use. A campuswide network can be accessed from student residence rooms and from off campus. At least one staffed computer lab available.

Student Life *Housing Options:* coed, disabled students. *Activities and Organizations:* drama/theater group, student-run newspaper, radio and television station, choral group, Program Council, Brothers and Sisters United, Hillel, Student Government Association, Residence Hall Association, national fraternities, national sororities. *Campus security:* 24-hour emergency response devices and patrols, late-night transport/escort service, controlled dormitory access, bicycle patrols. *Student Services:* health clinic, personal/psychological counseling, women's center, legal services.

Athletics Member NCAA. All Division I. *Intercollegiate sports:* baseball M(s), basketball M(s)/W(s), cross-country running M(s)/W(s), lacrosse M(s), rugby M(c), soccer M(s)/W(s), softball W(s), tennis M(s)/W(s), volleyball M(c)/W(s). *Intramural sports:* basketball M/W, racquetball M/W, soccer M/W, tennis M/W, volleyball M/W, water polo M/W.

Standardized Tests *Required:* SAT I or ACT (for admission).

Costs (2001–02) *Comprehensive fee:* $28,884 includes full-time tuition ($19,450), mandatory fees ($1360), and room and board ($8074). Part-time tuition: $290 per credit. Part-time tuition and fees vary according to course load. *Required fees:* $110 per term part-time. *Room and board:* College room only: $4980. Room and board charges vary according to board plan and housing facility. *Payment plans:* tuition prepayment, installment. *Waivers:* senior citizens and employees or children of employees.

Financial Aid Of all full-time matriculated undergraduates who enrolled in 2001, 2927 applied for aid, 2650 were judged to have need. 357 Federal Work-Study jobs (averaging $1427). 87 State and other part-time jobs (averaging $8305). In 2001, 974 non-need-based awards were made. *Average percent of need met:* 79%. *Average financial aid package:* $16,443. *Average need-based gift aid:* $10,746. *Average non-need based aid:* $5807. *Average indebtedness upon graduation:* $19,192.

Applying *Options:* common application, electronic application, early admission, deferred entrance. *Application fee:* $35. *Required:* high school transcript. *Recommended:* essay or personal statement, 2 letters of recommendation, interview. *Application deadline:* rolling (freshmen), rolling (transfers). *Notification:* continuous (freshmen).

Admissions Contact Mr. Richard Zeiser, Dean of Admissions, University of Hartford, 200 Bloomfield Avenue, West Hartford, CT 06117-1599. *Phone:* 860-768-4296. *Toll-free phone:* 800-947-4303. *Fax:* 860-768-4961. *E-mail:* admission@mail.hartford.edu.

UNIVERSITY OF NEW HAVEN

West Haven, Connecticut

- **Independent** comprehensive, founded 1920
- **Calendar** 4-1-4
- **Degrees** associate, bachelor's, master's, and postbachelor's certificates
- **Suburban** 78-acre campus with easy access to Hartford
- **Endowment** $6.0 million
- **Coed,** 2,532 undergraduate students, 67% full-time, 42% women, 58% men
- **Moderately difficult** entrance level, 76% of applicants were admitted

The University of New Haven is a comprehensive, independent, coeducational institution offering undergraduate and graduate degrees in arts and sciences, business, engineering, hospitality and tourism, and public safety and professional studies. Small classes, close student-faculty relationships, and preparation for successful careers in today's competitive global marketplace are the hallmarks of a UNH education.

Undergraduates 1,696 full-time, 836 part-time. Students come from 28 states and territories, 52 other countries, 30% are from out of state, 12% African American, 1% Asian American or Pacific Islander, 6% Hispanic American, 0.3% Native American, 5% international, 6% transferred in, 64% live on campus. *Retention:* 73% of 2001 full-time freshmen returned.

Freshmen *Admission:* 2,471 applied, 1,875 admitted, 554 enrolled. *Average high school GPA:* 2.80. *Test scores:* SAT verbal scores over 500: 44%; SAT math scores over 500: 42%; SAT verbal scores over 600: 9%; SAT math scores over 600: 7%; SAT verbal scores over 700: 1%; SAT math scores over 700: 1%.

Faculty *Total:* 464, 37% full-time. *Student/faculty ratio:* 11:1.

Majors Accounting; aerospace engineering technology; art; aviation management; biological technology; business administration; business economics; business marketing and marketing management; chemical engineering; chemistry; civil engineering; communications; computer/information sciences; criminal justice/law enforcement administration; dental hygiene; dietetics; economics; electrical engineering; engineering; English; environmental science; finance; fire protection/safety technology; forensic technology; general retailing/wholesaling; general studies; graphic design/commercial art/illustration; history; hospitality management; hotel and restaurant management; human resources management; industrial/manufacturing engineering; industrial technology; interior architecture; international business; liberal arts and sciences/liberal studies; marine biology; materials engineering; mathematics; mechanical engineering; mechanical engineering technology; medical technology; music; music business management/merchandising; occupational safety/health technology; political science; psychology; public administration; sport/fitness administration; travel/tourism management.

Academic Programs *Special study options:* academic remediation for entering students, accelerated degree program, adult/continuing education programs, advanced placement credit, cooperative education, double majors, English as a second language, honors programs, independent study, internships, part-time degree program, services for LD students, student-designed majors, summer session for credit. *ROTC:* Navy (c). *Unusual degree programs:* 3-2 environmental science.

University of New Haven (continued)

Library Marvin K. Peterson Library with 313,385 titles, 2,261 serial subscriptions, 601 audiovisual materials, an OPAC, a Web page.

Computers on Campus 800 computers available on campus for general student use. A campuswide network can be accessed from student residence rooms and from off campus that provide access to e-mail. Internet access, at least one staffed computer lab available.

Student Life *Housing:* on-campus residence required through sophomore year. *Options:* coed. *Activities and Organizations:* drama/theater group, student-run newspaper, radio and television station, choral group, intramural athletics, WNHU (radio station), USGA (Undergraduate Student Government Association), American Criminal Justice Association, Black Student Union, national fraternities. *Campus security:* 24-hour emergency response devices and patrols, late-night transport/escort service, escort service, vehicle, bicycle and foot patrols, crime prevention programs. *Student Services:* health clinic, personal/psychological counseling.

Athletics Member NCAA. All Division II. *Intercollegiate sports:* baseball M(s), basketball M(s)/W(s), cross-country running M(s)/W(s), football M(s), golf M/W, lacrosse M/W(s), soccer M(s)/W(s), softball W(s), tennis W(s), track and field M(s)/W(s), volleyball M(s)/W(s). *Intramural sports:* basketball M/W, cross-country running M/W, football M, racquetball M/W, soccer M/W, softball M/W, table tennis M/W, tennis M/W, volleyball M/W, weight lifting M/W.

Standardized Tests *Required:* SAT I or ACT (for admission). *Recommended:* SAT I (for admission).

Costs (2001–02) *Comprehensive fee:* $23,860 includes full-time tuition ($16,200), mandatory fees ($360), and room and board ($7300). Full-time tuition and fees vary according to course load and program. Part-time tuition: $540 per credit hour. Part-time tuition and fees vary according to class time, course load, location, and program. *Room and board:* College room only: $4400. Room and board charges vary according to board plan and housing facility. *Payment plan:* installment. *Waivers:* employees or children of employees.

Financial Aid Of all full-time matriculated undergraduates who enrolled in 2001, 1292 applied for aid, 1175 were judged to have need, 290 had their need fully met. 150 Federal Work-Study jobs (averaging $1006). In 2001, 166 non-need-based awards were made. *Average percent of need met:* 71%. *Average financial aid package:* $11,623. *Average need-based loan:* $4785. *Average need-based gift aid:* $7738. *Average indebtedness upon graduation:* $16,868.

Applying *Options:* common application, deferred entrance. *Application fee:* $25. *Required:* essay or personal statement, high school transcript. *Recommended:* minimum 2.75 GPA, interview. *Application deadline:* rolling (freshmen), rolling (transfers). *Notification:* continuous (freshmen).

Admissions Contact Ms. Jane C. Sangeloty, Director of Undergraduate Admissions and Financial Aid, University of New Haven, Bayer Hall, 300 Orange Avenue, West Haven, CT 06516. *Phone:* 203-932-7319. *Toll-free phone:* 800-DIAL-UNH. *Fax:* 203-931-6093. *E-mail:* adminfo@charger.newhaven.edu.

WESLEYAN UNIVERSITY

Middletown, Connecticut

- **Independent** university, founded 1831
- **Calendar** semesters
- **Degrees** bachelor's, master's, doctoral, and post-master's certificates
- **Small-town** 120-acre campus
- **Endowment** $520.7 million
- **Coed,** 2,792 undergraduate students, 99% full-time, 53% women, 47% men
- **Most difficult** entrance level, 26% of applicants were admitted

Undergraduates 2,776 full-time, 16 part-time. Students come from 51 states and territories, 45 other countries, 90% are from out of state, 8% African American, 6% Asian American or Pacific Islander, 6% Hispanic American, 0.3% Native American, 9% international, 2% transferred in, 93% live on campus. *Retention:* 95% of 2001 full-time freshmen returned.

Freshmen *Admission:* 7,014 applied, 1,796 admitted, 722 enrolled. *Test scores:* SAT verbal scores over 500: 98%; SAT math scores over 500: 98%; ACT scores over 18: 100%; SAT verbal scores over 600: 85%; SAT math scores over 600: 89%; ACT scores over 24: 100%; SAT verbal scores over 700: 48%; SAT math scores over 700: 44%; ACT scores over 30: 75%.

Faculty *Total:* 336, 93% full-time, 93% with terminal degrees. *Student/faculty ratio:* 9:1.

Majors African-American studies; American studies; anthropology; art history; astronomy; biochemistry; biology; chemistry; classics; computer science; dance; earth sciences; East Asian studies; Eastern European area studies; economics; English; environmental science; film studies; fine/studio arts; French; German; history; humanities; interdisciplinary studies; Italian; Latin American studies; mathematics; medieval/renaissance studies; molecular biology; music; neuroscience; philosophy; physics; political science; psychology; religious studies; romance languages; Russian; Russian/Slavic studies; science/technology and society; social sciences; sociology; Spanish; theater arts/drama; women's studies.

Academic Programs *Special study options:* accelerated degree program, adult/continuing education programs, advanced placement credit, double majors, English as a second language, independent study, internships, off-campus study, services for LD students, student-designed majors, study abroad, summer session for credit. *ROTC:* Air Force (c). *Unusual degree programs:* 3-2 engineering with Columbia University, California Institute of Technology.

Library Olin Memorial Library plus 3 others with 1.2 million titles, 2,719 serial subscriptions, 42,137 audiovisual materials, an OPAC, a Web page.

Computers on Campus 250 computers available on campus for general student use. A campuswide network can be accessed from student residence rooms and from off campus that provide access to electronic portfolio. Internet access, online (class) registration, at least one staffed computer lab available.

Student Life *Housing:* on-campus residence required for freshman year. *Options:* coed. *Activities and Organizations:* drama/theater group, student-run newspaper, radio station, choral group, community service, Students of Color groups, theater (student and faculty productions), campus publications, Intramurals, national fraternities, national sororities. *Campus security:* 24-hour emergency response devices and patrols, student patrols, late-night transport/escort service, controlled dormitory access. *Student Services:* health clinic, personal/psychological counseling, women's center.

Athletics Member NCAA. All Division III. *Intercollegiate sports:* baseball M, basketball M/W, crew M/W, cross-country running M/W, equestrian sports M(c)/W(c), field hockey W, football M, golf M/W, ice hockey M/W, lacrosse M/W, rugby M(c)/W(c), sailing M(c)/W(c), skiing (downhill) M(c)/W(c), soccer M/W, softball W, squash M/W, swimming M/W, table tennis M(c)/W(c), tennis M/W, track and field M/W, volleyball M(c)/W, water polo M(c)/W(c), wrestling M. *Intramural sports:* badminton M/W, basketball M/W, bowling M/W, crew M/W, cross-country running M/W, ice hockey M/W, racquetball M/W, soccer M/W, softball M/W, squash M/W, table tennis M/W, tennis M/W, track and field M/W, volleyball M/W.

Standardized Tests *Required:* SAT II: Writing Test (for admission).

Costs (2001–02) *Comprehensive fee:* $34,050 includes full-time tuition ($26,290), mandatory fees ($810), and room and board ($6950). Full-time tuition and fees vary according to program. Part-time tuition and fees vary according to program. *Room and board:* College room only: $4510. Room and board charges vary according to board plan and housing facility. *Payment plan:* installment. *Waivers:* employees or children of employees.

Financial Aid Of all full-time matriculated undergraduates who enrolled in 2001, 1389 applied for aid, 1266 were judged to have need, 1266 had their need fully met. 1246 Federal Work-Study jobs (averaging $1407). 40 State and other part-time jobs (averaging $1660). *Average percent of need met:* 100%. *Average financial aid package:* $23,549. *Average need-based loan:* $5449. *Average need-based gift aid:* $18,069. *Average indebtedness upon graduation:* $23,323. *Financial aid deadline:* 2/1.

Applying *Options:* common application, electronic application, early admission, early decision, deferred entrance. *Application fee:* $55. *Required:* essay or personal statement, high school transcript, 3 letters of recommendation. *Recommended:* interview. *Application deadlines:* 1/1 (freshmen), 3/15 (transfers). *Early decision:* 11/15 (for plan 1), 1/1 (for plan 2). *Notification:* 4/1 (freshmen), 12/15 (early decision plan 1), 2/20 (early decision plan 2).

Admissions Contact Mrs. Nancy Hargrave Meislahn, Dean of Admission and Financial Aid, Wesleyan University, Stewart M Reid House, 70 Wyllys Avenue, Middletown, CT 06459-0265. *Phone:* 860-685-3000. *Fax:* 860-685-3001. *E-mail:* admissions@wesleyan.edu.

WESTERN CONNECTICUT STATE UNIVERSITY

Danbury, Connecticut

- **State-supported** comprehensive, founded 1903, part of Connecticut State University System
- **Calendar** semesters
- **Degrees** associate, bachelor's, and master's
- **Urban** 340-acre campus with easy access to New York City
- **Coed,** 5,080 undergraduate students, 71% full-time, 53% women, 47% men
- **Moderately difficult** entrance level, 67% of applicants were admitted

Undergraduates 3,583 full-time, 1,497 part-time. Students come from 22 states and territories, 21 other countries, 11% are from out of state, 7% African American, 3% Asian American or Pacific Islander, 6% Hispanic American, 0.5% Native American, 0.7% international, 7% transferred in, 32% live on campus. *Retention:* 71% of 2001 full-time freshmen returned.

Freshmen *Admission:* 2,900 applied, 1,931 admitted, 871 enrolled. *Test scores:* SAT verbal scores over 500: 41%; SAT math scores over 500: 40%; SAT verbal scores over 600: 7%; SAT math scores over 600: 8%; SAT verbal scores over 700: 1%; SAT math scores over 700: 1%.

Faculty *Total:* 442, 43% full-time. *Student/faculty ratio:* 17:1.

Majors Accounting; American studies; anthropology; art; atmospheric sciences; biology; business administration; business marketing and marketing management; chemistry; community health liaison; computer science; earth sciences; economics; education; elementary education; English; environmental science; finance; graphic design/commercial art/illustration; health education; history; law enforcement/police science; liberal arts and sciences/liberal studies; management information systems/business data processing; mass communications; mathematics; medical technology; music; music history; music teacher education; nursing; political science; pre-dentistry; pre-medicine; psychology; secondary education; social sciences; social work; sociology; Spanish; theater arts/drama.

Academic Programs *Special study options:* academic remediation for entering students, accelerated degree program, adult/continuing education programs, advanced placement credit, cooperative education, distance learning, double majors, English as a second language, honors programs, independent study, internships, off-campus study, part-time degree program, services for LD students, student-designed majors, study abroad, summer session for credit. *ROTC:* Army (c), Air Force (c).

Library Ruth Haas Library plus 1 other with 261,328 titles, 2,538 serial subscriptions, 10,846 audiovisual materials, an OPAC, a Web page.

Computers on Campus 400 computers available on campus for general student use. A campuswide network can be accessed from student residence rooms and from off campus. Internet access, at least one staffed computer lab available.

Student Life *Housing Options:* coed, women-only. *Activities and Organizations:* drama/theater group, student-run newspaper, radio station, choral group, Black Student Alliance, Inter-Cultural Advisory Council, Greek Council, Education Club, History Society, national fraternities, national sororities. *Campus security:* 24-hour emergency response devices and patrols, student patrols, late-night transport/escort service, controlled dormitory access. *Student Services:* health clinic, personal/psychological counseling.

Athletics Member NCAA. All Division III. *Intercollegiate sports:* baseball M, basketball M/W, cross-country running W, football M, lacrosse W, soccer M/W, softball W, swimming W, tennis M/W, volleyball W. *Intramural sports:* basketball M/W, football M/W, ice hockey M(c), lacrosse M(c), rugby M(c), soccer M/W, softball M/W, volleyball M(c).

Standardized Tests *Required:* SAT I or ACT (for admission).

Costs (2002–03) *Tuition:* state resident $2321 full-time, $215 per semester hour part-time; nonresident $8540 full-time, $215 per semester hour part-time. Full-time tuition and fees vary according to reciprocity agreements. *Required fees:* $2134 full-time. *Room and board:* $6224; room only: $4120. Room and board charges vary according to housing facility. *Payment plan:* installment. *Waivers:* senior citizens and employees or children of employees.

Financial Aid Of all full-time matriculated undergraduates who enrolled in 2001, 2261 applied for aid, 1381 were judged to have need, 327 had their need fully met. 81 Federal Work-Study jobs (averaging $1497). 469 State and other part-time jobs (averaging $2187). In 2001, 51 non-need-based awards were made. *Average percent of need met:* 65%. *Average financial aid package:* $5655. *Average need-based loan:* $3155. *Average need-based gift aid:* $3281. *Average non-need based aid:* $3043. *Financial aid deadline:* 4/15.

Applying *Options:* common application, electronic application, early admission, deferred entrance. *Application fee:* $40. *Required:* high school transcript. *Recommended:* essay or personal statement, letters of recommendation, interview. *Application deadlines:* 5/1 (freshmen), 7/1 (transfers).

Admissions Contact Mr. William Hawkins, Enrollment Management Officer, Western Connecticut State University, 181 White Street, Danbury, CT 06810. *Phone:* 203-837-9000. *Toll-free phone:* 877-837-9278.

YALE UNIVERSITY

New Haven, Connecticut

- **Independent** university, founded 1701
- **Calendar** semesters
- **Degrees** bachelor's, master's, doctoral, first professional, and post-master's certificates
- **Urban** 200-acre campus with easy access to New York City
- **Endowment** $10.1 billion
- **Coed,** 5,286 undergraduate students, 99% full-time, 49% women, 51% men
- **Most difficult** entrance level, 14% of applicants were admitted

Undergraduates 5,253 full-time, 33 part-time. Students come from 55 states and territories, 74 other countries, 90% are from out of state, 8% African American, 14% Asian American or Pacific Islander, 6% Hispanic American, 0.7% Native American, 7% international, 0.5% transferred in, 83% live on campus. *Retention:* 98% of 2001 full-time freshmen returned.

Freshmen *Admission:* 14,809 applied, 2,038 admitted, 1,296 enrolled.

Faculty *Total:* 1,298, 75% full-time, 84% with terminal degrees. *Student/faculty ratio:* 7:1.

Majors African-American studies; African studies; American studies; anthropology; applied mathematics; archaeology; architecture; art; art history; astronomy; astrophysics; bioengineering; biology; cell and molecular biology related; chemical engineering; chemistry; Chinese; classics; cognitive psychology/psycholinguistics; computer/information sciences; cultural studies; East Asian studies; ecology; economics; electrical engineering; engineering physics; engineering science; English; environmental engineering; environmental science; ethnic/cultural studies related; evolutionary biology; film studies; foreign languages/literatures related; French; geological sciences related; German; Greek (ancient and medieval); history; humanities; Italian; Japanese; Judaic studies; Latin American studies; Latin (ancient and medieval); linguistics; literature; mathematics; mathematics/computer science; mechanical engineering; molecular biology; multi/interdisciplinary studies related; music; philosophy; physics; political science; Portuguese; psychology; religious studies; Russian; Russian/Slavic studies; sociology; South Asian languages; Spanish; systems science/theory; theater arts/drama; women's studies.

Academic Programs *Special study options:* accelerated degree program, advanced placement credit, double majors, English as a second language, honors programs, independent study, part-time degree program, student-designed majors, study abroad, summer session for credit. *ROTC:* Army (c), Air Force (c).

Library Sterling Memorial Library plus 20 others with 10.8 million titles, 57,377 serial subscriptions, an OPAC, a Web page.

Computers on Campus 350 computers available on campus for general student use. A campuswide network can be accessed from student residence rooms and from off campus. At least one staffed computer lab available.

Student Life *Housing:* on-campus residence required through sophomore year. *Options:* coed. *Activities and Organizations:* drama/theater group, student-run newspaper, radio station, choral group, marching band, community service, intramural sports, theater productions, music groups, campus publications, national fraternities, national sororities. *Campus security:* 24-hour emergency response devices and patrols, late-night transport/escort service, controlled dormitory access. *Student Services:* health clinic, personal/psychological counseling, women's center.

Athletics Member NCAA. All Division I except football (Division I-AA). *Intercollegiate sports:* baseball M, basketball M/W, crew M/W, cross-country running M/W, fencing M/W, field hockey W, golf M/W, gymnastics W, ice hockey M/W, lacrosse M/W, soccer M/W, softball W, squash M/W, swimming M/W, table tennis M(c), tennis M/W, track and field M/W, volleyball M(c)/W. *Intramural sports:* badminton M(c)/W(c), baseball M, basketball M/W, bowling M/W, crew M/W, cross-country running M/W, equestrian sports M(c)/W(c), field hockey W, football M/W, golf M/W, ice hockey M/W, racquetball M/W, riflery M(c)/W(c), rugby M(c)/W(c), sailing M(c)/W(c), skiing (cross-country) M(c)/W(c), skiing (downhill) M(c)/W(c), soccer M/W, softball M/W, squash M/W, swimming M/W, table tennis M/W, tennis M/W, volleyball M/W, water polo M/W, wrestling M(c).

Costs (2001–02) *Comprehensive fee:* $34,030 includes full-time tuition ($26,100) and room and board ($7930). *Payment plan:* installment. *Waivers:* employees or children of employees.

Financial Aid Of all full-time matriculated undergraduates who enrolled in 2001, 3475 applied for aid, 2052 were judged to have need, 2052 had their need fully met. *Average percent of need met:* 100%. *Average financial aid package:* $23,178. *Average need-based loan:* $5448. *Average need-based gift aid:* $17,246. *Average indebtedness upon graduation:* $18,786.

Applying *Options:* electronic application, early admission, early decision, deferred entrance. *Application fee:* $65. *Required:* essay or personal statement, high school transcript, 3 letters of recommendation. *Recommended:* interview. *Application deadlines:* 12/31 (freshmen), 3/1 (transfers). *Early decision:* 11/1. *Notification:* 4/1 (freshmen), 12/15 (early decision).

Admissions Contact Admissions Director, Yale University, PO Box 208234, New Haven, CT 06520-8324. *Phone:* 203-432-9300. *Fax:* 203-432-9392. *E-mail:* undergraduate.admissions@yale.edu.

DELAWARE

DELAWARE STATE UNIVERSITY

Dover, Delaware

- **State-supported** comprehensive, founded 1891, part of Delaware Higher Education Commission

Delaware State University (continued)
- **Calendar** semesters
- **Degrees** bachelor's and master's
- **Small-town** 400-acre campus
- **Endowment** $13.4 million
- **Coed,** 3,084 undergraduate students, 78% full-time, 57% women, 43% men
- **Moderately difficult** entrance level, 68% of applicants were admitted

Undergraduates 2,403 full-time, 681 part-time. Students come from 31 states and territories, 44% are from out of state, 79% African American, 1% Asian American or Pacific Islander, 2% Hispanic American, 0.5% Native American, 1% international, 6% transferred in, 46% live on campus. *Retention:* 68% of 2001 full-time freshmen returned.

Freshmen *Admission:* 2,712 applied, 1,844 admitted, 841 enrolled. *Average high school GPA:* 2.81.

Faculty *Total:* 249, 70% full-time. *Student/faculty ratio:* 15:1.

Majors Accounting; agricultural business; agricultural education; agricultural sciences; aircraft pilot (professional); animal sciences; architectural engineering technology; art; art education; aviation management; banking; biology; business administration; business economics; business education; business marketing and marketing management; chemistry; civil engineering; civil engineering technology; clothing/textiles; computer/information sciences; computer science; criminal justice/law enforcement administration; early childhood education; economics; education; electrical/electronic engineering technology; elementary education; engineering technology; English; environmental health; fish/game management; French; health education; health science; history; home economics; hotel and restaurant management; human services; information sciences/systems; journalism; mass communications; mathematics; mechanical engineering; mechanical engineering technology; music; music teacher education; natural resources management; nursing; nutrition science; physical education; physics; political science; pre-veterinary studies; psychology; recreation/leisure facilities management; recreation/leisure studies; science education; social work; sociology; Spanish; special education; sport/fitness administration; theater arts/drama; trade/industrial education; wildlife management.

Academic Programs *Special study options:* academic remediation for entering students, accelerated degree program, adult/continuing education programs, advanced placement credit, cooperative education, distance learning, double majors, English as a second language, honors programs, independent study, internships, off-campus study, part-time degree program, services for LD students, student-designed majors, summer session for credit. *ROTC:* Army (b), Air Force (b). *Unusual degree programs:* 3-2 engineering with University of Delaware.

Library William C. Jason Library with 204,127 titles, 3,094 serial subscriptions, 13,775 audiovisual materials, an OPAC.

Computers on Campus 641 computers available on campus for general student use. A campuswide network can be accessed from student residence rooms and from off campus that provide access to online grade access, e-mail. Internet access, online (class) registration, at least one staffed computer lab available.

Student Life *Activities and Organizations:* drama/theater group, student-run newspaper, radio and television station, choral group, marching band, NAACP, Women's Senate, Men's Council, national fraternities, national sororities. *Campus security:* 24-hour emergency response devices and patrols, student patrols, late-night transport/escort service, controlled dormitory access. *Student Services:* health clinic, personal/psychological counseling, women's center.

Athletics Member NCAA. All Division I except football (Division I-AA). *Intercollegiate sports:* baseball M, basketball M(s)/W(s), bowling W(s), cross-country running M(s)/W(s), softball W(s), tennis M(s)/W(s), track and field M(s)/W(s), volleyball W(s), wrestling M(s). *Intramural sports:* basketball M/W, bowling M/W, field hockey W, football M, racquetball M/W, swimming M/W, table tennis M/W, tennis M/W, volleyball M/W.

Standardized Tests *Required:* SAT I or ACT (for admission).

Costs (2001–02) *Tuition:* state resident $3422 full-time, $143 per credit hour part-time; nonresident $7696 full-time, $321 per credit hour part-time. Full-time tuition and fees vary according to course load. *Required fees:* $260 full-time, $40 per term part-time. *Room and board:* $5362. Room and board charges vary according to housing facility. *Payment plans:* installment, deferred payment. *Waivers:* senior citizens and employees or children of employees.

Financial Aid Of all full-time matriculated undergraduates who enrolled in 2001, 1855 applied for aid, 1660 were judged to have need, 708 had their need fully met. *Average percent of need met:* 73%. *Average financial aid package:* $5745.

Applying *Options:* common application, electronic application, early admission. *Application fee:* $15. *Required:* high school transcript, minimum 2.0 GPA, 2 letters of recommendation. *Recommended:* interview. *Application deadlines:* 4/1 (freshmen), 4/1 (transfers).

Admissions Contact Mr. Jethro C. Williams, Director of Admissions, Delaware State University, 1200 North Dupont Highway, Dover, DE 19901. *Phone:* 302-857-6353. *Fax:* 302-857-6352. *E-mail:* dadmiss@dsc.edu.

GOLDEY-BEACOM COLLEGE
Wilmington, Delaware

- **Independent** comprehensive, founded 1886
- **Calendar** semesters
- **Degrees** associate, bachelor's, and master's
- **Suburban** 27-acre campus with easy access to Philadelphia
- **Endowment** $1.7 million
- **Coed**
- **Moderately difficult** entrance level, 84% of applicants were admitted

Goldey-Beacom is a small, private, nationally accredited college offering challenging undergraduate degrees in business as well as a master's in business administration. The College is known for dedicated faculty members, small class size, and individual attention and is recognized regionally as a leader in the business field. Apartment-style housing is available on the safe, suburban campus located 15 minutes from downtown Wilmington.

Undergraduates Students come from 15 states and territories, 50 other countries, 50% are from out of state, 16% live on campus. *Retention:* 70% of 2001 full-time freshmen returned.

Freshmen *Admission:* 684 applied, 574 admitted. *Average high school GPA:* 2.97. *Test scores:* SAT verbal scores over 500: 33%; SAT math scores over 500: 32%; SAT verbal scores over 600: 6%; SAT math scores over 600: 6%; SAT verbal scores over 700: 1%; SAT math scores over 700: 2%.

Faculty *Total:* 49, 51% full-time, 43% with terminal degrees. *Student/faculty ratio:* 28:1.

Majors Accounting; business administration; business marketing and marketing management; finance; information sciences/systems; international business; management information systems/business data processing.

Academic Programs *Special study options:* academic remediation for entering students, accelerated degree program, advanced placement credit, cooperative education, honors programs, internships, part-time degree program, study abroad, summer session for credit.

Library J. Wilbur Hirons Library with 29,700 titles, 817 serial subscriptions, a Web page.

Computers on Campus 136 computers available on campus for general student use. A campuswide network can be accessed from student residence rooms and from off campus. Internet access, at least one staffed computer lab available.

Student Life *Housing Options:* coed. *Activities and Organizations:* drama/theater group, student-run newspaper, choral group, Marketing/Management Association, Circle K International, Data Processing Management Association, GBC singers, national fraternities, national sororities. *Campus security:* 24-hour emergency response devices. *Student Services:* health clinic.

Athletics Member NCAA. All Division II. *Intercollegiate sports:* basketball M(s)/W(s), field hockey W(c), soccer M(s)/W(s), softball W(s), volleyball W(s). *Intramural sports:* basketball M/W, football M, golf M/W, soccer M/W, softball M/W, tennis M/W, volleyball M/W.

Standardized Tests *Required:* SAT I (for admission).

Costs (2002–03) *Tuition:* $10,132 full-time, $298 per credit hour part-time. *Required fees:* $5 per credit hour. *Room only:* $3937. *Payment plans:* installment, deferred payment. *Waivers:* employees or children of employees.

Financial Aid Of all full-time matriculated undergraduates who enrolled in 2001, 523 applied for aid, 497 were judged to have need.

Applying *Options:* common application, electronic application, early admission, deferred entrance. *Application fee:* $30. *Required:* high school transcript, minimum 2.0 GPA. *Required for some:* 1 letter of recommendation, interview. *Application deadline:* rolling (freshmen), rolling (transfers). *Notification:* continuous until 8/15 (freshmen).

Admissions Contact Mr. Kevin M. McIntyre, Dean of Admissions, Goldey-Beacom College, 4701 Limestone Road, Wilmington, DE 19808-1999. *Phone:* 302-998-8814 Ext. 266. *Toll-free phone:* 800-833-4877. *Fax:* 302-996-5408. *E-mail:* mcintyrk@goldey.gbc.edu.

UNIVERSITY OF DELAWARE
Newark, Delaware

- **State-related** university, founded 1743
- **Calendar** 4-1-4

- **Degrees** associate, bachelor's, master's, and doctoral (enrollment data for undergraduate students does not include non-degree-seeking students)
- **Small-town** 1000-acre campus with easy access to Philadelphia and Baltimore
- **Endowment** $942.0 million
- **Coed,** 17,431 undergraduate students, 84% full-time, 58% women, 42% men
- **Moderately difficult** entrance level, 53% of applicants were admitted

Undergraduates 14,694 full-time, 2,737 part-time. Students come from 50 states and territories, 100 other countries, 59% are from out of state, 6% African American, 3% Asian American or Pacific Islander, 3% Hispanic American, 0.2% Native American, 1% international, 3% transferred in, 53% live on campus. *Retention:* 88% of 2001 full-time freshmen returned.

Freshmen *Admission:* 18,209 applied, 9,581 admitted, 3,320 enrolled. *Average high school GPA:* 3.45. *Test scores:* SAT verbal scores over 500: 87%; SAT math scores over 500: 90%; ACT scores over 18: 96%; SAT verbal scores over 600: 34%; SAT math scores over 600: 47%; ACT scores over 24: 55%; SAT verbal scores over 700: 4%; SAT math scores over 700: 7%; ACT scores over 30: 9%.

Faculty *Total:* 1,295, 85% full-time, 77% with terminal degrees. *Student/faculty ratio:* 13:1.

Majors Accounting; African-American studies; agribusiness; agricultural business; agricultural economics; agricultural education; agricultural engineering; agricultural sciences; agronomy/crop science; animal sciences; anthropology; applied art; architectural history; art; art history; astronomy; astrophysics; athletic training/sports medicine; bilingual/bicultural education; biochemistry; biological technology; biology; biology education; biotechnology research; botany; business administration; business economics; business marketing and marketing management; chemical engineering; chemistry; chemistry education; child care/development; civil engineering; classics; communications; community services; comparative literature; computer engineering; computer/information sciences; computer science; consumer economics; criminal justice/law enforcement administration; developmental/child psychology; dietetics; early childhood education; East Asian studies; ecology; economics; education; electrical engineering; elementary education; engineering; English; English education; entomology; environmental engineering; environmental science; environmental technology; exercise sciences; family/community studies; family/consumer studies; fashion design/illustration; fashion merchandising; film studies; finance; food sales operations; food sciences; foreign languages education; foreign languages/literatures; French; geography; geology; geophysics/seismology; German; graphic design/commercial art/illustration; health education; health/physical education; history; history education; horticulture science; hotel and restaurant management; individual/family development; international relations; Italian; journalism; Latin American studies; Latin (ancient and medieval); liberal arts and sciences/liberal studies; linguistics; mass communications; mathematics; mathematics education; mechanical engineering; medical technology; middle school education; music; music (piano and organ performance); music teacher education; music theory and composition; music (voice and choral/opera performance); natural resources management; neuroscience; nursing; nursing science; nutritional sciences; nutrition science; nutrition studies; operations management; ornamental horticulture; paleontology; philosophy; physical education; physics; physics education; plant protection; political science; pre-veterinary studies; psychology; public relations; recreation/leisure facilities management; Russian; science education; secondary education; sociology; soil conservation; soil sciences; Spanish; special education; teaching English as a second language; technical/business writing; theater design; wildlife management; women's studies.

Academic Programs *Special study options:* academic remediation for entering students, accelerated degree program, adult/continuing education programs, advanced placement credit, cooperative education, distance learning, double majors, English as a second language, honors programs, independent study, internships, part-time degree program, services for LD students, student-designed majors, study abroad, summer session for credit. *ROTC:* Army (b), Air Force (b).

Library Hugh Morris Library plus 3 others with 2.4 million titles, 12,633 serial subscriptions, 12,746 audiovisual materials, an OPAC, a Web page.

Computers on Campus 900 computers available on campus for general student use. A campuswide network can be accessed from student residence rooms and from off campus. At least one staffed computer lab available.

Student Life *Housing:* on-campus residence required for freshman year. *Options:* coed, women-only, disabled students. *Activities and Organizations:* drama/theater group, student-run newspaper, radio and television station, choral group, marching band, Undergraduate Student Congress, Resident Student Association, Black Student Union, HOLA (Hispanic Student Association), national fraternities, national sororities. *Campus security:* 24-hour emergency response devices and patrols, student patrols, late-night transport/escort service, controlled dormitory access. *Student Services:* health clinic, personal/psychological counseling, women's center.

Athletics Member NCAA. All Division I except football (Division I-AA). *Intercollegiate sports:* baseball M(s), basketball M(s)/W(s), bowling M(c)/W(c), crew M(c)/W(s), cross-country running M/W, equestrian sports M(c)/W(c), field hockey W(s), golf M, ice hockey M(c), lacrosse M(s)/W(s), rugby W(c), sailing M(c)/W(c), soccer M(s)/W(s), softball W(s), swimming M/W(s), tennis M/W, track and field M/W(s), volleyball W(s), wrestling M(c). *Intramural sports:* badminton M/W, basketball M/W, field hockey W(c), football M/W, golf M/W, lacrosse M(c)/W(c), racquetball M/W, soccer M/W(c), softball M/W, squash M/W, table tennis M/W, tennis M/W, volleyball M(c)/W(c), water polo M/W.

Standardized Tests *Required:* SAT I or ACT (for admission). *Recommended:* SAT II: Subject Tests (for admission), SAT II: Writing Test (for admission).

Costs (2001–02) *Tuition:* state resident $4770 full-time, $199 per credit hour part-time; nonresident $13,860 full-time, $578 per credit hour part-time. *Required fees:* $520 full-time, $15 per term part-time. *Room and board:* $5534; room only: $3064. Room and board charges vary according to housing facility. *Payment plans:* tuition prepayment, installment. *Waivers:* senior citizens and employees or children of employees.

Financial Aid Of all full-time matriculated undergraduates who enrolled in 2001, 8107 applied for aid, 5377 were judged to have need, 2930 had their need fully met. In 2001, 3069 non-need-based awards were made. *Average percent of need met:* 84%. *Average financial aid package:* $9277. *Average need-based loan:* $4410. *Average need-based gift aid:* $5425. *Average indebtedness upon graduation:* $13,993. *Financial aid deadline:* 3/15.

Applying *Options:* common application, electronic application, early admission, early decision, deferred entrance. *Application fee:* $55. *Required:* essay or personal statement, high school transcript, 1 letter of recommendation. *Application deadlines:* 2/15 (freshmen), 5/1 (transfers). *Early decision:* 11/15. *Notification:* 3/15 (freshmen), 12/15 (early decision).

Admissions Contact Mr. Larry Griffith, Director of Admissions, University of Delaware, 116 Hullihen Hall, Newark, DE 19716. *Phone:* 302-831-8123. *Fax:* 302-831-6905. *E-mail:* admissions@udel.edu.

WESLEY COLLEGE
Dover, Delaware

- **Independent United Methodist** comprehensive, founded 1873
- **Calendar** semesters
- **Degrees** certificates, associate, bachelor's, master's, and postbachelor's certificates
- **Small-town** 20-acre campus
- **Endowment** $5.0 million
- **Coed,** 1,424 undergraduate students, 78% full-time, 54% women, 46% men
- **Moderately difficult** entrance level, 77% of applicants were admitted

Undergraduates 1,110 full-time, 314 part-time. Students come from 12 states and territories, 9 other countries, 58% are from out of state, 18% African American, 2% Asian American or Pacific Islander, 2% Hispanic American, 0.4% Native American, 1% international, 4% transferred in, 62% live on campus. *Retention:* 58% of 2001 full-time freshmen returned.

Freshmen *Admission:* 1,532 applied, 1,185 admitted, 415 enrolled. *Average high school GPA:* 2.81. *Test scores:* SAT verbal scores over 500: 37%; SAT math scores over 500: 36%; SAT verbal scores over 600: 5%; SAT math scores over 600: 6%.

Faculty *Total:* 92, 62% full-time, 54% with terminal degrees. *Student/faculty ratio:* 18:1.

Majors Accounting; American studies; biology; business administration; business marketing and marketing management; education; elementary education; English; environmental science; exercise sciences; history; liberal arts and sciences/liberal studies; mass communications; medical technology; nursing; paralegal/legal assistant; physical education; psychology; secondary education.

Academic Programs *Special study options:* academic remediation for entering students, accelerated degree program, adult/continuing education programs, advanced placement credit, double majors, English as a second language, external degree program, independent study, internships, part-time degree program, study abroad, summer session for credit.

Library Robert H. Parker Library with 72,000 titles, 400 serial subscriptions, 1,814 audiovisual materials, an OPAC, a Web page.

Computers on Campus 115 computers available on campus for general student use. A campuswide network can be accessed from student residence rooms. Internet access, at least one staffed computer lab available.

Student Life *Housing:* on-campus residence required for freshman year. *Options:* coed, men-only, women-only. *Activities and Organizations:* drama/theater group, student-run newspaper, radio station, choral group, Student Activity Board, Student Government Association, National Coeducation Community

Wesley College (continued)
Service Organization, national fraternities, national sororities. *Campus security:* 24-hour patrols, controlled dormitory access. *Student Services:* health clinic, personal/psychological counseling.

Athletics Member NCAA. All Division III. *Intercollegiate sports:* baseball M, basketball M/W, field hockey W, football M, golf M, lacrosse M/W, soccer M/W, softball W, tennis M/W. *Intramural sports:* basketball M/W, cross-country running M/W, football M/W, soccer M/W, track and field M/W, volleyball M/W.

Standardized Tests *Required:* SAT I or ACT (for placement).

Costs (2002–03) *Comprehensive fee:* $18,933 includes full-time tuition ($12,418), mandatory fees ($705), and room and board ($5810). Full-time tuition and fees vary according to class time and program. Part-time tuition: $510 per credit hour. *Required fees:* $15 per term part-time. *Room and board:* College room only: $2910. Room and board charges vary according to board plan. *Payment plan:* installment. *Waivers:* senior citizens and employees or children of employees.

Applying *Options:* common application, electronic application, early admission, early decision, deferred entrance. *Application fee:* $20. *Required:* essay or personal statement, high school transcript, minimum 2.2 GPA, 1 letter of recommendation. *Recommended:* interview. *Application deadline:* rolling (freshmen), rolling (transfers). *Early decision:* 11/15. *Notification:* 12/1 (early decision).

Admissions Contact Mr. Art Jacobs, Director of Admissions, Wesley College, 120 North State Street, Dover, DE 19901-3875. *Phone:* 302-736-2400. *Toll-free phone:* 800-937-5398 Ext. 2400. *Fax:* 302-736-2301. *E-mail:* admissions@mail.wesley.edu.

WILMINGTON COLLEGE
New Castle, Delaware

- **Independent** comprehensive, founded 1967
- **Calendar** semesters
- **Degrees** certificates, associate, bachelor's, master's, doctoral, post-master's, and postbachelor's certificates
- **Suburban** 17-acre campus with easy access to Philadelphia
- **Endowment** $15.0 million
- **Coed,** 3,927 undergraduate students, 36% full-time, 69% women, 31% men
- **Noncompetitive** entrance level, 99% of applicants were admitted

Wilmington College is a small career-oriented college that specializes in offering a personal learning atmosphere to every student. Wilmington College encourages applications from students who, in its judgment, show promise of academic achievement, regardless of past performance. Applications are reviewed and accepted on a continuous basis. Freshmen and transfer students are admitted to the fall, spring, and summer terms.

Undergraduates 1,430 full-time, 2,497 part-time. Students come from 7 states and territories, 8 other countries, 12% African American, 0.5% Asian American or Pacific Islander, 2% Hispanic American, 0.2% Native American. *Retention:* 85% of 2001 full-time freshmen returned.

Freshmen *Admission:* 738 applied, 733 admitted, 1,046 enrolled. *Average high school GPA:* 2.50.

Faculty *Total:* 584, 8% full-time. *Student/faculty ratio:* 18:1.

Majors Accounting; aircraft mechanic/airframe; aviation management; aviation technology; behavioral sciences; business administration; communication equipment technology; criminal justice/law enforcement administration; early childhood education; elementary education; finance; human resources management; liberal arts and sciences/liberal studies; marketing management and research related; nursing; psychology related; sport/fitness administration.

Academic Programs *Special study options:* academic remediation for entering students, accelerated degree program, adult/continuing education programs, cooperative education, distance learning, double majors, external degree program, independent study, internships, part-time degree program, summer session for credit. *ROTC:* Army (c), Air Force (c).

Library Robert C. and Dorothy M. Peoples Library plus 1 other with 111,000 titles, 500 serial subscriptions, 6,795 audiovisual materials, an OPAC, a Web page.

Computers on Campus 100 computers available on campus for general student use. Internet access, at least one staffed computer lab available.

Student Life *Housing:* college housing not available. *Campus security:* 24-hour emergency response devices and patrols, late-night transport/escort service.

Athletics Member NAIA. *Intercollegiate sports:* baseball M(s), basketball M(s)/W(s), cross-country running M(s)/W(s), softball W(s), volleyball W(s).

Standardized Tests *Recommended:* SAT I or ACT (for placement).

Costs (2001–02) *Tuition:* $6480 full-time, $216 per credit part-time. Full-time tuition and fees vary according to degree level and location. Part-time tuition and fees vary according to degree level and location. *Required fees:* $50 full-time, $25 per term part-time. *Payment plan:* installment. *Waivers:* employees or children of employees.

Financial Aid Of all full-time matriculated undergraduates who enrolled in 2001, 862 applied for aid, 686 were judged to have need, 8 had their need fully met. 25 Federal Work-Study jobs (averaging $2000). In 2001, 125 non-need-based awards were made. *Average percent of need met:* 57%. *Average financial aid package:* $6166. *Average need-based loan:* $3628. *Average need-based gift aid:* $1033. *Average non-need based aid:* $4750. *Average indebtedness upon graduation:* $17,260.

Applying *Options:* early admission, deferred entrance. *Application fee:* $25. *Required:* high school transcript. *Recommended:* letters of recommendation, interview. *Application deadline:* rolling (freshmen), rolling (transfers). *Notification:* continuous (freshmen).

Admissions Contact Dr. JoAnn Ciuffetelli, Assistant Director of Admissions, Wilmington College, 320 DuPont Highway, New Castle, DE 19720-6491. *Phone:* 302-328-9407 Ext. 104. *Toll-free phone:* 877-967-5464. *Fax:* 302-328-5902. *E-mail:* jciuf@wilmcoll.edu.

DISTRICT OF COLUMBIA

AMERICAN UNIVERSITY
Washington, District of Columbia

- **Independent Methodist** university, founded 1893
- **Calendar** semesters
- **Degrees** certificates, associate, bachelor's, master's, doctoral, first professional, and postbachelor's certificates
- **Suburban** 77-acre campus with easy access to Baltimore
- **Endowment** $171.0 million
- **Coed,** 5,851 undergraduate students, 91% full-time, 62% women, 38% men
- **Moderately difficult** entrance level, 68% of applicants were admitted

American University attracts academically distinctive and intensely engaged students who want to understand how the world works. American's diverse campus community, location in Washington, D.C., study-abroad options, and emphasis on the practical application of knowledge prepare students to be major contributors in their fields.

Undergraduates 5,323 full-time, 528 part-time. Students come from 53 states and territories, 122 other countries, 93% are from out of state, 6% African American, 4% Asian American or Pacific Islander, 4% Hispanic American, 0.2% Native American, 11% international, 4% transferred in, 75% live on campus. *Retention:* 85% of 2001 full-time freshmen returned.

Freshmen *Admission:* 10,359 applied, 7,051 admitted, 1,422 enrolled. *Average high school GPA:* 3.23. *Test scores:* SAT verbal scores over 500: 95%; SAT math scores over 500: 94%; ACT scores over 18: 99%; SAT verbal scores over 600: 58%; SAT math scores over 600: 51%; ACT scores over 24: 78%; SAT verbal scores over 700: 13%; SAT math scores over 700: 8%; ACT scores over 30: 18%.

Faculty *Total:* 489. *Student/faculty ratio:* 14:1.

Majors African studies; American studies; anthropology; applied mathematics; art; art history; Asian studies; audio engineering; biochemistry; biology; broadcast journalism; business administration; business economics; business marketing and marketing management; business systems analysis/design; chemistry; computer science; criminal justice studies; development economics; economics; elementary education; enterprise management; environmental science; European studies; film/video production; finance; fine/studio arts; French; German; graphic design/commercial art/illustration; health science; history; human resources management; information sciences/systems; interdisciplinary studies; international business; international business marketing; international economics; international finance; international relations; Islamic studies; journalism; Judaic studies; Latin American studies; legal studies; liberal arts and sciences/liberal studies; literature; management information systems/business data processing; mathematical statistics; mathematics; Middle Eastern studies; multimedia; music; peace/conflict studies; philosophy; physics; political science; pre-dentistry; pre-law; pre-medicine; pre-pharmacy studies; pre-veterinary studies; psychology; public relations; Russian; Russian/Slavic studies; secondary education; sociology; Spanish; sport/fitness administration; theater arts/drama; women's studies.

Academic Programs *Special study options:* accelerated degree program, adult/continuing education programs, advanced placement credit, cooperative education, distance learning, double majors, English as a second language, honors programs, independent study, internships, off-campus study, part-time degree program, services for LD students, student-designed majors, study abroad, summer session for credit. *ROTC:* Army (c), Air Force (c). *Unusual degree programs:* 3-2 engineering with Washington University in St. Louis, University of Maryland College Park.

Library Bender Library plus 1 other with 725,000 titles, 3,600 serial subscriptions, 40,700 audiovisual materials, an OPAC, a Web page.

Computers on Campus 600 computers available on campus for general student use. A campuswide network can be accessed from student residence rooms and from off campus that provide access to online course support. Internet access, at least one staffed computer lab available.

Student Life *Housing Options:* coed. *Activities and Organizations:* drama/theater group, student-run newspaper, radio and television station, choral group, Kennedy Political Union, Student Confederation, Freshman Service Experience, Student Union Board, International Student Organization, national fraternities, national sororities. *Campus security:* 24-hour emergency response devices and patrols, late-night transport/escort service, controlled dormitory access. *Student Services:* health clinic, personal/psychological counseling.

Athletics Member NCAA. All Division I. *Intercollegiate sports:* basketball M(s)/W(s), cross-country running M(s)/W(s), field hockey W(s), golf M(s), lacrosse W(s), soccer M(s)/W(s), swimming M(s)/W(s), tennis M(s)/W(s), track and field M(s)/W(s), volleyball W(s), wrestling M(s). *Intramural sports:* badminton M(c)/W(c), baseball M(c), basketball M/W, crew M(c)/W(c), fencing M(c)/W(c), field hockey M(c)/W(c), golf M/W, ice hockey M(c)/W(c), lacrosse M, racquetball M/W, rugby M(c)/W(c), sailing M(c)/W(c), soccer M/W, softball M/W, squash M(c)/W(c), swimming M/W, tennis M/W, track and field M/W, volleyball M/W, water polo M/W.

Standardized Tests *Required:* SAT I or ACT (for admission). *Recommended:* SAT II: Subject Tests (for admission).

Costs (2001–02) *Comprehensive fee:* $31,544 includes full-time tuition ($22,116), mandatory fees ($365), and room and board ($9063). Part-time tuition: $737 per semester hour. *Required fees:* $65 per term part-time. *Room and board:* College room only: $5673. Room and board charges vary according to board plan and housing facility. *Payment plans:* tuition prepayment, installment, deferred payment. *Waivers:* senior citizens and employees or children of employees.

Financial Aid Of all full-time matriculated undergraduates who enrolled in 2001, 2906 applied for aid, 2298 were judged to have need, 879 had their need fully met. 1611 Federal Work-Study jobs (averaging $1848). In 2001, 514 non-need-based awards were made. *Average percent of need met:* 71%. *Average financial aid package:* $21,913. *Average need-based loan:* $4188. *Average need-based gift aid:* $12,321. *Average non-need based aid:* $10,246. *Financial aid deadline:* 3/1.

Applying *Options:* common application, electronic application, early admission, early decision, deferred entrance. *Application fee:* $45. *Required:* essay or personal statement, high school transcript, minimum 2.0 GPA, 2 letters of recommendation. *Recommended:* minimum 3.0 GPA, interview. *Application deadlines:* 2/1 (freshmen), 7/1 (transfers). *Early decision:* 11/15. *Notification:* 4/1 (freshmen), 12/31 (early decision).

Admissions Contact Dr. Sharon Alston, Director of Admissions, American University, 4400 Massachusetts Avenue, NW, Washington, DC 20016-8001. *Phone:* 202-885-6000. *Fax:* 202-885-1025. *E-mail:* afa@american.edu.

THE CATHOLIC UNIVERSITY OF AMERICA
Washington, District of Columbia

- **Independent** university, founded 1887, affiliated with Roman Catholic Church
- **Calendar** semesters
- **Degrees** bachelor's, master's, doctoral, first professional, and post-master's certificates
- **Urban** 144-acre campus
- **Endowment** $165.6 million
- **Coed,** 2,587 undergraduate students, 92% full-time, 54% women, 46% men
- **Moderately difficult** entrance level, 85% of applicants were admitted

Undergraduates 2,384 full-time, 203 part-time. Students come from 51 states and territories, 33 other countries, 94% are from out of state, 7% African American, 3% Asian American or Pacific Islander, 4% Hispanic American, 0.2% Native American, 3% international, 3% transferred in, 65% live on campus. *Retention:* 82% of 2001 full-time freshmen returned.

Freshmen *Admission:* 2,191 applied, 1,854 admitted, 614 enrolled. *Average high school GPA:* 3.34. *Test scores:* SAT verbal scores over 500: 85%; SAT math scores over 500: 83%; ACT scores over 18: 94%; SAT verbal scores over 600: 43%; SAT math scores over 600: 36%; ACT scores over 24: 53%; SAT verbal scores over 700: 9%; SAT math scores over 700: 5%; ACT scores over 30: 8%.

Faculty *Total:* 642, 56% full-time. *Student/faculty ratio:* 10:1.

Majors Accounting; anthropology; architecture; art; art education; art history; biochemistry; bioengineering; biology; biology education; business; business administration; chemical and atomic/molecular physics; chemistry; chemistry education; civil engineering; classics; communications; computer engineering; computer science; construction engineering; drama/dance education; early childhood education; ecology; economics; education; electrical engineering; elementary education; engineering; English; English education; finance; fine arts and art studies related; French; French language education; general studies; German; German language education; history; history education; human resources management; interdisciplinary studies; international economics; international finance; Latin (ancient and medieval); mathematics; mathematics education; mechanical engineering; medical technology; music; music (general performance); music history; music (piano and organ performance); music teacher education; music theory and composition; music (voice and choral/opera performance); nursing; painting; philosophy; physics; political science; psychology; religious education; religious studies; romance languages; sculpture; secondary education; social work; sociology; Spanish; Spanish language education; theater arts/drama.

Academic Programs *Special study options:* accelerated degree program, adult/continuing education programs, advanced placement credit, double majors, English as a second language, freshman honors college, honors programs, independent study, internships, off-campus study, part-time degree program, services for LD students, student-designed majors, study abroad, summer session for credit. *ROTC:* Army (c), Navy (c), Air Force (c).

Library Mullen Library plus 7 others with 1.4 million titles, 11,200 serial subscriptions, 38,200 audiovisual materials, an OPAC, a Web page.

Computers on Campus 450 computers available on campus for general student use. A campuswide network can be accessed from student residence rooms and from off campus. Internet access, online (class) registration, at least one staffed computer lab available.

Student Life *Housing:* on-campus residence required through sophomore year. *Options:* coed, men-only, women-only. *Activities and Organizations:* drama/theater group, student-run newspaper, radio station, choral group, Knights of Columbus, Students for Life, College Republicans, Habitat for Humanity, College Democrats, national fraternities, national sororities. *Campus security:* 24-hour emergency response devices and patrols, late-night transport/escort service, controlled dormitory access, controlled access of academic buildings. *Student Services:* health clinic, personal/psychological counseling, women's center, legal services.

Athletics Member NCAA. All Division III. *Intercollegiate sports:* baseball M, basketball M/W, cross-country running M/W, field hockey W, football M, lacrosse M/W, soccer M/W, softball W, swimming M/W, tennis M/W, track and field M/W, volleyball W. *Intramural sports:* basketball M/W, crew M(c)/W(c), equestrian sports M(c)/W(c), football M/W, ice hockey M(c), racquetball M/W, rugby M(c), soccer M/W, softball M/W, tennis M/W, track and field M/W, volleyball M/W.

Standardized Tests *Required:* SAT I or ACT (for admission). *Recommended:* SAT II: Subject Tests (for admission), SAT II: Writing Test (for admission).

Costs (2001–02) *One-time required fee:* $300. *Comprehensive fee:* $29,332 includes full-time tuition ($20,050), mandatory fees ($900), and room and board ($8382). Full-time tuition and fees vary according to program. Part-time tuition: $770 per course. *Required fees:* $465 per term part-time. *Room and board:* College room only: $4708. Room and board charges vary according to board plan and housing facility. *Payment plans:* installment, deferred payment. *Waivers:* employees or children of employees.

Financial Aid Of all full-time matriculated undergraduates who enrolled in 2001, 1988 applied for aid, 1380 were judged to have need, 883 had their need fully met. In 2001, 567 non-need-based awards were made. *Average percent of need met:* 78%. *Average financial aid package:* $14,234. *Average need-based loan:* $4604. *Average need-based gift aid:* $10,210. *Average non-need based aid:* $7544. *Financial aid deadline:* 2/1.

Applying *Options:* common application, electronic application, early admission, early action, deferred entrance. *Application fee:* $55. *Required:* essay or personal statement, high school transcript, 1 letter of recommendation. *Recommended:* minimum 2.8 GPA. *Application deadlines:* 2/15 (freshmen), 8/1 (transfers). *Notification:* 4/15 (freshmen), 12/15 (early action).

Admissions Contact Ms. Michelle D. Petro-Siraj, Executive Director of Undergraduate Admission, The Catholic University of America, 102 McMahon Hall, Washington, DC 20064. *Phone:* 202-319-5305. *Toll-free phone:* 202-319-5305 (in-state); 800-673-2772 (out-of-state). *Fax:* 202-319-6533. *E-mail:* cua-admissions@cua.edu.

CORCORAN COLLEGE OF ART AND DESIGN
Washington, District of Columbia

- **Independent** 4-year, founded 1890
- **Calendar** semesters

Corcoran College of Art and Design (continued)

- **Degrees** associate and bachelor's
- **Urban** 7-acre campus
- **Endowment** $29.5 million
- **Coed,** 372 undergraduate students, 90% full-time, 67% women, 33% men
- **Moderately difficult** entrance level, 62% of applicants were admitted

Undergraduates 335 full-time, 37 part-time. Students come from 19 states and territories, 21 other countries, 88% are from out of state, 7% African American, 12% Asian American or Pacific Islander, 7% Hispanic American, 15% transferred in, 19% live on campus. *Retention:* 65% of 2001 full-time freshmen returned.

Freshmen *Admission:* 198 applied, 123 admitted, 46 enrolled. *Average high school GPA:* 3.10. *Test scores:* SAT verbal scores over 500: 68%; SAT math scores over 500: 63%; ACT scores over 18: 84%; SAT verbal scores over 600: 35%; SAT math scores over 600: 18%; ACT scores over 24: 34%; SAT verbal scores over 700: 2%; SAT math scores over 700: 2%.

Faculty *Total:* 34, 76% full-time, 59% with terminal degrees. *Student/faculty ratio:* 8:1.

Majors Applied art; art; ceramic arts; drawing; fine/studio arts; graphic design/commercial art/illustration; photography; printmaking; sculpture.

Academic Programs *Special study options:* academic remediation for entering students, adult/continuing education programs, advanced placement credit, English as a second language, independent study, internships, off-campus study, summer session for credit.

Library Corcoran School of Art Library with 20,518 titles, 148 serial subscriptions, 45,175 audiovisual materials.

Computers on Campus 45 computers available on campus for general student use. Internet access, at least one staffed computer lab available.

Student Life *Activities and Organizations:* Student Government Association. *Campus security:* 24-hour patrols, ID check at all entrances. *Student Services:* personal/psychological counseling.

Standardized Tests *Required:* SAT I or ACT (for admission).

Costs (2001–02) *Comprehensive fee:* $23,800 includes full-time tuition ($16,970), mandatory fees ($30), and room and board ($6800). *Room and board:* College room only: $5000. *Payment plan:* installment.

Financial Aid Of all full-time matriculated undergraduates who enrolled in 2001, 293 applied for aid, 203 were judged to have need. 47 Federal Work-Study jobs (averaging $695). *Average percent of need met:* 27%. *Average financial aid package:* $7588. *Average need-based loan:* $4385. *Average need-based gift aid:* $3400.

Applying *Options:* early admission, deferred entrance. *Application fee:* $30. *Required:* high school transcript, minimum 2.5 GPA, portfolio. *Required for some:* essay or personal statement, 2 letters of recommendation, interview. *Recommended:* essay or personal statement, minimum 3.0 GPA, 2 letters of recommendation, interview. *Application deadline:* rolling (freshmen), rolling (transfers).

Admissions Contact Ms. Anne E. Bowman, Director of Admissions, Corcoran College of Art and Design, 500 17th Street, NW, Washington, DC 20006-4804. *Phone:* 202-639-1814. *Toll-free phone:* 888-CORCORAN. *Fax:* 202-639-1830. *E-mail:* admofc@corcoran.org.

GALLAUDET UNIVERSITY

Washington, District of Columbia

- **Independent** university, founded 1864
- **Calendar** semesters
- **Degrees** bachelor's, master's, doctoral, and post-master's certificates (all undergraduate programs open primarily to hearing-impaired)
- **Urban** 99-acre campus
- **Endowment** $126.6 million
- **Coed,** 1,200 undergraduate students, 94% full-time, 52% women, 48% men
- **Moderately difficult** entrance level, 70% of applicants were admitted

Undergraduates 99% are from out of state, 11% African American, 5% Asian American or Pacific Islander, 7% Hispanic American, 0.4% Native American, 12% international, 62% live on campus. *Retention:* 65% of 2001 full-time freshmen returned.

Freshmen *Admission:* 411 applied, 289 admitted.

Faculty *Total:* 223, 100% full-time, 77% with terminal degrees. *Student/faculty ratio:* 7:1.

Majors Accounting; American government; art; art education; art history; biology; business administration; chemical engineering technology; chemistry; child care/development; civil engineering; clothing/apparel/textile studies; communications; computer engineering; computer/information sciences; computer science; criminology; early childhood education; economics; education; electrical engineering; elementary education; engineering; engineering science; engineering technology; English; English composition; English education; family studies; fine/studio arts; French; graphic design/commercial art/illustration; history; information sciences/systems; international relations; mass communications; mathematics; mechanical engineering; nutrition science; philosophy; photography; physical education; physics; psychology; radio/television broadcasting; recreational therapy; secondary education; sign language interpretation; social work; sociology; Spanish; theater arts/drama.

Academic Programs *Special study options:* academic remediation for entering students, accelerated degree program, adult/continuing education programs, advanced placement credit, cooperative education, distance learning, double majors, English as a second language, honors programs, independent study, internships, off-campus study, part-time degree program, services for LD students, student-designed majors, study abroad, summer session for credit.

Library Merrill Learning Center with 159,142 titles, 1,649 serial subscriptions, 188,130 audiovisual materials, an OPAC, a Web page.

Computers on Campus 240 computers available on campus for general student use. A campuswide network can be accessed from student residence rooms and from off campus. Online (class) registration, at least one staffed computer lab available.

Student Life *Housing Options:* coed. *Activities and Organizations:* drama/theater group, student-run newspaper, Student Body Government, Delta Epsilon, Rainbow Society, Black Deaf Student Union, national fraternities, national sororities. *Campus security:* 24-hour emergency response devices and patrols, late-night transport/escort service, controlled dormitory access. *Student Services:* health clinic, personal/psychological counseling.

Athletics Member NCAA. All Division III. *Intercollegiate sports:* baseball M, basketball M/W, cross-country running M/W, football M, soccer M/W, softball W, swimming M/W, tennis M/W, track and field M/W, volleyball W, wrestling M. *Intramural sports:* badminton M/W, basketball M/W, bowling M/W, cross-country running M/W, football M/W, golf M/W, gymnastics M(c)/W(c), racquetball M/W, soccer M, softball W.

Standardized Tests *Required:* SAT I or ACT (for admission).

Costs (2001–02) *Comprehensive fee:* $16,554 includes full-time tuition ($7870), mandatory fees ($1120), and room and board ($7564). Part-time tuition: $394 per credit. *Room and board:* College room only: $4320. Room and board charges vary according to board plan. *Payment plan:* installment. *Waivers:* employees or children of employees.

Financial Aid Of all full-time matriculated undergraduates who enrolled in 2001, 791 applied for aid, 700 were judged to have need, 487 had their need fully met. 84 Federal Work-Study jobs (averaging $1548). In 2001, 49 non-need-based awards were made. *Average percent of need met:* 78%. *Average financial aid package:* $13,680. *Average need-based loan:* $2450. *Average need-based gift aid:* $10,840. *Average non-need based aid:* $9068. *Average indebtedness upon graduation:* $7492.

Applying *Options:* early admission, deferred entrance. *Application fee:* $35. *Required:* essay or personal statement, high school transcript, 2 letters of recommendation, audiogram. *Required for some:* interview. *Application deadlines:* 8/1 (freshmen), 8/1 (transfers). *Notification:* continuous (freshmen).

Admissions Contact Ms. Deborah E. DeStefano, Director of Admissions, Gallaudet University, 800 Florida Avenue, NE, Washington, DC 20002-3625. *Phone:* 202-651-5750. *Toll-free phone:* 800-995-0550. *Fax:* 202-651-5774. *E-mail:* admissions@gallua.gallaudet.edu.

GEORGETOWN UNIVERSITY

Washington, District of Columbia

- **Independent Roman Catholic (Jesuit)** university, founded 1789
- **Calendar** semesters
- **Degrees** bachelor's, master's, doctoral, and first professional
- **Urban** 110-acre campus
- **Endowment** $705.5 million
- **Coed,** 6,422 undergraduate students, 96% full-time, 53% women, 47% men
- **Most difficult** entrance level, 21% of applicants were admitted

The School of Nursing & Health Studies offers a program committed to values and education in the Jesuit tradition. Opportunities for study include the Bachelor or Science degree in nursing or health studies. Students at the School have a chance to study abroad as well as in some of the nation's most prestigious health-care centers.

Undergraduates 6,191 full-time, 231 part-time. Students come from 52 states and territories, 86 other countries, 99% are from out of state, 6% African American, 10% Asian American or Pacific Islander, 5% Hispanic American, 0.2%

Native American, 5% international, 3% transferred in, 66% live on campus. *Retention:* 98% of 2001 full-time freshmen returned.

Freshmen *Admission:* 15,327 applied, 3,194 admitted, 1,515 enrolled. *Test scores:* SAT verbal scores over 500: 99%; SAT math scores over 500: 100%; ACT scores over 18: 100%; SAT verbal scores over 600: 89%; SAT math scores over 600: 91%; ACT scores over 24: 93%; SAT verbal scores over 700: 46%; SAT math scores over 700: 47%; ACT scores over 30: 61%.

Faculty *Total:* 922, 69% full-time. *Student/faculty ratio:* 11:1.

Majors Accounting; American studies; Arabic; art; biochemistry; biology; business administration; business marketing and marketing management; chemistry; Chinese; classics; comparative literature; computer science; economics; English; finance; French; German; history; interdisciplinary studies; international business; international economics; international relations; Italian; Japanese; liberal arts and sciences/liberal studies; linguistics; mathematics; nursing; philosophy; physics; political science; Portuguese; psychology; religious studies; Russian; science/technology and society; social sciences and history related; sociology; Spanish; women's studies.

Academic Programs *Special study options:* academic remediation for entering students, adult/continuing education programs, advanced placement credit, double majors, English as a second language, honors programs, independent study, internships, services for LD students, student-designed majors, study abroad, summer session for credit. *ROTC:* Army (b), Navy (c), Air Force (c). *Unusual degree programs:* 3-2 foreign service.

Library Lauinger Library plus 6 others with 2.5 million titles, 28,547 serial subscriptions, 152,659 audiovisual materials, an OPAC, a Web page.

Computers on Campus 360 computers available on campus for general student use. A campuswide network can be accessed from student residence rooms and from off campus that provide access to online grade reports. Internet access, online (class) registration, at least one staffed computer lab available.

Student Life *Housing:* on-campus residence required through sophomore year. *Options:* coed, disabled students. *Activities and Organizations:* drama/theater group, student-run newspaper, radio station, choral group, University Choir, Mask and Bauble, The Hoya (student newspaper), International Relations Club, The Voice (weekly news magazine). *Campus security:* 24-hour emergency response devices and patrols, late-night transport/escort service, controlled dormitory access, student guards at residence halls and academic facilities. *Student Services:* health clinic, personal/psychological counseling.

Athletics Member NCAA. All Division I except football (Division I-AA). *Intercollegiate sports:* baseball M(s), basketball M(s)/W(s), crew M/W, cross-country running M(s)/W(s), field hockey W, golf M(s), ice hockey M(c), lacrosse M(s)/W(s), rugby M(c), sailing M/W, soccer M(s)/W(s), swimming M/W, tennis M/W(s), track and field M(s)/W(s), volleyball W(s). *Intramural sports:* basketball M/W, cross-country running M/W, football M/W, golf M/W, racquetball M/W, soccer M/W, softball M/W, squash M/W, table tennis M/W, tennis M/W, track and field M/W, volleyball M/W.

Standardized Tests *Required:* SAT I or ACT (for admission). *Recommended:* SAT II: Subject Tests (for admission), SAT II: Writing Test (for admission).

Costs (2001–02) *Comprehensive fee:* $34,847 includes full-time tuition ($25,152), mandatory fees ($273), and room and board ($9422). Part-time tuition: $1048 per credit hour. Part-time tuition and fees vary according to course load. *Room and board:* College room only: $6182. Room and board charges vary according to board plan and housing facility. *Payment plans:* installment, deferred payment. *Waivers:* employees or children of employees.

Financial Aid Of all full-time matriculated undergraduates who enrolled in 2001, 2796 applied for aid, 2354 were judged to have need, 2354 had their need fully met. 1088 Federal Work-Study jobs (averaging $2000). In 2001, 429 non-need-based awards were made. *Average percent of need met:* 100%. *Average financial aid package:* $20,302. *Average need-based loan:* $3885. *Average need-based gift aid:* $13,587.

Applying *Options:* electronic application, early admission, early action, deferred entrance. *Application fee:* $60. *Required:* essay or personal statement, high school transcript, 2 letters of recommendation, interview. *Application deadlines:* 1/10 (freshmen), 3/1 (transfers). *Notification:* 4/1 (freshmen), 12/15 (early action).

Admissions Contact Mr. Charles A. Deacon, Dean of Undergraduate Admissions, Georgetown University, 37th and O Street, NW, Washington, DC 20057. *Phone:* 202-687-3600. *Fax:* 202-687-6660.

The George Washington University
Washington, District of Columbia

- **Independent** university, founded 1821
- **Calendar** semesters
- **Degrees** certificates, associate, bachelor's, master's, doctoral, first professional, post-master's, and postbachelor's certificates
- **Urban** 36-acre campus
- **Endowment** $513.0 million
- **Coed,** 10,063 undergraduate students, 87% full-time, 56% women, 44% men
- **Very difficult** entrance level, 48% of applicants were admitted

Undergraduates 8,711 full-time, 1,352 part-time. Students come from 55 states and territories, 101 other countries, 96% are from out of state, 6% African American, 10% Asian American or Pacific Islander, 5% Hispanic American, 0.3% Native American, 5% international, 3% transferred in, 62% live on campus. *Retention:* 92% of 2001 full-time freshmen returned.

Freshmen *Admission:* 15,960 applied, 7,740 admitted, 2,578 enrolled. *Test scores:* SAT verbal scores over 500: 95%; SAT math scores over 500: 97%; ACT scores over 18: 99%; SAT verbal scores over 600: 64%; SAT math scores over 600: 67%; ACT scores over 24: 82%; SAT verbal scores over 700: 14%; SAT math scores over 700: 14%; ACT scores over 30: 16%.

Faculty *Total:* 1,626, 48% full-time, 61% with terminal degrees. *Student/faculty ratio:* 14:1.

Majors Accounting; American studies; anthropology; applied mathematics; archaeology; art; art history; Asian studies; biology; business administration; business economics; business marketing and marketing management; chemistry; Chinese; civil engineering; classics; computer engineering; computer/information sciences; computer science; criminal justice/law enforcement administration; dance; East Asian studies; economics; electrical engineering; emergency medical technology; engineering; English; environmental engineering; environmental science; European studies; exercise sciences; finance; fine/studio arts; French; geography; geology; German; history; humanities; human resources management; human services; industrial radiologic technology; interdisciplinary studies; international business; international relations; journalism; Judaic studies; Latin American studies; liberal arts and sciences/liberal studies; mass communications; mathematical statistics; mathematics; mechanical engineering; medical laboratory technician; medical laboratory technology; medical technology; Middle Eastern studies; music; nuclear medical technology; philosophy; physician assistant; physics; political science; pre-dentistry; pre-law; pre-medicine; psychology; public policy analysis; radiological science; radio/television broadcasting; religious studies; Russian; Russian/Slavic studies; sociology; Spanish; speech-language pathology/audiology; speech/rhetorical studies; systems engineering; theater arts/drama.

Academic Programs *Special study options:* accelerated degree program, adult/continuing education programs, advanced placement credit, cooperative education, distance learning, double majors, English as a second language, honors programs, independent study, internships, off-campus study, part-time degree program, services for LD students, student-designed majors, study abroad, summer session for credit. *ROTC:* Army (c), Navy (b), Air Force (c). *Unusual degree programs:* 3-2 chemical toxicology, art therapy, economics, engineering economics, operations research.

Library Gelman Library plus 2 others with 1.8 million titles, 14,729 serial subscriptions, 17,246 audiovisual materials, an OPAC, a Web page.

Computers on Campus 550 computers available on campus for general student use. A campuswide network can be accessed from student residence rooms and from off campus. At least one staffed computer lab available.

Student Life *Housing Options:* coed, men-only, women-only. *Activities and Organizations:* drama/theater group, student-run newspaper, radio and television station, choral group, marching band, Program Board, Student Association, Residence Hall Association, College Democrats, College Republicans, national fraternities, national sororities. *Campus security:* 24-hour emergency response devices and patrols, late-night transport/escort service, controlled dormitory access. *Student Services:* health clinic, personal/psychological counseling, legal services.

Athletics Member NCAA. All Division I. *Intercollegiate sports:* baseball M(s), basketball M(s)/W(s), crew M(s)/W(s), cross-country running M(s)/W(s), golf M(s), gymnastics W(s), soccer M(s)/W(s), swimming M(s)/W(s), tennis M(s)/W(s), volleyball W(s), water polo M(s). *Intramural sports:* badminton M(c)/W(c), basketball M/W, bowling M(c)/W(c), equestrian sports M(c)/W(c), fencing M(c)/W(c), football M/W, lacrosse M(c), racquetball M/W, rugby M(c), sailing M(c)/W(c), soccer M/W, softball M/W, squash M(c)/W, swimming M/W, tennis M/W, volleyball M(c)/W, water polo M/W.

Standardized Tests *Required:* SAT I or ACT (for admission). *Required for some:* SAT II: Subject Tests (for admission). *Recommended:* SAT I (for admission), SAT II: Writing Test (for admission).

Costs (2002–03) *Comprehensive fee:* $36,930 includes full-time tuition ($27,790), mandatory fees ($30), and room and board ($9110). Full-time tuition and fees vary according to student level. Part-time tuition: $879 per credit hour. *Required fees:* $1 per credit hour. *Room and board:* College room only: $6610. Room and board charges vary according to board plan and housing facility. *Payment plans:* installment, deferred payment. *Waivers:* employees or children of employees.

The George Washington University (continued)

Financial Aid Of all full-time matriculated undergraduates who enrolled in 2001, 4119 applied for aid, 3014 were judged to have need, 2562 had their need fully met. In 2001, 1600 non-need-based awards were made. *Average percent of need met:* 94%. *Average financial aid package:* $24,000. *Average need-based loan:* $4700. *Average need-based gift aid:* $12,560. *Average non-need based aid:* $9700. *Average indebtedness upon graduation:* $24,894.

Applying *Options:* common application, electronic application, early admission, early decision, deferred entrance. *Application fee:* $60. *Required:* essay or personal statement, high school transcript, 2 letters of recommendation. *Recommended:* interview. *Application deadlines:* 1/15 (freshmen), 6/1 (transfers). *Early decision:* 12/1 (for plan 1), 1/15 (for plan 2). *Notification:* 3/15 (freshmen), 12/15 (early decision plan 1), 2/1 (early decision plan 2).

Admissions Contact Dr. Kathryn M. Napper, Director of Admission, The George Washington University, 2121 I Street, NW, Suite 201, Washington, DC 20052. *Phone:* 202-994-6040. *Toll-free phone:* 800-447-3765. *Fax:* 202-944-0325. *E-mail:* gwadm@gwu.edu.

HOWARD UNIVERSITY
Washington, District of Columbia

- **Independent** university, founded 1867
- **Calendar** semesters
- **Degrees** certificates, bachelor's, master's, doctoral, first professional, post-master's, and first professional certificates
- **Urban** 242-acre campus
- **Endowment** $296.5 million
- **Coed,** 6,980 undergraduate students, 93% full-time, 65% women, 35% men
- **Moderately difficult** entrance level, 68% of applicants were admitted

Undergraduates 6,484 full-time, 496 part-time. Students come from 50 states and territories, 104 other countries, 90% are from out of state, 87% African American, 0.8% Asian American or Pacific Islander, 0.7% Hispanic American, 0.1% Native American, 11% international, 5% transferred in, 57% live on campus. *Retention:* 87% of 2001 full-time freshmen returned.

Freshmen *Admission:* 6,120 applied, 4,137 admitted, 1,524 enrolled. *Average high school GPA:* 3.12.

Faculty *Total:* 1,360, 83% full-time, 81% with terminal degrees. *Student/faculty ratio:* 8:1.

Majors Accounting; advertising; African-American studies; anatomy; anthropology; applied art; architecture; art; art therapy; biology; biomedical science; biophysics; botany; broadcast journalism; business administration; business marketing and marketing management; ceramic arts; chemical engineering; chemistry; civil engineering; classics; counselor education/guidance; dental hygiene; drama therapy; early childhood education; economics; education; electrical engineering; English; family/consumer studies; fashion design/illustration; film studies; finance; French; geology; German; graphic design/commercial art/illustration; history; hotel and restaurant management; industrial radiologic technology; information sciences/systems; insurance/risk management; interior design; international business; international economics; journalism; law enforcement/police science; mass communications; mathematics; mechanical engineering; medical technology; music; nursing; nutrition science; occupational therapy; pharmacy; philosophy; physical education; physical therapy; physician assistant; physics; political science; psychology; radio/television broadcasting; Russian; social work; sociology; Spanish; theater arts/drama; zoology.

Academic Programs *Special study options:* academic remediation for entering students, accelerated degree program, adult/continuing education programs, advanced placement credit, cooperative education, double majors, freshman honors college, honors programs, independent study, internships, off-campus study, part-time degree program, services for LD students, student-designed majors, study abroad, summer session for credit. *ROTC:* Army (b), Air Force (b).

Library Founders Library plus 8 others with 120,243 audiovisual materials.

Computers on Campus A campuswide network can be accessed from off campus. Internet access, online (class) registration, at least one staffed computer lab available.

Student Life *Housing:* on-campus residence required through sophomore year. *Options:* coed. *Activities and Organizations:* drama/theater group, student-run newspaper, radio and television station, choral group, marching band, Howard University Student Association, Undergraduate Student Assembly, Campus Pals, national fraternities, national sororities. *Campus security:* 24-hour emergency response devices and patrols, student patrols, late-night transport/escort service, controlled dormitory access, security lighting. *Student Services:* health clinic, personal/psychological counseling.

Athletics Member NCAA. All Division I except football (Division I-AA). *Intercollegiate sports:* baseball M(s)/W(s), basketball M(s)/W(s), bowling M/W, cross-country running M(s)/W(s), golf M(s), lacrosse W, soccer M(s), swimming M(s)/W(s), tennis M(s)/W(s), track and field M(s)/W(s), volleyball W(s), wrestling M(s). *Intramural sports:* basketball M/W, bowling M/W, football M, golf M, soccer M/W, softball W, swimming M/W, table tennis M/W, tennis M/W, track and field M/W, volleyball M/W, wrestling M.

Standardized Tests *Required:* SAT I or ACT (for admission), SAT II: Writing Test (for admission).

Costs (2001–02) *Comprehensive fee:* $15,070 includes full-time tuition ($9515), mandatory fees ($555), and room and board ($5000). Part-time tuition: $397 per credit hour. *Required fees:* $278 per term part-time. *Room and board:* College room only: $2712. Room and board charges vary according to board plan and housing facility. *Payment plan:* deferred payment. *Waivers:* employees or children of employees.

Applying *Options:* electronic application, early admission, early action, deferred entrance. *Application fee:* $45. *Required:* high school transcript. *Required for some:* 2 letters of recommendation. *Application deadlines:* 4/1 (freshmen), 4/1 (transfers). *Notification:* continuous (freshmen), 12/25 (early action).

Admissions Contact Ms. Linda Sanders-Hawkins, Interim Director of Admissions, Howard University, 2400 Sixth Street, NW, Washington, DC 20059-0002. *Phone:* 202-806-2700. *Toll-free phone:* 800-HOWARD-U. *Fax:* 202-806-4465. *E-mail:* admissions@howard.edu.

POTOMAC COLLEGE
Washington, District of Columbia

- **Proprietary** 4-year, founded 1991
- **Calendar** 6-week modules
- **Degree** bachelor's
- **Urban** campus
- **Coed,** 511 undergraduate students, 100% full-time, 57% women, 43% men
- **Noncompetitive** entrance level, 77% of applicants were admitted

Undergraduates Students come from 4 states and territories, 1 other country, 92% are from out of state, 68% African American, 2% Asian American or Pacific Islander, 3% Hispanic American. *Retention:* 76% of 2001 full-time freshmen returned.

Freshmen *Admission:* 167 applied, 128 admitted.

Faculty *Total:* 47, 30% full-time, 30% with terminal degrees. *Student/faculty ratio:* 11:1.

Majors Business administration; computer management.

Academic Programs *Special study options:* academic remediation for entering students, accelerated degree program, adult/continuing education programs, advanced placement credit, double majors, external degree program, independent study, internships, part-time degree program, services for LD students, summer session for credit.

Library Potomac College Library with 5,565 titles, 40 serial subscriptions, 100 audiovisual materials, an OPAC.

Computers on Campus 20 computers available on campus for general student use. A campuswide network can be accessed from off campus. Internet access, at least one staffed computer lab available.

Student Life *Housing:* college housing not available. *Activities and Organizations:* Student Government Association. *Campus security:* 24-hour emergency response devices. *Student Services:* personal/psychological counseling.

Costs (2002–03) *Tuition:* $11,160 full-time, $310 per credit hour part-time.

Financial Aid Of all full-time matriculated undergraduates who enrolled in 2001, 210 applied for aid, 210 were judged to have need. *Average financial aid package:* $5500.

Applying *Required:* high school transcript, interview, 4 years post high school work experience; minimum employment of 20 hours per week. *Application deadline:* rolling (freshmen), rolling (transfers). *Notification:* continuous (freshmen).

Admissions Contact Ms. Florence Tate, President, Potomac College, 4000 Chesapeake Street, NW, Washington, DC 20016. *Phone:* 202-686-0876. *Toll-free phone:* 888-686-0876. *Fax:* 202-686-0818. *E-mail:* cdresser@potomac.edu.

SOUTHEASTERN UNIVERSITY
Washington, District of Columbia

- **Independent** comprehensive, founded 1879
- **Calendar** quadmester (four 12-week semesters)
- **Degrees** certificates, associate, bachelor's, and master's
- **Urban** 1-acre campus
- **Endowment** $27,450

- **Coed,** 513 undergraduate students, 25% full-time, 69% women, 31% men
- **Noncompetitive** entrance level, 29% of applicants were admitted

Undergraduates 126 full-time, 387 part-time. Students come from 7 states and territories, 40 other countries, 25% are from out of state, 79% African American, 3% Asian American or Pacific Islander, 0.8% Hispanic American, 0.2% Native American, 14% international, 4% transferred in. *Retention:* 50% of 2001 full-time freshmen returned.

Freshmen *Admission:* 551 applied, 160 admitted, 105 enrolled.

Faculty *Total:* 89, 15% full-time, 52% with terminal degrees. *Student/faculty ratio:* 11:1.

Majors Accounting; banking; business administration; business marketing and marketing management; child care provider; computer science; finance; general studies; health services administration; information sciences/systems; legal studies; management information systems/business data processing; public administration.

Academic Programs *Special study options:* academic remediation for entering students, accelerated degree program, adult/continuing education programs, advanced placement credit, cooperative education, double majors, English as a second language, external degree program, honors programs, independent study, internships, part-time degree program, study abroad, summer session for credit.

Library The Learning Resources Center plus 1 other with 32,000 titles, 200 serial subscriptions, 250 audiovisual materials.

Computers on Campus 137 computers available on campus for general student use. A campuswide network can be accessed from off campus. At least one staffed computer lab available.

Student Life *Housing:* college housing not available. *Activities and Organizations:* SGA, national fraternities, national sororities. *Campus security:* late-night transport/escort service. *Student Services:* personal/psychological counseling.

Standardized Tests *Recommended:* SAT I or ACT (for admission).

Costs (2001–02) *Tuition:* $7980 full-time, $225 per credit hour part-time. *Required fees:* $525 full-time. *Payment plan:* installment. *Waivers:* employees or children of employees.

Financial Aid Of all full-time matriculated undergraduates who enrolled in 2001, 94 applied for aid, 94 were judged to have need, 89 had their need fully met. 30 Federal Work-Study jobs. *Average percent of need met:* 95%. *Average financial aid package:* $5500. *Average need-based gift aid:* $3200.

Applying *Options:* deferred entrance. *Application fee:* $45. *Required:* high school transcript. *Recommended:* essay or personal statement, interview. *Application deadline:* rolling (freshmen), rolling (transfers).

Admissions Contact Mr. Jack Flinter, Director of Admissions, Southeastern University, 501 I Street, SW, Washington, DC 20024-2788. *Phone:* 202-265-5343 Ext. 211. *Fax:* 202-488-8162. *E-mail:* jackf@admin.seu.edu.

STRAYER UNIVERSITY

Washington, District of Columbia

- **Proprietary** comprehensive, founded 1892
- **Calendar** quarters
- **Degrees** certificates, diplomas, associate, bachelor's, and master's
- **Urban** campus
- **Coed,** 11,785 undergraduate students, 21% full-time, 57% women, 43% men
- **Minimally difficult** entrance level

Undergraduates 2,508 full-time, 9,277 part-time. Students come from 26 states and territories, 124 other countries, 3% are from out of state, 43% African American, 5% Asian American or Pacific Islander, 4% Hispanic American, 0.4% Native American, 6% international.

Freshmen *Admission:* 2,430 admitted, 2,430 enrolled.

Faculty *Total:* 528, 22% full-time. *Student/faculty ratio:* 22:1.

Majors Accounting; business administration; business marketing and marketing management; computer/information sciences related; computer systems networking/telecommunications; economics; information sciences/systems; international business; Internet; liberal arts and sciences/liberal studies; purchasing/contracts management.

Academic Programs *Special study options:* academic remediation for entering students, accelerated degree program, adult/continuing education programs, advanced placement credit, cooperative education, distance learning, double majors, internships, off-campus study, part-time degree program, services for LD students, summer session for credit.

Library Wilkes Library plus 13 others with 29,500 titles, 460 serial subscriptions, 1,350 audiovisual materials, an OPAC, a Web page.

Computers on Campus 1000 computers available on campus for general student use. Internet access, online (class) registration, at least one staffed computer lab available.

Student Life *Housing:* college housing not available. *Activities and Organizations:* Honor Society, International Club, Association of Information Technology Professionals, Business Administration Club, Human Resource Management club. *Campus security:* patrols by trained personnel during operating hours.

Standardized Tests *Recommended:* SAT I (for admission).

Costs (2001–02) *Tuition:* $8789 full-time, $231 per quarter hour part-time. Full-time tuition and fees vary according to course load. Part-time tuition and fees vary according to course load. *Payment plan:* installment. *Waivers:* employees or children of employees.

Applying *Options:* electronic application, early admission, deferred entrance. *Application fee:* $35. *Required:* high school transcript. *Required for some:* 1 letter of recommendation. *Recommended:* essay or personal statement, 1 letter of recommendation, interview. *Application deadline:* rolling (freshmen), rolling (transfers). *Notification:* continuous (freshmen).

Admissions Contact Mr. Michael Williams, Regional Director, Strayer University, 1025 Fifteenth Street, NW, Washington, DC 20005. *Phone:* 703-339-2500. *Toll-free phone:* 888-4-STRAYER. *Fax:* 202-289-1831. *E-mail:* info40@strayer.edu.

TRINITY COLLEGE

Washington, District of Columbia

- **Independent Roman Catholic** comprehensive, founded 1897
- **Calendar** semesters
- **Degrees** bachelor's, master's, and postbachelor's certificates
- **Urban** 26-acre campus
- **Endowment** $10.0 million
- **Women only,** 930 undergraduate students, 61% full-time
- **Moderately difficult** entrance level, 74% of applicants were admitted

Trinity College offers women the Foundation for Leadership curriculum, combining liberal arts majors with professional focuses, mentor programs, and internship opportunities. Special programs include the Trinity Center for Women and Public Policy, Executive Women in Government Partnership, and a 5-year academic program combining a liberal arts undergraduate degree with a Master of Arts in Teaching.

Undergraduates 566 full-time, 364 part-time. Students come from 17 states and territories, 54% are from out of state, 65% African American, 1% Asian American or Pacific Islander, 9% Hispanic American, 0.1% Native American, 2% international, 3% transferred in, 30% live on campus. *Retention:* 58% of 2001 full-time freshmen returned.

Freshmen *Admission:* 316 applied, 235 admitted, 125 enrolled. *Average high school GPA:* 3.0. *Test scores:* SAT verbal scores over 500: 41%; SAT math scores over 500: 38%; SAT verbal scores over 600: 5%; SAT math scores over 600: 4%.

Faculty *Total:* 195, 30% full-time. *Student/faculty ratio:* 13:1.

Majors Art history; biochemistry; bioengineering; biology; business administration; chemistry; early childhood education; economics; education; elementary education; English; environmental science; French; history; individual/family development; interdisciplinary studies; international relations; liberal arts and sciences/liberal studies; mass communications; mathematics; political science; pre-law; pre-medicine; psychology; secondary education; Spanish; special education.

Academic Programs *Special study options:* academic remediation for entering students, accelerated degree program, adult/continuing education programs, advanced placement credit, cooperative education, double majors, English as a second language, honors programs, independent study, internships, off-campus study, part-time degree program, services for LD students, student-designed majors, study abroad, summer session for credit. *ROTC:* Army (c), Navy (c), Air Force (c). *Unusual degree programs:* 3-2 engineering with George Washington University; University of Maryland, College Park.

Library Sister Helen Sheehan Library plus 1 other with 210,285 titles, 537 serial subscriptions, 14,411 audiovisual materials, an OPAC, a Web page.

Computers on Campus 80 computers available on campus for general student use. A campuswide network can be accessed from student residence rooms and from off campus. Internet access, online (class) registration, at least one staffed computer lab available.

Student Life *Housing:* on-campus residence required through junior year. *Options:* women-only. *Activities and Organizations:* drama/theater group, student-run newspaper, choral group, Campus Ministry, Athletic Association, international club, Black Student Alliance, Young Democrats/Republicans. *Campus security:* 24-hour emergency response devices and patrols, late-night transport/escort service, controlled dormitory access. *Student Services:* health clinic, personal/psychological counseling.

Trinity College (continued)

Athletics Member NCAA. All Division III. *Intercollegiate sports:* basketball W(c), crew W, field hockey W, lacrosse W, soccer W, tennis W. *Intramural sports:* tennis W.

Standardized Tests *Recommended:* SAT I or ACT (for admission).

Costs (2002–03) *Comprehensive fee:* $22,570 includes full-time tuition ($15,450), mandatory fees ($150), and room and board ($6970). Part-time tuition: $500 per credit hour. Part-time tuition and fees vary according to class time. *Room and board:* College room only: $3100. Room and board charges vary according to board plan and housing facility. *Payment plans:* installment, deferred payment. *Waivers:* employees or children of employees.

Financial Aid Of all full-time matriculated undergraduates who enrolled in 2001, 395 applied for aid, 366 were judged to have need, 41 had their need fully met. In 2001, 7 non-need-based awards were made. *Average percent of need met:* 68%. *Average financial aid package:* $13,960. *Average need-based loan:* $4501. *Average need-based gift aid:* $9799. *Average non-need based aid:* $6951. *Average indebtedness upon graduation:* $28,534.

Applying *Options:* common application, electronic application, deferred entrance. *Application fee:* $35. *Required:* essay or personal statement, high school transcript, minimum 2.0 GPA, 1 letter of recommendation. *Recommended:* interview. *Application deadline:* 2/1 (freshmen), rolling (transfers).

Admissions Contact Ms. Wendy Kares, Director of Admissions, Trinity College, 125 Michigan Avenue, NE, Washington, DC 20017-1094. *Phone:* 202-884-9400. *Fax:* 202-884-9229.

UNIVERSITY OF THE DISTRICT OF COLUMBIA
Washington, District of Columbia

- **District-supported** comprehensive, founded 1976
- **Calendar** semesters
- **Degrees** associate, bachelor's, and master's
- **Urban** 28-acre campus
- **Endowment** $16.5 million
- **Coed,** 5,140 undergraduate students, 34% full-time, 62% women, 38% men
- **Noncompetitive** entrance level, 90% of applicants were admitted

Undergraduates 1,751 full-time, 3,389 part-time. Students come from 54 states and territories, 119 other countries, 19% are from out of state, 76% African American, 2% Asian American or Pacific Islander, 5% Hispanic American, 0.1% Native American, 7% international, 8% transferred in.

Freshmen *Admission:* 2,101 applied, 1,899 admitted, 1,320 enrolled.

Faculty *Total:* 479, 53% full-time. *Student/faculty ratio:* 13:1.

Majors Accounting; advertising; aerospace science; anthropology; architectural engineering technology; architecture; art; art education; aviation management; aviation technology; biological technology; biology; business administration; business education; business marketing and marketing management; ceramic arts; chemical engineering technology; chemistry; child care/development; city/community/regional planning; civil engineering; civil engineering technology; clothing/textiles; computer engineering technology; computer science; construction management; corrections; criminal justice/law enforcement administration; criminology; developmental/child psychology; early childhood education; economics; electrical/electronic engineering technology; electrical engineering; electromechanical technology; elementary education; emergency medical technology; engineering technology; English; environmental science; environmental technology; fashion merchandising; finance; fine/studio arts; fire science; food sciences; food services technology; forestry; French; geography; graphic design/commercial art/illustration; graphic/printing equipment; health education; history; home economics; home economics education; hospitality management; industrial arts; industrial radiologic technology; information sciences/systems; law enforcement/police science; legal administrative assistant; library science; marine science; mass communications; mathematics; mechanical engineering; mechanical engineering technology; medical laboratory technician; medical technology; mortuary science; music; music teacher education; nursing; nutritional sciences; ornamental horticulture; philosophy; physical education; physical sciences; physics; political science; practical nurse; psychology; public administration; purchasing/contracts management; recreation/leisure studies; respiratory therapy; secretarial science; social work; sociology; Spanish; special education; speech-language pathology/audiology; theater arts/drama; trade/industrial education; urban studies; water resources; water treatment technology.

Academic Programs *Special study options:* academic remediation for entering students, accelerated degree program, adult/continuing education programs, cooperative education, English as a second language, external degree program, honors programs, internships, off-campus study, part-time degree program, services for LD students, summer session for credit. *ROTC:* Army (c), Air Force (c).

Library Learning Resources Division Library plus 1 other with 544,412 titles, 591 serial subscriptions, 19,548 audiovisual materials, an OPAC, a Web page.

Computers on Campus 50 computers available on campus for general student use. At least one staffed computer lab available.

Student Life *Housing:* college housing not available. *Activities and Organizations:* drama/theater group, student-run newspaper, choral group, marching band, national fraternities, national sororities. *Campus security:* 24-hour patrols. *Student Services:* health clinic, personal/psychological counseling.

Athletics Member NCAA. All Division II. *Intercollegiate sports:* basketball M(s)/W(s), golf M(s), soccer M(s), tennis M(s)/W(s), track and field M(s)/W(s), volleyball W(s). *Intramural sports:* basketball M.

Costs (2001–02) *Tuition:* district resident $1800 full-time, $75 per semester hour part-time; nonresident $4440 full-time, $185 per semester hour part-time. Full-time tuition and fees vary according to course load. Part-time tuition and fees vary according to course load. *Required fees:* $270 full-time, $135 per term part-time. *Payment plans:* installment, deferred payment. *Waivers:* senior citizens and employees or children of employees.

Financial Aid Of all full-time matriculated undergraduates who enrolled in 2001, 1518 applied for aid, 987 were judged to have need, 226 had their need fully met. 110 Federal Work-Study jobs (averaging $2000). In 2001, 15 non-need-based awards were made. *Average need-based loan:* $3500. *Average non-need based aid:* $2500. *Average indebtedness upon graduation:* $19,000.

Applying *Options:* common application, deferred entrance. *Application fee:* $20. *Required:* high school transcript. *Required for some:* GED. *Application deadlines:* 8/1 (freshmen), 8/1 (transfers). *Notification:* continuous until 8/15 (freshmen).

Admissions Contact Mr. LaHugh Bankston, Registrar, University of the District of Columbia, 4200 Connecticut Avenue NW, Building 39—A-Level, Washington, DC 20008. *Phone:* 202-274-6200. *Fax:* 202-274-6067.

FLORIDA

AMERICAN COLLEGE OF PREHOSPITAL MEDICINE
Navarre, Florida

- **Proprietary** 4-year, founded 1991
- **Calendar** continuous
- **Degrees** associate and bachelor's (offers only distance learning degree programs)
- **Coed,** 240 undergraduate students
- **Moderately difficult** entrance level, 100% of applicants were admitted

Undergraduates Students come from 26 states and territories, 6 other countries.

Freshmen *Admission:* 40 applied, 40 admitted.

Faculty *Total:* 52, 50% with terminal degrees.

Majors Emergency medical technology.

Academic Programs *Special study options:* distance learning, external degree program, independent study, off-campus study.

Library American College of Prehospital Medicine Library plus 1 other with 700 titles, 14 serial subscriptions, an OPAC.

Student Life *Housing:* college housing not available.

Costs (2001–02) *Tuition:* $250 per semester hour part-time. Part-time tuition and fees vary according to course load and degree level. No tuition increase for student's term of enrollment. *Payment plan:* installment.

Applying *Options:* electronic application. *Application fee:* $50. *Required:* high school transcript, emergency medical technician certification or equivalent. *Application deadline:* rolling (freshmen), rolling (transfers). *Notification:* continuous (freshmen).

Admissions Contact Dr. Richard A. Clinchy, Chairman/CEO, American College of Prehospital Medicine, 7552 Navarre Parkway, Suite 1, Navarre, FL 32566-7312. *Phone:* 850-939-0840. *Toll-free phone:* 800-735-2276. *Fax:* 800-350-3870. *E-mail:* admit@acpm.edu.

AMERICAN INTERCONTINENTAL UNIVERSITY
Plantation, Florida

- **Proprietary** comprehensive
- **Degrees** associate, bachelor's, and master's

■ **Coed,** 714 undergraduate students

Undergraduates 43% African American, 4% Asian American or Pacific Islander, 33% Hispanic American, 0.6% Native American, 3% international.
Faculty *Total:* 26. *Student/faculty ratio:* 24:1.
Costs (2002–03) *Tuition:* Full-time tuition and fees vary according to program. Tuition per quarter: $1,980-$3,740.
Admissions Contact Joseph Rogalski, Director of Admissions, American InterContinental University, 8151 West Peters Road, Suite 1000, Plantation, FL 33324. *Phone:* 954-233-3990.

ARGOSY UNIVERSITY-SARASOTA
Sarasota, Florida

Admissions Contact 5250 17th Street, Sarasota, FL 34235-8246. *Toll-free phone:* 800-331-5995.

THE ART INSTITUTE OF FORT LAUDERDALE
Fort Lauderdale, Florida

- **Proprietary** 4-year, founded 1968
- **Calendar** quarters
- **Degrees** associate and bachelor's
- **Urban** campus with easy access to Miami
- **Coed,** 3,500 undergraduate students
- **Noncompetitive** entrance level, 72% of applicants were admitted

Freshmen *Admission:* 3,000 applied, 2,146 admitted.
Faculty *Total:* 110. *Student/faculty ratio:* 20:1.
Majors Applied art; clothing/textiles; computer graphics; culinary arts; fashion design/illustration; film/video production; graphic design/commercial art/illustration; industrial design; interior design; photography; radio/television broadcasting.
Academic Programs *Special study options:* academic remediation for entering students, accelerated degree program, adult/continuing education programs, advanced placement credit, cooperative education, internships, off-campus study, summer session for credit.
Library 16,200 titles, 270 serial subscriptions, an OPAC, a Web page.
Computers on Campus 125 computers available on campus for general student use. Internet access, at least one staffed computer lab available.
Student Life *Housing Options:* coed. *Student Services:* personal/psychological counseling.
Standardized Tests *Recommended:* SAT I or ACT (for placement).
Costs (2001–02) *Room and board:* $4480.
Applying *Options:* common application. *Application fee:* $50. *Required:* essay or personal statement, high school transcript. *Recommended:* interview. *Application deadline:* rolling (freshmen), rolling (transfers).
Admissions Contact Ms. Eileen L. Northrop, Vice President and Director of Admissions, The Art Institute of Fort Lauderdale, 1799 Southeast 17th Street Causeway, Fort Lauderdale, FL 33316-3000. *Phone:* 954-527-1799 Ext. 420. *Toll-free phone:* 800-275-7603. *Fax:* 954-728-8637.

THE BAPTIST COLLEGE OF FLORIDA
Graceville, Florida

- **Independent Southern Baptist** 4-year, founded 1943
- **Calendar** 4-4-2
- **Degrees** associate and bachelor's
- **Small-town** 165-acre campus
- **Endowment** $3.0 million
- **Coed,** 575 undergraduate students, 79% full-time, 34% women, 66% men
- **Noncompetitive** entrance level, 94% of applicants were admitted

Undergraduates 454 full-time, 121 part-time. Students come from 24 states and territories, 6 other countries, 28% are from out of state, 5% African American, 1% Asian American or Pacific Islander, 3% Hispanic American, 0.9% Native American, 1% international, 14% transferred in, 36% live on campus. *Retention:* 73% of 2001 full-time freshmen returned.
Freshmen *Admission:* 89 applied, 84 admitted, 50 enrolled.
Faculty *Total:* 50, 42% full-time, 40% with terminal degrees. *Student/faculty ratio:* 19:1.
Majors Biblical studies; child care/guidance; education; elementary education; pastoral counseling; religious education; religious music; theology.
Academic Programs *Special study options:* academic remediation for entering students, accelerated degree program, adult/continuing education programs, advanced placement credit, distance learning, double majors, independent study, internships, part-time degree program, services for LD students, summer session for credit.
Library Ida J. MacMillan Library with 47,117 titles, 2,227 serial subscriptions, 10,447 audiovisual materials, an OPAC, a Web page.
Computers on Campus 16 computers available on campus for general student use. Internet access, at least one staffed computer lab available.
Student Life *Housing:* on-campus residence required through sophomore year. *Options:* men-only, women-only. *Activities and Organizations:* drama/theater group, choral group, Baptist Collegiate Ministry, Student Government. *Campus security:* student patrols, patrols by police officers 11 p.m. to 7 a.m. *Student Services:* personal/psychological counseling.
Athletics *Intramural sports:* basketball M/W, football M/W, soccer M/W, softball M/W, table tennis M/W, volleyball M/W.
Standardized Tests *Required for some:* SAT I or ACT (for admission).
Costs (2002–03) *Comprehensive fee:* $8600 includes full-time tuition ($5250), mandatory fees ($200), and room and board ($3150). Part-time tuition: $180 per semester hour. Part-time tuition and fees vary according to course load. *Required fees:* $100 per term part-time. *Room and board:* Room and board charges vary according to board plan and housing facility. *Payment plan:* deferred payment. *Waivers:* employees or children of employees.
Financial Aid Of all full-time matriculated undergraduates who enrolled in 2001, 485 applied for aid, 363 were judged to have need, 9 had their need fully met. 36 Federal Work-Study jobs (averaging $1175). In 2001, 88 non-need-based awards were made. *Average percent of need met:* 59%. *Average financial aid package:* $3400. *Average need-based loan:* $2250. *Average non-need based aid:* $600. *Average indebtedness upon graduation:* $9513.
Applying *Options:* common application, electronic application, deferred entrance. *Application fee:* $20. *Required:* essay or personal statement, high school transcript, 3 letters of recommendation. *Required for some:* interview. *Application deadline:* rolling (freshmen), rolling (transfers). *Notification:* continuous (freshmen).
Admissions Contact Mr. Kyle S. Luke, Director of Admissions, The Baptist College of Florida, 5400 College Drive, Graceville, FL 32440-1898. *Phone:* 850-263-3261 Ext. 460. *Toll-free phone:* 800-328-2660 Ext. 460. *Fax:* 850-263-7506. *E-mail:* admissions@baptistcollege.edu.

BARRY UNIVERSITY
Miami Shores, Florida

- **Independent Roman Catholic** university, founded 1940
- **Calendar** semesters
- **Degrees** certificates, bachelor's, master's, doctoral, first professional, post-master's, postbachelor's, and first professional certificates
- **Suburban** 122-acre campus with easy access to Miami
- **Endowment** $15.8 million
- **Coed,** 5,907 undergraduate students, 55% full-time, 65% women, 35% men
- **Moderately difficult** entrance level, 73% of applicants were admitted

Barry University represents a personalized educational experience that encourages students to think critically, expand their skills, and find answers. With more than 60 undergraduate programs and more than 50 graduate programs, Barry offers superb opportunities for study, community service, and professional growth. Barry University is a coeducational, Catholic international university that is focused on quality academics, hands-on experience, and students' success.

Undergraduates 3,276 full-time, 2,631 part-time. Students come from 46 states and territories, 68 other countries, 24% are from out of state, 20% African American, 1% Asian American or Pacific Islander, 32% Hispanic American, 0.2% Native American, 6% international, 9% transferred in, 32% live on campus. *Retention:* 71% of 2001 full-time freshmen returned.
Freshmen *Admission:* 2,167 applied, 1,572 admitted, 437 enrolled. *Test scores:* SAT verbal scores over 500: 48%; SAT math scores over 500: 47%; SAT verbal scores over 600: 11%; SAT math scores over 600: 11%; SAT verbal scores over 700: 1%; SAT math scores over 700: 1%.
Faculty *Total:* 806, 40% full-time. *Student/faculty ratio:* 13:1.
Majors Accounting; acting/directing; advertising; biology; broadcast journalism; business administration; business marketing and marketing management; chemistry; communications; computer science; criminology; cytotechnology; early childhood education; ecology; economics; education; elementary education;

Barry University (continued)
engineering; English; English education; exercise sciences; finance; French; history; information sciences/systems; international business; international relations; journalism; liberal arts and sciences/liberal studies; literature; management information systems/business data processing; marine biology; mass communications; mathematics; medical laboratory technician; medical technology; music (piano and organ performance); music (voice and choral/opera performance); nuclear medical technology; nursing; philosophy; photography; physical education; political science; pre-dentistry; pre-law; pre-medicine; pre-pharmacy studies; pre-veterinary studies; psychology; public relations; radio/television broadcasting; sociology; Spanish; special education; sport/fitness administration; theater arts/drama; theology.

Academic Programs *Special study options:* academic remediation for entering students, accelerated degree program, adult/continuing education programs, advanced placement credit, distance learning, double majors, English as a second language, honors programs, independent study, internships, off-campus study, part-time degree program, services for LD students, study abroad, summer session for credit. *ROTC:* Air Force (c). *Unusual degree programs:* 3-2 engineering with University of Miami.

Library Monsignor William Barry Memorial Library plus 1 other with 233,938 titles, 2,880 serial subscriptions, 4,247 audiovisual materials, an OPAC, a Web page.

Computers on Campus 250 computers available on campus for general student use. A campuswide network can be accessed from student residence rooms and from off campus. Internet access, at least one staffed computer lab available.

Student Life *Housing:* on-campus residence required for freshman year. *Options:* coed, men-only, women-only, disabled students. *Activities and Organizations:* drama/theater group, student-run newspaper, radio and television station, choral group, Student Government Association, Campus Activities Board, Scuba Society, Caribbean Students Association, Jamaican Association, national fraternities, national sororities. *Campus security:* 24-hour emergency response devices and patrols, late-night transport/escort service. *Student Services:* health clinic, personal/psychological counseling.

Athletics Member NCAA. All Division II. *Intercollegiate sports:* baseball M(s), basketball M(s)/W(s), crew W(s), golf M(s)/W(s), soccer M(s)/W(s), softball W(s), tennis M(s)/W(s), volleyball W(s). *Intramural sports:* basketball M/W, football M/W, golf M/W, soccer M/W, softball M/W, volleyball M/W.

Standardized Tests *Required:* SAT I or ACT (for admission).

Costs (2001–02) *Comprehensive fee:* $24,100 includes full-time tuition ($17,500) and room and board ($6600). Full-time tuition and fees vary according to location and program. Part-time tuition: $505 per credit. Part-time tuition and fees vary according to course load, location, and program. *Room and board:* Room and board charges vary according to board plan. *Payment plans:* tuition prepayment, installment, deferred payment. *Waivers:* employees or children of employees.

Financial Aid Of all full-time matriculated undergraduates who enrolled in 2001, 2105 applied for aid, 1923 were judged to have need, 223 had their need fully met. 450 Federal Work-Study jobs (averaging $2305). In 2001, 523 non-need-based awards were made. *Average percent of need met:* 69%. *Average financial aid package:* $14,167. *Average need-based loan:* $3884. *Average need-based gift aid:* $4485. *Average non-need based aid:* $6139.

Applying *Options:* common application, electronic application, early admission, deferred entrance. *Application fee:* $30. *Required:* high school transcript, minimum 2.0 GPA. *Required for some:* essay or personal statement. *Recommended:* interview. *Application deadline:* rolling (freshmen), rolling (transfers). *Notification:* continuous (freshmen).

Admissions Contact Ms. Tracey Fontaine, Director of Admissions, Barry University, Kelly House, 11300 Northeast Second Avenue, Miami Shores, FL 33161. *Phone:* 308-699-3127. *Toll-free phone:* 800-695-2279. *Fax:* 305-899-2971. *E-mail:* admissions@mail.barry.edu.

BETHUNE-COOKMAN COLLEGE
Daytona Beach, Florida

- **Independent Methodist** 4-year, founded 1904
- **Calendar** semesters
- **Degree** bachelor's
- **Urban** 60-acre campus with easy access to Orlando
- **Endowment** $25.0 million
- **Coed,** 2,724 undergraduate students, 93% full-time, 58% women, 42% men
- **Minimally difficult** entrance level, 56% of applicants were admitted

Undergraduates 2,529 full-time, 195 part-time. Students come from 40 states and territories, 35 other countries, 28% are from out of state, 89% African American, 0.3% Asian American or Pacific Islander, 1% Hispanic American, 7% international, 3% transferred in, 61% live on campus. *Retention:* 76% of 2001 full-time freshmen returned.

Freshmen *Admission:* 3,098 applied, 1,721 admitted, 726 enrolled. *Average high school GPA:* 2.70. *Test scores:* SAT verbal scores over 500: 14%; SAT math scores over 500: 12%; ACT scores over 18: 27%; SAT verbal scores over 600: 3%; SAT math scores over 600: 3%; ACT scores over 24: 2%.

Faculty *Total:* 202, 68% full-time, 41% with terminal degrees. *Student/faculty ratio:* 18:1.

Majors Accounting; biology; biology education; business administration; business education; chemistry; chemistry education; computer science; criminal justice/law enforcement administration; education of the specific learning disabled; elementary education; English; English education; foreign languages education; foreign languages/literatures; gerontology; history; hotel and restaurant management; information sciences/systems; international business; international relations; liberal arts and sciences/liberal studies; mass communications; mathematics; mathematics education; medical technology; music; music teacher education; nursing; philosophy and religion related; physical education; physics; physics education; political science; psychology; recreation/leisure studies; social science education; sociology; special education.

Academic Programs *Special study options:* academic remediation for entering students, accelerated degree program, adult/continuing education programs, advanced placement credit, cooperative education, distance learning, double majors, honors programs, independent study, internships, part-time degree program, study abroad, summer session for credit. *ROTC:* Army (c), Air Force (c). *Unusual degree programs:* 3-2 engineering with Tuskegee University, University of Florida, Florida Atlantic University, Florida Agricultural and Mechanical University, University of Central Florida.

Library Carl S. Swisher Library plus 1 other with 160,518 titles, 771 serial subscriptions, 10,500 audiovisual materials, an OPAC, a Web page.

Computers on Campus 300 computers available on campus for general student use. A campuswide network can be accessed from student residence rooms and from off campus. Internet access, online (class) registration, at least one staffed computer lab available.

Student Life *Housing:* on-campus residence required for freshman year. *Options:* men-only, women-only. *Activities and Organizations:* drama/theater group, student-run newspaper, radio station, choral group, marching band, Greek organizations, concert chorale, marching band, inspirational gospel choir, SGA, national fraternities, national sororities. *Campus security:* 24-hour emergency response devices and patrols, student patrols, late-night transport/escort service. *Student Services:* health clinic, personal/psychological counseling.

Athletics Member NCAA. All Division I except football (Division I-AA). *Intercollegiate sports:* baseball M(s), basketball M(s)/W(s), cross-country running M(s)/W(s), golf M(s)/W(s), softball W(s), tennis M(s)/W(s), track and field M(s)/W(s), volleyball W(s). *Intramural sports:* basketball M/W, football M, racquetball M/W, soccer M, table tennis M/W, volleyball M/W.

Standardized Tests *Required:* SAT I or ACT (for admission).

Costs (2001–02) *Comprehensive fee:* $15,746 includes full-time tuition ($9617) and room and board ($6129). Part-time tuition: $401 per credit hour. *Waivers:* employees or children of employees.

Financial Aid Of all full-time matriculated undergraduates who enrolled in 2001, 2506 applied for aid, 2198 were judged to have need, 465 had their need fully met. 349 Federal Work-Study jobs (averaging $1442). In 2001, 56 non-need-based awards were made. *Average percent of need met:* 75%. *Average financial aid package:* $13,646. *Average need-based loan:* $3323. *Average need-based gift aid:* $6527. *Average non-need based aid:* $7830. *Average indebtedness upon graduation:* $23,750.

Applying *Options:* early admission, deferred entrance. *Application fee:* $25. *Required:* high school transcript, minimum 2.25 GPA, medical history. *Required for some:* interview. *Application deadlines:* 7/30 (freshmen), 7/30 (transfers). *Notification:* continuous (freshmen).

Admissions Contact Mr. Edwin Coffie, Director of Admissions, Bethune-Cookman College, 640 Dr. Mary McLeod Bethune Boulevard, Daytona Beach, FL 32114-3099. *Phone:* 386-255-1401 Ext. 676. *Toll-free phone:* 800-448-0228. *Fax:* 386-257-5338. *E-mail:* coffiee@cookman.edu.

CARLOS ALBIZU UNIVERSITY, MIAMI CAMPUS
Miami, Florida

- **Independent** upper-level, founded 1980, part of Carlos Albizu University
- **Calendar** trimesters
- **Degrees** bachelor's, master's, and doctoral
- **Urban** 2-acre campus
- **Coed, primarily women,** 144 undergraduate students, 50% full-time, 79% women, 21% men
- 77% of applicants were admitted

Undergraduates 72 full-time, 72 part-time. Students come from 3 states and territories, 17% African American, 75% Hispanic American, 63% transferred in.
Freshmen *Admission:* 26 applied, 20 admitted.
Faculty *Total:* 20, 15% full-time, 100% with terminal degrees. *Student/faculty ratio:* 10:1.
Majors Business administration/management related; elementary education; psychology.
Academic Programs *Special study options:* academic remediation for entering students, adult/continuing education programs, advanced placement credit, external degree program, independent study, internships, part-time degree program, services for LD students, summer session for credit.
Library Albizu Library with 16,634 titles, 220 serial subscriptions, 628 audiovisual materials, an OPAC, a Web page.
Computers on Campus 26 computers available on campus for general student use. A campuswide network can be accessed from off campus. Internet access, at least one staffed computer lab available.
Student Life *Housing:* college housing not available. *Activities and Organizations:* student-run newspaper, Student Council, Psi Chi, Students for Cross Cultural Advancement, Psychology Club. *Campus security:* 24-hour emergency response devices and patrols, late-night transport/escort service.
Costs (2002–03) *Tuition:* $7200 full-time, $240 per credit part-time. Full-time tuition and fees vary according to course load and program. Part-time tuition and fees vary according to course load and program. *Required fees:* $669 full-time, $223 per term part-time. *Payment plan:* installment. *Waivers:* minority students and employees or children of employees.
Financial Aid Of all full-time matriculated undergraduates who enrolled in 2001, 58 applied for aid, 58 were judged to have need. 16 Federal Work-Study jobs (averaging $2850). In 2001, 1 non-need-based awards were made. *Average percent of need met:* 48%. *Average financial aid package:* $6244. *Average need-based loan:* $3250. *Average need-based gift aid:* $3736. *Average non-need based aid:* $1000. *Average indebtedness upon graduation:* $13,293.
Applying *Options:* common application, deferred entrance. *Application fee:* $25. *Application deadline:* rolling (transfers).
Admissions Contact Ms. Miriam Matos, Admissions Officer, Carlos Albizu University, Miami Campus, 2173 N.W. 99th Avenue, Miami, FL 33172. *Phone:* 305-593-1223 Ext. 134. *Toll-free phone:* 800-672-3246. *Fax:* 305-593-1854. *E-mail:* msalva@albizu.edu.

CLEARWATER CHRISTIAN COLLEGE
Clearwater, Florida

- **Independent nondenominational** 4-year, founded 1966
- **Calendar** semesters
- **Degrees** associate and bachelor's
- **Suburban** 50-acre campus with easy access to Tampa-St. Petersburg
- **Endowment** $1.0 million
- **Coed,** 652 undergraduate students
- **Minimally difficult** entrance level, 86% of applicants were admitted

Undergraduates Students come from 40 states and territories, 15 other countries, 0% are from out of state, 70% live on campus. *Retention:* 59% of 2001 full-time freshmen returned.
Freshmen *Admission:* 503 applied, 432 admitted. *Test scores:* SAT verbal scores over 500: 64%; SAT math scores over 500: 53%; ACT scores over 18: 82%; SAT verbal scores over 600: 19%; SAT math scores over 600: 15%; ACT scores over 24: 33%; SAT verbal scores over 700: 2%; SAT math scores over 700: 1%; ACT scores over 30: 4%.
Faculty *Total:* 53, 68% full-time. *Student/faculty ratio:* 15:1.
Majors Accounting; banking; biblical studies; biology; biology education; business administration; business education; communications; education; education (K-12); elementary education; English; English education; general studies; history; history education; humanities; mathematics; mathematics education; music; music teacher education; pastoral counseling; physical education; pre-law; pre-medicine; psychology; religious music; science education; secondary education; secretarial science; social studies education; special education.
Academic Programs *Special study options:* academic remediation for entering students, advanced placement credit, double majors, internships, part-time degree program, services for LD students, summer session for credit. *ROTC:* Army (c), Air Force (c).
Library Easter Library with 106,000 titles, 700 serial subscriptions, an OPAC.
Computers on Campus 25 computers available on campus for general student use. A campuswide network can be accessed from student residence rooms and from off campus. Internet access, at least one staffed computer lab available.
Student Life *Housing:* on-campus residence required through senior year. *Options:* men-only, women-only. *Activities and Organizations:* drama/theater group, student-run newspaper, choral group, Drama Club, Alpha Chi, College Republicans, Science Club, Student Missionary Fellowship. *Campus security:* 24-hour emergency response devices and patrols. *Student Services:* personal/psychological counseling.
Athletics Member NCCAA. *Intercollegiate sports:* baseball M, basketball M/W, soccer M, softball W, volleyball W. *Intramural sports:* basketball M/W, tennis M/W, volleyball M/W.
Standardized Tests *Required:* SAT I or ACT (for admission).
Costs (2002–03) *Comprehensive fee:* $14,000 includes full-time tuition ($9080), mandatory fees ($630), and room and board ($4290). Full-time tuition and fees vary according to course load and program. Part-time tuition: $360 per credit hour. Part-time tuition and fees vary according to course load and program. *Required fees:* $150 per semester hour. *Payment plan:* installment.
Financial Aid Of all full-time matriculated undergraduates who enrolled in 2001, 638 applied for aid, 638 were judged to have need, 48 had their need fully met. *Average percent of need met:* 59%. *Average financial aid package:* $5712. *Average need-based loan:* $3508. *Average need-based gift aid:* $3076. *Average indebtedness upon graduation:* $13,819.
Applying *Options:* early admission, deferred entrance. *Application fee:* $35. *Required:* essay or personal statement, high school transcript, minimum 2.0 GPA, 2 letters of recommendation, Christian testimony. *Recommended:* interview. *Application deadline:* rolling (freshmen), rolling (transfers). *Notification:* continuous (freshmen).
Admissions Contact Mr. Benjamin J. Puckett, Dean of Enrollment Services, Clearwater Christian College, 3400 Gulf-to-Bay Boulevard, Clearwater, FL 33759-4595. *Phone:* 727-726-1153. *Toll-free phone:* 800-348-4463. *Fax:* 813-726-8597. *E-mail:* admissions@clearwater.edu.

COLLEGE FOR PROFESSIONAL STUDIES
Boca Raton, Florida

Admissions Contact Ms. Kristina Belanger, Dean, College for Professional Studies, 1801 Clint Moore Road, Suite 215, Boca Raton, FL 33487. *Phone:* 561-994-2522. *Toll-free phone:* 800-669-2555. *Fax:* 561-988-2223.

DEVRY UNIVERSITY
Orlando, Florida

- **Proprietary** 4-year, founded 2000, part of DeVry, Inc
- **Calendar** semesters
- **Degrees** associate and bachelor's
- **Coed,** 803 undergraduate students, 76% full-time, 23% women, 77% men
- **Minimally difficult** entrance level, 77% of applicants were admitted

Undergraduates 611 full-time, 192 part-time. Students come from 23 states and territories, 8 other countries, 8% are from out of state, 28% African American, 3% Asian American or Pacific Islander, 15% Hispanic American, 0.7% Native American, 3% international, 0.4% transferred in. *Retention:* 43% of 2001 full-time freshmen returned.
Freshmen *Admission:* 801 applied, 613 admitted, 464 enrolled.
Faculty *Total:* 43, 81% full-time. *Student/faculty ratio:* 19:1.
Majors Business administration/management related; business systems analysis/design; business systems networking/ telecommunications; computer engineering technology; electrical/electronic engineering technology; information sciences/systems.
Academic Programs *Special study options:* academic remediation for entering students, accelerated degree program, adult/continuing education programs, advanced placement credit, cooperative education, part-time degree program, services for LD students, summer session for credit.
Library Learning Resource Center with 3,300 titles, 2,800 serial subscriptions, 30 audiovisual materials, an OPAC.
Computers on Campus 175 computers available on campus for general student use. A campuswide network can be accessed from off campus. At least one staffed computer lab available.
Student Life *Housing:* college housing not available. *Activities and Organizations:* student-run newspaper, Association for Information Technology Professionals, DeVry Orlando Auto Club, Millenia Engineering Students Association, PBL, The Student Journal. *Campus security:* 24-hour emergency response devices and patrols, late-night transport/escort service, lighted pathways/sidewalks.
Standardized Tests *Recommended:* SAT I and SAT II or ACT (for admission).
Costs (2001–02) *Tuition:* $9800 full-time, $345 per credit hour part-time. Full-time tuition and fees vary according to course load. Part-time tuition and fees

DeVry University (continued)
vary according to course load. *Required fees:* $65 full-time. *Payment plans:* installment, deferred payment. *Waivers:* employees or children of employees.

Financial Aid Of all full-time matriculated undergraduates who enrolled in 2001, 1232 applied for aid, 1197 were judged to have need, 24 had their need fully met. In 2001, 35 non-need-based awards were made. *Average percent of need met:* 36%. *Average financial aid package:* $7111. *Average need-based loan:* $5048. *Average need-based gift aid:* $3693.

Applying *Options:* electronic application, deferred entrance. *Application fee:* $50. *Required:* high school transcript, interview. *Application deadline:* rolling (freshmen), rolling (transfers). *Notification:* continuous (freshmen).

Admissions Contact Ms. Laura Dorsey, New Student Coordinator, DeVry University, 4000 Millenia Boulevard, Orlando, FL 32839. *Phone:* 407-355-4833. *Toll-free phone:* 866-fl-devry. *Fax:* 407-370-3198.

ECKERD COLLEGE

St. Petersburg, Florida

- **Independent Presbyterian** 4-year, founded 1958
- **Calendar** 4-1-4
- **Degree** bachelor's
- **Suburban** 267-acre campus with easy access to Tampa
- **Endowment** $19.3 million
- **Coed,** 1,582 undergraduate students, 98% full-time, 56% women, 44% men
- **Moderately difficult** entrance level, 78% of applicants were admitted

Undergraduates 1,557 full-time, 25 part-time. Students come from 50 states and territories, 49 other countries, 73% are from out of state, 2% African American, 2% Asian American or Pacific Islander, 4% Hispanic American, 10% international, 11% transferred in, 68% live on campus. *Retention:* 77% of 2001 full-time freshmen returned.

Freshmen *Admission:* 1,930 applied, 1,496 admitted, 424 enrolled. *Average high school GPA:* 3.50. *Test scores:* SAT verbal scores over 500: 80%; SAT math scores over 500: 79%; ACT scores over 18: 97%; SAT verbal scores over 600: 32%; SAT math scores over 600: 29%; ACT scores over 24: 51%; SAT verbal scores over 700: 8%; SAT math scores over 700: 5%; ACT scores over 30: 8%.

Faculty *Total:* 134, 72% full-time, 76% with terminal degrees. *Student/faculty ratio:* 14:1.

Majors American studies; anthropology; art; biology; business administration; chemistry; communications; comparative literature; computer science; creative writing; economics; English; environmental science; French; German; history; humanities; human resources management; individual/family development; interdisciplinary studies; international business; international relations; literature; marine biology; mathematics; medical technology; modern languages; music; philosophy; physics; political science; pre-dentistry; pre-law; pre-medicine; pre-veterinary studies; psychology; religious studies; Russian; sociology; Spanish; theater arts/drama; women's studies.

Academic Programs *Special study options:* accelerated degree program, adult/continuing education programs, advanced placement credit, cooperative education, double majors, English as a second language, external degree program, honors programs, independent study, internships, off-campus study, part-time degree program, services for LD students, student-designed majors, study abroad, summer session for credit. *ROTC:* Army (c), Air Force (c). *Unusual degree programs:* 3-2 engineering with University of Miami, Columbia University, Washington University in St. Louis, Auburn University.

Library William Luther Cobb Library with 113,850 titles, 3,009 serial subscriptions, 1,941 audiovisual materials, an OPAC, a Web page.

Computers on Campus 144 computers available on campus for general student use. A campuswide network can be accessed from student residence rooms and from off campus. Internet access, at least one staffed computer lab available.

Student Life *Housing:* on-campus residence required for freshman year. *Options:* coed, men-only, women-only. *Activities and Organizations:* drama/theater group, student-run newspaper, radio and television station, choral group, Earth Society, Water Search and Rescue Team, Triton Tribune, College Choir, Organization of Students. *Campus security:* 24-hour emergency response devices and patrols, student patrols, late-night transport/escort service, controlled dormitory access. *Student Services:* health clinic, personal/psychological counseling, women's center.

Athletics Member NCAA. All Division II. *Intercollegiate sports:* baseball M(s), basketball M(s)/W(s), cross-country running W(s), golf M(s), sailing M/W, soccer M(s)/W(s), softball W(s), swimming M(c)/W(c), tennis M(s)/W(s), volleyball M(c)/W(s). *Intramural sports:* basketball M/W, bowling M/W, cross-country running M/W, football M, golf M/W, sailing M/W, soccer M/W, softball M/W, swimming M/W, table tennis M/W, tennis M/W, volleyball M/W, weight lifting M/W.

Standardized Tests *Required:* SAT I or ACT (for admission). *Recommended:* SAT II: Subject Tests (for admission), SAT II: Writing Test (for admission).

Costs (2001–02) *Comprehensive fee:* $25,500 includes full-time tuition ($19,870), mandatory fees ($215), and room and board ($5415). *Room and board:* College room only: $2865. Room and board charges vary according to board plan and housing facility. *Payment plan:* installment. *Waivers:* employees or children of employees.

Financial Aid Of all full-time matriculated undergraduates who enrolled in 2001, 1027 applied for aid, 899 were judged to have need, 764 had their need fully met. *Average percent of need met:* 85%. *Average financial aid package:* $17,608. *Average indebtedness upon graduation:* $17,500.

Applying *Options:* common application, electronic application, early admission, deferred entrance. *Application fee:* $25. *Required:* essay or personal statement, high school transcript, 1 letter of recommendation. *Recommended:* minimum 3.0 GPA, interview. *Application deadline:* rolling (freshmen), rolling (transfers). *Notification:* continuous (freshmen).

Admissions Contact Dr. Richard R. Hallin, Dean of Admissions, Eckerd College, 4200 54th Avenue South, St. Petersburg, FL 33711. *Phone:* 727-864-8331. *Toll-free phone:* 800-456-9009. *Fax:* 727-866-2304. *E-mail:* admissions@eckerd.edu.

EDUCATION AMERICA, TAMPA TECHNICAL INSTITUTE, TAMPA CAMPUS

Tampa, Florida

- **Proprietary** primarily 2-year, founded 1948, part of Education America Inc.
- **Calendar** quarters
- **Degrees** associate and bachelor's
- **Urban** 10-acre campus
- **Coed**
- **Noncompetitive** entrance level

Student Life *Campus security:* late-night transport/escort service.

Financial Aid Of all full-time matriculated undergraduates who enrolled in 2001, 12 Federal Work-Study jobs (averaging $8000).

Applying *Options:* common application, deferred entrance. *Application fee:* $50. *Required:* high school transcript, interview.

Admissions Contact Ms. Kathy Miller, Director of Admissions, Education America, Tampa Technical Institute, Tampa Campus, 2410 East Busch Boulevard, Tampa, FL 33612-8410. *Phone:* 813-935-5700. *Toll-free phone:* 800-992-4850. *E-mail:* rams@ix.netcom.com.

EDWARD WATERS COLLEGE

Jacksonville, Florida

- **Independent African Methodist Episcopal** 4-year, founded 1866
- **Calendar** semesters
- **Degree** bachelor's
- **Urban** 20-acre campus
- **Coed,** 1,320 undergraduate students, 97% full-time, 49% women, 51% men
- **Noncompetitive** entrance level

Undergraduates 1,284 full-time, 36 part-time. Students come from 15 states and territories, 91% African American, 0.8% Hispanic American, 2% international. *Retention:* 70% of 2001 full-time freshmen returned.

Freshmen *Admission:* 514 admitted, 552 enrolled.

Faculty *Total:* 49, 67% full-time.

Majors Biology; business administration; chemistry; criminal justice/law enforcement administration; early childhood education; education; elementary education; English; history; information sciences/systems; journalism; mathematics; physical education; psychology; public administration; secondary education; social sciences; social work; sociology.

Academic Programs *Special study options:* academic remediation for entering students, adult/continuing education programs, cooperative education, honors programs, internships, off-campus study, part-time degree program, student-designed majors, summer session for credit. *ROTC:* Army (c). *Unusual degree programs:* 3-2 engineering with University of Miami.

Library Centennial Library with 120,000 titles, 7,300 serial subscriptions.

Computers on Campus 125 computers available on campus for general student use.

Student Life *Housing Options:* coed. *Activities and Organizations:* student-run newspaper, radio station. *Campus security:* 24-hour emergency response devices and patrols, student patrols, late-night transport/escort service, controlled dormitory access.

Athletics Member NAIA. *Intercollegiate sports:* basketball M(s)/W(s), tennis M(s)/W(s), track and field M(s)/W(s). *Intramural sports:* basketball M/W, football M, golf M, tennis M/W, volleyball M/W.

Standardized Tests *Required:* CAT. *Recommended:* SAT I or ACT (for placement).

Costs (2001–02) *Comprehensive fee:* $6430 includes full-time tuition ($3100), mandatory fees ($595), and room and board ($2735). Part-time tuition: $315 per hour.

Applying *Options:* common application. *Application fee:* $15. *Required:* high school transcript, medical forms. *Application deadline:* rolling (freshmen), rolling (transfers). *Notification:* continuous (freshmen).

Admissions Contact Ms. Sadie Milliner-Smith, Director of Admissions, Edward Waters College, 1658 Kings Road, Jacksonville, FL 32209-6199. *Phone:* 904-366-2715.

EMBRY-RIDDLE AERONAUTICAL UNIVERSITY
Daytona Beach, Florida

- **Independent** comprehensive, founded 1926
- **Calendar** semesters
- **Degrees** associate, bachelor's, and master's
- **Urban** 178-acre campus with easy access to Orlando
- **Endowment** $34.8 million
- **Coed, primarily men,** 4,641 undergraduate students, 90% full-time, 16% women, 84% men
- **Moderately difficult** entrance level, 81% of applicants were admitted

Embry-Riddle teaches science, theory, and business to meet all the demands of employers in the world of aviation and aerospace; the University's impact on the industry through its graduates is significant. Founded just 22 years after the Wright brothers first flew, Embry-Riddle students learn to solve problems in engineering, business, computer science, technology, maintenance, psychology, communication, and flight. Whatever field students choose, they learn from educators and practitioners who are on the leading edge.

Undergraduates 4,156 full-time, 485 part-time. Students come from 55 states and territories, 99 other countries, 70% are from out of state, 5% African American, 3% Asian American or Pacific Islander, 5% Hispanic American, 0.6% Native American, 16% international, 6% transferred in, 42% live on campus. *Retention:* 79% of 2001 full-time freshmen returned.

Freshmen *Admission:* 2,631 applied, 2,119 admitted, 1,022 enrolled. *Average high school GPA:* 3.29. *Test scores:* SAT verbal scores over 500: 69%; SAT math scores over 500: 81%; ACT scores over 18: 95%; SAT verbal scores over 600: 23%; SAT math scores over 600: 35%; ACT scores over 24: 47%; SAT verbal scores over 700: 3%; SAT math scores over 700: 6%; ACT scores over 30: 6%.

Faculty *Total:* 272, 71% full-time, 50% with terminal degrees. *Student/faculty ratio:* 20:1.

Majors Aerospace engineering; aerospace engineering technology; aircraft mechanic/powerplant; aircraft pilot (professional); aviation/airway science; aviation management; business administration; civil engineering; communications; computer engineering; computer/information sciences; electrical/electronic engineering technologies related; electrical/electronic engineering technology; engineering; engineering physics; engineering technology; experimental psychology.

Academic Programs *Special study options:* academic remediation for entering students, adult/continuing education programs, advanced placement credit, cooperative education, distance learning, double majors, English as a second language, external degree program, independent study, internships, part-time degree program, services for LD students, study abroad, summer session for credit. *ROTC:* Army (b), Air Force (b).

Library Jack R. Hunt Memorial Library with 66,557 titles, 1,504 serial subscriptions, 6,484 audiovisual materials, an OPAC, a Web page.

Computers on Campus A campuswide network can be accessed from student residence rooms and from off campus. At least one staffed computer lab available.

Student Life *Housing:* on-campus residence required through sophomore year. *Options:* coed, disabled students. *Activities and Organizations:* drama/theater group, student-run newspaper, radio station, choral group, Eagle Wing, Future Professional Pilots Association, African Student Association, Caribbean Student Association, Sigma Gamma Tau, national fraternities, national sororities. *Campus security:* 24-hour emergency response devices and patrols, student patrols, late-night transport/escort service. *Student Services:* health clinic, personal/psychological counseling.

Athletics Member NAIA. *Intercollegiate sports:* baseball M(s), basketball M(s), cross-country running M/W, golf M(s), soccer M(s)/W(s), tennis M(s)/W, volleyball W(s). *Intramural sports:* badminton M/W, basketball M/W, bowling M(c)/W(c), crew M(c)/W(c), football M/W, golf M/W, ice hockey M(c), lacrosse M(c)/W(c), racquetball M/W, rugby M(c)/W(c), sailing M(c)/W(c), skiing (downhill) M/W, soccer M/W, softball M/W, swimming M/W, table tennis M/W, tennis M/W, volleyball M/W, water polo M/W, weight lifting M/W, wrestling M(c).

Standardized Tests *Required:* SAT I (for admission).

Costs (2002–03) *Comprehensive fee:* $24,160 includes full-time tuition ($17,850), mandatory fees ($550), and room and board ($5760). Full-time tuition and fees vary according to program. Part-time tuition: $745 per credit hour. Part-time tuition and fees vary according to program. *Room and board:* College room only: $3240. Room and board charges vary according to board plan. *Payment plans:* installment, deferred payment. *Waivers:* employees or children of employees.

Financial Aid Of all full-time matriculated undergraduates who enrolled in 2001, 2803 applied for aid, 2392 were judged to have need. 209 Federal Work-Study jobs (averaging $1117). *Average financial aid package:* $10,577. *Average need-based loan:* $4101. *Average need-based gift aid:* $6635. *Average indebtedness upon graduation:* $23,082. *Financial aid deadline:* 6/30.

Applying *Options:* common application, electronic application, early admission, early decision, deferred entrance. *Application fee:* $30. *Required:* high school transcript, minimum 2.0 GPA. *Required for some:* minimum 3.0 GPA, medical examination for flight students. *Recommended:* essay or personal statement, letters of recommendation, interview. *Application deadlines:* 7/1 (freshmen), 7/1 (transfers). *Early decision:* 12/1. *Notification:* continuous (freshmen), 12/31 (early decision).

Admissions Contact Mr. Michael Novak, Director of Admissions, Embry-Riddle Aeronautical University, 600 South Clyde Morris Boulevard, Daytona Beach, FL 32114-3900. *Phone:* 386-226-6112. *Toll-free phone:* 800-862-2416. *Fax:* 386-226-7070. *E-mail:* admit@db.erau.edu.

EMBRY-RIDDLE AERONAUTICAL UNIVERSITY, EXTENDED CAMPUS
Daytona Beach, Florida

- **Independent** comprehensive, founded 1970
- **Calendar** 5 9-week terms
- **Degrees** associate, bachelor's, and master's (programs offered at 100 military bases worldwide)
- **Endowment** $34.8 million
- **Coed, primarily men,** 6,568 undergraduate students, 3% full-time, 11% women, 89% men
- **Minimally difficult** entrance level

Undergraduates 167 full-time, 6,401 part-time. 8% African American, 3% Asian American or Pacific Islander, 7% Hispanic American, 1.0% Native American, 2% international.

Freshmen *Admission:* 195 enrolled.

Faculty *Total:* 2,947, 4% full-time, 21% with terminal degrees. *Student/faculty ratio:* 3:1.

Majors Aircraft mechanic/powerplant; aircraft pilot (professional); aviation/airway science; aviation management; business administration.

Academic Programs *Special study options:* adult/continuing education programs, advanced placement credit, cooperative education, distance learning, external degree program, independent study, off-campus study, part-time degree program, services for LD students.

Library Jack R. Hunt Memorial Library with 66,557 titles, 1,504 serial subscriptions, 6,484 audiovisual materials, an OPAC, a Web page.

Student Life *Housing:* college housing not available.

Costs (2001–02) *Tuition:* $4152 full-time, $173 per credit hour part-time. Full-time tuition and fees vary according to location and program. Part-time tuition and fees vary according to location. *Waivers:* employees or children of employees.

Financial Aid Of all full-time matriculated undergraduates who enrolled in 2001, 41 applied for aid, 41 were judged to have need. *Average financial aid package:* $5669. *Average need-based loan:* $4905. *Average need-based gift aid:* $2165. *Average indebtedness upon graduation:* $10,784. *Financial aid deadline:* 6/30.

Applying *Options:* deferred entrance. *Application fee:* $30. *Required for some:* essay or personal statement. *Application deadline:* rolling (freshmen), rolling (transfers). *Notification:* continuous (freshmen).

Admissions Contact Mrs. Pam Thomas, Director of Admissions, Records and Registration, Embry-Riddle Aeronautical University, Extended Campus, Daytona Beach, FL 32114-3900. *Phone:* 386-226-7610. *Toll-free phone:* 800-862-2416. *Fax:* 386-226-6984. *E-mail:* ecinfo@ec.db.erau.edu.

EVERGLADES COLLEGE

Ft. Lauderdale, Florida

- **Proprietary** 4-year
- **Degrees** associate and bachelor's
- **Coed,** 175 undergraduate students, 100% full-time, 41% women, 59% men
- 76% of applicants were admitted

Undergraduates 175 full-time.
Freshmen *Admission:* 66 applied, 50 admitted, 50 enrolled.
Faculty *Total:* 28, 11% full-time. *Student/faculty ratio:* 15:1.
Majors Aircraft pilot (professional); aviation management; business administration; information technology; management science.
Costs (2001–02) *Tuition:* $8600 full-time, $354 per credit hour part-time. *Required fees:* $400 full-time.
Applying *Application fee:* $55.
Admissions Contact Ms. Susan Ziegelhoffer, Vice President of Enrollment Management, Everglades College, 1500 NW 49th Street, Suite 600, Ft. Lauderdale, FL 33309. *Phone:* 954-772-2655.

FLAGLER COLLEGE

St. Augustine, Florida

- **Independent** 4-year, founded 1968
- **Calendar** semesters
- **Degree** bachelor's
- **Small-town** 36-acre campus with easy access to Jacksonville
- **Endowment** $34.9 million
- **Coed,** 1,852 undergraduate students, 97% full-time, 63% women, 37% men
- **Moderately difficult** entrance level, 28% of applicants were admitted

Size, cost, location, and excellent academics are the characteristics most often cited by students in their decision to enroll at Flagler. Interested students are encouraged to visit historic St. Augustine and learn how Flagler offers high-quality education in a beautiful setting at a reasonable cost. The cost of tuition, room, and board for the 2002-03 year is just $10,990.

Undergraduates 1,805 full-time, 47 part-time. Students come from 46 states and territories, 23 other countries, 33% are from out of state, 1% African American, 0.9% Asian American or Pacific Islander, 2% Hispanic American, 0.1% Native American, 3% international, 5% transferred in, 38% live on campus. *Retention:* 68% of 2001 full-time freshmen returned.
Freshmen *Admission:* 1,757 applied, 496 admitted, 423 enrolled. *Average high school GPA:* 3.54. *Test scores:* SAT verbal scores over 500: 87%; SAT math scores over 500: 82%; ACT scores over 18: 98%; SAT verbal scores over 600: 27%; SAT math scores over 600: 26%; ACT scores over 24: 40%; SAT verbal scores over 700: 4%; SAT math scores over 700: 1%; ACT scores over 30: 1%.
Faculty *Total:* 152, 41% full-time. *Student/faculty ratio:* 19:1.
Majors Accounting; art education; business administration; communications; education of the hearing impaired; education of the mentally handicapped; education of the specific learning disabled; elementary education; English; fine/studio arts; graphic design/commercial art/illustration; history; Latin American studies; philosophy; political science; psychology; religious studies; secondary education; social sciences; sociology; Spanish; Spanish language education; sport/fitness administration; theater arts/drama.
Academic Programs *Special study options:* academic remediation for entering students, advanced placement credit, distance learning, double majors, independent study, internships, off-campus study, services for LD students, study abroad, summer session for credit.
Library William L. Proctor Library with 63,791 titles, 472 serial subscriptions, 2,097 audiovisual materials, an OPAC, a Web page.
Computers on Campus 205 computers available on campus for general student use. A campuswide network can be accessed from off campus. Internet access, at least one staffed computer lab available.
Student Life *Housing:* on-campus residence required for freshman year. *Options:* men-only, women-only. *Activities and Organizations:* drama/theater group, student-run newspaper, radio station, choral group, Society for Advancement of Management, Student Government Association, Women's Club, Deaf Awareness Club, Sport Management Club. *Campus security:* 24-hour emergency response devices and patrols, late-night transport/escort service, controlled dormitory access. *Student Services:* health clinic, personal/psychological counseling.
Athletics Member NAIA. *Intercollegiate sports:* baseball M(s), basketball M(s)/W(s), cross-country running M(s)/W(s), golf M(s)/W, soccer M(s)/W(s), tennis M(s)/W(s), volleyball M(c)/W(s). *Intramural sports:* badminton M/W, basketball M/W, bowling M/W, football M/W, soccer M/W, softball M/W, swimming M/W, table tennis M/W, tennis M/W, volleyball M/W, weight lifting M/W.
Standardized Tests *Required:* SAT I or ACT (for admission).
Costs (2002–03) *Comprehensive fee:* $10,990 includes full-time tuition ($6870) and room and board ($4120). Part-time tuition: $225 per credit hour. *Waivers:* employees or children of employees.
Financial Aid Of all full-time matriculated undergraduates who enrolled in 2001, 1784 applied for aid, 763 were judged to have need, 262 had their need fully met. 231 Federal Work-Study jobs (averaging $485). 89 State and other part-time jobs (averaging $470). In 2001, 794 non-need-based awards were made. *Average percent of need met:* 74%. *Average financial aid package:* $6570. *Average need-based loan:* $3219. *Average need-based gift aid:* $2338. *Average non-need based aid:* $3870. *Average indebtedness upon graduation:* $15,669.
Applying *Options:* electronic application, early admission, early decision, deferred entrance. *Application fee:* $25. *Required:* essay or personal statement, high school transcript, 1 letter of recommendation. *Recommended:* minimum 2.75 GPA, interview, rank in upper 50% of high school class. *Application deadlines:* 3/1 (freshmen), 3/1 (transfers). *Early decision:* 12/1 (for plan 1), 1/15 (for plan 2). *Notification:* 3/15 (freshmen), 12/15 (early decision plan 1), 2/1 (early decision plan 2).
Admissions Contact Mr. Marc G. Williar, Director of Admissions, Flagler College, PO Box 1027, St. Augustine, FL 32085-1027. *Phone:* 904-829-6481 Ext. 220. *Toll-free phone:* 800-304-4208. *E-mail:* admiss@flagler.edu.

FLORIDA AGRICULTURAL AND MECHANICAL UNIVERSITY

Tallahassee, Florida

- **State-supported** university, founded 1887, part of State University System of Florida
- **Calendar** semesters
- **Degrees** associate, bachelor's, master's, doctoral, and first professional
- **Urban** 419-acre campus
- **Coed,** 10,853 undergraduate students, 88% full-time, 56% women, 44% men
- **Moderately difficult** entrance level, 71% of applicants were admitted

Undergraduates 9,513 full-time, 1,340 part-time. Students come from 47 states and territories, 50 other countries, 20% are from out of state, 95% African American, 0.5% Asian American or Pacific Islander, 0.8% Hispanic American, 0.0% Native American, 0.8% international, 4% transferred in. *Retention:* 80% of 2001 full-time freshmen returned.
Freshmen *Admission:* 5,820 applied, 4,160 admitted, 2,294 enrolled. *Average high school GPA:* 3.21.
Faculty *Total:* 488.
Majors Accounting; actuarial science; African-American studies; agricultural business; agricultural sciences; animal sciences; architectural engineering technology; architecture; art; art education; biology; business administration; business education; chemical engineering; chemistry; civil engineering; civil engineering technology; construction technology; criminal justice/law enforcement administration; early childhood education; economics; education; electrical/electronic engineering technology; electrical engineering; elementary education; English; entomology; finance; French; graphic design/commercial art/illustration; graphic/printing equipment; health education; health services administration; history; horticulture science; industrial arts; industrial/manufacturing engineering; information sciences/systems; journalism; landscape architecture; liberal arts and sciences/liberal studies; mass communications; mathematics; mechanical engineering; medical records administration; molecular biology; music; music teacher education; nursing; occupational therapy; ornamental horticulture; pharmacy; philosophy; physical education; physical therapy; physics; plant protection; political science; pre-dentistry; psychology; public administration; public relations; religious studies; respiratory therapy; secretarial science; social sciences; social work; sociology; Spanish; theater arts/drama; trade/industrial education.
Academic Programs *Special study options:* academic remediation for entering students, accelerated degree program, adult/continuing education programs, advanced placement credit, cooperative education, honors programs, internships, off-campus study, part-time degree program, services for LD students, summer session for credit. *ROTC:* Army (b), Navy (b), Air Force (c).
Library Coleman Memorial Library plus 5 others with 704,894 titles, 6,017 serial subscriptions, 73,209 audiovisual materials, an OPAC.
Computers on Campus A campuswide network can be accessed from student residence rooms and from off campus. Internet access, at least one staffed computer lab available.
Student Life *Housing:* on-campus residence required for freshman year. *Options:* men-only, women-only. *Activities and Organizations:* drama/theater

group, student-run newspaper, radio station, choral group, marching band, Gospel Choir, University Marching Band, Alpha Kappa Alpha, Alpha Phi Alpha, SBI, national fraternities, national sororities. *Campus security:* 24-hour emergency response devices and patrols, late-night transport/escort service. *Student Services:* health clinic, personal/psychological counseling, women's center.

Athletics Member NCAA. All Division I except football (Division I-AA). *Intercollegiate sports:* baseball M, basketball M(s)/W(s), cross-country running M(s)/W(s), golf M(s)/W(s), softball W, swimming M(s)/W(s), tennis M(s)/W(s), track and field M(s)/W(s), volleyball W(s). *Intramural sports:* basketball M/W, cross-country running M, football M, tennis M/W, volleyball M/W.

Standardized Tests *Required:* SAT I or ACT (for admission).

Costs (2001–02) *Tuition:* state resident $2458 full-time, $77 per credit hour part-time; nonresident $10,346 full-time, $321 per credit hour part-time. Full-time tuition and fees vary according to course load. Part-time tuition and fees vary according to course load. *Required fees:* $233 full-time. *Room and board:* $4742; room only: $2964. Room and board charges vary according to board plan and housing facility. *Payment plans:* tuition prepayment, deferred payment. *Waivers:* senior citizens and employees or children of employees.

Financial Aid Of all full-time matriculated undergraduates who enrolled in 2001, 8325 applied for aid, 7506 were judged to have need, 1319 had their need fully met. 407 Federal Work-Study jobs (averaging $1753). In 2001, 452 non-need-based awards were made. *Average percent of need met:* 55%. *Average financial aid package:* $6915. *Average need-based loan:* $3417. *Average need-based gift aid:* $3960. *Average non-need based aid:* $5972. *Average indebtedness upon graduation:* $22,428.

Applying *Options:* common application, electronic application, early admission, deferred entrance. *Application fee:* $20. *Required:* high school transcript, minimum 2.0 GPA. *Required for some:* essay or personal statement, letters of recommendation. *Recommended:* minimum 3.0 GPA. *Application deadlines:* 5/1 (freshmen), 5/1 (transfers). *Notification:* continuous until 8/1 (freshmen).

Admissions Contact Ms. Barbara R. Cox, Director of Admissions, Florida Agricultural and Mechanical University, Office of Admissions, Tallahassee, FL 32307. *Phone:* 850-599-3796. *Fax:* 850-599-3069. *E-mail:* barbara.cox@famu.edu.

FLORIDA ATLANTIC UNIVERSITY
Boca Raton, Florida

- **State-supported** university, founded 1961, part of State University System of Florida
- **Calendar** semesters
- **Degrees** associate, bachelor's, master's, and doctoral
- **Suburban** 850-acre campus with easy access to Miami
- **Endowment** $95.5 million
- **Coed,** 18,757 undergraduate students, 52% full-time, 61% women, 39% men
- **Moderately difficult** entrance level, 71% of applicants were admitted

Undergraduates 9,758 full-time, 8,999 part-time. Students come from 51 states and territories, 140 other countries, 9% are from out of state, 17% African American, 4% Asian American or Pacific Islander, 13% Hispanic American, 0.4% Native American, 6% international, 17% transferred in, 9% live on campus. *Retention:* 69% of 2001 full-time freshmen returned.

Freshmen *Admission:* 6,289 applied, 4,495 admitted, 2,258 enrolled. *Average high school GPA:* 3.40. *Test scores:* SAT verbal scores over 500: 59%; SAT math scores over 500: 64%; ACT scores over 18: 88%; SAT verbal scores over 600: 16%; SAT math scores over 600: 18%; ACT scores over 24: 30%; SAT verbal scores over 700: 3%; SAT math scores over 700: 2%; ACT scores over 30: 3%.

Faculty *Total:* 1,269, 54% full-time. *Student/faculty ratio:* 15:1.

Majors Accounting; anthropology; architecture; art; biology; business administration; business marketing and marketing management; chemistry; city/community/regional planning; civil engineering; computer engineering; computer/information sciences; criminal justice studies; economics; electrical engineering; elementary education; English; English education; exercise sciences; finance; French; geography; geology; German; health science; health services administration; history; human resources management; international business; Judaic studies; liberal arts and sciences/liberal studies; linguistics; management information systems/business data processing; mathematics; mathematics education; mechanical engineering; medical technology; music; music teacher education; nursing; ocean engineering; philosophy; physics; physiological psychology/psychobiology; political science; psychology; public administration; real estate; science education; social psychology; social science education; social sciences; social work; sociology; Spanish; special education; speech-language pathology/audiology; speech/rhetorical studies; theater arts/drama.

Academic Programs *Special study options:* accelerated degree program, adult/continuing education programs, advanced placement credit, cooperative education, distance learning, double majors, English as a second language, freshman honors college, honors programs, independent study, internships, off-campus study, part-time degree program, services for LD students, student-designed majors, study abroad, summer session for credit. *ROTC:* Army (c), Air Force (c).

Library S. E. Wimberly Library with 808,239 titles, 4,184 serial subscriptions, 9,511 audiovisual materials, an OPAC, a Web page.

Computers on Campus 400 computers available on campus for general student use. A campuswide network can be accessed from student residence rooms and from off campus. Internet access, online (class) registration, at least one staffed computer lab available.

Student Life *Housing:* on-campus residence required for freshman year. *Options:* coed, women-only. *Activities and Organizations:* drama/theater group, student-run newspaper, radio and television station, choral group, Latin American Student Organization, Alpha Tau Omega, Konbit Kreyol, Program Board, Owl Corral, national fraternities, national sororities. *Campus security:* 24-hour emergency response devices and patrols, student patrols, late-night transport/escort service. *Student Services:* health clinic, personal/psychological counseling, legal services.

Athletics Member NCAA. All Division I. *Intercollegiate sports:* baseball M(s), basketball M(s)/W(s), cross-country running M(s)/W(s), football M(s), golf M(s)/W(s), soccer M(s)/W(s), softball W(s), swimming M(s)/W(s), tennis M(s)/W(s), track and field W(s), volleyball W(s). *Intramural sports:* basketball M/W, bowling M/W, cross-country running M/W, fencing M(c)/W(c), football M/W, golf M/W, ice hockey M(c)/W(c), rugby M(c)/W(c), soccer M/W, softball M/W, swimming M/W, table tennis M/W, tennis M/W, track and field M/W, volleyball M/W, weight lifting M/W.

Standardized Tests *Required:* SAT I or ACT (for admission).

Costs (2001–02) *One-time required fee:* $10. *Tuition:* state resident $2699 full-time, $90 per credit part-time; nonresident $10,586 full-time, $353 per credit part-time. Full-time tuition and fees vary according to course load. Part-time tuition and fees vary according to course load. *Room and board:* $6134. Room and board charges vary according to board plan and housing facility. *Payment plans:* installment, deferred payment. *Waivers:* senior citizens and employees or children of employees.

Financial Aid Of all full-time matriculated undergraduates who enrolled in 2001, 196 Federal Work-Study jobs (averaging $3062). *Average financial aid package:* $2100. *Average need-based loan:* $3706. *Average need-based gift aid:* $1644. *Average non-need based aid:* $1887.

Applying *Options:* common application, electronic application, early admission, deferred entrance. *Application fee:* $20. *Required:* high school transcript, minimum 2.0 GPA. *Required for some:* 1 letter of recommendation. *Application deadlines:* rolling (freshmen), 6/1 (out-of-state freshmen), 6/1 (transfers). *Notification:* continuous (freshmen).

Admissions Contact Coordinator, Freshmen Recruitment, Florida Atlantic University, 777 Glades Road, PO Box 3091, Boca Raton, FL 33431-0991. *Phone:* 561-297-2458. *Toll-free phone:* 800-299-4FAU. *Fax:* 561-297-2758.

FLORIDA CHRISTIAN COLLEGE
Kissimmee, Florida

- **Independent** 4-year, founded 1976, affiliated with Christian Churches and Churches of Christ
- **Calendar** semesters
- **Degrees** diplomas, associate, and bachelor's
- **Small-town** 40-acre campus with easy access to Orlando
- **Endowment** $1.5 million
- **Coed,** 259 undergraduate students, 91% full-time, 50% women, 50% men
- **Minimally difficult** entrance level, 71% of applicants were admitted

Undergraduates Students come from 23 states and territories, 1 other country, 18% are from out of state, 3% African American, 2% Asian American or Pacific Islander, 5% Hispanic American, 0.4% international, 65% live on campus. *Retention:* 81% of 2001 full-time freshmen returned.

Freshmen *Admission:* 120 applied, 85 admitted. *Average high school GPA:* 2.75.

Faculty *Total:* 27, 37% full-time, 37% with terminal degrees. *Student/faculty ratio:* 12:1.

Majors Biblical studies; divinity/ministry; theology.

Academic Programs *Special study options:* academic remediation for entering students, adult/continuing education programs, advanced placement credit, internships, part-time degree program, study abroad, summer session for credit.

Library 31,000 titles, 285 serial subscriptions, an OPAC, a Web page.

Florida Christian College (continued)

Computers on Campus 11 computers available on campus for general student use. A campuswide network can be accessed from off campus. Internet access, at least one staffed computer lab available.

Student Life *Housing:* on-campus residence required for freshman year. *Activities and Organizations:* drama/theater group, student-run newspaper, choral group, Student Council, Camera Club, Timothy Club.

Athletics Member NCCAA. *Intercollegiate sports:* basketball M/W, volleyball W. *Intramural sports:* basketball W, bowling M/W, softball M/W, table tennis M/W, volleyball M/W.

Standardized Tests *Required:* ACT (for placement).

Costs (2001–02) *Tuition:* $5920 full-time, $185 per credit hour part-time. *Required fees:* $270 full-time. *Room only:* $1680. *Payment plan:* installment. *Waivers:* employees or children of employees.

Financial Aid Of all full-time matriculated undergraduates who enrolled in 2001, 183 applied for aid, 179 were judged to have need, 6 had their need fully met. 43 Federal Work-Study jobs (averaging $1044). In 2001, 17 non-need-based awards were made. *Average percent of need met:* 48%. *Average financial aid package:* $5950. *Average need-based loan:* $3231. *Average need-based gift aid:* $2479. *Average non-need based aid:* $2209. *Average indebtedness upon graduation:* $10,420. *Financial aid deadline:* 8/1.

Applying *Options:* early admission, deferred entrance. *Application fee:* $25. *Required:* high school transcript, 3 letters of recommendation. *Application deadlines:* 7/15 (freshmen), 7/15 (transfers). *Notification:* continuous until 8/25 (freshmen).

Admissions Contact Mr. Terry Davis, Admissions Director, Florida Christian College, 1011 Bill Beck Boulevard. *Phone:* 407-847-8966 Ext. 305.

FLORIDA COLLEGE
Temple Terrace, Florida

- **Independent** 4-year, founded 1944
- **Calendar** semesters
- **Degrees** associate and bachelor's
- **Small-town** 95-acre campus with easy access to Tampa
- **Endowment** $11.9 million
- **Coed,** 560 undergraduate students, 96% full-time, 51% women, 49% men
- **Moderately difficult** entrance level

Undergraduates 536 full-time, 24 part-time. Students come from 37 states and territories, 8 other countries, 70% are from out of state, 2% African American, 0.5% Asian American or Pacific Islander, 3% Hispanic American, 0.2% Native American, 1% international, 4% transferred in, 90% live on campus. *Retention:* 89% of 2001 full-time freshmen returned.

Freshmen *Admission:* 275 admitted, 270 enrolled. *Test scores:* SAT verbal scores over 500: 66%; SAT math scores over 500: 66%; ACT scores over 18: 88%; SAT verbal scores over 600: 23%; SAT math scores over 600: 26%; ACT scores over 24: 38%; SAT verbal scores over 700: 3%; SAT math scores over 700: 2%; ACT scores over 30: 4%.

Faculty *Total:* 41, 73% full-time, 29% with terminal degrees. *Student/faculty ratio:* 16:1.

Majors Biblical studies; elementary education; liberal arts and sciences/liberal studies.

Academic Programs *Special study options:* academic remediation for entering students, advanced placement credit, independent study. *ROTC:* Army (c), Air Force (c).

Library Chatlos Library with 72,943 titles, 395 serial subscriptions, 256 audiovisual materials, an OPAC, a Web page.

Computers on Campus 76 computers available on campus for general student use. A campuswide network can be accessed from off campus. Internet access, at least one staffed computer lab available.

Student Life *Housing:* on-campus residence required through sophomore year. *Options:* men-only, women-only. *Activities and Organizations:* drama/theater group, choral group, Drama Workshop, concert band, chorus, SBGA, YWTO. *Campus security:* controlled dormitory access, evening patrols by trained security personnel. *Student Services:* health clinic, personal/psychological counseling.

Athletics Member NJCAA. *Intercollegiate sports:* baseball M(s), basketball M(s), volleyball W(s). *Intramural sports:* basketball M/W, football M/W, soccer M/W, softball M/W, volleyball M/W.

Standardized Tests *Required:* SAT I or ACT (for admission).

Costs (2001–02) *Comprehensive fee:* $12,600 includes full-time tuition ($7660), mandatory fees ($240), and room and board ($4700). Part-time tuition: $340 per semester hour. *Required fees:* $75 per term part-time. *Room and board:* College room only: $2140. Room and board charges vary according to housing facility. *Payment plan:* installment. *Waivers:* employees or children of employees.

Financial Aid *Financial aid deadline:* 8/1.

Applying *Options:* electronic application. *Application fee:* $25. *Required:* high school transcript, minimum 2.0 GPA, letters of recommendation. *Required for some:* essay or personal statement. *Application deadlines:* 8/1 (freshmen), 8/1 (transfers). *Notification:* continuous (freshmen).

Admissions Contact Mrs. Mari Smith, Assistant Director of Admissions, Florida College, 119 North Glen Arven Avenue, Temple Terrace, FL 33617. *Phone:* 813-988-5131 Ext. 6716. *Toll-free phone:* 800-326-7655. *Fax:* 813-899-6772. *E-mail:* admissions@flcoll.edu.

FLORIDA GULF COAST UNIVERSITY
Fort Myers, Florida

- **State-supported** comprehensive, founded 1991, part of State University System of Florida
- **Calendar** semesters
- **Degrees** certificates, bachelor's, and master's
- **Suburban** 760-acre campus
- **Endowment** $14.3 million
- **Coed,** 3,403 undergraduate students, 60% full-time, 65% women, 35% men
- **Moderately difficult** entrance level, 73% of applicants were admitted

Undergraduates 2,039 full-time, 1,364 part-time. Students come from 23 states and territories, 60 other countries, 5% are from out of state, 4% African American, 2% Asian American or Pacific Islander, 8% Hispanic American, 0.5% Native American, 0.9% international, 18% transferred in, 19% live on campus. *Retention:* 69% of 2001 full-time freshmen returned.

Freshmen *Admission:* 1,615 applied, 1,178 admitted, 568 enrolled. *Average high school GPA:* 3.44. *Test scores:* SAT verbal scores over 500: 57%; SAT math scores over 500: 58%; ACT scores over 18: 85%; SAT verbal scores over 600: 15%; SAT math scores over 600: 14%; ACT scores over 24: 22%; SAT verbal scores over 700: 1%; SAT math scores over 700: 1%; ACT scores over 30: 1%.

Faculty *Total:* 163, 96% full-time, 83% with terminal degrees. *Student/faculty ratio:* 15:1.

Majors Accounting; business administration; business marketing and marketing management; criminal justice studies; early childhood education; elementary education; finance; health/medical diagnostic and treatment services related; human services; liberal arts and sciences/liberal studies; management information systems/business data processing; medical technology; nursing; occupational therapy; physical therapy; public health related; special education.

Academic Programs *Special study options:* academic remediation for entering students, accelerated degree program, advanced placement credit, cooperative education, distance learning, honors programs, independent study, internships, part-time degree program, services for LD students, study abroad, summer session for credit.

Library Library Services with 139,999 titles, 2,414 serial subscriptions, 1,655 audiovisual materials, an OPAC, a Web page.

Computers on Campus 323 computers available on campus for general student use. A campuswide network can be accessed from student residence rooms and from off campus that provide access to online admissions and advising. Internet access, online (class) registration, at least one staffed computer lab available.

Student Life *Housing Options:* coed. *Activities and Organizations:* drama/theater group, student-run newspaper, Golden Key National Honor Society, student government, Student Nurses Association, Student Council for Exceptional Children, Physical Therapy Association, national fraternities, national sororities. *Campus security:* 24-hour emergency response devices and patrols, late-night transport/escort service. *Student Services:* health clinic, personal/psychological counseling.

Athletics *Intercollegiate sports:* baseball M(s), cross-country running M/W, golf M(s)/W(s), softball W(s), tennis M(s)/W(s). *Intramural sports:* cross-country running M(c)/W(c), football M/W, soccer M/W, softball M/W, table tennis M/W, tennis M/W, volleyball M/W.

Standardized Tests *Required:* SAT I or ACT (for admission).

Costs (2001–02) *Tuition:* state resident $2453 full-time, $82 per credit part-time; nonresident $10,340 full-time, $345 per credit part-time. Full-time tuition and fees vary according to course load. Part-time tuition and fees vary according to course load. *Required fees:* $71 full-time, $36 per term part-time. *Room and board:* $7000; room only: $4000. Room and board charges vary according to board plan. *Waivers:* senior citizens and employees or children of employees.

Financial Aid Of all full-time matriculated undergraduates who enrolled in 2001, 1627 applied for aid, 868 were judged to have need, 137 had their need fully met. In 2001, 584 non-need-based awards were made. *Average percent of need*

met: 73%. *Average financial aid package:* $6411. *Average need-based loan:* $3688. *Average need-based gift aid:* $3657. *Average non-need based aid:* $3499. *Average indebtedness upon graduation:* $13,267.

Applying *Options:* electronic application, early admission, deferred entrance. *Application fee:* $20. *Required:* high school transcript, minimum 2.0 GPA. *Required for some:* essay or personal statement, letters of recommendation, interview. *Application deadline:* 8/15 (freshmen), rolling (transfers). *Notification:* continuous (freshmen).

Admissions Contact Ms. Michele Yovanovich, Director of Admissions, Florida Gulf Coast University, 10501 FGCU Boulevard South, Fort Myers, FL 33965-6565. *Phone:* 941-590-7878. *Toll-free phone:* 800-590-3428. *Fax:* 941-590-7894. *E-mail:* oar@fgcu.edu.

FLORIDA HOSPITAL COLLEGE OF HEALTH SCIENCES

Orlando, Florida

- **Independent** primarily 2-year
- **Calendar** semesters
- **Degrees** certificates, associate, and bachelor's
- **Urban** campus
- **Endowment** $153,800
- **Coed,** 746 undergraduate students, 55% full-time, 80% women, 20% men
- **Minimally difficult** entrance level

Undergraduates 408 full-time, 338 part-time. 14% African American, 9% Asian American or Pacific Islander, 18% Hispanic American, 0.9% Native American, 3% international, 16% live on campus.

Freshmen *Admission:* 102 enrolled. *Test scores:* ACT scores over 18: 60%; ACT scores over 24: 10%; ACT scores over 30: 1%.

Faculty *Total:* 55, 60% full-time, 18% with terminal degrees. *Student/faculty ratio:* 15:1.

Majors Diagnostic medical sonography; liberal arts and sciences/liberal studies; medical radiologic technology; nuclear medical technology; nursing; occupational therapy assistant; radiological science.

Academic Programs *Special study options:* academic remediation for entering students, adult/continuing education programs, distance learning, honors programs, independent study, services for LD students, student-designed majors, summer session for credit.

Library Florida plus 1 other with 17,152 titles, 163 serial subscriptions, 9 audiovisual materials.

Computers on Campus 10 computers available on campus for general student use. Internet access, at least one staffed computer lab available.

Student Life *Housing Options:* coed. *Activities and Organizations:* drama/theater group, student-run newspaper, choral group. *Campus security:* 24-hour emergency response devices and patrols, late-night transport/escort service, controlled dormitory access. *Student Services:* personal/psychological counseling.

Athletics *Intramural sports:* baseball M/W, soccer M/W, volleyball M/W.

Standardized Tests *Required:* ACT (for admission).

Costs (2001–02) *Tuition:* $3840 full-time, $160 per credit part-time. Full-time tuition and fees vary according to course load, degree level, and program. Part-time tuition and fees vary according to course load and program. *Required fees:* $550 full-time. *Room only:* $1400. Room and board charges vary according to housing facility.

Applying *Options:* common application, electronic application. *Application fee:* $20. *Required:* high school transcript, minimum 2.5 GPA, 2 letters of recommendation. *Required for some:* essay or personal statement, interview. *Application deadline:* 8/28 (freshmen).

Admissions Contact Joe Forton, Director of Admissions, Florida Hospital College of Health Sciences, 800 Lake Estelle Drive, Orlando, FL 32803. *Phone:* 407-303-9798 Ext. 5548. *Toll-free phone:* 800-500-7747. *Fax:* 407-303-9408. *E-mail:* joe_forton@fhchs.edu.

FLORIDA INSTITUTE OF TECHNOLOGY

Melbourne, Florida

- **Independent** university, founded 1958
- **Calendar** semesters
- **Degrees** associate, bachelor's, master's, doctoral, and post-master's certificates
- **Small-town** 130-acre campus with easy access to Orlando
- **Endowment** $25.3 million
- **Coed,** 2,191 undergraduate students, 93% full-time, 30% women, 70% men
- **Moderately difficult** entrance level, 82% of applicants were admitted

Undergraduates 2,032 full-time, 159 part-time. Students come from 54 states and territories, 82 other countries, 43% are from out of state, 4% African American, 2% Asian American or Pacific Islander, 5% Hispanic American, 0.2% Native American, 26% international, 7% transferred in, 46% live on campus. *Retention:* 77% of 2001 full-time freshmen returned.

Freshmen *Admission:* 2,156 applied, 1,763 admitted, 545 enrolled. *Average high school GPA:* 3.52. *Test scores:* SAT verbal scores over 500: 81%; SAT math scores over 500: 91%; ACT scores over 18: 100%; SAT verbal scores over 600: 34%; SAT math scores over 600: 53%; ACT scores over 24: 64%; SAT verbal scores over 700: 4%; SAT math scores over 700: 12%; ACT scores over 30: 18%.

Faculty *Total:* 242, 73% full-time, 81% with terminal degrees. *Student/faculty ratio:* 12:1.

Majors Aerospace engineering; aircraft pilot (professional); applied mathematics; astrophysics; atmospheric sciences; aviation/airway science; aviation management; biochemistry; biology; biology education; business administration; chemical engineering; chemistry; chemistry education; civil engineering; communications; computer education; computer engineering; computer science; ecology; electrical engineering; environmental science; humanities; information sciences/systems; interdisciplinary studies; marine biology; mathematics education; mechanical engineering; molecular biology; ocean engineering; oceanography; physics; physics education; psychology; science education.

Academic Programs *Special study options:* academic remediation for entering students, accelerated degree program, adult/continuing education programs, advanced placement credit, cooperative education, English as a second language, internships, part-time degree program, services for LD students, summer session for credit. *ROTC:* Army (b).

Library Evans Library with 138,503 titles, 5,325 serial subscriptions, 4,734 audiovisual materials, an OPAC, a Web page.

Computers on Campus 600 computers available on campus for general student use. A campuswide network can be accessed from student residence rooms and from off campus. Internet access, online (class) registration, at least one staffed computer lab available.

Student Life *Housing:* on-campus residence required for freshman year. *Options:* coed, men-only, women-only. *Activities and Organizations:* drama/theater group, student-run newspaper, television station, marching band, College Players, Caribbean Student Association, national fraternities, national sororities. *Campus security:* 24-hour emergency response devices and patrols, late-night transport/escort service, self-defense education. *Student Services:* health clinic, personal/psychological counseling, legal services.

Athletics Member NCAA. All Division II. *Intercollegiate sports:* baseball M(s), basketball M(s)/W(s), crew M(s)/W(s), cross-country running M/W, soccer M(s), softball W(s), volleyball W(s). *Intramural sports:* badminton M/W, basketball M/W, football M/W, golf M/W, racquetball M/W, soccer M/W, softball M/W, table tennis M/W, tennis M/W, volleyball M/W, water polo M/W, weight lifting M/W.

Standardized Tests *Required:* SAT I or ACT (for admission).

Costs (2001–02) *Comprehensive fee:* $25,250 includes full-time tuition ($19,700) and room and board ($5550). Full-time tuition and fees vary according to program. Part-time tuition: $600 per credit hour. Part-time tuition and fees vary according to program. *Room and board:* College room only: $2850. Room and board charges vary according to board plan and housing facility. *Payment plan:* installment. *Waivers:* senior citizens and employees or children of employees.

Financial Aid Of all full-time matriculated undergraduates who enrolled in 2001, 1616 applied for aid, 1149 were judged to have need, 332 had their need fully met. 415 Federal Work-Study jobs (averaging $1483). In 2001, 419 non-need-based awards were made. *Average percent of need met:* 84%. *Average financial aid package:* $16,864. *Average need-based loan:* $4647. *Average need-based gift aid:* $13,019. *Average non-need based aid:* $8400. *Average indebtedness upon graduation:* $25,137.

Applying *Options:* common application, electronic application, early admission, deferred entrance. *Application fee:* $40. *Required:* high school transcript, minimum 2.5 GPA. *Required for some:* minimum 3.0 GPA. *Recommended:* essay or personal statement, minimum 2.8 GPA, interview. *Application deadline:* rolling (freshmen), rolling (transfers). *Notification:* continuous (freshmen).

Admissions Contact Ms. Judith Marino, Director of Undergraduate Admissions, Florida Institute of Technology, 150 West University Boulevard, Mel-

Florida Institute of Technology (continued)
bourne, FL 32901-6975. *Phone:* 321-674-8030. *Toll-free phone:* 800-888-4348. *Fax:* 321-723-9468. *E-mail:* admissions@fit.edu.

FLORIDA INTERNATIONAL UNIVERSITY
Miami, Florida

- **State-supported** university, founded 1965, part of State University System of Florida
- **Calendar** semesters
- **Degrees** bachelor's, master's, and doctoral
- **Urban** 573-acre campus
- **Coed,** 25,971 undergraduate students, 58% full-time, 56% women, 44% men
- **Moderately difficult** entrance level, 47% of applicants were admitted

Undergraduates 15,144 full-time, 10,827 part-time. Students come from 52 states and territories, 115 other countries, 5% are from out of state, 14% African American, 4% Asian American or Pacific Islander, 55% Hispanic American, 0.2% Native American, 8% international, 4% transferred in, 7% live on campus. *Retention:* 88% of 2001 full-time freshmen returned.

Freshmen *Admission:* 6,561 applied, 3,059 admitted, 2,492 enrolled. *Average high school GPA:* 3.47. *Test scores:* SAT verbal scores over 500: 85%; SAT math scores over 500: 90%; ACT scores over 18: 100%; SAT verbal scores over 600: 28%; SAT math scores over 600: 28%; ACT scores over 24: 83%; SAT verbal scores over 700: 4%; SAT math scores over 700: 3%; ACT scores over 30: 6%.

Faculty *Total:* 1,394, 63% full-time, 70% with terminal degrees. *Student/faculty ratio:* 14:1.

Majors Accounting; applied mathematics; architectural environmental design; art education; art history; biology; broadcast journalism; business administration; business marketing and marketing management; chemical engineering; chemistry; civil engineering; communications; computer engineering; computer/information sciences; computer science; construction technology; criminal justice studies; dance; dietetics; economics; education of the emotionally handicapped; education of the mentally handicapped; education of the specific learning disabled; electrical engineering; elementary education; English; English education; environmental science; exercise sciences; finance; fine/studio arts; foreign languages education; French; geography; geology; German; health education; health science; health services administration; history; home economics education; hospitality management; humanities; human resources management; information sciences/systems; insurance/risk management; interior design; international business; international relations; Italian; liberal arts and sciences/liberal studies; mathematical statistics; mathematics; mathematics education; mechanical engineering; medical records administration; music; music teacher education; nursing; occupational therapy; orthotics/prosthetics; philosophy; physical education; physics; political science; Portuguese; psychology; public administration; real estate; recreation/leisure facilities management; religious studies; science education; social science education; social work; sociology; Spanish; systems engineering; theater arts/drama; trade/industrial education; urban studies; women's studies.

Academic Programs *Special study options:* accelerated degree program, adult/continuing education programs, advanced placement credit, cooperative education, distance learning, double majors, English as a second language, freshman honors college, honors programs, independent study, internships, off-campus study, part-time degree program, services for LD students, study abroad, summer session for credit. *ROTC:* Army (b), Air Force (b).

Library University Park Library plus 2 others with 2.2 million titles, 14,978 serial subscriptions, 121,173 audiovisual materials, an OPAC, a Web page.

Computers on Campus 600 computers available on campus for general student use. A campuswide network can be accessed from student residence rooms and from off campus. Internet access, online (class) registration, at least one staffed computer lab available.

Student Life *Housing Options:* coed. *Activities and Organizations:* drama/theater group, student-run newspaper, radio station, choral group, Students for Community Service, Black Student Leadership Council, Hospitality Management Student Club, Hispanic Students Association, Haitian Students Organization, national fraternities, national sororities. *Campus security:* 24-hour emergency response devices and patrols, late-night transport/escort service, controlled dormitory access. *Student Services:* health clinic, personal/psychological counseling, women's center, legal services.

Athletics Member NCAA. All Division I. *Intercollegiate sports:* baseball M(s), basketball M(s)/W(s), cross-country running M(s)/W(s), golf W(s), soccer M(s)/W(s), softball W(s), tennis W(s), track and field M(s)/W(s), volleyball W(s). *Intramural sports:* basketball M/W, bowling M/W, cross-country running M/W, football M, golf M/W, lacrosse M, racquetball M/W, rugby M, sailing M/W, soccer M/W, softball M/W, swimming M/W, table tennis M/W, tennis M/W, volleyball M/W, weight lifting M/W.

Standardized Tests *Required:* SAT I or ACT (for admission).

Costs (2001–02) *Tuition:* state resident $2394 full-time, $80 per credit hour part-time; nonresident $10,282 full-time, $343 per credit hour part-time. Full-time tuition and fees vary according to course load. Part-time tuition and fees vary according to course load. *Required fees:* $168 full-time, $168 per term part-time. *Room and board:* room only: $3504. Room and board charges vary according to housing facility. *Payment plan:* tuition prepayment. *Waivers:* senior citizens and employees or children of employees.

Financial Aid Of all full-time matriculated undergraduates who enrolled in 2001, 10227 applied for aid, 7143 were judged to have need, 1986 had their need fully met. 660 Federal Work-Study jobs (averaging $2558). 152 State and other part-time jobs (averaging $2234). In 2001, 2108 non-need-based awards were made. *Average percent of need met:* 61%. *Average need-based loan:* $3766. *Average need-based gift aid:* $2290. *Average non-need based aid:* $1860. *Average indebtedness upon graduation:* $2649.

Applying *Options:* common application, electronic application, early admission, deferred entrance. *Application fee:* $20. *Required:* high school transcript, minimum 3.0 GPA. *Required for some:* 1 letter of recommendation. *Application deadline:* rolling (freshmen), rolling (transfers). *Notification:* continuous until 8/1 (freshmen).

Admissions Contact Ms. Carmen Brown, Director of Admissions, Florida International University, University Park, PC 140, 11200 SW 8 Street, PC140, Miami, FL 33199. *Phone:* 305-348-3675. *Fax:* 305-348-3648. *E-mail:* admiss@fiu.edu.

FLORIDA MEMORIAL COLLEGE
Miami-Dade, Florida

Admissions Contact Mrs. Peggy Murray Martin, Director of Admissions and International Student Advisor, Florida Memorial College, 15800 NW 42nd Avenue, Miami-Dade, FL 33054. *Phone:* 305-626-3147. *Toll-free phone:* 800-822-1362.

FLORIDA METROPOLITAN UNIVERSITY-BRANDON CAMPUS
Tampa, Florida

- **Proprietary** comprehensive, founded 1890, part of Corinthian Colleges, Inc
- **Calendar** quarters
- **Degrees** associate, bachelor's, and master's
- **Urban** 5-acre campus
- **Coed**
- **Minimally difficult** entrance level

Faculty *Student/faculty ratio:* 14:1.

Student Life *Campus security:* 24-hour emergency response devices.

Applying *Options:* common application, early admission, deferred entrance. *Application fee:* $50. *Required:* high school transcript, interview, minimum CPAt score of 120.

Admissions Contact Mrs. Dee McKee, Director of Admissions, Florida Metropolitan University-Brandon Campus, 3924 Coconut Palm Drive, Tampa, FL 33619. *Phone:* 813-621-0041 Ext. 45. *Fax:* 813-623-5769. *E-mail:* dpearson@cci.edu.

FLORIDA METROPOLITAN UNIVERSITY-FORT LAUDERDALE CAMPUS
Fort Lauderdale, Florida

- **Proprietary** comprehensive, founded 1940, part of Corinthian Colleges, Inc
- **Calendar** quarters
- **Degrees** associate, bachelor's, and master's
- **Suburban** campus with easy access to Miami
- **Coed,** 1,300 undergraduate students
- **Minimally difficult** entrance level

Undergraduates Students come from 25 states and territories, 38 other countries.

Majors Accounting; business administration; business marketing and marketing management; computer programming; film studies; hotel and restaurant management; international business; management information systems/business data processing; paralegal/legal assistant.

Academic Programs *Special study options:* academic remediation for entering students, accelerated degree program, adult/continuing education programs, advanced placement credit, English as a second language, internships, part-time degree program, summer session for credit.
Library Florida Metropolitan University Library plus 1 other with 14,500 titles, 61 serial subscriptions, an OPAC.
Computers on Campus 92 computers available on campus for general student use. Internet access, at least one staffed computer lab available.
Student Life *Housing:* college housing not available. *Activities and Organizations:* student-run newspaper, American Marketing Association, International Business Club. *Campus security:* late-night transport/escort service, building security. *Student Services:* personal/psychological counseling.
Standardized Tests *Recommended:* SAT I or ACT (for admission).
Costs (2001–02) *Tuition:* $7488 full-time, $219 per quarter hour part-time. Full-time tuition and fees vary according to course load. *Required fees:* $150 full-time, $50 per term part-time. *Payment plan:* installment. *Waivers:* employees or children of employees.
Applying *Options:* common application, electronic application, deferred entrance. *Application fee:* $25. *Required:* essay or personal statement, high school transcript. *Required for some:* letters of recommendation. *Recommended:* interview. *Application deadline:* rolling (freshmen), rolling (transfers). *Notification:* continuous (freshmen).
Admissions Contact Mr. Tony Wallace, Director of Admissions, Florida Metropolitan University-Fort Lauderdale Campus, 1040 Bayview Drive, Fort Lauderdale, FL 33304-2522. *Phone:* 954-568-1600. *Toll-free phone:* 800-468-0168. *Fax:* 305-568-2008.

FLORIDA METROPOLITAN UNIVERSITY-JACKSONVILLE CAMPUS
Jacksonville, Florida

Admissions Contact 8226 Phillips Highway, Jacksonville, FL 32256. *Toll-free phone:* 888-741-4271.

FLORIDA METROPOLITAN UNIVERSITY-LAKELAND CAMPUS
Lakeland, Florida

- **Proprietary** comprehensive, founded 1890, part of Corinthian Colleges, Inc
- **Calendar** quarters
- **Degrees** associate, bachelor's, and master's (bachelor's degree in business administration only)
- **Suburban** campus with easy access to Orlando and Tampa-St. Petersburg
- **Coed,** 690 undergraduate students
- **Minimally difficult** entrance level, 91% of applicants were admitted

Undergraduates *Retention:* 70% of 2001 full-time freshmen returned.
Freshmen *Admission:* 660 applied, 600 admitted.
Faculty *Total:* 53, 25% full-time. *Student/faculty ratio:* 16:1.
Majors Accounting; business administration; business marketing and marketing management; computer programming; computer science; criminal justice studies; data processing technology; paralegal/legal assistant; secretarial science.
Academic Programs *Special study options:* academic remediation for entering students, adult/continuing education programs, advanced placement credit, internships, part-time degree program, summer session for credit.
Library Tampa College Library with 5,000 titles, 30 serial subscriptions.
Computers on Campus 50 computers available on campus for general student use. At least one staffed computer lab available.
Student Life *Housing:* college housing not available. *Activities and Organizations:* student-run newspaper. *Campus security:* 24-hour patrols.
Standardized Tests *Recommended:* SAT I (for admission), ACT (for admission).
Costs (2001–02) *Tuition:* $8388 full-time, $208 per credit hour part-time. Full-time tuition and fees vary according to course load and program. Part-time tuition and fees vary according to class time and program. *Required fees:* $75 full-time, $50 per term part-time. *Payment plan:* installment. *Waivers:* employees or children of employees.
Financial Aid Of all full-time matriculated undergraduates who enrolled in 2001, 816 applied for aid, 653 were judged to have need, 250 had their need fully met. 7 Federal Work-Study jobs (averaging $4309). In 2001, 206 non-need-based awards were made. *Average percent of need met:* 80%. *Average financial aid package:* $6500. *Average indebtedness upon graduation:* $18,000.
Applying *Options:* common application, early admission. *Required:* high school transcript.
Admissions Contact Joe Rostkowski, Director of Admissions, Florida Metropolitan University-Lakeland Campus, 995 East Memorial Boulevard, Suite 110, Lakeland, FL 33801. *Phone:* 863-686-1444. *Fax:* 863-686-1727. *E-mail:* dsimmons@cci.edu.

FLORIDA METROPOLITAN UNIVERSITY-MELBOURNE CAMPUS
Melbourne, Florida

- **Proprietary** comprehensive, founded 1953, part of Corinthian Colleges, Inc
- **Calendar** quarters
- **Degrees** associate, bachelor's, and master's
- **Small-town** 5-acre campus with easy access to Orlando
- **Coed**
- **Noncompetitive** entrance level

Faculty *Student/faculty ratio:* 13:1.
Student Life *Campus security:* 24-hour emergency response devices.
Costs (2001–02) *Tuition:* $9792 full-time. Full-time tuition and fees vary according to course load. Part-time tuition and fees vary according to course load. No tuition increase for student's term of enrollment. *Required fees:* $150 full-time. *Payment plans:* tuition prepayment, installment, deferred payment.
Financial Aid Of all full-time matriculated undergraduates who enrolled in 2001, 608 applied for aid, 516 were judged to have need. 8 Federal Work-Study jobs (averaging $3215). *Average percent of need met:* 70. *Average financial aid package:* $5500.
Applying *Options:* common application, deferred entrance. *Application fee:* $25. *Required:* high school transcript, interview.
Admissions Contact Ms. Teresa Stinson-Kumar, Director of Admissions, Florida Metropolitan University-Melbourne Campus, 2401 North Harbor City Boulevard, Melbourne, FL 32935-6657. *Phone:* 407-253-2929 Ext. 11.

FLORIDA METROPOLITAN UNIVERSITY-NORTH ORLANDO CAMPUS
Orlando, Florida

- **Proprietary** comprehensive, founded 1953, part of Corinthian Colleges, Inc
- **Calendar** quarters
- **Degrees** associate, bachelor's, and master's
- **Urban** 1-acre campus
- **Coed,** 826 undergraduate students, 57% full-time, 66% women, 34% men
- **Minimally difficult** entrance level

Undergraduates 32% African American, 4% Asian American or Pacific Islander, 18% Hispanic American, 0.5% Native American, 0.6% international.
Faculty *Total:* 79. *Student/faculty ratio:* 15:1.
Majors Accounting; business administration; business marketing and marketing management; computer/information sciences; computer programming; court reporting; data processing technology; film/video production; graphic design/commercial art/illustration; medical assistant; paralegal/legal assistant.
Academic Programs *Special study options:* advanced placement credit, double majors, external degree program, independent study, internships, part-time degree program, summer session for credit.
Library Orlando College Library with 10,000 titles, 105 serial subscriptions.
Computers on Campus 25 computers available on campus for general student use. Internet access, at least one staffed computer lab available.
Student Life *Housing:* college housing not available. *Campus security:* door alarms.
Costs (2001–02) *Tuition:* $7420 full-time, $212 per credit hour part-time. *Required fees:* $150 full-time, $50 per term part-time.
Applying *Options:* common application, deferred entrance. *Application fee:* $50. *Required:* high school transcript. *Application deadline:* rolling (freshmen), rolling (transfers). *Notification:* continuous (freshmen).
Admissions Contact Ms. Charlene Donnelly, Director of Admissions, Florida Metropolitan University-North Orlando Campus, 5421 Diplomat Circle, Orlando, FL 32810-5674. *Phone:* 407-628-5870 Ext. 108. *Toll-free phone:* 800-628-5870.

Florida Metropolitan University-North Orlando Campus (continued)

Student Life *Housing:* college housing not available. *Activities and Organizations:* Legal Network, Phi Beta Lambda, PC-MAC Users Group, international club, Art League. *Campus security:* evening and Saturday afternoon patrols by trained security personnel.

Standardized Tests *Required for some:* ACT (for admission).

Costs (2001–02) *Tuition:* $7488 full-time, $208 per credit part-time. Full-time tuition and fees vary according to program. Part-time tuition and fees vary according to program. *Required fees:* $150 full-time, $50 per term part-time. *Payment plan:* installment. *Waivers:* employees or children of employees.

Financial Aid Of all full-time matriculated undergraduates who enrolled in 2001, 733 applied for aid, 730 were judged to have need, 702 had their need fully met. *Average percent of need met:* 75%. *Average financial aid package:* $6000. *Average indebtedness upon graduation:* $12,000.

Applying *Options:* common application, deferred entrance. *Required:* high school transcript. *Application deadline:* rolling (freshmen), rolling (transfers). *Notification:* continuous (freshmen).

Admissions Contact Mr. Donnie Broughton, Director of Admissions, Florida Metropolitan University-Tampa Campus, 3319 W. Hillsborough Avenue, Tampa, FL 33614. *Phone:* 813-879-6000 Ext. 129. *Fax:* 813-871-2483.

FLORIDA METROPOLITAN UNIVERSITY-PINELLAS CAMPUS

Clearwater, Florida

Admissions Contact Mr. Wayne Childers, Director of Admissions, Florida Metropolitan University-Pinellas Campus, 2471 McMullen Booth Road, Suite 200, Clearwater, FL 33759. *Phone:* 727-725-2688 Ext. 702. *Toll-free phone:* 800-353-FMUS. *Fax:* 727-796-3722. *E-mail:* wchilder@cci.edu.

FLORIDA METROPOLITAN UNIVERSITY-SOUTH ORLANDO CAMPUS

Orlando, Florida

- **Proprietary** comprehensive
- **Calendar** quarters
- **Degrees** associate, bachelor's, and master's
- **Coed,** 1,509 undergraduate students, 90% full-time, 72% women, 28% men
- **Minimally difficult** entrance level

Undergraduates 1,358 full-time, 151 part-time. 32% African American, 2% Asian American or Pacific Islander, 28% Hispanic American, 0.8% Native American, 2% international.

Faculty *Total:* 77, 13% full-time, 21% with terminal degrees. *Student/faculty ratio:* 20:1.

Majors Accounting; business administration; computer/information sciences; criminal justice studies; health services administration; medical assistant; paralegal/legal assistant.

Academic Programs *Special study options:* academic remediation for entering students, accelerated degree program, cooperative education, distance learning, double majors, internships, services for LD students.

Student Life *Housing:* college housing not available.

Costs (2001–02) *Tuition:* $6656 full-time, $219 per quarter hour part-time. Full-time tuition and fees vary according to course load and program. Part-time tuition and fees vary according to program. *Required fees:* $150 full-time, $50 per term part-time.

Applying *Application fee:* $50. *Required:* high school transcript, interview. *Application deadline:* rolling (freshmen). *Notification:* continuous (freshmen).

Admissions Contact Ms. Annette Cloin, Director of Admissions, Florida Metropolitan University-South Orlando Campus, 2411 Sand Lake Road, Orlando, FL 32809. *Phone:* 407-851-2525 Ext. 111. *Toll-free phone:* 407-851 Ext. 2525 (in-state); 866-508 Ext. 0007 (out-of-state). *Fax:* 407-851-1477.

FLORIDA METROPOLITAN UNIVERSITY-TAMPA CAMPUS

Tampa, Florida

- **Proprietary** comprehensive, founded 1890, part of Corinthian Colleges, Inc
- **Calendar** quarters
- **Degrees** associate, bachelor's, and master's
- **Urban** 4-acre campus
- **Coed,** 1,125 undergraduate students, 62% full-time, 61% women, 39% men
- **Minimally difficult** entrance level

Undergraduates 698 full-time, 427 part-time. Students come from 10 states and territories, 35 other countries, 3% transferred in.

Freshmen *Admission:* 127 admitted, 127 enrolled.

Faculty *Total:* 54, 22% full-time, 13% with terminal degrees. *Student/faculty ratio:* 15:1.

Majors Accounting; business administration; business marketing and marketing management; computer programming; computer science; criminal justice/law enforcement administration; data processing technology; graphic design/commercial art/illustration; medical assistant; paralegal/legal assistant.

Academic Programs *Special study options:* accelerated degree program, adult/continuing education programs, advanced placement credit, cooperative education, distance learning, double majors, English as a second language, external degree program, independent study, internships, part-time degree program, student-designed majors, summer session for credit.

Library Tampa College Library with 4,000 titles, 125 serial subscriptions, 250 audiovisual materials, an OPAC, a Web page.

Computers on Campus 113 computers available on campus for general student use. Internet access, at least one staffed computer lab available.

FLORIDA SOUTHERN COLLEGE

Lakeland, Florida

- **Independent** comprehensive, founded 1885, affiliated with United Methodist Church
- **Calendar** semesters
- **Degrees** bachelor's and master's
- **Suburban** 100-acre campus with easy access to Tampa and Orlando
- **Endowment** $70.8 million
- **Coed,** 1,827 undergraduate students, 96% full-time, 61% women, 39% men
- **Moderately difficult** entrance level, 77% of applicants were admitted

Undergraduates 1,752 full-time, 75 part-time. Students come from 44 states and territories, 36 other countries, 22% are from out of state, 5% African American, 1% Asian American or Pacific Islander, 5% Hispanic American, 0.3% Native American, 4% international, 7% transferred in, 66% live on campus. *Retention:* 72% of 2001 full-time freshmen returned.

Freshmen *Admission:* 1,538 applied, 1,181 admitted, 515 enrolled. *Average high school GPA:* 3.37. *Test scores:* SAT verbal scores over 500: 64%; SAT math scores over 500: 63%; ACT scores over 18: 90%; SAT verbal scores over 600: 19%; SAT math scores over 600: 19%; ACT scores over 24: 41%; SAT verbal scores over 700: 3%; SAT math scores over 700: 3%; ACT scores over 30: 4%.

Faculty *Total:* 219, 49% full-time, 50% with terminal degrees. *Student/faculty ratio:* 16:1.

Majors Accounting; advertising; agricultural business; art; art education; athletic training/sports medicine; biology; broadcast journalism; business; business administration; business marketing and marketing management; chemistry; communications; computer science; criminal justice studies; early childhood education; economics; education; education of the specific learning disabled; elementary education; English; English composition; environmental science; finance; fine/studio arts; graphic design/commercial art/illustration; history; horticulture science; hotel and restaurant management; humanities; human resources management; international business; journalism; management information systems/business data processing; mathematics; music; music business management/merchandising; music teacher education; natural sciences; operations management; ornamental horticulture; physical education; physics; political science; pre-dentistry; pre-medicine; pre-veterinary studies; psychology; public relations; religious education; religious music; religious studies; secondary education; social sciences; sociology; Spanish; theater arts/drama.

Academic Programs *Special study options:* academic remediation for entering students, adult/continuing education programs, advanced placement credit, double majors, honors programs, independent study, internships, off-campus study, part-time degree program, study abroad, summer session for credit. *ROTC:* Army (b). *Unusual degree programs:* 3-2 engineering with Washington University in St. Louis, University of Miami; forestry with Duke University.

Library E. T. Roux Library plus 1 other with 167,633 titles, 667 serial subscriptions, 9,205 audiovisual materials, an OPAC, a Web page.

Computers on Campus 191 computers available on campus for general student use. A campuswide network can be accessed from student residence rooms and from off campus. Internet access, online (class) registration, at least one staffed computer lab available.

Student Life *Housing:* on-campus residence required through junior year. *Options:* men-only, women-only. *Activities and Organizations:* drama/theater group, student-run newspaper, choral group, Fellowship of Christian Athletes,

Student Government Association, Student Union Board, Shades of Color, International Student Association, national fraternities, national sororities. *Campus security:* 24-hour emergency response devices and patrols, student patrols, late-night transport/escort service, controlled dormitory access. *Student Services:* health clinic, personal/psychological counseling.

Athletics Member NCAA. All Division II. *Intercollegiate sports:* baseball M(s), basketball M(s)/W(s), cross-country running M(s)/W(s), golf M(s)/W(s), soccer M(s)/W(s), softball W(s), tennis M(s)/W(s), volleyball M(c)/W(s). *Intramural sports:* basketball M/W, football M/W, soccer W, softball M/W, tennis M/W, volleyball M/W.

Standardized Tests *Required:* SAT I or ACT (for admission).

Costs (2001–02) *Comprehensive fee:* $19,430 includes full-time tuition ($13,700), mandatory fees ($230), and room and board ($5500). Part-time tuition: $390 per credit hour. *Room and board:* College room only: $3050.

Financial Aid Of all full-time matriculated undergraduates who enrolled in 2001, 1581 applied for aid, 1266 were judged to have need, 407 had their need fully met. 311 Federal Work-Study jobs (averaging $1256). *Average percent of need met:* 64%. *Average financial aid package:* $13,229. *Average need-based loan:* $4309. *Average need-based gift aid:* $9972. *Average indebtedness upon graduation:* $13,658. *Financial aid deadline:* 8/1.

Applying *Options:* common application, electronic application, early admission, deferred entrance. *Application fee:* $30. *Required:* essay or personal statement, high school transcript, minimum 2.0 GPA, 3 letters of recommendation. *Recommended:* minimum 3.0 GPA, interview. *Application deadline:* rolling (transfers). *Notification:* continuous (freshmen).

Admissions Contact Mr. Barry Conners, Director of Admissions, Florida Southern College, 111 Lake Hollingsworth Drive. *Phone:* 863-680-3909. *Toll-free phone:* 800-274-4131. *Fax:* 863-680-4120. *E-mail:* fscadm@flsouthern.edu.

FLORIDA STATE UNIVERSITY

Tallahassee, Florida

- **State-supported** university, founded 1851, part of State University System of Florida
- **Calendar** semesters
- **Degrees** certificates, associate, bachelor's, master's, doctoral, first professional, post-master's, and postbachelor's certificates
- **Suburban** 456-acre campus
- **Endowment** $325.2 million
- **Coed,** 28,231 undergraduate students, 85% full-time, 57% women, 43% men
- **Very difficult** entrance level, 53% of applicants were admitted

Undergraduates 23,996 full-time, 4,235 part-time. Students come from 51 states and territories, 120 other countries, 19% are from out of state, 12% African American, 3% Asian American or Pacific Islander, 9% Hispanic American, 0.5% Native American, 0.8% international, 7% transferred in, 16% live on campus. *Retention:* 85% of 2001 full-time freshmen returned.

Freshmen *Admission:* 28,817 applied, 15,394 admitted, 5,763 enrolled. *Average high school GPA:* 3.63. *Test scores:* SAT verbal scores over 500: 87%; SAT math scores over 500: 89%; ACT scores over 18: 99%; SAT verbal scores over 600: 40%; SAT math scores over 600: 43%; ACT scores over 24: 58%; SAT verbal scores over 700: 7%; SAT math scores over 700: 6%; ACT scores over 30: 7%.

Faculty *Total:* 1,084. *Student/faculty ratio:* 22:1.

Majors Accounting; acting/directing; actuarial science; advertising; American studies; anthropology; applied economics; applied mathematics; art; art education; art history; Asian studies; atmospheric sciences; bilingual/bicultural education; biochemistry; bioengineering; biology; business; business administration; business communications; business marketing and marketing management; cell and molecular biology related; chemical engineering; chemistry; child care/development; civil engineering; classics; clothing/apparel/textile studies; communications; community health liaison; computer engineering; computer/information sciences; computer science; computer software engineering; creative writing; criminology; dance; dietetics; early childhood education; Eastern European area studies; ecology; economics; education of the emotionally handicapped; education of the mentally handicapped; education of the specific learning disabled; education of the visually handicapped; electrical engineering; elementary education; English; English education; entrepreneurship; environmental engineering; environmental science; evolutionary biology; family/consumer studies; fashion design/illustration; fashion merchandising; film studies; film/video production; finance; fine/studio arts; foreign languages education; French; genetics; geography; geology; German; graphic design/commercial art/illustration; Greek (modern); health education; history; home economics; home economics education; hospitality management; housing studies; humanities; human resources management; individual/family development; industrial/manufacturing engineering; insurance/risk management; interior design; international business; international relations; Italian; jazz; Latin American studies; Latin (ancient and medieval); liberal arts and sciences/liberal studies; library science; linguistics; literature; management information systems/business data processing; marine biology; mass communications; materials engineering; mathematical statistics; mathematics; mathematics education; mechanical engineering; music; music (general performance); music history; music (piano and organ performance); music teacher education; music theory and composition; music therapy; music (voice and choral/opera performance); nursing; nutrition science; nutrition studies; philosophy; physical education; physical sciences; physical sciences related; physics; physiology; plant physiology; political science; pre-dentistry; pre-law; pre-medicine; pre-pharmacy studies; pre-theology; pre-veterinary studies; psychology; public relations; radio/television broadcasting; real estate; recreation/leisure facilities management; religious studies; Russian; Russian/Slavic studies; science education; secondary education; social science education; social sciences; social work; sociology; Spanish; speech-language pathology/audiology; stringed instruments; theater arts/drama; theater design; vocational rehabilitation counseling; wind/percussion instruments; women's studies; zoology.

Academic Programs *Special study options:* accelerated degree program, adult/continuing education programs, advanced placement credit, cooperative education, distance learning, double majors, English as a second language, honors programs, independent study, internships, off-campus study, part-time degree program, services for LD students, study abroad, summer session for credit. *ROTC:* Army (b), Navy (c), Air Force (b).

Library Robert Manning Strozier Library plus 6 others with 2.3 million titles, 15,446 serial subscriptions, 43,275 audiovisual materials, an OPAC, a Web page.

Computers on Campus 1249 computers available on campus for general student use. A campuswide network can be accessed from student residence rooms and from off campus that provide access to Web pages. Internet access, online (class) registration, at least one staffed computer lab available.

Student Life *Housing Options:* coed, women-only, cooperative, disabled students. *Activities and Organizations:* drama/theater group, student-run newspaper, radio and television station, choral group, marching band, student government, honors program, Gold Key, Marching Chiefs, national fraternities, national sororities. *Campus security:* 24-hour emergency response devices and patrols, late-night transport/escort service, controlled dormitory access. *Student Services:* health clinic, personal/psychological counseling, women's center, legal services.

Athletics Member NCAA. All Division I except football (Division I-A). *Intercollegiate sports:* baseball M(s), basketball M(s)/W(s), bowling M(c)/W(c), cross-country running M(s)/W(s), golf M(s)/W(s), rugby M(c)/W(c), soccer W(s), softball W(s), swimming M(s)/W(s), table tennis M(c)/W(c), tennis M(s)/W(s), track and field M(s)/W(s), volleyball M(c)/W(s). *Intramural sports:* badminton M/W, basketball M/W, bowling M/W, crew M(c)/W(c), cross-country running M/W, fencing M(c)/W(c), football M/W, golf M/W, lacrosse M(c)/W(c), racquetball M/W, sailing M(c)/W(c), soccer M(c)/W(c), softball M/W, squash M/W, swimming M/W, table tennis M/W, tennis M/W, track and field M/W, volleyball M/W, water polo M(c)/W(c), wrestling M.

Standardized Tests *Required:* SAT I or ACT (for admission).

Costs (2001–02) *Tuition:* state resident $2513 full-time, $84 per credit hour part-time; nonresident $10,402 full-time, $347 per credit hour part-time. Full-time tuition and fees vary according to location. Part-time tuition and fees vary according to location. *Room and board:* $5322; room only: $2970. Room and board charges vary according to board plan and housing facility. *Payment plans:* tuition prepayment, installment. *Waivers:* senior citizens and employees or children of employees.

Financial Aid Of all full-time matriculated undergraduates who enrolled in 2001, 13619 applied for aid, 9452 were judged to have need, 343 had their need fully met. 551 Federal Work-Study jobs (averaging $1621). In 2001, 9931 non-need-based awards were made. *Average percent of need met:* 38%. *Average financial aid package:* $6807. *Average need-based loan:* $3287. *Average need-based gift aid:* $3329. *Average non-need based aid:* $1954. *Average indebtedness upon graduation:* $14,737.

Applying *Options:* common application, electronic application, early admission. *Application fee:* $20. *Required:* high school transcript. *Required for some:* audition. *Recommended:* essay or personal statement, minimum 3.0 GPA. *Application deadlines:* 3/1 (freshmen), 7/1 (transfers). *Notification:* continuous until 3/15 (freshmen).

Admissions Contact Office of Admissions, Florida State University, A2500 University Center, Tallahassee, FL 32306-2400. *Phone:* 850-644-6200. *Fax:* 850-644-0197. *E-mail:* admissions@admin.fsu.edu.

HOBE SOUND BIBLE COLLEGE

Hobe Sound, Florida

- **Independent nondenominational** 4-year, founded 1960
- **Calendar** semesters

Hobe Sound Bible College (continued)

- **Degrees** certificates, associate, and bachelor's
- **Small-town** 84-acre campus
- **Endowment** $433,096
- **Coed,** 146 undergraduate students, 70% full-time, 53% women, 47% men
- **Noncompetitive** entrance level, 63% of applicants were admitted

Undergraduates 102 full-time, 44 part-time. Students come from 23 states and territories, 8 other countries, 59% are from out of state, 0.8% African American, 0.8% Asian American or Pacific Islander, 2% Hispanic American, 15% international, 4% transferred in, 75% live on campus. *Retention:* 60% of 2001 full-time freshmen returned.

Freshmen *Admission:* 43 applied, 27 admitted, 28 enrolled. *Average high school GPA:* 2.89. *Test scores:* SAT verbal scores over 500: 77%; SAT math scores over 500: 54%; ACT scores over 18: 83%; SAT verbal scores over 600: 23%; SAT math scores over 600: 8%; ACT scores over 24: 50%; SAT verbal scores over 700: 8%.

Faculty *Total:* 21, 52% full-time, 19% with terminal degrees. *Student/faculty ratio:* 8:1.

Majors Biblical studies; elementary education; missionary studies; music teacher education; secondary education; secretarial science; teaching English as a second language; theology.

Academic Programs *Special study options:* academic remediation for entering students, advanced placement credit, distance learning, double majors, English as a second language, external degree program, independent study, internships, summer session for credit.

Library College Library with 35,468 titles, 119 serial subscriptions, 2,646 audiovisual materials, a Web page.

Computers on Campus 10 computers available on campus for general student use. Internet access, at least one staffed computer lab available.

Student Life *Housing:* on-campus residence required through senior year. *Options:* men-only, women-only. *Activities and Organizations:* choral group. *Campus security:* student patrols, late-night transport/escort service, controlled dormitory access.

Athletics *Intramural sports:* basketball M/W, football M, softball M/W, table tennis M/W, volleyball M/W.

Standardized Tests *Required:* SAT I or ACT (for placement).

Costs (2001–02) *Comprehensive fee:* $7735 includes full-time tuition ($4270), mandatory fees ($90), and room and board ($3375). *Room and board:* Room and board charges vary according to housing facility. *Payment plan:* installment. *Waivers:* employees or children of employees.

Financial Aid Of all full-time matriculated undergraduates who enrolled in 2001, 122 applied for aid, 76 were judged to have need, 33 had their need fully met. 4 Federal Work-Study jobs (averaging $1875). 30 State and other part-time jobs (averaging $3200). *Average percent of need met:* 85%. *Average financial aid package:* $3550. *Average need-based gift aid:* $875. *Average indebtedness upon graduation:* $7000.

Applying *Options:* common application, early admission. *Application fee:* $25. *Required:* high school transcript, 3 letters of recommendation, photograph, medical report. *Application deadline:* rolling (freshmen), rolling (transfers). *Notification:* continuous until 8/30 (freshmen).

Admissions Contact Mrs. Ann French, Director of Admissions, Hobe Sound Bible College, PO Box 1065, Hobe Sound, FL 33475-1065. *Phone:* 561-546-5534 Ext. 415. *Toll-free phone:* 800-881-5534. *Fax:* 561-545-1422. *E-mail:* hsbcuwin@aol.com.

INTERNATIONAL ACADEMY OF DESIGN & TECHNOLOGY

Tampa, Florida

- **Proprietary** 4-year, founded 1984, part of Career Education Corporation
- **Calendar** quarters
- **Degrees** associate and bachelor's
- **Urban** 1-acre campus
- **Coed,** 1,688 undergraduate students, 71% full-time, 54% women, 46% men
- **Noncompetitive** entrance level

Undergraduates 1,206 full-time, 482 part-time. Students come from 18 states and territories, 7 other countries, 18% are from out of state, 13% African American, 3% Asian American or Pacific Islander, 16% Hispanic American, 1% Native American, 4% international, 8% transferred in. *Retention:* 62% of 2001 full-time freshmen returned.

Freshmen *Admission:* 255 enrolled. *Average high school GPA:* 2.8.

Faculty *Total:* 126, 10% full-time, 15% with terminal degrees. *Student/faculty ratio:* 14:1.

Majors Computer graphics; design/visual communications; fashion design/illustration; graphic design/commercial art/illustration; interior design; multimedia.

Academic Programs *Special study options:* academic remediation for entering students, accelerated degree program, adult/continuing education programs, advanced placement credit, cooperative education, internships, study abroad, summer session for credit.

Library International Academy Library with 6,321 titles, 236 serial subscriptions, 421 audiovisual materials, an OPAC.

Computers on Campus 200 computers available on campus for general student use. Internet access, at least one staffed computer lab available.

Student Life *Housing:* college housing not available. *Activities and Organizations:* Student Chapter ASID, Dean's Team, Fashion Design International, computer animation club, marketing club. *Campus security:* 24-hour emergency response devices, late night patrols by trained security personnel.

Costs (2002–03) *Tuition:* $14,160 full-time, $295 per credit part-time. No tuition increase for student's term of enrollment. *Payment plans:* installment, deferred payment. *Waivers:* employees or children of employees.

Applying *Options:* common application, early admission, deferred entrance. *Application fee:* $100. *Required:* essay or personal statement, high school transcript, interview. *Recommended:* minimum 2.0 GPA. *Application deadline:* rolling (freshmen), rolling (transfers).

Admissions Contact Ms. Kristine Fescina, Vice President of Admissions and Marketing, International Academy of Design & Technology, 5225 Memorial Highway, Tampa, FL 33634-7350. *Phone:* 813-881-0007 Ext. 8095. *Toll-free phone:* 800-ACADEMY. *Fax:* 813-881-0008. *E-mail:* mpage@academy.edu.

INTERNATIONAL COLLEGE

Naples, Florida

- **Independent** comprehensive, founded 1990
- **Calendar** trimesters
- **Degrees** associate, bachelor's, master's, and postbachelor's certificates
- **Suburban** campus with easy access to Miami
- **Coed,** 1,100 undergraduate students, 71% full-time, 60% women, 40% men
- **Minimally difficult** entrance level, 67% of applicants were admitted

Undergraduates 777 full-time, 323 part-time. 0% are from out of state, 9% African American, 2% Asian American or Pacific Islander, 12% Hispanic American, 0.5% Native American, 0.2% international, 21% transferred in.

Freshmen *Admission:* 187 applied, 125 admitted, 130 enrolled.

Faculty *Total:* 85, 47% full-time, 49% with terminal degrees. *Student/faculty ratio:* 19:1.

Majors Accounting; business administration; computer/information sciences; criminal justice/law enforcement administration; criminal justice studies; medical assistant; medical records administration; paralegal/legal assistant.

Academic Programs *Special study options:* academic remediation for entering students, accelerated degree program, adult/continuing education programs, advanced placement credit, cooperative education, double majors, English as a second language, external degree program, internships, part-time degree program, services for LD students, summer session for credit.

Library Information Resource Center plus 1 other with 22,509 titles, 225 serial subscriptions, 175 audiovisual materials, an OPAC, a Web page.

Computers on Campus 150 computers available on campus for general student use. Internet access, at least one staffed computer lab available.

Student Life *Housing:* college housing not available. *Activities and Organizations:* Student Council, paralegal club, Institute of Managerial Accountants, running club. *Campus security:* late-night transport/escort service, building security. *Student Services:* personal/psychological counseling.

Standardized Tests *Recommended:* SAT I (for admission), ACT (for admission).

Costs (2001–02) *Tuition:* $6960 full-time, $290 per credit part-time. *Required fees:* $270 full-time, $135 per term part-time. *Payment plan:* installment. *Waivers:* employees or children of employees.

Financial Aid Of all full-time matriculated undergraduates who enrolled in 2001, 850 applied for aid, 790 were judged to have need, 415 had their need fully met. In 2001, 55 non-need-based awards were made. *Average financial aid package:* $7500. *Average need-based loan:* $3500. *Average need-based gift aid:* $1725. *Average non-need based aid:* $2686. *Average indebtedness upon graduation:* $15,000.

Applying *Options:* common application, electronic application, deferred entrance. *Application fee:* $20. *Required:* essay or personal statement, high school transcript, interview. *Application deadline:* rolling (freshmen), rolling (transfers). *Notification:* continuous (freshmen).

Admissions Contact Ms. Rita Lampus, Director of Admissions, International College, 2655 Northbrooke Drive, Naples, FL 34119. *Phone:* 941-513-1122 Ext. 104. *Toll-free phone:* 800-466-8017. *E-mail:* admit@internationalcollege.edu.

INTERNATIONAL FINE ARTS COLLEGE
Miami, Florida

- **Proprietary** comprehensive, founded 1965
- **Calendar** semesters
- **Degrees** associate, bachelor's, and master's
- **Urban** 4-acre campus
- **Coed**
- **Moderately difficult** entrance level

Faculty *Student/faculty ratio:* 18:1.
Student Life *Campus security:* 24-hour emergency response devices, student patrols, late-night transport/escort service, controlled dormitory access, security service.
Standardized Tests *Recommended:* SAT I and SAT II or ACT (for admission), SAT II: Writing Test (for admission).
Applying *Options:* common application, deferred entrance. *Application fee:* $50. *Required:* high school transcript, minimum 2.0 GPA, interview, 2 photographs, art portfolio. *Recommended:* essay or personal statement, 2 letters of recommendation.
Admissions Contact Ms. Elsia Suarez, Director of Admissions, International Fine Arts College, 1737 North Bayshore Drive, Miami, FL 33132-1121. *Phone:* 305-373-4684. *Toll-free phone:* 800-225-9023.

ITT TECHNICAL INSTITUTE
Tampa, Florida

- **Proprietary** primarily 2-year, founded 1981, part of ITT Educational Services, Inc
- **Calendar** quarters
- **Degrees** associate and bachelor's
- **Suburban** campus with easy access to St. Petersburg
- **Coed,** 649 undergraduate students
- **Minimally difficult** entrance level

Majors Computer/information sciences related; computer programming; design/applied arts related; drafting; electrical/electronic engineering technologies related; information technology.
Student Life *Housing:* college housing not available.
Costs (2001–02) *Tuition:* Full-time tuition and fees vary according to program. Part-time tuition and fees vary according to program. $260—$330 per credit hour.
Applying *Options:* deferred entrance. *Application fee:* $100. *Required:* high school transcript, interview. *Recommended:* letters of recommendation. *Application deadline:* rolling (freshmen), rolling (transfers). *Notification:* continuous (freshmen).
Admissions Contact Mr. Marty Baca, Director of Recruitment, ITT Technical Institute, 4809 Memorial Highway, Tampa, FL 33634-7151. *Phone:* 813-885-2244. *Toll-free phone:* 800-825-2831.

ITT TECHNICAL INSTITUTE
Fort Lauderdale, Florida

- **Proprietary** primarily 2-year, founded 1991, part of ITT Educational Services, Inc
- **Calendar** quarters
- **Degrees** associate and bachelor's
- **Suburban** campus with easy access to Miami
- **Coed,** 587 undergraduate students
- **Minimally difficult** entrance level

Majors Computer/information sciences related; computer programming; drafting; electrical/electronic engineering technologies related; information technology.
Student Life *Housing:* college housing not available.
Costs (2001–02) *Tuition:* Full-time tuition and fees vary according to program. Part-time tuition and fees vary according to program. $260—$330 per credit hour.
Applying *Options:* deferred entrance. *Application fee:* $100. *Required:* high school transcript, interview. *Recommended:* letters of recommendation. *Application deadline:* rolling (freshmen), rolling (transfers).
Admissions Contact Mr. Bob Bixler, Director of Recruitment, ITT Technical Institute, 3401 South University Drive, Ft. Lauderdale, FL 33328-2021. *Phone:* 954-476-9300. *Toll-free phone:* 800-488-7797. *Fax:* 954-476-6889.

ITT TECHNICAL INSTITUTE
Jacksonville, Florida

- **Proprietary** primarily 2-year, founded 1991, part of ITT Educational Services, Inc
- **Calendar** quarters
- **Degrees** associate and bachelor's
- **Urban** 1-acre campus
- **Coed,** 455 undergraduate students
- **Minimally difficult** entrance level

Majors Computer/information sciences related; computer programming; data processing technology; drafting; electrical/electronic engineering technologies related.
Student Life *Housing:* college housing not available.
Costs (2001–02) *Tuition:* Full-time tuition and fees vary according to program. Part-time tuition and fees vary according to program. $260—$330 per credit hour.
Financial Aid Of all full-time matriculated undergraduates who enrolled in 2001, 5 Federal Work-Study jobs.
Applying *Options:* deferred entrance. *Application fee:* $100. *Required:* high school transcript, interview. *Recommended:* letters of recommendation. *Application deadline:* rolling (freshmen), rolling (transfers).
Admissions Contact Mr. Del McCormick, Director of Recruitment, ITT Technical Institute, 6610-10 Youngerman Circle, Jacksonville, FL 32244. *Phone:* 904-573-9100. *Toll-free phone:* 800-318-1264.

ITT TECHNICAL INSTITUTE
Maitland, Florida

- **Proprietary** primarily 2-year, founded 1989, part of ITT Educational Services, Inc
- **Calendar** quarters
- **Degrees** associate and bachelor's
- **Suburban** 1-acre campus with easy access to Orlando
- **Coed,** 418 undergraduate students
- **Minimally difficult** entrance level

Majors Computer/information sciences related; computer programming; drafting; electrical/electronic engineering technologies related; electrical/electronic engineering technology; information technology.
Student Life *Housing:* college housing not available. *Activities and Organizations:* student-run newspaper.
Costs (2001–02) *Tuition:* Full-time tuition and fees vary according to program. Part-time tuition and fees vary according to program. $260—$330 per credit hour.
Applying *Options:* deferred entrance. *Application fee:* $100. *Required:* high school transcript, interview. *Recommended:* letters of recommendation. *Application deadline:* rolling (freshmen), rolling (transfers). *Notification:* continuous (freshmen).
Admissions Contact Ms. Sally Mills, Director of Recruitment, ITT Technical Institute, 2600 Lake Lucien Drive, Suite 140, Maitland, FL 32751-7234. *Phone:* 407-660-2900.

JACKSONVILLE UNIVERSITY
Jacksonville, Florida

- **Independent** comprehensive, founded 1934
- **Calendar** semesters
- **Degrees** bachelor's and master's
- **Suburban** 260-acre campus
- **Endowment** $29.5 million
- **Coed,** 2,040 undergraduate students, 86% full-time, 50% women, 50% men
- **Moderately difficult** entrance level, 74% of applicants were admitted

Undergraduates 1,760 full-time, 280 part-time. Students come from 44 states and territories, 55 other countries, 37% are from out of state, 15% African American, 2% Asian American or Pacific Islander, 4% Hispanic American, 0.6% Native American, 4% international, 9% transferred in, 50% live on campus. *Retention:* 74% of 2001 full-time freshmen returned.

Jacksonville University (continued)

Freshmen *Admission:* 1,470 applied, 1,085 admitted, 452 enrolled. *Average high school GPA:* 3.20. *Test scores:* SAT verbal scores over 500: 66%; SAT math scores over 500: 66%; ACT scores over 18: 93%; SAT verbal scores over 600: 26%; SAT math scores over 600: 23%; ACT scores over 24: 45%; SAT verbal scores over 700: 2%; SAT math scores over 700: 1%; ACT scores over 30: 4%.

Faculty *Total:* 225, 50% full-time. *Student/faculty ratio:* 14:1.

Majors Accounting; aircraft pilot (professional); art; art education; art history; aviation management; biology; business; business administration; business marketing and marketing management; chemistry; communications; computer/information sciences; dance; design/visual communications; drama/dance education; economics; education; electrical engineering; elementary education; engineering physics; English; environmental science; finance; fine/studio arts; French; geography; history; humanities; interdisciplinary studies; international business; international relations; liberal arts and sciences/liberal studies; management information systems/business data processing; marine science; mathematics; mechanical engineering; medical technology; music; music business management/merchandising; music (general performance); music teacher education; music theory and composition; music (voice and choral/opera performance); nursing; philosophy; physical education; physics; political science; pre-dentistry; pre-law; pre-medicine; pre-veterinary studies; psychology; secondary education; sociology; Spanish; special education; theater arts/drama; visual/performing arts.

Academic Programs *Special study options:* academic remediation for entering students, accelerated degree program, adult/continuing education programs, advanced placement credit, cooperative education, double majors, English as a second language, honors programs, independent study, internships, off-campus study, part-time degree program, services for LD students, student-designed majors, study abroad, summer session for credit. *Unusual degree programs:* 3-2 engineering with University of Florida, Georgia Institute of Technology, Columbia University, University of Miami, Stevens Institute of Technology, Washington University in St. Louis, Mercer University.

Library Carl S. Swisher Library with 306,090 titles, 780 serial subscriptions, a Web page.

Computers on Campus 300 computers available on campus for general student use. A campuswide network can be accessed from student residence rooms and from off campus. At least one staffed computer lab available.

Student Life *Housing:* on-campus residence required through junior year. *Options:* coed, men-only, women-only. *Activities and Organizations:* drama/theater group, student-run newspaper, radio and television station, choral group, marching band, Student Government Association, sororities, fraternities, Baptist Campus Ministry, national fraternities, national sororities. *Campus security:* 24-hour emergency response devices and patrols, student patrols, late-night transport/escort service, controlled dormitory access, code lock doors in residence halls, trained security patrols during evening hours. *Student Services:* health clinic, personal/psychological counseling.

Athletics Member NCAA. All Division I except football (Division I-AA). *Intercollegiate sports:* baseball M(s), basketball M(s), crew M(s)/W(s), cross-country running M(s)/W(s), golf M(s)/W(s), sailing M/W, soccer M(s)/W(s), tennis M(s)/W(s), track and field W(s), volleyball W(s). *Intramural sports:* archery M/W, badminton M/W, basketball M/W, bowling M/W, cross-country running M/W, football M/W, golf M/W, racquetball M/W, soccer M, softball M/W, swimming M/W, table tennis M/W, tennis M/W, track and field M, volleyball M/W.

Standardized Tests *Required:* SAT I or ACT (for admission).

Costs (2002–03) *Comprehensive fee:* $22,680 includes full-time tuition ($16,540), mandatory fees ($240), and room and board ($5900). Part-time tuition: $550 per hour. *Required fees:* $10 per hour. *Room and board:* College room only: $2700. Room and board charges vary according to board plan and housing facility. *Payment plan:* installment. *Waivers:* employees or children of employees.

Financial Aid Of all full-time matriculated undergraduates who enrolled in 2001, 1442 applied for aid, 978 were judged to have need. In 2001, 367 non-need-based awards were made. *Average percent of need met:* 85%. *Average financial aid package:* $14,442. *Average need-based loan:* $3256. *Average need-based gift aid:* $11,356. *Average non-need based aid:* $9402.

Applying *Options:* common application, electronic application, early admission. *Application fee:* $30. *Required:* essay or personal statement, high school transcript, minimum 2.0 GPA. *Recommended:* letters of recommendation, interview. *Application deadline:* rolling (freshmen), rolling (transfers).

Admissions Contact Mr. Jeff Hammer, Director of Admissions, Jacksonville University, 2800 University Boulevard North, Jacksonville, FL 32211. *Phone:* 904-745-7000. *Toll-free phone:* 800-225-2027. *Fax:* 904-745-7012. *E-mail:* admissions@ju.edu.

JOHNSON & WALES UNIVERSITY
North Miami, Florida

Admissions Contact Mr. Jeff Greenip, Director of Admissions, Johnson & Wales University, 1701 Northeast 127th Street, North Miami, FL 33181. *Phone:* 305-892-7002. *Toll-free phone:* 800-232-2433. *Fax:* 305-892-7020. *E-mail:* admissions@jwu.edu.

JONES COLLEGE
Jacksonville, Florida

- **Independent** 4-year, founded 1918
- **Calendar** trimesters
- **Degrees** associate and bachelor's
- **Urban** 5-acre campus
- **Coed,** 585 undergraduate students, 25% full-time, 76% women, 24% men
- **Noncompetitive** entrance level

Undergraduates Students come from 3 states and territories, 53% African American, 2% Asian American or Pacific Islander, 2% Hispanic American, 2% international. *Retention:* 68% of 2001 full-time freshmen returned.

Faculty *Total:* 48, 15% full-time, 25% with terminal degrees. *Student/faculty ratio:* 14:1.

Majors Accounting; business administration; information sciences/systems; interdisciplinary studies; medical assistant; paralegal/legal assistant; secretarial science.

Academic Programs *Special study options:* academic remediation for entering students, accelerated degree program, adult/continuing education programs, advanced placement credit, cooperative education, distance learning, double majors, internships, part-time degree program, student-designed majors, summer session for credit.

Library James V. Forrestal Library plus 2 others with 34,000 titles, 161 serial subscriptions, a Web page.

Computers on Campus 80 computers available on campus for general student use. Internet access, at least one staffed computer lab available.

Student Life *Housing:* college housing not available. *Activities and Organizations:* PBL, national fraternities. *Campus security:* late-night transport/escort service. *Student Services:* personal/psychological counseling.

Costs (2001–02) *Tuition:* $4800 full-time, $225 per credit hour part-time. *Required fees:* $90 full-time, $45 per term part-time.

Applying *Options:* early admission, deferred entrance. *Required:* high school transcript, interview. *Application deadline:* rolling (freshmen), rolling (transfers).

Admissions Contact Mr. Barry Durden, Director of Admissions, Jones College, 5355 Arlington Expressway, Jacksonville, FL 32211. *Phone:* 904-743-1122 Ext. 115. *Fax:* 904-743-4446. *E-mail:* bdurden@jones.edu.

LYNN UNIVERSITY
Boca Raton, Florida

- **Independent** comprehensive, founded 1962
- **Calendar** semesters
- **Degrees** certificates, associate, bachelor's, master's, and doctoral
- **Suburban** 123-acre campus with easy access to Fort Lauderdale
- **Coed,** 1,821 undergraduate students, 84% full-time, 52% women, 48% men
- **Minimally difficult** entrance level

The University, ideally located between Palm Beach and Fort Lauderdale, enrolls approximately 2,000 students. The faculty-student ratio of 1:17 provides an academic environment in which the well-being and development of the individual are assured. The University currently hosts students from 38 states and 78 nations, creating a community in which each student is provided with a rich multicultural experience and global awareness.

Undergraduates 1,522 full-time, 299 part-time. Students come from 38 states and territories, 70 other countries, 61% are from out of state, 5% African American, 0.8% Asian American or Pacific Islander, 6% Hispanic American, 0.2% Native American, 18% international, 8% transferred in, 50% live on campus. *Retention:* 53% of 2001 full-time freshmen returned.

Freshmen *Admission:* 466 enrolled.

Faculty *Total:* 170, 35% full-time. *Student/faculty ratio:* 19:1.

Majors Accounting; adult/continuing education; aircraft pilot (professional); aviation management; business administration; business marketing and marketing management; drafting; early childhood education; education; elementary education; English; environmental science; fashion design/illustration; fashion merchandising; food products retailing; gerontology; graphic design/commercial art/illustration; health services administration; history; hotel and restaurant management; humanities; international business; liberal arts and sciences/liberal studies; mass communications; middle school education; mortuary science; music; natural sciences; nursing; physical therapy; political science; pre-law; pre-medicine; psychology; recreation/leisure facilities management; secondary education; social sciences; sport/fitness administration; travel/tourism management.

Academic Programs *Special study options:* academic remediation for entering students, adult/continuing education programs, advanced placement credit, English as a second language, freshman honors college, honors programs, internships, part-time degree program, services for LD students, study abroad, summer session for credit.

Library Eugene M. and Christine E. Lynn Library with 80,341 titles, 840 serial subscriptions, an OPAC.

Computers on Campus 150 computers available on campus for general student use. A campuswide network can be accessed from student residence rooms and from off campus. At least one staffed computer lab available.

Student Life *Housing:* on-campus residence required through sophomore year. *Options:* coed, women-only. *Activities and Organizations:* drama/theater group, student-run newspaper, radio station, choral group, Knights of the Round Table, intramural group, student newspaper, Residence Hall Council, Activities Board, national fraternities, national sororities. *Campus security:* 24-hour patrols, late-night transport/escort service, video monitor at residence entrances. *Student Services:* health clinic, personal/psychological counseling.

Athletics Member NCAA. All Division II. *Intercollegiate sports:* baseball M(s), basketball M(s)/W(s), cross-country running M/W, golf M(s)/W(s), soccer M(s)/W(s), softball W, tennis M(s)/W(s), volleyball W. *Intramural sports:* baseball M, basketball M/W, bowling M/W, crew M, cross-country running M/W, equestrian sports M/W, football M/W, golf M/W, ice hockey M/W, lacrosse M/W, rugby M, soccer M/W, softball M/W, swimming M/W, table tennis M/W, tennis M/W, volleyball M/W, water polo M/W, weight lifting M/W.

Standardized Tests *Required:* SAT I or ACT (for admission).

Costs (2002–03) *Comprehensive fee:* $10,500 includes full-time tuition ($2100), mandatory fees ($750), and room and board ($7650). Part-time tuition: $630 per credit. Part-time tuition and fees vary according to class time. *Required fees:* $300 per year part-time. *Payment plans:* installment, deferred payment. *Waivers:* employees or children of employees.

Financial Aid Of all full-time matriculated undergraduates who enrolled in 2001, 493 applied for aid, 439 were judged to have need, 69 had their need fully met. 120 Federal Work-Study jobs (averaging $1200). 8 State and other part-time jobs (averaging $2500). *Average percent of need met:* 66%. *Average financial aid package:* $15,195. *Average need-based loan:* $4712. *Average need-based gift aid:* $11,097. *Average indebtedness upon graduation:* $14,426.

Applying *Options:* common application, electronic application, early admission, deferred entrance. *Application fee:* $25. *Required:* high school transcript, minimum 2.0 GPA, 2 letters of recommendation. *Recommended:* essay or personal statement, minimum 3.0 GPA, interview. *Application deadlines:* 8/15 (freshmen), 8/15 (transfers). *Notification:* continuous (freshmen).

Admissions Contact Mr. James P. Sullivan, Director of Admissions, Lynn University, 3601 North Military Trail, Boca Raton, FL 33431-5598. *Phone:* 561-237-7837. *Toll-free phone:* 800-888-LYNN (in-state); 800-544-8035 (out-of-state). *Fax:* 561-237-7100. *E-mail:* admission@lynn.edu.

NEW COLLEGE OF FLORIDA

Sarasota, Florida

- **State-supported** 4-year, founded 1960, part of State University System of Florida
- **Calendar** 4-1-4
- **Degree** bachelor's
- **Suburban** 140-acre campus with easy access to Tampa-St. Petersburg
- **Endowment** $29.3 million
- **Coed,** 634 undergraduate students, 100% full-time, 65% women, 35% men
- **Very difficult** entrance level, 61% of applicants were admitted

Undergraduates 634 full-time. Students come from 7 other countries, 25% are from out of state, 2% African American, 3% Asian American or Pacific Islander, 6% Hispanic American, 0.2% Native American, 2% international, 6% transferred in, 72% live on campus. *Retention:* 81% of 2001 full-time freshmen returned.

Freshmen *Admission:* 490 applied, 299 admitted, 150 enrolled. *Average high school GPA:* 3.90. *Test scores:* SAT verbal scores over 500: 100%; SAT math scores over 500: 100%; ACT scores over 18: 100%; SAT verbal scores over 600: 93%; SAT math scores over 600: 73%; ACT scores over 24: 94%; SAT verbal scores over 700: 60%; SAT math scores over 700: 19%; ACT scores over 30: 33%.

Faculty *Total:* 58, 100% full-time, 98% with terminal degrees. *Student/faculty ratio:* 11:1.

Majors Anthropology; art; biology; chemistry; classics; economics; environmental science; fine/studio arts; French; German; Greek (ancient and medieval); history; international relations; Latin (ancient and medieval); liberal arts and sciences/liberal studies; literature; mathematics; medieval/renaissance studies; music; natural sciences; philosophy; physics; political science; psychology; public policy analysis; religious studies; Russian; social sciences; sociology; Spanish; urban studies.

Academic Programs *Special study options:* accelerated degree program, double majors, honors programs, independent study, internships, off-campus study, services for LD students, student-designed majors, study abroad. *ROTC:* Army (c), Air Force (c).

Library Jane Bancroft Cook Library with 251,940 titles, 1,852 serial subscriptions, 4,132 audiovisual materials, an OPAC, a Web page.

Computers on Campus 34 computers available on campus for general student use. A campuswide network can be accessed from student residence rooms and from off campus. Internet access, at least one staffed computer lab available.

Student Life *Housing:* on-campus residence required for freshman year. *Options:* coed, disabled students. *Activities and Organizations:* drama/theater group, student-run newspaper, radio station, choral group, Amnesty International, multicultural club, New College Student Alliance, Gay/Lesbian Student Alliance, The Word (political action group). *Campus security:* 24-hour emergency response devices and patrols, late-night transport/escort service. *Student Services:* health clinic, personal/psychological counseling, women's center, legal services.

Athletics *Intramural sports:* basketball M/W, crew M/W, racquetball M/W, sailing M/W, soccer M/W, softball M/W, swimming M/W, table tennis M/W, tennis M/W, volleyball M/W.

Standardized Tests *Required:* SAT I or ACT (for admission).

Costs (2001–02) *Tuition:* state resident $2885 full-time; nonresident $12,350 full-time. Full-time tuition and fees vary according to student level. *Room and board:* $5120; room only: $3220. Room and board charges vary according to board plan and housing facility. *Payment plans:* tuition prepayment, installment.

Financial Aid Of all full-time matriculated undergraduates who enrolled in 2001, 314 applied for aid, 228 were judged to have need, 89 had their need fully met. In 2001, 305 non-need-based awards were made. *Average percent of need met:* 89%. *Average financial aid package:* $8192. *Average need-based loan:* $2276. *Average need-based gift aid:* $2061. *Average indebtedness upon graduation:* $14,693.

Applying *Options:* common application, early admission, deferred entrance. *Application fee:* $20. *Required:* essay or personal statement, high school transcript, 2 letters of recommendation. *Required for some:* interview. *Recommended:* minimum 3.0 GPA, interview, graded writing sample. *Application deadline:* 5/1 (freshmen), rolling (transfers). *Notification:* continuous (freshmen).

Admissions Contact Mr. Joel Bauman, Dean of Admissions and Financial Aid, New College of Florida, 5700 North Tamiami Trail, Sarasota, FL 34243-2197. *Phone:* 941-359-4269. *Fax:* 941-359-4435. *E-mail:* admissions@ncf.edu.

NEW WORLD SCHOOL OF THE ARTS

Miami, Florida

- **State-supported** 4-year, founded 1984
- **Calendar** semesters
- **Degrees** diplomas, associate, and bachelor's
- **Urban** 5-acre campus
- **Endowment** $3.2 million
- **Coed,** 370 undergraduate students, 100% full-time, 51% women, 49% men
- **Minimally difficult** entrance level, 50% of applicants were admitted

Undergraduates 370 full-time. 12% African American, 4% Asian American or Pacific Islander, 49% Hispanic American, 5% transferred in. *Retention:* 80% of 2001 full-time freshmen returned.

Freshmen *Admission:* 326 applied, 163 admitted, 135 enrolled. *Average high school GPA:* 2.80.

Faculty *Total:* 96, 21% full-time. *Student/faculty ratio:* 4:1.

Majors Applied art; art; dance; fine/studio arts; graphic design/commercial art/illustration; music; music (piano and organ performance); music (voice and choral/opera performance); photography; printmaking; sculpture; stringed instruments; theater arts/drama; wind/percussion instruments.

Academic Programs *Special study options:* academic remediation for entering students, advanced placement credit, cooperative education, distance learning, English as a second language, freshman honors college, honors programs, internships, services for LD students, summer session for credit.

Library Miami-Dade Community College library (Wolfson Campus) plus 1 other with an OPAC, a Web page.

New World School of the Arts (continued)

Computers on Campus 100 computers available on campus for general student use. A campuswide network can be accessed from student residence rooms. Internet access, online (class) registration, at least one staffed computer lab available.

Student Life *Housing:* college housing not available. *Activities and Organizations:* drama/theater group, student-run newspaper, student government. *Campus security:* 24-hour patrols.

Standardized Tests *Recommended:* SAT I or ACT (for placement).

Costs (2001–02) *Tuition:* state resident $1542 full-time, $51 per credit part-time; nonresident $5384 full-time, $179 per credit part-time. Full-time tuition and fees vary according to course load and student level. *Waivers:* employees or children of employees.

Applying *Application fee:* $20. *Required:* essay or personal statement, high school transcript, 2 letters of recommendation, interview, audition. *Notification:* continuous until 8/1 (freshmen).

Admissions Contact Ms. Pamela Neumann, Recruitment and Admissions Coordinator, New World School of the Arts, 300 NE Second Avenue, Miami, FL 33132. *Phone:* 305-237-7007. *Fax:* 305-237-3794. *E-mail:* pneumann@mdcc.edu.

NORTHWOOD UNIVERSITY, FLORIDA CAMPUS

West Palm Beach, Florida

- **Independent** 4-year, founded 1982
- **Calendar** quarters
- **Degrees** associate and bachelor's
- **Suburban** 90-acre campus with easy access to Miami
- **Endowment** $52.4 million
- **Coed,** 963 undergraduate students, 80% full-time, 48% women, 52% men
- **Moderately difficult** entrance level, 72% of applicants were admitted

Undergraduates 775 full-time, 188 part-time. Students come from 30 states and territories, 45 other countries, 50% are from out of state, 14% African American, 0.8% Asian American or Pacific Islander, 9% Hispanic American, 14% international, 13% transferred in, 50% live on campus. *Retention:* 66% of 2001 full-time freshmen returned.

Freshmen *Admission:* 557 applied, 399 admitted, 155 enrolled. *Average high school GPA:* 2.8.

Faculty *Total:* 45, 33% full-time, 40% with terminal degrees. *Student/faculty ratio:* 15:1.

Majors Accounting; advertising; business administration; business marketing and marketing management; computer management; finance; hotel and restaurant management; international business; management information systems/business data processing; vehicle marketing operations; vehicle parts/accessories marketing operations.

Academic Programs *Special study options:* academic remediation for entering students, accelerated degree program, adult/continuing education programs, advanced placement credit, distance learning, double majors, English as a second language, external degree program, honors programs, independent study, internships, part-time degree program, study abroad, summer session for credit.

Library Peter C. Cook Library with 27,000 titles, 285 serial subscriptions, an OPAC.

Computers on Campus 38 computers available on campus for general student use. A campuswide network can be accessed from off campus. Internet access, at least one staffed computer lab available.

Student Life *Housing:* on-campus residence required through sophomore year. *Options:* men-only, women-only. *Activities and Organizations:* drama/theater group, student-run newspaper. *Campus security:* 24-hour emergency response devices and patrols, student patrols. *Student Services:* health clinic, personal/psychological counseling.

Athletics Member NAIA. *Intercollegiate sports:* baseball M(s), cross-country running M/W, golf M(s)/W(s), soccer M(s)/W(s), softball W(s), tennis M(s)/W(s), volleyball W(s). *Intramural sports:* archery M, basketball M/W, racquetball M/W, softball M/W, table tennis M/W, tennis M/W, volleyball M/W.

Standardized Tests *Required:* SAT I or ACT (for admission).

Costs (2001–02) *Comprehensive fee:* $19,179 includes full-time tuition ($12,231), mandatory fees ($300), and room and board ($6648). Part-time tuition: $255 per credit. Part-time tuition and fees vary according to course load. *Room and board:* Room and board charges vary according to board plan. *Payment plan:* installment. *Waivers:* children of alumni and employees or children of employees.

Financial Aid Of all full-time matriculated undergraduates who enrolled in 2001, 327 applied for aid, 287 were judged to have need, 40 had their need fully met. 46 Federal Work-Study jobs (averaging $1633). In 2001, 121 non-need-based awards were made. *Average percent of need met:* 85%. *Average financial aid package:* $14,082. *Average need-based loan:* $3587. *Average need-based gift aid:* $8665. *Average non-need based aid:* $4365. *Average indebtedness upon graduation:* $16,248.

Applying *Options:* common application, electronic application, early admission, deferred entrance. *Application fee:* $25. *Required:* high school transcript, minimum 2.0 GPA. *Recommended:* essay or personal statement, 1 letter of recommendation, interview. *Application deadline:* rolling (freshmen), rolling (transfers).

Admissions Contact Mr. John M. Letvinchuck, Director of Admissions, Northwood University, Florida Campus, 2600 North Military Trail, West Palm Beach, FL 33409-2911. *Phone:* 561-478-5500. *Toll-free phone:* 800-458-8325. *Fax:* 561-640-3328. *E-mail:* fladmit@northwood.edu.

NOVA SOUTHEASTERN UNIVERSITY

Fort Lauderdale, Florida

- **Independent** university, founded 1964
- **Calendar** trimesters
- **Degrees** bachelor's, master's, doctoral, first professional, and first professional certificates
- **Suburban** 232-acre campus
- **Coed,** 4,014 undergraduate students, 59% full-time, 74% women, 26% men
- **Moderately difficult** entrance level, 67% of applicants were admitted

Nova Southeastern's Library, Research, and Information Technology Center accommodates 1,000 user seats, which are all equipped with Internet access; 700 workstations; a 500-seat Cultural Arts Auditorium; and twenty electronic classrooms. The Library will have the capacity to house 1.4 million volumes of reference materials, making it the largest in Florida.

Undergraduates 2,359 full-time, 1,655 part-time. 35% are from out of state, 26% African American, 2% Asian American or Pacific Islander, 23% Hispanic American, 0.4% Native American, 9% international, 4% transferred in, 6% live on campus. *Retention:* 75% of 2001 full-time freshmen returned.

Freshmen *Admission:* 585 applied, 394 admitted, 335 enrolled. *Average high school GPA:* 3.6. *Test scores:* SAT verbal scores over 500: 56%; SAT math scores over 500: 60%; ACT scores over 18: 86%; SAT verbal scores over 600: 12%; SAT math scores over 600: 15%; ACT scores over 24: 30%; SAT verbal scores over 700: 1%; SAT math scores over 700: 1%.

Faculty *Total:* 1,279, 37% full-time. *Student/faculty ratio:* 15:1.

Majors Accounting; biology; business administration; computer/information sciences; computer science; early childhood education; elementary education; general studies; hospitality management; hotel and restaurant management; humanities; information sciences/systems; interdisciplinary studies; legal studies; liberal arts and sciences/liberal studies; marine biology; mathematics education; multi/interdisciplinary studies related; oceanography; ophthalmic/optometric services; paralegal/legal assistant; physician assistant; pre-dentistry; pre-law; pre-medicine; pre-veterinary studies; psychology; secondary education; social studies education; special education; sport/fitness administration.

Academic Programs *Special study options:* academic remediation for entering students, accelerated degree program, adult/continuing education programs, advanced placement credit, cooperative education, distance learning, internships, part-time degree program, study abroad, summer session for credit. *Unusual degree programs:* 3-2 marine biology, occupational therapy.

Library Einstein Library plus 4 others with 362,611 titles, 8,821 serial subscriptions, 2,591 audiovisual materials, an OPAC, a Web page.

Computers on Campus 800 computers available on campus for general student use. A campuswide network can be accessed from student residence rooms and from off campus. Internet access, online (class) registration, at least one staffed computer lab available.

Student Life *Housing:* on-campus residence required through sophomore year. *Options:* coed. *Activities and Organizations:* drama/theater group, student-run newspaper, radio station, Pre-Med Society, Alpha Phi Omega, Salsa, national fraternities, national sororities. *Campus security:* 24-hour emergency response devices and patrols, shuttle bus service. *Student Services:* health clinic, personal/psychological counseling, women's center.

Athletics Member NAIA. *Intercollegiate sports:* baseball M(s), basketball M(s), cross-country running M(s)/W(s), golf M(s)/W(s), soccer M(s)/W(s), softball W(s), volleyball W(s). *Intramural sports:* basketball M, cross-country running M/W, golf M, soccer M/W, softball W, table tennis M/W, tennis M/W, volleyball W.

Standardized Tests *Required:* SAT I or ACT (for admission).

Costs (2001–02) *Tuition:* $12,180 full-time, $460 per credit hour part-time. Full-time tuition and fees vary according to class time and program. Part-time tuition and fees vary according to class time, course load, and program. *Required fees:* $25 per term part-time. *Room only:* Room and board charges vary according to board plan and housing facility. *Payment plan:* installment. *Waivers:* employees or children of employees.

Financial Aid Of all full-time matriculated undergraduates who enrolled in 2001, 2293 applied for aid, 1696 were judged to have need, 57 had their need fully met. In 2001, 372 non-need-based awards were made. *Average percent of need met:* 40%. *Average financial aid package:* $14,846. *Average need-based loan:* $5637. *Average need-based gift aid:* $8397. *Average non-need based aid:* $3849. *Average indebtedness upon graduation:* $23,405.

Applying *Options:* common application, electronic application, early admission, deferred entrance. *Application fee:* $35. *Required:* essay or personal statement, high school transcript. *Recommended:* minimum 2.5 GPA, letters of recommendation, interview. *Application deadline:* 7/1 (freshmen), rolling (transfers). *Notification:* 10/1 (freshmen).

Admissions Contact Ms. Zeida Roderiguez, Acting Director of Undergraduate Admissions, Nova Southeastern University, 3301 College Avenue, Ft. Lauderdale, FL 33314. *Phone:* 954-262-8000. *Toll-free phone:* 800-541-6682 Ext. 8000. *E-mail:* ncsinfo@nova.edu.

PALM BEACH ATLANTIC COLLEGE
West Palm Beach, Florida

- **Independent nondenominational** comprehensive, founded 1968
- **Calendar** semesters
- **Degrees** associate, bachelor's, master's, and first professional
- **Urban** 25-acre campus with easy access to Miami
- **Endowment** $51.9 million
- **Coed,** 2,216 undergraduate students, 89% full-time, 64% women, 36% men
- **Moderately difficult** entrance level, 50% of applicants were admitted

At the heart of the Palm Beach Atlantic experience is Workship, a program that combines work and worship and requires full-time students to contribute 45 hours annually to community service. PBA's Workship Program has recorded more than 1 million hours of service since the College was founded in 1968.

Undergraduates 25% are from out of state, 11% African American, 1% Asian American or Pacific Islander, 7% Hispanic American, 0.3% Native American, 4% international, 44% live on campus. *Retention:* 66% of 2001 full-time freshmen returned.

Freshmen *Admission:* 2,319 applied, 1,167 admitted. *Average high school GPA:* 3.45.

Faculty *Total:* 215, 43% full-time, 52% with terminal degrees. *Student/faculty ratio:* 17:1.

Majors Art; art education; biology; business administration; business marketing and marketing management; early childhood education; education; elementary education; English; finance; general studies; history; human resources management; information sciences/systems; international business; mathematics; music; music teacher education; music (voice and choral/opera performance); philosophy; physical education; political science; pre-law; pre-medicine; psychology; religious music; religious studies; secondary education; stringed instruments; theater arts/drama; wind/percussion instruments.

Academic Programs *Special study options:* academic remediation for entering students, adult/continuing education programs, advanced placement credit, double majors, English as a second language, freshman honors college, honors programs, independent study, internships, part-time degree program, student-designed majors, study abroad, summer session for credit.

Library E. C. Blomeyer Library with 81,016 titles, 2,144 serial subscriptions, 3,178 audiovisual materials, an OPAC, a Web page.

Computers on Campus A campuswide network can be accessed from student residence rooms and from off campus. At least one staffed computer lab available.

Student Life *Housing:* on-campus residence required through sophomore year. *Options:* men-only, women-only. *Activities and Organizations:* drama/theater group, student-run newspaper, radio and television station, choral group. *Campus security:* 24-hour emergency response devices and patrols, late-night transport/escort service, controlled dormitory access. *Student Services:* health clinic, personal/psychological counseling.

Athletics Member NAIA. *Intercollegiate sports:* baseball M(s), basketball M(s)/W(s), cross-country running M(s)/W(s), golf M(s)/W, soccer M(s)/W(s), softball W, tennis M(s)/W(s), volleyball W(s). *Intramural sports:* badminton M/W, basketball M/W, bowling M/W, football M/W, golf M/W, racquetball M/W, soccer M/W, softball M/W, table tennis M/W, tennis M/W, volleyball M/W, wrestling M.

Standardized Tests *Required:* SAT I or ACT (for admission).

Costs (2001–02) *Comprehensive fee:* $18,240 includes full-time tuition ($13,170) and room and board ($5070). Part-time tuition: $330 per credit hour. *Room and board:* College room only: $2748.

Applying *Options:* common application, electronic application, early admission, early decision, deferred entrance. *Application fee:* $25. *Required:* essay or personal statement, high school transcript, minimum 2.0 GPA, 2 letters of recommendation. *Recommended:* minimum 3.0 GPA, interview. *Application deadline:* rolling (freshmen), rolling (transfers). *Early decision:* 12/1. *Notification:* continuous (freshmen), 12/15 (early decision).

Admissions Contact Mr. Buck James, Vice President of Enrollment Services, Palm Beach Atlantic College, 901 South Flagler Dr, PO Box 24708, West Palm Beach, FL 33416-4708. *Phone:* 561-803-2100. *Toll-free phone:* 800-238-3998. *Fax:* 561-803-2115. *E-mail:* admit@pbac.edu.

RINGLING SCHOOL OF ART AND DESIGN
Sarasota, Florida

- **Independent** 4-year, founded 1931
- **Calendar** semesters
- **Degree** bachelor's
- **Urban** 35-acre campus with easy access to Tampa-St. Petersburg
- **Endowment** $7.0 million
- **Coed,** 969 undergraduate students, 98% full-time, 47% women, 53% men
- **Moderately difficult** entrance level, 44% of applicants were admitted

Undergraduates 951 full-time, 18 part-time. Students come from 46 states and territories, 32 other countries, 42% are from out of state, 2% African American, 3% Asian American or Pacific Islander, 7% Hispanic American, 0.4% Native American, 7% international, 12% transferred in, 47% live on campus. *Retention:* 73% of 2001 full-time freshmen returned.

Freshmen *Admission:* 701 applied, 309 admitted, 200 enrolled. *Average high school GPA:* 2.49. *Test scores:* SAT verbal scores over 500: 61%; SAT math scores over 500: 51%; SAT verbal scores over 600: 21%; SAT math scores over 600: 17%; ACT scores over 24: 100%; SAT verbal scores over 700: 5%; SAT math scores over 700: 2%.

Faculty *Total:* 108, 51% full-time, 12% with terminal degrees. *Student/faculty ratio:* 11:1.

Majors Design/applied arts related; fine/studio arts; graphic design/commercial art/illustration; interior design; photography.

Academic Programs *Special study options:* academic remediation for entering students, advanced placement credit, independent study, internships, off-campus study, part-time degree program, services for LD students, study abroad, summer session for credit.

Library Verman Kimbrough Memorial Library with 32,000 titles, 300 serial subscriptions, 65,600 audiovisual materials, an OPAC.

Computers on Campus 350 computers available on campus for general student use. A campuswide network can be accessed from student residence rooms and from off campus. Internet access, at least one staffed computer lab available.

Student Life *Housing Options:* coed. *Activities and Organizations:* drama/theater group, FEWS, Nontraditional Student Group, Phi Delta Theta, Sigma Sigma Sigma, Ringling Embassadors, national fraternities, national sororities. *Campus security:* 24-hour emergency response devices and patrols, late-night transport/escort service, controlled dormitory access. *Student Services:* personal/psychological counseling.

Athletics *Intramural sports:* basketball M/W, soccer M/W, softball M/W, volleyball M/W.

Standardized Tests *Recommended:* SAT I and SAT II or ACT (for placement).

Costs (2001–02) *One-time required fee:* $250. *Comprehensive fee:* $24,350 includes full-time tuition ($16,230), mandatory fees ($200), and room and board ($7920). Full-time tuition and fees vary according to course load and program. Part-time tuition: $800 per credit hour. Part-time tuition and fees vary according to course load and program. *Room and board:* College room only: $4310. Room and board charges vary according to board plan and housing facility. *Payment plan:* installment. *Waivers:* employees or children of employees.

Financial Aid Of all full-time matriculated undergraduates who enrolled in 2001, 622 applied for aid, 581 were judged to have need, 28 had their need fully met. 75 Federal Work-Study jobs (averaging $1786). In 2001, 114 non-need-based awards were made. *Average percent of need met:* 38%. *Average financial aid package:* $8151. *Average need-based loan:* $3789. *Average need-based gift aid:* $5784. *Average indebtedness upon graduation:* $20,453.

Applying *Options:* electronic application, deferred entrance. *Application fee:* $35. *Required:* essay or personal statement, high school transcript, minimum 2.0 GPA, 2 letters of recommendation, portfolio, resume. *Recommended:* interview. *Application deadline:* rolling (freshmen), rolling (transfers). *Notification:* continuous (freshmen).

Ringling School of Art and Design (continued)

Admissions Contact Ringling School of Art and Design, 2700 North Tamiami Trail, Sarasota, FL 34234. *Phone:* 937-351-5100 Ext. 7525. *Toll-free phone:* 800-255-7695. *Fax:* 937-359-7517. *E-mail:* admissions@rsad.edu.

ROLLINS COLLEGE

Winter Park, Florida

- **Independent** comprehensive, founded 1885
- **Calendar** semesters
- **Degrees** bachelor's and master's
- **Suburban** 67-acre campus with easy access to Orlando
- **Endowment** $152.6 million
- **Coed,** 1,676 undergraduate students, 100% full-time, 61% women, 39% men
- **Very difficult** entrance level, 65% of applicants were admitted

Supported by generosity of Rollins graduates such as George Cornell, who recently donated $10 million for endowed scholarships, Rollins is affordable and accessible for qualified students. More than 60% of Rollins students receive over $13 million annually to underwrite their education with demonstrated need-based awards, academic merit and leadership scholarships ranging from $3000 to $12,000 (academic scholarships include laptop computers), theater and music scholarships, and athletic grants in accordance with NCAA Division II standards.

Undergraduates 1,670 full-time, 6 part-time. Students come from 52 states and territories, 25 other countries, 47% are from out of state, 3% African American, 3% Asian American or Pacific Islander, 7% Hispanic American, 0.6% Native American, 4% international, 4% transferred in, 68% live on campus. *Retention:* 84% of 2001 full-time freshmen returned.

Freshmen *Admission:* 2,138 applied, 1,390 admitted, 472 enrolled. *Average high school GPA:* 3.40. *Test scores:* SAT verbal scores over 500: 88%; SAT math scores over 500: 87%; ACT scores over 18: 99%; SAT verbal scores over 600: 40%; SAT math scores over 600: 40%; ACT scores over 24: 60%; SAT verbal scores over 700: 5%; SAT math scores over 700: 5%; ACT scores over 30: 15%.

Faculty *Total:* 239, 70% full-time, 78% with terminal degrees. *Student/faculty ratio:* 12:1.

Majors Anthropology; art; art history; biology; chemistry; classics; computer science; economics; education; elementary education; English; environmental science; fine/studio arts; French; German; history; interdisciplinary studies; international business; international relations; Latin American studies; mathematics; music; music history; philosophy; physics; political science; pre-dentistry; pre-law; pre-medicine; pre-veterinary studies; psychology; religious studies; sociology; Spanish; theater arts/drama.

Academic Programs *Special study options:* academic remediation for entering students, accelerated degree program, adult/continuing education programs, advanced placement credit, double majors, honors programs, independent study, internships, off-campus study, part-time degree program, services for LD students, student-designed majors, study abroad. *Unusual degree programs:* 3-2 engineering with Washington University in St. Louis, Columbia University, Georgia Institute of Technology, Case Western Reserve University; forestry with Duke University; nursing with Emory University; medical technology, environmental management with Duke University.

Library Olin Library with 237,333 titles, 6,259 serial subscriptions, 4,853 audiovisual materials, an OPAC, a Web page.

Computers on Campus 200 computers available on campus for general student use. A campuswide network can be accessed from student residence rooms and from off campus. Internet access, at least one staffed computer lab available.

Student Life *Housing Options:* coed, disabled students. *Activities and Organizations:* drama/theater group, student-run newspaper, radio station, choral group, campus radio station, student government, student media, Residential Hall Association, national fraternities, national sororities. *Campus security:* 24-hour emergency response devices and patrols, late-night transport/escort service, controlled dormitory access. *Student Services:* health clinic, personal/psychological counseling.

Athletics Member NCAA. All Division II. *Intercollegiate sports:* baseball M(s), basketball M(s)/W(s), crew M/W, cross-country running M/W, golf M(s)/W(s), sailing M(c)/W(c), soccer M(s)/W(c), softball W, tennis M(s)/W(s), volleyball W(s). *Intramural sports:* basketball M/W, bowling M/W, football M/W, golf M/W, sailing M/W, soccer M/W, softball M, swimming M/W, table tennis M/W, tennis M/W, volleyball M/W.

Standardized Tests *Required:* SAT I or ACT (for admission). *Recommended:* SAT II: Subject Tests (for admission).

Costs (2001–02) *Comprehensive fee:* $31,223 includes full-time tuition ($23,205), mandatory fees ($677), and room and board ($7341). *Room and board:* College room only: $4229. *Payment plans:* tuition prepayment, installment. *Waivers:* employees or children of employees.

Financial Aid Of all full-time matriculated undergraduates who enrolled in 2001, 820 applied for aid, 724 were judged to have need, 357 had their need fully met. In 2001, 396 non-need-based awards were made. *Average percent of need met:* 93%. *Average financial aid package:* $23,243. *Average need-based loan:* $4066. *Average need-based gift aid:* $20,409. *Average indebtedness upon graduation:* $14,500.

Applying *Options:* common application, electronic application, early admission, early decision, deferred entrance. *Application fee:* $40. *Required:* essay or personal statement, high school transcript, 1 letter of recommendation. *Recommended:* interview. *Application deadlines:* 2/15 (freshmen), 4/15 (transfers). *Early decision:* 11/15 (for plan 1), 1/15 (for plan 2). *Notification:* 4/1 (freshmen), 12/15 (early decision plan 1), 2/1 (early decision plan 2).

Admissions Contact Mr. David Erdmann, Dean of Admissions and Student Financial Planning, Rollins College, 1000 Holt Avenue, Winter Park, FL 32789-4499. *Phone:* 407-646-2161. *Fax:* 407-646-1502. *E-mail:* admission@rollins.edu.

ST. JOHN VIANNEY COLLEGE SEMINARY

Miami, Florida

Admissions Contact Br. Edward Van Merrienboer, Academic Dean, St. John Vianney College Seminary, 2900 Southwest 87th Avenue, Miami, FL 33165-3244. *Phone:* 305-223-4561 Ext. 13. *E-mail:* academic@sjvcs.edu.

SAINT LEO UNIVERSITY

Saint Leo, Florida

- **Independent Roman Catholic** comprehensive, founded 1889
- **Calendar** semesters
- **Degrees** associate, bachelor's, and master's
- **Rural** 170-acre campus with easy access to Tampa and Orlando
- **Endowment** $7.1 million
- **Coed,** 912 undergraduate students, 94% full-time, 55% women, 45% men
- **Moderately difficult** entrance level, 81% of applicants were admitted

Undergraduates 854 full-time, 58 part-time. Students come from 35 states and territories, 27 other countries, 24% are from out of state, 8% African American, 1% Asian American or Pacific Islander, 9% Hispanic American, 0.7% Native American, 4% international, 12% transferred in, 61% live on campus. *Retention:* 70% of 2001 full-time freshmen returned.

Freshmen *Admission:* 793 applied, 644 admitted, 236 enrolled. *Average high school GPA:* 3.00. *Test scores:* SAT verbal scores over 500: 38%; SAT math scores over 500: 40%; ACT scores over 18: 69%; SAT verbal scores over 600: 7%; SAT math scores over 600: 7%; ACT scores over 24: 14%; SAT verbal scores over 700: 1%; SAT math scores over 700: 1%.

Faculty *Total:* 102, 54% full-time, 61% with terminal degrees. *Student/faculty ratio:* 15:1.

Majors Accounting; biology; business administration; business marketing and marketing management; creative writing; criminology; education; elementary education; English; English related; environmental science; health services administration; history; hotel and restaurant management; human resources management; human services; information sciences/systems; international business; international relations; liberal arts and sciences/liberal studies; literature; medical technology; physical education; political science; pre-dentistry; pre-law; pre-medicine; pre-veterinary studies; psychology; public administration; recreation/leisure facilities management; religious studies; secondary education; social work; sociology; special education; sport/fitness administration.

Academic Programs *Special study options:* academic remediation for entering students, accelerated degree program, adult/continuing education programs, advanced placement credit, cooperative education, distance learning, double majors, English as a second language, honors programs, independent study, internships, part-time degree program, services for LD students, study abroad, summer session for credit. *ROTC:* Army (c), Air Force (c).

Library Cannon Memorial Library with 103,938 titles, 750 serial subscriptions, 5,768 audiovisual materials, an OPAC, a Web page.

Computers on Campus 570 computers available on campus for general student use. A campuswide network can be accessed from student residence rooms and from off campus. Internet access, at least one staffed computer lab available.

Student Life *Housing:* on-campus residence required through junior year. *Options:* coed, men-only, women-only, disabled students. *Activities and Organizations:* drama/theater group, student-run newspaper, television station, choral group, Student Government Union, Circle K, Samaritans, American Marketing

Association, Phi Theta Kappa (Transfer Honor Society), national fraternities, national sororities. *Campus security:* 24-hour emergency response devices and patrols, late-night transport/escort service, controlled dormitory access. *Student Services:* health clinic, personal/psychological counseling.

Athletics Member NCAA. All Division II. *Intercollegiate sports:* baseball M(s), basketball M(s)/W(s), cross-country running M/W, golf M/W, soccer M(s)/W(s), softball W(s), tennis M(s)/W(s), volleyball W(s). *Intramural sports:* archery M/W, basketball M/W, football M, golf M/W, racquetball M/W, soccer M/W, softball M/W, swimming M/W, table tennis M/W, tennis M/W, volleyball M/W.

Standardized Tests *Required:* SAT I or ACT (for admission).

Costs (2001–02) *Comprehensive fee:* $19,250 includes full-time tuition ($12,350), mandatory fees ($420), and room and board ($6480). Part-time tuition: $6175 per term. *Room and board:* College room only: $3400. Room and board charges vary according to board plan and housing facility. *Payment plan:* installment. *Waivers:* employees or children of employees.

Financial Aid Of all full-time matriculated undergraduates who enrolled in 2001, 854 applied for aid, 769 were judged to have need, 452 had their need fully met. In 2001, 61 non-need-based awards were made. *Average percent of need met:* 87%. *Average financial aid package:* $13,500. *Average need-based loan:* $3925. *Average need-based gift aid:* $10,100. *Average non-need based aid:* $3850. *Average indebtedness upon graduation:* $12,000.

Applying *Options:* common application, electronic application, early admission, early decision, early action, deferred entrance. *Application fee:* $35. *Required:* essay or personal statement, high school transcript, minimum 2.3 GPA, 1 letter of recommendation. *Required for some:* interview. *Recommended:* minimum 3.0 GPA, interview. *Application deadlines:* 8/1 (freshmen), 8/1 (transfers). *Early decision:* 11/30. *Notification:* continuous until 11/30 (freshmen), 12/15 (early decision), 12/15 (early action).

Admissions Contact Saint Leo University, MC 2008, PO Box 6665, Saint Leo, FL 33574-6665. *Phone:* 352-588-8283. *Toll-free phone:* 800-334-5532. *Fax:* 352-588-8257. *E-mail:* admission@saintleo.edu.

ST. PETERSBURG COLLEGE

St. Petersburg, Florida

- **State and locally supported** primarily 2-year, founded 1927, part of Florida Community College System
- **Calendar** semesters
- **Degrees** certificates, diplomas, associate, and bachelor's
- **Suburban** campus
- **Coed,** 20,734 undergraduate students, 30% full-time, 60% women, 40% men
- **Noncompetitive** entrance level, 100% of applicants were admitted

Undergraduates 6,149 full-time, 14,585 part-time. Students come from 45 states and territories, 30 other countries, 4% are from out of state.

Freshmen *Admission:* 2,783 applied, 2,783 admitted, 2,783 enrolled. *Test scores:* SAT verbal scores over 500: 50%; SAT math scores over 500: 35%; SAT verbal scores over 600: 11%; SAT math scores over 600: 8%; SAT verbal scores over 700: 1%.

Faculty *Total:* 1,258, 21% full-time, 10% with terminal degrees.

Majors Accounting technician; alcohol/drug abuse counseling; architectural engineering technology; business administration; business marketing and marketing management; computer engineering technology; computer programming; computer systems networking/telecommunications; construction technology; corrections; dental hygiene; drafting/design technology; early childhood education; education; electrical/electronic engineering technology; emergency medical technology; engineering/industrial management; fire science; graphic design/commercial art/illustration; health services administration; hospitality management; human services; industrial radiologic technology; industrial technology; information sciences/systems; landscaping management; law enforcement/police science; legal administrative assistant; liberal arts and sciences/liberal studies; medical laboratory technician; medical records administration; mortuary science; natural resources management/protective services related; nursing; paralegal/legal assistant; physical therapy assistant; plastics technology; quality control technology; radiological science; respiratory therapy; sign language interpretation; telecommunications; travel/tourism management; veterinary technology; water resources; Web/multimedia management/webmaster.

Academic Programs *Special study options:* academic remediation for entering students, adult/continuing education programs, advanced placement credit, cooperative education, distance learning, English as a second language, freshman honors college, honors programs, internships, part-time degree program, services for LD students, summer session for credit.

Library M. M. Bennett Library plus 5 others with 219,799 titles, 1,346 serial subscriptions, 12,440 audiovisual materials, an OPAC, a Web page.

Computers on Campus 1060 computers available on campus for general student use. A campuswide network can be accessed from off campus. Internet access, online (class) registration, at least one staffed computer lab available.

Student Life *Housing:* college housing not available. *Activities and Organizations:* drama/theater group, student-run newspaper. *Campus security:* late-night transport/escort service. *Student Services:* women's center.

Athletics Member NJCAA. *Intercollegiate sports:* baseball M(s), basketball M(s)/W(s), softball W(s), volleyball W(s). *Intramural sports:* basketball M, bowling M/W, volleyball M/W.

Standardized Tests *Required for some:* SAT I and SAT II or ACT (for placement), SAT II: Writing Test (for placement), CPT.

Costs (2001–02) *Tuition:* state resident $1349 full-time, $45 per credit part-time; nonresident $5591 full-time, $186 per credit part-time. *Required fees:* $233 full-time, $8 per credit. *Payment plan:* deferred payment. *Waivers:* senior citizens and employees or children of employees.

Financial Aid Of all full-time matriculated undergraduates who enrolled in 2001, 350 Federal Work-Study jobs (averaging $2500).

Applying *Options:* common application, electronic application, early admission, deferred entrance. *Application fee:* $25. *Required:* high school transcript. *Application deadline:* rolling (freshmen). *Notification:* continuous (freshmen).

Admissions Contact Mr. Martyn Clay, Admissions Director/Registrar, St. Petersburg College, PO Box 13489, St. Petersburg, FL 33733-3489. *Phone:* 727-341-3322. *Fax:* 727-341-3150.

ST. THOMAS UNIVERSITY

Miami, Florida

- **Independent Roman Catholic** comprehensive, founded 1961
- **Calendar** semesters
- **Degrees** bachelor's, master's, and first professional
- **Suburban** 140-acre campus
- **Endowment** $9.1 million
- **Coed,** 1,286 undergraduate students, 85% full-time, 60% women, 40% men
- **Moderately difficult** entrance level, 65% of applicants were admitted

Undergraduates 1,091 full-time, 195 part-time. Students come from 25 states and territories, 58 other countries, 3% are from out of state, 26% African American, 0.6% Asian American or Pacific Islander, 48% Hispanic American, 0.1% Native American, 14% international, 11% transferred in, 10% live on campus. *Retention:* 71% of 2001 full-time freshmen returned.

Freshmen *Admission:* 824 applied, 532 admitted, 223 enrolled. *Average high school GPA:* 2.92. *Test scores:* SAT verbal scores over 500: 12%; SAT math scores over 500: 17%; ACT scores over 18: 35%; SAT verbal scores over 600: 1%; SAT math scores over 600: 2%; ACT scores over 24: 1%.

Faculty *Total:* 221, 38% full-time. *Student/faculty ratio:* 14:1.

Majors Accounting; biology; business administration; business marketing and marketing management; chemistry; computer science; criminal justice/law enforcement administration; elementary education; English; finance; history; hotel and restaurant management; information sciences/systems; international business; liberal arts and sciences/liberal studies; mass communications; pastoral counseling; political science; pre-dentistry; pre-law; pre-medicine; psychology; public administration; religious studies; secondary education; sociology; sport/fitness administration; travel/tourism management.

Academic Programs *Special study options:* academic remediation for entering students, adult/continuing education programs, advanced placement credit, cooperative education, English as a second language, external degree program, freshman honors college, honors programs, internships, part-time degree program, services for LD students, study abroad, summer session for credit. *ROTC:* Army (c), Air Force (c).

Library St. Thomas University Library plus 1 other with 125,000 titles, 900 serial subscriptions, a Web page.

Computers on Campus 60 computers available on campus for general student use. At least one staffed computer lab available.

Student Life *Housing Options:* men-only, women-only. *Activities and Organizations:* student-run newspaper, choral group, International Student Organization, Pre-Med Club, Hispanic Heritage Club, Inter-Dorm Council, Communicators Club. *Campus security:* 24-hour emergency response devices and patrols, late-night transport/escort service, controlled dormitory access. *Student Services:* health clinic, personal/psychological counseling.

Athletics Member NAIA. *Intercollegiate sports:* baseball M(s), cross-country running M(s)/W(s), golf M(s)/W(s), soccer M(s)/W(s), softball W(s), tennis M(s)/W(s), volleyball W(s). *Intramural sports:* baseball M, basketball M/W, cross-country running M/W, football M, golf M, soccer M/W, softball M/W, table tennis M/W, tennis M/W, volleyball M/W, water polo M/W, weight lifting M/W.

St. Thomas University (continued)

Standardized Tests *Recommended:* SAT I and SAT II or ACT (for admission).

Costs (2002–03) *Comprehensive fee:* $20,490 includes full-time tuition ($15,450) and room and board ($5040). Part-time tuition: $515 per credit. *Room and board:* Room and board charges vary according to housing facility. *Payment plan:* installment. *Waivers:* minority students, children of alumni, and employees or children of employees.

Financial Aid Of all full-time matriculated undergraduates who enrolled in 2001, 1002 applied for aid, 991 were judged to have need, 335 had their need fully met. 185 Federal Work-Study jobs (averaging $2250). In 2001, 175 non-need-based awards were made. *Average percent of need met:* 84%. *Average financial aid package:* $15,205. *Average non-need based aid:* $4836.

Applying *Options:* common application, electronic application, early admission, deferred entrance. *Application fee:* $45. *Required:* high school transcript, minimum 2.0 GPA. *Recommended:* essay or personal statement, 1 letter of recommendation, interview. *Application deadline:* rolling (freshmen), rolling (transfers). *Notification:* continuous (freshmen).

Admissions Contact Mr. Andre Lightbourne, Associate Director of Admissions, St. Thomas University, 16400 Northwest 32nd Avenue, Miami, FL 33054-6459. *Phone:* 305-628-6546. *Toll-free phone:* 800-367-9006 (in-state); 800-367-9010 (out-of-state). *Fax:* 305-628-6591. *E-mail:* signup@stu.edu.

SCHILLER INTERNATIONAL UNIVERSITY
Dunedin, Florida

- **Independent** comprehensive, founded 1991, part of Schiller International University
- **Calendar** semesters
- **Degrees** associate, bachelor's, and master's
- **Suburban** campus with easy access to Tampa
- **Coed,** 190 undergraduate students
- **Noncompetitive** entrance level

Schiller International University (SIU) is an independent American university with campuses in England, France, Germany, Spain, Switzerland, and the United States. In addition, students can transfer without loss of credit. English is the language of instruction at all campuses. SIU offers undergraduate and graduate students an American education in an international setting.

Undergraduates Students come from 60 other countries. *Retention:* 55% of 2001 full-time freshmen returned.

Faculty *Total:* 36, 22% full-time.

Majors Business marketing and marketing management; hotel and restaurant management; interdisciplinary studies; international business; international relations; liberal arts and sciences/liberal studies; travel/tourism management.

Academic Programs *Special study options:* accelerated degree program, adult/continuing education programs, advanced placement credit, English as a second language, internships, part-time degree program, student-designed majors, study abroad, summer session for credit.

Library SIU Library with 1,918 titles, 30 serial subscriptions.

Computers on Campus 17 computers available on campus for general student use. Internet access, at least one staffed computer lab available.

Student Life *Housing Options:* coed. *Activities and Organizations:* student-run newspaper, student government, student newspaper, yearbook staff, Model United Nations. *Campus security:* night patrols. *Student Services:* personal/psychological counseling.

Athletics *Intramural sports:* basketball M/W, sailing M/W, soccer M/W, softball M/W, swimming M/W, volleyball M/W.

Costs (2002–03) *Comprehensive fee:* $19,260 includes full-time tuition ($13,560) and room and board ($5700).

Applying *Options:* common application, deferred entrance. *Application fee:* $35. *Required:* essay or personal statement, high school transcript. *Recommended:* minimum 2.0 GPA. *Application deadline:* rolling (freshmen), rolling (transfers).

Admissions Contact Markus Leibrecht, Director of Admissions, Schiller International University, 453 Edgewater Drive, Dunedin, FL 34698-7532. *Phone:* 727-736-5082. *Toll-free phone:* 800-336-4133. *Fax:* 727-734-0359. *E-mail:* admissions@schiller.edu.

SOUTHEASTERN COLLEGE OF THE ASSEMBLIES OF GOD
Lakeland, Florida

- **Independent** 4-year, founded 1935, affiliated with Assemblies of God
- **Calendar** semesters
- **Degree** diplomas and bachelor's
- **Small-town** 62-acre campus with easy access to Tampa and Orlando
- **Endowment** $1.2 million
- **Coed,** 1,363 undergraduate students, 91% full-time, 53% women, 47% men
- **Minimally difficult** entrance level, 64% of applicants were admitted

Undergraduates 1,246 full-time, 117 part-time. Students come from 40 states and territories, 8 other countries, 52% are from out of state, 7% African American, 1% Asian American or Pacific Islander, 10% Hispanic American, 0.5% Native American, 0.5% international, 9% transferred in, 60% live on campus. *Retention:* 66% of 2001 full-time freshmen returned.

Freshmen *Admission:* 566 applied, 361 admitted, 281 enrolled.

Faculty *Total:* 80, 54% full-time. *Student/faculty ratio:* 21:1.

Majors Accounting; biblical studies; biology; business management/administrative services related; business marketing and marketing management; communications; elementary education; English; English education; interdisciplinary studies; mathematics education; missionary studies; music (general performance); music teacher education; pastoral counseling; pre-medicine; psychology; religious music; science education; social studies education; social work; theater arts/drama; theology/ministry related.

Academic Programs *Special study options:* advanced placement credit, internships, part-time degree program, summer session for credit. *ROTC:* Army (c), Air Force (c).

Library Steelman Library plus 3 others with 100,000 titles, 500 serial subscriptions, an OPAC.

Computers on Campus 26 computers available on campus for general student use. A campuswide network can be accessed from student residence rooms and from off campus that provide access to network programs. Internet access, at least one staffed computer lab available.

Student Life *Housing:* on-campus residence required through senior year. *Options:* men-only, women-only. *Activities and Organizations:* drama/theater group, student-run newspaper, radio and television station, choral group, Spanish Club, travel music groups, Impact (cross-cultural awareness), Psyche, Student Broadcast Organization. *Campus security:* 24-hour emergency response devices and patrols, late night transport/escort service, safety training and awareness sessions. *Student Services:* health clinic, personal/psychological counseling.

Athletics Member NCCAA. *Intercollegiate sports:* baseball M, basketball M/W, golf M, soccer M, tennis W, volleyball W. *Intramural sports:* basketball M, bowling M/W, football M, soccer M/W, softball M/W, tennis M/W, volleyball M/W, weight lifting M/W.

Standardized Tests *Required:* SAT I or ACT (for admission).

Costs (2002–03) *Comprehensive fee:* $12,853 includes full-time tuition ($8247) and room and board ($4606). Part-time tuition: $309 per credit. Part-time tuition and fees vary according to course load, program, and reciprocity agreements. *Required fees:* $32 per term part-time. *Room and board:* Room and board charges vary according to board plan and housing facility. *Payment plan:* installment. *Waivers:* employees or children of employees.

Financial Aid Of all full-time matriculated undergraduates who enrolled in 2001, 994 applied for aid, 853 were judged to have need, 123 had their need fully met. 94 Federal Work-Study jobs (averaging $1364). In 2001, 295 non-need-based awards were made. *Average percent of need met:* 66%. *Average financial aid package:* $6917. *Average need-based loan:* $3042. *Average need-based gift aid:* $4554. *Average indebtedness upon graduation:* $11,985.

Applying *Options:* electronic application, early admission, deferred entrance. *Application fee:* $40. *Required:* high school transcript, 2 letters of recommendation. *Required for some:* essay or personal statement, interview. *Application deadlines:* 8/1 (freshmen), 8/1 (transfers). *Notification:* continuous until 8/1 (freshmen).

Admissions Contact Mr. Omar Rashed, Director of Admission, Southeastern College of the Assemblies of God, 1000 Longfellow Boulevard, Lakeland, FL 33801. *Phone:* 863-667-5000. *Toll-free phone:* 800-500-8760. *Fax:* 863-667-5200. *E-mail:* admission@secollege.edu.

SOUTH UNIVERSITY
West Palm Beach, Florida

- **Proprietary** primarily 2-year, founded 1899
- **Calendar** quarters
- **Degrees** associate and bachelor's
- **Suburban** 1-acre campus with easy access to Miami
- **Coed**
- **Minimally difficult** entrance level

Faculty *Student/faculty ratio:* 8:1.

Student Life *Campus security:* evening security personnel.

Standardized Tests *Recommended:* SAT I and SAT II or ACT (for admission).
Financial Aid Of all full-time matriculated undergraduates who enrolled in 2001, 14 Federal Work-Study jobs (averaging $1530).
Applying *Options:* common application, electronic application, early admission, deferred entrance. *Application fee:* $25. *Required:* high school transcript. *Required for some:* letters of recommendation, interview.
Admissions Contact Mr. James W. Keeley III, Director of Admissions, South University, 1760 North Congress Avenue, West Palm Beach, FL 33409. *Phone:* 561-697-9200. *Fax:* 561-697-9944. *E-mail:* socowpb@icanect.net.

STETSON UNIVERSITY
DeLand, Florida

- **Independent** comprehensive, founded 1883
- **Calendar** semesters
- **Degrees** bachelor's, master's, first professional, and post-master's certificates
- **Small-town** 162-acre campus with easy access to Orlando
- **Endowment** $130.4 million
- **Coed,** 2,174 undergraduate students, 95% full-time, 57% women, 43% men
- **Moderately difficult** entrance level, 80% of applicants were admitted

As Florida's first private university, Stetson University sets a high standard for quality teaching and innovative, superior programs. Stetson maintains a more than century-old commitment to values and social responsibility for its students. Stetson is also committed to making top-quality, private education affordable to a diverse group of qualified students. With a more than $20-million donor-funded construction program, Stetson has added several new facilities and renovated others on the historic DeLand campus.

Undergraduates 2,063 full-time, 111 part-time. Students come from 43 states and territories, 47 other countries, 21% are from out of state, 4% African American, 2% Asian American or Pacific Islander, 6% Hispanic American, 0.6% Native American, 4% international, 6% transferred in, 67% live on campus. *Retention:* 77% of 2001 full-time freshmen returned.
Freshmen *Admission:* 1,942 applied, 1,545 admitted, 532 enrolled. *Average high school GPA:* 3.53. *Test scores:* SAT verbal scores over 500: 79%; SAT math scores over 500: 77%; ACT scores over 18: 98%; SAT verbal scores over 600: 31%; SAT math scores over 600: 34%; ACT scores over 24: 50%; SAT verbal scores over 700: 7%; SAT math scores over 700: 5%; ACT scores over 30: 7%.
Faculty *Total:* 260, 75% full-time. *Student/faculty ratio:* 10:1.
Majors Accounting; American studies; art; athletic training/sports medicine; biochemistry; biology; business administration; business economics; business marketing and marketing management; chemistry; computer science; economics; education; elementary education; English; environmental science; exercise sciences; finance; French; geography; German; history; humanities; information sciences/systems; international business; international relations; Latin American studies; management science; marine biology; mass communications; mathematics; medical technology; molecular biology; music; music (general performance); music (piano and organ performance); music teacher education; music theory and composition; music (voice and choral/opera performance); philosophy; physics; political science; pre-dentistry; pre-law; pre-medicine; pre-veterinary studies; psychology; religious music; religious studies; Russian/Slavic studies; social sciences; sociology; Spanish; speech/rhetorical studies; sport/fitness administration; theater arts/drama.
Academic Programs *Special study options:* accelerated degree program, adult/continuing education programs, advanced placement credit, double majors, honors programs, independent study, internships, off-campus study, part-time degree program, student-designed majors, study abroad, summer session for credit. *ROTC:* Army (c). *Unusual degree programs:* 3-2 engineering with Washington University in St. Louis, University of Florida, University of Miami; forestry with Duke University.
Library DuPont-Ball Library plus 2 others with 347,628 titles, 4,747 serial subscriptions, 18,760 audiovisual materials, an OPAC, a Web page.
Computers on Campus 262 computers available on campus for general student use. A campuswide network can be accessed from student residence rooms and from off campus. Internet access, at least one staffed computer lab available.
Student Life *Housing:* on-campus residence required through junior year. *Options:* coed, men-only, women-only. *Activities and Organizations:* drama/theater group, student-run newspaper, radio station, choral group, Into the Streets, Multi-Cultural Student Council, Black Student Association, Best Buddies, Habitat For Humanity, national fraternities, national sororities. *Campus security:* 24-hour emergency response devices and patrols, late-night transport/escort service. *Student Services:* health clinic, personal/psychological counseling, women's center.
Athletics Member NCAA. All Division I. *Intercollegiate sports:* baseball M(s), basketball M(s)/W(s), crew M/W, cross-country running M(s)/W(s), golf M(s)/W(s), soccer M(s)/W(s), softball W(s), tennis M(s)/W(s), volleyball W(s). *Intramural sports:* basketball M/W, bowling M/W, football M/W, racquetball M/W, rugby M(c), sailing M(c)/W(c), soccer M/W, softball M/W, swimming M/W, table tennis M/W, tennis M/W, volleyball M/W, water polo M/W.
Standardized Tests *Required:* SAT I or ACT (for admission).
Costs (2002–03) *One-time required fee:* $250. *Comprehensive fee:* $27,625 includes full-time tuition ($19,950), mandatory fees ($1025), and room and board ($6650). Part-time tuition: $650 per credit hour. Part-time tuition and fees vary according to course load. *Room and board:* College room only: $3730. Room and board charges vary according to board plan and housing facility. *Payment plan:* installment. *Waivers:* employees or children of employees.
Financial Aid Of all full-time matriculated undergraduates who enrolled in 2001, 1939 applied for aid, 1202 were judged to have need, 434 had their need fully met. 543 Federal Work-Study jobs. In 2001, 580 non-need-based awards were made. *Average percent of need met:* 85%. *Average financial aid package:* $18,988. *Average need-based loan:* $5883. *Average need-based gift aid:* $11,186. *Average non-need based aid:* $9775. *Average indebtedness upon graduation:* $18,000.
Applying *Options:* common application, electronic application, early admission, early decision. *Application fee:* $35. *Required:* essay or personal statement, high school transcript, letters of recommendation. *Recommended:* interview. *Application deadline:* 3/15 (freshmen), rolling (transfers). *Early decision:* 11/1. *Notification:* 11/15 (early decision).
Admissions Contact Ms. Deborah Thompson, Vice President for Admissions, Stetson University, Unit 8378, Griffith Hall, DeLand, FL 32723. *Phone:* 386-822-7100. *Toll-free phone:* 800-688-0101. *Fax:* 386-822-8832. *E-mail:* admissions@stetson.edu.

TALMUDIC COLLEGE OF FLORIDA
Miami Beach, Florida

Admissions Contact Ira Hill, Administrator, FAL, Talmudic College of Florida, 4014 Chase Avenue, Miami Beach, FL 33139. *Phone:* 305-534-7050.

TRINITY BAPTIST COLLEGE
Jacksonville, Florida

- **Independent Baptist** 4-year, founded 1974
- **Calendar** semesters
- **Degrees** diplomas, associate, and bachelor's
- **Urban** 148-acre campus
- **Coed,** 400 undergraduate students, 86% full-time, 49% women, 51% men
- **Moderately difficult** entrance level, 95% of applicants were admitted

Undergraduates 344 full-time, 56 part-time. Students come from 30 states and territories, 4 other countries, 35% are from out of state, 4% African American, 2% Asian American or Pacific Islander, 2% Hispanic American, 2% international, 7% transferred in, 48% live on campus.
Freshmen *Admission:* 139 applied, 132 admitted, 98 enrolled.
Faculty *Total:* 40, 30% full-time, 25% with terminal degrees. *Student/faculty ratio:* 10:1.
Majors Biblical studies; elementary education; missionary studies; pastoral counseling; secondary education; secretarial science.
Academic Programs *Special study options:* academic remediation for entering students, accelerated degree program, adult/continuing education programs, advanced placement credit, independent study, internships, part-time degree program, services for LD students, summer session for credit.
Library Travis Hudson Library with 33,000 titles, 210 serial subscriptions.
Computers on Campus 35 computers available on campus for general student use. Internet access, at least one staffed computer lab available.
Student Life *Housing:* on-campus residence required through senior year. *Options:* men-only, women-only. *Activities and Organizations:* drama/theater group, choral group. *Campus security:* 24-hour emergency response devices, controlled dormitory access, evening security. *Student Services:* health clinic, personal/psychological counseling.
Athletics Member NCCAA. *Intercollegiate sports:* basketball M, volleyball W. *Intramural sports:* basketball M/W, football M, softball M/W, volleyball M/W.
Standardized Tests *Required:* SAT I or ACT (for admission).
Costs (2001–02) *Comprehensive fee:* $7850 includes full-time tuition ($3950), mandatory fees ($500), and room and board ($3400). Full-time tuition and fees vary according to location. Part-time tuition: $165 per semester hour. Part-time tuition and fees vary according to course load and location. *Required fees:* $250

Trinity Baptist College (continued)

per term part-time. *Room and board:* College room only: $1800. Room and board charges vary according to board plan. *Payment plan:* installment. *Waivers:* employees or children of employees.

Financial Aid Of all full-time matriculated undergraduates who enrolled in 2001, 264 applied for aid, 168 were judged to have need, 37 had their need fully met. In 2001, 10 non-need-based awards were made. *Average percent of need met:* 55%. *Average financial aid package:* $4458. *Average need-based loan:* $2912. *Average need-based gift aid:* $2791. *Average non-need based aid:* $1279. *Average indebtedness upon graduation:* $6425. *Financial aid deadline:* 4/15.

Applying *Options:* common application. *Application fee:* $25. *Required:* essay or personal statement, high school transcript, minimum 2.0 GPA, 3 letters of recommendation. *Application deadline:* rolling (freshmen), rolling (transfers). *Notification:* continuous until 8/15 (freshmen).

Admissions Contact Mr. Larry Appleby, Administrative Dean, Trinity Baptist College, 800 Hammond Boulevard, Jacksonville, FL 32221. *Phone:* 904-596-2538. *Toll-free phone:* 800-786-2206. *Fax:* 904-596-2531. *E-mail:* trinity@tbc.edu.

TRINITY COLLEGE OF FLORIDA
New Port Richey, Florida

- **Independent nondenominational** 4-year, founded 1932
- **Calendar** semesters
- **Degrees** certificates, associate, and bachelor's
- **Small-town** 20-acre campus with easy access to Tampa
- **Endowment** $1.2 million
- **Coed,** 162 undergraduate students, 85% full-time, 44% women, 56% men
- **Minimally difficult** entrance level, 57% of applicants were admitted

Undergraduates 137 full-time, 25 part-time. Students come from 11 states and territories, 4 other countries, 9% are from out of state, 6% African American, 2% Asian American or Pacific Islander, 4% Hispanic American, 0.6% Native American, 4% international, 26% transferred in, 30% live on campus. *Retention:* 50% of 2001 full-time freshmen returned.

Freshmen *Admission:* 47 applied, 27 admitted, 25 enrolled.

Faculty *Total:* 19, 26% full-time, 32% with terminal degrees. *Student/faculty ratio:* 14:1.

Majors Biblical studies; elementary education; music; pastoral counseling.

Academic Programs *Special study options:* academic remediation for entering students, adult/continuing education programs, advanced placement credit, double majors, external degree program, independent study, internships, part-time degree program, services for LD students, summer session for credit.

Library Raymond H. Center, M.D. Library with 40,000 titles, 277 serial subscriptions, 2,300 audiovisual materials.

Computers on Campus 22 computers available on campus for general student use. Internet access, at least one staffed computer lab available.

Student Life *Housing Options:* men-only, women-only. *Activities and Organizations:* drama/theater group, student-run newspaper, choral group, Great Commission Missionary Fellowship, Men's Church League Basketball, music club. *Campus security:* controlled dormitory access, on-campus security personnel. *Student Services:* personal/psychological counseling.

Athletics Member NCCAA. *Intramural sports:* basketball M(c), soccer M(c), table tennis M/W, volleyball M/W.

Standardized Tests *Required:* SAT I or ACT (for admission).

Costs (2001–02) *Comprehensive fee:* $9372 includes full-time tuition ($5912), mandatory fees ($340), and room and board ($3120). Part-time tuition: $227 per credit hour. Part-time tuition and fees vary according to course load. *Required fees:* $170 per term part-time. *Payment plan:* deferred payment. *Waivers:* children of alumni, senior citizens, and employees or children of employees.

Applying *Options:* common application, electronic application, early admission, deferred entrance. *Application fee:* $25. *Required:* essay or personal statement, high school transcript, 3 letters of recommendation. *Required for some:* interview. *Application deadline:* rolling (freshmen), rolling (transfers). *Notification:* continuous (freshmen).

Admissions Contact Mr. Paul Heier, Director of Admissions, Trinity College of Florida, 2430 Welbilt Boulevard, New Port Richey, FL 34655. *Phone:* 727-376-6911 Ext. 1120. *Toll-free phone:* 888-776-4999. *Fax:* 727-376-0781. *E-mail:* admissions@trinitycollege.edu.

UNIVERSITY OF CENTRAL FLORIDA
Orlando, Florida

- **State-supported** university, founded 1963, part of State University System of Florida
- **Calendar** semesters
- **Degrees** certificates, associate, bachelor's, master's, and doctoral
- **Suburban** 1445-acre campus
- **Endowment** $55.1 million
- **Coed,** 30,036 undergraduate students, 73% full-time, 55% women, 45% men
- **Moderately difficult** entrance level, 65% of applicants were admitted

Undergraduates 22,039 full-time, 7,997 part-time. Students come from 52 states and territories, 107 other countries, 3% are from out of state, 8% African American, 5% Asian American or Pacific Islander, 11% Hispanic American, 0.7% Native American, 1% international, 10% transferred in, 18% live on campus. *Retention:* 79% of 2001 full-time freshmen returned.

Freshmen *Admission:* 17,043 applied, 11,143 admitted, 5,246 enrolled. *Average high school GPA:* 3.6. *Test scores:* SAT verbal scores over 500: 81%; SAT math scores over 500: 85%; ACT scores over 18: 99%; SAT verbal scores over 600: 29%; SAT math scores over 600: 33%; ACT scores over 24: 52%; SAT verbal scores over 700: 3%; SAT math scores over 700: 4%; ACT scores over 30: 5%.

Faculty *Total:* 1,454, 67% full-time, 68% with terminal degrees. *Student/faculty ratio:* 25:1.

Majors Accounting; advertising; aerospace engineering; anthropology; art; art education; biology; business; business administration; business economics; business education; business marketing and marketing management; chemistry; civil engineering; communications; computer engineering; computer/information sciences; criminal justice studies; early childhood education; economics; electrical/electronic engineering technology; electrical engineering; elementary education; engineering technology; English; English education; environmental engineering; film/video production; finance; fine/studio arts; foreign languages education; foreign languages/literatures; forensic technology; French; health science; health services administration; history; hospitality management; humanities; industrial/manufacturing engineering; journalism; liberal arts and sciences/liberal studies; management information systems/business data processing; mathematical statistics; mathematics; mathematics education; mechanical engineering; medical radiologic technology; medical records administration; medical technology; microbiology/bacteriology; multimedia; music (general performance); music teacher education; nursing; paralegal/legal assistant; philosophy; physical education; physics; political science; psychology; public administration; radio/television broadcasting; respiratory therapy; science education; social science education; social sciences; social work; sociology; Spanish; special education; speech-language pathology/audiology; speech/rhetorical studies; theater arts/drama; trade/industrial education.

Academic Programs *Special study options:* accelerated degree program, adult/continuing education programs, advanced placement credit, cooperative education, distance learning, double majors, English as a second language, external degree program, freshman honors college, honors programs, independent study, internships, off-campus study, part-time degree program, services for LD students, study abroad, summer session for credit. *ROTC:* Army (b), Air Force (b). *Unusual degree programs:* 3-2 physical therapy.

Library University Library with 865,527 titles, 7,423 serial subscriptions, 29,966 audiovisual materials, an OPAC, a Web page.

Computers on Campus 1191 computers available on campus for general student use. A campuswide network can be accessed from student residence rooms and from off campus. Internet access, online (class) registration, at least one staffed computer lab available.

Student Life *Housing Options:* coed, men-only, women-only. *Activities and Organizations:* drama/theater group, student-run newspaper, radio station, choral group, marching band, student government, Hispanic American Student Association, Volunteer UCF, Pre-Professional Medical Society and Student Nurses Association, African-American Student Union, national fraternities, national sororities. *Campus security:* 24-hour emergency response devices and patrols, late-night transport/escort service, controlled dormitory access. *Student Services:* health clinic, personal/psychological counseling, women's center, legal services.

Athletics Member NCAA. All Division I except football (Division I-A). *Intercollegiate sports:* baseball M(s), basketball M(s)/W(s), crew W, cross-country running M(s)/W(s), golf M(s)/W(s), soccer M(s)/W(s), tennis M(s)/W(s), track and field W, volleyball W(s). *Intramural sports:* baseball M(c), basketball M/W, crew M(c)/W(c), golf M/W, ice hockey M(c), lacrosse W(c), racquetball M/W, rugby M(c)/W(c), soccer M/W, softball M/W, swimming M(c)/W(c), tennis M(c)/W(c), volleyball M(c)/W(c), water polo M(c)/W(c), weight lifting M/W, wrestling M.

Standardized Tests *Required:* SAT I or ACT (for admission).

Costs (2001–02) *Tuition:* state resident $2402 full-time, $80 per credit part-time; nonresident $10,289 full-time, $343 per credit part-time. Full-time tuition and fees vary according to course load. Part-time tuition and fees vary according to course load. *Required fees:* $180 full-time, $6 per credit. *Room and board:* $5670; room only: $3300. Room and board charges vary according to board plan and housing facility. *Payment plans:* tuition prepayment, deferred payment. *Waivers:* senior citizens and employees or children of employees.

Financial Aid Of all full-time matriculated undergraduates who enrolled in 2001, 20194 applied for aid, 9684 were judged to have need, 3091 had their need fully met. 510 Federal Work-Study jobs. In 2001, 8962 non-need-based awards were made. *Average percent of need met:* 78%. *Average financial aid package:* $7029. *Average need-based loan:* $3843. *Average need-based gift aid:* $3041. *Average non-need based aid:* $4155. *Average indebtedness upon graduation:* $14,395. *Financial aid deadline:* 6/30.

Applying *Options:* electronic application, early admission. *Application fee:* $20. *Required:* high school transcript, minimum 2.0 GPA. *Required for some:* 1 letter of recommendation. *Recommended:* essay or personal statement. *Application deadlines:* 5/15 (freshmen), 5/15 (transfers). *Notification:* continuous until 8/15 (freshmen).

Admissions Contact Undergraduate Admissions Office, University of Central Florida, PO Box 160111, Orlando, FL 32816. *Phone:* 407-823-3000. *Fax:* 407-823-5625. *E-mail:* admission@mail.ucf.edu.

UNIVERSITY OF FLORIDA
Gainesville, Florida

- **State-supported** university, founded 1853, part of State University System of Florida
- **Calendar** semesters
- **Degrees** associate, bachelor's, master's, doctoral, and first professional
- **Suburban** 2000-acre campus with easy access to Jacksonville
- **Coed,** 32,680 undergraduate students, 90% full-time, 53% women, 47% men
- **Very difficult** entrance level, 60% of applicants were admitted

Undergraduates 29,452 full-time, 3,228 part-time. Students come from 52 states and territories, 114 other countries, 5% are from out of state, 8% African American, 7% Asian American or Pacific Islander, 11% Hispanic American, 0.5% Native American, 1% international, 6% transferred in, 21% live on campus. *Retention:* 92% of 2001 full-time freshmen returned.

Freshmen *Admission:* 18,625 applied, 11,186 admitted, 7,007 enrolled. *Average high school GPA:* 3.50. *Test scores:* SAT verbal scores over 500: 92%; SAT math scores over 500: 93%; ACT scores over 18: 95%; SAT verbal scores over 600: 55%; SAT math scores over 600: 60%; ACT scores over 24: 66%; SAT verbal scores over 700: 12%; SAT math scores over 700: 16%; ACT scores over 30: 16%.

Faculty *Total:* 1,646, 97% full-time, 96% with terminal degrees. *Student/faculty ratio:* 20:1.

Majors Accounting; advertising; aerospace engineering; agricultural economics; agricultural education; agricultural engineering; agronomy/crop science; American studies; animal sciences; anthropology; architecture; art education; art history; Asian studies; astronomy; botany; business administration; business marketing and marketing management; chemical engineering; chemistry; civil engineering; classics; computer engineering; computer/information sciences; construction technology; criminal justice studies; dairy science; dance; economics; electrical engineering; elementary education; engineering; English; entomology; environmental engineering; environmental science; exercise sciences; family/community studies; finance; fine/studio arts; food sciences; forestry; French; geography; geology; German; graphic design/commercial art/illustration; health education; health science; history; horticulture science; human resources management; industrial/manufacturing engineering; insurance/risk management; interdisciplinary studies; interior design; journalism; Judaic studies; landscape architecture; liberal arts and sciences/liberal studies; linguistics; management science; materials engineering; mathematical statistics; mathematics; mechanical engineering; microbiology/bacteriology; music; music teacher education; nuclear engineering; nursing; occupational therapy; pharmacy; philosophy; physical education; physical therapy; physics; plant pathology; plant sciences; political science; Portuguese; poultry science; psychology; public relations; radio/television broadcasting; real estate; recreation/leisure facilities management; rehabilitation therapy; religious studies; Russian; sociology; soil sciences; Spanish; special education; speech-language pathology/audiology; surveying; systems engineering; telecommunications; theater arts/drama; zoology.

Academic Programs *Special study options:* accelerated degree program, adult/continuing education programs, advanced placement credit, cooperative education, distance learning, double majors, English as a second language, external degree program, honors programs, independent study, internships, off-campus study, part-time degree program, services for LD students, student-designed majors, study abroad, summer session for credit. *ROTC:* Army (b), Navy (b), Air Force (b). *Unusual degree programs:* 3-2 mathematics.

Library George A. Smathers Library plus 15 others with 5.0 million titles, 28,103 serial subscriptions, 36,078 audiovisual materials, an OPAC, a Web page.

Computers on Campus 447 computers available on campus for general student use. A campuswide network can be accessed from student residence rooms and from off campus. At least one staffed computer lab available.

Student Life *Housing Options:* coed, women-only, cooperative, disabled students. *Activities and Organizations:* drama/theater group, student-run newspaper, choral group, marching band, Blue Key, student government, Black Student Union, Hispanic Student Association, Reitz Union Program Council, national fraternities, national sororities. *Campus security:* 24-hour emergency response devices and patrols, student patrols, late-night transport/escort service, controlled dormitory access, crime and rape prevention programs. *Student Services:* health clinic, personal/psychological counseling, women's center, legal services.

Athletics Member NCAA. All Division I except football (Division I-A). *Intercollegiate sports:* baseball M(s), basketball M(s)/W(s), cross-country running M(s)/W(s), golf M(s)/W(s), gymnastics W(s), soccer W(s), softball W(s), swimming M(s)/W(s), tennis M(s)/W(s), track and field M(s)/W(s), volleyball W(s). *Intramural sports:* archery M/W, badminton M/W, baseball M, basketball M/W, bowling M/W, crew M(c)/W(c), cross-country running M/W, fencing M/W, field hockey M/W, football M, golf M/W, gymnastics W, racquetball M/W, rugby M(c)/W(c), sailing M(c)/W(c), soccer W, softball W, swimming M/W, tennis M/W, track and field M/W, volleyball W, water polo M(c), weight lifting M.

Standardized Tests *Required:* SAT I or ACT (for admission).

Costs (2001–02) *Tuition:* state resident $2444 full-time, $81 per semester hour part-time; nonresident $10,332 full-time, $344 per semester hour part-time. *Room and board:* $5430; room only: $3290. Room and board charges vary according to board plan and housing facility. *Payment plan:* tuition prepayment. *Waivers:* senior citizens and employees or children of employees.

Financial Aid Of all full-time matriculated undergraduates who enrolled in 2001, 15039 applied for aid, 12229 were judged to have need, 3451 had their need fully met. 1508 Federal Work-Study jobs (averaging $1362). 5031 State and other part-time jobs (averaging $1477). In 2001, 14600 non-need-based awards were made. *Average percent of need met:* 82%. *Average financial aid package:* $8527. *Average need-based loan:* $3538. *Average need-based gift aid:* $3849. *Average non-need based aid:* $3415.

Applying *Options:* common application, electronic application, early admission, early decision. *Application fee:* $20. *Required:* high school transcript. *Application deadlines:* 1/16 (freshmen), 1/30 (transfers). *Early decision:* 10/1. *Notification:* continuous (freshmen), 12/1 (early decision).

Admissions Contact Office of Admissions, University of Florida, PO Box 114000, Gainesville, FL 32611-4000. *Phone:* 352-392-1365. *E-mail:* freshmen@ufl.edu.

UNIVERSITY OF MIAMI
Coral Gables, Florida

- **Independent** university, founded 1925
- **Calendar** semesters
- **Degrees** certificates, bachelor's, master's, doctoral, first professional, post-master's, and postbachelor's certificates
- **Suburban** 260-acre campus with easy access to Miami
- **Endowment** $457.8 million
- **Coed,** 9,359 undergraduate students, 92% full-time, 57% women, 43% men
- **Moderately difficult** entrance level, 46% of applicants were admitted

Undergraduates 8,618 full-time, 741 part-time. Students come from 52 states and territories, 99 other countries, 44% are from out of state, 10% African American, 5% Asian American or Pacific Islander, 25% Hispanic American, 0.3% Native American, 8% international, 6% transferred in, 40% live on campus. *Retention:* 82% of 2001 full-time freshmen returned.

Freshmen *Admission:* 14,724 applied, 6,809 admitted, 2,164 enrolled. *Average high school GPA:* 3.97. *Test scores:* SAT verbal scores over 500: 90%; SAT math scores over 500: 92%; ACT scores over 18: 100%; SAT verbal scores over 600: 48%; SAT math scores over 600: 53%; ACT scores over 24: 71%; SAT verbal scores over 700: 9%; SAT math scores over 700: 11%; ACT scores over 30: 13%.

Faculty *Total:* 1,129, 72% full-time, 74% with terminal degrees. *Student/faculty ratio:* 13:1.

Majors Accounting; advertising; aerospace engineering; African-American studies; American studies; anthropology; Arabic; architectural engineering; architecture; art; art history; athletic training/sports medicine; atmospheric sciences; biochemistry; bioengineering; biology; broadcast journalism; business administration; business economics; business marketing and marketing management; ceramic arts; chemistry; chemistry related; civil engineering; classics; communications; communications related; computer engineering; computer science; computer systems analysis; creative writing; criminology; dance; ecology; education; education administration/supervision related; electrical engineering; elementary education; engineering science; English; enterprise management; environmental

University of Miami (continued)
engineering; environmental health; environmental science; exercise sciences; film studies; film/video production; finance; fine/studio arts; French; general studies; geography; geological sciences related; geology; German; graphic design/commercial art/illustration; health/medical preparatory programs related; health professions and related sciences; history; human resources management; industrial/manufacturing engineering; information sciences/systems; international business; international relations; Italian; jazz; journalism; Judaic studies; Latin American studies; law and legal studies related; liberal arts and sciences/liberal studies; marine biology; mass communications; mathematics; mechanical engineering; medical microbiology; music; music business management/merchandising; music (general performance); musicology; music (piano and organ performance); music teacher education; music theory and composition; music therapy; music (voice and choral/opera performance); natural resources management; nursing; oceanography; painting; philosophy; photography; physical education; physics; physics related; physiological psychology/psychobiology; political science; Portuguese; pre-dentistry; pre-law; pre-medicine; pre-pharmacy studies; pre-veterinary studies; printmaking; psychology; public policy analysis; public relations; radio/television broadcasting; real estate; religious studies; Russian; sculpture; secondary education; social sciences and history related; sociology; Spanish; special education; stringed instruments; theater arts/drama; toxicology; visual/performing arts; wildlife management; wind/percussion instruments; women's studies.

Academic Programs *Special study options:* academic remediation for entering students, accelerated degree program, adult/continuing education programs, advanced placement credit, distance learning, double majors, English as a second language, honors programs, independent study, internships, part-time degree program, services for LD students, student-designed majors, study abroad, summer session for credit. *ROTC:* Army (c), Air Force (b). *Unusual degree programs:* 3-2 physical therapy, marine affairs policy, education.

Library Otto G. Richter Library plus 6 others with 1.3 million titles, 17,155 serial subscriptions, 109,633 audiovisual materials, an OPAC, a Web page.

Computers on Campus 2000 computers available on campus for general student use. A campuswide network can be accessed from student residence rooms and from off campus that provide access to online student account and grade information. Internet access, online (class) registration, at least one staffed computer lab available.

Student Life *Housing:* on-campus residence required for freshman year. *Options:* coed, disabled students. *Activities and Organizations:* drama/theater group, student-run newspaper, radio and television station, choral group, marching band, student government, international student organizations, sports and recreation clubs, Association of Commuter Students, United Black Students, national fraternities, national sororities. *Campus security:* 24-hour emergency response devices and patrols, student patrols, late-night transport/escort service, controlled dormitory access, crime prevention and safety workshops, residential college crime watch. *Student Services:* health clinic, personal/psychological counseling, women's center.

Athletics Member NCAA. All Division I except football (Division I-A). *Intercollegiate sports:* baseball M(s), basketball M(s)/W(s), crew W(s), cross-country running M(s)/W(s), golf W(s), racquetball M(c)/W(c), soccer W(s), squash M(c)/W(c), swimming W(s), tennis M(s)/W(s), track and field M(s)/W(s), volleyball M(c)/W(s). *Intramural sports:* badminton M(c)/W(c), basketball M/W, bowling M(c)/W(c), crew M(c)/W(c), equestrian sports M(c)/W(c), fencing M(c)/W(c), football M/W, golf M(c)/W(c), lacrosse M(c)/W(c), racquetball M/W, rugby M(c)/W(c), sailing M(c)/W(c), soccer M(c)/W(c), softball M/W(c), squash M/W, swimming M/W, table tennis M(c)/W(c), tennis M(c)/W(c), track and field M/W, volleyball M/W, water polo M(c)/W(c).

Standardized Tests *Required:* SAT I or ACT (for admission). *Required for some:* SAT II: Subject Tests (for admission).

Costs (2002–03) *Comprehensive fee:* $32,872 includes full-time tuition ($24,378), mandatory fees ($432), and room and board ($8062). Full-time tuition and fees vary according to course load, degree level, location, and program. Part-time tuition: $1010 per credit. Part-time tuition and fees vary according to course load, degree level, location, and program. *Room and board:* College room only: $4694. Room and board charges vary according to board plan and housing facility. *Payment plans:* tuition prepayment, installment. *Waivers:* employees or children of employees.

Financial Aid Of all full-time matriculated undergraduates who enrolled in 2001, 5341 applied for aid, 4554 were judged to have need, 1815 had their need fully met. 3013 Federal Work-Study jobs (averaging $2282). 309 State and other part-time jobs (averaging $3644). In 2001, 2295 non-need-based awards were made. *Average percent of need met:* 88%. *Average financial aid package:* $21,805. *Average need-based loan:* $5085. *Average need-based gift aid:* $15,081.

Applying *Options:* common application, electronic application, early admission, early decision, early action, deferred entrance. *Application fee:* $50. *Required:* essay or personal statement, high school transcript, 1 letter of recommendation. *Required for some:* interview. *Recommended:* minimum 3.0 GPA. *Application deadlines:* 2/15 (freshmen), 3/1 (transfers). *Early decision:* 11/15. *Notification:* 4/15 (freshmen), 12/15 (early decision), 1/15 (early action).

Admissions Contact University of Miami, PO Box 248025, Ashe Building Room 132, 1252 Memorial Drive, Coral Gables, FL 33146-4616. *Phone:* 305-284-4323. *Fax:* 305-284-2507. *E-mail:* admission@miami.edu.

UNIVERSITY OF NORTH FLORIDA
Jacksonville, Florida

- **State-supported** comprehensive, founded 1965, part of State University System of Florida
- **Calendar** semesters
- **Degrees** associate, bachelor's, master's, doctoral, post-master's, and postbachelor's certificates (doctoral degree in education only)
- **Urban** 1300-acre campus
- **Endowment** $35.1 million
- **Coed,** 11,134 undergraduate students, 65% full-time, 59% women, 41% men
- **Very difficult** entrance level, 71% of applicants were admitted

Undergraduates 7,205 full-time, 3,929 part-time. Students come from 47 states and territories, 96 other countries, 5% are from out of state, 10% African American, 6% Asian American or Pacific Islander, 5% Hispanic American, 0.4% Native American, 0.9% international, 9% transferred in, 18% live on campus. *Retention:* 76% of 2001 full-time freshmen returned.

Freshmen *Admission:* 6,314 applied, 4,461 admitted, 1,773 enrolled. *Average high school GPA:* 3.40. *Test scores:* SAT verbal scores over 500: 79%; SAT math scores over 500: 78%; ACT scores over 18: 93%; SAT verbal scores over 600: 27%; SAT math scores over 600: 25%; ACT scores over 24: 15%; SAT verbal scores over 700: 4%; SAT math scores over 700: 3%.

Faculty *Total:* 612, 62% full-time. *Student/faculty ratio:* 21:1.

Majors Accounting; anthropology; art; art education; banking; biological/physical sciences; biology; business administration; business economics; business marketing and marketing management; chemistry; civil engineering; communications; computer/information sciences; construction technology; criminal justice studies; economics; electrical engineering; elementary education; English; finance; fine/studio arts; general studies; health science; history; international business; international relations; jazz; liberal arts and sciences/liberal studies; mathematical statistics; mathematics; mathematics education; mechanical engineering; middle school education; music; music (general performance); music teacher education; nursing; philosophy; physical education; physics; political science; psychology; science education; secondary education; sociology; Spanish; special education; trade/industrial education.

Academic Programs *Special study options:* accelerated degree program, adult/continuing education programs, advanced placement credit, cooperative education, distance learning, double majors, freshman honors college, honors programs, independent study, internships, off-campus study, part-time degree program, services for LD students, study abroad, summer session for credit. *ROTC:* Navy (b).

Library Thomas G. Carpenter Library with 704,799 titles, 3,000 serial subscriptions, 60,776 audiovisual materials, an OPAC, a Web page.

Computers on Campus 700 computers available on campus for general student use. A campuswide network can be accessed from student residence rooms and from off campus that provide access to applications software. Internet access, online (class) registration, at least one staffed computer lab available.

Student Life *Housing Options:* coed, disabled students. *Activities and Organizations:* drama/theater group, student-run newspaper, radio and television station, choral group, International Student Association, Filipino Student Association, Student Physical Therapy Association, National Education Association, Student Government Association, national fraternities, national sororities. *Campus security:* 24-hour emergency response devices and patrols, student patrols, late-night transport/escort service, controlled dormitory access, electronic parking lot security. *Student Services:* health clinic, personal/psychological counseling, women's center.

Athletics Member NCAA. All Division II except golf (Division I), swimming (Division I). *Intercollegiate sports:* baseball M(s), basketball M(s)/W(s), cross-country running M(s)/W(s), golf M(s), soccer M(s)/W(s), softball W(s), swimming W(s), tennis M(s)/W(s), track and field M(s)/W(s), volleyball W(s). *Intramural sports:* badminton M/W, basketball M/W, bowling M/W, fencing M(c)/W(c), football M/W, golf M/W, lacrosse M(c)/W(c), racquetball M(c)/W(c), rugby M, sailing M(c)/W(c), soccer M/W, softball M/W, squash M/W, swimming M(c)/W(c), table tennis M/W, tennis M/W, track and field M/W, volleyball M(c)/W(c), water polo M/W, weight lifting M(c)/W(c).

Standardized Tests *Required:* SAT I or ACT (for admission).

Costs (2001–02) *Tuition:* state resident $2669 full-time, $89 per semester hour part-time; nonresident $10,557 full-time, $352 per semester hour part-time. *Room* *and board:* $5380; room only: $3120. Room and board charges vary according to board plan and housing facility. *Payment plan:* deferred payment. *Waivers:* senior citizens and employees or children of employees.

Financial Aid Of all full-time matriculated undergraduates who enrolled in 2001, 5389 applied for aid, 2669 were judged to have need, 931 had their need fully met. 61 Federal Work-Study jobs (averaging $3368). In 2001, 2404 non-need-based awards were made. *Average percent of need met:* 71%. *Average financial aid package:* $2228. *Average need-based loan:* $3637. *Average need-based gift aid:* $1836. *Average non-need based aid:* $2239. *Average indebtedness upon graduation:* $12,246.

Applying *Options:* common application, electronic application, early admission, early action, deferred entrance. *Application fee:* $20. *Required:* high school transcript, minimum 2.0 GPA. *Required for some:* essay or personal statement, letters of recommendation. *Recommended:* minimum 3.0 GPA. *Application deadlines:* 7/2 (freshmen), 7/2 (transfers). *Notification:* continuous (freshmen), 12/2 (early action).

Admissions Contact Ms. Sherry David, Director of Admissions, University of North Florida, 4567 St. Johns Bluff Road South, Jacksonville, FL 32224. *Phone:* 904-620-2624. *Fax:* 904-620-2414. *E-mail:* osprey@unf.edu.

UNIVERSITY OF PHOENIX-FORT LAUDERDALE CAMPUS

Plantation, Florida

- **Proprietary** comprehensive
- **Calendar** continuous
- **Degrees** certificates, associate, bachelor's, master's, doctoral, post-master's, and postbachelor's certificates (courses conducted at 54 campuses and learning centers in 13 states)
- **Coed,** 1,051 undergraduate students, 100% full-time, 63% women, 37% men
- **Noncompetitive** entrance level

Undergraduates Students come from 6 states and territories, 1% are from out of state.

Freshmen *Admission:* 11 admitted.

Faculty *Total:* 157, 4% full-time, 36% with terminal degrees. *Student/faculty ratio:* 13:1.

Majors Accounting; business administration; business marketing and marketing management; computer/information sciences; enterprise management; management information systems/business data processing; management science; nursing science.

Academic Programs *Special study options:* accelerated degree program, adult/continuing education programs, advanced placement credit, distance learning, external degree program, independent study.

Library University Library with 17.5 million titles, 9,000 serial subscriptions, an OPAC, a Web page.

Computers on Campus A campuswide network can be accessed from off campus. Internet access, at least one staffed computer lab available.

Student Life *Housing:* college housing not available.

Costs (2001–02) *Tuition:* $8100 full-time. Full-time tuition and fees vary according to location and program. *Payment plan:* deferred payment. *Waivers:* employees or children of employees.

Applying *Options:* deferred entrance. *Application fee:* $85. *Required:* 2 years of work experience. *Required for some:* high school transcript. *Application deadline:* rolling (freshmen), rolling (transfers).

Admissions Contact Ms. Beth Barilla, Director of Admissions, University of Phoenix-Fort Lauderdale Campus, 4615 East Elwood Street, Phoenix, AZ 85040-1958. *Phone:* 480-927-0099 Ext. 1218. *Toll-free phone:* 800-228-7240. *Fax:* 480-594-1758. *E-mail:* beth.barilla@apollogrp.edu.

UNIVERSITY OF PHOENIX-JACKSONVILLE CAMPUS

Jacksonville, Florida

- **Proprietary** comprehensive, founded 1976
- **Calendar** continuous
- **Degrees** certificates, associate, bachelor's, master's, doctoral, post-master's, and postbachelor's certificates (courses conducted at 54 campuses and learning centers in 13 states)
- **Coed,** 1,183 undergraduate students, 100% full-time, 60% women, 40% men
- **Noncompetitive** entrance level

Undergraduates Students come from 13 states and territories, 2% are from out of state.

Freshmen *Admission:* 14 admitted.

Faculty *Total:* 231, 3% full-time, 18% with terminal degrees. *Student/faculty ratio:* 13:1.

Majors Accounting; business administration; business marketing and marketing management; enterprise management; information sciences/systems; management information systems/business data processing; management science; nursing science.

Academic Programs *Special study options:* accelerated degree program, adult/continuing education programs, advanced placement credit, distance learning, external degree program, independent study.

Library University Library with 17.5 million titles, 9,000 serial subscriptions, an OPAC, a Web page.

Computers on Campus A campuswide network can be accessed from off campus. Internet access, at least one staffed computer lab available.

Student Life *Housing:* college housing not available.

Costs (2001–02) *Tuition:* $8100 full-time. Full-time tuition and fees vary according to location and program. *Payment plan:* deferred payment. *Waivers:* employees or children of employees.

Applying *Options:* deferred entrance. *Application fee:* $85. *Required:* 2 years of work experience. *Required for some:* high school transcript. *Application deadline:* rolling (freshmen), rolling (transfers).

Admissions Contact Ms. Beth Barilla, Director of Admissions, University of Phoenix-Jacksonville Campus, 4615 East Elwood Street, Phoenix, AZ 85040-1958. *Phone:* 480-927-0099 Ext. 1218. *Toll-free phone:* 800-228-7240. *Fax:* 480-594-1758. *E-mail:* beth.barilla@apollogrp.edu.

UNIVERSITY OF PHOENIX-ORLANDO CAMPUS

Maitland, Florida

- **Proprietary** comprehensive
- **Calendar** continuous
- **Degrees** certificates, associate, bachelor's, master's, doctoral, post-master's, and postbachelor's certificates (courses conducted at 54 campuses and learning centers in 13 states)
- **Coed,** 1,204 undergraduate students, 100% full-time, 59% women, 41% men
- **Noncompetitive** entrance level

Undergraduates Students come from 21 states and territories, 2% are from out of state.

Freshmen *Admission:* 36 admitted.

Faculty *Total:* 181, 4% full-time, 15% with terminal degrees. *Student/faculty ratio:* 13:1.

Majors Accounting; business administration; business marketing and marketing management; computer/information sciences; enterprise management; management information systems/business data processing; management science; nursing science.

Academic Programs *Special study options:* accelerated degree program, adult/continuing education programs, advanced placement credit, distance learning, external degree program, independent study.

Library University Library with 17.5 million titles, 9,000 serial subscriptions, an OPAC, a Web page.

Computers on Campus A campuswide network can be accessed from off campus. Internet access, at least one staffed computer lab available.

Student Life *Housing:* college housing not available.

Costs (2001–02) *Tuition:* $8100 full-time. Full-time tuition and fees vary according to location and program. *Payment plan:* deferred payment. *Waivers:* employees or children of employees.

Applying *Options:* deferred entrance. *Application fee:* $85. *Required:* 2 years of work experience. *Required for some:* high school transcript. *Application deadline:* rolling (freshmen), rolling (transfers).

Admissions Contact Ms. Beth Barilla, Director of Admissions, University of Phoenix-Orlando Campus, 4615 East Elwood Street, Phoenix, AZ 85040-1958. *Phone:* 480-927-0099 Ext. 1218. *Toll-free phone:* 800-228-7240. *Fax:* 480-594-1758. *E-mail:* beth.barilla@apollogrp.edu.

UNIVERSITY OF PHOENIX-TAMPA CAMPUS

Tampa, Florida

- **Proprietary** comprehensive
- **Calendar** continuous

University of Phoenix-Tampa Campus (continued)

- **Degrees** certificates, associate, bachelor's, master's, doctoral, post-master's, and postbachelor's certificates (courses conducted at 54 campuses and learning centers in 13 states)
- **Coed,** 878 undergraduate students, 100% full-time, 56% women, 44% men
- **Noncompetitive** entrance level

Undergraduates Students come from 10 states and territories, 1% are from out of state.

Freshmen *Admission:* 9 admitted.

Faculty *Total:* 180, 2% full-time, 9% with terminal degrees. *Student/faculty ratio:* 12:1.

Majors Accounting; business administration; business marketing and marketing management; computer/information sciences; management information systems/business data processing; management science; nursing science; public administration and services related.

Academic Programs *Special study options:* accelerated degree program, adult/continuing education programs, advanced placement credit, distance learning, external degree program, independent study.

Library University Library with 17.5 million titles, 9,000 serial subscriptions, an OPAC, a Web page.

Computers on Campus A campuswide network can be accessed from off campus. Internet access, at least one staffed computer lab available.

Student Life *Housing:* college housing not available.

Costs (2001–02) *Tuition:* $8100 full-time. Full-time tuition and fees vary according to location and program. *Payment plan:* deferred payment. *Waivers:* employees or children of employees.

Applying *Options:* deferred entrance. *Application fee:* $85. *Required:* 2 years of work experience. *Required for some:* high school transcript. *Application deadline:* rolling (freshmen), rolling (transfers).

Admissions Contact Ms. Beth Barilla, Director of Admissions, University of Phoenix-Tampa Campus, 4615 East Elwood Street, Phoenix, AZ 85040-1958. *Phone:* 480-927-0099 Ext. 1218. *Toll-free phone:* 800-228-7240. *Fax:* 480-594-1758. *E-mail:* beth.barilla@apollogrp.edu.

UNIVERSITY OF SOUTH FLORIDA
Tampa, Florida

- **State-supported** university, founded 1956
- **Calendar** semesters
- **Degrees** associate, bachelor's, master's, doctoral, first professional, and postbachelor's certificates
- **Urban** 1913-acre campus
- **Endowment** $220.9 million
- **Coed,** 28,769 undergraduate students, 63% full-time, 59% women, 41% men
- **Moderately difficult** entrance level, 67% of applicants were admitted

Undergraduates 18,001 full-time, 10,768 part-time. Students come from 52 states and territories, 116 other countries, 5% are from out of state, 12% African American, 6% Asian American or Pacific Islander, 10% Hispanic American, 0.4% Native American, 2% international, 14% transferred in, 13% live on campus.

Freshmen *Admission:* 12,403 applied, 8,294 admitted, 4,281 enrolled. *Average high school GPA:* 3.50. *Test scores:* SAT verbal scores over 500: 60%; SAT math scores over 500: 64%; ACT scores over 18: 87%; SAT verbal scores over 600: 18%; SAT math scores over 600: 20%; ACT scores over 24: 28%; SAT verbal scores over 700: 2%; SAT math scores over 700: 2%; ACT scores over 30: 2%.

Faculty *Total:* 1,973, 77% full-time. *Student/faculty ratio:* 16:1.

Majors Accounting; African-American studies; American studies; anthropology; art; art education; biological/physical sciences; biology; business; business administration; business economics; business education; business marketing and marketing management; chemical engineering; chemistry; civil engineering; classics; communications; computer engineering; computer/information sciences; computer/information sciences related; criminal justice studies; dance; drama/dance education; early childhood education; economics; education; education of the emotionally handicapped; education of the mentally handicapped; education of the specific learning disabled; electrical engineering; elementary education; engineering; English; English education; environmental science; finance; foreign languages education; French; general studies; geography; geology; German; gerontology; history; humanities; industrial/manufacturing engineering; information sciences/systems; international business; international relations; Italian; liberal arts and sciences/liberal studies; management science; mathematics; mathematics education; mechanical engineering; medical technology; microbiology/bacteriology; modern languages; music (general performance); music teacher education; nursing; philosophy; physical education; physics; political science; psychology; religious studies; Russian; science education; social science education; social sciences; social work; sociology; Spanish; special education; speech-language pathology/audiology; speech/rhetorical studies; theater arts/drama; trade/industrial education; women's studies.

Academic Programs *Special study options:* academic remediation for entering students, accelerated degree program, adult/continuing education programs, advanced placement credit, cooperative education, distance learning, double majors, external degree program, freshman honors college, honors programs, independent study, internships, off-campus study, part-time degree program, services for LD students, student-designed majors, study abroad, summer session for credit. *ROTC:* Army (b), Air Force (b).

Library Tampa Campus Library plus 2 others with 1.9 million titles, 9,607 serial subscriptions, 148,986 audiovisual materials, an OPAC, a Web page.

Computers on Campus 500 computers available on campus for general student use. A campuswide network can be accessed from student residence rooms and from off campus. Internet access, online (class) registration, at least one staffed computer lab available.

Student Life *Housing Options:* coed, men-only, women-only, cooperative, disabled students. *Activities and Organizations:* drama/theater group, student-run newspaper, radio and television station, choral group, marching band, student government, Campus Activities Board, USF Ambassadors, student admissions representatives, national fraternities, national sororities. *Campus security:* 24-hour emergency response devices and patrols, student patrols, late-night transport/escort service, controlled dormitory access, residence hall lobby personnel 8 p.m. to 6 a.m. *Student Services:* health clinic, personal/psychological counseling, women's center, legal services.

Athletics Member NCAA. All Division I. *Intercollegiate sports:* baseball M(s), basketball M(s)/W(s), cross-country running M(s)/W(s), football M(s), golf M(s)/W(s), soccer M(s)/W(s), softball W(s), tennis M(s)/W(s), track and field M(s)/W(s), volleyball W(s). *Intramural sports:* badminton M/W, basketball M/W, bowling M/W, cross-country running M/W, football M/W, golf M/W, racquetball M/W, soccer M/W, softball M/W, swimming M/W, tennis M/W, track and field M/W, volleyball M/W, wrestling M.

Standardized Tests *Required:* SAT I or ACT (for admission).

Costs (2001–02) *Tuition:* state resident $2520 full-time, $84 per credit hour part-time; nonresident $10,410 full-time, $347 per credit hour part-time. Full-time tuition and fees vary according to class time, course load, and location. Part-time tuition and fees vary according to class time, course load, and location. *Room and board:* $5600; room only: $3040. Room and board charges vary according to board plan, housing facility, and location. *Payment plans:* tuition prepayment, installment. *Waivers:* senior citizens.

Financial Aid Of all full-time matriculated undergraduates who enrolled in 2001, 10026 applied for aid, 8287 were judged to have need, 1802 had their need fully met. 1600 Federal Work-Study jobs. In 2001, 994 non-need-based awards were made. *Average percent of need met:* 83%. *Average financial aid package:* $8828. *Average need-based loan:* $4229. *Average need-based gift aid:* $3811. *Average non-need based aid:* $1586. *Average indebtedness upon graduation:* $16,715.

Applying *Options:* common application, electronic application, early admission. *Application fee:* $20. *Required:* high school transcript, minimum 2.0 GPA. *Required for some:* letters of recommendation. *Notification:* continuous (freshmen).

Admissions Contact Mr. Dewey Holleman, Director of Admissions, University of South Florida, 4202 East Fowler Avenue, SVC 1036, Tampa, FL 33620-9951. *Phone:* 813-974-3350. *Fax:* 813-974-9689. *E-mail:* bullseye@admin.usf.edu.

THE UNIVERSITY OF TAMPA
Tampa, Florida

- **Independent** comprehensive, founded 1931
- **Calendar** semesters
- **Degrees** certificates, associate, bachelor's, and master's
- **Urban** 75-acre campus with easy access to Orlando
- **Endowment** $22.0 million
- **Coed,** 3,327 undergraduate students, 86% full-time, 61% women, 39% men
- **Moderately difficult** entrance level, 81% of applicants were admitted

Undergraduates 2,862 full-time, 465 part-time. Students come from 50 states and territories, 85 other countries, 50% are from out of state, 7% African American, 2% Asian American or Pacific Islander, 9% Hispanic American, 0.6% Native American, 5% international, 8% transferred in, 50% live on campus. *Retention:* 76% of 2001 full-time freshmen returned.

Freshmen *Admission:* 3,335 applied, 2,713 admitted, 876 enrolled. *Average high school GPA:* 3.2. *Test scores:* SAT verbal scores over 500: 67%; SAT math scores over 500: 63%; ACT scores over 18: 97%; SAT verbal scores over 600:

15%; SAT math scores over 600: 15%; ACT scores over 24: 49%; SAT verbal scores over 700: 1%; SAT math scores over 700: 1%; ACT scores over 30: 4%.

Faculty *Total:* 310, 47% full-time, 60% with terminal degrees. *Student/faculty ratio:* 17:1.

Majors Accounting; art; biochemistry; biology; business administration; business marketing and marketing management; chemistry; computer graphics; computer programming; creative writing; criminology; economics; education (K-12); elementary education; English; environmental biology; environmental science; exercise sciences; finance; geography; history; information sciences/systems; international business; international relations; liberal arts and sciences/liberal studies; marine science; mass communications; mathematics; music; nursing; philosophy; physical education; political science; pre-dentistry; pre-law; pre-medicine; pre-veterinary studies; psychology; secondary education; social sciences; sociology; Spanish; theater arts/drama; urban studies; visual/performing arts.

Academic Programs *Special study options:* academic remediation for entering students, adult/continuing education programs, advanced placement credit, cooperative education, double majors, English as a second language, honors programs, independent study, internships, off-campus study, part-time degree program, services for LD students, study abroad, summer session for credit. *ROTC:* Army (b), Air Force (c).

Library Merl Kelce Library with 250,850 titles, 854 serial subscriptions, 3,733 audiovisual materials, an OPAC, a Web page.

Computers on Campus 250 computers available on campus for general student use. A campuswide network can be accessed from student residence rooms and from off campus. Internet access, at least one staffed computer lab available.

Student Life *Housing Options:* coed, women-only. *Activities and Organizations:* drama/theater group, student-run newspaper, radio and television station, choral group, student government, student productions, Interfraternity Council, Pannellenic Association, Residence Hall Association, national fraternities, national sororities. *Campus security:* 24-hour emergency response devices and patrols, late-night transport/escort service, controlled dormitory access. *Student Services:* health clinic, personal/psychological counseling.

Athletics Member NCAA. All Division II. *Intercollegiate sports:* baseball M(s), basketball M(s)/W(s), crew M/W(s), cross-country running M(s)/W(s), golf M(s), soccer M(s)/W(s), softball W(s), swimming M(s)/W(s), tennis W(s), volleyball W(s). *Intramural sports:* badminton M/W, baseball M/W, basketball M/W, bowling M/W, crew M/W, cross-country running M/W, equestrian sports W, field hockey W, football M, golf M/W, lacrosse M, racquetball M/W, rugby M, soccer M/W, softball M/W, swimming M/W, table tennis M/W, tennis W, volleyball M/W, weight lifting M/W.

Standardized Tests *Required:* SAT I or ACT (for admission).

Costs (2001–02) *Comprehensive fee:* $22,432 includes full-time tuition ($15,680), mandatory fees ($862), and room and board ($5890). Part-time tuition: $336 per hour. Part-time tuition and fees vary according to class time. *Required fees:* $35 per term part-time. *Room and board:* College room only: $3040. Room and board charges vary according to housing facility. *Payment plan:* installment. *Waivers:* employees or children of employees.

Financial Aid Of all full-time matriculated undergraduates who enrolled in 2001, 2168 applied for aid, 1617 were judged to have need, 342 had their need fully met. In 2001, 531 non-need-based awards were made. *Average percent of need met:* 76%. *Average financial aid package:* $14,098. *Average need-based loan:* $3711. *Average need-based gift aid:* $3744. *Average non-need based aid:* $6580. *Average indebtedness upon graduation:* $18,500.

Applying *Options:* common application, electronic application, early admission, deferred entrance. *Application fee:* $35. *Required:* essay or personal statement, high school transcript, minimum 2.0 GPA, 1 letter of recommendation. *Recommended:* interview. *Application deadline:* rolling (freshmen), rolling (transfers).

Admissions Contact The University of Tampa, 401 West Kennedy Boulevard, Tampa, FL 33606-1480. *Phone:* 813-253-6211. *Toll-free phone:* 888-646-2438. *Fax:* 813-258-7398. *E-mail:* admissions@ut.edu.

UNIVERSITY OF WEST FLORIDA

Pensacola, Florida

- **State-supported** comprehensive, founded 1963, part of State University System of Florida
- **Calendar** semesters
- **Degrees** bachelor's, master's, and doctoral
- **Suburban** 1600-acre campus
- **Endowment** $51.2 million
- **Coed,** 7,422 undergraduate students, 67% full-time, 57% women, 43% men
- **Moderately difficult** entrance level, 82% of applicants were admitted

The University of West Florida—near historic Pensacola and the world-famous beaches of the Gulf of Mexico—offers an inviting, environmentally friendly setting for study. Small classes, opportunities for individually tailored educational experiences, and scholarships for academic performance help make UWF an extraordinary value in higher education.

Undergraduates 5,002 full-time, 2,420 part-time. Students come from 48 states and territories, 82 other countries, 11% are from out of state, 10% African American, 5% Asian American or Pacific Islander, 4% Hispanic American, 1% Native American, 1% international, 14% transferred in, 11% live on campus. *Retention:* 73% of 2001 full-time freshmen returned.

Freshmen *Admission:* 2,345 applied, 1,932 admitted, 886 enrolled. *Average high school GPA:* 3.30. *Test scores:* SAT verbal scores over 500: 69%; SAT math scores over 500: 66%; ACT scores over 18: 94%; SAT verbal scores over 600: 23%; SAT math scores over 600: 20%; ACT scores over 24: 39%; SAT verbal scores over 700: 3%; SAT math scores over 700: 2%; ACT scores over 30: 4%.

Faculty *Total:* 532, 47% full-time. *Student/faculty ratio:* 19:1.

Majors Accounting; anthropology; art; art education; art history; biological/physical sciences; biology; business administration; business economics; business marketing and marketing management; chemistry; communications; community health liaison; computer engineering; computer/information sciences; criminal justice studies; early childhood education; elementary education; English; English education; environmental science; finance; fine/studio arts; foreign languages education; health/physical education; history; humanities; industrial technology; international relations; management information systems/business data processing; marine biology; mathematics; mathematics education; medical technology; middle school education; music (general performance); nursing; paralegal/legal assistant; philosophy; physical education; physics; political science; psychology; religious studies; science education; social science education; social sciences; social work; sociology; special education; theater arts/drama; trade/industrial education.

Academic Programs *Special study options:* advanced placement credit, cooperative education, distance learning, English as a second language, honors programs, independent study, internships, off-campus study, part-time degree program, services for LD students, study abroad, summer session for credit. *ROTC:* Army (b), Air Force (b).

Library Pace Library with 392,581 titles, 3,210 serial subscriptions, 10,182 audiovisual materials, an OPAC, a Web page.

Computers on Campus A campuswide network can be accessed from student residence rooms and from off campus. Internet access, online (class) registration, at least one staffed computer lab available.

Student Life *Housing Options:* coed. *Activities and Organizations:* drama/theater group, student-run newspaper, choral group, Marketing Association, Student Council for Exceptional Children, Intervarsity Christian Fellowship, Baptist Student Ministry, Golden Key Honor Society, national fraternities, national sororities. *Campus security:* 24-hour emergency response devices and patrols, student patrols, late-night transport/escort service, controlled dormitory access. *Student Services:* health clinic, personal/psychological counseling.

Athletics Member NCAA. All Division II. *Intercollegiate sports:* baseball M(s), basketball M(s)/W(s), cross-country running M(s)/W(s), golf M(s), soccer M(s)/W(s), softball W(s), tennis M(s)/W(s), volleyball W. *Intramural sports:* basketball M/W, bowling M/W, fencing M/W, football M/W, sailing M/W, soccer M/W, swimming M/W, tennis M/W, volleyball M/W.

Standardized Tests *Required:* SAT I or ACT (for admission).

Costs (2001–02) *Tuition:* state resident $1670 full-time, $56 per semester hour part-time; nonresident $9557 full-time, $319 per semester hour part-time. Full-time tuition and fees vary according to course load and location. Part-time tuition and fees vary according to course load and location. *Required fees:* $858 full-time, $29 per semester hour. *Room and board:* $5440. Room and board charges vary according to housing facility and location. *Waivers:* employees or children of employees.

Financial Aid Of all full-time matriculated undergraduates who enrolled in 2001, 2486 applied for aid, 2098 were judged to have need, 937 had their need fully met. 156 Federal Work-Study jobs (averaging $2350). 1460 State and other part-time jobs. In 2001, 377 non-need-based awards were made. *Average non-need based aid:* $3102.

Applying *Options:* electronic application, early admission, deferred entrance. *Application fee:* $20. *Required:* high school transcript, minimum 2.0 GPA. *Application deadlines:* 6/30 (freshmen), 6/30 (transfers). *Notification:* continuous (freshmen).

Admissions Contact Ms. Susie Neeley, Director of Admissions, University of West Florida, 11000 University Parkway, Pensacola, FL 32514-5750. *Phone:* 850-474-2230. *E-mail:* admissions@uwf.edu.

WARNER SOUTHERN COLLEGE
Lake Wales, Florida

- **Independent** comprehensive, founded 1968, affiliated with Church of God
- **Calendar** semesters
- **Degrees** certificates, associate, bachelor's, and master's
- **Rural** 320-acre campus with easy access to Tampa and Orlando
- **Endowment** $5.5 million
- **Coed,** 1,082 undergraduate students, 89% full-time, 60% women, 40% men
- **Minimally difficult** entrance level, 67% of applicants were admitted

Undergraduates 967 full-time, 115 part-time. Students come from 21 states and territories, 13 other countries, 30% are from out of state, 18% African American, 0.7% Asian American or Pacific Islander, 7% Hispanic American, 1% Native American, 5% international, 29% transferred in, 20% live on campus. *Retention:* 80% of 2001 full-time freshmen returned.

Freshmen *Admission:* 281 applied, 189 admitted, 90 enrolled. *Average high school GPA:* 3.23. *Test scores:* SAT verbal scores over 500: 42%; SAT math scores over 500: 41%; ACT scores over 18: 69%; SAT verbal scores over 600: 7%; SAT math scores over 600: 6%; ACT scores over 24: 8%; SAT math scores over 700: 1%.

Faculty *Total:* 77, 44% full-time, 55% with terminal degrees. *Student/faculty ratio:* 17:1.

Majors Accounting; biblical studies; biology; business administration; business education; business marketing and marketing management; communications; elementary education; English; English education; exercise sciences; finance; general studies; history; music teacher education; physical education; pre-law; pre-theology; psychology; recreation/leisure studies; religious music; science education; social science education; social sciences; social work; special education; sport/fitness administration.

Academic Programs *Special study options:* academic remediation for entering students, adult/continuing education programs, advanced placement credit, double majors, independent study, internships, part-time degree program, summer session for credit.

Library Learning Resource Center plus 1 other with 56,419 titles, 224 serial subscriptions, 14,935 audiovisual materials, an OPAC, a Web page.

Computers on Campus 30 computers available on campus for general student use. At least one staffed computer lab available.

Student Life *Housing:* on-campus residence required through junior year. *Options:* men-only, women-only. *Activities and Organizations:* choral group, Concert Choir, Fellowship of Christian Athletes, Young Americans, Student Government Association. *Campus security:* 24-hour emergency response devices and patrols, late-night transport/escort service, controlled dormitory access. *Student Services:* health clinic, personal/psychological counseling.

Athletics Member NAIA. *Intercollegiate sports:* baseball M(s), basketball M(s)/W(s), cross-country running M(s)/W(s), golf M(s), softball W(s), volleyball W(s). *Intramural sports:* basketball M, football M/W, golf M/W, racquetball M/W, table tennis M/W, tennis M/W, volleyball M/W.

Standardized Tests *Required:* SAT I or ACT (for admission).

Costs (2001–02) *Comprehensive fee:* $14,860 includes full-time tuition ($9950), mandatory fees ($90), and room and board ($4820). Full-time tuition and fees vary according to program. Part-time tuition: $260 per credit hour. Part-time tuition and fees vary according to course load. *Required fees:* $45 per term part-time. *Room and board:* College room only: $2310. Room and board charges vary according to board plan. *Payment plan:* installment. *Waivers:* children of alumni, senior citizens, and employees or children of employees.

Applying *Options:* common application, deferred entrance. *Application fee:* $20. *Required:* high school transcript, minimum 2.25 GPA, 1 letter of recommendation. *Required for some:* interview. *Recommended:* essay or personal statement. *Application deadline:* rolling (freshmen), rolling (transfers). *Notification:* continuous (freshmen).

Admissions Contact Mr. Jason Roe, Director of Admissions, Warner Southern College, Warner Southern Center, 13895 US 27, Lake Wales, FL 33859. *Phone:* 863-638-7212 Ext. 7213. *Toll-free phone:* 800-949-7248. *Fax:* 863-638-1472. *E-mail:* admissions@warner.edu.

WEBBER INTERNATIONAL UNIVERSITY
Babson Park, Florida

- **Independent** comprehensive, founded 1927
- **Calendar** semesters
- **Degrees** associate, bachelor's, and master's
- **Small-town** 110-acre campus with easy access to Orlando
- **Endowment** $5.7 million
- **Coed,** 451 undergraduate students, 86% full-time, 47% women, 53% men
- **Moderately difficult** entrance level, 71% of applicants were admitted

Webber International University celebrates its seventy-fifth anniversary with a name change that reflects the mission of the institution. The University attracts more than 140 international students from every continent except Antarctica. Worldwide business is the focus of the curriculum and successful employment is a key goal. Students are encouraged to follow careers as executives in established companies, leaders in their home countries, and groundbreaking entrepreneurs in the world of business.

Undergraduates 386 full-time, 65 part-time. Students come from 18 states and territories, 36 other countries, 8% are from out of state, 10% African American, 1% Asian American or Pacific Islander, 7% Hispanic American, 0.2% Native American, 27% international, 9% transferred in, 45% live on campus. *Retention:* 58% of 2001 full-time freshmen returned.

Freshmen *Admission:* 213 applied, 152 admitted, 96 enrolled. *Average high school GPA:* 3.02. *Test scores:* SAT verbal scores over 500: 16%; ACT scores over 18: 55%; SAT verbal scores over 600: 1%; ACT scores over 24: 6%; SAT math scores over 700: 1%.

Faculty *Total:* 30, 53% full-time, 53% with terminal degrees. *Student/faculty ratio:* 20:1.

Majors Accounting; business; business administration; business marketing and marketing management; finance; hotel and restaurant management; international business; pre-law; recreation/leisure facilities management; sport/fitness administration; travel/tourism management.

Academic Programs *Special study options:* academic remediation for entering students, accelerated degree program, adult/continuing education programs, advanced placement credit, cooperative education, internships, part-time degree program, services for LD students, study abroad, summer session for credit.

Library Grace and Roger Babson Library plus 1 other with 35,000 titles, 168 serial subscriptions, 11,073 audiovisual materials.

Computers on Campus 50 computers available on campus for general student use. Internet access, at least one staffed computer lab available.

Student Life *Housing:* on-campus residence required for freshman year. *Options:* men-only, women-only. *Activities and Organizations:* student-run newspaper, Fellowship of Christian Athletes, PBL, student government, Society of Hosteleurs, Webber Ambassadors. *Campus security:* 24-hour emergency response devices and patrols, late-night transport/escort service, controlled dormitory access. *Student Services:* health clinic, personal/psychological counseling.

Athletics Member NAIA. *Intercollegiate sports:* baseball M(s), basketball M(s)/W(s), cross-country running M(s)/W(s), golf M(s)/W(s), soccer M(s)/W(s), softball W(s), tennis M(s)/W(s), track and field M(s)/W(s). *Intramural sports:* basketball M/W, bowling M/W, football M/W, soccer M/W, softball W, swimming M/W, table tennis M/W, tennis M/W, volleyball M/W.

Standardized Tests *Required:* SAT I or ACT (for admission). *Required for some:* SAT I and SAT II or ACT (for admission).

Costs (2002–03) *Comprehensive fee:* $15,350 includes full-time tuition ($11,330) and room and board ($4020). Full-time tuition and fees vary according to class time. Part-time tuition: $160 per credit hour. *Room and board:* Room and board charges vary according to board plan. *Payment plan:* installment. *Waivers:* children of alumni, adult students, senior citizens, and employees or children of employees.

Financial Aid Of all full-time matriculated undergraduates who enrolled in 2001, 380 applied for aid, 196 were judged to have need, 23 had their need fully met. 24 Federal Work-Study jobs (averaging $1000). 39 State and other part-time jobs (averaging $774). *Average percent of need met:* 79%. *Average financial aid package:* $12,698. *Average need-based loan:* $3464. *Average need-based gift aid:* $9619. *Average indebtedness upon graduation:* $11,813. *Financial aid deadline:* 8/1.

Applying *Options:* early action. *Application fee:* $35. *Required:* essay or personal statement, high school transcript, minimum 2.0 GPA, letters of recommendation. *Recommended:* interview. *Application deadlines:* 8/1 (freshmen), 8/1 (out-of-state freshmen), 8/1 (transfers).

Admissions Contact Dr. Deborah Milliken, Executive Vice President, Webber International University, 1201 Scenic Highway, South, Babson Park, FL 33827. *Phone:* 863-638-2910. *Toll-free phone:* 800-741-1844. *Fax:* 863-638-1591. *E-mail:* admissions@webber.edu.

GEORGIA

AGNES SCOTT COLLEGE
Decatur, Georgia

- **Independent** comprehensive, founded 1889, affiliated with Presbyterian Church (U.S.A.)
- **Calendar** semesters
- **Degrees** bachelor's, master's, and postbachelor's certificates
- **Urban** 100-acre campus with easy access to Atlanta
- **Endowment** $347.0 million
- **Women only,** 869 undergraduate students, 95% full-time
- **Very difficult** entrance level, 74% of applicants were admitted

Undergraduates 829 full-time, 40 part-time. Students come from 39 states and territories, 24 other countries, 45% are from out of state, 22% African American, 5% Asian American or Pacific Islander, 4% Hispanic American, 0.2% Native American, 4% international, 2% transferred in, 90% live on campus. *Retention:* 75% of 2001 full-time freshmen returned.

Freshmen *Admission:* 223 enrolled. *Average high school GPA:* 3.66. *Test scores:* SAT verbal scores over 500: 88%; SAT math scores over 500: 88%; ACT scores over 18: 99%; SAT verbal scores over 600: 57%; SAT math scores over 600: 41%; ACT scores over 24: 72%; SAT verbal scores over 700: 18%; SAT math scores over 700: 6%; ACT scores over 30: 22%.

Faculty *Total:* 117, 69% full-time, 79% with terminal degrees. *Student/faculty ratio:* 10:1.

Majors Anthropology; art; astrophysics; biochemistry; biology; chemistry; classics; creative writing; economics; English; French; German; history; interdisciplinary studies; international relations; literature; mathematics; music; philosophy; physics; political science; psychology; religious studies; sociology; Spanish; theater arts/drama; women's studies.

Academic Programs *Special study options:* accelerated degree program, adult/continuing education programs, advanced placement credit, double majors, independent study, internships, off-campus study, part-time degree program, services for LD students, student-designed majors, study abroad, summer session for credit. *ROTC:* Navy (c), Air Force (c). *Unusual degree programs:* 3-2 engineering with Georgia Institute of Technology; art and architecture with Washington University in St. Louis.

Library McCain Library with 209,747 titles, 905 serial subscriptions, 17,187 audiovisual materials, an OPAC, a Web page.

Computers on Campus 263 computers available on campus for general student use. A campuswide network can be accessed from student residence rooms and from off campus. Internet access, at least one staffed computer lab available.

Student Life *Housing:* on-campus residence required through senior year. *Options:* women-only. *Activities and Organizations:* drama/theater group, student-run newspaper, choral group, marching band, Student Government Association, Blackfriars, Residence Hall Association, Witkaze, Volunteer Board. *Campus security:* 24-hour emergency response devices and patrols, late-night transport/escort service, shuttle bus service, security systems in apartments, public safety facility, surveillance equipment. *Student Services:* health clinic, personal/psychological counseling.

Athletics Member NCAA. All Division III. *Intercollegiate sports:* basketball W, cross-country running W, soccer W, softball W, swimming W, tennis W, volleyball W. *Intramural sports:* basketball W, field hockey W, soccer W, squash W, swimming W, tennis W, track and field W, volleyball W, weight lifting W.

Standardized Tests *Required:* SAT I or ACT (for admission). *Required for some:* SAT II: Subject Tests (for admission).

Costs (2001–02) *Comprehensive fee:* $24,950 includes full-time tuition ($17,500), mandatory fees ($170), and room and board ($7280). Part-time tuition: $730 per credit hour. Part-time tuition and fees vary according to course load. *Required fees:* $170 per year part-time. *Room and board:* Room and board charges vary according to board plan and housing facility. *Payment plans:* installment, deferred payment. *Waivers:* employees or children of employees.

Financial Aid Of all full-time matriculated undergraduates who enrolled in 2001, 644 applied for aid, 540 were judged to have need. 278 Federal Work-Study jobs (averaging $1576). 152 State and other part-time jobs. In 2001, 246 non-need-based awards were made. *Average percent of need met:* 99%. *Average financial aid package:* $17,749. *Average need-based loan:* $3658. *Average need-based gift aid:* $12,069. *Average non-need based aid:* $10,912. *Average indebtedness upon graduation:* $14,580.

Applying *Options:* common application, electronic application, early admission, early decision, deferred entrance. *Application fee:* $35. *Required:* essay or personal statement, high school transcript, 2 letters of recommendation. *Recommended:* minimum 3.0 GPA, interview. *Application deadlines:* 3/1 (freshmen), 3/1 (transfers). *Early decision:* 11/15. *Notification:* 3/1 (freshmen), 12/15 (early decision).

Admissions Contact Ms. Stephanie Balmer, Associate Vice President for Enrollment and Director of Admission, Agnes Scott College, 141 East College Avenue, Atlanta/Decatur, GA 30030-3797. *Phone:* 404-471-6285. *Toll-free phone:* 800-868-8602. *Fax:* 404-471-6414. *E-mail:* admission@agnesscott.edu.

ALBANY STATE UNIVERSITY
Albany, Georgia

- **State-supported** comprehensive, founded 1903, part of University System of Georgia
- **Calendar** semesters
- **Degrees** bachelor's, master's, and post-master's certificates
- **Urban** 144-acre campus
- **Endowment** $2.0 million
- **Coed,** 3,015 undergraduate students, 82% full-time, 67% women, 33% men
- **Minimally difficult** entrance level, 36% of applicants were admitted

Undergraduates 2,459 full-time, 556 part-time. 35% live on campus.

Freshmen *Admission:* 2,663 applied, 947 admitted, 417 enrolled. *Average high school GPA:* 2.89. *Test scores:* SAT verbal scores over 500: 21%; SAT math scores over 500: 22%; ACT scores over 18: 48%; SAT verbal scores over 600: 2%; SAT math scores over 600: 3%; ACT scores over 24: 5%.

Faculty *Total:* 190, 67% full-time, 52% with terminal degrees. *Student/faculty ratio:* 20:1.

Majors Accounting; art; biology; business administration; business education; business marketing and marketing management; chemistry; computer/information sciences; criminal justice studies; early childhood education; education related; English; French; health professions and related sciences; history; mathematics; middle school education; music; nursing; physical education; political science; psychology; science education; secretarial science; social work; sociology; Spanish; special education; speech/rhetorical studies.

Academic Programs *Special study options:* academic remediation for entering students, adult/continuing education programs, advanced placement credit, cooperative education, distance learning, double majors, honors programs, independent study, internships, off-campus study, part-time degree program, services for LD students, study abroad, summer session for credit. *ROTC:* Army (b). *Unusual degree programs:* 3-2 engineering with Georgia Institute of Technology.

Library James Pendergrast Memorial Library with 338,744 titles, 1,066 serial subscriptions, 3,301 audiovisual materials, an OPAC, a Web page.

Computers on Campus 1000 computers available on campus for general student use. A campuswide network can be accessed from student residence rooms and from off campus that provide access to email. Internet access, at least one staffed computer lab available.

Student Life *Housing Options:* coed, men-only, women-only. *Activities and Organizations:* drama/theater group, student-run newspaper, choral group, marching band, Gospel Choir, Religious Life Organization, Business Professionals of America, Concert Chorale, NAACP ASU Chapter, national fraternities, national sororities. *Campus security:* 24-hour emergency response devices and patrols, late-night transport/escort service, controlled dormitory access. *Student Services:* health clinic, personal/psychological counseling, women's center.

Athletics Member NCAA. All Division II. *Intercollegiate sports:* baseball M(s), basketball M(s)/W(s), cross-country running M(s)/W(s), football M(s), softball W(s), tennis M(s), track and field M(s)/W(s), volleyball W(s). *Intramural sports:* basketball M/W, softball M, swimming M/W.

Standardized Tests *Required:* SAT I or ACT (for admission).

Costs (2001–02) *Tuition:* state resident $1932 full-time, $81 per credit part-time; nonresident $7728 full-time, $322 per credit part-time. Full-time tuition and fees vary according to course load. Part-time tuition and fees vary according to course load. *Required fees:* $544 full-time, $544 per term part-time. *Room and board:* $3406; room only: $1690. Room and board charges vary according to housing facility.

Financial Aid Of all full-time matriculated undergraduates who enrolled in 2001, 2371 applied for aid, 1963 were judged to have need, 981 had their need fully met. 457 Federal Work-Study jobs. In 2001, 141 non-need-based awards were made. *Average percent of need met:* 69%. *Average financial aid package:* $6760. *Average need-based loan:* $2488. *Average need-based gift aid:* $2866. *Average non-need based aid:* $3041.

Applying *Options:* early admission, deferred entrance. *Application fee:* $20. *Required:* high school transcript, minimum 2.0 GPA. *Required for some:* interview. *Application deadlines:* 7/1 (freshmen), 7/1 (transfers).

Albany State University (continued)

Admissions Contact Mrs. Patricia Price, Assistant Director of Recruitment and Admissions, Albany State University, 504 College Drive, Albany, GA 31705. *Phone:* 229-430-4645. *Toll-free phone:* 800-822-RAMS. *Fax:* 229-430-3936. *E-mail:* fsuttles@asurams.edu.

AMERICAN INTERCONTINENTAL UNIVERSITY
Atlanta, Georgia

- **Proprietary** 4-year, founded 1977
- **Calendar** 5 10-week terms
- **Degrees** associate and bachelor's
- **Urban** campus
- **Coed,** 1,292 undergraduate students, 65% full-time, 64% women, 36% men
- **Noncompetitive** entrance level, 53% of applicants were admitted

Undergraduates Students come from 31 states and territories, 39 other countries, 39% are from out of state, 43% African American, 7% Asian American or Pacific Islander, 4% Hispanic American, 0.5% Native American, 8% international, 14% live on campus. *Retention:* 55% of 2001 full-time freshmen returned.

Freshmen *Admission:* 786 applied, 418 admitted. *Average high school GPA:* 2.5.

Faculty *Total:* 110, 13% full-time, 16% with terminal degrees. *Student/faculty ratio:* 14:1.

Majors Business administration; business marketing and marketing management; computer management; fashion design/illustration; fashion merchandising; film/video production; graphic design/commercial art/illustration; interior design; management information systems/business data processing; photography; travel/tourism management.

Academic Programs *Special study options:* academic remediation for entering students, accelerated degree program, adult/continuing education programs, cooperative education, double majors, English as a second language, external degree program, independent study, internships, part-time degree program, study abroad, summer session for credit.

Library American Intercontinental University Library-Backhead Campus with 21,691 titles, 244 serial subscriptions, 1,212 audiovisual materials, an OPAC.

Computers on Campus 86 computers available on campus for general student use. A campuswide network can be accessed from off campus. Internet access, at least one staffed computer lab available.

Student Life *Activities and Organizations:* student-run newspaper, Student Government Association, Positive Image (Black History), International Student Association, Ministries in Action, Fashion Association. *Campus security:* 24-hour patrols. *Student Services:* personal/psychological counseling.

Standardized Tests *Recommended:* SAT I or ACT (for admission), SAT II: Subject Tests (for admission).

Costs (2001–02) *One-time required fee:* $200. *Tuition:* $12,600 full-time, $1400 per course part-time. *Room only:* $4835. *Payment plan:* installment. *Waivers:* employees or children of employees.

Applying *Options:* early admission, deferred entrance. *Application fee:* $50. *Recommended:* essay or personal statement, high school transcript, minimum 2.0 GPA, 2 letters of recommendation, interview. *Application deadline:* 10/15 (freshmen), rolling (transfers). *Notification:* continuous (freshmen).

Admissions Contact Ms. Knitra Norwood, Director of Admissions, American InterContinental University, 3330 Peachtree Road, NE, Atlanta, GA 30326-1016. *Phone:* 404-965-5700. *Toll-free phone:* 888-999-4248. *Fax:* 404-965-5701. *E-mail:* acatl@ix.netcom.com.

AMERICAN INTERCONTINENTAL UNIVERSITY
Atlanta, Georgia

- **Proprietary** comprehensive, part of AIU is owned by Career Education Corporation
- **Degrees** associate, bachelor's, and master's
- **Coed,** 763 undergraduate students
- 44% of applicants were admitted

Freshmen *Admission:* 344 applied, 151 admitted. *Test scores:* SAT verbal scores over 500: 85%; SAT math scores over 500: 65%; ACT scores over 18: 81%; SAT verbal scores over 600: 10%; SAT math scores over 600: 15%; ACT scores over 24: 59%.

Faculty *Total:* 119, 33% full-time, 29% with terminal degrees. *Student/faculty ratio:* 18:1.

Majors Business marketing and marketing management; design/visual communications; information technology; international business.

Student Life *Housing:* college housing not available. *Student Services:* personal/psychological counseling.

Standardized Tests *Recommended:* SAT I or ACT (for admission).

Costs (2001–02) *Tuition:* $22,050 full-time, $11,025 per year part-time.

Applying *Application fee:* $50. *Required:* high school transcript, minimum 2.0 GPA, interview. *Required for some:* TOEFL or equivalent.

Admissions Contact Mr. Jeff Bostick, Director of Admissions, American InterContinental University, 6600 Peachtree-Dunwoody Road, 500 Embassy Row, Atlanta, GA 30328. *Phone:* 404-965-8050. *Toll-free phone:* 800-255-6839. *E-mail:* info@aiuniv.edu.

ARMSTRONG ATLANTIC STATE UNIVERSITY
Savannah, Georgia

- **State-supported** comprehensive, founded 1935, part of University System of Georgia
- **Calendar** semesters
- **Degrees** associate, bachelor's, and master's
- **Suburban** 250-acre campus
- **Coed,** 5,061 undergraduate students, 58% full-time, 68% women, 32% men
- **Minimally difficult** entrance level

Undergraduates 2,913 full-time, 2,148 part-time. Students come from 51 states and territories, 5% are from out of state, 9% transferred in, 2% live on campus. *Retention:* 61% of 2001 full-time freshmen returned.

Freshmen *Admission:* 859 enrolled. *Average high school GPA:* 2.70. *Test scores:* SAT verbal scores over 500: 57%; SAT math scores over 500: 52%; SAT verbal scores over 600: 13%; SAT math scores over 600: 9%; SAT verbal scores over 700: 1%; SAT math scores over 700: 1%.

Faculty *Total:* 361, 57% full-time. *Student/faculty ratio:* 16:1.

Majors Art; art education; biology; business education; chemistry; computer science; corrections; criminal justice/law enforcement administration; dental hygiene; early childhood education; economics; education; elementary education; English; health education; health science; history; industrial radiologic technology; information sciences/systems; law enforcement/police science; liberal arts and sciences/liberal studies; mathematics; medical technology; music; music teacher education; nursing; physical education; physical sciences; physical therapy; political science; psychology; recreation/leisure studies; respiratory therapy; science education; secondary education; special education; theater arts/drama.

Academic Programs *Special study options:* academic remediation for entering students, adult/continuing education programs, advanced placement credit, cooperative education, distance learning, double majors, honors programs, independent study, internships, off-campus study, part-time degree program, services for LD students, study abroad, summer session for credit. *ROTC:* Army (b). *Unusual degree programs:* 3-2 engineering with Georgia Institute of Technology.

Library Lane Library with 187,152 titles, 2,684 serial subscriptions, 3,946 audiovisual materials, an OPAC, a Web page.

Computers on Campus 160 computers available on campus for general student use. A campuswide network can be accessed from student residence rooms and from off campus. Internet access, online (class) registration, at least one staffed computer lab available.

Student Life *Housing Options:* coed. *Activities and Organizations:* drama/theater group, student-run newspaper, choral group, Women of Worth, Hispanic Student Society, Ebony Coalition, American Chemical Society, Phi Alpha Theta, national fraternities, national sororities. *Campus security:* 24-hour emergency response devices and patrols, student patrols, late-night transport/escort service. *Student Services:* personal/psychological counseling.

Athletics Member NCAA. All Division II. *Intercollegiate sports:* baseball M(s), basketball M(s)/W(s), cross-country running M(s)/W, tennis M(s)/W(s), volleyball W(s). *Intramural sports:* badminton M/W, basketball M/W, bowling M/W, football M/W, golf M/W, soccer M/W, softball M/W, table tennis M/W, tennis M/W, volleyball M/W, water polo M/W.

Standardized Tests *Required:* SAT I or ACT (for admission). *Required for some:* SAT II: Subject Tests (for admission).

Costs (2001–02) *Tuition:* state resident $1932 full-time, $81 per credit hour part-time; nonresident $7728 full-time, $322 per credit hour part-time. Part-time tuition and fees vary according to course load. *Required fees:* $382 full-time. *Room and board:* $4770; room only: $2840. *Waivers:* senior citizens and employees or children of employees.

Applying *Options:* early admission, early action, deferred entrance. *Application fee:* $20. *Required:* high school transcript, proof of immunization. *Application deadlines:* 7/1 (freshmen), 7/1 (transfers). *Notification:* continuous (freshmen).

Admissions Contact Ms. Melanie Mirande, Assistant Director of Recruitment, Armstrong Atlantic State University, Savannah, GA 31419. *Phone:* 912-925-5275. *Toll-free phone:* 800-633-2349. *Fax:* 912-921-5462.

THE ART INSTITUTE OF ATLANTA
Atlanta, Georgia

- **Proprietary** primarily 2-year, founded 1949, part of The Art Institutes
- **Calendar** quarters
- **Degrees** associate and bachelor's
- **Urban** 1-acre campus
- **Coed,** 2,237 undergraduate students, 83% full-time, 45% women, 55% men
- **Minimally difficult** entrance level

Undergraduates 1,866 full-time, 371 part-time. Students come from 29 states and territories, 37 other countries, 17% are from out of state, 30% African American, 2% Asian American or Pacific Islander, 2% Hispanic American, 0.4% Native American, 4% international, 14% live on campus.

Freshmen *Admission:* 519 enrolled.

Faculty *Total:* 127, 46% full-time, 43% with terminal degrees. *Student/faculty ratio:* 16:1.

Majors Computer graphics; culinary arts; film/video production; graphic design/commercial art/illustration; interior design; multimedia; photography.

Academic Programs *Special study options:* academic remediation for entering students, adult/continuing education programs, advanced placement credit, distance learning, independent study, internships, part-time degree program, services for LD students, study abroad, summer session for credit.

Library Library with 35,872 titles, 157 serial subscriptions, 2,548 audiovisual materials, an OPAC.

Computers on Campus 282 computers available on campus for general student use. A campuswide network can be accessed from that provide access to e-mail. Internet access, at least one staffed computer lab available.

Student Life *Housing Options:* coed. *Activities and Organizations:* Student Government Association, International Student Association, The Interactive Media Alliance, Talk N Design Group. *Campus security:* 24-hour patrols, controlled dormitory access. *Student Services:* personal/psychological counseling.

Athletics *Intramural sports:* basketball M, football M/W.

Financial Aid Of all full-time matriculated undergraduates who enrolled in 2001, 35 Federal Work-Study jobs (averaging $3000).

Applying *Options:* electronic application, early admission, deferred entrance. *Application fee:* $50. *Required:* essay or personal statement, minimum 2.0 GPA, interview. *Required for some:* high school transcript. *Application deadlines:* 9/29 (freshmen), 9/29 (transfers). *Notification:* continuous (freshmen).

Admissions Contact Dr. John Dietrich, Director of Admissions, The Art Institute of Atlanta, 6600 Peachtree Dunwoody Road, 100 Embassy Row, Atlanta, GA 30328. *Phone:* 770-394-8300 Ext. 2320. *Toll-free phone:* 800-275-4242. *Fax:* 770-394-8300. *E-mail:* aiaadm@aii.edu.

ATLANTA CHRISTIAN COLLEGE
East Point, Georgia

- **Independent Christian** 4-year, founded 1937
- **Calendar** semesters
- **Degrees** associate and bachelor's
- **Suburban** 52-acre campus with easy access to Atlanta
- **Endowment** $30.0 million
- **Coed,** 421 undergraduate students
- **Moderately difficult** entrance level, 77% of applicants were admitted

Undergraduates Students come from 12 states and territories, 13% are from out of state, 47% live on campus.

Freshmen *Admission:* 345 applied, 265 admitted. *Average high school GPA:* 2.8.

Faculty *Total:* 46, 50% full-time, 43% with terminal degrees. *Student/faculty ratio:* 16:1.

Majors Biblical studies; business; business administration; counseling psychology; early childhood education; humanities; music; pre-theology; theology.

Academic Programs *Special study options:* academic remediation for entering students, advanced placement credit, double majors, independent study, internships, part-time degree program, summer session for credit.

Library Atlanta Christian College Library with 50,000 titles, 187 serial subscriptions.

Computers on Campus 30 computers available on campus for general student use. A campuswide network can be accessed from student residence rooms and from off campus. Internet access, online (class) registration, at least one staffed computer lab available.

Student Life *Housing:* on-campus residence required for freshman year. *Options:* men-only, women-only. *Activities and Organizations:* drama/theater group, student-run radio station, choral group. *Campus security:* controlled dormitory access, 12-hour patrols by security personnel. *Student Services:* health clinic, personal/psychological counseling.

Athletics Member NCCAA. *Intercollegiate sports:* baseball M, basketball M/W, soccer M/W, softball W, tennis M(c)/W(c), volleyball W. *Intramural sports:* basketball M/W, golf M(c), table tennis M/W, tennis M/W, volleyball M/W.

Standardized Tests *Required:* SAT I or ACT (for admission).

Costs (2002–03) *Comprehensive fee:* $14,400 includes full-time tuition ($9950), mandatory fees ($500), and room and board ($3950). Full-time tuition and fees vary according to course load and student level. Part-time tuition: $415 per credit hour. Part-time tuition and fees vary according to course load and student level. *Room and board:* Room and board charges vary according to board plan. *Payment plan:* installment. *Waivers:* senior citizens and employees or children of employees.

Applying *Options:* early admission, early decision, deferred entrance. *Required:* high school transcript, minimum 2.0 GPA, 2 letters of recommendation, medical history. *Application deadline:* rolling (freshmen), rolling (transfers). *Early decision:* 11/15.

Admissions Contact Mr. Keith Wagner, Director of Admissions, Atlanta Christian College, 2605 Ben Hill Road, East Point, GA 30344-1999. *Phone:* 404-761-8861. *Toll-free phone:* 800-776-1ACC. *Fax:* 404-669-2024. *E-mail:* admissions@acc.edu.

ATLANTA COLLEGE OF ART
Atlanta, Georgia

- **Independent** 4-year, founded 1928
- **Calendar** semesters
- **Degree** bachelor's
- **Urban** 6-acre campus
- **Endowment** $3.6 million
- **Coed,** 388 undergraduate students, 100% full-time, 53% women, 47% men
- **Moderately difficult** entrance level, 72% of applicants were admitted

The Atlanta College of Art is a thriving artistic community that offers the Bachelor of Fine Arts degree in advertising design, computer animation, drawing, digital art, digital multimedia, digital video, graphic design, illustration, interior design, painting, photography, printmaking, and sculpture.

Undergraduates Students come from 30 states and territories, 17 other countries, 50% are from out of state, 23% African American, 6% Asian American or Pacific Islander, 3% Hispanic American, 0.3% Native American, 5% international, 30% live on campus. *Retention:* 66% of 2001 full-time freshmen returned.

Freshmen *Admission:* 206 applied, 148 admitted. *Average high school GPA:* 2.84. *Test scores:* SAT verbal scores over 500: 43%; SAT math scores over 500: 41%; ACT scores over 18: 70%; SAT verbal scores over 600: 19%; SAT math scores over 600: 6%; ACT scores over 24: 22%; SAT verbal scores over 700: 4%; SAT math scores over 700: 3%; ACT scores over 30: 3%.

Faculty *Total:* 81, 30% full-time, 59% with terminal degrees. *Student/faculty ratio:* 12:1.

Majors Computer graphics; design/visual communications; drawing; film/video production; fine/studio arts; graphic design/commercial art/illustration; interior design; painting; photography; printmaking; sculpture.

Academic Programs *Special study options:* advanced placement credit, independent study, internships, off-campus study, part-time degree program, student-designed majors, summer session for credit.

Library Atlanta College of Art Library with 30,000 titles, 200 serial subscriptions, 8,300 audiovisual materials.

Computers on Campus 80 computers available on campus for general student use. Internet access, at least one staffed computer lab available.

Student Life *Housing Options:* coed. *Activities and Organizations:* Cipher of Peace, Outing Club, Performance Art Club, Student Activities Club, Graphic Design Club. *Campus security:* 24-hour patrols, late-night transport/escort service, security cameras. *Student Services:* health clinic, personal/psychological counseling.

Standardized Tests *Required:* SAT I or ACT (for admission).

Costs (2002–03) *Tuition:* $15,400 full-time, $645 per credit hour part-time. Full-time tuition and fees vary according to course load. Part-time tuition and fees vary according to course load. *Required fees:* $500 full-time, $80 per year part-time. *Room only:* $4700. *Payment plan:* installment. *Waivers:* employees or children of employees.

Financial Aid Of all full-time matriculated undergraduates who enrolled in 2001, 254 applied for aid, 219 were judged to have need, 17 had their need fully met. 50 Federal Work-Study jobs (averaging $1815). *Average percent of need met:*

Atlanta College of Art (continued)

64%. *Average financial aid package:* $10,625. *Average need-based loan:* $3727. *Average need-based gift aid:* $6797. *Average indebtedness upon graduation:* $21,288.

Applying *Options:* electronic application, deferred entrance. *Application fee:* $30. *Required:* essay or personal statement, high school transcript, minimum 2.0 GPA, portfolio. *Required for some:* letters of recommendation. *Recommended:* letters of recommendation, interview. *Application deadline:* rolling (freshmen), rolling (transfers). *Notification:* continuous (freshmen).

Admissions Contact Ms. Lucy Leusch, Vice President of Enrollment Management, Atlanta College of Art, 1280 Peachtree Street, NE, Atlanta, GA 30309-3582. *Phone:* 404-733-5101. *Toll-free phone:* 800-832-2104. *Fax:* 404-733-5107. *E-mail:* acainfo@woodruff-arts.org.

AUGUSTA STATE UNIVERSITY
Augusta, Georgia

- **State-supported** comprehensive, founded 1925, part of University System of Georgia
- **Calendar** semesters
- **Degrees** associate, bachelor's, and master's
- **Urban** 72-acre campus
- **Endowment** $345,516
- **Coed,** 4,705 undergraduate students
- **Minimally difficult** entrance level, 68% of applicants were admitted

Undergraduates Students come from 34 states and territories, 59 other countries, 11% are from out of state. *Retention:* 49% of 2001 full-time freshmen returned.

Freshmen *Admission:* 1,653 applied, 1,123 admitted. *Average high school GPA:* 2.64. *Test scores:* SAT verbal scores over 500: 47%; SAT math scores over 500: 41%; SAT verbal scores over 600: 12%; SAT math scores over 600: 8%; SAT verbal scores over 700: 1%.

Faculty *Total:* 282, 69% full-time, 60% with terminal degrees. *Student/faculty ratio:* 17:1.

Majors Accounting; biology; business administration; business marketing and marketing management; chemistry; communications; computer/information sciences; criminal justice studies; early childhood education; education of the mentally handicapped; elementary education; English; finance; French; history; liberal arts and sciences/liberal studies; mathematics; medical technology; middle school education; multimedia; music; music (general performance); music teacher education; nursing; physical education; physical sciences; physics; political science; psychology; sociology; Spanish; special education.

Academic Programs *Special study options:* academic remediation for entering students, adult/continuing education programs, advanced placement credit, cooperative education, distance learning, double majors, English as a second language, honors programs, independent study, internships, off-campus study, part-time degree program, services for LD students, study abroad, summer session for credit. *ROTC:* Army (b).

Library Reese Library plus 1 other with 275,052 titles, 1,866 serial subscriptions, 7,185 audiovisual materials, an OPAC, a Web page.

Computers on Campus 160 computers available on campus for general student use. A campuswide network can be accessed from off campus. Internet access, online (class) registration, at least one staffed computer lab available.

Student Life *Housing:* college housing not available. *Activities and Organizations:* drama/theater group, student-run newspaper, choral group, SGAE, Baptist Student Union, Campus Outreach, College Republicans, Rowing Club, national fraternities, national sororities. *Campus security:* 24-hour patrols, late-night transport/escort service. *Student Services:* personal/psychological counseling.

Athletics Member NCAA, NAIA. All NCAA Division II. *Intercollegiate sports:* baseball M, basketball M(s)/W(s), cross-country running M(s)/W(s), soccer M(s), softball W, tennis M(s)/W(s), volleyball W(s). *Intramural sports:* softball W, volleyball M/W, weight lifting M/W.

Standardized Tests *Required:* SAT I or ACT (for admission).

Costs (2001–02) *Tuition:* state resident $1932 full-time, $81 per credit part-time; nonresident $7728 full-time, $322 per credit part-time. *Required fees:* $350 full-time, $175 per term part-time. *Waivers:* senior citizens and employees or children of employees.

Financial Aid Of all full-time matriculated undergraduates who enrolled in 2001, 1965 applied for aid, 1484 were judged to have need, 42 had their need fully met. 188 Federal Work-Study jobs (averaging $2245). In 2001, 168 non-need-based awards were made. *Average percent of need met:* 70%. *Average financial aid package:* $7046. *Average need-based loan:* $3019. *Average need-based gift aid:* $4595. *Average non-need based aid:* $1719. *Average indebtedness upon graduation:* $14,124.

Applying *Options:* early admission, deferred entrance. *Application fee:* $20. *Required:* high school transcript, minimum 2.0 GPA. *Application deadline:* 7/21 (freshmen), rolling (transfers). *Notification:* continuous (freshmen).

Admissions Contact Catherine R. Tuthill, Augusta State University, 2500 Walton Way, Augusta, GA 30904-2200. *Phone:* 706-737-1632. *Fax:* 706-667-4355. *E-mail:* admissions@ac.edu.

BEACON COLLEGE AND GRADUATE SCHOOL
Columbus, Georgia

- **Independent religious** comprehensive
- **Degrees** associate, bachelor's, and master's
- **Coed,** 70 undergraduate students, 67% full-time, 41% women, 59% men
- 89% of applicants were admitted

Undergraduates 47 full-time, 23 part-time. Students come from 4 states and territories, 2 other countries, 27% are from out of state, 44% African American, 3% Hispanic American, 3% international, 7% transferred in. *Retention:* 95% of 2001 full-time freshmen returned.

Freshmen *Admission:* 19 applied, 17 admitted, 17 enrolled. *Average high school GPA:* 2.90.

Faculty *Total:* 16, 19% full-time, 63% with terminal degrees. *Student/faculty ratio:* 5:1.

Majors Biblical studies; business administration; psychology.

Academic Programs *Special study options:* academic remediation for entering students, accelerated degree program, adult/continuing education programs, advanced placement credit, double majors, independent study, part-time degree program, summer session for credit.

Library Beacon College Library plus 1 other with 17,000 titles, 58 serial subscriptions.

Computers on Campus 15 computers available on campus for general student use. Internet access, at least one staffed computer lab available.

Student Life *Housing:* college housing not available. *Activities and Organizations:* student-run newspaper, Student Government Association, practical ministry. *Student Services:* personal/psychological counseling.

Standardized Tests *Recommended:* SAT I or ACT (for admission).

Costs (2001–02) *Tuition:* $2435 full-time, $115 per semester hour part-time. Full-time tuition and fees vary according to course load. *Required fees:* $100 full-time, $50 per term part-time. *Payment plan:* installment. *Waivers:* employees or children of employees.

Financial Aid Of all full-time matriculated undergraduates who enrolled in 2001, 23 applied for aid, 21 were judged to have need, 21 had their need fully met. *Average percent of need met:* 100%. *Average financial aid package:* $1500. *Average need-based gift aid:* $1500.

Applying *Options:* common application. *Application fee:* $25. *Required:* high school transcript, minimum 2.0 GPA, 3 letters of recommendation, interview. *Application deadline:* rolling (freshmen), rolling (transfers).

Admissions Contact Mrs. Paula Hardy, Director of Admissions and Student Records, Beacon College and Graduate School, 6003 Veterans Parkway, Columbus, GA 31909. *Phone:* 706-323-5364 Ext. 254. *Fax:* 706-323-5891.

BERRY COLLEGE
Mount Berry, Georgia

- **Independent interdenominational** comprehensive, founded 1902
- **Calendar** semesters
- **Degrees** bachelor's and master's
- **Small-town** 28,000-acre campus with easy access to Atlanta
- **Endowment** $567.9 million
- **Coed,** 1,846 undergraduate students, 98% full-time, 63% women, 37% men
- **Moderately difficult** entrance level, 82% of applicants were admitted

Undergraduates 1,808 full-time, 38 part-time. Students come from 34 states and territories, 27 other countries, 16% are from out of state, 2% African American, 0.8% Asian American or Pacific Islander, 1% Hispanic American, 0.1% Native American, 2% international, 4% transferred in, 69% live on campus. *Retention:* 75% of 2001 full-time freshmen returned.

Freshmen *Admission:* 1,948 applied, 1,593 admitted, 539 enrolled. *Average high school GPA:* 3.61. *Test scores:* SAT verbal scores over 500: 85%; SAT math scores over 500: 83%; ACT scores over 18: 99%; SAT verbal scores over 600: 43%; SAT math scores over 600: 35%; ACT scores over 24: 52%; SAT verbal scores over 700: 10%; SAT math scores over 700: 5%; ACT scores over 30: 14%.

Faculty *Total:* 179, 84% full-time, 76% with terminal degrees. *Student/faculty ratio:* 12:1.

Majors Accounting; animal sciences; anthropology; applied art; art; art education; art history; biochemistry; biology; biology education; broadcast journalism; business administration; business economics; business marketing and marketing management; chemistry; chemistry education; communications; computer/information sciences; computer science; early childhood education; economics; education; elementary education; English; English education; environmental science; finance; fine/studio arts; French; French language education; German; German language education; health education; history; history education; horticulture science; information sciences/systems; interdisciplinary studies; international relations; journalism; mass communications; mathematics; mathematics education; middle school education; music; music business management/merchandising; music (piano and organ performance); music teacher education; music (voice and choral/opera performance); philosophy; physical education; physics; physics education; political science; pre-dentistry; pre-law; pre-medicine; pre-veterinary studies; psychology; public relations; religious studies; science education; secondary education; social sciences; sociology; Spanish; Spanish language education; speech/rhetorical studies; theater arts/drama.

Academic Programs *Special study options:* accelerated degree program, adult/continuing education programs, advanced placement credit, cooperative education, double majors, honors programs, independent study, internships, part-time degree program, student-designed majors, study abroad, summer session for credit. *Unusual degree programs:* 3-2 engineering with Georgia Institute of Technology, Mercer University; nursing with Emory University.

Library Memorial Library plus 1 other with 264,714 titles, 1,364 serial subscriptions, an OPAC, a Web page.

Computers on Campus 100 computers available on campus for general student use. A campuswide network can be accessed from student residence rooms. Internet access, at least one staffed computer lab available.

Student Life *Housing:* on-campus residence required through sophomore year. *Options:* men-only, women-only. *Activities and Organizations:* drama/theater group, student-run newspaper, television station, choral group, Student Government Association, Baptist Student Union, equestrian, Campus Outreach. *Campus security:* 24-hour emergency response devices and patrols, late-night transport/escort service. *Student Services:* health clinic, personal/psychological counseling.

Athletics Member NAIA. *Intercollegiate sports:* baseball M(s), basketball M(s)/W(s), crew M(c)/W(c), cross-country running M(s)/W(s), equestrian sports M(c)/W(c), golf M(s)/W(s), rugby M(c), soccer M(s)/W(s), tennis M(s)/W(s), track and field M(s)/W(s). *Intramural sports:* badminton M/W, basketball M/W, bowling M/W, football M/W, golf M/W, racquetball M/W, soccer M/W, softball M/W, table tennis M/W, tennis M/W, track and field M/W, volleyball M/W, water polo M/W.

Standardized Tests *Required:* SAT I or ACT (for admission).

Costs (2001–02) *Comprehensive fee:* $19,180 includes full-time tuition ($13,450) and room and board ($5730). Part-time tuition: $448 per credit hour. *Room and board:* College room only: $3180. Room and board charges vary according to board plan and housing facility. *Payment plan:* installment. *Waivers:* senior citizens and employees or children of employees.

Financial Aid Of all full-time matriculated undergraduates who enrolled in 2001, 1808 applied for aid, 958 were judged to have need, 310 had their need fully met. 1240 State and other part-time jobs (averaging $2000). *Average percent of need met:* 90%. *Average financial aid package:* $12,500. *Average need-based loan:* $2500. *Average need-based gift aid:* $9400. *Average indebtedness upon graduation:* $12,500.

Applying *Options:* common application, electronic application, early admission, deferred entrance. *Application fee:* $25. *Required:* high school transcript. *Application deadlines:* 7/28 (freshmen), 7/28 (transfers). *Notification:* continuous (freshmen).

Admissions Contact Mr. George Gaddie, Dean of Admissions, Berry College, PO Box 490159, 2277 Martha Berry Highway, Mount Berry, GA 30149-0159. *Phone:* 706-236-2215. *Toll-free phone:* 800-237-7942. *Fax:* 706-290-2178. *E-mail:* admissions@berry.edu.

BEULAH HEIGHTS BIBLE COLLEGE
Atlanta, Georgia

- **Independent Pentecostal** 4-year, founded 1918
- **Calendar** semesters
- **Degrees** certificates, associate, and bachelor's
- **Urban** 10-acre campus
- **Endowment** $19,881
- **Coed,** 560 undergraduate students, 40% full-time, 56% women, 44% men
- **Noncompetitive** entrance level, 46% of applicants were admitted

Undergraduates 226 full-time, 334 part-time. Students come from 19 states and territories, 12 other countries, 30% are from out of state, 72% African American, 0.4% Asian American or Pacific Islander, 5% Hispanic American, 0.2% Native American, 16% international, 9% transferred in, 10% live on campus. *Retention:* 42% of 2001 full-time freshmen returned.

Freshmen *Admission:* 104 applied, 48 admitted, 104 enrolled. *Average high school GPA:* 3.1.

Faculty *Total:* 39, 26% full-time, 18% with terminal degrees. *Student/faculty ratio:* 17:1.

Majors Biblical studies; urban studies.

Academic Programs *Special study options:* academic remediation for entering students, accelerated degree program, adult/continuing education programs, advanced placement credit, cooperative education, distance learning, double majors, internships, part-time degree program, summer session for credit.

Library Barth Memorial Library with 53,400 titles, 150 serial subscriptions, a Web page.

Computers on Campus 28 computers available on campus for general student use. Internet access, at least one staffed computer lab available.

Student Life *Housing Options:* men-only, women-only. *Activities and Organizations:* choral group. *Campus security:* 24-hour emergency response devices, student patrols. *Student Services:* personal/psychological counseling.

Standardized Tests *Recommended:* SAT I or ACT (for admission), SAT II: Writing Test (for admission).

Costs (2001–02) *Tuition:* $3600 full-time, $150 per credit hour part-time. Full-time tuition and fees vary according to course load. *Required fees:* $80 full-time. *Room only:* $3000. *Waivers:* employees or children of employees.

Financial Aid Of all full-time matriculated undergraduates who enrolled in 2001, 150 applied for aid, 148 were judged to have need. 6 Federal Work-Study jobs (averaging $1878). In 2001, 1 non-need-based awards were made. *Average percent of need met:* 70%. *Average financial aid package:* $4015. *Average need-based loan:* $3510. *Average need-based gift aid:* $2300. *Average non-need based aid:* $2425. *Average indebtedness upon graduation:* $23,000.

Applying *Options:* common application, early admission. *Application fee:* $20. *Required:* high school transcript, minimum 2.0 GPA, 2 letters of recommendation. *Recommended:* interview. *Application deadline:* rolling (freshmen), rolling (transfers). *Notification:* continuous (freshmen).

Admissions Contact Ms. Dama Riles, Director of Admissions, Beulah Heights Bible College, 892 Berne Street, SE, PO Box 18145, Atlanta, GA 30316. *Phone:* 404-627-2681 Ext. 114. *Toll-free phone:* 888-777-BHBC. *Fax:* 404-627-0702. *E-mail:* cjkjr@aol.com.

BRENAU UNIVERSITY
Gainesville, Georgia

- **Independent** comprehensive, founded 1878
- **Calendar** semesters
- **Degrees** bachelor's and master's (also offers coed evening and weekend programs with significant enrollment not reflected in profile)
- **Small-town** 57-acre campus with easy access to Atlanta
- **Endowment** $47.8 million
- **Women only,** 572 undergraduate students, 88% full-time
- **Moderately difficult** entrance level, 81% of applicants were admitted

Undergraduates 505 full-time, 67 part-time. Students come from 19 states and territories, 20 other countries, 18% are from out of state, 9% African American, 2% Asian American or Pacific Islander, 2% Hispanic American, 0.3% Native American, 5% international, 15% transferred in, 45% live on campus. *Retention:* 61% of 2001 full-time freshmen returned.

Freshmen *Admission:* 375 applied, 303 admitted, 120 enrolled. *Average high school GPA:* 3.41. *Test scores:* SAT verbal scores over 500: 64%; SAT math scores over 500: 60%; SAT verbal scores over 600: 23%; SAT math scores over 600: 16%; SAT verbal scores over 700: 2%.

Faculty *Total:* 111, 69% full-time, 69% with terminal degrees. *Student/faculty ratio:* 7:1.

Majors Accounting; art education; arts management; biology; business administration; business communications; business marketing and marketing management; dance; drama/dance education; early childhood education; education; English; environmental science; fashion merchandising; fine/studio arts; general studies; graphic design/commercial art/illustration; history; interior design; international relations; mass communications; middle school education; music; music (piano and organ performance); music related; music teacher education; music (voice and choral/opera performance); nursing; occupational therapy; paralegal/legal assistant; political science; psychology; special education; theater arts/drama.

Brenau University (continued)

Academic Programs *Special study options:* academic remediation for entering students, advanced placement credit, cooperative education, distance learning, double majors, honors programs, independent study, internships, services for LD students, study abroad, summer session for credit.

Library Trustee Library with 99,678 titles, 527 serial subscriptions, 16,023 audiovisual materials, an OPAC, a Web page.

Computers on Campus 120 computers available on campus for general student use. A campuswide network can be accessed from student residence rooms and from off campus. Internet access, at least one staffed computer lab available.

Student Life *Housing:* on-campus residence required through junior year. *Options:* women-only. *Activities and Organizations:* drama/theater group, student-run newspaper, radio and television station, choral group, Student Government/Campus Activities Board, Silhouettes (diversity awareness), Recreation Association, Fellowship Association, International Club, national sororities. *Campus security:* 24-hour emergency response devices and patrols, late-night transport/escort service. *Student Services:* health clinic, personal/psychological counseling.

Athletics Member NAIA. *Intercollegiate sports:* cross-country running W(s), soccer W(s), tennis W(s), volleyball W(s).

Standardized Tests *Required:* SAT I or ACT (for admission).

Costs (2001–02) *Comprehensive fee:* $20,100 includes full-time tuition ($12,780) and room and board ($7320). Part-time tuition: $426 per semester hour. *Room and board:* Room and board charges vary according to board plan. *Payment plan:* installment. *Waivers:* employees or children of employees.

Financial Aid Of all full-time matriculated undergraduates who enrolled in 2001, 486 applied for aid, 294 were judged to have need, 119 had their need fully met. 100 Federal Work-Study jobs (averaging $1891). 18 State and other part-time jobs (averaging $1961). In 2001, 192 non-need-based awards were made. *Average percent of need met:* 81%. *Average financial aid package:* $13,658. *Average need-based loan:* $3699. *Average need-based gift aid:* $9981. *Average non-need based aid:* $7401. *Average indebtedness upon graduation:* $17,041.

Applying *Options:* electronic application, early admission, deferred entrance. *Application fee:* $35. *Required:* high school transcript, minimum 2.5 GPA, 1 letter of recommendation, minimum SAT I score of 900 or ACT score of 19. *Required for some:* essay or personal statement, interview. *Application deadline:* rolling (freshmen), rolling (transfers). *Notification:* continuous (freshmen).

Admissions Contact Ms. Christina Cochran, Coordinator of Women's College Admissions, Brenau University, Admissions, 1 Centennial Circle, Gainesville, GA 30501. *Phone:* 770-534-6100. *Toll-free phone:* 800-252-5119. *Fax:* 770-538-4306. *E-mail:* wcadmissions@lib.brenau.edu.

BREWTON-PARKER COLLEGE

Mt. Vernon, Georgia

- **Independent Southern Baptist** 4-year, founded 1904
- **Calendar** semesters
- **Degrees** associate and bachelor's
- **Rural** 280-acre campus
- **Endowment** $8.9 million
- **Coed,** 1,219 undergraduate students, 80% full-time, 63% women, 37% men
- **Minimally difficult** entrance level, 98% of applicants were admitted

Undergraduates 970 full-time, 249 part-time. Students come from 18 states and territories, 14 other countries, 4% are from out of state, 19% African American, 0.5% Asian American or Pacific Islander, 2% Hispanic American, 0.3% Native American, 3% international, 13% transferred in, 32% live on campus. *Retention:* 49% of 2001 full-time freshmen returned.

Freshmen *Admission:* 266 applied, 262 admitted, 250 enrolled. *Test scores:* SAT verbal scores over 500: 32%; SAT math scores over 500: 31%; ACT scores over 18: 57%; SAT verbal scores over 600: 3%; SAT math scores over 600: 3%; ACT scores over 24: 11%; SAT verbal scores over 700: 1%.

Faculty *Total:* 225, 20% full-time, 25% with terminal degrees. *Student/faculty ratio:* 10:1.

Majors Accounting; art; biology; business administration; business education; divinity/ministry; early childhood education; education; elementary education; English; history; information sciences/systems; liberal arts and sciences/liberal studies; management information systems/business data processing; mathematics; middle school education; music; music (piano and organ performance); music teacher education; music (voice and choral/opera performance); physical education; political science; pre-law; psychology; recreation/leisure studies; religious studies; science education; secondary education; social sciences; sociology.

Academic Programs *Special study options:* academic remediation for entering students, adult/continuing education programs, advanced placement credit, cooperative education, English as a second language, honors programs, internships, part-time degree program, services for LD students, summer session for credit.

Library Fountain-New Library with 70,000 titles, 410 serial subscriptions, 4,900 audiovisual materials.

Computers on Campus 75 computers available on campus for general student use. Internet access, at least one staffed computer lab available.

Student Life *Housing:* on-campus residence required through sophomore year. *Options:* men-only, women-only. *Activities and Organizations:* drama/theater group, student-run newspaper, choral group, Council of Intramural Activities, Student Activities Council, Rotaract, Circle K, Baptist Student Union. *Campus security:* 24-hour emergency response devices and patrols, controlled dormitory access. *Student Services:* health clinic, personal/psychological counseling.

Athletics Member NAIA. *Intercollegiate sports:* baseball M(s), basketball M(s)/W(s), soccer M(s)/W(s), softball W(s). *Intramural sports:* basketball M/W, football M/W, golf M/W, table tennis M/W, tennis M/W, volleyball M/W.

Standardized Tests *Required:* SAT I or ACT (for admission).

Costs (2001–02) *Comprehensive fee:* $11,700 includes full-time tuition ($7500), mandatory fees ($500), and room and board ($3700). Part-time tuition: $250 per credit hour. *Room and board:* College room only: $1850. *Payment plan:* installment. *Waivers:* employees or children of employees.

Financial Aid Of all full-time matriculated undergraduates who enrolled in 2001, 952 applied for aid, 823 were judged to have need, 145 had their need fully met. 139 Federal Work-Study jobs (averaging $1220). 28 State and other part-time jobs (averaging $1516). In 2001, 172 non-need-based awards were made. *Average percent of need met:* 63%. *Average financial aid package:* $7602. *Average need-based loan:* $2889. *Average need-based gift aid:* $5248. *Average non-need based aid:* $6889.

Applying *Options:* common application, early admission. *Application fee:* $25. *Required:* high school transcript, minimum 2.0 GPA. *Recommended:* interview. *Application deadline:* rolling (freshmen), rolling (transfers). *Notification:* continuous (freshmen).

Admissions Contact Mr. James E. Beall, Director of Admissions, Brewton-Parker College, Highway 280, Mt. Vernon, GA 30445-0197. *Phone:* 912-583-3268 Ext. 268. *Toll-free phone:* 800-342-1087. *Fax:* 912-583-4498.

CLARK ATLANTA UNIVERSITY

Atlanta, Georgia

- **Independent United Methodist** university, founded 1865
- **Calendar** semesters
- **Degrees** bachelor's, master's, doctoral, post-master's, and postbachelor's certificates
- **Urban** 113-acre campus
- **Endowment** $31.6 million
- **Coed,** 3,923 undergraduate students, 97% full-time, 71% women, 29% men
- **Moderately difficult** entrance level, 74% of applicants were admitted

Undergraduates 3,795 full-time, 128 part-time. Students come from 41 states and territories, 31 other countries, 60% are from out of state, 93% African American, 0.0% Asian American or Pacific Islander, 0.1% Hispanic American, 5% transferred in, 37% live on campus. *Retention:* 66% of 2001 full-time freshmen returned.

Freshmen *Admission:* 4,336 applied, 3,228 admitted, 1,014 enrolled. *Average high school GPA:* 3.39. *Test scores:* SAT verbal scores over 500: 23%; SAT math scores over 500: 19%; ACT scores over 18: 100%; SAT verbal scores over 600: 2%; SAT math scores over 600: 3%; ACT scores over 24: 10%; ACT scores over 30: 1%.

Faculty *Total:* 328, 99% full-time, 75% with terminal degrees. *Student/faculty ratio:* 15:1.

Majors Accounting; art; art education; biology; business administration; business education; chemistry; criminal justice/law enforcement administration; developmental/child psychology; early childhood education; economics; education; elementary education; engineering; English; fashion design/illustration; French; German; health education; history; information sciences/systems; interdisciplinary studies; mass communications; mathematics; medical illustrating; medical records administration; middle school education; music; music teacher education; philosophy; physical education; physics; political science; psychology; religious studies; science education; secondary education; social sciences; social work; sociology; Spanish; speech/rhetorical studies; theater arts/drama.

Academic Programs *Special study options:* academic remediation for entering students, accelerated degree program, adult/continuing education programs, advanced placement credit, cooperative education, English as a second language, freshman honors college, honors programs, internships, off-campus study, part-time degree program, services for LD students, study abroad, summer session for credit. *ROTC:* Army (b), Air Force (b). *Unusual degree programs:* 3-2 engineering with Georgia Institute of Technology, Boston University, North Carolina Agricultural and Technical State University.

Library Robert W. Woodruff Library with an OPAC, a Web page.
Computers on Campus 300 computers available on campus for general student use. A campuswide network can be accessed from off campus. At least one staffed computer lab available.
Student Life *Housing Options:* coed. *Activities and Organizations:* drama/theater group, student-run newspaper, radio and television station, choral group, marching band, student government, honors program, Pre-alumni Council, national fraternities, national sororities. *Campus security:* 24-hour emergency response devices and patrols, late-night transport/escort service. *Student Services:* health clinic, personal/psychological counseling.
Athletics Member NCAA. All Division II. *Intercollegiate sports:* basketball M(s)/W(s), cross-country running M(s)/W(s), football M(s), golf M(s), softball W, tennis M(s)/W(s), track and field M(s)/W, volleyball W. *Intramural sports:* basketball M/W, football M/W, swimming M/W, tennis M/W, track and field M/W, volleyball M/W.
Standardized Tests *Required:* SAT I or ACT (for admission).
Costs (2001–02) *Comprehensive fee:* $18,592 includes full-time tuition ($12,138), mandatory fees ($400), and room and board ($6054). Part-time tuition: $489 per credit. *Required fees:* $400 per term part-time. *Room and board:* College room only: $3534. Room and board charges vary according to board plan and housing facility. *Payment plan:* deferred payment. *Waivers:* employees or children of employees.
Applying *Options:* common application, early admission, deferred entrance. *Application fee:* $35. *Required:* essay or personal statement, high school transcript, minimum 2.0 GPA, 2 letters of recommendation. *Recommended:* minimum 2.5 GPA, interview. *Application deadlines:* 7/1 (freshmen), 7/1 (transfers). *Notification:* continuous (freshmen).
Admissions Contact Office of Admissions, Clark Atlanta University, 223 James P. Brawley Drive, SW, 101 Trevor Arnett Hall, Atlanta, GA 30314. *Phone:* 404-880-8784 Ext. 6650. *Toll-free phone:* 800-688-3228. *Fax:* 404-880-6174.

CLAYTON COLLEGE & STATE UNIVERSITY
Morrow, Georgia

- **State-supported** 4-year, founded 1969, part of University System of Georgia
- **Calendar** semesters
- **Degrees** certificates, associate, and bachelor's
- **Suburban** 163-acre campus with easy access to Atlanta
- **Coed,** 4,675 undergraduate students, 45% full-time, 65% women, 35% men
- **Minimally difficult** entrance level, 47% of applicants were admitted

Undergraduates 2% are from out of state. *Retention:* 57% of 2001 full-time freshmen returned.
Freshmen *Admission:* 1,454 applied, 689 admitted. *Average high school GPA:* 2.94. *Test scores:* SAT verbal scores over 500: 51%; SAT math scores over 500: 50%; ACT scores over 18: 79%; SAT verbal scores over 600: 11%; SAT math scores over 600: 9%; ACT scores over 24: 14%; SAT math scores over 700: 1%.
Faculty *Total:* 282, 51% full-time, 34% with terminal degrees. *Student/faculty ratio:* 16:1.
Majors Accounting; agricultural business; agricultural mechanization; agricultural sciences; aircraft mechanic/airframe; architectural engineering technology; art; art education; aviation management; aviation technology; biological/physical sciences; biology; business administration; business education; business marketing and marketing management; chemistry; computer engineering technology; computer science; criminal justice/law enforcement administration; data processing technology; dental hygiene; drafting; early childhood education; economics; education; electrical/electronic engineering technology; electromechanical technology; elementary education; emergency medical technology; engineering; engineering technology; English; finance; forestry; French; geology; health education; health services administration; history; home economics; information sciences/systems; instrumentation technology; journalism; legal administrative assistant; legal studies; management information systems/business data processing; mass communications; mathematics; mechanical design technology; medical assistant; medical illustrating; medical laboratory technician; medical records administration; medical technology; middle school education; music; nursing; occupational therapy; paralegal/legal assistant; pharmacy; philosophy; physical education; physical therapy; physics; political science; pre-engineering; psychology; radiological science; recreation/leisure studies; robotics; secretarial science; social sciences; sociology; Spanish; speech/rhetorical studies; telecommunications; theater arts/drama; urban studies; veterinary sciences.
Academic Programs *Special study options:* academic remediation for entering students, adult/continuing education programs, advanced placement credit, cooperative education, distance learning, double majors, freshman honors college, honors programs, independent study, internships, off-campus study, part-time degree program, services for LD students, student-designed majors, study abroad, summer session for credit. *ROTC:* Army (c).
Library Clayton College and State University Library plus 1 other with 77,043 titles, 4,250 serial subscriptions, 5,636 audiovisual materials, an OPAC, a Web page.
Computers on Campus 110 computers available on campus for general student use. A campuswide network can be accessed from off campus. Internet access, online (class) registration, at least one staffed computer lab available.
Student Life *Housing:* college housing not available. *Activities and Organizations:* drama/theater group, choral group, Accounting Club, International Awareness Club, Black Cultural Awareness Association, Student Government Association, Music Club. *Campus security:* 24-hour emergency response devices and patrols, late-night transport/escort service, lighted pathways. *Student Services:* personal/psychological counseling.
Athletics Member NCAA. All Division II. *Intercollegiate sports:* basketball M(s)/W(s), cross-country running M(s)/W(s), golf M(s), soccer M(s)/W(s), tennis W(s). *Intramural sports:* volleyball M/W.
Standardized Tests *Required:* SAT I or ACT (for admission). *Required for some:* SAT II: Subject Tests (for admission).
Costs (2001–02) *Tuition:* state resident $1932 full-time, $81 per hour part-time; nonresident $7728 full-time, $322 per hour part-time. Part-time tuition and fees vary according to program. *Required fees:* $390 full-time. *Waivers:* senior citizens and employees or children of employees.
Financial Aid Of all full-time matriculated undergraduates who enrolled in 2001, 1635 applied for aid, 910 were judged to have need, 405 had their need fully met. In 2001, 457 non-need-based awards were made.
Applying *Options:* early admission, deferred entrance. *Application fee:* $20. *Required:* high school transcript, proof of immunization. *Application deadline:* 7/17 (freshmen). *Notification:* continuous (freshmen).
Admissions Contact Ms. Carol S. Montgomery, Admissions, Clayton College & State University, 5900 North Lee Street, Morrow, GA 30260-0285. *Phone:* 770-961-3500. *Fax:* 770-961-3752. *E-mail:* csc-info@ce.clayton.peachnet.edu.

COLUMBUS STATE UNIVERSITY
Columbus, Georgia

- **State-supported** comprehensive, founded 1958, part of University System of Georgia
- **Calendar** semesters
- **Degrees** certificates, associate, bachelor's, master's, and post-master's certificates
- **Suburban** 132-acre campus with easy access to Atlanta
- **Coed,** 4,624 undergraduate students, 65% full-time, 62% women, 38% men
- **Minimally difficult** entrance level, 64% of applicants were admitted

Undergraduates Students come from 35 states and territories, 7% are from out of state, 26% African American, 2% Asian American or Pacific Islander, 4% Hispanic American, 0.5% Native American, 9% live on campus. *Retention:* 67% of 2001 full-time freshmen returned.
Freshmen *Admission:* 1,915 applied, 1,230 admitted. *Average high school GPA:* 2.99. *Test scores:* SAT verbal scores over 500: 47%; SAT math scores over 500: 40%; ACT scores over 18: 100%; SAT verbal scores over 600: 10%; SAT math scores over 600: 8%; ACT scores over 24: 49%; SAT verbal scores over 700: 1%.
Faculty *Total:* 350, 63% full-time, 53% with terminal degrees. *Student/faculty ratio:* 18:1.
Majors Accounting; art; art education; athletic training/sports medicine; biology; business administration; business economics; business marketing and marketing management; chemistry; computer management; computer programming; computer science; criminal justice/law enforcement administration; early childhood education; education; education (K-12); electrical/electronic engineering technology; elementary education; English; exercise sciences; finance; forestry; geology; health science; history; industrial radiologic technology; information sciences/systems; liberal arts and sciences/liberal studies; literature; mass communications; mathematics; medical laboratory technician; middle school education; music; music (piano and organ performance); music teacher education; music (voice and choral/opera performance); nursing; physical education; political science; pre-dentistry; pre-engineering; pre-law; pre-medicine; pre-veterinary studies; psychology; public relations; recreational therapy; recreation/leisure facilities management; science education; secondary education; sociology; special education; speech/theater education; stringed instruments; theater arts/drama; wind/percussion instruments.
Academic Programs *Special study options:* academic remediation for entering students, adult/continuing education programs, advanced placement credit, cooperative education, distance learning, freshman honors college, honors programs,

Columbus State University (continued)
independent study, internships, part-time degree program, services for LD students, study abroad, summer session for credit. *ROTC:* Army (b).
Library Simon Schwob Memorial Library with 250,000 titles, 1,400 serial subscriptions, 2,500 audiovisual materials, an OPAC, a Web page.
Computers on Campus 300 computers available on campus for general student use. A campuswide network can be accessed from student residence rooms and from off campus. Internet access, online (class) registration, at least one staffed computer lab available.
Student Life *Housing Options:* coed, men-only. *Activities and Organizations:* drama/theater group, student-run newspaper, choral group, Student Government Association, Student Programming Council, Greek Life, Baptist Student Union, national fraternities, national sororities. *Campus security:* 24-hour emergency response devices and patrols, late-night transport/escort service. *Student Services:* health clinic, personal/psychological counseling, women's center.
Athletics Member NCAA. All Division II. *Intercollegiate sports:* baseball M(s), basketball M(s)/W(s), cross-country running M(s)/W(s), golf M(s), softball W(s), tennis M(s)/W(s). *Intramural sports:* badminton M/W, basketball M/W, bowling M/W, cross-country running M/W, football M/W, golf M/W, racquetball M/W, skiing (downhill) M/W, soccer M/W, softball M/W, table tennis M/W, tennis M/W, volleyball M/W.
Standardized Tests *Required:* SAT I or ACT (for admission). *Required for some:* SAT II: Subject Tests (for admission).
Costs (2001–02) *Tuition:* state resident $1932 full-time, $81 per semester hour part-time; nonresident $7728 full-time, $322 per semester hour part-time. Part-time tuition and fees vary according to course load. *Required fees:* $420 full-time, $150 per semester hour. *Room and board:* $4876. Room and board charges vary according to board plan and housing facility. *Waivers:* senior citizens and employees or children of employees.
Financial Aid Of all full-time matriculated undergraduates who enrolled in 2001, 2757 applied for aid, 2044 were judged to have need, 19 had their need fully met. 110 Federal Work-Study jobs (averaging $1730). In 2001, 303 non-need-based awards were made. *Average percent of need met:* 37%. *Average financial aid package:* $4513. *Average need-based loan:* $3459. *Average need-based gift aid:* $2548. *Average non-need based aid:* $2816. *Average indebtedness upon graduation:* $10,778.
Applying *Options:* common application, electronic application, early admission, deferred entrance. *Application fee:* $25. *Required:* high school transcript, minimum 2.5 GPA, proof of immunization. *Application deadlines:* 8/2 (freshmen), 8/2 (transfers).
Admissions Contact Columbus State University, 4225 University Avenue, Columbus, GA 31907-5645. *Phone:* 706-568-2035 Ext. 1681. *Toll-free phone:* 866-264-2035. *Fax:* 706-568-2462.

COVENANT COLLEGE
Lookout Mountain, Georgia

- **Independent** comprehensive, founded 1955, affiliated with Presbyterian Church in America
- **Calendar** semesters
- **Degrees** associate, bachelor's, and master's (master's degree in education only)
- **Suburban** 250-acre campus
- **Endowment** $16.3 million
- **Coed,** 1,179 undergraduate students, 97% full-time, 61% women, 39% men
- **Moderately difficult** entrance level, 96% of applicants were admitted

Undergraduates 1,149 full-time, 30 part-time. Students come from 47 states and territories, 8 other countries, 77% are from out of state, 4% African American, 2% Asian American or Pacific Islander, 3% Hispanic American, 1% international, 5% transferred in, 81% live on campus. *Retention:* 83% of 2001 full-time freshmen returned.
Freshmen *Admission:* 544 applied, 520 admitted, 225 enrolled. *Average high school GPA:* 3.57. *Test scores:* SAT verbal scores over 500: 92%; SAT math scores over 500: 81%; ACT scores over 18: 98%; SAT verbal scores over 600: 49%; SAT math scores over 600: 37%; ACT scores over 24: 56%; SAT verbal scores over 700: 17%; SAT math scores over 700: 8%; ACT scores over 30: 16%.
Faculty *Total:* 72, 76% full-time, 67% with terminal degrees. *Student/faculty ratio:* 15:1.
Majors Biblical studies; biology; business administration; chemistry; computer science; economics; elementary education; English; health science; history; interdisciplinary studies; mathematics; music; natural sciences; nursing; philosophy; physics; pre-engineering; pre-law; pre-medicine; psychology; sociology.
Academic Programs *Special study options:* academic remediation for entering students, adult/continuing education programs, advanced placement credit, double majors, independent study, internships, off-campus study, part-time degree program, student-designed majors, study abroad, summer session for credit. *Unusual degree programs:* 3-2 nursing with Vanderbilt University.
Library Kresge Memorial Library with 61,502 titles, 554 serial subscriptions, 11,500 audiovisual materials, an OPAC, a Web page.
Computers on Campus 135 computers available on campus for general student use. A campuswide network can be accessed from off campus. Internet access, at least one staffed computer lab available.
Student Life *Housing:* on-campus residence required through junior year. *Options:* men-only, women-only. *Activities and Organizations:* drama/theater group, student-run newspaper, choral group, Psychology Club, Interpretive Dance Group, Drama Club, Backpacking Club, various ministries. *Campus security:* night security guards. *Student Services:* health clinic, personal/psychological counseling.
Athletics Member NAIA. *Intercollegiate sports:* basketball M(s)/W(s), cross-country running M(s)/W(s), soccer M(s)/W(s), volleyball W(s). *Intramural sports:* basketball M/W, football M, golf M, soccer M/W, tennis M/W, volleyball M/W.
Standardized Tests *Required:* SAT I or ACT (for admission). *Recommended:* SAT I (for admission).
Costs (2002–03) *Comprehensive fee:* $23,490 includes full-time tuition ($17,750), mandatory fees ($480), and room and board ($5260). Full-time tuition and fees vary according to course load. Part-time tuition: $740 per semester hour. Part-time tuition and fees vary according to course load. *Room and board:* Room and board charges vary according to board plan and housing facility. *Payment plan:* installment. *Waivers:* senior citizens and employees or children of employees.
Financial Aid Of all full-time matriculated undergraduates who enrolled in 2001, 814 applied for aid, 564 were judged to have need, 156 had their need fully met. 275 Federal Work-Study jobs (averaging $1933). 57 State and other part-time jobs (averaging $1574). In 2001, 202 non-need-based awards were made. *Average percent of need met:* 80%. *Average financial aid package:* $13,399. *Average need-based loan:* $3783. *Average need-based gift aid:* $9653. *Average non-need based aid:* $4054. *Average indebtedness upon graduation:* $12,319.
Applying *Options:* early admission, deferred entrance. *Application fee:* $25. *Required:* essay or personal statement, high school transcript, minimum 2.5 GPA, 2 letters of recommendation, interview. *Application deadline:* rolling (freshmen), rolling (transfers). *Notification:* continuous (freshmen).
Admissions Contact Ms. Leda Goodman, Regional Director, Covenant College, 14049 Scenic Highway, Lookout Mountain, GA 30750. *Phone:* 706-419-1644. *Toll-free phone:* 888-451-2683. *Fax:* 706-820-0893. *E-mail:* admissions@covenant.edu.

DALTON STATE COLLEGE
Dalton, Georgia

- **State-supported** 4-year, founded 1963, part of University System of Georgia
- **Calendar** semesters
- **Degrees** certificates, associate, and bachelor's
- **Small-town** 141-acre campus
- **Endowment** $9.5 million
- **Coed,** 3,647 undergraduate students, 40% full-time, 63% women, 37% men
- **Noncompetitive** entrance level, 62% of applicants were admitted

Undergraduates 1,456 full-time, 2,191 part-time. Students come from 2 states and territories, 1% are from out of state.
Freshmen *Admission:* 2,022 applied, 1,259 admitted, 612 enrolled. *Average high school GPA:* 2.64. *Test scores:* SAT verbal scores over 500: 42%; SAT math scores over 500: 36%; ACT scores over 18: 73%; SAT verbal scores over 600: 11%; SAT math scores over 600: 7%; ACT scores over 24: 14%; SAT verbal scores over 700: 1%; SAT math scores over 700: 1%; ACT scores over 30: 1%.
Faculty *Total:* 179, 80% full-time. *Student/faculty ratio:* 25:1.
Majors Agricultural sciences; biological/physical sciences; business; business administration; business computer facilities operation; business marketing and marketing management; chemistry; computer engineering technology; computer/information sciences; computer installation/repair; computer maintenance technology; computer science; criminal justice/law enforcement administration; dental hygiene; drafting; drafting/design technology; economics; education; electrical/electronic engineering technology; English; family/consumer studies; foreign languages/literatures; forestry; general studies; geology; health education; history; industrial arts; industrial electronics installation/repair; industrial machinery maintenance/repair; industrial technology; information sciences/systems; journalism; law enforcement/police science; machine shop assistant; management information systems/business data processing; marketing operations; mathematics; medical laboratory technician; medical office management; medical records

administration; medical technology; medical transcription; nuclear medical technology; nursing; occupational therapy; office management; operations management; philosophy; physical therapy; physician assistant; physics; political science; pre-pharmacy studies; psychology; radiological science; respiratory therapy; social work; sociology; speech/rhetorical studies.

Academic Programs *Special study options:* academic remediation for entering students, adult/continuing education programs, advanced placement credit, distance learning, English as a second language, internships, off-campus study, part-time degree program, services for LD students, study abroad, summer session for credit.

Library Derrell C. Roberts Library with 710 serial subscriptions, 6,064 audiovisual materials, an OPAC, a Web page.

Computers on Campus 559 computers available on campus for general student use. Internet access, at least one staffed computer lab available.

Student Life *Housing:* college housing not available. *Activities and Organizations:* student-run newspaper, Baptist Student Union, Phi Theta Kappa (PTK), International Students Association, Students in Free Enterprise, Spanish Club. *Campus security:* 24-hour emergency response devices and patrols.

Athletics *Intercollegiate sports:* basketball M(c)/W(c), golf W(c), softball M(c)/W(c), table tennis M(c)/W(c), tennis M(c)/W(c), volleyball M(c)/W(c). *Intramural sports:* badminton M/W, basketball M/W, football M/W, softball M/W, table tennis M/W, tennis M/W, volleyball M/W.

Standardized Tests *Required for some:* SAT I or ACT (for admission), SAT II: Subject Tests (for admission).

Costs (2001–02) *Tuition:* state resident $2046 full-time; nonresident $7842 full-time. Full-time tuition and fees vary according to program. *Required fees:* $114 full-time. *Waivers:* senior citizens.

Applying *Options:* common application, early admission. *Required:* high school transcript. *Application deadline:* rolling (freshmen), rolling (transfers). *Notification:* continuous (freshmen).

Admissions Contact Dr. Angela Harris, Assistant Director of Admissions, Dalton State College, 213 North College Drive, Dalton, GA 30720-3797. *Phone:* 706-272-4476. *Toll-free phone:* 800-829-4436. *Fax:* 706-272-2530. *E-mail:* aharris@em.daltonstate.edu.

DeVry University
Alphareta, Georgia

- **Proprietary** 4-year, founded 1997, part of DeVry, Inc
- **Calendar** semesters
- **Degrees** associate and bachelor's
- **Suburban** 9-acre campus with easy access to Atlanta
- **Coed,** 1,548 undergraduate students, 76% full-time, 32% women, 68% men
- **Minimally difficult** entrance level, 83% of applicants were admitted

Undergraduates 1,177 full-time, 371 part-time. Students come from 28 states and territories, 13 other countries, 18% are from out of state, 30% African American, 5% Asian American or Pacific Islander, 2% Hispanic American, 0.3% Native American, 3% international, 9% transferred in. *Retention:* 40% of 2001 full-time freshmen returned.

Freshmen *Admission:* 759 applied, 630 admitted, 268 enrolled.

Faculty *Total:* 86, 49% full-time. *Student/faculty ratio:* 21:1.

Majors Business administration/management related; business systems analysis/design; business systems networking/ telecommunications; computer engineering technology; electrical/electronic engineering technology; information sciences/systems; operations management.

Academic Programs *Special study options:* academic remediation for entering students, accelerated degree program, adult/continuing education programs, advanced placement credit, cooperative education, part-time degree program, services for LD students, summer session for credit.

Library Learning Resource Center with 7,659 titles, 73 serial subscriptions, 301 audiovisual materials, an OPAC.

Computers on Campus 218 computers available on campus for general student use. At least one staffed computer lab available.

Student Life *Housing:* college housing not available. *Activities and Organizations:* Epsilon Delta Pi, International Student Organization, Programming Club, Alpha Sigma Lambda, National Society of Black Engineers. *Campus security:* 24-hour emergency response devices, late-night transport/escort service, lighted pathways, video recorder (CCTV).

Athletics *Intramural sports:* basketball M/W, football M/W, softball M/W, volleyball M/W.

Standardized Tests *Recommended:* SAT I or ACT (for admission).

Costs (2001–02) *Tuition:* $8740 full-time, $310 per credit hour part-time. Full-time tuition and fees vary according to course load. Part-time tuition and fees vary according to course load. *Payment plans:* installment, deferred payment. *Waivers:* employees or children of employees.

Financial Aid Of all full-time matriculated undergraduates who enrolled in 2001, 1560 applied for aid, 1424 were judged to have need, 68 had their need fully met. In 2001, 136 non-need-based awards were made. *Average percent of need met:* 47%. *Average financial aid package:* $8267. *Average need-based loan:* $5199. *Average need-based gift aid:* $3891.

Applying *Options:* electronic application, deferred entrance. *Application fee:* $50. *Required:* high school transcript, interview. *Application deadline:* rolling (freshmen), rolling (transfers). *Notification:* continuous (freshmen).

Admissions Contact Ms. Kristi Franklin, New Student Coordinator, DeVry University, 2555 Northwinds Parkway, Alpharetta, GA 30004. *Phone:* 770-521-4900. *Fax:* 770-664-8824.

DeVry University
Decatur, Georgia

- **Proprietary** 4-year, founded 1969, part of DeVry, Inc
- **Calendar** semesters
- **Degrees** associate and bachelor's
- **Suburban** 21-acre campus with easy access to Atlanta
- **Coed,** 2,925 undergraduate students, 80% full-time, 41% women, 59% men
- **Minimally difficult** entrance level, 80% of applicants were admitted

Undergraduates 2,331 full-time, 594 part-time. Students come from 32 states and territories, 2 other countries, 18% are from out of state, 80% African American, 2% Asian American or Pacific Islander, 1% Hispanic American, 0.3% Native American, 2% international, 26% transferred in. *Retention:* 43% of 2001 full-time freshmen returned.

Freshmen *Admission:* 1,840 applied, 1,464 admitted, 309 enrolled.

Faculty *Total:* 225, 51% full-time. *Student/faculty ratio:* 13:1.

Majors Business administration/management related; business systems analysis/design; business systems networking/ telecommunications; computer engineering technology; electrical/electronic engineering technology; information sciences/systems; operations management.

Academic Programs *Special study options:* academic remediation for entering students, accelerated degree program, adult/continuing education programs, advanced placement credit, cooperative education, part-time degree program, services for LD students, summer session for credit.

Library Learning Resource Center with 18,849 titles, 80 serial subscriptions, 800 audiovisual materials, an OPAC.

Computers on Campus A campuswide network can be accessed from off campus. Internet access, at least one staffed computer lab available.

Student Life *Housing:* college housing not available. *Activities and Organizations:* Programming Club, Epsilon Delta Pi, Tau Alpha Pi, National Society of Black Engineers, International Student Organization. *Campus security:* 24-hour emergency response devices and patrols, late-night transport/escort service, lighted pathways/sidewalks.

Athletics *Intramural sports:* basketball M/W, football M/W, softball M/W, volleyball M/W.

Standardized Tests *Recommended:* SAT I or ACT (for admission).

Costs (2001–02) *Tuition:* $8740 full-time, $310 per credit hour part-time. Full-time tuition and fees vary according to course load. Part-time tuition and fees vary according to course load. *Required fees:* $65 full-time. *Payment plans:* installment, deferred payment. *Waivers:* employees or children of employees.

Financial Aid Of all full-time matriculated undergraduates who enrolled in 2001, 3286 applied for aid, 3196 were judged to have need, 95 had their need fully met. In 2001, 90 non-need-based awards were made. *Average percent of need met:* 45%. *Average financial aid package:* $8557. *Average need-based loan:* $5049. *Average need-based gift aid:* $4113.

Applying *Options:* electronic application, deferred entrance. *Application fee:* $50. *Required:* high school transcript, interview. *Application deadline:* rolling (freshmen), rolling (transfers). *Notification:* continuous (freshmen).

Admissions Contact Ms. Karen Krumenaker, New Student Coordinator, DeVry University, 250 North Arcadia Avenue, Decatur, GA 30030. *Phone:* 404-292-2645. *Toll-free phone:* 800-221-4771. *E-mail:* dwalters@admin.atl.devry.edu.

Emmanuel College
Franklin Springs, Georgia

- **Independent** 4-year, founded 1919, affiliated with Pentecostal Holiness Church

Emmanuel College (continued)
- **Calendar** semesters
- **Degrees** associate and bachelor's
- **Rural** 90-acre campus with easy access to Atlanta
- **Endowment** $1.5 million
- **Coed,** 762 undergraduate students, 93% full-time, 55% women, 45% men
- **Minimally difficult** entrance level, 52% of applicants were admitted

Undergraduates 709 full-time, 53 part-time. Students come from 21 states and territories, 10 other countries, 25% are from out of state, 14% African American, 2% Asian American or Pacific Islander, 0.5% Hispanic American, 0.4% Native American, 2% international, 9% transferred in, 51% live on campus. *Retention:* 58% of 2001 full-time freshmen returned.

Freshmen *Admission:* 1,102 applied, 573 admitted, 199 enrolled.

Faculty *Total:* 64, 80% full-time, 50% with terminal degrees. *Student/faculty ratio:* 14:1.

Majors Biblical studies; business administration; communications; divinity/ministry; elementary education; English; exercise sciences; history; information sciences/systems; liberal arts and sciences/liberal studies; middle school education; music; office management; pastoral counseling; pre-law; pre-pharmacy studies; psychology.

Academic Programs *Special study options:* academic remediation for entering students, advanced placement credit, distance learning, English as a second language, independent study, internships, part-time degree program, summer session for credit.

Library Shaw-Leslie Library with 44,966 titles, 187 serial subscriptions, 3,092 audiovisual materials, an OPAC.

Computers on Campus 50 computers available on campus for general student use. A campuswide network can be accessed from student residence rooms and from off campus. Internet access, at least one staffed computer lab available.

Student Life *Housing:* on-campus residence required through sophomore year. *Options:* men-only, women-only. *Activities and Organizations:* drama/theater group, student-run newspaper, choral group, SIFE. *Campus security:* 24-hour patrols, controlled dormitory access. *Student Services:* health clinic, personal/psychological counseling.

Athletics Member NAIA, NCCAA. *Intercollegiate sports:* baseball M(s), basketball M(s)/W(s), soccer M(s), softball W(s), tennis M(s)/W(s). *Intramural sports:* basketball M/W, football M/W, golf M/W, soccer M/W, tennis M/W, track and field M/W, volleyball M/W, weight lifting M/W.

Standardized Tests *Required:* SAT I or ACT (for admission).

Costs (2001–02) *Comprehensive fee:* $12,616 includes full-time tuition ($8242), mandatory fees ($220), and room and board ($4154). Part-time tuition: $285 per semester hour. *Required fees:* $75 per term part-time. *Room and board:* College room only: $1874. Room and board charges vary according to board plan. *Payment plan:* installment. *Waivers:* adult students, senior citizens, and employees or children of employees.

Financial Aid Of all full-time matriculated undergraduates who enrolled in 2001, 675 applied for aid, 519 were judged to have need, 117 had their need fully met. 171 Federal Work-Study jobs (averaging $1586). 105 State and other part-time jobs (averaging $1408). In 2001, 147 non-need-based awards were made. *Average percent of need met:* 43%. *Average financial aid package:* $7720. *Average need-based loan:* $3318. *Average need-based gift aid:* $2780. *Average non-need based aid:* $3567. *Average indebtedness upon graduation:* $16,575.

Applying *Options:* early admission, deferred entrance. *Application fee:* $25. *Required:* high school transcript. *Application deadlines:* 8/1 (freshmen), 8/1 (transfers). *Notification:* continuous until 8/1 (freshmen).

Admissions Contact Ms. Donna Quick, Associate Director of Admissions, Emmanuel College, PO Box 129, 181 Spring Street, Franklin Springs, GA 30639-0129. *Phone:* 706-245-7226 Ext. 2873. *Toll-free phone:* 800-860-8800. *Fax:* 706-245-4424. *E-mail:* admissions@emmanuel-college.edu.

EMORY UNIVERSITY
Atlanta, Georgia

- **Independent Methodist** university, founded 1836
- **Calendar** semesters
- **Degrees** bachelor's, master's, doctoral, and first professional (enrollment figures include Emory University, Oxford College; application data for main campus only)
- **Suburban** 631-acre campus
- **Endowment** $4.3 billion
- **Coed,** 6,374 undergraduate students, 98% full-time, 55% women, 45% men
- **Most difficult** entrance level, 43% of applicants were admitted

For information on Emory University's Oxford campus, please refer to Peterson's *Guide to Colleges in the South*. Oxford provides an intimate living-learning environment for students who want to begin their Emory education in a personalized setting with leadership opportunities. After completing the Oxford program, students automatically continue to Emory in Atlanta for their junior and senior years. See Oxford's Web site at http://www.emory.edu/OXFORD for additional information.

Undergraduates 6,248 full-time, 126 part-time. Students come from 52 states and territories, 59 other countries, 80% are from out of state, 10% African American, 15% Asian American or Pacific Islander, 3% Hispanic American, 0.2% Native American, 3% international, 1% transferred in, 63% live on campus. *Retention:* 94% of 2001 full-time freshmen returned.

Freshmen *Admission:* 9,607 applied, 4,096 admitted, 1,558 enrolled. *Average high school GPA:* 3.80. *Test scores:* SAT verbal scores over 500: 100%; SAT math scores over 500: 100%; ACT scores over 18: 100%; SAT verbal scores over 600: 83%; SAT math scores over 600: 91%; ACT scores over 24: 100%; SAT verbal scores over 700: 21%; SAT math scores over 700: 31%; ACT scores over 30: 40%.

Faculty *Total:* 1,848. *Student/faculty ratio:* 7:1.

Majors Accounting; African-American studies; African studies; anthropology; art history; Asian studies; biology; biomedical science; business administration; business economics; business marketing and marketing management; chemistry; classics; comparative literature; computer science; creative writing; dance; Eastern European area studies; economics; education; elementary education; English; film studies; finance; French; German; Greek (modern); history; human ecology; international relations; Italian; Judaic studies; Latin American studies; Latin (ancient and medieval); liberal arts and sciences/liberal studies; literature; mathematics; medieval/renaissance studies; music; neuroscience; nursing; philosophy; physics; political science; psychology; religious studies; Russian; secondary education; sociology; Spanish; theater arts/drama; women's studies.

Academic Programs *Special study options:* accelerated degree program, advanced placement credit, double majors, honors programs, internships, off-campus study, services for LD students, study abroad, summer session for credit. *ROTC:* Air Force (c). *Unusual degree programs:* 3-2 engineering with Georgia Institute of Technology.

Library Robert W. Woodruff Library plus 7 others with 2.3 million titles, 24,687 serial subscriptions, an OPAC, a Web page.

Computers on Campus 600 computers available on campus for general student use. A campuswide network can be accessed from student residence rooms and from off campus. Internet access, online (class) registration, at least one staffed computer lab available.

Student Life *Housing:* on-campus residence required for freshman year. *Options:* coed, women-only. *Activities and Organizations:* drama/theater group, student-run newspaper, radio and television station, choral group, Volunteer Emory, music/theater, student government, national fraternities, national sororities. *Campus security:* 24-hour emergency response devices and patrols, student patrols, late-night transport/escort service. *Student Services:* health clinic, personal/psychological counseling, women's center, legal services.

Athletics Member NCAA. All Division III. *Intercollegiate sports:* badminton M(c)/W(c), baseball M, basketball M/W, bowling M(c)/W(c), crew M(c)/W(c), cross-country running M/W, fencing M(c)/W(c), field hockey W(c), golf M, gymnastics M(c)/W(c), ice hockey M(c), lacrosse M(c), racquetball M(c)/W(c), rugby M(c), sailing M(c)/W(c), soccer M/W, softball W, swimming M/W, tennis M/W, track and field M/W, volleyball M(c)/W, wrestling M(c). *Intramural sports:* badminton M/W, baseball M, basketball M/W, bowling M/W, crew M/W, cross-country running M/W, fencing M/W, field hockey W, football M/W, golf M/W, ice hockey M, lacrosse M, racquetball M/W, rugby M, sailing M/W, soccer M/W, softball W, swimming M/W, tennis M/W, track and field M/W, volleyball M/W, water polo M/W, weight lifting M/W, wrestling M.

Standardized Tests *Required:* SAT I or ACT (for admission). *Recommended:* SAT II: Subject Tests (for admission).

Costs (2001–02) *Comprehensive fee:* $33,792 includes full-time tuition ($25,240), mandatory fees ($312), and room and board ($8240). *Room and board:* College room only: $5150. Room and board charges vary according to board plan, housing facility, and student level. *Payment plans:* tuition prepayment, installment. *Waivers:* employees or children of employees.

Financial Aid Of all full-time matriculated undergraduates who enrolled in 2001, 1885 applied for aid, 1545 were judged to have need, 1545 had their need fully met. In 2001, 666 non-need-based awards were made. *Average percent of need met:* 100%. *Average financial aid package:* $22,530. *Average need-based loan:* $4799. *Average need-based gift aid:* $16,728. *Average non-need based aid:* $8442. *Average indebtedness upon graduation:* $18,350. *Financial aid deadline:* 4/1.

Applying *Options:* common application, electronic application, early admission, early decision, deferred entrance. *Application fee:* $40. *Required:* essay or personal statement, high school transcript, 1 letter of recommendation. *Recom-*

mended: minimum 3.0 GPA. *Application deadlines:* 1/15 (freshmen), 6/1 (transfers). *Early decision:* 11/1 (for plan 1), 1/1 (for plan 2). *Notification:* 4/1 (freshmen), 12/15 (early decision plan 1), 2/1 (early decision plan 2).

Admissions Contact Mr. Daniel C. Walls, Dean of Admission, Emory University, Boisfeuillet Jones Center-Office of Admissions, Atlanta, GA 30322-1100. *Phone:* 404-727-6036. *Toll-free phone:* 800-727-6036. *E-mail:* admiss@unix.cc.emory.edu.

FORT VALLEY STATE UNIVERSITY

Fort Valley, Georgia

- **State-supported** comprehensive, founded 1895, part of University System of Georgia
- **Calendar** semesters
- **Degrees** associate, bachelor's, master's, doctoral, and first professional
- **Small-town** 1307-acre campus
- **Endowment** $5.0 million
- **Coed**
- **Moderately difficult** entrance level, 49% of applicants were admitted

Undergraduates Students come from 28 states and territories, 9 other countries, 59% live on campus. *Retention:* 74% of 2001 full-time freshmen returned.

Freshmen *Admission:* 2,329 applied, 1,146 admitted. *Average high school GPA:* 2.40.

Faculty *Total:* 174, 87% full-time, 63% with terminal degrees. *Student/faculty ratio:* 19:1.

Majors Accounting; agricultural economics; agricultural engineering; agronomy/crop science; animal sciences; biology; botany; business administration; business marketing and marketing management; chemistry; computer science; criminal justice/law enforcement administration; developmental/child psychology; early childhood education; economics; electrical/electronic engineering technology; French; health education; home economics education; mass communications; mathematics; nutrition science; ornamental horticulture; physical education; political science; pre-engineering; psychology; secretarial science; social sciences; social work; sociology; veterinary sciences; veterinary technology; zoology.

Academic Programs *Special study options:* academic remediation for entering students, adult/continuing education programs, advanced placement credit, cooperative education, distance learning, double majors, freshman honors college, honors programs, internships, off-campus study, part-time degree program, services for LD students, study abroad, summer session for credit. *ROTC:* Army (b). *Unusual degree programs:* 3-2 engineering with University of Nevada, Las Vegas; math, geological science with University of Oklahoma.

Library Henry A. Hunt Memorial Library plus 2 others with 186,365 titles, 1,213 serial subscriptions, an OPAC.

Computers on Campus 633 computers available on campus for general student use. A campuswide network can be accessed from off campus that provide access to on-line grade reports. At least one staffed computer lab available.

Student Life *Housing Options:* coed, men-only, women-only. *Activities and Organizations:* drama/theater group, student-run newspaper, radio and television station, choral group, marching band, Drama Group, Christian Student Organization, Habitat for Humanity, Debate Club, national fraternities, national sororities. *Campus security:* 24-hour emergency response devices and patrols, student patrols, late-night transport/escort service. *Student Services:* health clinic, personal/psychological counseling.

Athletics Member NCAA. All Division II. *Intercollegiate sports:* basketball M(s)/W(s), football M(s), golf M(s), tennis M(s)/W(s), track and field M(s)/W(s), volleyball W(s).

Standardized Tests *Required:* SAT I or ACT (for admission).

Costs (2001–02) *Tuition:* state resident $1234 full-time, $78 per credit part-time; nonresident $3149 full-time, $235 per credit part-time. Full-time tuition and fees vary according to course load. Part-time tuition and fees vary according to course load. *Required fees:* $536 full-time, $268 per term part-time. *Room and board:* $1915. Room and board charges vary according to board plan. *Waivers:* senior citizens and employees or children of employees.

Applying *Options:* common application, electronic application, early admission, deferred entrance. *Application fee:* $20. *Required:* high school transcript. *Application deadlines:* 8/1 (freshmen), 8/1 (transfers). *Notification:* continuous until 8/10 (freshmen).

Admissions Contact Mrs. Debra McGhee, Dean of Admissions and Enrollment Management, Fort Valley State University, 1005 State University Drive, Fort Valley, GA 31030. *Phone:* 478-825-6307. *Toll-free phone:* 800-248-7343. *Fax:* 478-825-6169. *E-mail:* admissap@mail.fusu.edu.

GEORGIA BAPTIST COLLEGE OF NURSING OF MERCER UNIVERSITY

Atlanta, Georgia

- **Independent Baptist** 4-year, founded 1988, part of Mercer University
- **Calendar** semesters
- **Degree** bachelor's
- **Urban** 20-acre campus
- **Endowment** $36.5 million
- **Coed, primarily women**
- **Moderately difficult** entrance level

Faculty *Student/faculty ratio:* 9:1.

Student Life *Campus security:* 24-hour emergency response devices and patrols, late-night transport/escort service, controlled dormitory access.

Standardized Tests *Required:* SAT I or ACT (for admission).

Financial Aid Of all full-time matriculated undergraduates who enrolled in 2001, 216 applied for aid, 199 were judged to have need, 28 had their need fully met. In 2001, 41. *Average percent of need met:* 62. *Average financial aid package:* $11,063. *Average need-based loan:* $4660. *Average need-based gift aid:* $3500. *Average non-need based aid:* $3500. *Average indebtedness upon graduation:* $16,148.

Applying *Application fee:* $35. *Required:* essay or personal statement, high school transcript, minimum 2.5 GPA. *Required for some:* letters of recommendation. *Recommended:* interview.

Admissions Contact Ms. Kim W. Hays, Associate Director of Admissions, Georgia Baptist College of Nursing of Mercer University, 274 Boulevard, NE, Atlanta, GA 30312. *Phone:* 673-547-6702. *Toll-free phone:* 800-551-8835. *Fax:* 673-547-6811. *E-mail:* gbcnadm@mindspring.com.

GEORGIA COLLEGE AND STATE UNIVERSITY

Milledgeville, Georgia

- **State-supported** comprehensive, founded 1889, part of University System of Georgia
- **Calendar** semesters
- **Degrees** bachelor's, master's, and post-master's certificates
- **Small-town** 666-acre campus
- **Endowment** $2.9 million
- **Coed,** 4,083 undergraduate students, 82% full-time, 62% women, 38% men
- **Moderately difficult** entrance level, 70% of applicants were admitted

Undergraduates 3,366 full-time, 717 part-time. Students come from 26 states and territories, 46 other countries, 1% are from out of state, 13% African American, 0.8% Asian American or Pacific Islander, 0.8% Hispanic American, 0.1% Native American, 3% international, 7% transferred in, 30% live on campus. *Retention:* 72% of 2001 full-time freshmen returned.

Freshmen *Admission:* 2,517 applied, 1,765 admitted, 764 enrolled. *Average high school GPA:* 3.13. *Test scores:* SAT verbal scores over 500: 67%; SAT math scores over 500: 61%; ACT scores over 18: 96%; SAT verbal scores over 600: 12%; SAT math scores over 600: 10%; ACT scores over 24: 10%; SAT verbal scores over 700: 1%.

Faculty *Total:* 364, 71% full-time. *Student/faculty ratio:* 14:1.

Majors Accounting; art; arts management; biology; business; business administration; business economics; business marketing and marketing management; business quantitative methods/management science related; chemistry; computer/information sciences; criminal justice/law enforcement administration; early childhood education; English; French; health education; history; journalism; liberal arts and sciences/liberal studies; logistics/materials management; mathematics; middle school education; music; music teacher education; music therapy; music (voice and choral/opera performance); nursing; office management; physical education; political science; psychology; recreation/leisure studies; sociology; Spanish; special education; theater arts/drama.

Academic Programs *Special study options:* academic remediation for entering students, accelerated degree program, advanced placement credit, cooperative education, distance learning, double majors, freshman honors college, honors programs, independent study, internships, part-time degree program, services for LD students, student-designed majors, study abroad, summer session for credit. *ROTC:* Army (c). *Unusual degree programs:* 3-2 engineering with Georgia Institute of Technology.

Library Ina Dillard Russell Library with 140,593 titles, 1,037 serial subscriptions, 4,169 audiovisual materials, an OPAC, a Web page.

Georgia College and State University (continued)

Computers on Campus 375 computers available on campus for general student use. A campuswide network can be accessed from student residence rooms and from off campus. Internet access, online (class) registration, at least one staffed computer lab available.

Student Life *Housing Options:* coed, men-only, women-only. *Activities and Organizations:* drama/theater group, student-run newspaper, radio and television station, choral group, Baptist Student Union, national fraternities, national sororities. *Campus security:* 24-hour emergency response devices and patrols, student patrols, late-night transport/escort service, controlled dormitory access. *Student Services:* health clinic, personal/psychological counseling.

Athletics Member NCAA. All Division II. *Intercollegiate sports:* baseball M(s), basketball M(s)/W(s), cross-country running M(s)/W(s), fencing M(c)/W(c), golf M(s), softball W(s), tennis M(s)/W(s). *Intramural sports:* basketball M/W, bowling M/W, football M/W, golf M, racquetball M/W, rugby M(c), soccer M/W, softball M/W, swimming M/W, tennis M/W, volleyball M/W.

Standardized Tests *Required:* SAT I or ACT (for admission).

Costs (2001–02) *Tuition:* state resident $2532 full-time, $106 per semester hour part-time; nonresident $10,128 full-time, $422 per semester hour part-time. Part-time tuition and fees vary according to course load. *Required fees:* $500 full-time, $500 per year part-time. *Room and board:* $4962; room only: $2748. Room and board charges vary according to board plan and housing facility. *Waivers:* senior citizens and employees or children of employees.

Financial Aid Of all full-time matriculated undergraduates who enrolled in 2001, 2771 applied for aid, 1192 were judged to have need. 149 Federal Work-Study jobs (averaging $1339). In 2001, 110 non-need-based awards were made. *Average indebtedness upon graduation:* $12,572.

Applying *Options:* electronic application, early admission, deferred entrance. *Application fee:* $25. *Required:* high school transcript, minimum 2.14 GPA, proof of immunization. *Recommended:* interview. *Application deadlines:* 7/15 (freshmen), 7/15 (transfers). *Notification:* continuous (freshmen).

Admissions Contact Ms. Maryllis Wolfgang, Director of Admissions, Georgia College and State University, CPO Box 023, Milledgeville, GA 31061. *Phone:* 478-445-6285. *Toll-free phone:* 800-342-0471. *Fax:* 478-445-1914. *E-mail:* gcsu@mail.gcsu.edu.

GEORGIA INSTITUTE OF TECHNOLOGY
Atlanta, Georgia

- **State-supported** university, founded 1885, part of University System of Georgia
- **Calendar** semesters
- **Degrees** bachelor's, master's, and doctoral
- **Urban** 360-acre campus
- **Endowment** $1.1 billion
- **Coed,** 11,043 undergraduate students, 92% full-time, 29% women, 71% men
- **Very difficult** entrance level, 56% of applicants were admitted

Undergraduates 10,163 full-time, 880 part-time. Students come from 55 states and territories, 87 other countries, 35% are from out of state, 8% African American, 14% Asian American or Pacific Islander, 3% Hispanic American, 0.1% Native American, 5% international, 4% transferred in, 58% live on campus. *Retention:* 90% of 2001 full-time freshmen returned.

Freshmen *Admission:* 9,255 applied, 5,158 admitted, 2,229 enrolled. *Average high school GPA:* 3.70. *Test scores:* SAT verbal scores over 500: 98%; SAT math scores over 500: 99%; SAT verbal scores over 600: 76%; SAT math scores over 600: 94%; SAT verbal scores over 700: 22%; SAT math scores over 700: 47%.

Faculty *Total:* 770, 98% full-time, 94% with terminal degrees. *Student/faculty ratio:* 14:1.

Majors Aerospace engineering; applied mathematics related; architecture; atmospheric sciences; biology; business administration; business economics; chemical engineering; chemistry; chemistry related; civil engineering; computer engineering; computer/information sciences; construction technology; earth sciences; electrical engineering; history of science and technology; industrial design; industrial/manufacturing engineering; international relations; management science; materials engineering; mathematics; mechanical engineering; modern languages; nuclear engineering; operations management; organizational psychology; physics; polymer chemistry; public policy analysis; science/technology and society; textile sciences/engineering.

Academic Programs *Special study options:* academic remediation for entering students, accelerated degree program, advanced placement credit, cooperative education, distance learning, double majors, English as a second language, honors programs, independent study, internships, off-campus study, part-time degree program, services for LD students, student-designed majors, study abroad, summer session for credit. *ROTC:* Army (b), Navy (b), Air Force (b).

Library Library and Information Center with 83,150 audiovisual materials, an OPAC, a Web page.

Computers on Campus 1450 computers available on campus for general student use. A campuswide network can be accessed from student residence rooms and from off campus. Internet access, online (class) registration, at least one staffed computer lab available.

Student Life *Housing:* on-campus residence required for freshman year. *Options:* coed. *Activities and Organizations:* drama/theater group, student-run newspaper, radio station, choral group, marching band, Christian Campus Fellowship, IEEE, Mechanical Engineering Graduate Student Association, Gamma Beta Phi Society, national fraternities, national sororities. *Campus security:* 24-hour emergency response devices and patrols, student patrols, late-night transport/escort service, controlled dormitory access. *Student Services:* health clinic, personal/psychological counseling, women's center, legal services.

Athletics Member NCAA. All Division I except football (Division I-A). *Intercollegiate sports:* baseball M(s), basketball M(s)/W(s), cross-country running M(s)/W(s), equestrian sports M(c)/W(c), golf M(s), ice hockey M(c), lacrosse M(c)/W(c), rugby M(c), softball W(s), swimming M(s)/W(s), tennis M(s)/W(s), track and field M(s)/W(s), volleyball W(s), wrestling M(c). *Intramural sports:* basketball M/W, bowling M(c)/W(c), crew M(c)/W(c), equestrian sports M/W, fencing M(c)/W(c), football M, golf M/W, gymnastics M/W, racquetball M(c)/W(c), sailing M(c)/W(c), skiing (cross-country) M(c)/W(c), skiing (downhill) M(c)/W(c), soccer M/W, softball W, squash M/W, swimming M/W, table tennis M(c)/W(c), tennis M/W, track and field M/W, volleyball M/W, water polo M(c)/W(c), weight lifting M(c)/W(c).

Standardized Tests *Required:* SAT I or ACT (for admission). *Required for some:* SAT II: Subject Tests (for admission). *Recommended:* SAT I (for admission).

Costs (2001–02) *Tuition:* state resident $2632 full-time, $110 per credit part-time; nonresident $11,528 full-time, $482 per credit part-time. Part-time tuition and fees vary according to course load. *Required fees:* $822 full-time, $38 per term part-time. *Room and board:* $5574; room only: $3088. Room and board charges vary according to board plan and housing facility.

Financial Aid Of all full-time matriculated undergraduates who enrolled in 2001, 7763 applied for aid, 2774 were judged to have need, 1276 had their need fully met. In 2001, 3067 non-need-based awards were made. *Average percent of need met:* 65%. *Average financial aid package:* $7261. *Average need-based loan:* $3756. *Average need-based gift aid:* $4607. *Average non-need based aid:* $4390. *Average indebtedness upon graduation:* $16,287.

Applying *Options:* electronic application, early admission. *Application fee:* $50. *Required:* essay or personal statement, high school transcript. *Application deadlines:* 1/15 (freshmen), 5/1 (transfers). *Notification:* 3/15 (freshmen).

Admissions Contact Ms. Deborah Smith, Director of Admissions, Georgia Institute of Technology, 225 North Avenue, NW, Atlanta, GA 30332-0320. *Phone:* 404-894-4154. *Fax:* 404-894-9511. *E-mail:* admissions@success.gatech.edu.

GEORGIA SOUTHERN UNIVERSITY
Statesboro, Georgia

- **State-supported** comprehensive, founded 1906, part of University System of Georgia
- **Calendar** semesters
- **Degrees** bachelor's, master's, doctoral, and post-master's certificates
- **Small-town** 601-acre campus
- **Endowment** $22.2 million
- **Coed,** 12,798 undergraduate students, 89% full-time, 52% women, 48% men
- **Moderately difficult** entrance level, 61% of applicants were admitted

Undergraduates Students come from 46 states and territories, 66 other countries, 5% are from out of state, 26% African American, 1% Asian American or Pacific Islander, 1% Hispanic American, 0.2% Native American, 1% international, 22% live on campus. *Retention:* 75% of 2001 full-time freshmen returned.

Freshmen *Admission:* 8,146 applied, 5,000 admitted. *Average high school GPA:* 3.01. *Test scores:* SAT verbal scores over 500: 58%; SAT math scores over 500: 58%; ACT scores over 18: 87%; SAT verbal scores over 600: 10%; SAT math scores over 600: 12%; ACT scores over 24: 13%; SAT verbal scores over 700: 1%.

Faculty *Total:* 717, 87% full-time, 74% with terminal degrees. *Student/faculty ratio:* 18:1.

Majors Accounting; anthropology; art; art education; athletic training/sports medicine; biology; biology education; business administration; business economics; business education; business marketing and marketing management; chemistry; chemistry education; civil engineering technology; clothing/apparel/textile studies; communications; computer/information sciences; construction technology; criminal justice studies; development economics; early childhood education;

economics; electrical/electronic engineering technology; English; English education; exercise sciences; finance; French; French language education; general studies; geography; geology; German; German language education; graphic/printing equipment; health/physical education; history; history education; home economics education; hotel and restaurant management; individual/family development; industrial arts education; industrial production technologies related; industrial technology; interior design; international business; international relations; journalism; logistics/materials management; management information systems/business data processing; mathematics; mathematics education; mechanical engineering technology; medical technology; middle school education; music; music (general performance); music teacher education; music theory and composition; nursing; nutrition studies; philosophy; physical education; physics; physics education; political science; psychology; public health education/promotion; public relations; radio/television broadcasting; recreation/leisure studies; sociology; Spanish; Spanish language education; special education; speech/rhetorical studies; sport/fitness administration; theater arts/drama.

Academic Programs *Special study options:* academic remediation for entering students, adult/continuing education programs, advanced placement credit, cooperative education, distance learning, double majors, English as a second language, honors programs, independent study, internships, off-campus study, part-time degree program, services for LD students, student-designed majors, study abroad, summer session for credit. *ROTC:* Army (b). *Unusual degree programs:* 3-2 physics with Georgia Institute of Technology.

Library Henderson Library with 3,511 serial subscriptions, 29,296 audiovisual materials, an OPAC, a Web page.

Computers on Campus 1100 computers available on campus for general student use. A campuswide network can be accessed from student residence rooms and from off campus. Internet access, at least one staffed computer lab available.

Student Life *Housing Options:* coed, men-only, women-only, disabled students. *Activities and Organizations:* drama/theater group, student-run newspaper, radio station, choral group, marching band, Baptist Student Union, United in Christ, Black Student Alliance, Wesley Foundation, Life Ministries, national fraternities, national sororities. *Campus security:* 24-hour emergency response devices and patrols, student patrols, late-night transport/escort service, residence hall security, locked residence hall entrances. *Student Services:* health clinic, personal/psychological counseling.

Athletics Member NCAA. All Division I except football (Division I-AA). *Intercollegiate sports:* baseball M(s), basketball M(s)/W(s), cross-country running W(s), equestrian sports M(c)/W(c), fencing M(c)/W(c), golf M(s), lacrosse M(c)/W(c), rugby M(c)/W(c), soccer M(s)(c)/W(s)(c), softball W(s), swimming M(c)/W(s)(c), tennis M(s)/W(s), track and field W(s)(c), volleyball M(c)/W(s)(c), weight lifting M(c)/W(c), wrestling M(c). *Intramural sports:* basketball M/W, bowling M/W, football M/W, golf M/W, soccer M/W, softball M/W, tennis M/W, volleyball M/W.

Standardized Tests *Required:* SAT I or ACT (for admission). *Required for some:* SAT II: Writing Test (for admission).

Costs (2001–02) *One-time required fee:* $50. *Tuition:* state resident $1932 full-time, $81 per semester hour part-time; nonresident $7728 full-time, $322 per semester hour part-time. Part-time tuition and fees vary according to course load. *Required fees:* $664 full-time. *Room and board:* $4382; room only: $2314. Room and board charges vary according to board plan and housing facility. *Waivers:* senior citizens.

Financial Aid Of all full-time matriculated undergraduates who enrolled in 2001, 9519 applied for aid, 5736 were judged to have need, 1261 had their need fully met. 445 Federal Work-Study jobs (averaging $1222). In 2001, 2710 non-need-based awards were made. *Average percent of need met:* 71%. *Average financial aid package:* $5630. *Average need-based loan:* $3352. *Average need-based gift aid:* $3410. *Average non-need based aid:* $2696. *Average indebtedness upon graduation:* $15,039.

Applying *Options:* common application, electronic application, early admission, deferred entrance. *Application fee:* $20. *Required:* high school transcript, minimum 2.0 GPA, proof of immunization. *Application deadline:* 8/1 (freshmen), rolling (transfers). *Notification:* continuous (freshmen).

Admissions Contact Georgia Southern University, GSU PO Box 8024, Building #805, Forest Drive, Statesboro, GA 30460. *Phone:* 912-681-5391. *Fax:* 912-486-7240. *E-mail:* admissions@gasou.edu.

GEORGIA SOUTHWESTERN STATE UNIVERSITY
Americus, Georgia

- **State-supported** comprehensive, founded 1906, part of University System of Georgia
- **Calendar** semesters
- **Degrees** associate, bachelor's, master's, and post-master's certificates
- **Small-town** 255-acre campus
- **Endowment** $24.9 million
- **Coed,** 1,947 undergraduate students, 74% full-time, 63% women, 37% men
- **Moderately difficult** entrance level, 69% of applicants were admitted

Undergraduates 1,449 full-time, 498 part-time. Students come from 19 states and territories, 33 other countries, 2% are from out of state, 10% transferred in, 38% live on campus. *Retention:* 71% of 2001 full-time freshmen returned.

Freshmen *Admission:* 979 applied, 672 admitted, 313 enrolled. *Average high school GPA:* 3.10. *Test scores:* SAT verbal scores over 500: 63%; SAT math scores over 500: 52%; ACT scores over 18: 100%; SAT verbal scores over 600: 15%; SAT math scores over 600: 13%; ACT scores over 24: 8%; SAT verbal scores over 700: 2%; SAT math scores over 700: 1%.

Faculty *Total:* 185, 69% full-time, 52% with terminal degrees. *Student/faculty ratio:* 15:1.

Majors Accounting; applied art; art; art education; auto body repair; aviation technology; behavioral sciences; biological/physical sciences; biology; business administration; business education; business marketing and marketing management; ceramic arts; chemistry; computer engineering technology; computer science; diesel engine mechanic; drafting; drawing; early childhood education; earth sciences; education; electrical/electronic engineering technology; elementary education; English; environmental biology; fine/studio arts; French; geology; graphic design/commercial art/illustration; heavy equipment maintenance; history; human resources management; industrial technology; information sciences/systems; machine technology; mathematics; medical assistant; middle school education; music; music teacher education; nursing; office management; physical education; physical sciences; political science; pre-dentistry; pre-law; pre-medicine; pre-veterinary studies; psychology; recreation/leisure studies; science education; secondary education; social sciences; sociology; Spanish; special education; wind/percussion instruments.

Academic Programs *Special study options:* academic remediation for entering students, adult/continuing education programs, advanced placement credit, cooperative education, distance learning, English as a second language, freshman honors college, honors programs, internships, off-campus study, part-time degree program, services for LD students, study abroad, summer session for credit. *Unusual degree programs:* 3-2 business administration with Georgia Institute of Technology; engineering with Georgia Institute of Technology; math, physics with Georgia Institute of Technology.

Library James Earl Carter Library with 190,000 titles, 59 serial subscriptions, 1,849 audiovisual materials, an OPAC, a Web page.

Computers on Campus 336 computers available on campus for general student use. A campuswide network can be accessed from off campus. Internet access, online (class) registration, at least one staffed computer lab available.

Student Life *Housing:* on-campus residence required through sophomore year. *Options:* coed, men-only, women-only. *Activities and Organizations:* drama/theater group, student-run newspaper, television station, choral group, Greek organizations, religious clubs and organizations, SABU (Black Student Organization), Biology Club, Gamma Beta Phi, national fraternities, national sororities. *Campus security:* 24-hour emergency response devices and patrols, late-night transport/escort service, controlled dormitory access. *Student Services:* health clinic, personal/psychological counseling, women's center.

Athletics Member NAIA. *Intercollegiate sports:* baseball M(s), basketball M(s)/W(s), softball W(s), tennis M(s)/W(s), volleyball W(s). *Intramural sports:* baseball M/W, basketball M/W, football M/W, golf M/W, soccer M, softball M/W, swimming M/W, tennis M/W, track and field M/W, volleyball M/W.

Standardized Tests *Required:* SAT I or ACT (for admission).

Costs (2001–02) *Tuition:* state resident $1932 full-time, $81 per semester hour part-time; nonresident $7728 full-time, $322 per semester hour part-time. Part-time tuition and fees vary according to course load. *Required fees:* $568 full-time, $291 per term part-time. *Room and board:* $3790. Room and board charges vary according to board plan and housing facility. *Waivers:* senior citizens.

Financial Aid Of all full-time matriculated undergraduates who enrolled in 2001, 1711 applied for aid, 1498 were judged to have need, 1498 had their need fully met. 106 Federal Work-Study jobs, 107 State and other part-time jobs (averaging $1621). *Average percent of need met:* 100%. *Average need-based loan:* $3875. *Average need-based gift aid:* $3900. *Average non-need based aid:* $3692. *Average indebtedness upon graduation:* $14,800.

Applying *Options:* common application, electronic application, early admission, early decision. *Application fee:* $20. *Required:* high school transcript, minimum 2.0 GPA, proof of immunization. *Recommended:* interview. *Application deadline:* rolling (freshmen), rolling (transfers). *Notification:* continuous until 8/1 (freshmen).

Admissions Contact Mr. Gary Fallis, Director of Admissions, Georgia Southwestern State University, 800 Wheatley Street. *Phone:* 229-928-1273. *Toll-free phone:* 800-338-0082. *Fax:* 229-931-2983. *E-mail:* gswapps@canes.gsw.edu.

GEORGIA STATE UNIVERSITY
Atlanta, Georgia

- **State-supported** university, founded 1913, part of University System of Georgia
- **Calendar** semesters
- **Degrees** certificates, bachelor's, master's, doctoral, first professional, and post-master's certificates
- **Urban** 24-acre campus
- **Endowment** $50.6 million
- **Coed,** 18,245 undergraduate students, 64% full-time, 61% women, 39% men
- **Moderately difficult** entrance level, 53% of applicants were admitted

Undergraduates 11,588 full-time, 6,657 part-time. Students come from 49 states and territories, 96 other countries, 4% are from out of state, 32% African American, 10% Asian American or Pacific Islander, 3% Hispanic American, 0.3% Native American, 3% international, 9% transferred in, 7% live on campus. *Retention:* 80% of 2001 full-time freshmen returned.

Freshmen *Admission:* 8,134 applied, 4,332 admitted, 2,200 enrolled. *Average high school GPA:* 3.23. *Test scores:* SAT verbal scores over 500: 65%; SAT math scores over 500: 67%; ACT scores over 18: 87%; SAT verbal scores over 600: 18%; SAT math scores over 600: 19%; ACT scores over 24: 24%; SAT verbal scores over 700: 2%; SAT math scores over 700: 2%; ACT scores over 30: 1%.

Faculty *Total:* 1,318, 74% full-time. *Student/faculty ratio:* 14:1.

Majors Accounting; actuarial science; African-American studies; anthropology; art education; biology; business administration; business economics; business marketing and marketing management; chemistry; classics; computer/information sciences; criminal justice studies; dietetics; drawing; early childhood education; economics; English; film studies; finance; French; geography; geology; German; history; hotel and restaurant management; human resources management; insurance/risk management; interdisciplinary studies; journalism; liberal arts and sciences/liberal studies; mathematics; medical records administration; medical technology; middle school education; music (general performance); nursing; operations research; philosophy; physical education; physical therapy; physics; political science; psychology; real estate; recreation/leisure facilities management; religious studies; respiratory therapy; social work; sociology; Spanish; speech/rhetorical studies; theater arts/drama; urban studies.

Academic Programs *Special study options:* academic remediation for entering students, adult/continuing education programs, cooperative education, distance learning, double majors, English as a second language, honors programs, independent study, internships, off-campus study, part-time degree program, services for LD students, student-designed majors, study abroad, summer session for credit. *ROTC:* Army (b), Navy (c).

Library Pullen Library plus 1 other with 12,053 serial subscriptions, 14,615 audiovisual materials, an OPAC, a Web page.

Computers on Campus 500 computers available on campus for general student use. A campuswide network can be accessed from student residence rooms and from off campus. At least one staffed computer lab available.

Student Life *Housing Options:* coed. *Activities and Organizations:* drama/theater group, student-run newspaper, radio and television station, choral group, Spotlight Programs Board, Sports Club Council, Student Government Association, national fraternities, national sororities. *Campus security:* 24-hour emergency response devices and patrols, late-night transport/escort service, controlled dormitory access. *Student Services:* health clinic, personal/psychological counseling, legal services.

Athletics Member NCAA. All Division I. *Intercollegiate sports:* baseball M(s), basketball M(s)/W(s), cross-country running M(s)/W(s), golf M(s)/W(s), soccer M(s), softball W(s), tennis M(s)/W(s), track and field M(s)/W, volleyball W(s). *Intramural sports:* archery M/W, badminton M(c)/W(c), basketball M/W, bowling M/W, crew M(c)/W(c), cross-country running M/W, equestrian sports M/W, fencing M(c)/W(c), football M/W, golf M/W, ice hockey M(c), racquetball M/W, rugby M(c), sailing M(c)/W(c), skiing (cross-country) M/W, skiing (downhill) M/W, soccer M/W(c), softball M/W, swimming M/W, table tennis M/W, tennis M/W, volleyball M/W, water polo M/W, weight lifting M/W.

Standardized Tests *Required:* SAT I or ACT (for admission). *Required for some:* SAT II: Subject Tests (for admission).

Costs (2001–02) *Tuition:* state resident $2632 full-time, $110 per credit part-time; nonresident $10,528 full-time, $440 per credit part-time. Full-time tuition and fees vary according to course load and program. Part-time tuition and fees vary according to course load and program. *Required fees:* $660 full-time, $330 per term part-time. *Room and board:* room only: $4500. Room and board charges vary according to housing facility. *Waivers:* employees or children of employees.

Financial Aid Of all full-time matriculated undergraduates who enrolled in 2001, 7365 applied for aid, 7232 were judged to have need. 258 Federal Work-Study jobs (averaging $1759).

Applying *Options:* deferred entrance. *Application fee:* $25. *Required:* high school transcript. *Required for some:* interview. *Recommended:* essay or personal statement, minimum 2.9 GPA. *Application deadlines:* 6/1 (freshmen), 6/1 (transfers). *Notification:* continuous (freshmen).

Admissions Contact Mr. Rob Sheinkopf, Dean of Admissions and Acting Dean for Enrollment Services, Georgia State University, PO Box 4009, Atlanta, GA 30302-4009. *Phone:* 404-651-2365. *Toll-free phone:* 404-651-2365. *Fax:* 404-651-4811.

HERZING COLLEGE
Atlanta, Georgia

- **Proprietary** primarily 2-year, founded 1949, part of Herzing Institutes, Inc
- **Calendar** semesters
- **Degrees** certificates, diplomas, associate, and bachelor's
- **Urban** campus
- **Coed**
- **Moderately difficult** entrance level

Faculty *Student/faculty ratio:* 8:1.

Student Life *Campus security:* 24-hour patrols.

Applying *Application fee:* $25. *Required:* high school transcript, interview.

Admissions Contact Stacy Johnston, Director of Admissions, Herzing College, 3355 Lenox Road, Suite 100, Atlanta, GA 30326. *Phone:* 404-816-4533. *Toll-free phone:* 800-573-4533. *Fax:* 404-816-5576. *E-mail:* leec@atl.herzing.edu.

KENNESAW STATE UNIVERSITY
Kennesaw, Georgia

- **State-supported** comprehensive, founded 1963, part of University System of Georgia
- **Calendar** semesters
- **Degrees** bachelor's and master's
- **Suburban** 185-acre campus with easy access to Atlanta
- **Coed**
- **Moderately difficult** entrance level, 72% of applicants were admitted

Undergraduates Students come from 118 other countries, 4% are from out of state. *Retention:* 67% of 2001 full-time freshmen returned.

Freshmen *Admission:* 3,026 applied, 2,186 admitted. *Average high school GPA:* 3.05. *Test scores:* SAT verbal scores over 500: 71%; SAT math scores over 500: 64%; SAT verbal scores over 600: 20%; SAT math scores over 600: 16%; SAT verbal scores over 700: 1%; SAT math scores over 700: 1%.

Faculty *Total:* 659, 59% full-time, 57% with terminal degrees. *Student/faculty ratio:* 24:1.

Majors Accounting; art; art education; biology; biology education; business administration; business economics; business marketing and marketing management; chemistry; chemistry education; communications; computer science; early childhood education; economics; education; elementary education; English; English education; exercise sciences; finance; fine/studio arts; French; French language education; health education; history; information sciences/systems; international relations; mathematics; mathematics education; middle school education; music; music teacher education; music (voice and choral/opera performance); nursing; operations management; physical education; political science; psychology; secondary education; social science education; social work; sociology; Spanish; Spanish language education; sport/fitness administration; theater arts/drama.

Academic Programs *Special study options:* academic remediation for entering students, adult/continuing education programs, advanced placement credit, cooperative education, double majors, English as a second language, freshman honors college, honors programs, independent study, internships, off-campus study, part-time degree program, services for LD students, study abroad, summer session for credit. *ROTC:* Army (b), Air Force (c).

Library Horace W. Sturgis Library with 565,000 titles, 3,500 serial subscriptions, an OPAC, a Web page.

Computers on Campus 542 computers available on campus for general student use. A campuswide network can be accessed from off campus. Internet access, online (class) registration, at least one staffed computer lab available.

Student Life *Housing:* college housing not available. *Activities and Organizations:* drama/theater group, student-run newspaper, choral group, Golden Key

National Honor Society, Student Government Association, Campus Activities Board, African-American Student Alliance, International Student Association, national fraternities, national sororities. *Campus security:* 24-hour emergency response devices and patrols, student patrols, late-night transport/escort service. *Student Services:* health clinic, personal/psychological counseling.

Athletics Member NCAA. All Division II. *Intercollegiate sports:* baseball M(s), basketball M(s)/W(s), cross-country running M(s)/W(s), golf M(s), softball W(s), tennis W(s). *Intramural sports:* basketball M/W, bowling M/W, football M/W, soccer M/W, softball M/W, swimming M/W, tennis M/W, volleyball M/W, weight lifting M/W.

Standardized Tests *Required:* SAT I or ACT (for admission).

Costs (2001–02) *Tuition:* state resident $2350 full-time, $78 per credit part-time; nonresident $7990 full-time, $313 per credit part-time. Part-time tuition and fees vary according to course load. *Required fees:* $478 full-time, $239 per term part-time. *Payment plan:* deferred payment. *Waivers:* senior citizens and employees or children of employees.

Financial Aid Of all full-time matriculated undergraduates who enrolled in 2001, 4443 applied for aid, 2732 were judged to have need, 1785 had their need fully met. 46 Federal Work-Study jobs (averaging $1501). 576 State and other part-time jobs (averaging $1600).

Applying *Options:* electronic application, early admission, deferred entrance. *Application fee:* $20. *Required:* high school transcript, minimum 2.0 GPA, proof of immunization. *Application deadlines:* 7/13 (freshmen), 7/13 (transfers). *Notification:* continuous (freshmen).

Admissions Contact Mr. Joe F. Head, Director of Admissions and Dean of Enrollment Services, Kennesaw State University, 1000 Chastain Road, Campus Box 0115, Kennesaw, GA 30144. *Phone:* 770-423-6300. *Fax:* 770-420-4435.

LaGrange College

LaGrange, Georgia

- **Independent United Methodist** comprehensive, founded 1831
- **Calendar** quarters
- **Degrees** associate, bachelor's, and master's
- **Small-town** 120-acre campus with easy access to Atlanta
- **Endowment** $62.1 million
- **Coed,** 902 undergraduate students, 84% full-time, 63% women, 37% men
- **Moderately difficult** entrance level, 79% of applicants were admitted

Undergraduates 759 full-time, 143 part-time. Students come from 18 states and territories, 9 other countries, 10% are from out of state, 15% African American, 1.0% Asian American or Pacific Islander, 0.7% Hispanic American, 0.7% Native American, 3% international, 6% transferred in, 52% live on campus. *Retention:* 74% of 2001 full-time freshmen returned.

Freshmen *Admission:* 519 applied, 408 admitted, 186 enrolled. *Average high school GPA:* 3.19. *Test scores:* SAT verbal scores over 500: 57%; SAT math scores over 500: 53%; ACT scores over 18: 83%; SAT verbal scores over 600: 15%; SAT math scores over 600: 12%; ACT scores over 24: 31%; SAT verbal scores over 700: 4%; ACT scores over 30: 1%.

Faculty *Total:* 101, 59% full-time, 59% with terminal degrees. *Student/faculty ratio:* 11:1.

Majors Accounting; art; art education; biochemistry; biology; business administration; business economics; chemistry; computer science; criminal justice/law enforcement administration; early childhood education; economics; education; elementary education; English; history; human services; international business; liberal arts and sciences/liberal studies; mathematics; middle school education; music; musical instrument technology; nursing; pastoral counseling; political science; pre-dentistry; pre-engineering; pre-law; pre-medicine; pre-veterinary studies; psychology; religious education; religious studies; science education; secondary education; social work; theater arts/drama.

Academic Programs *Special study options:* adult/continuing education programs, advanced placement credit, double majors, English as a second language, independent study, internships, part-time degree program, study abroad, summer session for credit. *Unusual degree programs:* 3-2 engineering with Georgia Institute of Technology, Auburn University.

Library William and Evelyn Banks Library with 135,522 titles, 7,294 serial subscriptions, 337 audiovisual materials, an OPAC, a Web page.

Computers on Campus 169 computers available on campus for general student use. A campuswide network can be accessed from student residence rooms and from off campus. At least one staffed computer lab available.

Student Life *Housing:* on-campus residence required through junior year. *Options:* coed, men-only, women-only. *Activities and Organizations:* drama/theater group, student-run newspaper, choral group, Student Government Association, Greek system, drama/theater groups, Habitat for Humanity, BSU/Wesley Fellowship, national fraternities, national sororities. *Campus security:* 24-hour patrols, controlled dormitory access. *Student Services:* health clinic, personal/psychological counseling.

Athletics Member NCAA, NAIA. All NCAA Division III. *Intercollegiate sports:* baseball M, basketball M/W, golf M, soccer M/W, softball W, swimming M/W, tennis M/W, volleyball W. *Intramural sports:* badminton M/W, basketball M/W, crew M(c)/W(c), football M, softball M/W, swimming M/W, tennis M/W, volleyball M/W, water polo M/W, weight lifting M.

Standardized Tests *Required:* SAT I or ACT (for admission).

Costs (2001–02) *Comprehensive fee:* $17,496 includes full-time tuition ($12,360) and room and board ($5136). Full-time tuition and fees vary according to location. Part-time tuition: $510 per credit hour. Part-time tuition and fees vary according to location. *Payment plan:* installment. *Waivers:* employees or children of employees.

Financial Aid Of all full-time matriculated undergraduates who enrolled in 2001, 681 applied for aid, 472 were judged to have need, 188 had their need fully met. 80 Federal Work-Study jobs (averaging $1481). 289 State and other part-time jobs (averaging $1569). In 2001, 209 non-need-based awards were made. *Average percent of need met:* 82%. *Average financial aid package:* $11,644. *Average need-based loan:* $3044. *Average need-based gift aid:* $8622. *Average indebtedness upon graduation:* $18,268. *Financial aid deadline:* 3/1.

Applying *Options:* common application, electronic application, early admission, deferred entrance. *Application fee:* $20. *Required:* essay or personal statement, high school transcript, minimum 2.0 GPA. *Required for some:* 1 letter of recommendation, interview. *Application deadlines:* 8/15 (freshmen), 8/15 (transfers). *Notification:* continuous (freshmen).

Admissions Contact LaGrange College, 601 Broad Street, LaGrange, GA 30240-2999. *Phone:* 706-880-8253. *Toll-free phone:* 800-593-2885. *Fax:* 706-880-8010. *E-mail:* lgcadmis@lgc.edu.

Life University

Marietta, Georgia

Admissions Contact Office of Admissions, Life University, 1269 Barclay Circle, Marietta, GA 30060-2903. *Phone:* 800-543-3202.

Luther Rice Bible College and Seminary

Lithonia, Georgia

- **Independent Baptist** comprehensive, founded 1962
- **Calendar** semesters
- **Degrees** bachelor's, master's, and doctoral
- **Urban** 5-acre campus with easy access to Atlanta
- **Endowment** $121,000
- **Coed**
- **Noncompetitive** entrance level

Student Life *Campus security:* 24-hour emergency response devices, late-night transport/escort service.

Costs (2001–02) *Tuition:* $2784 full-time, $348 per course part-time. *Required fees:* $50 full-time, $25 per term part-time.

Applying *Options:* common application, early admission. *Application fee:* $50. *Required:* high school transcript, letters of recommendation.

Admissions Contact Dr. Dennis Dieringer, Director of Admissions and Records, Luther Rice Bible College and Seminary, 3038 Evans Mill Road, Lithonia, GA 30038-2454. *Phone:* 770-484-1204. *Toll-free phone:* 800-442-1577. *E-mail:* lrs@lrs.edu.

Macon State College

Macon, Georgia

- **State-supported** 4-year, founded 1968, part of University System of Georgia
- **Calendar** semesters
- **Degrees** certificates, associate, and bachelor's
- **Urban** 167-acre campus
- **Endowment** $3.0 million
- **Coed,** 4,482 undergraduate students, 39% full-time, 64% women, 36% men
- **Minimally difficult** entrance level

Undergraduates Students come from 11 other countries, 32% African American, 2% Asian American or Pacific Islander, 1% Hispanic American, 0.4% Native American, 0.1% international.

Freshmen *Admission:* 1,696 admitted. *Average high school GPA:* 2.78.

Macon State College (continued)

Faculty *Total:* 215, 55% full-time, 49% with terminal degrees. *Student/faculty ratio:* 20:1.

Majors Accounting; agricultural sciences; art; biology; business; business administration; business computer programming; business education; chemistry; computer programming; computer science; corrections; criminal justice/law enforcement administration; data processing technology; dental hygiene; economics; education; elementary education; engineering technology; English; environmental science; food sciences; general studies; health science; health services administration; history; humanities; information sciences/systems; journalism; law enforcement/police science; liberal arts and sciences/liberal studies; mass communications; mathematics; medical laboratory technician; medical records administration; medical records technology; modern languages; music; nursing; physical education; physical therapy; physics; political science; postal management; pre-engineering; pre-pharmacy studies; psychology; public administration; respiratory therapy; secretarial science; sociology; speech/rhetorical studies; theater arts/drama.

Academic Programs *Special study options:* academic remediation for entering students, adult/continuing education programs, advanced placement credit, cooperative education, distance learning, honors programs, internships, part-time degree program, services for LD students, study abroad, summer session for credit.

Library Macon State College Library with 80,000 titles, 513 serial subscriptions, an OPAC, a Web page.

Computers on Campus 95 computers available on campus for general student use. A campuswide network can be accessed from off campus. At least one staffed computer lab available.

Student Life *Housing:* college housing not available. *Activities and Organizations:* drama/theater group, student-run newspaper, choral group, student government, Macon College Association of Nursing Students. *Campus security:* 24-hour patrols, late-night transport/escort service. *Student Services:* personal/psychological counseling.

Athletics *Intramural sports:* basketball M(c)/W(c), football M(c)/W(c), golf M(c)/W(c), softball M(c)/W(c), tennis M(c)/W(c), volleyball M(c)/W(c).

Standardized Tests *Required:* SAT I or ACT (for admission).

Costs (2001–02) *Tuition:* state resident $1280 full-time, $53 per semester hour part-time; nonresident $5120 full-time, $213 per semester hour part-time. Full-time tuition and fees vary according to class time, degree level, and student level. Part-time tuition and fees vary according to class time, course load, degree level, and student level. *Required fees:* $158 full-time, $79 per term part-time. *Waivers:* senior citizens.

Financial Aid Of all full-time matriculated undergraduates who enrolled in 2001, 102 Federal Work-Study jobs (averaging $1078).

Applying *Options:* common application, electronic application, early admission. *Application fee:* $10. *Required:* high school transcript. *Application deadline:* rolling (freshmen), rolling (transfers). *Notification:* continuous (freshmen).

Admissions Contact Macon State College, Macon, GA 31206. *Phone:* 912-471-2800 Ext. 2854. *Toll-free phone:* 800-272-7619.

MEDICAL COLLEGE OF GEORGIA
Augusta, Georgia

- **State-supported** upper-level, founded 1828, part of University System of Georgia
- **Calendar** semesters
- **Degrees** bachelor's, master's, doctoral, first professional, and postbachelor's certificates
- **Urban** 100-acre campus
- **Coed,** 669 undergraduate students, 92% full-time, 87% women, 13% men
- **Moderately difficult** entrance level

Undergraduates 616 full-time, 53 part-time. Students come from 12 states and territories, 10% are from out of state, 14% African American, 3% Asian American or Pacific Islander, 2% Hispanic American, 0.6% Native American, 12% transferred in, 13% live on campus.

Faculty *Total:* 722, 85% full-time, 85% with terminal degrees.

Majors Dental hygiene; diagnostic medical sonography; medical records administration; medical technology; nuclear medical technology; nursing; occupational therapy; physician assistant; radiological science; respiratory therapy.

Academic Programs *Special study options:* distance learning, off-campus study, summer session for credit.

Library Robert B. Greenblatt MD Library with 176,646 titles, 1,672 serial subscriptions, 12,928 audiovisual materials, an OPAC, a Web page.

Computers on Campus 58 computers available on campus for general student use. At least one staffed computer lab available.

Student Life *Housing Options:* coed. *Activities and Organizations:* student-run newspaper, Student Government Association, Baptist Student Union, International Club, Campus Outreach, Medical Student Auxiliary. *Campus security:* 24-hour emergency response devices and patrols, late-night transport/escort service, controlled dormitory access. *Student Services:* health clinic, personal/psychological counseling, legal services.

Athletics *Intramural sports:* basketball M/W, rugby M, soccer M.

Standardized Tests *Required for some:* SAT I or ACT (for admission).

Costs (2001–02) *Tuition:* state resident $2632 full-time, $110 per hour part-time; nonresident $10,528 full-time, $440 per hour part-time. Part-time tuition and fees vary according to course load. *Required fees:* $451 full-time, $218 per term, $218 per term part-time. *Room and board:* room only: $1302. Room and board charges vary according to housing facility. *Waivers:* senior citizens.

Financial Aid Of all full-time matriculated undergraduates who enrolled in 2001, 421 applied for aid, 365 were judged to have need, 63 had their need fully met. 35 Federal Work-Study jobs (averaging $1200). In 2001, 116 non-need-based awards were made. *Average percent of need met:* 57%. *Average financial aid package:* $7247. *Average need-based loan:* $5092. *Average need-based gift aid:* $3496. *Average indebtedness upon graduation:* $14,271.

Applying *Application fee:* $25. *Application deadline:* rolling (transfers). *Notification:* continuous (transfers).

Admissions Contact Ms. Carol S. Nobles, Director of Student Recruitment and Admissions, Medical College of Georgia, AA-170 Administration-Kelly Building, Augusta, GA 30912. *Phone:* 706-721-2725. *Fax:* 706-721-7279. *E-mail:* underadm@mail.mcg.edu.

MERCER UNIVERSITY
Macon, Georgia

- **Independent Baptist** comprehensive, founded 1833
- **Calendar** semesters
- **Degrees** bachelor's, master's, doctoral, first professional, post-master's, and postbachelor's certificates
- **Suburban** 130-acre campus with easy access to Atlanta
- **Endowment** $178.2 million
- **Coed,** 4,740 undergraduate students, 84% full-time, 67% women, 33% men
- **Moderately difficult** entrance level, 83% of applicants were admitted

Undergraduates 3,961 full-time, 779 part-time. Students come from 30 states and territories, 35 other countries, 16% are from out of state, 28% African American, 3% Asian American or Pacific Islander, 1% Hispanic American, 0.7% Native American, 4% international, 3% transferred in, 61% live on campus. *Retention:* 75% of 2001 full-time freshmen returned.

Freshmen *Admission:* 2,771 applied, 2,290 admitted, 803 enrolled. *Average high school GPA:* 3.50. *Test scores:* SAT verbal scores over 500: 86%; SAT math scores over 500: 89%; ACT scores over 18: 98%; SAT verbal scores over 600: 39%; SAT math scores over 600: 42%; ACT scores over 24: 60%; SAT verbal scores over 700: 7%; SAT math scores over 700: 6%; ACT scores over 30: 11%.

Faculty *Total:* 554, 57% full-time, 62% with terminal degrees. *Student/faculty ratio:* 15:1.

Majors Accounting; African-American studies; art; art education; bioengineering; biology; business; business administration; business marketing and marketing management; chemistry; classics; communications; computer engineering; computer/information sciences; computer science; criminal justice/law enforcement administration; early childhood education; earth sciences; economics; education of the specific learning disabled; electrical engineering; elementary education; engineering/industrial management; English; English education; environmental engineering; environmental science; finance; foreign languages education; French; German; history; history education; human services; industrial/manufacturing engineering; information sciences/systems; international business; Latin (ancient and medieval); mathematics; mathematics education; mechanical engineering; middle school education; multi/interdisciplinary studies related; music; music (general performance); music teacher education; nursing; philosophy; physics; political science; psychology; religious studies; science education; social sciences; social studies education; sociology; Spanish; theater arts/drama.

Academic Programs *Special study options:* academic remediation for entering students, accelerated degree program, adult/continuing education programs, advanced placement credit, cooperative education, double majors, English as a second language, honors programs, independent study, internships, off-campus study, part-time degree program, services for LD students, student-designed majors, study abroad, summer session for credit. *ROTC:* Army (b).

Library Jack Tarver Library plus 3 others with 439,121 titles, 9,567 serial subscriptions, 60,024 audiovisual materials, an OPAC, a Web page.

Computers on Campus 140 computers available on campus for general student use. A campuswide network can be accessed from student residence rooms and from off campus. Internet access, at least one staffed computer lab available.
Student Life *Housing:* on-campus residence required through sophomore year. *Options:* coed, men-only, women-only, disabled students. *Activities and Organizations:* drama/theater group, student-run newspaper, choral group, AGAPE, Baptist Student Union, Student Government Association, Reformed University Worship, Organization of Black Students, national fraternities, national sororities. *Campus security:* 24-hour emergency response devices and patrols, student patrols, late-night transport/escort service, controlled dormitory access, patrols by police officers. *Student Services:* health clinic, personal/psychological counseling.
Athletics Member NCAA. All Division I. *Intercollegiate sports:* baseball M(s), basketball M(s)/W(s), cross-country running M(s)/W(s), golf M(s)/W(s), riflery M(s)/W(s), soccer M(s)/W(s), softball W(s), tennis M(s)/W(s), volleyball W(s). *Intramural sports:* baseball M, basketball M/W, bowling M/W, football M/W, golf M/W, racquetball M/W, soccer M/W, softball M/W, tennis M/W, volleyball M/W.
Standardized Tests *Required:* SAT I or ACT (for admission).
Costs (2001–02) *Comprehensive fee:* $24,130 includes full-time tuition ($18,290) and room and board ($5840). Full-time tuition and fees vary according to class time, course load, and location. Part-time tuition: $610 per credit hour. Part-time tuition and fees vary according to class time, course load, and location. *Room and board:* College room only: $2880. Room and board charges vary according to board plan, housing facility, and location. *Payment plan:* installment. *Waivers:* employees or children of employees.
Financial Aid Of all full-time matriculated undergraduates who enrolled in 2001, 1931 applied for aid, 1578 were judged to have need, 782 had their need fully met. 462 Federal Work-Study jobs (averaging $1722). In 2001, 673 non-need-based awards were made. *Average percent of need met:* 86%. *Average financial aid package:* $18,388. *Average need-based loan:* $3766. *Average need-based gift aid:* $10,964. *Average non-need based aid:* $10,649. *Average indebtedness upon graduation:* $14,842.
Applying *Options:* common application, electronic application, early admission, deferred entrance. *Application fee:* $25. *Required:* high school transcript, minimum 2.8 GPA. *Required for some:* minimum 3.0 GPA, 2 letters of recommendation, interview, counselor's evaluation. *Recommended:* minimum 3.0 GPA, interview. *Application deadline:* 7/1 (freshmen), rolling (transfers). *Notification:* continuous (freshmen).
Admissions Contact Mr. Allen S. London, Associate Vice President for Freshman Admissions, Mercer University, 1400 Coleman Avenue, Macon, GA 31207-0003. *Phone:* 478-301-2650. *Toll-free phone:* 800-840-8577. *Fax:* 478-301-2828. *E-mail:* admissions@mercer.edu.

MOREHOUSE COLLEGE
Atlanta, Georgia

- **Independent** 4-year, founded 1867
- **Calendar** semesters
- **Degree** bachelor's
- **Urban** 61-acre campus
- **Endowment** $100.3 million
- **Men only,** 2,808 undergraduate students, 95% full-time
- **Moderately difficult** entrance level, 76% of applicants were admitted

Undergraduates 2,655 full-time, 153 part-time. Students come from 43 states and territories, 23 other countries, 67% are from out of state, 93% African American, 0.1% Asian American or Pacific Islander, 0.1% Hispanic American, 5% international, 1% transferred in, 50% live on campus. *Retention:* 85% of 2001 full-time freshmen returned.
Freshmen *Admission:* 656 enrolled. *Average high school GPA:* 3.08. *Test scores:* SAT verbal scores over 500: 61%; SAT math scores over 500: 57%; ACT scores over 18: 100%; SAT verbal scores over 600: 21%; SAT math scores over 600: 19%; ACT scores over 24: 24%; SAT verbal scores over 700: 3%; SAT math scores over 700: 2%; ACT scores over 30: 3%.
Faculty *Total:* 237, 73% full-time, 59% with terminal degrees. *Student/faculty ratio:* 15:1.
Majors Accounting; adult/continuing education; African-American studies; art; biology; business administration; business marketing and marketing management; chemistry; computer/information sciences; economics; elementary education; engineering; English; finance; French; German; history; interdisciplinary studies; international relations; mathematics; middle school education; music; philosophy; physical education; physics; political science; psychology; religious studies; secondary education; sociology; Spanish; theater arts/drama; urban studies.
Academic Programs *Special study options:* academic remediation for entering students, advanced placement credit, cooperative education, double majors, honors programs, internships, off-campus study, part-time degree program, services for LD students, study abroad, summer session for credit. *ROTC:* Army (b), Navy (b), Air Force (c). *Unusual degree programs:* 3-2 engineering with Georgia Institute of Technology, Boston University, Auburn University, Rensselaer Polytechnic University, Rochester Institute of Technology.
Library Woodruff Library with 560,000 titles, 1,000 serial subscriptions, an OPAC.
Computers on Campus 325 computers available on campus for general student use. A campuswide network can be accessed from student residence rooms and from off campus. Internet access, online (class) registration, at least one staffed computer lab available.
Student Life *Housing Options:* men-only. *Activities and Organizations:* drama/theater group, student-run newspaper, choral group, marching band, Glee Club, Political Science Club, STRIPES, national fraternities. *Campus security:* 24-hour emergency response devices and patrols, late-night transport/escort service. *Student Services:* health clinic, personal/psychological counseling.
Athletics Member NCAA. All Division II. *Intercollegiate sports:* basketball M(s), cross-country running M(s), football M(s), tennis M(s), track and field M(s). *Intramural sports:* baseball M, basketball M, bowling M, football M, table tennis M, tennis M.
Standardized Tests *Required:* SAT I or ACT (for admission).
Costs (2001–02) *Comprehensive fee:* $19,814 includes full-time tuition ($10,238), mandatory fees ($2194), and room and board ($7382). Full-time tuition and fees vary according to student level. Part-time tuition: $471 per semester hour. Part-time tuition and fees vary according to course load and student level. *Required fees:* $1088 per term part-time. *Room and board:* College room only: $4450. Room and board charges vary according to board plan. *Payment plan:* installment. *Waivers:* employees or children of employees.
Applying *Options:* common application, early admission, early decision, deferred entrance. *Application fee:* $45. *Required:* essay or personal statement, high school transcript, minimum 2.8 GPA, letters of recommendation. *Recommended:* minimum 3.0 GPA, interview. *Application deadlines:* 2/15 (freshmen), 2/15 (transfers). *Early decision:* 10/15. *Notification:* continuous until 4/1 (freshmen), 12/15 (early decision).
Admissions Contact Mr. Terrance Dixon, Associate Dean for Admissions and Recruitment, Morehouse College, 830 Westview Drive, SW, Atlanta, GA 30314. *Phone:* 404-215-2632. *Toll-free phone:* 800-851-1254. *Fax:* 404-524-5635. *E-mail:* admissions@morehouse.edu.

MORRIS BROWN COLLEGE
Atlanta, Georgia

- **Independent** 4-year, founded 1881, affiliated with African Methodist Episcopal Church
- **Calendar** semesters
- **Degree** bachelor's
- **Urban** 21-acre campus
- **Endowment** $15.1 million
- **Coed,** 2,874 undergraduate students, 97% full-time, 57% women, 43% men
- **Minimally difficult** entrance level, 67% of applicants were admitted

Undergraduates 2,792 full-time, 82 part-time. Students come from 40 states and territories, 16 other countries, 38% are from out of state, 95% African American, 0.2% Asian American or Pacific Islander, 0.1% Hispanic American, 0.0% Native American, 2% international, 4% transferred in, 35% live on campus. *Retention:* 61% of 2001 full-time freshmen returned.
Freshmen *Admission:* 3,278 applied, 2,188 admitted, 802 enrolled. *Average high school GPA:* 2.59. *Test scores:* SAT verbal scores over 500: 11%; SAT math scores over 500: 11%; ACT scores over 18: 29%; SAT verbal scores over 600: 3%; SAT math scores over 600: 1%; ACT scores over 24: 3%.
Faculty *Total:* 184, 57% full-time, 54% with terminal degrees. *Student/faculty ratio:* 21:1.
Majors Accounting; actuarial science; African-American studies; art; biology; business administration; business management/administrative services related; chemistry; computer/information sciences; computer/information sciences related; computer science; criminal justice/law enforcement administration; early childhood education; English; French; health education; history; hospitality management; mass communications; mathematics; music; philosophy; political science; psychology; religious studies; sociology; Spanish; speech/rhetorical studies; theater arts/drama.
Academic Programs *Special study options:* academic remediation for entering students, accelerated degree program, adult/continuing education programs, coop-

Morris Brown College (continued)
erative education, double majors, English as a second language, honors programs, internships, off-campus study, part-time degree program, services for LD students. *ROTC:* Navy (c). *Unusual degree programs:* 3-2 engineering with Georgia Institute of Technology, North Carolina Agricultural and Technical State University; nursing with Vanderbilt University, Tuskegee University; architecture with Georgia Institute of Technology.

Library Woodruff Library with 358,505 titles, 1,739 serial subscriptions, 4,506 audiovisual materials.

Computers on Campus 200 computers available on campus for general student use. A campuswide network can be accessed from student residence rooms. Internet access, at least one staffed computer lab available.

Student Life *Housing Options:* men-only, women-only. *Activities and Organizations:* student-run newspaper, choral group, marching band, national fraternities, national sororities. *Campus security:* 24-hour emergency response devices and patrols. *Student Services:* health clinic, personal/psychological counseling, legal services.

Athletics Member NCAA. All Division III. *Intercollegiate sports:* basketball M(s)/W(s), football M(s), golf M(s), tennis M/W, track and field M(s)/W(s). *Intramural sports:* basketball M/W, tennis M/W.

Standardized Tests *Required:* SAT I or ACT (for admission).

Costs (2001–02) *One-time required fee:* $1500. *Comprehensive fee:* $16,736 includes full-time tuition ($8786), mandatory fees ($2080), and room and board ($5870). Part-time tuition: $366 per semester hour. Part-time tuition and fees vary according to course load. *Room and board:* College room only: $2328. Room and board charges vary according to housing facility. *Payment plans:* installment, deferred payment. *Waivers:* employees or children of employees.

Financial Aid *Financial aid deadline:* 6/30.

Applying *Options:* common application, electronic application, early admission, deferred entrance. *Application fee:* $30. *Required:* high school transcript. *Recommended:* essay or personal statement, minimum 2.0 GPA. *Application deadline:* rolling (freshmen), rolling (transfers). *Notification:* 2/1 (freshmen).

Admissions Contact Ms. Karla Heyward, Interim Director, Morris Brown College, 643 Martin Luther King Jr. Drive, NW, Atlanta, GA 30314. *Phone:* 404-739-1560. *Fax:* 404-739-1565. *E-mail:* admissions@morrisbrown.edu.

NORTH GEORGIA COLLEGE & STATE UNIVERSITY
Dahlonega, Georgia

- **State-supported** comprehensive, founded 1873, part of University System of Georgia
- **Calendar** semesters
- **Degrees** certificates, associate, bachelor's, master's, post-master's, and postbachelor's certificates
- **Small-town** 140-acre campus with easy access to Atlanta
- **Endowment** $1.2 million
- **Coed,** 3,432 undergraduate students, 81% full-time, 65% women, 35% men
- **Moderately difficult** entrance level, 59% of applicants were admitted

Part of the University System of Georgia, NGCSU enrolls 3,900 undergraduate and graduate students and, as the Military College of Georgia, has a cadet corps of 550 men and women. Located an hour from Atlanta, NGCSU offers 50 academic programs in liberal arts and preprofessional programs on one of the safest campuses in America.

Undergraduates 2,775 full-time, 657 part-time. Students come from 28 states and territories, 41 other countries, 3% African American, 0.9% Asian American or Pacific Islander, 1% Hispanic American, 0.5% Native American, 1% international, 15% transferred in. *Retention:* 77% of 2001 full-time freshmen returned.

Freshmen *Admission:* 1,968 applied, 1,169 admitted, 687 enrolled. *Average high school GPA:* 3.33. *Test scores:* SAT verbal scores over 500: 74%; SAT math scores over 500: 63%; SAT verbal scores over 600: 18%; SAT math scores over 600: 17%; SAT verbal scores over 700: 3%; SAT math scores over 700: 2%.

Faculty *Total:* 313, 65% full-time, 53% with terminal degrees. *Student/faculty ratio:* 13:1.

Majors Accounting; art; art education; biology; business administration; business economics; business marketing and marketing management; chemistry; computer/information sciences; computer science; criminal justice/law enforcement administration; early childhood education; education; elementary education; English; finance; French; history; mathematics; middle school education; music; music teacher education; nursing; physical education; physics; political science; pre-dentistry; pre-medicine; pre-veterinary studies; psychology; secondary education; social sciences; sociology; Spanish; special education.

Academic Programs *Special study options:* academic remediation for entering students, advanced placement credit, cooperative education, distance learning, double majors, freshman honors college, honors programs, internships, part-time degree program, services for LD students, study abroad, summer session for credit. *ROTC:* Army (b). *Unusual degree programs:* 3-2 engineering with Georgia Institute of Technology, Clemson University; industrial management, computer science with Georgia Institute of Technology.

Library Stewart Library with 116,676 titles, 2,464 serial subscriptions, 4,496 audiovisual materials, an OPAC, a Web page.

Computers on Campus 500 computers available on campus for general student use. A campuswide network can be accessed from student residence rooms and from off campus. At least one staffed computer lab available.

Student Life *Housing:* on-campus residence required through sophomore year. *Options:* men-only, women-only. *Activities and Organizations:* drama/theater group, student-run newspaper, choral group, marching band, Student Government Association, Greek organizations, College Union Board, Resident Student Affairs Board, Baptist Student Union, national fraternities, national sororities. *Campus security:* 24-hour emergency response devices and patrols, late-night transport/escort service, controlled dormitory access. *Student Services:* health clinic, personal/psychological counseling.

Athletics Member NAIA. *Intercollegiate sports:* basketball M(s)/W(s), cross-country running M(c)/W(c), riflery M(s)/W(s), soccer M(c)/W(c), softball W, tennis M(s)/W(s), track and field M/W. *Intramural sports:* basketball M/W, football M(c)/W(c), golf M(c)/W(c), softball M(c), volleyball M(c)/W(c).

Standardized Tests *Required:* SAT I or ACT (for admission).

Costs (2001–02) *Tuition:* state resident $1932 full-time, $81 per semester hour part-time; nonresident $7728 full-time, $322 per semester hour part-time. Part-time tuition and fees vary according to course load. *Required fees:* $564 full-time, $273 per term part-time. *Room and board:* $3826. Room and board charges vary according to board plan and housing facility. *Waivers:* senior citizens and employees or children of employees.

Financial Aid Of all full-time matriculated undergraduates who enrolled in 2001, 96 Federal Work-Study jobs (averaging $1145). 360 State and other part-time jobs (averaging $1281). *Average indebtedness upon graduation:* $8619.

Applying *Options:* electronic application, early admission, deferred entrance. *Application fee:* $25. *Required:* high school transcript, minimum 2.0 GPA, proof of immunization. *Application deadline:* 7/1 (freshmen), rolling (transfers). *Notification:* continuous (freshmen).

Admissions Contact Robert J. LaVerriere, Director of Admissions and Recruitment, North Georgia College & State University, Admissions Center, 32 College Circle, Dahlonega, GA 30597. *Phone:* 706-864-1800. *Toll-free phone:* 800-498-9581. *Fax:* 706-864-1478. *E-mail:* admissions@ngcsu.edu.

OGLETHORPE UNIVERSITY
Atlanta, Georgia

- **Independent** comprehensive, founded 1835
- **Calendar** semesters
- **Degrees** bachelor's and master's
- **Suburban** 118-acre campus
- **Endowment** $17.5 million
- **Coed,** 1,169 undergraduate students, 81% full-time, 67% women, 33% men
- **Very difficult** entrance level, 70% of applicants were admitted

Undergraduates 942 full-time, 227 part-time. 10% transferred in, 70% live on campus. *Retention:* 81% of 2001 full-time freshmen returned.

Freshmen *Admission:* 761 applied, 529 admitted, 192 enrolled. *Average high school GPA:* 3.65. *Test scores:* SAT verbal scores over 500: 94%; SAT math scores over 500: 88%; ACT scores over 18: 100%; SAT verbal scores over 600: 55%; SAT math scores over 600: 43%; ACT scores over 24: 76%; SAT verbal scores over 700: 14%; SAT math scores over 700: 7%; ACT scores over 30: 20%.

Faculty *Total:* 122, 43% full-time, 89% with terminal degrees. *Student/faculty ratio:* 13:1.

Majors Accounting; American studies; art; biology; business administration; business economics; chemistry; computer science; early childhood education; economics; education; elementary education; English; history; interdisciplinary studies; international relations; mass communications; mathematics; middle school education; philosophy; physics; political science; pre-dentistry; pre-law; pre-medicine; pre-veterinary studies; psychology; secondary education; social work; sociology; urban studies.

Academic Programs *Special study options:* accelerated degree program, adult/continuing education programs, advanced placement credit, cooperative education, double majors, honors programs, independent study, internships, off-campus study, part-time degree program, services for LD students, student-designed majors, study abroad, summer session for credit. *Unusual degree programs:* 3-2 engineering with Auburn University, Georgia Institute of Technology, University of Florida, University of Southern California; art with Atlanta College of Art.

Library Philip Weltner Library with 135,000 titles, 950 serial subscriptions, 520 audiovisual materials, an OPAC, a Web page.

Computers on Campus 60 computers available on campus for general student use. A campuswide network can be accessed from student residence rooms and from off campus. At least one staffed computer lab available.

Student Life *Housing Options:* coed, men-only, women-only. *Activities and Organizations:* drama/theater group, student-run newspaper, radio station, choral group, Alpha Phi Omega, Christian Fellowship, International Club, Playmakers, national fraternities, national sororities. *Campus security:* 24-hour emergency response devices and patrols, student patrols, late-night transport/escort service, controlled dormitory access. *Student Services:* health clinic, personal/psychological counseling.

Athletics Member NCAA. All Division III. *Intercollegiate sports:* baseball M, basketball M/W, cross-country running M/W, golf M, soccer M/W, tennis M/W, track and field M/W, volleyball W. *Intramural sports:* badminton M/W, basketball M/W, football M/W, table tennis M/W, volleyball M/W.

Standardized Tests *Required:* SAT I or ACT (for admission).

Costs (2001–02) *Comprehensive fee:* $25,160 includes full-time tuition ($18,790), mandatory fees ($310), and room and board ($6060). Part-time tuition: $760 per course. Part-time tuition and fees vary according to class time. *Room and board:* Room and board charges vary according to board plan and housing facility. *Payment plans:* tuition prepayment, installment. *Waivers:* employees or children of employees.

Financial Aid Of all full-time matriculated undergraduates who enrolled in 2001, 708 applied for aid, 323 were judged to have need, 169 had their need fully met. In 2001, 335 non-need-based awards were made. *Average percent of need met:* 90%. *Average financial aid package:* $19,420. *Average need-based loan:* $3437. *Average need-based gift aid:* $11,820. *Average non-need based aid:* $9547. *Average indebtedness upon graduation:* $16,400.

Applying *Options:* common application, electronic application, early action, deferred entrance. *Application fee:* $30. *Required:* essay or personal statement, high school transcript, 1 letter of recommendation. *Required for some:* interview. *Recommended:* minimum 2.5 GPA, interview. *Application deadline:* rolling (freshmen), rolling (transfers). *Notification:* continuous until 2/1 (freshmen), 1/15 (early action).

Admissions Contact Mr. Dennis T. Matthews, Associate Dean for Enrollment Management, Oglethorpe University, 4484 Peachtree Road, NE, Atlanta, GA 30319-2797. *Phone:* 404-364-8307. *Toll-free phone:* 800-428-4484. *Fax:* 404-364-8500. *E-mail:* admission@oglethorpe.edu.

PAINE COLLEGE

Augusta, Georgia

- **Independent Methodist** 4-year, founded 1882
- **Calendar** semesters
- **Degree** bachelor's
- **Urban** 54-acre campus
- **Coed,** 888 undergraduate students, 84% full-time, 71% women, 29% men
- **Minimally difficult** entrance level, 28% of applicants were admitted

Undergraduates 746 full-time, 142 part-time. Students come from 29 states and territories, 2 other countries, 21% are from out of state, 98% African American, 0.1% Asian American or Pacific Islander, 0.3% Hispanic American, 0.2% international, 5% transferred in, 58% live on campus. *Retention:* 66% of 2001 full-time freshmen returned.

Freshmen *Admission:* 2,252 applied, 625 admitted, 207 enrolled. *Average high school GPA:* 2.79. *Test scores:* SAT verbal scores over 500: 47%; SAT math scores over 500: 40%; ACT scores over 18: 18%; SAT verbal scores over 600: 9%; SAT math scores over 600: 5%; ACT scores over 24: 1%; SAT verbal scores over 700: 1%.

Faculty *Total:* 80, 79% full-time, 53% with terminal degrees. *Student/faculty ratio:* 12:1.

Majors Biology; business administration; chemistry; early childhood education; elementary education; English; history; mass communications; mathematics; music teacher education; philosophy; pre-dentistry; pre-medicine; preveterinary studies; psychology; religious studies; secondary education; sociology.

Academic Programs *Special study options:* academic remediation for entering students, accelerated degree program, advanced placement credit, cooperative education, honors programs, independent study, internships, off-campus study, services for LD students, study abroad, summer session for credit. *ROTC:* Army (c). *Unusual degree programs:* 3-2 engineering with Georgia Institute of Technology, Florida Agricultural and Mechanical University.

Library Collins-Callaway Library with 76,120 titles, 4,350 serial subscriptions, 1,407 audiovisual materials.

Computers on Campus 71 computers available on campus for general student use. A campuswide network can be accessed from student residence rooms and from off campus. Internet access, at least one staffed computer lab available.

Student Life *Housing Options:* men-only, women-only. *Activities and Organizations:* drama/theater group, student-run newspaper, choral group, national fraternities, national sororities. *Campus security:* 24-hour patrols, late-night transport/escort service. *Student Services:* health clinic, personal/psychological counseling.

Athletics Member NCAA. All Division II. *Intercollegiate sports:* baseball M(s), basketball M(s)/W(s), cross-country running M(s)/W(s), softball W, track and field M(s)/W(s), volleyball W(s). *Intramural sports:* baseball M, basketball M/W, football M, softball M/W, table tennis M/W, tennis M/W, track and field M/W, volleyball M/W, weight lifting M/W.

Standardized Tests *Required:* SAT I or ACT (for admission).

Costs (2001–02) *Comprehensive fee:* $11,896 includes full-time tuition ($7736), mandatory fees ($554), and room and board ($3606). Full-time tuition and fees vary according to course load and reciprocity agreements. Part-time tuition: $322 per credit hour. Part-time tuition and fees vary according to course load, location, and reciprocity agreements. *Required fees:* $277 per term part-time. *Room and board:* Room and board charges vary according to board plan and housing facility. *Payment plan:* installment. *Waivers:* children of alumni and employees or children of employees.

Applying *Options:* early admission, deferred entrance. *Application fee:* $10. *Required:* essay or personal statement, high school transcript, minimum 2.0 GPA, medical history. *Recommended:* 2 letters of recommendation. *Application deadlines:* 8/1 (freshmen), 8/1 (transfers). *Notification:* continuous (freshmen).

Admissions Contact Mr. Joseph Tinsley, Director of Admissions, Paine College, 1235 15th Street, Augusta, GA 30901-3182. *Phone:* 706-821-8320. *Toll-free phone:* 800-476-7703. *Fax:* 706-821-8691. *E-mail:* tinsleyj@mail.paine.edu.

PIEDMONT COLLEGE

Demorest, Georgia

- **Independent** comprehensive, founded 1897, affiliated with Congregational Christian Church
- **Calendar** semesters
- **Degrees** bachelor's and master's
- **Rural** 115-acre campus with easy access to Atlanta
- **Endowment** $46.2 million
- **Coed,** 990 undergraduate students, 85% full-time, 63% women, 37% men
- **Moderately difficult** entrance level, 67% of applicants were admitted

Undergraduates 839 full-time, 151 part-time. Students come from 16 states and territories, 2% are from out of state, 8% African American, 0.9% Asian American or Pacific Islander, 2% Hispanic American, 0.2% Native American, 0.1% international, 12% transferred in, 16% live on campus. *Retention:* 75% of 2001 full-time freshmen returned.

Freshmen *Admission:* 377 applied, 251 admitted, 206 enrolled. *Average high school GPA:* 3.00. *Test scores:* SAT verbal scores over 500: 51%; SAT math scores over 500: 47%; SAT verbal scores over 600: 13%; SAT math scores over 600: 10%; SAT math scores over 700: 1%.

Faculty *Total:* 169, 50% full-time, 74% with terminal degrees. *Student/faculty ratio:* 12:1.

Majors Biology; business administration; chemistry; computer science; early childhood education; English; environmental science; fine/studio arts; history; information sciences/systems; interdisciplinary studies; journalism; mass communications; mathematics; middle school education; music; music (general performance); nursing; philosophy; psychology; religious music; religious studies; secondary education; social sciences; sociology; Spanish; special education; theater arts/drama.

Academic Programs *Special study options:* academic remediation for entering students, accelerated degree program, adult/continuing education programs, advanced placement credit, cooperative education, distance learning, double majors, freshman honors college, honors programs, independent study, internships, off-campus study, part-time degree program, services for LD students, student-designed majors, study abroad, summer session for credit. *Unusual degree programs:* 3-2 teacher education, public administration.

Library Arrendale Library with 110,000 titles, 346 serial subscriptions, 474 audiovisual materials, an OPAC, a Web page.

Piedmont College (continued)

Computers on Campus 100 computers available on campus for general student use. A campuswide network can be accessed from student residence rooms and from off campus that provide access to e-mail. Internet access, at least one staffed computer lab available.

Student Life *Housing:* on-campus residence required through junior year. *Options:* coed, men-only, women-only, disabled students. *Activities and Organizations:* drama/theater group, student-run newspaper, radio station, choral group, student government, Student Georgia Association of Educators, Students In Free Enterprise, psychology club, Alternatives. *Campus security:* 24-hour emergency response devices and patrols, late-night transport/escort service. *Student Services:* personal/psychological counseling.

Athletics Member NCAA, NCCAA. *Intercollegiate sports:* baseball M(s), basketball M(s)/W(s), cross-country running M/W, soccer M(s)/W(s), softball W(s), tennis M/W, volleyball W(s). *Intramural sports:* basketball M/W, crew M/W, cross-country running M/W, football M/W, soccer M/W, softball M/W, table tennis M/W, tennis M/W, volleyball M/W, weight lifting M/W.

Standardized Tests *Required:* SAT I or ACT (for admission).

Costs (2001–02) *Comprehensive fee:* $14,900 includes full-time tuition ($10,500) and room and board ($4400). Full-time tuition and fees vary according to course load and program. Part-time tuition: $438 per semester hour. Part-time tuition and fees vary according to course load and program. *Required fees:* $438 per semester hour. *Room and board:* College room only: $2250. Room and board charges vary according to board plan and housing facility. *Payment plan:* installment. *Waivers:* employees or children of employees.

Financial Aid Of all full-time matriculated undergraduates who enrolled in 2001, 834 applied for aid, 750 were judged to have need, 292 had their need fully met. 71 Federal Work-Study jobs (averaging $2439). In 2001, 85 non-need-based awards were made. *Average percent of need met:* 76%. *Average financial aid package:* $8410. *Average need-based loan:* $5730. *Average need-based gift aid:* $2990. *Average non-need based aid:* $2460. *Average indebtedness upon graduation:* $13,342.

Applying *Options:* common application, early admission, deferred entrance. *Application fee:* $20. *Required:* high school transcript, minimum 2.0 GPA. *Required for some:* interview. *Recommended:* essay or personal statement. *Application deadline:* rolling (freshmen), rolling (transfers).

Admissions Contact Ms. Kathy Edwards Rarey, Director of Undergraduate Admissions, Piedmont College, PO Box 10, Demorest, GA 30535-0010. *Phone:* 706-776-0103 Ext. 1299. *Toll-free phone:* 800-277-7020. *Fax:* 706-776-6635. *E-mail:* kedwards@piedmont.edu.

REINHARDT COLLEGE
Waleska, Georgia

- **Independent** 4-year, founded 1883, affiliated with United Methodist Church
- **Calendar** semesters
- **Degrees** associate and bachelor's
- **Rural** 600-acre campus with easy access to Atlanta
- **Endowment** $44.5 million
- **Coed,** 1,083 undergraduate students, 87% full-time, 59% women, 41% men
- **Moderately difficult** entrance level, 85% of applicants were admitted

Undergraduates 937 full-time, 146 part-time. Students come from 7 states and territories, 20 other countries, 5% are from out of state, 2% transferred in, 39% live on campus.

Freshmen *Admission:* 546 applied, 463 admitted, 235 enrolled.

Faculty *Total:* 106, 45% full-time. *Student/faculty ratio:* 15:1.

Majors Art; biology; business administration; early childhood education; education; health/physical education/fitness related; information sciences/systems; liberal arts and sciences/liberal studies; mass communications; middle school education; music; nursing; physical education; psychology; sociology; sport/fitness administration.

Academic Programs *Special study options:* academic remediation for entering students, adult/continuing education programs, advanced placement credit, cooperative education, double majors, external degree program, honors programs, independent study, internships, part-time degree program, services for LD students, study abroad, summer session for credit.

Library Hill Freeman Library with 41,032 titles, 351 serial subscriptions, 15,836 audiovisual materials, an OPAC, a Web page.

Computers on Campus 90 computers available on campus for general student use. A campuswide network can be accessed from student residence rooms and from off campus. Internet access, at least one staffed computer lab available.

Student Life *Housing:* on-campus residence required through sophomore year. *Options:* men-only, women-only. *Activities and Organizations:* student-run newspaper, television station, choral group, Real Deal, International & Historical Film Society, Student Government Association, SOAR-Student Orientation Leaders, Communication Club. *Campus security:* student patrols, late-night transport/escort service. *Student Services:* health clinic, personal/psychological counseling.

Athletics Member NAIA. *Intercollegiate sports:* basketball M(s)/W(s), golf M(s), soccer M(s)/W(s), tennis M(s)/W(s). *Intramural sports:* basketball M/W, football M/W, soccer M/W, softball M/W, volleyball M/W.

Standardized Tests *Required:* SAT I or ACT (for admission).

Costs (2002–03) *Comprehensive fee:* $13,585 includes full-time tuition ($8700) and room and board ($4885). Part-time tuition: $290 per credit hour. *Room and board:* College room only: $2300.

Financial Aid Of all full-time matriculated undergraduates who enrolled in 2001, 54 Federal Work-Study jobs (averaging $1351). 156 State and other part-time jobs (averaging $870). *Average financial aid package:* $7795.

Applying *Options:* common application, electronic application, early admission, deferred entrance. *Application fee:* $25. *Required:* high school transcript, minimum 2.0 GPA. *Recommended:* essay or personal statement, interview. *Application deadline:* rolling (freshmen), rolling (transfers). *Notification:* continuous (freshmen).

Admissions Contact Ms. Kathryn Smith, Director of Admissions, Reinhardt College, 7300 Reinhardt College Circle, Waleska, GA 30183-0128. *Phone:* 770-720-5526. *Toll-free phone:* 87-REINHARDT. *Fax:* 770-720-5602. *E-mail:* admissions@mail.reinhardt.edu.

SAVANNAH COLLEGE OF ART AND DESIGN
Savannah, Georgia

- **Independent** comprehensive, founded 1978
- **Calendar** quarters
- **Degrees** bachelor's and master's
- **Urban** campus
- **Coed,** 4,707 undergraduate students, 90% full-time, 46% women, 54% men
- **Moderately difficult** entrance level, 84% of applicants were admitted

The College is situated in Savannah's renowned historic district, a creative environment conducive to study, research, and artistic expression. The College exists to prepare talented students for careers, offering a well-rounded curriculum that emphasizes individual attention. The student body represents all 50 states and more than 75 countries.

Undergraduates 4,221 full-time, 486 part-time. Students come from 52 states and territories, 75 other countries, 79% are from out of state, 5% African American, 2% Asian American or Pacific Islander, 3% Hispanic American, 0.3% Native American, 7% international, 9% transferred in, 36% live on campus. *Retention:* 81% of 2001 full-time freshmen returned.

Freshmen *Admission:* 3,169 applied, 2,664 admitted, 1,038 enrolled. *Test scores:* SAT verbal scores over 500: 72%; SAT math scores over 500: 61%; ACT scores over 18: 93%; SAT verbal scores over 600: 29%; SAT math scores over 600: 21%; ACT scores over 24: 44%; SAT verbal scores over 700: 5%; SAT math scores over 700: 3%; ACT scores over 30: 5%.

Faculty *Total:* 285, 85% full-time, 84% with terminal degrees. *Student/faculty ratio:* 18:1.

Majors Applied art; architectural history; architecture; art; art history; computer graphics; fashion design/illustration; film/video production; graphic design/commercial art/illustration; industrial design; interior design; metal/jewelry arts; painting; photography; textile arts; visual/performing arts.

Academic Programs *Special study options:* advanced placement credit, double majors, English as a second language, independent study, internships, part-time degree program, services for LD students, study abroad, summer session for credit.

Library Savannah College of Art and Design Library plus 1 other with 72,000 titles, 900 serial subscriptions, 2,100 audiovisual materials, an OPAC, a Web page.

Computers on Campus 664 computers available on campus for general student use. A campuswide network can be accessed from student residence rooms and from off campus. Internet access, online (class) registration, at least one staffed computer lab available.

Student Life *Housing Options:* coed, men-only, women-only, disabled students. *Activities and Organizations:* drama/theater group, student-run newspaper, choral group, United Student Forum, Inter-Club Council, American Institute of Architecture Students, Intercultural Council, American Society of Interior Designers. *Campus security:* 24-hour emergency response devices and patrols, late-night transport/escort service, video camera surveillance. *Student Services:* health clinic, personal/psychological counseling.

Athletics Member NCAA. All Division III. *Intercollegiate sports:* baseball M, basketball M/W, crew M/W, equestrian sports M/W, golf M/W, sailing M(c)/W(c), soccer M/W, softball W, tennis M/W, volleyball W. *Intramural sports:* basketball M/W, bowling M/W, equestrian sports M(c)/W(c), football M.

Standardized Tests *Required:* SAT I or ACT (for admission).

Costs (2002–03) *One-time required fee:* $500. *Comprehensive fee:* $25,575 includes full-time tuition ($17,955) and room and board ($7620). Part-time tuition: $1995 per course. *Room and board:* College room only: $4800. Room and board charges vary according to board plan and housing facility. *Payment plan:* installment. *Waivers:* employees or children of employees.

Financial Aid Of all full-time matriculated undergraduates who enrolled in 2001, 2381 applied for aid, 1952 were judged to have need, 621 had their need fully met. 146 Federal Work-Study jobs (averaging $1000). 543 State and other part-time jobs (averaging $1000). In 2001, 304 non-need-based awards were made. *Average percent of need met:* 48%. *Average financial aid package:* $8614. *Average need-based loan:* $5500. *Average need-based gift aid:* $4010. *Average non-need based aid:* $1478. *Average indebtedness upon graduation:* $20,000.

Applying *Options:* electronic application, early admission. *Application fee:* $50. *Required:* high school transcript, 3 letters of recommendation. *Recommended:* interview. *Application deadline:* rolling (freshmen), rolling (transfers). *Notification:* continuous (freshmen).

Admissions Contact Ms. Pamela Afifi, Vice President for Admission, Savannah College of Art and Design, 342 Bull Street, PO Box 3146, Savannah, GA 31402-3146. *Phone:* 912-525-5100. *Toll-free phone:* 800-869-7223. *Fax:* 912-525-5983. *E-mail:* admission@scad.edu.

SAVANNAH STATE UNIVERSITY
Savannah, Georgia

- **State-supported** comprehensive, founded 1890, part of University System of Georgia
- **Calendar** semesters
- **Degrees** bachelor's and master's
- **Suburban** 165-acre campus
- **Endowment** $72,919
- **Coed,** 2,259 undergraduate students
- **Minimally difficult** entrance level, 27% of applicants were admitted

Undergraduates Students come from 28 states and territories, 18 other countries, 17% are from out of state, 45% live on campus. *Retention:* 68% of 2001 full-time freshmen returned.

Freshmen *Admission:* 2,500 applied, 670 admitted. *Average high school GPA:* 2.60.

Faculty *Total:* 138, 83% full-time, 66% with terminal degrees. *Student/faculty ratio:* 16:1.

Majors Accounting; African-American studies; biology; business administration; business marketing and marketing management; chemical engineering technology; chemistry; civil engineering; civil engineering technology; computer engineering; computer engineering technology; criminal justice/law enforcement administration; electrical/electronic engineering technology; English; environmental science; history; international business; management information systems/business data processing; marine biology; mass communications; mathematics; mechanical engineering technology; music; political science; recreation/leisure facilities management; social work; sociology.

Academic Programs *Special study options:* academic remediation for entering students, accelerated degree program, adult/continuing education programs, advanced placement credit, cooperative education, internships, off-campus study, part-time degree program, services for LD students, summer session for credit. *ROTC:* Army (b), Navy (b). *Unusual degree programs:* 3-2 engineering with Georgia Institute of Technology.

Library Asa H. Gordon Library with 187,916 titles, 812 serial subscriptions, an OPAC, a Web page.

Computers on Campus 440 computers available on campus for general student use. Internet access, at least one staffed computer lab available.

Student Life *Housing:* on-campus residence required through junior year. *Options:* men-only, women-only. *Activities and Organizations:* drama/theater group, student-run newspaper, radio station, choral group, marching band, marching band, gospel choir, concert chair, national fraternities, national sororities. *Campus security:* 24-hour patrols. *Student Services:* health clinic, personal/psychological counseling.

Athletics Member NCAA. All Division II. *Intercollegiate sports:* baseball M(s), basketball M(s)/W(s), cross-country running W(s), football M(s), tennis W(s), track and field M(s)/W(s), volleyball W(s). *Intramural sports:* basketball M/W, football M/W, softball M/W, swimming M/W, table tennis M/W, tennis M/W, track and field M/W, volleyball M/W, weight lifting M/W.

Standardized Tests *Required:* SAT I or ACT (for admission). *Required for some:* SAT II: Subject Tests (for admission). *Recommended:* SAT I (for admission).

Costs (2001–02) *Tuition:* state resident $1932 full-time, $492 per course part-time; nonresident $7728 full-time, $1215 per course part-time. *Required fees:* $618 full-time. *Room and board:* $4204; room only: $2120. Room and board charges vary according to student level.

Applying *Options:* common application, electronic application, early admission, deferred entrance. *Application fee:* $20. *Required:* high school transcript, minimum 2.0 GPA. *Application deadlines:* 6/1 (freshmen), 6/1 (transfers). *Notification:* continuous (freshmen).

Admissions Contact Mrs. Gwendolyn J. Moore, Associate Director of Admissions, Savannah State University, PO Box 20209, Savannah, GA 31404. *Phone:* 912-356-2181. *Toll-free phone:* 800-788-0478. *Fax:* 912-356-2566.

SHORTER COLLEGE
Rome, Georgia

- **Independent Baptist** comprehensive, founded 1873
- **Calendar** semesters
- **Degrees** associate and bachelor's
- **Small-town** 155-acre campus with easy access to Atlanta
- **Endowment** $28.5 million
- **Coed,** 970 undergraduate students, 95% full-time, 67% women, 33% men
- **Moderately difficult** entrance level, 86% of applicants were admitted

Undergraduates 920 full-time, 50 part-time. Students come from 18 states and territories, 18 other countries, 6% are from out of state, 4% African American, 0.6% Asian American or Pacific Islander, 1% Hispanic American, 0.5% Native American, 3% international, 6% transferred in, 60% live on campus. *Retention:* 68% of 2001 full-time freshmen returned.

Freshmen *Admission:* 687 applied, 592 admitted, 258 enrolled. *Average high school GPA:* 3.44. *Test scores:* SAT verbal scores over 500: 65%; SAT math scores over 500: 63%; ACT scores over 18: 90%; SAT verbal scores over 600: 23%; SAT math scores over 600: 16%; ACT scores over 24: 32%; SAT verbal scores over 700: 3%; SAT math scores over 700: 2%; ACT scores over 30: 1%.

Faculty *Total:* 115, 56% full-time, 44% with terminal degrees. *Student/faculty ratio:* 12:1.

Majors Accounting; art; art education; biology; broadcast journalism; business administration; chemistry; divinity/ministry; economics; elementary education; English; environmental science; fine/studio arts; French; history; humanities; journalism; liberal arts and sciences/liberal studies; mathematics; music; music (piano and organ performance); music teacher education; music (voice and choral/opera performance); natural sciences; psychology; public relations; recreational therapy; recreation/leisure studies; religious music; religious studies; science education; secondary education; social sciences; sociology; Spanish; theater arts/drama.

Academic Programs *Special study options:* academic remediation for entering students, accelerated degree program, adult/continuing education programs, advanced placement credit, distance learning, double majors, honors programs, independent study, internships, off-campus study, part-time degree program, services for LD students, student-designed majors, study abroad, summer session for credit.

Library Livingston Library with 82,597 titles, 612 serial subscriptions, 10,916 audiovisual materials, an OPAC, a Web page.

Computers on Campus 100 computers available on campus for general student use. A campuswide network can be accessed from student residence rooms that provide access to e-mail. Internet access, at least one staffed computer lab available.

Student Life *Housing:* on-campus residence required through senior year. *Options:* men-only, women-only, disabled students. *Activities and Organizations:* drama/theater group, student-run newspaper, radio and television station, choral group, marching band, Baptist Student Union, Student Government Association, Fellowship of Christian Athletes, Shorter Players, Habitat for Humanity. *Campus security:* 24-hour emergency response devices and patrols. *Student Services:* health clinic, personal/psychological counseling.

Athletics Member NAIA. *Intercollegiate sports:* baseball M(s), basketball M(s)/W(s), cross-country running M(s)/W(s), golf M(s)/W(s), soccer W(s), tennis M(s)/W(s), track and field M(s)/W(s). *Intramural sports:* basketball M/W, bowling M/W, soccer M, table tennis M/W, tennis M/W, volleyball M/W.

Standardized Tests *Required:* SAT I or ACT (for admission).

Costs (2001–02) *Comprehensive fee:* $15,185 includes full-time tuition ($9800), mandatory fees ($120), and room and board ($5265). Full-time tuition and fees vary according to course load. Part-time tuition: $240 per credit hour. *Room and*

Shorter College (continued)
board: College room only: $2985. Room and board charges vary according to board plan and housing facility. *Payment plan:* installment. *Waivers:* senior citizens and employees or children of employees.

Financial Aid Of all full-time matriculated undergraduates who enrolled in 2001, 811 applied for aid, 675 were judged to have need, 179 had their need fully met. 93 Federal Work-Study jobs (averaging $1445). 129 State and other part-time jobs (averaging $1296). In 2001, 136 non-need-based awards were made. *Average percent of need met:* 68%. *Average financial aid package:* $8905. *Average need-based loan:* $3266. *Average need-based gift aid:* $6602. *Average non-need based aid:* $7553. *Average indebtedness upon graduation:* $17,108.

Applying *Options:* early admission, deferred entrance. *Application fee:* $25. *Required:* essay or personal statement, high school transcript. *Required for some:* interview, audition for music and theater programs. *Recommended:* minimum 2.0 GPA, 1 letter of recommendation, interview. *Application deadlines:* 8/25 (freshmen), 8/25 (transfers).

Admissions Contact Ms. Wendy Sutton, Director of Admissions, Shorter College, 315 Shorter Avenue, Rome, GA 30165. *Phone:* 706-233-7342. *Toll-free phone:* 800-868-6980. *Fax:* 706-236-7224. *E-mail:* admissions@shorter.edu.

SOUTHERN POLYTECHNIC STATE UNIVERSITY
Marietta, Georgia

- **State-supported** comprehensive, founded 1948, part of University System of Georgia
- **Calendar** semesters
- **Degrees** certificates, associate, bachelor's, master's, and postbachelor's certificates
- **Suburban** 200-acre campus with easy access to Atlanta
- **Coed,** 2,943 undergraduate students, 60% full-time, 17% women, 83% men
- **Moderately difficult** entrance level, 61% of applicants were admitted

Undergraduates 1,753 full-time, 1,190 part-time. Students come from 40 states and territories, 4% are from out of state, 19% African American, 6% Asian American or Pacific Islander, 3% Hispanic American, 0.2% Native American, 4% international, 12% transferred in, 14% live on campus. *Retention:* 60% of 2001 full-time freshmen returned.

Freshmen *Admission:* 916 applied, 555 admitted, 403 enrolled. *Average high school GPA:* 3.15. *Test scores:* SAT verbal scores over 500: 72%; SAT math scores over 500: 85%; ACT scores over 18: 99%; SAT verbal scores over 600: 17%; SAT math scores over 600: 32%; ACT scores over 24: 31%; SAT verbal scores over 700: 2%; SAT math scores over 700: 4%; ACT scores over 30: 2%.

Faculty *Total:* 207, 67% full-time. *Student/faculty ratio:* 17:1.

Majors Architectural engineering technology; architecture; civil engineering technology; computer engineering technology; computer/information sciences; construction technology; electrical/electronic engineering technology; enterprise management; industrial technology; liberal arts and sciences/liberal studies; mathematics; mechanical engineering technology; physics; surveying; technical/business writing; telecommunications.

Academic Programs *Special study options:* adult/continuing education programs, advanced placement credit, cooperative education, distance learning, double majors, independent study, internships, part-time degree program, services for LD students, study abroad, summer session for credit. *ROTC:* Army (c), Navy (c), Air Force (c).

Library Lawrence V. Johnson Library with 194,302 titles, 1,415 serial subscriptions, 62 audiovisual materials, an OPAC.

Computers on Campus 500 computers available on campus for general student use. A campuswide network can be accessed from off campus. At least one staffed computer lab available.

Student Life *Housing Options:* coed. *Activities and Organizations:* student-run newspaper, radio station, International Student Association, Campus Activities Board, National Society of Black Engineers, Aerial Robotics Team, Intergreek Council, national fraternities, national sororities. *Campus security:* 24-hour emergency response devices and patrols, late-night transport/escort service, controlled dormitory access. *Student Services:* health clinic, personal/psychological counseling.

Athletics Member NAIA. *Intercollegiate sports:* baseball M(s), basketball M(s), tennis M(s). *Intramural sports:* badminton M/W, basketball M/W, bowling M/W, football M/W, golf M/W, racquetball M/W, soccer M/W, softball M/W, table tennis M/W, tennis M/W, volleyball M/W.

Standardized Tests *Required:* SAT I or ACT (for admission). *Required for some:* SAT II: Subject Tests (for admission).

Costs (2001–02) *Tuition:* state resident $1932 full-time, $81 per hour part-time; nonresident $7728 full-time, $322 per hour part-time. Part-time tuition and fees vary according to course load. *Required fees:* $422 full-time. *Room and board:* $4308; room only: $2102. *Waivers:* senior citizens.

Financial Aid Of all full-time matriculated undergraduates who enrolled in 2001, 1336 applied for aid, 1040 were judged to have need, 262 had their need fully met. 30 Federal Work-Study jobs (averaging $1774). In 2001, 269 non-need-based awards were made. *Average percent of need met:* 78%. *Average financial aid package:* $4082. *Average need-based loan:* $3572. *Average need-based gift aid:* $2270. *Average non-need based aid:* $4262. *Average indebtedness upon graduation:* $16,585.

Applying *Options:* early admission. *Application fee:* $20. *Required:* high school transcript, minimum 2.0 GPA, proof of immunization. *Application deadlines:* 8/1 (freshmen), 8/1 (transfers). *Notification:* continuous (freshmen).

Admissions Contact Ms. Virginia A. Head, Director of Admissions, Southern Polytechnic State University, Marietta, GA 30060-2896. *Phone:* 770-528-7281. *Toll-free phone:* 800-635-3204. *Fax:* 770-528-7292. *E-mail:* admissions@spsu.edu.

SOUTH UNIVERSITY
Savannah, Georgia

- **Proprietary** 4-year, founded 1899
- **Calendar** quarters
- **Degrees** associate and bachelor's
- **Suburban** 6-acre campus
- **Coed**
- **Minimally difficult** entrance level

Student Life *Campus security:* late-night transport/escort service.

Applying *Options:* deferred entrance. *Application fee:* $25. *Required:* high school transcript, interview. *Required for some:* essay or personal statement, 3 letters of recommendation.

Admissions Contact Ms. Deborah Welsh, Director of Admissions, South University, 709 Mall Boulevard, Savannah, GA 31406-4881. *Phone:* 912-691-6000. *Fax:* 912-691-6070. *E-mail:* southcollege@southcollege.edu.

SPELMAN COLLEGE
Atlanta, Georgia

- **Independent** 4-year, founded 1881
- **Calendar** semesters
- **Degree** bachelor's
- **Urban** 32-acre campus
- **Endowment** $228.9 million
- **Women only,** 2,139 undergraduate students, 97% full-time
- **Very difficult** entrance level, 49% of applicants were admitted

Spelman College is a historically black, privately endowed, 4-year liberal arts college for women. Founded in 1881 as the Atlanta Baptist Female Seminary, Spelman today is one of America's top liberal arts colleges, providing academic excellence for women as well as an environment that encourages leadership development and community service experience. Spelman's commitment to excellence is demonstrated by its dedicated, accessible faculty and low student-faculty ratio as well as by the outstanding success of students and alumnae.

Undergraduates Students come from 41 states and territories, 15 other countries, 70% are from out of state, 97% African American, 0.2% Hispanic American, 2% international, 53% live on campus. *Retention:* 91% of 2001 full-time freshmen returned.

Freshmen *Average high school GPA:* 3.30. *Test scores:* SAT verbal scores over 500: 73%; SAT math scores over 500: 65%; ACT scores over 18: 100%; SAT verbal scores over 600: 21%; SAT math scores over 600: 13%; ACT scores over 24: 47%; ACT scores over 30: 24%.

Faculty *Total:* 204, 76% full-time. *Student/faculty ratio:* 12:1.

Majors Art; biochemistry; biology; chemistry; computer science; developmental/child psychology; economics; engineering; English; environmental science; French; history; mathematics; music; natural sciences; philosophy; physics; political science; psychology; religious studies; sociology; Spanish; theater arts/drama; women's studies.

Academic Programs *Special study options:* academic remediation for entering students, adult/continuing education programs, advanced placement credit, double majors, honors programs, independent study, internships, off-campus study, part-time degree program, services for LD students, student-designed majors, study abroad. *ROTC:* Army (c), Navy (c), Air Force (c). *Unusual degree* *programs:* 3-2 engineering with North Carolina Agricultural and Technical State University, Rensselaer Polytechnic Institute, Georgia Institute of Technology, Boston University, The University of Alabama in Huntsville, Auburn University.

Library Robert Woodruff Library with 404,991 titles, 2,693 serial subscriptions, an OPAC.

Computers on Campus 105 computers available on campus for general student use. A campuswide network can be accessed from off campus. Internet access, online (class) registration, at least one staffed computer lab available.

Student Life *Housing Options:* women-only. *Activities and Organizations:* drama/theater group, student-run newspaper, choral group, Student Government Association, Spotlight (newspaper), Health Career Club, NAACP (campus organization), SHAPE (health organization), national sororities. *Campus security:* 24-hour emergency response devices and patrols, late-night transport/escort service, controlled dormitory access. *Student Services:* health clinic, personal/psychological counseling, women's center.

Athletics *Intercollegiate sports:* basketball W, cross-country running W, golf W, soccer W, tennis W, track and field W, volleyball W. *Intramural sports:* softball W, swimming W.

Standardized Tests *Required:* SAT I or ACT (for admission).

Costs (2001–02) *Comprehensive fee:* $18,930 includes full-time tuition ($10,150), mandatory fees ($1730), and room and board ($7050). Part-time tuition: $423 per hour. Part-time tuition and fees vary according to course load. *Payment plan:* deferred payment. *Waivers:* employees or children of employees.

Applying *Options:* common application, electronic application, early admission, early action, deferred entrance. *Application fee:* $35. *Required:* essay or personal statement, high school transcript, minimum 2.0 GPA, 2 letters of recommendation. *Required for some:* interview. *Application deadlines:* 2/1 (freshmen), 2/1 (transfers). *Notification:* 4/1 (freshmen), 12/31 (early action).

Admissions Contact Ms. Theodora Riley, Interim Director of Admissions and Orientation Services, Spelman College, 350 Spelman Lane, SW, Atlanta, GA 30314-4399. *Phone:* 404-681-3643 Ext. 2585. *Toll-free phone:* 800-982-2411. *Fax:* 404-215-7788. *E-mail:* admiss@spelman.edu.

STATE UNIVERSITY OF WEST GEORGIA

Carrollton, Georgia

- **State-supported** comprehensive, founded 1933, part of University System of Georgia
- **Calendar** semesters
- **Degrees** bachelor's, master's, doctoral, and post-master's certificates
- **Small-town** 400-acre campus with easy access to Atlanta
- **Coed,** 7,254 undergraduate students, 83% full-time, 61% women, 39% men
- **Minimally difficult** entrance level, 60% of applicants were admitted

Undergraduates Students come from 36 states and territories, 66 other countries, 5% are from out of state, 22% African American, 0.9% Asian American or Pacific Islander, 1% Hispanic American, 0.3% Native American, 1% international, 28% live on campus. *Retention:* 70% of 2001 full-time freshmen returned.

Freshmen *Admission:* 4,453 applied, 2,671 admitted. *Average high school GPA:* 2.99. *Test scores:* SAT verbal scores over 500: 49%; SAT math scores over 500: 48%; ACT scores over 18: 82%; SAT verbal scores over 600: 11%; SAT math scores over 600: 10%; ACT scores over 24: 14%; SAT verbal scores over 700: 1%; SAT math scores over 700: 1%; ACT scores over 30: 1%.

Faculty *Total:* 438, 79% full-time, 72% with terminal degrees. *Student/faculty ratio:* 19:1.

Majors Accounting; anthropology; art; art education; biology; biology education; business administration; business economics; business education; business marketing and marketing management; chemistry; chemistry education; computer science; criminal justice/law enforcement administration; earth sciences; ecology; economics; economics related; education of the mentally handicapped; elementary education; English; English education; environmental science; finance; foreign languages education; French; geography; geology; history; international economics; international relations; liberal arts and sciences/liberal studies; management information systems/business data processing; mass communications; mathematics; mathematics education; middle school education; music (general performance); music teacher education; music theory and composition; nursing; office management; philosophy; physical education; physics; physics education; political science; pre-law; pre-medicine; pre-veterinary studies; psychology; real estate; recreation/leisure facilities management; science education; secondary education; social studies education; sociology; Spanish; special education; speech-language pathology; theater arts/drama.

Academic Programs *Special study options:* academic remediation for entering students, accelerated degree program, adult/continuing education programs, advanced placement credit, cooperative education, distance learning, double majors, honors programs, independent study, internships, off-campus study, part-time degree program, services for LD students, study abroad, summer session for credit. *ROTC:* Army (b). *Unusual degree programs:* 3-2 engineering with Georgia Institute of Technology, Auburn University.

Library Irvine Sullivan Ingram Library with 292,883 titles, 2,095 serial subscriptions, an OPAC, a Web page.

Computers on Campus A campuswide network can be accessed from student residence rooms and from off campus. Internet access, online (class) registration, at least one staffed computer lab available.

Student Life *Housing:* on-campus residence required for freshman year. *Options:* coed, men-only, women-only. *Activities and Organizations:* drama/theater group, student-run newspaper, radio and television station, choral group, marching band, Black Student Alliance, Student Activities Council, Baptist Student Union, Campus Outreach, United Voices Gospel Choir, national fraternities, national sororities. *Campus security:* 24-hour emergency response devices and patrols, late-night transport/escort service, controlled dormitory access. *Student Services:* health clinic, personal/psychological counseling.

Athletics Member NCAA. All Division II. *Intercollegiate sports:* baseball M(s), basketball M(s)/W(s), cross-country running M(s)/W(s), football M(s), softball W(s), volleyball W(s). *Intramural sports:* badminton M/W, basketball M/W, bowling M/W, football M/W, golf M/W, racquetball M/W, soccer M/W, softball M/W, swimming M/W, table tennis M/W, tennis M/W, track and field M/W, volleyball M/W, water polo M/W, weight lifting M/W.

Standardized Tests *Required:* SAT I or ACT (for admission).

Costs (2001–02) *Tuition:* state resident $1932 full-time, $81 per semester hour part-time; nonresident $7728 full-time, $322 per semester hour part-time. Part-time tuition and fees vary according to course load. *Required fees:* $536 full-time, $14 per semester hour, $100 per term part-time. *Room and board:* $4100; room only: $2274. Room and board charges vary according to board plan and housing facility. *Waivers:* minority students, adult students, senior citizens, and employees or children of employees.

Financial Aid Of all full-time matriculated undergraduates who enrolled in 2001, 4959 applied for aid, 2930 were judged to have need, 688 had their need fully met. In 2001, 1209 non-need-based awards were made. *Average percent of need met:* 69%. *Average financial aid package:* $3939. *Average need-based loan:* $2628. *Average need-based gift aid:* $3923. *Average non-need based aid:* $3032.

Applying *Options:* early admission, deferred entrance. *Application fee:* $20. *Required:* high school transcript, proof of immunization. *Required for some:* 2 letters of recommendation, interview. *Application deadlines:* 7/31 (freshmen), 6/15 (transfers). *Notification:* continuous (freshmen).

Admissions Contact Dr. Robert Johnson, Director of Admissions, State University of West Georgia, 1600 Maple Street, Carrollton, GA 30118. *Phone:* 770-836-6416. *Fax:* 770-836-4659. *E-mail:* rjohnson@westga.edu.

THOMAS UNIVERSITY

Thomasville, Georgia

- **Independent** comprehensive, founded 1950
- **Calendar** semesters
- **Degrees** associate, bachelor's, master's, and postbachelor's certificates
- **Small-town** 24-acre campus
- **Endowment** $2.5 million
- **Coed,** 561 undergraduate students, 75% full-time, 69% women, 31% men
- **Noncompetitive** entrance level, 100% of applicants were admitted

Undergraduates 423 full-time, 138 part-time. Students come from 2 states and territories, 5 other countries, 5% are from out of state, 26% African American, 0.5% Asian American or Pacific Islander, 0.2% Native American, 4% international, 11% transferred in, 9% live on campus. *Retention:* 59% of 2001 full-time freshmen returned.

Freshmen *Admission:* 132 applied, 132 admitted, 59 enrolled. *Test scores:* SAT verbal scores over 500: 27%; SAT math scores over 500: 43%; ACT scores over 18: 25%; SAT verbal scores over 600: 2%; SAT math scores over 600: 8%; ACT scores over 24: 25%.

Faculty *Total:* 53, 68% full-time, 42% with terminal degrees. *Student/faculty ratio:* 10:1.

Majors Accounting; anthropology; art; biology; business; business administration; communications; criminal justice/law enforcement administration; early childhood education; English; history; humanities; liberal arts and sciences/liberal studies; mathematics; middle school education; music; music teacher education; nursing; political science; psychology; recreation/leisure facilities management; rehabilitation therapy; social sciences; social work; sociology.

Academic Programs *Special study options:* academic remediation for entering students, accelerated degree program, adult/continuing education programs,

Thomas University (continued)
advanced placement credit, cooperative education, double majors, internships, part-time degree program, services for LD students, summer session for credit. *ROTC:* Army (b).

Library Thomas University Library with 42,749 titles, 449 serial subscriptions, 546 audiovisual materials, an OPAC.

Computers on Campus 50 computers available on campus for general student use. At least one staffed computer lab available.

Student Life *Activities and Organizations:* student-run newspaper, choral group, Nursing Club, Psychology Club, Baptist Student Union, Equestrian Club, outdoor pursuits. *Campus security:* late-night transport/escort service, evening security guards. *Student Services:* personal/psychological counseling.

Athletics Member NAIA. *Intercollegiate sports:* baseball M(s), golf M(s), soccer M(s), softball W(s), tennis W(s). *Intramural sports:* equestrian sports M/W, football M/W, table tennis M/W, tennis M/W, volleyball M/W.

Standardized Tests *Required:* MAPS. *Recommended:* SAT I or ACT (for placement).

Costs (2001–02) *Tuition:* $7500 full-time, $250 per semester hour part-time. Full-time tuition and fees vary according to course load. No tuition increase for student's term of enrollment. *Required fees:* $370 full-time. *Room only:* $2400. Room and board charges vary according to board plan. *Payment plans:* installment, deferred payment. *Waivers:* senior citizens.

Financial Aid Of all full-time matriculated undergraduates who enrolled in 2001, 623 applied for aid, 623 were judged to have need, 290 had their need fully met. *Average percent of need met:* 29%. *Average financial aid package:* $5521. *Average need-based loan:* $3208. *Average need-based gift aid:* $2302.

Applying *Options:* early admission, deferred entrance. *Application fee:* $25. *Required:* high school transcript, minimum 2.0 GPA. *Application deadline:* rolling (freshmen), rolling (transfers).

Admissions Contact Darla M. Glass, Director of Student Affairs, Thomas University, 1501 Millpond Road, Thomasville, GA 31792-7499. *Phone:* 229-226-1621 Ext. 122. *Toll-free phone:* 800-538-9784. *Fax:* 229-227-1653.

TOCCOA FALLS COLLEGE
Toccoa Falls, Georgia

- **Independent interdenominational** 4-year, founded 1907
- **Calendar** 4-1-4
- **Degrees** certificates, diplomas, associate, and bachelor's
- **Small-town** 1100-acre campus
- **Endowment** $1.9 million
- **Coed,** 916 undergraduate students, 92% full-time, 57% women, 43% men
- **Moderately difficult** entrance level, 82% of applicants were admitted

Undergraduates 845 full-time, 71 part-time. Students come from 47 states and territories, 61% are from out of state, 2% African American, 4% Asian American or Pacific Islander, 2% Hispanic American, 0.1% Native American, 6% transferred in, 72% live on campus. *Retention:* 68% of 2001 full-time freshmen returned.

Freshmen *Admission:* 769 applied, 632 admitted, 235 enrolled. *Average high school GPA:* 3.20. *Test scores:* SAT verbal scores over 500: 54%; SAT math scores over 500: 47%; ACT scores over 18: 78%; SAT verbal scores over 600: 17%; SAT math scores over 600: 12%; ACT scores over 24: 44%; SAT verbal scores over 700: 2%; ACT scores over 30: 4%.

Faculty *Total:* 76, 71% full-time, 38% with terminal degrees. *Student/faculty ratio:* 14:1.

Majors Biblical languages/literatures; biblical studies; business administration; counseling psychology; early childhood education; elementary education; English; family/community studies; journalism; liberal arts and sciences/liberal studies; middle school education; music; music (piano and organ performance); music teacher education; music (voice and choral/opera performance); philosophy; public relations; radio/television broadcasting; religious education; religious music; religious studies; secondary education.

Academic Programs *Special study options:* academic remediation for entering students, accelerated degree program, advanced placement credit, double majors, independent study, internships, services for LD students, summer session for credit.

Library Seby Jones Library with 94,097 titles, 280 serial subscriptions, 5,161 audiovisual materials, a Web page.

Computers on Campus 50 computers available on campus for general student use. A campuswide network can be accessed from student residence rooms and from off campus. Internet access, at least one staffed computer lab available.

Student Life *Housing:* on-campus residence required through junior year. *Options:* men-only, women-only. *Activities and Organizations:* drama/theater group, student-run newspaper, radio station, choral group. *Campus security:* student patrols. *Student Services:* health clinic, personal/psychological counseling.

Athletics *Intercollegiate sports:* baseball M, basketball M/W, soccer M/W, volleyball W. *Intramural sports:* basketball M/W, golf M/W, soccer M/W, softball M/W.

Standardized Tests *Required:* SAT I or ACT (for admission).

Costs (2002–03) *One-time required fee:* $470. *Comprehensive fee:* $14,200 includes full-time tuition ($9900) and room and board ($4300). Full-time tuition and fees vary according to course load. Part-time tuition: $413 per credit hour. Part-time tuition and fees vary according to course load. *Room and board:* Room and board charges vary according to board plan and housing facility. *Waivers:* employees or children of employees.

Financial Aid Of all full-time matriculated undergraduates who enrolled in 2001, 597 applied for aid, 475 were judged to have need, 75 had their need fully met. In 2001, 74 non-need-based awards were made. *Average percent of need met:* 71%. *Average financial aid package:* $7671. *Average need-based loan:* $3534. *Average need-based gift aid:* $1569. *Average non-need based aid:* $2467.

Applying *Options:* common application, electronic application, early admission, deferred entrance. *Application fee:* $20. *Required:* essay or personal statement, high school transcript, minimum 2.0 GPA, 1 letter of recommendation. *Required for some:* interview. *Application deadline:* rolling (freshmen), rolling (transfers). *Notification:* continuous (freshmen).

Admissions Contact Director of Admissions, Toccoa Falls College, Office of Admissions, PO Box 899, Toccoa Falls, GA 30598-1000. *Phone:* 706-886-6831 Ext. 5380. *Toll-free phone:* 800-868-3257. *Fax:* 706-282-6012. *E-mail:* admissions@toccoafalls.edu.

UNIVERSITY OF GEORGIA
Athens, Georgia

- **State-supported** university, founded 1785, part of University System of Georgia
- **Calendar** semesters
- **Degrees** associate, bachelor's, master's, doctoral, and first professional
- **Suburban** 1289-acre campus with easy access to Atlanta
- **Endowment** $334.5 million
- **Coed,** 24,395 undergraduate students
- **Moderately difficult** entrance level, 62% of applicants were admitted

Undergraduates Students come from 53 states and territories, 131 other countries, 9% are from out of state, 6% African American, 3% Asian American or Pacific Islander, 1% Hispanic American, 0.2% Native American, 0.9% international, 26% live on campus. *Retention:* 90% of 2001 full-time freshmen returned.

Freshmen *Admission:* 13,393 applied, 8,275 admitted. *Average high school GPA:* 3.64. *Test scores:* SAT verbal scores over 500: 94%; SAT math scores over 500: 95%; ACT scores over 18: 100%; SAT verbal scores over 600: 51%; SAT math scores over 600: 52%; ACT scores over 24: 77%; SAT verbal scores over 700: 9%; SAT math scores over 700: 8%; ACT scores over 30: 18%.

Faculty *Total:* 2,038, 89% full-time, 95% with terminal degrees. *Student/faculty ratio:* 12:1.

Majors Accounting; advertising; African-American studies; agricultural business; agricultural economics; agricultural education; agricultural engineering; agronomy/crop science; animal sciences; anthropology; art; art education; art history; astronomy; biochemistry; biological/physical sciences; biology; botany; broadcast journalism; business; business administration; business economics; business education; business marketing and marketing management; cell biology; chemistry; classics; clothing/apparel/textile studies; cognitive psychology/psycholinguistics; communication disorders; comparative literature; computer/information sciences; consumer economics; criminal justice studies; dairy science; dietetics; drama/dance education; early childhood education; ecology; economics; English; English education; entomology; environmental health; fashion merchandising; finance; fine/studio arts; fishing sciences; food sciences; foreign languages education; foreign languages/literatures; forestry; forestry sciences; French; genetics; geography; geology; German; Greek (ancient and medieval); health education; history; home economics education; horticulture services; housing studies; individual/family development; industrial arts education; insurance/risk management; international business; Italian; Japanese; journalism; landscape architecture; landscaping management; Latin (ancient and medieval); liberal arts and sciences/liberal studies; linguistics; management information systems/business data processing; marketing/distribution education; mass communications; mathematical statistics; mathematics; mathematics education; microbiology/bacteriology; middle school education; music; music (general performance); music teacher education; music theory and composition; music therapy; nutrition studies; pharmacy; philosophy; physical education; physics;

plant protection; political science; poultry science; psychology; public relations; radio/television broadcasting technology; reading education; real estate; religious studies; Russian; science education; Slavic languages; social science education; social work; sociology; soil sciences; Spanish; special education; speech/rhetorical studies; sport/fitness administration; theater arts/drama; turf management; wildlife management; women's studies.

Academic Programs *Special study options:* academic remediation for entering students, accelerated degree program, adult/continuing education programs, advanced placement credit, cooperative education, distance learning, double majors, English as a second language, honors programs, independent study, internships, off-campus study, part-time degree program, services for LD students, student-designed majors, study abroad, summer session for credit. *ROTC:* Army (b), Air Force (b). *Unusual degree programs:* 3-2 engineering with Georgia Institute of Technology.

Library Ilah Dunlap Little Memorial Library plus 2 others with 3.8 million titles, 54,366 serial subscriptions, 201,184 audiovisual materials, an OPAC, a Web page.

Computers on Campus 2500 computers available on campus for general student use. A campuswide network can be accessed from student residence rooms and from off campus that provide access to e-mail, Web pages. Internet access, online (class) registration, at least one staffed computer lab available.

Student Life *Housing Options:* coed, men-only, women-only, disabled students. *Activities and Organizations:* drama/theater group, student-run newspaper, radio station, choral group, marching band, Intramurals, Recreational SportsP-program, Communiversity, University Union, Red Coat Band, national fraternities, national sororities. *Campus security:* 24-hour emergency response devices and patrols, late-night transport/escort service, controlled dormitory access. *Student Services:* health clinic, personal/psychological counseling, legal services.

Athletics Member NCAA. All Division I except football (Division I-A). *Intercollegiate sports:* baseball M(s), basketball M(s)/W(s), cross-country running M(s)/W(s), golf M(s)/W(s), gymnastics W(s), soccer M(c)/W(s), swimming M(s)/W(s), tennis M(s)/W(s), track and field M(s)/W(s), volleyball M(c)/W(s). *Intramural sports:* badminton M(c)/W(c), basketball M/W, bowling M/W, crew M(c), cross-country running M/W, equestrian sports M(c)/W(c), fencing M(c), football M/W, golf M/W, ice hockey M(c), lacrosse M(c)/W(c), racquetball M/W, rugby M(c), soccer M/W, softball M/W, swimming M/W, tennis M/W, track and field M/W, volleyball M/W, weight lifting M/W, wrestling M(c).

Standardized Tests *Required:* SAT I or ACT (for admission).

Costs (2001–02) *Tuition:* state resident $3418 full-time, $142 per credit part-time; nonresident $11,314 full-time, $471 per credit part-time. Full-time tuition and fees vary according to degree level and program. Part-time tuition and fees vary according to degree level and program. *Room and board:* $5388; room only: $3166. Room and board charges vary according to board plan and housing facility. *Waivers:* senior citizens and employees or children of employees.

Financial Aid Of all full-time matriculated undergraduates who enrolled in 2001, 19355 applied for aid, 6223 were judged to have need, 2083 had their need fully met. 316 Federal Work-Study jobs (averaging $2436). In 2001, 10713 non-need-based awards were made. *Average percent of need met:* 73%. *Average financial aid package:* $6451. *Average need-based loan:* $3651. *Average need-based gift aid:* $4824. *Average non-need based aid:* $4048. *Average indebtedness upon graduation:* $13,550.

Applying *Options:* electronic application, early admission, deferred entrance. *Application fee:* $50. *Required:* high school transcript. *Recommended:* essay or personal statement. *Application deadlines:* 1/15 (freshmen), 6/1 (transfers). *Notification:* 4/1 (freshmen).

Admissions Contact Dr. John Albright, Associate Director of Admissions, University of Georgia, Athens, GA 30602. *Phone:* 706-542-3000. *E-mail:* undergrad@admissions.uga.edu.

UNIVERSITY OF PHOENIX-ATLANTA CAMPUS

Atlanta, Georgia

- **Proprietary** comprehensive
- **Calendar** continuous
- **Degrees** certificates, associate, bachelor's, master's, doctoral, post-master's, and postbachelor's certificates (courses conducted at 54 campuses and learning centers in 13 states)
- **Coed**

Majors Accounting; business administration; business marketing and marketing management; computer/information sciences; enterprise management; management information systems/business data processing; management science; nursing science.

Student Life *Housing:* college housing not available.

Costs (2001–02) *Tuition:* $8550 full-time. Full-time tuition and fees vary according to location and program. *Payment plan:* deferred payment. *Waivers:* employees or children of employees.

Admissions Contact 7000 Central Parkway, Suite 1700, Atlanta, GA 30328.

VALDOSTA STATE UNIVERSITY

Valdosta, Georgia

- **State-supported** university, founded 1906, part of University System of Georgia
- **Calendar** semesters
- **Degrees** associate, bachelor's, master's, and doctoral
- **Small-town** 200-acre campus with easy access to Jacksonville
- **Endowment** $4.4 million
- **Coed,** 7,938 undergraduate students, 78% full-time, 60% women, 40% men
- **Moderately difficult** entrance level, 66% of applicants were admitted

Undergraduates 6,195 full-time, 1,743 part-time. Students come from 48 states and territories, 53 other countries, 8% are from out of state, 21% African American, 1% Asian American or Pacific Islander, 1% Hispanic American, 0.2% Native American, 2% international, 8% transferred in, 20% live on campus. *Retention:* 68% of 2001 full-time freshmen returned.

Freshmen *Admission:* 4,418 applied, 2,920 admitted, 1,573 enrolled. *Average high school GPA:* 3.00. *Test scores:* SAT verbal scores over 500: 53%; SAT math scores over 500: 53%; ACT scores over 18: 84%; SAT verbal scores over 600: 12%; SAT math scores over 600: 10%; ACT scores over 24: 14%; SAT verbal scores over 700: 1%; SAT math scores over 700: 1%; ACT scores over 30: 1%.

Faculty *Total:* 510, 80% full-time, 60% with terminal degrees. *Student/faculty ratio:* 19:1.

Majors Accounting; anthropology; applied art; applied mathematics; art; art education; astronomy; athletic training/sports medicine; biology; broadcast journalism; business administration; business economics; business education; business marketing and marketing management; chemistry; computer science; counselor education/guidance; criminal justice/law enforcement administration; data processing technology; early childhood education; economics; education; education administration; elementary education; emergency medical technology; English; environmental science; finance; fine/studio arts; French; health science; history; information sciences/systems; interior design; legal studies; liberal arts and sciences/liberal studies; mass communications; mathematics; medical technology; middle school education; music; music (piano and organ performance); music teacher education; music (voice and choral/opera performance); nursing; paralegal/legal assistant; philosophy; physical education; physics; political science; pre-dentistry; pre-engineering; pre-law; pre-medicine; psychology; public relations; radio/television broadcasting; secondary education; secretarial science; sociology; Spanish; special education; speech-language pathology/audiology; speech/rhetorical studies; theater arts/drama; trade/industrial education.

Academic Programs *Special study options:* academic remediation for entering students, accelerated degree program, adult/continuing education programs, advanced placement credit, cooperative education, distance learning, English as a second language, freshman honors college, honors programs, internships, off-campus study, part-time degree program, services for LD students, study abroad, summer session for credit. *ROTC:* Air Force (b). *Unusual degree programs:* 3-2 engineering with Georgia Institute of Technology.

Library Odom Library with 288,035 titles, 3,262 serial subscriptions, 62,677 audiovisual materials, an OPAC.

Computers on Campus 2400 computers available on campus for general student use. A campuswide network can be accessed from student residence rooms and from off campus. Internet access, online (class) registration, at least one staffed computer lab available.

Student Life *Housing:* on-campus residence required for freshman year. *Options:* coed, men-only, women-only, disabled students. *Activities and Organizations:* drama/theater group, student-run newspaper, radio and television station, choral group, marching band, Blazing Brigade (marching band), SGA (Student Government Association), Greek organizations, intramural athletics, Baptist Student Union, national fraternities, national sororities. *Campus security:* 24-hour emergency response devices and patrols, student patrols, late-night transport/escort service, controlled dormitory access, bicycle patrols, security cameras. *Student Services:* health clinic, personal/psychological counseling.

Athletics Member NCAA. All Division II. *Intercollegiate sports:* baseball M(s), basketball M(s)/W(s), cross-country running M(s)/W(s), football M(s), golf M(s), softball W(s), tennis M(s)/W(s), volleyball W(s). *Intramural sports:* badminton M/W, basketball M/W, bowling M/W, cross-country running M/W, field hockey M/W, football M/W, golf M/W, soccer M/W, softball M/W, swimming M/W, table tennis M/W, tennis M/W, volleyball M/W, weight lifting M/W.

Standardized Tests *Required:* SAT I or ACT (for admission).

Valdosta State University (continued)

Costs (2001–02) *Tuition:* state resident $1932 full-time, $81 per semester hour part-time; nonresident $7728 full-time, $322 per semester hour part-time. Part-time tuition and fees vary according to course load. *Required fees:* $594 full-time. *Room and board:* $4462; room only: $2178. Room and board charges vary according to board plan. *Waivers:* senior citizens and employees or children of employees.

Financial Aid Of all full-time matriculated undergraduates who enrolled in 2001, 5001 applied for aid, 3048 were judged to have need, 704 had their need fully met. 205 Federal Work-Study jobs (averaging $2412). In 2001, 913 non-need-based awards were made. *Average percent of need met:* 86%. *Average financial aid package:* $7050. *Average need-based loan:* $2950. *Average need-based gift aid:* $2050. *Average non-need based aid:* $3065. *Average indebtedness upon graduation:* $13,000.

Applying *Options:* electronic application, early admission, deferred entrance. *Application fee:* $20. *Required:* high school transcript, minimum 2.0 GPA, proof of immunization. *Application deadlines:* 8/1 (freshmen), 8/1 (transfers). *Notification:* continuous (freshmen).

Admissions Contact Mr. Walter Peacock, Director of Admissions, Valdosta State University, Valdosta, GA 31698. *Phone:* 229-333-5791. *Toll-free phone:* 800-618-1878 Ext. 1. *Fax:* 229-333-5482. *E-mail:* admissions@valdosta.edu.

WESLEYAN COLLEGE
Macon, Georgia

- **Independent United Methodist** comprehensive, founded 1836
- **Calendar** semesters
- **Degrees** bachelor's and master's
- **Suburban** 200-acre campus with easy access to Atlanta
- **Endowment** $35.1 million
- **Women only,** 674 undergraduate students, 78% full-time
- **Moderately difficult** entrance level, 74% of applicants were admitted

Undergraduates 529 full-time, 145 part-time. Students come from 24 states and territories, 22 other countries, 19% are from out of state, 28% African American, 3% Asian American or Pacific Islander, 2% Hispanic American, 0.3% Native American, 12% international, 4% transferred in, 75% live on campus. *Retention:* 73% of 2001 full-time freshmen returned.

Freshmen *Admission:* 193 enrolled. *Average high school GPA:* 3.67. *Test scores:* SAT verbal scores over 500: 84%; SAT math scores over 500: 86%; ACT scores over 18: 100%; SAT verbal scores over 600: 39%; SAT math scores over 600: 35%; ACT scores over 24: 55%; SAT verbal scores over 700: 10%; SAT math scores over 700: 3%; ACT scores over 30: 9%.

Faculty *Total:* 74, 62% full-time, 65% with terminal degrees. *Student/faculty ratio:* 11:1.

Majors Accounting; advertising; American studies; art history; biology; business administration; chemistry; communications; computer/information sciences; early childhood education; economics; education; English; fine/studio arts; history; humanities; interdisciplinary studies; international business; international relations; mathematics; middle school education; music; philosophy; physical sciences; physics; political science; psychology; religious studies; social sciences; sociology; Spanish.

Academic Programs *Special study options:* accelerated degree program, adult/continuing education programs, advanced placement credit, double majors, honors programs, independent study, internships, off-campus study, part-time degree program, student-designed majors, study abroad, summer session for credit. *Unusual degree programs:* 3-2 engineering with Georgia Institute of Technology, Mercer University, Auburn University.

Library Lucy Lester Willet Memorial Library with 140,923 titles, 650 serial subscriptions, 6,553 audiovisual materials, an OPAC, a Web page.

Computers on Campus 35 computers available on campus for general student use. A campuswide network can be accessed from student residence rooms and from off campus. Internet access, online (class) registration, at least one staffed computer lab available.

Student Life *Housing:* on-campus residence required through senior year. *Options:* women-only. *Activities and Organizations:* drama/theater group, student-run newspaper, choral group, Student Recreation Council, Campus Activities Board, Student Government Association, Council on Religious Concerns, Christian Fellowship. *Campus security:* 24-hour emergency response devices and patrols, late-night transport/escort service, controlled dormitory access. *Student Services:* health clinic, personal/psychological counseling, women's center.

Athletics Member NCAA. All Division III. *Intercollegiate sports:* basketball W, equestrian sports W, soccer W, softball W, tennis W, volleyball W. *Intramural sports:* basketball W, soccer W, softball W, volleyball W.

Standardized Tests *Required:* SAT I or ACT (for admission).

Costs (2001–02) *Comprehensive fee:* $17,050 includes full-time tuition ($8950), mandatory fees ($850), and room and board ($7250). Full-time tuition and fees vary according to class time and course load. Part-time tuition: $360 per semester hour. Part-time tuition and fees vary according to class time, course load, and program. *Room and board:* Room and board charges vary according to board plan and housing facility. *Waivers:* senior citizens and employees or children of employees.

Financial Aid Of all full-time matriculated undergraduates who enrolled in 2001, 412 applied for aid, 320 were judged to have need, 106 had their need fully met. 91 Federal Work-Study jobs (averaging $1100). 129 State and other part-time jobs (averaging $1322). In 2001, 192 non-need-based awards were made. *Average percent of need met:* 85%. *Average financial aid package:* $10,749. *Average need-based loan:* $3240. *Average need-based gift aid:* $8206. *Average indebtedness upon graduation:* $19,614.

Applying *Options:* common application, early admission, early decision, early action, deferred entrance. *Application fee:* $30. *Required:* essay or personal statement, high school transcript, 1 letter of recommendation. *Recommended:* 2 letters of recommendation, interview. *Application deadline:* 6/1 (freshmen), rolling (transfers). *Early decision:* 11/15 (for plan 1), 1/15 (for plan 2). *Notification:* continuous until 8/1 (freshmen), 12/15 (early decision plan 1), 2/15 (early decision plan 2), 3/1 (early action).

Admissions Contact Mr. Jonathan Stroud, Vice President for Enrollment and Marketing, Wesleyan College, 4760 Forsyth Road, Macon, GA 31210-4462. *Phone:* 478-757-5206. *Toll-free phone:* 800-447-6610. *Fax:* 478-757-4030. *E-mail:* admissions@wesleyancollege.edu.

HAWAII

BRIGHAM YOUNG UNIVERSITY-HAWAII
Laie, Hawaii

- **Independent Latter-day Saints** 4-year, founded 1955
- **Calendar** 4-4-2-2
- **Degrees** associate, bachelor's, and postbachelor's certificates
- **Small-town** 60-acre campus with easy access to Honolulu
- **Coed,** 2,278 undergraduate students, 96% full-time, 57% women, 43% men
- **Moderately difficult** entrance level, 10% of applicants were admitted

Undergraduates 2,177 full-time, 101 part-time. Students come from 43 states and territories, 58 other countries, 51% are from out of state, 0.4% African American, 16% Asian American or Pacific Islander, 2% Hispanic American, 0.3% Native American, 41% international, 13% transferred in, 62% live on campus.

Freshmen *Admission:* 3,207 applied, 325 admitted, 178 enrolled. *Average high school GPA:* 3.3. *Test scores:* ACT scores over 18: 89%; ACT scores over 24: 36%; ACT scores over 30: 1%.

Faculty *Total:* 183, 68% full-time. *Student/faculty ratio:* 21:1.

Majors Accounting; art; art education; biology; biology education; business administration; business education; chemistry; communications; computer programming; computer science; cultural studies; education; elementary education; English; English education; health/physical education; history; hotel and restaurant management; information sciences/systems; interdisciplinary studies; international business; mathematics; mathematics education; music; music (general performance); music (piano and organ performance); music (voice and choral/opera performance); Pacific area studies; physical education; physical sciences; political science; psychology; science education; secondary education; social work; special education; teaching English as a second language; theater arts/drama; travel/tourism management.

Academic Programs *Special study options:* academic remediation for entering students, accelerated degree program, adult/continuing education programs, advanced placement credit, cooperative education, double majors, English as a second language, freshman honors college, honors programs, internships, off-campus study, part-time degree program, services for LD students, summer session for credit. *ROTC:* Army (c), Navy (c), Air Force (c).

Library Joseph F. Smith Library with 319,400 titles, 2,100 serial subscriptions, 9,120 audiovisual materials, an OPAC, a Web page.

Computers on Campus 465 computers available on campus for general student use. A campuswide network can be accessed from student residence rooms. Internet access, online (class) registration, at least one staffed computer lab available.

Student Life *Housing:* on-campus residence required for freshman year. *Options:* men-only, women-only. *Activities and Organizations:* drama/theater group, student-run newspaper, choral group, Tonga Club, Samoa Club, Hawaiian

Club, Hong Kong Club, Singapore/Malaysia/Indonesia Club. *Campus security:* 24-hour patrols, late-night transport/escort service. *Student Services:* health clinic, personal/psychological counseling.

Athletics Member NCAA. All Division II. *Intercollegiate sports:* basketball M(s), cross-country running M(s)/W(s), soccer M(s), softball W(s), tennis M(s)/W(s), volleyball W(s). *Intramural sports:* archery M(c)/W(c), badminton M/W, basketball M/W, bowling M/W, cross-country running M/W, fencing M(c)/W(c), football M, golf M/W, racquetball M/W, rugby M(c), soccer M(c), swimming M/W, table tennis M/W, tennis M/W, track and field M/W, volleyball M/W, water polo M, weight lifting M/W.

Standardized Tests *Required:* ACT (for admission). *Recommended:* SAT I (for admission).

Costs (2002–03) *Comprehensive fee:* $6890 includes full-time tuition ($2490) and room and board ($4400). Full-time tuition and fees vary according to program. Part-time tuition: $160 per credit. Part-time tuition and fees vary according to program. *Room and board:* Room and board charges vary according to board plan and housing facility. *Payment plan:* installment. *Waivers:* employees or children of employees.

Applying *Options:* common application, electronic application, early admission, deferred entrance. *Application fee:* $25. *Required:* essay or personal statement, high school transcript, minimum 3.0 GPA, resume of activities, ecclesiastical endorsement. *Required for some:* letters of recommendation. *Application deadlines:* 2/15 (freshmen), 3/15 (transfers). *Notification:* continuous (freshmen).

Admissions Contact Mr. Jeffrey N. Bunker, Dean for Admissions and Records, Brigham Young University-Hawaii, 55-220 Kulanui Street, Laie, Oahu, HI 96762. *Phone:* 808-293-7010.

CHAMINADE UNIVERSITY OF HONOLULU
Honolulu, Hawaii

- **Independent Roman Catholic** comprehensive, founded 1955
- **Calendar** semesters
- **Degrees** associate, bachelor's, master's, and postbachelor's certificates
- **Urban** 62-acre campus
- **Endowment** $3.7 million
- **Coed,** 1,943 undergraduate students, 61% full-time, 60% women, 40% men
- **Moderately difficult** entrance level, 69% of applicants were admitted

Undergraduates 1,185 full-time, 758 part-time. Students come from 43 states and territories, 25 other countries, 43% are from out of state, 12% African American, 37% Asian American or Pacific Islander, 8% Hispanic American, 2% Native American, 2% international, 5% transferred in, 13% live on campus. *Retention:* 69% of 2001 full-time freshmen returned.

Freshmen *Admission:* 1,160 applied, 801 admitted, 223 enrolled. *Average high school GPA:* 3.05. *Test scores:* SAT verbal scores over 500: 31%; SAT math scores over 500: 35%; ACT scores over 18: 67%; SAT verbal scores over 600: 5%; SAT math scores over 600: 6%; ACT scores over 24: 4%.

Faculty *Total:* 318, 14% full-time. *Student/faculty ratio:* 16:1.

Majors Accounting; behavioral sciences; biology; business administration; business marketing and marketing management; chemistry; computer/information sciences; criminal justice/law enforcement administration; early childhood education; elementary education; English; forensic technology; history; humanities; interior design; international relations; mass communications; philosophy; political science; psychology; religious studies; social sciences.

Academic Programs *Special study options:* academic remediation for entering students, accelerated degree program, adult/continuing education programs, advanced placement credit, distance learning, double majors, independent study, internships, off-campus study, part-time degree program, student-designed majors, summer session for credit. *ROTC:* Army (c), Air Force (c). *Unusual degree programs:* 3-2 engineering with University of Dayton, St. Mary's University of San Antonio; mathematics with St. Mary's University of San Antonio.

Library Sullivan Library with 139,751 titles, 905 serial subscriptions, an OPAC.

Computers on Campus 50 computers available on campus for general student use. A campuswide network can be accessed from off campus. At least one staffed computer lab available.

Student Life *Housing Options:* coed, women-only. *Activities and Organizations:* drama/theater group, student-run newspaper, choral group, Chaminade University Student Association, Lumana O Samoa-Chaminade Somoan Club, Chaminade International Student Association, Kaimi Lalakea—Chaminade Hawaiian Club, Residence Hall Association. *Campus security:* 24-hour emergency response devices and patrols, late-night transport/escort service, controlled dormitory access. *Student Services:* personal/psychological counseling.

Athletics Member NCAA. All Division II. *Intercollegiate sports:* basketball M(s), cross-country running M(s)/W(s), softball W(s), tennis M(s)/W(s), volleyball W(s), water polo M(s). *Intramural sports:* basketball M/W, bowling M/W, football M/W, golf M/W, soccer M(c), table tennis M/W, tennis M/W, volleyball M/W, water polo M, weight lifting M/W.

Standardized Tests *Recommended:* SAT I or ACT (for admission).

Costs (2001–02) *Comprehensive fee:* $18,695 includes full-time tuition ($12,500), mandatory fees ($205), and room and board ($5990). Full-time tuition and fees vary according to class time. Part-time tuition: $415 per semester hour. Part-time tuition and fees vary according to class time and course load. *Room and board:* College room only: $3330. Room and board charges vary according to board plan and housing facility. *Payment plan:* deferred payment. *Waivers:* employees or children of employees.

Financial Aid Of all full-time matriculated undergraduates who enrolled in 2001, 748 applied for aid, 642 were judged to have need, 184 had their need fully met. In 2001, 49 non-need-based awards were made. *Average percent of need met:* 59%. *Average financial aid package:* $9160. *Average need-based loan:* $3180. *Average need-based gift aid:* $4440. *Average non-need based aid:* $3715.

Applying *Options:* common application, electronic application, deferred entrance. *Application fee:* $50. *Required:* essay or personal statement, high school transcript. *Required for some:* 3 letters of recommendation, interview. *Recommended:* minimum 2.0 GPA. *Application deadline:* rolling (freshmen), rolling (transfers). *Notification:* 9/8 (freshmen).

Admissions Contact Office of Admissions, Chaminade University of Honolulu, 3140 Waialae Avenue, Honolulu, HI 96816-1578. *Phone:* 808-735-4735. *Toll-free phone:* 800-735-3733. *Fax:* 808-739-4647. *E-mail:* admissions@chaminade.edu.

EDUCATION AMERICA, HONOLULU CAMPUS
Honolulu, Hawaii

Admissions Contact 1111 Bishop Street, Suite 400, Honolulu, HI 96813.

HAWAI'I PACIFIC UNIVERSITY
Honolulu, Hawaii

- **Independent** comprehensive, founded 1965
- **Calendar** 4-1-4
- **Degrees** certificates, associate, bachelor's, master's, and postbachelor's certificates
- **Urban** 140-acre campus
- **Endowment** $60.3 million
- **Coed,** 6,759 undergraduate students, 63% full-time, 55% women, 45% men
- **Moderately difficult** entrance level, 81% of applicants were admitted

Strategically situated at the crossroads of East and West, Hawai'i Pacific University is the ideal location for anyone interested in living and learning in an international setting. Approximately 8,000 students from all 50 states and more than 100 countries make HPU one of the most diverse universities in the United States.

Undergraduates 4,262 full-time, 2,497 part-time. Students come from 52 states and territories, 106 other countries, 34% are from out of state, 10% African American, 30% Asian American or Pacific Islander, 5% Hispanic American, 1.0% Native American, 22% international, 15% transferred in, 10% live on campus. *Retention:* 71% of 2001 full-time freshmen returned.

Freshmen *Admission:* 2,891 applied, 2,335 admitted, 625 enrolled. *Average high school GPA:* 3.14. *Test scores:* SAT verbal scores over 500: 49%; SAT math scores over 500: 55%; ACT scores over 18: 79%; SAT verbal scores over 600: 10%; SAT math scores over 600: 14%; ACT scores over 24: 29%; SAT verbal scores over 700: 1%; SAT math scores over 700: 1%; ACT scores over 30: 1%.

Faculty *Total:* 600, 51% full-time, 48% with terminal degrees. *Student/faculty ratio:* 17:1.

Majors Accounting; advertising; anthropology; applied mathematics; area studies; behavioral sciences; biology; business administration; business economics; business marketing and marketing management; communications; computer/information sciences; computer science; criminal justice/law enforcement administration; data processing technology; economics; entrepreneurship; environmental science; finance; history; humanities; human resources management; human services; individual/family development; information sciences/systems; interdisciplinary studies; international business; international relations; journalism; liberal arts and sciences/liberal studies; literature; management information systems/business data processing; marine biology; mass communications; military studies; nursing; oceanography; political science; pre-medicine; psychology; public administration; public relations; social sciences; social work; sociology; teaching English as a second language; travel/tourism management.

Hawai'i Pacific University (continued)

Academic Programs *Special study options:* academic remediation for entering students, accelerated degree program, adult/continuing education programs, advanced placement credit, cooperative education, distance learning, double majors, English as a second language, freshman honors college, honors programs, independent study, internships, part-time degree program, services for LD students, student-designed majors, study abroad, summer session for credit. *ROTC:* Army (c), Air Force (c). *Unusual degree programs:* 3-2 engineering with Washington University in St. Louis, University of Southern California.

Library Meader Library plus 2 others with 160,000 titles, 11,000 serial subscriptions, 8,695 audiovisual materials, an OPAC, a Web page.

Computers on Campus 418 computers available on campus for general student use. A campuswide network can be accessed from student residence rooms and from off campus. Internet access, at least one staffed computer lab available.

Student Life *Housing Options:* coed. *Activities and Organizations:* drama/theater group, student-run newspaper, choral group, Association of Students of HPU, Council of Countries, President's Hosts, Delta Mu Delta, Travel Industry Management Student Organization. *Campus security:* 24-hour emergency response devices and patrols, student patrols, late-night transport/escort service. *Student Services:* health clinic, personal/psychological counseling.

Athletics Member NCAA. All Division II. *Intercollegiate sports:* baseball M(s), basketball M(s), cross-country running M(s)/W(s), softball W(s), tennis M(s)/W(s), volleyball W(s). *Intramural sports:* soccer M/W, volleyball M/W.

Standardized Tests *Required:* SAT I or ACT (for admission). *Required for some:* SAT I or ACT (for admission).

Costs (2001–02) *Comprehensive fee:* $17,790 includes full-time tuition ($9360) and room and board ($8430). Full-time tuition and fees vary according to program and student level. Part-time tuition: $172 per credit. Part-time tuition and fees vary according to course load. *Room and board:* Room and board charges vary according to housing facility. *Payment plan:* installment. *Waivers:* employees or children of employees.

Financial Aid Of all full-time matriculated undergraduates who enrolled in 2001, 1832 applied for aid, 1526 were judged to have need, 346 had their need fully met. 125 Federal Work-Study jobs (averaging $3000). In 2001, 621 non-need-based awards were made. *Average percent of need met:* 72%. *Average financial aid package:* $11,429. *Average need-based loan:* $3742. *Average need-based gift aid:* $2990. *Average non-need based aid:* $3286. *Average indebtedness upon graduation:* $19,411.

Applying *Options:* common application, electronic application, early admission, deferred entrance. *Application fee:* $50. *Required:* high school transcript, minimum 2.5 GPA. *Required for some:* interview. *Recommended:* essay or personal statement, 2 letters of recommendation. *Application deadline:* rolling (freshmen), rolling (transfers).

Admissions Contact Mr. Scott Stensrud, Associate Vice President Enrollment Management, Hawai'i Pacific University, 1164 Bishop Street, Honolulu, HI 96813-2785. *Phone:* 808-544-0238. *Toll-free phone:* 800-669-4724. *Fax:* 808-544-1136. *E-mail:* admissions@hpu.edu.

INTERNATIONAL COLLEGE AND GRADUATE SCHOOL

Honolulu, Hawaii

- **Independent interdenominational** upper-level, founded 1967
- **Calendar** semesters
- **Degrees** certificates, bachelor's, master's, and first professional
- **Coed,** 19 undergraduate students, 21% full-time, 32% women, 68% men

Undergraduates 4 full-time, 15 part-time. Students come from 1 other state, 3 other countries, 0% are from out of state, 42% Asian American or Pacific Islander, 37% international.

Faculty *Total:* 40, 98% with terminal degrees. *Student/faculty ratio:* 12:1.

Majors Theology.

Academic Programs *Special study options:* adult/continuing education programs, advanced placement credit, independent study, internships, part-time degree program, study abroad, summer session for credit.

Library J. W. Cook Memorial Library with 16,669 titles, 65 serial subscriptions, 703 audiovisual materials.

Computers on Campus 6 computers available on campus for general student use. A campuswide network can be accessed from off campus.

Student Life *Housing:* college housing not available.

Costs (2002–03) *Tuition:* $4440 full-time, $185 per semester hour part-time. *Required fees:* $280 full-time, $130 per term part-time. *Payment plans:* installment, deferred payment.

Applying *Options:* deferred entrance. *Application fee:* $50. *Application deadline:* rolling (transfers). *Notification:* continuous (transfers).

Admissions Contact Mr. Jon Rawlings, Director of Admissions, International College and Graduate School, 20 Dowsett Avenue, Honolulu, HI 96817. *Phone:* 808-595-4247. *Fax:* 808-595-4779. *E-mail:* icgs@pixi.com.

UNIVERSITY OF HAWAII AT HILO

Hilo, Hawaii

- **State-supported** comprehensive, founded 1970, part of University of Hawaii System
- **Calendar** semesters
- **Degrees** certificates, bachelor's, and master's
- **Small-town** 115-acre campus
- **Coed,** 2,724 undergraduate students, 80% full-time, 60% women, 40% men
- **Moderately difficult** entrance level, 63% of applicants were admitted

Undergraduates 2,175 full-time, 549 part-time. Students come from 41 states and territories, 35 other countries, 21% are from out of state, 0.9% African American, 47% Asian American or Pacific Islander, 2% Hispanic American, 0.8% Native American, 17% transferred in, 29% live on campus. *Retention:* 58% of 2001 full-time freshmen returned.

Freshmen *Admission:* 1,663 applied, 1,040 admitted, 416 enrolled. *Average high school GPA:* 3.23. *Test scores:* SAT verbal scores over 500: 45%; SAT math scores over 500: 49%; SAT verbal scores over 600: 9%; SAT math scores over 600: 11%; SAT verbal scores over 700: 1%; SAT math scores over 700: 1%.

Faculty *Total:* 217, 75% full-time, 65% with terminal degrees. *Student/faculty ratio:* 14:1.

Majors Agricultural business; agricultural sciences; animal sciences; anthropology; art; biology; business administration; chemistry; computer science; economics; elementary education; English; geography; geology; history; horticulture science; interdisciplinary studies; Japanese; linguistics; mathematics; music; natural sciences; nursing; philosophy; physics; political science; psychology; secondary education; sociology.

Academic Programs *Special study options:* advanced placement credit, distance learning, double majors, English as a second language, freshman honors college, honors programs, independent study, internships, off-campus study, part-time degree program, services for LD students, student-designed majors, study abroad, summer session for credit. *ROTC:* Army (c).

Library Edwin H. Mookini Library with 250,000 titles, 2,500 serial subscriptions, an OPAC, a Web page.

Computers on Campus 200 computers available on campus for general student use. A campuswide network can be accessed from student residence rooms and from off campus. Internet access, online (class) registration, at least one staffed computer lab available.

Student Life *Housing Options:* coed. *Activities and Organizations:* drama/theater group, student-run newspaper, choral group, International Student Association, Hawaiian Leadership and Development, Delta Sigma Pi Business Fraternity, University Canoe Club, Samoan Club. *Campus security:* 24-hour emergency response devices and patrols, controlled dormitory access. *Student Services:* health clinic, personal/psychological counseling, women's center.

Athletics Member NCAA. All Division II except baseball (Division I). *Intercollegiate sports:* baseball M(s), basketball M(s), cross-country running M(s)/W(s), golf M(s), softball W(s), volleyball W(s). *Intramural sports:* archery M/W, badminton M/W, basketball M/W, bowling M/W, golf M/W, soccer M/W, softball M/W, table tennis M/W, tennis M/W, volleyball M/W, weight lifting M/W.

Standardized Tests *Required:* SAT I or ACT (for admission).

Costs (2002–03) *Tuition:* state resident $1608 full-time, $67 per credit hour part-time; nonresident $7224 full-time, $301 per credit hour part-time. Full-time tuition and fees vary according to class time and student level. Part-time tuition and fees vary according to class time and student level. *Required fees:* $50 full-time, $1 per credit hour, $10 per term part-time. *Room and board:* $4839; room only: $2248. Room and board charges vary according to board plan and housing facility.

Financial Aid Of all full-time matriculated undergraduates who enrolled in 2001, 1631 applied for aid, 974 were judged to have need, 310 had their need fully met. 135 Federal Work-Study jobs (averaging $2941). 319 State and other part-time jobs (averaging $2647). In 2001, 112 non-need-based awards were made. *Average percent of need met:* 76%. *Average financial aid package:* $6372. *Average need-based loan:* $3227. *Average need-based gift aid:* $3675. *Average non-need based aid:* $915. *Average indebtedness upon graduation:* $10,698.

Applying *Options:* common application, electronic application, deferred entrance. *Application fee:* $25. *Required:* high school transcript. *Required for some:* letters of recommendation. *Recommended:* minimum 3.0 GPA. *Application deadlines:* 7/1 (freshmen), 7/1 (transfers). *Notification:* 7/31 (freshmen).

Admissions Contact Mr. James Cromwell, UH Student Services Specialist III/Director of Admissions, University of Hawaii at Hilo, 200 West Kawili Street, Hilo, HI 96720-4091. *Phone:* 808-974-7414. *Toll-free phone:* 808-974-7414 (in-state); 800-897-4456 (out-of-state). *E-mail:* uhhao@hawaii.edu.

UNIVERSITY OF HAWAII AT MANOA
Honolulu, Hawaii

- **State-supported** university, founded 1907
- **Calendar** semesters
- **Degrees** bachelor's, master's, doctoral, first professional, and postbachelor's certificates
- **Urban** 300-acre campus
- **Endowment** $182.5 million
- **Coed,** 12,054 undergraduate students, 83% full-time, 56% women, 44% men
- **Moderately difficult** entrance level, 71% of applicants were admitted

Undergraduates 9,989 full-time, 2,065 part-time. Students come from 62 other countries, 17% are from out of state, 0.8% African American, 72% Asian American or Pacific Islander, 2% Hispanic American, 0.2% Native American, 6% international, 12% transferred in, 18% live on campus. *Retention:* 79% of 2001 full-time freshmen returned.

Freshmen *Admission:* 4,565 applied, 3,243 admitted, 1,650 enrolled. *Average high school GPA:* 3.34. *Test scores:* SAT verbal scores over 500: 64%; SAT math scores over 500: 82%; SAT verbal scores over 600: 18%; SAT math scores over 600: 32%; SAT verbal scores over 700: 2%; SAT math scores over 700: 5%.

Faculty *Total:* 1,142, 91% full-time, 82% with terminal degrees. *Student/faculty ratio:* 12:1.

Majors Accounting; agricultural economics; agricultural education; agricultural engineering; agricultural production; American studies; animal sciences; anthropology; applied history; archaeology; architectural environmental design; architectural history; architectural urban design; architecture; area, ethnic, and cultural studies related; art; art education; art history; Asian studies; astronomy; athletic training/sports medicine; atmospheric sciences; biochemistry; biological specializations related; biology; biophysics; biostatistics; botany; business; business administration; business administration/management related; business economics; business education; business marketing and marketing management; chemistry; Chinese; city/community/regional planning; civil engineering; classics; clothing/apparel/textile studies; communication disorders sciences/services related; communications; communications related; computer/information sciences; counselor education/guidance; curriculum and instruction; dance; dental hygiene; early childhood education; East and Southeast Asian languages related; East Asian studies; economics; education; education administration; educational media design; educational psychology; electrical engineering; elementary education; engineering; engineering related; English; English education; entomology; ethnic/cultural studies related; exercise sciences; family/consumer resource management related; family/consumer studies; finance; food sciences; foreign languages education; foreign languages/literatures related; French; genetics; geography; geological sciences related; geology; German; gerontology; Greek (ancient and medieval); health education; health/physical education; history; home economics; home economics education; horticulture science; horticulture services; hospitality services management related; human resources management; individual/family development; industrial arts education; interior architecture; international business; Japanese; journalism; landscape architecture; Latin (ancient and medieval); law and legal studies related; liberal arts and sciences/liberal studies; library science; linguistics; management information systems/business data processing; marketing/distribution education; mathematics; mathematics education; mechanical engineering; medical basic sciences related; medical molecular biology; medical technology; microbiology/bacteriology; multi/interdisciplinary studies related; music; music (general performance); music history; music teacher education; nursing; nursing related; nursing science; nutritional sciences; ocean engineering; oceanography; Pacific area studies; pharmacology; philosophy; physical education; physics; physiology; plant pathology; plant physiology; political science; pre-dentistry; pre-law; pre-medicine; pre-pharmacy studies; psychology; public administration; public health; public health related; real estate; recreation/leisure studies; religious studies; Russian; science education; secondary education; social/philosophical foundations of education; social science education; social sciences and history related; social studies education; social work; sociology; soil sciences; South Asian studies; Southeast Asian studies; Spanish; special education; speech-language pathology/audiology; speech/rhetorical studies; teacher education related; teacher education, specific programs related; teaching English as a second language; theater arts/drama; trade/industrial education; women's studies; zoology.

Academic Programs *Special study options:* accelerated degree program, adult/continuing education programs, advanced placement credit, cooperative education, distance learning, double majors, English as a second language, honors programs, independent study, internships, off-campus study, part-time degree program, services for LD students, student-designed majors, study abroad, summer session for credit. *ROTC:* Army (b), Air Force (b).

Library Hamilton Library plus 6 others with 3.1 million titles, 26,767 serial subscriptions, 47,992 audiovisual materials, an OPAC, a Web page.

Computers on Campus 1000 computers available on campus for general student use. A campuswide network can be accessed from student residence rooms and from off campus that provide access to telephone registration. Internet access, at least one staffed computer lab available.

Student Life *Housing Options:* coed, men-only, women-only, disabled students. *Activities and Organizations:* drama/theater group, student-run newspaper, radio station, choral group, marching band, Associated Students of University of Hawaii, Campus Center Board, Broadcast Communication Authority, Board of Publications, Student Activities and Program Fee Board, national fraternities, national sororities. *Campus security:* 24-hour emergency response devices and patrols, late-night transport/escort service, controlled dormitory access. *Student Services:* health clinic, personal/psychological counseling, women's center.

Athletics Member NCAA. All Division I except football (Division I-A). *Intercollegiate sports:* baseball M(s), basketball M(s)/W(s), cross-country running W(s), golf M(s)/W(s), rugby M(c), sailing M/W, soccer W(s), softball W(s), swimming M(s)/W(s), tennis M(s)/W(s), track and field W, volleyball M(s)/W(s), water polo W(s). *Intramural sports:* badminton M/W, basketball M/W, cross-country running M/W, golf M/W, soccer M/W, softball M/W, table tennis M/W, tennis M/W, track and field M/W, volleyball M/W, weight lifting M/W.

Standardized Tests *Required:* SAT I or ACT (for admission).

Costs (2002–03) *Tuition:* state resident $3216 full-time, $134 per credit part-time; nonresident $9696 full-time, $404 per credit part-time. Full-time tuition and fees vary according to class time, course load, and program. Part-time tuition and fees vary according to class time, course load, and program. *Room and board:* Room and board charges vary according to board plan and housing facility. *Waivers:* minority students and employees or children of employees.

Financial Aid Of all full-time matriculated undergraduates who enrolled in 2001, 4564 applied for aid, 3123 were judged to have need, 1041 had their need fully met. In 2001, 679 non-need-based awards were made. *Average percent of need met:* 75%. *Average financial aid package:* $5618. *Average need-based loan:* $2342. *Average need-based gift aid:* $3037. *Average indebtedness upon graduation:* $12,850.

Applying *Application fee:* $40 (non-residents). *Required:* high school transcript, minimum 2.8 GPA, minimum SAT I score of 510 for verbal and math sections. *Application deadlines:* 6/1 (freshmen), 6/1 (transfers). *Notification:* continuous (freshmen).

Admissions Contact Ms. Janice Heu, Interim Director of Admissions and Records, University of Hawaii at Manoa, 2600 Campus Road, Room 001, Honolulu, HI 96822. *Phone:* 808-956-8975. *Toll-free phone:* 800-823-9771. *Fax:* 808-956-4148. *E-mail:* ar-info@hawaii.edu.

UNIVERSITY OF HAWAII-WEST OAHU
Pearl City, Hawaii

- **State-supported** upper-level, founded 1976, part of University of Hawaii System
- **Calendar** semesters
- **Degree** bachelor's
- **Small-town** campus with easy access to Honolulu
- **Coed,** 740 undergraduate students, 42% full-time, 65% women, 35% men
- **Moderately difficult** entrance level, 77% of applicants were admitted

Undergraduates 313 full-time, 427 part-time. Students come from 16 states and territories, 1 other country, 8% are from out of state, 1% African American, 58% Asian American or Pacific Islander, 2% Hispanic American.

Freshmen *Admission:* 529 applied, 408 admitted.

Faculty *Total:* 58, 41% full-time, 100% with terminal degrees. *Student/faculty ratio:* 13:1.

Majors American studies; anthropology; Asian studies; business administration; criminal justice/law enforcement administration; economics; English; European studies; health services administration; history; humanities; international business; philosophy; political science; psychology; public administration; social sciences; sociology.

Academic Programs *Special study options:* internships, part-time degree program, summer session for credit. *ROTC:* Army (c).

Library University of Hawaii-West Oahu Library with 25,000 titles, 132 serial subscriptions.

University of Hawaii-West Oahu (continued)

Computers on Campus 18 computers available on campus for general student use. A campuswide network can be accessed from off campus. Internet access, at least one staffed computer lab available.

Student Life *Housing:* college housing not available. *Campus security:* 24-hour emergency response devices and patrols, late-night transport/escort service. *Student Services:* personal/psychological counseling.

Costs (2001–02) *Tuition:* state resident $1968 full-time, $82 per credit part-time; nonresident $7104 full-time, $296 per credit part-time. *Required fees:* $10 full-time, $5 per term part-time. *Waivers:* employees or children of employees.

Applying *Application fee:* $25. *Application deadline:* 8/1 (transfers). *Notification:* continuous until 8/31 (transfers).

Admissions Contact Jean M. Osumi, Dean of Student Services, University of Hawaii-West Oahu, 96-043 Ala Ike, Pearl City, HI 96782. *Phone:* 808-453-4700. *Fax:* 805-453-6076. *E-mail:* jeano@uhwo.hawaii.edu.

UNIVERSITY OF PHOENIX-HAWAII CAMPUS
Honolulu, Hawaii

- **Proprietary** comprehensive
- **Calendar** continuous
- **Degrees** certificates, associate, bachelor's, master's, doctoral, post-master's, and postbachelor's certificates (courses conducted at 54 campuses and learning centers in 13 states)
- **Coed,** 760 undergraduate students, 100% full-time, 57% women, 43% men
- **Noncompetitive** entrance level

Undergraduates Students come from 13 states and territories, 1 other country, 2% are from out of state.

Freshmen *Admission:* 4 admitted.

Faculty *Total:* 228, 2% full-time, 19% with terminal degrees. *Student/faculty ratio:* 10:1.

Majors Information technology ; management information systems/business data processing; management science; nursing; nursing science; public administration and services related.

Academic Programs *Special study options:* accelerated degree program, adult/continuing education programs, advanced placement credit, distance learning, external degree program, independent study.

Library University Library with 17.5 million titles, 9,000 serial subscriptions, an OPAC, a Web page.

Computers on Campus A campuswide network can be accessed from off campus. Internet access, at least one staffed computer lab available.

Student Life *Housing:* college housing not available.

Costs (2001–02) *Tuition:* $9360 full-time. Full-time tuition and fees vary according to location and program. *Payment plan:* deferred payment. *Waivers:* employees or children of employees.

Applying *Options:* deferred entrance. *Application fee:* $85. *Required:* 2 years of work experience. *Required for some:* high school transcript. *Application deadline:* rolling (freshmen), rolling (transfers).

Admissions Contact Ms. Beth Barilla, Director of Admissions, University of Phoenix-Hawaii Campus, 4615 East Elwood Street, Phoenix, AZ 85040-1958. *Phone:* 480-927-0099 Ext. 1218. *Toll-free phone:* 800-228-7240. *Fax:* 480-594-1758. *E-mail:* beth.barilla@apollogrp.edu.

IDAHO

ALBERTSON COLLEGE OF IDAHO
Caldwell, Idaho

- **Independent** 4-year, founded 1891
- **Calendar** 4-1-4
- **Degree** bachelor's
- **Small-town** 43-acre campus
- **Endowment** $54.9 million
- **Coed,** 778 undergraduate students, 97% full-time, 54% women, 46% men
- **Moderately difficult** entrance level, 98% of applicants were admitted

Undergraduates 756 full-time, 22 part-time. Students come from 18 states and territories, 11 other countries, 29% are from out of state, 0.5% African American, 4% Asian American or Pacific Islander, 4% Hispanic American, 0.8% Native American, 2% international, 4% transferred in, 56% live on campus. *Retention:* 73% of 2001 full-time freshmen returned.

Freshmen *Admission:* 631 applied, 616 admitted, 227 enrolled. *Average high school GPA:* 3.5. *Test scores:* SAT verbal scores over 500: 82%; SAT math scores over 500: 80%; ACT scores over 18: 96%; SAT verbal scores over 600: 33%; SAT math scores over 600: 39%; ACT scores over 24: 60%; SAT verbal scores over 700: 6%; SAT math scores over 700: 4%; ACT scores over 30: 7%.

Faculty *Total:* 77, 90% full-time, 92% with terminal degrees. *Student/faculty ratio:* 11:1.

Majors Accounting; anthropology; art; biology; business administration; chemistry; computer science; creative writing; economics; English; exercise sciences; history; international business; international economics; mathematics; music; philosophy; physical education; physics; political science; pre-medicine; psychology; religious studies; sociology; Spanish; sport/fitness administration; theater arts/drama.

Academic Programs *Special study options:* advanced placement credit, double majors, English as a second language, honors programs, independent study, internships, off-campus study, part-time degree program, services for LD students, student-designed majors, study abroad. *Unusual degree programs:* 3-2 engineering with University of Idaho, Columbia University, Washington University in St. Louis.

Library Terteling Library plus 1 other with 181,146 titles, 822 serial subscriptions, an OPAC, a Web page.

Computers on Campus 200 computers available on campus for general student use. A campuswide network can be accessed from student residence rooms and from off campus that provide access to online course syllabi, course assignments, course discussion. Internet access, at least one staffed computer lab available.

Student Life *Housing:* on-campus residence required through sophomore year. *Options:* coed, women-only. *Activities and Organizations:* drama/theater group, student-run newspaper, choral group, Scarlet Masque Drama Group, Latino American Students, International Studies Association, national fraternities, national sororities. *Campus security:* 24-hour emergency response devices and patrols, student patrols, late-night transport/escort service, controlled dormitory access. *Student Services:* health clinic, personal/psychological counseling.

Athletics Member NAIA. *Intercollegiate sports:* baseball M(s), basketball M(s)/W(s), golf M(s)/W(s), skiing (cross-country) M/W, skiing (downhill) M(s)/W(s), soccer M(s)/W(s), softball W, tennis W(s), volleyball W(s). *Intramural sports:* badminton M/W, basketball M/W, bowling M/W, football M/W, soccer M/W, softball M/W, swimming M/W, table tennis M/W, volleyball M/W.

Standardized Tests *Required:* SAT I or ACT (for admission).

Costs (2001–02) *Comprehensive fee:* $21,440 includes full-time tuition ($16,700), mandatory fees ($340), and room and board ($4400). Part-time tuition: $732 per credit. Part-time tuition and fees vary according to program. *Required fees:* $35 per term part-time. *Room and board:* College room only: $2100. Room and board charges vary according to board plan and housing facility. *Payment plan:* installment. *Waivers:* children of alumni, adult students, senior citizens, and employees or children of employees.

Financial Aid Of all full-time matriculated undergraduates who enrolled in 2001, 718 applied for aid, 480 were judged to have need, 104 had their need fully met. 199 Federal Work-Study jobs (averaging $947). 166 State and other part-time jobs (averaging $812). In 2001, 231 non-need-based awards were made. *Average percent of need met:* 88%. *Average financial aid package:* $14,327. *Average need-based loan:* $4041. *Average need-based gift aid:* $4461. *Average non-need based aid:* $8002. *Average indebtedness upon graduation:* $19,725.

Applying *Options:* common application, electronic application, early admission, early action, deferred entrance. *Application fee:* $25. *Required:* essay or personal statement, high school transcript, 1 letter of recommendation. *Recommended:* interview. *Application deadlines:* 6/1 (freshmen), 8/1 (transfers). *Notification:* 12/15 (early action).

Admissions Contact Brandie Allemand, Associate Dean of Admission, Albertson College of Idaho, 2112 Cleveland Boulevard, Caldwell, ID 83605-4494. *Phone:* 208-459-5305. *Toll-free phone:* 800-224-3246. *Fax:* 208-459-5757. *E-mail:* admission@albertson.edu.

BOISE BIBLE COLLEGE
Boise, Idaho

- **Independent nondenominational** 4-year, founded 1945
- **Calendar** semesters
- **Degrees** certificates, associate, and bachelor's
- **Suburban** 17-acre campus
- **Endowment** $507,870
- **Coed,** 111 undergraduate students, 88% full-time, 44% women, 56% men

■ **Minimally difficult** entrance level, 94% of applicants were admitted

Undergraduates 98 full-time, 13 part-time. Students come from 9 states and territories, 12% transferred in. *Retention:* 56% of 2001 full-time freshmen returned.
Freshmen *Admission:* 71 applied, 67 admitted, 29 enrolled. *Average high school GPA:* 3.17. *Test scores:* SAT verbal scores over 500: 38%; SAT math scores over 500: 38%; ACT scores over 18: 54%; SAT verbal scores over 600: 13%; SAT math scores over 600: 13%; ACT scores over 24: 16%.
Faculty *Total:* 13, 46% full-time. *Student/faculty ratio:* 13:1.
Majors Biblical studies; divinity/ministry; Greek (modern); pastoral counseling; religious education; religious music; religious studies.
Academic Programs *Special study options:* adult/continuing education programs, advanced placement credit, cooperative education, distance learning, double majors, independent study, internships, part-time degree program.
Library Boise Bible College Library with 29,431 titles, 115 serial subscriptions.
Computers on Campus 8 computers available on campus for general student use. Internet access, at least one staffed computer lab available.
Student Life *Housing:* on-campus residence required through sophomore year. *Options:* men-only, women-only. *Activities and Organizations:* choral group, Concert Choir, Missions, Women's TLC, Spiritual Families, Drama Club. *Campus security:* patrols by police officers. *Student Services:* personal/psychological counseling.
Athletics *Intramural sports:* basketball M/W, football M, volleyball M/W.
Costs (2002–03) *Comprehensive fee:* $9889 includes full-time tuition ($5600), mandatory fees ($89), and room and board ($4200). Part-time tuition: $235 per hour. *Required fees:* $3 per hour, $10 per year part-time.
Financial Aid Of all full-time matriculated undergraduates who enrolled in 2001, 95 applied for aid, 65 were judged to have need, 2 had their need fully met. 5 Federal Work-Study jobs (averaging $1561). In 2001, 14 non-need-based awards were made. *Average percent of need met:* 43%. *Average financial aid package:* $6216. *Average need-based loan:* $3360. *Average need-based gift aid:* $2764. *Average non-need based aid:* $3230. *Average indebtedness upon graduation:* $16,992.
Applying *Options:* deferred entrance. *Application fee:* $25. *Required:* essay or personal statement, high school transcript, minimum 2.0 GPA, 3 letters of recommendation. *Recommended:* interview. *Application deadline:* rolling (freshmen), rolling (transfers). *Notification:* continuous (freshmen).
Admissions Contact Mr. Ross Knudsen, Director of Admissions, Boise Bible College, 8695 Marigold Street, Boise, ID 83704. *Phone:* 208-376-7731. *Toll-free phone:* 800-893-7755. *Fax:* 208-376-7743. *E-mail:* boibible@micron.net.

BOISE STATE UNIVERSITY
Boise, Idaho

■ **State-supported** comprehensive, founded 1932, part of Idaho System of Higher Education
■ **Calendar** semesters
■ **Degrees** certificates, diplomas, associate, bachelor's, master's, and doctoral
■ **Urban** 130-acre campus
■ **Endowment** $42.1 million
■ **Coed,** 15,486 undergraduate students, 60% full-time, 54% women, 46% men
■ **Minimally difficult** entrance level, 92% of applicants were admitted

Undergraduates 9,323 full-time, 6,163 part-time. Students come from 53 states and territories, 53 other countries, 10% are from out of state, 1% African American, 2% Asian American or Pacific Islander, 5% Hispanic American, 1% Native American, 1% international, 8% transferred in, 8% live on campus. *Retention:* 58% of 2001 full-time freshmen returned.
Freshmen *Admission:* 4,034 applied, 3,714 admitted, 2,417 enrolled. *Average high school GPA:* 3.39. *Test scores:* SAT verbal scores over 500: 47%; SAT math scores over 500: 51%; ACT scores over 18: 79%; SAT verbal scores over 600: 12%; SAT math scores over 600: 15%; ACT scores over 24: 24%; SAT verbal scores over 700: 1%; SAT math scores over 700: 2%; ACT scores over 30: 2%.
Faculty *Total:* 912, 58% full-time, 74% with terminal degrees. *Student/faculty ratio:* 19:1.
Majors Accounting; advertising; anthropology; art; art education; art history; athletic training/sports medicine; auto mechanic/technician; bilingual/bicultural education; biology; business administration; business economics; business education; business machine repair; business marketing and marketing management; chemistry; child care/development; civil engineering; computer/information sciences; computer science; computer systems networking/telecommunications; construction management; criminal justice/law enforcement administration; culinary arts; cultural studies; drafting; drawing; early childhood education; earth sciences; economics; education; electrical/electronic engineering technologies related; electrical/electronic engineering technology; electrical engineering; elementary education; English; environmental health; environmental science; exercise sciences; finance; French; geology; geophysics/seismology; German; graphic design/commercial art/illustration; health science; heating/air conditioning/refrigeration; history; horticulture science; human resources management; industrial radiologic technology; industrial technology; information sciences/systems; interdisciplinary studies; international business; liberal arts and sciences/liberal studies; literature; machine technology; mass communications; mathematics; mechanical engineering technology; medical administrative assistant; medical records administration; medical technology; music; music business management/merchandising; music teacher education; nursing; operating room technician; operations management; paralegal/legal assistant; perfusion technology; philosophy; physical education; physician assistant; physics; political science; pre-dentistry; pre-engineering; pre-medicine; pre-veterinary studies; psychology; public administration; public health; radiological science; reading education; respiratory therapy; science education; secondary education; social sciences; social work; sociology; Spanish; special education; teacher assistant/aide; technical/business writing; theater arts/drama; welding technology.
Academic Programs *Special study options:* academic remediation for entering students, adult/continuing education programs, advanced placement credit, cooperative education, distance learning, double majors, English as a second language, freshman honors college, honors programs, independent study, internships, off-campus study, part-time degree program, services for LD students, student-designed majors, study abroad, summer session for credit. *ROTC:* Army (b).
Library Albertsons Library with 505,618 titles, 4,797 serial subscriptions, an OPAC, a Web page.
Computers on Campus 900 computers available on campus for general student use. A campuswide network can be accessed from student residence rooms and from off campus. Internet access, online (class) registration, at least one staffed computer lab available.
Student Life *Housing Options:* coed. *Activities and Organizations:* drama/theater group, student-run newspaper, choral group, marching band, Latter-Day Saints Student Association, Residence Hall Association, Organization of Student Social Workers, Marching Band Association, Teacher Education Association, national fraternities, national sororities. *Campus security:* 24-hour emergency response devices and patrols. *Student Services:* health clinic, personal/psychological counseling, women's center, legal services.
Athletics Member NCAA. All Division I except football (Division I-A). *Intercollegiate sports:* baseball M(c), basketball M(s)/W(s), cross-country running M(s)/W(s), golf M(s)/W(s), gymnastics W(s), soccer W, tennis M(s)/W(s), track and field M(s)/W(s), volleyball W(s), wrestling M(s). *Intramural sports:* basketball M/W, bowling M/W, lacrosse W(c), racquetball M/W, skiing (downhill) M(c)/W(c), soccer M/W, softball M/W, tennis M/W, volleyball M/W, weight lifting M/W.
Standardized Tests *Required for some:* SAT I or ACT (for admission).
Costs (2001–02) *Tuition:* state resident $2665 full-time, $135 per credit part-time; nonresident $8865 full-time, $135 per credit part-time. Part-time tuition and fees vary according to course load. *Room and board:* $3869. Room and board charges vary according to board plan and housing facility. *Payment plan:* deferred payment. *Waivers:* senior citizens and employees or children of employees.
Applying *Options:* electronic application. *Application fee:* $30. *Required for some:* high school transcript, minimum 2.0 GPA. *Application deadlines:* 7/17 (freshmen), 7/17 (transfers). *Notification:* continuous (freshmen).
Admissions Contact Mr. Mark Wheeler, Dean of Enrollment Services, Boise State University, Enrollment Services, 1910 University Drive, Boise, ID 83725. *Phone:* 208-426-1177. *Toll-free phone:* 800-632-6586 (in-state); 800-824-7017 (out-of-state). *E-mail:* bsuinfo@boisestate.edu.

IDAHO STATE UNIVERSITY
Pocatello, Idaho

■ **State-supported** university, founded 1901
■ **Calendar** semesters
■ **Degrees** certificates, diplomas, associate, bachelor's, master's, doctoral, first professional, post-master's, and postbachelor's certificates
■ **Small-town** 735-acre campus
■ **Coed,** 11,167 undergraduate students, 67% full-time, 55% women, 45% men
■ **Minimally difficult** entrance level, 71% of applicants were admitted

Located in a beautiful mountain valley, Idaho State University (ISU) is a comprehensive university granting certificates through doctoral degrees in a wide range of programs. ISU is recognized in the state as a center for health professions and supporting sciences as well as for educator preparation. In addition, the University emphasizes business, engineering, and the liberal arts, and has the largest vocational-technical school in Idaho.

Idaho State University (continued)

Undergraduates 7,535 full-time, 3,632 part-time. Students come from 35 states and territories, 52 other countries, 6% are from out of state, 0.7% African American, 1% Asian American or Pacific Islander, 3% Hispanic American, 2% Native American, 2% international, 8% transferred in, 6% live on campus. *Retention:* 61% of 2001 full-time freshmen returned.

Freshmen *Admission:* 4,122 applied, 2,921 admitted, 1,883 enrolled. *Average high school GPA:* 2.66. *Test scores:* SAT verbal scores over 500: 65%; SAT math scores over 500: 64%; ACT scores over 18: 78%; SAT verbal scores over 600: 21%; SAT math scores over 600: 32%; ACT scores over 24: 26%; SAT math scores over 700: 4%; ACT scores over 30: 2%.

Faculty *Total:* 633, 80% full-time, 62% with terminal degrees. *Student/faculty ratio:* 17:1.

Majors Accounting; aircraft mechanic/powerplant; American studies; anthropology; art; auto body repair; biochemistry; biology; botany; business; business administration; business computer programming; business marketing and marketing management; chemistry; child care provider; civil engineering technology; communications; communication systems installation/repair; computer/information sciences; criminal justice studies; data processing technology; dental hygiene; dental laboratory technician; diesel engine mechanic; drafting; drafting/design technology; early childhood education; ecology; economics; education; electrical/electronic engineering technology; electrical/electronics drafting; electrical equipment installation/repair; electromechanical technology; elementary education; engineering; engineering/industrial management; engineering-related technology; English; finance; French; general studies; geology; German; graphic/printing equipment; health education; health services administration; history; home economics; human resources management; information sciences/systems; instrumentation technology; instrument calibration/repair; interdisciplinary studies; international relations; laser/optical technology; machine shop assistant; machine technology; mass communications; mathematics; medical assistant; medical radiologic technology; medical records technology; medical technology; microbiology/bacteriology; middle school education; music; music (general performance); music teacher education; Native American languages; nursing; nutrition studies; pharmacy; philosophy; physical education; physical therapy assistant; physician assistant; physics; political science; psychology; secondary education; secretarial science; social work; sociology; Spanish; special education; speech-language pathology/audiology; speech/theater education; technical education; theater arts/drama; welding technology; zoology.

Academic Programs *Special study options:* academic remediation for entering students, adult/continuing education programs, advanced placement credit, distance learning, double majors, English as a second language, external degree program, honors programs, independent study, internships, off-campus study, part-time degree program, services for LD students, student-designed majors, study abroad, summer session for credit. *ROTC:* Army (c).

Library Eli M. Oboler Library with 345,066 titles, 3,336 serial subscriptions, 4,500 audiovisual materials, an OPAC, a Web page.

Computers on Campus 300 computers available on campus for general student use. A campuswide network can be accessed from student residence rooms and from off campus. At least one staffed computer lab available.

Student Life *Housing Options:* coed, men-only, women-only, disabled students. *Activities and Organizations:* drama/theater group, student-run newspaper, choral group, International Students Association, Vocational Industrial Clubs of America, Latter Day Saints Student Association, Student American Dental Hygienists Association, Academy of Students of Pharmacy, national fraternities, national sororities. *Campus security:* 24-hour emergency response devices and patrols, student patrols, late-night transport/escort service, controlled dormitory access. *Student Services:* health clinic, personal/psychological counseling, legal services.

Athletics Member NCAA. All Division I except football (Division I-AA). *Intercollegiate sports:* basketball M(s)/W(s), cross-country running M(s)/W(s), golf M(s)/W(s), skiing (downhill) M/W, tennis M(s)/W(s), track and field M(s)/W(s), volleyball W(s). *Intramural sports:* basketball M/W, bowling M/W, cross-country running M/W, field hockey M/W, football M, racquetball M/W, riflery M/W, rugby M, skiing (cross-country) M/W, skiing (downhill) M/W, soccer M/W, softball M/W, table tennis M/W, tennis M/W, track and field M/W, volleyball M/W, water polo M/W.

Standardized Tests *Required:* SAT I or ACT (for admission).

Costs (2001–02) *Tuition:* state resident $140 per credit hour part-time; nonresident $6240 full-time, $230 per credit hour part-time. Full-time tuition and fees vary according to reciprocity agreements. Part-time tuition and fees vary according to reciprocity agreements. *Required fees:* $2800 full-time. *Room and board:* $4230; room only: $1944. Room and board charges vary according to board plan and housing facility. *Payment plan:* deferred payment. *Waivers:* senior citizens and employees or children of employees.

Financial Aid Of all full-time matriculated undergraduates who enrolled in 2001, 3610 applied for aid, 3429 were judged to have need, 3326 had their need fully met. 2205 State and other part-time jobs. *Average percent of need met:* 80%. *Average financial aid package:* $7066. *Average need-based loan:* $4177. *Average need-based gift aid:* $2654. *Average indebtedness upon graduation:* $18,188.

Applying *Options:* common application, early admission, deferred entrance. *Application fee:* $35. *Required:* high school transcript, minimum 2.0 GPA. *Application deadlines:* 8/1 (freshmen), 8/1 (transfers).

Admissions Contact Linda Ann Barnier, Director of Recruitment, Idaho State University, Campus Box 8270, Pocatello, ID 83209. *Phone:* 208-282-3279. *Fax:* 208-282-4231. *E-mail:* info@isu.edu.

ITT Technical Institute
Boise, Idaho

- **Proprietary** primarily 2-year, founded 1906, part of ITT Educational Services, Inc
- **Calendar** quarters
- **Degrees** associate and bachelor's
- **Urban** 1-acre campus
- **Coed,** 382 undergraduate students
- **Minimally difficult** entrance level

Majors Administrative/secretarial services; computer/information sciences related; computer programming; drafting; electrical/electronic engineering technologies related; information technology.

Student Life *Housing:* college housing not available.

Costs (2001–02) *Tuition:* Full-time tuition and fees vary according to program. Part-time tuition and fees vary according to program. $260—$330 per credit hour.

Financial Aid Of all full-time matriculated undergraduates who enrolled in 2001, 9 Federal Work-Study jobs (averaging $5500).

Applying *Options:* deferred entrance. *Application fee:* $100. *Required:* high school transcript, interview. *Recommended:* letters of recommendation. *Application deadline:* rolling (freshmen), rolling (transfers). *Notification:* continuous (freshmen).

Admissions Contact Mr. Bart Van Ry, Director of Recruitment, ITT Technical Institute, 12302 West Explorer Drive, Boise, ID 83713. *Phone:* 208-322-8844. *Toll-free phone:* 800-666-4888. *Fax:* 208-322-0173.

Lewis-Clark State College
Lewiston, Idaho

- **State-supported** 4-year, founded 1893
- **Calendar** semesters
- **Degrees** certificates, diplomas, associate, and bachelor's
- **Small-town** 44-acre campus
- **Endowment** $509,158
- **Coed,** 2,953 undergraduate students, 74% full-time, 62% women, 38% men
- **Minimally difficult** entrance level, 64% of applicants were admitted

Undergraduates 2,176 full-time, 777 part-time. Students come from 19 states and territories, 23 other countries, 15% are from out of state, 0.6% African American, 0.9% Asian American or Pacific Islander, 2% Hispanic American, 5% Native American, 3% international, 10% transferred in, 10% live on campus. *Retention:* 50% of 2001 full-time freshmen returned.

Freshmen *Admission:* 1,099 applied, 700 admitted, 519 enrolled. *Average high school GPA:* 2.96. *Test scores:* SAT verbal scores over 500: 41%; SAT math scores over 500: 34%; ACT scores over 18: 80%; SAT verbal scores over 600: 4%; SAT math scores over 600: 11%; ACT scores over 24: 24%; ACT scores over 30: 1%.

Faculty *Total:* 248, 57% full-time, 42% with terminal degrees. *Student/faculty ratio:* 17:1.

Majors Accounting; agricultural mechanization; auto mechanic/technician; behavioral sciences; biological/physical sciences; biology; business administration; business marketing and marketing management; chemistry; child care provider; child care services management; computer engineering technology; criminal justice/law enforcement administration; drafting; drafting/design technology; earth sciences; education; education (K-12); electrical/electronic engineering technology; elementary education; engineering-related technology; English; environmental biology; exercise sciences; geology; graphic design/commercial art/illustration; graphic/printing equipment; heating/air conditioning/refrigeration; heavy equipment maintenance; history; hospitality management; hotel/motel services marketing operations; industrial electronics installation/repair; interdisciplinary studies; law enforcement/police science; legal administrative assistant; liberal arts and sciences/liberal studies; major appliance installation/repair; mass communications; mathematics; medical administrative assistant; medical laboratory technology; natural sciences; nursing; paralegal/legal assistant; physical education; pre-engineering; pre-law; psychology; radio/television broadcasting; restaurant operations; retail management; science education; secretarial science; social sciences; social work; special education; speech/rhetorical studies; speech/theater education; theater arts/drama; welding technology.

Academic Programs *Special study options:* academic remediation for entering students, accelerated degree program, adult/continuing education programs, advanced placement credit, cooperative education, distance learning, double majors, English as a second language, external degree program, honors programs, independent study, internships, off-campus study, part-time degree program, services for LD students, student-designed majors, summer session for credit. *ROTC:* Army (b), Navy (b), Air Force (c).

Library Lewis-Clark State College Library with 221,320 titles, 1,692 serial subscriptions, 6,884 audiovisual materials, an OPAC, a Web page.

Computers on Campus 88 computers available on campus for general student use. A campuswide network can be accessed from student residence rooms and from off campus. Internet access, at least one staffed computer lab available.

Student Life *Housing Options:* coed, cooperative. *Activities and Organizations:* drama/theater group, student-run newspaper, television station, choral group, Business Students Organization, Ambassadors Club, International Club, Honors Society, Explorers. *Campus security:* 24-hour emergency response devices and patrols, student patrols, late-night transport/escort service. *Student Services:* health clinic, personal/psychological counseling.

Athletics Member NAIA. *Intercollegiate sports:* baseball M(s), basketball M(s)/W(s), cross-country running M(s)/W(s), golf M(s)/W(s), tennis M(s)/W(s), volleyball W(s). *Intramural sports:* badminton M/W, baseball M/W, basketball M/W, bowling M/W, football M/W, golf M/W, skiing (downhill) M/W, soccer M/W, softball M/W, table tennis M/W, tennis M/W, volleyball M/W, weight lifting M/W.

Standardized Tests *Required for some:* SAT I or ACT (for admission). *Recommended:* ACT (for admission).

Costs (2001–02) *Tuition:* state resident $2550 full-time, $110 per credit part-time; nonresident $7988 full-time, $110 per credit part-time. *Required fees:* $2550 full-time. *Room and board:* $2970; room only: $1875. Room and board charges vary according to board plan and housing facility. *Payment plan:* deferred payment. *Waivers:* senior citizens and employees or children of employees.

Financial Aid Of all full-time matriculated undergraduates who enrolled in 2001, 2008 applied for aid, 1655 were judged to have need, 983 had their need fully met. 108 Federal Work-Study jobs (averaging $1600). 66 State and other part-time jobs (averaging $1693). In 2001, 239 non-need-based awards were made. *Average percent of need met:* 71%. *Average financial aid package:* $5489. *Average need-based loan:* $2481. *Average need-based gift aid:* $2289. *Average non-need based aid:* $1052. *Average indebtedness upon graduation:* $4187.

Applying *Options:* electronic application, early admission, early action, deferred entrance. *Application fee:* $20. *Required:* high school transcript, minimum 2.0 GPA. *Required for some:* essay or personal statement, interview. *Application deadline:* rolling (freshmen), rolling (transfers). *Notification:* continuous (freshmen).

Admissions Contact Ms. Rosanne English, Office Specialist II, Lewis-Clark State College, 500 8th Avenue, Lewiston, ID 83501. *Phone:* 208-792-2210. *Toll-free phone:* 800-933-LCSC Ext. 2210. *Fax:* 208-792-2876. *E-mail:* admoff@lcsc.edu.

NORTHWEST NAZARENE UNIVERSITY
Nampa, Idaho

- **Independent** comprehensive, founded 1913, affiliated with Church of the Nazarene
- **Calendar** quarters
- **Degrees** bachelor's and master's
- **Small-town** 85-acre campus
- **Endowment** $14.2 million
- **Coed,** 1,110 undergraduate students, 91% full-time, 55% women, 45% men
- **Moderately difficult** entrance level, 77% of applicants were admitted

NNU is consistently ranked by *U.S. News & World Report* as a top university and best value choice in the West. New and expanding undergraduate and graduate programs are a sign of growth at this progressive university. A new state-of-the-art business building is the latest addition to the campus complex.

Undergraduates 1,005 full-time, 105 part-time. Students come from 22 states and territories, 7 other countries, 56% are from out of state, 0.5% African American, 1% Asian American or Pacific Islander, 2% Hispanic American, 0.5% Native American, 0.2% international, 6% transferred in, 68% live on campus. *Retention:* 72% of 2001 full-time freshmen returned.

Freshmen *Admission:* 681 applied, 525 admitted, 262 enrolled. *Average high school GPA:* 3.38. *Test scores:* ACT scores over 18: 89%; ACT scores over 24: 43%; ACT scores over 30: 7%.

Faculty *Total:* 90, 98% full-time, 68% with terminal degrees. *Student/faculty ratio:* 12:1.

Majors Accounting; art; art education; athletic training/sports medicine; biblical languages/literatures; biology; biology education; business administration; business marketing and marketing management; ceramic arts; chemistry; chemistry education; computer science; divinity/ministry; elementary education; engineering physics; English; English education; finance; graphic design/commercial art/illustration; health/physical education; history; history education; international business; international relations; liberal arts and sciences/liberal studies; mass communications; mathematics; mathematics education; missionary studies; music; music (general performance); music teacher education; music theory and composition; nursing; painting; pastoral counseling; philosophy; physical education; physical therapy; physics; political science; pre-law; pre-medicine; psychology; public relations; recreation/leisure studies; religious education; religious music; religious studies; secondary education; social science education; social sciences; social work; Spanish; Spanish language education; speech-language pathology/audiology; theology.

Academic Programs *Special study options:* academic remediation for entering students, accelerated degree program, advanced placement credit, cooperative education, freshman honors college, honors programs, independent study, internships, off-campus study, part-time degree program, services for LD students, student-designed majors, study abroad, summer session for credit. *ROTC:* Army (b). *Unusual degree programs:* 3-2 engineering with University of Idaho, Boise State University, Walla Walla College.

Library John E. Riley Library with 100,966 titles, 821 serial subscriptions, an OPAC, a Web page.

Computers on Campus 400 computers available on campus for general student use. A campuswide network can be accessed from student residence rooms and from off campus that provide access to various software packages. Internet access, at least one staffed computer lab available.

Student Life *Housing:* on-campus residence required through junior year. *Options:* coed, men-only, women-only. *Activities and Organizations:* drama/theater group, student-run newspaper, choral group, student government, Are You Serving Him (RUSH), ministry clubs, service clubs, science clubs. *Campus security:* 24-hour patrols, student patrols, late-night transport/escort service, controlled dormitory access, residence hall check-in system. *Student Services:* health clinic, personal/psychological counseling.

Athletics Member NAIA. *Intercollegiate sports:* baseball M(s), basketball M(s)/W(s), cross-country running M(s)/W(s), golf M(s), soccer M(s)/W(s), track and field M(s)/W(s), volleyball M(c)/W(s). *Intramural sports:* basketball M/W, cross-country running M/W, fencing M/W, football M/W, golf M, softball M/W, table tennis M/W.

Standardized Tests *Required for some:* ACT (for admission). *Recommended:* ACT (for admission).

Costs (2002–03) *Comprehensive fee:* $19,345 includes full-time tuition ($14,520), mandatory fees ($540), and room and board ($4285). Part-time tuition: $631 per credit. Part-time tuition and fees vary according to course load. *Required fees:* $55 per term part-time. *Room and board:* Room and board charges vary according to student level. *Payment plan:* installment. *Waivers:* employees or children of employees.

Financial Aid Of all full-time matriculated undergraduates who enrolled in 2001, 1017 applied for aid, 791 were judged to have need, 304 had their need fully met. *Average percent of need met:* 75%. *Average financial aid package:* $11,063. *Average need-based loan:* $4361. *Average need-based gift aid:* $6652. *Average indebtedness upon graduation:* $20,159.

Applying *Options:* electronic application, early admission, deferred entrance. *Application fee:* $20. *Required:* high school transcript, minimum 2.5 GPA, 2 letters of recommendation. *Required for some:* interview. *Application deadlines:* 8/27 (freshmen), 8/27 (transfers). *Notification:* continuous (freshmen).

Admissions Contact Northwest Nazarene University, 623 Holly Street, Nampa, ID 83686. *Phone:* 208-467-8648. *Toll-free phone:* 877-NNU-4YOU. *Fax:* 208-467-8645. *E-mail:* admissions@nnu.edu.

UNIVERSITY OF IDAHO
Moscow, Idaho

- **State-supported** university, founded 1889
- **Calendar** semesters
- **Degrees** certificates, bachelor's, master's, doctoral, first professional, and post-master's certificates
- **Small-town** 1450-acre campus

University of Idaho (continued)
- **Endowment** $144.5 million
- **Coed,** 9,134 undergraduate students, 87% full-time, 46% women, 54% men
- **Moderately difficult** entrance level, 84% of applicants were admitted

Undergraduates 7,950 full-time, 1,184 part-time. Students come from 50 states and territories, 40 other countries, 19% are from out of state, 0.7% African American, 2% Asian American or Pacific Islander, 3% Hispanic American, 1% Native American, 2% international, 7% transferred in, 55% live on campus. *Retention:* 80% of 2001 full-time freshmen returned.

Freshmen *Admission:* 3,731 applied, 3,117 admitted, 1,679 enrolled. *Average high school GPA:* 3.45. *Test scores:* SAT verbal scores over 500: 70%; SAT math scores over 500: 74%; ACT scores over 18: 92%; SAT verbal scores over 600: 30%; SAT math scores over 600: 32%; ACT scores over 24: 47%; SAT verbal scores over 700: 6%; SAT math scores over 700: 6%; ACT scores over 30: 9%.

Faculty *Total:* 615, 92% full-time, 82% with terminal degrees. *Student/faculty ratio:* 17:1.

Majors Accounting; agricultural business; agricultural economics; agricultural education; agricultural engineering; agricultural mechanization; agricultural sciences; American studies; animal sciences; anthropology; applied mathematics; architecture; art; art education; athletic training/sports medicine; bioengineering; biology; botany; business education; business marketing and marketing management; cartography; chemical engineering; chemistry; child care/development; civil engineering; classics; clothing/apparel/textile studies; communications; computer engineering; computer science; criminal justice studies; dance; economics; electrical engineering; elementary education; engineering; English; entomology; environmental science; finance; fine/studio arts; fish/game management; food sciences; foreign languages/literatures; forestry; French; general studies; geography; geological engineering; geology; German; history; home economics education; horticulture science; human resources management; industrial arts education; industrial/manufacturing engineering; industrial technology; interior architecture; interior design; international relations; journalism; landscape architecture; Latin American studies; Latin (ancient and medieval); liberal arts and sciences/liberal studies; management information systems/business data processing; mathematics; mechanical engineering; medical technology; metallurgical engineering; microbiology/bacteriology; military technology; mining/mineral engineering; molecular biology; multi/interdisciplinary studies related; music business management/merchandising; music (general performance); music history; music teacher education; music theory and composition; music (voice and choral/opera performance); natural resources management; nutrition studies; operations management; philosophy; photography; physical education; physics; plant sciences; political science; pre-medicine; psychology; public relations; radio/television broadcasting; range management; recreation/leisure studies; secondary education; secretarial science; sociology; soil sciences; Spanish; special education; technical education; theater arts/drama; trade/industrial education; wildlife management; wood science/paper technology; zoology.

Academic Programs *Special study options:* academic remediation for entering students, accelerated degree program, adult/continuing education programs, advanced placement credit, cooperative education, distance learning, double majors, honors programs, independent study, internships, off-campus study, part-time degree program, services for LD students, student-designed majors, study abroad, summer session for credit. *ROTC:* Army (b), Navy (b), Air Force (c).

Library University of Idaho Library plus 1 other with 1.4 million titles, 14,230 serial subscriptions, 8,717 audiovisual materials, an OPAC, a Web page.

Computers on Campus 750 computers available on campus for general student use. A campuswide network can be accessed from student residence rooms and from off campus. Internet access, online (class) registration, at least one staffed computer lab available.

Student Life *Housing Options:* coed, men-only, women-only, cooperative. *Activities and Organizations:* drama/theater group, student-run newspaper, radio and television station, choral group, marching band, Alpha Phi Omega, Campus Crusade for Christ, Student International Association, OELA, Students of Human Resource Management, national fraternities, national sororities. *Campus security:* late-night transport/escort service, controlled dormitory access. *Student Services:* health clinic, personal/psychological counseling, women's center, legal services.

Athletics Member NCAA. All Division I except football (Division I-A). *Intercollegiate sports:* baseball M(c), basketball M(s)/W(s), cross-country running M(s)/W(s), golf M(s)/W(s), ice hockey M(c), riflery M(c)/W(c), rugby M(c)/W(c), skiing (cross-country) M(c)/W(c), skiing (downhill) M(c)/W(c), soccer M(c)/W(s), tennis M(s)/W(s), track and field M(s)/W(s), volleyball W(s). *Intramural sports:* baseball M, basketball M/W, equestrian sports M/W, football M/W, golf M/W, ice hockey M, racquetball M/W, riflery M/W, rugby M/W, skiing (cross-country) M/W, skiing (downhill) M/W, soccer M/W, softball M/W, squash M/W, swimming M/W, table tennis M/W, tennis M/W, track and field M/W, volleyball W, weight lifting M/W, wrestling M.

Standardized Tests *Required:* SAT I or ACT (for admission).

Costs (2001–02) *Tuition:* state resident $0 full-time; nonresident $6000 full-time, $95 per credit part-time. Full-time tuition and fees vary according to program and reciprocity agreements. Part-time tuition and fees vary according to course load. *Required fees:* $2720 full-time, $140 per credit. *Room and board:* $4306. Room and board charges vary according to board plan and housing facility. *Payment plan:* deferred payment. *Waivers:* senior citizens and employees or children of employees.

Financial Aid Of all full-time matriculated undergraduates who enrolled in 2001, 5004 applied for aid, 3883 were judged to have need, 1365 had their need fully met. 437 Federal Work-Study jobs (averaging $1294). 197 State and other part-time jobs (averaging $1434). In 2001, 1754 non-need-based awards were made. *Average percent of need met:* 80%. *Average financial aid package:* $7763. *Average need-based loan:* $5313. *Average need-based gift aid:* $2361. *Average non-need based aid:* $3136. *Average indebtedness upon graduation:* $18,710.

Applying *Options:* common application, electronic application, deferred entrance. *Application fee:* $30. *Required:* high school transcript, minimum 2.2 GPA. *Required for some:* essay or personal statement. *Application deadline:* 8/1 (freshmen), rolling (transfers). *Notification:* continuous (freshmen).

Admissions Contact Mr. Dan Davenport, Director of Admissions, University of Idaho, Admissions Office, PO Box 444264, Moscow, ID 83844-4264. *Phone:* 208-885-6326. *Toll-free phone:* 888-884-3246. *Fax:* 208-885-9119. *E-mail:* admappl@uidaho.edu.

University of Phoenix-Idaho Campus
Boise, Idaho

- **Proprietary** comprehensive
- **Calendar** continuous
- **Degrees** certificates, associate, bachelor's, master's, doctoral, post-master's, and postbachelor's certificates (courses conducted at 54 campuses and learning centers in 13 states)
- **Coed**

Majors Business administration/management related; computer/information sciences.

Student Life *Housing:* college housing not available.

Costs (2001–02) *Tuition:* $7860 full-time. Full-time tuition and fees vary according to location and program. *Payment plan:* deferred payment. *Waivers:* employees or children of employees.

Admissions Contact 6148 North Discovery Way, Suite 120, Boise, ID 83713.

ILLINOIS

American Academy of Art
Chicago, Illinois

- **Proprietary** 4-year, founded 1923
- **Calendar** trimesters
- **Degree** bachelor's
- **Urban** campus
- **Coed,** 360 undergraduate students, 76% full-time, 34% women, 66% men
- **Moderately difficult** entrance level, 100% of applicants were admitted

Undergraduates 272 full-time, 88 part-time. Students come from 8 states and territories, 2% are from out of state, 9% African American, 3% Asian American or Pacific Islander, 24% Hispanic American, 0.6% international, 7% transferred in. *Retention:* 82% of 2001 full-time freshmen returned.

Freshmen *Admission:* 87 applied, 87 admitted, 87 enrolled.

Faculty *Total:* 30, 87% full-time, 73% with terminal degrees. *Student/faculty ratio:* 13:1.

Majors Advertising; applied art; art; computer graphics; design/visual communications; drawing; fine/studio arts; graphic design/commercial art/illustration; painting; visual/performing arts.

Academic Programs *Special study options:* academic remediation for entering students, accelerated degree program, adult/continuing education programs, independent study, internships, part-time degree program, study abroad, summer session for credit.

Library Irving Shapiro Library with 1,730 titles, 62 serial subscriptions, 101 audiovisual materials.

Computers on Campus 2 computers available on campus for general student use.

Student Life *Housing:* college housing not available. *Campus security:* 24-hour emergency response devices.

Costs (2001–02) *Tuition:* $15,880 full-time, $3972 per term part-time. Full-time tuition and fees vary according to course load. Part-time tuition and fees vary according to course load. *Payment plan:* installment. *Waivers:* employees or children of employees.

Applying *Options:* electronic application. *Application fee:* $25. *Application deadline:* rolling (freshmen), rolling (transfers).

Admissions Contact Ms. Ione Fitzgerald, Director of Admissions, American Academy of Art, 332 South Michigan Ave, Suite 300, Chicago, IL 60604-4302. *Phone:* 312-461-0600 Ext. 143.

AMERICAN INTERCONTINENTAL UNIVERSITY ONLINE
Hoffman Estates, Illinois

- **Proprietary** comprehensive, part of American InterContinental University
- **Degrees** associate, bachelor's, and master's
- **Coed,** 196 undergraduate students, 100% full-time, 39% women, 61% men

Undergraduates 196 full-time. Students come from 24 states and territories, 1 other country, 24% African American, 6% Asian American or Pacific Islander, 6% Hispanic American, 3% Native American, 0.5% international, 15% transferred in.

Freshmen *Admission:* 19 enrolled.

Faculty *Total:* 21, 19% full-time, 24% with terminal degrees. *Student/faculty ratio:* 19:1.

Majors Business administration/management related; data processing technology.

Costs (2002–03) *Tuition:* $20,400 full-time. Full-time tuition and fees vary according to program. *Required fees:* $175 full-time. *Payment plan:* installment.

Applying *Application fee:* $50. *Required:* high school transcript, interview. *Recommended:* essay or personal statement. *Application deadline:* rolling (freshmen), rolling (transfers). *Notification:* continuous (freshmen).

Admissions Contact Mr. Steve Fireng, Vice President of Admissions, American InterContinental University Online, 2895 Greenspoint Parkway, Suite 400, Hoffman Estates, IL 60195. *Phone:* 877-701-3800. *Toll-free phone:* 877-221-5800 Ext. 2604 (in-state); 877-701-3800 (out-of-state). *E-mail:* info@aiu-online.com.

AUGUSTANA COLLEGE
Rock Island, Illinois

- **Independent** 4-year, founded 1860, affiliated with Evangelical Lutheran Church in America
- **Calendar** trimesters
- **Degree** bachelor's
- **Suburban** 115-acre campus
- **Endowment** $84.3 million
- **Coed,** 2,232 undergraduate students, 99% full-time, 57% women, 43% men
- **Moderately difficult** entrance level, 77% of applicants were admitted

Undergraduates 2,205 full-time, 27 part-time. Students come from 28 states and territories, 19 other countries, 12% are from out of state, 2% African American, 2% Asian American or Pacific Islander, 3% Hispanic American, 0.1% Native American, 0.6% international, 4% transferred in, 70% live on campus. *Retention:* 87% of 2001 full-time freshmen returned.

Freshmen *Admission:* 2,622 applied, 2,026 admitted, 552 enrolled. *Average high school GPA:* 3.50. *Test scores:* ACT scores over 18: 100%; ACT scores over 24: 67%; ACT scores over 30: 17%.

Faculty *Total:* 209, 68% full-time, 68% with terminal degrees. *Student/faculty ratio:* 12:1.

Majors Accounting; anthropology; art; art education; art history; Asian studies; biology; business administration; business marketing and marketing management; chemistry; classics; computer science; creative writing; earth sciences; economics; education; elementary education; engineering physics; English; environmental science; finance; fine/studio arts; French; geography; geology; German; history; jazz; Latin (ancient and medieval); liberal arts and sciences/liberal studies; literature; mass communications; mathematics; music; music (piano and organ performance); music teacher education; music (voice and choral/opera performance); occupational therapy; philosophy; physical education; physics; political science; pre-dentistry; pre-law; pre-medicine; pre-veterinary studies; psychology; public administration; religious music; religious studies; Scandinavian languages; secondary education; sociology; Spanish; speech-language pathology/audiology; speech/rhetorical studies; speech therapy; stringed instruments; theater arts/drama; wind/percussion instruments; women's studies.

Academic Programs *Special study options:* accelerated degree program, advanced placement credit, double majors, honors programs, independent study, internships, part-time degree program, services for LD students, study abroad, summer session for credit. *Unusual degree programs:* 3-2 engineering with Washington University in St. Louis, University of Illinois, Iowa State University of Science and Technology, Purdue University; forestry with Duke University; occupational therapy with Washington University in St. Louis, landscape architecture with University of Illinois, environmental studies with Duke University.

Library Augustana College Library plus 3 others with 227,357 titles, 1,870 serial subscriptions, 2,639 audiovisual materials, an OPAC, a Web page.

Computers on Campus 600 computers available on campus for general student use. A campuswide network can be accessed from student residence rooms and from off campus. Internet access, at least one staffed computer lab available.

Student Life *Housing:* on-campus residence required through junior year. *Options:* coed, men-only, women-only. *Activities and Organizations:* drama/theater group, student-run newspaper, radio station, choral group, College Union Board of Managers, Student Government Association, Literacy Council, student radio station. *Campus security:* 24-hour emergency response devices and patrols, late-night transport/escort service, controlled dormitory access. *Student Services:* health clinic, personal/psychological counseling, women's center.

Athletics Member NCAA. All Division III. *Intercollegiate sports:* baseball M, basketball M/W, cross-country running M/W, football M, golf M/W, soccer M/W, softball W, swimming M/W, tennis M/W, track and field M/W, volleyball M(c)/W, wrestling M. *Intramural sports:* badminton M/W, basketball M/W, bowling M/W, crew M, cross-country running M/W, football M/W, golf M/W, racquetball M/W, rugby M, skiing (cross-country) M/W, skiing (downhill) M/W, soccer M/W, softball M/W, swimming M/W, table tennis M/W, tennis M/W, track and field M/W, volleyball M/W, wrestling M.

Standardized Tests *Required:* SAT I or ACT (for admission).

Costs (2001–02) *Comprehensive fee:* $24,117 includes full-time tuition ($18,330), mandatory fees ($390), and room and board ($5397). Full-time tuition and fees vary according to course load. Part-time tuition: $765 per credit. *Room and board:* College room only: $2661. Room and board charges vary according to housing facility. *Payment plans:* tuition prepayment, installment. *Waivers:* employees or children of employees.

Financial Aid Of all full-time matriculated undergraduates who enrolled in 2001, 2142 applied for aid, 1464 were judged to have need, 502 had their need fully met. 1009 Federal Work-Study jobs (averaging $1241). In 2001, 642 non-need-based awards were made. *Average percent of need met:* 88%. *Average financial aid package:* $14,664. *Average need-based loan:* $4186. *Average need-based gift aid:* $10,372. *Average non-need based aid:* $6676. *Average indebtedness upon graduation:* $15,923.

Applying *Options:* common application, deferred entrance. *Application fee:* $25. *Required:* high school transcript. *Required for some:* essay or personal statement, 2 letters of recommendation, interview. *Application deadline:* rolling (freshmen), rolling (transfers). *Notification:* continuous (freshmen).

Admissions Contact Mr. Martin Sauer, Director of Admissions, Augustana College, 639 38th Street, Rock Island, IL 61201-2296. *Phone:* 309-794-7341. *Toll-free phone:* 800-798-8100. *Fax:* 309-794-7422. *E-mail:* admissions@augustana.edu.

AURORA UNIVERSITY
Aurora, Illinois

- **Independent** comprehensive, founded 1893
- **Calendar** trimesters
- **Degrees** certificates, diplomas, bachelor's, master's, doctoral, post-master's, and postbachelor's certificates
- **Suburban** 26-acre campus with easy access to Chicago
- **Endowment** $25.2 million
- **Coed,** 1,323 undergraduate students, 78% full-time, 60% women, 40% men
- **Moderately difficult** entrance level, 62% of applicants were admitted

Aurora University combines a residential and commuter population. Curriculum emphasizes human services offered through the College of Education and George Williams College (social work, nursing, human services), supplemented by University College, which houses Arts and Sciences and the John and Judy Dunham School of Business. The YMCA Senior Director Certificate Program is a supplemental major offered in cooperation with the YMCA of the USA.

Undergraduates 1,035 full-time, 288 part-time. Students come from 10 states and territories, 4% are from out of state, 17% African American, 2% Asian

Aurora University (continued)
American or Pacific Islander, 10% Hispanic American, 0.3% Native American, 20% transferred in, 30% live on campus. *Retention:* 76% of 2001 full-time freshmen returned.

Freshmen *Admission:* 778 applied, 484 admitted, 212 enrolled. *Average high school GPA:* 3.06. *Test scores:* SAT verbal scores over 500: 67%; SAT math scores over 500: 33%; ACT scores over 18: 81%; SAT math scores over 600: 33%; ACT scores over 24: 22%; ACT scores over 30: 1%.

Faculty *Total:* 88, 72% full-time, 57% with terminal degrees. *Student/faculty ratio:* 16:1.

Majors Accounting; biology; business; business economics; business marketing and marketing management; business systems networking/ telecommunications; chemistry; communications; computer/information sciences; criminal justice/law enforcement administration; criminal justice studies; economics; elementary education; engineering physics; English; English composition; environmental science; finance; health/medical preparatory programs related; history; humanities; management information systems/business data processing; mathematics; medical technology; nursing; operations management; philosophy; physical education; political science; psychology; social work; sociology.

Academic Programs *Special study options:* academic remediation for entering students, adult/continuing education programs, advanced placement credit, distance learning, double majors, independent study, internships, off-campus study, part-time degree program, services for LD students, student-designed majors, study abroad, summer session for credit. *ROTC:* Army (c).

Library Charles B. Phillips Library plus 1 other with 113,032 titles, 735 serial subscriptions, 5,880 audiovisual materials, an OPAC, a Web page.

Computers on Campus 90 computers available on campus for general student use. A campuswide network can be accessed from student residence rooms and from off campus. Internet access, at least one staffed computer lab available.

Student Life *Housing Options:* coed, men-only, women-only. *Activities and Organizations:* drama/theater group, student-run newspaper, television station, choral group, Black Student Association, Aurora University Student Association, Student Nursing Association, Social Work Association, national fraternities, national sororities. *Campus security:* 24-hour patrols, late-night transport/escort service, controlled dormitory access. *Student Services:* health clinic, personal/psychological counseling.

Athletics Member NCAA. All Division III. *Intercollegiate sports:* baseball M, basketball M/W, football M, golf M, soccer M/W, softball W, tennis M/W, volleyball W. *Intramural sports:* basketball M/W, football M/W, soccer M/W, softball M/W, volleyball M/W.

Standardized Tests *Recommended:* SAT I and SAT II or ACT (for admission).

Costs (2001–02) *Comprehensive fee:* $18,900 includes full-time tuition ($13,767) and room and board ($5133). Full-time tuition and fees vary according to course load, location, and program. Part-time tuition: $471 per semester hour. Part-time tuition and fees vary according to location and program. *Room and board:* Room and board charges vary according to board plan and housing facility. *Payment plans:* installment, deferred payment. *Waivers:* senior citizens and employees or children of employees.

Financial Aid Of all full-time matriculated undergraduates who enrolled in 2001, 929 applied for aid, 777 were judged to have need, 38 had their need fully met. 300 Federal Work-Study jobs (averaging $1452). In 2001, 127 non-need-based awards were made. *Average percent of need met:* 64%. *Average financial aid package:* $11,185. *Average need-based loan:* $3966. *Average need-based gift aid:* $6487. *Average non-need based aid:* $5214. *Average indebtedness upon graduation:* $10,903.

Applying *Options:* common application, electronic application, early admission, early action, deferred entrance. *Application fee:* $25. *Required:* high school transcript, minimum 2.0 GPA. *Required for some:* essay or personal statement, 2 letters of recommendation, interview. *Recommended:* essay or personal statement, interview. *Application deadline:* rolling (freshmen), rolling (transfers). *Notification:* continuous (freshmen).

Admissions Contact Mr. James Lancaster, Freshman Recruitment Coordinator, Aurora University, 347 South Gladstone Avenue, Aurora, IL 60506-4892. *Phone:* 630-844-5533. *Toll-free phone:* 800-742-5281. *Fax:* 630-844-5535. *E-mail:* admissions@aurora.edu.

BENEDICTINE UNIVERSITY
Lisle, Illinois

- **Independent Roman Catholic** comprehensive, founded 1887
- **Calendar** semesters
- **Degrees** associate, bachelor's, master's, and doctoral
- **Suburban** 108-acre campus with easy access to Chicago
- **Endowment** $11.1 million
- **Coed,** 1,986 undergraduate students, 69% full-time, 62% women, 38% men
- **Moderately difficult** entrance level, 66% of applicants were admitted

Undergraduates 1,363 full-time, 623 part-time. Students come from 22 states and territories, 3% are from out of state, 9% African American, 14% Asian American or Pacific Islander, 8% Hispanic American, 0.2% Native American, 11% transferred in, 23% live on campus. *Retention:* 75% of 2001 full-time freshmen returned.

Freshmen *Admission:* 852 applied, 565 admitted, 262 enrolled. *Average high school GPA:* 3.31. *Test scores:* SAT verbal scores over 500: 79%; SAT math scores over 500: 82%; ACT scores over 18: 95%; SAT verbal scores over 600: 34%; SAT math scores over 600: 40%; ACT scores over 24: 46%; SAT verbal scores over 700: 8%; ACT scores over 30: 5%.

Faculty *Total:* 218, 41% full-time, 66% with terminal degrees. *Student/faculty ratio:* 14:1.

Majors Accounting; arts management; biochemistry; biology; business; business administration; business economics; business management/administrative services related; business marketing and marketing management; chemistry; communications; computer science; economics; education; elementary education; engineering science; English; environmental science; finance; fine/studio arts; health science; health services administration; history; information sciences/systems; international business; international relations; mathematics; medical technology; molecular biology; music; music teacher education; nuclear medical technology; nursing science; nutritional sciences; organizational behavior; philosophy; physics; political science; pre-dentistry; pre-law; pre-medicine; pre-veterinary studies; psychology; publishing; science education; secondary education; social sciences; sociology; Spanish; special education.

Academic Programs *Special study options:* academic remediation for entering students, accelerated degree program, adult/continuing education programs, advanced placement credit, distance learning, double majors, English as a second language, honors programs, independent study, internships, off-campus study, part-time degree program, services for LD students, study abroad, summer session for credit. *ROTC:* Army (c). *Unusual degree programs:* 3-2 engineering with University of Illinois at Urbana-Champaign, Illinois Institute of Technology, Purdue University; nursing with Rush University.

Library Lownik Library with 170,450 titles, 4,781 serial subscriptions, 2,926 audiovisual materials, an OPAC, a Web page.

Computers on Campus 125 computers available on campus for general student use. A campuswide network can be accessed from student residence rooms and from off campus. At least one staffed computer lab available.

Student Life *Housing Options:* coed, men-only, women-only. *Activities and Organizations:* drama/theater group, student-run newspaper, television station, choral group, Student Government Association, Campus Ministry, choir/gospel choir. *Campus security:* 24-hour emergency response devices and patrols, late-night transport/escort service, controlled dormitory access. *Student Services:* health clinic, personal/psychological counseling.

Athletics Member NCAA. All Division III. *Intercollegiate sports:* baseball M, basketball M/W, cross-country running M/W, football M, golf M, soccer M/W, softball W, swimming M/W, tennis W, track and field M/W, volleyball W. *Intramural sports:* badminton M/W, baseball M, basketball M/W, bowling M/W, football M/W, racquetball M/W, soccer M/W, softball M/W, swimming M/W, table tennis M/W, tennis M/W, volleyball M/W, water polo M/W, weight lifting M/W.

Standardized Tests *Required:* SAT I or ACT (for admission).

Costs (2001–02) *Comprehensive fee:* $21,330 includes full-time tuition ($15,220), mandatory fees ($410), and room and board ($5700). Full-time tuition and fees vary according to class time and degree level. Part-time tuition: $510 per credit hour. Part-time tuition and fees vary according to class time and degree level. *Required fees:* $10 per credit hour. *Room and board:* Room and board charges vary according to board plan and housing facility. *Payment plan:* installment. *Waivers:* children of alumni and employees or children of employees.

Financial Aid *Financial aid deadline:* 6/30.

Applying *Options:* deferred entrance. *Application fee:* $30. *Required:* essay or personal statement, high school transcript, letters of recommendation. *Required for some:* interview. *Application deadline:* rolling (freshmen), rolling (transfers). *Notification:* continuous (freshmen).

Admissions Contact Benedictine University, Lisle, IL 60532-0900. *Phone:* 630-829-6306. *Toll-free phone:* 888-829-6363. *Fax:* 630-960-1126. *E-mail:* admissions@ben.edu.

BLACKBURN COLLEGE
Carlinville, Illinois

- **Independent Presbyterian** 4-year, founded 1837
- **Calendar** semesters

- **Degree** bachelor's
- **Small-town** 80-acre campus with easy access to St. Louis
- **Endowment** $10.4 million
- **Coed,** 571 undergraduate students, 97% full-time, 56% women, 44% men
- **Moderately difficult** entrance level, 68% of applicants were admitted

Undergraduates 556 full-time, 15 part-time. Students come from 12 states and territories, 8 other countries, 11% African American, 0.9% Asian American or Pacific Islander, 0.9% Hispanic American, 0.5% Native American, 3% international. *Retention:* 65% of 2001 full-time freshmen returned.

Freshmen *Admission:* 748 applied, 510 admitted, 163 enrolled. *Test scores:* ACT scores over 18: 89%; ACT scores over 24: 40%; ACT scores over 30: 1%.

Faculty *Total:* 53, 60% full-time, 49% with terminal degrees. *Student/faculty ratio:* 15:1.

Majors Art; art history; biology; business administration; chemistry; computer science; criminal justice/law enforcement administration; elementary education; English; history; interdisciplinary studies; liberal arts and sciences/liberal studies; literature; mathematics; medical technology; music; physical education; political science; pre-dentistry; pre-law; pre-medicine; pre-veterinary studies; psychology; public administration; secondary education; Spanish; speech/rhetorical studies.

Academic Programs *Special study options:* academic remediation for entering students, accelerated degree program, advanced placement credit, cooperative education, honors programs, internships, off-campus study, part-time degree program, student-designed majors, study abroad. *Unusual degree programs:* 3-2 engineering with Washington University in St. Louis; nursing with St. John's College.

Library Lumpkin Library with 82,000 titles, 389 serial subscriptions.

Computers on Campus 25 computers available on campus for general student use. Internet access, at least one staffed computer lab available.

Student Life *Housing:* on-campus residence required through junior year. *Options:* coed, men-only, women-only. *Activities and Organizations:* drama/theater group, student-run newspaper, choral group, Cultural Expressions, Residence Hall Association, New Student Orientation Committee, choral groups, student government. *Campus security:* student patrols, late-night transport/escort service. *Student Services:* personal/psychological counseling.

Athletics Member NCAA, NSCAA. All NCAA Division III. *Intercollegiate sports:* baseball M, basketball M/W, cross-country running M/W, football M, golf M/W, soccer M/W, softball W, tennis W, volleyball W. *Intramural sports:* badminton M/W, basketball M/W, bowling M/W, racquetball M/W, soccer M/W, tennis M/W, volleyball M/W.

Standardized Tests *Required:* SAT I or ACT (for admission).

Costs (2002–03) *Comprehensive fee:* $13,690 includes full-time tuition ($9200), mandatory fees ($220), and room and board ($4270). Full-time tuition and fees vary according to program. Part-time tuition: $375 per semester hour. *Payment plan:* installment. *Waivers:* employees or children of employees.

Applying *Options:* early admission, deferred entrance. *Required:* essay or personal statement, high school transcript, minimum 2.0 GPA. *Required for some:* 1 letter of recommendation, interview. *Application deadline:* rolling (freshmen), rolling (transfers).

Admissions Contact Mr. John Malin, Director of Admissions, Blackburn College, 700 College Avenue, Carlinville, IL 62626-1498. *Phone:* 217-854-3231 Ext. 4252. *Toll-free phone:* 800-233-3550. *Fax:* 217-854-3713. *E-mail:* admit@mail.blackburn.edu.

BLESSING-RIEMAN COLLEGE OF NURSING

Quincy, Illinois

- **Independent** 4-year, founded 1985
- **Calendar** semesters
- **Degree** bachelor's
- **Small-town** 1-acre campus
- **Endowment** $7.0 million
- **Coed, primarily women,** 153 undergraduate students, 78% full-time, 92% women, 8% men
- **Moderately difficult** entrance level, 49% of applicants were admitted

Undergraduates 119 full-time, 34 part-time. Students come from 3 states and territories, 36% are from out of state, 3% African American, 2% Hispanic American, 0.7% Native American, 20% transferred in, 79% live on campus. *Retention:* 67% of 2001 full-time freshmen returned.

Freshmen *Admission:* 140 applied, 68 admitted, 33 enrolled. *Average high school GPA:* 3.60. *Test scores:* ACT scores over 18: 100%; ACT scores over 24: 25%.

Faculty *Total:* 13, 100% full-time, 23% with terminal degrees. *Student/faculty ratio:* 10:1.

Majors Nursing.

Academic Programs *Special study options:* academic remediation for entering students, adult/continuing education programs, advanced placement credit, distance learning, double majors, honors programs, internships, part-time degree program, summer session for credit.

Library Blessing-Rieman Library plus 1 other with 4,275 titles, 112 serial subscriptions, an OPAC, a Web page.

Computers on Campus 10 computers available on campus for general student use. Internet access, at least one staffed computer lab available.

Student Life *Housing:* on-campus residence required through sophomore year. *Options:* coed. *Activities and Organizations:* drama/theater group, student-run newspaper, radio station, choral group, Student Nurses Organization, national fraternities, national sororities. *Campus security:* 24-hour patrols, late-night transport/escort service, controlled dormitory access. *Student Services:* health clinic, personal/psychological counseling.

Standardized Tests *Required:* SAT I or ACT (for admission).

Costs (2001–02) *Comprehensive fee:* $16,280 includes full-time tuition ($11,200), mandatory fees ($300), and room and board ($4780). Full-time tuition and fees vary according to student level. Part-time tuition: $310 per credit. *Room and board:* Room and board charges vary according to student level. *Waivers:* employees or children of employees.

Financial Aid Of all full-time matriculated undergraduates who enrolled in 2001, 79 applied for aid, 79 were judged to have need. *Average percent of need met:* 75%. *Average indebtedness upon graduation:* $11,000.

Applying *Options:* deferred entrance. *Required:* high school transcript, minimum 3.0 GPA. *Recommended:* essay or personal statement, interview. *Application deadline:* rolling (freshmen), rolling (transfers).

Admissions Contact Ms. Pam Brown, President/CEO, Blessing-Rieman College of Nursing, Broadway at 11th, Quincy, IL 62305-7005. *Phone:* 217-228-5520 Ext. 6963. *Toll-free phone:* 800-877-9140 Ext. 6964. *Fax:* 217-223-4661. *E-mail:* htourney@blessinghospital.com.

BRADLEY UNIVERSITY

Peoria, Illinois

- **Independent** comprehensive, founded 1897
- **Calendar** semesters
- **Degrees** bachelor's and master's
- **Urban** 65-acre campus
- **Endowment** $166.7 million
- **Coed,** 5,167 undergraduate students, 92% full-time, 54% women, 46% men
- **Moderately difficult** entrance level, 76% of applicants were admitted

Undergraduates 4,735 full-time, 432 part-time. Students come from 44 states and territories, 48 other countries, 14% are from out of state, 5% African American, 2% Asian American or Pacific Islander, 1% Hispanic American, 0.3% Native American, 2% international, 7% transferred in, 42% live on campus. *Retention:* 86% of 2001 full-time freshmen returned.

Freshmen *Admission:* 4,736 applied, 3,609 admitted, 1,110 enrolled. *Test scores:* SAT verbal scores over 500: 89%; SAT math scores over 500: 90%; ACT scores over 18: 98%; SAT verbal scores over 600: 50%; SAT math scores over 600: 54%; ACT scores over 24: 72%; SAT verbal scores over 700: 10%; SAT math scores over 700: 12%; ACT scores over 30: 14%.

Faculty *Total:* 516, 64% full-time, 52% with terminal degrees. *Student/faculty ratio:* 14:1.

Majors Accounting; actuarial science; advertising; art; art history; biochemistry; biology; broadcast journalism; business administration; business economics; business marketing and marketing management; chemistry; civil engineering; civil engineering related; communications; communications related; computer/information sciences; construction engineering; criminal justice/law enforcement administration; early childhood education; ecology; economics; education of the emotionally handicapped; education of the mentally handicapped; education of the specific learning disabled; electrical/electronic engineering technology; electrical engineering; elementary education; engineering physics; English; environmental engineering; family resource management studies; finance; fine/studio arts; French; geology; German; health professions and related sciences; health science; history; industrial/manufacturing engineering; industrial technology; information sciences/systems; insurance/risk management; international business; international relations; journalism; liberal arts and sciences/liberal studies; management information systems/business data processing; mathematics; mathematics related; mechanical engineering; medical technology; molecular biology; music; music business management/merchandising; music (general performance); music teacher education; music theory and composition; nursing; philosophy; physical therapy; physics; political science; psychology; public relations;

Bradley University (continued)
radio/television broadcasting; religious studies; social work; sociology; Spanish; speech/rhetorical studies; teacher education, specific programs related; theater arts/drama.

Academic Programs *Special study options:* academic remediation for entering students, accelerated degree program, adult/continuing education programs, advanced placement credit, cooperative education, distance learning, double majors, honors programs, independent study, internships, off-campus study, part-time degree program, student-designed majors, study abroad, summer session for credit. *ROTC:* Army (b).

Library Cullom-Davis Library with 524,945 titles, 1,965 serial subscriptions, 12,225 audiovisual materials, an OPAC, a Web page.

Computers on Campus 2000 computers available on campus for general student use. A campuswide network can be accessed from student residence rooms and from off campus. Internet access, at least one staffed computer lab available.

Student Life *Housing:* on-campus residence required through sophomore year. *Options:* coed. *Activities and Organizations:* drama/theater group, student-run newspaper, radio and television station, choral group, Alpha Phi Omega, Student Activities Council, Student Action for Environment, investment club, Student Senate, national fraternities, national sororities. *Campus security:* 24-hour emergency response devices and patrols, late-night transport/escort service, controlled dormitory access, bicycle patrol. *Student Services:* health clinic, personal/psychological counseling.

Athletics Member NCAA. All Division I. *Intercollegiate sports:* baseball M(s), basketball M(s)/W(s), cross-country running M(s)/W(s), fencing M(c)/W(c), golf M(s)/W(s), ice hockey M(c), soccer M(s)/W(c), softball W(s), table tennis M(c)/W(c), tennis M(s)/W(s), track and field W, volleyball W(s). *Intramural sports:* badminton M/W, basketball M/W, bowling M/W, football M/W, golf M/W, lacrosse M(c), racquetball M/W, soccer M/W, softball M/W, swimming M/W, table tennis M/W, tennis M/W, volleyball M/W, water polo M/W, wrestling M.

Standardized Tests *Required:* SAT I or ACT (for admission).

Costs (2001–02) *Comprehensive fee:* $20,970 includes full-time tuition ($15,230), mandatory fees ($110), and room and board ($5630). Full-time tuition and fees vary according to program. Part-time tuition: $415 per credit hour. Part-time tuition and fees vary according to course load. *Room and board:* Room and board charges vary according to board plan. *Payment plans:* installment, deferred payment. *Waivers:* senior citizens and employees or children of employees.

Financial Aid Of all full-time matriculated undergraduates who enrolled in 2001, 3707 applied for aid, 3029 were judged to have need, 1131 had their need fully met. In 2001, 1484 non-need-based awards were made. *Average percent of need met:* 82%. *Average financial aid package:* $12,131. *Average need-based loan:* $4793. *Average need-based gift aid:* $8292. *Average indebtedness upon graduation:* $17,054.

Applying *Options:* common application, electronic application, early admission, deferred entrance. *Application fee:* $35. *Required:* high school transcript. *Recommended:* essay or personal statement, minimum 3.0 GPA, letters of recommendation, interview. *Application deadline:* rolling (freshmen). *Notification:* continuous (freshmen).

Admissions Contact Ms. Nickie Roberson, Director of Admissions, Bradley University, 1501 West Bradley Avenue, 100 Swords Hall, Peoria, IL 61625-0002. *Phone:* 309-677-1000. *Toll-free phone:* 800-447-6460. *E-mail:* admissions@bradley.edu.

CHICAGO STATE UNIVERSITY
Chicago, Illinois

- **State-supported** comprehensive, founded 1867
- **Calendar** semesters
- **Degrees** bachelor's and master's
- **Urban** 161-acre campus
- **Coed,** 5,140 undergraduate students, 61% full-time, 74% women, 26% men
- **Moderately difficult** entrance level, 47% of applicants were admitted

Undergraduates 3,159 full-time, 1,981 part-time. Students come from 12 states and territories, 8 other countries, 1% are from out of state, 89% African American, 0.4% Asian American or Pacific Islander, 5% Hispanic American, 0.2% Native American, 0.0% international, 12% transferred in. *Retention:* 62% of 2001 full-time freshmen returned.

Freshmen *Admission:* 1,694 applied, 794 admitted, 441 enrolled. *Average high school GPA:* 2.56. *Test scores:* ACT scores over 18: 64%; ACT scores over 24: 3%.

Faculty *Total:* 439, 75% full-time. *Student/faculty ratio:* 13:1.

Majors Accounting; African studies; anthropology; applied art; art education; art history; bilingual/bicultural education; biology; broadcast journalism; business administration; business education; business marketing and marketing management; ceramic arts; chemistry; computer science; corrections; creative writing; criminal justice/law enforcement administration; data processing technology; drawing; early childhood education; economics; education; elementary education; English; finance; fine/studio arts; geography; graphic design/commercial art/illustration; health education; history; hotel and restaurant management; industrial arts; information sciences/systems; jazz; law enforcement/police science; literature; management information systems/business data processing; mathematics; medical records administration; modern languages; music; music teacher education; nursing; occupational therapy; physical education; political science; pre-dentistry; pre-law; pre-medicine; pre-veterinary studies; psychology; radio/television broadcasting; reading education; recreation/leisure studies; retail management; science education; secondary education; sociology; Spanish; special education; technical/business writing; wind/percussion instruments.

Academic Programs *Special study options:* academic remediation for entering students, accelerated degree program, adult/continuing education programs, advanced placement credit, cooperative education, distance learning, double majors, English as a second language, external degree program, honors programs, internships, part-time degree program, services for LD students, student-designed majors, study abroad, summer session for credit. *ROTC:* Army (b), Navy (c), Air Force (c).

Library Paul and Emily Douglas Library with 320,000 titles, 1,539 serial subscriptions.

Computers on Campus 40 computers available on campus for general student use. At least one staffed computer lab available.

Student Life *Housing Options:* coed. *Activities and Organizations:* drama/theater group, student-run newspaper, radio station, choral group, Math/Computer Science Club, Geographic Society Club, Gospel Choir, Movie Club, national fraternities, national sororities. *Campus security:* 24-hour emergency response devices and patrols, student patrols, controlled dormitory access. *Student Services:* health clinic, personal/psychological counseling, women's center.

Athletics Member NCAA, NAIA. All NCAA Division I. *Intercollegiate sports:* baseball M, basketball M(s)/W(s), cross-country running M(s)/W(s), golf M/W, tennis M/W, track and field M(s)/W(s), volleyball W(s).

Standardized Tests *Required:* SAT I or ACT (for admission).

Costs (2001–02) *Tuition:* state resident $2484 full-time, $104 per credit hour part-time; nonresident $7452 full-time, $311 per credit hour part-time. *Required fees:* $950 full-time. *Room and board:* $5825.

Applying *Application fee:* $20. *Required:* high school transcript. *Application deadlines:* 7/15 (freshmen), 7/15 (transfers). *Notification:* continuous (freshmen).

Admissions Contact Ms. Addie Epps, Director of Admissions, Chicago State University, 95th Street at King Drive, ADM 200, Chicago, IL 60628. *Phone:* 773-995-2513. *E-mail:* ug-admissions@csu.edu.

CHRISTIAN LIFE COLLEGE
Mount Prospect, Illinois

- **Independent religious** 4-year
- **Degrees** diplomas, associate, and bachelor's
- **Coed,** 80 undergraduate students, 59% full-time, 44% women, 56% men
- 57% of applicants were admitted

Undergraduates 47 full-time, 33 part-time. 4% African American, 4% Asian American or Pacific Islander, 8% Hispanic American, 9% international. *Retention:* 62% of 2001 full-time freshmen returned.

Freshmen *Admission:* 14 applied, 8 admitted, 8 enrolled.

Faculty *Total:* 15, 40% full-time, 27% with terminal degrees. *Student/faculty ratio:* 10:1.

Costs (2001–02) *Tuition:* $7100 full-time, $175 per credit hour part-time. *Required fees:* $500 full-time. *Room only:* $3300.

Admissions Contact Jim Spenner, Director of Admissions, Christian Life College, 400 East Gregory Street, Mount Prospect, IL 60056. *Phone:* 847-259-1840 Ext. 17.

COLUMBIA COLLEGE CHICAGO
Chicago, Illinois

- **Independent** comprehensive, founded 1890
- **Calendar** semesters
- **Degrees** bachelor's, master's, and postbachelor's certificates
- **Urban** campus
- **Endowment** $57.7 million
- **Coed,** 8,911 undergraduate students, 83% full-time, 51% women, 49% men

■ **Noncompetitive** entrance level, 90% of applicants were admitted

Undergraduates 7,372 full-time, 1,539 part-time. Students come from 50 states and territories, 51 other countries, 25% are from out of state, 18% African American, 4% Asian American or Pacific Islander, 11% Hispanic American, 0.6% Native American, 3% international, 15% transferred in, 3% live on campus.
Freshmen *Admission:* 2,831 applied, 2,548 admitted, 1,523 enrolled.
Faculty *Total:* 1,164, 22% full-time, 14% with terminal degrees. *Student/faculty ratio:* 13:1.
Majors Acting/directing; advertising; art; arts management; broadcast journalism; business administration; business marketing and marketing management; communications technologies related; computer graphics; computer/information sciences related; creative writing; dance; early childhood education; fashion design/illustration; film studies; film/video production; fine/studio arts; graphic design/commercial art/illustration; interdisciplinary studies; interior design; journalism; liberal arts and sciences/liberal studies; multimedia; music; music business management/merchandising; music (general performance); photography; play/screenwriting; public relations; radio/television broadcasting; sign language interpretation; theater arts/drama; theater design.
Academic Programs *Special study options:* academic remediation for entering students, advanced placement credit, English as a second language, independent study, internships, off-campus study, part-time degree program, services for LD students, student-designed majors, study abroad, summer session for credit.
Library Columbia College Library with 187,132 titles, 3,001 serial subscriptions, 127,494 audiovisual materials, an OPAC, a Web page.
Computers on Campus 730 computers available on campus for general student use. Internet access, at least one staffed computer lab available.
Student Life *Housing Options:* coed. *Activities and Organizations:* drama/theater group, student-run newspaper, radio and television station, choral group, CUMA (Columbia Urban Music Association), International Student Organization, Acianza Latina, Marketing Club. *Campus security:* 24-hour emergency response devices and patrols, late-night transport/escort service, controlled dormitory access, escort upon request. *Student Services:* personal/psychological counseling.
Standardized Tests *Recommended:* SAT I or ACT (for admission).
Costs (2001–02) *One-time required fee:* $25. *Tuition:* $12,524 full-time, $427 per semester hour part-time. Full-time tuition and fees vary according to program. *Required fees:* $320 full-time, $70 per term part-time. *Room only:* $5900. Room and board charges vary according to housing facility. *Payment plan:* deferred payment. *Waivers:* employees or children of employees.
Applying *Options:* deferred entrance. *Application fee:* $25. *Required:* essay or personal statement, high school transcript, letters of recommendation. *Required for some:* interview. *Recommended:* minimum 2.0 GPA, interview. *Application deadlines:* 8/15 (freshmen), 8/15 (transfers).
Admissions Contact Ms. Susan Greenwald, Director of Admissions and Recruitment, Columbia College Chicago, 600 South Michigan Avenue, Chicago, IL 60605-1996. *Phone:* 312-663-1600 Ext. 7133. *E-mail:* admissions@mail.colum.edu.

CONCORDIA UNIVERSITY
River Forest, Illinois

■ **Independent** comprehensive, founded 1864, affiliated with Lutheran Church-Missouri Synod, part of Concordia University System
■ **Calendar** semesters
■ **Degrees** certificates, bachelor's, master's, doctoral, post-master's, and postbachelor's certificates
■ **Suburban** 40-acre campus with easy access to Chicago
■ **Endowment** $8.3 million
■ **Coed,** 1,358 undergraduate students, 77% full-time, 68% women, 32% men
■ **Moderately difficult** entrance level, 28% of applicants were admitted

Undergraduates 1,043 full-time, 315 part-time. Students come from 35 states and territories, 6 other countries, 43% are from out of state, 9% African American, 2% Asian American or Pacific Islander, 4% Hispanic American, 0.1% Native American, 0.5% international, 6% transferred in, 65% live on campus.
Freshmen *Admission:* 863 applied, 245 admitted, 236 enrolled. *Test scores:* ACT scores over 18: 90%; ACT scores over 24: 42%; ACT scores over 30: 6%.
Faculty *Total:* 225, 34% full-time. *Student/faculty ratio:* 9:1.
Majors Accounting; art; art education; biblical languages/literatures; biological/physical sciences; biology; biology education; business administration; chemistry; communications; computer education; computer science; early childhood education; education; elementary education; English; English education; environmental science; exercise sciences; geography; graphic design/commercial art/illustration; history; history education; information sciences/systems; legal studies; mathematics; mathematics education; music; music (piano and organ performance); music teacher education; music (voice and choral/opera performance); natural sciences; nursing; pastoral counseling; philosophy; physical education; physical sciences; political science; pre-dentistry; pre-law; pre-medicine; pre-theology; psychology; religious education; religious music; science education; secondary education; social science education; social work; sociology; speech education; theater arts/drama; theology; wind/percussion instruments.
Academic Programs *Special study options:* academic remediation for entering students, accelerated degree program, adult/continuing education programs, advanced placement credit, distance learning, double majors, honors programs, independent study, internships, off-campus study, part-time degree program, services for LD students, study abroad, summer session for credit.
Library Klinck Memorial Library with 165,060 titles, 470 serial subscriptions, 5,834 audiovisual materials, an OPAC, a Web page.
Computers on Campus 70 computers available on campus for general student use. A campuswide network can be accessed from student residence rooms and from off campus. Internet access, at least one staffed computer lab available.
Student Life *Housing:* on-campus residence required through sophomore year. *Options:* coed, women-only. *Activities and Organizations:* drama/theater group, student-run newspaper, radio station, choral group, Concordia Youth Ministries, Kappelle Choir, Wind Symphony, student government, intramural sports. *Campus security:* 24-hour emergency response devices and patrols, student patrols, late-night transport/escort service, emergency call boxes. *Student Services:* health clinic, personal/psychological counseling, legal services.
Athletics Member NCAA. All Division III. *Intercollegiate sports:* baseball M, basketball M/W, cross-country running M/W, football M, golf M, soccer M/W, softball W, tennis M/W, track and field M/W, volleyball W. *Intramural sports:* badminton M/W, basketball M/W, bowling M/W, cross-country running M/W, football W, golf W, soccer M/W, softball M/W, swimming M/W, tennis M/W, track and field M/W, volleyball M/W.
Standardized Tests *Required:* SAT I or ACT (for admission).
Costs (2002–03) *Comprehensive fee:* $22,000 includes full-time tuition ($16,900) and room and board ($5100). Full-time tuition and fees vary according to program. Part-time tuition: $490 per semester hour. Part-time tuition and fees vary according to program. No tuition increase for student's term of enrollment. *Payment plan:* installment. *Waivers:* minority students, children of alumni, senior citizens, and employees or children of employees.
Financial Aid Of all full-time matriculated undergraduates who enrolled in 2001, 973 applied for aid, 778 were judged to have need, 642 had their need fully met. 70 Federal Work-Study jobs (averaging $1200). 54 State and other part-time jobs (averaging $1055). In 2001, 143 non-need-based awards were made. *Average percent of need met:* 75%. *Average financial aid package:* $10,000. *Average need-based loan:* $3900. *Average need-based gift aid:* $5700. *Average non-need based aid:* $5000. *Average indebtedness upon graduation:* $14,400. *Financial aid deadline:* 5/31.
Applying *Options:* electronic application, deferred entrance. *Application fee:* $25. *Required:* high school transcript, minimum 2.0 GPA, 1 letter of recommendation, minimum ACT score of 20 or SAT I score of 930. *Required for some:* essay or personal statement, interview. *Application deadline:* rolling (freshmen), rolling (transfers).
Admissions Contact Ms. Deborah A. Ness, Dean of Enrollment Services, Concordia University, 7400 Augusta Street, River Forest, IL 60305. *Phone:* 708-209-3100. *Toll-free phone:* 800-285-2668. *Fax:* 708-209-3473. *E-mail:* crfadmis@curf.edu.

DEPAUL UNIVERSITY
Chicago, Illinois

■ **Independent Roman Catholic** university, founded 1898
■ **Calendar** quarters
■ **Degrees** certificates, bachelor's, master's, doctoral, first professional, post-master's, and postbachelor's certificates
■ **Urban** 36-acre campus
■ **Coed,** 13,020 undergraduate students, 73% full-time, 59% women, 41% men
■ **Moderately difficult** entrance level, 72% of applicants were admitted

Undergraduates 9,476 full-time, 3,544 part-time. Students come from 50 states and territories, 44 other countries, 23% are from out of state, 11% African American, 10% Asian American or Pacific Islander, 13% Hispanic American, 0.3% Native American, 1% international, 10% transferred in, 20% live on campus. *Retention:* 85% of 2001 full-time freshmen returned.
Freshmen *Admission:* 8,374 applied, 6,070 admitted, 2,050 enrolled. *Average high school GPA:* 3.27. *Test scores:* SAT verbal scores over 500: 78%; SAT math scores over 500: 73%; ACT scores over 18: 99%; SAT verbal scores over 600:

DePaul University (continued)
33%; SAT math scores over 600: 27%; ACT scores over 24: 49%; SAT verbal scores over 700: 4%; SAT math scores over 700: 3%; ACT scores over 30: 8%.
Faculty *Total:* 2,205, 33% full-time, 26% with terminal degrees. *Student/faculty ratio:* 14:1.
Majors Accounting; acting/directing; adult/continuing education; advertising; African-American studies; African studies; American studies; anthropology; applied art; applied mathematics; art; art history; arts management; biochemistry; biology; business; business administration; business administration/management related; business computer programming; business economics; business marketing and marketing management; business systems networking/ telecommunications; chemistry; city/community/regional planning; communications; comparative literature; computer graphics; computer/information sciences; computer programming; computer science; counselor education/guidance; creative writing; drama/theater literature; drawing; early childhood education; East Asian studies; economics; education; elementary education; English; environmental science; finance; fine/studio arts; French; general studies; geography; German; graphic design/commercial art/illustration; health education; history; human resources management; information sciences/systems; interdisciplinary studies; international business; international relations; Italian; Japanese; jazz; Judaic studies; Latin American studies; literature; management information systems/business data processing; mass communications; mathematical statistics; mathematics; medical laboratory technician; medical technology; modern languages; music; music business management/merchandising; music (general performance); music (piano and organ performance); music teacher education; music theory and composition; music (voice and choral/opera performance); nursing; operations research; philosophy; physical education; physics; play/screenwriting; political science; pre-law; psychology; public policy analysis; religious studies; sculpture; secondary education; social sciences; sociology; Spanish; stringed instruments; theater arts/drama; theater arts/drama and stagecraft related; theater design; urban studies; wind/percussion instruments; women's studies.
Academic Programs *Special study options:* academic remediation for entering students, accelerated degree program, adult/continuing education programs, advanced placement credit, cooperative education, distance learning, double majors, English as a second language, freshman honors college, honors programs, independent study, internships, part-time degree program, services for LD students, study abroad, summer session for credit. *ROTC:* Army (b). *Unusual degree programs:* 3-2 engineering with University of Illinois at Urbana-Champaign, University of Illinois at Chicago, University of Detroit Mercy, University of Southern California, Northwestern University, Iowa State University, Ohio State University.
Library John T. Richardson Library plus 2 others with 1.4 million titles, 14,585 serial subscriptions, 96,669 audiovisual materials, a Web page.
Computers on Campus 850 computers available on campus for general student use. A campuswide network can be accessed from student residence rooms and from off campus. Internet access, online (class) registration, at least one staffed computer lab available.
Student Life *Housing Options:* coed. *Activities and Organizations:* drama/theater group, student-run newspaper, radio station, choral group, Student Ambassadors, DePaul Activities Board, DePaul Community Service Association, national fraternities, national sororities. *Campus security:* 24-hour emergency response devices and patrols, late-night transport/escort service, controlled dormitory access, Security lighting, prevention/awareness programs, on-campus police officers, video cameras, smoke detectors in residence halls. *Student Services:* health clinic, personal/psychological counseling, women's center, legal services.
Athletics Member NCAA. All Division I. *Intercollegiate sports:* basketball M(s)/W(s), cross-country running M(s)/W(s), golf M(s)/W, soccer M(s)/W(s), softball W(s), tennis M(s)/W(s), track and field M(s)/W(s), volleyball W(s). *Intramural sports:* badminton M/W, basketball M/W, racquetball M/W, skiing (downhill) M/W, softball W, table tennis M/W, tennis M/W, volleyball W, weight lifting M/W.
Standardized Tests *Required:* SAT I or ACT (for admission).
Costs (2001–02) *One-time required fee:* $100. *Comprehensive fee:* $23,130 includes full-time tuition ($16,140), mandatory fees ($30), and room and board ($6960). Full-time tuition and fees vary according to program. Part-time tuition: $319 per quarter hour. Part-time tuition and fees vary according to program. *Required fees:* $10 per term part-time. *Room and board:* College room only: $5220. Room and board charges vary according to board plan and housing facility. *Payment plans:* installment, deferred payment. *Waivers:* employees or children of employees.
Financial Aid Of all full-time matriculated undergraduates who enrolled in 2001, 6647 applied for aid, 5895 were judged to have need, 2483 had their need fully met. In 2001, 250 non-need-based awards were made. *Average percent of need met:* 75%. *Average financial aid package:* $14,750. *Average need-based loan:* $4200. *Average need-based gift aid:* $9100. *Average non-need based aid:* $6000. *Average indebtedness upon graduation:* $16,500. *Financial aid deadline:* 5/1.
Applying *Options:* common application, electronic application, early admission, early action, deferred entrance. *Application fee:* $35. *Required:* high school transcript, minimum 2.0 GPA, 1 letter of recommendation. *Required for some:* minimum 3.0 GPA, interview, audition. *Recommended:* minimum 3.0 GPA. *Application deadline:* rolling (freshmen), rolling (transfers). *Notification:* 1/15 (early action).
Admissions Contact Carlene Klaas, Undergraduate Admissions, DePaul University, Chicago, IL 60604. *Phone:* 312-362-8300. *Toll-free phone:* 800-4DE-PAUL. *E-mail:* admitdpu@depaul.edu.

DeVry University
Tinley Park, Illinois

- **Proprietary** 4-year, founded 2000, part of DeVry, Inc
- **Calendar** semesters
- **Degrees** associate and bachelor's
- **Coed,** 1,662 undergraduate students, 70% full-time, 27% women, 73% men
- **Minimally difficult** entrance level, 83% of applicants were admitted

Undergraduates 1,157 full-time, 505 part-time. Students come from 13 states and territories, 9 other countries, 7% are from out of state, 32% African American, 2% Asian American or Pacific Islander, 8% Hispanic American, 0.3% Native American, 0.8% international, 22% transferred in. *Retention:* 56% of 2001 full-time freshmen returned.
Freshmen *Admission:* 777 applied, 644 admitted, 436 enrolled.
Faculty *Total:* 83, 36% full-time. *Student/faculty ratio:* 20:1.
Majors Business administration/management related; business systems analysis/design; business systems networking/ telecommunications; computer engineering technology; electrical/electronic engineering technology; information sciences/systems; operations management.
Academic Programs *Special study options:* academic remediation for entering students, accelerated degree program, adult/continuing education programs, advanced placement credit, cooperative education, part-time degree program, services for LD students, summer session for credit.
Library Learning Resource Center with 1,450 titles, 60 serial subscriptions, 50 audiovisual materials, an OPAC.
Computers on Campus 306 computers available on campus for general student use. A campuswide network can be accessed from off campus. Online (class) registration, at least one staffed computer lab available.
Student Life *Housing:* college housing not available. *Activities and Organizations:* Institute of Electrical and Electronic Engineers (IEEE), Student Leadership, Hash Bang Slash, OGRE. *Campus security:* 24-hour emergency response devices, late-night transport/escort service, lighted pathways/sidewalks, security patrols.
Standardized Tests *Recommended:* SAT I or ACT (for admission).
Costs (2001–02) *Tuition:* $8740 full-time, $310 per credit hour part-time. Full-time tuition and fees vary according to course load. Part-time tuition and fees vary according to course load. *Required fees:* $65 full-time. *Payment plans:* installment, deferred payment. *Waivers:* employees or children of employees.
Financial Aid Of all full-time matriculated undergraduates who enrolled in 2001, 1466 applied for aid, 1343 were judged to have need, 39 had their need fully met. *Average percent of need met:* 54%. *Average financial aid package:* $8890. *Average need-based loan:* $4729. *Average need-based gift aid:* $6691.
Applying *Options:* electronic application, deferred entrance. *Application fee:* $50. *Required:* high school transcript, interview. *Application deadline:* rolling (freshmen), rolling (transfers). *Notification:* continuous (freshmen).
Admissions Contact Ms. Jane Miritello, Assistant New Student Coordinator, DeVry University, 18624 W. Creek Drive, Tinley Park, IL 60477. *Phone:* 708-342-3300. *Toll-free phone:* 877-305-8184.

DeVry University
Chicago, Illinois

- **Proprietary** 4-year, founded 1931, part of DeVry, Inc
- **Calendar** semesters
- **Degrees** associate and bachelor's
- **Urban** 17-acre campus
- **Coed,** 4,011 undergraduate students, 65% full-time, 36% women, 64% men
- **Minimally difficult** entrance level, 81% of applicants were admitted

Undergraduates 2,602 full-time, 1,409 part-time. Students come from 20 states and territories, 36 other countries, 3% are from out of state, 33% African

American, 14% Asian American or Pacific Islander, 25% Hispanic American, 0.3% Native American, 2% international, 0.2% transferred in. *Retention:* 45% of 2001 full-time freshmen returned.

Freshmen *Admission:* 1,360 applied, 1,107 admitted, 953 enrolled.

Faculty *Total:* 189, 44% full-time. *Student/faculty ratio:* 21:1.

Majors Business administration/management related; business systems analysis/ design; business systems networking/ telecommunications; computer engineering technology; electrical/electronic engineering technology; information sciences/ systems; operations management.

Academic Programs *Special study options:* academic remediation for entering students, accelerated degree program, adult/continuing education programs, advanced placement credit, cooperative education, English as a second language, part-time degree program, services for LD students, summer session for credit.

Library Learning Resource Center with 16,573 titles, 79 serial subscriptions, 1,047 audiovisual materials.

Computers on Campus 326 computers available on campus for general student use. A campuswide network can be accessed from off campus. Internet access, online (class) registration, at least one staffed computer lab available.

Student Life *Housing:* college housing not available. *Activities and Organizations:* drama/theater group, student-run newspaper, DeVry Student Government Association (DSGA), DeVry Telecommunications Society, Filipinos of a Culturally-Unified Society (FOCUS), Institute of Electrical and Electronics Engineering (IEEE), Society of Mexican-American Engineers and Scientists (MAES). *Campus security:* 24-hour emergency response devices and patrols, late-night transport/ escort service, lighted pathways/sidewalks.

Athletics *Intramural sports:* basketball M/W, bowling M/W, skiing (downhill) M/W, table tennis M/W, volleyball M/W.

Standardized Tests *Recommended:* SAT I or ACT (for admission).

Costs (2001–02) *Tuition:* $8740 full-time, $310 per credit hour part-time. Full-time tuition and fees vary according to course load. Part-time tuition and fees vary according to course load. *Required fees:* $65 full-time. *Payment plans:* installment, deferred payment. *Waivers:* employees or children of employees.

Financial Aid Of all full-time matriculated undergraduates who enrolled in 2001, 2851 applied for aid, 2785 were judged to have need, 60 had their need fully met. *Average percent of need met:* 58%. *Average financial aid package:* $11,155. *Average need-based loan:* $5286. *Average need-based gift aid:* $7122.

Applying *Options:* electronic application, deferred entrance. *Application fee:* $50. *Required:* high school transcript, interview. *Application deadline:* rolling (freshmen), rolling (transfers). *Notification:* continuous (freshmen).

Admissions Contact Ms. Christine Hierl, Director of Admissions, DeVry University, 3300 North Campbell Avenue, Chicago, IL 60618-5994. *Phone:* 773-929-6550. *Toll-free phone:* 800-383-3879. *Fax:* 773-929-8093.

DeVry University
Addison, Illinois

- **Proprietary** 4-year, founded 1982, part of DeVry, Inc
- **Calendar** semesters
- **Degrees** associate and bachelor's
- **Suburban** 14-acre campus with easy access to Chicago
- **Coed,** 3,543 undergraduate students, 65% full-time, 23% women, 77% men
- **Minimally difficult** entrance level, 88% of applicants were admitted

Undergraduates 2,306 full-time, 1,237 part-time. Students come from 26 states and territories, 30 other countries, 6% are from out of state, 10% African American, 16% Asian American or Pacific Islander, 9% Hispanic American, 0.5% Native American, 2% international, 2% transferred in. *Retention:* 46% of 2001 full-time freshmen returned.

Freshmen *Admission:* 1,181 applied, 1,038 admitted, 791 enrolled.

Faculty *Total:* 165, 41% full-time. *Student/faculty ratio:* 25:1.

Majors Business administration/management related; business systems analysis/ design; business systems networking/ telecommunications; computer engineering technology; electrical/electronic engineering technology; information sciences/ systems; operations management.

Academic Programs *Special study options:* academic remediation for entering students, accelerated degree program, adult/continuing education programs, advanced placement credit, cooperative education, part-time degree program, services for LD students, summer session for credit.

Library Learning Resource Center with 16,283 titles, 109 serial subscriptions, 676 audiovisual materials, an OPAC.

Computers on Campus 548 computers available on campus for general student use. A campuswide network can be accessed from off campus. Internet access, online (class) registration, at least one staffed computer lab available.

Student Life *Housing:* college housing not available. *Activities and Organizations:* student-run newspaper, Epsilon Delta Phi (EDP), International Student Organizations (ISO), Muslim Student Association (MSA), Institute for Electric and Electronic Engineers. *Campus security:* 24-hour emergency response devices, lighted pathways/sidewalks.

Athletics *Intramural sports:* basketball M, soccer M, softball M/W, table tennis M/W.

Standardized Tests *Recommended:* SAT I or ACT (for admission).

Costs (2001–02) *Tuition:* $8740 full-time, $310 per credit hour part-time. Full-time tuition and fees vary according to course load. Part-time tuition and fees vary according to course load. *Payment plans:* installment, deferred payment. *Waivers:* employees or children of employees.

Financial Aid Of all full-time matriculated undergraduates who enrolled in 2001, 2513 applied for aid, 2261 were judged to have need, 113 had their need fully met. *Average percent of need met:* 54%. *Average financial aid package:* $8720. *Average need-based loan:* $5285. *Average need-based gift aid:* $5822.

Applying *Options:* electronic application, deferred entrance. *Application fee:* $50. *Required:* high school transcript, interview. *Application deadline:* rolling (freshmen), rolling (transfers). *Notification:* continuous (freshmen).

Admissions Contact Ms. Jane Miritello, Assistant New Student Coordinator, DeVry University, 18624 W. Creek Drive, Tinley Park, IL 60477. *Phone:* 708-342-3300. *Toll-free phone:* 877-305-8184. *Fax:* 708-342-3120.

Dominican University
River Forest, Illinois

- **Independent Roman Catholic** comprehensive, founded 1901
- **Calendar** semesters
- **Degrees** certificates, bachelor's, master's, and post-master's certificates
- **Suburban** 30-acre campus with easy access to Chicago
- **Endowment** $11.5 million
- **Coed,** 1,189 undergraduate students, 80% full-time, 68% women, 32% men
- **Moderately difficult** entrance level, 83% of applicants were admitted

Undergraduates 957 full-time, 232 part-time. Students come from 21 states and territories, 15 other countries, 9% are from out of state, 5% African American, 2% Asian American or Pacific Islander, 15% Hispanic American, 0.1% Native American, 2% international, 14% transferred in, 35% live on campus. *Retention:* 84% of 2001 full-time freshmen returned.

Freshmen *Admission:* 603 applied, 499 admitted, 231 enrolled. *Average high school GPA:* 3.36. *Test scores:* ACT scores over 18: 91%; ACT scores over 24: 27%; ACT scores over 30: 4%.

Faculty *Total:* 223, 42% full-time, 60% with terminal degrees. *Student/faculty ratio:* 12:1.

Majors Accounting; American studies; art; art history; biochemistry; biology; business administration; chemistry; computer engineering; computer graphics; computer science; criminology; dietetics; economics; education (K-12); electrical engineering; elementary education; English; environmental science; fashion design/illustration; fashion merchandising; fine/studio arts; food products retailing; food sciences; French; gerontology; graphic design/commercial art/illustration; history; information sciences/systems; institutional food services; international business; Italian; Italian studies; mass communications; mathematics; medical technology; nutrition science; philosophy; photography; political science; pre-dentistry; pre-law; pre-medicine; pre-veterinary studies; psychology; religious studies; social sciences; sociology; Spanish; theater arts/drama.

Academic Programs *Special study options:* academic remediation for entering students, accelerated degree program, adult/continuing education programs, advanced placement credit, distance learning, double majors, English as a second language, honors programs, independent study, internships, off-campus study, part-time degree program, services for LD students, student-designed majors, study abroad, summer session for credit. *Unusual degree programs:* 3-2 engineering with with Illinois Institute of Technology; occupational therapy with Rush University.

Library Rebecca Crown Library with 280,475 titles, 4,422 serial subscriptions, 7,000 audiovisual materials, an OPAC, a Web page.

Computers on Campus 199 computers available on campus for general student use. A campuswide network can be accessed from student residence rooms and from off campus that provide access to email. Internet access, at least one staffed computer lab available.

Student Life *Housing Options:* coed, men-only, women-only. *Activities and Organizations:* drama/theater group, student-run newspaper, choral group, student government, Torch, Center Stage, Resident Student Association, International Club. *Campus security:* 24-hour emergency response devices and patrols, student patrols, late-night transport/escort service, controlled dormitory access, door alarms. *Student Services:* health clinic, personal/psychological counseling.

Dominican University (continued)

Athletics Member NCAA. All Division III. *Intercollegiate sports:* baseball M, basketball M/W, cross-country running M/W, golf M/W, soccer M/W, softball W, tennis M/W, volleyball M/W. *Intramural sports:* basketball M/W, football M/W, golf M/W, racquetball M/W, soccer M/W, softball W, tennis M/W, volleyball M/W, water polo M/W.

Standardized Tests *Required:* SAT I or ACT (for admission).

Costs (2001–02) *One-time required fee:* $100. *Comprehensive fee:* $20,800 includes full-time tuition ($15,600), mandatory fees ($100), and room and board ($5100). Part-time tuition: $520 per semester hour. Part-time tuition and fees vary according to location and program. *Required fees:* $10 per course. *Room and board:* Room and board charges vary according to board plan and housing facility. *Payment plan:* installment. *Waivers:* children of alumni and employees or children of employees.

Financial Aid Of all full-time matriculated undergraduates who enrolled in 2001, 676 applied for aid, 584 were judged to have need, 180 had their need fully met. 186 Federal Work-Study jobs (averaging $1929). 75 State and other part-time jobs (averaging $1997). In 2001, 164 non-need-based awards were made. *Average percent of need met:* 83%. *Average financial aid package:* $12,379. *Average need-based loan:* $3209. *Average need-based gift aid:* $8344. *Average non-need based aid:* $6616. *Average indebtedness upon graduation:* $12,409.

Applying *Options:* common application, deferred entrance. *Application fee:* $20. *Required:* essay or personal statement, high school transcript, minimum 2.5 GPA. *Required for some:* 2 letters of recommendation, interview. *Recommended:* letters of recommendation, interview. *Application deadline:* rolling (freshmen), rolling (transfers). *Notification:* continuous (freshmen).

Admissions Contact Ms. Hildegarde Schmidt, Dean of Admissions and Financial Aid, Dominican University, 7900 West Division Street, River Forest, IL 60305-1099. *Phone:* 708-524-6800. *Toll-free phone:* 800-828-8475. *Fax:* 708-366-5360. *E-mail:* domadmis@email.dom.edu.

EASTERN ILLINOIS UNIVERSITY
Charleston, Illinois

- **State-supported** comprehensive, founded 1895
- **Calendar** semesters
- **Degrees** bachelor's and master's
- **Small-town** 320-acre campus
- **Endowment** $21.3 million
- **Coed,** 9,115 undergraduate students, 90% full-time, 57% women, 43% men
- **Moderately difficult** entrance level, 70% of applicants were admitted

Undergraduates 8,203 full-time, 912 part-time. Students come from 37 states and territories, 38 other countries, 2% are from out of state, 7% African American, 0.8% Asian American or Pacific Islander, 2% Hispanic American, 0.2% Native American, 0.8% international, 10% transferred in, 43% live on campus.

Freshmen *Admission:* 6,237 applied, 4,388 admitted, 1,444 enrolled. *Test scores:* ACT scores over 18: 89%; ACT scores over 24: 14%; ACT scores over 30: 1%.

Faculty *Total:* 639, 90% full-time, 69% with terminal degrees. *Student/faculty ratio:* 16:1.

Majors Accounting; African-American studies; art; biology; business; business computer facilities operation; business marketing and marketing management; chemistry; communication disorders; early childhood education; economics; education related; elementary education; engineering related; English; family/community studies; finance; foreign languages/literatures; geography; geology; health education; history; home economics; industrial technology; journalism; liberal arts and sciences/liberal studies; management information systems/business data processing; mathematics; mathematics/computer science; medical technology; middle school education; multi/interdisciplinary studies related; music; philosophy; physical education; physics; political science; psychology; recreation/leisure facilities management; social science education; sociology; special education; speech/rhetorical studies; theater arts/drama.

Academic Programs *Special study options:* academic remediation for entering students, adult/continuing education programs, advanced placement credit, double majors, English as a second language, external degree program, honors programs, independent study, internships, part-time degree program, services for LD students, study abroad, summer session for credit. *ROTC:* Army (b). *Unusual degree programs:* 3-2 engineering with University of Illinois.

Library Booth Library with 486,300 titles, 2,922 serial subscriptions, 20,321 audiovisual materials, an OPAC, a Web page.

Computers on Campus 1202 computers available on campus for general student use. A campuswide network can be accessed from student residence rooms and from off campus. Internet access, online (class) registration, at least one staffed computer lab available.

Student Life *Housing:* on-campus residence required for freshman year. *Options:* coed, men-only, women-only. *Activities and Organizations:* drama/theater group, student-run newspaper, radio and television station, choral group, marching band, Greek organizations, Black Student Union, national fraternities, national sororities. *Campus security:* 24-hour emergency response devices and patrols, student patrols. *Student Services:* health clinic, personal/psychological counseling, women's center, legal services.

Athletics Member NCAA. All Division I except football (Division I-AA). *Intercollegiate sports:* baseball M(s), basketball M(s)/W(s), cross-country running M(s)/W(s), golf M(s)/W(s), rugby W(s), soccer M(s)/W(s), softball W(s), swimming M(s)/W(s), tennis M(s)/W(s), track and field M(s)/W(s), volleyball W(s), wrestling M(s). *Intramural sports:* baseball M, basketball M/W, bowling M/W, cross-country running M/W, football M, racquetball M/W, soccer M/W, softball M/W, swimming M/W, table tennis M/W, tennis M/W, track and field M/W, volleyball M/W, weight lifting M/W, wrestling M.

Standardized Tests *Required:* SAT I or ACT (for admission).

Costs (2002–03) *Tuition:* state resident $3143 full-time, $105 per semester hour part-time; nonresident $9428 full-time, $314 per semester hour part-time. Full-time tuition and fees vary according to course load. Part-time tuition and fees vary according to course load. *Required fees:* $1326 full-time, $56 per semester hour. *Room and board:* $5800. Room and board charges vary according to board plan. *Payment plan:* installment. *Waivers:* employees or children of employees.

Financial Aid Of all full-time matriculated undergraduates who enrolled in 2001, 6275 applied for aid, 4990 were judged to have need, 3320 had their need fully met. 361 Federal Work-Study jobs (averaging $1333). In 2001, 293 non-need-based awards were made. *Average percent of need met:* 19%. *Average financial aid package:* $7885. *Average need-based loan:* $2782. *Average need-based gift aid:* $2765. *Average non-need based aid:* $5457. *Average indebtedness upon graduation:* $12,824.

Applying *Application fee:* $30. *Required:* high school transcript, audition for music program. *Required for some:* essay or personal statement, 3 letters of recommendation. *Application deadline:* rolling (freshmen), rolling (transfers). *Notification:* continuous (freshmen).

Admissions Contact Mr. Dale W. Wolf, Director of Admissions, Eastern Illinois University, 600 Lincoln Avenue, Charleston, IL 61920-3099. *Phone:* 217-581-2223. *Toll-free phone:* 800-252-5711. *Fax:* 217-581-7060. *E-mail:* admissns@eiu.edu.

EAST-WEST UNIVERSITY
Chicago, Illinois

- **Independent** 4-year, founded 1978
- **Calendar** quarters
- **Degrees** associate and bachelor's
- **Urban** campus
- **Coed,** 1,076 undergraduate students, 99% full-time, 64% women, 36% men
- **Minimally difficult** entrance level, 82% of applicants were admitted

Undergraduates 1,065 full-time, 11 part-time. Students come from 10 other countries. *Retention:* 80% of 2001 full-time freshmen returned.

Freshmen *Admission:* 927 applied, 761 admitted, 767 enrolled.

Faculty *Total:* 78, 18% full-time, 14% with terminal degrees. *Student/faculty ratio:* 13:1.

Majors Accounting; behavioral sciences; biology; business administration; computer engineering technology; computer programming; computer science; electrical/electronic engineering technology; electrical engineering; English; finance; Islamic studies; liberal arts and sciences/liberal studies; mathematics; secretarial science; social sciences; sociology.

Academic Programs *Special study options:* academic remediation for entering students, part-time degree program, summer session for credit.

Library East-West University Library with 32,000 titles, 156 serial subscriptions.

Computers on Campus 30 computers available on campus for general student use. At least one staffed computer lab available.

Student Life *Housing:* college housing not available. *Activities and Organizations:* drama/theater group, student-run newspaper, choral group.

Standardized Tests *Recommended:* ACT (for placement).

Costs (2002–03) *Tuition:* $9300 full-time, $2480 per term part-time. *Required fees:* $435 full-time, $435 per term part-time.

Financial Aid Of all full-time matriculated undergraduates who enrolled in 2001, 54 Federal Work-Study jobs.

Applying *Options:* common application, electronic application. *Application fee:* $30. *Required:* high school transcript. *Required for some:* 1 letter of recommendation. *Application deadline:* rolling (freshmen), rolling (transfers).

Admissions Contact Mr. William Link, Director of Admissions, East-West University, 816 South Michigan Avenue, Chicago, IL 60605-2103. *Phone:* 312-939-0111 Ext. 1839. *Fax:* 312-939-0083.

ELMHURST COLLEGE
Elmhurst, Illinois

- **Independent** comprehensive, founded 1871, affiliated with United Church of Christ
- **Calendar** 4-1-4
- **Degrees** bachelor's and master's
- **Suburban** 38-acre campus with easy access to Chicago
- **Endowment** $69.8 million
- **Coed,** 2,410 undergraduate students, 81% full-time, 64% women, 36% men
- **Moderately difficult** entrance level, 77% of applicants were admitted

Undergraduates Students come from 28 states and territories, 28 other countries, 8% are from out of state, 7% African American, 2% Asian American or Pacific Islander, 5% Hispanic American, 0.3% Native American, 1% international, 40% live on campus. *Retention:* 86% of 2001 full-time freshmen returned.
Freshmen *Admission:* 1,210 applied, 933 admitted. *Average high school GPA:* 3.28. *Test scores:* ACT scores over 18: 91%; ACT scores over 24: 33%; ACT scores over 30: 4%.
Faculty *Total:* 267, 40% full-time, 49% with terminal degrees. *Student/faculty ratio:* 14:1.
Majors Accounting; actuarial science; American studies; art; art education; biology; biology education; business administration; business marketing and marketing management; chemistry; chemistry education; communications; computer science; cytotechnology; early childhood education; economics; education; elementary education; English; English education; environmental science; exercise sciences; finance; French; French language education; geography; German; German language education; health/physical education; history; history education; interdisciplinary studies; international business; logistics/materials management; management information systems/business data processing; mathematics; mathematics education; medical nutrition; medical technology; music; music business management/merchandising; music teacher education; nursing; occupational therapy; philosophy; physical education; physical therapy; physician assistant; physics; physics education; political science; pre-dentistry; pre-law; pre-medicine; pre-pharmacy studies; pre-veterinary studies; psychology; secondary education; sociology; Spanish; Spanish language education; special education; speech-language pathology/audiology; sport/fitness administration; theater arts/drama; theology; urban studies.
Academic Programs *Special study options:* academic remediation for entering students, accelerated degree program, adult/continuing education programs, advanced placement credit, cooperative education, double majors, honors programs, independent study, internships, off-campus study, part-time degree program, services for LD students, study abroad, summer session for credit. *ROTC:* Army (c), Air Force (c). *Unusual degree programs:* 3-2 engineering with Illinois Institute of Technology, Northwestern University, Washington University in St. Louis, University of Illinois at Chicago, University of Southern California.
Library Buehler Library with 211,151 titles, 2,000 serial subscriptions, 6,531 audiovisual materials, an OPAC, a Web page.
Computers on Campus 345 computers available on campus for general student use. A campuswide network can be accessed from student residence rooms and from off campus. At least one staffed computer lab available.
Student Life *Housing Options:* coed. *Activities and Organizations:* drama/theater group, student-run newspaper, radio station, choral group, Programming Board and Student Government, theater and music groups, Black Student Union, residence life groups, Hablamos, national fraternities, national sororities. *Campus security:* 24-hour emergency response devices and patrols, late-night transport/escort service, controlled dormitory access. *Student Services:* health clinic, personal/psychological counseling.
Athletics Member NCAA. All Division III. *Intercollegiate sports:* baseball M, basketball M/W, cross-country running M/W, football M, golf M/W, soccer W, softball W, tennis M/W, track and field M/W, volleyball W, wrestling M. *Intramural sports:* basketball M/W, football M, golf M/W, racquetball M/W, softball M/W, volleyball M/W.
Standardized Tests *Required:* SAT I or ACT (for admission).
Costs (2001–02) *Comprehensive fee:* $21,750 includes full-time tuition ($16,200) and room and board ($5550). Part-time tuition: $470 per credit hour. *Room and board:* College room only: $3200. Room and board charges vary according to board plan. *Payment plans:* installment, deferred payment. *Waivers:* senior citizens and employees or children of employees.
Financial Aid Of all full-time matriculated undergraduates who enrolled in 2001, 1455 applied for aid, 1255 were judged to have need, 1192 had their need fully met. 231 Federal Work-Study jobs (averaging $1131). 240 State and other part-time jobs (averaging $1166). In 2001, 141 non-need-based awards were made. *Average percent of need met:* 97%. *Average financial aid package:* $14,988. *Average need-based loan:* $4014. *Average need-based gift aid:* $10,682. *Average non-need based aid:* $6613. *Average indebtedness upon graduation:* $14,100.
Applying *Options:* electronic application, deferred entrance. *Application fee:* $25. *Required:* high school transcript. *Required for some:* essay or personal statement, letters of recommendation, interview. *Recommended:* essay or personal statement, interview. *Application deadlines:* 7/15 (freshmen), 8/1 (transfers). *Notification:* continuous (freshmen).
Admissions Contact Mr. Andrew B. Sison, Director of Admission, Elmhurst College, 190 Prospect Avenue, Elmhurst, IL 60126-3296. *Phone:* 630-617-3400 Ext. 3068. *Toll-free phone:* 800-697-1871. *Fax:* 630-617-5501. *E-mail:* admit@elmhurst.edu.

EUREKA COLLEGE
Eureka, Illinois

- **Independent** 4-year, founded 1855, affiliated with Christian Church (Disciples of Christ)
- **Calendar** 4 8-week terms
- **Degree** bachelor's
- **Small-town** 112-acre campus
- **Endowment** $6.8 million
- **Coed,** 544 undergraduate students, 93% full-time, 59% women, 41% men
- **Moderately difficult** entrance level, 72% of applicants were admitted

Undergraduates 506 full-time, 38 part-time. Students come from 17 states and territories, 2 other countries, 6% African American, 0.6% Asian American or Pacific Islander, 1% Hispanic American, 1% international, 8% transferred in, 84% live on campus. *Retention:* 67% of 2001 full-time freshmen returned.
Freshmen *Admission:* 799 applied, 578 admitted, 146 enrolled. *Average high school GPA:* 3.11. *Test scores:* ACT scores over 18: 82%; ACT scores over 24: 30%; ACT scores over 30: 1%.
Faculty *Total:* 65, 69% full-time. *Student/faculty ratio:* 13:1.
Majors Accounting; art; athletic training/sports medicine; biological/physical sciences; biology; business administration; chemistry; computer science; economics; education; education administration; elementary education; English; exercise sciences; finance; history; liberal arts and sciences/liberal studies; literature; management information systems/business data processing; mass communications; mathematics; medical technology; music; music teacher education; music (voice and choral/opera performance); natural sciences; nursing; philosophy; physical education; physical sciences; political science; pre-dentistry; pre-law; pre-medicine; pre-veterinary studies; psychology; religious studies; science education; secondary education; social sciences; sociology; theater arts/drama.
Academic Programs *Special study options:* advanced placement credit, double majors, honors programs, independent study, internships, part-time degree program, student-designed majors, study abroad. *Unusual degree programs:* 3-2 engineering with Illinois Institute of Technology; occupational therapy with Washington University in St. Louis.
Library Melick Library with 75,000 titles, 341 serial subscriptions, an OPAC.
Computers on Campus 55 computers available on campus for general student use. At least one staffed computer lab available.
Student Life *Housing:* on-campus residence required through senior year. *Options:* coed. *Activities and Organizations:* drama/theater group, student-run newspaper, choral group, College Choral, theater, Campus Activities Board, intercollegiate athletics, national fraternities, national sororities. *Campus security:* 24-hour emergency response devices, late night patrols. *Student Services:* health clinic, personal/psychological counseling.
Athletics Member NCAA. All Division III. *Intercollegiate sports:* baseball M, basketball M/W, football M, golf M/W, softball W, swimming M/W, tennis M/W, track and field M/W, volleyball W. *Intramural sports:* basketball M/W, football M, golf M/W, softball W, swimming M/W, tennis M/W, track and field M/W, volleyball M/W.
Standardized Tests *Required:* SAT I or ACT (for admission).
Costs (2001–02) *Comprehensive fee:* $22,200 includes full-time tuition ($16,600), mandatory fees ($300), and room and board ($5300). Part-time tuition: $485 per semester hour. *Room and board:* College room only: $2540. Room and board charges vary according to housing facility. *Payment plan:* installment. *Waivers:* children of alumni and employees or children of employees.
Financial Aid Of all full-time matriculated undergraduates who enrolled in 2001, 506 applied for aid, 504 were judged to have need, 428 had their need fully met. 61 Federal Work-Study jobs (averaging $1279). *Average percent of need met:*

Eureka College (continued)
91%. *Average financial aid package:* $12,741. *Average need-based loan:* $2865. *Average need-based gift aid:* $8115. *Average non-need based aid:* $7940. *Average indebtedness upon graduation:* $14,202.

Applying *Options:* electronic application, deferred entrance. *Application fee:* $15. *Required:* high school transcript, minimum 2.0 GPA, 1 letter of recommendation. *Required for some:* essay or personal statement, 3 letters of recommendation. *Recommended:* interview. *Application deadline:* rolling (freshmen), rolling (transfers). *Notification:* continuous (freshmen).

Admissions Contact Mr. John R. Clayton, Dean of Admissions and Financial Aid, Eureka College, 300 East College Avenue, Eureka, IL 61530-1500. *Phone:* 309-467-6350. *Toll-free phone:* 888-4-EUREKA. *Fax:* 309-467-6576. *E-mail:* admissions@eureka.edu.

FINCH UNIVERSITY OF HEALTH SCIENCES/THE CHICAGO MEDICAL SCHOOL

North Chicago, Illinois

- **Independent** upper-level, founded 1912
- **Calendar** quarters
- **Degrees** bachelor's, master's, doctoral, and first professional
- **Suburban** 50-acre campus with easy access to Chicago
- **Coed**
- **Minimally difficult** entrance level

Student Life *Campus security:* 24-hour patrols, late-night transport/escort service, outside doors have electric alarm active during evening hours.

Financial Aid *Financial aid deadline:* 6/30.

Applying *Options:* common application. *Application fee:* $20.

Admissions Contact Ms. Kristine A. Jones, Director of Admissions and Records, Finch University of Health Sciences/The Chicago Medical School, Undergraduate Admissions, 3333 Green Bay Road, North Chicago, IL 60064. *Phone:* 847-578-3204. *Fax:* 847-578-3284. *E-mail:* admissions@finchcms.edu.

GOVERNORS STATE UNIVERSITY

University Park, Illinois

- **State-supported** upper-level, founded 1969
- **Calendar** trimesters
- **Degrees** bachelor's and master's
- **Suburban** 750-acre campus with easy access to Chicago
- **Coed,** 2,980 undergraduate students, 29% full-time, 69% women, 31% men
- **Minimally difficult** entrance level, 66% of applicants were admitted

Undergraduates Students come from 9 states and territories, 16 other countries, 2% are from out of state, 29% African American, 1% Asian American or Pacific Islander, 6% Hispanic American, 0.3% Native American, 0.7% international.

Freshmen *Admission:* 2,286 applied, 1,505 admitted.

Faculty *Total:* 203, 86% full-time, 70% with terminal degrees. *Student/faculty ratio:* 16:1.

Majors Accounting; art; art history; biology; business administration; business marketing and marketing management; chemistry; computer science; criminal justice/law enforcement administration; drawing; early childhood education; elementary education; English; finance; fine/studio arts; health services administration; human resources management; labor/personnel relations; liberal arts and sciences/liberal studies; management information systems/business data processing; mass communications; mental health/rehabilitation; middle school education; nursing; photography; psychology; public administration; retail management; science education; social sciences; social work; speech-language pathology/audiology; speech/rhetorical studies.

Academic Programs *Special study options:* academic remediation for entering students, adult/continuing education programs, advanced placement credit, distance learning, external degree program, honors programs, independent study, internships, off-campus study, part-time degree program, services for LD students, student-designed majors, study abroad, summer session for credit. *ROTC:* Army (c), Air Force (c).

Library University Library with 246,000 titles, 2,200 serial subscriptions, 2,700 audiovisual materials, an OPAC, a Web page.

Computers on Campus 142 computers available on campus for general student use. A campuswide network can be accessed from off campus. At least one staffed computer lab available.

Student Life *Housing:* college housing not available. *Activities and Organizations:* student-run newspaper, choral group, Future Teachers of America, American College of Health Executives, Circle K, Counseling Club, African-American Student Association. *Campus security:* 24-hour emergency response devices and patrols, late-night transport/escort service. *Student Services:* personal/psychological counseling.

Athletics *Intramural sports:* badminton M/W, basketball M/W, racquetball M/W, skiing (cross-country) M/W, softball M/W, table tennis M/W, volleyball M/W.

Costs (2001–02) *One-time required fee:* $10. *Tuition:* state resident $2352 full-time, $98 per credit part-time; nonresident $7056 full-time, $294 per credit part-time. Full-time tuition and fees vary according to location. Part-time tuition and fees vary according to course load and location. *Required fees:* $280 full-time, $140 per term part-time. *Payment plans:* installment, deferred payment. *Waivers:* senior citizens and employees or children of employees.

Applying *Options:* deferred entrance. *Application deadline:* 7/15 (transfers).

Admissions Contact Mr. Larry Polselli, Executive Director of Enrollment Services, Governors State University, One University Parkway, University Park, IL 60466. *Phone:* 708-534-3148. *Fax:* 708-534-1640.

GREENVILLE COLLEGE

Greenville, Illinois

- **Independent Free Methodist** comprehensive, founded 1892
- **Calendar** 4-1-4
- **Degrees** bachelor's and master's
- **Small-town** 12-acre campus with easy access to St. Louis
- **Endowment** $6.9 million
- **Coed,** 1,121 undergraduate students, 96% full-time, 52% women, 48% men
- **Moderately difficult** entrance level, 73% of applicants were admitted

Undergraduates 1,081 full-time, 40 part-time. Students come from 37 states and territories, 32% are from out of state, 6% African American, 1% Asian American or Pacific Islander, 1% Hispanic American, 0.5% Native American, 1% international, 17% transferred in, 57% live on campus. *Retention:* 67% of 2001 full-time freshmen returned.

Freshmen *Admission:* 640 applied, 465 admitted, 223 enrolled. *Average high school GPA:* 3.26. *Test scores:* SAT verbal scores over 500: 91%; SAT math scores over 500: 54%; ACT scores over 18: 92%; SAT verbal scores over 600: 59%; SAT math scores over 600: 36%; ACT scores over 24: 54%; SAT verbal scores over 700: 9%; SAT math scores over 700: 9%; ACT scores over 30: 7%.

Faculty *Total:* 145, 41% full-time, 37% with terminal degrees. *Student/faculty ratio:* 13:1.

Majors Accounting; art; art education; biology; biology education; business administration; business marketing and marketing management; chemistry; chemistry education; computer science; divinity/ministry; drama/dance education; early childhood education; education; elementary education; English; English education; environmental biology; foreign languages education; history; liberal arts and sciences/liberal studies; management information systems/business data processing; mass communications; mathematics; mathematics education; modern languages; music; music teacher education; pastoral counseling; philosophy; physical education; physics; physics education; political science; pre-dentistry; pre-law; pre-medicine; pre-veterinary studies; psychology; public relations; recreation/leisure studies; religious music; religious studies; science education; secondary education; social studies education; social work; sociology; Spanish; Spanish language education; special education; speech education; speech/rhetorical studies; theater arts/drama; theology; Web page, digital/multimedia and information resources design.

Academic Programs *Special study options:* academic remediation for entering students, accelerated degree program, adult/continuing education programs, advanced placement credit, cooperative education, double majors, English as a second language, honors programs, independent study, internships, off-campus study, part-time degree program, student-designed majors, summer session for credit. *Unusual degree programs:* 3-2 engineering with University of Illinois at Urbana-Champaign; Washington University in St. Louis.

Library Ruby E. Dare Library with 126,210 titles, 490 serial subscriptions, 4,377 audiovisual materials, an OPAC, a Web page.

Computers on Campus 250 computers available on campus for general student use. A campuswide network can be accessed from student residence rooms and from off campus that provide access to intranet. Internet access, at least one staffed computer lab available.

Student Life *Housing:* on-campus residence required through senior year. *Options:* men-only, women-only. *Activities and Organizations:* drama/theater group, student-run newspaper, radio station, choral group, Campus Activity

Board, Intramurals, Greenville Student Outreach, Habitat for Humanity, Student Senate. *Campus security:* 24-hour emergency response devices, student patrols, late-night transport/escort service. *Student Services:* personal/psychological counseling.

Athletics Member NCAA, NCCAA. All NCAA Division III. *Intercollegiate sports:* baseball M, basketball M/W, cross-country running M/W, football M, soccer M/W, softball W, tennis M/W, track and field M/W, volleyball M(c)/W. *Intramural sports:* badminton M/W, basketball M/W, football M/W, soccer M/W, softball M/W, table tennis M/W, tennis M/W, volleyball M/W.

Standardized Tests *Required:* SAT I or ACT (for admission).

Costs (2001–02) *Comprehensive fee:* $19,186 includes full-time tuition ($13,490), mandatory fees ($510), and room and board ($5186). Part-time tuition: $283 per credit hour. Part-time tuition and fees vary according to course load. *Room and board:* College room only: $2450. Room and board charges vary according to housing facility. *Payment plan:* installment. *Waivers:* children of alumni, senior citizens, and employees or children of employees.

Financial Aid Of all full-time matriculated undergraduates who enrolled in 2001, 850 applied for aid, 767 were judged to have need, 171 had their need fully met. 126 Federal Work-Study jobs (averaging $1400). In 2001, 145 non-need-based awards were made. *Average percent of need met:* 84%. *Average financial aid package:* $13,157. *Average need-based loan:* $3874. *Average need-based gift aid:* $9143. *Average indebtedness upon graduation:* $13,349.

Applying *Options:* electronic application, early admission, deferred entrance. *Application fee:* $25. *Required:* essay or personal statement, high school transcript, minimum 2.25 GPA, 2 letters of recommendation, agreement to code of conduct. *Required for some:* interview. *Application deadline:* rolling (freshmen), rolling (transfers). *Notification:* continuous (freshmen).

Admissions Contact Mr. Randy Comfort, Dean of Admissions, Greenville College, 315 East College, PO Box 159, Greenville, IL 62246-0159. *Phone:* 618-664-7100. *Toll-free phone:* 800-248-2288 (in-state); 800-345-4440 (out-of-state). *Fax:* 618-664-9841. *E-mail:* admissions@greenville.edu.

HARRINGTON INSTITUTE OF INTERIOR DESIGN
Chicago, Illinois

- **Proprietary** 4-year, founded 1931
- **Calendar** semesters
- **Degrees** diplomas, associate, and bachelor's
- **Urban** campus
- **Coed, primarily women,** 820 undergraduate students
- **Noncompetitive** entrance level, 73% of applicants were admitted

Freshmen *Admission:* 411 applied, 302 admitted.

Faculty *Total:* 75, 4% full-time. *Student/faculty ratio:* 15:1.

Majors Interior design.

Academic Programs *Special study options:* adult/continuing education programs, internships, off-campus study, part-time degree program, study abroad.

Library Harrington Institute Design Library with 22,000 titles, 90 serial subscriptions, 26,000 audiovisual materials, an OPAC.

Computers on Campus 25 computers available on campus for general student use. Internet access, at least one staffed computer lab available.

Student Life *Housing:* college housing not available. *Activities and Organizations:* American Society of Interior Designers, International Interior Design Association.

Costs (2001–02) *Tuition:* $450 per semester hour part-time. *Required fees:* $150 per term part-time. *Payment plan:* installment.

Financial Aid Of all full-time matriculated undergraduates who enrolled in 2001, 167 applied for aid, 138 were judged to have need. In 2001, 1 non-need-based awards were made. *Average percent of need met:* 24%. *Average financial aid package:* $3910. *Average need-based loan:* $3142. *Average need-based gift aid:* $2039. *Average non-need based aid:* $250. *Average indebtedness upon graduation:* $21,375.

Applying *Options:* deferred entrance. *Application fee:* $60. *Required:* high school transcript, interview. *Application deadline:* rolling (freshmen). *Notification:* continuous (freshmen).

Admissions Contact Ms. Wendi Franczyk, Director of Admissions, Harrington Institute of Interior Design, 410 South Michigan Avenue, Chicago, IL 60605-1496. *Phone:* 877-939-4975. *Toll-free phone:* 877-939-4975. *Fax:* 312-939-8005. *E-mail:* harringtoninstitute@interiordesign.edu.

HEBREW THEOLOGICAL COLLEGE
Skokie, Illinois

Admissions Contact Office of Admissions, Hebrew Theological College, 7135 North Carpenter Road, Skokie, IL 60077-3263. *Phone:* 847-982-2500.

ILLINOIS COLLEGE
Jacksonville, Illinois

- **Independent interdenominational** 4-year, founded 1829
- **Calendar** semesters
- **Degree** bachelor's
- **Small-town** 62-acre campus with easy access to St. Louis
- **Endowment** $112.0 million
- **Coed,** 874 undergraduate students, 98% full-time, 55% women, 45% men
- **Moderately difficult** entrance level, 67% of applicants were admitted

Undergraduates 858 full-time, 16 part-time. Students come from 12 states and territories, 6 other countries, 2% are from out of state, 3% African American, 0.5% Asian American or Pacific Islander, 2% Hispanic American, 0.2% Native American, 0.7% international, 5% transferred in, 75% live on campus. *Retention:* 75% of 2001 full-time freshmen returned.

Freshmen *Admission:* 919 applied, 612 admitted, 205 enrolled. *Average high school GPA:* 3.25. *Test scores:* SAT verbal scores over 500: 75%; SAT math scores over 500: 80%; ACT scores over 18: 89%; SAT verbal scores over 600: 50%; ACT scores over 24: 36%; ACT scores over 30: 8%.

Faculty *Total:* 93, 63% full-time, 57% with terminal degrees. *Student/faculty ratio:* 14:1.

Majors Accounting; art; biology; business administration; business economics; chemistry; computer science; cytotechnology; economics; education; education (K-12); elementary education; English; environmental science; finance; French; German; history; information sciences/systems; interdisciplinary studies; international relations; liberal arts and sciences/liberal studies; management information systems/business data processing; mass communications; mathematics; medical technology; music; occupational therapy; philosophy; physical education; physics; political science; pre-dentistry; pre-law; pre-medicine; pre-veterinary studies; psychology; religious studies; secondary education; sociology; Spanish; speech/rhetorical studies; theater arts/drama.

Academic Programs *Special study options:* accelerated degree program, advanced placement credit, double majors, independent study, internships, study abroad, summer session for credit. *Unusual degree programs:* 3-2 engineering with University of Illinois at Urbana-Champaign, Washington University in St. Louis; nursing with Mennonite College of Nursing; occupational therapy with Washington University in St. Louis.

Library Schewe Library with 143,500 titles, 620 serial subscriptions, an OPAC, a Web page.

Computers on Campus 97 computers available on campus for general student use. A campuswide network can be accessed from student residence rooms and from off campus. At least one staffed computer lab available.

Student Life *Housing:* on-campus residence required through sophomore year. *Options:* coed, men-only, women-only. *Activities and Organizations:* drama/theater group, student-run newspaper, television station, choral group, Student Activity Board, Forum, Homecoming Committee, literary societies, B.A.S.I.C. (Brothers and Sisters in Christ). *Campus security:* 24-hour emergency response devices and patrols, late-night transport/escort service, controlled dormitory access. *Student Services:* health clinic, personal/psychological counseling.

Athletics Member NCAA. All Division III. *Intercollegiate sports:* baseball M, cross-country running M/W, football M, golf M/W, soccer M/W, softball W, tennis M/W, track and field M/W, volleyball W, wrestling M. *Intramural sports:* basketball M/W, fencing M/W, football M, softball M/W, volleyball M/W, weight lifting M/W.

Standardized Tests *Required:* SAT I or ACT (for admission).

Costs (2001–02) *Comprehensive fee:* $16,234 includes full-time tuition ($11,272) and room and board ($4962). Part-time tuition: $470 per credit hour. *Room and board:* Room and board charges vary according to housing facility. *Payment plans:* installment, deferred payment. *Waivers:* employees or children of employees.

Financial Aid Of all full-time matriculated undergraduates who enrolled in 2001, 813 applied for aid, 621 were judged to have need, 474 had their need fully met. In 2001, 112 non-need-based awards were made. *Average percent of need met:* 90%. *Average financial aid package:* $10,630. *Average need-based loan:* $3571. *Average need-based gift aid:* $6268. *Average non-need based aid:* $2846. *Average indebtedness upon graduation:* $8564.

Applying *Options:* common application, electronic application. *Application fee:* $10. *Required:* high school transcript, 2 letters of recommendation. *Required for some:* essay or personal statement. *Recommended:* interview. *Application deadlines:* 8/15 (freshmen), 12/15 (transfers). *Notification:* continuous until 8/15 (freshmen).

Admissions Contact Mr. Rick Bystry, Director of Admission, Illinois College, 1101 West College, Jacksonville, IL 62650. *Phone:* 217-245-3030. *Toll-free phone:* 866-464-5265. *Fax:* 217-245-3034. *E-mail:* admissions@ic.edu.

THE ILLINOIS INSTITUTE OF ART
Chicago, Illinois

- **Proprietary** 4-year, founded 1916, part of The Art Institutes
- **Calendar** quarters
- **Degrees** associate and bachelor's
- **Urban** campus
- **Coed,** 1,789 undergraduate students
- **Minimally difficult** entrance level, 93% of applicants were admitted

Undergraduates Students come from 42 states and territories, 26 other countries, 30% are from out of state. *Retention:* 70% of 2001 full-time freshmen returned.

Freshmen *Admission:* 535 applied, 495 admitted. *Average high school GPA:* 2.50.

Faculty *Total:* 108, 80% with terminal degrees. *Student/faculty ratio:* 18:1.

Majors Computer graphics; fashion design/illustration; fashion merchandising; graphic design/commercial art/illustration; interior design.

Academic Programs *Special study options:* academic remediation for entering students, accelerated degree program, adult/continuing education programs, advanced placement credit, cooperative education, independent study, internships, off-campus study, part-time degree program, services for LD students, summer session for credit.

Library The Illinois Institute of Art Library plus 1 other with 11,324 titles, 264 serial subscriptions, 502 audiovisual materials, an OPAC, a Web page.

Computers on Campus 150 computers available on campus for general student use. Internet access, at least one staffed computer lab available.

Student Life *Housing:* college housing not available. *Activities and Organizations:* student-run newspaper, Student Activities Committee, American Society of Interior Designers club, commercial art club, Student Ambassador Program, Fashion Focus. *Campus security:* 24-hour emergency response devices and patrols. *Student Services:* personal/psychological counseling.

Standardized Tests *Recommended:* SAT I or ACT (for placement).

Costs (2002–03) *Tuition:* $14,769 full-time.

Financial Aid *Average indebtedness upon graduation:* $15,800.

Applying *Options:* common application, electronic application, early admission, deferred entrance. *Application fee:* $50. *Required:* essay or personal statement, high school transcript, interview. *Required for some:* letters of recommendation, portfolio. *Recommended:* minimum 2.0 GPA. *Application deadline:* rolling (freshmen), rolling (transfers).

Admissions Contact Ms. Janis Anton, Director of Admissions, The Illinois Institute of Art, 350 North Orleans, Chicago, IL 60654. *Phone:* 312-280-3500 Ext. 132. *Toll-free phone:* 800-351-3450. *Fax:* 312-280-8562. *E-mail:* antonj@aii.edu.

THE ILLINOIS INSTITUTE OF ART-SCHAUMBURG
Schaumburg, Illinois

- **Proprietary** 4-year, part of The Arts Institutes International
- **Calendar** quarters
- **Degree** bachelor's
- **Coed,** 850 undergraduate students
- 75% of applicants were admitted

Undergraduates Students come from 9 states and territories, 2 other countries, 10% are from out of state, 3% African American, 9% Asian American or Pacific Islander, 7% Hispanic American, 1% international. *Retention:* 8% of 2001 full-time freshmen returned.

Freshmen *Admission:* 750 applied, 565 admitted. *Average high school GPA:* 2.70. *Test scores:* ACT scores over 18: 78%; ACT scores over 24: 20%.

Faculty *Total:* 55, 49% full-time, 18% with terminal degrees. *Student/faculty ratio:* 16:1.

Majors Design/visual communications; film/video production; interior design.

Student Life *Activities and Organizations:* student-run newspaper, animation club, ASID, newspaper, music club, A.I.G.A. (graphic design). *Campus security:* 24-hour emergency response devices and patrols, student patrols. *Student Services:* personal/psychological counseling.

Standardized Tests *Recommended:* SAT I and SAT II or ACT (for admission).

Costs (2001–02) *Tuition:* $13,000 full-time, $302 per credit hour part-time. No tuition increase for student's term of enrollment. *Required fees:* $100 full-time, $100 per year part-time. *Payment plans:* tuition prepayment, installment, deferred payment. *Waivers:* employees or children of employees.

Applying *Application fee:* $50. *Required:* essay or personal statement, high school transcript, minimum 2.0 GPA, letters of recommendation. *Required for some:* interview.

Admissions Contact Ms. Stephanie Schweihofer, Director of Admissions, The Illinois Institute of Art-Schaumburg, 1000 Plaza Drive, Schaumburg, IL 60173. *Phone:* 847-619-3450 Ext. 116. *Toll-free phone:* 800-314-3450. *Fax:* 847-619-3064 Ext. 3064.

ILLINOIS INSTITUTE OF TECHNOLOGY
Chicago, Illinois

- **Independent** university, founded 1890
- **Calendar** semesters
- **Degrees** certificates, bachelor's, master's, doctoral, first professional, and postbachelor's certificates
- **Urban** 128-acre campus
- **Endowment** $204.4 million
- **Coed,** 1,842 undergraduate students, 80% full-time, 25% women, 75% men
- **Very difficult** entrance level, 62% of applicants were admitted

IIT is a private, urban, research, PhD-granting university providing small class size, hands-on projects, undergraduate research, co-op learning, combined degree programs, and a distinguished faculty. Program offerings include architecture, engineering, computers, science, premed, and prelaw. IIT offers substantial need-based and merit-based scholarship programs. Job placement rates for graduates are over 90

.

Undergraduates 1,466 full-time, 376 part-time. Students come from 49 states and territories, 77 other countries, 46% are from out of state, 6% African American, 16% Asian American or Pacific Islander, 8% Hispanic American, 0.4% Native American, 19% international, 4% transferred in, 58% live on campus. *Retention:* 88% of 2001 full-time freshmen returned.

Freshmen *Admission:* 2,562 applied, 1,583 admitted, 294 enrolled. *Average high school GPA:* 3.75. *Test scores:* SAT verbal scores over 500: 98%; SAT math scores over 500: 99%; ACT scores over 18: 100%; SAT verbal scores over 600: 75%; SAT math scores over 600: 85%; ACT scores over 24: 95%; SAT verbal scores over 700: 23%; SAT math scores over 700: 47%; ACT scores over 30: 39%.

Faculty *Total:* 587, 54% full-time. *Student/faculty ratio:* 12:1.

Majors Aerospace engineering; applied mathematics; architectural engineering; architecture; bioengineering; biology; biophysics; chemical engineering; chemistry; civil engineering; computer engineering; computer science; electrical engineering; engineering/industrial management; industrial technology; information sciences/systems; materials engineering; mechanical engineering; metallurgical engineering; physics; political science; psychology.

Academic Programs *Special study options:* accelerated degree program, advanced placement credit, cooperative education, distance learning, double majors, English as a second language, internships, part-time degree program, services for LD students, study abroad, summer session for credit. *ROTC:* Army (b), Navy (b), Air Force (b).

Library Paul V. Galvin Library plus 5 others with 829,386 titles, 7,512 serial subscriptions, 52,251 audiovisual materials, an OPAC, a Web page.

Computers on Campus 450 computers available on campus for general student use. A campuswide network can be accessed from student residence rooms and from off campus. Internet access, online (class) registration, at least one staffed computer lab available.

Student Life *Housing Options:* coed, men-only, women-only. *Activities and Organizations:* drama/theater group, student-run newspaper, radio station, Union Board, Student Leadership Council, Residence Hall Association, Techmate Commuters, national fraternities, national sororities. *Campus security:* 24-hour emergency response devices and patrols, late-night transport/escort service, controlled dormitory access. *Student Services:* health clinic, personal/psychological counseling.

Athletics Member NAIA. *Intercollegiate sports:* baseball M(s), basketball M(s)/W(s), cross-country running M(s)/W(s), swimming M(s)/W(s), volleyball W(s). *Intramural sports:* basketball M/W, football M, golf M, racquetball M/W, sailing M/W, soccer M/W, softball M/W, swimming M/W, volleyball M/W, water polo M/W.

Standardized Tests *Required:* SAT I or ACT (for admission). *Recommended:* SAT II: Subject Tests (for admission).

Costs (2002–03) *Comprehensive fee:* $25,247 includes full-time tuition ($19,200), mandatory fees ($165), and room and board ($5882). Part-time tuition: $600 per credit hour. *Required fees:* $3 per credit hour. *Room and board:* Room and board charges vary according to board plan. *Payment plan:* installment. *Waivers:* employees or children of employees.

Financial Aid Of all full-time matriculated undergraduates who enrolled in 2001, 1403 applied for aid, 793 were judged to have need, 341 had their need fully met. In 2001, 605 non-need-based awards were made. *Average percent of need met:* 57%. *Average financial aid package:* $18,808. *Average need-based loan:* $5614. *Average need-based gift aid:* $8905. *Average non-need based aid:* $11,240. *Average indebtedness upon graduation:* $22,733.

Applying *Options:* common application, electronic application, deferred entrance. *Application fee:* $30. *Required:* high school transcript, minimum 3.0 GPA, 1 letter of recommendation. *Required for some:* essay or personal statement, interview. *Application deadlines:* rolling (freshmen), 7/1 (transfers). *Notification:* continuous (freshmen).

Admissions Contact Mr. Terry Miller, Dean of Undergraduate Admission, Illinois Institute of Technology, 10 West 33rd Street PH101, Chicago, IL 60616-3793. *Phone:* 312-567-3025. *Toll-free phone:* 800-448-2329. *Fax:* 312-567-6939. *E-mail:* admission@iit.edu.

ILLINOIS STATE UNIVERSITY
Normal, Illinois

- **State-supported** university, founded 1857
- **Calendar** semesters
- **Degrees** bachelor's, master's, doctoral, and post-master's certificates
- **Urban** 850-acre campus
- **Endowment** $26.6 million
- **Coed,** 18,472 undergraduate students, 92% full-time, 58% women, 42% men
- **Moderately difficult** entrance level, 77% of applicants were admitted

Undergraduates 17,032 full-time, 1,440 part-time. Students come from 45 states and territories, 49 other countries, 1% are from out of state, 6% African American, 2% Asian American or Pacific Islander, 2% Hispanic American, 0.3% Native American, 0.7% international, 11% transferred in, 40% live on campus. *Retention:* 80% of 2001 full-time freshmen returned.

Freshmen *Admission:* 10,211 applied, 7,905 admitted, 3,340 enrolled. *Test scores:* ACT scores over 18: 99%; ACT scores over 24: 40%; ACT scores over 30: 3%.

Faculty *Total:* 1,149, 75% full-time, 67% with terminal degrees. *Student/faculty ratio:* 19:1.

Majors Accounting; agribusiness; agricultural sciences; anthropology; art; biology; business administration; business education; business marketing and marketing management; business systems networking/ telecommunications; chemistry; computer science; criminal justice studies; early childhood education; economics; elementary education; English; environmental health; family/consumer studies; finance; French; geography; geology; German; health education; history; industrial arts education; industrial technology; information sciences/systems; insurance/risk management; international business; liberal arts and sciences/ liberal studies; mass communications; mathematics; medical records administration; medical technology; middle school education; music; music (general performance); music teacher education; nursing; occupational health/industrial hygiene; philosophy; physical education; physics; political science; psychology; public relations; recreation/leisure facilities management; social studies education; social work; sociology; Spanish; special education; speech-language pathology/audiology; speech/rhetorical studies; theater arts/drama; visual and performing arts related.

Academic Programs *Special study options:* academic remediation for entering students, accelerated degree program, adult/continuing education programs, advanced placement credit, cooperative education, distance learning, double majors, English as a second language, honors programs, independent study, internships, off-campus study, part-time degree program, services for LD students, student-designed majors, study abroad, summer session for credit. *ROTC:* Army (b). *Unusual degree programs:* 3-2 engineering with University of Illinois.

Library Milner Library with 1.5 million titles, 8,915 serial subscriptions, 59,272 audiovisual materials, an OPAC, a Web page.

Computers on Campus 2100 computers available on campus for general student use. A campuswide network can be accessed from student residence rooms and from off campus. Internet access, at least one staffed computer lab available.

Student Life *Housing:* on-campus residence required through sophomore year. *Options:* coed, women-only, disabled students. *Activities and Organizations:* drama/theater group, student-run newspaper, radio and television station, choral group, marching band, national fraternities, national sororities. *Campus security:* 24-hour emergency response devices and patrols, late-night transport/escort service, controlled dormitory access. *Student Services:* health clinic, personal/ psychological counseling, women's center, legal services.

Athletics Member NCAA. All Division I except football (Division I-AA). *Intercollegiate sports:* baseball M(s), basketball M(s)/W(s), cross-country running M(s)/W(s), golf M(s)/W(s), gymnastics W(s), soccer W(s), softball W(s), swimming W(s), tennis M(s)/W(s), track and field M(s)/W(s), volleyball W(s). *Intramural sports:* badminton M/W, baseball M, basketball M/W, bowling M(c)/ W(c), field hockey M/W, football M, golf M/W, gymnastics M(c), ice hockey M(c), lacrosse M(c), racquetball M/W, rugby M(c)/W(c), soccer M/W, softball M/W, tennis M/W, volleyball M(c)/W.

Standardized Tests *Required:* SAT I or ACT (for admission). *Recommended:* ACT (for admission).

Costs (2002–03) *Tuition:* state resident $3465 full-time, $116 per credit hour part-time; nonresident $7530 full-time, $251 per credit hour part-time. Full-time tuition and fees vary according to course load. Part-time tuition and fees vary according to course load. *Required fees:* $1464 full-time, $50 per credit hour, $573 per term part-time. *Room and board:* $4932; room only: $2427. Room and board charges vary according to board plan. *Payment plan:* installment. *Waivers:* minority students, senior citizens, and employees or children of employees.

Financial Aid Of all full-time matriculated undergraduates who enrolled in 2001, 11829 applied for aid, 7679 were judged to have need, 3077 had their need fully met. In 2001, 1121 non-need-based awards were made. *Average percent of need met:* 83%. *Average financial aid package:* $7522. *Average need-based loan:* $3775. *Average need-based gift aid:* $5794. *Average non-need based aid:* $3123. *Average indebtedness upon graduation:* $9612.

Applying *Options:* electronic application, early admission. *Application fee:* $30. *Required:* high school transcript. *Application deadline:* 3/1 (freshmen), rolling (transfers). *Notification:* continuous (freshmen).

Admissions Contact Mr. Steve Adams, Director of Admissions, Illinois State University, Campus Box 2200, Normal, IL 61790-2200. *Phone:* 309-438-2181. *Toll-free phone:* 800-366-2478. *Fax:* 309-438-3932. *E-mail:* ugradadm@ilstu.edu.

ILLINOIS WESLEYAN UNIVERSITY
Bloomington, Illinois

- **Independent** 4-year, founded 1850
- **Calendar** 4-4-1
- **Degree** bachelor's
- **Suburban** 70-acre campus
- **Endowment** $175.8 million
- **Coed,** 2,064 undergraduate students, 100% full-time, 56% women, 44% men
- **Very difficult** entrance level, 57% of applicants were admitted

Undergraduates 2,056 full-time, 8 part-time. Students come from 31 states and territories, 27 other countries, 11% are from out of state, 3% African American, 3% Asian American or Pacific Islander, 2% Hispanic American, 0.0% Native American, 3% international, 0.4% transferred in, 80% live on campus. *Retention:* 90% of 2001 full-time freshmen returned.

Freshmen *Admission:* 2,795 applied, 1,605 admitted, 567 enrolled. *Test scores:* SAT verbal scores over 500: 97%; SAT math scores over 500: 98%; ACT scores over 18: 100%; SAT verbal scores over 600: 67%; SAT math scores over 600: 72%; ACT scores over 24: 99%; SAT verbal scores over 700: 21%; SAT math scores over 700: 19%; ACT scores over 30: 28%.

Faculty *Total:* 182, 85% full-time, 95% with terminal degrees. *Student/faculty ratio:* 12:1.

Majors Accounting; applied art; art; art history; arts management; biology; business administration; chemistry; computer science; drawing; economics; education; elementary education; English; European studies; fine/studio arts; French; German; graphic design/commercial art/illustration; history; insurance/risk management; interdisciplinary studies; international business; international relations; Latin American studies; liberal arts and sciences/liberal studies; mathematics; medical technology; music; music business management/merchandising; music (piano and organ performance); music teacher education; music (voice and choral/opera performance); nursing; philosophy; physics; political science; pre-dentistry; pre-law; pre-medicine; pre-veterinary studies; psychology; religious studies; science education; secondary education; sociology; Spanish; stringed instruments; theater arts/drama; wind/percussion instruments.

Academic Programs *Special study options:* advanced placement credit, cooperative education, double majors, honors programs, independent study, internships, off-campus study, student-designed majors, study abroad, summer session for credit. *ROTC:* Army (c). *Unusual degree programs:* 3-2 engineering with Case Western Reserve University, Northwestern University, Washington University in St. Louis, Dartmouth College; forestry with Duke University; occupational therapy.

Library Sheean Library with 271,577 titles, 11,577 serial subscriptions, 10,402 audiovisual materials, an OPAC, a Web page.

Illinois Wesleyan University (continued)

Computers on Campus 450 computers available on campus for general student use. A campuswide network can be accessed from student residence rooms and from off campus. Internet access, online (class) registration, at least one staffed computer lab available.

Student Life *Housing:* on-campus residence required through sophomore year. *Options:* coed. *Activities and Organizations:* drama/theater group, student-run newspaper, radio and television station, choral group, International Club, InterVarsity, Circle K, Student Senate, Habitat for Humanity, national fraternities, national sororities. *Campus security:* 24-hour emergency response devices and patrols, student patrols, late-night transport/escort service, student/administration security committee. *Student Services:* health clinic, personal/psychological counseling.

Athletics Member NCAA. All Division III. *Intercollegiate sports:* baseball M, basketball M/W, cross-country running M/W, football M, golf M/W, sailing M(c)/W(c), soccer M/W, softball W, swimming M/W, tennis M/W, track and field M/W, volleyball W. *Intramural sports:* badminton M/W, basketball M/W, bowling M/W, golf M/W, lacrosse M, racquetball M/W, softball M, swimming M/W, table tennis M/W, tennis M/W, volleyball M/W.

Standardized Tests *Required:* SAT I or ACT (for admission).

Costs (2002–03) *Comprehensive fee:* $28,586 includes full-time tuition ($22,900), mandatory fees ($136), and room and board ($5550). *Room and board:* College room only: $3270. *Payment plan:* installment. *Waivers:* employees or children of employees.

Financial Aid Of all full-time matriculated undergraduates who enrolled in 2001, 1355 applied for aid, 1141 were judged to have need, 914 had their need fully met. 300 Federal Work-Study jobs (averaging $1957). 445 State and other part-time jobs (averaging $1847). In 2001, 665 non-need-based awards were made. *Average percent of need met:* 93%. *Average financial aid package:* $16,024. *Average need-based loan:* $4468. *Average need-based gift aid:* $11,163. *Average indebtedness upon graduation:* $18,103. *Financial aid deadline:* 3/1.

Applying *Options:* common application, electronic application, early admission, deferred entrance. *Required:* essay or personal statement, high school transcript, minimum 2.0 GPA. *Recommended:* minimum 3.0 GPA, 3 letters of recommendation, interview. *Application deadline:* 3/1 (freshmen), rolling (transfers). *Notification:* continuous (freshmen).

Admissions Contact Mr. James R. Ruoti, Dean of Admissions, Illinois Wesleyan University, PO Box 2900, Bloomington, IL 61702-2900. *Phone:* 309-556-3031. *Toll-free phone:* 800-332-2498. *Fax:* 309-556-3411. *E-mail:* iwuadmit@titan.iwu.edu.

INTERNATIONAL ACADEMY OF DESIGN & TECHNOLOGY

Chicago, Illinois

- **Proprietary** 4-year, founded 1977, part of Career Education Corporation
- **Calendar** quarters
- **Degrees** certificates, associate, and bachelor's
- **Urban** campus
- **Coed,** 2,063 undergraduate students, 83% full-time, 63% women, 37% men
- **Minimally difficult** entrance level, 55% of applicants were admitted

Undergraduates 1,716 full-time, 347 part-time. Students come from 21 states and territories, 5 other countries, 7% are from out of state, 35% African American, 4% Asian American or Pacific Islander, 23% Hispanic American, 0.0% Native American, 1% international, 6% transferred in. *Retention:* 70% of 2001 full-time freshmen returned.

Freshmen *Admission:* 1,071 applied, 589 admitted, 561 enrolled. *Average high school GPA:* 2.25.

Faculty *Total:* 178, 10% full-time, 2% with terminal degrees. *Student/faculty ratio:* 16:1.

Majors Computer graphics; design/visual communications; fashion design/illustration; fashion merchandising; interior design; multimedia.

Academic Programs *Special study options:* academic remediation for entering students, adult/continuing education programs, advanced placement credit, internships, part-time degree program, study abroad, summer session for credit.

Library International Academy of Merchandising & Design Library with 5,000 titles, 84 serial subscriptions, 350 audiovisual materials, an OPAC.

Computers on Campus 250 computers available on campus for general student use. Internet access, at least one staffed computer lab available.

Student Life *Housing:* college housing not available. *Activities and Organizations:* student-run newspaper, ASID/IDSA (Interior Design Student Organization), Byte-Me Club/AIGA (American Institute of Graphic Artists), International Club, Fashion Council, Adult Student Support Group. *Campus security:* building security during hours of operation. *Student Services:* personal/psychological counseling.

Standardized Tests *Recommended:* SAT I and SAT II or ACT (for placement), SAT II: Writing Test (for placement).

Costs (2002–03) *Tuition:* $13,038 full-time, $840 per course part-time. Full-time tuition and fees vary according to program. Part-time tuition and fees vary according to program. *Payment plans:* tuition prepayment, installment, deferred payment. *Waivers:* employees or children of employees.

Financial Aid Of all full-time matriculated undergraduates who enrolled in 2001, 15 Federal Work-Study jobs (averaging $2310).

Applying *Options:* common application, early admission, deferred entrance. *Application fee:* $50. *Required:* high school transcript, interview. *Required for some:* GED. *Recommended:* essay or personal statement, minimum 2.0 GPA. *Application deadline:* rolling (freshmen), rolling (transfers).

Admissions Contact Ms. Andrea Schmoyer, Director of Student Management, International Academy of Design & Technology, One North State Street, Suite 400, Chicago, IL 60602. *Phone:* 312-980-9200. *Toll-free phone:* 877-ACADEMY. *Fax:* 312-541-3929. *E-mail:* academy@iadtchicago.com.

ITT TECHNICAL INSTITUTE

Mount Prospect, Illinois

- **Proprietary** primarily 2-year, founded 1986, part of ITT Educational Services, Inc
- **Calendar** quarters
- **Degrees** associate and bachelor's
- **Suburban** 1-acre campus with easy access to Chicago
- **Coed,** 447 undergraduate students
- **Minimally difficult** entrance level

Majors Computer/information sciences related; drafting; electrical/electronic engineering technologies related; electrical/electronic engineering technology; information technology.

Student Life *Housing:* college housing not available.

Costs (2001–02) *Tuition:* Full-time tuition and fees vary according to program. Part-time tuition and fees vary according to program. $260—$330 per credit hour.

Applying *Options:* deferred entrance. *Application fee:* $100. *Required:* high school transcript, interview. *Recommended:* letters of recommendation. *Application deadline:* rolling (freshmen), rolling (transfers). *Notification:* continuous (freshmen).

Admissions Contact Mr. Ernest Lloyd, Director of Recruitment, ITT Technical Institute, 375 West Higgins Road, Hoffman Estates, IL 60195. *Phone:* 847-519-9300 Ext. 11.

JUDSON COLLEGE

Elgin, Illinois

- **Independent Baptist** 4-year, founded 1963
- **Calendar** 4-1-4
- **Degree** bachelor's
- **Suburban** 80-acre campus with easy access to Chicago
- **Endowment** $5.4 million
- **Coed,** 1,089 undergraduate students, 77% full-time, 57% women, 43% men
- **Moderately difficult** entrance level, 79% of applicants were admitted

Judson College, an evangelical Christian college of the liberal arts, sciences, and professions, emphasizes the integration of faith and learning, theory and practice. Judson is a caring community where faculty and staff members seek to facilitate each student's growth in all areas of life while equipping them for their careers, family life, and service to the community and church.

Undergraduates 835 full-time, 254 part-time. Students come from 21 states and territories, 18 other countries, 24% are from out of state, 5% African American, 0.8% Asian American or Pacific Islander, 3% Hispanic American, 5% international, 7% transferred in, 48% live on campus. *Retention:* 89% of 2001 full-time freshmen returned.

Freshmen *Admission:* 466 applied, 366 admitted, 154 enrolled. *Average high school GPA:* 3.14. *Test scores:* SAT verbal scores over 500: 68%; SAT math scores over 500: 68%; ACT scores over 18: 71%; SAT verbal scores over 600: 16%; SAT math scores over 600: 12%; ACT scores over 24: 25%; ACT scores over 30: 1%.

Faculty *Total:* 171, 34% full-time. *Student/faculty ratio:* 15:1.

Majors Accounting; anthropology; architecture; art; biblical studies; biological/physical sciences; biology; business administration; chemistry; computer graphics; computer science; criminal justice studies; drawing; early childhood education; education; elementary education; English; fine/studio arts; graphic design/commercial art/illustration; history; human resources management; human services; information sciences/systems; international business; journalism; linguistics; literature; management information systems/business data processing; mass communications; mathematics; music; music teacher education; music (voice and choral/opera performance); nursing; philosophy; physical education; physical sciences; pre-law; pre-medicine; psychology; religious studies; science education; secondary education; social sciences; sociology; speech/rhetorical studies; sport/fitness administration; theater arts/drama.

Academic Programs *Special study options:* academic remediation for entering students, accelerated degree program, adult/continuing education programs, advanced placement credit, distance learning, double majors, external degree program, honors programs, independent study, internships, off-campus study, part-time degree program, student-designed majors, study abroad.

Library Benjamin P. Browne Library plus 2 others with 104,331 titles, 450 serial subscriptions, 12,500 audiovisual materials, an OPAC, a Web page.

Computers on Campus 90 computers available on campus for general student use. A campuswide network can be accessed from student residence rooms. Internet access, at least one staffed computer lab available.

Student Life *Housing:* on-campus residence required through junior year. *Options:* men-only, women-only. *Activities and Organizations:* choral group, Judson Choir, Nowhere Near Broadway, philosophy and religion club, Phi Beta Lambda. *Campus security:* 24-hour emergency response devices and patrols, controlled dormitory access. *Student Services:* health clinic, personal/psychological counseling.

Athletics Member NAIA, NCCAA. *Intercollegiate sports:* baseball M(s), basketball M(s)/W(s), cross-country running M(s)/W(s), soccer M(s)/W(s), softball W(s), tennis M(s)/W(s), volleyball W(s). *Intramural sports:* badminton M/W, basketball M/W, football M, golf M, racquetball M/W, soccer M/W, softball W, tennis M/W, volleyball M/W.

Standardized Tests *Required:* SAT I or ACT (for admission). *Recommended:* ACT (for admission).

Costs (2002–03) *Comprehensive fee:* $20,950 includes full-time tuition ($14,900), mandatory fees ($250), and room and board ($5800). Part-time tuition: $500 per semester hour. Part-time tuition and fees vary according to course load. *Room and board:* Room and board charges vary according to board plan. *Payment plan:* installment. *Waivers:* senior citizens and employees or children of employees.

Financial Aid Of all full-time matriculated undergraduates who enrolled in 2001, 821 applied for aid, 521 were judged to have need.

Applying *Options:* early admission, deferred entrance. *Application fee:* $30. *Required:* essay or personal statement, high school transcript, minimum 2.0 GPA. *Required for some:* 2 letters of recommendation, interview. *Application deadline:* rolling (freshmen), rolling (transfers). *Notification:* continuous (freshmen).

Admissions Contact Mr. Billy Dean, Director of Admissions, Judson College, 1151 North State Street, Elgin, IL 60123-1498. *Phone:* 847-695-2500 Ext. 2322. *Toll-free phone:* 800-879-5376. *Fax:* 847-695-0216. *E-mail:* admission@judson-il.edu.

KENDALL COLLEGE
Evanston, Illinois

- **Independent United Methodist** 4-year, founded 1934
- **Calendar** quarters
- **Degrees** certificates, associate, and bachelor's
- **Suburban** 1-acre campus with easy access to Chicago
- **Endowment** $5.0 million
- **Coed,** 600 undergraduate students
- **Minimally difficult** entrance level, 83% of applicants were admitted

Undergraduates Students come from 18 states and territories, 13 other countries, 18% African American, 4% Asian American or Pacific Islander, 9% Hispanic American, 0.2% Native American, 3% international, 33% live on campus.

Freshmen *Admission:* 358 applied, 296 admitted. *Average high school GPA:* 2.50. *Test scores:* ACT scores over 18: 93%; ACT scores over 24: 13%; ACT scores over 30: 3%.

Faculty *Total:* 74, 41% with terminal degrees. *Student/faculty ratio:* 15:1.

Majors American studies; business administration; business marketing and marketing management; computer science; criminal justice studies; culinary arts; early childhood education; entrepreneurship; hospitality management; hotel and restaurant management; human services; information sciences/systems; interdisciplinary studies; liberal arts and sciences/liberal studies; psychology; social sciences.

Academic Programs *Special study options:* academic remediation for entering students, accelerated degree program, adult/continuing education programs, advanced placement credit, cooperative education, English as a second language, independent study, internships, part-time degree program, student-designed majors, study abroad, summer session for credit.

Library Kendall Library plus 1 other with 37,000 titles, 215 serial subscriptions, 150 audiovisual materials.

Computers on Campus 48 computers available on campus for general student use. A campuswide network can be accessed from student residence rooms and from off campus. Internet access, at least one staffed computer lab available.

Student Life *Housing Options:* coed. *Activities and Organizations:* drama/theater group, student-run newspaper, choral group, debate, mock trial, Students in Free Enterprise, culinary competitions, athletics. *Campus security:* student patrols, late night security in dorms. *Student Services:* personal/psychological counseling.

Athletics Member NAIA. *Intercollegiate sports:* basketball M/W, cross-country running M/W, soccer M/W, track and field M/W, volleyball M/W.

Standardized Tests *Required:* SAT I or ACT (for admission).

Costs (2001–02) *Comprehensive fee:* $18,519 includes full-time tuition ($12,840), mandatory fees ($150), and room and board ($5529). Full-time tuition and fees vary according to program. Part-time tuition: $388 per credit hour. Part-time tuition and fees vary according to program. *Room and board:* Room and board charges vary according to housing facility. *Payment plan:* installment. *Waivers:* employees or children of employees.

Financial Aid Of all full-time matriculated undergraduates who enrolled in 2001, 380 applied for aid, 301 were judged to have need, 218 had their need fully met. 50 Federal Work-Study jobs (averaging $1162). In 2001, 91 non-need-based awards were made. *Average financial aid package:* $15,136. *Average non-need based aid:* $1305. *Average indebtedness upon graduation:* $14,125.

Applying *Options:* common application, deferred entrance. *Application fee:* $30. *Required:* essay or personal statement, high school transcript, minimum ACT score of 18. *Required for some:* letters of recommendation, interview. *Recommended:* minimum 2.0 GPA, interview. *Application deadline:* rolling (freshmen), rolling (transfers). *Notification:* continuous (freshmen).

Admissions Contact Carl Goodmonson, Assistant Director of Admissions, Kendall College, 2408 Orrington Avenue, Evanston, IL 60201-2899. *Phone:* 847-866-1300 Ext. 1307. *Toll-free phone:* 877-588-8860. *Fax:* 847-866-1320. *E-mail:* admissions@kendall.edu.

KNOX COLLEGE
Galesburg, Illinois

- **Independent** 4-year, founded 1837
- **Calendar** three courses for each of three terms
- **Degree** bachelor's
- **Small-town** 82-acre campus with easy access to Peoria
- **Endowment** $45.7 million
- **Coed,** 1,143 undergraduate students, 97% full-time, 56% women, 44% men
- **Very difficult** entrance level, 72% of applicants were admitted

Undergraduates 1,110 full-time, 33 part-time. Students come from 48 states and territories, 37 other countries, 46% are from out of state, 4% African American, 4% Asian American or Pacific Islander, 4% Hispanic American, 0.8% Native American, 10% international, 4% transferred in, 96% live on campus. *Retention:* 88% of 2001 full-time freshmen returned.

Freshmen *Admission:* 1,428 applied, 1,027 admitted, 275 enrolled. *Test scores:* SAT verbal scores over 500: 91%; SAT math scores over 500: 88%; ACT scores over 18: 99%; SAT verbal scores over 600: 59%; SAT math scores over 600: 58%; ACT scores over 24: 77%; SAT verbal scores over 700: 21%; SAT math scores over 700: 9%; ACT scores over 30: 19%.

Faculty *Total:* 117, 79% full-time, 84% with terminal degrees. *Student/faculty ratio:* 12:1.

Majors African-American studies; American studies; anthropology; art; art history; biochemistry; biology; chemistry; classics; computer/information sciences; creative writing; economics; education; English; environmental science; foreign languages/literatures; French; German; history; international relations; mathematics; music; philosophy; physics; political science; psychology; Russian; Russian/Slavic studies; sociology; Spanish; theater arts/drama; Western European studies; women's studies.

Academic Programs *Special study options:* academic remediation for entering students, advanced placement credit, double majors, English as a second language, honors programs, independent study, internships, off-campus study, part-time degree program, services for LD students, student-designed majors, study abroad. *Unusual degree programs:* 3-2 engineering with Columbia University,

Knox College (continued)
Washington University in St. Louis, Rensselaer Polytechnic Institute, University of Illinois at Urbana-Champaign; forestry with Duke University; social work with University of Chicago; nursing, occupational therapy, medical technology with Columbia University, Rush University.

Library Seymour Library plus 2 others with 178,945 titles, 1,824 serial subscriptions, 5,692 audiovisual materials, an OPAC, a Web page.

Computers on Campus 171 computers available on campus for general student use. A campuswide network can be accessed from student residence rooms and from off campus that provide access to software applications. Internet access, at least one staffed computer lab available.

Student Life *Housing:* on-campus residence required through senior year. *Options:* coed, men-only, women-only. *Activities and Organizations:* drama/theater group, student-run newspaper, radio station, choral group, International Club, Allied Blacks for Liberty and Equality, Sexual Equality Awareness Coalition, Union Board, campus radio station, national fraternities, national sororities. *Campus security:* 24-hour emergency response devices and patrols, late-night transport/escort service. *Student Services:* personal/psychological counseling.

Athletics *Intercollegiate sports:* baseball M, basketball M/W, cross-country running M/W, football M, golf M/W, soccer M/W, softball W, swimming M/W, tennis M/W, track and field M/W, volleyball W, wrestling M. *Intramural sports:* badminton M/W, baseball M, basketball M/W, cross-country running M/W, fencing M/W, lacrosse M/W, soccer M/W, softball M/W, swimming M/W, tennis M/W, track and field M/W, volleyball M/W, water polo M/W, weight lifting M/W.

Standardized Tests *Required:* SAT I or ACT (for admission).

Costs (2001–02) *Comprehensive fee:* $28,230 includes full-time tuition ($22,380), mandatory fees ($240), and room and board ($5610). Part-time tuition: $830 per credit. *Room and board:* Room and board charges vary according to board plan and housing facility. *Payment plan:* installment. *Waivers:* employees or children of employees.

Financial Aid Of all full-time matriculated undergraduates who enrolled in 2001, 889 applied for aid, 805 were judged to have need, 752 had their need fully met. 551 Federal Work-Study jobs (averaging $1279). 127 State and other part-time jobs (averaging $1423). In 2001, 216 non-need-based awards were made. *Average percent of need met:* 99%. *Average financial aid package:* $19,669. *Average need-based loan:* $4687. *Average need-based gift aid:* $15,202. *Average non-need based aid:* $9336. *Average indebtedness upon graduation:* $17,096.

Applying *Options:* common application, electronic application, early admission, early action, deferred entrance. *Application fee:* $35. *Required:* essay or personal statement, high school transcript, 2 letters of recommendation. *Recommended:* interview. *Application deadlines:* 2/1 (freshmen), 4/1 (transfers). *Notification:* 3/31 (freshmen), 12/15 (early action).

Admissions Contact Paul Steenis, Director of Admissions, Knox College, Admission Office, Box K-148, Galesburg, IL 61401. *Phone:* 309-341-7100. *Toll-free phone:* 800-678-KNOX. *Fax:* 309-341-7070. *E-mail:* admission@knox.edu.

LAKE FOREST COLLEGE
Lake Forest, Illinois

- **Independent** comprehensive, founded 1857
- **Calendar** semesters
- **Degrees** bachelor's and master's
- **Suburban** 110-acre campus with easy access to Chicago
- **Endowment** $62.6 million
- **Coed,** 1,260 undergraduate students, 99% full-time, 58% women, 42% men
- **Very difficult** entrance level, 69% of applicants were admitted

Undergraduates 1,242 full-time, 18 part-time. Students come from 44 states and territories, 41 other countries, 50% are from out of state, 5% African American, 4% Asian American or Pacific Islander, 3% Hispanic American, 0.4% Native American, 8% international, 5% transferred in, 83% live on campus. *Retention:* 77% of 2001 full-time freshmen returned.

Freshmen *Admission:* 1,607 applied, 1,109 admitted, 336 enrolled. *Average high school GPA:* 3.40. *Test scores:* SAT verbal scores over 500: 79%; SAT math scores over 500: 79%; ACT scores over 18: 98%; SAT verbal scores over 600: 36%; SAT math scores over 600: 39%; ACT scores over 24: 68%; SAT verbal scores over 700: 5%; SAT math scores over 700: 6%; ACT scores over 30: 12%.

Faculty *Total:* 142, 58% full-time, 77% with terminal degrees. *Student/faculty ratio:* 12:1.

Majors African studies; American studies; anthropology; art history; Asian studies; biology; business economics; chemistry; communications; computer science; economics; education; elementary education; English; environmental science; European studies; finance; fine/studio arts; French; German; history; Latin American studies; mathematics; music; philosophy; physics; political science; pre-dentistry; pre-law; pre-medicine; pre-veterinary studies; psychology; secondary education; sociology; Spanish; women's studies.

Academic Programs *Special study options:* accelerated degree program, adult/continuing education programs, advanced placement credit, double majors, freshman honors college, honors programs, independent study, internships, off-campus study, part-time degree program, services for LD students, student-designed majors, study abroad, summer session for credit. *Unusual degree programs:* 3-2 engineering with Washington University in St. Louis.

Library Donnelley Library plus 1 other with 268,760 titles, 1,133 serial subscriptions, 11,911 audiovisual materials, an OPAC, a Web page.

Computers on Campus 120 computers available on campus for general student use. A campuswide network can be accessed from student residence rooms and from off campus. Internet access, at least one staffed computer lab available.

Student Life *Housing:* on-campus residence required for freshman year. *Options:* coed, women-only. *Activities and Organizations:* drama/theater group, student-run newspaper, radio station, choral group, Garrick Players Drama Group, League for Environmental Awareness and Protection, international student organization, Ambassadors Host Organization, national fraternities. *Campus security:* 24-hour emergency response devices and patrols, student patrols, late-night transport/escort service. *Student Services:* health clinic, personal/psychological counseling, women's center.

Athletics Member NCAA. All Division III. *Intercollegiate sports:* baseball M(c), basketball M/W, cross-country running M/W, fencing M(c)/W(c), football M, ice hockey M/W, lacrosse M(c)/W(c), rugby M(c), soccer M/W, softball W, swimming M/W, tennis M/W, volleyball M(c)/W, water polo M. *Intramural sports:* basketball M/W, football M, golf M/W, ice hockey M/W, racquetball M/W, sailing M/W, soccer M/W, squash M/W, tennis M/W, volleyball M/W.

Standardized Tests *Required:* SAT I or ACT (for admission).

Costs (2001–02) *One-time required fee:* $200. *Comprehensive fee:* $27,460 includes full-time tuition ($21,896), mandatory fees ($310), and room and board ($5254). Part-time tuition: $2740 per course. *Required fees:* $155 per term part-time. *Room and board:* College room only: $2870. Room and board charges vary according to housing facility. *Payment plan:* installment. *Waivers:* employees or children of employees.

Financial Aid Of all full-time matriculated undergraduates who enrolled in 2001, 1086 applied for aid, 867 were judged to have need, 867 had their need fully met. 373 Federal Work-Study jobs (averaging $1438). In 2001, 217 non-need-based awards were made. *Average percent of need met:* 100%. *Average financial aid package:* $19,050. *Average need-based loan:* $4208. *Average need-based gift aid:* $15,979. *Average indebtedness upon graduation:* $15,048.

Applying *Options:* common application, electronic application, early admission, early decision, early action, deferred entrance. *Application fee:* $40. *Required:* essay or personal statement, high school transcript, 2 letters of recommendation, graded paper. *Recommended:* interview. *Application deadline:* 3/1 (freshmen), rolling (transfers). *Early decision:* 1/1. *Notification:* 3/23 (freshmen), 1/21 (early decision), 12/20 (early action).

Admissions Contact Mr. William G. Motzer Jr., Director of Admissions, Lake Forest College, 555 North Sheridan Road, Lake Forest, IL 60045-2399. *Phone:* 847-735-5000. *Toll-free phone:* 800-828-4751. *Fax:* 847-735-6271. *E-mail:* admissions@lakeforest.edu.

LAKEVIEW COLLEGE OF NURSING
Danville, Illinois

- **Independent** upper-level, founded 1987
- **Calendar** semesters
- **Degree** bachelor's
- **Small-town** campus
- **Endowment** $6.2 million
- **Coed, primarily women,** 56 undergraduate students, 43% full-time, 93% women, 7% men
- **Moderately difficult** entrance level, 76% of applicants were admitted

Undergraduates 24 full-time, 32 part-time. Students come from 2 states and territories, 5% are from out of state, 7% African American, 2% Asian American or Pacific Islander, 4% Hispanic American, 30% transferred in.

Freshmen *Admission:* 29 applied, 22 admitted.

Faculty *Total:* 13, 46% full-time, 15% with terminal degrees. *Student/faculty ratio:* 4:1.

Majors Nursing.

Academic Programs *Special study options:* distance learning, part-time degree program, summer session for credit.

Library Lakeview College of Nursing Library with 1,500 titles, 85 serial subscriptions, 365 audiovisual materials, an OPAC.

Computers on Campus 12 computers available on campus for general student use. Internet access, at least one staffed computer lab available.

Student Life *Housing:* college housing not available. *Activities and Organizations:* student-run newspaper, Student Nurses Association, Nurses Christian Fellowship (NCF). *Campus security:* 24-hour emergency response devices. *Student Services:* personal/psychological counseling.

Costs (2001–02) *One-time required fee:* $120. *Tuition:* $250 per credit hour part-time. Part-time tuition and fees vary according to course load. *Payment plans:* installment, deferred payment.

Applying *Options:* common application, deferred entrance. *Application fee:* $50. *Application deadline:* rolling (transfers).

Admissions Contact Ms. Kelly Holden, Registrar, Lakeview College of Nursing, 903 North Logan Avenue, Danville, IL 61832. *Phone:* 217-443-5385. *Toll-free phone:* 217-443-5238 Ext. 5454 (in-state); 217-443-5238 (out-of-state). *Fax:* 217-431-4015. *E-mail:* kholden@lakeviewcol.edu.

LEWIS UNIVERSITY
Romeoville, Illinois

- **Independent** comprehensive, founded 1932, affiliated with Roman Catholic Church
- **Calendar** semesters
- **Degrees** certificates, associate, bachelor's, master's, and post-master's certificates
- **Small-town** 600-acre campus with easy access to Chicago
- **Endowment** $23.4 million
- **Coed,** 3,383 undergraduate students, 63% full-time, 58% women, 42% men
- **Moderately difficult** entrance level, 74% of applicants were admitted

Lewis University offers bachelor's degrees in more than 60 majors as well as graduate programs in business administration, counseling psychology, criminal/social justice, education, leadership studies, nursing, and school counseling and guidance. A Catholic and Lasallian university, Lewis is located in Romeoville, Illinois, just 35 minutes from Chicago on the interstate highways. Lewis has a widely recognized aviation program and an airport adjacent to the main campus.

Undergraduates 2,139 full-time, 1,244 part-time. Students come from 24 states and territories, 18 other countries, 3% are from out of state, 16% African American, 3% Asian American or Pacific Islander, 7% Hispanic American, 0.1% Native American, 4% international, 14% transferred in, 27% live on campus. *Retention:* 77% of 2001 full-time freshmen returned.

Freshmen *Admission:* 1,051 applied, 778 admitted, 387 enrolled. *Average high school GPA:* 2.91. *Test scores:* SAT verbal scores over 500: 64%; SAT math scores over 500: 72%; ACT scores over 18: 96%; SAT verbal scores over 600: 21%; SAT math scores over 600: 36%; ACT scores over 24: 26%; ACT scores over 30: 3%.

Faculty *Total:* 152, 93% full-time, 57% with terminal degrees. *Student/faculty ratio:* 15:1.

Majors Accounting; aircraft mechanic/airframe; aircraft pilot (professional); American studies; area studies related; art; art education; aviation management; aviation technology; biochemistry; biology; broadcast journalism; business administration; business economics; business information/data processing related; business marketing and marketing management; chemistry; computer science; criminal justice/law enforcement administration; drawing; economics; education; education (K-12); elementary education; English; environmental science; finance; fine/studio arts; graphic design/commercial art/illustration; health services administration; history; human resources management; journalism; liberal arts and sciences/liberal studies; management information systems/business data processing; mass communications; mathematics; medical technology; music; music business management/merchandising; nursing; painting; philosophy; physical education; physics; political science; pre-dentistry; pre-law; pre-medicine; pre-veterinary studies; protective services related; psychology; public administration; public relations; radio/television broadcasting technology; religious studies; secondary education; social work; sociology; special education; speech/rhetorical studies; speech/theater education; theater arts/drama.

Academic Programs *Special study options:* academic remediation for entering students, accelerated degree program, adult/continuing education programs, advanced placement credit, distance learning, double majors, English as a second language, honors programs, independent study, internships, part-time degree program, student-designed majors, study abroad, summer session for credit. *ROTC:* Army (b), Air Force (c).

Library Lewis University Library with 95,887 titles, 799 serial subscriptions, 2,818 audiovisual materials, an OPAC, a Web page.

Computers on Campus 287 computers available on campus for general student use. A campuswide network can be accessed from student residence rooms and from off campus. Internet access, online (class) registration, at least one staffed computer lab available.

Student Life *Housing Options:* coed, disabled students. *Activities and Organizations:* drama/theater group, student-run newspaper, radio and television station, choral group, Phi Kappa Theta, Scholars Academy, Black Student Union, Fellowship of Justice, Latin American Student Organization, national fraternities, national sororities. *Campus security:* 24-hour emergency response devices and patrols, student patrols, late-night transport/escort service, controlled dormitory access. *Student Services:* health clinic, personal/psychological counseling.

Athletics Member NCAA. All Division II. *Intercollegiate sports:* baseball M(s), basketball M(s)/W(s), cross-country running M(s)/W(s), golf M(s)/W(s), soccer M(s)/W(s), softball W(s), swimming M(s)/W(s), tennis M(s)/W(s), track and field M(s)/W(s), volleyball M(s)/W(s). *Intramural sports:* basketball M/W, bowling M/W, football M/W, golf M/W, racquetball M/W, softball M/W, table tennis M/W, tennis M/W, track and field M/W, volleyball M/W.

Standardized Tests *Required:* SAT I or ACT (for admission).

Costs (2001–02) *Comprehensive fee:* $20,960 includes full-time tuition ($14,040) and room and board ($6920). Full-time tuition and fees vary according to course load and program. Part-time tuition: $468 per credit hour. Part-time tuition and fees vary according to course load and program. *Room and board:* College room only: $3170. Room and board charges vary according to board plan and housing facility. *Payment plan:* installment. *Waivers:* children of alumni and employees or children of employees.

Financial Aid Of all full-time matriculated undergraduates who enrolled in 2001, 2019 applied for aid, 1395 were judged to have need, 591 had their need fully met. In 2001, 199 non-need-based awards were made. *Average percent of need met:* 86%. *Average financial aid package:* $14,850. *Average need-based loan:* $3600. *Average need-based gift aid:* $6460. *Average non-need based aid:* $4648. *Average indebtedness upon graduation:* $15,621.

Applying *Options:* common application, electronic application, deferred entrance. *Application fee:* $35. *Required:* high school transcript, minimum 2.0 GPA. *Required for some:* interview. *Application deadline:* rolling (freshmen), rolling (transfers).

Admissions Contact Ms. Arianne Martin, Assistant Director of Enrollment, Lewis University, Box 297, One University Parkway, Romeoville, IL 60446. *Phone:* 815-838-0500 Ext. 5237. *Toll-free phone:* 800-897-9000. *Fax:* 815-836-5002. *E-mail:* admissions@lewisu.edu.

LINCOLN CHRISTIAN COLLEGE
Lincoln, Illinois

- **Independent** 4-year, founded 1944, affiliated with Christian Churches and Churches of Christ
- **Calendar** semesters
- **Degrees** certificates, associate, and bachelor's
- **Small-town** 227-acre campus
- **Coed,** 670 undergraduate students, 82% full-time, 52% women, 48% men
- **Moderately difficult** entrance level, 80% of applicants were admitted

Undergraduates 547 full-time, 123 part-time. Students come from 25 states and territories, 8 other countries, 30% are from out of state, 2% African American, 1% Asian American or Pacific Islander, 0.9% Hispanic American, 1% Native American, 1% international, 5% transferred in, 50% live on campus. *Retention:* 71% of 2001 full-time freshmen returned.

Freshmen *Admission:* 232 applied, 186 admitted, 148 enrolled.

Faculty *Total:* 57, 46% full-time, 35% with terminal degrees. *Student/faculty ratio:* 13:1.

Majors Biblical studies; business administration; child care/development; divinity/ministry; early childhood education; elementary education; music (piano and organ performance); music (voice and choral/opera performance); religious education; religious music; secondary education; secretarial science; theology.

Academic Programs *Special study options:* academic remediation for entering students, adult/continuing education programs, advanced placement credit, distance learning, double majors, English as a second language, independent study, internships, off-campus study, part-time degree program, services for LD students, summer session for credit. *Unusual degree programs:* 3-2 teacher education.

Library Jessie Eury Library with 90,000 titles, 450 serial subscriptions, an OPAC, a Web page.

Computers on Campus 45 computers available on campus for general student use. A campuswide network can be accessed from student residence rooms and from off campus. Internet access, at least one staffed computer lab available.

Lincoln Christian College (continued)

Student Life *Housing:* on-campus residence required through senior year. *Options:* men-only, women-only. *Activities and Organizations:* drama/theater group, choral group. *Campus security:* 24-hour emergency response devices, student patrols. *Student Services:* health clinic, personal/psychological counseling.

Athletics Member NCCAA. *Intercollegiate sports:* baseball M, basketball M/W, soccer M/W, volleyball W. *Intramural sports:* basketball M, table tennis M/W, tennis M/W, volleyball M/W, weight lifting M/W.

Standardized Tests *Required:* ACT (for admission).

Costs (2001–02) *Comprehensive fee:* $12,228 includes full-time tuition ($7008), mandatory fees ($1120), and room and board ($4100). Part-time tuition: $219 per semester hour. Part-time tuition and fees vary according to course load. *Required fees:* $35 per semester hour. *Room and board:* College room only: $1845. *Payment plans:* installment, deferred payment. *Waivers:* employees or children of employees.

Financial Aid Of all full-time matriculated undergraduates who enrolled in 2001, 99 Federal Work-Study jobs (averaging $904). 144 State and other part-time jobs (averaging $895). *Average indebtedness upon graduation:* $16,632.

Applying *Options:* deferred entrance. *Application fee:* $20. *Required:* essay or personal statement, high school transcript, 3 letters of recommendation. *Required for some:* interview. *Application deadline:* rolling (freshmen), rolling (transfers).

Admissions Contact Mrs. Mary K. Davis, Assistant Director of Admissions, Lincoln Christian College, 100 Campus View Drive, Lincoln, IL 62656. *Phone:* 217-732-3168 Ext. 2251. *Toll-free phone:* 888-522-5228. *Fax:* 217-732-4199. *E-mail:* coladmis@lccs.edu.

LOYOLA UNIVERSITY CHICAGO
Chicago, Illinois

- **Independent Roman Catholic (Jesuit)** university, founded 1870
- **Calendar** semesters
- **Degrees** certificates, bachelor's, master's, doctoral, first professional, post-master's, and postbachelor's certificates (also offers adult part-time program with significant enrollment not reflected in profile)
- **Urban** 105-acre campus
- **Endowment** $227.1 million
- **Coed,** 7,497 undergraduate students, 73% full-time, 65% women, 35% men
- **Moderately difficult** entrance level, 77% of applicants were admitted

Undergraduates 5,446 full-time, 2,051 part-time. Students come from 50 states and territories, 60 other countries, 20% are from out of state, 9% African American, 12% Asian American or Pacific Islander, 10% Hispanic American, 0.1% Native American, 2% international, 6% transferred in, 29% live on campus. *Retention:* 85% of 2001 full-time freshmen returned.

Freshmen *Admission:* 8,746 applied, 6,722 admitted, 1,422 enrolled. *Test scores:* SAT verbal scores over 500: 88%; SAT math scores over 500: 84%; ACT scores over 18: 96%; SAT verbal scores over 600: 42%; SAT math scores over 600: 42%; ACT scores over 24: 61%; SAT verbal scores over 700: 7%; SAT math scores over 700: 7%; ACT scores over 30: 10%.

Faculty *Total:* 1,979, 47% full-time. *Student/faculty ratio:* 14:1.

Majors Accounting; anthropology; art; art history; biochemistry; biology; business administration; business economics; business marketing and marketing management; ceramic arts; chemistry; classics; communications; communications related; computer science; criminal justice studies; early childhood education; economics; elementary education; English; environmental science; finance; fine arts and art studies related; French; German; Greek (ancient and medieval); history; humanities; human resources management; information sciences/systems; international relations; Italian; journalism; Latin (ancient and medieval); management information systems/business data processing; mathematical statistics; mathematics; mathematics/computer science; metal/jewelry arts; music; natural sciences; nursing; nutrition studies; operations management; philosophy; photography; physics; political science; pre-dentistry; pre-law; pre-medicine; pre-theology; pre-veterinary studies; psychology; psychology related; social psychology; social work; sociology; Spanish; special education; theater arts/drama; theology.

Academic Programs *Special study options:* academic remediation for entering students, accelerated degree program, adult/continuing education programs, advanced placement credit, double majors, English as a second language, honors programs, internships, off-campus study, part-time degree program, services for LD students, study abroad, summer session for credit. *ROTC:* Army (c). *Unusual degree programs:* 3-2 engineering with University of Illinois at Urbana-Champaign, Washington University in St. Louis.

Library Cudahy Library plus 3 others with 983,023 titles, 110,502 serial subscriptions, 32,777 audiovisual materials, an OPAC, a Web page.

Computers on Campus 318 computers available on campus for general student use. A campuswide network can be accessed from student residence rooms and from off campus. Internet access, at least one staffed computer lab available.

Student Life *Housing Options:* coed. *Activities and Organizations:* drama/theater group, student-run newspaper, radio station, choral group, Campus Life Union Board, Activities Programming Board, Student Government, national fraternities, national sororities. *Campus security:* 24-hour emergency response devices and patrols, late-night transport/escort service, controlled dormitory access. *Student Services:* health clinic, personal/psychological counseling, women's center.

Athletics Member NCAA. All Division I. *Intercollegiate sports:* basketball M(s)/W(s), cross-country running M(s)/W(s), golf M(s)/W(s), soccer M(s)/W(s), softball W(s), track and field M(s)/W(s), volleyball M(s)/W(s). *Intramural sports:* badminton M/W, baseball M(c), basketball M/W, football M, racquetball M/W, rugby M(c), sailing M/W, soccer M/W, softball M/W, table tennis M/W, tennis M/W, volleyball M/W.

Standardized Tests *Required:* SAT I or ACT (for admission).

Costs (2001–02) *Comprehensive fee:* $26,540 includes full-time tuition ($18,814), mandatory fees ($460), and room and board ($7266). Part-time tuition: $371 per semester hour. Part-time tuition and fees vary according to course load. *Required fees:* $60 per term part-time. *Room and board:* Room and board charges vary according to board plan and housing facility. *Payment plan:* installment. *Waivers:* employees or children of employees.

Financial Aid Of all full-time matriculated undergraduates who enrolled in 2001, 4855 applied for aid, 3818 were judged to have need, 1586 had their need fully met. 2195 Federal Work-Study jobs (averaging $2086). In 2001, 280 non-need-based awards were made. *Average percent of need met:* 93%. *Average financial aid package:* $17,836. *Average need-based loan:* $4739. *Average need-based gift aid:* $12,292. *Average non-need based aid:* $7978. *Average indebtedness upon graduation:* $18,750.

Applying *Options:* common application, electronic application, early admission. *Application fee:* $25. *Required:* essay or personal statement, high school transcript. *Recommended:* interview. *Application deadlines:* 4/1 (freshmen), 7/9 (transfers). *Notification:* continuous until 8/15 (freshmen).

Admissions Contact Mr. Aaron Meis, Acting Director of Admissions, Loyola University Chicago, 820 North Michigan Avenue, Suite 613, Chicago, IL 60611. *Phone:* 312-915-6500. *Toll-free phone:* 800-262-2373. *Fax:* 312-915-7216. *E-mail:* admission@luc.edu.

MACMURRAY COLLEGE
Jacksonville, Illinois

- **Independent United Methodist** 4-year, founded 1846
- **Calendar** 4-1-4
- **Degrees** associate and bachelor's
- **Small-town** 60-acre campus
- **Endowment** $10.1 million
- **Coed,** 655 undergraduate students, 92% full-time, 53% women, 47% men
- **Moderately difficult** entrance level, 68% of applicants were admitted

Undergraduates 603 full-time, 52 part-time. Students come from 27 states and territories, 5 other countries, 15% are from out of state, 12% African American, 0.6% Asian American or Pacific Islander, 5% Hispanic American, 0.5% Native American, 0.9% international, 7% transferred in, 55% live on campus. *Retention:* 56% of 2001 full-time freshmen returned.

Freshmen *Admission:* 1,006 applied, 683 admitted, 144 enrolled. *Average high school GPA:* 3.16. *Test scores:* SAT verbal scores over 500: 36%; SAT math scores over 500: 42%; ACT scores over 18: 74%; SAT verbal scores over 600: 5%; SAT math scores over 600: 13%; ACT scores over 24: 20%; SAT math scores over 700: 5%; ACT scores over 30: 3%.

Faculty *Total:* 85, 71% full-time, 44% with terminal degrees. *Student/faculty ratio:* 12:1.

Majors Accounting; art; art history; biology; business administration; business marketing and marketing management; chemistry; computer science; criminal justice/law enforcement administration; elementary education; English; fine/studio arts; history; information sciences/systems; journalism; law enforcement/police science; liberal arts and sciences/liberal studies; management information systems/business data processing; mathematics; music; music teacher education; nursing; philosophy; physical education; physics; political science; pre-dentistry; pre-law; pre-medicine; pre-veterinary studies; psychology; religious studies; secondary education; sign language interpretation; social work; Spanish; special education; sport/fitness administration; theater arts/drama.

Academic Programs *Special study options:* academic remediation for entering students, advanced placement credit, double majors, honors programs, independent study, internships, off-campus study, part-time degree program, services for LD students, summer session for credit. *Unusual degree programs:* 3-2 engineering with Washington University in St. Louis, Columbia University, University of Missouri-Rolla.

Library Henry Pfeiffer Library with 146,000 titles, 103,519 serial subscriptions, 100 audiovisual materials, an OPAC, a Web page.

Computers on Campus 100 computers available on campus for general student use. A campuswide network can be accessed from student residence rooms that provide access to various software packages. Internet access, at least one staffed computer lab available.

Student Life *Housing:* on-campus residence required through junior year. *Options:* coed, men-only, women-only. *Activities and Organizations:* drama/theater group, student-run newspaper, choral group, Campus Activity Board, MacMurray Student Association, Sigma Tau Gamma, Alpha Phi Omega, Circle K, national fraternities. *Campus security:* 24-hour emergency response devices, student patrols, late-night transport/escort service, controlled dormitory access. *Student Services:* health clinic, personal/psychological counseling.

Athletics Member NCAA. All Division III. *Intercollegiate sports:* baseball M, basketball M/W, cross-country running M/W, football M, golf M/W, soccer M/W, softball W, swimming M/W, tennis M/W, volleyball W, wrestling M. *Intramural sports:* badminton M/W, basketball M/W, football M/W, soccer M/W, softball M/W, table tennis M/W, tennis M/W, volleyball M/W.

Standardized Tests *Required:* SAT I or ACT (for admission).

Costs (2002–03) *Comprehensive fee:* $19,665 includes full-time tuition ($14,500) and room and board ($5165). Part-time tuition: $225 per credit hour. *Room and board:* College room only: $2275. Room and board charges vary according to board plan and housing facility. *Payment plan:* installment. *Waivers:* minority students, children of alumni, senior citizens, and employees or children of employees.

Financial Aid Of all full-time matriculated undergraduates who enrolled in 2001, 600 applied for aid, 600 were judged to have need, 106 had their need fully met. 120 Federal Work-Study jobs (averaging $927). *Average percent of need met:* 83%. *Average financial aid package:* $14,335. *Average need-based loan:* $4541. *Average need-based gift aid:* $9603. *Average non-need based aid:* $3684. *Average indebtedness upon graduation:* $15,787.

Applying *Options:* common application, electronic application, early admission. *Required:* high school transcript. *Required for some:* essay or personal statement, minimum 2.5 GPA, letters of recommendation, interview. *Application deadline:* rolling (freshmen), rolling (transfers). *Notification:* continuous (freshmen).

Admissions Contact Mr. Tom McGinnis, Dean of Enrollment, MacMurray College, 447 East College Avenue, Jacksonville, IL 62650. *Phone:* 217-479-7056. *Toll-free phone:* 800-252-7485 (in-state); 217-479-7056 (out-of-state). *Fax:* 217-291-0702. *E-mail:* admiss@mac.edu.

McKendree College

Lebanon, Illinois

- **Independent** 4-year, founded 1828, affiliated with United Methodist Church
- **Calendar** semesters
- **Degree** bachelor's
- **Small-town** 80-acre campus with easy access to St. Louis
- **Endowment** $14.7 million
- **Coed,** 2,107 undergraduate students, 73% full-time, 62% women, 38% men
- **Moderately difficult** entrance level, 68% of applicants were admitted

Undergraduates 1,539 full-time, 568 part-time. Students come from 15 states and territories, 12 other countries, 31% are from out of state, 10% African American, 1.0% Asian American or Pacific Islander, 1% Hispanic American, 0.3% Native American, 2% international, 9% transferred in, 52% live on campus. *Retention:* 78% of 2001 full-time freshmen returned.

Freshmen *Admission:* 1,156 applied, 791 admitted, 323 enrolled. *Average high school GPA:* 3.60. *Test scores:* ACT scores over 18: 94%; ACT scores over 24: 45%; ACT scores over 30: 8%.

Faculty *Total:* 181, 36% full-time, 38% with terminal degrees. *Student/faculty ratio:* 17:1.

Majors Accounting; art; art education; athletic training/sports medicine; biology; biology education; business administration; business education; business marketing and marketing management; chemistry; computer science; criminal justice/law enforcement administration; distribution operations; economics; education (K-12); elementary education; English; English education; finance; history; history education; information sciences/systems; international relations; marketing operations; mass communications; mathematics; mathematics education; medical technology; music; nursing; philosophy; physical education; political science; pre-dentistry; pre-law; pre-medicine; pre-veterinary studies; psychology; public relations; religious studies; secondary education; social science education; social sciences; social work; sociology; speech/rhetorical studies; speech/theater education.

Academic Programs *Special study options:* academic remediation for entering students, accelerated degree program, advanced placement credit, double majors, honors programs, independent study, internships, off-campus study, part-time degree program, services for LD students, student-designed majors, study abroad, summer session for credit. *ROTC:* Army (c), Air Force (c). *Unusual degree programs:* 3-2 occupational therapy with Washington University in St. Louis.

Library Holman Library with 85,000 titles, 450 serial subscriptions, 4,558 audiovisual materials, an OPAC.

Computers on Campus 450 computers available on campus for general student use. A campuswide network can be accessed from student residence rooms and from off campus. At least one staffed computer lab available.

Student Life *Housing:* on-campus residence required for freshman year. *Options:* coed, men-only, women-only. *Activities and Organizations:* drama/theater group, student-run newspaper, choral group, marching band, Model United Nations, Campus Christian Fellowship, Residence Hall Association, Student Government Association, Students Against Social Injustice, national fraternities. *Campus security:* 24-hour emergency response devices and patrols, student patrols, late-night transport/escort service, controlled dormitory access. *Student Services:* health clinic, personal/psychological counseling.

Athletics Member NAIA. *Intercollegiate sports:* baseball M(s), basketball M(s)/W(s), bowling M(s)/W(s), cross-country running M(s)/W(s), football M(s), golf M(s)/W(s), soccer M(s)/W(s), softball W(s), tennis M(s)/W(s), track and field M(s)/W(s), volleyball W(s). *Intramural sports:* archery M/W, badminton M/W, basketball M/W, football M/W, soccer M/W, softball M/W, table tennis M/W, tennis M/W, volleyball M/W.

Standardized Tests *Required:* SAT I or ACT (for admission).

Costs (2001–02) *Comprehensive fee:* $18,300 includes full-time tuition ($13,350) and room and board ($4950). Full-time tuition and fees vary according to class time, course load, and location. Part-time tuition: $445 per credit hour. Part-time tuition and fees vary according to class time, course load, and location. *Room and board:* Room and board charges vary according to board plan and housing facility. *Payment plan:* installment. *Waivers:* employees or children of employees.

Financial Aid Of all full-time matriculated undergraduates who enrolled in 2001, 1199 applied for aid, 1038 were judged to have need, 531 had their need fully met. 441 Federal Work-Study jobs (averaging $1718). In 2001, 279 non-need-based awards were made. *Average percent of need met:* 95%. *Average financial aid package:* $10,607. *Average need-based loan:* $3250. *Average need-based gift aid:* $8554. *Average non-need based aid:* $5625. *Average indebtedness upon graduation:* $13,446.

Applying *Options:* common application, deferred entrance. *Required:* high school transcript, minimum 2.5 GPA, 1 letter of recommendation. *Required for some:* essay or personal statement, interview. *Application deadline:* rolling (freshmen), rolling (transfers). *Notification:* continuous (freshmen).

Admissions Contact Mr. Mark Campbell, Vice President for Admissions and Financial Aid, McKendree College, 701 College Road, Lebanon, IL 62254. *Phone:* 618-537-4481 Ext. 6835. *Toll-free phone:* 800-232-7228 Ext. 6835. *Fax:* 618-537-6496. *E-mail:* mecampbell@mckendree.edu.

Midstate College

Peoria, Illinois

Admissions Contact Ms. Meredith Bunch, Director of Enrollment Management, Midstate College, 411 West Northmoor Road, Peoria, IL 61614. *Phone:* 309-692-4092. *Fax:* 309-692-3893.

Millikin University

Decatur, Illinois

- **Independent** 4-year, founded 1901, affiliated with Presbyterian Church (U.S.A.)
- **Calendar** semesters
- **Degree** bachelor's
- **Suburban** 70-acre campus
- **Endowment** $60.0 million
- **Coed,** 2,389 undergraduate students, 97% full-time, 58% women, 42% men
- **Moderately difficult** entrance level, 76% of applicants were admitted

Undergraduates 2,316 full-time, 73 part-time. Students come from 33 states and territories, 13 other countries, 15% are from out of state, 7% African

Millikin University (continued)
American, 1% Asian American or Pacific Islander, 2% Hispanic American, 0.4% Native American, 0.6% international, 5% transferred in, 70% live on campus. *Retention:* 79% of 2001 full-time freshmen returned.

Freshmen *Admission:* 2,598 applied, 1,982 admitted, 652 enrolled. *Test scores:* SAT verbal scores over 500: 78%; SAT math scores over 500: 62%; SAT verbal scores over 600: 33%; SAT math scores over 600: 24%; SAT verbal scores over 700: 3%; SAT math scores over 700: 4%.

Faculty *Total:* 242, 64% full-time. *Student/faculty ratio:* 13:1.

Majors Accounting; American studies; art education; arts management; art therapy; athletic training/sports medicine; biology; business administration; business marketing and marketing management; chemistry; communications; computer/information sciences; creative writing; elementary education; English; experimental psychology; finance; fine/studio arts; foreign languages/literatures; French; German; graphic design/commercial art/illustration; history; human resources management; human services; interdisciplinary studies; international business; international relations; management information systems/business data processing; mathematics; music; music business management/merchandising; music (general performance); music teacher education; music (voice and choral/opera performance); nursing; philosophy; physical education; physics; political science; pre-dentistry; pre-law; pre-medicine; pre-veterinary studies; psychology; religious music; social science education; sociology; Spanish; sport/fitness administration; theater arts/drama.

Academic Programs *Special study options:* advanced placement credit, double majors, honors programs, independent study, internships, off-campus study, part-time degree program, services for LD students, student-designed majors, study abroad, summer session for credit. *Unusual degree programs:* 3-2 engineering with Washington University in St. Louis; physical therapy, occupational therapy, medical technology.

Library Staley Library with 183,000 titles, 965 serial subscriptions, 9,030 audiovisual materials, an OPAC, a Web page.

Computers on Campus 189 computers available on campus for general student use. A campuswide network can be accessed from student residence rooms that provide access to e-mail. Internet access, at least one staffed computer lab available.

Student Life *Housing:* on-campus residence required through junior year. *Options:* coed, men-only, women-only, disabled students. *Activities and Organizations:* drama/theater group, student-run newspaper, radio station, choral group, University Center Board, Millikin Marketing Association, Panhellenic Council, Interfraternity Council, Residence Hall Association, national fraternities, national sororities. *Campus security:* 24-hour emergency response devices and patrols, late-night transport/escort service, controlled dormitory access. *Student Services:* health clinic, personal/psychological counseling.

Athletics Member NCAA. All Division III. *Intercollegiate sports:* baseball M, basketball M/W, cross-country running M/W, football M, golf M/W, soccer M/W, softball W, swimming M/W, tennis M/W, track and field M/W, volleyball W, wrestling M. *Intramural sports:* basketball M/W, bowling M/W, softball M/W, table tennis M/W, tennis M/W, volleyball M/W.

Standardized Tests *Required:* SAT I or ACT (for admission).

Costs (2002–03) *Comprehensive fee:* $24,490 includes full-time tuition ($18,109), mandatory fees ($275), and room and board ($6106). Full-time tuition and fees vary according to course load. Part-time tuition: $500 per credit. *Room and board:* College room only: $3331. Room and board charges vary according to board plan and housing facility. *Payment plan:* installment. *Waivers:* employees or children of employees.

Financial Aid Of all full-time matriculated undergraduates who enrolled in 2001, 2123 applied for aid, 1783 were judged to have need, 1275 had their need fully met. *Average percent of need met:* 89%. *Average financial aid package:* $15,238. *Average need-based gift aid:* $9347. *Average non-need based aid:* $4342. *Financial aid deadline:* 6/1.

Applying *Options:* common application, electronic application, deferred entrance. *Required:* high school transcript, minimum 2.0 GPA, 2 letters of recommendation. *Required for some:* audition for school of music; portfolio review for art program. *Recommended:* interview. *Application deadline:* rolling (freshmen), rolling (transfers). *Notification:* continuous (freshmen).

Admissions Contact Mr. Lin Stoner, Dean of Admission, Millikin University, 1184 West Main Street, Decatur, IL 62522-2084. *Phone:* 217-424-6210. *Toll-free phone:* 800-373-7733 Ext. # 5. *Fax:* 217-425-4669. *E-mail:* admis@mail.millikin.edu.

MONMOUTH COLLEGE
Monmouth, Illinois

- **Independent** 4-year, founded 1853, affiliated with Presbyterian Church
- **Calendar** semesters
- **Degree** bachelor's
- **Small-town** 40-acre campus with easy access to Peoria
- **Endowment** $51.9 million
- **Coed,** 1,072 undergraduate students, 98% full-time, 54% women, 46% men
- **Moderately difficult** entrance level, 79% of applicants were admitted

Undergraduates 1,055 full-time, 17 part-time. Students come from 22 states and territories, 20 other countries, 7% are from out of state, 5% African American, 0.9% Asian American or Pacific Islander, 2% Hispanic American, 0.2% Native American, 3% international, 7% transferred in, 91% live on campus. *Retention:* 80% of 2001 full-time freshmen returned.

Freshmen *Admission:* 1,159 applied, 916 admitted, 261 enrolled. *Average high school GPA:* 3.20. *Test scores:* ACT scores over 18: 98%; ACT scores over 24: 32%; ACT scores over 30: 4%.

Faculty *Total:* 113, 66% full-time, 56% with terminal degrees. *Student/faculty ratio:* 12:1.

Majors Accounting; Army R.O.T.C./military science; art; biology; business administration; chemistry; classics; computer science; economics; education; elementary education; English; environmental science; French; Greek (modern); history; humanities; Latin (ancient and medieval); liberal arts and sciences/liberal studies; mass communications; mathematics; modern languages; music; natural sciences; philosophy; physical education; physics; political science; psychology; public relations; religious studies; secondary education; sociology; Spanish; special education; speech/rhetorical studies; theater arts/drama.

Academic Programs *Special study options:* advanced placement credit, double majors, honors programs, independent study, internships, off-campus study, part-time degree program, student-designed majors, study abroad. *ROTC:* Army (c). *Unusual degree programs:* 3-2 engineering with Case Western Reserve University, Washington University in St. Louis; nursing with Rush University.

Library Hewes Library with 177,974 titles, 1,709 serial subscriptions, 1,331 audiovisual materials, an OPAC, a Web page.

Computers on Campus 300 computers available on campus for general student use. A campuswide network can be accessed from student residence rooms and from off campus. Internet access, online (class) registration, at least one staffed computer lab available.

Student Life *Housing:* on-campus residence required through senior year. *Options:* coed, men-only, women-only. *Activities and Organizations:* drama/theater group, student-run newspaper, radio and television station, choral group, Student Service Organization, Student Association, M-Club, Greek life, Crimson Masque, national fraternities, national sororities. *Campus security:* 24-hour emergency response devices, late-night transport/escort service, night security. *Student Services:* personal/psychological counseling.

Athletics Member NCAA. All Division III. *Intercollegiate sports:* baseball M, basketball M/W, cross-country running M/W, football M, golf M/W, soccer M/W, softball W, tennis M/W, track and field M/W, volleyball W. *Intramural sports:* archery M/W, badminton M/W, basketball M/W, golf M/W, racquetball M/W, soccer M/W, softball M/W, swimming M/W, table tennis M/W, track and field M/W, volleyball M/W, wrestling M.

Standardized Tests *Required:* SAT I or ACT (for admission).

Costs (2002–03) *Comprehensive fee:* $22,490 includes full-time tuition ($17,760) and room and board ($4730). *Room and board:* College room only: $2500.

Financial Aid Of all full-time matriculated undergraduates who enrolled in 2001, 1083 applied for aid, 888 were judged to have need, 432 had their need fully met. 250 Federal Work-Study jobs. In 2001, 185 non-need-based awards were made. *Average percent of need met:* 95%. *Average financial aid package:* $14,937. *Average need-based loan:* $3970. *Average need-based gift aid:* $10,377. *Average non-need based aid:* $8811. *Average indebtedness upon graduation:* $16,088.

Applying *Options:* common application, electronic application, deferred entrance. *Required:* high school transcript. *Required for some:* essay or personal statement, 2 letters of recommendation. *Recommended:* interview. *Application deadline:* rolling (freshmen), rolling (transfers). *Notification:* continuous (freshmen).

Admissions Contact Monmouth College, 700 East Broadway, Monmouth, IL 61462-1998. *Phone:* 309-457-2131. *Toll-free phone:* 800-747-2687. *Fax:* 309-457-2141. *E-mail:* admit@monm.edu.

MOODY BIBLE INSTITUTE
Chicago, Illinois

- **Independent nondenominational** comprehensive, founded 1886
- **Calendar** semesters
- **Degrees** bachelor's, master's, and first professional
- **Urban** 25-acre campus

■ **Coed,** 1,396 undergraduate students, 93% full-time, 45% women, 55% men
■ **Moderately difficult** entrance level, 50% of applicants were admitted

Undergraduates 1,302 full-time, 94 part-time. Students come from 48 states and territories, 41 other countries, 69% are from out of state, 2% African American, 2% Asian American or Pacific Islander, 4% Hispanic American, 0.4% Native American, 7% international, 6% transferred in, 90% live on campus. *Retention:* 86% of 2001 full-time freshmen returned.

Freshmen *Admission:* 1,330 applied, 671 admitted, 428 enrolled. *Average high school GPA:* 3.46. *Test scores:* ACT scores over 18: 97%; ACT scores over 24: 61%; ACT scores over 30: 8%.

Faculty *Total:* 101, 88% full-time, 70% with terminal degrees. *Student/faculty ratio:* 20:1.

Majors Aviation technology; biblical studies; communications; linguistics; missionary studies; pre-theology; religious education; religious music; teaching English as a second language.

Academic Programs *Special study options:* adult/continuing education programs, advanced placement credit, distance learning, double majors, English as a second language, external degree program, independent study, internships, off-campus study, part-time degree program, study abroad, summer session for credit.

Library Henry Crowell Learning Center plus 1 other with 135,000 titles, 987 serial subscriptions.

Computers on Campus 26 computers available on campus for general student use. A campuswide network can be accessed from student residence rooms and from off campus. Internet access, at least one staffed computer lab available.

Student Life *Housing:* on-campus residence required through senior year. *Options:* men-only, women-only. *Activities and Organizations:* drama/theater group, student-run newspaper, radio station, choral group, Student Missionary Fellowship, Big Brother/Big Sister, music groups, Drama Group. *Campus security:* 24-hour emergency response devices and patrols, student patrols, late-night transport/escort service, controlled dormitory access. *Student Services:* health clinic, personal/psychological counseling.

Athletics Member NCCAA. *Intercollegiate sports:* basketball M/W, soccer M, volleyball M/W. *Intramural sports:* basketball M/W, cross-country running M/W, football M/W, golf M/W, soccer W, volleyball M/W, water polo M/W.

Costs (2001–02) *Comprehensive fee:* includes mandatory fees ($1382) and room and board ($6020). All students are awarded full-tuition scholarships. *Room and board:* College room only: $3420. Room and board charges vary according to housing facility. *Payment plan:* installment. *Waivers:* employees or children of employees.

Applying *Options:* early admission, early decision. *Application fee:* $35. *Required:* essay or personal statement, high school transcript, minimum 2.3 GPA, 4 letters of recommendation, Christian testimony. *Required for some:* interview. *Application deadlines:* 3/1 (freshmen), 3/1 (transfers). *Early decision:* 12/1. *Notification:* continuous until 8/1 (freshmen), 1/15 (early decision).

Admissions Contact Mrs. Marthe Campa, Application Coordinator, Moody Bible Institute, 820 North LaSalle Boulevard, Chicago, IL 60610. *Phone:* 312-329-4266. *Toll-free phone:* 800-967-4MBI. *Fax:* 312-329-8987. *E-mail:* admissions@moody.edu.

NAES College
Chicago, Illinois

■ **Independent** 4-year, founded 1974
■ **Calendar** semesters
■ **Degree** bachelor's
■ **Coed,** 70 undergraduate students, 66% full-time, 73% women, 27% men
■ **Noncompetitive** entrance level, 100% of applicants were admitted

Undergraduates 46 full-time, 24 part-time. 2% African American, 89% Native American.

Freshmen *Admission:* 1 applied, 1 admitted, 1 enrolled.

Faculty *Total:* 43, 9% full-time.

Majors Community services.

Academic Programs *Special study options:* accelerated degree program, advanced placement credit, cooperative education, summer session for credit.

Library 6,000 titles, 60 serial subscriptions.

Computers on Campus 10 computers available on campus for general student use. Internet access, at least one staffed computer lab available.

Student Life *Housing:* college housing not available.

Costs (2001–02) *Tuition:* $208 per semester hour part-time. *Required fees:* $35 per term part-time.

Financial Aid Of all full-time matriculated undergraduates who enrolled in 2001, 50 applied for aid, 50 were judged to have need, 48 had their need fully met. *Average percent of need met:* 88%. *Average financial aid package:* $5040.

Applying *Required:* high school transcript, interview, employment in an American Indian program. *Application deadline:* rolling (freshmen), rolling (transfers).

Admissions Contact Ms. Christine Redcloud, Registrar, NAES College, 2838 West Peterson Avenue, Chicago, IL 60659-3813. *Phone:* 773-761-5000. *Fax:* 773-761-3808.

National-Louis University
Evanston, Illinois

■ **Independent** university, founded 1886
■ **Calendar** quarters
■ **Degrees** bachelor's, master's, doctoral, post-master's, and postbachelor's certificates
■ 12-acre campus with easy access to Chicago
■ **Endowment** $13.6 million
■ **Coed,** 3,303 undergraduate students, 81% full-time, 72% women, 28% men
■ **Minimally difficult** entrance level, 77% of applicants were admitted

Undergraduates 2,680 full-time, 623 part-time. Students come from 19 states and territories, 1% are from out of state, 22% African American, 2% Asian American or Pacific Islander, 7% Hispanic American, 0.4% Native American, 0.2% international, 26% transferred in, 5% live on campus. *Retention:* 51% of 2001 full-time freshmen returned.

Freshmen *Admission:* 6,944 applied, 5,360 admitted, 199 enrolled. *Test scores:* ACT scores over 18: 47%; ACT scores over 24: 12%.

Faculty *Total:* 298, 100% full-time, 15% with terminal degrees. *Student/faculty ratio:* 18:1.

Majors Accounting; alcohol/drug abuse counseling; anthropology; art; behavioral sciences; biological/physical sciences; biology; business administration; computer management; early childhood education; elementary education; English; gerontology; health services administration; human services; individual/family development; industrial radiologic technology; information sciences/systems; international business; liberal arts and sciences/liberal studies; mathematics; medical technology; psychology; respiratory therapy; social sciences; theater arts/drama.

Academic Programs *Special study options:* academic remediation for entering students, accelerated degree program, adult/continuing education programs, advanced placement credit, English as a second language, external degree program, honors programs, independent study, internships, part-time degree program, services for LD students, summer session for credit.

Library NLU Library plus 5 others with 5,043 audiovisual materials, an OPAC.

Computers on Campus A campuswide network can be accessed from off campus. Internet access, at least one staffed computer lab available.

Student Life *Housing Options:* coed. *Activities and Organizations:* drama/theater group, choral group, Student Council, Nosotros Unidos, Accounting Club, African-American Club. *Campus security:* 24-hour emergency response devices and patrols. *Student Services:* health clinic, personal/psychological counseling.

Standardized Tests *Required for some:* SAT I or ACT (for admission).

Costs (2001–02) *Comprehensive fee:* $20,923 includes full-time tuition ($14,010), mandatory fees ($900), and room and board ($6013). Full-time tuition and fees vary according to location and program. Part-time tuition: $311 per quarter hour. Part-time tuition and fees vary according to location and program. *Room and board:* College room only: $2687. Room and board charges vary according to board plan. *Payment plans:* installment, deferred payment. *Waivers:* employees or children of employees.

Applying *Options:* deferred entrance. *Application fee:* $25. *Required:* high school transcript, minimum 2.0 GPA. *Required for some:* 2 letters of recommendation. *Recommended:* interview. *Application deadline:* rolling (freshmen), rolling (transfers). *Notification:* continuous (freshmen).

Admissions Contact Ms. Pat Petillo, Director of Admissions, National-Louis University, 2840 Sheridan Road, Evanston, IL 60201-1796. *Phone:* 888-NLU-TODAY. *Toll-free phone:* 888-NLU-TODAY Ext. 5151 (in-state); 800-443-5522 Ext. 5151 (out-of-state).

North Central College
Naperville, Illinois

■ **Independent United Methodist** comprehensive, founded 1861
■ **Calendar** trimesters
■ **Degrees** bachelor's and master's
■ **Suburban** 56-acre campus with easy access to Chicago
■ **Endowment** $53.1 million
■ **Coed,** 2,162 undergraduate students, 84% full-time, 57% women, 43% men

North Central College (continued)
■ **Moderately difficult** entrance level, 78% of applicants were admitted

Undergraduates 1,811 full-time, 351 part-time. Students come from 26 states and territories, 18 other countries, 11% are from out of state, 4% African American, 2% Asian American or Pacific Islander, 3% Hispanic American, 0.2% Native American, 1% international, 8% transferred in, 58% live on campus. *Retention:* 81% of 2001 full-time freshmen returned.

Freshmen *Admission:* 1,457 applied, 1,143 admitted, 444 enrolled. *Average high school GPA:* 3.40. *Test scores:* SAT verbal scores over 500: 75%; SAT math scores over 500: 80%; ACT scores over 18: 99%; SAT verbal scores over 600: 30%; SAT math scores over 600: 39%; ACT scores over 24: 58%; SAT verbal scores over 700: 3%; SAT math scores over 700: 8%; ACT scores over 30: 9%.

Faculty *Total:* 226, 53% full-time, 55% with terminal degrees. *Student/faculty ratio:* 14:1.

Majors Accounting; actuarial science; American history; anthropology; applied mathematics; art; art education; athletic training/sports medicine; biochemistry; biology; broadcast journalism; business administration; business education; business marketing and marketing management; chemistry; classics; computer science; early childhood education; economics; education; elementary education; English; exercise sciences; finance; French; German; health education; history; humanities; international business; international relations; Japanese; jazz; liberal arts and sciences/liberal studies; literature; management information systems/business data processing; mass communications; mathematics; modern languages; music; music (piano and organ performance); music (voice and choral/opera performance); natural sciences; philosophy; physical education; physics; political science; pre-dentistry; pre-law; pre-medicine; pre-veterinary studies; psychology; public relations; religious studies; science education; secondary education; social sciences; sociology; Spanish; speech/rhetorical studies; theater arts/drama.

Academic Programs *Special study options:* academic remediation for entering students, accelerated degree program, adult/continuing education programs, advanced placement credit, cooperative education, double majors, English as a second language, honors programs, independent study, internships, off-campus study, part-time degree program, services for LD students, student-designed majors, study abroad, summer session for credit. *ROTC:* Army (c), Air Force (c). *Unusual degree programs:* 3-2 engineering with Washington University in St. Louis; University of Illinois at Urbana-Champaign; Marquette University; University of Minnesota, Twin Cities Campus; medical technology with Rush University.

Library Oesterle Library with 132,322 titles, 736 serial subscriptions, 3,546 audiovisual materials, an OPAC, a Web page.

Computers on Campus 200 computers available on campus for general student use. A campuswide network can be accessed from student residence rooms and from off campus that provide access to software packages. Internet access, at least one staffed computer lab available.

Student Life *Housing Options:* coed, men-only, women-only. *Activities and Organizations:* drama/theater group, student-run newspaper, radio station, choral group, College Union Activities Board, student radio station, Cards in Action (service group), Black Student Organization, Residence Hall Association. *Campus security:* 24-hour emergency response devices and patrols, late-night transport/escort service. *Student Services:* health clinic, personal/psychological counseling.

Athletics Member NCAA. All Division III. *Intercollegiate sports:* baseball M, basketball M/W, cross-country running M/W, football M, golf M/W, soccer M/W, softball W, swimming M/W, tennis M/W, track and field M/W, volleyball W, wrestling M. *Intramural sports:* badminton M/W, basketball M/W, bowling M/W, cross-country running M/W, football M/W, golf M/W, racquetball M/W, skiing (cross-country) M/W, skiing (downhill) M/W, soccer M/W, swimming M/W, table tennis M/W, tennis M/W, track and field M/W, volleyball M/W, weight lifting M, wrestling M.

Standardized Tests *Required:* SAT I or ACT (for admission). *Recommended:* ACT (for admission).

Costs (2001–02) *Comprehensive fee:* $22,899 includes full-time tuition ($16,995), mandatory fees ($180), and room and board ($5724). Part-time tuition: $455 per semester hour. Part-time tuition and fees vary according to course load and program. *Room and board:* Room and board charges vary according to housing facility. *Payment plan:* installment. *Waivers:* senior citizens.

Financial Aid Of all full-time matriculated undergraduates who enrolled in 2001, 1324 applied for aid, 1151 were judged to have need, 600 had their need fully met. 184 Federal Work-Study jobs (averaging $682). 705 State and other part-time jobs (averaging $1156). In 2001, 395 non-need-based awards were made. *Average percent of need met:* 75%. *Average financial aid package:* $13,913. *Average need-based loan:* $3493. *Average need-based gift aid:* $8395. *Average non-need based aid:* $5213. *Average indebtedness upon graduation:* $12,909.

Applying *Options:* common application, early admission, deferred entrance. *Application fee:* $25. *Required:* high school transcript, minimum 2.0 GPA. *Required for some:* interview. *Recommended:* essay or personal statement, 1 letter of recommendation. *Application deadline:* rolling (freshmen), rolling (transfers). *Notification:* continuous (freshmen).

Admissions Contact Mr. Stephen Potts, Coordinator of Freshman Admission, North Central College, 30 North Brainard Street, PO Box 3063, Naperville, IL 60566-7063. *Phone:* 630-637-5815. *Toll-free phone:* 800-411-1861. *Fax:* 630-637-5819. *E-mail:* ncadm@noctrl.edu.

NORTHEASTERN ILLINOIS UNIVERSITY
Chicago, Illinois

■ **State-supported** comprehensive, founded 1961
■ **Calendar** semesters
■ **Degrees** bachelor's and master's
■ **Urban** 67-acre campus
■ **Endowment** $1.2 million
■ **Coed,** 8,382 undergraduate students, 57% full-time, 63% women, 37% men
■ **Minimally difficult** entrance level, 72% of applicants were admitted

Undergraduates 4,765 full-time, 3,617 part-time. Students come from 18 states and territories, 45 other countries, 1% are from out of state, 13% African American, 13% Asian American or Pacific Islander, 28% Hispanic American, 0.3% Native American, 1% international, 12% transferred in. *Retention:* 72% of 2001 full-time freshmen returned.

Freshmen *Admission:* 2,726 applied, 1,972 admitted, 1,056 enrolled. *Average high school GPA:* 2.76. *Test scores:* ACT scores over 18: 45%; ACT scores over 24: 5%.

Faculty *Total:* 590, 60% full-time, 56% with terminal degrees. *Student/faculty ratio:* 18:1.

Majors Accounting; anthropology; art; bilingual/bicultural education; biology; business; business marketing and marketing management; chemistry; computer/information sciences; criminal justice studies; early childhood education; earth sciences; economics; elementary education; English; environmental science; finance; French; geography; history; human resources management; liberal arts and sciences/liberal studies; linguistics; mathematics; music; philosophy; physical education; physics; political science; psychology; social work; sociology; Spanish; special education; speech/rhetorical studies; urban studies; women's studies.

Academic Programs *Special study options:* academic remediation for entering students, adult/continuing education programs, advanced placement credit, cooperative education, distance learning, double majors, English as a second language, external degree program, honors programs, independent study, internships, off-campus study, part-time degree program, services for LD students, study abroad, summer session for credit. *ROTC:* Army (c).

Library Ronald Williams Library with 498,940 titles, 3,451 serial subscriptions, 5,389 audiovisual materials, an OPAC, a Web page.

Computers on Campus 300 computers available on campus for general student use. A campuswide network can be accessed from off campus that provide access to productivity software. Internet access, online (class) registration, at least one staffed computer lab available.

Student Life *Housing:* college housing not available. *Activities and Organizations:* drama/theater group, student-run newspaper, radio station, choral group, student government, Chimexla, WZRD Radio Club, Business and Management Club, Black Heritage Gospel Choir, national sororities. *Campus security:* 24-hour emergency response devices and patrols, late-night transport/escort service. *Student Services:* health clinic, personal/psychological counseling, women's center.

Athletics *Intramural sports:* badminton M/W, baseball M, basketball M/W, cross-country running M/W, ice hockey M(c), racquetball M/W, soccer M/W, softball M/W, swimming M/W, table tennis M/W, tennis M/W, volleyball M/W, water polo M/W, weight lifting M/W.

Standardized Tests *Required:* ACT (for admission).

Costs (2001–02) *Tuition:* state resident $2424 full-time, $121 per credit hour part-time; nonresident $7272 full-time, $323 per credit hour part-time. *Required fees:* $474 full-time, $20 per credit hour. *Payment plan:* deferred payment. *Waivers:* senior citizens and employees or children of employees.

Financial Aid Of all full-time matriculated undergraduates who enrolled in 2001, 3317 applied for aid, 2508 were judged to have need, 464 had their need fully met. 224 Federal Work-Study jobs (averaging $1821). 535 State and other part-time jobs (averaging $1491). In 2001, 154 non-need-based awards were made. *Average percent of need met:* 69%. *Average financial aid package:* $5621. *Average need-based loan:* $2141. *Average need-based gift aid:* $5015. *Average non-need based aid:* $1582. *Average indebtedness upon graduation:* $10,918.

Applying *Options:* deferred entrance. *Required:* high school transcript. *Application deadlines:* 7/1 (freshmen), 7/1 (transfers).

Admissions Contact Ms. Kay D. Gulli, Administrative Assistant, Northeastern Illinois University, 500 North St. Louis Avenue, Chicago, IL 60625. *Phone:* 773-442-4000. *Fax:* 773-794-6243. *E-mail:* admrec@neiu.edu.

NORTHERN ILLINOIS UNIVERSITY
De Kalb, Illinois

- **State-supported** university, founded 1895
- **Calendar** semesters
- **Degrees** bachelor's, master's, doctoral, and first professional
- **Small-town** 589-acre campus with easy access to Chicago
- **Endowment** $870,857
- **Coed,** 17,468 undergraduate students, 89% full-time, 53% women, 47% men
- **Moderately difficult** entrance level, 64% of applicants were admitted

Undergraduates 15,555 full-time, 1,913 part-time. Students come from 50 states and territories, 105 other countries, 3% are from out of state, 13% African American, 6% Asian American or Pacific Islander, 6% Hispanic American, 0.3% Native American, 1% international, 13% transferred in, 36% live on campus. *Retention:* 76% of 2001 full-time freshmen returned.

Freshmen *Admission:* 13,421 applied, 8,633 admitted, 2,818 enrolled. *Test scores:* ACT scores over 18: 91%; ACT scores over 24: 38%; ACT scores over 30: 4%.

Faculty *Total:* 1,249, 81% full-time, 68% with terminal degrees. *Student/faculty ratio:* 17:1.

Majors Accounting; anthropology; art; art education; art history; atmospheric sciences; biology; business; business administration; business marketing and marketing management; chemistry; clothing/apparel/textile studies; communication disorders; communications; community health liaison; computer science; early childhood education; economics; education; electrical engineering; elementary education; engineering technology; English; finance; fine/studio arts; French; geography; geology; German; health education; health science; history; home economics education; individual/family development; industrial arts education; industrial/manufacturing engineering; industrial technology; journalism; liberal arts and sciences/liberal studies; mathematics; mechanical engineering; medical technology; music; music teacher education; nursing; nutrition studies; operations management; philosophy; physical education; physical therapy; physics; political science; psychology; Russian; social sciences; sociology; Spanish; special education; theater arts/drama.

Academic Programs *Special study options:* accelerated degree program, adult/continuing education programs, advanced placement credit, cooperative education, double majors, honors programs, independent study, internships, off-campus study, part-time degree program, services for LD students, student-designed majors, study abroad, summer session for credit. *ROTC:* Army (b), Air Force (c). *Unusual degree programs:* 3-2 engineering with University of Illinois.

Library Founders Memorial Library plus 8 others with 1.6 million titles, 17,000 serial subscriptions, 49,270 audiovisual materials, an OPAC, a Web page.

Computers on Campus 1200 computers available on campus for general student use. A campuswide network can be accessed from student residence rooms and from off campus. At least one staffed computer lab available.

Student Life *Housing:* on-campus residence required for freshman year. *Options:* coed. *Activities and Organizations:* drama/theater group, student-run newspaper, radio station, choral group, marching band, American Marketing Association, Delta Sigma Pi, Pi Sigma Epsilon, Black Choir, Student Volunteer Choir, national fraternities, national sororities. *Campus security:* 24-hour emergency response devices and patrols, student patrols, late-night transport/escort service, controlled dormitory access. *Student Services:* health clinic, personal/psychological counseling, women's center, legal services.

Athletics Member NCAA. All Division I except football (Division I-A). *Intercollegiate sports:* baseball M(s), basketball M(s)/W(s), cross-country running W, golf M(s)/W(s), gymnastics W(s), soccer M(s)/W(s), softball W(s), swimming M(s)/W(s), tennis M(s)/W(s), volleyball W(s), wrestling M(s). *Intramural sports:* archery M(c)/W(c), badminton M/W, basketball M/W, bowling M(c)/W(c), cross-country running W, football M/W, golf M/W, ice hockey M(c)/W(c), lacrosse M(c)/W(c), racquetball M/W, rugby M(c)/W(c), skiing (downhill) M(c)/W(c), soccer M/W, softball M/W, table tennis M/W, tennis M/W, track and field M(c)/W(c), volleyball M/W, water polo M(c)/W(c), weight lifting M(c)/W(c).

Standardized Tests *Required:* SAT I or ACT (for admission).

Costs (2001–02) *Tuition:* state resident $3293 full-time, $119 per credit hour part-time; nonresident $6585 full-time, $238 per credit hour part-time. Full-time tuition and fees vary according to course load. Part-time tuition and fees vary according to course load. *Required fees:* $1182 full-time, $49 per credit hour, $591 per term part-time. *Room and board:* $5070. Room and board charges vary according to board plan and housing facility. *Payment plan:* installment. *Waivers:* minority students and employees or children of employees.

Applying *Options:* electronic application. *Required:* high school transcript. *Application deadlines:* 8/1 (freshmen), 8/1 (transfers). *Notification:* continuous (freshmen).

Admissions Contact Dr. Robert Burk, Director of Admissions, Northern Illinois University, DeKalb, IL 60113-2857. *Phone:* 815-753-0446. *Toll-free phone:* 800-892-3050. *E-mail:* admission-info@niu.edu.

NORTH PARK UNIVERSITY
Chicago, Illinois

- **Independent** comprehensive, founded 1891, affiliated with Evangelical Covenant Church
- **Calendar** semesters
- **Degrees** bachelor's, master's, doctoral, and first professional
- **Urban** 30-acre campus
- **Endowment** $36.4 million
- **Coed,** 1,573 undergraduate students, 80% full-time, 62% women, 38% men
- **Moderately difficult** entrance level, 74% of applicants were admitted

North Park blends two traditions—faith and freedom—and two rich environments—the small, residential University and the large, complex city. North Park offers broad exposure to the liberal arts and specific education in a profession. Faculty members are superbly credentialed and devoted to teaching. North Park's Chicago location means unparalleled educational, cultural, recreational, spiritual, and artistic opportunities. Several hundred internships are available in every imaginable vocation. North Park's Outreach Ministries program has served as a national prototype for urban collegiate service opportunities. An outstanding scholars program includes generous scholarships, special courses, study abroad, and alumni mentors.

Undergraduates 1,252 full-time, 321 part-time. Students come from 38 states and territories, 32 other countries, 39% are from out of state, 12% African American, 5% Asian American or Pacific Islander, 10% Hispanic American, 0.4% Native American, 5% international, 12% transferred in. *Retention:* 70% of 2001 full-time freshmen returned.

Freshmen *Admission:* 1,068 applied, 791 admitted, 320 enrolled. *Test scores:* SAT verbal scores over 500: 82%; SAT math scores over 500: 80%; ACT scores over 18: 89%; SAT verbal scores over 600: 46%; SAT math scores over 600: 38%; ACT scores over 24: 42%; SAT verbal scores over 700: 11%; SAT math scores over 700: 9%; ACT scores over 30: 9%.

Faculty *Total:* 121, 73% full-time, 64% with terminal degrees. *Student/faculty ratio:* 16:1.

Majors Accounting; anthropology; art; art education; athletic training/sports medicine; biblical studies; biological/physical sciences; biology; business administration; business marketing and marketing management; chemistry; community services; divinity/ministry; early childhood education; economics; education; elementary education; English; exercise sciences; finance; fine/studio arts; French; history; international business; international relations; literature; mass communications; mathematics; medical technology; modern languages; music; music business management/merchandising; music teacher education; music (voice and choral/opera performance); natural sciences; nursing; philosophy; physical education; physics; political science; pre-dentistry; pre-law; pre-medicine; pre-veterinary studies; psychology; religious music; religious studies; Scandinavian languages; secondary education; social sciences; sociology; Spanish; speech/rhetorical studies; theater arts/drama; theology; urban studies.

Academic Programs *Special study options:* academic remediation for entering students, accelerated degree program, adult/continuing education programs, advanced placement credit, English as a second language, freshman honors college, honors programs, internships, off-campus study, part-time degree program, student-designed majors, study abroad, summer session for credit. *Unusual degree programs:* 3-2 engineering with University of Illinois at Urbana-Champaign, Case Western Reserve University, Washington University in St. Louis, University of Minnesota, Twin Cities Campus; physical therapy.

Library Consolidated Library plus 4 others with 260,685 titles, 1,178 serial subscriptions, an OPAC, a Web page.

Computers on Campus 105 computers available on campus for general student use. A campuswide network can be accessed from student residence rooms and from off campus. At least one staffed computer lab available.

Student Life *Housing:* on-campus residence required through junior year. *Options:* men-only, women-only. *Activities and Organizations:* drama/theater group, student-run newspaper, choral group, Student Association, Urban Out-

North Park University (continued)
reach, College Life, college music. *Campus security:* 24-hour emergency response devices and patrols, late-night transport/escort service. *Student Services:* health clinic, personal/psychological counseling.

Athletics Member NCAA. All Division III. *Intercollegiate sports:* baseball M, basketball M/W, cross-country running M/W, football M, golf M, soccer M/W, softball W, tennis W, track and field M/W, volleyball M/W. *Intramural sports:* basketball M/W, football M/W, golf M/W, volleyball M/W.

Standardized Tests *Required:* SAT I or ACT (for admission).

Costs (2001–02) *One-time required fee:* $220. *Comprehensive fee:* $23,620 includes full-time tuition ($17,790) and room and board ($5830). Full-time tuition and fees vary according to program. Part-time tuition: $355 per credit hour. Part-time tuition and fees vary according to program. *Room and board:* Room and board charges vary according to board plan, housing facility, and student level. *Payment plan:* installment. *Waivers:* adult students and employees or children of employees.

Financial Aid *Average indebtedness upon graduation:* $15,814.

Applying *Options:* early admission. *Application fee:* $20. *Required:* essay or personal statement, high school transcript, minimum 2.0 GPA, 1 letter of recommendation. *Required for some:* interview. *Recommended:* minimum 3.0 GPA. *Application deadline:* rolling (freshmen), rolling (transfers). *Notification:* continuous (freshmen).

Admissions Contact Office of Admissions, North Park University, 3225 West Foster Avenue, Chicago, IL 60625-4895. *Phone:* 773-244-5500. *Toll-free phone:* 800-888-NPC8. *Fax:* 773-583-0858. *E-mail:* afao@northpark.edu.

NORTHWESTERN UNIVERSITY
Evanston, Illinois

- **Independent** university, founded 1851
- **Calendar** semesters
- **Degrees** certificates, bachelor's, master's, doctoral, and first professional
- **Suburban** 250-acre campus with easy access to Chicago
- **Endowment** $3.3 billion
- **Coed,** 7,816 undergraduate students, 98% full-time, 53% women, 47% men
- **Most difficult** entrance level, 34% of applicants were admitted

Undergraduates 7,678 full-time, 138 part-time. Students come from 50 states and territories, 98 other countries, 78% are from out of state, 6% African American, 17% Asian American or Pacific Islander, 4% Hispanic American, 0.2% Native American, 4% international, 2% transferred in, 68% live on campus. *Retention:* 96% of 2001 full-time freshmen returned.

Freshmen *Admission:* 13,988 applied, 4,780 admitted, 1,952 enrolled. *Test scores:* SAT verbal scores over 500: 99%; SAT math scores over 500: 99%; ACT scores over 18: 100%; SAT verbal scores over 600: 90%; SAT math scores over 600: 94%; ACT scores over 24: 97%; SAT verbal scores over 700: 44%; SAT math scores over 700: 58%; ACT scores over 30: 68%.

Faculty *Total:* 1,103, 82% full-time, 100% with terminal degrees. *Student/faculty ratio:* 7:1.

Majors African-American studies; American studies; anthropology; applied mathematics; art; art history; Asian studies; astronomy; biochemistry; bioengineering; biological/physical sciences; biology; cell biology; chemical engineering; chemistry; civil engineering; classics; cognitive psychology/psycholinguistics; communication disorders; communications; community psychology; comparative literature; computer engineering; computer/information sciences; computer science; counseling psychology; dance; drama/theater literature; ecology; economics; education; education of the specific learning disabled; electrical engineering; engineering; engineering related; engineering science; English; environmental engineering; environmental science; film studies; French; geography; geology; German; hearing sciences; history; humanities; industrial/manufacturing engineering; interdisciplinary studies; international relations; Italian; jazz; journalism; liberal arts and sciences/liberal studies; linguistics; materials engineering; materials science; mathematical statistics; mathematics; mathematics education; mechanical engineering; molecular biology; music; music (general performance); music history; music (piano and organ performance); music related; music teacher education; music theory and composition; music (voice and choral/opera performance); neuroscience; organizational behavior; philosophy; physics; political science; pre-medicine; psychology; public policy analysis; radio/television broadcasting; religious studies; secondary education; Slavic languages; social/philosophical foundations of education; social sciences and history related; sociology; South Asian languages; Spanish; speech-language pathology; speech-language pathology/audiology; speech/rhetorical studies; speech therapy; theater arts/drama; urban studies; visual/performing arts; wind/percussion instruments; women's studies.

Academic Programs *Special study options:* accelerated degree program, adult/continuing education programs, advanced placement credit, cooperative education, double majors, honors programs, independent study, internships, off-campus study, part-time degree program, services for LD students, student-designed majors, study abroad, summer session for credit. *ROTC:* Army (c), Navy (b), Air Force (c).

Library University Library plus 6 others with 4.1 million titles, 37,467 serial subscriptions, 65,024 audiovisual materials, an OPAC, a Web page.

Computers on Campus 661 computers available on campus for general student use. A campuswide network can be accessed from student residence rooms and from off campus. Internet access, online (class) registration, at least one staffed computer lab available.

Student Life *Housing Options:* coed, men-only, women-only. *Activities and Organizations:* drama/theater group, student-run newspaper, radio and television station, choral group, marching band, Associated Student Government, Asian Christian Ministry, Activities and Organization Board, Special Olympics, national fraternities, national sororities. *Campus security:* 24-hour emergency response devices and patrols, late-night transport/escort service, controlled dormitory access. *Student Services:* health clinic, personal/psychological counseling, women's center.

Athletics Member NCAA. All Division I except football (Division I-A). *Intercollegiate sports:* baseball M(s), basketball M(s)/W(s), cross-country running W(s), fencing W(s), field hockey W(s), golf M(s)/W(s), soccer M(s)/W(s), softball W(s), swimming M(s)/W(s), tennis M(s)/W(s), volleyball W(s), wrestling M(s). *Intramural sports:* baseball M(c), basketball M/W, crew M(c)/W(c), equestrian sports M(c)/W(c), fencing M(c), football M, golf M/W, ice hockey M(c)/W(c), lacrosse M(c), racquetball M/W, rugby M(c)/W(c), sailing M(c)/W(c), skiing (cross-country) M/W, skiing (downhill) M/W, soccer M/W, softball W, squash M/W, swimming M/W, tennis M/W, volleyball M/W, water polo M(c)/W(c).

Standardized Tests *Required:* SAT I or ACT (for admission). *Required for some:* SAT II: Subject Tests (for admission). *Recommended:* SAT II: Subject Tests (for admission).

Costs (2002–03) *Comprehensive fee:* $35,674 includes full-time tuition ($27,108), mandatory fees ($120), and room and board ($8446). *Room and board:* College room only: $4851. Room and board charges vary according to board plan and housing facility. *Payment plan:* installment. *Waivers:* employees or children of employees.

Financial Aid Of all full-time matriculated undergraduates who enrolled in 2001, 3938 applied for aid, 3407 were judged to have need, 3407 had their need fully met. 1800 Federal Work-Study jobs (averaging $1611). 1038 State and other part-time jobs (averaging $2500). In 2001, 537 non-need-based awards were made. *Average percent of need met:* 100%. *Average financial aid package:* $21,314. *Average need-based loan:* $4130. *Average need-based gift aid:* $16,949. *Average non-need based aid:* $2268. *Average indebtedness upon graduation:* $13,253.

Applying *Options:* electronic application, early admission, early decision, deferred entrance. *Application fee:* $60. *Required:* essay or personal statement, high school transcript, 1 letter of recommendation. *Required for some:* audition for music program. *Recommended:* interview. *Application deadlines:* 1/1 (freshmen), 6/1 (transfers). *Early decision:* 11/1. *Notification:* 4/15 (freshmen), 12/15 (early decision).

Admissions Contact Ms. Carol Lunkenheimer, Director of Admissions, Northwestern University, PO Box 3060, Evanston, IL 60204-3060. *Phone:* 847-491-7271. *E-mail:* ug-admission@northwestern.edu.

OLIVET NAZARENE UNIVERSITY
Bourbonnais, Illinois

- **Independent** comprehensive, founded 1907, affiliated with Church of the Nazarene
- **Calendar** semesters
- **Degrees** bachelor's and master's
- **Small-town** 168-acre campus with easy access to Chicago
- **Endowment** $12.6 million
- **Coed,** 2,061 undergraduate students, 85% full-time, 57% women, 43% men
- **Moderately difficult** entrance level, 79% of applicants were admitted

Undergraduates 1,752 full-time, 309 part-time. Students come from 41 states and territories, 11 other countries, 60% are from out of state, 7% African American, 0.9% Asian American or Pacific Islander, 2% Hispanic American, 0.2% Native American, 0.7% international, 11% transferred in, 79% live on campus. *Retention:* 68% of 2001 full-time freshmen returned.

Freshmen *Admission:* 1,398 applied, 1,111 admitted, 548 enrolled. *Test scores:* ACT scores over 18: 85%; ACT scores over 24: 40%; ACT scores over 30: 9%.

Faculty *Total:* 108, 76% full-time. *Student/faculty ratio:* 20:1.

Majors Accounting; art; art education; athletic training/sports medicine; biblical studies; biochemistry; biological/physical sciences; biology; broadcast journalism; business administration; business economics; business marketing and marketing management; chemistry; child care/development; clothing/textiles; computer science; criminal justice/law enforcement administration; developmental/child psychology; dietetics; early childhood education; earth sciences; economics; education; elementary education; engineering; English; environmental science; exercise sciences; family/community studies; fashion merchandising; film studies; finance; food sciences; geology; graphic design/commercial art/illustration; history; home economics; home economics education; human resources management; information sciences/systems; interdisciplinary studies; journalism; liberal arts and sciences/liberal studies; literature; mass communications; mathematics; medical technology; modern languages; music; music (piano and organ performance); music teacher education; music (voice and choral/opera performance); natural sciences; nursing; pastoral counseling; philosophy; physical education; physical sciences; pre-dentistry; pre-law; pre-medicine; pre-veterinary studies; psychology; radio/television broadcasting; religious education; religious music; religious studies; romance languages; science education; secondary education; social sciences; Spanish; speech/rhetorical studies; sport/fitness administration; stringed instruments; theology; wind/percussion instruments; zoology.

Academic Programs *Special study options:* academic remediation for entering students, adult/continuing education programs, advanced placement credit, double majors, independent study, internships, part-time degree program, study abroad, summer session for credit. *ROTC:* Army (b).

Library Benner Library with 140,000 titles, 1,000 serial subscriptions, an OPAC, a Web page.

Computers on Campus 100 computers available on campus for general student use. Internet access, online (class) registration, at least one staffed computer lab available.

Student Life *Housing:* on-campus residence required through senior year. *Options:* men-only, women-only. *Activities and Organizations:* drama/theater group, student-run newspaper, radio station, choral group, Fellowship of Christian Athletes, C.A.U.S.E. College and University Serving and Enabling, Diakonia, Student Education Association, Women's Residence Association. *Campus security:* 24-hour patrols, late-night transport/escort service. *Student Services:* health clinic, personal/psychological counseling.

Athletics Member NAIA, NCCAA. *Intercollegiate sports:* baseball M(s), basketball M(s)/W(s), cross-country running M(s)/W(s), football M(s), golf M(s), soccer M(s)/W(s), softball W(s), tennis M(s)/W(s), track and field M(s)/W(s), volleyball W(s). *Intramural sports:* badminton M, baseball M, basketball M/W, cross-country running M, football M, golf M/W, racquetball M/W, soccer M/W, softball M/W, table tennis M/W, tennis M/W, track and field M/W, volleyball M/W.

Standardized Tests *Required:* ACT (for admission).

Costs (2001–02) *Comprehensive fee:* $18,444 includes full-time tuition ($12,644), mandatory fees ($820), and room and board ($4980). Full-time tuition and fees vary according to course load. Part-time tuition: $527 per hour. Part-time tuition and fees vary according to course load. *Required fees:* $10 per term part-time. *Room and board:* Room and board charges vary according to board plan. *Payment plan:* installment. *Waivers:* employees or children of employees.

Financial Aid Of all full-time matriculated undergraduates who enrolled in 2001, 1460 applied for aid, 1253 were judged to have need, 451 had their need fully met. In 2001, 455 non-need-based awards were made. *Average percent of need met:* 83%. *Average financial aid package:* $12,470. *Average need-based loan:* $4080. *Average need-based gift aid:* $5521. *Average non-need based aid:* $5771. *Average indebtedness upon graduation:* $13,479.

Applying *Options:* electronic application, deferred entrance. *Required:* high school transcript, minimum 2.0 GPA, 2 letters of recommendation. *Recommended:* interview. *Application deadline:* rolling (freshmen), rolling (transfers). *Notification:* continuous (freshmen).

Admissions Contact Mr. Brian Parker, Director of Admissions, Olivet Nazarene University, One University Avenue, Bourbonnais, IL 60914. *Phone:* 815-939-5203. *Toll-free phone:* 800-648-1463. *Fax:* 815-935-4998. *E-mail:* admissions@olivet.edu.

PRINCIPIA COLLEGE
Elsah, Illinois

- **Independent Christian Science** 4-year, founded 1910
- **Calendar** quarters
- **Degree** bachelor's
- **Rural** 2600-acre campus with easy access to St. Louis
- **Coed,** 554 undergraduate students, 96% full-time, 56% women, 44% men
- **Moderately difficult** entrance level, 93% of applicants were admitted

Undergraduates 533 full-time, 21 part-time. Students come from 46 states and territories, 25 other countries, 88% are from out of state, 1% African American, 1% Asian American or Pacific Islander, 2% Hispanic American, 12% international, 5% transferred in, 100% live on campus. *Retention:* 86% of 2001 full-time freshmen returned.

Freshmen *Admission:* 252 applied, 235 admitted, 125 enrolled. *Average high school GPA:* 3.32. *Test scores:* SAT verbal scores over 500: 79%; SAT math scores over 500: 81%; ACT scores over 18: 96%; SAT verbal scores over 600: 39%; SAT math scores over 600: 36%; ACT scores over 24: 55%; SAT verbal scores over 700: 13%; SAT math scores over 700: 4%; ACT scores over 30: 21%.

Faculty *Total:* 73, 66% full-time, 48% with terminal degrees. *Student/faculty ratio:* 9:1.

Majors Anthropology; art history; biology; business administration; chemistry; computer/information sciences; economics; elementary education; engineering related; English; environmental science; fine/studio arts; foreign languages/literatures; French; German; history; humanities; liberal arts and sciences/liberal studies; mass communications; mathematics; music; philosophy; physics; political science; religious studies; Russian; secondary education; sociology; Spanish; sport/fitness administration; theater arts/drama.

Academic Programs *Special study options:* accelerated degree program, adult/continuing education programs, advanced placement credit, double majors, English as a second language, honors programs, independent study, internships, student-designed majors, study abroad. *Unusual degree programs:* 3-2 engineering with Washington University in St. Louis, Southern Illinois University at Edwardsville, University of Southern California.

Library Marshall Brooks Library plus 1 other with 205,506 titles, 609 serial subscriptions, 6,584 audiovisual materials, an OPAC.

Computers on Campus 200 computers available on campus for general student use. A campuswide network can be accessed from student residence rooms and from off campus. Internet access, at least one staffed computer lab available.

Student Life *Housing:* on-campus residence required through senior year. *Options:* men-only, women-only. *Activities and Organizations:* drama/theater group, student-run newspaper, radio and television station, choral group, Christian Science Organization, student newspaper, International Students Association, student radio station, Rugby Club. *Campus security:* 24-hour patrols.

Athletics Member NCAA. All Division III. *Intercollegiate sports:* baseball M, basketball M/W, cross-country running M/W, football M, golf M/W, soccer M/W, softball W, swimming M/W, tennis M/W, track and field M/W, volleyball W. *Intramural sports:* baseball M, basketball M/W, football M, rugby M(c), soccer M/W, softball M/W, volleyball M/W.

Standardized Tests *Required:* SAT I or ACT (for admission). *Recommended:* SAT I (for admission).

Costs (2002–03) *Comprehensive fee:* $23,865 includes full-time tuition ($17,400), mandatory fees ($270), and room and board ($6195). *Room and board:* College room only: $3006. *Payment plan:* installment. *Waivers:* employees or children of employees.

Financial Aid Of all full-time matriculated undergraduates who enrolled in 2001, 344 applied for aid, 329 were judged to have need, 296 had their need fully met. 166 State and other part-time jobs (averaging $1500). In 2001, 106 non-need-based awards were made. *Average percent of need met:* 90%. *Average financial aid package:* $15,269. *Average need-based loan:* $3075. *Average need-based gift aid:* $8563. *Average non-need based aid:* $11,867.

Applying *Options:* deferred entrance. *Application fee:* $35. *Required:* essay or personal statement, high school transcript, minimum 2.0 GPA, 4 letters of recommendation, Christian Science commitment. *Required for some:* interview. *Recommended:* interview. *Application deadlines:* 3/1 (freshmen), 3/1 (transfers). *Notification:* continuous (freshmen).

Admissions Contact Martha Green Quirk, Dean of Admissions, Principia College, Office of Admissions and Enrollment, Elsah, IL 62028. *Phone:* 618-374-5180. *Toll-free phone:* 800-277-4648 Ext. 2802. *Fax:* 618-374-4000. *E-mail:* collegeadmissions@prin.edu.

QUINCY UNIVERSITY
Quincy, Illinois

- **Independent Roman Catholic** comprehensive, founded 1860
- **Calendar** semesters
- **Degrees** associate, bachelor's, and master's
- **Small-town** 75-acre campus
- **Coed,** 1,147 undergraduate students, 87% full-time, 56% women, 44% men
- **Moderately difficult** entrance level, 96% of applicants were admitted

Undergraduates 1,000 full-time, 147 part-time. Students come from 30 states and territories, 14 other countries, 25% are from out of state, 6% African

Quincy University (continued)
American, 0.6% Asian American or Pacific Islander, 2% Hispanic American, 0.2% Native American, 1.0% international, 11% transferred in, 57% live on campus. *Retention:* 74% of 2001 full-time freshmen returned.

Freshmen *Admission:* 898 applied, 862 admitted, 231 enrolled. *Average high school GPA:* 3.14. *Test scores:* SAT verbal scores over 500: 50%; SAT math scores over 500: 60%; ACT scores over 18: 88%; SAT verbal scores over 600: 20%; SAT math scores over 600: 20%; ACT scores over 24: 34%; ACT scores over 30: 4%.

Faculty *Total:* 122, 51% full-time, 55% with terminal degrees. *Student/faculty ratio:* 14:1.

Majors Accounting; art; art education; arts management; athletic training/sports medicine; aviation/airway science; aviation management; biology; business administration; business marketing and marketing management; chemistry; communications; computer science; criminal justice/law enforcement administration; education (K-12); elementary education; engineering-related technology; English; environmental science; finance; fine/studio arts; history; humanities; human services; information sciences/systems; interdisciplinary studies; journalism; mathematics; medical technology; music; music business management/ merchandising; music teacher education; nursing; philosophy; physical education; political science; pre-dentistry; pre-medicine; pre-veterinary studies; psychology; public relations; radio/television broadcasting; social work; sociology; special education; sport/fitness administration; theology.

Academic Programs *Special study options:* academic remediation for entering students, accelerated degree program, adult/continuing education programs, advanced placement credit, distance learning, double majors, English as a second language, honors programs, independent study, internships, part-time degree program, student-designed majors, study abroad, summer session for credit. *Unusual degree programs:* 3-2 engineering with Washington University in St. Louis.

Library Brenner Library with 239,983 titles, 814 serial subscriptions, 4,383 audiovisual materials, an OPAC, a Web page.

Computers on Campus 200 computers available on campus for general student use. A campuswide network can be accessed from student residence rooms and from off campus. Internet access, online (class) registration, at least one staffed computer lab available.

Student Life *Housing:* on-campus residence required through sophomore year. *Options:* coed, men-only, women-only. *Activities and Organizations:* drama/ theater group, student-run newspaper, radio station, choral group, Student Senate, campus ministry, student programming board, BACCHUS, Students in Free Enterprise, national fraternities, national sororities. *Campus security:* 24-hour emergency response devices and patrols, student patrols, late-night transport/ escort service, controlled dormitory access. *Student Services:* health clinic, personal/psychological counseling.

Athletics Member NCAA. All Division II. *Intercollegiate sports:* baseball M(s), basketball M(s)/W(s), football M(s), golf M(s)/W(s), soccer M(s)/W(s), softball W(s), tennis M(s)/W(s), track and field M/W, volleyball M(s)/W(s). *Intramural sports:* badminton M/W, baseball M, basketball M/W, bowling M/W, football M/W, golf M, soccer M/W, softball M/W, tennis M/W, volleyball M/W.

Standardized Tests *Required:* SAT I or ACT (for admission).

Costs (2002–03) *Comprehensive fee:* $21,680 includes full-time tuition ($15,910), mandatory fees ($450), and room and board ($5320). Part-time tuition: $455 per credit hour. No tuition increase for student's term of enrollment. *Room and board:* Room and board charges vary according to board plan and housing facility. *Payment plan:* installment. *Waivers:* senior citizens and employees or children of employees.

Financial Aid Of all full-time matriculated undergraduates who enrolled in 2001, 895 applied for aid, 750 were judged to have need, 275 had their need fully met. 343 Federal Work-Study jobs, 28 State and other part-time jobs (averaging $3000). In 2001, 209 non-need-based awards were made. *Average percent of need met:* 93%. *Average financial aid package:* $14,444. *Average need-based loan:* $4079. *Average need-based gift aid:* $6596. *Average non-need based aid:* $5586. *Average indebtedness upon graduation:* $15,152.

Applying *Options:* common application, electronic application, early admission, deferred entrance. *Application fee:* $25. *Required:* high school transcript. *Recommended:* minimum 2.0 GPA, interview. *Application deadline:* rolling (freshmen), rolling (transfers). *Notification:* continuous (freshmen).

Admissions Contact Mr. Kevin A. Brown, Director of Admissions, Quincy University, 1800 College Avenue, Quincy, IL 62301-2699. *Phone:* 217-222-8020 Ext. 5215. *Toll-free phone:* 800-688-4295. *E-mail:* admissions@quincy.edu.

ROBERT MORRIS COLLEGE
Chicago, Illinois

- **Independent** 4-year, founded 1913
- **Calendar** 5 ten-week academic sessions per year
- **Degree** certificates, diplomas, and bachelor's
- **Urban** campus
- **Endowment** $26.7 million
- **Coed,** 5,319 undergraduate students, 89% full-time, 68% women, 32% men
- **Minimally difficult** entrance level, 69% of applicants were admitted

Undergraduates 4,716 full-time, 603 part-time. Students come from 9 states and territories, 15 other countries, 1% are from out of state, 41% African American, 3% Asian American or Pacific Islander, 24% Hispanic American, 0.3% Native American, 0.4% international, 36% transferred in. *Retention:* 68% of 2001 full-time freshmen returned.

Freshmen *Admission:* 4,492 applied, 3,107 admitted, 1,204 enrolled. *Average high school GPA:* 2.44.

Faculty *Total:* 391, 30% full-time, 22% with terminal degrees. *Student/faculty ratio:* 27:1.

Majors Accounting technician; business administration; business computer programming; business systems networking/ telecommunications; computer/ information sciences; design/applied arts related; design/visual communications; drafting; film/video and photographic arts related; graphic design/commercial art/illustration; health/physical education/fitness related; interior design; legal administrative assistant; management information systems/business data processing; marketing operations; medical assistant; medical records technology; paralegal/ legal assistant; retailing operations; secretarial science; travel/tourism management.

Academic Programs *Special study options:* academic remediation for entering students, accelerated degree program, adult/continuing education programs, advanced placement credit, cooperative education, distance learning, honors programs, internships, study abroad, summer session for credit.

Library Thomas Jefferson Library plus 3 others with 101,130 titles, 9,800 audiovisual materials, an OPAC, a Web page.

Computers on Campus 980 computers available on campus for general student use. Internet access, at least one staffed computer lab available.

Student Life *Housing:* college housing not available. *Activities and Organizations:* drama/theater group, student-run newspaper, choral group, Alumni Association, Sigma Beta Delta (honor society), Eagle (newspaper), Accounting Club, Association for Medical Assistance. *Campus security:* 24-hour emergency response devices and patrols. *Student Services:* personal/psychological counseling.

Athletics Member NAIA, NSCAA. *Intercollegiate sports:* baseball M(s), basketball M(s)/W(s), cross-country running M(s)/W(s), soccer M(s)/W(s), softball W(s), volleyball W(s). *Intramural sports:* ice hockey M.

Costs (2002–03) *Tuition:* $12,750 full-time, $1060 per course part-time. *Payment plan:* installment. *Waivers:* employees or children of employees.

Financial Aid Of all full-time matriculated undergraduates who enrolled in 2001, 4279 applied for aid, 4171 were judged to have need, 209 had their need fully met. In 2001, 105 non-need-based awards were made. *Average percent of need met:* 60%. *Average financial aid package:* $9207. *Average need-based loan:* $2948. *Average need-based gift aid:* $7207. *Average indebtedness upon graduation:* $11,078.

Applying *Options:* common application, deferred entrance. *Application fee:* $20. *Required for some:* 2 letters of recommendation. *Application deadline:* rolling (freshmen), rolling (transfers). *Notification:* continuous (freshmen).

Admissions Contact Ms. Deb Dahlen, Senior Vice President for Institutional Advancement, Robert Morris College, 401 South State Street, Chicago, IL 60605. *Phone:* 312-935-6600. *Toll-free phone:* 800-225-1520. *Fax:* 312-935-6819. *E-mail:* enroll@rmcil.edu.

ROCKFORD COLLEGE
Rockford, Illinois

- **Independent** comprehensive, founded 1847
- **Calendar** semesters
- **Degrees** bachelor's and master's
- **Suburban** 130-acre campus with easy access to Chicago
- **Endowment** $13.6 million
- **Coed,** 1,056 undergraduate students, 77% full-time, 63% women, 37% men
- **Moderately difficult** entrance level, 61% of applicants were admitted

Rockford College, 1 of 11 colleges in Illinois with a Phi Beta Kappa chapter, is known for its integration of liberal arts and professional programs, community-based learning, and Regent's College in London. *U.S. News & World Report* named Rockford as one of the top tier universities in the Midwest. The North Central Association of Colleges and Schools reaccredited Rockford College through 2008-09, and the new President, Dr. Paul Pribbenow, joins the College on July 1, 2002, along with 10 new dynamic faculty members.

Undergraduates 818 full-time, 238 part-time. Students come from 8 states and territories, 10 other countries, 4% are from out of state, 8% African American, 2%

Asian American or Pacific Islander, 5% Hispanic American, 0.4% Native American, 1% international, 13% transferred in, 36% live on campus. *Retention:* 55% of 2001 full-time freshmen returned.

Freshmen *Admission:* 637 applied, 386 admitted, 131 enrolled. *Average high school GPA:* 3.03. *Test scores:* SAT verbal scores over 500: 60%; SAT math scores over 500: 63%; ACT scores over 18: 80%; SAT verbal scores over 600: 28%; SAT math scores over 600: 23%; ACT scores over 24: 33%; SAT verbal scores over 700: 14%; SAT math scores over 700: 5%; ACT scores over 30: 5%.

Faculty *Total:* 147, 54% full-time, 38% with terminal degrees. *Student/faculty ratio:* 10:1.

Majors Accounting; anthropology; art; art education; art history; biochemistry; biological/physical sciences; biology; business administration; business economics; business marketing and marketing management; chemistry; classics; computer science; criminal justice/law enforcement administration; developmental/child psychology; economics; education; elementary education; English; finance; fine/studio arts; French; German; Greek (modern); history; humanities; international economics; international relations; Latin (ancient and medieval); literature; management information systems/business data processing; mathematics; music history; nursing; philosophy; physical education; political science; pre-dentistry; pre-law; pre-medicine; pre-veterinary studies; psychology; science education; social sciences; social work; sociology; Spanish; theater arts/drama; urban studies.

Academic Programs *Special study options:* academic remediation for entering students, adult/continuing education programs, advanced placement credit, double majors, English as a second language, honors programs, internships, off-campus study, part-time degree program, student-designed majors, study abroad, summer session for credit. *ROTC:* Army (c). *Unusual degree programs:* 3-2 engineering with Washington University in St. Louis, University of Southern California, University of Illinois.

Library Howard Colman Library with 140,000 titles, 831 serial subscriptions, 9,723 audiovisual materials, an OPAC.

Computers on Campus 65 computers available on campus for general student use. A campuswide network can be accessed from student residence rooms. Internet access, at least one staffed computer lab available.

Student Life *Housing:* on-campus residence required through senior year. *Options:* coed, men-only, women-only. *Activities and Organizations:* drama/theater group, student-run newspaper, radio station, choral group, student government, intercultural club, 4Ts (Tomorrow's Teachers Together Today), psychology society, Nursing Student Organization. *Campus security:* 24-hour emergency response devices and patrols, late-night transport/escort service, controlled dormitory access. *Student Services:* health clinic, personal/psychological counseling.

Athletics Member NCAA. All Division III. *Intercollegiate sports:* baseball M, basketball M/W, football M, golf M, soccer M/W, softball W, tennis M/W, volleyball M(c)/W. *Intramural sports:* archery M/W, badminton M/W, basketball M/W, bowling M/W, football M/W, table tennis M/W, tennis M/W, volleyball M/W.

Standardized Tests *Required:* SAT I or ACT (for admission).

Costs (2001–02) *Comprehensive fee:* $23,080 includes full-time tuition ($17,450) and room and board ($5630). Part-time tuition: $460 per credit. *Required fees:* $20 per term part-time. *Room and board:* College room only: $3400. Room and board charges vary according to board plan and housing facility. *Payment plans:* installment, deferred payment. *Waivers:* employees or children of employees.

Financial Aid Of all full-time matriculated undergraduates who enrolled in 2001, 677 applied for aid, 677 were judged to have need, 677 had their need fully met. In 2001, 17 non-need-based awards were made. *Average percent of need met:* 99%. *Average indebtedness upon graduation:* $16,000.

Applying *Options:* common application, electronic application, early admission, deferred entrance. *Application fee:* $35. *Required:* high school transcript. *Required for some:* essay or personal statement, minimum 2.5 GPA, 2 letters of recommendation. *Recommended:* minimum 2.5 GPA, interview, campus visit. *Application deadline:* rolling (freshmen), rolling (transfers).

Admissions Contact Mr. William Laffey, Director of Admission, Rockford College, Nelson Hall, Rockford, IL 61108-2393. *Phone:* 815-226-4050 Ext. 3330. *Toll-free phone:* 800-892-2984. *Fax:* 815-226-2822. *E-mail:* admission@rockford.edu.

ROOSEVELT UNIVERSITY

Chicago, Illinois

- **Independent** comprehensive, founded 1945
- **Calendar** semesters
- **Degrees** bachelor's, master's, and doctoral
- **Urban** campus
- **Endowment** $34.0 million
- **Coed,** 4,628 undergraduate students, 41% full-time, 64% women, 36% men
- **Moderately difficult** entrance level, 71% of applicants were admitted

Inaugurated in 1998, Roosevelt Scholars is a distinctive honors program open to students who demonstrate outstanding scholarship along with leadership in school/community activities. In addition to enriched academic experiences and scholarship support that averages $6000 annually, students are mentored by Chicago's political, business, and social leaders and participate in internship and research opportunities in their areas of interest.

Undergraduates 1,882 full-time, 2,746 part-time. Students come from 24 states and territories, 70 other countries, 5% are from out of state, 27% African American, 4% Asian American or Pacific Islander, 12% Hispanic American, 0.5% Native American, 4% international, 18% transferred in, 5% live on campus. *Retention:* 63% of 2001 full-time freshmen returned.

Freshmen *Admission:* 846 applied, 598 admitted, 287 enrolled. *Average high school GPA:* 3.10. *Test scores:* ACT scores over 18: 66%; ACT scores over 24: 18%; ACT scores over 30: 3%.

Faculty *Total:* 640, 31% full-time. *Student/faculty ratio:* 16:1.

Majors Accounting; actuarial science; African-American studies; American studies; art history; biology; business administration; business economics; business marketing and marketing management; chemistry; community services; comparative literature; computer science; criminal justice studies; cytotechnology; early childhood education; economics; education; electrical/electronic engineering technology; elementary education; English; environmental science; finance; gerontology; health science; health services administration; history; hospitality management; human resources management; human services; insurance/risk management; international business; international relations; jazz; journalism; legal studies; liberal arts and sciences/liberal studies; literature; mass communications; mathematics; medical laboratory technology; medical technology; music; music history; music (piano and organ performance); music teacher education; music (voice and choral/opera performance); paralegal/legal assistant; philosophy; political science; pre-dentistry; pre-law; pre-medicine; psychology; public administration; public relations; secondary education; social sciences; sociology; Spanish; stringed instruments; telecommunications; theater arts/drama; urban studies; wind/percussion instruments; women's studies.

Academic Programs *Special study options:* academic remediation for entering students, accelerated degree program, adult/continuing education programs, advanced placement credit, distance learning, double majors, English as a second language, external degree program, honors programs, independent study, internships, off-campus study, part-time degree program, services for LD students, student-designed majors, summer session for credit.

Library Murray-Green Library plus 4 others with 300,000 titles, 1,200 serial subscriptions, 21,000 audiovisual materials, an OPAC, a Web page.

Computers on Campus 380 computers available on campus for general student use. A campuswide network can be accessed from off campus. Internet access, online (class) registration, at least one staffed computer lab available.

Student Life *Housing Options:* coed. *Activities and Organizations:* drama/theater group, student-run newspaper, radio station, choral group, International Student Union, RU 10%, Associacion de Latinos Unidos, Black Support Union, Residence Hall Council. *Campus security:* 24-hour emergency response devices and patrols, controlled dormitory access. *Student Services:* personal/psychological counseling.

Standardized Tests *Required:* SAT I or ACT (for admission).

Costs (2001–02) *Comprehensive fee:* $20,240 includes full-time tuition ($13,770), mandatory fees ($200), and room and board ($6270). Full-time tuition and fees vary according to course load, degree level, and program. Part-time tuition: $459 per credit hour. Part-time tuition and fees vary according to course load. *Required fees:* $100 per term part-time. *Room and board:* College room only: $4570. Room and board charges vary according to board plan. *Payment plans:* installment, deferred payment. *Waivers:* senior citizens and employees or children of employees.

Applying *Options:* common application, electronic application, early admission, deferred entrance. *Application fee:* $25. *Required:* essay or personal statement, high school transcript, minimum 2.0 GPA, audition for music and theater programs. *Required for some:* letters of recommendation, interview. *Application deadlines:* 8/15 (freshmen), 8/15 (transfers). *Notification:* continuous (freshmen).

Admissions Contact Mr. Brian Lynch, Director of Admission, Roosevelt University, Office of Admissions, 430 South Michigan Avenue, Room 576,

Roosevelt University (continued)
Chicago, IL 60605-1394. *Phone:* 312-341-2101. *Toll-free phone:* 877-APPLYRU. *Fax:* 312-341-3523. *E-mail:* applyru@roosevelt.edu.

RUSH UNIVERSITY
Chicago, Illinois

- **Independent** upper-level, founded 1969
- **Calendar** quarters
- **Degrees** bachelor's, master's, doctoral, first professional, and post-master's certificates
- **Urban** 35-acre campus
- **Endowment** $340.2 million
- **Coed,** 148 undergraduate students, 89% full-time, 88% women, 12% men
- **Moderately difficult** entrance level, 55% of applicants were admitted

Undergraduates 132 full-time, 16 part-time. Students come from 14 states and territories, 4 other countries, 6% are from out of state, 8% African American, 16% Asian American or Pacific Islander, 16% Hispanic American, 3% international, 64% transferred in, 27% live on campus.

Freshmen *Admission:* 184 applied, 101 admitted.

Faculty *Student/faculty ratio:* 8:1.

Majors Medical technology; nursing; perfusion technology.

Academic Programs *Special study options:* distance learning, part-time degree program. *Unusual degree programs:* 3-2 occupational therapy.

Library Library of Rush University with 120,042 titles, 1,992 serial subscriptions, an OPAC, a Web page.

Computers on Campus 39 computers available on campus for general student use. A campuswide network can be accessed from student residence rooms and from off campus. Internet access, at least one staffed computer lab available.

Student Life *Housing Options:* coed. *Campus security:* 24-hour emergency response devices and patrols, late-night transport/escort service, controlled dormitory access. *Student Services:* health clinic, personal/psychological counseling.

Costs (2001–02) *Tuition:* $14,175 full-time, $410 per quarter hour part-time. Full-time tuition and fees vary according to program. Part-time tuition and fees vary according to program. *Room only:* $7038. Room and board charges vary according to housing facility. *Payment plans:* installment, deferred payment. *Waivers:* employees or children of employees.

Financial Aid Of all full-time matriculated undergraduates who enrolled in 2001, 140 applied for aid, 139 were judged to have need, 130 had their need fully met. 15 Federal Work-Study jobs (averaging $1479). 64 State and other part-time jobs. *Average percent of need met:* 100%. *Average financial aid package:* $15,000. *Average need-based loan:* $5000. *Average need-based gift aid:* $9000. *Average indebtedness upon graduation:* $20,000. *Financial aid deadline:* 4/1.

Applying *Application fee:* $40. *Application deadline:* rolling (transfers).

Admissions Contact Ms. Hicela Castruita Woods, Director of College Admission Services, Rush University, 600 S. Paulina—Suite 440, College Admissions Services, Chicago, IL 60612-3878. *Phone:* 312-942-7100. *Fax:* 312-942-2219. *E-mail:* ruadmissions@rushu.rush.edu.

SAINT ANTHONY COLLEGE OF NURSING
Rockford, Illinois

- **Independent Roman Catholic** upper-level, founded 1915
- **Calendar** semesters
- **Degree** bachelor's
- **Urban** 17-acre campus with easy access to Chicago
- **Coed, primarily women,** 77 undergraduate students, 69% full-time, 95% women, 5% men
- **Moderately difficult** entrance level, 61% of applicants were admitted

Undergraduates 53 full-time, 24 part-time. Students come from 2 states and territories, 8% are from out of state, 3% African American, 3% Asian American or Pacific Islander, 3% Hispanic American, 31% transferred in.

Freshmen *Admission:* 38 applied, 23 admitted.

Faculty *Total:* 13, 77% full-time, 15% with terminal degrees. *Student/faculty ratio:* 6:1.

Majors Nursing.

Academic Programs *Special study options:* advanced placement credit, independent study, part-time degree program, services for LD students, summer session for credit.

Library Sister Mary Linus Learning Resource Center plus 1 other with 1,394 titles, 3,136 serial subscriptions, 163 audiovisual materials, an OPAC, a Web page.

Computers on Campus 10 computers available on campus for general student use. A campuswide network can be accessed from off campus. Internet access, at least one staffed computer lab available.

Student Life *Housing:* college housing not available. *Activities and Organizations:* student-run newspaper, Student Organization. *Campus security:* 24-hour emergency response devices and patrols, late-night transport/escort service. *Student Services:* health clinic, personal/psychological counseling.

Costs (2002–03) *One-time required fee:* $90. *Tuition:* $12,480 full-time, $390 per credit part-time. Full-time tuition and fees vary according to course load. Part-time tuition and fees vary according to course load. *Required fees:* $113 full-time, $56 per term. *Payment plans:* installment, deferred payment. *Waivers:* employees or children of employees.

Financial Aid Of all full-time matriculated undergraduates who enrolled in 2001, 73 applied for aid, 73 were judged to have need. *Average percent of need met:* 50%. *Average financial aid package:* $6800. *Average need-based loan:* $4790. *Average need-based gift aid:* $4217. *Average indebtedness upon graduation:* $13,000.

Applying *Options:* electronic application, deferred entrance. *Application fee:* $50. *Application deadline:* rolling (transfers). *Notification:* continuous (transfers).

Admissions Contact Saint Anthony College of Nursing, 5658 East State Street, Rockford, IL 61108-2468. *Phone:* 815-395-5100. *Fax:* 815-395 Ext. 2275. *E-mail:* nancysanders@sacn.edu.

ST. AUGUSTINE COLLEGE
Chicago, Illinois

- **Independent** 4-year, founded 1980
- **Calendar** semesters
- **Degrees** certificates, associate, and bachelor's (bilingual Spanish/English degree programs)
- **Urban** 4-acre campus
- **Endowment** $500,000
- **Coed,** 1,814 undergraduate students, 77% full-time, 78% women, 22% men
- **Noncompetitive** entrance level

Undergraduates 1,404 full-time, 410 part-time. Students come from 1 other state, 8% African American, 3% Asian American or Pacific Islander, 86% Hispanic American, 0.2% Native American, 0.7% transferred in. *Retention:* 68% of 2001 full-time freshmen returned.

Freshmen *Admission:* 586 enrolled.

Faculty *Total:* 131, 18% full-time, 13% with terminal degrees. *Student/faculty ratio:* 13:1.

Majors Accounting; business administration; early childhood education; liberal arts and sciences/liberal studies; management information systems/business data processing; mental health/rehabilitation; respiratory therapy; secretarial science; social work.

Academic Programs *Special study options:* academic remediation for entering students, cooperative education, English as a second language, independent study, internships, part-time degree program, summer session for credit.

Library 15,500 titles.

Computers on Campus Internet access, at least one staffed computer lab available.

Student Life *Housing:* college housing not available. *Activities and Organizations:* student-run newspaper, choral group. *Campus security:* late-night transport/escort service. *Student Services:* personal/psychological counseling.

Athletics *Intramural sports:* soccer M, volleyball M/W.

Costs (2001–02) *Tuition:* $6892 full-time, $283 per credit part-time. *Required fees:* $340 full-time, $80 per term.

Applying *Options:* deferred entrance. *Application deadline:* rolling (freshmen), rolling (transfers).

Admissions Contact Ms. Soledad Ruiz, Director of Admissions, St. Augustine College, 1333-1345 West Argyle, Chicago, IL 60640-3501. *Phone:* 773-878-8756 Ext. 243.

SAINT FRANCIS MEDICAL CENTER COLLEGE OF NURSING
Peoria, Illinois

- **Independent Roman Catholic** upper-level, founded 1986
- **Calendar** semesters
- **Degree** bachelor's

- **Urban** campus
- **Coed, primarily women,** 143 undergraduate students, 76% full-time, 94% women, 6% men
- **Moderately difficult** entrance level, 80% of applicants were admitted

Undergraduates Students come from 1 other state, 1% African American, 3% Asian American or Pacific Islander, 1% Hispanic American, 28% live on campus.
Freshmen *Admission:* 100 applied, 80 admitted.
Faculty *Total:* 19, 100% full-time. *Student/faculty ratio:* 8:1.
Majors Nursing.
Academic Programs *Special study options:* advanced placement credit, distance learning, independent study, part-time degree program, summer session for credit.
Library 6,215 titles, 125 serial subscriptions.
Computers on Campus 6 computers available on campus for general student use. Internet access, at least one staffed computer lab available.
Student Life *Housing Options:* coed. *Activities and Organizations:* choral group, Student Senate, SNAI. *Campus security:* 24-hour emergency response devices, controlled dormitory access. *Student Services:* health clinic, personal/psychological counseling.
Costs (2001–02) *Tuition:* $9048 full-time, $377 per semester hour part-time. Full-time tuition and fees vary according to course load. Part-time tuition and fees vary according to course load. *Required fees:* $324 full-time, $162 per term part-time. *Room only:* $1680. *Payment plans:* installment, deferred payment. *Waivers:* employees or children of employees.
Financial Aid Of all full-time matriculated undergraduates who enrolled in 2001, 110 applied for aid, 74 were judged to have need, 33 had their need fully met. In 2001, 36 non-need-based awards were made. *Average percent of need met:* 87%. *Average financial aid package:* $9002. *Average need-based loan:* $4641. *Average need-based gift aid:* $7248. *Average non-need based aid:* $5742.
Applying *Options:* common application, deferred entrance. *Application fee:* $25. *Application deadline:* rolling (transfers). *Notification:* continuous (transfers).
Admissions Contact Mrs. Janice Farquharson, Director of Admissions and Registrar, Saint Francis Medical Center College of Nursing, 511 Greenleaf Street, Peoria, IL 61603-3783. *Phone:* 309-655-2596. *Fax:* 309-624-8973. *E-mail:* janice.farquharson@osfhealthcare.org.

ST. JOHN'S COLLEGE
Springfield, Illinois

- **Independent Roman Catholic** upper-level, founded 1886
- **Calendar** semesters
- **Degree** bachelor's
- **Urban** campus
- **Endowment** $571,760
- **Coed, primarily women,** 58 undergraduate students, 95% full-time, 95% women, 5% men
- **Moderately difficult** entrance level, 74% of applicants were admitted

Undergraduates 55 full-time, 3 part-time. Students come from 1 other state, 0% are from out of state, 3% African American, 5% Hispanic American, 55% transferred in.
Freshmen *Admission:* 43 applied, 32 admitted.
Faculty *Total:* 15, 93% full-time, 7% with terminal degrees. *Student/faculty ratio:* 4:1.
Majors Nursing.
Academic Programs *Special study options:* part-time degree program, services for LD students.
Library St. John's Health Science Library with 7,129 titles, 365 serial subscriptions, 735 audiovisual materials, an OPAC.
Computers on Campus 10 computers available on campus for general student use. Internet access, at least one staffed computer lab available.
Student Life *Housing:* college housing not available. *Activities and Organizations:* NSNA, class/student government. *Campus security:* 24-hour emergency response devices and patrols, late-night transport/escort service. *Student Services:* health clinic, personal/psychological counseling.
Costs (2001–02) *One-time required fee:* $67. *Tuition:* $8282 full-time, $254 per credit hour part-time. Full-time tuition and fees vary according to course load and student level. Part-time tuition and fees vary according to course load and student level. *Required fees:* $239 full-time, $119 per term. *Payment plans:* installment, deferred payment.
Financial Aid Of all full-time matriculated undergraduates who enrolled in 2001, 51 applied for aid, 41 were judged to have need, 22 had their need fully met. 3 Federal Work-Study jobs (averaging $3970). *Average percent of need met:* 75%. *Average financial aid package:* $7500. *Average need-based loan:* $4006. *Average need-based gift aid:* $7361.
Applying *Options:* early action. *Application fee:* $25. *Notification:* continuous (transfers).
Admissions Contact Ms. Beth Beasley, Student Development Officer, St. John's College, 421 North Ninth Street, Springfield, IL 62702-5317. *Phone:* 217-525-5628 Ext. 45468.

SAINT XAVIER UNIVERSITY
Chicago, Illinois

- **Independent Roman Catholic** comprehensive, founded 1847
- **Calendar** semesters
- **Degrees** certificates, bachelor's, master's, post-master's, and postbachelor's certificates
- **Urban** 55-acre campus
- **Endowment** $6.8 million
- **Coed,** 2,815 undergraduate students, 71% full-time, 71% women, 29% men
- **Moderately difficult** entrance level, 73% of applicants were admitted

Undergraduates 1,989 full-time, 826 part-time. Students come from 15 states and territories, 7 other countries, 3% are from out of state, 16% African American, 2% Asian American or Pacific Islander, 12% Hispanic American, 0.4% Native American, 0.6% international, 16% transferred in, 17% live on campus. *Retention:* 81% of 2001 full-time freshmen returned.
Freshmen *Admission:* 1,411 applied, 1,037 admitted, 365 enrolled. *Average high school GPA:* 3.12. *Test scores:* ACT scores over 18: 90%; ACT scores over 24: 22%; ACT scores over 30: 1%.
Faculty *Total:* 347, 42% full-time, 46% with terminal degrees. *Student/faculty ratio:* 14:1.
Majors Accounting; art; art education; biological/physical sciences; biology; biology education; botany; business; chemistry; communications; computer/information sciences; computer science; counseling psychology; criminal justice studies; early childhood education; elementary education; English; English education; history; history education; international business; international relations; liberal arts and sciences/liberal studies; mathematics; mathematics education; music; music (general performance); music teacher education; nursing; organizational psychology; philosophy; political science; psychology; religious studies; social sciences; sociology; Spanish; Spanish language education; speech-language pathology.
Academic Programs *Special study options:* academic remediation for entering students, accelerated degree program, adult/continuing education programs, advanced placement credit, double majors, English as a second language, honors programs, independent study, internships, part-time degree program, services for LD students, student-designed majors, study abroad, summer session for credit. *ROTC:* Air Force (c).
Library Byrne Memorial Library with 123,325 titles, 2,199 serial subscriptions, 2,292 audiovisual materials, an OPAC, a Web page.
Computers on Campus 261 computers available on campus for general student use. A campuswide network can be accessed from student residence rooms and from off campus. Internet access, at least one staffed computer lab available.
Student Life *Housing Options:* coed. *Activities and Organizations:* drama/theater group, student-run newspaper, radio station, choral group, marching band, Student Activities Board, Black Student Union, UNIDOS (Hispanic Organization), Student Nurses Association, Business Students Association. *Campus security:* 24-hour emergency response devices and patrols, late-night transport/escort service. *Student Services:* health clinic, personal/psychological counseling, women's center.
Athletics Member NAIA. *Intercollegiate sports:* baseball M(s), basketball M(s), cross-country running W(s), football M(s), golf M(s), soccer M(s)/W(s), softball W(s), volleyball W(s). *Intramural sports:* basketball M, bowling M/W, volleyball M/W, weight lifting M.
Standardized Tests *Required:* SAT I or ACT (for admission).
Costs (2001–02) *Comprehensive fee:* $21,104 includes full-time tuition ($15,000), mandatory fees ($130), and room and board ($5974). Full-time tuition and fees vary according to course load. Part-time tuition: $500 per credit hour. Part-time tuition and fees vary according to course load. *Required fees:* $45 per term part-time. *Room and board:* College room only: $3408. Room and board charges vary according to board plan. *Payment plan:* installment. *Waivers:* senior citizens and employees or children of employees.
Financial Aid Of all full-time matriculated undergraduates who enrolled in 2001, 1956 applied for aid, 1587 were judged to have need, 561 had their need fully met. 1021 Federal Work-Study jobs (averaging $1998). In 2001, 325

Saint Xavier University (continued)
non-need-based awards were made. *Average percent of need met:* 88%. *Average financial aid package:* $13,262. *Average need-based loan:* $3665. *Average need-based gift aid:* $7091. *Average non-need based aid:* $3371. *Average indebtedness upon graduation:* $19,825.

Applying *Options:* common application, deferred entrance. *Application fee:* $25. *Required:* high school transcript. *Required for some:* interview. *Recommended:* essay or personal statement, minimum 2.5 GPA, interview. *Application deadlines:* 8/15 (freshmen), 8/15 (transfers). *Notification:* continuous until 8/30 (freshmen).

Admissions Contact Elizabeth A. Gierach, Director of Enrollment Services, Saint Xavier University, 3700 West 103rd Street, Chicago, IL 60655-3105. *Phone:* 773-298-3063. *Toll-free phone:* 800-462-9288. *Fax:* 773-298-3076 Ext. 3050. *E-mail:* admissions@sxu.edu.

SCHOLL COLLEGE OF PODIATRIC MEDICINE AT FINCH UNIVERSITY OF HEALTH SCIENCES/THE CHICAGO MEDICAL SCHOOL

Chicago, Illinois

- **Independent** upper-level, founded 1912, part of Finch University of Health Sciences/The Chicago Medical School.
- **Calendar** one 9 to 12 month term
- **Degrees** incidental bachelor's, doctoral, and first professional
- **Urban** campus
- **Endowment** $13.0 million
- **Coed**
- **Moderately difficult** entrance level

Undergraduates Students come from 33 states and territories, 3 other countries, 0% live on campus.

Freshmen *Admission:* 72 admitted.

Faculty *Total:* 35. *Student/faculty ratio:* 7:1.

Majors Biology.

Academic Programs *Special study options:* accelerated degree program, adult/continuing education programs, honors programs.

Library 8,000 titles, 285 serial subscriptions, an OPAC.

Computers on Campus 12 computers available on campus for general student use. At least one staffed computer lab available.

Student Life *Housing:* college housing not available. *Campus security:* motion detectors, night security guard. *Student Services:* health clinic, personal/psychological counseling.

Athletics *Intercollegiate sports:* basketball M(c)/W(c). *Intramural sports:* basketball M/W, cross-country running M/W, football M/W, golf M/W, swimming M/W, volleyball M/W.

Costs (2001–02) *Tuition:* $22,549 full-time. Full-time tuition and fees vary according to student level.

Applying *Options:* electronic application, deferred entrance. *Application fee:* $95. *Application deadline:* 8/1 (transfers).

Admissions Contact Mr. Thomas C. Taylor, Assistant Dean for Student Affairs, Scholl College of Podiatric Medicine at Finch University of Health Sciences/The Chicago Medical School, Office of Admissions, 3333 Green Bay Road, North Chicago, IL 60064-3095. *Phone:* 312-280-2940. *Toll-free phone:* 800-843-3059. *Fax:* 312-255-8169. *E-mail:* admiss@scholl.edu.

SCHOOL OF THE ART INSTITUTE OF CHICAGO

Chicago, Illinois

- **Independent** comprehensive, founded 1866
- **Calendar** semesters
- **Degrees** certificates, bachelor's, and master's
- **Urban** 1-acre campus
- **Endowment** $213.3 million
- **Coed,** 2,148 undergraduate students, 78% full-time, 64% women, 36% men
- **Moderately difficult** entrance level, 79% of applicants were admitted

Undergraduates 1,669 full-time, 479 part-time. Students come from 48 states and territories, 42 other countries, 77% are from out of state, 3% African American, 10% Asian American or Pacific Islander, 5% Hispanic American, 0.8% Native American, 12% international, 13% transferred in, 35% live on campus. *Retention:* 79% of 2001 full-time freshmen returned.

Freshmen *Admission:* 1,183 applied, 933 admitted, 330 enrolled.

Faculty *Total:* 455, 26% full-time. *Student/faculty ratio:* 13:1.

Majors Art; art education; art history; art therapy; computer graphics; drawing; fashion design/illustration; film studies; film/video production; fine/studio arts; graphic design/commercial art/illustration; printmaking; sculpture; textile arts.

Academic Programs *Special study options:* academic remediation for entering students, advanced placement credit, cooperative education, double majors, English as a second language, independent study, internships, off-campus study, part-time degree program, services for LD students, student-designed majors, study abroad, summer session for credit.

Library Flaxman Memorial Library plus 2 others with 66,325 titles, 345 serial subscriptions, 3,751 audiovisual materials, an OPAC, a Web page.

Computers on Campus 367 computers available on campus for general student use. A campuswide network can be accessed from student residence rooms and from off campus. Internet access, at least one staffed computer lab available.

Student Life *Housing Options:* coed. *Activities and Organizations:* drama/theater group, student-run newspaper, radio and television station, student government, N.I.A. (black student union), L.A.S.O. (Latin Art Student organization), Eye and Ear Clinic (film screening group), Student Union Galleries. *Campus security:* 24-hour emergency response devices and patrols, late-night transport/escort service, controlled dormitory access. *Student Services:* health clinic, personal/psychological counseling.

Standardized Tests *Required:* SAT I or ACT (for admission).

Costs (2001–02) *Tuition:* $21,300 full-time, $710 per credit hour part-time. *Room only:* $6500. *Payment plan:* installment. *Waivers:* employees or children of employees.

Applying *Options:* deferred entrance. *Application fee:* $55. *Required:* essay or personal statement, high school transcript, 1 letter of recommendation, portfolio. *Recommended:* interview. *Application deadlines:* 8/15 (freshmen), 8/15 (transfers). *Notification:* continuous (freshmen).

Admissions Contact Kendra E. Dane, Executive Director of Admissions and Marketing, School of the Art Institute of Chicago, 37 South Wabash, Chicago, IL 60603. *Phone:* 312-899-5219. *Toll-free phone:* 800-232-SAIC. *E-mail:* admiss@artic.edu.

SHIMER COLLEGE

Waukegan, Illinois

- **Independent** 4-year, founded 1853
- **Calendar** semesters
- **Degrees** bachelor's and postbachelor's certificates
- **Suburban** 3-acre campus with easy access to Chicago and Milwaukee
- **Coed,** 106 undergraduate students, 93% full-time, 49% women, 51% men
- **Moderately difficult** entrance level, 94% of applicants were admitted

Undergraduates 99 full-time, 7 part-time. Students come from 18 states and territories, 38% are from out of state, 7% African American, 0.9% Asian American or Pacific Islander, 3% Hispanic American, 0.9% Native American, 3% international, 7% transferred in, 50% live on campus. *Retention:* 66% of 2001 full-time freshmen returned.

Freshmen *Admission:* 47 applied, 44 admitted, 17 enrolled. *Average high school GPA:* 2.6. *Test scores:* SAT verbal scores over 500: 100%; SAT math scores over 500: 60%; ACT scores over 18: 85%; SAT verbal scores over 600: 100%; SAT math scores over 600: 20%; ACT scores over 24: 62%; ACT scores over 30: 15%.

Faculty *Total:* 12, 92% full-time, 83% with terminal degrees. *Student/faculty ratio:* 10:1.

Majors Humanities; liberal arts and sciences/liberal studies; literature; natural sciences; social sciences.

Academic Programs *Special study options:* academic remediation for entering students, accelerated degree program, adult/continuing education programs, cooperative education, double majors, independent study, off-campus study, part-time degree program, student-designed majors, study abroad, summer session for credit.

Library 200,000 titles, 200 serial subscriptions.

Computers on Campus 20 computers available on campus for general student use. Internet access, at least one staffed computer lab available.

Student Life *Housing Options:* coed. *Activities and Organizations:* drama/theater group, student-run newspaper, student government, drama group. *Campus security:* 24-hour emergency response devices, late-night transport/escort service. *Student Services:* personal/psychological counseling.

Athletics *Intramural sports:* basketball M/W, volleyball M/W.

Standardized Tests *Required for some:* SAT I or ACT (for admission). *Recommended:* SAT I or ACT (for admission).

Costs (2002–03) *Comprehensive fee:* $18,580 includes full-time tuition ($15,550), mandatory fees ($500), and room and board ($2530). Part-time tuition: $545 per credit hour. *Required fees:* $250 per term part-time.

Financial Aid Of all full-time matriculated undergraduates who enrolled in 2001, 55 Federal Work-Study jobs (averaging $2166). 29 State and other part-time jobs (averaging $722).

Applying *Options:* common application, electronic application, early admission, deferred entrance. *Application fee:* $10. *Required:* essay or personal statement, high school transcript, 1 letter of recommendation, interview. *Application deadlines:* 8/30 (freshmen), 8/30 (transfers). *Notification:* continuous (freshmen).

Admissions Contact Mr. David Buchanan, Admissions Counselor, Shimer College, PO Box 500, Waukegan, IL 60079-0500. *Phone:* 847-249-7174. *Toll-free phone:* 800-215-7173. *Fax:* 847-249-7171. *E-mail:* admissions@shimer.edu.

SOUTHERN ILLINOIS UNIVERSITY CARBONDALE

Carbondale, Illinois

- **State-supported** university, founded 1869, part of Southern Illinois University
- **Calendar** semesters
- **Degrees** associate, bachelor's, master's, doctoral, first professional, post-master's, postbachelor's, and first professional certificates
- **Small-town** 1128-acre campus
- **Endowment** $48.3 million
- **Coed,** 16,802 undergraduate students, 90% full-time, 44% women, 56% men
- **Moderately difficult** entrance level, 69% of applicants were admitted

Undergraduates 15,044 full-time, 1,758 part-time. Students come from 50 states and territories, 119 other countries, 20% are from out of state, 13% African American, 1% Asian American or Pacific Islander, 3% Hispanic American, 0.3% Native American, 4% international, 13% transferred in, 28% live on campus. *Retention:* 67% of 2001 full-time freshmen returned.

Freshmen *Admission:* 8,112 applied, 5,593 admitted, 2,248 enrolled. *Test scores:* ACT scores over 18: 99%; ACT scores over 24: 37%; ACT scores over 30: 4%.

Faculty *Total:* 1,126, 81% full-time, 70% with terminal degrees. *Student/faculty ratio:* 17:1.

Majors Accounting; agricultural economics; agricultural sciences; aircraft mechanic/airframe; aircraft pilot (professional); animal sciences; anthropology; architectural engineering technology; architecture; art; auto mechanic/technician; automotive engineering technology; aviation management; aviation technology; biology; botany; business; business administration; business computer programming; business economics; business marketing and marketing management; business systems analysis/design; chemistry; civil engineering; classics; clothing/apparel/textile studies; communication disorders; computer engineering; computer/information sciences; construction technology; criminal justice/law enforcement administration; dental hygiene; dental laboratory technician; design/visual communications; early childhood education; economics; electrical/electronic engineering technologies related; electrical/electronic engineering technology; electrical engineering; elementary education; emergency medical technology; engineering-related technology; engineering technology; English; family/consumer studies; film/video and photographic arts related; finance; fine/studio arts; fire services administration; foreign languages/literatures related; forestry; French; geography; geology; German; graphic design/commercial art/illustration; health education; health facilities administration; history; industrial technology; interior design; journalism; law enforcement/police science; liberal arts and sciences/liberal studies; linguistics; mathematics; mechanical engineering; medical radiologic technology; microbiology/bacteriology; mining/mineral engineering; mortuary science; music; nutrition studies; paralegal/legal assistant; philosophy; photographic technology; physical education; physical therapy assistant; physician assistant; physics; physiology; plant sciences; political science; psychology; radio/television broadcasting; recreation/leisure studies; rehabilitation/therapeutic services related; respiratory therapy; Russian; social sciences; social work; sociology; Spanish; special education; speech/rhetorical studies; theater arts/drama; tool/die making; trade/industrial education; zoology.

Academic Programs *Special study options:* academic remediation for entering students, accelerated degree program, adult/continuing education programs, advanced placement credit, cooperative education, distance learning, double majors, English as a second language, honors programs, independent study, internships, part-time degree program, services for LD students, study abroad, summer session for credit. *ROTC:* Army (b), Air Force (b).

Library Morris Library plus 1 other with 4.0 million titles, 20,450 serial subscriptions, 365,392 audiovisual materials, an OPAC, a Web page.

Computers on Campus 1426 computers available on campus for general student use. A campuswide network can be accessed from student residence rooms and from off campus. Internet access, online (class) registration, at least one staffed computer lab available.

Student Life *Housing:* on-campus residence required for freshman year. *Options:* coed, men-only, women-only, disabled students. *Activities and Organizations:* drama/theater group, student-run newspaper, radio and television station, choral group, marching band, Inter-Greek Council, International Student Council, Student Programming Council, Black Affairs Council, national fraternities, national sororities. *Campus security:* 24-hour emergency response devices and patrols, student patrols, late-night transport/escort service, well-lit pathways, night safety vans, student transit system. *Student Services:* health clinic, personal/psychological counseling, women's center, legal services.

Athletics Member NCAA. All Division I except football (Division I-AA). *Intercollegiate sports:* baseball M(s), basketball M(s)/W(s), cross-country running M(s)/W(s), golf M(s)/W(s), softball W(s), swimming M(s)/W(s), tennis M(s)/W(s), track and field M(s)/W(s), volleyball W(s). *Intramural sports:* badminton M(c)/W(c), baseball M(c), basketball M/W, bowling M(c), cross-country running M/W, equestrian sports M(c)/W(c), fencing M(c)/W(c), football M/W, golf M/W, lacrosse M(c), racquetball M(c)/W(c), rugby M(c)/W(c), sailing M(c)/W(c), soccer M(c)/W(c), softball M/W, squash M(c)/W, table tennis M(c)/W, tennis M/W, track and field M(c)/W(c), volleyball M(c)/W(c), water polo M(c)/W, weight lifting M(c)/W(c), wrestling M.

Standardized Tests *Required:* SAT I or ACT (for admission). *Recommended:* ACT (for admission).

Costs (2002–03) *Tuition:* state resident $3263 full-time, $109 per semester hour part-time; nonresident $6525 full-time, $218 per semester hour part-time. Full-time tuition and fees vary according to course load. Part-time tuition and fees vary according to course load. *Required fees:* $1205 full-time, $57 per semester hour. *Room and board:* $4610; room only: $2350. Room and board charges vary according to board plan and housing facility. *Payment plan:* installment. *Waivers:* senior citizens and employees or children of employees.

Financial Aid Of all full-time matriculated undergraduates who enrolled in 2001, 10586 applied for aid, 8434 were judged to have need, 3486 had their need fully met. 2019 Federal Work-Study jobs (averaging $978). 4526 State and other part-time jobs (averaging $1173). In 2001, 3902 non-need-based awards were made. *Average percent of need met:* 83%. *Average financial aid package:* $6621. *Average need-based loan:* $2957. *Average need-based gift aid:* $4720. *Average indebtedness upon graduation:* $12,413.

Applying *Options:* electronic application, early action, deferred entrance. *Application fee:* $30. *Required:* high school transcript. *Application deadline:* rolling (freshmen), rolling (transfers). *Notification:* continuous (freshmen).

Admissions Contact Mr. Walker Allen, Director of Admissions, Southern Illinois University Carbondale, Mail Code 4710, Carbondale, IL 62901-4710. *Phone:* 618-536-4405. *Fax:* 618-453-3250. *E-mail:* admrec@siu.edu.

SOUTHERN ILLINOIS UNIVERSITY EDWARDSVILLE

Edwardsville, Illinois

- **State-supported** comprehensive, founded 1957, part of Southern Illinois University
- **Calendar** semesters
- **Degrees** bachelor's, master's, first professional, post-master's, postbachelor's, and first professional certificates
- **Suburban** 2660-acre campus with easy access to St. Louis
- **Endowment** $7.5 million
- **Coed,** 9,799 undergraduate students, 82% full-time, 57% women, 43% men
- **Moderately difficult** entrance level, 87% of applicants were admitted

Undergraduates 8,032 full-time, 1,767 part-time. Students come from 43 states and territories, 65 other countries, 12% African American, 1% Asian American or Pacific Islander, 1% Hispanic American, 0.4% Native American, 1% international, 13% transferred in, 28% live on campus. *Retention:* 72% of 2001 full-time freshmen returned.

Freshmen *Admission:* 4,047 applied, 3,510 admitted, 1,611 enrolled. *Test scores:* ACT scores over 18: 85%; ACT scores over 24: 30%; ACT scores over 30: 3%.

Faculty *Total:* 751, 64% full-time. *Student/faculty ratio:* 17:1.

Majors Accounting; anthropology; art; biology; business; business economics; chemistry; civil engineering; computer engineering; computer/information sciences; construction technology; criminal justice studies; dance; early childhood education; economics; electrical engineering; elementary education; English; fine/studio arts; foreign languages/literatures; geography; health education; health/

Southern Illinois University Edwardsville (continued)
physical education; history; industrial/manufacturing engineering; liberal arts and sciences/liberal studies; management information systems/business data processing; mass communications; mathematics; mechanical engineering; music; nursing; philosophy; physics; political science; psychology; science education; social work; sociology; special education; speech-language pathology/audiology; speech/rhetorical studies; theater arts/drama.

Academic Programs *Special study options:* academic remediation for entering students, accelerated degree program, adult/continuing education programs, advanced placement credit, cooperative education, distance learning, double majors, English as a second language, honors programs, independent study, internships, off-campus study, part-time degree program, services for LD students, student-designed majors, study abroad, summer session for credit. *ROTC:* Army (b), Air Force (b).

Library Lovejoy Library with 763,443 titles, 12,174 serial subscriptions, 28,400 audiovisual materials, an OPAC, a Web page.

Computers on Campus 550 computers available on campus for general student use. A campuswide network can be accessed from student residence rooms and from off campus. Internet access, at least one staffed computer lab available.

Student Life *Housing Options:* coed, disabled students. *Activities and Organizations:* drama/theater group, student-run newspaper, radio station, choral group, student government, Greek Council, campus newspaper, University Center Board, International Student Council, national fraternities, national sororities. *Campus security:* 24-hour emergency response devices and patrols, student patrols, late-night transport/escort service, controlled dormitory access, 24-hour ID check at residence hall entrances, emergency call boxes located throughout campus. *Student Services:* health clinic, personal/psychological counseling, legal services.

Athletics Member NCAA. All Division II. *Intercollegiate sports:* baseball M(s), basketball M(s)/W(s), cross-country running M(s)/W(s), golf W, soccer M(s)/W(s), softball W(s), tennis M(s)/W(s), track and field M(s)/W(s), volleyball W, wrestling M(s). *Intramural sports:* badminton M/W, basketball M/W, bowling M/W, football M/W, golf M/W, racquetball M/W, soccer M/W, softball M/W, swimming M/W, table tennis M/W, tennis M/W, volleyball M/W, weight lifting M/W.

Standardized Tests *Required:* SAT I or ACT (for admission).

Costs (2002–03) *Tuition:* state resident $2850 full-time, $100 per semester hour part-time; nonresident $5700 full-time, $200 per semester hour part-time. Full-time tuition and fees vary according to course load. Part-time tuition and fees vary according to course load. *Required fees:* $723 full-time, $226 per term part-time. *Room and board:* $5016; room only: $2966. Room and board charges vary according to board plan and housing facility. *Payment plan:* installment. *Waivers:* employees or children of employees.

Financial Aid Of all full-time matriculated undergraduates who enrolled in 2001, 7315 applied for aid, 6237 were judged to have need, 5669 had their need fully met. 571 Federal Work-Study jobs (averaging $1348). 1219 State and other part-time jobs (averaging $1554). In 2001, 300 non-need-based awards were made. *Average percent of need met:* 74%. *Average financial aid package:* $2366. *Average need-based loan:* $1354. *Average need-based gift aid:* $434. *Average indebtedness upon graduation:* $13,351.

Applying *Options:* electronic application, early admission, deferred entrance. *Application fee:* $30. *Required:* high school transcript. *Application deadlines:* 5/31 (freshmen), 7/31 (transfers). *Notification:* continuous until 8/7 (freshmen).

Admissions Contact Mr. Boyd Bradshaw, Director of Admissions, Southern Illinois University Edwardsville, Box 1600. *Phone:* 618-650-3705. *Toll-free phone:* 800-447-SIUE. *Fax:* 618-650-5013. *E-mail:* admis@siue.edu.

TELSHE YESHIVA-CHICAGO
Chicago, Illinois

Admissions Contact Rosh Hayeshiva, Telshe Yeshiva-Chicago, 3535 West Foster Avenue, Chicago, IL 60625-5598. *Phone:* 773-463-7738.

TRINITY CHRISTIAN COLLEGE
Palos Heights, Illinois

- **Independent interdenominational** 4-year, founded 1959
- **Calendar** semesters
- **Degree** bachelor's
- **Suburban** 53-acre campus with easy access to Chicago
- **Endowment** $3.6 million
- **Coed,** 973 undergraduate students, 84% full-time, 63% women, 37% men
- **Moderately difficult** entrance level, 83% of applicants were admitted

Undergraduates 820 full-time, 153 part-time. Students come from 35 states and territories, 5 other countries, 45% are from out of state, 7% African American, 2% Asian American or Pacific Islander, 2% Hispanic American, 0.4% Native American, 2% international, 8% transferred in, 67% live on campus. *Retention:* 76% of 2001 full-time freshmen returned.

Freshmen *Admission:* 571 applied, 475 admitted, 208 enrolled. *Average high school GPA:* 3.21. *Test scores:* ACT scores over 18: 90%; ACT scores over 24: 44%; ACT scores over 30: 9%.

Faculty *Total:* 109, 46% full-time, 36% with terminal degrees. *Student/faculty ratio:* 13:1.

Majors Accounting; art; art education; biology; biology education; business; business administration; business administration/management related; business education; business marketing and marketing management; ceramic arts; chemistry; chemistry education; communications; computer science; drawing; education; education of the emotionally handicapped; education of the mentally handicapped; education of the specific learning disabled; elementary education; English; English education; entrepreneurship; financial planning; graphic design/commercial art/illustration; history; history education; human resources management; information sciences/systems; management information systems/business data processing; mathematics; mathematics education; middle school education; music; music (general performance); music (piano and organ performance); music teacher education; music (voice and choral/opera performance); nursing; painting; philosophy; photography; physical education; pre-dentistry; pre-medicine; pre-theology; pre-veterinary studies; printmaking; psychology; public relations; religious education; religious studies; science education; sculpture; secondary education; sociology; Spanish; special education; theology.

Academic Programs *Special study options:* academic remediation for entering students, adult/continuing education programs, advanced placement credit, double majors, honors programs, independent study, internships, off-campus study, part-time degree program, study abroad.

Library Jenny Huizenga Memorial Library with 56,713 titles, 434 serial subscriptions, 850 audiovisual materials, an OPAC, a Web page.

Computers on Campus 100 computers available on campus for general student use. A campuswide network can be accessed from student residence rooms and from off campus. Internet access, at least one staffed computer lab available.

Student Life *Housing:* on-campus residence required through senior year. *Options:* coed. *Activities and Organizations:* drama/theater group, student-run newspaper, choral group, Student Association, student ministries, student-run campus newspaper, Pro-Life Task Force, PACE (prison tutoring program). *Campus security:* 24-hour emergency response devices, student patrols, late-night transport/escort service. *Student Services:* personal/psychological counseling, women's center.

Athletics Member NAIA, NCCAA. *Intercollegiate sports:* baseball M(s), basketball M(s)/W(s), cross-country running M(s)/W(s), soccer M(s)/W(s), softball W(s), track and field M(s)/W(s), volleyball M(s)/W(s). *Intramural sports:* badminton M/W, basketball M/W, racquetball M/W, soccer M/W, table tennis M/W, tennis M/W, track and field M/W, volleyball M/W.

Standardized Tests *Required:* SAT I or ACT (for admission).

Costs (2001–02) *Comprehensive fee:* $19,416 includes full-time tuition ($13,970) and room and board ($5446). Part-time tuition: $465 per credit hour. Part-time tuition and fees vary according to course load. *Room and board:* College room only: $2800. Room and board charges vary according to board plan. *Payment plan:* installment. *Waivers:* senior citizens and employees or children of employees.

Financial Aid Of all full-time matriculated undergraduates who enrolled in 2001, 540 applied for aid, 477 were judged to have need, 121 had their need fully met. In 2001, 106 non-need-based awards were made. *Average percent of need met:* 66%. *Average financial aid package:* $9973. *Average need-based loan:* $3831. *Average need-based gift aid:* $2508. *Average non-need based aid:* $1250. *Average indebtedness upon graduation:* $15,000.

Applying *Options:* deferred entrance. *Application fee:* $20. *Required:* essay or personal statement, high school transcript, minimum 2.0 GPA, interview. *Required for some:* 1 letter of recommendation. *Application deadline:* rolling (freshmen), rolling (transfers). *Notification:* continuous (freshmen).

Admissions Contact Mr. Pete Hamstra, Dean of Admissions, Trinity Christian College, 6601 West College Drive, Palos Heights, IL 60463. *Phone:* 708-239-4709. *Toll-free phone:* 800-748-0085. *Fax:* 708-239-4826. *E-mail:* admissions@trnty.edu.

TRINITY COLLEGE OF NURSING AND HEALTH SCIENCES SCHOOLS
Moline, Illinois

- **Independent** 4-year, founded 1994
- **Calendar** semesters
- **Degrees** bachelor's (general education requirements are taken off campus, usually at Black Hawk College, Eastern Iowa Community College District and Western Illinois University)
- **Urban** 1-acre campus
- **Coed,** 98 undergraduate students, 50% full-time, 98% women, 2% men
- **Most difficult** entrance level, 60% of applicants were admitted

Undergraduates 49 full-time, 49 part-time. Students come from 2 states and territories, 28% are from out of state, 6% transferred in.

Freshmen *Admission:* 100 applied, 60 admitted, 5 enrolled. *Average high school GPA:* 2.50. *Test scores:* ACT scores over 18: 90%.

Faculty *Total:* 14, 86% full-time. *Student/faculty ratio:* 16:1.

Majors Nursing; nursing science.

Academic Programs *Special study options:* academic remediation for entering students, adult/continuing education programs, distance learning, honors programs, independent study, off-campus study, part-time degree program, services for LD students, summer session for credit.

Library Trinity Medical Center Library with a Web page.

Computers on Campus At least one staffed computer lab available.

Student Life *Activities and Organizations:* Student Nurses Association, student government, BSN Honor Society, Phi Theta Kappa. *Campus security:* 24-hour emergency response devices, controlled dormitory access. *Student Services:* personal/psychological counseling.

Standardized Tests *Required:* SAT I or ACT (for admission).

Costs (2002–03) *Tuition:* Full-time tuition and fees vary according to program and student level. Part-time tuition and fees vary according to program and student level. First year total: $4310, second year total: 5510, third year total: $4420, fourth year total: $4740. (Costs reflect Nursing Program).

Applying *Options:* common application. *Application fee:* $50. *Required:* high school transcript, minimum 2.5 GPA. *Application deadlines:* 6/1 (freshmen), 6/1 (transfers).

Admissions Contact Ms. Barbara Kimpe, Admissions Representative, Trinity College of Nursing and Health Sciences Schools, 555 6th Street, Moline, IL 61265-1216. *Phone:* 309-779-7812. *Fax:* 309-757-2194. *E-mail:* con@trinityqc.com.

TRINITY INTERNATIONAL UNIVERSITY
Deerfield, Illinois

- **Independent** university, founded 1897, affiliated with Evangelical Free Church of America
- **Calendar** semesters
- **Degrees** bachelor's, master's, doctoral, and first professional
- **Suburban** 108-acre campus with easy access to Chicago
- **Coed,** 1,200 undergraduate students, 92% full-time, 58% women, 42% men
- **Moderately difficult** entrance level, 82% of applicants were admitted

Undergraduates 1,099 full-time, 101 part-time. Students come from 32 states and territories, 5 other countries, 52% are from out of state, 10% African American, 3% Asian American or Pacific Islander, 4% Hispanic American, 0.3% Native American, 1% international, 7% transferred in, 80% live on campus. *Retention:* 88% of 2001 full-time freshmen returned.

Freshmen *Admission:* 458 applied, 377 admitted, 202 enrolled. *Average high school GPA:* 3.26. *Test scores:* SAT verbal scores over 500: 80%; SAT math scores over 500: 67%; ACT scores over 18: 96%; SAT verbal scores over 600: 37%; SAT math scores over 600: 20%; ACT scores over 24: 43%; SAT verbal scores over 700: 8%; ACT scores over 30: 6%.

Faculty *Total:* 82, 45% full-time, 43% with terminal degrees. *Student/faculty ratio:* 19:1.

Majors Accounting; athletic training/sports medicine; biblical studies; biology; business administration; business marketing and marketing management; chemistry; computer science; divinity/ministry; economics; education; education (K-12); elementary education; English; history; humanities; human resources management; liberal arts and sciences/liberal studies; mathematics; music; music teacher education; philosophy; physical education; pre-medicine; psychology; religious music; secondary education; social sciences; sociology.

Academic Programs *Special study options:* academic remediation for entering students, adult/continuing education programs, advanced placement credit, double majors, honors programs, independent study, internships, off-campus study, part-time degree program, study abroad.

Library Rolfing Memorial Library with 154,051 titles, 1,438 serial subscriptions, 3,888 audiovisual materials, an OPAC, a Web page.

Computers on Campus 80 computers available on campus for general student use. A campuswide network can be accessed from student residence rooms and from off campus. Internet access, at least one staffed computer lab available.

Student Life *Housing:* on-campus residence required through junior year. *Options:* men-only, women-only. *Activities and Organizations:* drama/theater group, student-run newspaper, choral group, Student Senate, college union, Trinity Summer Mission, student newspaper, yearbook. *Campus security:* 24-hour patrols, controlled dormitory access. *Student Services:* health clinic, personal/psychological counseling.

Athletics Member NAIA, NCCAA. *Intercollegiate sports:* baseball M, basketball M(s)/W(s), cross-country running M/W, football M(s), soccer M(s)/W(s), softball W(s), tennis M(s)/W(s), track and field M/W, volleyball M/W(s). *Intramural sports:* basketball M/W, football M, racquetball M/W, soccer M/W, table tennis M/W, tennis M/W.

Standardized Tests *Required:* SAT I or ACT (for admission), SAT I or ACT (for placement).

Costs (2001–02) *Comprehensive fee:* $20,640 includes full-time tuition ($15,100), mandatory fees ($250), and room and board ($5290). Part-time tuition: $630 per hour. No tuition increase for student's term of enrollment. *Required fees:* $63 per term part-time. *Room and board:* College room only: $2710. Room and board charges vary according to board plan and housing facility. *Payment plan:* installment. *Waivers:* employees or children of employees.

Financial Aid Of all full-time matriculated undergraduates who enrolled in 2001, 1043 applied for aid, 898 were judged to have need. 392 Federal Work-Study jobs (averaging $990). In 2001, 19 non-need-based awards were made. *Average percent of need met:* 68%. *Average financial aid package:* $12,174. *Average need-based loan:* $3928. *Average need-based gift aid:* $5245. *Average non-need based aid:* $1024. *Average indebtedness upon graduation:* $13,332.

Applying *Options:* electronic application, early admission. *Application fee:* $25. *Required:* essay or personal statement, high school transcript, minimum 2.5 GPA, 1 letter of recommendation. *Required for some:* interview. *Recommended:* minimum 3.0 GPA. *Application deadline:* rolling (freshmen), rolling (transfers). *Notification:* 9/1 (freshmen).

Admissions Contact Mr. Matt Yoder, Director of Undergraduate Admissions, Trinity International University, 2065 Half Day Road, Peterson Wing, McClennan Building, Deerfield, IL 60015-1284. *Phone:* 847-317-7000. *Toll-free phone:* 800-822-3225. *Fax:* 847-317-7081. *E-mail:* tcdadm@tiu.edu.

UNIVERSITY OF CHICAGO
Chicago, Illinois

- **Independent** university, founded 1891
- **Calendar** quarters
- **Degrees** bachelor's, master's, doctoral, and first professional
- **Urban** 203-acre campus
- **Endowment** $3.5 billion
- **Coed,** 4,075 undergraduate students, 99% full-time, 51% women, 49% men
- **Most difficult** entrance level, 44% of applicants were admitted

The Undergraduate College of the University of Chicago is at the heart of one of the world's great intellectual communities and centers of learning, where 73 Nobel laureates have researched, studied, or taught. The College offers fifty concentrations of study and the first established and most extensive general education curriculum.

Undergraduates 4,049 full-time, 26 part-time. Students come from 52 states and territories, 49 other countries, 78% are from out of state, 4% African American, 16% Asian American or Pacific Islander, 7% Hispanic American, 0.2% Native American, 7% international, 2% transferred in, 66% live on campus. *Retention:* 95% of 2001 full-time freshmen returned.

Freshmen *Admission:* 7,454 applied, 3,261 admitted, 1,081 enrolled. *Test scores:* SAT verbal scores over 500: 98%; SAT math scores over 500: 100%; ACT scores over 18: 100%; SAT verbal scores over 600: 91%; SAT math scores over 600: 92%; ACT scores over 24: 96%; SAT verbal scores over 700: 58%; SAT math scores over 700: 53%; ACT scores over 30: 65%.

University of Chicago (continued)

Faculty *Total:* 1,861, 86% full-time. *Student/faculty ratio:* 4:1.

Majors African-American studies; African studies; American studies; anthropology; applied mathematics; Arabic; art; art history; Asian studies; behavioral sciences; biblical languages/literatures; biochemistry; biology; chemistry; Chinese; classics; computer science; creative writing; East Asian studies; Eastern European area studies; economics; English; environmental science; film studies; fine/studio arts; French; geography; geophysics/seismology; German; Greek (ancient and medieval); history; history of science and technology; humanities; interdisciplinary studies; Italian; Japanese; Judaic studies; Latin American studies; Latin (ancient and medieval); liberal arts and sciences/liberal studies; linguistics; mathematical statistics; mathematics; medieval/renaissance studies; Middle Eastern studies; modern languages; music; music history; philosophy; physics; political science; psychology; public policy analysis; religious studies; romance languages; Russian; Russian/Slavic studies; Slavic languages; social sciences; sociology; South Asian studies; Southeast Asian studies; Spanish.

Academic Programs *Special study options:* accelerated degree program, adult/continuing education programs, advanced placement credit, double majors, independent study, internships, off-campus study, student-designed majors, study abroad, summer session for credit. *ROTC:* Army (c), Air Force (c). *Unusual degree programs:* 3-2 law, public policy, teacher education.

Library Joseph Regenstein Library plus 8 others with 5.8 million titles, 47,000 serial subscriptions, an OPAC, a Web page.

Computers on Campus 1000 computers available on campus for general student use. A campuswide network can be accessed from student residence rooms and from off campus. At least one staffed computer lab available.

Student Life *Housing:* on-campus residence required for freshman year. *Options:* coed. *Activities and Organizations:* drama/theater group, student-run newspaper, radio station, choral group, Model United Nations, university theater, Documentary Films Club, Major Activities Board, student radio station, national fraternities, national sororities. *Campus security:* 24-hour emergency response devices and patrols, late-night transport/escort service, controlled dormitory access. *Student Services:* health clinic, personal/psychological counseling, women's center.

Athletics Member NCAA. All Division III. *Intercollegiate sports:* baseball M, basketball M/W, cross-country running M/W, football M, soccer M/W, softball W, swimming M/W, tennis M/W, track and field M/W, volleyball W, wrestling M. *Intramural sports:* archery M/W, badminton M/W, basketball M/W, crew M(c)/W(c), cross-country running M/W, fencing M(c)/W(c), football M/W, gymnastics M(c)/W(c), ice hockey M(c), lacrosse M(c)/W(c), racquetball M/W, rugby M(c)/W(c), sailing M(c)/W(c), softball M/W, squash M(c)/W(c), swimming M/W, table tennis M/W, tennis M/W, track and field M/W, volleyball M(c).

Standardized Tests *Required:* SAT I or ACT (for admission).

Costs (2001–02) *Comprehensive fee:* $34,787 includes full-time tuition ($26,022), mandatory fees ($453), and room and board ($8312). Part-time tuition: $3645 per course. Part-time tuition and fees vary according to course load. *Required fees:* $453 per year part-time. *Payment plans:* tuition prepayment, installment. *Waivers:* employees or children of employees.

Financial Aid *Average indebtedness upon graduation:* $13,770.

Applying *Options:* electronic application, early admission, early action, deferred entrance. *Application fee:* $60. *Required:* essay or personal statement, high school transcript, 3 letters of recommendation. *Recommended:* interview. *Application deadlines:* 1/1 (freshmen), 4/11 (transfers). *Notification:* 4/1 (freshmen), 12/15 (early action).

Admissions Contact Mr. Theodore O'Neill, Dean of Admissions, University of Chicago, 1116 East 59th Street, Chicago, IL 60637-1513. *Phone:* 773-702-8650. *Fax:* 773-702-4199.

UNIVERSITY OF ILLINOIS AT CHICAGO
Chicago, Illinois

- **State-supported** university, founded 1946, part of University of Illinois System
- **Calendar** semesters
- **Degrees** bachelor's, master's, doctoral, first professional, and first professional certificates
- **Urban** 216-acre campus
- **Endowment** $107.7 million
- **Coed,** 15,887 undergraduate students, 89% full-time, 55% women, 45% men
- **Moderately difficult** entrance level, 64% of applicants were admitted

Undergraduates 14,085 full-time, 1,802 part-time. Students come from 52 states and territories, 81 other countries, 3% are from out of state, 9% African American, 24% Asian American or Pacific Islander, 17% Hispanic American, 0.3% Native American, 2% international, 10% transferred in, 11% live on campus. *Retention:* 79% of 2001 full-time freshmen returned.

Freshmen *Admission:* 9,512 applied, 6,049 admitted, 2,692 enrolled. *Test scores:* ACT scores over 18: 93%; ACT scores over 24: 44%; ACT scores over 30: 6%.

Faculty *Total:* 1,549, 81% full-time, 81% with terminal degrees. *Student/faculty ratio:* 14:1.

Majors Accounting; African-American studies; anthropology; architecture; art education; art history; biochemistry; bioengineering; biology; biology education; business administration; business marketing and marketing management; chemical engineering; chemistry; chemistry education; civil engineering; classics; computer engineering; computer/information sciences; criminal justice studies; economics; electrical engineering; elementary education; engineering/industrial management; engineering physics; English; English education; film/video production; finance; fine/studio arts; foreign languages education; French; French language education; geography; geology; German; German language education; graphic design/commercial art/illustration; health/physical education; history; history education; industrial design; industrial/manufacturing engineering; Italian; Latin American studies; management information systems/business data processing; mathematical statistics; mathematics; mathematics/computer science; mathematics education; mechanical engineering; medical dietician; medical records administration; medical technology; music; nursing; philosophy; photography; physical therapy; physics; physics education; political science; pre-dentistry; pre-law; psychology; Russian; science education; secondary education; Slavic languages; social science education; social work; sociology; Spanish; Spanish language education; speech/rhetorical studies; theater arts/drama.

Academic Programs *Special study options:* academic remediation for entering students, accelerated degree program, advanced placement credit, cooperative education, distance learning, double majors, English as a second language, honors programs, independent study, internships, off-campus study, part-time degree program, services for LD students, student-designed majors, study abroad, summer session for credit. *ROTC:* Army (b), Navy (c), Air Force (c).

Library University Library plus 8 others with 2.1 million titles, 20,875 serial subscriptions, 27,856 audiovisual materials, an OPAC, a Web page.

Computers on Campus 600 computers available on campus for general student use. A campuswide network can be accessed from student residence rooms and from off campus. At least one staffed computer lab available.

Student Life *Housing Options:* coed. *Activities and Organizations:* drama/theater group, student-run newspaper, radio station, choral group, Golden Key National Honor Society, Chinese Students and Scholars Friendship Association, Muslim Student Association, MBA Association, Alternative Spring Break, national fraternities, national sororities. *Campus security:* 24-hour emergency response devices and patrols, student patrols, late-night transport/escort service, controlled dormitory access, housing ID stickers, guest escort policy, 24-hour closed circuit videos for exits and entrances, security screen for first floor. *Student Services:* health clinic, personal/psychological counseling, women's center, legal services.

Athletics Member NCAA. All Division I. *Intercollegiate sports:* baseball M(s), basketball M(s)/W(s), cross-country running M(s)/W(s), gymnastics M(s)/W(s), soccer M(s), softball W(s), swimming M(s)/W(s), tennis M(s)/W(s), track and field M(s)/W(s), volleyball W(s). *Intramural sports:* badminton M/W, basketball M/W, cross-country running M/W, fencing M(c)/W(c), field hockey M/W, football M/W, golf M/W, lacrosse M(c)/W(c), racquetball M/W, rugby M(c)/W(c), soccer M/W, softball M/W, squash M/W, table tennis M/W, tennis M/W, volleyball M(c)/W, water polo M(c)/W(c), wrestling M.

Standardized Tests *Required:* SAT I or ACT (for admission).

Costs (2001–02) *Tuition:* state resident $3330 full-time; nonresident $9990 full-time. Full-time tuition and fees vary according to program. Part-time tuition and fees vary according to course load and program. *Required fees:* $1614 full-time. *Room and board:* $6058. Room and board charges vary according to board plan and housing facility. *Waivers:* senior citizens and employees or children of employees.

Financial Aid Of all full-time matriculated undergraduates who enrolled in 2001, 10000 applied for aid, 8500 were judged to have need, 4100 had their need fully met. 600 Federal Work-Study jobs (averaging $1290). 2800 State and other part-time jobs (averaging $2247). In 2001, 3200 non-need-based awards were made. *Average percent of need met:* 86%. *Average financial aid package:* $11,800. *Average need-based loan:* $3300. *Average need-based gift aid:* $5200.

Applying *Options:* electronic application, early admission. *Application fee:* $40. *Required:* high school transcript. *Required for some:* essay or personal statement, interview. *Application deadlines:* 2/28 (freshmen), 6/1 (transfers). *Notification:* continuous (freshmen).

Admissions Contact University of Illinois at Chicago, Box 5220, Chicago, IL 60680-5220. *Phone:* 312-996-4350. *Fax:* 312-413-7628. *E-mail:* uic.admit@uic.edu.

UNIVERSITY OF ILLINOIS AT SPRINGFIELD

Springfield, Illinois

- **State-supported** upper-level, founded 1969
- **Calendar** semesters
- **Degrees** bachelor's and master's
- **Suburban** 746-acre campus
- **Coed,** 2,300 undergraduate students, 53% full-time, 64% women, 36% men
- **Minimally difficult** entrance level, 51% of applicants were admitted

Undergraduates 1,219 full-time, 1,081 part-time. Students come from 13 states and territories, 35 other countries, 2% are from out of state, 8% African American, 2% Asian American or Pacific Islander, 1% Hispanic American, 0.1% Native American, 1% international, 12% live on campus.

Freshmen *Admission:* 1,406 applied, 722 admitted.

Faculty *Total:* 260, 68% full-time. *Student/faculty ratio:* 15:1.

Majors Accounting; anthropology; art; biology; business administration; chemistry; child care/development; computer science; criminal justice/law enforcement administration; economics; elementary education; English; health services administration; history; home economics education; interdisciplinary studies; legal studies; liberal arts and sciences/liberal studies; mass communications; mathematics; medical laboratory technology; nursing; political science; psychology; secondary education; social work; sociology.

Academic Programs *Special study options:* academic remediation for entering students, adult/continuing education programs, cooperative education, external degree program, internships, off-campus study, part-time degree program, student-designed majors, summer session for credit.

Library Brookens Library with 39,536 audiovisual materials, an OPAC, a Web page.

Computers on Campus 160 computers available on campus for general student use. A campuswide network can be accessed from student residence rooms and from off campus. Internet access, at least one staffed computer lab available.

Student Life *Housing Options:* coed. *Activities and Organizations:* student-run newspaper, radio and television station, International Student Association, Model United Nations, Model Illinois Government, African-American Student Organization. *Campus security:* 24-hour patrols, late-night transport/escort service. *Student Services:* health clinic, personal/psychological counseling, women's center.

Athletics Member NAIA. *Intercollegiate sports:* basketball W(s), soccer M(s), tennis M(s)/W(s), volleyball W(s). *Intramural sports:* basketball M/W, bowling M/W, football M/W, golf M/W, softball M/W, tennis M/W, volleyball M/W.

Costs (2001–02) *Tuition:* state resident $2985 full-time, $100 per credit hour part-time; nonresident $8955 full-time, $299 per credit hour part-time. *Required fees:* $626 full-time, $183 per semester part-time. *Room and board:* room only: $3060. Room and board charges vary according to housing facility. *Payment plan:* installment. *Waivers:* senior citizens and employees or children of employees.

Financial Aid *Financial aid deadline:* 11/15.

Applying *Options:* deferred entrance. *Application deadline:* rolling (transfers). *Notification:* continuous (transfers).

Admissions Contact Office of Enrollment Services, University of Illinois at Springfield, Building SAB. *Phone:* 217-206-6626. *Toll-free phone:* 800-252-8533. *Fax:* 217-206-6620.

UNIVERSITY OF ILLINOIS AT URBANA-CHAMPAIGN

Champaign, Illinois

- **State-supported** university, founded 1867, part of University of Illinois System
- **Calendar** semesters
- **Degrees** bachelor's, master's, doctoral, and first professional
- **Small-town** 1470-acre campus
- **Endowment** $596.5 million
- **Coed,** 28,746 undergraduate students, 96% full-time, 48% women, 52% men
- **Very difficult** entrance level, 62% of applicants were admitted

Undergraduates 27,624 full-time, 1,122 part-time. Students come from 50 states and territories, 121 other countries, 7% are from out of state, 7% African American, 13% Asian American or Pacific Islander, 6% Hispanic American, 0.2% Native American, 2% international, 4% transferred in, 30% live on campus. *Retention:* 93% of 2001 full-time freshmen returned.

Freshmen *Admission:* 19,930 applied, 12,351 admitted, 6,247 enrolled. *Test scores:* SAT verbal scores over 500: 90%; SAT math scores over 500: 95%; ACT scores over 18: 99%; SAT verbal scores over 600: 57%; SAT math scores over 600: 78%; ACT scores over 24: 84%; SAT verbal scores over 700: 12%; SAT math scores over 700: 32%; ACT scores over 30: 29%.

Faculty *Total:* 2,652, 84% full-time, 85% with terminal degrees. *Student/faculty ratio:* 15:1.

Majors Accounting; actuarial science; advertising; aerospace engineering; agricultural economics; agricultural education; agricultural engineering; agricultural/food products processing; agricultural mechanization; agricultural sciences; agronomy/crop science; aircraft pilot (professional); animal sciences; anthropology; architecture related; area studies related; art education; art history; Asian studies; astronomy; biochemistry; bioengineering; biology; biophysics; botany; broadcast journalism; business; cell and molecular biology related; cell biology; chemical engineering; chemistry; city/community/regional planning; civil engineering; classics; comparative literature; computer education; computer engineering; computer/information sciences; consumer economics; craft/folk art; dance; early childhood education; ecology; economics; electrical engineering; elementary education; engineering; engineering mechanics; engineering physics; English; English composition; English education; entomology; environmental science; finance; food sciences; foreign languages education; forestry; French; French language education; geography; geology; German; German language education; graphic design/commercial art/illustration; health/physical education; history; horticulture science; humanities; individual/family development; industrial design; industrial/manufacturing engineering; Italian; journalism; landscape architecture; Latin American studies; liberal arts and sciences/liberal studies; linguistics; marketing operations; mass communications; materials science; mathematical statistics; mathematics; mathematics/computer science; mechanical engineering; microbiology/bacteriology; music; music (general performance); music history; music teacher education; music theory and composition; music (voice and choral/opera performance); nuclear engineering; ornamental horticulture; painting; philosophy; photography; physics; physiology; political science; Portuguese; pre-veterinary studies; psychology; public health related; recreation/leisure studies; religious studies; Russian; Russian/Slavic studies; sculpture; sociology; Spanish; Spanish language education; special education; speech-language pathology/audiology; speech/rhetorical studies; theater arts/drama.

Academic Programs *Special study options:* accelerated degree program, advanced placement credit, cooperative education, distance learning, double majors, honors programs, internships, off-campus study, services for LD students, student-designed majors, study abroad, summer session for credit. *ROTC:* Army (b), Air Force (b). *Unusual degree programs:* 3-2 accounting.

Library University Library plus 40 others with 9.5 million titles, 90,962 serial subscriptions, 868,538 audiovisual materials, an OPAC, a Web page.

Computers on Campus 3000 computers available on campus for general student use. A campuswide network can be accessed from student residence rooms and from off campus. Internet access, online (class) registration, at least one staffed computer lab available.

Student Life *Housing:* on-campus residence required for freshman year. *Options:* coed, men-only, women-only, disabled students. *Activities and Organizations:* drama/theater group, student-run newspaper, radio and television station, choral group, marching band, Volunteer Illini Project, Alpha Phi Omega, Indian Student Organization, Panhel IFC, Residence Hall Association, national fraternities, national sororities. *Campus security:* 24-hour emergency response devices and patrols, student patrols, late-night transport/escort service, controlled dormitory access, safety training classes, ID cards with safety numbers. *Student Services:* health clinic, personal/psychological counseling, women's center, legal services.

Athletics Member NCAA. All Division I except football (Division I-A). *Intercollegiate sports:* baseball M(s), basketball M(s)/W(s), cross-country running M(s)/W(s), golf M(s)/W(s), gymnastics M(s)/W(s), soccer W(s), swimming W(s), tennis M(s)/W(s), track and field M(s)/W(s), volleyball W(s), wrestling M(s). *Intramural sports:* badminton M/W, basketball M/W, bowling M/W, cross-country running M/W, equestrian sports M(c)/W(c), fencing M(c)/W(c), field hockey W(c), football M/W, golf M/W, gymnastics M(c)/W(c), ice hockey M/W, lacrosse M(c)/W(c), racquetball M/W, riflery M(c)/W(c), rugby M(c)/W(c), sailing M(c)/W(c), skiing (cross-country) M(c)/W(c), skiing (downhill) M(c)/W(c), soccer M/W, softball M/W, squash M(c)/W(c), swimming M/W, table tennis M/W, tennis M/W, volleyball M/W, water polo M/W, weight lifting M(c)/W(c), wrestling M/W.

Standardized Tests *Required:* SAT I or ACT (for admission).

Costs (2001–02) *Tuition:* state resident $4410 full-time, $1470 per term part-time; nonresident $12,230 full-time, $4077 per term part-time. Full-time tuition and fees vary according to course load and student level. Part-time tuition and fees vary according to program and student level. *Required fees:* $1384 full-time, $317 per term part-time. *Room and board:* $6090. Room and board charges vary according to board plan and housing facility. *Payment plan:* installment. *Waivers:* senior citizens and employees or children of employees.

Financial Aid Of all full-time matriculated undergraduates who enrolled in 2001, 15333 applied for aid, 10705 were judged to have need, 4811 had their need

University of Illinois at Urbana-Champaign (continued)
fully met. 1595 Federal Work-Study jobs. In 2001, 5404 non-need-based awards were made. *Average percent of need met:* 89%. *Average financial aid package:* $8419. *Average need-based loan:* $3448. *Average need-based gift aid:* $5267. *Average indebtedness upon graduation:* $14,791.

Applying *Options:* deferred entrance. *Application fee:* $40. *Required:* essay or personal statement, high school transcript. *Required for some:* audition, statement of professional interest. *Application deadlines:* 1/1 (freshmen), 3/15 (transfers). *Notification:* continuous (freshmen).

Admissions Contact Mr. Abel Mandujano, Assistant Director of Admissions, University of Illinois at Urbana-Champaign, 901 West Illinois, Urbana, IL 61801. *Phone:* 217-333-0302. *E-mail:* admissions@oar.uiuc.edu.

UNIVERSITY OF ST. FRANCIS
Joliet, Illinois

- **Independent Roman Catholic** comprehensive, founded 1920
- **Calendar** semesters
- **Degrees** bachelor's and master's
- **Suburban** 16-acre campus with easy access to Chicago
- **Endowment** $8.0 million
- **Coed,** 1,376 undergraduate students, 79% full-time, 67% women, 33% men
- **Moderately difficult** entrance level, 80% of applicants were admitted

Founded in 1920, the University of St. Francis offers a rich tradition of excellence in higher education. With more than 60 programs of study, the University's academic quality is matched only by its commitment to technology and innovation in course delivery, as well as a long-standing belief in providing the best service to St. Francis students.

Undergraduates 1,084 full-time, 292 part-time. Students come from 8 states and territories, 10% are from out of state, 7% African American, 2% Asian American or Pacific Islander, 6% Hispanic American, 0.2% Native American, 0.1% international, 17% transferred in, 24% live on campus. *Retention:* 76% of 2001 full-time freshmen returned.

Freshmen *Admission:* 811 applied, 646 admitted, 177 enrolled. *Average high school GPA:* 3.30. *Test scores:* ACT scores over 18: 95%; ACT scores over 24: 33%; ACT scores over 30: 2%.

Faculty *Total:* 168, 45% full-time. *Student/faculty ratio:* 11:1.

Majors Accounting; actuarial science; biology; broadcast journalism; business administration; business marketing and marketing management; business systems networking/ telecommunications; computer programming; computer science; elementary education; English; environmental science; finance; health science; history; liberal arts and sciences/liberal studies; mass communications; mathematics; medical radiologic technology; medical technology; nuclear medical technology; nursing; operations management; political science; pre-dentistry; premedicine; pre-veterinary studies; psychology; radiological science; recreational therapy; recreation/leisure studies; social studies education; social work; special education; theology; visual/performing arts.

Academic Programs *Special study options:* accelerated degree program, adult/continuing education programs, advanced placement credit, cooperative education, distance learning, double majors, external degree program, independent study, internships, part-time degree program, student-designed majors, study abroad, summer session for credit. *Unusual degree programs:* 3-2 computer science engineering with Illinois Institute of Technology.

Library University of St. Francis Library with 184,000 titles, 710 serial subscriptions, 2,800 audiovisual materials, an OPAC, a Web page.

Computers on Campus 147 computers available on campus for general student use. A campuswide network can be accessed from student residence rooms. Internet access, online (class) registration, at least one staffed computer lab available.

Student Life *Housing Options:* coed. *Activities and Organizations:* drama/ theater group, student-run newspaper, radio and television station, choral group, Student Business Association, Ethnic Affairs Council, Campus Ministry Poverellos, Student Activity Board, Recreation Club. *Campus security:* 24-hour emergency response devices and patrols, late-night transport/escort service, controlled dormitory access, First Response trained security personnel. *Student Services:* health clinic, personal/psychological counseling.

Athletics Member NAIA. *Intercollegiate sports:* baseball M(s), basketball M(s)/W(s), cross-country running W(s), football M(s), golf M(s)/W(s), soccer M(s)/W(s), softball W(s), tennis M(s)/W(s), volleyball W(s). *Intramural sports:* badminton M/W, basketball M/W, bowling M/W, golf M/W, racquetball M/W, skiing (downhill) M/W, table tennis M/W, tennis M/W, volleyball M/W.

Standardized Tests *Required:* SAT I or ACT (for admission). *Recommended:* ACT (for admission).

Costs (2001–02) *Comprehensive fee:* $20,570 includes full-time tuition ($14,680), mandatory fees ($310), and room and board ($5580). Part-time tuition: $440 per credit. Part-time tuition and fees vary according to course load. *Required fees:* $15 per term part-time. *Payment plan:* installment. *Waivers:* children of alumni and employees or children of employees.

Financial Aid Of all full-time matriculated undergraduates who enrolled in 2001, 1037 applied for aid, 711 were judged to have need, 498 had their need fully met. 135 Federal Work-Study jobs (averaging $1762). In 2001, 227 non-need-based awards were made. *Average percent of need met:* 90%. *Average financial aid package:* $12,063. *Average need-based loan:* $3554. *Average need-based gift aid:* $5953. *Average non-need based aid:* $4563. *Average indebtedness upon graduation:* $15,556.

Applying *Options:* common application, deferred entrance. *Application fee:* $20. *Required:* high school transcript, minimum 2.5 GPA. *Required for some:* essay or personal statement, 2 letters of recommendation, interview. *Application deadline:* rolling (freshmen), rolling (transfers). *Notification:* continuous (freshmen).

Admissions Contact Mr. Mike Rodewald, Director of Freshman Admission, University of St. Francis, 500 North Wilcox Street, Joliet, IL 60435-6188. *Phone:* 815-740-5037. *Toll-free phone:* 800-735-7500. *Fax:* 815-740-5078. *E-mail:* admissions@stfrancis.edu.

VANDERCOOK COLLEGE OF MUSIC
Chicago, Illinois

- **Independent** comprehensive, founded 1909
- **Calendar** semesters
- **Degrees** bachelor's and master's
- **Urban** 1-acre campus
- **Endowment** $112,363
- **Coed,** 152 undergraduate students, 51% full-time, 38% women, 63% men
- **Moderately difficult** entrance level

Undergraduates 78 full-time, 74 part-time. Students come from 10 states and territories, 2 other countries, 31% are from out of state, 17% African American, 17% Hispanic American, 2% international, 3% transferred in. *Retention:* 85% of 2001 full-time freshmen returned.

Freshmen *Admission:* 19 enrolled. *Average high school GPA:* 2.74. *Test scores:* ACT scores over 18: 50%; ACT scores over 24: 12%; ACT scores over 30: 6%.

Faculty *Total:* 24, 38% full-time, 21% with terminal degrees. *Student/faculty ratio:* 7:1.

Majors Music teacher education.

Academic Programs *Special study options:* adult/continuing education programs, advanced placement credit, independent study, internships, summer session for credit.

Library Harry Ruppel Memorial Library with 5,521 titles, 93 serial subscriptions, an OPAC, a Web page.

Computers on Campus 20 computers available on campus for general student use. A campuswide network can be accessed from student residence rooms and from off campus. Internet access, at least one staffed computer lab available.

Student Life *Housing Options:* coed. *Activities and Organizations:* choral group, MENC (Music Educators Natural Conference), national fraternities, national sororities. *Campus security:* 24-hour emergency response devices and patrols, late-night transport/escort service, controlled dormitory access.

Standardized Tests *Required:* SAT I or ACT (for admission).

Costs (2001–02) *Comprehensive fee:* $19,410 includes full-time tuition ($13,440), mandatory fees ($370), and room and board ($5600). Full-time tuition and fees vary according to degree level. Part-time tuition: $560 per credit. Part-time tuition and fees vary according to class time and course load. *Required fees:* $185 per term part-time. *Room and board:* Room and board charges vary according to board plan. *Payment plan:* installment. *Waivers:* employees or children of employees.

Financial Aid *Financial aid deadline:* 7/1.

Applying *Options:* early decision, deferred entrance. *Application fee:* $35. *Required:* essay or personal statement, high school transcript, 3 letters of recommendation, interview, audition. *Required for some:* minimum 3.0 GPA. *Recommended:* minimum 3.0 GPA. *Application deadlines:* 5/1 (freshmen), 5/1 (transfers). *Early decision:* 12/1.

Admissions Contact Mr. James Malley, Director of Undergraduate Admission, VanderCook College of Music, 3140 South Federal Street, Chicago, IL 60616. *Phone:* 800-448-2655 Ext. 241. *Toll-free phone:* 800-448-2655. *Fax:* 312-225-5211. *E-mail:* admissions@vandercook.edu.

Western Illinois University
Macomb, Illinois

- **State-supported** comprehensive, founded 1899
- **Calendar** semesters
- **Degrees** bachelor's and master's
- **Small-town** 1050-acre campus
- **Endowment** $14.1 million
- **Coed,** 10,755 undergraduate students, 86% full-time, 51% women, 49% men
- **Moderately difficult** entrance level, 61% of applicants were admitted

Western Illinois University guarantees a fixed rate of tuition, fees, room, and board for all new undergraduate students. The program establishes and freezes a per-semester-hour cost for students for 4 years as long as they maintain continuous enrollment at Western. All new undergraduate students entering the University are automatically included.

Undergraduates 9,300 full-time, 1,455 part-time. Students come from 46 states and territories, 54 other countries, 9% are from out of state, 7% African American, 1% Asian American or Pacific Islander, 3% Hispanic American, 0.2% Native American, 2% international, 13% transferred in, 51% live on campus. *Retention:* 75% of 2001 full-time freshmen returned.

Freshmen *Admission:* 8,115 applied, 4,952 admitted, 1,709 enrolled. *Test scores:* ACT scores over 18: 91%; ACT scores over 24: 28%; ACT scores over 30: 2%.

Faculty *Total:* 684, 90% full-time, 63% with terminal degrees. *Student/faculty ratio:* 17:1.

Majors Accounting; agricultural sciences; art; bilingual/bicultural education; biology; business; business economics; business marketing and marketing management; chemistry; communication disorders; communications; computer/information sciences; criminal justice/law enforcement administration; economics; educational media design; elementary education; English; finance; fine/studio arts; French; geography; geology; health education; history; home economics; human resources management; industrial technology; journalism; liberal arts and sciences/liberal studies; management information systems/business data processing; mathematics; medical technology; music; philosophy; physical education; physics; political science; psychology; recreation/leisure facilities management; social work; sociology; Spanish; special education; theater arts/drama; trade/industrial education; women's studies.

Academic Programs *Special study options:* academic remediation for entering students, adult/continuing education programs, advanced placement credit, distance learning, double majors, English as a second language, external degree program, freshman honors college, honors programs, independent study, internships, off-campus study, part-time degree program, services for LD students, student-designed majors, study abroad, summer session for credit. *ROTC:* Army (b). *Unusual degree programs:* 3-2 engineering with University of Illinois at Urbana-Champaign, Case Western Reserve University.

Library Western Illinois University Library plus 4 others with 998,041 titles, 3,200 serial subscriptions, 3,445 audiovisual materials, an OPAC, a Web page.

Computers on Campus 700 computers available on campus for general student use. A campuswide network can be accessed from off campus that provide access to course registration. At least one staffed computer lab available.

Student Life *Housing:* on-campus residence required through sophomore year. *Options:* coed, men-only, women-only. *Activities and Organizations:* drama/theater group, student-run newspaper, radio and television station, choral group, marching band, Student Government Association, Black Student Association, University Union Board, International Friendship Club, Bureau of Cultural Affairs, national fraternities, national sororities. *Campus security:* 24-hour emergency response devices and patrols, student patrols, late-night transport/escort service, controlled dormitory access. *Student Services:* health clinic, personal/psychological counseling, women's center, legal services.

Athletics Member NCAA. All Division I except football (Division I-AA). *Intercollegiate sports:* baseball M(s), basketball M(s)/W(s), cross-country running M(s)/W(s), golf M(s), soccer M(s), softball W(s), swimming M(s)/W(s), tennis M(s)/W(s), track and field M(s)/W(s), volleyball W(s). *Intramural sports:* badminton M/W, basketball M/W, bowling M/W, cross-country running M/W, football M/W, golf M/W, racquetball M/W, soccer M/W, softball M/W, table tennis M/W, tennis M/W, volleyball M/W.

Standardized Tests *Required:* SAT I or ACT (for admission).

Costs (2002–03) *Tuition:* state resident $3165 full-time, $106 per credit hour part-time; nonresident $6330 full-time, $211 per credit hour part-time. No tuition increase for student's term of enrollment. *Required fees:* $1344 full-time, $34 per credit hour. *Room and board:* $5062; room only: $3032. Room and board charges vary according to board plan. *Waivers:* senior citizens and employees or children of employees.

Financial Aid Of all full-time matriculated undergraduates who enrolled in 2001, 8207 applied for aid, 4871 were judged to have need, 1855 had their need fully met. 367 Federal Work-Study jobs (averaging $1500). 1762 State and other part-time jobs (averaging $842). In 2001, 3162 non-need-based awards were made. *Average percent of need met:* 74%. *Average financial aid package:* $7265. *Average need-based loan:* $3266. *Average need-based gift aid:* $4717. *Average indebtedness upon graduation:* $12,900.

Applying *Options:* electronic application, deferred entrance. *Required:* high school transcript. *Application deadline:* 8/1 (freshmen), rolling (transfers). *Notification:* continuous until 8/3 (freshmen).

Admissions Contact Ms. Karen Helmers, Director of Admissions, Western Illinois University, 1 University Circle, 115 Sherman Hall, Macomb, IL 61455-1390. *Phone:* 309-298-3157. *Toll-free phone:* 877-742-5948. *Fax:* 309-298-3111. *E-mail:* karen_helmers@wiu.edu.

West Suburban College of Nursing
Oak Park, Illinois

- **Independent** 4-year, founded 1982
- **Calendar** semesters
- **Degrees** bachelor's (jointly with Concordia University [IL])
- **Suburban** 10-acre campus with easy access to Chicago
- **Coed,** 121 undergraduate students, 100% full-time, 98% women, 2% men
- **Moderately difficult** entrance level, 35% of applicants were admitted

Undergraduates 121 full-time. Students come from 5 states and territories, 3% are from out of state, 14% African American, 7% Asian American or Pacific Islander, 7% Hispanic American, 23% transferred in, 50% live on campus.

Freshmen *Admission:* 40 applied, 14 admitted, 14 enrolled. *Average high school GPA:* 3.3. *Test scores:* ACT scores over 18: 100%; ACT scores over 24: 44%; ACT scores over 30: 11%.

Faculty *Total:* 11, 73% full-time. *Student/faculty ratio:* 10:1.

Majors Nursing.

Academic Programs *Special study options:* academic remediation for entering students, adult/continuing education programs, advanced placement credit, external degree program, part-time degree program, summer session for credit.

Library Professional Library with 4,000 titles, 310 serial subscriptions.

Computers on Campus 20 computers available on campus for general student use. Internet access, at least one staffed computer lab available.

Student Life *Housing Options:* coed, men-only, women-only. *Activities and Organizations:* drama/theater group, student-run newspaper, choral group. *Campus security:* 24-hour emergency response devices and patrols, late-night transport/escort service, controlled dormitory access. *Student Services:* personal/psychological counseling.

Athletics Member NCAA. All Division III. *Intercollegiate sports:* basketball M/W, football M, golf M, tennis W, volleyball W.

Standardized Tests *Required:* SAT I or ACT (for admission).

Costs (2002–03) *Comprehensive fee:* $22,099 includes full-time tuition ($16,999) and room and board ($5100). No tuition increase for student's term of enrollment. *Payment plan:* installment.

Applying *Options:* common application, electronic application, deferred entrance. *Required:* essay or personal statement, high school transcript, minimum 2.5 GPA, 1 letter of recommendation. *Application deadline:* rolling (freshmen), rolling (transfers). *Notification:* continuous until 8/21 (freshmen).

Admissions Contact Ms. Dara P. Lawyer, Interim Director of Admission, West Suburban College of Nursing, 3 Erie Court, Oak Park, IL 60302. *Phone:* 708-763-6530. *Fax:* 708-763-1531. *E-mail:* wsadmis@crf.cuis.edu.

Wheaton College
Wheaton, Illinois

- **Independent nondenominational** comprehensive, founded 1860
- **Calendar** semesters
- **Degrees** bachelor's, master's, doctoral, and postbachelor's certificates
- **Suburban** 80-acre campus with easy access to Chicago
- **Endowment** $261.7 million
- **Coed,** 2,386 undergraduate students, 98% full-time, 51% women, 49% men
- **Very difficult** entrance level, 57% of applicants were admitted

Undergraduates 2,336 full-time, 50 part-time. Students come from 50 states and territories, 17 other countries, 79% are from out of state, 2% African American, 4% Asian American or Pacific Islander, 3% Hispanic American, 0.3%

Wheaton College (continued)
Native American, 1% international, 4% transferred in, 90% live on campus. *Retention:* 92% of 2001 full-time freshmen returned.

Freshmen *Admission:* 1,870 applied, 1,057 admitted, 574 enrolled. *Average high school GPA:* 3.69. *Test scores:* SAT verbal scores over 500: 98%; SAT math scores over 500: 96%; ACT scores over 18: 99%; SAT verbal scores over 600: 80%; SAT math scores over 600: 80%; ACT scores over 24: 92%; SAT verbal scores over 700: 32%; SAT math scores over 700: 30%; ACT scores over 30: 42%.

Faculty *Total:* 273, 66% full-time, 73% with terminal degrees. *Student/faculty ratio:* 11:1.

Majors Anthropology; archaeology; art; biblical studies; biology; business economics; chemistry; computer science; economics; elementary education; engineering related; English; environmental science; exercise sciences; French; geology; German; history; international relations; mathematics; multi/interdisciplinary studies related; music; music business management/merchandising; music (general performance); music history; music related; music teacher education; music theory and composition; nursing related; philosophy; physical sciences; physics; political science; psychology; religious education; religious studies; social studies education; sociology; Spanish; speech/rhetorical studies; theology/ministry related.

Academic Programs *Special study options:* advanced placement credit, double majors, independent study, internships, off-campus study, services for LD students, student-designed majors, study abroad, summer session for credit. *ROTC:* Army (b), Air Force (c). *Unusual degree programs:* 3-2 engineering with University of Illinois, Case Western Reserve University, Washington University in St. Louis, Illinois Institute of Technology; nursing with Rush University, Emory University, Goshen College, University of Rochester.

Library Buswell Memorial Library plus 1 other with 342,746 titles, 3,264 serial subscriptions, 32,761 audiovisual materials, an OPAC, a Web page.

Computers on Campus 150 computers available on campus for general student use. A campuswide network can be accessed from student residence rooms and from off campus. Internet access, at least one staffed computer lab available.

Student Life *Housing:* on-campus residence required through senior year. *Options:* men-only, women-only, cooperative. *Activities and Organizations:* drama/theater group, student-run newspaper, radio and television station, choral group, Intramurals, Discipleship Small Groups, Christian Service Council, Orientation Committee, Resident Assistant Staff. *Campus security:* 24-hour patrols, late-night transport/escort service, controlled dormitory access. *Student Services:* health clinic, personal/psychological counseling.

Athletics Member NCAA. All Division III. *Intercollegiate sports:* baseball M, basketball M/W, crew M(c)/W(c), cross-country running M/W, field hockey W(c), football M, golf M/W, ice hockey M(c), lacrosse M(c)/W(c), soccer M/W, softball W, swimming M/W, tennis M/W, track and field M/W, volleyball M(c)/W, wrestling M. *Intramural sports:* badminton M/W, basketball M/W, football M/W, golf M/W, soccer M/W, softball M/W, table tennis M/W, tennis M/W, volleyball M/W, weight lifting M/W.

Standardized Tests *Required:* SAT I or ACT (for admission). *Recommended:* SAT II: Writing Test (for admission).

Costs (2001–02) *Comprehensive fee:* $21,934 includes full-time tuition ($16,390) and room and board ($5544). Part-time tuition: $683 per hour. *Room and board:* College room only: $3240. Room and board charges vary according to board plan and housing facility. *Payment plans:* installment, deferred payment. *Waivers:* employees or children of employees.

Financial Aid Of all full-time matriculated undergraduates who enrolled in 2001, 1673 applied for aid, 1115 were judged to have need, 232 had their need fully met. 381 Federal Work-Study jobs (averaging $1295). In 2001, 473 non-need-based awards were made. *Average percent of need met:* 85%. *Average financial aid package:* $14,176. *Average need-based loan:* $4530. *Average need-based gift aid:* $9096. *Average indebtedness upon graduation:* $14,595.

Applying *Options:* early action, deferred entrance. *Application fee:* $35. *Required:* essay or personal statement, high school transcript, 2 letters of recommendation. *Recommended:* interview. *Application deadlines:* 1/15 (freshmen), 3/1 (transfers). *Notification:* 4/10 (freshmen), 12/31 (early action).

Admissions Contact Ms. Shawn Leftwich, Director of Admissions, Wheaton College, 501 College Avenue, Wheaton, IL 60187-5593. *Phone:* 630-752-5011. *Toll-free phone:* 800-222-2419. *Fax:* 630-752-5285. *E-mail:* admissions@wheaton.edu.

INDIANA

ANDERSON UNIVERSITY
Anderson, Indiana

- **Independent** comprehensive, founded 1917, affiliated with Church of God
- **Calendar** semesters
- **Degrees** associate, bachelor's, master's, doctoral, and first professional
- **Suburban** 100-acre campus with easy access to Indianapolis
- **Endowment** $7.1 million
- **Coed,** 2,093 undergraduate students, 90% full-time, 58% women, 42% men
- **Moderately difficult** entrance level, 76% of applicants were admitted

Undergraduates 1,881 full-time, 212 part-time. Students come from 43 states and territories, 15 other countries, 37% are from out of state, 5% African American, 1% Asian American or Pacific Islander, 0.7% Hispanic American, 0.3% Native American, 0.8% international, 6% transferred in, 63% live on campus. *Retention:* 73% of 2001 full-time freshmen returned.

Freshmen *Admission:* 1,839 applied, 1,391 admitted, 475 enrolled. *Average high school GPA:* 3.22. *Test scores:* SAT verbal scores over 500: 56%; SAT math scores over 500: 56%; ACT scores over 18: 88%; SAT verbal scores over 600: 17%; SAT math scores over 600: 23%; ACT scores over 24: 40%; SAT verbal scores over 700: 2%; SAT math scores over 700: 2%; ACT scores over 30: 7%.

Faculty *Total:* 223, 61% full-time, 35% with terminal degrees. *Student/faculty ratio:* 13:1.

Majors Accounting; art education; athletic training/sports medicine; biblical studies; biology; business; business administration; business economics; business marketing and marketing management; chemistry; computer science; criminal justice/law enforcement administration; education; elementary education; English; English education; family studies; finance; fine/studio arts; French; French language education; general studies; German; German language education; graphic design/commercial art/illustration; health education; health/physical education; history; information sciences/systems; mass communications; mathematics; mathematics/computer science; mathematics education; mathematics related; medical technology; music business management/merchandising; music (general performance); music teacher education; nursing; organizational behavior; philosophy; physical education; physics; political science; pre-dentistry; pre-engineering; pre-law; pre-medicine; pre-veterinary studies; psychology; religious music; religious studies; science education; social studies education; social work; sociology; Spanish; Spanish language education; speech education; theater arts/drama; theology.

Academic Programs *Special study options:* academic remediation for entering students, accelerated degree program, adult/continuing education programs, advanced placement credit, double majors, honors programs, independent study, internships, part-time degree program, services for LD students, student-designed majors, study abroad, summer session for credit. *Unusual degree programs:* 3-2 engineering with Purdue University.

Library Robert A. Nicholson Library with 245,019 titles, 937 serial subscriptions, 372 audiovisual materials, an OPAC, a Web page.

Computers on Campus 200 computers available on campus for general student use. A campuswide network can be accessed from student residence rooms and from off campus that provide access to microcomputer software. At least one staffed computer lab available.

Student Life *Housing:* on-campus residence required through junior year. *Options:* men-only, women-only. *Activities and Organizations:* drama/theater group, student-run newspaper, radio station, choral group, Social Clubs, Adult and Continuing Education Students Association, Multicultural Student Union, Campus Ministries, Intramurals. *Campus security:* 24-hour emergency response devices and patrols, student patrols, late-night transport/escort service, 24-hour crime line. *Student Services:* health clinic, personal/psychological counseling.

Athletics Member NCAA. All Division III. *Intercollegiate sports:* baseball M, basketball M/W, cross-country running M/W, football M, golf M/W, soccer M/W, softball W, tennis M/W, track and field M/W, volleyball W. *Intramural sports:* basketball M/W, rugby M(c), softball M/W, swimming M(c)/W(c), tennis M/W, volleyball M/W.

Standardized Tests *Required:* SAT I or ACT (for admission).

Costs (2001–02) *Comprehensive fee:* $20,400 includes full-time tuition ($15,380) and room and board ($5020). Part-time tuition: $641 per credit hour.

Part-time tuition and fees vary according to course load. *Room and board:* College room only: $2960. Room and board charges vary according to board plan. *Payment plan:* installment. *Waivers:* adult students and employees or children of employees.

Financial Aid Of all full-time matriculated undergraduates who enrolled in 2001, 1493 applied for aid, 1319 were judged to have need, 646 had their need fully met. 820 Federal Work-Study jobs (averaging $2185). 12 State and other part-time jobs (averaging $500). In 2001, 425 non-need-based awards were made. *Average percent of need met:* 96%. *Average financial aid package:* $14,449. *Average need-based loan:* $5033. *Average need-based gift aid:* $8348. *Average non-need based aid:* $5751. *Average indebtedness upon graduation:* $17,192.

Applying *Options:* deferred entrance. *Application fee:* $20. *Required:* high school transcript, minimum 2.0 GPA, 2 letters of recommendation, lifestyle statement. *Required for some:* interview. *Recommended:* essay or personal statement. *Application deadlines:* 7/1 (freshmen), 8/25 (transfers). *Notification:* continuous until 9/1 (freshmen).

Admissions Contact Mr. Jim King, Director of Admissions, Anderson University, 1100 East 5th Street, Anderson, IN 46012-3495. *Phone:* 765-641-4080. *Toll-free phone:* 800-421-3014 (in-state); 800-428-6414 (out-of-state). *Fax:* 765-641-3851. *E-mail:* info@anderson.edu.

BALL STATE UNIVERSITY

Muncie, Indiana

- **State-supported** university, founded 1918
- **Calendar** semesters
- **Degrees** associate, bachelor's, master's, doctoral, post-master's, and postbachelor's certificates
- **Suburban** 955-acre campus with easy access to Indianapolis
- **Coed,** 16,535 undergraduate students, 92% full-time, 53% women, 47% men
- **Moderately difficult** entrance level, 76% of applicants were admitted

Undergraduates 15,131 full-time, 1,404 part-time. Students come from 49 states and territories, 86 other countries, 8% are from out of state, 6% African American, 0.7% Asian American or Pacific Islander, 1% Hispanic American, 0.3% Native American, 0.0% international, 5% transferred in, 42% live on campus. *Retention:* 77% of 2001 full-time freshmen returned.

Freshmen *Admission:* 10,462 applied, 7,961 admitted, 3,777 enrolled. *Test scores:* SAT verbal scores over 500: 59%; SAT math scores over 500: 61%; ACT scores over 18: 91%; SAT verbal scores over 600: 16%; SAT math scores over 600: 19%; ACT scores over 24: 39%; SAT verbal scores over 700: 2%; SAT math scores over 700: 2%; ACT scores over 30: 5%.

Faculty *Total:* 1,097, 76% full-time, 63% with terminal degrees. *Student/faculty ratio:* 14:1.

Majors Accounting; actuarial science; advertising; anthropology; architectural environmental design; architecture; art; art education; athletic training/sports medicine; biology; botany; business administration; business economics; business education; business marketing and marketing management; cartography; cell biology; ceramic arts; chemical engineering technology; chemistry; city/community/regional planning; classics; computer science; criminal justice/law enforcement administration; criminology; dance; dietetics; drawing; early childhood education; ecology; economics; education; educational media design; elementary education; emergency medical technology; English; environmental science; exercise sciences; family/consumer studies; fashion merchandising; finance; fine/studio arts; food products retailing; French; genetics; geography; geology; German; graphic design/commercial art/illustration; graphic/printing equipment; Greek (modern); health education; health science; history; home economics; home economics education; human resources management; industrial arts; industrial radiologic technology; industrial technology; information sciences/systems; insurance/risk management; Japanese; journalism; landscape architecture; Latin American studies; Latin (ancient and medieval); legal administrative assistant; liberal arts and sciences/liberal studies; management information systems/business data processing; marine biology; mathematics; medical technology; microbiology/bacteriology; modern languages; molecular biology; music; musical instrument technology; music (piano and organ performance); music teacher education; music (voice and choral/opera performance); natural resources management; nuclear medical technology; nursing; occupational safety/health technology; paralegal/legal assistant; philosophy; photography; physical education; physics; plastics engineering; plastics technology; political science; pre-dentistry; pre-law; pre-medicine; printmaking; psychology; public relations; real estate; recreation/leisure facilities management; religious studies; respiratory therapy; science education; sculpture; secondary education; secretarial science; social sciences; social work; sociology; soil conservation; Spanish; special education; speech-language pathology/audiology; speech/rhetorical studies; sport/fitness administration; stringed instruments; telecommunications; theater arts/drama; trade/industrial education; travel/tourism management; wildlife biology; wind/percussion instruments; zoology.

Academic Programs *Special study options:* academic remediation for entering students, adult/continuing education programs, advanced placement credit, cooperative education, distance learning, double majors, English as a second language, freshman honors college, honors programs, independent study, internships, part-time degree program, study abroad, summer session for credit. *ROTC:* Army (b). *Unusual degree programs:* 3-2 engineering with Purdue University, Tri-State University.

Library Bracken Library plus 3 others with 1.1 million titles, 4,091 serial subscriptions, 501,621 audiovisual materials, an OPAC, a Web page.

Computers on Campus 1500 computers available on campus for general student use. A campuswide network can be accessed from student residence rooms and from off campus. At least one staffed computer lab available.

Student Life *Housing:* on-campus residence required for freshman year. *Options:* coed. *Activities and Organizations:* drama/theater group, student-run newspaper, radio and television station, choral group, marching band, Student Association, Excellence in Leadership, fraternities/sororities, Black Student Association, Student Voluntary Services, national fraternities, national sororities. *Campus security:* 24-hour emergency response devices and patrols, late-night transport/escort service, controlled dormitory access. *Student Services:* health clinic, personal/psychological counseling, women's center, legal services.

Athletics Member NCAA. All Division I except football (Division I-A). *Intercollegiate sports:* baseball M(s), basketball M(s)/W(s), cross-country running M(s)/W(s), equestrian sports M(c)/W(c), field hockey W(s), golf M(s), gymnastics W(s), ice hockey M(c), rugby M(c)/W(c), sailing M(c)/W(c), soccer M(c)/W, softball W(s), swimming M(s)/W(s), tennis M(s)/W(s), track and field M(s)/W(s), volleyball M(s)/W(s), water polo M(c), wrestling M(c). *Intramural sports:* archery M/W, badminton M(c)/W(c), basketball M/W, bowling M(c)/W(c), cross-country running M/W, fencing M(c)/W(c), football M, golf M, lacrosse M(c), racquetball M/W, soccer M, softball M/W, squash M/W, swimming M/W, table tennis M(c)/W(c), tennis M/W, track and field M/W, volleyball M/W, weight lifting M(c)/W(c).

Standardized Tests *Required:* SAT I or ACT (for admission).

Costs (2001–02) *Tuition:* state resident $3924 full-time; nonresident $10,800 full-time. Part-time tuition and fees vary according to course load. *Required fees:* $110 full-time. *Room and board:* $5100; room only: $3915. Room and board charges vary according to board plan and housing facility. *Payment plan:* installment. *Waivers:* employees or children of employees.

Financial Aid Of all full-time matriculated undergraduates who enrolled in 2001, 10754 applied for aid, 7402 were judged to have need, 3686 had their need fully met. In 2001, 3933 non-need-based awards were made. *Average percent of need met:* 73%. *Average financial aid package:* $6031. *Average need-based loan:* $2881. *Average need-based gift aid:* $3786. *Average indebtedness upon graduation:* $16,197.

Applying *Options:* deferred entrance. *Application fee:* $25. *Required:* high school transcript. *Required for some:* essay or personal statement, letters of recommendation, interview. *Application deadline:* rolling (freshmen), rolling (transfers).

Admissions Contact Dr. Lawrence Waters, Dean of Admissions and Financial Aid, Ball State University, 2000 University Avenue, Muncie, IN 47306. *Phone:* 765-285-8300. *Toll-free phone:* 800-482-4BSU. *Fax:* 765-285-1632. *E-mail:* askus@wp.bsu.edu.

BETHEL COLLEGE

Mishawaka, Indiana

- **Independent** comprehensive, founded 1947, affiliated with Missionary Church
- **Calendar** semesters
- **Degrees** associate, bachelor's, and master's
- **Suburban** 70-acre campus
- **Endowment** $3.8 million
- **Coed,** 1,541 undergraduate students, 73% full-time, 64% women, 36% men
- **Moderately difficult** entrance level, 69% of applicants were admitted

Undergraduates 1,129 full-time, 412 part-time. Students come from 27 states and territories, 14 other countries, 27% are from out of state, 9% African American, 1% Asian American or Pacific Islander, 1% Hispanic American, 0.4% Native American, 2% international, 12% transferred in, 49% live on campus. *Retention:* 86% of 2001 full-time freshmen returned.

Freshmen *Admission:* 716 applied, 497 admitted, 277 enrolled. *Average high school GPA:* 3.27. *Test scores:* SAT verbal scores over 500: 63%; SAT math scores over 500: 65%; ACT scores over 18: 84%; SAT verbal scores over 600: 26%; SAT

Bethel College (continued)
math scores over 600: 26%; ACT scores over 24: 40%; SAT verbal scores over 700: 4%; SAT math scores over 700: 2%; ACT scores over 30: 12%.
Faculty *Total:* 106, 71% full-time, 63% with terminal degrees. *Student/faculty ratio:* 18:1.
Majors Accounting; art; biblical languages/literatures; biblical studies; biology; business administration; business education; chemistry; communications; computer/information sciences; computer science; criminal justice studies; design/visual communications; divinity/ministry; early childhood education; education; elementary education; engineering; English; English education; environmental biology; exercise sciences; history; human services; interior design; international business; journalism; liberal arts and sciences/liberal studies; mathematics; mathematics/computer science; mathematics education; middle school education; missionary studies; music; music (general performance); music (piano and organ performance); music teacher education; music (voice and choral/opera performance); nursing; philosophy; physical education; physics; pre-dentistry; pre-law; pre-medicine; psychology; religious music; science education; sign language interpretation; social sciences; social studies education; sociology; sport/fitness administration; theater arts/drama.
Academic Programs *Special study options:* academic remediation for entering students, accelerated degree program, adult/continuing education programs, advanced placement credit, double majors, freshman honors college, honors programs, independent study, internships, off-campus study, part-time degree program, study abroad, summer session for credit. *ROTC:* Army (c), Air Force (c). *Unusual degree programs:* 3-2 engineering with University of Notre Dame.
Library Otis and Elizabeth Bowen Library with 99,381 titles, 3,450 serial subscriptions, 3,740 audiovisual materials, an OPAC, a Web page.
Computers on Campus 110 computers available on campus for general student use. A campuswide network can be accessed from student residence rooms and from off campus. Internet access, at least one staffed computer lab available.
Student Life *Housing:* on-campus residence required through sophomore year. *Options:* men-only, women-only. *Activities and Organizations:* drama/theater group, student-run newspaper, radio station, choral group, "Task Force" Mission Teams, Student Council, Center for Community Service, Fellowship of Christian Athletes. *Campus security:* 24-hour patrols, student patrols, controlled dormitory access. *Student Services:* health clinic, personal/psychological counseling.
Athletics Member NAIA, NCCAA. *Intercollegiate sports:* baseball M(s), basketball M(s)/W(s), cross-country running M(s)/W(s), golf M(s), soccer M(s)/W(s), softball W(s), tennis M(s)/W(s), track and field M(s)/W(s), volleyball W(s), wrestling M(c). *Intramural sports:* basketball M/W, bowling M/W, football M/W, racquetball M/W, soccer M/W, softball M/W, table tennis M/W, tennis M/W, track and field M/W, volleyball M/W, weight lifting M/W.
Standardized Tests *Required:* SAT I or ACT (for admission).
Costs (2001–02) *One-time required fee:* $400. *Comprehensive fee:* $17,750 includes full-time tuition ($13,300), mandatory fees ($100), and room and board ($4350). Part-time tuition: $250 per hour. Part-time tuition and fees vary according to course load. *Required fees:* $40 per year. *Room and board:* Room and board charges vary according to board plan and housing facility. *Payment plan:* installment. *Waivers:* employees or children of employees.
Financial Aid Of all full-time matriculated undergraduates who enrolled in 2001, 1110 applied for aid, 1072 were judged to have need, 600 had their need fully met. *Average percent of need met:* 90%. *Average financial aid package:* $10,895. *Average need-based loan:* $3722. *Average need-based gift aid:* $3018. *Average non-need based aid:* $7075. *Average indebtedness upon graduation:* $14,330.
Applying *Options:* common application, electronic application, early admission, deferred entrance. *Application fee:* $25. *Required:* essay or personal statement, high school transcript, minimum 2.0 GPA, 1 letter of recommendation. *Recommended:* minimum 2.5 GPA, interview. *Application deadlines:* 8/1 (freshmen), 8/1 (transfers). *Notification:* continuous (freshmen).
Admissions Contact Ms. Andrea M. Helmuth, Director of Admissions, Bethel College, 1001 West McKinley Avenue, Mishawaka, IN 46545-5591. *Phone:* 574-257-3319. *Toll-free phone:* 800-422-4101. *Fax:* 574-257-3335. *E-mail:* admissions@bethelcollege.edu.

BUTLER UNIVERSITY
Indianapolis, Indiana

- **Independent** comprehensive, founded 1855
- **Calendar** semesters
- **Degrees** associate, bachelor's, master's, first professional, and postbachelor's certificates
- **Urban** 290-acre campus
- **Endowment** $139.0 million
- **Coed,** 3,424 undergraduate students, 97% full-time, 63% women, 37% men
- **Moderately difficult** entrance level, 85% of applicants were admitted

With an undergraduate population of 3,500, Butler University is committed to the interactive learning in each of its five colleges. Students take practical classroom knowledge and apply it to professional experiences in Indianapolis that are tailored to individual interests and talents.

Undergraduates 3,337 full-time, 87 part-time. Students come from 43 states and territories, 40 other countries, 40% are from out of state, 4% African American, 2% Asian American or Pacific Islander, 1% Hispanic American, 0.1% Native American, 2% international, 3% transferred in, 62% live on campus. *Retention:* 81% of 2001 full-time freshmen returned.
Freshmen *Admission:* 3,168 applied, 2,677 admitted, 933 enrolled. *Average high school GPA:* 3.60. *Test scores:* SAT verbal scores over 500: 88%; SAT math scores over 500: 90%; ACT scores over 18: 100%; SAT verbal scores over 600: 40%; SAT math scores over 600: 49%; ACT scores over 24: 77%; SAT verbal scores over 700: 5%; SAT math scores over 700: 8%; ACT scores over 30: 16%.
Faculty *Total:* 438, 59% full-time, 58% with terminal degrees. *Student/faculty ratio:* 13:1.
Majors Accounting; actuarial science; anthropology; arts management; athletic training/sports medicine; biology; business administration; business economics; business marketing and marketing management; chemistry; computer science; criminal justice studies; dance; economics; elementary education; English; finance; French; German; Greek (modern); history; international business; international relations; journalism; Latin (ancient and medieval); liberal arts and sciences/liberal studies; mathematics; medicinal/pharmaceutical chemistry; music; music business management/merchandising; music history; music (piano and organ performance); music teacher education; music (voice and choral/opera performance); pharmacy; philosophy; physician assistant; physics; political science; psychology; public relations; religious studies; secondary education; sociology; Spanish; speech-language pathology/audiology; speech/rhetorical studies; stringed instruments; telecommunications; theater arts/drama; wind/percussion instruments.
Academic Programs *Special study options:* accelerated degree program, adult/continuing education programs, advanced placement credit, cooperative education, double majors, English as a second language, honors programs, independent study, internships, off-campus study, part-time degree program, study abroad, summer session for credit. *ROTC:* Army (c), Air Force (c). *Unusual degree programs:* 3-2 engineering with Indiana University-Purdue University Indianapolis; forestry with Duke University.
Library Irwin Library System plus 1 other with 345,415 titles, 2,202 serial subscriptions, 13,316 audiovisual materials, an OPAC, a Web page.
Computers on Campus 250 computers available on campus for general student use. A campuswide network can be accessed from student residence rooms and from off campus that provide access to e-mail. Internet access, at least one staffed computer lab available.
Student Life *Housing:* on-campus residence required for freshman year. *Options:* coed, women-only. *Activities and Organizations:* drama/theater group, student-run newspaper, radio and television station, choral group, marching band, University YMCA, Student Government Association, Academic Service Honoraries, Alpha Phi Omega, Mortar Board, national fraternities, national sororities. *Campus security:* 24-hour emergency response devices and patrols, late-night transport/escort service, controlled dormitory access. *Student Services:* health clinic, personal/psychological counseling.
Athletics Member NCAA. All Division I except football (Division III). *Intercollegiate sports:* baseball M(s), basketball M(s)/W(s), crew M(c)/W(c), cross-country running M(s)/W(s), football M, golf M(s)/W(s), ice hockey M(c), lacrosse M(s), rugby M(c), soccer M(s)/W(s), softball W(s), swimming M(s)/W(s), tennis M(s)/W(s), track and field M/W, volleyball W(s). *Intramural sports:* badminton M/W, baseball M, basketball M/W, bowling M/W, football M, soccer M/W, softball M/W, swimming M/W, table tennis M/W, tennis M/W, track and field M/W, volleyball M/W, weight lifting M/W.
Standardized Tests *Required:* SAT I or ACT (for admission). *Recommended:* SAT II: Subject Tests (for admission).
Costs (2001–02) *Comprehensive fee:* $25,580 includes full-time tuition ($18,940), mandatory fees ($190), and room and board ($6450). Full-time tuition and fees vary according to program. Part-time tuition: $800 per credit. Part-time tuition and fees vary according to program. *Room and board:* Room and board charges vary according to board plan and housing facility. *Payment plans:* tuition prepayment, installment. *Waivers:* employees or children of employees.
Financial Aid Of all full-time matriculated undergraduates who enrolled in 2001, 3136 applied for aid, 2098 were judged to have need, 517 had their need fully met. In 2001, 936 non-need-based awards were made. *Average financial aid package:* $14,900. *Average need-based loan:* $5129. *Average need-based gift aid:* $10,500. *Average non-need based aid:* $7990.

Applying *Options:* common application, electronic application, early action, deferred entrance. *Application fee:* $25. *Required:* essay or personal statement, high school transcript. *Required for some:* interview, audition. *Application deadlines:* 8/15 (freshmen), 8/15 (transfers). *Notification:* continuous (freshmen), 1/15 (early action).

Admissions Contact Mr. William Preble, Dean of Admissions, Butler University, 4600 Sunset Avenue, Indianapolis, IN 46208-3485. *Phone:* 317-940-8100 Ext. 8124. *Toll-free phone:* 888-940-8100. *Fax:* 317-940-8150. *E-mail:* admission@butler.edu.

CALUMET COLLEGE OF SAINT JOSEPH
Whiting, Indiana

Admissions Contact Mr. Thomas A. Clark, Vice President for Enrollment Management, Calumet College of Saint Joseph, 2400 New York Avenue, Whiting, IN 46394-2195. *Phone:* 219-473-4215. *Toll-free phone:* 877-700-9100. *Fax:* 219-473-4259.

CROSSROADS BIBLE COLLEGE
Indianapolis, Indiana

Admissions Contact 601 North Shortridge Road, Indianapolis, IN 46219. *Toll-free phone:* 800-273-2224.

DEPAUW UNIVERSITY
Greencastle, Indiana

- **Independent** 4-year, founded 1837, affiliated with United Methodist Church
- **Calendar** 4-1-4
- **Degree** bachelor's
- **Small-town** 175-acre campus with easy access to Indianapolis
- **Endowment** $445.1 million
- **Coed,** 2,219 undergraduate students, 98% full-time, 56% women, 44% men
- **Moderately difficult** entrance level, 53% of applicants were admitted

Undergraduates 2,178 full-time, 41 part-time. Students come from 43 states and territories, 16 other countries, 46% are from out of state, 6% African American, 2% Asian American or Pacific Islander, 2% Hispanic American, 0.4% Native American, 1% international, 0.6% transferred in, 94% live on campus. *Retention:* 92% of 2001 full-time freshmen returned.

Freshmen *Admission:* 3,004 applied, 1,591 admitted, 620 enrolled. *Average high school GPA:* 3.59. *Test scores:* SAT verbal scores over 500: 94%; SAT math scores over 500: 93%; ACT scores over 18: 100%; SAT verbal scores over 600: 48%; SAT math scores over 600: 53%; ACT scores over 24: 77%; SAT verbal scores over 700: 11%; SAT math scores over 700: 10%; ACT scores over 30: 17%.

Faculty *Total:* 254, 82% full-time, 82% with terminal degrees. *Student/faculty ratio:* 10:1.

Majors Anthropology; art history; athletic training/sports medicine; biology; chemistry; classics; computer science; earth sciences; East Asian studies; economics; elementary education; English; English composition; fine/studio arts; French; geography; geology; German; Greek (modern); history; interdisciplinary studies; Latin (ancient and medieval); mass communications; mathematics; medical technology; music; music business management/merchandising; music (general performance); music teacher education; music theory and composition; peace/conflict studies; philosophy; physics; political science; psychology; religious studies; romance languages; Russian/Slavic studies; sociology; Spanish; women's studies.

Academic Programs *Special study options:* advanced placement credit, double majors, honors programs, independent study, internships, off-campus study, part-time degree program, student-designed majors, study abroad. *ROTC:* Army (c), Air Force (c). *Unusual degree programs:* 3-2 engineering with Columbia University, Washington University in St. Louis, Case Western Reserve University; nursing with Rush University; medical technology with Methodist Hospital, National-Louis University.

Library Roy O. West Library plus 3 others with 545,736 titles, 2,134 serial subscriptions, 12,126 audiovisual materials, an OPAC, a Web page.

Computers on Campus 235 computers available on campus for general student use. A campuswide network can be accessed from student residence rooms and from off campus. Internet access, online (class) registration, at least one staffed computer lab available.

Student Life *Housing:* on-campus residence required through senior year. *Options:* coed. *Activities and Organizations:* drama/theater group, student-run newspaper, radio and television station, choral group, Community Service Program, Union Board, Student Congress, national fraternities, national sororities. *Campus security:* 24-hour emergency response devices and patrols, late-night transport/escort service, controlled dormitory access. *Student Services:* health clinic, personal/psychological counseling.

Athletics Member NCAA. All Division III. *Intercollegiate sports:* baseball M, basketball M/W, cross-country running M/W, field hockey W, football M, golf M/W, soccer M/W, softball W, swimming M/W, tennis M/W, track and field M/W, volleyball W. *Intramural sports:* badminton M/W, basketball M/W, bowling M/W, football M, golf M, racquetball M/W, soccer M/W, softball M/W, swimming M/W, table tennis M/W, tennis M/W, track and field M/W, volleyball M/W, wrestling M.

Standardized Tests *Required:* SAT I or ACT (for admission).

Costs (2001–02) *Comprehensive fee:* $28,000 includes full-time tuition ($21,100), mandatory fees ($400), and room and board ($6500). Part-time tuition: $630 per semester hour. *Payment plans:* tuition prepayment, installment, deferred payment. *Waivers:* employees or children of employees.

Financial Aid Of all full-time matriculated undergraduates who enrolled in 2001, 1400 applied for aid, 1167 were judged to have need, 1167 had their need fully met. 678 Federal Work-Study jobs (averaging $1533). 41 State and other part-time jobs (averaging $1232). In 2001, 998 non-need-based awards were made. *Average percent of need met:* 100%. *Average financial aid package:* $18,740. *Average need-based loan:* $3179. *Average need-based gift aid:* $16,789. *Average non-need based aid:* $11,403. *Average indebtedness upon graduation:* $14,481.

Applying *Options:* common application, electronic application, early admission, early decision, early action, deferred entrance. *Required:* essay or personal statement, high school transcript, 1 letter of recommendation. *Recommended:* minimum 3.0 GPA, interview. *Application deadlines:* 2/1 (freshmen), 3/1 (transfers). *Early decision:* 11/1. *Notification:* 1/1 (early decision), 2/15 (early action).

Admissions Contact Director of Admission, DePauw University, 101 East Seminary Street, Greencastle, IN 46135-0037. *Phone:* 765-658-4006. *Toll-free phone:* 800-447-2495. *Fax:* 765-658-4007. *E-mail:* admission@depauw.edu.

EARLHAM COLLEGE
Richmond, Indiana

- **Independent** comprehensive, founded 1847, affiliated with Society of Friends
- **Calendar** semesters
- **Degrees** bachelor's and master's
- **Small-town** 800-acre campus with easy access to Cincinnati, Indianapolis, and Dayton
- **Endowment** $353.4 million
- **Coed,** 1,078 undergraduate students, 98% full-time, 55% women, 45% men
- **Moderately difficult** entrance level, 80% of applicants were admitted

Undergraduates 1,054 full-time, 24 part-time. Students come from 48 states and territories, 30 other countries, 72% are from out of state, 8% African American, 2% Asian American or Pacific Islander, 2% Hispanic American, 0.1% Native American, 5% international, 3% transferred in, 84% live on campus. *Retention:* 89% of 2001 full-time freshmen returned.

Freshmen *Admission:* 1,153 applied, 923 admitted, 267 enrolled. *Average high school GPA:* 3.35. *Test scores:* SAT verbal scores over 500: 89%; SAT math scores over 500: 79%; ACT scores over 18: 97%; SAT verbal scores over 600: 66%; SAT math scores over 600: 46%; ACT scores over 24: 67%; SAT verbal scores over 700: 20%; SAT math scores over 700: 11%; ACT scores over 30: 23%.

Faculty *Total:* 107, 86% full-time, 90% with terminal degrees. *Student/faculty ratio:* 11:1.

Majors African-American studies; art; Asian studies; biology; business administration; chemistry; classics; computer science; economics; education; English; environmental science; French; geology; German; history; interdisciplinary studies; international relations; Latin American studies; mathematics; music; peace/conflict studies; philosophy; physics; political science; pre-law; pre-medicine; psychology; religious studies; sociology; Spanish; theater arts/drama; women's studies.

Academic Programs *Special study options:* accelerated degree program, advanced placement credit, double majors, independent study, internships, off-campus study, student-designed majors, study abroad. *Unusual degree programs:* 3-2 business administration with Washington University in St. Louis; engineering with Columbia University, University of Michigan, Rensselaer Polytechnic Institute; forestry with Duke University; nursing with Case Western Reserve University, Washington University in St. Louis, Emory University, Columbia University; architecture with Washington University in St. Louis.

Library Lilly Library plus 1 other with 389,000 titles, 1,195 serial subscriptions, an OPAC, a Web page.

Earlham College (continued)

Computers on Campus 116 computers available on campus for general student use. A campuswide network can be accessed from student residence rooms. Internet access, online (class) registration, at least one staffed computer lab available.

Student Life *Housing:* on-campus residence required through senior year. *Options:* coed, men-only, women-only, cooperative. *Activities and Organizations:* drama/theater group, student-run newspaper, radio station, choral group, Gospel Revelations Chorus, Dance Alloy, club sports, student government, Black Leadership Action Coalition. *Campus security:* 24-hour emergency response devices and patrols, student patrols, late-night transport/escort service, controlled dormitory access. *Student Services:* health clinic, personal/psychological counseling, women's center.

Athletics Member NCAA. All Division III. *Intercollegiate sports:* baseball M, basketball M/W, cross-country running M/W, equestrian sports M(c)/W(c), field hockey W, football M, lacrosse M(c)/W, rugby M(c), soccer M/W, swimming M(c)/W(c), tennis M/W, track and field M/W, volleyball M(c)/W. *Intramural sports:* basketball M/W, football M/W, racquetball M/W, soccer M/W, softball M/W, tennis M/W, volleyball M/W.

Standardized Tests *Required:* SAT I or ACT (for admission). *Recommended:* SAT I (for admission).

Costs (2001–02) *Comprehensive fee:* $27,446 includes full-time tuition ($21,700), mandatory fees ($608), and room and board ($5138). Part-time tuition: $723 per credit hour. *Room and board:* College room only: $2500. Room and board charges vary according to board plan. *Payment plans:* tuition prepayment, installment, deferred payment. *Waivers:* employees or children of employees.

Financial Aid Of all full-time matriculated undergraduates who enrolled in 2001, 780 applied for aid, 710 were judged to have need, 175 had their need fully met. In 2001, 145 non-need-based awards were made. *Average percent of need met:* 94%. *Average financial aid package:* $19,343. *Average need-based loan:* $4170. *Average need-based gift aid:* $12,200. *Average non-need based aid:* $5600. *Average indebtedness upon graduation:* $14,918.

Applying *Options:* common application, electronic application, early admission, early decision, early action, deferred entrance. *Application fee:* $30. *Required:* essay or personal statement, high school transcript, minimum 3.0 GPA, 2 letters of recommendation. *Recommended:* interview. *Application deadlines:* 2/15 (freshmen), 4/1 (transfers). *Early decision:* 12/1. *Notification:* 3/15 (freshmen), 12/15 (early decision), 2/1 (early action).

Admissions Contact Director of Admissions, Earlham College, 801 National Road West, Richmond, IN 47374. *Phone:* 765-983-1600. *Toll-free phone:* 800-327-5426. *Fax:* 765-983-1560. *E-mail:* admission@earlham.edu.

FRANKLIN COLLEGE OF INDIANA
Franklin, Indiana

- **Independent** 4-year, founded 1834, affiliated with American Baptist Churches in the U.S.A.
- **Calendar** 4-1-4
- **Degree** bachelor's
- **Small-town** 74-acre campus with easy access to Indianapolis
- **Endowment** $73.9 million
- **Coed,** 1,028 undergraduate students, 93% full-time, 55% women, 45% men
- **Moderately difficult** entrance level, 77% of applicants were admitted

A Franklin College education combines traditional liberal arts learning with career-oriented preparation in order to create a solid foundation for lifelong leadership skills and professional success. The College's nationally recognized Leadership and Professional Development Programs are distinguishing features of the Franklin curriculum and serve as proof of their commitment to developing students' broad-based communication, professional, and problem-solving skills. Students are offered a wide variety of diverse opportunities for creative learning and benefit from the small class sizes and personalized relationships with the faculty.

Undergraduates 959 full-time, 69 part-time. Students come from 19 states and territories, 5 other countries, 7% are from out of state, 3% African American, 0.4% Asian American or Pacific Islander, 0.8% Hispanic American, 0.6% international, 3% transferred in, 74% live on campus. *Retention:* 72% of 2001 full-time freshmen returned.

Freshmen *Admission:* 918 applied, 703 admitted, 284 enrolled. *Test scores:* SAT verbal scores over 500: 60%; SAT math scores over 500: 66%; ACT scores over 18: 72%; SAT verbal scores over 600: 18%; SAT math scores over 600: 17%; ACT scores over 24: 31%; SAT verbal scores over 700: 2%; SAT math scores over 700: 1%; ACT scores over 30: 4%.

Faculty *Total:* 103, 56% full-time, 53% with terminal degrees. *Student/faculty ratio:* 12:1.

Majors Accounting; American studies; applied mathematics; athletic training/sports medicine; biology; biology education; broadcast journalism; business; business administration; business marketing and marketing management; Canadian studies; chemistry; chemistry education; computer/information sciences; computer science; economics; education (K-12); elementary education; English; English education; finance; French; French language education; history; history education; international business; journalism; mathematics; mathematics education; philosophy; physical education; physics; political science; psychology; recreation/leisure studies; religious studies; social studies education; sociology; Spanish; Spanish language education; teacher education, specific programs related; theater arts/drama.

Academic Programs *Special study options:* academic remediation for entering students, advanced placement credit, double majors, independent study, internships, off-campus study, part-time degree program, services for LD students, study abroad, summer session for credit. *ROTC:* Army (c). *Unusual degree programs:* 3-2 engineering with Washington University in St. Louis; forestry with Duke University; nursing with Rush University; public health with University of South Florida.

Library Hamilton Library plus 1 other with 110,258 titles, 843 serial subscriptions, 5,910 audiovisual materials, an OPAC, a Web page.

Computers on Campus 105 computers available on campus for general student use. A campuswide network can be accessed from student residence rooms and from off campus. At least one staffed computer lab available.

Student Life *Housing:* on-campus residence required through junior year. *Options:* coed, men-only, women-only, disabled students. *Activities and Organizations:* drama/theater group, student-run newspaper, radio and television station, choral group, Intervarsity, FC Volunteers, Education Club, Student Congress, Society of Professional Journalist, national fraternities, national sororities. *Campus security:* 24-hour emergency response devices and patrols, late-night transport/escort service. *Student Services:* health clinic, personal/psychological counseling.

Athletics Member NCAA. All Division III. *Intercollegiate sports:* baseball M, basketball M/W, cross-country running M/W, football M, golf M/W, soccer M/W, softball W, tennis M/W, track and field M/W, volleyball W. *Intramural sports:* basketball M/W, football M, softball M/W, volleyball M/W.

Standardized Tests *Required:* SAT I or ACT (for admission).

Costs (2002–03) *Comprehensive fee:* $19,905 includes full-time tuition ($14,750), mandatory fees ($135), and room and board ($5020). Part-time tuition and fees vary according to course load. *Room and board:* College room only: $3090. Room and board charges vary according to board plan and housing facility. *Payment plan:* installment. *Waivers:* senior citizens and employees or children of employees.

Financial Aid Of all full-time matriculated undergraduates who enrolled in 2001, 877 applied for aid, 745 were judged to have need, 282 had their need fully met. 267 Federal Work-Study jobs (averaging $1270). 29 State and other part-time jobs (averaging $950). In 2001, 221 non-need-based awards were made. *Average percent of need met:* 91%. *Average financial aid package:* $12,821. *Average need-based loan:* $3570. *Average need-based gift aid:* $9892. *Average non-need based aid:* $9131. *Average indebtedness upon graduation:* $4980. *Financial aid deadline:* 3/1.

Applying *Options:* common application, electronic application, deferred entrance. *Application fee:* $30. *Required:* essay or personal statement, high school transcript, 1 letter of recommendation. *Recommended:* interview. *Application deadline:* 5/1 (freshmen). *Notification:* continuous (freshmen).

Admissions Contact Alan Hill, Vice President for Enrollment Management, Franklin College of Indiana, 501 East Monroe Street, Franklin, IN 46131-2598. *Phone:* 317-738-8062. *Toll-free phone:* 800-852-0232. *Fax:* 317-738-8274. *E-mail:* admissions@franklincollege.edu.

GOSHEN COLLEGE
Goshen, Indiana

- **Independent Mennonite** 4-year, founded 1894
- **Calendar** semesters
- **Degree** bachelor's
- **Small-town** 135-acre campus
- **Endowment** $88.8 million
- **Coed,** 986 undergraduate students, 86% full-time, 61% women, 39% men
- **Moderately difficult** entrance level, 68% of applicants were admitted

Undergraduates 851 full-time, 135 part-time. Students come from 37 states and territories, 36 other countries, 51% are from out of state, 2% African American, 1% Asian American or Pacific Islander, 3% Hispanic American, 10% international, 6% transferred in, 64% live on campus. *Retention:* 77% of 2001 full-time freshmen returned.

Freshmen *Admission:* 414 applied, 283 admitted, 177 enrolled. *Average high school GPA:* 3.39. *Test scores:* SAT verbal scores over 500: 77%; SAT math scores over 500: 74%; ACT scores over 18: 96%; SAT verbal scores over 600: 43%; SAT math scores over 600: 37%; ACT scores over 24: 68%; SAT verbal scores over 700: 13%; SAT math scores over 700: 13%; ACT scores over 30: 26%.

Faculty *Total:* 120, 62% full-time, 40% with terminal degrees. *Student/faculty ratio:* 11:1.

Majors Accounting; art; art education; art therapy; biblical studies; bilingual/bicultural education; biology; broadcast journalism; business administration; business education; chemistry; child care/development; computer science; early childhood education; economics; education; elementary education; English; environmental science; family/community studies; German; Hispanic-American studies; history; information sciences/systems; journalism; liberal arts and sciences/liberal studies; mass communications; mathematics; music; music teacher education; natural sciences; nursing; peace/conflict studies; physical education; physical sciences; physics; political science; pre-dentistry; pre-law; pre-medicine; pre-veterinary studies; psychology; religious studies; science education; secondary education; sign language interpretation; social work; sociology; Spanish; teaching English as a second language; theater arts/drama.

Academic Programs *Special study options:* academic remediation for entering students, accelerated degree program, adult/continuing education programs, advanced placement credit, cooperative education, distance learning, double majors, English as a second language, freshman honors college, honors programs, independent study, internships, off-campus study, part-time degree program, services for LD students, student-designed majors, study abroad, summer session for credit. *Unusual degree programs:* 3-2 engineering with Case Western Reserve University, Washington University in St. Louis, Pennsylvania State University University Park Campus, University of Illinois.

Library Harold and Wilma Good Library plus 2 others with 124,000 titles, 750 serial subscriptions, 1,800 audiovisual materials, an OPAC, a Web page.

Computers on Campus 160 computers available on campus for general student use. A campuswide network can be accessed from student residence rooms and from off campus that provide access to online services. Internet access, at least one staffed computer lab available.

Student Life *Housing:* on-campus residence required through junior year. *Options:* coed, women-only. *Activities and Organizations:* drama/theater group, student-run newspaper, radio and television station, choral group, Business Club, Black Student Union, Nontraditional Student Network, Goshen Student Women's Organization, International Student Club. *Campus security:* 24-hour emergency response devices and patrols, late-night transport/escort service. *Student Services:* health clinic, personal/psychological counseling, women's center.

Athletics Member NAIA. *Intercollegiate sports:* baseball M(s), basketball M(s)/W(s), cross-country running M(s)/W(s), golf M(s), soccer M(s)/W(s), softball W(s), tennis M(s)/W(s), track and field M(s)/W(s), volleyball W(s). *Intramural sports:* badminton M/W, basketball M/W, cross-country running M/W, racquetball M/W, skiing (cross-country) M/W, soccer M/W, softball W, swimming M/W, table tennis M/W, tennis M/W, volleyball M/W, weight lifting M/W.

Standardized Tests *Required:* SAT I or ACT (for admission).

Costs (2002–03) *Comprehensive fee:* $20,450 includes full-time tuition ($14,700), mandatory fees ($300), and room and board ($5450). Part-time tuition and fees vary according to course load. *Room and board:* College room only: $2780. Room and board charges vary according to board plan and student level. *Payment plan:* installment. *Waivers:* employees or children of employees.

Financial Aid Of all full-time matriculated undergraduates who enrolled in 2001, 849 applied for aid, 559 were judged to have need, 264 had their need fully met. 387 Federal Work-Study jobs (averaging $1050). 16 State and other part-time jobs (averaging $1701). In 2001, 228 non-need-based awards were made. *Average percent of need met:* 93%. *Average financial aid package:* $12,961. *Average need-based loan:* $4366. *Average need-based gift aid:* $7449. *Average indebtedness upon graduation:* $13,471.

Applying *Options:* common application, electronic application, early admission, deferred entrance. *Application fee:* $25. *Required:* high school transcript, minimum 2.0 GPA, 2 letters of recommendation, interview, rank in upper 50% of high school class, minimum SAT score of 920, ACT score of 19. *Recommended:* essay or personal statement. *Application deadlines:* 8/15 (freshmen), 8/15 (transfers). *Notification:* continuous (freshmen).

Admissions Contact Director of Admissions, Goshen College, 1700 South Main Street, Goshen, IN 46526-4794. *Phone:* 574-535-7535. *Toll-free phone:* 800-348-7422. *Fax:* 574-535-7609. *E-mail:* admissions@goshen.edu.

GRACE COLLEGE
Winona Lake, Indiana

- **Independent** comprehensive, founded 1948, affiliated with Fellowship of Grace Brethren Churches
- **Calendar** semesters
- **Degrees** associate, bachelor's, and master's
- **Small-town** 160-acre campus
- **Endowment** $4.0 million
- **Coed,** 1,145 undergraduate students, 91% full-time, 52% women, 48% men
- **Moderately difficult** entrance level, 81% of applicants were admitted

Grace College is a 4-year Christian liberal arts college that applies biblical values in strengthening character, sharpening competence, and preparing for service. Grace offers a variety of academic majors and programs, coupled with many ministry and service opportunities, to equip students to make an impact in whatever career they choose.

Undergraduates 1,040 full-time, 105 part-time. Students come from 37 states and territories, 7 other countries, 60% are from out of state, 5% African American, 0.3% Asian American or Pacific Islander, 1% Hispanic American, 0.3% Native American, 0.7% international, 5% transferred in, 74% live on campus. *Retention:* 80% of 2001 full-time freshmen returned.

Freshmen *Admission:* 745 applied, 603 admitted, 243 enrolled. *Average high school GPA:* 3.43. *Test scores:* SAT verbal scores over 500: 66%; SAT math scores over 500: 61%; ACT scores over 18: 89%; SAT verbal scores over 600: 22%; SAT math scores over 600: 18%; ACT scores over 24: 38%; SAT verbal scores over 700: 2%; SAT math scores over 700: 2%; ACT scores over 30: 2%.

Faculty *Total:* 84, 50% full-time, 39% with terminal degrees. *Student/faculty ratio:* 19:1.

Majors Accounting; art; art education; biblical studies; biology; business; business administration; counseling psychology; criminal justice/law enforcement administration; divinity/ministry; drawing; elementary education; English; English education; French; French language education; German; German language education; graphic design/commercial art/illustration; international business; management information systems/business data processing; mass communications; mathematics; mathematics education; music (piano and organ performance); music teacher education; painting; pastoral counseling; physical education; psychology; science education; secretarial science; social work; sociology; Spanish; Spanish language education.

Academic Programs *Special study options:* academic remediation for entering students, accelerated degree program, advanced placement credit, distance learning, double majors, independent study, internships, off-campus study, part-time degree program, services for LD students, study abroad, summer session for credit.

Library Morgan Library with 140,202 titles, 7,178 serial subscriptions, 850 audiovisual materials, an OPAC, a Web page.

Computers on Campus 45 computers available on campus for general student use. A campuswide network can be accessed from student residence rooms and from off campus. Internet access, at least one staffed computer lab available.

Student Life *Housing:* on-campus residence required through senior year. *Options:* men-only, women-only. *Activities and Organizations:* drama/theater group, student-run newspaper, choral group, Grace Ministries in Action, Student Activities Board, Funfest, Women's Ministries, Breakout. *Campus security:* student patrols, late-night transport/escort service, controlled dormitory access, evening patrols by trained security personnel. *Student Services:* health clinic, personal/psychological counseling.

Athletics Member NAIA, NCCAA. *Intercollegiate sports:* baseball M(s), basketball M(s)/W(s), cross-country running M(s)/W(s), golf M(s), soccer M(s)/W(s), softball W(s), tennis M(s)/W(s), track and field M(s)/W(s), volleyball W(s). *Intramural sports:* basketball M/W, football M, soccer M/W, softball M/W, table tennis M/W, tennis M/W, volleyball M/W.

Standardized Tests *Required:* SAT I or ACT (for admission).

Costs (2001–02) *Comprehensive fee:* $16,728 includes full-time tuition ($11,400), mandatory fees ($320), and room and board ($5008). Part-time tuition: $4090 per term. Part-time tuition and fees vary according to course load. *Required fees:* $155 per term. *Room and board:* College room only: $2394. Room and board charges vary according to board plan and housing facility. *Payment plan:* installment. *Waivers:* employees or children of employees.

Financial Aid Of all full-time matriculated undergraduates who enrolled in 2001, 762 applied for aid, 680 were judged to have need, 232 had their need fully

Grace College (continued)
met. In 2001, 178 non-need-based awards were made. *Average percent of need met:* 88%. *Average financial aid package:* $11,119. *Average need-based loan:* $4891. *Average need-based gift aid:* $6580. *Average non-need based aid:* $6045. *Average indebtedness upon graduation:* $14,456.

Applying *Options:* electronic application, early admission, deferred entrance. *Application fee:* $20. *Required:* high school transcript, minimum 2.3 GPA, 2 letters of recommendation. *Required for some:* interview. *Application deadlines:* 8/1 (freshmen), 8/1 (transfers). *Notification:* continuous until 8/15 (freshmen).

Admissions Contact Rebecca E. Gehrke, Administrative Assistant to Director of Admissions, Grace College, Winona Lake, TX 46590. *Phone:* 219-372-5100 Ext. 6008. *Toll-free phone:* 800-54-GRACE (in-state); 800-54 GRACE (out-of-state). *E-mail:* enroll@grace.edu.

HANOVER COLLEGE
Hanover, Indiana

- **Independent Presbyterian** 4-year, founded 1827
- **Calendar** 4-4-1
- **Degree** bachelor's
- **Rural** 630-acre campus with easy access to Louisville
- **Endowment** $133.6 million
- **Coed,** 1,111 undergraduate students, 99% full-time, 54% women, 46% men
- **Moderately difficult** entrance level, 80% of applicants were admitted

Hanover College, the oldest private college in Indiana, offers a classic liberal arts education in a value-based environment. Nestled among 650 acres overlooking the Ohio River, Hanover is home to 1,100 students from 36 states and 22 countries who want a challenging college experience. Hanover has been consistently ranked as one of the best buys among private liberal arts colleges in the nation.

Undergraduates 1,100 full-time, 11 part-time. Students come from 36 states and territories, 18 other countries, 34% are from out of state, 2% African American, 2% Asian American or Pacific Islander, 2% Hispanic American, 0.4% Native American, 3% international, 2% transferred in, 93% live on campus. *Retention:* 78% of 2001 full-time freshmen returned.

Freshmen *Admission:* 1,171 applied, 940 admitted, 306 enrolled. *Test scores:* SAT verbal scores over 500: 76%; SAT math scores over 500: 78%; ACT scores over 18: 97%; SAT verbal scores over 600: 33%; SAT math scores over 600: 37%; ACT scores over 24: 57%; SAT verbal scores over 700: 5%; SAT math scores over 700: 5%; ACT scores over 30: 15%.

Faculty *Total:* 106, 89% full-time, 83% with terminal degrees. *Student/faculty ratio:* 11:1.

Majors Anthropology; art; art history; biology; business administration; chemistry; classics; computer science; economics; elementary education; English; French; geology; German; history; international relations; Latin American studies; mass communications; mathematics; medieval/renaissance studies; music; philosophy; physical education; physics; political science; psychology; sociology; Spanish; theater arts/drama; theology.

Academic Programs *Special study options:* accelerated degree program, advanced placement credit, double majors, honors programs, independent study, internships, off-campus study, study abroad. *Unusual degree programs:* 3-2 engineering with Washington University in St. Louis.

Library Duggan Library with 256,909 titles, 1,743 serial subscriptions, 5,983 audiovisual materials, an OPAC, a Web page.

Computers on Campus 90 computers available on campus for general student use. A campuswide network can be accessed from student residence rooms and from off campus. Internet access, at least one staffed computer lab available.

Student Life *Housing:* on-campus residence required through senior year. *Options:* coed, men-only, women-only. *Activities and Organizations:* drama/theater group, student-run newspaper, television station, choral group, marching band, Christian Life, Baptist Collegiate Ministries, Student Programming Board, Link, American Chemical Society, national fraternities, national sororities. *Campus security:* 24-hour emergency response devices and patrols, late-night transport/escort service, controlled dormitory access. *Student Services:* health clinic, personal/psychological counseling.

Athletics Member NCAA. All Division III. *Intercollegiate sports:* baseball M, basketball M/W, cross-country running M/W, field hockey W, football M, golf M/W, soccer M/W, softball W, tennis M/W, track and field M/W, volleyball W. *Intramural sports:* basketball M/W, football M/W, soccer M/W, volleyball M/W.

Standardized Tests *Required:* SAT I or ACT (for admission).

Costs (2001–02) *Comprehensive fee:* $17,560 includes full-time tuition ($12,000), mandatory fees ($370), and room and board ($5190). Part-time tuition: $1335 per unit. Part-time tuition and fees vary according to course load. *Room and board:* College room only: $2420. Room and board charges vary according to housing facility. *Payment plan:* installment. *Waivers:* senior citizens and employees or children of employees.

Financial Aid Of all full-time matriculated undergraduates who enrolled in 2001, 752 applied for aid, 605 were judged to have need, 259 had their need fully met. In 2001, 349 non-need-based awards were made. *Average percent of need met:* 87%. *Average financial aid package:* $10,156. *Average need-based loan:* $2968. *Average need-based gift aid:* $8352. *Average indebtedness upon graduation:* $14,582. *Financial aid deadline:* 3/1.

Applying *Options:* common application, electronic application, early admission, early action, deferred entrance. *Application fee:* $25. *Required:* essay or personal statement, high school transcript, 1 letter of recommendation. *Recommended:* interview. *Application deadline:* 3/1 (freshmen), rolling (transfers). *Notification:* continuous (freshmen), 12/20 (early action).

Admissions Contact Mr. Kenneth Moyer Jr., Dean of Admissions, Hanover College, Box 108, Hanover, IN 47243-0108. *Phone:* 812-866-7021. *Toll-free phone:* 800-213-2178. *Fax:* 812-866-7098. *E-mail:* admissions@hanover.edu.

HUNTINGTON COLLEGE
Huntington, Indiana

- **Independent** comprehensive, founded 1897, affiliated with Church of the United Brethren in Christ
- **Calendar** 4-1-4
- **Degrees** diplomas, bachelor's, master's, and postbachelor's certificates
- **Small-town** 200-acre campus
- **Endowment** $13.5 million
- **Coed,** 968 undergraduate students, 92% full-time, 59% women, 41% men
- **Moderately difficult** entrance level, 95% of applicants were admitted

Huntington College is all about academic leadership and Christian maturity. Since 1897, Huntington has been educating men and women to impact the world for Christ. Huntington offers more than 50 areas of study, including nationally recognized programs in youth ministry and theater. Huntington is ranked as a top 15 Midwest Comprehensive College by *U.S. News & World Report.*

Undergraduates 888 full-time, 80 part-time. Students come from 22 states and territories, 44% are from out of state, 0.6% African American, 0.4% Asian American or Pacific Islander, 0.6% Hispanic American, 0.1% Native American, 2% international, 5% transferred in, 69% live on campus. *Retention:* 75% of 2001 full-time freshmen returned.

Freshmen *Admission:* 677 applied, 640 admitted, 219 enrolled. *Average high school GPA:* 3.58. *Test scores:* SAT verbal scores over 500: 63%; SAT math scores over 500: 66%; ACT scores over 18: 89%; SAT verbal scores over 600: 26%; SAT math scores over 600: 25%; ACT scores over 24: 43%; SAT verbal scores over 700: 5%; SAT math scores over 700: 3%; ACT scores over 30: 7%.

Faculty *Total:* 88, 64% full-time. *Student/faculty ratio:* 16:1.

Majors Accounting; art; art education; biblical studies; biological/physical sciences; biology; broadcast journalism; business administration; business economics; business education; chemistry; computer science; divinity/ministry; economics; education; elementary education; English; exercise sciences; graphic design/commercial art/illustration; history; mass communications; mathematics; music; music (piano and organ performance); music teacher education; music (voice and choral/opera performance); natural resources management; philosophy; physical education; pre-dentistry; pre-law; pre-medicine; pre-veterinary studies; psychology; recreation/leisure studies; religious studies; science education; secondary education; sociology; special education; theater arts/drama; theology.

Academic Programs *Special study options:* academic remediation for entering students, adult/continuing education programs, advanced placement credit, distance learning, double majors, English as a second language, independent study, off-campus study, part-time degree program, summer session for credit.

Library RichLyn Library with 76,954 titles, 553 serial subscriptions.

Computers on Campus 75 computers available on campus for general student use. A campuswide network can be accessed from student residence rooms. Internet access, at least one staffed computer lab available.

Student Life *Housing:* on-campus residence required through junior year. *Options:* men-only, women-only. *Activities and Organizations:* drama/theater group, student-run newspaper, radio and television station, choral group, Joe Mertz Volunteer Center, Chapel Worship Team, student newspaper, ministry groups, Dormitory Council, national fraternities, national sororities. *Campus security:* 24-hour emergency response devices, late-night transport/escort service, night patrols by trained security personnel. *Student Services:* health clinic, personal/psychological counseling.

Athletics Member NAIA. *Intercollegiate sports:* baseball M(s), basketball M(s)/W(s), cross-country running M(s)/W(s), golf M(s)/W(s), soccer M(s)/W(s), softball W(s), tennis M(s)/W(s), track and field M(s)/W(s), volleyball W(s). *Intramural sports:* basketball M/W, bowling M/W, football M, racquetball M/W, soccer M/W, softball W, tennis M/W, volleyball M/W, weight lifting M/W.
Standardized Tests *Required:* SAT I or ACT (for admission).
Costs (2001–02) *Comprehensive fee:* $20,480 includes full-time tuition ($14,270), mandatory fees ($760), and room and board ($5450). Part-time tuition: $450 per semester hour. Part-time tuition and fees vary according to course load. No tuition increase for student's term of enrollment. *Required fees:* $185 per term part-time. *Room and board:* College room only: $2500. Room and board charges vary according to board plan. *Payment plan:* installment. *Waivers:* minority students, children of alumni, adult students, senior citizens, and employees or children of employees.
Financial Aid Of all full-time matriculated undergraduates who enrolled in 2001, 775 applied for aid, 559 were judged to have need, 547 had their need fully met. 168 Federal Work-Study jobs (averaging $1702). In 2001, 192 non-need-based awards were made. *Average percent of need met:* 97%. *Average financial aid package:* $11,357. *Average need-based loan:* $4086. *Average need-based gift aid:* $7321. *Average indebtedness upon graduation:* $14,747.
Applying *Options:* electronic application, deferred entrance. *Application fee:* $20. *Required:* essay or personal statement, high school transcript, minimum 2.3 GPA. *Recommended:* interview. *Application deadline:* 8/1 (freshmen), rolling (transfers). *Notification:* continuous (freshmen).
Admissions Contact Mr. Jeff Berggren, Dean of Enrollment, Huntington College, 2303 College Avenue, Huntington, IN 46750-1299. *Phone:* 260-356-6000 Ext. 4016. *Toll-free phone:* 800-642-6493. *Fax:* 260-356-9448. *E-mail:* admissions@huntington.edu.

INDIANA INSTITUTE OF TECHNOLOGY
Fort Wayne, Indiana

- **Independent** comprehensive, founded 1930
- **Calendar** semesters
- **Degrees** associate, bachelor's, and master's
- **Urban** 25-acre campus
- **Endowment** $18.3 million
- **Coed,** 2,476 undergraduate students, 47% full-time, 54% women, 46% men
- **Moderately difficult** entrance level, 15% of applicants were admitted

Undergraduates 1,157 full-time, 1,319 part-time. Students come from 33 states and territories, 9 other countries, 16% are from out of state, 22% African American, 2% Asian American or Pacific Islander, 2% Hispanic American, 1% Native American, 5% international, 2% transferred in, 50% live on campus.
Freshmen *Admission:* 1,353 applied, 209 admitted, 908 enrolled.
Faculty *Total:* 162, 26% full-time, 50% with terminal degrees. *Student/faculty ratio:* 22:1.
Majors Accounting; business administration; business marketing and marketing management; civil engineering; computer engineering; computer science; electrical engineering; finance; human resources management; human services; information sciences/systems; mechanical engineering; recreational therapy; recreation/leisure facilities management.
Academic Programs *Special study options:* academic remediation for entering students, accelerated degree program, adult/continuing education programs, advanced placement credit, distance learning, double majors, English as a second language, external degree program, independent study, internships, part-time degree program, services for LD students, student-designed majors, summer session for credit.
Library McMillen Library with 60,000 titles, 175 serial subscriptions, an OPAC, a Web page.
Computers on Campus 79 computers available on campus for general student use. A campuswide network can be accessed from off campus. At least one staffed computer lab available.
Student Life *Housing:* on-campus residence required through sophomore year. *Options:* coed. *Activities and Organizations:* national fraternities. *Campus security:* 24-hour emergency response devices and patrols, controlled dormitory access. *Student Services:* personal/psychological counseling.
Athletics Member NAIA. *Intercollegiate sports:* baseball M(s), basketball M(s)/W(s), soccer M(s)/W(s), softball W(s). *Intramural sports:* basketball M/W, bowling M/W, football M/W, golf M/W, table tennis M/W, volleyball M/W, weight lifting M/W.
Standardized Tests *Required:* SAT I or ACT (for admission).
Costs (2001–02) *Comprehensive fee:* $19,806 includes full-time tuition ($13,560), mandatory fees ($1000), and room and board ($5246). Full-time tuition and fees vary according to course load. Part-time tuition and fees vary according to class time and course load. *Room and board:* Room and board charges vary according to housing facility and student level. *Payment plan:* deferred payment. *Waivers:* employees or children of employees.
Financial Aid Of all full-time matriculated undergraduates who enrolled in 2001, 529 applied for aid, 480 were judged to have need, 81 had their need fully met. In 2001, 41 non-need-based awards were made. *Average percent of need met:* 70%. *Average financial aid package:* $9125. *Average need-based loan:* $3035. *Average need-based gift aid:* $6789. *Average indebtedness upon graduation:* $16,500.
Applying *Options:* electronic application, early admission, deferred entrance. *Application fee:* $25. *Required:* high school transcript. *Recommended:* minimum 3.0 GPA, interview, 2 references. *Application deadline:* 9/1 (freshmen).
Admissions Contact Indiana Institute of Technology, 1600 East Washington Boulevard, Fort Wayne, IN 46803. *Phone:* 219-422-5561 Ext. 2251. *Toll-free phone:* 800-937-2448 (in-state); 888-666-TECH (out-of-state). *Fax:* 219-422-7696. *E-mail:* filus@indtech.edu.

INDIANA STATE UNIVERSITY
Terre Haute, Indiana

- **State-supported** university, founded 1865
- **Calendar** semesters
- **Degrees** associate, bachelor's, master's, doctoral, and first professional
- **Suburban** 91-acre campus with easy access to Indianapolis
- **Endowment** $1.1 million
- **Coed,** 9,734 undergraduate students, 86% full-time, 53% women, 47% men
- **Moderately difficult** entrance level, 86% of applicants were admitted

Undergraduates 8,396 full-time, 1,338 part-time. Students come from 51 states and territories, 77 other countries, 7% are from out of state, 11% African American, 0.7% Asian American or Pacific Islander, 1% Hispanic American, 0.3% Native American, 2% international, 7% transferred in, 37% live on campus. *Retention:* 71% of 2001 full-time freshmen returned.
Freshmen *Admission:* 5,540 applied, 4,780 admitted, 2,211 enrolled. *Average high school GPA:* 2.88. *Test scores:* SAT verbal scores over 500: 35%; SAT math scores over 500: 36%; ACT scores over 18: 69%; SAT verbal scores over 600: 7%; SAT math scores over 600: 7%; ACT scores over 24: 15%; SAT math scores over 700: 1%; ACT scores over 30: 1%.
Faculty *Student/faculty ratio:* 15:1.
Majors Accounting; African-American studies; aircraft pilot (professional); anthropology; architectural drafting; architectural engineering technology; art; art education; art history; athletic training/sports medicine; automotive engineering technology; aviation/airway science; aviation management; biology; biomedical engineering-related technology; business administration; business education; business marketing and marketing management; business quantitative methods/management science related; chemistry; clothing/apparel/textile studies; communications; communications related; community health liaison; computer engineering technology; computer/information sciences; computer science related; criminology; early childhood education; economics; educational media design; electrical/electronic engineering technology; elementary education; English; environmental health; finance; fine arts and art studies related; fine/studio arts; foreign languages/literatures; French; general studies; geography; geology; German; graphic/printing equipment; health education; history; home economics; humanities; human resources management; individual/family development; industrial production technologies related; industrial technology; instrumentation technology; insurance/risk management; interior architecture; journalism; liberal arts and sciences/liberal studies; management information systems/business data processing; mathematics; mechanical engineering technologies related; medical technology; music; music related; nursing; nutrition studies; occupational safety/health technology; office management; operations management; philosophy; physical education; physics; political science; psychology; radio/television broadcasting; recreation/leisure facilities management; robotics technology; science education; secretarial science; social studies education; social work; sociology; Spanish; special education; speech-language pathology; speech-language pathology/audiology; theater arts/drama; trade/industrial education.
Academic Programs *Special study options:* academic remediation for entering students, accelerated degree program, adult/continuing education programs, advanced placement credit, cooperative education, distance learning, double majors, English as a second language, honors programs, independent study, internships, off-campus study, part-time degree program, services for LD students, study abroad, summer session for credit. *ROTC:* Army (b), Air Force (b).
Library Cunningham Memorial Library plus 2 others with 2.5 million titles, 2,827 serial subscriptions, an OPAC, a Web page.

Indiana State University (continued)

Computers on Campus A campuswide network can be accessed from student residence rooms and from off campus. Internet access, at least one staffed computer lab available.

Student Life *Housing:* on-campus residence required through sophomore year. *Options:* coed, men-only, women-only. *Activities and Organizations:* drama/theater group, student-run newspaper, radio station, choral group, marching band, Hulman Memorial Union and Junior Union Boards, Student Government Association, Sycamore Ambassadors, Student Alumni Association, Panhellenic, National Panhellenic, and Interfraternity Council, national fraternities, national sororities. *Campus security:* 24-hour emergency response devices and patrols, student patrols, late-night transport/escort service, controlled dormitory access. *Student Services:* health clinic, personal/psychological counseling, women's center, legal services.

Athletics Member NCAA. All Division I except football (Division I-AA). *Intercollegiate sports:* baseball M(s), basketball M(s)/W(s), bowling M(c)/W(c), cross-country running M(s)/W(s), soccer M(c)/W(c), softball W(s), swimming M(c)/W(c), tennis M(s)/W(s), track and field M(s)/W(s), volleyball M(c)/W(s). *Intramural sports:* badminton M/W, basketball M/W, bowling M/W, cross-country running M/W, golf M/W, racquetball M/W, soccer M/W, softball M/W, swimming M/W, table tennis M/W, tennis M/W, track and field M/W, volleyball M(c)/W, weight lifting M/W.

Standardized Tests *Required:* SAT I or ACT (for admission).

Costs (2001–02) *Tuition:* state resident $3672 full-time, $132 per credit part-time; nonresident $9166 full-time, $323 per credit part-time. Full-time tuition and fees vary according to course load. Part-time tuition and fees vary according to course load. *Required fees:* $50 full-time. *Room and board:* $4789; room only: $2448. Room and board charges vary according to board plan and housing facility. *Payment plans:* installment, deferred payment. *Waivers:* employees or children of employees.

Financial Aid Of all full-time matriculated undergraduates who enrolled in 2001, 5723 applied for aid, 4417 were judged to have need, 1163 had their need fully met. 528 Federal Work-Study jobs (averaging $1300). In 2001, 389 non-need-based awards were made. *Average percent of need met:* 76%. *Average financial aid package:* $5838. *Average need-based loan:* $4376. *Average need-based gift aid:* $3926. *Average non-need based aid:* $2455. *Average indebtedness upon graduation:* $15,352.

Applying *Options:* electronic application, deferred entrance. *Application fee:* $25. *Required:* high school transcript, minimum 2.0 GPA. *Required for some:* letters of recommendation, interview. *Recommended:* essay or personal statement. *Application deadline:* 8/15 (freshmen), rolling (transfers). *Notification:* continuous (freshmen).

Admissions Contact Mr. Ronald Brown, Director of Admissions, Indiana State University, Tirey Hall 134, 217 North 7th Street, Terre Haute, IN 47809. *Phone:* 812-237-2121. *Toll-free phone:* 800-742-0891. *Fax:* 812-237-8023. *E-mail:* admisu@amber.indstate.edu.

INDIANA UNIVERSITY BLOOMINGTON

Bloomington, Indiana

- **State-supported** university, founded 1820, part of Indiana University System
- **Calendar** semesters
- **Degrees** certificates, diplomas, associate, bachelor's, master's, doctoral, first professional, post-master's, postbachelor's, and first professional certificates
- **Small-town** 1931-acre campus with easy access to Indianapolis
- **Endowment** $588.7 million
- **Coed,** 30,157 undergraduate students, 92% full-time, 53% women, 47% men
- **Moderately difficult** entrance level, 83% of applicants were admitted

Undergraduates 27,879 full-time, 2,278 part-time. Students come from 56 states and territories, 135 other countries, 28% are from out of state, 4% African American, 3% Asian American or Pacific Islander, 2% Hispanic American, 0.2% Native American, 4% international, 3% transferred in, 37% live on campus. *Retention:* 87% of 2001 full-time freshmen returned.

Freshmen *Admission:* 20,228 applied, 16,777 admitted, 6,815 enrolled. *Test scores:* SAT verbal scores over 500: 71%; SAT math scores over 500: 75%; ACT scores over 18: 96%; SAT verbal scores over 600: 26%; SAT math scores over 600: 32%; ACT scores over 24: 60%; SAT verbal scores over 700: 4%; SAT math scores over 700: 5%; ACT scores over 30: 9%.

Faculty *Total:* 1,881, 88% full-time, 73% with terminal degrees. *Student/faculty ratio:* 20:1.

Majors Accounting; African-American studies; African studies; anthropology; applied art; art; art education; art history; Asian studies; astronomy; astrophysics; athletic training/sports medicine; bilingual/bicultural education; biochemistry; biology; biology education; broadcast journalism; business; business administration; business economics; business marketing and marketing management; ceramic arts; chemistry; chemistry education; child care/development; Chinese; city/community/regional planning; classics; clothing/apparel/textile studies; clothing/textiles; cognitive psychology/psycholinguistics; communications; comparative literature; computer/information sciences; criminal justice studies; dance; dietetics; drawing; early childhood education; East Asian studies; Eastern European area studies; economics; education; elementary education; English; English education; environmental science; family/consumer studies; fashion design/illustration; fashion merchandising; finance; fine/studio arts; folklore; forensic technology; French; French language education; general studies; geography; geology; German; German language education; graphic design/commercial art/illustration; Greek (ancient and medieval); hearing sciences; history; individual/family development; interior design; Italian; Japanese; jazz; journalism; Judaic studies; labor/personnel relations; laser/optical technology; Latin American studies; Latin (ancient and medieval); linguistics; literature; management information systems/business data processing; mass communications; mathematics; mathematics education; metal/jewelry arts; microbiology/bacteriology; Middle Eastern studies; music; musical instrument technology; music history; music (piano and organ performance); music teacher education; music (voice and choral/opera performance); nutrition science; occupational safety/health technology; ophthalmic/optometric services; optical technician; optometric/ophthalmic laboratory technician; philosophy; photography; physical education; physics; physics education; political science; Portuguese; pre-dentistry; pre-law; pre-medicine; psychology; public administration; public health; public policy analysis; radio/television broadcasting; real estate; recreational therapy; recreation/leisure facilities management; recreation/leisure studies; religious studies; retail management; Russian; Russian/Slavic studies; science education; sculpture; secondary education; Slavic languages; social studies education; social work; sociology; Spanish; Spanish language education; special education; speech education; speech-language pathology/audiology; speech/rhetorical studies; speech therapy; sport/fitness administration; systems science/theory; telecommunications; theater arts/drama; theater design; urban studies; wind/percussion instruments; women's studies.

Academic Programs *Special study options:* academic remediation for entering students, accelerated degree program, adult/continuing education programs, advanced placement credit, cooperative education, distance learning, double majors, English as a second language, external degree program, freshman honors college, honors programs, independent study, internships, off-campus study, part-time degree program, services for LD students, student-designed majors, study abroad, summer session for credit. *ROTC:* Army (b), Air Force (b). *Unusual degree programs:* 3-2 accounting.

Library Indiana University Library plus 32 others with 6.3 million titles, 45,596 serial subscriptions, 635,574 audiovisual materials, an OPAC, a Web page.

Computers on Campus 1500 computers available on campus for general student use. A campuswide network can be accessed from student residence rooms and from off campus that provide access to various software packages. Internet access, at least one staffed computer lab available.

Student Life *Housing Options:* coed, men-only, women-only. *Activities and Organizations:* drama/theater group, student-run newspaper, radio and television station, choral group, marching band, Union Board, Student Association, Student Foundation, Habitat for Humanity, Student Athletic Board, national fraternities, national sororities. *Campus security:* 24-hour emergency response devices and patrols, late-night transport/escort service, safety seminars, lighted pathways, escort service, shuttle bus service, emergency telephones. *Student Services:* health clinic, personal/psychological counseling, women's center, legal services.

Athletics Member NCAA. All Division I except football (Division I-A). *Intercollegiate sports:* baseball M(s), basketball M(s)/W(s), crew W(s), cross-country running M(s)/W(s), golf M(s)/W(s), soccer M(s)/W(s), softball W(s), swimming M(s)/W(s), tennis M(s)/W(s), track and field M(s)/W(s), volleyball W(s), water polo W(s), wrestling M(s). *Intramural sports:* archery M/W, badminton M(c)/W(c), baseball M/W, basketball M/W, bowling M(c)/W(c), crew M(c)/W(c), cross-country running M/W, equestrian sports M(c)/W(c), fencing M(c)/W(c), field hockey W(c), golf M/W, gymnastics M/W, ice hockey M/W, lacrosse M(c)/W, racquetball M(c)/W(c), riflery M(c)/W(c), rugby M(c)/W(c), sailing M(c)/W(c), skiing (downhill) M(c)/W(c), soccer M/W(c), softball M/W, squash M/W, swimming M/W, table tennis M/W, tennis M(c)/W, track and field M/W, volleyball M/W, water polo M(c)/W, weight lifting M(c)/W(c), wrestling M(c).

Standardized Tests *Required:* SAT I or ACT (for admission).

Costs (2001–02) *Tuition:* state resident $4196 full-time, $131 per credit hour part-time; nonresident $13,930 full-time, $435 per credit hour part-time. Full-time tuition and fees vary according to program. Part-time tuition and fees vary according to course load and program. *Required fees:* $539 full-time. *Room and board:* $5978; room only: $3128. Room and board charges vary according to board plan and housing facility. *Payment plan:* deferred payment. *Waivers:* employees or children of employees.

Financial Aid Of all full-time matriculated undergraduates who enrolled in 2001, 15863 applied for aid, 9954 were judged to have need, 1229 had their need

fully met. 1770 Federal Work-Study jobs (averaging $1823). In 2001, 5379 non-need-based awards were made. *Average percent of need met:* 59%. *Average financial aid package:* $5654. *Average need-based loan:* $2812. *Average need-based gift aid:* $4047. *Average non-need based aid:* $2733.

Applying *Options:* electronic application, deferred entrance. *Application fee:* $40. *Required:* high school transcript. *Recommended:* interview. *Application deadline:* 2/1 (freshmen), rolling (transfers). *Notification:* continuous (freshmen).

Admissions Contact Mr. Don Hossler, Vice Chancellor for Enrollment Services, Indiana University Bloomington, 300 North Jordan Avenue, Bloomington, IN 47405-1106. *Phone:* 812-855-0661. *Toll-free phone:* 812-855-0661. *Fax:* 812-855-5102. *E-mail:* iuadmit@indiana.edu.

INDIANA UNIVERSITY EAST

Richmond, Indiana

- **State-supported** 4-year, founded 1971, part of Indiana University System
- **Calendar** semesters
- **Degrees** associate, bachelor's, and postbachelor's certificates
- **Small-town** 194-acre campus with easy access to Indianapolis
- **Endowment** $2.5 million
- **Coed,** 2,405 undergraduate students, 47% full-time, 71% women, 29% men
- **Moderately difficult** entrance level, 79% of applicants were admitted

Undergraduates 1,126 full-time, 1,279 part-time. Students come from 7 states and territories, 5% are from out of state, 4% African American, 0.5% Asian American or Pacific Islander, 0.5% Hispanic American, 0.6% Native American, 0.1% international, 6% transferred in. *Retention:* 56% of 2001 full-time freshmen returned.

Freshmen *Admission:* 546 applied, 433 admitted, 466 enrolled. *Test scores:* SAT verbal scores over 500: 32%; SAT math scores over 500: 27%; ACT scores over 18: 68%; SAT verbal scores over 600: 4%; SAT math scores over 600: 3%; ACT scores over 24: 20%; SAT math scores over 700: 1%.

Faculty *Total:* 177, 39% full-time, 24% with terminal degrees. *Student/faculty ratio:* 15:1.

Majors Biological/physical sciences; biology; business; communications; computer programming; criminal justice studies; earth sciences; education; elementary education; English; general studies; history; human services; mathematics; medical technology; nursing; psychology; secondary education; social work; sociology; visual/performing arts.

Academic Programs *Special study options:* academic remediation for entering students, adult/continuing education programs, advanced placement credit, cooperative education, distance learning, double majors, external degree program, independent study, internships, off-campus study, part-time degree program, services for LD students, summer session for credit.

Library Library and Media Services plus 1 other with 65,888 titles, 425 serial subscriptions, 9,477 audiovisual materials.

Computers on Campus 110 computers available on campus for general student use. A campuswide network can be accessed from off campus. Internet access, at least one staffed computer lab available.

Student Life *Housing:* college housing not available. *Activities and Organizations:* drama/theater group, student-run newspaper, television station, Student Government Association, Phi Beta Lambda, Multicultural Awareness Association, psychology club, sociology club. *Campus security:* 24-hour emergency response devices, late-night transport/escort service, safety awareness, lighted pathways, 14-hour foot and vehicle patrol. *Student Services:* personal/psychological counseling.

Athletics *Intramural sports:* basketball M(c)/W(c), soccer M/W, softball M/W, volleyball M/W.

Standardized Tests *Recommended:* SAT I or ACT (for admission).

Costs (2001–02) *Tuition:* state resident $3221 full-time, $107 per credit hour part-time; nonresident $8520 full-time, $284 per credit hour part-time. Full-time tuition and fees vary according to course load. Part-time tuition and fees vary according to course load. *Required fees:* $194 full-time. *Payment plan:* deferred payment. *Waivers:* employees or children of employees.

Financial Aid Of all full-time matriculated undergraduates who enrolled in 2001, 903 applied for aid, 789 were judged to have need, 53 had their need fully met. 79 Federal Work-Study jobs (averaging $3525). In 2001, 47 non-need-based awards were made. *Average percent of need met:* 51%. *Average financial aid package:* $4773. *Average need-based loan:* $2610. *Average need-based gift aid:* $3500. *Average non-need based aid:* $1029.

Applying *Options:* early admission, deferred entrance. *Application fee:* $25. *Required:* high school transcript. *Recommended:* minimum 2.0 GPA. *Application deadline:* rolling (freshmen), rolling (transfers). *Notification:* continuous (freshmen).

Admissions Contact Ms. Susanna Tanner, Admissions Counselor, Indiana University East, 2325 Chester Boulevard, WZ 116, Richmond, IN 47374-1289. *Phone:* 765-973-8415. *Toll-free phone:* 800-959-EAST. *Fax:* 765-973-8288. *E-mail:* eaadmit@indiana.edu.

INDIANA UNIVERSITY KOKOMO

Kokomo, Indiana

- **State-supported** comprehensive, founded 1945, part of Indiana University System
- **Calendar** semesters
- **Degrees** certificates, associate, bachelor's, master's, and postbachelor's certificates
- **Small-town** 51-acre campus with easy access to Indianapolis
- **Endowment** $2.4 million
- **Coed,** 2,519 undergraduate students, 47% full-time, 70% women, 30% men
- **Minimally difficult** entrance level, 87% of applicants were admitted

Undergraduates 1,176 full-time, 1,343 part-time. Students come from 3 states and territories, 1% are from out of state, 3% African American, 0.6% Asian American or Pacific Islander, 2% Hispanic American, 0.4% Native American, 0.2% international, 6% transferred in. *Retention:* 53% of 2001 full-time freshmen returned.

Freshmen *Admission:* 699 applied, 609 admitted, 515 enrolled. *Test scores:* SAT verbal scores over 500: 41%; SAT math scores over 500: 33%; ACT scores over 18: 69%; SAT verbal scores over 600: 7%; SAT math scores over 600: 7%; ACT scores over 24: 11%; SAT verbal scores over 700: 1%; ACT scores over 30: 1%.

Faculty *Total:* 151, 50% full-time, 36% with terminal degrees. *Student/faculty ratio:* 16:1.

Majors Behavioral sciences; biological/physical sciences; biology; business; communications; criminal justice studies; data processing technology; elementary education; English; general studies; humanities; labor/personnel relations; mathematics; medical technology; nursing; psychology; sociology.

Academic Programs *Special study options:* academic remediation for entering students, adult/continuing education programs, advanced placement credit, distance learning, external degree program, freshman honors college, honors programs, independent study, internships, part-time degree program, services for LD students, study abroad, summer session for credit. *ROTC:* Army (c).

Library Main Library plus 1 other with 132,064 titles, 1,707 serial subscriptions, 5,979 audiovisual materials.

Computers on Campus 120 computers available on campus for general student use. Internet access, at least one staffed computer lab available.

Student Life *Housing:* college housing not available. *Activities and Organizations:* drama/theater group, student-run newspaper, choral group. *Campus security:* 24-hour patrols, late-night transport/escort service, campus police, lighted pathways. *Student Services:* personal/psychological counseling.

Athletics *Intramural sports:* basketball M, softball W, volleyball W.

Standardized Tests *Required:* SAT I or ACT (for admission).

Costs (2001–02) *Tuition:* state resident $3221 full-time, $107 per credit hour part-time; nonresident $8520 full-time, $284 per credit hour part-time. Full-time tuition and fees vary according to course load. Part-time tuition and fees vary according to course load. *Required fees:* $201 full-time. *Waivers:* employees or children of employees.

Financial Aid Of all full-time matriculated undergraduates who enrolled in 2001, 736 applied for aid, 479 were judged to have need, 52 had their need fully met. 38 Federal Work-Study jobs (averaging $1754). In 2001, 173 non-need-based awards were made. *Average percent of need met:* 63%. *Average financial aid package:* $4436. *Average need-based loan:* $2385. *Average need-based gift aid:* $3376. *Average non-need based aid:* $1461.

Applying *Options:* early admission, deferred entrance. *Application fee:* $30. *Required:* high school transcript. *Application deadlines:* 8/3 (freshmen), 8/3 (transfers). *Notification:* continuous (freshmen).

Admissions Contact Ms. Patty Young, Admissions Director, Indiana University Kokomo, PO Box 9003, Kelley Student Center 230A, Kokomo, IN 46904-9003. *Phone:* 765-455-9217. *Toll-free phone:* 888-875-4485. *Fax:* 765-455-9537. *E-mail:* iuadmis@iuk.edu.

INDIANA UNIVERSITY NORTHWEST

Gary, Indiana

- **State-supported** comprehensive, founded 1959, part of Indiana University System

Indiana University Northwest (continued)
- **Calendar** semesters
- **Degrees** certificates, associate, bachelor's, master's, and postbachelor's certificates
- **Urban** 38-acre campus with easy access to Chicago
- **Endowment** $5.1 million
- **Coed,** 4,027 undergraduate students, 51% full-time, 70% women, 30% men
- **Minimally difficult** entrance level, 79% of applicants were admitted

Undergraduates 2,067 full-time, 1,960 part-time. Students come from 6 states and territories, 1% are from out of state, 24% African American, 1% Asian American or Pacific Islander, 11% Hispanic American, 0.4% Native American, 0.2% international, 6% transferred in. *Retention:* 60% of 2001 full-time freshmen returned.

Freshmen *Admission:* 1,135 applied, 891 admitted, 657 enrolled. *Test scores:* SAT verbal scores over 500: 30%; SAT math scores over 500: 24%; ACT scores over 18: 75%; SAT verbal scores over 600: 5%; SAT math scores over 600: 5%; ACT scores over 24: 16%.

Faculty *Total:* 311, 48% full-time, 33% with terminal degrees. *Student/faculty ratio:* 14:1.

Majors Accounting; actuarial science; African-American studies; art; biology; biology education; business administration; chemistry; chemistry education; criminal justice/law enforcement administration; data processing technology; dental hygiene; economics; education; elementary education; English; English education; French; French language education; general studies; geology; health services administration; history; labor/personnel relations; mass communications; mathematics; mathematics education; medical laboratory technician; medical radiologic technology; medical records administration; nursing; philosophy; political science; psychology; public administration; public relations; radiological science; respiratory therapy; secondary education; social studies education; sociology; Spanish; Spanish language education; theater arts/drama.

Academic Programs *Special study options:* academic remediation for entering students, accelerated degree program, adult/continuing education programs, advanced placement credit, cooperative education, distance learning, double majors, external degree program, honors programs, independent study, internships, off-campus study, part-time degree program, services for LD students, student-designed majors, study abroad, summer session for credit. *ROTC:* Army (b).

Library IUN Library with 242,667 titles, 1,786 serial subscriptions, 1,224 audiovisual materials, an OPAC, a Web page.

Computers on Campus 250 computers available on campus for general student use. A campuswide network can be accessed from off campus. Internet access, online (class) registration, at least one staffed computer lab available.

Student Life *Housing:* college housing not available. *Activities and Organizations:* drama/theater group, student-run newspaper, choral group, Student Government Association, Student Guides Organization, Nursing Association, Dental Association, international affairs club, national fraternities, national sororities. *Campus security:* 24-hour emergency response devices and patrols, late-night transport/escort service, lighted pathways. *Student Services:* personal/psychological counseling.

Athletics Member NAIA. *Intercollegiate sports:* baseball M, basketball M, golf M, softball W. *Intramural sports:* basketball M(c), bowling M(c)/W(c), fencing M(c)/W(c), soccer M(c), softball M(c)/W(c), table tennis M(c)/W(c), tennis M(c)/W(c), volleyball M(c)/W(c).

Standardized Tests *Required:* SAT I or ACT (for admission).

Costs (2001–02) *Tuition:* state resident $3221 full-time, $107 per credit hour part-time; nonresident $8520 full-time, $284 per credit hour part-time. Full-time tuition and fees vary according to class time. Part-time tuition and fees vary according to class time. *Required fees:* $226 full-time. *Payment plans:* installment, deferred payment. *Waivers:* senior citizens and employees or children of employees.

Financial Aid Of all full-time matriculated undergraduates who enrolled in 2001, 1376 applied for aid, 935 were judged to have need, 67 had their need fully met. 96 Federal Work-Study jobs (averaging $2265). In 2001, 171 non-need-based awards were made. *Average percent of need met:* 54%. *Average financial aid package:* $4299. *Average need-based loan:* $2384. *Average need-based gift aid:* $3070. *Average non-need based aid:* $1310.

Applying *Options:* early admission, deferred entrance. *Application fee:* $25. *Required:* high school transcript, minimum 2.0 GPA. *Application deadline:* 8/1 (freshmen). *Notification:* continuous (freshmen).

Admissions Contact Charmaine Connelly, Assistant Director of Admissions, Indiana University Northwest, Hawthorne 100, 3400 Broadway, Gary, IN 46408-1197. *Phone:* 219-980-6991. *Toll-free phone:* 800-968-7486. *Fax:* 219-981-4219. *E-mail:* pkeshei@iun.edu.

Indiana University-Purdue University Fort Wayne

Fort Wayne, Indiana

- **State-supported** comprehensive, founded 1917, part of Indiana University System and Purdue University System
- **Calendar** semesters
- **Degrees** certificates, associate, bachelor's, master's, and postbachelor's certificates
- **Urban** 565-acre campus
- **Endowment** $17.7 million
- **Coed,** 10,282 undergraduate students, 56% full-time, 57% women, 43% men
- **Minimally difficult** entrance level, 97% of applicants were admitted

Undergraduates 5,725 full-time, 4,557 part-time. Students come from 39 states and territories, 66 other countries, 6% are from out of state, 5% African American, 2% Asian American or Pacific Islander, 2% Hispanic American, 0.4% Native American, 1% international, 9% transferred in, 0% live on campus. *Retention:* 61% of 2001 full-time freshmen returned.

Freshmen *Admission:* 2,479 applied, 2,393 admitted, 1,722 enrolled. *Average high school GPA:* 2.88. *Test scores:* SAT verbal scores over 500: 41%; SAT math scores over 500: 42%; ACT scores over 18: 77%; SAT verbal scores over 600: 9%; SAT math scores over 600: 10%; ACT scores over 24: 20%; SAT verbal scores over 700: 1%; SAT math scores over 700: 1%; ACT scores over 30: 2%.

Faculty *Total:* 634, 53% full-time, 51% with terminal degrees. *Student/faculty ratio:* 17:1.

Majors Accounting; anthropology; architectural engineering technology; biology; biology education; business administration; business economics; business marketing and marketing management; chemical technology; chemistry; chemistry education; civil engineering technology; computer science; construction technology; criminal justice studies; dental hygiene; dental laboratory technician; drama/dance education; early childhood education; economics; education; electrical/electronic engineering technology; electrical engineering; elementary education; engineering; English; finance; fine/studio arts; French; French language education; general studies; geology; German; German language education; graphic design/commercial art/illustration; health services administration; history; hospitality management; hotel and restaurant management; industrial technology; information sciences/systems; interior design; labor/personnel relations; mathematics; mathematics education; mechanical engineering; mechanical engineering technology; medical technology; music; music (piano and organ performance); music teacher education; music therapy; music (voice and choral/opera performance); nursing; operations management; philosophy; physics; physics education; political science; pre-dentistry; pre-medicine; psychology; public administration; public relations; science education; secondary education; social studies education; sociology; Spanish; Spanish language education; speech education; speech-language pathology/audiology; theater arts/drama; women's studies.

Academic Programs *Special study options:* academic remediation for entering students, accelerated degree program, adult/continuing education programs, advanced placement credit, cooperative education, distance learning, double majors, English as a second language, honors programs, independent study, internships, off-campus study, part-time degree program, services for LD students, student-designed majors, study abroad, summer session for credit.

Library Helmke Library with 451,969 titles, 3,079 serial subscriptions, 962 audiovisual materials, an OPAC, a Web page.

Computers on Campus 285 computers available on campus for general student use. A campuswide network can be accessed from off campus that provide access to students academic records. Internet access, online (class) registration, at least one staffed computer lab available.

Student Life *Housing:* college housing not available. *Activities and Organizations:* drama/theater group, student-run newspaper, television station, choral group, Campus Ministry, Hispanos Unidos, Sigma Phi Epsilon, Psi Chi, United Sexualities, national fraternities, national sororities. *Campus security:* 24-hour emergency response devices and patrols, late-night transport/escort service. *Student Services:* health clinic, personal/psychological counseling, women's center.

Athletics Member NCAA. All Division II. *Intercollegiate sports:* baseball M(s), basketball M(s)/W(s), cross-country running M(s)/W(s), soccer M(s)/W(s), softball W(s), tennis M(s)/W(s), track and field M(s)/W(s), volleyball M(s)/W(s). *Intramural sports:* badminton M/W, basketball M/W, football M, golf M/W, racquetball M/W, softball M/W, table tennis M/W, tennis M/W, volleyball M/W.

Standardized Tests *Required:* SAT I or ACT (for admission).

Costs (2001–02) *Tuition:* state resident $2960 full-time, $123 per semester hour part-time; nonresident $7169 full-time, $299 per semester hour part-time. Full-time tuition and fees vary according to course load. Part-time tuition and fees vary according to course load. *Required fees:* $206 full-time, $9 per semester hour. *Payment plans:* installment, deferred payment. *Waivers:* senior citizens and employees or children of employees.

Financial Aid Of all full-time matriculated undergraduates who enrolled in 2001, 2399 applied for aid, 1699 were judged to have need, 571 had their need fully met. 477 Federal Work-Study jobs (averaging $416). *Average percent of need met:* 83%. *Average indebtedness upon graduation:* $8088.

Applying *Options:* electronic application, early admission, deferred entrance. *Application fee:* $30. *Required:* high school transcript. *Recommended:* rank in upper 50% of high school class. *Application deadlines:* 8/1 (freshmen), 8/1 (transfers). *Notification:* continuous (freshmen).

Admissions Contact Ms. Carol Isaacs, Director of Admissions, Indiana University-Purdue University Fort Wayne, Admissions Office, 2101 East Coliseum Boulevard, Fort Wayne, IN 46805-1499. *Phone:* 219-481-6812. *Toll-free phone:* 800-324-4739. *Fax:* 219-481-6880. *E-mail:* ipfwadms@ipfw.edu.

INDIANA UNIVERSITY-PURDUE UNIVERSITY INDIANAPOLIS

Indianapolis, Indiana

- **State-supported** university, founded 1969, part of Indiana University System
- **Calendar** semesters
- **Degrees** certificates, associate, bachelor's, master's, doctoral, first professional, and postbachelor's certificates
- **Urban** 511-acre campus
- **Endowment** $292.1 million
- **Coed,** 20,695 undergraduate students, 58% full-time, 59% women, 41% men
- **Moderately difficult** entrance level, 73% of applicants were admitted

Undergraduates 11,957 full-time, 8,738 part-time. Students come from 40 states and territories, 3% are from out of state, 11% African American, 2% Asian American or Pacific Islander, 2% Hispanic American, 0.3% Native American, 2% international, 8% transferred in. *Retention:* 62% of 2001 full-time freshmen returned.

Freshmen *Admission:* 6,060 applied, 4,405 admitted, 2,978 enrolled. *Test scores:* SAT verbal scores over 500: 44%; SAT math scores over 500: 42%; ACT scores over 18: 75%; SAT verbal scores over 600: 10%; SAT math scores over 600: 10%; ACT scores over 24: 22%; SAT verbal scores over 700: 1%; SAT math scores over 700: 1%; ACT scores over 30: 1%.

Faculty *Total:* 2,630, 68% full-time, 66% with terminal degrees. *Student/faculty ratio:* 19:1.

Majors Anthropology; architectural drafting; architectural engineering technology; art education; art history; bioengineering; biology; biomedical engineering-related technology; business; chemistry; civil engineering technology; communications; computer engineering; computer/information sciences; criminal justice studies; cytotechnology; dental hygiene; early childhood education; economics; education; electrical/electronic engineering technology; electrical engineering; elementary education; emergency medical technology; engineering; English; English education; fine/studio arts; French; French language education; general studies; geography; geology; German; German language education; health education; health services administration; history; hospitality services management related; hotel and restaurant management; interior design; journalism; labor/personnel relations; mathematics; mechanical drafting; mechanical engineering; mechanical engineering technology; medical radiologic technology; medical records administration; medical technology; nuclear medical technology; nursing; occupational therapy; operations management; philosophy; physical education; physical therapy; physics; political science; pre-dentistry; pre-law; pre-medicine; pre-veterinary studies; psychology; public administration; public health; religious studies; respiratory therapy; robotics technology; secondary education; sign language interpretation; social studies education; social work; sociology; Spanish; Spanish language education; speech education.

Academic Programs *Special study options:* academic remediation for entering students, adult/continuing education programs, advanced placement credit, cooperative education, distance learning, double majors, English as a second language, external degree program, honors programs, independent study, internships, off-campus study, part-time degree program, services for LD students, study abroad, summer session for credit. *ROTC:* Army (b).

Library University Library plus 5 others with 1.4 million titles, 14,931 serial subscriptions, 434,863 audiovisual materials, an OPAC, a Web page.

Computers on Campus 500 computers available on campus for general student use. A campuswide network can be accessed from off campus. Internet access, at least one staffed computer lab available.

Student Life *Housing Options:* coed. *Activities and Organizations:* drama/theater group, student-run newspaper, choral group, Undergraduate Student Assembly, Black Student Union, Student Activities Programming Board, national fraternities, national sororities. *Campus security:* 24-hour emergency response devices and patrols, late-night transport/escort service, controlled dormitory access, lighted pathways, self-defense education. *Student Services:* health clinic, personal/psychological counseling, women's center.

Athletics Member NCAA. All Division I. *Intercollegiate sports:* baseball M(s), basketball M(s)/W(s), cross-country running M(s)/W(s), golf M(s), soccer M(s)/W(s), softball W(s), swimming M(s)/W(s), tennis M(s)/W(s), volleyball W(s). *Intramural sports:* badminton M/W, baseball M, basketball M/W, cross-country running M/W, football M, golf M/W, racquetball M/W, soccer M/W, softball M/W, swimming M/W, table tennis M/W, tennis M/W, track and field M/W, volleyball M/W, water polo M/W.

Standardized Tests *Required:* SAT I or ACT (for admission). *Recommended:* SAT I (for admission).

Costs (2001–02) *Tuition:* state resident $3839 full-time, $128 per credit hour part-time; nonresident $11,940 full-time, $398 per credit hour part-time. Full-time tuition and fees vary according to course load. Part-time tuition and fees vary according to course load. *Required fees:* $333 full-time. *Room and board:* $5302. Room and board charges vary according to board plan and housing facility. *Payment plans:* installment, deferred payment. *Waivers:* employees or children of employees.

Financial Aid Of all full-time matriculated undergraduates who enrolled in 2001, 7905 applied for aid, 6563 were judged to have need, 328 had their need fully met. 403 Federal Work-Study jobs (averaging $3049). In 2001, 812 non-need-based awards were made. *Average percent of need met:* 45%. *Average financial aid package:* $4944. *Average need-based loan:* $3018. *Average need-based gift aid:* $3423. *Average non-need based aid:* $1915.

Applying *Options:* electronic application, early admission, deferred entrance. *Application fee:* $35. *Required:* high school transcript. *Required for some:* interview. *Recommended:* portfolio for art program. *Application deadline:* rolling (freshmen), rolling (transfers). *Notification:* continuous (freshmen).

Admissions Contact Michael Donahue, Director of Admissions, Indiana University-Purdue University Indianapolis, 425 N. University Boulevard, Cavanaugh Hall Room 129, Indianapolis, IN 46202-5143. *Phone:* 317-274-4591. *Fax:* 317-278-1862. *E-mail:* apply@iupui.edu.

INDIANA UNIVERSITY SOUTH BEND

South Bend, Indiana

- **State-supported** comprehensive, founded 1922, part of Indiana University System
- **Calendar** semesters
- **Degrees** certificates, diplomas, associate, bachelor's, master's, and postbachelor's certificates
- **Suburban** 73-acre campus with easy access to Chicago
- **Endowment** $4.5 million
- **Coed,** 6,070 undergraduate students, 52% full-time, 64% women, 36% men
- **Moderately difficult** entrance level, 88% of applicants were admitted

Undergraduates 3,157 full-time, 2,913 part-time. Students come from 13 states and territories, 3% are from out of state, 7% African American, 1% Asian American or Pacific Islander, 3% Hispanic American, 0.5% Native American, 2% international, 7% transferred in. *Retention:* 64% of 2001 full-time freshmen returned.

Freshmen *Admission:* 1,600 applied, 1,409 admitted, 1,029 enrolled. *Test scores:* SAT verbal scores over 500: 44%; SAT math scores over 500: 39%; ACT scores over 18: 68%; SAT verbal scores over 600: 11%; SAT math scores over 600: 9%; ACT scores over 24: 23%; ACT scores over 30: 4%.

Faculty *Total:* 496, 51% full-time, 38% with terminal degrees. *Student/faculty ratio:* 14:1.

Majors Applied mathematics; art; biology; biology education; business; business marketing and marketing management; chemistry; chemistry education; computer science; criminal justice/law enforcement administration; dental hygiene; early childhood education; economics; education; elementary education; English; English education; film studies; finance; fine/studio arts; French; French language education; general studies; German; German language education; health services administration; history; jazz; labor/personnel relations; mass communications; mathematics; mathematics education; medical radiologic technology; music (general performance); music teacher education; nursing; paralegal/legal assistant; philosophy; physics; physics education; political science; psychology; public administration; science education; secondary education; social studies education; sociology; Spanish; Spanish language education; special education; speech/rhetorical studies; theater arts/drama; women's studies.

Academic Programs *Special study options:* accelerated degree program, adult/continuing education programs, distance learning, double majors, English

Indiana University South Bend (continued)
as a second language, external degree program, honors programs, internships, off-campus study, part-time degree program, study abroad, summer session for credit. *ROTC:* Army (c), Navy (c), Air Force (c).
Library Franklin D. Schurz Library plus 1 other with 592,095 titles, 2,116 serial subscriptions, 29,613 audiovisual materials.
Computers on Campus 200 computers available on campus for general student use. Internet access, at least one staffed computer lab available.
Student Life *Housing:* college housing not available. *Activities and Organizations:* drama/theater group, student-run newspaper, choral group, national fraternities. *Campus security:* 24-hour emergency response devices and patrols, late-night transport/escort service, safety seminars, lighted pathways. *Student Services:* personal/psychological counseling, women's center.
Athletics Member NAIA. *Intercollegiate sports:* basketball M(s)/W(s), soccer M, table tennis M/W, volleyball M/W. *Intramural sports:* baseball M, basketball M/W, cross-country running M/W, golf M/W, soccer W.
Standardized Tests *Required:* SAT I or ACT (for admission).
Costs (2001–02) *Tuition:* state resident $3278 full-time, $109 per credit hour part-time; nonresident $9147 full-time, $305 per credit hour part-time. Full-time tuition and fees vary according to course load. Part-time tuition and fees vary according to course load. *Required fees:* $237 full-time. *Payment plans:* installment, deferred payment. *Waivers:* employees or children of employees.
Financial Aid Of all full-time matriculated undergraduates who enrolled in 2001, 2116 applied for aid, 1545 were judged to have need, 145 had their need fully met. 145 Federal Work-Study jobs (averaging $2387). In 2001, 191 non-need-based awards were made. *Average percent of need met:* 53%. *Average financial aid package:* $4033. *Average need-based loan:* $2351. *Average need-based gift aid:* $2640. *Average non-need based aid:* $1808.
Applying *Options:* deferred entrance. *Application fee:* $40. *Required:* high school transcript, minimum 2.0 GPA. *Application deadlines:* 7/1 (freshmen), 6/1 (transfers). *Notification:* continuous (freshmen).
Admissions Contact Jeff Johnston, Director of Recruitment/Admissions, Indiana University South Bend, 1700 Mishawaka Avenue, Administration Building, Room 169, PO Box 7111, South Bend, IN 46634-7111. *Phone:* 219-237-4480. *Fax:* 219-237-4834. *E-mail:* admissions@iusb.edu.

INDIANA UNIVERSITY SOUTHEAST
New Albany, Indiana

- **State-supported** comprehensive, founded 1941, part of Indiana University System
- **Calendar** semesters
- **Degrees** certificates, associate, bachelor's, master's, and postbachelor's certificates
- **Suburban** 177-acre campus with easy access to Louisville
- **Endowment** $4.3 million
- **Coed,** 5,668 undergraduate students, 54% full-time, 63% women, 37% men
- **Minimally difficult** entrance level, 87% of applicants were admitted

Undergraduates 3,069 full-time, 2,599 part-time. Students come from 3 states and territories, 15% are from out of state, 2% African American, 0.4% Asian American or Pacific Islander, 0.5% Hispanic American, 0.2% Native American, 0.3% international, 6% transferred in. *Retention:* 64% of 2001 full-time freshmen returned.
Freshmen *Admission:* 1,352 applied, 1,173 admitted, 915 enrolled. *Test scores:* SAT verbal scores over 500: 41%; SAT math scores over 500: 36%; ACT scores over 18: 76%; SAT verbal scores over 600: 8%; SAT math scores over 600: 6%; ACT scores over 24: 18%; SAT verbal scores over 700: 1%.
Faculty *Total:* 410, 41% full-time, 38% with terminal degrees. *Student/faculty ratio:* 17:1.
Majors Art; biology; biology education; business; business economics; chemistry; communications; computer science; cytotechnology; economics; education; elementary education; English; English education; fine/studio arts; French; general studies; geography; German; history; journalism; labor/personnel relations; mathematics; mathematics education; medical technology; music; nursing; philosophy; political science; psychology; recreation/leisure facilities management; science education; secondary education; social studies education; sociology; Spanish; special education.
Academic Programs *Special study options:* academic remediation for entering students, accelerated degree program, adult/continuing education programs, advanced placement credit, double majors, external degree program, independent study, internships, off-campus study, part-time degree program, services for LD students, study abroad, summer session for credit. *ROTC:* Army (c), Air Force (c).
Library Main Library plus 1 other with 202,111 titles, 1,037 serial subscriptions, 15,676 audiovisual materials.
Computers on Campus 200 computers available on campus for general student use. A campuswide network can be accessed from off campus. Internet access available.
Student Life *Housing:* college housing not available. *Activities and Organizations:* drama/theater group, student-run newspaper, choral group, national fraternities, national sororities. *Campus security:* 24-hour emergency response devices and patrols, self-defense education, lighted pathways, police department on campus. *Student Services:* personal/psychological counseling.
Athletics Member NAIA. *Intercollegiate sports:* basketball M(s)/W(s), volleyball W(s). *Intramural sports:* basketball M/W, bowling M/W, cross-country running M/W, softball M/W, tennis M/W, volleyball W.
Standardized Tests *Required:* SAT I or ACT (for admission).
Costs (2001–02) *Tuition:* state resident $3221 full-time, $107 per credit hour part-time; nonresident $8520 full-time, $284 per credit hour part-time. Full-time tuition and fees vary according to course load. Part-time tuition and fees vary according to course load. *Required fees:* $239 full-time. *Waivers:* employees or children of employees.
Financial Aid Of all full-time matriculated undergraduates who enrolled in 2001, 1911 applied for aid, 1353 were judged to have need, 105 had their need fully met. 121 Federal Work-Study jobs (averaging $1872). In 2001, 323 non-need-based awards were made. *Average percent of need met:* 54%. *Average financial aid package:* $4158. *Average need-based loan:* $2447. *Average need-based gift aid:* $3273. *Average non-need based aid:* $1465.
Applying *Options:* early admission, deferred entrance. *Application fee:* $30. *Required:* high school transcript. *Required for some:* interview. *Application deadlines:* 7/15 (freshmen), 7/1 (transfers). *Notification:* continuous (freshmen).
Admissions Contact Mr. David B. Campbell, Director of Admissions, Indiana University Southeast, University Center Building, Room 100, 4201 Grant Line Road, New Albany, IN 47150. *Phone:* 812-941-2212. *Toll-free phone:* 800-852-8835. *Fax:* 812-941-2595. *E-mail:* admissions@ius.edu.

INDIANA WESLEYAN UNIVERSITY
Marion, Indiana

- **Independent Wesleyan** comprehensive, founded 1920
- **Calendar** 4-4-1
- **Degrees** associate, bachelor's, master's, and post-master's certificates (also offers adult program with significant enrollment not reflected in profile)
- **Small-town** 132-acre campus with easy access to Indianapolis
- **Endowment** $15.6 million
- **Coed,** 5,725 undergraduate students
- **Moderately difficult** entrance level, 79% of applicants were admitted

Undergraduates Students come from 42 states and territories, 17 other countries, 20% are from out of state, 10% African American, 0.6% Asian American or Pacific Islander, 1.0% Hispanic American, 0.5% Native American, 1.0% international, 70% live on campus. *Retention:* 74% of 2001 full-time freshmen returned.
Freshmen *Admission:* 1,702 applied, 1,352 admitted. *Average high school GPA:* 3.40. *Test scores:* SAT verbal scores over 500: 63%; SAT math scores over 500: 73%; ACT scores over 18: 93%; SAT verbal scores over 600: 28%; SAT math scores over 600: 25%; ACT scores over 24: 51%; SAT verbal scores over 700: 4%; SAT math scores over 700: 4%; ACT scores over 30: 9%.
Faculty *Total:* 175, 59% full-time, 33% with terminal degrees. *Student/faculty ratio:* 17:1.
Majors Accounting; alcohol/drug abuse counseling; art; art education; athletic training/sports medicine; biblical languages/literatures; biblical studies; biology; business administration; business marketing and marketing management; ceramic arts; chemistry; communications; computer graphics; computer/information sciences; creative writing; criminal justice studies; cultural studies; economics; education; education (K-12); elementary education; English; English education; exercise sciences; finance; general studies; history; mathematics; mathematics education; medical technology; middle school education; music; music teacher education; music theory and composition; nursing; painting; pastoral counseling; philosophy; photography; physical education; political science; pre-dentistry; pre-law; pre-medicine; pre-veterinary studies; printmaking; psychology; recreation/leisure facilities management; religious education; religious music; science education; secondary education; social sciences; social studies education; social work; sociology; Spanish; special education; sport/fitness administration; theology.
Academic Programs *Special study options:* academic remediation for entering students, accelerated degree program, adult/continuing education programs, advanced placement credit, distance learning, double majors, freshman honors college, honors programs, independent study, internships, off-campus study,

part-time degree program, services for LD students, student-designed majors, study abroad, summer session for credit.

Library Goodman Library with 106,362 titles, 5,343 serial subscriptions, 8,553 audiovisual materials, an OPAC, a Web page.

Computers on Campus 163 computers available on campus for general student use. A campuswide network can be accessed from student residence rooms. Internet access, at least one staffed computer lab available.

Student Life *Housing:* on-campus residence required through junior year. *Options:* men-only, women-only. *Activities and Organizations:* drama/theater group, student-run newspaper, radio and television station, choral group, Student Government Organization, Student Activities Council, University Players, World Christian Fellowship, International Student Association. *Campus security:* 24-hour emergency response devices and patrols, late-night transport/escort service, controlled dormitory access. *Student Services:* health clinic, personal/psychological counseling.

Athletics Member NAIA, NCCAA. *Intercollegiate sports:* baseball M(s), basketball M(s)/W(s), cross-country running M(s)/W(s), golf M(s), soccer M(s)/W(s), softball W(s), tennis M(s)/W(s), track and field M(s)/W(s), volleyball W(s). *Intramural sports:* badminton M/W, basketball M/W, bowling M/W, football M/W, golf M/W, racquetball M/W, soccer M/W, softball M, table tennis M/W, tennis M/W, volleyball M/W, weight lifting M/W.

Standardized Tests *Required:* SAT I or ACT (for admission).

Costs (2001–02) *Comprehensive fee:* $17,680 includes full-time tuition ($12,740) and room and board ($4940). Part-time tuition: $270 per credit hour. Part-time tuition and fees vary according to course load. *Room and board:* College room only: $1095. Room and board charges vary according to board plan. *Payment plan:* installment. *Waivers:* employees or children of employees.

Applying *Options:* electronic application, deferred entrance. *Application fee:* $25. *Required:* essay or personal statement, high school transcript, minimum 2.0 GPA, 1 letter of recommendation. *Required for some:* interview. *Application deadline:* rolling (freshmen), rolling (transfers). *Notification:* continuous (freshmen).

Admissions Contact Ms. Gaytha Holloway, Director of Admissions, Indiana Wesleyan University, 4201 South Washington Street, Marion, IN 46953. *Phone:* 765-677-2138. *Toll-free phone:* 800-332-6901. *Fax:* 765-677-2333. *E-mail:* admissions@indwes.edu.

INTERNATIONAL BUSINESS COLLEGE

Fort Wayne, Indiana

- **Proprietary** primarily 2-year, founded 1889, part of Bradford Schools, Inc
- **Calendar** semesters
- **Degrees** diplomas, associate, and bachelor's
- **Suburban** 2-acre campus
- **Coed, primarily women,** 659 undergraduate students
- **Minimally difficult** entrance level, 96% of applicants were admitted

Freshmen *Admission:* 1,053 applied, 1,011 admitted.

Faculty *Total:* 44, 25% full-time. *Student/faculty ratio:* 24:1.

Majors Accounting; business administration; computer engineering technology; computer programming; engineering/industrial management; finance; graphic design/commercial art/illustration; hospitality management; legal administrative assistant; medical assistant; paralegal/legal assistant; retail management; secretarial science; travel/tourism management.

Academic Programs *Special study options:* adult/continuing education programs, independent study, internships, part-time degree program.

Library 2,100 titles, 100 serial subscriptions.

Computers on Campus 150 computers available on campus for general student use. At least one staffed computer lab available.

Student Life *Activities and Organizations:* Student Senate, Collegiate Secretarial Institute, Accounting Club. *Campus security:* controlled dormitory access.

Costs (2001–02) *Tuition:* $9200 full-time. No tuition increase for student's term of enrollment. *Room only:* $3900.

Applying *Options:* deferred entrance. *Application fee:* $50. *Required:* high school transcript. *Application deadline:* 9/3 (freshmen).

Admissions Contact Mr. Steve Kinzer, School Director, International Business College, 3811 Illinois Road, Fort Wayne, IN 46804. *Phone:* 219-459-4513. *Toll-free phone:* 800-589-6363. *Fax:* 219-436-1896.

ITT TECHNICAL INSTITUTE

Newburgh, Indiana

- **Proprietary** primarily 2-year, founded 1966, part of ITT Educational Services, Inc
- **Calendar** quarters
- **Degrees** associate and bachelor's
- **Coed,** 364 undergraduate students
- **Minimally difficult** entrance level

Majors Computer/information sciences related; computer programming; drafting; electrical/electronic engineering technologies related; information technology; robotics technology.

Student Life *Housing:* college housing not available.

Costs (2001–02) *Tuition:* Full-time tuition and fees vary according to program. Part-time tuition and fees vary according to program. $260—$330 per credit hour.

Financial Aid *Financial aid deadline:* 3/1.

Applying *Options:* deferred entrance. *Application fee:* $100. *Required:* high school transcript, interview. *Recommended:* letters of recommendation. *Application deadline:* rolling (freshmen), rolling (transfers). *Notification:* continuous (freshmen).

Admissions Contact Mr. Jim Smolinski, Director of Recruitment, ITT Technical Institute, 10999 Stahl Road, Newburgh, IN 47630-7430. *Phone:* 812-858-1600.

ITT TECHNICAL INSTITUTE

Fort Wayne, Indiana

- **Proprietary** primarily 2-year, founded 1967, part of ITT Educational Services, Inc
- **Calendar** quarters
- **Degrees** associate and bachelor's
- **Coed,** 509 undergraduate students
- **Minimally difficult** entrance level

Majors Computer/information sciences related; computer programming; drafting; industrial design; information technology; robotics technology.

Student Life *Housing:* college housing not available.

Costs (2001–02) *Tuition:* Full-time tuition and fees vary according to program. Part-time tuition and fees vary according to program. $260—$330 per credit hour.

Applying *Options:* deferred entrance. *Application fee:* $100. *Required:* high school transcript, interview. *Recommended:* letters of recommendation. *Application deadline:* rolling (freshmen), rolling (transfers). *Notification:* continuous (freshmen).

Admissions Contact Mr. Jack Young, Director of Recruitment, ITT Technical Institute, 4919 Coldwater Road, Fort Wayne, IN 46825-5532. *Phone:* 260-484-4107 Ext. 244. *Toll-free phone:* 800-866-4488.

ITT TECHNICAL INSTITUTE

Indianapolis, Indiana

- **Proprietary** founded 1966, part of ITT Educational Services, Inc
- **Calendar** quarters
- **Degrees** diplomas, associate, bachelor's, and master's
- **Suburban** 10-acre campus
- **Coed,** 798 undergraduate students
- **Minimally difficult** entrance level

Majors Computer/information sciences related; computer programming; design/applied arts related; drafting; electrical/electronic engineering technologies related; information technology; robotics technology.

Student Life *Housing:* college housing not available. *Activities and Organizations:* student-run newspaper.

Costs (2001–02) *Tuition:* Full-time tuition and fees vary according to program. Part-time tuition and fees vary according to program. $260—$330 per credit hour.

Applying *Options:* deferred entrance. *Application fee:* $100. *Required:* high school transcript, interview. *Recommended:* letters of recommendation. *Application deadline:* rolling (freshmen), rolling (transfers). *Notification:* continuous (freshmen).

Admissions Contact Mr. Byron Ratclife, Director of Recruitment, ITT Technical Institute, 9511 Angola Court, Indianapolis, IN 46268-1119. *Phone:* 317-875-8640. *Toll-free phone:* 800-937-4488. *Fax:* 317-875-8641.

MANCHESTER COLLEGE

North Manchester, Indiana

- **Independent** comprehensive, founded 1889, affiliated with Church of the Brethren

Manchester College (continued)

- **Calendar** 4-1-4
- **Degrees** associate, bachelor's, and master's
- **Small-town** 125-acre campus
- **Endowment** $26.4 million
- **Coed,** 1,135 undergraduate students, 97% full-time, 55% women, 45% men
- **Moderately difficult** entrance level, 81% of applicants were admitted

Undergraduates 1,102 full-time, 33 part-time. Students come from 23 states and territories, 29 other countries, 11% are from out of state, 3% transferred in, 77% live on campus. *Retention:* 76% of 2001 full-time freshmen returned.

Freshmen *Admission:* 1,103 applied, 896 admitted, 334 enrolled. *Test scores:* SAT verbal scores over 500: 54%; SAT math scores over 500: 58%; ACT scores over 18: 83%; SAT verbal scores over 600: 14%; SAT math scores over 600: 19%; ACT scores over 24: 35%; SAT verbal scores over 700: 2%; SAT math scores over 700: 2%; ACT scores over 30: 5%.

Faculty *Total:* 87, 78% full-time, 76% with terminal degrees. *Student/faculty ratio:* 14:1.

Majors Accounting; art; art education; athletic training/sports medicine; biology; broadcast journalism; business; business administration; business marketing and marketing management; chemistry; computer science; creative writing; criminal justice studies; early childhood education; ecology; economics; education; elementary education; engineering science; English; environmental science; exercise sciences; finance; fine/studio arts; French; German; gerontology; health education; health science; history; interdisciplinary studies; journalism; literature; mass communications; mathematics; medical technology; music; music teacher education; nonprofit/public management; peace/conflict studies; philosophy; physical education; physics; political science; pre-dentistry; pre-law; pre-medicine; pre-theology; pre-veterinary studies; psychology; religious studies; science education; secondary education; social work; sociology; Spanish; special education; speech/rhetorical studies; theater arts/drama.

Academic Programs *Special study options:* adult/continuing education programs, advanced placement credit, double majors, honors programs, independent study, internships, off-campus study, part-time degree program, services for LD students, student-designed majors, study abroad, summer session for credit. *Unusual degree programs:* 3-2 engineering with Washington University in St. Louis; nursing with Goshen College; physical therapy, occupational therapy.

Library Funderburg Library with 172,822 titles, 740 serial subscriptions, 5,278 audiovisual materials, an OPAC, a Web page.

Computers on Campus 165 computers available on campus for general student use. A campuswide network can be accessed from student residence rooms and from off campus. Internet access, at least one staffed computer lab available.

Student Life *Housing:* on-campus residence required through junior year. *Options:* coed, men-only, women-only, disabled students. *Activities and Organizations:* drama/theater group, student-run newspaper, radio station, choral group, volunteer services, Campus Ministry Board, accounting club, Manchester Admissions Recruiting Corps, Student Alumni Council. *Campus security:* 24-hour emergency response devices and patrols, student patrols, late-night transport/escort service, alarm system, locked residence hall entrances. *Student Services:* health clinic, personal/psychological counseling.

Athletics Member NCAA. All Division III. *Intercollegiate sports:* baseball M, basketball M/W, cross-country running M/W, football M, golf M/W, soccer M/W, softball W, tennis M/W, track and field M/W, volleyball W, wrestling M. *Intramural sports:* badminton M/W, basketball M/W, bowling M/W, football M/W, racquetball M/W, soccer M/W, table tennis M/W, tennis M/W, track and field M/W, volleyball M/W.

Standardized Tests *Required:* SAT I or ACT (for admission).

Costs (2002–03) *Comprehensive fee:* $19,800 includes full-time tuition ($15,980), mandatory fees ($100), and room and board ($3720). Part-time tuition: $530 per credit hour. *Room and board:* College room only: $2210. Room and board charges vary according to board plan and housing facility. *Payment plan:* installment. *Waivers:* employees or children of employees.

Financial Aid Of all full-time matriculated undergraduates who enrolled in 2001, 1103 applied for aid, 930 were judged to have need, 647 had their need fully met. In 2001, 191 non-need-based awards were made. *Average percent of need met:* 95%. *Average financial aid package:* $15,286. *Average need-based loan:* $4175. *Average need-based gift aid:* $10,616. *Average non-need based aid:* $7311. *Average indebtedness upon graduation:* $13,461.

Applying *Options:* common application, electronic application, deferred entrance. *Application fee:* $20. *Required:* high school transcript, 1 letter of recommendation, rank in upper 50% of high school class. *Required for some:* essay or personal statement, minimum 3.0 GPA, interview. *Recommended:* minimum 2.3 GPA, interview. *Application deadline:* rolling (freshmen), rolling (transfers). *Notification:* continuous (freshmen).

Admissions Contact Ms. Jolane Rohr, Director of Admissions, Manchester College, 604 East College Avenue, North Manchester, IN 46962-1225. *Phone:* 219-982-5055. *Toll-free phone:* 800-852-3648. *Fax:* 260-982-5239. *E-mail:* admitinfo@manchester.edu.

MARIAN COLLEGE
Indianapolis, Indiana

- **Independent Roman Catholic** comprehensive, founded 1851
- **Calendar** semesters
- **Degrees** associate, bachelor's, and master's
- **Urban** 114-acre campus
- **Endowment** $5.4 million
- **Coed,** 1,260 undergraduate students, 69% full-time, 75% women, 25% men
- **Moderately difficult** entrance level, 79% of applicants were admitted

Undergraduates 872 full-time, 388 part-time. Students come from 22 states and territories, 15 other countries, 7% are from out of state, 17% African American, 1% Asian American or Pacific Islander, 2% Hispanic American, 0.5% Native American, 2% international, 9% transferred in, 41% live on campus. *Retention:* 69% of 2001 full-time freshmen returned.

Freshmen *Admission:* 700 applied, 556 admitted, 191 enrolled. *Average high school GPA:* 3.04. *Test scores:* SAT verbal scores over 500: 42%; SAT math scores over 500: 42%; ACT scores over 18: 50%; SAT verbal scores over 600: 11%; SAT math scores over 600: 12%; ACT scores over 24: 10%; SAT verbal scores over 700: 3%; SAT math scores over 700: 1%.

Faculty *Total:* 145, 48% full-time. *Student/faculty ratio:* 12:1.

Majors Accounting; art; art education; art history; biology; business administration; chemistry; early childhood education; education; elementary education; English; finance; fine/studio arts; French; history; interior design; liberal arts and sciences/liberal studies; mass communications; mathematics; music; music teacher education; nursing; philosophy; physical education; pre-dentistry; pre-engineering; pre-law; pre-medicine; pre-veterinary studies; psychology; religious education; secondary education; sociology; Spanish; special education; theology.

Academic Programs *Special study options:* academic remediation for entering students, accelerated degree program, adult/continuing education programs, advanced placement credit, cooperative education, double majors, honors programs, independent study, internships, off-campus study, part-time degree program, services for LD students, study abroad, summer session for credit. *ROTC:* Army (c), Air Force (c).

Library Mother Theresa Hackelmeier Memorial Library with 132,000 titles, an OPAC, a Web page.

Computers on Campus 130 computers available on campus for general student use. A campuswide network can be accessed from student residence rooms. Internet access, at least one staffed computer lab available.

Student Life *Housing:* on-campus residence required through senior year. *Options:* coed. *Activities and Organizations:* drama/theater group, student-run newspaper, choral group, Fellowship of Christian Athletics, Marian College Student Association, Residence Hall Council, business club, BBB. *Campus security:* 24-hour patrols, late-night transport/escort service. *Student Services:* health clinic, personal/psychological counseling.

Athletics Member NAIA. *Intercollegiate sports:* baseball M(s), basketball M(s)/W(s), cross-country running M(s)/W(s), golf M(s)/W(s), soccer M(s)/W(s), softball W(s), tennis M(s)/W(s), track and field M(s)/W(s), volleyball W(s). *Intramural sports:* basketball M/W, football M/W, racquetball M/W, table tennis M/W, tennis M/W, volleyball M/W.

Standardized Tests *Required:* SAT I or ACT (for admission).

Costs (2001–02) *Comprehensive fee:* $21,060 includes full-time tuition ($15,266), mandatory fees ($404), and room and board ($5390). Part-time tuition: $658 per credit. Part-time tuition and fees vary according to class time and course load. *Required fees:* $250 per credit. *Room and board:* Room and board charges vary according to board plan and housing facility. *Payment plans:* installment, deferred payment. *Waivers:* senior citizens and employees or children of employees.

Financial Aid Of all full-time matriculated undergraduates who enrolled in 2001, 832 applied for aid, 685 were judged to have need, 372 had their need fully met. In 2001, 121 non-need-based awards were made. *Average percent of need met:* 85%. *Average financial aid package:* $13,727. *Average need-based loan:* $3620. *Average need-based gift aid:* $7317. *Average non-need based aid:* $7446. *Average indebtedness upon graduation:* $16,571.

Applying *Options:* common application, electronic application, early admission, deferred entrance. *Application fee:* $20. *Required:* high school transcript, minimum 2.00 GPA. *Application deadlines:* 8/15 (freshmen), 8/1 (transfers). *Notification:* continuous until 8/24 (freshmen).

Admissions Contact Ms. Karen Kist, Director of Admission, Marian College, 3200 Cold Spring Road, Indianapolis, IN 46222-1997. *Phone:* 317-955-6300. *Toll-free phone:* 800-772-7264.

MARTIN UNIVERSITY
Indianapolis, Indiana

- **Independent** comprehensive, founded 1977
- **Calendar** semesters
- **Degrees** bachelor's and master's
- **Urban** 5-acre campus
- **Coed**
- **Noncompetitive** entrance level

Faculty *Student/faculty ratio:* 20:1.
Student Life *Campus security:* building security, security personnel from 7 a.m. to 9:30 p.m.
Standardized Tests *Required for some:* Wonderlic aptitude test, Wide Range Achievement Test.
Financial Aid Of all full-time matriculated undergraduates who enrolled in 2001, 475 applied for aid, 300 were judged to have need. *Average percent of need met:* 80. *Average financial aid package:* $12,924. *Average need-based gift aid:* $7164.
Applying *Options:* early admission, deferred entrance. *Application fee:* $25. *Required:* essay or personal statement, high school transcript, interview, writing sample.
Admissions Contact Ms. Brenda Shaheed, Director of Enrollment Management, Martin University, 2171 Avondale Place, PO Box 18567, Indianapolis, IN 46218-3867. *Phone:* 317-543-3237. *Fax:* 317-543-4790.

OAKLAND CITY UNIVERSITY
Oakland City, Indiana

- **Independent General Baptist** comprehensive, founded 1885
- **Calendar** semesters
- **Degrees** certificates, diplomas, associate, bachelor's, master's, doctoral, and first professional
- **Rural** 20-acre campus
- **Endowment** $1.3 million
- **Coed,** 1,487 undergraduate students, 82% full-time, 54% women, 46% men
- **Minimally difficult** entrance level, 100% of applicants were admitted

Undergraduates 1,213 full-time, 274 part-time. Students come from 5 states and territories, 23% are from out of state, 11% African American, 0.4% Asian American or Pacific Islander, 2% Hispanic American, 0.6% Native American, 8% transferred in, 42% live on campus. *Retention:* 91% of 2001 full-time freshmen returned.
Freshmen *Admission:* 332 applied, 332 admitted, 332 enrolled. *Average high school GPA:* 3.10.
Faculty *Total:* 162, 22% full-time, 17% with terminal degrees. *Student/faculty ratio:* 15:1.
Majors Accounting; applied art; applied mathematics; art; art education; auto mechanic/technician; biblical studies; biological/physical sciences; biology; business administration; business education; chemistry; computer engineering technology; computer graphics; computer management; computer programming; computer science; criminal justice/law enforcement administration; culinary arts; divinity/ministry; education; elementary education; English; English education; heating/air conditioning/refrigeration; humanities; human resources management; industrial design; information sciences/systems; interdisciplinary studies; liberal arts and sciences/liberal studies; management science; mathematics; mathematics education; middle school education; music; music teacher education; organizational behavior; physical education; pre-law; pre-medicine; preveterinary studies; religious education; religious studies; science education; secondary education; secretarial science; social sciences; social studies education; theology; welding technology.
Academic Programs *Special study options:* academic remediation for entering students, accelerated degree program, adult/continuing education programs, advanced placement credit, external degree program, part-time degree program, services for LD students, summer session for credit.
Library Founders Memorial Library with 75,000 titles, 350 serial subscriptions, an OPAC.
Computers on Campus 70 computers available on campus for general student use. Internet access, at least one staffed computer lab available.
Student Life *Housing:* on-campus residence required for freshman year. *Activities and Organizations:* drama/theater group, student-run newspaper, choral group, Student Government Association, Good News Players, Art Guild. *Campus security:* 24-hour patrols, student patrols. *Student Services:* personal/psychological counseling.
Athletics Member NAIA, NCCAA, NSCAA. *Intercollegiate sports:* baseball M(s), basketball M(s)/W(s), cross-country running M(s)/W(s), golf M/W, soccer M/W, softball W(s), volleyball W(s). *Intramural sports:* archery M/W, badminton M/W, basketball M/W, bowling M/W, golf M/W, soccer M/W, softball M/W, table tennis M/W, tennis M/W, volleyball M/W.
Standardized Tests *Required:* SAT I or ACT (for placement). *Recommended:* SAT I or ACT (for admission).
Costs (2002–03) *Comprehensive fee:* $16,138 includes full-time tuition ($11,490), mandatory fees ($318), and room and board ($4330). Full-time tuition and fees vary according to location and program. Part-time tuition: $383 per hour. Part-time tuition and fees vary according to location and program. *Room and board:* College room only: $1390. Room and board charges vary according to housing facility. *Payment plans:* installment, deferred payment. *Waivers:* minority students and employees or children of employees.
Applying *Options:* common application, early admission, deferred entrance. *Application fee:* $35. *Required:* essay or personal statement, high school transcript, minimum 2.0 GPA, 1 letter of recommendation. *Recommended:* interview. *Application deadline:* rolling (freshmen). *Notification:* continuous (freshmen).
Admissions Contact Jeff Main, Director of Admissions, Oakland City University, 143 North Lucretia Street, Oakland City, IN 47660-1099. *Phone:* 812-749-1222. *Toll-free phone:* 800-737-5125.

PURDUE UNIVERSITY
West Lafayette, Indiana

- **State-supported** university, founded 1869, part of Purdue University System
- **Calendar** semesters
- **Degrees** certificates, associate, bachelor's, master's, doctoral, and first professional
- **Suburban** 1579-acre campus with easy access to Indianapolis
- **Endowment** $1.2 billion
- **Coed,** 30,987 undergraduate students, 94% full-time, 42% women, 58% men
- **Moderately difficult** entrance level, 77% of applicants were admitted

Undergraduates 29,238 full-time, 1,749 part-time. Students come from 52 states and territories, 105 other countries, 23% are from out of state, 3% African American, 4% Asian American or Pacific Islander, 2% Hispanic American, 0.4% Native American, 6% international, 3% transferred in, 39% live on campus. *Retention:* 89% of 2001 full-time freshmen returned.
Freshmen *Admission:* 21,760 applied, 16,727 admitted, 6,504 enrolled. *Test scores:* SAT verbal scores over 500: 75%; SAT math scores over 500: 82%; ACT scores over 18: 99%; SAT verbal scores over 600: 27%; SAT math scores over 600: 43%; ACT scores over 24: 67%; SAT verbal scores over 700: 4%; SAT math scores over 700: 9%; ACT scores over 30: 13%.
Faculty *Total:* 1,891, 98% full-time, 98% with terminal degrees. *Student/faculty ratio:* 16:1.
Majors Accounting; aerospace engineering; aerospace engineering technology; African-American studies; agricultural economics; agricultural education; agricultural engineering; agricultural mechanization; agricultural sciences; agronomy/crop science; aircraft pilot (professional); animal sciences; aquaculture operations/production management; architectural engineering technology; art; aviation/airway science; biochemistry; biological/physical sciences; biology; botany; business administration; chemical engineering; chemistry; civil engineering; clothing/apparel/textile studies; communications; computer engineering; computer/information sciences; design/visual communications; early childhood education; economics; education; electrical/electronic engineering technology; electrical engineering; elementary education; engineering; English; entomology; food sciences; foreign languages/literatures; forestry; geology; history; home economics; horticulture science; hotel and restaurant management; humanities; individual/family development; industrial arts education; industrial/manufacturing engineering; industrial technology; interdisciplinary studies; landscape architecture; materials engineering; mathematical statistics; mathematics; mechanical drafting; mechanical engineering; medical technology; natural resources conservation; nuclear engineering; nursing; nutrition studies; operations management; pharmacy; philosophy; physical education; physical sciences; physics; political science; pre-medicine; pre-veterinary studies; psychology; robotics technology; social sciences; sociology; speech-language pathology/audiology; surveying; theater arts/drama; trade/industrial education; veterinarian assistant; wildlife management.
Academic Programs *Special study options:* accelerated degree program, adult/continuing education programs, advanced placement credit, cooperative

Purdue University (continued)

education, distance learning, double majors, freshman honors college, honors programs, independent study, internships, part-time degree program, services for LD students, student-designed majors, study abroad, summer session for credit. *ROTC:* Army (b), Navy (b), Air Force (b).

Library Hicks Undergraduate Library plus 14 others with 1.1 million titles, 18,635 serial subscriptions, 10,666 audiovisual materials, an OPAC, a Web page.

Computers on Campus 2100 computers available on campus for general student use. A campuswide network can be accessed from student residence rooms and from off campus. Internet access, at least one staffed computer lab available.

Student Life *Housing Options:* coed, men-only, women-only. *Activities and Organizations:* drama/theater group, student-run newspaper, radio station, choral group, marching band, student government, Alpha Phi Omega, Society of Women Engineers, ballroom dancing, Golden Key National Honor Society, national fraternities, national sororities. *Campus security:* 24-hour emergency response devices and patrols, student patrols, late-night transport/escort service, controlled dormitory access. *Student Services:* health clinic, personal/psychological counseling, women's center.

Athletics Member NCAA. All Division I except football (Division I-A). *Intercollegiate sports:* archery M(c)/W(c), badminton M(c)/W(c), baseball M(s), basketball M(s)/W(s), crew M(c)/W(c), cross-country running M(s)/W(s), equestrian sports M(c)/W(c), fencing M(c)/W(c), golf M(s)/W(s), gymnastics M(c)/W(c), ice hockey M(c), lacrosse M(c)/W(c), racquetball M(c)/W(c), riflery M(c)/W(c), rugby M(c)/W(c), sailing M(c)/W(c), skiing (downhill) M(c)/W(c), soccer M(c)/W(s), softball W(s), squash M(c)/W(c), swimming M(s)/W(s), table tennis M(c)/W(c), tennis M(s)/W(s), track and field M(s)/W(s), volleyball M(c)/W(s), water polo M(c)/W(c), weight lifting M(c)/W(c), wrestling M(s). *Intramural sports:* archery M/W, badminton M/W, basketball M/W, bowling M/W, cross-country running M/W, football M, golf M/W, racquetball M/W, riflery M/W, soccer M/W, softball M/W, squash M, swimming M/W, table tennis M/W, tennis M/W, track and field M/W, volleyball M/W, water polo M/W.

Standardized Tests *Required:* SAT I or ACT (for admission).

Costs (2001–02) *Tuition:* state resident $4164 full-time, $145 per semester hour part-time; nonresident $13,872 full-time, $454 per semester hour part-time. Full-time tuition and fees vary according to course load. Part-time tuition and fees vary according to course load. *Room and board:* $6120. Room and board charges vary according to board plan and housing facility. *Payment plan:* installment. *Waivers:* senior citizens and employees or children of employees.

Financial Aid Of all full-time matriculated undergraduates who enrolled in 2001, 16542 applied for aid, 10751 were judged to have need, 4596 had their need fully met. 971 Federal Work-Study jobs (averaging $1626). In 2001, 3468 non-need-based awards were made. *Average percent of need met:* 91%. *Average financial aid package:* $7621. *Average need-based loan:* $3724. *Average need-based gift aid:* $5389. *Average indebtedness upon graduation:* $15,486.

Applying *Options:* electronic application, early admission, deferred entrance. *Application fee:* $30. *Required:* high school transcript. *Application deadline:* rolling (freshmen), rolling (transfers).

Admissions Contact Director of Admissions, Purdue University, Schleman Hall, West Lafayette, IN 47907-1080. *Phone:* 765-494-1776. *E-mail:* admissions@purdue.edu.

PURDUE UNIVERSITY CALUMET
Hammond, Indiana

- **State-supported** comprehensive, founded 1951, part of Purdue University System
- **Calendar** semesters
- **Degrees** certificates, associate, bachelor's, master's, and postbachelor's certificates
- **Urban** 167-acre campus with easy access to Chicago
- **Coed**
- **Minimally difficult** entrance level, 99% of applicants were admitted

Freshmen *Admission:* 1,642 applied, 1,630 admitted.

Faculty *Total:* 480, 63% full-time, 41% with terminal degrees.

Majors Accounting; architectural engineering technology; Army R.O.T.C./military science; behavioral sciences; biological/physical sciences; biological technology; biology; botany; business administration; business marketing and marketing management; chemistry; child care/development; civil engineering technology; clinical psychology; computer engineering; computer engineering technology; computer/information sciences; computer programming; computer science; construction technology; counselor education/guidance; criminal justice/law enforcement administration; culinary arts; dietetics; early childhood education; economics; education; education administration; electrical/electronic engineering technology; electrical engineering; elementary education; engineering; engineering technology; English; food products retailing; food services technology; French; German; history; hotel and restaurant management; humanities; human resources management; industrial/manufacturing engineering; industrial technology; information sciences/systems; journalism; law enforcement/police science; liberal arts and sciences/liberal studies; literature; mass communications; mathematics; mechanical engineering; mechanical engineering technology; medical laboratory technician; medical technology; metallurgical technology; microbiology/bacteriology; nursing; philosophy; physics; political science; pre-dentistry; pre-law; pre-medicine; pre-veterinary studies; psychology; public relations; radio/television broadcasting; science education; secondary education; social work; sociology; Spanish; special education; wildlife management; women's studies.

Academic Programs *Special study options:* academic remediation for entering students, adult/continuing education programs, advanced placement credit, cooperative education, honors programs, internships, part-time degree program, services for LD students, summer session for credit. *ROTC:* Army (c).

Library Purdue Calumet Library with 215,830 titles, 1,736 serial subscriptions.

Computers on Campus 250 computers available on campus for general student use. Internet access, at least one staffed computer lab available.

Student Life *Housing:* college housing not available. *Activities and Organizations:* drama/theater group, student-run newspaper, choral group, Los Latinos, student government, Theater Club, Black Student Union, Song Company, national fraternities, national sororities. *Campus security:* 24-hour emergency response devices and patrols, student patrols, late-night transport/escort service. *Student Services:* personal/psychological counseling.

Athletics Member NAIA. *Intercollegiate sports:* basketball M(s)/W(s), soccer M(s), volleyball W(s). *Intramural sports:* football M/W, golf M/W, racquetball M/W, softball M/W, volleyball M/W, weight lifting M/W.

Standardized Tests *Required for some:* SAT I or ACT (for admission).

Costs (2001–02) *Tuition:* state resident $3053 full-time, $109 per credit hour part-time; nonresident $7679 full-time, $274 per credit hour part-time. Full-time tuition and fees vary according to program. Part-time tuition and fees vary according to course load and program. *Required fees:* $286 full-time, $10 per credit hour. *Payment plan:* deferred payment. *Waivers:* senior citizens and employees or children of employees.

Financial Aid Of all full-time matriculated undergraduates who enrolled in 2001, 2647 applied for aid, 2023 were judged to have need, 18 had their need fully met. 130 Federal Work-Study jobs. In 2001, 368 non-need-based awards were made. *Average percent of need met:* 33%. *Average financial aid package:* $2900. *Average need-based loan:* $2500. *Average need-based gift aid:* $2200. *Average indebtedness upon graduation:* $10,500.

Applying *Options:* common application, early admission. *Required:* high school transcript. *Application deadline:* rolling (freshmen), rolling (transfers).

Admissions Contact Mr. Paul McGuinness, Director of Admissions, Purdue University Calumet, 173rd and Woodmar Avenue, Hammond, IN 46323-2094. *Phone:* 219-989-2213. *Toll-free phone:* 800-447-8738. *E-mail:* adms@calumet.purdue.edu.

PURDUE UNIVERSITY NORTH CENTRAL
Westville, Indiana

- **State-supported** comprehensive, founded 1967, part of Purdue University System
- **Calendar** semesters
- **Degrees** certificates, associate, bachelor's, and master's
- **Rural** 264-acre campus with easy access to Chicago
- **Endowment** $442,108
- **Coed**, 3,467 undergraduate students, 55% full-time, 60% women, 40% men
- **Noncompetitive** entrance level, 100% of applicants were admitted

Undergraduates 1,917 full-time, 1,550 part-time. Students come from 5 states and territories, 1% are from out of state, 4% African American, 0.8% Asian American or Pacific Islander, 3% Hispanic American, 1% Native American, 0.2% international, 15% transferred in. *Retention:* 54% of 2001 full-time freshmen returned.

Freshmen *Admission:* 1,049 applied, 1,046 admitted, 725 enrolled. *Average high school GPA:* 2.79. *Test scores:* SAT verbal scores over 500: 27%; SAT math scores over 500: 30%; ACT scores over 18: 65%; SAT verbal scores over 600: 4%; SAT math scores over 600: 4%; ACT scores over 24: 13%.

Faculty *Total:* 242, 38% full-time, 29% with terminal degrees. *Student/faculty ratio:* 17:1.

Majors Accounting; architectural engineering technology; biology; business administration; business marketing and marketing management; civil engineering technology; computer engineering technology; computer programming; construction technology; electrical/electronic engineering technology; elementary education; engineering technology; English; health services administration; hotel and restaurant management; industrial technology; information sciences/systems; liberal arts and sciences/liberal studies; marketing operations; mechanical engineering technology; medical laboratory technology; medical technology; nursing; pre-engineering.

Academic Programs *Special study options:* academic remediation for entering students, adult/continuing education programs, advanced placement credit, cooperative education, honors programs, internships, part-time degree program, services for LD students, student-designed majors, summer session for credit.

Library Purdue University North Central Library with 88,156 titles, 417 serial subscriptions, 541 audiovisual materials, an OPAC, a Web page.

Computers on Campus 382 computers available on campus for general student use. At least one staffed computer lab available.

Student Life *Housing:* college housing not available. *Activities and Organizations:* drama/theater group, student-run newspaper, Student Cultural Society, Student Education Association, construction club. *Campus security:* 24-hour emergency response devices, late-night transport/escort service. *Student Services:* personal/psychological counseling.

Athletics Member NAIA. *Intercollegiate sports:* baseball M(c), basketball M(c), cross-country running M(c). *Intramural sports:* basketball M/W, cross-country running M/W, football M/W, golf M/W, skiing (cross-country) M/W, skiing (downhill) M/W, softball M/W, table tennis M/W, tennis M/W, volleyball M/W.

Standardized Tests *Required for some:* SAT I or ACT (for admission). *Recommended:* SAT I (for admission), ACT (for admission).

Costs (2001–02) *Tuition:* state resident $3271 full-time, $110 per credit hour part-time; nonresident $8301 full-time, $277 per credit hour part-time. Full-time tuition and fees vary according to course load. Part-time tuition and fees vary according to course load. *Required fees:* $318 full-time, $11 per credit hour. *Payment plan:* deferred payment. *Waivers:* senior citizens.

Financial Aid Of all full-time matriculated undergraduates who enrolled in 2001, 1313 applied for aid, 989 were judged to have need, 270 had their need fully met. 60 Federal Work-Study jobs (averaging $1600). In 2001, 25 non-need-based awards were made. *Average percent of need met:* 61%. *Average financial aid package:* $4577. *Average need-based loan:* $2912. *Average need-based gift aid:* $3762. *Average non-need based aid:* $1109. *Average indebtedness upon graduation:* $4873.

Applying *Options:* early admission. *Required:* high school transcript. *Required for some:* essay or personal statement, minimum 2.0 GPA, interview. *Application deadlines:* 8/6 (freshmen), 8/1 (transfers). *Notification:* continuous (freshmen).

Admissions Contact Ms. Cathy Buckman, Director of Admissions, Purdue University North Central, 1401 South U.S. Highway 421, Westville, IN 46391. *Phone:* 219-785-5458. *Toll-free phone:* 800-872-1231. *E-mail:* cbuckman@purduenc.edu.

ROSE-HULMAN INSTITUTE OF TECHNOLOGY

Terre Haute, Indiana

- **Independent** comprehensive, founded 1874
- **Calendar** quarters
- **Degrees** bachelor's and master's
- **Rural** 130-acre campus with easy access to Indianapolis
- **Endowment** $174.0 million
- **Coed, primarily men,** 1,573 undergraduate students, 98% full-time, 18% women, 82% men
- **Very difficult** entrance level, 67% of applicants were admitted

Undergraduates 1,544 full-time, 29 part-time. Students come from 51 states and territories, 3 other countries, 50% are from out of state, 1% African American, 3% Asian American or Pacific Islander, 1% Hispanic American, 0.1% Native American, 1% international, 1% transferred in, 55% live on campus. *Retention:* 93% of 2001 full-time freshmen returned.

Freshmen *Admission:* 3,034 applied, 2,040 admitted, 404 enrolled. *Test scores:* SAT verbal scores over 500: 95%; SAT math scores over 500: 99%; ACT scores over 18: 100%; SAT verbal scores over 600: 60%; SAT math scores over 600: 88%; ACT scores over 24: 91%; SAT verbal scores over 700: 14%; SAT math scores over 700: 40%; ACT scores over 30: 35%.

Faculty *Total:* 136, 90% full-time, 97% with terminal degrees. *Student/faculty ratio:* 13:1.

Majors Biology; chemical engineering; chemistry; civil engineering; computer engineering; computer science; economics; electrical engineering; mathematics; mechanical engineering; optics; physics.

Academic Programs *Special study options:* adult/continuing education programs, advanced placement credit, cooperative education, double majors, honors programs, independent study, internships, off-campus study, study abroad, summer session for credit. *ROTC:* Army (b), Air Force (b).

Library Logan Library with 74,525 titles, 589 serial subscriptions, 325 audiovisual materials, an OPAC, a Web page.

Computers on Campus 100 computers available on campus for general student use. A campuswide network can be accessed from student residence rooms and from off campus. Internet access, online (class) registration, at least one staffed computer lab available.

Student Life *Housing:* on-campus residence required for freshman year. *Options:* coed, men-only, women-only. *Activities and Organizations:* drama/theater group, student-run newspaper, radio station, choral group, Intramurals, Band, Drama Club, Student Government, national fraternities, national sororities. *Campus security:* 24-hour emergency response devices and patrols, late-night transport/escort service, controlled dormitory access. *Student Services:* health clinic, personal/psychological counseling.

Athletics Member NCAA. All Division III. *Intercollegiate sports:* baseball M, basketball M/W, cross-country running M/W, football M, golf M, riflery M/W, soccer M/W, softball W, swimming M/W, tennis M/W, track and field M/W, volleyball W, wrestling M. *Intramural sports:* basketball M/W, bowling M/W, cross-country running M/W, football M/W, golf M/W, racquetball M/W, soccer M/W, softball M/W, tennis M/W, volleyball M/W.

Standardized Tests *Required:* SAT I or ACT (for admission).

Costs (2001–02) *One-time required fee:* $3300. *Comprehensive fee:* $27,707 includes full-time tuition ($21,263), mandatory fees ($405), and room and board ($6039). Full-time tuition and fees vary according to course load and student level. Part-time tuition: $615 per credit. Part-time tuition and fees vary according to course load. *Room and board:* College room only: $3360. Room and board charges vary according to board plan. *Payment plans:* tuition prepayment, installment. *Waivers:* employees or children of employees.

Financial Aid Of all full-time matriculated undergraduates who enrolled in 2001, 1285 applied for aid, 1195 were judged to have need, 187 had their need fully met. 300 Federal Work-Study jobs (averaging $1500). *Average percent of need met:* 73%. *Average financial aid package:* $14,839. *Average need-based loan:* $4112. *Average need-based gift aid:* $5011. *Average non-need based aid:* $6005. *Average indebtedness upon graduation:* $26,000.

Applying *Options:* common application, electronic application, deferred entrance. *Application fee:* $40. *Required:* high school transcript, 1 letter of recommendation. *Recommended:* essay or personal statement, interview. *Application deadlines:* 3/1 (freshmen), 6/15 (transfers). *Notification:* continuous (freshmen).

Admissions Contact Mr. Charles G. Howard, Dean of Admissions/Vice President, Rose-Hulman Institute of Technology, 5500 Wabash Avenue, Terre Haute, IN 47803-3920. *Phone:* 812-877-8213. *Toll-free phone:* 800-552-0725 (in-state); 800-248-7448 (out-of-state). *Fax:* 812-877-8941. *E-mail:* admis.ofc@rose-hulman.edu.

SAINT JOSEPH'S COLLEGE

Rensselaer, Indiana

- **Independent Roman Catholic** comprehensive, founded 1889
- **Calendar** semesters
- **Degrees** certificates, diplomas, associate, bachelor's, and master's
- **Small-town** 340-acre campus with easy access to Chicago
- **Endowment** $8.8 million
- **Coed,** 914 undergraduate students, 86% full-time, 56% women, 44% men
- **Moderately difficult** entrance level, 74% of applicants were admitted

Undergraduates 788 full-time, 126 part-time. Students come from 19 states and territories, 2 other countries, 28% are from out of state, 4% African American, 0.4% Asian American or Pacific Islander, 3% Hispanic American, 0.2% Native American, 0.4% international, 3% transferred in, 73% live on campus. *Retention:* 69% of 2001 full-time freshmen returned.

Freshmen *Admission:* 1,019 applied, 755 admitted, 213 enrolled. *Average high school GPA:* 2.91. *Test scores:* SAT verbal scores over 500: 49%; SAT math scores over 500: 48%; ACT scores over 18: 91%; SAT verbal scores over 600: 9%; SAT math scores over 600: 15%; ACT scores over 24: 36%; SAT verbal scores over 700: 2%; SAT math scores over 700: 1%; ACT scores over 30: 2%.

Faculty *Total:* 95, 56% full-time, 65% with terminal degrees. *Student/faculty ratio:* 14:1.

Majors Accounting; applied economics; applied mathematics; biochemistry; biology; business administration; business education; business marketing and marketing management; chemistry; communications; computer/information sciences; computer programming; computer science; creative writing; criminal justice studies; early childhood education; economics; elementary education; English; environmental science; finance; history; humanities; international busi-

Saint Joseph's College (continued)
ness; international relations; management information systems/business data processing; mass communications; mathematics; mathematics/computer science; medical technology; music; music history; music teacher education; nursing science; philosophy; physical education; political science; psychology; religious music; religious studies; secondary education; social sciences; sociology.

Academic Programs *Special study options:* academic remediation for entering students, accelerated degree program, advanced placement credit, double majors, honors programs, independent study, internships, part-time degree program, services for LD students, student-designed majors, study abroad, summer session for credit. *Unusual degree programs:* 3-2 engineering with various universities.

Library Robinson Memorial Library with 147,434 titles, 559 serial subscriptions, 22,724 audiovisual materials, an OPAC.

Computers on Campus 69 computers available on campus for general student use. A campuswide network can be accessed from student residence rooms. At least one staffed computer lab available.

Student Life *Housing:* on-campus residence required through senior year. *Options:* men-only, women-only, disabled students. *Activities and Organizations:* drama/theater group, student-run newspaper, radio and television station, choral group, marching band, Minority Student Union, Student Senate, Student Union, marching band, Alpha Lambda Delta. *Campus security:* 24-hour emergency response devices and patrols, student patrols, late-night transport/escort service. *Student Services:* health clinic, personal/psychological counseling.

Athletics Member NCAA. All Division II. *Intercollegiate sports:* baseball M(s), basketball M(s)/W(s), cross-country running M(s)/W(s), football M(s), golf M(s)/W(s), soccer M(s)/W(s), softball W(s), tennis M(s)/W(s), track and field M(s)/W(s), volleyball W(s). *Intramural sports:* basketball M/W, bowling M/W, football M/W, softball M/W, volleyball M/W.

Standardized Tests *Required:* SAT I or ACT (for admission).

Costs (2001–02) *Comprehensive fee:* $21,640 includes full-time tuition ($15,880), mandatory fees ($160), and room and board ($5600). Full-time tuition and fees vary according to reciprocity agreements. Part-time tuition: $530 per credit. Part-time tuition and fees vary according to course load and program. *Required fees:* $5 per credit hour, $30 per term part-time. *Payment plan:* installment. *Waivers:* minority students, children of alumni, and employees or children of employees.

Financial Aid Of all full-time matriculated undergraduates who enrolled in 2001, 763 applied for aid, 641 were judged to have need, 295 had their need fully met. 114 Federal Work-Study jobs (averaging $782). In 2001, 46 non-need-based awards were made. *Average percent of need met:* 85%. *Average financial aid package:* $12,500. *Average need-based loan:* $3700. *Average need-based gift aid:* $9000. *Average non-need based aid:* $5500. *Average indebtedness upon graduation:* $18,000.

Applying *Options:* electronic application, early admission, early decision, deferred entrance. *Application fee:* $25. *Required:* high school transcript, minimum 2.0 GPA. *Required for some:* interview. *Recommended:* essay or personal statement, letters of recommendation. *Application deadline:* rolling (freshmen), rolling (transfers). *Early decision:* 10/1. *Notification:* continuous (freshmen), 10/15 (early decision).

Admissions Contact Mr. Frank P. Bevec, Director of Admissions, Saint Joseph's College, PO Box 815, Rensselaer, IN 47978-0850. *Phone:* 219-866-6170. *Toll-free phone:* 800-447-8781. *Fax:* 219-866-6122. *E-mail:* admissions@saintjoe.edu.

SAINT MARY-OF-THE-WOODS COLLEGE
Saint Mary-of-the-Woods, Indiana

- **Independent Roman Catholic** comprehensive, founded 1840
- **Calendar** semesters
- **Degrees** certificates, associate, bachelor's, and master's (also offers external degree program with significant enrollment reflected in profile)
- **Rural** 67-acre campus with easy access to Indianapolis
- **Endowment** $9.4 million
- **Women only,** 1,380 undergraduate students, 28% full-time
- **Moderately difficult** entrance level, 89% of applicants were admitted

Undergraduates 391 full-time, 989 part-time. Students come from 22 states and territories, 6 other countries, 30% are from out of state, 3% African American, 0.5% Asian American or Pacific Islander, 1% Hispanic American, 0.8% Native American, 0.2% international, 67% live on campus. *Retention:* 68% of 2001 full-time freshmen returned.

Freshmen *Admission:* 167 enrolled. *Average high school GPA:* 3.1. *Test scores:* SAT verbal scores over 500: 46%; SAT math scores over 500: 32%; ACT scores over 18: 77%; SAT verbal scores over 600: 14%; SAT math scores over 600: 10%; ACT scores over 24: 45%; SAT verbal scores over 700: 2%; ACT scores over 30: 3%.

Faculty *Total:* 62, 97% full-time, 69% with terminal degrees. *Student/faculty ratio:* 12:1.

Majors Accounting; accounting related; agricultural animal husbandry/production management; art; art education; biological/physical sciences; biology; business administration; business administration/management related; business marketing and marketing management; child care services management; communication equipment technology; communications technologies related; computer/information sciences; cultural studies; design/visual communications; early childhood education; education; education (K-12); elementary education; English; English related; equestrian studies; fine/studio arts; French; gerontological services; gerontology; history; humanities; human resources management; human services; information sciences/systems; journalism; liberal arts and sciences/liberal studies; mass communications; mathematics; medical technology; music; music (piano and organ performance); music teacher education; music therapy; music (voice and choral/opera performance); nonprofit/public management; paralegal/legal assistant; pastoral counseling; photography; pre-dentistry; pre-law; pre-medicine; pre-pharmacy studies; pre-veterinary studies; professional studies; psychology; public relations; religious education; religious studies; secondary education; social sciences; Spanish; special education; theater arts/drama; theology.

Academic Programs *Special study options:* academic remediation for entering students, accelerated degree program, adult/continuing education programs, advanced placement credit, distance learning, double majors, external degree program, independent study, internships, off-campus study, part-time degree program, student-designed majors, study abroad, summer session for credit. *ROTC:* Army (c), Air Force (c).

Library College Library with 152,162 titles, 301 serial subscriptions, 522 audiovisual materials, an OPAC.

Computers on Campus 65 computers available on campus for general student use. A campuswide network can be accessed from student residence rooms and from off campus. Internet access, at least one staffed computer lab available.

Student Life *Housing:* on-campus residence required through senior year. *Options:* women-only. *Activities and Organizations:* drama/theater group, student-run newspaper, choral group, Student Senate, In-Law, student newspaper, chorale, Green Day. *Campus security:* 24-hour patrols. *Student Services:* health clinic, personal/psychological counseling.

Athletics Member NSCAA. *Intercollegiate sports:* basketball W(s), equestrian sports W, soccer W(s), softball W(s). *Intramural sports:* soccer W, softball W.

Standardized Tests *Required for some:* SAT I or ACT (for admission).

Costs (2001–02) *One-time required fee:* $70. *Comprehensive fee:* $21,310 includes full-time tuition ($15,090), mandatory fees ($470), and room and board ($5750). Part-time tuition: $298 per hour. Part-time tuition and fees vary according to course load and program. *Required fees:* $25 per term part-time. *Payment plan:* installment. *Waivers:* minority students, children of alumni, and employees or children of employees.

Applying *Options:* common application, electronic application, early admission, deferred entrance. *Application fee:* $30. *Required:* minimum 2.0 GPA, 1 letter of recommendation. *Required for some:* essay or personal statement, high school transcript, interview. *Application deadlines:* 8/15 (freshmen), 8/15 (transfers). *Notification:* continuous (freshmen).

Admissions Contact Mr. Joel Wincowski, Director of Admission, Saint Mary-of-the-Woods College, Guerin Hall, Saint Mary-of-the-Woods, IN 47876. *Phone:* 812-535-5106. *Toll-free phone:* 800-926-SMWC. *Fax:* 812-535-4900. *E-mail:* smwcadms@smwc.edu.

SAINT MARY'S COLLEGE
Notre Dame, Indiana

- **Independent Roman Catholic** 4-year, founded 1844
- **Calendar** semesters
- **Degree** bachelor's
- **Suburban** 275-acre campus
- **Endowment** $87.6 million
- **Women only,** 1,523 undergraduate students, 98% full-time
- **Moderately difficult** entrance level, 82% of applicants were admitted

Undergraduates 1,485 full-time, 38 part-time. Students come from 49 states and territories, 5 other countries, 72% are from out of state, 1% African American, 2% Asian American or Pacific Islander, 5% Hispanic American, 0.3% Native American, 0.6% international, 3% transferred in, 78% live on campus. *Retention:* 82% of 2001 full-time freshmen returned.

Freshmen *Admission:* 436 enrolled. *Average high school GPA:* 3.60. *Test scores:* SAT verbal scores over 500: 82%; SAT math scores over 500: 80%; ACT scores over 18: 98%; SAT verbal scores over 600: 34%; SAT math scores over 600: 34%; ACT scores over 24: 65%; SAT verbal scores over 700: 4%; SAT math scores over 700: 4%; ACT scores over 30: 7%.

Faculty *Total:* 181, 60% full-time. *Student/faculty ratio:* 11:1.

Majors Accounting; anthropology; applied mathematics; art; art education; biology; business administration; business education; business marketing and marketing management; chemistry; communications; creative writing; cytotechnology; economics; education; elementary education; English; finance; French; history; humanities; interdisciplinary studies; international business; management information systems/business data processing; mathematics; mathematics/computer science; medical technology; music; music (piano and organ performance); music teacher education; music (voice and choral/opera performance); nursing; philosophy; political science; psychology; religious studies; social work; sociology; Spanish; theater arts/drama.

Academic Programs *Special study options:* academic remediation for entering students, accelerated degree program, advanced placement credit, double majors, independent study, internships, off-campus study, part-time degree program, services for LD students, student-designed majors, study abroad. *ROTC:* Army (c), Navy (c), Air Force (c). *Unusual degree programs:* 3-2 engineering with University of Notre Dame.

Library Cushwa-Leighton Library with 209,375 titles, 776 serial subscriptions, 3,399 audiovisual materials, an OPAC, a Web page.

Computers on Campus 193 computers available on campus for general student use. A campuswide network can be accessed from student residence rooms and from off campus. At least one staffed computer lab available.

Student Life *Housing Options:* women-only. *Activities and Organizations:* drama/theater group, student-run newspaper, radio station, choral group, marching band, Circle K, Toastmasters, volunteers in support of admissions (VISA), student government association, academic clubs. *Campus security:* 24-hour emergency response devices and patrols, late-night transport/escort service, controlled dormitory access. *Student Services:* health clinic, personal/psychological counseling, women's center.

Athletics Member NCAA. All Division III. *Intercollegiate sports:* basketball W, crew W(c), cross-country running W(c), equestrian sports W(c), gymnastics W(c), sailing W(c), skiing (downhill) W(c), soccer W, softball W, swimming W, tennis W, track and field W, volleyball W. *Intramural sports:* basketball W, cross-country running W, football W, golf W, racquetball W, skiing (cross-country) W, soccer W, softball W, tennis W, volleyball W.

Costs (2001–02) *Comprehensive fee:* $25,939 includes full-time tuition ($19,240), mandatory fees ($150), and room and board ($6549). Full-time tuition and fees vary according to location. Part-time tuition: $760 per semester hour. *Room and board:* Room and board charges vary according to housing facility. *Payment plans:* installment, deferred payment. *Waivers:* adult students, senior citizens, and employees or children of employees.

Financial Aid Of all full-time matriculated undergraduates who enrolled in 2001, 1095 applied for aid, 909 were judged to have need, 295 had their need fully met. 282 Federal Work-Study jobs (averaging $994). In 2001, 324 non-need-based awards were made. *Average percent of need met:* 86%. *Average financial aid package:* $15,527. *Average need-based loan:* $3913. *Average need-based gift aid:* $11,823. *Average non-need based aid:* $6338. *Average indebtedness upon graduation:* $16,346.

Applying *Options:* electronic application, early admission, early decision, deferred entrance. *Application fee:* $30. *Required:* essay or personal statement, high school transcript, 1 letter of recommendation. *Recommended:* interview. *Application deadline:* 3/1 (freshmen), rolling (transfers). *Early decision:* 11/15. *Notification:* continuous (freshmen), 12/15 (early decision).

Admissions Contact Ms. Mary Pat Nolan, Director of Admissions, Saint Mary's College, Notre Dame, IN 46556. *Phone:* 574-284-4587. *Toll-free phone:* 800-551-7621 (in-state); 574-284-4716 (out-of-state). *E-mail:* admission@saintmarys.edu.

TAYLOR UNIVERSITY

Upland, Indiana

- **Independent interdenominational** 4-year, founded 1846
- **Calendar** 4-1-4
- **Degrees** certificates, associate, and bachelor's
- **Rural** 250-acre campus with easy access to Indianapolis
- **Endowment** $32.0 million
- **Coed,** 1,861 undergraduate students, 98% full-time, 52% women, 48% men
- **Very difficult** entrance level, 78% of applicants were admitted

Taylor University is anchored by 3 distinctive traditions: Scholarship—students value academic excellence and enjoy personal attention from highly credentialed faculty members; Leadership—Taylor's nationally recognized leadership development program equips students for leadership in career, community, and church; Christian Commitment—every aspect of Taylor life is fully integrated with an active faith in Jesus Christ.

Undergraduates 1,827 full-time, 34 part-time. Students come from 48 states and territories, 17 other countries, 69% are from out of state, 2% transferred in, 83% live on campus. *Retention:* 89% of 2001 full-time freshmen returned.

Freshmen *Admission:* 1,389 applied, 1,078 admitted, 492 enrolled. *Average high school GPA:* 3.70. *Test scores:* SAT verbal scores over 500: 87%; SAT math scores over 500: 90%; ACT scores over 18: 99%; SAT verbal scores over 600: 56%; SAT math scores over 600: 55%; ACT scores over 24: 78%; SAT verbal scores over 700: 9%; SAT math scores over 700: 11%; ACT scores over 30: 16%.

Faculty *Total:* 172, 78% full-time, 58% with terminal degrees. *Student/faculty ratio:* 15:1.

Majors Accounting; art; art education; athletic training/sports medicine; biblical languages/literatures; biblical studies; biology; business administration; business marketing and marketing management; chemistry; computer engineering; computer programming; computer science; creative writing; early childhood education; economics; education; elementary education; engineering physics; English; environmental biology; environmental science; finance; French; graphic design/commercial art/illustration; history; human resources management; information sciences/systems; international business; international economics; international relations; literature; management information systems/business data processing; mass communications; mathematics; medical technology; middle school education; music; music business management/merchandising; music (piano and organ performance); music teacher education; music (voice and choral/opera performance); natural sciences; philosophy; physical education; physics; political science; pre-dentistry; pre-law; pre-medicine; pre-veterinary studies; psychology; recreation/leisure studies; religious education; religious music; religious studies; science education; secondary education; social sciences; social work; sociology; Spanish; sport/fitness administration; theater arts/drama; theology.

Academic Programs *Special study options:* academic remediation for entering students, accelerated degree program, advanced placement credit, double majors, honors programs, independent study, internships, off-campus study, part-time degree program, services for LD students, student-designed majors, study abroad, summer session for credit. *Unusual degree programs:* 3-2 engineering with Washington University in St. Louis; medical technology.

Library Zondervan Library with 188,000 titles, 737 serial subscriptions, 6,288 audiovisual materials, an OPAC, a Web page.

Computers on Campus 235 computers available on campus for general student use. A campuswide network can be accessed from student residence rooms and from off campus. At least one staffed computer lab available.

Student Life *Housing:* on-campus residence required through sophomore year. *Options:* men-only, women-only. *Activities and Organizations:* drama/theater group, student-run newspaper, radio and television station, choral group, Student Activities Council, World Outreach, Student Organization. *Campus security:* 24-hour patrols, student patrols, late-night transport/escort service. *Student Services:* health clinic, personal/psychological counseling.

Athletics Member NAIA, NCCAA. *Intercollegiate sports:* baseball M(s), basketball M(s)/W(s), cross-country running M(s)/W(s), equestrian sports M(c)/W(c), football M(s), golf M(s), lacrosse M(c)/W(c), soccer M(s)/W(s), softball W(s), tennis M(s)/W(s), track and field M(s)/W(s), volleyball M(c)/W(s). *Intramural sports:* badminton M/W, basketball M/W, cross-country running M/W, football M/W, golf M, racquetball M/W, soccer M/W, softball M/W, table tennis M/W, tennis M/W, track and field M/W, volleyball W.

Standardized Tests *Required:* SAT I or ACT (for admission).

Costs (2001–02) *Comprehensive fee:* $21,562 includes full-time tuition ($16,350), mandatory fees ($222), and room and board ($4990). Part-time tuition: $585 per credit. Part-time tuition and fees vary according to course load. *Room and board:* Room and board charges vary according to board plan and housing facility. *Payment plan:* installment. *Waivers:* employees or children of employees.

Financial Aid Of all full-time matriculated undergraduates who enrolled in 2001, 1213 applied for aid, 1008 were judged to have need, 230 had their need fully met. 803 Federal Work-Study jobs (averaging $988). In 2001, 520 non-need-based awards were made. *Average percent of need met:* 81%. *Average financial aid package:* $11,835. *Average need-based loan:* $3122. *Average need-based gift aid:* $8637. *Average non-need based aid:* $3470. *Average indebtedness upon graduation:* $14,877. *Financial aid deadline:* 3/1.

Applying *Options:* electronic application, deferred entrance. *Application fee:* $20. *Required:* essay or personal statement, high school transcript, 2 letters of recommendation, interview. *Recommended:* minimum 2.8 GPA. *Application deadline:* rolling (freshmen), rolling (transfers). *Notification:* continuous (freshmen).

Taylor University (continued)

Admissions Contact Mr. Stephen R. Mortland, Director of Admissions, Taylor University, 236 West Reade Avenue, Upland, IN 46989-1001. *Phone:* 765-998-5134. *Toll-free phone:* 800-882-3456. *Fax:* 765-998-4925. *E-mail:* admissions_u@tayloru.edu.

TAYLOR UNIVERSITY, FORT WAYNE CAMPUS

Fort Wayne, Indiana

- **Independent interdenominational** 4-year, founded 1992, part of Taylor University
- **Calendar** 4-1-4
- **Degrees** associate and bachelor's
- **Suburban** 32-acre campus
- **Endowment** $3.7 million
- **Coed,** 515 undergraduate students, 73% full-time, 58% women, 42% men
- **Moderately difficult** entrance level, 76% of applicants were admitted

Undergraduates 378 full-time, 137 part-time. Students come from 25 states and territories, 5 other countries, 28% are from out of state, 6% African American, 0.9% Asian American or Pacific Islander, 2% Hispanic American, 0.2% Native American, 1% international, 5% transferred in, 55% live on campus. *Retention:* 76% of 2001 full-time freshmen returned.

Freshmen *Admission:* 480 applied, 365 admitted, 145 enrolled. *Average high school GPA:* 3.06. *Test scores:* SAT verbal scores over 500: 48%; SAT math scores over 500: 46%; ACT scores over 18: 82%; SAT verbal scores over 600: 25%; SAT math scores over 600: 14%; ACT scores over 24: 49%; SAT verbal scores over 700: 3%; SAT math scores over 700: 1%; ACT scores over 30: 4%.

Faculty *Total:* 55, 53% full-time, 38% with terminal degrees. *Student/faculty ratio:* 14:1.

Majors Biblical studies; business administration; communications related; computer science; criminal justice/law enforcement administration; criminal justice studies; divinity/ministry; early childhood education; elementary education; English; interdisciplinary studies; international business; liberal arts and sciences/liberal studies; music; pastoral counseling; pre-law; psychology; public relations; religious education; social work; urban studies.

Academic Programs *Special study options:* academic remediation for entering students, accelerated degree program, advanced placement credit, cooperative education, distance learning, double majors, independent study, internships, off-campus study, part-time degree program, services for LD students, student-designed majors, study abroad, summer session for credit.

Library S. A. Lehman Memorial Library with 75,419 titles, 733 serial subscriptions, 4,699 audiovisual materials, an OPAC, a Web page.

Computers on Campus 50 computers available on campus for general student use. A campuswide network can be accessed from off campus. Internet access, at least one staffed computer lab available.

Student Life *Housing:* on-campus residence required through junior year. *Options:* men-only, women-only. *Activities and Organizations:* drama/theater group, student-run newspaper, choral group, Taylor Student Organization, Youth Conference Committee, Multicultrual Activities Council, World Outreach, Student Activities Council. *Campus security:* student patrols, late-night transport/escort service, controlled dormitory access, 12-hour night patrols by trained personnel. *Student Services:* health clinic, personal/psychological counseling.

Athletics Member NCCAA. *Intercollegiate sports:* basketball M/W, soccer M, softball W(c), volleyball W. *Intramural sports:* badminton M/W, baseball M(c), basketball M/W, football M/W, soccer M/W, table tennis M/W, tennis M/W, volleyball M/W, weight lifting M/W.

Standardized Tests *Required:* SAT I or ACT (for admission).

Costs (2001–02) *Comprehensive fee:* $18,690 includes full-time tuition ($14,090), mandatory fees ($110), and room and board ($4490). Part-time tuition: $175 per hour. Part-time tuition and fees vary according to course load. *Required fees:* $25 per hour. *Room and board:* College room only: $1920. Room and board charges vary according to board plan. *Payment plan:* installment. *Waivers:* senior citizens and employees or children of employees.

Financial Aid Of all full-time matriculated undergraduates who enrolled in 2001, 337 applied for aid, 306 were judged to have need, 60 had their need fully met. In 2001, 46 non-need-based awards were made. *Average percent of need met:* 87%. *Average financial aid package:* $13,470. *Average need-based loan:* $2693. *Average need-based gift aid:* $10,676. *Average non-need based aid:* $3043. *Average indebtedness upon graduation:* $15,400.

Applying *Options:* electronic application, deferred entrance. *Application fee:* $20. *Required:* essay or personal statement, high school transcript, minimum 2.0 GPA, 2 letters of recommendation. *Recommended:* minimum 3.0 GPA, interview. *Application deadline:* rolling (freshmen), rolling (transfers).

Admissions Contact Mr. Leo Gonot, Director of Admissions, Taylor University, Fort Wayne Campus, 1025 West Rudisill Boulevard, Fort Wayne, IN 46807-2197. *Phone:* 219-744-8689. *Toll-free phone:* 800-233-3922. *Fax:* 219-744-8660. *E-mail:* admissions_f@tayloru.edu.

TRI-STATE UNIVERSITY

Angola, Indiana

- **Independent** 4-year, founded 1884
- **Calendar** semesters
- **Degrees** associate and bachelor's
- **Small-town** 400-acre campus
- **Endowment** $12.8 million
- **Coed,** 1,268 undergraduate students, 89% full-time, 34% women, 66% men
- **Moderately difficult** entrance level, 76% of applicants were admitted

Within six months of graduation, 90% of Tri-State University's graduates in engineering, technology, business, education, mathematics, computer science, science, criminal justice, psychology, sport management, golf management, and communications have accepted full-time positions in their major areas, with average salaries at or above national averages for their disciplines.

Undergraduates 1,127 full-time, 141 part-time. Students come from 21 states and territories, 23 other countries, 40% are from out of state, 2% African American, 0.6% Asian American or Pacific Islander, 0.2% Hispanic American, 0.3% Native American, 5% international, 3% transferred in, 48% live on campus. *Retention:* 68% of 2001 full-time freshmen returned.

Freshmen *Admission:* 1,433 applied, 1,086 admitted, 317 enrolled. *Average high school GPA:* 3.10. *Test scores:* SAT verbal scores over 500: 46%; SAT math scores over 500: 64%; ACT scores over 18: 90%; SAT verbal scores over 600: 6%; SAT math scores over 600: 22%; ACT scores over 24: 33%; SAT verbal scores over 700: 1%; SAT math scores over 700: 2%; ACT scores over 30: 3%.

Faculty *Total:* 88, 66% full-time, 52% with terminal degrees. *Student/faculty ratio:* 17:1.

Majors Accounting; biological/physical sciences; biology; business administration; business marketing and marketing management; chemical engineering; chemistry; civil engineering; communications; computer/information sciences; computer science; construction technology; criminal justice/law enforcement administration; drafting; drafting/design technology; education; electrical engineering; elementary education; engineering/industrial management; engineering-related technology; English education; enterprise management; environmental science; industrial technology; liberal arts and sciences/liberal studies; management information systems/business data processing; mathematics; mathematics education; mechanical engineering; operations management; physical education; physical sciences; pre-law; pre-medicine; pre-veterinary studies; psychology; recreation/leisure facilities management; science education; secondary education; social sciences; social studies education; sport/fitness administration.

Academic Programs *Special study options:* academic remediation for entering students, adult/continuing education programs, advanced placement credit, cooperative education, distance learning, double majors, internships, part-time degree program, study abroad, summer session for credit.

Library Perry Ford Library with 188,564 titles, 349 serial subscriptions, 3,533 audiovisual materials, an OPAC, a Web page.

Computers on Campus 150 computers available on campus for general student use. A campuswide network can be accessed from student residence rooms and from off campus. Internet access, at least one staffed computer lab available.

Student Life *Housing:* on-campus residence required through sophomore year. *Options:* coed. *Activities and Organizations:* drama/theater group, student-run newspaper, radio station, choral group, Circle K, drama club, International Student Association, student newspaper, student radio station, national fraternities. *Campus security:* 24-hour emergency response devices, late-night transport/escort service. *Student Services:* personal/psychological counseling.

Athletics Member NAIA. *Intercollegiate sports:* baseball M(s), basketball M(s)/W(s), cross-country running M(s)/W(s), football M(s), golf M(s)/W(s), soccer M(s)/W(s), softball W(s), swimming M(s)/W(s), tennis M(s)/W(s), track and field M(s)/W(s), volleyball M(s)/W(s). *Intramural sports:* badminton M/W, basketball M/W, football M, golf M/W, racquetball M/W, softball M/W, table tennis M/W, volleyball M/W.

Standardized Tests *Required:* SAT I or ACT (for admission).

Costs (2001–02) *Comprehensive fee:* $21,200 includes full-time tuition ($15,950) and room and board ($5250). Part-time tuition: $498 per semester hour. *Payment plan:* installment. *Waivers:* employees or children of employees.

Financial Aid Of all full-time matriculated undergraduates who enrolled in 2001, 1126 applied for aid, 1047 were judged to have need, 531 had their need

fully met. 200 Federal Work-Study jobs (averaging $702). In 2001, 35 non-need-based awards were made. *Average percent of need met:* 78%. *Average financial aid package:* $9419. *Average need-based gift aid:* $8574. *Average non-need based aid:* $5924. *Average indebtedness upon graduation:* $14,050.

Applying *Options:* common application, electronic application. *Application fee:* $20. *Required:* high school transcript, minimum 2.0 GPA. *Recommended:* letters of recommendation, interview. *Application deadlines:* 6/1 (freshmen), 8/15 (transfers). *Notification:* continuous until 8/15 (freshmen).

Admissions Contact Ms. Sara Yarian, Admissions Officer, Tri-State University, Angola, IN 46703. *Phone:* 219-665-4365. *Toll-free phone:* 800-347-4TSU. *Fax:* 219-665-4578. *E-mail:* admit@tristate.edu.

UNIVERSITY OF EVANSVILLE

Evansville, Indiana

- **Independent** comprehensive, founded 1854, affiliated with United Methodist Church
- **Calendar** semesters
- **Degrees** associate, bachelor's, and master's
- **Suburban** 75-acre campus
- **Endowment** $59.9 million
- **Coed,** 2,674 undergraduate students, 86% full-time, 61% women, 39% men
- **Moderately difficult** entrance level, 91% of applicants were admitted

For 9 consecutive years, the University of Evansville has been ranked by *U.S. News & World Report* as one of the top 15 outstanding Midwest regional universities and as one of the best values in the Midwest.

Undergraduates 2,298 full-time, 376 part-time. Students come from 46 states and territories, 42 other countries, 34% are from out of state, 2% African American, 0.6% Asian American or Pacific Islander, 0.7% Hispanic American, 0.2% Native American, 6% international, 4% transferred in, 70% live on campus. *Retention:* 81% of 2001 full-time freshmen returned.

Freshmen *Admission:* 1,870 applied, 1,693 admitted, 513 enrolled. *Average high school GPA:* 3.58. *Test scores:* SAT verbal scores over 500: 77%; SAT math scores over 500: 81%; ACT scores over 18: 100%; SAT verbal scores over 600: 33%; SAT math scores over 600: 34%; ACT scores over 24: 70%; SAT verbal scores over 700: 6%; SAT math scores over 700: 5%; ACT scores over 30: 15%.

Faculty *Total:* 178, 97% full-time. *Student/faculty ratio:* 13:1.

Majors Accounting; anthropology; archaeology; art; art education; art history; arts management; athletic training/sports medicine; biblical studies; biochemistry; biology; business administration; business economics; business marketing and marketing management; ceramic arts; chemistry; civil engineering; classics; computer engineering; computer science; creative writing; criminal justice/law enforcement administration; drawing; economics; electrical engineering; elementary education; engineering/industrial management; English; environmental science; exercise sciences; finance; French; German; gerontology; graphic design/commercial art/illustration; health services administration; history; international business; international relations; legal studies; liberal arts and sciences/liberal studies; literature; mass communications; mathematics; mechanical engineering; medical technology; music; music business management/merchandising; music teacher education; music therapy; nursing; philosophy; physical education; physical therapy; physical therapy assistant; physics; physiological psychology/psychobiology; political science; pre-dentistry; pre-law; pre-medicine; pre-veterinary studies; psychology; religious studies; science education; sculpture; secondary education; sociology; Spanish; special education; theater arts/drama.

Academic Programs *Special study options:* adult/continuing education programs, advanced placement credit, cooperative education, English as a second language, freshman honors college, honors programs, internships, part-time degree program, services for LD students, study abroad, summer session for credit.

Library Bower Suhrheinrich Library plus 1 other with 268,402 titles, 1,352 serial subscriptions, 10,000 audiovisual materials, an OPAC.

Computers on Campus 360 computers available on campus for general student use. A campuswide network can be accessed from student residence rooms and from off campus. At least one staffed computer lab available.

Student Life *Housing:* on-campus residence required for freshman year. *Options:* coed. *Activities and Organizations:* drama/theater group, student-run newspaper, radio station, choral group, Kappa Chi, Admission Ambassadors, Student Activities Board, Phi Eta Sigma, Mortar Board, national fraternities, national sororities. *Campus security:* 24-hour emergency response devices and patrols, late-night transport/escort service. *Student Services:* health clinic, personal/psychological counseling.

Athletics Member NCAA. All Division I. *Intercollegiate sports:* baseball M(s), basketball M(s)/W(s), cross-country running M(s)/W(s), football M, golf M(s), soccer M(s)/W, softball W, swimming M(s)/W(s), tennis M(s)/W(s), volleyball W(s). *Intramural sports:* badminton W, basketball M/W, bowling M/W, cross-country running M/W, football M, golf M/W, soccer M/W, swimming M/W, table tennis M/W, tennis M/W, track and field M/W, volleyball M/W, wrestling M.

Standardized Tests *Required:* SAT I or ACT (for admission).

Costs (2001–02) *Comprehensive fee:* $22,865 includes full-time tuition ($17,050), mandatory fees ($345), and room and board ($5470). *Room and board:* College room only: $2620. *Payment plan:* installment. *Waivers:* minority students, children of alumni, and employees or children of employees.

Financial Aid Of all full-time matriculated undergraduates who enrolled in 2001, 2132 applied for aid, 1495 were judged to have need, 453 had their need fully met. 413 Federal Work-Study jobs (averaging $1246). 65 State and other part-time jobs (averaging $1214). In 2001, 508 non-need-based awards were made. *Average percent of need met:* 87%. *Average financial aid package:* $14,836. *Average need-based loan:* $4285. *Average need-based gift aid:* $9911. *Average non-need based aid:* $5956. *Average indebtedness upon graduation:* $13,030.

Applying *Options:* common application, electronic application, early admission, early action, deferred entrance. *Application fee:* $35. *Required:* high school transcript, minimum 2.0 GPA, 1 letter of recommendation. *Required for some:* essay or personal statement, interview. *Recommended:* minimum 3.0 GPA, interview. *Application deadlines:* 2/15 (freshmen), 7/1 (transfers). *Notification:* 3/1 (freshmen), 12/15 (early action).

Admissions Contact Mr. Tom Bear, Dean of Admission, University of Evansville, 1800 Lincoln Avenue, Evansville, IN 47722-0002. *Phone:* 812-479-2468. *Toll-free phone:* 800-992-5877 (in-state); 800-423-8633 (out-of-state). *Fax:* 812-474-4076. *E-mail:* admission@evansville.edu.

UNIVERSITY OF INDIANAPOLIS

Indianapolis, Indiana

- **Independent** comprehensive, founded 1902, affiliated with United Methodist Church
- **Calendar** 4-4-1
- **Degrees** associate, bachelor's, master's, and doctoral
- **Suburban** 60-acre campus
- **Endowment** $58.3 million
- **Coed,** 2,854 undergraduate students, 71% full-time, 66% women, 34% men
- **Moderately difficult** entrance level, 80% of applicants were admitted

Undergraduates 2,020 full-time, 834 part-time. Students come from 28 states and territories, 60 other countries, 8% are from out of state, 8% African American, 0.9% Asian American or Pacific Islander, 1% Hispanic American, 0.3% Native American, 6% international, 4% transferred in, 31% live on campus. *Retention:* 80% of 2001 full-time freshmen returned.

Freshmen *Admission:* 2,289 applied, 1,822 admitted, 610 enrolled. *Average high school GPA:* 3.01. *Test scores:* SAT verbal scores over 500: 56%; SAT math scores over 500: 56%; ACT scores over 18: 82%; SAT verbal scores over 600: 15%; SAT math scores over 600: 19%; ACT scores over 24: 31%; SAT verbal scores over 700: 1%; SAT math scores over 700: 1%; ACT scores over 30: 2%.

Faculty *Total:* 367, 44% full-time, 49% with terminal degrees. *Student/faculty ratio:* 14:1.

Majors Accounting; anatomy; anthropology; archaeology; art; art education; art history; art therapy; athletic training/sports medicine; banking; biology; business administration; business economics; business education; business marketing and marketing management; chemistry; communications; computer programming; computer science; corrections; criminal justice/law enforcement administration; earth sciences; education; electrical engineering; elementary education; English; English education; environmental science; fine/studio arts; French; French language education; German; graphic design/commercial art/illustration; history; human resources management; information sciences/systems; international business; international relations; liberal arts and sciences/liberal studies; mathematics; mathematics education; medical technology; music; music (general performance); music teacher education; nursing; operations management; paralegal/legal assistant; philosophy; physical education; physical therapy assistant; physics; political science; pre-dentistry; pre-law; pre-medicine; pre-theology; pre-veterinary studies; psychology; religious studies; science education; secondary education; social studies education; social work; sociology; Spanish; Spanish language education; speech education; theater arts/drama.

Academic Programs *Special study options:* academic remediation for entering students, accelerated degree program, adult/continuing education programs, advanced placement credit, cooperative education, distance learning, double majors, English as a second language, honors programs, independent study, internships, off-campus study, part-time degree program, services for LD students, student-designed majors, study abroad, summer session for credit. *ROTC:*

University of Indianapolis (continued)
Army (c). *Unusual degree programs:* 3-2 engineering with Indiana University-Purdue University Indianapolis; physical therapy, occupational therapy.
Library Krannert Memorial Library with 168,247 titles, 1,001 serial subscriptions, 8,152 audiovisual materials, an OPAC, a Web page.
Computers on Campus 218 computers available on campus for general student use. A campuswide network can be accessed from student residence rooms and from off campus. Internet access, at least one staffed computer lab available.
Student Life *Housing Options:* coed, women-only. *Activities and Organizations:* drama/theater group, student-run newspaper, radio station, choral group, Fellowship of Christian Athletes, Intercultural Association, Circle K, Indianapolis Student Government, Residence Hall Association. *Campus security:* 24-hour emergency response devices and patrols, student patrols, late-night transport/escort service, emergency call boxes. *Student Services:* health clinic, personal/psychological counseling.
Athletics Member NCAA. All Division II. *Intercollegiate sports:* baseball M(s), basketball M(s)/W(s), cross-country running M(s)/W(s), football M(s), golf M(s)/W(s), soccer M(s)/W(s), softball W(s), swimming M(s)/W(s), tennis M(s)/W(s), track and field M(s)/W(s), volleyball W(s), wrestling M(s). *Intramural sports:* badminton M/W, basketball M/W, football M/W, racquetball M/W, softball M/W, table tennis M/W, tennis M/W, volleyball M/W.
Standardized Tests *Required:* SAT I or ACT (for admission).
Costs (2001–02) *Comprehensive fee:* $20,840 includes full-time tuition ($15,350) and room and board ($5490). Full-time tuition and fees vary according to course load and program. Part-time tuition: $660 per credit hour. Part-time tuition and fees vary according to class time and course load. *Room and board:* Room and board charges vary according to board plan. *Payment plans:* installment, deferred payment. *Waivers:* senior citizens and employees or children of employees.
Financial Aid Of all full-time matriculated undergraduates who enrolled in 2001, 1642 applied for aid, 1409 were judged to have need, 409 had their need fully met. 971 Federal Work-Study jobs (averaging $222). In 2001, 298 non-need-based awards were made. *Average percent of need met:* 83%. *Average financial aid package:* $13,319. *Average need-based loan:* $2694. *Average need-based gift aid:* $7569. *Average non-need based aid:* $6427. *Average indebtedness upon graduation:* $17,152.
Applying *Options:* electronic application, deferred entrance. *Application fee:* $20. *Required:* high school transcript, minimum 2.0 GPA. *Required for some:* interview. *Application deadline:* rolling (freshmen), rolling (transfers). *Notification:* continuous (freshmen).
Admissions Contact Mr. Ronald Wilks, Director of Admissions, University of Indianapolis, 1400 East Hanna Avenue, Indianapolis, IN 46227-3697. *Phone:* 317-788-3216. *Toll-free phone:* 800-232-8634 Ext. 3216. *Fax:* 317-778-3300. *E-mail:* admissions@uindy.edu.

UNIVERSITY OF NOTRE DAME
Notre Dame, Indiana

- **Independent Roman Catholic** university, founded 1842
- **Calendar** semesters
- **Degrees** bachelor's, master's, doctoral, and first professional
- **Suburban** 1250-acre campus
- **Endowment** $2.8 billion
- **Coed,** 8,208 undergraduate students, 100% full-time, 46% women, 54% men
- **Most difficult** entrance level, 36% of applicants were admitted

Undergraduates 8,193 full-time, 15 part-time. Students come from 55 states and territories, 64 other countries, 88% are from out of state, 3% African American, 4% Asian American or Pacific Islander, 7% Hispanic American, 0.5% Native American, 3% international, 2% transferred in, 77% live on campus.
Freshmen *Admission:* 9,385 applied, 3,338 admitted, 2,036 enrolled. *Test scores:* SAT verbal scores over 500: 97%; SAT math scores over 500: 99%; ACT scores over 18: 100%; SAT verbal scores over 600: 84%; SAT math scores over 600: 90%; ACT scores over 24: 98%; SAT verbal scores over 700: 37%; SAT math scores over 700: 48%; ACT scores over 30: 79%.
Majors Accounting; aerospace engineering; American studies; anthropology; Arabic; architecture; art history; biochemistry; biology; business; business administration/management related; business marketing and marketing management; chemical engineering; chemistry; chemistry related; Chinese; civil engineering; classics; computer engineering; computer/information sciences; computer/information sciences related; design/visual communications; economics; electrical engineering; English; environmental engineering; environmental science; finance; fine/studio arts; French; geology; German; Greek (ancient and medieval); history; Italian; Japanese; Latin (ancient and medieval); liberal arts and sciences/liberal studies; management information systems/business data processing; mathematics; mechanical engineering; medieval/renaissance studies; music; philosophy; philosophy and religion related; physics; physics related; political science; pre-medicine; psychology; religious studies; Russian; science education; sociology; Spanish; theater arts/drama; theology.
Academic Programs *Special study options:* advanced placement credit, cooperative education, distance learning, double majors, English as a second language, honors programs, independent study, internships, off-campus study, services for LD students, student-designed majors, study abroad, summer session for credit. *ROTC:* Army (b), Navy (b), Air Force (b). *Unusual degree programs:* 3-2 business administration.
Library University Libraries of Notre Dame plus 8 others with 2.6 million titles, 19,100 serial subscriptions, 18,416 audiovisual materials, an OPAC, a Web page.
Computers on Campus 880 computers available on campus for general student use. A campuswide network can be accessed from student residence rooms and from off campus. Internet access, at least one staffed computer lab available.
Student Life *Housing:* on-campus residence required for freshman year. *Options:* men-only, women-only. *Activities and Organizations:* drama/theater group, student-run newspaper, radio station, choral group, marching band, marching band, Circle K, finance club, Notre Dame/St. Mary's Right to Life. *Campus security:* 24-hour emergency response devices and patrols, late-night transport/escort service, controlled dormitory access. *Student Services:* health clinic, personal/psychological counseling, women's center, legal services.
Athletics Member NCAA. All Division I except football (Division I-A). *Intercollegiate sports:* baseball M(s), basketball M(s)/W(s), bowling M(c)/W(c), crew M(c)/W(s), cross-country running M(s)/W(s), equestrian sports M(c)/W(c), fencing M(s)/W(s), field hockey M(c)/W(c), golf M(s)/W(s), gymnastics M(c)/W(c), ice hockey M(s), lacrosse M(s)/W(s), sailing M(c)/W(c), skiing (downhill) M(c)/W(c), soccer M(s)/W(s), softball W(s), squash M(c)/W(c), swimming M(s)/W(s), tennis M(s)/W(s), track and field M(s)/W(s), volleyball M(c)/W(s), water polo M(c)/W(c). *Intramural sports:* baseball M, basketball M/W, cross-country running M/W, football M/W, golf M/W, gymnastics M/W, ice hockey M, lacrosse M/W, racquetball M/W, sailing M/W, skiing (cross-country) M/W, skiing (downhill) M/W, soccer M/W, softball M/W, squash M/W, table tennis M/W, tennis M/W, volleyball M/W, water polo M/W.
Standardized Tests *Required:* SAT I or ACT (for admission).
Costs (2001–02) *Comprehensive fee:* $30,707 includes full-time tuition ($24,320), mandatory fees ($177), and room and board ($6210). Part-time tuition: $1013 per credit. Part-time tuition and fees vary according to course load and program. *Required fees:* $100 per year part-time. *Room and board:* Room and board charges vary according to housing facility. *Payment plan:* installment.
Financial Aid Of all full-time matriculated undergraduates who enrolled in 2001, 4257 applied for aid, 3263 were judged to have need, 3247 had their need fully met. 1438 Federal Work-Study jobs (averaging $1794). 2728 State and other part-time jobs (averaging $2278). In 2001, 954 non-need-based awards were made. *Average percent of need met:* 100%. *Average financial aid package:* $22,031. *Average need-based loan:* $5028. *Average need-based gift aid:* $15,841. *Average non-need based aid:* $8049. *Average indebtedness upon graduation:* $22,270. *Financial aid deadline:* 2/15.
Applying *Options:* electronic application, early action, deferred entrance. *Application fee:* $50. *Required:* essay or personal statement, high school transcript, 1 letter of recommendation. *Application deadlines:* 1/9 (freshmen), 4/15 (transfers). *Notification:* 4/1 (freshmen), 12/15 (early action).
Admissions Contact Mr. Daniel J. Saracino, Assistant Provost for Enrollment, University of Notre Dame, 220 Main Building, Notre Dame, IN 46556-5612. *Phone:* 574-631-7505. *Fax:* 574-631-8865. *E-mail:* admissions.admissio.1@nd.edu.

UNIVERSITY OF SAINT FRANCIS
Fort Wayne, Indiana

- **Independent Roman Catholic** comprehensive, founded 1890
- **Calendar** semesters
- **Degrees** certificates, associate, bachelor's, master's, and postbachelor's certificates
- **Suburban** 73-acre campus
- **Endowment** $3.4 million
- **Coed,** 1,484 undergraduate students, 75% full-time, 68% women, 32% men
- **Moderately difficult** entrance level, 84% of applicants were admitted

Undergraduates 1,115 full-time, 369 part-time. Students come from 13 states and territories, 9% are from out of state, 6% African American, 0.5% Asian American or Pacific Islander, 2% Hispanic American, 0.3% Native American, 0.3% international, 12% transferred in, 25% live on campus. *Retention:* 78% of 2001 full-time freshmen returned.

Freshmen *Admission:* 600 applied, 503 admitted, 276 enrolled. *Average high school GPA:* 3.04. *Test scores:* ACT scores over 18: 76%; ACT scores over 24: 18%.
Faculty *Total:* 161, 63% full-time, 31% with terminal degrees. *Student/faculty ratio:* 11:1.
Majors Accounting; art; art education; biological/physical sciences; biology; business administration; business education; business marketing and marketing management; chemistry; communications; design/applied arts related; divinity/ministry; economics; education; elementary education; English; environmental science; finance; fine arts and art studies related; graphic design/commercial art/illustration; health education; health science; history; human resources management; human services; international business; liberal arts and sciences/liberal studies; mass communications; medical technology; nursing; pre-dentistry; pre-law; pre-medicine; pre-veterinary studies; psychology; religious studies; science education; secondary education; social work; special education.
Academic Programs *Special study options:* academic remediation for entering students, adult/continuing education programs, advanced placement credit, cooperative education, distance learning, double majors, honors programs, independent study, internships, part-time degree program, services for LD students, summer session for credit.
Library University Library plus 1 other with 85,544 titles, 580 serial subscriptions, an OPAC, a Web page.
Computers on Campus 135 computers available on campus for general student use. Internet access, at least one staffed computer lab available.
Student Life *Housing:* on-campus residence required through sophomore year. *Options:* coed. *Activities and Organizations:* drama/theater group, student-run newspaper, marching band, Student Activities Council, art club, student government organization, honors club, Residence Hall Council. *Campus security:* 24-hour emergency response devices and patrols, late-night transport/escort service. *Student Services:* personal/psychological counseling.
Athletics Member NAIA. *Intercollegiate sports:* baseball M(s), basketball M(s)/W(s), cross-country running M(s)/W(s), football M(s), golf M(s), soccer M(s)/W(s), softball W(s), tennis W(s), track and field M(s)/W(s), volleyball W(s). *Intramural sports:* basketball M/W, bowling M/W, field hockey M/W, volleyball M/W.
Standardized Tests *Recommended:* SAT I or ACT (for admission).
Costs (2001–02) *Comprehensive fee:* $18,640 includes full-time tuition ($13,100), mandatory fees ($540), and room and board ($5000). Full-time tuition and fees vary according to class time. Part-time tuition: $410 per semester hour. Part-time tuition and fees vary according to class time and course load. *Required fees:* $10 per semester hour, $75 per term part-time. *Payment plan:* installment. *Waivers:* children of alumni, senior citizens, and employees or children of employees.
Financial Aid Of all full-time matriculated undergraduates who enrolled in 2001, 1073 applied for aid, 922 were judged to have need, 308 had their need fully met. In 2001, 156 non-need-based awards were made. *Average percent of need met:* 80%. *Average financial aid package:* $11,401. *Average need-based loan:* $3264. *Average need-based gift aid:* $8116. *Average indebtedness upon graduation:* $5500.
Applying *Options:* common application, electronic application, deferred entrance. *Application fee:* $20. *Required:* high school transcript. *Required for some:* letters of recommendation, interview. *Recommended:* essay or personal statement, minimum 2.0 GPA. *Application deadline:* rolling (freshmen), rolling (transfers). *Notification:* continuous until 8/15 (freshmen).
Admissions Contact Mr. David McMahan, Director of Admissions, University of Saint Francis, 2701 Spring Street, Fort Wayne, IN 46808. *Phone:* 219-434-3279. *Toll-free phone:* 800-729-4732. *E-mail:* admiss@sfc.edu.

UNIVERSITY OF SOUTHERN INDIANA
Evansville, Indiana

- **State-supported** comprehensive, founded 1965, part of Indiana Commission for Higher Education
- **Calendar** semesters
- **Degrees** certificates, associate, bachelor's, master's, post-master's, and postbachelor's certificates
- **Suburban** 300-acre campus
- **Coed,** 8,783 undergraduate students, 77% full-time, 60% women, 40% men
- **Noncompetitive** entrance level, 93% of applicants were admitted

Undergraduates 6,777 full-time, 2,006 part-time. Students come from 28 states and territories, 28 other countries, 10% are from out of state, 4% African American, 0.6% Asian American or Pacific Islander, 0.5% Hispanic American, 0.2% Native American, 0.5% international, 7% transferred in, 31% live on campus. *Retention:* 62% of 2001 full-time freshmen returned.
Freshmen *Admission:* 4,105 applied, 3,834 admitted, 2,039 enrolled. *Average high school GPA:* 2.86. *Test scores:* SAT verbal scores over 500: 38%; SAT math scores over 500: 39%; ACT scores over 18: 70%; SAT verbal scores over 600: 9%; SAT math scores over 600: 9%; ACT scores over 24: 16%; SAT verbal scores over 700: 1%; SAT math scores over 700: 1%; ACT scores over 30: 1%.
Faculty *Total:* 507, 54% full-time. *Student/faculty ratio:* 18:1.
Majors Accounting; advertising; art; biological/physical sciences; biology; biophysics; business; business administration; business education; business marketing and marketing management; chemistry; civil engineering technology; communications; computer/information sciences; data processing technology; dental assistant; dental hygiene; economics; education; electrical/electronic engineering technologies related; electrical/electronic engineering technology; elementary education; English; exercise sciences; finance; French; geology; German; health services administration; history; journalism; liberal arts and sciences/liberal studies; mathematics; mechanical engineering technologies related; mechanical engineering technology; medical radiologic technology; nursing; occupational therapy; occupational therapy assistant; philosophy; physical education; political science; psychology; public relations; radiological science; radio/television broadcasting; respiratory therapy; secretarial science; social sciences; social work; sociology; Spanish; theater arts/drama.
Academic Programs *Special study options:* academic remediation for entering students, adult/continuing education programs, advanced placement credit, cooperative education, distance learning, double majors, honors programs, independent study, internships, part-time degree program, services for LD students, study abroad, summer session for credit.
Library David L. Rice Library plus 1 other with 248,546 titles, 3,302 serial subscriptions, 7,563 audiovisual materials, an OPAC, a Web page.
Computers on Campus 750 computers available on campus for general student use. A campuswide network can be accessed from student residence rooms and from off campus. Internet access, online (class) registration, at least one staffed computer lab available.
Student Life *Housing Options:* coed. *Activities and Organizations:* drama/theater group, student-run newspaper, radio station, choral group, student government, national fraternities, national sororities. *Campus security:* 24-hour emergency response devices and patrols, student patrols, late-night transport/escort service. *Student Services:* health clinic, personal/psychological counseling.
Athletics Member NCAA. All Division II. *Intercollegiate sports:* baseball M(s), basketball M(s)/W(s), cross-country running M(s)/W(s), golf M(s)/W(s), soccer M(s)/W(s), softball W(s), tennis M(s)/W(s), volleyball W(s). *Intramural sports:* badminton M/W, basketball M/W, bowling M/W, cross-country running M/W, football M/W, golf M/W, soccer M, softball M/W, table tennis M/W, tennis M/W, volleyball M/W.
Standardized Tests *Required:* SAT I or ACT (for admission).
Costs (2001–02) *One-time required fee:* $62. *Tuition:* state resident $3083 full-time, $103 per semester hour part-time; nonresident $7545 full-time, $252 per semester hour part-time. Part-time tuition and fees vary according to course load. *Required fees:* $60 full-time, $23 per term part-time. *Room and board:* $5512; room only: $2520. Room and board charges vary according to board plan and housing facility. *Payment plan:* installment. *Waivers:* senior citizens and employees or children of employees.
Financial Aid Of all full-time matriculated undergraduates who enrolled in 2001, 5174 applied for aid, 3844 were judged to have need, 618 had their need fully met. 135 Federal Work-Study jobs (averaging $1737). In 2001, 1806 non-need-based awards were made. *Average percent of need met:* 45%. *Average financial aid package:* $5326. *Average need-based loan:* $3753. *Average need-based gift aid:* $3685. *Average indebtedness upon graduation:* $12,611.
Applying *Options:* common application, electronic application. *Application fee:* $25. *Required:* high school transcript. *Required for some:* interview. *Recommended:* essay or personal statement, minimum 2.0 GPA. *Application deadlines:* 8/15 (freshmen), 8/15 (transfers). *Notification:* continuous until 8/27 (freshmen).
Admissions Contact Mr. Eric Otto, Director of Admission, University of Southern Indiana, 8600 University Boulevard, Evansville, IN 47712-3590. *Phone:* 812-464-1765. *Toll-free phone:* 800-467-1965. *Fax:* 812-465-7154. *E-mail:* enroll@usi.edu.

VALPARAISO UNIVERSITY
Valparaiso, Indiana

- **Independent** comprehensive, founded 1859, affiliated with Lutheran Church
- **Calendar** semesters
- **Degrees** certificates, associate, bachelor's, master's, first professional, and post-master's certificates
- **Small-town** 310-acre campus with easy access to Chicago
- **Endowment** $132.9 million

Valparaiso University (continued)
■ **Coed,** 2,873 undergraduate students, 94% full-time, 53% women, 47% men
■ **Moderately difficult** entrance level, 80% of applicants were admitted

Undergraduates 2,687 full-time, 186 part-time. Students come from 47 states and territories, 48 other countries, 65% are from out of state, 3% African American, 2% Asian American or Pacific Islander, 3% Hispanic American, 0.5% Native American, 4% international, 3% transferred in, 64% live on campus. *Retention:* 86% of 2001 full-time freshmen returned.

Freshmen *Admission:* 3,173 applied, 2,537 admitted, 663 enrolled. *Test scores:* SAT verbal scores over 500: 87%; SAT math scores over 500: 89%; ACT scores over 18: 100%; SAT verbal scores over 600: 46%; SAT math scores over 600: 44%; ACT scores over 24: 78%; SAT verbal scores over 700: 10%; SAT math scores over 700: 13%; ACT scores over 30: 24%.

Faculty *Total:* 340, 63% full-time, 71% with terminal degrees. *Student/faculty ratio:* 13:1.

Majors Accounting; American studies; art; art education; art history; astronomy; athletic training/sports medicine; atmospheric sciences; biological/physical sciences; biology; business administration; business marketing and marketing management; chemistry; civil engineering; classics; communications; computer science; criminology; East Asian studies; economics; education; electrical engineering; elementary education; engineering; English; environmental science; European studies; exercise sciences; finance; fine/studio arts; French; geography; geology; German; health/physical education; history; interdisciplinary studies; international business; international economics; international relations; liberal arts and sciences/liberal studies; mathematics; mechanical engineering; music; music business management/merchandising; music (general performance); music teacher education; music theory and composition; nursing; philosophy; physical education; physics; political science; pre-theology; psychology; religious music; secondary education; social sciences; social work; sociology; Spanish; sport/fitness administration; theater arts/drama; theology.

Academic Programs *Special study options:* accelerated degree program, adult/continuing education programs, advanced placement credit, cooperative education, double majors, freshman honors college, honors programs, independent study, internships, off-campus study, part-time degree program, student-designed majors, study abroad, summer session for credit. *ROTC:* Air Force (b).

Library Moellering Library plus 1 other with 714,657 titles, 16,158 serial subscriptions, 84,570 audiovisual materials, an OPAC, a Web page.

Computers on Campus 580 computers available on campus for general student use. A campuswide network can be accessed from student residence rooms and from off campus. Internet access, at least one staffed computer lab available.

Student Life *Housing:* on-campus residence required through junior year. *Options:* coed, women-only. *Activities and Organizations:* drama/theater group, student-run newspaper, radio station, choral group, Union Board, student government, Student Volunteer Organization, Chapel programs, national fraternities. *Campus security:* 24-hour emergency response devices and patrols, late-night transport/escort service, controlled dormitory access. *Student Services:* health clinic, personal/psychological counseling.

Athletics Member NCAA. All Division I. *Intercollegiate sports:* baseball M(s), basketball M(s)/W(s), cross-country running M(s)/W(s), football M, soccer M(s)/W(s), softball W(s), swimming M(s)/W(s), tennis M(s)/W(s), volleyball W(s). *Intramural sports:* badminton M/W, baseball M, basketball M/W, bowling M/W, football M/W, golf M/W, racquetball M/W, rugby M(c), soccer M/W, softball M/W, swimming M/W, table tennis M/W, tennis M/W, track and field M/W, volleyball M/W, water polo M.

Standardized Tests *Required:* SAT I or ACT (for admission).

Costs (2001–02) *Comprehensive fee:* $23,570 includes full-time tuition ($18,100), mandatory fees ($600), and room and board ($4870). Full-time tuition and fees vary according to program. Part-time tuition: $770 per credit. Part-time tuition and fees vary according to course load. *Required fees:* $50 per term part-time. *Room and board:* College room only: $3100. Room and board charges vary according to board plan and housing facility. *Payment plan:* installment. *Waivers:* employees or children of employees.

Financial Aid Of all full-time matriculated undergraduates who enrolled in 2001, 1997 applied for aid, 1677 were judged to have need, 1083 had their need fully met. 380 Federal Work-Study jobs (averaging $1013). In 2001, 704 non-need-based awards were made. *Average percent of need met:* 86%. *Average financial aid package:* $15,250. *Average need-based loan:* $4414. *Average need-based gift aid:* $10,040. *Average non-need based aid:* $7952. *Average indebtedness upon graduation:* $18,762.

Applying *Options:* common application, electronic application, early action, deferred entrance. *Application fee:* $30. *Required:* high school transcript. *Required for some:* interview. *Recommended:* essay or personal statement, 2 letters of recommendation. *Application deadline:* 8/15 (freshmen), rolling (transfers). *Notification:* 12/1 (early action).

Admissions Contact Ms. Karen Foust, Director of Admissions, Valparaiso University, 651 South College Avenue, Valparaiso, IN 46383-6493. *Phone:* 219-464-5011. *Toll-free phone:* 888-GO-VALPO. *Fax:* 219-464-6898. *E-mail:* undergrad.admissions@valpo.edu.

WABASH COLLEGE
Crawfordsville, Indiana

■ **Independent** 4-year, founded 1832
■ **Calendar** semesters
■ **Degree** bachelor's
■ **Small-town** 50-acre campus with easy access to Indianapolis
■ **Endowment** $319.0 million
■ **Men only,** 849 undergraduate students, 99% full-time
■ **Moderately difficult** entrance level, 55% of applicants were admitted

Undergraduates 840 full-time, 9 part-time. Students come from 35 states and territories, 14 other countries, 25% are from out of state, 7% African American, 3% Asian American or Pacific Islander, 5% Hispanic American, 0.4% Native American, 4% international, 0.6% transferred in, 94% live on campus. *Retention:* 86% of 2001 full-time freshmen returned.

Freshmen *Admission:* 232 enrolled. *Average high school GPA:* 3.57. *Test scores:* SAT verbal scores over 500: 86%; SAT math scores over 500: 94%; ACT scores over 18: 100%; SAT verbal scores over 600: 46%; SAT math scores over 600: 58%; ACT scores over 24: 73%; SAT verbal scores over 700: 10%; SAT math scores over 700: 11%; ACT scores over 30: 17%.

Faculty *Total:* 80, 99% full-time, 99% with terminal degrees. *Student/faculty ratio:* 11:1.

Majors Art; biology; chemistry; classics; economics; English; French; German; Greek (modern); history; Latin (ancient and medieval); mathematics; music; philosophy; physics; political science; pre-law; pre-medicine; pre-veterinary studies; psychology; religious studies; Spanish; speech/rhetorical studies; theater arts/drama.

Academic Programs *Special study options:* accelerated degree program, advanced placement credit, cooperative education, double majors, independent study, internships, off-campus study, services for LD students, study abroad. *ROTC:* Army (c). *Unusual degree programs:* 3-2 engineering with Columbia University, Washington University in St. Louis.

Library Lilly Library with 416,798 titles, 1,422 serial subscriptions, 9,325 audiovisual materials, an OPAC, a Web page.

Computers on Campus 131 computers available on campus for general student use. A campuswide network can be accessed from student residence rooms and from off campus. Internet access, at least one staffed computer lab available.

Student Life *Housing:* on-campus residence required through sophomore year. *Options:* men-only. *Activities and Organizations:* drama/theater group, student-run newspaper, radio station, choral group, Sphinx Club, Alpha Phi Omega, The Bachelor, Malcolm X Institute, Christian Fellowship, national fraternities. *Campus security:* 24-hour emergency response devices and patrols, late-night transport/escort service. *Student Services:* health clinic, personal/psychological counseling.

Athletics Member NCAA. All Division III. *Intercollegiate sports:* baseball M, basketball M, crew M(c), cross-country running M, football M, golf M, lacrosse M(c), rugby M(c), sailing M(c), soccer M, swimming M, tennis M, track and field M, water polo M(c), wrestling M. *Intramural sports:* badminton M, basketball M, bowling M, cross-country running M, football M, golf M, racquetball M, soccer M, softball M, swimming M, table tennis M, tennis M, track and field M, volleyball M, weight lifting M, wrestling M.

Standardized Tests *Required:* SAT I or ACT (for admission).

Costs (2001–02) *Comprehensive fee:* $25,335 includes full-time tuition ($18,893), mandatory fees ($350), and room and board ($6092). Part-time tuition: $3148 per course. Part-time tuition and fees vary according to course load. *Room and board:* College room only: $2254. Room and board charges vary according to board plan and housing facility. *Payment plans:* tuition prepayment, installment. *Waivers:* employees or children of employees.

Financial Aid Of all full-time matriculated undergraduates who enrolled in 2001, 654 applied for aid, 604 were judged to have need, 604 had their need fully met. 362 State and other part-time jobs (averaging $1648). In 2001, 242 non-need-based awards were made. *Average percent of need met:* 100%. *Average financial aid package:* $18,472. *Average need-based loan:* $3613. *Average need-based gift aid:* $13,349. *Average indebtedness upon graduation:* $16,504. *Financial aid deadline:* 3/1.

Applying *Options:* common application, electronic application, early admission, early decision, early action, deferred entrance. *Application fee:* $30. *Required:* essay or personal statement, high school transcript, minimum 2.0 GPA, 1 letter of recommendation. *Recommended:* minimum 3.0 GPA, interview. *Application* *deadlines:* 3/15 (freshmen), 3/15 (transfers). *Early decision:* 11/15. *Notification:* continuous until 4/1 (freshmen), 12/15 (early decision), 1/15 (early action).

Admissions Contact Mr. Steve Klein, Director of Admissions, Wabash College, PO Box 362, Crawfordsville, IN 47933-0352. *Phone:* 765-361-6225. *Toll-free phone:* 800-345-5385. *Fax:* 765-361-6437. *E-mail:* admissions@wabash.edu.

IOWA

ALLEN COLLEGE
Waterloo, Iowa

- **Independent** comprehensive, founded 1989
- **Calendar** semesters
- **Degrees** associate, bachelor's, and master's
- **Suburban** 20-acre campus
- **Endowment** $837,668
- **Coed, primarily women,** 233 undergraduate students, 78% full-time, 94% women, 6% men
- **Moderately difficult** entrance level, 53% of applicants were admitted

Undergraduates 182 full-time, 51 part-time. Students come from 4 states and territories, 2% are from out of state, 2% African American, 0.9% Hispanic American, 0.9% Native American, 20% transferred in, 11% live on campus. *Retention:* 80% of 2001 full-time freshmen returned.

Freshmen *Admission:* 38 applied, 20 admitted, 19 enrolled. *Average high school GPA:* 3.45. *Test scores:* ACT scores over 18: 85%; ACT scores over 24: 15%.

Faculty *Total:* 25, 72% full-time, 4% with terminal degrees. *Student/faculty ratio:* 8:1.

Majors Nursing; radiological science.

Academic Programs *Special study options:* advanced placement credit, distance learning, independent study, off-campus study, part-time degree program. *ROTC:* Army (c).

Library Barrett Library with 2,951 titles, 188 serial subscriptions, 478 audiovisual materials, a Web page.

Computers on Campus 14 computers available on campus for general student use. Internet access, at least one staffed computer lab available.

Student Life *Housing Options:* coed, men-only, women-only. *Activities and Organizations:* student-run newspaper, Allen Student Nurses' Association, Nurses' Christian Fellowship, Allen Student Organization. *Campus security:* 24-hour patrols. *Student Services:* health clinic, personal/psychological counseling, women's center.

Costs (2001–02) *One-time required fee:* $250. *Comprehensive fee:* $12,982 includes full-time tuition ($7812), mandatory fees ($760), and room and board ($4410). Full-time tuition and fees vary according to course load, location, program, and student level. Part-time tuition: $308 per credit hour. Part-time tuition and fees vary according to program and student level. *Required fees:* $19 per credit hour, $185 per credit hour part-time. *Room and board:* College room only: $2205. Room and board charges vary according to housing facility. *Payment plan:* installment.

Financial Aid Of all full-time matriculated undergraduates who enrolled in 2001, 146 applied for aid, 124 were judged to have need, 32 had their need fully met. 5 Federal Work-Study jobs (averaging $2000). 2 State and other part-time jobs (averaging $1464). In 2001, 26 non-need-based awards were made. *Average percent of need met:* 72%. *Average financial aid package:* $7678. *Average need-based loan:* $3251. *Average need-based gift aid:* $4927. *Average non-need based aid:* $609. *Average indebtedness upon graduation:* $15,737.

Applying *Options:* electronic application. *Application fee:* $20. *Required:* essay or personal statement, high school transcript, 1 letter of recommendation. *Required for some:* interview. *Recommended:* minimum 2.3 GPA. *Application deadlines:* 8/1 (freshmen), 8/1 (transfers). *Notification:* continuous until 8/20 (freshmen).

Admissions Contact Ms. Lois Hagedorn, Student Services Assistant, Allen College, Barrett Forum, 1825 Logan Avenue, Waterloo, IA 50703. *Phone:* 319-226-2000. *Fax:* 319-226-2051. *E-mail:* hagedole@ihs.org.

BRIAR CLIFF UNIVERSITY
Sioux City, Iowa

- **Independent Roman Catholic** comprehensive, founded 1930
- **Calendar** (3 10-week terms plus 2 5-week summer sessions)
- **Degrees** associate, bachelor's, and master's
- **Suburban** 70-acre campus
- **Endowment** $9.1 million
- **Coed,** 969 undergraduate students, 75% full-time, 62% women, 38% men
- **Moderately difficult** entrance level, 73% of applicants were admitted

Career success for Briar Cliff College (BCC)students begins in the classroom, where a low student-teacher ratio translates into quality time for each individual. A solid grounding in the liberal arts and a strong emphasis on internship opportunities results in extraordinarily high placement rates. Of the BCC students who responded to a recent survey, 95 percent had found a job within the field of their choice or were accepted to graduate school within six months of graduation.

Undergraduates 724 full-time, 245 part-time. Students come from 32 states and territories, 6 other countries, 27% are from out of state, 3% African American, 1% Asian American or Pacific Islander, 3% Hispanic American, 0.6% Native American, 0.6% international, 11% transferred in, 42% live on campus. *Retention:* 70% of 2001 full-time freshmen returned.

Freshmen *Admission:* 920 applied, 673 admitted, 195 enrolled. *Average high school GPA:* 3.16. *Test scores:* SAT verbal scores over 500: 50%; SAT math scores over 500: 50%; ACT scores over 18: 88%; SAT verbal scores over 600: 50%; SAT math scores over 600: 50%; ACT scores over 24: 29%; ACT scores over 30: 3%.

Faculty *Total:* 88, 59% full-time, 56% with terminal degrees. *Student/faculty ratio:* 14:1.

Majors Accounting; art; art education; biology; business administration; chemistry; computer/information systems security; computer science; creative writing; criminal justice/law enforcement administration; education; education (K-12); elementary education; English; environmental science; graphic design/commercial art/illustration; health education; health/physical education/fitness related; history; human resources management; industrial radiologic technology; interdisciplinary studies; liberal arts and sciences/liberal studies; management information systems/business data processing; mass communications; mathematics; medical technology; music; nursing; pharmacy; physical education; political science; pre-dentistry; pre-engineering; pre-law; pre-medicine; pre-veterinary studies; professional studies; psychology; secondary education; social work; sociology; Spanish; special education related; speech/theater education; theater arts/drama; theology.

Academic Programs *Special study options:* academic remediation for entering students, accelerated degree program, adult/continuing education programs, advanced placement credit, distance learning, double majors, English as a second language, independent study, internships, off-campus study, part-time degree program, services for LD students, student-designed majors, summer session for credit.

Library Mueller Library with 82,293 titles, 8,529 serial subscriptions, 9,769 audiovisual materials, an OPAC, a Web page.

Computers on Campus 114 computers available on campus for general student use. A campuswide network can be accessed from student residence rooms and from off campus. Internet access, at least one staffed computer lab available.

Student Life *Housing:* on-campus residence required through junior year. *Options:* coed. *Activities and Organizations:* drama/theater group, student-run newspaper, radio and television station, choral group, Student Government Association, Ethnic Relations Club, Residence Hall Association, Vision: Campus Programming Board, Peer Advising Leaders. *Campus security:* 24-hour emergency response devices and patrols, student patrols, late-night transport/escort service, controlled dormitory access. *Student Services:* health clinic, personal/psychological counseling.

Athletics Member NAIA. *Intercollegiate sports:* baseball M(s), basketball M(s)/W(s), cross-country running M(s)/W(s), football M(s), golf M(s)/W(s), soccer M(s)/W(s), softball W(s), track and field M(s)/W(s), volleyball W(s), wrestling M(s). *Intramural sports:* basketball M/W, bowling M/W, cross-country running M/W, football M, golf M/W, racquetball M/W, skiing (cross-country) M/W, soccer M/W, softball W, table tennis M/W, tennis M/W, volleyball M/W, weight lifting M/W.

Standardized Tests *Required:* SAT I or ACT (for admission).

Costs (2001–02) *Comprehensive fee:* $19,406 includes full-time tuition ($14,200), mandatory fees ($295), and room and board ($4911). Part-time tuition: $474 per credit hour. Part-time tuition and fees vary according to class time and course load. *Required fees:* $12 per credit hour. *Room and board:* College room only: $2433. Room and board charges vary according to board plan and housing facility. *Payment plan:* deferred payment. *Waivers:* adult students, senior citizens, and employees or children of employees.

Financial Aid Of all full-time matriculated undergraduates who enrolled in 2001, 676 applied for aid, 638 were judged to have need, 328 had their need fully met. 378 Federal Work-Study jobs (averaging $1500). 15 State and other part-time jobs (averaging $1000). In 2001, 5 non-need-based awards were made. *Average*

Briar Cliff University (continued)
percent of need met: 92%. *Average financial aid package:* $13,650. *Average non-need based aid:* $7844. *Average indebtedness upon graduation:* $15,540.

Applying *Options:* common application, early admission, deferred entrance. *Application fee:* $20. *Required:* high school transcript, minimum 2.0 GPA, ACT-18. *Required for some:* 3 letters of recommendation, interview. *Recommended:* essay or personal statement. *Application deadline:* rolling (freshmen), rolling (transfers).

Admissions Contact Ms. Tammy Namminga, Applications Specialist, Briar Cliff University, 3303 Rebecca Street, Sioux City, IA 51106. *Phone:* 712-279-5200 Ext. 5460. *Toll-free phone:* 800-662-3303 Ext. 5200. *Fax:* 712-279-1632. *E-mail:* admissions@briarcliff.edu.

BUENA VISTA UNIVERSITY
Storm Lake, Iowa

- **Independent** comprehensive, founded 1891, affiliated with Presbyterian Church (U.S.A.)
- **Calendar** 4-1-4
- **Degrees** bachelor's and master's
- **Small-town** 60-acre campus
- **Endowment** $115.9 million
- **Coed,** 1,292 undergraduate students, 97% full-time, 51% women, 49% men
- **Moderately difficult** entrance level, 85% of applicants were admitted

Undergraduates 1,252 full-time, 40 part-time. Students come from 18 states and territories, 6 other countries, 15% are from out of state, 1% African American, 2% Asian American or Pacific Islander, 1% Hispanic American, 0.3% Native American, 2% international, 5% transferred in, 86% live on campus. *Retention:* 72% of 2001 full-time freshmen returned.

Freshmen *Admission:* 1,172 applied, 1,000 admitted, 380 enrolled. *Average high school GPA:* 3.36. *Test scores:* ACT scores over 18: 94%; ACT scores over 24: 37%; ACT scores over 30: 4%.

Faculty *Total:* 115, 71% full-time, 52% with terminal degrees. *Student/faculty ratio:* 15:1.

Majors Accounting; art; arts management; athletic training/sports medicine; biological/physical sciences; biology; business administration; business economics; business education; business marketing and marketing management; chemistry; communications; computer science; criminal justice/law enforcement administration; economics; education; elementary education; English; finance; graphic design/commercial art/illustration; history; information sciences/systems; international business; liberal arts and sciences/liberal studies; management information systems/business data processing; mass communications; mathematics; modern languages; music; music teacher education; natural sciences; philosophy; physical education; physics; political science; pre-dentistry; pre-law; pre-medicine; pre-veterinary studies; psychology; public administration; public relations; radio/television broadcasting; religious studies; science education; secondary education; social sciences; social work; Spanish; special education; speech/rhetorical studies; theater arts/drama.

Academic Programs *Special study options:* academic remediation for entering students, adult/continuing education programs, advanced placement credit, distance learning, double majors, English as a second language, freshman honors college, honors programs, independent study, internships, off-campus study, part-time degree program, services for LD students, student-designed majors, study abroad, summer session for credit. *Unusual degree programs:* 3-2 engineering with Washington University in St. Louis.

Library BVU Library with 153,084 titles, 698 serial subscriptions, 4,158 audiovisual materials, an OPAC, a Web page.

Computers on Campus 400 computers available on campus for general student use. A campuswide network can be accessed from student residence rooms and from off campus. Internet access, online (class) registration, at least one staffed computer lab available.

Student Life *Housing:* on-campus residence required through senior year. *Options:* coed. *Activities and Organizations:* drama/theater group, student-run newspaper, radio and television station, choral group, marching band, Student Activities Board, student orientation staff, Esprit De Corps, Student Senate, Marketing Association. *Campus security:* 24-hour emergency response devices, late-night transport/escort service, controlled dormitory access, night security patrols. *Student Services:* health clinic, personal/psychological counseling.

Athletics Member NCAA. All Division III. *Intercollegiate sports:* baseball M, basketball M/W, cross-country running M/W, football M, golf M/W, soccer M/W, softball W, swimming M/W, tennis M/W, track and field M/W, volleyball W, wrestling M. *Intramural sports:* baseball M, basketball M/W, football M/W, racquetball M/W, softball M/W, swimming M/W, tennis M/W, volleyball M/W, weight lifting M/W.

Standardized Tests *Required:* SAT I or ACT (for admission).

Costs (2001–02) *Comprehensive fee:* $22,828 includes full-time tuition ($17,846) and room and board ($4982). Part-time tuition: $600 per semester hour. Part-time tuition and fees vary according to course load. *Room and board:* Room and board charges vary according to board plan, housing facility, and location. *Payment plan:* installment. *Waivers:* employees or children of employees.

Financial Aid Of all full-time matriculated undergraduates who enrolled in 2001, 1194 applied for aid, 1124 were judged to have need, 344 had their need fully met. 602 Federal Work-Study jobs (averaging $1065). In 2001, 87 non-need-based awards were made. *Average percent of need met:* 93%. *Average financial aid package:* $17,618. *Average need-based loan:* $4278. *Average need-based gift aid:* $7659. *Average non-need based aid:* $7795. *Average indebtedness upon graduation:* $19,708.

Applying *Options:* common application, electronic application, early admission, deferred entrance. *Application fee:* $25. *Required:* high school transcript, letters of recommendation. *Required for some:* essay or personal statement, interview. *Recommended:* minimum 3.0 GPA. *Application deadlines:* 6/1 (freshmen), 6/1 (transfers). *Notification:* continuous (freshmen).

Admissions Contact Ms. Louise Cummings-Simmons, Director of Admissions, Buena Vista University, 610 West Fourth Street, Storm Lake, IA 50588. *Toll-free phone:* 800-383-9600. *E-mail:* admissions@bvu.edu.

CENTRAL COLLEGE
Pella, Iowa

- **Independent** 4-year, founded 1853, affiliated with Reformed Church in America
- **Calendar** semesters
- **Degree** bachelor's
- **Small-town** 133-acre campus with easy access to Des Moines
- **Endowment** $49.0 million
- **Coed,** 1,425 undergraduate students, 96% full-time, 58% women, 42% men
- **Moderately difficult** entrance level, 87% of applicants were admitted

Undergraduates 1,375 full-time, 50 part-time. Students come from 34 states and territories, 16% are from out of state, 0.4% African American, 0.9% Asian American or Pacific Islander, 1% Hispanic American, 0.1% Native American, 0.7% international, 3% transferred in, 87% live on campus. *Retention:* 80% of 2001 full-time freshmen returned.

Freshmen *Admission:* 1,438 applied, 1,258 admitted, 412 enrolled. *Average high school GPA:* 3.47. *Test scores:* ACT scores over 18: 95%; ACT scores over 24: 49%; ACT scores over 30: 5%.

Faculty *Total:* 135, 66% full-time, 70% with terminal degrees. *Student/faculty ratio:* 13:1.

Majors Accounting; art; biology; business administration; chemistry; communications; computer science; economics; elementary education; English; environmental science; exercise sciences; French; general studies; German; history; information sciences/systems; interdisciplinary studies; international business; Latin American studies; linguistics; mathematics; mathematics/computer science; music; music teacher education; philosophy; physics; political science; psychology; religious studies; secondary education; social sciences; sociology; Spanish; theater arts/drama; Western European studies.

Academic Programs *Special study options:* academic remediation for entering students, advanced placement credit, English as a second language, freshman honors college, honors programs, internships, off-campus study, part-time degree program, student-designed majors, study abroad, summer session for credit. *Unusual degree programs:* 3-2 engineering with Washington University in St. Louis, Iowa State University of Science and Technology, The University of Iowa; occupational therapy with Washington University in St. Louis.

Library Geisler Library plus 3 others with 198,000 titles, 924 serial subscriptions, an OPAC, a Web page.

Computers on Campus 168 computers available on campus for general student use. A campuswide network can be accessed from student residence rooms and from off campus. At least one staffed computer lab available.

Student Life *Housing:* on-campus residence required through senior year. *Options:* coed. *Activities and Organizations:* drama/theater group, student-run newspaper, radio station, choral group, Students Concerned About the Environment, Intervarsity, FCA, Coalition for Multicultural Campus, Student Senate. *Campus security:* 24-hour emergency response devices, student patrols, late-night transport/escort service, controlled dormitory access. *Student Services:* health clinic, personal/psychological counseling.

Athletics Member NCAA. All Division III. *Intercollegiate sports:* baseball M, basketball M/W, cross-country running M/W, football M, golf M/W, soccer M/W, softball W, tennis M/W, track and field M/W, volleyball W, wrestling M.

Intramural sports: basketball M/W, bowling M/W, football M/W, racquetball M/W, rugby M/W, soccer M/W, softball M/W, table tennis M/W, tennis M/W, track and field M/W, volleyball M/W, weight lifting M/W, wrestling M.

Standardized Tests *Required:* SAT I or ACT (for admission).

Costs (2001–02) *Comprehensive fee:* $21,206 includes full-time tuition ($15,598), mandatory fees ($116), and room and board ($5492). Full-time tuition and fees vary according to location. Part-time tuition: $541 per credit hour. Part-time tuition and fees vary according to course load. *Required fees:* $116 per year part-time. *Room and board:* College room only: $2684. Room and board charges vary according to board plan. *Payment plan:* installment. *Waivers:* employees or children of employees.

Financial Aid Of all full-time matriculated undergraduates who enrolled in 2001, 1456 applied for aid, 905 were judged to have need, 201 had their need fully met. 662 Federal Work-Study jobs (averaging $1300). 526 State and other part-time jobs (averaging $994). In 2001, 224 non-need-based awards were made. *Average percent of need met:* 78%. *Average financial aid package:* $13,111. *Average need-based loan:* $3179. *Average need-based gift aid:* $11,411. *Average non-need based aid:* $8415.

Applying *Options:* common application, early admission, deferred entrance. *Application fee:* $25. *Required:* high school transcript. *Required for some:* essay or personal statement, 3 letters of recommendation, interview. *Recommended:* minimum 2.0 GPA, interview. *Application deadline:* rolling (freshmen), rolling (transfers). *Notification:* continuous until 8/15 (freshmen).

Admissions Contact John Olsen, Vice President for Admission and Student Enrollment Services, Central College, 812 University Street, Pella, IA 50219-1999. *Phone:* 641-628-7600. *Toll-free phone:* 800-458-5503. *Fax:* 641-628-5316. *E-mail:* admissions@central.edu.

CLARKE COLLEGE
Dubuque, Iowa

- **Independent Roman Catholic** comprehensive, founded 1843
- **Calendar** semesters
- **Degrees** associate, bachelor's, and master's
- **Urban** 55-acre campus
- **Endowment** $12.5 million
- **Coed,** 1,052 undergraduate students, 73% full-time, 67% women, 33% men
- **Moderately difficult** entrance level, 58% of applicants were admitted

Undergraduates 771 full-time, 281 part-time. Students come from 27 states and territories, 14 other countries, 41% are from out of state, 0.8% African American, 0.3% Asian American or Pacific Islander, 2% Hispanic American, 0.3% Native American, 2% international, 9% transferred in, 70% live on campus. *Retention:* 83% of 2001 full-time freshmen returned.

Freshmen *Admission:* 871 applied, 508 admitted, 133 enrolled. *Average high school GPA:* 3.32. *Test scores:* SAT verbal scores over 500: 68%; SAT math scores over 500: 79%; ACT scores over 18: 100%; SAT verbal scores over 600: 14%; SAT math scores over 600: 19%; ACT scores over 24: 62%; SAT math scores over 700: 3%; ACT scores over 30: 3%.

Faculty *Total:* 137, 64% full-time, 36% with terminal degrees. *Student/faculty ratio:* 9:1.

Majors Accounting; advertising; art; art education; art history; athletic training/sports medicine; biology; business administration; business marketing and marketing management; chemistry; computer science; early childhood education; economics; education; elementary education; English; fine/studio arts; French; history; information sciences/systems; international business; liberal arts and sciences/liberal studies; management information systems/business data processing; mass communications; mathematics; middle school education; music; music teacher education; music (voice and choral/opera performance); nursing science; philosophy; physical education; physical therapy; psychology; public relations; religious studies; secondary education; social work; sociology; Spanish; special education; theater arts/drama.

Academic Programs *Special study options:* adult/continuing education programs, advanced placement credit, cooperative education, distance learning, double majors, English as a second language, honors programs, independent study, internships, off-campus study, part-time degree program, student-designed majors, study abroad, summer session for credit. *Unusual degree programs:* 3-2 engineering with University of Southern California.

Library Nicholas J. Schrupp Library with 115,562 titles, 936 serial subscriptions, 1,171 audiovisual materials, an OPAC, a Web page.

Computers on Campus 197 computers available on campus for general student use. A campuswide network can be accessed from student residence rooms and from off campus. Internet access, at least one staffed computer lab available.

Student Life *Housing:* on-campus residence required through junior year. *Options:* coed, men-only, women-only. *Activities and Organizations:* drama/theater group, student-run newspaper, radio station, choral group, Admissions Student Team, Student Multicultural Organization, Concert Choir, Campus Ministry, student government. *Campus security:* 24-hour emergency response devices and patrols, late-night transport/escort service, controlled dormitory access. *Student Services:* health clinic, personal/psychological counseling.

Athletics Member NCAA. All Division III. *Intercollegiate sports:* baseball M, basketball M/W, cross-country running M/W, golf M/W, skiing (downhill) M/W, soccer M/W, softball W, tennis M/W, volleyball M/W. *Intramural sports:* badminton M/W, basketball M/W, bowling M/W, equestrian sports M/W, football M/W, golf M/W, racquetball M/W, skiing (cross-country) M/W, skiing (downhill) M/W, softball M/W, swimming M/W, table tennis M/W, tennis M/W, track and field M/W, volleyball M/W, water polo M/W, weight lifting M/W.

Standardized Tests *Required:* SAT I or ACT (for admission).

Costs (2001–02) *Comprehensive fee:* $20,625 includes full-time tuition ($14,685), mandatory fees ($435), and room and board ($5505). Full-time tuition and fees vary according to class time. Part-time tuition: $375 per credit hour. Part-time tuition and fees vary according to class time. *Room and board:* College room only: $2675. Room and board charges vary according to board plan and housing facility. *Payment plans:* installment, deferred payment. *Waivers:* children of alumni, adult students, senior citizens, and employees or children of employees.

Financial Aid Of all full-time matriculated undergraduates who enrolled in 2001, 643 applied for aid, 526 were judged to have need, 154 had their need fully met. 211 Federal Work-Study jobs (averaging $1345). 182 State and other part-time jobs (averaging $1033). In 2001, 162 non-need-based awards were made. *Average percent of need met:* 100%. *Average financial aid package:* $12,797. *Average need-based loan:* $4002. *Average need-based gift aid:* $8977. *Average indebtedness upon graduation:* $16,778.

Applying *Options:* common application, electronic application, deferred entrance. *Application fee:* $25. *Required:* high school transcript, minimum 2.0 GPA, rank in upper 50% of high school class, minimum ACT score of 21 or SAT score of 1000. *Required for some:* interview. *Application deadline:* rolling (freshmen), rolling (transfers). *Notification:* continuous until 7/15 (freshmen).

Admissions Contact Clarke College, 1550 Clarke Drive, Dubuque, IA 52001-3198. *Phone:* 563-588-6316. *Toll-free phone:* 800-383-2345. *Fax:* 319-588-6789. *E-mail:* admissions@clarke.edu.

COE COLLEGE
Cedar Rapids, Iowa

- **Independent** comprehensive, founded 1851, affiliated with Presbyterian Church
- **Calendar** 4-1-4
- **Degrees** bachelor's and master's
- **Urban** 55-acre campus
- **Endowment** $54.7 million
- **Coed,** 1,280 undergraduate students, 89% full-time, 56% women, 44% men
- **Moderately difficult** entrance level, 77% of applicants were admitted

Listed among the top 100 liberal arts colleges in America, Coe College is a private, coeducational, liberal arts college located in Cedar Rapids, Iowa. Coe offers 41 majors, 65 student clubs, and NCAA Division III Iowa Conference competition in 11 men's and 10 women's sports. Ninety-eight percent of Coe graduates are in jobs or graduate school within 6 months of graduation.

Undergraduates 1,142 full-time, 138 part-time. Students come from 40 states and territories, 20 other countries, 38% are from out of state, 2% African American, 0.9% Asian American or Pacific Islander, 1% Hispanic American, 0.1% Native American, 5% international, 4% transferred in, 85% live on campus. *Retention:* 79% of 2001 full-time freshmen returned.

Freshmen *Admission:* 1,219 applied, 941 admitted, 302 enrolled. *Average high school GPA:* 3.59. *Test scores:* SAT verbal scores over 500: 84%; SAT math scores over 500: 82%; ACT scores over 18: 98%; SAT verbal scores over 600: 35%; SAT math scores over 600: 41%; ACT scores over 24: 59%; SAT verbal scores over 700: 6%; SAT math scores over 700: 4%; ACT scores over 30: 7%.

Faculty *Total:* 119, 61% full-time, 73% with terminal degrees. *Student/faculty ratio:* 12:1.

Majors Accounting; African-American studies; American studies; architecture; art; art education; Asian studies; athletic training/sports medicine; biochemistry; biological/physical sciences; biology; business administration; chemistry; classics; computer science; economics; education; elementary education; English; environmental science; fine/studio arts; French; German; history; interdisciplinary studies; liberal arts and sciences/liberal studies; literature; mathematics; molecular biology; music; music teacher education; nursing; philosophy; physical education; physical sciences; physics; political science; pre-dentistry; pre-law;

Coe College (continued)
pre-medicine; pre-veterinary studies; psychology; public relations; religious studies; science education; secondary education; sociology; Spanish; speech/rhetorical studies; theater arts/drama.

Academic Programs *Special study options:* accelerated degree program, adult/continuing education programs, advanced placement credit, double majors, English as a second language, honors programs, independent study, internships, off-campus study, part-time degree program, services for LD students, student-designed majors, study abroad, summer session for credit. *ROTC:* Army (c), Air Force (c). *Unusual degree programs:* 3-2 social service administration with University of Chicago.

Library Stewart Memorial Library plus 1 other with 206,290 titles, 818 serial subscriptions, 9,782 audiovisual materials, an OPAC, a Web page.

Computers on Campus 189 computers available on campus for general student use. A campuswide network can be accessed from student residence rooms and from off campus. Internet access, at least one staffed computer lab available.

Student Life *Housing:* on-campus residence required through senior year. *Options:* coed, men-only, women-only. *Activities and Organizations:* drama/theater group, student-run newspaper, radio station, choral group, Student Activities Committee, International Club, Student Alumni Association, C-Club, Coe Alliance, national fraternities, national sororities. *Campus security:* 24-hour emergency response devices and patrols, late-night transport/escort service, controlled dormitory access. *Student Services:* health clinic, personal/psychological counseling.

Athletics Member NCAA. All Division III. *Intercollegiate sports:* baseball M, basketball M/W, cross-country running M/W, football M, golf M/W, soccer M/W, softball W, swimming M/W, tennis M/W, track and field M/W, volleyball W, wrestling M. *Intramural sports:* basketball M/W, football M/W, racquetball M/W, rugby M/W, soccer M/W, softball M/W, squash M/W, table tennis M/W, tennis M/W, volleyball M/W.

Standardized Tests *Required:* SAT I or ACT (for admission).

Costs (2001–02) *Comprehensive fee:* $24,750 includes full-time tuition ($19,140), mandatory fees ($200), and room and board ($5410). Part-time tuition: $950 per course. *Room and board:* College room only: $2540. Room and board charges vary according to board plan and housing facility. *Payment plan:* installment. *Waivers:* children of alumni, adult students, and employees or children of employees.

Financial Aid Of all full-time matriculated undergraduates who enrolled in 2001, 1112 applied for aid, 984 were judged to have need, 651 had their need fully met. In 2001, 148 non-need-based awards were made. *Average percent of need met:* 96%. *Average financial aid package:* $18,813. *Average need-based loan:* $4952. *Average need-based gift aid:* $13,066. *Average non-need based aid:* $9553. *Average indebtedness upon graduation:* $18,901.

Applying *Options:* common application, electronic application, early admission, early action, deferred entrance. *Required:* essay or personal statement, high school transcript, 1 letter of recommendation. *Recommended:* minimum 3.0 GPA, interview. *Application deadline:* 3/1 (freshmen), rolling (transfers). *Notification:* 3/15 (freshmen), 1/15 (early action).

Admissions Contact Mr. Dennis Trotter, Vice President of Admission and Financial Aid, Coe College, 1220 1st Avenue, NE, Cedar Rapids, IA 52402-5070. *Phone:* 319-399-8500. *Toll-free phone:* 877-225-5263. *Fax:* 319-399-8816. *E-mail:* admission@coe.edu.

CORNELL COLLEGE
Mount Vernon, Iowa

- **Independent Methodist** 4-year, founded 1853
- **Calendar** 9 3½-week terms
- **Degree** bachelor's
- **Small-town** 129-acre campus
- **Endowment** $68.2 million
- **Coed,** 986 undergraduate students, 99% full-time, 58% women, 42% men
- **Moderately difficult** entrance level, 70% of applicants were admitted

Undergraduates 977 full-time, 9 part-time. Students come from 38 states and territories, 7 other countries, 70% are from out of state, 3% African American, 1% Asian American or Pacific Islander, 2% Hispanic American, 0.4% Native American, 2% international, 4% transferred in, 92% live on campus. *Retention:* 79% of 2001 full-time freshmen returned.

Freshmen *Admission:* 1,182 applied, 826 admitted, 302 enrolled. *Average high school GPA:* 3.49. *Test scores:* SAT verbal scores over 500: 73%; SAT math scores over 500: 83%; ACT scores over 18: 98%; SAT verbal scores over 600: 48%; SAT math scores over 600: 46%; ACT scores over 24: 59%; SAT verbal scores over 700: 9%; SAT math scores over 700: 11%; ACT scores over 30: 11%.

Faculty *Total:* 109, 78% full-time, 83% with terminal degrees. *Student/faculty ratio:* 11:1.

Majors Anthropology; architecture; art; art education; art history; biochemistry; biology; business economics; business education; chemistry; classics; computer science; cultural studies; economics; education; elementary education; English; environmental science; exercise sciences; French; geology; German; Greek (modern); history; interdisciplinary studies; international business; international relations; Latin American studies; Latin (ancient and medieval); liberal arts and sciences/liberal studies; mathematics; medieval/renaissance studies; modern languages; music; music teacher education; philosophy; physical education; physics; political science; psychology; religious studies; Russian; Russian/Slavic studies; secondary education; sociology; Spanish; speech/rhetorical studies; theater arts/drama; women's studies.

Academic Programs *Special study options:* adult/continuing education programs, advanced placement credit, double majors, English as a second language, independent study, internships, off-campus study, student-designed majors, study abroad. *Unusual degree programs:* 3-2 engineering with Washington University in St. Louis; forestry with Duke University; environmental management with Duke University, architecture with Washington University in St. Louis.

Library Cole Library with 128,098 titles, 731 serial subscriptions, 7,743 audiovisual materials, an OPAC, a Web page.

Computers on Campus 100 computers available on campus for general student use. A campuswide network can be accessed from student residence rooms and from off campus. Internet access, at least one staffed computer lab available.

Student Life *Housing:* on-campus residence required through senior year. *Options:* coed, men-only, women-only. *Activities and Organizations:* drama/theater group, student-run newspaper, radio station, choral group, social groups, Student-initiated Living-learning Community, Lunch Buddies/Youth Mentoring, Chess and Games Club, Black Awareness Cultural Organization. *Campus security:* 24-hour emergency response devices and patrols. *Student Services:* health clinic, personal/psychological counseling, women's center.

Athletics Member NCAA. All Division III. *Intercollegiate sports:* baseball M, basketball M/W, cross-country running M/W, football M, golf M/W, soccer M/W, softball W, tennis M/W, track and field M/W, volleyball M(c)/W, wrestling M. *Intramural sports:* badminton M/W, basketball M/W, bowling M/W, cross-country running M/W, fencing M/W, football M, golf M/W, racquetball M/W, soccer M/W, softball M/W, table tennis M/W, tennis M/W, track and field M/W, volleyball M/W, wrestling M/W.

Standardized Tests *Required:* SAT I or ACT (for admission).

Costs (2001–02) *Comprehensive fee:* $25,850 includes full-time tuition ($20,090), mandatory fees ($160), and room and board ($5600). Full-time tuition and fees vary according to reciprocity agreements. Part-time tuition: $2531 per course. Part-time tuition and fees vary according to course load. *Room and board:* College room only: $2620. Room and board charges vary according to board plan. *Payment plan:* installment. *Waivers:* adult students, senior citizens, and employees or children of employees.

Financial Aid Of all full-time matriculated undergraduates who enrolled in 2001, 824 applied for aid, 729 were judged to have need, 325 had their need fully met. 452 Federal Work-Study jobs (averaging $1080). 192 State and other part-time jobs (averaging $1050). In 2001, 136 non-need-based awards were made. *Average percent of need met:* 90%. *Average financial aid package:* $19,500. *Average need-based loan:* $4435. *Average need-based gift aid:* $6130. *Average non-need based aid:* $10,485. *Average indebtedness upon graduation:* $17,260.

Applying *Options:* common application, electronic application, early admission, deferred entrance. *Application fee:* $25. *Required:* essay or personal statement, high school transcript, 1 letter of recommendation. *Recommended:* minimum 2.80 GPA, interview. *Application deadlines:* 2/1 (freshmen), 2/1 (transfers). *Notification:* continuous (freshmen).

Admissions Contact Cornell College, 600 First Street West, Mount Vernon, IA 52314-1098. *Phone:* 319-895-4477. *Toll-free phone:* 800-747-1112. *Fax:* 319-895-4451. *E-mail:* admissions@cornellcollege.edu.

DIVINE WORD COLLEGE
Epworth, Iowa

Admissions Contact Br. Dennis Newton SVD, Vice President of Recruitment/Director of Admissions, Divine Word College, 102 Jacoby Drive SW, Epworth, IA 52045-0380. *Phone:* 319-876-3332. *Toll-free phone:* 800-553-3321. *Fax:* 319-876-3407.

DORDT COLLEGE
Sioux Center, Iowa

- **Independent Christian Reformed** comprehensive, founded 1955
- **Calendar** semesters
- **Degrees** associate, bachelor's, and master's
- **Small-town** 65-acre campus
- **Endowment** $16.0 million
- **Coed,** 1,396 undergraduate students, 95% full-time, 56% women, 44% men
- **Moderately difficult** entrance level, 94% of applicants were admitted

Undergraduates 1,331 full-time, 65 part-time. Students come from 37 states and territories, 18 other countries, 58% are from out of state, 0.6% African American, 0.6% Asian American or Pacific Islander, 0.4% Hispanic American, 12% international, 2% transferred in, 90% live on campus. *Retention:* 87% of 2001 full-time freshmen returned.

Freshmen *Admission:* 793 applied, 742 admitted, 308 enrolled. *Average high school GPA:* 3.34. *Test scores:* SAT verbal scores over 500: 83%; SAT math scores over 500: 81%; ACT scores over 18: 98%; SAT verbal scores over 600: 45%; SAT math scores over 600: 43%; ACT scores over 24: 54%; SAT verbal scores over 700: 8%; SAT math scores over 700: 10%; ACT scores over 30: 8%.

Faculty *Total:* 117, 73% full-time, 63% with terminal degrees. *Student/faculty ratio:* 15:1.

Majors Accounting; agricultural animal husbandry/production management; agricultural business; agricultural sciences; animal sciences; art; biology; business administration; business education; chemistry; computer science; criminal justice/law enforcement administration; data processing technology; education; education (K-12); electrical engineering; elementary education; engineering; engineering mechanics; engineering-related technology; English; environmental science; exercise sciences; German; graphic design/commercial art/illustration; history; journalism; management information systems/business data processing; mass communications; mathematics; medical technology; music; music teacher education; natural sciences; nursing; pastoral counseling; philosophy; physical education; physics; political science; pre-dentistry; pre-medicine; pre-veterinary studies; psychology; recreation/leisure studies; religious studies; secondary education; secretarial science; social sciences; social work; sociology; Spanish; teacher assistant/aide; theater arts/drama; theology.

Academic Programs *Special study options:* academic remediation for entering students, advanced placement credit, distance learning, double majors, English as a second language, independent study, internships, off-campus study, part-time degree program, services for LD students, student-designed majors, study abroad.

Library Dordt College Library plus 1 other with 107,000 titles, 6,597 serial subscriptions, 1,989 audiovisual materials, an OPAC, a Web page.

Computers on Campus 205 computers available on campus for general student use. A campuswide network can be accessed from student residence rooms and from off campus. Internet access, at least one staffed computer lab available.

Student Life *Housing:* on-campus residence required through senior year. *Options:* coed, men-only, women-only, disabled students. *Activities and Organizations:* drama/theater group, student-run newspaper, radio station, choral group, PLIA, Future Teachers, Ag Club, Lacrosse Club, Defenders of Life. *Campus security:* 24-hour emergency response devices, student patrols, late-night transport/escort service, controlled dormitory access. *Student Services:* health clinic, personal/psychological counseling.

Athletics Member NAIA. *Intercollegiate sports:* basketball M(s)/W(s), cross-country running M(s)/W(s), golf M(s), ice hockey M, soccer M(s)/W(s), softball W(s), tennis M(s)/W(s), track and field M(s)/W(s), volleyball W(s). *Intramural sports:* baseball M, basketball M/W, bowling M/W, field hockey M/W, gymnastics M/W, ice hockey M, lacrosse M, racquetball M/W, skiing (cross-country) M/W, soccer M/W, softball M/W, swimming M/W, table tennis M/W, tennis M/W, track and field M/W, volleyball M/W, weight lifting M/W.

Standardized Tests *Required:* SAT I or ACT (for admission).

Costs (2001–02) *Comprehensive fee:* $18,100 includes full-time tuition ($13,950), mandatory fees ($150), and room and board ($4000). Part-time tuition: $585 per credit hour. *Required fees:* $75 per term part-time. *Room and board:* College room only: $1990. Room and board charges vary according to board plan and housing facility. *Payment plan:* installment. *Waivers:* children of alumni, senior citizens, and employees or children of employees.

Financial Aid Of all full-time matriculated undergraduates who enrolled in 2001, 1237 applied for aid, 1110 were judged to have need, 231 had their need fully met. *Average percent of need met:* 78%. *Average financial aid package:* $12,916. *Average need-based loan:* $4233. *Average need-based gift aid:* $7188. *Average indebtedness upon graduation:* $15,243.

Applying *Options:* electronic application, deferred entrance. *Application fee:* $25. *Required:* high school transcript, minimum 2.25 GPA, minimum ACT composite score of 19 or combined SAT I score of 920. *Required for some:* interview. *Application deadlines:* 8/1 (freshmen), 8/1 (transfers). *Notification:* continuous until 9/1 (freshmen).

Admissions Contact Mr. Quentin Van Essen, Executive Director of Admissions, Dordt College, 498 4th Avenue, NE, Sioux Center, IA 51250-1697. *Phone:* 712-722-6080. *Toll-free phone:* 800-343-6738. *Fax:* 712-722-1967. *E-mail:* admissions@dordt.edu.

DRAKE UNIVERSITY
Des Moines, Iowa

- **Independent** university, founded 1881
- **Calendar** semesters
- **Degrees** bachelor's, master's, doctoral, and first professional
- **Suburban** 120-acre campus
- **Endowment** $114.3 million
- **Coed,** 3,577 undergraduate students, 92% full-time, 61% women, 39% men
- **Moderately difficult** entrance level, 87% of applicants were admitted

Undergraduates 3,295 full-time, 282 part-time. Students come from 43 states and territories, 57 other countries, 60% are from out of state, 3% African American, 5% Asian American or Pacific Islander, 2% Hispanic American, 0.3% Native American, 5% international, 7% transferred in, 60% live on campus. *Retention:* 81% of 2001 full-time freshmen returned.

Freshmen *Admission:* 2,735 applied, 2,392 admitted, 757 enrolled. *Average high school GPA:* 3.58. *Test scores:* SAT verbal scores over 500: 84%; SAT math scores over 500: 77%; ACT scores over 18: 99%; SAT verbal scores over 600: 47%; SAT math scores over 600: 38%; ACT scores over 24: 67%; SAT verbal scores over 700: 11%; SAT math scores over 700: 6%; ACT scores over 30: 16%.

Faculty *Total:* 375, 68% full-time. *Student/faculty ratio:* 13:1.

Majors Accounting; actuarial science; advertising; anthropology; Army R.O.T.C./military science; art; art history; astronomy; biology; broadcast journalism; business; business administration; business education; business marketing and marketing management; chemistry; computer science; drawing; economics; elementary education; English; environmental science; finance; fine/studio arts; graphic design/commercial art/illustration; history; information sciences/systems; international business; international relations; journalism; mass communications; mathematics; music; music business management/merchandising; music (piano and organ performance); music teacher education; music (voice and choral/opera performance); pharmacy; pharmacy administration/pharmaceutics; philosophy; physics; political science; pre-dentistry; pre-law; pre-medicine; pre-veterinary studies; psychology; public relations; radio/television broadcasting; religious music; religious studies; science education; sculpture; secondary education; sociology; speech/rhetorical studies; theater arts/drama.

Academic Programs *Special study options:* advanced placement credit, cooperative education, distance learning, double majors, English as a second language, honors programs, independent study, internships, off-campus study, part-time degree program, services for LD students, student-designed majors, study abroad, summer session for credit. *ROTC:* Army (b), Air Force (c). *Unusual degree programs:* 3-2 engineering with Washington University in St. Louis, Cornell University.

Library Cowles Library plus 1 other with 559,764 titles, 2,120 serial subscriptions, 165 audiovisual materials, an OPAC, a Web page.

Computers on Campus 1081 computers available on campus for general student use. A campuswide network can be accessed from student residence rooms and from off campus. Internet access, at least one staffed computer lab available.

Student Life *Housing:* on-campus residence required through sophomore year. *Options:* coed. *Activities and Organizations:* drama/theater group, student-run newspaper, radio and television station, choral group, marching band, Student Activities Board, international student organizations, Coalition of Black Students, Alpha Phi Omega Service Organization, Residence Hall Association, national fraternities, national sororities. *Campus security:* 24-hour emergency response devices and patrols, late-night transport/escort service, 24-hour desk attendants in residence halls. *Student Services:* health clinic, personal/psychological counseling, women's center, legal services.

Athletics Member NCAA. All Division I except football (Division I-AA). *Intercollegiate sports:* basketball M(s)/W(s), crew W, cross-country running M(s)/W(s), golf M(s), rugby M(c)/W(c), soccer M(s)/W, softball W(s), tennis M(s)/W(s), track and field M(s)/W(s), volleyball W(s). *Intramural sports:* badminton M/W, basketball M/W, football M/W, golf M/W, racquetball M/W, soccer M/W, softball M/W, swimming M/W, table tennis M/W, tennis M/W, track and field M/W, volleyball M/W.

Standardized Tests *Required:* SAT I or ACT (for admission).

Costs (2001–02) *Comprehensive fee:* $22,830 includes full-time tuition ($17,580), mandatory fees ($210), and room and board ($5040). Full-time tuition

Drake University (continued)
and fees vary according to student level. Part-time tuition: $350 per semester hour. Part-time tuition and fees vary according to class time. *Required fees:* $20 per term part-time. *Room and board:* College room only: $2580. Room and board charges vary according to board plan. *Payment plan:* installment. *Waivers:* children of alumni, senior citizens, and employees or children of employees.
Financial Aid Of all full-time matriculated undergraduates who enrolled in 2001, 2192 applied for aid, 1843 were judged to have need, 271 had their need fully met. 768 Federal Work-Study jobs (averaging $1332). 575 State and other part-time jobs (averaging $1222). *Average percent of need met:* 87%. *Average financial aid package:* $15,118. *Average need-based loan:* $5457. *Average need-based gift aid:* $10,395. *Average indebtedness upon graduation:* $21,422.
Applying *Options:* common application, electronic application, early admission, deferred entrance. *Application fee:* $25. *Required:* high school transcript. *Recommended:* essay or personal statement, interview. *Application deadline:* rolling (freshmen), rolling (transfers). *Notification:* continuous until 8/1 (freshmen).
Admissions Contact Mr. Thomas F. Willoughby, Dean of Admission and Financial Aid, Drake University, 2507 University Avenue, Des Moines, IA 50311. *Phone:* 515-271-3181. *Toll-free phone:* 800-44DRAKE. *Fax:* 515-271-2831. *E-mail:* admission@drake.edu.

EMMAUS BIBLE COLLEGE
Dubuque, Iowa

- **Independent nondenominational** 4-year, founded 1941
- **Calendar** semesters
- **Degrees** certificates, associate, and bachelor's
- **Small-town** 22-acre campus
- **Endowment** $1.2 million
- **Coed,** 284 undergraduate students, 90% full-time, 50% women, 50% men
- **Noncompetitive** entrance level

Undergraduates 256 full-time, 28 part-time. Students come from 42 states and territories, 7 other countries, 72% are from out of state, 1% African American, 2% Asian American or Pacific Islander, 2% Hispanic American, 1% Native American, 6% international, 15% transferred in, 79% live on campus. *Retention:* 86% of 2001 full-time freshmen returned.
Freshmen *Admission:* 73 enrolled. *Average high school GPA:* 3.35. *Test scores:* SAT verbal scores over 500: 94%; SAT math scores over 500: 70%; ACT scores over 18: 87%; SAT verbal scores over 600: 47%; SAT math scores over 600: 35%; ACT scores over 24: 30%; SAT verbal scores over 700: 12%; ACT scores over 30: 4%.
Faculty *Total:* 25, 60% full-time, 36% with terminal degrees. *Student/faculty ratio:* 14:1.
Majors Biblical studies; computer/information sciences; elementary education; missionary studies; pre-theology.
Academic Programs *Special study options:* advanced placement credit, double majors, independent study, internships, off-campus study, part-time degree program.
Library The Emmaus Bible College Library plus 1 other with 86,000 titles, 330 serial subscriptions.
Computers on Campus 60 computers available on campus for general student use. A campuswide network can be accessed from off campus. Internet access, at least one staffed computer lab available.
Student Life *Housing:* on-campus residence required through senior year. *Options:* men-only, women-only. *Activities and Organizations:* drama/theater group, student-run radio station, choral group. *Campus security:* 24-hour emergency response devices, student patrols, controlled dormitory access. *Student Services:* personal/psychological counseling.
Athletics Member NCCAA. *Intercollegiate sports:* basketball M/W. *Intramural sports:* badminton M/W, basketball M/W, cross-country running M/W, football M/W, golf M/W, racquetball M/W, skiing (cross-country) M/W, skiing (downhill) M/W, soccer M/W, softball M/W, table tennis M/W, tennis M/W, volleyball M/W, weight lifting M/W.
Standardized Tests *Required:* SAT I or ACT (for placement).
Costs (2002–03) *Comprehensive fee:* $9816 includes full-time tuition ($6116), mandatory fees ($210), and room and board ($3490). Full-time tuition and fees vary according to program. Part-time tuition: $185 per credit hour. Part-time tuition and fees vary according to course load. *Required fees:* $9 per credit hour. *Payment plan:* installment. *Waivers:* employees or children of employees.
Financial Aid Of all full-time matriculated undergraduates who enrolled in 2001, 244 applied for aid, 223 were judged to have need, 22 had their need fully met. *Average percent of need met:* 68%. *Average financial aid package:* $2732. *Average need-based gift aid:* $2150. *Average indebtedness upon graduation:* $17,125. *Financial aid deadline:* 6/10.
Applying *Options:* deferred entrance. *Application fee:* $10. *Required:* essay or personal statement, high school transcript, 3 letters of recommendation. *Application deadlines:* 8/1 (freshmen), 8/1 (transfers). *Notification:* continuous (freshmen).
Admissions Contact Emmaus Bible College, 2570 Asbury Road, Dubuque, IA 52001-3097. *Phone:* 563-588-8000 Ext. 1310. *Toll-free phone:* 800-397-2425. *Fax:* 563-588-1216. *E-mail:* registrar@emmausl.edu.

FAITH BAPTIST BIBLE COLLEGE AND THEOLOGICAL SEMINARY
Ankeny, Iowa

- **Independent** comprehensive, founded 1921, affiliated with General Association of Regular Baptist Churches
- **Calendar** semesters
- **Degrees** certificates, associate, bachelor's, master's, and first professional
- **Small-town** 52-acre campus
- **Endowment** $5.5 million
- **Coed,** 372 undergraduate students, 91% full-time, 57% women, 43% men
- **Minimally difficult** entrance level, 91% of applicants were admitted

Undergraduates 337 full-time, 35 part-time. Students come from 28 states and territories, 12 other countries, 49% are from out of state, 0.8% African American, 1% Asian American or Pacific Islander, 0.8% Hispanic American, 0.8% international, 12% transferred in, 81% live on campus. *Retention:* 76% of 2001 full-time freshmen returned.
Freshmen *Admission:* 196 applied, 179 admitted, 111 enrolled. *Average high school GPA:* 3.41. *Test scores:* SAT verbal scores over 500: 43%; SAT math scores over 500: 29%; ACT scores over 18: 82%; SAT verbal scores over 600: 29%; ACT scores over 24: 33%; ACT scores over 30: 7%.
Faculty *Total:* 31, 48% full-time, 52% with terminal degrees. *Student/faculty ratio:* 18:1.
Majors Biblical studies; divinity/ministry; elementary education; English education; missionary studies; music teacher education; pastoral counseling; religious education; religious music; secretarial science.
Academic Programs *Special study options:* adult/continuing education programs, advanced placement credit, double majors, internships, part-time degree program, summer session for credit.
Library Patten Hall plus 1 other with 60,700 titles, 423 serial subscriptions, 3,768 audiovisual materials, an OPAC.
Computers on Campus 41 computers available on campus for general student use. A campuswide network can be accessed from student residence rooms. Internet access, at least one staffed computer lab available.
Student Life *Housing:* on-campus residence required through senior year. *Options:* men-only, women-only. *Activities and Organizations:* drama/theater group, student-run newspaper, choral group, Student Association, Student Missions Fellowship. *Campus security:* 24-hour emergency response devices and patrols, late-night transport/escort service. *Student Services:* personal/psychological counseling.
Athletics Member NCCAA. *Intercollegiate sports:* basketball M/W, soccer M, volleyball W. *Intramural sports:* basketball M/W, cross-country running M/W, football M, soccer W, softball M/W, table tennis M/W, volleyball M/W.
Standardized Tests *Required:* SAT I or ACT (for admission).
Costs (2001–02) *Comprehensive fee:* $12,476 includes full-time tuition ($8690), mandatory fees ($320), and room and board ($3466). Full-time tuition and fees vary according to course load. Part-time tuition: $315 per semester hour. Part-time tuition and fees vary according to course load. *Required fees:* $70 per term part-time. *Room and board:* College room only: $1616. Room and board charges vary according to housing facility. *Payment plan:* installment. *Waivers:* employees or children of employees.
Financial Aid Of all full-time matriculated undergraduates who enrolled in 2001, 337 applied for aid, 305 were judged to have need, 17 had their need fully met. In 2001, 35 non-need-based awards were made. *Average percent of need met:* 39%. *Average financial aid package:* $4635. *Average need-based loan:* $2977. *Average need-based gift aid:* $3498. *Average non-need based aid:* $2593. *Average indebtedness upon graduation:* $9778.
Applying *Options:* early admission, deferred entrance. *Application fee:* $25. *Required:* essay or personal statement, high school transcript, 2 letters of recommendation. *Required for some:* interview. *Application deadlines:* 8/1 (freshmen), 8/1 (transfers).

Admissions Contact Mrs. Sherie Bartlett, Admissions Office Secretary, Faith Baptist Bible College and Theological Seminary, 1900 NW 4th Street, Ankeny, IA 50021. *Phone:* 515-964-0601 Ext. 233. *Toll-free phone:* 888-FAITH 4U. *Fax:* 515-964-1638. *E-mail:* admissions@faith.edu.

GRACELAND UNIVERSITY
Lamoni, Iowa

- **Independent Reorganized Latter Day Saints** comprehensive, founded 1895
- **Calendar** 4-1-4
- **Degrees** bachelor's, master's, and post-master's certificates
- **Small-town** 169-acre campus
- **Endowment** $75.4 million
- **Coed,** 2,283 undergraduate students, 56% full-time, 69% women, 31% men
- **Moderately difficult** entrance level, 61% of applicants were admitted

Undergraduates 1,276 full-time, 1,007 part-time. Students come from 50 states and territories, 22 other countries, 71% are from out of state, 3% African American, 2% Asian American or Pacific Islander, 3% Hispanic American, 0.7% Native American, 4% international, 4% transferred in, 59% live on campus. *Retention:* 75% of 2001 full-time freshmen returned.

Freshmen *Admission:* 981 applied, 601 admitted, 251 enrolled. *Average high school GPA:* 3.19. *Test scores:* SAT verbal scores over 500: 52%; SAT math scores over 500: 49%; ACT scores over 18: 80%; SAT verbal scores over 600: 24%; SAT math scores over 600: 27%; ACT scores over 24: 32%; SAT verbal scores over 700: 9%; SAT math scores over 700: 3%; ACT scores over 30: 5%.

Faculty *Total:* 104, 82% full-time, 45% with terminal degrees. *Student/faculty ratio:* 16:1.

Majors Accounting; alcohol/drug abuse counseling; art; art education; athletic training/sports medicine; biology; business administration; chemistry; computer science; criminal justice/law enforcement administration; economics; education; education (K-12); elementary education; English; English composition; fine/studio arts; foreign languages/literatures; German; graphic design/commercial art/illustration; health education; health science; history; human services; international business; international relations; liberal arts and sciences/liberal studies; literature; management information systems/business data processing; mathematics; medical technology; music; music teacher education; nursing; philosophy and religion related; physical education; physical sciences; pre-dentistry; pre-law; pre-medicine; psychology; publishing; recreation/leisure studies; religious studies; science education; secondary education; social sciences; social work; sociology; Spanish; speech/rhetorical studies; speech/theater education; sport/fitness administration; theater arts/drama.

Academic Programs *Special study options:* academic remediation for entering students, accelerated degree program, adult/continuing education programs, advanced placement credit, distance learning, double majors, English as a second language, external degree program, honors programs, independent study, internships, off-campus study, part-time degree program, services for LD students, student-designed majors, study abroad, summer session for credit.

Library Frederick Madison Smith Library with 110,862 titles, 567 serial subscriptions, 2,827 audiovisual materials, an OPAC, a Web page.

Computers on Campus 138 computers available on campus for general student use. A campuswide network can be accessed from student residence rooms and from off campus. Internet access, at least one staffed computer lab available.

Student Life *Housing:* on-campus residence required through sophomore year. *Options:* men-only, women-only. *Activities and Organizations:* drama/theater group, student-run newspaper, choral group, marching band, Student Activities Organization, Nontraditional Students (OASIS), "Choices Alcohol" Free Night Spot, International Club, Students in Free Enterprise. *Campus security:* 24-hour emergency response devices and patrols, controlled dormitory access. *Student Services:* health clinic, personal/psychological counseling.

Athletics Member NAIA. *Intercollegiate sports:* baseball M(s), basketball M(s)/W(s), cross-country running M(s)/W(s), football M(s), golf M(s)/W(s), soccer M(s)/W(s), softball W(s), tennis M(s)/W(s), track and field M(s)/W(s), volleyball M(s)/W(s). *Intramural sports:* baseball M/W, basketball M/W, cross-country running M/W, football M/W, golf M/W, racquetball M/W, soccer M/W, softball M/W, swimming M/W, table tennis M/W, tennis M/W, track and field M/W, volleyball M/W, weight lifting M/W, wrestling M.

Standardized Tests *Required:* SAT I or ACT (for admission).

Costs (2001–02) *One-time required fee:* $100. *Comprehensive fee:* $17,450 includes full-time tuition ($13,025), mandatory fees ($120), and room and board ($4305). Full-time tuition and fees vary according to course load. Part-time tuition: $410 per semester hour. Part-time tuition and fees vary according to location. *Required fees:* $60 per term part-time. *Room and board:* College room only: $1605. Room and board charges vary according to board plan, housing facility, and location. *Payment plan:* installment. *Waivers:* senior citizens and employees or children of employees.

Financial Aid Of all full-time matriculated undergraduates who enrolled in 2001, 1034 applied for aid, 893 were judged to have need, 293 had their need fully met. 254 Federal Work-Study jobs (averaging $1161). In 2001, 193 non-need-based awards were made. *Average percent of need met:* 87%. *Average financial aid package:* $12,760. *Average need-based loan:* $4951. *Average need-based gift aid:* $8280. *Average non-need based aid:* $6019. *Average indebtedness upon graduation:* $15,472.

Applying *Options:* common application, electronic application, early admission, deferred entrance. *Application fee:* $50. *Required:* high school transcript, minimum 2.0 GPA. *Required for some:* essay or personal statement, 2 letters of recommendation, interview. *Application deadline:* rolling (freshmen), rolling (transfers). *Notification:* continuous (freshmen).

Admissions Contact Ms. Bonita A. Booth, Vice Provost for Enrollment and Dean of Admissions, Graceland University, 1 University Place. *Phone:* 641-784-5118. *Toll-free phone:* 888-472-235263 (in-state); 800-472-235263 (out-of-state). *Fax:* 641-784-5480. *E-mail:* admissions@graceland.edu.

GRAND VIEW COLLEGE
Des Moines, Iowa

- **Independent** 4-year, founded 1896, affiliated with Evangelical Lutheran Church in America
- **Calendar** semesters
- **Degrees** certificates, associate, bachelor's, and postbachelor's certificates
- **Urban** 25-acre campus
- **Endowment** $7.9 million
- **Coed,** 1,402 undergraduate students, 69% full-time, 67% women, 33% men
- **Noncompetitive** entrance level, 99% of applicants were admitted

Undergraduates 971 full-time, 431 part-time. Students come from 17 states and territories, 12 other countries, 5% are from out of state, 3% African American, 2% Asian American or Pacific Islander, 0.9% Hispanic American, 0.4% Native American, 1% international, 15% transferred in, 19% live on campus. *Retention:* 63% of 2001 full-time freshmen returned.

Freshmen *Admission:* 365 applied, 361 admitted, 196 enrolled. *Average high school GPA:* 3.03. *Test scores:* SAT verbal scores over 500: 25%; SAT math scores over 500: 50%; ACT scores over 18: 81%; SAT verbal scores over 600: 25%; SAT math scores over 600: 25%; ACT scores over 24: 22%; ACT scores over 30: 1%.

Faculty *Total:* 131, 50% full-time, 47% with terminal degrees. *Student/faculty ratio:* 15:1.

Majors Accounting; applied mathematics; art; art education; biological/physical sciences; biology; business administration; business education; computer science; computer software and media applications related; criminal justice/law enforcement administration; education; elementary education; English; fine/studio arts; graphic design/commercial art/illustration; history; human services; information sciences/systems; interdisciplinary studies; journalism; liberal arts and sciences/liberal studies; management information systems/business data processing; mass communications; middle school education; music; nursing; physical sciences related; political science; pre-engineering; pre-law; professional studies; psychology; radio/television broadcasting; religious studies; science education; secondary education; sociology; special education; theater arts/drama.

Academic Programs *Special study options:* academic remediation for entering students, accelerated degree program, advanced placement credit, cooperative education, distance learning, double majors, freshman honors college, honors programs, independent study, internships, off-campus study, part-time degree program, services for LD students, student-designed majors, study abroad, summer session for credit. *ROTC:* Army (c), Air Force (c). *Unusual degree programs:* 3-2 engineering with Iowa State University; hospital administration with The University of Iowa.

Library Grand View College Library with 101,094 titles, 3,412 serial subscriptions, 6,323 audiovisual materials, an OPAC.

Computers on Campus 210 computers available on campus for general student use. A campuswide network can be accessed from student residence rooms and from off campus. Internet access, at least one staffed computer lab available.

Student Life *Housing Options:* coed, men-only, women-only. *Activities and Organizations:* drama/theater group, student-run newspaper, radio and television station, choral group, Nursing Student Association (NSA), Art Club, Science Club, Education Club, Business Club. *Campus security:* 24-hour emergency response devices, night security patrols. *Student Services:* health clinic, personal/psychological counseling.

Grand View College (continued)

Athletics Member NAIA. *Intercollegiate sports:* baseball M(s), basketball M(s)/W(s), soccer M(s)/W(s), softball W(s), volleyball W(s). *Intramural sports:* basketball M/W, football M/W, golf M/W, soccer M/W, softball W, table tennis M/W, tennis M/W, volleyball M/W.

Standardized Tests *Required:* SAT I or ACT (for admission).

Costs (2001–02) *Comprehensive fee:* $17,596 includes full-time tuition ($13,340), mandatory fees ($90), and room and board ($4166). Part-time tuition: $380 per credit hour. Part-time tuition and fees vary according to class time. *Room and board:* Room and board charges vary according to board plan, housing facility, and student level. *Payment plans:* installment, deferred payment. *Waivers:* senior citizens and employees or children of employees.

Financial Aid Of all full-time matriculated undergraduates who enrolled in 2001, 915 applied for aid, 836 were judged to have need, 170 had their need fully met. *Average percent of need met:* 81%. *Average financial aid package:* $11,812. *Average need-based loan:* $3764. *Average need-based gift aid:* $8393. *Average indebtedness upon graduation:* $18,133.

Applying *Options:* common application, electronic application. *Required:* high school transcript. *Recommended:* minimum 2.0 GPA. *Application deadline:* 8/15 (freshmen), rolling (transfers). *Notification:* 9/15 (freshmen).

Admissions Contact Ms. Diane Johnson, Director of Admission, Grand View College, 1200 Grandview Avenue, Des Moines, IA 50316-1599. *Phone:* 515-263-6149. *Toll-free phone:* 800-444-6083. *Fax:* 515-263-2974. *E-mail:* admiss@gvc.edu.

GRINNELL COLLEGE

Grinnell, Iowa

- **Independent** 4-year, founded 1846
- **Calendar** semesters
- **Degree** bachelor's
- **Small-town** 95-acre campus
- **Endowment** $1.0 billion
- **Coed,** 1,338 undergraduate students, 97% full-time, 54% women, 46% men
- **Very difficult** entrance level, 65% of applicants were admitted

For the past fifteen years, Grinnell College has been named one of the 15 best liberal arts colleges by *U.S. News & World Report* and was ranked 11th in 2001. Grinnell has an open curriculum, with no general education, core, or distribution requirements. The College has a $1-billion endowment and awarded more than $14 million in grants and scholarships last year.

Undergraduates 1,301 full-time, 37 part-time. Students come from 51 states and territories, 53 other countries, 86% are from out of state, 4% African American, 4% Asian American or Pacific Islander, 4% Hispanic American, 0.5% Native American, 10% international, 3% transferred in, 85% live on campus. *Retention:* 92% of 2001 full-time freshmen returned.

Freshmen *Admission:* 1,980 applied, 1,281 admitted, 358 enrolled. *Test scores:* SAT verbal scores over 500: 96%; SAT math scores over 500: 101%; ACT scores over 18: 99%; SAT verbal scores over 600: 86%; SAT math scores over 600: 86%; ACT scores over 24: 92%; SAT verbal scores over 700: 43%; SAT math scores over 700: 34%; ACT scores over 30: 54%.

Faculty *Total:* 140, 98% full-time, 94% with terminal degrees. *Student/faculty ratio:* 10:1.

Majors African-American studies; American studies; anthropology; art; biochemistry; biological/physical sciences; biology; chemistry; Chinese; classics; computer science; economics; English; environmental science; French; German; history; interdisciplinary studies; Latin American studies; linguistics; mathematics; music; philosophy; physics; political science; psychology; religious studies; Russian; science/technology and society; sociology; Spanish; theater arts/drama; Western European studies; women's studies.

Academic Programs *Special study options:* accelerated degree program, advanced placement credit, double majors, independent study, internships, off-campus study, services for LD students, student-designed majors, study abroad. *Unusual degree programs:* 3-2 engineering with Columbia University, California Institute of Technology, Rensselaer Polytechnic Institute, Washington University in St. Louis; architecture with Washington University in St. Louis, law at Columbia University.

Library Burling Library plus 2 others with 970,403 titles, 3,400 serial subscriptions, 26,122 audiovisual materials, an OPAC, a Web page.

Computers on Campus 240 computers available on campus for general student use. A campuswide network can be accessed from student residence rooms and from off campus that provide access to e-mail. Internet access, at least one staffed computer lab available.

Student Life *Housing:* on-campus residence required through sophomore year. *Options:* coed, cooperative. *Activities and Organizations:* drama/theater group, student-run newspaper, radio station, choral group, Environmental Action Group, Chalutzim, Stonewall Coalition, International Student Organization, Campus Democrats. *Campus security:* 24-hour emergency response devices and patrols, student patrols, late-night transport/escort service, controlled dormitory access. *Student Services:* health clinic, personal/psychological counseling.

Athletics Member NCAA. All Division III. *Intercollegiate sports:* baseball M, basketball M/W, cross-country running M/W, football M, golf M/W, soccer M/W, softball W, swimming M/W, tennis M/W, track and field M/W, volleyball W. *Intramural sports:* badminton M/W, basketball M/W, fencing M(c)/W(c), field hockey M/W, lacrosse M(c)/W(c), rugby M(c)/W(c), soccer M/W, softball M/W, tennis M/W, volleyball M(c)/W(c), water polo M/W.

Standardized Tests *Required:* SAT I or ACT (for admission).

Costs (2001–02) *Comprehensive fee:* $28,300 includes full-time tuition ($21,700), mandatory fees ($550), and room and board ($6050). Part-time tuition: $678 per credit hour. *Room and board:* College room only: $2820. Room and board charges vary according to board plan. *Payment plans:* tuition prepayment, installment. *Waivers:* employees or children of employees.

Financial Aid Of all full-time matriculated undergraduates who enrolled in 2001, 1295 applied for aid, 817 were judged to have need, 817 had their need fully met. 386 Federal Work-Study jobs (averaging $1620). 389 State and other part-time jobs (averaging $1772). In 2001, 430 non-need-based awards were made. *Average percent of need met:* 100%. *Average financial aid package:* $18,711. *Average need-based loan:* $4461. *Average need-based gift aid:* $14,314. *Average non-need based aid:* $7762. *Average indebtedness upon graduation:* $13,324. *Financial aid deadline:* 2/1.

Applying *Options:* common application, electronic application, early admission, early decision, deferred entrance. *Application fee:* $30. *Required:* essay or personal statement, high school transcript, 3 letters of recommendation. *Recommended:* interview. *Application deadlines:* 1/20 (freshmen), 5/1 (transfers). *Early decision:* 11/20. *Notification:* 4/1 (freshmen), 12/20 (early decision).

Admissions Contact Mr. James Sumner, Dean for Admission and Financial Aid, Grinnell College, 1103 Park Street, Grinnell, IA 50112-1690. *Phone:* 641-269-3600. *Toll-free phone:* 800-247-0113. *Fax:* 641-269-4800. *E-mail:* askgrin@grinnell.edu.

HAMILTON COLLEGE

Cedar Rapids, Iowa

- **Proprietary** primarily 2-year, founded 1900
- **Calendar** quarters
- **Degrees** certificates, diplomas, associate, and bachelor's (branch locations in Des Moines, Mason City with significant enrollment reflected in profile)
- **Suburban** 4-acre campus
- **Coed**
- **Moderately difficult** entrance level

Faculty *Student/faculty ratio:* 25:1.

Student Life *Campus security:* 24-hour emergency response devices.

Financial Aid Of all full-time matriculated undergraduates who enrolled in 2001, 121 Federal Work-Study jobs (averaging $152558). 3 State and other part-time jobs (averaging $1885).

Applying *Options:* common application, early admission, deferred entrance. *Application fee:* $25. *Required:* high school transcript, minimum 2.0 GPA, interview.

Admissions Contact Ms. Bonnie Flyte, Director of Admissions, Hamilton College, 1924 D Street SW, Cedar Rapids, IA 52404. *Phone:* 563-355-3500. *Toll-free phone:* 800-728-0481. *Fax:* 319-363-3812.

HAMILTON TECHNICAL COLLEGE

Davenport, Iowa

- **Proprietary** 4-year, founded 1969
- **Calendar** continuous
- **Degrees** diplomas, associate, and bachelor's
- **Urban** campus
- **Coed,** 420 undergraduate students
- **Noncompetitive** entrance level

Freshmen *Admission:* 393 admitted.

Faculty *Total:* 18. *Student/faculty ratio:* 20:1.

Majors Drafting; electrical/electronic engineering technology.

Academic Programs *Special study options:* accelerated degree program.

Library Hamilton Technical College Library with 4,500 titles, 30 serial subscriptions.

Computers on Campus 110 computers available on campus for general student use. Internet access, at least one staffed computer lab available.

Student Life *Housing:* college housing not available. *Campus security:* 24-hour emergency response devices.

Costs (2001–02) *Tuition:* $6300 full-time. No tuition increase for student's term of enrollment. *Payment plan:* installment.

Applying *Options:* common application, deferred entrance. *Application fee:* $25. *Required:* high school transcript, interview. *Application deadline:* rolling (freshmen), rolling (transfers).

Admissions Contact Mr. Chad Nelson, Admissions, Hamilton Technical College, 1011 East 53rd Street, Davenport, IA 52807. *Phone:* 563-386-3570. *Fax:* 319-386-6756.

IOWA STATE UNIVERSITY OF SCIENCE AND TECHNOLOGY

Ames, Iowa

- **State-supported** university, founded 1858
- **Calendar** semesters
- **Degrees** bachelor's, master's, doctoral, first professional, and post-master's certificates
- **Suburban** 1788-acre campus
- **Endowment** $368.3 million
- **Coed,** 23,060 undergraduate students, 92% full-time, 44% women, 56% men
- **Moderately difficult** entrance level, 90% of applicants were admitted

Undergraduates 21,232 full-time, 1,828 part-time. Students come from 54 states and territories, 116 other countries, 19% are from out of state, 3% African American, 3% Asian American or Pacific Islander, 2% Hispanic American, 0.3% Native American, 5% international, 7% transferred in, 36% live on campus. *Retention:* 84% of 2001 full-time freshmen returned.

Freshmen *Admission:* 10,658 applied, 9,604 admitted, 4,654 enrolled. *Average high school GPA:* 3.50. *Test scores:* SAT verbal scores over 500: 80%; SAT math scores over 500: 87%; ACT scores over 18: 97%; SAT verbal scores over 600: 46%; SAT math scores over 600: 60%; ACT scores over 24: 57%; SAT verbal scores over 700: 17%; SAT math scores over 700: 23%; ACT scores over 30: 12%.

Faculty *Total:* 1,644, 85% full-time, 87% with terminal degrees. *Student/faculty ratio:* 16:1.

Majors Accounting; advertising; aerospace engineering; agricultural business; agricultural education; agricultural engineering; agricultural mechanization; agricultural sciences; agronomy/crop science; animal sciences; anthropology; architecture; art; atmospheric sciences; biochemistry; biology; biophysics; botany; business administration; business management/administrative services related; business marketing and marketing management; ceramic sciences/engineering; chemical engineering; chemistry; city/community/regional planning; civil engineering; clothing/apparel/textile studies; community services; computer engineering; computer science; consumer services; dairy science; design/visual communications; developmental/child psychology; dietetics; early childhood education; earth sciences; ecology; economics; education; electrical engineering; elementary education; engineering; engineering related; engineering science; English; enterprise management; entomology; environmental science; family/community studies; family/consumer studies; family resource management studies; farm/ranch management; fashion design/illustration; finance; fish/game management; food products retailing; food services technology; forestry; French; genetics; geology; German; graphic design/commercial art/illustration; health education; health/physical education; history; home economics; home economics education; horticulture science; horticulture services; hotel and restaurant management; housing studies; industrial/manufacturing engineering; interdisciplinary studies; interior design; international agriculture; international business; international relations; journalism; landscape architecture; liberal arts and sciences/liberal studies; linguistics; logistics/materials management; management information systems/business data processing; mass communications; mathematical statistics; mathematics; mechanical engineering; medical illustrating; metallurgical engineering; microbiology/bacteriology; music; music teacher education; natural resources management; nutrition science; ornamental horticulture; philosophy; physics; plant protection; political science; pre-dentistry; pre-law; pre-medicine; preveterinary studies; psychology; public administration; religious studies; Russian; secondary education; sociology; Spanish; speech/rhetorical studies; technical/business writing; theater arts/drama; trade/industrial education; transportation technology; visual/performing arts; wildlife biology; women's studies; zoology.

Academic Programs *Special study options:* academic remediation for entering students, accelerated degree program, adult/continuing education programs, advanced placement credit, cooperative education, distance learning, double majors, English as a second language, external degree program, freshman honors college, honors programs, independent study, internships, off-campus study, part-time degree program, services for LD students, student-designed majors, study abroad, summer session for credit. *ROTC:* Army (b), Navy (b), Air Force (b). *Unusual degree programs:* 3-2 engineering with William Penn College.

Library University Library plus 1 other with 2.3 million titles, 21,239 serial subscriptions, 925,593 audiovisual materials, an OPAC, a Web page.

Computers on Campus 2600 computers available on campus for general student use. A campuswide network can be accessed from student residence rooms and from off campus that provide access to e-mail, network services. At least one staffed computer lab available.

Student Life *Housing Options:* coed, men-only, women-only, disabled students. *Activities and Organizations:* drama/theater group, student-run newspaper, radio and television station, choral group, marching band, student government, Student Alumni Association, Residence Hall Associations, national fraternities, national sororities. *Campus security:* 24-hour emergency response devices and patrols, student patrols, late-night transport/escort service, controlled dormitory access, crime prevention programs, threat assessment team, motor vehicle help van. *Student Services:* health clinic, personal/psychological counseling, women's center, legal services.

Athletics Member NCAA. All Division I except football (Division I-A). *Intercollegiate sports:* baseball M(s), basketball M(s)/W(s), cross-country running M(s)/W(s), golf M(s)/W(s), gymnastics W(s), soccer W(s), softball W(s), swimming M(s)/W(s), tennis W(s), track and field M(s)/W(s), volleyball W(s), wrestling M(s). *Intramural sports:* archery M(c)/W(c), badminton M(c)/W(c), basketball M/W, bowling M(c)/W(c), cross-country running M/W, equestrian sports M(c)/W(c), fencing M(c)/W(c), football M/W, golf M/W, ice hockey M(c)/W(c), lacrosse M(c)/W(c), racquetball M(c)/W(c), riflery M(c)/W(c), rugby M(c)/W(c), sailing M(c)/W(c), skiing (cross-country) M(c)/W(c), skiing (downhill) M(c)/W(c), soccer M(c)/W(c), softball M/W, squash M/W, swimming M/W, table tennis M(c)/W(c), tennis M/W, volleyball M(c)/W(c), water polo M(c)/W(c), weight lifting M(c)/W(c), wrestling M/W.

Standardized Tests *Required:* SAT I or ACT (for admission).

Costs (2001–02) *Tuition:* state resident $3116 full-time, $130 per semester hour part-time; nonresident $10,450 full-time, $436 per semester hour part-time. Full-time tuition and fees vary according to class time, degree level, and program. Part-time tuition and fees vary according to class time, course load, degree level, and program. *Required fees:* $326 full-time, $20 per semester hour, $100 per term part-time. *Room and board:* $4666; room only: $2592. Room and board charges vary according to board plan and housing facility. *Payment plans:* installment, deferred payment.

Financial Aid Of all full-time matriculated undergraduates who enrolled in 2001, 12915 applied for aid, 9648 were judged to have need, 4965 had their need fully met. 1282 Federal Work-Study jobs (averaging $1586). 786 State and other part-time jobs (averaging $874). In 2001, 4698 non-need-based awards were made. *Average percent of need met:* 100%. *Average financial aid package:* $6428. *Average need-based loan:* $3915. *Average need-based gift aid:* $2487. *Average non-need based aid:* $2604. *Average indebtedness upon graduation:* $16,979.

Applying *Options:* common application, electronic application, early admission, deferred entrance. *Application fee:* $20. *Required:* high school transcript, rank in upper 50% of high school class. *Application deadline:* 8/21 (freshmen), rolling (transfers). *Notification:* continuous (freshmen).

Admissions Contact Mr. Phil Caffrey, Associate Director for Freshman Admissions, Iowa State University of Science and Technology, 100 Alumni Hall, Ames, IA 50011-2010. *Phone:* 515-294-5836. *Toll-free phone:* 800-262-3810. *Fax:* 515-294-2592. *E-mail:* admissions@iastate.edu.

IOWA WESLEYAN COLLEGE

Mount Pleasant, Iowa

- **Independent United Methodist** 4-year, founded 1842
- **Calendar** 4-1-4
- **Degree** bachelor's
- **Small-town** 60-acre campus
- **Endowment** $8.9 million
- **Coed,** 777 undergraduate students, 62% full-time, 60% women, 40% men
- **Moderately difficult** entrance level, 82% of applicants were admitted

Undergraduates 482 full-time, 295 part-time. Students come from 22 states and territories, 6 other countries, 17% are from out of state, 9% African American, 1% Asian American or Pacific Islander, 4% Hispanic American, 0.1% Native American, 3% international, 57% live on campus. *Retention:* 55% of 2001 full-time freshmen returned.

Freshmen *Admission:* 491 applied, 404 admitted, 131 enrolled. *Average high school GPA:* 2.72. *Test scores:* ACT scores over 18: 57%; ACT scores over 24: 10%; ACT scores over 30: 2%.

Iowa Wesleyan College (continued)

Faculty *Total:* 57, 74% full-time, 42% with terminal degrees. *Student/faculty ratio:* 11:1.

Majors Accounting; adult/continuing education; applied art; art; art education; biological/physical sciences; biology; business administration; chemistry; computer programming; computer science; criminal justice/law enforcement administration; early childhood education; education; elementary education; English; environmental biology; environmental health; exercise sciences; film/video production; fine/studio arts; graphic design/commercial art/illustration; history; information sciences/systems; liberal arts and sciences/liberal studies; mass communications; mathematics; music; music teacher education; natural resources conservation; natural sciences; nursing; physical education; pre-dentistry; pre-law; pre-medicine; pre-veterinary studies; psychology; secondary education; social work; sport/fitness administration.

Academic Programs *Special study options:* academic remediation for entering students, adult/continuing education programs, advanced placement credit, distance learning, double majors, English as a second language, independent study, internships, off-campus study, part-time degree program, services for LD students, student-designed majors, study abroad, summer session for credit. *Unusual degree programs:* 3-2 forestry with Iowa State University of Science and Technology, Duke University.

Library Chadwick Library plus 1 other with 107,227 titles, 431 serial subscriptions, 6,553 audiovisual materials, an OPAC, a Web page.

Computers on Campus 72 computers available on campus for general student use. Internet access, at least one staffed computer lab available.

Student Life *Housing:* on-campus residence required through junior year. *Options:* men-only, women-only. *Activities and Organizations:* student-run newspaper, radio station, choral group, Commuter Club, Student Senate, International Club, Behavioral Science Club, Blue Key, national fraternities, national sororities. *Campus security:* 24-hour patrols, late-night transport/escort service, controlled dormitory access. *Student Services:* health clinic, personal/psychological counseling.

Athletics Member NAIA. *Intercollegiate sports:* baseball M(s), basketball M(s)/W(s), football M(s), soccer M(s)/W(s), softball W(s), track and field M(s)/W(s), volleyball W(s). *Intramural sports:* badminton M/W, basketball M/W, bowling M/W, football M/W, soccer M/W, softball M/W, swimming M/W, table tennis M/W, tennis M/W, track and field M/W, volleyball M/W, water polo M/W, weight lifting M/W.

Standardized Tests *Required:* SAT I or ACT (for admission).

Costs (2002–03) *One-time required fee:* $100. *Comprehensive fee:* $18,740 includes full-time tuition ($14,280) and room and board ($4460). Part-time tuition: $345 per credit hour. Part-time tuition and fees vary according to class time. *Room and board:* College room only: $1860. Room and board charges vary according to board plan and housing facility. *Payment plans:* installment, deferred payment. *Waivers:* employees or children of employees.

Financial Aid Of all full-time matriculated undergraduates who enrolled in 2001, 471 applied for aid, 450 were judged to have need, 172 had their need fully met. 20 State and other part-time jobs (averaging $1000). In 2001, 11 non-need-based awards were made. *Average percent of need met:* 92%. *Average financial aid package:* $14,476. *Average need-based loan:* $4327. *Average need-based gift aid:* $9570. *Average non-need based aid:* $8562. *Average indebtedness upon graduation:* $15,115.

Applying *Options:* common application, electronic application, early admission, deferred entrance. *Required:* high school transcript, minimum 2.0 GPA. *Required for some:* essay or personal statement, letters of recommendation. *Recommended:* interview. *Application deadlines:* 8/15 (freshmen), 8/15 (transfers).

Admissions Contact Mr. David File, Associate Vice President and Dean, Iowa Wesleyan College, 601 North Main Street, Mount Pleasant, IA 52641-1398. *Phone:* 319-385-6230. *Toll-free phone:* 800-582-2383. *Fax:* 319-385-6296. *E-mail:* admitrwl@iwc.edu.

LORAS COLLEGE
Dubuque, Iowa

- **Independent Roman Catholic** comprehensive, founded 1839
- **Calendar** semesters
- **Degrees** associate, bachelor's, and master's
- **Suburban** 60-acre campus
- **Endowment** $28.0 million
- **Coed,** 1,636 undergraduate students, 93% full-time, 51% women, 49% men
- **Moderately difficult** entrance level, 80% of applicants were admitted

Undergraduates 1,527 full-time, 109 part-time. Students come from 27 states and territories, 13 other countries, 42% are from out of state, 1% African American, 0.3% Asian American or Pacific Islander, 2% Hispanic American, 0.2% Native American, 2% international, 6% transferred in, 66% live on campus. *Retention:* 76% of 2001 full-time freshmen returned.

Freshmen *Admission:* 1,286 applied, 1,029 admitted, 359 enrolled. *Average high school GPA:* 3.24. *Test scores:* SAT verbal scores over 500: 62%; SAT math scores over 500: 62%; ACT scores over 18: 92%; SAT verbal scores over 600: 14%; SAT math scores over 600: 10%; ACT scores over 24: 42%; SAT verbal scores over 700: 14%; ACT scores over 30: 3%.

Faculty *Total:* 178, 69% full-time, 53% with terminal degrees. *Student/faculty ratio:* 12:1.

Majors Accounting; art education; athletic training/sports medicine; biochemistry; biological sciences/life sciences related; biology; business; business administration; business marketing and marketing management; chemistry; classics; computer science; creative writing; criminal justice studies; early childhood education; economics; education; education of the emotionally handicapped; education of the mentally handicapped; elementary education; engineering physics; English; exercise sciences; finance; fine/studio arts; French; history; human resources management; international business; international relations; journalism; liberal arts and sciences/liberal studies; management information systems/business data processing; mass communications; mathematics; music; philosophy; physical education; physical sciences; physics; political science; polymer chemistry; pre-theology; psychology; public relations; religious studies; secondary education; social work; sociology; Spanish; sport/fitness administration.

Academic Programs *Special study options:* adult/continuing education programs, advanced placement credit, cooperative education, double majors, English as a second language, honors programs, independent study, internships, off-campus study, part-time degree program, services for LD students, student-designed majors, study abroad, summer session for credit. *Unusual degree programs:* 3-2 engineering with Iowa State University of Science and Technology, University of Illinois, University of Notre Dame, University of Iowa; nursing with University of Iowa.

Library Wahlert Memorial Library plus 1 other with 283,000 titles, 963 serial subscriptions, an OPAC, a Web page.

Computers on Campus 100 computers available on campus for general student use. A campuswide network can be accessed from student residence rooms and from off campus. Internet access, at least one staffed computer lab available.

Student Life *Housing:* on-campus residence required through junior year. *Options:* coed. *Activities and Organizations:* drama/theater group, student-run newspaper, radio and television station, choral group, Student Senate, Campus Ministry, College Activities Board, Residence Hall Councils, national fraternities, national sororities. *Campus security:* 24-hour emergency response devices and patrols, late-night transport/escort service, controlled dormitory access. *Student Services:* health clinic, personal/psychological counseling.

Athletics Member NCAA. All Division III. *Intercollegiate sports:* baseball M, basketball M/W, cross-country running M/W, football M, golf M/W, ice hockey M(c), rugby M(c), skiing (downhill) M(c), soccer M/W, softball W, swimming M/W, tennis M/W, track and field M/W, volleyball M(c)/W, wrestling M. *Intramural sports:* badminton M/W, baseball M, basketball M/W, cross-country running M/W, football M/W, golf M/W, ice hockey M, racquetball M/W, rugby M, skiing (cross-country) M/W, skiing (downhill) M/W, soccer M/W, softball M/W, swimming M/W, table tennis M/W, tennis M/W, track and field M/W, volleyball M/W, water polo M/W, weight lifting M/W, wrestling M.

Standardized Tests *Required:* SAT I or ACT (for admission).

Costs (2001–02) *Comprehensive fee:* $22,994 includes full-time tuition ($15,980), mandatory fees ($1089), and room and board ($5925). Part-time tuition: $350 per credit. *Room and board:* College room only: $2840. Room and board charges vary according to board plan and housing facility. *Payment plan:* installment. *Waivers:* children of alumni, senior citizens, and employees or children of employees.

Financial Aid Of all full-time matriculated undergraduates who enrolled in 2001, 1304 applied for aid, 1167 were judged to have need, 207 had their need fully met. In 2001, 68 non-need-based awards were made. *Average percent of need met:* 63%. *Average financial aid package:* $10,887. *Average need-based loan:* $4413. *Average need-based gift aid:* $4669. *Average non-need based aid:* $4062. *Average indebtedness upon graduation:* $16,693.

Applying *Options:* common application, electronic application, deferred entrance. *Application fee:* $25. *Required:* high school transcript, minimum 2.5 GPA. *Required for some:* interview. *Recommended:* essay or personal statement, 1 letter of recommendation. *Application deadline:* rolling (freshmen), rolling (transfers). *Notification:* continuous (freshmen).

Admissions Contact Mr. Tim Hauber, Director of Admissions, Loras College, 1450 Alta Vista, Dubuque, IA 52004-0178. *Phone:* 563-588-7829. *Toll-free phone:* 800-245-6727. *Fax:* 563-588-7119. *E-mail:* adms@loras.edu.

LUTHER COLLEGE
Decorah, Iowa

- **Independent** 4-year, founded 1861, affiliated with Evangelical Lutheran Church in America
- **Calendar** 4-1-4
- **Degree** bachelor's
- **Small-town** 800-acre campus
- **Endowment** $58.6 million
- **Coed,** 2,575 undergraduate students, 97% full-time, 60% women, 40% men
- **Moderately difficult** entrance level, 83% of applicants were admitted

Undergraduates 2,495 full-time, 80 part-time. Students come from 39 states and territories, 44 other countries, 63% are from out of state, 0.6% African American, 1% Asian American or Pacific Islander, 0.6% Hispanic American, 0.2% Native American, 6% international, 3% transferred in, 82% live on campus. *Retention:* 84% of 2001 full-time freshmen returned.

Freshmen *Admission:* 1,911 applied, 1,595 admitted, 636 enrolled. *Average high school GPA:* 3.60. *Test scores:* SAT verbal scores over 500: 93%; SAT math scores over 500: 90%; ACT scores over 18: 99%; SAT verbal scores over 600: 62%; SAT math scores over 600: 58%; ACT scores over 24: 65%; SAT verbal scores over 700: 15%; SAT math scores over 700: 11%; ACT scores over 30: 16%.

Faculty *Total:* 232, 78% full-time, 66% with terminal degrees. *Student/faculty ratio:* 13:1.

Majors Accounting; African-American studies; African studies; anthropology; art; art education; arts management; biblical languages/literatures; biology; biology education; business; business administration; business computer programming; business marketing and marketing management; chemistry; chemistry education; classics; computer/information sciences; computer management; computer programming; computer science; cytotechnology; dance; drama/dance education; early childhood education; economics; education; elementary education; English; English composition; English education; environmental biology; foreign languages education; French; French language education; German; German language education; Greek (modern); health education; health/physical education; Hebrew; history; history education; interdisciplinary studies; international business; international relations; Latin American studies; Latin (ancient and medieval); management information systems/business data processing; mass communications; mathematical statistics; mathematics; mathematics education; medical technology; middle school education; modern languages; museum studies; music; music business management/merchandising; music conducting; music (general performance); music history; music (piano and organ performance); music teacher education; music theory and composition; music (voice and choral/opera performance); nursing; philosophy; physical education; physics; physics education; physiological psychology/psychobiology; political science; pre-dentistry; pre-law; pre-medicine; pre-theology; pre-veterinary studies; psychology; reading education; religious studies; Scandinavian languages; Scandinavian studies; science education; secondary education; social science education; social work; sociology; Spanish; Spanish language education; special education; sport/fitness administration; stringed instruments; theater arts/drama; theology; wind/percussion instruments.

Academic Programs *Special study options:* academic remediation for entering students, advanced placement credit, double majors, honors programs, independent study, internships, off-campus study, part-time degree program, student-designed majors, study abroad, summer session for credit. *Unusual degree programs:* 3-2 engineering with Washington University in St. Louis; University of Minnesota, Twin Cities Campus; environmental management, resource management with Duke University.

Library Preus Library with 345,743 titles, 1,663 serial subscriptions, 23,983 audiovisual materials, an OPAC, a Web page.

Computers on Campus 526 computers available on campus for general student use. A campuswide network can be accessed from student residence rooms and from off campus. Internet access, online (class) registration, at least one staffed computer lab available.

Student Life *Housing:* on-campus residence required through senior year. *Options:* coed. *Activities and Organizations:* drama/theater group, student-run newspaper, radio station, choral group, National Service Organization, Student Activities Council, intramural clubs and organizations, Campus Ministry, national fraternities. *Campus security:* 24-hour emergency response devices and patrols, late-night transport/escort service, controlled dormitory access. *Student Services:* health clinic, personal/psychological counseling.

Athletics Member NCAA. All Division III. *Intercollegiate sports:* baseball M, basketball M/W, cross-country running M/W, football M, golf M/W, soccer M/W, softball W, swimming M/W, tennis M/W, track and field M/W, volleyball W, wrestling M. *Intramural sports:* archery M/W, badminton M/W, basketball M/W, bowling M/W, football M/W, golf M/W, racquetball M/W, rugby M(c)/W(c), skiing (downhill) M(c)/W(c), soccer M/W, softball M/W, table tennis M/W, tennis M/W, track and field M/W, volleyball M(c)/W, water polo M/W.

Standardized Tests *Required:* SAT I or ACT (for admission).

Costs (2001–02) *Comprehensive fee:* $23,300 includes full-time tuition ($19,325) and room and board ($3975). Full-time tuition and fees vary according to course load. Part-time tuition: $690 per semester hour. Part-time tuition and fees vary according to course load. *Room and board:* College room only: $1935. Room and board charges vary according to housing facility. *Payment plan:* installment. *Waivers:* employees or children of employees.

Financial Aid Of all full-time matriculated undergraduates who enrolled in 2001, 2111 applied for aid, 1565 were judged to have need, 584 had their need fully met. 662 Federal Work-Study jobs (averaging $1310). 1239 State and other part-time jobs (averaging $1235). In 2001, 630 non-need-based awards were made. *Average percent of need met:* 86%. *Average financial aid package:* $15,639. *Average need-based loan:* $4139. *Average need-based gift aid:* $10,502. *Average non-need based aid:* $6656. *Average indebtedness upon graduation:* $16,495.

Applying *Options:* common application, electronic application, early admission, deferred entrance. *Application fee:* $25. *Required:* essay or personal statement, high school transcript, 1 letter of recommendation. *Recommended:* interview. *Notification:* continuous (freshmen).

Admissions Contact Mr. Jon Lund, Vice President for Enrollment and Marketing, Luther College, 700 College Drive, Decorah, IA 52101. *Phone:* 563-387-1287. *Toll-free phone:* 800-458-8437. *Fax:* 563-387-2159. *E-mail:* admissions@luther.edu.

MAHARISHI UNIVERSITY OF MANAGEMENT
Fairfield, Iowa

- **Independent** university, founded 1971
- **Calendar** semesters
- **Degrees** certificates, associate, bachelor's, master's, and doctoral
- **Small-town** 262-acre campus
- **Endowment** $10.2 million
- **Coed,** 210 undergraduate students, 94% full-time, 49% women, 51% men
- **Moderately difficult** entrance level, 62% of applicants were admitted

Undergraduates 197 full-time, 13 part-time. Students come from 27 states and territories, 19 other countries, 40% are from out of state, 4% African American, 3% Asian American or Pacific Islander, 2% Hispanic American, 36% international, 8% transferred in, 87% live on campus. *Retention:* 66% of 2001 full-time freshmen returned.

Freshmen *Admission:* 94 applied, 58 admitted, 58 enrolled. *Average high school GPA:* 3.46. *Test scores:* SAT verbal scores over 500: 81%; SAT math scores over 500: 73%; ACT scores over 18: 95%; SAT verbal scores over 600: 58%; SAT math scores over 600: 46%; ACT scores over 24: 67%; SAT verbal scores over 700: 8%; SAT math scores over 700: 12%; ACT scores over 30: 19%.

Faculty *Total:* 80, 70% full-time, 68% with terminal degrees. *Student/faculty ratio:* 9:1.

Majors Acting/directing; agricultural sciences; agricultural sciences related; art; biochemistry; biology; British literature; business; business administration; ceramic arts; chemistry; computer graphics; computer science; creative writing; design/visual communications; drawing; ecology; education; electrical/electronic engineering technology; electrical engineering; English; environmental biology; environmental science; exercise sciences; film/video production; graphic design/commercial art/illustration; health professions and related sciences; interdisciplinary studies; literature; management science; mathematics; multimedia; painting; pre-law; pre-medicine; psychology; sculpture; theater arts/drama; theater design; visual/performing arts; Web page, digital/multimedia and information resources design.

Academic Programs *Special study options:* academic remediation for entering students, adult/continuing education programs, advanced placement credit, cooperative education, distance learning, double majors, English as a second language, honors programs, independent study, internships, services for LD students, student-designed majors, study abroad.

Library Maharishi University of Management Library plus 1 other with 111,022 titles, 846 serial subscriptions, 13,276 audiovisual materials, an OPAC, a Web page.

Computers on Campus 120 computers available on campus for general student use. A campuswide network can be accessed from student residence rooms and from off campus. Internet access, at least one staffed computer lab available.

Student Life *Housing:* on-campus residence required through senior year. *Options:* men-only, women-only, disabled students. *Activities and Organizations:* drama/theater group, student-run newspaper, radio station, choral group, Permaculture Club, Organization of New Earth, World Congress, Yogic Flying Club. *Campus security:* 24-hour emergency response devices and patrols, late-night

Maharishi University of Management (continued)
transport/escort service, controlled dormitory access. *Student Services:* health clinic, personal/psychological counseling, legal services.

Athletics *Intercollegiate sports:* basketball M, golf M, soccer M(c)/W(c), tennis M(c). *Intramural sports:* badminton M/W, basketball M/W, golf M/W, gymnastics M/W, sailing M/W, skiing (cross-country) M/W, skiing (downhill) M/W, soccer M/W, softball M/W, swimming M/W, table tennis M/W, tennis M/W, volleyball M/W, weight lifting M/W.

Standardized Tests *Required:* SAT I or ACT (for admission).

Costs (2002–03) *Tuition:* $24,030 full-time, $275 per credit part-time. Full-time tuition and fees vary according to program. Part-time tuition and fees vary according to program. *Required fees:* $430 full-time. *Room only:* Room and board charges vary according to housing facility. *Payment plan:* installment. *Waivers:* children of alumni and employees or children of employees.

Financial Aid Of all full-time matriculated undergraduates who enrolled in 2001, 183 applied for aid, 181 were judged to have need, 125 had their need fully met. 88 Federal Work-Study jobs (averaging $1590). 72 State and other part-time jobs (averaging $2718). In 2001, 4 non-need-based awards were made. *Average percent of need met:* 84%. *Average financial aid package:* $20,597. *Average need-based loan:* $6682. *Average need-based gift aid:* $12,427. *Average non-need based aid:* $12,602.

Applying *Options:* common application, electronic application, early admission, deferred entrance. *Application fee:* $25. *Required:* essay or personal statement, high school transcript, minimum 2.5 GPA, 2 letters of recommendation, minimum SAT score of 950 or ACT score of 19. *Recommended:* interview. *Application deadlines:* 8/1 (freshmen), 8/1 (transfers). *Notification:* continuous (freshmen).

Admissions Contact Mr. Brad Mylett, Director of Admissions, Maharishi University of Management, 1000 North 4th Street, Fairfield, IA 52557. *Phone:* 641-472-1110. *Fax:* 641-472-1179. *E-mail:* admissions@mum.edu.

MERCY COLLEGE OF HEALTH SCIENCES
Des Moines, Iowa

- **Independent** 4-year, founded 1995, affiliated with Roman Catholic Church
- **Degrees** certificates, associate, and bachelor's
- **Coed, primarily women,** 442 undergraduate students, 56% full-time, 93% women, 7% men
- 52% of applicants were admitted

Undergraduates 0% are from out of state, 2% African American, 1% Asian American or Pacific Islander, 1% Hispanic American, 0.5% Native American.

Freshmen *Admission:* 536 applied, 280 admitted.

Faculty *Total:* 56, 32% full-time. *Student/faculty ratio:* 11:1.

Majors Diagnostic medical sonography; health services administration; medical radiologic technology; nursing; nursing science; operating room technician.

Student Life *Campus security:* 24-hour emergency response devices, late-night transport/escort service.

Standardized Tests *Required:* ACT (for admission).

Costs (2001–02) *Tuition:* $8900 full-time, $250 per credit part-time. *Required fees:* $25 full-time. *Payment plan:* installment. *Waivers:* employees or children of employees.

Financial Aid Of all full-time matriculated undergraduates who enrolled in 2001, 15 Federal Work-Study jobs (averaging $1666). 94 State and other part-time jobs (averaging $1762).

Applying *Options:* common application. *Application fee:* $10. *Required:* high school transcript, minimum 3.2 GPA. *Required for some:* interview. *Application deadline:* rolling (freshmen). *Notification:* continuous (freshmen).

Admissions Contact Ms. Sandi Nagel, Admissions Representative, Mercy College of Health Sciences, IA. *Phone:* 515-643-6605. *Toll-free phone:* 800-637-2994.

MORNINGSIDE COLLEGE
Sioux City, Iowa

- **Independent United Methodist** comprehensive, founded 1894
- **Calendar** semesters
- **Degrees** bachelor's and master's
- **Suburban** 41-acre campus
- **Endowment** $29.2 million
- **Coed,** 850 undergraduate students, 88% full-time, 63% women, 37% men
- **Moderately difficult** entrance level, 73% of applicants were admitted

The Morningside College experience cultivates a passion for lifelong learning and a dedication to ethical leadership and civic responsibility. Students develop various dimensions of themselves through the liberal arts core curriculum, a complete range of majors, internships, independent study, and career and graduate school advising services. Typical merit scholarship candidates are students who make a difference in a variety of areas, both in and out of the classroom; those who have an alumni connection; or students with a tie to the United Methodist Church. Within 6 months of graduation, more than 95% are employed or admitted to graduate school.

Undergraduates 744 full-time, 106 part-time. Students come from 22 states and territories, 7 other countries, 23% are from out of state, 3% African American, 2% Asian American or Pacific Islander, 3% Hispanic American, 0.5% Native American, 2% international, 7% transferred in, 64% live on campus. *Retention:* 63% of 2001 full-time freshmen returned.

Freshmen *Admission:* 904 applied, 664 admitted, 183 enrolled. *Average high school GPA:* 3.22. *Test scores:* ACT scores over 18: 84%; ACT scores over 24: 31%; ACT scores over 30: 3%.

Faculty *Total:* 114, 57% full-time, 57% with terminal degrees. *Student/faculty ratio:* 10:1.

Majors Accounting; art; art education; biology; biopsychology; business administration; business communications; business education; business marketing and marketing management; chemistry; computer science; counseling psychology; education; elementary education; engineering physics; English; fine/studio arts; graphic design/commercial art/illustration; history; interdisciplinary studies; literature; management information systems/business data processing; mass communications; mathematics; medical technology; music; music teacher education; nursing; philosophy; photography; physics; political science; pre-dentistry; pre-law; pre-medicine; pre-veterinary studies; psychology; religious studies; science education; secondary education; Spanish; special education; theater arts/drama.

Academic Programs *Special study options:* academic remediation for entering students, accelerated degree program, adult/continuing education programs, advanced placement credit, double majors, English as a second language, honors programs, independent study, internships, off-campus study, part-time degree program, services for LD students, student-designed majors, study abroad, summer session for credit. *Unusual degree programs:* 3-2 engineering with Washington University in St. Louis, Iowa State University of Science and Technology, South Dakota State University.

Library Hickman-Johnson-Furrow Library with 114,288 titles, 607 serial subscriptions, 5,332 audiovisual materials, an OPAC, a Web page.

Computers on Campus 800 computers available on campus for general student use. A campuswide network can be accessed from student residence rooms and from off campus. Internet access, at least one staffed computer lab available.

Student Life *Housing:* on-campus residence required through junior year. *Options:* coed. *Activities and Organizations:* drama/theater group, student-run newspaper, radio and television station, choral group, Student Government/Activities Council, Student Ambassadors, fraternities and sororities, Homecoming Committee, New Student Orientation, national fraternities, national sororities. *Campus security:* 24-hour emergency response devices, student patrols, late-night transport/escort service, controlled dormitory access, 18-hour patrols by trained security personnel. *Student Services:* health clinic, personal/psychological counseling, women's center.

Athletics Member NAIA. *Intercollegiate sports:* baseball M(s), basketball M(s)/W(s), cross-country running M(s)/W(s), football M(s), golf M(s)/W(s), soccer M/W(s), softball W(s), track and field M(s)/W(s), volleyball W(s). *Intramural sports:* basketball M/W, bowling M/W, cross-country running M/W, volleyball M/W.

Standardized Tests *Required:* SAT I or ACT (for admission).

Costs (2001–02) *Comprehensive fee:* $19,124 includes full-time tuition ($13,930), mandatory fees ($280), and room and board ($4914). Part-time tuition: $460 per semester hour. Part-time tuition and fees vary according to course load and location. *Room and board:* College room only: $2580. Room and board charges vary according to board plan and housing facility. *Payment plan:* installment. *Waivers:* senior citizens and employees or children of employees.

Financial Aid Of all full-time matriculated undergraduates who enrolled in 2001, 711 applied for aid, 659 were judged to have need, 393 had their need fully met. 270 Federal Work-Study jobs, 123 State and other part-time jobs (averaging $1616). In 2001, 76 non-need-based awards were made. *Average percent of need met:* 88%. *Average financial aid package:* $14,863. *Average need-based loan:* $4082. *Average need-based gift aid:* $5926. *Average non-need based aid:* $6930. *Average indebtedness upon graduation:* $17,140.

Applying *Options:* electronic application, early admission, deferred entrance. *Application fee:* $25. *Required:* high school transcript, minimum SAT score of 840 or ACT score of 20 and rank in top 50% of high school class or have achieved

GPA of 2.5 or better. *Required for some:* 2 letters of recommendation. *Recommended:* interview. *Application deadline:* rolling (freshmen), rolling (transfers). *Notification:* continuous (freshmen).

Admissions Contact Joel Weyand, Director of Admissions, Morningside College, 1501 Morningside Avenue, Sioux City, IA 51106-1751. *Phone:* 712-274-5111. *Toll-free phone:* 800-831-0806 Ext. 5111. *Fax:* 712-274-5101. *E-mail:* mscadm@morningside.edu.

MOUNT MERCY COLLEGE

Cedar Rapids, Iowa

- **Independent Roman Catholic** 4-year, founded 1928
- **Calendar** 4-1-4
- **Degree** bachelor's
- **Suburban** 36-acre campus
- **Endowment** $13.5 million
- **Coed,** 1,387 undergraduate students, 66% full-time, 68% women, 32% men
- **Moderately difficult** entrance level, 86% of applicants were admitted

Undergraduates 919 full-time, 468 part-time. Students come from 15 states and territories, 10 other countries, 9% are from out of state, 1% African American, 1% Asian American or Pacific Islander, 1% Hispanic American, 0.2% Native American, 0.6% international, 17% transferred in, 40% live on campus. *Retention:* 80% of 2001 full-time freshmen returned.

Freshmen *Admission:* 448 applied, 386 admitted, 181 enrolled. *Average high school GPA:* 3.41. *Test scores:* ACT scores over 18: 97%; ACT scores over 24: 48%; ACT scores over 30: 2%.

Faculty *Total:* 121, 55% full-time, 39% with terminal degrees. *Student/faculty ratio:* 14:1.

Majors Accounting; art; art education; biology; business administration; business marketing and marketing management; communications; computer/information sciences; computer science; criminal justice/law enforcement administration; education; elementary education; English; history; international relations; liberal arts and sciences/liberal studies; mathematics; medical technology; middle school education; music; music teacher education; music (voice and choral/opera performance); nursing; political science; pre-dentistry; pre-law; pre-medicine; pre-veterinary studies; psychology; religious studies; science education; secondary education; social work; sociology; speech/rhetorical studies; theater arts/drama; urban studies.

Academic Programs *Special study options:* academic remediation for entering students, accelerated degree program, adult/continuing education programs, advanced placement credit, double majors, freshman honors college, honors programs, independent study, internships, off-campus study, part-time degree program, services for LD students, student-designed majors, summer session for credit.

Library Busse Center with 107,000 titles, 660 serial subscriptions, an OPAC, a Web page.

Computers on Campus 70 computers available on campus for general student use. A campuswide network can be accessed from student residence rooms and from off campus. Internet access, at least one staffed computer lab available.

Student Life *Housing Options:* coed. *Activities and Organizations:* drama/theater group, student-run newspaper, choral group, Student Government Association, Business Club, Nursing Club, Student Teachers club, Biology Club. *Campus security:* 24-hour emergency response devices and patrols, student patrols, late-night transport/escort service, controlled dormitory access. *Student Services:* personal/psychological counseling, legal services.

Athletics Member NAIA. *Intercollegiate sports:* baseball M, basketball M/W, cross-country running M/W, golf M/W, soccer M/W, softball W, track and field M/W, volleyball W. *Intramural sports:* baseball M, basketball M/W, football M/W, racquetball M/W, tennis M/W, volleyball M/W, weight lifting M/W.

Standardized Tests *Required:* SAT I or ACT (for admission).

Costs (2001–02) *Comprehensive fee:* $19,390 includes full-time tuition ($14,560) and room and board ($4830). Full-time tuition and fees vary according to course load. Part-time tuition: $405 per credit hour. Part-time tuition and fees vary according to course load. *Room and board:* College room only: $1960. Room and board charges vary according to board plan. *Payment plan:* installment. *Waivers:* employees or children of employees.

Financial Aid Of all full-time matriculated undergraduates who enrolled in 2001, 860 applied for aid, 784 were judged to have need, 308 had their need fully met. 289 Federal Work-Study jobs (averaging $1361). In 2001, 126 non-need-based awards were made. *Average percent of need met:* 86%. *Average financial aid package:* $13,219. *Average need-based loan:* $4551. *Average need-based gift aid:* $8679. *Average non-need based aid:* $9560. *Average indebtedness upon graduation:* $16,956.

Applying *Options:* electronic application, early admission, deferred entrance. *Application fee:* $20. *Required:* high school transcript, minimum 2.5 GPA, 1 letter of recommendation. *Required for some:* interview. *Recommended:* essay or personal statement, minimum 3.0 GPA. *Application deadlines:* 8/30 (freshmen), 8/30 (transfers). *Notification:* continuous (freshmen).

Admissions Contact Ms. Margaret M. Jackson, Dean of Admission, Mount Mercy College, 1330 Elmhurst Drive, NE, Cedar Rapids, IA 52402. *Phone:* 319-368-6460. *Toll-free phone:* 800-248-4504. *Fax:* 319-363-5270. *E-mail:* admission@mmc.mtmercy.edu.

MOUNT ST. CLARE COLLEGE

Clinton, Iowa

- **Independent Roman Catholic** 4-year, founded 1918
- **Calendar** semesters
- **Degrees** associate and bachelor's (offers some graduate classes)
- **Small-town** 24-acre campus with easy access to Chicago
- **Endowment** $1.1 million
- **Coed,** 479 undergraduate students, 84% full-time, 56% women, 44% men
- **Minimally difficult** entrance level, 75% of applicants were admitted

Mount St. Clare College holds an annual academic scholarship competition in February. At stake are renewable scholarships that range from $1500 to full tuition in 22 academic areas: accounting, athletic administration, biology, business administration, information systems, criminal justice, cytotechnology, education (elementary and secondary), environmental studies, health-care management, literature, marketing communications, mathematics, music, pre-medical studies, pre-physical therapy, prelaw, psychology, religious studies, social science, and visual arts.

Undergraduates 401 full-time, 78 part-time. Students come from 12 states and territories, 10 other countries, 41% are from out of state, 7% African American, 0.8% Asian American or Pacific Islander, 2% Hispanic American, 3% international, 16% transferred in, 36% live on campus. *Retention:* 63% of 2001 full-time freshmen returned.

Freshmen *Admission:* 357 applied, 268 admitted, 92 enrolled. *Average high school GPA:* 2.96. *Test scores:* SAT verbal scores over 500: 17%; SAT math scores over 500: 17%; ACT scores over 18: 74%; ACT scores over 24: 23%; ACT scores over 30: 1%.

Faculty *Total:* 53, 43% full-time, 32% with terminal degrees. *Student/faculty ratio:* 14:1.

Majors Accounting; athletic training/sports medicine; biology; business administration; business education; communications related; computer/information sciences; criminal justice studies; cytotechnology; early childhood education; education; elementary education; English; general studies; health services administration; history related; humanities; human services; journalism; liberal arts and sciences/liberal studies; middle school education; multi/interdisciplinary studies related; music; music teacher education; pre-law; pre-medicine; psychology; religious studies; science education; secondary education; social sciences; visual/performing arts.

Academic Programs *Special study options:* academic remediation for entering students, adult/continuing education programs, advanced placement credit, double majors, English as a second language, external degree program, freshman honors college, honors programs, independent study, internships, part-time degree program, student-designed majors, study abroad, summer session for credit.

Library Mount St. Clare Library with 76,639 titles, 1,151 serial subscriptions, 1,640 audiovisual materials, an OPAC, a Web page.

Computers on Campus 46 computers available on campus for general student use. Internet access, at least one staffed computer lab available.

Student Life *Housing:* on-campus residence required through junior year. *Options:* coed, women-only. *Activities and Organizations:* drama/theater group, student-run newspaper, choral group, Student Senate, Student Ambassadors, Hall Council, Black Student Union, Student Iowa State Education Association. *Campus security:* 24-hour emergency response devices and patrols, student patrols, late-night transport/escort service, controlled dormitory access, self-defense education, lighted pathways. *Student Services:* health clinic, personal/psychological counseling.

Athletics Member NAIA. *Intercollegiate sports:* baseball M(s), basketball M(s)/W(s), cross-country running M(s)/W(s), golf M(s), soccer M(s)/W(s), softball W(s), tennis M(s)/W(s), track and field M(s)/W(s), volleyball W(s), wrestling M(s). *Intramural sports:* football M/W, golf M, skiing (downhill) M/W, tennis M/W, track and field M/W, volleyball M/W.

Standardized Tests *Required:* SAT I or ACT (for admission).

Costs (2001–02) *One-time required fee:* $20. *Comprehensive fee:* $19,300 includes full-time tuition ($14,050), mandatory fees ($250), and room and board

Mount St. Clare College (continued)
($5000). Part-time tuition: $405 per credit hour. Part-time tuition and fees vary according to course load. No tuition increase for student's term of enrollment. *Required fees:* $8 per credit hour. *Room and board:* College room only: $2500. Room and board charges vary according to board plan and housing facility. *Payment plan:* installment. *Waivers:* children of alumni, senior citizens, and employees or children of employees.

Financial Aid Of all full-time matriculated undergraduates who enrolled in 2001, 355 applied for aid, 306 were judged to have need, 136 had their need fully met. 72 Federal Work-Study jobs (averaging $1165). 36 State and other part-time jobs (averaging $1350). In 2001, 64 non-need-based awards were made. *Average percent of need met:* 88%. *Average financial aid package:* $11,063. *Average need-based loan:* $3562. *Average need-based gift aid:* $8355. *Average indebtedness upon graduation:* $15,223. *Financial aid deadline:* 8/1.

Applying *Options:* common application, electronic application, early admission. *Application fee:* $20. *Required:* high school transcript. *Required for some:* letters of recommendation, interview. *Recommended:* minimum 2.0 GPA. *Application deadline:* 8/15 (freshmen), rolling (transfers). *Notification:* continuous (freshmen).

Admissions Contact Ms. Waunita M. Sullivan, Director of Enrollment, Mount St. Clare College, 400 North Bluff Boulevard, PO Box 2967, Clinton, IA 52733-2967. *Phone:* 563-242-4023 Ext. 3401. *Toll-free phone:* 800-242-4153 Ext. 3400. *Fax:* 563-243-6102. *E-mail:* admissns@clare.edu.

NORTHWESTERN COLLEGE
Orange City, Iowa

- **Independent** 4-year, founded 1882, affiliated with Reformed Church in America
- **Calendar** semesters
- **Degrees** associate and bachelor's
- **Rural** 45-acre campus
- **Endowment** $33.4 million
- **Coed,** 1,294 undergraduate students, 96% full-time, 62% women, 38% men
- **Moderately difficult** entrance level, 86% of applicants were admitted

Northwestern College combines academic rigor with a Christian perspective and opportunities for service and extracurricular preparation. Named the best value among Midwestern colleges by *U.S. News and World Report* and a "most wired" college by *Yahoo Internet Life*, Northwestern has set enrollment records for three consecutive years.

Undergraduates 1,243 full-time, 51 part-time. Students come from 27 states and territories, 14 other countries, 41% are from out of state, 0.4% African American, 0.6% Asian American or Pacific Islander, 0.7% Hispanic American, 0.2% Native American, 2% international, 5% transferred in, 89% live on campus. *Retention:* 76% of 2001 full-time freshmen returned.

Freshmen *Admission:* 1,105 applied, 948 admitted, 374 enrolled. *Average high school GPA:* 3.52. *Test scores:* SAT verbal scores over 500: 62%; ACT scores over 18: 97%; SAT verbal scores over 600: 12%; ACT scores over 24: 57%; SAT verbal scores over 700: 6%; ACT scores over 30: 11%.

Faculty *Total:* 115, 63% full-time, 54% with terminal degrees. *Student/faculty ratio:* 15:1.

Majors Accounting; agribusiness; art; art education; biology; business administration; business education; chemistry; computer science; economics; education; education (K-12); elementary education; English; environmental science; exercise sciences; history; humanities; mass communications; mathematics; medical technology; music; music teacher education; philosophy; physical education; political science; psychology; religious education; religious studies; secondary education; secretarial science; social work; sociology; Spanish; speech/rhetorical studies; speech/theater education; theater arts/drama; theology.

Academic Programs *Special study options:* academic remediation for entering students, accelerated degree program, advanced placement credit, cooperative education, double majors, English as a second language, freshman honors college, honors programs, independent study, internships, off-campus study, part-time degree program, student-designed majors, study abroad, summer session for credit. *Unusual degree programs:* 3-2 engineering with Washington University in St. Louis; nursing with Trinity Christian College, Briar Cliff College.

Library Ramaker Library plus 1 other with 108,527 titles, 563 serial subscriptions, 5,385 audiovisual materials, an OPAC.

Computers on Campus 250 computers available on campus for general student use. A campuswide network can be accessed from student residence rooms and from off campus. Internet access, at least one staffed computer lab available.

Student Life *Housing:* on-campus residence required through senior year. *Options:* men-only, women-only, disabled students. *Activities and Organizations:* drama/theater group, student-run newspaper, radio station, choral group, Phi Beta Lambda, Student Ministries Board, Student Iowa State Education Association, Fellowship of Christian Athletes, International Club. *Campus security:* 24-hour emergency response devices, controlled dormitory access. *Student Services:* health clinic, personal/psychological counseling.

Athletics Member NAIA. *Intercollegiate sports:* baseball M(s), basketball M(s)/W(s), cross-country running M(s)/W(s), football M(s), golf M(s)/W(s), soccer M(s)/W(s), softball W(s), tennis M(s)/W(s), track and field M(s)/W(s), volleyball W(s), wrestling M(s). *Intramural sports:* badminton M/W, basketball M/W, bowling M/W, cross-country running M/W, football M/W, golf M/W, racquetball M/W, softball M, table tennis M/W, tennis M/W, volleyball M/W.

Standardized Tests *Required:* SAT I or ACT (for admission).

Costs (2001–02) *Comprehensive fee:* $17,630 includes full-time tuition ($13,750) and room and board ($3880). Part-time tuition: $285 per credit hour. Part-time tuition and fees vary according to course load. *Room and board:* College room only: $1600. *Payment plan:* installment. *Waivers:* employees or children of employees.

Financial Aid Of all full-time matriculated undergraduates who enrolled in 2001, 1208 applied for aid, 1109 were judged to have need, 170 had their need fully met. 377 Federal Work-Study jobs, 286 State and other part-time jobs (averaging $900). In 2001, 45 non-need-based awards were made. *Average percent of need met:* 75%. *Average financial aid package:* $11,012. *Average need-based loan:* $4810. *Average need-based gift aid:* $4445. *Average non-need based aid:* $2049. *Average indebtedness upon graduation:* $13,805.

Applying *Options:* common application, electronic application, deferred entrance. *Application fee:* $25. *Required:* essay or personal statement, high school transcript, minimum 2.0 GPA, 1 letter of recommendation. *Recommended:* minimum 2.5 GPA, interview. *Application deadline:* rolling (freshmen), rolling (transfers). *Notification:* continuous until 8/30 (freshmen).

Admissions Contact Mr. Ronald K. DeJong, Director of Admissions, Northwestern College, 101 College Lane, Orange City, IA 51041-1996. *Phone:* 712-737-7130. *Toll-free phone:* 800-747-4757. *Fax:* 712-707-7164. *E-mail:* markb@nwciowa.edu.

PALMER COLLEGE OF CHIROPRACTIC
Davenport, Iowa

- **Independent** comprehensive, founded 1897, part of Palmer Chiropractic University System
- **Calendar** trimesters
- **Degrees** certificates, associate, incidental bachelor's, master's, and first professional
- **Urban** 3-acre campus
- **Endowment** $8.9 million
- **Coed,** 47 undergraduate students, 87% full-time, 91% women, 9% men
- **Moderately difficult** entrance level, 85% of applicants were admitted

Undergraduates *Retention:* 94% of 2001 full-time freshmen returned.

Freshmen *Admission:* 13 applied, 11 admitted. *Average high school GPA:* 2.8.

Faculty *Total:* 97, 100% full-time. *Student/faculty ratio:* 17:1.

Majors Biological/physical sciences; medical assistant.

Academic Programs *Special study options:* academic remediation for entering students, internships, services for LD students, summer session for credit.

Library D. D. Palmer Health Sciences Library with 51,445 titles, 894 serial subscriptions, 4,077 audiovisual materials, an OPAC.

Computers on Campus 75 computers available on campus for general student use. A campuswide network can be accessed from off campus. Internet access, at least one staffed computer lab available.

Student Life *Housing:* college housing not available. *Activities and Organizations:* student-run newspaper, Gonstead Club, intramural sports, Campus Guides, Student International Chiropractic Association, Palmer Student Alumni Foundation. *Campus security:* 24-hour emergency response devices and patrols, late-night transport/escort service. *Student Services:* health clinic, personal/psychological counseling.

Athletics *Intramural sports:* baseball M(c), basketball M(c)/W(c), golf M/W, ice hockey M(c), rugby M, skiing (downhill) M/W, soccer M, softball M/W, table tennis M/W, tennis M/W, volleyball M/W.

Costs (2001–02) *One-time required fee:* $150. *Tuition:* $17,490 full-time, $225 per credit hour part-time. Full-time tuition and fees vary according to degree level. Part-time tuition and fees vary according to degree level. *Required fees:* $60 full-time, $20 per term part-time. *Payment plan:* deferred payment. *Waivers:* employees or children of employees.

Applying *Options:* common application, electronic application, deferred entrance. *Application fee:* $50. *Required:* high school transcript, minimum 2.0 GPA, minimum 2.0 in math, sciences, and English courses. *Required for some:* essay or personal statement, interview. *Application deadline:* rolling (freshmen). *Notification:* continuous (freshmen).

Admissions Contact Dr. David Anderson, Director of Admissions, Palmer College of Chiropractic, 1000 Brady Street, Davenport, IA 52803-5287. *Phone:* 563-884-5656. *Toll-free phone:* 800-722-3648. *Fax:* 563-884-5414. *E-mail:* pcadmit@palmer.edu.

ST. AMBROSE UNIVERSITY

Davenport, Iowa

- **Independent Roman Catholic** comprehensive, founded 1882
- **Calendar** 4-1-4
- **Degrees** certificates, bachelor's, master's, doctoral, post-master's, and postbachelor's certificates
- **Urban** 11-acre campus
- **Endowment** $23.1 million
- **Coed,** 2,271 undergraduate students, 77% full-time, 59% women, 41% men
- **Moderately difficult** entrance level, 87% of applicants were admitted

Undergraduates 1,755 full-time, 516 part-time. Students come from 22 states and territories, 13 other countries, 48% are from out of state, 3% African American, 1% Asian American or Pacific Islander, 4% Hispanic American, 0.4% Native American, 0.8% international, 13% transferred in, 45% live on campus. *Retention:* 80% of 2001 full-time freshmen returned.

Freshmen *Admission:* 1,112 applied, 971 admitted, 414 enrolled. *Average high school GPA:* 3.11. *Test scores:* ACT scores over 18: 87%; ACT scores over 24: 26%; ACT scores over 30: 2%.

Faculty *Total:* 289, 54% full-time, 39% with terminal degrees. *Student/faculty ratio:* 16:1.

Majors Accounting; adapted physical education; advertising; art; art education; athletic training/sports medicine; biology; biology education; business; business administration; business education; business marketing and marketing management; chemistry; chemistry education; computer science; computer systems analysis; criminal justice studies; design/visual communications; early childhood education; economics; education; education (K-12); elementary education; engineering physics; English; English education; finance; fine/studio arts; French; French language education; German; German language education; health education; history; history education; industrial/manufacturing engineering; information sciences/systems; international business; journalism; mass communications; mathematics; mathematics education; music; music teacher education; nursing; organizational behavior; philosophy; physical education; physics; physics education; political science; psychology; public administration; public relations; radio/television broadcasting; science education; secondary education; social science education; sociology; Spanish; Spanish language education; speech/theater education; sport/fitness administration; theater arts/drama; theology.

Academic Programs *Special study options:* academic remediation for entering students, accelerated degree program, adult/continuing education programs, advanced placement credit, cooperative education, distance learning, double majors, independent study, internships, off-campus study, part-time degree program, services for LD students, student-designed majors, study abroad, summer session for credit. *Unusual degree programs:* 3-2 physical therapy, occupational therapy, special education.

Library O'Keefe Library plus 1 other with 198,391 titles, 3,261 serial subscriptions, 1,953 audiovisual materials, an OPAC, a Web page.

Computers on Campus 190 computers available on campus for general student use. A campuswide network can be accessed from student residence rooms and from off campus that provide access to on-line course syllabi, class listings. Internet access, online (class) registration, at least one staffed computer lab available.

Student Life *Housing:* on-campus residence required through sophomore year. *Options:* coed, men-only, women-only, disabled students. *Activities and Organizations:* drama/theater group, student-run newspaper, radio and television station, choral group, Student Government Association, Student Alumni Association, Social Action Group, College Activities Board, Ambrosian's for Peace and Justice. *Campus security:* 24-hour emergency response devices and patrols, late-night transport/escort service, controlled dormitory access, police officer on campus 10 p.m. to 6 a.m. *Student Services:* health clinic, personal/psychological counseling, women's center.

Athletics Member NAIA. *Intercollegiate sports:* baseball M(s), basketball M(s)/W(s), cross-country running M(s)/W(s), football M(s), golf M(s)/W(s), soccer M(s)/W(s), softball W(s), tennis M(s)/W(s), track and field M(s)/W(s), volleyball M(s)/W(s). *Intramural sports:* basketball M/W, football M/W, skiing (downhill) M/W, softball M/W, volleyball M/W.

Standardized Tests *Required:* SAT I or ACT (for admission).

Costs (2002–03) *One-time required fee:* $100. *Comprehensive fee:* $21,310 includes full-time tuition ($15,750) and room and board ($5560). Full-time tuition and fees vary according to course load and location. Part-time tuition: $490 per credit. Part-time tuition and fees vary according to course load and location. *Room and board:* College room only: $2580. Room and board charges vary according to board plan and housing facility. *Payment plan:* installment. *Waivers:* minority students, children of alumni, senior citizens, and employees or children of employees.

Financial Aid Of all full-time matriculated undergraduates who enrolled in 2001, 1557 applied for aid, 1329 were judged to have need, 327 had their need fully met. In 2001, 205 non-need-based awards were made. *Average financial aid package:* $12,184. *Average need-based loan:* $3999. *Average need-based gift aid:* $4848. *Average non-need based aid:* $4819. *Average indebtedness upon graduation:* $19,625.

Applying *Options:* common application, electronic application, deferred entrance. *Application fee:* $25. *Required:* high school transcript, minimum 2.5 GPA, minimum ACT score of 20 or rank in top 50% of high school class. *Required for some:* letters of recommendation, interview. *Recommended:* interview. *Application deadline:* rolling (freshmen), rolling (transfers).

Admissions Contact Ms. Meg Flaherty, Director of Admissions, St. Ambrose University, 518 West Locust, Davenport, IA 52803-2898. *Phone:* 563-333-6300 Ext. 6311. *Toll-free phone:* 800-383-2627. *Fax:* 563-333-6297. *E-mail:* mflahery@sau.edu.

SIMPSON COLLEGE

Indianola, Iowa

- **Independent United Methodist** 4-year, founded 1860
- **Calendar** 4-4-1
- **Degree** bachelor's
- **Small-town** 68-acre campus
- **Endowment** $66.3 million
- **Coed,** 1,816 undergraduate students, 72% full-time, 58% women, 42% men
- **Moderately difficult** entrance level, 86% of applicants were admitted

Simpson is more than a beautiful campus. The College has an outstanding faculty and renowned curricula, including more than 40 majors, minors, and preprofessional programs. A 4-4-1 calendar provides students with many learning opportunities, including internships, career observations, and study programs both abroad and in the United States. Located just 12 miles from Des Moines, Iowa's capital and largest metropolitan area, Simpson's ideal location allows students the opportunity to enjoy both city sophistication and small-town charm.

Undergraduates 1,307 full-time, 509 part-time. Students come from 27 states and territories, 11 other countries, 12% are from out of state, 0.8% African American, 0.7% Asian American or Pacific Islander, 0.9% Hispanic American, 0.6% Native American, 1% international, 4% transferred in, 83% live on campus. *Retention:* 82% of 2001 full-time freshmen returned.

Freshmen *Admission:* 1,185 applied, 1,024 admitted, 299 enrolled. *Test scores:* ACT scores over 18: 99%; ACT scores over 24: 51%; ACT scores over 30: 6%.

Faculty *Total:* 140, 60% full-time, 54% with terminal degrees. *Student/faculty ratio:* 14:1.

Majors Accounting; advertising; art; art education; athletic training/sports medicine; biochemistry; biological/physical sciences; biology; business administration; business communications; chemistry; computer management; computer science; criminal justice/law enforcement administration; early childhood education; economics; education; elementary education; English; environmental biology; French; German; graphic design/commercial art/illustration; history; information sciences/systems; international business; international relations; mass communications; mathematics; medical technology; music; music (general performance); music teacher education; philosophy; physical education; physical therapy; political science; pre-dentistry; pre-law; pre-medicine; pre-veterinary studies; psychology; religious studies; secondary education; social sciences; sociology; Spanish; speech/rhetorical studies; sport/fitness administration; theater arts/drama.

Academic Programs *Special study options:* academic remediation for entering students, accelerated degree program, adult/continuing education programs, advanced placement credit, cooperative education, double majors, freshman honors college, honors programs, independent study, internships, off-campus study, part-time degree program, services for LD students, student-designed majors, study abroad, summer session for credit. *Unusual degree programs:* 3-2 engineering with Washington University in St. Louis.

Library Dunn Library plus 1 other with 174,739 titles, 722 serial subscriptions, 4,377 audiovisual materials, an OPAC, a Web page.

Simpson College (continued)

Computers on Campus 265 computers available on campus for general student use. A campuswide network can be accessed from student residence rooms and from off campus. Internet access, at least one staffed computer lab available.

Student Life *Housing:* on-campus residence required through junior year. *Options:* coed, men-only, women-only. *Activities and Organizations:* drama/theater group, student-run newspaper, radio station, choral group, Intramurals, Religious Life Council, Campus Activities Board, Student Government, national fraternities, national sororities. *Campus security:* 24-hour emergency response devices and patrols, student patrols, late-night transport/escort service, controlled dormitory access. *Student Services:* health clinic, personal/psychological counseling.

Athletics Member NCAA. All Division III. *Intercollegiate sports:* baseball M, basketball M/W, cross-country running M/W, football M, golf M/W, rugby M(c)/W(c), soccer M/W, softball W, swimming M(c)/W, tennis M/W, track and field M/W, volleyball W, wrestling M. *Intramural sports:* badminton M/W, basketball M/W, bowling M/W, football M/W, racquetball M/W, soccer M/W, softball M/W, swimming M/W, volleyball M/W, water polo M/W.

Standardized Tests *Required:* SAT I or ACT (for admission).

Costs (2001–02) *Comprehensive fee:* $21,200 includes full-time tuition ($15,766), mandatory fees ($142), and room and board ($5292). Part-time tuition: $205 per credit. Part-time tuition and fees vary according to class time and course load. *Room and board:* College room only: $2515. Room and board charges vary according to board plan and housing facility. *Payment plan:* installment. *Waivers:* employees or children of employees.

Financial Aid Of all full-time matriculated undergraduates who enrolled in 2001, 1289 applied for aid, 1112 were judged to have need, 298 had their need fully met. 348 Federal Work-Study jobs (averaging $732). 390 State and other part-time jobs (averaging $994). In 2001, 124 non-need-based awards were made. *Average percent of need met:* 88%. *Average financial aid package:* $16,147. *Average need-based loan:* $3535. *Average need-based gift aid:* $10,800. *Average non-need based aid:* $7184. *Average indebtedness upon graduation:* $19,053.

Applying *Options:* electronic application, early admission, deferred entrance. *Required:* high school transcript, 1 letter of recommendation. *Recommended:* interview, rank in upper 50% of high school class. *Application deadlines:* 8/15 (freshmen), 8/15 (transfers). *Notification:* continuous (freshmen).

Admissions Contact Ms. Deborah Tierney, Vice President for Enrollment, Simpson College, 701 North C Street, Indianola, IA 50125-1297. *Phone:* 515-961-1624. *Toll-free phone:* 800-362-2454. *Fax:* 515-961-1870. *E-mail:* admiss@simpson.edu.

UNIVERSITY OF DUBUQUE

Dubuque, Iowa

- **Independent Presbyterian** comprehensive, founded 1852
- **Calendar** semesters
- **Degrees** certificates, associate, bachelor's, master's, and first professional
- **Suburban** 56-acre campus
- **Endowment** $20.0 million
- **Coed,** 756 undergraduate students, 92% full-time, 37% women, 63% men
- **Moderately difficult** entrance level, 82% of applicants were admitted

Undergraduates 695 full-time, 61 part-time. Students come from 24 states and territories, 8 other countries, 39% are from out of state, 11% African American, 1% Asian American or Pacific Islander, 3% Hispanic American, 1% Native American, 0.9% international, 12% transferred in, 45% live on campus. *Retention:* 75% of 2001 full-time freshmen returned.

Freshmen *Admission:* 551 applied, 451 admitted, 256 enrolled. *Average high school GPA:* 3.00. *Test scores:* SAT verbal scores over 500: 43%; SAT math scores over 500: 60%; ACT scores over 18: 77%; SAT verbal scores over 600: 12%; SAT math scores over 600: 9%; ACT scores over 24: 20%; SAT verbal scores over 700: 3%; ACT scores over 30: 1%.

Faculty *Total:* 86, 40% full-time, 53% with terminal degrees. *Student/faculty ratio:* 14:1.

Majors Accounting; aircraft pilot (professional); aviation management; biological/physical sciences; biology; business administration; computer graphics; computer science; criminal justice/law enforcement administration; elementary education; English; environmental biology; environmental science; mass communications; philosophy; professional studies; psychology; religious studies; sociology; speech/rhetorical studies; theology.

Academic Programs *Special study options:* academic remediation for entering students, accelerated degree program, adult/continuing education programs, advanced placement credit, distance learning, double majors, English as a second language, independent study, internships, off-campus study, part-time degree program, services for LD students, student-designed majors, study abroad, summer session for credit. *Unusual degree programs:* communications.

Library Charles C. Myer's Library with 139,513 titles, 700 serial subscriptions, 525 audiovisual materials, an OPAC, a Web page.

Computers on Campus 100 computers available on campus for general student use. A campuswide network can be accessed from off campus that provide access to intranet. Internet access, at least one staffed computer lab available.

Student Life *Housing:* on-campus residence required through junior year. *Options:* men-only, women-only. *Activities and Organizations:* drama/theater group, student-run newspaper, choral group, Alpha Phi Omega, Students in Free Enterprise, Student Activities Board, Student Government Association, Web of Life (environmental science). *Campus security:* 24-hour patrols, late-night transport/escort service, controlled dormitory access. *Student Services:* health clinic, personal/psychological counseling.

Athletics Member NCAA. All Division III. *Intercollegiate sports:* baseball M, basketball M/W, cross-country running M/W, football M, golf M/W, soccer M/W, softball W, tennis M/W, track and field M/W, volleyball W, wrestling M. *Intramural sports:* archery M/W, badminton M/W, baseball M, basketball M/W, football M, golf M/W, racquetball M/W, soccer M/W, softball M/W, table tennis M/W, tennis M/W, track and field M/W, volleyball M/W, wrestling M.

Standardized Tests *Required:* SAT I or ACT (for admission).

Costs (2001–02) *Comprehensive fee:* $19,930 includes full-time tuition ($14,770), mandatory fees ($140), and room and board ($5020). Full-time tuition and fees vary according to program. Part-time tuition: $310 per credit. *Room and board:* College room only: $2420. Room and board charges vary according to board plan and housing facility. *Payment plans:* installment, deferred payment. *Waivers:* children of alumni and employees or children of employees.

Financial Aid Of all full-time matriculated undergraduates who enrolled in 2001, 556 applied for aid, 529 were judged to have need, 193 had their need fully met. 172 Federal Work-Study jobs (averaging $720). In 2001, 33 non-need-based awards were made. *Average percent of need met:* 82%. *Average financial aid package:* $13,294. *Average need-based loan:* $6015. *Average need-based gift aid:* $7819. *Average non-need based aid:* $4500. *Average indebtedness upon graduation:* $17,622.

Applying *Options:* electronic application. *Application fee:* $25. *Required:* essay or personal statement, high school transcript, minimum 2.0 GPA, 2 letters of recommendation. *Recommended:* interview. *Application deadline:* rolling (freshmen), rolling (transfers). *Notification:* continuous (freshmen).

Admissions Contact Mr. Jesse James, Director of Admissions and Records, University of Dubuque, 2000 University Avenue, Dubuque, IA 52001-5099. *Phone:* 319-589-3214. *Toll-free phone:* 800-722-5583. *Fax:* 319-589-3690. *E-mail:* admssns@dbq.edu.

THE UNIVERSITY OF IOWA

Iowa City, Iowa

- **State-supported** university, founded 1847
- **Calendar** semesters
- **Degrees** bachelor's, master's, doctoral, and first professional
- **Small-town** 1900-acre campus
- **Endowment** $697.7 million
- **Coed,** 19,603 undergraduate students, 88% full-time, 55% women, 45% men
- **Moderately difficult** entrance level, 85% of applicants were admitted

Undergraduates Students come from 52 states and territories, 70 other countries, 31% are from out of state, 2% African American, 3% Asian American or Pacific Islander, 2% Hispanic American, 0.4% Native American, 2% international, 29% live on campus. *Retention:* 82% of 2001 full-time freshmen returned.

Freshmen *Admission:* 11,836 applied, 10,089 admitted. *Average high school GPA:* 3.49. *Test scores:* SAT verbal scores over 500: 87%; SAT math scores over 500: 87%; ACT scores over 18: 98%; SAT verbal scores over 600: 49%; SAT math scores over 600: 54%; ACT scores over 24: 58%; SAT verbal scores over 700: 13%; SAT math scores over 700: 15%; ACT scores over 30: 10%.

Faculty *Total:* 1,707, 95% full-time. *Student/faculty ratio:* 14:1.

Majors Accounting; actuarial science; African-American studies; African studies; Air Force R.O.T.C./air science; American history; American studies; anthropology; Army R.O.T.C./military science; art; art education; art history; arts management; Asian studies; astronomy; athletic training/sports medicine; biochemistry; bioengineering; biology; broadcast journalism; business administration; business economics; business marketing and marketing management; ceramic arts; chemical engineering; chemistry; chemistry education; Chinese; civil engineering; classics; comparative literature; computer engineering; computer science; creative writing; dance; drama/dance education; drawing; earth sciences; Eastern European area studies; economics; education; electrical engineering;

elementary education; engineering; engineering/industrial management; English; entrepreneurship; environmental engineering; environmental science; exercise sciences; film studies; film/video production; finance; fine/studio arts; French; French language education; geography; geology; German; German language education; Greek (modern); health education; history; history education; human resources management; industrial/manufacturing engineering; information sciences/systems; interdisciplinary studies; international business; international relations; Italian; Japanese; jazz; journalism; labor/personnel relations; Latin American studies; Latin (ancient and medieval); linguistics; literature; management information systems/business data processing; management science; mass communications; materials engineering; mathematical statistics; mathematics; mathematics education; mechanical engineering; medical technology; medieval/renaissance studies; metal/jewelry arts; microbiology/bacteriology; museum studies; music; music history; music (piano and organ performance); music teacher education; music therapy; music (voice and choral/opera performance); Native American studies; nuclear medical technology; nursing; painting; pharmacy; philosophy; photography; physics; political science; Portuguese; pre-dentistry; pre-law; pre-medicine; pre-pharmacy studies; pre-veterinary studies; printmaking; psychology; public relations; radio/television broadcasting; recreational therapy; recreation/leisure studies; religious studies; Russian; science education; sculpture; secondary education; social sciences; social studies education; social work; sociology; Spanish; Spanish language education; speech education; speech-language pathology/audiology; speech/rhetorical studies; speech therapy; sport/fitness administration; stringed instruments; theater arts/drama; wind/percussion instruments; women's studies.

Academic Programs *Special study options:* academic remediation for entering students, accelerated degree program, adult/continuing education programs, advanced placement credit, cooperative education, distance learning, double majors, English as a second language, external degree program, honors programs, independent study, internships, off-campus study, part-time degree program, services for LD students, student-designed majors, study abroad, summer session for credit. *ROTC:* Army (b), Air Force (b). *Unusual degree programs:* 3-2 hospital and health administration.

Library Main Library plus 12 others with 4.0 million titles, 44,644 serial subscriptions, 267,192 audiovisual materials, an OPAC, a Web page.

Computers on Campus 1200 computers available on campus for general student use. A campuswide network can be accessed from student residence rooms and from off campus that provide access to online degree process, grades, financial aid summary. Internet access, online (class) registration, at least one staffed computer lab available.

Student Life *Housing Options:* coed. *Activities and Organizations:* drama/theater group, student-run newspaper, radio station, choral group, marching band, Association of Students of Engineering, Association of Residence Halls, Newman Center, Friendship Association of Chinese Scholars, May Co., national fraternities, national sororities. *Campus security:* 24-hour emergency response devices and patrols, late-night transport/escort service, controlled dormitory access. *Student Services:* health clinic, personal/psychological counseling, women's center, legal services.

Athletics Member NCAA. All Division I except football (Division I-A). *Intercollegiate sports:* badminton M(c)/W(c), baseball M(s), basketball M(s)/W(s), bowling M(c)/W(c), crew M(c)/W(s), cross-country running M(s)/W(s), field hockey W(s), golf M(s)/W(s), gymnastics M(s)/W(s), ice hockey M(c)/W(c), lacrosse M(c)/W(c), rugby M(c)/W(c), sailing M(c)/W(c), soccer M(c)/W(s), softball W(s), swimming M(s)/W(s), table tennis M(c)/W(c), tennis M(s)/W(s), track and field M(s)/W(s), volleyball M(c)/W(s), wrestling M(s). *Intramural sports:* badminton M/W, basketball M/W, bowling M/W, fencing M(c)/W(c), football M/W, golf M/W, racquetball M/W, riflery M/W, rugby M(c)/W(c), sailing M(c)/W(c), skiing (cross-country) M(c)/W(c), skiing (downhill) M(c)/W(c), soccer M/W, softball M/W, squash M(c)/W(c), swimming M/W, table tennis M/W, tennis M/W, track and field M/W, volleyball M/W, water polo M(c)/W(c), wrestling M.

Standardized Tests *Required:* SAT I or ACT (for admission).

Costs (2002–03) *Tuition:* state resident $3692 full-time, $154 per semester hour part-time; nonresident $13,334 full-time, $556 per semester hour part-time. Full-time tuition and fees vary according to course load. Part-time tuition and fees vary according to course load. *Required fees:* $499 full-time, $250 per term part-time. *Room and board:* $5440. Room and board charges vary according to board plan and housing facility. *Payment plan:* installment.

Financial Aid Of all full-time matriculated undergraduates who enrolled in 2001, 10536 applied for aid, 7536 were judged to have need, 3887 had their need fully met. 1100 Federal Work-Study jobs (averaging $2800). 660 State and other part-time jobs (averaging $2000). In 2001, 3745 non-need-based awards were made. *Average percent of need met:* 99%. *Average financial aid package:* $6020. *Average need-based loan:* $2959. *Average need-based gift aid:* $2069. *Average non-need based aid:* $3542. *Average indebtedness upon graduation:* $15,752.

Applying *Options:* electronic application, early admission, deferred entrance. *Application fee:* $30. *Required:* high school transcript. *Application deadlines:* 5/15 (freshmen), 5/15 (transfers). *Notification:* continuous (freshmen).

Admissions Contact Mr. Michael Barron, Director of Admissions, The University of Iowa, 107 Calvin Hall, Iowa City, IA 52242. *Phone:* 319-335-3847. *Toll-free phone:* 800-553-4692. *Fax:* 319-335-1535. *E-mail:* admissions@uiowa.edu.

UNIVERSITY OF NORTHERN IOWA
Cedar Falls, Iowa

- **State-supported** comprehensive, founded 1876, part of Iowa State Board of Regents
- **Calendar** semesters
- **Degrees** bachelor's, master's, and doctoral
- **Small-town** 940-acre campus
- **Endowment** $37.4 million
- **Coed,** 12,680 undergraduate students, 88% full-time, 58% women, 42% men
- **Moderately difficult** entrance level, 81% of applicants were admitted

Undergraduates 11,208 full-time, 1,472 part-time. Students come from 43 states and territories, 64 other countries, 4% are from out of state, 2% African American, 1% Asian American or Pacific Islander, 1% Hispanic American, 0.2% Native American, 2% international, 10% transferred in, 38% live on campus. *Retention:* 84% of 2001 full-time freshmen returned.

Freshmen *Admission:* 4,688 applied, 3,786 admitted, 2,097 enrolled. *Test scores:* SAT verbal scores over 500: 63%; SAT math scores over 500: 61%; ACT scores over 18: 94%; SAT verbal scores over 600: 28%; SAT math scores over 600: 31%; ACT scores over 24: 41%; SAT verbal scores over 700: 4%; SAT math scores over 700: 7%; ACT scores over 30: 5%.

Faculty *Total:* 852, 83% full-time, 65% with terminal degrees. *Student/faculty ratio:* 16:1.

Majors Accounting; acting/directing; actuarial science; American studies; anthropology; applied economics; art; art education; art history; Asian studies; biochemistry; biological/physical sciences; biology; broadcast journalism; business administration; business education; business marketing and marketing management; chemistry; clothing/apparel/textile studies; communications; community health liaison; computer/information sciences; computer science; criminology; dietetics; drama/theater literature; early childhood education; economics; education of the mentally handicapped; education of the multiple handicapped; elementary education; engineering physics; English; English education; environmental science; European studies; family/community studies; family/consumer studies; finance; fine/studio arts; foreign languages education; foreign languages/literatures; French; geography; geology; German; health education; history; housing studies; humanities; industrial arts education; industrial technology; information sciences/systems; interior design; Latin American studies; liberal arts and sciences/liberal studies; linguistics; management information systems/business data processing; mathematics; mathematics education; middle school education; music; music (general performance); music teacher education; music theory and composition; nutrition science; nutrition studies; philosophy; physical education; physics; political science; psychology; public administration; public relations; quantitative economics; radio/television broadcasting; reading education; real estate; recreation/leisure studies; religious studies; Russian; Russian/Slavic studies; science education; social science education; social work; sociology; Spanish; special education; speech-language pathology; teaching English as a second language; theater arts/drama; theater design; trade/industrial education.

Academic Programs *Special study options:* academic remediation for entering students, accelerated degree program, adult/continuing education programs, advanced placement credit, cooperative education, distance learning, double majors, English as a second language, honors programs, independent study, internships, off-campus study, part-time degree program, services for LD students, student-designed majors, study abroad, summer session for credit. *ROTC:* Army (b). *Unusual degree programs:* 3-2 nursing with University of Iowa.

Library Rod Library plus 1 other with 731,256 titles, 6,781 serial subscriptions, 18,452 audiovisual materials, an OPAC, a Web page.

Computers on Campus 884 computers available on campus for general student use. A campuswide network can be accessed from student residence rooms and from off campus that provide access to course registration, student account and grade information. Internet access, online (class) registration, at least one staffed computer lab available.

Student Life *Housing Options:* coed, men-only, women-only. *Activities and Organizations:* drama/theater group, student-run newspaper, radio station, choral group, marching band, American Marketing Association, Public Relations Student Society, Iowa State Education Association, Greek system, United Students of Iowa, national fraternities, national sororities. *Campus security:* 24-hour emer-

University of Northern Iowa (continued)
gency response devices and patrols, student patrols, late-night transport/escort service, controlled dormitory access. *Student Services:* health clinic, personal/psychological counseling.

Athletics Member NCAA. All Division I except football (Division I-AA). *Intercollegiate sports:* baseball M(s), basketball M(s)/W(s), cross-country running M(s)/W(s), golf M(s)/W(s), soccer W, softball W(s), swimming M(s)/W(s), tennis M/W(s), track and field M(s)/W(s), volleyball W(s), wrestling M(s). *Intramural sports:* badminton M/W, basketball M/W, bowling M(c)/W(c), crew M(c)/W(c), football M/W, golf M/W, ice hockey M(c), racquetball M(c)/W(c), rugby M(c)/W(c), skiing (cross-country) M(c)/W(c), skiing (downhill) M(c)/W(c), soccer M(c)/W(c), softball M/W, swimming M/W, table tennis M/W, tennis M/W, track and field M/W, volleyball M(c)/W(c), weight lifting M/W, wrestling M.

Standardized Tests *Required:* SAT I or ACT (for admission).

Costs (2001–02) *Tuition:* state resident $3116 full-time, $130 per hour part-time; nonresident $8438 full-time, $352 per hour part-time. Part-time tuition and fees vary according to course load. *Required fees:* $324 full-time, $27 per term part-time. *Room and board:* $4410; room only: $2022. Room and board charges vary according to board plan and housing facility. *Payment plan:* installment.

Financial Aid Of all full-time matriculated undergraduates who enrolled in 2001, 8272 applied for aid, 6142 were judged to have need, 1903 had their need fully met. 539 Federal Work-Study jobs (averaging $1846). In 2001, 1092 non-need-based awards were made. *Average percent of need met:* 77%. *Average financial aid package:* $5943. *Average need-based loan:* $3864. *Average need-based gift aid:* $2807. *Average non-need based aid:* $2247. *Average indebtedness upon graduation:* $17,812.

Applying *Options:* electronic application, deferred entrance. *Application fee:* $20. *Required:* high school transcript. *Required for some:* interview. *Application deadlines:* 8/15 (freshmen), 8/15 (transfers). *Notification:* continuous (freshmen).

Admissions Contact Mr. Clark Elmer, Director of Enrollment Management and Admissions, University of Northern Iowa, 120 Gilchrist Hall, Cedar Falls, IA 50614-0018. *Phone:* 319-273-2281. *Toll-free phone:* 800-772-2037. *Fax:* 319-273-2885. *E-mail:* admissions@uni.edu.

UPPER IOWA UNIVERSITY
Fayette, Iowa

- **Independent** comprehensive, founded 1857
- **Calendar** 8-8-3-8-8
- **Degrees** associate, bachelor's, and master's (also offers continuing education program with significant enrollment not reflected in profile)
- **Rural** 80-acre campus
- **Coed,** 718 undergraduate students, 100% full-time, 39% women, 61% men
- **Moderately difficult** entrance level, 65% of applicants were admitted

Undergraduates 718 full-time. Students come from 20 states and territories, 3 other countries, 42% are from out of state, 12% African American, 8% Asian American or Pacific Islander, 5% Hispanic American, 0.6% Native American, 0.4% international, 15% transferred in, 70% live on campus. *Retention:* 3% of 2001 full-time freshmen returned.

Freshmen *Admission:* 507 applied, 329 admitted, 138 enrolled. *Average high school GPA:* 2.71. *Test scores:* ACT scores over 18: 74%; ACT scores over 24: 25%.

Faculty *Total:* 46, 89% full-time, 78% with terminal degrees. *Student/faculty ratio:* 16:1.

Majors Accounting; American studies; art; art education; arts management; athletic training/sports medicine; biological/physical sciences; biology; business administration; business education; business marketing and marketing management; chemistry; criminology; education; elementary education; English; exercise sciences; graphic design/commercial art/illustration; health education; human services; liberal arts and sciences/liberal studies; management information systems/business data processing; mass communications; mathematics; middle school education; music; music teacher education; natural resources conservation; physical education; pre-dentistry; pre-medicine; pre-veterinary studies; psychology; public administration; reading education; recreation/leisure studies; science education; secondary education; social sciences; sociology; special education.

Academic Programs *Special study options:* academic remediation for entering students, accelerated degree program, adult/continuing education programs, advanced placement credit, distance learning, double majors, external degree program, independent study, internships, part-time degree program, student-designed majors, summer session for credit.

Library Henderson Wilder Library with 132,175 titles, 287 serial subscriptions, 4,040 audiovisual materials, a Web page.

Computers on Campus 75 computers available on campus for general student use. Internet access, at least one staffed computer lab available.

Student Life *Housing:* on-campus residence required through sophomore year. *Options:* coed, men-only, women-only. *Activities and Organizations:* drama/theater group, student-run newspaper, choral group, Outdoor Pursuits, Sigma Delta Phi, Alpha Nu Omega, psychology club, Campus Events Council. *Campus security:* late-night transport/escort service, controlled dormitory access. *Student Services:* health clinic, personal/psychological counseling.

Athletics Member NCAA. All Division III. *Intercollegiate sports:* baseball M, basketball M/W, cross-country running M/W, football M, golf M/W, soccer M/W, softball W, tennis M/W, track and field M/W, volleyball W, wrestling M. *Intramural sports:* basketball M/W, bowling M/W, football M, skiing (cross-country) M/W, softball M/W, tennis M/W, volleyball M/W.

Standardized Tests *Required:* SAT I or ACT (for admission).

Costs (2001–02) *Comprehensive fee:* $17,438 includes full-time tuition ($12,856) and room and board ($4582). Part-time tuition: $400 per semester hour. *Room and board:* Room and board charges vary according to board plan and housing facility. *Payment plan:* installment. *Waivers:* employees or children of employees.

Financial Aid Of all full-time matriculated undergraduates who enrolled in 2001, 3700 applied for aid, 3700 were judged to have need. 219 Federal Work-Study jobs (averaging $1650). 29 State and other part-time jobs (averaging $1650). *Average percent of need met:* 50%. *Average financial aid package:* $6000. *Average need-based loan:* $3500. *Average need-based gift aid:* $4000. *Average indebtedness upon graduation:* $17,125.

Applying *Options:* common application, early admission, deferred entrance. *Application fee:* $15. *Required:* high school transcript, minimum 2.0 GPA. *Required for some:* essay or personal statement, letters of recommendation, interview. *Application deadline:* rolling (freshmen), rolling (transfers).

Admissions Contact Mr. Kent McElvania, Director of Admissions, Upper Iowa University, Box 1859, Fayette, IA 52142-1857. *Phone:* 563-425-5281 Ext. 5279. *Toll-free phone:* 800-553-4150 Ext. 2. *Fax:* 563-425-5277. *E-mail:* admission@uiu.edu.

WALDORF COLLEGE
Forest City, Iowa

- **Independent Lutheran** 4-year, founded 1903
- **Calendar** semesters
- **Degrees** associate and bachelor's
- **Small-town** 29-acre campus
- **Coed,** 642 undergraduate students, 84% full-time, 46% women, 54% men
- **Moderately difficult** entrance level

Undergraduates Students come from 36 states and territories, 16 other countries, 39% are from out of state, 3% African American, 1% Asian American or Pacific Islander, 0.8% Hispanic American, 0.3% Native American, 7% international, 93% live on campus. *Retention:* 75% of 2001 full-time freshmen returned.

Freshmen *Average high school GPA:* 3.00.

Faculty *Total:* 53, 68% full-time, 30% with terminal degrees. *Student/faculty ratio:* 13:1.

Majors Accounting; art; art education; behavioral sciences; biblical studies; biological/physical sciences; biology; broadcast journalism; business administration; chemistry; child care/development; community services; computer programming; computer science; data processing technology; developmental/child psychology; divinity/ministry; early childhood education; education; engineering; English; film/video production; finance; German; graphic design/commercial art/illustration; health education; health science; history; home economics; humanities; human services; information sciences/systems; journalism; law enforcement/police science; liberal arts and sciences/liberal studies; mass communications; mathematics; medical assistant; music; music (piano and organ performance); music teacher education; music (voice and choral/opera performance); natural sciences; nursing; physical education; physical sciences; physics; pre-engineering; psychology; religious education; religious studies; social sciences; social work; sociology; Spanish; speech/rhetorical studies; telecommunications; theater arts/drama; theology; veterinary sciences; wildlife biology; wildlife management.

Academic Programs *Special study options:* academic remediation for entering students, accelerated degree program, adult/continuing education programs, advanced placement credit, cooperative education, double majors, English as a second language, freshman honors college, honors programs, internships, part-time degree program, services for LD students, study abroad, summer session for credit.

Library Voss Memorial Library with 33,422 titles, 55,989 serial subscriptions, 274 audiovisual materials, an OPAC.

Computers on Campus A campuswide network can be accessed from student residence rooms. Internet access, at least one staffed computer lab available.

Student Life *Housing:* on-campus residence required through sophomore year. *Options:* coed, men-only, women-only. *Activities and Organizations:* drama/theater group, student-run newspaper, radio and television station, choral group, Student Government, FCA, Drama Club, Intramurals, Amnesty International. *Campus security:* late-night transport/escort service, evening and night patrols by trained security personnel. *Student Services:* health clinic, personal/psychological counseling.

Athletics Member NJCAA. *Intercollegiate sports:* baseball M(s), basketball M(s)/W(s), football M(s), golf M(s)/W(s), soccer M(s)/W(s), softball W(s), volleyball W(s), wrestling M(s). *Intramural sports:* basketball M/W, football M, racquetball M/W, skiing (cross-country) M/W, skiing (downhill) M/W, soccer M/W, softball M/W, tennis M/W, volleyball M/W.

Standardized Tests *Required:* SAT I or ACT (for admission).

Costs (2001–02) *Comprehensive fee:* $19,580 includes full-time tuition ($13,708), mandatory fees ($620), and room and board ($5252). Part-time tuition: $150 per credit.

Applying *Options:* electronic application, early admission. *Application fee:* $20. *Required:* high school transcript, 1 letter of recommendation, SAT or ACT. *Required for some:* interview. *Recommended:* minimum 2.0 GPA. *Application deadline:* rolling (freshmen), rolling (transfers). *Notification:* continuous (freshmen).

Admissions Contact Mr. Steve Hall, Assistant Dean of Admission, Waldorf College, 106 South 6th Street, Forest City, IA 50436. *Phone:* 641-585-8119. *Toll-free phone:* 800-292-1903. *Fax:* 641-585-8194. *E-mail:* admissions@waldorf.edu.

WARTBURG COLLEGE

Waverly, Iowa

- **Independent Lutheran** 4-year, founded 1852
- **Calendar** 4-4-1
- **Degree** bachelor's
- **Small-town** 118-acre campus
- **Endowment** $37.7 million
- **Coed,** 1,649 undergraduate students, 95% full-time, 58% women, 42% men
- **Moderately difficult** entrance level, 88% of applicants were admitted

Wartburg's integrated approach to education combines the liberal arts with an emphasis on leadership education, global and multicultural studies, and hands-on learning. Cultural immersion programs offer academic credit and give students the opportunity to live and work for one month, one term, or the entire year in settings throughout the world.

Undergraduates 1,562 full-time, 87 part-time. Students come from 25 states and territories, 32 other countries, 21% are from out of state, 4% African American, 1% Asian American or Pacific Islander, 0.8% Hispanic American, 0.1% Native American, 4% international, 4% transferred in, 83% live on campus. *Retention:* 75% of 2001 full-time freshmen returned.

Freshmen *Admission:* 1,562 applied, 1,373 admitted, 470 enrolled. *Average high school GPA:* 3.50. *Test scores:* SAT verbal scores over 500: 78%; SAT math scores over 500: 81%; ACT scores over 18: 94%; SAT verbal scores over 600: 36%; SAT math scores over 600: 51%; ACT scores over 24: 57%; SAT verbal scores over 700: 18%; SAT math scores over 700: 15%; ACT scores over 30: 11%.

Faculty *Total:* 153, 59% full-time, 54% with terminal degrees. *Student/faculty ratio:* 14:1.

Majors Accounting; art; art education; arts management; biochemistry; biology; broadcast journalism; business administration; business marketing and marketing management; chemistry; computer science; early childhood education; economics; elementary education; engineering; English; English composition; finance; French; German; graphic design/commercial art/illustration; history; history education; information sciences/systems; international business; international relations; journalism; mass communications; mathematics; mathematics education; medical technology; music; music (general performance); music teacher education; music theory and composition; music therapy; occupational therapy; philosophy; physical education; physics; political science; psychology; public relations; religious music; religious studies; secondary education; social science education; social work; sociology; Spanish; speech/theater education; sport/fitness administration.

Academic Programs *Special study options:* academic remediation for entering students, accelerated degree program, advanced placement credit, double majors, English as a second language, honors programs, independent study, internships, off-campus study, part-time degree program, student-designed majors, study abroad, summer session for credit. *Unusual degree programs:* 3-2 engineering with Iowa State University of Science and Technology, University of Iowa, University of Illinois at Urbana-Champaign, Washington University in St. Louis; occupational therapy with Washington University in St. Louis.

Library Vogel Library with 165,515 titles, 718 serial subscriptions, 2,765 audiovisual materials, an OPAC, a Web page.

Computers on Campus 200 computers available on campus for general student use. A campuswide network can be accessed from student residence rooms and from off campus. Internet access, at least one staffed computer lab available.

Student Life *Housing:* on-campus residence required through senior year. *Options:* coed, men-only, women-only, disabled students. *Activities and Organizations:* drama/theater group, student-run newspaper, radio and television station, choral group, Entertainment To Knight, choir, Student Senate, Campus Ministry, band. *Campus security:* 24-hour emergency response devices and patrols, late-night transport/escort service, controlled dormitory access. *Student Services:* health clinic, personal/psychological counseling.

Athletics Member NCAA. All Division III. *Intercollegiate sports:* baseball M, basketball M/W, cross-country running M/W, football M, golf M/W, soccer M/W, softball W, tennis M/W, track and field M/W, volleyball W, wrestling M. *Intramural sports:* badminton M/W, basketball M/W, golf M/W, racquetball M/W, rugby W, softball M/W, tennis M/W, volleyball M/W.

Standardized Tests *Required:* SAT I or ACT (for admission).

Costs (2001–02) *Comprehensive fee:* $21,165 includes full-time tuition ($16,210), mandatory fees ($355), and room and board ($4600). Part-time tuition: $600 per credit. Part-time tuition and fees vary according to class time and course load. *Required fees:* $15 per term part-time. *Room and board:* College room only: $2200. Room and board charges vary according to board plan and housing facility. *Payment plan:* installment. *Waivers:* senior citizens and employees or children of employees.

Financial Aid Of all full-time matriculated undergraduates who enrolled in 2001, 1556 applied for aid, 1075 were judged to have need, 331 had their need fully met. 468 Federal Work-Study jobs (averaging $1551). 547 State and other part-time jobs (averaging $911). In 2001, 453 non-need-based awards were made. *Average percent of need met:* 88%. *Average financial aid package:* $15,215. *Average need-based loan:* $3973. *Average need-based gift aid:* $10,053. *Average non-need based aid:* $7036. *Average indebtedness upon graduation:* $17,366.

Applying *Options:* common application, early action, deferred entrance. *Application fee:* $20. *Required:* high school transcript, minimum 2.0 GPA. *Required for some:* interview. *Recommended:* letters of recommendation, secondary school report. *Notification:* continuous (freshmen), 12/15 (early action).

Admissions Contact Doug Bowman, Dean of Admissions/Financial Aid, Wartburg College, 100 Wartburg Boulevard, PO Box 1003, Waverly, IA 50677-0903. *Phone:* 319-352-8264. *Toll-free phone:* 800-772-2085. *Fax:* 319-352-8579. *E-mail:* admissions@wartburg.edu.

WILLIAM PENN UNIVERSITY

Oskaloosa, Iowa

- **Independent** 4-year, founded 1873, affiliated with Society of Friends
- **Calendar** semesters
- **Degrees** associate and bachelor's
- **Rural** 40-acre campus with easy access to Des Moines
- **Endowment** $4.4 million
- **Coed,** 1,547 undergraduate students, 89% full-time, 48% women, 52% men
- **Moderately difficult** entrance level, 72% of applicants were admitted

Undergraduates 1,378 full-time, 169 part-time. Students come from 41 states and territories, 10 other countries, 27% are from out of state, 9% African American, 0.4% Asian American or Pacific Islander, 3% Hispanic American, 0.7% Native American, 0.7% international, 11% transferred in, 40% live on campus. *Retention:* 55% of 2001 full-time freshmen returned.

Freshmen *Admission:* 756 applied, 544 admitted, 265 enrolled. *Average high school GPA:* 2.88. *Test scores:* ACT scores over 18: 90%; ACT scores over 24: 15%; ACT scores over 30: 1%.

Faculty *Total:* 65, 66% full-time, 26% with terminal degrees. *Student/faculty ratio:* 14:1.

Majors Accounting; biology; business administration; business education; communications; computer science; criminology; driver/safety education; education; elementary education; engineering technology; English education; environmental biology; health education; health/physical education; history; human services; industrial arts; industrial technology; mathematics education; mechanical engineering; physical education; political science; pre-dentistry; pre-law; pre-medicine; psychology; recreation/leisure studies; science education; secondary education; social science education; sociology; special education; sport/fitness administration.

William Penn University (continued)

Academic Programs *Special study options:* academic remediation for entering students, accelerated degree program, adult/continuing education programs, advanced placement credit, cooperative education, distance learning, double majors, English as a second language, independent study, internships, off-campus study, part-time degree program, services for LD students, student-designed majors, summer session for credit. *Unusual degree programs:* 3-2 engineering with Washington University in St. Louis, Iowa State University of Science and Technology.

Library Wilcox Library with 72,907 titles, 354 serial subscriptions, 738 audiovisual materials, an OPAC, a Web page.

Computers on Campus 85 computers available on campus for general student use. A campuswide network can be accessed from student residence rooms and from off campus. Internet access, at least one staffed computer lab available.

Student Life *Housing:* on-campus residence required through junior year. *Options:* coed, women-only. *Activities and Organizations:* drama/theater group, student-run newspaper, radio station, choral group, Fellowship of Christian Athletes, Lettermen's Club, Literacy Tutoring Project, student government. *Campus security:* 24-hour emergency response devices and patrols, controlled dormitory access. *Student Services:* health clinic, personal/psychological counseling.

Athletics Member NCAA. All Division III. *Intercollegiate sports:* baseball M, basketball M/W, cross-country running M/W, football M, golf M/W, soccer M/W, softball W, track and field M/W, volleyball W, wrestling M. *Intramural sports:* basketball M/W, bowling M/W, football M, golf M/W, table tennis M/W, tennis M/W, volleyball M/W, weight lifting M/W.

Standardized Tests *Required:* SAT I or ACT (for admission).

Costs (2001–02) *Comprehensive fee:* $17,575 includes full-time tuition ($12,900), mandatory fees ($370), and room and board ($4305). Part-time tuition: $210 per credit hour. Part-time tuition and fees vary according to course load. *Room and board:* College room only: $1685. Room and board charges vary according to board plan and housing facility. *Payment plan:* installment. *Waivers:* senior citizens and employees or children of employees.

Financial Aid Of all full-time matriculated undergraduates who enrolled in 2001, 554 applied for aid, 548 were judged to have need, 502 had their need fully met. 335 Federal Work-Study jobs (averaging $639). 33 State and other part-time jobs (averaging $1252). In 2001, 9 non-need-based awards were made. *Average percent of need met:* 92%. *Average financial aid package:* $9305. *Average need-based loan:* $4833. *Average need-based gift aid:* $4434. *Average non-need based aid:* $5800.

Applying *Options:* electronic application, deferred entrance. *Application fee:* $20. *Required:* high school transcript, minimum 2.0 GPA. *Required for some:* essay or personal statement, letters of recommendation, interview. *Notification:* continuous (freshmen).

Admissions Contact Mrs. Mary Boyd, Director of Admissions, William Penn University, 201 Trueblood Avenue, Oskaloosa, IA 52577. *Phone:* 641-673-1012. *Toll-free phone:* 800-779-7366. *Fax:* 641-673-1396. *E-mail:* admissions@wmpenn.edu.

KANSAS

BAKER UNIVERSITY
Baldwin City, Kansas

- **Independent United Methodist** comprehensive, founded 1858
- **Calendar** 4-1-4, semesters for nursing program
- **Degree** bachelor's
- **Small-town** 26-acre campus with easy access to Kansas City
- **Endowment** $30.2 million
- **Coed,** 1,002 undergraduate students, 94% full-time, 59% women, 41% men
- **Moderately difficult** entrance level, 88% of applicants were admitted

Undergraduates 946 full-time, 56 part-time. Students come from 18 states and territories, 3 other countries, 25% are from out of state, 4% African American, 0.8% Asian American or Pacific Islander, 2% Hispanic American, 1% Native American, 0.9% international, 4% transferred in, 90% live on campus. *Retention:* 81% of 2001 full-time freshmen returned.

Freshmen *Admission:* 931 applied, 820 admitted, 250 enrolled. *Average high school GPA:* 3.45. *Test scores:* SAT verbal scores over 500: 57%; SAT math scores over 500: 73%; ACT scores over 18: 96%; SAT verbal scores over 600: 35%; SAT math scores over 600: 27%; ACT scores over 24: 45%; SAT verbal scores over 700: 5%; SAT math scores over 700: 5%; ACT scores over 30: 3%.

Faculty *Total:* 109, 69% full-time, 53% with terminal degrees. *Student/faculty ratio:* 11:1.

Majors Accounting; art education; art history; biology; business administration; chemistry; computer science; economics; elementary education; engineering; English; fine/studio arts; French; German; history; information sciences/systems; international business; mass communications; mathematics; music; music teacher education; nursing; philosophy; physical education; physics; political science; pre-dentistry; pre-law; pre-medicine; pre-veterinary studies; psychology; sociology; Spanish; speech/rhetorical studies; theater arts/drama; theology; wildlife biology.

Academic Programs *Special study options:* academic remediation for entering students, advanced placement credit, double majors, English as a second language, honors programs, independent study, internships, services for LD students, student-designed majors, study abroad, summer session for credit. *ROTC:* Army (c). *Unusual degree programs:* 3-2 engineering with Washington University in St. Louis, University of Kansas; forestry with Duke University.

Library Collins Library with 84,114 titles, 507 serial subscriptions, 1,139 audiovisual materials, an OPAC, a Web page.

Computers on Campus 151 computers available on campus for general student use. A campuswide network can be accessed from student residence rooms and from off campus. Internet access, at least one staffed computer lab available.

Student Life *Housing:* on-campus residence required through senior year. *Options:* coed, men-only, women-only, disabled students. *Activities and Organizations:* drama/theater group, student-run newspaper, radio station, choral group, Delta Sigma Pi, Earth We Are, Mungano, Fellowship of Christian Athletes, national fraternities, national sororities. *Campus security:* 24-hour emergency response devices and patrols, student patrols. *Student Services:* health clinic, personal/psychological counseling.

Athletics Member NAIA. *Intercollegiate sports:* baseball M(s), basketball M(s)/W(s), cross-country running M(s)/W(s), football M(s), golf M(s)/W(s), soccer M(s)/W(s), softball W(s), tennis M(s)/W(s), track and field M(s)/W(s), volleyball W(s). *Intramural sports:* badminton M/W, basketball M/W, fencing M/W, football M/W, racquetball M/W, soccer M/W, softball M/W, table tennis M/W, tennis M/W, volleyball M/W.

Standardized Tests *Required:* SAT I or ACT (for admission).

Costs (2001–02) *One-time required fee:* $80. *Comprehensive fee:* $17,780 includes full-time tuition ($12,900) and room and board ($4880). Full-time tuition and fees vary according to location and program. Part-time tuition: $455 per credit hour. Part-time tuition and fees vary according to course load. *Room and board:* College room only: $2200. Room and board charges vary according to board plan and housing facility. *Payment plan:* installment. *Waivers:* senior citizens and employees or children of employees.

Financial Aid Of all full-time matriculated undergraduates who enrolled in 2001, 816 applied for aid, 646 were judged to have need. 222 Federal Work-Study jobs (averaging $1397). 342 State and other part-time jobs (averaging $1403). *Average financial aid package:* $10,586. *Average need-based loan:* $4281. *Average need-based gift aid:* $4905.

Applying *Options:* electronic application, deferred entrance. *Application fee:* $20. *Required:* high school transcript, minimum 3.0 GPA, 1 letter of recommendation. *Required for some:* essay or personal statement, interview. *Application deadline:* rolling (freshmen), rolling (transfers).

Admissions Contact Ms. Cheryl McCracy, Director of Admission, Baker University, PO Box 65, Baldwin City, KS 66006-0065. *Phone:* 785-594-6451 Ext. 458. *Toll-free phone:* 800-873-4282. *Fax:* 785-594-8372. *E-mail:* admission@bakeru.edu.

BARCLAY COLLEGE
Haviland, Kansas

- **Independent** 4-year, founded 1917, affiliated with Society of Friends
- **Calendar** semesters
- **Degrees** certificates, associate, and bachelor's
- **Rural** 13-acre campus
- **Endowment** $1.4 million
- **Coed,** 196 undergraduate students, 87% full-time, 59% women, 41% men
- **Minimally difficult** entrance level, 30% of applicants were admitted

Barclay College is a coed, 4-year, interdenominational, accredited college located in Haviland, Kansas. Founded in 1917 by the Evangelical Friends, Barclay offers bachelor's degrees in bible/theology, business administration, Christian school elementary education, church music, pastorial ministries, psychology/family counseling, and youth ministries, along with associate degrees. Tuition, room and board, and fees total $11,200.

Undergraduates 171 full-time, 25 part-time. Students come from 14 states and territories, 2 other countries, 36% are from out of state, 6% African American,

0.5% Asian American or Pacific Islander, 2% Hispanic American, 2% Native American, 2% international, 4% transferred in. *Retention:* 41% of 2001 full-time freshmen returned.

Freshmen *Admission:* 66 applied, 20 admitted, 20 enrolled. *Average high school GPA:* 3.13. *Test scores:* SAT verbal scores over 500: 100%; SAT math scores over 500: 75%; ACT scores over 18: 53%; SAT verbal scores over 600: 50%; SAT math scores over 600: 25%; ACT scores over 24: 7%; SAT verbal scores over 700: 25%.

Faculty *Total:* 38, 24% full-time, 8% with terminal degrees. *Student/faculty ratio:* 7:1.

Majors Biblical studies; business administration; divinity/ministry; elementary education; pastoral counseling; psychology; religious education; religious music.

Academic Programs *Special study options:* academic remediation for entering students, accelerated degree program, adult/continuing education programs, advanced placement credit, distance learning, double majors, external degree program, independent study, internships, part-time degree program, student-designed majors.

Library Worden Memorial Library with 55,637 titles, 183 serial subscriptions, 1,549 audiovisual materials, an OPAC.

Computers on Campus 20 computers available on campus for general student use. A campuswide network can be accessed from off campus that provide access to on-line library catalog. Internet access, at least one staffed computer lab available.

Student Life *Housing:* on-campus residence required through senior year. *Options:* men-only, women-only. *Activities and Organizations:* drama/theater group, choral group, Pep Club, Drama Club, Missions Club. *Campus security:* student patrols. *Student Services:* personal/psychological counseling.

Athletics Member NSCAA. *Intercollegiate sports:* baseball M, basketball M/W, soccer M, tennis M/W, volleyball W. *Intramural sports:* baseball M/W, basketball M/W, volleyball M/W.

Standardized Tests *Required:* SAT I or ACT (for admission).

Costs (2002–03) *Comprehensive fee:* $12,200 includes full-time tuition ($8200) and room and board ($4000). Part-time tuition: $340 per credit hour. Part-time tuition and fees vary according to course load. *Room and board:* College room only: $1450. Room and board charges vary according to board plan. *Payment plan:* installment. *Waivers:* employees or children of employees.

Financial Aid Of all full-time matriculated undergraduates who enrolled in 2001, 155 applied for aid, 145 were judged to have need, 23 had their need fully met. 42 Federal Work-Study jobs (averaging $1191). In 2001, 3 non-need-based awards were made. *Average percent of need met:* 79%. *Average financial aid package:* $6016. *Average need-based loan:* $3029. *Average need-based gift aid:* $2690. *Average non-need based aid:* $1467. *Average indebtedness upon graduation:* $10,000.

Applying *Options:* early admission, deferred entrance. *Application fee:* $15. *Required:* essay or personal statement, high school transcript, minimum 2.3 GPA, 2 letters of recommendation. *Application deadlines:* 9/1 (freshmen), 9/1 (transfers).

Admissions Contact Ryan Haase, Director of Admissions, Barclay College, 607 North Kingman, Haviland, KS 67059. *Phone:* 620-862-5252 Ext. 41. *Toll-free phone:* 800-862-0226. *Fax:* 620-862-5242. *E-mail:* admissions@barclaycollege.edu.

BENEDICTINE COLLEGE
Atchison, Kansas

- **Independent Roman Catholic** comprehensive, founded 1859
- **Calendar** semesters
- **Degrees** associate, bachelor's, and master's
- **Small-town** 225-acre campus with easy access to Kansas City
- **Endowment** $10.0 million
- **Coed,** 1,297 undergraduate students, 68% full-time, 52% women, 48% men
- **Moderately difficult** entrance level, 88% of applicants were admitted

Benedictine College, America's Discovery College, is a 4-year Catholic, residential, liberal arts Benedictine college that provides an outstanding education for students of all backgrounds and faiths. Benedictine is distinguished by its distinctive student-centered academic program that offers students exceptional opportunities for research and personal growth.

Undergraduates 879 full-time, 418 part-time. Students come from 35 states and territories, 15 other countries, 54% are from out of state, 5% African American, 0.5% Asian American or Pacific Islander, 7% Hispanic American, 0.6% Native American, 3% international, 6% transferred in, 78% live on campus. *Retention:* 71% of 2001 full-time freshmen returned.

Freshmen *Admission:* 648 applied, 569 admitted, 240 enrolled. *Average high school GPA:* 3.27. *Test scores:* SAT verbal scores over 500: 51%; SAT math scores over 500: 54%; ACT scores over 18: 96%; SAT verbal scores over 600: 17%; SAT math scores over 600: 22%; ACT scores over 24: 40%; SAT verbal scores over 700: 5%; SAT math scores over 700: 2%; ACT scores over 30: 8%.

Faculty *Total:* 84, 68% full-time, 60% with terminal degrees. *Student/faculty ratio:* 15:1.

Majors Accounting; arts management; astronomy; biochemistry; biological/physical sciences; biology; business administration; business marketing and marketing management; chemistry; computer science; criminal justice/law enforcement administration; economics; elementary education; English; finance; French; history; journalism; liberal arts and sciences/liberal studies; mathematics; modern languages; music; music business management/merchandising; music (piano and organ performance); music teacher education; music (voice and choral/opera performance); natural sciences; philosophy; physical education; physics; political science; pre-law; psychology; religious studies; science education; secondary education; social sciences; sociology; Spanish; special education; sport/fitness administration; stringed instruments; theater arts/drama; theology.

Academic Programs *Special study options:* academic remediation for entering students, advanced placement credit, cooperative education, English as a second language, independent study, internships, off-campus study, part-time degree program, student-designed majors, study abroad, summer session for credit. *ROTC:* Army (b). *Unusual degree programs:* 3-2 engineering with Kansas State University, University of Missouri-Columbia, South Dakota School of Mines and Technology; occupational therapy with Washington University in St. Louis.

Library Benedictine College Library with 366,212 titles, 501 serial subscriptions, 831 audiovisual materials, an OPAC, a Web page.

Computers on Campus 80 computers available on campus for general student use. A campuswide network can be accessed from student residence rooms and from off campus. Internet access, at least one staffed computer lab available.

Student Life *Housing:* on-campus residence required through junior year. *Options:* men-only, women-only. *Activities and Organizations:* drama/theater group, student-run newspaper, choral group, student government, Students in Free Enterprise, Knights of Columbus, Concert Chorale/Chamber Singers, Campus Activities Board. *Campus security:* 24-hour emergency response devices and patrols, late-night transport/escort service. *Student Services:* health clinic, personal/psychological counseling.

Athletics Member NAIA. *Intercollegiate sports:* baseball M(s), basketball M(s)/W(s), cross-country running M(s)/W(s), football M(s), golf M(s)/W(s), soccer M(s)/W(s), softball W(s), tennis M(s)/W(s), track and field M(s)/W(s), volleyball W(s). *Intramural sports:* basketball M/W, football M/W, racquetball M/W, soccer M/W, softball M/W, table tennis M/W, volleyball M/W.

Standardized Tests *Required:* SAT I or ACT (for admission).

Costs (2002–03) *Comprehensive fee:* $19,095 includes full-time tuition ($13,515), mandatory fees ($280), and room and board ($5300). Full-time tuition and fees vary according to course load and degree level. Part-time tuition: $250 per credit hour. Part-time tuition and fees vary according to course load and degree level. *Room and board:* College room only: $2370. Room and board charges vary according to board plan and housing facility. *Payment plan:* installment. *Waivers:* senior citizens and employees or children of employees.

Financial Aid Of all full-time matriculated undergraduates who enrolled in 2001, 790 applied for aid, 714 were judged to have need, 143 had their need fully met. In 2001, 54 non-need-based awards were made. *Average percent of need met:* 69%. *Average financial aid package:* $12,329. *Average need-based loan:* $4453. *Average need-based gift aid:* $3869. *Average non-need based aid:* $4408. *Average indebtedness upon graduation:* $20,822.

Applying *Options:* common application, electronic application, deferred entrance. *Application fee:* $25. *Required:* high school transcript, minimum 2.0 GPA. *Required for some:* interview. *Notification:* continuous (freshmen).

Admissions Contact Ms. Kelly Vowels, Dean of Enrollment Management, Benedictine College, 1020 N. 2nd Street, Atchison, KS 66002. *Phone:* 913-367-5340 Ext. 2476. *Toll-free phone:* 800-467-5340. *Fax:* 913-367-5462. *E-mail:* bcadmiss@benedictine.edu.

BETHANY COLLEGE
Lindsborg, Kansas

- **Independent Lutheran** 4-year, founded 1881
- **Calendar** 4-1-4
- **Degree** bachelor's
- **Small-town** 80-acre campus
- **Endowment** $14.3 million
- **Coed,** 622 undergraduate students, 92% full-time, 47% women, 53% men
- **Moderately difficult** entrance level, 76% of applicants were admitted

Bethany College (continued)

Undergraduates 571 full-time, 51 part-time. Students come from 24 states and territories, 6 other countries, 38% are from out of state, 6% African American, 2% Asian American or Pacific Islander, 4% Hispanic American, 1% Native American, 1% international, 10% transferred in, 74% live on campus. *Retention:* 73% of 2001 full-time freshmen returned.

Freshmen *Admission:* 560 applied, 423 admitted, 158 enrolled. *Average high school GPA:* 3.38. *Test scores:* ACT scores over 18: 86%; ACT scores over 24: 34%; ACT scores over 30: 4%.

Faculty *Total:* 69, 61% full-time, 46% with terminal degrees. *Student/faculty ratio:* 11:1.

Majors Accounting; art; art education; athletic training/sports medicine; biology; biology education; business administration; business economics; business education; ceramic arts; chemistry; chemistry education; communications; criminal justice studies; drawing; education; elementary education; English; English education; financial planning; history; international business; law and legal studies related; mathematics; mathematics education; music; music teacher education; painting; philosophy; physical education; political science; psychology; recreation/leisure studies; religious studies; sculpture; social studies education; social work; sociology.

Academic Programs *Special study options:* accelerated degree program, advanced placement credit, double majors, independent study, internships, off-campus study, services for LD students, student-designed majors, summer session for credit. *Unusual degree programs:* 3-2 engineering with Wichita State University.

Library Wallerstedt Library plus 1 other with 609 serial subscriptions, 3,518 audiovisual materials.

Computers on Campus 41 computers available on campus for general student use. Internet access, at least one staffed computer lab available.

Student Life *Housing:* on-campus residence required through senior year. *Options:* coed, women-only. *Activities and Organizations:* drama/theater group, student-run newspaper, choral group, Business Club, Bethany Student Education Association, Multicultural Student Association. *Campus security:* 24-hour emergency response devices, student patrols, late-night transport/escort service, controlled dormitory access, night patrols by security personnel. *Student Services:* health clinic, personal/psychological counseling.

Athletics Member NAIA. *Intercollegiate sports:* baseball M(s), basketball M(s)/W(s), cross-country running M(s)/W(s), football M(s), golf M(s), soccer M(s)/W(s), softball W(s), tennis M(s)/W(s), track and field M(s)/W(s), volleyball W(s). *Intramural sports:* archery M/W, badminton M/W, basketball M/W, bowling M/W, cross-country running M/W, football M/W, golf M/W, racquetball M/W, soccer M/W, softball M/W, table tennis M/W, tennis M/W, track and field M/W, volleyball M/W, weight lifting M/W.

Standardized Tests *Required:* SAT I or ACT (for admission).

Costs (2001–02) *Comprehensive fee:* $16,543 includes full-time tuition ($12,943) and room and board ($3600). Full-time tuition and fees vary according to location. Part-time tuition: $210 per credit hour. Part-time tuition and fees vary according to course load. *Room and board:* College room only: $1650. Room and board charges vary according to board plan and housing facility. *Payment plan:* installment. *Waivers:* employees or children of employees.

Financial Aid Of all full-time matriculated undergraduates who enrolled in 2001, 540 applied for aid, 425 were judged to have need, 193 had their need fully met. 163 Federal Work-Study jobs (averaging $595). In 2001, 36 non-need-based awards were made. *Average percent of need met:* 95%. *Average financial aid package:* $13,158. *Average need-based loan:* $4252. *Average need-based gift aid:* $4658. *Average non-need based aid:* $4116. *Average indebtedness upon graduation:* $12,698.

Applying *Options:* deferred entrance. *Application fee:* $20. *Required:* high school transcript, minimum 2.5 GPA. *Required for some:* essay or personal statement, letters of recommendation, interview. *Application deadline:* 7/1 (freshmen), rolling (transfers). *Notification:* continuous (freshmen).

Admissions Contact Daniel McKinney, Dean of Admissions and Financial Aid, Bethany College, 421 North First Street, Lindsborg, KS 67456-1897. *Phone:* 785-227-3311 Ext. 8108. *Toll-free phone:* 800-826-2281. *Fax:* 785-227-2004. *E-mail:* admissions@bethanylb.edu.

BETHEL COLLEGE
North Newton, Kansas

- **Independent** 4-year, founded 1887, affiliated with General Conference Mennonite Church
- **Calendar** 4-1-4
- **Degree** bachelor's
- **Small-town** 60-acre campus with easy access to Wichita
- **Endowment** $16.3 million
- **Coed,** 525 undergraduate students, 92% full-time, 50% women, 50% men
- **Moderately difficult** entrance level, 75% of applicants were admitted

Undergraduates 482 full-time, 43 part-time. Students come from 25 states and territories, 15 other countries, 31% are from out of state, 6% African American, 2% Asian American or Pacific Islander, 6% Hispanic American, 1.0% Native American, 4% international, 11% transferred in, 75% live on campus. *Retention:* 72% of 2001 full-time freshmen returned.

Freshmen *Admission:* 432 applied, 323 admitted, 126 enrolled. *Average high school GPA:* 3.36. *Test scores:* SAT verbal scores over 500: 43%; SAT math scores over 500: 57%; ACT scores over 18: 92%; SAT verbal scores over 600: 14%; SAT math scores over 600: 14%; ACT scores over 24: 49%; SAT verbal scores over 700: 7%; SAT math scores over 700: 7%; ACT scores over 30: 13%.

Faculty *Total:* 67, 75% full-time, 40% with terminal degrees. *Student/faculty ratio:* 11:1.

Majors Accounting; art; biology; business administration; chemistry; communications; computer/information technology services administration and management related; computer science; criminal justice studies; elementary education; English; German; health/physical education; history; mathematics; music; natural sciences; nursing; peace/conflict studies; physics; psychology; religious studies; social sciences; social sciences and history related; social work; Spanish; visual/performing arts.

Academic Programs *Special study options:* academic remediation for entering students, advanced placement credit, cooperative education, distance learning, double majors, independent study, internships, off-campus study, part-time degree program, services for LD students, study abroad, summer session for credit. *Unusual degree programs:* 3-2 engineering with Kansas State University, University of Kansas, Washington University in St. Louis, Wichita State University.

Library Mantz Library plus 1 other with 95,668 titles, 629 serial subscriptions, 154,354 audiovisual materials, an OPAC, a Web page.

Computers on Campus 40 computers available on campus for general student use. A campuswide network can be accessed from student residence rooms and from off campus. Internet access, at least one staffed computer lab available.

Student Life *Housing:* on-campus residence required through senior year. *Options:* coed, disabled students. *Activities and Organizations:* drama/theater group, student-run newspaper, radio station, choral group, Bethel College Service Corps, The Collegian (newspaper), Student Alumni Association, Student Senate, Student Activities Board. *Campus security:* 24-hour emergency response devices, student patrols, community police patrols. *Student Services:* health clinic, personal/psychological counseling.

Athletics Member NAIA. *Intercollegiate sports:* basketball M(s)/W(s), football M(s), soccer M(s)/W(s), tennis M(s)/W(s), track and field M(s)/W(s), volleyball W(s). *Intramural sports:* badminton M/W, baseball M, basketball M/W, bowling M/W, cross-country running M/W, golf M/W, soccer M/W, softball M/W, table tennis M/W, tennis M/W, volleyball M/W.

Standardized Tests *Required:* SAT I or ACT (for admission).

Costs (2002–03) *Comprehensive fee:* $18,500 includes full-time tuition ($13,000) and room and board ($5500). Full-time tuition and fees vary according to course load. Part-time tuition: $480 per credit hour. Part-time tuition and fees vary according to course load. *Room and board:* Room and board charges vary according to board plan and housing facility. *Payment plans:* installment, deferred payment. *Waivers:* children of alumni, senior citizens, and employees or children of employees.

Financial Aid Of all full-time matriculated undergraduates who enrolled in 2001, 396 applied for aid, 365 were judged to have need, 147 had their need fully met. 202 Federal Work-Study jobs (averaging $2121). 140 State and other part-time jobs (averaging $1145). In 2001, 79 non-need-based awards were made. *Average percent of need met:* 90%. *Average financial aid package:* $13,878. *Average need-based loan:* $4300. *Average need-based gift aid:* $4147. *Average non-need based aid:* $5192. *Average indebtedness upon graduation:* $11,839.

Applying *Options:* deferred entrance. *Application fee:* $20. *Required:* high school transcript, minimum 2.5 GPA. *Required for some:* essay or personal statement, 2 letters of recommendation. *Recommended:* interview. *Application deadlines:* 8/1 (freshmen), 8/1 (transfers). *Notification:* continuous (freshmen).

Admissions Contact Dr. Shirley King, Dean of Enrollment Services, Bethel College, 300 East 27th Street, North Newton, KS 67117-0531. *Phone:* 316-284-5230. *Toll-free phone:* 800-522-1887 Ext. 230. *Fax:* 316-284-5870. *E-mail:* admissions@bethelks.edu.

CENTRAL CHRISTIAN COLLEGE OF KANSAS
McPherson, Kansas

- **Independent Free Methodist** 4-year, founded 1884
- **Calendar** 4-1-4

- **Degrees** certificates, associate, and bachelor's
- **Small-town** 16-acre campus
- **Endowment** $4.1 million
- **Coed,** 314 undergraduate students, 88% full-time, 52% women, 48% men
- **Moderately difficult** entrance level, 99% of applicants were admitted

Undergraduates Students come from 29 states and territories, 63% are from out of state, 9% African American, 5% Asian American or Pacific Islander, 7% Hispanic American, 1% Native American, 82% live on campus. *Retention:* 67% of 2001 full-time freshmen returned.

Freshmen *Admission:* 341 applied, 336 admitted. *Average high school GPA:* 3.20. *Test scores:* ACT scores over 18: 65%; ACT scores over 24: 21%; ACT scores over 30: 3%.

Faculty *Total:* 31, 55% full-time, 13% with terminal degrees. *Student/faculty ratio:* 15:1.

Majors Accounting; acting/directing; agricultural business; aircraft pilot (private); aircraft pilot (professional); American history; architectural engineering technology; architecture; art; art education; athletic training/sports medicine; behavioral sciences; biblical studies; biological/physical sciences; biology; business administration; business communications; business economics; business education; business marketing and marketing management; carpentry; chemistry; computer science; construction technology; counseling psychology; counselor education/guidance; criminal justice studies; data processing; developmental/child psychology; divinity/ministry; drafting; drawing; early childhood education; economics; education; elementary education; engineering; English; English composition; family/community studies; finance; general studies; health education; health/physical education; history; humanities; human resources management; industrial arts; journalism; legal studies; liberal arts and sciences/liberal studies; marriage/family counseling; mass communications; mathematics; missionary studies; music; musical instrument technology; music business management/merchandising; music conducting; music (general performance); music history; music (piano and organ performance); music teacher education; music theory and composition; music (voice and choral/opera performance); natural sciences; nurse assistant/aide; nursing; painting; pastoral counseling; photography; physical education; physical sciences; physical therapy; physical therapy assistant; physician assistant; practical nurse; pre-dentistry; pre-law; pre-medicine; pre-pharmacy studies; pre-theology; pre-veterinary studies; psychology; recreation/leisure studies; religious studies; science education; social psychology; social sciences; social work; sociology; Spanish; sport/fitness administration; theater arts/drama; theology; western civilization; wildlife biology; zoology.

Academic Programs *Special study options:* academic remediation for entering students, adult/continuing education programs, advanced placement credit, cooperative education, double majors, independent study, internships, off-campus study, part-time degree program, services for LD students, student-designed majors.

Library Briner Library with 25,767 titles, 157 serial subscriptions, 1,547 audiovisual materials, an OPAC, a Web page.

Computers on Campus 22 computers available on campus for general student use. Internet access, online (class) registration, at least one staffed computer lab available.

Student Life *Housing:* on-campus residence required through junior year. *Options:* men-only, women-only. *Activities and Organizations:* drama/theater group, student-run newspaper, choral group, C.O.L.O.R.S. (Cross Over Lines of Racial Stereotype), Performing Arts Club, Student Activities Committee, Fellowship of Christian Athletes, Phi Beta Lambda Business Club. *Campus security:* controlled dormitory access. *Student Services:* health clinic, personal/psychological counseling.

Athletics Member NAIA, NCCAA. *Intercollegiate sports:* baseball M(s), basketball M(s)/W(s), cross-country running M(s)/W(s), golf M(s)/W(s), soccer M(s)/W(s), softball W(s), tennis M(s)/W(s), volleyball W(s). *Intramural sports:* basketball M/W, soccer M/W, table tennis M/W, volleyball M/W.

Standardized Tests *Required:* SAT I or ACT (for admission).

Costs (2002–03) *Comprehensive fee:* $15,700 includes full-time tuition ($11,200), mandatory fees ($500), and room and board ($4000). Part-time tuition and fees vary according to course load and program. *Room and board:* College room only: $1400. Room and board charges vary according to board plan and gender. *Payment plan:* installment. *Waivers:* employees or children of employees.

Financial Aid Of all full-time matriculated undergraduates who enrolled in 2001, 264 applied for aid, 228 were judged to have need, 16 had their need fully met. In 2001, 31 non-need-based awards were made. *Average percent of need met:* 88%. *Average financial aid package:* $10,671. *Average need-based loan:* $4694. *Average need-based gift aid:* $3487. *Average non-need based aid:* $4103. *Average indebtedness upon graduation:* $20,000.

Applying *Options:* electronic application, early admission, deferred entrance. *Application fee:* $15. *Required:* high school transcript, minimum 2.0 GPA, 2 letters of recommendation. *Recommended:* essay or personal statement, interview. *Application deadline:* rolling (freshmen), rolling (transfers). *Notification:* continuous (freshmen).

Admissions Contact Dr. David Ferrell, Dean of Admissions, Central Christian College of Kansas, PO Box 1403, McPherson, KS 67460. *Phone:* 620-241-0723 Ext. 380. *Toll-free phone:* 800-835-0078. *Fax:* 620-241-6032. *E-mail:* admissions@centralchristian.edu.

EMPORIA STATE UNIVERSITY
Emporia, Kansas

- **State-supported** comprehensive, founded 1863, part of Kansas Board of Regents
- **Calendar** semesters
- **Degrees** bachelor's, master's, doctoral, and post-master's certificates
- **Small-town** 207-acre campus with easy access to Wichita
- **Endowment** $40.3 million
- **Coed,** 4,287 undergraduate students, 86% full-time, 61% women, 39% men
- **Noncompetitive** entrance level, 90% of applicants were admitted

Undergraduates 3,695 full-time, 592 part-time. Students come from 41 states and territories, 54 other countries, 2% are from out of state, 4% African American, 0.9% Asian American or Pacific Islander, 4% Hispanic American, 0.7% Native American, 3% international, 10% transferred in, 31% live on campus. *Retention:* 69% of 2001 full-time freshmen returned.

Freshmen *Admission:* 1,275 applied, 1,152 admitted, 723 enrolled.

Faculty *Total:* 344, 71% full-time, 66% with terminal degrees. *Student/faculty ratio:* 18:1.

Majors Accounting; art; art education; biology; business administration; business education; business marketing and marketing management; chemistry; communications; computer/information sciences; earth sciences; economics; elementary education; English; foreign languages/literatures; general studies; health education; history; information sciences/systems; mathematics; music; music teacher education; nursing science; physical education; physical sciences; physics; political science; psychology; recreation/leisure studies; science education; secondary education; social sciences; sociology; speech education; theater arts/drama; vocational rehabilitation counseling.

Academic Programs *Special study options:* academic remediation for entering students, accelerated degree program, adult/continuing education programs, advanced placement credit, cooperative education, distance learning, double majors, English as a second language, honors programs, independent study, internships, off-campus study, part-time degree program, services for LD students, student-designed majors, study abroad, summer session for credit. *Unusual degree programs:* 3-2 engineering with Kansas State University, University of Kansas, Wichita State University.

Library William Allen White Library with 620,077 titles, 1,405 serial subscriptions, 8,340 audiovisual materials, an OPAC, a Web page.

Computers on Campus 283 computers available on campus for general student use. A campuswide network can be accessed from student residence rooms and from off campus that provide access to various software packages. Internet access, online (class) registration, at least one staffed computer lab available.

Student Life *Housing:* on-campus residence required for freshman year. *Options:* coed, men-only, women-only, disabled students. *Activities and Organizations:* drama/theater group, student-run newspaper, choral group, marching band, Associated Student Government, Union Activities Council, Black Student Union, Residence Hall Association, Interfraternity Council, national fraternities, national sororities. *Campus security:* 24-hour emergency response devices and patrols, late-night transport/escort service, controlled dormitory access, 24-hour residence hall monitoring, safety and self-awareness programs. *Student Services:* health clinic, personal/psychological counseling, women's center, legal services.

Athletics Member NCAA. All Division II. *Intercollegiate sports:* baseball M(s), basketball M(s)/W(s), cross-country running M(s)/W(s), football M(s), soccer W(s), softball W(s), tennis M(s)/W(s), track and field M(s)/W(s), volleyball W(s). *Intramural sports:* badminton M/W, basketball M/W, bowling M/W, football M/W, racquetball M/W, rugby M(c), soccer M(c)/W(c), softball M/W, swimming M(c)/W(c), table tennis M/W, tennis M/W, volleyball M/W, weight lifting M/W.

Standardized Tests *Required:* SAT I or ACT (for admission).

Costs (2001–02) *Tuition:* state resident $1740 full-time, $58 per credit hour part-time; nonresident $6594 full-time, $220 per credit hour part-time. *Required fees:* $544 full-time, $32 per credit hour. *Room and board:* $3914; room only: $1916. Room and board charges vary according to board plan and housing facility. *Payment plans:* installment, deferred payment. *Waivers:* senior citizens and employees or children of employees.

Financial Aid Of all full-time matriculated undergraduates who enrolled in 2001, 3213 applied for aid, 2114 were judged to have need. 30 State and other

Emporia State University (continued)

part-time jobs. *Average financial aid package:* $5075. *Average need-based loan:* $3026. *Average need-based gift aid:* $2093. *Average indebtedness upon graduation:* $12,439.

Applying *Options:* early admission, deferred entrance. *Application fee:* $25. *Required:* high school transcript. *Recommended:* minimum 2.0 GPA. *Application deadline:* rolling (freshmen), rolling (transfers).

Admissions Contact Ms. Susan Brinkman, Director of Admissions, Emporia State University, 1200 Commercial, Emporia, KS 66801-5087. *Phone:* 620-341-5465. *Toll-free phone:* 877-GOTOESU (in-state); 877-468-6378 (out-of-state). *Fax:* 620-341-5599. *E-mail:* go2esu@emporia.edu.

FORT HAYS STATE UNIVERSITY

Hays, Kansas

- **State-supported** comprehensive, founded 1902, part of Kansas Board of Regents
- **Calendar** semesters
- **Degrees** associate, bachelor's, and master's
- **Small-town** 200-acre campus
- **Endowment** $30.2 million
- **Coed,** 4,565 undergraduate students, 81% full-time, 54% women, 46% men
- **Noncompetitive** entrance level, 86% of applicants were admitted

Undergraduates Students come from 36 states and territories, 22 other countries, 1% African American, 0.5% Asian American or Pacific Islander, 2% Hispanic American, 0.7% Native American, 2% international, 19% live on campus. *Retention:* 65% of 2001 full-time freshmen returned.

Freshmen *Admission:* 1,446 applied, 1,238 admitted. *Average high school GPA:* 3.26. *Test scores:* ACT scores over 18: 85%; ACT scores over 24: 35%; ACT scores over 30: 3%.

Faculty *Total:* 273, 94% full-time. *Student/faculty ratio:* 17:1.

Majors Accounting; agricultural business; agricultural sciences; agronomy/crop science; animal sciences; art; art education; biological/physical sciences; biology; business administration; business economics; business education; business marketing and marketing management; chemistry; criminal justice studies; early childhood education; economics; elementary education; English; finance; French; geology; German; graphic design/commercial art/illustration; history; industrial arts; industrial radiologic technology; information sciences/systems; journalism; liberal arts and sciences/liberal studies; mass communications; mathematics; medical technology; music; music teacher education; natural resources management; nursing; philosophy; physical education; physical sciences; physics; political science; pre-law; psychology; public relations; radio/television broadcasting; range management; school psychology; science education; secretarial science; social work; sociology; Spanish; speech-language pathology/audiology; wildlife management.

Academic Programs *Special study options:* academic remediation for entering students, adult/continuing education programs, advanced placement credit, distance learning, double majors, English as a second language, external degree program, internships, off-campus study, part-time degree program, services for LD students, summer session for credit. *Unusual degree programs:* 3-2 engineering with Kansas State University, University of Kansas.

Library Forsyth Library with 195,000 titles, 3,400 serial subscriptions, an OPAC, a Web page.

Computers on Campus 550 computers available on campus for general student use. A campuswide network can be accessed from student residence rooms and from off campus. Internet access, at least one staffed computer lab available.

Student Life *Housing:* on-campus residence required for freshman year. *Options:* coed, men-only, women-only. *Activities and Organizations:* drama/theater group, student-run newspaper, radio and television station, choral group, marching band, Student Government Association, University Activities Board, Residence Hall Association, International Student Union, Block and Bridle, national fraternities, national sororities. *Campus security:* 24-hour emergency response devices and patrols, late-night transport/escort service, controlled dormitory access. *Student Services:* health clinic, personal/psychological counseling, women's center.

Athletics Member NCAA. All Division II. *Intercollegiate sports:* baseball M(s), basketball M(s)/W(s), cross-country running M(s)/W(s), football M(s), golf M(s), softball W, tennis W(s), track and field M(s)/W(s), volleyball W(s), wrestling M(s). *Intramural sports:* archery M/W, badminton M/W, basketball M/W, bowling M/W, cross-country running M/W, fencing M, field hockey M/W, football M/W, golf M/W, racquetball M/W, rugby M/W, soccer M/W, softball M/W, swimming M/W, table tennis M/W, tennis M/W, track and field M/W, volleyball M/W, water polo M/W, weight lifting M/W, wrestling M.

Costs (2001–02) *Tuition:* state resident $2217 full-time, $74 per credit hour part-time; nonresident $7070 full-time, $236 per credit hour part-time. Full-time tuition and fees vary according to course load, location, and reciprocity agreements. Part-time tuition and fees vary according to course load and location. *Room and board:* $4077; room only: $2072. Room and board charges vary according to board plan, housing facility, and student level. *Payment plan:* installment. *Waivers:* senior citizens.

Financial Aid Of all full-time matriculated undergraduates who enrolled in 2001, 2790 applied for aid, 2360 were judged to have need, 1702 had their need fully met. 400 Federal Work-Study jobs. *Average percent of need met:* 89%. *Average financial aid package:* $6563. *Average need-based loan:* $4104. *Average need-based gift aid:* $3884. *Average indebtedness upon graduation:* $12,907.

Applying *Options:* common application, electronic application. *Application fee:* $25. *Required:* high school transcript. *Application deadline:* rolling (freshmen), rolling (transfers). *Notification:* continuous (freshmen).

Admissions Contact Christy Befort, Senior Administrative Assistant, Office of Admissions, Fort Hays State University, 600 Park Street, Hays, KS 67601-4099. *Phone:* 785-628-5830. *Toll-free phone:* 800-628-FHSU. *Fax:* 785-628-4187. *E-mail:* tigers@fhsu.edu.

FRIENDS UNIVERSITY

Wichita, Kansas

- **Independent** comprehensive, founded 1898
- **Calendar** semesters
- **Degrees** associate, bachelor's, and master's
- **Urban** 45-acre campus
- **Coed,** 2,629 undergraduate students
- **Moderately difficult** entrance level, 93% of applicants were admitted

Undergraduates Students come from 30 states and territories, 25 other countries, 10% are from out of state, 18% live on campus. *Retention:* 63% of 2001 full-time freshmen returned.

Freshmen *Admission:* 668 applied, 620 admitted. *Average high school GPA:* 3.23.

Faculty *Total:* 225, 33% full-time.

Majors Accounting; applied art; art; art education; biblical studies; biology; business administration; business education; ceramic arts; chemistry; child care/development; communications; computer/information sciences; computer programming; computer science; dance; divinity/ministry; early childhood education; ecology; education; elementary education; English; graphic design/commercial art/illustration; health education; health services administration; history; human resources management; human services; industrial radiologic technology; interdisciplinary studies; international business; liberal arts and sciences/liberal studies; literature; marriage/family counseling; mathematics; medical laboratory technician; music; music business management/merchandising; music (piano and organ performance); music teacher education; music (voice and choral/opera performance); philosophy; physical education; political science; pre-dentistry; pre-engineering; pre-medicine; pre-veterinary studies; psychology; religious music; religious studies; science education; secondary education; social sciences; sociology; Spanish; speech/rhetorical studies; stringed instruments; theology.

Academic Programs *Special study options:* academic remediation for entering students, accelerated degree program, adult/continuing education programs, advanced placement credit, cooperative education, external degree program, honors programs, internships, off-campus study, part-time degree program, student-designed majors, summer session for credit.

Library Edmund Stanley Library plus 3 others with 105,989 titles, 857 serial subscriptions, an OPAC.

Computers on Campus 190 computers available on campus for general student use. A campuswide network can be accessed from student residence rooms and from off campus. At least one staffed computer lab available.

Student Life *Housing Options:* men-only, women-only. *Activities and Organizations:* drama/theater group, choral group, Singing Quakers, Phi Beta Lambda, Student Association. *Campus security:* 24-hour patrols, late-night transport/escort service. *Student Services:* health clinic, personal/psychological counseling.

Athletics Member NAIA. *Intercollegiate sports:* baseball M(s), basketball M(s)/W(s), cross-country running M(s)/W(s), football M(s), golf M(s), soccer M(s)/W(s), softball W(s), tennis M(s)/W(s), track and field M(s)/W(s), volleyball W(s). *Intramural sports:* basketball M/W, football M, racquetball M/W, soccer M/W, table tennis M/W, tennis M/W, volleyball M/W.

Standardized Tests *Required:* SAT I or ACT (for admission).

Costs (2001–02) *One-time required fee:* $40. *Comprehensive fee:* $15,280 includes full-time tuition ($11,620), mandatory fees ($120), and room and board ($3540). Full-time tuition and fees vary according to course load. Part-time tuition: $382 per credit hour. Part-time tuition and fees vary according to course load. *Required fees:* $3 per credit hour, $30 per year part-time. *Room and board:* College room only: $1610. Room and board charges vary according to student level. *Payment plan:* installment. *Waivers:* senior citizens and employees or children of employees.

Financial Aid Of all full-time matriculated undergraduates who enrolled in 2001, 1519 applied for aid, 1402 were judged to have need, 210 had their need fully met. 179 Federal Work-Study jobs (averaging $1250). In 2001, 194 non-need-based awards were made. *Average percent of need met:* 55%. *Average financial aid package:* $6925. *Average need-based loan:* $3741. *Average need-based gift aid:* $4311. *Average indebtedness upon graduation:* $15,069.

Applying *Options:* early admission. *Application fee:* $15. *Required:* high school transcript. *Required for some:* essay or personal statement, 1 letter of recommendation. *Recommended:* interview. *Application deadline:* rolling (freshmen), rolling (transfers). *Notification:* continuous (freshmen).

Admissions Contact Mr. Tony Myers, Director of Admissions, Friends University, 2100 West University Street, Wichita, KS 67213. *Phone:* 316-295-5100. *Toll-free phone:* 800-577-2233. *Fax:* 316-262-5027. *E-mail:* tmyers@friends.edu.

Haskell Indian Nations University
Lawrence, Kansas

- **Federally supported** 4-year, founded 1884
- **Calendar** semesters
- **Degrees** associate and bachelor's
- **Suburban** 320-acre campus
- **Coed,** 1,028 undergraduate students, 90% full-time, 47% women, 53% men
- **Minimally difficult** entrance level, 74% of applicants were admitted

Undergraduates 922 full-time, 106 part-time. Students come from 37 states and territories, 100% Native American, 9% transferred in.

Freshmen *Admission:* 353 applied, 262 admitted, 350 enrolled.

Faculty *Total:* 48, 100% full-time. *Student/faculty ratio:* 15:1.

Majors Accounting; business administration; computer engineering technology; elementary education; liberal arts and sciences/liberal studies; natural resources management; physical education; secretarial science.

Academic Programs *Special study options:* academic remediation for entering students, advanced placement credit, distance learning, independent study, off-campus study, part-time degree program, services for LD students, student-designed majors, summer session for credit. *ROTC:* Air Force (c).

Library 50,000 titles, 400 serial subscriptions, an OPAC.

Computers on Campus 35 computers available on campus for general student use. At least one staffed computer lab available.

Student Life *Housing Options:* coed, men-only, women-only. *Activities and Organizations:* drama/theater group, student-run newspaper, choral group, Phi Beta Lambda, Aises, H-Club, Navajo club, Unity. *Campus security:* 24-hour patrols. *Student Services:* health clinic, personal/psychological counseling.

Athletics Member NAIA. *Intercollegiate sports:* basketball M/W, cross-country running M/W, football M, golf M, softball W, track and field M/W, volleyball W. *Intramural sports:* golf W, racquetball M/W, weight lifting M/W.

Standardized Tests *Required:* SAT I or ACT (for placement).

Costs (2002–03) *One-time required fee:* $10. *Tuition:* state resident $0 full-time; nonresident $0 full-time. *Required fees:* $210 full-time, $70 per term part-time. *Room and board:* $70.

Financial Aid Of all full-time matriculated undergraduates who enrolled in 2001, 11 Federal Work-Study jobs.

Applying *Options:* common application, electronic application. *Application fee:* $5. *Required:* high school transcript, minimum 2.0 GPA. *Required for some:* 2 letters of recommendation. *Application deadlines:* 7/15 (freshmen), 7/15 (transfers). *Notification:* continuous (freshmen).

Admissions Contact Ms. Patty Grant, Recruitment Officer, Haskell Indian Nations University, 155 Indian Avenue, #5031. *Phone:* 785-749-8437 Ext. 437. *Fax:* 785-749-8429.

Kansas State University
Manhattan, Kansas

- **State-supported** university, founded 1863
- **Calendar** semesters
- **Degrees** associate, bachelor's, master's, doctoral, and first professional
- **Suburban** 668-acre campus with easy access to Kansas City
- **Coed,** 18,770 undergraduate students, 86% full-time, 47% women, 53% men
- **Noncompetitive** entrance level, 62% of applicants were admitted

Undergraduates 16,105 full-time, 2,665 part-time. Students come from 50 states and territories, 98 other countries, 9% are from out of state, 3% African American, 1% Asian American or Pacific Islander, 2% Hispanic American, 0.6% Native American, 1% international, 9% transferred in, 33% live on campus. *Retention:* 79% of 2001 full-time freshmen returned.

Freshmen *Admission:* 8,077 applied, 5,006 admitted, 3,562 enrolled. *Average high school GPA:* 3.47. *Test scores:* ACT scores over 18: 93%; ACT scores over 24: 47%; ACT scores over 30: 9%.

Faculty *Total:* 858. *Student/faculty ratio:* 15:1.

Majors Accounting; agricultural business; agricultural economics; agricultural engineering; agricultural/food products processing; agricultural mechanization; agronomy/crop science; aircraft mechanic/airframe; aircraft mechanic/powerplant; aircraft pilot (professional); animal sciences; anthropology; architectural engineering; architecture; art; aviation/airway science; biochemistry; biology; business administration; business marketing and marketing management; chemical engineering; chemical engineering technology; chemistry; child care/development; civil engineering; civil engineering technology; clothing/apparel/textile studies; communication disorders; communications; computer engineering; computer engineering technology; computer/information sciences; computer programming; computer systems analysis; dietetics; economics; electrical/electronic engineering technology; electrical engineering; elementary education; English; environmental technology; exercise sciences; finance; food sciences; foreign languages/literatures; geography; geology; geophysics/seismology; health science; history; horticulture science; hotel and restaurant management; human ecology; humanities; individual/family development; industrial/manufacturing engineering; industrial technology; information sciences/systems; interdisciplinary studies; interior architecture; interior design; journalism; landscape architecture; mathematical statistics; mathematics; mechanical engineering; mechanical engineering technology; medical technology; microbiology/bacteriology; music; music teacher education; nuclear engineering; nutrition studies; philosophy; physical sciences; physics; political science; pre-dentistry; pre-medicine; pre-veterinary studies; psychology; recreation/leisure facilities management; recreation/leisure studies; secondary education; social sciences; social work; sociology; surveying; theater arts/drama; wildlife biology; women's studies.

Academic Programs *Special study options:* academic remediation for entering students, accelerated degree program, adult/continuing education programs, advanced placement credit, cooperative education, distance learning, double majors, English as a second language, external degree program, freshman honors college, honors programs, independent study, internships, off-campus study, part-time degree program, services for LD students, study abroad, summer session for credit. *ROTC:* Army (b), Air Force (b). *Unusual degree programs:* 3-2 agriculture.

Library Hale Library plus 3 others with 1.5 million titles, 9,443 serial subscriptions, 3,899 audiovisual materials, an OPAC, a Web page.

Computers on Campus 556 computers available on campus for general student use. A campuswide network can be accessed from student residence rooms and from off campus. Internet access, online (class) registration, at least one staffed computer lab available.

Student Life *Housing Options:* coed, men-only, women-only, cooperative. *Activities and Organizations:* drama/theater group, student-run newspaper, radio station, choral group, marching band, athletic department groups, marching band, Union Governing Board, theater productions, debate team, national fraternities, national sororities. *Campus security:* 24-hour emergency response devices and patrols, late-night transport/escort service, controlled dormitory access. *Student Services:* health clinic, personal/psychological counseling, women's center, legal services.

Athletics Member NCAA. All Division I except football (Division I-A). *Intercollegiate sports:* baseball M(s), basketball M(s)/W(s), crew W(s), cross-country running M(s)/W(s), golf M(s)/W(s), tennis W(s), track and field M(s)/W(s), volleyball W(s). *Intramural sports:* badminton M/W, basketball M/W, bowling M/W, crew M/W, cross-country running M/W, football M/W, golf M/W, ice hockey M, lacrosse M, racquetball M/W, rugby M/W, soccer M/W, softball M/W, table tennis M/W, tennis M/W, track and field M/W, volleyball M/W, water polo M/W, weight lifting M/W, wrestling M.

Standardized Tests *Required:* ACT (for admission), SAT I or ACT (for admission).

Costs (2001–02) *Tuition:* state resident $2333 full-time, $78 per semester hour part-time; nonresident $9260 full-time, $309 per semester hour part-time. Full-time tuition and fees vary according to degree level and location. Part-time tuition and fees vary according to degree level and location. *Room and board:* $4662; room only: $2331. *Payment plans:* installment, deferred payment.

Financial Aid Of all full-time matriculated undergraduates who enrolled in 2001, 12373 applied for aid, 9196 were judged to have need, 1863 had their need fully met. In 2001, 999 non-need-based awards were made. *Average percent of*

Kansas State University (continued)
need met: 67%. *Average financial aid package:* $6023. *Average need-based loan:* $3267. *Average need-based gift aid:* $2361. *Average non-need based aid:* $1807. *Average indebtedness upon graduation:* $17,000.

Applying *Options:* common application, electronic application, early admission, deferred entrance. *Application fee:* $25. *Required:* minimum 2.0 GPA. *Required for some:* high school transcript. *Application deadline:* rolling (freshmen), rolling (transfers). *Notification:* continuous (freshmen).

Admissions Contact Mr. Larry Moeder, Interim Director of Admissions, Kansas State University, 119 Anderson Hall, Manhattan, KS 66506. *Phone:* 785-532-6250. *Toll-free phone:* 800-432-8270. *Fax:* 785-532-6393. *E-mail:* kstate@ksu.edu.

KANSAS WESLEYAN UNIVERSITY
Salina, Kansas

- **Independent United Methodist** comprehensive, founded 1886
- **Calendar** 2 semesters with a summer term
- **Degrees** associate, bachelor's, and master's
- **Urban** 28-acre campus
- **Endowment** $12.3 million
- **Coed,** 722 undergraduate students, 68% full-time, 62% women, 38% men
- **Moderately difficult** entrance level, 68% of applicants were admitted

Undergraduates 490 full-time, 232 part-time. Students come from 33 states and territories, 4 other countries, 39% are from out of state, 14% transferred in, 52% live on campus. *Retention:* 74% of 2001 full-time freshmen returned.

Freshmen *Admission:* 531 applied, 363 admitted, 99 enrolled. *Average high school GPA:* 3.29. *Test scores:* ACT scores over 18: 94%; ACT scores over 24: 34%; ACT scores over 30: 2%.

Faculty *Total:* 59, 71% full-time, 54% with terminal degrees. *Student/faculty ratio:* 14:1.

Majors Accounting; alcohol/drug abuse counseling; art; art education; arts management; biology; business administration; chemistry; computer science; criminal justice/law enforcement administration; early childhood education; education; elementary education; engineering; English; German; health education; history; information sciences/systems; liberal arts and sciences/liberal studies; literature; mass communications; mathematics; mental health/rehabilitation; nursing; physical education; physics; pre-dentistry; pre-law; pre-medicine; pre-veterinary studies; psychology; religious education; religious studies; social sciences; sociology; Spanish; special education; speech/rhetorical studies; theater arts/drama.

Academic Programs *Special study options:* academic remediation for entering students, adult/continuing education programs, advanced placement credit, distance learning, double majors, English as a second language, external degree program, independent study, internships, off-campus study, part-time degree program, student-designed majors, study abroad, summer session for credit. *Unusual degree programs:* 3-2 engineering with Columbia University, Washington University in St. Louis; agriculture with Kansas State University.

Library Memorial Library with 370 serial subscriptions, 1,055 audiovisual materials, an OPAC, a Web page.

Computers on Campus 72 computers available on campus for general student use. A campuswide network can be accessed from student residence rooms and from off campus. Internet access, at least one staffed computer lab available.

Student Life *Housing:* on-campus residence required through sophomore year. *Options:* men-only, women-only. *Activities and Organizations:* drama/theater group, student-run newspaper, choral group, Fellowship of Christian Athletes, student government, Wesleyan Chorale, Multicultural Student Association, Business Club. *Campus security:* 24-hour emergency response devices, student patrols, late-night transport/escort service, controlled dormitory access, evening patrols by security. *Student Services:* personal/psychological counseling.

Athletics Member NAIA, NSCAA. *Intercollegiate sports:* baseball M(s), basketball M(s)/W(s), cross-country running M(s)/W(s), football M(s), golf M(s)/W(s), soccer M(s)/W(s), softball W(s), tennis M(s)/W(s), track and field M(s)/W(s), volleyball W(s). *Intramural sports:* basketball M/W, bowling M/W, fencing M/W, football W, golf M/W, racquetball M/W, softball M/W, table tennis M/W, volleyball M/W, weight lifting M/W.

Standardized Tests *Required:* SAT I or ACT (for admission). *Recommended:* SAT I (for admission), ACT (for admission).

Costs (2001–02) *Comprehensive fee:* $18,000 includes full-time tuition ($13,400) and room and board ($4600). Part-time tuition: $160 per credit. Part-time tuition and fees vary according to course load. *Payment plan:* installment. *Waivers:* children of alumni, senior citizens, and employees or children of employees.

Financial Aid Of all full-time matriculated undergraduates who enrolled in 2001, 497 applied for aid, 452 were judged to have need, 429 had their need fully met. 100 Federal Work-Study jobs (averaging $790). 62 State and other part-time jobs (averaging $790). In 2001, 45 non-need-based awards were made. *Average percent of need met:* 95%. *Average financial aid package:* $15,495. *Average need-based loan:* $3739. *Average need-based gift aid:* $4346. *Average non-need based aid:* $6553.

Applying *Options:* common application, electronic application, deferred entrance. *Application fee:* $20. *Required:* high school transcript, minimum 2.5 GPA, minimum ACT composite score of 18. *Required for some:* essay or personal statement, 2 letters of recommendation, interview. *Application deadline:* rolling (freshmen), rolling (transfers). *Notification:* continuous (freshmen).

Admissions Contact Kansas Wesleyan University, 100 East Claflin, Salina, KS 67401-6196. *Phone:* 785-829-5541 Ext. 1283. *Toll-free phone:* 800-874-1154 Ext. 1285. *Fax:* 785-827-0927. *E-mail:* admissions@diamond.kwu.edu.

MANHATTAN CHRISTIAN COLLEGE
Manhattan, Kansas

- **Independent** 4-year, founded 1927, affiliated with Christian Churches and Churches of Christ
- **Calendar** semesters
- **Degrees** associate and bachelor's
- **Small-town** 10-acre campus
- **Endowment** $939,895
- **Coed,** 412 undergraduate students, 70% full-time, 55% women, 45% men
- **Minimally difficult** entrance level, 71% of applicants were admitted

Undergraduates 290 full-time, 122 part-time. Students come from 17 states and territories, 24% are from out of state, 2% African American, 0.3% Asian American or Pacific Islander, 1% Hispanic American, 0.3% Native American, 0.3% international, 8% transferred in, 65% live on campus. *Retention:* 63% of 2001 full-time freshmen returned.

Freshmen *Admission:* 116 applied, 82 admitted, 82 enrolled. *Average high school GPA:* 3.34. *Test scores:* SAT verbal scores over 500: 55%; SAT math scores over 500: 55%; ACT scores over 18: 94%; SAT verbal scores over 600: 22%; SAT math scores over 600: 22%; ACT scores over 24: 45%; ACT scores over 30: 4%.

Faculty *Total:* 31, 39% full-time, 10% with terminal degrees. *Student/faculty ratio:* 16:1.

Majors Biblical studies; business administration; divinity/ministry; missionary studies; pastoral counseling; religious education; religious music; religious studies; theology.

Academic Programs *Special study options:* academic remediation for entering students, advanced placement credit, internships, off-campus study, student-designed majors, summer session for credit. *Unusual degree programs:* 3-2 engineering with Kansas State University; nursing with Wichita State University, Washburn University, Kansas Wesleyan University; social work with Kansas State University.

Library Manhattan Christian College Library with 2,500 titles, 45 serial subscriptions.

Computers on Campus 12 computers available on campus for general student use. A campuswide network can be accessed from student residence rooms. Internet access, at least one staffed computer lab available.

Student Life *Housing:* on-campus residence required through sophomore year. *Options:* men-only, women-only. *Activities and Organizations:* drama/theater group, choral group, Student Council, Unspoken Message (drama and dance team), praise bands, Drama Team, Prison Ministry. *Student Services:* personal/psychological counseling.

Athletics Member NCCAA. *Intercollegiate sports:* basketball M/W, soccer M/W, tennis M/W, volleyball W. *Intramural sports:* softball M/W.

Standardized Tests *Required:* SAT I or ACT (for admission).

Costs (2002–03) *Comprehensive fee:* $11,920 includes full-time tuition ($7936), mandatory fees ($30), and room and board ($3954). Part-time tuition: $331 per hour. *Room and board:* Room and board charges vary according to board plan. *Payment plan:* installment. *Waivers:* senior citizens and employees or children of employees.

Financial Aid Of all full-time matriculated undergraduates who enrolled in 2001, 378 applied for aid, 299 were judged to have need, 14 had their need fully met. 42 Federal Work-Study jobs (averaging $1740). In 2001, 76 non-need-based awards were made. *Average financial aid package:* $5643. *Average need-based loan:* $3630. *Average need-based gift aid:* $2475. *Average non-need based aid:* $3380.

Applying *Application fee:* $25. *Required:* essay or personal statement, high school transcript, minimum 2.0 GPA, 3 letters of recommendation. *Required for some:* interview. *Application deadlines:* 8/1 (freshmen), 8/1 (transfers). *Notification:* continuous (freshmen).

Admissions Contact Mr. Scott Jenkins, Director of Admissions, Manhattan Christian College, 1415 Anderson, Manhattan, KS 66502-4081. *Phone:* 785-539-3571. *Toll-free phone:* 877-246-4622. *Fax:* 785-539-0832. *E-mail:* admit@mccks.edu.

McPherson College
McPherson, Kansas

- **Independent** 4-year, founded 1887, affiliated with Church of the Brethren
- **Calendar** 4-1-4
- **Degrees** associate and bachelor's
- **Small-town** 26-acre campus
- **Endowment** $31.4 million
- **Coed,** 397 undergraduate students, 91% full-time, 48% women, 52% men
- **Moderately difficult** entrance level, 78% of applicants were admitted

Undergraduates 362 full-time, 35 part-time. Students come from 30 states and territories, 5 other countries, 56% are from out of state, 12% African American, 0.8% Asian American or Pacific Islander, 10% Hispanic American, 0.8% Native American, 2% international, 7% transferred in, 70% live on campus. *Retention:* 45% of 2001 full-time freshmen returned.

Freshmen *Admission:* 461 applied, 359 admitted, 121 enrolled. *Average high school GPA:* 3.18. *Test scores:* SAT verbal scores over 500: 46%; SAT math scores over 500: 37%; ACT scores over 18: 81%; SAT verbal scores over 600: 6%; SAT math scores over 600: 10%; ACT scores over 24: 18%; SAT verbal scores over 700: 3%; ACT scores over 30: 1%.

Faculty *Total:* 48, 83% full-time, 58% with terminal degrees. *Student/faculty ratio:* 10:1.

Majors Accounting; agricultural business; agricultural economics; art; art education; auto mechanic/technician; behavioral sciences; biology; business administration; business education; chemistry; computer programming; computer science; early childhood education; education; education (K-12); elementary education; English; environmental science; finance; history; industrial arts; interdisciplinary studies; international business; mathematics; music; music teacher education; philosophy; physical education; physical sciences; pre-dentistry; pre-engineering; pre-law; pre-medicine; pre-pharmacy studies; pre-veterinary studies; psychology; religious studies; secondary education; social sciences; sociology; Spanish; special education; speech/theater education; theater arts/drama.

Academic Programs *Special study options:* academic remediation for entering students, adult/continuing education programs, advanced placement credit, cooperative education, double majors, English as a second language, independent study, internships, off-campus study, part-time degree program, services for LD students, student-designed majors, study abroad, summer session for credit.

Library Miller Library with 90,535 titles, 308 serial subscriptions, 4,484 audiovisual materials, an OPAC, a Web page.

Computers on Campus 60 computers available on campus for general student use. A campuswide network can be accessed from student residence rooms and from off campus. Internet access, at least one staffed computer lab available.

Student Life *Housing:* on-campus residence required through senior year. *Options:* coed, men-only, disabled students. *Activities and Organizations:* drama/theater group, student-run newspaper, choral group, Today's Educators, Spectator (newspaper), drama productions, athletics, choir. *Campus security:* student patrols, controlled dormitory access. *Student Services:* health clinic, personal/psychological counseling.

Athletics Member NAIA. *Intercollegiate sports:* basketball M/W, cross-country running M/W, football M, softball W, track and field M/W, volleyball W. *Intramural sports:* basketball M/W, football M/W, racquetball M/W, soccer M/W, softball M/W, table tennis M/W, volleyball M/W.

Standardized Tests *Required:* SAT I or ACT (for admission).

Costs (2002–03) *Comprehensive fee:* $18,545 includes full-time tuition ($13,125), mandatory fees ($220), and room and board ($5200). Part-time tuition: $450 per credit hour. Part-time tuition and fees vary according to course load. *Required fees:* $30 per term part-time. *Room and board:* College room only: $2205. Room and board charges vary according to board plan. *Payment plan:* installment. *Waivers:* senior citizens and employees or children of employees.

Financial Aid Of all full-time matriculated undergraduates who enrolled in 2001, 351 applied for aid, 306 were judged to have need, 47 had their need fully met. 196 Federal Work-Study jobs. In 2001, 52 non-need-based awards were made. *Average percent of need met:* 97%. *Average financial aid package:* $13,447. *Average need-based loan:* $4600. *Average need-based gift aid:* $4599. *Average non-need based aid:* $4649. *Average indebtedness upon graduation:* $19,910.

Applying *Options:* electronic application, deferred entrance. *Application fee:* $25. *Required:* high school transcript, minimum 2.0 GPA. *Application deadline:* rolling (freshmen), rolling (transfers). *Notification:* continuous (freshmen).

Admissions Contact Mr. Fred Schmidt, Dean of Enrollment, McPherson College, 1600 East Euclid, PO Box 1402, McPherson, KS 67460-1402. *Phone:* 316-241-0731 Ext. 1270. *Toll-free phone:* 800-365-7402 Ext. 1270. *Fax:* 316-241-8443 Ext. 1270. *E-mail:* admiss@mcpherson.edu.

MidAmerica Nazarene University
Olathe, Kansas

- **Independent** comprehensive, founded 1966, affiliated with Church of the Nazarene
- **Calendar** semesters
- **Degrees** associate, bachelor's, and master's
- **Suburban** 112-acre campus with easy access to Kansas City
- **Endowment** $16.1 million
- **Coed,** 1,290 undergraduate students, 89% full-time, 53% women, 47% men
- **Minimally difficult** entrance level, 51% of applicants were admitted

MidAmerica is a comprehensive, Christian liberal arts university committed to transforming students for a life of service to God, their country, and their world. The University offers undergraduate and graduate degrees with 44 majors in such areas as business, education, nursing, psychology, and criminal justice. The University is located just 20 miles from Kansas City.

Undergraduates 1,154 full-time, 136 part-time. Students come from 34 states and territories, 8 other countries, 39% are from out of state, 6% African American, 1% Asian American or Pacific Islander, 1% Hispanic American, 0.6% Native American, 0.5% international, 5% transferred in, 62% live on campus. *Retention:* 76% of 2001 full-time freshmen returned.

Freshmen *Admission:* 504 applied, 258 admitted, 294 enrolled. *Average high school GPA:* 3.30. *Test scores:* SAT verbal scores over 500: 71%; SAT math scores over 500: 67%; ACT scores over 18: 87%; SAT verbal scores over 600: 26%; SAT math scores over 600: 19%; ACT scores over 24: 37%; SAT verbal scores over 700: 7%; ACT scores over 30: 8%.

Faculty *Total:* 151, 26% with terminal degrees. *Student/faculty ratio:* 18:1.

Majors Accounting; agricultural business; athletic training/sports medicine; biology; business administration; business education; chemistry; chemistry education; computer science; criminal justice/law enforcement administration; divinity/ministry; elementary education; English; English education; exercise sciences; graphic design/commercial art/illustration; health education; history; human resources management; international agriculture; liberal arts and sciences/liberal studies; mass communications; mathematics; mathematics education; middle school education; missionary studies; modern languages; music; music teacher education; music (voice and choral/opera performance); nursing; physical education; physics; psychology; public relations; religious education; religious music; religious studies; science education; secondary education; social studies education; sociology; Spanish; Spanish language education; sport/fitness administration.

Academic Programs *Special study options:* academic remediation for entering students, accelerated degree program, adult/continuing education programs, advanced placement credit, double majors, independent study, internships, off-campus study, part-time degree program, services for LD students, study abroad, summer session for credit. *ROTC:* Army (c), Air Force (c).

Library Mabee Library with 80,560 titles, 1,025 serial subscriptions, an OPAC, a Web page.

Computers on Campus 85 computers available on campus for general student use. A campuswide network can be accessed from student residence rooms and from off campus. Internet access, at least one staffed computer lab available.

Student Life *Housing:* on-campus residence required through senior year. *Options:* men-only, women-only. *Activities and Organizations:* drama/theater group, student-run newspaper, radio and television station, choral group, Associated Student Government, Residence Hall Government, ministry groups, Intramurals, gospel station. *Campus security:* 24-hour emergency response devices and patrols, student patrols, late-night transport/escort service, controlled dormitory access. *Student Services:* health clinic, personal/psychological counseling.

Athletics Member NAIA, NCCAA. *Intercollegiate sports:* baseball M(s), basketball M(s)/W(s), cross-country running M(s)/W(s), football M(s), softball W(s), track and field M(s)/W(s), volleyball W(s). *Intramural sports:* basketball M/W, football M/W, softball M/W, table tennis M/W, tennis M/W, volleyball M/W.

MidAmerica Nazarene University (continued)

Standardized Tests *Required:* SAT I or ACT (for admission).

Costs (2002–03) *Comprehensive fee:* $17,894 includes full-time tuition ($11,270), mandatory fees ($1010), and room and board ($5614). Full-time tuition and fees vary according to course load. Part-time tuition: $380 per semester hour. Part-time tuition and fees vary according to course load. *Required fees:* $365 per term part-time. *Room and board:* Room and board charges vary according to board plan and housing facility. *Waivers:* senior citizens and employees or children of employees.

Financial Aid Of all full-time matriculated undergraduates who enrolled in 2001, 924 applied for aid, 834 were judged to have need, 34 had their need fully met. 93 Federal Work-Study jobs (averaging $1764). In 2001, 179 non-need-based awards were made. *Average percent of need met:* 60%. *Average financial aid package:* $8613. *Average need-based loan:* $4604. *Average need-based gift aid:* $4973. *Average non-need based aid:* $2707.

Applying *Options:* early admission, deferred entrance. *Application fee:* $15. *Required:* high school transcript, minimum 2.0 GPA, 1 letter of recommendation. *Application deadlines:* 8/1 (freshmen), 8/1 (transfers). *Notification:* continuous (freshmen).

Admissions Contact Mr. Mike Redwine, Vice President for Enrollment Development, MidAmerica Nazarene University, 2030 East College Way, Olathe, KS 66062-1899. *Phone:* 913-791-3380 Ext. 481. *Toll-free phone:* 800-800-8887. *Fax:* 913-791-3481. *E-mail:* admissions@mnu.edu.

NEWMAN UNIVERSITY
Wichita, Kansas

- **Independent Roman Catholic** comprehensive, founded 1933
- **Calendar** semesters
- **Degrees** associate, bachelor's, and master's
- **Urban** 53-acre campus
- **Endowment** $18.3 million
- **Coed,** 1,660 undergraduate students, 57% full-time, 66% women, 34% men
- **Minimally difficult** entrance level, 99% of applicants were admitted

Undergraduates 952 full-time, 708 part-time. Students come from 25 states and territories, 26 other countries, 13% are from out of state, 8% African American, 2% Asian American or Pacific Islander, 5% Hispanic American, 2% Native American, 3% international, 15% transferred in, 14% live on campus. *Retention:* 63% of 2001 full-time freshmen returned.

Freshmen *Admission:* 430 applied, 426 admitted, 144 enrolled. *Average high school GPA:* 3.35. *Test scores:* SAT verbal scores over 500: 75%; SAT math scores over 500: 75%; ACT scores over 18: 86%; SAT verbal scores over 600: 38%; SAT math scores over 600: 13%; ACT scores over 24: 38%; SAT verbal scores over 700: 13%; ACT scores over 30: 4%.

Faculty *Total:* 181, 38% full-time, 18% with terminal degrees. *Student/faculty ratio:* 14:1.

Majors Accounting; alcohol/drug abuse counseling; athletic training/sports medicine; biology; business administration; business marketing and marketing management; chemistry; education; elementary education; English; health science; history; industrial radiologic technology; information sciences/systems; liberal arts and sciences/liberal studies; mass communications; mathematics; mental health/rehabilitation; nursing; occupational therapy; pastoral counseling; pre-dentistry; pre-engineering; pre-law; pre-medicine; pre-veterinary studies; psychology; respiratory therapy; secondary education; sociology; theology.

Academic Programs *Special study options:* academic remediation for entering students, accelerated degree program, adult/continuing education programs, advanced placement credit, cooperative education, distance learning, double majors, external degree program, independent study, internships, off-campus study, part-time degree program, services for LD students, study abroad, summer session for credit. *Unusual degree programs:* 3-2 physical therapy with Washington University in St. Louis.

Library Ryan Library with 88,000 titles, 450 serial subscriptions.

Computers on Campus 90 computers available on campus for general student use. At least one staffed computer lab available.

Student Life *Housing:* on-campus residence required through sophomore year. *Options:* coed, women-only. *Activities and Organizations:* drama/theater group, student-run newspaper, choral group, Student Activities Board, chorale, International Club, Chemistry/Pre-Med Club, Newman Occupational Therapy Student Association. *Campus security:* 24-hour patrols, late-night transport/escort service. *Student Services:* personal/psychological counseling.

Athletics Member NAIA. *Intercollegiate sports:* baseball M(s), basketball M(s)/W(s), cross-country running M(s)/W(s), golf M(s)/W(s), soccer M(s)/W(s), softball W(s), volleyball M(s)/W(s). *Intramural sports:* baseball M, basketball M/W, bowling M/W, cross-country running M/W, football M/W, golf M/W, soccer M/W, softball M/W, table tennis M/W, volleyball M/W, weight lifting M/W.

Standardized Tests *Required:* SAT I or ACT (for admission).

Costs (2002–03) *Comprehensive fee:* $16,630 includes full-time tuition ($11,890), mandatory fees ($150), and room and board ($4590). Part-time tuition: $396 per credit hour. *Required fees:* $5 per credit hour.

Financial Aid Of all full-time matriculated undergraduates who enrolled in 2001, 954 applied for aid, 782 were judged to have need, 214 had their need fully met. 88 Federal Work-Study jobs (averaging $982). 89 State and other part-time jobs (averaging $1267). In 2001, 193 non-need-based awards were made. *Average percent of need met:* 75%. *Average financial aid package:* $9260. *Average need-based loan:* $1743. *Average need-based gift aid:* $1122. *Average non-need based aid:* $3329. *Average indebtedness upon graduation:* $17,168.

Applying *Options:* early admission, deferred entrance. *Application fee:* $20. *Required:* high school transcript, minimum 2.0 GPA. *Recommended:* interview. *Application deadline:* rolling (freshmen), rolling (transfers). *Notification:* continuous (freshmen).

Admissions Contact Mrs. Marla Sexson, Dean of Admissions, Newman University, 3100 McCormick Avenue, Wichita, KS 67213. *Phone:* 316-942-4291 Ext. 144. *Toll-free phone:* 877-NEWMANU Ext. 144. *Fax:* 316-942-4483. *E-mail:* admissions@newmanu.edu.

OTTAWA UNIVERSITY
Ottawa, Kansas

- **Independent American Baptist Churches in the USA** comprehensive, founded 1865
- **Calendar** semesters
- **Degrees** bachelor's and master's (also offers adult, international and on-line education programs with significant enrollment not reflected in profile)
- **Small-town** 60-acre campus with easy access to Kansas City
- **Endowment** $12.7 million
- **Coed,** 433 undergraduate students, 94% full-time, 45% women, 55% men
- **Moderately difficult** entrance level, 68% of applicants were admitted

At Ottawa University, the residence halls are considered the student's home away from home. Choices of campus housing include a traditional coed residence hall as well as suite arrangements in New Hall and Martin Hall. Within these suites, 3-7 students share a common living room as well as a bathroom, 2-3 bedrooms, and a small kitchen area.

Undergraduates 409 full-time, 24 part-time. Students come from 19 states and territories, 4 other countries, 61% are from out of state, 11% African American, 0.5% Asian American or Pacific Islander, 4% Hispanic American, 2% Native American, 4% international, 10% transferred in, 52% live on campus. *Retention:* 54% of 2001 full-time freshmen returned.

Freshmen *Admission:* 451 applied, 305 admitted, 115 enrolled. *Average high school GPA:* 3.22. *Test scores:* ACT scores over 18: 83%; ACT scores over 24: 26%.

Faculty *Total:* 32, 56% full-time, 47% with terminal degrees. *Student/faculty ratio:* 14:1.

Majors Art; art education; biology; business administration; elementary education; English; history; human services; information sciences/systems; mass communications; mathematics; music; music teacher education; physical education; political science; psychology; religious studies; sociology; theater arts/drama.

Academic Programs *Special study options:* advanced placement credit, double majors, English as a second language, independent study, internships, part-time degree program, student-designed majors, summer session for credit. *Unusual degree programs:* 3-2 engineering with Kansas State University.

Library Myers Library with 80,500 titles, 310 serial subscriptions.

Computers on Campus 71 computers available on campus for general student use. A campuswide network can be accessed from student residence rooms and from off campus. Internet access, online (class) registration, at least one staffed computer lab available.

Student Life *Housing:* on-campus residence required through junior year. *Options:* men-only, women-only. *Activities and Organizations:* drama/theater group, student-run newspaper, radio station, choral group, Christian Faith In Action, Student Activities Force, education club, Whole Earth club, Fellowship of Christian Athletes. *Campus security:* 24-hour emergency response devices and patrols, locked residence hall entrances. *Student Services:* health clinic, personal/psychological counseling.

Athletics Member NAIA. *Intercollegiate sports:* baseball M(s), basketball M(s)/W(s), cross-country running M(s)/W(s), football M(s), golf M(s), soccer M(s)/W(s), softball W(s), track and field M(s)/W(s), volleyball W(s). *Intramural sports:* badminton M/W, basketball M/W, bowling M/W, golf M/W, racquetball M/W, tennis M/W, volleyball M/W, weight lifting M/W.

Standardized Tests *Required:* SAT I or ACT (for admission).
Costs (2001–02) *Comprehensive fee:* $16,960 includes full-time tuition ($11,550), mandatory fees ($250), and room and board ($5160). Full-time tuition and fees vary according to course load. Part-time tuition: $285 per credit hour. Part-time tuition and fees vary according to course load. *Required fees:* $65 per term part-time. *Room and board:* College room only: $2400. Room and board charges vary according to board plan and housing facility. *Payment plans:* installment, deferred payment. *Waivers:* senior citizens and employees or children of employees.
Applying *Options:* electronic application. *Application fee:* $15. *Required:* high school transcript, minimum 2.5 GPA. *Required for some:* essay or personal statement. *Recommended:* 2 letters of recommendation, interview. *Application deadline:* rolling (freshmen), rolling (transfers). *Notification:* continuous (freshmen).
Admissions Contact Ms. Lanette Stineman, Director of Admissions, Ottawa University, 1001 South Cedar, Ottawa, KS 66067-3399. *Phone:* 785-242-5200 Ext. 1051. *Toll-free phone:* 800-755-5200. *Fax:* 785-242-7429. *E-mail:* wwwadmiss@ottawa.edu.

PITTSBURG STATE UNIVERSITY
Pittsburg, Kansas

- **State-supported** comprehensive, founded 1903, part of Kansas Board of Regents
- **Calendar** semesters
- **Degrees** certificates, associate, bachelor's, and master's
- **Small-town** 233-acre campus
- **Endowment** $29.1 million
- **Coed,** 5,470 undergraduate students, 89% full-time, 48% women, 52% men
- **Noncompetitive** entrance level, 66% of applicants were admitted

Undergraduates Students come from 50 states and territories, 57 other countries, 13% are from out of state, 20% live on campus. *Retention:* 87% of 2001 full-time freshmen returned.
Freshmen *Admission:* 1,585 applied, 1,052 admitted. *Average high school GPA:* 3.28. *Test scores:* ACT scores over 18: 79%; ACT scores over 24: 26%; ACT scores over 30: 4%.
Faculty *Total:* 269. *Student/faculty ratio:* 23:1.
Majors Accounting; adult/continuing education; advertising; art; art education; art therapy; auto mechanic/technician; biology; broadcast journalism; business administration; business economics; business marketing and marketing management; chemistry; child care/development; computer programming; computer science; construction management; construction technology; counselor education/guidance; criminal justice/law enforcement administration; criminal justice studies; early childhood education; economics; education; electrical/electronic engineering technology; elementary education; engineering technology; English; environmental biology; environmental science; fashion merchandising; finance; fine/studio arts; fish/game management; French; geography; graphic design/commercial art/illustration; graphic/printing equipment; health education; heavy equipment maintenance; history; home economics; home economics education; industrial arts; industrial design; industrial technology; information sciences/systems; interior design; journalism; liberal arts and sciences/liberal studies; mass communications; mathematics; mechanical design technology; mechanical engineering technology; medical technology; mental health/rehabilitation; music; music (piano and organ performance); music teacher education; music (voice and choral/opera performance); nursing; physical education; physical sciences; physical therapy; physics; plastics technology; political science; pre-dentistry; pre-law; pre-medicine; pre-veterinary studies; psychology; public relations; radio/television broadcasting; recreational therapy; recreation/leisure studies; science education; secondary education; social sciences; social work; sociology; Spanish; speech/rhetorical studies; stringed instruments; trade/industrial education; wildlife management; wind/percussion instruments; wood science/paper technology.
Academic Programs *Special study options:* academic remediation for entering students, adult/continuing education programs, advanced placement credit, cooperative education, double majors, English as a second language, external degree program, freshman honors college, honors programs, independent study, internships, part-time degree program, services for LD students, student-designed majors, study abroad, summer session for credit. *ROTC:* Army (b). *Unusual degree programs:* 3-2 engineering with Kansas State University, University of Kansas.
Library Leonard H. Axe Library plus 2 others with 290,798 titles, 1,368 serial subscriptions, an OPAC, a Web page.
Computers on Campus 213 computers available on campus for general student use. A campuswide network can be accessed from student residence rooms and from off campus. Internet access, online (class) registration, at least one staffed computer lab available.
Student Life *Housing:* on-campus residence required for freshman year. *Options:* coed. *Activities and Organizations:* drama/theater group, student-run newspaper, radio and television station, choral group, marching band, Student Government Association, student yearbook, student newspaper, national fraternities, national sororities. *Campus security:* 24-hour emergency response devices and patrols, student patrols, controlled dormitory access. *Student Services:* health clinic, personal/psychological counseling, legal services.
Athletics Member NCAA. All Division II. *Intercollegiate sports:* baseball M(s), basketball M(s)/W(s), cross-country running M(s)/W, football M(s), golf M(s), softball W(s), track and field M(s)/W(s), volleyball W(s). *Intramural sports:* archery M/W, badminton M/W, basketball M/W, cross-country running M/W, football M/W, racquetball M/W, rugby M(c), soccer M(c), softball M/W, swimming M/W, table tennis M/W, tennis M/W, track and field M/W, volleyball M/W, water polo M/W, weight lifting M.
Standardized Tests *Required:* ACT (for admission).
Costs (2001–02) *Tuition:* state resident $2338 full-time, $85 per credit hour part-time; nonresident $7192 full-time, $247 per credit hour part-time. *Room and board:* $3890. Room and board charges vary according to board plan. *Payment plan:* installment. *Waivers:* employees or children of employees.
Financial Aid Of all full-time matriculated undergraduates who enrolled in 2001, 3375 applied for aid, 2769 were judged to have need, 478 had their need fully met. 292 Federal Work-Study jobs, 1191 State and other part-time jobs (averaging $2117). In 2001, 761 non-need-based awards were made. *Average percent of need met:* 84%. *Average financial aid package:* $6098. *Average need-based loan:* $3677. *Average need-based gift aid:* $3499. *Average non-need based aid:* $1883. *Average indebtedness upon graduation:* $10,860.
Applying *Options:* common application, electronic application, early admission, deferred entrance. *Application fee:* $25. *Required:* high school transcript. *Required for some:* minimum 2.0 GPA, ACT. *Application deadline:* rolling (freshmen), rolling (transfers).
Admissions Contact Ms. Ange Peterson, Director of Admission and Retention, Pittsburg State University, Pittsburg, KS 66762. *Phone:* 620-235-4251. *Toll-free phone:* 800-854-7488 Ext. 1. *Fax:* 316-235-6003. *E-mail:* psuadmit@pittstate.edu.

SAINT MARY COLLEGE
Leavenworth, Kansas

- **Independent Roman Catholic** comprehensive, founded 1923
- **Calendar** semesters
- **Degrees** associate, bachelor's, and master's
- **Small-town** 240-acre campus with easy access to Kansas City
- **Endowment** $10.6 million
- **Coed,** 484 undergraduate students, 70% full-time, 62% women, 38% men
- **Moderately difficult** entrance level, 29% of applicants were admitted

Undergraduates 337 full-time, 147 part-time. Students come from 20 states and territories, 1 other country, 24% are from out of state, 8% African American, 2% Asian American or Pacific Islander, 4% Hispanic American, 1% Native American, 0.7% international, 14% transferred in. *Retention:* 64% of 2001 full-time freshmen returned.
Freshmen *Admission:* 498 applied, 145 admitted, 86 enrolled. *Average high school GPA:* 3.34. *Test scores:* ACT scores over 18: 84%; ACT scores over 24: 15%.
Faculty *Total:* 112, 40% full-time, 43% with terminal degrees. *Student/faculty ratio:* 12:1.
Majors Accounting; art; biology; business administration; chemistry; community psychology; community services; elementary education; English; history; information sciences/systems; interdisciplinary studies; liberal arts and sciences/liberal studies; mass communications; mathematics; political science; psychology; sociology; Spanish; theater arts/drama; theology; visual/performing arts.
Academic Programs *Special study options:* adult/continuing education programs, advanced placement credit, double majors, honors programs, independent study, internships, off-campus study, part-time degree program, student-designed majors, study abroad, summer session for credit. *ROTC:* Army (c).
Library De Paul Library with 114,175 titles, 363 serial subscriptions, 1,742 audiovisual materials, an OPAC, a Web page.
Computers on Campus 95 computers available on campus for general student use. A campuswide network can be accessed from student residence rooms. Internet access, at least one staffed computer lab available.
Student Life *Housing:* on-campus residence required through senior year. *Options:* coed. *Activities and Organizations:* drama/theater group, student-run newspaper, choral group, Student Government Association, BACCHUS, Theatrical Union, Campus Ministry, Amnesty International. *Campus security:* late-

Saint Mary College (continued)
night transport/escort service, controlled dormitory access. *Student Services:* health clinic, personal/psychological counseling.

Athletics Member NAIA. *Intercollegiate sports:* baseball M(s), basketball M(s)/W(s), football M(s), soccer M(s)/W(s), softball W(s), tennis M(s)/W(s), volleyball W(s). *Intramural sports:* badminton M/W, basketball M/W, bowling M/W, cross-country running M/W, football M/W, racquetball M/W, soccer M/W, softball M/W, swimming M/W, table tennis M/W, tennis M/W, volleyball M/W, weight lifting M/W.

Standardized Tests *Required:* SAT I or ACT (for admission).

Costs (2002–03) *Comprehensive fee:* $18,250 includes full-time tuition ($12,928), mandatory fees ($200), and room and board ($5122). Part-time tuition: $418 per credit hour. Part-time tuition and fees vary according to course load. *Required fees:* $55 per term part-time. *Payment plan:* installment. *Waivers:* minority students, adult students, senior citizens, and employees or children of employees.

Financial Aid Of all full-time matriculated undergraduates who enrolled in 2001, 258 applied for aid, 186 were judged to have need, 79 had their need fully met. 108 Federal Work-Study jobs (averaging $644). In 2001, 72 non-need-based awards were made. *Average percent of need met:* 86%. *Average financial aid package:* $10,851. *Average need-based loan:* $3225. *Average need-based gift aid:* $3725. *Average indebtedness upon graduation:* $13,275.

Applying *Options:* common application, electronic application, early admission, deferred entrance. *Application fee:* $20. *Required:* high school transcript, minimum 2.2 GPA, 1 letter of recommendation. *Recommended:* interview. *Application deadline:* rolling (freshmen), rolling (transfers). *Notification:* continuous (freshmen).

Admissions Contact Mr. Todd Moore, Enrollment Services Director, Saint Mary College, 4100 South Fourth Street, Leavenworth, KS 66048. *Phone:* 913-682-5151 Ext. 6118. *Toll-free phone:* 800-758-6140. *E-mail:* admis@hub.smcks.edu.

SOUTHWESTERN COLLEGE
Winfield, Kansas

- **Independent United Methodist** comprehensive, founded 1885
- **Calendar** semesters
- **Degrees** bachelor's and master's
- **Small-town** 70-acre campus with easy access to Wichita
- **Endowment** $19.3 million
- **Coed,** 1,175 undergraduate students, 50% full-time, 50% women, 50% men
- **Moderately difficult** entrance level, 72% of applicants were admitted

Undergraduates 583 full-time, 592 part-time. Students come from 18 states and territories, 9 other countries, 18% are from out of state, 63% live on campus. *Retention:* 64% of 2001 full-time freshmen returned.

Freshmen *Admission:* 398 applied, 285 admitted, 131 enrolled. *Average high school GPA:* 3.48. *Test scores:* ACT scores over 18: 80%; ACT scores over 24: 36%; ACT scores over 30: 2%.

Faculty *Total:* 100, 49% full-time. *Student/faculty ratio:* 13:1.

Majors Athletic training/sports medicine; biochemistry; biology; business administration; chemistry; communications; computer/information sciences; computer/information sciences related; criminal justice studies; drama/dance education; early childhood education; elementary education; English; English education; foreign languages education; foreign languages/literatures; general studies; health/physical education; history; human resources management; industrial production technologies related; industrial technology; liberal arts and sciences/liberal studies; management information systems/business data processing; management science; marine biology; mathematics; mathematics education; music; music teacher education; nursing; philosophy and religion related; physical education; physics; pre-theology; psychology; science education; sport/fitness administration; theater arts/drama.

Academic Programs *Special study options:* academic remediation for entering students, adult/continuing education programs, advanced placement credit, double majors, external degree program, honors programs, independent study, internships, part-time degree program, student-designed majors, study abroad, summer session for credit. *Unusual degree programs:* 3-2 engineering with Washington University in St. Louis.

Library Memorial Library plus 1 other with 75,000 titles, 300 serial subscriptions, an OPAC, a Web page.

Computers on Campus 55 computers available on campus for general student use. A campuswide network can be accessed from student residence rooms and from off campus. Internet access, at least one staffed computer lab available.

Student Life *Housing:* on-campus residence required for freshman year. *Options:* coed, men-only, women-only. *Activities and Organizations:* drama/theater group, student-run newspaper, radio and television station, choral group, Student Activities Association, student government, Fellowship of Christian Athletes, Campus Council on Ministries, international club, national fraternities, national sororities. *Campus security:* 24-hour emergency response devices, late-night transport/escort service. *Student Services:* health clinic, personal/psychological counseling.

Athletics Member NAIA. *Intercollegiate sports:* basketball M(s)/W(s), cross-country running M(s)/W(s), football M(s), golf M(s)/W(s), soccer M(s)/W(s), tennis M(s)/W(s), track and field M(s)/W(s), volleyball W(s). *Intramural sports:* baseball M/W, basketball M/W, bowling M/W, softball M/W.

Standardized Tests *Required:* SAT I or ACT (for admission).

Costs (2001–02) *Comprehensive fee:* $17,656 includes full-time tuition ($12,090), mandatory fees ($986), and room and board ($4580). Full-time tuition and fees vary according to degree level and location. Part-time tuition: $507 per semester hour. Part-time tuition and fees vary according to degree level and location. *Room and board:* College room only: $1980. Room and board charges vary according to board plan, housing facility, and location. *Payment plan:* installment. *Waivers:* senior citizens and employees or children of employees.

Financial Aid Of all full-time matriculated undergraduates who enrolled in 2001, 539 applied for aid, 479 were judged to have need, 207 had their need fully met. In 2001, 99 non-need-based awards were made. *Average percent of need met:* 88%. *Average financial aid package:* $12,576. *Average need-based loan:* $5203. *Average need-based gift aid:* $7931. *Average non-need based aid:* $4400. *Average indebtedness upon graduation:* $15,206. *Financial aid deadline:* 8/1.

Applying *Options:* deferred entrance. *Application fee:* $20. *Required:* essay or personal statement, high school transcript, minimum 2.0 GPA. *Required for some:* interview. *Application deadlines:* 8/1 (freshmen), 8/1 (transfers). *Notification:* continuous (freshmen).

Admissions Contact Ms. Brenda D. Hicks, Director of Admission, Southwestern College, Winfield, KS 67156-2499. *Phone:* 620-229-6236. *Toll-free phone:* 800-846-1543. *Fax:* 620-229-6344. *E-mail:* scadmit@sckans.edu.

STERLING COLLEGE
Sterling, Kansas

- **Independent Presbyterian** 4-year, founded 1887
- **Calendar** 4-1-4
- **Degree** bachelor's
- **Small-town** 46-acre campus
- **Endowment** $7.0 million
- **Coed,** 461 undergraduate students, 95% full-time, 52% women, 48% men
- **Minimally difficult** entrance level, 59% of applicants were admitted

Undergraduates 439 full-time, 22 part-time. Students come from 29 states and territories, 35% are from out of state, 5% African American, 0.7% Asian American or Pacific Islander, 5% Hispanic American, 0.7% Native American, 2% international, 12% transferred in, 79% live on campus. *Retention:* 65% of 2001 full-time freshmen returned.

Freshmen *Admission:* 437 applied, 257 admitted, 106 enrolled. *Average high school GPA:* 3.34. *Test scores:* SAT verbal scores over 500: 44%; SAT math scores over 500: 56%; ACT scores over 18: 85%; SAT verbal scores over 600: 31%; SAT math scores over 600: 12%; ACT scores over 24: 46%; ACT scores over 30: 6%.

Faculty *Total:* 50, 72% full-time, 42% with terminal degrees. *Student/faculty ratio:* 12:1.

Majors Art; athletic training/sports medicine; behavioral sciences; biology; business administration; communications related; computer/information sciences; elementary education; English; history; interdisciplinary studies; mathematics; music; music teacher education; philosophy and religion related; physical education; religious education; theater arts/drama.

Academic Programs *Special study options:* advanced placement credit, double majors, honors programs, independent study, internships, off-campus study, student-designed majors, study abroad.

Library Mabee Library with 92,304 titles, 403 serial subscriptions, 1,982 audiovisual materials, an OPAC.

Computers on Campus 86 computers available on campus for general student use. Internet access, at least one staffed computer lab available.

Student Life *Housing:* on-campus residence required through senior year. *Options:* men-only, women-only. *Activities and Organizations:* drama/theater group, student-run newspaper, choral group, Fellowship of Christian Athletes, Student Activities Council, My Brother's Keeper, Habitat for Humanity, Youth Ministries. *Campus security:* controlled dormitory access, late night security patrol. *Student Services:* personal/psychological counseling.

Athletics Member NAIA. *Intercollegiate sports:* baseball M(s), basketball M(s)/W(s), cross-country running M(s)/W(s), football M(s), soccer M(s)/W(s), softball W(s), tennis M(s)/W(s), track and field M(s)/W(s), volleyball W(s). *Intramural sports:* basketball M/W, golf M/W, soccer M/W, softball M/W, tennis M/W, volleyball M/W.

Standardized Tests *Required:* SAT I or ACT (for admission).

Costs (2001–02) *One-time required fee:* $100. *Comprehensive fee:* $17,120 includes full-time tuition ($12,100) and room and board ($5020). Full-time tuition and fees vary according to course load. Part-time tuition: $265 per credit. Part-time tuition and fees vary according to course load. *Room and board:* College room only: $2080. Room and board charges vary according to board plan and housing facility. *Payment plan:* installment. *Waivers:* senior citizens and employees or children of employees.

Financial Aid Of all full-time matriculated undergraduates who enrolled in 2001, 407 applied for aid, 307 were judged to have need, 109 had their need fully met. 143 Federal Work-Study jobs (averaging $589). 175 State and other part-time jobs (averaging $717). In 2001, 97 non-need-based awards were made. *Average percent of need met:* 92%. *Average financial aid package:* $11,927. *Average need-based loan:* $3590. *Average need-based gift aid:* $6488. *Average non-need based aid:* $4488. *Average indebtedness upon graduation:* $14,296.

Applying *Options:* common application, electronic application, early action, deferred entrance. *Application fee:* $25. *Required:* high school transcript, minimum 2.2 GPA. *Required for some:* letters of recommendation. *Recommended:* essay or personal statement. *Application deadline:* rolling (freshmen), rolling (transfers). *Notification:* continuous (freshmen), 12/1 (early action).

Admissions Contact Mr. Calvin White, Vice President for Enrollment Services, Sterling College, PO Box 98, Sterling, KS 67579-0098. *Phone:* 620-278-4364 Ext. 364. *Toll-free phone:* 800-346-1017. *Fax:* 620-278-4416. *E-mail:* admissions@sterling.edu.

TABOR COLLEGE
Hillsboro, Kansas

- **Independent Mennonite Brethren** comprehensive, founded 1908
- **Calendar** 4-1-4
- **Degrees** associate, bachelor's, and master's
- **Small-town** 26-acre campus with easy access to Wichita
- **Endowment** $3.6 million
- **Coed,** 572 undergraduate students, 71% full-time, 51% women, 49% men
- **Moderately difficult** entrance level, 35% of applicants were admitted

Undergraduates 406 full-time, 166 part-time. Students come from 22 states and territories, 4 other countries, 33% are from out of state, 6% African American, 0.8% Asian American or Pacific Islander, 2% Hispanic American, 0.8% Native American, 1% international, 4% transferred in, 81% live on campus. *Retention:* 69% of 2001 full-time freshmen returned.

Freshmen *Admission:* 280 applied, 98 admitted, 99 enrolled. *Average high school GPA:* 3.37. *Test scores:* ACT scores over 18: 89%; ACT scores over 24: 39%; ACT scores over 30: 3%.

Faculty *Total:* 55, 47% full-time, 36% with terminal degrees. *Student/faculty ratio:* 13:1.

Majors Accounting; actuarial science; adult/continuing education; agricultural business; art education; athletic training/sports medicine; biblical studies; biological/physical sciences; biology; business administration; business education; business marketing and marketing management; chemistry; communications; computer science; divinity/ministry; early childhood education; education; education (K-12); elementary education; English; environmental biology; health education; history; humanities; interdisciplinary studies; international relations; journalism; legal administrative assistant; mass communications; mathematics; medical administrative assistant; medical technology; music; music business management/merchandising; music (piano and organ performance); music teacher education; music (voice and choral/opera performance); natural sciences; pastoral counseling; philosophy; physical education; pre-dentistry; pre-medicine; psychology; public relations; religious studies; science education; secondary education; secretarial science; social sciences; sociology; special education.

Academic Programs *Special study options:* academic remediation for entering students, accelerated degree program, adult/continuing education programs, advanced placement credit, cooperative education, distance learning, double majors, external degree program, honors programs, independent study, internships, off-campus study, part-time degree program, services for LD students, student-designed majors, study abroad, summer session for credit.

Library Tabor College Library with 80,754 titles, 265 serial subscriptions, 945 audiovisual materials, an OPAC, a Web page.

Computers on Campus 57 computers available on campus for general student use. A campuswide network can be accessed from student residence rooms and from off campus. Internet access, at least one staffed computer lab available.

Student Life *Housing:* on-campus residence required through senior year. *Options:* men-only, women-only, disabled students. *Activities and Organizations:* drama/theater group, student-run newspaper, choral group, Student Activities Board, Student Senate, Campus Ministries Council, Fellowship of Christian Athletes, Share, Prayer, and Dare. *Campus security:* student patrols. *Student Services:* personal/psychological counseling.

Athletics Member NAIA. *Intercollegiate sports:* baseball M(s), basketball M(s)/W(s), cross-country running M(s)/W(s), football M(s), golf M(s)/W(s), soccer M(s)/W(s), softball W(s), tennis M(s)/W(s), track and field M(s)/W(s), volleyball W(s). *Intramural sports:* basketball M/W, football M/W, golf M/W, racquetball M/W, soccer M/W, table tennis M/W, tennis M/W, track and field M/W, volleyball M/W, weight lifting M/W.

Standardized Tests *Required:* SAT I or ACT (for admission).

Costs (2001–02) *Comprehensive fee:* $17,900 includes full-time tuition ($12,680), mandatory fees ($320), and room and board ($4900). Part-time tuition: $528 per credit hour. Part-time tuition and fees vary according to course load and location. *Required fees:* $320 per term part-time. *Room and board:* College room only: $1700. Room and board charges vary according to board plan, housing facility, and location. *Payment plan:* installment. *Waivers:* children of alumni, adult students, senior citizens, and employees or children of employees.

Financial Aid Of all full-time matriculated undergraduates who enrolled in 2001, 390 applied for aid, 343 were judged to have need, 117 had their need fully met. 183 Federal Work-Study jobs (averaging $608). 135 State and other part-time jobs (averaging $719). In 2001, 87 non-need-based awards were made. *Average percent of need met:* 90%. *Average financial aid package:* $12,540. *Average need-based loan:* $4536. *Average need-based gift aid:* $3322. *Average non-need based aid:* $3938. *Average indebtedness upon graduation:* $16,851. *Financial aid deadline:* 8/15.

Applying *Options:* common application, electronic application, deferred entrance. *Application fee:* $20. *Required:* essay or personal statement, high school transcript, minimum 2.0 GPA, 2 letters of recommendation, ACT-18. *Recommended:* minimum 3.0 GPA, interview. *Application deadlines:* 8/1 (freshmen), 8/1 (transfers). *Notification:* continuous (freshmen).

Admissions Contact Ms. Cara Mars, Director of Admissions, Tabor College, 400 South Jefferson, Hillsboro, KS 67063. *Phone:* 620-947-3121 Ext. 1727. *Toll-free phone:* 800-822-6799. *Fax:* 620-947-2607. *E-mail:* admissions@tabor.edu.

UNIVERSITY OF KANSAS
Lawrence, Kansas

- **State-supported** university, founded 1866
- **Calendar** semesters
- **Degrees** bachelor's, master's, doctoral, first professional, post-master's, and first professional certificates (University of Kansas is a single institution with academic programs and facilities at two primary locations: Lawrence and Kansas City. Undergraduate, graduate, and professional education are the principal missions of the Lawrence campus, with medicine and related professional education the focus of the Kansas City campus)
- **Suburban** 1000-acre campus with easy access to Kansas City
- **Endowment** $1.1 billion
- **Coed,** 20,062 undergraduate students, 90% full-time, 53% women, 47% men
- **Moderately difficult** entrance level, 69% of applicants were admitted

Undergraduates Students come from 53 states and territories, 116 other countries, 24% are from out of state, 3% African American, 3% Asian American or Pacific Islander, 3% Hispanic American, 0.9% Native American, 4% international, 23% live on campus. *Retention:* 80% of 2001 full-time freshmen returned.

Freshmen *Admission:* 8,479 applied, 5,861 admitted. *Average high school GPA:* 3.44. *Test scores:* ACT scores over 18: 96%; ACT scores over 24: 58%; ACT scores over 30: 13%.

Faculty *Total:* 1,749, 78% full-time, 84% with terminal degrees. *Student/faculty ratio:* 15:1.

Majors Accounting; advertising; aerospace engineering; African-American studies; African studies; American studies; anthropology; archaeology; architectural engineering; architecture; architecture related; art; art education; art history; astronomy; atmospheric sciences; biochemistry; biological/physical sciences; biology; broadcast journalism; business; chemical engineering; chemistry; Chinese; civil engineering; classics; cognitive psychology/psycholinguistics; communication disorders; computer engineering; computer/information sciences; cytotechnology; dance; design/visual communications; developmental/child psychology; East and Southeast Asian languages related; economics; electrical engineering; elementary education; engineering physics; English; European studies; fine/studio arts; French; geography; geology; German; health education; health/physical education; history; humanities; international relations; Japanese;

University of Kansas (continued)
journalism; Latin American studies; liberal arts and sciences/liberal studies; linguistics; mathematics; mechanical engineering; medical records administration; medical technology; microbiology/bacteriology; middle school education; music; music history; music (piano and organ performance); music teacher education; music theory and composition; music therapy; music (voice and choral/opera performance); nursing science; painting; petroleum engineering; philosophy; physical education; physics; political science; printmaking; psychology; radio/television broadcasting; religious studies; respiratory therapy; Russian; Russian/Slavic studies; sculpture; secondary education; social work; sociology; Spanish; speech/rhetorical studies; stringed instruments; systems science/theory; theater arts/drama; theater design; wind/percussion instruments; women's studies.

Academic Programs *Special study options:* academic remediation for entering students, accelerated degree program, adult/continuing education programs, advanced placement credit, cooperative education, distance learning, double majors, English as a second language, honors programs, independent study, internships, part-time degree program, services for LD students, student-designed majors, study abroad, summer session for credit. *ROTC:* Army (b), Navy (b), Air Force (b).

Library Watson Library plus 11 others with 4.4 million titles, 32,722 serial subscriptions, 48,554 audiovisual materials, an OPAC, a Web page.

Computers on Campus 938 computers available on campus for general student use. A campuswide network can be accessed from student residence rooms and from off campus. Internet access, at least one staffed computer lab available.

Student Life *Housing Options:* coed, women-only, cooperative. *Activities and Organizations:* drama/theater group, student-run newspaper, radio and television station, choral group, marching band, Center for Community Outreach, Graduate and Professional Association, St. Lawrence Catholic Campus Center, Panhellenic, International Student Association, national fraternities, national sororities. *Campus security:* 24-hour emergency response devices and patrols, late-night transport/escort service, controlled dormitory access, KU has a police department; security guards are included. *Student Services:* health clinic, personal/psychological counseling, women's center, legal services.

Athletics Member NCAA. All Division I except football (Division I-A). *Intercollegiate sports:* baseball M(s), basketball M(s)/W(s), crew M(c)/W(s), cross-country running M(s)/W(s), fencing M(c)/W(c), golf M(s)/W(s), rugby M(c)/W(c), soccer M(c)/W(s), softball W(s), swimming W(s), tennis W(s), track and field M(s)/W(s), volleyball W(s). *Intramural sports:* badminton M(c)/W(c), basketball M/W, bowling M/W, crew M(c)/W(c), football M/W, golf M/W, ice hockey M(c)/W(c), lacrosse W(c), racquetball M/W, sailing M(c)/W(c), soccer M/W, softball M/W, swimming M/W, table tennis M/W, tennis M/W, water polo M(c)/W(c), wrestling M(c).

Standardized Tests *Required:* SAT I or ACT (for admission).

Costs (2001–02) *Tuition:* state resident $2333 full-time, $78 per credit hour part-time; nonresident $9260 full-time, $309 per credit hour part-time. Full-time tuition and fees vary according to course load and program. Part-time tuition and fees vary according to course load and program. *Required fees:* $551 full-time, $46 per credit hour. *Room and board:* $4348. Room and board charges vary according to board plan and housing facility. *Payment plan:* installment. *Waivers:* senior citizens and employees or children of employees.

Financial Aid Of all full-time matriculated undergraduates who enrolled in 2001, 8600 applied for aid, 6104 were judged to have need, 1928 had their need fully met. 606 Federal Work-Study jobs (averaging $1630). 86 State and other part-time jobs (averaging $3879). In 2001, 2429 non-need-based awards were made. *Average percent of need met:* 75%. *Average financial aid package:* $6118. *Average need-based loan:* $3622. *Average need-based gift aid:* $3248. *Average indebtedness upon graduation:* $17,002.

Applying *Options:* electronic application, deferred entrance. *Application fee:* $25. *Required:* high school transcript, minimum 2.0 GPA, Kansas Board of Regents admissions criteria with GPA of 2.0/2.5, top third of high school class. *Required for some:* minimum 2.5 GPA. *Application deadline:* 4/1 (freshmen), rolling (transfers). *Notification:* continuous (freshmen).

Admissions Contact Mr. Alan Cerveny, Director of Admissions and Scholarships, University of Kansas, KU Visitor Center, 1502 Iowa Street, Lawrence, KS 66045-1910. *Phone:* 785-864-3911. *Toll-free phone:* 888-686-7323. *Fax:* 785-864-5006. *E-mail:* adm@ku.edu.

WASHBURN UNIVERSITY OF TOPEKA

Topeka, Kansas

- **City-supported** comprehensive, founded 1865
- **Calendar** semesters
- **Degrees** associate, bachelor's, master's, and first professional
- **Urban** 160-acre campus with easy access to Kansas City
- **Endowment** $99.5 million
- **Coed,** 5,098 undergraduate students, 61% full-time, 62% women, 38% men
- **Noncompetitive** entrance level, 100% of applicants were admitted

Undergraduates Students come from 45 states and territories, 4% are from out of state, 6% African American, 2% Asian American or Pacific Islander, 4% Hispanic American, 1% Native American, 13% live on campus. *Retention:* 67% of 2001 full-time freshmen returned.

Freshmen *Admission:* 1,238 applied, 1,238 admitted. *Average high school GPA:* 3.2. *Test scores:* ACT scores over 18: 83%; ACT scores over 24: 34%; ACT scores over 30: 4%.

Faculty *Total:* 457, 50% full-time. *Student/faculty ratio:* 15:1.

Majors Accounting; actuarial science; anthropology; art; art education; art history; biological/physical sciences; biology; business administration; business marketing and marketing management; chemistry; child care/development; corrections; court reporting; criminal justice/law enforcement administration; early childhood education; economics; education; electrical/electronic engineering technology; elementary education; English; finance; fine/studio arts; food products retailing; French; German; health education; history; hospitality management; humanities; industrial radiologic technology; information sciences/systems; journalism; law enforcement/police science; legal administrative assistant; liberal arts and sciences/liberal studies; mass communications; mathematics; medical administrative assistant; medical records administration; medical technology; mental health/rehabilitation; music; music teacher education; nursing; occupational safety/health technology; paralegal/legal assistant; philosophy; physical education; physical therapy; physics; political science; postal management; pre-engineering; pre-law; pre-medicine; psychology; public administration; radiological science; radio/television broadcasting; religious studies; respiratory therapy; secretarial science; social work; sociology; Spanish; speech/rhetorical studies; theater arts/drama.

Academic Programs *Special study options:* academic remediation for entering students, adult/continuing education programs, advanced placement credit, cooperative education, distance learning, double majors, English as a second language, honors programs, independent study, internships, off-campus study, part-time degree program, services for LD students, student-designed majors, study abroad, summer session for credit. *ROTC:* Army (b), Air Force (c). *Unusual degree programs:* 3-2 engineering with University of Kansas, Kansas State University.

Library Mabee Library plus 2 others with 1.5 million titles, 14,000 serial subscriptions, an OPAC, a Web page.

Computers on Campus 200 computers available on campus for general student use. A campuswide network can be accessed from off campus. Internet access, online (class) registration, at least one staffed computer lab available.

Student Life *Housing Options:* coed. *Activities and Organizations:* drama/theater group, student-run newspaper, television station, choral group, marching band, Washburn Student Association, Campus Activities Board, Student Alumni Association, Learning in the Community, Washburn Education Association, national fraternities, national sororities. *Campus security:* 24-hour emergency response devices and patrols, late-night transport/escort service. *Student Services:* health clinic, personal/psychological counseling, legal services.

Athletics Member NCAA. All Division II. *Intercollegiate sports:* baseball M(s), basketball M(s)/W(s), crew M(c)/W(c), football M(s), golf M(s), softball W(s), tennis M(s)/W(s), volleyball W(s), wrestling M(c). *Intramural sports:* basketball M/W, bowling M/W, crew M/W, football M, golf M, racquetball M/W, swimming M/W, tennis M/W, volleyball M/W, wrestling M.

Standardized Tests *Required:* ACT (for admission).

Costs (2001–02) *Tuition:* state resident $3300 full-time, $110 per credit hour part-time; nonresident $7440 full-time, $248 per credit hour part-time. Part-time tuition and fees vary according to course load. *Required fees:* $56 full-time, $28 per term part-time. *Room and board:* $4300. Room and board charges vary according to housing facility. *Payment plan:* installment. *Waivers:* employees or children of employees.

Financial Aid Of all full-time matriculated undergraduates who enrolled in 2001, 2257 applied for aid, 1915 were judged to have need, 402 had their need fully met. 6 State and other part-time jobs (averaging $1932). In 2001, 97 non-need-based awards were made. *Average percent of need met:* 67%. *Average financial aid package:* $2275. *Average need-based loan:* $3316. *Average need-based gift aid:* $530. *Average non-need based aid:* $575. *Average indebtedness upon graduation:* $11,000.

Applying *Options:* electronic application, early admission. *Application fee:* $20. *Required:* high school transcript. *Application deadlines:* rolling (freshmen), 8/8 (transfers). *Notification:* continuous (freshmen).

Admissions Contact Ms. April Hansen, Director of Admission, Washburn University of Topeka, 1700 SW College Avenue, Topeka, KS 66621. *Phone:*

785-231-1010 Ext. 1293. *Toll-free phone:* 800-332-0291. *Fax:* 785-231-1089. *E-mail:* zzhansen@acc.washburn.edu.

WICHITA STATE UNIVERSITY
Wichita, Kansas

- **State-supported** university, founded 1895, part of Kansas Board of Regents
- **Calendar** semesters
- **Degrees** associate, bachelor's, master's, doctoral, post-master's, and postbachelor's certificates
- **Urban** 335-acre campus
- **Endowment** $135.8 million
- **Coed,** 11,303 undergraduate students, 60% full-time, 56% women, 44% men
- **Noncompetitive** entrance level, 73% of applicants were admitted

Undergraduates 6,731 full-time, 4,572 part-time. Students come from 49 states and territories, 98 other countries, 3% are from out of state, 7% African American, 8% Asian American or Pacific Islander, 5% Hispanic American, 1% Native American, 6% international, 44% transferred in, 8% live on campus. *Retention:* 67% of 2001 full-time freshmen returned.

Freshmen *Admission:* 3,229 applied, 2,358 admitted, 1,309 enrolled. *Average high school GPA:* 3.10. *Test scores:* ACT scores over 18: 82%; ACT scores over 24: 29%; ACT scores over 30: 3%.

Faculty *Total:* 522, 90% full-time, 71% with terminal degrees. *Student/faculty ratio:* 17:1.

Majors Accounting; aerospace engineering; anthropology; art; art education; art history; biology; business administration; business marketing and marketing management; chemistry; communications; computer engineering; computer/information sciences; criminal justice studies; dental hygiene; economics; electrical/electronic engineering technology; electrical engineering; elementary education; English; entrepreneurship; finance; French; geology; gerontology; graphic design/commercial art/illustration; health services administration; history; humanities; human resources management; industrial/manufacturing engineering; international business; Latin (ancient and medieval); liberal arts and sciences/liberal studies; management information systems/business data processing; mathematics; mechanical engineering; medical technology; music; music teacher education; nursing science; occupational therapy assistant; paralegal/legal assistant; philosophy; physical education; physical therapy assistant; physician assistant; physics; political science; psychology; science education; secondary education; social work; sociology; Spanish; speech-language pathology/audiology; theater arts/drama; visual/performing arts; women's studies.

Academic Programs *Special study options:* academic remediation for entering students, accelerated degree program, advanced placement credit, cooperative education, distance learning, double majors, English as a second language, freshman honors college, honors programs, independent study, internships, off-campus study, part-time degree program, services for LD students, student-designed majors, study abroad, summer session for credit. *Unusual degree programs:* 3-2 accounting.

Library Ablah Library plus 2 others with 1.1 million titles, 12,055 serial subscriptions, 2,572 audiovisual materials, an OPAC, a Web page.

Computers on Campus 1500 computers available on campus for general student use. A campuswide network can be accessed from student residence rooms and from off campus. Internet access, at least one staffed computer lab available.

Student Life *Housing:* on-campus residence required for freshman year. *Options:* coed. *Activities and Organizations:* drama/theater group, student-run newspaper, radio and television station, choral group, Association of Malaysian Students, Organization of Pakistani Students, psychology club, nursing students, Institute of Aeronautics, national fraternities, national sororities. *Campus security:* 24-hour emergency response devices and patrols, student patrols, late-night transport/escort service, controlled dormitory access, bicycle patrols by campus security. *Student Services:* health clinic, personal/psychological counseling, women's center, legal services.

Athletics Member NCAA. All Division I. *Intercollegiate sports:* baseball M(s), basketball M(s)/W(s), bowling M(c)/W(c), crew M(c)/W(c), cross-country running M(s)/W(s), golf M(s)/W(s), ice hockey M(c)/W(c), racquetball M(c)/W(c), rugby M(c), soccer M(c)/W(c), softball W(s), swimming M(c)/W(c), tennis M(s)/W(s), track and field M(s)/W(s), volleyball M(c)/W(s), wrestling M(c). *Intramural sports:* badminton M/W, basketball M/W, bowling M/W, football M/W, golf M/W, racquetball M/W, soccer M/W, softball M/W, swimming M/W, table tennis M/W, tennis M/W, volleyball M/W, weight lifting M/W.

Standardized Tests *Required for some:* ACT (for admission).

Costs (2001–02) *Tuition:* state resident $2823 full-time, $94 per credit hour part-time; nonresident $9600 full-time, $320 per credit hour part-time. Full-time tuition and fees vary according to course load. *Required fees:* $34 full-time, $17 per term part-time. *Room and board:* $4260. Room and board charges vary according to board plan and housing facility. *Payment plan:* installment. *Waivers:* senior citizens and employees or children of employees.

Financial Aid Of all full-time matriculated undergraduates who enrolled in 2001, 4584 applied for aid, 3768 were judged to have need, 314 had their need fully met. 191 Federal Work-Study jobs (averaging $1981). In 2001, 846 non-need-based awards were made. *Average percent of need met:* 63%. *Average financial aid package:* $5065. *Average need-based loan:* $3652. *Average need-based gift aid:* $2575. *Average non-need based aid:* $2101. *Average indebtedness upon graduation:* $15,980.

Applying *Options:* electronic application, deferred entrance. *Application fee:* $25. *Required:* high school transcript. *Required for some:* minimum 2.0 GPA. *Application deadline:* rolling (transfers).

Admissions Contact Ms. Christine Schneikart-Luebbe, Director of Admissions, Wichita State University, 1845 North Fairmount, Wichita, KS 67260. *Phone:* 316-978-3085. *Toll-free phone:* 800-362-2594. *Fax:* 316-978-3174. *E-mail:* admissions@wichita.edu.

KENTUCKY

ALICE LLOYD COLLEGE
Pippa Passes, Kentucky

- **Independent** 4-year, founded 1923
- **Calendar** semesters
- **Degree** bachelor's
- **Rural** 175-acre campus
- **Endowment** $15.8 million
- **Coed,** 565 undergraduate students, 95% full-time, 55% women, 45% men
- **Moderately difficult** entrance level, 58% of applicants were admitted

Undergraduates 539 full-time, 26 part-time. Students come from 6 states and territories, 5 other countries, 6% are from out of state, 0.5% African American, 0.4% Asian American or Pacific Islander, 0.9% Hispanic American, 0.4% Native American, 1% international, 8% transferred in, 76% live on campus. *Retention:* 62% of 2001 full-time freshmen returned.

Freshmen *Admission:* 802 applied, 463 admitted, 163 enrolled. *Average high school GPA:* 3.39. *Test scores:* ACT scores over 18: 53%; ACT scores over 24: 18%; ACT scores over 30: 6%.

Faculty *Total:* 33, 82% full-time, 45% with terminal degrees. *Student/faculty ratio:* 19:1.

Majors Biological/physical sciences; biology; business administration; elementary education; English; history; interdisciplinary studies; physical education; pre-dentistry; pre-law; pre-medicine; pre-veterinary studies; science education; secondary education.

Academic Programs *Special study options:* academic remediation for entering students, advanced placement credit, double majors, independent study, part-time degree program.

Library McGaw Library and Learning Center with 80,000 titles, 400 serial subscriptions, an OPAC.

Computers on Campus 40 computers available on campus for general student use. Internet access, at least one staffed computer lab available.

Student Life *Housing:* on-campus residence required through senior year. *Activities and Organizations:* drama/theater group, student-run newspaper, radio station, choral group, choral group, Phi Beta Lambda, All Scholastic Society, Math/Science Club, Allied Health Sciences Club. *Campus security:* 24-hour patrols, late-night transport/escort service. *Student Services:* health clinic, personal/psychological counseling.

Athletics Member NAIA. *Intercollegiate sports:* baseball M(s), basketball M(s)/W(s), golf M, softball W. *Intramural sports:* badminton M/W, basketball M/W, bowling M/W, cross-country running M/W, football M, racquetball M/W, soccer M/W, softball M/W, swimming M/W, table tennis M/W, tennis M/W, volleyball M/W, weight lifting M/W.

Standardized Tests *Required:* SAT I or ACT (for admission).

Costs (2002–03) *Comprehensive fee:* includes mandatory fees ($660) and room and board ($3120). Full-time tuition and fees vary according to reciprocity agreements. Part-time tuition: $125 per hour. *Payment plan:* installment. *Waivers:* minority students and employees or children of employees.

Financial Aid Of all full-time matriculated undergraduates who enrolled in 2001, 539 applied for aid, 345 were judged to have need, 90 had their need fully met. 185 State and other part-time jobs (averaging $1648). In 2001, 194 non-need-based awards were made. *Average percent of need met:* 74%. *Average financial*

Alice Lloyd College (continued)
aid package: $8328. *Average need-based loan:* $2000. *Average need-based gift aid:* $6680. *Average indebtedness upon graduation:* $2558.

Applying *Options:* deferred entrance. *Required:* high school transcript. *Required for some:* essay or personal statement, 1 letter of recommendation, interview. *Application deadline:* 8/1 (freshmen), rolling (transfers). *Notification:* continuous until 8/1 (freshmen).

Admissions Contact Sean Damron, Director of Admissions, Alice Lloyd College, 100 Purpose Road, Pippa Passes, KY 41844. *Phone:* 606-368-2101 Ext. 6134. *Fax:* 606-368-2125. *E-mail:* admissions@alc.edu.

ASBURY COLLEGE
Wilmore, Kentucky

- **Independent nondenominational** comprehensive, founded 1890
- **Calendar** semesters
- **Degrees** bachelor's and master's
- **Small-town** 400-acre campus with easy access to Lexington
- **Endowment** $25.9 million
- **Coed,** 1,328 undergraduate students, 96% full-time, 59% women, 41% men
- **Moderately difficult** entrance level, 84% of applicants were admitted

Undergraduates 1,273 full-time, 55 part-time. Students come from 42 states and territories, 14 other countries, 73% are from out of state, 1% African American, 0.6% Asian American or Pacific Islander, 1% Hispanic American, 0.3% Native American, 1% international, 4% transferred in, 88% live on campus. *Retention:* 81% of 2001 full-time freshmen returned.

Freshmen *Admission:* 848 applied, 713 admitted, 331 enrolled. *Average high school GPA:* 3.54. *Test scores:* SAT verbal scores over 500: 81%; SAT math scores over 500: 76%; ACT scores over 18: 99%; SAT verbal scores over 600: 47%; SAT math scores over 600: 35%; ACT scores over 24: 58%; SAT verbal scores over 700: 11%; SAT math scores over 700: 6%; ACT scores over 30: 13%.

Faculty *Total:* 153, 59% full-time, 53% with terminal degrees. *Student/faculty ratio:* 12:1.

Majors Accounting; applied mathematics; art education; biblical studies; biochemistry; biology; business; chemistry; classics; computer/information sciences; elementary education; English; fine/studio arts; French; Greek (ancient and medieval); health/physical education; history; interdisciplinary studies; journalism; Latin (ancient and medieval); mathematics; middle school education; missionary studies; music; music teacher education; philosophy; physical education; physical sciences; psychology; radio/television broadcasting technology; recreation/leisure facilities management; religious education; social sciences; social work; sociology; Spanish; speech/rhetorical studies.

Academic Programs *Special study options:* academic remediation for entering students, advanced placement credit, double majors, independent study, internships, part-time degree program, study abroad, summer session for credit. *ROTC:* Army (c), Air Force (c). *Unusual degree programs:* 3-2 engineering with University of Kentucky; nursing with University of Kentucky; computer science with University of Kentucky.

Library Morrison Kenyon Library with 150,449 titles, 5,203 serial subscriptions, 8,466 audiovisual materials, an OPAC, a Web page.

Computers on Campus 290 computers available on campus for general student use. A campuswide network can be accessed from student residence rooms and from off campus. At least one staffed computer lab available.

Student Life *Housing:* on-campus residence required through senior year. *Options:* men-only, women-only, disabled students. *Activities and Organizations:* drama/theater group, student-run newspaper, radio and television station, choral group, Fellowship of Christian Athletes, Impact (community service), Christian Service Association, ministry teams, Student-Faculty Council. *Campus security:* 24-hour emergency response devices, late-night transport/escort service, controlled dormitory access, late night security personnel. *Student Services:* health clinic, personal/psychological counseling.

Athletics Member NAIA, NCCAA. *Intercollegiate sports:* baseball M, basketball M/W, cross-country running M/W, soccer M/W, softball W, swimming M/W, tennis M/W, volleyball W. *Intramural sports:* basketball M/W, football M/W, gymnastics M/W, soccer M/W, softball M/W, swimming M/W, tennis M/W, volleyball M/W, weight lifting M/W.

Standardized Tests *Required:* SAT I or ACT (for admission).

Costs (2001–02) *Comprehensive fee:* $18,558 includes full-time tuition ($14,624), mandatory fees ($140), and room and board ($3794). Full-time tuition and fees vary according to course load. Part-time tuition: $562 per semester hour. Part-time tuition and fees vary according to course load. *Room and board:* College room only: $2002. Room and board charges vary according to board plan, housing facility, and location. *Payment plans:* installment, deferred payment. *Waivers:* senior citizens and employees or children of employees.

Financial Aid Of all full-time matriculated undergraduates who enrolled in 2001, 717 applied for aid, 597 were judged to have need, 183 had their need fully met. 477 Federal Work-Study jobs (averaging $1226). In 2001, 120 non-need-based awards were made. *Average percent of need met:* 86%. *Average financial aid package:* $10,591. *Average need-based loan:* $3901. *Average need-based gift aid:* $5657. *Average non-need based aid:* $6737. *Average indebtedness upon graduation:* $15,994.

Applying *Options:* early admission, deferred entrance. *Application fee:* $30. *Required:* essay or personal statement, high school transcript, minimum 2.5 GPA, 3 letters of recommendation. *Required for some:* interview. *Application deadline:* rolling (freshmen), rolling (transfers). *Notification:* continuous (freshmen).

Admissions Contact Mr. Stan F. Wiggam, Dean of Admissions, Asbury College, 1 Macklem Drive, Wilmore, KY 40390. *Phone:* 859-858-3511 Ext. 2142. *Toll-free phone:* 800-888-1818. *Fax:* 859-858-3921. *E-mail:* admissions@asbury.edu.

BELLARMINE UNIVERSITY
Louisville, Kentucky

- **Independent Roman Catholic** comprehensive, founded 1950
- **Calendar** semesters
- **Degrees** certificates, bachelor's, and master's
- **Suburban** 120-acre campus
- **Endowment** $17.2 million
- **Coed,** 1,735 undergraduate students
- **Moderately difficult** entrance level, 84% of applicants were admitted

Undergraduates Students come from 19 states and territories, 12 other countries, 31% are from out of state, 3% African American, 2% Asian American or Pacific Islander, 1.0% Hispanic American, 0.3% Native American, 1% international, 37% live on campus. *Retention:* 81% of 2001 full-time freshmen returned.

Freshmen *Admission:* 1,291 applied, 1,080 admitted. *Average high school GPA:* 3.49. *Test scores:* SAT verbal scores over 500: 77%; SAT math scores over 500: 83%; ACT scores over 18: 97%; SAT verbal scores over 600: 39%; SAT math scores over 600: 43%; ACT scores over 24: 46%; SAT verbal scores over 700: 7%; SAT math scores over 700: 8%; ACT scores over 30: 5%.

Faculty *Total:* 235, 46% full-time, 46% with terminal degrees. *Student/faculty ratio:* 14:1.

Majors Accounting; actuarial science; art; arts management; biology; business administration; business economics; chemistry; communications; community services; computer engineering; computer/information sciences; computer science; criminal justice studies; economics; education; elementary education; English; French; German; history; human resources management; international business; international relations; liberal arts and sciences/liberal studies; mathematics; middle school education; music; musical instrument technology; music business management/merchandising; music (voice and choral/opera performance); nursing; painting; pastoral counseling; philosophy; political science; pre-dentistry; pre-law; pre-medicine; pre-pharmacy studies; pre-veterinary studies; psychology; sculpture; secondary education; sociology; Spanish; special education; theology.

Academic Programs *Special study options:* accelerated degree program, adult/continuing education programs, advanced placement credit, double majors, honors programs, independent study, internships, off-campus study, part-time degree program, services for LD students, student-designed majors, study abroad, summer session for credit. *ROTC:* Army (c), Air Force (c).

Library W.L. Lyons Brown Library with 97,737 titles, 401 serial subscriptions, 3,853 audiovisual materials, an OPAC, a Web page.

Computers on Campus 160 computers available on campus for general student use. A campuswide network can be accessed from student residence rooms. Internet access, at least one staffed computer lab available.

Student Life *Housing:* on-campus residence required through sophomore year. *Options:* coed, men-only, women-only, disabled students. *Activities and Organizations:* drama/theater group, student-run newspaper, choral group, student government, Delta Sigma Pi, Fellowship of Christian Athletes, Campus Ministry, Residence Hall Council, national fraternities, national sororities. *Campus security:* 24-hour emergency response devices and patrols, late-night transport/escort service, 24-hour locked residence hall entrances, security cameras. *Student Services:* health clinic, personal/psychological counseling.

Athletics Member NCAA. All Division II. *Intercollegiate sports:* baseball M(s), basketball M(s)/W(s), cross-country running M(s)/W(s), field hockey W(s), golf M(s)/W(s), soccer M(s)/W(s), softball W(s), tennis M(s)/W(s), track and field M(s)/W(s), volleyball W(s). *Intramural sports:* basketball M/W, football M/W, golf M/W, soccer M/W, table tennis M/W, tennis M/W, volleyball M/W, weight lifting M/W.

Standardized Tests *Required:* SAT I or ACT (for admission).

Costs (2002–03) *Comprehensive fee:* $22,310 includes full-time tuition ($16,340), mandatory fees ($670), and room and board ($5300). Part-time tuition: $385 per credit.

Applying *Options:* common application, electronic application, early admission, early action, deferred entrance. *Application fee:* $25. *Required:* essay or personal statement, high school transcript, minimum 2.5 GPA, letters of recommendation. *Recommended:* interview. *Application deadlines:* 8/15 (freshmen), 8/15 (transfers). *Notification:* 12/1 (early action).

Admissions Contact Mr. Timothy A. Sturgeon, Dean of Admission, Bellarmine University, 2001 Newburg Road, Louisville, KY 40205-0671. *Phone:* 502-452-8131. *Toll-free phone:* 800-274-4723 Ext. 8131. *Fax:* 502-452-8002. *E-mail:* admissions@bellarmine.edu.

BEREA COLLEGE

Berea, Kentucky

- **Independent** 4-year, founded 1855
- **Calendar** 4-1-4
- **Degree** bachelor's
- **Small-town** 140-acre campus
- **Endowment** $788.3 million
- **Coed,** 1,674 undergraduate students, 97% full-time, 56% women, 44% men
- **Very difficult** entrance level, 32% of applicants were admitted

Berea College is a small, residential, nonsectarian Christian college recognized for its distinctive academic and work programs and for its special interest in Appalachia. Financial need is an absolute prerequisite for admission. Every accepted student is awarded a full tuition scholarship that is currently worth $19,900 per year. All students participate in a work program on campus for 10-15 hours per week.

Undergraduates 1,619 full-time, 55 part-time. Students come from 45 states and territories, 64 other countries, 57% are from out of state, 15% African American, 1% Asian American or Pacific Islander, 0.6% Hispanic American, 0.7% Native American, 2% transferred in, 79% live on campus. *Retention:* 83% of 2001 full-time freshmen returned.

Freshmen *Admission:* 1,871 applied, 603 admitted, 425 enrolled. *Average high school GPA:* 3.35. *Test scores:* SAT verbal scores over 500: 76%; SAT math scores over 500: 71%; ACT scores over 18: 96%; SAT verbal scores over 600: 32%; SAT math scores over 600: 27%; ACT scores over 24: 49%; SAT verbal scores over 700: 5%; SAT math scores over 700: 3%; ACT scores over 30: 5%.

Faculty *Total:* 150, 87% full-time. *Student/faculty ratio:* 11:1.

Majors Agricultural business; agricultural sciences; art; art education; art history; biology; biology education; business administration; chemistry; child care/development; classics; developmental/child psychology; dietetics; early childhood education; economics; education; elementary education; English; English education; family/consumer studies; fine/studio arts; foreign languages education; French; French language education; German; German language education; history; home economics education; hotel and restaurant management; industrial arts; industrial technology; mathematics; mathematics education; middle school education; music; music teacher education; nursing; philosophy; physical education; physics; political science; pre-dentistry; pre-medicine; pre-veterinary studies; psychology; religious studies; secondary education; sociology; Spanish; Spanish language education; theater arts/drama; women's studies.

Academic Programs *Special study options:* academic remediation for entering students, advanced placement credit, double majors, honors programs, independent study, internships, off-campus study, services for LD students, student-designed majors, study abroad, summer session for credit. *Unusual degree programs:* 3-2 engineering with Washington University in St. Louis, University of Kentucky.

Library Hutchins Library plus 2 others with 242,893 titles, 2,029 serial subscriptions, 5,172 audiovisual materials, an OPAC, a Web page.

Computers on Campus 260 computers available on campus for general student use. A campuswide network can be accessed from student residence rooms and from off campus. Internet access, at least one staffed computer lab available.

Student Life *Housing:* on-campus residence required through senior year. *Options:* men-only, women-only. *Activities and Organizations:* drama/theater group, student-run newspaper, choral group, Campus Activities Board, Cosmopolitan Club, Students for Appalachia, Flag Football and Basketball Intramurals, Baptist Student Union. *Campus security:* 24-hour emergency response devices and patrols, late-night transport/escort service, controlled dormitory access, crime prevention programs. *Student Services:* health clinic, personal/psychological counseling, women's center.

Athletics Member NAIA. *Intercollegiate sports:* baseball M, basketball M/W, cross-country running M/W, golf M, soccer M/W, softball W, swimming M/W, tennis M/W, track and field M/W, volleyball W. *Intramural sports:* badminton M/W, basketball M/W, racquetball M/W, soccer M/W, softball M/W, table tennis M/W, volleyball M/W, weight lifting M/W.

Standardized Tests *Required:* SAT I or ACT (for admission).

Costs (2001–02) *Comprehensive fee:* includes mandatory fees ($205) and room and board ($4099). Financial aid is provided to all students for tuition costs. *Payment plan:* deferred payment.

Financial Aid Of all full-time matriculated undergraduates who enrolled in 2001, 1625 applied for aid, 1625 were judged to have need. 284 State and other part-time jobs. *Average percent of need met:* 87%. *Average financial aid package:* $20,849. *Average need-based gift aid:* $19,540. *Average indebtedness upon graduation:* $3567.

Applying *Required:* essay or personal statement, high school transcript, interview, financial aid application. *Recommended:* 2 letters of recommendation. *Application deadline:* rolling (transfers). *Notification:* 4/20 (freshmen).

Admissions Contact Mr. Joseph Bagnoli, Director of Admissions, Berea College, CPO 2220, Berea, KY 40404. *Phone:* 859-985-3500. *Toll-free phone:* 800-326-5948. *Fax:* 859-985-3512. *E-mail:* admissions@berea.edu.

BRESCIA UNIVERSITY

Owensboro, Kentucky

- **Independent Roman Catholic** comprehensive, founded 1950
- **Calendar** semesters
- **Degrees** certificates, associate, bachelor's, and master's
- **Urban** 6-acre campus
- **Endowment** $9.0 million
- **Coed,** 756 undergraduate students, 71% full-time, 61% women, 39% men
- **Moderately difficult** entrance level, 80% of applicants were admitted

Undergraduates 534 full-time, 222 part-time. Students come from 18 states and territories, 19 other countries, 16% are from out of state, 4% African American, 0.5% Asian American or Pacific Islander, 0.8% Hispanic American, 0.3% Native American, 5% international, 11% transferred in, 34% live on campus. *Retention:* 67% of 2001 full-time freshmen returned.

Freshmen *Admission:* 264 applied, 210 admitted, 117 enrolled. *Average high school GPA:* 3.24. *Test scores:* ACT scores over 18: 87%; ACT scores over 24: 33%; ACT scores over 30: 2%.

Faculty *Total:* 70, 59% full-time, 53% with terminal degrees. *Student/faculty ratio:* 14:1.

Majors Accounting; applied mathematics; art; art education; art therapy; biological/physical sciences; biology; business; business marketing and marketing management; chemistry; education; elementary education; engineering; English; finance; graphic design/commercial art/illustration; history; human resources management; liberal arts and sciences/liberal studies; mathematics/computer science; medical technology; middle school education; pre-engineering; psychology; religious studies; secondary education; social sciences; social studies education; social work; Spanish; special education; speech-language pathology/audiology; theology/ministry related.

Academic Programs *Special study options:* academic remediation for entering students, adult/continuing education programs, advanced placement credit, double majors, English as a second language, honors programs, independent study, internships, off-campus study, part-time degree program, services for LD students, student-designed majors, study abroad, summer session for credit.

Library Brescia University Library with 62,607 titles, 2,466 serial subscriptions, 6,717 audiovisual materials, an OPAC, a Web page.

Computers on Campus 41 computers available on campus for general student use. A campuswide network can be accessed from student residence rooms and from off campus. Internet access, at least one staffed computer lab available.

Student Life *Housing:* on-campus residence required for freshman year. *Options:* coed, men-only, women-only. *Activities and Organizations:* drama/theater group, student-run newspaper, choral group, Student Government Association, Ichabod Society, National Student Speech-Language-Hearing Association, Social Work Club, Spanish Club. *Campus security:* late-night transport/escort service, controlled dormitory access. *Student Services:* personal/psychological counseling, women's center.

Athletics Member NAIA. *Intercollegiate sports:* baseball M(s), basketball M(s)/W(s), golf M(s)/W(s), soccer M(s)/W(s), softball W(s), tennis W(s), volleyball W(s). *Intramural sports:* badminton M/W, basketball M/W, bowling M/W, racquetball M/W, table tennis M/W, volleyball M/W.

Standardized Tests *Required:* SAT I or ACT (for admission).

Costs (2001–02) *Comprehensive fee:* $14,225 includes full-time tuition ($9690), mandatory fees ($155), and room and board ($4380). Part-time tuition: $325 per credit hour. Part-time tuition and fees vary according to course load. *Room and*

Brescia University (continued)
board: Room and board charges vary according to board plan and housing facility. *Payment plan:* deferred payment. *Waivers:* children of alumni, senior citizens, and employees or children of employees.

Financial Aid Of all full-time matriculated undergraduates who enrolled in 2001, 390 applied for aid, 388 were judged to have need, 59 had their need fully met. 84 Federal Work-Study jobs (averaging $1236). In 2001, 59 non-need-based awards were made. *Average percent of need met:* 100%. *Average financial aid package:* $8720. *Average need-based loan:* $3354. *Average need-based gift aid:* $5571. *Average non-need based aid:* $5150.

Applying *Options:* common application, electronic application, deferred entrance. *Application fee:* $25. *Required:* essay or personal statement, high school transcript, minimum 2.5 GPA. *Required for some:* 1 letter of recommendation, interview. *Application deadline:* rolling (freshmen), rolling (transfers). *Notification:* continuous (freshmen).

Admissions Contact Sr. Mary Austin Blank, Director of Admissions, Brescia University, 717 Frederica Street, Owensboro, KY 42301-3023. *Phone:* 270-686-4241 Ext. 241. *Toll-free phone:* 877-BRESCIA. *Fax:* 270-686-4201. *E-mail:* admissions@brescia.edu.

CAMPBELLSVILLE UNIVERSITY
Campbellsville, Kentucky

- **Independent** comprehensive, founded 1906, affiliated with Kentucky Baptist Convention
- **Calendar** semesters
- **Degrees** certificates, associate, bachelor's, master's, and postbachelor's certificates
- **Small-town** 70-acre campus
- **Endowment** $7.8 million
- **Coed,** 1,630 undergraduate students, 71% full-time, 58% women, 42% men
- **Moderately difficult** entrance level, 79% of applicants were admitted

Undergraduates 1,152 full-time, 478 part-time. Students come from 26 states and territories, 25 other countries, 12% are from out of state, 5% African American, 0.2% Asian American or Pacific Islander, 0.7% Hispanic American, 0.2% Native American, 4% international, 7% transferred in, 50% live on campus. *Retention:* 67% of 2001 full-time freshmen returned.

Freshmen *Admission:* 1,130 applied, 889 admitted, 334 enrolled. *Average high school GPA:* 3.20. *Test scores:* SAT verbal scores over 500: 76%; SAT math scores over 500: 58%; ACT scores over 18: 78%; SAT verbal scores over 600: 28%; SAT math scores over 600: 20%; ACT scores over 24: 32%; SAT verbal scores over 700: 12%; SAT math scores over 700: 12%; ACT scores over 30: 2%.

Faculty *Total:* 188, 37% full-time. *Student/faculty ratio:* 16:1.

Majors Accounting; art; art education; athletic training/sports medicine; biblical studies; biology; business administration; business economics; business education; business marketing and marketing management; chemistry; criminal justice/law enforcement administration; data processing technology; divinity/ministry; economics; elementary education; English; health education; history; information sciences/systems; journalism; mass communications; mathematics; medical technology; music; music (piano and organ performance); music teacher education; music (voice and choral/opera performance); pastoral counseling; physical education; political science; pre-dentistry; pre-law; pre-medicine; pre-veterinary studies; psychology; recreation/leisure studies; religious education; religious music; religious studies; science education; secondary education; secretarial science; social sciences; social work; sociology.

Academic Programs *Special study options:* academic remediation for entering students, accelerated degree program, adult/continuing education programs, advanced placement credit, distance learning, double majors, English as a second language, honors programs, independent study, internships, off-campus study, part-time degree program, study abroad, summer session for credit. *Unusual degree programs:* 3-2 engineering with University of Kentucky; nursing with Eastern Kentucky University.

Library Montgomery Library plus 2 others with 110,000 titles, 25,000 serial subscriptions, 8,000 audiovisual materials, a Web page.

Computers on Campus 120 computers available on campus for general student use. Internet access, at least one staffed computer lab available.

Student Life *Housing:* on-campus residence required through sophomore year. *Options:* men-only, women-only. *Activities and Organizations:* drama/theater group, student-run newspaper, radio and television station, choral group, marching band, Student Government Association, Baptist Student Union, Phi Beta Lambda, African-American Leadership League, Fellowship of Christian Athletics. *Campus security:* 24-hour emergency response devices and patrols, student patrols, late-night transport/escort service, controlled dormitory access. *Student Services:* health clinic, personal/psychological counseling.

Athletics Member NAIA. *Intercollegiate sports:* baseball M(s), basketball M(s)/W(s), cross-country running M(s)/W(s), football M(s), golf M(s)/W(s), soccer M(s)/W(s), softball W(s), tennis M(s)/W(s), volleyball W(s). *Intramural sports:* basketball M/W, football M/W, racquetball M/W, soccer M/W, swimming M/W, table tennis M/W, tennis M/W, volleyball M/W, weight lifting M/W.

Standardized Tests *Required:* SAT I or ACT (for admission).

Costs (2001–02) *Comprehensive fee:* $14,470 includes full-time tuition ($9800), mandatory fees ($270), and room and board ($4400). Full-time tuition and fees vary according to class time and course load. Part-time tuition: $408 per credit. Part-time tuition and fees vary according to class time and course load. *Required fees:* $35 per term part-time. *Room and board:* College room only: $1940. Room and board charges vary according to board plan and housing facility. *Payment plans:* installment, deferred payment. *Waivers:* minority students, senior citizens, and employees or children of employees.

Financial Aid Of all full-time matriculated undergraduates who enrolled in 2001, 995 applied for aid, 905 were judged to have need, 149 had their need fully met. 265 Federal Work-Study jobs (averaging $1328). 101 State and other part-time jobs (averaging $1411). In 2001, 253 non-need-based awards were made. *Average percent of need met:* 66%. *Average financial aid package:* $8549. *Average need-based loan:* $2930. *Average need-based gift aid:* $5969. *Average non-need based aid:* $5253. *Average indebtedness upon graduation:* $11,180.

Applying *Options:* common application, electronic application, deferred entrance. *Application fee:* $20. *Required:* high school transcript, minimum 2.0 GPA. *Recommended:* essay or personal statement, minimum 3.0 GPA, letters of recommendation, interview. *Application deadline:* rolling (freshmen), rolling (transfers). *Notification:* continuous (freshmen).

Admissions Contact Mr. R. Trent Argo, Director of Admissions, Campbellsville University, 1 University Drive, Campbellsville, KY 42718-2799. *Phone:* 270-789-5552. *Toll-free phone:* 800-264-6014. *Fax:* 270-789-5071. *E-mail:* admissions@campbellsvil.edu.

CENTRE COLLEGE
Danville, Kentucky

- **Independent** 4-year, founded 1819, affiliated with Presbyterian Church (U.S.A.)
- **Calendar** 4-2-4
- **Degree** bachelor's
- **Small-town** 100-acre campus
- **Endowment** $140.0 million
- **Coed,** 1,070 undergraduate students, 99% full-time, 55% women, 45% men
- **Very difficult** entrance level, 82% of applicants were admitted

Undergraduates 1,056 full-time, 14 part-time. Students come from 37 states and territories, 7 other countries, 28% are from out of state, 3% African American, 2% Asian American or Pacific Islander, 0.5% Hispanic American, 0.3% Native American, 1% international, 1% transferred in, 94% live on campus. *Retention:* 89% of 2001 full-time freshmen returned.

Freshmen *Admission:* 1,265 applied, 1,041 admitted, 299 enrolled. *Average high school GPA:* 3.73. *Test scores:* SAT verbal scores over 500: 95%; SAT math scores over 500: 97%; ACT scores over 18: 100%; SAT verbal scores over 600: 68%; SAT math scores over 600: 66%; ACT scores over 24: 89%; SAT verbal scores over 700: 25%; SAT math scores over 700: 19%; ACT scores over 30: 24%.

Faculty *Total:* 104, 87% full-time, 88% with terminal degrees. *Student/faculty ratio:* 11:1.

Majors Anthropology; art; art history; biochemistry; biology; chemistry; classics; computer science; economics; elementary education; English; French; German; history; international relations; mathematics; molecular biology; music; philosophy; physics; physiological psychology/psychobiology; political science; pre-dentistry; pre-law; pre-medicine; psychology; religious studies; secondary education; sociology; Spanish; theater arts/drama.

Academic Programs *Special study options:* advanced placement credit, double majors, independent study, internships, off-campus study, part-time degree program, services for LD students, student-designed majors, study abroad. *ROTC:* Army (c), Air Force (c). *Unusual degree programs:* 3-2 engineering with Washington University in St. Louis, Columbia University, Vanderbilt University, University of Kentucky.

Library Doherty Library plus 1 other with 152,721 titles, 2,076 serial subscriptions, an OPAC, a Web page.

Computers on Campus 150 computers available on campus for general student use. A campuswide network can be accessed from student residence rooms and from off campus. Internet access, at least one staffed computer lab available.

Student Life *Housing:* on-campus residence required through sophomore year. *Options:* coed, men-only, women-only. *Activities and Organizations:* drama/

theater group, student-run newspaper, choral group, CARE (Centre Action Reaches Everyone), Christian Fellowship, College Democrats and Republicans, Student Congress, Outdoors Club, national fraternities, national sororities. *Campus security:* 24-hour emergency response devices and patrols, late-night transport/escort service, controlled dormitory access. *Student Services:* health clinic, personal/psychological counseling.

Athletics Member NCAA. All Division III. *Intercollegiate sports:* baseball M, basketball M/W, cross-country running M/W, field hockey W, football M, golf M/W, soccer M/W, softball W, swimming M/W, tennis M/W, track and field M/W, volleyball W. *Intramural sports:* badminton M/W, basketball M/W, bowling M/W, equestrian sports M/W, football M/W, golf M/W, racquetball M/W, soccer M/W, softball M/W, swimming M/W, table tennis M/W, tennis M/W, track and field M/W, volleyball M/W, weight lifting M/W, wrestling M.

Standardized Tests *Required:* SAT I or ACT (for admission).

Costs (2001–02) *Comprehensive fee:* $24,000 includes full-time tuition ($18,000) and room and board ($6000). Part-time tuition: $560 per credit hour. Part-time tuition and fees vary according to course load. *Room and board:* College room only: $3030. Room and board charges vary according to board plan. *Payment plan:* installment. *Waivers:* children of alumni and employees or children of employees.

Financial Aid Of all full-time matriculated undergraduates who enrolled in 2001, 745 applied for aid, 657 were judged to have need, 258 had their need fully met. 349 Federal Work-Study jobs (averaging $1250). In 2001, 101 non-need-based awards were made. *Average percent of need met:* 100%. *Average financial aid package:* $18,519. *Average need-based loan:* $3887. *Average need-based gift aid:* $12,057. *Average non-need based aid:* $8911. *Average indebtedness upon graduation:* $13,900. *Financial aid deadline:* 3/1.

Applying *Options:* common application, electronic application, early admission, early decision, early action, deferred entrance. *Application fee:* $35. *Required:* essay or personal statement, high school transcript, 1 letter of recommendation. *Recommended:* interview. *Application deadlines:* 2/1 (freshmen), 6/1 (transfers). *Early decision:* 11/15. *Notification:* 3/1 (freshmen), 12/15 (early decision), 1/1 (early action).

Admissions Contact Mr. J. Carey Thompson, Dean of Admission and Financial Aid, Centre College, 600 West Walnut Street, Danville, KY 40422-1394. *Phone:* 859-238-5350. *Toll-free phone:* 800-423-6236. *Fax:* 859-238-5373. *E-mail:* admission@centre.edu.

CLEAR CREEK BAPTIST BIBLE COLLEGE
Pineville, Kentucky

- **Independent Southern Baptist** 4-year, founded 1926
- **Calendar** semesters
- **Degrees** certificates, diplomas, associate, and bachelor's
- **Rural** 700-acre campus
- **Coed, primarily men,** 198 undergraduate students, 81% full-time, 12% women, 88% men
- **Noncompetitive** entrance level, 90% of applicants were admitted

Undergraduates Students come from 15 states and territories, 2 other countries. *Retention:* 83% of 2001 full-time freshmen returned.

Freshmen *Admission:* 48 applied, 43 admitted.

Faculty *Total:* 22, 91% full-time, 64% with terminal degrees. *Student/faculty ratio:* 13:1.

Majors Biblical studies; divinity/ministry.

Academic Programs *Special study options:* academic remediation for entering students, off-campus study, part-time degree program, services for LD students, summer session for credit.

Library Carolyn Boatman Brooks Memorial Library with 38,000 titles, 271 serial subscriptions, an OPAC.

Computers on Campus 4 computers available on campus for general student use. Internet access, at least one staffed computer lab available.

Student Life *Housing Options:* coed. *Activities and Organizations:* choral group. *Campus security:* 24-hour emergency response devices, student patrols. *Student Services:* health clinic, personal/psychological counseling.

Athletics *Intramural sports:* basketball M/W, table tennis M/W, tennis M/W, volleyball M/W.

Costs (2001–02) *Comprehensive fee:* $7776 includes full-time tuition ($4046), mandatory fees ($350), and room and board ($3380). Part-time tuition: $168 per semester hour. *Required fees:* $145 per term part-time. *Room and board:* Room and board charges vary according to housing facility. *Payment plan:* installment.

Financial Aid Of all full-time matriculated undergraduates who enrolled in 2001, 184 applied for aid, 142 were judged to have need. 35 Federal Work-Study jobs (averaging $816). 35 State and other part-time jobs (averaging $272). In 2001, 39 non-need-based awards were made. *Average percent of need met:* 42%. *Average financial aid package:* $4123. *Average need-based gift aid:* $5650. *Average non-need based aid:* $1973.

Applying *Options:* common application, electronic application, deferred entrance. *Application fee:* $40. *Required:* essay or personal statement, 4 letters of recommendation. *Recommended:* high school transcript, interview. *Application deadlines:* 7/15 (freshmen), 7/15 (transfers). *Notification:* continuous (freshmen).

Admissions Contact Mr. Donnie Fox, Director of Admissions, Clear Creek Baptist Bible College, 300 Clear Creek Road, Pineville, KY 40977-9754. *Phone:* 606-337-3196 Ext. 103. *Fax:* 606-337-2372. *E-mail:* ccbbc@ccbbc.edu.

CUMBERLAND COLLEGE
Williamsburg, Kentucky

- **Independent Kentucky Baptist** comprehensive, founded 1889
- **Calendar** semesters
- **Degrees** bachelor's and master's
- **Rural** 30-acre campus with easy access to Knoxville
- **Endowment** $45.8 million
- **Coed,** 1,569 undergraduate students, 86% full-time, 53% women, 47% men
- **Moderately difficult** entrance level, 70% of applicants were admitted

Cumberland College is a 4-year, private, liberal arts college situated in the foothills of the Kentucky mountains. Founded in 1889, the College strives to provide a high-quality education at a reasonable cost while maintaining a strong commitment to the Christian values established by its founders.

Undergraduates 1,344 full-time, 225 part-time. Students come from 39 states and territories, 16 other countries, 45% are from out of state, 5% African American, 0.3% Asian American or Pacific Islander, 1% Hispanic American, 0.1% Native American, 2% international, 4% transferred in, 53% live on campus. *Retention:* 63% of 2001 full-time freshmen returned.

Freshmen *Admission:* 1,074 applied, 754 admitted, 416 enrolled. *Average high school GPA:* 3.34. *Test scores:* SAT verbal scores over 500: 47%; SAT math scores over 500: 53%; ACT scores over 18: 98%; SAT verbal scores over 600: 5%; SAT math scores over 600: 15%; ACT scores over 24: 25%; SAT math scores over 700: 1%; ACT scores over 30: 3%.

Faculty *Total:* 100, 98% full-time, 63% with terminal degrees. *Student/faculty ratio:* 17:1.

Majors Accounting; art education; biology; business; business education; chemistry; communications; community health liaison; computer/information sciences; elementary education; English; executive assistant; fine/studio arts; general studies; health education; history; mathematics; medical technology; middle school education; music; music teacher education; physical education; physics; political science; psychology; religious education; social studies education; social work; special education; speech/rhetorical studies; theater arts/drama.

Academic Programs *Special study options:* academic remediation for entering students, accelerated degree program, adult/continuing education programs, advanced placement credit, double majors, English as a second language, freshman honors college, honors programs, internships, part-time degree program, student-designed majors, study abroad, summer session for credit.

Library Norma Perkins Hagan Memorial Library with 159,068 titles, 2,020 serial subscriptions, 6,906 audiovisual materials, an OPAC, a Web page.

Computers on Campus 300 computers available on campus for general student use. A campuswide network can be accessed from student residence rooms and from off campus. Internet access, online (class) registration, at least one staffed computer lab available.

Student Life *Housing:* on-campus residence required through junior year. *Options:* men-only, women-only. *Activities and Organizations:* drama/theater group, student-run television station, choral group, marching band, Baptist Student Union, Student Government Association, Campus Activity Board, Mountain Outreach, Fellowship of Christian Athletes. *Campus security:* 24-hour emergency response devices, student patrols, late-night transport/escort service. *Student Services:* health clinic, personal/psychological counseling.

Athletics Member NAIA. *Intercollegiate sports:* baseball M(s), basketball M(s)/W(s), cross-country running M(s)/W(s), football M(s), golf M(s)/W(s), soccer M(s)/W(s), softball W(s), swimming M(s)/W(s), tennis M(s)/W(s), track and field M(s)/W(s), volleyball W(s), wrestling M(s)/W(s). *Intramural sports:* basketball M/W, football M/W, soccer M/W, softball M/W, table tennis M/W, tennis M/W, volleyball M/W.

Standardized Tests *Required:* SAT I or ACT (for admission).

Costs (2002–03) *Comprehensive fee:* $15,634 includes full-time tuition ($10,598), mandatory fees ($360), and room and board ($4676). Part-time tuition: $355 per hour. Part-time tuition and fees vary according to course load. *Required fees:* $49 per term part-time. *Payment plan:* installment. *Waivers:* employees or children of employees.

Cumberland College (continued)

Financial Aid Of all full-time matriculated undergraduates who enrolled in 2001, 1208 applied for aid, 1050 were judged to have need, 421 had their need fully met. 397 Federal Work-Study jobs (averaging $1615). 151 State and other part-time jobs (averaging $1652). In 2001, 190 non-need-based awards were made. *Average percent of need met:* 90%. *Average financial aid package:* $10,422. *Average need-based loan:* $3692. *Average need-based gift aid:* $5374. *Average non-need based aid:* $3516. *Average indebtedness upon graduation:* $14,275.

Applying *Options:* common application. *Application fee:* $25. *Required:* essay or personal statement, high school transcript, minimum 2.0 GPA, 1 letter of recommendation. *Recommended:* interview. *Application deadline:* rolling (freshmen), rolling (transfers). *Notification:* continuous (freshmen).

Admissions Contact Mrs. Erica Harris, Coordinator of Admissions, Cumberland College, 6178 College Station Drive, Williamsburg, KY 40769. *Phone:* 606-539-4241. *Toll-free phone:* 800-343-1609. *Fax:* 606-539-4303. *E-mail:* admiss@cc.cumber.edu.

EASTERN KENTUCKY UNIVERSITY
Richmond, Kentucky

- **State-supported** comprehensive, founded 1906, part of Kentucky Council on Post Secondary Education
- **Calendar** semesters
- **Degrees** certificates, associate, bachelor's, master's, post-master's, and postbachelor's certificates
- **Small-town** 500-acre campus with easy access to Lexington
- **Coed,** 12,804 undergraduate students, 75% full-time, 59% women, 41% men
- **Noncompetitive** entrance level, 79% of applicants were admitted

Undergraduates 9,642 full-time, 3,162 part-time. Students come from 44 states and territories, 40 other countries, 7% are from out of state, 5% African American, 0.9% Asian American or Pacific Islander, 0.5% Hispanic American, 0.2% Native American, 0.5% international, 7% transferred in, 33% live on campus. *Retention:* 64% of 2001 full-time freshmen returned.

Freshmen *Admission:* 4,744 applied, 3,760 admitted, 2,151 enrolled. *Test scores:* ACT scores over 18: 75%; ACT scores over 24: 18%; ACT scores over 30: 2%.

Faculty *Total:* 575. *Student/faculty ratio:* 16:1.

Majors Accounting; agricultural business; agricultural mechanization; agricultural sciences; aircraft pilot (professional); anthropology; applied mathematics; art; art education; athletic training/sports medicine; aviation management; biochemistry; biology; broadcast journalism; business administration; business economics; business education; business marketing and marketing management; ceramic arts; chemistry; child care/development; city/community/regional planning; clothing/textiles; computer engineering technology; computer science; construction technology; corrections; criminal justice/law enforcement administration; cytotechnology; dairy science; dance; dietetics; drafting; drawing; early childhood education; earth sciences; ecology; economics; education; electrical/electronic engineering technology; elementary education; emergency medical technology; English; environmental biology; environmental health; environmental science; exercise sciences; family/community studies; farm/ranch management; fashion merchandising; finance; fire protection/safety technology; fire science; forensic technology; French; geography; geology; German; graphic design/commercial art/illustration; health education; health services administration; history; home economics; home economics education; horticulture science; industrial arts; industrial technology; information sciences/systems; insurance/risk management; interdisciplinary studies; interior design; journalism; landscape architecture; landscaping management; law enforcement/police science; liberal arts and sciences/liberal studies; literature; mass communications; mathematical statistics; mathematics; medical assistant; medical laboratory technician; medical records administration; medical technology; metal/jewelry arts; microbiology/bacteriology; middle school education; music; music teacher education; natural sciences; nursing; nutrition science; occupational therapy; ornamental horticulture; paralegal/legal assistant; philosophy; physical education; physics; political science; pre-dentistry; pre-engineering; pre-law; pre-medicine; pre-veterinary studies; psychology; public health; public relations; quality control technology; radio/television broadcasting; real estate; recreational therapy; recreation/leisure facilities management; recreation/leisure studies; retail management; safety/security technology; science education; sculpture; secondary education; secretarial science; sign language interpretation; social work; sociology; Spanish; special education; speech-language pathology/audiology; speech/rhetorical studies; speech therapy; theater arts/drama; trade/industrial education; transportation technology; travel/tourism management; wildlife management.

Academic Programs *Special study options:* academic remediation for entering students, accelerated degree program, adult/continuing education programs, advanced placement credit, cooperative education, distance learning, double majors, English as a second language, external degree program, honors programs, independent study, internships, part-time degree program, services for LD students, student-designed majors, summer session for credit. *ROTC:* Army (b), Air Force (c). *Unusual degree programs:* 3-2 engineering with Georgia Institute of Technology, University of Kentucky, Auburn University.

Library John Grant Crabbe Library plus 2 others with 832,663 titles, 3,564 serial subscriptions, an OPAC, a Web page.

Computers on Campus 500 computers available on campus for general student use. Internet access, at least one staffed computer lab available.

Student Life *Housing:* on-campus residence required through senior year. *Options:* coed, men-only, women-only. *Activities and Organizations:* drama/theater group, student-run newspaper, radio station, choral group, marching band, fraternities, sororities, honor society, regular society, national fraternities, national sororities. *Campus security:* 24-hour emergency response devices and patrols, student patrols, late-night transport/escort service. *Student Services:* health clinic, personal/psychological counseling.

Athletics Member NCAA. All Division I except football (Division I-AA). *Intercollegiate sports:* baseball M(s), basketball M(s)/W(s), cross-country running M(s)/W(s), golf M(s), softball W(s), tennis M(s)/W(s), track and field M(s)/W(s), volleyball W(s). *Intramural sports:* archery W(c), basketball M/W, bowling M(c)/W(c), equestrian sports M(c)/W(c), football M/W, rugby M(c), soccer M(c)/W(c), softball M/W, tennis M/W, track and field M/W, volleyball M/W, weight lifting M/W.

Standardized Tests *Required:* ACT (for admission).

Costs (2001–02) *Tuition:* state resident $2558 full-time, $114 per credit hour part-time; nonresident $7670 full-time, $309 per credit hour part-time. Part-time tuition and fees vary according to course load. *Required fees:* $370 full-time. *Room and board:* $2924; room only: $1526. Room and board charges vary according to board plan and housing facility. *Payment plan:* deferred payment. *Waivers:* senior citizens and employees or children of employees.

Financial Aid Of all full-time matriculated undergraduates who enrolled in 2001, 6498 applied for aid, 5406 were judged to have need, 2012 had their need fully met. *Average percent of need met:* 86%. *Average financial aid package:* $7410. *Average need-based loan:* $2785. *Average need-based gift aid:* $3518. *Average indebtedness upon graduation:* $14,976.

Applying *Options:* deferred entrance. *Application fee:* $25. *Required:* high school transcript, minimum 2.0 GPA. *Application deadline:* rolling (freshmen), rolling (transfers). *Notification:* continuous (freshmen).

Admissions Contact Stephen A. Byrn, Director of Admissions, Eastern Kentucky University, Coates 2A, 521 Lancaster Avenue, Richmond, KY 40475-3102. *Phone:* 859-622-2106. *Toll-free phone:* 800-465-9191.

GEORGETOWN COLLEGE
Georgetown, Kentucky

- **Independent** comprehensive, founded 1829, affiliated with Baptist Church
- **Calendar** semesters
- **Degrees** bachelor's and master's
- **Suburban** 110-acre campus with easy access to Cincinnati
- **Endowment** $33.3 million
- **Coed,** 1,361 undergraduate students, 96% full-time, 57% women, 43% men
- **Moderately difficult** entrance level, 95% of applicants were admitted

Undergraduates 1,304 full-time, 57 part-time. Students come from 25 states and territories, 16 other countries, 16% are from out of state, 2% African American, 0.3% Asian American or Pacific Islander, 0.2% Hispanic American, 0.1% Native American, 1% international, 3% transferred in, 91% live on campus. *Retention:* 79% of 2001 full-time freshmen returned.

Freshmen *Admission:* 827 applied, 782 admitted, 357 enrolled. *Average high school GPA:* 3.56. *Test scores:* SAT verbal scores over 500: 70%; SAT math scores over 500: 68%; ACT scores over 18: 97%; SAT verbal scores over 600: 22%; SAT math scores over 600: 22%; ACT scores over 24: 50%; SAT verbal scores over 700: 2%; SAT math scores over 700: 2%; ACT scores over 30: 7%.

Faculty *Total:* 126, 73% full-time, 75% with terminal degrees. *Student/faculty ratio:* 13:1.

Majors Accounting; American studies; art; biology; business administration; business marketing and marketing management; chemistry; computer science; early childhood education; ecology; education; elementary education; English; environmental science; European studies; finance; French; German; history; information sciences/systems; international business; management information systems/business data processing; mass communications; mathematics; medical technology; music; music (piano and organ performance); music teacher education; music (voice and choral/opera performance); philosophy; physical education; physics; political science; pre-dentistry; pre-law; pre-medicine; psychology; recreation/leisure studies; religious studies; secondary education; sociology; Spanish; speech/rhetorical studies; theater arts/drama.

Academic Programs *Special study options:* accelerated degree program, advanced placement credit, cooperative education, double majors, internships, off-campus study, part-time degree program, student-designed majors, study abroad, summer session for credit. *ROTC:* Army (b), Air Force (c). *Unusual degree programs:* 3-2 engineering with University of Kentucky, Washington University in St. Louis; nursing with University of Kentucky.

Library Anna Ashcraft Ensor Learning Resource Center plus 1 other with 145,794 titles, 833 serial subscriptions, 3,009 audiovisual materials, an OPAC, a Web page.

Computers on Campus 150 computers available on campus for general student use. A campuswide network can be accessed from student residence rooms and from off campus. Internet access, at least one staffed computer lab available.

Student Life *Housing:* on-campus residence required through senior year. *Options:* men-only, women-only. *Activities and Organizations:* drama/theater group, student-run newspaper, radio station, choral group, Campus Ministries, Association of Georgetown Students, Harper-Gatton Leadership Center, President's Ambassadors, Phi Beta Lambda, national fraternities, national sororities. *Campus security:* 24-hour patrols, late-night transport/escort service. *Student Services:* health clinic, personal/psychological counseling.

Athletics Member NAIA. *Intercollegiate sports:* baseball M(s), basketball M(s)/W(s), cross-country running M(s)/W(s), football M(s), golf M(s)/W(s), soccer M(s)/W(s), softball W(s), tennis M(s)/W(s), volleyball W(s). *Intramural sports:* basketball M/W, football M/W, golf M/W, racquetball M/W, soccer M/W, softball M/W, table tennis M/W, tennis M/W, volleyball M/W.

Standardized Tests *Required:* SAT I or ACT (for admission). *Recommended:* ACT (for admission).

Costs (2002–03) *Comprehensive fee:* $19,690 includes full-time tuition ($14,260), mandatory fees ($380), and room and board ($5050). Part-time tuition: $580 per hour. *Room and board:* College room only: $2430. Room and board charges vary according to board plan and housing facility. *Payment plans:* installment, deferred payment. *Waivers:* employees or children of employees.

Financial Aid Of all full-time matriculated undergraduates who enrolled in 2001, 1274 applied for aid, 808 were judged to have need, 642 had their need fully met. 218 Federal Work-Study jobs (averaging $785). In 2001, 427 non-need-based awards were made. *Average percent of need met:* 93%. *Average financial aid package:* $14,780. *Average need-based loan:* $3436. *Average need-based gift aid:* $8813. *Average indebtedness upon graduation:* $14,735.

Applying *Options:* electronic application, early decision. *Application fee:* $25. *Required:* essay or personal statement, high school transcript, minimum 2.5 GPA. *Required for some:* letters of recommendation, interview. *Application deadline:* 7/1 (freshmen), rolling (transfers). *Early decision:* 9/15. *Notification:* continuous (freshmen), 10/15 (early decision).

Admissions Contact Mr. Brian Taylor, Director of Admissions, Georgetown College, 400 East College Street, Georgetown, KY 40324. *Phone:* 502-863-8009. *Toll-free phone:* 800-788-9985. *Fax:* 502-868-7733. *E-mail:* admissions@georgetowncollege.edu.

KENTUCKY CHRISTIAN COLLEGE
Grayson, Kentucky

- **Independent** comprehensive, founded 1919, affiliated with Christian Churches and Churches of Christ
- **Calendar** semesters
- **Degrees** certificates, associate, bachelor's, and master's
- **Rural** 124-acre campus
- **Endowment** $4.2 million
- **Coed,** 578 undergraduate students, 97% full-time, 52% women, 48% men
- **Moderately difficult** entrance level, 83% of applicants were admitted

Undergraduates 558 full-time, 20 part-time. Students come from 25 states and territories, 8 other countries, 66% are from out of state, 2% African American, 0.2% Asian American or Pacific Islander, 0.3% Hispanic American, 0.5% Native American, 3% international, 6% transferred in, 92% live on campus. *Retention:* 68% of 2001 full-time freshmen returned.

Freshmen *Admission:* 273 applied, 226 admitted, 159 enrolled. *Average high school GPA:* 3.20. *Test scores:* SAT verbal scores over 500: 32%; SAT math scores over 500: 48%; ACT scores over 18: 82%; SAT verbal scores over 600: 16%; SAT math scores over 600: 4%; ACT scores over 24: 33%; ACT scores over 30: 7%.

Faculty *Total:* 52, 58% full-time, 58% with terminal degrees. *Student/faculty ratio:* 18:1.

Majors Business administration; elementary education; history; interdisciplinary studies; middle school education; music; music teacher education; nursing; pastoral counseling; psychology; religious education; secretarial science; social work.

Academic Programs *Special study options:* academic remediation for entering students, accelerated degree program, advanced placement credit, cooperative education, double majors, independent study, internships, off-campus study, part-time degree program, services for LD students, summer session for credit.

Library Young Library with 101,859 titles, 439 serial subscriptions, 634 audiovisual materials.

Computers on Campus 50 computers available on campus for general student use. A campuswide network can be accessed from student residence rooms and from off campus. Internet access, at least one staffed computer lab available.

Student Life *Housing:* on-campus residence required through senior year. *Options:* men-only, women-only. *Activities and Organizations:* drama/theater group, student-run newspaper, choral group, Rotaract, SIFE, Matheteuo, Pi Chi Delta, Laos Alpha. *Campus security:* 24-hour emergency response devices, late-night transport/escort service, controlled dormitory access, late night security patrols. *Student Services:* health clinic, personal/psychological counseling.

Athletics Member NCCAA. *Intercollegiate sports:* basketball M/W, cross-country running M/W, soccer M/W, tennis M/W, volleyball W. *Intramural sports:* basketball M/W, bowling M/W, football M/W, racquetball M/W, soccer M/W, softball M/W, table tennis M/W, volleyball M/W.

Standardized Tests *Required:* SAT I or ACT (for admission).

Costs (2001–02) *One-time required fee:* $125. *Comprehensive fee:* $12,220 includes full-time tuition ($7872), mandatory fees ($70), and room and board ($4278). Part-time tuition: $246 per credit hour. *Room and board:* Room and board charges vary according to board plan. *Payment plans:* tuition prepayment, installment. *Waivers:* minority students and employees or children of employees.

Financial Aid Of all full-time matriculated undergraduates who enrolled in 2001, 549 applied for aid, 405 were judged to have need, 49 had their need fully met. 218 Federal Work-Study jobs (averaging $1895). 50 State and other part-time jobs (averaging $1604). In 2001, 99 non-need-based awards were made. *Average percent of need met:* 54%. *Average financial aid package:* $7820. *Average need-based loan:* $3594. *Average need-based gift aid:* $3333. *Average non-need based aid:* $5076. *Average indebtedness upon graduation:* $19,497.

Applying *Options:* common application, deferred entrance. *Application fee:* $25. *Required:* essay or personal statement, high school transcript, 3 letters of recommendation. *Required for some:* interview. *Recommended:* minimum 2.0 GPA. *Application deadline:* rolling (freshmen), rolling (transfers). *Notification:* continuous (freshmen).

Admissions Contact Sandra Deakins, Director of Admissions, Kentucky Christian College, 100 Academic Parkway, Grayson, KY 41143-2205. *Phone:* 606-474-3266. *Toll-free phone:* 800-522-3181. *Fax:* 606-474-3155. *E-mail:* knights@email.kcc.edu.

KENTUCKY MOUNTAIN BIBLE COLLEGE
Vancleve, Kentucky

- **Independent interdenominational** 4-year, founded 1931
- **Calendar** semesters
- **Degrees** associate and bachelor's
- **Rural** 35-acre campus
- **Endowment** $350,000
- **Coed,** 82 undergraduate students, 78% full-time, 40% women, 60% men
- **Moderately difficult** entrance level, 51% of applicants were admitted

Undergraduates 64 full-time, 18 part-time. Students come from 14 states and territories, 5 other countries, 60% are from out of state, 1% African American, 1% Hispanic American, 9% international, 6% transferred in, 93% live on campus. *Retention:* 64% of 2001 full-time freshmen returned.

Freshmen *Admission:* 41 applied, 21 admitted, 25 enrolled. *Average high school GPA:* 3.33. *Test scores:* SAT verbal scores over 500: 50%; SAT math scores over 500: 50%; ACT scores over 18: 77%; SAT verbal scores over 600: 17%; SAT math scores over 600: 17%; ACT scores over 24: 54%; ACT scores over 30: 8%.

Faculty *Total:* 14, 64% full-time. *Student/faculty ratio:* 6:1.

Majors Mass communications; missionary studies; pre-theology; religious education; religious studies.

Academic Programs *Special study options:* academic remediation for entering students, adult/continuing education programs, advanced placement credit, internships, part-time degree program.

Library Gibson Library with 23,520 titles, 175 serial subscriptions, 1,263 audiovisual materials, an OPAC.

Computers on Campus 12 computers available on campus for general student use. Internet access, at least one staffed computer lab available.

Kentucky Mountain Bible College (continued)

Student Life *Housing:* on-campus residence required through senior year. *Options:* men-only, women-only. *Activities and Organizations:* choral group, Drama Team, choral groups, Student Council, Band, Student Involvement (missionary group). *Campus security:* student patrols. *Student Services:* personal/psychological counseling.

Standardized Tests *Required:* SAT I or ACT (for admission).

Costs (2002–03) *Comprehensive fee:* $7180 includes full-time tuition ($3750), mandatory fees ($430), and room and board ($3000). Full-time tuition and fees vary according to course load. Part-time tuition: $125 per credit hour. Part-time tuition and fees vary according to course load. *Required fees:* $88 per term part-time. *Room and board:* College room only: $950. Room and board charges vary according to housing facility. *Payment plan:* installment. *Waivers:* employees or children of employees.

Financial Aid Of all full-time matriculated undergraduates who enrolled in 2001, 55 applied for aid, 55 were judged to have need. 40 Federal Work-Study jobs (averaging $480). In 2001, 2 non-need-based awards were made. *Average percent of need met:* 30%. *Average financial aid package:* $2000. *Average need-based loan:* $2600. *Average need-based gift aid:* $1500. *Average non-need based aid:* $3800. *Average indebtedness upon graduation:* $2000.

Applying *Options:* deferred entrance. *Application fee:* $25. *Required:* essay or personal statement, high school transcript, minimum 2.0 GPA, letters of recommendation. *Recommended:* interview. *Application deadline:* rolling (freshmen), rolling (transfers). *Notification:* continuous (freshmen).

Admissions Contact Mr. James Nelson, Director of Recruiting, Kentucky Mountain Bible College, PO Box 10, Vancleve, KY 41385. *Phone:* 606-666-5000 Ext. 130. *Toll-free phone:* 800-879-KMBC Ext. 130. *Fax:* 606-666-7744. *E-mail:* jnelson@kmbc.edu.

KENTUCKY STATE UNIVERSITY

Frankfort, Kentucky

- **State-related** comprehensive, founded 1886
- **Calendar** semesters
- **Degrees** associate, bachelor's, and master's
- **Small-town** 485-acre campus with easy access to Louisville
- **Coed,** 2,129 undergraduate students, 71% full-time, 56% women, 44% men
- **Minimally difficult** entrance level, 45% of applicants were admitted

Undergraduates 1,520 full-time, 609 part-time. Students come from 35 states and territories, 23 other countries, 34% are from out of state, 4% transferred in, 36% live on campus. *Retention:* 74% of 2001 full-time freshmen returned.

Freshmen *Admission:* 1,134 applied, 511 admitted, 339 enrolled. *Average high school GPA:* 2.7.

Faculty *Total:* 130, 95% full-time. *Student/faculty ratio:* 15:1.

Majors Applied mathematics; art education; biology; business administration; chemistry; clothing/apparel/textile studies; computer/information sciences; criminal justice studies; drafting/design technology; electrical/electronic engineering technology; elementary education; English; executive assistant; fine/studio arts; health/physical education; history; individual/family development; liberal arts and sciences/liberal studies; mathematics; medical technology; music (general performance); music teacher education; nursing; physical education; political science; psychology; public administration; secondary education; social studies education; social work; sociology.

Academic Programs *Special study options:* academic remediation for entering students, accelerated degree program, adult/continuing education programs, advanced placement credit, cooperative education, English as a second language, honors programs, independent study, internships, off-campus study, part-time degree program, services for LD students, student-designed majors, study abroad, summer session for credit. *ROTC:* Army (c). *Unusual degree programs:* 3-2 engineering with University of Kentucky, University of Maryland College Park.

Library Blazer Library with 296,631 titles, 1,097 serial subscriptions, 3,025 audiovisual materials, an OPAC.

Computers on Campus 230 computers available on campus for general student use. A campuswide network can be accessed from off campus that provide access to e-mail. Internet access, at least one staffed computer lab available.

Student Life *Housing Options:* men-only, women-only. *Activities and Organizations:* drama/theater group, student-run newspaper, choral group, marching band, Baptist Student Union, student government, national fraternities, national sororities. *Campus security:* 24-hour patrols, controlled dormitory access. *Student Services:* health clinic, personal/psychological counseling.

Athletics Member NCAA. All Division II. *Intercollegiate sports:* baseball M, basketball M(s)/W(s), cross-country running M(s)/W(s), football M(s), golf M(s), softball W, tennis M(s)/W(s), track and field M(s)/W(s), volleyball W(s). *Intramural sports:* archery M/W, basketball M/W, bowling M/W, football M/W, soccer M/W, swimming M/W, tennis M/W, track and field M/W, volleyball M/W.

Standardized Tests *Required:* SAT I or ACT (for admission). *Recommended:* ACT (for admission).

Costs (2002–03) *Tuition:* state resident $2448 full-time, $102 per credit hour part-time; nonresident $7350 full-time, $306 per credit hour part-time. *Required fees:* $398 full-time, $11 per credit hour, $38 per term part-time. *Room and board:* $4214; room only: $2000. *Payment plans:* installment, deferred payment. *Waivers:* senior citizens and employees or children of employees.

Financial Aid Of all full-time matriculated undergraduates who enrolled in 2001, 1679 applied for aid, 1595 were judged to have need, 338 had their need fully met. 1000 Federal Work-Study jobs. *Average percent of need met:* 85%. *Average financial aid package:* $7200. *Average non-need based aid:* $4000. *Financial aid deadline:* 5/31.

Applying *Options:* early admission. *Application fee:* $15. *Required:* high school transcript. *Required for some:* essay or personal statement, minimum 3.0 GPA, 2 letters of recommendation, interview. *Recommended:* minimum 2.0 GPA. *Application deadline:* rolling (freshmen), rolling (transfers).

Admissions Contact Mr. Vory Billaps, Director of Records, Registration, and Admission, Kentucky State University, 400 East Main, Frankfort, KY 40601. *Phone:* 502-597-6340. *Toll-free phone:* 800-633-9415 (in-state); 800-325-1716 (out-of-state). *Fax:* 502-597-6239. *E-mail:* jburrell@qwmail.kysu.edu.

KENTUCKY WESLEYAN COLLEGE

Owensboro, Kentucky

- **Independent Methodist** 4-year, founded 1858
- **Calendar** semesters
- **Degree** bachelor's
- **Suburban** 52-acre campus
- **Endowment** $20.9 million
- **Coed,** 671 undergraduate students, 94% full-time, 46% women, 54% men
- **Moderately difficult** entrance level, 81% of applicants were admitted

Undergraduates 631 full-time, 40 part-time. Students come from 12 states and territories, 3 other countries, 29% are from out of state, 7% African American, 0.5% Asian American or Pacific Islander, 0.3% Hispanic American, 0.5% international, 6% transferred in, 47% live on campus. *Retention:* 77% of 2001 full-time freshmen returned.

Freshmen *Admission:* 554 applied, 450 admitted, 164 enrolled. *Average high school GPA:* 3.25. *Test scores:* SAT verbal scores over 500: 34%; SAT math scores over 500: 43%; ACT scores over 18: 78%; SAT verbal scores over 600: 17%; SAT math scores over 600: 13%; ACT scores over 24: 33%; ACT scores over 30: 2%.

Faculty *Total:* 80, 54% full-time, 48% with terminal degrees. *Student/faculty ratio:* 13:1.

Majors Accounting; art education; biology; business administration; chemistry; communications; computer science; criminal justice studies; elementary education; English; environmental science; fine arts and art studies related; foreign languages/literatures; history; human services; interdisciplinary studies; mathematics; medical technology; middle school education; music teacher education; philosophy; philosophy and religion related; physical education; physics; political science; pre-dentistry; pre-law; pre-medicine; pre-veterinary studies; psychology; public administration and services related; secondary education; sociology; sport/fitness administration.

Academic Programs *Special study options:* academic remediation for entering students, advanced placement credit, double majors, independent study, internships, off-campus study, part-time degree program, student-designed majors, study abroad, summer session for credit. *Unusual degree programs:* 3-2 engineering with Auburn University, University of Kentucky.

Library Library Learning Center with 78,781 titles, 362 serial subscriptions, 3,510 audiovisual materials, a Web page.

Computers on Campus A campuswide network can be accessed from student residence rooms. At least one staffed computer lab available.

Student Life *Housing:* on-campus residence required through junior year. *Options:* coed, men-only, women-only. *Activities and Organizations:* drama/theater group, student-run newspaper, radio station, choral group, Student Government Association, student activities programming board, Leadership KWC, Pre-Professional Society, Wesley club, national fraternities, national sororities. *Campus security:* late-night transport/escort service, 12-hour patrols by trained security personnel. *Student Services:* health clinic, personal/psychological counseling.

Athletics Member NCAA. All Division II. *Intercollegiate sports:* baseball M(s), basketball M(s)/W(s), football M(s), golf M(s)/W(s), soccer M(s)/W(s), softball W(s), tennis W, volleyball W(s). *Intramural sports:* basketball M/W, racquetball M/W, soccer M/W, softball M, table tennis M/W, volleyball M/W.

Standardized Tests *Required:* SAT I or ACT (for admission).
Costs (2001–02) *Comprehensive fee:* $15,900 includes full-time tuition ($10,570), mandatory fees ($350), and room and board ($4980). Full-time tuition and fees vary according to course load. Part-time tuition: $340 per semester hour. Part-time tuition and fees vary according to course load. *Required fees:* $50 per term part-time. *Room and board:* College room only: $2320. *Payment plans:* installment, deferred payment. *Waivers:* children of alumni, senior citizens, and employees or children of employees.
Financial Aid Of all full-time matriculated undergraduates who enrolled in 2001, 608 applied for aid, 496 were judged to have need, 183 had their need fully met. In 2001, 113 non-need-based awards were made. *Average percent of need met:* 83%. *Average financial aid package:* $9855. *Average need-based gift aid:* $8251. *Average non-need based aid:* $8167.
Applying *Options:* common application, electronic application, early admission, deferred entrance. *Application fee:* $20. *Required:* essay or personal statement, high school transcript. *Required for some:* letters of recommendation. *Recommended:* letters of recommendation. *Application deadlines:* 9/1 (freshmen), 9/1 (transfers). *Notification:* continuous (freshmen).
Admissions Contact Mr. Ken Rasp, Dean of Admission, Kentucky Wesleyan College, 3000 Frederica Street, PO Box 1039, Owensboro, KY 42302-1039. *Phone:* 270-852-3120. *Toll-free phone:* 800-999-0592 (in-state); 270-926-3111 (out-of-state). *Fax:* 270-926-3196. *E-mail:* admission@kwc.edu.

LINDSEY WILSON COLLEGE
Columbia, Kentucky

- **Independent United Methodist** comprehensive, founded 1903
- **Calendar** semesters
- **Degrees** associate, bachelor's, and master's
- **Rural** 40-acre campus
- **Endowment** $28.0 million
- **Coed,** 1,255 undergraduate students, 89% full-time, 61% women, 39% men
- **Minimally difficult** entrance level, 94% of applicants were admitted

Undergraduates Students come from 18 states and territories, 22 other countries, 8% are from out of state, 7% African American, 0.2% Asian American or Pacific Islander, 2% Hispanic American, 0.3% Native American, 7% international, 44% live on campus. *Retention:* 54% of 2001 full-time freshmen returned.
Freshmen *Admission:* 1,340 applied, 1,254 admitted. *Average high school GPA:* 2.90. *Test scores:* ACT scores over 18: 80%; ACT scores over 24: 10%; ACT scores over 30: 5%.
Faculty *Total:* 87, 68% full-time, 41% with terminal degrees. *Student/faculty ratio:* 20:1.
Majors Accounting; agricultural business; American studies; art; biology; business administration; business education; chemistry; computer programming; criminal justice/law enforcement administration; education; elementary education; English; history; human services; liberal arts and sciences/liberal studies; management information systems/business data processing; mass communications; mathematics; physical education; pre-dentistry; pre-engineering; pre-law; pre-medicine; social sciences; social work.
Academic Programs *Special study options:* academic remediation for entering students, accelerated degree program, adult/continuing education programs, advanced placement credit, cooperative education, double majors, English as a second language, independent study, internships, off-campus study, part-time degree program, services for LD students, student-designed majors, summer session for credit. *ROTC:* Army (c).
Library Katie Murrell Library with 80,000 titles, 1,500 serial subscriptions.
Computers on Campus 80 computers available on campus for general student use. A campuswide network can be accessed from student residence rooms and from off campus. Internet access, at least one staffed computer lab available.
Student Life *Housing:* on-campus residence required through senior year. *Options:* men-only, women-only, disabled students. *Activities and Organizations:* drama/theater group, student-run newspaper, choral group. *Campus security:* 24-hour emergency response devices and patrols. *Student Services:* health clinic, personal/psychological counseling.
Athletics Member NAIA. *Intercollegiate sports:* baseball M(s), basketball M(s)/W(s), bowling M(s)/W(s), cross-country running M(s)/W(s), golf M(s)/W(s), soccer M(s)/W(s), softball W(s), tennis M(s)/W(s), track and field M(s)/W(s), volleyball W(s). *Intramural sports:* basketball M, football M/W, softball M/W, table tennis M/W, tennis M/W, volleyball M/W, weight lifting M/W.
Standardized Tests *Required:* ACT (for admission).
Costs (2002–03) *Comprehensive fee:* $17,372 includes full-time tuition ($11,952), mandatory fees ($146), and room and board ($5274). Part-time tuition: $498 per credit hour. *Room and board:* College room only: $1946. *Payment plan:* installment. *Waivers:* employees or children of employees.
Applying *Options:* common application, electronic application, early admission, deferred entrance. *Required:* high school transcript. *Required for some:* 3 letters of recommendation. *Recommended:* interview. *Application deadline:* rolling (freshmen), rolling (transfers). *Notification:* continuous (freshmen).
Admissions Contact Mr. Claude Bacon, Director of Admissions, Lindsey Wilson College, 210 Lindsey Wilson Street, Columbia, KY 42728-1298. *Phone:* 270-384-8100 Ext. 8008. *Toll-free phone:* 800-264-0138. *Fax:* 270-384-8200. *E-mail:* baconc@lindsey.edu.

MID-CONTINENT COLLEGE
Mayfield, Kentucky

- **Independent Southern Baptist** 4-year, founded 1949
- **Calendar** semesters
- **Degree** certificates, diplomas, and bachelor's
- **Small-town** 60-acre campus
- **Endowment** $2.1 million
- **Coed,** 265 undergraduate students, 85% full-time, 37% women, 63% men
- **Minimally difficult** entrance level, 85% of applicants were admitted

Undergraduates 224 full-time, 41 part-time. Students come from 15 states and territories, 10 other countries, 21% are from out of state, 58% transferred in. *Retention:* 58% of 2001 full-time freshmen returned.
Freshmen *Admission:* 156 applied, 133 admitted, 90 enrolled. *Average high school GPA:* 2.89. *Test scores:* SAT verbal scores over 500: 17%; SAT math scores over 500: 17%; ACT scores over 18: 68%; SAT math scores over 600: 17%; ACT scores over 24: 7%.
Faculty *Total:* 48, 46% full-time, 33% with terminal degrees. *Student/faculty ratio:* 14:1.
Majors Behavioral sciences; biblical languages/literatures; biblical studies; counseling psychology; elementary education; English; general studies; missionary studies; organizational behavior; religious education; social sciences and history related.
Academic Programs *Special study options:* academic remediation for entering students, accelerated degree program, advanced placement credit, double majors, English as a second language, independent study, part-time degree program, study abroad, summer session for credit.
Library Anne P. Markham Library with 30,158 titles, 148 serial subscriptions, 1,865 audiovisual materials.
Computers on Campus 24 computers available on campus for general student use. A campuswide network can be accessed from student residence rooms and from off campus. Internet access, at least one staffed computer lab available.
Student Life *Housing:* on-campus residence required for freshman year. *Options:* men-only, women-only. *Activities and Organizations:* student-run newspaper. *Campus security:* student patrols. *Student Services:* personal/psychological counseling.
Athletics Member NAIA, NCCAA. *Intercollegiate sports:* baseball M(s), basketball M(s), golf M/W, soccer M(s), softball W(s).
Standardized Tests *Required:* SAT I or ACT (for admission).
Costs (2001–02) *Comprehensive fee:* $11,680 includes full-time tuition ($6880) and room and board ($4800). Full-time tuition and fees vary according to course load and program. Part-time tuition: $215 per credit hour. Part-time tuition and fees vary according to course load and program. *Room and board:* College room only: $2600. Room and board charges vary according to board plan and housing facility. *Waivers:* employees or children of employees.
Financial Aid Of all full-time matriculated undergraduates who enrolled in 2001, 540 applied for aid, 525 were judged to have need, 175 had their need fully met. 6 Federal Work-Study jobs (averaging $2144). In 2001, 9 non-need-based awards were made. *Average percent of need met:* 65%. *Average financial aid package:* $6000. *Average need-based loan:* $4000. *Average need-based gift aid:* $1500. *Average non-need based aid:* $500. *Average indebtedness upon graduation:* $12,000.
Applying *Options:* common application, early admission. *Application fee:* $20. *Required:* essay or personal statement, high school transcript, minimum 2.0 GPA, 2 letters of recommendation. *Recommended:* minimum 2.0 GPA, 1 letter of recommendation. *Application deadline:* rolling (freshmen), rolling (transfers). *Notification:* continuous (freshmen).
Admissions Contact Mrs. Darla Zakowicz, Director of Enrollment and Retention Management, Mid-Continent College, 99 Powell Road East, Mayfield, KY 42068. *Phone:* 270-247-8521 Ext. 311. *E-mail:* mcc@midcontinent.edu.

MIDWAY COLLEGE
Midway, Kentucky

- **Independent** 4-year, founded 1847, affiliated with Christian Church (Disciples of Christ)
- **Calendar** semesters
- **Degrees** associate and bachelor's
- **Small-town** 105-acre campus with easy access to Louisville and Lexington
- **Endowment** $11.2 million
- **Women only,** 874 undergraduate students, 73% full-time
- **Minimally difficult** entrance level, 71% of applicants were admitted

Undergraduates 639 full-time, 235 part-time. Students come from 31 states and territories, 5 other countries, 12% are from out of state, 7% African American, 0.7% Hispanic American, 0.6% Native American, 0.8% international, 7% transferred in, 21% live on campus. *Retention:* 64% of 2001 full-time freshmen returned.

Freshmen *Admission:* 358 applied, 255 admitted, 132 enrolled. *Average high school GPA:* 3.03. *Test scores:* SAT verbal scores over 500: 57%; SAT math scores over 500: 43%; ACT scores over 18: 74%; SAT verbal scores over 600: 29%; ACT scores over 24: 8%.

Faculty *Total:* 82, 46% full-time, 37% with terminal degrees. *Student/faculty ratio:* 15:1.

Majors Biology; business administration; child care/development; early childhood education; education; elementary education; English; environmental biology; equestrian studies; farm/ranch management; information sciences/systems; liberal arts and sciences/liberal studies; middle school education; nursing; paralegal/legal assistant; physical therapy; psychology.

Academic Programs *Special study options:* academic remediation for entering students, adult/continuing education programs, advanced placement credit, distance learning, honors programs, independent study, internships, off-campus study, part-time degree program, services for LD students, study abroad, summer session for credit. *ROTC:* Army (c).

Library Little Memorial Library with 96,236 titles, 427 serial subscriptions, 9,141 audiovisual materials, an OPAC, a Web page.

Computers on Campus 60 computers available on campus for general student use. A campuswide network can be accessed from student residence rooms and from off campus. Internet access, at least one staffed computer lab available.

Student Life *Housing:* on-campus residence required through sophomore year. *Options:* women-only. *Activities and Organizations:* student-run newspaper, choral group, student government, Midway Chorale, Midway Association of Nursing Students, Council on Religious Activities, Midway Horse Women's Association. *Campus security:* 24-hour emergency response devices and patrols, late-night transport/escort service. *Student Services:* health clinic, personal/psychological counseling, women's center.

Athletics Member NAIA. *Intercollegiate sports:* basketball W(s), cross-country running W(s), equestrian sports W(s), soccer W(s), softball W(s), tennis W(s), track and field W(s), volleyball W(s). *Intramural sports:* basketball W, equestrian sports W, softball W, tennis W, volleyball W.

Standardized Tests *Required:* SAT I or ACT (for admission).

Costs (2001–02) *Comprehensive fee:* $15,715 includes full-time tuition ($10,100), mandatory fees ($75), and room and board ($5540). Full-time tuition and fees vary according to program. Part-time tuition: $340 per semester hour. Part-time tuition and fees vary according to class time and course load. *Required fees:* $4 per semester hour. *Room and board:* College room only: $2800. Room and board charges vary according to board plan and housing facility. *Payment plan:* deferred payment. *Waivers:* senior citizens and employees or children of employees.

Financial Aid Of all full-time matriculated undergraduates who enrolled in 2001, 517 applied for aid, 491 were judged to have need, 215 had their need fully met. 118 Federal Work-Study jobs (averaging $1582). 38 State and other part-time jobs (averaging $1547). In 2001, 19 non-need-based awards were made. *Average percent of need met:* 77%. *Average financial aid package:* $11,446. *Average need-based loan:* $3551. *Average need-based gift aid:* $4984. *Average non-need based aid:* $4009. *Average indebtedness upon graduation:* $10,023.

Applying *Options:* common application, electronic application, early admission, deferred entrance. *Application fee:* $15. *Required:* high school transcript. *Required for some:* essay or personal statement, letters of recommendation, interview. *Recommended:* minimum 2.2 GPA. *Application deadline:* rolling (freshmen), rolling (transfers). *Notification:* continuous (freshmen).

Admissions Contact Mr. K. Bryan, Director of Admissions, Midway College, 512 East Stephens Street, Pinkerton Building, Midway, KY 40347-1120. *Phone:* 859-846-5346. *Toll-free phone:* 800-755-0031. *Fax:* 859-846-5823. *E-mail:* admissions@midway.edu.

MOREHEAD STATE UNIVERSITY
Morehead, Kentucky

- **State-supported** comprehensive, founded 1922
- **Calendar** semesters
- **Degrees** associate, bachelor's, master's, and post-master's certificates
- **Small-town** 809-acre campus
- **Coed,** 7,199 undergraduate students, 85% full-time, 61% women, 39% men
- **Minimally difficult** entrance level, 73% of applicants were admitted

Undergraduates Students come from 41 states and territories, 29 other countries, 15% are from out of state, 4% African American, 0.3% Asian American or Pacific Islander, 0.4% Hispanic American, 0.4% Native American, 0.7% international, 36% live on campus.

Freshmen *Admission:* 5,180 applied, 3,772 admitted. *Average high school GPA:* 3.11.

Faculty *Total:* 469, 74% full-time. *Student/faculty ratio:* 18:1.

Majors Accounting; agribusiness; agricultural education; agricultural sciences; biology; business administration; business economics; business education; business marketing and marketing management; chemistry; communications; early childhood education; ecology; elementary education; English; enterprise management; finance; fine/studio arts; French; general studies; geography; geology; health education; history; home economics; home economics education; industrial arts education; industrial technology; mathematics; mathematics/computer science; mathematics education; medical radiologic technology; medical technology; middle school education; music; music teacher education; nursing; paralegal/legal assistant; philosophy; physical education; physics; political science; psychology; real estate; recreation/leisure facilities management; science education; secretarial science; social sciences; social work; sociology; Spanish; special education; speech/rhetorical studies; theater arts/drama; trade/industrial education; veterinarian assistant.

Academic Programs *Special study options:* academic remediation for entering students, accelerated degree program, adult/continuing education programs, advanced placement credit, cooperative education, distance learning, double majors, English as a second language, honors programs, independent study, internships, off-campus study, part-time degree program, services for LD students, student-designed majors, study abroad, summer session for credit. *ROTC:* Army (b).

Library Camden Carroll Library with 299,290 titles, 13,570 serial subscriptions, 21,033 audiovisual materials, an OPAC, a Web page.

Computers on Campus 1000 computers available on campus for general student use. A campuswide network can be accessed from student residence rooms and from off campus. Internet access, online (class) registration, at least one staffed computer lab available.

Student Life *Housing:* on-campus residence required through sophomore year. *Options:* coed, men-only, women-only, disabled students. *Activities and Organizations:* drama/theater group, student-run newspaper, radio and television station, choral group, marching band, national fraternities, national sororities. *Campus security:* 24-hour emergency response devices and patrols, late-night transport/escort service. *Student Services:* health clinic, personal/psychological counseling.

Athletics Member NCAA. All Division I except football (Division I-AA). *Intercollegiate sports:* baseball M(s), basketball M(s)/W(s), bowling M(c)/W(c), cross-country running M(s)/W(s), equestrian sports M(c)/W(c), golf M(s), riflery M(s)/W(s), soccer W, softball W(s), tennis M(s)/W(s), track and field M(s)/W(s), volleyball W(s). *Intramural sports:* archery M/W, badminton M/W, basketball M/W, football M/W, golf M/W, racquetball M/W, soccer M(c)/W(c), table tennis M/W, tennis M/W, track and field M/W, volleyball M/W.

Standardized Tests *Required:* SAT I or ACT (for admission). *Recommended:* ACT (for admission).

Costs (2001–02) *Tuition:* state resident $2710 full-time, $113 per credit hour part-time; nonresident $7204 full-time, $300 per credit hour part-time. *Room and board:* $3800; room only: $1900. Room and board charges vary according to board plan and housing facility. *Payment plans:* installment, deferred payment. *Waivers:* senior citizens and employees or children of employees.

Financial Aid Of all full-time matriculated undergraduates who enrolled in 2001, 4777 applied for aid, 3882 were judged to have need, 1782 had their need fully met. 650 Federal Work-Study jobs (averaging $1508). 626 State and other part-time jobs (averaging $1045). In 2001, 1176 non-need-based awards were made. *Average percent of need met:* 91%. *Average financial aid package:* $6122. *Average need-based loan:* $2596. *Average need-based gift aid:* $3771. *Average non-need based aid:* $2224. *Average indebtedness upon graduation:* $12,604.

Applying *Options:* electronic application, early admission, deferred entrance. *Required:* high school transcript. *Required for some:* letters of recommendation. *Application deadline:* rolling (freshmen), rolling (transfers). *Notification:* continuous (freshmen).

Admissions Contact Mr. Tim Rhodes, Assistant Vice President of Admissions, Financial Aid and Housing, Morehead State University, Howell McDowell 301, Morehead, KY 40351. *Phone:* 606-783-2000. *Toll-free phone:* 800-585-6781. *Fax:* 606-783-5038. *E-mail:* admissions@morehead-st.edu.

MURRAY STATE UNIVERSITY
Murray, Kentucky

- **State-supported** comprehensive, founded 1922, part of Kentucky Council on Post Secondary Education
- **Calendar** semesters
- **Degrees** associate, bachelor's, master's, post-master's, and postbachelor's certificates
- **Small-town** 238-acre campus
- **Endowment** $25.1 million
- **Coed,** 7,763 undergraduate students, 85% full-time, 58% women, 42% men
- **Moderately difficult** entrance level, 88% of applicants were admitted

Undergraduates 6,622 full-time, 1,141 part-time. Students come from 48 states and territories, 66 other countries, 28% are from out of state, 6% African American, 0.6% Asian American or Pacific Islander, 0.6% Hispanic American, 0.3% Native American, 3% international, 9% transferred in, 40% live on campus. *Retention:* 78% of 2001 full-time freshmen returned.

Freshmen *Admission:* 2,743 applied, 2,411 admitted, 1,411 enrolled. *Test scores:* ACT scores over 18: 100%; ACT scores over 24: 47%; ACT scores over 30: 5%.

Faculty *Total:* 509, 74% full-time, 61% with terminal degrees. *Student/faculty ratio:* 17:1.

Majors Accounting; advertising; agricultural business; agricultural economics; agricultural education; agricultural engineering; agricultural sciences; agronomy/crop science; applied mathematics; art; art education; biology; business; business administration; business education; business marketing and marketing management; chemistry; civil engineering technology; clothing/apparel/textile studies; computer engineering technology; computer/information sciences; construction technology; corrections; criminal justice studies; data processing technology; drafting; earth sciences; economics; electrical/electronic engineering technology; elementary education; engineering physics; English; equestrian studies; exercise sciences; family/consumer studies; finance; fine/studio arts; fishing sciences; French; geography; geology; German; graphic/printing equipment; health education; history; home economics education; horticulture science; individual/family development; industrial arts; industrial technology; information sciences/systems; institutional food workers; interior environments; international business; international relations; journalism; liberal arts and sciences/liberal studies; library science; management information systems/business data processing; mathematics; mechanical engineering technology; medical technology; middle school education; music; music teacher education; nursing; nutrition studies; occupational safety/health technology; philosophy; physical education; physics; political science; psychology; public relations; radio/television broadcasting; recreation/leisure facilities management; secretarial science; social work; sociology; Spanish; special education; speech-language pathology/audiology; speech/rhetorical studies; speech therapy; teaching English as a second language; telecommunications; theater arts/drama; trade/industrial education; veterinarian assistant; water treatment technology; wildlife management.

Academic Programs *Special study options:* academic remediation for entering students, accelerated degree program, adult/continuing education programs, advanced placement credit, cooperative education, distance learning, double majors, English as a second language, external degree program, freshman honors college, honors programs, independent study, internships, off-campus study, part-time degree program, services for LD students, study abroad, summer session for credit. *ROTC:* Army (c). *Unusual degree programs:* 3-2 engineering with University of Louisville, University of Kentucky; social work with University of Louisville.

Library Harry Lee Waterfield Library plus 1 other with 470,000 titles, 3,000 serial subscriptions, an OPAC, a Web page.

Computers on Campus 1500 computers available on campus for general student use. A campuswide network can be accessed from student residence rooms and from off campus. Internet access, at least one staffed computer lab available.

Student Life *Housing:* on-campus residence required through sophomore year. *Options:* coed, women-only. *Activities and Organizations:* drama/theater group, student-run newspaper, radio and television station, choral group, marching band, student government, Student Alumni, Phi Mu Alpha, national fraternities, national sororities. *Campus security:* 24-hour emergency response devices and patrols, student patrols, late-night transport/escort service, controlled dormitory access. *Student Services:* health clinic, personal/psychological counseling, women's center, legal services.

Athletics Member NCAA. All Division I except football (Division I-AA). *Intercollegiate sports:* baseball M(s), basketball M(s)/W(s), bowling M/W, crew M/W, cross-country running M(s)/W(s), equestrian sports M/W, golf M(s)/W(s), riflery M(s)/W(s), soccer W, tennis M(s)/W(s), track and field M(s)/W(s), volleyball W(s). *Intramural sports:* archery M/W, badminton M/W, basketball M/W, bowling M/W, crew M/W, cross-country running M/W, equestrian sports M/W, fencing M/W, football M, golf M/W, gymnastics W, racquetball M/W, riflery M/W, rugby M/W, sailing M/W, soccer M/W, softball M/W, swimming M/W, tennis M/W, track and field M/W, volleyball M/W, weight lifting M/W.

Standardized Tests *Required:* ACT (for admission).

Costs (2001–02) *Tuition:* state resident $2335 full-time, $119 per hour part-time; nonresident $7000 full-time, $314 per hour part-time. *Required fees:* $420 full-time. *Room and board:* $4150; room only: $2020. Room and board charges vary according to board plan. *Payment plan:* installment. *Waivers:* children of alumni and employees or children of employees.

Financial Aid Of all full-time matriculated undergraduates who enrolled in 2001, 4948 applied for aid, 2974 were judged to have need, 2686 had their need fully met. 429 Federal Work-Study jobs (averaging $1229). 2093 State and other part-time jobs (averaging $1528). In 2001, 2036 non-need-based awards were made. *Average percent of need met:* 90%. *Average financial aid package:* $4575. *Average need-based loan:* $1835. *Average need-based gift aid:* $2140. *Average indebtedness upon graduation:* $13,423.

Applying *Options:* electronic application, early admission, deferred entrance. *Application fee:* $25. *Required:* high school transcript, rank in top 50% of graduating class. *Required for some:* letters of recommendation. *Recommended:* interview. *Application deadlines:* rolling (freshmen), 8/1 (out-of-state freshmen), rolling (transfers). *Notification:* continuous (freshmen).

Admissions Contact Mrs. Stacy Bell, Admission Clerk, Murray State University, PO Box 9, Murray, KY 42071-0009. *Phone:* 270-762-3035. *Toll-free phone:* 800-272-4678. *Fax:* 270-762-3050. *E-mail:* admissions@murraystate.edu.

NORTHERN KENTUCKY UNIVERSITY
Highland Heights, Kentucky

- **State-supported** comprehensive, founded 1968
- **Calendar** semesters
- **Degrees** certificates, associate, bachelor's, master's, first professional, and post-master's certificates
- **Suburban** 300-acre campus with easy access to Cincinnati
- **Endowment** $1.5 million
- **Coed,** 11,269 undergraduate students, 72% full-time, 59% women, 41% men
- **Noncompetitive** entrance level, 95% of applicants were admitted

Undergraduates 8,158 full-time, 3,111 part-time. Students come from 32 states and territories, 11 other countries, 23% are from out of state, 4% African American, 0.8% Asian American or Pacific Islander, 0.7% Hispanic American, 0.3% Native American, 1% international, 5% transferred in, 25% live on campus. *Retention:* 72% of 2001 full-time freshmen returned.

Freshmen *Admission:* 3,222 applied, 3,046 admitted, 1,867 enrolled. *Test scores:* SAT verbal scores over 500: 47%; SAT math scores over 500: 44%; ACT scores over 18: 71%; SAT verbal scores over 600: 13%; SAT math scores over 600: 12%; ACT scores over 24: 16%; SAT verbal scores over 700: 2%; SAT math scores over 700: 3%; ACT scores over 30: 1%.

Faculty *Total:* 878, 54% full-time. *Student/faculty ratio:* 17:1.

Majors Accounting; anthropology; architectural engineering technology; art; aviation management; biology; business; business administration; business education; business marketing and marketing management; chemistry; computer/information sciences; computer science; criminal justice/law enforcement administration; criminal justice studies; early childhood education; economics; education; electrical/electronic engineering technology; elementary education; English; environmental science; exercise sciences; finance; fine/studio arts; French; geography; geology; graphic design/commercial art/illustration; history; human services; industrial/manufacturing engineering; industrial radiologic technology; industrial technology; information sciences/systems; international relations; journalism; labor/personnel relations; law enforcement/police science; management information systems/business data processing; mathematics; mathematics education; medical radiologic technology; mental health/rehabilitation; middle school education; music; nursing; nursing (adult health); operations management; organizational behavior; philosophy; physical education; physics; political science; pre-dentistry; pre-law; pre-medicine; pre-veterinary studies; psychiatric/mental health services; psychology; public administration; radio/television broadcasting; respiratory therapy; science education; social sciences; social work; sociology; Spanish; special education; speech/rhetorical studies; technical education; theater arts/drama; trade/industrial education.

Academic Programs *Special study options:* academic remediation for entering students, adult/continuing education programs, advanced placement credit, coop-

Northern Kentucky University (continued)
erative education, distance learning, double majors, honors programs, independent study, internships, off-campus study, part-time degree program, services for LD students, study abroad, summer session for credit. *ROTC:* Army (c), Air Force (c). *Unusual degree programs:* 3-2 engineering with University of Kentucky, University of Louisville, University of Cincinnati.
Library Steely Library plus 2 others with 524,802 titles, 3,554 serial subscriptions, 1,490 audiovisual materials, an OPAC, a Web page.
Computers on Campus 600 computers available on campus for general student use. A campuswide network can be accessed from student residence rooms and from off campus. Internet access, online (class) registration, at least one staffed computer lab available.
Student Life *Housing Options:* coed, men-only, women-only, disabled students. *Activities and Organizations:* drama/theater group, student-run newspaper, radio and television station, choral group, Greek organizations, campus ministries, academic organizations, student government, activities program board, national fraternities, national sororities. *Campus security:* 24-hour emergency response devices and patrols, late-night transport/escort service, controlled dormitory access. *Student Services:* health clinic, personal/psychological counseling, women's center.
Athletics Member NCAA. All Division II. *Intercollegiate sports:* baseball M(s), basketball M(s)/W(s), cross-country running M(s)/W(s), golf M(s)/W(s), soccer M(s)/W(s), softball W(s), tennis M(s)/W(s), volleyball W(s). *Intramural sports:* basketball M/W, football M/W, racquetball M/W, rugby M(c), soccer M/W, softball M/W, swimming M/W, table tennis M/W, tennis M/W, volleyball M/W.
Standardized Tests *Required:* SAT I or ACT (for admission).
Costs (2001–02) *Tuition:* $103 per credit hour part-time; state resident $2886 full-time, $149 per credit hour part-time; nonresident $7134 full-time, $267 per credit hour part-time. Full-time tuition and fees vary according to reciprocity agreements. Part-time tuition and fees vary according to location and reciprocity agreements. *Required fees:* $15 per credit hour. *Room and board:* $4460; room only: $2460. Room and board charges vary according to board plan and housing facility. *Payment plan:* installment. *Waivers:* senior citizens and employees or children of employees.
Financial Aid Of all full-time matriculated undergraduates who enrolled in 2001, 8373 applied for aid, 6360 were judged to have need. 362 Federal Work-Study jobs (averaging $1439). 1113 State and other part-time jobs (averaging $1028). In 2001, 362 non-need-based awards were made. *Average percent of need met:* 85%. *Average financial aid package:* $5414. *Average need-based loan:* $5108. *Average need-based gift aid:* $3162. *Average non-need based aid:* $2772. *Average indebtedness upon graduation:* $19,186.
Applying *Options:* early admission, early action, deferred entrance. *Application fee:* $25. *Required:* high school transcript. *Application deadlines:* 8/21 (freshmen), 8/1 (transfers). *Notification:* continuous (freshmen).
Admissions Contact Mrs. Debbie Poweleit, Associate Director of Admissions, Northern Kentucky University, Administrative Center 400, Highland Heights, KY 41099-7010. *Phone:* 606-572-5220 Ext. 5154. *Toll-free phone:* 800-637-9948. *Fax:* 859-572-6665. *E-mail:* admitnku@nku.edu.

PIKEVILLE COLLEGE
Pikeville, Kentucky

- **Independent** comprehensive, founded 1889, affiliated with Presbyterian Church (U.S.A.)
- **Calendar** semesters
- **Degrees** associate, bachelor's, and first professional
- **Small-town** 25-acre campus
- **Endowment** $14.7 million
- **Coed,** 948 undergraduate students, 94% full-time, 59% women, 41% men
- **Noncompetitive** entrance level, 100% of applicants were admitted

Undergraduates 891 full-time, 57 part-time. Students come from 19 states and territories, 18% are from out of state, 9% African American, 0.5% Asian American or Pacific Islander, 2% Hispanic American, 10% transferred in, 50% live on campus. *Retention:* 61% of 2001 full-time freshmen returned.
Freshmen *Admission:* 641 applied, 641 admitted, 261 enrolled. *Average high school GPA:* 3.35. *Test scores:* SAT verbal scores over 500: 8%; ACT scores over 18: 58%; ACT scores over 24: 15%.
Faculty *Total:* 92, 88% full-time, 52% with terminal degrees. *Student/faculty ratio:* 15:1.
Majors Art; biology; biology education; business administration; chemistry; communications; computer science; criminal justice studies; education (K-12); elementary education; English; English education; history; human services; mathematics; mathematics education; medical technology; middle school education; nursing; psychology; religious studies; science education; social sciences; social studies education; sociology.
Academic Programs *Special study options:* academic remediation for entering students, advanced placement credit, double majors, independent study, internships, off-campus study, part-time degree program, services for LD students, summer session for credit. *Unusual degree programs:* medical technology.
Library Allara Library plus 1 other with 60,052 titles, 3,234 serial subscriptions, 1,518 audiovisual materials, an OPAC, a Web page.
Computers on Campus 170 computers available on campus for general student use. A campuswide network can be accessed from student residence rooms and from off campus. Internet access, at least one staffed computer lab available.
Student Life *Housing Options:* coed, men-only, women-only. *Activities and Organizations:* drama/theater group, student-run newspaper, choral group, Pre-Professional, Phi Beta Lambda, Rotaract, Psychology Round Table, nursing club. *Campus security:* 24-hour patrols, controlled dormitory access. *Student Services:* personal/psychological counseling.
Athletics Member NAIA. *Intercollegiate sports:* baseball M(s), basketball M(s)/W(s), bowling M(s)/W(s), cross-country running M(s)/W(s), football M(s), golf M(s), softball W(s), tennis M(s)/W(s), volleyball W(s). *Intramural sports:* badminton M/W, basketball M/W, bowling M/W, football M/W, softball M/W, table tennis M/W, tennis M/W, volleyball M/W.
Standardized Tests *Required:* SAT I or ACT (for placement).
Costs (2002–03) *Comprehensive fee:* $12,000 includes full-time tuition ($8200) and room and board ($3800). Part-time tuition: $342 per credit hour. *Room and board:* College room only: $1700. *Payment plan:* installment. *Waivers:* senior citizens and employees or children of employees.
Financial Aid Of all full-time matriculated undergraduates who enrolled in 2001, 864 applied for aid, 851 were judged to have need, 797 had their need fully met. 211 Federal Work-Study jobs (averaging $1200). 5 State and other part-time jobs (averaging $800). *Average percent of need met:* 96%. *Average financial aid package:* $8600. *Average need-based loan:* $3200. *Average need-based gift aid:* $3500. *Average non-need based aid:* $3500. *Average indebtedness upon graduation:* $12,500.
Applying *Options:* electronic application, early admission, deferred entrance. *Required:* high school transcript. *Recommended:* interview. *Application deadlines:* 8/24 (freshmen), 8/24 (transfers). *Notification:* continuous (freshmen).
Admissions Contact Ms. Melinda Lynch, Director of Admissions, Pikeville College, 147 Sycamore Street, Pikeville, KY 41501. *Phone:* 606-218-5251. *Toll-free phone:* 866-232-7700. *Fax:* 606-218-5255. *E-mail:* wewantyou@pc.edu.

SOUTHERN BAPTIST THEOLOGICAL SEMINARY
Louisville, Kentucky

Admissions Contact 2825 Lexington Road, Louisville, KY 40280-0004.

SPALDING UNIVERSITY
Louisville, Kentucky

- **Independent** comprehensive, founded 1814, affiliated with Roman Catholic Church
- **Calendar** semesters
- **Degrees** certificates, associate, bachelor's, master's, and doctoral
- **Urban** 5-acre campus
- **Endowment** $3.6 million
- **Coed**
- **Moderately difficult** entrance level

Faculty *Student/faculty ratio:* 16:1.
Student Life *Campus security:* 24-hour emergency response devices and patrols, late-night transport/escort service.
Athletics Member NAIA.
Standardized Tests *Required:* SAT I or ACT (for admission).
Financial Aid Of all full-time matriculated undergraduates who enrolled in 2001, 609 applied for aid, 523 were judged to have need, 153 had their need fully met. 36 Federal Work-Study jobs (averaging $1073). 77 State and other part-time jobs (averaging $1268). In 2001, 59. *Average percent of need met:* 75. *Average financial aid package:* $9547. *Average need-based loan:* $3018. *Average need-based gift aid:* $7477. *Average non-need based aid:* $6150. *Average indebtedness upon graduation:* $48,000.
Applying *Options:* common application, electronic application, early admission, deferred entrance. *Application fee:* $20. *Required:* high school transcript, minimum 2.0 GPA. *Recommended:* minimum 3.0 GPA, interview.

Admissions Contact Spalding University, Louisville, KY 40203. *Phone:* 502-585-7111 Ext. 2226. *Toll-free phone:* 800-896-8941 Ext. 2111. *Fax:* 502-992-2148. *E-mail:* admissions@spalding.edu.

SULLIVAN UNIVERSITY
Louisville, Kentucky

- **Proprietary** comprehensive, founded 1864
- **Calendar** quarters
- **Degrees** certificates, diplomas, associate, bachelor's, and master's (master's degree in business administration only)
- **Suburban** 10-acre campus
- **Coed,** 4,245 undergraduate students, 66% full-time, 61% women, 39% men
- **Minimally difficult** entrance level

Undergraduates 2,808 full-time, 1,437 part-time. Students come from 19 states and territories, 23 other countries, 11% are from out of state, 17% African American, 2% Hispanic American, 0.4% Native American, 1% international, 8% transferred in, 9% live on campus. *Retention:* 60% of 2001 full-time freshmen returned.

Freshmen *Admission:* 2,851 enrolled.

Faculty *Total:* 120, 43% full-time, 10% with terminal degrees. *Student/faculty ratio:* 18:1.

Majors Accounting; business administration; business marketing and marketing management; computer science; culinary arts; hotel and restaurant management; legal administrative assistant; medical administrative assistant; paralegal/legal assistant; retail management; secretarial science; travel/tourism management.

Academic Programs *Special study options:* academic remediation for entering students, accelerated degree program, adult/continuing education programs, advanced placement credit, cooperative education, independent study, part-time degree program, summer session for credit.

Library McWhorter Library with 22,000 titles, 217 serial subscriptions.

Computers on Campus 125 computers available on campus for general student use. Internet access, at least one staffed computer lab available.

Student Life *Housing Options:* coed. *Activities and Organizations:* student government, Travel Club, Sullivan Student Paralegal Association, American Marketing Association, Society of Hosteurs. *Campus security:* 24-hour patrols.

Athletics *Intramural sports:* basketball M/W, bowling M/W, softball M/W, volleyball M/W.

Standardized Tests *Recommended:* ACT (for admission).

Costs (2002–03) *Tuition:* $11,280 full-time, $188 per credit part-time. Full-time tuition and fees vary according to program. Part-time tuition and fees vary according to program. No tuition increase for student's term of enrollment. *Required fees:* $415 full-time, $20 per course. *Room only:* $3555. *Payment plan:* installment. *Waivers:* employees or children of employees.

Applying *Application fee:* $90. *Required:* high school transcript, interview. *Application deadline:* rolling (freshmen), rolling (transfers). *Notification:* continuous (freshmen).

Admissions Contact Mr. Greg Cawthon, Director of Admissions, Sullivan University, 3101 Bardstown Road, Louisville, KY 40205. *Phone:* 502-456-6505 Ext. 370. *Toll-free phone:* 800-844-1354. *Fax:* 502-456-0040. *E-mail:* admissions@sullivan.edu.

THOMAS MORE COLLEGE
Crestview Hills, Kentucky

- **Independent Roman Catholic** comprehensive, founded 1921
- **Calendar** semesters
- **Degrees** certificates, associate, bachelor's, and master's
- **Suburban** 100-acre campus with easy access to Cincinnati
- **Endowment** $8.8 million
- **Coed,** 1,422 undergraduate students, 70% full-time, 53% women, 47% men
- **Moderately difficult** entrance level, 76% of applicants were admitted

Thomas More College is dedicated to the individual learning experience, offering majors and preprofessional programs. The College provides an outstanding liberal arts education that is carefully combined with practical professional training through cooperative education. The Thomas More experience is an education for all seasons of life.

Undergraduates Students come from 12 states and territories, 9 other countries, 34% are from out of state, 20% live on campus. *Retention:* 63% of 2001 full-time freshmen returned.

Freshmen *Admission:* 1,288 applied, 981 admitted. *Average high school GPA:* 2.88. *Test scores:* SAT verbal scores over 500: 42%; SAT math scores over 500: 46%; ACT scores over 18: 75%; SAT verbal scores over 600: 11%; SAT math scores over 600: 8%; ACT scores over 24: 16%; SAT verbal scores over 700: 3%; SAT math scores over 700: 1%; ACT scores over 30: 1%.

Faculty *Total:* 136, 57% full-time, 43% with terminal degrees. *Student/faculty ratio:* 12:1.

Majors Accounting; art education; art history; biology; business; business education; chemistry; communications; computer/information sciences; criminal justice/law enforcement administration; data processing technology; economics; elementary education; English; exercise sciences; fine/studio arts; gerontology; history; international relations; liberal arts and sciences/liberal studies; mathematics; medical technology; middle school education; music; nursing; nursing related; philosophy; physics; political science; pre-law; psychology; religious studies; social studies education; sociology; Spanish; speech/rhetorical studies; teacher education, specific programs related; theater arts/drama; visual/performing arts.

Academic Programs *Special study options:* academic remediation for entering students, accelerated degree program, adult/continuing education programs, advanced placement credit, cooperative education, double majors, external degree program, honors programs, independent study, internships, off-campus study, part-time degree program, services for LD students, student-designed majors, study abroad, summer session for credit. *ROTC:* Army (c), Air Force (c). *Unusual degree programs:* 3-2 engineering with University of Dayton, University of Kentucky, University of Detroit Mercy, University of Cincinnati, University of Notre Dame, University of Louisville.

Library Thomas More Library with 131,694 titles, 571 serial subscriptions, 1,756 audiovisual materials, a Web page.

Computers on Campus 100 computers available on campus for general student use. A campuswide network can be accessed from student residence rooms and from off campus. At least one staffed computer lab available.

Student Life *Housing Options:* men-only, women-only. *Activities and Organizations:* drama/theater group, Student Government Association, orientation team, ACT More Program Board, outdoors club, Business Society. *Campus security:* 24-hour patrols, late-night transport/escort service, controlled dormitory access. *Student Services:* health clinic, personal/psychological counseling.

Athletics Member NCAA. All Division III. *Intercollegiate sports:* baseball M, basketball M/W, football M, soccer M/W, softball W, tennis M/W, volleyball W. *Intramural sports:* basketball M/W, football M/W, golf M, racquetball M/W, softball M/W, volleyball M/W.

Standardized Tests *Required:* SAT I or ACT (for admission).

Costs (2001–02) *Comprehensive fee:* $17,700 includes full-time tuition ($13,200), mandatory fees ($350), and room and board ($4150). Part-time tuition: $350 per credit hour. Part-time tuition and fees vary according to course load and program. *Required fees:* $10 per credit hour, $10 per term part-time. *Room and board:* College room only: $2400. Room and board charges vary according to board plan and housing facility. *Payment plans:* installment, deferred payment. *Waivers:* children of alumni and employees or children of employees.

Financial Aid Of all full-time matriculated undergraduates who enrolled in 2001, 626 applied for aid, 512 were judged to have need, 461 had their need fully met. 108 Federal Work-Study jobs (averaging $1614). 162 State and other part-time jobs (averaging $1318). In 2001, 71 non-need-based awards were made. *Average percent of need met:* 91%. *Average financial aid package:* $10,156. *Average need-based loan:* $4377. *Average need-based gift aid:* $5472. *Average non-need based aid:* $5250. *Average indebtedness upon graduation:* $18,869.

Applying *Options:* common application, electronic application, deferred entrance. *Application fee:* $25. *Required:* high school transcript, minimum 2.0 GPA, Rank in top 50%, admissions committee may consider those not meeting criteria. *Required for some:* essay or personal statement, 2 letters of recommendation. *Recommended:* interview. *Application deadlines:* 8/15 (freshmen), 8/15 (transfers). *Notification:* continuous (freshmen).

Admissions Contact Mr. Robert A. McDermott, Director of Admissions, Thomas More College, 333 Thomas More Parkway, Crestview Hills, KY 41017. *Phone:* 606-344-3332. *Toll-free phone:* 800-825-4557. *Fax:* 606-344-3444. *E-mail:* robert.mcdermott@thomasmore.edu.

TRANSYLVANIA UNIVERSITY
Lexington, Kentucky

- **Independent** 4-year, founded 1780, affiliated with Christian Church (Disciples of Christ)
- **Calendar** 4-4-1
- **Degree** bachelor's
- **Urban** 35-acre campus with easy access to Cincinnati and Louisville

Transylvania University (continued)
- **Endowment** $122.5 million
- **Coed,** 1,052 undergraduate students, 99% full-time, 57% women, 43% men
- **Very difficult** entrance level, 88% of applicants were admitted

Undergraduates 1,045 full-time, 7 part-time. Students come from 30 states and territories, 2 other countries, 18% are from out of state, 3% African American, 2% Asian American or Pacific Islander, 1.0% Hispanic American, 0.3% Native American, 0.5% international, 0.7% transferred in, 80% live on campus. *Retention:* 80% of 2001 full-time freshmen returned.

Freshmen *Admission:* 1,092 applied, 964 admitted, 306 enrolled. *Average high school GPA:* 3.60. *Test scores:* SAT verbal scores over 500: 85%; SAT math scores over 500: 83%; ACT scores over 18: 100%; SAT verbal scores over 600: 49%; SAT math scores over 600: 51%; ACT scores over 24: 73%; SAT verbal scores over 700: 15%; SAT math scores over 700: 11%; ACT scores over 30: 18%.

Faculty *Total:* 97, 78% full-time, 78% with terminal degrees. *Student/faculty ratio:* 13:1.

Majors Accounting; anthropology; art; art education; biology; business administration; chemistry; computer science; economics; education (K-12); elementary education; English; exercise sciences; fine/studio arts; French; history; mathematics; middle school education; music (general performance); music teacher education; philosophy; physical education; physics; political science; psychology; religious studies; sociology; Spanish; theater arts/drama.

Academic Programs *Special study options:* advanced placement credit, double majors, independent study, internships, off-campus study, part-time degree program, student-designed majors, study abroad, summer session for credit. *ROTC:* Army (c), Air Force (c). *Unusual degree programs:* 3-2 engineering with Washington University in St. Louis, University of Kentucky, Vanderbilt University.

Library Transylvania Library with 93,019 titles, 500 serial subscriptions, 1,860 audiovisual materials, an OPAC, a Web page.

Computers on Campus 240 computers available on campus for general student use. A campuswide network can be accessed from student residence rooms and from off campus. Internet access, at least one staffed computer lab available.

Student Life *Housing:* on-campus residence required through junior year. *Options:* coed, men-only, women-only. *Activities and Organizations:* drama/theater group, student-run newspaper, radio station, choral group, Student Alumni Association, Student Government Association, Student Activities Board, Crimson Crew, Alternative Spring Break, national fraternities, national sororities. *Campus security:* 24-hour emergency response devices and patrols, late-night transport/escort service. *Student Services:* health clinic, personal/psychological counseling.

Athletics Member NCAA. All Division III. *Intercollegiate sports:* baseball M, basketball M/W, cross-country running M/W, field hockey W, golf M/W, soccer M/W, softball W, swimming M/W, tennis M/W, volleyball W. *Intramural sports:* badminton M/W, basketball M/W, bowling M/W, cross-country running M/W, football M/W, golf M/W, racquetball M/W, softball M/W, swimming M/W, table tennis M/W, tennis M/W, volleyball M/W.

Standardized Tests *Required:* SAT I or ACT (for admission).

Costs (2001–02) *Comprehensive fee:* $21,780 includes full-time tuition ($15,420), mandatory fees ($590), and room and board ($5770). Part-time tuition: $1714 per course. *Required fees:* $60 per course. *Room and board:* College room only: $3220. Room and board charges vary according to board plan and housing facility. *Payment plans:* installment, deferred payment. *Waivers:* employees or children of employees.

Financial Aid Of all full-time matriculated undergraduates who enrolled in 2001, 747 applied for aid, 628 were judged to have need, 186 had their need fully met. 322 Federal Work-Study jobs (averaging $1210). In 2001, 395 non-need-based awards were made. *Average percent of need met:* 89%. *Average financial aid package:* $14,071. *Average need-based loan:* $3517. *Average need-based gift aid:* $10,583. *Average non-need based aid:* $9289. *Average indebtedness upon graduation:* $13,910.

Applying *Options:* common application, electronic application, early admission, early action, deferred entrance. *Application fee:* $30. *Required:* essay or personal statement, high school transcript, minimum 2.75 GPA, 2 letters of recommendation. *Required for some:* interview. *Recommended:* interview. *Application deadline:* 2/1 (freshmen), rolling (transfers). *Notification:* 3/1 (freshmen), 12/24 (early action).

Admissions Contact Ms. Sarah Coen, Director of Admissions, Transylvania University, 300 North Broadway, Lexington, KY 40508-1797. *Phone:* 859-233-8242. *Toll-free phone:* 800-872-6798. *Fax:* 859-233-8797. *E-mail:* admissions@transy.edu.

UNION COLLEGE
Barbourville, Kentucky

- **Independent United Methodist** comprehensive, founded 1879
- **Calendar** semesters
- **Degrees** bachelor's and master's
- **Small-town** 110-acre campus
- **Endowment** $16.0 million
- **Coed,** 576 undergraduate students, 91% full-time, 52% women, 48% men
- **Moderately difficult** entrance level, 75% of applicants were admitted

With the implementation of the new core curriculum and both current and planned technological facilities and equipment, Union College has embraced the latest trends in education methods: interdisciplinary teaching and learning, engagement of students in the learning process and continuous goal setting and self-assessment, and integration of technology.

Undergraduates 524 full-time, 52 part-time. Students come from 25 states and territories, 10 other countries, 27% are from out of state, 13% transferred in, 48% live on campus. *Retention:* 56% of 2001 full-time freshmen returned.

Freshmen *Admission:* 391 applied, 292 admitted, 102 enrolled. *Average high school GPA:* 2.93. *Test scores:* SAT verbal scores over 500: 56%; SAT math scores over 500: 56%; ACT scores over 18: 66%; SAT verbal scores over 600: 6%; SAT math scores over 600: 11%; ACT scores over 24: 8%; SAT math scores over 700: 6%.

Faculty *Total:* 85, 54% full-time, 44% with terminal degrees. *Student/faculty ratio:* 11:1.

Majors Accounting; biology; business administration; business education; chemistry; communications; criminal justice/law enforcement administration; education; elementary education; English; health education; history; mathematics; middle school education; music; music business management/merchandising; music teacher education; music (voice and choral/opera performance); physical education; physics; pre-dentistry; pre-law; pre-medicine; pre-veterinary studies; psychology; recreation/leisure facilities management; religious education; religious studies; secondary education; special education; sport/fitness administration; theater arts/drama.

Academic Programs *Special study options:* academic remediation for entering students, accelerated degree program, advanced placement credit, cooperative education, double majors, honors programs, independent study, internships, off-campus study, part-time degree program, study abroad, summer session for credit. *Unusual degree programs:* 3-2 engineering with University of Kentucky.

Library Weeks-Townsend Memorial Library plus 1 other with 105,210 titles, 2,469 serial subscriptions, 5,004 audiovisual materials, an OPAC, a Web page.

Computers on Campus 100 computers available on campus for general student use. A campuswide network can be accessed from student residence rooms and from off campus. Internet access, at least one staffed computer lab available.

Student Life *Housing:* on-campus residence required through sophomore year. *Options:* coed, men-only, women-only. *Activities and Organizations:* drama/theater group, student-run newspaper, choral group, Fellowship of Christian Athletes, Baptist Student Union, Thespian Society, Newman Club, Dawg Pound. *Campus security:* 24-hour emergency response devices and patrols, late-night transport/escort service, controlled dormitory access. *Student Services:* health clinic, personal/psychological counseling.

Athletics Member NAIA. *Intercollegiate sports:* baseball M(s), basketball M(s)/W(s), football M(s), golf M(s)/W(s), soccer M(s)/W(s), softball W(s), tennis M/W, volleyball W(s). *Intramural sports:* basketball M/W, football M, softball M/W, table tennis M/W, tennis M/W, volleyball M/W, weight lifting M/W.

Standardized Tests *Required:* SAT I or ACT (for admission).

Costs (2001–02) *Comprehensive fee:* $17,370 includes full-time tuition ($11,720) and room and board ($5650). Part-time tuition: $225 per hour.

Financial Aid Of all full-time matriculated undergraduates who enrolled in 2001, 530 applied for aid, 514 were judged to have need, 166 had their need fully met. 184 Federal Work-Study jobs (averaging $1000). In 2001, 8 non-need-based awards were made. *Average percent of need met:* 86%. *Average financial aid package:* $8507. *Average need-based loan:* $2775. *Average need-based gift aid:* $6000. *Average non-need based aid:* $6619. *Average indebtedness upon graduation:* $11,253.

Applying *Options:* common application, electronic application, early admission, deferred entrance. *Application fee:* $20. *Required:* high school transcript, minimum 2.0 GPA. *Required for some:* essay or personal statement, letters of recommendation. *Recommended:* interview. *Application deadlines:* 8/1 (freshmen), 8/31 (transfers). *Notification:* continuous (freshmen).

Admissions Contact Joretta Nelson, Vice President for Enrollment and Recruitment, Union College, 310 College Street, Barbourville, KY 40906. *Phone:* 606-546-1220. *Toll-free phone:* 800-489-8646. *Fax:* 606-546-1667. *E-mail:* enroll@unionky.edu.

UNIVERSITY OF KENTUCKY
Lexington, Kentucky

- **State-supported** university, founded 1865
- **Calendar** semesters
- **Degrees** bachelor's, master's, doctoral, first professional, and post-master's certificates
- **Urban** 685-acre campus with easy access to Cincinnati and Louisville
- **Endowment** $420.8 million
- **Coed,** 17,138 undergraduate students, 89% full-time, 52% women, 48% men
- **Moderately difficult** entrance level, 82% of applicants were admitted

Undergraduates 15,244 full-time, 1,894 part-time. Students come from 53 states and territories, 123 other countries, 12% are from out of state, 6% African American, 2% Asian American or Pacific Islander, 0.9% Hispanic American, 0.2% Native American, 2% international, 8% transferred in, 31% live on campus. *Retention:* 77% of 2001 full-time freshmen returned.

Freshmen *Admission:* 8,449 applied, 6,914 admitted, 3,140 enrolled. *Average high school GPA:* 3.53. *Test scores:* SAT verbal scores over 500: 78%; SAT math scores over 500: 81%; ACT scores over 18: 99%; SAT verbal scores over 600: 31%; SAT math scores over 600: 39%; ACT scores over 24: 53%; SAT verbal scores over 700: 6%; SAT math scores over 700: 8%; ACT scores over 30: 9%.

Faculty *Total:* 1,231. *Student/faculty ratio:* 17:1.

Majors Accounting; advertising; agricultural economics; agricultural engineering; agricultural sciences related; agronomy/crop science; animal sciences; anthropology; architecture; art education; art history; arts management; biology; business; business economics; business marketing and marketing management; cell and molecular biology related; chemical engineering; chemistry; civil engineering; classics; clothing/apparel/textile studies; communications; computer/information sciences; early childhood education; economics; electrical engineering; elementary education; English; finance; fine/studio arts; food sciences; forestry sciences; French; geography; geology; German; health education; health services administration; history; home economics; hospitality management; interdisciplinary studies; interior design; journalism; landscape architecture; Latin American studies; linguistics; management science; materials engineering; mathematics; mechanical engineering; medical technology; middle school education; mining/mineral engineering; multi/interdisciplinary studies related; music (general performance); music history; music teacher education; natural resources conservation; nursing; nursing related; nutrition science; nutrition studies; philosophy; physical education; physical therapy; physics; political science; psychology; radio/television broadcasting; Russian; science education; social sciences; social work; sociology; Spanish; special education; speech-language pathology/audiology; teacher education, specific programs related; theater arts/drama.

Academic Programs *Special study options:* academic remediation for entering students, accelerated degree program, adult/continuing education programs, advanced placement credit, cooperative education, distance learning, double majors, English as a second language, honors programs, independent study, internships, off-campus study, part-time degree program, services for LD students, student-designed majors, study abroad, summer session for credit. *ROTC:* Army (b), Air Force (b).

Library William T. Young Library plus 15 others with 2.9 million titles, 29,850 serial subscriptions, 78,136 audiovisual materials, an OPAC, a Web page.

Computers on Campus 1400 computers available on campus for general student use. A campuswide network can be accessed from student residence rooms and from off campus that provide access to various software packages. Internet access, online (class) registration, at least one staffed computer lab available.

Student Life *Housing Options:* coed, men-only, women-only, disabled students. *Activities and Organizations:* drama/theater group, student-run newspaper, radio station, choral group, marching band, Student Activities Board, Student Government Association, Campus Progressive Coalition, Ski and Snowboard Club, Society of Women Engineers, national fraternities, national sororities. *Campus security:* 24-hour emergency response devices and patrols, late-night transport/escort service, controlled dormitory access. *Student Services:* health clinic, personal/psychological counseling, women's center, legal services.

Athletics Member NCAA. All Division I except football (Division I-A). *Intercollegiate sports:* baseball M(s), basketball M(s)/W(s), cross-country running M(s)/W(s), golf M(s)/W(s), gymnastics W(s), riflery M(s)/W(s), soccer M(s)/W(s), softball W(s), swimming M(s)/W(s), tennis M(s)/W(s), track and field M(s)/W(s), volleyball W(s). *Intramural sports:* archery M/W, badminton M/W, basketball M/W, fencing M/W, football M/W, golf M/W, ice hockey M, lacrosse M, rugby M, soccer M/W, softball M/W, swimming M/W, table tennis M/W, tennis M/W, track and field M/W, volleyball M/W.

Standardized Tests *Required:* SAT I or ACT (for admission).

Costs (2001–02) *Tuition:* state resident $3270 full-time, $136 per semester hour part-time; nonresident $9810 full-time, $409 per semester hour part-time. Full-time tuition and fees vary according to reciprocity agreements. Part-time tuition and fees vary according to course load and reciprocity agreements. *Required fees:* $464 full-time, $16 per semester hour. *Room and board:* $3980; room only: $2600. Room and board charges vary according to board plan and housing facility. *Payment plan:* installment. *Waivers:* senior citizens and employees or children of employees.

Financial Aid Of all full-time matriculated undergraduates who enrolled in 2001, 7493 applied for aid, 5267 were judged to have need, 2733 had their need fully met. 769 Federal Work-Study jobs (averaging $1708). *Average percent of need met:* 85%. *Average financial aid package:* $7766. *Average need-based loan:* $3329. *Average need-based gift aid:* $3570. *Average indebtedness upon graduation:* $20,823.

Applying *Options:* electronic application, early admission. *Application fee:* $20. *Required:* high school transcript, minimum 2.0 GPA. *Application deadlines:* 2/15 (freshmen), 8/1 (transfers). *Notification:* continuous (freshmen).

Admissions Contact Ms. Michelle Nordin, Associate Director of Admissions, University of Kentucky, 100 W.D. Funkhouser Building, Lexington, KY 40506-0054. *Phone:* 859-257-2000. *Toll-free phone:* 800-432-0967. *E-mail:* admissio@uky.edu.

UNIVERSITY OF LOUISVILLE
Louisville, Kentucky

- **State-supported** university, founded 1798
- **Calendar** semesters
- **Degrees** certificates, diplomas, associate, bachelor's, master's, doctoral, first professional, post-master's, and postbachelor's certificates
- **Urban** 169-acre campus
- **Endowment** $503.2 million
- **Coed,** 14,109 undergraduate students, 70% full-time, 54% women, 46% men
- **Moderately difficult** entrance level, 68% of applicants were admitted

Undergraduates 9,842 full-time, 4,267 part-time. Students come from 50 states and territories, 77 other countries, 13% are from out of state, 13% African American, 3% Asian American or Pacific Islander, 1% Hispanic American, 0.3% Native American, 2% international, 7% transferred in, 16% live on campus. *Retention:* 72% of 2001 full-time freshmen returned.

Freshmen *Admission:* 5,814 applied, 3,955 admitted, 2,331 enrolled. *Average high school GPA:* 3.30. *Test scores:* ACT scores over 18: 92%; ACT scores over 24: 38%; ACT scores over 30: 6%.

Faculty *Total:* 1,231, 58% full-time, 65% with terminal degrees. *Student/faculty ratio:* 13:1.

Majors Accounting; African-American studies; anthropology; art history; biology; business administration; business economics; business marketing and marketing management; chemical engineering; chemistry; civil engineering; communications; computer engineering; computer systems analysis; criminal justice/law enforcement administration; cytotechnology; dental hygiene; economics; electrical engineering; elementary education; engineering; English; equestrian studies; finance; fine/studio arts; French; geography; German; health/medical preparatory programs related; health occupations education; health/physical education; history; industrial/manufacturing engineering; interior design; liberal arts and sciences/liberal studies; liberal arts and studies related; management information systems/business data processing; mathematics; mechanical engineering; medical radiologic technology; medical technology; middle school education; music; music (general performance); music history; music teacher education; music theory and composition; music therapy; nuclear medical technology; nursing; paralegal/legal assistant; philosophy; physical therapy; physics; political science; psychology; respiratory therapy; Russian; Russian/Slavic studies; sign language interpretation; sociology; Spanish; sport/fitness administration; theater arts/drama; trade/industrial education; women's studies; zoology.

Academic Programs *Special study options:* academic remediation for entering students, accelerated degree program, adult/continuing education programs, advanced placement credit, cooperative education, distance learning, double majors, English as a second language, external degree program, honors programs, independent study, internships, off-campus study, part-time degree program, services for LD students, student-designed majors, study abroad, summer session for credit. *ROTC:* Army (b), Air Force (b).

Library William F. Ekstrom Library plus 5 others with 969,925 titles, 13,333 serial subscriptions, an OPAC, a Web page.

University of Louisville (continued)

Computers on Campus 250 computers available on campus for general student use. A campuswide network can be accessed from student residence rooms and from off campus. Internet access, at least one staffed computer lab available.

Student Life *Housing Options:* coed, disabled students. *Activities and Organizations:* drama/theater group, student-run newspaper, radio station, choral group, marching band, Spirit Club, Baptist Student Union, Golden Key, Sigma Chi, Phi Eta Sigma, national fraternities, national sororities. *Campus security:* 24-hour emergency response devices and patrols, late-night transport/escort service, controlled dormitory access. *Student Services:* health clinic, personal/psychological counseling, women's center, legal services.

Athletics Member NCAA. All Division I except football (Division I-A). *Intercollegiate sports:* baseball M(s), basketball M(s)/W(s), crew W(s), cross-country running M(s)/W(s), field hockey W(s), golf M(s)/W(s), soccer M(s)/W(s), softball W(s), swimming M(s)/W(s), tennis M(s)/W(s), track and field M(s)/W(s), volleyball W(s). *Intramural sports:* badminton M/W, basketball M/W, bowling M/W, cross-country running M/W, fencing M/W, football M/W, golf M/W, racquetball M/W, soccer M/W, softball M/W, swimming M/W, table tennis M/W, tennis M/W, track and field M/W, volleyball M/W, weight lifting M(c)/W(c).

Standardized Tests *Required:* SAT I or ACT (for admission).

Costs (2001–02) *Tuition:* state resident $3794 full-time, $162 per hour part-time; nonresident $10,472 full-time, $442 per hour part-time. Part-time tuition and fees vary according to course load. *Room and board:* $3608; room only: $2208. Room and board charges vary according to board plan and housing facility. *Payment plan:* installment. *Waivers:* senior citizens and employees or children of employees.

Financial Aid Of all full-time matriculated undergraduates who enrolled in 2001, 6232 applied for aid, 4321 were judged to have need, 1235 had their need fully met. In 2001, 1369 non-need-based awards were made. *Average percent of need met:* 72%. *Average financial aid package:* $6488. *Average non-need based aid:* $2014.

Applying *Options:* electronic application, early admission, deferred entrance. *Application fee:* $25. *Required:* high school transcript, minimum 2.50 GPA. *Application deadline:* rolling (freshmen), rolling (transfers). *Notification:* continuous (freshmen).

Admissions Contact Ms. Jenny Sawyer, Executive Director for Admissions, University of Louisville, 2211 South Brook, Louisville, KY 40292. *Phone:* 502-852-6531. *Toll-free phone:* 502-852-6531 (in-state); 800-334-8635 (out-of-state). *Fax:* 502-852-4776 Ext. 6531. *E-mail:* admitme@gwise.louisville.edu.

WESTERN KENTUCKY UNIVERSITY

Bowling Green, Kentucky

- **State-supported** comprehensive, founded 1906
- **Calendar** semesters
- **Degrees** certificates, associate, bachelor's, and master's
- **Suburban** 223-acre campus with easy access to Nashville
- **Endowment** $40.7 million
- **Coed,** 14,135 undergraduate students, 76% full-time, 59% women, 41% men
- **Moderately difficult** entrance level, 85% of applicants were admitted

Undergraduates 10,701 full-time, 3,434 part-time. Students come from 46 states and territories, 54 other countries, 16% are from out of state, 8% African American, 1% Asian American or Pacific Islander, 0.7% Hispanic American, 0.2% Native American, 0.6% international, 6% transferred in. *Retention:* 75% of 2001 full-time freshmen returned.

Freshmen *Admission:* 5,105 applied, 4,332 admitted, 2,726 enrolled. *Average high school GPA:* 3.11. *Test scores:* SAT verbal scores over 500: 58%; SAT math scores over 500: 61%; ACT scores over 18: 81%; SAT verbal scores over 600: 18%; SAT math scores over 600: 17%; ACT scores over 24: 27%; SAT verbal scores over 700: 4%; SAT math scores over 700: 1%; ACT scores over 30: 3%.

Faculty *Total:* 1,008, 59% full-time. *Student/faculty ratio:* 18:1.

Majors Accounting; advertising; agricultural production; agricultural sciences; anthropology; architectural drafting; art education; biochemistry; biology; business administration; business economics; business education; business marketing and marketing management; chemistry; civil engineering; clothing/apparel/textile studies; communications; communications related; community health liaison; computer/information sciences; data processing technology; dental hygiene; early childhood education; economics; education of the speech impaired; electrical engineering; elementary education; emergency medical technology; engineering technologies related; English; English related; environmental technology; executive assistant; finance; fine/studio arts; French; general studies; geography; geology; German; graphic design/commercial art/illustration; health services administration; history; home economics education; hotel and restaurant management; housing studies; industrial production technologies related; industrial technology; journalism; management information systems/business data processing; mathematics; mechanical engineering; medical records technology; medical technology; middle school education; multi/interdisciplinary studies related; music; music related; music teacher education; nursing; nursing related; nutrition studies; paralegal/legal assistant; philosophy; physical education; physical science technologies related; physics; political science; psychology; public relations; radio/television broadcasting; recreation/leisure facilities management; religious studies; respiratory therapy; science education; social sciences; social work; sociology; Spanish; special education; speech/rhetorical studies; technical education; theater arts/drama; trade/industrial education; visual/performing arts.

Academic Programs *Special study options:* academic remediation for entering students, accelerated degree program, adult/continuing education programs, advanced placement credit, cooperative education, distance learning, double majors, English as a second language, honors programs, internships, part-time degree program, services for LD students, student-designed majors, study abroad, summer session for credit. *ROTC:* Army (b), Air Force (c). *Unusual degree programs:* 3-2 engineering with University of Kentucky, University of Louisville.

Library Helm-Cravens Library plus 3 others with 967,067 titles, 10,156 serial subscriptions, 90,955 audiovisual materials, an OPAC, a Web page.

Computers on Campus 100 computers available on campus for general student use. A campuswide network can be accessed from student residence rooms and from off campus that provide access to on-line grade reports. Internet access, online (class) registration, at least one staffed computer lab available.

Student Life *Housing:* on-campus residence required through sophomore year. *Options:* coed, men-only, women-only, disabled students. *Activities and Organizations:* drama/theater group, student-run newspaper, radio and television station, choral group, marching band, Student Government Association, Campus Activities Board, Campus Crusade for Christ, campus ministries, Residence Hall Association, national fraternities, national sororities. *Campus security:* 24-hour emergency response devices and patrols, student patrols, late-night transport/escort service, controlled dormitory access. *Student Services:* health clinic, personal/psychological counseling.

Athletics Member NCAA. All Division I except football (Division I-AA). *Intercollegiate sports:* baseball M(s), basketball M(s)/W(s), cross-country running M(s)/W(s), golf M(s)/W(s), riflery M(c)/W(c), soccer M(s), softball W(s), swimming M(s)/W(s), tennis M(s)/W(s), track and field M(s)/W(s), volleyball W(s). *Intramural sports:* archery M/W, badminton M/W, basketball M/W, bowling M/W, equestrian sports M/W, fencing M(c)/W(c), golf M/W, lacrosse M(c)/W(c), racquetball M/W, rugby M(c)/W(c), soccer M/W, softball M/W(c), swimming M(c)/W(c), table tennis M/W, volleyball M(c)/W(c), water polo M/W, wrestling M.

Standardized Tests *Required:* SAT I or ACT (for admission).

Costs (2001–02) *Tuition:* state resident $2290 full-time, $117 per credit hour part-time; nonresident $6870 full-time, $308 per credit hour part-time. Full-time tuition and fees vary according to reciprocity agreements. Part-time tuition and fees vary according to course load and reciprocity agreements. *Required fees:* $554 full-time, $1 per credit. *Room and board:* $3990; room only: $1890. Room and board charges vary according to board plan and housing facility. *Payment plans:* installment, deferred payment. *Waivers:* children of alumni, senior citizens, and employees or children of employees.

Financial Aid Of all full-time matriculated undergraduates who enrolled in 2001, 7320 applied for aid, 5282 were judged to have need, 2221 had their need fully met. 716 Federal Work-Study jobs (averaging $1318). 1479 State and other part-time jobs. In 2001, 2926 non-need-based awards were made. *Average percent of need met:* 43%. *Average financial aid package:* $5194. *Average need-based loan:* $2853. *Average need-based gift aid:* $3218. *Average indebtedness upon graduation:* $12,175.

Applying *Application fee:* $30. *Required:* high school transcript, minimum 2.5 GPA. *Application deadlines:* 8/1 (freshmen), 6/1 (out-of-state freshmen), 8/1 (transfers). *Notification:* continuous (freshmen), continuous (out-of-state freshmen).

Admissions Contact Ms. Sharon Dyrsen, Director of Admissions and Academic Services, Western Kentucky University, Potter Hall 117, 1 Big Red Way, Bowling Green, KY 42101-3576. *Phone:* 270-745-4241. *Toll-free phone:* 800-495-8463. *Fax:* 270-745-6133. *E-mail:* admission@wku.edu.

LOUISIANA

CENTENARY COLLEGE OF LOUISIANA

Shreveport, Louisiana

- **Independent United Methodist** comprehensive, founded 1825
- **Calendar** 4-4-1

- **Degrees** bachelor's and master's
- **Suburban** 65-acre campus
- **Coed,** 910 undergraduate students, 98% full-time, 62% women, 38% men
- **Moderately difficult** entrance level, 86% of applicants were admitted

Undergraduates 888 full-time, 22 part-time. Students come from 38 states and territories, 18 other countries, 6% African American, 1% Asian American or Pacific Islander, 3% Hispanic American, 1% Native American, 3% international, 4% transferred in, 60% live on campus. *Retention:* 74% of 2001 full-time freshmen returned.

Freshmen *Admission:* 737 applied, 634 admitted, 261 enrolled. *Test scores:* SAT verbal scores over 500: 79%; SAT math scores over 500: 85%; ACT scores over 18: 99%; SAT verbal scores over 600: 45%; SAT math scores over 600: 45%; ACT scores over 24: 68%; SAT verbal scores over 700: 9%; SAT math scores over 700: 10%; ACT scores over 30: 16%.

Faculty *Total:* 115, 64% full-time, 71% with terminal degrees. *Student/faculty ratio:* 12:1.

Majors Accounting; art; art education; arts management; biochemistry; biology; biophysics; business administration; business economics; chemistry; dance; drawing; early childhood education; economics; education; education (K-12); elementary education; English; environmental science; film studies; fine/studio arts; French; geology; German; health education; health science; history; interdisciplinary studies; Latin (ancient and medieval); liberal arts and sciences/liberal studies; literature; mass communications; mathematics; middle school education; music; music (piano and organ performance); music teacher education; music (voice and choral/opera performance); occupational therapy; philosophy; physical education; physical sciences; physical therapy; physics; political science; pre-dentistry; pre-law; pre-medicine; pre-veterinary studies; psychology; religious music; religious studies; science education; secondary education; social sciences; sociology; Spanish; speech-language pathology/audiology; speech/rhetorical studies; stringed instruments; theater arts/drama; wind/percussion instruments.

Academic Programs *Special study options:* adult/continuing education programs, advanced placement credit, double majors, honors programs, independent study, internships, off-campus study, part-time degree program, student-designed majors, study abroad, summer session for credit. *Unusual degree programs:* 3-2 engineering with Columbia University, Tulane University, Case Western Reserve University, Texas A&M University, Louisiana Tech University, Southern Methodist University, University of Arkansas, Washington University in St. Louis; forestry with Duke University; computer science with Southern Methodist University, communication disorders with Louisiana State University Medical Center School of Medicine in Shreveport.

Library Magale Library plus 1 other with 186,564 titles, 59,899 serial subscriptions, 5,945 audiovisual materials, an OPAC, a Web page.

Computers on Campus A campuswide network can be accessed from student residence rooms and from off campus. Internet access, at least one staffed computer lab available.

Student Life *Housing:* on-campus residence required through senior year. *Options:* coed, men-only, women-only. *Activities and Organizations:* drama/theater group, student-run newspaper, radio station, choral group, intramural sports, Student Activities Board, crew, Church Career/Campus Ministries, student media, national fraternities, national sororities. *Campus security:* 24-hour emergency response devices and patrols, late-night transport/escort service, controlled dormitory access. *Student Services:* health clinic, personal/psychological counseling.

Athletics Member NCAA. All Division I. *Intercollegiate sports:* baseball M(s), basketball M(s)/W(s), crew M(c)/W(c), cross-country running M(s)/W(s), golf M(s)/W(s), gymnastics W(s), riflery M(s)/W(s), sailing M(c)/W(c), soccer M(s)/W(s), softball W(s), tennis M(s)/W(s), volleyball W(s). *Intramural sports:* basketball M/W, football M/W, golf M, soccer M/W, softball M/W, table tennis M/W, tennis M/W, volleyball M/W.

Standardized Tests *Required:* SAT I or ACT (for admission). *Required for some:* SAT II: Subject Tests (for admission).

Costs (2001–02) *Comprehensive fee:* $20,600 includes full-time tuition ($15,400), mandatory fees ($400), and room and board ($4800). Part-time tuition: $525 per semester hour. *Required fees:* $30 per term part-time. *Room and board:* College room only: $2200. Room and board charges vary according to board plan and housing facility. *Payment plans:* installment, deferred payment. *Waivers:* employees or children of employees.

Financial Aid Of all full-time matriculated undergraduates who enrolled in 2001, 865 applied for aid, 521 were judged to have need, 200 had their need fully met. 186 Federal Work-Study jobs (averaging $1478). 54 State and other part-time jobs (averaging $1244). In 2001, 237 non-need-based awards were made. *Average percent of need met:* 76%. *Average financial aid package:* $11,397. *Average need-based loan:* $3407. *Average need-based gift aid:* $9476. *Average non-need based aid:* $9514. *Average indebtedness upon graduation:* $14,700.

Applying *Options:* common application, early admission, early decision, deferred entrance. *Application fee:* $30. *Required:* essay or personal statement, high school transcript, minimum 2.0 GPA, 1 letter of recommendation. *Recommended:* interview, class rank. *Application deadlines:* 2/15 (freshmen), 8/1 (transfers). *Early decision:* 12/1. *Notification:* 3/15 (freshmen), 1/1 (early decision).

Admissions Contact Dr. Eugene Gregory, Vice President of College Relations, Centenary College of Louisiana, 2911 Centenary Blvd, PO Box 41188, Shreveport, LA 71134-1188. *Phone:* 318-869-5131. *Toll-free phone:* 800-234-4448. *Fax:* 318-869-5005. *E-mail:* jtmartin@centenary.edu.

DILLARD UNIVERSITY

New Orleans, Louisiana

- **Independent interdenominational** 4-year, founded 1869
- **Calendar** semesters
- **Degree** bachelor's
- **Urban** 46-acre campus
- **Endowment** $53.1 million
- **Coed,** 2,137 undergraduate students, 92% full-time, 77% women, 23% men
- **Moderately difficult** entrance level, 65% of applicants were admitted

Undergraduates Students come from 35 states and territories, 46% are from out of state, 99% African American, 0.1% Hispanic American, 0.0% international, 30% live on campus. *Retention:* 70% of 2001 full-time freshmen returned.

Freshmen *Admission:* 3,020 applied, 1,968 admitted. *Average high school GPA:* 3.20. *Test scores:* SAT verbal scores over 500: 24%; SAT math scores over 500: 29%; ACT scores over 18: 63%; SAT verbal scores over 600: 4%; SAT math scores over 600: 5%; ACT scores over 24: 8%.

Faculty *Total:* 187, 73% full-time, 50% with terminal degrees. *Student/faculty ratio:* 16:1.

Majors Accounting; art; art education; biology; biology education; business administration; chemistry; computer science; early childhood education; economics; education; elementary education; English; English composition; French; German; health education; health services administration; history; information sciences/systems; international business; Japanese; mass communications; mathematics; modern languages; music; music (general performance); music (piano and organ performance); music teacher education; music therapy; nursing; physical education; physics; political science; pre-dentistry; pre-law; pre-medicine; pre-veterinary studies; psychology; public health; public health education/promotion; religious studies; science education; secondary education; social work; sociology; Spanish; special education; speech/rhetorical studies; theater arts/drama; urban studies.

Academic Programs *Special study options:* academic remediation for entering students, advanced placement credit, cooperative education, double majors, honors programs, internships, part-time degree program, services for LD students, study abroad, summer session for credit. *ROTC:* Army (c), Navy (c), Air Force (c). *Unusual degree programs:* 3-2 engineering with Auburn University, Columbia University, Georgia Institute of Technology; urban studies with Columbia University, allied health with Howard University, Tuskegee University.

Library Will W. Alexander Library with 116,187 titles, 7,789 serial subscriptions, an OPAC, a Web page.

Computers on Campus 220 computers available on campus for general student use. A campuswide network can be accessed from student residence rooms and from off campus. Internet access, at least one staffed computer lab available.

Student Life *Housing Options:* men-only, women-only. *Activities and Organizations:* drama/theater group, student-run newspaper, radio station, choral group, national fraternities, national sororities. *Campus security:* 24-hour patrols. *Student Services:* health clinic, personal/psychological counseling.

Athletics Member NAIA. *Intercollegiate sports:* basketball M(s)/W(s). *Intramural sports:* basketball M/W, bowling M/W, gymnastics M/W, swimming M/W, tennis M/W, track and field M/W, volleyball M/W, weight lifting M.

Standardized Tests *Required:* SAT I or ACT (for admission). *Recommended:* SAT II: Subject Tests (for admission).

Costs (2001–02) *Comprehensive fee:* $16,326 includes full-time tuition ($9660), mandatory fees ($370), and room and board ($6296). Full-time tuition and fees vary according to program. Part-time tuition: $403 per credit hour. Part-time tuition and fees vary according to class time and program. *Required fees:* $185 per term part-time. *Room and board:* College room only: $3750. Room and board charges vary according to board plan and housing facility. *Payment plan:* installment.

Financial Aid Of all full-time matriculated undergraduates who enrolled in 2001, 2082 applied for aid, 1948 were judged to have need, 1948 had their need fully met. 230 State and other part-time jobs. In 2001, 53 non-need-based awards were made. *Average percent of need met:* 85%. *Average financial aid package:*

Dillard University (continued)
$12,685. *Average need-based loan:* $3298. *Average need-based gift aid:* $2838. *Average non-need based aid:* $4039. *Average indebtedness upon graduation:* $18,679.

Applying *Options:* common application, electronic application. *Application fee:* $10. *Required:* essay or personal statement, high school transcript, minimum 2.0 GPA, 2 letters of recommendation. *Recommended:* interview. *Application deadlines:* 7/1 (freshmen), 7/1 (transfers). *Notification:* continuous until 8/1 (freshmen).

Admissions Contact Mr. Darrin Q. Rankin, Assistant Vice President, Enrollment Management, Dillard University, 2601 Gentilly Boulevard, New Orleans, LA 70122. *Phone:* 504-286-4670. *Fax:* 504-286-4895.

GRAMBLING STATE UNIVERSITY
Grambling, Louisiana

- **State-supported** comprehensive, founded 1901, part of University of Louisiana System
- **Calendar** semesters
- **Degrees** associate, bachelor's, master's, and doctoral
- **Small-town** 340-acre campus
- **Endowment** $1.8 million
- **Coed,** 4,052 undergraduate students, 92% full-time, 57% women, 43% men
- **Noncompetitive** entrance level, 58% of applicants were admitted

Undergraduates 3,730 full-time, 322 part-time. Students come from 42 states and territories, 10 other countries, 36% are from out of state, 97% African American, 0.2% Asian American or Pacific Islander, 0.5% Hispanic American, 0.0% Native American, 0.5% international, 4% transferred in.

Freshmen *Admission:* 2,661 applied, 1,549 admitted, 814 enrolled. *Average high school GPA:* 2.00. *Test scores:* ACT scores over 18: 62%.

Faculty *Total:* 259, 98% full-time. *Student/faculty ratio:* 17:1.

Majors Accounting; architectural engineering technology; art; art education; automotive engineering technology; biology; business administration; business economics; business education; business marketing and marketing management; chemistry; child care/development; computer science; construction technology; criminal justice/law enforcement administration; drafting; early childhood education; electrical/electronic engineering technology; elementary education; English; English education; French; French language education; geography; history; home economics education; hotel and restaurant management; industrial arts education; industrial technology; information sciences/systems; institutional food workers; law enforcement/police science; mass communications; mathematics; music (general performance); music teacher education; nursing; paralegal/legal assistant; physical education; physics; political science; pre-law; psychology; public administration; science education; secondary education; social science education; social work; sociology; Spanish; special education; speech-language pathology; speech/theater education; theater arts/drama.

Academic Programs *Special study options:* academic remediation for entering students, adult/continuing education programs, advanced placement credit, cooperative education, honors programs, internships, off-campus study, part-time degree program, study abroad, summer session for credit. *ROTC:* Army (b), Air Force (b).

Library A. C. Lewis Memorial Library with 256,743 titles, 1,360 serial subscriptions, an OPAC, a Web page.

Computers on Campus 250 computers available on campus for general student use. A campuswide network can be accessed from student residence rooms and from off campus. Internet access, at least one staffed computer lab available.

Student Life *Housing:* on-campus residence required for freshman year. *Options:* men-only, women-only. *Activities and Organizations:* drama/theater group, student-run newspaper, radio station, choral group, marching band, national fraternities, national sororities. *Campus security:* 24-hour patrols, student patrols, controlled dormitory access. *Student Services:* health clinic, personal/psychological counseling.

Athletics Member NCAA. All Division I except football (Division I-AA). *Intercollegiate sports:* baseball M(s), basketball M(s)/W(s), bowling W(s), cross-country running M/W, golf M(s)/W(s), tennis M(s)/W(s), track and field M(s)/W(s), volleyball W(s). *Intramural sports:* bowling W, gymnastics M/W, softball M/W, swimming M/W, table tennis M/W, tennis M, track and field M/W, volleyball M/W, weight lifting M/W.

Standardized Tests *Required:* SAT I or ACT (for admission).

Costs (2001–02) *Tuition:* state resident $2589 full-time, $789 per term part-time; nonresident $7939 full-time, $2127 per term part-time. Part-time tuition and fees vary according to course load. *Room and board:* $2712; room only: $1400. *Waivers:* children of alumni, senior citizens, and employees or children of employees.

Financial Aid Of all full-time matriculated undergraduates who enrolled in 2001, 3691 applied for aid, 3325 were judged to have need. *Average percent of need met:* 80%. *Average financial aid package:* $6800. *Average need-based loan:* $3875. *Average need-based gift aid:* $6300. *Average indebtedness upon graduation:* $18,500.

Applying *Options:* common application, early admission, early decision, deferred entrance. *Application fee:* $20. *Required:* high school transcript. *Application deadlines:* 7/15 (freshmen), 7/15 (transfers). *Early decision:* 4/15. *Notification:* continuous until 8/1 (freshmen), 4/20 (early decision).

Admissions Contact Mr. Martin Lemelle, Head Recruiter/Admission Officer, Grambling State University, PO Box 607, Grambling, LA 71245. *Phone:* 318-274-3395. *E-mail:* bingamann@medgar.gram.edu.

GRANTHAM COLLEGE OF ENGINEERING
Slidell, Louisiana

- **Proprietary** 4-year, founded 1951
- **Calendar** continuous
- **Degrees** associate and bachelor's (offers only external degree programs)
- **Small-town** campus
- **Coed, primarily men**
- **Noncompetitive** entrance level

Admissions Contact Mrs. Maria Adcock, Student Services Manager, Grantham College of Engineering, PO Box 5700, Slidell, LA 70460-6815. *Phone:* 504-649-4191. *Toll-free phone:* 800-955-2527. *Fax:* 504-649-4183. *E-mail:* gce@grantham.edu.

HERZING COLLEGE
Kenner, Louisiana

- **Proprietary** primarily 2-year, founded 1996
- **Calendar** semesters
- **Degrees** diplomas, associate, and bachelor's
- **Coed**
- **Moderately difficult** entrance level

Admissions Contact Genny Bordelon, Director of Admissions, Herzing College, 2400 Veterans Boulevard, Kenner, LA 70062. *Phone:* 504-733-0074.

LOUISIANA COLLEGE
Pineville, Louisiana

- **Independent Southern Baptist** 4-year, founded 1906
- **Calendar** semesters
- **Degree** bachelor's
- **Small-town** 81-acre campus
- **Endowment** $27.6 million
- **Coed,** 1,204 undergraduate students, 88% full-time, 58% women, 42% men
- **Moderately difficult** entrance level, 70% of applicants were admitted

Undergraduates 1,055 full-time, 149 part-time. Students come from 18 states and territories, 7 other countries, 10% are from out of state, 8% African American, 2% Asian American or Pacific Islander, 1% Hispanic American, 0.7% Native American, 0.7% international, 5% transferred in, 50% live on campus. *Retention:* 60% of 2001 full-time freshmen returned.

Freshmen *Admission:* 332 applied, 234 admitted, 294 enrolled. *Average high school GPA:* 3.30. *Test scores:* ACT scores over 18: 95%; ACT scores over 24: 46%; ACT scores over 30: 2%.

Faculty *Total:* 102, 66% full-time. *Student/faculty ratio:* 16:1.

Majors Accounting; adult/continuing education; advertising; art; art education; athletic training/sports medicine; biology; broadcast journalism; business administration; business education; business marketing and marketing management; chemistry; criminal justice/law enforcement administration; early childhood education; economics; elementary education; English; exercise sciences; family/consumer studies; finance; fine/studio arts; French; graphic design/commercial art/illustration; health education; history; interdisciplinary studies; journalism; law enforcement/police science; liberal arts and sciences/liberal studies; mass communications; mathematics; medical technology; modern languages; music; music (piano and organ performance); music teacher education; music (voice and choral/opera performance); nursing; philosophy; physical education; physics; pre-law; psychology; public administration; religious education; religious music;

religious studies; science education; secondary education; social work; sociology; Spanish; special education; speech/rhetorical studies; theater arts/drama; theology.

Academic Programs *Special study options:* academic remediation for entering students, accelerated degree program, adult/continuing education programs, advanced placement credit, honors programs, internships, part-time degree program, services for LD students, student-designed majors, study abroad, summer session for credit.

Library Richard W. Morton Memorial Library with 131,000 titles, 600 serial subscriptions, an OPAC, a Web page.

Computers on Campus 142 computers available on campus for general student use. A campuswide network can be accessed from off campus. Internet access, at least one staffed computer lab available.

Student Life *Housing:* on-campus residence required through senior year. *Options:* men-only, women-only. *Activities and Organizations:* drama/theater group, student-run newspaper, radio and television station, choral group, Baptist Student Union, Delta Xi Omega, Student Government Association, Union Board, Lambda Chi Beta. *Campus security:* 24-hour patrols, student patrols, late-night transport/escort service, controlled dormitory access. *Student Services:* health clinic, personal/psychological counseling.

Athletics Member NCAA, NCCAA. All NCAA Division III. *Intercollegiate sports:* baseball M, basketball M/W, cross-country running M/W, football M, golf M/W, sailing M/W, soccer M/W, softball M/W, swimming M/W, tennis W. *Intramural sports:* badminton M/W, basketball M/W, bowling M/W, football M/W, golf M/W, softball M/W, swimming M/W, table tennis M/W, tennis M/W, volleyball M/W, weight lifting M/W.

Standardized Tests *Required:* SAT I or ACT (for admission).

Costs (2002–03) *Comprehensive fee:* $11,516 includes full-time tuition ($7800), mandatory fees ($400), and room and board ($3316). Part-time tuition: $260 per hour. No tuition increase for student's term of enrollment. *Room and board:* Room and board charges vary according to board plan and housing facility. *Payment plan:* installment. *Waivers:* senior citizens and employees or children of employees.

Applying *Options:* early admission. *Application fee:* $25. *Required:* high school transcript, letters of recommendation. *Required for some:* minimum 2.0 GPA, 3 letters of recommendation, class rank. *Recommended:* interview. *Application deadlines:* 8/1 (freshmen), 8/1 (transfers). *Notification:* continuous (freshmen).

Admissions Contact Mrs. Mary Wagner, Director of Admissions, Louisiana College, Box 560, Pineville, LA 71359-0001. *Phone:* 318-487-7259 Ext. 7301. *Toll-free phone:* 800-487-1906. *Fax:* 318-487-7550. *E-mail:* admissions@lacollege.edu.

Louisiana State University and Agricultural and Mechanical College
Baton Rouge, Louisiana

- **State-supported** university, founded 1860, part of Louisiana State University System
- **Calendar** semesters
- **Degrees** bachelor's, master's, doctoral, first professional, and post-master's certificates
- **Urban** 2000-acre campus with easy access to New Orleans
- **Endowment** $197.9 million
- **Coed,** 26,518 undergraduate students, 90% full-time, 53% women, 47% men
- **Moderately difficult** entrance level, 79% of applicants were admitted

Undergraduates 23,873 full-time, 2,645 part-time. Students come from 49 states and territories, 99 other countries, 8% are from out of state, 9% African American, 4% Asian American or Pacific Islander, 2% Hispanic American, 0.3% Native American, 3% international, 3% transferred in, 23% live on campus. *Retention:* 83% of 2001 full-time freshmen returned.

Freshmen *Admission:* 10,536 applied, 8,336 admitted, 5,301 enrolled. *Average high school GPA:* 3.36. *Test scores:* ACT scores over 18: 98%; ACT scores over 24: 47%; ACT scores over 30: 7%.

Faculty *Total:* 1,415, 92% full-time, 77% with terminal degrees. *Student/faculty ratio:* 21:1.

Majors Accounting; agricultural business; animal sciences; anthropology; architectural engineering technology; architecture; biochemistry; bioengineering; biological sciences/life sciences related; business administration; business economics; business marketing and marketing management; chemical engineering; chemistry; civil engineering; computer engineering; computer science; dietetics; economics; electrical engineering; elementary education; English; environmental engineering; environmental science; fashion merchandising; finance; fine/studio arts; food sciences; forest management; French; general studies; geography; geology; German; history; individual/family development; industrial/manufacturing engineering; interior architecture; international business; landscape architecture; Latin (ancient and medieval); liberal arts and sciences/liberal studies; management information systems/business data processing; mass communications; mathematics; mechanical engineering; multi/interdisciplinary studies related; music; music (general performance); music teacher education; petroleum engineering; philosophy; physical education; physics; plant sciences; political science; psychology; Russian/Slavic studies; secondary education; sociology; Spanish; speech-language pathology/audiology; speech/rhetorical studies; teacher education, specific programs related; theater arts/drama; wildlife management.

Academic Programs *Special study options:* academic remediation for entering students, accelerated degree program, adult/continuing education programs, advanced placement credit, cooperative education, distance learning, double majors, English as a second language, freshman honors college, honors programs, independent study, internships, off-campus study, part-time degree program, services for LD students, student-designed majors, study abroad, summer session for credit. *ROTC:* Army (b), Navy (c), Air Force (b).

Library Troy H. Middleton Library plus 7 others with 1.1 million titles, 17,975 serial subscriptions, 2,043 audiovisual materials, an OPAC, a Web page.

Computers on Campus 7000 computers available on campus for general student use. A campuswide network can be accessed from student residence rooms and from off campus that provide access to e-mail. Internet access, online (class) registration, at least one staffed computer lab available.

Student Life *Housing Options:* coed, men-only, women-only, disabled students. *Activities and Organizations:* drama/theater group, student-run newspaper, radio and television station, choral group, marching band, intramural athletics, student political organizations, Greek organizations, student professional organizations, religious organizations, national fraternities, national sororities. *Campus security:* 24-hour emergency response devices and patrols, late-night transport/escort service, controlled dormitory access, self-defense education, crime prevention programs. *Student Services:* health clinic, personal/psychological counseling, women's center, legal services.

Athletics Member NCAA. All Division I except football (Division I-A). *Intercollegiate sports:* baseball M(s), basketball M(s)/W(s), cross-country running M(s)/W(s), golf M(s)/W(s), gymnastics W(s), soccer W(s), softball W(s), swimming M(s)/W(s), tennis M(s)/W(s), track and field M(s)/W(s), volleyball W(s). *Intramural sports:* badminton M/W, basketball M/W, cross-country running M/W, fencing M(c)/W(c), football M/W, golf M/W, lacrosse M(c), racquetball M/W, rugby M(c)/W(c), sailing M(c)/W(c), soccer M/W, softball M/W, squash M, swimming M/W, table tennis M/W, tennis M/W, track and field M/W, volleyball M/W, weight lifting M(c), wrestling M(c).

Standardized Tests *Required:* SAT I or ACT (for admission). *Required for some:* SAT I and SAT II or ACT (for admission).

Costs (2001–02) *Tuition:* state resident $2551 full-time; nonresident $7851 full-time. Part-time tuition and fees vary according to course load. *Required fees:* $917 full-time. *Room and board:* $4546; room only: $2650. Room and board charges vary according to board plan and housing facility. *Payment plan:* deferred payment. *Waivers:* children of alumni, senior citizens, and employees or children of employees.

Financial Aid Of all full-time matriculated undergraduates who enrolled in 2001, 18273 applied for aid, 10700 were judged to have need, 2484 had their need fully met. 1048 Federal Work-Study jobs (averaging $1336). 6147 State and other part-time jobs (averaging $2017). In 2001, 8274 non-need-based awards were made. *Average percent of need met:* 69%. *Average financial aid package:* $6177. *Average need-based loan:* $3636. *Average need-based gift aid:* $2481. *Average non-need based aid:* $3573. *Average indebtedness upon graduation:* $17,818.

Applying *Options:* early admission. *Application fee:* $25. *Required:* high school transcript, minimum 2.8 GPA, minimum ACT score of 20 or SAT I score of 950. *Required for some:* essay or personal statement, 3 letters of recommendation, interview. *Application deadlines:* 4/15 (freshmen), 4/15 (transfers). *Notification:* continuous (freshmen).

Admissions Contact Cleve Brooks, Director of Admissions, Louisiana State University and Agricultural and Mechanical College, 110 Thomas Boyd Hall, Baton Rouge, LA 70803. *Phone:* 225-578-1175. *Fax:* 225-578-4433. *E-mail:* admissions@lsu.edu.

Louisiana State University Health Sciences Center
New Orleans, Louisiana

- **State-supported** university, founded 1931, part of Louisiana State University System
- **Calendar** semesters
- **Degrees** associate, bachelor's, master's, doctoral, and first professional

Louisiana State University Health Sciences Center (continued)
- **Urban** campus
- **Coed,** 784 undergraduate students

Undergraduates Students come from 14 states and territories, 1% are from out of state, 9% African American, 5% Asian American or Pacific Islander, 2% Hispanic American, 0.3% Native American, 0.3% international.
Faculty *Total:* 3,000.
Majors Dental hygiene; dental laboratory technician; medical technology; mental health/rehabilitation; nursing; optometric/ophthalmic laboratory technician; physician assistant; respiratory therapy.
Academic Programs *Special study options:* academic remediation for entering students, advanced placement credit, independent study, internships, services for LD students, summer session for credit.
Library John P. Ische Library plus 2 others with 389,486 titles, 3,500 serial subscriptions, 9,454 audiovisual materials, an OPAC, a Web page.
Computers on Campus 100 computers available on campus for general student use. A campuswide network can be accessed from student residence rooms and from off campus. At least one staffed computer lab available.
Student Life *Housing Options:* coed. *Campus security:* 24-hour patrols, late-night transport/escort service, controlled dormitory access. *Student Services:* health clinic, personal/psychological counseling.
Athletics *Intramural sports:* baseball M, football M, golf M, soccer M, softball M, volleyball M/W.
Costs (2001–02) *Tuition:* state resident $3875 full-time; nonresident $6895 full-time. Full-time tuition and fees vary according to degree level, location, program, and student level. Part-time tuition and fees vary according to course load, location, and program. *Room and board:* room only: $1975. Room and board charges vary according to housing facility. *Payment plan:* deferred payment. *Waivers:* children of alumni, senior citizens, and employees or children of employees.
Applying *Application fee:* $50. *Application deadline:* 3/1 (transfers).
Admissions Contact Mr. Edmund A. Vidacovich, Registrar, Louisiana State University Health Sciences Center, 433 Bolivar Street, New Orleans, LA 70112-2223. *Phone:* 504-568-4829.

LOUISIANA STATE UNIVERSITY IN SHREVEPORT

Shreveport, Louisiana

- **State-supported** comprehensive, founded 1965, part of Louisiana State University System
- **Calendar** semesters
- **Degrees** bachelor's and master's
- **Urban** 200-acre campus
- **Endowment** $3.8 million
- **Coed,** 3,419 undergraduate students, 67% full-time, 62% women, 38% men
- **Noncompetitive** entrance level, 59% of applicants were admitted

Undergraduates 2,281 full-time, 1,138 part-time. Students come from 45 states and territories, 10 other countries, 4% are from out of state, 20% African American, 2% Asian American or Pacific Islander, 2% Hispanic American, 0.9% Native American, 0.4% international, 12% transferred in, 5% live on campus. *Retention:* 58% of 2001 full-time freshmen returned.
Freshmen *Admission:* 845 applied, 496 admitted, 496 enrolled. *Average high school GPA:* 3.16. *Test scores:* ACT scores over 18: 77%; ACT scores over 24: 24%; ACT scores over 30: 1%.
Faculty *Total:* 230, 57% full-time, 53% with terminal degrees. *Student/faculty ratio:* 19:1.
Majors Accounting; art; art education; biological/physical sciences; biology; biology education; business administration; business marketing and marketing management; chemistry; chemistry education; computer science; criminal justice studies; elementary education; English; English education; environmental science; finance; French; French language education; general studies; geography; history; mass communications; mathematics; mathematics education; physical education; physics; physics education; political science; psychology; social studies education; sociology; Spanish; special education; speech-language pathology/audiology; speech/rhetorical studies.
Academic Programs *Special study options:* academic remediation for entering students, accelerated degree program, adult/continuing education programs, advanced placement credit, cooperative education, distance learning, double majors, honors programs, independent study, internships, off-campus study, part-time degree program, services for LD students, student-designed majors, summer session for credit. *ROTC:* Army (b).
Library Noel Memorial Library with 279,821 titles, 1,190 serial subscriptions, 1,914 audiovisual materials, an OPAC, a Web page.
Computers on Campus A campuswide network can be accessed from off campus. Internet access, at least one staffed computer lab available.
Student Life *Housing Options:* coed, men-only, women-only. *Activities and Organizations:* student-run newspaper, choral group, American Humanics, The Louisiana Association of Educators, Catholic Student Union, Biology/Health Club, Psychology Club, national fraternities, national sororities. *Campus security:* 24-hour patrols, student patrols, controlled dormitory access. *Student Services:* personal/psychological counseling.
Athletics Member NAIA. *Intercollegiate sports:* baseball M(s). *Intramural sports:* archery M, basketball M/W, football M/W, lacrosse M, racquetball M/W, softball M/W, table tennis M/W, volleyball M/W.
Standardized Tests *Recommended:* ACT (for admission), SAT I or ACT (for admission), SAT II: Subject Tests (for admission).
Costs (2001–02) *Tuition:* state resident $2300 full-time, $85 per credit part-time; nonresident $6630 full-time, $260 per credit part-time. Full-time tuition and fees vary according to course load. Part-time tuition and fees vary according to course load and location. *Required fees:* $250 full-time, $5 per credit. *Room and board:* Room and board charges vary according to housing facility. *Payment plan:* deferred payment. *Waivers:* senior citizens and employees or children of employees.
Applying *Options:* early admission, deferred entrance. *Application fee:* $10. *Required:* high school transcript, minimum 2.0 GPA. *Required for some:* minimum ACT score of 17 for nonresidents. *Application deadlines:* 8/1 (freshmen), 8/1 (transfers). *Notification:* continuous (freshmen).
Admissions Contact Ms. Julie Wilkins, Assistant Director of Admissions and Records, Louisiana State University in Shreveport, One University Place, Shreveport, LA 71115-2399. *Phone:* 318-797-5061. *Toll-free phone:* 800-229-5957. *Fax:* 318-797-5286. *E-mail:* admissions@pilot.lsus.edu.

LOUISIANA TECH UNIVERSITY

Ruston, Louisiana

- **State-supported** university, founded 1894, part of University of Louisiana System
- **Calendar** quarters
- **Degrees** associate, bachelor's, master's, and doctoral
- **Small-town** 247-acre campus
- **Endowment** $39.1 million
- **Coed,** 9,060 undergraduate students, 83% full-time, 48% women, 52% men
- **Moderately difficult** entrance level, 93% of applicants were admitted

Louisiana Tech University is known for high graduation rates, entrance exam scores, and overall academic quality. Quarter terms provide flexible scheduling. Family atmosphere enhances creativity and opportunity for participation in the many student organizations.

Undergraduates 7,485 full-time, 1,575 part-time. Students come from 49 states and territories, 51 other countries, 13% are from out of state, 15% African American, 0.9% Asian American or Pacific Islander, 1% Hispanic American, 0.6% Native American, 2% international, 6% transferred in, 30% live on campus.
Freshmen *Admission:* 3,289 applied, 3,067 admitted, 1,880 enrolled. *Average high school GPA:* 3.50. *Test scores:* ACT scores over 18: 87%; ACT scores over 24: 36%; ACT scores over 30: 4%.
Faculty *Total:* 442, 84% full-time, 71% with terminal degrees. *Student/faculty ratio:* 24:1.
Majors Accounting; agricultural business; animal sciences; architecture; art; art education; aviation/airway science; aviation management; bioengineering; biology; business administration; business economics; business marketing and marketing management; chemical engineering; chemistry; child care/development; civil engineering; civil engineering technology; computer science; consumer economics; dietetics; early childhood education; education of the speech impaired; electrical/electronic engineering technology; electrical engineering; elementary education; English; environmental science; finance; forestry; French; French language education; general studies; geography; geology; graphic design/commercial art/illustration; health/physical education; history; human resources management; industrial/manufacturing engineering; interior architecture; journalism; management information systems/business data processing; management science; mathematics; mechanical engineering; medical records administration; medical records technology; medical technology; music; music (general performance); music teacher education; natural resources conservation; nursing; operations management; photography; physical education; physics; plant sciences; political science; psychology; secondary education; sociology; Spanish; special education; speech education; speech-language pathology/audiology; speech/rhetorical studies.

Academic Programs *Special study options:* academic remediation for entering students, adult/continuing education programs, advanced placement credit, cooperative education, distance learning, double majors, English as a second language, honors programs, independent study, internships, off-campus study, part-time degree program, study abroad, summer session for credit. *ROTC:* Army (c), Air Force (b).

Library Prescott Memorial Library with 3,319 titles, 2,469 serial subscriptions, 14,532 audiovisual materials, an OPAC, a Web page.

Computers on Campus 1800 computers available on campus for general student use. A campuswide network can be accessed from student residence rooms and from off campus. At least one staffed computer lab available.

Student Life *Housing:* on-campus residence required through sophomore year. *Options:* men-only, women-only, disabled students. *Activities and Organizations:* drama/theater group, student-run newspaper, radio station, choral group, marching band, Student Government Association, Association of Women's Studies, Union Board, national fraternities, national sororities. *Campus security:* 24-hour emergency response devices and patrols, student patrols, late-night transport/escort service, controlled dormitory access. *Student Services:* health clinic, personal/psychological counseling, legal services.

Athletics Member NCAA. All Division I except football (Division I-A). *Intercollegiate sports:* baseball M(s), basketball M(s)/W(s), cross-country running M(s)/W(s), golf M(s), softball W(s), tennis W(s), track and field M(s)/W(s), volleyball W(s), weight lifting M/W. *Intramural sports:* basketball M/W, bowling M/W, cross-country running M/W, football M/W, golf M, racquetball M/W, soccer M, softball M/W, tennis M/W, track and field M/W, volleyball M/W.

Standardized Tests *Required:* SAT I or ACT (for admission). *Recommended:* ACT (for admission).

Costs (2001–02) *Tuition:* state resident $2922 full-time; nonresident $7827 full-time. Full-time tuition and fees vary according to program. Part-time tuition and fees vary according to course load and program. *Required fees:* $119 full-time. *Room and board:* $3465; room only: $1785. Room and board charges vary according to board plan and housing facility. *Waivers:* children of alumni, senior citizens, and employees or children of employees.

Financial Aid Of all full-time matriculated undergraduates who enrolled in 2001, 4915 applied for aid, 2909 were judged to have need, 486 had their need fully met. 376 Federal Work-Study jobs (averaging $1516). 1066 State and other part-time jobs. In 2001, 1270 non-need-based awards were made. *Average percent of need met:* 69%. *Average financial aid package:* $5974. *Average need-based loan:* $2748. *Average need-based gift aid:* $4262. *Average indebtedness upon graduation:* $11,016.

Applying *Options:* common application, early admission. *Application fee:* $20. *Required:* high school transcript, minimum 2.2 GPA. *Application deadline:* 7/3 (freshmen), rolling (transfers). *Notification:* continuous (freshmen).

Admissions Contact Mrs. Jan B. Albritton, Director of Admissions, Louisiana Tech University, PO Box 3178, Ruston, LA 71272. *Phone:* 318-257-3036. *Toll-free phone:* 800-528-3241. *Fax:* 318-257-2499. *E-mail:* bulldog@latech.edu.

LOYOLA UNIVERSITY NEW ORLEANS
New Orleans, Louisiana

- **Independent Roman Catholic (Jesuit)** comprehensive, founded 1912
- **Calendar** semesters
- **Degrees** bachelor's, master's, and first professional
- **Urban** 26-acre campus
- **Endowment** $304.7 million
- **Coed,** 3,792 undergraduate students, 85% full-time, 64% women, 36% men
- **Moderately difficult** entrance level, 69% of applicants were admitted

Academic excellence, ideal size, and a rich Jesuit tradition—a unique combination of quality faculty and academic programs and facilities, an ideal size that fosters a positive learning environment and individual student attention, and the centuries-old Jesuit tradition of educating the whole person distinguishes Loyola from other institutions.

Undergraduates 3,235 full-time, 557 part-time. Students come from 50 states and territories, 44 other countries, 47% are from out of state, 11% African American, 4% Asian American or Pacific Islander, 10% Hispanic American, 0.5% Native American, 3% international, 4% transferred in, 39% live on campus. *Retention:* 81% of 2001 full-time freshmen returned.

Freshmen *Admission:* 3,419 applied, 2,373 admitted, 872 enrolled. *Average high school GPA:* 3.54. *Test scores:* SAT verbal scores over 500: 90%; SAT math scores over 500: 88%; ACT scores over 18: 99%; SAT verbal scores over 600: 47%; SAT math scores over 600: 35%; ACT scores over 24: 67%; SAT verbal scores over 700: 10%; SAT math scores over 700: 3%; ACT scores over 30: 9%.

Faculty *Total:* 408, 64% full-time, 70% with terminal degrees. *Student/faculty ratio:* 14:1.

Majors Accounting; art; behavioral sciences; biology; business administration; business economics; business marketing and marketing management; chemistry; classics; communications; computer/information sciences; creative writing; criminal justice studies; economics; education; elementary education; English; finance; forensic technology; French; general studies; German; graphic design/commercial art/illustration; history; humanities; information sciences/systems; international business; jazz; mathematics; music; music business management/merchandising; music (general performance); music (piano and organ performance); music teacher education; music theory and composition; music therapy; nursing; philosophy; physics; political science; psychology; religious education; religious music; religious studies; Russian; social sciences; sociology; Spanish; theater arts/drama; visual/performing arts.

Academic Programs *Special study options:* academic remediation for entering students, accelerated degree program, adult/continuing education programs, advanced placement credit, distance learning, double majors, English as a second language, honors programs, independent study, internships, off-campus study, part-time degree program, services for LD students, student-designed majors, study abroad, summer session for credit. *ROTC:* Army (c), Air Force (c). *Unusual degree programs:* 3-2 engineering with Tulane University.

Library University Library plus 1 other with 384,774 titles, 5,111 serial subscriptions, 13,829 audiovisual materials, an OPAC, a Web page.

Computers on Campus 300 computers available on campus for general student use. A campuswide network can be accessed from student residence rooms and from off campus. Internet access, online (class) registration, at least one staffed computer lab available.

Student Life *Housing:* on-campus residence required for freshman year. *Options:* coed, women-only, disabled students. *Activities and Organizations:* drama/theater group, student-run newspaper, radio and television station, choral group, University Programming Board, Community Action Program, Black Student Union, Student Government Association, national fraternities, national sororities. *Campus security:* 24-hour emergency response devices and patrols, late-night transport/escort service, controlled dormitory access, self-defense education, bicycle patrols, closed circuit TV monitors, door alarms, crime prevention programs. *Student Services:* health clinic, personal/psychological counseling, women's center.

Athletics Member NAIA. *Intercollegiate sports:* baseball M, basketball M/W, bowling M(c), crew M(c)/W(c), cross-country running M/W, golf M(c)/W(c), lacrosse M(c), rugby M(c)/W(c), soccer M(c)/W, swimming M(c)/W(c), tennis M(c)/W(c), track and field M/W, volleyball W, wrestling M(c). *Intramural sports:* basketball M/W, golf M/W, racquetball M/W, soccer M/W, softball M/W, swimming M/W, tennis M/W, volleyball M/W, water polo M/W, weight lifting M/W.

Standardized Tests *Required:* SAT I or ACT (for admission).

Costs (2002–03) *Comprehensive fee:* $26,120 includes full-time tuition ($18,700), mandatory fees ($512), and room and board ($6908). Full-time tuition and fees vary according to student level. Part-time tuition: $601 per credit hour. *Required fees:* $662 per year part-time. *Room and board:* College room only: $4400. Room and board charges vary according to board plan and housing facility. *Payment plan:* installment. *Waivers:* senior citizens and employees or children of employees.

Financial Aid Of all full-time matriculated undergraduates who enrolled in 2001, 2266 applied for aid, 1726 were judged to have need, 676 had their need fully met. 783 Federal Work-Study jobs (averaging $1860). In 2001, 965 non-need-based awards were made. *Average percent of need met:* 85%. *Average financial aid package:* $14,084. *Average need-based loan:* $3821. *Average need-based gift aid:* $10,043. *Average non-need based aid:* $7428. *Average indebtedness upon graduation:* $17,981.

Applying *Options:* common application, electronic application, deferred entrance. *Application fee:* $20. *Required:* essay or personal statement, high school transcript, 1 letter of recommendation. *Required for some:* interview. *Recommended:* interview. *Application deadline:* 1/15 (freshmen), rolling (transfers). *Notification:* continuous (freshmen).

Admissions Contact Ms. Deborah C. Stieffel, Dean of Admission and Enrollment Management, Loyola University New Orleans, 6363 Saint Charles Avenue, Box 18, New Orleans, LA 70118-6195. *Phone:* 504-865-3240. *Toll-free phone:* 800-4-LOYOLA. *Fax:* 504-865-3383. *E-mail:* admit@loyno.edu.

MCNEESE STATE UNIVERSITY
Lake Charles, Louisiana

- **State-supported** comprehensive, founded 1939, part of University of Louisiana System
- **Calendar** semesters
- **Degrees** associate, bachelor's, master's, and postbachelor's certificates
- **Suburban** 580-acre campus

McNeese State University (continued)

- **Endowment** $29.3 million
- **Coed,** 6,845 undergraduate students, 83% full-time, 59% women, 41% men
- **Moderately difficult** entrance level, 86% of applicants were admitted

Undergraduates 5,697 full-time, 1,148 part-time. Students come from 31 states and territories, 38 other countries, 6% are from out of state, 17% African American, 0.7% Asian American or Pacific Islander, 1% Hispanic American, 1% Native American, 1% international, 4% transferred in, 12% live on campus. *Retention:* 58% of 2001 full-time freshmen returned.

Freshmen *Admission:* 2,033 applied, 1,741 admitted, 1,383 enrolled. *Average high school GPA:* 3.05. *Test scores:* ACT scores over 18: 70%; ACT scores over 24: 15%; ACT scores over 30: 1%.

Faculty *Total:* 392, 73% full-time, 52% with terminal degrees. *Student/faculty ratio:* 20:1.

Majors Accounting; agricultural sciences; applied art; biology; business administration; business marketing and marketing management; ceramic arts; chemistry; child care/development; computer science; computer typography/composition; criminal justice studies; drawing; early childhood education; education; education administration; electrical/electronic engineering technology; electrical engineering; elementary education; engineering; English; environmental science; finance; French; history; home economics; home economics education; instrumentation technology; liberal arts and sciences/liberal studies; mass communications; mathematics; medical radiologic technology; medical technology; music; music teacher education; nursing; nutrition science; paralegal/legal assistant; petroleum technology; photography; physical education; physics; political science; printmaking; psychology; secondary education; secretarial science; sociology; Spanish; special education; speech/rhetorical studies; theater arts/drama; wildlife management.

Academic Programs *Special study options:* academic remediation for entering students, accelerated degree program, adult/continuing education programs, advanced placement credit, cooperative education, distance learning, double majors, English as a second language, freshman honors college, honors programs, independent study, internships, off-campus study, part-time degree program, services for LD students, study abroad, summer session for credit.

Library Frazer Memorial Library plus 2 others with 365,259 titles, 1,679 serial subscriptions, 1,395 audiovisual materials, an OPAC, a Web page.

Computers on Campus 354 computers available on campus for general student use. A campuswide network can be accessed from off campus. Internet access, online (class) registration, at least one staffed computer lab available.

Student Life *Housing:* on-campus residence required for freshman year. *Options:* coed, men-only, women-only. *Activities and Organizations:* drama/theater group, student-run newspaper, radio station, choral group, marching band, Student Government Association, International Students Association, Resident Student Association, national fraternities, national sororities. *Campus security:* 24-hour emergency response devices and patrols, late-night transport/escort service, controlled dormitory access. *Student Services:* health clinic, personal/psychological counseling, women's center.

Athletics Member NCAA. All Division I except football (Division I-AA). *Intercollegiate sports:* baseball M(s), basketball M(s)/W(s), cross-country running M(s)/W(s), golf M(s), riflery M/W, soccer W, softball W(s), tennis W(s), track and field M(s)/W(s), volleyball W(s), weight lifting M(c)/W(c). *Intramural sports:* badminton M/W, baseball M, basketball M/W, football M/W, golf M/W, racquetball M/W, soccer M/W, softball W, swimming M/W, table tennis M/W, tennis M/W, volleyball M/W, water polo M/W, weight lifting M/W.

Standardized Tests *Required:* SAT I or ACT (for admission).

Costs (2002–03) *Tuition:* state resident $1974 full-time, $499 per term part-time; nonresident $8114 full-time, $499 per term part-time. Full-time tuition and fees vary according to degree level. Part-time tuition and fees vary according to degree level. *Required fees:* $571 full-time, $208 per term part-time. *Room and board:* $3720; room only: $1370. Room and board charges vary according to board plan and housing facility. *Payment plans:* installment, deferred payment. *Waivers:* senior citizens and employees or children of employees.

Applying *Options:* electronic application, early admission. *Application fee:* $20. *Required:* high school transcript. *Required for some:* minimum 2.0 GPA. *Application deadline:* rolling (freshmen), rolling (transfers). *Notification:* continuous (freshmen).

Admissions Contact Ms. Tammie Pettis, Director of Admissions, McNeese State University, PO Box 92495, Kaufman Hall, 4100 Ryan Street, Lake Charles, LA 70609-2495. *Phone:* 337-475-5148. *Toll-free phone:* 800-622-3352. *Fax:* 337-475-5189. *E-mail:* jmartin@mail.mcneese.edu.

New Orleans Baptist Theological Seminary

New Orleans, Louisiana

- **Independent Southern Baptist** comprehensive, founded 1917
- **Calendar** semesters
- **Degrees** associate, bachelor's, master's, doctoral, and first professional
- **Suburban** 81-acre campus
- **Coed, primarily men,** 1,063 undergraduate students, 30% full-time, 19% women, 81% men
- **Minimally difficult** entrance level, 82% of applicants were admitted

Undergraduates Students come from 29 states and territories, 5 other countries, 18% African American, 2% Asian American or Pacific Islander, 11% Hispanic American, 0.2% Native American, 4% international. *Retention:* 70% of 2001 full-time freshmen returned.

Freshmen *Admission:* 85 applied, 70 admitted.

Faculty *Total:* 84, 12% full-time, 83% with terminal degrees.

Majors Religious studies.

Academic Programs *Special study options:* academic remediation for entering students, adult/continuing education programs, English as a second language, independent study, internships, off-campus study, part-time degree program, summer session for credit.

Library John Christian Library plus 1 other with 206,321 titles.

Computers on Campus 10 computers available on campus for general student use.

Student Life *Activities and Organizations:* student-run radio station, choral group. *Campus security:* 24-hour emergency response devices and patrols. *Student Services:* health clinic, personal/psychological counseling.

Athletics *Intramural sports:* badminton M, basketball M, football M, golf M, softball M, swimming M/W, table tennis M/W, tennis M/W, volleyball M/W, weight lifting M/W.

Costs (2002–03) *Tuition:* $2950 full-time, $100 per hour part-time. *Required fees:* $100 full-time.

Financial Aid *Financial aid deadline:* 4/30.

Applying *Options:* deferred entrance. *Application fee:* $25. *Recommended:* minimum 2.0 GPA. *Application deadline:* 8/9 (freshmen). *Notification:* continuous (freshmen).

Admissions Contact Dr. Paul E. Gregoire Jr., Registrar/Director of Admissions, New Orleans Baptist Theological Seminary, 3939 Gentilly Boulevard, New Orleans, LA 70126-4858. *Phone:* 504-282-4455 Ext. 3337. *Toll-free phone:* 800-662-8701.

Nicholls State University

Thibodaux, Louisiana

- **State-supported** comprehensive, founded 1948, part of University of Louisiana System
- **Calendar** semesters
- **Degrees** certificates, associate, bachelor's, master's, and post-master's certificates
- **Small-town** 210-acre campus with easy access to New Orleans
- **Endowment** $5.9 million
- **Coed,** 6,534 undergraduate students, 83% full-time, 63% women, 37% men
- **Noncompetitive** entrance level, 99% of applicants were admitted

Undergraduates 5,395 full-time, 1,139 part-time. Students come from 32 states and territories, 29 other countries, 3% are from out of state, 16% African American, 0.6% Asian American or Pacific Islander, 1% Hispanic American, 2% Native American, 0.8% international, 5% transferred in, 15% live on campus. *Retention:* 57% of 2001 full-time freshmen returned.

Freshmen *Admission:* 2,459 applied, 2,434 admitted, 1,488 enrolled. *Average high school GPA:* 2.87. *Test scores:* SAT verbal scores over 500: 57%; SAT math scores over 500: 45%; ACT scores over 18: 70%; SAT verbal scores over 600: 18%; SAT math scores over 600: 15%; ACT scores over 24: 12%; ACT scores over 30: 1%.

Faculty *Total:* 275, 100% full-time. *Student/faculty ratio:* 22:1.

Majors Accounting; agricultural business; art; art education; biology; business; business administration; business education; business marketing and marketing management; chemistry; computer science; dietetics; early childhood education; education; elementary education; emergency medical technology; English; finance; French; general studies; health education; history; home economics; institutional food workers; law enforcement/police science; management information systems/business data processing; marine biology; mass communications; mathematics; middle school education; music; music teacher education; nursing; paralegal/legal assistant; petroleum technology; physical education; political science; pre-dentistry; pre-medicine; psychology; respiratory therapy; science education; secondary education; secretarial science; sociology; special education; speech-language pathology/audiology.

Academic Programs *Special study options:* academic remediation for entering students, accelerated degree program, adult/continuing education programs, advanced placement credit, cooperative education, distance learning, double majors, English as a second language, honors programs, independent study, internships, off-campus study, part-time degree program, services for LD students, study abroad, summer session for credit.

Library Allen J. Ellender Memorial Library with 303,962 titles, 1,341 serial subscriptions, 3,374 audiovisual materials, an OPAC, a Web page.

Computers on Campus 204 computers available on campus for general student use. A campuswide network can be accessed from student residence rooms and from off campus. Internet access, at least one staffed computer lab available.

Student Life *Housing Options:* coed, men-only, women-only, disabled students. *Activities and Organizations:* drama/theater group, student-run newspaper, radio station, choral group, marching band, Student Government Association, Student Programming Association, Residence Hall Association, Food Advisory Association, Intrafraternity Council, national fraternities, national sororities. *Campus security:* 24-hour emergency response devices and patrols, student patrols, late-night transport/escort service. *Student Services:* health clinic, personal/psychological counseling, women's center, legal services.

Athletics Member NCAA. All Division I except football (Division I-AA). *Intercollegiate sports:* baseball M(s), basketball M(s)/W(s), cross-country running M(s)/W(s), golf M(s), soccer M/W, softball W(s), tennis W(s), track and field M(s)/W(s), volleyball W(s). *Intramural sports:* badminton M/W, baseball M, basketball M/W, bowling M/W, cross-country running M/W, football M/W, golf M/W, racquetball M/W, soccer M/W, softball M/W, swimming M/W, table tennis M/W, tennis M/W, track and field M/W, volleyball M/W, weight lifting M/W.

Standardized Tests *Required for some:* ACT (for placement). *Recommended:* ACT (for placement).

Costs (2001–02) *Tuition:* state resident $1965 full-time, $509 per term part-time; nonresident $7413 full-time, $1871 per term part-time. Part-time tuition and fees vary according to course load. *Required fees:* $475 full-time, $78 per term part-time. *Room and board:* $3002. *Payment plan:* deferred payment. *Waivers:* senior citizens and employees or children of employees.

Financial Aid Of all full-time matriculated undergraduates who enrolled in 2001, 4214 applied for aid, 2313 were judged to have need, 249 had their need fully met. In 2001, 947 non-need-based awards were made. *Average percent of need met:* 45%. *Average financial aid package:* $2714. *Average need-based gift aid:* $1678.

Applying *Options:* electronic application, early admission, deferred entrance. *Application fee:* $20. *Required:* high school transcript. *Application deadline:* rolling (freshmen), rolling (transfers). *Notification:* continuous until 8/24 (freshmen).

Admissions Contact Mrs. Becky L. Durocher, Director of Admissions, Nicholls State University, PO Box 2004-NSU, Thibodaux, LA 70310. *Phone:* 985-448-4507. *Toll-free phone:* 877-NICHOLLS. *Fax:* 985-448-4929. *E-mail:* nicholls@nicholls.edu.

NORTHWESTERN STATE UNIVERSITY OF LOUISIANA

Natchitoches, Louisiana

- **State-supported** comprehensive, founded 1884
- **Calendar** semesters
- **Degrees** associate, bachelor's, and master's
- **Small-town** 1000-acre campus
- **Coed,** 8,373 undergraduate students, 79% full-time, 65% women, 35% men
- **Noncompetitive** entrance level, 100% of applicants were admitted

Undergraduates 6,584 full-time, 1,789 part-time. Students come from 38 states and territories, 23 other countries, 6% are from out of state, 5% transferred in, 35% live on campus. *Retention:* 67% of 2001 full-time freshmen returned.

Freshmen *Admission:* 3,576 applied, 3,576 admitted, 1,686 enrolled. *Average high school GPA:* 3.01. *Test scores:* ACT scores over 18: 67%; ACT scores over 24: 17%; ACT scores over 30: 1%.

Faculty *Total:* 256, 98% full-time, 53% with terminal degrees. *Student/faculty ratio:* 30:1.

Majors Accounting; anthropology; art; biology; business administration; chemistry; criminal justice studies; design/visual communications; early childhood education; electrical/electronic engineering technology; elementary education; English; general studies; history; home economics; home economics related; industrial technology; information sciences/systems; journalism; law enforcement/police science; liberal arts and sciences/liberal studies; mathematics; medical radiologic technology; medical technology; music; music teacher education; nursing; physical education; physics; political science; psychology; secondary education; secretarial science; social sciences; social work; sociology; special education; theater arts/drama; veterinary technology.

Academic Programs *Special study options:* academic remediation for entering students, adult/continuing education programs, advanced placement credit, cooperative education, distance learning, double majors, freshman honors college, honors programs, independent study, internships, off-campus study, part-time degree program, study abroad, summer session for credit. *ROTC:* Army (b).

Library Eugene P. Watson Memorial Library with 330,145 titles, 1,749 serial subscriptions, 5,282 audiovisual materials, an OPAC.

Computers on Campus 687 computers available on campus for general student use. A campuswide network can be accessed from student residence rooms and from off campus. Internet access, online (class) registration, at least one staffed computer lab available.

Student Life *Housing:* on-campus residence required through junior year. *Options:* men-only, women-only. *Activities and Organizations:* drama/theater group, student-run newspaper, radio and television station, choral group, marching band, national fraternities, national sororities. *Campus security:* 24-hour emergency response devices and patrols, late-night transport/escort service, controlled dormitory access. *Student Services:* health clinic, personal/psychological counseling.

Athletics Member NCAA. All Division I except football (Division I-AA). *Intercollegiate sports:* baseball M(s), basketball M(s)/W(s), cross-country running M(s)/W(s), golf M(s), soccer W(s), softball W(s), tennis W(s), track and field M(s)/W(s), volleyball W(s). *Intramural sports:* badminton M/W, basketball M/W, bowling M/W, crew M/W, cross-country running M/W, football M/W, golf M/W, racquetball M/W, riflery M/W, soccer M/W, softball M/W, swimming M/W, tennis M/W, track and field M/W, volleyball M/W, weight lifting M/W.

Standardized Tests *Required:* ACT (for admission).

Costs (2001–02) *Tuition:* state resident $1970 full-time; nonresident $7640 full-time. Part-time tuition and fees vary according to course load. *Required fees:* $459 full-time. *Room and board:* $3132; room only: $1675. Room and board charges vary according to board plan and housing facility. *Payment plan:* installment. *Waivers:* children of alumni and employees or children of employees.

Applying *Options:* early admission. *Application fee:* $20. *Required:* high school transcript. *Application deadline:* rolling (freshmen), rolling (transfers). *Notification:* continuous (freshmen).

Admissions Contact Ms. Jana Lucky, Director of Recruiting and Admissions, Northwestern State University of Louisiana, Roy Hall, Room 101. *Phone:* 318-357-4503. *Toll-free phone:* 800-426-3754 (in-state); 800-327-1903 (out-of-state). *E-mail:* admissions@alpha.nsula.edu.

OUR LADY OF HOLY CROSS COLLEGE

New Orleans, Louisiana

- **Independent Roman Catholic** comprehensive, founded 1916
- **Calendar** semesters
- **Degrees** associate, bachelor's, master's, and postbachelor's certificates
- **Suburban** 40-acre campus
- **Endowment** $6.3 million
- **Coed,** 1,250 undergraduate students, 57% full-time, 75% women, 25% men
- **Minimally difficult** entrance level, 37% of applicants were admitted

Our Lady of Holy Cross College, a Catholic, coeducational liberal arts college, was founded in 1916. With a low student-faculty ratio, Our Lady of Holy Cross College provides high-quality education at reasonable tuition rates. Associate, baccalaureate, and master's programs are offered, and financial aid is available.

Undergraduates 711 full-time, 539 part-time. Students come from 4 states and territories, 3 other countries, 0% are from out of state, 13% African American, 3% Asian American or Pacific Islander, 5% Hispanic American, 0.6% Native American, 0.4% international, 12% transferred in. *Retention:* 64% of 2001 full-time freshmen returned.

Freshmen *Admission:* 342 applied, 128 admitted, 128 enrolled. *Average high school GPA:* 2.8. *Test scores:* ACT scores over 18: 71%; ACT scores over 24: 4%.

Our Lady of Holy Cross College (continued)

Faculty *Total:* 110, 33% full-time, 58% with terminal degrees. *Student/faculty ratio:* 21:1.

Majors Accounting; behavioral sciences; biology; business administration; business education; counselor education/guidance; education; education (K-12); elementary education; English; general studies; health science; history; marketing operations; mathematics; medical technology; nursing; reading education; respiratory therapy; science education; secondary education; social sciences; teacher assistant/aide; tourism promotion operations; travel/tourism management.

Academic Programs *Special study options:* academic remediation for entering students, adult/continuing education programs, advanced placement credit, cooperative education, internships, off-campus study, part-time degree program, study abroad, summer session for credit. *ROTC:* Army (c), Navy (c), Air Force (c). *Unusual degree programs:* 3-2 social work with Tulane University.

Library Blaine Kern Library with 85,404 titles, 970 serial subscriptions, 14,513 audiovisual materials, an OPAC, a Web page.

Computers on Campus 65 computers available on campus for general student use. At least one staffed computer lab available.

Student Life *Housing:* college housing not available. *Activities and Organizations:* drama/theater group, student-run newspaper, Innovators, student government, Association of Student Nurses, Delta Sigma Pi, Louisiana Association of Educators/Student Programs. *Campus security:* 24-hour patrols. *Student Services:* personal/psychological counseling.

Athletics *Intramural sports:* baseball M, football M, golf M, volleyball M/W.

Standardized Tests *Recommended:* SAT I or ACT (for placement).

Costs (2001–02) *Tuition:* $5270 full-time, $205 per semester hour part-time. *Required fees:* $350 full-time, $195 per term part-time. *Payment plan:* installment. *Waivers:* employees or children of employees.

Financial Aid Of all full-time matriculated undergraduates who enrolled in 2001, 1005 applied for aid, 861 were judged to have need, 78 had their need fully met. 43 Federal Work-Study jobs (averaging $1359). In 2001, 241 non-need-based awards were made. *Average percent of need met:* 40%. *Average financial aid package:* $4058. *Average need-based loan:* $3290. *Average need-based gift aid:* $2458. *Average indebtedness upon graduation:* $18,500.

Applying *Options:* common application, electronic application, deferred entrance. *Application fee:* $15. *Required:* high school transcript. *Recommended:* minimum 2.0 GPA. *Application deadline:* rolling (freshmen), rolling (transfers). *Notification:* continuous (freshmen).

Admissions Contact Ms. Kristine Hatfield Kopecky, Vice President for Student Affairs and Admissions, Our Lady of Holy Cross College, 4123 Woodland Drive, New Orleans, LA 70131-7399. *Phone:* 504-394-7744 Ext. 185. *Toll-free phone:* 800-259-7744 Ext. 175. *Fax:* 504-391-2421.

OUR LADY OF THE LAKE COLLEGE

Baton Rouge, Louisiana

Admissions Contact Dr. James B. Davis, Director of Admissions and Records, Our Lady of the Lake College, 5345 Brittany Drive, Baton Rouge, LA 70808. *Phone:* 225-768-1700 Ext. 1720. *Toll-free phone:* 877-242-3509. *E-mail:* admission@ololcollege.edu.

SAINT JOSEPH SEMINARY COLLEGE

Saint Benedict, Louisiana

- **Independent Roman Catholic** 4-year, founded 1891
- **Calendar** semesters
- **Degree** bachelor's
- **Rural** 1300-acre campus with easy access to New Orleans
- **Coed, primarily men,** 194 undergraduate students, 100% full-time, 27% women, 73% men
- **Minimally difficult** entrance level, 100% of applicants were admitted

Undergraduates 194 full-time. Students come from 8 states and territories, 5% transferred in, 100% live on campus. *Retention:* 85% of 2001 full-time freshmen returned.

Freshmen *Admission:* 12 applied, 12 admitted, 10 enrolled. *Average high school GPA:* 2.92.

Faculty *Total:* 51, 24% full-time, 20% with terminal degrees. *Student/faculty ratio:* 7:1.

Majors Liberal arts and sciences/liberal studies.

Academic Programs *Special study options:* academic remediation for entering students, adult/continuing education programs, advanced placement credit, English as a second language.

Library Pere Rouquette Library with 62,672 titles, 157 serial subscriptions.

Computers on Campus 6 computers available on campus for general student use. At least one staffed computer lab available.

Student Life *Housing:* on-campus residence required through senior year. *Options:* men-only. *Activities and Organizations:* drama/theater group, choral group, student government. *Campus security:* 24-hour emergency response devices, controlled dormitory access, entrance gate. *Student Services:* health clinic, personal/psychological counseling.

Athletics *Intramural sports:* baseball M, basketball M, football M, golf M, racquetball M, soccer M, softball M, squash M, swimming M, table tennis M, tennis M, volleyball M, water polo M, weight lifting M.

Standardized Tests *Required:* ACT (for admission), ACT (for placement), Michigan Test of English Language Proficiency.

Costs (2001–02) *Comprehensive fee:* $13,150 includes full-time tuition ($7450) and room and board ($5700). Part-time tuition: $75 per hour. *Required fees:* $25 per term. *Payment plan:* installment. *Waivers:* senior citizens.

Financial Aid Of all full-time matriculated undergraduates who enrolled in 2001, 33 applied for aid, 19 were judged to have need, 19 had their need fully met. 15 Federal Work-Study jobs (averaging $1000). 8 State and other part-time jobs (averaging $700). In 2001, 13 non-need-based awards were made. *Average percent of need met:* 100%. *Average financial aid package:* $12,386. *Average need-based loan:* $1614. *Average need-based gift aid:* $9530. *Average non-need based aid:* $2285. *Average indebtedness upon graduation:* $12,400.

Applying *Options:* early admission, deferred entrance. *Application fee:* $10. *Required:* high school transcript, minimum 2.0 GPA, letters of recommendation, interview. *Application deadline:* rolling (freshmen), rolling (transfers). *Notification:* continuous (freshmen).

Admissions Contact Br. Bernard Boudreaux OSB, Academic Assistant, Saint Joseph Seminary College, 75376 River Road, St. Benedict, LA 70457. *Phone:* 985-867-2248. *E-mail:* asec@stjosephabbey.org.

SOUTHEASTERN LOUISIANA UNIVERSITY

Hammond, Louisiana

- **State-supported** comprehensive, founded 1925, part of University of Louisiana System
- **Calendar** semesters
- **Degrees** associate, bachelor's, and master's
- **Small-town** 375-acre campus with easy access to New Orleans
- **Endowment** $20.0 million
- **Coed,** 12,821 undergraduate students, 84% full-time, 63% women, 37% men
- **Minimally difficult** entrance level, 87% of applicants were admitted

Undergraduates 10,824 full-time, 1,997 part-time. Students come from 35 states and territories, 39 other countries, 1% are from out of state, 14% African American, 0.4% Asian American or Pacific Islander, 2% Hispanic American, 0.5% Native American, 0.7% international, 5% transferred in, 12% live on campus. *Retention:* 66% of 2001 full-time freshmen returned.

Freshmen *Admission:* 3,421 applied, 2,963 admitted, 2,194 enrolled. *Test scores:* ACT scores over 18: 72%; ACT scores over 24: 12%; ACT scores over 30: 1%.

Faculty *Total:* 655, 74% full-time, 50% with terminal degrees. *Student/faculty ratio:* 25:1.

Majors Accounting; art; art education; arts management; biology; business administration; business marketing and marketing management; chemistry; communications; computer science; consumer economics; criminal justice studies; education of the speech impaired; elementary education; English; English education; finance; French; French language education; general studies; history; horticulture science; humanities; industrial technology; law enforcement/police science; mathematics; mathematics education; music (general performance); music teacher education; nursing; physical education; physics; political science; psychology; science education; secretarial science; social studies education; social work; sociology; Spanish; Spanish language education; special education; speech education.

Academic Programs *Special study options:* academic remediation for entering students, adult/continuing education programs, advanced placement credit, distance learning, double majors, honors programs, independent study, internships, off-campus study, part-time degree program, services for LD students, study abroad, summer session for credit. *ROTC:* Army (c).

Library Sims Memorial Library with 554,523 titles, 2,122 serial subscriptions, 48,081 audiovisual materials, an OPAC, a Web page.

Computers on Campus 702 computers available on campus for general student use. A campuswide network can be accessed from off campus. Internet access, online (class) registration, at least one staffed computer lab available.

Student Life *Housing:* on-campus residence required through sophomore year. *Options:* coed, men-only, women-only. *Activities and Organizations:* drama/theater group, student-run newspaper, radio station, choral group, Gamma Beta Phi, Phi Kappa Phi, Southeastern Oaks Residential Community Organization, Sigma Sigma Sigma, Phi Mu, national fraternities, national sororities. *Campus security:* 24-hour emergency response devices and patrols, late-night transport/escort service, controlled dormitory access. *Student Services:* health clinic, personal/psychological counseling, legal services.

Athletics Member NCAA. All Division I. *Intercollegiate sports:* baseball M(s), basketball M(s)/W(s), cross-country running M(s)/W(s), golf M(s), soccer W(s), softball W(s), tennis M(s)/W(s), track and field M(s)/W(s), volleyball W(s). *Intramural sports:* basketball M/W, football M/W, golf M/W, racquetball M/W, rugby M/W, soccer M/W, softball M/W, tennis M/W, volleyball M/W.

Standardized Tests *Required:* ACT (for admission).

Costs (2001–02) *Tuition:* state resident $2607 full-time, $109 per credit hour part-time; nonresident $7935 full-time, $331 per credit hour part-time. Part-time tuition and fees vary according to course load. *Room and board:* $3440; room only: $1650. Room and board charges vary according to board plan and housing facility. *Payment plans:* installment, deferred payment. *Waivers:* senior citizens and employees or children of employees.

Financial Aid Of all full-time matriculated undergraduates who enrolled in 2001, 8029 applied for aid, 6799 were judged to have need. 615 Federal Work-Study jobs (averaging $1298). In 2001, 448 non-need-based awards were made. *Average financial aid package:* $4647. *Average need-based loan:* $3309. *Average need-based gift aid:* $2620. *Average non-need based aid:* $1984.

Applying *Options:* electronic application, early admission, deferred entrance. *Application fee:* $20. *Required:* high school transcript, proof of immunization. *Required for some:* minimum 2.0 GPA. *Application deadline:* 7/15 (freshmen), rolling (transfers). *Notification:* continuous (freshmen).

Admissions Contact Ms. Pat Duplessis, University Admissions Analyst, Southeastern Louisiana University, SLU 10752, North Campus-Basic Studies, Hammond, LA 70402. *Phone:* 985-549-2066. *Toll-free phone:* 800-222-7358. *Fax:* 985-549-5632. *E-mail:* jmercante@selu.edu.

SOUTHERN UNIVERSITY AND AGRICULTURAL AND MECHANICAL COLLEGE
Baton Rouge, Louisiana

- **State-supported** comprehensive, founded 1880, part of Southern University System
- **Calendar** semesters
- **Degrees** associate, bachelor's, master's, doctoral, and first professional
- **Suburban** 964-acre campus
- **Endowment** $5.1 million
- **Coed,** 7,472 undergraduate students, 90% full-time, 59% women, 41% men
- **Noncompetitive** entrance level, 44% of applicants were admitted

Undergraduates 6,728 full-time, 744 part-time. Students come from 38 states and territories, 29 other countries, 14% are from out of state, 98% African American, 0.6% Asian American or Pacific Islander, 0.0% Hispanic American, 0.7% international, 2% transferred in, 31% live on campus. *Retention:* 60% of 2001 full-time freshmen returned.

Freshmen *Admission:* 3,336 applied, 1,460 admitted, 1,221 enrolled. *Average high school GPA:* 2.84. *Test scores:* ACT scores over 18: 35%; ACT scores over 24: 2%.

Faculty *Total:* 548, 75% full-time, 59% with terminal degrees. *Student/faculty ratio:* 17:1.

Majors Accounting; adapted physical education; agricultural economics; agricultural sciences; architecture; art; biology; business administration; business economics; business marketing and marketing management; chemistry; civil engineering; computer science; criminal justice studies; electrical/electronic engineering technology; electrical engineering; elementary education; English; forest products technology; French; history; individual/family development; jazz; law enforcement/police science; mass communications; mathematics; mechanical engineering; music (general performance); music teacher education; nursing; physics; political science; psychology; rehabilitation therapy; secondary education; social work; sociology; Spanish; special education; speech-language pathology/audiology; speech/rhetorical studies; theater arts/drama.

Academic Programs *Special study options:* academic remediation for entering students, adult/continuing education programs, advanced placement credit, cooperative education, distance learning, honors programs, internships, off-campus study, part-time degree program, services for LD students, study abroad, summer session for credit. *ROTC:* Army (b), Air Force (c).

Library John B. Cade Library plus 2 others with 672,448 titles, 17,016 serial subscriptions, 27,620 audiovisual materials, an OPAC, a Web page.

Computers on Campus 835 computers available on campus for general student use. A campuswide network can be accessed from student residence rooms and from off campus. Internet access, online (class) registration, at least one staffed computer lab available.

Student Life *Housing Options:* men-only, women-only. *Activities and Organizations:* drama/theater group, student-run newspaper, choral group, marching band, Student Government Association, Pan Hellenic Council, Association for Women Students (AWS), Men's Federation, Honor's Association, national fraternities, national sororities. *Campus security:* 24-hour emergency response devices and patrols. *Student Services:* health clinic, personal/psychological counseling, women's center, legal services.

Athletics Member NCAA. All Division I except football (Division I-AA). *Intercollegiate sports:* baseball M, basketball M(s)/W(s), bowling W(s), cross-country running M(s), golf M(s)/W(s), softball W(s), tennis M(s)/W(s), track and field M(s)/W(s), volleyball W(s). *Intramural sports:* archery M/W, basketball M/W, football M/W, track and field M/W, volleyball M/W, weight lifting M/W.

Standardized Tests *Required:* SAT I or ACT (for admission), SAT I or ACT (for placement).

Costs (2001–02) *One-time required fee:* $20. *Tuition:* state resident $2682 full-time, $772 per term part-time; nonresident $8474 full-time. Part-time tuition and fees vary according to course load and location. *Room and board:* $3683. Room and board charges vary according to board plan and housing facility. *Waivers:* children of alumni, senior citizens, and employees or children of employees.

Financial Aid Of all full-time matriculated undergraduates who enrolled in 2001, 5466 applied for aid, 4684 were judged to have need, 357 had their need fully met. In 2001, 216 non-need-based awards were made. *Average percent of need met:* 63%. *Average financial aid package:* $6848. *Average need-based gift aid:* $3426. *Average non-need based aid:* $4280. *Average indebtedness upon graduation:* $17,000.

Applying *Options:* common application, early admission. *Application fee:* $5. *Required:* high school transcript, minimum 2.3 GPA. *Application deadlines:* 7/1 (freshmen), 7/1 (transfers). *Notification:* continuous (freshmen).

Admissions Contact Ms. Velva Thomas, Director of Admissions, Southern University and Agricultural and Mechanical College, PO Box 9901, Baton Rouge, LA 70813. *Phone:* 225-771-2430. *Toll-free phone:* 800-256-1531. *Fax:* 225-771-2500. *E-mail:* admit@subr.edu.

SOUTHERN UNIVERSITY AT NEW ORLEANS
New Orleans, Louisiana

Admissions Contact Registrar/Director of Admissions, Southern University at New Orleans, 6400 Press Drive, New Orleans, LA 70126-1009. *Phone:* 504-286-5314.

TULANE UNIVERSITY
New Orleans, Louisiana

- **Independent** university, founded 1834
- **Calendar** semesters
- **Degrees** associate, bachelor's, master's, doctoral, first professional, and postbachelor's certificates
- **Urban** 110-acre campus
- **Endowment** $636.3 million
- **Coed,** 7,522 undergraduate students, 76% full-time, 53% women, 47% men
- **Very difficult** entrance level, 61% of applicants were admitted

Undergraduates 5,741 full-time, 1,781 part-time. Students come from 59 states and territories, 108 other countries, 64% are from out of state, 9% African American, 5% Asian American or Pacific Islander, 4% Hispanic American, 0.3% Native American, 3% international, 2% transferred in, 42% live on campus. *Retention:* 83% of 2001 full-time freshmen returned.

Freshmen *Admission:* 10,862 applied, 6,638 admitted, 1,517 enrolled. *Test scores:* SAT verbal scores over 500: 97%; SAT math scores over 500: 97%; SAT verbal scores over 600: 85%; SAT math scores over 600: 78%; SAT verbal scores over 700: 33%; SAT math scores over 700: 24%.

Faculty *Total:* 1,105, 49% full-time, 57% with terminal degrees. *Student/faculty ratio:* 12:1.

Majors Accounting; African studies; American studies; anthropology; architecture; art; art history; Asian studies; biochemistry; bioengineering; biology; business administration; business marketing and marketing management; cell biology; chemical engineering; chemistry; civil engineering; classics; cognitive psychology/psycholinguistics; computer engineering; computer/information sciences; com-

Tulane University (continued)
puter science; earth sciences; ecology; economics; electrical engineering; engineering science; English; environmental biology; environmental engineering; environmental science; evolutionary biology; exercise sciences; finance; fine/studio arts; French; geology; German; Greek (modern); Hispanic-American studies; history; information sciences/systems; international relations; Italian; Judaic studies; Latin American studies; Latin (ancient and medieval); liberal arts and sciences/liberal studies; linguistics; mass communications; mathematics; mechanical engineering; medical illustrating; medieval/renaissance studies; molecular biology; music; paralegal/legal assistant; philosophy; physics; political science; Portuguese; psychology; religious studies; Russian; Russian/Slavic studies; sociology; Spanish; sport/fitness administration; theater arts/drama; women's studies.

Academic Programs *Special study options:* accelerated degree program, adult/continuing education programs, advanced placement credit, cooperative education, double majors, English as a second language, freshman honors college, honors programs, independent study, internships, off-campus study, part-time degree program, services for LD students, student-designed majors, study abroad, summer session for credit. *ROTC:* Army (b), Navy (b), Air Force (b). *Unusual degree programs:* 3-2 public health, tropical medicine.

Library Howard Tilton Memorial Library plus 8 others with 1.3 million titles, 15,286 serial subscriptions, 83,774 audiovisual materials, an OPAC, a Web page.

Computers on Campus A campuswide network can be accessed from student residence rooms and from off campus. At least one staffed computer lab available.

Student Life *Housing:* on-campus residence required for freshman year. *Options:* coed, women-only. *Activities and Organizations:* drama/theater group, student-run newspaper, radio and television station, choral group, Community Action Council, Campus Programming, African-American Congress, club sports, Tsunami, national fraternities, national sororities. *Campus security:* 24-hour emergency response devices and patrols, student patrols, late-night transport/escort service, controlled dormitory access, on and off-campus shuttle service, crime prevention programs. *Student Services:* health clinic, personal/psychological counseling, women's center, legal services.

Athletics Member NCAA. All Division I. *Intercollegiate sports:* baseball M(s), basketball M(s)/W(s), crew M(c)/W(c), cross-country running M(s)/W(s), equestrian sports M(c)/W(c), fencing M(c)/W(c), field hockey M(c)/W(c), football M(s), golf M(s)/W(s), gymnastics M(c)/W(c), ice hockey M(c)/W(c), lacrosse M(c)/W(c), riflery M(c)/W(c), rugby M(c), sailing M(c)/W(c), soccer M(c)/W(s), softball W(c), swimming M(c)/W(c), tennis M(s)/W(s), track and field M(s)/W(s), volleyball M(c)/W(s), water polo M(c)/W(c). *Intramural sports:* badminton M/W, basketball M/W, bowling M/W, crew M(c)/W(c), cross-country running M, equestrian sports M(c)/W(c), fencing M(c)/W(c), field hockey M(c)/W(c), football M/W, golf M/W, gymnastics M(c)/W(c), ice hockey M(c), lacrosse M(c)/W(c), racquetball M/W, riflery M(c)/W(c), rugby M(c), sailing M(c)/W(c), soccer M(c)/W(c), softball M/W(c), swimming M(c)/W(c), tennis M(c)/W(c), track and field M/W, volleyball M(c)/W(c), water polo M(c)/W(c), wrestling M.

Standardized Tests *Required:* SAT I (for admission), SAT I or ACT (for admission). *Required for some:* SAT II: Subject Tests (for admission). *Recommended:* SAT II: Subject Tests (for admission).

Costs (2001–02) *Comprehensive fee:* $34,014 includes full-time tuition ($24,676), mandatory fees ($2210), and room and board ($7128). Part-time tuition: $1091 per credit hour. *Required fees:* $215 per credit hour. *Room and board:* College room only: $4128. Room and board charges vary according to board plan and housing facility. *Payment plan:* installment. *Waivers:* employees or children of employees.

Financial Aid Of all full-time matriculated undergraduates who enrolled in 2001, 3137 applied for aid, 2528 were judged to have need, 1736 had their need fully met. In 2001, 1303 non-need-based awards were made. *Average percent of need met:* 94%. *Average financial aid package:* $22,948. *Average need-based loan:* $5217. *Average need-based gift aid:* $16,286. *Average non-need based aid:* $13,797. *Average indebtedness upon graduation:* $20,040. *Financial aid deadline:* 2/1.

Applying *Options:* common application, electronic application, early admission, early decision, early action, deferred entrance. *Application fee:* $55. *Required:* essay or personal statement, high school transcript, 1 letter of recommendation. *Application deadlines:* 1/15 (freshmen), 6/1 (transfers). *Early decision:* 11/1. *Notification:* continuous until 4/1 (freshmen), 1/15 (early decision), 12/15 (early action).

Admissions Contact Mr. Richard Whiteside, Vice President of Enrollment Management and Institutional Research, Tulane University, 6823 St Charles Avenue, New Orleans, LA 70118-5669. *Phone:* 504-865-5731. *Toll-free phone:* 800-873-9283. *Fax:* 504-862-8715. *E-mail:* undergrad.admission@tulane.edu.

UNIVERSITY OF LOUISIANA AT LAFAYETTE
Lafayette, Louisiana

- **State-supported** university, founded 1898, part of University of Louisiana System
- **Calendar** semesters
- **Degrees** associate, bachelor's, master's, doctoral, and post-master's certificates
- **Urban** 1375-acre campus
- **Endowment** $85.0 million
- **Coed,** 13,913 undergraduate students, 83% full-time, 57% women, 43% men
- **Minimally difficult** entrance level, 82% of applicants were admitted

Undergraduates 11,486 full-time, 2,427 part-time. Students come from 47 states and territories, 95 other countries, 4% are from out of state, 18% African American, 2% Asian American or Pacific Islander, 2% Hispanic American, 0.5% Native American, 2% international, 4% transferred in, 11% live on campus. *Retention:* 72% of 2001 full-time freshmen returned.

Freshmen *Admission:* 4,762 applied, 3,911 admitted, 2,413 enrolled. *Average high school GPA:* 3.05. *Test scores:* ACT scores over 18: 84%; ACT scores over 24: 21%; ACT scores over 30: 1%.

Faculty *Total:* 672, 81% full-time, 59% with terminal degrees. *Student/faculty ratio:* 23:1.

Majors Accounting; agricultural sciences; anthropology; architecture related; art; biological specializations related; biology; business administration; business economics; business marketing and marketing management; business systems analysis/design; chemical engineering; chemistry; civil engineering; communications; computer engineering; computer science; conservation and renewable natural resources related; criminal justice studies; dental hygiene; dietetics; electrical engineering; elementary education; English; fashion merchandising; finance; general studies; geology; history; hospitality services management related; individual/family development related; industrial design; industrial technology; insurance/risk management; interior architecture; mass communications; mathematics; mechanical engineering; medical records administration; microbiology/bacteriology; modern languages; music (general performance); music teacher education; nursing; petroleum engineering; philosophy; physical education; physics; political science; pre-law; psychology; public relations; secondary education; sociology; special education; speech-language pathology/audiology; teacher education, specific programs related; visual/performing arts.

Academic Programs *Special study options:* academic remediation for entering students, adult/continuing education programs, advanced placement credit, cooperative education, double majors, honors programs, independent study, internships, part-time degree program, services for LD students, study abroad, summer session for credit. *ROTC:* Army (b).

Library Edith Garland Dupre Library with 425,034 titles, 5,174 serial subscriptions, 5,755 audiovisual materials, an OPAC, a Web page.

Computers on Campus 548 computers available on campus for general student use. A campuswide network can be accessed from off campus. Internet access, online (class) registration, at least one staffed computer lab available.

Student Life *Housing:* on-campus residence required for freshman year. *Options:* men-only, women-only. *Activities and Organizations:* drama/theater group, student-run newspaper, choral group, marching band, national fraternities, national sororities. *Campus security:* 24-hour emergency response devices and patrols, late-night transport/escort service. *Student Services:* health clinic, personal/psychological counseling, women's center, legal services.

Athletics Member NCAA. All Division I except football (Division I-A). *Intercollegiate sports:* baseball M(s), basketball M(s)/W(s), cross-country running M(s)/W(s), golf M(s), soccer W, softball W(s), tennis M(s)/W(s), track and field M(s)/W(s), volleyball W(s). *Intramural sports:* badminton M(c)/W(c), baseball M, basketball M/W, bowling M(c)/W(c), cross-country running M/W, football M/W, golf M/W, racquetball M/W, rugby M(c)/W(c), sailing M(c)/W(c), soccer M(c)/W(c), softball M/W, swimming M/W, table tennis M/W, tennis M/W, track and field M/W, volleyball M/W, water polo M/W, weight lifting M/W.

Standardized Tests *Required:* SAT I or ACT (for admission).

Costs (2001–02) *Tuition:* state resident $2316 full-time, $79 per credit part-time; nonresident $8881 full-time, $337 per credit part-time. Part-time tuition and fees vary according to course load. *Room and board:* $2886. Room and board charges vary according to board plan. *Payment plan:* deferred payment. *Waivers:* children of alumni, senior citizens, and employees or children of employees.

Financial Aid Of all full-time matriculated undergraduates who enrolled in 2001, 10665 applied for aid, 7785 were judged to have need. *Average percent of need met:* 92%. *Average financial aid package:* $5400.

Applying *Options:* early admission, deferred entrance. *Application fee:* $20. *Required:* high school transcript, minimum 2.0 GPA. *Application deadline:* rolling (freshmen), rolling (transfers).

Admissions Contact Mr. Leroy Broussard Jr., Director of Admissions, University of Louisiana at Lafayette, PO Drawer 41210, Lafayette, LA 70504. *Phone:* 337-482-6473. *Toll-free phone:* 800-752-6553. *Fax:* 337-482-6195. *E-mail:* admissions@louisiana.edu.

UNIVERSITY OF LOUISIANA AT MONROE

Monroe, Louisiana

- **State-supported** university, founded 1931
- **Calendar** semesters
- **Degrees** certificates, associate, bachelor's, master's, doctoral, first professional, post-master's, and postbachelor's certificates
- **Urban** 238-acre campus
- **Coed,** 7,802 undergraduate students, 82% full-time, 63% women, 37% men
- **Noncompetitive** entrance level

Undergraduates 6,372 full-time, 1,430 part-time. Students come from 39 states and territories, 44 other countries, 5% are from out of state, 27% African American, 2% Asian American or Pacific Islander, 0.9% Hispanic American, 0.3% Native American, 1% international, 7% transferred in, 22% live on campus. *Retention:* 64% of 2001 full-time freshmen returned.

Freshmen *Admission:* 1,301 enrolled. *Test scores:* ACT scores over 18: 63%; ACT scores over 24: 16%; ACT scores over 30: 1%.

Majors Accounting; agricultural business; art; art education; atmospheric sciences; biology; business administration; business economics; business marketing and marketing management; chemistry; computer/information sciences; computer science; construction technology; criminal justice studies; dental hygiene; early childhood education; elementary education; English; English education; finance; flight attendant; foreign languages education; French; general studies; geography; geology; health/physical education; history; home economics; insurance/risk management; journalism; law enforcement/police science; mathematics; mathematics education; medical radiologic technology; medical technology; music; music (general performance); music teacher education; nursing; occupational therapy; occupational therapy assistant; pharmacy; physical education; physics; political science; pre-dentistry; pre-law; psychology; radio/television broadcasting; science education; social studies education; social work; sociology; Spanish; special education; speech education; speech-language pathology/audiology; speech/rhetorical studies; toxicology; wood science/paper technology.

Academic Programs *Special study options:* academic remediation for entering students, accelerated degree program, advanced placement credit, cooperative education, distance learning, English as a second language, honors programs, internships, off-campus study, part-time degree program, summer session for credit. *ROTC:* Army (b).

Library Sandel Library with 355,748 titles, 2,912 serial subscriptions, 331 audiovisual materials, an OPAC.

Computers on Campus 1400 computers available on campus for general student use. A campuswide network can be accessed from off campus. At least one staffed computer lab available.

Student Life *Housing:* on-campus residence required through senior year. *Options:* coed, men-only, women-only. *Activities and Organizations:* drama/theater group, student-run newspaper, radio station, choral group, marching band, Panhellenic Council, Intrafraternity Council, Union Board, Student Government Association, national fraternities, national sororities. *Campus security:* 24-hour emergency response devices and patrols, student patrols, late-night transport/escort service. *Student Services:* health clinic, personal/psychological counseling.

Athletics Member NCAA. All Division I except football (Division I-A). *Intercollegiate sports:* baseball M(s), basketball M(s)/W(s), cross-country running M(s)/W(s), golf M(s)/W, soccer W(s), softball W(s), swimming M(s)/W(s), tennis M(s)/W(s), track and field M(s)/W(s), volleyball W(s). *Intramural sports:* badminton M/W, basketball M/W, bowling M/W, cross-country running M/W, football M/W, golf M/W, softball M/W, table tennis M/W, tennis M/W, track and field M/W, volleyball M/W.

Standardized Tests *Required:* ACT (for placement).

Costs (2001–02) *Tuition:* state resident $1894 full-time, $79 per credit hour part-time; nonresident $5952 full-time, $248 per credit hour part-time. Part-time tuition and fees vary according to course load. *Required fees:* $413 full-time, $17 per credit hour. *Room and board:* $5740. Room and board charges vary according to board plan and housing facility. *Waivers:* children of alumni and employees or children of employees.

Applying *Application fee:* $15. *Required for some:* high school transcript. *Application deadline:* rolling (freshmen), rolling (transfers). *Notification:* continuous (freshmen).

Admissions Contact Ms. Carlette Browder, Associate Registrar, University of Louisiana at Monroe, Monroe, LA 71209-1115. *Phone:* 318-342-5252. *Toll-free phone:* 800-372-5127. *Fax:* 318-342-5274. *E-mail:* rebrowder@ulm.edu.

UNIVERSITY OF NEW ORLEANS

New Orleans, Louisiana

- **State-supported** university, founded 1958, part of Louisiana State University System
- **Calendar** semesters
- **Degrees** certificates, bachelor's, master's, doctoral, and postbachelor's certificates
- **Urban** 345-acre campus
- **Endowment** $12.8 million
- **Coed,** 12,967 undergraduate students, 72% full-time, 57% women, 43% men
- **Moderately difficult** entrance level, 80% of applicants were admitted

Undergraduates 9,369 full-time, 3,598 part-time. Students come from 47 states and territories, 84 other countries, 5% are from out of state, 23% African American, 5% Asian American or Pacific Islander, 6% Hispanic American, 0.5% Native American, 3% international, 10% transferred in, 5% live on campus. *Retention:* 64% of 2001 full-time freshmen returned.

Freshmen *Admission:* 4,527 applied, 3,614 admitted, 2,204 enrolled. *Test scores:* SAT verbal scores over 500: 56%; SAT math scores over 500: 56%; ACT scores over 18: 79%; SAT verbal scores over 600: 22%; SAT math scores over 600: 22%; ACT scores over 24: 18%; SAT verbal scores over 700: 5%; SAT math scores over 700: 5%; ACT scores over 30: 1%.

Faculty *Total:* 578, 79% full-time, 67% with terminal degrees. *Student/faculty ratio:* 24:1.

Majors Accounting; anthropology; art history; biological/physical sciences; biology; business administration; business economics; business marketing and marketing management; chemistry; civil engineering; communications; computer science; economics; electrical engineering; elementary education; English; English education; finance; foreign languages education; French; general studies; geography; geology; geophysics/seismology; history; hospitality management; management information systems/business data processing; mathematics; mathematics education; mechanical engineering; medical technology; music; music teacher education; naval architecture/marine engineering; philosophy; physical education; physics; political science; pre-dentistry; pre-medicine; pre-veterinary studies; psychology; reading education; real estate; science education; secondary education; social studies education; sociology; Spanish; theater arts/drama.

Academic Programs *Special study options:* academic remediation for entering students, adult/continuing education programs, advanced placement credit, cooperative education, distance learning, double majors, English as a second language, honors programs, independent study, internships, off-campus study, part-time degree program, services for LD students, student-designed majors, study abroad, summer session for credit. *ROTC:* Army (c), Air Force (c). *Unusual degree programs:* 3-2 engineering with Xavier University of Louisiana, Southern University at New Orleans, Loyola University, New Orleans.

Library Earl K. Long Library with 864,442 titles, 3,909 serial subscriptions, 123,120 audiovisual materials, an OPAC, a Web page.

Computers on Campus 1084 computers available on campus for general student use. A campuswide network can be accessed from student residence rooms and from off campus. Internet access, at least one staffed computer lab available.

Student Life *Housing Options:* coed. *Activities and Organizations:* drama/theater group, student-run newspaper, radio station, choral group, Student Government Association, Student Government Activities Council, Circle K International, International Student Organization, Progressive Black Student Union, national fraternities, national sororities. *Campus security:* 24-hour emergency response devices and patrols, late-night transport/escort service, controlled dormitory access. *Student Services:* health clinic, personal/psychological counseling, women's center, legal services.

Athletics Member NCAA. All Division I. *Intercollegiate sports:* baseball M(s), basketball M(s)/W(s), cross-country running M(s)/W(s), golf M(s)/W(s), swimming M, tennis M(s)/W(s), track and field M(s)/W(s), volleyball W(s). *Intramural sports:* basketball M/W, bowling M/W, football M/W, racquetball M/W, soccer M/W, softball M/W, table tennis M/W, tennis M/W, volleyball M/W.

Standardized Tests *Required:* SAT I or ACT (for admission).

Costs (2001–02) *Tuition:* state resident $3402 full-time, $429 per course part-time; nonresident $10,996 full-time, $1767 per course part-time. Part-time tuition and fees vary according to course load. *Required fees:* $200 full-time, $5

University of New Orleans (continued)
per semester hour, $10 per term part-time. *Room and board:* $3900. Room and board charges vary according to board plan and housing facility. *Payment plan:* deferred payment. *Waivers:* senior citizens and employees or children of employees.

Financial Aid Of all full-time matriculated undergraduates who enrolled in 2001, 6952 applied for aid, 5119 were judged to have need, 106 had their need fully met. 282 Federal Work-Study jobs (averaging $2220). In 2001, 212 non-need-based awards were made. *Average percent of need met:* 63%. *Average financial aid package:* $4493. *Average need-based loan:* $3292. *Average need-based gift aid:* $2360. *Average non-need based aid:* $1648.

Applying *Options:* common application, electronic application, early admission, deferred entrance. *Application fee:* $20. *Required:* high school transcript. *Required for some:* essay or personal statement, minimum 2.0 GPA, 3 letters of recommendation, interview, 2.0 high school GPA on high school core program. *Application deadline:* rolling (freshmen), rolling (transfers). *Notification:* continuous (freshmen).

Admissions Contact Ms. Roslyn S. Sheley, Director of Admissions, University of New Orleans, Lake Front, New Orleans, LA 70148. *Phone:* 504-280-6595. *Toll-free phone:* 888-514-4275. *Fax:* 504-280-5522. *E-mail:* admission@uno.edu.

UNIVERSITY OF PHOENIX-LOUISIANA CAMPUS
Metairie, Louisiana

- **Proprietary** comprehensive, founded 1976
- **Calendar** continuous
- **Degrees** certificates, associate, bachelor's, master's, doctoral, post-master's, and postbachelor's certificates (courses conducted at 54 campuses and learning centers in 13 states)
- **Coed,** 1,377 undergraduate students, 100% full-time, 63% women, 37% men
- **Noncompetitive** entrance level

Undergraduates Students come from 15 states and territories, 3% are from out of state.

Freshmen *Admission:* 27 admitted.

Faculty *Total:* 303, 2% full-time, 14% with terminal degrees. *Student/faculty ratio:* 13:1.

Majors Accounting; business administration; computer/information sciences; enterprise management; management information systems/business data processing; nursing science.

Academic Programs *Special study options:* accelerated degree program, adult/continuing education programs, advanced placement credit, distance learning, external degree program, independent study.

Library University Library with 17.5 million titles, 9,000 serial subscriptions, an OPAC, a Web page.

Computers on Campus A campuswide network can be accessed from off campus. Internet access, at least one staffed computer lab available.

Student Life *Housing:* college housing not available.

Costs (2001–02) *Tuition:* $7350 full-time. Full-time tuition and fees vary according to location and program. *Payment plan:* deferred payment. *Waivers:* employees or children of employees.

Applying *Options:* deferred entrance. *Application fee:* $85. *Required:* 2 years of work experience. *Required for some:* high school transcript. *Application deadline:* rolling (freshmen), rolling (transfers).

Admissions Contact Ms. Beth Barilla, Director of Admissions, University of Phoenix-Louisiana Campus, 4615 East Elwood Street, Phoenix, AZ 85040-1958. *Phone:* 480-927-0099 Ext. 1218. *Toll-free phone:* 800-228-7240. *Fax:* 480-594-1758. *E-mail:* beth.barilla@apollogrp.edu.

XAVIER UNIVERSITY OF LOUISIANA
New Orleans, Louisiana

- **Independent Roman Catholic** comprehensive, founded 1925
- **Calendar** semesters
- **Degrees** bachelor's, master's, and first professional
- **Urban** 23-acre campus
- **Endowment** $27.5 million
- **Coed,** 3,295 undergraduate students, 96% full-time, 74% women, 26% men
- **Moderately difficult** entrance level, 86% of applicants were admitted

Undergraduates 3,164 full-time, 131 part-time. Students come from 48 states and territories, 27 other countries, 51% are from out of state, 92% African American, 2% Asian American or Pacific Islander, 0.3% Hispanic American, 0.7% international, 5% transferred in, 35% live on campus. *Retention:* 73% of 2001 full-time freshmen returned.

Freshmen *Admission:* 3,970 applied, 3,399 admitted, 893 enrolled. *Average high school GPA:* 3.03. *Test scores:* SAT verbal scores over 500: 49%; SAT math scores over 500: 46%; ACT scores over 18: 82%; SAT verbal scores over 600: 13%; SAT math scores over 600: 11%; ACT scores over 24: 21%; SAT verbal scores over 700: 2%; SAT math scores over 700: 1%; ACT scores over 30: 1%.

Faculty *Total:* 259, 85% full-time. *Student/faculty ratio:* 15:1.

Majors Accounting; art; art education; biochemistry; biology; business administration; business economics; business marketing and marketing management; chemistry; computer science; early childhood education; economics; education; elementary education; English; environmental science; French; health education; history; information sciences/systems; mass communications; mathematical statistics; mathematics; microbiology/bacteriology; middle school education; music; music (piano and organ performance); music teacher education; philosophy; physical education; physics; political science; pre-dentistry; pre-law; pre-medicine; pre-veterinary studies; psychology; science education; secondary education; sociology; Spanish; special education; speech-language pathology/audiology; speech therapy; stringed instruments; theology; wind/percussion instruments.

Academic Programs *Special study options:* academic remediation for entering students, accelerated degree program, adult/continuing education programs, advanced placement credit, cooperative education, distance learning, double majors, freshman honors college, honors programs, independent study, internships, off-campus study, part-time degree program, services for LD students, study abroad, summer session for credit. *ROTC:* Air Force (c). *Unusual degree programs:* 3-2 business administration with Tulane University; engineering with Tulane University, University of Maryland, University of New Orleans, Georgia Institute of Technology, University of Wisconsin-Madison, Morgan State University, Southern University and Agricultural and Mechanical College; biostatistics with Louisiana State University Medical Center.

Library Xavier Library plus 1 other with 108,583 titles, 2,339 serial subscriptions, 4,984 audiovisual materials.

Computers on Campus 250 computers available on campus for general student use. A campuswide network can be accessed from student residence rooms and from off campus. At least one staffed computer lab available.

Student Life *Housing Options:* coed, men-only, women-only. *Activities and Organizations:* student-run newspaper, television station, choral group, Mobilization at Xavier, AWARE, NAACP, California club, Beta Beta Beta, national fraternities, national sororities. *Campus security:* 24-hour emergency response devices and patrols, student patrols, bicycle patrols. *Student Services:* health clinic, personal/psychological counseling.

Athletics Member NAIA. *Intercollegiate sports:* basketball M(s)/W(s), cross-country running M/W, tennis M(s)/W(s). *Intramural sports:* badminton M/W, basketball M/W, bowling M/W, football M/W, golf M/W, softball M/W, swimming M/W, table tennis M/W, tennis M/W, track and field M/W, volleyball M/W.

Standardized Tests *Required:* SAT I or ACT (for admission).

Costs (2001–02) *Comprehensive fee:* $16,200 includes full-time tuition ($9700), mandatory fees ($800), and room and board ($5700). Full-time tuition and fees vary according to program. Part-time tuition: $410 per credit hour. Part-time tuition and fees vary according to course load and program.

Financial Aid Of all full-time matriculated undergraduates who enrolled in 2001, 2826 applied for aid, 2533 were judged to have need, 546 had their need fully met. In 2001, 146 non-need-based awards were made. *Average percent of need met:* 13%. *Average financial aid package:* $9114. *Average need-based loan:* $6186. *Average need-based gift aid:* $3427. *Average non-need based aid:* $4608.

Applying *Options:* common application, early admission, early action. *Application fee:* $25. *Required:* high school transcript, minimum 2.0 GPA, 1 letter of recommendation. *Required for some:* interview. *Application deadlines:* 3/1 (freshmen), 6/1 (transfers). *Notification:* 4/15 (freshmen), 2/1 (early action).

Admissions Contact Mr. Winston Brown, Dean of Admissions, Xavier University of Louisiana, 1 Drexel Drive, New Orleans, LA 70125. *Phone:* 504-483-7388. *E-mail:* apply@xula.edu.

MAINE

BATES COLLEGE
Lewiston, Maine

- **Independent** 4-year, founded 1855
- **Calendar** 4-4-1
- **Degree** bachelor's

■ **Suburban** 109-acre campus
■ **Endowment** $173.1 million
■ **Coed,** 1,767 undergraduate students, 100% full-time, 51% women, 49% men
■ **Most difficult** entrance level, 33% of applicants were admitted

Undergraduates 1,767 full-time. Students come from 50 states and territories, 68 other countries, 89% are from out of state, 2% African American, 3% Asian American or Pacific Islander, 2% Hispanic American, 0.2% Native American, 5% international, 0.8% transferred in, 90% live on campus. *Retention:* 93% of 2001 full-time freshmen returned.

Freshmen *Admission:* 4,264 applied, 1,397 admitted, 582 enrolled. *Test scores:* SAT verbal scores over 500: 99%; SAT math scores over 500: 100%; SAT verbal scores over 600: 91%; SAT math scores over 600: 94%; SAT verbal scores over 700: 30%; SAT math scores over 700: 31%.

Faculty *Total:* 183, 89% full-time. *Student/faculty ratio:* 10:1.

Majors African studies; American studies; anthropology; art; biochemistry; biology; chemistry; Chinese; classics; East Asian studies; economics; English; environmental science; French; geology; German; history; interdisciplinary studies; Japanese; mathematics; medieval/renaissance studies; music; neuroscience; philosophy; physics; political science; psychology; religious studies; Russian; sociology; Spanish; speech/rhetorical studies; theater arts/drama; women's studies.

Academic Programs *Special study options:* accelerated degree program, advanced placement credit, double majors, honors programs, independent study, internships, off-campus study, services for LD students, student-designed majors, study abroad. *Unusual degree programs:* 3-2 engineering with Columbia University, Rensselaer Polytechnic Institute, Case Western Reserve University, Washington University in St. Louis, Dartmouth College.

Library Ladd Library with 524,830 titles, 2,012 serial subscriptions, an OPAC, a Web page.

Computers on Campus 1150 computers available on campus for general student use. A campuswide network can be accessed from student residence rooms and from off campus. Internet access, online (class) registration, at least one staffed computer lab available.

Student Life *Housing:* on-campus residence required for freshman year. *Options:* coed, men-only, women-only. *Activities and Organizations:* drama/theater group, student-run newspaper, radio and television station, choral group, Representative Assembly, International Club, Outing Club (outdoor recreation), student radio station, The Student (newspaper). *Campus security:* 24-hour emergency response devices and patrols, student patrols, late-night transport/escort service, controlled dormitory access. *Student Services:* health clinic, personal/psychological counseling, women's center.

Athletics Member NCAA. All Division III. *Intercollegiate sports:* badminton M(c)/W(c), baseball M, basketball M/W, crew M/W, cross-country running M/W, equestrian sports M(c)/W(c), fencing M(c)/W(c), field hockey W, football M, golf M/W, ice hockey M(c)/W(c), lacrosse M/W, rugby M(c)/W(c), sailing M(c)/W(c), skiing (cross-country) M/W, skiing (downhill) M/W, soccer M/W, softball W, squash M/W, swimming M/W, tennis M/W, track and field M/W, volleyball M(c)/W, water polo M(c)/W(c). *Intramural sports:* badminton M/W, basketball M/W, golf M/W, ice hockey M/W, racquetball M/W, rugby M/W, sailing M/W, soccer M/W, softball M/W, squash M/W, swimming M/W, table tennis M/W, tennis M/W, volleyball M/W, water polo M/W.

Costs (2001–02) *Payment plan:* installment. *Waivers:* employees or children of employees.

Financial Aid Of all full-time matriculated undergraduates who enrolled in 2001, 874 applied for aid, 726 were judged to have need, 676 had their need fully met. 518 Federal Work-Study jobs (averaging $1574). 56 State and other part-time jobs (averaging $1621). *Average percent of need met:* 100%. *Average financial aid package:* $22,434. *Average need-based loan:* $3107. *Average need-based gift aid:* $19,015. *Average indebtedness upon graduation:* $18,946. *Financial aid deadline:* 1/15.

Applying *Options:* common application, electronic application, early admission, early decision, deferred entrance. *Application fee:* $50. *Required:* essay or personal statement, high school transcript, 3 letters of recommendation. *Recommended:* interview. *Application deadlines:* 1/15 (freshmen), 3/1 (transfers). *Early decision:* 1/1 (for plan 1), 11/15 (for plan 2). *Notification:* 3/31 (freshmen), 2/1 (early decision plan 1), 12/20 (early decision plan 2).

Admissions Contact Mr. Wylie L. Mitchell, Dean of Admissions, Bates College, 23 Campus Avenue, Lewiston, ME 04240-6028. *Phone:* 207-786-6000. *Fax:* 207-786-6025. *E-mail:* admissions@bates.edu.

BOWDOIN COLLEGE

Brunswick, Maine

■ **Independent** 4-year, founded 1794
■ **Calendar** semesters
■ **Degree** bachelor's
■ **Small-town** 110-acre campus with easy access to Portland
■ **Endowment** $433.2 million
■ **Coed,** 1,635 undergraduate students, 99% full-time, 49% women, 51% men
■ **Most difficult** entrance level, 24% of applicants were admitted

Undergraduates 1,621 full-time, 14 part-time. Students come from 52 states and territories, 29 other countries, 86% are from out of state, 3% African American, 7% Asian American or Pacific Islander, 3% Hispanic American, 0.6% Native American, 3% international, 0.1% transferred in, 88% live on campus. *Retention:* 94% of 2001 full-time freshmen returned.

Freshmen *Admission:* 4,536 applied, 1,080 admitted, 452 enrolled. *Test scores:* SAT verbal scores over 500: 98%; SAT math scores over 500: 99%; SAT verbal scores over 600: 90%; SAT math scores over 600: 91%; SAT verbal scores over 700: 47%; SAT math scores over 700: 38%.

Faculty *Total:* 186, 81% full-time, 90% with terminal degrees. *Student/faculty ratio:* 10:1.

Majors African-American studies; African studies; anthropology; archaeology; art; art history; Asian studies; biochemistry; biology; chemistry; classics; computer science; economics; English; environmental science; fine/studio arts; French; geology; German; history; interdisciplinary studies; Latin American studies; mathematics; music; neuroscience; philosophy; physics; political science; premedicine; psychology; religious studies; romance languages; Russian; sociology; Spanish; women's studies.

Academic Programs *Special study options:* accelerated degree program, advanced placement credit, double majors, independent study, off-campus study, services for LD students, student-designed majors, study abroad. *Unusual degree programs:* 3-2 engineering with California Institute of Technology, Columbia University.

Library Hawthorne-Longfellow Library plus 6 others with 914,339 titles, 2,742 serial subscriptions, 18,202 audiovisual materials, an OPAC, a Web page.

Computers on Campus 462 computers available on campus for general student use. A campuswide network can be accessed from student residence rooms and from off campus. Internet access, at least one staffed computer lab available.

Student Life *Housing:* on-campus residence required through sophomore year. *Options:* coed. *Activities and Organizations:* drama/theater group, student-run newspaper, radio and television station, choral group, Outing Club, Men's and Women's Rugby, volunteer programs, Ballroom Dance Club, Campus Activities Board. *Campus security:* 24-hour emergency response devices and patrols, student patrols, late-night transport/escort service, controlled dormitory access, self-defense education, whistle program. *Student Services:* health clinic, personal/psychological counseling, women's center.

Athletics Member NCAA. All Division III except men's and women's skiing (cross-country) (Division I), men's and women's skiing (downhill) (Division I). *Intercollegiate sports:* baseball M, basketball M/W, cross-country running M/W, field hockey W, football M, golf M/W, ice hockey M/W, lacrosse M/W, sailing M/W, skiing (cross-country) M/W, skiing (downhill) M/W, soccer M/W, softball W, squash M/W, swimming M/W, tennis M/W, track and field M/W, volleyball W. *Intramural sports:* basketball M/W, crew M(c)/W(c), cross-country running M/W, equestrian sports M(c)/W(c), field hockey M/W, football M, ice hockey M/W, rugby M(c)/W(c), sailing M/W, soccer M/W, softball M/W, volleyball M/W, water polo M(c)/W(c).

Costs (2001–02) *Comprehensive fee:* $34,280 includes full-time tuition ($26,700), mandatory fees ($580), and room and board ($7000). *Room and board:* College room only: $3095. Room and board charges vary according to board plan and housing facility. *Payment plans:* installment, deferred payment. *Waivers:* employees or children of employees.

Financial Aid Of all full-time matriculated undergraduates who enrolled in 2001, 748 applied for aid, 627 were judged to have need, 627 had their need fully met. 153 Federal Work-Study jobs (averaging $1378). In 2001, 27 non-need-based awards were made. *Average percent of need met:* 100%. *Average financial aid package:* $22,919. *Average need-based loan:* $2731. *Average need-based gift aid:* $19,354. *Average non-need based aid:* $1031. *Average indebtedness upon graduation:* $14,682. *Financial aid deadline:* 2/15.

Bowdoin College (continued)

Applying *Options:* common application, early admission, early decision, deferred entrance. *Application fee:* $55. *Required:* essay or personal statement, high school transcript, 3 letters of recommendation. *Recommended:* interview. *Application deadlines:* 1/1 (freshmen), 3/1 (transfers). *Early decision:* 11/15 (for plan 1), 1/1 (for plan 2). *Notification:* 4/5 (freshmen), 12/15 (early decision plan 1), 2/15 (early decision plan 2).

Admissions Contact Ms. Rose Woodd, Receptionist, Bowdoin College, 5000 College Station, Brunswick, ME 04011-8441. *Phone:* 207-725-3958. *Fax:* 207-725-3101. *E-mail:* admissions@bowdoin.edu.

COLBY COLLEGE
Waterville, Maine

- **Independent** 4-year, founded 1813
- **Calendar** 4-1-4
- **Degree** bachelor's
- **Small-town** 714-acre campus
- **Endowment** $353.4 million
- **Coed,** 1,809 undergraduate students, 100% full-time, 52% women, 48% men
- **Most difficult** entrance level, 34% of applicants were admitted

Colby combines a challenging academic program, an emphasis on undergraduate research, and a friendly, supportive atmosphere on one of the nation's most beautiful campuses. Colby's reach is global in its recruitment of diverse students and faculty members, the scope of its curriculum, and its ambitious study-abroad program.

Undergraduates 1,808 full-time, 1 part-time. Students come from 47 states and territories, 50 other countries, 89% are from out of state, 2% African American, 4% Asian American or Pacific Islander, 2% Hispanic American, 0.3% Native American, 5% international, 0.7% transferred in, 94% live on campus. *Retention:* 94% of 2001 full-time freshmen returned.

Freshmen *Admission:* 3,909 applied, 1,323 admitted, 488 enrolled. *Test scores:* SAT verbal scores over 500: 98%; SAT math scores over 500: 100%; ACT scores over 18: 100%; SAT verbal scores over 600: 84%; SAT math scores over 600: 90%; ACT scores over 24: 93%; SAT verbal scores over 700: 31%; SAT math scores over 700: 35%; ACT scores over 30: 28%.

Faculty *Total:* 187, 84% full-time, 93% with terminal degrees. *Student/faculty ratio:* 11:1.

Majors African-American studies; American studies; anthropology; art; art history; biochemistry; biology; cell biology; chemistry; classics; computer science; earth sciences; East Asian studies; economics; English; environmental science; French; geology; German; history; international relations; Latin American studies; mathematics; molecular biology; music; philosophy; physics; political science; psychology; religious studies; Russian/Slavic studies; sociology; Spanish; theater arts/drama; women's studies.

Academic Programs *Special study options:* advanced placement credit, double majors, English as a second language, honors programs, independent study, internships, off-campus study, part-time degree program, services for LD students, student-designed majors, study abroad. *ROTC:* Army (c). *Unusual degree programs:* 3-2 engineering with Case Western Reserve University, Dartmouth College, University of Rochester.

Library Miller Library plus 2 others with 620,705 titles, 1,835 serial subscriptions, 20,645 audiovisual materials, an OPAC, a Web page.

Computers on Campus 300 computers available on campus for general student use. A campuswide network can be accessed from student residence rooms and from off campus. Internet access, online (class) registration, at least one staffed computer lab available.

Student Life *Housing:* on-campus residence required through senior year. *Options:* coed. *Activities and Organizations:* drama/theater group, student-run newspaper, radio station, choral group, Outing Club, Volunteer Center, WMHB-FM, student government, Powder and Wig (theater). *Campus security:* 24-hour emergency response devices and patrols, late-night transport/escort service, controlled dormitory access, campus lighting, student emergency response team, self-defense education, property id program, party monitors. *Student Services:* health clinic, personal/psychological counseling, women's center.

Athletics Member NCAA. All Division III except men's and women's skiing (cross-country) (Division I), men's and women's skiing (downhill) (Division I). *Intercollegiate sports:* badminton M(c)/W(c), baseball M, basketball M/W, crew M/W, cross-country running M/W, equestrian sports M(c)/W(c), fencing M(c)/W(c), field hockey W, football M, golf M/W, ice hockey M/W, lacrosse M/W, rugby M(c)/W(c), sailing M(c)/W(c), skiing (cross-country) M/W, skiing (downhill) M/W, soccer M/W, softball W, squash M/W, swimming M/W, tennis M/W, track and field M/W, volleyball M(c)/W, water polo M(c)/W(c). *Intramural sports:* badminton M/W, basketball M/W, cross-country running M/W, equestrian sports M/W, fencing M/W, football M/W, golf M/W, ice hockey M/W, skiing (cross-country) M/W, soccer M/W, softball M/W, squash M/W, swimming M/W, table tennis M/W, tennis M/W, volleyball M/W.

Standardized Tests *Required:* SAT I or ACT (for admission).

Costs (2001–02) *Payment plan:* installment. *Waivers:* adult students, senior citizens, and employees or children of employees.

Financial Aid Of all full-time matriculated undergraduates who enrolled in 2001, 880 applied for aid, 650 were judged to have need, 650 had their need fully met. 428 Federal Work-Study jobs (averaging $1500). 46 State and other part-time jobs (averaging $1600). *Average percent of need met:* 100%. *Average financial aid package:* $20,792. *Average need-based loan:* $2928. *Average need-based gift aid:* $19,123. *Average indebtedness upon graduation:* $17,400. *Financial aid deadline:* 2/1.

Applying *Options:* common application, electronic application, early admission, early decision, deferred entrance. *Application fee:* $55. *Required:* essay or personal statement, high school transcript, 2 letters of recommendation. *Recommended:* interview. *Application deadlines:* 1/1 (freshmen), 3/1 (transfers). *Early decision:* 11/15 (for plan 1), 1/1 (for plan 2). *Notification:* 4/1 (freshmen), 12/15 (early decision plan 1), 2/1 (early decision plan 2).

Admissions Contact Dean of Admissions and Financial Aid, Colby College, Office of Admissions and Financial Aid, 4800 Mayflower Hill, Waterville, ME 04901-8848. *Phone:* 207-872-3168. *Toll-free phone:* 800-723-3032. *Fax:* 207-872-3474. *E-mail:* admissions@colby.edu.

COLLEGE OF THE ATLANTIC
Bar Harbor, Maine

- **Independent** comprehensive, founded 1969
- **Calendar** 3 10-week terms
- **Degrees** bachelor's and master's
- **Small-town** 25-acre campus
- **Endowment** $8.6 million
- **Coed,** 269 undergraduate students, 97% full-time, 59% women, 41% men
- **Very difficult** entrance level, 75% of applicants were admitted

Undergraduates 260 full-time, 9 part-time. Students come from 33 states and territories, 19 other countries, 78% are from out of state, 0.7% African American, 0.4% Asian American or Pacific Islander, 10% international, 8% transferred in, 40% live on campus. *Retention:* 90% of 2001 full-time freshmen returned.

Freshmen *Admission:* 233 applied, 174 admitted, 69 enrolled. *Average high school GPA:* 3.53. *Test scores:* SAT verbal scores over 500: 100%; SAT math scores over 500: 89%; ACT scores over 18: 100%; SAT verbal scores over 600: 63%; SAT math scores over 600: 49%; ACT scores over 24: 100%; SAT verbal scores over 700: 20%; SAT math scores over 700: 9%; ACT scores over 30: 22%.

Faculty *Total:* 29, 76% full-time, 90% with terminal degrees. *Student/faculty ratio:* 10:1.

Majors Architectural environmental design; art; biological/physical sciences; biology; botany; ceramic arts; computer graphics; drawing; ecology; economics; education; elementary education; English; environmental biology; environmental education; environmental science; evolutionary biology; human ecology; interdisciplinary studies; landscape architecture; legal studies; liberal arts and sciences/liberal studies; literature; marine biology; maritime science; middle school education; museum studies; music; natural sciences; philosophy; pre-veterinary studies; psychology; public policy analysis; science education; secondary education; wildlife biology; zoology.

Academic Programs *Special study options:* accelerated degree program, advanced placement credit, cooperative education, independent study, internships, off-campus study, part-time degree program, student-designed majors, study abroad.

Library Thorndike Library with 35,000 titles, 475 serial subscriptions, 1,579 audiovisual materials, an OPAC, a Web page.

Computers on Campus 48 computers available on campus for general student use. A campuswide network can be accessed from student residence rooms and from off campus. At least one staffed computer lab available.

Student Life *Housing Options:* coed. *Activities and Organizations:* drama/theater group, student-run newspaper, choral group, Outing Club, Environmental Awareness Club, Students for a Free Tibet, All-Campus Meeting, Choral Group. *Campus security:* 24-hour emergency response devices and patrols, late-night transport/escort service. *Student Services:* health clinic, personal/psychological counseling, women's center.

Athletics *Intercollegiate sports:* soccer M(c)/W(c). *Intramural sports:* basketball M, bowling M/W, sailing M/W, skiing (cross-country) M/W, volleyball M/W, water polo M/W.

Standardized Tests *Recommended:* SAT I and SAT II or ACT (for admission).
Costs (2001–02) *One-time required fee:* $300. *Comprehensive fee:* $26,994 includes full-time tuition ($21,138), mandatory fees ($246), and room and board ($5610). Part-time tuition: $2819 per term. *Required fees:* $82 per term part-time. *Room and board:* College room only: $3450. Room and board charges vary according to board plan. *Payment plan:* installment. *Waivers:* adult students, senior citizens, and employees or children of employees.
Financial Aid Of all full-time matriculated undergraduates who enrolled in 2001, 210 applied for aid, 191 were judged to have need, 90 had their need fully met. 147 Federal Work-Study jobs (averaging $1932). 24 State and other part-time jobs (averaging $1189). *Average percent of need met:* 89%. *Average financial aid package:* $17,425. *Average need-based loan:* $3077. *Average need-based gift aid:* $11,008. *Average indebtedness upon graduation:* $12,985.
Applying *Options:* common application, electronic application, early admission, early decision, deferred entrance. *Application fee:* $45. *Required:* essay or personal statement, high school transcript, 3 letters of recommendation. *Required for some:* interview. *Recommended:* minimum 3.0 GPA, interview. *Application deadlines:* 3/1 (freshmen), 4/1 (transfers). *Early decision:* 12/1 (for plan 1), 1/10 (for plan 2). *Notification:* 4/1 (freshmen), 12/15 (early decision plan 1), 1/25 (early decision plan 2).
Admissions Contact Ms. Sarah G. Baker, Director of Admission, College of the Atlantic, 105 Eden Street, Bar Harbor, ME 04609-1198. *Phone:* 207-288-5015 Ext. 233. *Toll-free phone:* 800-528-0025. *Fax:* 207-288-4126. *E-mail:* inquiry@ecology.coa.edu.

HUSSON COLLEGE

Bangor, Maine

- **Independent** comprehensive, founded 1898
- **Calendar** semesters
- **Degrees** associate, bachelor's, master's, post-master's, and postbachelor's certificates
- **Suburban** 170-acre campus
- **Endowment** $2.4 million
- **Coed,** 1,536 undergraduate students, 59% full-time, 66% women, 34% men
- **Moderately difficult** entrance level, 98% of applicants were admitted

Undergraduates 910 full-time, 626 part-time. Students come from 23 states and territories, 6 other countries, 15% are from out of state, 1% African American, 1% Asian American or Pacific Islander, 1.0% Hispanic American, 0.7% Native American, 4% international, 7% transferred in, 40% live on campus. *Retention:* 68% of 2001 full-time freshmen returned.
Freshmen *Admission:* 450 applied, 443 admitted, 190 enrolled. *Average high school GPA:* 3.06. *Test scores:* SAT verbal scores over 500: 25%; SAT math scores over 500: 28%; ACT scores over 18: 100%; SAT verbal scores over 600: 3%; SAT math scores over 600: 6%; ACT scores over 24: 40%; SAT verbal scores over 700: 1%; SAT math scores over 700: 1%.
Faculty *Total:* 90, 46% full-time, 56% with terminal degrees. *Student/faculty ratio:* 19:1.
Majors Accounting; banking; biology; biology education; business administration; business computer programming; business education; business marketing and marketing management; clinical psychology; computer programming; criminology; elementary education; entrepreneurship; finance; hospitality management; information sciences/systems; international business; legal administrative assistant; liberal arts and sciences/liberal studies; management information systems/business data processing; medical administrative assistant; medical assistant; nursing; occupational therapy; organizational psychology; paralegal/legal assistant; physical education; physical therapy; secretarial science; sport/fitness administration.
Academic Programs *Special study options:* academic remediation for entering students, adult/continuing education programs, advanced placement credit, cooperative education, distance learning, double majors, English as a second language, independent study, internships, part-time degree program, services for LD students, student-designed majors, summer session for credit. *ROTC:* Army (c), Navy (c).
Library Husson College Library with 35,411 titles, 500 serial subscriptions, 219 audiovisual materials, an OPAC, a Web page.
Computers on Campus 135 computers available on campus for general student use. A campuswide network can be accessed from student residence rooms and from off campus. Internet access, at least one staffed computer lab available.
Student Life *Housing:* on-campus residence required through senior year. *Options:* coed. *Activities and Organizations:* drama/theater group, student-run newspaper, radio station, student government, Organization of Student Nurses, Organization of Physical Therapy Students, Accounting Society, Phi Beta Lambda, national fraternities. *Campus security:* 24-hour emergency response devices and patrols. *Student Services:* health clinic, personal/psychological counseling.
Athletics Member NCAA, NAIA. All NCAA Division III. *Intercollegiate sports:* baseball M, basketball M/W, cross-country running M/W, field hockey W, golf M/W, soccer M/W, softball W, tennis M/W, volleyball W. *Intramural sports:* baseball M, basketball M/W, football M, lacrosse M, soccer M/W, softball M/W, swimming M/W, volleyball M/W, water polo M/W, wrestling M.
Standardized Tests *Required:* SAT I or ACT (for admission).
Costs (2001–02) *Comprehensive fee:* $15,340 includes full-time tuition ($9840), mandatory fees ($150), and room and board ($5350). Full-time tuition and fees vary according to class time. Part-time tuition: $328 per credit hour. Part-time tuition and fees vary according to class time and course load. *Payment plans:* tuition prepayment, installment. *Waivers:* senior citizens and employees or children of employees.
Financial Aid Of all full-time matriculated undergraduates who enrolled in 2001, 810 applied for aid, 753 were judged to have need, 84 had their need fully met. In 2001, 128 non-need-based awards were made. *Average percent of need met:* 79%. *Average financial aid package:* $8329. *Average need-based loan:* $3578. *Average need-based gift aid:* $5075. *Average indebtedness upon graduation:* $17,125.
Applying *Options:* common application, electronic application, early admission, early action, deferred entrance. *Application fee:* $25. *Required:* essay or personal statement, high school transcript, 1 letter of recommendation. *Recommended:* interview. *Application deadlines:* 9/1 (freshmen), 9/1 (transfers). *Notification:* continuous (freshmen), 1/2 (early action).
Admissions Contact Mrs. Jane Goodwin, Director of Admissions, Husson College, One College Circle, Bangor, ME 04401-2999. *Phone:* 207-941-7100. *Toll-free phone:* 800-4-HUSSON. *Fax:* 207-941-7935. *E-mail:* admit@husson.edu.

MAINE COLLEGE OF ART

Portland, Maine

- **Independent** comprehensive, founded 1882
- **Calendar** semesters
- **Degrees** bachelor's and master's
- **Urban** campus with easy access to Boston
- **Endowment** $2.3 million
- **Coed,** 410 undergraduate students, 92% full-time, 57% women, 43% men
- **Moderately difficult** entrance level, 90% of applicants were admitted

Undergraduates 377 full-time, 33 part-time. Students come from 21 states and territories, 52% are from out of state, 0.5% African American, 0.7% Asian American or Pacific Islander, 1% Hispanic American, 0.5% Native American, 0.2% international, 12% transferred in, 25% live on campus. *Retention:* 52% of 2001 full-time freshmen returned.
Freshmen *Admission:* 408 applied, 368 admitted, 103 enrolled. *Average high school GPA:* 3.20. *Test scores:* SAT verbal scores over 500: 62%; SAT math scores over 500: 39%; ACT scores over 18: 83%; SAT verbal scores over 600: 21%; SAT math scores over 600: 6%; ACT scores over 24: 33%; SAT verbal scores over 700: 2%.
Faculty *Total:* 56, 54% full-time, 93% with terminal degrees. *Student/faculty ratio:* 10:1.
Majors Ceramic arts; design/applied arts related; graphic design/commercial art/illustration; metal/jewelry arts; painting; photography; printmaking; sculpture.
Academic Programs *Special study options:* adult/continuing education programs, advanced placement credit, cooperative education, double majors, independent study, internships, off-campus study, part-time degree program, services for LD students, student-designed majors.
Library Joanne Waxman Library at the Main College of Art with 20,797 titles, 98 serial subscriptions, 182 audiovisual materials, an OPAC, a Web page.
Computers on Campus 40 computers available on campus for general student use. Internet access, at least one staffed computer lab available.
Student Life *Housing Options:* coed. *Activities and Organizations:* student-run newspaper, Student Representative Association, Outdoor Group, The Canvas—student newspaper, Ski and Snowboard Club, Movie Club. *Campus security:* 24-hour emergency response devices and patrols, controlled dormitory access. *Student Services:* health clinic, personal/psychological counseling.
Standardized Tests *Required:* SAT I or ACT (for admission).
Costs (2001–02) *One-time required fee:* $15. *Comprehensive fee:* $26,352 includes full-time tuition ($18,360), mandatory fees ($450), and room and board ($7542). Full-time tuition and fees vary according to course load. Part-time tuition: $765 per credit hour. Part-time tuition and fees vary according to course

Maine College of Art (continued)
load. *Room and board:* College room only: $4996. Room and board charges vary according to board plan and housing facility. *Payment plan:* installment. *Waivers:* employees or children of employees.

Financial Aid Of all full-time matriculated undergraduates who enrolled in 2001, 366 applied for aid, 296 were judged to have need, 31 had their need fully met. 89 Federal Work-Study jobs (averaging $1344). In 2001, 87 non-need-based awards were made. *Average percent of need met:* 59%. *Average financial aid package:* $12,135. *Average need-based loan:* $3944. *Average need-based gift aid:* $8310. *Average indebtedness upon graduation:* $23,634.

Applying *Options:* common application, electronic application, early admission, deferred entrance. *Application fee:* $40. *Required:* essay or personal statement, high school transcript, 2 letters of recommendation, portfolio. *Recommended:* minimum 2.0 GPA, interview. *Application deadline:* rolling (freshmen), rolling (transfers). *Notification:* continuous until 8/31 (freshmen).

Admissions Contact Kathryn Quin-Easter, Admissions Assistant, Maine College of Art, 97 Spring Street, Portland, ME 04101-3987. *Phone:* 207-775-3052 Ext. 226. *Toll-free phone:* 800-639-4808. *Fax:* 207-772-5069. *E-mail:* admissions@meca.edu.

MAINE MARITIME ACADEMY
Castine, Maine

- **State-supported** comprehensive, founded 1941
- **Calendar** semesters
- **Degrees** bachelor's and master's
- **Small-town** 35-acre campus
- **Endowment** $8.0 million
- **Coed, primarily men,** 721 undergraduate students, 98% full-time, 15% women, 85% men
- **Moderately difficult** entrance level, 78% of applicants were admitted

Maine Maritime is a college awarding associate and bachelor's degrees in marine engineering, marine transportation, ocean studies, international business, and logistics. A 500-foot training ship, a fleet of 90 vessels, annual cruises, high-tech simulation, 4 USCG licenses. Telephone: 800-464-6565 (toll-free, in-state); 800-227-8465 (toll-free, out-of-state). Web site: http://www.mainemaritime.edu.

Undergraduates 708 full-time, 13 part-time. Students come from 37 states and territories, 6 other countries, 48% are from out of state, 0.3% African American, 0.3% Asian American or Pacific Islander, 0.7% Hispanic American, 0.7% Native American, 4% international, 0.1% transferred in, 80% live on campus. *Retention:* 75% of 2001 full-time freshmen returned.

Freshmen *Admission:* 465 applied, 365 admitted, 146 enrolled. *Average high school GPA:* 2.8.

Faculty *Total:* 74, 88% full-time, 51% with terminal degrees. *Student/faculty ratio:* 12:1.

Majors Business administration; engineering; engineering technology; international business; logistics/materials management; marine biology; marine science; maritime science; naval architecture/marine engineering; oceanography; systems engineering; transportation technology.

Academic Programs *Special study options:* academic remediation for entering students, adult/continuing education programs, advanced placement credit, distance learning, internships. *ROTC:* Navy (b).

Library Nutting Memorial Library with 68,200 titles, 453 serial subscriptions, an OPAC, a Web page.

Computers on Campus 40 computers available on campus for general student use. A campuswide network can be accessed from student residence rooms. Internet access, online (class) registration, at least one staffed computer lab available.

Student Life *Housing:* on-campus residence required through junior year. *Options:* coed. *Activities and Organizations:* drama/theater group, choral group, Alpha Phi Omega, yacht club, outing club, Social Council, drill team. *Campus security:* 24-hour patrols, student patrols. *Student Services:* health clinic, personal/psychological counseling, women's center.

Athletics Member NCAA. All Division III. *Intercollegiate sports:* basketball M/W, cross-country running M/W, football M, lacrosse M, sailing M/W, soccer M/W, softball W. *Intramural sports:* basketball M/W, football M/W, golf M/W, ice hockey M, racquetball M/W, riflery M/W, rugby M, sailing M/W, skiing (downhill) M/W, softball M/W, squash M/W, swimming M/W, tennis M/W, volleyball M/W, weight lifting M/W.

Standardized Tests *Required:* SAT I or ACT (for admission).

Costs (2002–03) *Tuition:* state resident $4739 full-time, $158 per credit part-time; nonresident $8774 full-time, $293 per credit part-time. *Required fees:* $645 full-time. *Room and board:* $5327.

Financial Aid Of all full-time matriculated undergraduates who enrolled in 2001, 510 applied for aid, 434 were judged to have need, 91 had their need fully met. 305 Federal Work-Study jobs (averaging $657). In 2001, 76 non-need-based awards were made. *Average percent of need met:* 80%. *Average financial aid package:* $8006. *Average need-based loan:* $4540. *Average need-based gift aid:* $4283. *Average indebtedness upon graduation:* $15,650.

Applying *Options:* electronic application, early admission, early decision, deferred entrance. *Application fee:* $15. *Required:* high school transcript, 1 letter of recommendation, physical examination. *Recommended:* interview. *Application deadlines:* 7/1 (freshmen), 7/1 (transfers). *Early decision:* 12/20. *Notification:* 1/1 (early decision).

Admissions Contact Jeffrey C. Wright, Director of Admissions, Maine Maritime Academy, Castine, ME 04420. *Phone:* 207-326-2215. *Toll-free phone:* 800-464-6565 (in-state); 800-227-8465 (out-of-state). *Fax:* 207-326-2515. *E-mail:* admissions@bell.mma.edu.

NEW ENGLAND SCHOOL OF COMMUNICATIONS
Bangor, Maine

- **Private** 4-year, founded 1981
- **Calendar** semesters
- **Degrees** certificates, associate, and bachelor's
- **Coed,** 168 undergraduate students, 96% full-time, 31% women, 69% men
- **Noncompetitive** entrance level, 69% of applicants were admitted

Undergraduates 162 full-time, 6 part-time. Students come from 5 states and territories, 3 other countries, 9% are from out of state, 0.6% African American, 0.6% Native American, 2% international, 4% transferred in, 42% live on campus.

Freshmen *Admission:* 270 applied, 186 admitted, 101 enrolled.

Faculty *Total:* 28, 21% full-time, 79% with terminal degrees. *Student/faculty ratio:* 12:1.

Majors Advertising; audio engineering; broadcast journalism; business marketing and marketing management; communications; communications related; communications technologies related; computer graphics; computer software and media applications related; film/video and photographic arts related; film/video production; marketing operations; multimedia; public relations; radio/television broadcasting; radio/television broadcasting technology; speech/rhetorical studies; Web/multimedia management/webmaster; Web page, digital/multimedia and information resources design.

Academic Programs *Special study options:* adult/continuing education programs, advanced placement credit, double majors, English as a second language, independent study, internships, part-time degree program, services for LD students, student-designed majors.

Library Husson College Library plus 1 other with a Web page.

Computers on Campus 150 computers available on campus for general student use. A campuswide network can be accessed from student residence rooms and from off campus. Internet access, at least one staffed computer lab available.

Student Life *Housing Options:* coed. *Activities and Organizations:* drama/theater group, student-run newspaper, radio station, choral group, drama, Greek organizations, newspaper, Student Government, Radio Station, national fraternities, national sororities. *Campus security:* 24-hour emergency response devices and patrols, late-night transport/escort service. *Student Services:* health clinic, personal/psychological counseling.

Athletics *Intramural sports:* basketball M/W, lacrosse M/W, soccer M/W, softball M/W, swimming M/W, table tennis M/W, tennis M/W, volleyball M/W.

Standardized Tests *Recommended:* SAT I or ACT (for admission).

Costs (2002–03) *Comprehensive fee:* $14,370 includes full-time tuition ($7990), mandatory fees ($990), and room and board ($5390). Part-time tuition and fees vary according to course load. *Payment plan:* installment. *Waivers:* employees or children of employees.

Financial Aid Of all full-time matriculated undergraduates who enrolled in 2001, 148 applied for aid, 148 were judged to have need, 72 had their need fully met. *Average percent of need met:* 92%. *Average financial aid package:* $6320. *Average need-based loan:* $3100. *Average need-based gift aid:* $6000. *Average indebtedness upon graduation:* $12,000.

Applying *Options:* electronic application, early admission, deferred entrance. *Application fee:* $15. *Required:* high school transcript, 2 letters of recommendation, interview, Wonderlic Scholastic Test. *Recommended:* essay or personal statement. *Application deadline:* rolling (freshmen). *Notification:* continuous (freshmen).

Admissions Contact Ms. Louise G. Grant, Director of Admissions, New England School of Communications, 1 College Circle, Bangor, ME 04401. *Phone:* 207-941-7176 Ext. 1093. *Toll-free phone:* 888-877-1876. *Fax:* 207-947-3987. *E-mail:* info@nescom.edu.

SAINT JOSEPH'S COLLEGE
Standish, Maine

- **Independent** comprehensive, founded 1912, affiliated with Roman Catholic Church
- **Calendar** semesters
- **Degrees** associate, bachelor's, and master's (profile does not include enrollment in distance learning master's program)
- **Small-town** 330-acre campus
- **Endowment** $4.1 million
- **Coed,** 892 undergraduate students, 96% full-time, 65% women, 35% men
- **Moderately difficult** entrance level, 87% of applicants were admitted

Saint Joseph's College of Maine, the only Catholic college in Maine, offers a liberal arts education in a values-centered environment. Sponsored by the Sisters of Mercy since 1912, Saint Joseph's College endeavors to engage the minds, bodies, and spirits of men and women of all ages and faiths. More than 40 majors and concentrations prepare students for life and careers.

Undergraduates 860 full-time, 32 part-time. Students come from 15 states and territories, 37% are from out of state, 1% African American, 0.7% Asian American or Pacific Islander, 0.9% Hispanic American, 0.3% Native American, 4% transferred in, 81% live on campus. *Retention:* 70% of 2001 full-time freshmen returned.

Freshmen *Admission:* 1,109 applied, 969 admitted, 318 enrolled. *Average high school GPA:* 3.0.

Faculty *Total:* 110, 54% full-time, 84% with terminal degrees. *Student/faculty ratio:* 12:1.

Majors Accounting; advertising; biology; biology education; business administration; business marketing and marketing management; chemistry; chemistry education; criminal justice studies; education; elementary education; English; English education; environmental science; exercise sciences; finance; international business; journalism; liberal arts and sciences/liberal studies; marine biology; mathematics; mathematics education; medical radiologic technology; nursing; philosophy; physical education; psychology; religious studies; science education; social studies education; social work; sociology; sport/fitness administration.

Academic Programs *Special study options:* accelerated degree program, adult/continuing education programs, advanced placement credit, cooperative education, distance learning, external degree program, freshman honors college, honors programs, independent study, internships, off-campus study, part-time degree program, services for LD students, study abroad, summer session for credit. *ROTC:* Army (c). *Unusual degree programs:* pharmacy, Massachusetts College of Pharmacy.

Library Wellehan Library with 77,446 titles, 474 serial subscriptions, an OPAC, a Web page.

Computers on Campus 71 computers available on campus for general student use. A campuswide network can be accessed from student residence rooms and from off campus. Internet access, at least one staffed computer lab available.

Student Life *Housing Options:* coed, men-only, women-only. *Activities and Organizations:* drama/theater group, student-run newspaper, radio station, Campus Ministry, Superkids, Student Government Association and Senate, Business Club, Inter-Hall Council. *Campus security:* 24-hour emergency response devices and patrols, late-night transport/escort service, controlled dormitory access. *Student Services:* health clinic, personal/psychological counseling.

Athletics Member NCAA, NAIA. All NCAA Division III. *Intercollegiate sports:* baseball M, basketball M/W, cross-country running M/W, field hockey W, golf M, soccer M/W, softball W, volleyball W. *Intramural sports:* basketball M/W, cross-country running M/W, football M, golf M/W, ice hockey M/W, skiing (cross-country) M/W, skiing (downhill) M/W, soccer M/W, softball M/W, swimming M/W, volleyball M/W, water polo M/W, weight lifting M/W.

Standardized Tests *Required:* SAT I or ACT (for admission).

Costs (2002–03) *Comprehensive fee:* $23,720 includes full-time tuition ($16,150), mandatory fees ($590), and room and board ($6980). Part-time tuition: $275 per credit hour. *Required fees:* $50 per term part-time.

Financial Aid Of all full-time matriculated undergraduates who enrolled in 2001, 850 applied for aid, 785 were judged to have need, 116 had their need fully met. 367 Federal Work-Study jobs (averaging $1157). In 2001, 65 non-need-based awards were made. *Average percent of need met:* 89%. *Average financial aid package:* $12,736. *Average need-based loan:* $4576. *Average need-based gift aid:* $8762. *Average non-need based aid:* $3367. *Average indebtedness upon graduation:* $17,687.

Applying *Options:* common application, electronic application, early admission, deferred entrance. *Required:* essay or personal statement, high school transcript, minimum 2.0 GPA. *Recommended:* letters of recommendation, interview. *Application deadline:* rolling (freshmen), rolling (transfers). *Notification:* continuous (freshmen).

Admissions Contact Mr. Alexander Popovics, Vice President for Enrollment and Dean of Admission and Financial Aid, Saint Joseph's College, 278 Whites Bridge Road, Standish, ME 04084-5263. *Phone:* 207-893-7746 Ext. 7741. *Toll-free phone:* 800-338-7057. *Fax:* 207-893-7862. *E-mail:* admissions@sjcme.edu.

THOMAS COLLEGE
Waterville, Maine

- **Independent** comprehensive, founded 1894
- **Calendar** semesters
- **Degrees** associate, bachelor's, and master's
- **Small-town** 70-acre campus
- **Endowment** $1.1 million
- **Coed,** 658 undergraduate students, 71% full-time, 55% women, 45% men
- **Minimally difficult** entrance level, 94% of applicants were admitted

Undergraduates 465 full-time, 193 part-time. Students come from 13 states and territories, 2 other countries, 9% are from out of state, 0.3% African American, 0.5% Hispanic American, 0.3% Native American, 0.2% international, 4% transferred in, 60% live on campus. *Retention:* 63% of 2001 full-time freshmen returned.

Freshmen *Admission:* 431 applied, 406 admitted, 178 enrolled. *Average high school GPA:* 2.85. *Test scores:* SAT verbal scores over 500: 30%; SAT math scores over 500: 38%; SAT verbal scores over 600: 5%; SAT math scores over 600: 7%.

Faculty *Total:* 67, 28% full-time, 34% with terminal degrees. *Student/faculty ratio:* 17:1.

Majors Accounting; business administration; business education; business marketing and marketing management; computer/information sciences; computer management; computer programming; computer science; criminal justice/law enforcement administration; education (K-12); elementary education; entrepreneurship; fashion merchandising; finance; hotel and restaurant management; human resources management; international business; legal administrative assistant; management information systems/business data processing; mathematics education; medical administrative assistant; paralegal/legal assistant; professional studies; psychology; retail management; secretarial science; sport/fitness administration.

Academic Programs *Special study options:* academic remediation for entering students, adult/continuing education programs, advanced placement credit, cooperative education, internships, off-campus study, part-time degree program, study abroad, summer session for credit.

Library Marriner Library with 20,000 titles, 1,000 serial subscriptions, 300 audiovisual materials, an OPAC, a Web page.

Computers on Campus 90 computers available on campus for general student use. A campuswide network can be accessed from student residence rooms and from off campus. Internet access, online (class) registration, at least one staffed computer lab available.

Student Life *Housing:* on-campus residence required through senior year. *Options:* coed. *Activities and Organizations:* drama/theater group, student-run newspaper, Phi Beta Lambda, students club, GLOBE, Campus Activity Board, peer advisors, national fraternities, national sororities. *Campus security:* 24-hour emergency response devices and patrols, student patrols. *Student Services:* health clinic, personal/psychological counseling.

Athletics Member NCAA, NAIA. All NCAA Division III. *Intercollegiate sports:* baseball M, basketball M/W, field hockey W, golf M, soccer M/W, softball W, volleyball W. *Intramural sports:* baseball M, basketball M/W, bowling M/W, football M/W, ice hockey M(c), lacrosse M(c), skiing (cross-country) M/W, skiing (downhill) M/W, soccer M/W, softball M/W, tennis M/W, volleyball M/W, weight lifting M/W.

Standardized Tests *Required for some:* SAT I or ACT (for admission).

Costs (2001–02) *One-time required fee:* $75. *Comprehensive fee:* $19,175 includes full-time tuition ($12,980), mandatory fees ($310), and room and board ($5885). Part-time tuition: $811 per course. Part-time tuition and fees vary according to class time and course load. *Required fees:* $155 per term part-time. *Room and board:* College room only: $2940. Room and board charges vary according to housing facility. *Payment plan:* installment. *Waivers:* employees or children of employees.

Financial Aid Of all full-time matriculated undergraduates who enrolled in 2001, 441 applied for aid, 404 were judged to have need, 19 had their need fully met. 103 Federal Work-Study jobs (averaging $1500). In 2001, 37 non-need-based awards were made. *Average percent of need met:* 85%. *Average financial*

Thomas College (continued)
aid package: $11,233. *Average need-based loan:* $5016. *Average need-based gift aid:* $5562. *Average non-need based aid:* $7245. *Average indebtedness upon graduation:* $19,125.

Applying *Options:* electronic application, early action, deferred entrance. *Application fee:* $25. *Required:* essay or personal statement, high school transcript, 1 letter of recommendation. *Recommended:* minimum 2.0 GPA, interview, rank in upper 50% of high school class. *Application deadline:* rolling (freshmen), rolling (transfers). *Notification:* continuous (freshmen), 12/30 (early action).

Admissions Contact Ms. Jennifer Quinlan, Director of Admissions, Thomas College, 180 West River Road, Waterville, ME 04901. *Phone:* 207-859-1101. *Toll-free phone:* 800-339-7001. *Fax:* 207-859-1114. *E-mail:* admiss@thomas.edu.

UNITY COLLEGE
Unity, Maine

- **Independent** 4-year, founded 1965
- **Calendar** semesters
- **Degrees** associate and bachelor's
- **Rural** 205-acre campus
- **Endowment** $2.4 million
- **Coed,** 510 undergraduate students, 95% full-time, 32% women, 68% men
- **Moderately difficult** entrance level, 69% of applicants were admitted

Unity College's Learning Resource Center provides academic support services for students who need academic improvement. The center offers courses, advising, tutoring, study skills workshops, and counseling. The staff consists of 5 full-time faculty members, including a learning disabilities specialist.

Undergraduates 487 full-time, 23 part-time. Students come from 21 states and territories, 2 other countries, 62% are from out of state, 0.4% African American, 0.4% Hispanic American, 0.4% international, 9% transferred in, 72% live on campus. *Retention:* 64% of 2001 full-time freshmen returned.

Freshmen *Admission:* 367 applied, 252 admitted, 136 enrolled. *Average high school GPA:* 3.42. *Test scores:* SAT verbal scores over 500: 22%; SAT math scores over 500: 18%; SAT verbal scores over 600: 9%; SAT math scores over 600: 9%.

Faculty *Total:* 61, 59% full-time, 59% with terminal degrees. *Student/faculty ratio:* 16:1.

Majors Ecology; environmental biology; environmental education; environmental science; environmental technology; fishing sciences; forestry; interdisciplinary studies; marine biology; natural resources conservation; natural resources management; natural resources protective services; recreation/leisure facilities management; wildlife biology.

Academic Programs *Special study options:* academic remediation for entering students, accelerated degree program, advanced placement credit, cooperative education, English as a second language, honors programs, independent study, internships, off-campus study, part-time degree program, services for LD students, student-designed majors, summer session for credit. *ROTC:* Army (c).

Library Dorothy Webb Quimby Library with 46,000 titles, 650 serial subscriptions, a Web page.

Computers on Campus 42 computers available on campus for general student use. A campuswide network can be accessed from student residence rooms and from off campus. At least one staffed computer lab available.

Student Life *Housing:* on-campus residence required through sophomore year. *Options:* coed. *Activities and Organizations:* drama/theater group, student-run newspaper. *Campus security:* 24-hour patrols. *Student Services:* health clinic, personal/psychological counseling.

Athletics Member NSCAA. *Intercollegiate sports:* basketball M(s), cross-country running M(s)/W(s), soccer M(s), volleyball W(s). *Intramural sports:* badminton M/W, baseball M, basketball M/W, cross-country running M/W, football M/W, golf M/W, ice hockey M/W, lacrosse M/W, skiing (cross-country) M/W, skiing (downhill) M/W, soccer W, softball M/W, table tennis M/W, tennis M/W, volleyball M/W, weight lifting M/W.

Standardized Tests *Recommended:* SAT I or ACT (for placement).

Costs (2001–02) *One-time required fee:* $150. *Comprehensive fee:* $19,230 includes full-time tuition ($13,200), mandatory fees ($530), and room and board ($5500). Part-time tuition: $440 per credit. Part-time tuition and fees vary according to course load. *Payment plan:* installment. *Waivers:* employees or children of employees.

Financial Aid Of all full-time matriculated undergraduates who enrolled in 2001, 425 applied for aid, 372 were judged to have need, 97 had their need fully met. 299 Federal Work-Study jobs (averaging $1838). 17 State and other part-time jobs (averaging $1235). In 2001, 70 non-need-based awards were made. *Average percent of need met:* 81%. *Average financial aid package:* $10,902. *Average need-based loan:* $3954. *Average need-based gift aid:* $6319. *Average indebtedness upon graduation:* $21,268.

Applying *Options:* common application, electronic application, early admission, early action, deferred entrance. *Application fee:* $25. *Required:* essay or personal statement, high school transcript, 2 letters of recommendation. *Required for some:* interview. *Recommended:* minimum 2.0 GPA, interview. *Application deadline:* rolling (freshmen), rolling (transfers). *Notification:* 2/1 (early action).

Admissions Contact Ms. Kay Fiedler, Director of Admissions, Unity College, PO Box 532, Unity, ME 04988-0532. *Phone:* 800-624-1024. *Fax:* 207-948-6277.

UNIVERSITY OF MAINE
Orono, Maine

- **State-supported** university, founded 1865, part of University of Maine System
- **Calendar** semesters
- **Degrees** bachelor's, master's, doctoral, post-master's, and postbachelor's certificates
- **Small-town** 3298-acre campus
- **Endowment** $135.0 million
- **Coed,** 8,511 undergraduate students, 81% full-time, 53% women, 47% men
- **Moderately difficult** entrance level, 80% of applicants were admitted

Undergraduates 6,875 full-time, 1,636 part-time. Students come from 45 states and territories, 74 other countries, 14% are from out of state, 0.9% African American, 1.0% Asian American or Pacific Islander, 0.8% Hispanic American, 2% Native American, 2% international, 6% transferred in, 45% live on campus. *Retention:* 79% of 2001 full-time freshmen returned.

Freshmen *Admission:* 4,811 applied, 3,854 admitted, 1,590 enrolled. *Average high school GPA:* 3.15. *Test scores:* SAT verbal scores over 500: 71%; SAT math scores over 500: 69%; ACT scores over 18: 91%; SAT verbal scores over 600: 24%; SAT math scores over 600: 26%; ACT scores over 24: 43%; SAT verbal scores over 700: 3%; SAT math scores over 700: 4%; ACT scores over 30: 5%.

Faculty *Total:* 720, 72% full-time, 70% with terminal degrees. *Student/faculty ratio:* 14:1.

Majors Agricultural economics; agricultural engineering; animal sciences; anthropology; art; art education; art history; biochemistry; biology; botany; business administration; chemical engineering; chemistry; child care/development; civil engineering; classics; communication disorders; communications; computer engineering; computer science; construction technology; drafting/design technology; early childhood education; economics; education; educational media technology; education (K-12); electrical/electronic engineering technology; electrical engineering; elementary education; engineering physics; engineering-related technology; engineering technology; English; fine/studio arts; food sciences; forest engineering; forestry; French; geology; German; health education; history; individual/family development; international relations; journalism; landscaping management; Latin (ancient and medieval); marine biology; mass communications; mathematics; mechanical engineering; mechanical engineering technology; medical technology; microbiology/bacteriology; modern languages; molecular biology; music; music teacher education; natural resources management; nursing; nutrition science; philosophy; physical education; physics; political science; pre-medicine; pre-veterinary studies; psychology; public administration; recreation/leisure facilities management; romance languages; secondary education; social work; sociology; soil sciences; Spanish; speech/theater education; surveying; theater arts/drama; wildlife management; women's studies; wood science/paper technology; zoology.

Academic Programs *Special study options:* adult/continuing education programs, advanced placement credit, cooperative education, distance learning, double majors, English as a second language, external degree program, honors programs, independent study, internships, off-campus study, part-time degree program, services for LD students, student-designed majors, study abroad, summer session for credit. *ROTC:* Army (b), Navy (b).

Library Fogler Library with 854,000 titles, 16,700 serial subscriptions, 25,000 audiovisual materials, an OPAC, a Web page.

Computers on Campus 520 computers available on campus for general student use. A campuswide network can be accessed from student residence rooms and from off campus that provide access to on-line grade information, e-mail. Internet access, online (class) registration, at least one staffed computer lab available.

Student Life *Housing:* on-campus residence required for freshman year. *Options:* coed, women-only, disabled students. *Activities and Organizations:* drama/theater group, student-run newspaper, radio station, choral group, marching band, Volunteers in Community Efforts/VOICE, Circle K, Campus Crusade for Christ, Outing Club, Wilde Stein, national fraternities, national sororities. *Campus security:* 24-hour emergency response devices and patrols, late-night transport/escort service, controlled dormitory access. *Student Services:* health clinic, personal/psychological counseling, women's center, legal services.

Athletics Member NCAA. All Division I except football (Division I-A). *Intercollegiate sports:* baseball M(s), basketball M(s)/W(s), cross-country running M(s)/W(s), field hockey W(s), golf M, ice hockey M(s)/W(s), soccer M(s)/W(s), softball W(s), swimming M/W(s), track and field M(s)/W(s), volleyball W(s). *Intramural sports:* badminton M/W, basketball M/W, cross-country running M/W, fencing M(c)/W(c), field hockey W, golf M/W, lacrosse M(c)/W(c), racquetball M/W, rugby M(c)/W(c), skiing (cross-country) M/W, skiing (downhill) M(c)/W(c), soccer M/W, softball M/W, squash M/W, swimming M/W, table tennis M/W, tennis M/W, track and field M/W, volleyball M/W, water polo M/W, weight lifting M/W, wrestling M(c).

Standardized Tests *Required:* SAT I or ACT (for admission).

Costs (2002–03) *One-time required fee:* $15. *Tuition:* state resident $4350 full-time, $145 per credit hour part-time; nonresident $12,390 full-time, $413 per credit hour part-time. Full-time tuition and fees vary according to course load and reciprocity agreements. Part-time tuition and fees vary according to course load and reciprocity agreements. *Required fees:* $900 full-time, $171 per term part-time. *Room and board:* $6014; room only: $3106. Room and board charges vary according to board plan and housing facility. *Payment plan:* installment. *Waivers:* employees or children of employees.

Financial Aid Of all full-time matriculated undergraduates who enrolled in 2001, 5434 applied for aid, 3852 were judged to have need, 1477 had their need fully met. In 2001, 788 non-need-based awards were made. *Average percent of need met:* 83%. *Average financial aid package:* $7800. *Average need-based loan:* $4003. *Average need-based gift aid:* $4727. *Average non-need based aid:* $4259. *Average indebtedness upon graduation:* $17,816.

Applying *Options:* electronic application, early admission, deferred entrance. *Application fee:* $25. *Required:* essay or personal statement, high school transcript, 1 letter of recommendation. *Application deadline:* rolling (freshmen), rolling (transfers). *Notification:* continuous (freshmen).

Admissions Contact Mr. Jonathan H. Henry, Director, University of Maine, 5713 Chadbourne Hall, Orono, ME 04469-5713. *Phone:* 207-581-1561. *Toll-free phone:* 877-486-2364. *Fax:* 207-581-1213. *E-mail:* um-admit@maine.edu.

THE UNIVERSITY OF MAINE AT AUGUSTA
Augusta, Maine

- **State-supported** 4-year, founded 1965, part of University of Maine System
- **Calendar** semesters
- **Degrees** certificates, associate, bachelor's, and postbachelor's certificates (also offers some graduate courses and continuing education program with significant enrollment not reflected in profile)
- **Small-town** 165-acre campus
- **Endowment** $1.0 million
- **Coed,** 5,575 undergraduate students, 26% full-time, 75% women, 25% men
- **Noncompetitive** entrance level, 52% of applicants were admitted

Undergraduates 1,476 full-time, 4,099 part-time. Students come from 25 states and territories, 2% are from out of state, 0.7% African American, 0.4% Asian American or Pacific Islander, 0.5% Hispanic American, 3% Native American, 0.0% international, 8% transferred in.

Freshmen *Admission:* 2,491 applied, 1,286 admitted, 587 enrolled. *Average high school GPA:* 3.1.

Faculty *Total:* 235, 40% full-time. *Student/faculty ratio:* 20:1.

Majors Accounting; applied art; architectural engineering technology; biological/physical sciences; business administration; criminal justice/law enforcement administration; English; graphic design/commercial art/illustration; human services; information sciences/systems; jazz; liberal arts and sciences/liberal studies; library science; mathematics; medical laboratory technician; nursing; photography; public administration; social sciences.

Academic Programs *Special study options:* academic remediation for entering students, adult/continuing education programs, advanced placement credit, cooperative education, double majors, honors programs, independent study, internships, off-campus study, part-time degree program, services for LD students, student-designed majors, study abroad, summer session for credit.

Library The Bennett D. Katz Library with 44,000 titles, 560 serial subscriptions, an OPAC.

Computers on Campus 142 computers available on campus for general student use. A campuswide network can be accessed from off campus. At least one staffed computer lab available.

Student Life *Housing:* college housing not available. *Activities and Organizations:* student-run newspaper, Honors Program Student Association, Arts and Architecture Students of UMA, Student Nurse Association, Student-American Dental Hygiene Association, UMA Computer Club. *Campus security:* late-night transport/escort service. *Student Services:* personal/psychological counseling.

Athletics *Intercollegiate sports:* basketball M/W(c), fencing M(c)/W(c), soccer M(c)/W(c), softball W(s)(c). *Intramural sports:* golf M/W, racquetball M/W, skiing (cross-country) M/W, skiing (downhill) M/W, soccer M/W, softball M/W, volleyball M/W.

Standardized Tests *Required for some:* SAT I (for placement). *Recommended:* SAT I (for placement).

Costs (2001–02) *One-time required fee:* $15. *Tuition:* state resident $3270 full-time, $109 per credit part-time; nonresident $7980 full-time, $266 per credit part-time. Full-time tuition and fees vary according to reciprocity agreements. Part-time tuition and fees vary according to reciprocity agreements. *Required fees:* $658 full-time, $375 per term part-time. *Payment plan:* installment. *Waivers:* senior citizens and employees or children of employees.

Financial Aid Of all full-time matriculated undergraduates who enrolled in 2001, 1446 applied for aid, 1314 were judged to have need, 204 had their need fully met. In 2001, 37 non-need-based awards were made. *Average percent of need met:* 71%. *Average financial aid package:* $7312. *Average need-based loan:* $3409. *Average need-based gift aid:* $4520. *Average non-need based aid:* $3057. *Average indebtedness upon graduation:* $10,533.

Applying *Options:* common application, electronic application, early admission, early action, deferred entrance. *Application fee:* $25. *Required:* high school transcript. *Application deadline:* rolling (freshmen), rolling (transfers). *Notification:* 12/1 (early action).

Admissions Contact Mr. William Clark Ketcham, Director of Enrollment Services, The University of Maine at Augusta, 46 University Drive, Robinson Hall, Augusta, ME 04330. *Phone:* 207-621-3185. *Toll-free phone:* 800-696-6000 Ext. 3185. *Fax:* 207-621-3116. *E-mail:* umaar@maine.maine.edu.

UNIVERSITY OF MAINE AT FARMINGTON
Farmington, Maine

- **State-supported** 4-year, founded 1863, part of University of Maine System
- **Calendar** semesters
- **Degree** certificates and bachelor's
- **Small-town** 50-acre campus
- **Endowment** $5.3 million
- **Coed,** 2,435 undergraduate students, 86% full-time, 67% women, 33% men
- **Moderately difficult** entrance level, 68% of applicants were admitted

Undergraduates 2,095 full-time, 340 part-time. Students come from 23 states and territories, 15 other countries, 17% are from out of state, 0.4% African American, 0.5% Asian American or Pacific Islander, 0.4% Hispanic American, 0.9% Native American, 1% international, 6% transferred in, 43% live on campus. *Retention:* 74% of 2001 full-time freshmen returned.

Freshmen *Admission:* 1,468 applied, 993 admitted, 489 enrolled. *Test scores:* SAT verbal scores over 500: 62%; SAT math scores over 500: 57%; SAT verbal scores over 600: 19%; SAT math scores over 600: 18%; SAT verbal scores over 700: 3%; SAT math scores over 700: 1%.

Faculty *Total:* 151, 77% full-time, 69% with terminal degrees. *Student/faculty ratio:* 16:1.

Majors Anthropology; art; biology; biology education; business economics; chemistry; computer science; creative writing; early childhood education; economics; education of the emotionally handicapped; education of the mentally handicapped; education of the specific learning disabled; elementary education; English; English education; environmental science; general studies; geography; geology; health education; health occupations education; history; interdisciplinary studies; international relations; liberal arts and sciences/liberal studies; mathematics; mathematics education; mental health/rehabilitation; music; philosophy; political science; psychology; rehabilitation therapy; religious studies; science education; secondary education; social science education; sociology; special education; theater arts/drama; women's studies.

Academic Programs *Special study options:* academic remediation for entering students, accelerated degree program, advanced placement credit, distance learning, double majors, honors programs, independent study, internships, off-campus study, part-time degree program, services for LD students, student-designed majors, study abroad, summer session for credit.

Library Mantor Library with 104,313 titles, 2,399 serial subscriptions, 8,572 audiovisual materials, an OPAC, a Web page.

Computers on Campus 175 computers available on campus for general student use. A campuswide network can be accessed from student residence rooms and from off campus. Internet access, at least one staffed computer lab available.

Student Life *Housing Options:* coed, women-only. *Activities and Organizations:* drama/theater group, student-run newspaper, radio station, choral group, Program Board, Intramural Board, Campus Residence Council, campus radio station, Commuter Council. *Campus security:* 24-hour emergency response

University of Maine at Farmington (continued)
devices and patrols, late-night transport/escort service, controlled dormitory access, safety whistles. *Student Services:* health clinic, personal/psychological counseling.

Athletics Member NCAA, NAIA. All NCAA Division III. *Intercollegiate sports:* baseball M, basketball M/W, cross-country running M/W, field hockey W, golf M/W, ice hockey M(c), lacrosse M(c), soccer M/W, softball W, volleyball W. *Intramural sports:* basketball M/W, football M/W, ice hockey M(c)/W(c), rugby M(c)/W(c), skiing (downhill) M(c)/W(c), soccer M/W, softball M/W, swimming M(c)/W(c), tennis M(c)/W(c), volleyball M/W.

Standardized Tests *Recommended:* SAT I or ACT (for placement).

Costs (2001–02) *One-time required fee:* $15. *Tuition:* state resident $3735 full-time, $124 per credit part-time; nonresident $9120 full-time, $304 per credit part-time. Full-time tuition and fees vary according to course load, reciprocity agreements, and student level. Part-time tuition and fees vary according to course load, reciprocity agreements, and student level. *Required fees:* $582 full-time, $8 per credit, $126 per term part-time. *Room and board:* $4846; room only: $2596. Room and board charges vary according to board plan and housing facility. *Payment plan:* installment. *Waivers:* minority students, senior citizens, and employees or children of employees.

Financial Aid Of all full-time matriculated undergraduates who enrolled in 2001, 1591 applied for aid, 1308 were judged to have need, 390 had their need fully met. 523 Federal Work-Study jobs (averaging $1047). 561 State and other part-time jobs (averaging $1662). In 2001, 79 non-need-based awards were made. *Average percent of need met:* 85%. *Average financial aid package:* $8312. *Average need-based loan:* $3387. *Average need-based gift aid:* $3415. *Average non-need based aid:* $2114. *Average indebtedness upon graduation:* $14,435.

Applying *Options:* electronic application, early admission, early action, deferred entrance. *Application fee:* $25. *Required:* essay or personal statement, high school transcript, minimum 2.0 GPA, 1 letter of recommendation. *Recommended:* interview. *Notification:* continuous (freshmen), 1/8 (early action).

Admissions Contact Mr. James G. Collins, Associate Director of Admissions, University of Maine at Farmington, 246 Main Street, Farmington, ME 04938-1994. *Phone:* 207-778-7050. *Fax:* 207-778-8182. *E-mail:* umfadmit@maine.edu.

UNIVERSITY OF MAINE AT FORT KENT
Fort Kent, Maine

- **State-supported** 4-year, founded 1878, part of University of Maine System
- **Calendar** semesters
- **Degrees** associate and bachelor's
- **Rural** 52-acre campus
- **Endowment** $1.6 million
- **Coed,** 897 undergraduate students, 66% full-time, 64% women, 36% men
- **Moderately difficult** entrance level, 83% of applicants were admitted

Undergraduates 592 full-time, 305 part-time. Students come from 18 states and territories, 12 other countries, 32% are from out of state, 0.2% African American, 0.2% Asian American or Pacific Islander, 0.2% Hispanic American, 0.8% Native American, 2% international, 18% transferred in, 11% live on campus. *Retention:* 81% of 2001 full-time freshmen returned.

Freshmen *Admission:* 288 applied, 238 admitted, 102 enrolled. *Average high school GPA:* 2.70. *Test scores:* SAT verbal scores over 500: 39%; SAT math scores over 500: 37%; SAT verbal scores over 600: 8%; SAT math scores over 600: 7%.

Faculty *Total:* 36. *Student/faculty ratio:* 14:1.

Majors Behavioral sciences; biology; business administration; computer science; criminal justice/law enforcement administration; education; education (K-12); elementary education; English; environmental science; forest products technology; forestry; French; human services; liberal arts and sciences/liberal studies; nursing; public administration; social sciences.

Academic Programs *Special study options:* academic remediation for entering students, advanced placement credit, distance learning, double majors, English as a second language, external degree program, honors programs, independent study, internships, part-time degree program, services for LD students, student-designed majors, summer session for credit.

Library Waneta Blake Library plus 1 other with 64,898 titles, 382 serial subscriptions, 3,858 audiovisual materials, an OPAC, a Web page.

Computers on Campus 100 computers available on campus for general student use. A campuswide network can be accessed from student residence rooms and from off campus that provide access to e-mail. Internet access, online (class) registration, at least one staffed computer lab available.

Student Life *Housing Options:* coed. *Activities and Organizations:* drama/theater group, student-run newspaper, radio station, choral group, Performing Arts, Student Teachers Educational Professional Society, Student Nurses Organization, Ice Hockey Club, Dorm Council, national fraternities, national sororities. *Campus security:* controlled dormitory access, 8-hour night patrols by security personnel 11pm-7am. *Student Services:* health clinic, personal/psychological counseling.

Athletics Member NAIA. *Intercollegiate sports:* basketball M/W, cross-country running M/W, golf M/W, skiing (cross-country) M/W, skiing (downhill) M/W, soccer M/W. *Intramural sports:* baseball M, basketball M/W, cross-country running M/W, golf M/W, ice hockey M, racquetball M/W, skiing (cross-country) M/W, skiing (downhill) M/W, soccer M/W, softball M/W, table tennis M/W, tennis M/W, volleyball M/W, weight lifting M/W.

Standardized Tests *Recommended:* SAT I and SAT II or ACT (for admission).

Costs (2001–02) *One-time required fee:* $15. *Tuition:* state resident $3290 full-time, $109 per credit hour part-time; nonresident $7980 full-time, $266 per credit hour part-time. Full-time tuition and fees vary according to course load and reciprocity agreements. Part-time tuition and fees vary according to course load and reciprocity agreements. *Required fees:* $300 full-time, $10 per credit hour. *Room and board:* $4224; room only: $2132. Room and board charges vary according to board plan. *Payment plan:* installment. *Waivers:* senior citizens and employees or children of employees.

Financial Aid Of all full-time matriculated undergraduates who enrolled in 2001, 454 applied for aid, 396 were judged to have need, 97 had their need fully met. 209 Federal Work-Study jobs (averaging $1012). 41 State and other part-time jobs (averaging $943). In 2001, 28 non-need-based awards were made. *Average percent of need met:* 87%. *Average financial aid package:* $5003. *Average need-based loan:* $3190. *Average need-based gift aid:* $3560. *Average indebtedness upon graduation:* $10,483.

Applying *Options:* common application, electronic application, early admission, early decision, deferred entrance. *Application fee:* $25. *Required:* essay or personal statement, high school transcript. *Required for some:* interview. *Recommended:* letters of recommendation. *Application deadline:* rolling (freshmen), rolling (transfers).

Admissions Contact Mr. Melik Peter Khoury, Director of Admissions, University of Maine at Fort Kent, 23 University Drive. *Phone:* 207-834-7600 Ext. 608. *Toll-free phone:* 888-TRY-UMFK. *Fax:* 207-834-7609. *E-mail:* umfkadm@maine.maine.edu.

UNIVERSITY OF MAINE AT MACHIAS
Machias, Maine

- **State-supported** 4-year, founded 1909, part of University of Maine System
- **Calendar** semesters
- **Degrees** associate and bachelor's
- **Rural** 42-acre campus
- **Endowment** $859,304
- **Coed,** 1,017 undergraduate students, 53% full-time, 69% women, 31% men
- **Moderately difficult** entrance level, 81% of applicants were admitted

Undergraduates 542 full-time, 475 part-time. Students come from 23 states and territories, 17 other countries, 22% are from out of state, 0.6% African American, 0.6% Asian American or Pacific Islander, 0.4% Hispanic American, 3% Native American, 7% international, 5% transferred in, 42% live on campus. *Retention:* 71% of 2001 full-time freshmen returned.

Freshmen *Admission:* 521 applied, 423 admitted, 169 enrolled. *Average high school GPA:* 3.10. *Test scores:* SAT verbal scores over 500: 60%; SAT math scores over 500: 58%; ACT scores over 18: 96%; SAT verbal scores over 600: 12%; SAT math scores over 600: 11%; ACT scores over 24: 38%; SAT verbal scores over 700: 3%; SAT math scores over 700: 2%; ACT scores over 30: 5%.

Faculty *Total:* 74, 50% full-time, 45% with terminal degrees. *Student/faculty ratio:* 13:1.

Majors Accounting; behavioral sciences; biology; business administration; business education; business marketing and marketing management; ecology; education; elementary education; English; environmental education; environmental science; general studies; history; hotel and restaurant management; human services; liberal arts and sciences/liberal studies; marine biology; middle school education; psychology; recreation/leisure facilities management; recreation/leisure studies; secretarial science; travel/tourism management; visual/performing arts.

Academic Programs *Special study options:* academic remediation for entering students, accelerated degree program, adult/continuing education programs, advanced placement credit, cooperative education, distance learning, double majors, external degree program, independent study, internships, off-campus study, part-time degree program, services for LD students, student-designed majors, study abroad, summer session for credit.

Library Merrill Library plus 1 other with 80,633 titles, 491 serial subscriptions, 3,259 audiovisual materials, an OPAC, a Web page.

Computers on Campus 185 computers available on campus for general student use. A campuswide network can be accessed from student residence rooms and from off campus. Internet access, online (class) registration, at least one staffed computer lab available.

Student Life *Housing Options:* coed. *Activities and Organizations:* drama/theater group, student-run radio station, choral group, national fraternities, national sororities. *Campus security:* 24-hour emergency response devices, late-night transport/escort service, controlled dormitory access, night security guard until 3:00 a.m., day security 8-5 p.m. *Student Services:* health clinic, personal/psychological counseling.

Athletics Member NAIA. *Intercollegiate sports:* basketball M/W, cross-country running M/W, lacrosse M(c)/W(c), soccer M/W, volleyball W. *Intramural sports:* basketball M/W, football M/W, ice hockey M/W, racquetball M/W, softball M/W, table tennis M/W, tennis M/W, volleyball M/W.

Standardized Tests *Required for some:* SAT I or ACT (for admission).

Costs (2001–02) *One-time required fee:* $15. *Tuition:* state resident $3270 full-time, $109 per credit hour part-time; nonresident $8250 full-time, $275 per credit hour part-time. Full-time tuition and fees vary according to course load and reciprocity agreements. Part-time tuition and fees vary according to course load and reciprocity agreements. *Required fees:* $485 full-time. *Room and board:* $4644. *Payment plans:* installment, deferred payment. *Waivers:* senior citizens and employees or children of employees.

Financial Aid Of all full-time matriculated undergraduates who enrolled in 2001, 491 applied for aid, 460 were judged to have need, 95 had their need fully met. 198 Federal Work-Study jobs (averaging $1024). 199 State and other part-time jobs (averaging $1327). *Average percent of need met:* 83%. *Average financial aid package:* $6322. *Average need-based loan:* $3040. *Average need-based gift aid:* $4404. *Average indebtedness upon graduation:* $14,775.

Applying *Options:* common application, electronic application, early admission, early action, deferred entrance. *Application fee:* $25. *Required:* essay or personal statement, high school transcript, 1 letter of recommendation. *Required for some:* minimum 2.0 GPA. *Recommended:* 2 letters of recommendation, interview. *Application deadline:* rolling (freshmen), rolling (transfers). *Notification:* continuous (freshmen).

Admissions Contact Mr. David Baldwin, Director of Admissions, University of Maine at Machias, 9 O'Brien Avenue, Machias, ME 04654. *Phone:* 207-255-1318. *Toll-free phone:* 888-GOTOUMM. *Fax:* 207-255-1363. *E-mail:* admissions@acad.umm.maine.edu.

UNIVERSITY OF MAINE AT PRESQUE ISLE

Presque Isle, Maine

- **State-supported** 4-year, founded 1903, part of University of Maine System
- **Calendar** semesters
- **Degrees** certificates, associate, and bachelor's
- **Small-town** 150-acre campus
- **Endowment** $938,310
- **Coed,** 1,367 undergraduate students, 70% full-time, 64% women, 36% men
- **Minimally difficult** entrance level, 90% of applicants were admitted

Undergraduates 953 full-time, 414 part-time. Students come from 26 states and territories, 6 other countries, 5% are from out of state, 0.3% African American, 0.9% Asian American or Pacific Islander, 0.7% Hispanic American, 3% Native American, 16% international, 9% transferred in, 27% live on campus. *Retention:* 64% of 2001 full-time freshmen returned.

Freshmen *Admission:* 300 applied, 270 admitted, 232 enrolled. *Average high school GPA:* 3.0.

Faculty *Total:* 118, 52% full-time, 56% with terminal degrees. *Student/faculty ratio:* 14:1.

Majors Accounting; applied art; art; art education; athletic training/sports medicine; behavioral sciences; biology; business administration; communications; creative writing; criminal justice/law enforcement administration; education; elementary education; English; environmental science; fine/studio arts; forest management; French; geology; health education; history; international relations; liberal arts and sciences/liberal studies; mathematics; medical laboratory technician; nursing; nutrition studies; physical education; political science; recreation/leisure studies; science education; secondary education; social work; sociology.

Academic Programs *Special study options:* academic remediation for entering students, accelerated degree program, adult/continuing education programs, advanced placement credit, distance learning, double majors, honors programs, independent study, internships, off-campus study, part-time degree program, services for LD students, student-designed majors, study abroad, summer session for credit.

Library UMPI Library with 239,410 titles, 416 serial subscriptions, 1,281 audiovisual materials, an OPAC, a Web page.

Computers on Campus 90 computers available on campus for general student use. A campuswide network can be accessed from off campus. Internet access, online (class) registration, at least one staffed computer lab available.

Student Life *Housing Options:* coed. *Activities and Organizations:* drama/theater group, student-run newspaper, radio station, choral group, Student Senate, OAPI-Outdoor Adventure Program International, Student Activities Board, Student Organization of Social Work, Campus Crusade for Christ, national fraternities, national sororities. *Campus security:* student patrols, late-night transport/escort service, crime prevention programs, lighted pathways. *Student Services:* health clinic, personal/psychological counseling.

Athletics Member NAIA. *Intercollegiate sports:* baseball M, basketball M/W, cross-country running M/W, golf M, soccer M/W, softball W, volleyball W. *Intramural sports:* archery M/W, badminton M/W, basketball M/W, bowling M/W, cross-country running M/W, football M/W, ice hockey M/W, skiing (downhill) M/W, soccer M/W, softball M/W, table tennis M/W, tennis M/W, track and field M/W, volleyball M/W, weight lifting M/W.

Standardized Tests *Required for some:* SAT I or ACT (for admission).

Costs (2001–02) *One-time required fee:* $15. *Tuition:* state resident $3270 full-time, $109 per credit hour part-time; nonresident $7980 full-time, $266 per credit hour part-time. Full-time tuition and fees vary according to course load and reciprocity agreements. Part-time tuition and fees vary according to course load and reciprocity agreements. *Required fees:* $430 full-time, $6 per credit hour, $20 per credit hour part-time. *Room and board:* $4264; room only: $2206. Room and board charges vary according to board plan. *Payment plans:* installment, deferred payment. *Waivers:* minority students, senior citizens, and employees or children of employees.

Financial Aid Of all full-time matriculated undergraduates who enrolled in 2001, 755 applied for aid, 676 were judged to have need, 264 had their need fully met. 257 Federal Work-Study jobs (averaging $1533). In 2001, 68 non-need-based awards were made. *Average percent of need met:* 88%. *Average financial aid package:* $6719. *Average need-based loan:* $2830. *Average need-based gift aid:* $4399. *Average indebtedness upon graduation:* $11,251.

Applying *Options:* common application, electronic application, early admission, deferred entrance. *Application fee:* $25. *Required:* essay or personal statement, high school transcript, minimum 2.0 GPA. *Required for some:* 1 letter of recommendation, interview. *Application deadline:* rolling (freshmen), rolling (transfers). *Notification:* continuous (freshmen).

Admissions Contact University of Maine at Presque Isle, 181 Main Street, Presque Isle, ME 04769. *Phone:* 207-768-9536. *Fax:* 207-768-9608. *E-mail:* infoumpi@polaris.umpi.maine.edu.

UNIVERSITY OF NEW ENGLAND

Biddeford, Maine

- **Independent** comprehensive, founded 1831
- **Calendar** semesters
- **Degrees** certificates, associate, bachelor's, master's, first professional, post-master's, and postbachelor's certificates
- **Small-town** 410-acre campus
- **Endowment** $18.8 million
- **Coed,** 1,389 undergraduate students, 79% full-time, 76% women, 24% men
- **Moderately difficult** entrance level, 76% of applicants were admitted

Undergraduates 1,100 full-time, 289 part-time. Students come from 34 states and territories, 3 other countries, 53% are from out of state, 0.8% African American, 0.8% Asian American or Pacific Islander, 0.9% Hispanic American, 0.1% Native American, 0.4% international, 8% transferred in, 35% live on campus.

Freshmen *Admission:* 1,432 applied, 1,090 admitted, 321 enrolled. *Average high school GPA:* 3.14. *Test scores:* SAT verbal scores over 500: 65%; SAT math scores over 500: 65%; SAT verbal scores over 600: 17%; SAT math scores over 600: 19%; SAT verbal scores over 700: 1%.

Faculty *Total:* 210, 62% full-time. *Student/faculty ratio:* 16:1.

Majors American studies; art education; biochemistry; biology; business administration; dental hygiene; developmental/child psychology; education; elementary education; English; environmental biology; environmental science; health science; health services administration; history; humanities; human services; individual/family development; liberal arts and sciences/liberal studies; marine biology; medical laboratory technician; medical laboratory technology; medical technology; nursing; occupational therapy; organizational behavior; physical therapy; physician assistant; physiological psychology/psychobiology; pre-dentistry; pre-law; pre-medicine; pre-veterinary studies; psychology; science education; secondary education; social sciences; sport/fitness administration.

University of New England (continued)

Academic Programs *Special study options:* academic remediation for entering students, accelerated degree program, adult/continuing education programs, advanced placement credit, cooperative education, distance learning, double majors, English as a second language, honors programs, independent study, internships, part-time degree program, services for LD students, student-designed majors, study abroad, summer session for credit. *ROTC:* Army (c). *Unusual degree programs:* 3-2 physician assistant.

Library Ketchum Library plus 1 other with 46,030 titles, 1,210 serial subscriptions, 9,536 audiovisual materials, an OPAC, a Web page.

Computers on Campus 76 computers available on campus for general student use. A campuswide network can be accessed from off campus. Internet access, at least one staffed computer lab available.

Student Life *Housing:* on-campus residence required through sophomore year. *Options:* coed, women-only. *Activities and Organizations:* student-run newspaper, choral group, Student Senate, Earth's Eco, Campus Programming Board, Rotoract, outing club. *Campus security:* 24-hour patrols, late-night transport/escort service, controlled dormitory access. *Student Services:* health clinic, personal/psychological counseling.

Athletics Member NCAA. All Division III. *Intercollegiate sports:* basketball M/W, cross-country running M/W, lacrosse M, soccer M/W, softball W, volleyball W. *Intramural sports:* badminton M/W, basketball M/W, field hockey W, lacrosse W, racquetball M/W, skiing (cross-country) M/W, soccer M/W, softball M/W, table tennis M/W, tennis M/W, volleyball M/W, weight lifting M/W.

Standardized Tests *Required:* SAT I or ACT (for admission).

Costs (2001–02) *Comprehensive fee:* $24,030 includes full-time tuition ($16,740), mandatory fees ($520), and room and board ($6770). Part-time tuition: $600 per credit. Part-time tuition and fees vary according to course load. *Room and board:* Room and board charges vary according to housing facility. *Payment plans:* installment, deferred payment. *Waivers:* employees or children of employees.

Financial Aid Of all full-time matriculated undergraduates who enrolled in 2001, 969 applied for aid, 894 were judged to have need, 125 had their need fully met. 348 Federal Work-Study jobs (averaging $1409). In 2001, 134 non-need-based awards were made. *Average percent of need met:* 71%. *Average financial aid package:* $13,024. *Average need-based loan:* $4954. *Average need-based gift aid:* $3508. *Average non-need based aid:* $5966. *Average indebtedness upon graduation:* $17,500.

Applying *Options:* early decision, deferred entrance. *Application fee:* $40. *Required:* high school transcript, 2 letters of recommendation. *Required for some:* interview. *Recommended:* interview. *Application deadline:* rolling (freshmen), rolling (transfers). *Early decision:* 11/15. *Notification:* continuous (freshmen), 12/15 (early decision).

Admissions Contact Ms. Patricia Cribby, Dean of Admissions, University of New England, Hills Beach Road, Biddeford, ME 04005-9526. *Phone:* 207-283-0170 Ext. 2240. *Toll-free phone:* 800-477-4UNE. *E-mail:* jshae@mailbox.une.edu.

UNIVERSITY OF SOUTHERN MAINE
Portland, Maine

- **State-supported** comprehensive, founded 1878, part of University of Maine System
- **Calendar** semesters
- **Degrees** associate, bachelor's, master's, doctoral, first professional, and post-master's certificates
- **Suburban** 144-acre campus
- **Endowment** $13.4 million
- **Coed,** 8,831 undergraduate students, 50% full-time, 61% women, 39% men
- **Moderately difficult** entrance level, 75% of applicants were admitted

Combining a small-school atmosphere with the choices of a larger university, USM is just 2 hours from Boston, with access to the ocean, lakes, and ski resorts. Features include dedicated faculty members, small class sizes, a diverse student body, internships and cooperative education, a new field house and ice arena, and a dual residential campus (urban and rural). USM provides students with real value: a high-quality education at an affordable cost.

Undergraduates 4,424 full-time, 4,407 part-time. Students come from 36 states and territories, 9% are from out of state, 8% transferred in, 40% live on campus. *Retention:* 69% of 2001 full-time freshmen returned.

Freshmen *Admission:* 3,202 applied, 2,410 admitted, 1,038 enrolled. *Average high school GPA:* 2.85. *Test scores:* SAT verbal scores over 500: 61%; SAT math scores over 500: 59%; ACT scores over 18: 85%; SAT verbal scores over 600: 17%; SAT math scores over 600: 14%; ACT scores over 24: 17%; SAT verbal scores over 700: 2%; SAT math scores over 700: 1%.

Faculty *Total:* 696, 57% full-time, 41% with terminal degrees. *Student/faculty ratio:* 13:1.

Majors Accounting; anthropology; art; art education; athletic training/sports medicine; biology; biotechnology research; business administration; chemistry; classics; communications; computer science; criminology; economics; electrical engineering; English; environmental health; environmental science; French; geography; geology; health science; Hispanic-American studies; history; industrial arts; international relations; linguistics; mass communications; mathematics; modern languages; music; music (general performance); music teacher education; nursing; philosophy; physics; political science; psychology; recreational therapy; Russian/Slavic studies; social sciences; social work; sociology; theater arts/drama; trade/industrial education; women's studies.

Academic Programs *Special study options:* academic remediation for entering students, adult/continuing education programs, advanced placement credit, cooperative education, double majors, English as a second language, external degree program, honors programs, independent study, internships, off-campus study, part-time degree program, services for LD students, student-designed majors, study abroad, summer session for credit. *ROTC:* Air Force (c).

Library University of Southern Maine Library plus 4 others with 620,000 titles, 7,600 serial subscriptions, 2,500 audiovisual materials, an OPAC, a Web page.

Computers on Campus 440 computers available on campus for general student use. A campuswide network can be accessed from student residence rooms and from off campus. Internet access, online (class) registration, at least one staffed computer lab available.

Student Life *Housing Options:* coed. *Activities and Organizations:* drama/theater group, student-run newspaper, radio and television station, choral group, Outing and Ski Clubs, fraternities and sororities, Gorham Events Board, Commuter Student Group, Circle K, national fraternities, national sororities. *Campus security:* 24-hour emergency response devices and patrols, student patrols, late-night transport/escort service, controlled dormitory access, security lighting, preventative programs within residence halls. *Student Services:* health clinic, personal/psychological counseling, women's center, legal services.

Athletics Member NCAA. All Division III. *Intercollegiate sports:* baseball M, basketball M/W, cross-country running M/W, field hockey W, golf M/W, ice hockey M/W, sailing M/W, soccer M/W, softball W, tennis M/W, track and field M/W, volleyball W, wrestling M. *Intramural sports:* basketball M/W, bowling M/W, football M/W, ice hockey M/W, lacrosse M(c)/W(c), racquetball M/W, skiing (downhill) M(c)/W(c), soccer M/W, softball M/W, squash M/W, table tennis M/W, tennis M/W, volleyball M/W, weight lifting M/W.

Standardized Tests *Required:* SAT I or ACT (for admission).

Costs (2001–02) *One-time required fee:* $15. *Tuition:* state resident $3855 full-time, $129 per credit hour part-time; nonresident $10,770 full-time, $359 per credit hour part-time. Full-time tuition and fees vary according to course load, degree level, location, and reciprocity agreements. Part-time tuition and fees vary according to course load, degree level, location, and reciprocity agreements. *Required fees:* $841 full-time, $13 per credit hour. *Room and board:* $5873; room only: $2762. Room and board charges vary according to board plan, housing facility, and location. *Payment plan:* installment. *Waivers:* minority students, senior citizens, and employees or children of employees.

Financial Aid Of all full-time matriculated undergraduates who enrolled in 2001, 3688 applied for aid, 3168 were judged to have need, 940 had their need fully met. 1761 Federal Work-Study jobs (averaging $2700). In 2001, 404 non-need-based awards were made. *Average percent of need met:* 84%. *Average financial aid package:* $8494. *Average need-based loan:* $4049. *Average need-based gift aid:* $3594. *Average indebtedness upon graduation:* $18,296.

Applying *Options:* common application, electronic application, early admission, deferred entrance. *Application fee:* $50. *Required:* essay or personal statement, high school transcript, interview. *Required for some:* audition. *Recommended:* minimum 2.7 GPA, 1 letter of recommendation. *Application deadlines:* 2/1 (freshmen), 2/1 (transfers). *Notification:* continuous (freshmen).

Admissions Contact Mr. Jon Barker, Assistant Director, University of Southern Maine, 37 College Avenue, Gorham, ME 04038. *Phone:* 207-780-5724. *Toll-free phone:* 800-800-4USM Ext. 5670. *Fax:* 207-780-5640. *E-mail:* usmadm@usm.maine.edu.

MARYLAND

BALTIMORE HEBREW UNIVERSITY
Baltimore, Maryland

- **Independent** comprehensive, founded 1919
- **Calendar** semesters

- **Degrees** associate, bachelor's, master's, and doctoral
- **Urban** 2-acre campus
- **Endowment** $2.4 million
- **Coed,** 107 undergraduate students, 50% full-time, 71% women, 29% men
- **Moderately difficult** entrance level, 100% of applicants were admitted

Undergraduates 54 full-time, 53 part-time. Students come from 2 other countries, 3% African American, 5% international.

Freshmen *Admission:* 2 applied, 2 admitted, 6 enrolled.

Faculty *Total:* 30, 33% full-time, 50% with terminal degrees. *Student/faculty ratio:* 4:1.

Majors Archaeology; biblical languages/literatures; biblical studies; computer typography/composition; cultural studies; Eastern European area studies; education; Hebrew; Judaic studies; Middle Eastern studies; philosophy; rabbinical/Talmudic studies; religious education; religious studies.

Academic Programs *Special study options:* accelerated degree program, adult/continuing education programs, advanced placement credit, cooperative education, distance learning, double majors, English as a second language, honors programs, off-campus study, part-time degree program, study abroad, summer session for credit.

Library Joseph Meyerhoff Library with 100,000 titles, 250 serial subscriptions, 30,000 audiovisual materials.

Computers on Campus 15 computers available on campus for general student use. Internet access, at least one staffed computer lab available.

Student Life *Housing:* college housing not available. *Activities and Organizations:* Israeli Dance, Chug Ivri Club for Advanced Hebrew Speakers, Yiddish Club. *Campus security:* 24-hour patrols, guards on duty during class hours, patrols by security, well-lit parking lots.

Costs (2002–03) *Tuition:* $7200 full-time, $900 per course part-time. *Required fees:* $30 full-time.

Financial Aid Of all full-time matriculated undergraduates who enrolled in 2001, 80 applied for aid, 80 were judged to have need, 80 had their need fully met. *Average percent of need met:* 100%. *Average financial aid package:* $8000.

Applying *Options:* common application, early admission, deferred entrance. *Application fee:* $20. *Required:* high school transcript, interview. *Required for some:* 3 letters of recommendation. *Application deadline:* rolling (freshmen), rolling (transfers). *Notification:* continuous (freshmen).

Admissions Contact Essie Keyser, Director of Admissions, Baltimore Hebrew University, 5800 Park Heights Avenue, Baltimore, MD 21215-3996. *Phone:* 410-578-6967. *Toll-free phone:* 888-248-7420. *Fax:* 410-578-6940. *E-mail:* bhu@bhu.edu.

BALTIMORE INTERNATIONAL COLLEGE
Baltimore, Maryland

- **Independent** 4-year, founded 1972
- **Calendar** semesters
- **Degrees** certificates, associate, and bachelor's
- **Urban** 6-acre campus with easy access to Washington, DC
- **Endowment** $704,390
- **Coed,** 456 undergraduate students, 95% full-time, 46% women, 54% men
- **Minimally difficult** entrance level, 49% of applicants were admitted

Undergraduates 435 full-time, 21 part-time. Students come from 22 states and territories, 4 other countries, 44% African American, 0.9% Asian American or Pacific Islander, 5% Hispanic American, 0.2% Native American, 0.9% international, 7% transferred in, 24% live on campus.

Freshmen *Admission:* 463 applied, 228 admitted, 140 enrolled. *Average high school GPA:* 2.50.

Faculty *Total:* 34, 53% full-time, 24% with terminal degrees. *Student/faculty ratio:* 21:1.

Majors Business administration; culinary arts; hospitality management; hotel and restaurant management.

Academic Programs *Special study options:* academic remediation for entering students, accelerated degree program, adult/continuing education programs, advanced placement credit, cooperative education, double majors, honors programs, internships, off-campus study, study abroad.

Library George A. Piendak Library with 13,000 titles, 200 serial subscriptions, 1,000 audiovisual materials.

Computers on Campus 35 computers available on campus for general student use. A campuswide network can be accessed from off campus. Internet access, at least one staffed computer lab available.

Student Life *Housing:* on-campus residence required for freshman year. *Options:* coed. *Activities and Organizations:* student-run newspaper, American Culinary Federation, Beta Iota Kappa. *Campus security:* late-night transport/escort service, controlled dormitory access. *Student Services:* health clinic, personal/psychological counseling.

Standardized Tests *Required for some:* SAT I or ACT (for admission).

Costs (2002–03) *Comprehensive fee:* $22,562 includes full-time tuition ($12,742), mandatory fees ($4196), and room and board ($5624). Part-time tuition: $378 per credit hour. *Room and board:* Room and board charges vary according to housing facility. *Payment plans:* tuition prepayment, installment. *Waivers:* employees or children of employees.

Applying *Options:* common application, electronic application, deferred entrance. *Application fee:* $35. *Required:* high school transcript. *Recommended:* interview. *Application deadline:* rolling (freshmen), rolling (transfers). *Notification:* continuous until 8/15 (freshmen).

Admissions Contact Ms. Lori Makowski, Director of Admissions, Baltimore International College, Commerce Exchange, 17 Commerce Street, Baltimore, MD 21202-3230. *Phone:* 410-752-4710 Ext. 125. *Toll-free phone:* 800-624-9926 Ext. 120. *Fax:* 410-752-3730. *E-mail:* admissions@bic.edu.

BOWIE STATE UNIVERSITY
Bowie, Maryland

- **State-supported** comprehensive, founded 1865, part of University System of Maryland
- **Calendar** semesters
- **Degrees** certificates, bachelor's, master's, and doctoral
- **Small-town** 312-acre campus with easy access to Baltimore and Washington, DC
- **Endowment** $2.8 million
- **Coed,** 3,542 undergraduate students, 74% full-time, 62% women, 38% men
- **Minimally difficult** entrance level, 53% of applicants were admitted

Undergraduates 2,635 full-time, 907 part-time. Students come from 36 states and territories, 7% are from out of state, 89% African American, 1% Asian American or Pacific Islander, 1% Hispanic American, 0.3% Native American, 1% international, 14% transferred in, 26% live on campus. *Retention:* 73% of 2001 full-time freshmen returned.

Freshmen *Admission:* 2,031 applied, 1,073 admitted, 612 enrolled. *Average high school GPA:* 2.75. *Test scores:* SAT verbal scores over 500: 23%; SAT math scores over 500: 18%; SAT verbal scores over 600: 3%; SAT math scores over 600: 2%; SAT verbal scores over 700: 1%.

Faculty *Total:* 312, 50% full-time, 53% with terminal degrees. *Student/faculty ratio:* 18:1.

Majors Accounting; American government; applied mathematics; art; biology; broadcast journalism; business administration; business marketing and marketing management; computer graphics; computer/information sciences; creative writing; criminal justice/law enforcement administration; early childhood education; economics; education; elementary education; English; history; mass communications; mathematics; mathematics education; musical instrument technology; nursing; political science; psychology; science education; secondary education; social work; sociology; special education.

Academic Programs *Special study options:* academic remediation for entering students, accelerated degree program, adult/continuing education programs, advanced placement credit, cooperative education, distance learning, double majors, external degree program, honors programs, independent study, internships, off-campus study, part-time degree program, services for LD students, summer session for credit. *ROTC:* Army (b). *Unusual degree programs:* 3-2 engineering with George Washington University, University of Maryland College Park, Howard University.

Library Thurgood Marshall Library with 232,888 titles, 1,319 serial subscriptions, an OPAC, a Web page.

Computers on Campus A campuswide network can be accessed from student residence rooms and from off campus. Internet access, online (class) registration, at least one staffed computer lab available.

Student Life *Housing Options:* coed, men-only, women-only. *Activities and Organizations:* drama/theater group, student-run newspaper, radio and television station, choral group, marching band, national fraternities, national sororities. *Campus security:* 24-hour emergency response devices and patrols, student patrols, late-night transport/escort service, controlled dormitory access. *Student Services:* health clinic, personal/psychological counseling.

Athletics Member NCAA. All Division II. *Intercollegiate sports:* basketball M(s)/W(s), bowling W, cross-country running M/W, football M(s), softball W(s), track and field M(s)/W(s), volleyball W(s).

Standardized Tests *Required:* SAT I or ACT (for admission).

Costs (2001–02) *Tuition:* state resident $2941 full-time, $129 per credit part-time; nonresident $9023 full-time, $379 per credit part-time. Part-time tuition

Bowie State University (continued)
and fees vary according to course load. *Required fees:* $841 full-time, $123 per term part-time. *Room and board:* $5440; room only: $3500. Room and board charges vary according to board plan and housing facility. *Payment plans:* installment, deferred payment. *Waivers:* senior citizens and employees or children of employees.

Financial Aid Of all full-time matriculated undergraduates who enrolled in 2001, 2159 applied for aid, 1585 were judged to have need, 256 had their need fully met. 108 Federal Work-Study jobs (averaging $2180). In 2001, 231 non-need-based awards were made. *Average percent of need met:* 66%. *Average financial aid package:* $7124. *Average need-based loan:* $3810. *Average need-based gift aid:* $3887. *Average non-need based aid:* $4290. *Average indebtedness upon graduation:* $18,951.

Applying *Options:* electronic application. *Application fee:* $40. *Required:* high school transcript, minimum 2.2 GPA. *Required for some:* letters of recommendation. *Recommended:* letters of recommendation. *Application deadlines:* 4/1 (freshmen), 4/1 (transfers). *Notification:* continuous (freshmen).

Admissions Contact Shingiral Chanaiwa, Coordinator of Undergraduate Enrollment, Bowie State University, 14000 Jericho Park Road, Henry Building, Bowie, MD 20715-9465. *Phone:* 301-860-3425. *Toll-free phone:* 877-772-6943. *Fax:* 301-860-3438. *E-mail:* dkiah@bowiestate.edu.

CAPITOL COLLEGE
Laurel, Maryland

- **Independent** comprehensive, founded 1964
- **Calendar** semesters
- **Degrees** certificates, associate, bachelor's, master's, and postbachelor's certificates
- **Suburban** 52-acre campus with easy access to Baltimore and Washington, DC
- **Endowment** $3.0 million
- **Coed,** 630 undergraduate students, 51% full-time, 23% women, 77% men
- **Minimally difficult** entrance level, 90% of applicants were admitted

Capitol College specializes in focused quality degree programs that include both in-depth theory and extensive hands-on experience. A new computer science program offers students a broad range of theoretical and practical knowledge. Courses include programming with the latest computer languages, techniques, networks, and security.

Undergraduates 319 full-time, 311 part-time. Students come from 15 states and territories, 21 other countries, 14% are from out of state, 37% African American, 7% Asian American or Pacific Islander, 2% Hispanic American, 0.4% Native American, 4% international, 5% transferred in, 17% live on campus.

Freshmen *Admission:* 213 applied, 191 admitted, 61 enrolled. *Average high school GPA:* 2.74. *Test scores:* SAT verbal scores over 500: 33%; SAT math scores over 500: 56%; SAT verbal scores over 600: 2%; SAT math scores over 600: 13%; SAT verbal scores over 700: 1%; SAT math scores over 700: 1%.

Faculty *Total:* 54, 28% full-time, 24% with terminal degrees. *Student/faculty ratio:* 12:1.

Majors Computer engineering; computer engineering technology; electrical/electronic engineering technology; electrical engineering; laser/optical technology; management information systems/business data processing; telecommunications.

Academic Programs *Special study options:* academic remediation for entering students, accelerated degree program, adult/continuing education programs, advanced placement credit, cooperative education, English as a second language, part-time degree program, summer session for credit. *ROTC:* Army (c), Navy (c), Air Force (c).

Library Puente Library with 10,000 titles, 100 serial subscriptions, 117 audiovisual materials, an OPAC.

Computers on Campus 42 computers available on campus for general student use. A campuswide network can be accessed from off campus. Internet access, at least one staffed computer lab available.

Student Life *Housing Options:* coed. *Activities and Organizations:* student-run newspaper, IEEE, NSDE, SWE. *Campus security:* night security patrols. *Student Services:* personal/psychological counseling.

Athletics *Intercollegiate sports:* basketball M/W, soccer M. *Intramural sports:* basketball M, bowling M/W, football M, soccer M, table tennis M/W, volleyball M/W.

Standardized Tests *Required:* SAT I or ACT (for admission).

Costs (2001–02) *Tuition:* $14,472 full-time, $482 per semester hour part-time. Full-time tuition and fees vary according to course load and location. Part-time tuition and fees vary according to location. No tuition increase for student's term of enrollment. *Required fees:* $550 full-time, $10 per semester hour, $7 per term part-time. *Room only:* $3440. *Payment plan:* deferred payment. *Waivers:* employees or children of employees.

Financial Aid Of all full-time matriculated undergraduates who enrolled in 2001, 324 applied for aid, 304 were judged to have need, 25 had their need fully met. 34 Federal Work-Study jobs (averaging $2200). 15 State and other part-time jobs (averaging $4000). In 2001, 43 non-need-based awards were made. *Average percent of need met:* 46%. *Average financial aid package:* $7146. *Average need-based loan:* $3252. *Average need-based gift aid:* $4921.

Applying *Options:* electronic application, deferred entrance. *Application fee:* $25. *Required:* high school transcript. *Required for some:* essay or personal statement, 2 letters of recommendation, interview. *Recommended:* minimum 2.2 GPA, interview. *Application deadline:* rolling (freshmen), rolling (transfers).

Admissions Contact Director of Admissions, Capitol College, 11301 Springfield Road, Laurel, MD 20708-9759. *Phone:* 301-953-3200. *Toll-free phone:* 800-950-1992. *E-mail:* admissions@capitol-college.edu.

COLLEGE OF NOTRE DAME OF MARYLAND
Baltimore, Maryland

- **Independent Roman Catholic** comprehensive, founded 1873
- **Calendar** 4-1-4
- **Degrees** bachelor's, master's, post-master's, and postbachelor's certificates
- **Suburban** 58-acre campus
- **Endowment** $36.0 million
- **Women only,** 1,938 undergraduate students
- **Moderately difficult** entrance level, 80% of applicants were admitted

The vision of the College of Notre Dame of Maryland as it charts its 2nd century is to become a learning community of excellence for the 21st-century woman. Excellence in learning means a liberal education that liberates minds, hearts, and spirits to think critically, communicate effectively, and develop holistically. Essential components of a Notre Dame education are the integration of a global perspective and the development of leadership skills.

Undergraduates Students come from 23 states and territories, 8% are from out of state, 21% African American, 2% Asian American or Pacific Islander, 2% Hispanic American, 0.3% Native American, 2% international, 57% live on campus. *Retention:* 82% of 2001 full-time freshmen returned.

Freshmen *Admission:* 383 applied, 308 admitted. *Average high school GPA:* 3.28. *Test scores:* SAT verbal scores over 500: 67%; SAT math scores over 500: 46%; SAT verbal scores over 600: 16%; SAT math scores over 600: 13%; SAT verbal scores over 700: 3%; SAT math scores over 700: 1%.

Faculty *Total:* 90, 91% full-time, 67% with terminal degrees. *Student/faculty ratio:* 12:1.

Majors Art; biology; business administration; chemistry; classics; computer science; early childhood education; economics; education; elementary education; engineering science; English; history; human services; information sciences/systems; interdisciplinary studies; international business; international relations; liberal arts and sciences/liberal studies; mass communications; mathematics; modern languages; music; nursing; physics; physiological psychology/psychobiology; political science; pre-law; pre-medicine; pre-veterinary studies; psychology; religious studies; special education.

Academic Programs *Special study options:* accelerated degree program, adult/continuing education programs, advanced placement credit, double majors, English as a second language, honors programs, independent study, internships, off-campus study, part-time degree program, services for LD students, student-designed majors, study abroad, summer session for credit. *ROTC:* Army (c). *Unusual degree programs:* 3-2 engineering with University of Maryland College Park, Johns Hopkins University; nursing with Johns Hopkins University; radiological science with Johns Hopkins University.

Library Loyola/Notre Dame Library with an OPAC, a Web page.

Computers on Campus 80 computers available on campus for general student use. A campuswide network can be accessed from student residence rooms and from off campus that provide access to online classroom assignments and information. Internet access, at least one staffed computer lab available.

Student Life *Housing:* on-campus residence required through sophomore year. *Options:* women-only. *Activities and Organizations:* drama/theater group, student-run newspaper, radio and television station, choral group, Black Student Association, Kymry, Commuter Association, Community Service Organization, campus ministry. *Campus security:* 24-hour emergency response devices and patrols, late-night transport/escort service, controlled dormitory access, emergency call boxes. *Student Services:* health clinic, personal/psychological counseling, women's center.

Athletics Member NCAA. All Division III. *Intercollegiate sports:* basketball W, field hockey W, lacrosse W, soccer W, swimming W, tennis W, volleyball W.

Intramural sports: badminton W, basketball W, cross-country running W, field hockey W, golf W, lacrosse W, racquetball W, soccer W, softball W, swimming W, tennis W, volleyball W.

Standardized Tests *Required:* SAT I or ACT (for admission).

Costs (2001–02) *Comprehensive fee:* $25,325 includes full-time tuition ($17,600), mandatory fees ($325), and room and board ($7400). *Required fees:* $30 per term part-time. *Payment plan:* installment. *Waivers:* employees or children of employees.

Financial Aid Of all full-time matriculated undergraduates who enrolled in 2001, 493 applied for aid, 403 were judged to have need, 244 had their need fully met. 213 Federal Work-Study jobs (averaging $731). In 2001, 45 non-need-based awards were made. *Average percent of need met:* 100%. *Average financial aid package:* $15,000. *Average need-based loan:* $4075. *Average need-based gift aid:* $11,891. *Average indebtedness upon graduation:* $17,000.

Applying *Options:* common application, electronic application, early admission, early action, deferred entrance. *Application fee:* $25. *Required:* essay or personal statement, high school transcript, minimum 2.0 GPA, 2 letters of recommendation. *Recommended:* minimum 3.0 GPA, interview, resume. *Application deadline:* rolling (freshmen), rolling (transfers). *Notification:* continuous until 6/30 (freshmen), 1/1 (early action).

Admissions Contact Mrs. Karen Stakem Hornig, Vice President for Enrollment Management, College of Notre Dame of Maryland, 4701 North Charles Street, Baltimore, MD 21210. *Phone:* 410-532-5330. *Toll-free phone:* 800-435-0200 (in-state); 800-435-0300 (out-of-state). *Fax:* 410-532-6287. *E-mail:* admiss@ndm.edu.

COLUMBIA UNION COLLEGE
Takoma Park, Maryland

- **Independent Seventh-day Adventist** comprehensive, founded 1904
- **Calendar** semesters
- **Degrees** associate, bachelor's, and master's
- **Suburban** 19-acre campus with easy access to Washington, DC
- **Endowment** $4.2 million
- **Coed,** 1,069 undergraduate students, 60% full-time, 61% women, 39% men
- **Minimally difficult** entrance level, 46% of applicants were admitted

Undergraduates 641 full-time, 428 part-time. Students come from 40 states and territories, 38% are from out of state, 45% African American, 6% Asian American or Pacific Islander, 9% Hispanic American, 0.2% Native American, 4% international, 15% transferred in, 61% live on campus. *Retention:* 52% of 2001 full-time freshmen returned.

Freshmen *Admission:* 712 applied, 329 admitted, 160 enrolled. *Average high school GPA:* 3.02. *Test scores:* SAT verbal scores over 500: 39%; SAT math scores over 500: 31%; ACT scores over 18: 74%; SAT verbal scores over 600: 12%; SAT math scores over 600: 7%; ACT scores over 24: 19%; SAT verbal scores over 700: 1%.

Faculty *Total:* 50, 96% full-time, 48% with terminal degrees. *Student/faculty ratio:* 13:1.

Majors Accounting; biochemistry; biology; broadcast journalism; business administration; chemistry; computer science; early childhood education; elementary education; engineering; English; English education; exercise sciences; health services administration; history; information sciences/systems; journalism; liberal arts and sciences/liberal studies; mass communications; mathematics; mathematics education; music; music (general performance); music teacher education; nursing; political science; pre-dentistry; pre-law; pre-medicine; pre-veterinary studies; psychology; religious studies; respiratory therapy; theology.

Academic Programs *Special study options:* academic remediation for entering students, accelerated degree program, adult/continuing education programs, advanced placement credit, cooperative education, distance learning, double majors, external degree program, honors programs, independent study, internships, off-campus study, part-time degree program, student-designed majors, study abroad, summer session for credit. *Unusual degree programs:* 3-2 engineering with University of Maryland College Park.

Library Theofield G. Weis Library with 130,000 titles, 2,309 serial subscriptions, 7,500 audiovisual materials, an OPAC, a Web page.

Computers on Campus 50 computers available on campus for general student use. A campuswide network can be accessed from off campus. At least one staffed computer lab available.

Student Life *Housing:* on-campus residence required through senior year. *Options:* men-only, women-only. *Activities and Organizations:* drama/theater group, student-run newspaper, radio station, choral group, Student Association. *Campus security:* 24-hour emergency response devices, student patrols, late-night transport/escort service. *Student Services:* health clinic, personal/psychological counseling.

Athletics Member NCAA. All Division II. *Intercollegiate sports:* baseball M, basketball M(s)/W(s), cross-country running M(s)/W(s), soccer M(s)/W(s), softball W(s), track and field M(s)/W(s). *Intramural sports:* basketball M/W, cross-country running M/W, football M, golf M, gymnastics M/W, racquetball M/W, soccer M/W, track and field M/W.

Standardized Tests *Required:* SAT I or ACT (for admission).

Costs (2001–02) *Comprehensive fee:* $18,809 includes full-time tuition ($13,450), mandatory fees ($510), and room and board ($4849). Part-time tuition: $560 per semester hour. *Required fees:* $255 per term part-time. *Room and board:* College room only: $2634. *Payment plan:* installment. *Waivers:* senior citizens and employees or children of employees.

Financial Aid *Financial aid deadline:* 5/1.

Applying *Options:* early admission, deferred entrance. *Application fee:* $25. *Required:* high school transcript, minimum 2.50 GPA, 2 letters of recommendation. *Required for some:* essay or personal statement, interview. *Application deadline:* rolling (freshmen), rolling (transfers). *Notification:* continuous (freshmen).

Admissions Contact Mr. Emil John, Director of Admissions, Columbia Union College, Takoma Park, MD 20912. *Phone:* 301-891-4080. *Toll-free phone:* 800-835-4212. *Fax:* 301-891-4230. *E-mail:* enroll@cuc.edu.

COPPIN STATE COLLEGE
Baltimore, Maryland

- **State-supported** comprehensive, founded 1900, part of University System of Maryland
- **Calendar** semesters
- **Degrees** bachelor's and master's
- **Urban** 33-acre campus
- **Coed,** 3,092 undergraduate students
- **Moderately difficult** entrance level, 47% of applicants were admitted

Undergraduates Students come from 20 states and territories, 19 other countries, 95% African American, 0.2% Asian American or Pacific Islander, 0.6% Hispanic American, 0.4% Native American, 2% international, 10% live on campus.

Freshmen *Admission:* 2,270 applied, 1,078 admitted. *Average high school GPA:* 2.76.

Faculty *Total:* 202, 54% full-time. *Student/faculty ratio:* 17:1.

Majors Biology; business administration; chemistry; computer science; criminal justice/law enforcement administration; early childhood education; education; elementary education; English; history; liberal arts and sciences/liberal studies; mathematics; natural sciences; nursing; philosophy; physical education; physical therapy; pre-dentistry; pre-law; pre-medicine; psychology; science education; secondary education; social sciences; social work; special education.

Academic Programs *Special study options:* academic remediation for entering students, adult/continuing education programs, advanced placement credit, cooperative education, double majors, English as a second language, external degree program, freshman honors college, honors programs, internships, off-campus study, part-time degree program, services for LD students, summer session for credit. *ROTC:* Army (b). *Unusual degree programs:* 3-2 engineering with University of Maryland College Park.

Library Parlett L. Moore Library with 134,983 titles, 665 serial subscriptions, an OPAC.

Computers on Campus 130 computers available on campus for general student use. A campuswide network can be accessed from off campus. Internet access, at least one staffed computer lab available.

Student Life *Housing Options:* coed. *Activities and Organizations:* drama/theater group, student-run newspaper, choral group, International Students Association, class government, Nursing Students' Association, Coppin Models Fashion Club, Student Honors Association, national fraternities, national sororities. *Campus security:* 24-hour emergency response devices and patrols, late-night transport/escort service, controlled dormitory access. *Student Services:* health clinic, personal/psychological counseling.

Athletics Member NCAA. All Division I. *Intercollegiate sports:* baseball M(s), basketball M(s)/W(s), bowling M/W, cross-country running M(s)/W(s), rugby M(c), softball W, tennis M(s)/W(s), track and field M(s)/W(s), volleyball W(s), weight lifting M(s)/W(s), wrestling M(s). *Intramural sports:* basketball M/W, bowling M/W, softball W, tennis M/W, track and field M/W, volleyball W, weight lifting M/W, wrestling M.

Standardized Tests *Required:* SAT I or ACT (for admission).

Costs (2001–02) *Tuition:* state resident $2582 full-time, $117 per credit hour part-time; nonresident $7709 full-time, $270 per credit hour part-time. *Required fees:* $895 full-time, $20 per credit hour, $71 per term part-time. *Room and board:* $5734; room only: $3626.

Coppin State College (continued)

Financial Aid Of all full-time matriculated undergraduates who enrolled in 2001, 2097 applied for aid, 1798 were judged to have need, 120 had their need fully met. 100 Federal Work-Study jobs (averaging $2174). In 2001, 120 non-need-based awards were made. *Average percent of need met:* 56%. *Average financial aid package:* $6316. *Average need-based loan:* $3396. *Average need-based gift aid:* $3937. *Average non-need based aid:* $3248. *Average indebtedness upon graduation:* $13,905.

Applying *Options:* common application, electronic application, early admission, deferred entrance. *Application fee:* $35. *Required:* high school transcript. *Required for some:* 2 letters of recommendation. *Recommended:* minimum 2.5 GPA, interview. *Application deadlines:* 7/15 (freshmen), 7/15 (transfers). *Notification:* continuous (freshmen).

Admissions Contact Ms. Michelle Gross, Director of Admissions, Coppin State College, 2500 W North Avenue, Baltimore, MD 21216. *Phone:* 410-951-3600. *Toll-free phone:* 800-635-3674. *E-mail:* mgross@coppin.edu.

FROSTBURG STATE UNIVERSITY
Frostburg, Maryland

- **State-supported** comprehensive, founded 1898, part of University System of Maryland
- **Calendar** semesters
- **Degrees** bachelor's and master's
- **Small-town** 260-acre campus with easy access to Baltimore and Washington, DC
- **Endowment** $6.6 million
- **Coed,** 4,354 undergraduate students, 92% full-time, 52% women, 48% men
- **Moderately difficult** entrance level, 75% of applicants were admitted

Undergraduates 4,027 full-time, 327 part-time. Students come from 27 states and territories, 16 other countries, 12% are from out of state, 13% African American, 2% Asian American or Pacific Islander, 2% Hispanic American, 0.4% Native American, 0.4% international, 9% transferred in, 41% live on campus. *Retention:* 70% of 2001 full-time freshmen returned.

Freshmen *Admission:* 2,872 applied, 2,161 admitted, 926 enrolled. *Average high school GPA:* 3.03. *Test scores:* SAT verbal scores over 500: 49%; SAT math scores over 500: 54%; ACT scores over 18: 73%; SAT verbal scores over 600: 10%; SAT math scores over 600: 13%; ACT scores over 24: 7%; SAT verbal scores over 700: 1%; SAT math scores over 700: 1%.

Faculty *Total:* 346, 72% full-time, 85% with terminal degrees. *Student/faculty ratio:* 16:1.

Majors Accounting; actuarial science; art education; biology; business administration; business education; cartography; chemistry; computer/information sciences; criminal justice studies; dance; early childhood education; earth sciences; ecology; economics; education; electrical engineering; elementary education; English; environmental science; exercise sciences; foreign languages/literatures; geography; health services administration; history; international relations; land use management; liberal arts and sciences/liberal studies; mass communications; mathematics; mechanical engineering; music; philosophy; physical education; physics; political science; pre-law; psychology; recreation/leisure studies; secondary education; social sciences; social work; sociology; speech/rhetorical studies; theater arts/drama; visual/performing arts; wildlife management.

Academic Programs *Special study options:* adult/continuing education programs, advanced placement credit, distance learning, double majors, freshman honors college, honors programs, independent study, internships, off-campus study, part-time degree program, services for LD students, study abroad, summer session for credit. *Unusual degree programs:* 3-2 engineering with University of Maryland, College Park.

Library Lewis J. Ort Library with 256,977 titles, 3,353 serial subscriptions, 72,490 audiovisual materials, an OPAC, a Web page.

Computers on Campus 577 computers available on campus for general student use. A campuswide network can be accessed from student residence rooms and from off campus. Internet access, online (class) registration, at least one staffed computer lab available.

Student Life *Housing Options:* coed, men-only, women-only. *Activities and Organizations:* drama/theater group, student-run newspaper, radio and television station, choral group, marching band, Student Government Association, Black Student Association, Campus Activities Board, Residence Hall Association, national fraternities, national sororities. *Campus security:* 24-hour emergency response devices and patrols, student patrols, late-night transport/escort service, controlled dormitory access, bicycle patrols. *Student Services:* health clinic, personal/psychological counseling, women's center.

Athletics Member NCAA. All Division III. *Intercollegiate sports:* baseball M, basketball M/W, cross-country running M/W, field hockey W, football M, lacrosse W, soccer M/W, softball W, swimming M/W, tennis M/W, track and field M/W, volleyball W. *Intramural sports:* badminton M/W, basketball M/W, field hockey M/W, football M/W, golf M/W, lacrosse M(c)/W, racquetball M/W, rugby M(c), soccer M/W, softball M/W, squash M/W, table tennis M/W, tennis M/W, volleyball M(c)/W, water polo M/W, weight lifting M/W, wrestling M.

Standardized Tests *Required:* SAT I or ACT (for admission).

Costs (2002–03) *Tuition:* state resident $3566 full-time, $147 per credit hour part-time; nonresident $9232 full-time, $260 per credit hour part-time. Full-time tuition and fees vary according to course load and program. Part-time tuition and fees vary according to course load and program. *Required fees:* $866 full-time, $38 per credit hour, $9 per term part-time. *Room and board:* $5424; room only: $2730. Room and board charges vary according to board plan and housing facility. *Payment plans:* installment, deferred payment. *Waivers:* senior citizens and employees or children of employees.

Financial Aid Of all full-time matriculated undergraduates who enrolled in 2001, 2882 applied for aid, 2009 were judged to have need, 592 had their need fully met. 213 Federal Work-Study jobs (averaging $934). 423 State and other part-time jobs (averaging $468). In 2001, 227 non-need-based awards were made. *Average percent of need met:* 79%. *Average financial aid package:* $6395. *Average need-based loan:* $3297. *Average need-based gift aid:* $3720. *Average non-need based aid:* $3545. *Average indebtedness upon graduation:* $13,278.

Applying *Options:* electronic application, early admission. *Application fee:* $30. *Required:* high school transcript, minimum 2.0 GPA. *Required for some:* essay or personal statement. *Recommended:* letters of recommendation, interview. *Application deadline:* rolling (freshmen), rolling (transfers).

Admissions Contact Ms. Trish Gregory, Associate Director for Admissions, Frostburg State University, 101 Braddock Road, Frostburg, MD 21532-1099. *Phone:* 301-687-4201. *Fax:* 301-687-7074. *E-mail:* fsuadmissions@frostburg.edu.

GOUCHER COLLEGE
Baltimore, Maryland

- **Independent** comprehensive, founded 1885
- **Calendar** semesters
- **Degrees** bachelor's, master's, and postbachelor's certificates
- **Suburban** 287-acre campus
- **Endowment** $167.0 million
- **Coed,** 1,221 undergraduate students, 96% full-time, 72% women, 28% men
- **Moderately difficult** entrance level, 73% of applicants were admitted

Undergraduates 1,175 full-time, 46 part-time. Students come from 43 states and territories, 21 other countries, 60% are from out of state, 7% African American, 3% Asian American or Pacific Islander, 3% Hispanic American, 0.3% Native American, 1% international, 4% transferred in, 71% live on campus. *Retention:* 83% of 2001 full-time freshmen returned.

Freshmen *Admission:* 2,146 applied, 1,557 admitted, 343 enrolled. *Average high school GPA:* 3.19. *Test scores:* SAT verbal scores over 500: 92%; SAT math scores over 500: 88%; ACT scores over 18: 100%; SAT verbal scores over 600: 58%; SAT math scores over 600: 40%; ACT scores over 24: 80%; SAT verbal scores over 700: 13%; SAT math scores over 700: 5%; ACT scores over 30: 8%.

Faculty *Total:* 154, 51% full-time, 66% with terminal degrees. *Student/faculty ratio:* 10:1.

Majors American studies; architectural history; art; biology; chemistry; computer science; dance; economics; education; elementary education; English; French; history; interdisciplinary studies; international relations; management science; mass communications; mathematics; music; philosophy; physics; political science; psychology; religious studies; Russian; sociology; Spanish; theater arts/drama; women's studies.

Academic Programs *Special study options:* accelerated degree program, adult/continuing education programs, advanced placement credit, distance learning, double majors, honors programs, independent study, internships, off-campus study, part-time degree program, services for LD students, student-designed majors, study abroad. *Unusual degree programs:* 3-2 engineering with Johns Hopkins University.

Library Julia Rogers Library with 295,593 titles, 1,138 serial subscriptions, 8,532 audiovisual materials, an OPAC, a Web page.

Computers on Campus 150 computers available on campus for general student use. A campuswide network can be accessed from student residence rooms and from off campus. Internet access, at least one staffed computer lab available.

Student Life *Housing:* on-campus residence required through sophomore year. *Options:* coed, women-only. *Activities and Organizations:* drama/theater group, student-run newspaper, choral group, CAUSE (Community Auxiliary for Service), Umoja: The African Alliance, Quindecim (newspaper), BGlad, Hillel.

Campus security: 24-hour emergency response devices and patrols, late-night transport/escort service. *Student Services:* health clinic, personal/psychological counseling, women's center.

Athletics Member NCAA. All Division III. *Intercollegiate sports:* basketball M/W, cross-country running M/W, equestrian sports M/W, field hockey W, lacrosse M/W, soccer M/W, swimming M/W, tennis M/W, volleyball W. *Intramural sports:* basketball M/W, cross-country running M/W, equestrian sports M(c)/W(c), fencing M(c)/W(c), football M/W, golf M/W, racquetball M/W, soccer M/W, softball M/W(c), squash M/W, tennis M/W, volleyball M/W.

Standardized Tests *Required:* SAT I or ACT (for admission). *Recommended:* SAT II: Subject Tests (for admission), SAT II: Writing Test (for admission).

Costs (2001–02) *Comprehensive fee:* $30,050 includes full-time tuition ($22,000), mandatory fees ($300), and room and board ($7750). Part-time tuition: $780 per credit hour. Part-time tuition and fees vary according to course load. *Room and board:* College room only: $5150. Room and board charges vary according to board plan. *Payment plan:* installment. *Waivers:* adult students and employees or children of employees.

Financial Aid Of all full-time matriculated undergraduates who enrolled in 2001, 851 applied for aid, 733 were judged to have need, 166 had their need fully met. 320 State and other part-time jobs (averaging $1114). In 2001, 118 non-need-based awards were made. *Average percent of need met:* 82%. *Average financial aid package:* $16,737. *Average need-based loan:* $3549. *Average need-based gift aid:* $13,660. *Average non-need based aid:* $8500. *Average indebtedness upon graduation:* $14,500.

Applying *Options:* common application, electronic application, early admission, early decision, early action, deferred entrance. *Application fee:* $40. *Required:* essay or personal statement, high school transcript, minimum 2.0 GPA, 3 letters of recommendation. *Recommended:* minimum 3.0 GPA, interview. *Application deadlines:* 2/1 (freshmen), 4/1 (transfers). *Early decision:* 11/15. *Notification:* 4/1 (freshmen), 1/15 (early decision), 1/15 (early action).

Admissions Contact Mr. Carlton E. Surbeck III, Director of Admissions, Goucher College, 1021 Dulaney Valley Road, Baltimore, MD 21204-2794. *Phone:* 410-337-6100. *Toll-free phone:* 800-GOUCHER. *Fax:* 410-337-6354. *E-mail:* admission@goucher.edu.

GRIGGS UNIVERSITY
Silver Spring, Maryland

- **Independent Seventh-day Adventist** 4-year, founded 1990, part of Seventh-day Adventist Parochial School System
- **Calendar** continuous
- **Degrees** associate and bachelor's (offers only external degree programs)
- **Suburban** campus
- **Coed, primarily men,** 372 undergraduate students
- **Minimally difficult** entrance level

Faculty *Total:* 40, 55% with terminal degrees.

Majors Business administration; religious education; religious studies; theology.

Academic Programs *Special study options:* accelerated degree program, adult/continuing education programs, advanced placement credit, distance learning, double majors, external degree program, independent study, part-time degree program, summer session for credit.

Student Life *Housing:* college housing not available.

Costs (2001–02) *Tuition:* $5700 full-time, $190 per semester hour part-time. Full-time tuition and fees vary according to course load. *Required fees:* $60 full-time, $60 per year part-time. *Payment plan:* installment. *Waivers:* senior citizens and employees or children of employees.

Applying *Options:* common application, early admission, deferred entrance. *Application fee:* $50. *Required:* essay or personal statement, high school transcript, minimum 2.0 GPA. *Application deadline:* rolling (freshmen), rolling (transfers).

Admissions Contact Ms. Eva Michel, Enrollment Officer, Griggs University, PO Box 4437, Silver Spring, MD 20914-4437. *Phone:* 301-680-6593. *Toll-free phone:* 800-782-4769. *Fax:* 301-680-6577. *E-mail:* emichel@hsi.edu.

HOOD COLLEGE
Frederick, Maryland

- **Independent** comprehensive, founded 1893
- **Calendar** semesters
- **Degrees** bachelor's, master's, and postbachelor's certificates (also offers adult program with significant enrollment not reflected in profile)
- **Suburban** 50-acre campus with easy access to Baltimore and Washington, DC
- **Endowment** $65.3 million
- **Women only,** 784 undergraduate students, 76% full-time
- **Moderately difficult** entrance level, 74% of applicants were admitted

Undergraduates 595 full-time, 189 part-time. Students come from 20 states and territories, 22 other countries, 23% are from out of state, 12% African American, 2% Asian American or Pacific Islander, 3% Hispanic American, 0.3% Native American, 5% international, 8% transferred in, 52% live on campus. *Retention:* 85% of 2001 full-time freshmen returned.

Freshmen *Admission:* 502 applied, 372 admitted, 113 enrolled. *Average high school GPA:* 3.47. *Test scores:* SAT verbal scores over 500: 83%; SAT math scores over 500: 81%; ACT scores over 18: 95%; SAT verbal scores over 600: 42%; SAT math scores over 600: 32%; ACT scores over 24: 45%; SAT verbal scores over 700: 7%; SAT math scores over 700: 7%; ACT scores over 30: 6%.

Faculty *Total:* 179, 40% full-time, 59% with terminal degrees. *Student/faculty ratio:* 9:1.

Majors Art; biochemistry; biology; business administration; chemistry; computer/information sciences; computer science; early childhood education; economics; engineering; English; environmental science; French; German; history; Latin American studies; legal studies; mass communications; mathematics; music; philosophy; political science; pre-dentistry; pre-law; pre-medicine; pre-veterinary studies; psychology; religious studies; social work; sociology; Spanish; special education.

Academic Programs *Special study options:* academic remediation for entering students, accelerated degree program, adult/continuing education programs, advanced placement credit, double majors, English as a second language, honors programs, independent study, internships, off-campus study, part-time degree program, services for LD students, student-designed majors, study abroad, summer session for credit. *ROTC:* Army (c). *Unusual degree programs:* 3-2 engineering with George Washington University; computer science, biomedical science.

Library Beneficial-Hodson Library and Information Technology Center with 200,000 titles, 6,300 serial subscriptions, 3,293 audiovisual materials, an OPAC, a Web page.

Computers on Campus 222 computers available on campus for general student use. A campuswide network can be accessed from student residence rooms and from off campus. Internet access, at least one staffed computer lab available.

Student Life *Housing:* on-campus residence required through sophomore year. *Options:* women-only, disabled students. *Activities and Organizations:* drama/theater group, student-run newspaper, choral group, Education Club, Black Student Union, Campus Activities Board, International Club, Hood Today (newspaper). *Campus security:* 24-hour emergency response devices and patrols, late-night transport/escort service, controlled dormitory access, residence hall security. *Student Services:* health clinic, personal/psychological counseling, women's center.

Athletics Member NCAA. All Division III. *Intercollegiate sports:* basketball W, cross-country running W(c), field hockey W, lacrosse W, soccer W, softball W, swimming W, tennis W, volleyball W. *Intramural sports:* football W, golf W.

Standardized Tests *Required:* SAT I or ACT (for admission). *Recommended:* SAT II: Subject Tests (for admission).

Costs (2001–02) *Comprehensive fee:* $26,020 includes full-time tuition ($18,795), mandatory fees ($325), and room and board ($6900). Part-time tuition: $540 per credit. Part-time tuition and fees vary according to course load. *Required fees:* $100 per term part-time. *Room and board:* College room only: $3600. Room and board charges vary according to board plan. *Payment plans:* tuition prepayment, installment, deferred payment. *Waivers:* employees or children of employees.

Financial Aid Of all full-time matriculated undergraduates who enrolled in 2001, 562 applied for aid, 404 were judged to have need, 160 had their need fully met. 142 Federal Work-Study jobs (averaging $1662). In 2001, 154 non-need-based awards were made. *Average percent of need met:* 88%. *Average financial aid package:* $15,409. *Average need-based loan:* $4223. *Average need-based gift aid:* $12,164. *Average non-need based aid:* $13,586. *Average indebtedness upon graduation:* $15,642. *Financial aid deadline:* 2/15.

Applying *Options:* common application, electronic application, early admission, early action, deferred entrance. *Application fee:* $35. *Required:* essay or personal statement, high school transcript, 2 letters of recommendation. *Recommended:* minimum 3.0 GPA, interview. *Application deadline:* 2/15 (freshmen), rolling (transfers). *Notification:* 3/15 (freshmen), 1/1 (early action).

Admissions Contact Dr. Susan Hallenbeck, Dean of Admissions, Hood College, 401 Rosemont Avenue, Frederick, MD 21701. *Phone:* 301-696-3400. *Toll-free phone:* 800-922-1599. *Fax:* 301-696-3819. *E-mail:* admissions@hood.edu.

JOHNS HOPKINS UNIVERSITY
Baltimore, Maryland

- **Independent** university, founded 1876
- **Calendar** 4-1-4
- **Degrees** certificates, diplomas, bachelor's, master's, doctoral, first professional, post-master's, and postbachelor's certificates
- **Urban** 140-acre campus with easy access to Washington, DC
- **Endowment** $1.8 billion
- **Coed,** 3,961 undergraduate students, 99% full-time, 41% women, 59% men
- **Most difficult** entrance level, 34% of applicants were admitted

Since its founding in 1876 as America's first great research university, Johns Hopkins University has been attracting brilliant thinkers. Johns Hopkins puts the power of education directly into the hands of students through opportunities to engage with professors and peers in the areas of humanities, social and behavioral sciences, engineering, and natural sciences. This, combined with a small undergraduate enrollment, affords unparalleled exposure to creative investigation and discovery beginning in the freshman year.

Undergraduates 3,933 full-time, 28 part-time. Students come from 55 states and territories, 53 other countries, 78% are from out of state, 4% African American, 19% Asian American or Pacific Islander, 2% Hispanic American, 0.2% Native American, 8% international, 0.5% transferred in, 54% live on campus. *Retention:* 96% of 2001 full-time freshmen returned.

Freshmen *Admission:* 9,127 applied, 3,132 admitted, 1,015 enrolled. *Average high school GPA:* 3.84. *Test scores:* SAT verbal scores over 500: 99%; SAT math scores over 500: 100%; ACT scores over 18: 100%; SAT verbal scores over 600: 91%; SAT math scores over 600: 97%; ACT scores over 24: 97%; SAT verbal scores over 700: 47%; SAT math scores over 700: 67%; ACT scores over 30: 66%.

Faculty *Total:* 1,104, 37% full-time, 80% with terminal degrees. *Student/faculty ratio:* 9:1.

Majors American studies; anthropology; applied mathematics; art history; behavioral sciences; bioengineering; biological/physical sciences; biology; biophysics; business; chemical engineering; chemistry; civil engineering; classics; cognitive psychology/psycholinguistics; computer engineering; computer/information sciences; creative writing; earth sciences; East Asian studies; economics; electrical engineering; electroencephalograph technology; engineering; engineering mechanics; English; environmental engineering; environmental science; film studies; French; geography; German; history; history of science and technology; industrial/manufacturing engineering; interdisciplinary studies; international relations; Italian; Latin American studies; liberal arts and sciences/liberal studies; liberal arts and studies related; literature; materials engineering; materials science; mathematics; mechanical engineering; Middle Eastern studies; music; music (general performance); music teacher education; music theory and composition; natural sciences; neuroscience; nursing; philosophy; physics; physiological psychology/psychobiology; political science; psychology; public administration; public health; social sciences; sociology; Spanish.

Academic Programs *Special study options:* accelerated degree program, adult/continuing education programs, advanced placement credit, cooperative education, distance learning, double majors, English as a second language, honors programs, independent study, internships, off-campus study, part-time degree program, services for LD students, student-designed majors, study abroad, summer session for credit. *ROTC:* Army (b), Air Force (c). *Unusual degree programs:* 3-2 international studies with Johns Hopkins University, School of Advanced International Studies (Washington, DC); education.

Library Milton S. Eisenhower Library plus 6 others with 3.4 million titles, 23,043 serial subscriptions, 295,952 audiovisual materials, an OPAC, a Web page.

Computers on Campus 185 computers available on campus for general student use. A campuswide network can be accessed from student residence rooms and from off campus. Internet access, at least one staffed computer lab available.

Student Life *Housing:* on-campus residence required through sophomore year. *Options:* coed, men-only, women-only, disabled students. *Activities and Organizations:* drama/theater group, student-run newspaper, radio station, choral group, marching band, The Outdoors Club, The Hopkins Organization for Programs, The Barn Stormers, Inter Asian Council, national fraternities, national sororities. *Campus security:* 24-hour emergency response devices and patrols, student patrols, late-night transport/escort service, controlled dormitory access. *Student Services:* health clinic, personal/psychological counseling, women's center.

Athletics Member NCAA. All Division III except men's and women's lacrosse (Division I). *Intercollegiate sports:* baseball M, basketball M/W, crew M/W, cross-country running M/W, fencing M/W, field hockey W, football M, golf M(c)/W(c), ice hockey M(c), lacrosse M(s)/W(s), rugby M(c)/W(c), soccer M/W, softball W(c), swimming M/W, table tennis M(c)/W(c), tennis M/W, track and field M/W, volleyball W, water polo M, wrestling M. *Intramural sports:* basketball M/W, football M/W, lacrosse M/W, soccer M/W, tennis M(c)/W(c), volleyball M/W.

Standardized Tests *Required:* SAT II: Writing Test (for admission).

Costs (2002–03) *Comprehensive fee:* $36,560 includes full-time tuition ($27,190), mandatory fees ($500), and room and board ($8870). Part-time tuition: $906 per credit. *Room and board:* College room only: $5195. Room and board charges vary according to board plan and housing facility. *Payment plans:* tuition prepayment, installment. *Waivers:* employees or children of employees.

Financial Aid Of all full-time matriculated undergraduates who enrolled in 2001, 2337 applied for aid, 1763 were judged to have need, 1454 had their need fully met. In 2001, 235 non-need-based awards were made. *Average percent of need met:* 95%. *Average financial aid package:* $24,285. *Average need-based loan:* $3986. *Average need-based gift aid:* $18,894. *Average non-need based aid:* $13,968. *Average indebtedness upon graduation:* $16,300. *Financial aid deadline:* 2/15.

Applying *Options:* common application, electronic application, early admission, early decision, deferred entrance. *Application fee:* $60. *Required:* essay or personal statement, high school transcript, 1 letter of recommendation. *Required for some:* interview. *Application deadlines:* 1/1 (freshmen), 3/15 (transfers). *Early decision:* 11/15. *Notification:* 3/31 (freshmen), 12/15 (early decision).

Admissions Contact Johns Hopkins University, 140 Garland Hall, 3400 North Charles Street, Baltimore, MD 21218-2699. *Phone:* 410-516-8341. *Fax:* 410-516-6025. *E-mail:* gotojhu@jhu.edu.

LOYOLA COLLEGE IN MARYLAND
Baltimore, Maryland

- **Independent Roman Catholic (Jesuit)** comprehensive, founded 1852
- **Calendar** semesters
- **Degrees** bachelor's, master's, doctoral, and post-master's certificates
- **Urban** 89-acre campus with easy access to Washington, DC
- **Endowment** $146.4 million
- **Coed,** 3,477 undergraduate students, 98% full-time, 57% women, 43% men
- **Moderately difficult** entrance level, 61% of applicants were admitted

Undergraduates 3,408 full-time, 69 part-time. Students come from 41 states and territories, 6 other countries, 77% are from out of state, 5% African American, 2% Asian American or Pacific Islander, 1% Hispanic American, 0.0% Native American, 0.2% international, 2% transferred in, 75% live on campus. *Retention:* 89% of 2001 full-time freshmen returned.

Freshmen *Admission:* 6,577 applied, 4,014 admitted, 884 enrolled. *Average high school GPA:* 3.40. *Test scores:* SAT verbal scores over 500: 96%; SAT math scores over 500: 96%; SAT verbal scores over 600: 53%; SAT math scores over 600: 60%; SAT verbal scores over 700: 9%; SAT math scores over 700: 9%.

Faculty *Total:* 413, 54% full-time. *Student/faculty ratio:* 13:1.

Majors Accounting; applied mathematics; art; biology; business; chemistry; classics; communications; computer/information sciences; creative writing; economics; education; electrical engineering; elementary education; engineering; English; finance; French; German; history; interdisciplinary studies; international business; mathematics; philosophy; physics; political science; psychology; religious studies; sociology; Spanish; special education; speech-language pathology.

Academic Programs *Special study options:* accelerated degree program, advanced placement credit, double majors, honors programs, independent study, internships, off-campus study, part-time degree program, services for LD students, study abroad, summer session for credit. *ROTC:* Army (b), Air Force (c).

Library Loyola/Notre Dame Library with 380,000 titles, 2,100 serial subscriptions, 30,000 audiovisual materials, an OPAC, a Web page.

Computers on Campus 292 computers available on campus for general student use. A campuswide network can be accessed from student residence rooms and from off campus. Internet access, at least one staffed computer lab available.

Student Life *Housing:* on-campus residence required for freshman year. *Options:* coed. *Activities and Organizations:* drama/theater group, student-run newspaper, choral group. *Campus security:* 24-hour emergency response devices and patrols, late-night transport/escort service, controlled dormitory access. *Student Services:* health clinic, personal/psychological counseling.

Athletics Member NCAA. All Division I.

Standardized Tests *Required:* SAT I (for admission).

Costs (2001–02) *Comprehensive fee:* $30,900 includes full-time tuition ($22,930), mandatory fees ($570), and room and board ($7400). Full-time tuition and fees vary according to student level. Part-time tuition: $400 per credit. *Required fees:* $25 per term part-time. *Room and board:* College room only: $5400. Room and board charges vary according to board plan. *Waivers:* employees or children of employees.

Financial Aid Of all full-time matriculated undergraduates who enrolled in 2001, 2061 applied for aid, 1534 were judged to have need, 1474 had their need fully met. 348 Federal Work-Study jobs (averaging $1890). 65 State and other part-time jobs (averaging $8172). In 2001, 572 non-need-based awards were made. *Average percent of need met:* 98%. *Average financial aid package:* $15,280. *Average need-based loan:* $4940. *Average need-based gift aid:* $8440. *Average non-need based aid:* $8360. *Average indebtedness upon graduation:* $15,210. *Financial aid deadline:* 2/10.
Applying *Options:* common application, early admission, deferred entrance. *Application fee:* $30. *Required:* essay or personal statement, high school transcript. *Recommended:* interview. *Application deadlines:* 1/15 (freshmen), 7/15 (transfers). *Notification:* 4/15 (freshmen).
Admissions Contact Mr. William Bossemeyer, Dean of Admissions, Loyola College in Maryland, 4501 North Charles Street, Baltimore, MD 21210. *Phone:* 410-617-2000 Ext. 2252. *Toll-free phone:* 800-221-9107 Ext. 2252. *Fax:* 410-617-2176.

MAPLE SPRINGS BAPTIST BIBLE COLLEGE AND SEMINARY
Capitol Heights, Maryland

Admissions Contact Ms. Mazie Murphy, Assistant Director of Admissions and Records, Maple Springs Baptist Bible College and Seminary, 4130 Belt Road, Capitol Heights, MD 20743. *Phone:* 301-736-3631. *Fax:* 301-735-6507.

MARYLAND INSTITUTE, COLLEGE OF ART
Baltimore, Maryland

- **Independent** comprehensive, founded 1826
- **Calendar** semesters
- **Degrees** bachelor's, master's, and postbachelor's certificates
- **Urban** 12-acre campus with easy access to Washington, DC
- **Endowment** $32.7 million
- **Coed,** 1,195 undergraduate students, 99% full-time, 61% women, 39% men
- **Very difficult** entrance level, 46% of applicants were admitted

Undergraduates 1,178 full-time, 17 part-time. Students come from 46 states and territories, 50 other countries, 74% are from out of state, 4% African American, 6% Asian American or Pacific Islander, 4% Hispanic American, 0.5% Native American, 5% international, 5% transferred in, 88% live on campus. *Retention:* 82% of 2001 full-time freshmen returned.
Freshmen *Admission:* 1,693 applied, 775 admitted, 321 enrolled. *Average high school GPA:* 3.58. *Test scores:* SAT verbal scores over 500: 82%; SAT math scores over 500: 73%; SAT verbal scores over 600: 41%; SAT math scores over 600: 31%; SAT verbal scores over 700: 8%; SAT math scores over 700: 3%.
Faculty *Total:* 231, 49% full-time, 36% with terminal degrees. *Student/faculty ratio:* 10:1.
Majors Art; art education; ceramic arts; drawing; fine/studio arts; graphic design/commercial art/illustration; interior design; multimedia; painting; photography; printmaking; sculpture; textile arts; visual/performing arts.
Academic Programs *Special study options:* academic remediation for entering students, accelerated degree program, adult/continuing education programs, advanced placement credit, distance learning, double majors, independent study, internships, off-campus study, services for LD students, student-designed majors, study abroad, summer session for credit. *ROTC:* Army (c).
Library Decker Library plus 1 other with 50,000 titles, 305 serial subscriptions, 4,600 audiovisual materials, an OPAC, a Web page.
Computers on Campus 240 computers available on campus for general student use. A campuswide network can be accessed from student residence rooms and from off campus that provide access to email. Internet access, at least one staffed computer lab available.
Student Life *Housing Options:* coed, disabled students. *Activities and Organizations:* drama/theater group, student-run newspaper, Anime Club, soccer teams, Black Student Union, Koinonia (Christian Fellowship), Hip-Hop Club. *Campus security:* 24-hour emergency response devices and patrols, student patrols, late-night transport/escort service, controlled dormitory access, self-defense education, 24-hour building security, safety awareness programs, campus patrols by city police. *Student Services:* health clinic, personal/psychological counseling, legal services.
Athletics *Intramural sports:* soccer M/W.
Standardized Tests *Required for some:* SAT I or ACT (for admission).
Costs (2001–02) *Comprehensive fee:* $27,720 includes full-time tuition ($20,640), mandatory fees ($440), and room and board ($6640). Part-time tuition: $860 per credit. *Required fees:* $220 per term part-time. *Room and board:* College room only: $4600. Room and board charges vary according to board plan and housing facility. *Payment plan:* installment. *Waivers:* employees or children of employees.
Applying *Options:* electronic application, early admission, early decision, deferred entrance. *Application fee:* $45. *Required:* essay or personal statement, high school transcript, art portfolio. *Recommended:* 3 letters of recommendation, interview. *Application deadlines:* 1/15 (freshmen), 3/15 (transfers). *Early decision:* 11/15. *Notification:* 3/15 (freshmen), 12/15 (early decision).
Admissions Contact Mr. Hans Ever, Director of Undergraduate Admission, Maryland Institute, College of Art, 1300 Mount Royal Avenue, Baltimore, MD 21217-4191. *Phone:* 410-225-2222. *Fax:* 410-225-2337. *E-mail:* admissions@mica.edu.

MORGAN STATE UNIVERSITY
Baltimore, Maryland

- **State-supported** university, founded 1867
- **Calendar** semesters
- **Degrees** bachelor's, master's, and doctoral
- **Urban** 140-acre campus with easy access to Washington, DC
- **Coed,** 6,543 undergraduate students, 82% full-time, 57% women, 43% men
- **Moderately difficult** entrance level, 35% of applicants were admitted

Undergraduates 5,340 full-time, 1,203 part-time. Students come from 47 states and territories, 30 other countries, 92% African American, 0.3% Asian American or Pacific Islander, 0.5% Hispanic American, 0.2% Native American, 5% international, 4% transferred in, 30% live on campus. *Retention:* 76% of 2001 full-time freshmen returned.
Freshmen *Admission:* 11,112 applied, 3,911 admitted, 1,315 enrolled. *Average high school GPA:* 3.10.
Faculty *Total:* 576, 63% full-time. *Student/faculty ratio:* 14:1.
Majors Accounting; African-American studies; African studies; art; art history; behavioral sciences; biology; business administration; business economics; business education; business marketing and marketing management; chemistry; civil engineering; computer science; dietetics; economics; education; electrical engineering; elementary education; engineering; engineering physics; English; finance; health education; history; home economics; hospitality management; hotel and restaurant management; human ecology; industrial/manufacturing engineering; information sciences/systems; management information systems/business data processing; mass communications; mathematics; medical laboratory technician; medical technology; mental health/rehabilitation; music; nutrition science; philosophy; physical education; physics; political science; pre-dentistry; pre-law; pre-medicine; psychology; recreation/leisure studies; religious studies; secondary education; social work; sociology; speech/rhetorical studies; sport/fitness administration; telecommunications; theater arts/drama.
Academic Programs *Special study options:* academic remediation for entering students, accelerated degree program, adult/continuing education programs, advanced placement credit, cooperative education, honors programs, independent study, internships, off-campus study, part-time degree program, services for LD students, summer session for credit. *ROTC:* Army (b).
Library Morris Soper Library with 333,101 titles, 2,526 serial subscriptions, an OPAC.
Computers on Campus 65 computers available on campus for general student use. A campuswide network can be accessed from student residence rooms and from off campus that provide access to engineering lab supercomputer. Internet access, online (class) registration, at least one staffed computer lab available.
Student Life *Housing Options:* coed. *Activities and Organizations:* drama/theater group, student-run newspaper, radio station, choral group, marching band, Student Government Association, choir, band, national fraternities, national sororities. *Campus security:* 24-hour emergency response devices and patrols, late-night transport/escort service, controlled dormitory access. *Student Services:* health clinic, personal/psychological counseling.
Athletics Member NCAA. All Division I except football (Division I-AA). *Intercollegiate sports:* basketball M(s)/W(s), bowling W, cross-country running M(s)/W(s), softball W, tennis M(s)/W(s), track and field M(s)/W(s), volleyball W. *Intramural sports:* badminton M/W, basketball M/W, bowling M/W, cross-country running M/W, field hockey M/W, football M, golf M/W, gymnastics M/W, racquetball M/W, soccer M/W, softball M/W, swimming M/W, table tennis M/W, tennis M/W, track and field M/W, volleyball M/W, weight lifting M/W.
Standardized Tests *Required:* SAT I or ACT (for admission).
Costs (2001–02) *Tuition:* state resident $3150 full-time, $143 per credit part-time; nonresident $9360 full-time, $332 per credit part-time. *Required fees:* $1358 full-time, $40 per credit. *Room and board:* $5980; room only: $3900.

Morgan State University (continued)
Room and board charges vary according to board plan and housing facility. *Payment plans:* installment, deferred payment. *Waivers:* senior citizens and employees or children of employees.

Applying *Options:* common application, electronic application, early admission, deferred entrance. *Application fee:* $25. *Required:* high school transcript, minimum 2.0 GPA. *Required for some:* 2 letters of recommendation, interview. *Recommended:* essay or personal statement. *Application deadline:* rolling (freshmen), rolling (transfers). *Notification:* continuous (freshmen).

Admissions Contact Mr. Edwin T. Johnson, Director of Admissions and Recruitment, Morgan State University, 1700 East Cold Spring Lane, Baltimore, MD 21251. *Phone:* 443-885-3000. *Toll-free phone:* 800-332-6674.

Mount Saint Mary's College and Seminary
Emmitsburg, Maryland

- **Independent Roman Catholic** comprehensive, founded 1808
- **Calendar** semesters
- **Degrees** bachelor's, master's, first professional, and postbachelor's certificates
- **Rural** 1400-acre campus with easy access to Baltimore and Washington, DC
- **Endowment** $30.1 million
- **Coed,** 1,542 undergraduate students, 86% full-time, 59% women, 41% men
- **Moderately difficult** entrance level, 79% of applicants were admitted

The Mount has expanded the concentrations in the business administration major to include sports management as well as finance, international business, management, and marketing. The sports management concentration includes courses in sport history, marketing, economics, and a required internship in the field. More than one half of Mount students enhance their majors with internships and study abroad programs. The Mount is proud to award academic scholarships ranging from $7000 to more than $19,000 per year for qualified students.

Undergraduates 1,329 full-time, 213 part-time. Students come from 30 states and territories, 10 other countries, 44% are from out of state, 5% African American, 2% Asian American or Pacific Islander, 3% Hispanic American, 0.2% Native American, 0.8% international, 3% transferred in, 83% live on campus. *Retention:* 80% of 2001 full-time freshmen returned.

Freshmen *Admission:* 1,946 applied, 1,542 admitted, 355 enrolled. *Average high school GPA:* 3.20. *Test scores:* SAT verbal scores over 500: 73%; SAT math scores over 500: 72%; SAT verbal scores over 600: 22%; SAT math scores over 600: 21%; SAT verbal scores over 700: 2%; SAT math scores over 700: 2%.

Faculty *Total:* 166, 61% full-time, 64% with terminal degrees. *Student/faculty ratio:* 14:1.

Majors Accounting; biochemistry; biology; business administration; chemistry; communications; computer science; creative writing; economics; elementary education; English; French; general studies; German; history; interdisciplinary studies; international relations; mathematics; philosophy; political science; psychology; secondary education; sociology; Spanish; speech/rhetorical studies; theology; visual/performing arts.

Academic Programs *Special study options:* academic remediation for entering students, accelerated degree program, adult/continuing education programs, advanced placement credit, cooperative education, double majors, English as a second language, honors programs, independent study, internships, off-campus study, part-time degree program, services for LD students, student-designed majors, study abroad, summer session for credit. *ROTC:* Army (c). *Unusual degree programs:* 3-2 nursing with Johns Hopkins University.

Library Phillips Library with 207,557 titles, 920 serial subscriptions, 4,440 audiovisual materials, an OPAC, a Web page.

Computers on Campus 118 computers available on campus for general student use. A campuswide network can be accessed from student residence rooms and from off campus. Internet access, online (class) registration, at least one staffed computer lab available.

Student Life *Housing:* on-campus residence required for freshman year. *Options:* coed. *Activities and Organizations:* drama/theater group, student-run newspaper, radio station, choral group, Campus Ministry, Rugby Team Club, Ice Hockey Club, Circle K, International Affairs Organization. *Campus security:* 24-hour emergency response devices and patrols, late-night transport/escort service, controlled dormitory access. *Student Services:* health clinic, personal/psychological counseling.

Athletics Member NCAA. All Division I. *Intercollegiate sports:* baseball M(s), basketball M(s)/W(s), cross-country running M(s)/W(s), equestrian sports M(c)/W(c), golf M(s)/W(s), ice hockey M(c), lacrosse M(s)/W(s), rugby M(c)/W(c), soccer M(s)/W(s), softball W(s), tennis M(s)/W(s), track and field M(s)/W(s). *Intramural sports:* basketball M/W, field hockey W, football M/W, racquetball M/W, skiing (downhill) M/W, softball M, swimming M(c)/W(c), tennis M/W, track and field M/W, volleyball M/W, weight lifting M/W.

Standardized Tests *Required:* SAT I or ACT (for admission).

Costs (2001–02) *Comprehensive fee:* $25,740 includes full-time tuition ($18,480), mandatory fees ($200), and room and board ($7060). Part-time tuition: $616 per credit. Part-time tuition and fees vary according to course load. *Required fees:* $5 per credit. *Room and board:* College room only: $3500. Room and board charges vary according to board plan. *Payment plans:* tuition prepayment, installment. *Waivers:* employees or children of employees.

Financial Aid Of all full-time matriculated undergraduates who enrolled in 2001, 973 applied for aid, 825 were judged to have need, 264 had their need fully met. 226 Federal Work-Study jobs (averaging $1295). In 2001, 306 non-need-based awards were made. *Average percent of need met:* 76%. *Average financial aid package:* $13,650. *Average need-based loan:* $4800. *Average need-based gift aid:* $9530. *Average non-need based aid:* $8550. *Average indebtedness upon graduation:* $15,860.

Applying *Options:* early admission, early action, deferred entrance. *Application fee:* $35. *Required:* high school transcript, minimum 2.0 GPA, 1 letter of recommendation. *Recommended:* essay or personal statement, minimum 3.0 GPA, interview. *Application deadlines:* rolling (freshmen), 6/1 (transfers). *Notification:* continuous (freshmen), 12/15 (early action).

Admissions Contact Mr. Stephen Neitz, Executive Director of Admissions and Financial Aid, Mount Saint Mary's College and Seminary, 16300 Old Emmitsburg Road, Emmitsburg, MD 21727. *Phone:* 301-447-5214. *Toll-free phone:* 800-448-4347. *Fax:* 301-447-5860. *E-mail:* admissions@msmary.edu.

Ner Israel Rabbinical College
Baltimore, Maryland

Admissions Contact Rabbi Berel Weisbord, Dean of Admissions, Ner Israel Rabbinical College, Mount Wilson Lane, Baltimore, MD 21208. *Phone:* 410-484-7200.

Peabody Conservatory of Music of The Johns Hopkins University
Baltimore, Maryland

- **Independent** comprehensive, founded 1857
- **Calendar** semesters
- **Degrees** bachelor's, master's, and doctoral
- **Urban** campus with easy access to Washington, DC
- **Endowment** $62.0 million
- **Coed,** 343 undergraduate students, 95% full-time, 49% women, 51% men
- **Very difficult** entrance level, 42% of applicants were admitted

Undergraduates 326 full-time, 17 part-time. Students come from 40 states and territories, 22 other countries, 92% are from out of state, 4% African American, 11% Asian American or Pacific Islander, 4% Hispanic American, 16% international, 5% transferred in. *Retention:* 98% of 2001 full-time freshmen returned.

Freshmen *Admission:* 608 applied, 255 admitted, 68 enrolled. *Test scores:* SAT verbal scores over 500: 81%; SAT math scores over 500: 90%; SAT verbal scores over 600: 53%; SAT math scores over 600: 49%; SAT verbal scores over 700: 10%; SAT math scores over 700: 14%.

Faculty *Total:* 166, 20% with terminal degrees. *Student/faculty ratio:* 4:1.

Majors Audio engineering; music; music (piano and organ performance); music teacher education; music (voice and choral/opera performance); stringed instruments; wind/percussion instruments.

Academic Programs *Special study options:* academic remediation for entering students, accelerated degree program, advanced placement credit, double majors, English as a second language, honors programs, independent study, internships, off-campus study, services for LD students.

Library Arthur Friedheim Library with 76,606 titles, 255 serial subscriptions, 21,693 audiovisual materials, an OPAC, a Web page.

Computers on Campus 35 computers available on campus for general student use. A campuswide network can be accessed from student residence rooms and from off campus that provide access to word processing, music processing. Internet access, at least one staffed computer lab available.

Student Life *Housing:* on-campus residence required through sophomore year. *Options:* coed, women-only. *Activities and Organizations:* choral group. *Campus* *security:* 24-hour emergency response devices, late-night transport/escort service, controlled dormitory access. *Student Services:* health clinic, personal/psychological counseling.

Standardized Tests *Required for some:* SAT I or ACT (for admission).

Costs (2001–02) *One-time required fee:* $500. *Comprehensive fee:* $32,775 includes full-time tuition ($23,700), mandatory fees ($275), and room and board ($8800). Part-time tuition: $680 per semester hour. Part-time tuition and fees vary according to course load. *Room and board:* Room and board charges vary according to board plan and housing facility. *Waivers:* employees or children of employees.

Financial Aid Of all full-time matriculated undergraduates who enrolled in 2001, 221 applied for aid, 195 were judged to have need, 39 had their need fully met. 83 Federal Work-Study jobs (averaging $990). 110 State and other part-time jobs (averaging $484). In 2001, 85 non-need-based awards were made. *Average percent of need met:* 71%. *Average financial aid package:* $16,145. *Average need-based loan:* $4773. *Average need-based gift aid:* $5010. *Average non-need based aid:* $10,540. *Average indebtedness upon graduation:* $17,573.

Applying *Application fee:* $55. *Required:* high school transcript, 3 letters of recommendation, interview, audition. *Required for some:* essay or personal statement. *Application deadlines:* 12/15 (freshmen), 12/15 (transfers). *Notification:* 4/1 (freshmen).

Admissions Contact Mr. David Lane, Director of Admissions, Peabody Conservatory of Music of The Johns Hopkins University, 1 East Mount Vernon Place, Baltimore, MD 21202-2397. *Phone:* 410-659-8110. *Toll-free phone:* 800-368-2521.

ST. JOHN'S COLLEGE
Annapolis, Maryland

- **Independent** comprehensive, founded 1784
- **Calendar** semesters
- **Degrees** bachelor's and master's
- **Small-town** 36-acre campus with easy access to Baltimore and Washington, DC
- **Endowment** $59.0 million
- **Coed,** 477 undergraduate students, 99% full-time, 45% women, 55% men
- **Moderately difficult** entrance level, 78% of applicants were admitted

Undergraduates 474 full-time, 3 part-time. Students come from 47 states and territories, 8 other countries, 85% are from out of state, 0.4% African American, 3% Asian American or Pacific Islander, 3% Hispanic American, 0.4% Native American, 2% international, 75% live on campus. *Retention:* 81% of 2001 full-time freshmen returned.

Freshmen *Admission:* 464 applied, 363 admitted, 112 enrolled. *Test scores:* SAT verbal scores over 500: 99%; SAT math scores over 500: 94%; SAT verbal scores over 600: 89%; SAT math scores over 600: 71%; SAT verbal scores over 700: 54%; SAT math scores over 700: 18%.

Faculty *Total:* 72, 92% full-time, 71% with terminal degrees. *Student/faculty ratio:* 8:1.

Majors Interdisciplinary studies; liberal arts and sciences/liberal studies; western civilization.

Academic Programs *Special study options:* internships, off-campus study.

Library Greenfield Library plus 1 other with 92,806 titles, 114 serial subscriptions, 1,873 audiovisual materials, an OPAC, a Web page.

Computers on Campus 16 computers available on campus for general student use. A campuswide network can be accessed from off campus. Internet access, at least one staffed computer lab available.

Student Life *Housing:* on-campus residence required for freshman year. *Options:* coed. *Activities and Organizations:* drama/theater group, student-run newspaper, choral group, King William Players, Project Politaca, Political Forum, Student Committee on Instruction, rowing club. *Campus security:* 24-hour emergency response devices and patrols, late-night transport/escort service, controlled dormitory access. *Student Services:* health clinic, personal/psychological counseling.

Athletics *Intercollegiate sports:* crew M(c)/W(c), fencing M(c)/W(c). *Intramural sports:* badminton M/W, basketball M/W, fencing M/W, football M, golf M/W, racquetball M/W, sailing M/W, soccer M/W, softball M/W, squash M/W, table tennis M/W, tennis M/W, track and field M/W, volleyball M/W, weight lifting M/W.

Standardized Tests *Required for some:* SAT I or ACT (for admission). *Recommended:* SAT I or ACT (for admission).

Costs (2001–02) *Comprehensive fee:* $32,760 includes full-time tuition ($25,790), mandatory fees ($200), and room and board ($6770). *Room and board:* College room only: $3400. Room and board charges vary according to board plan. *Payment plans:* tuition prepayment, installment. *Waivers:* employees or children of employees.

Financial Aid Of all full-time matriculated undergraduates who enrolled in 2001, 278 applied for aid, 268 were judged to have need, 240 had their need fully met. *Average percent of need met:* 90%. *Average financial aid package:* $21,512. *Average need-based loan:* $4860. *Average need-based gift aid:* $16,635. *Average indebtedness upon graduation:* $18,125.

Applying *Options:* common application, early admission, deferred entrance. *Required:* essay or personal statement, high school transcript, 2 letters of recommendation. *Recommended:* interview. *Application deadline:* rolling (freshmen), rolling (transfers). *Notification:* continuous (freshmen).

Admissions Contact Mr. John Christensen, Director of Admissions, St. John's College, PO Box 2800, 60 College Avenue, Annapolis, MD 21404. *Phone:* 410-626-2522. *Toll-free phone:* 800-727-9238. *Fax:* 410-269-7916. *E-mail:* admissions@sjca.edu.

ST. MARY'S COLLEGE OF MARYLAND
St. Mary's City, Maryland

- **State-supported** 4-year, founded 1840, part of Maryland State Colleges and Universities System
- **Calendar** semesters
- **Degree** bachelor's
- **Rural** 275-acre campus
- **Endowment** $23.7 million
- **Coed,** 1,688 undergraduate students, 90% full-time, 61% women, 39% men
- **Moderately difficult** entrance level, 71% of applicants were admitted

St. Mary's College, with its distinctive identity as Maryland's Public Honors College, is emerging as one of the finest liberal arts and sciences colleges in the country. A lively academic atmosphere combines with the serene yet stunning natural beauty of the riverfront campus to create a challenging and memorable college experience. Recent construction includes the completion of a new Campus Center, baseball field complex, and suite-style residence halls.

Undergraduates 1,524 full-time, 164 part-time. Students come from 31 states and territories, 24 other countries, 14% are from out of state, 7% African American, 4% Asian American or Pacific Islander, 2% Hispanic American, 0.5% Native American, 0.8% international, 4% transferred in, 78% live on campus. *Retention:* 87% of 2001 full-time freshmen returned.

Freshmen *Admission:* 1,447 applied, 1,027 admitted, 456 enrolled. *Average high school GPA:* 3.48. *Test scores:* SAT verbal scores over 500: 93%; SAT math scores over 500: 93%; SAT verbal scores over 600: 65%; SAT math scores over 600: 54%; SAT verbal scores over 700: 18%; SAT math scores over 700: 8%.

Faculty *Total:* 184, 65% full-time, 76% with terminal degrees. *Student/faculty ratio:* 11:1.

Majors Anthropology; art; biology; chemistry; computer science; economics; educational psychology; English; history; interdisciplinary studies; mathematics; modern languages; music; natural sciences; philosophy; physics; political science; psychology; public policy analysis; religious studies; sociology; theater arts/drama.

Academic Programs *Special study options:* adult/continuing education programs, advanced placement credit, cooperative education, double majors, freshman honors college, honors programs, independent study, internships, off-campus study, part-time degree program, services for LD students, student-designed majors, study abroad, summer session for credit.

Library Baltimore Hall with 116,267 titles, 7,286 serial subscriptions, 15,612 audiovisual materials, an OPAC, a Web page.

Computers on Campus 165 computers available on campus for general student use. A campuswide network can be accessed from student residence rooms and from off campus that provide access to e-mail. Internet access, at least one staffed computer lab available.

Student Life *Housing Options:* coed, men-only, women-only, disabled students. *Activities and Organizations:* drama/theater group, student-run newspaper, radio and television station, choral group, For Goodness Sake (community service), Economics Club, Amnesty International, Black Student Union, Inter Varsity Christian Fellowship. *Campus security:* 24-hour emergency response devices and patrols, student patrols, late-night transport/escort service, controlled dormitory access. *Student Services:* health clinic, personal/psychological counseling.

Athletics Member NCAA. All Division III. *Intercollegiate sports:* baseball M, basketball M/W, crew M(c)/W(c), fencing M(c)/W(c), field hockey W, golf M(c)/W(c), lacrosse M/W, rugby M(c)/W(c), sailing M/W, soccer M/W, swimming M/W, tennis M/W, volleyball M(c)/W, wrestling M(c). *Intramural sports:*

St. Mary's College of Maryland (continued)
basketball M/W, bowling M/W, cross-country running M(c)/W(c), equestrian sports M(c)/W(c), football M/W, lacrosse M/W, sailing M/W, soccer M/W, softball M/W, swimming M/W, tennis M/W, track and field M(c)/W(c), volleyball M/W, water polo M/W.

Standardized Tests *Required:* SAT I or ACT (for admission).

Costs (2002–03) *Tuition:* state resident $6925 full-time, $110 per credit part-time; nonresident $12,260 full-time, $110 per credit part-time. Part-time tuition and fees vary according to course load. *Required fees:* $1157 full-time, $250 per term part-time. *Room and board:* $6613; room only: $3775. Room and board charges vary according to board plan, housing facility, and student level. *Payment plan:* installment. *Waivers:* senior citizens and employees or children of employees.

Financial Aid Of all full-time matriculated undergraduates who enrolled in 2001, 1089 applied for aid, 626 were judged to have need. 65 Federal Work-Study jobs (averaging $1100). 105 State and other part-time jobs (averaging $1000). In 2001, 419 non-need-based awards were made. *Average percent of need met:* 69%. *Average financial aid package:* $6908. *Average need-based loan:* $4000. *Average need-based gift aid:* $5208. *Average non-need based aid:* $4500. *Average indebtedness upon graduation:* $15,500. *Financial aid deadline:* 2/15.

Applying *Options:* early admission, early decision. *Application fee:* $25. *Required:* essay or personal statement, high school transcript, minimum 2.0 GPA. *Recommended:* 2 letters of recommendation, interview. *Application deadlines:* 1/15 (freshmen), 3/15 (transfers). *Early decision:* 12/1 (for plan 1), 1/15 (for plan 2). *Notification:* 4/1 (freshmen), 1/1 (early decision plan 1), 2/15 (early decision plan 2).

Admissions Contact Mr. Richard J. Edgar, Director of Admissions, St. Mary's College of Maryland, 18952 East Fisher Road, St. Mary's City, MD 20686-3001. *Phone:* 240-895-5000. *Toll-free phone:* 800-492-7181. *Fax:* 240-895-5001. *E-mail:* admissions@smcm.edu.

SALISBURY UNIVERSITY
Salisbury, Maryland

- **State-supported** comprehensive, founded 1925, part of University System of Maryland
- **Calendar** 4-1-4
- **Degrees** bachelor's and master's
- **Small-town** 140-acre campus
- **Endowment** $14.7 million
- **Coed,** 6,060 undergraduate students, 87% full-time, 57% women, 43% men
- **Moderately difficult** entrance level, 52% of applicants were admitted

Salisbury University, formerly Salisbury State University, is a rarity among public institutions in Maryland—all 4 of its schools are endowed. These multimillion-dollar gifts have expanded scholarships and other opportunities for students. With an emphasis on active learning, including undergraduate research, internships, community service, and travel abroad, SU is earning a national reputation for educating undergraduates. Publications such as *U.S. News & World Report, Kiplinger's,* and *Princeton Review* rank SU among the nation's best schools.

Undergraduates 5,280 full-time, 780 part-time. Students come from 34 states and territories, 28 other countries, 18% are from out of state, 6% African American, 2% Asian American or Pacific Islander, 1% Hispanic American, 0.3% Native American, 0.7% international, 9% transferred in, 32% live on campus. *Retention:* 83% of 2001 full-time freshmen returned.

Freshmen *Admission:* 4,978 applied, 2,598 admitted, 942 enrolled. *Average high school GPA:* 3.38. *Test scores:* SAT verbal scores over 500: 80%; SAT math scores over 500: 87%; SAT verbal scores over 600: 24%; SAT math scores over 600: 32%; SAT verbal scores over 700: 2%; SAT math scores over 700: 2%.

Faculty *Total:* 454, 64% full-time, 56% with terminal degrees. *Student/faculty ratio:* 18:1.

Majors Accounting; art; athletic training/sports medicine; biology; business administration; business marketing and marketing management; chemistry; communications; computer/information sciences; economics; education; elementary education; English; environmental health; French; geography; health education; health/physical education; history; liberal arts and sciences/liberal studies; management information systems/business data processing; mathematics; medical technology; music; nursing; peace/conflict studies; philosophy; physical education; physics; political science; psychology; respiratory therapy; secondary education; social work; sociology; Spanish; theater arts/drama.

Academic Programs *Special study options:* academic remediation for entering students, adult/continuing education programs, advanced placement credit, double majors, English as a second language, honors programs, independent study, internships, off-campus study, part-time degree program, services for LD students, student-designed majors, study abroad, summer session for credit. *ROTC:* Army (c). *Unusual degree programs:* 3-2 engineering with University of Maryland College Park, Old Dominion University, Widener University; social work with University of Maryland Eastern Shore; environmental marine science with University of Maryland Eastern Shore.

Library Blackwell Library plus 1 other with 249,710 titles, 1,762 serial subscriptions, 10,663 audiovisual materials, an OPAC, a Web page.

Computers on Campus 200 computers available on campus for general student use. A campuswide network can be accessed from student residence rooms and from off campus. Internet access, at least one staffed computer lab available.

Student Life *Housing Options:* coed, men-only, women-only. *Activities and Organizations:* drama/theater group, student-run newspaper, radio and television station, choral group, Student Government Association, campus radio station, Programming Board, Greek Council, Union of African-American Students, national fraternities, national sororities. *Campus security:* 24-hour emergency response devices and patrols, student patrols, late-night transport/escort service, controlled dormitory access. *Student Services:* health clinic, personal/psychological counseling.

Athletics Member NCAA. All Division III. *Intercollegiate sports:* baseball M, basketball M/W, cross-country running M/W, field hockey W, football M, lacrosse M/W, soccer M/W, softball W, swimming M/W, tennis M/W, track and field M/W, volleyball W. *Intramural sports:* basketball M/W, cross-country running M/W, fencing M(c)/W(c), field hockey W(c), football M/W, golf M(c)/W(c), ice hockey M(c), lacrosse M(c)/W, racquetball M/W, rugby M(c)/W(c), sailing M(c)/W(c), soccer M(c)/W(c), softball M/W, swimming M/W, tennis M/W, volleyball M(c)/W, water polo M/W, weight lifting M(c)/W(c).

Standardized Tests *Required:* SAT I or ACT (for admission).

Costs (2002–03) *Tuition:* state resident $3346 full-time, $140 per credit hour part-time; nonresident $9030 full-time, $370 per credit hour part-time. *Required fees:* $1310 full-time, $4 per credit hour. *Room and board:* $6340; room only: $3300. Room and board charges vary according to board plan and housing facility. *Payment plan:* installment. *Waivers:* senior citizens and employees or children of employees.

Financial Aid Of all full-time matriculated undergraduates who enrolled in 2001, 3107 applied for aid, 2061 were judged to have need, 532 had their need fully met. 84 Federal Work-Study jobs (averaging $1305). In 2001, 331 non-need-based awards were made. *Average percent of need met:* 66%. *Average financial aid package:* $5362. *Average need-based loan:* $3464. *Average need-based gift aid:* $3115. *Average non-need based aid:* $2770. *Average indebtedness upon graduation:* $14,000.

Applying *Options:* common application, electronic application, early admission, early decision. *Application fee:* $30. *Required:* high school transcript, minimum 2.0 GPA. *Application deadline:* 1/15 (freshmen), rolling (transfers). *Early decision:* 12/15. *Notification:* 3/15 (freshmen), 1/15 (early decision).

Admissions Contact Mrs. Jane H. Dané, Dean of Admissions, Salisbury University, Admissions House, 1101 Camden Avenue, Salisbury, MD 21801. *Phone:* 410-543-6161. *Toll-free phone:* 888-543-0148. *Fax:* 410-546-6016. *E-mail:* admissions@salisbury.edu.

SOJOURNER-DOUGLASS COLLEGE
Baltimore, Maryland

- **Independent** comprehensive, founded 1980
- **Calendar** trimesters
- **Degrees** bachelor's and master's (offers only evening and weekend programs)
- **Urban** 15-acre campus
- **Coed, primarily women,** 1,060 undergraduate students, 67% full-time, 84% women, 16% men
- **Noncompetitive** entrance level

Undergraduates 714 full-time, 346 part-time. 98% African American, 0.8% Hispanic American, 0.1% Native American. *Retention:* 78% of 2001 full-time freshmen returned.

Freshmen *Admission:* 169 enrolled.

Faculty *Total:* 136, 26% full-time, 24% with terminal degrees. *Student/faculty ratio:* 10:1.

Majors Accounting; behavioral sciences; business administration; city/community/regional planning; criminal justice/law enforcement administration; early childhood education; economics; gerontology; health services administration; hospitality management; human resources management; human services; individual/family development; psychology; public administration; social work; sociology; urban studies.

Academic Programs *Special study options:* academic remediation for entering students, accelerated degree program, adult/continuing education programs, external degree program, honors programs, internships, part-time degree program, services for LD students, student-designed majors, summer session for credit.

Library 10,000 titles, 25 serial subscriptions.

Computers on Campus 16 computers available on campus for general student use. A campuswide network can be accessed from off campus. Internet access, at least one staffed computer lab available.

Student Life *Housing:* college housing not available. *Student Services:* personal/psychological counseling.

Costs (2001–02) *Tuition:* $4794 full-time. *Required fees:* $190 full-time. *Payment plans:* installment, deferred payment. *Waivers:* employees or children of employees.

Applying *Options:* common application, deferred entrance. *Required:* essay or personal statement, high school transcript, 2 letters of recommendation, interview, resume. *Application deadline:* rolling (freshmen), rolling (transfers).

Admissions Contact Ms. Diana Samuels, Manager, Office of Admissions, Sojourner-Douglass College, 500 North Caroline Street, Baltimore, MD 21205-1814. *Phone:* 410-276-0306 Ext. 251. *Fax:* 410-675-1810.

TOWSON UNIVERSITY
Towson, Maryland

- **State-supported** comprehensive, founded 1866, part of University System of Maryland
- **Calendar** 4-1-4
- **Degrees** bachelor's, master's, doctoral, post-master's, and postbachelor's certificates
- **Suburban** 321-acre campus with easy access to Baltimore and Washington, DC
- **Coed,** 13,959 undergraduate students, 84% full-time, 60% women, 40% men
- **Moderately difficult** entrance level, 59% of applicants were admitted

Undergraduates 11,757 full-time, 2,202 part-time. Students come from 46 states and territories, 92 other countries, 18% are from out of state, 10% African American, 3% Asian American or Pacific Islander, 2% Hispanic American, 0.3% Native American, 3% international, 11% transferred in, 25% live on campus. *Retention:* 82% of 2001 full-time freshmen returned.

Freshmen *Admission:* 9,448 applied, 5,550 admitted, 1,927 enrolled. *Average high school GPA:* 3.43. *Test scores:* SAT verbal scores over 500: 75%; SAT math scores over 500: 80%; SAT verbal scores over 600: 20%; SAT math scores over 600: 24%; SAT verbal scores over 700: 2%; SAT math scores over 700: 2%.

Faculty *Total:* 1,219, 47% full-time, 52% with terminal degrees. *Student/faculty ratio:* 18:1.

Majors Accounting; alcohol/drug abuse counseling; American studies; anthropology; art; art education; athletic training/sports medicine; biochemistry; biological/physical sciences; biology; business administration; business administration/management related; chemistry; communications; computer/information sciences; dance; early childhood education; ecology; economics; elementary education; English; exercise sciences; family/consumer studies; French; geography; geology; German; gerontology; health science; health services administration; history; information sciences/systems; interdisciplinary studies; international relations; mass communications; mathematics; molecular biology; music; music teacher education; nursing; occupational therapy; philosophy; physical education; physics; political science; psychology; radio/television broadcasting technology; religious studies; social sciences; social sciences and history related; sociology; Spanish; special education; speech-language pathology; speech-language pathology/audiology; sport/fitness administration; theater arts/drama; urban studies; women's studies.

Academic Programs *Special study options:* academic remediation for entering students, adult/continuing education programs, advanced placement credit, cooperative education, distance learning, double majors, English as a second language, freshman honors college, honors programs, independent study, internships, off-campus study, part-time degree program, services for LD students, student-designed majors, study abroad, summer session for credit. *ROTC:* Army (c). *Unusual degree programs:* 3-2 engineering with University of Maryland College Park; law with University of Baltimore.

Library Cook Library with 363,430 titles, 2,227 serial subscriptions, an OPAC, a Web page.

Computers on Campus 1013 computers available on campus for general student use. A campuswide network can be accessed from student residence rooms and from off campus. Internet access, at least one staffed computer lab available.

Student Life *Housing Options:* coed, disabled students. *Activities and Organizations:* drama/theater group, student-run newspaper, radio and television station, choral group, marching band, Black Student Union, Student Government Association, Habitat for Humanity, Circle K, University Residence Government, national fraternities, national sororities. *Campus security:* 24-hour emergency response devices and patrols, late-night transport/escort service, controlled dormitory access. *Student Services:* health clinic, personal/psychological counseling, women's center.

Athletics Member NCAA. All Division I except football (Division I-AA). *Intercollegiate sports:* baseball M(s), basketball M(s)/W(s), cross-country running M(s)/W(s), field hockey W(s), golf M(s), gymnastics W(s), lacrosse M(s)/W(s), soccer M(s)/W(s), softball W(s), swimming M(s)/W(s), tennis M(s)/W(s), track and field M(s)/W(s), volleyball M/W(s). *Intramural sports:* archery M(c)/W(c), badminton M(c)/W(c), basketball M/W, bowling M(c)/W(c), equestrian sports M(c)/W(c), football M/W, golf M(c)/W(c), ice hockey M, lacrosse M/W, racquetball M(c)/W(c), rugby M, skiing (downhill) M/W, soccer M/W(c), softball M/W, table tennis M/W, tennis M/W, volleyball M/W, water polo M(c)/W(c), wrestling M.

Standardized Tests *Required:* SAT I or ACT (for admission).

Costs (2001–02) *Tuition:* state resident $3605 full-time, $156 per credit part-time; nonresident $10,491 full-time, $384 per credit part-time. *Required fees:* $1379 full-time, $51 per credit. *Room and board:* $6030; room only: $3480. Room and board charges vary according to board plan and housing facility. *Payment plan:* installment. *Waivers:* senior citizens and employees or children of employees.

Financial Aid Of all full-time matriculated undergraduates who enrolled in 2001, 6822 applied for aid, 4626 were judged to have need, 2071 had their need fully met. In 2001, 1360 non-need-based awards were made. *Average percent of need met:* 78%. *Average financial aid package:* $6920. *Average need-based loan:* $3972. *Average need-based gift aid:* $3843. *Average non-need based aid:* $4117. *Average indebtedness upon graduation:* $14,960.

Applying *Options:* electronic application, early admission, deferred entrance. *Application fee:* $35. *Required:* high school transcript. *Required for some:* interview. *Recommended:* essay or personal statement, minimum 2.75 GPA, letters of recommendation, interview. *Application deadline:* 5/1 (freshmen), rolling (transfers). *Notification:* 10/1 (freshmen).

Admissions Contact Ms. Louise Shulack, Director of Admissions, Towson University, 8000 York Road, Towson, MD 21252. *Phone:* 410-704-3687. *Toll-free phone:* 888-4TOWSON. *Fax:* 410-830-3030. *E-mail:* admissions@towson.edu.

UNITED STATES NAVAL ACADEMY
Annapolis, Maryland

- **Federally supported** 4-year, founded 1845
- **Calendar** semesters
- **Degree** bachelor's
- **Small-town** 329-acre campus with easy access to Baltimore and Washington, DC
- **Endowment** $36.3 million
- **Coed,** 4,297 undergraduate students, 100% full-time, 15% women, 85% men
- **Very difficult** entrance level, 13% of applicants were admitted

Undergraduates 4,297 full-time. Students come from 54 states and territories, 17 other countries, 96% are from out of state, 6% African American, 4% Asian American or Pacific Islander, 8% Hispanic American, 1% Native American, 0.7% international, 100% live on campus. *Retention:* 96% of 2001 full-time freshmen returned.

Freshmen *Admission:* 11,558 applied, 1,471 admitted, 1,182 enrolled. *Test scores:* SAT verbal scores over 500: 100%; SAT math scores over 500: 100%; SAT verbal scores over 600: 77%; SAT math scores over 600: 88%; SAT verbal scores over 700: 22%; SAT math scores over 700: 30%.

Faculty *Total:* 554, 100% full-time, 58% with terminal degrees. *Student/faculty ratio:* 7:1.

Majors Aerospace engineering; chemistry; computer science; economics; electrical engineering; engineering; English; history; mathematics; mechanical engineering; naval architecture/marine engineering; ocean engineering; oceanography; physics; political science; quantitative economics; systems engineering.

Academic Programs *Special study options:* academic remediation for entering students, advanced placement credit, double majors, English as a second language, honors programs, independent study, summer session for credit.

Library Nimitz Library plus 1 other with 800,000 titles, 1,892 serial subscriptions, an OPAC.

Computers on Campus 6100 computers available on campus for general student use. A campuswide network can be accessed from student residence rooms and from off campus. Internet access, online (class) registration, at least one staffed computer lab available.

Student Life *Housing:* on-campus residence required through senior year. *Options:* coed. *Activities and Organizations:* drama/theater group, student-run

United States Naval Academy (continued)
radio station, choral group, marching band, Mountaineering Club, Semper Fi, Black Studies Club, Midshipmen Action Club, Martial Arts Club. *Campus security:* 24-hour emergency response devices and patrols, student patrols, front gate security. *Student Services:* health clinic, personal/psychological counseling, legal services.

Athletics Member NCAA. All Division I except football (Division I-A). *Intercollegiate sports:* baseball M, basketball M/W, crew M/W, cross-country running M/W, golf M, gymnastics M/W(c), ice hockey M(c), lacrosse M/W(c), riflery M/W, rugby M(c)/W(c), sailing M/W, skiing (downhill) M(c)/W(c), soccer M/W, softball W(c), squash M, swimming M/W, tennis M/W(c), track and field M/W, volleyball M(c)/W, water polo M, weight lifting M(c)/W(c), wrestling M. *Intramural sports:* basketball M/W, football M, lacrosse M(c), racquetball M/W, sailing M/W, skiing (cross-country) M/W, soccer M/W, softball M/W, squash M/W, tennis M/W, volleyball M/W, water polo M, weight lifting M/W, wrestling M.

Standardized Tests *Required:* SAT I or ACT (for admission).

Applying *Required:* essay or personal statement, high school transcript, minimum 2.0 GPA, 2 letters of recommendation, interview, authorized nomination. *Application deadline:* 2/15 (freshmen). *Notification:* 4/15 (freshmen).

Admissions Contact Col. David A. Vetter, Dean of Admissions, United States Naval Academy, 117 Decatur Road, Annapolis, MD 21402-5000. *Phone:* 410-293-4361. *Fax:* 410-293-4348. *E-mail:* webmail@gwmail.usna.edu.

UNIVERSITY OF BALTIMORE
Baltimore, Maryland

- **State-supported** upper-level, founded 1925, part of University System of Maryland
- **Calendar** semesters
- **Degrees** bachelor's, master's, doctoral, first professional, post-master's, and postbachelor's certificates
- **Urban** 49-acre campus
- **Endowment** $18.9 million
- **Coed,** 1,993 undergraduate students, 45% full-time, 61% women, 39% men
- **Noncompetitive** entrance level, 88% of applicants were admitted

Undergraduates 890 full-time, 1,103 part-time. Students come from 7 states and territories, 59 other countries, 19% are from out of state, 30% African American, 2% Asian American or Pacific Islander, 2% Hispanic American, 1.0% Native American, 4% international, 28% transferred in.

Freshmen *Admission:* 857 applied, 752 admitted.

Faculty *Total:* 332, 49% full-time, 70% with terminal degrees. *Student/faculty ratio:* 14:1.

Majors Accounting; business administration; business marketing and marketing management; computer/information sciences; criminal justice/law enforcement administration; economics; English; entrepreneurship; finance; forensic technology; health/medical administrative services related; history; human resources management; human services; information sciences/systems; interdisciplinary studies; international business; journalism; legal studies; liberal arts and sciences/ liberal studies; literature; mass communications; political science; psychology; technical/business writing.

Academic Programs *Special study options:* academic remediation for entering students, accelerated degree program, adult/continuing education programs, advanced placement credit, cooperative education, honors programs, independent study, internships, off-campus study, part-time degree program, services for LD students, student-designed majors, summer session for credit. *ROTC:* Army (c). *Unusual degree programs:* law school.

Library Langsdale Library plus 1 other with 258,747 titles, 10,738 serial subscriptions, 883 audiovisual materials, an OPAC, a Web page.

Computers on Campus 135 computers available on campus for general student use. A campuswide network can be accessed from off campus. Internet access, at least one staffed computer lab available.

Student Life *Housing:* college housing not available. *Activities and Organizations:* student-run newspaper, Project Hunger, Student Events Board, student government association. *Campus security:* 24-hour emergency response devices and patrols, late-night transport/escort service. *Student Services:* health clinic, personal/psychological counseling, women's center.

Athletics *Intramural sports:* badminton M/W, basketball M/W, crew M/W(c), golf M/W, racquetball M/W, soccer M, softball M, table tennis M/W, tennis M/W, volleyball M/W, weight lifting M/W.

Costs (2001–02) *Tuition:* state resident $4504 full-time, $169 per credit part-time; nonresident $12,594 full-time, $491 per credit part-time. Full-time tuition and fees vary according to class time. *Required fees:* $820 full-time, $30 per credit, $60 per credit part-time. *Payment plan:* deferred payment. *Waivers:* senior citizens and employees or children of employees.

Financial Aid *Average indebtedness upon graduation:* $22,441.

Applying *Options:* electronic application. *Application fee:* $20. *Application deadline:* rolling (transfers). *Notification:* continuous (transfers).

Admissions Contact Mr. Daryl Minus, Assistant Director of Admissions, University of Baltimore, 1420 North Charles St., Baltimore, MD 21201-5779. *Phone:* 410-837-4777. *Toll-free phone:* 877-APPLYUB. *Fax:* 410-837-4793. *E-mail:* admissions@ubmail.ubalt.edu.

UNIVERSITY OF MARYLAND, BALTIMORE COUNTY
Baltimore, Maryland

- **State-supported** university, founded 1963, part of University System of Maryland
- **Calendar** semesters
- **Degrees** bachelor's, master's, doctoral, and postbachelor's certificates
- **Suburban** 500-acre campus
- **Endowment** $17.4 million
- **Coed,** 9,328 undergraduate students, 81% full-time, 50% women, 50% men
- **Moderately difficult** entrance level, 66% of applicants were admitted

Some of the most exciting students and best teaching talents anywhere are coming together at a young university located in the suburbs of Baltimore that has approximately 9,100 undergraduates. UMBC's leadership in technology, its friendly campus climate, business and industry partnerships, and ability to place students in leading graduate programs and promising careers are just a few of the reasons why students who could attend any college are choosing UMBC.

Undergraduates 7,572 full-time, 1,756 part-time. Students come from 39 states and territories, 91 other countries, 8% are from out of state, 16% African American, 18% Asian American or Pacific Islander, 3% Hispanic American, 0.5% Native American, 5% international, 12% transferred in, 38% live on campus. *Retention:* 82% of 2001 full-time freshmen returned.

Freshmen *Admission:* 5,282 applied, 3,460 admitted, 1,309 enrolled. *Average high school GPA:* 3.44. *Test scores:* SAT verbal scores over 500: 89%; SAT math scores over 500: 96%; ACT scores over 18: 96%; SAT verbal scores over 600: 46%; SAT math scores over 600: 58%; ACT scores over 24: 50%; SAT verbal scores over 700: 9%; SAT math scores over 700: 14%; ACT scores over 30: 10%.

Faculty *Total:* 754, 59% full-time, 68% with terminal degrees. *Student/faculty ratio:* 17:1.

Majors African-American studies; American studies; anthropology; applied mathematics; art; art history; biochemistry; biology; chemical engineering; chemistry; classics; computer engineering; computer science; dance; economics; emergency medical technology; engineering science; English; environmental science; film studies; French; geography; German; health science; health services administration; history; information sciences/systems; interdisciplinary studies; linguistics; mathematical statistics; mathematics; mechanical engineering; modern languages; music; philosophy; photography; physics; political science; pre-dentistry; pre-law; pre-medicine; pre-veterinary studies; psychology; Russian; social work; sociology; Spanish; theater arts/drama; visual/performing arts.

Academic Programs *Special study options:* academic remediation for entering students, adult/continuing education programs, advanced placement credit, cooperative education, distance learning, double majors, English as a second language, external degree program, freshman honors college, honors programs, independent study, internships, off-campus study, part-time degree program, services for LD students, student-designed majors, study abroad, summer session for credit. *ROTC:* Army (c), Air Force (c).

Library Albin O. Kuhn Library and Gallery plus 1 other with 4,508 serial subscriptions, 1.5 million audiovisual materials, an OPAC, a Web page.

Computers on Campus 500 computers available on campus for general student use. A campuswide network can be accessed from student residence rooms and from off campus that provide access to student account and grade information. Internet access, online (class) registration, at least one staffed computer lab available.

Student Life *Housing Options:* coed. *Activities and Organizations:* drama/ theater group, student-run newspaper, radio and television station, choral group, marching band, Student Government Association, Student Events Board, Retriever Weekly, Resident Student Association, Black Student Union, national fraternities, national sororities. *Campus security:* 24-hour emergency response devices and patrols, late-night transport/escort service. *Student Services:* health clinic, personal/ psychological counseling, women's center, legal services.

Athletics Member NCAA. All Division I. *Intercollegiate sports:* baseball M(s), basketball M(s)/W(s), bowling M(c)/W(c), crew M(c)/W(c), cross-country running M(s)/W(s), fencing M(c)/W(c), field hockey W(c), golf M(s)/W(s), ice hockey M(c), lacrosse M(s)/W(s), rugby M(c)/W(c), sailing M(c)/W(c), skiing (downhill) M(c)/W(c), soccer M(s)/W(s), softball W(s), swimming M(s)/W(s), tennis M(s)/W(s), track and field M(s)/W(s), volleyball M(c)/W(s), wrestling M(c). *Intramural sports:* badminton M/W, basketball M/W, cross-country running M/W, football M/W, lacrosse M/W, soccer M/W, softball M/W, swimming M/W, tennis M/W, track and field M/W, volleyball M/W.

Standardized Tests *Required:* SAT I or ACT (for admission). *Recommended:* SAT I (for admission).

Costs (2001–02) *Tuition:* state resident $4374 full-time, $182 per credit part-time; nonresident $9754 full-time, $406 per credit part-time. Part-time tuition and fees vary according to course load. *Required fees:* $1536 full-time, $59 per credit. *Room and board:* $6280; room only: $3840. Room and board charges vary according to board plan and housing facility. *Payment plan:* installment. *Waivers:* senior citizens and employees or children of employees.

Financial Aid Of all full-time matriculated undergraduates who enrolled in 2001, 5813 applied for aid, 4840 were judged to have need, 2023 had their need fully met. In 2001, 1213 non-need-based awards were made. *Average percent of need met:* 62%. *Average financial aid package:* $6214. *Average need-based loan:* $4201. *Average need-based gift aid:* $3602. *Average non-need based aid:* $5794. *Average indebtedness upon graduation:* $13,100.

Applying *Options:* common application, electronic application, early admission, deferred entrance. *Application fee:* $45. *Required:* essay or personal statement, high school transcript, minimum 2.0 GPA. *Application deadline:* 3/15 (freshmen), rolling (transfers). *Notification:* continuous (freshmen).

Admissions Contact Ms. Yvette Mozie-Ross, Director of Admissions, University of Maryland, Baltimore County, 1000 Hilltop Circle, Baltimore, MD 21250-5398. *Phone:* 410-455-3799. *Toll-free phone:* 800-UMBC-4U2 (in-state); 800-862-2402 (out-of-state). *Fax:* 410-455-1094. *E-mail:* admissions@umbc.edu.

UNIVERSITY OF MARYLAND, COLLEGE PARK

College Park, Maryland

- **State-supported** university, founded 1856, part of University System of Maryland
- **Calendar** semesters
- **Degrees** certificates, bachelor's, master's, doctoral, first professional, post-master's, and postbachelor's certificates
- **Suburban** 3650-acre campus with easy access to Baltimore and Washington, DC
- **Endowment** $221.0 million
- **Coed,** 25,099 undergraduate students, 89% full-time, 49% women, 51% men
- **Moderately difficult** entrance level, 55% of applicants were admitted

Undergraduates 22,412 full-time, 2,687 part-time. Students come from 53 states and territories, 154 other countries, 25% are from out of state, 13% African American, 14% Asian American or Pacific Islander, 5% Hispanic American, 0.2% Native American, 3% international, 7% transferred in, 39% live on campus. *Retention:* 91% of 2001 full-time freshmen returned.

Freshmen *Admission:* 19,647 applied, 10,801 admitted, 4,374 enrolled. *Average high school GPA:* 3.76. *Test scores:* SAT verbal scores over 500: 93%; SAT math scores over 500: 98%; SAT verbal scores over 600: 59%; SAT math scores over 600: 74%; SAT verbal scores over 700: 14%; SAT math scores over 700: 22%.

Faculty *Total:* 2,136, 72% full-time, 79% with terminal degrees. *Student/faculty ratio:* 13:1.

Majors Accounting; aerospace engineering; African-American studies; agricultural economics; agricultural sciences; agronomy/crop science; American studies; animal sciences; anthropology; architecture; art education; art history; astronomy; biochemistry; biology; broadcast journalism; business; business administration/management related; business marketing and marketing management; cartography; chemical engineering; chemistry; Chinese; civil engineering; classics; communications; computer engineering; computer/information sciences; computer science; criminology; dance; dietetics; drama/dance education; early childhood education; ecology; economics; education; electrical engineering; elementary education; engineering; engineering related; English; English education; environmental science; family/community studies; finance; fine/studio arts; food sciences; foreign languages education; French; geography; geology; German; health education; history; horticulture science; human resources management; Italian; Japanese; journalism; Judaic studies; landscape architecture; linguistics; mass communications; materials engineering; mathematics; mathematics education; mechanical engineering; microbiology/bacteriology; music; music (general performance); music teacher education; natural resources conservation; nuclear engineering; nutrition science; operations management; philosophy; physical education; physical sciences; physics; plant sciences; political science; pre-veterinary studies; psychology; Russian; Russian/Slavic studies; science education; secondary education; social studies education; sociology; Spanish; special education; speech-language pathology; theater arts/drama; turf management; women's studies.

Academic Programs *Special study options:* academic remediation for entering students, accelerated degree program, adult/continuing education programs, advanced placement credit, cooperative education, distance learning, double majors, English as a second language, honors programs, independent study, internships, off-campus study, part-time degree program, services for LD students, student-designed majors, study abroad, summer session for credit. *ROTC:* Army (c), Navy (c), Air Force (b).

Library McKeldin Library plus 6 others with 2.9 million titles, 32,290 serial subscriptions, 244,336 audiovisual materials, an OPAC, a Web page.

Computers on Campus 899 computers available on campus for general student use. A campuswide network can be accessed from student residence rooms and from off campus that provide access to student account information, financial aid summary. Internet access, online (class) registration, at least one staffed computer lab available.

Student Life *Housing Options:* coed, men-only, women-only, disabled students. *Activities and Organizations:* drama/theater group, student-run newspaper, radio and television station, choral group, marching band, Student Government Association, Residence Hall Association, Black Student Union, Asian-American Student Union/Jewish Student Union, national fraternities, national sororities. *Campus security:* 24-hour emergency response devices and patrols, student patrols, late-night transport/escort service, controlled dormitory access, campus police, video camera surveillance. *Student Services:* health clinic, personal/psychological counseling, women's center, legal services.

Athletics Member NCAA. All Division I except football (Division I-A). *Intercollegiate sports:* baseball M(s), basketball M(s)/W(s), cross-country running M/W, field hockey W(s), golf M(s)/W(s), gymnastics W(s), lacrosse M(s)/W(s), soccer M(s)/W(s), softball W(s), swimming M(s)/W(s), tennis M/W(s), track and field M(s)/W(s), volleyball W(s), wrestling M(s). *Intramural sports:* badminton M(c)/W(c), basketball M/W, bowling M(c)/W(c), cross-country running M/W, equestrian sports M(c)/W(c), fencing M(c)/W(c), field hockey W(c), football M/W, golf M/W, ice hockey M(c)/W(c), lacrosse M(c)/W(c), racquetball M(c)/W(c), rugby M(c), sailing M(c)/W(c), soccer M(c)/W(c), softball M/W, squash M(c)/W(c), swimming M(c)/W(c), table tennis M/W, tennis M/W, track and field M/W, volleyball M(c)/W, water polo M(c)/W(c), weight lifting M/W, wrestling M.

Standardized Tests *Required:* SAT I or ACT (for admission).

Costs (2001–02) *Tuition:* state resident $4334 full-time, $181 per semester hour part-time; nonresident $12,406 full-time, $517 per semester hour part-time. *Required fees:* $1007 full-time, $227 per term part-time. *Room and board:* $6618; room only: $3814. Room and board charges vary according to board plan. *Payment plans:* installment, deferred payment. *Waivers:* senior citizens and employees or children of employees.

Financial Aid Of all full-time matriculated undergraduates who enrolled in 2001, 16209 applied for aid, 10136 were judged to have need, 2478 had their need fully met. 841 Federal Work-Study jobs (averaging $1444). In 2001, 3266 non-need-based awards were made. *Average percent of need met:* 67%. *Average financial aid package:* $7740. *Average need-based loan:* $3575. *Average need-based gift aid:* $3596. *Average non-need based aid:* $3880. *Average indebtedness upon graduation:* $14,076.

Applying *Options:* electronic application, early admission, early action. *Application fee:* $45. *Required:* essay or personal statement, high school transcript, 1 letter of recommendation. *Required for some:* interview. *Recommended:* 2 letters of recommendation, resume of activities, auditions. *Application deadlines:* 2/15 (freshmen), 7/1 (transfers). *Notification:* continuous until 4/1 (freshmen), 2/1 (early action).

Admissions Contact Barbara Gill, Director of Undergraduate Admissions, University of Maryland, College Park, Mitchell Building, College Park, MD 20742-5235. *Phone:* 301-314-8385. *Toll-free phone:* 800-422-5867. *Fax:* 301-314-9693. *E-mail:* um-admit@uga.umd.edu.

UNIVERSITY OF MARYLAND EASTERN SHORE

Princess Anne, Maryland

- **State-supported** university, founded 1886, part of University System of Maryland
- **Calendar** semesters
- **Degrees** bachelor's, master's, and doctoral
- **Rural** 700-acre campus

University of Maryland Eastern Shore (continued)

- **Coed,** 3,134 undergraduate students, 82% full-time, 58% women, 42% men
- **Moderately difficult** entrance level, 66% of applicants were admitted

Undergraduates Students come from 30 states and territories, 50 other countries, 28% are from out of state, 75% African American, 1% Asian American or Pacific Islander, 1% Hispanic American, 0.4% Native American, 11% international, 52% live on campus. *Retention:* 74% of 2001 full-time freshmen returned.

Freshmen *Admission:* 1,905 applied, 1,264 admitted. *Average high school GPA:* 2.75. *Test scores:* SAT verbal scores over 500: 23%; SAT math scores over 500: 18%; SAT verbal scores over 600: 4%; SAT math scores over 600: 2%; SAT verbal scores over 700: 1%.

Faculty *Total:* 280, 77% full-time. *Student/faculty ratio:* 20:1.

Majors Accounting; agricultural business; agricultural education; agricultural sciences; air traffic control; art education; biology; business administration; business education; chemistry; child care/development; computer science; construction management; construction technology; criminal justice/law enforcement administration; dietetics; early childhood education; ecology; education; electrical/electronic engineering technology; elementary education; engineering technology; English; environmental science; family/consumer studies; fashion design/illustration; fashion merchandising; food products retailing; history; home economics; home economics education; hotel and restaurant management; human ecology; industrial arts; industrial radiologic technology; liberal arts and sciences/liberal studies; marine biology; mass communications; mathematics; medical laboratory technician; medical technology; music teacher education; physical education; physical therapy; poultry science; pre-dentistry; pre-law; pre-medicine; rehabilitation therapy; social sciences; social work; sociology; special education.

Academic Programs *Special study options:* academic remediation for entering students, accelerated degree program, adult/continuing education programs, advanced placement credit, cooperative education, honors programs, internships, off-campus study, part-time degree program, services for LD students, student-designed majors, summer session for credit.

Library Frederick Douglass Library with 150,000 titles, 1,260 serial subscriptions, an OPAC, a Web page.

Computers on Campus 120 computers available on campus for general student use. At least one staffed computer lab available.

Student Life *Housing Options:* coed, men-only, women-only. *Activities and Organizations:* drama/theater group, student-run newspaper, choral group, national fraternities, national sororities. *Campus security:* 24-hour emergency response devices and patrols, student patrols, late-night transport/escort service, controlled dormitory access. *Student Services:* health clinic, personal/psychological counseling.

Athletics Member NCAA. All Division I. *Intercollegiate sports:* baseball M(s), basketball M(s)/W(s), cross-country running M/W, softball W, tennis M(s)/W, track and field M/W, volleyball W, wrestling M. *Intramural sports:* basketball M/W, bowling W, cross-country running M/W, soccer M/W, softball W, swimming M/W, table tennis M/W, tennis M/W, track and field M/W, volleyball M/W, wrestling M.

Standardized Tests *Required:* SAT I or ACT (for admission).

Costs (2001–02) *Tuition:* state resident $4128 full-time, $124 per credit part-time; nonresident $8612 full-time, $265 per credit part-time. *Room and board:* $5130; room only: $2830. Room and board charges vary according to board plan and housing facility. *Payment plans:* installment, deferred payment. *Waivers:* senior citizens and employees or children of employees.

Financial Aid Of all full-time matriculated undergraduates who enrolled in 2001, 2065 applied for aid, 1652 were judged to have need, 330 had their need fully met. 318 Federal Work-Study jobs (averaging $723). In 2001, 300 non-need-based awards were made. *Average percent of need met:* 70%. *Average financial aid package:* $10,150. *Average need-based loan:* $3700. *Average need-based gift aid:* $7950. *Average non-need based aid:* $2000. *Average indebtedness upon graduation:* $8000.

Applying *Options:* common application, electronic application, early admission, early action, deferred entrance. *Application fee:* $25. *Required:* essay or personal statement, high school transcript, minimum 2.5 GPA, 2 letters of recommendation. *Recommended:* interview. *Application deadline:* 7/15 (freshmen), rolling (transfers).

Admissions Contact Ms. Cheryll Collier-Mills, Director of Admissions and Recruitment, University of Maryland Eastern Shore, Princess Anne, MD 21853-1299. *Phone:* 410-651-8410. *Fax:* 410-651-7922. *E-mail:* umesadmissions@mail.umes.edu.

UNIVERSITY OF MARYLAND UNIVERSITY COLLEGE
Adelphi, Maryland

- **State-supported** comprehensive, founded 1947, part of University System of Maryland
- **Calendar** semesters
- **Degrees** certificates, associate, bachelor's, master's, doctoral, post-master's, and postbachelor's certificates (offers primarily part-time evening and weekend degree programs at more than 30 off-campus locations in Maryland and the Washington, DC area, and more than 180 military communities in Europe and Asia with military enrollment not reflected in this profile; associate of arts program available to military students only)
- **Suburban** campus with easy access to Washington, DC
- **Coed,** 16,062 undergraduate students, 14% full-time, 58% women, 42% men
- **Noncompetitive** entrance level, 100% of applicants were admitted

Undergraduates 2,181 full-time, 13,881 part-time. Students come from 54 states and territories, 41 other countries, 28% are from out of state, 32% African American, 7% Asian American or Pacific Islander, 5% Hispanic American, 0.7% Native American, 2% international, 7% transferred in.

Freshmen *Admission:* 1,172 applied, 1,172 admitted, 646 enrolled.

Faculty *Total:* 962, 8% full-time, 57% with terminal degrees. *Student/faculty ratio:* 23:1.

Majors Accounting; business administration; business marketing and marketing management; communications; computer/information sciences; computer science; criminal justice/law enforcement administration; English; environmental science; fire science; history; humanities; human resources management; information sciences/systems; management science; multi/interdisciplinary studies related; paralegal/legal assistant; psychology; social sciences.

Academic Programs *Special study options:* accelerated degree program, adult/continuing education programs, advanced placement credit, cooperative education, distance learning, external degree program, independent study, off-campus study, part-time degree program, services for LD students, summer session for credit.

Library Information and Library Services plus 1 other with 4,623 titles, 65 serial subscriptions, an OPAC, a Web page.

Computers on Campus 375 computers available on campus for general student use. A campuswide network can be accessed from off campus. At least one staffed computer lab available.

Student Life *Housing:* college housing not available. *Campus security:* 24-hour emergency response devices and patrols, late-night transport/escort service.

Costs (2001–02) *Tuition:* state resident $4728 full-time, $197 per semester hour part-time; nonresident $8736 full-time, $364 per semester hour part-time. *Waivers:* senior citizens and employees or children of employees.

Financial Aid Of all full-time matriculated undergraduates who enrolled in 2001, 1287 applied for aid, 1133 were judged to have need, 30 had their need fully met. In 2001, 16 non-need-based awards were made. *Average percent of need met:* 24%. *Average financial aid package:* $1601. *Average need-based loan:* $1925. *Average need-based gift aid:* $1058. *Average non-need based aid:* $701. *Average indebtedness upon graduation:* $1846.

Applying *Options:* electronic application, deferred entrance. *Application fee:* $30. *Required:* high school transcript. *Application deadline:* rolling (freshmen), rolling (transfers). *Notification:* continuous (freshmen).

Admissions Contact Ms. Anne Rahill, Technical Director, Admissions, University of Maryland University College, 3501 University Boulevard, East, Adelphi, MD 20783. *Phone:* 301-985-7000. *Toll-free phone:* 800-888-UMUC. *Fax:* 301-985-7364. *E-mail:* umucinfo@nova.umuc.edu.

UNIVERSITY OF PHOENIX-MARYLAND CAMPUS
Columbia, Maryland

- **Proprietary** comprehensive
- **Calendar** continuous
- **Degrees** certificates, associate, bachelor's, master's, doctoral, post-master's, and postbachelor's certificates (courses conducted at 54 campuses and learning centers in 13 states)
- **Coed,** 458 undergraduate students, 187% full-time, 107% women, 81% men
- **Noncompetitive** entrance level

Undergraduates Students come from 8 states and territories, 5% are from out of state.

Freshmen *Admission:* 21 admitted.

Faculty *Total:* 6. *Student/faculty ratio:* 13:1.

Majors Accounting; business administration; information technology; management information systems/business data processing; management science.

Academic Programs *Special study options:* accelerated degree program, adult/continuing education programs, advanced placement credit, distance learning, external degree program, independent study.

Library University Library with 17.5 million titles, 9,000 serial subscriptions, an OPAC, a Web page.

Computers on Campus A campuswide network can be accessed from off campus. Internet access, at least one staffed computer lab available.

Student Life *Housing:* college housing not available.

Costs (2001–02) *Tuition:* $9000 full-time. Full-time tuition and fees vary according to location and program. *Payment plan:* deferred payment. *Waivers:* employees or children of employees.

Applying *Options:* deferred entrance. *Application fee:* $85. *Required:* 2 years of work experience. *Required for some:* high school transcript. *Application deadline:* rolling (freshmen), rolling (transfers).

Admissions Contact Ms. Beth Barilla, Director of Admissions, University of Phoenix-Maryland Campus, 4615 East Elwood Street, Phoenix, AZ 85040-1958. *Phone:* 480-927-0099 Ext. 1218. *Toll-free phone:* 800-228-7240. *Fax:* 480-894-1758. *E-mail:* beth.barilla@apollogrp.edu.

VILLA JULIE COLLEGE

Stevenson, Maryland

- **Independent** comprehensive, founded 1952
- **Calendar** semesters
- **Degrees** certificates, associate, bachelor's, and master's
- **Suburban** 60-acre campus with easy access to Baltimore
- **Coed,** 2,376 undergraduate students, 75% full-time, 72% women, 28% men
- **Moderately difficult** entrance level, 84% of applicants were admitted

Undergraduates 1,781 full-time, 595 part-time. Students come from 7 states and territories, 4 other countries, 3% are from out of state, 10% African American, 3% Asian American or Pacific Islander, 1% Hispanic American, 0.2% Native American, 0.3% international, 8% transferred in, 17% live on campus. *Retention:* 76% of 2001 full-time freshmen returned.

Freshmen *Admission:* 1,430 applied, 1,202 admitted, 521 enrolled. *Average high school GPA:* 3.34. *Test scores:* SAT verbal scores over 500: 61%; SAT math scores over 500: 60%; SAT verbal scores over 600: 16%; SAT math scores over 600: 17%; SAT verbal scores over 700: 1%; SAT math scores over 700: 1%.

Faculty *Total:* 264, 32% full-time, 51% with terminal degrees. *Student/faculty ratio:* 12:1.

Majors Accounting; applied art; art; biological/physical sciences; biological technology; biology; business administration; chemistry; child care/development; computer graphics; computer/information sciences; computer programming; court reporting; developmental/child psychology; early childhood education; elementary education; English; environmental science; film/video production; graphic design/commercial art/illustration; history; humanities; information sciences/systems; interdisciplinary studies; journalism; legal studies; liberal arts and sciences/liberal studies; management information systems/business data processing; mass communications; medical laboratory technician; medical laboratory technology; medical technology; middle school education; nursing; paralegal/legal assistant; photography; physical sciences; physical therapy; political science; pre-dentistry; pre-law; pre-medicine; pre-veterinary studies; psychology; science education; social sciences; sociology; theater arts/drama.

Academic Programs *Special study options:* academic remediation for entering students, accelerated degree program, adult/continuing education programs, advanced placement credit, cooperative education, double majors, English as a second language, freshman honors college, honors programs, independent study, internships, off-campus study, part-time degree program, student-designed majors, summer session for credit. *ROTC:* Army (c). *Unusual degree programs:* 3-2 physical therapy with University of Maryland, Baltimore County.

Library Villa Julie College Library with 124,417 titles, 720 serial subscriptions, 2,288 audiovisual materials, an OPAC, a Web page.

Computers on Campus 230 computers available on campus for general student use. A campuswide network can be accessed from student residence rooms and from off campus. Internet access, at least one staffed computer lab available.

Student Life *Housing Options:* coed. *Activities and Organizations:* drama/theater group, student-run newspaper, choral group, Student Government Association, Wilderness Club, Black Student Union, National Student Nurses Association, Phi Sigma, national sororities. *Campus security:* 24-hour emergency response devices, late-night transport/escort service, controlled dormitory access, patrols by trained security personnel during campus hours. *Student Services:* personal/psychological counseling.

Athletics Member NCAA. All Division III. *Intercollegiate sports:* basketball M/W, cross-country running M/W, field hockey W, golf M/W, lacrosse M/W, soccer M/W, tennis M/W, volleyball W. *Intramural sports:* badminton M/W, baseball M, basketball M/W, fencing M/W, field hockey W, football M/W, sailing M/W, skiing (cross-country) M/W, skiing (downhill) M/W, softball W, table tennis M/W, tennis M/W, volleyball M.

Standardized Tests *Required:* SAT I or ACT (for admission).

Costs (2001–02) *Tuition:* $11,300 full-time, $320 per credit part-time. *Required fees:* $776 full-time, $30 per term part-time. *Room only:* $3950. *Payment plan:* installment. *Waivers:* employees or children of employees.

Financial Aid Of all full-time matriculated undergraduates who enrolled in 2001, 1283 applied for aid, 978 were judged to have need. 90 Federal Work-Study jobs (averaging $1400). In 2001, 424 non-need-based awards were made. *Average percent of need met:* 50%. *Average financial aid package:* $12,431. *Average need-based loan:* $3424. *Average need-based gift aid:* $2220. *Average non-need based aid:* $11,095. *Average indebtedness upon graduation:* $14,562.

Applying *Options:* electronic application, early admission, deferred entrance. *Application fee:* $25. *Required:* essay or personal statement, high school transcript, 2 letters of recommendation, interview. *Recommended:* minimum 3.0 GPA. *Application deadlines:* 7/15 (freshmen), 7/15 (transfers). *Notification:* continuous (freshmen).

Admissions Contact Mr. Mark Hergan, Dean of Admissions, Villa Julie College, 125 Greenspring Valley Road, Stevenson, MD 21153. *Phone:* 410-486-7001. *Toll-free phone:* 877-468-6852 (in-state); 877-468-3852 (out-of-state). *Fax:* 410-602-6600. *E-mail:* admissions@vjc.edu.

WASHINGTON BIBLE COLLEGE

Lanham, Maryland

- **Independent nondenominational** 4-year, founded 1938
- **Calendar** semesters
- **Degrees** certificates, associate, and bachelor's
- **Suburban** 63-acre campus with easy access to Washington, DC
- **Coed,** 331 undergraduate students, 56% full-time, 47% women, 53% men
- **Moderately difficult** entrance level, 65% of applicants were admitted

Since 1938, Washington Bible College has been preparing students for God-centered lives and careers through programs that include biblical, general, and professional studies. Located on a 63-acre campus in suburban Maryland, near Washington, D.C., WBC fosters an environment that enables students to grow spiritually, socially, and intellectually.

Undergraduates Students come from 14 states and territories, 9 other countries, 24% are from out of state, 39% African American, 8% Asian American or Pacific Islander, 2% Hispanic American, 2% international, 28% live on campus. *Retention:* 70% of 2001 full-time freshmen returned.

Freshmen *Admission:* 167 applied, 108 admitted. *Average high school GPA:* 2.80.

Faculty *Total:* 14, 100% full-time, 14% with terminal degrees. *Student/faculty ratio:* 13:1.

Majors Biblical studies; early childhood education; elementary education; music; music teacher education; religious education; religious studies; theology.

Academic Programs *Special study options:* academic remediation for entering students, accelerated degree program, adult/continuing education programs, advanced placement credit, cooperative education, double majors, English as a second language, internships, off-campus study, part-time degree program, summer session for credit.

Library Oyer Memorial Library plus 1 other with 78,000 titles, 525 serial subscriptions, 3,824 audiovisual materials, a Web page.

Computers on Campus 25 computers available on campus for general student use. Internet access, at least one staffed computer lab available.

Student Life *Housing:* on-campus residence required through senior year. *Options:* men-only, women-only. *Activities and Organizations:* drama/theater group, choral group, Student Missions Fellowship, School Choir and Ensemble, Korean Student Fellowship. *Campus security:* 24-hour patrols, student patrols, late-night transport/escort service, secured campus entrances, trained guards on duty. *Student Services:* health clinic, personal/psychological counseling.

Athletics Member NCCAA. *Intercollegiate sports:* basketball M/W, soccer M, volleyball W. *Intramural sports:* basketball M, football M, racquetball M/W, soccer M, table tennis M/W, tennis M/W, volleyball M/W.

Standardized Tests *Required:* SAT I or ACT (for admission).

Washington Bible College (continued)

Costs (2002–03) *Comprehensive fee:* $13,205 includes full-time tuition ($7840), mandatory fees ($365), and room and board ($5000). Part-time tuition: $285 per credit hour. Part-time tuition and fees vary according to course load and location. *Room and board:* College room only: $3000. Room and board charges vary according to board plan. *Payment plans:* installment, deferred payment. *Waivers:* employees or children of employees.

Applying *Options:* early admission, deferred entrance. *Application fee:* $15. *Required:* essay or personal statement, high school transcript, 2 letters of recommendation, Christian testimony. *Required for some:* interview. *Application deadline:* rolling (freshmen), rolling (transfers). *Notification:* continuous until 8/15 (freshmen).

Admissions Contact Barbara Fox, Director of Enrollment Management, Washington Bible College, 6511 Princess Garden Parkway, Lanham, MD 20706. *Phone:* 301-552-1400 Ext. 213. *Toll-free phone:* 800-787-0256 Ext. 212. *Fax:* 301-552-2775 Ext. 212. *E-mail:* admissions@bible.edu.

WASHINGTON COLLEGE
Chestertown, Maryland

- **Independent** comprehensive, founded 1782
- **Calendar** semesters
- **Degrees** bachelor's and master's
- **Small-town** 120-acre campus with easy access to Baltimore and Washington, DC
- **Endowment** $104.0 million
- **Coed,** 1,208 undergraduate students, 95% full-time, 62% women, 38% men
- **Moderately difficult** entrance level, 73% of applicants were admitted

Washington College has initiated a $40,000 scholarship program expressly for National Honor Society and Cum Laude Society members. Washington College NHS/CLS Scholarships are $10,000 annual awards renewable through the completion of 8 semesters. To be eligible for scholarship consideration, a student must apply for freshman aid no later than February 15 of the senior year. For more information, students should contact the Admissions Office or visit the WC Web Site at http://www.washcoll.edu.

Undergraduates 1,153 full-time, 55 part-time. Students come from 37 states and territories, 38 other countries, 50% are from out of state, 3% African American, 2% Asian American or Pacific Islander, 1% Hispanic American, 0.3% Native American, 5% international, 3% transferred in, 80% live on campus. *Retention:* 82% of 2001 full-time freshmen returned.

Freshmen *Admission:* 1,914 applied, 1,391 admitted, 338 enrolled. *Average high school GPA:* 3.37. *Test scores:* SAT verbal scores over 500: 84%; SAT math scores over 500: 85%; ACT scores over 18: 92%; SAT verbal scores over 600: 40%; SAT math scores over 600: 34%; ACT scores over 24: 54%; SAT verbal scores over 700: 7%; SAT math scores over 700: 4%; ACT scores over 30: 8%.

Faculty *Total:* 126, 64% full-time, 64% with terminal degrees. *Student/faculty ratio:* 12:1.

Majors American studies; anthropology; art; biology; business administration; chemistry; economics; English; environmental science; French; German; history; humanities; international relations; Latin American studies; liberal arts and sciences/liberal studies; mathematics; music; philosophy; physics; physiological psychology/psychobiology; political science; pre-dentistry; pre-law; pre-medicine; pre-veterinary studies; psychology; sociology; Spanish; theater arts/drama.

Academic Programs *Special study options:* advanced placement credit, cooperative education, double majors, English as a second language, independent study, internships, off-campus study, part-time degree program, services for LD students, student-designed majors, study abroad. *Unusual degree programs:* 3-2 engineering with University of Maryland, College Park; nursing with Johns Hopkins University.

Library Clifton M. Miller Library with 231,576 titles, 4,635 serial subscriptions, 5,561 audiovisual materials, an OPAC, a Web page.

Computers on Campus 100 computers available on campus for general student use. A campuswide network can be accessed from student residence rooms and from off campus that provide access to e-mail. Internet access, at least one staffed computer lab available.

Student Life *Housing:* on-campus residence required through sophomore year. *Options:* coed, men-only, women-only. *Activities and Organizations:* drama/theater group, student-run newspaper, choral group, Writers Union, Student Government Association, Hands Out, Omicron Delta Kappa, Dale Adams Society, national fraternities, national sororities. *Campus security:* 24-hour emergency response devices and patrols, student patrols, late-night transport/escort service, controlled dormitory access. *Student Services:* health clinic, personal/psychological counseling.

Athletics Member NCAA. All Division III. *Intercollegiate sports:* baseball M, basketball M/W, crew M/W, field hockey W, ice hockey M(c), lacrosse M/W, rugby M(c), sailing M(c)/W(c), soccer M/W, softball W, swimming M/W, tennis M/W, volleyball W. *Intramural sports:* basketball M/W, golf M, racquetball M/W, rugby M, sailing M/W, softball M, squash M/W, tennis M/W, volleyball M/W.

Standardized Tests *Required:* SAT I or ACT (for admission).

Costs (2002–03) *Comprehensive fee:* $29,040 includes full-time tuition ($22,750), mandatory fees ($550), and room and board ($5740). Full-time tuition and fees vary according to program. Part-time tuition: $3791 per course. Part-time tuition and fees vary according to course load and program. *Required fees:* $92 per course. *Room and board:* College room only: $2600. Room and board charges vary according to board plan and housing facility. *Payment plans:* tuition prepayment, installment. *Waivers:* minority students and employees or children of employees.

Financial Aid Of all full-time matriculated undergraduates who enrolled in 2001, 689 applied for aid, 571 were judged to have need, 241 had their need fully met. 253 Federal Work-Study jobs (averaging $1258). In 2001, 408 non-need-based awards were made. *Average percent of need met:* 88%. *Average financial aid package:* $18,409. *Average need-based loan:* $3500. *Average need-based gift aid:* $14,402. *Average non-need based aid:* $12,357. *Average indebtedness upon graduation:* $17,711.

Applying *Options:* common application, electronic application, early admission, early decision, early action, deferred entrance. *Application fee:* $40. *Required:* essay or personal statement, high school transcript, 1 letter of recommendation. *Required for some:* interview. *Recommended:* interview. *Application deadline:* 2/15 (freshmen), rolling (transfers). *Early decision:* 11/15. *Notification:* continuous until 4/1 (freshmen), 12/15 (early decision), 12/19 (early action).

Admissions Contact Mr. Kevin Coveney, Vice President for Admissions, Washington College, 300 Washington Avenue, Chestertown, MD 21620-1197. *Phone:* 410-778-7700. *Toll-free phone:* 800-422-1782. *E-mail:* admissions_office@washcoll.edu.

WESTERN MARYLAND COLLEGE
(now known as McDaniel College)
Westminster, Maryland

- **Independent** comprehensive, founded 1867
- **Calendar** 4-1-4
- **Degrees** bachelor's and master's
- **Small-town** 160-acre campus with easy access to Baltimore and Washington, DC
- **Endowment** $59.5 million
- **Coed,** 1,641 undergraduate students, 96% full-time, 56% women, 44% men
- **Moderately difficult** entrance level, 77% of applicants were admitted

Undergraduates 1,569 full-time, 72 part-time. Students come from 28 states and territories, 24 other countries, 29% are from out of state, 8% African American, 2% Asian American or Pacific Islander, 2% Hispanic American, 0.1% Native American, 4% international, 3% transferred in, 72% live on campus. *Retention:* 86% of 2001 full-time freshmen returned.

Freshmen *Admission:* 1,885 applied, 1,443 admitted, 370 enrolled. *Average high school GPA:* 3.40. *Test scores:* SAT verbal scores over 500: 82%; SAT math scores over 500: 81%; SAT verbal scores over 600: 29%; SAT math scores over 600: 30%; SAT verbal scores over 700: 6%; SAT math scores over 700: 3%.

Faculty *Total:* 153, 61% full-time, 64% with terminal degrees. *Student/faculty ratio:* 12:1.

Majors Art; art history; biochemistry; biology; business administration; chemistry; communications; economics; English; exercise sciences; French; German; history; mathematics; music; philosophy; physics; political science; psychology; religious studies; social work; sociology; Spanish; theater arts/drama.

Academic Programs *Special study options:* academic remediation for entering students, adult/continuing education programs, advanced placement credit, double majors, honors programs, independent study, internships, off-campus study, part-time degree program, services for LD students, student-designed majors, study abroad, summer session for credit. *ROTC:* Army (b), Air Force (c). *Unusual degree programs:* 3-2 engineering with University of Maryland College Park, Washington University in St. Louis; forestry with Duke University.

Library Hoover Library with 214,259 titles, 1,090 serial subscriptions, 9,968 audiovisual materials, an OPAC, a Web page.

Computers on Campus 162 computers available on campus for general student use. A campuswide network can be accessed from student residence rooms and from off campus. Internet access, at least one staffed computer lab available.

Student Life *Housing:* on-campus residence required through junior year. *Options:* coed, men-only, women-only. *Activities and Organizations:* drama/

theater group, student-run newspaper, radio and television station, choral group, Christian Fellowship, Beta Beta Beta, Cap Board, SERVE, Black Student Union, national fraternities, national sororities. *Campus security:* 24-hour emergency response devices and patrols, student patrols, late-night transport/escort service, controlled dormitory access. *Student Services:* health clinic, personal/psychological counseling.

Athletics Member NCAA. All Division III. *Intercollegiate sports:* baseball M, basketball M/W, cross-country running M/W, equestrian sports M(c), field hockey W, football M, golf M, lacrosse M/W, soccer M/W, softball W, swimming M/W, tennis M/W, track and field M/W, volleyball W, wrestling M. *Intramural sports:* badminton M/W, basketball M/W, football M, golf M/W, racquetball M/W, soccer M/W, softball M/W, swimming M/W, tennis M/W, volleyball M/W, weight lifting M/W.

Standardized Tests *Required:* SAT I or ACT (for admission). *Recommended:* SAT II: Subject Tests (for admission).

Costs (2002–03) *Comprehensive fee:* $27,390 includes full-time tuition ($21,760), mandatory fees ($350), and room and board ($5280). Part-time tuition: $680 per credit. *Room and board:* College room only: $2690. Room and board charges vary according to board plan and housing facility. *Payment plans:* tuition prepayment, installment. *Waivers:* employees or children of employees.

Financial Aid Of all full-time matriculated undergraduates who enrolled in 2001, 1091 applied for aid, 951 were judged to have need, 285 had their need fully met. 193 Federal Work-Study jobs (averaging $1109). 118 State and other part-time jobs (averaging $827). In 2001, 451 non-need-based awards were made. *Average percent of need met:* 94%. *Average financial aid package:* $17,188. *Average need-based loan:* $4906. *Average need-based gift aid:* $7564. *Average non-need based aid:* $5498. *Average indebtedness upon graduation:* $17,490.

Applying *Options:* common application, electronic application, early admission, early action, deferred entrance. *Application fee:* $40. *Required:* essay or personal statement, high school transcript, minimum 2.5 GPA. *Required for some:* interview. *Recommended:* letters of recommendation, interview. *Application deadlines:* 3/15 (freshmen), 7/1 (transfers). *Notification:* 4/1 (freshmen), 12/15 (early action).

Admissions Contact Ms. M. Martha O'Connell, Dean of Admissions, Western Maryland College, 2 College Hill, Westminster, MD 21157-4390. *Phone:* 410-857-2230. *Toll-free phone:* 800-638-5005. *Fax:* 410-857-2757. *E-mail:* admissio@wmdc.edu.

MASSACHUSETTS

AMERICAN INTERNATIONAL COLLEGE
Springfield, Massachusetts

- **Independent** comprehensive, founded 1885
- **Calendar** semesters
- **Degrees** certificates, associate, bachelor's, master's, doctoral, and post-master's certificates
- **Urban** 58-acre campus
- **Endowment** $11.0 million
- **Coed,** 1,068 undergraduate students, 83% full-time, 53% women, 47% men
- **Moderately difficult** entrance level, 77% of applicants were admitted

Undergraduates Students come from 26 states and territories, 52 other countries, 41% are from out of state, 24% African American, 2% Asian American or Pacific Islander, 6% Hispanic American, 0.3% Native American, 6% international, 58% live on campus. *Retention:* 62% of 2001 full-time freshmen returned.

Freshmen *Admission:* 1,025 applied, 790 admitted. *Average high school GPA:* 2.75.

Faculty *Total:* 155, 48% full-time, 54% with terminal degrees. *Student/faculty ratio:* 13:1.

Majors Accounting; adult/continuing education; biochemistry; biology; business administration; business economics; business education; business marketing and marketing management; chemistry; criminal justice/law enforcement administration; early childhood education; economics; education; elementary education; English; finance; history; human resources management; human services; information sciences/systems; international business; international relations; law enforcement/police science; liberal arts and sciences/liberal studies; management information systems/business data processing; mass communications; mathematics; medical technology; middle school education; nursing; occupational therapy; philosophy; political science; pre-dentistry; pre-law; pre-medicine; pre-veterinary studies; psychology; public administration; secondary education; social sciences; sociology; Spanish; special education.

Academic Programs *Special study options:* academic remediation for entering students, accelerated degree program, adult/continuing education programs, advanced placement credit, double majors, English as a second language, freshman honors college, honors programs, independent study, internships, off-campus study, part-time degree program, services for LD students, study abroad, summer session for credit. *ROTC:* Army (c), Air Force (c).

Library James J. Shea Jr. Library with 118,000 titles, 390 serial subscriptions, an OPAC, a Web page.

Computers on Campus 100 computers available on campus for general student use. Internet access, at least one staffed computer lab available.

Student Life *Housing:* on-campus residence required through sophomore year. *Options:* coed, men-only, women-only. *Activities and Organizations:* drama/theater group, student-run newspaper, radio station, choral group, Student Activities Committee, Golden Key Society, PRIDE (Persons Ready in Defense of Ebony), student government, national fraternities, national sororities. *Campus security:* 24-hour emergency response devices and patrols, student patrols, late-night transport/escort service, controlled dormitory access. *Student Services:* health clinic, personal/psychological counseling.

Athletics Member NCAA. All Division II. *Intercollegiate sports:* baseball M(s), basketball M(s)/W(s), field hockey W(s), football M(s), golf M, ice hockey M(s), lacrosse M/W(s), soccer M/W(s), softball W(s), tennis M/W, volleyball W(s), wrestling M. *Intramural sports:* archery M/W, basketball M/W, equestrian sports M/W, football M, golf M, skiing (cross-country) M/W, skiing (downhill) M/W, soccer M/W, swimming M/W, table tennis M/W, tennis M/W, volleyball M/W, wrestling W(c).

Standardized Tests *Required:* SAT I or ACT (for admission).

Costs (2001–02) *Comprehensive fee:* $22,268 includes full-time tuition ($14,800) and room and board ($7468). Full-time tuition and fees vary according to course load and program. Part-time tuition: $345 per credit. *Required fees:* $25 per term part-time. *Room and board:* Room and board charges vary according to board plan. *Payment plans:* tuition prepayment, installment, deferred payment. *Waivers:* senior citizens and employees or children of employees.

Financial Aid Of all full-time matriculated undergraduates who enrolled in 2001, 764 applied for aid, 712 were judged to have need, 279 had their need fully met. 250 Federal Work-Study jobs. In 2001, 16 non-need-based awards were made. *Average percent of need met:* 83%. *Average financial aid package:* $16,755. *Average need-based loan:* $5763. *Average need-based gift aid:* $6622. *Average non-need based aid:* $4104. *Average indebtedness upon graduation:* $17,125.

Applying *Options:* common application, electronic application, early admission, early decision, deferred entrance. *Application fee:* $20. *Required:* high school transcript, 1 letter of recommendation. *Required for some:* interview. *Recommended:* interview. *Application deadline:* rolling (freshmen), rolling (transfers). *Early decision:* 11/15. *Notification:* continuous (freshmen), 12/15 (early decision).

Admissions Contact Dean of Admissions, American International College, 1000 State Street, Springfield, MA 01109-3189. *Phone:* 413-205-3201. *Toll-free phone:* 800-242-3142. *Fax:* 413-205-3051. *E-mail:* inquiry@acad.aic.edu.

AMHERST COLLEGE
Amherst, Massachusetts

- **Independent** 4-year, founded 1821
- **Calendar** semesters
- **Degree** bachelor's
- **Small-town** 964-acre campus
- **Endowment** $890.5 million
- **Coed,** 1,631 undergraduate students, 100% full-time, 49% women, 51% men
- **Most difficult** entrance level, 19% of applicants were admitted

Undergraduates 1,631 full-time. Students come from 56 states and territories, 29 other countries, 84% are from out of state, 9% African American, 11% Asian American or Pacific Islander, 8% Hispanic American, 4% international, 0.3% transferred in, 98% live on campus. *Retention:* 97% of 2001 full-time freshmen returned.

Freshmen *Admission:* 5,175 applied, 973 admitted, 430 enrolled. *Test scores:* SAT verbal scores over 500: 100%; SAT math scores over 500: 99%; ACT scores over 18: 100%; SAT verbal scores over 600: 92%; SAT math scores over 600: 91%; ACT scores over 24: 91%; SAT verbal scores over 700: 61%; SAT math scores over 700: 57%; ACT scores over 30: 58%.

Faculty *Total:* 207, 86% full-time, 90% with terminal degrees. *Student/faculty ratio:* 9:1.

Majors African-American studies; American studies; anthropology; art; Asian studies; astronomy; biology; chemistry; classics; computer science; dance; eco-

Amherst College (continued)
nomics; English; European studies; fine/studio arts; French; geology; German; Greek (ancient and medieval); history; interdisciplinary studies; Latin (ancient and medieval); legal studies; mathematics; music; neuroscience; philosophy; physics; political science; psychology; religious studies; Russian; sociology; Spanish; theater arts/drama; women's studies.

Academic Programs *Special study options:* double majors, honors programs, independent study, off-campus study, student-designed majors, study abroad.

Library Robert Frost Library plus 5 others with 916,830 titles, 5,878 serial subscriptions, 56,494 audiovisual materials, an OPAC, a Web page.

Computers on Campus 161 computers available on campus for general student use. A campuswide network can be accessed from student residence rooms and from off campus. Internet access, at least one staffed computer lab available.

Student Life *Housing:* on-campus residence required for freshman year. *Options:* coed, cooperative. *Activities and Organizations:* drama/theater group, student-run newspaper, radio station, choral group, choral groups, WAMH (campus radio station), OUTREACH (Community Service), literary magazines, The Amherst Student (school newspaper). *Campus security:* 24-hour emergency response devices and patrols, student patrols, late-night transport/escort service, controlled dormitory access. *Student Services:* health clinic, personal/psychological counseling, women's center.

Athletics Member NCAA. All Division III. *Intercollegiate sports:* baseball M, basketball M/W, crew M(c)/W(c), cross-country running M/W, equestrian sports M(c)/W(c), fencing M(c)/W(c), field hockey W, football M, golf M/W, ice hockey M/W, lacrosse M/W, rugby M(c)/W(c), sailing M(c)/W(c), skiing (downhill) M(c)/W(c), soccer M/W, softball W, squash M/W, swimming M/W, tennis M/W, track and field M/W, volleyball M(c)/W, water polo M(c)/W(c). *Intramural sports:* badminton M/W, basketball M/W, golf M/W, ice hockey M/W, soccer M/W, softball M/W, squash M/W, swimming M/W, tennis M/W, track and field M/W, volleyball M/W.

Standardized Tests *Required:* SAT I or ACT (for admission).

Costs (2001–02) *Comprehensive fee:* $34,358 includes full-time tuition ($26,760), mandatory fees ($498), and room and board ($7100). *Room and board:* College room only: $3800. *Payment plans:* installment, deferred payment.

Financial Aid Of all full-time matriculated undergraduates who enrolled in 2001, 874 applied for aid, 763 were judged to have need, 763 had their need fully met. 557 Federal Work-Study jobs (averaging $1322). 90 State and other part-time jobs (averaging $1363). In 2001, 150 non-need-based awards were made. *Average percent of need met:* 100%. *Average financial aid package:* $24,229. *Average need-based loan:* $2904. *Average need-based gift aid:* $22,904. *Average non-need based aid:* $5615. *Average indebtedness upon graduation:* $12,270.

Applying *Options:* common application, electronic application, early decision, deferred entrance. *Application fee:* $55. *Required:* essay or personal statement, high school transcript, 3 letters of recommendation. *Application deadlines:* 12/31 (freshmen), 12/31 (transfers). *Early decision:* 11/15. *Notification:* 4/5 (freshmen), 12/15 (early decision).

Admissions Contact Mr. Thomas Parker, Dean of Admission and Financial Aid, Amherst College, PO Box 5000, Amherst, MA 01002. *Phone:* 413-542-2328. *Fax:* 413-542-2040. *E-mail:* admission@amherst.edu.

ANNA MARIA COLLEGE
Paxton, Massachusetts

- **Independent Roman Catholic** comprehensive, founded 1946
- **Calendar** semesters
- **Degrees** associate, bachelor's, master's, post-master's, and postbachelor's certificates
- **Rural** 180-acre campus with easy access to Boston
- **Endowment** $1.7 million
- **Coed,** 832 undergraduate students, 69% full-time, 63% women, 37% men
- **Moderately difficult** entrance level, 87% of applicants were admitted

Undergraduates 576 full-time, 256 part-time. Students come from 13 states and territories, 4 other countries, 14% are from out of state, 3% African American, 1% Asian American or Pacific Islander, 3% Hispanic American, 0.4% Native American, 0.8% international, 6% transferred in, 59% live on campus. *Retention:* 75% of 2001 full-time freshmen returned.

Freshmen *Admission:* 508 applied, 440 admitted, 149 enrolled. *Average high school GPA:* 2.75. *Test scores:* SAT verbal scores over 500: 41%; SAT math scores over 500: 36%; ACT scores over 18: 57%; SAT verbal scores over 600: 7%; SAT math scores over 600: 7%; SAT verbal scores over 700: 1%.

Faculty *Total:* 163, 21% full-time, 23% with terminal degrees. *Student/faculty ratio:* 11:1.

Majors Art; art education; art therapy; behavioral sciences; biology; business administration; computer/information sciences related; criminal justice/law enforcement administration; early childhood education; elementary education; English; fine/studio arts; fire science; history; interdisciplinary studies; medical illustrating; music; music (piano and organ performance); music teacher education; music therapy; music (voice and choral/opera performance); nursing; paralegal/legal assistant; philosophy; political science; psychology; religious studies; social sciences; social work.

Academic Programs *Special study options:* academic remediation for entering students, accelerated degree program, adult/continuing education programs, advanced placement credit, double majors, English as a second language, internships, off-campus study, part-time degree program, services for LD students, student-designed majors, study abroad, summer session for credit. *ROTC:* Army (c). *Unusual degree programs:* 3-2 engineering with Worcester Polytechnic Institute.

Library Mondor-Eagen Library with 65,794 titles, 364 serial subscriptions, 1,247 audiovisual materials, an OPAC, a Web page.

Computers on Campus 57 computers available on campus for general student use. A campuswide network can be accessed from student residence rooms and from off campus that provide access to on-line class schedules, student account information. Internet access, at least one staffed computer lab available.

Student Life *Housing Options:* coed. *Activities and Organizations:* drama/theater group, student-run newspaper, choral group, Student Government Association, Drama Club, Ski Club, chorus, Criminal Justice Club. *Campus security:* 24-hour emergency response devices and patrols, late-night transport/escort service, controlled dormitory access. *Student Services:* health clinic, personal/psychological counseling.

Athletics Member NCAA. All Division III. *Intercollegiate sports:* baseball M, basketball M/W, cross-country running M/W, field hockey W, golf M, soccer M/W, softball W, volleyball W. *Intramural sports:* basketball M/W, field hockey W, football M, softball M/W, volleyball M/W, weight lifting M.

Standardized Tests *Required:* SAT I or ACT (for admission).

Costs (2001–02) *Comprehensive fee:* $22,800 includes full-time tuition ($15,250), mandatory fees ($1250), and room and board ($6300). Part-time tuition: $600 per course. No tuition increase for student's term of enrollment. *Room and board:* Room and board charges vary according to board plan. *Payment plan:* installment. *Waivers:* children of alumni, senior citizens, and employees or children of employees.

Financial Aid Of all full-time matriculated undergraduates who enrolled in 2001, 495 applied for aid, 431 were judged to have need, 118 had their need fully met. 133 Federal Work-Study jobs (averaging $1000). In 2001, 70 non-need-based awards were made. *Average percent of need met:* 82%. *Average financial aid package:* $12,155. *Average need-based loan:* $4167. *Average need-based gift aid:* $8300. *Average indebtedness upon graduation:* $18,000.

Applying *Options:* early admission, deferred entrance. *Application fee:* $30. *Required:* essay or personal statement, high school transcript, 2 letters of recommendation. *Required for some:* audition for music programs, portfolio for art programs. *Recommended:* minimum 2.0 GPA, interview. *Application deadline:* rolling (freshmen), rolling (transfers). *Notification:* continuous (freshmen).

Admissions Contact Ms. Jane Fidler, Director of Admissions, Anna Maria College, Box O, Sunset Lane, Paxton, MA 01612. *Phone:* 508-849-3360. *Toll-free phone:* 800-344-4586 Ext. 360. *Fax:* 508-849-3362. *E-mail:* admission@annamaria.edu.

THE ART INSTITUTE OF BOSTON AT LESLEY UNIVERSITY
Boston, Massachusetts

- **Independent** comprehensive, founded 1912
- **Calendar** semesters
- **Degrees** certificates, diplomas, bachelor's, and master's
- **Urban** campus
- **Endowment** $29.0 million
- **Coed,** 554 undergraduate students, 91% full-time, 56% women, 44% men
- **Moderately difficult** entrance level, 76% of applicants were admitted

Undergraduates 503 full-time, 51 part-time. Students come from 35 states and territories, 25 other countries, 58% are from out of state, 3% African American, 3% Asian American or Pacific Islander, 3% Hispanic American, 11% international, 11% transferred in, 22% live on campus. *Retention:* 85% of 2001 full-time freshmen returned.

Freshmen *Admission:* 483 applied, 368 admitted, 89 enrolled. *Average high school GPA:* 2.96. *Test scores:* SAT verbal scores over 500: 70%; SAT math scores over 500: 66%; SAT verbal scores over 600: 27%; SAT math scores over 600: 18%; SAT verbal scores over 700: 3%; SAT math scores over 700: 1%.

Faculty *Total:* 102, 22% full-time, 65% with terminal degrees. *Student/faculty ratio:* 11:1.

Majors Art; graphic design/commercial art/illustration; photography.

Academic Programs *Special study options:* academic remediation for entering students, adult/continuing education programs, advanced placement credit, English as a second language, honors programs, internships, off-campus study, part-time degree program, services for LD students, student-designed majors, study abroad, summer session for credit.

Library The Art Institute of Boston Library plus 1 other with 9,015 titles, 77 serial subscriptions, 365 audiovisual materials.

Computers on Campus 50 computers available on campus for general student use. A campuswide network can be accessed from that provide access to graphics programs, software applications. Internet access, at least one staffed computer lab available.

Student Life *Housing Options:* coed. *Activities and Organizations:* Peer Advisors, International Student Association, Student Gallery Committee, Literary Journal. *Campus security:* 24-hour emergency response devices, student patrols, controlled dormitory access. *Student Services:* health clinic, personal/psychological counseling.

Athletics Member NCAA. All Division III. *Intercollegiate sports:* basketball W, crew W, cross-country running W, soccer W, softball W, volleyball W. *Intramural sports:* tennis W, volleyball W.

Standardized Tests *Required:* SAT I or ACT (for admission).

Costs (2002–03) *Comprehensive fee:* $24,940 includes full-time tuition ($15,000), mandatory fees ($740), and room and board ($9200). Full-time tuition and fees vary according to program. Part-time tuition: $640 per credit. Part-time tuition and fees vary according to program. *Required fees:* $230 per term part-time. *Room and board:* Room and board charges vary according to housing facility. *Payment plan:* installment. *Waivers:* adult students, senior citizens, and employees or children of employees.

Financial Aid Of all full-time matriculated undergraduates who enrolled in 2001, 338 applied for aid, 246 were judged to have need. In 2001, 35 non-need-based awards were made. *Average percent of need met:* 66%. *Average financial aid package:* $8130. *Average need-based loan:* $4721. *Average need-based gift aid:* $4159. *Average non-need based aid:* $3500. *Average indebtedness upon graduation:* $13,350.

Applying *Options:* common application, deferred entrance. *Application fee:* $40. *Required:* essay or personal statement, high school transcript, interview, portfolio. *Recommended:* minimum 2.0 GPA, letters of recommendation. *Application deadline:* rolling (freshmen), rolling (transfers). *Notification:* continuous (freshmen).

Admissions Contact Bradford White, Director of Admissions, The Art Institute of Boston at Lesley University, 700 Beacon Street, Boston, MA 02215-2598. *Phone:* 617-585-6700. *Toll-free phone:* 800-773-0494. *Fax:* 617-437-1226. *E-mail:* admissions@aiboston.edu.

ASSUMPTION COLLEGE
Worcester, Massachusetts

- **Independent Roman Catholic** comprehensive, founded 1904
- **Calendar** semesters
- **Degrees** bachelor's, master's, and post-master's certificates
- **Urban** 145-acre campus with easy access to Boston
- **Endowment** $38.3 million
- **Coed,** 2,094 undergraduate students, 99% full-time, 61% women, 39% men
- **Moderately difficult** entrance level, 75% of applicants were admitted

Undergraduates 2,068 full-time, 26 part-time. Students come from 23 states and territories, 16 other countries, 32% are from out of state, 0.9% African American, 1% Asian American or Pacific Islander, 2% Hispanic American, 0.9% international, 1% transferred in, 88% live on campus. *Retention:* 82% of 2001 full-time freshmen returned.

Freshmen *Admission:* 2,804 applied, 2,113 admitted, 606 enrolled. *Average high school GPA:* 3.18. *Test scores:* SAT verbal scores over 500: 73%; SAT math scores over 500: 71%; ACT scores over 18: 92%; SAT verbal scores over 600: 18%; SAT math scores over 600: 19%; ACT scores over 24: 31%; SAT verbal scores over 700: 1%; SAT math scores over 700: 2%; ACT scores over 30: 2%.

Faculty *Total:* 193, 66% full-time, 79% with terminal degrees. *Student/faculty ratio:* 14:1.

Majors Accounting; biology; biotechnology research; business administration; business communications; business marketing and marketing management; chemistry; classics; computer science; economics; education; elementary education; English; environmental science; foreign languages/literatures; French; history; human services; international business; international economics; international relations; Latin American studies; mathematics; molecular biology; philosophy; political science; psychology; public relations; secondary education; sociology; Spanish; theology; visual/performing arts.

Academic Programs *Special study options:* adult/continuing education programs, advanced placement credit, double majors, honors programs, independent study, internships, off-campus study, part-time degree program, services for LD students, student-designed majors, summer session for credit. *ROTC:* Air Force (c). *Unusual degree programs:* 3-2 engineering with Worcester Polytechnic Institute.

Library Emmanuel d'Alzon Library with 104,586 titles, 1,119 serial subscriptions, 1,450 audiovisual materials, an OPAC, a Web page.

Computers on Campus 190 computers available on campus for general student use. A campuswide network can be accessed from student residence rooms and from off campus. Internet access, at least one staffed computer lab available.

Student Life *Housing Options:* coed, women-only. *Activities and Organizations:* drama/theater group, student-run newspaper, television station, choral group, Volunteer Center, Campus Activities Board, student government, Campus Ministry, resident assistants. *Campus security:* 24-hour emergency response devices and patrols, student patrols, late-night transport/escort service, front gate security, well-lit pathways. *Student Services:* health clinic, personal/psychological counseling.

Athletics Member NCAA. All Division II. *Intercollegiate sports:* baseball M, basketball M(s)/W(s), crew M/W, cross-country running M/W, field hockey W, football M, golf M, ice hockey M, lacrosse M/W, soccer M/W, softball W, tennis M/W, track and field M(c)/W(c), volleyball W. *Intramural sports:* basketball M/W, football M, racquetball M/W, skiing (downhill) M/W, soccer M/W, softball M/W, volleyball M/W.

Standardized Tests *Required:* SAT I or ACT (for admission).

Costs (2001–02) *Comprehensive fee:* $26,320 includes full-time tuition ($18,800), mandatory fees ($145), and room and board ($7375). Full-time tuition and fees vary according to course load, program, and reciprocity agreements. Part-time tuition: $627 per credit hour. Part-time tuition and fees vary according to course load. *Required fees:* $145 per year part-time. *Room and board:* College room only: $4575. Room and board charges vary according to board plan and housing facility. *Payment plan:* installment. *Waivers:* minority students and employees or children of employees.

Financial Aid Of all full-time matriculated undergraduates who enrolled in 2001, 1642 applied for aid, 1407 were judged to have need, 482 had their need fully met. 429 Federal Work-Study jobs (averaging $1020). In 2001, 435 non-need-based awards were made. *Average percent of need met:* 82%. *Average financial aid package:* $13,404. *Average need-based loan:* $4672. *Average need-based gift aid:* $9208. *Average indebtedness upon graduation:* $18,523. *Financial aid deadline:* 3/1.

Applying *Options:* common application, electronic application, early decision, deferred entrance. *Application fee:* $40. *Required:* essay or personal statement, high school transcript, 1 letter of recommendation. *Recommended:* interview. *Application deadlines:* 3/1 (freshmen), 5/1 (transfers). *Early decision:* 11/15. *Notification:* continuous until 5/1 (freshmen), 12/15 (early decision).

Admissions Contact Ms. Mary Bresnahan, Dean of Admission, Assumption College, 500 Salisbury Street, Worcester, MA 01609-1296. *Phone:* 508-767-7362. *Toll-free phone:* 888-882-7786. *Fax:* 508-799-4412. *E-mail:* admiss@assumption.edu.

ATLANTIC UNION COLLEGE
South Lancaster, Massachusetts

- **Independent Seventh-day Adventist** comprehensive, founded 1882
- **Calendar** semesters
- **Degrees** certificates, associate, bachelor's, and master's
- **Small-town** 314-acre campus with easy access to Boston
- **Endowment** $2.0 million
- **Coed,** 637 undergraduate students, 75% full-time, 59% women, 41% men
- **Moderately difficult** entrance level, 19% of applicants were admitted

Undergraduates 477 full-time, 160 part-time. Students come from 15 states and territories, 45% are from out of state, 49% African American, 2% Asian American or Pacific Islander, 21% Hispanic American, 0.4% Native American, 68% live on campus. *Retention:* 75% of 2001 full-time freshmen returned.

Freshmen *Admission:* 621 applied, 118 admitted, 88 enrolled.

Faculty *Total:* 47, 85% full-time, 57% with terminal degrees. *Student/faculty ratio:* 12:1.

Majors Accounting; adult/continuing education; art; art education; biochemistry; biological/physical sciences; biology; business administration; business education; chemistry; computer programming; computer science; divinity/ministry; early childhood education; education; elementary education; English; exercise sciences; French; history; information sciences/systems; interior design; mathematics; medical technology; modern languages; music; music teacher education;

Atlantic Union College (continued)
natural sciences; nursing; paralegal/legal assistant; physical education; pre-dentistry; pre-engineering; pre-law; pre-medicine; pre-veterinary studies; psychology; religious music; religious studies; secondary education; secretarial science; social work; sociology; Spanish; theology.

Academic Programs *Special study options:* academic remediation for entering students, adult/continuing education programs, advanced placement credit, cooperative education, English as a second language, external degree program, freshman honors college, honors programs, internships, part-time degree program, study abroad, summer session for credit.

Library G. Eric Jones Library with 136,744 titles, 531 serial subscriptions, 827 audiovisual materials, an OPAC, a Web page.

Computers on Campus 74 computers available on campus for general student use. Internet access, at least one staffed computer lab available.

Student Life *Housing:* on-campus residence required through senior year. *Options:* coed, men-only, women-only. *Activities and Organizations:* drama/theater group, student-run newspaper, radio station, choral group, Student Association, Black Christian Union, choir, CHISPA (Hispanic group). *Campus security:* 24-hour patrols, late-night transport/escort service. *Student Services:* health clinic, personal/psychological counseling.

Athletics Member NAIA. *Intercollegiate sports:* basketball M(s)/W(s), soccer M, volleyball M/W(s). *Intramural sports:* basketball M/W, football M/W, golf M/W, skiing (downhill) M/W, soccer M/W, softball M/W, volleyball M/W.

Standardized Tests *Required:* ACT (for placement). *Recommended:* SAT I (for placement).

Costs (2001–02) *Comprehensive fee:* $18,280 includes full-time tuition ($12,600), mandatory fees ($980), and room and board ($4700). Full-time tuition and fees vary according to class time and program. Part-time tuition: $511 per hour. *Room and board:* College room only: $2600. Room and board charges vary according to board plan and gender. *Payment plan:* installment. *Waivers:* senior citizens and employees or children of employees.

Financial Aid Of all full-time matriculated undergraduates who enrolled in 2001, 515 applied for aid, 482 were judged to have need, 36 had their need fully met. In 2001, 124 non-need-based awards were made. *Average percent of need met:* 67%. *Average financial aid package:* $8784. *Average need-based loan:* $4851. *Average need-based gift aid:* $4937. *Average indebtedness upon graduation:* $18,500.

Applying *Options:* common application. *Application fee:* $25. *Required:* high school transcript, minimum 2.0 GPA, 2 letters of recommendation. *Required for some:* essay or personal statement, interview. *Application deadlines:* 8/1 (freshmen), 8/1 (transfers). *Notification:* continuous (freshmen).

Admissions Contact Mrs. Rosita Lashley, Associate Director for Admissions, Atlantic Union College, PO Box 1000, South Lancaster, MA 01561. *Phone:* 978-368-2239. *Toll-free phone:* 800-282-2030. *Fax:* 978-368-2015. *E-mail:* enroll@math.atlanticuc.edu.

BABSON COLLEGE
Wellesley, Massachusetts

- **Independent** comprehensive, founded 1919
- **Calendar** semesters
- **Degrees** bachelor's and master's
- **Suburban** 450-acre campus with easy access to Boston
- **Endowment** $181.2 million
- **Coed,** 1,719 undergraduate students, 100% full-time, 37% women, 63% men
- **Very difficult** entrance level, 35% of applicants were admitted

Undergraduates 1,719 full-time. Students come from 42 states and territories, 64 other countries, 53% are from out of state, 3% African American, 8% Asian American or Pacific Islander, 4% Hispanic American, 0.3% Native American, 19% international, 3% transferred in, 87% live on campus. *Retention:* 89% of 2001 full-time freshmen returned.

Freshmen *Admission:* 3,127 applied, 1,081 admitted, 398 enrolled. *Average high school GPA:* 2.83. *Test scores:* SAT verbal scores over 500: 97%; SAT math scores over 500: 99%; SAT verbal scores over 600: 53%; SAT math scores over 600: 80%; SAT verbal scores over 700: 5%; SAT math scores over 700: 17%.

Faculty *Total:* 201, 81% full-time, 90% with terminal degrees. *Student/faculty ratio:* 9:1.

Majors Accounting; business administration; business communications; business marketing and marketing management; economics; entrepreneurship; finance; international business; investments and securities; management information systems/business data processing; operations research.

Academic Programs *Special study options:* advanced placement credit, freshman honors college, honors programs, independent study, internships, off-campus study, services for LD students, student-designed majors, study abroad, summer session for credit. *ROTC:* Army (c), Navy (c), Air Force (c).

Library Horn Library plus 1 other with 129,401 titles, 1,224 serial subscriptions, 4,053 audiovisual materials, an OPAC, a Web page.

Computers on Campus 350 computers available on campus for general student use. A campuswide network can be accessed from student residence rooms and from off campus. Internet access, online (class) registration, at least one staffed computer lab available.

Student Life *Housing Options:* coed, men-only, disabled students. *Activities and Organizations:* drama/theater group, student-run newspaper, radio station, choral group, student government, Free Press, Dance Ensemble, Asian Pacific Student Association, college radio, national fraternities, national sororities. *Campus security:* 24-hour emergency response devices and patrols, late-night transport/escort service, controlled dormitory access. *Student Services:* health clinic, personal/psychological counseling.

Athletics Member NCAA. All Division III. *Intercollegiate sports:* baseball M, basketball M/W, cross-country running M/W, field hockey W, golf M/W, ice hockey M, lacrosse M/W, rugby M(c)/W(c), sailing M(c)/W(c), skiing (downhill) M/W, soccer M/W, softball W, squash M(c)/W(c), swimming M/W, tennis M/W, track and field M/W, volleyball M(c)/W. *Intramural sports:* basketball M/W, football M, ice hockey M/W, racquetball M/W, soccer M/W, squash M/W, swimming M/W, tennis M/W, volleyball M/W, water polo M/W.

Standardized Tests *Required:* SAT I or ACT (for admission). *Recommended:* SAT II: Writing Test (for admission).

Costs (2001–02) *Comprehensive fee:* $33,290 includes full-time tuition ($24,544) and room and board ($8746). *Room and board:* College room only: $5950. Room and board charges vary according to board plan and housing facility. *Payment plan:* installment. *Waivers:* employees or children of employees.

Financial Aid Of all full-time matriculated undergraduates who enrolled in 2001, 742 applied for aid, 701 were judged to have need, 660 had their need fully met. 271 Federal Work-Study jobs (averaging $1443). In 2001, 90 non-need-based awards were made. *Average percent of need met:* 99%. *Average financial aid package:* $19,475. *Average need-based loan:* $4059. *Average need-based gift aid:* $14,200. *Average non-need based aid:* $6600. *Average indebtedness upon graduation:* $23,000. *Financial aid deadline:* 2/15.

Applying *Options:* common application, electronic application, early decision, early action, deferred entrance. *Application fee:* $50. *Required:* essay or personal statement, high school transcript, 2 letters of recommendation. *Application deadlines:* 2/1 (freshmen), 4/1 (transfers). *Early decision:* 12/1. *Notification:* 4/1 (freshmen), 1/1 (early decision), 1/15 (early action).

Admissions Contact Mrs. Monica Inzer, Dean of Undergraduate Admission and Student Financial Services, Babson College, Office of Undergraduate Admission, Mustard Hall, Babson Park, MA 02457-0310. *Phone:* 800-488-3696. *Toll-free phone:* 800-488-3696. *Fax:* 781-239-4006. *E-mail:* ugradadmission@babson.edu.

BAPTIST BIBLE COLLEGE EAST
Boston, Massachusetts

- **Independent Baptist** primarily 2-year, founded 1976
- **Calendar** semesters
- **Degrees** certificates, diplomas, associate, and bachelor's
- **Suburban** 8-acre campus with easy access to Providence
- **Coed**
- **Moderately difficult** entrance level

Student Life *Campus security:* 24-hour emergency response devices, student patrols.

Standardized Tests *Required:* SAT I or ACT (for admission).

Costs (2001–02) *Comprehensive fee:* $8530 includes full-time tuition ($3350), mandatory fees ($980), and room and board ($4200). Part-time tuition: $150 per credit hour. *Required fees:* $50 per credit hour.

Applying *Options:* common application. *Application fee:* $25. *Required:* essay or personal statement, high school transcript, letters of recommendation. *Recommended:* interview.

Admissions Contact Mr. James Thomasson, Director of Admissions and Records, Baptist Bible College East, 950 Metropolitan Avenue, Boston, MA 02136. *Phone:* 617-364-3510. *Toll-free phone:* 888-235-2014. *Fax:* 617-364-0723.

BAY PATH COLLEGE
Longmeadow, Massachusetts

- **Independent** comprehensive, founded 1897
- **Calendar** semesters

- **Degrees** certificates, associate, bachelor's, and master's
- **Suburban** 44-acre campus with easy access to Boston
- **Endowment** $16.7 million
- **Women only,** 918 undergraduate students, 73% full-time
- **Moderately difficult** entrance level, 72% of applicants were admitted

Undergraduates 669 full-time, 249 part-time. Students come from 15 states and territories, 17 other countries, 40% are from out of state, 11% African American, 2% Asian American or Pacific Islander, 5% Hispanic American, 0.1% Native American, 5% international, 2% transferred in, 40% live on campus. *Retention:* 79% of 2001 full-time freshmen returned.

Freshmen *Admission:* 162 enrolled. *Average high school GPA:* 3.02. *Test scores:* SAT verbal scores over 500: 47%; SAT math scores over 500: 39%; SAT verbal scores over 600: 11%; SAT math scores over 600: 4%; SAT verbal scores over 700: 1%; SAT math scores over 700: 1%.

Faculty *Total:* 118, 28% full-time, 34% with terminal degrees. *Student/faculty ratio:* 13:1.

Majors Business; business administration; communications; criminal justice/law enforcement administration; early childhood education; elementary education; fine/studio arts; health services administration; history; hospitality management; human resources management; information technology; international business; legal studies; liberal arts and sciences/liberal studies; occupational therapy; occupational therapy assistant; paralegal/legal assistant; psychology; travel/tourism management.

Academic Programs *Special study options:* academic remediation for entering students, adult/continuing education programs, advanced placement credit, English as a second language, freshman honors college, honors programs, independent study, internships, off-campus study, part-time degree program, services for LD students, student-designed majors, study abroad, summer session for credit. *ROTC:* Army (c), Air Force (c).

Library Frank and Marion Hatch Library with 43,997 titles, 317 serial subscriptions, 2,153 audiovisual materials, an OPAC.

Computers on Campus 114 computers available on campus for general student use. A campuswide network can be accessed from student residence rooms and from off campus. At least one staffed computer lab available.

Student Life *Housing Options:* women-only. *Activities and Organizations:* drama/theater group, choral group, student government, All Women Excel, Golden Z Service Club, Phi Beta Lambda, Women of Culture. *Campus security:* 24-hour emergency response devices and patrols, late-night transport/escort service, controlled dormitory access. *Student Services:* health clinic, personal/psychological counseling, women's center.

Athletics Member NCAA. All Division III. *Intercollegiate sports:* basketball W, cross-country running W(c), soccer W, softball W, volleyball W(c).

Standardized Tests *Required:* SAT I or ACT (for admission).

Costs (2001–02) *Comprehensive fee:* $21,621 includes full-time tuition ($14,754) and room and board ($6867). Full-time tuition and fees vary according to course load. Part-time tuition: $408 per credit. Part-time tuition and fees vary according to course load. *Room and board:* Room and board charges vary according to board plan. *Payment plans:* tuition prepayment, installment, deferred payment. *Waivers:* employees or children of employees.

Financial Aid Of all full-time matriculated undergraduates who enrolled in 2001, 486 applied for aid, 431 were judged to have need, 61 had their need fully met. 98 Federal Work-Study jobs (averaging $1719). In 2001, 112 non-need-based awards were made. *Average percent of need met:* 75%. *Average financial aid package:* $10,893. *Average need-based loan:* $4102. *Average need-based gift aid:* $6780. *Average indebtedness upon graduation:* $18,000.

Applying *Options:* common application, electronic application, early admission, early action, deferred entrance. *Application fee:* $25. *Required:* essay or personal statement, high school transcript, 2 letters of recommendation. *Required for some:* minimum 3.0 GPA, interview. *Recommended:* minimum 2.0 GPA, interview. *Application deadline:* rolling (freshmen), rolling (transfers). *Notification:* continuous (freshmen), 1/2 (early action).

Admissions Contact Ms. Brenda Wishart, Director of Admissions, Bay Path College, 588 Longmeadow Street, Longmeadow, MA 01106-2292. *Phone:* 413-565-1000 Ext. 229. *Toll-free phone:* 800-782-7284 Ext. 331. *Fax:* 413-565-1105. *E-mail:* admiss@baypath.edu.

BECKER COLLEGE
Worcester, Massachusetts

- **Independent** 4-year, founded 1784
- **Calendar** semesters
- **Degrees** certificates, associate, and bachelor's (also includes Leicester, MA small town campus)
- **Urban** campus with easy access to Boston
- **Coed,** 1,298 undergraduate students, 57% full-time, 79% women, 21% men
- **Minimally difficult** entrance level, 90% of applicants were admitted

The innovative programs at Becker College are a carefully crafted blend of professional and liberal arts courses that contribute to the development of competent professionals and informed citizens. The two beautiful campuses offer students a choice as to the living environment that best suits their personal taste.

Undergraduates 740 full-time, 558 part-time. Students come from 17 states and territories, 32% are from out of state, 4% transferred in, 65% live on campus. *Retention:* 87% of 2001 full-time freshmen returned.

Freshmen *Admission:* 1,309 applied, 1,181 admitted, 394 enrolled. *Average high school GPA:* 2.70.

Faculty *Total:* 107, 36% full-time, 16% with terminal degrees. *Student/faculty ratio:* 15:1.

Majors Accounting; administration of special education; animal sciences; business administration; business marketing and marketing management; child care/development; computer systems analysis; criminal justice/law enforcement administration; developmental/child psychology; early childhood education; elementary education; exercise sciences; graphic design/commercial art/illustration; hospitality management; hotel and restaurant management; humanities; human resources management; human services; interior design; law enforcement/police science; legal studies; liberal arts and sciences/liberal studies; mass communications; nursing; occupational therapy assistant; paralegal/legal assistant; physical therapy assistant; psychology; sport/fitness administration; veterinary sciences; veterinary technology.

Academic Programs *Special study options:* academic remediation for entering students, accelerated degree program, adult/continuing education programs, advanced placement credit, cooperative education, distance learning, English as a second language, internships, off-campus study, part-time degree program, services for LD students, study abroad, summer session for credit. *ROTC:* Army (c), Navy (c), Air Force (c). *Unusual degree programs:* 3-2 law, Massachusetts School of Law.

Library Ruska Library plus 1 other with 65,000 titles, 400 serial subscriptions, 2,900 audiovisual materials, an OPAC.

Computers on Campus 155 computers available on campus for general student use. A campuswide network can be accessed from student residence rooms and from off campus. Internet access, at least one staffed computer lab available.

Student Life *Housing Options:* coed, men-only, women-only. *Activities and Organizations:* drama/theater group, student-run newspaper, radio station, student government, Student Activities Committee, Travel Club, Ski Club, Drama Club. *Campus security:* 24-hour emergency response devices and patrols, late-night transport/escort service, controlled dormitory access. *Student Services:* health clinic, personal/psychological counseling.

Athletics Member NCAA. *Intercollegiate sports:* baseball M, basketball M/W, cross-country running M/W, equestrian sports M/W, field hockey W, golf M, ice hockey M(c)/W(c), lacrosse M, soccer M/W, softball W, tennis M, volleyball W. *Intramural sports:* badminton M/W, basketball M/W, bowling M(c)/W(c), skiing (downhill) M(c)/W(c), soccer M/W, table tennis M/W, volleyball M/W, weight lifting M/W.

Standardized Tests *Required:* SAT I or ACT (for admission).

Costs (2001–02) *Comprehensive fee:* $20,930 includes full-time tuition ($13,530), mandatory fees ($220), and room and board ($7180). Full-time tuition and fees vary according to class time, course load, and program. Part-time tuition: $451 per credit. Part-time tuition and fees vary according to class time, course load, and program. *Payment plan:* installment. *Waivers:* senior citizens and employees or children of employees.

Financial Aid Of all full-time matriculated undergraduates who enrolled in 2001, 636 applied for aid, 574 were judged to have need, 124 had their need fully met. 388 Federal Work-Study jobs. In 2001, 68 non-need-based awards were made. *Average percent of need met:* 65%. *Average financial aid package:* $9737. *Average need-based loan:* $4373. *Average need-based gift aid:* $5087. *Average indebtedness upon graduation:* $8303.

Applying *Options:* common application, electronic application, deferred entrance. *Application fee:* $25. *Required:* high school transcript, minimum 2.0 GPA. *Required for some:* minimum 2.5 GPA, interview. *Recommended:* essay or personal statement, letters of recommendation. *Application deadline:* rolling (freshmen), rolling (transfers). *Notification:* continuous (freshmen).

Admissions Contact Admissions Receptionist, Becker College, 61 Sever Street, Worcester, MA 01609. *Phone:* 508-791-9241 Ext. 245. *Toll-free phone:* 877-5BECKER Ext. 245. *Fax:* 508-890-1500. *E-mail:* admissions@beckercollege.edu.

BENJAMIN FRANKLIN INSTITUTE OF TECHNOLOGY

Boston, Massachusetts

- **Independent** primarily 2-year, founded 1908
- **Calendar** semesters
- **Degrees** certificates, associate, and bachelor's
- **Urban** 3-acre campus
- **Endowment** $8.0 million
- **Coed, primarily men**
- **Minimally difficult** entrance level

Faculty *Student/faculty ratio:* 11:1.
Student Life *Campus security:* 24-hour emergency response devices, student patrols.
Standardized Tests *Recommended:* SAT I or ACT (for admission).
Costs (2001–02) *Tuition:* $10,125 full-time, $422 per credit part-time. *Required fees:* $265 full-time, $422 per credit. *Room only:* Room and board charges vary according to board plan and housing facility.
Applying *Options:* common application, electronic application, deferred entrance. *Application fee:* $20. *Required:* high school transcript. *Recommended:* essay or personal statement, minimum 2.0 GPA, letters of recommendation, interview.
Admissions Contact Wildolfo Arvelo, Dean of Enrollment Services, Benjamin Franklin Institute of Technology, 41 Berkeley Street, Boston, MA 02116-6296. *Phone:* 617-423-4630 Ext. 122. *Fax:* 617-482-3706. *E-mail:* fibadm@fib.edu.

BENTLEY COLLEGE

Waltham, Massachusetts

- **Independent** comprehensive, founded 1917
- **Calendar** semesters
- **Degrees** associate, bachelor's, master's, post-master's, and postbachelor's certificates
- **Suburban** 143-acre campus with easy access to Boston
- **Endowment** $166.6 million
- **Coed,** 4,256 undergraduate students, 87% full-time, 43% women, 57% men
- **Moderately difficult** entrance level, 38% of applicants were admitted

Undergraduates 3,710 full-time, 546 part-time. Students come from 43 states and territories, 63 other countries, 38% are from out of state, 3% African American, 7% Asian American or Pacific Islander, 3% Hispanic American, 0.1% Native American, 8% international, 4% transferred in, 78% live on campus. *Retention:* 93% of 2001 full-time freshmen returned.
Freshmen *Admission:* 5,906 applied, 2,250 admitted, 851 enrolled. *Test scores:* SAT verbal scores over 500: 84%; SAT math scores over 500: 97%; ACT scores over 18: 95%; SAT verbal scores over 600: 24%; SAT math scores over 600: 51%; ACT scores over 24: 55%; SAT verbal scores over 700: 2%; SAT math scores over 700: 6%; ACT scores over 30: 6%.
Faculty *Total:* 422, 58% full-time. *Student/faculty ratio:* 14:1.
Majors Accounting; business; business administration; business communications; business economics; business marketing and marketing management; computer/information sciences; economics; English; finance; history; interdisciplinary studies; international economics; liberal arts and sciences/liberal studies; mathematics; philosophy.
Academic Programs *Special study options:* academic remediation for entering students, accelerated degree program, adult/continuing education programs, advanced placement credit, distance learning, English as a second language, honors programs, internships, off-campus study, part-time degree program, services for LD students, student-designed majors, study abroad, summer session for credit. *ROTC:* Army (c).
Library Soloman R. Baker Library with 208,986 titles, 9,319 serial subscriptions, an OPAC, a Web page.
Computers on Campus 3349 computers available on campus for general student use. A campuswide network can be accessed from student residence rooms and from off campus. Internet access, online (class) registration, at least one staffed computer lab available.
Student Life *Activities and Organizations:* drama/theater group, student-run newspaper, radio station, choral group, Student Government Association, Campus Activities Board, Hall Council Advisory Board, Greek Council, WBTY, national fraternities, national sororities. *Campus security:* 24-hour emergency response devices and patrols, late-night transport/escort service, controlled dormitory access, security cameras. *Student Services:* health clinic, personal/psychological counseling.
Athletics Member NCAA. All Division II. *Intercollegiate sports:* baseball M(s), basketball M(s)/W(s), cross-country running M(s)/W(s), field hockey W(s), football M, ice hockey M(s), lacrosse M(s), soccer M(s)/W(s), softball W(s), swimming M(s)/W(s), tennis M/W, track and field M(s)/W(s), volleyball W(s). *Intramural sports:* basketball M/W, field hockey W, football M, racquetball M/W, soccer M/W, softball M/W, volleyball M/W.
Standardized Tests *Required:* SAT I or ACT (for admission).
Costs (2001–02) *Comprehensive fee:* $29,071 includes full-time tuition ($19,876), mandatory fees ($185), and room and board ($9010). Part-time tuition and fees vary according to class time. *Room and board:* College room only: $5130. Room and board charges vary according to board plan and housing facility. *Payment plan:* installment. *Waivers:* employees or children of employees.
Financial Aid Of all full-time matriculated undergraduates who enrolled in 2001, 2386 applied for aid, 1863 were judged to have need, 745 had their need fully met. In 2001, 349 non-need-based awards were made. *Average percent of need met:* 97%. *Average financial aid package:* $19,633. *Average need-based loan:* $4094. *Average need-based gift aid:* $11,706. *Average non-need based aid:* $8946. *Average indebtedness upon graduation:* $17,811. *Financial aid deadline:* 2/1.
Applying *Options:* common application, electronic application, early admission, early decision, early action, deferred entrance. *Application fee:* $50. *Required:* essay or personal statement, high school transcript, 2 letters of recommendation. *Recommended:* interview. *Application deadlines:* 2/1 (freshmen), 5/15 (transfers). *Early decision:* 12/1. *Notification:* 4/1 (freshmen), 12/28 (early decision), 1/15 (early action).
Admissions Contact Ms. Judith A. Pearson, Director of Admission, Bentley College, 175 Forest Street, Waltham, MA 02452-4705. *Phone:* 781-891-2244. *Toll-free phone:* 800-523-2354. *Fax:* 781-891-3414. *E-mail:* ugadmission@bentley.edu.

BERKLEE COLLEGE OF MUSIC

Boston, Massachusetts

- **Independent** 4-year, founded 1945
- **Calendar** semesters
- **Degree** diplomas and bachelor's
- **Urban** campus
- **Endowment** $139.8 million
- **Coed,** 3,415 undergraduate students
- **Moderately difficult** entrance level, 35% of applicants were admitted

Undergraduates Students come from 55 states and territories, 81 other countries, 80% are from out of state, 4% African American, 3% Asian American or Pacific Islander, 3% Hispanic American, 0.4% Native American, 30% international, 22% live on campus.
Freshmen *Admission:* 2,582 applied, 916 admitted.
Faculty *Total:* 498, 42% full-time. *Student/faculty ratio:* 14:1.
Majors Audio engineering; jazz; music; music business management/merchandising; music (general performance); music (piano and organ performance); music teacher education; music theory and composition; music therapy; music (voice and choral/opera performance); stringed instruments; wind/percussion instruments.
Academic Programs *Special study options:* accelerated degree program, advanced placement credit, double majors, English as a second language, internships, off-campus study, services for LD students, student-designed majors, study abroad, summer session for credit.
Library The Stan Getz Media Center and Library with 30,208 titles, 77 serial subscriptions, 19,480 audiovisual materials, an OPAC, a Web page.
Computers on Campus 45 computers available on campus for general student use. A campuswide network can be accessed from student residence rooms. Internet access, at least one staffed computer lab available.
Student Life *Housing Options:* coed. *Activities and Organizations:* drama/theater group, student-run newspaper, choral group, Musical Theater at Berklee Club, Yoga Society, Black Student Union, Christian Fellowship. *Campus security:* 24-hour patrols. *Student Services:* personal/psychological counseling.
Athletics *Intramural sports:* basketball M/W, ice hockey M/W, soccer M/W, table tennis M/W.
Standardized Tests *Required for some:* SAT I or ACT (for admission).
Costs (2002–03) *Comprehensive fee:* $28,559 includes full-time tuition ($18,290), mandatory fees ($479), and room and board ($9790). *Payment plan:* installment. *Waivers:* employees or children of employees.
Financial Aid Of all full-time matriculated undergraduates who enrolled in 2001, 1304 applied for aid, 1175 were judged to have need. In 2001, 621 non-need-based awards were made. *Average percent of need met:* 81%. *Average financial aid package:* $15,500. *Average need-based loan:* $4249. *Average need-based gift aid:* $1834.

Applying *Options:* electronic application, deferred entrance. *Application fee:* $75. *Required:* essay or personal statement, high school transcript, 2 letters of recommendation, 2 years of formal music study. *Required for some:* interview. *Recommended:* interview. *Application deadline:* rolling (freshmen), rolling (out-of-state freshmen), rolling (transfers). *Notification:* continuous (freshmen), continuous (out-of-state freshmen).

Admissions Contact Ms. Marsha Ginn, Director of Admissions, Berklee College of Music, 1140 Boylston Street, Boston, MA 02215-3693. *Phone:* 617-747-2222. *Toll-free phone:* 800-BERKLEE. *Fax:* 617-747-2047. *E-mail:* admissions@berklee.edu.

BOSTON ARCHITECTURAL CENTER
Boston, Massachusetts

- **Independent** comprehensive, founded 1889
- **Calendar** semesters
- **Degrees** certificates, bachelor's, and master's
- **Urban** campus
- **Endowment** $59.4 million
- **Coed,** 458 undergraduate students, 85% full-time, 25% women, 75% men
- **Noncompetitive** entrance level, 95% of applicants were admitted

Undergraduates 391 full-time, 67 part-time. Students come from 43 states and territories, 47% are from out of state, 2% African American, 2% Asian American or Pacific Islander, 5% Hispanic American, 3% Native American, 14% transferred in. *Retention:* 53% of 2001 full-time freshmen returned.

Freshmen *Admission:* 330 applied, 315 admitted, 103 enrolled.

Faculty *Total:* 189, 37% with terminal degrees. *Student/faculty ratio:* 10:1.

Majors Architecture; interior design.

Academic Programs *Special study options:* adult/continuing education programs, advanced placement credit, cooperative education, independent study, internships, off-campus study, summer session for credit.

Library Shaw and Stone Library plus 1 other with 25,000 titles, 140 serial subscriptions, a Web page.

Computers on Campus 50 computers available on campus for general student use. Internet access, at least one staffed computer lab available.

Student Life *Housing:* college housing not available. *Activities and Organizations:* student-run newspaper, student government. *Campus security:* 24-hour emergency response devices and patrols, electronically operated building access.

Costs (2001–02) *Tuition:* $7016 full-time, $585 per credit part-time. Full-time tuition and fees vary according to course load and program. Part-time tuition and fees vary according to course load and program. *Required fees:* $10 full-time, $10 per term part-time. *Payment plans:* installment, deferred payment.

Applying *Application fee:* $50. *Required:* high school transcript. *Application deadline:* rolling (freshmen), rolling (transfers).

Admissions Contact Mr. Will Dunfey, Director of Admissions, Boston Architectural Center, 320 Newbury Street, Boston, MA 02115-2795. *Phone:* 617-585-0202. *Toll-free phone:* 877-585-0100. *Fax:* 617-585-0121. *E-mail:* admissions@the-bac.edu.

BOSTON COLLEGE
Chestnut Hill, Massachusetts

- **Independent Roman Catholic (Jesuit)** university, founded 1863
- **Calendar** semesters
- **Degrees** bachelor's, master's, doctoral, first professional, and post-master's certificates (also offers continuing education program with significant enrollment not reflected in profile)
- **Suburban** 240-acre campus with easy access to Boston
- **Endowment** $1.1 billion
- **Coed,** 9,000 undergraduate students, 100% full-time, 53% women, 47% men
- **Very difficult** entrance level, 34% of applicants were admitted

Boston College's international stature is strengthened by the more than 450-year tradition of Jesuit education. Students are challenged to fulfill their potential as scholars through honors programs, research with faculty members, independent study, study abroad, and service learning. Students are also challenged to fulfill their potential as caring, thoughtful individuals and future leaders in society with artistic, cultural, service, social, religious, and athletic opportunities that abound on campus and throughout Boston.

Undergraduates 9,000 full-time. Students come from 53 states and territories, 63 other countries, 72% are from out of state, 4% African American, 8% Asian American or Pacific Islander, 5% Hispanic American, 0.3% Native American, 1% international, 1% transferred in, 73% live on campus. *Retention:* 95% of 2001 full-time freshmen returned.

Freshmen *Admission:* 19,059 applied, 6,401 admitted, 2,103 enrolled. *Test scores:* SAT verbal scores over 500: 96%; SAT math scores over 500: 98%; SAT verbal scores over 600: 78%; SAT math scores over 600: 85%; SAT verbal scores over 700: 22%; SAT math scores over 700: 30%.

Faculty *Total:* 1,120, 58% full-time. *Student/faculty ratio:* 13:1.

Majors Accounting; art history; biochemistry; biology; business administration; business marketing and marketing management; chemistry; classics; computer science; early childhood education; economics; elementary education; English; environmental science; finance; fine/studio arts; French; geology; geophysics/seismology; German; Hispanic-American studies; history; human resources management; individual/family development; interdisciplinary studies; Italian; management information systems/business data processing; mass communications; mathematics; music; nursing; operations research; philosophy; physics; political science; pre-medicine; psychology; Russian; Russian/Slavic studies; secondary education; Slavic languages; sociology; special education; theater arts/drama; theology.

Academic Programs *Special study options:* accelerated degree program, adult/continuing education programs, advanced placement credit, double majors, freshman honors college, honors programs, independent study, internships, off-campus study, part-time degree program, services for LD students, student-designed majors, study abroad, summer session for credit. *ROTC:* Army (c), Navy (c), Air Force (c). *Unusual degree programs:* 3-2 engineering with Boston University; education.

Library Thomas P. O'Neill Library plus 6 others with 2.0 million titles, 21,121 serial subscriptions, 121,969 audiovisual materials, an OPAC, a Web page.

Computers on Campus 200 computers available on campus for general student use. A campuswide network can be accessed from student residence rooms and from off campus. At least one staffed computer lab available.

Student Life *Housing Options:* coed, women-only. *Activities and Organizations:* drama/theater group, student-run newspaper, radio and television station, choral group, marching band, Ski Club, The Bostonians, Boston College Bop. *Campus security:* 24-hour emergency response devices and patrols, late-night transport/escort service, controlled dormitory access. *Student Services:* health clinic, personal/psychological counseling, women's center.

Athletics Member NCAA. All Division I except football (Division I-A). *Intercollegiate sports:* baseball M, basketball M(s)/W(s), crew M(c)/W(c), cross-country running M/W(s), fencing M/W, field hockey W(s), golf M/W, ice hockey M(s)/W, lacrosse M/W(s), rugby M(c)/W(c), sailing M/W, skiing (downhill) M/W, soccer M(s)/W(s), softball W(s), swimming M/W(s), tennis M/W(s), track and field M(s)/W(s), volleyball W(s), water polo M, wrestling M. *Intramural sports:* basketball M/W, cross-country running M/W, football M/W, ice hockey M/W, lacrosse M(c)/W(c), racquetball M/W, sailing M(c)/W(c), skiing (downhill) M(c)/W(c), softball M/W, squash M/W, swimming M/W, tennis M/W, track and field M/W, volleyball M/W, water polo M.

Standardized Tests *Required:* SAT II: Writing Test (for admission).

Costs (2001–02) *Comprehensive fee:* $33,330 includes full-time tuition ($24,050), mandatory fees ($420), and room and board ($8860). *Room and board:* Room and board charges vary according to housing facility. *Payment plans:* tuition prepayment, installment. *Waivers:* employees or children of employees.

Financial Aid Of all full-time matriculated undergraduates who enrolled in 2001, 6251 applied for aid, 3760 were judged to have need, 3722 had their need fully met. In 2001, 360 non-need-based awards were made. *Average percent of need met:* 100%. *Average financial aid package:* $18,830. *Average need-based loan:* $4692. *Average need-based gift aid:* $13,275. *Average non-need based aid:* $5585. *Average indebtedness upon graduation:* $16,732.

Applying *Options:* common application, electronic application, early admission, early action, deferred entrance. *Application fee:* $55. *Required:* essay or personal statement, high school transcript, 2 letters of recommendation. *Application deadlines:* 1/2 (freshmen), 4/15 (transfers). *Notification:* 4/15 (freshmen), 12/24 (early action).

Admissions Contact Mr. John L. Mahoney Jr., Director of Undergraduate Admission, Boston College, 140 Commonwealth Avenue, Devlin Hall 208, 140 Commonwealth Avenue, Chestnut Hill, MA 02167-3809. *Phone:* 617-552-3100. *Toll-free phone:* 800-360-2522. *Fax:* 617-552-0798. *E-mail:* ugadmis@bc.edu.

THE BOSTON CONSERVATORY
Boston, Massachusetts

- **Independent** comprehensive, founded 1867
- **Calendar** semesters
- **Degrees** diplomas, bachelor's, and master's

The Boston Conservatory (continued)
- **Urban** campus
- **Coed,** 373 undergraduate students, 99% full-time, 62% women, 38% men
- **Moderately difficult** entrance level, 16% of applicants were admitted

Undergraduates 368 full-time, 5 part-time. Students come from 42 states and territories, 80% are from out of state, 5% African American, 5% Asian American or Pacific Islander, 5% Hispanic American, 0.8% Native American, 8% international. *Retention:* 86% of 2001 full-time freshmen returned.
Freshmen *Admission:* 907 applied, 146 admitted, 120 enrolled.
Faculty *Total:* 164, 28% full-time. *Student/faculty ratio:* 6:1.
Majors Dance; music; music (piano and organ performance); music teacher education; music theory and composition; music (voice and choral/opera performance); stringed instruments; theater arts/drama; wind/percussion instruments.
Academic Programs *Special study options:* adult/continuing education programs, advanced placement credit, double majors, English as a second language, off-campus study, summer session for credit.
Library The Albert Alphin Music Library with 40,000 titles, 92 serial subscriptions.
Computers on Campus 16 computers available on campus for general student use. Internet access, at least one staffed computer lab available.
Student Life *Housing:* on-campus residence required for freshman year. *Options:* coed, women-only. *Activities and Organizations:* drama/theater group, student-run newspaper, choral group, Student Government Association, Korean Student Association, Chinese Student Association, Sigma Alpha Iota, national fraternities, national sororities. *Campus security:* 24-hour emergency response devices and patrols, controlled dormitory access. *Student Services:* health clinic, personal/psychological counseling.
Standardized Tests *Required:* SAT I or ACT (for admission).
Costs (2002–03) *Comprehensive fee:* $31,565 includes full-time tuition ($20,310), mandatory fees ($1775), and room and board ($9480). Full-time tuition and fees vary according to course load, degree level, and program. Part-time tuition: $830 per credit. Part-time tuition and fees vary according to course load, degree level, and program.
Financial Aid Of all full-time matriculated undergraduates who enrolled in 2001, 306 applied for aid, 215 were judged to have need, 21 had their need fully met. 67 Federal Work-Study jobs (averaging $971). 24 State and other part-time jobs (averaging $1250). In 2001, 71 non-need-based awards were made. *Average percent of need met:* 50%. *Average financial aid package:* $11,050. *Average need-based loan:* $4884. *Average need-based gift aid:* $4088. *Average non-need based aid:* $6322. *Average indebtedness upon graduation:* $15,000. *Financial aid deadline:* 3/1.
Applying *Options:* deferred entrance. *Application fee:* $60. *Required:* essay or personal statement, high school transcript, minimum 2.7 GPA, 4 letters of recommendation, audition. *Required for some:* interview. *Application deadline:* 3/1 (freshmen), rolling (transfers). *Notification:* 4/1 (freshmen).
Admissions Contact Ms. Halley Shefler, Dean of Enrollment, The Boston Conservatory, 8 The Fenway, Boston, MA 02215. *Phone:* 617-912-9153. *Fax:* 617-536-3176.

BOSTON UNIVERSITY
Boston, Massachusetts

- **Independent** university, founded 1839
- **Calendar** semesters
- **Degrees** bachelor's, master's, doctoral, first professional, and post-master's certificates
- **Urban** 132-acre campus
- **Endowment** $674.1 million
- **Coed,** 17,602 undergraduate students, 89% full-time, 60% women, 40% men
- **Very difficult** entrance level, 48% of applicants were admitted

Boston University (BU) is a private teaching and research institution with a strong emphasis on undergraduate education. The University is committed to providing the highest level of teaching excellence and fulfillment of this pledge is its highest priority. BU has 11 undergraduate schools and colleges offering 250 major and minor areas of concentration. Students may choose from programs of study in areas as diverse as biochemistry, theater arts, physical therapy, elementary education, broadcast journalism, international relations, business, and computer engineering. BU has an international student body, with students from every state and more than 100 countries. In addition, opportunities to study abroad exist through 34 different programs, spanning 16 countries on 6 continents.

Undergraduates 15,600 full-time, 2,002 part-time. Students come from 52 states and territories, 102 other countries, 76% are from out of state, 3% African American, 12% Asian American or Pacific Islander, 5% Hispanic American, 0.3% Native American, 7% international, 1% transferred in, 59% live on campus. *Retention:* 85% of 2001 full-time freshmen returned.
Freshmen *Admission:* 27,562 applied, 13,270 admitted, 3,601 enrolled. *Average high school GPA:* 3.5. *Test scores:* SAT verbal scores over 500: 100%; SAT math scores over 500: 100%; ACT scores over 18: 100%; SAT verbal scores over 600: 75%; SAT math scores over 600: 83%; ACT scores over 24: 91%; SAT verbal scores over 700: 20%; SAT math scores over 700: 22%; ACT scores over 30: 29%.
Faculty *Total:* 3,283, 72% full-time. *Student/faculty ratio:* 12:1.
Majors Accounting; acting/directing; aerospace engineering; American studies; anthropology; archaeology; area studies related; art education; art history; astronomy; astrophysics; athletic training/sports medicine; bilingual/bicultural education; biochemistry; bioengineering; biological sciences/life sciences related; biology; business administration; business marketing and marketing management; chemistry; chemistry education; classics; communication disorders; communications; computer engineering; computer science; dental laboratory technician; drama/dance education; drama/theater literature; drawing; early childhood education; earth sciences; East Asian studies; ecology; economics; education; education of the hearing impaired; electrical engineering; elementary education; engineering; engineering related; English; English education; environmental science; ethnic/cultural studies related; exercise sciences; film/video production; finance; foreign languages education; foreign languages/literatures; French; geography; geology; German; graphic design/commercial art/illustration; Greek (ancient and medieval); Greek (modern); health science; history; hospitality management; hotel and restaurant management; industrial/manufacturing engineering; information sciences/systems; interdisciplinary studies; international business; international finance; international relations; Italian; journalism; journalism and mass communication related; Latin American studies; Latin (ancient and medieval); linguistics; management information systems/business data processing; marine biology; marketing research; mass communications; mathematics; mathematics/computer science; mathematics education; mechanical engineering; medical technology; molecular biology; music (general performance); music history; music (piano and organ performance); music teacher education; music theory and composition; music (voice and choral/opera performance); neuroscience; nutritional sciences; occupational therapy; operations management; organizational behavior; painting; paralegal/legal assistant; philosophy; physical education; physical therapy; physics; physiology; political science; pre-dentistry; psychology; public relations; radio/television broadcasting; recreation/leisure studies; rehabilitation therapy; religious studies; Russian; Russian/Slavic studies; science education; sculpture; social sciences and history related; social studies education; sociology; Spanish; special education; speech/theater education; systems engineering; teacher education related; theater design; urban studies.
Academic Programs *Special study options:* accelerated degree program, adult/continuing education programs, advanced placement credit, cooperative education, double majors, English as a second language, honors programs, independent study, internships, off-campus study, part-time degree program, services for LD students, student-designed majors, study abroad, summer session for credit. *ROTC:* Army (b), Navy (b), Air Force (b). *Unusual degree programs:* 3-2 over 30 other programs.
Library Mugar Memorial Library plus 18 others with 2.3 million titles, 30,689 serial subscriptions, 71,678 audiovisual materials, an OPAC, a Web page.
Computers on Campus 750 computers available on campus for general student use. A campuswide network can be accessed from student residence rooms and from off campus that provide access to research and educational networks. Internet access, at least one staffed computer lab available.
Student Life *Housing:* on-campus residence required for freshman year. *Options:* coed, women-only, cooperative. *Activities and Organizations:* drama/theater group, student-run newspaper, radio station, choral group, marching band, performing and acappella groups, cultural organizations, service organizations, student government, residence hall associations, national fraternities, national sororities. *Campus security:* 24-hour emergency response devices and patrols, late-night transport/escort service, controlled dormitory access, security personnel at residence hall entrances, self-defense education, well-lit sidewalks. *Student Services:* health clinic, personal/psychological counseling, women's center.
Athletics Member NCAA. All Division I. *Intercollegiate sports:* badminton M(c)/W(c), baseball M(c), basketball M(s)/W(s), crew M(s)/W(s), cross-country running M(s)/W(s), equestrian sports M(c)/W(c), fencing M(c)/W(c), field hockey W(s), golf M/W, gymnastics M(c)/W(c), ice hockey M(s)/W(c), lacrosse M(c)/W(s), rugby M(c)/W(c), sailing M(c)/W(c), skiing (downhill) M(c)/W(c), soccer M(s)/W(s), softball W(s), swimming M(s)/W(s), table tennis M(c)/W(c), tennis M/W(s), track and field M(s)/W(s), volleyball M(c)/W(c), water polo W(c), wrestling M(s). *Intramural sports:* basketball M/W, field hockey W, football M/W, ice hockey M, soccer M/W, softball M/W, swimming M/W, tennis M/W, volleyball M/W, water polo W, wrestling M.
Standardized Tests *Required:* SAT I or ACT (for admission). *Required for some:* SAT II: Subject Tests (for admission), SAT II: Writing Test (for admission).

Costs (2001–02) *Comprehensive fee:* $34,978 includes full-time tuition ($25,872), mandatory fees ($356), and room and board ($8750). Part-time tuition: $809 per credit. *Required fees:* $40 per term part-time. *Room and board:* College room only: $3280. Room and board charges vary according to board plan and housing facility. *Payment plans:* tuition prepayment, installment. *Waivers:* senior citizens and employees or children of employees.

Financial Aid Of all full-time matriculated undergraduates who enrolled in 2001, 7513 applied for aid, 6919 were judged to have need, 4323 had their need fully met. 4051 Federal Work-Study jobs (averaging $2265). 186 State and other part-time jobs (averaging $8892). In 2001, 1904 non-need-based awards were made. *Average percent of need met:* 93%. *Average financial aid package:* $23,838. *Average need-based loan:* $4374. *Average need-based gift aid:* $15,980. *Average indebtedness upon graduation:* $17,808.

Applying *Options:* common application, electronic application, early admission, early decision, deferred entrance. *Application fee:* $60. *Required:* essay or personal statement, high school transcript, 2 letters of recommendation. *Required for some:* interview, audition, portfolio. *Recommended:* minimum 3.0 GPA. *Application deadlines:* 1/1 (freshmen), 4/1 (transfers). *Early decision:* 11/1. *Notification:* continuous until 4/15 (freshmen), 12/15 (early decision).

Admissions Contact Ms. Kelly A. Walter, Director of Undergraduate Admissions, Boston University, 121 Bay State Road, Boston, MA 02215. *Phone:* 617-353-2300. *Fax:* 617-353-9695. *E-mail:* admissions@bu.edu.

BRANDEIS UNIVERSITY
Waltham, Massachusetts

- **Independent** university, founded 1948
- **Calendar** semesters
- **Degrees** bachelor's, master's, doctoral, and postbachelor's certificates
- **Suburban** 235-acre campus with easy access to Boston
- **Endowment** $397.0 million
- **Coed,** 3,081 undergraduate students, 99% full-time, 56% women, 44% men
- **Most difficult** entrance level, 41% of applicants were admitted

A recent major study ranked Brandeis 9th among all United States private research universities, based on the faculty's contribution to the generation of new knowledge. To assist students of exceptional scholarly achievement and promise to study with this teaching faculty, Brandeis offers a significant number of academic merit-based scholarships of up to 75% of tuition.

Undergraduates 3,051 full-time, 30 part-time. Students come from 52 states and territories, 54 other countries, 75% are from out of state, 2% African American, 10% Asian American or Pacific Islander, 2% Hispanic American, 0.2% Native American, 6% international, 1% transferred in, 82% live on campus. *Retention:* 93% of 2001 full-time freshmen returned.

Freshmen *Admission:* 6,653 applied, 2,708 admitted, 736 enrolled. *Average high school GPA:* 3.50. *Test scores:* SAT verbal scores over 500: 99%; SAT math scores over 500: 99%; SAT verbal scores over 600: 87%; SAT math scores over 600: 85%; SAT verbal scores over 700: 32%; SAT math scores over 700: 37%.

Faculty *Total:* 470, 69% full-time, 90% with terminal degrees. *Student/faculty ratio:* 8:1.

Majors African-American studies; African studies; American studies; anthropology; area, ethnic, and cultural studies related; art; biochemistry; biological sciences/life sciences related; biology; biophysics; cell and molecular biology related; chemistry; classical and ancient Near Eastern languages related; comparative literature; computer science; economics; engineering physics; English; European studies; fine/studio arts; French; German; Greek (ancient and medieval); history; Islamic studies; Judaic studies; Latin American studies; Latin (ancient and medieval); linguistics; mathematics; Middle Eastern studies; multi/interdisciplinary studies related; music; neuroscience; philosophy; physics; political science; psychology; Russian; Russian/Slavic studies; sociology; Spanish; theater arts/drama.

Academic Programs *Special study options:* adult/continuing education programs, advanced placement credit, double majors, English as a second language, independent study, internships, off-campus study, part-time degree program, services for LD students, student-designed majors, study abroad, summer session for credit. *ROTC:* Army (c), Air Force (c).

Library Goldfarb Library plus 2 others with 1.1 million titles, 16,119 serial subscriptions, 32,996 audiovisual materials, an OPAC, a Web page.

Computers on Campus 104 computers available on campus for general student use. A campuswide network can be accessed from student residence rooms and from off campus that provide access to educational software. Internet access, online (class) registration, at least one staffed computer lab available.

Student Life *Housing Options:* coed, disabled students. *Activities and Organizations:* drama/theater group, student-run newspaper, radio and television station, choral group, Waltham Group, Student Programming Board, performing groups, student government. *Campus security:* 24-hour emergency response devices and patrols, late-night transport/escort service, controlled dormitory access. *Student Services:* health clinic, personal/psychological counseling, women's center.

Athletics Member NCAA. All Division III. *Intercollegiate sports:* baseball M, basketball M/W, crew M(c), cross-country running M/W, fencing M/W, field hockey W(c), golf M, lacrosse M(c)/W(c), rugby M(c)/W(c), sailing M/W, skiing (downhill) M(c)/W(c), soccer W, softball W, squash M(c), swimming M/W, tennis M/W, track and field M/W, volleyball W. *Intramural sports:* basketball M/W, equestrian sports M/W, football M, golf M/W, ice hockey M, lacrosse M, softball M/W, squash M/W, table tennis M/W, tennis M/W, volleyball M/W, water polo M/W, weight lifting M/W.

Costs (2001–02) *Comprehensive fee:* $34,481 includes full-time tuition ($26,281), mandatory fees ($795), and room and board ($7405). Full-time tuition and fees vary according to degree level and reciprocity agreements. Part-time tuition: $3285 per course. Part-time tuition and fees vary according to course load, degree level, and program. *Room and board:* College room only: $4160. Room and board charges vary according to board plan and housing facility. *Payment plans:* tuition prepayment, installment. *Waivers:* employees or children of employees.

Financial Aid Of all full-time matriculated undergraduates who enrolled in 2001, 1532 applied for aid, 1368 were judged to have need, 350 had their need fully met. 1016 Federal Work-Study jobs (averaging $1336). 274 State and other part-time jobs (averaging $1290). In 2001, 547 non-need-based awards were made. *Average percent of need met:* 84%. *Average financial aid package:* $21,076. *Average need-based loan:* $5827. *Average need-based gift aid:* $14,776.

Applying *Options:* common application, electronic application, early decision, deferred entrance. *Application fee:* $55. *Required:* essay or personal statement, high school transcript, 2 letters of recommendation. *Recommended:* minimum 3.0 GPA, interview. *Application deadlines:* 1/31 (freshmen), 4/1 (transfers). *Early decision:* 1/1. *Notification:* 4/15 (freshmen), 2/1 (early decision).

Admissions Contact Mr. Michael Kalafatas, Director of Admissions, Brandeis University, 415 South Street, Waltham, MA 02254-9110. *Phone:* 781-736-3500. *Toll-free phone:* 800-622-0622. *Fax:* 781-736-3536. *E-mail:* sendinfo@brandeis.edu.

BRIDGEWATER STATE COLLEGE
Bridgewater, Massachusetts

- **State-supported** comprehensive, founded 1840, part of Massachusetts Public Higher Education System
- **Calendar** semesters
- **Degrees** bachelor's, master's, post-master's, and postbachelor's certificates
- **Suburban** 235-acre campus with easy access to Boston
- **Endowment** $7.2 million
- **Coed,** 7,199 undergraduate students, 78% full-time, 61% women, 39% men
- **Moderately difficult** entrance level, 74% of applicants were admitted

Undergraduates 5,604 full-time, 1,595 part-time. Students come from 22 states and territories, 32 other countries, 3% are from out of state, 4% African American, 1% Asian American or Pacific Islander, 2% Hispanic American, 0.3% Native American, 2% international, 9% transferred in. *Retention:* 74% of 2001 full-time freshmen returned.

Freshmen *Admission:* 4,681 applied, 3,485 admitted, 1,171 enrolled. *Average high school GPA:* 2.92. *Test scores:* SAT verbal scores over 500: 55%; SAT math scores over 500: 53%; ACT scores over 18: 69%; SAT verbal scores over 600: 14%; SAT math scores over 600: 10%; ACT scores over 24: 22%; SAT verbal scores over 700: 1%; SAT math scores over 700: 1%; ACT scores over 30: 4%.

Faculty *Total:* 462, 54% full-time, 48% with terminal degrees. *Student/faculty ratio:* 19:1.

Majors Accounting; adapted physical education; aircraft pilot (professional); American government; anthropology; archaeology; art; athletic training/sports medicine; aviation management; biochemistry; biology; business administration; business marketing and marketing management; chemistry; city/community/regional planning; clinical psychology; communication disorders; computer science; craft/folk art; creative writing; criminal justice studies; criminology; drama/dance education; early childhood education; earth sciences; economics; education; elementary education; English; enterprise management; environmental biology; exercise sciences; finance; fine/studio arts; geochemistry; geography; geology; graphic design/commercial art/illustration; health education; health/physical education; history; international business; international relations; management information systems/business data processing; mathematics; middle school education; molecular biology; music; organizational psychology; philosophy; physical education; physics; political science; pre-law; psychology; recreation/leisure studies; social work; sociology; Spanish; special education; theater arts/drama.

Bridgewater State College (continued)

Academic Programs *Special study options:* academic remediation for entering students, adult/continuing education programs, advanced placement credit, distance learning, double majors, English as a second language, honors programs, independent study, internships, off-campus study, part-time degree program, services for LD students, student-designed majors, study abroad, summer session for credit. *ROTC:* Army (c), Air Force (b).

Library Clement Maxwell Library with 280,000 titles, 1,600 serial subscriptions, 9,700 audiovisual materials, an OPAC, a Web page.

Computers on Campus 534 computers available on campus for general student use. A campuswide network can be accessed from student residence rooms and from off campus that provide access to student account information, application software. Internet access, online (class) registration, at least one staffed computer lab available.

Student Life *Housing Options:* coed, women-only, disabled students. *Activities and Organizations:* drama/theater group, student-run newspaper, radio station, choral group, Greek life, Children's Developmental Clinic, Student Government Association, Afro-American/Latino Club, Program Committee, national fraternities, national sororities. *Campus security:* 24-hour emergency response devices and patrols, late-night transport/escort service, controlled dormitory access. *Student Services:* health clinic, personal/psychological counseling, women's center.

Athletics Member NCAA. All Division III. *Intercollegiate sports:* baseball M, basketball M/W, cross-country running M/W, field hockey W, football M, lacrosse M(c)/W, soccer M/W, softball W, swimming M/W, tennis M/W, track and field M/W, volleyball W, water polo M(c)/W(c), wrestling M. *Intramural sports:* basketball M/W, football M/W, soccer M/W, softball M/W, tennis M/W, volleyball M/W.

Standardized Tests *Required:* SAT I or ACT (for admission).

Costs (2001–02) *Tuition:* state resident $910 full-time, $38 per credit part-time; nonresident $7050 full-time, $294 per credit part-time. *Required fees:* $1913 full-time. *Room and board:* $4996; room only: $2818. Room and board charges vary according to board plan and housing facility. *Payment plan:* installment. *Waivers:* employees or children of employees.

Financial Aid Of all full-time matriculated undergraduates who enrolled in 2001, 2312 applied for aid, 1610 were judged to have need, 862 had their need fully met. In 2001, 581 non-need-based awards were made. *Average percent of need met:* 75%. *Average financial aid package:* $6450. *Average need-based loan:* $2765. *Average need-based gift aid:* $3198. *Average indebtedness upon graduation:* $9348.

Applying *Options:* common application, electronic application, early admission, early action, deferred entrance. *Application fee:* $20. *Required:* essay or personal statement, high school transcript, minimum 2.7 GPA. *Recommended:* letters of recommendation. *Application deadlines:* 3/1 (freshmen), 4/1 (transfers). *Notification:* continuous until 4/15 (freshmen), 12/15 (early action).

Admissions Contact Mr. Steve King, Director of Admissions, Bridgewater State College, Admission Office, Bridgewater, MA 02325-0001. *Phone:* 508-531-1237. *Fax:* 508-531-1746. *E-mail:* admission@bridgew.edu.

CAMBRIDGE COLLEGE
Cambridge, Massachusetts

- **Independent** comprehensive, founded 1971
- **Calendar** trimesters
- **Degrees** certificates, bachelor's, and master's
- **Urban** campus with easy access to Boston
- **Coed,** 450 undergraduate students
- **Minimally difficult** entrance level, 100% of applicants were admitted

Cambridge College's innovative Bachelor of Arts in psychology program is designed for working adults. It offers an empowering learning model, emphasizes peer support and assessment, and encourages personal and professional development. Students may choose a concentration in educational psychology, family and community systems: human services, organizational psychology and management, juvenile justice, educational psychology, or medical interpreter training.

Undergraduates Students come from 6 states and territories, 5 other countries, 2% are from out of state.

Freshmen *Admission:* 100 applied, 100 admitted.

Faculty *Total:* 50, 44% full-time, 100% with terminal degrees. *Student/faculty ratio:* 18:1.

Majors Psychology.

Academic Programs *Special study options:* accelerated degree program, adult/continuing education programs, English as a second language, independent study, internships, part-time degree program, study abroad, summer session for credit.

Library Gutman Library with an OPAC, a Web page.

Computers on Campus Internet access, at least one staffed computer lab available.

Student Life *Housing:* college housing not available.

Standardized Tests *Required:* ACCUPLACER.

Costs (2001–02) *Tuition:* $9000 full-time, $300 per credit part-time. *Required fees:* $150 full-time, $75 per term part-time. *Payment plan:* installment.

Applying *Options:* deferred entrance. *Application fee:* $30. *Required:* essay or personal statement, high school transcript, letters of recommendation, interview. *Application deadline:* rolling (freshmen), rolling (transfers). *Notification:* continuous (freshmen).

Admissions Contact Cambridge College, 1000 Massachusetts Avenue, Cambridge, MA 02138-5304. *Phone:* 617-868-1000. *Toll-free phone:* 800-877-4723. *Fax:* 617-349-3545. *E-mail:* enroll@idea.cambridge.edu.

CLARK UNIVERSITY
Worcester, Massachusetts

- **Independent** university, founded 1887
- **Calendar** semesters
- **Degrees** certificates, bachelor's, master's, doctoral, post-master's, and postbachelor's certificates
- **Urban** 50-acre campus with easy access to Boston
- **Endowment** $153.4 million
- **Coed,** 2,138 undergraduate students, 89% full-time, 60% women, 40% men
- **Moderately difficult** entrance level, 68% of applicants were admitted

Undergraduates 1,896 full-time, 242 part-time. Students come from 44 states and territories, 57 other countries, 60% are from out of state, 3% African American, 4% Asian American or Pacific Islander, 3% Hispanic American, 0.2% Native American, 8% international, 2% transferred in, 75% live on campus. *Retention:* 84% of 2001 full-time freshmen returned.

Freshmen *Admission:* 3,704 applied, 2,536 admitted, 515 enrolled. *Average high school GPA:* 3.31. *Test scores:* SAT verbal scores over 500: 87%; SAT math scores over 500: 90%; ACT scores over 18: 98%; SAT verbal scores over 600: 48%; SAT math scores over 600: 42%; ACT scores over 24: 64%; SAT verbal scores over 700: 9%; SAT math scores over 700: 5%; ACT scores over 30: 15%.

Faculty *Total:* 251, 65% full-time. *Student/faculty ratio:* 10:1.

Majors Art; art history; Asian studies; biochemistry; biology; business administration; chemistry; classics; comparative literature; computer science; cultural studies; development economics; earth sciences; ecology; economics; education; elementary education; engineering; English; environmental science; film studies; fine/studio arts; French; geography; graphic design/commercial art/illustration; history; interdisciplinary studies; international relations; Judaic studies; literature; mass communications; mathematics; middle school education; modern languages; molecular biology; music; natural resources management; neuroscience; peace/conflict studies; philosophy; physics; political science; pre-dentistry; pre-law; pre-medicine; pre-veterinary studies; psychology; secondary education; sociology; Spanish; theater arts/drama.

Academic Programs *Special study options:* academic remediation for entering students, accelerated degree program, adult/continuing education programs, advanced placement credit, double majors, English as a second language, honors programs, independent study, internships, off-campus study, part-time degree program, services for LD students, student-designed majors, study abroad, summer session for credit. *ROTC:* Army (c), Navy (c), Air Force (c). *Unusual degree programs:* 3-2 engineering with Columbia University, Washington University in St. Louis, Worcester Polytechnic Institute; environmental studies, international development, biology, chemistry, physics, economics, history, communication, public administration.

Library Robert Hutchings Goddard Library plus 4 others with 285,656 titles, 1,496 serial subscriptions, 970 audiovisual materials, an OPAC, a Web page.

Computers on Campus 70 computers available on campus for general student use. A campuswide network can be accessed from student residence rooms and from off campus that provide access to on-line course support. Internet access, at least one staffed computer lab available.

Student Life *Housing:* on-campus residence required through sophomore year. *Options:* coed, women-only, disabled students. *Activities and Organizations:* drama/theater group, student-run newspaper, radio and television station, choral group, Big Brother/Big Sister, Student Council, Student Activities Board, Massachusetts PIRG, Caribbean African Student Association. *Campus security:* 24-hour emergency response devices and patrols, student patrols, late-night transport/escort service, controlled dormitory access. *Student Services:* health clinic, personal/psychological counseling.

Athletics Member NCAA. All Division III. *Intercollegiate sports:* baseball M, basketball M/W, crew M/W, cross-country running M/W, field hockey W, lacrosse M, soccer M/W, softball W, swimming M/W, tennis M/W, volleyball W. *Intramural sports:* badminton M/W, basketball M/W, bowling M/W, equestrian sports M(c)/W(c), football M/W, golf M(c)/W(c), ice hockey M(c), lacrosse W(c), racquetball M/W, rugby M(c)/W(c), sailing M(c)/W(c), soccer M/W, softball M/W, squash M/W, table tennis M/W, track and field M(c)/W(c), volleyball M/W, water polo M/W, weight lifting M(c)/W(c).

Standardized Tests *Required:* SAT I or ACT (for admission). *Recommended:* SAT II: Subject Tests (for admission).

Costs (2001–02) *Comprehensive fee:* $29,170 includes full-time tuition ($24,400), mandatory fees ($220), and room and board ($4550). Part-time tuition: $3050 per course. *Room and board:* College room only: $2750. Room and board charges vary according to board plan and housing facility. *Payment plans:* tuition prepayment, installment. *Waivers:* employees or children of employees.

Financial Aid Of all full-time matriculated undergraduates who enrolled in 2001, 1540 applied for aid, 1080 were judged to have need, 702 had their need fully met. 750 Federal Work-Study jobs (averaging $1500). *Average percent of need met:* 86%. *Average financial aid package:* $20,685. *Average need-based loan:* $4464. *Average need-based gift aid:* $12,050. *Average indebtedness upon graduation:* $17,650.

Applying *Options:* common application, early admission, early decision, deferred entrance. *Application fee:* $50. *Required:* essay or personal statement, high school transcript, 2 letters of recommendation. *Recommended:* interview. *Application deadlines:* 2/1 (freshmen), 4/15 (transfers). *Early decision:* 11/15. *Notification:* 4/1 (freshmen), 12/15 (early decision).

Admissions Contact Mr. Harold M. Wingood, Dean of Admissions, Clark University, 950 Main Street, Worcester, MA 01610-1477. *Phone:* 508-793-7431. *Toll-free phone:* 800-GO-CLARK. *E-mail:* admissions@clarku.edu.

COLLEGE OF THE HOLY CROSS
Worcester, Massachusetts

- **Independent Roman Catholic (Jesuit)** 4-year, founded 1843
- **Calendar** semesters
- **Degree** bachelor's
- **Suburban** 174-acre campus with easy access to Boston
- **Endowment** $377.6 million
- **Coed,** 2,811 undergraduate students, 99% full-time, 52% women, 48% men
- **Very difficult** entrance level, 43% of applicants were admitted

Undergraduates 2,782 full-time, 29 part-time. Students come from 47 states and territories, 17 other countries, 66% are from out of state, 3% African American, 4% Asian American or Pacific Islander, 5% Hispanic American, 0.3% Native American, 0.8% international, 0.7% transferred in, 78% live on campus. *Retention:* 95% of 2001 full-time freshmen returned.

Freshmen *Admission:* 4,753 applied, 2,037 admitted, 691 enrolled. *Test scores:* SAT verbal scores over 500: 98%; SAT math scores over 500: 98%; SAT verbal scores over 600: 71%; SAT math scores over 600: 74%; SAT verbal scores over 700: 17%; SAT math scores over 700: 14%.

Faculty *Total:* 268, 83% full-time, 81% with terminal degrees. *Student/faculty ratio:* 12:1.

Majors Accounting; African-American studies; African studies; art history; Asian studies; biochemistry; biology; biopsychology; chemistry; classics; economics; English; environmental science; fine/studio arts; French; German; gerontology; history; Italian; Latin American studies; literature; mathematics; Middle Eastern studies; music; peace/conflict studies; philosophy; physics; political science; pre-dentistry; pre-law; pre-medicine; psychology; religious studies; Russian; sociology; Spanish; theater arts/drama; women's studies.

Academic Programs *Special study options:* accelerated degree program, advanced placement credit, double majors, honors programs, independent study, internships, off-campus study, student-designed majors, study abroad. *ROTC:* Army (c), Navy (b), Air Force (c). *Unusual degree programs:* 3-2 engineering with Washington University in St. Louis, Columbia University, Dartmouth College.

Library Dinand Library plus 2 others with 566,900 titles, 10,139 serial subscriptions, 23,355 audiovisual materials, an OPAC, a Web page.

Computers on Campus 267 computers available on campus for general student use. A campuswide network can be accessed from student residence rooms and from off campus. Internet access, at least one staffed computer lab available.

Student Life *Housing Options:* coed. *Activities and Organizations:* drama/theater group, student-run newspaper, radio station, choral group, marching band, SPUD (community service organization), choral and music groups, Campus Activities Board, Student Government Association, Purple Key Society. *Campus security:* 24-hour emergency response devices and patrols, late-night transport/escort service, controlled dormitory access. *Student Services:* health clinic, personal/psychological counseling, women's center.

Athletics Member NCAA. All Division I except football (Division I-AA). *Intercollegiate sports:* baseball M, basketball M(s)/W(s), crew M/W, cross-country running M/W, field hockey W, golf M/W, ice hockey M/W, lacrosse M/W, soccer M/W, softball W, swimming M/W, tennis M/W, track and field M/W, volleyball W. *Intramural sports:* basketball M/W, equestrian sports M(c)/W(c), field hockey W, football M, ice hockey M, rugby M(c)/W(c), soccer M(c)/W(c), softball M/W, volleyball W, water polo M(c)/W(c).

Standardized Tests *Required:* SAT II: Writing Test (for admission).

Costs (2002–03) *Comprehensive fee:* $34,440 includes full-time tuition ($26,000), mandatory fees ($440), and room and board ($8000). *Room and board:* College room only: $4000. Room and board charges vary according to board plan and housing facility. *Payment plans:* tuition prepayment, installment. *Waivers:* employees or children of employees.

Financial Aid Of all full-time matriculated undergraduates who enrolled in 2001, 1682 applied for aid, 1364 were judged to have need, 1364 had their need fully met. In 2001, 183 non-need-based awards were made. *Average percent of need met:* 100%. *Average financial aid package:* $18,419. *Average need-based loan:* $5384. *Average need-based gift aid:* $13,682. *Average non-need based aid:* $8791. *Average indebtedness upon graduation:* $16,063. *Financial aid deadline:* 2/1.

Applying *Options:* common application, electronic application, early admission, early decision, deferred entrance. *Application fee:* $50. *Required:* essay or personal statement, high school transcript, 2 letters of recommendation. *Recommended:* interview. *Application deadlines:* 1/15 (freshmen), 5/1 (transfers). *Early decision:* 12/15. *Notification:* 4/1 (freshmen), 2/15 (early decision).

Admissions Contact Ms. Ann Bowe McDermott, Director of Admissions, College of the Holy Cross, 1 College Street, Worcester, MA 01610. *Phone:* 508-793-2443. *Toll-free phone:* 800-442-2421. *E-mail:* admissions@holycross.edu.

CURRY COLLEGE
Milton, Massachusetts

- **Independent** comprehensive, founded 1879
- **Calendar** semesters
- **Degrees** certificates, bachelor's, and master's
- **Suburban** 131-acre campus with easy access to Boston
- **Endowment** $3.5 million
- **Coed,** 2,287 undergraduate students, 61% full-time, 50% women, 50% men
- **Moderately difficult** entrance level, 79% of applicants were admitted

Undergraduates 1,403 full-time, 884 part-time. Students come from 31 states and territories, 12 other countries, 32% are from out of state, 4% transferred in, 65% live on campus. *Retention:* 65% of 2001 full-time freshmen returned.

Freshmen *Admission:* 2,066 applied, 1,624 admitted, 459 enrolled. *Average high school GPA:* 2.60. *Test scores:* SAT verbal scores over 500: 29%; SAT math scores over 500: 16%; SAT verbal scores over 600: 7%; SAT math scores over 600: 3%; SAT verbal scores over 700: 1%; SAT math scores over 700: 1%.

Faculty *Total:* 393, 21% full-time. *Student/faculty ratio:* 12:1.

Majors Art; biology; business administration; chemistry; criminal justice/law enforcement administration; early childhood education; education; elementary education; English; environmental science; film studies; graphic design/commercial art/illustration; health education; history; journalism; mass communications; nursing; philosophy; physics; political science; pre-law; psychology; public relations; radio/television broadcasting; sociology; special education; women's studies.

Academic Programs *Special study options:* academic remediation for entering students, accelerated degree program, adult/continuing education programs, advanced placement credit, cooperative education, double majors, external degree program, honors programs, independent study, internships, off-campus study, part-time degree program, services for LD students, student-designed majors, study abroad, summer session for credit. *ROTC:* Army (c).

Library Levin Library plus 1 other with 90,000 titles, 675 serial subscriptions, 1,050 audiovisual materials, an OPAC, a Web page.

Computers on Campus 100 computers available on campus for general student use. A campuswide network can be accessed from student residence rooms and from off campus that provide access to Library online catalog. Internet access, at least one staffed computer lab available.

Student Life *Housing Options:* coed, men-only, women-only. *Activities and Organizations:* drama/theater group, student-run newspaper, radio station, choral

Curry College (continued)
group, student radio station, student government, Community Service Organization, student newspaper, Drama Club. *Campus security:* 24-hour emergency response devices and patrols, late-night transport/escort service, controlled dormitory access. *Student Services:* health clinic, personal/psychological counseling.

Athletics Member NCAA. All Division III. *Intercollegiate sports:* baseball M, basketball M/W, cross-country running W, football M, ice hockey M, lacrosse M/W, soccer M/W, softball W, tennis M/W. *Intramural sports:* basketball M/W, rugby M/W, softball M/W, tennis M/W, volleyball M/W.

Standardized Tests *Required for some:* SAT I or ACT (for admission).

Costs (2002–03) *Comprehensive fee:* $25,805 includes full-time tuition ($18,020), mandatory fees ($575), and room and board ($7210). Part-time tuition: $600 per credit. *Required fees:* $120 per year part-time. *Room and board:* Room and board charges vary according to board plan. *Payment plan:* installment. *Waivers:* children of alumni, senior citizens, and employees or children of employees.

Financial Aid Of all full-time matriculated undergraduates who enrolled in 2001, 1000 applied for aid, 825 were judged to have need. *Average percent of need met:* 68%. *Average financial aid package:* $14,250. *Average need-based loan:* $4500. *Average need-based gift aid:* $5000. *Average indebtedness upon graduation:* $17,000.

Applying *Options:* common application, electronic application, early admission, early decision, deferred entrance. *Application fee:* $40. *Required:* essay or personal statement, high school transcript, minimum 2.0 GPA, 1 letter of recommendation. *Required for some:* interview. *Recommended:* interview. *Application deadlines:* 4/1 (freshmen), 7/1 (transfers). *Early decision:* 12/1. *Notification:* continuous until 5/1 (freshmen), 12/15 (early decision).

Admissions Contact Mr. Michael Poll, Dean of Admission and Financial Aid, Curry College, 1071 Blue Hill Avenue, Milton, MA 02186. *Phone:* 617-333-2210. *Toll-free phone:* 800-669-0686. *Fax:* 617-333-2114. *E-mail:* curryadm@curry.edu.

EASTERN NAZARENE COLLEGE
Quincy, Massachusetts

- **Independent** comprehensive, founded 1918, affiliated with Church of the Nazarene
- **Calendar** 4-1-4
- **Degrees** associate, bachelor's, and master's
- **Suburban** 15-acre campus with easy access to Boston
- **Endowment** $8.0 million
- **Coed,** 1,075 undergraduate students, 98% full-time, 60% women, 40% men
- **Moderately difficult** entrance level, 61% of applicants were admitted

Undergraduates 1,058 full-time, 17 part-time. Students come from 32 states and territories, 18 other countries, 57% are from out of state, 3% transferred in, 82% live on campus. *Retention:* 71% of 2001 full-time freshmen returned.

Freshmen *Admission:* 560 applied, 342 admitted, 178 enrolled. *Average high school GPA:* 3.10. *Test scores:* SAT verbal scores over 500: 88%; SAT math scores over 500: 82%; ACT scores over 18: 99%; SAT verbal scores over 600: 48%; SAT math scores over 600: 39%; ACT scores over 24: 46%; SAT verbal scores over 700: 22%; SAT math scores over 700: 20%; ACT scores over 30: 15%.

Faculty *Total:* 48, 92% full-time, 71% with terminal degrees. *Student/faculty ratio:* 15:1.

Majors Advertising; aerospace engineering; bioengineering; biological/physical sciences; biology; business; business administration; chemistry; clinical psychology; computer engineering; computer science; early childhood education; education; electrical engineering; elementary education; engineering physics; English; general studies; health science; history; industrial/manufacturing engineering; journalism; liberal arts and sciences/liberal studies; mass communications; mathematics; mechanical engineering; middle school education; music; music (general performance); music teacher education; pharmacy; physical education; physical therapy; physics; pre-law; pre-medicine; psychology; radio/television broadcasting; religious education; religious music; religious studies; secondary education; social work; sociology; special education; systems engineering; theater arts/drama.

Academic Programs *Special study options:* academic remediation for entering students, accelerated degree program, adult/continuing education programs, advanced placement credit, double majors, English as a second language, honors programs, independent study, internships, off-campus study, part-time degree program, services for LD students, study abroad, summer session for credit. *ROTC:* Army (c). *Unusual degree programs:* 3-2 engineering with Boston University; nursing with Boston College; pharmacy with Massachusetts College of Pharmacy and Allied Health Sciences.

Library Nease Library with 117,540 titles, 466 serial subscriptions, 1,290 audiovisual materials, an OPAC.

Computers on Campus 98 computers available on campus for general student use. A campuswide network can be accessed from student residence rooms and from off campus. Internet access, at least one staffed computer lab available.

Student Life *Housing:* on-campus residence required through senior year. *Options:* men-only, women-only, disabled students. *Activities and Organizations:* drama/theater group, student-run newspaper, radio station, choral group, AMS Associated Men Students, AWS Associated Women Students, Gospel Choir, ACTS Actors Christians Teachers Singers, Kid's Club. *Campus security:* 24-hour emergency response devices and patrols, student patrols, late-night transport/escort service, controlled dormitory access. *Student Services:* health clinic, personal/psychological counseling.

Athletics Member NCAA. All Division III. *Intercollegiate sports:* baseball M, basketball M/W, cross-country running M/W, lacrosse M(c), soccer M/W, softball W, tennis M/W, volleyball M(c)/W. *Intramural sports:* baseball M, basketball M/W, cross-country running M/W, lacrosse M, skiing (downhill) M(c)/W(c), soccer M/W, softball W, tennis M/W, volleyball M/W.

Standardized Tests *Required:* SAT I or ACT (for admission).

Costs (2002–03) *Comprehensive fee:* $20,530 includes full-time tuition ($14,850), mandatory fees ($465), and room and board ($5215).

Financial Aid Of all full-time matriculated undergraduates who enrolled in 2001, 572 applied for aid, 456 were judged to have need, 110 had their need fully met. 179 Federal Work-Study jobs (averaging $1362). In 2001, 106 non-need-based awards were made. *Average percent of need met:* 69%. *Average financial aid package:* $10,394. *Average need-based loan:* $4122. *Average need-based gift aid:* $3144. *Average non-need based aid:* $4275.

Applying *Options:* early admission, deferred entrance. *Application fee:* $25. *Required:* essay or personal statement, high school transcript, minimum 2.3 GPA, 2 letters of recommendation, interview. *Application deadline:* rolling (freshmen), rolling (transfers). *Notification:* continuous (freshmen).

Admissions Contact Mr. James F. Heyward II, Director of Admissions, Eastern Nazarene College, 23 East Elm Avenue, Quincy, MA 02170. *Phone:* 617-745-3868. *Toll-free phone:* 800-88-ENC88. *Fax:* 617-745-3929. *E-mail:* admissions@enc.edu.

ELMS COLLEGE
Chicopee, Massachusetts

- **Independent Roman Catholic** comprehensive, founded 1928
- **Calendar** semesters
- **Degrees** associate, bachelor's, master's, and postbachelor's certificates
- **Suburban** 32-acre campus
- **Endowment** $6.7 million
- **Coed, primarily women,** 630 undergraduate students, 66% full-time, 86% women, 14% men
- **Moderately difficult** entrance level, 70% of applicants were admitted

Undergraduates 418 full-time, 212 part-time. Students come from 10 states and territories, 3 other countries, 15% are from out of state, 4% African American, 2% Asian American or Pacific Islander, 4% Hispanic American, 0.6% international, 7% transferred in, 39% live on campus. *Retention:* 86% of 2001 full-time freshmen returned.

Freshmen *Admission:* 323 applied, 226 admitted, 63 enrolled. *Average high school GPA:* 2.81. *Test scores:* SAT verbal scores over 500: 49%; SAT math scores over 500: 43%; SAT verbal scores over 600: 8%; SAT math scores over 600: 6%; SAT math scores over 700: 2%.

Faculty *Total:* 96, 45% full-time, 48% with terminal degrees. *Student/faculty ratio:* 11:1.

Majors Accounting; American studies; applied art; applied mathematics; art; art education; art therapy; bilingual/bicultural education; biology; business administration; business marketing and marketing management; chemistry; computer science; early childhood education; education; elementary education; English; English education; French; graphic design/commercial art/illustration; history; interdisciplinary studies; international relations; legal studies; liberal arts and sciences/liberal studies; mathematics; mathematics education; medical technology; molecular biology; natural sciences; nursing; paralegal/legal assistant; pre-dentistry; pre-law; pre-medicine; pre-veterinary studies; psychology; religious studies; science education; secondary education; social work; sociology; Spanish; special education; speech-language pathology/audiology; speech therapy; teaching English as a second language.

Academic Programs *Special study options:* academic remediation for entering students, accelerated degree program, adult/continuing education programs, advanced placement credit, double majors, English as a second language, honors programs, internships, off-campus study, part-time degree program, student-designed majors, study abroad, summer session for credit. *ROTC:* Army (c), Air Force (c).

Library Alumnae Library with 116,889 titles, 503 serial subscriptions, 10,286 audiovisual materials, an OPAC.

Computers on Campus 76 computers available on campus for general student use. A campuswide network can be accessed from student residence rooms and from off campus. Internet access, at least one staffed computer lab available.

Student Life *Housing Options:* coed, women-only. *Activities and Organizations:* drama/theater group, student-run newspaper, choral group, Student Government Association, Zonta, Elmscript, Umoja, social work club. *Campus security:* 24-hour emergency response devices and patrols, late-night transport/escort service, controlled dormitory access. *Student Services:* health clinic, personal/psychological counseling.

Athletics Member NCAA. All Division III. *Intercollegiate sports:* basketball M/W, cross-country running M/W, equestrian sports W, field hockey W, golf M, lacrosse W, soccer M/W, softball W, swimming M/W, volleyball M/W. *Intramural sports:* basketball M/W, bowling M/W, cross-country running M/W, equestrian sports W, field hockey W, golf W, lacrosse M/W, racquetball M/W, skiing (cross-country) M/W, soccer M/W, softball M/W, swimming M/W, volleyball M/W, water polo M/W, weight lifting M/W.

Standardized Tests *Required:* SAT I or ACT (for admission). *Recommended:* SAT II: Subject Tests (for admission).

Costs (2002–03) *Comprehensive fee:* $23,650 includes full-time tuition ($16,490), mandatory fees ($670), and room and board ($6490). Part-time tuition: $330 per credit. *Room and board:* Room and board charges vary according to board plan. *Waivers:* senior citizens and employees or children of employees.

Financial Aid Of all full-time matriculated undergraduates who enrolled in 2001, 395 applied for aid, 364 were judged to have need, 106 had their need fully met. 128 Federal Work-Study jobs (averaging $1354). In 2001, 33 non-need-based awards were made. *Average percent of need met:* 79%. *Average financial aid package:* $12,125. *Average need-based loan:* $4784. *Average need-based gift aid:* $7480. *Average indebtedness upon graduation:* $18,600.

Applying *Options:* common application, early admission, deferred entrance. *Application fee:* $30. *Required:* essay or personal statement, high school transcript, minimum 2.0 GPA, 2 letters of recommendation. *Recommended:* interview. *Application deadline:* rolling (freshmen), rolling (transfers). *Notification:* continuous (freshmen).

Admissions Contact Mr. Joseph P. Wagner, Director of Admissions, Elms College, Chicopee, MA 01013-2839. *Phone:* 413-592-3189 Ext. 350. *Toll-free phone:* 800-255-ELMS. *Fax:* 413-594-2781. *E-mail:* admissions@elms.edu.

EMERSON COLLEGE
Boston, Massachusetts

- **Independent** comprehensive, founded 1880
- **Calendar** semesters
- **Degrees** bachelor's, master's, and doctoral
- **Urban** campus
- **Endowment** $29.0 million
- **Coed,** 3,412 undergraduate students, 84% full-time, 60% women, 40% men
- **Very difficult** entrance level, 47% of applicants were admitted

Founded in 1880, Emerson is one of the premier colleges in the U.S. for studying communication and the arts. Located on Boston Common in the city's Theatre District, the College's 2,700 students participate in internships, study abroad, and more than 50 student organizations, performance groups, NCAA teams, student publications, and honor societies. More information can be found online at http://www.emerson.edu.

Undergraduates 2,857 full-time, 555 part-time. Students come from 51 states and territories, 3 other countries, 65% are from out of state, 2% African American, 3% Asian American or Pacific Islander, 4% Hispanic American, 0.3% Native American, 5% international, 7% transferred in, 45% live on campus. *Retention:* 84% of 2001 full-time freshmen returned.

Freshmen *Admission:* 4,071 applied, 1,914 admitted, 639 enrolled. *Average high school GPA:* 3.45. *Test scores:* SAT verbal scores over 500: 97%; SAT math scores over 500: 92%; ACT scores over 18: 99%; SAT verbal scores over 600: 61%; SAT math scores over 600: 41%; ACT scores over 24: 74%; SAT verbal scores over 700: 14%; SAT math scores over 700: 5%; ACT scores over 30: 12%.

Faculty *Total:* 356, 35% full-time, 47% with terminal degrees. *Student/faculty ratio:* 15:1.

Majors Acting/directing; advertising; broadcast journalism; business marketing and marketing management; communication disorders; communications; creative writing; dance; drama/dance education; education of the speech impaired; film studies; film/video production; interdisciplinary studies; journalism; mass communications; multimedia; play/screenwriting; public relations; publishing; radio/television broadcasting; radio/television broadcasting technology; speech-language pathology; speech-language pathology/audiology; speech/rhetorical studies; speech therapy; theater arts/drama; theater design; visual/performing arts.

Academic Programs *Special study options:* adult/continuing education programs, advanced placement credit, double majors, honors programs, independent study, internships, off-campus study, part-time degree program, services for LD students, student-designed majors, study abroad, summer session for credit.

Library Emerson Library plus 1 other with 193,000 titles, 7,430 serial subscriptions, 8,579 audiovisual materials, an OPAC, a Web page.

Computers on Campus 265 computers available on campus for general student use. A campuswide network can be accessed from student residence rooms and from off campus. Internet access, online (class) registration, at least one staffed computer lab available.

Student Life *Housing Options:* coed. *Activities and Organizations:* drama/theater group, student-run newspaper, radio and television station, Independent Video, WERS 88.0 FM, Musical Theatre Society, Berkeley Beacon, International Student Association, national fraternities, national sororities. *Campus security:* 24-hour emergency response devices and patrols, late-night transport/escort service, controlled dormitory access. *Student Services:* health clinic, personal/psychological counseling.

Athletics Member NCAA. All Division III. *Intercollegiate sports:* baseball M, basketball M/W, cross-country running M/W, lacrosse M, soccer M/W, softball W, tennis M/W, volleyball W. *Intramural sports:* basketball M/W, lacrosse W, tennis M/W, volleyball W.

Standardized Tests *Required:* SAT I or ACT (for admission).

Costs (2001–02) *Comprehensive fee:* $30,008 includes full-time tuition ($20,224), mandatory fees ($494), and room and board ($9290). Full-time tuition and fees vary according to course load and program. Part-time tuition: $632 per credit hour. Part-time tuition and fees vary according to course load and program. *Room and board:* College room only: $5540. Room and board charges vary according to board plan. *Payment plans:* installment, deferred payment. *Waivers:* employees or children of employees.

Financial Aid Of all full-time matriculated undergraduates who enrolled in 2001, 1588 applied for aid, 1359 were judged to have need, 927 had their need fully met. 340 Federal Work-Study jobs (averaging $2000). In 2001, 97 non-need-based awards were made. *Average percent of need met:* 68%. *Average financial aid package:* $12,500. *Average need-based loan:* $4600. *Average need-based gift aid:* $9400. *Average indebtedness upon graduation:* $17,125.

Applying *Options:* electronic application, early admission, early action, deferred entrance. *Application fee:* $45. *Required:* essay or personal statement, high school transcript, 2 letters of recommendation. *Required for some:* interview, audition, portfolio, or resume for performing arts applicants. *Application deadlines:* 2/1 (freshmen), 3/1 (transfers). *Notification:* 4/1 (freshmen), 12/15 (early action).

Admissions Contact Ms. Sara Ramirez, Director of Admission, Emerson College, 120 Boylston Street, Boston, MA 02116-4624. *Phone:* 617-824-8600. *Fax:* 617-824-8609. *E-mail:* admission@emerson.edu.

EMMANUEL COLLEGE
Boston, Massachusetts

- **Independent Roman Catholic** comprehensive, founded 1919
- **Calendar** semesters
- **Degrees** bachelor's and master's
- **Urban** 16-acre campus
- **Endowment** $4.1 million
- **Coed,** 1,309 undergraduate students, 67% full-time, 83% women, 17% men
- **Moderately difficult** entrance level, 19% of applicants were admitted

Undergraduates 883 full-time, 426 part-time. Students come from 23 states and territories, 40 other countries, 22% are from out of state, 10% African American, 3% Asian American or Pacific Islander, 5% Hispanic American, 0.3% Native American, 6% international, 3% transferred in, 65% live on campus. *Retention:* 79% of 2001 full-time freshmen returned.

Freshmen *Admission:* 1,333 applied, 259 admitted, 278 enrolled. *Average high school GPA:* 3.20. *Test scores:* SAT verbal scores over 500: 57%; SAT math scores over 500: 48%; ACT scores over 18: 75%; SAT verbal scores over 600: 19%; SAT math scores over 600: 11%; ACT scores over 24: 50%.

Faculty *Total:* 76, 63% full-time, 63% with terminal degrees. *Student/faculty ratio:* 12:1.

Majors Accounting; art; art education; art history; art therapy; biochemistry; biology; business administration; business economics; chemistry; economics; education; elementary education; English; fine/studio arts; graphic design/

Emmanuel College (continued)
commercial art/illustration; history; interdisciplinary studies; liberal arts and sciences/liberal studies; literature; mass communications; mathematics; nursing administration; physics; political science; pre-dentistry; pre-law; pre-medicine; printmaking; psychology; secondary education; sociology; Spanish.

Academic Programs *Special study options:* academic remediation for entering students, accelerated degree program, adult/continuing education programs, advanced placement credit, double majors, English as a second language, honors programs, independent study, internships, off-campus study, part-time degree program, student-designed majors, study abroad, summer session for credit. *ROTC:* Army (c). *Unusual degree programs:* 3-2 engineering with Wentworth Institute of Technology.

Library Cardinal Cushing Library with 98,513 titles, 876 serial subscriptions, 515 audiovisual materials, an OPAC, a Web page.

Computers on Campus 115 computers available on campus for general student use. A campuswide network can be accessed from student residence rooms that provide access to software applications. Internet access, at least one staffed computer lab available.

Student Life *Housing Options:* women-only. *Activities and Organizations:* drama/theater group, student-run newspaper, choral group, Hellas, Student Government Association, Peace and Justice Club, Theatre Guild, L.E.A.D.E.R.S. *Campus security:* 24-hour emergency response devices and patrols, late-night transport/escort service, controlled dormitory access, 24-hour security personnel on duty at front desk in residence halls. *Student Services:* personal/psychological counseling.

Athletics Member NCAA. All Division III. *Intercollegiate sports:* basketball M/W, cross-country running M/W, soccer M/W, softball W, tennis W, track and field M/W, volleyball M/W. *Intramural sports:* basketball M/W, field hockey W, soccer M/W, volleyball W.

Standardized Tests *Required:* SAT I or ACT (for admission).

Costs (2001–02) *Comprehensive fee:* $26,715 includes full-time tuition ($16,800), mandatory fees ($300), and room and board ($9615). Part-time tuition: $894 per course. Part-time tuition and fees vary according to program. *Payment plan:* installment.

Financial Aid Of all full-time matriculated undergraduates who enrolled in 2001, 466 applied for aid, 378 were judged to have need, 43 had their need fully met. 260 Federal Work-Study jobs (averaging $1885). In 2001, 55 non-need-based awards were made. *Average percent of need met:* 65%. *Average financial aid package:* $17,461. *Average need-based loan:* $4649. *Average need-based gift aid:* $8807. *Average non-need based aid:* $11,912. *Average indebtedness upon graduation:* $14,131.

Applying *Options:* common application, electronic application, early admission, early decision, deferred entrance. *Application fee:* $40. *Required:* essay or personal statement, high school transcript, minimum 2.0 GPA, 2 letters of recommendation. *Required for some:* interview. *Application deadline:* rolling (freshmen), rolling (transfers). *Early decision:* 11/1. *Notification:* continuous (freshmen), 12/1 (early decision).

Admissions Contact Ms. Sandra Robbins, Dean of Admissions, Emmanuel College, 400 The Fenway, Boston, MA 02115. *Phone:* 617-735-9715. *Fax:* 617-735-9801. *E-mail:* enroll@emmanuel.edu.

ENDICOTT COLLEGE
Beverly, Massachusetts

- **Independent** comprehensive, founded 1939
- **Calendar** semesters
- **Degrees** certificates, associate, bachelor's, and master's
- **Suburban** 200-acre campus with easy access to Boston
- **Endowment** $9.4 million
- **Coed,** 1,584 undergraduate students, 89% full-time, 66% women, 34% men
- **Moderately difficult** entrance level, 61% of applicants were admitted

Undergraduates 1,415 full-time, 169 part-time. Students come from 26 states and territories, 32 other countries, 47% are from out of state, 1% African American, 0.6% Asian American or Pacific Islander, 2% Hispanic American, 0.4% Native American, 6% international, 5% transferred in, 84% live on campus. *Retention:* 67% of 2001 full-time freshmen returned.

Freshmen *Admission:* 2,115 applied, 1,282 admitted, 511 enrolled. *Test scores:* SAT verbal scores over 500: 59%; SAT math scores over 500: 57%; ACT scores over 18: 87%; SAT verbal scores over 600: 10%; SAT math scores over 600: 5%; ACT scores over 24: 4%; SAT verbal scores over 700: 1%.

Faculty *Total:* 124, 40% full-time, 40% with terminal degrees. *Student/faculty ratio:* 14:1.

Majors Athletic training/sports medicine; business administration; communications; computer/information sciences; criminal justice studies; early childhood education; education; elementary education; fine/studio arts; general studies; graphic design/commercial art/illustration; hospitality management; interior design; liberal arts and sciences/liberal studies; nursing; physical therapy assistant; psychology; sport/fitness administration.

Academic Programs *Special study options:* academic remediation for entering students, accelerated degree program, adult/continuing education programs, advanced placement credit, distance learning, English as a second language, honors programs, independent study, internships, off-campus study, part-time degree program, services for LD students, study abroad, summer session for credit.

Library Endicott College Library with 115,000 titles, 2,100 serial subscriptions, 500 audiovisual materials, an OPAC, a Web page.

Computers on Campus 100 computers available on campus for general student use. A campuswide network can be accessed from student residence rooms and from off campus that provide access to e-mail, on-line instructional courses. Internet access, at least one staffed computer lab available.

Student Life *Housing:* on-campus residence required through senior year. *Options:* coed, women-only. *Activities and Organizations:* drama/theater group, student-run newspaper, television station, choral group, Student Activities Committee, student government, yearbook, Admissions Ambassadors, Adventure Base Council. *Campus security:* 24-hour emergency response devices and patrols, late-night transport/escort service, controlled dormitory access. *Student Services:* health clinic, personal/psychological counseling.

Athletics Member NCAA, NCCAA. All NCAA Division III. *Intercollegiate sports:* baseball M, basketball M/W, cross-country running M/W, equestrian sports M/W, field hockey W, golf M/W, lacrosse M/W, soccer M/W, softball W, tennis M/W, volleyball M/W. *Intramural sports:* basketball M/W, football M/W, ice hockey M, racquetball M/W, soccer M/W, softball M/W, tennis M/W, volleyball M/W.

Standardized Tests *Required:* SAT I or ACT (for admission).

Costs (2001–02) *Comprehensive fee:* $23,704 includes full-time tuition ($15,130), mandatory fees ($574), and room and board ($8000). Part-time tuition: $464 per credit. Part-time tuition and fees vary according to program. *Required fees:* $75 per term part-time. *Room and board:* College room only: $5610. Room and board charges vary according to board plan and housing facility. *Payment plan:* installment. *Waivers:* senior citizens and employees or children of employees.

Financial Aid Of all full-time matriculated undergraduates who enrolled in 2001, 993 applied for aid, 843 were judged to have need, 107 had their need fully met. 234 Federal Work-Study jobs (averaging $1400). *Average percent of need met:* 66%. *Average financial aid package:* $10,710. *Average need-based loan:* $3983. *Average need-based gift aid:* $6866. *Average indebtedness upon graduation:* $17,125.

Applying *Options:* common application, electronic application, deferred entrance. *Application fee:* $25. *Required:* essay or personal statement, high school transcript, minimum 2.0 GPA, 2 letters of recommendation. *Required for some:* interview. *Recommended:* interview. *Application deadline:* rolling (freshmen), rolling (transfers). *Notification:* continuous (freshmen).

Admissions Contact Mr. Thomas J. Redman, Vice President of Admissions and Financial Aid, Endicott College, 376 Hale Street, Beverly, MA 01915. *Phone:* 978-921-1000. *Toll-free phone:* 800-325-1114. *Fax:* 978-232-2520. *E-mail:* admissio@endicott.edu.

FISHER COLLEGE
Boston, Massachusetts

- **Independent** primarily 2-year, founded 1903
- **Calendar** semesters
- **Degrees** certificates, associate, and bachelor's
- **Urban** 3-acre campus
- **Endowment** $14.7 million
- **Coed,** 526 undergraduate students, 98% full-time, 69% women, 31% men
- **Minimally difficult** entrance level, 57% of applicants were admitted

Undergraduates 516 full-time, 10 part-time. 21% African American, 4% Asian American or Pacific Islander, 10% Hispanic American, 0.2% Native American, 17% international, 18% transferred in, 50% live on campus.

Freshmen *Admission:* 1,046 applied, 594 admitted, 168 enrolled.

Faculty *Total:* 55, 44% full-time, 24% with terminal degrees. *Student/faculty ratio:* 18:1.

Majors Accounting; business administration; data processing technology; early childhood education; fashion design/illustration; fashion merchandising; hospitality management; humanities; liberal arts and sciences/liberal studies; office management; paralegal/legal assistant; psychology; travel/tourism management.

Academic Programs *Special study options:* academic remediation for entering students, adult/continuing education programs, advanced placement credit, English as a second language, internships, off-campus study, part-time degree program, summer session for credit.

Library Fisher College Library plus 1 other with 30,000 titles, 160 serial subscriptions, an OPAC.

Computers on Campus 112 computers available on campus for general student use. A campuswide network can be accessed from off campus. Internet access, at least one staffed computer lab available.

Student Life *Housing Options:* coed, women-only. *Activities and Organizations:* drama/theater group, choral group, Drama Club, student government, Student Activity Club, Intercultural Club. *Campus security:* 24-hour emergency response devices and patrols, controlled dormitory access. *Student Services:* health clinic, personal/psychological counseling, women's center.

Athletics Member NAIA. *Intercollegiate sports:* baseball M, basketball M/W, soccer M/W, softball W, volleyball W.

Costs (2002–03) *Comprehensive fee:* $23,100 includes full-time tuition ($13,800), mandatory fees ($1400), and room and board ($7900). Part-time tuition and fees vary according to class time, course load, and program.

Applying *Options:* deferred entrance. *Application fee:* $25. *Required:* high school transcript. *Required for some:* essay or personal statement, letters of recommendation, interview. *Recommended:* minimum 2.0 GPA. *Application deadline:* rolling (freshmen), rolling (transfers). *Notification:* continuous (freshmen).

Admissions Contact Ms. Marietta Baier, Associate Director Admissions, Fisher College, 118 Beacon Street, Boston, MA 02116. *Phone:* 617-236-8800 Ext. 818. *Toll-free phone:* 800-821-3050 (in-state); 800-446-1226 (out-of-state). *Fax:* 617-236-5473. *E-mail:* admissions@fisher.edu.

FITCHBURG STATE COLLEGE
Fitchburg, Massachusetts

- **State-supported** comprehensive, founded 1894, part of Massachusetts Public Higher Education System
- **Calendar** semesters
- **Degrees** certificates, bachelor's, master's, and post-master's certificates
- **Small-town** 45-acre campus with easy access to Boston
- **Endowment** $7.5 million
- **Coed,** 3,219 undergraduate students, 70% full-time, 57% women, 43% men
- **Moderately difficult** entrance level, 61% of applicants were admitted

Undergraduates 2,245 full-time, 974 part-time. Students come from 14 states and territories, 10 other countries, 8% are from out of state, 3% African American, 2% Asian American or Pacific Islander, 3% Hispanic American, 0.1% Native American, 0.8% international, 10% transferred in, 35% live on campus. *Retention:* 75% of 2001 full-time freshmen returned.

Freshmen *Admission:* 2,094 applied, 1,273 admitted, 431 enrolled. *Average high school GPA:* 2.90. *Test scores:* SAT verbal scores over 500: 57%; SAT math scores over 500: 53%; SAT verbal scores over 600: 13%; SAT math scores over 600: 9%; SAT verbal scores over 700: 1%.

Faculty *Total:* 326, 62% full-time. *Student/faculty ratio:* 11:1.

Majors Accounting; architectural engineering technology; biology; business administration; business marketing and marketing management; communications; computer science; construction technology; criminal justice/law enforcement administration; developmental/child psychology; development economics; early childhood education; earth sciences; economics; education; electrical/electronic engineering technology; elementary education; energy management technology; engineering-related technology; English; environmental science; exercise sciences; film/video production; general studies; geography; graphic design/commercial art/illustration; history; human services; industrial arts; industrial technology; information sciences/systems; literature; mathematics; medical microbiology; medical technology; middle school education; nursing; organizational psychology; photography; political science; psychology; secondary education; sociology; special education; technical/business writing; theater arts/drama.

Academic Programs *Special study options:* academic remediation for entering students, accelerated degree program, adult/continuing education programs, advanced placement credit, distance learning, double majors, freshman honors college, honors programs, independent study, internships, off-campus study, part-time degree program, services for LD students, student-designed majors, study abroad, summer session for credit.

Library Hammond Library with 229,505 titles, 11,799 serial subscriptions, 2,159 audiovisual materials, an OPAC, a Web page.

Computers on Campus 500 computers available on campus for general student use. A campuswide network can be accessed from student residence rooms and from off campus. Internet access, at least one staffed computer lab available.

Student Life *Housing Options:* coed, disabled students. *Activities and Organizations:* drama/theater group, student-run newspaper, radio station, choral group, Student Government Association, Residence Hall Council, student radio station, student newspaper, Programs Committee, national fraternities, national sororities. *Campus security:* 24-hour emergency response devices and patrols, late-night transport/escort service, controlled dormitory access. *Student Services:* health clinic, personal/psychological counseling, legal services.

Athletics Member NCAA. All Division III. *Intercollegiate sports:* baseball M, basketball M/W, cross-country running M/W, field hockey W, football M, ice hockey M, soccer M/W, softball W, track and field M/W, volleyball W. *Intramural sports:* basketball M/W, football M, ice hockey M, soccer M/W, softball M/W, volleyball M/W.

Standardized Tests *Required:* SAT I or ACT (for admission).

Costs (2001–02) *Tuition:* state resident $970 full-time, $40 per semester hour part-time; nonresident $7050 full-time, $294 per semester hour part-time. Full-time tuition and fees vary according to class time, course load, and reciprocity agreements. Part-time tuition and fees vary according to class time, course load, and reciprocity agreements. *Required fees:* $2018 full-time, $84 per semester hour. *Room and board:* $4838. Room and board charges vary according to board plan and housing facility. *Payment plan:* installment. *Waivers:* senior citizens and employees or children of employees.

Financial Aid Of all full-time matriculated undergraduates who enrolled in 2001, 336 Federal Work-Study jobs (averaging $885).

Applying *Options:* common application, early admission, deferred entrance. *Application fee:* $10. *Required:* essay or personal statement, high school transcript, minimum 3.0 GPA. *Required for some:* interview. *Recommended:* letters of recommendation. *Application deadline:* 4/1 (freshmen), rolling (transfers). *Notification:* continuous (freshmen).

Admissions Contact Mr. Robert McGann, Dean of Enrollment Management, Fitchburg State College, Fitchburg, MA 01420-2697. *Phone:* 978-665-3144. *Toll-free phone:* 800-705-9692. *Fax:* 978-665-4540. *E-mail:* admissions@fsc.edu.

FRAMINGHAM STATE COLLEGE
Framingham, Massachusetts

- **State-supported** comprehensive, founded 1839, part of Massachusetts Public Higher Education System
- **Calendar** semesters
- **Degrees** bachelor's, master's, and postbachelor's certificates
- **Suburban** 73-acre campus with easy access to Boston
- **Endowment** $6.0 million
- **Coed,** 4,041 undergraduate students, 77% full-time, 64% women, 36% men
- **Moderately difficult** entrance level, 60% of applicants were admitted

Framingham State College has launched an initiative making it the first Massachusetts state college to provide wireless computing for all students. Beginning in 2002, all entering freshmen must purchase a laptop computer.

Undergraduates 3,123 full-time, 918 part-time. Students come from 17 states and territories, 17 other countries, 8% are from out of state, 4% African American, 3% Asian American or Pacific Islander, 3% Hispanic American, 0.5% Native American, 4% international, 9% transferred in, 45% live on campus. *Retention:* 73% of 2001 full-time freshmen returned.

Freshmen *Admission:* 3,730 applied, 2,252 admitted, 679 enrolled. *Average high school GPA:* 2.90. *Test scores:* SAT verbal scores over 500: 69%; SAT math scores over 500: 59%; SAT verbal scores over 600: 14%; SAT math scores over 600: 9%; SAT verbal scores over 700: 2%; SAT math scores over 700: 1%.

Faculty *Total:* 332, 48% full-time, 51% with terminal degrees. *Student/faculty ratio:* 15:1.

Majors Accounting; anthropology; art education; art history; biological/physical sciences; biology; biology education; biomedical science; business administration; business economics; business marketing and marketing management; chemistry; chemistry education; city/community/regional planning; clothing/textiles; community services; computer science; developmental/child psychology; dietetics; drawing; early childhood education; earth sciences; economics; education; elementary education; English; English education; environmental biology; environmental science; family/consumer studies; fashion design/illustration; fashion merchandising; finance; fine/studio arts; food sciences; French; French language education; geography; gerontology; history; history education; home economics; home economics communications; home economics education; humanities; human resources management; human services; interdisciplinary studies; international business; international economics; journalism; liberal arts and sciences/liberal studies; literature; mass communications; mathematical statistics; mathematics; medical technology; microbiology/bacteriology; modern

Framingham State College (continued)
languages; museum studies; natural sciences; nursing administration; nutrition science; nutrition studies; physical sciences; political science; pre-dentistry; pre-law; pre-medicine; pre-veterinary studies; printmaking; psychology; public administration; public relations; science education; sculpture; secondary education; social sciences; sociology; Spanish; Spanish language education; urban studies; wildlife biology; wildlife management.

Academic Programs *Special study options:* adult/continuing education programs, advanced placement credit, distance learning, double majors, English as a second language, honors programs, independent study, internships, off-campus study, part-time degree program, study abroad, summer session for credit. *ROTC:* Army (c).

Library Whittemore Library with 198,263 titles, 1,123 serial subscriptions, 2,421 audiovisual materials, an OPAC, a Web page.

Computers on Campus 575 computers available on campus for general student use. A campuswide network can be accessed from student residence rooms and from off campus that provide access to TELNET. Internet access, online (class) registration, at least one staffed computer lab available.

Student Life *Housing Options:* coed, women-only. *Activities and Organizations:* drama/theater group, student-run newspaper, radio station, choral group, Student Union Activities Board, Student Government Association, Gatepost (student newspaper), Hilltop Players, literary magazine. *Campus security:* 24-hour emergency response devices and patrols, student patrols, late-night transport/escort service, controlled dormitory access. *Student Services:* health clinic, personal/psychological counseling.

Athletics Member NCAA. All Division III. *Intercollegiate sports:* baseball M, basketball M/W, cross-country running M/W, equestrian sports M/W, field hockey W, football M, ice hockey M, soccer M/W, softball W, volleyball W. *Intramural sports:* basketball M/W, football M, golf M/W, racquetball M/W, rugby M/W, softball M/W, volleyball W.

Standardized Tests *Required:* SAT I or ACT (for admission).

Costs (2001–02) *One-time required fee:* $2. *Tuition:* state resident $970 full-time, $162 per course part-time; nonresident $7050 full-time, $1175 per course part-time. Full-time tuition and fees vary according to class time. Part-time tuition and fees vary according to class time and course load. *Required fees:* $1800 full-time, $47 per course. *Room and board:* $4403. Room and board charges vary according to board plan. *Payment plan:* installment. *Waivers:* senior citizens and employees or children of employees.

Financial Aid Of all full-time matriculated undergraduates who enrolled in 2001, 1802 applied for aid, 1319 were judged to have need, 703 had their need fully met. 150 Federal Work-Study jobs (averaging $1200). In 2001, 366 non-need-based awards were made. *Average percent of need met:* 93%. *Average financial aid package:* $5025. *Average need-based loan:* $3058. *Average need-based gift aid:* $1832. *Average non-need based aid:* $3885. *Average indebtedness upon graduation:* $12,339.

Applying *Options:* electronic application, early admission, early action, deferred entrance. *Application fee:* $25. *Required:* high school transcript. *Required for some:* essay or personal statement, interview. *Recommended:* essay or personal statement, minimum 2.9 GPA, letters of recommendation. *Application deadlines:* 3/1 (freshmen), 3/1 (transfers). *Notification:* 5/1 (freshmen), 12/15 (early action).

Admissions Contact Dr. Philip Dooher, Vice President, Enrollment Management and Dean of Admissions, Framingham State College, P.O. Box 9101, Dwight Hall, Room 209, Framingham, MA 01701-9101. *Phone:* 508-626-4500. *E-mail:* admiss@frc.mass.edu.

GORDON COLLEGE
Wenham, Massachusetts

- **Independent nondenominational** comprehensive, founded 1889
- **Calendar** semesters
- **Degrees** bachelor's and master's
- **Small-town** 500-acre campus with easy access to Boston
- **Endowment** $23.9 million
- **Coed,** 1,624 undergraduate students, 97% full-time, 66% women, 34% men
- **Moderately difficult** entrance level, 78% of applicants were admitted

Undergraduates 1,572 full-time, 52 part-time. Students come from 42 states and territories, 21 other countries, 73% are from out of state, 0.7% African American, 1% Asian American or Pacific Islander, 2% Hispanic American, 0.1% Native American, 2% international, 4% transferred in, 88% live on campus. *Retention:* 88% of 2001 full-time freshmen returned.

Freshmen *Admission:* 1,089 applied, 850 admitted, 441 enrolled. *Average high school GPA:* 3.56. *Test scores:* SAT verbal scores over 500: 93%; SAT math scores over 500: 92%; ACT scores over 18: 100%; SAT verbal scores over 600: 53%; SAT math scores over 600: 51%; ACT scores over 24: 86%; SAT verbal scores over 700: 11%; SAT math scores over 700: 5%; ACT scores over 30: 19%.

Faculty *Total:* 130, 67% full-time, 61% with terminal degrees. *Student/faculty ratio:* 15:1.

Majors Accounting; art; biblical studies; biology; business administration; chemistry; communications; computer science; early childhood education; economics; education; elementary education; English; exercise sciences; foreign languages/literatures; French; German; history; international relations; mass communications; mathematics; modern languages; music; music (general performance); music teacher education; philosophy; physics; political science; psychology; recreation/leisure studies; religious education; social work; sociology; Spanish; special education.

Academic Programs *Special study options:* academic remediation for entering students, advanced placement credit, cooperative education, double majors, honors programs, independent study, internships, off-campus study, part-time degree program, services for LD students, student-designed majors, study abroad. *ROTC:* Army (c), Air Force (c). *Unusual degree programs:* 3-2 engineering with University of Massachusetts Lowell; nursing with Thomas Jefferson University.

Library Jenks Learning Resource Center with 136,625 titles, 563 serial subscriptions, 9,078 audiovisual materials, an OPAC.

Computers on Campus 75 computers available on campus for general student use. A campuswide network can be accessed from student residence rooms and from off campus. Internet access, online (class) registration, at least one staffed computer lab available.

Student Life *Housing:* on-campus residence required through senior year. *Options:* coed, men-only, women-only, disabled students. *Activities and Organizations:* drama/theater group, student-run newspaper, choral group, Student Government Association, student ministries, diverse music ensembles. *Campus security:* 24-hour emergency response devices and patrols, late-night transport/escort service, controlled dormitory access. *Student Services:* health clinic, personal/psychological counseling.

Athletics Member NCAA. All Division III. *Intercollegiate sports:* baseball M, basketball M/W, cross-country running M/W, field hockey W, lacrosse M/W, soccer M/W, softball W, swimming M(c)/W, tennis M/W, volleyball W. *Intramural sports:* basketball M/W, football M/W, golf M/W, racquetball M/W, soccer M/W, softball M/W, table tennis M/W, tennis M/W, track and field M/W, volleyball M/W.

Standardized Tests *Required:* SAT I or ACT (for admission).

Costs (2001–02) *Comprehensive fee:* $23,594 includes full-time tuition ($17,378), mandatory fees ($756), and room and board ($5460). Part-time tuition: $4722 per term. Part-time tuition and fees vary according to course load. *Required fees:* $189 per term part-time. *Room and board:* College room only: $3692. Room and board charges vary according to board plan and housing facility. *Payment plans:* tuition prepayment, installment. *Waivers:* employees or children of employees.

Financial Aid Of all full-time matriculated undergraduates who enrolled in 2001, 1217 applied for aid, 1069 were judged to have need, 180 had their need fully met. 114 State and other part-time jobs (averaging $1658). In 2001, 440 non-need-based awards were made. *Average percent of need met:* 79%. *Average financial aid package:* $13,825. *Average need-based loan:* $4347. *Average need-based gift aid:* $9215.

Applying *Options:* electronic application, early admission, early decision, deferred entrance. *Application fee:* $40. *Required:* essay or personal statement, high school transcript, 2 letters of recommendation, interview, pastoral recommendation, statement of Christian faith. *Recommended:* minimum 3.0 GPA. *Application deadline:* rolling (freshmen), rolling (transfers). *Early decision:* 12/1. *Notification:* continuous (freshmen), 1/1 (early decision).

Admissions Contact Mr. Silvio E. Vazquez, Dean of Admissions, Gordon College, 255 Grapevine Road, Wenham, MA 01984-1899. *Phone:* 978-927-2300 Ext. 4218. *Toll-free phone:* 800-343-1379. *Fax:* 978-524-3722. *E-mail:* admissions@hope.gordon.edu.

HAMPSHIRE COLLEGE
Amherst, Massachusetts

- **Independent** 4-year, founded 1965
- **Calendar** 4-1-4
- **Degrees** associate and bachelor's
- **Rural** 800-acre campus
- **Endowment** $30.5 million
- **Coed,** 1,219 undergraduate students, 100% full-time, 58% women, 42% men
- **Moderately difficult** entrance level, 59% of applicants were admitted

Hampshire College's bold, innovative approach to the liberal arts creates an academic atmosphere that energizes students to work hard and grow tremendously, both personally and intellectually. Students have the freedom to design an individualized course of study in a graduate school-like environment, culminating in original final projects such as science or social science research, academic study, or a body of work in writing, performing, visual, or media arts. Students work closely with faculty mentors, often integrating different disciplines. Independent thinking is expected. Hampshire students and faculty agree: if students incorporate what they love into their education, they will love their education.

Undergraduates 1,219 full-time. Students come from 46 states and territories, 25 other countries, 81% are from out of state, 4% African American, 4% Asian American or Pacific Islander, 5% Hispanic American, 0.4% Native American, 3% international, 4% transferred in, 94% live on campus. *Retention:* 77% of 2001 full-time freshmen returned.

Freshmen *Admission:* 1,974 applied, 1,158 admitted, 343 enrolled. *Average high school GPA:* 3.28. *Test scores:* SAT verbal scores over 500: 97%; SAT math scores over 500: 89%; ACT scores over 18: 100%; SAT verbal scores over 600: 76%; SAT math scores over 600: 49%; ACT scores over 24: 88%; SAT verbal scores over 700: 30%; SAT math scores over 700: 7%; ACT scores over 30: 24%.

Faculty *Total:* 118, 87% full-time, 82% with terminal degrees. *Student/faculty ratio:* 11:1.

Majors African-American studies; African studies; agricultural sciences; American studies; anatomy; animal sciences; anthropology; applied mathematics; archaeology; architectural environmental design; architecture; art; art history; Asian studies; astronomy; astrophysics; behavioral sciences; biochemistry; biological/physical sciences; biology; biophysics; botany; business economics; Canadian studies; cell biology; chemistry; child care/development; city/community/regional planning; cognitive psychology/psycholinguistics; community services; comparative literature; computer graphics; computer/information sciences; computer programming; computer science; creative writing; cultural studies; dance; developmental/child psychology; drawing; early childhood education; earth sciences; East Asian studies; Eastern European area studies; ecology; economics; education; elementary education; English; environmental biology; environmental health; environmental science; European studies; evolutionary biology; exercise sciences; family/consumer studies; film studies; film/video production; fine/studio arts; genetics; geochemistry; geography; geology; geophysics/seismology; graphic design/commercial art/illustration; health science; Hispanic-American studies; history; history of philosophy; history of science and technology; humanities; individual/family development; interdisciplinary studies; international business; international economics; international relations; Islamic studies; jazz; journalism; Judaic studies; labor/personnel relations; Latin American studies; legal studies; liberal arts and sciences/liberal studies; linguistics; literature; marine biology; mass communications; mathematical statistics; mathematics; medieval/renaissance studies; Mexican-American studies; microbiology/bacteriology; Middle Eastern studies; molecular biology; music; music history; Native American studies; natural sciences; neuroscience; nutrition science; oceanography; peace/conflict studies; philosophy; photography; physical sciences; physics; physiological psychology/psychobiology; physiology; political science; pre-medicine; pre-veterinary studies; psychology; public health; public policy analysis; radio/television broadcasting; religious studies; Russian/Slavic studies; sculpture; secondary education; social sciences; sociobiology; sociology; solar technology; South Asian studies; Southeast Asian studies; telecommunications; theater arts/drama; urban studies; women's studies.

Academic Programs *Special study options:* accelerated degree program, advanced placement credit, double majors, independent study, internships, off-campus study, services for LD students, student-designed majors, study abroad. *ROTC:* Army (c).

Library Harold F. Johnson Library with 105,809 titles, 750 serial subscriptions, 35,657 audiovisual materials, an OPAC, a Web page.

Computers on Campus 125 computers available on campus for general student use. A campuswide network can be accessed from student residence rooms and from off campus. At least one staffed computer lab available.

Student Life *Housing:* on-campus residence required through senior year. *Options:* coed, disabled students. *Activities and Organizations:* drama/theater group, student-run newspaper, television station, choral group, SOURCE groups, Human Rights, Student Action, Sports Co-op, Women's Center organizations. *Campus security:* 24-hour emergency response devices and patrols, student patrols, late-night transport/escort service. *Student Services:* health clinic, personal/psychological counseling, women's center.

Athletics Member NSCAA. *Intercollegiate sports:* basketball M(c)/W(c), fencing M/W, soccer M(c)/W(c). *Intramural sports:* archery M(c)/W(c), lacrosse W(c).

Costs (2001–02) *One-time required fee:* $90. *Comprehensive fee:* $33,881 includes full-time tuition ($26,455), mandatory fees ($416), and room and board ($7010). *Room and board:* College room only: $4455. Room and board charges vary according to board plan. *Waivers:* employees or children of employees.

Financial Aid Of all full-time matriculated undergraduates who enrolled in 2001, 737 applied for aid, 637 were judged to have need, 588 had their need fully met. 510 Federal Work-Study jobs (averaging $2300). 176 State and other part-time jobs (averaging $2300). In 2001, 26 non-need-based awards were made. *Average percent of need met:* 100%. *Average financial aid package:* $22,465. *Average need-based loan:* $4000. *Average need-based gift aid:* $16,100. *Average indebtedness upon graduation:* $16,200.

Applying *Options:* common application, electronic application, early admission, early decision, early action, deferred entrance. *Application fee:* $50. *Required:* essay or personal statement, high school transcript, 2 letters of recommendation. *Recommended:* interview. *Application deadlines:* 2/1 (freshmen), 3/1 (transfers). *Early decision:* 11/15. *Notification:* 4/1 (freshmen), 12/15 (early decision), 2/1 (early action).

Admissions Contact Ms. Karen S. Parker, Director of Admissions, Hampshire College, 839 West Street, Amherst, MA 01002. *Phone:* 413-559-5471. *Toll-free phone:* 877-937-4267. *Fax:* 413-559-5631. *E-mail:* admissions@hampshire.edu.

HARVARD UNIVERSITY

Cambridge, Massachusetts

- **Independent** university, founded 1636
- **Calendar** semesters
- **Degrees** bachelor's, master's, doctoral, and first professional
- **Urban** 380-acre campus with easy access to Boston
- **Endowment** $18.3 billion
- **Coed,** 6,660 undergraduate students
- **Most difficult** entrance level, 11% of applicants were admitted

Undergraduates Students come from 53 states and territories, 82 other countries, 8% African American, 17% Asian American or Pacific Islander, 8% Hispanic American, 0.7% Native American, 7% international, 96% live on campus. *Retention:* 97% of 2001 full-time freshmen returned.

Freshmen *Admission:* 19,014 applied, 2,110 admitted.

Faculty *Total:* 760, 100% with terminal degrees. *Student/faculty ratio:* 8:1.

Majors African-American studies; African languages; African studies; American studies; anthropology; applied mathematics; Arabic; archaeology; architectural engineering; architectural environmental design; art; art history; Asian studies; astronomy; astrophysics; atmospheric sciences; behavioral sciences; biblical languages/literatures; biblical studies; biochemistry; bioengineering; biological/physical sciences; biological technology; biology; biomedical science; biometrics; biophysics; cell biology; chemical engineering; chemistry; Chinese; city/community/regional planning; civil engineering; classics; cognitive psychology/psycholinguistics; comparative literature; computer engineering; computer engineering technology; computer graphics; computer/information sciences; computer programming; computer science; creative writing; cultural studies; earth sciences; East Asian studies; Eastern European area studies; ecology; economics; electrical engineering; engineering; engineering physics; engineering science; English; entomology; environmental biology; environmental engineering; environmental science; European studies; evolutionary biology; film studies; fine/studio arts; fluid/thermal sciences; folklore; French; genetics; geochemistry; geological engineering; geology; geophysical engineering; geophysics/seismology; German; Greek (modern); Hebrew; Hispanic-American studies; history; history of philosophy; history of science and technology; humanities; individual/family development; information sciences/systems; interdisciplinary studies; international economics; international relations; Islamic studies; Italian; Japanese; Judaic studies; Latin American studies; Latin (ancient and medieval); liberal arts and sciences/liberal studies; linguistics; literature; marine biology; materials engineering; materials science; mathematical statistics; mathematics; mechanical engineering; medieval/renaissance studies; metallurgical engineering; microbiology/bacteriology; Middle Eastern studies; modern languages; molecular biology; music; music history; natural resources conservation; neuroscience; nuclear physics; philosophy; physical sciences; physics; physiological psychology/psychobiology; political science; polymer chemistry; Portuguese; pre-dentistry; pre-law; pre-medicine; pre-veterinary studies; psychology; public policy analysis; religious studies; robotics; romance languages; Russian; Russian/Slavic studies; Scandinavian languages; Slavic languages; social sciences; sociobiology; sociology; South Asian studies; Southeast Asian studies; Spanish; systems engineering; theater arts/drama; urban studies; western civilization; women's studies.

Academic Programs *Special study options:* academic remediation for entering students, accelerated degree program, adult/continuing education programs, advanced placement credit, double majors, English as a second language, honors programs, independent study, internships, off-campus study, services for LD students, student-designed majors, study abroad, summer session for credit. *ROTC:* Army (c), Navy (c), Air Force (c).

Harvard University (continued)

Library Widener Library plus 90 others with 13.4 million titles, 97,568 serial subscriptions.

Computers on Campus A campuswide network can be accessed from student residence rooms and from off campus. Internet access, at least one staffed computer lab available.

Student Life *Housing:* on-campus residence required for freshman year. *Options:* coed. *Activities and Organizations:* drama/theater group, student-run newspaper, radio and television station, choral group, marching band, Phillips Brooks House, Asian-American Association, International Relations Council, Harvard Crimson (newspaper), Harvard/Radcliffe Chorus. *Campus security:* 24-hour emergency response devices and patrols, late-night transport/escort service, controlled dormitory access, required and optional safety courses. *Student Services:* health clinic, personal/psychological counseling, women's center, legal services.

Athletics Member NCAA. All Division I except football (Division I-AA). *Intercollegiate sports:* baseball M, basketball M/W, crew M/W, cross-country running M/W, fencing M/W, field hockey W, golf M/W, ice hockey M/W, lacrosse M/W, sailing M/W, skiing (cross-country) M/W, skiing (downhill) M/W, soccer M/W, softball W, squash M/W, swimming M/W, tennis M/W, track and field M/W, volleyball M/W, water polo M/W, wrestling M. *Intramural sports:* badminton M(c)/W(c), baseball M, basketball M/W, crew M/W, cross-country running M/W, equestrian sports M(c)/W(c), fencing M/W, field hockey M/W, football M, gymnastics M(c)/W(c), ice hockey M/W, racquetball M/W, rugby M(c)/W(c), soccer M/W, softball W, squash M/W, swimming M/W, table tennis M(c)/W(c), tennis M/W, track and field M/W, volleyball M/W.

Standardized Tests *Required:* SAT I or ACT (for admission), SAT II: Subject Tests (for admission).

Costs (2001–02) *Comprehensive fee:* $34,269 includes full-time tuition ($23,457), mandatory fees ($2562), and room and board ($8250). *Room and board:* College room only: $4331. *Payment plans:* tuition prepayment, installment.

Financial Aid Of all full-time matriculated undergraduates who enrolled in 2001, 3530 applied for aid, 3216 were judged to have need, 3216 had their need fully met. 867 Federal Work-Study jobs (averaging $1262). 2587 State and other part-time jobs (averaging $1540). In 2001, 1075 non-need-based awards were made. *Average percent of need met:* 100%. *Average financial aid package:* $23,064. *Average need-based loan:* $3619. *Average need-based gift aid:* $19,031. *Average non-need based aid:* $4999. *Average indebtedness upon graduation:* $13,360.

Applying *Options:* common application, early action, deferred entrance. *Application fee:* $60. *Required:* essay or personal statement, high school transcript, 2 letters of recommendation, interview. *Application deadlines:* 1/1 (freshmen), 2/1 (transfers). *Notification:* 4/1 (freshmen), 12/15 (early action).

Admissions Contact Office of Admissions and Financial Aid, Harvard University, Byerly Hall, 8 Garden Street, Cambridge, MA 02138. *Phone:* 617-495-1551. *E-mail:* college@harvard.edu.

HEBREW COLLEGE
Newton Centre, Massachusetts

- **Independent Jewish** comprehensive, founded 1921
- **Calendar** semesters
- **Degrees** bachelor's and master's
- **Suburban** 3-acre campus with easy access to Boston
- **Endowment** $8.0 million
- **Coed**
- **Minimally difficult** entrance level

Standardized Tests *Required:* SAT I (for placement).

Financial Aid *Financial aid deadline:* 8/15.

Applying *Options:* common application, early decision, deferred entrance. *Application fee:* $25. *Required:* essay or personal statement, high school transcript, minimum 2.0 GPA, 2 letters of recommendation. *Recommended:* interview.

Admissions Contact Mrs. Norma Frankel, Registrar, Hebrew College, 160 Herrick Road, Newton Centre, MA 02459. *Phone:* 617-278-4944. *Toll-free phone:* 800-866-4814. *Fax:* 617-734-9769. *E-mail:* nfrankel@lynx.neu.edu.

HELLENIC COLLEGE
Brookline, Massachusetts

- **Independent Greek Orthodox** 4-year, founded 1937
- **Calendar** semesters
- **Degrees** bachelor's and master's
- **Suburban** 52-acre campus with easy access to Boston
- **Endowment** $19.4 million
- **Coed,** 58 undergraduate students, 97% full-time, 34% women, 66% men
- **Minimally difficult** entrance level, 60% of applicants were admitted

Undergraduates 56 full-time, 2 part-time. Students come from 29 states and territories, 6 other countries, 87% are from out of state, 21% international, 5% transferred in, 90% live on campus. *Retention:* 100% of 2001 full-time freshmen returned.

Freshmen *Admission:* 40 applied, 24 admitted, 13 enrolled. *Average high school GPA:* 2.71. *Test scores:* SAT verbal scores over 500: 66%; SAT math scores over 500: 45%; SAT verbal scores over 600: 33%; SAT math scores over 600: 20%.

Faculty *Total:* 28, 29% full-time. *Student/faculty ratio:* 7:1.

Majors Classics; elementary education; individual/family development; religious studies; theology.

Academic Programs *Special study options:* academic remediation for entering students, advanced placement credit, double majors, independent study, internships, off-campus study, part-time degree program, summer session for credit.

Library Archbishop Iakoros Library with 119,000 titles, 770 serial subscriptions, 1,415 audiovisual materials, an OPAC, a Web page.

Computers on Campus 9 computers available on campus for general student use. At least one staffed computer lab available.

Student Life *Housing:* on-campus residence required through senior year. *Options:* coed. *Activities and Organizations:* drama/theater group, student-run newspaper, choral group. *Campus security:* controlled dormitory access. *Student Services:* health clinic, personal/psychological counseling.

Athletics *Intramural sports:* baseball M, basketball M/W, football M, golf M, soccer M, table tennis M/W, volleyball M/W.

Standardized Tests *Required:* SAT I or ACT (for admission). *Required for some:* SAT II: Writing Test (for admission).

Costs (2001–02) *Comprehensive fee:* $17,015 includes full-time tuition ($9450), mandatory fees ($215), and room and board ($7350). Part-time tuition: $395 per credit. *Required fees:* $40 per term part-time. *Room and board:* Room and board charges vary according to housing facility. *Waivers:* minority students, children of alumni, and employees or children of employees.

Financial Aid Of all full-time matriculated undergraduates who enrolled in 2001, 18 applied for aid, 18 were judged to have need, 15 had their need fully met. 8 Federal Work-Study jobs (averaging $1000). *Average percent of need met:* 75%. *Average financial aid package:* $8000. *Average need-based gift aid:* $2100. *Average indebtedness upon graduation:* $15,000.

Applying *Options:* common application, electronic application, deferred entrance. *Application fee:* $35. *Required:* essay or personal statement, high school transcript, minimum 2.0 GPA, letters of recommendation, interview, health certificate. *Application deadline:* rolling (freshmen), rolling (transfers). *Notification:* continuous (freshmen).

Admissions Contact Rev. James Katinas, Director of Admissions and Records, Hellenic College, 50 Goddard Avenue, Brookline, MA 02445-7496. *Phone:* 617-731-3500 Ext. 1260. *Fax:* 617-850-1460. *E-mail:* admissions@hchc.edu.

LASELL COLLEGE
Newton, Massachusetts

- **Independent** comprehensive, founded 1851
- **Calendar** semesters
- **Degrees** associate and bachelor's
- **Suburban** 50-acre campus with easy access to Boston
- **Endowment** $12.1 million
- **Coed,** 894 undergraduate students, 95% full-time, 74% women, 26% men
- **Moderately difficult** entrance level, 78% of applicants were admitted

The Lasell Plan of Education is distinguished by a philosophy called connected learning. In connected learning, students practice classroom theory in practical settings. In addition to off-campus internship sites, students gain practical experience in on-campus labs, which include 2 renowned child-study centers, a state-of-the-art business technology center, bed and breakfast, fashion design and merchandising center, allied health labs, CADD lab, and an art center.

Undergraduates 851 full-time, 43 part-time. Students come from 20 states and territories, 8 other countries, 34% are from out of state, 10% African American, 5% Asian American or Pacific Islander, 6% Hispanic American, 3% international, 5% transferred in, 80% live on campus. *Retention:* 82% of 2001 full-time freshmen returned.

Freshmen *Admission:* 1,638 applied, 1,281 admitted, 278 enrolled. *Average high school GPA:* 2.60. *Test scores:* SAT verbal scores over 500: 41%; SAT math scores over 500: 36%; SAT verbal scores over 600: 4%; SAT math scores over 600: 5%.

Faculty *Total:* 130, 34% full-time, 15% with terminal degrees. *Student/faculty ratio:* 10:1.

Majors Accounting; business administration; business marketing and marketing management; child care/development; communications; criminal justice studies; early childhood education; education; elementary education; exercise sciences; fashion design/illustration; fashion merchandising; finance; graphic design/commercial art/illustration; hotel and restaurant management; human services; information sciences/systems; interdisciplinary studies; international business; liberal arts and sciences/liberal studies; paralegal/legal assistant; physical therapy; psychology; retail management; sociology; special education; travel/tourism management.

Academic Programs *Special study options:* advanced placement credit, cooperative education, double majors, English as a second language, honors programs, independent study, internships, part-time degree program, services for LD students, study abroad.

Library Brennan Library with 51,219 titles, 521 serial subscriptions, 2,145 audiovisual materials, an OPAC.

Computers on Campus 150 computers available on campus for general student use. A campuswide network can be accessed from student residence rooms and from off campus. At least one staffed computer lab available.

Student Life *Housing Options:* coed, women-only. *Activities and Organizations:* drama/theater group, student-run newspaper, choral group, Center for Public Service, student government, Umoja-Nia, yearbook, fashion board. *Campus security:* 24-hour emergency response devices and patrols, late-night transport/escort service, controlled dormitory access. *Student Services:* health clinic, personal/psychological counseling.

Athletics Member NCAA. All Division III. *Intercollegiate sports:* basketball M/W, cross-country running M/W, field hockey W, lacrosse M/W, soccer M/W, softball W, volleyball M/W. *Intramural sports:* basketball M/W, crew M/W, soccer M/W, volleyball M/W.

Standardized Tests *Required:* SAT I (for admission).

Costs (2001–02) *Comprehensive fee:* $24,100 includes full-time tuition ($15,300), mandatory fees ($800), and room and board ($8000). Full-time tuition and fees vary according to program. Part-time tuition: $510 per credit hour. Part-time tuition and fees vary according to course load and program. *Required fees:* $200 per term part-time. *Room and board:* Room and board charges vary according to housing facility. *Payment plan:* installment. *Waivers:* children of alumni and employees or children of employees.

Financial Aid Of all full-time matriculated undergraduates who enrolled in 2001, 782 applied for aid, 780 were judged to have need, 76 had their need fully met. *Average percent of need met:* 78%. *Average financial aid package:* $15,488. *Average need-based loan:* $3569. *Average need-based gift aid:* $11,490. *Average indebtedness upon graduation:* $18,050.

Applying *Options:* electronic application, deferred entrance. *Application fee:* $25. *Required:* high school transcript, minimum 2.0 GPA, 1 letter of recommendation. *Recommended:* essay or personal statement, interview. *Application deadline:* rolling (freshmen), rolling (transfers). *Notification:* continuous (freshmen).

Admissions Contact Mr. Darryl Tiggle, Director of Admission, Lasell College, 1844 Commonwealth Avenue, Newton, MA 02466. *Phone:* 617-243-2225. *Toll-free phone:* 888-LASELL-4. *Fax:* 617-796-4343. *E-mail:* info@lasell.edu.

LESLEY UNIVERSITY

Cambridge, Massachusetts

- **Independent** comprehensive, founded 1909
- **Calendar** semesters
- **Degrees** certificates, diplomas, associate, bachelor's, master's, doctoral, and post-master's certificates
- **Urban** 5-acre campus with easy access to Boston
- **Endowment** $29.0 million
- **Coed, primarily women,** 1,115 undergraduate students, 95% full-time, 78% women, 22% men
- **Moderately difficult** entrance level, 83% of applicants were admitted

Located on Lesley University's main campus in Cambridge, Massachusetts, Lesley College offers a small, residential college experience to 600 undergraduate women. Academic programs in the areas of education, human services, management, and the arts integrate the liberal arts with professional course work and hands-on internship experience.

Undergraduates 1,064 full-time, 51 part-time. Students come from 31 states and territories, 11 other countries, 34% are from out of state, 9% African American, 5% Asian American or Pacific Islander, 7% Hispanic American, 0.2% Native American, 6% international, 5% transferred in, 63% live on campus. *Retention:* 76% of 2001 full-time freshmen returned.

Freshmen *Admission:* 357 applied, 298 admitted, 130 enrolled. *Average high school GPA:* 2.73. *Test scores:* SAT verbal scores over 500: 52%; SAT math scores over 500: 39%; SAT verbal scores over 600: 10%; SAT math scores over 600: 10%; SAT verbal scores over 700: 1%; SAT math scores over 700: 2%.

Faculty *Total:* 70, 44% full-time, 37% with terminal degrees. *Student/faculty ratio:* 12:1.

Majors Business administration; child care/development; early childhood education; education; elementary education; humanities; human services; liberal arts and sciences/liberal studies; middle school education; natural sciences; social sciences; special education.

Academic Programs *Special study options:* academic remediation for entering students, adult/continuing education programs, advanced placement credit, distance learning, English as a second language, external degree program, independent study, internships, off-campus study, part-time degree program, services for LD students, study abroad, summer session for credit. *Unusual degree programs:* 3-2 counseling psychology, clinical mental health counseling, elementary education, special education, management.

Library Eleanor DeWolfe Ludcke Library with 100,992 titles, 91,873 serial subscriptions, 1,308 audiovisual materials, an OPAC, a Web page.

Computers on Campus 150 computers available on campus for general student use. A campuswide network can be accessed from student residence rooms and from off campus. Internet access, at least one staffed computer lab available.

Student Life *Housing Options:* women-only. *Activities and Organizations:* drama/theater group, student-run newspaper, choral group, Student Senate, Gay/Straight/Bisexual Alliance, Education Council, LINC (Learning in Neighborhood Communities), Spirit Club. *Campus security:* 24-hour emergency response devices and patrols, late-night transport/escort service. *Student Services:* health clinic, personal/psychological counseling.

Athletics Member NCAA. All Division III. *Intercollegiate sports:* basketball W, crew W, cross-country running W, soccer W, softball W, volleyball W. *Intramural sports:* tennis W.

Standardized Tests *Required:* SAT I or ACT (for admission).

Costs (2002–03) *Comprehensive fee:* $26,775 includes full-time tuition ($18,300), mandatory fees ($175), and room and board ($8300). Full-time tuition and fees vary according to course load. Part-time tuition: $538 per credit. *Payment plan:* installment. *Waivers:* employees or children of employees.

Financial Aid Of all full-time matriculated undergraduates who enrolled in 2001, 441 applied for aid, 374 were judged to have need, 61 had their need fully met. 166 Federal Work-Study jobs (averaging $900). 135 State and other part-time jobs (averaging $1100). In 2001, 40 non-need-based awards were made. *Average percent of need met:* 94%. *Average financial aid package:* $14,345. *Average need-based loan:* $4681. *Average need-based gift aid:* $9003. *Average non-need based aid:* $7505. *Average indebtedness upon graduation:* $13,550.

Applying *Options:* electronic application, early decision, deferred entrance. *Application fee:* $35. *Required:* essay or personal statement, high school transcript, 3 letters of recommendation. *Recommended:* interview. *Application deadlines:* 3/15 (freshmen), 6/1 (transfers). *Early decision:* 12/1. *Notification:* 1/15 (freshmen), 12/15 (early decision).

Admissions Contact Jane A. Raley, Director of Women's College Admissions, Lesley University, 29 Everett Street, Cambridge, MA 02138-2790. *Phone:* 617-349-8800. *Toll-free phone:* 800-999-1959 Ext. 8800. *Fax:* 617-349-8810. *E-mail:* ugadm@mail.lesley.edu.

MASSACHUSETTS COLLEGE OF ART

Boston, Massachusetts

- **State-supported** comprehensive, founded 1873, part of Massachusetts Public Higher Education System
- **Calendar** semesters
- **Degrees** certificates, bachelor's, master's, and postbachelor's certificates
- **Urban** 5-acre campus
- **Endowment** $1.4 million
- **Coed,** 2,133 undergraduate students, 59% full-time, 65% women, 35% men
- **Very difficult** entrance level, 46% of applicants were admitted

Undergraduates 1,267 full-time, 866 part-time. Students come from 26 states and territories, 58 other countries, 22% are from out of state, 3% African American, 3% Asian American or Pacific Islander, 4% Hispanic American, 0.1% Native American, 5% international, 8% transferred in, 15% live on campus. *Retention:* 86% of 2001 full-time freshmen returned.

Freshmen *Admission:* 1,133 applied, 526 admitted, 236 enrolled. *Average high school GPA:* 3.23. *Test scores:* SAT verbal scores over 500: 83%; SAT math scores

Massachusetts College of Art (continued)
over 500: 67%; SAT verbal scores over 600: 35%; SAT math scores over 600: 23%; SAT verbal scores over 700: 8%; SAT math scores over 700: 2%.

Faculty *Total:* 207, 32% full-time, 24% with terminal degrees. *Student/faculty ratio:* 13:1.

Majors Architecture; art education; art history; ceramic arts; fashion design/illustration; film/video production; fine/studio arts; graphic design/commercial art/illustration; industrial design; metal/jewelry arts; multimedia; painting; photography; printmaking; sculpture; textile arts.

Academic Programs *Special study options:* double majors, external degree program, independent study, internships, off-campus study, part-time degree program, student-designed majors, study abroad, summer session for credit.

Library Morton R. Godine Library with 231,586 titles, 757 serial subscriptions, 125,000 audiovisual materials.

Computers on Campus 250 computers available on campus for general student use. A campuswide network can be accessed from off campus. At least one staffed computer lab available.

Student Life *Housing Options:* coed. *Activities and Organizations:* drama/theater group, student-run newspaper, radio station, international students, Design Research Unit, Spectrum, film society, Event Works. *Campus security:* 24-hour emergency response devices and patrols, late-night transport/escort service, security lighting, self-defense workshops. *Student Services:* health clinic, personal/psychological counseling, women's center.

Athletics *Intramural sports:* basketball M/W, ice hockey M, table tennis M/W, volleyball M/W.

Standardized Tests *Required:* SAT I or ACT (for admission).

Costs (2001–02) *Tuition:* state resident $1030 full-time, $129 per course part-time; nonresident $10,160 full-time, $1457 per course part-time. Full-time tuition and fees vary according to reciprocity agreements. Part-time tuition and fees vary according to class time, course load, and reciprocity agreements. *Required fees:* $3038 full-time, $1064 per term part-time. *Room and board:* $7742. Room and board charges vary according to housing facility. *Payment plan:* installment. *Waivers:* senior citizens and employees or children of employees.

Financial Aid Of all full-time matriculated undergraduates who enrolled in 2001, 120 Federal Work-Study jobs (averaging $1000). *Average indebtedness upon graduation:* $18,337.

Applying *Options:* early admission, early decision, deferred entrance. *Application fee:* $65 (non-residents). *Required:* essay or personal statement, high school transcript, minimum 2.9 GPA, portfolio. *Recommended:* letters of recommendation. *Application deadlines:* 3/1 (freshmen), 4/1 (transfers). *Early decision:* 12/1. *Notification:* continuous until 4/20 (freshmen).

Admissions Contact Ms. Kay Ransdell, Dean of Admissions, Massachusetts College of Art, 621 Huntington Avenue, Boston, MA 02115-5882. *Phone:* 617-232-1555 Ext. 235. *Fax:* 617-879-7250. *E-mail:* admissions@massart.edu.

MASSACHUSETTS COLLEGE OF LIBERAL ARTS
North Adams, Massachusetts

- **State-supported** comprehensive, founded 1894, part of Massachusetts Public Higher Education System
- **Calendar** semesters
- **Degrees** bachelor's, master's, and postbachelor's certificates
- **Small-town** 80-acre campus
- **Endowment** $3.9 million
- **Coed,** 1,401 undergraduate students, 79% full-time, 59% women, 41% men
- **Moderately difficult** entrance level, 100% of applicants were admitted

North Adams State College changed its name to Massachusetts College of Liberal Arts to officially recognize the institution's liberal arts character. With this new designation, Massachusetts College joins the 2 other specialized institutions in the public sector (Massachusetts College of Art and Massachusetts Maritime Academy) in providing a distinctive educational experience.

Undergraduates 1,109 full-time, 292 part-time. 17% are from out of state, 5% African American, 2% Asian American or Pacific Islander, 3% Hispanic American, 0.3% Native American, 0.7% international, 9% transferred in, 50% live on campus. *Retention:* 71% of 2001 full-time freshmen returned.

Freshmen *Admission:* 284 applied, 284 admitted, 277 enrolled. *Average high school GPA:* 2.98. *Test scores:* SAT verbal scores over 500: 73%; SAT math scores over 500: 54%; ACT scores over 18: 100%; SAT verbal scores over 600: 19%; SAT math scores over 600: 13%; ACT scores over 24: 100%; SAT verbal scores over 700: 4%; SAT math scores over 700: 1%.

Faculty *Total:* 121, 68% full-time, 56% with terminal degrees. *Student/faculty ratio:* 13:1.

Majors Accounting; adult/continuing education; anthropology; art; athletic training/sports medicine; biological/physical sciences; biology; broadcast journalism; business administration; business marketing and marketing management; chemistry; computer/information sciences; computer science; creative writing; early childhood education; economics; education; elementary education; English; environmental science; finance; history; interdisciplinary studies; journalism; literature; mass communications; mathematics; medical laboratory technician; medical technology; middle school education; multi/interdisciplinary studies related; music; philosophy; physics; pre-law; psychology; secondary education; social work; sociology; theater arts/drama; visual/performing arts.

Academic Programs *Special study options:* academic remediation for entering students, advanced placement credit, distance learning, double majors, honors programs, independent study, internships, off-campus study, part-time degree program, services for LD students, student-designed majors, study abroad, summer session for credit.

Library Freel Library with 541 serial subscriptions, 4,567 audiovisual materials, an OPAC, a Web page.

Computers on Campus A campuswide network can be accessed from student residence rooms and from off campus. Internet access, at least one staffed computer lab available.

Student Life *Housing:* on-campus residence required through junior year. *Options:* coed, disabled students. *Activities and Organizations:* drama/theater group, student-run newspaper, radio and television station, choral group, Student Activities Council, Weightlifting Club, Non-Traditional Student Organization, Outing Club, Lacrosse Club, national fraternities, national sororities. *Campus security:* 24-hour emergency response devices and patrols, late-night transport/escort service, controlled dormitory access. *Student Services:* health clinic, personal/psychological counseling, women's center.

Athletics Member NCAA. All Division III. *Intercollegiate sports:* baseball M, basketball M/W, cross-country running M/W, golf M, ice hockey M/W, soccer M/W, softball W, tennis W, volleyball W. *Intramural sports:* basketball M/W, cross-country running M/W, football M, golf M/W, ice hockey M, lacrosse M(c)/W(c), racquetball M/W, rugby M(c)/W(c), skiing (cross-country) M(c)/W(c), skiing (downhill) M(c)/W(c), soccer M/W, softball M/W, squash M/W, swimming M/W, tennis M/W, volleyball M/W, water polo M/W, weight lifting M(c)/W(c), wrestling M(c)/W(c).

Standardized Tests *Required:* SAT I (for admission).

Costs (2002–03) *Tuition:* state resident $1030 full-time, $43 per credit part-time; nonresident $9975 full-time, $391 per credit part-time. Full-time tuition and fees vary according to reciprocity agreements. Part-time tuition and fees vary according to reciprocity agreements. *Required fees:* $2867 full-time, $141 per credit. *Room and board:* $5846; room only: $2579. Room and board charges vary according to board plan and housing facility. *Payment plan:* installment. *Waivers:* senior citizens and employees or children of employees.

Financial Aid Of all full-time matriculated undergraduates who enrolled in 2001, 924 applied for aid, 716 were judged to have need, 314 had their need fully met. In 2001, 181 non-need-based awards were made. *Average percent of need met:* 77%. *Average financial aid package:* $6642. *Average need-based loan:* $3377. *Average need-based gift aid:* $3844. *Average indebtedness upon graduation:* $15,867.

Applying *Options:* common application, electronic application, early action, deferred entrance. *Application fee:* $10. *Required:* essay or personal statement, high school transcript, minimum 3.0 GPA. *Required for some:* interview. *Recommended:* letters of recommendation, interview. *Application deadline:* rolling (freshmen), rolling (transfers). *Notification:* continuous (freshmen), 12/15 (early action).

Admissions Contact Ms. Denise Richardello, Dean of Enrollment Management, Massachusetts College of Liberal Arts, 375 Church Street, North Adams, MA 01247-4100. *Phone:* 413-662-5410 Ext. 5416. *Toll-free phone:* 800-292-6632. *Fax:* 413-662-5179. *E-mail:* admissions@mcla.mass.edu.

MASSACHUSETTS COLLEGE OF PHARMACY AND HEALTH SCIENCES
Boston, Massachusetts

- **Independent** university, founded 1823
- **Calendar** semesters
- **Degrees** bachelor's, master's, doctoral, first professional, and first professional certificates (bachelor of science in nursing program for registered nurses only)
- **Urban** 2-acre campus
- **Endowment** $25.5 million
- **Coed,** 1,165 undergraduate students, 89% full-time, 67% women, 33% men
- **Moderately difficult** entrance level, 33% of applicants were admitted

Dedicated solely to health education, the College is a highly respected institution in Boston's world-renowned Longwood Medical Academic Area. The Fennell-Iorio Wing, completed in 1996, houses new residence halls, dining commons, sophisticated research facilities, laboratories, offices, and classrooms. MCPHS offers the following undergraduate degrees and programs: Bachelor of Science degrees in pharmacy, pharmacy/chemistry (dual degree), pharmaceutical sciences, chemistry, health psychology, premedical and health studies, radiologic sciences (accelerated BS degree program in nuclear medicine, radiography, or radiation therapy), and dental hygiene (Forsyth School for Dental Hygienists). Students admitted to the College are directly enrolled in the Doctor of Pharmacy (Pharm.D.) program.

Undergraduates 1,034 full-time, 131 part-time. Students come from 32 states and territories, 30 other countries, 53% are from out of state, 19% transferred in, 15% live on campus. *Retention:* 86% of 2001 full-time freshmen returned.

Freshmen *Admission:* 346 applied, 115 admitted, 112 enrolled. *Average high school GPA:* 3.20. *Test scores:* SAT verbal scores over 500: 56%; SAT math scores over 500: 79%; SAT verbal scores over 600: 12%; SAT math scores over 600: 17%; SAT verbal scores over 700: 2%; SAT math scores over 700: 3%.

Faculty *Total:* 128, 93% full-time, 100% with terminal degrees. *Student/faculty ratio:* 14:1.

Majors Chemistry; health professions and related sciences; nuclear medical technology; pharmacy; pharmacy related; pre-medicine; radiological science.

Academic Programs *Special study options:* adult/continuing education programs, advanced placement credit, double majors, English as a second language, independent study, internships, off-campus study, part-time degree program, services for LD students, summer session for credit. *ROTC:* Army (c), Navy (c), Air Force (c).

Library Shepard Library with 60,000 titles, 790 serial subscriptions, 750 audiovisual materials, an OPAC, a Web page.

Computers on Campus 60 computers available on campus for general student use. A campuswide network can be accessed from student residence rooms and from off campus. Internet access, at least one staffed computer lab available.

Student Life *Housing Options:* coed. *Activities and Organizations:* drama/theater group, student-run newspaper, radio station, choral group, Black Student Union, Alpha Zeta Omega, Vietnamese Student Association, Outing Club, Lambda Kappa Sigma, national fraternities, national sororities. *Campus security:* 24-hour emergency response devices and patrols, controlled dormitory access, electronically operated academic area entrances, security guards at entrance. *Student Services:* health clinic, personal/psychological counseling, women's center.

Athletics *Intramural sports:* baseball M, basketball M/W, bowling M/W, cross-country running M/W, field hockey W, golf M, skiing (downhill) M/W, soccer M, squash M/W, table tennis M/W, volleyball M/W, weight lifting M/W.

Standardized Tests *Required:* SAT I or ACT (for admission).

Costs (2001–02) *One-time required fee:* $150. *Comprehensive fee:* $27,131 includes full-time tuition ($17,721), mandatory fees ($500), and room and board ($8910). Full-time tuition and fees vary according to class time, course load, location, and program. Part-time tuition: $537 per semester hour. Part-time tuition and fees vary according to class time and program. *Required fees:* $50 per term part-time. *Payment plan:* installment. *Waivers:* employees or children of employees.

Financial Aid Of all full-time matriculated undergraduates who enrolled in 2001, 922 applied for aid, 863 were judged to have need, 25 had their need fully met. In 2001, 80 non-need-based awards were made. *Average percent of need met:* 47%. *Average financial aid package:* $11,852. *Average need-based loan:* $6247. *Average need-based gift aid:* $6447.

Applying *Options:* common application, electronic application, early admission, early decision, deferred entrance. *Application fee:* $70. *Required:* essay or personal statement, high school transcript, 2 letters of recommendation. *Required for some:* 3 letters of recommendation, interview. *Recommended:* interview. *Application deadlines:* 2/1 (freshmen), 3/1 (transfers). *Early decision:* 11/1. *Notification:* continuous until 8/1 (freshmen), 12/1 (early decision).

Admissions Contact Jim Zarakas, Admissions Assistant, Massachusetts College of Pharmacy and Health Sciences, 179 Longwood Avenue, Boston, MA 02115. *Phone:* 617-732-2846. *Toll-free phone:* 617-732-2850 (in-state); 800-225-5506 (out-of-state). *Fax:* 617-732-2801. *E-mail:* admissions@mcp.edu.

MASSACHUSETTS INSTITUTE OF TECHNOLOGY
Cambridge, Massachusetts

- **Independent** university, founded 1861
- **Calendar** 4-1-4
- **Degrees** bachelor's, master's, and doctoral
- **Urban** 154-acre campus with easy access to Boston
- **Endowment** $6.1 billion
- **Coed,** 4,220 undergraduate students, 98% full-time, 42% women, 58% men
- **Most difficult** entrance level, 17% of applicants were admitted

Undergraduates 4,154 full-time, 66 part-time. Students come from 55 states and territories, 88 other countries, 90% are from out of state, 6% African American, 28% Asian American or Pacific Islander, 11% Hispanic American, 2% Native American, 8% international, 0.9% transferred in, 97% live on campus. *Retention:* 97% of 2001 full-time freshmen returned.

Freshmen *Admission:* 10,490 applied, 1,787 admitted, 1,030 enrolled. *Test scores:* SAT verbal scores over 500: 99%; SAT math scores over 500: 100%; ACT scores over 18: 100%; SAT verbal scores over 600: 95%; SAT math scores over 600: 100%; ACT scores over 24: 99%; SAT verbal scores over 700: 63%; SAT math scores over 700: 89%; ACT scores over 30: 80%.

Faculty *Total:* 1,760, 74% full-time. *Student/faculty ratio:* 7:1.

Majors Aerospace engineering; American studies; anthropology; applied mathematics; archaeology; architecture; bioengineering; biology; business administration; chemical engineering; chemistry; city/community/regional planning; civil engineering; cognitive psychology/psycholinguistics; computer engineering; computer science; earth sciences; East Asian studies; economics; electrical engineering; engineering; environmental engineering; environmental science; foreign languages/literatures; German; history; humanities; interdisciplinary studies; Latin American studies; liberal arts and sciences/liberal studies; linguistics; literature; materials engineering; materials science; mathematics; mechanical engineering; music; naval architecture/marine engineering; Navy/Marine Corps R.O.T.C./naval science; nuclear engineering; ocean engineering; philosophy; physics; political science; pre-dentistry; pre-law; pre-medicine; pre-veterinary studies; Russian; Russian/Slavic studies; science/technology and society; Spanish; theater arts/drama; women's studies.

Academic Programs *Special study options:* accelerated degree program, advanced placement credit, cooperative education, English as a second language, internships, off-campus study, student-designed majors, summer session for credit. *ROTC:* Army (b), Navy (b), Air Force (b).

Library Main Library plus 10 others with 2.6 million titles, 20,207 serial subscriptions, 590,664 audiovisual materials, an OPAC, a Web page.

Computers on Campus 950 computers available on campus for general student use. A campuswide network can be accessed from student residence rooms and from off campus. At least one staffed computer lab available.

Student Life *Housing:* on-campus residence required for freshman year. *Options:* coed, women-only. *Activities and Organizations:* drama/theater group, student-run newspaper, radio and television station, choral group, marching band, Tech Catholic Community, Outing Club, Society of Women Engineers, Hillel, South Asian American Students, national fraternities, national sororities. *Campus security:* 24-hour emergency response devices and patrols, student patrols, late-night transport/escort service, controlled dormitory access. *Student Services:* health clinic, personal/psychological counseling.

Athletics Member NCAA. All Division III except men's and women's crew (Division I), men's and women's fencing (Division I), men's and women's riflery (Division I), men's and women's sailing (Division I), men's and women's skiing (cross-country) (Division I), men's and women's skiing (downhill) (Division I), squash (Division I). *Intercollegiate sports:* baseball M, basketball M/W, crew M/W, cross-country running M/W, fencing M/W, field hockey W, football M, golf M, gymnastics M/W, ice hockey M(c)/W, lacrosse M/W, riflery M/W, sailing M/W, skiing (cross-country) M/W, skiing (downhill) M/W, soccer M/W, softball W, squash M, swimming M/W, tennis M/W, track and field M/W, volleyball M/W, water polo M, wrestling M. *Intramural sports:* archery M/W, badminton M(c)/W(c), baseball M/W, basketball M/W, crew M(c)/W(c), cross-country running M/W, equestrian sports M(c)/W(c), football M/W, ice hockey M/W, rugby M(c)/W(c), soccer M/W, softball M/W, table tennis M(c)/W(c), volleyball M(c)/W(c), water polo M/W(c).

Standardized Tests *Required:* SAT I or ACT (for admission), SAT II: Subject Tests (for admission).

Costs (2001–02) *Comprehensive fee:* $34,460 includes full-time tuition ($26,960) and room and board ($7500). *Room and board:* Room and board charges vary according to board plan and housing facility. *Waivers:* employees or children of employees.

Financial Aid Of all full-time matriculated undergraduates who enrolled in 2001, 2622 applied for aid, 2133 were judged to have need, 2133 had their need fully met. In 2001, 111 non-need-based awards were made. *Average percent of need met:* 100%. *Average financial aid package:* $24,417. *Average need-based loan:* $5280. *Average need-based gift aid:* $17,464. *Average non-need based aid:* $4949. *Average indebtedness upon graduation:* $20,484. *Financial aid deadline:* 2/8.

Applying *Options:* electronic application, early action, deferred entrance. *Application fee:* $60. *Required:* essay or personal statement, high school transcript, 2

Massachusetts Institute of Technology (continued)

letters of recommendation, interview. *Application deadlines:* 1/1 (freshmen), 3/15 (transfers). *Notification:* 3/22 (freshmen), 12/15 (early action).

Admissions Contact Ms. Marilee Jones, Dean of Admissions, Massachusetts Institute of Technology, 77 Massachusetts Avenue, Cambridge, MA 02139-4307. *Phone:* 617-253-4791.

MASSACHUSETTS MARITIME ACADEMY

Buzzards Bay, Massachusetts

- **State-supported** 4-year, founded 1891, part of Massachusetts Public Higher Education System
- **Calendar** semesters
- **Degree** bachelor's
- **Small-town** 55-acre campus with easy access to Boston
- **Endowment** $4.1 million
- **Coed, primarily men,** 831 undergraduate students, 94% full-time, 13% women, 87% men
- **Moderately difficult** entrance level, 72% of applicants were admitted

Engineering, international business, transportation, and environmental science are all majors at Massachusetts Maritime Academy. The semester at sea takes students on an international odyssey to more than a dozen countries. Paid cooperatives and internships provide the opportunity to learn and earn, while a regimented lifestyle prepares students to lead in industry or, at the student's option, the US armed services. Web site: www.mma.mass.edu.

Undergraduates 781 full-time, 50 part-time. Students come from 24 states and territories, 4 other countries, 27% are from out of state, 4% transferred in. *Retention:* 79% of 2001 full-time freshmen returned.

Freshmen *Admission:* 625 applied, 450 admitted, 212 enrolled. *Average high school GPA:* 2.8. *Test scores:* SAT verbal scores over 500: 52%; SAT math scores over 500: 64%; SAT verbal scores over 600: 10%; SAT math scores over 600: 17%; SAT verbal scores over 700: 1%; SAT math scores over 700: 1%.

Faculty *Total:* 70, 84% full-time, 61% with terminal degrees. *Student/faculty ratio:* 12:1.

Majors Engineering; engineering technology; environmental engineering; environmental science; international business; marine science; maritime science; naval architecture/marine engineering.

Academic Programs *Special study options:* academic remediation for entering students, adult/continuing education programs, advanced placement credit, cooperative education, double majors, independent study, internships, services for LD students, summer session for credit. *ROTC:* Army (c).

Library Hurley Library with 42,000 titles, 505 serial subscriptions, a Web page.

Computers on Campus 110 computers available on campus for general student use. A campuswide network can be accessed from student residence rooms. Internet access, at least one staffed computer lab available.

Student Life *Housing:* on-campus residence required through senior year. *Options:* coed. *Activities and Organizations:* drama/theater group, student-run newspaper, choral group, marching band, Club Hockey, water sports, sailing/cruising, Rugby Club, Scuba Club. *Campus security:* 24-hour emergency response devices and patrols, late-night transport/escort service. *Student Services:* health clinic, personal/psychological counseling.

Athletics Member NCAA. All Division III. *Intercollegiate sports:* baseball M, crew M/W, cross-country running M/W, football M, lacrosse M, riflery M/W, sailing M/W, soccer M, softball W, volleyball W. *Intramural sports:* basketball M, crew M, football M, golf M/W, ice hockey M, racquetball M/W, rugby M, soccer M/W, swimming M/W, table tennis M/W, volleyball M/W, water polo M/W, weight lifting M/W, wrestling M.

Standardized Tests *Required:* SAT I (for admission). *Recommended:* SAT II: Subject Tests (for admission).

Costs (2002–03) *Tuition:* $210 per credit part-time.

Applying *Options:* early decision, deferred entrance. *Application fee:* $40 (non-residents). *Required:* essay or personal statement, high school transcript, 2 letters of recommendation, interview, physical examination. *Application deadline:* rolling (freshmen), rolling (transfers). *Early decision:* 11/1. *Notification:* continuous (freshmen), 12/15 (early decision).

Admissions Contact Roy Fulgueras, Director of Admissions, Massachusetts Maritime Academy, 101 Academy Drive, Buzzards Bay, MA 02532-1803. *Phone:* 508-830-5031. *Toll-free phone:* 800-544-3411. *Fax:* 508-830-5077. *E-mail:* admissions@mma.mass.edu.

MERRIMACK COLLEGE

North Andover, Massachusetts

- **Independent Roman Catholic** comprehensive, founded 1947
- **Calendar** semesters
- **Degrees** certificates, associate, bachelor's, and master's
- **Suburban** 220-acre campus with easy access to Boston
- **Endowment** $27.3 million
- **Coed,** 2,568 undergraduate students, 82% full-time, 53% women, 47% men
- **Moderately difficult** entrance level, 63% of applicants were admitted

Undergraduates 2,099 full-time, 469 part-time. Students come from 27 states and territories, 17 other countries, 26% are from out of state, 0.8% African American, 1% Asian American or Pacific Islander, 2% Hispanic American, 0.1% Native American, 1% international, 4% transferred in, 70% live on campus. *Retention:* 82% of 2001 full-time freshmen returned.

Freshmen *Admission:* 3,407 applied, 2,141 admitted, 598 enrolled. *Average high school GPA:* 3.20. *Test scores:* SAT verbal scores over 500: 94%; SAT math scores over 500: 94%; ACT scores over 18: 99%; SAT verbal scores over 600: 24%; SAT math scores over 600: 24%; ACT scores over 24: 28%; SAT verbal scores over 700: 2%; SAT math scores over 700: 4%.

Faculty *Total:* 210, 68% full-time, 74% with terminal degrees. *Student/faculty ratio:* 14:1.

Majors Accounting; athletic training/sports medicine; biochemistry; biology; business administration; business economics; business marketing and marketing management; chemistry; civil engineering; communications; computer engineering; computer science; economics; electrical/electronic engineering technology; electrical engineering; elementary education; engineering physics; engineering science; English; environmental science; finance; fine/studio arts; French; health science; history; human services; interdisciplinary studies; international business; liberal arts and sciences/liberal studies; mathematics; middle school education; modern languages; paralegal/legal assistant; philosophy; physical therapy; physics; political science; pre-dentistry; pre-law; pre-medicine; psychology; religious studies; secondary education; sociology; Spanish.

Academic Programs *Special study options:* academic remediation for entering students, adult/continuing education programs, advanced placement credit, cooperative education, double majors, English as a second language, honors programs, independent study, internships, off-campus study, part-time degree program, services for LD students, student-designed majors, study abroad, summer session for credit. *ROTC:* Air Force (c).

Library McQuade Library with 120,369 titles, 967 serial subscriptions, 1,300 audiovisual materials, an OPAC, a Web page.

Computers on Campus 175 computers available on campus for general student use. A campuswide network can be accessed from student residence rooms and from off campus. Internet access, at least one staffed computer lab available.

Student Life *Housing Options:* coed. *Activities and Organizations:* drama/theater group, student-run newspaper, television station, choral group, Merrimaction Community Outreach, MORE Retreat Program, Merrimack Marketing Association, Orientation Committee Coordinators, Developing Leaders Program, national fraternities, national sororities. *Campus security:* 24-hour emergency response devices and patrols, student patrols, late-night transport/escort service, controlled dormitory access. *Student Services:* health clinic, personal/psychological counseling.

Athletics Member NCAA. All Division II except ice hockey (Division I). *Intercollegiate sports:* baseball M, basketball M(s)/W(s), cross-country running M/W(s), field hockey W(s), football M, ice hockey M(s), lacrosse M/W(s), soccer M/W(s), softball W(s), tennis M/W(s), track and field M(c)/W(c), volleyball M(c)/W(s). *Intramural sports:* basketball M/W, ice hockey M/W, lacrosse M/W, racquetball M/W, skiing (downhill) M(c)/W(c), softball M/W, tennis M/W, volleyball M/W.

Standardized Tests *Required:* SAT I or ACT (for admission).

Costs (2001–02) *One-time required fee:* $135. *Comprehensive fee:* $25,725 includes full-time tuition ($17,445), mandatory fees ($200), and room and board ($8080). Part-time tuition: $645 per credit. Part-time tuition and fees vary according to class time and course load. *Required fees:* $75 per term part-time. *Room and board:* College room only: $4530. Room and board charges vary according to board plan and housing facility. *Payment plans:* installment, deferred payment. *Waivers:* senior citizens and employees or children of employees.

Financial Aid Of all full-time matriculated undergraduates who enrolled in 2001, 1700 applied for aid, 1525 were judged to have need, 1100 had their need fully met. 200 State and other part-time jobs (averaging $1500). In 2001, 175 non-need-based awards were made. *Average percent of need met:* 70%. *Average financial aid package:* $15,000. *Average need-based loan:* $7000. *Average need-based gift aid:* $8500. *Average indebtedness upon graduation:* $17,000. *Financial aid deadline:* 2/15.

Applying *Options:* common application, electronic application, early admission, early action, deferred entrance. *Application fee:* $40. *Required:* essay or personal statement, high school transcript. *Required for some:* interview. *Recommended:* minimum 2.8 GPA, 1 letter of recommendation, interview. *Application deadlines:* 2/15 (freshmen), 6/1 (transfers). *Notification:* continuous until 3/20 (freshmen), 12/15 (early action).

Admissions Contact Ms. MaryLou Retelle, Dean of Admissions and Financial Aid, Merrimack College, Austin Hall, A22, North Andover, MA 01845. *Phone:* 978-837-5100 Ext. 5120. *Fax:* 978-837-5133. *E-mail:* admission@merrimack.edu.

MONTSERRAT COLLEGE OF ART
Beverly, Massachusetts

- **Independent** 4-year, founded 1970
- **Calendar** semesters
- **Degree** diplomas and bachelor's
- **Suburban** 10-acre campus with easy access to Boston
- **Endowment** $449,000
- **Coed,** 392 undergraduate students, 93% full-time, 58% women, 42% men
- **Moderately difficult** entrance level, 84% of applicants were admitted

Undergraduates 365 full-time, 27 part-time. Students come from 21 states and territories, 3 other countries, 50% are from out of state, 0.5% African American, 3% Asian American or Pacific Islander, 2% Hispanic American, 1% Native American, 1% international, 3% transferred in, 63% live on campus. *Retention:* 71% of 2001 full-time freshmen returned.

Freshmen *Admission:* 365 applied, 305 admitted, 92 enrolled. *Average high school GPA:* 2.70. *Test scores:* SAT verbal scores over 500: 60%; SAT math scores over 500: 28%; SAT verbal scores over 600: 16%; SAT math scores over 600: 4%; SAT verbal scores over 700: 3%.

Faculty *Total:* 68, 31% full-time, 53% with terminal degrees. *Student/faculty ratio:* 11:1.

Majors Art; art education; drawing; fine/studio arts; graphic design/commercial art/illustration; photography; printmaking; sculpture.

Academic Programs *Special study options:* adult/continuing education programs, advanced placement credit, double majors, English as a second language, independent study, internships, off-campus study, part-time degree program, services for LD students, student-designed majors, study abroad, summer session for credit. *ROTC:* Air Force (c).

Library Paul Scott Library plus 1 other with 12,000 titles, 70 serial subscriptions, 41,000 audiovisual materials, an OPAC.

Computers on Campus 90 computers available on campus for general student use. Internet access, at least one staffed computer lab available.

Student Life *Housing Options:* coed. *Activities and Organizations:* student-run newspaper, radio station, Student Council, Language Partners, Peer Leaders, Fashion Show Committee, coed intramural sports. *Campus security:* late-night transport/escort service. *Student Services:* personal/psychological counseling.

Standardized Tests *Required for some:* SAT I or ACT (for admission).

Costs (2001–02) *Tuition:* $14,980 full-time, $625 per credit part-time. Full-time tuition and fees vary according to course load. Part-time tuition and fees vary according to course load. *Required fees:* $510 full-time, $56 per course. *Room only:* $4258. Room and board charges vary according to housing facility. *Payment plan:* installment. *Waivers:* employees or children of employees.

Financial Aid Of all full-time matriculated undergraduates who enrolled in 2001, 426 applied for aid, 383 were judged to have need, 8 had their need fully met. 33 Federal Work-Study jobs (averaging $1000). In 2001, 59 non-need-based awards were made. *Average percent of need met:* 39%. *Average financial aid package:* $6527. *Average need-based loan:* $3464. *Average need-based gift aid:* $4566. *Average indebtedness upon graduation:* $6567.

Applying *Options:* deferred entrance. *Application fee:* $40. *Required:* essay or personal statement, high school transcript, minimum 2.0 GPA, 2 letters of recommendation, portfolio. *Recommended:* minimum 3.0 GPA, interview. *Application deadlines:* 8/1 (freshmen), 8/1 (transfers). *Notification:* continuous until 8/20 (freshmen).

Admissions Contact Mr. Stephen M. Negron, Director of Admissions, Montserrat College of Art, 41 Essex Street, Beverly, MA 01945. *Phone:* 978-921-4242 Ext. 1153. *Toll-free phone:* 800-836-0487. *Fax:* 978-921-4241. *E-mail:* admiss@montserrat.edu.

MOUNT HOLYOKE COLLEGE
South Hadley, Massachusetts

- **Independent** comprehensive, founded 1837
- **Calendar** 4-1-4
- **Degrees** bachelor's, master's, and postbachelor's certificates
- **Small-town** 800-acre campus
- **Endowment** $399.7 million
- **Women only,** 2,037 undergraduate students, 97% full-time
- **Very difficult** entrance level, 49% of applicants were admitted

Undergraduates 1,966 full-time, 71 part-time. Students come from 47 states and territories, 77 other countries, 76% are from out of state, 5% African American, 10% Asian American or Pacific Islander, 4% Hispanic American, 0.5% Native American, 17% international, 3% transferred in, 89% live on campus. *Retention:* 97% of 2001 full-time freshmen returned.

Freshmen *Admission:* 488 enrolled. *Average high school GPA:* 3.65. *Test scores:* SAT verbal scores over 500: 98%; SAT math scores over 500: 97%; ACT scores over 18: 99%; SAT verbal scores over 600: 77%; SAT math scores over 600: 65%; ACT scores over 24: 86%; SAT verbal scores over 700: 22%; SAT math scores over 700: 13%; ACT scores over 30: 26%.

Faculty *Total:* 238, 80% full-time, 86% with terminal degrees. *Student/faculty ratio:* 10:1.

Majors African-American studies; American studies; anthropology; art history; Asian studies; astronomy; biochemistry; biology; chemistry; classics; computer science; dance; economics; education; English; environmental science; European studies; film studies; fine/studio arts; French; geography; geology; German; Greek (modern); history; interdisciplinary studies; international relations; Italian; Judaic studies; Latin American studies; Latin (ancient and medieval); mathematical statistics; mathematics; medieval/renaissance studies; music; philosophy; physics; political science; psychology; religious studies; romance languages; Russian; Russian/Slavic studies; social sciences; sociology; Spanish; theater arts/drama; women's studies.

Academic Programs *Special study options:* adult/continuing education programs, advanced placement credit, double majors, honors programs, independent study, internships, off-campus study, part-time degree program, services for LD students, student-designed majors, study abroad. *ROTC:* Army (c), Air Force (c). *Unusual degree programs:* 3-2 engineering with Dartmouth College; nursing with Johns Hopkins University.

Library Williston Memorial Library plus 1 other with 724,634 titles, 3,189 serial subscriptions, 3,443 audiovisual materials, an OPAC, a Web page.

Computers on Campus 245 computers available on campus for general student use. A campuswide network can be accessed from student residence rooms and from off campus that provide access to personal Web pages. Internet access, at least one staffed computer lab available.

Student Life *Housing:* on-campus residence required through senior year. *Options:* women-only. *Activities and Organizations:* drama/theater group, student-run newspaper, radio station, choral group, APAU, MHACASA, ALE, MASSPIRG, WMHC (radio station). *Campus security:* 24-hour emergency response devices and patrols, student patrols, late-night transport/escort service, controlled dormitory access, police officers on-campus. *Student Services:* health clinic, personal/psychological counseling, women's center.

Athletics Member NCAA. All Division III. *Intercollegiate sports:* basketball W, crew W, cross-country running W, equestrian sports W, field hockey W, golf W, ice hockey W(c), lacrosse W, rugby W(c), soccer W, softball W, squash W, swimming W, tennis W, track and field W, volleyball W, water polo W(c). *Intramural sports:* basketball W, equestrian sports W, fencing W, ice hockey W, soccer W, tennis W, volleyball W.

Costs (2001–02) *Comprehensive fee:* $34,128 includes full-time tuition ($26,250), mandatory fees ($158), and room and board ($7720). Part-time tuition: $820 per credit hour. *Required fees:* $158 per year part-time. *Room and board:* College room only: $3780. Room and board charges vary according to board plan and housing facility. *Payment plans:* tuition prepayment, installment. *Waivers:* employees or children of employees.

Financial Aid Of all full-time matriculated undergraduates who enrolled in 2001, 1573 applied for aid, 1393 were judged to have need, 1393 had their need fully met. 775 Federal Work-Study jobs (averaging $1650). 500 State and other part-time jobs. *Average percent of need met:* 100%. *Average financial aid package:* $22,800. *Average need-based loan:* $4850. *Average need-based gift aid:* $17,830. *Average indebtedness upon graduation:* $13,000. *Financial aid deadline:* 2/1.

Applying *Options:* common application, electronic application, early admission, early decision, deferred entrance. *Application fee:* $55. *Required:* essay or personal statement, high school transcript, 2 letters of recommendation. *Recommended:* interview. *Application deadlines:* 1/15 (freshmen), 5/15 (transfers). *Early decision:* 11/15 (for plan 1), 1/1 (for plan 2). *Notification:* 4/1 (freshmen), 1/1 (early decision plan 1), 2/1 (early decision plan 2).

Admissions Contact Ms. Diane Anci, Dean of Admission, Mount Holyoke College, 50 College Street, South Hadley, MA 01075. *Phone:* 413-538-2023. *Fax:* 413-538-2409. *E-mail:* admission@mtholyoke.edu.

MOUNT IDA COLLEGE
Newton Center, Massachusetts

- **Independent** 4-year, founded 1899
- **Calendar** semesters
- **Degrees** certificates, associate, bachelor's, and postbachelor's certificates
- **Suburban** 85-acre campus with easy access to Boston
- **Endowment** $9.4 million
- **Coed,** 1,165 undergraduate students, 85% full-time, 61% women, 39% men
- **Minimally difficult** entrance level, 31% of applicants were admitted

Undergraduates Students come from 29 states and territories, 42 other countries, 18% African American, 5% Asian American or Pacific Islander, 6% Hispanic American, 0.8% Native American, 10% international, 38% live on campus.

Freshmen *Admission:* 1,798 applied, 550 admitted. *Average high school GPA:* 2.55. *Test scores:* SAT verbal scores over 500: 24%; SAT math scores over 500: 16%; SAT verbal scores over 600: 5%; SAT math scores over 600: 2%; SAT verbal scores over 700: 2%; SAT math scores over 700: 1%.

Faculty *Total:* 153, 35% full-time, 18% with terminal degrees. *Student/faculty ratio:* 15:1.

Majors Accounting; animal sciences; biological/physical sciences; business administration; business marketing and marketing management; child care/development; computer management; criminal justice/law enforcement administration; dental hygiene; developmental/child psychology; early childhood education; equestrian studies; fashion design/illustration; fashion merchandising; graphic design/commercial art/illustration; hotel and restaurant management; human services; interior design; legal studies; liberal arts and sciences/liberal studies; mass communications; mortuary science; retail management; social work; teacher assistant/aide; travel/tourism management; veterinary technology.

Academic Programs *Special study options:* academic remediation for entering students, accelerated degree program, adult/continuing education programs, cooperative education, English as a second language, freshman honors college, honors programs, internships, part-time degree program, services for LD students, student-designed majors, study abroad.

Library Wadsworth Learning Resource Center plus 1 other with 100,695 titles, 533 serial subscriptions, a Web page.

Computers on Campus 101 computers available on campus for general student use. Internet access, at least one staffed computer lab available.

Student Life *Housing Options:* coed, men-only, women-only. *Activities and Organizations:* drama/theater group, student-run newspaper, radio station, choral group, Leadership Students, student government, Phi Theta Kappa, Residence Council, Alpha Chi. *Campus security:* 24-hour emergency response devices and patrols, student patrols, late-night transport/escort service, controlled residence hall entrances, secured campus entrance. *Student Services:* health clinic, personal/psychological counseling.

Athletics Member NCAA. except men's and women's basketball (Division III), men's and women's cross-country running (Division III), football (Division III), lacrosse (Division III), soccer (Division III), softball (Division III), men's and women's volleyball (Division III) *Intercollegiate sports:* baseball M, basketball M/W, cross-country running M/W, equestrian sports M/W, football M, lacrosse M, soccer M/W, softball W, volleyball M/W. *Intramural sports:* basketball M/W, football W, golf M/W, lacrosse W, skiing (downhill) M/W, soccer M/W, softball M/W, tennis M/W, volleyball M/W, weight lifting M/W.

Standardized Tests *Required:* SAT I or ACT (for admission), SAT I or ACT (for placement).

Costs (2001–02) *Comprehensive fee:* $24,780 includes full-time tuition ($15,300), mandatory fees ($530), and room and board ($8950). Part-time tuition: $1050 per course. *Required fees:* $100 per year part-time.

Financial Aid Of all full-time matriculated undergraduates who enrolled in 2001, 861 applied for aid, 804 were judged to have need, 56 had their need fully met. 12 State and other part-time jobs (averaging $1476). In 2001, 96 non-need-based awards were made. *Average percent of need met:* 55%. *Average financial aid package:* $11,457. *Average need-based loan:* $3328. *Average need-based gift aid:* $8117.

Applying *Options:* common application, electronic application, early action, deferred entrance. *Application fee:* $35. *Required:* high school transcript, 2 letters of recommendation. *Recommended:* essay or personal statement, minimum 2.0 GPA, interview. *Application deadline:* rolling (freshmen), rolling (transfers). *Notification:* continuous (freshmen).

Admissions Contact Ms. Nancy Lemelman, Director of Admissions, Mount Ida College, 777 Dedham Street, Newton, MA 02459. *Phone:* 617-928-4500 Ext. 4508. *E-mail:* admissions@mountida.edu.

NEWBURY COLLEGE
Brookline, Massachusetts

- **Independent** primarily 2-year, founded 1962
- **Calendar** semesters
- **Degrees** certificates, associate, and bachelor's
- **Suburban** 10-acre campus with easy access to Boston
- **Endowment** $4.5 million
- **Coed,** 1,689 undergraduate students, 39% full-time, 64% women, 36% men
- **Minimally difficult** entrance level, 88% of applicants were admitted

Just minutes from Boston, Newbury College features an ideal collegiate setting in a safe, elite neighborhood with easy access to public transportation. Skilled and experienced faculty members, small classes, personalized attention, and hands-on training opportunities make Newbury graduates among the most employable. Students may pursue bachelor's and associate degrees.

Undergraduates 654 full-time, 1,035 part-time. Students come from 22 states and territories, 41 other countries, 34% are from out of state, 11% African American, 4% Asian American or Pacific Islander, 5% Hispanic American, 6% international, 35% live on campus. *Retention:* 80% of 2001 full-time freshmen returned.

Freshmen *Admission:* 964 applied, 850 admitted, 340 enrolled. *Average high school GPA:* 2.70. *Test scores:* SAT verbal scores over 500: 28%; SAT math scores over 500: 28%; ACT scores over 18: 75%; SAT verbal scores over 600: 9%; SAT math scores over 600: 6%; ACT scores over 24: 25%; SAT verbal scores over 700: 1%; SAT math scores over 700: 1%.

Faculty *Total:* 89, 39% full-time. *Student/faculty ratio:* 16:1.

Majors Accounting; business administration; business marketing and marketing management; computer programming; computer science; criminal justice/law enforcement administration; culinary arts; culinary arts and services related; fashion merchandising; finance; food products retailing; graphic design/commercial art/illustration; health services administration; hotel and restaurant management; humanities; human resources management; interior design; international business; legal studies; marketing research; mass communications; paralegal/legal assistant; pre-law; psychology; radio/television broadcasting; retail management; social sciences; sociology; travel/tourism management.

Academic Programs *Special study options:* academic remediation for entering students, accelerated degree program, adult/continuing education programs, advanced placement credit, cooperative education, double majors, English as a second language, freshman honors college, honors programs, independent study, internships, off-campus study, part-time degree program, services for LD students, study abroad, summer session for credit.

Library Newbury College Library plus 1 other with 32,459 titles, 1,109 serial subscriptions, an OPAC.

Computers on Campus 75 computers available on campus for general student use. A campuswide network can be accessed from off campus. At least one staffed computer lab available.

Student Life *Housing Options:* coed, women-only. *Activities and Organizations:* student-run newspaper, radio station, student government, Newbury College Programming Board, Inn Keepers Club, Speech and Debate Team, International Student Organization. *Campus security:* 24-hour emergency response devices and patrols, late-night transport/escort service, controlled dormitory access. *Student Services:* personal/psychological counseling.

Athletics Member NCAA. All Division III. *Intercollegiate sports:* basketball M/W, cross-country running M/W, golf M/W, soccer M, softball W, tennis M/W, volleyball M/W. *Intramural sports:* basketball M/W, football M/W, softball W, swimming M/W, volleyball M/W, weight lifting M/W.

Standardized Tests *Required for some:* SAT I or ACT (for admission). *Recommended:* SAT I or ACT (for admission).

Costs (2001–02) *One-time required fee:* $300. *Comprehensive fee:* $21,700 includes full-time tuition ($13,650), mandatory fees ($650), and room and board ($7400). Full-time tuition and fees vary according to class time, course load, and program. Part-time tuition: $195 per credit. Part-time tuition and fees vary according to class time, course load, and program. *Required fees:* $195 per credit. *Room and board:* Room and board charges vary according to board plan. *Payment plan:* installment. *Waivers:* employees or children of employees.

Applying *Options:* electronic application, early admission, early action, deferred entrance. *Application fee:* $50. *Required:* essay or personal statement, high school transcript, letters of recommendation. *Recommended:* minimum 2.0 GPA, interview. *Application deadline:* 3/1 (freshmen), rolling (transfers). *Notification:* 4/1 (freshmen), 1/1 (early action).

Admissions Contact Ms. Jacqueline Giordano, Dean of Admission, Newbury College, 129 Fisher Avenue, Brookline, MA 02445-5796. *Phone:* 617-730-7007. *Toll-free phone:* 800-NEWBURY. *Fax:* 617-731-9618. *E-mail:* info@newbury.edu.

NEW ENGLAND COLLEGE OF FINANCE
Boston, Massachusetts

Admissions Contact Ms. Judith Marley, Vice President and Director of Academic Affairs, New England College of Finance, 1 Lincoln Plaza, Boston, MA 02111-2645. *Phone:* 617-951-2350 Ext. 227. *Toll-free phone:* 888-696-NECF. *Fax:* 617-951-2533.

NEW ENGLAND CONSERVATORY OF MUSIC
Boston, Massachusetts

- **Independent** comprehensive, founded 1867
- **Calendar** semesters
- **Degrees** certificates, diplomas, bachelor's, master's, doctoral, and postbachelor's certificates
- **Urban** campus
- **Endowment** $47.8 million
- **Coed,** 381 undergraduate students, 93% full-time, 47% women, 53% men
- **Very difficult** entrance level, 56% of applicants were admitted

Undergraduates 356 full-time, 25 part-time. Students come from 44 states and territories, 36 other countries, 75% are from out of state, 4% African American, 9% Asian American or Pacific Islander, 3% Hispanic American, 0.6% Native American, 19% international, 5% transferred in, 40% live on campus.

Freshmen *Admission:* 731 applied, 408 admitted, 97 enrolled. *Average high school GPA:* 3.05.

Faculty *Total:* 206, 37% full-time. *Student/faculty ratio:* 7:1.

Majors Jazz; music history; music (piano and organ performance); music theory and composition; music (voice and choral/opera performance); stringed instruments; wind/percussion instruments.

Academic Programs *Special study options:* adult/continuing education programs, advanced placement credit, double majors, English as a second language, independent study, internships, off-campus study, part-time degree program, services for LD students, summer session for credit.

Library Spaulding Library plus 1 other with 75,674 titles, 255 serial subscriptions, 1,238 audiovisual materials, an OPAC, a Web page.

Computers on Campus 48 computers available on campus for general student use. Internet access, at least one staffed computer lab available.

Student Life *Housing:* on-campus residence required for freshman year. *Options:* coed. *Activities and Organizations:* NEC Student Association, Chinese Student Association, Christian Fellowship, Vegetarian Club, Soccer Club. *Campus security:* 24-hour patrols, late-night transport/escort service. *Student Services:* health clinic, personal/psychological counseling.

Standardized Tests *Required:* SAT I or ACT (for admission).

Costs (2001–02) *Comprehensive fee:* $31,200 includes full-time tuition ($21,550), mandatory fees ($250), and room and board ($9400). Full-time tuition and fees vary according to program. Part-time tuition: $700 per credit hour. Part-time tuition and fees vary according to program. *Required fees:* $250 per year part-time. *Room and board:* Room and board charges vary according to housing facility. *Payment plan:* installment. *Waivers:* employees or children of employees.

Financial Aid Of all full-time matriculated undergraduates who enrolled in 2001, 222 applied for aid, 184 were judged to have need, 40 had their need fully met. 140 Federal Work-Study jobs (averaging $1936). In 2001, 61 non-need-based awards were made. *Average percent of need met:* 71%. *Average financial aid package:* $16,467. *Average need-based loan:* $4497. *Average need-based gift aid:* $11,582. *Average non-need based aid:* $9753.

Applying *Options:* deferred entrance. *Application fee:* $100. *Required:* essay or personal statement, high school transcript, minimum 2.75 GPA, 2 letters of recommendation, audition. *Application deadlines:* 12/3 (freshmen), 12/3 (transfers). *Notification:* 4/1 (freshmen).

Admissions Contact Dean of Enrollment Services, New England Conservatory of Music, 290 Huntington Avenue, Boston, MA 02115-5000. *Phone:* 617-585-1101. *Fax:* 617-585-1115. *E-mail:* admissions@newenglandconservatory.edu.

NICHOLS COLLEGE
Dudley, Massachusetts

- **Independent** comprehensive, founded 1815
- **Calendar** semesters
- **Degrees** associate, bachelor's, and master's
- **Rural** 210-acre campus with easy access to Boston
- **Coed**
- **Moderately difficult** entrance level

Faculty *Student/faculty ratio:* 18:1.

Student Life *Campus security:* 24-hour patrols, late-night transport/escort service.

Athletics Member NCAA. All Division III.

Standardized Tests *Required:* SAT I or ACT (for admission).

Financial Aid Of all full-time matriculated undergraduates who enrolled in 2001, 780 applied for aid, 588 were judged to have need, 186 had their need fully met. 436 Federal Work-Study jobs (averaging $1414). In 2001, 184. *Average percent of need met:* 74. *Average financial aid package:* $12,583. *Average need-based loan:* $5266. *Average need-based gift aid:* $7213. *Average indebtedness upon graduation:* $14,867.

Applying *Options:* electronic application, early admission, deferred entrance. *Application fee:* $25. *Required:* essay or personal statement, high school transcript, 1 letter of recommendation. *Required for some:* interview.

Admissions Contact Susan Montville, Admissions Assistant, Nichols College, P.O. Box 5000, Office of Admissions, Dudley, MA 01571. *Phone:* 508-943-2055. *Toll-free phone:* 800-470-3379. *Fax:* 508-943-9885. *E-mail:* admissions@nichols.edu.

NORTHEASTERN UNIVERSITY
Boston, Massachusetts

- **Independent** university, founded 1898
- **Calendar** quarters
- **Degrees** certificates, associate, bachelor's, master's, doctoral, first professional, post-master's, and postbachelor's certificates
- **Urban** 60-acre campus
- **Endowment** $511.3 million
- **Coed,** 13,963 undergraduate students, 100% full-time, 49% women, 51% men
- **Moderately difficult** entrance level, 63% of applicants were admitted

Northeastern University is a world leader in practice-oriented education with one of the oldest cooperative education program in the U.S. Students alternate between an academic curriculum and co-op employment. With an appealing campus, a full range of student activities, and a location in the center of Boston, Northeastern offers virtually everything students need in a place where they live, learn, and complete their undergraduate degrees.

Undergraduates Students come from 50 states and territories, 113 other countries, 60% are from out of state, 5% African American, 7% Asian American or Pacific Islander, 4% Hispanic American, 0.3% Native American, 7% international. *Retention:* 84% of 2001 full-time freshmen returned.

Freshmen *Admission:* 16,173 applied, 10,155 admitted. *Average high school GPA:* 3.15. *Test scores:* SAT verbal scores over 500: 85%; SAT math scores over 500: 92%; ACT scores over 18: 97%; SAT verbal scores over 600: 36%; SAT math scores over 600: 47%; ACT scores over 24: 62%; SAT verbal scores over 700: 5%; SAT math scores over 700: 8%; ACT scores over 30: 7%.

Faculty *Total:* 1,105, 70% full-time. *Student/faculty ratio:* 16:1.

Majors Accounting; advertising; aerospace engineering technology; African-American studies; anthropology; architecture; art; athletic training/sports medicine; behavioral sciences; biochemistry; biological technology; biology; business; business administration; business marketing and marketing management; chemical engineering; chemistry; civil engineering; communications; computer engineering; computer engineering technology; computer science; corrections; criminal justice studies; dental hygiene; early childhood education; economics; education; electrical/electronic engineering technology; electrical engineering; elementary education; energy management technology; engineering; engineering technology; English; enterprise management; environmental science; environmental technology; finance; French; geology; German; graphic design/commercial art/illustration; health science; health services administration; history; hotel and restaurant management; human resources management; human services; industrial/manufacturing engineering; industrial technology; information sciences/systems; international business; international relations; Italian; journalism; law enforcement/police science; legal studies; liberal arts and sciences/liberal studies; linguistics; logistics/materials management; management information systems/business data processing; management science; marine biology; mass communications; mathematics; mechanical engineering; mechanical engineering technology; medical laboratory technician; medical toxicology; modern languages; music; music business management/merchandising; music history; nursing related; pharmacy; philosophy; physical education; physical therapy; physician assistant; physics; political science; pre-law; psychology; public administration; public relations; purchasing/contracts management; radio/television broadcasting; recreational therapy; rehabilitation therapy; Russian; sign language interpretation; sociology; Spanish; speech-language pathology/audiology; surveying; technical/business writing; telecommunications; theater arts/drama.

Northeastern University (continued)

Academic Programs *Special study options:* academic remediation for entering students, accelerated degree program, adult/continuing education programs, advanced placement credit, cooperative education, distance learning, double majors, English as a second language, honors programs, independent study, internships, off-campus study, part-time degree program, services for LD students, student-designed majors, study abroad, summer session for credit. *ROTC:* Army (b), Navy (c), Air Force (c).

Library Snell Library plus 6 others with 681,972 titles, 8,590 serial subscriptions, 15,928 audiovisual materials, an OPAC, a Web page.

Computers on Campus A campuswide network can be accessed from student residence rooms and from off campus. Internet access, at least one staffed computer lab available.

Student Life *Housing Options:* coed, women-only. *Activities and Organizations:* drama/theater group, student-run newspaper, radio station, choral group, Student Government Association, NU Hus-kiers and Outing Club, International Student Association, Council for University Programs, Resident Student Association, national fraternities, national sororities. *Campus security:* 24-hour emergency response devices and patrols, late-night transport/escort service. *Student Services:* health clinic, personal/psychological counseling, women's center.

Athletics Member NCAA. All Division I except football (Division I-AA). *Intercollegiate sports:* baseball M(s), basketball M(s)/W(s), crew M(s)/W(s), cross-country running M(s)/W(s), field hockey W(s), ice hockey M(s)/W(s), soccer M(s)/W(s), swimming W(s), track and field M(s)/W(s), volleyball W(s). *Intramural sports:* basketball M/W, football M/W, ice hockey M/W, lacrosse M(c), racquetball M/W, rugby M(c)/W(c), soccer M/W, softball M/W, tennis M/W, volleyball M/W.

Standardized Tests *Required:* SAT I or ACT (for admission).

Costs (2001–02) *Comprehensive fee:* $30,078 includes full-time tuition ($20,535), mandatory fees ($198), and room and board ($9345). Full-time tuition and fees vary according to student level. *Room and board:* College room only: $5010. Room and board charges vary according to board plan and housing facility. *Payment plans:* installment, deferred payment. *Waivers:* senior citizens and employees or children of employees.

Financial Aid Of all full-time matriculated undergraduates who enrolled in 2001, 9672 applied for aid, 8628 were judged to have need, 921 had their need fully met. 4143 Federal Work-Study jobs (averaging $2010). In 2001, 1302 non-need-based awards were made. *Average percent of need met:* 71%. *Average financial aid package:* $13,627. *Average need-based loan:* $4653. *Average need-based gift aid:* $9110.

Applying *Options:* electronic application, early admission, deferred entrance. *Application fee:* $50. *Required:* essay or personal statement, high school transcript. *Required for some:* interview. *Recommended:* minimum 2.0 GPA, 2 letters of recommendation. *Application deadline:* rolling (freshmen), rolling (transfers). *Notification:* continuous (freshmen).

Admissions Contact Ronne A. Patrick, Director of Admissions, Northeastern University, 150 Richards Hall, Boston, MA 02115. *Phone:* 617-373-2200. *Fax:* 617-373-8780. *E-mail:* admissions@neu.edu.

PINE MANOR COLLEGE
Chestnut Hill, Massachusetts

- **Independent** 4-year, founded 1911
- **Calendar** semesters
- **Degrees** certificates, associate, and bachelor's
- **Suburban** 65-acre campus with easy access to Boston
- **Endowment** $16.3 million
- **Women only,** 406 undergraduate students, 96% full-time
- **Moderately difficult** entrance level, 73% of applicants were admitted

Undergraduates 390 full-time, 16 part-time. Students come from 25 states and territories, 27 other countries, 32% are from out of state, 21% African American, 3% Asian American or Pacific Islander, 14% Hispanic American, 0.7% Native American, 11% international, 7% transferred in, 75% live on campus. *Retention:* 60% of 2001 full-time freshmen returned.

Freshmen *Admission:* 168 enrolled. *Average high school GPA:* 2.31. *Test scores:* SAT verbal scores over 500: 31%; SAT math scores over 500: 23%; ACT scores over 18: 53%; SAT verbal scores over 600: 8%; SAT math scores over 600: 4%; ACT scores over 24: 16%.

Faculty *Total:* 56, 52% full-time. *Student/faculty ratio:* 13:1.

Majors American studies; art history; biology; business administration; communications; creative writing; early childhood education; elementary education; English; fine/studio arts; history; liberal arts and sciences/liberal studies; mass communications; political science; psychology; secondary education.

Academic Programs *Special study options:* academic remediation for entering students, adult/continuing education programs, advanced placement credit, double majors, English as a second language, external degree program, honors programs, independent study, internships, off-campus study, part-time degree program, services for LD students, student-designed majors, study abroad, summer session for credit.

Library Annenberg Library with 64,647 titles, 1,645 serial subscriptions, 4,085 audiovisual materials, an OPAC, a Web page.

Computers on Campus 135 computers available on campus for general student use. A campuswide network can be accessed from student residence rooms and from off campus. Internet access, at least one staffed computer lab available.

Student Life *Housing Options:* women-only. *Activities and Organizations:* drama/theater group, student-run newspaper, radio station, choral group, Student Government Association, ALANA, business club, Pine Manor Post, Campus Activities Board. *Campus security:* 24-hour emergency response devices and patrols, student patrols, late-night transport/escort service, controlled dormitory access. *Student Services:* health clinic, personal/psychological counseling, women's center.

Athletics Member NCAA. All Division III. *Intercollegiate sports:* basketball W, cross-country running W, soccer W, softball W, tennis W, volleyball W. *Intramural sports:* basketball W, cross-country running W, golf W(c), skiing (cross-country) W, skiing (downhill) W, soccer W, softball W, tennis W, track and field W(c), volleyball W, weight lifting W.

Standardized Tests *Required:* SAT I or ACT (for admission).

Costs (2001–02) *Comprehensive fee:* $20,118 includes full-time tuition ($12,370) and room and board ($7748). Part-time tuition: $386 per credit. *Room and board:* Room and board charges vary according to housing facility. *Payment plans:* tuition prepayment, installment. *Waivers:* children of alumni, adult students, senior citizens, and employees or children of employees.

Financial Aid Of all full-time matriculated undergraduates who enrolled in 2001, 303 applied for aid, 277 were judged to have need, 51 had their need fully met. In 2001, 45 non-need-based awards were made. *Average percent of need met:* 86%. *Average financial aid package:* $14,228. *Average need-based loan:* $3271. *Average need-based gift aid:* $10,725. *Average indebtedness upon graduation:* $14,543.

Applying *Options:* common application, electronic application, early admission, deferred entrance. *Application fee:* $25. *Required:* essay or personal statement, high school transcript, 1 letter of recommendation. *Recommended:* minimum 2.0 GPA, interview. *Application deadline:* rolling (freshmen), rolling (transfers). *Notification:* continuous (freshmen).

Admissions Contact Mr. Bill Nichols, Dean of Admissions, Pine Manor College, 400 Heath Street, Chestnut Hill, MA 02167-2332. *Phone:* 617-731-7104. *Toll-free phone:* 800-762-1357. *Fax:* 617-731-7199. *E-mail:* admission@pmc.edu.

REGIS COLLEGE
Weston, Massachusetts

- **Independent Roman Catholic** comprehensive, founded 1927
- **Calendar** semesters
- **Degrees** associate, bachelor's, master's, and post-master's certificates
- **Small-town** 168-acre campus with easy access to Boston
- **Endowment** $25.2 million
- **Women only,** 851 undergraduate students, 76% full-time
- **Moderately difficult** entrance level, 82% of applicants were admitted

Undergraduates 643 full-time, 208 part-time. Students come from 25 states and territories, 19 other countries, 17% are from out of state, 6% African American, 5% Asian American or Pacific Islander, 7% Hispanic American, 3% international, 6% transferred in, 54% live on campus. *Retention:* 73% of 2001 full-time freshmen returned.

Freshmen *Admission:* 183 enrolled. *Average high school GPA:* 3.20. *Test scores:* SAT verbal scores over 500: 51%; SAT math scores over 500: 42%; SAT verbal scores over 600: 16%; SAT math scores over 600: 7%; SAT verbal scores over 700: 3%; SAT math scores over 700: 1%.

Faculty *Total:* 117, 55% full-time, 64% with terminal degrees. *Student/faculty ratio:* 10:1.

Majors Art; biochemistry; biology; business; chemistry; communications; computer/information sciences; economics; English; French; history; interdisciplinary studies; mathematics; museum studies; nursing; political science; psychology; social work; sociology; Spanish; theater arts/drama.

Academic Programs *Special study options:* academic remediation for entering students, adult/continuing education programs, advanced placement credit, double majors, English as a second language, honors programs, independent study, internships, off-campus study, part-time degree program, services for LD students, student-designed majors, study abroad, summer session for credit. *ROTC:* Army (c). *Unusual degree programs:* 3-2 engineering with Worcester Polytechnic Institute.

Library Regis College Library with 133,565 titles, 968 serial subscriptions, 5,684 audiovisual materials, an OPAC, a Web page.

Computers on Campus 133 computers available on campus for general student use. A campuswide network can be accessed from student residence rooms. Internet access, at least one staffed computer lab available.

Student Life *Housing Options:* women-only. *Activities and Organizations:* drama/theater group, student-run radio station, choral group, Board of Programmers, student government, glee club, orientation committee, AHANA Club. *Campus security:* 24-hour emergency response devices and patrols, late-night transport/escort service, controlled dormitory access. *Student Services:* health clinic, personal/psychological counseling.

Athletics Member NCAA. All Division III. *Intercollegiate sports:* basketball W, crew W, cross-country running W, field hockey W, soccer W, softball W, swimming W, tennis W, track and field W, volleyball W. *Intramural sports:* badminton W, basketball W, field hockey W, soccer W, softball W, tennis W, volleyball W.

Standardized Tests *Required:* SAT I or ACT (for admission). *Recommended:* SAT II: Subject Tests (for admission).

Costs (2001–02) *Comprehensive fee:* $26,750 includes full-time tuition ($18,400) and room and board ($8350). Part-time tuition: $1960 per course. Part-time tuition and fees vary according to class time and course load. *Payment plans:* tuition prepayment, installment, deferred payment. *Waivers:* employees or children of employees.

Financial Aid Of all full-time matriculated undergraduates who enrolled in 2001, 611 applied for aid, 552 were judged to have need, 93 had their need fully met. 274 Federal Work-Study jobs (averaging $1500). 83 State and other part-time jobs (averaging $1500). In 2001, 36 non-need-based awards were made. *Average percent of need met:* 87%. *Average financial aid package:* $17,046. *Average need-based loan:* $4844. *Average need-based gift aid:* $4760. *Average non-need based aid:* $6527. *Average indebtedness upon graduation:* $22,741.

Applying *Options:* common application, electronic application, deferred entrance. *Application fee:* $30. *Required:* essay or personal statement, high school transcript, minimum 2.5 GPA, 2 letters of recommendation. *Required for some:* interview. *Recommended:* minimum 3.0 GPA, interview, rank in upper 50% of high school class. *Application deadline:* rolling (freshmen), rolling (transfers).

Admissions Contact Dr. Leona McCaughey-Oreszak, Director of Admission, Regis College, 235 Wellesley Street, Weston, MA 02493. *Phone:* 781-768-7100. *Toll-free phone:* 800-456-1820. *Fax:* 781-768-7071. *E-mail:* admission@regiscollege.edu.

SAINT JOHN'S SEMINARY COLLEGE OF LIBERAL ARTS
Brighton, Massachusetts

- **Independent Roman Catholic** 4-year, founded 1884
- **Calendar** semesters
- **Degree** bachelor's
- **Urban** 70-acre campus with easy access to Boston
- **Endowment** $9.2 million
- **Men only,** 26 undergraduate students, 100% full-time
- **Minimally difficult** entrance level

Undergraduates 26 full-time. Students come from 6 states and territories, 48% are from out of state, 8% Asian American or Pacific Islander, 8% Hispanic American, 8% transferred in, 100% live on campus.

Freshmen *Admission:* 10 enrolled.

Faculty *Total:* 13, 69% full-time, 62% with terminal degrees. *Student/faculty ratio:* 4:1.

Majors Philosophy.

Academic Programs *Special study options:* academic remediation for entering students, double majors, English as a second language, independent study, off-campus study, services for LD students, student-designed majors.

Library Saint John's Library with 150,000 titles, 345 serial subscriptions, an OPAC.

Computers on Campus 9 computers available on campus for general student use. A campuswide network can be accessed from off campus. Internet access, at least one staffed computer lab available.

Student Life *Housing:* on-campus residence required through senior year. *Options:* men-only. *Activities and Organizations:* drama/theater group, choral group, national fraternities. *Campus security:* 24-hour patrols. *Student Services:* personal/psychological counseling.

Athletics *Intramural sports:* basketball M, football M, racquetball M, softball M, table tennis M, tennis M, volleyball M.

Standardized Tests *Required:* SAT I (for admission).

Costs (2002–03) *Comprehensive fee:* $15,000 includes full-time tuition ($11,000) and room and board ($4000). *Payment plan:* installment.

Applying *Required:* essay or personal statement, high school transcript, 4 letters of recommendation, interview. *Required for some:* bishop's sponsorship. *Application deadlines:* 8/1 (freshmen), 8/1 (transfers). *Notification:* continuous (freshmen).

Admissions Contact Rev. Robert W. Flagg, Dean of the College, Saint John's Seminary College of Liberal Arts, 127 Lake Street, Brighton, MA 02135. *Phone:* 617-746-5460. *Fax:* 617-746-5499.

SALEM STATE COLLEGE
Salem, Massachusetts

- **State-supported** comprehensive, founded 1854, part of Massachusetts Public Higher Education System
- **Calendar** semesters
- **Degrees** bachelor's, master's, and post-master's certificates
- **Small-town** 62-acre campus with easy access to Boston
- **Endowment** $5.2 million
- **Coed,** 6,317 undergraduate students, 68% full-time, 63% women, 37% men
- **Minimally difficult** entrance level, 69% of applicants were admitted

Undergraduates 4,311 full-time, 2,006 part-time. Students come from 18 states and territories, 16% are from out of state, 4% African American, 1% Asian American or Pacific Islander, 3% Hispanic American, 1.0% Native American, 4% international, 11% transferred in, 22% live on campus. *Retention:* 70% of 2001 full-time freshmen returned.

Freshmen *Admission:* 3,932 applied, 2,699 admitted, 853 enrolled. *Average high school GPA:* 2.88. *Test scores:* SAT verbal scores over 500: 36%; SAT math scores over 500: 30%; SAT verbal scores over 600: 6%; SAT math scores over 600: 5%; SAT verbal scores over 700: 1%; SAT math scores over 700: 1%.

Faculty *Total:* 533, 57% full-time, 45% with terminal degrees. *Student/faculty ratio:* 16:1.

Majors Accounting; applied mathematics; art; art education; aviation management; biology; business administration; business economics; business education; business marketing and marketing management; cartography; chemistry; city/community/regional planning; comparative literature; computer science; criminal justice/law enforcement administration; drawing; early childhood education; earth sciences; Eastern European area studies; economics; education; elementary education; English; European studies; exercise sciences; finance; geography; geology; graphic design/commercial art/illustration; health education; history; journalism; liberal arts and sciences/liberal studies; literature; management information systems/business data processing; marine biology; marine science; mass communications; mathematics; medical technology; nuclear medical technology; nursing; photography; physical education; political science; pre-dentistry; pre-law; pre-medicine; pre-veterinary studies; psychology; public relations; recreation/leisure studies; retail management; secretarial science; social sciences; social work; sociology; sport/fitness administration; theater arts/drama; travel/tourism management.

Academic Programs *Special study options:* academic remediation for entering students, adult/continuing education programs, advanced placement credit, double majors, English as a second language, honors programs, independent study, internships, off-campus study, part-time degree program, services for LD students, student-designed majors, study abroad, summer session for credit.

Library Salem State College Library with 236,337 titles, 1,360 serial subscriptions.

Computers on Campus 150 computers available on campus for general student use.

Student Life *Housing Options:* coed. *Activities and Organizations:* drama/theater group, student-run newspaper, radio and television station, choral group, Student Government Association, Program Council, Hispanic American Student Association, GLBT Alliance, WMWM Radio. *Campus security:* 24-hour emergency response devices and patrols, late-night transport/escort service. *Student Services:* health clinic, personal/psychological counseling, women's center, legal services.

Athletics Member NCAA. All Division III except ice hockey (Division II). *Intercollegiate sports:* baseball M, basketball M/W, cross-country running M/W,

Salem State College (continued)

field hockey W, golf M, ice hockey M, sailing M/W, soccer M/W, softball W, swimming M/W, tennis M/W, track and field M/W, volleyball W. *Intramural sports:* archery M/W, badminton M/W, basketball M/W, cross-country running M/W, fencing M/W, field hockey W, football M, golf M/W, gymnastics M/W, ice hockey M/W, lacrosse M/W, racquetball M/W, sailing M/W, skiing (cross-country) M/W, skiing (downhill) M/W, soccer M/W, squash M/W, swimming M/W, tennis M/W, volleyball M/W, water polo M/W, weight lifting M/W, wrestling M.

Standardized Tests *Required:* SAT I or ACT (for admission).

Costs (2002–03) *Tuition:* state resident $910 full-time, $38 per credit part-time; nonresident $7050 full-time, $294 per credit part-time. Full-time tuition and fees vary according to class time. Part-time tuition and fees vary according to class time. *Required fees:* $2828 full-time, $120 per credit. *Room and board:* $5428; room only: $3198. Room and board charges vary according to board plan and housing facility. *Payment plans:* installment, deferred payment. *Waivers:* minority students, senior citizens, and employees or children of employees.

Financial Aid Of all full-time matriculated undergraduates who enrolled in 2001, 2992 applied for aid, 2453 were judged to have need, 840 had their need fully met. 495 Federal Work-Study jobs (averaging $1130). 581 State and other part-time jobs (averaging $1135). In 2001, 447 non-need-based awards were made. *Average percent of need met:* 84%. *Average financial aid package:* $7748. *Average need-based loan:* $2159. *Average need-based gift aid:* $4448.

Applying *Options:* early admission. *Application fee:* $10. *Required:* high school transcript, minimum 2.9 GPA, letters of recommendation. *Required for some:* interview. *Recommended:* essay or personal statement. *Application deadline:* rolling (freshmen), rolling (transfers). *Notification:* continuous (freshmen).

Admissions Contact Mr. Nate Bryant, Director of Admissions, Salem State College, 352 Lafayette Street, Salem, MA 01970-5353. *Phone:* 978-542-6200.

School of the Museum of Fine Arts
Boston, Massachusetts

- **Independent** comprehensive, founded 1876
- **Calendar** semesters
- **Degrees** certificates, diplomas, bachelor's, master's, and postbachelor's certificates
- **Urban** 14-acre campus
- **Endowment** $9.6 million
- **Coed,** 1,085 undergraduate students
- **Moderately difficult** entrance level

Undergraduates Students come from 33 states and territories, 30 other countries, 40% are from out of state, 1% African American, 6% Asian American or Pacific Islander, 3% Hispanic American, 0.4% Native American, 9% international, 47% live on campus.

Faculty *Total:* 104, 55% full-time.

Majors Applied art; art; art education; ceramic arts; computer graphics; drawing; film studies; film/video production; fine/studio arts; graphic design/commercial art/illustration; metal/jewelry arts; photography; printmaking; sculpture.

Academic Programs *Special study options:* adult/continuing education programs, double majors, independent study, internships, off-campus study, part-time degree program, student-designed majors, study abroad, summer session for credit. *ROTC:* Army (c), Navy (c), Air Force (c). *Unusual degree programs:* 3-2 fine arts, art education with Tufts University.

Library William Morris Hunt Memorial Library plus 1 other with 657 serial subscriptions, 220 audiovisual materials, an OPAC, a Web page.

Computers on Campus 46 computers available on campus for general student use. A campuswide network can be accessed from off campus. Internet access, at least one staffed computer lab available.

Student Life *Activities and Organizations:* Gay/Lesbian/Bisexual Alliance. *Campus security:* 24-hour emergency response devices and patrols, late-night transport/escort service. *Student Services:* personal/psychological counseling.

Standardized Tests *Required for some:* SAT I or ACT (for admission).

Costs (2001–02) *Comprehensive fee:* $28,916 includes full-time tuition ($18,996), mandatory fees ($680), and room and board ($9240). Full-time tuition and fees vary according to program. Part-time tuition: $1185 per course. Part-time tuition and fees vary according to program. *Payment plan:* installment. *Waivers:* employees or children of employees.

Financial Aid Of all full-time matriculated undergraduates who enrolled in 2001, 362 applied for aid, 310 were judged to have need. 40 Federal Work-Study jobs (averaging $2003). *Average percent of need met:* 61%. *Average financial aid package:* $14,090. *Average need-based gift aid:* $7537. *Average indebtedness upon graduation:* $17,125.

Applying *Options:* deferred entrance. *Application fee:* $35. *Required:* essay or personal statement, high school transcript, portfolio. *Required for some:* interview. *Application deadline:* 3/1 (freshmen), rolling (transfers). *Notification:* continuous (freshmen).

Admissions Contact Mr. John A. Williamson, Director of Enrollment and Student Services, School of the Museum of Fine Arts, 230 The Fenway, Boston, MA 02115. *Phone:* 617-369-3626. *Toll-free phone:* 800-643-6078. *Fax:* 617-369-3679. *E-mail:* admissions@smfa.edu.

Simmons College
Boston, Massachusetts

- **Independent** comprehensive, founded 1899
- **Calendar** semesters
- **Degrees** bachelor's, master's, doctoral, post-master's, and postbachelor's certificates
- **Urban** 12-acre campus
- **Endowment** $149.0 million
- **Women only,** 1,275 undergraduate students, 88% full-time, 100% women
- **Moderately difficult** entrance level, 68% of applicants were admitted

Undergraduates 1,127 full-time, 148 part-time. Students come from 38 states and territories, 26 other countries, 40% are from out of state, 7% African American, 5% Asian American or Pacific Islander, 4% Hispanic American, 0.2% Native American, 4% international, 5% transferred in, 70% live on campus. *Retention:* 83% of 2001 full-time freshmen returned.

Freshmen *Admission:* 294 enrolled. *Average high school GPA:* 3.20. *Test scores:* SAT verbal scores over 500: 84%; SAT math scores over 500: 71%; SAT verbal scores over 600: 36%; SAT math scores over 600: 24%; SAT verbal scores over 700: 5%; SAT math scores over 700: 1%.

Faculty *Total:* 351, 50% full-time. *Student/faculty ratio:* 10:1.

Majors Accounting; advertising; African-American studies; art; arts management; biochemistry; biology; business administration; business marketing and marketing management; chemistry; comparative literature; computer science; dietetics; early childhood education; East Asian studies; economics; education; elementary education; English; environmental science; finance; French; graphic design/commercial art/illustration; history; human services; information technology; international relations; management information systems/business data processing; mass communications; mathematics; music; music history; nursing; nutrition science; pharmacy; philosophy; physical therapy; physiological psychology/psychobiology; political science; pre-dentistry; pre-law; pre-medicine; psychology; public policy analysis; public relations; retail management; secondary education; sociology; Spanish; special education; teaching English as a second language; women's studies.

Academic Programs *Special study options:* academic remediation for entering students, accelerated degree program, adult/continuing education programs, advanced placement credit, double majors, English as a second language, freshman honors college, honors programs, independent study, internships, off-campus study, part-time degree program, services for LD students, student-designed majors, study abroad, summer session for credit. *ROTC:* Army (c). *Unusual degree programs:* 3-2 pharmacy with Massachusetts College of Pharmacy and Allied Health Sciences, nutrition with Boston University.

Library Beatley Library plus 5 others with 285,698 titles, 1,861 serial subscriptions, 5,725 audiovisual materials, an OPAC, a Web page.

Computers on Campus 250 computers available on campus for general student use. A campuswide network can be accessed from student residence rooms and from off campus. Internet access, at least one staffed computer lab available.

Student Life *Housing Options:* women-only, disabled students. *Activities and Organizations:* drama/theater group, student-run newspaper, choral group, Student Government Association, Simmons Community Outreach, Campus Activities Board, Class Councils, Simmons Voice. *Campus security:* 24-hour emergency response devices and patrols, late-night transport/escort service, controlled dormitory access. *Student Services:* health clinic, personal/psychological counseling, women's center.

Athletics Member NCAA. All Division III. *Intercollegiate sports:* basketball W, crew W, field hockey W, sailing W, soccer W, softball W, swimming W, tennis W, track and field W, volleyball W. *Intramural sports:* basketball W, golf W, racquetball W, skiing (cross-country) W, skiing (downhill) W, soccer W, softball W, tennis W, volleyball W.

Standardized Tests *Required:* SAT I or ACT (for admission).

Costs (2001–02) *Comprehensive fee:* $30,418 includes full-time tuition ($21,020), mandatory fees ($648), and room and board ($8750). Full-time tuition and fees vary according to course load. Part-time tuition: $663 per semester hour.

Part-time tuition and fees vary according to course load. *Payment plan:* installment. *Waivers:* adult students, senior citizens, and employees or children of employees.

Financial Aid Of all full-time matriculated undergraduates who enrolled in 2001, 827 applied for aid, 716 were judged to have need. In 2001, 23 non-need-based awards were made. *Average percent of need met:* 95%. *Average financial aid package:* $20,181. *Average need-based loan:* $6734. *Average need-based gift aid:* $11,632. *Average non-need based aid:* $12,208. *Average indebtedness upon graduation:* $19,820.

Applying *Options:* common application, early admission, early action, deferred entrance. *Application fee:* $35. *Required:* essay or personal statement, high school transcript, 2 letters of recommendation. *Recommended:* minimum 3.0 GPA, interview. *Application deadlines:* 2/1 (freshmen), 4/1 (transfers). *Notification:* 4/15 (freshmen), 1/20 (early action).

Admissions Contact Ms. Jennifer O'Loughlin Hieber, Interim Director of Undergraduate Admissions, Simmons College, 300 The Fenway, Boston, MA 02115. *Phone:* 617-521-2051. *Toll-free phone:* 800-345-8468. *Fax:* 617-521-3190. *E-mail:* ugadm@simmons.edu.

SIMON'S ROCK COLLEGE OF BARD

Great Barrington, Massachusetts

- **Independent** 4-year, founded 1964
- **Calendar** semesters
- **Degrees** associate and bachelor's
- **Rural** 275-acre campus with easy access to Albany and Springfield
- **Endowment** $8.5 million
- **Coed,** 414 undergraduate students, 96% full-time, 57% women, 43% men
- **Very difficult** entrance level, 42% of applicants were admitted

Undergraduates 396 full-time, 18 part-time. Students come from 28 states and territories, 3 other countries, 85% are from out of state, 3% African American, 7% Asian American or Pacific Islander, 3% Hispanic American, 0.7% Native American, 1% international, 0.2% transferred in, 78% live on campus. *Retention:* 81% of 2001 full-time freshmen returned.

Freshmen *Admission:* 562 applied, 234 admitted, 162 enrolled. *Test scores:* SAT verbal scores over 500: 96%; SAT math scores over 500: 74%; ACT scores over 18: 100%; SAT verbal scores over 600: 63%; SAT math scores over 600: 40%; ACT scores over 24: 50%; SAT verbal scores over 700: 24%; SAT math scores over 700: 10%; ACT scores over 30: 10%.

Faculty *Total:* 60, 60% full-time, 88% with terminal degrees. *Student/faculty ratio:* 9:1.

Majors Acting/directing; African-American studies; agricultural business; American studies; anthropology; applied mathematics; art history; Asian studies; biology; ceramic arts; chemistry; cognitive psychology/psycholinguistics; computer graphics; computer science; creative writing; cultural studies; dance; developmental/child psychology; drawing; ecology; environmental science; European studies; fine/studio arts; foreign languages/literatures; French; geography; geology; German; interdisciplinary studies; jazz; Latin American studies; liberal arts and sciences/liberal studies; literature; mathematics; metal/jewelry arts; music; music theory and composition; natural sciences; painting; philosophy; photography; physics; play/screenwriting; political science; pre-law; pre-medicine; printmaking; psychology; religious studies; sculpture; Spanish; theater arts/drama; visual/performing arts; women's studies.

Academic Programs *Special study options:* adult/continuing education programs, double majors, external degree program, independent study, internships, off-campus study, part-time degree program, student-designed majors, study abroad.

Library Alumni Library with 71,000 titles, 380 serial subscriptions, 3,400 audiovisual materials, an OPAC, a Web page.

Computers on Campus 25 computers available on campus for general student use. A campuswide network can be accessed from student residence rooms and from off campus. Internet access, at least one staffed computer lab available.

Student Life *Housing:* on-campus residence required through sophomore year. *Options:* coed. *Activities and Organizations:* drama/theater group, student-run newspaper, radio station, choral group, women's center, math and sciences club, multicultural student organization, Community Health Institute, Community Service Program. *Campus security:* 24-hour emergency response devices, late-night transport/escort service, controlled dormitory access, 24-hour weekend patrols by trained security personnel. *Student Services:* health clinic, personal/psychological counseling, women's center.

Athletics *Intercollegiate sports:* basketball M/W, soccer M/W, tennis M/W. *Intramural sports:* baseball M, basketball M/W, bowling M/W, cross-country running M/W, football M, racquetball M/W, skiing (cross-country) M/W, skiing (downhill) M/W, soccer M/W, softball M/W, squash M/W, swimming M/W, table tennis M/W, tennis M/W, volleyball M/W, weight lifting M/W.

Standardized Tests *Required:* SAT I (for admission). *Recommended:* ACT (for admission).

Costs (2001–02) *One-time required fee:* $575. *Comprehensive fee:* $32,450 includes full-time tuition ($22,870), mandatory fees ($2740), and room and board ($6840). Full-time tuition and fees vary according to course load. Part-time tuition: $950 per credit hour. Part-time tuition and fees vary according to course load. *Required fees:* $170 per term part-time. *Room and board:* College room only: $3340. Room and board charges vary according to board plan and housing facility. *Payment plan:* installment. *Waivers:* employees or children of employees.

Financial Aid Of all full-time matriculated undergraduates who enrolled in 2001, 296 applied for aid, 228 were judged to have need, 64 had their need fully met. 142 Federal Work-Study jobs (averaging $1338). In 2001, 78 non-need-based awards were made. *Average percent of need met:* 71%. *Average financial aid package:* $14,775. *Average need-based loan:* $4366. *Average need-based gift aid:* $11,280. *Average non-need based aid:* $11,808. *Average indebtedness upon graduation:* $17,000.

Applying *Options:* electronic application, early admission, deferred entrance. *Application fee:* $40. *Required:* essay or personal statement, high school transcript, minimum 2.0 GPA, 2 letters of recommendation, interview, parent application. *Recommended:* minimum 3.0 GPA. *Application deadlines:* 6/15 (freshmen), 7/15 (transfers). *Notification:* continuous (freshmen).

Admissions Contact Ms. Mary King Austin, Director of Admissions, Simon's Rock College of Bard, 84 Alford Road, Great Barrington, MA 01230-9702. *Phone:* 413-528-7317. *Toll-free phone:* 800-235-7186. *Fax:* 413-528-7334. *E-mail:* admit@simons-rock.edu.

SMITH COLLEGE

Northampton, Massachusetts

- **Independent** comprehensive, founded 1871
- **Calendar** semesters
- **Degrees** bachelor's, master's, doctoral, post-master's, and postbachelor's certificates
- **Urban** 125-acre campus with easy access to Hartford
- **Endowment** $917.0 million
- **Women only,** 2,665 undergraduate students, 98% full-time
- **Very difficult** entrance level, 54% of applicants were admitted

Undergraduates 2,623 full-time, 42 part-time. Students come from 53 states and territories, 53 other countries, 76% are from out of state, 5% African American, 9% Asian American or Pacific Islander, 5% Hispanic American, 0.9% Native American, 6% international, 3% transferred in, 91% live on campus. *Retention:* 91% of 2001 full-time freshmen returned.

Freshmen *Admission:* 660 enrolled. *Average high school GPA:* 3.80. *Test scores:* SAT verbal scores over 500: 95%; SAT math scores over 500: 95%; ACT scores over 18: 98%; SAT verbal scores over 600: 74%; SAT math scores over 600: 61%; ACT scores over 24: 88%; SAT verbal scores over 700: 28%; SAT math scores over 700: 15%; ACT scores over 30: 35%.

Faculty *Total:* 300, 93% full-time, 96% with terminal degrees. *Student/faculty ratio:* 9:1.

Majors African-American studies; American studies; anthropology; architecture; art; art history; astronomy; biochemistry; biology; chemistry; classics; comparative literature; computer science; dance; East Asian studies; economics; education; English; fine/studio arts; French; geology; German; Greek (ancient and medieval); history; interdisciplinary studies; Italian; Latin American studies; Latin (ancient and medieval); mathematics; medieval/renaissance studies; Middle Eastern studies; music; neuroscience; philosophy; physics; political science; Portuguese; psychology; religious studies; Russian; Russian/Slavic studies; sociology; Spanish; theater arts/drama; women's studies.

Academic Programs *Special study options:* accelerated degree program, adult/continuing education programs, advanced placement credit, double majors, honors programs, independent study, internships, off-campus study, part-time degree program, services for LD students, student-designed majors, study abroad. *ROTC:* Army (c), Air Force (c).

Library Neilson Library plus 3 others with 1.2 million titles, 5,119 serial subscriptions, 62,517 audiovisual materials, an OPAC, a Web page.

Computers on Campus 550 computers available on campus for general student use. A campuswide network can be accessed from student residence rooms and from off campus that provide access to e-mail. Internet access, online (class) registration, at least one staffed computer lab available.

Student Life *Housing:* on-campus residence required through senior year. *Options:* women-only, cooperative. *Activities and Organizations:* drama/theater

Smith College (continued)
group, student-run newspaper, radio station, choral group, Recreation Council, Service Organizations of Smith, glee club and choirs, Athletic Association, Black Student Alliance. *Campus security:* 24-hour emergency response devices and patrols, late-night transport/escort service, self-defense workshops, emergency telephones, programs in crime and sexual assault prevention. *Student Services:* health clinic, personal/psychological counseling, women's center.

Athletics Member NCAA. All Division III. *Intercollegiate sports:* basketball W, crew W, cross-country running W, equestrian sports W, field hockey W, lacrosse W, skiing (downhill) W, soccer W, softball W, squash W, swimming W, tennis W, track and field W, volleyball W. *Intramural sports:* badminton W(c), crew W, cross-country running W, equestrian sports W(c), fencing W(c), golf W(c), ice hockey W(c), rugby W(c), sailing W(c), skiing (cross-country) W(c), soccer W, softball W, squash W, swimming W, tennis W, track and field W, volleyball W, water polo W.

Standardized Tests *Required:* SAT I or ACT (for admission). *Recommended:* SAT II: Subject Tests (for admission), SAT II: Writing Test (for admission).

Costs (2001–02) *Comprehensive fee:* $33,110 includes full-time tuition ($24,550) and room and board ($8560). *Room and board:* Room and board charges vary according to housing facility. *Payment plans:* tuition prepayment, installment. *Waivers:* employees or children of employees.

Financial Aid Of all full-time matriculated undergraduates who enrolled in 2001, 1881 applied for aid, 1567 were judged to have need, 1567 had their need fully met. 1266 Federal Work-Study jobs (averaging $1960). 219 State and other part-time jobs (averaging $1961). In 2001, 108 non-need-based awards were made. *Average percent of need met:* 100%. *Average financial aid package:* $23,172. *Average need-based loan:* $3928. *Average need-based gift aid:* $17,467. *Average non-need based aid:* $6506. *Average indebtedness upon graduation:* $19,546. *Financial aid deadline:* 2/1.

Applying *Options:* common application, electronic application, early admission, early decision, deferred entrance. *Application fee:* $50. *Required:* essay or personal statement, high school transcript, 3 letters of recommendation. *Recommended:* interview. *Application deadlines:* 1/15 (freshmen), 6/1 (transfers). *Early decision:* 11/15 (for plan 1), 1/2 (for plan 2). *Notification:* 4/1 (freshmen), 12/15 (early decision plan 1), 2/1 (early decision plan 2).

Admissions Contact Ms. Audrey Y. Smith, Director of Admissions, Smith College, 7 College Lane, Northampton, MA 01063. *Phone:* 413-585-2500. *Fax:* 413-585-2527. *E-mail:* admission@smith.edu.

SPRINGFIELD COLLEGE
Springfield, Massachusetts

- **Independent** comprehensive, founded 1885
- **Calendar** semesters
- **Degrees** bachelor's, master's, doctoral, and post-master's certificates
- **Suburban** 167-acre campus
- **Coed,** 2,077 undergraduate students
- **Moderately difficult** entrance level, 72% of applicants were admitted

Founded in 1885, Springfield College emphasizes the education of leaders in the allied health sciences, human and social services, sports and movement activities, and the arts and sciences. Through its distintive humanistics philosophy—the education of the whole person, consisting of spirit, mind, and body—Springfield College prepares students for leadership in service to others.

Undergraduates Students come from 37 states and territories, 4% African American, 1% Asian American or Pacific Islander, 3% Hispanic American, 0.4% Native American, 1% international, 85% live on campus. *Retention:* 83% of 2001 full-time freshmen returned.

Freshmen *Admission:* 2,337 applied, 1,671 admitted.

Faculty *Total:* 346, 61% full-time, 82% with terminal degrees. *Student/faculty ratio:* 12:1.

Majors Applied art; art therapy; athletic training/sports medicine; biology; business administration; chemistry; community services; computer graphics; computer science; early childhood education; ecology; education; elementary education; emergency medical technology; English; environmental health; environmental science; exercise sciences; general studies; gerontology; health education; health services administration; history; human resources management; human services; information sciences/systems; management information systems/business data processing; mathematics; medical laboratory technology; medical records administration; medical technology; mental health/rehabilitation; middle school education; natural resources conservation; physical education; physical therapy; physician assistant; political science; pre-dentistry; pre-law; pre-medicine; psychology; public health; recreational therapy; recreation/leisure facilities management; recreation/leisure studies; rehabilitation therapy; science education; secondary education; sociology; special education; sport/fitness administration.

Academic Programs *Special study options:* accelerated degree program, adult/continuing education programs, advanced placement credit, cooperative education, English as a second language, honors programs, internships, off-campus study, part-time degree program, services for LD students, study abroad, summer session for credit. *ROTC:* Army (c), Air Force (c). *Unusual degree programs:* 3-2 physical therapy.

Library Babson Library with 125,000 titles, 850 serial subscriptions.

Computers on Campus 95 computers available on campus for general student use. A campuswide network can be accessed from student residence rooms and from off campus. Internet access available.

Student Life *Housing:* on-campus residence required through junior year. *Options:* coed, men-only, women-only. *Activities and Organizations:* drama/theater group, student-run newspaper, radio station. *Student Services:* health clinic, personal/psychological counseling.

Athletics Member NCAA. All Division III. *Intercollegiate sports:* baseball M, basketball M/W, cross-country running M/W, field hockey W, football M, golf M/W, gymnastics M/W, lacrosse M/W, soccer M/W, softball W, swimming M/W, tennis M/W, track and field M/W, volleyball M/W, wrestling M. *Intramural sports:* baseball M, basketball M/W, crew M/W, equestrian sports M/W, field hockey W, football M/W, golf M/W, racquetball M/W, riflery M/W, rugby M/W, soccer M/W, softball M/W, squash M/W, swimming M/W, tennis M/W, track and field M/W, volleyball M/W, water polo M/W, weight lifting M/W, wrestling M.

Standardized Tests *Required:* SAT I (for admission).

Costs (2002–03) *Comprehensive fee:* $25,430 includes full-time tuition ($18,490), mandatory fees ($200), and room and board ($6740). Part-time tuition: $560 per credit. *Room and board:* College room only: $3640. Room and board charges vary according to board plan and housing facility.

Financial Aid Of all full-time matriculated undergraduates who enrolled in 2001, 1779 applied for aid, 1572 were judged to have need, 277 had their need fully met. 323 Federal Work-Study jobs (averaging $1392). 622 State and other part-time jobs (averaging $1180). In 2001, 49 non-need-based awards were made. *Average percent of need met:* 76%. *Average financial aid package:* $12,964. *Average need-based loan:* $4056. *Average need-based gift aid:* $8997. *Average non-need based aid:* $5765. *Average indebtedness upon graduation:* $17,500.

Applying *Options:* common application, electronic application, early admission, early decision, deferred entrance. *Application fee:* $30. *Required:* essay or personal statement, high school transcript, 2 letters of recommendation, interview. *Required for some:* portfolio. *Application deadlines:* 4/1 (freshmen), 5/1 (transfers). *Early decision:* 12/1. *Notification:* continuous until 4/15 (freshmen), 2/1 (early decision).

Admissions Contact Mary N. DeAngelo, Director of Undergraduate Admissions, Springfield College, 263 Alden Street, Box M, Springfield, MA 01109. *Phone:* 413-748-3136. *Toll-free phone:* 800-343-1257. *Fax:* 413-748-3694. *E-mail:* admissions@spfldcol.edu.

STONEHILL COLLEGE
Easton, Massachusetts

- **Independent Roman Catholic** comprehensive, founded 1948
- **Calendar** semesters
- **Degrees** bachelor's and master's
- **Suburban** 375-acre campus with easy access to Boston
- **Endowment** $93.1 million
- **Coed,** 2,613 undergraduate students, 83% full-time, 60% women, 40% men
- **Very difficult** entrance level, 43% of applicants were admitted

Located 20 miles south of Boston, Stonehill combines a community atmosphere and a beautiful 375-acre campus with easy access to America's premier college town. Exciting special programs, such as full-time international internships, study abroad, domestic internships, and Stonehill Undergraduate Research Experience (SURE), complement the College's rigorous education in the liberal arts, sciences, and business. More than 70% of graduating students take advantage of these enriching programs.

Undergraduates 2,179 full-time, 434 part-time. Students come from 31 states and territories, 11 other countries, 40% are from out of state, 2% African American, 2% Asian American or Pacific Islander, 2% Hispanic American, 0.3% Native American, 0.9% international, 0.5% transferred in, 85% live on campus. *Retention:* 90% of 2001 full-time freshmen returned.

Freshmen *Admission:* 4,936 applied, 2,120 admitted, 588 enrolled. *Average high school GPA:* 3.51. *Test scores:* SAT verbal scores over 500: 92%; SAT math scores over 500: 95%; SAT verbal scores over 600: 41%; SAT math scores over 600: 47%; SAT verbal scores over 700: 3%; SAT math scores over 700: 5%.

Faculty *Total:* 230, 55% full-time, 62% with terminal degrees. *Student/faculty ratio:* 14:1.

Majors Accounting; American studies; biochemistry; biology; business administration; business economics; business marketing and marketing management; chemistry; communications; computer engineering; computer science; criminal justice studies; early childhood education; economics; education; elementary education; English; finance; fine/studio arts; foreign languages/literatures; health services administration; history; international relations; mathematics; medical technology; multi/interdisciplinary studies related; philosophy; political science; pre-dentistry; pre-law; pre-medicine; pre-veterinary studies; psychology; public administration; religious studies; sociology.

Academic Programs *Special study options:* adult/continuing education programs, advanced placement credit, double majors, honors programs, independent study, internships, off-campus study, part-time degree program, services for LD students, student-designed majors, study abroad, summer session for credit. *ROTC:* Army (b). *Unusual degree programs:* 3-2 computer engineering with University of Notre Dame.

Library Bartley MacPhaidin, C.S.C. Library plus 1 other with 188,980 titles, 1,800 serial subscriptions, 4,335 audiovisual materials, an OPAC, a Web page.

Computers on Campus 210 computers available on campus for general student use. A campuswide network can be accessed from student residence rooms and from off campus that provide access to online class schedules, assignments, grades; student account. Internet access, at least one staffed computer lab available.

Student Life *Housing Options:* coed, women-only, disabled students. *Activities and Organizations:* drama/theater group, student-run newspaper, radio station, choral group, Into the Streets, student radio station, student government, Summit (student newspaper), sports clubs. *Campus security:* 24-hour emergency response devices and patrols, late-night transport/escort service. *Student Services:* health clinic, personal/psychological counseling.

Athletics Member NCAA. All Division II. *Intercollegiate sports:* baseball M(s), basketball M(s)/W(s), bowling M(c)/W(c), cross-country running M(s)/W(s), equestrian sports W, fencing M(c)/W(c), field hockey W(s), football M(s), golf M(c)/W(c), ice hockey M(s), lacrosse M(c)/W(s), rugby M(c)/W(c), soccer M(s)/W(s), softball W(s), tennis M(s)/W(s), track and field M(s)/W(s), volleyball M(c)/W(s). *Intramural sports:* basketball M/W, field hockey M/W, football M/W, racquetball M/W, soccer M/W, softball M/W, tennis M/W, volleyball M/W.

Standardized Tests *Required:* SAT I or ACT (for admission).

Costs (2001–02) *One-time required fee:* $50. *Comprehensive fee:* $26,852 includes full-time tuition ($17,680), mandatory fees ($680), and room and board ($8492). Full-time tuition and fees vary according to class time and course load. Part-time tuition: $1768 per course. Part-time tuition and fees vary according to class time. *Required fees:* $68 per course. *Room and board:* Room and board charges vary according to board plan. *Payment plans:* tuition prepayment, installment. *Waivers:* minority students, senior citizens, and employees or children of employees.

Financial Aid Of all full-time matriculated undergraduates who enrolled in 2001, 1694 applied for aid, 1353 were judged to have need, 503 had their need fully met. 541 Federal Work-Study jobs (averaging $1200). 327 State and other part-time jobs (averaging $750). In 2001, 537 non-need-based awards were made. *Average percent of need met:* 88%. *Average financial aid package:* $13,648. *Average need-based loan:* $4720. *Average need-based gift aid:* $9595. *Average indebtedness upon graduation:* $15,670.

Applying *Options:* common application, electronic application, early admission, early decision, deferred entrance. *Application fee:* $50. *Required:* essay or personal statement, high school transcript, 2 letters of recommendation. *Required for some:* interview. *Recommended:* campus visit. *Application deadlines:* 1/15 (freshmen), 4/1 (transfers). *Early decision:* 11/1. *Notification:* 4/1 (freshmen), 12/31 (early decision).

Admissions Contact Mr. Brian P. Murphy, Dean of Admissions and Enrollment, Stonehill College, 320 Washington Street, Easton, MA 02357-5610. *Phone:* 508-565-1373. *Fax:* 508-565-1545. *E-mail:* admissions@stonehill.edu.

SUFFOLK UNIVERSITY
Boston, Massachusetts

- **Independent** comprehensive, founded 1906
- **Calendar** semesters
- **Degrees** certificates, diplomas, associate, bachelor's, master's, doctoral, first professional, post-master's, and postbachelor's certificates (doctoral degree in law)
- **Urban** 2-acre campus
- **Endowment** $51.0 million
- **Coed,** 3,437 undergraduate students, 80% full-time, 57% women, 43% men
- **Moderately difficult** entrance level, 83% of applicants were admitted

Undergraduates 2,740 full-time, 697 part-time. Students come from 34 states and territories, 97 other countries, 15% are from out of state, 4% African American, 6% Asian American or Pacific Islander, 5% Hispanic American, 0.2% Native American, 13% international, 9% transferred in, 18% live on campus. *Retention:* 77% of 2001 full-time freshmen returned.

Freshmen *Admission:* 3,283 applied, 2,738 admitted, 721 enrolled. *Average high school GPA:* 2.90. *Test scores:* SAT verbal scores over 500: 54%; SAT math scores over 500: 48%; SAT verbal scores over 600: 12%; SAT math scores over 600: 9%; SAT verbal scores over 700: 1%; SAT math scores over 700: 1%.

Faculty *Total:* 550, 43% full-time, 50% with terminal degrees. *Student/faculty ratio:* 12:1.

Majors Accounting; African-American studies; art; biochemistry; biological technology; biology; biomedical science; biomedical technology; biophysics; broadcast journalism; business administration; business education; business marketing and marketing management; chemistry; computer engineering; computer/information sciences; computer science; criminal justice/law enforcement administration; cytotechnology; developmental/child psychology; economics; education; electrical engineering; elementary education; English; environmental biology; environmental science; finance; French; graphic design/commercial art/illustration; history; humanities; human services; information sciences/systems; interdisciplinary studies; interior design; international economics; journalism; legal studies; liberal arts and sciences/liberal studies; management information systems/business data processing; marine biology; marine science; mass communications; mathematics; medical technology; modern languages; paralegal/legal assistant; philosophy; physics; political science; pre-dentistry; pre-law; pre-medicine; pre-veterinary studies; psychology; public administration; public policy analysis; public relations; radiological science; secondary education; secretarial science; social sciences; social work; sociology; Spanish; speech/rhetorical studies; theater arts/drama; women's studies.

Academic Programs *Special study options:* academic remediation for entering students, accelerated degree program, adult/continuing education programs, advanced placement credit, cooperative education, distance learning, double majors, English as a second language, freshman honors college, honors programs, independent study, internships, off-campus study, part-time degree program, services for LD students, study abroad, summer session for credit. *ROTC:* Army (c). *Unusual degree programs:* 3-2 engineering with Boston University, Case Western Reserve University.

Library Mildred Sawyer Library plus 3 others with 279,000 titles, 6,900 serial subscriptions, 16,000 audiovisual materials, an OPAC, a Web page.

Computers on Campus 300 computers available on campus for general student use. A campuswide network can be accessed from student residence rooms and from off campus. Internet access, at least one staffed computer lab available.

Student Life *Housing Options:* coed. *Activities and Organizations:* drama/theater group, student-run newspaper, radio and television station, choral group, Student Government Association, Program Council, Black Student Union, Evening Student Association, International Student Association, national fraternities. *Campus security:* 24-hour emergency response devices, late-night transport/escort service, controlled dormitory access. *Student Services:* health clinic, personal/psychological counseling, women's center.

Athletics Member NCAA. All Division III. *Intercollegiate sports:* baseball M, basketball M/W, cross-country running M/W, golf M, ice hockey M, soccer M, softball W, tennis M/W, volleyball W. *Intramural sports:* basketball M/W, soccer W, volleyball M/W.

Standardized Tests *Required:* SAT I or ACT (for admission).

Costs (2001–02) *Comprehensive fee:* $26,606 includes full-time tuition ($16,536), mandatory fees ($80), and room and board ($9990). Part-time tuition: $437 per semester hour. *Required fees:* $10 per term part-time. *Room and board:* Room and board charges vary according to housing facility. *Payment plans:* installment, deferred payment. *Waivers:* senior citizens and employees or children of employees.

Financial Aid Of all full-time matriculated undergraduates who enrolled in 2001, 2035 applied for aid, 1509 were judged to have need, 322 had their need fully met. In 2001, 257 non-need-based awards were made. *Average percent of need met:* 76%. *Average financial aid package:* $12,404. *Average need-based loan:* $4515. *Average need-based gift aid:* $6222. *Average non-need based aid:* $2682.

Applying *Options:* common application, early admission, early action, deferred entrance. *Application fee:* $40. *Required:* essay or personal statement, high school transcript, 2 letters of recommendation. *Required for some:* interview. *Recommended:* minimum 2.5 GPA. *Application deadline:* rolling (freshmen), rolling (transfers). *Notification:* continuous (freshmen), 12/1 (early action).

Suffolk University (continued)

Admissions Contact Mr. Walter Caffey, Dean of Enrollment Management, Suffolk University, Boston, MA 02108. *Phone:* 617-573-8460. *Toll-free phone:* 800-6-SUFFOLK. *Fax:* 617-742-4291. *E-mail:* admission@admin.suffolk.edu.

TUFTS UNIVERSITY
Medford, Massachusetts

- **Independent** university, founded 1852
- **Calendar** semesters
- **Degrees** bachelor's, master's, doctoral, first professional, and post-master's certificates
- **Suburban** 150-acre campus with easy access to Boston
- **Endowment** $592.0 million
- **Coed,** 4,755 undergraduate students, 98% full-time, 54% women, 46% men
- **Most difficult** entrance level, 23% of applicants were admitted

Undergraduates 4,679 full-time, 76 part-time. Students come from 52 states and territories, 70 other countries, 77% are from out of state, 7% African American, 13% Asian American or Pacific Islander, 8% Hispanic American, 0.2% Native American, 7% international, 1% transferred in, 75% live on campus. *Retention:* 96% of 2001 full-time freshmen returned.

Freshmen *Admission:* 13,700 applied, 3,178 admitted, 1,161 enrolled. *Test scores:* SAT verbal scores over 500: 95%; SAT math scores over 500: 99%; ACT scores over 18: 100%; SAT verbal scores over 600: 75%; SAT math scores over 600: 86%; ACT scores over 24: 89%; SAT verbal scores over 700: 26%; SAT math scores over 700: 39%; ACT scores over 30: 37%.

Faculty *Total:* 1,103, 62% full-time. *Student/faculty ratio:* 9:1.

Majors African-American studies; American studies; anthropology; archaeology; architectural engineering; art history; Asian studies; astronomy; behavioral sciences; biology; chemical engineering; chemistry; child care/development; Chinese; civil engineering; classics; computer engineering; computer science; developmental/child psychology; early childhood education; ecology; economics; electrical engineering; elementary education; engineering; engineering design; engineering physics; engineering science; English; environmental engineering; environmental science; experimental psychology; French; geology; geophysical engineering; German; Greek (modern); history; industrial/manufacturing engineering; international relations; Judaic studies; Latin (ancient and medieval); mathematics; mechanical engineering; mental health/rehabilitation; music; philosophy; physics; political science; psychology; public health; romance languages; Russian; Russian/Slavic studies; secondary education; sociobiology; sociology; Southeast Asian studies; Spanish; special education; theater arts/drama; urban studies; women's studies.

Academic Programs *Special study options:* adult/continuing education programs, advanced placement credit, double majors, honors programs, independent study, internships, off-campus study, services for LD students, student-designed majors, study abroad, summer session for credit. *ROTC:* Army (c), Navy (c), Air Force (c). *Unusual degree programs:* 3-2 music with New England Conservatory of Music, fine arts with School of the Museum of Fine Arts.

Library Tisch Library plus 1 other with 1.6 million titles, 5,329 serial subscriptions, 32,200 audiovisual materials, an OPAC, a Web page.

Computers on Campus 254 computers available on campus for general student use. A campuswide network can be accessed from student residence rooms and from off campus. Internet access, online (class) registration, at least one staffed computer lab available.

Student Life *Housing:* on-campus residence required through sophomore year. *Options:* coed, women-only, cooperative. *Activities and Organizations:* drama/theater group, student-run newspaper, radio and television station, choral group, marching band, Leonard Carmichael Society, Mountain Club, Environmental Consciousness Outreach, national fraternities, national sororities. *Campus security:* 24-hour emergency response devices and patrols, late-night transport/escort service, controlled dormitory access, security lighting, call boxes to campus police. *Student Services:* health clinic, personal/psychological counseling, women's center, legal services.

Athletics Member NCAA. All Division III. *Intercollegiate sports:* baseball M, basketball M/W, crew M/W, cross-country running M/W, fencing W, field hockey W, football M, golf M, ice hockey M, lacrosse M/W, sailing M/W, soccer M/W, softball W, squash M/W, swimming M/W, tennis M/W, track and field M/W, volleyball W. *Intramural sports:* basketball M/W, cross-country running M/W, equestrian sports M/W, fencing M, football M, racquetball M/W, rugby M/W, skiing (downhill) M/W, soccer M/W, softball M/W, squash M/W, tennis M/W, track and field M/W, volleyball M, water polo M.

Standardized Tests *Required for some:* SAT II: Writing Test (for admission).

Costs (2001–02) *Comprehensive fee:* $34,879 includes full-time tuition ($26,213), mandatory fees ($679), and room and board ($7987). *Room and board:* College room only: $4087. Room and board charges vary according to board plan. *Payment plans:* tuition prepayment, installment. *Waivers:* employees or children of employees.

Financial Aid Of all full-time matriculated undergraduates who enrolled in 2001, 2066 applied for aid, 1852 were judged to have need, 1852 had their need fully met. 1413 Federal Work-Study jobs (averaging $1670). 37 State and other part-time jobs (averaging $1525). In 2001, 94 non-need-based awards were made. *Average percent of need met:* 100%. *Average financial aid package:* $22,109. *Average need-based loan:* $4446. *Average need-based gift aid:* $17,148. *Average non-need based aid:* $2818. *Average indebtedness upon graduation:* $15,169. *Financial aid deadline:* 2/15.

Applying *Options:* common application, electronic application, early admission, early decision, deferred entrance. *Application fee:* $60. *Required:* essay or personal statement, high school transcript, 1 letter of recommendation. *Recommended:* interview. *Application deadlines:* 1/1 (freshmen), 3/1 (transfers). *Early decision:* 11/15 (for plan 1), 1/1 (for plan 2). *Notification:* 4/1 (freshmen), 12/15 (early decision plan 1), 2/1 (early decision plan 2).

Admissions Contact Mr. David D. Cuttino, Dean of Undergraduate Admissions, Tufts University, Bendetson Hall, Medford, MA 02155. *Phone:* 617-627-3170. *Fax:* 617-627-3860. *E-mail:* admissions.inquiry@ase.tufts.edu.

UNIVERSITY OF MASSACHUSETTS AMHERST
Amherst, Massachusetts

- **State-supported** university, founded 1863, part of University of Massachusetts
- **Calendar** semesters
- **Degrees** associate, bachelor's, master's, doctoral, and post-master's certificates
- **Small-town** 1463-acre campus with easy access to Hartford
- **Coed,** 19,368 undergraduate students, 92% full-time, 51% women, 49% men
- **Moderately difficult** entrance level, 73% of applicants were admitted

The Commonwealth College Honors Program combines an innovative curriculum, rigorous standards, and a residential academic experience. The College encourages creativity, initiative, responsibility, collaboration, and independent thought. Profile of first-year honors students: median SAT, 1315; median weighted GPA, 4.0; on average in top 5% of their high school class.

Undergraduates 17,885 full-time, 1,483 part-time. Students come from 50 states and territories, 70 other countries, 24% are from out of state, 4% African American, 6% Asian American or Pacific Islander, 3% Hispanic American, 0.4% Native American, 2% international, 6% transferred in, 58% live on campus. *Retention:* 84% of 2001 full-time freshmen returned.

Freshmen *Admission:* 18,625 applied, 13,518 admitted, 4,199 enrolled. *Average high school GPA:* 3.35. *Test scores:* SAT verbal scores over 500: 76%; SAT math scores over 500: 81%; SAT verbal scores over 600: 31%; SAT math scores over 600: 36%; SAT verbal scores over 700: 5%; SAT math scores over 700: 7%.

Faculty *Total:* 1,276, 90% full-time, 91% with terminal degrees. *Student/faculty ratio:* 18:1.

Majors Accounting; African-American studies; animal sciences; anthropology; applied economics; architectural environmental design; art history; astronomy; biochemistry; biological/physical sciences; biology; business administration; business marketing and marketing management; chemical engineering; chemistry; Chinese; civil engineering; classics; communication disorders; communications; comparative literature; computer engineering; computer science; crop production management; dance; earth sciences; economics; education; electrical engineering; English; environmental science; equestrian studies; exercise sciences; finance; fine/studio arts; food sciences; forestry; French; general studies; geography; geology; German; history; horticulture services; horticulture services related; hospitality management; humanities; industrial/manufacturing engineering; interdisciplinary studies; interior design; Italian; Japanese; journalism; Judaic studies; landscape architecture; landscaping management; legal studies; linguistics; mathematics; mechanical engineering; medical technology; microbiology/bacteriology; Middle Eastern studies; music; music (general performance); natural resources management; nursing; nutrition studies; ornamental horticulture; philosophy; physics; plant sciences; political science; Portuguese; pre-dentistry; pre-medicine; pre-veterinary studies; psychology; Russian/Slavic studies; social sciences and history related; sociology; Spanish; sport/fitness administration; theater arts/drama; turf management; wildlife management; women's studies; wood science/paper technology.

Academic Programs *Special study options:* academic remediation for entering students, adult/continuing education programs, advanced placement credit, cooperative education, distance learning, double majors, English as a second language, freshman honors college, honors programs, independent study, internships, off-campus study, part-time degree program, services for LD students, student-designed majors, study abroad, summer session for credit. *ROTC:* Army (b), Air Force (b).

Library W. E. B. Du Bois Library plus 3 others with 3.0 million titles, 15,362 serial subscriptions, 16,420 audiovisual materials, an OPAC, a Web page.

Computers on Campus A campuswide network can be accessed from student residence rooms and from off campus that provide access to on-line course and grade information. At least one staffed computer lab available.

Student Life *Housing:* on-campus residence required through sophomore year. *Options:* coed, men-only, women-only, disabled students. *Activities and Organizations:* drama/theater group, student-run newspaper, radio and television station, choral group, marching band, Minutemen Marching Band, Theater Guild, Ski Club, Outing Club, student newspaper, national fraternities, national sororities. *Campus security:* 24-hour emergency response devices and patrols, student patrols, late-night transport/escort service, controlled dormitory access, residence halls locked nights and weekends. *Student Services:* health clinic, personal/psychological counseling, women's center, legal services.

Athletics Member NCAA. All Division I except football (Division I-A). *Intercollegiate sports:* baseball M(s), basketball M(s)/W(s), crew W(s), cross-country running M(s)/W(s), field hockey W(s), gymnastics M(s)/W(s), ice hockey M(s), lacrosse M(s)/W(s), skiing (downhill) M(s)/W(s), soccer M(s)/W(s), softball W(s), swimming M(s)/W(s), tennis M(s)/W(s), track and field M(s)/W(s), volleyball W(s), water polo M(s)/W(s). *Intramural sports:* basketball M/W, crew M(c)/W(c), cross-country running M/W, equestrian sports M(c)/W(c), fencing M(c)/W(c), field hockey W, football M/W, ice hockey M/W, lacrosse M(c)/W, rugby M(c)/W(c), soccer M/W, softball M/W, swimming M/W, tennis M/W, track and field M/W, volleyball M/W, wrestling M/W.

Standardized Tests *Required:* SAT I or ACT (for admission).

Costs (2001–02) *One-time required fee:* $173. *Tuition:* state resident $1714 full-time, $72 per credit part-time; nonresident $9937 full-time, $414 per credit part-time. Full-time tuition and fees vary according to reciprocity agreements and student level. Part-time tuition and fees vary according to course load and reciprocity agreements. *Required fees:* $4166 full-time, $619 per term part-time. *Room and board:* $5115; room only: $2872. Room and board charges vary according to board plan. *Payment plan:* installment. *Waivers:* senior citizens and employees or children of employees.

Financial Aid Of all full-time matriculated undergraduates who enrolled in 2001, 13224 applied for aid, 8689 were judged to have need, 3730 had their need fully met. In 2001, 1223 non-need-based awards were made. *Average percent of need met:* 90%. *Average financial aid package:* $8167. *Average need-based loan:* $3474. *Average need-based gift aid:* $5248. *Average non-need based aid:* $3628. *Average indebtedness upon graduation:* $15,256.

Applying *Options:* common application, electronic application, early admission, deferred entrance. *Application fee:* $50 (non-residents). *Required:* essay or personal statement, high school transcript. *Recommended:* minimum 3.0 GPA, letters of recommendation. *Application deadlines:* 2/1 (freshmen), 5/1 (transfers). *Notification:* continuous (freshmen).

Admissions Contact Mr. Joseph Marshall, Assistant Dean for Enrollment Services, University of Massachusetts Amherst, 37 Mather Drive, Amherst, MA 01003-9291. *Phone:* 413-545-0222. *Fax:* 413-545-4312. *E-mail:* mail@admissions.umass.edu.

UNIVERSITY OF MASSACHUSETTS BOSTON
Boston, Massachusetts

- **State-supported** university, founded 1964, part of University of Massachusetts
- **Calendar** semesters
- **Degrees** certificates, bachelor's, master's, doctoral, and post-master's certificates
- **Urban** 177-acre campus
- **Endowment** $9.3 million
- **Coed,** 10,565 undergraduate students, 56% full-time, 56% women, 44% men
- **Moderately difficult** entrance level, 58% of applicants were admitted

The University of Massachusetts Boston is a public urban university, located on a peninsula in Boston Harbor, just 3 miles south of the city and adjacent to the John F. Kennedy Library and Museum. Established in 1964, the University enrolls more than 13,000 students in both undergraduate and graduate programs.

Undergraduates 5,930 full-time, 4,635 part-time. Students come from 38 states and territories, 97 other countries, 96% are from out of state, 14% African American, 11% Asian American or Pacific Islander, 6% Hispanic American, 0.4% Native American, 7% international, 15% transferred in. *Retention:* 69% of 2001 full-time freshmen returned.

Freshmen *Admission:* 2,652 applied, 1,539 admitted, 701 enrolled. *Average high school GPA:* 2.80. *Test scores:* SAT verbal scores over 500: 46%; SAT math scores over 500: 53%; SAT verbal scores over 600: 16%; SAT math scores over 600: 19%; SAT verbal scores over 700: 2%; SAT math scores over 700: 2%.

Faculty *Total:* 885, 53% full-time. *Student/faculty ratio:* 15:1.

Majors African-American studies; American studies; anthropology; applied mathematics; art; biochemistry; biology; business administration; chemistry; classics; community services; computer science; criminal justice studies; economics; engineering physics; English; French; geography; German; gerontology; history; human services; interdisciplinary studies; Italian; labor/personnel relations; Latin (ancient and medieval); legal studies; mathematics; medical technology; music; nursing; philosophy; physical education; physics; political science; psychology; public administration; public policy analysis; Russian; social work; sociology; Spanish; theater arts/drama; women's studies.

Academic Programs *Special study options:* academic remediation for entering students, accelerated degree program, adult/continuing education programs, advanced placement credit, cooperative education, distance learning, double majors, English as a second language, freshman honors college, honors programs, independent study, internships, off-campus study, part-time degree program, services for LD students, student-designed majors, study abroad, summer session for credit. *Unusual degree programs:* 3-2 engineering with University of Massachusetts Lowell, University of Massachusetts Amherst, Northeastern University.

Library Joseph P. Healey Library with 440,396 titles, 2,772 serial subscriptions, 1,885 audiovisual materials, an OPAC, a Web page.

Computers on Campus 260 computers available on campus for general student use. A campuswide network can be accessed from off campus. Internet access, online (class) registration, at least one staffed computer lab available.

Student Life *Housing:* college housing not available. *Activities and Organizations:* drama/theater group, student-run newspaper, radio station, choral group, women's center, black student center, Asian student center, veterans student center, disabilities student center. *Campus security:* 24-hour emergency response devices and patrols, late-night transport/escort service, crime prevention program, bicycle patrols. *Student Services:* health clinic, personal/psychological counseling, women's center, legal services.

Athletics Member NCAA. All Division III. *Intercollegiate sports:* baseball M, basketball M/W, cross-country running M/W, golf M, ice hockey M, lacrosse M, soccer M/W, softball W, tennis M/W, track and field M/W, volleyball W. *Intramural sports:* basketball M/W, ice hockey M, racquetball M/W, sailing M/W, soccer M/W, softball M/W, squash M/W, swimming M/W, tennis M/W, volleyball M/W, weight lifting M/W.

Standardized Tests *Required:* SAT I or ACT (for admission), SAT I or ACT (for placement).

Costs (2001–02) *One-time required fee:* $150. *Tuition:* state resident $1714 full-time, $108 per credit hour part-time; nonresident $9758 full-time, $407 per credit hour part-time. Part-time tuition and fees vary according to course load. *Required fees:* $2508 full-time, $481 per term part-time. *Payment plan:* installment. *Waivers:* senior citizens and employees or children of employees.

Financial Aid Of all full-time matriculated undergraduates who enrolled in 2001, 2488 applied for aid, 2125 were judged to have need, 364 had their need fully met. In 2001, 364 non-need-based awards were made. *Average percent of need met:* 76%. *Average financial aid package:* $7663. *Average need-based loan:* $2378. *Average need-based gift aid:* $4688. *Average indebtedness upon graduation:* $4886.

Applying *Options:* common application, electronic application, deferred entrance. *Application fee:* $40. *Required:* high school transcript, minimum 2.75 GPA. *Required for some:* essay or personal statement, letters of recommendation, interview. *Recommended:* essay or personal statement. *Application deadline:* rolling (freshmen), rolling (transfers). *Notification:* continuous (freshmen).

Admissions Contact Office of Admissions Information Service, University of Massachusetts Boston, Office of Undergraduate Admissions, 100 Morrissey Boulevard, Boston, MA 02125-3393. *Phone:* 617-287-6100. *Fax:* 617-287-6242. *E-mail:* enrollment.info@umb.edu.

UNIVERSITY OF MASSACHUSETTS DARTMOUTH
North Dartmouth, Massachusetts

- **State-supported** comprehensive, founded 1895, part of University of Massachusetts
- **Calendar** semesters
- **Degrees** certificates, bachelor's, master's, doctoral, post-master's, and postbachelor's certificates
- **Suburban** 710-acre campus with easy access to Boston and Providence
- **Endowment** $11.7 million
- **Coed,** 6,638 undergraduate students, 81% full-time, 53% women, 47% men

University of Massachusetts Dartmouth (continued)

■ **Moderately difficult** entrance level, 67% of applicants were admitted

The University of Massachusetts Dartmouth enrolls more than 5,800 students on its 710-acre campus in southeastern Massachusetts. Five colleges offer 42 undergraduate and 18 graduate programs. Publicly supported, the University provides affordable options in professional and preprofessional programs as well as in a variety of cocurricular activities, organizations, and teams.

Undergraduates 5,344 full-time, 1,294 part-time. Students come from 26 states and territories, 28 other countries, 6% are from out of state, 6% African American, 2% Asian American or Pacific Islander, 2% Hispanic American, 0.7% Native American, 1% international, 7% transferred in, 40% live on campus. *Retention:* 80% of 2001 full-time freshmen returned.

Freshmen *Admission:* 5,070 applied, 3,400 admitted, 1,190 enrolled. *Average high school GPA:* 3.04. *Test scores:* SAT verbal scores over 500: 64%; SAT math scores over 500: 68%; SAT verbal scores over 600: 19%; SAT math scores over 600: 21%; SAT verbal scores over 700: 2%; SAT math scores over 700: 2%.

Faculty *Total:* 475, 76% full-time, 65% with terminal degrees. *Student/faculty ratio:* 13:1.

Majors Accounting; art; art education; art history; biology; business administration; business marketing and marketing management; ceramic arts; chemistry; civil engineering; computer engineering; computer/information sciences; design/visual communications; economics; electrical/electronic engineering technology; electrical engineering; English; finance; French; graphic design/commercial art/illustration; history; interdisciplinary studies; liberal arts and sciences/liberal studies; management information systems/business data processing; mathematics; mechanical engineering; mechanical engineering technology; medical technology; metal/jewelry arts; multimedia; music; nursing; painting; philosophy; photography; physics; political science; Portuguese; printmaking; psychology; sculpture; sociology; Spanish; textile arts; textile sciences/engineering.

Academic Programs *Special study options:* academic remediation for entering students, adult/continuing education programs, advanced placement credit, cooperative education, distance learning, double majors, honors programs, independent study, internships, off-campus study, part-time degree program, services for LD students, student-designed majors, study abroad, summer session for credit. *ROTC:* Army (c).

Library University of Massachusetts Dartmouth Library with 288,189 titles, 2,925 serial subscriptions, 12,980 audiovisual materials, an OPAC, a Web page.

Computers on Campus 368 computers available on campus for general student use. A campuswide network can be accessed from student residence rooms and from off campus. Internet access, online (class) registration, at least one staffed computer lab available.

Student Life *Housing Options:* coed, disabled students. *Activities and Organizations:* drama/theater group, student-run newspaper, radio station, choral group, Student Activities Board, Outing Club, Phi Sigma Sigma, Portuguese Language Club, United Brothers and Sisters, national fraternities, national sororities. *Campus security:* 24-hour emergency response devices and patrols, student patrols, late-night transport/escort service, controlled dormitory access. *Student Services:* health clinic, personal/psychological counseling, women's center, legal services.

Athletics Member NCAA. All Division III. *Intercollegiate sports:* baseball M, basketball M/W, cross-country running M/W, equestrian sports M(c)/W(c), field hockey W, football M, golf M, ice hockey M, lacrosse M, soccer M/W, softball W, swimming M/W, tennis M/W, track and field M/W, volleyball W. *Intramural sports:* basketball M/W, cross-country running M/W, softball M/W, swimming M/W, tennis M/W, volleyball M/W, water polo M/W.

Standardized Tests *Required:* SAT I or ACT (for admission).

Costs (2001–02) *One-time required fee:* $50. *Tuition:* state resident $1417 full-time, $59 per credit hour part-time; nonresident $8099 full-time, $337 per credit hour part-time. Part-time tuition and fees vary according to course load and program. *Required fees:* $2712 full-time, $113 per credit hour. *Room and board:* $5723; room only: $3043. Room and board charges vary according to board plan and housing facility. *Payment plan:* installment. *Waivers:* senior citizens and employees or children of employees.

Financial Aid Of all full-time matriculated undergraduates who enrolled in 2001, 3781 applied for aid, 2886 were judged to have need, 2291 had their need fully met. In 2001, 368 non-need-based awards were made. *Average percent of need met:* 89%. *Average financial aid package:* $6707. *Average need-based loan:* $3337. *Average need-based gift aid:* $4056. *Average indebtedness upon graduation:* $14,015.

Applying *Options:* common application, early admission, early decision, deferred entrance. *Application fee:* $45 (non-residents). *Required:* essay or personal statement, high school transcript, minimum 2.0 GPA. *Recommended:* minimum 3.0 GPA, letters of recommendation. *Application deadline:* rolling (freshmen), rolling (transfers). *Early decision:* 11/15. *Notification:* continuous (freshmen), 12/15 (early decision).

Admissions Contact Mr. Steven Briggs, Director of Admissions, University of Massachusetts Dartmouth, 285 Old Westport Road, North Dartmouth, MA 02747-2300. *Phone:* 508-999-8606. *Fax:* 508-999-8755. *E-mail:* admissions@umassd.edu.

UNIVERSITY OF MASSACHUSETTS LOWELL

Lowell, Massachusetts

■ **State-supported** university, founded 1894, part of University of Massachusetts

■ **Calendar** semesters

■ **Degrees** associate, bachelor's, master's, and doctoral

■ **Urban** 100-acre campus with easy access to Boston

■ **Endowment** $6.6 million

■ **Coed,** 9,650 undergraduate students, 67% full-time, 41% women, 59% men

■ **Moderately difficult** entrance level, 70% of applicants were admitted

Undergraduates Students come from 36 states and territories, 73 other countries, 14% are from out of state, 2% African American, 7% Asian American or Pacific Islander, 3% Hispanic American, 0.1% Native American, 3% international, 32% live on campus. *Retention:* 74% of 2001 full-time freshmen returned.

Freshmen *Admission:* 3,286 applied, 2,284 admitted. *Average high school GPA:* 2.98. *Test scores:* SAT verbal scores over 500: 62%; SAT math scores over 500: 72%; SAT verbal scores over 600: 17%; SAT math scores over 600: 22%; SAT verbal scores over 700: 2%; SAT math scores over 700: 3%.

Faculty *Total:* 553, 73% full-time. *Student/faculty ratio:* 15:1.

Majors Accounting; American studies; applied mathematics; biology; business; business administration; chemical engineering; chemical technology; chemistry; civil engineering; civil engineering technology; computer science; criminal justice/law enforcement administration; economics; electrical/electronic engineering technology; electrical engineering; English; enterprise management; exercise sciences; foreign languages/literatures; health education; history; information sciences/systems; liberal arts and sciences/liberal studies; mathematics; mechanical engineering; medical technology; music (general performance); nursing; philosophy; physics; plastics engineering; political science; psychology; sociology.

Academic Programs *Special study options:* accelerated degree program, adult/continuing education programs, advanced placement credit, cooperative education, distance learning, double majors, honors programs, internships, off-campus study, part-time degree program, services for LD students, study abroad, summer session for credit. *ROTC:* Air Force (b). *Unusual degree programs:* 3-2 engineering with Saint Anselm College.

Library O'Leary Library plus 2 others with 549,243 titles, 7,855 serial subscriptions, an OPAC, a Web page.

Computers on Campus 4000 computers available on campus for general student use. A campuswide network can be accessed from student residence rooms and from off campus. At least one staffed computer lab available.

Student Life *Housing Options:* coed, men-only, women-only. *Activities and Organizations:* drama/theater group, student-run newspaper, radio station, choral group, marching band. *Campus security:* 24-hour emergency response devices and patrols, late-night transport/escort service, controlled dormitory access. *Student Services:* health clinic, personal/psychological counseling, women's center.

Athletics Member NCAA. All Division II except ice hockey (Division I). *Intercollegiate sports:* basketball M(s)/W(s), crew M/W, cross-country running M(s)/W(s), field hockey W(s), football M, golf M, ice hockey M(s), soccer M, swimming M(s), tennis M(s)/W(s), track and field M(s)/W(s), volleyball W(s), wrestling M(s). *Intramural sports:* badminton M/W, basketball M/W, bowling M/W, golf M/W, ice hockey M/W, racquetball M/W, soccer M/W, squash M/W, table tennis M/W, tennis M/W, volleyball M/W, water polo M/W.

Standardized Tests *Required:* SAT I or ACT (for admission).

Costs (2001–02) *Tuition:* state resident $1454 full-time, $61 per credit part-time; nonresident $8567 full-time, $357 per credit part-time. *Required fees:* $2801 full-time, $127 per credit. *Room and board:* $5095; room only: $3020. Room and board charges vary according to board plan and housing facility. *Payment plan:* installment. *Waivers:* senior citizens and employees or children of employees.

Financial Aid Of all full-time matriculated undergraduates who enrolled in 2001, 3414 applied for aid, 2258 were judged to have need, 1887 had their need fully met. 94 Federal Work-Study jobs (averaging $3073). In 2001, 238 non-need-based awards were made. *Average percent of need met:* 95%. *Average financial aid package:* $6795. *Average need-based loan:* $2715. *Average need-based gift aid:* $3772. *Average non-need based aid:* $3329. *Average indebtedness upon graduation:* $15,569.

Applying *Options:* electronic application, deferred entrance. *Application fee:* $35 (non-residents). *Required:* essay or personal statement, high school transcript, 1 letter of recommendation. *Required for some:* interview. *Application deadline:* rolling (freshmen), rolling (transfers). *Notification:* continuous (freshmen).

Admissions Contact Ms. Lisa Johnson, Assistant Vice Chancellor of Enrollment Management, University of Massachusetts Lowell, 883 Broadway Street, Room 110, Lowell, MA 01854-5104. *Phone:* 978-934-3944. *Toll-free phone:* 800-410-4607. *Fax:* 978-934-3086. *E-mail:* admissions@uml.edu.

UNIVERSITY OF PHOENIX-BOSTON CAMPUS
Braintree, Massachusetts

- **Proprietary** 4-year, founded 2001
- **Calendar** continuous
- **Degrees** certificates, associate, bachelor's, master's, doctoral, post-master's, and postbachelor's certificates (courses conducted at 54 campuses and learning centers in 13 states)
- **Coed,** 59 undergraduate students, 100% full-time, 75% women, 25% men

Undergraduates Students come from 3 states and territories, 4% are from out of state.

Freshmen *Admission:* 3 admitted.

Faculty *Total:* 37, 5% full-time, 19% with terminal degrees. *Student/faculty ratio:* 8:1.

Majors Business administration; management information systems/business data processing.

Student Life *Housing:* college housing not available.

Costs (2001–02) *Tuition:* $10,350 full-time. Full-time tuition and fees vary according to location and program. *Payment plan:* deferred payment. *Waivers:* employees or children of employees.

Applying *Application fee:* $85. *Required:* 2 years of work experience. *Required for some:* high school transcript. *Application deadline:* rolling (freshmen), rolling (transfers).

Admissions Contact Ms. Beth Barilla, Director of Admissions, University of Phoenix-Boston Campus, 4615 East Elwood Street, Phoenix, AZ 85040-1958. *Phone:* 480-927-0099 Ext. 1218. *Toll-free phone:* 800-228-7240. *Fax:* 480-594-1758. *E-mail:* beth.barilla@apollogrp.edu.

WELLESLEY COLLEGE
Wellesley, Massachusetts

- **Independent** 4-year, founded 1870
- **Calendar** semesters
- **Degrees** bachelor's (double bachelor's degree with Massachusetts Institute of Technology)
- **Suburban** 500-acre campus with easy access to Boston
- **Endowment** $1.1 billion
- **Women only,** 2,273 undergraduate students, 97% full-time
- **Most difficult** entrance level, 43% of applicants were admitted

Undergraduates 2,201 full-time, 72 part-time. Students come from 52 states and territories, 77 other countries, 81% are from out of state, 6% African American, 25% Asian American or Pacific Islander, 5% Hispanic American, 0.4% Native American, 7% international, 1% transferred in, 93% live on campus. *Retention:* 96% of 2001 full-time freshmen returned.

Freshmen *Admission:* 3,006 applied, 1,299 admitted, 578 enrolled. *Test scores:* SAT verbal scores over 500: 99%; SAT math scores over 500: 98%; ACT scores over 18: 100%; SAT verbal scores over 600: 88%; SAT math scores over 600: 85%; ACT scores over 24: 88%; SAT verbal scores over 700: 46%; SAT math scores over 700: 33%; ACT scores over 30: 47%.

Faculty *Total:* 315, 71% full-time, 92% with terminal degrees. *Student/faculty ratio:* 9:1.

Majors African-American studies; African studies; American studies; anthropology; archaeology; architecture; art history; astronomy; astrophysics; biochemistry; biology; chemistry; Chinese; classics; cognitive psychology/psycholinguistics; comparative literature; computer science; East Asian studies; economics; English; environmental science; ethnic/cultural studies related; film studies; fine/studio arts; French; geology; German; Greek (ancient and medieval); history; international relations; Islamic studies; Italian; Italian studies; Japanese; Judaic studies; Latin American studies; Latin (ancient and medieval); linguistics; mathematics; medieval/renaissance studies; music; neuroscience; peace/conflict studies; philosophy; physics; political science; psychology; religious studies; Russian; Russian/Slavic studies; sociology; Spanish; theater arts/drama; women's studies.

Academic Programs *Special study options:* adult/continuing education programs, advanced placement credit, double majors, independent study, internships, off-campus study, part-time degree program, services for LD students, student-designed majors, study abroad, summer session for credit. *ROTC:* Army (c), Air Force (c). *Unusual degree programs:* 3-2 in over 20 fields with Massachusetts Institute of Technology.

Library Margaret Clapp Library plus 3 others with 689,627 titles, 4,756 serial subscriptions, 20,532 audiovisual materials, an OPAC, a Web page.

Computers on Campus 200 computers available on campus for general student use. A campuswide network can be accessed from student residence rooms and from off campus that provide access to electronic bulletin boards. Internet access, at least one staffed computer lab available.

Student Life *Housing Options:* women-only, cooperative, disabled students. *Activities and Organizations:* drama/theater group, student-run newspaper, radio station, choral group, student government, radio station, cultural clubs, rugby club, theater groups. *Campus security:* 24-hour emergency response devices and patrols, late-night transport/escort service, controlled dormitory access. *Student Services:* health clinic, personal/psychological counseling, women's center.

Athletics Member NCAA. All Division III. *Intercollegiate sports:* basketball W, crew W, cross-country running W, fencing W, field hockey W, golf W, lacrosse W, rugby W(c), sailing W(c), skiing (downhill) W(c), soccer W, softball W(c), squash W, swimming W, tennis W, track and field W(c), volleyball W. *Intramural sports:* archery W, badminton W, basketball W, crew W, cross-country running W, equestrian sports W, ice hockey W, racquetball W, sailing W(c), skiing (cross-country) W, soccer W, squash W, swimming W, table tennis W, tennis W, volleyball W, water polo W, weight lifting W.

Costs (2001–02) *Comprehensive fee:* $33,394 includes full-time tuition ($25,022), mandatory fees ($482), and room and board ($7890). *Room and board:* College room only: $3996. Room and board charges vary according to board plan. *Payment plans:* tuition prepayment, installment. *Waivers:* employees or children of employees.

Financial Aid Of all full-time matriculated undergraduates who enrolled in 2001, 1383 applied for aid, 1179 were judged to have need, 1179 had their need fully met. 821 Federal Work-Study jobs, 201 State and other part-time jobs (averaging $1128). *Average percent of need met:* 100%. *Average financial aid package:* $20,891. *Average need-based loan:* $3129. *Average need-based gift aid:* $18,435. *Average indebtedness upon graduation:* $15,467.

Applying *Options:* common application, early admission, early decision, deferred entrance. *Application fee:* $50. *Required:* essay or personal statement, high school transcript, 3 letters of recommendation. *Required for some:* interview. *Recommended:* interview. *Application deadlines:* 1/15 (freshmen), 2/10 (transfers). *Early decision:* 11/1. *Notification:* 4/1 (freshmen), 12/15 (early decision).

Admissions Contact Ms. Janet Lavin Rapelye, Dean of Admission, Wellesley College, 106 Central Street, Wellesley, MA 02481-8203. *Phone:* 781-283-2270. *Fax:* 781-283-3678. *E-mail:* admission@wellesley.edu.

WENTWORTH INSTITUTE OF TECHNOLOGY
Boston, Massachusetts

- **Independent** 4-year, founded 1904
- **Calendar** semesters for freshmen and sophomores, trimesters for juniors and seniors
- **Degrees** certificates, associate, and bachelor's
- **Urban** 35-acre campus
- **Endowment** $74.8 million
- **Coed,** 3,273 undergraduate students, 77% full-time, 18% women, 82% men
- **Moderately difficult** entrance level, 70% of applicants were admitted

Founded in 1904, Wentworth Institute of Technology offers bachelor's degrees in architecture, computer science, design, engineering, engineering technology, and management of technology. Wentworth provides an education that balances classroom theory with laboratory/studio practice and work experience through its strong co-op program. Approximately 3,000 students attend this private coeducational institution, located on a 35-acre campus on Huntington Avenue, across from Boston's Museum of Fine Arts.

Undergraduates 2,535 full-time, 738 part-time. 5% African American, 6% Asian American or Pacific Islander, 4% Hispanic American, 0.3% Native American, 6% international, 4% transferred in, 50% live on campus.

Freshmen *Admission:* 3,623 applied, 2,548 admitted, 1,064 enrolled. *Test scores:* SAT verbal scores over 500: 42%; SAT math scores over 500: 61%; SAT verbal scores over 600: 10%; SAT math scores over 600: 17%; SAT verbal scores over 700: 1%; SAT math scores over 700: 2%.

Faculty *Total:* 239, 48% full-time. *Student/faculty ratio:* 24:1.

Majors Aircraft mechanic/airframe; architectural engineering technology; architecture; aviation technology; biomedical technology; business administration;

Wentworth Institute of Technology (continued)
civil engineering technology; computer engineering technology; computer science; construction management; construction technology; electrical/electronic engineering technology; electrical engineering; engineering mechanics; engineering technology; environmental engineering; environmental technology; industrial design; industrial technology; interior design; mechanical engineering technology.

Academic Programs *Special study options:* academic remediation for entering students, accelerated degree program, advanced placement credit, cooperative education, English as a second language, freshman honors college, internships, off-campus study, part-time degree program, services for LD students, study abroad, summer session for credit. *ROTC:* Army (c), Air Force (c).

Library Wentworth Alumni Library with 77,000 titles, 500 serial subscriptions, an OPAC, a Web page.

Computers on Campus 400 computers available on campus for general student use. A campuswide network can be accessed from student residence rooms and from off campus. At least one staffed computer lab available.

Student Life *Housing Options:* coed. *Activities and Organizations:* drama/theater group, student-run newspaper, radio station, intramural sports, Wentworth Events Board, Asian Students Association, ski and adventure club. *Campus security:* 24-hour emergency response devices and patrols, student patrols, late-night transport/escort service, controlled dormitory access. *Student Services:* health clinic, personal/psychological counseling, women's center.

Athletics Member NCAA. All Division III. *Intercollegiate sports:* baseball M, basketball M/W, golf M/W, ice hockey M, lacrosse M, riflery M/W, rugby M(c), soccer M/W, softball W, tennis M/W, volleyball M/W. *Intramural sports:* archery M/W, badminton M/W, baseball M, basketball M/W, cross-country running M/W, golf M, ice hockey M, lacrosse M, riflery M/W, rugby M, skiing (downhill) M(c)/W(c), soccer M/W, softball W, tennis M/W, volleyball M/W, weight lifting M(c)/W(c).

Standardized Tests *Required:* SAT I or ACT (for admission).

Costs (2001–02) *Comprehensive fee:* $21,050 includes full-time tuition ($13,650) and room and board ($7400). Part-time tuition: $425 per credit. Part-time tuition and fees vary according to class time. *Room and board:* College room only: $5600. Room and board charges vary according to board plan and housing facility. *Payment plan:* installment. *Waivers:* employees or children of employees.

Financial Aid Of all full-time matriculated undergraduates who enrolled in 2001, 2276 applied for aid, 2011 were judged to have need, 56 had their need fully met. *Average percent of need met:* 65%. *Average financial aid package:* $8146. *Average need-based loan:* $4957. *Average need-based gift aid:* $1814. *Average indebtedness upon graduation:* $6139.

Applying *Options:* common application, electronic application, deferred entrance. *Application fee:* $30. *Required:* high school transcript. *Recommended:* essay or personal statement, minimum 2.0 GPA, letters of recommendation, interview. *Application deadline:* rolling (freshmen), rolling (transfers). *Notification:* continuous (freshmen).

Admissions Contact Ms. Keiko S. Broomhead, Director of Admissions, Wentworth Institute of Technology, 550 Huntington Avenue, Boston, MA 02115-5998. *Phone:* 617-989-4009. *Toll-free phone:* 800-556-0610. *Fax:* 617-989-4010. *E-mail:* admissions@wit.edu.

WESTERN NEW ENGLAND COLLEGE
Springfield, Massachusetts

- **Independent** comprehensive, founded 1919
- **Calendar** semesters
- **Degrees** associate, bachelor's, master's, and first professional
- **Suburban** 185-acre campus
- **Endowment** $34.7 million
- **Coed,** 3,091 undergraduate students, 67% full-time, 36% women, 64% men
- **Moderately difficult** entrance level, 74% of applicants were admitted

Undergraduates 2,060 full-time, 1,031 part-time. Students come from 27 states and territories, 14 other countries, 56% are from out of state, 3% transferred in, 79% live on campus. *Retention:* 74% of 2001 full-time freshmen returned.

Freshmen *Admission:* 4,068 applied, 3,029 admitted, 740 enrolled. *Average high school GPA:* 3.06. *Test scores:* SAT verbal scores over 500: 57%; SAT math scores over 500: 67%; SAT verbal scores over 600: 12%; SAT math scores over 600: 20%; SAT verbal scores over 700: 1%; SAT math scores over 700: 2%.

Faculty *Total:* 351, 44% full-time, 38% with terminal degrees. *Student/faculty ratio:* 17:1.

Majors Accounting; advertising; bioengineering; biology; business administration; business marketing and marketing management; chemistry; communications; computer science; criminal justice/law enforcement administration; economics; electrical engineering; engineering; English; environmental science; finance; history; industrial/manufacturing engineering; information sciences/systems; international business; international relations; liberal arts and sciences/liberal studies; mathematics; mechanical engineering; political science; political science/government related; psychology; social work; sociology; sport/fitness administration.

Academic Programs *Special study options:* adult/continuing education programs, advanced placement credit, double majors, honors programs, independent study, internships, off-campus study, part-time degree program, services for LD students, student-designed majors, study abroad, summer session for credit. *ROTC:* Army (b), Air Force (b).

Library D'Amour Library plus 1 other with 118,364 titles, 2,260 serial subscriptions, 2,989 audiovisual materials, an OPAC, a Web page.

Computers on Campus 250 computers available on campus for general student use. A campuswide network can be accessed from student residence rooms and from off campus. Internet access, at least one staffed computer lab available.

Student Life *Housing Options:* coed, men-only, women-only. *Activities and Organizations:* drama/theater group, student-run newspaper, radio station, choral group, Student Senate, Residence Hall Association, Campus Activities Board, student radio station, Management Association. *Campus security:* 24-hour emergency response devices and patrols, student patrols, late-night transport/escort service, controlled dormitory access, security cameras. *Student Services:* health clinic, personal/psychological counseling.

Athletics Member NCAA. All Division III. *Intercollegiate sports:* baseball M, basketball M/W, bowling M/W, cross-country running M/W, field hockey W, football M, golf M, ice hockey M, lacrosse M/W, soccer M/W, softball W, swimming W, tennis M/W, volleyball W, wrestling M. *Intramural sports:* basketball M/W, football M, racquetball M/W, softball M/W, squash M/W, tennis M/W, volleyball M/W.

Standardized Tests *Required:* SAT I or ACT (for admission).

Costs (2001–02) *Comprehensive fee:* $23,882 includes full-time tuition ($15,244), mandatory fees ($1250), and room and board ($7388). Full-time tuition and fees vary according to program. Part-time tuition: $356 per semester hour. Part-time tuition and fees vary according to program. *Required fees:* $10 per semester hour, $20 per term part-time. *Room and board:* Room and board charges vary according to board plan and housing facility. *Payment plans:* tuition prepayment, installment, deferred payment. *Waivers:* senior citizens and employees or children of employees.

Financial Aid Of all full-time matriculated undergraduates who enrolled in 2001, 1553 applied for aid, 1359 were judged to have need, 170 had their need fully met. In 2001, 106 non-need-based awards were made. *Average percent of need met:* 69%. *Average financial aid package:* $10,000. *Average need-based loan:* $2507. *Average need-based gift aid:* $4265. *Average non-need based aid:* $4268. *Average indebtedness upon graduation:* $17,552.

Applying *Options:* common application, electronic application. *Application fee:* $30. *Required:* high school transcript, minimum 2.2 GPA, 1 letter of recommendation. *Recommended:* essay or personal statement, interview. *Application deadline:* rolling (freshmen), rolling (transfers). *Notification:* continuous (freshmen).

Admissions Contact Dr. Charles R. Pollock, Vice President of Enrollment Management, Western New England College, 1215 Wilbraham Road, Springfield, MA 01119. *Phone:* 413-782-1321. *Toll-free phone:* 800-325-1122 Ext. 1321. *Fax:* 413-782-1777. *E-mail:* ugradmis@wnec.edu.

WESTFIELD STATE COLLEGE
Westfield, Massachusetts

- **State-supported** comprehensive, founded 1838, part of Massachusetts Public Higher Education System
- **Calendar** semesters
- **Degrees** bachelor's, master's, post-master's, and postbachelor's certificates
- **Small-town** 227-acre campus
- **Endowment** $3.5 million
- **Coed,** 4,378 undergraduate students, 83% full-time, 56% women, 44% men
- **Moderately difficult** entrance level, 67% of applicants were admitted

Undergraduates 3,628 full-time, 750 part-time. Students come from 14 states and territories, 1 other country, 8% are from out of state, 3% African American, 0.8% Asian American or Pacific Islander, 2% Hispanic American, 0.2% Native American, 0.1% international, 5% transferred in, 59% live on campus. *Retention:* 74% of 2001 full-time freshmen returned.

Freshmen *Admission:* 3,528 applied, 2,354 admitted, 968 enrolled. *Average high school GPA:* 2.96. *Test scores:* SAT verbal scores over 500: 58%; SAT math scores over 500: 57%; SAT verbal scores over 600: 12%; SAT math scores over 600: 11%.

Faculty *Total:* 262, 65% full-time, 57% with terminal degrees. *Student/faculty ratio:* 18:1.

Majors Accounting; art; art education; biology; business administration; business education; business marketing and marketing management; city/community/regional planning; computer science; corrections; counselor education/guidance; criminal justice/law enforcement administration; early childhood education; economics; education; elementary education; English; environmental biology; finance; geography; graphic design/commercial art/illustration; history; information sciences/systems; jazz; liberal arts and sciences/liberal studies; literature; management information systems/business data processing; mass communications; mathematics; medical technology; music; music business management/merchandising; music history; music teacher education; music (voice and choral/opera performance); physical education; physical sciences; political science; pre-law; pre-medicine; psychology; radio/television broadcasting; reading education; recreation/leisure studies; science education; secondary education; social sciences; sociology; special education.

Academic Programs *Special study options:* accelerated degree program, adult/continuing education programs, advanced placement credit, cooperative education, distance learning, double majors, honors programs, independent study, internships, off-campus study, part-time degree program, services for LD students, student-designed majors, study abroad, summer session for credit. *ROTC:* Army (c).

Library Ely Library with 124,363 titles, 819 serial subscriptions, 2,379 audiovisual materials, an OPAC, a Web page.

Computers on Campus 230 computers available on campus for general student use. A campuswide network can be accessed from student residence rooms and from off campus. Internet access, at least one staffed computer lab available.

Student Life *Housing Options:* coed, disabled students. *Activities and Organizations:* drama/theater group, student-run newspaper, radio and television station, choral group. *Campus security:* 24-hour emergency response devices and patrols, student patrols, late-night transport/escort service. *Student Services:* health clinic, personal/psychological counseling, legal services.

Athletics Member NCAA. All Division III. *Intercollegiate sports:* baseball M, basketball M/W, cross-country running M/W, field hockey W, football M, soccer M/W, softball W, swimming W, track and field M/W, volleyball W. *Intramural sports:* baseball M, basketball M/W, bowling M/W, cross-country running M/W, football M/W, golf M/W, ice hockey M/W, racquetball M/W, soccer M/W, softball M/W, swimming M/W, tennis M/W, track and field M/W, volleyball M/W, water polo M/W.

Standardized Tests *Required:* SAT I (for admission).

Costs (2001–02) *Tuition:* state resident $970 full-time, $145 per credit part-time; nonresident $7050 full-time, $155 per credit part-time. Full-time tuition and fees vary according to reciprocity agreements and student level. Part-time tuition and fees vary according to course load. *Required fees:* $1986 full-time. *Room and board:* $4789; room only: $2963. Room and board charges vary according to board plan and housing facility. *Payment plan:* installment. *Waivers:* senior citizens and employees or children of employees.

Financial Aid Of all full-time matriculated undergraduates who enrolled in 2001, 2416 applied for aid, 1468 were judged to have need, 642 had their need fully met. In 2001, 944 non-need-based awards were made. *Average percent of need met:* 82%. *Average financial aid package:* $4935. *Average need-based loan:* $2193. *Average need-based gift aid:* $3756.

Applying *Options:* deferred entrance. *Application fee:* $40 (non-residents). *Required:* high school transcript, minimum 2.0 GPA. *Recommended:* letters of recommendation. *Application deadlines:* 3/1 (freshmen), 4/1 (transfers). *Notification:* continuous (freshmen).

Admissions Contact Ms. Michelle Mattie, Director of Student Administrative Services, Westfield State College, 333 Western Avenue. *Phone:* 413-572-5218. *Toll-free phone:* 800-322-8401. *Fax:* 413-572-0520. *E-mail:* admission@wsc.mass.edu.

WHEATON COLLEGE
Norton, Massachusetts

- **Independent** 4-year, founded 1834
- **Calendar** semesters
- **Degree** bachelor's
- **Small-town** 385-acre campus with easy access to Boston
- **Endowment** $150.6 million
- **Coed,** 1,551 undergraduate students, 99% full-time, 65% women, 35% men
- **Moderately difficult** entrance level, 61% of applicants were admitted

Undergraduates 1,532 full-time, 19 part-time. Students come from 43 states and territories, 26 other countries, 65% are from out of state, 3% African American, 2% Asian American or Pacific Islander, 3% Hispanic American, 0.3% Native American, 3% international, 0.5% transferred in, 98% live on campus. *Retention:* 80% of 2001 full-time freshmen returned.

Freshmen *Admission:* 3,249 applied, 1,974 admitted, 494 enrolled. *Average high school GPA:* 3.40. *Test scores:* SAT verbal scores over 500: 95%; SAT math scores over 500: 94%; SAT verbal scores over 600: 61%; SAT math scores over 600: 49%; SAT verbal scores over 700: 10%; SAT math scores over 700: 4%.

Faculty *Total:* 150, 80% full-time, 84% with terminal degrees. *Student/faculty ratio:* 12:1.

Majors American studies; anthropology; art; art history; Asian studies; astronomy; biochemistry; biology; chemistry; classics; computer science; economics; English; environmental science; fine/studio arts; French; German; Hispanic-American studies; history; interdisciplinary studies; international relations; literature; mathematics; music; philosophy; physics; physiological psychology/psychobiology; political science; pre-medicine; psychology; religious studies; Russian; Russian/Slavic studies; sociology; theater arts/drama; women's studies.

Academic Programs *Special study options:* academic remediation for entering students, accelerated degree program, adult/continuing education programs, advanced placement credit, double majors, honors programs, independent study, internships, off-campus study, part-time degree program, student-designed majors, study abroad. *ROTC:* Army (c). *Unusual degree programs:* 3-2 business administration with University of Rochester, Clark University; engineering with Dartmouth College, George Washington University, Worcester Polytechnic Institute; theology with Andover Newton Theological School, optometry with New England College of Optometry, communications with Emerson College, studio art with School of the Museum of Fine Arts.

Library Madeleine Clark Wallace Library plus 1 other with 381,749 titles, 2,781 serial subscriptions, 9,103 audiovisual materials, an OPAC, a Web page.

Computers on Campus 157 computers available on campus for general student use. A campuswide network can be accessed from student residence rooms and from off campus. Internet access, online (class) registration, at least one staffed computer lab available.

Student Life *Housing:* on-campus residence required through senior year. *Options:* coed, men-only, women-only. *Activities and Organizations:* drama/theater group, student-run newspaper, radio station, choral group, Student Government Association, Community Service Network, Amnesty International, a cappella singing groups, Programming Council. *Campus security:* 24-hour emergency response devices and patrols, student patrols, late-night transport/escort service, controlled dormitory access. *Student Services:* health clinic, personal/psychological counseling, women's center.

Athletics Member NCAA. All Division III. *Intercollegiate sports:* baseball M, basketball M/W, cross-country running M/W, field hockey W, lacrosse M/W, soccer M/W, softball W, swimming M/W, tennis M/W, track and field M/W, volleyball W. *Intramural sports:* archery M/W, badminton M/W, basketball M/W, cross-country running M/W, equestrian sports M(c)/W(c), fencing M/W, field hockey W, golf M/W, ice hockey M(c)/W(c), lacrosse M/W, rugby M(c), sailing M(c)/W(c), skiing (cross-country) M/W, skiing (downhill) M(c)/W(c), soccer M/W, table tennis M/W, tennis M/W, track and field W(c), volleyball M/W, water polo M/W, weight lifting M/W.

Costs (2001–02) *Comprehensive fee:* $32,940 includes full-time tuition ($25,565), mandatory fees ($225), and room and board ($7150). Part-time tuition: $3196 per course. *Room and board:* College room only: $3770. *Payment plans:* tuition prepayment, installment, deferred payment. *Waivers:* employees or children of employees.

Financial Aid Of all full-time matriculated undergraduates who enrolled in 2001, 981 applied for aid, 892 were judged to have need, 478 had their need fully met. 773 Federal Work-Study jobs (averaging $1731). 208 State and other part-time jobs (averaging $2104). In 2001, 157 non-need-based awards were made. *Average percent of need met:* 95%. *Average financial aid package:* $19,408. *Average need-based loan:* $4623. *Average need-based gift aid:* $14,252. *Average non-need based aid:* $6749. *Average indebtedness upon graduation:* $16,903. *Financial aid deadline:* 1/15.

Applying *Options:* common application, electronic application, early admission, early decision, deferred entrance. *Application fee:* $50. *Required:* essay or personal statement, high school transcript, 2 letters of recommendation. *Recommended:* interview. *Application deadlines:* 1/15 (freshmen), 4/1 (transfers). *Early decision:* 11/15 (for plan 1), 1/15 (for plan 2). *Notification:* 4/1 (freshmen), 12/15 (early decision plan 1), 2/15 (early decision plan 2).

Wheaton College (continued)

Admissions Contact Ms. Lynne M. Stack, Director of Admission, Wheaton College, Norton, MA 02766. *Phone:* 508-286-8251. *Toll-free phone:* 800-394-6003. *Fax:* 508-286-8271. *E-mail:* admission@wheatoncollege.edu.

WHEELOCK COLLEGE
Boston, Massachusetts

- **Independent** comprehensive, founded 1888
- **Calendar** semesters
- **Degrees** bachelor's and master's
- **Urban** 5-acre campus
- **Endowment** $39.4 million
- **Coed, primarily women,** 616 undergraduate students, 99% full-time, 94% women, 6% men
- **Moderately difficult** entrance level, 81% of applicants were admitted

Undergraduates 608 full-time, 8 part-time. Students come from 20 states and territories, 46% are from out of state, 5% African American, 2% Asian American or Pacific Islander, 4% Hispanic American, 0.7% Native American, 0.7% international, 8% transferred in, 70% live on campus. *Retention:* 82% of 2001 full-time freshmen returned.

Freshmen *Admission:* 447 applied, 361 admitted, 155 enrolled. *Average high school GPA:* 2.80. *Test scores:* SAT verbal scores over 500: 62%; SAT math scores over 500: 52%; SAT verbal scores over 600: 15%; SAT math scores over 600: 15%; SAT math scores over 700: 1%.

Faculty *Total:* 221, 29% full-time, 37% with terminal degrees. *Student/faculty ratio:* 11:1.

Majors Child care/development; early childhood education; education; elementary education; individual/family development; social work; special education.

Academic Programs *Special study options:* academic remediation for entering students, advanced placement credit, double majors, honors programs, independent study, internships, off-campus study, part-time degree program, services for LD students.

Library Wheelock College Library with 96,500 titles, 546 serial subscriptions, an OPAC, a Web page.

Computers on Campus 120 computers available on campus for general student use. A campuswide network can be accessed from student residence rooms and from off campus. Internet access, at least one staffed computer lab available.

Student Life *Housing Options:* coed, women-only, cooperative. *Activities and Organizations:* drama/theater group, choral group, Student Government Association, theatre club, AHANA Club, residence hall councils, class councils. *Campus security:* 24-hour patrols, late-night transport/escort service, controlled dormitory access, self-defense education. *Student Services:* health clinic, personal/psychological counseling, women's center.

Athletics Member NCAA. All Division III. *Intercollegiate sports:* basketball W, cross-country running W, field hockey W, softball W, swimming W. *Intramural sports:* basketball M/W, ice hockey M/W, racquetball M/W, soccer M/W, softball M/W, squash M/W, volleyball M/W, weight lifting M/W.

Standardized Tests *Required:* SAT I or ACT (for admission).

Costs (2001–02) *Comprehensive fee:* $25,520 includes full-time tuition ($18,195) and room and board ($7325). Part-time tuition: $575 per credit. *Payment plan:* installment. *Waivers:* employees or children of employees.

Financial Aid Of all full-time matriculated undergraduates who enrolled in 2001, 488 applied for aid, 440 were judged to have need, 72 had their need fully met. 156 Federal Work-Study jobs (averaging $980). In 2001, 83 non-need-based awards were made. *Average percent of need met:* 77%. *Average financial aid package:* $14,343. *Average need-based loan:* $4664. *Average need-based gift aid:* $9632. *Average indebtedness upon graduation:* $19,445.

Applying *Options:* common application, electronic application, early decision, deferred entrance. *Application fee:* $30. *Required:* essay or personal statement, high school transcript, 2 letters of recommendation. *Recommended:* minimum 2.0 GPA, interview. *Application deadlines:* 3/1 (freshmen), 4/15 (transfers). *Early decision:* 12/1. *Notification:* continuous until 4/15 (freshmen), 1/1 (early decision).

Admissions Contact Ms. Lynne E. Dailey, Dean of Admissions, Wheelock College, 200 The Riverway, Boston, MA 02215. *Phone:* 617-879-2204. *Toll-free phone:* 800-734-5212. *Fax:* 617-566-4453. *E-mail:* undergrad@wheelock.edu.

WILLIAMS COLLEGE
Williamstown, Massachusetts

- **Independent** comprehensive, founded 1793
- **Calendar** 4-1-4
- **Degrees** bachelor's and master's
- **Small-town** 450-acre campus with easy access to Albany
- **Endowment** $980.2 million
- **Coed,** 1,997 undergraduate students, 98% full-time, 48% women, 52% men
- **Most difficult** entrance level, 24% of applicants were admitted

Undergraduates 1,959 full-time, 38 part-time. Students come from 51 states and territories, 32 other countries, 85% are from out of state, 7% African American, 8% Asian American or Pacific Islander, 7% Hispanic American, 0.4% Native American, 5% international, 0.5% transferred in, 96% live on campus. *Retention:* 97% of 2001 full-time freshmen returned.

Freshmen *Admission:* 4,656 applied, 1,130 admitted, 520 enrolled. *Test scores:* SAT verbal scores over 500: 100%; SAT math scores over 500: 99%; SAT verbal scores over 600: 92%; SAT math scores over 600: 92%; SAT verbal scores over 700: 59%; SAT math scores over 700: 58%.

Faculty *Total:* 250, 92% full-time, 94% with terminal degrees. *Student/faculty ratio:* 9:1.

Majors American studies; anthropology; art history; Asian studies; astronomy; astrophysics; biology; chemistry; Chinese; classics; computer science; economics; English; fine/studio arts; French; geology; German; history; Japanese; literature; mathematics; music; philosophy; physics; political science; psychology; religious studies; Russian; sociology; Spanish; theater arts/drama.

Academic Programs *Special study options:* accelerated degree program, advanced placement credit, double majors, honors programs, independent study, internships, off-campus study, services for LD students, student-designed majors, study abroad. *Unusual degree programs:* 3-2 engineering with Columbia University, Washington University in St. Louis.

Library Sawyer Library plus 9 others with 420,144 titles, 2,853 serial subscriptions, 31,569 audiovisual materials, an OPAC, a Web page.

Computers on Campus 150 computers available on campus for general student use. A campuswide network can be accessed from student residence rooms and from off campus. At least one staffed computer lab available.

Student Life *Housing:* on-campus residence required through senior year. *Options:* coed. *Activities and Organizations:* drama/theater group, student-run newspaper, radio station, choral group, marching band. *Campus security:* 24-hour emergency response devices and patrols, student patrols, late-night transport/escort service, controlled dormitory access. *Student Services:* health clinic, personal/psychological counseling, women's center.

Athletics Member NCAA. All Division III except men's and women's skiing (cross-country) (Division I), men's and women's skiing (downhill) (Division I). *Intercollegiate sports:* baseball M, basketball M/W, crew M/W, cross-country running M/W, equestrian sports M(c)/W(c), field hockey W, football M, golf M/W(c), ice hockey M/W, lacrosse M/W, rugby M(c)/W(c), sailing M(c)/W(c), skiing (cross-country) M/W, skiing (downhill) M/W, soccer M/W, softball W, squash M/W, swimming M/W, tennis M/W, track and field M/W, volleyball M(c)/W, water polo M(c)/W(c), wrestling M. *Intramural sports:* badminton M/W, baseball M(c), basketball M/W, fencing M(c)/W(c), ice hockey M/W, skiing (cross-country) M/W, skiing (downhill) M/W, soccer M/W, softball M/W, volleyball M/W, water polo M/W.

Costs (2001–02) *Comprehensive fee:* $32,470 includes full-time tuition ($25,352), mandatory fees ($188), and room and board ($6930). *Room and board:* College room only: $3440. Room and board charges vary according to board plan. *Payment plan:* installment. *Waivers:* employees or children of employees.

Financial Aid Of all full-time matriculated undergraduates who enrolled in 2001, 888 applied for aid, 825 were judged to have need, 825 had their need fully met. 376 Federal Work-Study jobs (averaging $1593). 325 State and other part-time jobs (averaging $1645). *Average percent of need met:* 100%. *Average financial aid package:* $23,215. *Average need-based loan:* $2848. *Average need-based gift aid:* $20,355. *Average indebtedness upon graduation:* $15,520. *Financial aid deadline:* 2/1.

Applying *Options:* common application, electronic application, early admission, early decision, deferred entrance. *Application fee:* $50. *Required:* essay or personal statement, high school transcript, 2 letters of recommendation. *Application deadlines:* 1/1 (freshmen), 3/1 (transfers). *Early decision:* 11/15. *Notification:* 4/8 (freshmen), 12/15 (early decision).

Admissions Contact Mr. Richard L. Nesbitt, Director of Admission, Williams College, 988 Main Street, Williamstown, MA 01267. *Phone:* 413-597-2211. *Fax:* 413-597-4052. *E-mail:* admission@williams.edu.

WORCESTER POLYTECHNIC INSTITUTE
Worcester, Massachusetts

- **Independent** university, founded 1865
- **Calendar** 4 7-week terms

- **Degrees** bachelor's, master's, and doctoral
- **Suburban** 80-acre campus with easy access to Boston
- **Endowment** $213.3 million
- **Coed,** 2,823 undergraduate students, 96% full-time, 23% women, 77% men
- **Very difficult** entrance level, 74% of applicants were admitted

Undergraduates 2,715 full-time, 108 part-time. Students come from 51 states and territories, 40 other countries, 1% African American, 7% Asian American or Pacific Islander, 3% Hispanic American, 0.3% Native American, 5% international, 3% transferred in, 50% live on campus. *Retention:* 92% of 2001 full-time freshmen returned.

Freshmen *Admission:* 3,316 applied, 2,460 admitted, 700 enrolled. *Test scores:* SAT verbal scores over 500: 93%; SAT math scores over 500: 100%; SAT verbal scores over 600: 58%; SAT math scores over 600: 83%; SAT verbal scores over 700: 13%; SAT math scores over 700: 29%.

Faculty *Total:* 341, 68% full-time, 64% with terminal degrees. *Student/faculty ratio:* 13:1.

Majors Actuarial science; aerospace engineering; applied mathematics; biochemistry; bioengineering; biological technology; biology; biomedical science; business administration; cell biology; chemical engineering; chemistry; civil engineering; computer engineering; computer/information sciences; computer science; economics; electrical engineering; engineering design; engineering/industrial management; engineering mechanics; engineering physics; environmental engineering; environmental science; fluid/thermal sciences; genetics; history; history of science and technology; humanities; industrial/manufacturing engineering; information sciences/systems; interdisciplinary studies; management information systems/business data processing; materials engineering; materials science; mathematics; mechanical engineering; medicinal/pharmaceutical chemistry; metallurgy; microbiology/bacteriology; molecular biology; music; nuclear engineering; philosophy; physics; science/technology and society; social sciences; technical/business writing.

Academic Programs *Special study options:* accelerated degree program, adult/continuing education programs, advanced placement credit, cooperative education, double majors, English as a second language, independent study, off-campus study, part-time degree program, services for LD students, student-designed majors, study abroad, summer session for credit. *ROTC:* Army (b), Navy (c), Air Force (b).

Library Gordon Library with 170,000 titles, 1,400 serial subscriptions, an OPAC, a Web page.

Computers on Campus 1000 computers available on campus for general student use. A campuswide network can be accessed from student residence rooms and from off campus. Internet access, online (class) registration, at least one staffed computer lab available.

Student Life *Housing Options:* coed, men-only. *Activities and Organizations:* drama/theater group, student-run newspaper, radio station, choral group, student government, Masque (Drama Group), music groups, intramural sports, ethnic clubs, national fraternities, national sororities. *Campus security:* 24-hour emergency response devices and patrols, student patrols, late-night transport/escort service. *Student Services:* health clinic, personal/psychological counseling, women's center.

Athletics Member NCAA. All Division III. *Intercollegiate sports:* baseball M, basketball M/W, bowling M(c)/W(c), crew M(c)/W(c), cross-country running M/W, fencing M(c)/W(c), field hockey W, football M, golf M, ice hockey M(c), lacrosse M(c)/W(c), rugby M(c)/W(c), sailing M(c)/W(c), skiing (downhill) M(c)/W(c), soccer M/W, softball W, swimming M/W, tennis M/W, track and field M/W, volleyball M(c)/W, water polo M(c)/W(c), wrestling M. *Intramural sports:* basketball M/W, bowling M/W, cross-country running M/W, football M, golf M/W, ice hockey M, soccer M/W, softball M/W, swimming M/W, table tennis M/W, track and field M/W, volleyball M/W, wrestling M.

Costs (2001–02) *Comprehensive fee:* $32,790 includes full-time tuition ($24,740), mandatory fees ($150), and room and board ($7900). Part-time tuition: $2062 per course. *Room and board:* College room only: $4530. Room and board charges vary according to board plan and housing facility. *Waivers:* employees or children of employees.

Financial Aid Of all full-time matriculated undergraduates who enrolled in 2001, 1932 applied for aid, 1815 were judged to have need, 910 had their need fully met. 688 Federal Work-Study jobs. In 2001, 153 non-need-based awards were made. *Average percent of need met:* 83%. *Average financial aid package:* $22,375. *Average need-based loan:* $6993. *Average need-based gift aid:* $11,924. *Average non-need based aid:* $10,036. *Average indebtedness upon graduation:* $17,500.

Applying *Options:* common application, electronic application, early admission, early decision, early action, deferred entrance. *Application fee:* $60. *Required:* essay or personal statement, high school transcript, 1 letter of recommendation. *Recommended:* interview. *Application deadlines:* 2/1 (freshmen), 4/15 (transfers). *Early decision:* 11/15 (for plan 1), 12/15 (for plan 2). *Notification:* 4/1 (freshmen), 12/15 (early decision plan 1), 1/15 (early decision plan 2), 12/15 (early action).

Admissions Contact Ms. Kristin Tichenor, Director of Admissions, Worcester Polytechnic Institute, 100 Institute Road, Worcester, MA 01609-2280. *Phone:* 508-831-5286. *Fax:* 508-831-5875. *E-mail:* admissions@wpi.edu.

WORCESTER STATE COLLEGE

Worcester, Massachusetts

- **State-supported** comprehensive, founded 1874, part of Massachusetts Public Higher Education System
- **Calendar** semesters
- **Degrees** bachelor's and master's
- **Urban** 53-acre campus with easy access to Boston
- **Endowment** $6.3 million
- **Coed,** 4,915 undergraduate students, 63% full-time, 62% women, 38% men
- **Moderately difficult** entrance level, 54% of applicants were admitted

Undergraduates 3,108 full-time, 1,807 part-time. Students come from 20 states and territories, 84 other countries, 4% are from out of state, 8% transferred in, 16% live on campus. *Retention:* 75% of 2001 full-time freshmen returned.

Freshmen *Admission:* 2,987 applied, 1,613 admitted, 578 enrolled. *Average high school GPA:* 2.83. *Test scores:* SAT verbal scores over 500: 51%; SAT math scores over 500: 48%; ACT scores over 18: 80%; SAT verbal scores over 600: 8%; SAT math scores over 600: 8%; ACT scores over 24: 19%; SAT verbal scores over 700: 1%; SAT math scores over 700: 1%.

Faculty *Total:* 258, 65% full-time. *Student/faculty ratio:* 19:1.

Majors Accounting; biological/physical sciences; biological technology; biology; business administration; business marketing and marketing management; chemistry; community health liaison; computer science; early childhood education; economics; elementary education; English; geography; health facilities administration; health services administration; history; human resources management; mass communications; mathematics; natural sciences; nonprofit/public management; nursing; occupational therapy; operations management; psychology; public health education/promotion; sociology; Spanish; speech-language pathology/audiology; urban studies.

Academic Programs *Special study options:* accelerated degree program, adult/continuing education programs, advanced placement credit, double majors, honors programs, independent study, internships, off-campus study, part-time degree program, study abroad, summer session for credit. *ROTC:* Army (c), Navy (c), Air Force (c).

Library Learning Resources Center with 1,137 serial subscriptions, 11,963 audiovisual materials, an OPAC, a Web page.

Computers on Campus 250 computers available on campus for general student use. A campuswide network can be accessed from student residence rooms. Internet access, at least one staffed computer lab available.

Student Life *Housing Options:* men-only, women-only, disabled students. *Activities and Organizations:* drama/theater group, student-run newspaper, radio and television station, choral group, Third World Alliance, ski club, Program Council, pep club. *Campus security:* 24-hour emergency response devices and patrols, late-night transport/escort service, controlled dormitory access, well-lit campus, limited access to campus at night. *Student Services:* personal/psychological counseling, women's center.

Athletics Member NCAA, NAIA. All NCAA Division III. *Intercollegiate sports:* baseball M, basketball M/W, crew M(c)/W(c), cross-country running M/W, equestrian sports W(c), field hockey W, football M, golf M, ice hockey M, rugby M(c), soccer M/W, softball W, tennis M/W, track and field M/W, volleyball W. *Intramural sports:* baseball M, basketball M/W, crew M/W, cross-country running M/W, equestrian sports W, field hockey W, football M, golf M, ice hockey M, rugby M, soccer M/W, softball W, tennis M/W, track and field M/W, volleyball W.

Standardized Tests *Required for some:* SAT I or ACT (for admission).

Costs (2001–02) *Tuition:* state resident $970 full-time, $40 per credit hour part-time; nonresident $7050 full-time, $294 per credit hour part-time. Full-time tuition and fees vary according to reciprocity agreements. Part-time tuition and fees vary according to reciprocity agreements. *Required fees:* $1460 full-time, $68 per credit hour. *Room and board:* $5186; room only: $3226. Room and board charges vary according to board plan and housing facility. *Payment plan:* deferred payment. *Waivers:* senior citizens and employees or children of employees.

Applying *Options:* electronic application, early admission, deferred entrance. *Application fee:* $40 (non-residents). *Required:* high school transcript, minimum 2.9 GPA. *Application deadlines:* 8/1 (freshmen), 8/1 (transfers). *Notification:* continuous (freshmen).

Worcester State College (continued)

Admissions Contact Ms. Elizabeth Axelson, Associate Director, Admissions, Worcester State College, 486 Chandler Street, Administration Building, Room 204, Worcester, MA 01602-2597. *Phone:* 508-929-8040. *Fax:* 508-929-8131. *E-mail:* admissions@worcester.edu.

MICHIGAN

ADRIAN COLLEGE
Adrian, Michigan

- **Independent** 4-year, founded 1859, affiliated with United Methodist Church
- **Calendar** semesters
- **Degrees** associate and bachelor's
- **Small-town** 100-acre campus with easy access to Detroit and Toledo
- **Endowment** $37.8 million
- **Coed,** 1,055 undergraduate students, 95% full-time, 57% women, 43% men
- **Moderately difficult** entrance level, 90% of applicants were admitted

Adrian College offers more than 40 majors and programs that are complemented by a liberal arts core. Academic and cocurricular opportunities develop students' fullest potential. Students have free Internet and e-mail access, internships, and study-abroad options, and there is a 90% placement record for graduates.

Undergraduates 1,002 full-time, 53 part-time. Students come from 17 states and territories, 9 other countries, 5% African American, 0.9% Asian American or Pacific Islander, 1% Hispanic American, 0.1% Native American, 1% international, 4% transferred in, 75% live on campus. *Retention:* 86% of 2001 full-time freshmen returned.

Freshmen *Admission:* 1,215 applied, 1,096 admitted, 276 enrolled. *Average high school GPA:* 3.20. *Test scores:* ACT scores over 18: 87%; ACT scores over 24: 33%; ACT scores over 30: 1%.

Faculty *Total:* 108, 61% full-time, 58% with terminal degrees. *Student/faculty ratio:* 15:1.

Majors Accounting; art; art education; arts management; bilingual/bicultural education; biology; broadcast journalism; business administration; business education; chemistry; criminal justice/law enforcement administration; earth sciences; economics; education; education (K-12); elementary education; English; environmental science; exercise sciences; French; German; history; human services; interior design; international business; international relations; mass communications; mathematics; music; music teacher education; physical education; physics; political science; pre-medicine; pre-veterinary studies; psychology; religious studies; science education; secondary education; social sciences; social work; sociology; Spanish; theater arts/drama.

Academic Programs *Special study options:* academic remediation for entering students, adult/continuing education programs, advanced placement credit, cooperative education, double majors, English as a second language, honors programs, independent study, internships, off-campus study, part-time degree program, services for LD students, student-designed majors, study abroad, summer session for credit. *Unusual degree programs:* 3-2 engineering with University of Detroit Mercy, Washington University in St. Louis.

Library Shipman Library with 82,687 titles, 622 serial subscriptions, 956 audiovisual materials, an OPAC, a Web page.

Computers on Campus 100 computers available on campus for general student use. A campuswide network can be accessed from student residence rooms and from off campus. Internet access, at least one staffed computer lab available.

Student Life *Housing:* on-campus residence required through junior year. *Options:* coed, women-only. *Activities and Organizations:* drama/theater group, student-run newspaper, radio station, choral group, student government, volunteerism, Greek organizations, Adrian College Theatre, musical ensembles, national fraternities, national sororities. *Campus security:* 24-hour patrols, student patrols, late-night transport/escort service. *Student Services:* health clinic, personal/psychological counseling.

Athletics Member NCAA. All Division III. *Intercollegiate sports:* baseball M, basketball M/W, cross-country running M/W, football M, golf M/W, soccer M/W, softball W, tennis M/W, track and field M/W, volleyball W. *Intramural sports:* badminton M/W, basketball M/W, football M/W, golf M, racquetball M/W, soccer M/W, softball M/W, tennis M/W, volleyball M/W.

Standardized Tests *Required:* SAT I or ACT (for admission). *Recommended:* ACT (for admission).

Costs (2001–02) *Comprehensive fee:* $19,700 includes full-time tuition ($14,750), mandatory fees ($100), and room and board ($4850). Part-time tuition: $460 per semester hour. *Room and board:* College room only: $2200. Room and board charges vary according to board plan. *Payment plan:* installment. *Waivers:* employees or children of employees.

Financial Aid Of all full-time matriculated undergraduates who enrolled in 2001, 964 applied for aid, 732 were judged to have need, 610 had their need fully met. In 2001, 212 non-need-based awards were made. *Average percent of need met:* 99%. *Average financial aid package:* $13,811. *Average need-based loan:* $4081. *Average need-based gift aid:* $7946. *Average non-need based aid:* $7040. *Average indebtedness upon graduation:* $15,326.

Applying *Options:* common application, electronic application, deferred entrance. *Application fee:* $20. *Required:* high school transcript. *Required for some:* essay or personal statement. *Recommended:* interview. *Application deadlines:* 8/1 (freshmen), 8/1 (transfers). *Notification:* continuous (freshmen).

Admissions Contact Ms. Janel Sutkus, Director of Admissions, Adrian College, 110 South Madison Street, Adrian, MI 49221. *Phone:* 517-265-5161 Ext. 4326. *Toll-free phone:* 800-877-2246. *Fax:* 517-264-3331. *E-mail:* admissions@adrian.edu.

ALBION COLLEGE
Albion, Michigan

- **Independent Methodist** 4-year, founded 1835
- **Calendar** semesters
- **Degree** bachelor's
- **Small-town** 225-acre campus with easy access to Detroit
- **Endowment** $166.9 million
- **Coed,** 1,548 undergraduate students, 100% full-time, 56% women, 44% men
- **Moderately difficult** entrance level, 87% of applicants were admitted

Undergraduates 1,543 full-time, 5 part-time. Students come from 28 states and territories, 19 other countries, 11% are from out of state, 2% African American, 2% Asian American or Pacific Islander, 0.8% Hispanic American, 0.3% Native American, 1% international, 2% transferred in, 99% live on campus. *Retention:* 86% of 2001 full-time freshmen returned.

Freshmen *Admission:* 1,297 applied, 1,127 admitted, 451 enrolled. *Average high school GPA:* 3.50. *Test scores:* SAT verbal scores over 500: 85%; SAT math scores over 500: 82%; ACT scores over 18: 99%; SAT verbal scores over 600: 40%; SAT math scores over 600: 41%; ACT scores over 24: 62%; SAT verbal scores over 700: 6%; SAT math scores over 700: 9%; ACT scores over 30: 12%.

Faculty *Total:* 125, 97% full-time, 90% with terminal degrees. *Student/faculty ratio:* 12:1.

Majors American studies; anthropology; art; biology; business administration; chemistry; computer science; economics; education; elementary education; English; environmental science; French; geology; German; history; human services; international relations; mass communications; mathematics; modern languages; music; philosophy; physical education; physics; political science; pre-law; pre-medicine; pre-veterinary studies; psychology; public policy analysis; religious studies; secondary education; sociology; Spanish; theater arts/drama; women's studies.

Academic Programs *Special study options:* advanced placement credit, double majors, honors programs, independent study, internships, off-campus study, services for LD students, student-designed majors, study abroad, summer session for credit. *Unusual degree programs:* 3-2 engineering with Columbia University, University of Michigan, Case Western Reserve University, Michigan Technological University, Washington University in St. Louis; forestry with Duke University, Washington University in St. Louis; nursing with Case Western Reserve University; public policy studies with University of Michigan, fine arts with Bank Street College of Education.

Library Stockwell Mudd Libraries with 348,542 titles, 1,528 serial subscriptions, 5,539 audiovisual materials, an OPAC, a Web page.

Computers on Campus 257 computers available on campus for general student use. A campuswide network can be accessed from student residence rooms and from off campus. Internet access, at least one staffed computer lab available.

Student Life *Housing:* on-campus residence required through senior year. *Options:* coed, women-only, cooperative, disabled students. *Activities and Organizations:* drama/theater group, student-run newspaper, radio station, choral group, marching band, Alpha Phi Omega, Union Board, Inter Varsity Christian Fellowship, Student Senate, national fraternities, national sororities. *Campus security:* 24-hour emergency response devices and patrols, student patrols, late-night transport/escort service, controlled dormitory access. *Student Services:* health clinic, personal/psychological counseling, women's center.

Athletics Member NCAA. All Division III. *Intercollegiate sports:* baseball M, basketball M/W, cross-country running M/W, football M, golf M/W, soccer M/W, softball W, swimming M/W, tennis M/W, track and field M/W, volleyball M(c)/W. *Intramural sports:* badminton M/W, basketball M/W, bowling M/W, equestrian sports M/W, field hockey W, football M, golf M/W, ice hockey M(c), lacrosse M/W, rugby M(c)/W(c), sailing M(c)/W(c), soccer M/W, softball M/W, swimming M/W, table tennis M/W, tennis M/W, track and field M/W, volleyball M/W, water polo M(c)/W(c).

Costs (2001–02) *Comprehensive fee:* $25,224 includes full-time tuition ($19,390), mandatory fees ($230), and room and board ($5604). Part-time tuition: $825 per credit. *Room and board:* College room only: $2742. *Payment plan:* deferred payment. *Waivers:* children of alumni and senior citizens.

Financial Aid Of all full-time matriculated undergraduates who enrolled in 2001, 1072 applied for aid, 911 were judged to have need, 662 had their need fully met. 355 Federal Work-Study jobs (averaging $1235). In 2001, 521 non-need-based awards were made. *Average percent of need met:* 96%. *Average financial aid package:* $16,620. *Average need-based loan:* $3602. *Average need-based gift aid:* $13,452. *Average non-need based aid:* $8970. *Average indebtedness upon graduation:* $16,244.

Applying *Options:* common application, electronic application, early admission, early decision, early action, deferred entrance. *Application fee:* $20. *Required:* essay or personal statement, high school transcript, 1 letter of recommendation. *Required for some:* interview. *Recommended:* minimum 3.0 GPA. *Application deadline:* 5/1 (freshmen), rolling (transfers). *Early decision:* 11/15. *Notification:* continuous (freshmen), 12/15 (early decision), 1/15 (early action).

Admissions Contact Doug Kellar, Associate Vice President for Enrollment, Albion College, 611 East Porter Street, Albion, MI 49224. *Phone:* 517-629-0600. *Toll-free phone:* 800-858-6770. *E-mail:* admissions@albion.edu.

ALMA COLLEGE
Alma, Michigan

- **Independent Presbyterian** 4-year, founded 1886
- **Calendar** 4-4-1
- **Degree** bachelor's
- **Small-town** 100-acre campus
- **Endowment** $102.7 million
- **Coed,** 1,366 undergraduate students, 97% full-time, 59% women, 41% men
- **Moderately difficult** entrance level, 82% of applicants were admitted

Undergraduates 1,325 full-time, 41 part-time. Students come from 21 states and territories, 19 other countries, 3% are from out of state, 1% African American, 1% Asian American or Pacific Islander, 2% Hispanic American, 0.7% Native American, 1% international, 2% transferred in, 85% live on campus. *Retention:* 85% of 2001 full-time freshmen returned.

Freshmen *Admission:* 1,237 applied, 1,016 admitted, 308 enrolled. *Average high school GPA:* 3.50. *Test scores:* ACT scores over 18: 98%; ACT scores over 24: 59%; ACT scores over 30: 9%.

Faculty *Total:* 119, 69% full-time, 63% with terminal degrees. *Student/faculty ratio:* 13:1.

Majors Accounting; art; art education; athletic training/sports medicine; biochemistry; biological/physical sciences; biology; business administration; business marketing and marketing management; chemistry; computer science; dance; drawing; early childhood education; ecology; economics; education; elementary education; English; exercise sciences; French; German; gerontology; health science; history; humanities; information sciences/systems; international business; liberal arts and sciences/liberal studies; literature; mass communications; mathematics; medical illustrating; modern languages; music; music teacher education; music (voice and choral/opera performance); occupational therapy; philosophy; physics; political science; pre-dentistry; pre-law; pre-medicine; pre-theology; pre-veterinary studies; psychology; public health; religious studies; secondary education; social sciences; sociology; Spanish; stringed instruments; theater arts/drama; wind/percussion instruments.

Academic Programs *Special study options:* academic remediation for entering students, accelerated degree program, adult/continuing education programs, advanced placement credit, double majors, English as a second language, independent study, internships, off-campus study, services for LD students, student-designed majors, study abroad, summer session for credit. *ROTC:* Army (c). *Unusual degree programs:* 3-2 engineering with University of Michigan, Michigan Technological University, Washington University in St. Louis; occupational therapy with Washington University in St. Louis.

Library Kerhl Building-Monteith Library with 176,278 titles, 1,178 serial subscriptions, an OPAC, a Web page.

Computers on Campus 621 computers available on campus for general student use. A campuswide network can be accessed from student residence rooms and from off campus. Internet access, at least one staffed computer lab available.

Student Life *Housing:* on-campus residence required through senior year. *Options:* coed, women-only. *Activities and Organizations:* drama/theater group, student-run newspaper, radio station, choral group, marching band, Ambassadors, Almanian (student newspaper), MEGA-Mentoring Program, student government, SOS (Students Offering Service), national fraternities, national sororities. *Campus security:* 24-hour emergency response devices and patrols. *Student Services:* health clinic, personal/psychological counseling, women's center.

Athletics Member NCAA. All Division III. *Intercollegiate sports:* baseball M, basketball M/W, cross-country running M/W, football M, golf M/W, soccer M/W, softball W, swimming M/W, tennis M/W, track and field M/W, volleyball W. *Intramural sports:* badminton M/W, basketball M/W, football M/W, lacrosse W(c), racquetball M/W, soccer M/W, softball M/W, swimming M/W, tennis M/W, volleyball M/W, water polo M/W.

Standardized Tests *Required:* SAT I or ACT (for admission).

Costs (2001–02) *Comprehensive fee:* $22,586 includes full-time tuition ($16,442), mandatory fees ($160), and room and board ($5984). Part-time tuition: $631 per credit. Part-time tuition and fees vary according to course load. *Room and board:* College room only: $2964. Room and board charges vary according to board plan and housing facility. *Payment plans:* installment, deferred payment. *Waivers:* employees or children of employees.

Financial Aid Of all full-time matriculated undergraduates who enrolled in 2001, 1289 applied for aid, 967 were judged to have need, 292 had their need fully met. 140 Federal Work-Study jobs (averaging $950). 30 State and other part-time jobs (averaging $1000). In 2001, 312 non-need-based awards were made. *Average percent of need met:* 91%. *Average financial aid package:* $15,010. *Average need-based loan:* $4287. *Average need-based gift aid:* $11,466. *Average non-need based aid:* $9581. *Average indebtedness upon graduation:* $10,125.

Applying *Options:* early admission, early action, deferred entrance. *Application fee:* $25. *Required:* high school transcript, minimum 3.0 GPA, 2 letters of recommendation. *Recommended:* essay or personal statement, interview. *Application deadline:* rolling (freshmen), rolling (transfers). *Notification:* continuous (freshmen), 12/15 (early action).

Admissions Contact Alma College, Admissions Office, Alma, MI 48801-1599. *Phone:* 989-463-7139. *Toll-free phone:* 800-321-ALMA. *Fax:* 989-463-7057. *E-mail:* admissions@alma.edu.

ANDREWS UNIVERSITY
Berrien Springs, Michigan

- **Independent Seventh-day Adventist** university, founded 1874
- **Calendar** quarters
- **Degrees** associate, bachelor's, master's, doctoral, and first professional
- **Small-town** 1650-acre campus
- **Endowment** $18.3 million
- **Coed,** 1,643 undergraduate students, 81% full-time, 56% women, 44% men
- **Moderately difficult** entrance level, 55% of applicants were admitted

Undergraduates 1,329 full-time, 314 part-time. Students come from 49 states and territories, 51 other countries, 51% are from out of state, 21% African American, 8% Asian American or Pacific Islander, 11% Hispanic American, 0.2% Native American, 15% international, 11% transferred in, 53% live on campus. *Retention:* 74% of 2001 full-time freshmen returned.

Freshmen *Admission:* 886 applied, 489 admitted, 271 enrolled. *Average high school GPA:* 3.14. *Test scores:* SAT verbal scores over 500: 57%; SAT math scores over 500: 49%; ACT scores over 18: 77%; SAT verbal scores over 600: 24%; SAT math scores over 600: 20%; ACT scores over 24: 35%; SAT verbal scores over 700: 7%; SAT math scores over 700: 2%; ACT scores over 30: 8%.

Faculty *Total:* 261, 93% full-time, 64% with terminal degrees. *Student/faculty ratio:* 10:1.

Majors Accounting; adult/continuing education; agricultural business; agricultural education; agricultural mechanization; agricultural sciences; agronomy/crop science; aircraft pilot (professional); anatomy; animal sciences; architectural engineering; architectural engineering technology; architecture; art; art education; art history; auto mechanic/technician; aviation technology; behavioral sciences; biblical studies; biochemistry; biology; biomedical technology; biophysics; botany; business administration; business economics; business marketing and marketing management; carpentry; chemistry; computer engineering technology; computer/information sciences; computer programming; computer science; construction engineering; construction management; construction technology; dietetics; drafting; economics; education; electrical/electronic engineering technology; elementary education; engineering technology; English; exercise sciences; family/community studies; family/consumer studies; French; graphic design/commercial art/illustration; graphic/printing equipment; history; horticulture science; industrial arts; industrial radiologic technology; industrial technology; information sciences/systems; journalism; landscaping management; liberal arts and sciences/liberal studies; mass communications; mathematics; mechanical engineering; mechanical engineering technology; medical laboratory technician; medical technology; music; music (piano and organ performance); music teacher education;

Andrews University (continued)
music (voice and choral/opera performance); nursing; nutrition science; photography; physical education; physical therapy; physics; political science; pre-law; pre-medicine; pre-veterinary studies; psychology; public relations; religious education; religious studies; science education; secondary education; social sciences; social work; sociology; Spanish; speech-language pathology/audiology; theology; zoology.

Academic Programs *Special study options:* academic remediation for entering students, accelerated degree program, adult/continuing education programs, advanced placement credit, cooperative education, distance learning, double majors, English as a second language, external degree program, freshman honors college, honors programs, internships, part-time degree program, student-designed majors, study abroad, summer session for credit. *Unusual degree programs:* 3-2 physical therapy.

Library James White Library plus 2 others with 684,686 titles, 3,060 serial subscriptions, 79,225 audiovisual materials, an OPAC, a Web page.

Computers on Campus 130 computers available on campus for general student use. A campuswide network can be accessed from student residence rooms and from off campus. Internet access, at least one staffed computer lab available.

Student Life *Housing:* on-campus residence required through senior year. *Options:* men-only, women-only. *Activities and Organizations:* drama/theater group, student-run newspaper, radio station, choral group. *Campus security:* 24-hour emergency response devices and patrols, controlled dormitory access. *Student Services:* health clinic, personal/psychological counseling.

Athletics *Intramural sports:* basketball M/W, football M/W, golf M/W, gymnastics M/W, racquetball M/W, soccer M/W, softball M/W, volleyball M/W, water polo M/W.

Standardized Tests *Required:* SAT I or ACT (for admission). *Recommended:* ACT (for admission).

Costs (2001–02) *Comprehensive fee:* $18,096 includes full-time tuition ($13,350), mandatory fees ($326), and room and board ($4420). Full-time tuition and fees vary according to course load. Part-time tuition: $445 per credit hour. Part-time tuition and fees vary according to course load. *Room and board:* College room only: $2360. Room and board charges vary according to board plan. *Payment plan:* installment. *Waivers:* senior citizens and employees or children of employees.

Financial Aid Of all full-time matriculated undergraduates who enrolled in 2001, 1308 applied for aid, 881 were judged to have need, 143 had their need fully met. 348 Federal Work-Study jobs (averaging $1632). 241 State and other part-time jobs (averaging $1516). *Average percent of need met:* 78%. *Average financial aid package:* $14,760. *Average need-based loan:* $4742. *Average need-based gift aid:* $5706. *Average indebtedness upon graduation:* $15,636.

Applying *Options:* deferred entrance. *Application fee:* $30. *Required:* high school transcript, minimum 2.25 GPA, 2 letters of recommendation. *Application deadline:* rolling (freshmen), rolling (transfers). *Notification:* continuous (freshmen).

Admissions Contact Ms. Charlotte Coy, Admissions Supervisor, Andrews University, Berrien Springs, MI 49104. *Toll-free phone:* 800-253-2874. *Fax:* 616-471-3228. *E-mail:* enroll@andrews.edu.

AQUINAS COLLEGE
Grand Rapids, Michigan

- **Independent Roman Catholic** comprehensive, founded 1886
- **Calendar** semesters
- **Degrees** associate, bachelor's, and master's
- **Suburban** 107-acre campus with easy access to Detroit
- **Endowment** $16.6 million
- **Coed,** 2,016 undergraduate students, 78% full-time, 68% women, 32% men
- **Moderately difficult** entrance level, 89% of applicants were admitted

Undergraduates 1,578 full-time, 438 part-time. Students come from 23 states and territories, 1 other country, 7% are from out of state, 4% African American, 0.8% Asian American or Pacific Islander, 3% Hispanic American, 0.4% Native American, 0.0% international, 4% transferred in, 51% live on campus. *Retention:* 75% of 2001 full-time freshmen returned.

Freshmen *Admission:* 1,208 applied, 1,073 admitted, 321 enrolled. *Average high school GPA:* 3.38. *Test scores:* ACT scores over 18: 93%; ACT scores over 24: 43%; ACT scores over 30: 4%.

Faculty *Total:* 206, 49% full-time, 42% with terminal degrees. *Student/faculty ratio:* 16:1.

Majors Accounting; art; art education; art history; athletic training/sports medicine; biological/physical sciences; biology; business administration; chemistry; communications; community services; drawing; economics; education of the specific learning disabled; elementary education; English; environmental science; fine/studio arts; French; geography; German; health education; history; information sciences/systems; international business; international relations; jazz; liberal arts and sciences/liberal studies; mathematics; medical technology; music; music history; music (piano and organ performance); music teacher education; music (voice and choral/opera performance); nuclear medical technology; philosophy; physical education; political science; pre-dentistry; pre-law; pre-medicine; pre-veterinary studies; psychology; reading education; religious education; religious music; religious studies; sculpture; secondary education; social sciences; sociology; Spanish; special education; stringed instruments; urban studies.

Academic Programs *Special study options:* academic remediation for entering students, accelerated degree program, adult/continuing education programs, advanced placement credit, cooperative education, distance learning, double majors, honors programs, independent study, internships, off-campus study, part-time degree program, services for LD students, student-designed majors, study abroad, summer session for credit.

Library Woodhouse Library with 104,564 titles, 843 serial subscriptions, 6,170 audiovisual materials, an OPAC, a Web page.

Computers on Campus 85 computers available on campus for general student use. At least one staffed computer lab available.

Student Life *Housing:* on-campus residence required through sophomore year. *Options:* coed. *Activities and Organizations:* drama/theater group, student-run newspaper, radio station, choral group, Community Senate Programming Board, Aquinas Times, JAMMIN (multicultural group). *Campus security:* 24-hour emergency response devices and patrols, student patrols, late-night transport/escort service, controlled dormitory access. *Student Services:* health clinic, personal/psychological counseling, women's center.

Athletics Member NAIA. *Intercollegiate sports:* baseball M(s), basketball M(s)/W(s), cross-country running M(s)/W(s), golf M(s)/W(s), soccer M(s)/W(s), softball W(s), tennis M(s)/W(s), track and field M(s)/W(s), volleyball W(s). *Intramural sports:* basketball M/W, bowling M/W, football M/W, golf M, ice hockey M, skiing (cross-country) M/W, skiing (downhill) M/W, soccer M/W, softball M/W, tennis M/W, volleyball M/W.

Standardized Tests *Required:* ACT (for admission).

Costs (2001–02) *Comprehensive fee:* $20,052 includes full-time tuition ($14,876) and room and board ($5176). Full-time tuition and fees vary according to course load. Part-time tuition: $300 per credit. Part-time tuition and fees vary according to course load. *Room and board:* College room only: $2390. Room and board charges vary according to board plan and housing facility. *Payment plans:* installment, deferred payment. *Waivers:* children of alumni and employees or children of employees.

Financial Aid Of all full-time matriculated undergraduates who enrolled in 2001, 1134 applied for aid, 990 were judged to have need, 482 had their need fully met. 183 Federal Work-Study jobs (averaging $956). 34 State and other part-time jobs (averaging $758). In 2001, 364 non-need-based awards were made. *Average percent of need met:* 95%. *Average financial aid package:* $13,856. *Average need-based loan:* $3240. *Average need-based gift aid:* $10,616. *Average non-need based aid:* $7987. *Average indebtedness upon graduation:* $12,200.

Applying *Options:* electronic application, early admission, deferred entrance. *Application fee:* $25. *Required:* high school transcript, minimum 2.5 GPA. *Required for some:* essay or personal statement, interview. *Application deadline:* rolling (freshmen), rolling (transfers).

Admissions Contact Ms. Amy Sprouse, Applications Specialist, Aquinas College, Grand Rapids, MI 49506-1799. *Phone:* 616-732-4460 Ext. 5150. *Toll-free phone:* 800-678-9593. *Fax:* 616-732-4469. *E-mail:* admissions@aquinas.edu.

AVE MARIA COLLEGE
Ypsilanti, Michigan

- **Independent Roman Catholic** 4-year, founded 1998
- **Calendar** semesters
- **Degree** bachelor's
- **Coed,** 187 undergraduate students, 84% full-time, 58% women, 42% men
- **Very difficult** entrance level, 83% of applicants were admitted

Undergraduates 157 full-time, 30 part-time. Students come from 27 states and territories, 16 other countries, 62% are from out of state, 0.6% African American, 3% Hispanic American, 21% international, 18% transferred in, 95% live on campus.

Freshmen *Admission:* 125 applied, 104 admitted, 52 enrolled. *Average high school GPA:* 3.20.

Faculty *Total:* 23, 57% full-time, 65% with terminal degrees. *Student/faculty ratio:* 10:1.

Majors Classics; economics; history; literature; mathematics; philosophy; political science; theology.

Student Life *Housing:* on-campus residence required through senior year. *Options:* men-only, women-only, disabled students. *Activities and Organizations:* drama/theater group, student-run newspaper, choral group, Pro-Life Organization, Student Government, Yearbook, Newspaper, Liturgical Ministries. *Campus security:* 24-hour emergency response devices, late-night transport/escort service, controlled dormitory access, 12-hour evening patrols. *Student Services:* personal/psychological counseling.

Standardized Tests *Required:* SAT I or ACT (for admission).

Costs (2002–03) *Comprehensive fee:* $13,550 includes full-time tuition ($8300), mandatory fees ($250), and room and board ($5000). Full-time tuition and fees vary according to program. Part-time tuition: $300 per credit. Part-time tuition and fees vary according to program. *Payment plan:* installment. *Waivers:* employees or children of employees.

Financial Aid Of all full-time matriculated undergraduates who enrolled in 2001, 151 applied for aid, 89 were judged to have need, 31 had their need fully met. 6 State and other part-time jobs (averaging $317). In 2001, 74 non-need-based awards were made. *Average percent of need met:* 82%. *Average financial aid package:* $7619. *Average need-based loan:* $3614. *Average need-based gift aid:* $8700. *Average non-need based aid:* $4652.

Applying *Application fee:* $25. *Required:* essay or personal statement, high school transcript, minimum 2.4 GPA, 2 letters of recommendation. *Recommended:* interview.

Admissions Contact Admissions Office Manager, Ave Maria College, 300 West Forest, Ypsilanti, MI 48197. *Phone:* 734-337-4545. *Toll-free phone:* 866-866-3030. *Fax:* 734-337-4140. *E-mail:* admissions@avemaria.edu.

BAKER COLLEGE OF AUBURN HILLS
Auburn Hills, Michigan

- **Independent** 4-year, founded 1911, part of Baker College System
- **Calendar** quarters
- **Degrees** certificates, diplomas, associate, bachelor's, and postbachelor's certificates
- **Urban** 7-acre campus with easy access to Detroit
- **Coed,** 2,192 undergraduate students, 54% full-time, 65% women, 35% men
- **Noncompetitive** entrance level, 100% of applicants were admitted

Undergraduates Students come from 1 other state.

Freshmen *Admission:* 1,007 applied, 1,007 admitted.

Faculty *Total:* 115, 8% full-time, 10% with terminal degrees. *Student/faculty ratio:* 22:1.

Majors Accounting; business administration; business marketing and marketing management; computer typography/composition; data processing technology; drafting; graphic design/commercial art/illustration; health services administration; interior design; legal administrative assistant; medical administrative assistant; medical assistant; medical records administration; secretarial science.

Academic Programs *Special study options:* academic remediation for entering students, accelerated degree program, advanced placement credit, cooperative education, distance learning, double majors, external degree program, independent study, internships, part-time degree program, services for LD students, summer session for credit.

Library Baker College of Auburn Hills Library with 5,400 titles, 95 serial subscriptions, an OPAC, a Web page.

Computers on Campus 110 computers available on campus for general student use. A campuswide network can be accessed from off campus. Internet access, online (class) registration, at least one staffed computer lab available.

Student Life *Housing:* college housing not available. *Activities and Organizations:* Baker Business Club, Interior Design Society, Students Action in Engineering, Marketing Club. *Campus security:* 24-hour emergency response devices.

Standardized Tests *Recommended:* SAT I or ACT (for placement).

Costs (2001–02) *One-time required fee:* $50. *Tuition:* $5580 full-time, $155 per quarter hour part-time. *Payment plan:* installment. *Waivers:* employees or children of employees.

Applying *Options:* early admission, deferred entrance. *Application fee:* $20. *Required:* high school transcript. *Application deadline:* rolling (freshmen), rolling (transfers).

Admissions Contact Ms. Jan Bohlen, Vice President for Admissions, Baker College of Auburn Hills, 1500 University Drive, Auburn Hills, MI 48326-1586. *Phone:* 248-340-0600. *Toll-free phone:* 888-429-0410. *Fax:* 248-340-0608. *E-mail:* bohlen_j@auburnhills.baker.edu.

BAKER COLLEGE OF CADILLAC
Cadillac, Michigan

- **Independent** 4-year, founded 1986, part of Baker College System
- **Calendar** quarters
- **Degrees** certificates, diplomas, associate, and bachelor's
- **Small-town** 40-acre campus
- **Coed,** 1,021 undergraduate students, 57% full-time, 72% women, 28% men
- **Noncompetitive** entrance level, 100% of applicants were admitted

Undergraduates Students come from 4 states and territories, 0.1% African American, 0.1% Asian American or Pacific Islander, 0.4% Hispanic American, 0.1% Native American. *Retention:* 69% of 2001 full-time freshmen returned.

Freshmen *Admission:* 448 applied, 448 admitted.

Faculty *Total:* 73, 5% full-time. *Student/faculty ratio:* 16:1.

Majors Accounting; architectural engineering technology; business administration; business marketing and marketing management; computer graphics; computer typography/composition; data processing technology; drafting; electrical/electronic engineering technology; emergency medical technology; information sciences/systems; medical administrative assistant; medical assistant; medical records administration; quality control technology; secretarial science.

Academic Programs *Special study options:* academic remediation for entering students, advanced placement credit, cooperative education, distance learning, double majors, external degree program, independent study, internships, part-time degree program, services for LD students, summer session for credit.

Library Baker College of Cadillac Library with 4,000 titles, 78 serial subscriptions, an OPAC, a Web page.

Computers on Campus 77 computers available on campus for general student use. A campuswide network can be accessed from off campus. Internet access, online (class) registration, at least one staffed computer lab available.

Student Life *Housing:* college housing not available. *Campus security:* 24-hour emergency response devices.

Standardized Tests *Recommended:* SAT I or ACT (for placement).

Costs (2001–02) *One-time required fee:* $50. *Tuition:* $5580 full-time, $155 per quarter hour part-time. Full-time tuition and fees vary according to program. Part-time tuition and fees vary according to program. *Payment plan:* installment. *Waivers:* employees or children of employees.

Applying *Options:* early admission, deferred entrance. *Application fee:* $20. *Required:* high school transcript. *Recommended:* interview. *Application deadline:* rolling (freshmen), rolling (transfers).

Admissions Contact Eric Runstrom, Vice President for Admissions, Baker College of Cadillac, 9600 East 13th Street, Cadillac, MI 49601. *Phone:* 616-775-8458. *Toll-free phone:* 888-313-3463 (in-state); 231-876-3100 (out-of-state). *Fax:* 231-775-8505. *E-mail:* runstr_e@cadillac.baker.edu.

BAKER COLLEGE OF CLINTON TOWNSHIP
Clinton Township, Michigan

- **Independent** 4-year, founded 1990, part of Baker College System
- **Calendar** quarters
- **Degrees** certificates, diplomas, associate, and bachelor's
- **Urban** campus with easy access to Detroit
- **Coed,** 3,091 undergraduate students, 54% full-time, 77% women, 23% men
- **Noncompetitive** entrance level, 100% of applicants were admitted

Undergraduates 16% African American, 2% Asian American or Pacific Islander, 0.5% Hispanic American, 0.6% Native American.

Freshmen *Admission:* 1,516 applied, 1,516 admitted.

Faculty *Total:* 133, 6% full-time. *Student/faculty ratio:* 19:1.

Majors Accounting; architectural engineering technology; business administration; business marketing and marketing management; computer typography/composition; data processing; data processing technology; drafting; early childhood education; emergency medical technology; graphic design/commercial art/illustration; human services; information sciences/systems; interior design; legal administrative assistant; medical administrative assistant; medical assistant; medical records administration; operating room technician; secretarial science.

Academic Programs *Special study options:* academic remediation for entering students, advanced placement credit, cooperative education, external degree program, internships, part-time degree program, services for LD students, summer session for credit.

Library Baker College of Mt. Clemens Library with 8,000 titles, 97 serial subscriptions, an OPAC, a Web page.

Computers on Campus 127 computers available on campus for general student use. A campuswide network can be accessed from off campus. Internet access, at least one staffed computer lab available.

Baker College of Clinton Township (continued)

Student Life *Housing:* college housing not available. *Campus security:* evening security guard. *Student Services:* personal/psychological counseling.

Standardized Tests *Recommended:* SAT I or ACT (for placement).

Costs (2001–02) *One-time required fee:* $50. *Tuition:* $5580 full-time, $155 per quarter hour part-time. Full-time tuition and fees vary according to program. Part-time tuition and fees vary according to program. *Payment plan:* installment. *Waivers:* employees or children of employees.

Applying *Options:* electronic application, early admission, deferred entrance. *Application fee:* $20. *Required:* high school transcript. *Application deadline:* rolling (freshmen), rolling (transfers).

Admissions Contact Ms. Annette M. Looser, Vice President for Admissions, Baker College of Clinton Township, 34950 Little Mack Avenue, Clinton Township, MI 48035. *Phone:* 810-791-6610. *Toll-free phone:* 888-272-2842. *Fax:* 810-791-6611. *E-mail:* looser_a@mtclemens.baker.edu.

BAKER COLLEGE OF FLINT
Flint, Michigan

- **Independent** 4-year, founded 1911, part of Baker College System
- **Calendar** quarters
- **Degrees** certificates, diplomas, associate, and bachelor's
- **Urban** 30-acre campus with easy access to Detroit
- **Coed,** 4,399 undergraduate students
- **Noncompetitive** entrance level, 100% of applicants were admitted

Undergraduates Students come from 5 states and territories, 1% are from out of state, 22% African American, 2% Asian American or Pacific Islander, 2% Hispanic American, 1.0% Native American, 2% live on campus.

Freshmen *Admission:* 1,970 applied, 1,970 admitted.

Faculty *Total:* 173, 15% full-time, 10% with terminal degrees. *Student/faculty ratio:* 37:1.

Majors Accounting; accounting technician; aircraft pilot (professional); architectural drafting; auto mechanic/technician; aviation technology; biomedical technology; business; business administration; business marketing and marketing management; business systems networking/ telecommunications; computer education; computer graphics; computer programming; computer systems analysis; computer typography/composition; construction management; data processing technology; drafting; energy management technology; enterprise management; entrepreneurship; environmental technology; executive assistant; family/ community studies; graphic design/commercial art/illustration; health services administration; hospitality management; human services; industrial technology; information sciences/systems; interior design; legal administrative assistant; management information systems/business data processing; mechanical drafting; mechanical engineering; mechanical engineering technology; medical administrative assistant; medical assistant; medical records administration; medical records technology; medical transcription; occupational therapy; office management; operating room technician; operations management; pharmacy technician/ assistant; physical therapy assistant; quality control technology; secretarial science; transportation technology; travel/tourism management; vehicle/equipment operation.

Academic Programs *Special study options:* academic remediation for entering students, accelerated degree program, advanced placement credit, cooperative education, distance learning, double majors, external degree program, independent study, internships, part-time degree program, services for LD students, summer session for credit.

Library Marianne Jewell Library with 168,700 titles, an OPAC, a Web page.

Computers on Campus 412 computers available on campus for general student use. A campuswide network can be accessed from off campus. At least one staffed computer lab available.

Student Life *Housing Options:* coed. *Activities and Organizations:* Occupational Therapy Club, Interior Design Society, Medical Assistants Student Organization, Physical Therapist Aassistant Club. *Campus security:* 24-hour patrols, late-night transport/escort service, controlled dormitory access, video monitoring of high traffic areas. *Student Services:* personal/psychological counseling.

Standardized Tests *Recommended:* SAT I or ACT (for placement).

Costs (2001–02) *One-time required fee:* $50. *Tuition:* $5580 full-time, $155 per quarter hour part-time. Full-time tuition and fees vary according to program. Part-time tuition and fees vary according to program. *Room only:* $1950. *Payment plan:* installment. *Waivers:* employees or children of employees.

Applying *Options:* early admission, deferred entrance. *Application fee:* $20. *Required:* high school transcript. *Application deadlines:* 9/20 (freshmen), 9/20 (transfers).

Admissions Contact Mr. Mark Heaton, Vice President for Admissions, Baker College of Flint, 1050 West Bristol Road, Flint, MI 48507-5508. *Phone:* 810-766-4015. *Toll-free phone:* 800-964-4299. *Fax:* 810-766-4049. *E-mail:* heaton_m@ fafl.baker.edu.

BAKER COLLEGE OF JACKSON
Jackson, Michigan

- **Independent** 4-year, founded 1994, part of Baker College System
- **Calendar** quarters
- **Degrees** certificates, diplomas, associate, and bachelor's
- **Urban** 42-acre campus with easy access to Lansing
- **Coed,** 1,238 undergraduate students
- **Noncompetitive** entrance level, 100% of applicants were admitted

Undergraduates Students come from 2 states and territories, 1% are from out of state, 7% African American, 0.6% Asian American or Pacific Islander, 2% Hispanic American, 0.7% Native American.

Freshmen *Admission:* 627 applied, 627 admitted.

Faculty *Total:* 90, 10% full-time, 10% with terminal degrees. *Student/faculty ratio:* 13:1.

Majors Accounting; business; business administration; business marketing and marketing management; communications; computer typography/composition; data processing technology; entrepreneurship; information sciences/systems; legal administrative assistant; marketing research; medical administrative assistant; medical assistant; medical records administration; medical records technology; medical transcription; office management; operating room technician; pharmacy technician/assistant; secretarial science.

Academic Programs *Special study options:* academic remediation for entering students, accelerated degree program, advanced placement credit, cooperative education, distance learning, double majors, external degree program, independent study, internships, part-time degree program, services for LD students, summer session for credit.

Library Baker College of Jackson Library with 7,000 titles, 150 serial subscriptions, an OPAC, a Web page.

Computers on Campus 110 computers available on campus for general student use. A campuswide network can be accessed from off campus. Internet access, online (class) registration, at least one staffed computer lab available.

Student Life *Campus security:* 24-hour emergency response devices. *Student Services:* personal/psychological counseling.

Standardized Tests *Recommended:* SAT I or ACT (for placement).

Costs (2001–02) *One-time required fee:* $50. *Tuition:* $5580 full-time, $155 per quarter hour part-time. Full-time tuition and fees vary according to program. Part-time tuition and fees vary according to program. *Room only:* $1950. *Payment plan:* installment. *Waivers:* employees or children of employees.

Applying *Options:* electronic application, early admission, deferred entrance. *Application fee:* $20. *Required:* high school transcript. *Application deadline:* 9/19 (freshmen), rolling (transfers). *Notification:* continuous (freshmen).

Admissions Contact Ms. Kelli Hoban, Director of Admissions, Baker College of Jackson, 2800 Springport Road, Jackson, MI 49202. *Phone:* 517-788-7800. *Toll-free phone:* 888-343-3683. *Fax:* 517-789-7331. *E-mail:* hoban_k@ jackson.baker.edu.

BAKER COLLEGE OF MUSKEGON
Muskegon, Michigan

- **Independent** 4-year, founded 1888, part of Baker College System
- **Calendar** quarters
- **Degrees** certificates, diplomas, associate, and bachelor's
- **Suburban** 40-acre campus with easy access to Grand Rapids
- **Coed,** 2,924 undergraduate students
- **Noncompetitive** entrance level, 100% of applicants were admitted

Undergraduates Students come from 13 states and territories, 1% are from out of state, 13% African American, 1% Asian American or Pacific Islander, 4% Hispanic American, 0.8% Native American, 11% live on campus.

Freshmen *Admission:* 1,199 applied, 1,199 admitted.

Faculty *Total:* 145, 10% full-time, 6% with terminal degrees. *Student/faculty ratio:* 30:1.

Majors Accounting; aircraft pilot (professional); architectural drafting; aviation management; business administration; business marketing and marketing management; computer/information sciences; computer programming; computer science; corrections; culinary arts; data processing technology; drafting; early childhood education; electrical/electronic engineering technology; emergency medical technology; graphic design/commercial art/illustration; health services administration; hotel and restaurant management; human services; industrial technology; information sciences/systems; interior design; legal administrative assistant; medical administrative assistant; medical assistant; occupational therapy assistant; operating room technician; pharmacy technician/assistant; physical therapy assistant; quality control technology; rehabilitation therapy; secretarial science; speech-language pathology; travel/tourism management.

Academic Programs *Special study options:* academic remediation for entering students, accelerated degree program, adult/continuing education programs, advanced placement credit, cooperative education, distance learning, double majors, external degree program, independent study, internships, part-time degree program, services for LD students, summer session for credit.

Library Marianne Jewell Library with 32,000 titles, 140 serial subscriptions, an OPAC, a Web page.

Computers on Campus 165 computers available on campus for general student use. A campuswide network can be accessed from student residence rooms and from off campus that provide access to e-mail. Internet access, at least one staffed computer lab available.

Student Life *Housing:* on-campus residence required for freshman year. *Options:* coed, disabled students. *Activities and Organizations:* Accounting Club, Rehab Club, Travel Club, Culinary Club. *Campus security:* 24-hour patrols, late-night transport/escort service, controlled dormitory access, 24-hour security camera surveillance. *Student Services:* personal/psychological counseling.

Standardized Tests *Recommended:* SAT I or ACT (for placement).

Costs (2001–02) *One-time required fee:* $50. *Tuition:* $5580 full-time, $155 per quarter hour part-time. Full-time tuition and fees vary according to program. Part-time tuition and fees vary according to program. *Room only:* $1950. Room and board charges vary according to housing facility. *Payment plans:* installment, deferred payment. *Waivers:* employees or children of employees.

Applying *Options:* electronic application, early admission, deferred entrance. *Application fee:* $20. *Required:* high school transcript. *Application deadline:* 9/24 (freshmen), rolling (transfers). *Notification:* continuous (freshmen).

Admissions Contact Ms. Kathy Jacobson, Director of Admissions, Baker College of Muskegon, 1903 Marquette Avenue, Muskegon, MI 49442-3497. *Phone:* 231-777-5207. *Toll-free phone:* 800-937-0337. *Fax:* 231-777-5201. *E-mail:* jacobs_k@muskegon.baker.edu.

BAKER COLLEGE OF OWOSSO

Owosso, Michigan

- **Independent** 4-year, founded 1984, part of Baker College System
- **Calendar** quarters
- **Degrees** certificates, diplomas, associate, and bachelor's
- **Small-town** 32-acre campus
- **Coed,** 2,062 undergraduate students, 61% full-time, 66% women, 34% men
- **Noncompetitive** entrance level, 100% of applicants were admitted

Undergraduates Students come from 4 states and territories, 1% are from out of state, 1% African American, 0.2% Asian American or Pacific Islander, 2% Hispanic American, 0.7% Native American, 15% live on campus.

Freshmen *Admission:* 1,046 applied, 1,046 admitted.

Faculty *Total:* 103, 5% full-time, 11% with terminal degrees. *Student/faculty ratio:* 38:1.

Majors Accounting; architectural engineering technology; business administration; business marketing and marketing management; computer engineering technology; computer programming; computer science; construction technology; data processing technology; diagnostic medical sonography; drafting; early childhood education; electrical/electronic engineering technology; environmental technology; graphic design/commercial art/illustration; health services administration; hospitality management; hotel and restaurant management; human resources management; industrial radiologic technology; information sciences/systems; interior design; legal administrative assistant; medical administrative assistant; medical assistant; medical laboratory technician; retail management; secretarial science.

Academic Programs *Special study options:* academic remediation for entering students, accelerated degree program, adult/continuing education programs, advanced placement credit, cooperative education, external degree program, internships, part-time degree program, services for LD students, summer session for credit.

Library Baker College of Owosso Library with 35,424 titles, 215 serial subscriptions, 344 audiovisual materials.

Computers on Campus 190 computers available on campus for general student use. A campuswide network can be accessed from off campus. Internet access, at least one staffed computer lab available.

Student Life *Housing Options:* coed. *Activities and Organizations:* student-run newspaper, Accounting Club, Travel Club, Management Club, Baker Health Information Management Club, RAD Club. *Campus security:* 24-hour emergency response devices and patrols, late-night transport/escort service. *Student Services:* personal/psychological counseling.

Standardized Tests *Recommended:* SAT I or ACT (for placement).

Costs (2001–02) *One-time required fee:* $50. *Tuition:* $5580 full-time, $155 per quarter hour part-time. Full-time tuition and fees vary according to program. Part-time tuition and fees vary according to program. *Room only:* Room and board charges vary according to location. *Waivers:* employees or children of employees.

Applying *Options:* common application, early admission, deferred entrance. *Application fee:* $20. *Required:* high school transcript. *Application deadline:* rolling (freshmen), rolling (transfers).

Admissions Contact Mr. Michael Konopacke, Director, Baker College of Owosso, 1020 South Washington Street, Owosso, MI 48867-4400. *Phone:* 517-729-3353. *Toll-free phone:* 800-879-3797. *Fax:* 517-729-3359. *E-mail:* konopa-_m@owosso.baker.edu.

BAKER COLLEGE OF PORT HURON

Port Huron, Michigan

- **Independent** 4-year, founded 1990, part of Baker College System
- **Calendar** quarters
- **Degrees** certificates, diplomas, associate, and bachelor's
- **Urban** 10-acre campus with easy access to Detroit
- **Coed,** 1,301 undergraduate students, 52% full-time, 77% women, 23% men
- **Noncompetitive** entrance level, 100% of applicants were admitted

Undergraduates 10% are from out of state, 4% African American, 0.5% Asian American or Pacific Islander, 2% Hispanic American, 0.9% Native American.

Freshmen *Admission:* 498 applied, 498 admitted.

Faculty *Total:* 95, 11% full-time, 9% with terminal degrees. *Student/faculty ratio:* 13:1.

Majors Accounting; architectural engineering technology; business administration; business marketing and marketing management; computer programming; data processing technology; dental hygiene; drafting; environmental technology; graphic design/commercial art/illustration; health services administration; hotel and restaurant management; information sciences/systems; interior design; legal administrative assistant; medical administrative assistant; medical assistant; medical records administration; secretarial science.

Academic Programs *Special study options:* academic remediation for entering students, accelerated degree program, advanced placement credit, cooperative education, distance learning, double majors, external degree program, independent study, internships, part-time degree program, services for LD students, summer session for credit.

Library Baker College of Port Huron Library with 16,823 titles, 181 serial subscriptions, 135 audiovisual materials, an OPAC, a Web page.

Computers on Campus 145 computers available on campus for general student use. A campuswide network can be accessed from off campus that provide access to software. Internet access, online (class) registration, at least one staffed computer lab available.

Student Life *Housing:* college housing not available. *Activities and Organizations:* Travel Club, Student Association Dental Hygienists of America. *Campus security:* 24-hour emergency response devices, late-night transport/escort service. *Student Services:* personal/psychological counseling.

Costs (2001–02) *Tuition:* $5580 full-time, $155 per quarter hour part-time. Full-time tuition and fees vary according to program. Part-time tuition and fees vary according to program. *Payment plans:* installment, deferred payment. *Waivers:* employees or children of employees.

Applying *Options:* early admission, deferred entrance. *Application fee:* $20. *Required:* high school transcript, interview. *Application deadline:* 9/24 (freshmen), rolling (transfers). *Notification:* continuous (freshmen).

Admissions Contact Mr. Daniel Kenny, Director of Admissions, Baker College of Port Huron, 3403 Lapeer Road, Port Huron, MI 48060-2597. *Phone:* 810-985-7000. *Toll-free phone:* 888-262-2442. *Fax:* 810-985-7066. *E-mail:* kenny_d@porthuron.baker.edu.

CALVIN COLLEGE

Grand Rapids, Michigan

- **Independent** comprehensive, founded 1876, affiliated with Christian Reformed Church
- **Calendar** 4-1-4

Calvin College (continued)

- **Degrees** bachelor's, master's, and postbachelor's certificates
- **Suburban** 370-acre campus
- **Endowment** $51.8 million
- **Coed,** 4,221 undergraduate students, 95% full-time, 56% women, 44% men
- **Moderately difficult** entrance level, 98% of applicants were admitted

Academic excellence, Christian commitment, reasonable cost, 4,300 students, 100 academic options. Calvin College is recognized by *U.S. News & World Report's* America's Best Colleges, *The National Review College Guide*, the *Templeton Guide: Colleges that Encourage Character Development*, the *Fiske Guide to Colleges*, and *Barron's Best Buys in College Education*.

Undergraduates 4,008 full-time, 213 part-time. Students come from 48 states and territories, 33 other countries, 39% are from out of state, 0.9% African American, 2% Asian American or Pacific Islander, 1% Hispanic American, 0.4% Native American, 8% international, 3% transferred in, 58% live on campus. *Retention:* 86% of 2001 full-time freshmen returned.

Freshmen *Admission:* 1,920 applied, 1,891 admitted, 1,031 enrolled. *Average high school GPA:* 3.5. *Test scores:* SAT verbal scores over 500: 85%; SAT math scores over 500: 85%; ACT scores over 18: 98%; SAT verbal scores over 600: 43%; SAT math scores over 600: 52%; ACT scores over 24: 71%; SAT verbal scores over 700: 13%; SAT math scores over 700: 15%; ACT scores over 30: 16%.

Faculty *Total:* 353, 80% full-time, 74% with terminal degrees. *Student/faculty ratio:* 15:1.

Majors Accounting; American history; art; art education; art history; athletic training/sports medicine; biblical studies; bilingual/bicultural education; biochemistry; biological/physical sciences; biology; biotechnology research; business administration; business communications; chemical engineering; chemistry; civil engineering; classics; computer science; criminal justice/law enforcement administration; design/visual communications; economics; electrical engineering; elementary education; engineering; English; environmental science; European history; exercise sciences; film studies; fine/studio arts; French; geography; geology; German; Greek (modern); history; interdisciplinary studies; international relations; Latin (ancient and medieval); mass communications; mathematics; mechanical engineering; music; music conducting; music (general performance); music history; music (piano and organ performance); music teacher education; music theory and composition; music (voice and choral/opera performance); natural sciences; nursing; occupational therapy; philosophy; physical education; physical sciences; physics; political science; pre-dentistry; pre-law; pre-medicine; preveterinary studies; psychology; public administration; recreation/leisure studies; religious music; religious studies; science education; secondary education; social sciences; social work; sociology; Spanish; special education; speech-language pathology/audiology; speech/rhetorical studies; teaching English as a second language; theater arts/drama; theology.

Academic Programs *Special study options:* academic remediation for entering students, accelerated degree program, adult/continuing education programs, advanced placement credit, cooperative education, distance learning, double majors, English as a second language, honors programs, independent study, internships, off-campus study, part-time degree program, services for LD students, student-designed majors, study abroad, summer session for credit. *ROTC:* Army (c). *Unusual degree programs:* 3-2 occupational therapy with Washington University in St. Louis.

Library Hekman Library with 700,000 titles, 2,660 serial subscriptions, 21,260 audiovisual materials, an OPAC, a Web page.

Computers on Campus 659 computers available on campus for general student use. A campuswide network can be accessed from student residence rooms and from off campus. Internet access, online (class) registration, at least one staffed computer lab available.

Student Life *Housing:* on-campus residence required through sophomore year. *Options:* men-only, women-only. *Activities and Organizations:* drama/theater group, student-run newspaper, radio station, choral group, Association for Supervision and Curriculum Development, Environmental Stewardship Coalition, China Club, Young Life, Dance Guild. *Campus security:* 24-hour emergency response devices and patrols, student patrols, late-night transport/escort service, controlled dormitory access, crime prevention programs, crime alert bulletins. *Student Services:* health clinic, personal/psychological counseling.

Athletics Member NCAA. All Division III. *Intercollegiate sports:* baseball M, basketball M/W, crew M(c)/W(c), cross-country running M/W, golf M/W, ice hockey M(c), lacrosse M(c)/W(c), soccer M/W, softball W, swimming M/W, tennis M/W, track and field M/W, volleyball M(c)/W. *Intramural sports:* badminton M/W, basketball M/W, cross-country running M/W, football M/W, golf M/W, racquetball M/W, soccer M/W, softball M/W, swimming M/W, tennis M/W, track and field M/W, volleyball M/W, water polo M/W.

Standardized Tests *Required:* SAT I or ACT (for admission). *Recommended:* ACT (for admission).

Costs (2001–02) *Comprehensive fee:* $20,050 includes full-time tuition ($14,870) and room and board ($5180). Part-time tuition: $360 per credit hour. Part-time tuition and fees vary according to course load. *Room and board:* College room only: $2820. Room and board charges vary according to board plan. *Payment plans:* tuition prepayment, installment. *Waivers:* employees or children of employees.

Financial Aid Of all full-time matriculated undergraduates who enrolled in 2001, 2810 applied for aid, 2390 were judged to have need, 802 had their need fully met. 676 Federal Work-Study jobs (averaging $1160). 1340 State and other part-time jobs (averaging $1060). In 2001, 1101 non-need-based awards were made. *Average percent of need met:* 88%. *Average financial aid package:* $11,390. *Average need-based loan:* $5000. *Average need-based gift aid:* $7750. *Average non-need based aid:* $3650. *Average indebtedness upon graduation:* $15,000.

Applying *Options:* common application, deferred entrance. *Application fee:* $35. *Required:* essay or personal statement, high school transcript, minimum 2.5 GPA, 1 letter of recommendation. *Application deadline:* 8/15 (freshmen), rolling (transfers). *Notification:* continuous (freshmen).

Admissions Contact Mr. Dale D. Kuiper, Director of Admissions, Calvin College, 3201 Burton Street, SE, Grand Rapids, MI 49546-4388. *Phone:* 616-957-6106. *Toll-free phone:* 800-688-0122. *Fax:* 616-957-6777. *E-mail:* admissions@calvin.edu.

CENTRAL MICHIGAN UNIVERSITY

Mount Pleasant, Michigan

- **State-supported** university, founded 1892
- **Calendar** semesters
- **Degrees** bachelor's, master's, doctoral, post-master's, and postbachelor's certificates
- **Small-town** 854-acre campus
- **Endowment** $42.2 million
- **Coed,** 19,530 undergraduate students, 85% full-time, 60% women, 40% men
- **Moderately difficult** entrance level, 83% of applicants were admitted

Undergraduates 16,600 full-time, 2,930 part-time. Students come from 42 states and territories, 78 other countries, 2% are from out of state, 6% African American, 0.9% Asian American or Pacific Islander, 2% Hispanic American, 0.7% Native American, 1% international, 6% transferred in, 35% live on campus. *Retention:* 79% of 2001 full-time freshmen returned.

Freshmen *Admission:* 12,100 applied, 10,016 admitted, 3,690 enrolled. *Average high school GPA:* 3.34. *Test scores:* SAT verbal scores over 500: 61%; SAT math scores over 500: 67%; ACT scores over 18: 92%; SAT verbal scores over 600: 22%; SAT math scores over 600: 21%; ACT scores over 24: 33%; SAT verbal scores over 700: 2%; SAT math scores over 700: 3%; ACT scores over 30: 3%.

Faculty *Total:* 1,072, 58% full-time, 61% with terminal degrees. *Student/faculty ratio:* 23:1.

Majors Accounting; actuarial science; adapted physical education; advertising; anthropology; art; art education; astronomy; athletic training/sports medicine; automotive engineering technology; banking; biology; biology education; business; business administration; business education; business marketing and marketing management; chemistry; chemistry education; child care/guidance; community services; computer education; computer engineering technology; computer/information sciences; construction technology; court reporting; creative writing; criminology; dietetics; earth sciences; economics; education of the emotionally handicapped; education of the mentally handicapped; electrical/electronic engineering technology; elementary education; English; English education; entrepreneurship; environmental science; European studies; family resource management studies; family studies; fashion merchandising; finance; financial planning; French; French language education; geography; geology; German; German language education; graphic design/commercial art/illustration; health education; health facilities administration; health/physical education; history; history education; home economics; home economics education; hospitality management; hotel and restaurant management; human resources management; industrial arts education; industrial/manufacturing engineering; interdisciplinary studies; interior architecture; international business; international relations; journalism; logistics/materials management; management information systems/business data processing; marketing/distribution education; mathematical statistics; mathematics; mathematics education; mechanical engineering technology; medical technology; microbiology/bacteriology; music; music history; music teacher education; music theory and composition; natural resources conservation; neuroscience; oceanography; office management; operations management; philosophy; physical education; physical sciences; physics; physics education; political science; psychology; public health; public relations; radio/television broadcasting; recreation/leisure facilities management; recreation/leisure studies; rehabilitation/

therapeutic services related; religious studies; science education; social science education; social sciences; social studies education; social work; sociology; Spanish; Spanish language education; speech education; speech-language pathology/audiology; speech/rhetorical studies; technical/business writing; theater arts/drama.

Academic Programs *Special study options:* academic remediation for entering students, accelerated degree program, adult/continuing education programs, advanced placement credit, distance learning, double majors, English as a second language, external degree program, freshman honors college, honors programs, internships, part-time degree program, student-designed majors, study abroad, summer session for credit. *ROTC:* Army (b).

Library Park Library plus 1 other with 941,543 titles, 4,358 serial subscriptions, 24,630 audiovisual materials, an OPAC, a Web page.

Computers on Campus 1500 computers available on campus for general student use. A campuswide network can be accessed from student residence rooms and from off campus. Internet access, online (class) registration, at least one staffed computer lab available.

Student Life *Housing:* on-campus residence required through sophomore year. *Options:* coed, men-only, women-only, disabled students. *Activities and Organizations:* drama/theater group, student-run newspaper, radio and television station, choral group, marching band, Residence Hall Assembly, Student Government Association, Big Brothers/Big Sisters, Organization for Black Unity, Program Board, national fraternities, national sororities. *Campus security:* 24-hour patrols, late-night transport/escort service. *Student Services:* health clinic, personal/psychological counseling, women's center, legal services.

Athletics Member NCAA. All Division I except football (Division I-A). *Intercollegiate sports:* baseball M(s), basketball M(s)/W(s), cross-country running M(s)/W(s), field hockey W(s), gymnastics W(s), soccer W(s), softball W(s), track and field M(s)/W(s), volleyball W(s), wrestling M(s). *Intramural sports:* basketball M/W, bowling M/W, cross-country running M/W, fencing M(c)/W(c), football M/W, golf M/W, ice hockey M(c), lacrosse M/W(c), racquetball M/W, rugby M(c)/W(c), skiing (cross-country) M(c)/W(c), skiing (downhill) M(c)/W(c), soccer M/W, softball M/W, swimming M/W, table tennis M/W, tennis M/W, track and field M/W, volleyball M/W, weight lifting M(c)/W(c), wrestling M.

Standardized Tests *Required:* ACT (for admission).

Costs (2001–02) *Tuition:* state resident $3686 full-time, $119 per credit part-time; nonresident $9567 full-time, $309 per credit part-time. *Required fees:* $680 full-time, $133 per term part-time. *Room and board:* $5220. Room and board charges vary according to board plan and housing facility. *Waivers:* senior citizens and employees or children of employees.

Financial Aid Of all full-time matriculated undergraduates who enrolled in 2001, 10919 applied for aid, 7903 were judged to have need, 2114 had their need fully met. 1029 Federal Work-Study jobs (averaging $1771). 3337 State and other part-time jobs (averaging $1865). In 2001, 5460 non-need-based awards were made. *Average percent of need met:* 91%. *Average financial aid package:* $7232. *Average need-based loan:* $3309. *Average need-based gift aid:* $3060. *Average indebtedness upon graduation:* $15,795.

Applying *Options:* electronic application, early admission, deferred entrance. *Application fee:* $25. *Required:* high school transcript. *Required for some:* essay or personal statement, letters of recommendation, interview. *Recommended:* minimum 3.0 GPA. *Application deadline:* rolling (freshmen), rolling (transfers).

Admissions Contact Mrs. Betty J. Wagner, Director of Admissions, Central Michigan University, Office of Admissions, 105 Warriner Hall, Mt. Pleasant, MI 48859. *Phone:* 989-774-3076. *Fax:* 989-774-7267. *E-mail:* cmuadmit@cmich.edu.

CLEARY COLLEGE
Ann Arbor, Michigan

- **Independent** comprehensive, founded 1883
- **Calendar** quarters
- **Degrees** certificates, associate, and bachelor's
- **Small-town** 27-acre campus with easy access to Detroit and Lansing
- **Endowment** $1.1 million
- **Coed,** 900 undergraduate students
- **Moderately difficult** entrance level

Undergraduates Students come from 2 states and territories, 1% are from out of state, 7% African American, 0.8% Asian American or Pacific Islander, 0.5% Hispanic American, 0.6% Native American.

Faculty *Total:* 85, 13% full-time. *Student/faculty ratio:* 10:1.

Majors Accounting; business administration; business marketing and marketing management; computer programming; data processing technology; finance; health services administration; human resources management; information sciences/systems; management information systems/business data processing.

Academic Programs *Special study options:* accelerated degree program, adult/continuing education programs, advanced placement credit, cooperative education, distance learning, external degree program, independent study, internships, part-time degree program, summer session for credit. *ROTC:* Navy (c), Air Force (c).

Library Cleary College Library plus 1 other with 6,000 titles, 35 serial subscriptions, 20 audiovisual materials, an OPAC, a Web page.

Computers on Campus 60 computers available on campus for general student use. A campuswide network can be accessed from student residence rooms and from off campus. Internet access, online (class) registration, at least one staffed computer lab available.

Student Life *Housing:* college housing not available. *Campus security:* 24-hour emergency response devices. *Student Services:* personal/psychological counseling.

Costs (2002–03) *Payment plan:* deferred payment. *Waivers:* senior citizens and employees or children of employees.

Financial Aid Of all full-time matriculated undergraduates who enrolled in 2001, 473 applied for aid, 473 were judged to have need. 5 Federal Work-Study jobs (averaging $1913). 2 State and other part-time jobs (averaging $2500). In 2001, 13 non-need-based awards were made. *Average percent of need met:* 60%. *Average financial aid package:* $3927. *Average need-based loan:* $2495. *Average need-based gift aid:* $1431. *Average indebtedness upon graduation:* $10,500.

Applying *Options:* common application, electronic application, early admission, deferred entrance. *Application fee:* $25. *Required:* high school transcript, minimum 2.5 GPA. *Required for some:* essay or personal statement, 2 letters of recommendation. *Recommended:* interview. *Application deadline:* rolling (freshmen), rolling (transfers).

Admissions Contact Ms. Mary Krowleski, Admissions Representative, Cleary College, 3750 Cleary College Drive, Howell, MI 48843. *Phone:* 517-548-3670 Ext. 2215. *Toll-free phone:* 888-5-CLEARY (in-state); 888-5-CLEARY Ext. 2249 (out-of-state). *Fax:* 517-552-7805. *E-mail:* admissions@cleary.edu.

COLLEGE FOR CREATIVE STUDIES
Detroit, Michigan

- **Independent** 4-year, founded 1926
- **Calendar** semesters
- **Degree** bachelor's
- **Urban** 11-acre campus
- **Coed,** 1,152 undergraduate students, 84% full-time, 41% women, 59% men
- **Moderately difficult** entrance level, 79% of applicants were admitted

Undergraduates 973 full-time, 179 part-time. Students come from 31 states and territories, 15 other countries, 17% are from out of state, 7% African American, 5% Asian American or Pacific Islander, 3% Hispanic American, 0.2% Native American, 6% international, 14% transferred in, 23% live on campus. *Retention:* 69% of 2001 full-time freshmen returned.

Freshmen *Admission:* 405 applied, 321 admitted, 193 enrolled. *Average high school GPA:* 3.02.

Faculty *Total:* 199, 22% full-time. *Student/faculty ratio:* 9:1.

Majors Applied art; architectural environmental design; art; ceramic arts; computer graphics; drawing; film/video and photographic arts related; fine/studio arts; graphic design/commercial art/illustration; industrial design; interior design; metal/jewelry arts; photography; sculpture; textile arts.

Academic Programs *Special study options:* academic remediation for entering students, advanced placement credit, cooperative education, double majors, English as a second language, independent study, internships, off-campus study, part-time degree program, services for LD students, summer session for credit.

Library Center for Creative Studies Library with 24,000 titles, 75 serial subscriptions.

Computers on Campus A campuswide network can be accessed from student residence rooms and from off campus. Internet access, at least one staffed computer lab available.

Student Life *Housing Options:* coed. *Campus security:* 24-hour patrols. *Student Services:* personal/psychological counseling.

Standardized Tests *Required:* SAT I or ACT (for admission).

Costs (2002–03) *Tuition:* $17,520 full-time, $584 per credit hour part-time. Part-time tuition and fees vary according to course load. *Required fees:* $1078 full-time, $424 per term part-time. *Room only:* $3300. Room and board charges vary according to housing facility. *Payment plans:* installment, deferred payment. *Waivers:* employees or children of employees.

Applying *Options:* electronic application, deferred entrance. *Application fee:* $35. *Required:* essay or personal statement, high school transcript, portfolio. *Required for some:* letters of recommendation, interview. *Recommended:* minimum 2.5 GPA. *Application deadline:* rolling (freshmen), rolling (transfers).

College for Creative Studies (continued)

Admissions Contact Office of Admissions, College for Creative Studies, 201 East Kirby, Detroit, MI 48202-4034. *Phone:* 313-664-7425. *Toll-free phone:* 800-952-ARTS. *Fax:* 313-872-2739. *E-mail:* admissions@ccscad.edu.

CONCORDIA UNIVERSITY

Ann Arbor, Michigan

- **Independent** comprehensive, founded 1963, affiliated with Lutheran Church-Missouri Synod, part of Concordia University System
- **Calendar** semesters
- **Degrees** associate, bachelor's, and master's
- **Suburban** 234-acre campus with easy access to Detroit
- **Endowment** $5.9 million
- **Coed,** 533 undergraduate students, 86% full-time, 56% women, 44% men
- **Moderately difficult** entrance level, 86% of applicants were admitted

Undergraduates 458 full-time, 75 part-time. Students come from 23 states and territories, 3 other countries, 23% are from out of state, 9% African American, 0.4% Asian American or Pacific Islander, 2% Hispanic American, 1% Native American, 0.9% international, 11% transferred in, 60% live on campus. *Retention:* 77% of 2001 full-time freshmen returned.

Freshmen *Admission:* 298 applied, 256 admitted, 101 enrolled. *Average high school GPA:* 3.29. *Test scores:* ACT scores over 18: 82%; ACT scores over 24: 41%; ACT scores over 30: 9%.

Faculty *Total:* 71, 51% full-time. *Student/faculty ratio:* 11:1.

Majors Aircraft pilot (professional); art; biblical languages/literatures; biological/physical sciences; biology; business administration; communications; criminal justice/law enforcement administration; elementary education; English; health services administration; individual/family development; information sciences/systems; liberal arts and sciences/liberal studies; mathematics; music; music (piano and organ performance); physical education; pre-law; pre-medicine; psychology; religious music; religious studies; secondary education; social sciences; sociology; sport/fitness administration.

Academic Programs *Special study options:* academic remediation for entering students, accelerated degree program, adult/continuing education programs, advanced placement credit, distance learning, double majors, independent study, internships, off-campus study, part-time degree program, services for LD students, student-designed majors, study abroad, summer session for credit. *ROTC:* Army (c), Air Force (c).

Library Zimmerman Library with 120,000 titles, 3,950 serial subscriptions, 10,500 audiovisual materials, an OPAC, a Web page.

Computers on Campus 65 computers available on campus for general student use. A campuswide network can be accessed from student residence rooms and from off campus. Internet access, at least one staffed computer lab available.

Student Life *Housing:* on-campus residence required through sophomore year. *Options:* men-only, women-only. *Activities and Organizations:* drama/theater group, student-run newspaper, choral group, Student Activities Committee, Drama Club, Student Senate, Spiritual Life Committee, Off-Campus Ministries. *Campus security:* student patrols, late-night transport/escort service. *Student Services:* personal/psychological counseling.

Athletics Member NAIA, NCCAA. *Intercollegiate sports:* baseball M(s), basketball M(s)/W(s), cross-country running M(s)/W(s), soccer M(s)/W(s), softball W(s), track and field M(s)/W(s), volleyball W(s). *Intramural sports:* badminton M/W, basketball M/W, football M/W, golf M/W, softball M/W, tennis M/W, volleyball M/W.

Standardized Tests *Required:* SAT I or ACT (for admission). *Recommended:* ACT (for admission).

Costs (2001–02) *One-time required fee:* $100. *Comprehensive fee:* $20,500 includes full-time tuition ($14,250), mandatory fees ($450), and room and board ($5800). Full-time tuition and fees vary according to class time and program. Part-time tuition: $475 per semester hour. Part-time tuition and fees vary according to class time, course load, and program. *Payment plans:* installment, deferred payment. *Waivers:* employees or children of employees.

Financial Aid Of all full-time matriculated undergraduates who enrolled in 2001, 437 applied for aid, 399 were judged to have need. In 2001, 58 non-need-based awards were made. *Average percent of need met:* 87%. *Average financial aid package:* $12,347. *Average non-need based aid:* $5599. *Average indebtedness upon graduation:* $20,026.

Applying *Options:* electronic application, deferred entrance. *Application fee:* $25. *Required:* high school transcript, minimum 2.5 GPA. *Required for some:* essay or personal statement, interview. *Recommended:* 1 letter of recommendation. *Application deadline:* rolling (freshmen), rolling (transfers).

Admissions Contact Ms. Kathleen Rowe, Director of Admissions, Concordia University, 4090 Geddes Road, Ann Arbor, MI 48105. *Phone:* 734-995-7322 Ext. 7311. *Toll-free phone:* 800-253-0680. *Fax:* 734-995-7455. *E-mail:* admissions@cuaa.edu.

CORNERSTONE UNIVERSITY

Grand Rapids, Michigan

- **Independent Baptist** 4-year, founded 1941
- **Calendar** semesters
- **Degrees** diplomas, associate, and bachelor's
- **Suburban** 132-acre campus
- **Endowment** $5.4 million
- **Coed,** 1,716 undergraduate students, 89% full-time, 61% women, 39% men
- **Moderately difficult** entrance level, 96% of applicants were admitted

Undergraduates 1,532 full-time, 184 part-time. Students come from 31 states and territories, 20% are from out of state, 7% African American, 0.4% Asian American or Pacific Islander, 2% Hispanic American, 0.3% Native American, 0.7% international, 10% transferred in. *Retention:* 64% of 2001 full-time freshmen returned.

Freshmen *Admission:* 841 applied, 805 admitted, 379 enrolled. *Average high school GPA:* 3.34. *Test scores:* ACT scores over 18: 96%; ACT scores over 24: 35%; ACT scores over 30: 5%.

Faculty *Total:* 136, 50% full-time, 45% with terminal degrees. *Student/faculty ratio:* 16:1.

Majors Accounting; adult/continuing education; aircraft pilot (professional); biblical languages/literatures; biblical studies; biology; broadcast journalism; business administration; business education; business marketing and marketing management; divinity/ministry; early childhood education; education; elementary education; English; history; information sciences/systems; interdisciplinary studies; mass communications; mathematics; music; music teacher education; pastoral counseling; physical education; pre-dentistry; pre-law; pre-medicine; pre-veterinary studies; psychology; religious education; religious studies; science education; secondary education; social work; sociology; Spanish; speech/rhetorical studies; sport/fitness administration.

Academic Programs *Special study options:* academic remediation for entering students, accelerated degree program, adult/continuing education programs, advanced placement credit, double majors, independent study, internships, off-campus study, part-time degree program, summer session for credit. *ROTC:* Army (c).

Library Miller Library with 119,943 titles, 1,107 serial subscriptions, 3,761 audiovisual materials, an OPAC, a Web page.

Computers on Campus 531 computers available on campus for general student use. A campuswide network can be accessed from student residence rooms and from off campus. Internet access, at least one staffed computer lab available.

Student Life *Housing:* on-campus residence required through junior year. *Options:* men-only, women-only, disabled students. *Activities and Organizations:* drama/theater group, student-run newspaper, choral group, student government, Student Education Association, Breakpoint, Student Activities Council. *Campus security:* 24-hour emergency response devices and patrols, student patrols, late-night transport/escort service, controlled dormitory access. *Student Services:* health clinic, personal/psychological counseling.

Athletics Member NAIA. *Intercollegiate sports:* basketball M(s)/W(s), cross-country running M(s)/W(s), golf M(s), soccer M(s)/W(s), softball W(s), tennis M(s), volleyball W(s). *Intramural sports:* basketball M/W, football M, soccer M/W, softball M/W, volleyball M/W.

Standardized Tests *Required:* SAT I or ACT (for admission).

Costs (2002–03) *Comprehensive fee:* $18,092 includes full-time tuition ($13,070) and room and board ($5022). Part-time tuition: $6535 per term. Part-time tuition and fees vary according to course load. *Room and board:* College room only: $2290. *Payment plan:* installment. *Waivers:* employees or children of employees.

Financial Aid Of all full-time matriculated undergraduates who enrolled in 2001, 1133 applied for aid, 889 were judged to have need, 299 had their need fully met. 114 Federal Work-Study jobs (averaging $1527). 34 State and other part-time jobs (averaging $1172). *Average percent of need met:* 79%. *Average financial aid package:* $10,395. *Average need-based loan:* $3743. *Average need-based gift aid:* $3642. *Average indebtedness upon graduation:* $15,795.

Applying *Options:* deferred entrance. *Application fee:* $25. *Required:* essay or personal statement, high school transcript, minimum 2.25 GPA, 1 letter of recommendation. *Recommended:* interview. *Application deadline:* rolling (freshmen), rolling (transfers).

Admissions Contact Mr. Brent Rudin, Director of Admissions, Cornerstone University, 1001 East Beltline Avenue, NE, Grand Rapids, MI 49525. *Phone:* 616-222-1426. *Toll-free phone:* 800-787-9778. *Fax:* 616-222-1400. *E-mail:* admissions@cornerstone.edu.

DAVENPORT UNIVERSITY
Kalamazoo, Michigan

- **Independent** 4-year, founded 1866, part of Davenport Educational System
- **Calendar** quarters
- **Degrees** certificates, diplomas, associate, bachelor's, and postbachelor's certificates
- **Suburban** 5-acre campus
- **Endowment** $500,000
- **Coed,** 1,063 undergraduate students, 33% full-time, 75% women, 25% men
- **Noncompetitive** entrance level, 100% of applicants were admitted

Undergraduates 355 full-time, 708 part-time. Students come from 2 states and territories, 6 other countries, 1% are from out of state, 16% African American, 2% Asian American or Pacific Islander, 1% Hispanic American, 1.0% Native American, 0.2% international.

Freshmen *Admission:* 161 applied, 161 admitted, 161 enrolled.

Faculty *Total:* 110, 22% full-time, 13% with terminal degrees. *Student/faculty ratio:* 13:1.

Majors Accounting; business administration; business marketing and marketing management; computer programming; data processing technology; health services administration; information sciences/systems; legal administrative assistant; medical administrative assistant; medical assistant; medical records administration; paralegal/legal assistant; secretarial science.

Academic Programs *Special study options:* academic remediation for entering students, adult/continuing education programs, cooperative education, distance learning, English as a second language, independent study, internships, off-campus study, part-time degree program, study abroad, summer session for credit.

Library T. F. Reed Library with 10,257 titles, 949 audiovisual materials.

Computers on Campus 100 computers available on campus for general student use. Internet access, at least one staffed computer lab available.

Student Life *Housing:* college housing not available. *Activities and Organizations:* Management/Marketing Club, Institute of Management Accountants, Paralegal Association, Data Processing Management Association. *Campus security:* late-night transport/escort service. *Student Services:* personal/psychological counseling.

Costs (2001–02) *One-time required fee:* $50. *Tuition:* $9540 full-time, $212 per credit part-time. Full-time tuition and fees vary according to location. Part-time tuition and fees vary according to location. *Required fees:* $105 full-time, $35 per term part-time. *Payment plans:* installment, deferred payment. *Waivers:* employees or children of employees.

Applying *Options:* common application, electronic application, early admission, deferred entrance. *Application fee:* $25. *Required:* essay or personal statement, high school transcript. *Application deadline:* rolling (freshmen), rolling (transfers).

Admissions Contact Ms. Gloria Stender, Admissions Director, Davenport University, 4123 West Main Street, Kalamazoo, MI 49006-2791. *Phone:* 616-382-2835 Ext. 3309. *Toll-free phone:* 800-632-8928 Ext. 3308. *Fax:* 616-382-2661.

DAVENPORT UNIVERSITY
Lansing, Michigan

- **Independent** 4-year, founded 1979, part of Davenport Educational System
- **Calendar** quarters
- **Degrees** certificates, diplomas, associate, and bachelor's
- **Suburban** 2-acre campus with easy access to Detroit
- **Coed,** 1,209 undergraduate students, 39% full-time, 72% women, 28% men
- **Noncompetitive** entrance level

Undergraduates 475 full-time, 734 part-time. Students come from 1 other state, 0% are from out of state, 18% African American, 2% Asian American or Pacific Islander, 5% Hispanic American, 0.6% Native American, 0.2% international, 27% transferred in. *Retention:* 43% of 2001 full-time freshmen returned.

Freshmen *Admission:* 270 enrolled.

Faculty *Total:* 79, 14% full-time. *Student/faculty ratio:* 15:1.

Majors Accounting; business administration; computer management; finance; human resources management; information sciences/systems; medical administrative assistant; medical assistant; physical therapy; secretarial science.

Academic Programs *Special study options:* academic remediation for entering students, accelerated degree program, adult/continuing education programs, advanced placement credit, cooperative education, distance learning, external degree program, independent study, internships, part-time degree program, services for LD students, student-designed majors, summer session for credit. *ROTC:* Army (c).

Library 10,680 titles, 850 serial subscriptions, an OPAC, a Web page.

Computers on Campus 65 computers available on campus for general student use. At least one staffed computer lab available.

Student Life *Housing:* college housing not available. *Activities and Organizations:* Student Accounting Society, Management Marketing Association, Student Leadership Council, Data Processing Management Association, Professional Secretaries International. *Campus security:* 24-hour emergency response devices, late-night transport/escort service.

Standardized Tests *Required for some:* ACT (for placement).

Costs (2002–03) *Tuition:* $8586 full-time, $212 per credit hour part-time. *Required fees:* $70 full-time, $35 per term part-time. *Payment plan:* installment. *Waivers:* senior citizens.

Financial Aid *Average indebtedness upon graduation:* $3280.

Applying *Options:* common application, electronic application, early admission, deferred entrance. *Application fee:* $25. *Required:* high school transcript. *Recommended:* interview. *Application deadlines:* 9/15 (freshmen), 9/15 (transfers). *Notification:* continuous until 9/15 (freshmen).

Admissions Contact Mr. Tom Woods, Associate Dean of Enrollment, Davenport University, 220 East Kalamazoo, Lansing, MI 48933-2197. *Phone:* 517-484-2600 Ext. 288. *Toll-free phone:* 800-331-3306. *Fax:* 517-484-9719. *E-mail:* laadmissions@davenport.edu.

DAVENPORT UNIVERSITY
Grand Rapids, Michigan

- **Independent** comprehensive, founded 1866, part of Davenport University
- **Calendar** quarters
- **Degrees** certificates, diplomas, associate, bachelor's, and master's
- **Urban** 5-acre campus
- **Coed,** 1,679 undergraduate students, 43% full-time, 63% women, 37% men
- **Noncompetitive** entrance level, 65% of applicants were admitted

Undergraduates 718 full-time, 961 part-time. Students come from 11 states and territories, 27 other countries, 9% African American, 4% Asian American or Pacific Islander, 4% Hispanic American, 1% Native American, 2% international, 12% transferred in, 10% live on campus. *Retention:* 51% of 2001 full-time freshmen returned.

Freshmen *Admission:* 452 applied, 295 admitted, 181 enrolled.

Faculty *Total:* 129, 16% full-time, 11% with terminal degrees. *Student/faculty ratio:* 19:1.

Majors Accounting; business administration; business marketing and marketing management; computer programming; emergency medical technology; finance; health services administration; hotel and restaurant management; information sciences/systems; international business; legal administrative assistant; medical administrative assistant; medical assistant; paralegal/legal assistant; secretarial science.

Academic Programs *Special study options:* academic remediation for entering students, accelerated degree program, adult/continuing education programs, advanced placement credit, cooperative education, distance learning, English as a second language, external degree program, independent study, internships, part-time degree program, study abroad, summer session for credit.

Library Sneden Library plus 1 other with 40,810 titles, 1,500 serial subscriptions, an OPAC.

Computers on Campus 122 computers available on campus for general student use. A campuswide network can be accessed from student residence rooms and from off campus. Internet access, at least one staffed computer lab available.

Student Life *Housing Options:* coed. *Campus security:* 24-hour emergency response devices and patrols, late-night transport/escort service, controlled dormitory access. *Student Services:* personal/psychological counseling.

Athletics *Intramural sports:* basketball M/W, golf M/W, racquetball M/W, soccer M/W, softball M/W, tennis M/W, volleyball M/W.

Standardized Tests *Recommended:* ACT (for placement).

Costs (2001–02) *One-time required fee:* $105. *Tuition:* $8586 full-time, $212 per credit part-time. Full-time tuition and fees vary according to course load, degree level, location, and reciprocity agreements. Part-time tuition and fees vary according to course load, degree level, location, and reciprocity agreements. *Required fees:* $105 full-time. *Room only:* $7335. Room and board charges vary according to housing facility. *Payment plan:* installment. *Waivers:* employees or children of employees.

Davenport University (continued)

Applying *Options:* common application, early admission, deferred entrance. *Application fee:* $25. *Required:* high school transcript. *Recommended:* essay or personal statement, interview. *Application deadlines:* rolling (freshmen), 9/15 (out-of-state freshmen), rolling (transfers). *Notification:* continuous (freshmen), continuous (out-of-state freshmen).

Admissions Contact Mr. Paul David, Director of Admissions, Davenport University, 415 East Fulton, Grand Rapids, MI 49503. *Phone:* 616-732-1200. *Toll-free phone:* 800-632-9569.

DAVENPORT UNIVERSITY
Dearborn, Michigan

- **Independent** comprehensive, founded 1962
- **Calendar** quarters
- **Degrees** certificates, associate, bachelor's, and master's
- **Suburban** 17-acre campus with easy access to Detroit
- **Coed,** 2,862 undergraduate students, 54% full-time, 75% women, 25% men
- **Noncompetitive** entrance level, 100% of applicants were admitted

Undergraduates 1,542 full-time, 1,320 part-time. Students come from 4 states and territories, 10 other countries, 1% are from out of state, 60% African American, 2% Asian American or Pacific Islander, 2% Hispanic American, 0.7% Native American, 1% international, 14% transferred in.

Freshmen *Admission:* 625 applied, 625 admitted, 351 enrolled.

Faculty *Total:* 190, 15% full-time. *Student/faculty ratio:* 24:1.

Majors Accounting; business administration; business marketing and marketing management; business systems networking/ telecommunications; enterprise management; finance; health services administration; international business; legal administrative assistant; management information systems/business data processing; medical administrative assistant; nonprofit/public management; office management; secretarial science.

Academic Programs *Special study options:* academic remediation for entering students, advanced placement credit, cooperative education, double majors, independent study, internships, part-time degree program, summer session for credit.

Library Dearborn Campus Library plus 1 other with 33,560 titles, 224 serial subscriptions, 299 audiovisual materials, an OPAC.

Computers on Campus 295 computers available on campus for general student use. Internet access, at least one staffed computer lab available.

Student Life *Housing:* college housing not available. *Activities and Organizations:* student-run newspaper, Health Occupations Students of America (HOSA), student newspaper, student council, Allman Rafiki Society (ARS), President's Council. *Campus security:* late-night transport/escort service.

Athletics *Intramural sports:* bowling M/W, golf M, softball M/W.

Costs (2001–02) *Tuition:* $7344 full-time, $204 per quarter hour part-time. Full-time tuition and fees vary according to course load and location. Part-time tuition and fees vary according to course load and location. *Required fees:* $105 full-time, $35 per quarter hour. *Payment plans:* installment, deferred payment. *Waivers:* children of alumni and employees or children of employees.

Financial Aid Of all full-time matriculated undergraduates who enrolled in 2001, 1387 applied for aid, 1360 were judged to have need, 96 had their need fully met. 51 Federal Work-Study jobs (averaging $1847). 79 State and other part-time jobs (averaging $2807). In 2001, 87 non-need-based awards were made. *Average percent of need met:* 37%. *Average financial aid package:* $6786. *Average need-based loan:* $3859. *Average need-based gift aid:* $4070. *Average non-need based aid:* $1863. *Average indebtedness upon graduation:* $5789.

Applying *Options:* early admission, deferred entrance. *Application fee:* $20. *Required:* high school transcript. *Recommended:* interview. *Application deadline:* rolling (freshmen), rolling (transfers). *Notification:* continuous (freshmen).

Admissions Contact Ms. Jennifer Salloum, Director of Admissions, Davenport University, 4801 Oakman Boulevard, Dearborn, MI 48126-3799. *Phone:* 313-581-4400. *Fax:* 313-581-1985. *E-mail:* jennifer.salloum@davenport.edu.

DAVENPORT UNIVERSITY
Warren, Michigan

- **Independent** comprehensive, founded 1962
- **Calendar** quarters
- **Degrees** certificates, associate, bachelor's, and master's
- **Suburban** 9-acre campus with easy access to Detroit
- **Coed,** 2,350 undergraduate students, 55% full-time, 78% women, 22% men
- **Noncompetitive** entrance level, 100% of applicants were admitted

Undergraduates 1,292 full-time, 1,058 part-time. Students come from 3 states and territories, 2 other countries, 1% are from out of state, 45% African American, 2% Asian American or Pacific Islander, 1% Hispanic American, 0.5% Native American, 0.2% international, 15% transferred in.

Freshmen *Admission:* 300 applied, 300 admitted, 299 enrolled.

Faculty *Total:* 114, 13% full-time. *Student/faculty ratio:* 24:1.

Majors Accounting; business administration; business marketing and marketing management; business systems analysis/design; business systems networking/ telecommunications; enterprise management; finance; international business; legal administrative assistant; management information systems/business data processing; nonprofit/public management.

Academic Programs *Special study options:* academic remediation for entering students, advanced placement credit, cooperative education, double majors, internships, part-time degree program, summer session for credit.

Library Detroit College of Business-Warren Library plus 1 other with 95,000 titles, 185 serial subscriptions, 237 audiovisual materials, an OPAC.

Computers on Campus 110 computers available on campus for general student use. At least one staffed computer lab available.

Student Life *Housing:* college housing not available. *Activities and Organizations:* student-run newspaper, Business Olympics, Marketing Club, Management Club, campus newspaper, Accounting Club. *Campus security:* late-night transport/ escort service. *Student Services:* personal/psychological counseling.

Athletics *Intramural sports:* bowling M/W.

Costs (2001–02) *Tuition:* $7344 full-time, $204 per quarter hour part-time. Full-time tuition and fees vary according to course load. Part-time tuition and fees vary according to course load. *Required fees:* $105 full-time, $35 per quarter hour. *Payment plans:* installment, deferred payment. *Waivers:* children of alumni and employees or children of employees.

Financial Aid Of all full-time matriculated undergraduates who enrolled in 2001, 915 applied for aid, 897 were judged to have need, 63 had their need fully met. 34 Federal Work-Study jobs (averaging $1829). 52 State and other part-time jobs (averaging $2875). In 2001, 57 non-need-based awards were made. *Average percent of need met:* 23%. *Average financial aid package:* $6315. *Average need-based loan:* $3120. *Average need-based gift aid:* $4097. *Average non-need based aid:* $1250. *Average indebtedness upon graduation:* $5789.

Applying *Options:* early admission, deferred entrance. *Application fee:* $20. *Required:* high school transcript. *Application deadline:* rolling (freshmen), rolling (transfers). *Notification:* continuous (freshmen).

Admissions Contact Ms. Gerri Pavone, Director of Admissions, Davenport University, 27650 Dequindre Road, Warren, MI 48092-5209. *Phone:* 586-558-8700. *Fax:* 810-558-7868. *E-mail:* gerripavone@davenport.edu.

DAVENPORT UNIVERSITY
Midland, Michigan

- **Independent** primarily 2-year, founded 1907, part of Davenport Educational System
- **Calendar** semesters
- **Degrees** certificates, associate, and bachelor's
- **Urban** campus
- **Coed**
- **Noncompetitive** entrance level

Student Life *Campus security:* 24-hour emergency response devices.

Standardized Tests *Required:* ACT ASSET.

Applying *Options:* early admission, deferred entrance. *Application fee:* $20. *Required:* high school transcript.

Admissions Contact Davenport University, 3555 East Patrick Road, Midland, MI 48642. *Toll-free phone:* 800-968-4860. *Fax:* 517-752-3453.

EASTERN MICHIGAN UNIVERSITY
Ypsilanti, Michigan

- **State-supported** comprehensive, founded 1849
- **Calendar** semesters
- **Degrees** bachelor's, master's, doctoral, and post-master's certificates
- **Suburban** 460-acre campus with easy access to Detroit
- **Endowment** $33.7 million
- **Coed,** 18,502 undergraduate students, 70% full-time, 61% women, 39% men
- **Moderately difficult** entrance level, 75% of applicants were admitted

Undergraduates 13,003 full-time, 5,499 part-time. Students come from 47 states and territories, 66 other countries, 10% are from out of state, 17% African

American, 2% Asian American or Pacific Islander, 2% Hispanic American, 0.7% Native American, 2% international, 10% transferred in, 23% live on campus. *Retention:* 71% of 2001 full-time freshmen returned.

Freshmen *Admission:* 9,212 applied, 6,868 admitted, 2,810 enrolled. *Average high school GPA:* 3.02. *Test scores:* SAT verbal scores over 500: 49%; SAT math scores over 500: 48%; ACT scores over 18: 80%; SAT verbal scores over 600: 14%; SAT math scores over 600: 18%; ACT scores over 24: 23%; SAT verbal scores over 700: 2%; SAT math scores over 700: 2%; ACT scores over 30: 2%.

Faculty *Total:* 1,166, 65% full-time. *Student/faculty ratio:* 19:1.

Majors Accounting; actuarial science; adapted physical education; aerospace engineering technology; African-American studies; anthropology; architecture; area studies; art; art education; art history; arts management; athletic training/sports medicine; bilingual/bicultural education; biochemistry; biological/physical sciences; biology; biology education; broadcast journalism; business; business administration; business economics; business education; business marketing and marketing management; chemistry; chemistry education; city/community/regional planning; communication equipment technology; computer education; computer engineering; computer/information sciences; criminal justice/law enforcement administration; criminology; cytotechnology; dance; data processing; dietetics; drama/dance education; earth sciences; economics; education of the emotionally handicapped; education of the hearing impaired; education of the mentally handicapped; education of the physically handicapped; education of the speech impaired; education of the visually handicapped; elementary education; energy management technology; English; English composition; English education; executive assistant; family resource management studies; fashion merchandising; finance; foreign languages education; French; French language education; geography; geology; geophysics/seismology; German; German language education; health/physical education; health services administration; history; history education; home economics education; hospitality management; human resources management; individual/family development; industrial arts education; industrial technology; information sciences/systems; interdisciplinary studies; interior design; international business; international business marketing; Japanese; journalism; legal administrative assistant; linguistics; management information systems/business data processing; marketing/distribution education; mathematical statistics; mathematics; mathematics education; medical technology; metallurgy; music; music (general performance); music teacher education; music therapy; nursing; nutrition studies; occupational therapy; philosophy; physical education; physical sciences; physics; physics education; plastics engineering; plastics technology; political science; pre-medicine; psychology; public administration; public relations; purchasing/contracts management; radio/television broadcasting technology; real estate; recreation/leisure facilities management; religious studies; science education; secondary education; social science education; social sciences; social studies education; social work; sociology; Spanish; Spanish language education; special education; speech/rhetorical studies; theater arts/drama; tourism promotion operations; tourism/travel marketing; toxicology; women's studies.

Academic Programs *Special study options:* academic remediation for entering students, accelerated degree program, adult/continuing education programs, advanced placement credit, cooperative education, distance learning, double majors, English as a second language, honors programs, independent study, internships, part-time degree program, services for LD students, student-designed majors, study abroad, summer session for credit. *ROTC:* Army (b), Navy (c), Air Force (c).

Library Bruce T. Halle Library with 951,062 titles, 6,244 serial subscriptions, 7,229 audiovisual materials, an OPAC, a Web page.

Computers on Campus 525 computers available on campus for general student use. A campuswide network can be accessed from student residence rooms and from off campus. Internet access, at least one staffed computer lab available.

Student Life *Housing:* on-campus residence required through sophomore year. *Options:* coed, women-only, disabled students. *Activities and Organizations:* drama/theater group, student-run newspaper, radio and television station, choral group, marching band, national fraternities, national sororities. *Campus security:* 24-hour emergency response devices and patrols, student patrols, late-night transport/escort service, controlled dormitory access, bicycle patrols, local police in dormitories, self defense education, lighted pathways, bike lock lease program. *Student Services:* health clinic, personal/psychological counseling, women's center.

Athletics Member NCAA. All Division I except football (Division I-A). *Intercollegiate sports:* baseball M(s), basketball M(s)/W(s), crew W, cross-country running M(s)/W(s), golf M(s)/W(s), gymnastics W(s), soccer W(s), softball W(s), swimming M(s)/W(s), tennis W(s), track and field M(s)/W(s), volleyball W(s), wrestling M(s). *Intramural sports:* badminton M/W, basketball M/W, bowling M/W, cross-country running M/W, fencing M(c)/W(c), golf M/W, gymnastics M(c)/W(c), ice hockey M(c), lacrosse M(c)/W(c), racquetball M/W, skiing (cross-country) M/W, soccer M/W, softball M/W, swimming M/W, table tennis M/W, tennis M/W, track and field M/W, volleyball M/W, water polo W(c), weight lifting M/W.

Standardized Tests *Required:* SAT I or ACT (for admission).

Costs (2001–02) *Tuition:* state resident $3623 full-time, $121 per credit hour part-time; nonresident $11,250 full-time, $375 per credit hour part-time. Full-time tuition and fees vary according to reciprocity agreements. Part-time tuition and fees vary according to reciprocity agreements. *Required fees:* $980 full-time, $30 per credit hour, $40 per term part-time. *Room and board:* $5252. Room and board charges vary according to housing facility and location. *Payment plan:* installment. *Waivers:* employees or children of employees.

Financial Aid Of all full-time matriculated undergraduates who enrolled in 2001, 9453 applied for aid, 6428 were judged to have need, 2088 had their need fully met. In 2001, 1552 non-need-based awards were made. *Average percent of need met:* 86%. *Average financial aid package:* $9901. *Average need-based loan:* $3718. *Average need-based gift aid:* $3331. *Average non-need based aid:* $1798. *Average indebtedness upon graduation:* $12,018.

Applying *Options:* deferred entrance. *Application fee:* $25. *Required:* high school transcript, minimum 2.0 GPA. *Required for some:* 1 letter of recommendation, interview. *Application deadlines:* 6/30 (freshmen), 6/30 (transfers). *Notification:* continuous (freshmen).

Admissions Contact Ms. Judy Benfield-Tatum, Director of Admissions, Eastern Michigan University, Ypsilanti, MI 48197. *Phone:* 734-487-3060. *Toll-free phone:* 800-GO TO EMU. *Fax:* 734-487-1484.

FERRIS STATE UNIVERSITY
Big Rapids, Michigan

- **State-supported** comprehensive, founded 1884
- **Calendar** semesters
- **Degrees** certificates, associate, bachelor's, master's, and first professional
- **Small-town** 600-acre campus with easy access to Grand Rapids
- **Endowment** $20.3 million
- **Coed,** 10,092 undergraduate students, 79% full-time, 46% women, 54% men
- **Minimally difficult** entrance level, 51% of applicants were admitted

Undergraduates 7,961 full-time, 2,131 part-time. Students come from 45 states and territories, 76 other countries, 6% are from out of state, 9% African American, 2% Asian American or Pacific Islander, 2% Hispanic American, 0.7% Native American, 2% international, 12% transferred in, 38% live on campus. *Retention:* 59% of 2001 full-time freshmen returned.

Freshmen *Admission:* 6,409 applied, 3,263 admitted, 2,204 enrolled. *Average high school GPA:* 3.51. *Test scores:* ACT scores over 18: 69%; ACT scores over 24: 20%; ACT scores over 30: 2%.

Faculty *Total:* 510, 91% full-time. *Student/faculty ratio:* 18:1.

Majors Accounting; advertising; applied mathematics; architectural engineering technology; auto mechanic/technician; biological technology; biology; business administration; business economics; business education; business marketing and marketing management; chemical engineering technology; child care/development; civil engineering technology; communication equipment technology; computer programming; construction management; construction technology; criminal justice/law enforcement administration; dental hygiene; drafting; education; educational media design; electrical/electronic engineering technology; energy management technology; environmental health; finance; fine/studio arts; food products retailing; furniture design; graphic design/commercial art/illustration; graphic/printing equipment; health services administration; heating/air conditioning/refrigeration; heavy equipment maintenance; home economics education; hospitality management; industrial design; industrial/manufacturing engineering; industrial radiologic technology; industrial technology; information sciences/systems; insurance/risk management; interior design; international business; labor/personnel relations; law enforcement/police science; legal administrative assistant; liberal arts and sciences/liberal studies; machine technology; management information systems/business data processing; mass communications; mathematics; mechanical design technology; mechanical engineering technology; medical laboratory technician; medical laboratory technology; medical records administration; medical technology; music business management/merchandising; nuclear medical technology; nursing; occupational safety/health technology; ophthalmic/optometric services; ornamental horticulture; paralegal/legal assistant; pharmacy; plastics engineering; plastics technology; pre-engineering; public administration; public relations; quality control technology; real estate; recreation/leisure studies; respiratory therapy; retail management; science education; secondary education; social work; speech/rhetorical studies; surveying; technical/business writing; telecommunications; welding technology.

Academic Programs *Special study options:* academic remediation for entering students, accelerated degree program, adult/continuing education programs, advanced placement credit, cooperative education, distance learning, double majors, English as a second language, external degree program, freshman honors college, honors programs, internships, off-campus study, part-time degree program, summer session for credit. *ROTC:* Army (c).

Ferris State University (continued)

Library Ferris Library for Information, Technology and Education with 339,164 titles, 10,000 serial subscriptions, 10,136 audiovisual materials, an OPAC, a Web page.

Computers on Campus 276 computers available on campus for general student use. A campuswide network can be accessed from student residence rooms and from off campus. Internet access, online (class) registration, at least one staffed computer lab available.

Student Life *Housing:* on-campus residence required through sophomore year. *Options:* coed, men-only, women-only. *Activities and Organizations:* drama/theater group, student-run newspaper, radio and television station, choral group, Associated Student Government, intramural sports club, University Theatre, Music Club, Forensics Club, national fraternities, national sororities. *Campus security:* 24-hour emergency response devices, student patrols, late-night transport/escort service. *Student Services:* health clinic, personal/psychological counseling.

Athletics Member NCAA. All Division II except ice hockey (Division I). *Intercollegiate sports:* basketball M(s)/W(s), cross-country running W(s), football M(s), golf M(s)/W(s), ice hockey M(s), softball W(s), tennis M(s)/W(s), track and field M(s)/W(s), volleyball W(s). *Intramural sports:* badminton M/W, basketball M/W, bowling M/W, cross-country running M/W, football M, golf M/W, ice hockey M, racquetball M/W, softball M/W, swimming M/W, table tennis M/W, tennis M/W, track and field M/W, volleyball M/W, water polo M/W, wrestling M.

Standardized Tests *Required:* ACT (for admission).

Costs (2001–02) *Tuition:* state resident $4670 full-time, $196 per credit hour part-time; nonresident $9890 full-time, $414 per credit hour part-time. Part-time tuition and fees vary according to course load. *Required fees:* $400 full-time, $15 per credit hour part-time. *Room and board:* $5628. Room and board charges vary according to board plan and housing facility. *Payment plans:* installment, deferred payment. *Waivers:* employees or children of employees.

Financial Aid Of all full-time matriculated undergraduates who enrolled in 2001, 6454 applied for aid, 5744 were judged to have need, 382 had their need fully met. In 2001, 596 non-need-based awards were made. *Average percent of need met:* 80%. *Average financial aid package:* $7880. *Average need-based loan:* $3400. *Average need-based gift aid:* $3300. *Average non-need based aid:* $1900. *Average indebtedness upon graduation:* $18,287.

Applying *Options:* electronic application, deferred entrance. *Application fee:* $30. *Required:* high school transcript, minimum 2.0 GPA. *Required for some:* interview. *Recommended:* interview. *Application deadline:* rolling (freshmen), rolling (transfers). *Notification:* continuous (freshmen).

Admissions Contact Mr. Ronnie Higgs, Assistant Vice President/Dean of Enrollment Services, Ferris State University, PRK 110, Big Rapids, MI 49307-2742. *Phone:* 231-591-2100. *Toll-free phone:* 800-433-7747. *Fax:* 616-592-2978. *E-mail:* admissions@ferris.edu.

FINLANDIA UNIVERSITY
Hancock, Michigan

- **Independent** 4-year, founded 1896, affiliated with Evangelical Lutheran Church in America
- **Calendar** semesters
- **Degrees** associate and bachelor's
- **Small-town** 25-acre campus
- **Endowment** $2.5 million
- **Coed,** 418 undergraduate students, 83% full-time, 66% women, 34% men
- **Minimally difficult** entrance level, 52% of applicants were admitted

Undergraduates 349 full-time, 69 part-time. Students come from 8 states and territories, 4 other countries, 9% are from out of state, 1.0% African American, 0.2% Asian American or Pacific Islander, 1% Native American, 6% international, 8% transferred in, 25% live on campus. *Retention:* 54% of 2001 full-time freshmen returned.

Freshmen *Admission:* 195 applied, 101 admitted, 101 enrolled. *Average high school GPA:* 2.81. *Test scores:* ACT scores over 18: 72%; ACT scores over 24: 23%; ACT scores over 30: 2%.

Faculty *Total:* 62, 52% full-time. *Student/faculty ratio:* 11:1.

Majors Art; business administration; ceramic arts; criminal justice/law enforcement administration; education; education (K-12); fine/studio arts; general studies; human services; industrial design; international business; liberal arts and sciences/liberal studies; nursing; physical therapy assistant; textile arts.

Academic Programs *Special study options:* academic remediation for entering students, accelerated degree program, adult/continuing education programs, advanced placement credit, distance learning, English as a second language, independent study, internships, part-time degree program, services for LD students, study abroad, summer session for credit. *ROTC:* Army (c), Air Force (c).

Library Sulo and Aileen Maki Library with 61,631 titles, 313 serial subscriptions, 15,694 audiovisual materials, an OPAC.

Computers on Campus 65 computers available on campus for general student use. Internet access, at least one staffed computer lab available.

Student Life *Housing:* on-campus residence required through junior year. *Options:* coed. *Activities and Organizations:* drama/theater group, choral group, Student Senate, community service club, Suomi business group, Campus Enrichment, hall government. *Campus security:* 24-hour patrols, late-night transport/escort service. *Student Services:* personal/psychological counseling.

Athletics Member NSCAA. *Intercollegiate sports:* basketball M/W. *Intramural sports:* basketball M/W, bowling M/W, equestrian sports M/W, ice hockey M/W, skiing (cross-country) M/W, softball M/W, table tennis M/W, tennis M/W, volleyball M/W.

Standardized Tests *Recommended:* SAT I or ACT (for admission).

Costs (2002–03) *One-time required fee:* $75. *Comprehensive fee:* $17,280 includes full-time tuition ($12,600) and room and board ($4680). Full-time tuition and fees vary according to degree level. Part-time tuition: $420 per credit. Part-time tuition and fees vary according to course load and reciprocity agreements. *Room and board:* Room and board charges vary according to housing facility. *Payment plan:* installment. *Waivers:* employees or children of employees.

Financial Aid Of all full-time matriculated undergraduates who enrolled in 2001, 318 applied for aid, 308 were judged to have need. 288 Federal Work-Study jobs (averaging $880). 31 State and other part-time jobs (averaging $830). In 2001, 11 non-need-based awards were made. *Average non-need based aid:* $2400. *Average indebtedness upon graduation:* $17,000.

Applying *Options:* common application, early admission. *Application fee:* $20. *Required:* high school transcript, minimum 2.25 GPA. *Required for some:* essay or personal statement, letters of recommendation, interview. *Application deadlines:* 8/15 (freshmen), 8/15 (transfers). *Notification:* continuous (freshmen).

Admissions Contact Mr. Ben Larson, Executive Director of Admissions, Finlandia University, 601 Quincy Street, Hancock, MI 49930. *Phone:* 906-487-7311 Ext. 311. *Toll-free phone:* 877-202-5491. *Fax:* 906-487-7383. *E-mail:* admissions@finlandia.edu.

GRACE BIBLE COLLEGE
Grand Rapids, Michigan

- **Independent** 4-year, founded 1945, affiliated with Grace Gospel Fellowship
- **Calendar** semesters
- **Degrees** associate and bachelor's
- **Suburban** 16-acre campus
- **Endowment** $1.2 million
- **Coed,** 149 undergraduate students, 89% full-time, 48% women, 52% men
- **Minimally difficult** entrance level, 51% of applicants were admitted

Undergraduates 133 full-time, 16 part-time. Students come from 15 states and territories, 2 other countries, 32% are from out of state, 2% African American, 2% Asian American or Pacific Islander, 0.7% Hispanic American, 0.7% Native American, 1% international, 8% transferred in, 64% live on campus. *Retention:* 83% of 2001 full-time freshmen returned.

Freshmen *Admission:* 122 applied, 62 admitted, 31 enrolled. *Average high school GPA:* 3.13. *Test scores:* ACT scores over 18: 71%; ACT scores over 24: 19%.

Faculty *Total:* 29, 31% full-time, 21% with terminal degrees. *Student/faculty ratio:* 11:1.

Majors Biblical studies; business administration; early childhood education; elementary education; human services; liberal arts and sciences/liberal studies; multi/interdisciplinary studies related; music; music business management/merchandising; music teacher education; pastoral counseling; religious education; religious studies; secondary education; theology.

Academic Programs *Special study options:* academic remediation for entering students, advanced placement credit, English as a second language, independent study, internships, off-campus study.

Library Bultema Memorial Library with 40,013 titles, 160 serial subscriptions, 1,641 audiovisual materials, an OPAC.

Computers on Campus 25 computers available on campus for general student use. Internet access, at least one staffed computer lab available.

Student Life *Housing:* on-campus residence required through sophomore year. *Options:* men-only, women-only. *Activities and Organizations:* drama/theater group, choral group, Ambassador Fellowship, Student Activities Committee, Student Council, Ambassador Staff, Campus Ministry Team. *Campus security:* student patrols, controlled dormitory access. *Student Services:* personal/psychological counseling.

Athletics Member NCCAA. *Intercollegiate sports:* basketball M/W, soccer M, volleyball W. *Intramural sports:* basketball M, football M, golf M, racquetball

M/W, skiing (cross-country) M/W, skiing (downhill) M/W, soccer M/W, table tennis M/W, tennis M/W, volleyball M, weight lifting M/W.

Standardized Tests *Required:* ACT (for admission).

Costs (2001–02) *Comprehensive fee:* $12,600 includes full-time tuition ($7600), mandatory fees ($350), and room and board ($4650). Part-time tuition: $320 per semester hour. Part-time tuition and fees vary according to course load. *Room and board:* College room only: $2000. Room and board charges vary according to housing facility. *Payment plan:* installment. *Waivers:* employees or children of employees.

Financial Aid Of all full-time matriculated undergraduates who enrolled in 2001, 131 applied for aid, 102 were judged to have need. 28 Federal Work-Study jobs (averaging $1171). 13 State and other part-time jobs (averaging $483). *Average percent of need met:* 73%. *Average financial aid package:* $7706. *Average need-based loan:* $4453. *Average need-based gift aid:* $10,724. *Average non-need based aid:* $1041. *Average indebtedness upon graduation:* $12,122.

Applying *Options:* early admission, deferred entrance. *Required:* high school transcript, 2 letters of recommendation. *Required for some:* interview. *Recommended:* minimum 2.5 GPA. *Application deadline:* 7/15 (freshmen). *Notification:* continuous until 8/1 (freshmen).

Admissions Contact Mr. Kevin Gilliam, Director of Enrollment, Grace Bible College, 1101 Aldon Street, SW, PO Box 910, Grand Rapids, MI 49509. *Phone:* 616-538-2330. *Toll-free phone:* 800-968-1887. *Fax:* 616-538-0599. *E-mail:* gbc@gbcol.edu.

GRAND VALLEY STATE UNIVERSITY
Allendale, Michigan

- **State-supported** comprehensive, founded 1960
- **Calendar** semesters
- **Degrees** bachelor's, master's, post-master's, and postbachelor's certificates
- **Small-town** 900-acre campus with easy access to Grand Rapids
- **Endowment** $39.4 million
- **Coed,** 16,385 undergraduate students, 82% full-time, 60% women, 40% men
- **Moderately difficult** entrance level, 78% of applicants were admitted

Undergraduates 13,371 full-time, 3,014 part-time. Students come from 40 states and territories, 38 other countries, 3% are from out of state, 5% African American, 2% Asian American or Pacific Islander, 2% Hispanic American, 0.6% Native American, 0.5% international, 7% transferred in, 27% live on campus. *Retention:* 78% of 2001 full-time freshmen returned.

Freshmen *Admission:* 9,593 applied, 7,506 admitted, 3,009 enrolled. *Average high school GPA:* 3.30. *Test scores:* ACT scores over 18: 97%; ACT scores over 24: 40%; ACT scores over 30: 4%.

Faculty *Total:* 1,146, 60% full-time, 42% with terminal degrees. *Student/faculty ratio:* 22:1.

Majors Accounting; advertising; anthropology; applied mathematics; art; art education; art history; athletic training/sports medicine; behavioral sciences; biological/physical sciences; biology; biomedical science; broadcast journalism; business administration; business marketing and marketing management; ceramic arts; chemistry; computer/information sciences; computer programming; computer science; creative writing; criminal justice/law enforcement administration; drawing; earth sciences; economics; education; electrical engineering; elementary education; engineering; engineering/industrial management; English; film studies; film/video production; finance; fine/studio arts; French; geology; German; graphic design/commercial art/illustration; health science; history; hotel and restaurant management; humanities; human resources management; industrial/manufacturing engineering; information sciences/systems; interdisciplinary studies; international business; international relations; journalism; labor/personnel relations; land use management; law enforcement/police science; legal studies; liberal arts and sciences/liberal studies; literature; management information systems/business data processing; mass communications; mathematical statistics; mathematics; mechanical engineering; medical technology; metal/jewelry arts; music; music (piano and organ performance); music teacher education; music (voice and choral/opera performance); natural resources management; natural sciences; nursing; occupational safety/health technology; occupational therapy assistant; paralegal/legal assistant; philosophy; photography; physical education; physical sciences; physical therapy; physician assistant; physics; physiological psychology/psychobiology; political science; pre-dentistry; pre-law; pre-medicine; pre-veterinary studies; printmaking; psychology; public administration; public health; public policy analysis; public relations; radio/television broadcasting; reading education; recreational therapy; recreation/leisure facilities management; Russian/Slavic studies; sanitation technology; science education; sculpture; secondary education; social sciences; social work; sociology; Spanish; special education; stringed instruments; technical/business writing; telecommunications; theater arts/drama; travel/tourism management; water resources; western civilization; wildlife biology; wildlife management; wind/percussion instruments; women's studies.

Academic Programs *Special study options:* academic remediation for entering students, accelerated degree program, adult/continuing education programs, advanced placement credit, cooperative education, distance learning, double majors, English as a second language, honors programs, independent study, internships, part-time degree program, services for LD students, study abroad, summer session for credit.

Library James H. Zumberge Library plus 2 others with 620,000 titles, 3,207 serial subscriptions, an OPAC, a Web page.

Computers on Campus 2600 computers available on campus for general student use. A campuswide network can be accessed from student residence rooms and from off campus that provide access to transcript, degree audit. Internet access, online (class) registration, at least one staffed computer lab available.

Student Life *Housing Options:* coed. *Activities and Organizations:* drama/theater group, student-run newspaper, choral group, marching band, Black Student Union, Residence Hall Association, Crew Club, student senate, Student Organization Network, national fraternities, national sororities. *Campus security:* 24-hour emergency response devices and patrols, student patrols, late-night transport/escort service. *Student Services:* health clinic, personal/psychological counseling, women's center.

Athletics Member NCAA. All Division II. *Intercollegiate sports:* baseball M(s), basketball M(s)/W(s), crew M(c)/W(c), cross-country running M(s)/W(s), football M(s), golf M(s)/W(s), ice hockey M(c), skiing (downhill) M(c)/W(c), soccer M(c)/W(s), softball W(s), swimming M(s)/W(s), tennis M(s)/W(s), track and field M(s)/W(s), volleyball M(c)/W(s), wrestling M(c). *Intramural sports:* archery M/W, badminton M/W, basketball M/W, bowling M/W, crew M/W, cross-country running M/W, fencing M/W, field hockey M/W, football M/W, golf M/W, gymnastics M/W, racquetball M/W, skiing (cross-country) M/W, skiing (downhill) M/W, soccer M/W, softball M/W, squash M/W, swimming M/W, tennis M/W, volleyball M/W, water polo M/W, weight lifting M/W, wrestling M.

Standardized Tests *Required:* SAT I or ACT (for admission).

Costs (2001–02) *Tuition:* state resident $4660 full-time, $205 per semester hour part-time; nonresident $10,080 full-time, $431 per semester hour part-time. Full-time tuition and fees vary according to student level. Part-time tuition and fees vary according to course load. *Room and board:* $5380. Room and board charges vary according to board plan, housing facility, and location. *Payment plans:* installment, deferred payment. *Waivers:* employees or children of employees.

Financial Aid Of all full-time matriculated undergraduates who enrolled in 2001, 8230 applied for aid, 5942 were judged to have need, 5431 had their need fully met. In 2001, 1603 non-need-based awards were made. *Average percent of need met:* 92%. *Average financial aid package:* $5986. *Average need-based loan:* $3263. *Average need-based gift aid:* $2824. *Average non-need based aid:* $1210. *Average indebtedness upon graduation:* $12,200.

Applying *Options:* electronic application. *Application fee:* $20. *Required:* high school transcript. *Required for some:* essay or personal statement, interview. *Application deadlines:* 7/25 (freshmen), 7/25 (transfers). *Notification:* continuous until 8/25 (freshmen).

Admissions Contact Ms. Jodi Chycinski, Director of Admissions, Grand Valley State University, 1 Campus Drive, Allendale, MI 49401. *Phone:* 616-895-2025. *Toll-free phone:* 800-748-0246. *Fax:* 616-895-2000. *E-mail:* go2gvsu@gvsu.edu.

GREAT LAKES CHRISTIAN COLLEGE
Lansing, Michigan

- **Independent** 4-year, founded 1949, affiliated with Christian Churches and Churches of Christ
- **Calendar** semesters
- **Degrees** associate and bachelor's
- **Suburban** 50-acre campus
- **Coed,** 220 undergraduate students
- **Moderately difficult** entrance level, 64% of applicants were admitted

Undergraduates Students come from 8 states and territories, 3 other countries, 68% live on campus.

Freshmen *Admission:* 138 applied, 89 admitted. *Average high school GPA:* 3.00.

Faculty *Total:* 16, 63% full-time. *Student/faculty ratio:* 17:1.

Majors Biblical studies; divinity/ministry; education; music; religious education; theology.

Academic Programs *Special study options:* adult/continuing education programs, advanced placement credit, double majors, external degree program,

Great Lakes Christian College (continued)
independent study, internships, off-campus study, part-time degree program. *Unusual degree programs:* 3-2 business administration with Davenport College of Business; education with Michigan State University.

Library Louis M. Detro Memorial Library with 34,000 titles, 213 serial subscriptions.

Computers on Campus 10 computers available on campus for general student use. Internet access, at least one staffed computer lab available.

Student Life *Housing:* on-campus residence required through senior year. *Options:* men-only, women-only. *Activities and Organizations:* choral group. *Campus security:* evening security patrols. *Student Services:* personal/psychological counseling.

Athletics *Intercollegiate sports:* baseball M, soccer M/W. *Intramural sports:* basketball M/W, volleyball W.

Costs (2002–03) *Comprehensive fee:* $12,500 includes full-time tuition ($6600), mandatory fees ($1400), and room and board ($4500). Part-time tuition: $220 per hour.

Applying *Options:* early admission, deferred entrance. *Application fee:* $30. *Required:* essay or personal statement, high school transcript, minimum 2.25 GPA, 3 letters of recommendation. *Application deadlines:* 8/1 (freshmen), 8/1 (transfers). *Notification:* continuous until 8/15 (freshmen).

Admissions Contact Mr. Mike Klauka, Director of Admissions, Great Lakes Christian College, 6211 West Willow Highway, Lansing, MI 48917-1299. *Phone:* 517-321-0242 Ext. 221. *Toll-free phone:* 800-YES-GLCC. *Fax:* 517-321-5902.

HILLSDALE COLLEGE
Hillsdale, Michigan

- **Independent** 4-year, founded 1844
- **Calendar** semesters
- **Degree** bachelor's
- **Small-town** 200-acre campus
- **Endowment** $200.0 million
- **Coed,** 1,168 undergraduate students, 97% full-time, 51% women, 49% men
- **Very difficult** entrance level, 85% of applicants were admitted

Undergraduates 1,128 full-time, 40 part-time. Students come from 47 states and territories, 10 other countries, 51% are from out of state, 3% transferred in, 85% live on campus. *Retention:* 87% of 2001 full-time freshmen returned.

Freshmen *Admission:* 925 applied, 783 admitted, 355 enrolled. *Average high school GPA:* 3.56. *Test scores:* SAT verbal scores over 500: 94%; SAT math scores over 500: 91%; ACT scores over 18: 100%; SAT verbal scores over 600: 63%; SAT math scores over 600: 55%; ACT scores over 24: 72%; SAT verbal scores over 700: 26%; SAT math scores over 700: 13%; ACT scores over 30: 19%.

Faculty *Total:* 130, 68% full-time, 90% with terminal degrees. *Student/faculty ratio:* 11:1.

Majors Accounting; American studies; art; biology; business administration; business marketing and marketing management; chemistry; classics; comparative literature; computer science; drafting/design technology; early childhood education; economics; education; education (K-12); elementary education; English; European studies; finance; French; German; history; interdisciplinary studies; international relations; mathematics; music; philosophy; physical education; physics; political science; pre-dentistry; pre-medicine; pre-veterinary studies; psychology; religious studies; secondary education; sociology; Spanish; speech/rhetorical studies; theater arts/drama.

Academic Programs *Special study options:* accelerated degree program, advanced placement credit, double majors, honors programs, independent study, internships, part-time degree program, study abroad, summer session for credit. *Unusual degree programs:* 3-2 engineering with Northwestern University, Tri-State University.

Library Mossey Learning Center plus 3 others with 205,000 titles, 1,623 serial subscriptions, 7,900 audiovisual materials, an OPAC, a Web page.

Computers on Campus 175 computers available on campus for general student use. A campuswide network can be accessed from student residence rooms and from off campus. Internet access, at least one staffed computer lab available.

Student Life *Housing:* on-campus residence required through sophomore year. *Options:* men-only, women-only. *Activities and Organizations:* drama/theater group, student-run newspaper, choral group, Intervarsity Christian Fellowship, H-Club, Student Federation, Prelaw Society, national fraternities, national sororities. *Campus security:* 24-hour emergency response devices and patrols, late-night transport/escort service, controlled dormitory access. *Student Services:* health clinic, personal/psychological counseling.

Athletics Member NCAA. All Division II. *Intercollegiate sports:* baseball M(s), basketball M(s)/W(s), cross-country running M(s)/W(s), equestrian sports W, football M(s), golf M(s), ice hockey M, soccer M(s)/W(s), softball W(s), swimming M(s)/W(s), tennis M(s)/W(s), track and field M(s)/W(s), volleyball W(s). *Intramural sports:* basketball M/W, cross-country running M/W, equestrian sports W(c), football M/W, golf M/W, ice hockey M(c), racquetball M/W, skiing (downhill) M(c)/W(c), soccer M/W, softball M/W, squash M/W, swimming M/W, table tennis M/W, tennis M/W, track and field M/W, volleyball M/W.

Standardized Tests *Required:* SAT I or ACT (for admission). *Recommended:* SAT II: Subject Tests (for admission), SAT II: Writing Test (for admission).

Costs (2001–02) *Comprehensive fee:* $20,586 includes full-time tuition ($14,400), mandatory fees ($300), and room and board ($5886). Part-time tuition: $570 per semester hour. Part-time tuition and fees vary according to course load. *Room and board:* College room only: $2886. Room and board charges vary according to board plan. *Payment plan:* installment. *Waivers:* employees or children of employees.

Financial Aid Of all full-time matriculated undergraduates who enrolled in 2001, 1024 applied for aid, 602 were judged to have need, 270 had their need fully met. *Average percent of need met:* 77%. *Average financial aid package:* $14,000. *Average need-based loan:* $2500. *Average need-based gift aid:* $9500. *Average non-need based aid:* $6000. *Average indebtedness upon graduation:* $14,000.

Applying *Options:* common application, electronic application, early admission, deferred entrance. *Application fee:* $15. *Required:* essay or personal statement, high school transcript, minimum 3.1 GPA, 1 letter of recommendation. *Required for some:* interview. *Recommended:* interview. *Application deadline:* rolling (freshmen), rolling (transfers). *Notification:* continuous until 7/15 (freshmen).

Admissions Contact Mr. Jeffrey S. Lantis, Director of Admissions, Hillsdale College, 33 East College Street, Hillsdale, MI 49242-1298. *Phone:* 517-607-2327 Ext. 2327. *Fax:* 517-607-2298. *E-mail:* admissions@hillsdale.edu.

HOPE COLLEGE
Holland, Michigan

- **Independent** 4-year, founded 1866, affiliated with Reformed Church in America
- **Calendar** semesters
- **Degree** bachelor's
- **Small-town** 45-acre campus with easy access to Grand Rapids
- **Endowment** $115.2 million
- **Coed,** 2,999 undergraduate students, 96% full-time, 60% women, 40% men
- **Moderately difficult** entrance level, 89% of applicants were admitted

Undergraduates 2,871 full-time, 128 part-time. Students come from 38 states and territories, 40 other countries, 23% are from out of state, 1% African American, 2% Asian American or Pacific Islander, 2% Hispanic American, 0.2% Native American, 2% international, 2% transferred in, 76% live on campus. *Retention:* 87% of 2001 full-time freshmen returned.

Freshmen *Admission:* 2,110 applied, 1,869 admitted, 763 enrolled. *Average high school GPA:* 3.69. *Test scores:* SAT verbal scores over 500: 88%; SAT math scores over 500: 87%; ACT scores over 18: 98%; SAT verbal scores over 600: 49%; SAT math scores over 600: 57%; ACT scores over 24: 64%; SAT verbal scores over 700: 12%; SAT math scores over 700: 16%; ACT scores over 30: 15%.

Faculty *Total:* 295, 71% full-time, 80% with terminal degrees. *Student/faculty ratio:* 14:1.

Majors Accounting; art history; athletic training/sports medicine; biochemistry; biology; business administration; chemistry; classics; communications; computer science; dance; economics; education of the emotionally handicapped; education of the specific learning disabled; elementary education; engineering; engineering physics; English; environmental science; exercise sciences; fine/studio arts; French; geology; geophysics/seismology; German; history; humanities; interdisciplinary studies; Latin (ancient and medieval); mathematics; music; music (general performance); music history; music teacher education; music theory and composition; nursing; philosophy; physical education; physics; political science; psychology; religious studies; secondary education; social work; sociology; Spanish; theater arts/drama.

Academic Programs *Special study options:* advanced placement credit, double majors, English as a second language, independent study, internships, off-campus study, part-time degree program, services for LD students, student-designed majors, study abroad, summer session for credit. *Unusual degree programs:* 3-2 engineering with University of Michigan, Columbia University, Rensselaer Polytechnic Institute, Case Western Reserve University, Washington University in St. Louis, University of Southern California.

Library Van Wylen Library plus 1 other with 330,408 titles, 2,250 serial subscriptions, 10,786 audiovisual materials, an OPAC, a Web page.

Computers on Campus 300 computers available on campus for general student use. A campuswide network can be accessed from student residence rooms and from off campus. Internet access, at least one staffed computer lab available.
Student Life *Housing:* on-campus residence required through junior year. *Options:* coed, men-only, women-only, disabled students. *Activities and Organizations:* drama/theater group, student-run newspaper, radio and television station, choral group, Fellowship of Christian Athletes, Social Activities Committee. *Campus security:* 24-hour emergency response devices and patrols, late-night transport/escort service, controlled dormitory access, deputized sheriffs. *Student Services:* health clinic, personal/psychological counseling.
Athletics Member NCAA. All Division III. *Intercollegiate sports:* baseball M, basketball M/W, cross-country running M/W, football M, golf M/W, ice hockey M(c), lacrosse M(c), soccer M/W, softball W, swimming M/W, tennis M/W, track and field M/W, volleyball M(c)/W, water polo M(c)/W(c). *Intramural sports:* basketball M/W, bowling M/W, cross-country running M/W, football M/W, lacrosse W, racquetball M/W, sailing M(c)/W(c), skiing (cross-country) M(c)/W(c), skiing (downhill) M(c)/W(c), soccer M/W, softball M/W, swimming M/W, tennis M/W, track and field M/W, volleyball M/W, water polo M/W.
Standardized Tests *Required:* SAT I or ACT (for admission).
Costs (2001–02) *Comprehensive fee:* $22,922 includes full-time tuition ($17,348), mandatory fees ($100), and room and board ($5474). Part-time tuition: $610 per credit. Part-time tuition and fees vary according to course load. *Room and board:* College room only: $2496. Room and board charges vary according to board plan and housing facility. *Payment plan:* installment. *Waivers:* employees or children of employees.
Financial Aid Of all full-time matriculated undergraduates who enrolled in 2001, 2001 applied for aid, 1649 were judged to have need, 484 had their need fully met. 280 Federal Work-Study jobs. In 2001, 720 non-need-based awards were made. *Average percent of need met:* 88%. *Average financial aid package:* $14,670. *Average need-based loan:* $4103. *Average need-based gift aid:* $9923. *Average non-need based aid:* $6328. *Average indebtedness upon graduation:* $16,675.
Applying *Options:* common application, electronic application, early admission, deferred entrance. *Application fee:* $25. *Required:* essay or personal statement, high school transcript. *Required for some:* 1 letter of recommendation. *Recommended:* interview. *Application deadline:* rolling (freshmen), rolling (transfers). *Notification:* continuous (freshmen).
Admissions Contact Hope College, 69 East 10th Street, PO Box 9000, Holland, MI 49422-9000. *Phone:* 616-395-7955. *Toll-free phone:* 800-968-7850. *Fax:* 616-395-7130. *E-mail:* admissions@hope.edu.

KALAMAZOO COLLEGE
Kalamazoo, Michigan

- **Independent** 4-year, founded 1833, affiliated with American Baptist Churches in the U.S.A.
- **Calendar** quarters
- **Degree** bachelor's
- **Suburban** 60-acre campus
- **Endowment** $115.0 million
- **Coed,** 1,384 undergraduate students, 100% full-time, 56% women, 44% men
- **Very difficult** entrance level, 78% of applicants were admitted

Undergraduates 1,384 full-time. Students come from 42 states and territories, 16 other countries, 24% are from out of state, 2% African American, 4% Asian American or Pacific Islander, 2% Hispanic American, 0.1% Native American, 2% international, 1% transferred in, 74% live on campus. *Retention:* 88% of 2001 full-time freshmen returned.
Freshmen *Admission:* 1,328 applied, 1,038 admitted, 341 enrolled. *Average high school GPA:* 3.67. *Test scores:* SAT verbal scores over 500: 99%; SAT math scores over 500: 99%; ACT scores over 18: 100%; SAT verbal scores over 600: 72%; SAT math scores over 600: 68%; ACT scores over 24: 94%; SAT verbal scores over 700: 20%; SAT math scores over 700: 16%; ACT scores over 30: 31%.
Faculty *Total:* 107, 91% full-time, 86% with terminal degrees. *Student/faculty ratio:* 12:1.
Majors Anthropology; art; art history; biology; business economics; chemistry; classics; computer science; English; French; German; health science; history; interdisciplinary studies; mathematics; music; philosophy; physics; political science; psychology; religious studies; sociology; Spanish; theater arts/drama.
Academic Programs *Special study options:* adult/continuing education programs, advanced placement credit, cooperative education, double majors, English as a second language, independent study, internships, off-campus study, services for LD students, study abroad. *ROTC:* Army (c). *Unusual degree programs:* 3-2 engineering with University of Michigan, Washington University in St. Louis; architecture with Washington University in St. Louis.
Library Upjohn Library plus 1 other with 346,484 titles, 1,331 serial subscriptions, 8,166 audiovisual materials, an OPAC, a Web page.
Computers on Campus 130 computers available on campus for general student use. A campuswide network can be accessed from student residence rooms and from off campus. Internet access, at least one staffed computer lab available.
Student Life *Housing:* on-campus residence required for freshman year. *Options:* coed. *Activities and Organizations:* drama/theater group, student-run newspaper, radio station, choral group, Student Activities Committee, Student Commission, Index (college newspaper), Intervarsity Christian Fellowship, Project Brave volunteer organization. *Campus security:* 24-hour emergency response devices and patrols, late-night transport/escort service, controlled dormitory access. *Student Services:* health clinic, personal/psychological counseling, women's center.
Athletics Member NCAA. All Division III. *Intercollegiate sports:* baseball M, basketball M/W, cross-country running M/W, football M, golf M/W, soccer M/W, softball W, swimming M/W, tennis M/W, volleyball W. *Intramural sports:* badminton M/W, basketball M/W, gymnastics W(c), racquetball M/W, rugby M(c)/W(c), skiing (downhill) M(c)/W(c), soccer M(c)/W(c), softball M/W, swimming M/W, table tennis M/W, tennis M/W, track and field M(c)/W(c), volleyball W, water polo M/W.
Standardized Tests *Required:* SAT I or ACT (for admission).
Costs (2001–02) *One-time required fee:* $75. *Comprehensive fee:* $26,880 includes full-time tuition ($20,652) and room and board ($6228). Part-time tuition and fees vary according to course load. *Room and board:* College room only: $3084. Room and board charges vary according to board plan and housing facility. *Payment plans:* installment, deferred payment. *Waivers:* employees or children of employees.
Financial Aid Of all full-time matriculated undergraduates who enrolled in 2001, 818 applied for aid, 655 were judged to have need. 350 Federal Work-Study jobs (averaging $1469). In 2001, 675 non-need-based awards were made. *Average financial aid package:* $17,775. *Average need-based loan:* $5170. *Average need-based gift aid:* $13,200. *Average non-need based aid:* $7800. *Average indebtedness upon graduation:* $17,400.
Applying *Options:* common application, electronic application, early decision, early action, deferred entrance. *Application fee:* $35. *Required:* essay or personal statement, high school transcript, 2 letters of recommendation. *Recommended:* minimum 3.0 GPA, interview. *Application deadlines:* 2/15 (freshmen), 2/15 (transfers). *Early decision:* 11/15. *Notification:* 4/1 (freshmen), 12/1 (early decision), 12/20 (early action).
Admissions Contact Mrs. Linda Wirgau, Records Manager, Kalamazoo College, Mandelle Hall, 1200 Academy Street, Kalamazoo, MI 49006-3295. *Phone:* 616-337-7166. *Toll-free phone:* 800-253-3602. *E-mail:* admission@kzoo.edu.

KENDALL COLLEGE OF ART AND DESIGN OF FERRIS STATE UNIVERSITY
Grand Rapids, Michigan

- **Independent** comprehensive, founded 1928
- **Calendar** semesters
- **Degree** bachelor's
- **Urban** campus
- **Endowment** $2.5 million
- **Coed,** 738 undergraduate students, 73% full-time, 57% women, 43% men
- **Minimally difficult** entrance level

Kendall was founded as a living memorial to one of America's most renowned and innovative furniture designers. David Wolcott Kendall was considered truly avant-garde in arts education. The College today continues to push the envelope, offering leading-edge professional programs that blur the distinction between making art and making a living.

Undergraduates 536 full-time, 202 part-time. Students come from 17 states and territories, 5 other countries, 6% are from out of state, 4% African American, 2% Asian American or Pacific Islander, 2% Hispanic American, 0.1% Native American, 1% international, 13% transferred in. *Retention:* 70% of 2001 full-time freshmen returned.
Freshmen *Admission:* 111 admitted, 115 enrolled. *Average high school GPA:* 2.80. *Test scores:* SAT verbal scores over 500: 50%; SAT math scores over 500: 35%; SAT verbal scores over 600: 7%; SAT math scores over 600: 7%.
Faculty *Total:* 83, 40% full-time. *Student/faculty ratio:* 13:1.
Majors Art history; design/visual communications; fine/studio arts; graphic design/commercial art/illustration; industrial design; interior design.

Kendall College of Art and Design of Ferris State University (continued)

Academic Programs *Special study options:* adult/continuing education programs, advanced placement credit, independent study, internships, off-campus study, part-time degree program, services for LD students, study abroad, summer session for credit.

Library Van Steenburg Library with 21,324 titles, 111 serial subscriptions, 311 audiovisual materials.

Computers on Campus 100 computers available on campus for general student use. At least one staffed computer lab available.

Student Life *Housing:* college housing not available. *Activities and Organizations:* Student Government Association, Graphics Club, American Society of Interior Designers, Industrial Designers Society of America. *Campus security:* 24-hour emergency response devices, late-night transport/escort service. *Student Services:* personal/psychological counseling.

Standardized Tests *Required:* ACT (for admission).

Costs (2001–02) *Tuition:* state resident $8460 full-time; nonresident $13,640 full-time. Full-time tuition and fees vary according to course load and program. Part-time tuition and fees vary according to course load and program. *Required fees:* $360 full-time. *Payment plans:* installment, deferred payment. *Waivers:* employees or children of employees.

Financial Aid Of all full-time matriculated undergraduates who enrolled in 2001, 470 applied for aid, 357 were judged to have need, 98 had their need fully met. In 2001, 113 non-need-based awards were made. *Average percent of need met:* 83%. *Average financial aid package:* $10,526. *Average need-based loan:* $3580. *Average need-based gift aid:* $3931. *Average indebtedness upon graduation:* $18,804.

Applying *Options:* common application, early admission, early decision, deferred entrance. *Application fee:* $35. *Required:* essay or personal statement, high school transcript, minimum 2.5 GPA, portfolio. *Recommended:* interview. *Application deadline:* rolling (freshmen), rolling (transfers).

Admissions Contact Ms. Amy Packard, Director of Admissions, Kendall College of Art and Design of Ferris State University, 111 Division Avenue North, Grand Rapids, MI 49503-3194. *Phone:* 616-451-2787 Ext. 109. *Toll-free phone:* 800-676-2787. *Fax:* 616-831-9689.

KETTERING UNIVERSITY

Flint, Michigan

- **Independent** comprehensive, founded 1919
- **Calendar** alternating 12-week terms of school and co-operative work experience
- **Degrees** bachelor's and master's
- **Suburban** 45-acre campus with easy access to Detroit
- **Endowment** $43.3 million
- **Coed,** 2,653 undergraduate students, 100% full-time, 19% women, 81% men
- **Very difficult** entrance level, 71% of applicants were admitted

Kettering University (formerly GMI Engineering & Management Institute) will jump-start your career in engineering, math, applied sciences, or business. With our renowned professional co-op program, students alternate 3-month class terms with 3-month paid work experience terms with one of more than 750 corporate employers. Ninety-nine percent of seniors receive job offers or are accepted by graduate schools before they receive their diplomas. Kettering University provides an "Education for the Real World."

Undergraduates 2,653 full-time. Students come from 48 states and territories, 18 other countries, 40% are from out of state, 7% African American, 4% Asian American or Pacific Islander, 2% Hispanic American, 0.3% Native American, 3% international, 2% transferred in, 43% live on campus. *Retention:* 87% of 2001 full-time freshmen returned.

Freshmen *Admission:* 2,413 applied, 1,708 admitted, 593 enrolled. *Average high school GPA:* 3.53. *Test scores:* SAT verbal scores over 500: 91%; SAT math scores over 500: 99%; ACT scores over 18: 99%; SAT verbal scores over 600: 43%; SAT math scores over 600: 79%; ACT scores over 24: 84%; SAT verbal scores over 700: 7%; SAT math scores over 700: 19%; ACT scores over 30: 12%.

Faculty *Total:* 162, 90% full-time, 82% with terminal degrees. *Student/faculty ratio:* 9:1.

Majors Accounting; applied mathematics; business administration; business marketing and marketing management; chemistry; computer engineering; computer science; electrical engineering; engineering/industrial management; environmental science; finance; industrial/manufacturing engineering; information sciences/systems; mathematical statistics; mechanical engineering; operations management; physics; plastics engineering.

Academic Programs *Special study options:* accelerated degree program, advanced placement credit, cooperative education, distance learning, double majors, independent study, internships, services for LD students, study abroad.

Library Kettering University Library plus 1 other with 100,339 titles, 1,011 serial subscriptions, 778 audiovisual materials, an OPAC, a Web page.

Computers on Campus 300 computers available on campus for general student use. A campuswide network can be accessed from student residence rooms and from off campus. Internet access, online (class) registration, at least one staffed computer lab available.

Student Life *Housing:* on-campus residence required for freshman year. *Options:* coed. *Activities and Organizations:* drama/theater group, student-run newspaper, radio station, choral group, student government, Society of Automotive Engineers, National Society of Black Engineers, Outdoors Club, Christians in Action, national fraternities, national sororities. *Campus security:* 24-hour emergency response devices and patrols, late-night transport/escort service, controlled dormitory access. *Student Services:* health clinic, personal/psychological counseling, women's center.

Athletics *Intercollegiate sports:* ice hockey M(c), soccer M(c), volleyball M(c). *Intramural sports:* basketball M/W, bowling M/W, cross-country running M/W, football M/W, golf M/W, ice hockey M, lacrosse M, racquetball M/W, soccer M/W, softball M/W, squash M/W, swimming M/W, table tennis M/W, tennis M/W, track and field M/W, volleyball M/W, water polo M/W.

Standardized Tests *Required:* SAT I or ACT (for admission). *Recommended:* SAT II: Subject Tests (for admission).

Costs (2001–02) *Comprehensive fee:* $23,256 includes full-time tuition ($18,500), mandatory fees ($156), and room and board ($4600). Full-time tuition and fees vary according to student level. Part-time tuition: $578 per credit. Part-time tuition and fees vary according to student level. *Room and board:* College room only: $2900. Room and board charges vary according to student level. *Payment plan:* installment. *Waivers:* employees or children of employees.

Financial Aid Of all full-time matriculated undergraduates who enrolled in 2001, 1879 applied for aid, 1710 were judged to have need. 264 Federal Work-Study jobs (averaging $549). In 2001, 417 non-need-based awards were made. *Average percent of need met:* 64%. *Average financial aid package:* $13,078. *Average need-based loan:* $4037. *Average need-based gift aid:* $6490. *Average non-need based aid:* $5094.

Applying *Options:* electronic application, deferred entrance. *Application fee:* $25. *Required:* high school transcript. *Required for some:* essay or personal statement. *Recommended:* minimum 3.0 GPA, interview. *Application deadline:* rolling (freshmen), rolling (transfers). *Notification:* continuous (freshmen).

Admissions Contact Mr. Rawlan Lillard II, Director of Admissions, Kettering University, 1700 West Third Avenue, Flint, MI 48504-4898. *Phone:* 810-762-7865. *Toll-free phone:* 800-955-4464 Ext. 7865 (in-state); 800-955-4464 (out-of-state). *Fax:* 810-762-9837. *E-mail:* admissions@kettering.edu.

LAKE SUPERIOR STATE UNIVERSITY

Sault Sainte Marie, Michigan

- **State-supported** 4-year, founded 1946
- **Calendar** semesters
- **Degrees** certificates, associate, and bachelor's
- **Small-town** 121-acre campus
- **Endowment** $5.3 million
- **Coed,** 3,186 undergraduate students, 77% full-time, 52% women, 48% men
- **Moderately difficult** entrance level, 66% of applicants were admitted

Undergraduates 2,458 full-time, 728 part-time. Students come from 20 states and territories, 12 other countries, 5% are from out of state, 1% African American, 0.6% Asian American or Pacific Islander, 0.7% Hispanic American, 8% Native American, 14% international, 12% transferred in, 29% live on campus. *Retention:* 68% of 2001 full-time freshmen returned.

Freshmen *Admission:* 1,396 applied, 925 admitted, 583 enrolled. *Average high school GPA:* 2.99. *Test scores:* ACT scores over 18: 81%; ACT scores over 24: 26%; ACT scores over 30: 2%.

Faculty *Total:* 221, 55% full-time. *Student/faculty ratio:* 18:1.

Majors Accounting; accounting technician; athletic training/sports medicine; biology; business administration; business economics; chemistry; computer engineering technology; computer science; construction technology; corrections; criminal justice/law enforcement administration; data processing technology; drafting; early childhood education; economics; education; education (multiple levels); electrical/electronic engineering technology; electrical engineering; elementary education; engineering; engineering/industrial management; engineering technology; English; environmental science; environmental technology; exercise sciences; finance; fire science; fish/game management; geology; history; human services; industrial technology; interdisciplinary studies; law enforcement/police science; legal studies; liberal arts and sciences/liberal studies; literature; machine technology; management information systems/business data processing; mathematics; mathematics/computer science; mechanical engineering; mechanical engineering technology; medical technology; mental health/rehabilitation; middle school education; Native American studies; natural resources management; nursing; office management; paralegal/legal assistant; political science; pre-dentistry; pre-law; pre-medicine; pre-veterinary studies; psychiatric/mental health services; psychology; recreational therapy; recreation/leisure facilities management; recreation/leisure studies; robotics technology; secondary education; secretarial science; social sciences; sociology; sport/fitness administration; water resources; water treatment technology; wildlife management.

Academic Programs *Special study options:* academic remediation for entering students, adult/continuing education programs, advanced placement credit, cooperative education, distance learning, double majors, freshman honors college, honors programs, independent study, internships, part-time degree program, services for LD students, student-designed majors, summer session for credit.

Library Kenneth Shouldice Library with 112,920 titles, 714 serial subscriptions, an OPAC.

Computers on Campus 350 computers available on campus for general student use. A campuswide network can be accessed from off campus. Internet access, at least one staffed computer lab available.

Student Life *Housing:* on-campus residence required through sophomore year. *Options:* coed, men-only, women-only. *Activities and Organizations:* drama/theater group, student-run newspaper, radio station, choral group, national fraternities, national sororities. *Campus security:* 24-hour patrols, student patrols, late-night transport/escort service. *Student Services:* health clinic, personal/psychological counseling.

Athletics Member NCAA. All Division II except ice hockey (Division I). *Intercollegiate sports:* basketball M(s)/W(s), cross-country running M(s)/W(s), golf M, ice hockey M(s), softball W, tennis M(s)/W(s), track and field M(s)/W(s), volleyball W(s). *Intramural sports:* basketball M/W, football M/W, ice hockey M, racquetball M/W, riflery M/W, tennis M/W, track and field M/W, volleyball M/W, water polo M/W, wrestling M.

Standardized Tests *Required:* ACT (for admission).

Costs (2001–02) *Tuition:* state resident $4128 full-time, $172 per credit hour part-time; nonresident $8106 full-time, $338 per credit hour part-time. Full-time tuition and fees vary according to reciprocity agreements. Part-time tuition and fees vary according to reciprocity agreements. *Required fees:* $206 full-time. *Room and board:* $5281; room only: $4708. Room and board charges vary according to board plan. *Waivers:* minority students, children of alumni, senior citizens, and employees or children of employees.

Financial Aid Of all full-time matriculated undergraduates who enrolled in 2001, 1925 applied for aid, 1925 were judged to have need, 863 had their need fully met. In 2001, 376 non-need-based awards were made. *Average percent of need met:* 80%. *Average financial aid package:* $5360. *Average need-based loan:* $3017. *Average need-based gift aid:* $2508. *Average non-need based aid:* $2396. *Average indebtedness upon graduation:* $5909.

Applying *Options:* deferred entrance. *Application fee:* $20. *Required:* high school transcript. *Required for some:* minimum 2.0 GPA. *Application deadline:* 8/15 (freshmen), rolling (transfers).

Admissions Contact Mr. Kevin Pollock, Director of Admissions, Lake Superior State University, 650 West Easterday Avenue, Sault Saint Marie, MI 49783-1699. *Phone:* 906-635-2670. *Toll-free phone:* 888-800-LSSU Ext. 2231. *Fax:* 906-635-6669. *E-mail:* admissions@gw.lssu.edu.

LAWRENCE TECHNOLOGICAL UNIVERSITY
Southfield, Michigan

- **Independent** comprehensive, founded 1932
- **Calendar** semesters
- **Degrees** associate, bachelor's, and master's
- **Suburban** 110-acre campus with easy access to Detroit
- **Endowment** $14.0 million
- **Coed,** 2,979 undergraduate students
- **Moderately difficult** entrance level, 78% of applicants were admitted

Undergraduates Students come from 39 states and territories, 34 other countries, 8% are from out of state, 9% live on campus. *Retention:* 75% of 2001 full-time freshmen returned.

Freshmen *Admission:* 2,250 applied, 1,750 admitted. *Average high school GPA:* 3.50. *Test scores:* ACT scores over 18: 99%; ACT scores over 24: 72%; ACT scores over 30: 37%.

Faculty *Student/faculty ratio:* 12:1.

Majors Architecture; business administration; chemical engineering technology; chemistry; civil engineering; civil engineering technology; computer science; construction engineering; construction technology; electrical/electronic engineering technology; electrical engineering; engineering design; engineering technology; humanities; industrial/manufacturing engineering; industrial technology; information sciences/systems; interior architecture; mathematics; mechanical engineering; mechanical engineering technology; physics; technical/business writing.

Academic Programs *Special study options:* academic remediation for entering students, adult/continuing education programs, advanced placement credit, cooperative education, distance learning, double majors, honors programs, independent study, internships, part-time degree program, student-designed majors, summer session for credit. *ROTC:* Army (c), Air Force (c).

Library Lawrence Technological University Library plus 1 other with 107,000 titles, 665 serial subscriptions, an OPAC, a Web page.

Computers on Campus 400 computers available on campus for general student use. A campuswide network can be accessed from student residence rooms and from off campus. At least one staffed computer lab available.

Student Life *Housing Options:* coed. *Activities and Organizations:* drama/theater group, student-run newspaper, Society of Automotive Engineers, Institute of Electric and Electronic Engineers, Michigan Society of Professional Engineers, American Institute of Architecture Students, American Society of Civil Engineers, national fraternities, national sororities. *Campus security:* 24-hour patrols, late-night transport/escort service, controlled dormitory access. *Student Services:* personal/psychological counseling.

Athletics *Intramural sports:* badminton M/W, basketball M(c)/W, bowling M(c)/W(c), football M, golf M/W, ice hockey M(c), skiing (cross-country) M/W, skiing (downhill) M/W, soccer M/W, softball M/W, table tennis M/W, tennis M/W, volleyball M/W.

Standardized Tests *Required:* SAT I or ACT (for admission).

Costs (2001–02) *Tuition:* $10,950 full-time, $365 per credit hour part-time. Full-time tuition and fees vary according to program and student level. Part-time tuition and fees vary according to program and student level. *Required fees:* $1300 full-time, $650 per term part-time. *Room only:* $2475. Room and board charges vary according to housing facility. *Payment plan:* installment. *Waivers:* employees or children of employees.

Financial Aid Of all full-time matriculated undergraduates who enrolled in 2001, 1191 applied for aid, 1064 were judged to have need, 136 had their need fully met. 30 State and other part-time jobs (averaging $1224). In 2001, 104 non-need-based awards were made. *Average percent of need met:* 95%. *Average need-based loan:* $5500. *Average need-based gift aid:* $6850. *Average non-need based aid:* $2000. *Average indebtedness upon graduation:* $15,400.

Applying *Options:* common application, electronic application, early admission, deferred entrance. *Application fee:* $30. *Required:* high school transcript, minimum 2.5 GPA. *Required for some:* essay or personal statement, letters of recommendation, interview. *Recommended:* essay or personal statement. *Application deadlines:* 4/15 (freshmen), 8/15 (transfers). *Notification:* continuous until 8/26 (freshmen).

Admissions Contact Mrs. Lisa Kujawa, Director of Admissions, Lawrence Technological University, 2100 West 10 Mile Road, Southfield, MI 48075. *Phone:* 248-204-3180. *Toll-free phone:* 800-225-5588. *Fax:* 248-204-3188. *E-mail:* admissions@ltu.edu.

MADONNA UNIVERSITY
Livonia, Michigan

- **Independent Roman Catholic** comprehensive, founded 1947
- **Calendar** semesters
- **Degrees** associate, bachelor's, and master's
- **Suburban** 49-acre campus with easy access to Detroit
- **Endowment** $31.9 million
- **Coed**
- **Moderately difficult** entrance level

Faculty *Student/faculty ratio:* 17:1.

Student Life *Campus security:* 24-hour emergency response devices and patrols, late-night transport/escort service.

Athletics Member NAIA.

Standardized Tests *Required:* ACT (for admission).

Costs (2001–02) *Comprehensive fee:* $12,714 includes full-time tuition ($7560), mandatory fees ($100), and room and board ($5054). Part-time tuition: $257 per credit hour. *Required fees:* $50 per term part-time. *Room and board:* College room only: $2318. Room and board charges vary according to board plan.

Financial Aid Of all full-time matriculated undergraduates who enrolled in 2001, 2575 applied for aid, 2512 were judged to have need. *Average percent of need met:* 80. *Average financial aid package:* $1800. *Average need-based gift aid:* $3000. *Average non-need based aid:* $750.

Madonna University (continued)

Applying *Options:* early admission, deferred entrance. *Required:* high school transcript, minimum 2.75 GPA. *Required for some:* 2 letters of recommendation.

Admissions Contact Mr. Frank J. Hribar, Director of Enrollment Management, Madonna University, 36600 Schoolcraft Road, Livonia, MI 48150-1173. *Phone:* 734-432-5317. *Toll-free phone:* 800-852-4951. *Fax:* 734-432-5393. *E-mail:* muinfo@smtp.munet.edu.

MARYGROVE COLLEGE
Detroit, Michigan

- **Independent Roman Catholic** comprehensive, founded 1905
- **Calendar** semesters
- **Degrees** certificates, diplomas, associate, bachelor's, and master's
- **Urban** 50-acre campus
- **Endowment** $13.0 million
- **Coed, primarily women,** 879 undergraduate students, 47% full-time, 81% women, 19% men
- **Moderately difficult** entrance level, 15% of applicants were admitted

Undergraduates 410 full-time, 469 part-time. Students come from 2 states and territories, 3 other countries, 1% are from out of state, 75% African American, 0.2% Asian American or Pacific Islander, 0.8% Hispanic American, 0.2% Native American, 0.8% international, 11% transferred in, 4% live on campus. *Retention:* 67% of 2001 full-time freshmen returned.

Freshmen *Admission:* 272 applied, 42 admitted, 42 enrolled. *Average high school GPA:* 2.70. *Test scores:* ACT scores over 18: 36%.

Faculty *Total:* 75, 81% full-time, 67% with terminal degrees. *Student/faculty ratio:* 15:1.

Majors Accounting; applied art; art; art therapy; biological/physical sciences; biology; business; business administration; business marketing and marketing management; chemistry; computer/information sciences; corrections; dance; early childhood education; education of the emotionally handicapped; English; environmental science; fashion merchandising; fine/studio arts; history; international business; liberal arts and sciences/liberal studies; mathematics; medical radiologic technology; music; music (general performance); nutrition studies; political science; psychology; religious studies; respiratory therapy; social sciences; social work.

Academic Programs *Special study options:* academic remediation for entering students, advanced placement credit, cooperative education, distance learning, double majors, internships, off-campus study, part-time degree program, student-designed majors, summer session for credit. *Unusual degree programs:* 3-2 social work with Wayne State University, Eastern Michigan University.

Library 160,230 titles, 550 serial subscriptions, an OPAC.

Computers on Campus 115 computers available on campus for general student use. At least one staffed computer lab available.

Student Life *Housing Options:* coed. *Activities and Organizations:* choral group, Association of Black Social Workers, Council of Student Organization, Political Science Club, United Brotherhood, Marygrove Business Association. *Campus security:* 24-hour emergency response devices and patrols, late-night transport/escort service. *Student Services:* personal/psychological counseling.

Athletics *Intercollegiate sports:* basketball M/W.

Standardized Tests *Required:* ACT (for admission).

Costs (2001–02) *Comprehensive fee:* $15,950 includes full-time tuition ($10,500), mandatory fees ($250), and room and board ($5200). Part-time tuition: $380 per credit. *Required fees:* $10 per credit. *Payment plan:* installment. *Waivers:* senior citizens and employees or children of employees.

Applying *Options:* early admission, deferred entrance. *Application fee:* $25. *Required:* high school transcript, minimum 2.7 GPA. *Required for some:* letters of recommendation, interview. *Application deadlines:* 8/15 (freshmen), 8/15 (transfers). *Notification:* continuous until 9/1 (freshmen).

Admissions Contact Fred A. Schebor, Dean of Admissions, Marygrove College, Office of Admissions, Detroit, MI 48221-2599. *Phone:* 313-927-1570. *Toll-free phone:* 866-313-1297. *Fax:* 313-927-1345. *E-mail:* info@marygrove.edu.

MICHIGAN STATE UNIVERSITY
East Lansing, Michigan

- **State-supported** university, founded 1855
- **Calendar** semesters
- **Degrees** certificates, bachelor's, master's, doctoral, and first professional
- **Suburban** campus with easy access to Detroit
- **Coed,** 34,874 undergraduate students, 88% full-time, 53% women, 47% men
- **Moderately difficult** entrance level, 65% of applicants were admitted

Undergraduates 30,583 full-time, 4,291 part-time. Students come from 54 states and territories, 93 other countries, 6% are from out of state, 9% African American, 5% Asian American or Pacific Islander, 3% Hispanic American, 0.7% Native American, 3% international, 5% transferred in, 44% live on campus. *Retention:* 89% of 2001 full-time freshmen returned.

Freshmen *Admission:* 24,246 applied, 15,812 admitted, 6,914 enrolled. *Average high school GPA:* 3.52. *Test scores:* SAT verbal scores over 500: 75%; SAT math scores over 500: 81%; ACT scores over 18: 96%; SAT verbal scores over 600: 33%; SAT math scores over 600: 43%; ACT scores over 24: 55%; SAT verbal scores over 700: 7%; SAT math scores over 700: 11%; ACT scores over 30: 8%.

Faculty *Total:* 2,673, 88% full-time, 89% with terminal degrees. *Student/faculty ratio:* 18:1.

Majors Accounting; advertising; agribusiness; agricultural business; agricultural business and production related; agricultural economics; agricultural engineering; agricultural/food products processing; agronomy/crop science; American literature; animal sciences; anthropology; applied mathematics; art; art education; art history; astrophysics; biochemistry; bioengineering; biological/physical sciences; biology; botany; business administration; business marketing and marketing management; chemical engineering; chemistry; chemistry education; Chinese; city/community/regional planning; civil engineering; clothing/apparel/textile studies; communications; computer engineering; computer/information sciences; criminal justice studies; dietetics; earth sciences; East and Southeast Asian languages related; economics; electrical engineering; elementary education; engineering; engineering mechanics; English; entomology; family resource management studies; family studies; finance; food sciences; forestry; French; geography; geology; German; history; home economics; home economics education; horticulture science; hotel and restaurant management; humanities; human resources management; interior architecture; international relations; journalism; landscape architecture; Latin (ancient and medieval); law enforcement/police science; liberal arts and sciences/liberal studies; linguistics; logistics/materials management; materials science; mathematical statistics; mathematics; mechanical engineering; medical technology; microbiology/bacteriology; music teacher education; music theory and composition; music therapy; natural resources conservation; nursing; nutrition science; operations management; philosophy; physical education; physical sciences; physical/theoretical chemistry; physics; physiology; plant pathology; political science; psychology; public administration; purchasing/contracts management; recreation/leisure facilities management; religious studies; Russian; social science education; social sciences; social work; sociology; soil sciences; Spanish; special education; speech-language pathology/audiology; telecommunications; theater arts/drama; veterinarian assistant; veterinary technology; wildlife management; women's studies; zoology.

Academic Programs *Special study options:* academic remediation for entering students, accelerated degree program, adult/continuing education programs, advanced placement credit, cooperative education, distance learning, double majors, English as a second language, freshman honors college, honors programs, independent study, internships, off-campus study, part-time degree program, services for LD students, student-designed majors, study abroad, summer session for credit. *ROTC:* Army (b), Air Force (b).

Library Main Library plus 14 others with 4.4 million titles, 27,324 serial subscriptions, 278,968 audiovisual materials, an OPAC, a Web page.

Computers on Campus 2000 computers available on campus for general student use. A campuswide network can be accessed from student residence rooms and from off campus. Internet access, online (class) registration, at least one staffed computer lab available.

Student Life *Housing:* on-campus residence required for freshman year. *Options:* coed, women-only, disabled students. *Activities and Organizations:* drama/theater group, student-run newspaper, radio and television station, choral group, marching band, national fraternities, national sororities. *Campus security:* 24-hour emergency response devices and patrols, late-night transport/escort service, self-defense workshops. *Student Services:* health clinic, personal/psychological counseling, women's center, legal services.

Athletics Member NCAA. All Division I except football (Division I-A). *Intercollegiate sports:* baseball M, basketball M(s)/W(s), crew W(s), cross-country running M(s)/W(s), equestrian sports M(c)/W(c), field hockey W(s), golf M(s)/W(s), gymnastics M(s)/W(s), ice hockey M(s), lacrosse M(c), soccer M(s), softball W, swimming M(s)/W(s), tennis M(s)/W(s), track and field M(s)/W(s), volleyball W(s), wrestling M(s). *Intramural sports:* archery M/W, badminton M/W, baseball M, basketball M/W, crew M/W, cross-country running M/W, fencing M/W, football M/W, golf M/W, gymnastics M/W, ice hockey M/W, lacrosse M, racquetball M/W, rugby M/W, sailing M/W, skiing (cross-country) M/W, skiing (downhill) M/W, soccer M/W, softball W, squash M/W, swimming M/W, table tennis M/W, tennis M/W, track and field M/W, volleyball M/W, water polo M/W, weight lifting M/W, wrestling M.

Standardized Tests *Required:* SAT I or ACT (for admission).

Costs (2001–02) *Tuition:* state resident $4973 full-time, $166 per semester hour part-time; nonresident $13,320 full-time, $444 per semester hour part-time. Full-time tuition and fees vary according to course load, program, and student level. Part-time tuition and fees vary according to course load, program, and student level. *Required fees:* $654 full-time, $654 per year part-time. *Room and board:* $4678; room only: $2026. Room and board charges vary according to board plan and housing facility. *Payment plan:* deferred payment. *Waivers:* employees or children of employees.

Financial Aid Of all full-time matriculated undergraduates who enrolled in 2001, 17512 applied for aid, 11752 were judged to have need, 4561 had their need fully met. 2159 Federal Work-Study jobs (averaging $2498). 623 State and other part-time jobs (averaging $2644). In 2001, 7048 non-need-based awards were made. *Average percent of need met:* 87%. *Average financial aid package:* $7746. *Average need-based loan:* $3752. *Average need-based gift aid:* $4704. *Average indebtedness upon graduation:* $17,876.

Applying *Options:* electronic application, deferred entrance. *Application fee:* $30. *Required:* high school transcript. *Application deadlines:* 7/30 (freshmen), 7/30 (transfers).

Admissions Contact Dr. Gordon Stanley, Assistant to the Provost for Enrollment and Director of Admissions, Michigan State University, 250 Administration Building, East Lansing, MI 48824. *Phone:* 517-355-8332. *Fax:* 517-353-1647. *E-mail:* admis@msu.edu.

MICHIGAN TECHNOLOGICAL UNIVERSITY
Houghton, Michigan

- **State-supported** university, founded 1885
- **Calendar** quarters
- **Degrees** certificates, associate, bachelor's, master's, and doctoral
- **Small-town** 240-acre campus
- **Endowment** $26.7 million
- **Coed,** 5,666 undergraduate students, 87% full-time, 26% women, 74% men
- **Moderately difficult** entrance level, 94% of applicants were admitted

Undergraduates 4,933 full-time, 733 part-time. Students come from 36 states and territories, 60 other countries, 18% are from out of state, 2% African American, 1% Asian American or Pacific Islander, 0.8% Hispanic American, 0.9% Native American, 5% international, 4% transferred in, 43% live on campus. *Retention:* 82% of 2001 full-time freshmen returned.

Freshmen *Admission:* 3,111 applied, 2,938 admitted, 1,275 enrolled. *Average high school GPA:* 3.5. *Test scores:* SAT verbal scores over 500: 82%; SAT math scores over 500: 95%; ACT scores over 18: 97%; SAT verbal scores over 600: 38%; SAT math scores over 600: 64%; ACT scores over 24: 68%; SAT verbal scores over 700: 10%; SAT math scores over 700: 21%; ACT scores over 30: 13%.

Faculty *Total:* 415, 90% full-time, 85% with terminal degrees. *Student/faculty ratio:* 12:1.

Majors Accounting; applied mathematics; biochemistry; biological technology; biology; business administration; business economics; business marketing and marketing management; chemical engineering; chemical engineering technology; chemistry; civil engineering; civil engineering technology; communications; computer engineering; computer programming; computer science; construction engineering; earth sciences; ecology; electrical/electronic engineering technology; electrical engineering; electromechanical technology; engineering; engineering mechanics; engineering physics; English; environmental engineering; finance; forest harvesting production technology; forestry; general studies; geological engineering; geology; geophysics/seismology; history; humanities; industrial/manufacturing engineering; information sciences/systems; management information systems/business data processing; materials engineering; mathematical statistics; mathematics; mechanical engineering; mechanical engineering technology; medical technology; metallurgical engineering; microbiology/bacteriology; mining/mineral engineering; operations management; physical sciences; physics; pre-dentistry; pre-medicine; pre-veterinary studies; science education; secondary education; social sciences; surveying; technical/business writing.

Academic Programs *Special study options:* advanced placement credit, cooperative education, distance learning, double majors, English as a second language, internships, off-campus study, part-time degree program, services for LD students, student-designed majors, study abroad, summer session for credit. *ROTC:* Army (b), Air Force (b).

Library J. R. Van Pelt Library with 992,197 titles, 10,585 serial subscriptions, 3,790 audiovisual materials, an OPAC, a Web page.

Computers on Campus 1235 computers available on campus for general student use. A campuswide network can be accessed from student residence rooms and from off campus. Internet access, online (class) registration, at least one staffed computer lab available.

Student Life *Housing:* on-campus residence required for freshman year. *Options:* coed, men-only, women-only. *Activities and Organizations:* drama/theater group, student-run newspaper, radio station, choral group, Film Board, undergraduate student government, Inter-Residence Hall Council, Blue Key National Honor Fraternity, national fraternities, national sororities. *Campus security:* 24-hour emergency response devices and patrols, late-night transport/escort service. *Student Services:* health clinic, personal/psychological counseling.

Athletics Member NCAA. All Division II except ice hockey (Division I). *Intercollegiate sports:* basketball M(s)/W(s), cross-country running M/W, fencing M(c)/W(c), football M(s), ice hockey M(s)/W(c), racquetball M(c)/W(c), riflery M(c)/W(c), skiing (cross-country) M/W, skiing (downhill) M(c)/W(c), soccer M(c)/W(c), squash M(c)/W(c), swimming M(c)/W(c), table tennis M(c)/W(c), tennis M/W(s), track and field M/W, volleyball W(s), water polo M(c)/W(c). *Intramural sports:* badminton M/W, basketball M/W, bowling M/W, cross-country running M/W, football M/W, golf M/W, ice hockey M/W, racquetball M/W, riflery M/W, skiing (cross-country) M(c)/W(c), soccer M/W, softball M/W, squash M/W, swimming M/W, table tennis M/W, tennis M/W, track and field M(c)/W(c), volleyball M(c)/W(c), water polo M/W, weight lifting M/W, wrestling M.

Standardized Tests *Required:* SAT I or ACT (for admission).

Costs (2001–02) *Tuition:* state resident $5028 full-time, $210 per credit hour part-time; nonresident $12,306 full-time, $513 per credit hour part-time. Full-time tuition and fees vary according to student level. Part-time tuition and fees vary according to course load and student level. *Required fees:* $859 full-time, $68 per term part-time. *Room and board:* $5181. Room and board charges vary according to board plan and housing facility. *Payment plan:* installment. *Waivers:* children of alumni, senior citizens, and employees or children of employees.

Financial Aid Of all full-time matriculated undergraduates who enrolled in 2001, 5239 applied for aid, 2375 were judged to have need, 1061 had their need fully met. 234 Federal Work-Study jobs (averaging $1452). In 2001, 1298 non-need-based awards were made. *Average percent of need met:* 80%. *Average financial aid package:* $7451. *Average need-based loan:* $4024. *Average need-based gift aid:* $4613. *Average non-need based aid:* $4064. *Average indebtedness upon graduation:* $11,636.

Applying *Options:* common application, electronic application, deferred entrance. *Application fee:* $30. *Required:* high school transcript. *Recommended:* interview. *Application deadline:* rolling (freshmen), rolling (transfers).

Admissions Contact Ms. Nancy Rehling, Director of Undergraduate Admissions, Michigan Technological University, 1400 Townsend Drive, Houghton, MI 49931-1295. *Phone:* 906-487-2335. *Fax:* 906-487-3343. *E-mail:* mtu4u@mtu.edu.

NORTHERN MICHIGAN UNIVERSITY
Marquette, Michigan

- **State-supported** comprehensive, founded 1899, part of Michigan Department of Education
- **Calendar** semesters
- **Degrees** certificates, diplomas, associate, bachelor's, master's, post-master's, and postbachelor's certificates
- **Small-town** 300-acre campus
- **Endowment** $19.4 million
- **Coed,** 7,724 undergraduate students, 87% full-time, 53% women, 47% men
- **Minimally difficult** entrance level, 99% of applicants were admitted

Undergraduates 6,724 full-time, 1,000 part-time. Students come from 46 states and territories, 15% are from out of state, 1% African American, 0.4% Asian American or Pacific Islander, 0.9% Hispanic American, 2% Native American, 1% international, 6% transferred in, 38% live on campus. *Retention:* 69% of 2001 full-time freshmen returned.

Freshmen *Admission:* 3,820 applied, 3,776 admitted, 1,806 enrolled. *Average high school GPA:* 3.22. *Test scores:* ACT scores over 18: 83%; ACT scores over 24: 34%; ACT scores over 30: 4%.

Faculty *Total:* 399, 74% full-time, 74% with terminal degrees. *Student/faculty ratio:* 20:1.

Majors Accounting; applied art; architectural engineering technology; architectural environmental design; art; art education; athletic training/sports medicine; auto mechanic/technician; aviation technology; biochemistry; biology; botany; broadcast journalism; business administration; business education; business marketing and marketing management; ceramic arts; chemistry; child care/development; city/community/regional planning; computer graphics; computer programming; computer science; computer typography/composition; construction technology; creative writing; criminal justice/law enforcement administration; culinary arts; cytotechnology; data processing technology; dietetics; drafting; drawing; earth sciences; ecology; economics; education; electrical/electronic

Northern Michigan University (continued)
engineering technology; electromechanical technology; elementary education; English; environmental science; exercise sciences; family/consumer studies; film studies; film/video production; finance; fine/studio arts; food products retailing; French; geography; graphic design/commercial art/illustration; health education; heating/air conditioning/refrigeration; history; industrial design; industrial technology; information sciences/systems; international relations; land use management; law enforcement/police science; legal administrative assistant; liberal arts and sciences/liberal studies; management information systems/business data processing; mass communications; mathematics; medical administrative assistant; medical laboratory technician; medical technology; metal/jewelry arts; microbiology/bacteriology; music; music (piano and organ performance); music teacher education; music (voice and choral/opera performance); natural resources conservation; nursing; philosophy; photography; physical education; physics; physiology; political science; pre-dentistry; pre-law; pre-medicine; pre-veterinary studies; printmaking; psychology; public administration; public relations; recreation/leisure studies; retail management; science education; sculpture; secondary education; social sciences; social work; sociology; Spanish; special education; speech-language pathology/audiology; speech/rhetorical studies; stringed instruments; textile arts; theater arts/drama; water resources; wildlife biology; wind/percussion instruments; zoology.

Academic Programs *Special study options:* academic remediation for entering students, accelerated degree program, adult/continuing education programs, advanced placement credit, distance learning, double majors, independent study, internships, off-campus study, part-time degree program, services for LD students, student-designed majors, study abroad, summer session for credit. *ROTC:* Army (b).

Library Lydia Olson Library plus 1 other with 1,492 titles, 1,748 serial subscriptions, 39,924 audiovisual materials, an OPAC, a Web page.

Computers on Campus 450 computers available on campus for general student use. A campuswide network can be accessed from student residence rooms and from off campus. Internet access, online (class) registration, at least one staffed computer lab available.

Student Life *Housing:* on-campus residence required through sophomore year. *Options:* coed, disabled students. *Activities and Organizations:* drama/theater group, student-run newspaper, radio and television station, choral group, marching band, Associated Students of Northern Michigan University, Platform Personalities, Campus Cinema, Northern Arts and Entertainment, Student Leader Fellowship Program, national fraternities, national sororities. *Campus security:* 24-hour emergency response devices and patrols, student patrols, late-night transport/escort service. *Student Services:* health clinic, personal/psychological counseling.

Athletics Member NCAA. All Division II. *Intercollegiate sports:* basketball M(s)/W(s), crew M(c)/W(c), cross-country running W(s), football M(s), golf M(s), ice hockey M(s)/W(c), rugby M(c)/W(c), skiing (cross-country) M(s)/W(s), skiing (downhill) M(c)/W(s), soccer W(s), swimming W(s), tennis W(s), volleyball W(s). *Intramural sports:* basketball M/W, field hockey W, football M, ice hockey M, lacrosse M, skiing (downhill) M/W, soccer M/W, softball M/W.

Standardized Tests *Required:* SAT I or ACT (for admission).

Costs (2001–02) *One-time required fee:* $100. *Tuition:* state resident $3192 full-time, $133 per credit hour part-time; nonresident $5976 full-time, $249 per credit hour part-time. Part-time tuition and fees vary according to course load. *Required fees:* $1065 full-time. *Room and board:* $5436; room only: $2324. Room and board charges vary according to housing facility. *Payment plan:* installment. *Waivers:* children of alumni, senior citizens, and employees or children of employees.

Financial Aid Of all full-time matriculated undergraduates who enrolled in 2001, 5967 applied for aid, 3588 were judged to have need, 696 had their need fully met. In 2001, 13 non-need-based awards were made. *Average percent of need met:* 82%. *Average financial aid package:* $6106. *Average need-based loan:* $3161. *Average need-based gift aid:* $2660. *Average non-need based aid:* $1477. *Average indebtedness upon graduation:* $13,784.

Applying *Options:* common application, electronic application, deferred entrance. *Application fee:* $25. *Required:* high school transcript. *Required for some:* minimum 2.25 GPA. *Application deadline:* rolling (freshmen), rolling (transfers). *Notification:* continuous (freshmen).

Admissions Contact Ms. Gerri Daniels, Northern Michigan University, 1401 Presque Isle Avenue, Marquette, MI 49855. *Phone:* 906-227-2650. *Toll-free phone:* 800-682-9797 Ext. 1 (in-state); 800-682-9797 (out-of-state). *Fax:* 906-227-1747. *E-mail:* admiss@nmu.edu.

NORTHWOOD UNIVERSITY
Midland, Michigan

- **Independent** comprehensive, founded 1959
- **Calendar** quarters
- **Degrees** associate, bachelor's, and master's
- **Small-town** 434-acre campus
- **Endowment** $52.4 million
- **Coed,** 3,414 undergraduate students, 66% full-time, 46% women, 54% men
- **Moderately difficult** entrance level, 88% of applicants were admitted

Exciting programs: a major in international business; an honors program for the most capable students; automotive aftermarket management and hotel, restaurant, and resort management majors at the BBA and associate degree levels; new entertainment, sports and promotion management curriculum. Through the EXCEL Program, students participate in valuable, documentable activities and receive a Student Development Transcript in addition to an academic transcript. Potential employers of Northwood graduates see the experiences, attitudes, and leadership abilities gained by these students.

Undergraduates 2,254 full-time, 1,160 part-time. Students come from 30 states and territories, 33 other countries, 20% are from out of state, 9% African American, 0.5% Asian American or Pacific Islander, 2% Hispanic American, 0.1% Native American, 7% international, 8% transferred in, 55% live on campus. *Retention:* 78% of 2001 full-time freshmen returned.

Freshmen *Admission:* 1,341 applied, 1,186 admitted, 484 enrolled. *Average high school GPA:* 2.90. *Test scores:* SAT verbal scores over 500: 25%; SAT math scores over 500: 38%; ACT scores over 18: 90%; SAT verbal scores over 600: 3%; SAT math scores over 600: 11%; ACT scores over 24: 30%; SAT math scores over 700: 1%; ACT scores over 30: 1%.

Faculty *Total:* 113, 39% full-time. *Student/faculty ratio:* 30:1.

Majors Accounting; advertising; business administration; business economics; business marketing and marketing management; computer management; economics; enterprise management; fashion merchandising; finance; hotel and restaurant management; international business; vehicle marketing operations; vehicle parts/accessories marketing operations.

Academic Programs *Special study options:* academic remediation for entering students, accelerated degree program, adult/continuing education programs, advanced placement credit, distance learning, double majors, English as a second language, external degree program, honors programs, independent study, internships, off-campus study, part-time degree program, study abroad, summer session for credit.

Library Strosacker Library with 45,913 titles, 410 serial subscriptions, an OPAC, a Web page.

Computers on Campus 95 computers available on campus for general student use. A campuswide network can be accessed from student residence rooms and from off campus. Internet access, at least one staffed computer lab available.

Student Life *Housing:* on-campus residence required for freshman year. *Options:* men-only, women-only. *Activities and Organizations:* drama/theater group, student-run newspaper, choral group, fraternities/sororities, student senate, intramural sports, campus art, Investment Club, national fraternities, national sororities. *Campus security:* 24-hour emergency response devices and patrols. *Student Services:* health clinic, personal/psychological counseling.

Athletics Member NCAA. All Division II. *Intercollegiate sports:* baseball M(s), basketball M(s)/W(s), cross-country running M(s)/W(s), football M(s), golf M(s), ice hockey M(c), soccer M(s)/W(s), softball W(s), tennis M(s)/W(s), track and field M(s)/W(s), volleyball W(s). *Intramural sports:* basketball M/W, bowling M/W, football M, golf M, ice hockey M, skiing (downhill) M(c)/W(c), soccer M/W, softball M/W, table tennis M/W, tennis M/W, volleyball M/W, weight lifting M/W.

Standardized Tests *Required:* SAT I or ACT (for admission).

Costs (2001–02) *Comprehensive fee:* $18,360 includes full-time tuition ($12,231), mandatory fees ($300), and room and board ($5829). Part-time tuition: $255 per credit. Part-time tuition and fees vary according to course load. *Room and board:* Room and board charges vary according to board plan. *Payment plan:* installment. *Waivers:* children of alumni and employees or children of employees.

Financial Aid Of all full-time matriculated undergraduates who enrolled in 2001, 1137 applied for aid, 964 were judged to have need, 187 had their need fully met. In 2001, 338 non-need-based awards were made. *Average percent of need met:* 92%. *Average financial aid package:* $16,621. *Average need-based loan:*

$3500. *Average need-based gift aid:* $5461. *Average non-need based aid:* $4537. *Average indebtedness upon graduation:* $10,770.

Applying *Options:* common application, electronic application, early admission, deferred entrance. *Application fee:* $25. *Required:* high school transcript. *Recommended:* essay or personal statement, minimum 2.0 GPA, 1 letter of recommendation, interview. *Application deadline:* rolling (freshmen), rolling (transfers). *Notification:* continuous (freshmen).

Admissions Contact Daniel F. Toland, Director of Admission, Northwood University, 4000 Whiting Drive, Midland, MI 48640. *Phone:* 989-837-4273. *Toll-free phone:* 800-457-7878. *Fax:* 989-837-4490. *E-mail:* admissions@northwood.edu.

OAKLAND UNIVERSITY
Rochester, Michigan

- **State-supported** university, founded 1957
- **Calendar** semesters
- **Degrees** bachelor's, master's, doctoral, post-master's, and postbachelor's certificates
- **Suburban** 1444-acre campus with easy access to Detroit
- **Endowment** $26.3 million
- **Coed,** 12,529 undergraduate students, 69% full-time, 63% women, 37% men
- **Moderately difficult** entrance level, 77% of applicants were admitted

Undergraduates 8,587 full-time, 3,942 part-time. Students come from 37 states and territories, 49 other countries, 2% are from out of state, 8% African American, 3% Asian American or Pacific Islander, 2% Hispanic American, 0.4% Native American, 0.9% international, 10% transferred in, 12% live on campus. *Retention:* 74% of 2001 full-time freshmen returned.

Freshmen *Admission:* 5,468 applied, 4,220 admitted, 1,905 enrolled. *Average high school GPA:* 3.13. *Test scores:* ACT scores over 18: 82%; ACT scores over 24: 29%; ACT scores over 30: 2%.

Faculty *Total:* 803, 55% full-time. *Student/faculty ratio:* 21:1.

Majors Accounting; African studies; anthropology; art history; biochemistry; biology; business administration; business marketing and marketing management; chemistry; communications; computer engineering; computer/information sciences; criminal justice/law enforcement administration; cytotechnology; dance; East Asian studies; economics; electrical engineering; elementary education; engineering physics; English; environmental health; exercise sciences; finance; foreign languages/literatures; French; German; health science; history; human resources management; interdisciplinary studies; international relations; journalism; Latin American studies; liberal arts and sciences/liberal studies; linguistics; management information systems/business data processing; mathematical statistics; mathematics; mechanical engineering; medical laboratory technology; medical technology; modern languages; music; music (piano and organ performance); music teacher education; music theory and composition; music (voice and choral/opera performance); nuclear medical technology; nursing; occupational health/industrial hygiene; philosophy; physical therapy; physics; political science; pre-dentistry; pre-law; pre-medicine; pre-veterinary studies; psychology; public administration; Russian; Russian/Slavic studies; secondary education; sociology; South Asian studies; Spanish; systems engineering; theater arts/drama; visual/performing arts; women's studies.

Academic Programs *Special study options:* academic remediation for entering students, accelerated degree program, advanced placement credit, cooperative education, distance learning, double majors, English as a second language, honors programs, independent study, internships, off-campus study, part-time degree program, services for LD students, student-designed majors, study abroad, summer session for credit. *Unusual degree programs:* 3-2 physical therapy.

Library Kresge Library plus 1 other with 688,000 titles, 2,600 serial subscriptions, 4,361 audiovisual materials, an OPAC, a Web page.

Computers on Campus 640 computers available on campus for general student use. A campuswide network can be accessed from student residence rooms and from off campus. At least one staffed computer lab available.

Student Life *Housing:* on-campus residence required for freshman year. *Options:* coed, disabled students. *Activities and Organizations:* drama/theater group, student-run newspaper, radio station, choral group, Golden Key National Honor Society, Association of Black Students, SATE (Student Association for Teacher Education), Psi Chi Psychology Club, Student Nurses Association, national fraternities, national sororities. *Campus security:* 24-hour emergency response devices and patrols, student patrols, late-night transport/escort service, controlled dormitory access, security lighting, self defense classes. *Student Services:* health clinic, personal/psychological counseling.

Athletics Member NCAA. All Division I. *Intercollegiate sports:* baseball M(s), basketball M(s)/W(s), cross-country running M(s)/W(s), golf M(s)/W(s), ice hockey M(c)/W(c), soccer M(s)/W(s), softball W, swimming M(s)/W(s), tennis W(s), volleyball W(s). *Intramural sports:* badminton M/W, basketball M/W, football M, racquetball M/W, soccer M/W, softball M/W, table tennis M/W, tennis M/W, volleyball M/W.

Costs (2001–02) *Tuition:* state resident $4166 full-time, $132 per credit hour part-time; nonresident $11,340 full-time, $364 per credit hour part-time. Full-time tuition and fees vary according to program and student level. Part-time tuition and fees vary according to program and student level. *Required fees:* $472 full-time, $236 per term part-time. *Room and board:* $4978. Room and board charges vary according to housing facility. *Payment plans:* installment, deferred payment. *Waivers:* employees or children of employees.

Financial Aid Of all full-time matriculated undergraduates who enrolled in 2001, 3872 applied for aid, 2651 were judged to have need, 754 had their need fully met. 788 Federal Work-Study jobs (averaging $2150). In 2001, 1650 non-need-based awards were made. *Average percent of need met:* 90%. *Average financial aid package:* $5866. *Average need-based loan:* $3377. *Average need-based gift aid:* $2932.

Applying *Options:* common application, electronic application, early action, deferred entrance. *Application fee:* $25. *Required:* high school transcript, minimum 2.5 GPA. *Required for some:* minimum 3.0 GPA, letters of recommendation, interview. *Application deadline:* rolling (freshmen). *Notification:* continuous (freshmen).

Admissions Contact Mr. Robert E. Johnson, Associate Vice President for Enrollment Management, Oakland University, 101 North Foundation Hall, Rochester, MI 48309-4401. *Phone:* 248-370-3360. *Toll-free phone:* 800-OAK-UNIV. *Fax:* 248-370-4462. *E-mail:* ouinfo@oakland.edu.

OLIVET COLLEGE
Olivet, Michigan

- **Independent** comprehensive, founded 1844, affiliated with Congregational Christian Church
- **Calendar** 4-4-1
- **Degrees** bachelor's and master's
- **Small-town** 92-acre campus
- **Endowment** $10.7 million
- **Coed,** 746 undergraduate students, 92% full-time, 47% women, 53% men
- **Minimally difficult** entrance level, 93% of applicants were admitted

Undergraduates 687 full-time, 59 part-time. Students come from 19 states and territories, 23% are from out of state, 19% African American, 0.8% Asian American or Pacific Islander, 2% Hispanic American, 1% Native American, 7% international, 10% transferred in, 66% live on campus. *Retention:* 56% of 2001 full-time freshmen returned.

Freshmen *Admission:* 793 applied, 740 admitted, 177 enrolled. *Average high school GPA:* 2.70. *Test scores:* SAT verbal scores over 500: 38%; SAT math scores over 500: 37%; ACT scores over 18: 65%; SAT verbal scores over 600: 19%; ACT scores over 24: 14%; SAT verbal scores over 700: 5%; ACT scores over 30: 1%.

Faculty *Total:* 119, 37% full-time. *Student/faculty ratio:* 14:1.

Majors Accounting; applied art; art; art education; athletic training/sports medicine; biochemistry; biology; business administration; business marketing and marketing management; chemistry; computer science; criminal justice studies; economics; education; elementary education; English; environmental science; finance; fine/studio arts; graphic design/commercial art/illustration; health/physical education; history; insurance/risk management; international relations; journalism; liberal arts and sciences/liberal studies; mass communications; mathematics; medical illustrating; physical education; pre-dentistry; pre-law; pre-medicine; pre-veterinary studies; psychology; radio/television broadcasting; secondary education; social sciences; sociology; sport/fitness administration.

Academic Programs *Special study options:* accelerated degree program, advanced placement credit, cooperative education, double majors, honors programs, independent study, internships, part-time degree program, services for LD students, student-designed majors, study abroad, summer session for credit. *Unusual degree programs:* engineering with Michigan Technological University.

Library Burrage Library with 90,000 titles, 415 serial subscriptions, an OPAC.

Computers on Campus 60 computers available on campus for general student use. A campuswide network can be accessed from student residence rooms and from off campus. Internet access, online (class) registration available.

Student Life *Housing:* on-campus residence required through junior year. *Options:* coed, men-only, women-only. *Activities and Organizations:* drama/theater group, student-run newspaper, radio station, choral group, Campus Activities Board, Black Student Union, international club, non-traditional student organization, Omicron Delta Kappa. *Campus security:* 24-hour emergency response devices and patrols, late-night transport/escort service. *Student Services:* health clinic, personal/psychological counseling, women's center.

Olivet College (continued)

Athletics Member NCAA. All Division III. *Intercollegiate sports:* baseball M, basketball M/W, cross-country running M/W, football M, golf M/W, soccer M/W, softball W, swimming W, tennis M/W, track and field M/W, volleyball W, wrestling M. *Intramural sports:* basketball M/W, football M, softball M/W, volleyball M/W.

Standardized Tests *Required for some:* SAT I or ACT (for admission).

Costs (2002–03) *Comprehensive fee:* $19,300 includes full-time tuition ($14,332), mandatory fees ($266), and room and board ($4702). Part-time tuition: $480 per credit. Part-time tuition and fees vary according to course load. *Required fees:* $133 per term part-time. *Room and board:* College room only: $2614. Room and board charges vary according to board plan and housing facility. *Payment plan:* installment. *Waivers:* employees or children of employees.

Financial Aid Of all full-time matriculated undergraduates who enrolled in 2001, 775 applied for aid, 739 were judged to have need, 129 had their need fully met. 165 Federal Work-Study jobs (averaging $1020). 443 State and other part-time jobs (averaging $896). In 2001, 131 non-need-based awards were made. *Average percent of need met:* 81%. *Average financial aid package:* $11,643. *Average need-based loan:* $3671. *Average need-based gift aid:* $7681. *Average indebtedness upon graduation:* $6587.

Applying *Options:* common application, electronic application, deferred entrance. *Application fee:* $25. *Required:* high school transcript. *Required for some:* essay or personal statement, letters of recommendation, interview. *Recommended:* minimum 2.6 GPA. *Application deadline:* rolling (freshmen), rolling (transfers). *Notification:* continuous (freshmen).

Admissions Contact Mr. Kevin Leonard, Director of Admissions, Olivet College, 320 South Main Street, Olivet, MI 49076. *Phone:* 616-749-7635. *Toll-free phone:* 800-456-7189. *Fax:* 616-749-3821. *E-mail:* admissions@olivetcollege.edu.

REFORMED BIBLE COLLEGE
Grand Rapids, Michigan

- **Independent religious** 4-year, founded 1939
- **Calendar** semesters
- **Degrees** certificates, associate, bachelor's, and postbachelor's certificates
- **Suburban** 27-acre campus
- **Endowment** $5.8 million
- **Coed,** 294 undergraduate students, 73% full-time, 48% women, 52% men
- **Moderately difficult** entrance level, 59% of applicants were admitted

Reformed Bible College is dedicated academic excellence, on-campus spiritual nurturing, and practical ministry application for all fields of study. This interdenominational college equips students from around the world for effective careers in Christian service. RBC offers a variety of bachelor's degrees, including programs in social work, youth ministry, education, and nursing. The College is located on a 34-acre suburban campus.

Undergraduates 216 full-time, 78 part-time. Students come from 20 states and territories, 11 other countries, 7% are from out of state, 4% African American, 1% Hispanic American, 0.4% Native American, 8% international, 14% transferred in, 40% live on campus.

Freshmen *Admission:* 96 applied, 57 admitted, 56 enrolled. *Average high school GPA:* 3.01. *Test scores:* ACT scores over 18: 95%; ACT scores over 24: 48%; ACT scores over 30: 3%.

Faculty *Total:* 25, 52% full-time, 36% with terminal degrees. *Student/faculty ratio:* 16:1.

Majors Accounting; biblical studies; broadcast journalism; business administration; child care/development; child guidance; communications; computer/information sciences; cultural studies; divinity/ministry; elementary education; interdisciplinary studies; liberal arts and sciences/liberal studies; missionary studies; music teacher education; pastoral counseling; pre-theology; religious education; secondary education; secretarial science; social work; theology.

Academic Programs *Special study options:* academic remediation for entering students, adult/continuing education programs, advanced placement credit, cooperative education, double majors, independent study, internships, off-campus study, part-time degree program, services for LD students, study abroad, summer session for credit. *Unusual degree programs:* 3-2 education.

Library Zondervan Library with 55,760 titles, 234 serial subscriptions, 3,855 audiovisual materials, an OPAC, a Web page.

Computers on Campus 27 computers available on campus for general student use. A campuswide network can be accessed from student residence rooms. Internet access, at least one staffed computer lab available.

Student Life *Housing:* on-campus residence required through sophomore year. *Activities and Organizations:* drama/theater group, choral group, Bible study and prayer groups, Student Council, yearbook, Student Activities, Wellspring drama club. *Campus security:* student patrols, controlled dormitory access. *Student Services:* health clinic, personal/psychological counseling.

Athletics *Intercollegiate sports:* soccer M/W. *Intramural sports:* basketball M/W, volleyball M/W.

Standardized Tests *Required:* SAT I or ACT (for admission).

Costs (2001–02) *Comprehensive fee:* $13,425 includes full-time tuition ($8400), mandatory fees ($425), and room and board ($4600). Part-time tuition: $350 per credit hour. Part-time tuition and fees vary according to course load. *Required fees:* $127 per year part-time. *Payment plan:* deferred payment. *Waivers:* employees or children of employees.

Financial Aid Of all full-time matriculated undergraduates who enrolled in 2001, 175 applied for aid, 140 were judged to have need, 25 had their need fully met. 29 Federal Work-Study jobs (averaging $1500). 6 State and other part-time jobs (averaging $1500). In 2001, 101 non-need-based awards were made. *Average percent of need met:* 49%. *Average financial aid package:* $7494. *Average need-based loan:* $4000. *Average need-based gift aid:* $3994. *Average non-need based aid:* $500. *Average indebtedness upon graduation:* $14,250.

Applying *Options:* common application, electronic application, deferred entrance. *Application fee:* $25. *Required:* essay or personal statement, high school transcript, minimum 2.5 GPA, 2 letters of recommendation, interview. *Application deadline:* rolling (freshmen), rolling (transfers).

Admissions Contact Ms. Jeanine Kopaska Brock, Assistant Director of Admissions, Reformed Bible College, 3333 East Beltline North East, Grand Rapids, MI 49525. *Phone:* 616-222-3000 Ext. 631. *Toll-free phone:* 800-511-3749. *Fax:* 616-222-3045. *E-mail:* admissions@reformed.edu.

ROCHESTER COLLEGE
Rochester Hills, Michigan

- **Independent** 4-year, founded 1959, affiliated with Church of Christ
- **Calendar** semesters
- **Degrees** associate and bachelor's
- **Suburban** 83-acre campus with easy access to Detroit
- **Endowment** $900,953
- **Coed,** 927 undergraduate students, 68% full-time, 57% women, 43% men
- **Minimally difficult** entrance level, 83% of applicants were admitted

Undergraduates Students come from 19 states and territories, 10 other countries, 13% are from out of state, 11% African American, 0.6% Asian American or Pacific Islander, 0.6% Hispanic American, 0.8% Native American, 3% international, 51% live on campus. *Retention:* 69% of 2001 full-time freshmen returned.

Freshmen *Admission:* 277 applied, 231 admitted.

Faculty *Total:* 83, 39% full-time, 28% with terminal degrees. *Student/faculty ratio:* 19:1.

Majors Accounting; behavioral sciences; biblical studies; biological/physical sciences; business administration; business communications; business marketing and marketing management; child guidance; communications; computer management; counseling psychology; English; English composition; history; interdisciplinary studies; liberal arts and sciences/liberal studies; literature; mathematics; music; music teacher education; music (voice and choral/opera performance); pastoral counseling; psychology; sport/fitness administration.

Academic Programs *Special study options:* academic remediation for entering students, accelerated degree program, adult/continuing education programs, advanced placement credit, distance learning, double majors, external degree program, independent study, internships, off-campus study, part-time degree program, study abroad, summer session for credit.

Library Muirhead Library with 43,032 titles, 307 serial subscriptions, 913 audiovisual materials.

Computers on Campus 29 computers available on campus for general student use. A campuswide network can be accessed from student residence rooms and from off campus. Internet access, at least one staffed computer lab available.

Student Life *Housing:* on-campus residence required through sophomore year. *Options:* men-only, women-only, disabled students. *Activities and Organizations:* drama/theater group, student-run newspaper, choral group. *Campus security:* 24-hour emergency response devices, late-night transport/escort service, controlled dormitory access, evening security guards. *Student Services:* personal/psychological counseling.

Athletics Member NCCAA. *Intercollegiate sports:* baseball M(s), basketball M(s)/W(s), cross-country running M(s)/W(s), soccer M(s), softball W(s), track and field M(s)/W(s), volleyball W(s). *Intramural sports:* basketball M/W, cross-country running M/W, football M/W, softball M/W, track and field M/W, volleyball M/W.

Standardized Tests *Required:* SAT I or ACT (for admission).

Costs (2001–02) *Comprehensive fee:* $15,354 includes full-time tuition ($9462), mandatory fees ($708), and room and board ($5184). Part-time tuition: $296 per credit hour. Part-time tuition and fees vary according to course load. *Required fees:* $131 per term part-time. *Payment plan:* installment. *Waivers:* children of alumni, senior citizens, and employees or children of employees.

Financial Aid Of all full-time matriculated undergraduates who enrolled in 2001, 87 Federal Work-Study jobs (averaging $805). 127 State and other part-time jobs (averaging $1220). *Average indebtedness upon graduation:* $11,283.

Applying *Options:* electronic application, early admission, deferred entrance. *Application fee:* $25. *Required:* high school transcript. *Required for some:* interview. *Recommended:* essay or personal statement, minimum 2.25 GPA, 1 letter of recommendation. *Application deadline:* rolling (freshmen), rolling (transfers). *Notification:* continuous (freshmen).

Admissions Contact Mr. Larry Norman, Vice President for Enrollment Management, Rochester College, 800 West Avon Road, Rochester Hills, MI 48307-2764. *Phone:* 248-218-2032. *Toll-free phone:* 800-521-6010. *Fax:* 248-218-2005. *E-mail:* admissions@rc.edu.

SACRED HEART MAJOR SEMINARY

Detroit, Michigan

- **Independent Roman Catholic** comprehensive, founded 1919
- **Calendar** semesters
- **Degrees** certificates, associate, bachelor's, master's, and first professional
- **Urban** 24-acre campus
- **Endowment** $2.3 million
- **Coed,** 294 undergraduate students, 11% full-time, 48% women, 52% men
- **Moderately difficult** entrance level, 100% of applicants were admitted

Undergraduates 32 full-time, 262 part-time. Students come from 3 states and territories, 2 other countries, 31% are from out of state, 3% African American, 9% Asian American or Pacific Islander, 12% Hispanic American, 2% transferred in. *Retention:* 100% of 2001 full-time freshmen returned.

Freshmen *Admission:* 5 applied, 5 admitted, 5 enrolled. *Average high school GPA:* 3.47.

Faculty *Total:* 33, 64% full-time, 55% with terminal degrees. *Student/faculty ratio:* 8:1.

Majors Divinity/ministry; philosophy.

Academic Programs *Special study options:* academic remediation for entering students, advanced placement credit, honors programs, independent study, off-campus study, part-time degree program, services for LD students.

Library Szoka Library with 120,000 titles, 495 serial subscriptions.

Computers on Campus 8 computers available on campus for general student use. At least one staffed computer lab available.

Student Life *Housing:* on-campus residence required through senior year. *Options:* men-only. *Activities and Organizations:* choral group. *Campus security:* 24-hour emergency response devices, late-night transport/escort service. *Student Services:* personal/psychological counseling.

Standardized Tests *Required:* SAT I or ACT (for admission).

Costs (2001–02) *One-time required fee:* $100. *Comprehensive fee:* $11,490 includes full-time tuition ($6792), mandatory fees ($40), and room and board ($4658). Full-time tuition and fees vary according to course load. Part-time tuition: $196 per credit hour. Part-time tuition and fees vary according to course load. *Payment plans:* installment, deferred payment. *Waivers:* employees or children of employees.

Financial Aid Of all full-time matriculated undergraduates who enrolled in 2001, 20 applied for aid, 17 were judged to have need. 4 Federal Work-Study jobs (averaging $600). 5 State and other part-time jobs (averaging $1000). In 2001, 1 non-need-based awards were made. *Average percent of need met:* 60%. *Average financial aid package:* $3000. *Average non-need based aid:* $1000.

Applying *Options:* deferred entrance. *Application fee:* $30. *Required:* essay or personal statement, high school transcript, minimum 2.0 GPA, 1 letter of recommendation, interview. *Application deadlines:* 7/31 (freshmen), 7/31 (transfers). *Notification:* continuous until 8/15 (freshmen).

Admissions Contact Fr. Patrick Halfpenny, Vice Rector, Sacred Heart Major Seminary, 2701 Chicago Boulevard, Detroit, MI 48206. *Phone:* 313-883-8552.

SAGINAW VALLEY STATE UNIVERSITY

University Center, Michigan

- **State-supported** comprehensive, founded 1963
- **Calendar** semesters
- **Degrees** bachelor's, master's, and post-master's certificates
- **Rural** 782-acre campus
- **Endowment** $20.7 million
- **Coed,** 7,320 undergraduate students, 69% full-time, 60% women, 40% men
- **Moderately difficult** entrance level, 45% of applicants were admitted

Undergraduates 5,036 full-time, 2,284 part-time. Students come from 15 states and territories, 49 other countries, 53% are from out of state, 6% African American, 0.8% Asian American or Pacific Islander, 3% Hispanic American, 0.4% Native American, 4% international, 9% transferred in, 14% live on campus. *Retention:* 65% of 2001 full-time freshmen returned.

Freshmen *Admission:* 7,551 applied, 3,370 admitted, 1,090 enrolled. *Average high school GPA:* 3.11. *Test scores:* ACT scores over 18: 76%; ACT scores over 24: 24%; ACT scores over 30: 3%.

Faculty *Total:* 228, 100% full-time, 77% with terminal degrees. *Student/faculty ratio:* 24:1.

Majors Accounting; art; biochemistry; biological/physical sciences; biology; business; business administration; business economics; chemistry; communications; computer/information sciences; computer systems analysis; criminal justice studies; design/visual communications; economics; electrical engineering; elementary education; English; finance; fine/studio arts; French; general studies; history; industrial technology; interdisciplinary studies; international relations; marketing research; mathematics; mathematics/computer science; mechanical engineering; medical technology; music; nursing; occupational therapy; operations management; optics; physical education; physics; political science; psychology; public administration; science education; social work; sociology; Spanish; special education; theater arts/drama.

Academic Programs *Special study options:* academic remediation for entering students, accelerated degree program, advanced placement credit, cooperative education, distance learning, double majors, English as a second language, honors programs, independent study, internships, part-time degree program, services for LD students, student-designed majors, study abroad, summer session for credit.

Library Zahnow Library with 3,119 serial subscriptions, 19,231 audiovisual materials, an OPAC, a Web page.

Computers on Campus 408 computers available on campus for general student use. A campuswide network can be accessed from off campus. Internet access, at least one staffed computer lab available.

Student Life *Housing Options:* coed, disabled students. *Activities and Organizations:* drama/theater group, student-run newspaper, choral group, marching band, Alpha Sigma Alpha, Sigma Pi, Organization of Black Unity, International Students Association, University Residence Association, national fraternities, national sororities. *Campus security:* 24-hour emergency response devices, late-night transport/escort service, controlled dormitory access, rape prevention program. *Student Services:* health clinic, personal/psychological counseling.

Athletics Member NCAA. except baseball (Division II), men's and women's basketball (Division II), men's and women's cross-country running (Division II), football (Division II), golf (Division II), men's and women's soccer (Division II), softball (Division II), tennis (Division II), men's and women's track and field (Division II), volleyball (Division II) *Intercollegiate sports:* baseball M(s), basketball M(s)/W(s), bowling M(s), cross-country running M(s)/W(s), football M(s), golf M(s), soccer M(s)/W(s), softball W(s), tennis W(s), track and field M(s)/W(s), volleyball W(s). *Intramural sports:* archery M/W, basketball M/W, bowling M/W, equestrian sports M(c)/W(c), ice hockey M(c), racquetball M/W, skiing (cross-country) M/W, soccer M/W, softball M/W, table tennis M/W, tennis M/W, volleyball M/W.

Standardized Tests *Required:* SAT I or ACT (for admission).

Costs (2001–02) *Tuition:* state resident $3897 full-time, $115 per credit hour part-time; nonresident $8160 full-time, $257 per credit hour part-time. Full-time tuition and fees vary according to course load, location, and program. Part-time tuition and fees vary according to course load, location, and program. *Required fees:* $443 full-time, $17 per credit hour. *Room and board:* $5200. Room and board charges vary according to board plan and housing facility. *Payment plan:* installment. *Waivers:* employees or children of employees.

Applying *Options:* deferred entrance. *Application fee:* $25. *Required:* high school transcript. *Recommended:* minimum 2.5 GPA. *Application deadline:* rolling (freshmen), rolling (transfers).

Saginaw Valley State University (continued)

Admissions Contact Mr. James P. Dwyer, Director of Admissions, Saginaw Valley State University, 7400 Bay Road, University Center, HI 48710-0001. *Phone:* 989-790-4200. *Toll-free phone:* 800-968-9500. *Fax:* 517-790-0180. *E-mail:* admissions@svsu.edu.

SAINT MARY'S COLLEGE OF AVE MARIA UNIVERSITY

Orchard Lake, Michigan

- **Independent Roman Catholic** 4-year, founded 1885
- **Calendar** semesters
- **Degree** bachelor's
- **Suburban** 120-acre campus with easy access to Detroit
- **Coed,** 513 undergraduate students, 50% full-time, 46% women, 54% men
- **Moderately difficult** entrance level, 62% of applicants were admitted

Undergraduates 256 full-time, 257 part-time. Students come from 8 states and territories, 11 other countries, 2% are from out of state, 7% African American, 1.0% Asian American or Pacific Islander, 0.7% Hispanic American, 0.2% Native American, 41% international, 16% transferred in, 29% live on campus. *Retention:* 56% of 2001 full-time freshmen returned.

Freshmen *Admission:* 160 applied, 99 admitted, 61 enrolled. *Average high school GPA:* 2.90. *Test scores:* ACT scores over 18: 99%; ACT scores over 24: 21%; ACT scores over 30: 4%.

Faculty *Total:* 60, 42% full-time, 50% with terminal degrees. *Student/faculty ratio:* 12:1.

Majors Accounting; biology; business administration; business marketing and marketing management; chemistry; English; environmental science; human resources management; industrial radiologic technology; information sciences/systems; mass communications; pastoral counseling; philosophy; psychology; Slavic languages; social sciences; sociology; theology.

Academic Programs *Special study options:* academic remediation for entering students, accelerated degree program, advanced placement credit, cooperative education, double majors, English as a second language, independent study, internships, off-campus study, part-time degree program, study abroad.

Library Alumni Memorial Library with 79,103 titles, 335 serial subscriptions, 1,400 audiovisual materials, an OPAC, a Web page.

Computers on Campus 20 computers available on campus for general student use. Internet access, at least one staffed computer lab available.

Student Life *Housing Options:* men-only, women-only. *Activities and Organizations:* choral group, Campus Ministry, student government. *Campus security:* 24-hour emergency response devices, security patrols until 2 a.m. *Student Services:* personal/psychological counseling.

Athletics Member NSCAA. *Intercollegiate sports:* baseball M, basketball M, soccer M/W.

Standardized Tests *Required:* SAT I or ACT (for admission).

Costs (2001–02) *Comprehensive fee:* $11,932 includes full-time tuition ($6504), mandatory fees ($288), and room and board ($5140). Full-time tuition and fees vary according to course load. Part-time tuition: $271 per credit hour. Part-time tuition and fees vary according to course load. *Room and board:* College room only: $2000. Room and board charges vary according to board plan and housing facility. *Payment plan:* installment. *Waivers:* employees or children of employees.

Financial Aid Of all full-time matriculated undergraduates who enrolled in 2001, 233 applied for aid, 233 were judged to have need. 13 Federal Work-Study jobs (averaging $1131). In 2001, 23 non-need-based awards were made. *Average financial aid package:* $4752. *Average need-based loan:* $3455. *Average need-based gift aid:* $5787. *Average non-need based aid:* $3761. *Average indebtedness upon graduation:* $13,027. *Financial aid deadline:* 4/30.

Applying *Options:* early admission. *Application fee:* $25. *Required:* essay or personal statement, high school transcript, minimum 2.5 GPA, minimum ACT score of 19 or SAT I score of 900. *Required for some:* interview. *Recommended:* 2 letters of recommendation. *Application deadline:* rolling (freshmen), rolling (transfers).

Admissions Contact Mr. James Bass, Director of Admissions, Saint Mary's College of Ave Maria University, 3535 Indian Trail. *Phone:* 248-683-0523. *Toll-free phone:* 877-252-3131. *Fax:* 248-683-1756. *E-mail:* admissions@stmarys.avemaria.edu.

SIENA HEIGHTS UNIVERSITY

Adrian, Michigan

- **Independent Roman Catholic** comprehensive, founded 1919
- **Calendar** semesters
- **Degrees** associate, bachelor's, and master's
- **Small-town** 140-acre campus with easy access to Detroit
- **Coed,** 1,746 undergraduate students
- **Moderately difficult** entrance level, 78% of applicants were admitted

Siena Heights University students integrate liberal arts and career preparation. Siena has introduced a new field of study, sport management. The curriculum combines a strong business foundation with a specialized knowledge in sport. The program features an outstanding practicum experience along with great career opportunities.

Undergraduates Students come from 8 states and territories, 33% live on campus.

Freshmen *Admission:* 594 applied, 464 admitted. *Test scores:* ACT scores over 18: 88%; ACT scores over 24: 25%; ACT scores over 30: 1%.

Faculty *Total:* 65. *Student/faculty ratio:* 14:1.

Majors Accounting; art; art education; biology; business administration; business education; business marketing and marketing management; chemistry; child guidance; community services; criminal justice/law enforcement administration; early childhood education; elementary education; English; general studies; gerontology; history; hospitality management; humanities; human services; information sciences/systems; mathematics; music; music teacher education; natural sciences; philosophy; pre-engineering; pre-law; psychology; public administration; religious studies; secondary education; social sciences; social work; Spanish; theater arts/drama.

Academic Programs *Special study options:* academic remediation for entering students, accelerated degree program, adult/continuing education programs, advanced placement credit, cooperative education, double majors, external degree program, independent study, internships, off-campus study, part-time degree program, services for LD students, student-designed majors, study abroad, summer session for credit.

Library 120,407 titles, 451 serial subscriptions.

Computers on Campus 75 computers available on campus for general student use. A campuswide network can be accessed from student residence rooms and from off campus. Internet access, at least one staffed computer lab available.

Student Life *Housing:* on-campus residence required through sophomore year. *Options:* coed. *Activities and Organizations:* drama/theater group, student-run newspaper, choral group, Student Programming Association, Residence Hall Counsel, Student Senate, Siena Heights African American Knowledge Association, Greek Council, national fraternities, national sororities. *Campus security:* 24-hour patrols, student patrols, late-night transport/escort service. *Student Services:* health clinic, personal/psychological counseling.

Athletics Member NAIA. *Intercollegiate sports:* baseball M(s), basketball M(s)/W(s), cross-country running M(s)/W(s), golf M(s), soccer M(s)/W(s), softball W(s), track and field M(s)/W(s), volleyball W(s). *Intramural sports:* basketball M/W, football M, softball M/W, volleyball M/W.

Standardized Tests *Required:* SAT I or ACT (for admission).

Costs (2002–03) *Comprehensive fee:* $18,760 includes full-time tuition ($13,330), mandatory fees ($300), and room and board ($5130). Part-time tuition: $350 per credit. Part-time tuition and fees vary according to course load. *Required fees:* $50 per term part-time. *Room and board:* Room and board charges vary according to board plan and housing facility. *Payment plans:* installment, deferred payment. *Waivers:* children of alumni and employees or children of employees.

Applying *Options:* common application, electronic application, deferred entrance. *Application fee:* $25. *Required:* high school transcript. *Required for some:* essay or personal statement, letters of recommendation, interview. *Recommended:* minimum 2.3 GPA, interview. *Application deadline:* rolling (freshmen), rolling (transfers).

Admissions Contact Mr. Kevin Kucera, Dean of Admissions and Enrollment Services, Siena Heights University, 1247 East Siena Heights Drive, Adrian, MI 49221-1796. *Phone:* 517-264-7180. *Toll-free phone:* 800-521-0009. *Fax:* 517-264-7745. *E-mail:* admissions@sienahts.edu.

SPRING ARBOR UNIVERSITY

Spring Arbor, Michigan

- **Independent Free Methodist** comprehensive, founded 1873
- **Calendar** 4-1-4
- **Degrees** associate, bachelor's, and master's
- **Small-town** 70-acre campus
- **Endowment** $8.2 million
- **Coed,** 2,173 undergraduate students, 83% full-time, 67% women, 33% men
- **Moderately difficult** entrance level, 86% of applicants were admitted

Undergraduates 1,805 full-time, 368 part-time. Students come from 14 other countries, 13% are from out of state, 11% African American, 0.7% Asian

American or Pacific Islander, 1% Hispanic American, 0.5% Native American, 1% international, 5% transferred in, 70% live on campus. *Retention:* 83% of 2001 full-time freshmen returned.

Freshmen *Admission:* 571 applied, 490 admitted, 225 enrolled. *Average high school GPA:* 3.37. *Test scores:* ACT scores over 18: 86%; ACT scores over 24: 39%; ACT scores over 30: 6%.

Faculty *Total:* 84, 82% full-time, 48% with terminal degrees. *Student/faculty ratio:* 15:1.

Majors Accounting; art; biochemistry; biology; business administration; chemistry; communications; computer science; early childhood education; elementary education; English; family studies; health/physical education; health services administration; history; history of philosophy; human resources management; journalism; liberal arts and sciences/liberal studies; management information systems/business data processing; mathematics; music; music (piano and organ performance); music teacher education; philosophy; physical education; psychology; radio/television broadcasting; religious studies; secondary education; social sciences; social work; sociology; Spanish; sport/fitness administration.

Academic Programs *Special study options:* academic remediation for entering students, accelerated degree program, adult/continuing education programs, advanced placement credit, double majors, English as a second language, external degree program, honors programs, independent study, internships, off-campus study, part-time degree program, services for LD students, student-designed majors, summer session for credit. *Unusual degree programs:* 3-2 engineering with University of Michigan, Michigan State University, Western Michigan University, Tri-State University.

Library Hugh A. White Library plus 1 other with 84,225 titles, 5,120 audiovisual materials.

Computers on Campus 85 computers available on campus for general student use. Internet access, at least one staffed computer lab available.

Student Life *Housing:* on-campus residence required through senior year. *Options:* men-only, women-only, disabled students. *Activities and Organizations:* drama/theater group, student-run newspaper, radio station, choral group, Action Jackson, Cougarettes, Multicultural Organization. *Campus security:* late-night transport/escort service. *Student Services:* health clinic, personal/psychological counseling.

Athletics Member NAIA. *Intercollegiate sports:* baseball M(s), basketball M(s)/W(s), cross-country running M(s)/W(s), golf M(s), soccer M(s)/W(s), softball W(s), tennis M(s)/W(s), track and field M(s)/W(s), volleyball W(s). *Intramural sports:* basketball M/W, soccer M/W, softball M/W, tennis M/W, volleyball M/W.

Standardized Tests *Required:* SAT I or ACT (for admission).

Costs (2001–02) *Comprehensive fee:* $17,976 includes full-time tuition ($12,920), mandatory fees ($216), and room and board ($4840). Part-time tuition: $270 per credit. Part-time tuition and fees vary according to course load. *Required fees:* $25 per term part-time. *Room and board:* College room only: $2180. *Payment plans:* installment, deferred payment. *Waivers:* senior citizens and employees or children of employees.

Financial Aid Of all full-time matriculated undergraduates who enrolled in 2001, 1781 applied for aid, 1479 were judged to have need, 553 had their need fully met. 294 Federal Work-Study jobs (averaging $704). In 2001, 690 non-need-based awards were made. *Average percent of need met:* 80%. *Average financial aid package:* $9703. *Average need-based loan:* $2001. *Average need-based gift aid:* $2852. *Average non-need based aid:* $936. *Average indebtedness upon graduation:* $9140.

Applying *Options:* early admission, deferred entrance. *Application fee:* $30. *Required:* high school transcript. *Required for some:* letters of recommendation. *Recommended:* essay or personal statement, interview, guidance counselor's evaluation form. *Application deadline:* rolling (freshmen), rolling (transfers). *Notification:* continuous (freshmen).

Admissions Contact Mr. Jim Weidman, Director of Admissions, Spring Arbor University, 106 East Main Street, Spring Arbor, MI 49283-9799. *Phone:* 517-750-1200 Ext. 1475. *Toll-free phone:* 800-968-0011. *Fax:* 517-750-6620. *E-mail:* shellya@admin.arbor.edu.

UNIVERSITY OF DETROIT MERCY

Detroit, Michigan

Admissions Contact Ms. Colleen Ezzeddine, Admissions Counselor, University of Detroit Mercy, PO Box 19900, Detroit, MI 48219-0900. *Phone:* 313-993-1245. *Toll-free phone:* 800-635-5020. *Fax:* 313-993-3326. *E-mail:* admissions@udmercy.edu.

UNIVERSITY OF MICHIGAN

Ann Arbor, Michigan

- **State-supported** university, founded 1817
- **Calendar** trimesters
- **Degrees** certificates, bachelor's, master's, doctoral, first professional, and post-master's certificates
- **Suburban** 2861-acre campus with easy access to Detroit
- **Endowment** $3.1 billion
- **Coed,** 24,547 undergraduate students, 94% full-time, 50% women, 50% men
- **Very difficult** entrance level, 52% of applicants were admitted

Undergraduates 23,189 full-time, 1,358 part-time. Students come from 54 states and territories, 87 other countries, 32% are from out of state, 8% African American, 12% Asian American or Pacific Islander, 4% Hispanic American, 0.7% Native American, 4% international, 4% transferred in, 37% live on campus. *Retention:* 95% of 2001 full-time freshmen returned.

Freshmen *Admission:* 24,141 applied, 12,594 admitted, 5,540 enrolled. *Average high school GPA:* 3.80. *Test scores:* SAT verbal scores over 500: 93%; SAT math scores over 500: 97%; ACT scores over 18: 99%; SAT verbal scores over 600: 64%; SAT math scores over 600: 81%; ACT scores over 24: 88%; SAT verbal scores over 700: 17%; SAT math scores over 700: 33%; ACT scores over 30: 31%.

Faculty *Total:* 2,678, 79% full-time, 88% with terminal degrees. *Student/faculty ratio:* 16:1.

Majors Accounting; aerospace engineering; African-American studies; African studies; American studies; anthropology; applied art; applied mathematics; Arabic; archaeology; architecture; art education; art history; Asian studies; astronomy; athletic training/sports medicine; atmospheric sciences; biblical studies; biochemistry; biology; biomedical science; biometrics; biophysics; botany; business administration; cell biology; ceramic arts; chemical engineering; chemistry; Chinese; civil engineering; classics; comparative literature; computer engineering; computer science; creative writing; dance; dental hygiene; design/visual communications; drawing; ecology; economics; education; electrical engineering; elementary education; engineering; engineering physics; engineering science; English; environmental engineering; environmental science; European studies; exercise sciences; film studies; French; general studies; geography; geology; German; graphic design/commercial art/illustration; Greek (modern); Hebrew; Hispanic-American studies; history; humanities; industrial design; industrial/manufacturing engineering; interdisciplinary studies; interior design; international relations; Islamic studies; Italian; Japanese; jazz; journalism; Judaic studies; landscape architecture; Latin American studies; Latin (ancient and medieval); liberal arts and sciences/liberal studies; linguistics; literature; mass communications; materials engineering; materials science; mathematical statistics; mathematics; mechanical engineering; medical technology; medieval/renaissance studies; metal/jewelry arts; metallurgical engineering; Mexican-American studies; microbiology/bacteriology; Middle Eastern studies; molecular biology; multimedia; music; music history; music (piano and organ performance); music teacher education; music theory and composition; music (voice and choral/opera performance); natural resources management; naval architecture/marine engineering; nuclear engineering; nursing; nutrition science; oceanography; painting; pharmacy; philosophy; photography; physical education; physics; play/screenwriting; political science; printmaking; psychology; radiological science; recreation/leisure studies; religious studies; romance languages; Russian; Russian/Slavic studies; Scandinavian studies; sculpture; secondary education; social sciences; sociology; South Asian studies; Southeast Asian studies; Spanish; speech/rhetorical studies; sport/fitness administration; stringed instruments; textile arts; theater arts/drama; theater design; visual/performing arts; wildlife biology; wind/percussion instruments; women's studies; zoology.

Academic Programs *Special study options:* accelerated degree program, adult/continuing education programs, advanced placement credit, cooperative education, distance learning, double majors, English as a second language, honors programs, independent study, internships, off-campus study, part-time degree program, services for LD students, student-designed majors, study abroad, summer session for credit. *ROTC:* Army (b), Navy (b), Air Force (b). *Unusual degree programs:* 3-2 architecture, public policy.

Library University Library plus 20 others with 7.2 million titles, 68,798 serial subscriptions, 56,512 audiovisual materials, an OPAC, a Web page.

Computers on Campus A campuswide network can be accessed from student residence rooms and from off campus. At least one staffed computer lab available.

Student Life *Housing Options:* coed, women-only, cooperative, disabled students. *Activities and Organizations:* drama/theater group, student-run newspaper, radio and television station, choral group, marching band, University Activities Center, Hillel, Project Serve, Residence Hall Association, Black Student Union, national fraternities, national sororities. *Campus security:* 24-hour emergency response devices and patrols, student patrols, late-night transport/escort

University of Michigan (continued)
service, controlled dormitory access, bicycle patrols. *Student Services:* health clinic, personal/psychological counseling, women's center, legal services.

Athletics Member NCAA. All Division I except football (Division I-A). *Intercollegiate sports:* baseball M(s), basketball M(s)/W(s), crew W, cross-country running M(s)/W(s), field hockey W(s), golf M(s)/W(s), gymnastics M(s)/W(s), ice hockey M(s), soccer W(s), softball W(s), swimming M(s)/W(s), tennis M(s)/W(s), track and field M(s)/W(s), volleyball W(s), water polo W, wrestling M(s). *Intramural sports:* archery M(c)/W(c), badminton M/W, basketball M/W, crew M(c)/W(c), cross-country running M/W, fencing M(c)/W(c), football M/W, golf M/W, ice hockey M/W, lacrosse M(c)/W(c), racquetball M/W, rugby M(c)/W(c), sailing M(c)/W(c), skiing (cross-country) M(c)/W(c), skiing (downhill) M(c)/W(c), soccer M/W, softball M/W, swimming M/W, table tennis M/W, tennis M/W, track and field M/W, volleyball M/W, water polo M(c)/W(c), wrestling M/W.

Standardized Tests *Required:* SAT I or ACT (for admission). *Required for some:* SAT II: Subject Tests (for admission), SAT II: Writing Test (for admission).

Costs (2001–02) *Tuition:* state resident $6750 full-time, $256 per credit part-time; nonresident $21,460 full-time, $869 per credit part-time. Full-time tuition and fees vary according to program and student level. Part-time tuition and fees vary according to course load, program, and student level. *Required fees:* $185 full-time. *Room and board:* $6068. Room and board charges vary according to board plan and housing facility. *Payment plan:* installment. *Waivers:* senior citizens and employees or children of employees.

Financial Aid Of all full-time matriculated undergraduates who enrolled in 2001, 11147 applied for aid, 8360 were judged to have need, 7524 had their need fully met. 5721 Federal Work-Study jobs (averaging $1940). 1122 State and other part-time jobs (averaging $2498). In 2001, 4931 non-need-based awards were made. *Average percent of need met:* 90%. *Average financial aid package:* $10,969. *Average need-based loan:* $4485. *Average need-based gift aid:* $6709. *Average non-need based aid:* $4330. *Average indebtedness upon graduation:* $16,024.

Applying *Options:* electronic application, deferred entrance. *Application fee:* $40. *Required:* essay or personal statement, high school transcript. *Required for some:* letters of recommendation, interview. *Application deadlines:* 2/1 (freshmen), 3/1 (transfers). *Notification:* continuous until 4/1 (freshmen).

Admissions Contact Mr. Ted Spencer, Director of Undergraduate Admissions, University of Michigan, Ann Arbor, MI 48109-1316. *Phone:* 734-764-7433. *Fax:* 734-936-0740. *E-mail:* ugadmiss@umich.edu.

UNIVERSITY OF MICHIGAN-DEARBORN
Dearborn, Michigan

- **State-supported** comprehensive, founded 1959, part of University of Michigan System
- **Calendar** semesters
- **Degrees** bachelor's, master's, and postbachelor's certificates
- **Suburban** 210-acre campus with easy access to Detroit
- **Coed,** 6,326 undergraduate students, 60% full-time, 54% women, 46% men
- **Moderately difficult** entrance level, 65% of applicants were admitted

Undergraduates 3,771 full-time, 2,555 part-time. Students come from 25 states and territories, 22 other countries, 1% are from out of state, 7% African American, 6% Asian American or Pacific Islander, 2% Hispanic American, 0.6% Native American, 1% international, 10% transferred in. *Retention:* 86% of 2001 full-time freshmen returned.

Freshmen *Admission:* 2,334 applied, 1,509 admitted, 707 enrolled. *Average high school GPA:* 3.42.

Faculty *Total:* 493, 53% full-time, 65% with terminal degrees. *Student/faculty ratio:* 15:1.

Majors American studies; anthropology; art education; art history; arts management; behavioral sciences; bilingual/bicultural education; biochemistry; biological/physical sciences; biology; business administration; business marketing and marketing management; chemistry; child care/development; communication equipment technology; comparative literature; computer/information sciences; computer science; developmental/child psychology; early childhood education; economics; education; electrical engineering; elementary education; engineering; English; environmental science; finance; French; German; health services administration; Hispanic-American studies; history; humanities; industrial/manufacturing engineering; information sciences/systems; interdisciplinary studies; international relations; liberal arts and sciences/liberal studies; mathematics; mechanical engineering; medieval/renaissance studies; microbiology/bacteriology; middle school education; music; music history; natural sciences; philosophy; physical sciences; physics; political science; psychology; public administration; science education; secondary education; social sciences; sociology; Spanish; speech/rhetorical studies; women's studies.

Academic Programs *Special study options:* academic remediation for entering students, accelerated degree program, adult/continuing education programs, cooperative education, honors programs, independent study, internships, off-campus study, part-time degree program, services for LD students, student-designed majors, study abroad, summer session for credit. *ROTC:* Army (b), Navy (c), Air Force (c).

Library Mardigian Library with 214,909 titles, 1,244 serial subscriptions, 3,241 audiovisual materials, an OPAC, a Web page.

Computers on Campus 350 computers available on campus for general student use. A campuswide network can be accessed from off campus. Internet access, at least one staffed computer lab available.

Student Life *Housing:* college housing not available. *Activities and Organizations:* drama/theater group, student-run newspaper, radio station, Dearborn Campus Engineers, student radio station, Association for African-American Students, national fraternities, national sororities. *Campus security:* 24-hour emergency response devices and patrols, late-night transport/escort service. *Student Services:* health clinic, personal/psychological counseling, women's center.

Athletics Member NAIA. *Intercollegiate sports:* basketball M(s)/W(s), volleyball W(s). *Intramural sports:* basketball M/W, cross-country running M(c)/W(c), fencing M(c)/W(c), ice hockey M(c), racquetball M/W, soccer M(c), table tennis M/W, tennis M/W, volleyball M/W.

Standardized Tests *Required:* SAT I or ACT (for admission).

Costs (2001–02) *Tuition:* state resident $4915 full-time, $187 per credit hour part-time; nonresident $11,883 full-time, $466 per credit hour part-time. Full-time tuition and fees vary according to class time, course load, program, and student level. Part-time tuition and fees vary according to class time, course load, program, and student level. *Required fees:* $180 full-time. *Payment plan:* installment. *Waivers:* senior citizens and employees or children of employees.

Financial Aid Of all full-time matriculated undergraduates who enrolled in 2001, 2432 applied for aid, 1323 were judged to have need, 477 had their need fully met. 25 Federal Work-Study jobs (averaging $729). 12 State and other part-time jobs (averaging $1414). In 2001, 536 non-need-based awards were made. *Average percent of need met:* 75%. *Average financial aid package:* $5816. *Average need-based gift aid:* $3049. *Average non-need based aid:* $3565. *Average indebtedness upon graduation:* $14,673.

Applying *Application fee:* $30. *Required:* high school transcript, minimum 3.0 GPA. *Required for some:* interview. *Application deadline:* rolling (freshmen), rolling (transfers). *Notification:* continuous until 9/15 (freshmen).

Admissions Contact Mr. David Placey, Director of Admissions, University of Michigan-Dearborn, 4901 Evergreen Road, Dearborn, MI 48128-1491. *Phone:* 313-593-5100. *E-mail:* umdgoblu@umd.umich.edu.

UNIVERSITY OF MICHIGAN-FLINT
Flint, Michigan

- **State-supported** comprehensive, founded 1956, part of University of Michigan System
- **Calendar** semesters
- **Degrees** bachelor's, master's, and postbachelor's certificates
- **Urban** 72-acre campus with easy access to Detroit
- **Coed,** 5,879 undergraduate students, 58% full-time, 65% women, 35% men
- **Moderately difficult** entrance level, 81% of applicants were admitted

Undergraduates 3,424 full-time, 2,455 part-time. Students come from 21 states and territories, 1% are from out of state, 11% African American, 1% Asian American or Pacific Islander, 2% Hispanic American, 0.7% Native American, 0.3% international, 10% transferred in. *Retention:* 70% of 2001 full-time freshmen returned.

Freshmen *Admission:* 1,540 applied, 1,248 admitted, 649 enrolled. *Average high school GPA:* 3.31. *Test scores:* SAT verbal scores over 500: 50%; SAT math scores over 500: 64%; ACT scores over 18: 85%; SAT verbal scores over 600: 6%; SAT math scores over 600: 27%; ACT scores over 24: 28%; ACT scores over 30: 2%.

Faculty *Total:* 392, 47% full-time, 49% with terminal degrees. *Student/faculty ratio:* 17:1.

Majors Accounting; actuarial science; African-American studies; anthropology; art; art education; biology; business administration; chemistry; city/community/regional planning; clinical psychology; computer science; criminal justice/law enforcement administration; early childhood education; earth sciences; economics; education; elementary education; engineering; engineering science; English; environmental health; environmental science; finance; French; geography; German; health services administration; history; human resources management; liberal arts and sciences/liberal studies; mass communications; mathematics; medical technology; music; music teacher education; natural resources management; nursing; operations research; philosophy; physical sciences; physics; political science; psychology; public administration; secondary education; social sciences; social work; sociology; Spanish; theater arts/drama; urban studies.

Academic Programs *Special study options:* academic remediation for entering students, adult/continuing education programs, advanced placement credit, cooperative education, double majors, honors programs, independent study, internships, part-time degree program, student-designed majors, summer session for credit.

Library Frances Willson Thompson Library with 194,772 titles, 1,215 serial subscriptions, 22,278 audiovisual materials, an OPAC, a Web page.

Computers on Campus 160 computers available on campus for general student use. A campuswide network can be accessed from off campus. Internet access, online (class) registration, at least one staffed computer lab available.

Student Life *Housing:* college housing not available. *Activities and Organizations:* drama/theater group, student-run newspaper, television station, choral group, national fraternities, national sororities. *Campus security:* 24-hour emergency response devices and patrols, student patrols, late-night transport/escort service. *Student Services:* health clinic, personal/psychological counseling.

Athletics *Intramural sports:* badminton M/W, basketball M/W, bowling M/W, football M, golf M/W, racquetball M/W, soccer M/W, softball M/W, tennis M/W, volleyball M/W.

Standardized Tests *Required:* SAT I or ACT (for admission).

Costs (2001–02) *Tuition:* state resident $4102 full-time, $171 per credit part-time; nonresident $8430 full-time, $342 per credit part-time. Full-time tuition and fees vary according to program and student level. Part-time tuition and fees vary according to program and student level. *Required fees:* $226 full-time, $113 per term part-time. *Payment plan:* deferred payment. *Waivers:* minority students and senior citizens.

Applying *Options:* deferred entrance. *Application fee:* $30. *Required:* high school transcript. *Recommended:* essay or personal statement. *Application deadlines:* 9/2 (freshmen), 8/21 (transfers). *Notification:* continuous (freshmen).

Admissions Contact Dr. Virginia R. Allen, Vice Chancellor for Student Services and Enrollment, University of Michigan-Flint, 303 East Kearsley Street, Flint, MI 48502-1950. *Phone:* 810-762-3434. *Toll-free phone:* 800-942-5636. *Fax:* 810-762-3272. *E-mail:* admissions@list.flint.umich.edu.

University of Phoenix-Metro Detroit Campus

Troy, Michigan

- **Proprietary** comprehensive
- **Calendar** continuous
- **Degrees** certificates, associate, bachelor's, master's, doctoral, post-master's, and postbachelor's certificates (courses conducted at 54 campuses and learning centers in 13 states)
- **Coed,** 791 undergraduate students, 100% full-time, 57% women, 43% men
- **Noncompetitive** entrance level

Undergraduates Students come from 15 states and territories, 1% are from out of state.

Faculty *Total:* 424, 3% full-time, 21% with terminal degrees. *Student/faculty ratio:* 13:1.

Majors Accounting; business administration; business marketing and marketing management; enterprise management; information technology; management information systems/business data processing; management science; nursing science.

Academic Programs *Special study options:* accelerated degree program, advanced placement credit, distance learning, external degree program, independent study.

Library University Library with 17.5 million titles, 9,000 serial subscriptions, an OPAC, a Web page.

Computers on Campus A campuswide network can be accessed from off campus. Internet access, at least one staffed computer lab available.

Student Life *Housing:* college housing not available.

Costs (2001–02) *Tuition:* $8700 full-time. Full-time tuition and fees vary according to location and program. *Payment plan:* deferred payment. *Waivers:* employees or children of employees.

Applying *Options:* deferred entrance. *Application fee:* $85. *Required:* 2 years of work experience. *Required for some:* high school transcript. *Application deadline:* rolling (freshmen), rolling (transfers).

Admissions Contact Ms. Beth Barilla, Director of Admissions, University of Phoenix-Metro Detroit Campus, 4615 East Elwood Street, Phoenix, AZ 85040-1958. *Phone:* 480-927-0099 Ext. 1218. *Toll-free phone:* 800-834-2438. *Fax:* 480-594-1758. *E-mail:* beth.barilla@apollogrp.edu.

University of Phoenix-West Michigan Campus

Grand Rapids, Michigan

- **Proprietary** comprehensive
- **Calendar** continuous
- **Degrees** certificates, associate, bachelor's, master's, doctoral, post-master's, and postbachelor's certificates (courses conducted at 54 campuses and learning centers in 13 states)
- **Coed,** 472 undergraduate students, 100% full-time, 50% women, 50% men
- **Noncompetitive** entrance level

Undergraduates Students come from 6 states and territories, 1% are from out of state.

Freshmen *Admission:* 23 admitted.

Faculty *Total:* 46, 9% full-time, 20% with terminal degrees. *Student/faculty ratio:* 11:1.

Majors Business administration; information technology; management information systems/business data processing; nursing science; public administration and services related.

Academic Programs *Special study options:* accelerated degree program, adult/continuing education programs, advanced placement credit, distance learning, external degree program, independent study.

Library University Library with 17.5 million titles, 9,000 serial subscriptions, an OPAC, a Web page.

Computers on Campus A campuswide network can be accessed from off campus. Internet access, at least one staffed computer lab available.

Student Life *Housing:* college housing not available.

Costs (2001–02) *Tuition:* $8700 full-time. Full-time tuition and fees vary according to location and program. *Payment plan:* deferred payment. *Waivers:* employees or children of employees.

Applying *Options:* deferred entrance. *Application fee:* $85. *Required:* 2 years of work experience. *Required for some:* high school transcript. *Application deadline:* rolling (freshmen), rolling (transfers).

Admissions Contact Ms. Beth Barilla, Director of Admissions, University of Phoenix-West Michigan Campus, 4615 East Elwood Street, Phoenix, AZ 85040-1958. *Phone:* 480-927-0099 Ext. 1218. *Toll-free phone:* 800-228-7240. *Fax:* 480-594-1758. *E-mail:* beth.barilla@apollogrp.edu.

Walsh College of Accountancy and Business Administration

Troy, Michigan

- **Independent** upper-level, founded 1922
- **Calendar** trimesters
- **Degrees** bachelor's and master's
- **Suburban** 29-acre campus with easy access to Detroit
- **Endowment** $1.8 million
- **Coed,** 1,192 undergraduate students, 17% full-time, 60% women, 40% men
- **Noncompetitive** entrance level, 65% of applicants were admitted

Undergraduates Students come from 1 other state, 24 other countries, 5% African American, 3% Asian American or Pacific Islander, 0.8% Hispanic American, 0.3% Native American, 4% international.

Freshmen *Admission:* 415 applied, 271 admitted.

Faculty *Total:* 131, 13% full-time, 27% with terminal degrees. *Student/faculty ratio:* 20:1.

Majors Accounting; business administration; business marketing and marketing management; computer/information sciences; finance.

Academic Programs *Special study options:* adult/continuing education programs, advanced placement credit, distance learning, double majors, independent study, internships, off-campus study, part-time degree program, services for LD students, summer session for credit.

Library Vollbrecht Library with 33,100 titles, 450 serial subscriptions, 70 audiovisual materials, an OPAC, a Web page.

Computers on Campus 298 computers available on campus for general student use. A campuswide network can be accessed from off campus. Internet access, at least one staffed computer lab available.

Student Life *Housing:* college housing not available. *Activities and Organizations:* student government, American Marketing Association, economics/finance club, accounting club, National Association of Black Accountants. *Campus security:* 24-hour emergency response devices.

Costs (2001–02) *Tuition:* $5232 full-time, $218 per credit part-time. Full-time tuition and fees vary according to course load. Part-time tuition and fees vary

Walsh College of Accountancy and Business Administration (continued)
according to course load. *Required fees:* $220 full-time, $110 per term part-time. *Payment plan:* deferred payment. *Waivers:* employees or children of employees.

Financial Aid Of all full-time matriculated undergraduates who enrolled in 2001, 114 applied for aid, 106 were judged to have need1 State and other part-time jobs (averaging $3600). In 2001, 51 non-need-based awards were made. *Average percent of need met:* 21%. *Average financial aid package:* $7367. *Average need-based loan:* $4817. *Average need-based gift aid:* $2550. *Average non-need based aid:* $1000. *Average indebtedness upon graduation:* $12,700.

Applying *Options:* electronic application, deferred entrance. *Application fee:* $25. *Application deadline:* rolling (transfers). *Notification:* continuous (transfers).

Admissions Contact Ms. Karen Mahaffy, Director of Admissions, Walsh College of Accountancy and Business Administration, 3838 Livernois, PO Box 7006, Troy, MI 48007-7006. *Phone:* 248-823-1610. *Toll-free phone:* 800-925-7401. *Fax:* 248-524-2520. *E-mail:* admissions@walshcollege.edu.

WAYNE STATE UNIVERSITY
Detroit, Michigan

- **State-supported** university, founded 1868
- **Calendar** semesters
- **Degrees** certificates, bachelor's, master's, doctoral, first professional, post-master's, and postbachelor's certificates
- **Urban** 203-acre campus
- **Endowment** $157.6 million
- **Coed,** 18,489 undergraduate students, 50% full-time, 60% women, 40% men
- **Moderately difficult** entrance level, 72% of applicants were admitted

Undergraduates 9,272 full-time, 9,217 part-time. Students come from 30 states and territories, 55 other countries, 1% are from out of state, 31% African American, 5% Asian American or Pacific Islander, 2% Hispanic American, 0.4% Native American, 5% international.

Freshmen *Admission:* 5,972 applied, 4,311 admitted, 2,585 enrolled. *Test scores:* ACT scores over 18: 71%; ACT scores over 24: 26%; ACT scores over 30: 2%.

Faculty *Total:* 1,754, 51% full-time, 52% with terminal degrees. *Student/faculty ratio:* 11:1.

Majors Accounting; African-American studies; American studies; anthropology; art; art education; art history; Asian studies; biology; business administration; business marketing and marketing management; chemical engineering; chemistry; civil engineering; classics; clothing/apparel/textile; communications; computer/information sciences; criminal justice studies; dance; dietetics; East Asian studies; economics; education of the speech impaired; electrical/electronic engineering technology; electrical engineering; electromechanical technology; elementary education; English; English education; film studies; finance; foreign languages/literatures; French; geography; geology; German; health/medical assistants related; health science; Hispanic-American studies; history; industrial/manufacturing engineering; industrial production technologies related; industrial technology; information sciences/systems; interdisciplinary studies; international relations; Italian; journalism; labor/personnel relations; linguistics; logistics/materials management; management information systems/business data processing; mathematics; mathematics education; mechanical engineering; mechanical engineering technology; medical radiologic technology; mortuary science; music; nursing; nutrition studies; occupational therapy; organizational behavior; peace/conflict studies; pharmacy; philosophy; physical education; physics; political science; psychology; public administration; public relations; radio/television broadcasting; recreation/leisure studies; Russian; science education; Slavic languages; social studies education; social work; sociology; Spanish; special education; speech-language pathology; technical education; theater arts/drama; urban studies; women's studies.

Academic Programs *Special study options:* academic remediation for entering students, accelerated degree program, adult/continuing education programs, advanced placement credit, cooperative education, distance learning, double majors, English as a second language, honors programs, independent study, internships, off-campus study, part-time degree program, services for LD students, student-designed majors, study abroad, summer session for credit. *ROTC:* Air Force (c).

Library David Adamany Undergraduate Library plus 6 others with 3.1 million titles, 18,236 serial subscriptions, 38,110 audiovisual materials, an OPAC, a Web page.

Computers on Campus 1000 computers available on campus for general student use. A campuswide network can be accessed from student residence rooms and from off campus. Internet access, online (class) registration, at least one staffed computer lab available.

Student Life *Housing Options:* coed. *Activities and Organizations:* drama/theater group, student-run newspaper, choral group, marching band, Indian Student Association, Golden Key Honor Society, Campus Crusade for Christ, Friendship Association of Chinese Students, Project Volunteer/Students of Service, national fraternities, national sororities. *Campus security:* 24-hour emergency response devices and patrols, late-night transport/escort service. *Student Services:* health clinic, personal/psychological counseling, women's center, legal services.

Athletics Member NCAA. All Division II. *Intercollegiate sports:* baseball M, basketball M(s)/W(s), cross-country running M(s)/W(s), fencing M(s)/W(s), football M(s), golf M(s), ice hockey M/W, softball W(s), swimming M(s)/W(s), tennis M(s)/W(s), volleyball W(s). *Intramural sports:* badminton M/W, basketball M/W, cross-country running M/W, fencing M/W, racquetball M/W, soccer M/W, softball M/W, squash M/W, swimming M/W, tennis M/W, volleyball M/W.

Standardized Tests *Required:* SAT I or ACT (for admission).

Costs (2001–02) *Tuition:* state resident $3888 full-time, $130 per semester hour part-time; nonresident $8910 full-time, $297 per semester hour part-time. Full-time tuition and fees vary according to class time and student level. Part-time tuition and fees vary according to class time and student level. *Required fees:* $442 full-time, $12 per semester hour, $80 per term part-time. *Room and board:* Room and board charges vary according to housing facility. *Payment plan:* installment. *Waivers:* senior citizens and employees or children of employees.

Financial Aid Of all full-time matriculated undergraduates who enrolled in 2001, 5909 applied for aid, 5152 were judged to have need, 430 had their need fully met. In 2001, 356 non-need-based awards were made. *Average percent of need met:* 60%. *Average financial aid package:* $5870. *Average need-based loan:* $4154. *Average need-based gift aid:* $3347. *Average non-need based aid:* $3758. *Average indebtedness upon graduation:* $16,073.

Applying *Application fee:* $20. *Required:* high school transcript, minimum 2.0 GPA. *Required for some:* letters of recommendation, interview, portfolio. *Application deadlines:* 8/1 (freshmen), 8/1 (transfers). *Notification:* continuous until 9/1 (freshmen).

Admissions Contact Mr. Michael Wood, Interim Director of University Admissions, Wayne State University, 3E HNJ, Detroit, MI 48202. *Phone:* 313-577-3581. *Fax:* 313-577-7536. *E-mail:* admissions@wayne.edu.

WESTERN MICHIGAN UNIVERSITY
Kalamazoo, Michigan

- **State-supported** university, founded 1903
- **Calendar** semesters
- **Degrees** certificates, bachelor's, master's, doctoral, and post-master's certificates
- **Urban** 504-acre campus
- **Endowment** $107.9 million
- **Coed,** 23,156 undergraduate students, 86% full-time, 52% women, 48% men
- **Moderately difficult** entrance level, 84% of applicants were admitted

Undergraduates 19,895 full-time, 3,261 part-time. Students come from 53 states and territories, 104 other countries, 6% are from out of state, 5% African American, 1% Asian American or Pacific Islander, 2% Hispanic American, 0.4% Native American, 4% international, 8% transferred in, 28% live on campus. *Retention:* 77% of 2001 full-time freshmen returned.

Freshmen *Admission:* 13,517 applied, 11,362 admitted, 4,601 enrolled. *Average high school GPA:* 3.28. *Test scores:* ACT scores over 18: 90%; ACT scores over 24: 32%; ACT scores over 30: 2%.

Faculty *Total:* 1,142, 83% full-time. *Student/faculty ratio:* 16:1.

Majors Accounting; aerospace engineering; African-American studies; aircraft pilot (professional); air transportation related; American studies; anthropology; applied history; applied mathematics; art; art education; art history; Asian studies; automotive engineering technology; aviation/airway science; aviation management; aviation technology; biochemistry; biology; biomedical science; business; business administration; business computer programming; business education; business marketing and marketing management; business statistics; chemical engineering; chemistry; child care/development; communications; community health liaison; computer engineering; computer/information sciences; computer science; construction engineering; construction management; creative writing; criminal justice studies; criminology; dance; dietetics; drafting; earth sciences; economics; education of the emotionally handicapped; education of the mentally handicapped; education of the visually handicapped; electrical engineering; elementary education; engineering/industrial management; engineering related; engineering technologies related; English; environmental engineering; environmental science; European studies; exercise sciences; family studies; finance; food systems administration; French; geography; geological sciences related; geology; geophysics/seismology; German; gerontology; graphic design/commercial art/

illustration; health education; history; home economics education; human resources management; industrial design; industrial/manufacturing engineering; industrial technology; interior design; journalism; Latin (ancient and medieval); logistics/materials management; management information systems/business data processing; marketing/distribution education; marketing management and research related; materials engineering; mathematical statistics; mathematics; mechanical engineering; music; music (general performance); music history; music teacher education; music theory and composition; music therapy; music (voice and choral/opera performance); nursing; nutrition studies; occupational therapy; philosophy; physical education; physics; political science; psychology; public administration; public relations; radio/television broadcasting; recreation/leisure studies; religious studies; Russian/Slavic studies; sculpture; social work; sociology; Spanish; speech-language pathology/audiology; telecommunications; theater arts/drama; theater design; travel/tourism management; women's studies.

Academic Programs *Special study options:* academic remediation for entering students, accelerated degree program, adult/continuing education programs, advanced placement credit, cooperative education, distance learning, double majors, English as a second language, freshman honors college, honors programs, independent study, internships, off-campus study, part-time degree program, services for LD students, student-designed majors, study abroad, summer session for credit. *ROTC:* Army (b).

Library Waldo Library plus 4 others with 937,095 titles, 7,262 serial subscriptions, 125,347 audiovisual materials, an OPAC, a Web page.

Computers on Campus 2000 computers available on campus for general student use. A campuswide network can be accessed from student residence rooms and from off campus. At least one staffed computer lab available.

Student Life *Housing Options:* coed, men-only, women-only, disabled students. *Activities and Organizations:* drama/theater group, student-run newspaper, radio station, choral group, marching band, Intrafraternity Council, National Panhellenic Conference, Golden Key, Inter-Varsity Christian Fellowship, Malaysian Student Organization, national fraternities, national sororities. *Campus security:* 24-hour emergency response devices and patrols, student patrols, late-night transport/escort service, controlled dormitory access. *Student Services:* health clinic, personal/psychological counseling, women's center, legal services.

Athletics Member NCAA. All Division I except football (Division I-A). *Intercollegiate sports:* baseball M(s), basketball M(s)/W(s), cross-country running M(s)/W(s), golf W(s), gymnastics W(s), ice hockey M(s), soccer M(s)/W(s), softball W(s), tennis M(s)/W(s), track and field M(s)/W(s), volleyball W(s). *Intramural sports:* badminton M/W, basketball M/W, bowling M/W, equestrian sports M(c)/W(c), fencing M(c)/W(c), football M/W, golf M, ice hockey M(c)/W(c), lacrosse M(c)/W(c), racquetball M/W, rugby M(c)/W, sailing M(c)/W(c), soccer M/W, softball M/W, swimming M/W, table tennis M/W, tennis M/W, volleyball M/W.

Standardized Tests *Required:* SAT I or ACT (for admission).

Costs (2001–02) *Tuition:* state resident $3897 full-time, $130 per credit hour part-time; nonresident $9653 full-time, $322 per credit hour part-time. Full-time tuition and fees vary according to course load and student level. Part-time tuition and fees vary according to course load and student level. *Required fees:* $602 full-time, $132 per term part-time. *Room and board:* $5517. Room and board charges vary according to board plan. *Payment plan:* installment. *Waivers:* senior citizens and employees or children of employees.

Financial Aid Of all full-time matriculated undergraduates who enrolled in 2001, 16944 applied for aid, 16129 were judged to have need, 2991 had their need fully met. In 2001, 3766 non-need-based awards were made. *Average percent of need met:* 64%. *Average financial aid package:* $6642. *Average need-based loan:* $3526. *Average need-based gift aid:* $4330. *Average non-need based aid:* $3268. *Average indebtedness upon graduation:* $12,297.

Applying *Options:* electronic application, early admission. *Application fee:* $25. *Required:* high school transcript. *Required for some:* interview. *Application deadlines:* rolling (freshmen), 8/1 (transfers). *Notification:* continuous (freshmen).

Admissions Contact Mr. John Fraire, Dean, Office of Admissions and Orientation, Western Michigan University, 1903 West Michigan Avenue, Kalamazoo, MI 49008. *Phone:* 616-387-2000. *Toll-free phone:* 800-400-4968. *Fax:* 616-387-2096. *E-mail:* ask-wmu@wmich.edu.

WILLIAM TYNDALE COLLEGE
Farmington Hills, Michigan

- **Independent religious** 4-year, founded 1945
- **Calendar** semesters
- **Degrees** certificates, associate, and bachelor's
- **Suburban** 28-acre campus with easy access to Detroit
- **Coed,** 608 undergraduate students, 52% full-time, 54% women, 46% men
- **Minimally difficult** entrance level, 77% of applicants were admitted

Undergraduates 316 full-time, 292 part-time. Students come from 2 states and territories, 13 other countries, 31% African American, 2% Asian American or Pacific Islander, 0.7% Hispanic American, 0.5% Native American, 2% international, 18% transferred in, 7% live on campus. *Retention:* 60% of 2001 full-time freshmen returned.

Freshmen *Admission:* 60 applied, 46 admitted, 67 enrolled. *Average high school GPA:* 3.27. *Test scores:* SAT verbal scores over 500: 75%; SAT math scores over 500: 50%; ACT scores over 18: 90%; SAT verbal scores over 600: 25%; ACT scores over 24: 41%; ACT scores over 30: 2%.

Faculty *Total:* 82, 5% full-time, 30% with terminal degrees. *Student/faculty ratio:* 7:1.

Majors Biblical studies; business administration; early childhood education; English; history; liberal arts and sciences/liberal studies; mathematics; Middle Eastern studies; music; music (general performance); music (piano and organ performance); music (voice and choral/opera performance); pastoral counseling; pre-law; psychology; religious education; religious music; social sciences; theology.

Academic Programs *Special study options:* academic remediation for entering students, accelerated degree program, adult/continuing education programs, advanced placement credit, double majors, independent study, internships, part-time degree program, summer session for credit.

Library Boll Mindlab with 63,500 titles, 230 serial subscriptions, 3,300 audiovisual materials.

Computers on Campus 21 computers available on campus for general student use. A campuswide network can be accessed from off campus. Internet access, at least one staffed computer lab available.

Student Life *Housing Options:* coed. *Activities and Organizations:* drama/theater group, choral group, choir, Drama Club, Student Executive Board. *Student Services:* personal/psychological counseling.

Athletics *Intercollegiate sports:* soccer M(c).

Standardized Tests *Required:* SAT I or ACT (for admission).

Costs (2001–02) *Comprehensive fee:* $11,150 includes full-time tuition ($7950) and room and board ($3200). Part-time tuition: $265 per credit. *Room and board:* Room and board charges vary according to housing facility. *Payment plan:* deferred payment. *Waivers:* senior citizens and employees or children of employees.

Financial Aid Of all full-time matriculated undergraduates who enrolled in 2001, 429 applied for aid, 429 were judged to have need, 93 had their need fully met. In 2001, 5 non-need-based awards were made. *Average percent of need met:* 90%. *Average financial aid package:* $2747. *Average need-based loan:* $2318. *Average need-based gift aid:* $2472. *Average non-need based aid:* $4000. *Average indebtedness upon graduation:* $4000. *Financial aid deadline:* 6/30.

Applying *Options:* electronic application, early admission, deferred entrance. *Application fee:* $50. *Required:* high school transcript, minimum 2.25 GPA. *Required for some:* essay or personal statement, letters of recommendation, interview. *Recommended:* minimum 3.0 GPA. *Application deadline:* rolling (freshmen), rolling (transfers). *Notification:* continuous until 9/1 (freshmen).

Admissions Contact William Tyndale College, 37500 West Twelve Mile Road, Farmington Hills, MI 48331. *Phone:* 248-553-7200 Ext. 204. *Toll-free phone:* 800-483-0707. *Fax:* 248-553-5963. *E-mail:* admissions@williamtyndale.edu.

YESHIVA GEDDOLAH OF GREATER DETROIT RABBINICAL COLLEGE
Oak Park, Michigan

Admissions Contact Mr. Eric Krohner, Executive Director, Yeshiva Geddolah of Greater Detroit Rabbinical College, 24600 Greenfield, Oak Park, MI 48237-1544.

MINNESOTA

THE ART INSTITUTES INTERNATIONAL MINNESOTA
Minneapolis, Minnesota

- **Proprietary** primarily 2-year, founded 1964, part of The Art Institute
- **Calendar** quarters
- **Degrees** certificates, associate, and bachelor's

The Art Institutes International Minnesota (continued)
- **Urban** campus
- **Coed,** 948 undergraduate students
- **Minimally difficult** entrance level, 55% of applicants were admitted

Undergraduates Students come from 27 states and territories, 8 other countries, 1% African American, 2% Asian American or Pacific Islander, 0.8% Hispanic American, 0.4% Native American, 13% live on campus.
Freshmen *Admission:* 572 applied, 316 admitted. *Average high school GPA:* 2.53.
Faculty *Total:* 57, 44% full-time. *Student/faculty ratio:* 20:1.
Majors Computer graphics; culinary arts; graphic design/commercial art/illustration; interior design; multimedia.
Academic Programs *Special study options:* academic remediation for entering students, advanced placement credit, cooperative education, internships, part-time degree program, services for LD students, summer session for credit.
Library Learning Resource Center with 1,450 titles, 25 serial subscriptions.
Computers on Campus 75 computers available on campus for general student use. Internet access, at least one staffed computer lab available.
Student Life *Housing Options:* coed. *Campus security:* security personnel during hours of operation. *Student Services:* personal/psychological counseling.
Standardized Tests *Recommended:* ACT (for admission).
Costs (2001–02) *One-time required fee:* $100. *Tuition:* $19,136 full-time, $299 per credit part-time. Full-time tuition and fees vary according to program. No tuition increase for student's term of enrollment. *Room only:* $5220. Room and board charges vary according to housing facility. *Payment plan:* installment. *Waivers:* employees or children of employees.
Applying *Options:* common application, electronic application, deferred entrance. *Application fee:* $50. *Required:* essay or personal statement, high school transcript, interview. *Application deadline:* rolling (freshmen), rolling (transfers).
Admissions Contact Mr. Jeff Marcus, Director of Admissions, The Art Institutes International Minnesota, 15 South 9th Street, Minneapolis, MN 55402. *Phone:* 612-332-3361 Ext. 120. *Toll-free phone:* 800-777-3643. *Fax:* 612-332-3934. *E-mail:* kozela@aii.edu.

AUGSBURG COLLEGE
Minneapolis, Minnesota

- **Independent Lutheran** comprehensive, founded 1869
- **Calendar** 4-1-4
- **Degrees** bachelor's, master's, and postbachelor's certificates
- **Urban** 23-acre campus
- **Endowment** $24.8 million
- **Coed,** 2,780 undergraduate students, 82% full-time, 58% women, 42% men
- **Moderately difficult** entrance level, 79% of applicants were admitted

Augsburg College, an urban liberal arts college, draws upon the cultural and corporate resources of Minneapolis to complement the campus and classroom learning experience. A college of diversity, it serves people of all colors and nationalities and of many religions. Affiliated with the Evangelical Lutheran Church of America, Augsburg is a college of intellectual challenge, academic excellence, and career preparation.

Undergraduates 2,275 full-time, 505 part-time. Students come from 38 states and territories, 39 other countries, 10% are from out of state, 5% African American, 3% Asian American or Pacific Islander, 1% Hispanic American, 1.0% Native American, 2% international, 12% transferred in, 53% live on campus. *Retention:* 76% of 2001 full-time freshmen returned.
Freshmen *Admission:* 910 applied, 718 admitted, 354 enrolled. *Average high school GPA:* 3.28. *Test scores:* SAT verbal scores over 500: 68%; SAT math scores over 500: 76%; ACT scores over 18: 94%; SAT verbal scores over 600: 34%; SAT math scores over 600: 24%; ACT scores over 24: 44%; SAT verbal scores over 700: 4%; SAT math scores over 700: 4%; ACT scores over 30: 6%.
Faculty *Total:* 296, 47% full-time, 60% with terminal degrees. *Student/faculty ratio:* 15:1.
Majors Accounting; aerospace science; art; art education; art history; astrophysics; athletic training/sports medicine; behavioral sciences; biological/physical sciences; biology; business administration; business economics; business marketing and marketing management; chemistry; computer science; criminal justice studies; early childhood education; East Asian studies; economics; education; elementary education; English; fine/studio arts; French; German; health education; history; humanities; interdisciplinary studies; international business; international relations; liberal arts and sciences/liberal studies; management information systems/business data processing; mass communications; mathematics; music; music teacher education; music therapy; natural sciences; nursing; philosophy; physical education; physician assistant; physics; political science; pre-dentistry; pre-law; pre-medicine; pre-veterinary studies; psychology; religious studies; Scandinavian languages; secondary education; social sciences; social work; sociology; Spanish; speech/rhetorical studies; theater arts/drama; theology; urban studies; women's studies.
Academic Programs *Special study options:* academic remediation for entering students, adult/continuing education programs, advanced placement credit, cooperative education, double majors, English as a second language, freshman honors college, honors programs, independent study, internships, off-campus study, part-time degree program, services for LD students, student-designed majors, study abroad, summer session for credit. *ROTC:* Army (c), Air Force (c). *Unusual degree programs:* 3-2 engineering with Michigan Technological University, Washington University in St. Louis, University of Minnesota, Twin Cities Campus; occupational therapy with Washington University in St. Louis.
Library James G. Lindell Library with 142,739 titles, 1,007 serial subscriptions, 2,355 audiovisual materials, an OPAC, a Web page.
Computers on Campus 224 computers available on campus for general student use. A campuswide network can be accessed from student residence rooms and from off campus. Internet access, online (class) registration, at least one staffed computer lab available.
Student Life *Housing Options:* coed, men-only, women-only, disabled students. *Activities and Organizations:* drama/theater group, student-run newspaper, radio station, choral group, Student Activities Council, Student Government, Newspaper/Yearbook, Campus Ministry, Intramurals. *Campus security:* 24-hour emergency response devices and patrols, late-night transport/escort service, controlled dormitory access. *Student Services:* health clinic, personal/psychological counseling.
Athletics Member NCAA. All Division III. *Intercollegiate sports:* baseball M, basketball M/W, cross-country running M/W, football M, golf M/W, ice hockey M/W, soccer M/W, softball W, track and field M/W, volleyball W, wrestling M. *Intramural sports:* basketball M/W, football M, skiing (cross-country) M(c)/W(c), skiing (downhill) M(c)/W(c), softball M/W, volleyball M/W, wrestling M.
Standardized Tests *Required:* SAT I or ACT (for admission).
Costs (2001–02) *Comprehensive fee:* $22,978 includes full-time tuition ($17,070), mandatory fees ($368), and room and board ($5540). Part-time tuition: $1844 per course. Part-time tuition and fees vary according to course load. *Required fees:* $97 per term part-time. *Room and board:* College room only: $2820. Room and board charges vary according to board plan and housing facility. *Payment plans:* installment, deferred payment. *Waivers:* children of alumni and senior citizens.
Financial Aid Of all full-time matriculated undergraduates who enrolled in 2001, 1739 applied for aid, 1480 were judged to have need, 680 had their need fully met. 371 State and other part-time jobs (averaging $2168). In 2001, 174 non-need-based awards were made. *Average percent of need met:* 100%. *Average financial aid package:* $12,569. *Average need-based loan:* $4476. *Average need-based gift aid:* $8218. *Average non-need based aid:* $4420. *Average indebtedness upon graduation:* $21,456. *Financial aid deadline:* 4/15.
Applying *Options:* deferred entrance. *Application fee:* $25. *Required:* essay or personal statement, high school transcript, minimum 2.5 GPA. *Required for some:* 2 letters of recommendation. *Recommended:* interview. *Application deadlines:* 8/15 (freshmen), 8/10 (transfers). *Notification:* continuous (freshmen).
Admissions Contact Ms. Sally Daniels, Director of Undergraduate Day Admissions, Augsburg College, 2211 Riverside Avenue, Minneapolis, MN 55454-1351. *Phone:* 612-330-1001. *Toll-free phone:* 800-788-5678. *Fax:* 612-330-1590. *E-mail:* admissions@augsburg.edu.

BEMIDJI STATE UNIVERSITY
Bemidji, Minnesota

- **State-supported** comprehensive, founded 1919, part of Minnesota State Colleges and Universities System
- **Calendar** semesters
- **Degrees** associate, bachelor's, and master's
- **Small-town** 89-acre campus
- **Endowment** $7.0 million
- **Coed,** 4,448 undergraduate students, 77% full-time, 57% women, 43% men
- **Moderately difficult** entrance level, 76% of applicants were admitted

Undergraduates 3,438 full-time, 1,010 part-time. Students come from 28 states and territories, 39 other countries, 5% are from out of state, 0.5% African American, 0.4% Asian American or Pacific Islander, 0.4% Hispanic American, 3% Native American, 6% international, 11% transferred in, 26% live on campus. *Retention:* 72% of 2001 full-time freshmen returned.

Freshmen *Admission:* 1,759 applied, 1,333 admitted, 706 enrolled. *Average high school GPA:* 3.33. *Test scores:* ACT scores over 18: 88%; ACT scores over 24: 26%; ACT scores over 30: 2%.

Faculty *Total:* 257, 83% full-time, 68% with terminal degrees. *Student/faculty ratio:* 20:1.

Majors Accounting; applied art; art; art education; behavioral sciences; biological/physical sciences; biology; broadcast journalism; business administration; chemistry; community services; computer science; construction technology; criminal justice/law enforcement administration; data processing technology; earth sciences; ecology; economics; education; elementary education; engineering physics; English; environmental science; fine/studio arts; geography; geology; German; graphic design/commercial art/illustration; health education; history; humanities; industrial arts; industrial technology; information sciences/systems; journalism; law enforcement/police science; liberal arts and sciences/liberal studies; marine biology; mass communications; mathematics; medical technology; modern languages; music; music teacher education; Native American languages; Native American studies; natural sciences; nursing; philosophy; physical education; physical sciences; physics; political science; pre-law; pre-medicine; pre-veterinary studies; professional studies; psychology; radio/television broadcasting; recreation/leisure studies; religious studies; science education; secondary education; social sciences; social work; sociology; Spanish; speech/rhetorical studies; speech/theater education; sport/fitness administration; theater arts/drama; trade/industrial education.

Academic Programs *Special study options:* academic remediation for entering students, adult/continuing education programs, advanced placement credit, cooperative education, distance learning, double majors, English as a second language, external degree program, honors programs, independent study, internships, off-campus study, part-time degree program, services for LD students, study abroad, summer session for credit.

Library A. C. Clark Library with 554,087 titles, 991 serial subscriptions, 4,673 audiovisual materials, an OPAC, a Web page.

Computers on Campus 400 computers available on campus for general student use. A campuswide network can be accessed from student residence rooms and from off campus. Internet access, online (class) registration, at least one staffed computer lab available.

Student Life *Housing Options:* coed, disabled students. *Activities and Organizations:* drama/theater group, student-run newspaper, radio and television station, choral group, national fraternities, national sororities. *Campus security:* 24-hour emergency response devices and patrols, late-night transport/escort service, controlled dormitory access. *Student Services:* health clinic, personal/psychological counseling, women's center.

Athletics Member NCAA. All Division II. *Intercollegiate sports:* baseball M(s), basketball M(s)/W(s), cross-country running W, football M(s), golf M/W, ice hockey M(s)/W(s), soccer W(s), softball W(s), tennis W(s), track and field M(s)/W(s), volleyball W(s). *Intramural sports:* basketball M/W, football M, ice hockey M/W, racquetball M/W, soccer M/W, softball M/W, tennis M/W, track and field M/W, volleyball M/W, wrestling M.

Standardized Tests *Required:* ACT (for admission).

Costs (2001–02) *Tuition:* state resident $3470 full-time, $125 per credit part-time; nonresident $7360 full-time, $275 per credit part-time. Full-time tuition and fees vary according to reciprocity agreements. Part-time tuition and fees vary according to course load and reciprocity agreements. *Required fees:* $694 full-time, $75 per credit. *Room and board:* $4158; room only: $2238. Room and board charges vary according to board plan and housing facility. *Payment plan:* installment. *Waivers:* senior citizens and employees or children of employees.

Financial Aid Of all full-time matriculated undergraduates who enrolled in 2001, 2679 applied for aid, 2609 were judged to have need, 2417 had their need fully met. 201 Federal Work-Study jobs (averaging $1268). In 2001, 348 non-need-based awards were made. *Average percent of need met:* 86%. *Average financial aid package:* $5083. *Average need-based loan:* $2794. *Average need-based gift aid:* $3489. *Average non-need based aid:* $4534. *Average indebtedness upon graduation:* $13,950.

Applying *Options:* common application, electronic application, deferred entrance. *Application fee:* $20. *Required:* high school transcript. *Required for some:* essay or personal statement, letters of recommendation, interview. *Application deadline:* rolling (freshmen), rolling (transfers). *Notification:* continuous (freshmen).

Admissions Contact Mr. Kevin Drexel, Director of Admissions, Bemidji State University, Deputy-102, Bemidji, MN 56601. *Phone:* 218-755-2040. *Toll-free phone:* 800-475-2001 (in-state); 800-652-9747 (out-of-state). *Fax:* 218-755-2074. *E-mail:* admissions@bemidjistate.edu.

BETHANY LUTHERAN COLLEGE
Mankato, Minnesota

- **Independent Lutheran** primarily 2-year, founded 1927
- **Calendar** semesters
- **Degrees** associate and bachelor's
- **Small-town** 50-acre campus with easy access to Minneapolis-St. Paul
- **Endowment** $21.7 million
- **Coed,** 420 undergraduate students, 100% full-time, 52% women, 48% men
- **Moderately difficult** entrance level, 90% of applicants were admitted

Undergraduates 420 full-time. Students come from 22 states and territories, 11 other countries, 26% are from out of state, 2% African American, 1% Asian American or Pacific Islander, 1.0% Hispanic American, 0.2% Native American, 4% international, 3% transferred in, 88% live on campus. *Retention:* 83% of 2001 full-time freshmen returned.

Freshmen *Admission:* 296 applied, 267 admitted, 185 enrolled. *Average high school GPA:* 3.20. *Test scores:* ACT scores over 18: 87%; ACT scores over 24: 32%; ACT scores over 30: 1%.

Faculty *Total:* 65, 49% full-time, 23% with terminal degrees. *Student/faculty ratio:* 9:1.

Majors Art; biology; business administration; chemistry; communications; liberal arts and sciences/liberal studies; music; religious music.

Academic Programs *Special study options:* academic remediation for entering students, advanced placement credit, honors programs, services for LD students. *ROTC:* Army (c).

Library Memorial Library plus 1 other with 52,000 titles, 275 serial subscriptions, 2,652 audiovisual materials, an OPAC, a Web page.

Computers on Campus 40 computers available on campus for general student use. A campuswide network can be accessed from student residence rooms and from off campus. Internet access, at least one staffed computer lab available.

Student Life *Housing:* on-campus residence required through sophomore year. *Options:* men-only, women-only. *Activities and Organizations:* drama/theater group, student-run newspaper, television station, choral group, Student Senate, Paul Vluisaker Center, Phi Theta Kappa, AAL the Lutheran Brotherhood Branch, Lutherans for Life. *Campus security:* 24-hour emergency response devices and patrols, late-night transport/escort service, controlled dormitory access. *Student Services:* personal/psychological counseling.

Athletics Member NJCAA. *Intercollegiate sports:* baseball M, basketball M(s)/W(s), cross-country running M(s)/W(s), golf M(s)/W(s), soccer M(s)/W(s), softball W(s), tennis M(s)/W(s), volleyball W(s). *Intramural sports:* basketball M/W, football M/W, racquetball M/W, soccer M/W, softball M/W, volleyball M/W.

Standardized Tests *Required:* SAT I or ACT (for admission).

Costs (2002–03) *One-time required fee:* $50. *Comprehensive fee:* $17,208 includes full-time tuition ($12,260), mandatory fees ($260), and room and board ($4688). *Room and board:* College room only: $1718.

Financial Aid Of all full-time matriculated undergraduates who enrolled in 2001, 65 Federal Work-Study jobs (averaging $566). 199 State and other part-time jobs (averaging $556). *Financial aid deadline:* 7/15.

Applying *Options:* common application, electronic application. *Application fee:* $20. *Required:* essay or personal statement, high school transcript, minimum 2.0 GPA. *Required for some:* interview. *Recommended:* minimum 3.0 GPA, interview. *Application deadline:* 7/15 (freshmen), rolling (transfers).

Admissions Contact Mr. Donald Westphal, Dean of Admissions, Bethany Lutheran College, 700 Luther Drive, Mankato, MN 56001. *Phone:* 507-344-7320. *Toll-free phone:* 800-944-3066. *Fax:* 507-344-7376. *E-mail:* admiss@blc.edu.

BETHEL COLLEGE
St. Paul, Minnesota

- **Independent** comprehensive, founded 1871, affiliated with Baptist General Conference
- **Calendar** 4-1-4
- **Degrees** associate, bachelor's, and master's
- **Suburban** 231-acre campus
- **Endowment** $16.5 million
- **Coed,** 2,700 undergraduate students, 90% full-time, 61% women, 39% men
- **Moderately difficult** entrance level, 67% of applicants were admitted

Bethel College (continued)

Bethel College provides academic excellence in a dynamic Christian environment. *U.S. News and World Report* has recognized Bethel as one of the top liberal arts colleges in the Midwest. What makes Bethel outstanding are its excellent students, expert faculty, and dedicated staff. Bethel is committed to providing a high-quality liberal arts education to prepare tomorrow's leaders to make a difference in their community, the church, and the world.

Undergraduates 2,435 full-time, 265 part-time. Students come from 38 states and territories, 28% are from out of state, 0.8% African American, 2% Asian American or Pacific Islander, 0.9% Hispanic American, 0.3% Native American, 0.3% international, 4% transferred in, 73% live on campus. *Retention:* 86% of 2001 full-time freshmen returned.

Freshmen *Admission:* 1,580 applied, 1,055 admitted, 638 enrolled. *Test scores:* SAT verbal scores over 500: 91%; SAT math scores over 500: 85%; ACT scores over 18: 95%; SAT verbal scores over 600: 50%; SAT math scores over 600: 45%; ACT scores over 24: 57%; SAT verbal scores over 700: 10%; SAT math scores over 700: 10%; ACT scores over 30: 10%.

Faculty *Total:* 288, 51% full-time, 38% with terminal degrees. *Student/faculty ratio:* 16:1.

Majors Accounting; adult/continuing education; art; art education; art history; athletic training/sports medicine; biblical studies; biochemistry; biology; business administration; chemistry; child care/development; computer science; creative writing; cultural studies; early childhood education; economics; education; elementary education; English; environmental science; finance; fine/studio arts; health education; history; international relations; liberal arts and sciences/liberal studies; literature; management information systems/business data processing; mass communications; mathematics; molecular biology; music; music teacher education; nursing; philosophy; physical education; physics; political science; pre-dentistry; pre-law; pre-medicine; pre-veterinary studies; psychology; religious music; science education; secondary education; social work; Spanish; speech/rhetorical studies; teaching English as a second language; theater arts/drama.

Academic Programs *Special study options:* accelerated degree program, adult/continuing education programs, advanced placement credit, double majors, English as a second language, external degree program, freshman honors college, honors programs, independent study, internships, off-campus study, part-time degree program, services for LD students, student-designed majors, study abroad, summer session for credit. *ROTC:* Army (c), Navy (c), Air Force (c). *Unusual degree programs:* 3-2 engineering with Washington University in St. Louis, Case Western Reserve University, University of Minnesota.

Library Bethel College Library plus 1 other with 156,000 titles, 4,045 serial subscriptions, 6,970 audiovisual materials, an OPAC, a Web page.

Computers on Campus 367 computers available on campus for general student use. A campuswide network can be accessed from student residence rooms and from off campus. Internet access, at least one staffed computer lab available.

Student Life *Housing:* on-campus residence required through sophomore year. *Options:* coed, disabled students. *Activities and Organizations:* drama/theater group, student-run newspaper, radio and television station, choral group, United Cultures, Student Senate, Student Association, Habitat for Humanity, Tri Beta. *Campus security:* 24-hour emergency response devices and patrols, student patrols, late-night transport/escort service, controlled dormitory access. *Student Services:* health clinic, personal/psychological counseling.

Athletics Member NCAA. All Division III. *Intercollegiate sports:* baseball M, basketball M/W, cross-country running M/W, football M, golf M, ice hockey M/W, soccer M/W, softball W, tennis M/W, track and field M/W, volleyball M(c)/W. *Intramural sports:* badminton M/W, basketball M/W, football M/W, golf M/W, lacrosse M/W, racquetball M/W, softball M/W, table tennis M/W, tennis M/W, track and field M/W, volleyball M/W, weight lifting M/W.

Costs (2002–03) *Comprehensive fee:* $23,935 includes full-time tuition ($17,700), mandatory fees ($35), and room and board ($6200). Part-time tuition: $670 per credit. Part-time tuition and fees vary according to course load. *Room and board:* College room only: $3680. Room and board charges vary according to board plan. *Payment plan:* installment. *Waivers:* senior citizens and employees or children of employees.

Financial Aid Of all full-time matriculated undergraduates who enrolled in 2001, 2333 applied for aid, 1649 were judged to have need, 508 had their need fully met. 315 Federal Work-Study jobs (averaging $1812). 510 State and other part-time jobs (averaging $1771). In 2001, 551 non-need-based awards were made. *Average percent of need met:* 86%. *Average financial aid package:* $13,986. *Average need-based loan:* $4143. *Average need-based gift aid:* $8195. *Average non-need based aid:* $3593. *Average indebtedness upon graduation:* $18,741.

Applying *Options:* electronic application, early action, deferred entrance. *Application fee:* $25. *Required:* essay or personal statement, high school transcript, 2 letters of recommendation. *Required for some:* interview. *Recommended:* interview. *Application deadlines:* 3/1 (freshmen), 12/1 (transfers). *Notification:* 4/1 (freshmen), 1/15 (early action).

Admissions Contact Mr. Jay Fedje, Director of Admissions, Bethel College, 3900 Bethel Drive, St. Paul, MN 55112. *Phone:* 651-638-6242. *Toll-free phone:* 800-255-8706 Ext. 6242. *Fax:* 651-635-1490. *E-mail:* bcoll-admit@bethel.edu.

CAPELLA UNIVERSITY
Minneapolis, Minnesota

- **Proprietary** upper-level, founded 1993
- **Calendar** quarters
- **Degrees** certificates, bachelor's, master's, doctoral, first professional, and first professional certificates (offers only distance learning degree programs)
- **Coed,** 200 undergraduate students
- 48% of applicants were admitted

Undergraduates 75% are from out of state.

Freshmen *Admission:* 330 applied, 160 admitted.

Faculty *Total:* 317, 13% full-time, 89% with terminal degrees. *Student/faculty ratio:* 12:1.

Majors Business; computer graphics; computer/information technology services administration and management related; computer systems networking/telecommunications; human resources management related; information technology; management science; marketing management and research related; Web page, digital/multimedia and information resources design.

Academic Programs *Special study options:* adult/continuing education programs, distance learning, double majors, external degree program, independent study, internships, off-campus study, part-time degree program, services for LD students, student-designed majors, summer session for credit.

Library University of Alabama in Huntsville.

Costs (2002–03) *Tuition:* $1,425 per course. Full-time tuition and fees vary according to degree level and program. Part-time tuition and fees vary according to degree level and program.

Applying *Options:* common application, electronic application.

Admissions Contact Ms. Liz Krumman, Associate Director, Enrollment Services, Capella University, 222 South 9th Street, 2nd Floor, Minneapolis, MN 55402. *Phone:* 612-252-4286. *Toll-free phone:* 888-CAPELLA. *Fax:* 612-339-8022. *E-mail:* info@capella.edu.

CARLETON COLLEGE
Northfield, Minnesota

- **Independent** 4-year, founded 1866
- **Calendar** three courses for each of three terms
- **Degree** bachelor's
- **Small-town** 955-acre campus with easy access to Minneapolis-St. Paul
- **Endowment** $543.5 million
- **Coed,** 1,948 undergraduate students, 99% full-time, 52% women, 48% men
- **Very difficult** entrance level, 37% of applicants were admitted

Undergraduates 1,932 full-time, 16 part-time. Students come from 50 states and territories, 26 other countries, 77% are from out of state, 4% African American, 9% Asian American or Pacific Islander, 4% Hispanic American, 0.4% Native American, 2% international, 0.3% transferred in, 89% live on campus. *Retention:* 96% of 2001 full-time freshmen returned.

Freshmen *Admission:* 4,065 applied, 1,511 admitted, 516 enrolled. *Test scores:* SAT verbal scores over 500: 98%; SAT math scores over 500: 99%; ACT scores over 18: 99%; SAT verbal scores over 600: 90%; SAT math scores over 600: 88%; ACT scores over 24: 94%; SAT verbal scores over 700: 49%; SAT math scores over 700: 42%; ACT scores over 30: 51%.

Faculty *Total:* 223, 83% full-time, 91% with terminal degrees. *Student/faculty ratio:* 10:1.

Majors African studies; American studies; anthropology; art history; Asian studies; biology; chemistry; classics; computer science; economics; English; fine/studio arts; French; geology; German; Greek (ancient and medieval); history; interdisciplinary studies; international relations; Latin American studies; Latin (ancient and medieval); mathematics; music; philosophy; physics; political science; psychology; religious studies; romance languages; Russian; sociology; Spanish; women's studies.

Academic Programs *Special study options:* accelerated degree program, advanced placement credit, double majors, independent study, internships, off-campus study, services for LD students, student-designed majors, study abroad.

Unusual degree programs: 3-2 engineering with Columbia University, Washington University in St. Louis; nursing with Rush University.

Library Laurence McKinley Gould Library plus 1 other with 629,099 titles, 1,555 serial subscriptions, 2,037 audiovisual materials, an OPAC, a Web page.

Computers on Campus 275 computers available on campus for general student use. A campuswide network can be accessed from student residence rooms and from off campus. Internet access, at least one staffed computer lab available.

Student Life *Housing:* on-campus residence required through senior year. *Options:* coed, disabled students. *Activities and Organizations:* drama/theater group, student-run newspaper, radio station, choral group, CANOE (Carleton Association of Nature and Outdoor Enthusiasts), Farm Club, Amnesty International, WHIMS (Women in Math and Science), Ebony II. *Campus security:* 24-hour emergency response devices and patrols, student patrols, late-night transport/escort service, controlled dormitory access. *Student Services:* health clinic, personal/psychological counseling, women's center.

Athletics Member NCAA. All Division III. *Intercollegiate sports:* baseball M, basketball M/W, crew M(c)/W(c), cross-country running M/W, fencing M(c)/W(c), field hockey W(c), football M, golf M/W, ice hockey M(c)/W(c), lacrosse M(c)/W(c), rugby M(c)/W(c), skiing (cross-country) M/W, skiing (downhill) M/W, soccer M/W, softball W, swimming M/W, tennis M/W, track and field M/W, volleyball M(c)/W, water polo M(c)/W(c), wrestling M. *Intramural sports:* badminton M/W, basketball M/W, equestrian sports M(c)/W(c), gymnastics W(c), ice hockey M/W, racquetball M/W, soccer M/W, softball M/W, table tennis M/W, tennis M/W, volleyball M/W.

Standardized Tests *Required:* SAT I or ACT (for admission). *Recommended:* SAT II: Subject Tests (for admission), SAT II: Writing Test (for admission).

Costs (2001–02) *Comprehensive fee:* $30,780 includes full-time tuition ($25,371), mandatory fees ($159), and room and board ($5250). *Room and board:* Room and board charges vary according to board plan. *Payment plans:* tuition prepayment, installment. *Waivers:* employees or children of employees.

Financial Aid Of all full-time matriculated undergraduates who enrolled in 2001, 1731 applied for aid, 973 were judged to have need, 973 had their need fully met. In 2001, 105 non-need-based awards were made. *Average percent of need met:* 100%. *Average financial aid package:* $18,334. *Average need-based loan:* $3304. *Average need-based gift aid:* $14,544. *Average non-need based aid:* $2127. *Average indebtedness upon graduation:* $14,882.

Applying *Options:* common application, electronic application, early admission, early decision, deferred entrance. *Application fee:* $30. *Required:* essay or personal statement, high school transcript, 2 letters of recommendation. *Recommended:* interview. *Application deadlines:* 1/15 (freshmen), 3/31 (transfers). *Early decision:* 11/15 (for plan 1), 1/15 (for plan 2). *Notification:* 4/15 (freshmen), 12/15 (early decision plan 1), 2/15 (early decision plan 2).

Admissions Contact Carleton College, 100 South College Street, Northfield, MN 55057. *Phone:* 507-646-4190. *Toll-free phone:* 800-995-2275. *Fax:* 507-646-4526. *E-mail:* admissions@acs.carleton.edu.

COLLEGE OF SAINT BENEDICT

Saint Joseph, Minnesota

- **Independent Roman Catholic** 4-year, founded 1887
- **Calendar** 4-1-4
- **Degrees** bachelor's (Coordinate with Saint John's University for men)
- **Small-town** 315-acre campus with easy access to Minneapolis-St. Paul
- **Endowment** $20.0 million
- **Coed,** 2,100 undergraduate students, 97% full-time, 100% women
- **Moderately difficult** entrance level, 82% of applicants were admitted

Undergraduates 2,029 full-time, 71 part-time. Students come from 31 states and territories, 24 other countries, 14% are from out of state, 0.5% African American, 2% Asian American or Pacific Islander, 1% Hispanic American, 0.2% Native American, 4% international, 3% transferred in, 74% live on campus. *Retention:* 88% of 2001 full-time freshmen returned.

Freshmen *Admission:* 556 enrolled. *Average high school GPA:* 3.7. *Test scores:* SAT verbal scores over 500: 82%; SAT math scores over 500: 84%; ACT scores over 18: 99%; SAT verbal scores over 600: 56%; SAT math scores over 600: 53%; ACT scores over 24: 66%; SAT verbal scores over 700: 15%; SAT math scores over 700: 7%; ACT scores over 30: 14%.

Faculty *Total:* 160, 86% full-time, 70% with terminal degrees. *Student/faculty ratio:* 14:1.

Majors Accounting; art; art education; art history; biochemistry; biology; business administration; chemistry; classics; computer science; dietetics; economics; education; elementary education; English; fine/studio arts; forestry; French; German; history; humanities; liberal arts and sciences/liberal studies; mathematics; mathematics/computer science; music; music teacher education; natural sciences; nursing; nutrition science; occupational therapy; peace/conflict studies; philosophy; physical therapy; physics; political science; pre-dentistry; pre-law; pre-medicine; pre-pharmacy studies; pre-theology; pre-veterinary studies; psychology; religious education; secondary education; social sciences; social work; sociology; Spanish; speech/rhetorical studies; theater arts/drama; theology.

Academic Programs *Special study options:* accelerated degree program, advanced placement credit, double majors, English as a second language, honors programs, independent study, internships, off-campus study, services for LD students, student-designed majors, study abroad. *ROTC:* Army (c). *Unusual degree programs:* 3-2 engineering with University of Minnesota, Twin Cities Campus.

Library Clemens Library plus 2 others with 853,351 titles, 8,916 serial subscriptions, 20,319 audiovisual materials, an OPAC, a Web page.

Computers on Campus 350 computers available on campus for general student use. A campuswide network can be accessed from student residence rooms and from off campus. Internet access, online (class) registration, at least one staffed computer lab available.

Student Life *Housing:* on-campus residence required through sophomore year. *Options:* women-only. *Activities and Organizations:* drama/theater group, student-run newspaper, radio station, choral group, Volunteers in Service to Others, ultimate Frisbee, Joint Events Council, Students in Free Enterprise, Cultural Affairs Board. *Campus security:* 24-hour emergency response devices and patrols, student patrols, late-night transport/escort service, controlled dormitory access, well-lit pathways. *Student Services:* health clinic, personal/psychological counseling.

Athletics Member NCAA. All Division III. *Intercollegiate sports:* basketball W, crew W(c), cross-country running W, golf W, gymnastics W, lacrosse W(c), rugby W(c), skiing (cross-country) W, soccer W, softball W, swimming W, tennis W, track and field W, volleyball W. *Intramural sports:* badminton W, basketball W, football W, racquetball W, riflery W(c), skiing (cross-country) W(c), skiing (downhill) W(c), soccer W, softball W, tennis W, volleyball W, water polo W(c).

Standardized Tests *Required:* SAT I or ACT (for admission).

Costs (2001–02) *Comprehensive fee:* $23,921 includes full-time tuition ($18,015), mandatory fees ($300), and room and board ($5606). Part-time tuition: $750 per credit. *Required fees:* $150 per term part-time. *Room and board:* College room only: $2950. Room and board charges vary according to board plan and housing facility. *Payment plans:* tuition prepayment, installment, deferred payment.

Financial Aid Of all full-time matriculated undergraduates who enrolled in 2001, 1948 applied for aid, 1310 were judged to have need, 1158 had their need fully met. 502 Federal Work-Study jobs (averaging $1900). In 2001, 551 non-need-based awards were made. *Average percent of need met:* 78%. *Average financial aid package:* $15,507. *Average need-based loan:* $4399. *Average need-based gift aid:* $10,233. *Average non-need based aid:* $5216. *Average indebtedness upon graduation:* $19,480.

Applying *Options:* common application, electronic application, early admission, deferred entrance. *Application fee:* $25. *Required:* essay or personal statement, high school transcript. *Required for some:* letters of recommendation. *Recommended:* minimum 3.0 GPA, interview. *Application deadline:* rolling (freshmen), rolling (transfers). *Notification:* continuous (freshmen).

Admissions Contact Ms. Mary Milbert, Dean of Admissions, College of Saint Benedict, 37 South College Avenue, St. Joseph, MN 56374. *Phone:* 320-363-5308. *Toll-free phone:* 800-544-1489. *Fax:* 320-363-5010. *E-mail:* admissions@csbsju.edu.

COLLEGE OF ST. CATHERINE

St. Paul, Minnesota

- **Independent Roman Catholic** comprehensive, founded 1905
- **Calendar** 4-1-4
- **Degrees** certificates, associate, bachelor's, master's, and postbachelor's certificates
- **Urban** 110-acre campus with easy access to Minneapolis
- **Endowment** $38.1 million
- **Women only,** 3,610 undergraduate students, 64% full-time
- **Moderately difficult** entrance level, 82% of applicants were admitted

Undergraduates 2,303 full-time, 1,307 part-time. Students come from 36 states and territories, 30 other countries, 10% are from out of state, 6% African American, 5% Asian American or Pacific Islander, 2% Hispanic American, 0.6% Native American, 2% international, 21% transferred in, 38% live on campus. *Retention:* 76% of 2001 full-time freshmen returned.

Freshmen *Admission:* 814 applied, 671 admitted, 369 enrolled. *Average high school GPA:* 3.37. *Test scores:* SAT verbal scores over 500: 70%; SAT math scores over 500: 82%; ACT scores over 18: 85%; SAT verbal scores over 600: 40%; SAT

College of St. Catherine (continued)
math scores over 600: 46%; ACT scores over 24: 36%; SAT verbal scores over 700: 6%; SAT math scores over 700: 9%; ACT scores over 30: 5%.

Faculty *Total:* 443, 42% full-time, 52% with terminal degrees. *Student/faculty ratio:* 10:1.

Majors Accounting; art; art education; art history; biochemistry; biology; biology education; business administration; business marketing and marketing management; chemistry; chemistry education; computer/information sciences; creative writing; diagnostic medical sonography; dietetics; drama/dance education; early childhood education; economics; education; elementary education; English; English education; fashion merchandising; fine/studio arts; French; French language education; health/physical education; history; home economics; home economics education; international business; international economics; international relations; journalism; liberal arts and sciences/liberal studies; literature; management information systems/business data processing; mass communications; mathematics; mathematics education; medical radiologic technology; medical records technology; medical technology; music; music teacher education; nursing; nutrition science; occupational therapy; occupational therapy assistant; philosophy; physical education; physical therapy assistant; physics; political science; pre-dentistry; pre-law; pre-medicine; pre-veterinary studies; psychology; respiratory therapy; secondary education; sign language interpretation; social sciences; social studies education; social work; sociology; Spanish; Spanish language education; speech education; speech/rhetorical studies; theater arts/drama; theology; women's studies.

Academic Programs *Special study options:* academic remediation for entering students, adult/continuing education programs, advanced placement credit, distance learning, double majors, English as a second language, external degree program, honors programs, independent study, internships, off-campus study, part-time degree program, services for LD students, student-designed majors, study abroad, summer session for credit. *ROTC:* Air Force (c). *Unusual degree programs:* 3-2 engineering with Washington University in St. Louis, University of Minnesota, Twin Cities Campus; optometry with Illinois College of Optometry.

Library St. Catherine Library plus 2 others with 263,495 titles, 1,141 serial subscriptions, 13,627 audiovisual materials, an OPAC, a Web page.

Computers on Campus 350 computers available on campus for general student use. A campuswide network can be accessed from student residence rooms and from off campus that provide access to transcript. Internet access, at least one staffed computer lab available.

Student Life *Housing Options:* women-only. *Activities and Organizations:* drama/theater group, student-run newspaper, choral group, student government, Residence Hall Association, Women Helping Women, Student Nursing Association, social work club. *Campus security:* 24-hour emergency response devices and patrols, student patrols, late-night transport/escort service, controlled dormitory access. *Student Services:* health clinic, personal/psychological counseling, women's center.

Athletics Member NCAA. All Division III. *Intercollegiate sports:* basketball W, cross-country running W, ice hockey W, soccer W, softball W, swimming W, tennis W, track and field W, volleyball W. *Intramural sports:* badminton W, basketball W, cross-country running W, football W, golf W, lacrosse W, racquetball W, soccer W, softball W, swimming W, tennis W, track and field W, volleyball W.

Standardized Tests *Required:* SAT I or ACT (for admission).

Costs (2001–02) *Comprehensive fee:* $22,324 includes full-time tuition ($17,280), mandatory fees ($122), and room and board ($4922). Full-time tuition and fees vary according to class time and degree level. Part-time tuition: $540 per credit. Part-time tuition and fees vary according to class time and degree level. *Required fees:* $61 per term part-time. *Room and board:* College room only: $2782. Room and board charges vary according to board plan and housing facility. *Payment plan:* installment. *Waivers:* senior citizens and employees or children of employees.

Financial Aid Of all full-time matriculated undergraduates who enrolled in 2001, 1238 applied for aid, 1089 were judged to have need, 612 had their need fully met. 500 Federal Work-Study jobs. In 2001, 203 non-need-based awards were made. *Average percent of need met:* 93%. *Average financial aid package:* $17,615. *Average need-based loan:* $4735. *Average need-based gift aid:* $6663. *Average non-need based aid:* $9354. *Average indebtedness upon graduation:* $22,642.

Applying *Options:* common application, deferred entrance. *Application fee:* $20. *Required:* high school transcript, 1 letter of recommendation. *Required for some:* essay or personal statement, interview. *Recommended:* interview. *Application deadline:* 8/15 (freshmen), rolling (transfers). *Notification:* continuous (freshmen).

Admissions Contact Ms. Cory Piper-Hauswirth, Associate Director of Admission and Financial Aid, College of St. Catherine, 2004 Randolph Avenue, St. Paul, MN 55105-1789. *Phone:* 651-690-6047. *Toll-free phone:* 800-945-4599. *Fax:* 651-690-8824. *E-mail:* admissions@stkate.edu.

COLLEGE OF ST. CATHERINE-MINNEAPOLIS
Minneapolis, Minnesota

Admissions Contact Ms. Pamela A. Johnson, Director of Admissions and Financial Aid, College of St. Catherine-Minneapolis, Minneapolis, MN 55454-1494. *Phone:* 651-690-8600. *Fax:* 651-690-8119. *E-mail:* career-info@stkate.edu.

THE COLLEGE OF ST. SCHOLASTICA
Duluth, Minnesota

- **Independent** comprehensive, founded 1912, affiliated with Roman Catholic Church
- **Calendar** semesters
- **Degrees** bachelor's and master's
- **Suburban** 160-acre campus
- **Endowment** $16.2 million
- **Coed,** 1,700 undergraduate students, 88% full-time, 70% women, 30% men
- **Moderately difficult** entrance level, 31% of applicants were admitted

Undergraduates 1,497 full-time, 203 part-time. Students come from 22 states and territories, 11% are from out of state, 1% African American, 0.9% Asian American or Pacific Islander, 0.6% Hispanic American, 1% Native American, 0.5% international, 16% transferred in, 39% live on campus. *Retention:* 76% of 2001 full-time freshmen returned.

Freshmen *Admission:* 960 applied, 300 admitted, 298 enrolled. *Average high school GPA:* 3.55. *Test scores:* SAT verbal scores over 500: 86%; SAT math scores over 500: 86%; ACT scores over 18: 96%; SAT verbal scores over 600: 29%; SAT math scores over 600: 36%; ACT scores over 24: 48%; SAT verbal scores over 700: 7%; SAT math scores over 700: 7%; ACT scores over 30: 5%.

Faculty *Total:* 175, 65% full-time, 34% with terminal degrees. *Student/faculty ratio:* 12:1.

Majors Accounting; biochemistry; biology; business communications; business management/administrative services related; chemistry; communications; computer/information sciences; economics; education; educational media design; education (K-12); English; exercise sciences; health science; health services administration; history; humanities; international business; international relations; liberal arts and sciences/liberal studies; management science; mathematics; medical laboratory technology; music; natural sciences; nursing; occupational therapy; physical therapy; psychology; religious studies; social science education; social work.

Academic Programs *Special study options:* academic remediation for entering students, accelerated degree program, adult/continuing education programs, advanced placement credit, distance learning, double majors, external degree program, honors programs, independent study, internships, off-campus study, part-time degree program, services for LD students, student-designed majors, study abroad, summer session for credit. *ROTC:* Army (c), Air Force (c).

Library College of St. Scholastica Library plus 1 other with 122,492 titles, 828 serial subscriptions, an OPAC, a Web page.

Computers on Campus 160 computers available on campus for general student use. A campuswide network can be accessed from student residence rooms and from off campus. Internet access, at least one staffed computer lab available.

Student Life *Housing Options:* coed. *Activities and Organizations:* drama/theater group, student-run newspaper, choral group, Campus Activity Board (CAB), Intervarsity, SOTA, SHIMA, Social Work Club. *Campus security:* 24-hour emergency response devices and patrols, late-night transport/escort service, controlled dormitory access, student door monitor at night. *Student Services:* health clinic, personal/psychological counseling.

Athletics Member NCAA, NAIA. All NCAA Division III. *Intercollegiate sports:* baseball M, basketball M/W, cross-country running M/W, ice hockey M, soccer M/W, softball W, tennis M/W, volleyball W. *Intramural sports:* basketball M(c)/W(c), field hockey M(c)/W(c), football M(c)/W(c), ice hockey W, racquetball M/W, soccer M/W, track and field W, volleyball M/W.

Standardized Tests *Required:* SAT I or ACT (for admission).

Costs (2001–02) *Comprehensive fee:* $22,378 includes full-time tuition ($17,080), mandatory fees ($100), and room and board ($5198). Part-time tuition: $535 per credit. Part-time tuition and fees vary according to course load. *Required fees:* $50 per term part-time. *Room and board:* Room and board charges vary according to board plan. *Payment plan:* installment. *Waivers:* employees or children of employees.

Financial Aid Of all full-time matriculated undergraduates who enrolled in 2001, 1094 applied for aid, 1004 were judged to have need, 843 had their need

fully met. 220 Federal Work-Study jobs (averaging $1782). 278 State and other part-time jobs (averaging $1662). In 2001, 145 non-need-based awards were made. *Average percent of need met:* 84%. *Average financial aid package:* $15,050. *Average need-based loan:* $2867. *Average need-based gift aid:* $5782. *Average non-need based aid:* $6302. *Average indebtedness upon graduation:* $26,826.

Applying *Options:* common application, electronic application, early admission, deferred entrance. *Application fee:* $25. *Required:* high school transcript. *Required for some:* minimum 2.0 GPA, interview. *Recommended:* essay or personal statement, letters of recommendation, interview. *Application deadline:* rolling (freshmen), rolling (transfers). *Notification:* continuous (freshmen).

Admissions Contact Mr. Brian Dalton, Vice President for Enrollment Management, The College of St. Scholastica, 1200 Kenwood Avenue, Duluth, MN 55811-4199. *Phone:* 218-723-6053. *Toll-free phone:* 800-249-6412. *Fax:* 218-723-6290. *E-mail:* admissions@css.edu.

COLLEGE OF VISUAL ARTS
St. Paul, Minnesota

- **Independent** 4-year, founded 1924
- **Calendar** semesters
- **Degree** bachelor's
- **Urban** 2-acre campus with easy access to Minneapolis
- **Coed,** 269 undergraduate students, 89% full-time, 58% women, 42% men
- **Minimally difficult** entrance level, 84% of applicants were admitted

Undergraduates Students come from 9 states and territories, 4 other countries, 11% are from out of state, 1% African American, 4% Asian American or Pacific Islander, 2% Hispanic American, 1% Native American, 2% international. *Retention:* 77% of 2001 full-time freshmen returned.

Freshmen *Admission:* 126 applied, 106 admitted. *Average high school GPA:* 3.00.

Faculty *Total:* 58, 19% full-time. *Student/faculty ratio:* 8:1.

Majors Art; drawing; graphic design/commercial art/illustration; painting; photography; printmaking; sculpture.

Academic Programs *Special study options:* academic remediation for entering students, advanced placement credit, double majors, independent study, internships, part-time degree program, study abroad, summer session for credit.

Library College of Visual Arts Library with 6,000 titles, 35 serial subscriptions, 15,000 audiovisual materials, a Web page.

Computers on Campus 30 computers available on campus for general student use. Internet access, at least one staffed computer lab available.

Student Life *Housing:* college housing not available. *Activities and Organizations:* AIGA Student Chapter. *Campus security:* 24-hour patrols, late-night transport/escort service, controlled dormitory access. *Student Services:* personal/psychological counseling.

Standardized Tests *Required:* SAT I or ACT (for admission).

Costs (2002–03) *Tuition:* $12,998 full-time, $650 per credit part-time. Full-time tuition and fees vary according to course load. Part-time tuition and fees vary according to course load. *Required fees:* $450 full-time. *Payment plan:* installment. *Waivers:* children of alumni and employees or children of employees.

Financial Aid Of all full-time matriculated undergraduates who enrolled in 2001, 189 applied for aid, 153 were judged to have need. 13 Federal Work-Study jobs (averaging $3207). 44 State and other part-time jobs (averaging $2111). In 2001, 15 non-need-based awards were made. *Average financial aid package:* $5919. *Average need-based loan:* $2734. *Average need-based gift aid:* $2579. *Average non-need based aid:* $1991. *Average indebtedness upon graduation:* $34,070.

Applying *Options:* common application, electronic application, deferred entrance. *Application fee:* $40. *Required:* essay or personal statement, high school transcript, minimum 2.6 GPA, interview, portfolio. *Recommended:* minimum 3.0 GPA, letters of recommendation. *Application deadline:* rolling (freshmen), rolling (transfers). *Notification:* continuous (freshmen).

Admissions Contact Ms. Lynn E. Tanaka, Director of Admissions, College of Visual Arts, 344 Summit Avenue, St. Paul, MN 55102-2124. *Phone:* 651-224-3416. *Toll-free phone:* 800-224-1536. *Fax:* 651-224-8854. *E-mail:* info@cva.edu.

CONCORDIA COLLEGE
Moorhead, Minnesota

- **Independent** 4-year, founded 1891, affiliated with Evangelical Lutheran Church in America
- **Calendar** semesters
- **Degrees** bachelor's and master's
- **Suburban** 120-acre campus
- **Endowment** $74.3 million
- **Coed,** 2,766 undergraduate students, 98% full-time, 62% women, 38% men
- **Moderately difficult** entrance level, 86% of applicants were admitted

Concordia College is distinctive as a nationally ranked liberal arts college that successfully blends career preparation, off-campus cooperative education, cocurricular activities, and international study-abroad programs. Offering nearly 100 majors and preprofessional programs, Concordia encourages students to explore all of the options that their future holds. Concordia is noted for the friendliness of its student body and the personal attention of its faculty members. The approximately 2,900 students at Concordia College in Moorehead, Minnesota, are the beneficiaries of a top-quality educational experience that comes at a cost below that of comparable private colleges.

Undergraduates 2,712 full-time, 54 part-time. Students come from 31 states and territories, 41 other countries, 39% are from out of state, 0.6% African American, 1% Asian American or Pacific Islander, 0.7% Hispanic American, 0.5% Native American, 6% international, 3% transferred in, 60% live on campus. *Retention:* 81% of 2001 full-time freshmen returned.

Freshmen *Admission:* 2,326 applied, 2,000 admitted, 773 enrolled. *Test scores:* SAT verbal scores over 500: 85%; SAT math scores over 500: 84%; ACT scores over 18: 95%; SAT verbal scores over 600: 39%; SAT math scores over 600: 38%; ACT scores over 24: 52%; SAT verbal scores over 700: 5%; SAT math scores over 700: 5%; ACT scores over 30: 6%.

Faculty *Total:* 255, 78% full-time, 64% with terminal degrees. *Student/faculty ratio:* 14:1.

Majors Accounting; advertising; apparel marketing; architecture; art; art education; art history; biology; biology education; broadcast journalism; business; business administration; business education; chemistry; chemistry education; child care/development; classics; clothing/apparel/textile; clothing/textiles; communications; computer science; creative writing; criminal justice studies; dietetics; early childhood education; economics; education; elementary education; English; English education; environmental science; exercise sciences; family/consumer studies; fine/studio arts; French; French language education; German; German language education; health education; health/physical education; health services administration; history; history education; humanities; international business; international relations; journalism; Latin (ancient and medieval); mass communications; mathematics; mathematics education; medical laboratory technology; medical technology; music; music (general performance); music (piano and organ performance); music teacher education; music theory and composition; music (voice and choral/opera performance); nursing; nutrition science; occupational therapy; office management; ophthalmic/optometric services related; philosophy; physical education; physical therapy; physics; physics education; political science; pre-dentistry; pre-engineering; pre-law; pre-medicine; pre-theology; pre-veterinary studies; psychology; public relations; radio/television broadcasting; religious studies; respiratory therapy; Russian/Slavic studies; Scandinavian languages; science education; secondary education; social studies education; social work; sociology; Spanish; Spanish language education; speech/rhetorical studies; theater arts/drama.

Academic Programs *Special study options:* adult/continuing education programs, advanced placement credit, cooperative education, double majors, English as a second language, honors programs, independent study, internships, off-campus study, part-time degree program, services for LD students, study abroad, summer session for credit. *ROTC:* Army (c), Air Force (c). *Unusual degree programs:* 3-2 engineering with North Dakota State University; architecture with North Dakota State University.

Library Carl B. Ylvisaker Library with 300,000 titles, 1,440 serial subscriptions, an OPAC, a Web page.

Computers on Campus 185 computers available on campus for general student use. A campuswide network can be accessed from student residence rooms and from off campus. At least one staffed computer lab available.

Student Life *Housing:* on-campus residence required through sophomore year. *Options:* coed, men-only, women-only. *Activities and Organizations:* drama/theater group, student-run newspaper, radio and television station, choral group, Sources of Service, Habitat for Humanity, Student Minnesota Education Association, language clubs, Health Professions Interest Club. *Campus security:* 24-hour emergency response devices and patrols, student patrols, late-night transport/escort service, well-lit campus, 24-hour locked wing doors. *Student Services:* health clinic, personal/psychological counseling, women's center.

Athletics Member NCAA. All Division III. *Intercollegiate sports:* baseball M, basketball M/W, cross-country running M/W, football M, golf M/W, ice hockey M/W, skiing (cross-country) M(c)/W(c), soccer M/W, softball W, swimming W, tennis M/W, track and field M/W, volleyball M(c)/W, wrestling M. *Intramural*

Concordia College (continued)
sports: badminton M/W, baseball M/W, basketball M/W, bowling M/W, cross-country running M/W, football M/W, golf M/W, ice hockey M/W, racquetball M/W, rugby M/W, skiing (cross-country) M/W, soccer M/W, softball M/W, swimming M/W, table tennis M/W, tennis M/W, track and field M/W, volleyball M/W, water polo M/W, weight lifting M/W.

Standardized Tests *Required:* SAT I or ACT (for admission). *Recommended:* ACT (for admission).

Costs (2002–03) *Comprehensive fee:* $19,945 includes full-time tuition ($15,503), mandatory fees ($132), and room and board ($4310). Part-time tuition: $2435 per course. Part-time tuition and fees vary according to course load. *Room and board:* College room only: $1960. Room and board charges vary according to board plan and housing facility. *Payment plan:* installment. *Waivers:* employees or children of employees.

Financial Aid Of all full-time matriculated undergraduates who enrolled in 2001, 2211 applied for aid, 1928 were judged to have need, 1700 had their need fully met. 1012 Federal Work-Study jobs (averaging $1257). In 2001, 688 non-need-based awards were made. *Average percent of need met:* 92%. *Average financial aid package:* $12,400. *Average need-based loan:* $6076. *Average need-based gift aid:* $8152. *Average indebtedness upon graduation:* $19,823.

Applying *Options:* common application, electronic application, early admission, deferred entrance. *Application fee:* $20. *Required:* high school transcript, 2 letters of recommendation. *Application deadline:* rolling (freshmen), rolling (transfers).

Admissions Contact Mr. Scott E. Ellingson, Director of Admissions, Concordia College, 901 8th Street South, Moorhead, MN 56562. *Phone:* 218-299-3004. *Toll-free phone:* 800-699-9897. *Fax:* 218-299-3947. *E-mail:* admissions@cord.edu.

CONCORDIA UNIVERSITY
St. Paul, Minnesota

- **Independent** comprehensive, founded 1893, affiliated with Lutheran Church-Missouri Synod, part of Concordia University System
- **Calendar** semesters
- **Degrees** certificates, associate, bachelor's, and master's
- **Urban** 37-acre campus
- **Coed,** 1,511 undergraduate students, 91% full-time, 60% women, 40% men
- **Minimally difficult** entrance level, 54% of applicants were admitted

Undergraduates 1,372 full-time, 139 part-time. Students come from 45 states and territories, 4 other countries, 25% are from out of state, 5% African American, 4% Asian American or Pacific Islander, 0.8% Hispanic American, 0.4% Native American, 0.1% international, 8% transferred in, 48% live on campus. *Retention:* 61% of 2001 full-time freshmen returned.

Freshmen *Admission:* 937 applied, 503 admitted, 200 enrolled. *Average high school GPA:* 3.10. *Test scores:* SAT verbal scores over 500: 70%; SAT math scores over 500: 62%; ACT scores over 18: 86%; SAT verbal scores over 600: 36%; SAT math scores over 600: 27%; ACT scores over 24: 31%; SAT verbal scores over 700: 6%; SAT math scores over 700: 2%; ACT scores over 30: 1%.

Faculty *Total:* 310, 28% full-time. *Student/faculty ratio:* 12:1.

Majors Accounting; art history; biology; business administration; early childhood education; economics; education; elementary education; English; environmental education; environmental science; finance; health education; history; interdisciplinary studies; liberal arts and sciences/liberal studies; literature; management information systems/business data processing; mass communications; middle school education; music; music teacher education; natural sciences; pastoral counseling; physical education; physical sciences; psychology; religious education; religious music; religious studies; science education; secondary education; social sciences; sociology; teacher assistant/aide; theater arts/drama; theology.

Academic Programs *Special study options:* academic remediation for entering students, accelerated degree program, adult/continuing education programs, advanced placement credit, cooperative education, distance learning, double majors, English as a second language, external degree program, independent study, internships, off-campus study, part-time degree program, services for LD students, student-designed majors, study abroad, summer session for credit. *ROTC:* Army (c), Navy (c), Air Force (c).

Library Buenger Memorial Library plus 1 other with 125,000 titles, 1,400 serial subscriptions, 6,000 audiovisual materials, an OPAC, a Web page.

Computers on Campus 1200 computers available on campus for general student use. A campuswide network can be accessed from student residence rooms and from off campus. Internet access, at least one staffed computer lab available.

Student Life *Housing:* on-campus residence required for freshman year. *Options:* coed, men-only, women-only, disabled students. *Activities and Organizations:* drama/theater group, student-run newspaper, choral group, church vocations, Minority Students, ministry, community based outreach. *Campus security:* 24-hour emergency response devices and patrols, student patrols, late-night transport/escort service. *Student Services:* health clinic, personal/psychological counseling.

Athletics Member NCAA. All Division II. *Intercollegiate sports:* baseball M(s), basketball M(s)/W(s), cross-country running M(s)/W(s), football M(s), soccer M/W(s), softball W(s), track and field M(s)/W(s), volleyball W(s). *Intramural sports:* basketball M/W, cross-country running M/W, football M/W, racquetball M/W, skiing (downhill) M/W, soccer M/W, table tennis M/W, tennis M/W, track and field M/W, volleyball M/W.

Standardized Tests *Required:* ACT (for admission).

Costs (2002–03) *Comprehensive fee:* $22,856 includes full-time tuition ($17,326) and room and board ($5530). Part-time tuition: $362 per credit. Part-time tuition and fees vary according to course load. *Payment plan:* installment. *Waivers:* senior citizens and employees or children of employees.

Financial Aid Of all full-time matriculated undergraduates who enrolled in 2001, 1078 applied for aid, 927 were judged to have need, 273 had their need fully met. 167 Federal Work-Study jobs (averaging $1600). 264 State and other part-time jobs (averaging $1652). In 2001, 112 non-need-based awards were made. *Average percent of need met:* 75%. *Average financial aid package:* $10,643. *Average need-based loan:* $3852. *Average need-based gift aid:* $7697. *Average non-need based aid:* $5024.

Applying *Options:* common application, electronic application, early admission, deferred entrance. *Application fee:* $20. *Required:* high school transcript, 2 letters of recommendation. *Required for some:* essay or personal statement. *Recommended:* minimum 2.0 GPA, interview. *Application deadlines:* 8/15 (freshmen), 8/15 (transfers). *Notification:* continuous (freshmen).

Admissions Contact Ms. Rhonda Behm-Severeid, Director of Freshman Admissions, Concordia University, 275 Syndicate North, St. Paul, MN 55104-5494. *Phone:* 651-641-8230. *Toll-free phone:* 800-333-4705. *Fax:* 651-659-0207. *E-mail:* admiss@luther.csp.edu.

CROWN COLLEGE
St. Bonifacius, Minnesota

- **Independent** comprehensive, founded 1916, affiliated with The Christian and Missionary Alliance
- **Calendar** semesters
- **Degrees** certificates, associate, bachelor's, and master's
- **Suburban** 193-acre campus with easy access to Minneapolis-St. Paul
- **Endowment** $3.9 million
- **Coed,** 862 undergraduate students, 81% full-time, 55% women, 45% men
- **Minimally difficult** entrance level, 75% of applicants were admitted

Undergraduates 701 full-time, 161 part-time. Students come from 33 states and territories, 25% are from out of state, 2% African American, 3% Asian American or Pacific Islander, 2% Hispanic American, 0.3% Native American, 6% transferred in, 69% live on campus. *Retention:* 70% of 2001 full-time freshmen returned.

Freshmen *Admission:* 417 applied, 311 admitted, 160 enrolled. *Average high school GPA:* 3.19. *Test scores:* ACT scores over 18: 87%; ACT scores over 24: 30%; ACT scores over 30: 3%.

Faculty *Total:* 57, 68% full-time, 53% with terminal degrees. *Student/faculty ratio:* 14:1.

Majors Biblical studies; biological/physical sciences; biology; business; business administration; business systems networking/ telecommunications; child care/development; early childhood education; elementary education; English; English education; general studies; history; history education; individual/family development; liberal arts and sciences/liberal studies; linguistics; missionary studies; music; music teacher education; pastoral counseling; physical education; psychology; religious education; social sciences; social studies education; sport/fitness administration; theology.

Academic Programs *Special study options:* academic remediation for entering students, adult/continuing education programs, advanced placement credit, distance learning, double majors, English as a second language, honors programs, independent study, internships, part-time degree program, services for LD students, study abroad, summer session for credit.

Library Peter Watne Memorial Library with 190,000 titles, 1,780 serial subscriptions, 2,400 audiovisual materials, an OPAC, a Web page.

Computers on Campus 50 computers available on campus for general student use. A campuswide network can be accessed from student residence rooms and from off campus. Internet access, at least one staffed computer lab available.

Student Life *Housing:* on-campus residence required through senior year. *Options:* men-only, women-only. *Activities and Organizations:* drama/theater group, student-run newspaper, choral group, Global Impact Team, Hmong Student Fellowship, Married Student Fellowship, Senate/Student Services Board, newspaper/yearbook staff. *Campus security:* 24-hour emergency response devices, late-night transport/escort service, controlled dormitory access. *Student Services:* health clinic, personal/psychological counseling.

Athletics Member NAIA, NCCAA. *Intercollegiate sports:* baseball M, basketball M/W, cross-country running M/W, football M, golf M/W, soccer M/W, softball W, volleyball W. *Intramural sports:* basketball M/W, football M, soccer M, table tennis M/W, tennis M/W, volleyball M/W, weight lifting M/W.

Standardized Tests *Required:* SAT I or ACT (for admission).

Costs (2001–02) *Comprehensive fee:* $16,066 includes full-time tuition ($10,600), mandatory fees ($746), and room and board ($4720). Part-time tuition: $442 per credit. Part-time tuition and fees vary according to course load. *Required fees:* $28 per credit hour. *Room and board:* College room only: $2192. Room and board charges vary according to board plan. *Payment plan:* installment. *Waivers:* employees or children of employees.

Financial Aid Of all full-time matriculated undergraduates who enrolled in 2001, 537 applied for aid, 500 were judged to have need. In 2001, 33 non-need-based awards were made. *Average financial aid package:* $8589. *Average need-based loan:* $4011. *Average need-based gift aid:* $3976. *Average non-need based aid:* $933. *Average indebtedness upon graduation:* $17,067.

Applying *Options:* early admission, deferred entrance. *Application fee:* $35. *Required:* essay or personal statement, high school transcript, minimum 2.0 GPA, 2 letters of recommendation. *Required for some:* interview. *Application deadline:* rolling (freshmen), rolling (transfers).

Admissions Contact Ms. Kimberely LaQuay, Application Coordinator/Office Systems Manager, Crown College, 6425 County Road 30, St. Bonifacius, MN 55375-9001. *Phone:* 952-446-4143. *Toll-free phone:* 800-68-CROWN. *Fax:* 952-446-4149. *E-mail:* info@crown.edu.

GLOBE COLLEGE
Oakdale, Minnesota

- **Private** primarily 2-year, founded 1885
- **Calendar** quarters
- **Degrees** diplomas, associate, and bachelor's
- 665 undergraduate students, 45% full-time

Faculty *Student/faculty ratio:* 14:1.

Costs (2001–02) *Tuition:* $11,075 full-time, $235 per credit part-time.

Admissions Contact Mr. Mike Hughes, Director of Admissions, Globe College, 7166 10th Street North, Oakdale, MN 55128. *Phone:* 651-730-5100 Ext. 311. *Fax:* 651-730-5151. *E-mail:* admissions@globecollege.com.

GUSTAVUS ADOLPHUS COLLEGE
St. Peter, Minnesota

- **Independent** 4-year, founded 1862, affiliated with Evangelical Lutheran Church in America
- **Calendar** 4-1-4
- **Degree** bachelor's
- **Small-town** 330-acre campus with easy access to Minneapolis-St. Paul
- **Endowment** $79.3 million
- **Coed,** 2,592 undergraduate students, 99% full-time, 58% women, 42% men
- **Very difficult** entrance level, 76% of applicants were admitted

Additions to the 340-acre campus include an international education center and residence hall, a 9-lane outdoor track with access to an indoor track facility, an international soccer field, Campus Center housing, the Market Place and Courtyard Café, a diversity center, a student activities and ticket office, a bookstore, a health center, and student organization offices.

Undergraduates 2,568 full-time, 24 part-time. Students come from 39 states and territories, 22 other countries, 22% are from out of state, 1% African American, 3% Asian American or Pacific Islander, 0.9% Hispanic American, 0.2% Native American, 2% international, 2% transferred in, 85% live on campus. *Retention:* 89% of 2001 full-time freshmen returned.

Freshmen *Admission:* 2,163 applied, 1,637 admitted, 670 enrolled. *Average high school GPA:* 3.62. *Test scores:* SAT verbal scores over 500: 85%; SAT math scores over 500: 90%; ACT scores over 18: 100%; SAT verbal scores over 600: 50%; SAT math scores over 600: 56%; ACT scores over 24: 70%; SAT verbal scores over 700: 16%; SAT math scores over 700: 15%; ACT scores over 30: 18%.

Faculty *Total:* 231, 75% full-time, 68% with terminal degrees. *Student/faculty ratio:* 13:1.

Majors Accounting; anthropology; art; art education; art history; athletic training/sports medicine; biochemistry; biology; biology education; business administration; business economics; chemistry; chemistry education; classics; computer science; criminal justice/law enforcement administration; dance; economics; education; elementary education; English; environmental science; French; geography; geology; German; health education; history; interdisciplinary studies; international business; Japanese; Latin American studies; mass communications; mathematics; mathematics education; music; music teacher education; nursing; occupational therapy; philosophy; physical education; physical therapy; physics; physics education; political science; pre-dentistry; pre-law; pre-medicine; pre-veterinary studies; psychology; religious music; religious studies; Russian; Russian/Slavic studies; Scandinavian languages; secondary education; social sciences; social studies education; sociology; Spanish; speech/rhetorical studies; theater arts/drama; trade/industrial education.

Academic Programs *Special study options:* accelerated degree program, advanced placement credit, cooperative education, double majors, honors programs, independent study, internships, off-campus study, services for LD students, student-designed majors, study abroad, summer session for credit. *ROTC:* Army (c). *Unusual degree programs:* 3-2 engineering with Minnesota State University, Mankato; University of Minnesota; environmental studies with Duke University.

Library Folke Bernadotte Memorial Library plus 4 others with 267,677 titles, 1,088 serial subscriptions, 14,993 audiovisual materials, an OPAC, a Web page.

Computers on Campus 441 computers available on campus for general student use. A campuswide network can be accessed from student residence rooms and from off campus. Internet access, at least one staffed computer lab available.

Student Life *Housing:* on-campus residence required through senior year. *Options:* coed. *Activities and Organizations:* drama/theater group, student-run newspaper, radio station, choral group, Campus Activity Board, Gustavus Choir, Greens, Fellowship of Christian Athletes, Big Partner/Little Partner. *Campus security:* 24-hour emergency response devices and patrols, late-night transport/escort service, controlled dormitory access. *Student Services:* health clinic, personal/psychological counseling, women's center.

Athletics Member NCAA. All Division III. *Intercollegiate sports:* baseball M, basketball M/W, cross-country running M/W, football M, golf M/W, gymnastics W, ice hockey M/W, lacrosse M(c), rugby M(c)/W(c), skiing (cross-country) M/W, soccer M/W, softball W, swimming M/W, tennis M/W, track and field M/W, volleyball M(c)/W. *Intramural sports:* basketball M/W, bowling M/W, football M, ice hockey M, racquetball M/W, skiing (cross-country) M/W, skiing (downhill) M/W, soccer M/W, softball M/W, swimming M/W, tennis M/W, volleyball W, water polo M/W, weight lifting M/W.

Standardized Tests *Required:* SAT I or ACT (for admission).

Costs (2001–02) *One-time required fee:* $50. *Comprehensive fee:* $24,255 includes full-time tuition ($18,940), mandatory fees ($415), and room and board ($4900). Full-time tuition and fees vary according to student level. Part-time tuition: $2050 per course. No tuition increase for student's term of enrollment. *Required fees:* $175 per year part-time. *Room and board:* College room only: $2530. Room and board charges vary according to board plan, housing facility, and student level. *Payment plans:* tuition prepayment, installment. *Waivers:* senior citizens and employees or children of employees.

Financial Aid Of all full-time matriculated undergraduates who enrolled in 2001, 1957 applied for aid, 1578 were judged to have need. 591 Federal Work-Study jobs (averaging $1785). 1101 State and other part-time jobs (averaging $1775). In 2001, 751 non-need-based awards were made. *Average percent of need met:* 91%. *Average financial aid package:* $14,694. *Average need-based loan:* $4015. *Average need-based gift aid:* $10,252. *Average non-need based aid:* $6170. *Average indebtedness upon graduation:* $17,300.

Applying *Options:* common application, electronic application, early admission, early decision, early action, deferred entrance. *Application fee:* $25. *Required:* essay or personal statement, high school transcript, 2 letters of recommendation. *Recommended:* interview. *Application deadlines:* 4/1 (freshmen), 4/1 (transfers). *Early decision:* 11/15. *Notification:* continuous until 5/1 (freshmen), 12/1 (early decision), 1/15 (early action).

Admissions Contact Mr. Mark H. Anderson, Dean of Admission, Gustavus Adolphus College, 800 West College Avenue, St. Peter, MN 56082-1498. *Phone:* 507-933-7676. *Toll-free phone:* 800-GUSTAVU(S). *Fax:* 507-933-7474. *E-mail:* admission@gac.edu.

HAMLINE UNIVERSITY
St. Paul, Minnesota

- **Independent** comprehensive, founded 1854, affiliated with United Methodist Church
- **Calendar** 4-1-4

Hamline University (continued)

- **Degrees** certificates, bachelor's, master's, doctoral, first professional, post-master's, postbachelor's, and first professional certificates
- **Urban** 50-acre campus
- **Endowment** $51.8 million
- **Coed,** 1,873 undergraduate students, 94% full-time, 64% women, 36% men
- **Moderately difficult** entrance level, 79% of applicants were admitted

Undergraduates 1,767 full-time, 106 part-time. Students come from 35 states and territories, 32 other countries, 34% are from out of state, 4% African American, 4% Asian American or Pacific Islander, 1% Hispanic American, 0.7% Native American, 3% international, 7% transferred in, 47% live on campus. *Retention:* 81% of 2001 full-time freshmen returned.

Freshmen *Admission:* 1,461 applied, 1,160 admitted, 421 enrolled. *Average high school GPA:* 3.4. *Test scores:* ACT scores over 18: 97%; ACT scores over 24: 63%; ACT scores over 30: 12%.

Faculty *Total:* 354, 47% full-time, 67% with terminal degrees. *Student/faculty ratio:* 13:1.

Majors Anthropology; art; art history; Asian studies; athletic training/sports medicine; biology; business administration; chemistry; criminal justice/law enforcement administration; East Asian studies; Eastern European area studies; economics; education; education (K-12); elementary education; English; environmental science; European studies; exercise sciences; fine/studio arts; French; German; health education; history; international business; international economics; international relations; Judaic studies; Latin American studies; legal studies; mass communications; mathematics; music; music teacher education; occupational therapy; paralegal/legal assistant; philosophy; physical education; physical therapy; physics; political science; pre-dentistry; pre-law; pre-medicine; pre-veterinary studies; psychology; public administration; religious studies; Russian/Slavic studies; science education; secondary education; social sciences; sociology; Spanish; speech/theater education; theater arts/drama; urban studies; women's studies.

Academic Programs *Special study options:* academic remediation for entering students, adult/continuing education programs, advanced placement credit, cooperative education, double majors, English as a second language, honors programs, independent study, internships, off-campus study, part-time degree program, services for LD students, student-designed majors, study abroad, summer session for credit. *ROTC:* Air Force (c). *Unusual degree programs:* 3-2 engineering with University of Minnesota, Washington University in St. Louis; occupational therapy with Washington University in St. Louis.

Library Bush Library plus 1 other with 445,902 titles, 3,803 serial subscriptions, 2,040 audiovisual materials, an OPAC, a Web page.

Computers on Campus 326 computers available on campus for general student use. A campuswide network can be accessed from student residence rooms and from off campus. Internet access, online (class) registration, at least one staffed computer lab available.

Student Life *Housing Options:* coed. *Activities and Organizations:* drama/theater group, student-run newspaper, choral group, Student Congress (HUSC), Acting in the Community Together, Minnesota Public Interest Research Group, Residential Hall Councils, Affordable Arts. *Campus security:* 24-hour emergency response devices and patrols, student patrols, late-night transport/escort service, controlled dormitory access. *Student Services:* health clinic, personal/psychological counseling, women's center.

Athletics Member NCAA. All Division III. *Intercollegiate sports:* baseball M, basketball M/W, cross-country running M/W, football M, gymnastics W, ice hockey M, soccer M/W, softball W, swimming M/W, tennis M/W, track and field M/W, volleyball W. *Intramural sports:* basketball M/W, bowling M/W, football M/W, golf M/W, ice hockey W, lacrosse M, racquetball M/W, skiing (cross-country) M/W, softball M/W, swimming M/W, table tennis M/W, tennis M/W, volleyball M/W, water polo M/W, weight lifting M/W.

Standardized Tests *Required:* SAT I or ACT (for admission).

Costs (2001–02) *Comprehensive fee:* $23,489 includes full-time tuition ($17,414), mandatory fees ($188), and room and board ($5887). Part-time tuition: $545 per credit. Part-time tuition and fees vary according to course load. *Required fees:* $163 per term part-time. *Room and board:* College room only: $2951. Room and board charges vary according to board plan. *Payment plan:* installment. *Waivers:* employees or children of employees.

Financial Aid Of all full-time matriculated undergraduates who enrolled in 2001, 1557 applied for aid, 1179 were judged to have need, 297 had their need fully met. 551 Federal Work-Study jobs (averaging $2272). In 2001, 340 non-need-based awards were made. *Average percent of need met:* 71%. *Average financial aid package:* $17,200. *Average need-based loan:* $1216. *Average need-based gift aid:* $9948. *Average indebtedness upon graduation:* $18,860.

Applying *Options:* electronic application, early admission, early action, deferred entrance. *Required:* essay or personal statement, high school transcript, 2 letters of recommendation. *Recommended:* interview. *Application deadline:* rolling (freshmen), rolling (transfers). *Notification:* continuous (freshmen), 12/15 (early action).

Admissions Contact Mr. Steven Bjork, Director of Undergraduate Admission, Hamline University, 1536 Hewitt Avenue C1930, St. Paul, MN 55104-1284. *Phone:* 651-523-2207. *Toll-free phone:* 800-753-9753. *Fax:* 651-523-2458. *E-mail:* cla-admis@gw.hamline.edu.

MACALESTER COLLEGE
St. Paul, Minnesota

- **Independent Presbyterian** 4-year, founded 1874
- **Calendar** semesters
- **Degree** bachelor's
- **Urban** 53-acre campus
- **Endowment** $500.4 million
- **Coed,** 1,822 undergraduate students, 97% full-time, 58% women, 42% men
- **Very difficult** entrance level, 50% of applicants were admitted

Undergraduates 1,769 full-time, 53 part-time. Students come from 50 states and territories, 88 other countries, 73% are from out of state, 3% African American, 5% Asian American or Pacific Islander, 3% Hispanic American, 0.8% Native American, 14% international, 1% transferred in, 73% live on campus. *Retention:* 91% of 2001 full-time freshmen returned.

Freshmen *Admission:* 3,480 applied, 1,749 admitted, 505 enrolled. *Test scores:* SAT verbal scores over 500: 100%; SAT math scores over 500: 100%; ACT scores over 18: 100%; SAT verbal scores over 600: 92%; SAT math scores over 600: 83%; ACT scores over 24: 98%; SAT verbal scores over 700: 46%; SAT math scores over 700: 31%; ACT scores over 30: 48%.

Faculty *Total:* 205, 72% full-time, 84% with terminal degrees. *Student/faculty ratio:* 11:1.

Majors Anthropology; art history; Asian studies; biology; chemistry; classics; communications; computer science; economics; English; environmental science; fine/studio arts; French; geography; geology; Greek (modern); history; humanities; interdisciplinary studies; international relations; Latin American studies; Latin (ancient and medieval); linguistics; mathematics; music; neuroscience; philosophy; physics; political science; psychology; religious studies; Russian; Russian/Slavic studies; sociology; Spanish; theater arts/drama; urban studies; women's studies.

Academic Programs *Special study options:* honors programs, independent study, internships, off-campus study, part-time degree program, student-designed majors, study abroad. *ROTC:* Army (c), Air Force (c). *Unusual degree programs:* 3-2 engineering with Washington University in St. Louis, University of Minnesota; nursing with Rush University; architecture with Washington University in St. Louis.

Library DeWitt Wallace Library with 407,321 titles, 2,459 serial subscriptions, 9,208 audiovisual materials, an OPAC, a Web page.

Computers on Campus 350 computers available on campus for general student use. A campuswide network can be accessed from student residence rooms and from off campus. Internet access, online (class) registration, at least one staffed computer lab available.

Student Life *Housing:* on-campus residence required through sophomore year. *Options:* coed, cooperative. *Activities and Organizations:* drama/theater group, student-run newspaper, radio and television station, choral group, Community Service Organization, student publications, multicultural organization, International Organization, outing club. *Campus security:* 24-hour emergency response devices and patrols, late-night transport/escort service, controlled dormitory access. *Student Services:* health clinic, personal/psychological counseling.

Athletics Member NCAA. All Division III. *Intercollegiate sports:* baseball M, basketball M/W, crew M(c)/W(c), cross-country running M/W, fencing M(c)/W(c), football M, golf M/W, ice hockey M(c)/W(c), rugby M(c)/W(c), skiing (cross-country) M/W, soccer M/W, softball W, swimming M/W, tennis M/W, track and field M/W, volleyball M(c)/W, water polo M(c)/W. *Intramural sports:* badminton M/W, basketball M/W, bowling M/W, football M/W, golf M/W, racquetball M/W, soccer M/W, softball M/W, table tennis M/W, tennis M/W, volleyball M/W, water polo M/W, weight lifting M/W.

Standardized Tests *Required:* SAT I or ACT (for admission).

Costs (2001–02) *Comprehensive fee:* $28,814 includes full-time tuition ($22,480), mandatory fees ($128), and room and board ($6206). Part-time tuition: $705 per semester hour. *Required fees:* $82 per term part-time. *Room and board:* College room only: $3222. Room and board charges vary according to board plan and housing facility. *Payment plan:* installment. *Waivers:* employees or children of employees.

Financial Aid Of all full-time matriculated undergraduates who enrolled in 2001, 1359 applied for aid, 1316 were judged to have need, 1316 had their need

fully met. 484 Federal Work-Study jobs (averaging $1711). 854 State and other part-time jobs (averaging $1730). In 2001, 82 non-need-based awards were made. *Average percent of need met:* 100%. *Average financial aid package:* $18,194. *Average need-based loan:* $3595. *Average need-based gift aid:* $14,662. *Average non-need based aid:* $4130.

Applying *Options:* common application, electronic application, early admission, early decision, deferred entrance. *Application fee:* $40. *Required:* essay or personal statement, high school transcript, 3 letters of recommendation. *Recommended:* interview. *Application deadlines:* 1/15 (freshmen), 4/1 (transfers). *Early decision:* 11/15 (for plan 1), 1/15 (for plan 2). *Notification:* 4/1 (freshmen), 12/15 (early decision plan 1), 2/7 (early decision plan 2).

Admissions Contact Mr. Lorne T. Robinson, Dean of Admissions and Financial Aid, Macalester College, 1600 Grand Avenue, St. Paul, MN 55105-1899. *Phone:* 651-696-6357. *Toll-free phone:* 800-231-7974. *Fax:* 651-696-6724. *E-mail:* admissions@macalester.edu.

MARTIN LUTHER COLLEGE
New Ulm, Minnesota

- **Independent** 4-year, founded 1995, affiliated with Wisconsin Evangelical Lutheran Synod
- **Calendar** semesters
- **Degree** bachelor's
- **Small-town** 50-acre campus
- **Coed,** 1,060 undergraduate students, 98% full-time, 51% women, 49% men
- **Moderately difficult** entrance level, 95% of applicants were admitted

Undergraduates 1,043 full-time, 17 part-time. Students come from 35 states and territories, 9 other countries, 73% are from out of state, 0.6% African American, 0.9% Asian American or Pacific Islander, 0.7% Hispanic American, 0.4% Native American, 2% international, 3% transferred in, 82% live on campus. *Retention:* 83% of 2001 full-time freshmen returned.

Freshmen *Admission:* 343 applied, 327 admitted, 255 enrolled. *Average high school GPA:* 3.38. *Test scores:* ACT scores over 18: 98%; ACT scores over 24: 51%; ACT scores over 30: 9%.

Faculty *Total:* 99, 88% full-time, 43% with terminal degrees. *Student/faculty ratio:* 13:1.

Majors Early childhood education; education (multiple levels); elementary education; interdisciplinary studies; pre-theology; theology.

Academic Programs *Special study options:* academic remediation for entering students, advanced placement credit, double majors, independent study, internships, summer session for credit.

Library Martin Luther College Library with 120,375 titles, 464 serial subscriptions, 5,688 audiovisual materials, an OPAC.

Computers on Campus 125 computers available on campus for general student use. A campuswide network can be accessed from student residence rooms. At least one staffed computer lab available.

Student Life *Housing:* on-campus residence required through junior year. *Options:* men-only, women-only. *Activities and Organizations:* drama/theater group, student-run newspaper, choral group, Drama Club, Color Guard, Pom Poms. *Campus security:* 24-hour emergency response devices, student patrols, controlled dormitory access. *Student Services:* health clinic, personal/psychological counseling.

Athletics Member NCAA, NAIA. All NCAA Division III. *Intercollegiate sports:* baseball M, basketball M/W, cross-country running M/W, football M, golf M, soccer M/W, softball W, tennis M/W, track and field M/W, volleyball W. *Intramural sports:* badminton M/W, basketball M/W, bowling M/W, football M, soccer M/W, softball M/W, tennis M/W, volleyball M/W.

Standardized Tests *Required:* ACT (for admission).

Costs (2002–03) *Comprehensive fee:* $13,560 includes full-time tuition ($11,080), mandatory fees ($630), and room and board ($1850). Part-time tuition: $150 per credit hour. *Room and board:* College room only: $680. *Payment plan:* installment.

Financial Aid Of all full-time matriculated undergraduates who enrolled in 2001, 957 applied for aid, 890 were judged to have need, 213 had their need fully met. 49 Federal Work-Study jobs (averaging $871). 7 State and other part-time jobs (averaging $841). *Average percent of need met:* 70%. *Average financial aid package:* $6146. *Average need-based loan:* $2106. *Average need-based gift aid:* $5585. *Average indebtedness upon graduation:* $8510. *Financial aid deadline:* 4/15.

Applying *Options:* deferred entrance. *Application fee:* $25. *Required:* high school transcript, minimum 2.0 GPA, letters of recommendation. *Application deadlines:* 4/15 (freshmen), 5/1 (transfers). *Notification:* continuous (freshmen).

Admissions Contact Prof. Ronald B. Brutlag, Associate Director of Admissions, Martin Luther College, 1995 Luther Court, New Ulm, MN 56073. *Phone:* 507-354-8221 Ext. 280. *Fax:* 507-354-8225. *E-mail:* mlcadmit@mlc-wels.edu.

MAYO SCHOOL OF HEALTH SCIENCES
Rochester, Minnesota

- **Independent** upper-level, founded 1973
- **Calendar** semesters
- **Degrees** certificates, associate, bachelor's, master's, and postbachelor's certificates
- **Urban** campus
- **Coed,** 515 undergraduate students, 100% full-time, 22% women, 78% men
- **Moderately difficult** entrance level

Majors Cytotechnology; medical technology; radiological science; respiratory therapy.

Academic Programs *Special study options:* cooperative education, independent study, internships, off-campus study.

Library Mayo Medical Library plus 3 others.

Computers on Campus A campuswide network can be accessed from off campus. Internet access, at least one staffed computer lab available.

Student Life *Housing:* college housing not available. *Campus security:* 24-hour emergency response devices, late-night transport/escort service. *Student Services:* health clinic, personal/psychological counseling, women's center, legal services.

Costs (2001–02) *Tuition:* $13,500 full-time. Full-time tuition and fees vary according to program.

Financial Aid Of all full-time matriculated undergraduates who enrolled in 2001, 42 applied for aid, 42 were judged to have need. *Average percent of need met:* 75%. *Average financial aid package:* $5740. *Average need-based loan:* $4016. *Average need-based gift aid:* $4245.

Applying *Options:* common application.

Admissions Contact Ms. Kate Ray, Enrollment and Student Services, Mayo School of Health Sciences, Siebins Building, 200 First Street, SW, Rochester, MN 55905. *Phone:* 507-266-4077. *Toll-free phone:* 800-626-9041. *Fax:* 507-284-0656. *E-mail:* kray@mayo.edu.

METROPOLITAN STATE UNIVERSITY
St. Paul, Minnesota

- **State-supported** comprehensive, founded 1971, part of Minnesota State Colleges and Universities System
- **Calendar** semesters
- **Degrees** certificates, bachelor's, and master's (offers primarily part-time evening degree programs)
- **Urban** campus
- **Endowment** $735,412
- **Coed,** 5,662 undergraduate students, 27% full-time, 61% women, 39% men
- **Minimally difficult** entrance level

Undergraduates 1,539 full-time, 4,123 part-time. Students come from 12 states and territories, 53 other countries, 2% are from out of state, 7% African American, 5% Asian American or Pacific Islander, 1% Hispanic American, 0.5% Native American, 3% international, 17% transferred in. *Retention:* 51% of 2001 full-time freshmen returned.

Freshmen *Admission:* 167 admitted, 112 enrolled.

Faculty *Total:* 587, 17% full-time, 26% with terminal degrees. *Student/faculty ratio:* 12:1.

Majors Accounting; advertising; alcohol/drug abuse counseling; applied mathematics; biology; business administration; business marketing and marketing management; business systems analysis/design; communications; computer science; criminal justice studies; culinary arts; developmental/child psychology; economics; English; English composition; ethnic/cultural studies related; finance; general studies; history; hospitality management; human resources management; human services; information sciences/systems; international business; law enforcement/police science; liberal arts and sciences/liberal studies; management information systems/business data processing; nursing related; operations management; philosophy; play/screenwriting; psychology; public administration; social sciences; social work; technical/business writing; theater arts/drama; women's studies.

Academic Programs *Special study options:* adult/continuing education programs, double majors, English as a second language, external degree program, independent study, internships, off-campus study, part-time degree program, student-designed majors, summer session for credit.

Metropolitan State University (continued)

Computers on Campus 150 computers available on campus for general student use. A campuswide network can be accessed from off campus. Internet access, at least one staffed computer lab available.

Student Life *Housing:* college housing not available. *Activities and Organizations:* student-run newspaper, Psychology Club, Lavender Bridge, International Student Organization, Voices of Indian Council for Educational Success, Metro Theater Underground. *Campus security:* late-night transport/escort service. *Student Services:* personal/psychological counseling.

Standardized Tests *Required for some:* SAT I or ACT (for admission).

Costs (2001–02) *Tuition:* state resident $2919 full-time, $97 per credit part-time; nonresident $6642 full-time, $221 per credit part-time. Full-time tuition and fees vary according to reciprocity agreements. Part-time tuition and fees vary according to course load and reciprocity agreements. *Required fees:* $192 full-time, $6 per credit. *Payment plan:* installment. *Waivers:* senior citizens and employees or children of employees.

Financial Aid Of all full-time matriculated undergraduates who enrolled in 2001, 700 applied for aid, 600 were judged to have need. 40 State and other part-time jobs (averaging $3000). In 2001, 5 non-need-based awards were made. *Average percent of need met:* 85%. *Average financial aid package:* $12,000. *Average need-based loan:* $4000. *Average need-based gift aid:* $2400. *Average non-need based aid:* $500. *Average indebtedness upon graduation:* $10,000.

Applying *Options:* deferred entrance. *Application fee:* $20. *Required:* high school transcript, minimum 2.0 GPA. *Application deadline:* rolling (freshmen), rolling (transfers). *Notification:* continuous (freshmen).

Admissions Contact Metropolitan State University, 700 East 7th Street, St. Paul, MN 55106-5000. *Phone:* 651-772-7660. *Fax:* 651-772-7572. *E-mail:* admissionsmetro@metrostate.edu.

MINNEAPOLIS COLLEGE OF ART AND DESIGN
Minneapolis, Minnesota

- **Independent** comprehensive, founded 1886
- **Calendar** semesters
- **Degrees** bachelor's, master's, and postbachelor's certificates
- **Urban** 7-acre campus
- **Endowment** $37.4 million
- **Coed,** 591 undergraduate students, 91% full-time, 43% women, 57% men
- **Moderately difficult** entrance level, 80% of applicants were admitted

Located in a culturally supportive city, the Minneapolis College of Art and Design (MCAD) offers a rigorous BFA curriculum that teaches students to think conceptually and creatively and to explore various techniques and technology. In addition, MCAD also offers a BS in visualization, which offers course work in visual persuasion and information techniques. MCAD's facilities are extensive and include individual studio spaces, state-of-the-art computer and media areas, and student galleries.

Undergraduates 539 full-time, 52 part-time. Students come from 30 states and territories, 39% are from out of state, 2% African American, 4% Asian American or Pacific Islander, 2% Hispanic American, 0.7% Native American, 9% transferred in, 45% live on campus. *Retention:* 79% of 2001 full-time freshmen returned.

Freshmen *Admission:* 279 applied, 223 admitted, 98 enrolled. *Average high school GPA:* 3.20. *Test scores:* SAT verbal scores over 500: 70%; SAT math scores over 500: 63%; ACT scores over 18: 89%; SAT verbal scores over 600: 57%; SAT math scores over 600: 25%; ACT scores over 24: 46%; SAT verbal scores over 700: 13%; ACT scores over 30: 3%.

Faculty *Total:* 92, 39% full-time, 29% with terminal degrees. *Student/faculty ratio:* 15:1.

Majors Advertising; drawing; film/video production; fine/studio arts; graphic design/commercial art/illustration; interdisciplinary studies; interior architecture; multimedia; painting; photography; printmaking; sculpture.

Academic Programs *Special study options:* adult/continuing education programs, advanced placement credit, cooperative education, distance learning, independent study, internships, off-campus study, part-time degree program, services for LD students, study abroad, summer session for credit.

Library Minneapolis College of Art and Design Library with 47,166 titles, 196 serial subscriptions, 139,245 audiovisual materials, a Web page.

Computers on Campus 110 computers available on campus for general student use. A campuswide network can be accessed from off campus. Internet access, at least one staffed computer lab available.

Student Life *Housing Options:* coed. *Activities and Organizations:* drama/theater group. *Campus security:* 24-hour emergency response devices and patrols, late-night transport/escort service. *Student Services:* personal/psychological counseling.

Athletics *Intramural sports:* basketball M(c), soccer M(c)/W(c), softball M(c)/W(c).

Standardized Tests *Required:* SAT I or ACT (for admission).

Costs (2001–02) *Tuition:* $20,190 full-time, $673 per credit part-time. *Required fees:* $300 full-time, $4 per term part-time. *Room only:* $3880. Room and board charges vary according to housing facility. *Payment plan:* installment. *Waivers:* children of alumni and employees or children of employees.

Financial Aid Of all full-time matriculated undergraduates who enrolled in 2001, 471 applied for aid, 402 were judged to have need, 42 had their need fully met. 29 State and other part-time jobs (averaging $1850). *Average percent of need met:* 63%. *Average financial aid package:* $11,758. *Average need-based loan:* $4167. *Average need-based gift aid:* $6043. *Average non-need based aid:* $3906. *Average indebtedness upon graduation:* $27,954.

Applying *Options:* common application, early admission, deferred entrance. *Application fee:* $35. *Required:* essay or personal statement, high school transcript, 1 letter of recommendation, interview. *Required for some:* portfolio. *Application deadline:* rolling (freshmen), rolling (transfers). *Notification:* 7/1 (freshmen).

Admissions Contact Mr. Brad Nuorala, Director of Admissions, Minneapolis College of Art and Design, 2501 Stevens Avenue South, Minneapolis, MN 55404-4347. *Phone:* 612-874-3762. *Toll-free phone:* 800-874-6223. *E-mail:* admissions@mn.mcad.edu.

MINNESOTA BIBLE COLLEGE
Rochester, Minnesota

- **Independent** 4-year, founded 1913, affiliated with Christian Churches and Churches of Christ
- **Calendar** semesters
- **Degrees** associate and bachelor's
- **Urban** 40-acre campus with easy access to Minneapolis-St. Paul
- **Endowment** $708,000
- **Coed,** 109 undergraduate students, 83% full-time, 45% women, 55% men
- **Noncompetitive** entrance level, 56% of applicants were admitted

Undergraduates 90 full-time, 19 part-time. Students come from 9 states and territories, 5 other countries, 33% are from out of state, 2% Asian American or Pacific Islander, 2% Hispanic American, 6% international, 8% transferred in, 78% live on campus. *Retention:* 61% of 2001 full-time freshmen returned.

Freshmen *Admission:* 50 applied, 28 admitted, 19 enrolled. *Average high school GPA:* 3.01. *Test scores:* SAT verbal scores over 500: 67%; SAT math scores over 500: 33%; ACT scores over 18: 72%; ACT scores over 24: 39%; ACT scores over 30: 6%.

Faculty *Total:* 20, 45% full-time, 50% with terminal degrees. *Student/faculty ratio:* 8:1.

Majors Biblical studies; counseling psychology; liberal arts and sciences/liberal studies; religious education; religious music; theology.

Academic Programs *Special study options:* academic remediation for entering students, advanced placement credit, double majors, independent study, internships, off-campus study, student-designed majors.

Library G. H. Cachiaras Memorial Library with 34,440 titles, 240 serial subscriptions, 1,294 audiovisual materials.

Computers on Campus 15 computers available on campus for general student use. Internet access available.

Student Life *Housing:* on-campus residence required through senior year. *Options:* men-only, women-only. *Activities and Organizations:* drama/theater group, choral group, Christian Outdoors, Musical Outreach, Ambassadors Mission Group. *Campus security:* student patrols, late-night transport/escort service. *Student Services:* personal/psychological counseling.

Athletics *Intercollegiate sports:* baseball M, basketball M/W, golf M/W, softball W, tennis M/W, volleyball M/W. *Intramural sports:* basketball M/W, field hockey M/W, football M/W, golf M/W, racquetball M/W, skiing (cross-country) M/W, softball M, swimming M/W, tennis M/W, volleyball M/W, weight lifting M/W.

Standardized Tests *Required:* SAT I or ACT (for admission).

Costs (2002–03) *Tuition:* $6900 full-time, $230 per semester hour part-time. Full-time tuition and fees vary according to course load. Part-time tuition and fees vary according to course load. *Required fees:* $110 full-time. *Room only:* $1750. Room and board charges vary according to housing facility. *Payment plan:* installment. *Waivers:* senior citizens and employees or children of employees.

Financial Aid Of all full-time matriculated undergraduates who enrolled in 2001, 97 applied for aid, 78 were judged to have need, 39 had their need fully met. 11 Federal Work-Study jobs (averaging $985). 6 State and other part-time jobs (averaging $1237). In 2001, 14 non-need-based awards were made. *Average percent of need met:* 73%. *Average financial aid package:* $4939. *Average need-based loan:* $3340. *Average need-based gift aid:* $6496. *Average non-need based aid:* $4247. *Average indebtedness upon graduation:* $18,185.

Applying *Options:* deferred entrance. *Application fee:* $30. *Required:* essay or personal statement, high school transcript, 3 letters of recommendation. *Required for some:* interview. *Application deadlines:* 8/15 (freshmen), 8/15 (transfers). *Notification:* continuous until 9/1 (freshmen).

Admissions Contact Mr. Michael Golembiesky, Director of Admissions, Minnesota Bible College, 920 Mayowood Road, SW, Rochester, MN 55902-2382. *Phone:* 507-288-4563 Ext. 313. *Toll-free phone:* 800-456-7651. *Fax:* 507-288-9046. *E-mail:* admissions@mnbc.edu.

MINNESOTA SCHOOL OF BUSINESS

Richfield, Minnesota

- **Proprietary** primarily 2-year, founded 1877
- **Calendar** quarters
- **Degrees** certificates, diplomas, associate, and bachelor's
- **Urban** 3-acre campus with easy access to Minneapolis-St. Paul
- **Coed**
- **Minimally difficult** entrance level

Costs (2001–02) *Tuition:* $10,125 full-time, $225 per credit part-time. Full-time tuition and fees vary according to course load and program.

Applying *Options:* common application. *Application fee:* $50. *Required:* high school transcript, interview. *Required for some:* essay or personal statement.

Admissions Contact Mr. Roger Kuhl, Director of Marketing, Minnesota School of Business, 1401 West 76th Street, Richfield, MN 55430. *Phone:* 612-861-2000 Ext. 712. *Toll-free phone:* 800-752-4223. *Fax:* 612-861-5548. *E-mail:* rkuhl@msbcollege.com.

MINNESOTA STATE UNIVERSITY, MANKATO

Mankato, Minnesota

- **State-supported** comprehensive, founded 1868, part of Minnesota State Colleges and Universities System
- **Calendar** semesters
- **Degrees** associate, bachelor's, master's, and post-master's certificates
- **Small-town** 303-acre campus with easy access to Minneapolis-St. Paul
- **Endowment** $1.5 million
- **Coed,** 11,640 undergraduate students, 89% full-time, 52% women, 48% men
- **Moderately difficult** entrance level, 82% of applicants were admitted

Undergraduates 10,311 full-time, 1,329 part-time. Students come from 39 states and territories, 57 other countries, 13% are from out of state, 1% African American, 1% Asian American or Pacific Islander, 0.7% Hispanic American, 0.2% Native American, 4% international, 9% transferred in, 25% live on campus. *Retention:* 77% of 2001 full-time freshmen returned.

Freshmen *Admission:* 5,402 applied, 4,423 admitted, 2,203 enrolled. *Test scores:* ACT scores over 18: 89%; ACT scores over 24: 25%; ACT scores over 30: 2%.

Faculty *Total:* 600, 76% full-time, 60% with terminal degrees. *Student/faculty ratio:* 23:1.

Majors Accounting; anatomy; anthropology; applied art; Army R.O.T.C./military science; art; art education; art history; astronomy; athletic training/sports medicine; automotive engineering technology; aviation management; behavioral sciences; biochemistry; biological/physical sciences; biological technology; biology; botany; business administration; business marketing and marketing management; ceramic arts; chemistry; child care/development; city/community/regional planning; civil engineering; clothing/textiles; communication disorders; computer engineering; computer engineering technology; computer programming; computer science; construction management; corrections; creative writing; cultural studies; data processing technology; dental hygiene; developmental/child psychology; dietetics; drawing; early childhood education; earth sciences; ecology; economics; education; electrical/electronic engineering technology; electrical engineering; elementary education; English; environmental biology; environmental science; family/consumer studies; fashion design/illustration; finance; fine/studio arts; French; geography; German; graphic design/commercial art/illustration; health education; health science; history; home economics; home economics education; humanities; industrial arts; industrial technology; information sciences/systems; insurance/risk management; interior design; international business; international relations; journalism; law enforcement/police science; liberal arts and sciences/liberal studies; literature; management science; mass communications; mathematics; mechanical engineering; medical technology; microbiology/bacteriology; modern languages; music; music business management/merchandising; music (piano and organ performance); music teacher education; music (voice and choral/opera performance); natural sciences; nursing; nutrition science; philosophy; physical education; physical sciences; physics; physiology; political science; pre-dentistry; pre-engineering; pre-law; pre-medicine; pre-theology; pre-veterinary studies; psychology; public administration; public health; public relations; real estate; recreational therapy; recreation/leisure facilities management; recreation/leisure studies; science education; sculpture; secondary education; social sciences; social studies education; social work; sociology; Spanish; speech-language pathology/audiology; speech/rhetorical studies; sport/fitness administration; theater arts/drama; toxicology; urban studies; wind/percussion instruments; women's studies.

Academic Programs *Special study options:* academic remediation for entering students, accelerated degree program, adult/continuing education programs, advanced placement credit, double majors, English as a second language, honors programs, independent study, internships, off-campus study, part-time degree program, services for LD students, student-designed majors, study abroad, summer session for credit. *ROTC:* Army (b).

Library Memorial Library with 1.1 million titles, 4,396 serial subscriptions, 129,006 audiovisual materials, an OPAC, a Web page.

Computers on Campus 525 computers available on campus for general student use. A campuswide network can be accessed from student residence rooms and from off campus. Internet access, online (class) registration, at least one staffed computer lab available.

Student Life *Housing Options:* coed. *Activities and Organizations:* drama/theater group, student-run newspaper, radio station, choral group, marching band, national fraternities, national sororities. *Campus security:* 24-hour emergency response devices and patrols, student patrols, late-night transport/escort service, Night Owl security program in residence halls, closed circuit cameras in parking lots. *Student Services:* health clinic, personal/psychological counseling, women's center, legal services.

Athletics Member NCAA. All Division II except ice hockey (Division I). *Intercollegiate sports:* baseball M(s), basketball M(s)/W(s), cross-country running M(s)/W(s), football M(s), golf M(s)/W(s), ice hockey M(s)/W(s), soccer W(s), softball W(s), swimming M(s)/W(s), tennis M(s)/W(s), track and field M(s)/W(s), volleyball W(s), wrestling M(s). *Intramural sports:* archery M/W, basketball M/W, bowling M/W, fencing M/W, football M, ice hockey M/W, lacrosse M/W, racquetball M/W, rugby M/W, sailing M/W, skiing (cross-country) M/W, skiing (downhill) M/W, soccer M, softball M/W, swimming M/W, tennis M/W, track and field M/W, volleyball M/W, wrestling M.

Standardized Tests *Required:* ACT (for admission).

Costs (2001–02) *Tuition:* state resident $3050 full-time, $122 per credit part-time; nonresident $6465 full-time, $259 per credit part-time. Full-time tuition and fees vary according to course load and reciprocity agreements. Part-time tuition and fees vary according to course load and reciprocity agreements. *Required fees:* $569 full-time, $23 per credit. *Room and board:* $3677. Room and board charges vary according to board plan. *Payment plan:* installment. *Waivers:* senior citizens and employees or children of employees.

Financial Aid Of all full-time matriculated undergraduates who enrolled in 2001, 6581 applied for aid, 4480 were judged to have need, 1744 had their need fully met. 485 Federal Work-Study jobs (averaging $2885). 464 State and other part-time jobs (averaging $2510). In 2001, 681 non-need-based awards were made. *Average percent of need met:* 86%. *Average financial aid package:* $5320. *Average need-based loan:* $3149. *Average need-based gift aid:* $2928. *Average non-need based aid:* $1361.

Applying *Options:* electronic application, deferred entrance. *Application fee:* $20. *Required:* high school transcript. *Required for some:* essay or personal statement, 3 letters of recommendation. *Application deadline:* rolling (freshmen), rolling (transfers). *Notification:* continuous (freshmen).

Admissions Contact Mr. Walt Wolff, Director of Admissions, Minnesota State University, Mankato, 122 Taylor Center, Mankato, MN 56001. *Phone:* 507-389-6670. *Toll-free phone:* 800-722-0544. *Fax:* 507-389-1511. *E-mail:* admissions@mnsu.edu.

MINNESOTA STATE UNIVERSITY MOORHEAD

Moorhead, Minnesota

- **State-supported** comprehensive, founded 1885, part of Minnesota State Colleges and Universities System
- **Calendar** semesters

Minnesota State University Moorhead (continued)

- **Degrees** associate, bachelor's, master's, and post-master's certificates
- **Urban** 118-acre campus
- **Coed,** 7,048 undergraduate students, 82% full-time, 62% women, 38% men
- **Moderately difficult** entrance level

Undergraduates Students come from 39 states and territories, 25 other countries, 39% are from out of state, 0.5% African American, 0.8% Asian American or Pacific Islander, 1% Hispanic American, 1% Native American, 2% international, 27% live on campus. *Retention:* 68% of 2001 full-time freshmen returned.

Freshmen *Test scores:* ACT scores over 18: 88%; ACT scores over 24: 31%; ACT scores over 30: 2%.

Faculty *Total:* 334, 90% full-time. *Student/faculty ratio:* 18:1.

Majors Accounting; advertising; American studies; anthropology; applied art; archaeology; art; art education; art history; biology; broadcast journalism; business administration; business marketing and marketing management; ceramic arts; chemistry; commercial photography; community health liaison; computer/information sciences; computer science; construction technology; criminal justice studies; cytotechnology; drama/dance education; early childhood education; economics; education of the emotionally handicapped; education of the mentally handicapped; education of the specific learning disabled; elementary education; English; English education; finance; fine/studio arts; foreign languages/literatures; graphic design/commercial art/illustration; health education; health/physical education; health services administration; history; industrial technology; interdisciplinary studies; international business; journalism; liberal arts and sciences/liberal studies; management information systems/business data processing; mass communications; mathematics; mathematics education; medical technology; middle school education; music; music business management/merchandising; music (piano and organ performance); music teacher education; music theory and composition; music (voice and choral/opera performance); nursing; painting; paralegal/legal assistant; philosophy; physical education; physics; political science; pre-dentistry; pre-law; pre-medicine; pre-veterinary studies; printmaking; psychology; public relations; science education; sculpture; secondary education; social studies education; social work; sociology; Spanish; Spanish language education; special education; speech education; speech-language pathology/audiology; speech/rhetorical studies; sport/fitness administration; theater arts/drama; wind/percussion instruments.

Academic Programs *Special study options:* academic remediation for entering students, adult/continuing education programs, advanced placement credit, distance learning, double majors, external degree program, freshman honors college, honors programs, independent study, internships, off-campus study, part-time degree program, services for LD students, student-designed majors, study abroad, summer session for credit. *ROTC:* Army (c), Air Force (c).

Library Livingston Lord Library with 367,334 titles, 1,539 serial subscriptions, an OPAC, a Web page.

Computers on Campus 450 computers available on campus for general student use. A campuswide network can be accessed from student residence rooms and from off campus. Internet access, online (class) registration, at least one staffed computer lab available.

Student Life *Housing Options:* coed, men-only, women-only. *Activities and Organizations:* drama/theater group, student-run newspaper, radio station, choral group, Residence Hall Associations, Campus Activities Board, Pi Sigma Epsilon, Campus Crusade for Christ, Transfer Club, national fraternities, national sororities. *Campus security:* 24-hour emergency response devices and patrols, student patrols, late-night transport/escort service, controlled dormitory access. *Student Services:* health clinic, personal/psychological counseling, women's center.

Athletics Member NCAA. All Division II. *Intercollegiate sports:* basketball M(s)/W(s), cross-country running M/W, football M(s), golf M/W, soccer W(s), softball W(s), tennis W, track and field M(s)/W(s), volleyball W(s), wrestling M(s). *Intramural sports:* archery M/W, badminton M/W, basketball M/W, bowling M/W, football M/W, golf M/W, ice hockey M, racquetball M/W, skiing (cross-country) M/W, soccer M/W, softball W, swimming M/W, tennis W, track and field M/W, volleyball M/W, wrestling M.

Standardized Tests *Required:* SAT I or ACT (for admission).

Costs (2001–02) *Tuition:* state resident $3377 full-time, $117 per credit part-time; nonresident $6936 full-time, $236 per credit part-time. Full-time tuition and fees vary according to reciprocity agreements. Part-time tuition and fees vary according to reciprocity agreements. *Required fees:* $21 per credit hour. *Room and board:* $3706; room only: $2016. Room and board charges vary according to board plan. *Payment plan:* deferred payment. *Waivers:* senior citizens and employees or children of employees.

Financial Aid Of all full-time matriculated undergraduates who enrolled in 2001, 239 Federal Work-Study jobs (averaging $1973). 1471 State and other part-time jobs (averaging $1287). *Average indebtedness upon graduation:* $16,584.

Applying *Options:* early admission, deferred entrance. *Application fee:* $20. *Required:* high school transcript. *Application deadlines:* 8/7 (freshmen), 8/7 (transfers). *Notification:* continuous (freshmen).

Admissions Contact Ms. Gina Monson, Director of Admissions, Minnesota State University Moorhead, Owens Hall, Moorhead, MN 56563-0002. *Phone:* 218-236-2161. *Toll-free phone:* 800-593-7246. *Fax:* 218-236-2168.

NATIONAL AMERICAN UNIVERSITY-ST. PAUL CAMPUS

St. Paul, Minnesota

- **Proprietary** 4-year, founded 1974, part of National American University
- **Calendar** quarters
- **Degrees** diplomas, associate, and bachelor's
- **Urban** 1-acre campus
- **Coed,** 446 undergraduate students, 49% full-time, 48% women, 52% men
- **Noncompetitive** entrance level, 100% of applicants were admitted

Undergraduates 220 full-time, 226 part-time. Students come from 5 states and territories, 18% African American, 16% Asian American or Pacific Islander, 3% Hispanic American, 0.4% Native American, 5% international. *Retention:* 52% of 2001 full-time freshmen returned.

Freshmen *Admission:* 259 applied, 259 admitted, 45 enrolled.

Faculty *Total:* 32, 16% full-time, 22% with terminal degrees. *Student/faculty ratio:* 10:1.

Majors Accounting; business administration; hospitality management; information sciences/systems; management information systems/business data processing.

Academic Programs *Special study options:* academic remediation for entering students, accelerated degree program, advanced placement credit, cooperative education, distance learning, double majors, independent study, internships, part-time degree program, summer session for credit.

Library National College Library plus 1 other with 1,500 titles, 25 serial subscriptions, an OPAC, a Web page.

Computers on Campus Internet access, at least one staffed computer lab available.

Student Life *Housing:* college housing not available. *Activities and Organizations:* student-run newspaper, Southeast Asian Student Organization, Phi Beta Lambda/Lambda Beta Omicron, Student Government Association, International Student Organization. *Campus security:* late-night transport/escort service.

Costs (2001–02) *Tuition:* $8640 full-time, $240 per credit hour part-time. *Required fees:* $105 full-time, $40 per term part-time.

Applying *Options:* common application, deferred entrance. *Application fee:* $25. *Required:* high school transcript. *Required for some:* essay or personal statement. *Recommended:* minimum 2.0 GPA, interview. *Application deadline:* rolling (freshmen), rolling (transfers). *Notification:* continuous (freshmen).

Admissions Contact Mr. Steve Grunlan, Director of Admissions, National American University-St. Paul Campus, 1500 West Highway 36, Roseville, MN. *Phone:* 651-644-1265.

NORTH CENTRAL UNIVERSITY

Minneapolis, Minnesota

- **Independent** 4-year, founded 1930, affiliated with Assemblies of God
- **Calendar** semesters
- **Degrees** certificates, diplomas, associate, and bachelor's
- **Urban** 9-acre campus
- **Endowment** $969,948
- **Coed**
- **Noncompetitive** entrance level

Faculty *Student/faculty ratio:* 18:1.

Student Life *Campus security:* 24-hour emergency response devices and patrols, late-night transport/escort service, controlled dormitory access.

Athletics Member NCCAA.

Standardized Tests *Required:* SAT I or ACT (for admission).

Applying *Options:* common application, deferred entrance. *Application fee:* $25. *Required:* essay or personal statement, high school transcript, minimum 2.2 GPA, letters of recommendation, Christian testimony.

Admissions Contact Ms. Mary Jo Meier, Admissions Secretary, North Central University, 910 Elliot Avenue, Minneapolis, MN 55404. *Phone:* 612-343-4401. *Toll-free phone:* 800-289-6222. *Fax:* 612-343-4146. *E-mail:* admissions@northcentral.edu.

NORTHWESTERN COLLEGE
St. Paul, Minnesota

- **Independent nondenominational** 4-year, founded 1902
- **Calendar** semesters
- **Degrees** certificates, associate, and bachelor's
- **Suburban** 100-acre campus
- **Endowment** $5.0 million
- **Coed,** 2,278 undergraduate students, 79% full-time, 63% women, 37% men
- **Moderately difficult** entrance level, 99% of applicants were admitted

Northwestern Collge is a nondenominational Christian college where students earn an equivalent of a double major in an academic area and the Bible. More than 1,600 students enjoy a Christian community atmosphere, music, athletics, drama, and missions opportunities. Daily chapel services, 44 academic majors, and the Minneapolis-St. Paul location are benefits of NWC.

Undergraduates 1,801 full-time, 477 part-time. Students come from 32 states and territories, 27 other countries, 37% are from out of state, 3% African American, 2% Asian American or Pacific Islander, 1% Hispanic American, 0.2% Native American, 0.6% international, 4% transferred in, 61% live on campus. *Retention:* 78% of 2001 full-time freshmen returned.

Freshmen *Admission:* 742 applied, 733 admitted, 431 enrolled. *Average high school GPA:* 3.48. *Test scores:* SAT verbal scores over 500: 81%; SAT math scores over 500: 75%; ACT scores over 18: 97%; SAT verbal scores over 600: 53%; SAT math scores over 600: 35%; ACT scores over 24: 50%; SAT verbal scores over 700: 12%; SAT math scores over 700: 19%; ACT scores over 30: 6%.

Faculty *Total:* 182, 37% full-time, 40% with terminal degrees. *Student/faculty ratio:* 15:1.

Majors Accounting; art education; athletic training/sports medicine; biblical studies; biology; business administration; business marketing and marketing management; communications; creative writing; criminal justice studies; early childhood education; elementary education; English; English education; finance; fine/studio arts; graphic design/commercial art/illustration; history; international business; journalism; liberal arts and sciences/liberal studies; management information systems/business data processing; mathematics; mathematics education; missionary studies; music; music (general performance); music (piano and organ performance); music teacher education; music (voice and choral/opera performance); organizational behavior; pastoral counseling; physical education; pretheology; psychology; public relations; radio/television broadcasting; religious education; social sciences; social studies education; Spanish; sport/fitness administration; teaching English as a second language; technical/business writing; theater arts/drama; theology/ministry related.

Academic Programs *Special study options:* academic remediation for entering students, adult/continuing education programs, advanced placement credit, distance learning, double majors, English as a second language, independent study, internships, off-campus study, part-time degree program, study abroad, summer session for credit. *ROTC:* Army (c), Air Force (c).

Library Berntsen Resource Center with 74,857 titles, 1,695 serial subscriptions, an OPAC.

Computers on Campus 130 computers available on campus for general student use. A campuswide network can be accessed from off campus. Internet access, online (class) registration, at least one staffed computer lab available.

Student Life *Housing:* on-campus residence required through sophomore year. *Options:* men-only, women-only, disabled students. *Activities and Organizations:* drama/theater group, student-run newspaper, radio station, choral group, NWSA (student government association), Edge (religious group), Transfer Connection, Guardian Angels, Mu Kappa. *Campus security:* 24-hour patrols, late-night transport/escort service, controlled dormitory access. *Student Services:* health clinic, personal/psychological counseling.

Athletics Member NAIA, NCCAA. *Intercollegiate sports:* baseball M, basketball M/W, cross-country running M/W, football M, golf M/W, ice hockey M(c), soccer M/W, softball W, tennis M/W, track and field M/W, volleyball W. *Intramural sports:* badminton M/W, basketball M/W, bowling M/W, cross-country running M/W, football M/W, golf M/W, racquetball M/W, skiing (cross-country) M/W, soccer W, softball M/W, table tennis M/W, tennis M/W, volleyball M/W, weight lifting M/W.

Standardized Tests *Required:* SAT I or ACT (for admission).

Costs (2002–03) *Comprehensive fee:* $21,830 includes full-time tuition ($16,500) and room and board ($5330). Full-time tuition and fees vary according to course load and program. Part-time tuition: $695 per credit. Part-time tuition and fees vary according to program. *Room and board:* College room only: $2830. Room and board charges vary according to board plan. *Payment plan:* installment. *Waivers:* senior citizens and employees or children of employees.

Financial Aid Of all full-time matriculated undergraduates who enrolled in 2001, 1503 applied for aid, 1250 were judged to have need, 118 had their need fully met. 205 Federal Work-Study jobs (averaging $1607). 190 State and other part-time jobs (averaging $1500). In 2001, 251 non-need-based awards were made. *Average percent of need met:* 76%. *Average financial aid package:* $12,025. *Average need-based loan:* $3892. *Average need-based gift aid:* $8386. *Average non-need based aid:* $4367. *Average indebtedness upon graduation:* $16,500. *Financial aid deadline:* 7/1.

Applying *Options:* electronic application, early admission, deferred entrance. *Application fee:* $25. *Required:* essay or personal statement, high school transcript, minimum 2.0 GPA, 2 letters of recommendation, lifestyle agreement, statement of Christian faith. *Required for some:* interview. *Recommended:* minimum 3.0 GPA, interview. *Application deadlines:* 8/1 (freshmen), 8/1 (transfers). *Notification:* continuous until 8/15 (freshmen).

Admissions Contact Mr. Kenneth K. Faffler, Director of Recruitment, Northwestern College, 3003 Snelling Avenue North, Nazareth Hall, Room 229, St. Paul, MN 55113-1598. *Phone:* 651-631-5209. *Toll-free phone:* 800-827-6827. *Fax:* 651-631-5680. *E-mail:* admissions@nwc.edu.

OAK HILLS CHRISTIAN COLLEGE
Bemidji, Minnesota

- **Independent interdenominational** 4-year, founded 1946
- **Calendar** semesters
- **Degrees** certificates, diplomas, associate, and bachelor's
- **Rural** 180-acre campus
- **Endowment** $205,117
- **Coed,** 178 undergraduate students, 85% full-time, 53% women, 47% men
- **Minimally difficult** entrance level, 32% of applicants were admitted

Undergraduates 151 full-time, 27 part-time. Students come from 12 states and territories, 100% are from out of state, 4% African American, 0.6% Asian American or Pacific Islander, 1% Hispanic American, 2% Native American, 20% transferred in, 80% live on campus. *Retention:* 58% of 2001 full-time freshmen returned.

Freshmen *Admission:* 103 applied, 33 admitted, 33 enrolled. *Average high school GPA:* 3.10. *Test scores:* ACT scores over 18: 72%; ACT scores over 24: 12%.

Faculty *Total:* 20, 35% full-time, 35% with terminal degrees. *Student/faculty ratio:* 8:1.

Majors Biblical studies; business administration; liberal arts and sciences/liberal studies; missionary studies; music; psychology; recreation/leisure facilities management; religious music.

Academic Programs *Special study options:* academic remediation for entering students, advanced placement credit, honors programs, independent study, internships, off-campus study, part-time degree program, services for LD students.

Library Cummings Library with 22,343 titles, 144 serial subscriptions, 1,251 audiovisual materials, an OPAC, a Web page.

Computers on Campus 13 computers available on campus for general student use. At least one staffed computer lab available.

Student Life *Housing:* on-campus residence required through sophomore year. *Options:* men-only, women-only. *Activities and Organizations:* choral group, Student Council, Students Older Than Average. *Campus security:* 24-hour emergency response devices, evening patrols by trained security personnel. *Student Services:* health clinic, personal/psychological counseling.

Athletics *Intercollegiate sports:* basketball M, volleyball W. *Intramural sports:* basketball M/W, football M/W, golf M/W, racquetball M/W, soccer M/W, softball M/W, table tennis M/W, tennis M/W, volleyball M/W, weight lifting M/W.

Standardized Tests *Required:* ACT (for admission).

Costs (2001–02) *Comprehensive fee:* $12,860 includes full-time tuition ($9450) and room and board ($3410). Full-time tuition and fees vary according to course load. Part-time tuition: $275 per semester hour. Part-time tuition and fees vary according to course load. *Room and board:* College room only: $1330. Room and board charges vary according to housing facility. *Payment plan:* installment. *Waivers:* employees or children of employees.

Financial Aid Of all full-time matriculated undergraduates who enrolled in 2001, 151 applied for aid, 144 were judged to have need, 12 had their need fully met. 20 Federal Work-Study jobs (averaging $1157). 59 State and other part-time jobs (averaging $2151). *Average percent of need met:* 66%. *Average financial aid package:* $8410. *Average need-based loan:* $3002. *Average need-based gift aid:* $5743. *Average indebtedness upon graduation:* $16,303.

Applying *Options:* deferred entrance. *Application fee:* $20. *Required:* essay or personal statement, high school transcript, 2 letters of recommendation. *Required for some:* minimum 2.0 GPA. *Application deadline:* rolling (freshmen), rolling (transfers). *Notification:* continuous (freshmen).

Oak Hills Christian College (continued)

Admissions Contact Mr. Dan Hovestol, Admissions Director, Oak Hills Christian College, Bemidji, MN 56601. *Phone:* 218-751-8670 Ext. 220. *Toll-free phone:* 888-751-8670 Ext. 285. *Fax:* 218-751-8825. *E-mail:* admissions@oakhill.edu.

PILLSBURY BAPTIST BIBLE COLLEGE

Owatonna, Minnesota

- **Independent Baptist** 4-year, founded 1957
- **Calendar** semesters
- **Degrees** associate and bachelor's
- **Small-town** 14-acre campus with easy access to Minneapolis-St. Paul
- **Endowment** $453,020
- **Coed,** 222 undergraduate students, 90% full-time, 58% women, 42% men
- **Noncompetitive** entrance level, 70% of applicants were admitted

Undergraduates 199 full-time, 23 part-time. Students come from 31 states and territories, 2 other countries, 0.9% African American, 0.5% Asian American or Pacific Islander, 1% Hispanic American, 0.5% Native American, 1% international, 7% transferred in, 83% live on campus. *Retention:* 67% of 2001 full-time freshmen returned.

Freshmen *Admission:* 108 applied, 76 admitted, 79 enrolled. *Test scores:* ACT scores over 18: 75%; ACT scores over 24: 36%; ACT scores over 30: 3%.

Faculty *Total:* 27, 63% full-time, 4% with terminal degrees. *Student/faculty ratio:* 10:1.

Majors Biblical studies; biological/physical sciences; business administration; business education; divinity/ministry; education; elementary education; English; health/physical education; history; music; music teacher education; pastoral counseling; religious education; religious music; science education; secondary education; secretarial science; speech/rhetorical studies.

Academic Programs *Special study options:* academic remediation for entering students, accelerated degree program, adult/continuing education programs, advanced placement credit, internships, part-time degree program, services for LD students, student-designed majors, summer session for credit.

Library Pillsbury College Library with 55,000 titles, 280 serial subscriptions.

Computers on Campus 27 computers available on campus for general student use. At least one staffed computer lab available.

Student Life *Housing:* on-campus residence required through senior year. *Options:* men-only, women-only. *Activities and Organizations:* drama/theater group, student-run newspaper, choral group. *Campus security:* student patrols. *Student Services:* personal/psychological counseling.

Athletics Member NCCAA. *Intercollegiate sports:* baseball M, basketball M/W, golf M/W, soccer M, softball W, volleyball W. *Intramural sports:* basketball M/W, football M, table tennis M/W, volleyball M/W.

Standardized Tests *Required:* ACT (for admission).

Costs (2002–03) *Comprehensive fee:* $11,120 includes full-time tuition ($6240), mandatory fees ($1440), and room and board ($3440). Part-time tuition: $195 per credit hour. *Required fees:* $876 per year part-time.

Financial Aid Of all full-time matriculated undergraduates who enrolled in 2001, 162 applied for aid, 97 were judged to have need. In 2001, 22 non-need-based awards were made. *Average percent of need met:* 50%. *Average financial aid package:* $5030. *Average non-need based aid:* $1200.

Applying *Options:* deferred entrance. *Application fee:* $25. *Required:* essay or personal statement, high school transcript, 2 letters of recommendation, 2 photographs. *Recommended:* interview. *Application deadlines:* 9/1 (freshmen), 9/1 (transfers). *Notification:* continuous until 9/4 (freshmen).

Admissions Contact Mr. Gene Young, Director of Admissions, Pillsbury Baptist Bible College, 315 South Grove, Owatonna, MN 55060-3097. *Phone:* 507-451-2710 Ext. 279. *Toll-free phone:* 800-747-4557. *Fax:* 507-451-6459.

ST. CLOUD STATE UNIVERSITY

St. Cloud, Minnesota

- **State-supported** comprehensive, founded 1869, part of Minnesota State Colleges and Universities System
- **Calendar** semesters
- **Degrees** certificates, diplomas, associate, bachelor's, master's, doctoral, postbachelor's, and first professional certificates
- **Suburban** 108-acre campus with easy access to Minneapolis-St. Paul
- **Endowment** $19.8 million
- **Coed,** 14,714 undergraduate students, 81% full-time, 54% women, 46% men
- **Moderately difficult** entrance level, 84% of applicants were admitted

Undergraduates 11,885 full-time, 2,829 part-time. Students come from 50 states and territories, 77 other countries, 12% are from out of state, 0.9% African American, 1% Asian American or Pacific Islander, 0.6% Hispanic American, 0.5% Native American, 5% international, 10% transferred in, 19% live on campus. *Retention:* 71% of 2001 full-time freshmen returned.

Freshmen *Admission:* 5,312 applied, 4,468 admitted, 2,427 enrolled. *Test scores:* ACT scores over 18: 83%; ACT scores over 24: 25%; ACT scores over 30: 2%.

Faculty *Total:* 733, 83% full-time, 70% with terminal degrees. *Student/faculty ratio:* 20:1.

Majors Accounting; acting/directing; actuarial science; adapted physical education; advertising; aircraft pilot (professional); air traffic control; alcohol/drug abuse counseling; American studies; anthropology; applied art; art; art education; art history; atmospheric sciences; aviation management; behavioral sciences; biological technology; biology; biomedical science; botany; broadcast journalism; business administration; business marketing and marketing management; ceramic arts; chemistry; child care/development; city/community/regional planning; comparative literature; computer engineering; computer science; corrections; counselor education/guidance; creative writing; criminal justice/law enforcement administration; criminology; drawing; early childhood education; earth sciences; ecology; economics; education; education administration; educational media design; education (K-12); electrical/electronic engineering technology; electrical engineering; elementary education; engineering; engineering-related technology; engineering technology; English; environmental biology; exercise sciences; film studies; finance; fine/studio arts; French; genetics; geography; German; gerontology; graphic design/commercial art/illustration; health education; history; human resources management; industrial arts; industrial/manufacturing engineering; information sciences/systems; insurance/risk management; interdisciplinary studies; international business; international relations; journalism; Latin American studies; liberal arts and sciences/liberal studies; library science; linguistics; marketing operations; mass communications; mathematical statistics; mathematics; mechanical engineering; medical technology; mental health/rehabilitation; microbiology/bacteriology; middle school education; music; music history; music teacher education; music (voice and choral/opera performance); natural sciences; nuclear medical technology; nursing; optical technician; philosophy; physical education; physical sciences; physical therapy; physics; physiology; political science; pre-law; pre-medicine; pre-veterinary studies; psychoanalysis; psychology; public administration; public policy analysis; public relations; radio/television broadcasting; reading education; real estate; science education; secondary education; social sciences; social work; sociology; Spanish; special education; speech-language pathology/audiology; speech/rhetorical studies; speech/theater education; speech therapy; theater arts/drama; tourism promotion operations; travel/tourism management; urban studies; wildlife biology; zoology.

Academic Programs *Special study options:* academic remediation for entering students, accelerated degree program, adult/continuing education programs, advanced placement credit, double majors, English as a second language, freshman honors college, honors programs, independent study, internships, off-campus study, part-time degree program, services for LD students, student-designed majors, study abroad, summer session for credit. *ROTC:* Army (b).

Library Miller Learning Center with 622,316 titles, 8,324 serial subscriptions, 28,148 audiovisual materials, an OPAC, a Web page.

Computers on Campus 1045 computers available on campus for general student use. A campuswide network can be accessed from student residence rooms and from off campus. Online (class) registration, at least one staffed computer lab available.

Student Life *Housing Options:* coed. *Activities and Organizations:* drama/theater group, student-run newspaper, radio and television station, choral group, American Marketing Association, Z Club, Residence Hall Association, university program committees, national fraternities, national sororities. *Campus security:* 24-hour emergency response devices and patrols, late-night transport/escort service. *Student Services:* health clinic, personal/psychological counseling, women's center.

Athletics Member NCAA. All Division II except ice hockey (Division I). *Intercollegiate sports:* baseball M, basketball M(s)/W(s), bowling M(c)/W(c), crew M(c)/W(c), cross-country running M(s)/W, fencing M(c)/W(c), football M(s), golf M/W, ice hockey M(s)/W, rugby M(c)/W(c), skiing (cross-country) M(c)/W(c), skiing (downhill) M(c)/W(c), soccer M(c)/W(s), softball W, swimming M(s)/W(s), tennis M/W, track and field M(s)/W(s), volleyball M(c)/W(s), wrestling M(s). *Intramural sports:* badminton M/W, baseball M, basketball M/W, bowling M/W, crew M/W, field hockey M/W, football M/W, ice hockey M/W, lacrosse M/W, racquetball M/W, rugby W, sailing M/W, soccer M/W, softball W, squash M/W, swimming M/W, tennis M/W, volleyball M/W, water polo M/W, weight lifting M/W, wrestling M.

Standardized Tests *Required:* ACT (for admission).

Costs (2001–02) *Tuition:* state resident $3385 full-time, $102 per credit part-time; nonresident $6648 full-time, $222 per credit part-time. Full-time tuition and fees vary according to course load, location, and reciprocity agreements. Part-time tuition and fees vary according to course load, location, and reciprocity agreements. *Required fees:* $498 full-time, $20 per credit. *Room and board:* $3614; room only: $2324. Room and board charges vary according to board plan and housing facility. *Payment plan:* deferred payment. *Waivers:* senior citizens and employees or children of employees.

Financial Aid Of all full-time matriculated undergraduates who enrolled in 2001, 7975 applied for aid, 5393 were judged to have need, 5393 had their need fully met. In 2001, 2582 non-need-based awards were made. *Average percent of need met:* 96%. *Average financial aid package:* $6097. *Average need-based loan:* $2521. *Average need-based gift aid:* $2652. *Average indebtedness upon graduation:* $14,864.

Applying *Options:* electronic application, early admission, deferred entrance. *Application fee:* $20. *Required:* high school transcript. *Required for some:* letters of recommendation. *Application deadlines:* 7/31 (freshmen), 8/1 (transfers). *Notification:* continuous (freshmen).

Admissions Contact Ms. Debbie Tamte-Horan, Director of Admissions, St. Cloud State University, 720 4th Avenue South, St. Cloud, MN 56301-4498. *Phone:* 320-255-2286. *Toll-free phone:* 877-654-7278. *Fax:* 320-255-2243. *E-mail:* scsu4u@stcloudstate.edu.

SAINT JOHN'S UNIVERSITY
Collegeville, Minnesota

- **Independent Roman Catholic** comprehensive, founded 1857
- **Calendar** 4-1-4
- **Degrees** bachelor's, master's, and first professional (Coordinate with College of Saint Benedicts for women)
- **Rural** 2400-acre campus with easy access to Minneapolis-St. Paul
- **Endowment** $103.4 million
- **Coed,** 1,888 undergraduate students, 98% full-time, 100% men
- **Moderately difficult** entrance level, 85% of applicants were admitted

Undergraduates 1,853 full-time, 35 part-time. Students come from 31 states and territories, 21 other countries, 14% are from out of state, 0.2% African American, 2% Asian American or Pacific Islander, 1% Hispanic American, 0.3% Native American, 3% international, 2% transferred in, 78% live on campus. *Retention:* 92% of 2001 full-time freshmen returned.

Freshmen *Admission:* 502 enrolled. *Average high school GPA:* 3.53. *Test scores:* SAT verbal scores over 500: 86%; SAT math scores over 500: 92%; ACT scores over 18: 100%; SAT verbal scores over 600: 42%; SAT math scores over 600: 56%; ACT scores over 24: 68%; SAT verbal scores over 700: 9%; SAT math scores over 700: 17%; ACT scores over 30: 11%.

Faculty *Total:* 198, 79% full-time, 78% with terminal degrees. *Student/faculty ratio:* 11:1.

Majors Accounting; art; art education; art history; biochemistry; biology; business administration; chemistry; classics; computer science; dietetics; economics; education; elementary education; English; fine/studio arts; forestry; French; German; history; humanities; mathematics; mathematics/computer science; music; music teacher education; natural sciences; nursing; nutrition science; occupational therapy; peace/conflict studies; philosophy; physical therapy; physics; political science; pre-dentistry; pre-law; pre-medicine; pre-pharmacy studies; pre-theology; pre-veterinary studies; psychology; religious education; secondary education; social sciences; social work; sociology; Spanish; speech/rhetorical studies; theater arts/drama; theology.

Academic Programs *Special study options:* accelerated degree program, advanced placement credit, double majors, English as a second language, honors programs, independent study, internships, off-campus study, services for LD students, student-designed majors, study abroad. *ROTC:* Army (b). *Unusual degree programs:* 3-2 engineering with University of Minnesota, Washington University in St. Louis.

Library Alcuin Library plus 2 others with 726,844 titles, 8,564 serial subscriptions, 18,824 audiovisual materials, an OPAC, a Web page.

Computers on Campus 350 computers available on campus for general student use. A campuswide network can be accessed from student residence rooms and from off campus. Internet access, online (class) registration, at least one staffed computer lab available.

Student Life *Housing:* on-campus residence required through sophomore year. *Options:* men-only. *Activities and Organizations:* drama/theater group, student-run newspaper, radio station, choral group, Volunteers in Service to Others, Joint Events Council, Cultural Affairs Board, Students in Free Enterprise, ultimate Frisbee. *Campus security:* 24-hour emergency response devices and patrols, late-night transport/escort service, well-lit pathways, 911 center on campus, closed circuit TV monitors. *Student Services:* health clinic, personal/psychological counseling.

Athletics Member NCAA. All Division III. *Intercollegiate sports:* baseball M, basketball M, crew M(c), cross-country running M, football M, golf M, ice hockey M, lacrosse M(c), riflery M(c), rugby M(c), skiing (cross-country) M, soccer M, swimming M, tennis M, track and field M, volleyball M(c), water polo M(c), wrestling M. *Intramural sports:* badminton M, basketball M, fencing M(c), football M, ice hockey M, racquetball M, skiing (cross-country) M(c), skiing (downhill) M(c), soccer M, softball M, volleyball M.

Standardized Tests *Required:* SAT I or ACT (for admission).

Costs (2001–02) *Comprehensive fee:* $23,931 includes full-time tuition ($18,015), mandatory fees ($310), and room and board ($5606). Part-time tuition: $750 per credit. *Required fees:* $155 per term part-time. *Room and board:* College room only: $2593. Room and board charges vary according to board plan and housing facility. *Payment plans:* tuition prepayment, installment, deferred payment.

Financial Aid Of all full-time matriculated undergraduates who enrolled in 2001, 1759 applied for aid, 1097 were judged to have need, 767 had their need fully met. 238 Federal Work-Study jobs (averaging $1680). In 2001, 532 non-need-based awards were made. *Average percent of need met:* 80%. *Average financial aid package:* $16,168. *Average need-based loan:* $4313. *Average need-based gift aid:* $7662. *Average non-need based aid:* $4827. *Average indebtedness upon graduation:* $18,835.

Applying *Options:* common application, electronic application, early admission, deferred entrance. *Application fee:* $25. *Required:* essay or personal statement, high school transcript. *Required for some:* 3 letters of recommendation. *Recommended:* minimum 3.0 GPA, interview. *Application deadline:* rolling (freshmen), rolling (transfers). *Notification:* continuous (freshmen).

Admissions Contact Ms. Mary Milbert, Dean of Admissions, Saint John's University, PO Box 7155, Collegeville, MN 56321-7155. *Phone:* 320-363-2196. *Toll-free phone:* 800-24JOHNS. *Fax:* 320-363-3206. *E-mail:* admissions@csbsju.edu.

SAINT MARY'S UNIVERSITY OF MINNESOTA
Winona, Minnesota

- **Independent Roman Catholic** comprehensive, founded 1912
- **Calendar** semesters
- **Degrees** certificates, bachelor's, master's, doctoral, post-master's, and postbachelor's certificates
- **Small-town** 350-acre campus
- **Endowment** $23.0 million
- **Coed,** 1,621 undergraduate students, 82% full-time, 54% women, 46% men
- **Moderately difficult** entrance level, 86% of applicants were admitted

Undergraduates 1,336 full-time, 285 part-time. Students come from 27 states and territories, 18 other countries, 38% are from out of state, 1% African American, 1% Asian American or Pacific Islander, 1% Hispanic American, 0.2% Native American, 1% international, 3% transferred in, 85% live on campus. *Retention:* 77% of 2001 full-time freshmen returned.

Freshmen *Admission:* 1,055 applied, 910 admitted, 397 enrolled. *Average high school GPA:* 3.10. *Test scores:* ACT scores over 18: 95%; ACT scores over 24: 40%; ACT scores over 30: 5%.

Faculty *Total:* 146, 72% full-time, 58% with terminal degrees. *Student/faculty ratio:* 14:1.

Majors Accounting; biological specializations related; biology; biophysics; business; business administration; business management/administrative services related; business marketing and marketing management; chemical and atomic/molecular physics; chemistry; chemistry education; communications technologies related; computer/information sciences related; computer science; criminal justice/law enforcement administration; cytotechnology; early childhood education; engineering physics; English; English education; fine/studio arts; French; French language education; graphic design/commercial art/illustration; health services administration; history; history related; human resources management; individual/family development related; industrial technology; information sciences/systems; international business; journalism; journalism and mass communication related; law enforcement/police science; mathematics; mathematics/computer science; mathematics education; medical technology; music; music business management/merchandising; music (general performance); music related; music teacher education; nuclear medical technology; pastoral counseling; philosophy; physical therapy; physics education; political science; psychology; public administration; public relations; science education; social science education; social sciences; social sciences and history related; sociology; Spanish; Spanish language education; theater arts/drama; theology.

Saint Mary's University of Minnesota (continued)

Academic Programs *Special study options:* academic remediation for entering students, accelerated degree program, adult/continuing education programs, advanced placement credit, double majors, English as a second language, honors programs, independent study, internships, off-campus study, part-time degree program, services for LD students, student-designed majors, study abroad, summer session for credit.

Library Fitzgerald Library with 160,712 titles, 1,650 serial subscriptions, 8,952 audiovisual materials, an OPAC, a Web page.

Computers on Campus 356 computers available on campus for general student use. A campuswide network can be accessed from student residence rooms and from off campus. Internet access, at least one staffed computer lab available.

Student Life *Housing:* on-campus residence required through sophomore year. *Options:* coed, men-only, women-only. *Activities and Organizations:* drama/theater group, student-run newspaper, radio station, choral group, Student Activity Committee, Good Times Committee (chapter of BACCHUS), Volunteers in Service to Others, Serving Others United in Love (Soul), concert choir/chamber singers, national fraternities, national sororities. *Campus security:* 24-hour emergency response devices and patrols, late-night transport/escort service, controlled dormitory access. *Student Services:* health clinic, personal/psychological counseling, women's center.

Athletics Member NCAA. All Division III. *Intercollegiate sports:* baseball M, basketball M/W, cross-country running M/W, golf M/W, ice hockey M/W, skiing (cross-country) M/W, soccer M/W, softball W, swimming M/W, tennis M/W, track and field M/W, volleyball W. *Intramural sports:* basketball M/W, field hockey M/W, football M/W, ice hockey M, lacrosse M(c)/W(c), rugby M(c)/W(c), skiing (downhill) M(c)/W(c), soccer M/W, softball M/W, tennis M/W, volleyball W, water polo M(c)/W(c).

Standardized Tests *Required:* SAT I or ACT (for admission).

Costs (2001–02) *One-time required fee:* $100. *Comprehensive fee:* $19,975 includes full-time tuition ($14,830), mandatory fees ($365), and room and board ($4780). Part-time tuition: $495 per credit. *Room and board:* Room and board charges vary according to housing facility. *Payment plan:* installment. *Waivers:* employees or children of employees.

Applying *Options:* common application, electronic application, early admission, deferred entrance. *Application fee:* $25. *Required:* essay or personal statement, high school transcript, minimum 2.5 GPA. *Required for some:* interview. *Recommended:* 2 letters of recommendation. *Application deadline:* 5/1 (freshmen), rolling (transfers). *Notification:* continuous (freshmen).

Admissions Contact Mr. Anthony M. Piscitiello, Vice President for Admission, Saint Mary's University of Minnesota, Winona, MN 55987-1399. *Phone:* 507-457-1700. *Toll-free phone:* 800-635-5987. *Fax:* 507-457-1722. *E-mail:* admissions@smumn.edu.

ST. OLAF COLLEGE

Northfield, Minnesota

- **Independent Lutheran** 4-year, founded 1874
- **Calendar** 4-1-4
- **Degree** bachelor's
- **Small-town** 350-acre campus with easy access to Minneapolis-St. Paul
- **Endowment** $156.6 million
- **Coed,** 3,011 undergraduate students, 98% full-time, 58% women, 42% men
- **Very difficult** entrance level, 76% of applicants were admitted

Undergraduates 2,941 full-time, 70 part-time. Students come from 47 states and territories, 20 other countries, 46% are from out of state, 1.0% African American, 3% Asian American or Pacific Islander, 1% Hispanic American, 0.2% Native American, 1% international, 1% transferred in, 96% live on campus. *Retention:* 93% of 2001 full-time freshmen returned.

Freshmen *Admission:* 2,463 applied, 1,882 admitted, 745 enrolled. *Average high school GPA:* 3.71. *Test scores:* SAT verbal scores over 500: 95%; SAT math scores over 500: 96%; ACT scores over 18: 99%; SAT verbal scores over 600: 66%; SAT math scores over 600: 64%; ACT scores over 24: 85%; SAT verbal scores over 700: 19%; SAT math scores over 700: 16%; ACT scores over 30: 24%.

Faculty *Total:* 322, 61% full-time, 73% with terminal degrees. *Student/faculty ratio:* 13:1.

Majors American studies; art; art history; Asian studies; biology; chemistry; classics; cultural studies; dance; economics; English; environmental science; ethnic/cultural studies related; French; German; Greek (ancient and medieval); Hispanic-American studies; history; individual/family development; Latin (ancient and medieval); liberal arts and sciences/liberal studies; mathematics; multi/interdisciplinary studies related; music; music (general performance); musicology; music related; music teacher education; nursing; philosophy; physics; political science; psychology; religious studies; Russian; Russian/Slavic studies; Scandinavian languages; social studies education; social work; sociology; Spanish; theater arts/drama; visual/performing arts; women's studies.

Academic Programs *Special study options:* academic remediation for entering students, accelerated degree program, adult/continuing education programs, advanced placement credit, double majors, English as a second language, independent study, internships, off-campus study, part-time degree program, services for LD students, student-designed majors, study abroad, summer session for credit. *Unusual degree programs:* 3-2 engineering with Washington University in St. Louis.

Library Rolvaag Memorial Library plus 3 others with 521,383 titles, 1,805 serial subscriptions, 13,476 audiovisual materials, an OPAC, a Web page.

Computers on Campus 1100 computers available on campus for general student use. A campuswide network can be accessed from student residence rooms. Internet access, at least one staffed computer lab available.

Student Life *Housing:* on-campus residence required through senior year. *Options:* coed, disabled students. *Activities and Organizations:* drama/theater group, student-run newspaper, radio station, choral group, Student Congregation, Student Government Association, Fellowship of Christian Athletes, Alpha Phi Omega, Habitat for Humanity. *Campus security:* 24-hour emergency response devices and patrols, late-night transport/escort service, controlled dormitory access. *Student Services:* health clinic, personal/psychological counseling, women's center.

Athletics Member NCAA. All Division III. *Intercollegiate sports:* baseball M, basketball M/W, cross-country running M/W, football M, golf M/W, ice hockey M/W, skiing (cross-country) M/W, skiing (downhill) M/W, soccer M/W, softball W, swimming M/W, tennis M/W, track and field M/W, volleyball W, wrestling M. *Intramural sports:* badminton M/W, basketball M/W, football M/W, lacrosse M(c)/W(c), racquetball M/W, skiing (cross-country) M/W, skiing (downhill) M/W, soccer M/W, softball M/W, swimming M/W, table tennis M/W, tennis M/W, volleyball M/W, water polo M/W.

Standardized Tests *Required:* SAT I or ACT (for admission).

Costs (2002–03) *Comprehensive fee:* $26,950 includes full-time tuition ($22,200) and room and board ($4750). Part-time tuition: $695 per credit hour. *Room and board:* College room only: $2200. Room and board charges vary according to board plan. *Payment plans:* tuition prepayment, installment. *Waivers:* adult students, senior citizens, and employees or children of employees.

Financial Aid Of all full-time matriculated undergraduates who enrolled in 2001, 2619 applied for aid, 1785 were judged to have need, 1775 had their need fully met. 971 Federal Work-Study jobs (averaging $1835). 1066 State and other part-time jobs (averaging $1511). In 2001, 600 non-need-based awards were made. *Average percent of need met:* 100%. *Average financial aid package:* $16,354. *Average need-based loan:* $4545. *Average need-based gift aid:* $11,562. *Average non-need based aid:* $4518. *Average indebtedness upon graduation:* $15,490.

Applying *Options:* common application, electronic application, early decision, early action, deferred entrance. *Application fee:* $35. *Required:* essay or personal statement, high school transcript, minimum 3.0 GPA, 2 letters of recommendation. *Recommended:* interview. *Application deadline:* rolling (freshmen), rolling (transfers). *Early decision:* 11/15. *Notification:* continuous (freshmen), 12/15 (early decision), 2/1 (early action).

Admissions Contact Jeff McLaughlin, Acting Director of Admissions, St. Olaf College, 1520 St. Olaf Avenue, Northfield, MN 55057. *Phone:* 507-646-3025. *Toll-free phone:* 800-800-3025. *Fax:* 507-646-3832. *E-mail:* admiss@stolaf.edu.

SOUTHWEST STATE UNIVERSITY

Marshall, Minnesota

- **State-supported** comprehensive, founded 1963, part of Minnesota State Colleges and Universities System
- **Calendar** semesters
- **Degrees** associate, bachelor's, and master's
- **Small-town** 216-acre campus
- **Endowment** $5.4 million
- **Coed,** 4,408 undergraduate students, 50% full-time, 60% women, 40% men
- **Minimally difficult** entrance level, 52% of applicants were admitted

Undergraduates 2,224 full-time, 2,184 part-time. Students come from 26 states and territories, 27 other countries, 20% are from out of state, 0.8% African American, 0.7% Asian American or Pacific Islander, 0.3% Hispanic American, 0.2% Native American, 3% international, 5% transferred in, 53% live on campus. *Retention:* 86% of 2001 full-time freshmen returned.

Freshmen *Admission:* 1,078 applied, 563 admitted, 515 enrolled. *Average high school GPA:* 3.1. *Test scores:* ACT scores over 18: 91%; ACT scores over 24: 27%; ACT scores over 30: 2%.

Faculty *Total:* 156, 83% full-time, 59% with terminal degrees. *Student/faculty ratio:* 18:1.

Majors Accounting; agricultural business; agronomy/crop science; art; art education; biology; biology education; business administration; business marketing and marketing management; chemistry; chemistry education; communications; computer science; creative writing; criminal justice studies; drama/dance education; early childhood education; education; elementary education; English; English education; environmental science; fine/studio arts; health education; health/physical education; history; interdisciplinary studies; literature; mathematics; mathematics education; music; music teacher education; philosophy; physical education; physical sciences; political science; pre-dentistry; pre-law; pre-medicine; pre-veterinary studies; psychology; public administration; radio/television broadcasting; secondary education; social work; sociology; Spanish; speech education; speech/theater education; theater arts/drama.

Academic Programs *Special study options:* academic remediation for entering students, accelerated degree program, adult/continuing education programs, advanced placement credit, distance learning, double majors, external degree program, freshman honors college, honors programs, independent study, internships, off-campus study, part-time degree program, services for LD students, student-designed majors, study abroad, summer session for credit.

Library Southwest State University with 188,861 titles, 748 serial subscriptions, 9,819 audiovisual materials, an OPAC, a Web page.

Computers on Campus 350 computers available on campus for general student use. A campuswide network can be accessed from student residence rooms and from off campus. Internet access, online (class) registration, at least one staffed computer lab available.

Student Life *Housing Options:* coed, men-only, women-only. *Activities and Organizations:* drama/theater group, student-run newspaper, radio and television station, choral group, marching band. *Campus security:* 24-hour emergency response devices and patrols, student patrols, late-night transport/escort service. *Student Services:* health clinic, personal/psychological counseling, women's center.

Athletics Member NCAA. All Division II. *Intercollegiate sports:* baseball M(s), basketball M(s)/W(s), football M(s), golf W(s), soccer W(s), softball W(s), tennis W(s), volleyball W(s), wrestling M(s). *Intramural sports:* badminton M/W, basketball M/W, football M, ice hockey M, racquetball M/W, softball M/W, tennis M/W, volleyball M/W.

Standardized Tests *Required:* SAT I or ACT (for admission).

Costs (2001–02) *Tuition:* state resident $3067 full-time, $102 per credit part-time; nonresident $3067 full-time, $102 per credit part-time. Full-time tuition and fees vary according to course load, location, and reciprocity agreements. Part-time tuition and fees vary according to course load, location, and reciprocity agreements. *Required fees:* $649 full-time, $26 per credit. *Room and board:* $3934; room only: $2710. Room and board charges vary according to board plan and housing facility. *Payment plans:* installment, deferred payment. *Waivers:* senior citizens and employees or children of employees.

Financial Aid Of all full-time matriculated undergraduates who enrolled in 2001, 1773 applied for aid, 1560 were judged to have need, 858 had their need fully met. In 2001, 289 non-need-based awards were made. *Average percent of need met:* 80%. *Average financial aid package:* $4162. *Average need-based loan:* $2718. *Average need-based gift aid:* $2846. *Average non-need based aid:* $1689. *Average indebtedness upon graduation:* $12,080.

Applying *Options:* common application, electronic application, early admission, deferred entrance. *Application fee:* $20. *Required:* essay or personal statement, high school transcript. *Application deadline:* rolling (freshmen), rolling (transfers).

Admissions Contact Richard Shearer, Director of Enrollment Services, Southwest State University, 1501 State Street, Marshall, MN 56258-1598. *Phone:* 507-537-6286. *Toll-free phone:* 800-642-0684. *Fax:* 507-537-7154. *E-mail:* shearerr@southwest.msus.edu.

UNIVERSITY OF MINNESOTA, CROOKSTON
Crookston, Minnesota

- **State-supported** 4-year, founded 1966, part of University of Minnesota System
- **Calendar** semesters
- **Degrees** associate and bachelor's
- **Rural** 95-acre campus
- **Endowment** $4.3 million
- **Coed,** 2,529 undergraduate students, 44% full-time, 56% women, 44% men
- **Moderately difficult** entrance level, 88% of applicants were admitted

Undergraduates 1,108 full-time, 1,421 part-time. Students come from 21 states and territories, 18 other countries, 5% transferred in. *Retention:* 65% of 2001 full-time freshmen returned.

Freshmen *Admission:* 529 applied, 467 admitted, 269 enrolled.

Faculty *Student/faculty ratio:* 18:1.

Majors Accounting; agricultural business; agricultural sciences; agronomy/crop science; aircraft pilot (professional); animal sciences; aviation technology; business administration; child care/development; dietetics; early childhood education; environmental science; equestrian studies; food products retailing; horticulture science; hospitality management; hotel and restaurant management; information sciences/systems; interdisciplinary studies; liberal arts and sciences/liberal studies; natural resources conservation; natural resources management; retail management; soil conservation; wildlife management.

Academic Programs *Special study options:* academic remediation for entering students, adult/continuing education programs, advanced placement credit, internships, part-time degree program, services for LD students, summer session for credit. *ROTC:* Air Force (c).

Library 30,000 titles, 700 serial subscriptions.

Computers on Campus 900 computers available on campus for general student use. A campuswide network can be accessed from student residence rooms and from off campus. At least one staffed computer lab available.

Student Life *Housing Options:* coed. *Activities and Organizations:* drama/theater group, choral group. *Campus security:* student patrols, controlled dormitory access. *Student Services:* health clinic, personal/psychological counseling.

Athletics Member NCAA. All Division II. *Intercollegiate sports:* baseball M(s), basketball M(s)/W(s), football M(s), golf M(s)/W, ice hockey M(s), soccer W(s), softball W(s), tennis W(s), volleyball W(s). *Intramural sports:* basketball M/W, football M, racquetball M/W, softball M/W, table tennis M, tennis M/W, volleyball M/W.

Standardized Tests *Required:* ACT (for admission).

Costs (2002–03) *Tuition:* $161 per credit part-time; state resident $5116 full-time, $161 per credit part-time; nonresident $5116 full-time. Full-time tuition and fees vary according to reciprocity agreements. Part-time tuition and fees vary according to course load. No tuition increase for student's term of enrollment. *Required fees:* $1306 full-time. *Room and board:* $4464. Room and board charges vary according to board plan and housing facility. *Payment plan:* installment. *Waivers:* senior citizens.

Financial Aid Of all full-time matriculated undergraduates who enrolled in 2001, 821 applied for aid, 681 were judged to have need, 309 had their need fully met. In 2001, 51 non-need-based awards were made. *Average percent of need met:* 87%. *Average financial aid package:* $8069. *Average need-based loan:* $4163. *Average need-based gift aid:* $4453. *Average non-need based aid:* $1982.

Applying *Options:* common application, electronic application, deferred entrance. *Required:* high school transcript. *Application deadlines:* 8/1 (freshmen), 8/1 (transfers). *Notification:* 8/15 (freshmen).

Admissions Contact Mr. Russell L. Kreager, Director of Admissions, University of Minnesota, Crookston, 2900 University Avenue, 170 Owen Hall, Crookston, MN 56716-5001. *Phone:* 218-281-8569. *Toll-free phone:* 800-232-6466. *Fax:* 218-281-8575. *E-mail:* info@mail.crk.umn.edu.

UNIVERSITY OF MINNESOTA, DULUTH
Duluth, Minnesota

- **State-supported** comprehensive, founded 1947, part of University of Minnesota System
- **Calendar** quarters
- **Degrees** bachelor's, master's, and first professional
- **Suburban** 250-acre campus
- **Endowment** $46.3 million
- **Coed,** 8,774 undergraduate students, 87% full-time, 51% women, 49% men
- **Moderately difficult** entrance level, 79% of applicants were admitted

Undergraduates 7,654 full-time, 1,120 part-time. Students come from 26 states and territories, 36 other countries, 1% African American, 2% Asian American or Pacific Islander, 1% Hispanic American, 1% Native American, 2% international, 5% transferred in, 38% live on campus. *Retention:* 78% of 2001 full-time freshmen returned.

Freshmen *Admission:* 6,339 applied, 5,018 admitted, 2,153 enrolled. *Average high school GPA:* 3.10. *Test scores:* ACT scores over 18: 99%; ACT scores over 24: 35%; ACT scores over 30: 3%.

Faculty *Total:* 445, 78% full-time, 65% with terminal degrees. *Student/faculty ratio:* 20:1.

Majors Accounting; actuarial science; anthropology; art; art education; art history; biochemistry; biology; business administration; business marketing and

University of Minnesota, Duluth (continued)
marketing management; cell biology; chemical engineering; chemistry; computer engineering; computer science; criminology; early childhood education; economics; education; electrical engineering; elementary education; English; environmental science; exercise sciences; finance; fine/studio arts; fish/game management; French language education; geography; geology; German language education; graphic design/commercial art/illustration; health education; history; human resources management; industrial/manufacturing engineering; interdisciplinary studies; international relations; jazz; mathematics; mathematics education; middle school education; molecular biology; music; music (piano and organ performance); music teacher education; Native American studies; philosophy; physical education; physics; political science; pre-dentistry; pre-law; pre-medicine; pre-pharmacy studies; pre-veterinary studies; psychology; recreation/leisure studies; science education; social studies education; sociology; Spanish; Spanish language education; special education; speech-language pathology/audiology; theater arts/drama; urban studies; women's studies.

Academic Programs *Special study options:* academic remediation for entering students, adult/continuing education programs, advanced placement credit, distance learning, double majors, English as a second language, honors programs, independent study, internships, off-campus study, part-time degree program, services for LD students, student-designed majors, study abroad, summer session for credit. *ROTC:* Air Force (b).

Library University of Minnesota Duluth Library plus 1 other with 614,367 titles, 4,500 serial subscriptions, 13,000 audiovisual materials, an OPAC, a Web page.

Computers on Campus 525 computers available on campus for general student use. A campuswide network can be accessed from student residence rooms and from off campus. Internet access, online (class) registration, at least one staffed computer lab available.

Student Life *Housing Options:* coed, men-only, women-only. *Activities and Organizations:* drama/theater group, student-run newspaper, choral group, recreational sports, departmental clubs, outdoor recreation clubs, national fraternities, national sororities. *Campus security:* 24-hour emergency response devices and patrols, late-night transport/escort service. *Student Services:* health clinic, personal/psychological counseling, women's center, legal services.

Athletics Member NCAA. All Division II except men's and women's ice hockey (Division I). *Intercollegiate sports:* baseball M(s), basketball M(s)/W(s), bowling M(c)/W(c), cross-country running M(s)/W(s), football M(s), ice hockey M(s)/W, lacrosse M(c)/W(c), rugby M(c)/W(c), skiing (downhill) M(c)/W(c), soccer M(c)/W(s), softball W(s), tennis M(s)/W(s), track and field M(s)/W(s), volleyball M(c)/W(s), weight lifting M(c)/W(c). *Intramural sports:* basketball M/W, cross-country running M/W, field hockey M/W, football M/W, golf M/W, ice hockey M, riflery M/W, skiing (cross-country) M/W, skiing (downhill) M/W, soccer M/W, softball M/W, swimming M/W, tennis M/W, track and field M/W, volleyball M/W.

Standardized Tests *Required:* SAT I or ACT (for admission).

Costs (2001–02) *Tuition:* state resident $4920 full-time, $164 per credit part-time; nonresident $13,957 full-time, $465 per credit part-time. Full-time tuition and fees vary according to class time and course load. Part-time tuition and fees vary according to class time and course load. *Required fees:* $924 full-time, $462 per term part-time. *Room and board:* $4592. Room and board charges vary according to board plan and housing facility. *Payment plan:* installment. *Waivers:* children of alumni, senior citizens, and employees or children of employees.

Financial Aid Of all full-time matriculated undergraduates who enrolled in 2001, 5271 applied for aid, 3740 were judged to have need, 402 had their need fully met. 192 Federal Work-Study jobs (averaging $1957). 243 State and other part-time jobs (averaging $1898). In 2001, 1547 non-need-based awards were made. *Average percent of need met:* 70%. *Average financial aid package:* $5777. *Average need-based loan:* $2868. *Average need-based gift aid:* $4136. *Average indebtedness upon graduation:* $7063.

Applying *Options:* electronic application. *Application fee:* $25. *Required:* high school transcript. *Application deadlines:* 2/1 (freshmen), 8/1 (transfers). *Notification:* continuous (freshmen).

Admissions Contact Ms. Beth Esselstrom, Director of Admissions, University of Minnesota, Duluth, 23 Solon Campus Center, 1117 University Drive, Duluth, MN 55812-3000. *Phone:* 218-726-7171. *Toll-free phone:* 800-232-1339. *Fax:* 218-726-6394. *E-mail:* umdadmis@d.umn.edu.

UNIVERSITY OF MINNESOTA, MORRIS
Morris, Minnesota

- **State-supported** 4-year, founded 1959, part of University of Minnesota System
- **Calendar** semesters
- **Degree** bachelor's
- **Small-town** 130-acre campus
- **Endowment** $5.6 million
- **Coed,** 1,924 undergraduate students, 95% full-time, 59% women, 41% men
- **Moderately difficult** entrance level, 84% of applicants were admitted

Undergraduates 1,829 full-time, 95 part-time. Students come from 32 states and territories, 15 other countries, 21% are from out of state, 5% African American, 3% Asian American or Pacific Islander, 2% Hispanic American, 7% Native American, 4% transferred in, 49% live on campus. *Retention:* 84% of 2001 full-time freshmen returned.

Freshmen *Admission:* 1,268 applied, 1,064 admitted, 480 enrolled. *Test scores:* SAT verbal scores over 500: 83%; SAT math scores over 500: 78%; ACT scores over 18: 99%; SAT verbal scores over 600: 44%; SAT math scores over 600: 34%; ACT scores over 24: 63%; SAT verbal scores over 700: 12%; SAT math scores over 700: 8%; ACT scores over 30: 15%.

Faculty *Total:* 120, 100% full-time. *Student/faculty ratio:* 14:1.

Majors Art history; biology; business administration; chemistry; computer science; economics; education; education (K-12); elementary education; English; European studies; fine/studio arts; French; geology; German; history; human services; Latin American studies; liberal arts and sciences/liberal studies; management science; mass communications; mathematical statistics; mathematics; music; philosophy; physical therapy; physics; political science; pre-dentistry; pre-law; pre-medicine; pre-pharmacy studies; pre-veterinary studies; psychology; secondary education; social sciences; sociology; Spanish; speech/rhetorical studies; speech/theater education; theater arts/drama; women's studies.

Academic Programs *Special study options:* accelerated degree program, adult/continuing education programs, advanced placement credit, distance learning, double majors, English as a second language, external degree program, freshman honors college, honors programs, internships, off-campus study, part-time degree program, services for LD students, student-designed majors, study abroad, summer session for credit. *Unusual degree programs:* 3-2 engineering with University of Minnesota, Twin Cities Campus.

Library Rodney A. Briggs Library plus 1 other with 1,100 serial subscriptions, 4,522 audiovisual materials, an OPAC, a Web page.

Computers on Campus 190 computers available on campus for general student use. A campuswide network can be accessed from student residence rooms and from off campus. At least one staffed computer lab available.

Student Life *Housing Options:* coed. *Activities and Organizations:* drama/theater group, student-run newspaper, radio station, choral group, student radio station, Intervarsity Christian Fellowship, jazz ensemble/concert choir, Big Friend, Little Friend, student newspaper. *Campus security:* 24-hour emergency response devices and patrols, late-night transport/escort service, controlled dormitory access. *Student Services:* health clinic, personal/psychological counseling, women's center, legal services.

Athletics Member NCAA. All Division II. *Intercollegiate sports:* baseball M, basketball M/W, cross-country running W, football M, golf M/W, soccer W, softball W, tennis M/W, track and field M/W, volleyball W, wrestling M/W. *Intramural sports:* basketball M/W, equestrian sports M(c)/W(c), fencing M(c)/W(c), football M/W, ice hockey M(c)/W(c), soccer M(c)/W(c), softball M/W, table tennis M/W, tennis M/W, volleyball M(c)/W(c).

Standardized Tests *Required:* SAT I or ACT (for admission).

Costs (2001–02) *Tuition:* state resident $5548 full-time, $185 per credit part-time; nonresident $10,065 full-time, $370 per credit part-time. Part-time tuition and fees vary according to course load. *Required fees:* $698 full-time, $349 per term part-time. *Room and board:* $4470; room only: $2080. Room and board charges vary according to board plan and housing facility. *Payment plans:* installment, deferred payment.

Financial Aid Of all full-time matriculated undergraduates who enrolled in 2001, 1580 applied for aid, 1580 were judged to have need, 732 had their need fully met. 258 Federal Work-Study jobs (averaging $1609). 435 State and other part-time jobs (averaging $1920). In 2001, 213 non-need-based awards were made. *Average financial aid package:* $7763. *Average need-based loan:* $2550. *Average need-based gift aid:* $5111. *Average non-need based aid:* $4000. *Average indebtedness upon graduation:* $9208.

Applying *Options:* electronic application, early admission, deferred entrance. *Application fee:* $25. *Required:* essay or personal statement, high school transcript. *Required for some:* interview. *Recommended:* minimum 3.0 GPA. *Application deadlines:* 3/15 (freshmen), 5/1 (transfers). *Notification:* 4/1 (freshmen).

Admissions Contact Mr. Scott K. Hagg, Acting Director of Admissions, University of Minnesota, Morris, 600 East 4th Street, Morris, MN 56267-2199. *Phone:* 320-539-6035. *Toll-free phone:* 800-992-8863. *Fax:* 320-589-1673. *E-mail:* admissions@mrs.umn.edu.

UNIVERSITY OF MINNESOTA, TWIN CITIES CAMPUS

Minneapolis, Minnesota

- **State-supported** university, founded 1851, part of University of Minnesota System
- **Calendar** quarters
- **Degrees** certificates, diplomas, bachelor's, master's, doctoral, first professional, post-master's, and postbachelor's certificates
- **Urban** 2000-acre campus
- **Coed,** 32,136 undergraduate students, 75% full-time, 53% women, 47% men
- **Moderately difficult** entrance level, 76% of applicants were admitted

Undergraduates 23,949 full-time, 8,187 part-time. Students come from 55 states and territories, 85 other countries, 26% are from out of state, 4% African American, 8% Asian American or Pacific Islander, 2% Hispanic American, 0.7% Native American, 2% international, 6% transferred in, 22% live on campus. *Retention:* 82% of 2001 full-time freshmen returned.

Freshmen *Admission:* 15,436 applied, 11,673 admitted, 5,344 enrolled. *Test scores:* SAT verbal scores over 500: 86%; SAT math scores over 500: 89%; ACT scores over 18: 95%; SAT verbal scores over 600: 50%; SAT math scores over 600: 61%; ACT scores over 24: 61%; SAT verbal scores over 700: 12%; SAT math scores over 700: 20%; ACT scores over 30: 11%.

Faculty *Total:* 3,079, 88% full-time, 95% with terminal degrees.

Majors Accounting; actuarial science; aerospace engineering; African-American studies; African studies; agricultural business; agricultural education; agricultural engineering; agricultural sciences; agronomy/crop science; American studies; animal sciences; anthropology; architecture; art; art education; art history; astronomy; astrophysics; biochemistry; biology; botany; business education; business marketing and marketing management; cell biology; chemical engineering; chemistry; Chinese; civil engineering; clothing/textiles; comparative literature; computer science; construction management; dance; dental hygiene; developmental/child psychology; early childhood education; East Asian studies; ecology; economics; education; electrical engineering; elementary education; emergency medical technology; English; English education; environmental science; European studies; family/community studies; film studies; finance; fish/game management; foreign languages education; forest management; forestry; French; genetics; geography; geological engineering; geology; geophysics/seismology; German; graphic design/commercial art/illustration; Greek (modern); Hebrew; history; home economics education; industrial/manufacturing engineering; insurance/risk management; interior design; international business; international relations; Italian; Japanese; journalism; Judaic studies; landscape architecture; Latin American studies; Latin (ancient and medieval); linguistics; management information systems/business data processing; mass communications; materials engineering; materials science; mathematics; mathematics education; mechanical engineering; medical technology; Mexican-American studies; microbiology/bacteriology; Middle Eastern studies; mortuary science; music; music teacher education; music therapy; Native American studies; natural resources management; neuroscience; nursing; nutrition science; occupational therapy; philosophy; physical education; physical therapy; physics; physiology; plant sciences; political science; Portuguese; pre-dentistry; pre-law; pre-medicine; pre-veterinary studies; psychology; public health; recreation/leisure facilities management; religious studies; Russian; Russian/Slavic studies; Scandinavian languages; science education; social science education; sociology; socio-psychological sports studies; soil sciences; South Asian studies; Spanish; speech-language pathology/audiology; theater arts/drama; urban studies; women's studies; wood science/paper technology.

Academic Programs *Special study options:* academic remediation for entering students, accelerated degree program, adult/continuing education programs, advanced placement credit, cooperative education, distance learning, double majors, English as a second language, external degree program, freshman honors college, honors programs, independent study, internships, off-campus study, part-time degree program, services for LD students, student-designed majors, study abroad, summer session for credit. *ROTC:* Army (b), Navy (b), Air Force (b).

Library Wilson Library plus 17 others with 5.6 million titles, 46,989 serial subscriptions, 1.2 million audiovisual materials, an OPAC, a Web page.

Computers on Campus A campuswide network can be accessed from student residence rooms and from off campus that provide access to e-mail. At least one staffed computer lab available.

Student Life *Housing Options:* coed, cooperative, disabled students. *Activities and Organizations:* drama/theater group, student-run newspaper, radio and television station, choral group, marching band, sports clubs, student government, religious organizations, departmental/professional organizations, national fraternities, national sororities. *Campus security:* 24-hour emergency response devices and patrols, student patrols, late-night transport/escort service, controlled dormitory access, safety/security orientation, security lighting. *Student Services:* health clinic, personal/psychological counseling, women's center, legal services.

Athletics Member NCAA. All Division I except football (Division I-A). *Intercollegiate sports:* baseball M(s), basketball M(s)/W(s), cross-country running M(s)/W(s), golf M(s)/W(s), gymnastics M(s)/W(s), ice hockey M(s)/W(s), soccer W(s), softball W(s), swimming M(s)/W(s), tennis M(s)/W(s), track and field M(s)/W(s), volleyball W(s), wrestling M(s). *Intramural sports:* baseball M/W, basketball M/W, bowling M/W, crew M/W, football M/W, golf M/W, ice hockey M/W, rugby M/W, skiing (cross-country) M/W, skiing (downhill) M/W, soccer M/W, softball M/W, tennis M/W, volleyball M/W, water polo M/W, wrestling M/W.

Standardized Tests *Required:* SAT I or ACT (for admission).

Costs (2001–02) *Tuition:* state resident $4852 full-time, $180 per credit part-time; nonresident $14,318 full-time, $530 per credit part-time. Full-time tuition and fees vary according to program, reciprocity agreements, and student level. Part-time tuition and fees vary according to course load, program, reciprocity agreements, and student level. No tuition increase for student's term of enrollment. *Required fees:* $684 full-time. *Room and board:* $5582; room only: $5086. Room and board charges vary according to board plan, housing facility, and location. *Payment plan:* installment. *Waivers:* senior citizens and employees or children of employees.

Financial Aid Of all full-time matriculated undergraduates who enrolled in 2001, 13466 applied for aid, 10329 were judged to have need, 4053 had their need fully met. In 2001, 844 non-need-based awards were made. *Average percent of need met:* 79%. *Average financial aid package:* $7893. *Average need-based loan:* $4053. *Average need-based gift aid:* $3582. *Average non-need based aid:* $3249.

Applying *Options:* electronic application, early admission, deferred entrance. *Application fee:* $35. *Required:* high school transcript. *Recommended:* minimum 2.0 GPA. *Application deadlines:* rolling (freshmen), 3/1 (transfers). *Notification:* continuous (freshmen).

Admissions Contact Ms. Patricia Jones Whyte, Associate Director of Admissions, University of Minnesota, Twin Cities Campus, 240 Williamson Hall, Minneapolis, MN 55455-0115. *Phone:* 612-625-2008. *Toll-free phone:* 800-752-1000. *Fax:* 612-626-1693. *E-mail:* admissions@tc.umn.edu.

UNIVERSITY OF ST. THOMAS

St. Paul, Minnesota

- **Independent Roman Catholic** university, founded 1885
- **Calendar** 4-1-4
- **Degrees** certificates, bachelor's, master's, doctoral, first professional, post-master's, and postbachelor's certificates
- **Urban** 78-acre campus with easy access to Minneapolis
- **Endowment** $254.4 million
- **Coed,** 5,416 undergraduate students, 87% full-time, 53% women, 47% men
- **Moderately difficult** entrance level, 81% of applicants were admitted

St. Thomas, a coeducational, Catholic liberal arts university with more than 11,000 undergraduate and graduate students—the largest independent university in Minnesota—is located in a quiet neighborhood only 10 minutes from the downtown areas of both St. Paul and Minneapolis. St. Thomas offers more than 80 majors, including business administration, computer science, journalism, biology, engineering, and pre-professional programs. St. Thomas emphasizes values-centered, career-oriented education.

Undergraduates 4,720 full-time, 696 part-time. Students come from 42 states and territories, 48 other countries, 18% are from out of state, 2% African American, 5% Asian American or Pacific Islander, 2% Hispanic American, 0.7% Native American, 1% international, 5% transferred in, 43% live on campus. *Retention:* 84% of 2001 full-time freshmen returned.

Freshmen *Admission:* 3,257 applied, 2,639 admitted, 1,083 enrolled. *Average high school GPA:* 3.55. *Test scores:* SAT verbal scores over 500: 81%; SAT math scores over 500: 84%; ACT scores over 18: 100%; SAT verbal scores over 600: 40%; SAT math scores over 600: 50%; ACT scores over 24: 64%; SAT verbal scores over 700: 9%; SAT math scores over 700: 6%; ACT scores over 30: 10%.

Faculty *Total:* 799, 48% full-time, 59% with terminal degrees. *Student/faculty ratio:* 14:1.

Majors Accounting; actuarial science; advertising; alcohol/drug abuse counseling; art history; behavioral sciences; biochemistry; biology; broadcast journalism; business administration; business administration/management related; business communications; business marketing and marketing management; chemistry; classics; communications; comparative literature; computer/information sciences; creative writing; criminology; drama/dance education; East Asian studies; economics; education (K-12); electrical engineering; elementary education;

University of St. Thomas (continued)
English; enterprise management; environmental science; finance; French; geography; geology; German; Greek (ancient and medieval); health education; health/physical education; health science; history; human resources management; interdisciplinary studies; international business; international relations; journalism; journalism and mass communication related; Latin (ancient and medieval); mass communications; mathematics; mathematics education; mechanical engineering; music; music business management/merchandising; music related; music teacher education; operations management; peace/conflict studies; philosophy; physical education; physics; political science; psychology; public health education/promotion; public relations; publishing; real estate; religious studies; Russian; Russian/Slavic studies; science education; secondary education; social sciences; social studies education; social work; sociology; Spanish; speech/theater education; teacher education, specific programs related; theater arts/drama; theology; women's studies.

Academic Programs *Special study options:* adult/continuing education programs, advanced placement credit, double majors, English as a second language, honors programs, independent study, internships, off-campus study, part-time degree program, services for LD students, student-designed majors, study abroad, summer session for credit. *ROTC:* Army (c), Navy (c), Air Force (b). *Unusual degree programs:* 3-2 engineering with University of Notre Dame; Washington University in St. Louis; University of Minnesota, Twin Cities Campus; Kettering University.

Library O'Shaughnessy-Frey Library plus 2 others with 312,092 titles, 2,528 serial subscriptions, 6,158 audiovisual materials, an OPAC, a Web page.

Computers on Campus 843 computers available on campus for general student use. A campuswide network can be accessed from student residence rooms and from off campus. Internet access, online (class) registration, at least one staffed computer lab available.

Student Life *Housing Options:* men-only, women-only, disabled students. *Activities and Organizations:* drama/theater group, student-run newspaper, choral group. *Campus security:* 24-hour emergency response devices and patrols, late-night transport/escort service, controlled dormitory access. *Student Services:* health clinic, personal/psychological counseling, women's center, legal services.

Athletics Member NCAA. All Division III. *Intercollegiate sports:* baseball M, basketball M/W, crew M(c)/W(c), cross-country running M/W, football M, golf M/W, ice hockey M/W, lacrosse M(c)/W(c), skiing (downhill) M(c)/W(c), soccer M/W, softball W, swimming M/W, tennis M/W, track and field M/W, volleyball W. *Intramural sports:* basketball M/W, racquetball M/W, soccer M/W, softball M/W, squash M/W, table tennis M/W, tennis M/W, volleyball M/W.

Standardized Tests *Required:* SAT I or ACT (for admission). *Recommended:* ACT (for admission).

Costs (2001–02) *Comprehensive fee:* $24,044 includes full-time tuition ($18,096), mandatory fees ($325), and room and board ($5623). Full-time tuition and fees vary according to course load. Part-time tuition: $566 per credit. Part-time tuition and fees vary according to course load. *Required fees:* $82 per term part-time. *Room and board:* College room only: $3339. Room and board charges vary according to board plan and housing facility. *Payment plans:* installment, deferred payment. *Waivers:* senior citizens and employees or children of employees.

Financial Aid Of all full-time matriculated undergraduates who enrolled in 2001, 3190 applied for aid, 2603 were judged to have need, 668 had their need fully met. 629 Federal Work-Study jobs (averaging $2165). 1827 State and other part-time jobs (averaging $2280). In 2001, 417 non-need-based awards were made. *Average percent of need met:* 84%. *Average financial aid package:* $14,266. *Average need-based loan:* $3662. *Average need-based gift aid:* $8137. *Average non-need based aid:* $5471. *Average indebtedness upon graduation:* $19,708.

Applying *Options:* electronic application, deferred entrance. *Application fee:* $30. *Required:* essay or personal statement, high school transcript. *Recommended:* letters of recommendation, interview. *Application deadlines:* rolling (freshmen), 8/1 (transfers). *Notification:* continuous (freshmen).

Admissions Contact Ms. Marla Friederichs, Associate Vice President of Enrollment Management, University of St. Thomas, Mail #32F-1, 2115 Summit Avenue, St. Paul, MN 55105-1096. *Phone:* 651-962-6150. *Toll-free phone:* 800-328-6819 Ext. 26150. *Fax:* 651-962-6160. *E-mail:* admissions@stthomas.edu.

WINONA STATE UNIVERSITY
Winona, Minnesota

- **State-supported** comprehensive, founded 1858, part of Minnesota State Colleges and Universities System
- **Calendar** semesters
- **Degrees** associate, bachelor's, master's, and post-master's certificates
- **Small-town** 40-acre campus
- **Endowment** $3.1 million
- **Coed,** 7,114 undergraduate students, 88% full-time, 63% women, 37% men
- **Moderately difficult** entrance level, 85% of applicants were admitted

Undergraduates Students come from 40 states and territories, 53 other countries, 40% are from out of state, 0.4% African American, 1.0% Asian American or Pacific Islander, 0.7% Hispanic American, 0.2% Native American, 4% international, 28% live on campus. *Retention:* 75% of 2001 full-time freshmen returned.

Freshmen *Admission:* 4,032 applied, 3,420 admitted. *Average high school GPA:* 3.30. *Test scores:* ACT scores over 18: 99%; ACT scores over 24: 59%; ACT scores over 30: 3%.

Faculty *Total:* 357, 88% full-time, 62% with terminal degrees. *Student/faculty ratio:* 19:1.

Majors Accounting; advertising; aircraft pilot (professional); applied art; applied mathematics; art; art education; athletic training/sports medicine; aviation management; biological/physical sciences; biology; broadcast journalism; business administration; business economics; business education; business marketing and marketing management; chemical engineering; chemistry; city/community/regional planning; computer/information sciences; computer programming; computer science; corrections; criminal justice/law enforcement administration; cytotechnology; drawing; early childhood education; earth sciences; ecology; economics; education; elementary education; engineering; English; environmental biology; exercise sciences; finance; fine/studio arts; fish/game management; forestry; French; geology; German; gerontology; graphic design/commercial art/illustration; health education; health science; health services administration; history; human resources management; information sciences/systems; international relations; Japanese; journalism; labor/personnel relations; law enforcement/police science; legal studies; liberal arts and sciences/liberal studies; management information systems/business data processing; mass communications; materials engineering; mathematical statistics; mathematics; mechanical engineering; medical laboratory technician; medical technology; middle school education; music; music business management/merchandising; music teacher education; music (voice and choral/opera performance); natural resources conservation; natural sciences; nursing; paralegal/legal assistant; physical education; physical sciences; physical therapy; physics; plastics engineering; political science; polymer chemistry; pre-dentistry; pre-engineering; pre-law; pre-medicine; pre-veterinary studies; psychology; public administration; public health; public relations; quality control technology; radio/television broadcasting; reading education; recreational therapy; recreation/leisure facilities management; recreation/leisure studies; retail management; science education; secondary education; secretarial science; social sciences; social work; sociology; Spanish; special education; speech/rhetorical studies; sport/fitness administration; telecommunications; theater arts/drama; wildlife biology; wildlife management; zoology.

Academic Programs *Special study options:* academic remediation for entering students, accelerated degree program, adult/continuing education programs, advanced placement credit, distance learning, double majors, English as a second language, external degree program, honors programs, independent study, internships, off-campus study, part-time degree program, services for LD students, student-designed majors, study abroad, summer session for credit. *ROTC:* Army (c).

Library Maxwell Library with 243,500 titles, 1,950 serial subscriptions, an OPAC, a Web page.

Computers on Campus 1400 computers available on campus for general student use. A campuswide network can be accessed from student residence rooms and from off campus. Internet access, at least one staffed computer lab available.

Student Life *Housing Options:* coed, men-only, women-only. *Activities and Organizations:* drama/theater group, student-run newspaper, radio station, choral group, marching band, University Program Activities Committee, student senate, Inter-residence Hall Council, national fraternities, national sororities. *Campus security:* 24-hour emergency response devices and patrols, student patrols, late-night transport/escort service, controlled dormitory access, security cameras. *Student Services:* health clinic, personal/psychological counseling, women's center, legal services.

Athletics Member NCAA. All Division II. *Intercollegiate sports:* baseball M(s), basketball M(s)/W(s), bowling M(c)/W(c), cross-country running M(c)/W(s), fencing M(c)/W(c), football M(s), golf M(s)/W(s), gymnastics W(s), ice hockey M(c), rugby M(c)/W(c), skiing (downhill) M(c)/W(c), soccer M(c)/W(s), softball W(s), tennis M(s)/W(s), track and field W(s), volleyball M(c)/W(s), wrestling M(c). *Intramural sports:* archery M/W, badminton M/W, baseball M, basketball M/W, bowling M/W, cross-country running M/W, fencing M/W, field hockey M/W, football M/W, golf M/W, gymnastics W, ice hockey M/W, racquetball M/W, riflery M/W, rugby M/W, skiing (cross-country) M/W, skiing (downhill) M/W, soccer M/W, softball M/W, swimming M/W, table tennis M/W, tennis M/W, track and field W, volleyball M/W, weight lifting M/W, wrestling M.

Standardized Tests *Required:* SAT I or ACT (for admission).

Costs (2001–02) *Tuition:* state resident $3130 full-time; nonresident $6860 full-time. Full-time tuition and fees vary according to course load and reciprocity agreements. Part-time tuition and fees vary according to course load and reciprocity agreements. *Required fees:* $500 full-time. *Room and board:* $3940. Room and board charges vary according to board plan, housing facility, and location. *Waivers:* senior citizens and employees or children of employees.

Financial Aid Of all full-time matriculated undergraduates who enrolled in 2001, 4625 applied for aid, 3425 were judged to have need, 859 had their need fully met. 216 Federal Work-Study jobs (averaging $1457). In 2001, 316 non-need-based awards were made. *Average percent of need met:* 65%. *Average financial aid package:* $4829. *Average need-based loan:* $3059. *Average need-based gift aid:* $2479. *Average non-need based aid:* $1193. *Average indebtedness upon graduation:* $10,102.

Applying *Options:* common application, electronic application, early admission, early action, deferred entrance. *Application fee:* $20. *Required:* high school transcript, class rank. *Required for some:* essay or personal statement, letters of recommendation, interview. *Application deadlines:* rolling (freshmen), 8/1 (transfers). *Notification:* continuous (freshmen).

Admissions Contact Mr. Douglas Schacke, Director of Admissions, Winona State University, PO Box 5838, Winona, MN 55987. *Phone:* 507-457-5100. *Toll-free phone:* 800-DIAL WSU. *Fax:* 507-457-5620. *E-mail:* admissions@vax2.winona.msus.edu.

MISSISSIPPI

ALCORN STATE UNIVERSITY
Alcorn State, Mississippi

- **State-supported** comprehensive, founded 1871, part of Mississippi Institutions of Higher Learning
- **Calendar** semesters
- **Degrees** associate, bachelor's, master's, and post-master's certificates
- **Rural** 1756-acre campus
- **Endowment** $209,871
- **Coed,** 2,543 undergraduate students, 89% full-time, 60% women, 40% men
- **Minimally difficult** entrance level, 40% of applicants were admitted

Undergraduates 2,269 full-time, 274 part-time. Students come from 31 states and territories, 7 other countries, 16% are from out of state, 93% African American, 0.1% Asian American or Pacific Islander, 0.2% Hispanic American, 0.0% Native American, 1% international, 7% transferred in, 66% live on campus.

Freshmen *Admission:* 3,780 applied, 1,507 admitted, 505 enrolled. *Average high school GPA:* 2.0. *Test scores:* ACT scores over 18: 45%; ACT scores over 24: 1%.

Faculty *Total:* 196, 85% full-time, 61% with terminal degrees. *Student/faculty ratio:* 13:1.

Majors Accounting; agricultural business; agricultural economics; agricultural sciences; agronomy/crop science; animal sciences; biology; business administration; chemistry; child guidance; computer/information sciences; criminal justice studies; economics; educational psychology; elementary education; English; health professions and related sciences; history; home economics; industrial arts education; industrial technology; liberal arts and sciences/liberal studies; mass communications; mathematics; medical technology; music (general performance); music teacher education; nursing; nutrition studies; physical education; physical therapy; political science; recreation/leisure studies; secondary education; secretarial science; sociology; special education.

Academic Programs *Special study options:* academic remediation for entering students, advanced placement credit, cooperative education, distance learning, double majors, honors programs, independent study, internships, part-time degree program. *ROTC:* Army (b).

Library John Dewey Boyd Library with 195,433 titles, 1,046 serial subscriptions, 9,908 audiovisual materials, an OPAC.

Computers on Campus 400 computers available on campus for general student use. A campuswide network can be accessed from student residence rooms and from off campus. Online (class) registration, at least one staffed computer lab available.

Student Life *Housing Options:* men-only, women-only. *Activities and Organizations:* drama/theater group, student-run newspaper, radio station, choral group, marching band, Panhellenic Council, intramural sports, Marching Band, Gospel Choir, Interfaith Choir, national fraternities, national sororities. *Campus security:* 24-hour patrols. *Student Services:* health clinic, personal/psychological counseling.

Athletics Member NCAA. All Division I. *Intercollegiate sports:* baseball M(s), basketball M(s)/W(s), cross-country running M(s)/W(s), football M(s), golf M(s)/W(s), soccer W(s), softball W(s), tennis M(s)/W(s), track and field M(s)/W(s), volleyball W(s). *Intramural sports:* basketball M/W, football M, golf M, gymnastics M/W, softball W, swimming M/W, table tennis M/W, tennis M/W, track and field M/W, volleyball M/W, wrestling M/W.

Standardized Tests *Required:* SAT I or ACT (for admission).

Costs (2001–02) *Tuition:* state resident $2294 full-time, $124 per semester hour part-time; nonresident $8104 full-time, $298 per semester hour part-time. *Required fees:* $909 full-time. *Room and board:* $3090. *Waivers:* employees or children of employees.

Financial Aid Of all full-time matriculated undergraduates who enrolled in 2001, 2209 applied for aid, 2091 were judged to have need. 295 Federal Work-Study jobs (averaging $1311). *Average percent of need met:* 73%. *Average financial aid package:* $9250. *Average need-based gift aid:* $3370. *Average non-need based aid:* $3857.

Applying *Options:* early admission, deferred entrance. *Required:* high school transcript, minimum 2.0 GPA. *Application deadline:* rolling (freshmen), rolling (transfers). *Notification:* continuous (freshmen).

Admissions Contact Mr. Emanuel Barnes, Director of Admissions, Alcorn State University, 1000 ASU Drive, Alcorn State, MS 39096-7500. *Phone:* 601-877-6147. *Toll-free phone:* 800-222-6790. *Fax:* 601-877-6347. *E-mail:* ebarnes@loman.alcorn.edu.

BELHAVEN COLLEGE
Jackson, Mississippi

- **Independent Presbyterian** comprehensive, founded 1883
- **Calendar** semesters
- **Degrees** certificates, bachelor's, and master's
- **Urban** 42-acre campus
- **Endowment** $2.3 million
- **Coed,** 1,666 undergraduate students, 91% full-time, 63% women, 37% men
- **Moderately difficult** entrance level, 67% of applicants were admitted

A nationally recognized leader in Christian higher education, Belhaven prepares students to serve Christ Jesus. Twenty-five majors characterized by an intellectual foundation of a biblical world view include dance, theater, communications, sports medicine, and sports ministry. Scholarships are available, including a $1000 campus visit voucher for freshmen who enroll. Apply online at www.belhaven.edu.

Undergraduates 1,510 full-time, 156 part-time. Students come from 35 states and territories, 11 other countries, 31% are from out of state, 34% African American, 0.7% Asian American or Pacific Islander, 1% Hispanic American, 0.8% Native American, 1% international, 19% transferred in, 32% live on campus. *Retention:* 58% of 2001 full-time freshmen returned.

Freshmen *Admission:* 538 applied, 361 admitted, 225 enrolled. *Average high school GPA:* 3.34. *Test scores:* SAT verbal scores over 500: 73%; SAT math scores over 500: 64%; ACT scores over 18: 87%; SAT verbal scores over 600: 44%; SAT math scores over 600: 24%; ACT scores over 24: 37%; SAT verbal scores over 700: 9%; SAT math scores over 700: 7%; ACT scores over 30: 7%.

Faculty *Total:* 193, 25% full-time, 38% with terminal degrees. *Student/faculty ratio:* 15:1.

Majors Accounting; art; athletic training/sports medicine; biblical studies; biology; business administration; chemistry; communications; computer science; dance; elementary education; English; history; humanities; information sciences/systems; mathematics; music; pastoral counseling; philosophy; psychology; sport/fitness administration; theater arts/drama.

Academic Programs *Special study options:* academic remediation for entering students, accelerated degree program, adult/continuing education programs, advanced placement credit, double majors, English as a second language, honors programs, independent study, internships, off-campus study, part-time degree program, study abroad, summer session for credit. *Unusual degree programs:* 3-2 engineering with Mississippi State University.

Library Hood Library with 108,042 titles, 541 serial subscriptions, 3,444 audiovisual materials, an OPAC, a Web page.

Computers on Campus 45 computers available on campus for general student use. A campuswide network can be accessed from student residence rooms and from off campus. Internet access, at least one staffed computer lab available.

Student Life *Housing:* on-campus residence required through sophomore year. *Options:* men-only, women-only. *Activities and Organizations:* drama/theater

Belhaven College (continued)
group, student-run newspaper, choral group, Student Government Association, Reformed University Fellowship, Kappa Delta Epsilon, Black Student Association, Math/Computer Science Club. *Campus security:* 24-hour emergency response devices and patrols, late-night transport/escort service, controlled dormitory access. *Student Services:* health clinic, personal/psychological counseling.

Athletics Member NAIA. *Intercollegiate sports:* baseball M(s), basketball M(s)/W(s), cross-country running M(s)/W(s), football M(s), golf M(s)/W(s), soccer M(s)/W(s), softball W(s), tennis M(s)/W(s), volleyball W(s). *Intramural sports:* basketball M/W, football M/W, soccer M/W, softball M/W, volleyball M/W.

Standardized Tests *Required:* SAT I or ACT (for admission).

Costs (2001–02) *One-time required fee:* $30. *Comprehensive fee:* $16,040 includes full-time tuition ($10,990), mandatory fees ($610), and room and board ($4440). Part-time tuition: $315 per semester hour. Part-time tuition and fees vary according to course load. *Required fees:* $70 per term part-time. *Room and board:* Room and board charges vary according to housing facility. *Payment plan:* installment. *Waivers:* senior citizens and employees or children of employees.

Financial Aid Of all full-time matriculated undergraduates who enrolled in 2001, 1389 applied for aid, 1292 were judged to have need, 121 had their need fully met. 124 Federal Work-Study jobs (averaging $1507). In 2001, 144 non-need-based awards were made. *Average percent of need met:* 58%. *Average financial aid package:* $9300. *Average need-based loan:* $4750. *Average need-based gift aid:* $3200. *Average non-need based aid:* $4800. *Average indebtedness upon graduation:* $17,800.

Applying *Options:* early admission, deferred entrance. *Application fee:* $25. *Required:* high school transcript, minimum 2.0 GPA, 1 letter of recommendation, 1 academic reference. *Required for some:* essay or personal statement, interview. *Application deadline:* rolling (freshmen), rolling (transfers). *Notification:* continuous (freshmen).

Admissions Contact Suzanne Teel, Director of Admissions, Belhaven College, 150 Peachtree Street, Jackson, MS 39202. *Phone:* 601-968-5940. *Toll-free phone:* 800-960-5940. *Fax:* 601-968-8946. *E-mail:* admissions@belhaven.edu.

BLUE MOUNTAIN COLLEGE
Blue Mountain, Mississippi

- **Independent Southern Baptist** 4-year, founded 1873
- **Calendar** semesters
- **Degrees** bachelor's (also offers a coordinate academic program for men preparing for church-related vocations)
- **Rural** 44-acre campus with easy access to Memphis
- **Women only,** 395 undergraduate students, 78% full-time
- **Noncompetitive** entrance level, 80% of applicants were admitted

Undergraduates 309 full-time, 86 part-time. Students come from 10 states and territories, 1 other country, 11% are from out of state, 11% African American, 0.3% Asian American or Pacific Islander, 0.3% Hispanic American, 0.3% Native American, 0.3% international, 23% transferred in, 23% live on campus. *Retention:* 74% of 2001 full-time freshmen returned.

Freshmen *Admission:* 109 applied, 87 admitted, 48 enrolled. *Average high school GPA:* 2.97. *Test scores:* ACT scores over 18: 68%; ACT scores over 24: 17%.

Faculty *Total:* 30, 70% full-time, 43% with terminal degrees. *Student/faculty ratio:* 14:1.

Majors Biblical studies; biology; biology education; business; business administration; business education; chemistry; chemistry education; elementary education; English; English education; French; French language education; history; mathematics; mathematics education; medical technology; modern languages; music; music (piano and organ performance); music teacher education; music (voice and choral/opera performance); natural sciences; physical education; pre-dentistry; pre-law; pre-medicine; pre-pharmacy studies; pre-theology; pre-veterinary studies; psychology; science education; social science education; social sciences; Spanish; Spanish language education; speech/rhetorical studies; theater arts/drama.

Academic Programs *Special study options:* accelerated degree program, advanced placement credit, double majors, honors programs, internships, part-time degree program, summer session for credit.

Library Guyton Library with 59,732 titles, 197 serial subscriptions, 4,334 audiovisual materials.

Computers on Campus 12 computers available on campus for general student use. At least one staffed computer lab available.

Student Life *Housing:* on-campus residence required through senior year. *Options:* women-only. *Activities and Organizations:* drama/theater group, choral group, Baptist Student Union, Student Government Association, Athletic Association, Commuter Club, Mississippi Association of Educators/Student Program. *Campus security:* 24-hour patrols.

Athletics Member NAIA. *Intercollegiate sports:* basketball W(s), tennis W(s). *Intramural sports:* basketball W, softball W, swimming W, table tennis W, tennis W, track and field W, volleyball W.

Standardized Tests *Required:* SAT I or ACT (for admission).

Costs (2001–02) *Comprehensive fee:* $9320 includes full-time tuition ($5700), mandatory fees ($500), and room and board ($3120). Full-time tuition and fees vary according to course load. Part-time tuition: $190 per semester hour. Part-time tuition and fees vary according to course load. *Required fees:* $75 per term part-time. *Room and board:* College room only: $1020. Room and board charges vary according to board plan and housing facility. *Payment plan:* installment. *Waivers:* employees or children of employees.

Financial Aid Of all full-time matriculated undergraduates who enrolled in 2001, 259 applied for aid, 216 were judged to have need, 41 had their need fully met. 57 Federal Work-Study jobs (averaging $1400). 40 State and other part-time jobs (averaging $1400). In 2001, 22 non-need-based awards were made. *Average need-based loan:* $1594. *Average need-based gift aid:* $938. *Average non-need based aid:* $980. *Average indebtedness upon graduation:* $10,000.

Applying *Options:* early admission. *Application fee:* $10. *Required:* high school transcript. *Required for some:* 2 letters of recommendation, interview. *Recommended:* minimum 2.0 GPA. *Application deadline:* rolling (freshmen), rolling (transfers). *Notification:* continuous (freshmen).

Admissions Contact Ms. Tina Barkley, Director of Admissions, Blue Mountain College, PO Box 160, Blue Mountain, MS 38610-0160. *Phone:* 662-685-4161 Ext. 176. *Toll-free phone:* 800-235-0136. *E-mail:* tbarkley@bmc.edu.

DELTA STATE UNIVERSITY
Cleveland, Mississippi

- **State-supported** comprehensive, founded 1924, part of Mississippi Institutions of Higher Learning
- **Calendar** semesters
- **Degrees** bachelor's, master's, doctoral, and post-master's certificates
- **Small-town** 332-acre campus
- **Endowment** $7.8 million
- **Coed,** 3,292 undergraduate students, 86% full-time, 60% women, 40% men
- **Minimally difficult** entrance level

Undergraduates 2,822 full-time, 470 part-time. Students come from 23 states and territories, 8% are from out of state, 30% African American, 0.3% Asian American or Pacific Islander, 0.4% Hispanic American, 0.2% Native American, 18% transferred in, 38% live on campus. *Retention:* 68% of 2001 full-time freshmen returned.

Freshmen *Admission:* 430 enrolled. *Average high school GPA:* 3.01. *Test scores:* ACT scores over 18: 72%; ACT scores over 24: 16%; ACT scores over 30: 1%.

Faculty *Total:* 278, 68% full-time, 56% with terminal degrees. *Student/faculty ratio:* 14:1.

Majors Accounting; aircraft pilot (professional); art education; aviation/airway science; biological/physical sciences; biology; biology education; business; business administration; business education; business marketing and marketing management; chemistry; chemistry education; criminal justice studies; early childhood education; education; elementary education; English; English education; fashion merchandising; finance; foreign languages education; foreign languages/literatures; history; home economics; home economics education; hospitality management; insurance/risk management; journalism; management information systems/business data processing; mathematics; mathematics education; medical technology; music; music teacher education; nursing; office management; physical education; political science; psychology; science education; secondary education; social science education; social sciences; social work; special education; speech-language pathology/audiology; visual/performing arts.

Academic Programs *Special study options:* academic remediation for entering students, advanced placement credit, cooperative education, double majors, honors programs, independent study, internships, part-time degree program, services for LD students, summer session for credit. *ROTC:* Air Force (b).

Library W. B. Roberts Library plus 1 other with 203,045 titles, 1,337 serial subscriptions, 15,523 audiovisual materials, an OPAC, a Web page.

Computers on Campus 268 computers available on campus for general student use. A campuswide network can be accessed from student residence rooms and from off campus that provide access to e-mail. Internet access, online (class) registration, at least one staffed computer lab available.

Student Life *Housing Options:* men-only, women-only. *Activities and Organizations:* drama/theater group, student-run newspaper, choral group, marching band, Student Government Association, Student Alumni Association, Baptist Student Union, Fellowship of Christian Athletes, Delta Volunteers, national fraternities, national sororities. *Campus security:* 24-hour emergency response devices and patrols, late-night transport/escort service, controlled dormitory access. *Student Services:* health clinic, personal/psychological counseling.

Athletics Member NCAA. All Division II. *Intercollegiate sports:* baseball M(s), basketball M(s)/W(s), cross-country running W(s), football M(s), golf M(s), softball W, swimming M(s)/W(s), tennis M(s)/W(s). *Intramural sports:* archery M/W, badminton M/W, basketball M/W, bowling M/W, cross-country running M/W, football M/W, golf M/W, racquetball M/W, riflery M/W, soccer M/W, softball M/W, swimming M/W, table tennis M/W, tennis M/W, track and field M/W, volleyball M/W.

Standardized Tests *Required:* SAT I or ACT (for admission).

Costs (2001–02) *Tuition:* state resident $3100 full-time, $110 per semester hour part-time; nonresident $7174 full-time, $288 per semester hour part-time. *Room and board:* $2920. *Payment plan:* installment. *Waivers:* children of alumni, senior citizens, and employees or children of employees.

Financial Aid *Average indebtedness upon graduation:* $11,178.

Applying *Options:* electronic application, deferred entrance. *Required:* high school transcript. *Required for some:* interview for art, music majors. *Application deadline:* 8/1 (freshmen), rolling (transfers). *Notification:* continuous (freshmen).

Admissions Contact Delta State University, Highway 8 West, Cleveland, MS 38733. *Phone:* 662-846-4018. *Toll-free phone:* 800-468-6378. *Fax:* 662-846-4683. *E-mail:* dheslep@dsu.deltast.edu.

JACKSON STATE UNIVERSITY

Jackson, Mississippi

- **State-supported** university, founded 1877, part of Mississippi Institutions of Higher Learning
- **Calendar** semesters
- **Degrees** bachelor's, master's, doctoral, and post-master's certificates
- **Urban** 128-acre campus
- **Endowment** $5.1 million
- **Coed,** 5,741 undergraduate students, 86% full-time, 61% women, 39% men
- **Minimally difficult** entrance level

Undergraduates 4,941 full-time, 800 part-time. Students come from 40 states and territories, 34 other countries, 23% are from out of state, 97% African American, 0.2% Asian American or Pacific Islander, 0.1% Hispanic American, 0.0% Native American, 0.8% international, 8% transferred in, 47% live on campus. *Retention:* 58% of 2001 full-time freshmen returned.

Freshmen *Admission:* 998 enrolled. *Average high school GPA:* 2.50.

Faculty *Total:* 423, 81% full-time, 67% with terminal degrees. *Student/faculty ratio:* 16:1.

Majors Accounting; art; art education; atmospheric sciences; biology; business administration; business economics; business education; business marketing and marketing management; chemistry; child care/development; computer/information sciences; computer science; criminal justice/law enforcement administration; criminal justice studies; economics; electrical/electronic engineering technology; elementary education; engineering technology; English; finance; fire science; health education; history; industrial arts; industrial arts education; industrial technology; journalism; law enforcement/police science; mass communications; mathematics; mathematics education; medical records administration; medical technology; music (general performance); music (piano and organ performance); music teacher education; office management; physical education; physics; political science; pre-dentistry; pre-law; pre-medicine; pre-veterinary studies; psychology; recreational therapy; science education; secondary education; secretarial science; social science education; social sciences; social work; sociology; Spanish; special education; speech-language pathology/audiology; speech/rhetorical studies; urban studies; visual/performing arts.

Academic Programs *Special study options:* academic remediation for entering students, accelerated degree program, adult/continuing education programs, advanced placement credit, cooperative education, English as a second language, honors programs, internships, off-campus study, part-time degree program, services for LD students, summer session for credit. *ROTC:* Army (b). *Unusual degree programs:* 3-2 engineering with Mississippi State University, Auburn University, Tuskegee University, University of Mississippi, Georgia Institute of Technology, Southern University and Agricultural and Mechanical College, University of Minnesota.

Library H. T. Sampson Library plus 1 other with 435,552 titles, 1,589 serial subscriptions, an OPAC.

Computers on Campus A campuswide network can be accessed from off campus. Internet access, at least one staffed computer lab available.

Student Life *Activities and Organizations:* drama/theater group, student-run newspaper, radio station, choral group, marching band, national fraternities, national sororities. *Campus security:* 24-hour emergency response devices and patrols, late-night transport/escort service, controlled dormitory access. *Student Services:* health clinic, personal/psychological counseling.

Athletics Member NCAA. All Division I except football (Division I-AA). *Intercollegiate sports:* baseball M(s), basketball M(s)/W(s), cross-country running M/W, golf M(s), tennis M(s), track and field M(s)/W(s), volleyball W. *Intramural sports:* archery M/W, badminton M/W, baseball M, basketball M/W, bowling M/W, football M, soccer M, tennis M/W, volleyball M/W.

Standardized Tests *Required:* ACT (for admission). *Required for some:* SAT I (for admission).

Costs (2001–02) *Tuition:* state resident $3206 full-time, $134 per credit hour part-time; nonresident $7376 full-time, $174 per credit hour part-time. *Room and board:* $4014; room only: $2428. Room and board charges vary according to board plan and housing facility. *Payment plans:* installment, deferred payment. *Waivers:* employees or children of employees.

Applying *Options:* common application, electronic application, early admission, deferred entrance. *Required:* high school transcript, minimum 3.0 GPA. *Required for some:* 3 letters of recommendation. *Application deadlines:* 8/1 (freshmen), 8/1 (transfers). *Notification:* continuous until 8/15 (freshmen).

Admissions Contact Mrs. Linda Rush, Admissions Counselor, Jackson State University, PO Box 17330, 1400 John R. Lynch Street, Jackson, MS 39217. *Phone:* 601-968-2911. *Toll-free phone:* 800-682-5390 (in-state); 800-848-6817 (out-of-state). *E-mail:* schatman@ccaix.jsums.edu.

MAGNOLIA BIBLE COLLEGE

Kosciusko, Mississippi

- **Independent** 4-year, founded 1976, affiliated with Church of Christ
- **Calendar** semesters
- **Degree** bachelor's
- **Small-town** 5-acre campus
- **Endowment** $471,035
- **Coed, primarily men,** 37 undergraduate students, 57% full-time, 35% women, 65% men
- **Noncompetitive** entrance level, 100% of applicants were admitted

Undergraduates 21 full-time, 16 part-time. Students come from 2 states and territories, 1 other country, 5% are from out of state, 33% African American, 3% Asian American or Pacific Islander, 3% Hispanic American, 16% transferred in, 35% live on campus. *Retention:* 100% of 2001 full-time freshmen returned.

Freshmen *Admission:* 10 applied, 10 admitted, 3 enrolled.

Faculty *Total:* 10, 20% full-time, 20% with terminal degrees. *Student/faculty ratio:* 6:1.

Majors Biblical studies.

Academic Programs *Special study options:* academic remediation for entering students, independent study, internships, part-time degree program, summer session for credit.

Library John and Phillip Gaunt Library with 36,650 titles, 278 serial subscriptions, 1,403 audiovisual materials.

Computers on Campus 8 computers available on campus for general student use. At least one staffed computer lab available.

Student Life *Housing:* on-campus residence required through sophomore year. *Student Services:* personal/psychological counseling.

Standardized Tests *Recommended:* SAT I or ACT (for placement).

Costs (2002–03) *Tuition:* $4500 full-time, $150 per semester hour part-time. *Required fees:* $90 full-time, $90 per term part-time. *Room only:* $1120. Room and board charges vary according to housing facility. *Payment plan:* deferred payment. *Waivers:* employees or children of employees.

Financial Aid Of all full-time matriculated undergraduates who enrolled in 2001, 19 applied for aid, 10 were judged to have need, 2 had their need fully met. 5 Federal Work-Study jobs (averaging $1915). In 2001, 7 non-need-based awards were made. *Average percent of need met:* 64%. *Average financial aid package:* $5870. *Average need-based loan:* $2625. *Average need-based gift aid:* $3753. *Average non-need based aid:* $3197.

Applying *Required:* essay or personal statement, high school transcript, 3 letters of recommendation. *Application deadlines:* 8/31 (freshmen), 8/31 (transfers). *Notification:* continuous (freshmen).

Admissions Contact Mr. Allen Coker, Director of Admissions, Magnolia Bible College, PO Box 1109, Kosciusko, MS 39090-1109. *Phone:* 601-289-2896 Ext. 106. *Toll-free phone:* 800-748-8655. *Fax:* 601-289-1850. *E-mail:* mbcadmissions@hotmail.com.

MILLSAPS COLLEGE
Jackson, Mississippi

- **Independent United Methodist** comprehensive, founded 1890
- **Calendar** semesters
- **Degrees** bachelor's and master's
- **Urban** 100-acre campus
- **Endowment** $84.9 million
- **Coed,** 1,221 undergraduate students, 95% full-time, 55% women, 45% men
- **Moderately difficult** entrance level, 86% of applicants were admitted

Undergraduates 1,165 full-time, 56 part-time. Students come from 25 states and territories, 10 other countries, 42% are from out of state, 11% African American, 2% Asian American or Pacific Islander, 0.7% Hispanic American, 0.3% Native American, 0.6% international, 4% transferred in, 82% live on campus. *Retention:* 83% of 2001 full-time freshmen returned.

Freshmen *Admission:* 952 applied, 815 admitted, 324 enrolled. *Average high school GPA:* 3.54. *Test scores:* SAT verbal scores over 500: 92%; SAT math scores over 500: 88%; ACT scores over 18: 100%; SAT verbal scores over 600: 53%; SAT math scores over 600: 49%; ACT scores over 24: 73%; SAT verbal scores over 700: 12%; SAT math scores over 700: 10%; ACT scores over 30: 21%.

Faculty *Total:* 100, 93% full-time, 89% with terminal degrees. *Student/faculty ratio:* 13:1.

Majors Accounting; anthropology; art; biology; business administration; chemistry; classics; computer science; economics; education; English; European studies; French; geology; German; history; mathematics; music; philosophy; physics; political science; psychology; religious studies; sociology; Spanish; theater arts/drama.

Academic Programs *Special study options:* adult/continuing education programs, advanced placement credit, double majors, English as a second language, honors programs, internships, off-campus study, part-time degree program, study abroad, summer session for credit. *ROTC:* Army (c). *Unusual degree programs:* 3-2 engineering with Auburn University, Columbia University, Vanderbilt University, Washington University in St. Louis.

Library Millsaps Wilson Library with 117,640 titles, 3,087 serial subscriptions, 7,643 audiovisual materials, an OPAC, a Web page.

Computers on Campus 117 computers available on campus for general student use. A campuswide network can be accessed from student residence rooms. Internet access, at least one staffed computer lab available.

Student Life *Housing:* on-campus residence required through sophomore year. *Options:* coed, men-only, women-only. *Activities and Organizations:* drama/theater group, student-run newspaper, choral group, Campus Ministry Team, National Leadership Organization, Habitat for Humanity, Student Body Association, national fraternities, national sororities. *Campus security:* 24-hour emergency response devices and patrols, student patrols, late-night transport/escort service, controlled dormitory access, self-defense education, lighted pathways. *Student Services:* health clinic, personal/psychological counseling, women's center.

Athletics Member NCAA. All Division III. *Intercollegiate sports:* baseball M, basketball M/W, cross-country running M/W, football M, golf M/W, soccer M/W, softball W, tennis M/W, volleyball W. *Intramural sports:* basketball M/W, racquetball M/W, soccer M/W, softball M/W, tennis M/W, track and field M/W, volleyball M/W, weight lifting M/W.

Standardized Tests *Required:* SAT I or ACT (for admission).

Costs (2001–02) *Comprehensive fee:* $22,608 includes full-time tuition ($15,586), mandatory fees ($960), and room and board ($6062). Part-time tuition: $486 per semester hour. Part-time tuition and fees vary according to course load. *Required fees:* $26 per semester hour. *Room and board:* Room and board charges vary according to housing facility. *Payment plan:* installment. *Waivers:* employees or children of employees.

Financial Aid Of all full-time matriculated undergraduates who enrolled in 2001, 834 applied for aid, 692 were judged to have need, 253 had their need fully met. 261 Federal Work-Study jobs (averaging $1143). 93 State and other part-time jobs (averaging $941). In 2001, 435 non-need-based awards were made. *Average percent of need met:* 90%. *Average financial aid package:* $15,670. *Average need-based loan:* $4006. *Average need-based gift aid:* $12,240. *Average non-need based aid:* $11,395. *Average indebtedness upon graduation:* $16,000.

Applying *Options:* common application, electronic application, early admission, early action, deferred entrance. *Application fee:* $25. *Required:* essay or personal statement, high school transcript, minimum 2.5 GPA. *Recommended:* letters of recommendation, interview. *Application deadline:* 2/1 (freshmen), rolling (transfers). *Notification:* 1/15 (freshmen), 12/20 (early action).

Admissions Contact Millsaps College, 1701 North State Street, Jackson, MS 39210-0001. *Phone:* 601-974-1050. *Toll-free phone:* 800-352-1050. *Fax:* 601-974-1059. *E-mail:* admissions@millsaps.edu.

MISSISSIPPI COLLEGE
Clinton, Mississippi

- **Independent Southern Baptist** comprehensive, founded 1826
- **Calendar** semesters
- **Degrees** bachelor's, master's, first professional, and postbachelor's certificates
- **Suburban** 320-acre campus
- **Endowment** $40.5 million
- **Coed,** 2,289 undergraduate students, 88% full-time, 59% women, 41% men
- **Moderately difficult** entrance level, 87% of applicants were admitted

Founded in 1826 and located in Clinton, Mississippi College is the state's oldest institution of higher learning and the second-oldest Baptist university in the nation. With an undergraduate enrollment of more than 2,400, Mississippi College is also the largest private university in the state. At Mississippi College, more than 175 years of tradition blends with state-of-the-art technology to provide a 4-year liberal arts education of unrivaled quality.

Undergraduates 2,017 full-time, 272 part-time. Students come from 31 states and territories, 18% are from out of state, 11% African American, 0.8% Asian American or Pacific Islander, 0.3% Hispanic American, 0.2% Native American, 0.1% international, 14% transferred in, 61% live on campus. *Retention:* 79% of 2001 full-time freshmen returned.

Freshmen *Admission:* 525 applied, 457 admitted, 300 enrolled. *Test scores:* ACT scores over 18: 96%; ACT scores over 24: 48%; ACT scores over 30: 8%.

Faculty *Total:* 247, 61% full-time, 61% with terminal degrees. *Student/faculty ratio:* 16:1.

Majors Accounting; applied art; art; art education; art history; biology; business administration; business education; business marketing and marketing management; chemistry; communications; computer/information sciences; computer science; criminal justice/law enforcement administration; education; elementary education; English; family/consumer studies; fashion merchandising; foreign languages/literatures; French; graphic design/commercial art/illustration; history; home economics education; interior design; law enforcement/police science; liberal arts and sciences/liberal studies; mathematics; modern languages; music; music (general performance); music (piano and organ performance); music teacher education; music (voice and choral/opera performance); nursing; paralegal/legal assistant; physics; political science; pre-dentistry; pre-law; pre-medicine; psychology; religious music; religious studies; science education; social science education; social sciences; social studies education; social work; sociology; Spanish; special education.

Academic Programs *Special study options:* academic remediation for entering students, adult/continuing education programs, advanced placement credit, cooperative education, double majors, freshman honors college, honors programs, independent study, internships, part-time degree program, services for LD students, study abroad, summer session for credit. *ROTC:* Army (c). *Unusual degree programs:* 3-2 engineering with Auburn University, University of Mississippi.

Library Leland Speed Library plus 1 other with 276,245 titles, 5,305 serial subscriptions, 15,210 audiovisual materials, an OPAC, a Web page.

Computers on Campus 160 computers available on campus for general student use. A campuswide network can be accessed from student residence rooms and from off campus. At least one staffed computer lab available.

Student Life *Housing:* on-campus residence required through senior year. *Options:* men-only, women-only, disabled students. *Activities and Organizations:* drama/theater group, student-run newspaper, radio and television station, choral group, marching band, Baptist Student Union, Nenamoosha Social Tribe, Laguna Social Tribe, Civitan Service Club, Shawreth Service Club. *Campus security:* 24-hour emergency response devices and patrols, late-night transport/escort service, controlled dormitory access. *Student Services:* health clinic, personal/psychological counseling.

Athletics Member NCAA. All Division III. *Intercollegiate sports:* baseball M, basketball M/W, cross-country running M/W, football M, soccer M/W, softball W, tennis M/W, volleyball W. *Intramural sports:* basketball M/W, football M/W, soccer M/W, softball M/W, volleyball M/W.

Standardized Tests *Required:* SAT I or ACT (for admission).

Costs (2002–03) *Comprehensive fee:* $15,392 includes full-time tuition ($10,140), mandatory fees ($572), and room and board ($4680). Full-time tuition and fees vary according to course load. Part-time tuition: $338 per credit hour. Part-time tuition and fees vary according to course load. *Required fees:* $69 per term part-time. *Room and board:* College room only: $2260. Room and board charges vary according to board plan and housing facility. *Payment plans:* installment, deferred payment. *Waivers:* employees or children of employees.

Financial Aid Of all full-time matriculated undergraduates who enrolled in 2001, 1611 applied for aid, 858 were judged to have need, 343 had their need fully met. 257 Federal Work-Study jobs (averaging $1224). In 2001, 728 non-need-based awards were made. *Average percent of need met:* 82%. *Average financial aid package:* $12,769. *Average need-based loan:* $6135. *Average need-based gift aid:* $7738. *Average non-need based aid:* $9343.

Applying *Options:* early admission, deferred entrance. *Application fee:* $25. *Required:* essay or personal statement, high school transcript. *Application deadline:* rolling (freshmen), rolling (transfers). *Notification:* continuous (freshmen).

Admissions Contact Mr. Chad Phillips, Director of Admissions, Mississippi College, PO Box 4026, South Capitol Street, Clinton, MS 39058. *Phone:* 601-925-3800. *Toll-free phone:* 800-738-1236. *Fax:* 601-925-3804. *E-mail:* enrollment-services@mc.edu.

MISSISSIPPI STATE UNIVERSITY

Mississippi State, Mississippi

- **State-supported** university, founded 1878
- **Calendar** semesters
- **Degrees** bachelor's, master's, doctoral, first professional, and post-master's certificates
- **Small-town** 4200-acre campus
- **Endowment** $144.6 million
- **Coed,** 13,604 undergraduate students, 88% full-time, 47% women, 53% men
- **Moderately difficult** entrance level, 72% of applicants were admitted

Undergraduates 11,917 full-time, 1,687 part-time. Students come from 50 states and territories, 49 other countries, 21% are from out of state, 19% African American, 1% Asian American or Pacific Islander, 0.8% Hispanic American, 0.4% Native American, 1% international, 12% transferred in, 21% live on campus. *Retention:* 80% of 2001 full-time freshmen returned.

Freshmen *Admission:* 5,447 applied, 3,911 admitted, 1,777 enrolled. *Average high school GPA:* 3.33. *Test scores:* ACT scores over 18: 92%; ACT scores over 24: 46%; ACT scores over 30: 12%.

Faculty *Total:* 1,065, 83% full-time, 72% with terminal degrees. *Student/faculty ratio:* 18:1.

Majors Accounting; aerospace engineering; agribusiness; agricultural economics; agricultural education; agricultural engineering; agricultural sciences; agronomy/crop science; animal sciences; anthropology; architecture; biochemistry; bioengineering; biological/physical sciences; biology; business administration; business economics; business education; business marketing and marketing management; chemical engineering; chemistry; civil engineering; communications; computer engineering; computer/information sciences; computer software engineering; construction management; economics; educational psychology; electrical engineering; elementary education; English; finance; food sciences; foreign languages/literatures; forestry; geology; history; home economics; horticulture science; industrial arts education; industrial/manufacturing engineering; industrial technology; insurance/risk management; landscape architecture; landscaping management; liberal arts and sciences/liberal studies; management information systems/business data processing; marine biology; mathematics; mechanical engineering; medical technology; microbiology/bacteriology; multi/interdisciplinary studies related; music teacher education; philosophy; physical education; physics; plant protection; political science; poultry science; psychology; real estate; secondary education; social work; sociology; special education; technical education; visual/performing arts; wildlife management; wood science/paper technology.

Academic Programs *Special study options:* academic remediation for entering students, accelerated degree program, adult/continuing education programs, advanced placement credit, cooperative education, distance learning, double majors, English as a second language, freshman honors college, honors programs, independent study, internships, off-campus study, part-time degree program, services for LD students, student-designed majors, study abroad, summer session for credit. *ROTC:* Army (b), Air Force (b). *Unusual degree programs:* 3-2 engineering with Armstrong State College, Belhaven College, Jackson State University.

Library Mitchell Memorial Library plus 2 others with 1.6 million titles, 15,574 serial subscriptions, 14,665 audiovisual materials, an OPAC, a Web page.

Computers on Campus 2000 computers available on campus for general student use. A campuswide network can be accessed from student residence rooms and from off campus. Internet access, online (class) registration, at least one staffed computer lab available.

Student Life *Housing Options:* coed, men-only, women-only, disabled students. *Activities and Organizations:* drama/theater group, student-run newspaper, radio and television station, choral group, marching band, Student Association, Black Student Alliance, Residence Hall Association, Fashion Board, Campus Activities Board, national fraternities, national sororities. *Campus security:* 24-hour emergency response devices, late-night transport/escort service, controlled dormitory access, bicycle patrols, crime prevention program, RAD program, general law enforcement services. *Student Services:* health clinic, personal/psychological counseling.

Athletics Member NCAA. All Division I except football (Division I-A). *Intercollegiate sports:* baseball M(s), basketball M(s)/W(s), cross-country running W(s), golf M(s)/W(s), soccer W(s), softball W(s), tennis M(s)/W(s), track and field M(s)/W(s), volleyball W(s). *Intramural sports:* badminton M/W, basketball M/W, fencing M(c)/W(c), football M/W, golf M/W, lacrosse M(c), racquetball M/W, rugby M(c)/W(c), soccer M(c)/W(c), softball M/W, swimming M/W, table tennis M/W, tennis M/W, volleyball M(c)/W, water polo M/W, weight lifting M/W.

Standardized Tests *Required:* SAT I or ACT (for admission).

Costs (2001–02) *Tuition:* state resident $3586 full-time, $150 per credit hour part-time; nonresident $8128 full-time, $339 per credit hour part-time. Full-time tuition and fees vary according to location. Part-time tuition and fees vary according to course load and location. *Room and board:* $5704; room only: $2669. Room and board charges vary according to board plan and housing facility. *Waivers:* children of alumni, senior citizens, and employees or children of employees.

Financial Aid Of all full-time matriculated undergraduates who enrolled in 2001, 11334 applied for aid, 8091 were judged to have need, 3161 had their need fully met. 1058 Federal Work-Study jobs (averaging $2278). *Average percent of need met:* 70%. *Average financial aid package:* $6525. *Average need-based loan:* $3306. *Average need-based gift aid:* $2763. *Average indebtedness upon graduation:* $13,499.

Applying *Options:* electronic application, early admission, deferred entrance. *Application fee:* $25 (non-residents). *Required:* high school transcript, minimum 2.0 GPA. *Required for some:* letters of recommendation, interview. *Application deadlines:* 5/1 (freshmen), 8/1 (transfers). *Notification:* continuous (freshmen).

Admissions Contact Mr. Jerry Inmon, Director of Admissions, Mississippi State University, PO Box 6305, Mississippi State, MS 39762. *Phone:* 662-325-2224. *Fax:* 662-325-7360. *E-mail:* admit@admissions.msstate.edu.

MISSISSIPPI UNIVERSITY FOR WOMEN

Columbus, Mississippi

- **State-supported** comprehensive, founded 1884, part of Mississippi Institutions of Higher Learning
- **Calendar** semesters
- **Degrees** associate, bachelor's, and master's
- **Small-town** 110-acre campus
- **Endowment** $16.2 million
- **Coed, primarily women,** 2,166 undergraduate students, 68% full-time, 83% women, 17% men
- **Moderately difficult** entrance level, 65% of applicants were admitted

Undergraduates Students come from 26 states and territories, 36 other countries, 11% are from out of state, 28% African American, 1.0% Asian American or Pacific Islander, 0.7% Hispanic American, 0.4% Native American, 2% international, 21% live on campus. *Retention:* 70% of 2001 full-time freshmen returned.

Freshmen *Admission:* 609 applied, 395 admitted. *Average high school GPA:* 3.2. *Test scores:* ACT scores over 18: 90%; ACT scores over 24: 56%; ACT scores over 30: 8%.

Faculty *Total:* 214, 63% full-time. *Student/faculty ratio:* 13:1.

Majors Accounting; art; art education; biological/physical sciences; biology; business administration; business marketing and marketing management; chemistry; clothing/textiles; communications; culinary arts; drawing; education; elementary education; English; exercise sciences; history; individual/family development; information sciences/systems; mathematics; microbiology/bacteriology; music business management/merchandising; music teacher education; nursing; paralegal/legal assistant; physical education; physical sciences; political science; printmaking; psychology; recreation/leisure studies; science education; secondary education; social sciences; Spanish; special education; speech-language pathology/audiology; sport/fitness administration; theater arts/drama.

Academic Programs *Special study options:* academic remediation for entering students, accelerated degree program, adult/continuing education programs, advanced placement credit, cooperative education, distance learning, double majors, English as a second language, freshman honors college, honors programs, internships, off-campus study, part-time degree program, services for LD students, study abroad, summer session for credit. *ROTC:* Army (c), Air Force (c). *Unusual degree programs:* 3-2 engineering with Auburn University, Mississippi State University.

Library John Clayton Fant Memorial Library with 426,543 titles, 1,629 serial subscriptions, 164 audiovisual materials, an OPAC.

Mississippi University for Women (continued)

Computers on Campus 250 computers available on campus for general student use. A campuswide network can be accessed from student residence rooms and from off campus that provide access to various software packages. Internet access, at least one staffed computer lab available.

Student Life *Housing Options:* men-only, women-only. *Activities and Organizations:* drama/theater group, student-run newspaper, radio station, choral group, Student Government Association, Union Advisory Cabinet, Black Student Council, W Angels, Student Alumni Ambassadors, national fraternities, national sororities. *Campus security:* 24-hour patrols, student patrols, late-night transport/escort service. *Student Services:* health clinic, personal/psychological counseling.

Athletics Member NCAA. All Division II. *Intercollegiate sports:* basketball W(s), softball W(s), tennis W(s), volleyball W(s). *Intramural sports:* basketball M/W, football M/W, golf M/W, racquetball M/W, softball M/W, swimming M/W, table tennis M/W, tennis M/W, volleyball M/W.

Standardized Tests *Required for some:* SAT I or ACT (for admission). *Recommended:* SAT I or ACT (for admission).

Costs (2001–02) *Tuition:* state resident $3054 full-time, $127 per semester hour part-time; nonresident $7375 full-time, $307 per semester hour part-time. *Room and board:* $3030. Room and board charges vary according to board plan. *Payment plans:* installment, deferred payment. *Waivers:* minority students, children of alumni, adult students, and employees or children of employees.

Applying *Options:* common application, electronic application, early admission. *Application fee:* $25 (non-residents). *Required:* high school transcript. *Required for some:* minimum 2.0 GPA, letters of recommendation, rank in upper 50% of high school class. *Application deadlines:* 9/6 (freshmen), 9/6 (transfers). *Notification:* continuous (freshmen).

Admissions Contact Ms. Terri Heath, Director of Admissions, Mississippi University for Women, PO Box 1613, Columbus, MS 39701-9998. *Phone:* 601-329-7106. *Toll-free phone:* 877-GO 2 THE W. *Fax:* 601-241-7481. *E-mail:* admissions@muw.edu.

MISSISSIPPI VALLEY STATE UNIVERSITY

Itta Bena, Mississippi

- **State-supported** comprehensive, founded 1946, part of Mississippi Institutions of Higher Learning
- **Calendar** semesters
- **Degrees** bachelor's and master's
- **Small-town** 450-acre campus
- **Endowment** $1.5 million
- **Coed,** 2,636 undergraduate students, 81% full-time, 69% women, 31% men
- **Minimally difficult** entrance level, 16% of applicants were admitted

Undergraduates 2,146 full-time, 490 part-time. Students come from 24 states and territories, 7 other countries, 6% are from out of state, 95% African American, 0.1% Asian American or Pacific Islander, 0.0% Hispanic American, 8% transferred in, 53% live on campus. *Retention:* 74% of 2001 full-time freshmen returned.

Freshmen *Admission:* 3,122 applied, 506 admitted, 263 enrolled. *Average high school GPA:* 2.69. *Test scores:* ACT scores over 18: 31%; ACT scores over 24: 1%.

Faculty *Total:* 162, 73% full-time, 44% with terminal degrees. *Student/faculty ratio:* 19:1.

Majors Accounting; art; biology; business administration; chemistry; computer science; criminal justice/law enforcement administration; early childhood education; education; elementary education; English; English education; history; industrial technology; mass communications; mathematics; mathematics education; music; music teacher education; office management; physical education; political science; public administration; science education; social science education; social work; sociology; speech/rhetorical studies; water treatment technology.

Academic Programs *Special study options:* academic remediation for entering students, adult/continuing education programs, cooperative education, freshman honors college, honors programs, internships, part-time degree program, summer session for credit. *ROTC:* Army (b), Air Force (b).

Library James H. White Library with 130,918 titles, 599 serial subscriptions, 3,525 audiovisual materials, an OPAC, a Web page.

Computers on Campus 250 computers available on campus for general student use. A campuswide network can be accessed from student residence rooms and from off campus. Internet access, at least one staffed computer lab available.

Student Life *Housing:* on-campus residence required through senior year. *Options:* men-only, women-only. *Activities and Organizations:* drama/theater group, student-run newspaper, radio and television station, choral group, marching band, Student Government Association, Baptist Student Union, Black Student Fellowship, Panhellenic Council, National Education Association, national fraternities, national sororities. *Campus security:* 24-hour emergency response devices and patrols, controlled dormitory access. *Student Services:* health clinic, personal/psychological counseling.

Athletics Member NCAA. All Division I except football (Division I-AA). *Intercollegiate sports:* baseball M(s), basketball M(s)/W(s), bowling W, cross-country running M(s)/W(s), golf M(s), tennis M(s), track and field M(s)/W(s). *Intramural sports:* baseball M, basketball M/W, cross-country running M/W, football M, golf M/W, softball M/W, tennis M/W, track and field M/W.

Standardized Tests *Required:* SAT I or ACT (for admission).

Costs (2001–02) *Tuition:* state resident $3158 full-time, $132 per semester hour part-time; nonresident $7375 full-time, $307 per semester hour part-time. Full-time tuition and fees vary according to course load. Part-time tuition and fees vary according to course load. *Room and board:* $3187. *Payment plan:* installment. *Waivers:* children of alumni and employees or children of employees.

Applying *Options:* deferred entrance. *Required:* high school transcript. *Recommended:* interview. *Application deadline:* rolling (freshmen), rolling (transfers). *Notification:* continuous (freshmen).

Admissions Contact Mr. Wilson Lee, Director of Admissions and Recruitment, Mississippi Valley State University, 14000 Highway 82 West, Itta Bena, MS 38941-1400. *Phone:* 662-254-3344. *Toll-free phone:* 800-844-6885. *Fax:* 662-254-7900.

RUST COLLEGE

Holly Springs, Mississippi

- **Independent United Methodist** 4-year, founded 1866
- **Calendar** semesters
- **Degrees** associate and bachelor's
- **Rural** 126-acre campus with easy access to Memphis
- **Endowment** $20.7 million
- **Coed,** 801 undergraduate students, 74% full-time, 65% women, 35% men
- **Moderately difficult** entrance level, 43% of applicants were admitted

Undergraduates 595 full-time, 206 part-time. Students come from 21 states and territories, 6 other countries, 31% are from out of state, 93% African American, 7% international, 4% transferred in, 56% live on campus. *Retention:* 48% of 2001 full-time freshmen returned.

Freshmen *Admission:* 1,760 applied, 752 admitted, 154 enrolled. *Average high school GPA:* 2.40. *Test scores:* ACT scores over 18: 19%; ACT scores over 24: 1%.

Faculty *Total:* 46, 91% full-time, 41% with terminal degrees. *Student/faculty ratio:* 17:1.

Majors Biology; biology education; broadcast journalism; business administration; business education; chemistry; computer science; early childhood education; elementary education; English composition; English education; journalism; mathematics; mathematics education; music; political science; recreation/leisure facilities management; social science education; social work; sociology.

Academic Programs *Special study options:* academic remediation for entering students, accelerated degree program, adult/continuing education programs, cooperative education, honors programs, independent study, internships, part-time degree program, study abroad, summer session for credit. *ROTC:* Army (b). *Unusual degree programs:* 3-2 engineering with Memphis State University, Tuskegee University; nursing with Alcorn State University; Mehary Medical College, Tennessee State University.

Library Leontyne Price Library with 119,375 titles, 347 serial subscriptions, 1,308 audiovisual materials, an OPAC.

Computers on Campus 150 computers available on campus for general student use. A campuswide network can be accessed from student residence rooms and from off campus. Internet access, at least one staffed computer lab available.

Student Life *Housing Options:* men-only, women-only. *Activities and Organizations:* drama/theater group, student-run newspaper, radio and television station, choral group, national fraternities, national sororities. *Campus security:* 24-hour emergency response devices and patrols, late-night transport/escort service, controlled dormitory access.

Athletics Member NCAA. All Division III. *Intercollegiate sports:* baseball M, basketball M/W, cross-country running M/W, tennis M/W, track and field M/W.

Standardized Tests *Required:* ACT (for admission).

Costs (2001–02) *One-time required fee:* $100. *Comprehensive fee:* $8000 includes full-time tuition ($5600) and room and board ($2400). Part-time tuition: $242 per credit hour. Part-time tuition and fees vary according to course load. *Room and board:* College room only: $1061. *Payment plan:* deferred payment. *Waivers:* employees or children of employees.

Financial Aid Of all full-time matriculated undergraduates who enrolled in 2001, 592 applied for aid, 592 were judged to have need, 390 had their need fully

met. 465 Federal Work-Study jobs (averaging $821). 96 State and other part-time jobs (averaging $1025). *Average percent of need met:* 48%. *Average financial aid package:* $6882. *Average need-based loan:* $3105. *Average need-based gift aid:* $4542. *Average indebtedness upon graduation:* $7868.

Applying *Options:* common application, deferred entrance. *Application fee:* $10. *Required:* high school transcript, minimum 2.0 GPA, letters of recommendation. *Required for some:* essay or personal statement. *Recommended:* minimum X GPA. *Application deadlines:* 7/15 (freshmen), 7/15 (transfers). *Notification:* 7/15 (freshmen).

Admissions Contact Mr. Johnny McDonald, Director of Enrollment Services, Rust College, 150 Rust Avenue, Holly Springs, MS 38635-2328. *Phone:* 601-252-8000 Ext. 4065. *Toll-free phone:* 888-886-8492 Ext. 4065. *Fax:* 662-252-8895. *E-mail:* admissions@rustcollege.edu.

SOUTHEASTERN BAPTIST COLLEGE
Laurel, Mississippi

Admissions Contact Mrs. Emma Bond, Director of Admissions, Southeastern Baptist College, 4229 Highway 15 North, Laurel, MS 39440-1096. *Phone:* 601-426-6346.

TOUGALOO COLLEGE
Tougaloo, Mississippi

- **Independent** 4-year, founded 1869, affiliated with United Church of Christ
- **Calendar** semesters
- **Degrees** associate and bachelor's
- **Suburban** 500-acre campus
- **Endowment** $4.7 million
- **Coed,** 950 undergraduate students, 91% full-time, 71% women, 29% men
- **Minimally difficult** entrance level, 99% of applicants were admitted

Undergraduates 861 full-time, 89 part-time. Students come from 24 states and territories, 1 other country, 14% are from out of state, 100% African American, 0.2% international, 5% transferred in. *Retention:* 68% of 2001 full-time freshmen returned.

Freshmen *Admission:* 627 applied, 621 admitted, 201 enrolled. *Average high school GPA:* 3.00. *Test scores:* ACT scores over 18: 53%; ACT scores over 24: 10%; ACT scores over 30: 2%.

Faculty *Total:* 103, 68% full-time. *Student/faculty ratio:* 18:1.

Majors Accounting; African-American studies; art; biology; business administration; chemistry; child guidance; computer science; early childhood education; economics; education; elementary education; English; history; interdisciplinary studies; mathematics; music; physics; political science; pre-dentistry; psychology; secondary education; sociology.

Academic Programs *Special study options:* academic remediation for entering students, accelerated degree program, adult/continuing education programs, cooperative education, honors programs, internships, off-campus study, part-time degree program, student-designed majors, study abroad. *ROTC:* Army (b). *Unusual degree programs:* 3-2 engineering with Brown University, Georgia Institute of Technology.

Library L. Zenobiz Coleman Library with 137,000 titles, 432 serial subscriptions.

Computers on Campus 43 computers available on campus for general student use. Internet access, at least one staffed computer lab available.

Student Life *Housing Options:* men-only, women-only. *Activities and Organizations:* drama/theater group, student-run newspaper, choral group, Concert Choir, Student Government Association, Gospel Choir, NAACP, Pre-Alumni, national fraternities, national sororities. *Campus security:* 24-hour emergency response devices and patrols. *Student Services:* health clinic, personal/psychological counseling.

Athletics Member NAIA. *Intercollegiate sports:* basketball M(s)/W(s), cross-country running M(s)/W(s), golf M, softball W. *Intramural sports:* basketball M/W, bowling M, cross-country running M/W, golf M/W, softball M/W, tennis M/W, volleyball M/W.

Standardized Tests *Required:* SAT I or ACT (for admission).

Costs (2001–02) *Comprehensive fee:* $10,725 includes full-time tuition ($6900), mandatory fees ($425), and room and board ($3400). Part-time tuition: $240 per hour. *Payment plans:* installment, deferred payment. *Waivers:* adult students, senior citizens, and employees or children of employees.

Applying *Options:* common application, early admission. *Application fee:* $5. *Required:* high school transcript, minimum 2.0 GPA. *Application deadline:* rolling (freshmen), rolling (transfers). *Notification:* continuous (freshmen).

Admissions Contact Ms. Adriene W. Walls, Data Entry Specialist, Tougaloo College, Student Enrollment Management Center, 500 West County Line Road, Tougaloo, MS 39174. *Phone:* 601-977-7768. *Toll-free phone:* 888-42GALOO. *E-mail:* carolyn.evans@tougaloo.edu.

UNIVERSITY OF MISSISSIPPI
Oxford, Mississippi

- **State-supported** university, founded 1844, part of Mississippi Institutions of Higher Learning
- **Calendar** semesters
- **Degrees** bachelor's, master's, doctoral, and first professional
- **Small-town** 2500-acre campus with easy access to Memphis
- **Endowment** $17.1 million
- **Coed,** 2,091 undergraduate students, 99% full-time, 52% women, 48% men
- **Moderately difficult** entrance level, 80% of applicants were admitted

Undergraduates 2,061 full-time, 30 part-time. Students come from 47 states and territories, 46 other countries, 35% are from out of state, 37% transferred in, 33% live on campus.

Freshmen *Admission:* 6,601 applied, 5,287 admitted, 2,091 enrolled. *Average high school GPA:* 3.34. *Test scores:* ACT scores over 18: 94%; ACT scores over 24: 46%; ACT scores over 30: 11%.

Faculty *Student/faculty ratio:* 19:1.

Majors Accounting; advertising; American studies; anthropology; art; art history; biology; biomedical science; business; business administration; business economics; business marketing and marketing management; chemical engineering; chemistry; civil engineering; classics; computer/information sciences; court reporting; economics; electrical engineering; elementary education; engineering; English; English education; exercise sciences; finance; forensic technology; French; geological engineering; geology; German; history; home economics; insurance/risk management; international business; international relations; journalism; liberal arts and sciences/liberal studies; linguistics; management information systems/business data processing; mathematics; mathematics education; mechanical engineering; medical technology; music; pharmacy; philosophy; physics; political science; psychology; public administration; radio/television broadcasting; real estate; recreation/leisure studies; science education; secondary education; social studies education; social work; sociology; Spanish; special education; speech-language pathology/audiology; theater arts/drama.

Academic Programs *Special study options:* academic remediation for entering students, accelerated degree program, adult/continuing education programs, advanced placement credit, double majors, English as a second language, freshman honors college, honors programs, independent study, internships, part-time degree program, services for LD students, study abroad, summer session for credit. *ROTC:* Army (b), Navy (b), Air Force (b).

Library J. D. Williams Library plus 3 others with 951,259 titles, 8,495 serial subscriptions, 143,717 audiovisual materials, an OPAC, a Web page.

Computers on Campus 3500 computers available on campus for general student use. A campuswide network can be accessed from student residence rooms and from off campus. At least one staffed computer lab available.

Student Life *Housing:* on-campus residence required for freshman year. *Activities and Organizations:* drama/theater group, student-run newspaper, radio and television station, choral group, marching band, Associated Student Body, School Spirit, sport clubs, Black Student Union, Student Programming Board, national fraternities, national sororities. *Campus security:* 24-hour emergency response devices and patrols, late-night transport/escort service, controlled dormitory access, crime prevention programs. *Student Services:* health clinic, personal/psychological counseling, women's center, legal services.

Athletics Member NCAA. All Division I except football (Division I-A). *Intercollegiate sports:* baseball M(s), basketball M(s)/W(s), cross-country running M(s)/W(s), fencing M(c)/W(c), golf M(s)/W(s), lacrosse M(c), riflery W(s), rugby M(c), soccer M(c)/W(s), softball W(s), tennis M(s)/W(s), track and field M(s)/W(s), volleyball M(c)/W(s). *Intramural sports:* badminton M/W, basketball M/W, football M/W, golf M/W, racquetball M/W, riflery M(c), soccer M/W, softball M/W, swimming M/W, table tennis M(c)/W(c), tennis M/W, track and field M/W, volleyball M/W, water polo M/W.

Standardized Tests *Recommended:* SAT I or ACT (for admission).

Costs (2001–02) *Tuition:* state resident $3626 full-time, $151 per credit hour part-time; nonresident $8172 full-time, $341 per credit hour part-time. Part-time tuition and fees vary according to course load. *Room and board:* $4040; room only: $2340. Room and board charges vary according to board plan and housing facility. *Payment plans:* tuition prepayment, deferred payment. *Waivers:* children of alumni, senior citizens, and employees or children of employees.

Financial Aid Of all full-time matriculated undergraduates who enrolled in 2001, 4728 applied for aid, 3463 were judged to have need, 1427 had their need

University of Mississippi (continued)

fully met. In 2001, 1242 non-need-based awards were made. *Average percent of need met:* 76%. *Average financial aid package:* $7570. *Average need-based loan:* $4097. *Average need-based gift aid:* $4729. *Average non-need based aid:* $6327. *Average indebtedness upon graduation:* $14,459.

Applying *Options:* electronic application, early admission. *Application fee:* $25 (non-residents). *Required:* high school transcript, minimum 2.0 GPA. *Application deadlines:* 7/20 (freshmen), 7/24 (transfers). *Notification:* continuous until 8/16 (freshmen).

Admissions Contact Mr. Beckett Howorth, Director of Admissions, University of Mississippi, Office of Admissions, 145 Martindale Student Services Center, University, MS 38677. *Phone:* 662-915-7226. *Toll-free phone:* 800-653-6477. *Fax:* 662-915-5869. *E-mail:* admissions@olemiss.edu.

UNIVERSITY OF MISSISSIPPI MEDICAL CENTER
Jackson, Mississippi

- **State-supported** upper-level, founded 1955, part of University of Mississippi
- **Calendar** semesters
- **Degrees** certificates, bachelor's, master's, doctoral, and first professional
- **Urban** 164-acre campus
- **Endowment** $37.3 million
- **Coed,** 421 undergraduate students, 100% full-time, 85% women, 15% men
- **Moderately difficult** entrance level

Undergraduates 421 full-time. Students come from 4 states and territories, 0% are from out of state, 22% African American, 2% Asian American or Pacific Islander, 0.5% Hispanic American, 37% transferred in.

Faculty *Total:* 2,301, 26% full-time, 75% with terminal degrees. *Student/faculty ratio:* 2:1.

Majors Cytotechnology; dental hygiene; medical records administration; medical technology; nursing; occupational therapy.

Academic Programs *Special study options:* internships, services for LD students, summer session for credit.

Library Rowland Medical Library with 244,460 titles, 2,371 serial subscriptions, 17,084 audiovisual materials, an OPAC, a Web page.

Computers on Campus 120 computers available on campus for general student use. A campuswide network can be accessed from off campus. Internet access, at least one staffed computer lab available.

Student Life *Housing Options:* women-only. *Activities and Organizations:* student-run newspaper. *Campus security:* 24-hour emergency response devices and patrols, late-night transport/escort service, controlled dormitory access. *Student Services:* health clinic, personal/psychological counseling.

Athletics *Intramural sports:* basketball M/W, football M/W, golf M, rugby M, soccer M/W, softball M/W, volleyball M/W.

Standardized Tests *Required for some:* ACT (for admission).

Costs (2001–02) *Tuition:* state resident $2850 full-time; nonresident $5669 full-time. *Room and board:* room only: $1836.

Financial Aid Of all full-time matriculated undergraduates who enrolled in 2001, 328 applied for aid, 197 were judged to have need, 62 had their need fully met. *Average percent of need met:* 47%. *Average financial aid package:* $6500. *Average need-based loan:* $3500. *Average need-based gift aid:* $2500.

Applying *Application fee:* $10. *Application deadline:* 2/15 (transfers). *Notification:* continuous until 5/1 (transfers).

Admissions Contact Director of Student Services and Records, University of Mississippi Medical Center, 2500 North State Street, Jackson, MS 39216-4505. *Phone:* 601-984-1080. *Fax:* 601-984-1079.

UNIVERSITY OF SOUTHERN MISSISSIPPI
Hattiesburg, Mississippi

- **State-supported** university, founded 1910
- **Calendar** semesters
- **Degrees** bachelor's, master's, and doctoral
- **Suburban** 1090-acre campus with easy access to New Orleans
- **Coed,** 12,844 undergraduate students, 85% full-time, 61% women, 39% men
- **Moderately difficult** entrance level, 51% of applicants were admitted

Undergraduates 10,865 full-time, 1,979 part-time. Students come from 50 states and territories, 61 other countries, 10% are from out of state, 24% African American, 1% Asian American or Pacific Islander, 1.0% Hispanic American, 0.3% Native American, 1% international, 15% transferred in, 34% live on campus. *Retention:* 73% of 2001 full-time freshmen returned.

Freshmen *Admission:* 5,608 applied, 2,852 admitted, 1,505 enrolled. *Average high school GPA:* 3.23. *Test scores:* ACT scores over 18: 77%; ACT scores over 24: 26%; ACT scores over 30: 2%.

Faculty *Total:* 757, 82% full-time, 68% with terminal degrees. *Student/faculty ratio:* 20:1.

Majors Accounting; advertising; American studies; anthropology; architectural engineering technology; biology; business administration; business economics; business education; business marketing and marketing management; chemistry; chemistry related; city/community/regional planning; clothing/apparel/textile studies; communications; communications related; computer engineering technology; computer/information sciences; criminal justice studies; dance; data processing technology; dietetics; education of the hearing impaired; electrical/electronic engineering technology; elementary education; English; family studies; finance; foreign languages/literatures; geography; geology; health/physical education; history; home economics; hotel and restaurant management; industrial arts education; industrial technology; interdisciplinary studies; interior architecture; international business; international relations; journalism; library science; management information systems/business data processing; marine biology; mathematics; mechanical engineering technology; medical technology; museum studies; music; music teacher education; nursing; paralegal/legal assistant; philosophy; physical education; physics; political science; psychology; public health; radio/television broadcasting; recreation/leisure studies; social work; special education; speech-language pathology/audiology; theater arts/drama; visual/performing arts.

Academic Programs *Special study options:* academic remediation for entering students, accelerated degree program, adult/continuing education programs, advanced placement credit, cooperative education, distance learning, double majors, English as a second language, honors programs, off-campus study, part-time degree program, services for LD students, study abroad, summer session for credit. *ROTC:* Army (b), Air Force (b).

Library Cook Memorial Library plus 4 others with 217,634 titles, 21,134 audiovisual materials, an OPAC, a Web page.

Computers on Campus 600 computers available on campus for general student use. Internet access, at least one staffed computer lab available.

Student Life *Housing Options:* men-only, women-only, disabled students. *Activities and Organizations:* drama/theater group, student-run newspaper, radio station, choral group, marching band, University Activities Council, residence halls associations, Greek life, Student Government Association, national fraternities, national sororities. *Campus security:* 24-hour emergency response devices and patrols, late-night transport/escort service, controlled dormitory access. *Student Services:* health clinic, personal/psychological counseling, women's center, legal services.

Athletics Member NCAA. All Division I except football (Division I-A). *Intercollegiate sports:* baseball M(s), basketball M(s)/W(s), cross-country running M(s)/W(s), golf M(s)/W(s), tennis M(s)/W(s), track and field M(s)/W(s), volleyball W(s). *Intramural sports:* badminton M/W, basketball M/W, bowling M/W, cross-country running M/W, fencing M/W, football M/W, golf M/W, racquetball M/W, rugby M, soccer M/W, softball M/W, squash M/W, swimming M/W, table tennis M/W, tennis M/W, track and field M/W, volleyball M/W, weight lifting M/W.

Standardized Tests *Required:* SAT I or ACT (for admission).

Costs (2001–02) *Tuition:* state resident $3416 full-time, $143 per credit hour part-time; nonresident $4518 full-time, $189 per credit hour part-time. Part-time tuition and fees vary according to course load. *Room and board:* $4450; room only: $2760. Room and board charges vary according to housing facility. *Payment plans:* tuition prepayment, installment. *Waivers:* children of alumni, senior citizens, and employees or children of employees.

Financial Aid Of all full-time matriculated undergraduates who enrolled in 2001, 9706 applied for aid, 6741 were judged to have need, 3707 had their need fully met. In 2001, 2150 non-need-based awards were made. *Average percent of need met:* 88%. *Average financial aid package:* $7050. *Average need-based loan:* $3300. *Average need-based gift aid:* $2980. *Average non-need based aid:* $1050. *Average indebtedness upon graduation:* $17,350.

Applying *Options:* electronic application, early admission, deferred entrance. *Required:* high school transcript, minimum 2.0 GPA. *Required for some:* interview. *Application deadline:* rolling (freshmen), rolling (transfers). *Notification:* continuous (freshmen).

Admissions Contact Dr. Homer Wesley, Dean of Admissions, University of Southern Mississippi, Box 5166, Hattiesburg, MS 39406-5166. *Phone:* 601-266-5000. *Fax:* 601-266-5148. *E-mail:* admissions@usm.edu.

WESLEY COLLEGE
Florence, Mississippi

- **Independent Congregational Methodist** 4-year, founded 1944
- **Calendar** semesters

- **Degree** certificates and bachelor's
- **Small-town** 40-acre campus with easy access to Jackson
- **Endowment** $353,038
- **Coed,** 101 undergraduate students, 70% full-time, 41% women, 59% men
- **Noncompetitive** entrance level, 97% of applicants were admitted

Undergraduates 71 full-time, 30 part-time. Students come from 10 states and territories, 3 other countries, 35% are from out of state, 10% transferred in, 69% live on campus.

Freshmen *Admission:* 30 applied, 29 admitted, 29 enrolled. *Test scores:* SAT verbal scores over 500: 100%; ACT scores over 18: 77%; ACT scores over 24: 23%.

Faculty *Total:* 16, 63% full-time, 19% with terminal degrees. *Student/faculty ratio:* 5:1.

Majors Biblical studies; religious education.

Academic Programs *Special study options:* academic remediation for entering students, adult/continuing education programs, advanced placement credit, double majors, independent study, internships, part-time degree program.

Library 25,000 titles, 96 serial subscriptions, 51 audiovisual materials.

Computers on Campus 2 computers available on campus for general student use. At least one staffed computer lab available.

Student Life *Housing Options:* men-only, women-only. *Activities and Organizations:* drama/theater group, choral group, Missionary Prayer Band, Ministerial Union. *Campus security:* 24-hour emergency response devices.

Athletics Member NCCAA. *Intercollegiate sports:* basketball M. *Intramural sports:* basketball M, table tennis M/W, volleyball M/W, weight lifting M/W.

Standardized Tests *Required:* SAT I or ACT (for admission).

Costs (2001–02) *Comprehensive fee:* $6600 includes full-time tuition ($3500), mandatory fees ($400), and room and board ($2700). Part-time tuition: $150 per credit hour. *Required fees:* $100 per semester hour. *Room and board:* College room only: $1150.

Applying *Application fee:* $20. *Required:* essay or personal statement, high school transcript, 3 letters of recommendation. *Recommended:* interview. *Application deadline:* rolling (freshmen), rolling (transfers). *Notification:* continuous (freshmen).

Admissions Contact Rev. Chris Lohrstorfer, Director of Admissions, Wesley College, PO Box 1070, Florence, MS 39073-1070. *Phone:* 601-845-2265 Ext. 21. *Toll-free phone:* 800-748-9972. *Fax:* 601-845-2266. *E-mail:* wcadmit@aol.com.

WILLIAM CAREY COLLEGE
Hattiesburg, Mississippi

- **Independent Southern Baptist** comprehensive, founded 1906
- **Calendar** trimesters
- **Degrees** bachelor's and master's
- **Small-town** 64-acre campus with easy access to New Orleans
- **Endowment** $5.2 million
- **Coed,** 1,582 undergraduate students, 79% full-time, 68% women, 32% men
- **Moderately difficult** entrance level, 52% of applicants were admitted

Undergraduates Students come from 30 states and territories, 21 other countries, 29% African American, 0.6% Asian American or Pacific Islander, 2% Hispanic American, 0.4% Native American, 2% international, 35% live on campus. *Retention:* 64% of 2001 full-time freshmen returned.

Freshmen *Admission:* 409 applied, 211 admitted.

Faculty *Total:* 172, 47% full-time.

Majors Applied art; art; art education; biblical studies; biological/physical sciences; biology; business administration; chemistry; drawing; economics; education; education administration; elementary education; English; finance; fine/studio arts; health education; history; industrial radiologic technology; liberal arts and sciences/liberal studies; mass communications; mathematics; medical technology; modern languages; music; music teacher education; music therapy; music (voice and choral/opera performance); nursing; physical education; physical therapy; pre-dentistry; pre-law; pre-medicine; pre-veterinary studies; psychology; religious music; religious studies; secondary education; social sciences; Spanish; theater arts/drama.

Academic Programs *Special study options:* academic remediation for entering students, accelerated degree program, adult/continuing education programs, honors programs, off-campus study, part-time degree program, services for LD students, summer session for credit. *ROTC:* Army (c), Air Force (c).

Library I. E. Rouse Library with 109,746 titles, 587 serial subscriptions.

Computers on Campus 30 computers available on campus for general student use. Internet access, at least one staffed computer lab available.

Student Life *Housing:* on-campus residence required through senior year. *Options:* men-only, women-only. *Activities and Organizations:* drama/theater group, student-run newspaper, choral group, Student Government Association, Baptist Student Union, Phi Beta Lambda. *Campus security:* 24-hour patrols, controlled dormitory access. *Student Services:* personal/psychological counseling.

Athletics Member NAIA. *Intercollegiate sports:* baseball M(s), basketball M(s)/W(s), golf M, soccer M(s)/W(s), softball W. *Intramural sports:* badminton M/W, basketball M/W, football M, golf M, softball M/W, table tennis M/W, volleyball M/W.

Standardized Tests *Required:* SAT I or ACT (for admission).

Costs (2002–03) *Comprehensive fee:* $8505 includes full-time tuition ($6345), mandatory fees ($170), and room and board ($1990). Part-time tuition: $235 per hour. *Required fees:* $85 per term part-time. *Room and board:* College room only: $830. Room and board charges vary according to board plan and housing facility. *Payment plan:* deferred payment.

Financial Aid Of all full-time matriculated undergraduates who enrolled in 2001, 1610 applied for aid, 1207 were judged to have need, 1100 had their need fully met. 340 Federal Work-Study jobs (averaging $1500). *Average percent of need met:* 75%. *Average financial aid package:* $8200. *Average need-based loan:* $4300. *Average need-based gift aid:* $5500. *Average indebtedness upon graduation:* $15,000.

Applying *Options:* common application, electronic application, early admission, deferred entrance. *Application fee:* $20. *Required:* high school transcript. *Required for some:* letters of recommendation. *Recommended:* minimum 2.0 GPA. *Application deadline:* rolling (freshmen), rolling (transfers). *Notification:* continuous until 8/15 (freshmen).

Admissions Contact Mr. David Armstrong, Director of Admissions, William Carey College, 498 Tuscan Avenue, Hattiesburg, MS 39401-5499. *Phone:* 601-318-5051 Ext. 103. *Toll-free phone:* 800-962-5991. *E-mail:* admiss@mail.wmcarey.edu.

MISSOURI

AVILA COLLEGE
Kansas City, Missouri

- **Independent Roman Catholic** comprehensive, founded 1916
- **Calendar** semesters
- **Degrees** certificates, bachelor's, and master's
- **Suburban** 50-acre campus
- **Endowment** $4.9 million
- **Coed,** 1,235 undergraduate students, 64% full-time, 66% women, 34% men
- **Minimally difficult** entrance level, 60% of applicants were admitted

Undergraduates 795 full-time, 440 part-time. Students come from 17 states and territories, 20 other countries, 27% are from out of state, 14% African American, 2% Asian American or Pacific Islander, 3% Hispanic American, 0.7% Native American, 3% international, 14% transferred in, 14% live on campus. *Retention:* 80% of 2001 full-time freshmen returned.

Freshmen *Admission:* 645 applied, 390 admitted, 163 enrolled. *Average high school GPA:* 3.03. *Test scores:* SAT verbal scores over 500: 43%; SAT math scores over 500: 50%; ACT scores over 18: 82%; SAT verbal scores over 600: 14%; ACT scores over 24: 21%; ACT scores over 30: 2%.

Faculty *Total:* 174, 33% full-time, 52% with terminal degrees. *Student/faculty ratio:* 13:1.

Majors Accounting; art; art education; art therapy; behavioral sciences; biology; business administration; business education; business marketing and marketing management; cardiovascular technology; chemistry; communications; computer science; criminal justice studies; elementary education; English; exercise sciences; finance; general studies; gerontology; graphic design/commercial art/illustration; history; humanities; information sciences/systems; international business; marketing operations; mathematics; medical radiologic technology; medical technology; middle school education; music; natural sciences; nursing; occupational therapy; paralegal/legal assistant; physical therapy; political science; pre-medicine; psychology; social work; sociology; special education; theater arts/drama; theology.

Academic Programs *Special study options:* academic remediation for entering students, accelerated degree program, adult/continuing education programs, advanced placement credit, cooperative education, distance learning, double majors, English as a second language, independent study, internships, off-campus study, part-time degree program, services for LD students, study abroad, summer session for credit. *ROTC:* Army (c). *Unusual degree programs:* 3-2 occupational therapy, physical therapy, law with Rockhurst University, University of Missouri-Kansas City.

Avila College (continued)

Library Hooley Bundshu Library with 75,505 titles, 7,179 serial subscriptions, 3,094 audiovisual materials, an OPAC, a Web page.

Computers on Campus 68 computers available on campus for general student use. A campuswide network can be accessed from student residence rooms and from off campus. Internet access, at least one staffed computer lab available.

Student Life *Housing:* on-campus residence required through sophomore year. *Options:* coed, women-only. *Activities and Organizations:* drama/theater group, student-run newspaper, television station, choral group, Group Activities Programming, Avila Student Nurses Association, Residence Hall Association, Student Senate, Avila Education Association. *Campus security:* student patrols, late-night transport/escort service, controlled dormitory access, 8-hour patrols by trained security personnel; 24-hour security personnel on-call. *Student Services:* health clinic, personal/psychological counseling.

Athletics Member NAIA. *Intercollegiate sports:* baseball M(s), basketball M(s)/W(s), soccer M(s)/W(s), softball W(s), volleyball W(s). *Intramural sports:* basketball M/W, bowling M/W, football M/W, golf M/W, soccer M/W, softball M/W, table tennis M/W, tennis M/W, volleyball M/W, weight lifting M/W.

Standardized Tests *Required:* SAT I or ACT (for admission).

Costs (2001–02) *Comprehensive fee:* $18,570 includes full-time tuition ($13,150), mandatory fees ($270), and room and board ($5150). Full-time tuition and fees vary according to course load. Part-time tuition: $290 per credit hour. Part-time tuition and fees vary according to course load. *Required fees:* $5 per credit hour. *Room and board:* Room and board charges vary according to board plan and housing facility. *Payment plans:* installment, deferred payment. *Waivers:* children of alumni, senior citizens, and employees or children of employees.

Financial Aid Of all full-time matriculated undergraduates who enrolled in 2001, 439 applied for aid, 373 were judged to have need. 150 Federal Work-Study jobs (averaging $946). *Average indebtedness upon graduation:* $17,125.

Applying *Options:* common application, early admission. *Required:* high school transcript, minimum 2.5 GPA. *Required for some:* essay or personal statement, letters of recommendation. *Recommended:* interview. *Application deadline:* rolling (freshmen), rolling (transfers). *Notification:* continuous (freshmen).

Admissions Contact Ms. Paige Illum, Director of Admissions, Avila College, 11901 Wornall Rd, Kansas City, MO 64145. *Phone:* 816-501-3773. *Toll-free phone:* 800-GO-AVILA. *Fax:* 816-501-2453. *E-mail:* admissions@mail.avila.edu.

BAPTIST BIBLE COLLEGE
Springfield, Missouri

- **Independent Baptist** comprehensive, founded 1950
- **Calendar** semesters
- **Degrees** associate, bachelor's, and master's
- 38-acre campus
- **Coed,** 727 undergraduate students
- **Noncompetitive** entrance level, 100% of applicants were admitted

Undergraduates Students come from 46 states and territories, 5 other countries, 80% are from out of state, 0.8% African American, 0.3% Asian American or Pacific Islander, 4% Hispanic American, 0.7% Native American, 1.0% international, 61% live on campus.

Freshmen *Admission:* 224 applied, 224 admitted.

Faculty *Total:* 41, 85% full-time.

Majors Business administration; divinity/ministry; elementary education; music; music teacher education; pastoral counseling; religious education; secretarial science.

Academic Programs *Special study options:* academic remediation for entering students, internships, part-time degree program, summer session for credit. *ROTC:* Army (c).

Library 36,844 titles, 226 serial subscriptions.

Computers on Campus 50 computers available on campus for general student use. At least one staffed computer lab available.

Student Life *Housing:* on-campus residence required through senior year. *Options:* men-only, women-only. *Activities and Organizations:* drama/theater group, student-run radio station, choral group. *Student Services:* health clinic, personal/psychological counseling.

Athletics Member NAIA. *Intercollegiate sports:* basketball M/W, soccer M, volleyball W. *Intramural sports:* basketball M/W, soccer M, table tennis M/W, volleyball M/W.

Standardized Tests *Required:* ACT (for placement).

Costs (2001–02) *Comprehensive fee:* $7730 includes full-time tuition ($2998), mandatory fees ($482), and room and board ($4250). Full-time tuition and fees vary according to program. Part-time tuition: $128 per hour.

Applying *Options:* early admission, deferred entrance. *Application fee:* $40. *Required:* high school transcript, 1 letter of recommendation. *Application deadline:* rolling (freshmen), rolling (transfers). *Notification:* continuous (freshmen).

Admissions Contact Dr. Joseph Gleason, Director of Admissions, Baptist Bible College, 628 East Kearney, Springfield, MO 65803-3498. *Phone:* 417-268-6000 Ext. 6013. *Fax:* 417-268-6694.

CALVARY BIBLE COLLEGE AND THEOLOGICAL SEMINARY
Kansas City, Missouri

- **Independent interdenominational** comprehensive, founded 1932
- **Calendar** 4-4-1
- **Degrees** certificates, diplomas, associate, bachelor's, master's, and first professional
- **Suburban** 55-acre campus
- **Coed,** 212 undergraduate students, 65% full-time, 47% women, 53% men
- **Minimally difficult** entrance level

Undergraduates 137 full-time, 75 part-time. Students come from 25 states and territories, 5 other countries, 47% are from out of state, 7% African American, 4% Asian American or Pacific Islander, 0.9% Hispanic American, 0.4% international.

Freshmen *Admission:* 41 enrolled.

Faculty *Total:* 31, 19% full-time, 19% with terminal degrees. *Student/faculty ratio:* 7:1.

Majors Aircraft mechanic/powerplant; aircraft pilot (private); aircraft pilot (professional); biblical studies; broadcast journalism; business administration; computer science; divinity/ministry; education; elementary education; Greek (ancient and medieval); Hebrew; human resources management; mass communications; music; music (piano and organ performance); music teacher education; music (voice and choral/opera performance); paralegal/legal assistant; pastoral counseling; religious education; religious music; secondary education; theology.

Academic Programs *Special study options:* academic remediation for entering students, accelerated degree program, adult/continuing education programs, advanced placement credit, distance learning, double majors, independent study, off-campus study, part-time degree program, summer session for credit.

Library Hilda Kroeker Library with 59,000 titles, 307 serial subscriptions, an OPAC, a Web page.

Computers on Campus 10 computers available on campus for general student use. At least one staffed computer lab available.

Student Life *Housing:* on-campus residence required through senior year. *Options:* men-only, women-only. *Activities and Organizations:* student-run radio station, choral group. *Campus security:* night patrols by trained security personnel. *Student Services:* health clinic, personal/psychological counseling.

Athletics Member NCCAA. *Intercollegiate sports:* basketball M/W, soccer M, volleyball W. *Intramural sports:* basketball M/W.

Standardized Tests *Required:* SAT I or ACT (for admission).

Costs (2001–02) *Comprehensive fee:* $8050 includes full-time tuition ($4600), mandatory fees ($410), and room and board ($3040). Part-time tuition: $180 per semester hour. *Required fees:* $18 per semester hour. *Room and board:* College room only: $1290. *Payment plans:* installment, deferred payment. *Waivers:* children of alumni, senior citizens, and employees or children of employees.

Financial Aid *Financial aid deadline:* 3/31.

Applying *Options:* early admission, deferred entrance. *Application fee:* $25. *Required:* essay or personal statement, high school transcript, 2 letters of recommendation, statement of faith. *Recommended:* interview. *Application deadline:* rolling (freshmen), rolling (transfers).

Admissions Contact Mr. Timothy Smith, Director of Admissions, Calvary Bible College and Theological Seminary, 15800 Calvary Road, Kansas City, MO 64147-1341. *Phone:* 816-322-0110 Ext. 1326. *Toll-free phone:* 800-326-3960. *Fax:* 816-331-4474. *E-mail:* admissions@calvary.edu.

CENTRAL BIBLE COLLEGE
Springfield, Missouri

- **Independent** 4-year, founded 1922, affiliated with Assemblies of God
- **Calendar** semesters
- **Degrees** certificates, diplomas, associate, and bachelor's
- **Suburban** 108-acre campus
- **Coed,** 805 undergraduate students, 90% full-time, 41% women, 59% men
- **Moderately difficult** entrance level, 65% of applicants were admitted

Undergraduates 722 full-time, 83 part-time. Students come from 47 states and territories, 75% are from out of state, 2% African American, 2% Asian American or Pacific Islander, 3% Hispanic American, 1% Native American, 0.5% international, 4% transferred in, 65% live on campus. *Retention:* 75% of 2001 full-time freshmen returned.

Freshmen *Admission:* 210 applied, 137 admitted, 137 enrolled. *Average high school GPA:* 3.16. *Test scores:* SAT verbal scores over 500: 74%; SAT math scores over 500: 63%; ACT scores over 18: 85%; SAT verbal scores over 600: 31%; SAT math scores over 600: 31%; ACT scores over 24: 42%; SAT verbal scores over 700: 5%; SAT math scores over 700: 5%; ACT scores over 30: 4%.

Faculty *Total:* 56, 66% full-time, 23% with terminal degrees. *Student/faculty ratio:* 21:1.

Majors Biblical languages/literatures; biblical studies; pastoral counseling; religious education; religious music; religious studies; theology.

Academic Programs *Special study options:* academic remediation for entering students, advanced placement credit, double majors, independent study, internships, part-time degree program, services for LD students, summer session for credit.

Library Meyer Pearlman Library with 166,795 titles, 994 serial subscriptions, 11,736 audiovisual materials, an OPAC, a Web page.

Computers on Campus 20 computers available on campus for general student use. Internet access, at least one staffed computer lab available.

Student Life *Housing:* on-campus residence required through senior year. *Options:* men-only, women-only. *Activities and Organizations:* drama/theater group, student-run newspaper, radio station, choral group. *Campus security:* 24-hour emergency response devices and patrols, student patrols, controlled dormitory access. *Student Services:* health clinic, personal/psychological counseling.

Athletics Member NCCAA. *Intercollegiate sports:* basketball M/W, soccer M, volleyball W. *Intramural sports:* basketball M/W, softball M/W, volleyball W.

Standardized Tests *Required:* SAT I or ACT (for placement).

Costs (2002–03) *Comprehensive fee:* $10,480 includes full-time tuition ($6340), mandatory fees ($540), and room and board ($3600). Full-time tuition and fees vary according to course load. Part-time tuition: $245 per credit. Part-time tuition and fees vary according to course load. *Required fees:* $90 per term part-time. *Payment plan:* installment. *Waivers:* senior citizens and employees or children of employees.

Financial Aid Of all full-time matriculated undergraduates who enrolled in 2001, 765 applied for aid, 700 were judged to have need, 55 had their need fully met. 140 Federal Work-Study jobs (averaging $1183). In 2001, 65 non-need-based awards were made. *Average percent of need met:* 51%. *Average financial aid package:* $5857. *Average need-based loan:* $3869. *Average need-based gift aid:* $3111. *Average indebtedness upon graduation:* $10,500.

Applying *Options:* early admission, deferred entrance. *Application fee:* $25. *Required:* essay or personal statement, high school transcript, 3 letters of recommendation. *Required for some:* interview. *Recommended:* minimum 2.0 GPA. *Application deadline:* rolling (freshmen), rolling (transfers).

Admissions Contact Mrs. Eunice A. Bruegman, Director of Admissions and Records, Central Bible College, 3000 North Grant Avenue, Springfield, MO 65803-1096. *Phone:* 417-833-2551 Ext. 1184. *Toll-free phone:* 800-831-4222 Ext. 1184. *Fax:* 417-833-5141. *E-mail:* info@cbcag.edu.

CENTRAL CHRISTIAN COLLEGE OF THE BIBLE
Moberly, Missouri

- **Independent** 4-year, founded 1957, affiliated with Christian Churches and Churches of Christ
- **Calendar** semesters
- **Degrees** associate and bachelor's
- **Small-town** 40-acre campus
- **Coed,** 191 undergraduate students, 94% full-time, 42% women, 58% men
- **Noncompetitive** entrance level

Undergraduates Students come from 10 states and territories, 1 other country, 40% are from out of state, 0.5% African American, 0.5% Asian American or Pacific Islander, 1% Hispanic American, 75% live on campus.

Faculty *Total:* 18, 28% full-time, 28% with terminal degrees. *Student/faculty ratio:* 19:1.

Majors Biblical studies; divinity/ministry; music; religious education; religious music; religious studies; social work; theology.

Academic Programs *Special study options:* academic remediation for entering students, internships, off-campus study, part-time degree program, student-designed majors.

Library 35,000 titles, 196 serial subscriptions.

Computers on Campus 25 computers available on campus for general student use. At least one staffed computer lab available.

Student Life *Housing:* on-campus residence required through senior year. *Options:* men-only, women-only. *Activities and Organizations:* choral group, Harvesters. *Student Services:* personal/psychological counseling.

Athletics *Intercollegiate sports:* basketball M/W, golf M/W, tennis M/W, volleyball W. *Intramural sports:* basketball M/W, bowling M/W, football M/W, golf M/W, tennis M/W, volleyball M/W.

Standardized Tests *Required:* SAT I or ACT (for admission).

Costs (2001–02) *Comprehensive fee:* $7890 includes full-time tuition ($4200), mandatory fees ($500), and room and board ($3190). Part-time tuition: $140 per credit hour. Part-time tuition and fees vary according to course load. *Required fees:* $200 per term. *Room and board:* Room and board charges vary according to board plan. *Payment plan:* deferred payment. *Waivers:* children of alumni and employees or children of employees.

Financial Aid Of all full-time matriculated undergraduates who enrolled in 2001, 101 applied for aid, 98 were judged to have need, 2 had their need fully met. 7 Federal Work-Study jobs (averaging $1248). In 2001, 2 non-need-based awards were made. *Average percent of need met:* 36%. *Average financial aid package:* $6155. *Average need-based loan:* $4094. *Average need-based gift aid:* $1952. *Average non-need based aid:* $2380. *Average indebtedness upon graduation:* $10,884. *Financial aid deadline:* 3/15.

Applying *Options:* early admission, deferred entrance. *Application fee:* $25. *Required:* high school transcript, 3 letters of recommendation. *Application deadline:* rolling (freshmen), rolling (transfers).

Admissions Contact Ms. Misty Rodda, Director of Admissions, Central Christian College of the Bible, 911 Urbandale Drive East, Moberly, MO 65270-1997. *Phone:* 660-263-3900. *Toll-free phone:* 888-263-3900. *Fax:* 660-263-3936. *E-mail:* iwant2be@cccb.edu.

CENTRAL METHODIST COLLEGE
Fayette, Missouri

- **Independent Methodist** comprehensive, founded 1854
- **Calendar** 4-1-4
- **Degrees** associate, bachelor's, and master's
- **Small-town** 52-acre campus
- **Endowment** $18.0 million
- **Coed,** 1,226 undergraduate students, 88% full-time, 61% women, 39% men
- **Moderately difficult** entrance level, 83% of applicants were admitted

Undergraduates 1,077 full-time, 149 part-time. Students come from 20 states and territories, 6% are from out of state, 6% African American, 0.8% Asian American or Pacific Islander, 1% Hispanic American, 0.7% Native American, 0.2% international, 8% transferred in, 45% live on campus. *Retention:* 61% of 2001 full-time freshmen returned.

Freshmen *Admission:* 1,056 applied, 880 admitted, 246 enrolled. *Average high school GPA:* 3.14. *Test scores:* ACT scores over 18: 72%; ACT scores over 24: 23%; ACT scores over 30: 2%.

Faculty *Total:* 97, 58% full-time, 42% with terminal degrees. *Student/faculty ratio:* 14:1.

Majors Accounting; applied mathematics; athletic training/sports medicine; biology; biology education; business administration; chemistry; chemistry education; communications; computer science; criminal justice studies; early childhood education; economics; education; elementary education; English; environmental biology; environmental science; foreign languages education; foreign languages/literatures; French; history; interdisciplinary studies; management science; mathematics; middle school education; music; music (general performance); music teacher education; nursing; nursing administration; philosophy; physical education; physics; physics education; political science; psychology; public administration; religious studies; science education; secondary education; social science education; sociology; Spanish; sport/fitness administration; theater arts/drama.

Academic Programs *Special study options:* academic remediation for entering students, advanced placement credit, distance learning, double majors, honors programs, independent study, internships, off-campus study, part-time degree program, services for LD students, student-designed majors, study abroad, summer session for credit. *ROTC:* Army (c). *Unusual degree programs:* 3-2 engineering with University of Missouri-Rolla.

Library Smiley Library plus 1 other with 94,841 titles, 3,100 serial subscriptions, 3,654 audiovisual materials, an OPAC, a Web page.

Computers on Campus 72 computers available on campus for general student use. A campuswide network can be accessed from student residence rooms and from off campus. Internet access, at least one staffed computer lab available.

Central Methodist College (continued)

Student Life *Housing:* on-campus residence required through senior year. *Options:* coed, men-only, women-only. *Activities and Organizations:* drama/theater group, student-run newspaper, radio and television station, choral group, marching band, Student Government Association, Wesley Foundation, Alpha Phi Omega, Christian Students United in Christ, Big Brothers/Big Sisters program. *Campus security:* 24-hour emergency response devices, late-night transport/escort service, controlled dormitory access. *Student Services:* health clinic, personal/psychological counseling.

Athletics Member NAIA. *Intercollegiate sports:* baseball M(s), basketball M(s)/W(s), cross-country running M(s)/W(s), football M(s), golf M(s)/W(s), soccer M(s)/W(s), softball W(s), track and field M(s)/W(s), volleyball W(s). *Intramural sports:* basketball M/W, football M/W, golf M/W, racquetball M/W, soccer M/W, softball M/W, tennis M/W, track and field M/W, volleyball M/W, water polo M/W.

Standardized Tests *Required:* SAT I or ACT (for admission). *Recommended:* ACT (for admission).

Costs (2002–03) *Comprehensive fee:* $17,610 includes full-time tuition ($12,420), mandatory fees ($370), and room and board ($4820). Part-time tuition: $135 per credit hour. Part-time tuition and fees vary according to course load. *Required fees:* $17 per credit hour. *Payment plan:* installment. *Waivers:* employees or children of employees.

Financial Aid Of all full-time matriculated undergraduates who enrolled in 2001, 1026 applied for aid, 1008 were judged to have need, 530 had their need fully met. 163 Federal Work-Study jobs (averaging $937). *Average percent of need met:* 65%. *Average financial aid package:* $14,200. *Average need-based loan:* $4300. *Average need-based gift aid:* $5423. *Average non-need based aid:* $5000. *Average indebtedness upon graduation:* $17,618.

Applying *Options:* common application, electronic application, early admission, deferred entrance. *Application fee:* $20. *Required:* high school transcript, minimum 2.0 GPA. *Required for some:* 2 letters of recommendation. *Application deadline:* 8/1 (freshmen), rolling (transfers). *Notification:* continuous (freshmen).

Admissions Contact Mr. Don Hapward, Dean of Admissions and Financial Assistance, Central Methodist College, 411 Central Methodist Square, Fayette, MO 65248-1198. *Phone:* 660-248-6247. *Toll-free phone:* 888-262-1854. *Fax:* 660-248-1872. *E-mail:* admissions@cmc.edu.

CENTRAL MISSOURI STATE UNIVERSITY

Warrensburg, Missouri

- **State-supported** comprehensive, founded 1871
- **Calendar** semesters
- **Degrees** associate, bachelor's, master's, post-master's, and postbachelor's certificates
- **Small-town** 1240-acre campus with easy access to Kansas City
- **Endowment** $1.3 million
- **Coed,** 9,068 undergraduate students, 81% full-time, 53% women, 47% men
- **Moderately difficult** entrance level, 72% of applicants were admitted

Central Missouri State University offers outstanding career-oriented programs in more than 150 areas of study within the arts and sciences, applied sciences and technology, business and economics, and education and human services. A friendly environment, an excellent faculty, and state-of-the-art facilities make the 1,240-acre campus an exciting place to learn and live.

Undergraduates 7,387 full-time, 1,681 part-time. Students come from 41 states and territories, 65 other countries, 6% are from out of state, 5% African American, 1% Asian American or Pacific Islander, 1% Hispanic American, 0.6% Native American, 4% international, 9% transferred in, 32% live on campus. *Retention:* 74% of 2001 full-time freshmen returned.

Freshmen *Admission:* 3,720 applied, 2,664 admitted, 1,502 enrolled. *Test scores:* ACT scores over 18: 92%; ACT scores over 24: 28%; ACT scores over 30: 4%.

Faculty *Total:* 561, 78% full-time, 64% with terminal degrees. *Student/faculty ratio:* 17:1.

Majors Accounting; actuarial science; aerospace engineering technology; agribusiness; agricultural business; agricultural economics; agricultural education; agricultural mechanization; architectural engineering technology; art education; auto mechanic/technician; automotive engineering technology; biology; biology education; business administration; business education; business marketing and marketing management; chemistry; chemistry education; child care/guidance; clothing/apparel/textile studies; computer/information sciences; construction technology; criminal justice/law enforcement administration; dietetics; drafting; earth sciences; economics; education; electrical/electronic engineering technology; elementary education; English; English education; fashion merchandising; finance; fine/studio arts; French; French language education; geography; geology; German; German language education; graphic design/commercial art/illustration; graphic/printing equipment; heating/air conditioning/refrigeration technology; history; home economics; home economics education; hotel and restaurant management; human resources management; industrial arts education; industrial technology; interior architecture; interior design; journalism; legal administrative assistant; management information systems/business data processing; mass communications; mathematics; mathematics education; medical technology; middle school education; music; music teacher education; music theory and composition; nursing; occupational safety/health technology; office management; photography; physical education; physics; physics education; political science; predentistry; pre-medicine; pre-pharmacy studies; pre-veterinary studies; psychology; public relations; radio/television broadcasting; reading education; recreation/leisure studies; science education; secondary education; secretarial science; social studies education; social work; sociology; Spanish; Spanish language education; special education; speech education; speech-language pathology; speech/rhetorical studies; theater arts/drama; tourism/travel marketing.

Academic Programs *Special study options:* academic remediation for entering students, adult/continuing education programs, advanced placement credit, distance learning, double majors, English as a second language, honors programs, internships, off-campus study, part-time degree program, services for LD students, student-designed majors, study abroad, summer session for credit. *ROTC:* Army (b). *Unusual degree programs:* 3-2 engineering with University of Missouri-Columbia, University of Missouri-Rolla, University of Missouri-Kansas City.

Library James C. Kirkpatrick Library with 850,973 titles, 3,570 serial subscriptions, 23,412 audiovisual materials, an OPAC, a Web page.

Computers on Campus 1007 computers available on campus for general student use. A campuswide network can be accessed from student residence rooms and from off campus. Internet access, online (class) registration, at least one staffed computer lab available.

Student Life *Housing:* on-campus residence required for freshman year. *Options:* coed, men-only, women-only, disabled students. *Activities and Organizations:* drama/theater group, student-run newspaper, radio and television station, choral group, marching band, Student Government Association, University Program Council, Association of Black Collegiates, University Student Housing Council, International Student Organization, national fraternities, national sororities. *Campus security:* 24-hour emergency response devices and patrols, student patrols, late-night transport/escort service, controlled dormitory access. *Student Services:* health clinic, personal/psychological counseling, women's center.

Athletics Member NCAA. All Division II. *Intercollegiate sports:* baseball M(s), basketball M(s)/W(s), bowling M(c)/W(c), cross-country running M(s)/W(s), football M(s), golf M(s), rugby M(c)/W(c), soccer M(c)/W(s), softball W(s), track and field M(s)/W(s), volleyball W(s), wrestling M(s). *Intramural sports:* archery M, badminton M/W, basketball M/W, bowling M/W, cross-country running M/W, football M/W, golf M/W, racquetball M/W, riflery M/W, rugby M/W, soccer M/W, softball M/W, swimming M/W, table tennis M/W, tennis M/W, track and field M/W, volleyball M/W, water polo M/W, weight lifting M, wrestling M.

Standardized Tests *Required:* ACT (for admission).

Costs (2001–02) *Tuition:* state resident $3450 full-time, $115 per credit part-time; nonresident $6900 full-time, $230 per credit part-time. Full-time tuition and fees vary according to course load and location. Part-time tuition and fees vary according to course load and location. *Required fees:* $60 full-time, $2 per credit. *Room and board:* $4410; room only: $2790. Room and board charges vary according to board plan and housing facility. *Payment plans:* installment, deferred payment. *Waivers:* children of alumni, senior citizens, and employees or children of employees.

Financial Aid Of all full-time matriculated undergraduates who enrolled in 2001, 5576 applied for aid, 4300 were judged to have need, 1876 had their need fully met. 374 Federal Work-Study jobs (averaging $1328). 1383 State and other part-time jobs (averaging $1422). In 2001, 2140 non-need-based awards were made. *Average percent of need met:* 96%. *Average financial aid package:* $6192. *Average need-based loan:* $3785. *Average need-based gift aid:* $2911. *Average non-need based aid:* $2340. *Average indebtedness upon graduation:* $8950.

Applying *Options:* common application, electronic application, deferred entrance. *Application fee:* $25. *Required:* high school transcript, rank in upper two-thirds of high school class, minimum ACT score of 20. *Required for some:* letters of recommendation. *Application deadline:* rolling (freshmen), rolling (transfers). *Notification:* continuous (freshmen).

Admissions Contact Ms. Susan Duggins, Director of Admissions, Central Missouri State University, Administration Building Room 104, Warrensburg, MO 64093. *Phone:* 660-543-4290. *Toll-free phone:* 800-729-2678. *Fax:* 660-543-8517. *E-mail:* admit@cmsuvmb.cmsu.edu.

CLEVELAND CHIROPRACTIC COLLEGE-KANSAS CITY CAMPUS

Kansas City, Missouri

- **Independent** upper-level, founded 1922
- **Calendar** trimesters
- **Degrees** bachelor's and first professional
- **Coed**

Faculty *Student/faculty ratio:* 15:1.

Applying *Options:* deferred entrance. *Application fee:* $35.

Admissions Contact Ms. Melissa Denton, Director of Admissions, Cleveland Chiropractic College-Kansas City Campus, 6401 Rockhill Road, Kansas City, MO 64131. *Phone:* 816-501-0100. *Toll-free phone:* 800-467-2252. *Fax:* 816-501-0205. *E-mail:* kc.admissions@cleveland.edu.

COLLEGE OF THE OZARKS

Point Lookout, Missouri

- **Independent Presbyterian** 4-year, founded 1906
- **Calendar** semesters
- **Degree** bachelor's
- **Small-town** 1000-acre campus
- **Endowment** $273.4 million
- **Coed,** 1,395 undergraduate students, 92% full-time, 56% women, 44% men
- **Moderately difficult** entrance level, 15% of applicants were admitted

Undergraduates 1,286 full-time, 109 part-time. Students come from 26 states and territories, 22 other countries, 33% are from out of state, 0.4% African American, 0.6% Asian American or Pacific Islander, 1% Hispanic American, 0.5% Native American, 3% international, 5% transferred in, 68% live on campus. *Retention:* 81% of 2001 full-time freshmen returned.

Freshmen *Admission:* 2,129 applied, 311 admitted, 275 enrolled. *Average high school GPA:* 2.89. *Test scores:* ACT scores over 18: 90%; ACT scores over 24: 25%; ACT scores over 30: 3%.

Faculty *Total:* 123, 72% full-time. *Student/faculty ratio:* 14:1.

Majors Accounting; agribusiness; agricultural education; agricultural mechanization; agronomy/crop science; animal sciences; art education; aviation technology; biology; biology education; broadcast journalism; business administration; business education; business marketing and marketing management; chemistry; chemistry education; child care/development; child guidance; clothing/apparel/textile studies; computer/information sciences; computer science; consumer services; corrections; criminal justice/law enforcement administration; criminology; dietetics; education; elementary education; English; English education; fine/studio arts; forensic technology; French; German; gerontology; health/physical education; health science; history; history education; home economics; home economics education; horticulture science; hotel and restaurant management; industrial arts; industrial arts education; interdisciplinary studies; international business; journalism; law enforcement/police science; mass communications; mathematics; mathematics education; medical technology; middle school education; music; music business management/merchandising; music teacher education; nutrition science; philosophy; physical education; political science; poultry science; pre-medicine; pre-pharmacy studies; pre-veterinary studies; psychology; public relations; recreation/leisure facilities management; religious music; religious studies; science education; secondary education; social work; sociology; Spanish; speech/rhetorical studies; theater arts/drama.

Academic Programs *Special study options:* academic remediation for entering students, accelerated degree program, advanced placement credit, cooperative education, honors programs, internships, part-time degree program, student-designed majors, study abroad, summer session for credit. *ROTC:* Army (b). *Unusual degree programs:* 3-2 engineering with various colleges.

Library Lyons Memorial Library plus 1 other with 116,680 titles, 508 serial subscriptions, 4,764 audiovisual materials.

Computers on Campus 80 computers available on campus for general student use. A campuswide network can be accessed from student residence rooms and from off campus. Internet access, at least one staffed computer lab available.

Student Life *Housing:* on-campus residence required through senior year. *Options:* men-only, women-only. *Activities and Organizations:* drama/theater group, student-run newspaper, radio station, choral group, Aviation Club, Student Senate, Baptist Student Union, Aggie Club, Business Undergraduate Society. *Campus security:* 24-hour emergency response devices and patrols, controlled dormitory access, front gate closed 1 a.m. to 6 a.m., gate security 5:30 p.m. to 1 a.m. *Student Services:* health clinic, personal/psychological counseling.

Athletics Member NAIA. *Intercollegiate sports:* baseball M(s), basketball M(s)/W(s), volleyball W(s). *Intramural sports:* basketball M/W, fencing M/W, football M/W, golf M/W, racquetball M/W, soccer M, softball M/W, volleyball M/W, water polo M/W, weight lifting M/W.

Standardized Tests *Required:* SAT I or ACT (for admission).

Costs (2001–02) *Comprehensive fee:* includes mandatory fees ($150) and room and board ($2500). Part-time tuition: $125 per credit hour. *Required fees:* $75 per term part-time.

Financial Aid Of all full-time matriculated undergraduates who enrolled in 2001, 1288 applied for aid, 1159 were judged to have need, 326 had their need fully met. *Average percent of need met:* 80%. *Average financial aid package:* $10,380. *Average need-based gift aid:* $6616. *Average indebtedness upon graduation:* $8514.

Applying *Options:* early admission. *Required:* high school transcript, 2 letters of recommendation, interview, medical history, financial statement. *Recommended:* essay or personal statement, minimum 2.0 GPA. *Application deadlines:* 2/15 (freshmen), 2/1 (transfers). *Notification:* continuous (freshmen).

Admissions Contact Mrs. Gayle Groves, Admissions Secretary, College of the Ozarks, PO Box 17, Point Lookout, MO 65726. *Phone:* 417-334-6411 Ext. 4217. *Toll-free phone:* 800-222-0525. *Fax:* 417-335-2618. *E-mail:* admiss4@cofo.edu.

COLUMBIA COLLEGE

Columbia, Missouri

- **Independent** comprehensive, founded 1851, affiliated with Christian Church (Disciples of Christ)
- **Calendar** semesters
- **Degrees** associate, bachelor's, and master's (offers continuing education program with significant enrollment not reflected in profile)
- **Small-town** 29-acre campus
- **Endowment** $7.0 million
- **Coed,** 855 undergraduate students, 78% full-time, 57% women, 43% men
- **Minimally difficult** entrance level, 56% of applicants were admitted

Undergraduates 669 full-time, 186 part-time. Students come from 18 states and territories, 28 other countries, 6% are from out of state, 5% African American, 1% Asian American or Pacific Islander, 2% Hispanic American, 0.8% Native American, 8% international, 16% transferred in, 38% live on campus. *Retention:* 61% of 2001 full-time freshmen returned.

Freshmen *Admission:* 707 applied, 394 admitted, 166 enrolled. *Average high school GPA:* 3.14. *Test scores:* SAT verbal scores over 500: 100%; SAT math scores over 500: 100%; ACT scores over 18: 84%; SAT verbal scores over 600: 50%; SAT math scores over 600: 50%; ACT scores over 24: 30%; SAT math scores over 700: 50%; ACT scores over 30: 2%.

Faculty *Total:* 81, 62% full-time, 58% with terminal degrees. *Student/faculty ratio:* 12:1.

Majors Accounting; applied art; art; art education; behavioral sciences; biology; business administration; business education; business marketing and marketing management; chemistry; computer graphics; criminal justice/law enforcement administration; drawing; education; education (K-12); elementary education; English; finance; fine/studio arts; forensic technology; geology; graphic design/commercial art/illustration; history; humanities; information sciences/systems; international business; liberal arts and sciences/liberal studies; mathematics; middle school education; nursing; photography; physics; political science; pre-dentistry; pre-engineering; pre-law; pre-medicine; pre-veterinary studies; psychology; science education; secondary education; social work; sociology.

Academic Programs *Special study options:* academic remediation for entering students, accelerated degree program, adult/continuing education programs, advanced placement credit, cooperative education, distance learning, double majors, English as a second language, honors programs, independent study, internships, off-campus study, part-time degree program, student-designed majors, study abroad, summer session for credit. *ROTC:* Army (c), Navy (c), Air Force (c).

Library Stafford Library with 56,169 titles, 619 serial subscriptions, 3,366 audiovisual materials, an OPAC, a Web page.

Computers on Campus 125 computers available on campus for general student use. Internet access, at least one staffed computer lab available.

Student Life *Housing:* on-campus residence required through sophomore year. *Options:* coed, women-only. *Activities and Organizations:* student-run newspaper, choral group, Students in Free Enterprise, Campus Community Government, Student Leaders Advocating Teaching Excellence, Spanish Club, Criminal Justice Association. *Campus security:* 24-hour emergency response devices and patrols, late-night transport/escort service, controlled dormitory access. *Student Services:* health clinic, personal/psychological counseling.

Athletics Member NAIA. *Intercollegiate sports:* basketball M(s)/W(s), soccer M(s), softball W(s), volleyball W(s). *Intramural sports:* basketball M/W, softball M/W, table tennis M/W, volleyball M/W.

Columbia College (continued)

Standardized Tests *Required:* ACT (for admission). *Recommended:* SAT I (for admission).

Costs (2001–02) *Comprehensive fee:* $15,082 includes full-time tuition ($10,506) and room and board ($4576). Full-time tuition and fees vary according to class time and course load. Part-time tuition: $195 per credit hour. Part-time tuition and fees vary according to class time, course load, and location. *Room and board:* College room only: $2878. Room and board charges vary according to board plan. *Payment plan:* deferred payment. *Waivers:* children of alumni, senior citizens, and employees or children of employees.

Financial Aid Of all full-time matriculated undergraduates who enrolled in 2001, 549 applied for aid, 324 were judged to have need, 50 had their need fully met. 83 Federal Work-Study jobs (averaging $2121). In 2001, 133 non-need-based awards were made. *Average percent of need met:* 66%. *Average financial aid package:* $8031. *Average need-based loan:* $3718. *Average need-based gift aid:* $3127. *Average non-need based aid:* $8909. *Average indebtedness upon graduation:* $16,185.

Applying *Options:* common application, early admission, deferred entrance. *Application fee:* $25. *Required:* high school transcript, minimum 2.0 GPA. *Required for some:* essay or personal statement, letters of recommendation, interview. *Recommended:* rank in upper 50% of high school class. *Application deadline:* rolling (freshmen), rolling (transfers). *Notification:* continuous (freshmen).

Admissions Contact Ms. Regina Morin, Director of Admissions, Columbia College, 1001 Rogers Street, Columbia, MO 65216. *Phone:* 573-875-7352. *Toll-free phone:* 800-231-2391 Ext. 7366. *Fax:* 573-875-7506. *E-mail:* admissions@email.ccis.edu.

CONCEPTION SEMINARY COLLEGE

Conception, Missouri

- **Independent Roman Catholic** 4-year, founded 1886
- **Calendar** semesters
- **Degree** certificates and bachelor's
- **Rural** 30-acre campus
- **Men only,** 90 undergraduate students, 91% full-time
- **Noncompetitive** entrance level, 100% of applicants were admitted

Undergraduates 82 full-time, 8 part-time. Students come from 18 states and territories, 5 other countries, 84% are from out of state, 1% African American, 16% Asian American or Pacific Islander, 6% Hispanic American, 7% international, 29% transferred in, 100% live on campus. *Retention:* 82% of 2001 full-time freshmen returned.

Freshmen *Admission:* 10 enrolled. *Average high school GPA:* 3.26. *Test scores:* ACT scores over 18: 70%; ACT scores over 24: 30%.

Faculty *Total:* 24, 88% full-time, 96% with terminal degrees. *Student/faculty ratio:* 4:1.

Majors Liberal arts and sciences/liberal studies.

Academic Programs *Special study options:* academic remediation for entering students, advanced placement credit, double majors, English as a second language, independent study, off-campus study.

Library Conception Seminary College Library with 115,000 titles, 300 serial subscriptions, 5,000 audiovisual materials, a Web page.

Computers on Campus 12 computers available on campus for general student use. A campuswide network can be accessed from off campus. Internet access, at least one staffed computer lab available.

Student Life *Housing:* on-campus residence required through senior year. *Options:* men-only. *Activities and Organizations:* drama/theater group, student-run newspaper, choral group, Vocation Committee, Drama Club, Apostolics, Fine Arts Committee, Social Concerns Committee. *Student Services:* health clinic, personal/psychological counseling.

Athletics *Intramural sports:* basketball M, bowling M, cross-country running M, football M, golf M, gymnastics M, racquetball M, soccer M, softball M, swimming M, table tennis M, tennis M, track and field M, volleyball M, weight lifting M.

Standardized Tests *Required:* ACT (for admission).

Costs (2001–02) *Comprehensive fee:* $14,686 includes full-time tuition ($9170), mandatory fees ($142), and room and board ($5374). Part-time tuition: $100 per credit. *Room and board:* College room only: $2204. Room and board charges vary according to board plan. *Payment plan:* installment.

Financial Aid Of all full-time matriculated undergraduates who enrolled in 2001, 57 applied for aid, 54 were judged to have need, 28 had their need fully met. 25 Federal Work-Study jobs (averaging $803). 31 State and other part-time jobs (averaging $801). In 2001, 15 non-need-based awards were made. *Average percent of need met:* 91%. *Average financial aid package:* $8864. *Average need-based loan:* $2539. *Average need-based gift aid:* $4305. *Average non-need based aid:* $8593. *Average indebtedness upon graduation:* $8963.

Applying *Options:* electronic application. *Required:* essay or personal statement, high school transcript, minimum 2.0 GPA, 2 letters of recommendation, church certificate, medical history. *Application deadlines:* 7/31 (freshmen), 7/31 (transfers). *Notification:* continuous until 8/15 (freshmen).

Admissions Contact Mr. Keith Jiron, Director of Recruitment and Admissions, Conception Seminary College, PO Box 502, Highway 136 & VV, 37174 State Highway VV, Conception, MO 64433. *Phone:* 660-944-2886. *E-mail:* vocations@conception.edu.

CULVER-STOCKTON COLLEGE

Canton, Missouri

- **Independent** 4-year, founded 1853, affiliated with Christian Church (Disciples of Christ)
- **Calendar** semesters
- **Degree** bachelor's
- **Rural** 143-acre campus
- **Endowment** $21.8 million
- **Coed,** 821 undergraduate students, 91% full-time, 55% women, 45% men
- **Moderately difficult** entrance level, 86% of applicants were admitted

Undergraduates 745 full-time, 76 part-time. Students come from 28 states and territories, 8 other countries, 46% are from out of state, 6% African American, 0.5% Asian American or Pacific Islander, 3% Hispanic American, 0.1% Native American, 1% international, 10% transferred in, 70% live on campus. *Retention:* 64% of 2001 full-time freshmen returned.

Freshmen *Admission:* 727 applied, 625 admitted, 199 enrolled. *Average high school GPA:* 3.22. *Test scores:* ACT scores over 18: 85%; ACT scores over 24: 24%; ACT scores over 30: 3%.

Faculty *Total:* 71, 79% full-time, 55% with terminal degrees. *Student/faculty ratio:* 12:1.

Majors Accounting; art; art education; arts management; athletic training/sports medicine; biology; business administration; chemistry; criminal justice/law enforcement administration; elementary education; English; English education; finance; history; history education; information sciences/systems; mass communications; mathematics; mathematics education; medical technology; music; music teacher education; nursing; parks, recreation, leisure and fitness studies related; physical education; psychology; religious studies; science education; sociology; special education; speech/theater education; theater arts/drama.

Academic Programs *Special study options:* accelerated degree program, advanced placement credit, double majors, honors programs, independent study, internships, off-campus study, part-time degree program, student-designed majors, study abroad, summer session for credit. *Unusual degree programs:* 3-2 engineering with Washington University in St. Louis; occupational therapy with Washington University in St. Louis.

Library Johann Memorial Library with 151,979 titles, 777 serial subscriptions, 3,722 audiovisual materials, an OPAC, a Web page.

Computers on Campus 70 computers available on campus for general student use. A campuswide network can be accessed from student residence rooms and from off campus. Internet access, at least one staffed computer lab available.

Student Life *Housing:* on-campus residence required through senior year. *Options:* coed, men-only, women-only. *Activities and Organizations:* drama/theater group, student-run newspaper, radio station, choral group, C-S Teachers Organization, Varsity Club, Christian Fellowship Group, Student Government Association, Student Nurses Organization, national fraternities, national sororities. *Campus security:* 24-hour emergency response devices, late-night transport/escort service. *Student Services:* health clinic, personal/psychological counseling.

Athletics Member NAIA. *Intercollegiate sports:* baseball M(s), basketball M(s)/W(s), football M(s), golf M(s)/W(s), soccer M(s)/W(s), softball W(s), volleyball W(s). *Intramural sports:* basketball M/W, bowling M/W, racquetball M/W, soccer M/W, softball M/W, table tennis M/W, tennis M/W, volleyball M/W.

Standardized Tests *Required:* SAT I or ACT (for admission).

Costs (2002–03) *Comprehensive fee:* $17,000 includes full-time tuition ($11,800) and room and board ($5200). Part-time tuition: $325 per credit hour. *Room and board:* College room only: $2400. Room and board charges vary according to board plan. *Payment plan:* installment. *Waivers:* senior citizens and employees or children of employees.

Financial Aid Of all full-time matriculated undergraduates who enrolled in 2001, 655 applied for aid, 588 were judged to have need, 212 had their need fully met. 90 Federal Work-Study jobs (averaging $1155). 221 State and other part-time jobs (averaging $1452). In 2001, 59 non-need-based awards were made. *Average*

percent of need met: 86%. *Average financial aid package:* $12,475. *Average need-based loan:* $3430. *Average need-based gift aid:* $7932. *Average non-need based aid:* $4928. *Average indebtedness upon graduation:* $12,100. *Financial aid deadline:* 6/15.

Applying *Options:* electronic application, deferred entrance. *Application fee:* $25. *Required:* high school transcript, minimum 2.0 GPA. *Required for some:* interview. *Recommended:* essay or personal statement, letters of recommendation, interview.

Admissions Contact Mr. Ron Cronacher, Director of Enrollment Services, Culver-Stockton College, One College Hill, Canton, MO 63435-1299. *Phone:* 800-537-1883. *Toll-free phone:* 800-537-1883. *Fax:* 217-231-6618. *E-mail:* enrollment@culver.edu.

DEACONESS COLLEGE OF NURSING
St. Louis, Missouri

- **Proprietary** 4-year, founded 1889
- **Calendar** semesters
- **Degrees** associate and bachelor's
- **Urban** 15-acre campus
- **Coed,** 244 undergraduate students, 63% full-time, 96% women, 4% men
- **Moderately difficult** entrance level, 92% of applicants were admitted

Undergraduates 153 full-time, 91 part-time. Students come from 15 states and territories, 30% African American, 1% Asian American or Pacific Islander, 2% Hispanic American, 4% transferred in, 21% live on campus. *Retention:* 58% of 2001 full-time freshmen returned.

Freshmen *Admission:* 74 applied, 68 admitted, 61 enrolled. *Average high school GPA:* 3.06. *Test scores:* ACT scores over 18: 54%; ACT scores over 24: 39%.

Faculty *Total:* 14, 100% full-time, 100% with terminal degrees. *Student/faculty ratio:* 9:1.

Majors Nursing.

Academic Programs *Special study options:* academic remediation for entering students, advanced placement credit, English as a second language, off-campus study, part-time degree program, summer session for credit. *ROTC:* Army (c).

Library Drusch Professional Library with 8,700 titles, 233 serial subscriptions, an OPAC.

Computers on Campus 20 computers available on campus for general student use. Internet access, at least one staffed computer lab available.

Student Life *Housing Options:* coed, women-only. *Activities and Organizations:* student-run newspaper, Deaconess Ambassadors, National Student Nurses Association, Student Government Association, Campus Crusade for Christ. *Campus security:* 24-hour patrols, late-night transport/escort service, controlled dormitory access. *Student Services:* personal/psychological counseling.

Standardized Tests *Required:* ACT (for admission).

Costs (2001–02) *Comprehensive fee:* $13,400 includes full-time tuition ($9250), mandatory fees ($160), and room and board ($3990). Part-time tuition: $365 per credit. *Required fees:* $80 per term part-time. *Room and board:* Room and board charges vary according to housing facility. *Payment plans:* installment, deferred payment.

Financial Aid Of all full-time matriculated undergraduates who enrolled in 2001, 149 applied for aid, 117 were judged to have need, 19 had their need fully met. 22 Federal Work-Study jobs (averaging $1136). In 2001, 15 non-need-based awards were made. *Average percent of need met:* 60%. *Average financial aid package:* $7081. *Average need-based loan:* $3950. *Average need-based gift aid:* $2013. *Average non-need based aid:* $5638. *Average indebtedness upon graduation:* $20,900.

Applying *Options:* deferred entrance. *Application fee:* $30. *Required:* essay or personal statement, high school transcript. *Required for some:* letters of recommendation, interview. *Recommended:* minimum 2.5 GPA. *Application deadline:* rolling (freshmen), rolling (transfers). *Notification:* continuous (freshmen).

Admissions Contact Ms. Andrea Gordon, Admissions Coordinator, Deaconess College of Nursing, 6150 Oakland Avenue, St. Louis, MO 63139-3215. *Phone:* 314-768-3044. *Toll-free phone:* 800-942-4310. *Fax:* 314-768-5673.

DEVRY UNIVERSITY
Kansas City, Missouri

- **Proprietary** 4-year, founded 1931, part of DeVry, Inc
- **Calendar** semesters
- **Degrees** associate and bachelor's
- **Urban** 12-acre campus
- **Coed,** 2,620 undergraduate students, 70% full-time, 25% women, 75% men
- **Minimally difficult** entrance level, 90% of applicants were admitted

Undergraduates 1,844 full-time, 776 part-time. Students come from 30 states and territories, 3 other countries, 42% are from out of state, 14% African American, 3% Asian American or Pacific Islander, 3% Hispanic American, 0.8% Native American, 0.7% international, 18% transferred in. *Retention:* 46% of 2001 full-time freshmen returned.

Freshmen *Admission:* 841 applied, 760 admitted, 498 enrolled.

Faculty *Total:* 143, 54% full-time. *Student/faculty ratio:* 20:1.

Majors Business administration/management related; business systems analysis/design; business systems networking/ telecommunications; computer engineering technology; electrical/electronic engineering technology; information sciences/systems; operations management.

Academic Programs *Special study options:* academic remediation for entering students, accelerated degree program, adult/continuing education programs, advanced placement credit, cooperative education, part-time degree program, services for LD students, summer session for credit.

Library James E. Lovan Library with 8,752 titles, 121 serial subscriptions, 333 audiovisual materials, an OPAC.

Computers on Campus 313 computers available on campus for general student use. A campuswide network can be accessed from off campus. At least one staffed computer lab available.

Student Life *Housing:* college housing not available. *Activities and Organizations:* student-run newspaper, Phi Beta Lambda, Institution of Electrical and Electronic Engineers, Tau Alpha Pi, Association of Information Technology Professionals, Cutting Edge Bible Club. *Campus security:* 24-hour emergency response devices and patrols, lighted pathways/sidewalks.

Athletics *Intramural sports:* basketball M/W, football M, golf M, volleyball M/W.

Standardized Tests *Recommended:* SAT I or ACT (for admission).

Costs (2001–02) *Tuition:* $8740 full-time, $310 per credit hour part-time. Full-time tuition and fees vary according to course load. Part-time tuition and fees vary according to course load. *Payment plans:* installment, deferred payment. *Waivers:* employees or children of employees.

Financial Aid Of all full-time matriculated undergraduates who enrolled in 2001, 2203 applied for aid, 2065 were judged to have need, 76 had their need fully met. In 2001, 137 non-need-based awards were made. *Average percent of need met:* 44%. *Average financial aid package:* $7500. *Average need-based loan:* $5815. *Average need-based gift aid:* $4093.

Applying *Options:* electronic application, deferred entrance. *Application fee:* $50. *Required:* high school transcript, interview. *Application deadline:* rolling (freshmen), rolling (transfers). *Notification:* continuous (freshmen).

Admissions Contact Ms. Anna Diamond, New Student Coordinator, DeVry University, 11224 Holmes Street, Kansas City, MO 64131. *Phone:* 816-941-0430. *Toll-free phone:* 800-821-3766.

DRURY UNIVERSITY
Springfield, Missouri

- **Independent** comprehensive, founded 1873
- **Calendar** semesters
- **Degrees** bachelor's and master's (also offers evening program with significant enrollment not reflected in profile)
- **Urban** 60-acre campus
- **Endowment** $86.0 million
- **Coed,** 1,450 undergraduate students, 98% full-time, 56% women, 44% men
- **Moderately difficult** entrance level, 85% of applicants were admitted

Undergraduates 1,415 full-time, 35 part-time. Students come from 35 states and territories, 50 other countries, 20% are from out of state, 0.9% African American, 1% Asian American or Pacific Islander, 1% Hispanic American, 0.6% Native American, 6% international, 6% transferred in, 48% live on campus. *Retention:* 81% of 2001 full-time freshmen returned.

Freshmen *Admission:* 974 applied, 826 admitted, 335 enrolled. *Average high school GPA:* 3.55. *Test scores:* SAT verbal scores over 500: 70%; SAT math scores over 500: 86%; ACT scores over 18: 100%; SAT verbal scores over 600: 21%; SAT math scores over 600: 25%; ACT scores over 24: 64%; SAT verbal scores over 700: 2%; SAT math scores over 700: 9%; ACT scores over 30: 16%.

Faculty *Total:* 141, 74% full-time, 75% with terminal degrees. *Student/faculty ratio:* 11:1.

Majors Accounting; architecture; art; art education; art history; behavioral sciences; biology; business administration; chemistry; computer/information sciences; computer science; criminology; economics; education; elementary educa-

Drury University (continued)
tion; English; environmental science; exercise sciences; fine/studio arts; French; German; history; international business; mass communications; mathematics; music; music teacher education; nursing; philosophy; physical education; physics; political science; pre-dentistry; pre-law; pre-medicine; pre-veterinary studies; psychology; religious studies; secondary education; sociology; Spanish; theater arts/drama.

Academic Programs *Special study options:* accelerated degree program, adult/continuing education programs, advanced placement credit, cooperative education, distance learning, double majors, English as a second language, freshman honors college, honors programs, independent study, internships, off-campus study, part-time degree program, services for LD students, student-designed majors, study abroad, summer session for credit. *ROTC:* Army (c). *Unusual degree programs:* 3-2 engineering with Washington University in St. Louis; international management with American Graduate School of International Management, occupational therapy with Washington University in St. Louis.

Library F. W. Olin Library plus 1 other with 244,000 titles, 797 serial subscriptions, 56,583 audiovisual materials, an OPAC, a Web page.

Computers on Campus 205 computers available on campus for general student use. A campuswide network can be accessed from student residence rooms and from off campus that provide access to digital imaging lab. Internet access, online (class) registration, at least one staffed computer lab available.

Student Life *Housing:* on-campus residence required for freshman year. *Options:* coed, men-only, women-only. *Activities and Organizations:* drama/theater group, student-run newspaper, radio station, choral group, Student Union Board, Community Service Coalition, choral groups and bands, International Student Organization, academic department clubs, national fraternities, national sororities. *Campus security:* 24-hour emergency response devices and patrols, student patrols, late-night transport/escort service, controlled dormitory access, security cameras in parking areas. *Student Services:* health clinic, personal/psychological counseling.

Athletics Member NCAA. All Division II. *Intercollegiate sports:* basketball M(s), cross-country running M/W, golf M(s), soccer M(s)/W(s), swimming M(s)/W(s), tennis M(s)/W(s), volleyball W(s). *Intramural sports:* basketball M/W, bowling M/W, football M/W, racquetball M/W, soccer M/W, softball M/W, table tennis M/W, tennis M/W, volleyball M/W.

Standardized Tests *Required:* SAT I or ACT (for admission).

Costs (2002–03) *Comprehensive fee:* $17,025 includes full-time tuition ($12,290), mandatory fees ($275), and room and board ($4460). Part-time tuition: $405 per semester hour. *Room and board:* Room and board charges vary according to board plan and housing facility. *Payment plans:* tuition prepayment, installment, deferred payment. *Waivers:* children of alumni, senior citizens, and employees or children of employees.

Financial Aid Of all full-time matriculated undergraduates who enrolled in 2001, 1383 applied for aid, 1361 were judged to have need, 1236 had their need fully met. 161 Federal Work-Study jobs (averaging $1800). 78 State and other part-time jobs (averaging $2000). *Average percent of need met:* 83%. *Average financial aid package:* $7892. *Average need-based loan:* $4683. *Average need-based gift aid:* $7080. *Average non-need based aid:* $2480. *Average indebtedness upon graduation:* $12,800.

Applying *Options:* electronic application, deferred entrance. *Application fee:* $20. *Required:* essay or personal statement, high school transcript, minimum 2.7 GPA, 1 letter of recommendation, minimum ACT score of 21. *Recommended:* interview. *Application deadline:* 3/15 (freshmen), rolling (transfers). *Notification:* continuous (freshmen).

Admissions Contact Mr. Michael Thomas, Director of Admission, Drury University, 900 North Benton, Bay Hall, Springfield, MO 65802. *Phone:* 417-873-7205. *Toll-free phone:* 800-922-2274. *Fax:* 417-866-3873. *E-mail:* druryad@drury.edu.

EVANGEL UNIVERSITY
Springfield, Missouri

- **Independent Assemblies of God** comprehensive, founded 1955, affiliated with Assemblies of God
- **Calendar** semesters
- **Degrees** associate, bachelor's, and master's
- **Urban** 80-acre campus
- **Endowment** $3.6 million
- **Coed,** 1,529 undergraduate students, 95% full-time, 56% women, 44% men
- **Moderately difficult** entrance level, 89% of applicants were admitted

Prominent Evangel University alumni include Admiral Vern Clerk, Chief of Naval Operations for the U.S. Navy; Congressman Todd Tiahrt (R-KS); Dr. Fred Mihm, Professor of Anesthesiology, Director of ICU, Stanford University Medical School; Steve Poppen, VP/CFO, Minnesota Vikings (NFL); Beverly Lewis, best-selling author of inspirational fiction (*October Song, The Shunning*); and Phil Stanton, founding member of Blue Man Group.

Undergraduates 1,450 full-time, 79 part-time. Students come from 46 states and territories, 7 other countries, 61% are from out of state, 7% transferred in, 82% live on campus. *Retention:* 72% of 2001 full-time freshmen returned.

Freshmen *Admission:* 813 applied, 720 admitted, 402 enrolled. *Average high school GPA:* 3.20. *Test scores:* ACT scores over 18: 96%; ACT scores over 24: 33%; ACT scores over 30: 2%.

Faculty *Total:* 141, 67% full-time, 38% with terminal degrees. *Student/faculty ratio:* 18:1.

Majors Accounting; art; art education; behavioral sciences; biblical studies; biology; broadcast journalism; business administration; business education; business marketing and marketing management; chemistry; child care/development; computer science; criminal justice/law enforcement administration; early childhood education; education; elementary education; English; history; journalism; mass communications; mathematics; medical laboratory technology; medical technology; mental health/rehabilitation; music; music teacher education; physical education; political science; pre-dentistry; pre-law; pre-medicine; pre-veterinary studies; psychology; public administration; radio/television broadcasting; recreation/leisure studies; religious music; science education; secondary education; secretarial science; social sciences; social work; sociology; Spanish; special education; speech/rhetorical studies.

Academic Programs *Special study options:* academic remediation for entering students, advanced placement credit, part-time degree program, services for LD students, summer session for credit. *ROTC:* Army (b). *Unusual degree programs:* 3-2 engineering with Washington University in St. Louis, University of Missouri-Rolla.

Library Claude Kendrick Library with 96,487 titles, 748 serial subscriptions, an OPAC.

Computers on Campus 77 computers available on campus for general student use. At least one staffed computer lab available.

Student Life *Housing:* on-campus residence required through senior year. *Options:* coed. *Activities and Organizations:* drama/theater group, student-run newspaper, radio station, choral group. *Campus security:* 24-hour emergency response devices and patrols, student patrols, late-night transport/escort service, controlled dormitory access. *Student Services:* health clinic, personal/psychological counseling.

Athletics Member NAIA. *Intercollegiate sports:* baseball M(s), basketball M(s)/W(s), cross-country running M(s)/W(s), football M(s), golf M(s)/W(s), softball W(s), tennis M(s)/W(s), track and field M(s)/W(s), volleyball W(s). *Intramural sports:* baseball M, basketball M/W, football M, golf M/W, soccer M/W, softball W, tennis M/W, volleyball W.

Standardized Tests *Required:* SAT I or ACT (for admission).

Costs (2002–03) *Comprehensive fee:* $14,770 includes full-time tuition ($10,100), mandatory fees ($670), and room and board ($4000). Full-time tuition and fees vary according to course load. Part-time tuition: $394 per credit hour. *Required fees:* $210 per term part-time. *Room and board:* College room only: $1890. Room and board charges vary according to board plan. *Payment plan:* installment. *Waivers:* employees or children of employees.

Financial Aid Of all full-time matriculated undergraduates who enrolled in 2001, 1036 applied for aid, 931 were judged to have need, 97 had their need fully met. 390 Federal Work-Study jobs, 72 State and other part-time jobs. In 2001, 274 non-need-based awards were made. *Average percent of need met:* 60%. *Average financial aid package:* $7824. *Average need-based loan:* $4240. *Average need-based gift aid:* $4266. *Average indebtedness upon graduation:* $13,563.

Applying *Options:* deferred entrance. *Application fee:* $25. *Required:* high school transcript. *Recommended:* minimum 2.0 GPA. *Application deadlines:* 8/1 (freshmen), 8/1 (transfers). *Notification:* continuous (freshmen).

Admissions Contact Andrew Denton, Director of Admissions, Evangel University, 1111 North Glenstone, Springfield, MO 65802-2191. *Phone:* 417-865-2811 Ext. 7342. *Toll-free phone:* 800-382-6435. *Fax:* 417-865-9599. *E-mail:* admissions@mail4.evangel.edu.

FONTBONNE UNIVERSITY
St. Louis, Missouri

- **Independent Roman Catholic** comprehensive, founded 1917
- **Calendar** semesters
- **Degrees** bachelor's and master's
- **Suburban** 13-acre campus
- **Endowment** $9.0 million
- **Coed,** 1,516 undergraduate students, 78% full-time, 73% women, 27% men

■ **Moderately difficult** entrance level, 84% of applicants were admitted

Undergraduates 1,189 full-time, 327 part-time. Students come from 17 states and territories, 18 other countries, 13% are from out of state, 23% African American, 0.7% Asian American or Pacific Islander, 0.8% Hispanic American, 1.0% Native American, 2% international, 9% transferred in, 35% live on campus. *Retention:* 75% of 2001 full-time freshmen returned.

Freshmen *Admission:* 426 applied, 357 admitted, 177 enrolled. *Average high school GPA:* 3.20. *Test scores:* ACT scores over 18: 91%; ACT scores over 24: 35%; ACT scores over 30: 5%.

Faculty *Total:* 185, 32% full-time, 40% with terminal degrees. *Student/faculty ratio:* 12:1.

Majors Accounting; art; art education; arts management; biology; broadcast journalism; business administration; business marketing and marketing management; civil engineering technology; computer programming; computer science; dietetics; early childhood education; education; elementary education; engineering; English; fashion merchandising; finance; fine/studio arts; graphic design/commercial art/illustration; history; home economics; home economics education; human services; information sciences/systems; liberal arts and sciences/liberal studies; management information systems/business data processing; mathematics; middle school education; pre-law; pre-medicine; psychology; public relations; retail management; secondary education; social sciences; special education; speech-language pathology/audiology; speech therapy; theater arts/drama.

Academic Programs *Special study options:* academic remediation for entering students, accelerated degree program, adult/continuing education programs, advanced placement credit, cooperative education, distance learning, double majors, English as a second language, honors programs, independent study, internships, off-campus study, services for LD students, student-designed majors, study abroad, summer session for credit. *ROTC:* Army (c). *Unusual degree programs:* 3-2 engineering with Washington University in St. Louis; social work with Washington University in St. Louis.

Library Fontbonne Library with 109,411 titles, 3,640 serial subscriptions, 15,234 audiovisual materials, an OPAC, a Web page.

Computers on Campus 50 computers available on campus for general student use. A campuswide network can be accessed from student residence rooms and from off campus. Internet access, online (class) registration, at least one staffed computer lab available.

Student Life *Housing Options:* coed. *Activities and Organizations:* drama/theater group, student-run newspaper, choral group, Student Government Association, Residents Hall Council. *Campus security:* 24-hour patrols, late-night transport/escort service, controlled dormitory access. *Student Services:* health clinic, personal/psychological counseling.

Athletics Member NCAA. All Division III. *Intercollegiate sports:* baseball M, basketball M/W, cross-country running M/W, golf M/W, soccer M/W, softball W, tennis M/W, volleyball W. *Intramural sports:* basketball M/W, volleyball M/W.

Standardized Tests *Required:* SAT I or ACT (for admission).

Costs (2001–02) *Comprehensive fee:* $18,396 includes full-time tuition ($12,596), mandatory fees ($300), and room and board ($5500). Full-time tuition and fees vary according to class time, program, and reciprocity agreements. Part-time tuition: $351 per credit hour. Part-time tuition and fees vary according to class time, course load, program, and reciprocity agreements. *Required fees:* $7 per hour. *Room and board:* Room and board charges vary according to board plan and housing facility. *Payment plans:* installment, deferred payment. *Waivers:* senior citizens and employees or children of employees.

Financial Aid Of all full-time matriculated undergraduates who enrolled in 2001, 801 applied for aid, 537 were judged to have need, 135 had their need fully met. In 2001, 264 non-need-based awards were made. *Average percent of need met:* 76%. *Average financial aid package:* $8500. *Average non-need based aid:* $4000. *Financial aid deadline:* 7/1.

Applying *Options:* common application, electronic application, early admission, deferred entrance. *Application fee:* $25. *Required:* essay or personal statement, high school transcript, minimum 2.5 GPA. *Recommended:* 2 letters of recommendation, interview. *Application deadline:* 8/1 (freshmen), rolling (transfers). *Notification:* continuous (freshmen).

Admissions Contact Ms. Peggy Musen, Associate Dean for Enrollment Management, Fontbonne University, 6800 Wydown Boulevard, St. Louis, MO 63105-3098. *Phone:* 314-889-1400. *Fax:* 314-719-8021. *E-mail:* pmusen@fontbonne.edu.

Global University of the Assemblies of God

Springfield, Missouri

■ **Independent** comprehensive, founded 1948, affiliated with Assemblies of God
■ **Calendar** continuous
■ **Degrees** associate, bachelor's, and master's (offers only external degree programs)
■ **Endowment** $521,736
■ **Coed,** 4,145 undergraduate students, 7% full-time, 32% women, 68% men
■ **Noncompetitive** entrance level

Undergraduates Students come from 50 states and territories, 121 other countries, 97% are from out of state.

Faculty *Total:* 473, 12% full-time, 31% with terminal degrees.

Majors Biblical studies; divinity/ministry; missionary studies; pastoral counseling; religious education; religious studies; theology.

Academic Programs *Special study options:* academic remediation for entering students, accelerated degree program, adult/continuing education programs, advanced placement credit, cooperative education, distance learning, external degree program, honors programs, independent study, internships, part-time degree program.

Library Global University Library with 180 serial subscriptions, 3,000 audiovisual materials, a Web page.

Student Life *Housing:* college housing not available. *Campus security:* 24-hour emergency response devices.

Costs (2001–02) *Tuition:* $1800 full-time, $75 per credit hour part-time. Full-time tuition and fees vary according to location and reciprocity agreements. Part-time tuition and fees vary according to course load, location, and reciprocity agreements. *Payment plan:* installment. *Waivers:* employees or children of employees.

Applying *Application fee:* $35. *Required:* high school transcript. *Required for some:* 1 letter of recommendation. *Recommended:* essay or personal statement. *Application deadline:* rolling (freshmen), rolling (transfers).

Admissions Contact Odell Jones, Dean of Student Affairs, Global University of the Assemblies of God, 1211 South Glenstone Avenue, Springfield, MO 65804. *Phone:* 800-443-1083. *Toll-free phone:* 800-443-1083.

Hannibal-LaGrange College

Hannibal, Missouri

■ **Independent Southern Baptist** 4-year, founded 1858
■ **Calendar** semesters
■ **Degrees** associate and bachelor's
■ **Small-town** 110-acre campus
■ **Endowment** $3.4 million
■ **Coed,** 1,099 undergraduate students, 64% full-time, 63% women, 37% men
■ **Moderately difficult** entrance level, 38% of applicants were admitted

Undergraduates 706 full-time, 393 part-time. Students come from 24 states and territories, 8 other countries, 24% are from out of state, 2% African American, 0.9% Asian American or Pacific Islander, 0.7% Hispanic American, 0.1% Native American, 2% international, 7% transferred in, 35% live on campus. *Retention:* 71% of 2001 full-time freshmen returned.

Freshmen *Admission:* 584 applied, 221 admitted, 169 enrolled. *Average high school GPA:* 3.10. *Test scores:* ACT scores over 18: 97%; ACT scores over 24: 42%; ACT scores over 30: 7%.

Faculty *Total:* 87, 59% full-time, 30% with terminal degrees. *Student/faculty ratio:* 13:1.

Majors Accounting; agricultural business; art; art education; biblical studies; biology; business administration; business marketing and marketing management; computer programming; criminal justice/law enforcement administration; data processing technology; divinity/ministry; early childhood education; education; elementary education; emergency medical technology; English; history; human services; information sciences/systems; law enforcement/police science; legal administrative assistant; liberal arts and sciences/liberal studies; mass communications; mathematics; medical administrative assistant; music; music (piano and organ performance); music teacher education; music (voice and choral/opera performance); nursing; pastoral counseling; physical education; pre-engineering; psychology; recreation/leisure facilities management; recreation/leisure studies; religious education; religious music; religious studies; secondary education; secretarial science; speech/rhetorical studies; theater arts/drama; theology.

Academic Programs *Special study options:* academic remediation for entering students, accelerated degree program, adult/continuing education programs, advanced placement credit, cooperative education, double majors, freshman honors college, honors programs, independent study, internships, part-time degree program, services for LD students, student-designed majors, study abroad, summer session for credit.

Hannibal-LaGrange College (continued)

Library L. A. Foster Library with 71,680 titles, 516 serial subscriptions, 6,605 audiovisual materials, an OPAC.

Computers on Campus 76 computers available on campus for general student use. A campuswide network can be accessed from student residence rooms and from off campus. Internet access, at least one staffed computer lab available.

Student Life *Housing:* on-campus residence required through senior year. *Options:* men-only, women-only. *Activities and Organizations:* drama/theater group, student-run newspaper, choral group, Phi Beta Lambda, Baptist Student Union, Alpha Chi Honor Society, Phi Beta Delta, politically affiliated clubs. *Campus security:* 24-hour emergency response devices, late-night transport/escort service, controlled dormitory access. *Student Services:* health clinic, personal/psychological counseling.

Athletics Member NAIA, NCCAA. *Intercollegiate sports:* baseball M(s), basketball M(s)/W(s), golf M(s), softball W(s), volleyball W(s). *Intramural sports:* basketball M/W, racquetball M/W, tennis M/W, volleyball M/W.

Standardized Tests *Required:* SAT I or ACT (for admission).

Costs (2001–02) *Comprehensive fee:* $12,530 includes full-time tuition ($8850), mandatory fees ($280), and room and board ($3400). Full-time tuition and fees vary according to course load and program. Part-time tuition: $295 per credit hour. Part-time tuition and fees vary according to course load and program. *Required fees:* $70 per term part-time. *Room and board:* Room and board charges vary according to board plan and housing facility. *Payment plan:* deferred payment. *Waivers:* senior citizens and employees or children of employees.

Financial Aid Of all full-time matriculated undergraduates who enrolled in 2001, 649 applied for aid, 521 were judged to have need, 110 had their need fully met. 83 Federal Work-Study jobs (averaging $550). *Average percent of need met:* 50%. *Average financial aid package:* $5160. *Average need-based loan:* $3548. *Average need-based gift aid:* $1281. *Average indebtedness upon graduation:* $15,281.

Applying *Options:* early admission, deferred entrance. *Application fee:* $25. *Required:* high school transcript, 2 letters of recommendation. *Application deadline:* 8/26 (freshmen), rolling (transfers). *Notification:* continuous (freshmen).

Admissions Contact Mr. Raymond Carty, Dean of Enrollment Management, Hannibal-LaGrange College, Hannibal, MO 63401-1999. *Phone:* 573-221-3113. *Toll-free phone:* 800-HLG-1119. *E-mail:* admissio@hlg.edu.

HARRIS-STOWE STATE COLLEGE

St. Louis, Missouri

- **State-supported** 4-year, founded 1857, part of Missouri Coordinating Board for Higher Education
- **Calendar** semesters
- **Degree** bachelor's
- **Urban** 22-acre campus
- **Coed,** 1,306 undergraduate students, 42% full-time, 70% women, 30% men
- **Moderately difficult** entrance level, 61% of applicants were admitted

Undergraduates 553 full-time, 753 part-time. Students come from 5 states and territories, 21 other countries, 8% are from out of state, 70% African American, 1% Asian American or Pacific Islander, 2% Hispanic American, 3% international, 23% transferred in. *Retention:* 60% of 2001 full-time freshmen returned.

Freshmen *Admission:* 402 applied, 247 admitted, 472 enrolled. *Average high school GPA:* 2.80. *Test scores:* SAT verbal scores over 500: 26%; SAT math scores over 500: 31%; ACT scores over 18: 56%; SAT verbal scores over 600: 5%; SAT math scores over 600: 5%; ACT scores over 24: 8%.

Faculty *Total:* 61, 66% with terminal degrees. *Student/faculty ratio:* 18:1.

Majors Accounting; business administration; criminal justice/law enforcement administration; early childhood education; elementary education; health services administration; information sciences/systems; interdisciplinary studies; middle school education; secondary education; urban studies.

Academic Programs *Special study options:* academic remediation for entering students, advanced placement credit, internships, off-campus study, part-time degree program, services for LD students, summer session for credit. *ROTC:* Air Force (c).

Library Southwestern Bell Library and Technology Center with 60,000 titles, 340 serial subscriptions, an OPAC.

Computers on Campus 84 computers available on campus for general student use. Internet access available.

Student Life *Housing:* college housing not available. *Activities and Organizations:* drama/theater group, choral group, Drama Club, concert chorale, Student Government Association, national fraternities, national sororities. *Campus security:* 24-hour emergency response devices, late-night transport/escort service, 16-hour patrols by trained security personnel Monday through Friday, 24-hour weekend and holiday patrols. *Student Services:* health clinic, personal/psychological counseling.

Athletics Member NAIA. *Intercollegiate sports:* baseball M(s), basketball M(s)/W(s), soccer M(s)/W(s), track and field W(s), volleyball W(s).

Standardized Tests *Required:* SAT I or ACT (for admission).

Costs (2001–02) *Tuition:* state resident $2280 full-time, $95 per credit hour part-time; nonresident $4491 full-time, $187 per credit hour part-time. *Required fees:* $30 full-time. *Payment plan:* installment. *Waivers:* employees or children of employees.

Financial Aid Of all full-time matriculated undergraduates who enrolled in 2001, 581 applied for aid, 567 were judged to have need, 119 had their need fully met. 234 Federal Work-Study jobs. In 2001, 78 non-need-based awards were made. *Average percent of need met:* 88%. *Average need-based loan:* $4862. *Average need-based gift aid:* $2969. *Average non-need based aid:* $1800. *Average indebtedness upon graduation:* $12,957.

Applying *Options:* early admission, deferred entrance. *Required:* high school transcript, minimum 2.0 GPA. *Application deadline:* rolling (freshmen), rolling (transfers).

Admissions Contact Jo Henderson, Director of Admissions, Harris-Stowe State College, 3026 Laclede Avenue, St. Louis, MO 63103. *Phone:* 314-340-3300. *Fax:* 314-340-3555. *E-mail:* currierd@mail1.hssc.edu.

ITT TECHNICAL INSTITUTE

Earth City, Missouri

- **Proprietary** primarily 2-year, founded 1936, part of ITT Educational Services, Inc
- **Calendar** quarters
- **Degrees** associate and bachelor's
- **Suburban** 2-acre campus with easy access to St. Louis
- **Coed,** 600 undergraduate students
- **Minimally difficult** entrance level

Majors Computer/information sciences related; computer programming; drafting; electrical/electronic engineering technologies related; information sciences/systems; information technology.

Student Life *Housing:* college housing not available.

Costs (2001–02) *Tuition:* Full-time tuition and fees vary according to program. Part-time tuition and fees vary according to program. $260—$330 per credit hour.

Applying *Options:* common application, deferred entrance. *Application fee:* $100. *Required:* high school transcript, interview. *Recommended:* letters of recommendation. *Application deadline:* rolling (freshmen), rolling (transfers). *Notification:* continuous (freshmen).

Admissions Contact Ms. Karen Finkenkeller, Director, ITT Technical Institute, 13505 Lakefront Drive, Earth City, MO 63045. *Phone:* 314-298-7800. *Toll-free phone:* 800-235-5488. *Fax:* 314-298-0559.

JEWISH HOSPITAL COLLEGE OF NURSING AND ALLIED HEALTH

St. Louis, Missouri

- **Independent** comprehensive, founded 1902
- **Calendar** semesters
- **Degrees** certificates, associate, bachelor's, master's, post-master's, and postbachelor's certificates
- **Urban** campus
- **Endowment** $4.1 million
- **Coed, primarily women,** 395 undergraduate students, 32% full-time, 89% women, 11% men
- **Moderately difficult** entrance level, 100% of applicants were admitted

Undergraduates 128 full-time, 267 part-time. Students come from 8 states and territories, 19% African American, 2% Asian American or Pacific Islander, 1% Hispanic American, 0.5% Native American, 8% live on campus. *Retention:* 86% of 2001 full-time freshmen returned.

Freshmen *Admission:* 18 applied, 18 admitted, 9 enrolled. *Average high school GPA:* 3.10. *Test scores:* ACT scores over 18: 100%; ACT scores over 24: 26%.

Faculty *Total:* 43, 77% full-time, 40% with terminal degrees. *Student/faculty ratio:* 10:1.

Majors Cytotechnology; medical technology; nursing.

Academic Programs *Special study options:* advanced placement credit, double majors, independent study, off-campus study, part-time degree program, services for LD students, summer session for credit.

Library George and Juanita Way Library plus 4 others with 2,801 titles, 187 serial subscriptions, an OPAC.

Computers on Campus 21 computers available on campus for general student use. A campuswide network can be accessed from off campus that provide access to software, research databases. At least one staffed computer lab available.

Student Life *Housing Options:* coed. *Activities and Organizations:* Student Council. *Campus security:* 24-hour patrols, late-night transport/escort service, controlled dormitory access. *Student Services:* personal/psychological counseling.

Athletics *Intramural sports:* soccer W, volleyball M/W.

Standardized Tests *Required:* SAT I or ACT (for admission).

Costs (2001–02) *Tuition:* $10,890 full-time, $330 per credit hour part-time. Full-time tuition and fees vary according to program. Part-time tuition and fees vary according to course load and program. *Required fees:* $200 full-time, $35 per term part-time. *Room only:* $2385. Room and board charges vary according to housing facility. *Payment plans:* installment, deferred payment.

Financial Aid Of all full-time matriculated undergraduates who enrolled in 2001, 8 Federal Work-Study jobs (averaging $2735). *Average financial aid package:* $8000. *Average indebtedness upon graduation:* $10,000.

Applying *Application fee:* $25. *Required:* essay or personal statement, high school transcript, minimum 2.5 GPA, 2 letters of recommendation. *Required for some:* interview. *Application deadline:* rolling (freshmen), rolling (transfers).

Admissions Contact Ms. Christie Schneider, Chief Admissions Officer, Jewish Hospital College of Nursing and Allied Health, 306 South Kingshighway, St. Louis, MO 63110-1091. *Phone:* 314-454-7538. *Toll-free phone:* 800-832-9009. *Fax:* 314-454-5239. *E-mail:* jxi4885@bjcmail.carenet.org.

KANSAS CITY ART INSTITUTE

Kansas City, Missouri

- **Independent** 4-year, founded 1885
- **Calendar** semesters
- **Degree** bachelor's
- **Urban** 12-acre campus
- **Endowment** $18.9 million
- **Coed,** 537 undergraduate students, 98% full-time, 53% women, 47% men
- **Moderately difficult** entrance level, 79% of applicants were admitted

Undergraduates 525 full-time, 12 part-time. Students come from 40 states and territories, 10 other countries, 62% are from out of state, 3% African American, 2% Asian American or Pacific Islander, 6% Hispanic American, 0.6% Native American, 2% international, 12% transferred in, 25% live on campus. *Retention:* 79% of 2001 full-time freshmen returned.

Freshmen *Admission:* 441 applied, 348 admitted, 109 enrolled. *Average high school GPA:* 3.13. *Test scores:* SAT verbal scores over 500: 75%; SAT math scores over 500: 61%; ACT scores over 18: 88%; SAT verbal scores over 600: 36%; SAT math scores over 600: 24%; ACT scores over 24: 42%; SAT verbal scores over 700: 7%; SAT math scores over 700: 4%; ACT scores over 30: 3%.

Faculty *Total:* 75, 56% full-time, 80% with terminal degrees. *Student/faculty ratio:* 10:1.

Majors Art history; ceramic arts; graphic design/commercial art/illustration; industrial design; painting; photography; printmaking; sculpture; textile arts.

Academic Programs *Special study options:* academic remediation for entering students, adult/continuing education programs, advanced placement credit, cooperative education, double majors, English as a second language, independent study, internships, off-campus study, services for LD students, study abroad, summer session for credit.

Library Charles T. and Marion M. Thompson Library with 30,000 titles, 125 serial subscriptions, an OPAC.

Computers on Campus 80 computers available on campus for general student use. A campuswide network can be accessed from student residence rooms and from off campus. Online (class) registration, at least one staffed computer lab available.

Student Life *Housing:* on-campus residence required for freshman year. *Options:* coed. *Activities and Organizations:* Student Union, Student Gallery Committee, Ethnic Student Association. *Campus security:* 24-hour emergency response devices and patrols, late-night transport/escort service, controlled dormitory access. *Student Services:* personal/psychological counseling.

Standardized Tests *Required:* SAT I or ACT (for admission).

Costs (2002–03) *Comprehensive fee:* $25,880 includes full-time tuition ($18,544), mandatory fees ($1036), and room and board ($6300). Part-time tuition: $770 per credit hour. *Room and board:* College room only: $3900. Room and board charges vary according to board plan and housing facility. *Waivers:* employees or children of employees.

Financial Aid Of all full-time matriculated undergraduates who enrolled in 2001, 395 applied for aid, 346 were judged to have need, 63 had their need fully met. 120 Federal Work-Study jobs (averaging $1500). In 2001, 157 non-need-based awards were made. *Average percent of need met:* 69%. *Average financial aid package:* $14,565. *Average need-based loan:* $6117. *Average need-based gift aid:* $8626. *Average indebtedness upon graduation:* $17,125.

Applying *Options:* deferred entrance. *Application fee:* $25. *Required:* essay or personal statement, high school transcript, minimum 2.5 GPA, 2 letters of recommendation, portfolio, statement of purpose. *Recommended:* interview. *Application deadline:* rolling (freshmen), rolling (transfers). *Notification:* continuous until 8/1 (freshmen).

Admissions Contact Mr. Gerald Valet, Director of Admission Technology, Kansas City Art Institute, 4415 Warwick Boulevard, Kansas City, MO 64111-1874. *Phone:* 816-474-5224. *Toll-free phone:* 800-522-5224. *Fax:* 816-802-3309. *E-mail:* admiss@kcai.edu.

KANSAS CITY COLLEGE OF LEGAL STUDIES

Kansas City, Missouri

- **Proprietary** 4-year
- **Calendar** trimesters
- **Degrees** associate and bachelor's
- **Coed,** 123 undergraduate students
- 90% of applicants were admitted

Freshmen *Admission:* 42 applied, 38 admitted.

Faculty *Total:* 15, 13% full-time. *Student/faculty ratio:* 19:1.

Majors Court reporting; paralegal/legal assistant.

Student Life *Housing:* college housing not available.

Standardized Tests *Required for some:* ACT (for admission).

Costs (2001–02) *Tuition:* $23,958 per degree program part-time. No tuition increase for student's term of enrollment. *Payment plans:* tuition prepayment, installment, deferred payment. *Waivers:* employees or children of employees.

Applying *Application fee:* $50. *Required:* high school transcript, interview. *Application deadline:* 9/24 (freshmen).

Admissions Contact Mrs. Rosemary Velez, Admissions Director, Kansas City College of Legal Studies, 402 East Bannister Road, Suite A, Kansas City, MO 64131. *Phone:* 816-444-2232. *Toll-free phone:* 816-444-2232 (in-state); 816-444-3142 (out-of-state).

LESTER L. COX COLLEGE OF NURSING AND HEALTH SCIENCES

Springfield, Missouri

- **Independent** 4-year
- **Degrees** certificates, associate, and bachelor's
- **Coed, primarily women,** 312 undergraduate students, 56% full-time, 94% women, 6% men
- 93% of applicants were admitted

Undergraduates 176 full-time, 136 part-time. Students come from 4 states and territories, 77% are from out of state, 1% African American, 1% Asian American or Pacific Islander, 2% Hispanic American, 0.7% Native American, 25% transferred in, 15% live on campus. *Retention:* 60% of 2001 full-time freshmen returned.

Freshmen *Admission:* 192 applied, 178 admitted, 37 enrolled. *Average high school GPA:* 3.48. *Test scores:* ACT scores over 18: 100%; ACT scores over 24: 36%; ACT scores over 30: 1%.

Faculty *Total:* 22, 73% full-time, 5% with terminal degrees. *Student/faculty ratio:* 15:1.

Majors Nursing.

Academic Programs *Special study options:* adult/continuing education programs, part-time degree program.

Library The Cox Health Systems Libraries.

Computers on Campus 28 computers available on campus for general student use. Internet access, at least one staffed computer lab available.

Student Life *Housing Options:* coed. *Activities and Organizations:* student-run newspaper, Student Nurses Association, National Student Nurses Association, Student Council, Residence Hall Council, Christian Fellowship. *Campus security:* 24-hour patrols, late-night transport/escort service. *Student Services:* personal/psychological counseling.

Standardized Tests *Required:* ACT (for admission).

Lester L. Cox College of Nursing and Health Sciences (continued)

Costs (2002–03) *Tuition:* $3300 full-time, $275 per credit hour part-time. Full-time tuition and fees vary according to course load and program. Part-time tuition and fees vary according to course load and program. *Room only:* $1925. *Payment plan:* deferred payment. *Waivers:* employees or children of employees.

Applying *Options:* common application, early decision. *Application fee:* $30. *Required:* high school transcript, minimum 2.5 GPA. *Application deadline:* 2/1 (freshmen). *Early decision:* 11/1. *Notification:* 3/1 (freshmen), 12/1 (early decision).

Admissions Contact Ms. Virginia Mace, Admission Counselor, Lester L. Cox College of Nursing and Health Sciences, 1423 North Jefferson, Springfield, MO 65802. *Phone:* 417-269-3069. *Fax:* 417-269-3581. *E-mail:* vsmace@coxnet.org.

LINCOLN UNIVERSITY

Jefferson City, Missouri

- **State-supported** comprehensive, founded 1866, part of Missouri Coordinating Board for Higher Education
- **Calendar** semesters
- **Degrees** associate, bachelor's, and master's
- **Small-town** 152-acre campus
- **Coed,** 3,124 undergraduate students, 67% full-time, 59% women, 41% men
- **Noncompetitive** entrance level, 99% of applicants were admitted

Undergraduates 2,080 full-time, 1,044 part-time. 15% are from out of state, 35% African American, 0.5% Asian American or Pacific Islander, 1.0% Hispanic American, 0.8% Native American, 5% international, 7% transferred in, 73% live on campus.

Freshmen *Admission:* 1,280 applied, 1,269 admitted, 535 enrolled. *Test scores:* ACT scores over 18: 43%; ACT scores over 24: 6%; ACT scores over 30: 1%.

Faculty *Total:* 153, 95% full-time, 54% with terminal degrees. *Student/faculty ratio:* 15:1.

Majors Accounting; agricultural business; agricultural sciences; art; art education; biology; business administration; business education; business marketing and marketing management; chemistry; computer science; criminal justice/law enforcement administration; data processing technology; drafting; economics; electrical/electronic engineering technology; elementary education; English; fashion merchandising; French; history; industrial arts; information sciences/systems; journalism; mathematics; mechanical design technology; medical technology; music teacher education; nursing; philosophy; physical education; physics; political science; psychology; public administration; science education; secretarial science; social sciences; sociology; special education.

Academic Programs *Special study options:* academic remediation for entering students, accelerated degree program, adult/continuing education programs, advanced placement credit, cooperative education, freshman honors college, honors programs, internships, part-time degree program, services for LD students, student-designed majors, summer session for credit. *ROTC:* Army (b).

Library Inman Page Library with 151,595 titles, 761 serial subscriptions.

Computers on Campus 175 computers available on campus for general student use. A campuswide network can be accessed from off campus. Internet access, at least one staffed computer lab available.

Student Life *Housing:* on-campus residence required through sophomore year. *Options:* men-only, women-only. *Activities and Organizations:* drama/theater group, student-run newspaper, radio and television station, choral group, marching band, national fraternities, national sororities. *Campus security:* 24-hour emergency response devices and patrols, student patrols, late-night transport/escort service, controlled dormitory access. *Student Services:* health clinic, personal/psychological counseling.

Athletics Member NCAA. All Division II. *Intercollegiate sports:* baseball M(s), basketball M(s)/W(s), cross-country running M(s)/W(s), football M(s), golf M(s), soccer M(s), softball W(s), tennis W(s), track and field M(s)/W(s). *Intramural sports:* baseball M, basketball M/W, bowling M/W, track and field M/W.

Standardized Tests *Required:* ACT (for admission).

Costs (2001–02) *Tuition:* state resident $3210 full-time, $107 per credit part-time; nonresident $6420 full-time, $214 per credit part-time. *Required fees:* $428 full-time. *Room and board:* $3790; room only: $1850. *Waivers:* senior citizens and employees or children of employees.

Financial Aid Of all full-time matriculated undergraduates who enrolled in 2001, 3329 applied for aid, 2930 were judged to have need, 1786 had their need fully met. *Average percent of need met:* 85%. *Average financial aid package:* $8625. *Average need-based loan:* $5500. *Average need-based gift aid:* $4229. *Average indebtedness upon graduation:* $17,125.

Applying *Options:* common application, early admission, deferred entrance. *Application fee:* $17. *Required:* high school transcript, 1 letter of recommendation. *Application deadlines:* 7/15 (freshmen), 6/15 (transfers). *Notification:* continuous (freshmen).

Admissions Contact Executive Director of Enrollment Management, Lincoln University, 820 Chestnut, Jefferson City, MO 65102. *Phone:* 573-681-5599. *Toll-free phone:* 800-521-5052.

LINDENWOOD UNIVERSITY

St. Charles, Missouri

- **Independent Presbyterian** comprehensive, founded 1827
- **Calendar** semesters
- **Degrees** bachelor's, master's, and post-master's certificates
- **Suburban** 358-acre campus with easy access to St. Louis
- **Endowment** $22.6 million
- **Coed,** 4,199 undergraduate students, 89% full-time, 57% women, 43% men
- **Moderately difficult** entrance level

Undergraduates 3,725 full-time, 474 part-time. Students come from 60 other countries, 25% are from out of state, 9% African American, 0.9% Asian American or Pacific Islander, 1% Hispanic American, 0.1% Native American, 6% international, 14% transferred in, 48% live on campus. *Retention:* 89% of 2001 full-time freshmen returned.

Freshmen *Admission:* 2,186 applied, 568 enrolled. *Average high school GPA:* 3.01. *Test scores:* ACT scores over 18: 89%; ACT scores over 24: 29%; ACT scores over 30: 7%.

Faculty *Total:* 327, 47% full-time. *Student/faculty ratio:* 17:1.

Majors Accounting; applied art; art; art education; art history; athletic training/sports medicine; biology; broadcast journalism; business administration; business education; business marketing and marketing management; cell biology; chemistry; computer science; criminal justice/law enforcement administration; criminology; dance; drawing; early childhood education; economics; education; education administration; education (K-12); elementary education; English; fashion design/illustration; fashion merchandising; finance; fine/studio arts; food products retailing; French; gerontology; health services administration; history; human resources management; human services; international relations; journalism; liberal arts and sciences/liberal studies; management information systems/business data processing; mass communications; mathematics; medical technology; middle school education; mortuary science; music; music teacher education; music (voice and choral/opera performance); physical education; political science; pre-dentistry; pre-law; pre-medicine; pre-veterinary studies; psychology; public administration; public relations; radio/television broadcasting; religious studies; retail management; secondary education; social work; sociology; Spanish; special education; stringed instruments; theater arts/drama.

Academic Programs *Special study options:* academic remediation for entering students, accelerated degree program, adult/continuing education programs, advanced placement credit, cooperative education, double majors, external degree program, freshman honors college, honors programs, independent study, internships, off-campus study, part-time degree program, services for LD students, student-designed majors, summer session for credit. *ROTC:* Army (c), Air Force (c). *Unusual degree programs:* 3-2 engineering with Washington University in St. Louis, University of Missouri-St. Louis.

Library Butler Library with 222,071 titles, 519 serial subscriptions.

Computers on Campus 160 computers available on campus for general student use. At least one staffed computer lab available.

Student Life *Housing Options:* men-only, women-only. *Activities and Organizations:* drama/theater group, student-run newspaper, radio station, choral group, marching band, Lindenwood Student Government, American Humanics, Circle K, International Club, Honors Club, national fraternities, national sororities. *Campus security:* 24-hour emergency response devices and patrols, late-night transport/escort service, controlled dormitory access. *Student Services:* personal/psychological counseling.

Athletics Member NAIA. *Intercollegiate sports:* baseball M, basketball M/W, bowling M/W, cross-country running M/W, fencing M(c)/W(c), field hockey W, football M, golf M/W, lacrosse M/W, soccer M/W, softball W, swimming M/W, tennis M/W, track and field M/W, volleyball M/W, wrestling M. *Intramural sports:* badminton M/W, basketball M/W, bowling M/W, cross-country running M/W, fencing M/W, football M, soccer M/W, softball M/W, swimming M/W, table tennis M/W, tennis M/W, track and field M/W, volleyball M/W, weight lifting M/W, wrestling M.

Standardized Tests *Required:* SAT I or ACT (for admission).

Costs (2002–03) *One-time required fee:* $200. *Comprehensive fee:* $17,250 includes full-time tuition ($11,200), mandatory fees ($450), and room and board

($5600). Part-time tuition: $300 per credit hour. Part-time tuition and fees vary according to course load. *Room and board:* College room only: $2800. *Payment plans:* installment, deferred payment. *Waivers:* senior citizens and employees or children of employees.

Applying *Options:* early admission, deferred entrance. *Application fee:* $25. *Required:* high school transcript, minimum 2.0 GPA. *Required for some:* essay or personal statement, letters of recommendation, interview. *Application deadline:* rolling (freshmen), rolling (transfers).

Admissions Contact John Guffey, Dean of Admissions, Lindenwood University, 209 South Kingshighway, St. Charles, MO 63301-1695. *Phone:* 636-949-4933. *Fax:* 636-949-4910.

LOGAN UNIVERSITY-COLLEGE OF CHIROPRACTIC

Chesterfield, Missouri

- **Independent** upper-level, founded 1935
- **Calendar** trimesters
- **Degrees** incidental bachelor's and first professional
- **Suburban** 100-acre campus with easy access to St. Louis
- **Endowment** $9.8 million
- **Coed**
- **Moderately difficult** entrance level

Student Life *Campus security:* 24-hour patrols.

Financial Aid Of all full-time matriculated undergraduates who enrolled in 2001, 160 applied for aid, 160 were judged to have need, 130 had their need fully met. 130 Federal Work-Study jobs (averaging $2693). *Average percent of need met:* 100. *Average need-based loan:* $3500. *Average need-based gift aid:* $3000.

Applying *Options:* electronic application, deferred entrance. *Application fee:* $50.

Admissions Contact Dr. Patrick Browne, Dean of Admissions, Logan University-College of Chiropractic, 1851 Schoettler Road, Box 1065, Chesterfield, MO 63006-1065. *Phone:* 636-227-2100 Ext. 149. *Toll-free phone:* 800-533-9210. *E-mail:* loganadm@logan.edu.

MARYVILLE UNIVERSITY OF SAINT LOUIS

St. Louis, Missouri

- **Independent** comprehensive, founded 1872
- **Calendar** semesters
- **Degrees** bachelor's and master's
- **Suburban** 130-acre campus
- **Endowment** $38.2 million
- **Coed,** 2,632 undergraduate students, 54% full-time, 74% women, 26% men
- **Moderately difficult** entrance level, 82% of applicants were admitted

Undergraduates 1,418 full-time, 1,214 part-time. Students come from 16 states and territories, 33 other countries, 8% are from out of state, 5% African American, 0.9% Asian American or Pacific Islander, 0.8% Hispanic American, 0.3% Native American, 3% international, 15% transferred in, 25% live on campus. *Retention:* 80% of 2001 full-time freshmen returned.

Freshmen *Admission:* 791 applied, 646 admitted, 268 enrolled. *Average high school GPA:* 3.42. *Test scores:* SAT verbal scores over 500: 60%; SAT math scores over 500: 60%; ACT scores over 18: 95%; SAT verbal scores over 600: 33%; SAT math scores over 600: 33%; ACT scores over 24: 44%; SAT verbal scores over 700: 6%; SAT math scores over 700: 13%; ACT scores over 30: 8%.

Faculty *Total:* 290, 30% full-time, 54% with terminal degrees. *Student/faculty ratio:* 13:1.

Majors Accounting; accounting related; actuarial science; applied mathematics; art education; biological/physical sciences; biology; business; business administration; business marketing and marketing management; chemistry; communications; computer science; criminology; early childhood education; elementary education; English; environmental science; fine/studio arts; graphic design/commercial art/illustration; health science; health services administration; history; humanities; interdisciplinary studies; interior design; liberal arts and sciences/liberal studies; management information systems/business data processing; marketing management and research related; mathematics; medical technology; middle school education; music; music therapy; nursing; organizational psychology; paralegal/legal assistant; philosophy; political science; psychology; public health; religious studies; secondary education; social psychology; sociology.

Academic Programs *Special study options:* accelerated degree program, adult/continuing education programs, advanced placement credit, cooperative education, distance learning, double majors, English as a second language, freshman honors college, honors programs, independent study, internships, off-campus study, part-time degree program, services for LD students, study abroad, summer session for credit. *ROTC:* Army (c). *Unusual degree programs:* 3-2 engineering with Washington University in St. Louis; social work with Saint Louis University; education.

Library Maryville University Library with 125,742 titles, 7,721 serial subscriptions, 10,039 audiovisual materials, an OPAC, a Web page.

Computers on Campus 260 computers available on campus for general student use. A campuswide network can be accessed from student residence rooms and from off campus that provide access to e-mail, specialized software. Internet access, at least one staffed computer lab available.

Student Life *Housing Options:* coed. *Activities and Organizations:* drama/theater group, student-run newspaper, choral group, Ambassadors, Physical Therapy Club, Campus Activity Board, Maryville University Student Occupational Therapy Association, Drama Club. *Campus security:* 24-hour emergency response devices and patrols, late-night transport/escort service, controlled dormitory access, video security system in residence halls, self-defense and education programs. *Student Services:* health clinic, personal/psychological counseling.

Athletics Member NCAA. All Division III. *Intercollegiate sports:* baseball M, basketball M/W, cross-country running M/W, golf M, soccer M/W, softball W, tennis M/W, volleyball W. *Intramural sports:* basketball M/W, football M/W, soccer M/W, table tennis M/W, volleyball M/W.

Standardized Tests *Required:* SAT I or ACT (for admission).

Costs (2001–02) *Comprehensive fee:* $19,770 includes full-time tuition ($13,650), mandatory fees ($120), and room and board ($6000). Part-time tuition: $389 per credit hour. Part-time tuition and fees vary according to class time. *Required fees:* $30 per term part-time. *Payment plans:* installment, deferred payment. *Waivers:* senior citizens and employees or children of employees.

Financial Aid Of all full-time matriculated undergraduates who enrolled in 2001, 1126 applied for aid, 989 were judged to have need, 276 had their need fully met. 174 Federal Work-Study jobs (averaging $1100). 195 State and other part-time jobs (averaging $1456). In 2001, 137 non-need-based awards were made. *Average percent of need met:* 62%. *Average financial aid package:* $8056. *Average need-based loan:* $4695. *Average need-based gift aid:* $6351. *Average non-need based aid:* $6378. *Average indebtedness upon graduation:* $12,638.

Applying *Options:* common application, electronic application, early admission, deferred entrance. *Application fee:* $20. *Required:* high school transcript, minimum 2.5 GPA. *Required for some:* essay or personal statement, letters of recommendation, interview, audition, portfolio. *Application deadline:* 8/15 (freshmen), rolling (transfers). *Notification:* continuous (freshmen).

Admissions Contact Ms. Teresa Bont, Admissions Director, Maryville University of Saint Louis, 13550 Conway Road, St. Louis, MO 63141-7299. *Phone:* 314-529-9350. *Toll-free phone:* 800-627-9855. *Fax:* 314-529-9927. *E-mail:* admissions@maryville.edu.

MESSENGER COLLEGE

Joplin, Missouri

- **Independent Pentecostal** 4-year, founded 1987
- **Calendar** semesters
- **Degrees** associate and bachelor's
- **Small-town** 16-acre campus with easy access to Springfield
- **Endowment** $289,532
- **Coed**
- **Moderately difficult** entrance level

Student Life *Campus security:* 24-hour emergency response devices.

Athletics Member NCCAA.

Standardized Tests *Required:* SAT I or ACT (for admission).

Financial Aid Of all full-time matriculated undergraduates who enrolled in 2001, 84 applied for aid, 84 were judged to have need, 2 had their need fully met. *Average percent of need met:* 83.

Applying *Options:* common application. *Application fee:* $10. *Required:* essay or personal statement, high school transcript, minimum 2.0 GPA, 2 letters of recommendation. *Required for some:* interview.

Admissions Contact Gwen Minor, Vice President of Academic Affairs, Messenger College, 300 East 50th, PO Box 4050, Joplin, MO 64803. *Phone:* 417-624-7070 Ext. 102. *Toll-free phone:* 800-385-8940. *Fax:* 417-624-5070. *E-mail:* mc@pcg.org.

METRO BUSINESS COLLEGE

Cape Girardeau, Missouri

- **Private** primarily 2-year
- **Calendar** quarters
- **Degrees** certificates, diplomas, associate, and bachelor's
- 90 undergraduate students

Admissions Contact Mr. Ken Hovis, Admissions Director, Metro Business College, 1732 North Kings Highway, Cape Girardeau, MO 63701. *Phone:* 573-334-9181.

MISSOURI BAPTIST COLLEGE

St. Louis, Missouri

- **Independent Southern Baptist** comprehensive, founded 1964
- **Calendar** semesters
- **Degrees** associate, bachelor's, master's, and postbachelor's certificates (also offers some graduate courses)
- **Suburban** 65-acre campus
- **Endowment** $2.7 million
- **Coed,** 2,734 undergraduate students, 35% full-time, 62% women, 38% men
- **Moderately difficult** entrance level, 77% of applicants were admitted

Undergraduates 958 full-time, 1,776 part-time. Students come from 20 states and territories, 22 other countries, 11% are from out of state, 6% African American, 0.6% Asian American or Pacific Islander, 2% Hispanic American, 0.3% Native American, 3% international, 8% transferred in, 23% live on campus. *Retention:* 67% of 2001 full-time freshmen returned.

Freshmen *Admission:* 378 applied, 290 admitted, 176 enrolled. *Average high school GPA:* 3.05. *Test scores:* ACT scores over 18: 87%; ACT scores over 24: 28%; ACT scores over 30: 5%.

Faculty *Total:* 141, 26% full-time, 23% with terminal degrees. *Student/faculty ratio:* 18:1.

Majors Accounting; athletic training/sports medicine; biology; business administration; business administration/management related; business education; business marketing and marketing management; chemistry; child care/development; communications; community services; computer/information sciences; criminal justice studies; early childhood education; elementary education; English; health education; history; mathematics; middle school education; multi/interdisciplinary studies related; music (general performance); music teacher education; nursing science; operations management; physical education; psychology; religious education; religious music; religious studies; science education; social sciences; sport/fitness administration; theological studies/religious vocations related.

Academic Programs *Special study options:* accelerated degree program, adult/continuing education programs, advanced placement credit, distance learning, double majors, independent study, internships, off-campus study, part-time degree program, services for LD students, student-designed majors, study abroad, summer session for credit. *ROTC:* Army (c). *Unusual degree programs:* 3-2 engineering with University of Missouri-Columbia.

Library Jung-Kellogg Library with 90,387 titles, 610 serial subscriptions, 4,181 audiovisual materials, an OPAC.

Computers on Campus 78 computers available on campus for general student use. A campuswide network can be accessed from student residence rooms and from off campus. Internet access, at least one staffed computer lab available.

Student Life *Housing Options:* men-only, women-only. *Activities and Organizations:* drama/theater group, student-run newspaper, choral group, Baptist Collegiate Ministry, Students in Free Enterprise (SIFE), Missouri State Teacher's Association, Fellowship of Christian Athletes, Ministerial Alliance. *Campus security:* 24-hour patrols, late-night transport/escort service, controlled dormitory access, self-defense classes. *Student Services:* personal/psychological counseling.

Athletics Member NAIA. *Intercollegiate sports:* baseball M(s), basketball M(s)/W(s), cross-country running M(s)/W(s), golf M(s), soccer M(s)/W(s), softball W(s), volleyball M(s)(c)/W(s), wrestling M(s). *Intramural sports:* basketball M/W, soccer M/W, softball M/W, volleyball M/W.

Standardized Tests *Required:* SAT I or ACT (for admission).

Costs (2001–02) *Comprehensive fee:* $15,762 includes full-time tuition ($10,290), mandatory fees ($392), and room and board ($5080). Full-time tuition and fees vary according to course load and location. Part-time tuition: $360 per credit hour. Part-time tuition and fees vary according to course load and location. *Required fees:* $6 per credit hour, $15 per term part-time. *Room and board:* Room and board charges vary according to housing facility. *Payment plan:* installment. *Waivers:* children of alumni, senior citizens, and employees or children of employees.

Financial Aid Of all full-time matriculated undergraduates who enrolled in 2001, 928 applied for aid, 928 were judged to have need, 12 had their need fully met. 47 Federal Work-Study jobs (averaging $1105). 17 State and other part-time jobs (averaging $1780). In 2001, 126 non-need-based awards were made. *Average percent of need met:* 32%. *Average financial aid package:* $5990. *Average need-based loan:* $3212. *Average need-based gift aid:* $4400. *Average non-need based aid:* $1590. *Financial aid deadline:* 11/15.

Applying *Options:* electronic application. *Application fee:* $25. *Required:* high school transcript, minimum 2.0 GPA, letters of recommendation, interview. *Application deadline:* rolling (freshmen), rolling (transfers). *Notification:* continuous (freshmen).

Admissions Contact Mr. Robert Cornwell, Associate Director of Admissions, Missouri Baptist College, One College Park Drive, St. Louis, MO 63141-8660. *Phone:* 314-392-2296. *Toll-free phone:* 877-434-1115 Ext. 2290. *Fax:* 314-434-7596. *E-mail:* admissions@mobap.edu.

MISSOURI SOUTHERN STATE COLLEGE

Joplin, Missouri

- **State-supported** 4-year, founded 1937
- **Calendar** semesters
- **Degrees** certificates, associate, and bachelor's
- **Small-town** 350-acre campus
- **Coed,** 5,899 undergraduate students, 65% full-time, 57% women, 43% men
- **Moderately difficult** entrance level, 79% of applicants were admitted

Undergraduates 3,863 full-time, 2,036 part-time. Students come from 37 states and territories, 42 other countries, 13% are from out of state, 2% African American, 0.9% Asian American or Pacific Islander, 2% Hispanic American, 3% Native American, 1% international, 7% transferred in, 10% live on campus. *Retention:* 64% of 2001 full-time freshmen returned.

Freshmen *Admission:* 1,772 applied, 1,399 admitted, 875 enrolled. *Test scores:* ACT scores over 18: 85%; ACT scores over 24: 31%; ACT scores over 30: 3%.

Faculty *Total:* 294, 69% full-time, 48% with terminal degrees. *Student/faculty ratio:* 19:1.

Majors Accounting; biology; biotechnology research; business administration; business marketing and marketing management; chemistry; computer/information sciences; computer science; criminal justice/law enforcement administration; data processing technology; dental hygiene; drafting; early childhood education; ecology; education; elementary education; English; environmental health; exercise sciences; finance; French; genetics; German; graphic design/commercial art/illustration; history; information sciences/systems; international business; international relations; law enforcement/police science; machine technology; marine biology; mass communications; mathematics; medical radiologic technology; medical technology; microbiology/bacteriology; middle school education; music; music teacher education; nursing; physical education; physics; political science; pre-dentistry; pre-engineering; pre-medicine; pre-pharmacy studies; preveterinary studies; professional studies; psychology; respiratory therapy; secondary education; sociology; Spanish; special education; theater arts/drama.

Academic Programs *Special study options:* academic remediation for entering students, accelerated degree program, adult/continuing education programs, advanced placement credit, distance learning, double majors, English as a second language, honors programs, independent study, internships, off-campus study, part-time degree program, services for LD students, study abroad, summer session for credit.

Library Spiva Library with 425,116 titles, 1,235 serial subscriptions, 13,724 audiovisual materials, an OPAC, a Web page.

Computers on Campus 577 computers available on campus for general student use. A campuswide network can be accessed from student residence rooms and from off campus. Internet access, at least one staffed computer lab available.

Student Life *Housing:* on-campus residence required through sophomore year. *Options:* men-only, women-only, disabled students. *Activities and Organizations:* drama/theater group, student-run newspaper, radio and television station, choral group, marching band, Koinonia, Campus Activities Board, Residence Hall Association, Baptist Student Union, Student Senate, national fraternities, national sororities. *Campus security:* 24-hour emergency response devices and patrols, late-night transport/escort service, controlled dormitory access. *Student Services:* health clinic, personal/psychological counseling.

Athletics Member NCAA. All Division II. *Intercollegiate sports:* baseball M(s), basketball M(s)/W(s), cross-country running M(s)/W(s), football M(s), golf M(s), soccer M(s)/W(s), softball W(s), tennis W(s), track and field M(s)/W(s), volleyball W(s). *Intramural sports:* basketball M/W, bowling M/W, football M/W, golf M/W, racquetball M/W, soccer M/W, softball M/W, swimming M/W, table tennis M/W, tennis M/W, volleyball M/W.

Standardized Tests *Required:* SAT I or ACT (for admission). *Required for some:* ACT (for admission).
Costs (2001–02) *Tuition:* state resident $2700 full-time, $90 per credit part-time; nonresident $5400 full-time, $180 per credit part-time. Full-time tuition and fees vary according to course load. *Required fees:* $166 full-time, $53 per term part-time. *Room and board:* $3800. Room and board charges vary according to housing facility. *Payment plan:* deferred payment. *Waivers:* senior citizens and employees or children of employees.
Financial Aid Of all full-time matriculated undergraduates who enrolled in 2001, 3761 applied for aid, 3210 were judged to have need, 226 had their need fully met. 130 Federal Work-Study jobs (averaging $1710). 382 State and other part-time jobs (averaging $1571). *Average percent of need met:* 82%. *Average financial aid package:* $4049. *Average need-based loan:* $3317. *Average need-based gift aid:* $2074. *Average indebtedness upon graduation:* $11,570.
Applying *Options:* common application, electronic application, deferred entrance. *Application fee:* $15. *Required:* high school transcript. *Application deadlines:* 8/1 (freshmen), 8/1 (transfers). *Notification:* continuous (freshmen).
Admissions Contact Mr. Derek Skaggs, Director of Enrollment Services, Missouri Southern State College, 3950 East Newman Road, Joplin, MO 64801-1595. *Phone:* 417-625-9537. *Toll-free phone:* 800-606-MSSC. *Fax:* 417-659-4429. *E-mail:* admissions@mail.mssc.edu.

MISSOURI TECH
St. Louis, Missouri

- **Proprietary** 4-year, founded 1932
- **Calendar** semesters
- **Degrees** associate and bachelor's
- **Suburban** campus
- **Coed, primarily men,** 266 undergraduate students, 23% full-time, 12% women, 88% men
- **Moderately difficult** entrance level

Undergraduates Students come from 4 states and territories, 8 other countries, 6% live on campus.
Faculty *Total:* 20, 35% with terminal degrees. *Student/faculty ratio:* 10:1.
Majors Computer engineering; computer engineering technology; electrical/electronic engineering technology; electrical engineering; engineering/industrial management; engineering-related technology; systems engineering.
Academic Programs *Special study options:* accelerated degree program, adult/continuing education programs, advanced placement credit, internships, part-time degree program, summer session for credit.
Computers on Campus 100 computers available on campus for general student use. A campuswide network can be accessed from off campus. Internet access, at least one staffed computer lab available.
Student Life *Housing Options:* men-only, women-only. *Campus security:* 24-hour emergency response devices.
Standardized Tests *Recommended:* ACT (for admission).
Costs (2001–02) *Tuition:* $325 per credit part-time. *Required fees:* $160 full-time, $325 per credit. *Room only:* $375.
Applying *Options:* common application, electronic application. *Required:* high school transcript. *Required for some:* interview, minimum ACT score of 20. *Application deadline:* rolling (freshmen).
Admissions Contact Mr. Phil Eberle, Director of Admissions, Missouri Tech, 1167 Corporate Lake Drive, St. Louis, MO 63132. *Phone:* 314-569-3600. *Toll-free phone:* 800-960-8324. *Fax:* 314-569-1167.

MISSOURI VALLEY COLLEGE
Marshall, Missouri

- **Independent** 4-year, founded 1889, affiliated with Presbyterian Church
- **Calendar** 4-1-4
- **Degrees** associate and bachelor's
- **Small-town** 140-acre campus with easy access to Kansas City
- **Endowment** $2.3 million
- **Coed,** 1,577 undergraduate students, 83% full-time, 42% women, 58% men
- **Moderately difficult** entrance level, 62% of applicants were admitted

Undergraduates 1,305 full-time, 272 part-time. Students come from 43 states and territories, 22 other countries, 40% are from out of state, 13% African American, 4% Asian American or Pacific Islander, 4% Hispanic American, 1% Native American, 7% international, 10% transferred in, 75% live on campus. *Retention:* 49% of 2001 full-time freshmen returned.
Freshmen *Admission:* 1,085 applied, 678 admitted, 414 enrolled. *Average high school GPA:* 2.70. *Test scores:* SAT verbal scores over 500: 22%; SAT math scores over 500: 24%; ACT scores over 18: 68%; SAT verbal scores over 600: 1%; SAT math scores over 600: 2%; ACT scores over 24: 12%; ACT scores over 30: 1%.
Faculty *Total:* 92, 68% full-time, 27% with terminal degrees. *Student/faculty ratio:* 22:1.
Majors Accounting; actuarial science; agricultural business; art; biology; business administration; business marketing and marketing management; computer science; criminal justice/law enforcement administration; economics; education; elementary education; English; health education; history; human services; liberal arts and sciences/liberal studies; mass communications; mathematics; philosophy; physical education; political science; pre-law; pre-medicine; pre-veterinary studies; psychology; public administration; recreation/leisure facilities management; recreation/leisure studies; religious studies; science education; secondary education; sociology; special education; speech/rhetorical studies; theater arts/drama.
Academic Programs *Special study options:* adult/continuing education programs, advanced placement credit, cooperative education, double majors, English as a second language, independent study, internships, part-time degree program, services for LD students, summer session for credit. *ROTC:* Army (c).
Library Murrell Memorial Library plus 1 other with 61,003 titles, 391 serial subscriptions, 1,333 audiovisual materials, an OPAC, a Web page.
Computers on Campus 250 computers available on campus for general student use. A campuswide network can be accessed from student residence rooms and from off campus. Internet access, at least one staffed computer lab available.
Student Life *Housing Options:* coed, men-only, women-only. *Activities and Organizations:* drama/theater group, student-run newspaper, radio and television station, choral group, V Club, fraternities, sororities, Rodeo Club, Musical Theatre, national fraternities, national sororities. *Campus security:* 24-hour emergency response devices, student patrols, controlled dormitory access. *Student Services:* health clinic.
Athletics Member NAIA. *Intercollegiate sports:* baseball M(s), basketball M(s)/W(s), cross-country running M(s)/W(s), football M(s), golf M(s)/W, soccer M(s)/W(s), softball W(s), track and field M(s)/W(s), volleyball M(s)/W(s), wrestling M(s)/W(s). *Intramural sports:* badminton M/W, baseball M, basketball M/W, bowling M/W, football M/W, soccer M/W, softball M/W, table tennis M/W, tennis M/W, volleyball W.
Standardized Tests *Required:* ACT (for admission). *Recommended:* SAT II: Writing Test (for admission).
Costs (2002–03) *Comprehensive fee:* $17,950 includes full-time tuition ($12,300), mandatory fees ($450), and room and board ($5200). Part-time tuition: $350 per credit hour. *Payment plan:* installment. *Waivers:* children of alumni, senior citizens, and employees or children of employees.
Financial Aid Of all full-time matriculated undergraduates who enrolled in 2001, 1198 applied for aid, 1148 were judged to have need. 655 State and other part-time jobs (averaging $1860). In 2001, 184 non-need-based awards were made. *Average percent of need met:* 80%. *Average financial aid package:* $12,034. *Average need-based loan:* $2401. *Average need-based gift aid:* $9915. *Average indebtedness upon graduation:* $12,100. *Financial aid deadline:* 9/15.
Applying *Options:* common application, electronic application, early admission, deferred entrance. *Application fee:* $15. *Required:* high school transcript. *Required for some:* essay or personal statement, 3 letters of recommendation. *Recommended:* minimum 2.0 GPA, interview. *Application deadline:* rolling (freshmen), rolling (transfers). *Notification:* continuous (freshmen).
Admissions Contact Ms. Debbie Bultman, Admissions, Missouri Valley College, 500 East College, Marshall, MO 65340-3197. *Phone:* 660-831-4114. *Fax:* 660-831-4039. *E-mail:* admissions@moval.edu.

MISSOURI WESTERN STATE COLLEGE
St. Joseph, Missouri

- **State-supported** 4-year, founded 1915
- **Calendar** semesters
- **Degrees** certificates, associate, and bachelor's
- **Suburban** 744-acre campus with easy access to Kansas City
- **Endowment** $5.9 million
- **Coed,** 5,102 undergraduate students, 77% full-time, 61% women, 39% men
- **Noncompetitive** entrance level, 100% of applicants were admitted

Missouri Western State College affords quality instruction in a wide range of programs, reasonable costs, scholarships, and a well-rounded college experience. A friendly, personal atmosphere pervades both classroom and campus. The College serves a four-state area and attracts students nationwide. Its small student-faculty ratio allows hands-on emphasis in all academic areas.

Missouri Western State College (continued)

Undergraduates 3,914 full-time, 1,188 part-time. Students come from 38 states and territories, 7 other countries, 10% are from out of state, 9% African American, 0.6% Asian American or Pacific Islander, 2% Hispanic American, 0.9% Native American, 0.2% international, 6% transferred in, 20% live on campus. *Retention:* 56% of 2001 full-time freshmen returned.

Freshmen *Admission:* 2,453 applied, 2,453 admitted, 1,176 enrolled. *Test scores:* ACT scores over 18: 66%; ACT scores over 24: 16%; ACT scores over 30: 1%.

Faculty *Total:* 323, 59% full-time, 47% with terminal degrees. *Student/faculty ratio:* 19:1.

Majors Accounting; art; art education; biology; business administration; business marketing and marketing management; chemistry; civil engineering technology; computer/information sciences; criminal justice studies; economics; electrical/electronic engineering technology; elementary education; English; English education; exercise sciences; finance; French; French language education; general studies; graphic design/commercial art/illustration; history; industrial technology; information sciences/systems; mathematics; medical records technology; medical technology; music; music teacher education; nursing; paralegal/legal assistant; physical therapy assistant; political science; psychology; recreation/leisure facilities management; social work; Spanish; Spanish language education; speech/rhetorical studies; speech/theater education.

Academic Programs *Special study options:* academic remediation for entering students, accelerated degree program, adult/continuing education programs, advanced placement credit, distance learning, double majors, freshman honors college, honors programs, internships, part-time degree program, summer session for credit. *ROTC:* Army (b).

Library Warren E. Hearnes Library with 147,509 titles, 1,068 serial subscriptions, 13,705 audiovisual materials, an OPAC, a Web page.

Computers on Campus 250 computers available on campus for general student use. A campuswide network can be accessed from student residence rooms and from off campus. Internet access, online (class) registration, at least one staffed computer lab available.

Student Life *Housing Options:* coed. *Activities and Organizations:* drama/theater group, student-run newspaper, choral group, marching band, national fraternities, national sororities. *Campus security:* 24-hour emergency response devices and patrols, student patrols, late-night transport/escort service, controlled dormitory access. *Student Services:* health clinic, personal/psychological counseling, women's center.

Athletics Member NCAA. All Division II. *Intercollegiate sports:* baseball M(s), basketball M(s)/W(s), football M(s), golf M(s), softball W(s), tennis W(s), volleyball W(s). *Intramural sports:* basketball M/W, bowling M/W, football M, golf M/W, ice hockey M, racquetball M/W, rugby M, soccer M, swimming M/W, table tennis M/W, tennis M/W, volleyball M/W.

Standardized Tests *Required:* ACT (for placement).

Costs (2001–02) *One-time required fee:* $15. *Tuition:* state resident $2928 full-time, $107 per credit hour part-time; nonresident $5394 full-time, $191 per credit hour part-time. *Required fees:* $296 full-time, $11 per credit hour, $10 per term part-time. *Room and board:* $3636. Room and board charges vary according to board plan and housing facility. *Payment plans:* installment, deferred payment. *Waivers:* senior citizens and employees or children of employees.

Financial Aid Of all full-time matriculated undergraduates who enrolled in 2001, 337 Federal Work-Study jobs (averaging $1192). 483 State and other part-time jobs (averaging $1793). *Average indebtedness upon graduation:* $15,200.

Applying *Options:* early admission. *Application fee:* $15. *Required:* high school transcript. *Application deadlines:* 7/30 (freshmen), 7/30 (transfers). *Notification:* continuous until 8/10 (freshmen).

Admissions Contact Mr. Howard McCauley, Director of Admissions, Missouri Western State College, 4525 Downs Drive, St. Joseph, MO 64507-2294. *Phone:* 816-271-4267. *Toll-free phone:* 800-662-7041 Ext. 60. *Fax:* 816-271-5833. *E-mail:* admissn@mwsc.edu.

NATIONAL AMERICAN UNIVERSITY
Kansas City, Missouri

- **Proprietary** 4-year, founded 1941, part of National College
- **Calendar** quarters
- **Degrees** diplomas, associate, and bachelor's
- **Urban** 1-acre campus
- **Coed**
- **Noncompetitive** entrance level

Faculty *Student/faculty ratio:* 12:1.

Student Life *Campus security:* 24-hour patrols.

Athletics Member NAIA.

Costs (2001–02) *One-time required fee:* $35. *Tuition:* $9360 full-time, $195 per credit hour part-time. Full-time tuition and fees vary according to course load and location. Part-time tuition and fees vary according to course load and location.

Applying *Options:* early admission, deferred entrance. *Application fee:* $25. *Required:* high school transcript, interview.

Admissions Contact Janet Miller, Director of Admissions, National American University, 4200 Blue Ridge Boulevard, Kansas City, MO 64133-1612. *Phone:* 816-353-4554. *Fax:* 816-353-1176.

NORTHWEST MISSOURI STATE UNIVERSITY
Maryville, Missouri

- **State-supported** comprehensive, founded 1905, part of Missouri Coordinating Board for Higher Education
- **Calendar** trimesters
- **Degrees** bachelor's and master's
- **Small-town** 240-acre campus with easy access to Kansas City
- **Coed,** 5,905 undergraduate students, 84% full-time, 56% women, 44% men
- **Moderately difficult** entrance level, 90% of applicants were admitted

Undergraduates 4,976 full-time, 929 part-time. Students come from 35 states and territories, 10 other countries, 28% are from out of state, 6% transferred in, 49% live on campus. *Retention:* 72% of 2001 full-time freshmen returned.

Freshmen *Admission:* 2,951 applied, 2,663 admitted, 1,197 enrolled. *Average high school GPA:* 3.20. *Test scores:* ACT scores over 18: 94%; ACT scores over 24: 37%; ACT scores over 30: 7%.

Faculty *Total:* 242, 98% full-time, 70% with terminal degrees. *Student/faculty ratio:* 24:1.

Majors Accounting; advertising; agricultural business; agricultural economics; agricultural education; agricultural mechanization; agricultural sciences; agronomy/crop science; animal sciences; Army R.O.T.C./military science; art; art education; behavioral sciences; biological/physical sciences; biology; biomedical technology; botany; broadcast journalism; business administration; business economics; business education; business marketing and marketing management; chemistry; child care/development; clothing/textiles; computer management; computer programming; computer science; counselor education/guidance; data processing technology; developmental/child psychology; dietetics; drawing; early childhood education; earth sciences; ecology; economics; education; education administration; elementary education; English; family/consumer studies; farm/ranch management; fashion design/illustration; fashion merchandising; finance; fine/studio arts; food sales operations; food sciences; forestry; French; geography; geology; graphic design/commercial art/illustration; health education; health science; history; home economics; home economics education; horticulture science; humanities; information sciences/systems; interior design; international business; journalism; landscape architecture; legal administrative assistant; literature; management information systems/business data processing; mass communications; mathematics; medical laboratory technician; medical technology; metal/jewelry arts; middle school education; music; music business management/merchandising; music (piano and organ performance); music teacher education; music (voice and choral/opera performance); natural resources conservation; nutrition science; philosophy; physical education; physical sciences; physics; political science; pre-dentistry; pre-law; pre-medicine; pre-veterinary studies; psychology; public administration; public relations; radio/television broadcasting; reading education; recreational therapy; recreation/leisure studies; retail management; romance languages; science education; sculpture; secondary education; secretarial science; social sciences; sociology; Spanish; special education; speech/rhetorical studies; sport/fitness administration; stringed instruments; textile arts; theater arts/drama; wildlife biology; wildlife management; wind/percussion instruments; zoology.

Academic Programs *Special study options:* academic remediation for entering students, accelerated degree program, advanced placement credit, English as a second language, internships, off-campus study, part-time degree program, services for LD students, study abroad, summer session for credit. *ROTC:* Army (b). *Unusual degree programs:* 3-2 engineering with University of Missouri-Rolla, University of Missouri-Columbia.

Library B. D. Owens Library plus 1 other with 305,982 titles, 1,469 serial subscriptions, an OPAC, a Web page.

Computers on Campus 2450 computers available on campus for general student use. A campuswide network can be accessed from student residence rooms and from off campus. Internet access, at least one staffed computer lab available.

Student Life *Housing:* on-campus residence required for freshman year. *Options:* coed. *Activities and Organizations:* drama/theater group, student-run newspaper, radio and television station, choral group, marching band, Greek system, student government, national fraternities, national sororities. *Campus* *security:* 24-hour patrols, student patrols, late-night transport/escort service. *Student Services:* health clinic, personal/psychological counseling, women's center.

Athletics Member NCAA. All Division II. *Intercollegiate sports:* baseball M(s), basketball M(s)/W(s), cross-country running M(s)/W(s), football M(s), golf M(s), soccer W(s), softball W(s), tennis M(s)/W(s), track and field M(s)/W(s), volleyball W(s). *Intramural sports:* badminton M/W, basketball M/W, cross-country running M/W, football M/W, golf M/W, racquetball M/W, soccer M(c), swimming M/W, table tennis M/W, tennis M/W, track and field M/W, volleyball M/W, water polo M/W, weight lifting M/W.

Standardized Tests *Required:* SAT I or ACT (for admission).

Costs (2001–02) *Tuition:* state resident $3450 full-time, $115 per credit hour part-time; nonresident $5918 full-time, $197 per credit hour part-time. *Required fees:* $150 full-time, $5 per credit hour. *Room and board:* $4322. Room and board charges vary according to board plan and housing facility. *Payment plan:* installment. *Waivers:* senior citizens and employees or children of employees.

Financial Aid Of all full-time matriculated undergraduates who enrolled in 2001, 3320 applied for aid, 2455 were judged to have need, 838 had their need fully met. 402 Federal Work-Study jobs (averaging $1374). 595 State and other part-time jobs (averaging $970). In 2001, 398 non-need-based awards were made. *Average percent of need met:* 82%. *Average financial aid package:* $6047. *Average need-based loan:* $3252. *Average need-based gift aid:* $2560. *Average non-need based aid:* $1706. *Average indebtedness upon graduation:* $13,799.

Applying *Options:* electronic application, deferred entrance. *Application fee:* $15. *Required:* high school transcript, minimum 2.0 GPA. *Required for some:* interview. *Application deadline:* rolling (freshmen), rolling (transfers). *Notification:* continuous until 8/15 (freshmen).

Admissions Contact Ms. Beverly Schenkel, Associate Director of Admission, Northwest Missouri State University, 800 University Drive, Maryville, MO 64468-6001. *Phone:* 660-562-1149. *Toll-free phone:* 800-633-1175. *Fax:* 660-562-1121. *E-mail:* admissions@acad.nwmissouri.edu.

OZARK CHRISTIAN COLLEGE

Joplin, Missouri

- **Independent Christian** 4-year, founded 1942
- **Calendar** semesters
- **Degrees** certificates, associate, and bachelor's
- **Suburban** 110-acre campus
- **Coed,** 757 undergraduate students, 83% full-time, 50% women, 50% men
- **Noncompetitive** entrance level, 100% of applicants were admitted

Undergraduates Students come from 32 states and territories, 8 other countries, 57% are from out of state, 1% African American, 0.9% Asian American or Pacific Islander, 2% Hispanic American, 2% Native American, 1% international, 63% live on campus. *Retention:* 70% of 2001 full-time freshmen returned.

Freshmen *Admission:* 287 applied, 287 admitted. *Average high school GPA:* 3.38.

Faculty *Total:* 33, 67% full-time, 27% with terminal degrees. *Student/faculty ratio:* 21:1.

Majors Biblical languages/literatures; biblical studies; elementary education; religious education; religious music; sign language interpretation; theology.

Academic Programs *Special study options:* academic remediation for entering students, adult/continuing education programs, double majors, English as a second language, internships, part-time degree program, services for LD students, summer session for credit.

Library Seth Wilson Library with 54,881 titles, 366 serial subscriptions, 20,017 audiovisual materials, an OPAC, a Web page.

Computers on Campus 28 computers available on campus for general student use. Internet access, at least one staffed computer lab available.

Student Life *Housing:* on-campus residence required through senior year. *Options:* men-only, women-only. *Activities and Organizations:* drama/theater group, student-run radio station, choral group, Family Outreach Group, God's Spokesman, Imagine. *Campus security:* 24-hour emergency response devices, 12-hour patrols by trained security personnel. *Student Services:* health clinic, personal/psychological counseling.

Athletics Member NCCAA. *Intercollegiate sports:* basketball M/W, soccer M, volleyball W. *Intramural sports:* basketball M, racquetball M/W, soccer M, softball M/W, volleyball M/W.

Standardized Tests *Required:* SAT I or ACT (for admission).

Costs (2002–03) *Comprehensive fee:* $9625 includes full-time tuition ($5280), mandatory fees ($515), and room and board ($3830). Part-time tuition: $165 per credit. *Room and board:* College room only: $1880. Room and board charges vary according to board plan. *Payment plans:* installment, deferred payment. *Waivers:* senior citizens and employees or children of employees.

Financial Aid Of all full-time matriculated undergraduates who enrolled in 2001, 46 Federal Work-Study jobs (averaging $1089). *Financial aid deadline:* 4/1.

Applying *Options:* electronic application. *Application fee:* $30. *Required:* essay or personal statement, high school transcript, 4 letters of recommendation. *Required for some:* interview. *Application deadline:* 8/15 (freshmen), rolling (transfers).

Admissions Contact Jim Marcum, Executive Director of Admissions, Ozark Christian College, 1111 North Main Street, Joplin, MO 64801-4804. *Phone:* 417-624-2518 Ext. 2021. *Toll-free phone:* 800-299-4622. *Fax:* 417-624-0090. *E-mail:* occadmin@occ.edu.

PARK UNIVERSITY

Parkville, Missouri

- **Independent** comprehensive, founded 1875
- **Calendar** semesters
- **Degrees** associate, bachelor's, and master's
- **Suburban** 800-acre campus with easy access to Kansas City
- **Endowment** $24.5 million
- **Coed,** 9,262 undergraduate students, 10% full-time, 48% women, 52% men
- **Moderately difficult** entrance level, 68% of applicants were admitted

Undergraduates 949 full-time, 8,313 part-time. Students come from 37 states and territories, 58 other countries, 86% are from out of state, 21% African American, 2% Asian American or Pacific Islander, 14% Hispanic American, 0.7% Native American, 2% international, 22% transferred in, 12% live on campus. *Retention:* 73% of 2001 full-time freshmen returned.

Freshmen *Admission:* 405 applied, 274 admitted, 141 enrolled. *Average high school GPA:* 3.00. *Test scores:* ACT scores over 18: 67%; ACT scores over 24: 14%; ACT scores over 30: 1%.

Faculty *Total:* 651, 8% full-time. *Student/faculty ratio:* 14:1.

Majors Accounting; accounting related; athletic training/sports medicine; aviation management; biological sciences/life sciences related; biology; building maintenance/management; business administration; business economics; business management/administrative services related; business marketing and marketing management; chemistry; communications; computer/information sciences; computer/information sciences related; computer science; criminal justice/law enforcement administration; early childhood education; economics; education related; elementary education; engineering related; English; financial management and services related; fine/studio arts; graphic design/commercial art/illustration; history; human resources management related; human services; interior design; legal studies; liberal arts and sciences/liberal studies; logistics/materials management; management information systems/business data processing; mathematics; medical records administration; natural sciences; nursing; office management; political science; psychology; public administration; social psychology; sociology; Spanish.

Academic Programs *Special study options:* academic remediation for entering students, adult/continuing education programs, advanced placement credit, distance learning, double majors, English as a second language, external degree program, honors programs, independent study, internships, off-campus study, part-time degree program, services for LD students, student-designed majors, summer session for credit. *ROTC:* Army (b).

Library McAfee Memorial Library with 139,202 titles, 775 serial subscriptions, 750 audiovisual materials, an OPAC.

Computers on Campus 116 computers available on campus for general student use. A campuswide network can be accessed from student residence rooms. Internet access, online (class) registration, at least one staffed computer lab available.

Student Life *Housing:* on-campus residence required through junior year. *Options:* coed. *Activities and Organizations:* drama/theater group, student-run newspaper, radio station, choral group, World Student Union, Student Senate, radio club, Latin American Student Organization, marketing club. *Campus security:* 24-hour patrols, student patrols, late-night transport/escort service. *Student Services:* health clinic, personal/psychological counseling.

Athletics Member NAIA. *Intercollegiate sports:* baseball M(s), basketball M(s)/W(s), cross-country running M(s)/W(s), soccer M(s)/W(s), softball W(s), track and field M(s)/W(s), volleyball M(s)/W(s). *Intramural sports:* basketball M/W, softball M/W, volleyball M/W.

Standardized Tests *Required:* SAT I or ACT (for admission).

Costs (2001–02) *Comprehensive fee:* $10,160 includes full-time tuition ($5160) and room and board ($5000). Part-time tuition: $172 per credit hour. *Room and board:* Room and board charges vary according to board plan and housing facility. *Payment plan:* installment. *Waivers:* senior citizens and employees or children of employees.

Park University (continued)

Financial Aid Of all full-time matriculated undergraduates who enrolled in 2001, 3357 applied for aid, 2744 were judged to have need, 553 had their need fully met. 186 Federal Work-Study jobs (averaging $2044). 165 State and other part-time jobs (averaging $3210). In 2001, 338 non-need-based awards were made. *Average percent of need met:* 62%. *Average financial aid package:* $4557. *Average need-based loan:* $3949. *Average need-based gift aid:* $2640. *Average non-need based aid:* $3508. *Average indebtedness upon graduation:* $10,500.

Applying *Options:* electronic application, early admission, deferred entrance. *Application fee:* $25. *Required:* high school transcript, minimum 2.0 GPA. *Required for some:* 2 letters of recommendation, interview. *Recommended:* essay or personal statement. *Application deadlines:* 8/1 (freshmen), 8/1 (transfers). *Notification:* continuous (freshmen).

Admissions Contact Dr. Ron Carruth, Director of Student Recruiting and Marketing, Park University, 8700 NW River Park Drive, Campus Box 1, Parkville, MO 64152. *Phone:* 816-584-6215. *Toll-free phone:* 800-745-7275. *Fax:* 816-741-4462. *E-mail:* admissions@mail.park.edu.

RESEARCH COLLEGE OF NURSING

Kansas City, Missouri

- **Independent** comprehensive, founded 1980, part of Rockhurst University
- **Calendar** semesters
- **Degrees** bachelor's and master's (jointly with Rockhurst College)
- **Urban** 66-acre campus
- **Coed, primarily women,** 219 undergraduate students, 93% full-time, 94% women, 6% men
- **Moderately difficult** entrance level, 78% of applicants were admitted

Undergraduates 204 full-time, 15 part-time. Students come from 7 states and territories, 14% African American, 3% Asian American or Pacific Islander, 7% Hispanic American, 1% Native American, 5% transferred in.

Freshmen *Admission:* 65 applied, 51 admitted, 20 enrolled. *Average high school GPA:* 3.40. *Test scores:* ACT scores over 18: 100%; ACT scores over 24: 80%; ACT scores over 30: 30%.

Faculty *Total:* 35, 71% full-time. *Student/faculty ratio:* 7:1.

Majors Nursing.

Academic Programs *Special study options:* accelerated degree program, advanced placement credit, double majors, honors programs, independent study, services for LD students, study abroad, summer session for credit. *ROTC:* Army (c).

Library Greenlease Library with 150,000 titles, 675 serial subscriptions, an OPAC, a Web page.

Computers on Campus 125 computers available on campus for general student use. A campuswide network can be accessed from student residence rooms and from off campus. Internet access, at least one staffed computer lab available.

Student Life *Housing:* on-campus residence required for freshman year. *Options:* coed, men-only, women-only. *Activities and Organizations:* drama/theater group, student-run newspaper, radio station, choral group, national fraternities, national sororities. *Campus security:* 24-hour emergency response devices and patrols, late-night transport/escort service, controlled dormitory access. *Student Services:* health clinic, personal/psychological counseling.

Athletics Member NCAA. All Division II. *Intercollegiate sports:* baseball M(s), basketball M(s)/W(s), cross-country running M/W, soccer M(s)/W(s), tennis M(c)/W(c), volleyball W(s). *Intramural sports:* badminton M/W, basketball M/W, cross-country running M/W, field hockey M/W, football M/W, golf M/W, lacrosse M/W, racquetball M/W, rugby M/W, soccer M/W, softball M/W, table tennis M/W, tennis M/W, volleyball M/W, weight lifting M.

Standardized Tests *Required:* SAT I or ACT (for admission).

Costs (2001–02) *One-time required fee:* $40. *Comprehensive fee:* $20,200 includes full-time tuition ($14,800), mandatory fees ($450), and room and board ($4950). Full-time tuition and fees vary according to program. Part-time tuition: $490 per credit hour. Part-time tuition and fees vary according to class time and program. *Required fees:* $15 per term part-time. *Room and board:* Room and board charges vary according to housing facility. *Payment plans:* installment, deferred payment. *Waivers:* senior citizens and employees or children of employees.

Financial Aid Of all full-time matriculated undergraduates who enrolled in 2001, 97 applied for aid, 85 were judged to have need, 25 had their need fully met. In 2001, 9 non-need-based awards were made. *Average percent of need met:* 50%. *Average financial aid package:* $8700. *Average need-based loan:* $7000. *Average need-based gift aid:* $5100. *Average non-need based aid:* $8455. *Average indebtedness upon graduation:* $8600.

Applying *Options:* common application, electronic application, deferred entrance. *Application fee:* $20. *Required:* high school transcript, 1 letter of recommendation. *Recommended:* minimum 2.7 GPA, interview, minimum ACT score of 2.0. *Application deadlines:* 6/30 (freshmen), 1/31 (transfers). *Notification:* continuous until 8/15 (freshmen).

Admissions Contact Ms. Marisa Ferrara, Rockhurst College Admission Office, Research College of Nursing, 1100 Rockhurst Road, Kansas City, MO 64110. *Phone:* 816-501-4100 Ext. 4654. *Toll-free phone:* 800-842-6776. *Fax:* 816-501-4588. *E-mail:* mendenhall@vax2.rockhurst.edu.

ROCKHURST UNIVERSITY

Kansas City, Missouri

- **Independent Roman Catholic (Jesuit)** comprehensive, founded 1910
- **Calendar** semesters
- **Degrees** certificates, bachelor's, master's, and postbachelor's certificates
- **Urban** 35-acre campus
- **Endowment** $29.0 million
- **Coed,** 2,011 undergraduate students, 60% full-time, 56% women, 44% men
- **Moderately difficult** entrance level, 87% of applicants were admitted

With its proximity to the new Stowers Institute, one of the world's largest molecular and genetic research facilities, Rockhurst University has elevated its opportunities for molecular biology to a full program. Students have the opportunity to be involved in investigative techniques used in modern molecular and cell studies.

Undergraduates 1,214 full-time, 797 part-time. Students come from 24 states and territories, 19 other countries, 33% are from out of state, 9% African American, 2% Asian American or Pacific Islander, 5% Hispanic American, 0.7% Native American, 2% international, 7% transferred in, 52% live on campus. *Retention:* 79% of 2001 full-time freshmen returned.

Freshmen *Admission:* 973 applied, 846 admitted, 298 enrolled. *Average high school GPA:* 3.24. *Test scores:* SAT verbal scores over 500: 72%; SAT math scores over 500: 58%; ACT scores over 18: 95%; SAT verbal scores over 600: 24%; SAT math scores over 600: 18%; ACT scores over 24: 46%; SAT verbal scores over 700: 2%; SAT math scores over 700: 4%; ACT scores over 30: 6%.

Faculty *Total:* 225, 58% full-time, 60% with terminal degrees. *Student/faculty ratio:* 11:1.

Majors Accounting; biology; business; business administration; business communications; business marketing and marketing management; chemistry; communications; community services; computer programming; computer science; computer systems analysis; creative writing; economics; education; elementary education; English; finance; French; history; human resources management; information sciences/systems; international relations; labor/personnel relations; management science; mathematics; medical laboratory technology; nursing; philosophy; physics; political science; psychology; public relations; secondary education; social sciences; sociology; Spanish; speech-language pathology; theater arts/drama; theology.

Academic Programs *Special study options:* academic remediation for entering students, accelerated degree program, adult/continuing education programs, advanced placement credit, cooperative education, double majors, freshman honors college, honors programs, independent study, internships, off-campus study, part-time degree program, services for LD students, study abroad, summer session for credit. *ROTC:* Army (c). *Unusual degree programs:* 3-2 engineering with University of Missouri-Rolla, University of Detroit Mercy, Marquette University.

Library Greenlease Library with 53,720 titles, 100 serial subscriptions, 2,730 audiovisual materials, an OPAC, a Web page.

Computers on Campus 500 computers available on campus for general student use. A campuswide network can be accessed from student residence rooms and from off campus. Internet access, at least one staffed computer lab available.

Student Life *Housing:* on-campus residence required through sophomore year. *Options:* coed, men-only, women-only. *Activities and Organizations:* drama/theater group, student-run newspaper, radio station, choral group, Student Activities Board, Organization of Collegiate Women, Black Student Union, Student Organization of Latinos, College Players, national fraternities, national sororities. *Campus security:* 24-hour emergency response devices and patrols, student patrols, late-night transport/escort service, controlled dormitory access, closed circuit TV monitors. *Student Services:* health clinic, personal/psychological counseling.

Athletics Member NCAA. All Division II. *Intercollegiate sports:* baseball M(s), basketball M(s)/W(s), golf M(s)/W(s), soccer M(s)/W(s), tennis M(s)/W(s), volleyball W(s). *Intramural sports:* badminton M/W, basketball M/W, cross-country running M/W, field hockey M/W, football M/W, golf M/W, racquetball M/W, soccer M/W, softball M/W, tennis M/W, volleyball M/W, weight lifting M, wrestling M.

Standardized Tests *Required:* SAT I or ACT (for admission).

Costs (2001–02) *One-time required fee:* $40. *Comprehensive fee:* $20,060 includes full-time tuition ($14,800), mandatory fees ($340), and room and board ($4920). Full-time tuition and fees vary according to course load. Part-time tuition: $490 per semester hour. Part-time tuition and fees vary according to class time, course load, and program. *Required fees:* $15 per term part-time. *Room and board:* Room and board charges vary according to gender and housing facility. *Payment plans:* installment, deferred payment. *Waivers:* children of alumni, senior citizens, and employees or children of employees.

Financial Aid Of all full-time matriculated undergraduates who enrolled in 2001, 1198 applied for aid, 937 were judged to have need, 25 had their need fully met. In 2001, 147 non-need-based awards were made. *Average percent of need met:* 81%. *Average financial aid package:* $14,467. *Average need-based loan:* $6780. *Average need-based gift aid:* $6813. *Average non-need based aid:* $5081. *Average indebtedness upon graduation:* $16,000.

Applying *Options:* common application, early admission, early action, deferred entrance. *Application fee:* $20. *Required:* high school transcript, minimum 2.0 GPA, 1 letter of recommendation. *Required for some:* essay or personal statement, interview. *Application deadline:* 6/30 (freshmen), rolling (transfers). *Notification:* continuous (freshmen), 7/1 (early action).

Admissions Contact Mr. Phillip Gebauer, Director of Undergraduate Admissions, Rockhurst University, 1100 Rockhurst Road, Kansas City, MO 64110-2561. *Phone:* 816-501-4100. *Toll-free phone:* 800-842-6776. *Fax:* 816-501-4142. *E-mail:* admission@rockhurst.edu.

ST. LOUIS CHRISTIAN COLLEGE

Florissant, Missouri

- **Independent Christian** 4-year, founded 1956
- **Calendar** semesters
- **Degrees** associate and bachelor's
- **Suburban** 20-acre campus with easy access to St. Louis
- **Endowment** $577,910
- **Coed,** 223 undergraduate students, 57% full-time, 39% women, 61% men
- **Minimally difficult** entrance level, 62% of applicants were admitted

Undergraduates 128 full-time, 95 part-time. Students come from 11 states and territories, 3 other countries, 37% are from out of state, 26% African American, 0.4% Asian American or Pacific Islander, 0.9% Hispanic American, 0.4% Native American, 1% international, 5% transferred in, 38% live on campus.

Freshmen *Admission:* 79 applied, 49 admitted, 33 enrolled. *Average high school GPA:* 3.10. *Test scores:* ACT scores over 18: 91%; ACT scores over 24: 48%; ACT scores over 30: 2%.

Faculty *Total:* 30, 30% full-time. *Student/faculty ratio:* 10:1.

Majors Biblical studies; divinity/ministry; liberal arts and sciences/liberal studies; religious education; religious music; theology.

Academic Programs *Special study options:* academic remediation for entering students, accelerated degree program, adult/continuing education programs, advanced placement credit, internships, part-time degree program, services for LD students.

Library St. Louis Christian College Library with 39,728 titles, 144 serial subscriptions, a Web page.

Computers on Campus 11 computers available on campus for general student use. Internet access, at least one staffed computer lab available.

Student Life *Housing:* on-campus residence required through senior year. *Options:* men-only, women-only. *Activities and Organizations:* drama/theater group, choral group, World Christians Unlimited, drama club, pep band. *Campus security:* 24-hour emergency response devices and patrols, controlled dormitory access, night security. *Student Services:* personal/psychological counseling.

Athletics Member NCCAA. *Intercollegiate sports:* baseball M, basketball M, volleyball W. *Intramural sports:* basketball M/W, volleyball W.

Standardized Tests *Required:* ACT (for admission).

Costs (2001–02) *Comprehensive fee:* $9604 includes full-time tuition ($5824) and room and board ($3780). Part-time tuition: $182 per credit hour. *Room and board:* Room and board charges vary according to housing facility. *Payment plan:* installment. *Waivers:* employees or children of employees.

Financial Aid Of all full-time matriculated undergraduates who enrolled in 2001, 103 applied for aid, 78 were judged to have need, 16 had their need fully met. 9 Federal Work-Study jobs (averaging $1013). In 2001, 19 non-need-based awards were made. *Average percent of need met:* 82%. *Average financial aid package:* $6643. *Average need-based loan:* $2796. *Average need-based gift aid:* $4472. *Average non-need based aid:* $755.

Applying *Options:* early admission. *Required:* essay or personal statement, high school transcript, 2 letters of recommendation. *Required for some:* interview. *Recommended:* minimum 2.0 GPA. *Application deadlines:* 8/15 (freshmen), 8/15 (transfers). *Notification:* continuous (freshmen).

Admissions Contact Mr. Richard Fordyce, Registrar, St. Louis Christian College, 1360 Grandview Drive, Florissant, MO 63033-6499. *Phone:* 314-837-6777 Ext. 1500. *Toll-free phone:* 800-887-SLCC. *Fax:* 314-837-8291. *E-mail:* questions@slcc4ministry.edu.

ST. LOUIS COLLEGE OF PHARMACY

St. Louis, Missouri

- **Independent** comprehensive, founded 1864
- **Calendar** semesters
- **Degrees** bachelor's, master's, and first professional (BS Degree program in pharmaceutical studies cannot be applied to directly; students have the option to transfer in after their second year in the PharmD program. Bachelor's degree candidates are not eligible to take the pharmacist's licensing exam)
- **Urban** 5-acre campus
- **Endowment** $50.5 million
- **Coed,** 814 undergraduate students, 98% full-time, 66% women, 34% men
- **Moderately difficult** entrance level, 66% of applicants were admitted

Undergraduates 796 full-time, 18 part-time. Students come from 26 states and territories, 50% are from out of state, 5% African American, 13% Asian American or Pacific Islander, 1% Hispanic American, 0.1% international, 7% transferred in, 26% live on campus. *Retention:* 89% of 2001 full-time freshmen returned.

Freshmen *Admission:* 432 applied, 286 admitted, 170 enrolled. *Average high school GPA:* 3.56. *Test scores:* ACT scores over 18: 100%; ACT scores over 24: 62%; ACT scores over 30: 6%.

Faculty *Total:* 100, 64% full-time, 67% with terminal degrees. *Student/faculty ratio:* 13:1.

Majors Pharmacy.

Academic Programs *Special study options:* adult/continuing education programs, advanced placement credit, internships, summer session for credit.

Library O. J. Cloughly Alumni Library with 56,636 titles, 282 serial subscriptions, 1,003 audiovisual materials, an OPAC, a Web page.

Computers on Campus 80 computers available on campus for general student use. A campuswide network can be accessed from student residence rooms and from off campus. Internet access, at least one staffed computer lab available.

Student Life *Housing:* on-campus residence required for freshman year. *Options:* coed. *Activities and Organizations:* drama/theater group, student-run newspaper, choral group, Gateway Academy of Student Pharmacists, Student Council, International Student Council, Student Ambassadors, Student Alumni Association, national fraternities, national sororities. *Campus security:* 24-hour emergency response devices and patrols, late-night transport/escort service, controlled dormitory access. *Student Services:* personal/psychological counseling.

Athletics Member NAIA. *Intercollegiate sports:* basketball M, cross-country running M/W, volleyball W. *Intramural sports:* basketball M, cross-country running M/W, football M/W, golf M/W, soccer M/W, table tennis M/W, tennis M/W, volleyball M/W, weight lifting M/W.

Standardized Tests *Required:* SAT I or ACT (for admission).

Costs (2001–02) *Comprehensive fee:* $19,139 includes full-time tuition ($13,650), mandatory fees ($125), and room and board ($5364). Full-time tuition and fees vary according to student level. Part-time tuition: $590 per credit. *Required fees:* $200 per term part-time. *Room and board:* Room and board charges vary according to housing facility. *Payment plan:* deferred payment. *Waivers:* employees or children of employees.

Financial Aid Of all full-time matriculated undergraduates who enrolled in 2001, 713 applied for aid, 650 were judged to have need, 2 had their need fully met. 111 Federal Work-Study jobs (averaging $1200). In 2001, 94 non-need-based awards were made. *Average percent of need met:* 31%. *Average financial aid package:* $11,324. *Average need-based loan:* $5340. *Average need-based gift aid:* $1498. *Average non-need based aid:* $7279. *Average indebtedness upon graduation:* $64,500. *Financial aid deadline:* 11/15.

Applying *Options:* electronic application. *Application fee:* $35. *Required:* essay or personal statement, high school transcript, minimum 2.5 GPA, letters of recommendation. *Required for some:* interview. *Recommended:* minimum 3.0 GPA. *Application deadlines:* rolling (freshmen), 2/1 (transfers). *Notification:* continuous until 8/1 (freshmen).

Admissions Contact Ms. Penny Bryant, Director of Admissions/Registrar, St. Louis College of Pharmacy, 4588 Parkview Place, St. Louis, MO 63110-1088. *Phone:* 314-367-8700 Ext. 1067. *Toll-free phone:* 800-278-5267. *Fax:* 314-367-2784. *E-mail:* pbryant@stlcop.edu.

SAINT LOUIS UNIVERSITY

St. Louis, Missouri

- **Independent Roman Catholic (Jesuit)** university, founded 1818
- **Calendar** semesters
- **Degrees** certificates, bachelor's, master's, doctoral, first professional, post-master's, and postbachelor's certificates
- **Urban** 279-acre campus
- **Endowment** $824.5 million
- **Coed,** 7,228 undergraduate students, 91% full-time, 55% women, 45% men
- **Moderately difficult** entrance level, 69% of applicants were admitted

Undergraduates 6,545 full-time, 683 part-time. Students come from 50 states and territories, 80 other countries, 48% are from out of state, 8% African American, 4% Asian American or Pacific Islander, 2% Hispanic American, 0.3% Native American, 4% international, 6% transferred in, 50% live on campus. *Retention:* 86% of 2001 full-time freshmen returned.

Freshmen *Admission:* 5,547 applied, 3,834 admitted, 1,479 enrolled. *Average high school GPA:* 3.47. *Test scores:* SAT verbal scores over 500: 88%; SAT math scores over 500: 88%; ACT scores over 18: 99%; SAT verbal scores over 600: 50%; SAT math scores over 600: 55%; ACT scores over 24: 78%; SAT verbal scores over 700: 8%; SAT math scores over 700: 12%; ACT scores over 30: 23%.

Faculty *Total:* 878, 65% full-time. *Student/faculty ratio:* 12:1.

Majors Accounting; aerospace engineering; aerospace engineering technology; aircraft pilot (professional); American studies; applied mathematics; art history; atmospheric sciences; aviation management; bioengineering; biology; business administration; business economics; business marketing and marketing management; chemistry; classics; communications; communications related; computer/information sciences; computer/information sciences related; computer software engineering; corrections; criminal justice studies; dietetics; economics; education (multiple levels); electrical engineering; engineering/industrial management; English; environmental science; exercise sciences; finance; fine/studio arts; French; geology; geophysics/seismology; German; Greek (ancient and medieval); health/medical laboratory technologies related; health services administration; history; humanities; human resources management; international business; international relations; management information systems/business data processing; management science; mathematics; mechanical engineering; music; nuclear medical technology; nursing; occupational therapy; philosophy; physician assistant; physics; political science; psychology; public relations; Russian; social sciences; social work; sociology; Spanish; theater arts/drama; theology; urban studies.

Academic Programs *Special study options:* academic remediation for entering students, accelerated degree program, adult/continuing education programs, advanced placement credit, cooperative education, distance learning, double majors, English as a second language, external degree program, freshman honors college, honors programs, independent study, internships, off-campus study, part-time degree program, services for LD students, student-designed majors, study abroad, summer session for credit. *ROTC:* Army (c), Air Force (b). *Unusual degree programs:* 3-2 engineering with Washington University in St. Louis.

Library Pius XII Memorial Library plus 3 others with 1.3 million titles, 14,724 serial subscriptions, 200,400 audiovisual materials, a Web page.

Computers on Campus 6500 computers available on campus for general student use. A campuswide network can be accessed from student residence rooms and from off campus. Internet access, online (class) registration, at least one staffed computer lab available.

Student Life *Housing Options:* coed, women-only, disabled students. *Activities and Organizations:* drama/theater group, student-run newspaper, radio and television station, choral group, Student Government Association, Student Activities Board, Black Student Alliance, International Student Federation, national fraternities, national sororities. *Campus security:* 24-hour emergency response devices and patrols, student patrols, late-night transport/escort service, controlled dormitory access, crime prevention program, bicycle patrols. *Student Services:* health clinic, personal/psychological counseling, legal services.

Athletics Member NCAA. All Division I. *Intercollegiate sports:* baseball M(s), basketball M(s)/W(s), crew M(c)/W(c), cross-country running M(s)/W(s), field hockey W(s), golf M(s), ice hockey M(c), lacrosse M(c)/W(c), riflery M(s)/W(s), rugby M(c), soccer M(s)(c)/W(s)(c), softball W(s), swimming M(s)/W(s), tennis M(s)/W(s), volleyball M(c)/W(s)(c). *Intramural sports:* badminton M/W, basketball M/W, lacrosse M, racquetball M/W, soccer M/W, softball M/W, tennis M/W, volleyball M/W, water polo M/W.

Standardized Tests *Required:* SAT I or ACT (for admission).

Costs (2001–02) *Comprehensive fee:* $26,590 includes full-time tuition ($19,670), mandatory fees ($160), and room and board ($6760). Part-time tuition: $690 per credit hour. Part-time tuition and fees vary according to class time and program. *Room and board:* College room only: $3650. Room and board charges vary according to board plan and housing facility. *Payment plan:* installment. *Waivers:* employees or children of employees.

Financial Aid Of all full-time matriculated undergraduates who enrolled in 2001, 5776 applied for aid, 4466 were judged to have need, 741 had their need fully met. 878 Federal Work-Study jobs (averaging $2741). In 2001, 1013 non-need-based awards were made. *Average percent of need met:* 69%. *Average financial aid package:* $19,526. *Average need-based loan:* $5959. *Average need-based gift aid:* $12,377. *Average non-need based aid:* $7762. *Average indebtedness upon graduation:* $14,231.

Applying *Options:* common application, electronic application, early admission, deferred entrance. *Application fee:* $25. *Required:* essay or personal statement, high school transcript, secondary school report form. *Recommended:* 2 letters of recommendation, interview. *Application deadlines:* 8/1 (freshmen), 8/1 (transfers). *Notification:* 8/1 (freshmen).

Admissions Contact Saint Louis University, 221 North Grand Boulevard, St. Louis, MO 63103-2097. *Phone:* 314-977-2500. *Toll-free phone:* 800-758-3678. *Fax:* 314-977-7136. *E-mail:* admitme@slu.edu.

SAINT LUKE'S COLLEGE

Kansas City, Missouri

- **Independent Episcopal** upper-level, founded 1903
- **Calendar** semesters
- **Degree** bachelor's
- **Urban** 3-acre campus
- **Endowment** $1.8 million
- **Coed, primarily women,** 129 undergraduate students, 89% full-time, 95% women, 5% men
- **Very difficult** entrance level

Undergraduates 115 full-time, 14 part-time. 4% African American, 0.9% Asian American or Pacific Islander, 2% Hispanic American, 43% transferred in, 4% live on campus.

Freshmen *Admission:* 55 admitted.

Faculty *Total:* 19, 89% full-time, 5% with terminal degrees. *Student/faculty ratio:* 7:1.

Majors Nursing.

Academic Programs *Special study options:* cooperative education, summer session for credit.

Library Health Sciences Library.

Computers on Campus 10 computers available on campus for general student use. At least one staffed computer lab available.

Student Life *Housing Options:* coed. *Activities and Organizations:* Saint Luke's Student Nurse Association. *Campus security:* 24-hour emergency response devices and patrols, late-night transport/escort service, controlled dormitory access. *Student Services:* health clinic, personal/psychological counseling.

Costs (2001–02) *Tuition:* $8250 full-time, $275 per credit hour part-time. Part-time tuition and fees vary according to course load. *Required fees:* $450 full-time, $225 per term part-time. *Room only:* $1600. *Payment plans:* installment, deferred payment.

Financial Aid Of all full-time matriculated undergraduates who enrolled in 2001, 3 Federal Work-Study jobs. *Average indebtedness upon graduation:* $21,000.

Applying *Options:* common application. *Application fee:* $20. *Application deadline:* 12/31 (transfers). *Notification:* continuous until 2/15 (transfers).

Admissions Contact Ms. Marsha Thomas, Director of Admissions, Saint Luke's College, 4426 Wornall Road, Kansas City, MO 64111. *Phone:* 816-932-2073. *E-mail:* mjthomas@saint-lukes.org.

SOUTHEAST MISSOURI STATE UNIVERSITY

Cape Girardeau, Missouri

- **State-supported** comprehensive, founded 1873, part of Missouri Coordinating Board for Higher Education
- **Calendar** semesters
- **Degrees** certificates, associate, bachelor's, and master's
- **Small-town** 693-acre campus with easy access to St. Louis
- **Endowment** $29.6 million
- **Coed,** 8,098 undergraduate students, 76% full-time, 60% women, 40% men
- **Moderately difficult** entrance level, 55% of applicants were admitted

Undergraduates 6,126 full-time, 1,972 part-time. Students come from 37 states and territories, 41 other countries, 10% are from out of state, 6% African

American, 0.6% Asian American or Pacific Islander, 0.7% Hispanic American, 0.4% Native American, 2% international, 6% transferred in, 28% live on campus. *Retention:* 70% of 2001 full-time freshmen returned.

Freshmen *Admission:* 3,390 applied, 1,859 admitted, 1,606 enrolled. *Average high school GPA:* 3.25. *Test scores:* ACT scores over 18: 97%; ACT scores over 24: 33%; ACT scores over 30: 5%.

Faculty *Total:* 544, 68% full-time, 64% with terminal degrees. *Student/faculty ratio:* 17:1.

Majors Accounting; advertising; agricultural business; agricultural sciences; agronomy/crop science; animal sciences; anthropology; applied mathematics; art; art education; athletic training/sports medicine; banking; biological/physical sciences; biology; business administration; business economics; business education; business marketing and marketing management; chemistry; child care/development; child care/guidance; clothing/apparel/textile studies; computer engineering technology; computer/information sciences; computer programming; corrections; criminal justice/law enforcement administration; criminal justice studies; early childhood education; earth sciences; economics; electrical/electronic engineering technology; electromechanical instrumentation and maintenance technologies related; elementary education; emergency medical technology; engineering physics; English; environmental science; family/consumer studies; fashion merchandising; finance; French; geography; geology; German; health/physical education; history; home economics; home economics education; horticulture science; housing studies; human resources management; individual/family development; industrial arts education; industrial technology; information sciences/systems; interdisciplinary studies; journalism; law enforcement/police science; liberal arts and sciences/liberal studies; management information systems/business data processing; marketing operations/marketing and distribution related; mass communications; mathematics; mathematics education; medical technology; music; music (general performance); music teacher education; music theory and composition; nursing; nutrition science; office management; operations management; paleontology; philosophy; physical education; physics; political science; psychology; public relations; radio/television broadcasting; recreation/leisure facilities management; recreation/leisure studies; science education; secondary education; secretarial science; social studies education; social work; sociology; Spanish; special education; speech education; speech-language pathology; speech/rhetorical studies; speech therapy; sport/fitness administration; theater arts/drama.

Academic Programs *Special study options:* academic remediation for entering students, adult/continuing education programs, advanced placement credit, cooperative education, distance learning, double majors, English as a second language, honors programs, independent study, internships, part-time degree program, services for LD students, student-designed majors, study abroad, summer session for credit. *ROTC:* Air Force (b).

Library Kent Library with 429,421 titles, 6,264 serial subscriptions, 7,955 audiovisual materials, an OPAC, a Web page.

Computers on Campus 650 computers available on campus for general student use. A campuswide network can be accessed from student residence rooms and from off campus. Internet access, online (class) registration, at least one staffed computer lab available.

Student Life *Housing:* on-campus residence required through sophomore year. *Options:* coed. *Activities and Organizations:* drama/theater group, student-run newspaper, radio station, choral group, marching band, student government, Greek life, Residence Hall Association, marketing club, national fraternities, national sororities. *Campus security:* 24-hour emergency response devices and patrols, late-night transport/escort service, controlled dormitory access. *Student Services:* health clinic, personal/psychological counseling.

Athletics Member NCAA. All Division I except football (Division I-AA). *Intercollegiate sports:* baseball M(s), basketball M(s)/W(s), cross-country running M(s)/W(s), golf M(s), gymnastics W(s), soccer W(s), softball W(s), tennis W(s), track and field M(s)/W(s), volleyball W(s). *Intramural sports:* badminton M/W, basketball M/W, bowling M/W, cross-country running M/W, fencing M/W, football M/W, golf M/W, lacrosse M/W, racquetball M/W, soccer M/W, softball M/W, swimming M/W, table tennis M/W, tennis M/W, track and field M/W, volleyball M/W, water polo M/W, weight lifting M/W, wrestling M/W.

Standardized Tests *Required:* SAT I or ACT (for admission).

Costs (2001–02) *Tuition:* state resident $3234 full-time, $118 per credit part-time; nonresident $6069 full-time, $212 per credit part-time. *Required fees:* $291 full-time. *Room and board:* $4842; room only: $2960. Room and board charges vary according to board plan, housing facility, and location. *Payment plans:* installment, deferred payment. *Waivers:* senior citizens and employees or children of employees.

Financial Aid Of all full-time matriculated undergraduates who enrolled in 2001, 4407 applied for aid, 2591 were judged to have need, 1404 had their need fully met. 266 Federal Work-Study jobs (averaging $1049). 1835 State and other part-time jobs (averaging $1160). In 2001, 1729 non-need-based awards were made. *Average percent of need met:* 82%. *Average financial aid package:* $5574. *Average need-based loan:* $3481. *Average need-based gift aid:* $2588. *Average indebtedness upon graduation:* $14,301.

Applying *Options:* common application, electronic application, early admission, deferred entrance. *Application fee:* $20. *Required:* high school transcript, minimum 2.0 GPA. *Application deadline:* 8/1 (freshmen). *Notification:* 10/1 (freshmen).

Admissions Contact Deborah Below, Director of Admissions, Southeast Missouri State University, MS 3550, Cape Girardeau, MO 63701. *Phone:* 573-651-2590. *Fax:* 573-651-5936. *E-mail:* admissions@semovm.semo.edu.

SOUTHWEST BAPTIST UNIVERSITY
Bolivar, Missouri

- **Independent Southern Baptist** comprehensive, founded 1878
- **Calendar** 4-1-4
- **Degrees** diplomas, associate, bachelor's, and master's
- **Small-town** 152-acre campus
- **Endowment** $10.9 million
- **Coed,** 2,714 undergraduate students, 69% full-time, 66% women, 34% men
- **Moderately difficult** entrance level, 70% of applicants were admitted

SBU is a Christ-centered, caring academic community preparing students to be servant leaders in a global society. SBU is a fully accredited university located in a thriving small-town environment just minutes from a metropolitan area. Academic programs include both liberal arts and professional degrees. Graduate degrees in administration, business, education, and physical therapy are offered. Popular majors include biology, business, education, music, and religious studies.

Undergraduates 1,869 full-time, 845 part-time. Students come from 39 states and territories, 7 other countries, 51% are from out of state, 4% transferred in, 35% live on campus. *Retention:* 70% of 2001 full-time freshmen returned.

Freshmen *Admission:* 1,136 applied, 790 admitted, 420 enrolled. *Average high school GPA:* 3.36. *Test scores:* SAT verbal scores over 500: 77%; SAT math scores over 500: 49%; ACT scores over 18: 89%; SAT verbal scores over 600: 10%; SAT math scores over 600: 4%; ACT scores over 24: 48%; ACT scores over 30: 8%.

Faculty *Total:* 212, 41% full-time, 26% with terminal degrees. *Student/faculty ratio:* 19:1.

Majors Accounting; art; art education; athletic training/sports medicine; biblical studies; biology; business; business administration; business education; chemistry; communications; computer science; criminal justice/law enforcement administration; education (K-12); elementary education; emergency medical technology; English; English education; general studies; graphic design/commercial art/illustration; history; human services; information sciences/systems; mathematics; medical technology; middle school education; music; music teacher education; nursing; occupational safety/health technology; physical education; political science; psychology; recreation/leisure studies; religious studies; secondary education; secretarial science; social sciences; sociology; Spanish; speech/theater education; sport/fitness administration; theater arts/drama.

Academic Programs *Special study options:* academic remediation for entering students, accelerated degree program, advanced placement credit, cooperative education, double majors, English as a second language, honors programs, independent study, internships, part-time degree program, study abroad, summer session for credit. *ROTC:* Army (c). *Unusual degree programs:* 3-2 engineering with University of Missouri-Rolla.

Library Harriett K. Hutchens Library with 108,128 titles, 2,518 serial subscriptions, 9,370 audiovisual materials, an OPAC, a Web page.

Computers on Campus 130 computers available on campus for general student use. A campuswide network can be accessed from off campus. Internet access, at least one staffed computer lab available.

Student Life *Housing:* on-campus residence required through senior year. *Options:* men-only, women-only. *Activities and Organizations:* drama/theater group, student-run newspaper, choral group, small group ministries, Christian Service Organization, Student Government Association, Student Missouri State Teachers Association, revival teams. *Campus security:* 24-hour emergency response devices and patrols. *Student Services:* health clinic, personal/psychological counseling.

Athletics Member NCAA. All Division II. *Intercollegiate sports:* baseball M(s), basketball M(s)/W(s), cross-country running M(s)/W(s), football M(s), golf M(s), soccer M(s)/W(s), softball W(s), tennis M(s)/W(s), volleyball W(s). *Intramural sports:* basketball M/W, bowling M/W, football M, golf M, softball M/W, table tennis M/W, volleyball M/W.

Standardized Tests *Required:* SAT I or ACT (for admission).

Costs (2001–02) *Comprehensive fee:* $13,426 includes full-time tuition ($10,000), mandatory fees ($326), and room and board ($3100). Part-time tuition:

Southwest Baptist University (continued)
$420 per credit hour. Part-time tuition and fees vary according to course load. *Required fees:* $9 per credit hour, $50 per year part-time. *Room and board:* College room only: $1600. Room and board charges vary according to board plan and housing facility. *Payment plan:* installment. *Waivers:* employees or children of employees.

Financial Aid Of all full-time matriculated undergraduates who enrolled in 2001, 1805 applied for aid, 1592 were judged to have need, 359 had their need fully met. 626 Federal Work-Study jobs (averaging $1016). In 2001, 175 non-need-based awards were made. *Average percent of need met:* 71%. *Average financial aid package:* $8513. *Average need-based loan:* $3826. *Average need-based gift aid:* $3233. *Average non-need based aid:* $3922. *Average indebtedness upon graduation:* $11,590.

Applying *Options:* electronic application, early action. *Application fee:* $25. *Required:* high school transcript. *Recommended:* interview. *Application deadline:* rolling (freshmen), rolling (transfers). *Notification:* continuous (freshmen).

Admissions Contact Mr. Rob Harris, Director of Admissions, Southwest Baptist University, 1600 University Avenue, Bolivar, MO 65613-2597. *Phone:* 417-328-1809. *Toll-free phone:* 800-526-5859. *Fax:* 417-328-1514. *E-mail:* rharris@sbuniv.edu.

SOUTHWEST MISSOURI STATE UNIVERSITY
Springfield, Missouri

- **State-supported** comprehensive, founded 1905
- **Calendar** semesters
- **Degrees** bachelor's, master's, and postbachelor's certificates
- **Suburban** 225-acre campus
- **Endowment** $28.9 million
- **Coed,** 15,147 undergraduate students, 80% full-time, 54% women, 46% men
- **Moderately difficult** entrance level, 86% of applicants were admitted

Southwest Missouri State University (SMSU) is Missouri's second-largest university, with more than 18,000 students from 49 states and 80 countries. As Missouri's public affairs university, SMSU offers 140 undergraduate programs, 40 graduate programs, an Honors College, one of the largest cooperative education programs in the Midwest, NCAA Division I athletics, 250 student organizations, and much more. The compact SMSU campus, with a comfortable blend of traditional modern buildings and outstanding residence halls, is in Springfield, Missouri's third-largest city. Springfield and the surrounding Ozarks region offer abundant opportunities for recreation, entertainment, and employment.

Undergraduates 12,090 full-time, 3,057 part-time. Students come from 48 states and territories, 85 other countries, 9% are from out of state, 3% African American, 1% Asian American or Pacific Islander, 1% Hispanic American, 1% Native American, 2% international, 7% transferred in, 27% live on campus. *Retention:* 73% of 2001 full-time freshmen returned.

Freshmen *Admission:* 5,786 applied, 4,985 admitted, 2,570 enrolled. *Average high school GPA:* 3.50. *Test scores:* ACT scores over 18: 98%; ACT scores over 24: 47%; ACT scores over 30: 7%.

Faculty *Total:* 979, 73% full-time, 62% with terminal degrees. *Student/faculty ratio:* 18:1.

Majors Accounting; agribusiness; agricultural education; agricultural sciences; agronomy/crop science; animal sciences; anthropology; art; art education; athletic training/sports medicine; biology; biology education; business; business administration; business education; business marketing and marketing management; cartography; cell biology; chemistry; chemistry education; city/community/regional planning; clothing/apparel/textile studies; communications; computer science; construction technology; criminal justice studies; dance; design/visual communications; dietetics; drafting; early childhood education; economics; electrical/electronic engineering technology; elementary education; engineering physics; English; English education; finance; foreign languages education; French; French language education; geography; geology; German; German language education; gerontology; history; history education; home economics education; horticulture science; hotel and restaurant management; housing studies; humanities; individual/family development; industrial arts education; insurance/risk management; journalism; Latin (ancient and medieval); management information systems/business data processing; mass communications; mathematics; mathematics education; mechanical engineering technology; medical radiologic technology; medical technology; middle school education; molecular biology; music; music (general performance); music teacher education; nursing; philosophy; physical education; physics; physics education; political science; psychology; public administration; recreation/leisure studies; religious studies; respiratory therapy; science education; social work; sociology; Spanish; Spanish language education; special education; speech education; speech-language pathology/audiology; technical/business writing; theater arts/drama; visual/performing arts; wildlife management.

Academic Programs *Special study options:* accelerated degree program, adult/continuing education programs, advanced placement credit, cooperative education, distance learning, double majors, English as a second language, freshman honors college, honors programs, independent study, internships, off-campus study, part-time degree program, services for LD students, student-designed majors, study abroad, summer session for credit. *ROTC:* Army (b).

Library Meyer Library plus 3 others with 771,382 titles, 891,319 serial subscriptions, 32,773 audiovisual materials, an OPAC, a Web page.

Computers on Campus 3500 computers available on campus for general student use. A campuswide network can be accessed from student residence rooms and from off campus. At least one staffed computer lab available.

Student Life *Housing:* on-campus residence required through sophomore year. *Options:* coed, disabled students. *Activities and Organizations:* drama/theater group, student-run newspaper, radio station, choral group, marching band, Residence Hall Association, Campus Crusade, Gamma Sigma Sigma, Student Government Association, national fraternities, national sororities. *Campus security:* 24-hour emergency response devices and patrols, late-night transport/escort service, controlled dormitory access, on-campus police substation. *Student Services:* health clinic, personal/psychological counseling, legal services.

Athletics Member NCAA. All Division I except football (Division I-AA). *Intercollegiate sports:* baseball M(s), basketball M(s)/W(s), bowling M(c)/W(c), cross-country running M(s)/W(s), equestrian sports M(c)/W(c), field hockey W(s), golf M(s)/W(s), racquetball M(c)/W(c), riflery M(c)/W(c), soccer M(s)/W(s), softball W(s), swimming M(s)/W(s), tennis M(s)/W(s), track and field M(s)/W(s), volleyball W(s). *Intramural sports:* badminton M/W, basketball M/W, bowling M/W, football M/W, golf M/W, racquetball M/W, soccer M/W, softball M/W, table tennis M/W, tennis M/W, track and field M/W, volleyball M/W, weight lifting M/W.

Standardized Tests *Required:* SAT I or ACT (for admission). *Recommended:* ACT (for admission).

Costs (2001–02) *Tuition:* state resident $3330 full-time, $111 per credit hour part-time; nonresident $6660 full-time, $222 per credit hour part-time. Full-time tuition and fees vary according to class time and course load. Part-time tuition and fees vary according to class time and course load. *Required fees:* $418 full-time. *Room and board:* $4284; room only: $2814. Room and board charges vary according to board plan and housing facility. *Payment plan:* deferred payment. *Waivers:* senior citizens and employees or children of employees.

Financial Aid Of all full-time matriculated undergraduates who enrolled in 2001, 8945 applied for aid, 5679 were judged to have need, 2172 had their need fully met. In 2001, 1941 non-need-based awards were made. *Average percent of need met:* 87%. *Average financial aid package:* $7147. *Average need-based loan:* $3609. *Average need-based gift aid:* $4554. *Average non-need based aid:* $2963.

Applying *Options:* electronic application, deferred entrance. *Application fee:* $25. *Required:* high school transcript. *Required for some:* essay or personal statement, interview. *Application deadlines:* 8/1 (freshmen), 8/1 (transfers). *Notification:* continuous (freshmen).

Admissions Contact Ms. Jill Duncan, Associate Director of Admissions, Southwest Missouri State University, 901 South National, Springfield, MO 65804-0094. *Phone:* 417-836-5517. *Toll-free phone:* 800-492-7900. *Fax:* 417-836-6334. *E-mail:* smsuinfo@smsu.edu.

STEPHENS COLLEGE
Columbia, Missouri

- **Independent** comprehensive, founded 1833
- **Calendar** semesters
- **Degrees** associate, bachelor's, and master's
- **Urban** 202-acre campus
- **Endowment** $19.7 million
- **Women only,** 618 undergraduate students, 71% full-time
- **Moderately difficult** entrance level, 85% of applicants were admitted

Undergraduates 436 full-time, 182 part-time. Students come from 41 states and territories, 3 other countries, 52% are from out of state, 8% African American, 1% Asian American or Pacific Islander, 2% Hispanic American, 0.7% Native American, 3% international, 4% transferred in, 75% live on campus. *Retention:* 68% of 2001 full-time freshmen returned.

Freshmen *Admission:* 337 applied, 285 admitted, 128 enrolled. *Average high school GPA:* 3.38. *Test scores:* SAT verbal scores over 500: 85%; SAT math scores over 500: 71%; ACT scores over 18: 93%; SAT verbal scores over 600: 36%; SAT math scores over 600: 11%; ACT scores over 24: 41%; SAT verbal scores over 700: 2%; SAT math scores over 700: 2%; ACT scores over 30: 3%.

Faculty *Total:* 74, 69% full-time, 61% with terminal degrees. *Student/faculty ratio:* 10:1.

Majors Accounting; advertising; biology; biomedical science; broadcast journalism; business administration; business marketing and marketing management; child care/development; creative writing; dance; early childhood education; elementary education; English; environmental science; equestrian studies; fashion design/illustration; fashion merchandising; history; interdisciplinary studies; international relations; liberal arts and sciences/liberal studies; mass communications; mathematics; modern languages; natural sciences; occupational therapy; philosophy; political science; pre-law; pre-medicine; pre-veterinary studies; psychology; public relations; radio/television broadcasting; social sciences; theater arts/drama.

Academic Programs *Special study options:* academic remediation for entering students, accelerated degree program, adult/continuing education programs, advanced placement credit, cooperative education, distance learning, double majors, English as a second language, external degree program, freshman honors college, honors programs, independent study, internships, off-campus study, part-time degree program, services for LD students, student-designed majors, study abroad. *ROTC:* Army (c), Air Force (c). *Unusual degree programs:* 3-2 animal science with University of Missouri-Columbia, occupational therapy with Washington University in St. Louis.

Library Hugh Stephens Library with 121,084 titles, 534 serial subscriptions, 4,764 audiovisual materials, an OPAC, a Web page.

Computers on Campus 64 computers available on campus for general student use. A campuswide network can be accessed from student residence rooms and from off campus. Internet access, at least one staffed computer lab available.

Student Life *Housing:* on-campus residence required through senior year. *Options:* women-only. *Activities and Organizations:* drama/theater group, student-run newspaper, radio and television station, choral group, Student Government Association, Martin Luther King Jr. Student Union, Stephens Ambassadors Association, Stephens Christian Fellowship, Young Women's Political Caucus, national sororities. *Campus security:* 24-hour emergency response devices and patrols, student patrols, late-night transport/escort service, controlled dormitory access. *Student Services:* health clinic, personal/psychological counseling, women's center.

Athletics Member NCAA. All Division III. *Intercollegiate sports:* basketball W, soccer W, swimming W, tennis W, volleyball W. *Intramural sports:* basketball W, soccer W, swimming W, tennis W, volleyball W.

Standardized Tests *Required:* SAT I or ACT (for admission).

Costs (2001–02) *Comprehensive fee:* $22,295 includes full-time tuition ($16,245) and room and board ($6050). Part-time tuition: $14 per credit. *Room and board:* College room only: $3025. Room and board charges vary according to board plan. *Payment plan:* installment. *Waivers:* employees or children of employees.

Financial Aid Of all full-time matriculated undergraduates who enrolled in 2001, 414 applied for aid, 310 were judged to have need, 109 had their need fully met. 40 Federal Work-Study jobs (averaging $1500). 214 State and other part-time jobs (averaging $1200). In 2001, 104 non-need-based awards were made. *Average percent of need met:* 83%. *Average financial aid package:* $16,270. *Average need-based loan:* $3519. *Average need-based gift aid:* $5040. *Average non-need based aid:* $8396.

Applying *Options:* common application, electronic application, early admission, early decision, deferred entrance. *Application fee:* $25. *Required:* essay or personal statement, high school transcript, minimum 2.5 GPA, 1 letter of recommendation. *Recommended:* interview. *Application deadlines:* 7/31 (freshmen), 7/31 (transfers). *Early decision:* 12/15. *Notification:* continuous until 8/15 (freshmen), 1/20 (early decision).

Admissions Contact Stephens College, Box 2121, Columbia, MO 65215-0002. *Phone:* 573-876-7207. *Toll-free phone:* 800-876-7207. *Fax:* 573-876-7237. *E-mail:* apply@stephens.edu.

TRUMAN STATE UNIVERSITY
Kirksville, Missouri

- **State-supported** comprehensive, founded 1867
- **Calendar** semesters
- **Degrees** bachelor's and master's
- **Small-town** 140-acre campus
- **Endowment** $15.0 million
- **Coed,** 5,685 undergraduate students, 97% full-time, 58% women, 42% men
- **Moderately difficult** entrance level, 82% of applicants were admitted

Undergraduates 5,516 full-time, 169 part-time. Students come from 43 states and territories, 50 other countries, 24% are from out of state, 3% African American, 2% Asian American or Pacific Islander, 2% Hispanic American, 0.4% Native American, 4% international, 2% transferred in, 46% live on campus.

Freshmen *Admission:* 5,002 applied, 4,107 admitted, 1,459 enrolled. *Average high school GPA:* 3.73. *Test scores:* SAT verbal scores over 500: 92%; SAT math scores over 500: 90%; ACT scores over 18: 100%; SAT verbal scores over 600: 55%; SAT math scores over 600: 50%; ACT scores over 24: 84%; SAT verbal scores over 700: 17%; SAT math scores over 700: 10%; ACT scores over 30: 27%.

Faculty *Total:* 403, 92% full-time, 74% with terminal degrees. *Student/faculty ratio:* 15:1.

Majors Accounting; agricultural economics; agricultural sciences; agronomy/crop science; animal sciences; applied art; art; art history; biology; business administration; chemistry; classics; communication disorders; computer science; criminal justice/law enforcement administration; economics; English; equestrian studies; exercise sciences; finance; fine/studio arts; French; German; graphic design/commercial art/illustration; health science; history; journalism; law enforcement/police science; mass communications; mathematics; music; music (piano and organ performance); music (voice and choral/opera performance); nursing; philosophy; physics; political science; pre-dentistry; pre-law; pre-medicine; pre-veterinary studies; psychology; public health; religious studies; Russian; sociology; Spanish; speech/rhetorical studies; theater arts/drama.

Academic Programs *Special study options:* accelerated degree program, advanced placement credit, double majors, English as a second language, honors programs, internships, off-campus study, part-time degree program, services for LD students, study abroad, summer session for credit. *ROTC:* Army (b).

Library Pickler Memorial Library plus 1 other with 472,652 titles, 3,665 serial subscriptions, 33,694 audiovisual materials, an OPAC, a Web page.

Computers on Campus 769 computers available on campus for general student use. A campuswide network can be accessed from student residence rooms and from off campus. Internet access, at least one staffed computer lab available.

Student Life *Housing:* on-campus residence required for freshman year. *Options:* coed, women-only. *Activities and Organizations:* drama/theater group, student-run newspaper, radio and television station, choral group, marching band, Campus Christian Fellowship, Alpha Phi Omega, Student Ambassadors, Phi Sigma Pi, Alpha Gamma Sigma, national fraternities, national sororities. *Campus security:* 24-hour emergency response devices and patrols, student patrols, late-night transport/escort service, patrols by commissioned officers. *Student Services:* health clinic, personal/psychological counseling, women's center.

Athletics Member NCAA. All Division II. *Intercollegiate sports:* baseball M(s), basketball M(s)/W(s), cross-country running M(s)/W(s), equestrian sports M(c)/W(c), football M(s), golf M(s)/W(s), lacrosse M(c)/W(c), rugby M(c)/W(c), soccer M(s)/W(s), softball W(s), swimming M(s)/W(s), tennis M(s)/W(s), track and field M(s)/W(s), volleyball M(c)/W(s), wrestling M(s). *Intramural sports:* badminton M/W, basketball M/W, bowling M/W, cross-country running M/W, golf M/W, racquetball M/W, rugby M(c)/W(c), soccer M/W, softball M/W, swimming M/W, table tennis M/W, tennis M/W, track and field M/W, volleyball M/W, weight lifting M/W, wrestling M.

Standardized Tests *Required:* SAT I or ACT (for admission). *Recommended:* ACT (for admission).

Costs (2002–03) *Tuition:* state resident $4144 full-time, $172 per credit hour part-time; nonresident $7544 full-time, $314 per credit hour part-time. Part-time tuition and fees vary according to course load. *Required fees:* $56 full-time. *Room and board:* $4928. Room and board charges vary according to board plan and housing facility. *Payment plan:* installment. *Waivers:* senior citizens and employees or children of employees.

Financial Aid Of all full-time matriculated undergraduates who enrolled in 2001, 3292 applied for aid, 2173 were judged to have need, 1041 had their need fully met. 278 Federal Work-Study jobs (averaging $912). In 2001, 1784 non-need-based awards were made. *Average percent of need met:* 83%. *Average financial aid package:* $4782. *Average need-based loan:* $3485. *Average need-based gift aid:* $2766. *Average non-need based aid:* $3940. *Average indebtedness upon graduation:* $14,382.

Applying *Options:* electronic application, early admission, early action, deferred entrance. *Required:* essay or personal statement, high school transcript. *Recommended:* minimum 3.0 GPA, interview. *Application deadlines:* 3/1 (freshmen), 5/1 (transfers). *Notification:* continuous (freshmen), 12/15 (early action).

Admissions Contact Mr. Brad Chambers, Co-Director of Admissions, Truman State University, 205 McClain Hall, Kirksville, MO 63501-4221. *Phone:* 660-785-4114. *Toll-free phone:* 800-892-7792. *Fax:* 660-785-7456. *E-mail:* admissions@truman.edu.

UNIVERSITY OF MISSOURI-COLUMBIA
Columbia, Missouri

- **State-supported** university, founded 1839, part of University of Missouri System

University of Missouri-Columbia (continued)

- **Calendar** semesters
- **Degrees** bachelor's, master's, doctoral, first professional, and post-master's certificates
- **Small-town** 1348-acre campus
- **Endowment** $353.0 million
- **Coed,** 18,431 undergraduate students, 94% full-time, 52% women, 48% men
- **Moderately difficult** entrance level, 64% of applicants were admitted

Undergraduates 17,379 full-time, 1,052 part-time. Students come from 51 states and territories, 99 other countries, 12% are from out of state, 6% African American, 3% Asian American or Pacific Islander, 1% Hispanic American, 0.5% Native American, 1% international, 6% transferred in, 42% live on campus. *Retention:* 85% of 2001 full-time freshmen returned.

Freshmen *Admission:* 9,678 applied, 6,197 admitted, 4,166 enrolled. *Test scores:* ACT scores over 18: 99%; ACT scores over 24: 70%; ACT scores over 30: 18%.

Faculty *Total:* 1,761, 96% full-time, 86% with terminal degrees. *Student/faculty ratio:* 18:1.

Majors Accounting; advertising; agricultural business; agricultural economics; agricultural education; agricultural mechanization; agricultural sciences; animal sciences; anthropology; archaeology; art; art education; atmospheric sciences; biochemistry; bioengineering; biology; broadcast journalism; business administration; business economics; business marketing and marketing management; chemical engineering; chemistry; civil engineering; classics; clothing/apparel/textile studies; communications; computer engineering; computer science; developmental/child psychology; dietetics; early childhood education; economics; education; electrical engineering; elementary education; English; family/consumer studies; finance; fish/game management; food sciences; forestry; French; geography; geology; German; history; hotel and restaurant management; housing studies; individual/family development; industrial/manufacturing engineering; interdisciplinary studies; international business; journalism; liberal arts and sciences/liberal studies; linguistics; mass communications; mathematical statistics; mathematics; mechanical engineering; microbiology/bacteriology; middle school education; music; music teacher education; nuclear medical technology; nursing; nutrition science; occupational therapy; philosophy; physical therapy; physics; plant sciences; political science; psychology; publishing; radiological science; radio/television broadcasting; real estate; recreation/leisure studies; religious studies; respiratory therapy; Russian; Russian/Slavic studies; science education; social work; sociology; South Asian studies; Spanish; theater arts/drama.

Academic Programs *Special study options:* academic remediation for entering students, accelerated degree program, adult/continuing education programs, advanced placement credit, cooperative education, distance learning, double majors, English as a second language, external degree program, freshman honors college, honors programs, independent study, internships, off-campus study, part-time degree program, services for LD students, student-designed majors, study abroad, summer session for credit. *ROTC:* Army (b), Navy (b), Air Force (b). *Unusual degree programs:* 3-2 accountancy.

Library Ellis Library plus 11 others with 4.7 million titles, 20,524 serial subscriptions, an OPAC, a Web page.

Computers on Campus 1150 computers available on campus for general student use. A campuswide network can be accessed from student residence rooms and from off campus that provide access to telephone registration. Internet access, online (class) registration, at least one staffed computer lab available.

Student Life *Housing:* on-campus residence required for freshman year. *Options:* coed, men-only, women-only, disabled students. *Activities and Organizations:* drama/theater group, student-run newspaper, radio and television station, choral group, marching band, Students Association, Residence Hall Association, Honors International Organization, national fraternities, national sororities. *Campus security:* 24-hour emergency response devices and patrols, late-night transport/escort service, controlled dormitory access. *Student Services:* health clinic, personal/psychological counseling, women's center, legal services.

Athletics Member NCAA. All Division I except football (Division I-A). *Intercollegiate sports:* baseball M(s), basketball M(s)/W(s), cross-country running M(s)/W(s), golf M(s)/W(s), gymnastics W(s), soccer W(s), softball W(s), swimming M(s)/W(s), tennis W(s), track and field M(s)/W(s), volleyball W(s), wrestling M(s). *Intramural sports:* basketball M/W, bowling M(c)/W(c), cross-country running M/W, fencing M(c)/W(c), football M/W, golf M/W, gymnastics W, lacrosse M(c)/W(c), racquetball M(c)/W, rugby M(c)/W(c), soccer W(c), softball M/W, swimming M/W, table tennis M(c)/W(c), tennis M/W, track and field M/W, volleyball M(c)/W(c).

Standardized Tests *Required:* ACT (for admission).

Costs (2001–02) *Tuition:* state resident $3396 full-time, $142 per credit hour part-time; nonresident $9818 full-time, $423 per credit hour part-time. Full-time tuition and fees vary according to course load. Part-time tuition and fees vary according to course load. *Required fees:* $589 full-time, $19 per credit hour. *Room and board:* $5043. Room and board charges vary according to board plan and housing facility. *Waivers:* senior citizens and employees or children of employees.

Financial Aid Of all full-time matriculated undergraduates who enrolled in 2001, 9646 applied for aid, 6803 were judged to have need, 3837 had their need fully met. 1278 Federal Work-Study jobs (averaging $1608). In 2001, 5975 non-need-based awards were made. *Average percent of need met:* 86%. *Average financial aid package:* $6216. *Average need-based loan:* $4298. *Average need-based gift aid:* $4691. *Average non-need based aid:* $2831. *Average indebtedness upon graduation:* $15,096.

Applying *Options:* electronic application, deferred entrance. *Application fee:* $25. *Required:* high school transcript, specific high school curriculum. *Application deadline:* rolling (freshmen), rolling (transfers). *Notification:* continuous (freshmen).

Admissions Contact Ms. Georgeanne Porter, Director of Admissions, University of Missouri-Columbia, 225 Jesse Hall, Columbia, MO 65211. *Phone:* 573-882-7786. *Toll-free phone:* 800-225-6075. *Fax:* 573-882-7887. *E-mail:* mu4u@missouri.edu.

UNIVERSITY OF MISSOURI-KANSAS CITY
Kansas City, Missouri

- **State-supported** university, founded 1929, part of University of Missouri System
- **Calendar** semesters
- **Degrees** bachelor's, master's, doctoral, first professional, and first professional certificates
- **Urban** 191-acre campus
- **Coed,** 8,299 undergraduate students, 53% full-time, 58% women, 42% men
- **Moderately difficult** entrance level, 73% of applicants were admitted

Undergraduates 4,368 full-time, 3,931 part-time. Students come from 47 states and territories, 118 other countries, 12% are from out of state, 13% African American, 6% Asian American or Pacific Islander, 4% Hispanic American, 0.9% Native American, 5% international, 13% transferred in, 5% live on campus. *Retention:* 72% of 2001 full-time freshmen returned.

Freshmen *Admission:* 2,523 applied, 1,853 admitted, 773 enrolled. *Test scores:* ACT scores over 18: 95%; ACT scores over 24: 58%; ACT scores over 30: 16%.

Faculty *Total:* 769, 68% full-time, 76% with terminal degrees. *Student/faculty ratio:* 8:1.

Majors Accounting; American studies; art; art history; biology; business administration; chemistry; civil engineering; computer science; criminal justice/law enforcement administration; dance; dental hygiene; early childhood education; earth sciences; economics; education; electrical engineering; elementary education; English; fine/studio arts; French; geography; geology; German; health/physical education; history; information sciences/systems; interdisciplinary studies; Judaic studies; liberal arts and sciences/liberal studies; mass communications; mathematical statistics; mathematics; mechanical engineering; medical laboratory technician; music; music (piano and organ performance); music teacher education; music therapy; music (voice and choral/opera performance); nursing; pharmacy; philosophy; physical education; physics; political science; psychology; secondary education; sociology; Spanish; stringed instruments; theater arts/drama; urban studies; wind/percussion instruments.

Academic Programs *Special study options:* accelerated degree program, adult/continuing education programs, advanced placement credit, cooperative education, English as a second language, honors programs, internships, off-campus study, part-time degree program, services for LD students, student-designed majors, study abroad, summer session for credit. *ROTC:* Army (b). *Unusual degree programs:* 3-2 education.

Library Miller-Nichols Library plus 3 others with 1.6 million titles, 12,472 serial subscriptions, 363,933 audiovisual materials, an OPAC, a Web page.

Computers on Campus 400 computers available on campus for general student use. A campuswide network can be accessed from student residence rooms and from off campus. Internet access, online (class) registration, at least one staffed computer lab available.

Student Life *Housing Options:* coed. *Activities and Organizations:* drama/theater group, student-run newspaper, choral group, African-American Student Association, International Student Council, Alpha Phi Omega, Activities and Programs Council, national fraternities, national sororities. *Campus security:* 24-hour emergency response devices and patrols, late-night transport/escort service, controlled dormitory access. *Student Services:* health clinic, personal/psychological counseling, women's center, legal services.

Athletics Member NCAA. All Division I. *Intercollegiate sports:* basketball M(s)/W(s), cross-country running M(s)/W(s), golf M(s)/W(s), riflery M(s)/W(s), soccer M(s), softball W(s), tennis M(s)/W(s), track and field M(s)/W(s), volleyball W(s). *Intramural sports:* badminton M/W, basketball M/W, fencing M/W, football M/W, golf M/W, racquetball M/W, soccer M/W, softball M/W, squash M/W, swimming M/W, tennis M/W, track and field M/W, volleyball M/W, weight lifting M/W.

Standardized Tests *Required:* ACT (for admission).

Costs (2001–02) *Tuition:* state resident $5000 full-time, $142 per credit hour part-time; nonresident $13,445 full-time, $423 per credit hour part-time. Full-time tuition and fees vary according to course load, program, and student level. Part-time tuition and fees vary according to course load, program, and student level. *Required fees:* $50 full-time, $23 per credit, $30 per term part-time. *Room and board:* $4950. Room and board charges vary according to board plan and housing facility. *Payment plan:* installment. *Waivers:* employees or children of employees.

Financial Aid Of all full-time matriculated undergraduates who enrolled in 2001, 3593 applied for aid, 2377 were judged to have need, 1541 had their need fully met. 673 Federal Work-Study jobs (averaging $4206). In 2001, 773 non-need-based awards were made. *Average percent of need met:* 66%. *Average financial aid package:* $10,674. *Average need-based loan:* $5667. *Average need-based gift aid:* $4797. *Average non-need based aid:* $4386. *Average indebtedness upon graduation:* $15,498.

Applying *Application fee:* $25. *Required:* high school transcript. *Application deadline:* rolling (freshmen), rolling (transfers). *Notification:* continuous (freshmen).

Admissions Contact Mr. Melvin C. Tyler, Director of Admissions, University of Missouri-Kansas City, 5100 Rockhill Road, Kansas City, MO 64110-2499. *Phone:* 816-235-1111. *Fax:* 816-235-5544. *E-mail:* admit@umkc.edu.

UNIVERSITY OF MISSOURI-ROLLA

Rolla, Missouri

- **State-supported** university, founded 1870, part of University of Missouri System
- **Calendar** semesters
- **Degrees** bachelor's, master's, and doctoral
- **Small-town** 284-acre campus
- **Endowment** $63.8 million
- **Coed,** 3,756 undergraduate students, 89% full-time, 23% women, 77% men
- **Very difficult** entrance level, 96% of applicants were admitted

Undergraduates 3,346 full-time, 410 part-time. Students come from 47 states and territories, 38 other countries, 22% are from out of state, 5% African American, 3% Asian American or Pacific Islander, 1% Hispanic American, 0.7% Native American, 3% international, 6% transferred in, 56% live on campus. *Retention:* 83% of 2001 full-time freshmen returned.

Freshmen *Admission:* 1,789 applied, 1,716 admitted, 702 enrolled. *Average high school GPA:* 3.46. *Test scores:* ACT scores over 18: 100%; ACT scores over 24: 80%; ACT scores over 30: 30%.

Faculty *Total:* 385, 77% full-time, 86% with terminal degrees. *Student/faculty ratio:* 14:1.

Majors Aerospace engineering; applied mathematics; architectural engineering; biology; business; business administration; ceramic sciences/engineering; chemical engineering; chemistry; civil engineering; computer engineering; computer/information sciences related; computer science; economics; electrical engineering; engineering/industrial management; English; geological engineering; geology; geophysics/seismology; history; information sciences/systems; mechanical engineering; metallurgical engineering; mining/mineral engineering; nuclear engineering; petroleum engineering; philosophy; physics; pre-dentistry; pre-law; pre-medicine; psychology; secondary education.

Academic Programs *Special study options:* academic remediation for entering students, accelerated degree program, adult/continuing education programs, advanced placement credit, cooperative education, distance learning, double majors, English as a second language, freshman honors college, honors programs, independent study, internships, off-campus study, part-time degree program, services for LD students, study abroad, summer session for credit. *ROTC:* Army (b), Air Force (b).

Library Curtis Laws Wilson Library with 255,768 titles, 1,495 serial subscriptions, 6,353 audiovisual materials, an OPAC, a Web page.

Computers on Campus 800 computers available on campus for general student use. A campuswide network can be accessed from student residence rooms and from off campus. Internet access, online (class) registration, at least one staffed computer lab available.

Student Life *Housing:* on-campus residence required through sophomore year. *Options:* coed, men-only, women-only. *Activities and Organizations:* drama/theater group, student-run newspaper, radio station, choral group, marching band, student government, service organizations, academic organizations, national fraternities, national sororities. *Campus security:* 24-hour emergency response devices and patrols, student patrols, late-night transport/escort service, controlled dormitory access, crime prevention programs. *Student Services:* health clinic, personal/psychological counseling, legal services.

Athletics Member NCAA. All Division II. *Intercollegiate sports:* baseball M(s), basketball M(s)/W(s), cross-country running M(s)/W(s), football M(s), golf M(s), soccer M(s)/W(s), softball W(s), swimming M(s), tennis M(s), track and field M(s)/W(s). *Intramural sports:* badminton M/W, basketball M/W, bowling M/W, cross-country running M/W, football M, golf M/W, racquetball M/W, soccer M/W, softball M/W, swimming M/W, table tennis M/W, tennis M/W, track and field M/W, volleyball M/W, water polo M, weight lifting M/W.

Standardized Tests *Required:* SAT I or ACT (for admission).

Costs (2001–02) *Tuition:* state resident $4245 full-time, $142 per credit hour part-time; nonresident $12,690 full-time, $423 per credit hour part-time. Full-time tuition and fees vary according to course load, program, and reciprocity agreements. Part-time tuition and fees vary according to course load, program, and reciprocity agreements. *Required fees:* $729 full-time, $25 per credit hour, $68 per term part-time. *Room and board:* $5060; room only: $3060. Room and board charges vary according to board plan and housing facility. *Payment plan:* installment. *Waivers:* minority students, children of alumni, and employees or children of employees.

Financial Aid Of all full-time matriculated undergraduates who enrolled in 2001, 2134 applied for aid, 1653 were judged to have need, 635 had their need fully met. 257 Federal Work-Study jobs (averaging $1079). 1148 State and other part-time jobs (averaging $1051). In 2001, 1101 non-need-based awards were made. *Average percent of need met:* 86%. *Average financial aid package:* $8330. *Average need-based loan:* $4451. *Average need-based gift aid:* $4922. *Average non-need based aid:* $5220. *Average indebtedness upon graduation:* $15,000.

Applying *Options:* common application, electronic application, early admission, deferred entrance. *Application fee:* $25. *Required:* high school transcript. *Application deadlines:* 7/1 (freshmen), 7/1 (transfers). *Notification:* continuous (freshmen).

Admissions Contact Mr. Jay W. Goff, Acting Director of Admission and Dean of Enrollment Management, University of Missouri-Rolla, 106 Parker Hall, Rolla, MO 65409. *Phone:* 573-341-4164. *Toll-free phone:* 800-522-0938. *Fax:* 573-341-4082. *E-mail:* umrolla@umr.edu.

UNIVERSITY OF MISSOURI-ST. LOUIS

St. Louis, Missouri

- **State-supported** university, founded 1963, part of University of Missouri System
- **Calendar** semesters
- **Degrees** bachelor's, master's, doctoral, first professional, and postbachelor's certificates
- **Suburban** 250-acre campus
- **Endowment** $32.6 million
- **Coed,** 12,251 undergraduate students, 45% full-time, 60% women, 40% men
- **Moderately difficult** entrance level, 52% of applicants were admitted

Undergraduates 5,486 full-time, 6,765 part-time. Students come from 47 states and territories, 77 other countries, 4% are from out of state, 14% African American, 3% Asian American or Pacific Islander, 1% Hispanic American, 0.3% Native American, 3% international, 15% transferred in, 8% live on campus. *Retention:* 61% of 2001 full-time freshmen returned.

Freshmen *Admission:* 2,165 applied, 1,136 admitted, 634 enrolled. *Test scores:* SAT verbal scores over 500: 67%; SAT math scores over 500: 69%; ACT scores over 18: 96%; SAT verbal scores over 600: 31%; SAT math scores over 600: 29%; ACT scores over 24: 43%; SAT verbal scores over 700: 5%; SAT math scores over 700: 5%; ACT scores over 30: 6%.

Faculty *Total:* 657, 47% full-time, 60% with terminal degrees. *Student/faculty ratio:* 22:1.

Majors Accounting; anthropology; applied mathematics; art; art history; astrophysics; behavioral sciences; biochemistry; biological technology; biology; business administration; business education; business marketing and marketing management; chemistry; child care/development; civil engineering; clinical psychology; communications; computer science; criminal justice/law enforcement administration; criminology; cytotechnology; early childhood education; ecology; economics; education; education related; electrical engineering; elementary education; English; finance; fine/studio arts; French; general studies; German; gerontology; graphic design/commercial art/illustration; health science; history; humanities; interdisciplinary studies; international relations; liberal arts and sciences/liberal studies; linguistics; literature; management information systems/business data processing; mass communications; mathematics; mechanical engi-

University of Missouri-St. Louis (continued)
neering; medical technology; middle school education; modern languages; music; music history; music teacher education; nursing; philosophy; photography; physical education; physical sciences; physics; political science; pre-dentistry; pre-law; pre-medicine; pre-veterinary studies; printmaking; psychology; public administration; public policy analysis; reading education; science education; secondary education; social sciences; social work; sociology; Spanish; special education; urban studies.

Academic Programs *Special study options:* accelerated degree program, adult/continuing education programs, advanced placement credit, cooperative education, distance learning, double majors, English as a second language, freshman honors college, honors programs, independent study, internships, off-campus study, part-time degree program, services for LD students, student-designed majors, study abroad, summer session for credit. *ROTC:* Army (c), Air Force (c).

Library Thomas Jefferson Library plus 2 others with 1.1 million titles, 3,807 serial subscriptions, 3,871 audiovisual materials, an OPAC, a Web page.

Computers on Campus 750 computers available on campus for general student use. A campuswide network can be accessed from student residence rooms and from off campus. Internet access, at least one staffed computer lab available.

Student Life *Housing Options:* coed. *Activities and Organizations:* student-run newspaper, choral group, Student Government Association, Associated Black Collegians, Pierre laclede Honors College Student Association, Residence Hall Council, International Student Association, national fraternities, national sororities. *Campus security:* 24-hour emergency response devices and patrols, late-night transport/escort service, controlled dormitory access. *Student Services:* health clinic, personal/psychological counseling, women's center.

Athletics Member NCAA. All Division II. *Intercollegiate sports:* baseball M(s), basketball M(s)/W(s), golf M(s)/W(s), ice hockey M(c), soccer M(s)/W(s), softball W(s), tennis M(s)/W(s), volleyball W(s). *Intramural sports:* badminton M/W, basketball M/W, bowling M/W, cross-country running M/W, football M/W, golf M/W, ice hockey M, racquetball M/W, soccer M/W, softball M/W, swimming M/W, table tennis M/W, tennis M/W, volleyball M/W, weight lifting M/W.

Standardized Tests *Required:* SAT I or ACT (for admission).

Costs (2002–03) *Tuition:* state resident $3682 full-time, $153 per credit hour part-time; nonresident $11,004 full-time, $458 per credit hour part-time. Full-time tuition and fees vary according to reciprocity agreements. Part-time tuition and fees vary according to course load. *Required fees:* $884 full-time, $37 per credit hour. *Room and board:* $5400; room only: $4100. Room and board charges vary according to board plan and housing facility. *Payment plan:* installment. *Waivers:* employees or children of employees.

Financial Aid Of all full-time matriculated undergraduates who enrolled in 2001, 4367 had their need fully met. In 2001, 1602 non-need-based awards were made. *Average percent of need met:* 98%. *Average financial aid package:* $6214. *Average need-based loan:* $3460. *Average need-based gift aid:* $4615. *Average non-need based aid:* $3129.

Applying *Options:* electronic application, early admission. *Application fee:* $25. *Required:* high school transcript. *Application deadline:* rolling (freshmen), rolling (transfers).

Admissions Contact Mr. Curtis C. Coonrod, Director of Admissions, University of Missouri-St. Louis, 351 Millennuim Student Center, St. Louis, MO 63121-4499. *Phone:* 314-516-5460. *Toll-free phone:* 888-GO2-UMSL. *Fax:* 314-516-5310. *E-mail:* curt_coonrod@umsl.edu.

UNIVERSITY OF PHOENIX-SAINT LOUIS CAMPUS
St. Louis, Missouri

- **Proprietary** comprehensive
- **Calendar** continuous
- **Degrees** certificates, associate, bachelor's, master's, doctoral, post-master's, and postbachelor's certificates (courses conducted at 54 campuses and learning centers in 13 states)
- **Coed,** 226 undergraduate students, 100% full-time, 63% women, 37% men
- **Noncompetitive** entrance level

Undergraduates Students come from 3 states and territories, 11% are from out of state.

Freshmen *Admission:* 4 admitted.

Faculty *Total:* 87, 3% full-time, 11% with terminal degrees. *Student/faculty ratio:* 11:1.

Majors Business administration; management information systems/business data processing.

Academic Programs *Special study options:* accelerated degree program, adult/continuing education programs, advanced placement credit, distance learning, external degree program, independent study.

Library University Library with 17.5 million titles, 9,000 serial subscriptions, an OPAC, a Web page.

Computers on Campus A campuswide network can be accessed from off campus. Internet access, at least one staffed computer lab available.

Student Life *Housing:* college housing not available.

Costs (2001–02) *Tuition:* $9600 full-time. Full-time tuition and fees vary according to location and program. *Payment plan:* deferred payment. *Waivers:* employees or children of employees.

Applying *Options:* deferred entrance. *Application fee:* $85. *Required:* 2 years of work experience. *Required for some:* high school transcript. *Application deadline:* rolling (freshmen), rolling (transfers). *Notification:* continuous (freshmen).

Admissions Contact Ms. Beth Barilla, Director of Admissions, University of Phoenix-Saint Louis Campus, 4615 East Elwood Street, Phoenix, AZ 85040-1958. *Phone:* 480-927-0099 Ext. 1218. *Toll-free phone:* 888-326-7737 (in-state); 800-228-7240 (out-of-state). *Fax:* 480-594-1758. *E-mail:* beth.barilla@apollogrp.edu.

WASHINGTON UNIVERSITY IN ST. LOUIS
St. Louis, Missouri

- **Independent** university, founded 1853
- **Calendar** semesters
- **Degrees** certificates, bachelor's, master's, doctoral, first professional, and postbachelor's certificates
- **Suburban** 169-acre campus
- **Endowment** $4.0 billion
- **Coed,** 6,772 undergraduate students, 87% full-time, 51% women, 49% men
- **Most difficult** entrance level, 23% of applicants were admitted

Undergraduates 5,909 full-time, 863 part-time. Students come from 52 states and territories, 104 other countries, 89% are from out of state, 8% African American, 10% Asian American or Pacific Islander, 3% Hispanic American, 0.1% Native American, 5% international, 3% transferred in, 80% live on campus. *Retention:* 96% of 2001 full-time freshmen returned.

Freshmen *Admission:* 20,834 applied, 4,888 admitted, 1,272 enrolled. *Test scores:* SAT verbal scores over 500: 99%; SAT math scores over 500: 100%; ACT scores over 18: 100%; SAT verbal scores over 600: 92%; SAT math scores over 600: 97%; ACT scores over 24: 98%; SAT verbal scores over 700: 44%; SAT math scores over 700: 59%; ACT scores over 30: 63%.

Faculty *Total:* 1,056, 75% full-time. *Student/faculty ratio:* 7:1.

Majors Accounting; advertising; African-American studies; African studies; American literature; American studies; anthropology; applied art; applied mathematics; Arabic; archaeology; architectural engineering technology; architecture; architecture related; area, ethnic, and cultural studies related; art; art education; art history; Asian studies; biochemistry; bioengineering; biological/physical sciences; biological sciences/life sciences related; biology; biology education; biophysics; biopsychology; British literature; business; business administration; business economics; business marketing and marketing management; ceramic arts; chemical engineering; chemistry; chemistry education; Chinese; civil engineering; civil engineering technology; classics; cognitive psychology/psycholinguistics; communications; comparative literature; computer engineering; computer/information sciences; computer/information sciences related; computer science; creative writing; cultural studies; dance; design/visual communications; drama/dance education; drama/theater literature; drawing; earth sciences; East and Southeast Asian languages related; East Asian studies; economics; education; education (K-12); electrical engineering; elementary education; engineering; engineering physics; engineering science; English; English related; environmental science; ethnic/cultural studies related; European studies; fashion design/illustration; film studies; finance; fine/studio arts; French; French language education; German; German language education; graphic design/commercial art/illustration; Greek (ancient and medieval); health professions and related sciences; Hebrew; history; history education; human resources management; information sciences/systems; interdisciplinary studies; international business; international economics; international finance; international relations; Islamic studies; Italian; Japanese; Judaic studies; Latin American studies; Latin (ancient and medieval); liberal arts and sciences/liberal studies; literature; marketing management and research related; marketing operations/marketing and distribution related; mathematical statistics; mathematics; mathematics/computer science; mathematics education; mechanical engineering; medieval/renaissance studies; Middle Eastern studies; middle school education; modern languages; multi/interdisciplinary studies related; music; music history; music theory and composition; music (voice and choral/opera performance); natural resources conservation; natural sciences; neuroscience; operations management; painting; philosophy; philosophy and religion related; photography; physical sciences; physics; physics education; political science; pre-dentistry; pre-medicine; pre-pharmacy studies; pre-veterinary studies; printmaking; psychology; religious studies; romance languages; Russian; Russian/Slavic studies; science education; science/technology and society; sculpture; secondary education; social/philosophical foundations of education; social science education; social sciences; social studies education; Spanish; Spanish language education; systems engineering; systems science/theory; theater arts/drama; urban studies; women's studies.

Academic Programs *Special study options:* accelerated degree program, adult/continuing education programs, advanced placement credit, cooperative education, double majors, English as a second language, independent study, internships, off-campus study, part-time degree program, services for LD students, student-designed majors, study abroad, summer session for credit. *ROTC:* Army (b), Air Force (c). *Unusual degree programs:* 3-2 art, occupational therapy, physical therapy, business, engineering, social work.

Library John M. Olin Library plus 13 others with 1.5 million titles, 21,017 serial subscriptions, 42,799 audiovisual materials, an OPAC, a Web page.

Computers on Campus 2500 computers available on campus for general student use. A campuswide network can be accessed from student residence rooms and from off campus that provide access to e-mail. Internet access, online (class) registration, at least one staffed computer lab available.

Student Life *Housing:* on-campus residence required for freshman year. *Options:* coed, men-only, women-only. *Activities and Organizations:* drama/theater group, student-run newspaper, radio and television station, choral group, community service organizations, student government/programming groups, performing arts groups, multicultural interest groups, national fraternities, national sororities. *Campus security:* 24-hour emergency response devices and patrols, student patrols, late-night transport/escort service, controlled dormitory access. *Student Services:* health clinic, personal/psychological counseling, women's center.

Athletics Member NCAA. All Division III. *Intercollegiate sports:* baseball M, basketball M/W, crew M(c)/W(c), cross-country running M/W, field hockey W(c), football M, golf M(c)/W(c), gymnastics W(c), ice hockey M(c), lacrosse M(c)/W(c), racquetball M(c)/W(c), rugby M(c), soccer M/W, softball W, swimming M/W, tennis M/W, track and field M/W, volleyball M(c)/W. *Intramural sports:* badminton M/W, basketball M/W, bowling M/W, cross-country running M/W, fencing M/W, football M/W, golf M/W, racquetball M/W, soccer M/W, softball M/W, squash M/W, swimming M/W, table tennis M/W, tennis M/W, track and field M/W, volleyball M/W, water polo M/W.

Standardized Tests *Required:* SAT I or ACT (for admission).

Costs (2002–03) *Comprehensive fee:* $36,297 includes full-time tuition ($26,900), mandatory fees ($719), and room and board ($8678). Part-time tuition and fees vary according to class time. *Room and board:* College room only: $5044. Room and board charges vary according to board plan and housing facility. *Payment plans:* tuition prepayment, installment. *Waivers:* employees or children of employees.

Financial Aid Of all full-time matriculated undergraduates who enrolled in 2001, 4209 applied for aid, 2710 were judged to have need, 2673 had their need fully met. 1287 Federal Work-Study jobs (averaging $1873). *Average percent of need met:* 100%. *Average financial aid package:* $22,173. *Average need-based loan:* $5799. *Average need-based gift aid:* $17,517. *Financial aid deadline:* 2/15.

Applying *Options:* common application, electronic application, early admission, early decision, deferred entrance. *Application fee:* $55. *Required:* essay or personal statement, high school transcript, 2 letters of recommendation. *Recommended:* minimum 3.0 GPA, portfolio for art and architecture programs. *Application deadlines:* 1/15 (freshmen), 4/15 (transfers). *Early decision:* 11/15 (for plan 1), 1/1 (for plan 2). *Notification:* 4/1 (freshmen), 12/15 (early decision plan 1), 1/15 (early decision plan 2).

Admissions Contact Ms. Nanette Tarbouni, Director of Admissions, Washington University in St. Louis, Campus Box 1089, One Brookings Drive, St. Louis, MO 63130-4899. *Phone:* 314-935-6000. *Toll-free phone:* 800-638-0700. *Fax:* 314-935-4290. *E-mail:* admissions@wustl.edu.

WEBSTER UNIVERSITY
St. Louis, Missouri

- **Independent** comprehensive, founded 1915
- **Calendar** semesters
- **Degrees** certificates, bachelor's, master's, and doctoral
- **Suburban** 47-acre campus
- **Endowment** $38.2 million
- **Coed,** 3,760 undergraduate students, 64% full-time, 63% women, 37% men
- **Moderately difficult** entrance level, 56% of applicants were admitted

Undergraduates 2,391 full-time, 1,369 part-time. Students come from 43 states and territories, 93 other countries, 28% are from out of state, 10% African American, 2% Asian American or Pacific Islander, 2% Hispanic American, 0.4% Native American, 3% international, 12% transferred in, 25% live on campus. *Retention:* 79% of 2001 full-time freshmen returned.

Freshmen *Admission:* 1,104 applied, 613 admitted, 457 enrolled. *Average high school GPA:* 3.40. *Test scores:* SAT verbal scores over 500: 90%; SAT math scores over 500: 75%; ACT scores over 18: 93%; SAT verbal scores over 600: 43%; SAT math scores over 600: 26%; ACT scores over 24: 53%; SAT verbal scores over 700: 10%; SAT math scores over 700: 2%; ACT scores over 30: 10%.

Faculty *Total:* 1,862, 8% full-time, 37% with terminal degrees. *Student/faculty ratio:* 13:1.

Majors Accounting; advertising; anthropology; art; art history; art therapy; audio engineering; biology; broadcast journalism; business; business administration; business marketing and marketing management; ceramic arts; computer management; computer science; creative writing; dance; drawing; early childhood education; economics; education; elementary education; English; environmental science; film studies; film/video production; fine/studio arts; French; German; graphic design/commercial art/illustration; health services administration; history; human resources management; information sciences/systems; interdisciplinary studies; international business; international relations; jazz; journalism; legal studies; liberal arts and sciences/liberal studies; literature; management information systems/business data processing; mathematics; middle school education; music; music (general performance); music (piano and organ performance); music teacher education; music theory and composition; music (voice and choral/opera performance); nursing; nursing (anesthetist); painting; philosophy; photography; political science; printmaking; psychology; public relations; radio/television broadcasting; real estate; religious studies; sculpture; secondary education; social sciences; sociology; Spanish; special education; theater arts/drama; theater design.

Academic Programs *Special study options:* academic remediation for entering students, accelerated degree program, adult/continuing education programs, advanced placement credit, cooperative education, distance learning, double majors, English as a second language, independent study, internships, off-campus study, part-time degree program, services for LD students, student-designed majors, study abroad, summer session for credit. *ROTC:* Army (c), Air Force (c). *Unusual degree programs:* 3-2 engineering with University of Missouri-Columbia, Washington University in St. Louis; architecture with Washington University in St. Louis.

Library Eden-Webster Library with 250,000 titles, 1,400 serial subscriptions, 8,700 audiovisual materials, an OPAC, a Web page.

Computers on Campus 185 computers available on campus for general student use. Internet access, online (class) registration, at least one staffed computer lab available.

Student Life *Housing:* on-campus residence required for freshman year. *Options:* coed. *Activities and Organizations:* drama/theater group, student-run newspaper, radio station, choral group, Student Government Association, Student Activities Council, Thai Students Association, International Student Association, Women in Media. *Campus security:* 24-hour emergency response devices and patrols, student patrols, late-night transport/escort service. *Student Services:* health clinic, personal/psychological counseling, women's center.

Athletics Member NCAA. All Division III. *Intercollegiate sports:* baseball M, basketball M/W, cross-country running W, golf M, soccer M/W, softball W, swimming W, tennis M/W, volleyball W. *Intramural sports:* bowling M(c)/W(c), soccer M(c)/W(c), swimming M(c), table tennis M(c)/W(c), volleyball M(c)/W(c).

Standardized Tests *Required:* SAT I or ACT (for admission).

Costs (2001–02) *Comprehensive fee:* $19,809 includes full-time tuition ($13,720), mandatory fees ($200), and room and board ($5889). Full-time tuition and fees vary according to program. Part-time tuition: $390 per credit hour. Part-time tuition and fees vary according to location. *Room and board:* Room and board charges vary according to board plan and housing facility. *Payment plan:* installment. *Waivers:* employees or children of employees.

Financial Aid Of all full-time matriculated undergraduates who enrolled in 2001, 2009 applied for aid, 1521 were judged to have need. 439 Federal Work-Study jobs (averaging $2252). 400 State and other part-time jobs. In 2001, 397 non-need-based awards were made. *Average financial aid package:* $14,389. *Average need-based loan:* $4415. *Average need-based gift aid:* $4135. *Average non-need based aid:* $6272.

Applying *Options:* common application, electronic application, early admission, deferred entrance. *Application fee:* $25. *Required:* essay or personal statement, high school transcript, minimum 2.5 GPA, 1 letter of recommendation. *Required for some:* audition. *Recommended:* minimum 3.0 GPA, interview. *Application deadlines:* 7/1 (freshmen), 8/1 (transfers). *Notification:* continuous (freshmen).

Webster University (continued)

Admissions Contact Mr. Andrew Laue, Associate Director of Undergraduate Admission, Webster University, 470 East Lockwood Avenue, St. Louis, MO 63119-3194. *Phone:* 314-961-2660 Ext. 7712. *Toll-free phone:* 800-75-ENROL. *Fax:* 314-968-7115. *E-mail:* admit@webster.edu.

WESTMINSTER COLLEGE

Fulton, Missouri

- **Independent** 4-year, founded 1851, affiliated with Presbyterian Church
- **Calendar** semesters
- **Degree** bachelor's
- **Small-town** 65-acre campus
- **Endowment** $33.3 million
- **Coed,** 768 undergraduate students, 97% full-time, 42% women, 58% men
- **Moderately difficult** entrance level, 88% of applicants were admitted

Undergraduates 747 full-time, 21 part-time. Students come from 24 states and territories, 20 other countries, 26% are from out of state, 2% African American, 0.8% Asian American or Pacific Islander, 1% Hispanic American, 1% Native American, 7% international, 3% transferred in, 80% live on campus. *Retention:* 80% of 2001 full-time freshmen returned.

Freshmen *Admission:* 666 applied, 584 admitted, 248 enrolled. *Average high school GPA:* 3.23. *Test scores:* ACT scores over 18: 98%; ACT scores over 24: 52%; ACT scores over 30: 8%.

Faculty *Total:* 73, 68% full-time, 66% with terminal degrees. *Student/faculty ratio:* 11:1.

Majors Accounting; anthropology; athletic training/sports medicine; biology; business administration; business marketing and marketing management; chemistry; classics; computer science; creative writing; early childhood education; economics; education; elementary education; English; environmental science; finance; French; history; international business; international relations; literature; management information systems/business data processing; mathematics; middle school education; philosophy; physical education; physics; political science; pre-dentistry; pre-law; pre-medicine; pre-veterinary studies; psychology; public administration; religious studies; secondary education; sociology; Spanish.

Academic Programs *Special study options:* academic remediation for entering students, advanced placement credit, double majors, English as a second language, independent study, internships, off-campus study, part-time degree program, services for LD students, student-designed majors, study abroad, summer session for credit. *ROTC:* Army (c), Air Force (c). *Unusual degree programs:* 3-2 engineering with Washington University in St. Louis, University of Missouri-Columbia.

Library Reeves Memorial Library plus 1 other with 97,268 titles, 2,943 serial subscriptions, 7,059 audiovisual materials, an OPAC, a Web page.

Computers on Campus 112 computers available on campus for general student use. A campuswide network can be accessed from student residence rooms and from off campus that provide access to on-line registration. Internet access, at least one staffed computer lab available.

Student Life *Housing:* on-campus residence required through junior year. *Options:* coed, women-only. *Activities and Organizations:* drama/theater group, student-run newspaper, choral group, Student Government Association, Environmentally Concerned Students, International Student Club, Habitat for Humanity, Little Brother/Little Sister, national fraternities, national sororities. *Campus security:* 24-hour emergency response devices and patrols, late-night transport/escort service, controlled dormitory access, well-lit campus. *Student Services:* health clinic, personal/psychological counseling, women's center.

Athletics Member NCAA. All Division III. *Intercollegiate sports:* baseball M, basketball M/W, football M, golf M/W, soccer M/W, softball W, tennis M/W, volleyball W. *Intramural sports:* badminton M/W, basketball M/W, bowling M/W, football M/W, racquetball M/W, softball M/W, table tennis M/W, tennis M/W, volleyball M/W, water polo M/W.

Standardized Tests *Required:* SAT I or ACT (for admission).

Costs (2001–02) *Comprehensive fee:* $19,990 includes full-time tuition ($14,630), mandatory fees ($240), and room and board ($5120). Part-time tuition: $610 per credit hour. Part-time tuition and fees vary according to course load. *Required fees:* $120 per term part-time. *Room and board:* College room only: $2580. Room and board charges vary according to board plan. *Payment plan:* installment. *Waivers:* employees or children of employees.

Financial Aid Of all full-time matriculated undergraduates who enrolled in 2001, 732 applied for aid, 411 were judged to have need, 272 had their need fully met. 131 Federal Work-Study jobs (averaging $763). 144 State and other part-time jobs (averaging $798). *Average percent of need met:* 83%. *Average financial aid package:* $14,423. *Average need-based loan:* $3133. *Average need-based gift aid:* $11,014. *Average indebtedness upon graduation:* $17,043.

Applying *Options:* common application, electronic application, early admission, early decision, deferred entrance. *Application fee:* $25. *Required:* high school transcript, 1 letter of recommendation. *Required for some:* interview. *Recommended:* essay or personal statement. *Application deadline:* rolling (freshmen), rolling (transfers). *Early decision:* 11/1. *Notification:* continuous (freshmen), 12/1 (early decision).

Admissions Contact Dr. Patrick Kirby, Dean of Enrollment Services, Westminster College, 501 Westminster Avenue, Fulton, MO 65251-1299. *Phone:* 573-592-5251. *Toll-free phone:* 800-475-3361. *Fax:* 573-592-5255. *E-mail:* admissions@jaynet.wcmo.edu.

WILLIAM JEWELL COLLEGE

Liberty, Missouri

- **Independent Baptist** 4-year, founded 1849
- **Calendar** semesters
- **Degrees** bachelor's (also offers evening program with significant enrollment not reflected in profile)
- **Small-town** 149-acre campus with easy access to Kansas City
- **Endowment** $84.9 million
- **Coed,** 1,089 undergraduate students, 97% full-time, 59% women, 41% men
- **Moderately difficult** entrance level, 80% of applicants were admitted

The Oxbridge Honors Program, a program of tutorials and examinations through which a small number of academically outstanding students may pursue their areas of concentration, is available at William Jewell College. As its name implies, the propgram is an American adaptation of the educational method of the great English universities, Oxford and Cambridge.

Undergraduates 1,054 full-time, 35 part-time. Students come from 32 states and territories, 12 other countries, 20% are from out of state, 2% African American, 0.5% Asian American or Pacific Islander, 1% Hispanic American, 0.5% Native American, 2% international, 5% transferred in, 67% live on campus. *Retention:* 75% of 2001 full-time freshmen returned.

Freshmen *Admission:* 635 applied, 508 admitted, 243 enrolled. *Average high school GPA:* 3.66. *Test scores:* SAT verbal scores over 500: 80%; SAT math scores over 500: 81%; ACT scores over 18: 98%; SAT verbal scores over 600: 34%; SAT math scores over 600: 48%; ACT scores over 24: 55%; SAT verbal scores over 700: 14%; SAT math scores over 700: 7%; ACT scores over 30: 12%.

Faculty *Total:* 133, 63% full-time, 58% with terminal degrees. *Student/faculty ratio:* 11:1.

Majors Accounting; art; biochemistry; biology; business administration; cell biology; chemistry; computer science; drama/dance education; economics; education; elementary education; English; French; history; information sciences/systems; interdisciplinary studies; international business; international relations; mathematics; medical technology; molecular biology; music; music (general performance); music teacher education; music theory and composition; nursing; philosophy; physics; political science; pre-dentistry; pre-law; pre-medicine; pre-veterinary studies; psychology; religious music; religious studies; secondary education; Spanish; speech education; speech/rhetorical studies; theater arts/drama.

Academic Programs *Special study options:* academic remediation for entering students, adult/continuing education programs, advanced placement credit, cooperative education, double majors, honors programs, independent study, internships, part-time degree program, student-designed majors, study abroad, summer session for credit. *Unusual degree programs:* 3-2 engineering with Columbia University, Washington University in St. Louis, University of Kansas; forestry with Duke University.

Library Charles F. Curry Library with 248,749 titles, 899 serial subscriptions, 26,334 audiovisual materials, an OPAC, a Web page.

Computers on Campus 160 computers available on campus for general student use. A campuswide network can be accessed from student residence rooms and from off campus. Internet access, at least one staffed computer lab available.

Student Life *Housing:* on-campus residence required through junior year. *Options:* coed, men-only, women-only. *Activities and Organizations:* drama/theater group, student-run newspaper, radio station, choral group, Christian Student Ministries, college union activities, Fellowship of Christian Athletes, Alpha Omega, Earth Rocks, national fraternities, national sororities. *Campus security:* 24-hour emergency response devices and patrols, late-night transport/escort service, controlled dormitory access. *Student Services:* health clinic, personal/psychological counseling.

Athletics Member NAIA. *Intercollegiate sports:* baseball M(s), basketball M(s)/W(s), cross-country running M(s)/W(s), football M(s), golf M(s)/W(s), soccer M(s)/W(s), softball W(s), tennis M(s)/W(s), track and field M(s)/W(s), volleyball W(s). *Intramural sports:* archery M/W, badminton M/W, baseball M, basketball M/W, bowling M/W, cross-country running M/W, football M/W, golf M/W, racquetball M/W, soccer M/W, softball M/W, swimming M/W, table tennis M/W, tennis M/W, track and field M/W, volleyball M/W, weight lifting M/W.

Standardized Tests *Required:* SAT I or ACT (for admission).

Costs (2001–02) *Comprehensive fee:* $19,140 includes full-time tuition ($14,750) and room and board ($4390). Full-time tuition and fees vary according to class time and course load. Part-time tuition: $555 per semester hour. Part-time tuition and fees vary according to class time. *Room and board:* Room and board charges vary according to board plan and housing facility. *Payment plans:* tuition prepayment, installment, deferred payment. *Waivers:* senior citizens and employees or children of employees.

Financial Aid Of all full-time matriculated undergraduates who enrolled in 2001, 738 applied for aid, 635 were judged to have need. 421 Federal Work-Study jobs (averaging $1580). 95 State and other part-time jobs (averaging $1352). *Average need-based loan:* $4612. *Average need-based gift aid:* $9036. *Average indebtedness upon graduation:* $17,500.

Applying *Options:* common application, electronic application, early action, deferred entrance. *Application fee:* $25. *Required:* high school transcript, minimum 2.0 GPA. *Recommended:* essay or personal statement, minimum 2.5 GPA, 2 letters of recommendation, interview. *Application deadline:* rolling (freshmen), rolling (transfers). *Notification:* continuous (freshmen), 12/1 (early action).

Admissions Contact Mr. Chad Jolly, Dean of Enrollment Development, William Jewell College, 500 College Hill, Liberty, MO 64068. *Phone:* 816-781-7700. *Toll-free phone:* 800-753-7009. *Fax:* 816-415-5027. *E-mail:* admission@william.jewell.edu.

WILLIAM WOODS UNIVERSITY
Fulton, Missouri

- **Independent** comprehensive, founded 1870, affiliated with Christian Church (Disciples of Christ)
- **Calendar** semesters
- **Degrees** associate, bachelor's, and master's
- **Small-town** 170-acre campus with easy access to St. Louis
- **Endowment** $11.4 million
- **Coed,** 989 undergraduate students, 86% full-time, 71% women, 29% men
- **Moderately difficult** entrance level, 96% of applicants were admitted

Undergraduates 846 full-time, 143 part-time. Students come from 36 states and territories, 16 other countries, 25% are from out of state, 4% African American, 5% Asian American or Pacific Islander, 1% Hispanic American, 0.6% Native American, 6% transferred in, 88% live on campus.

Freshmen *Admission:* 513 applied, 494 admitted, 202 enrolled. *Average high school GPA:* 3.23. *Test scores:* SAT verbal scores over 500: 70%; SAT math scores over 500: 64%; ACT scores over 18: 84%; SAT verbal scores over 600: 15%; SAT math scores over 600: 12%; ACT scores over 24: 47%; ACT scores over 30: 9%.

Faculty *Total:* 98, 63% full-time, 61% with terminal degrees. *Student/faculty ratio:* 10:1.

Majors Accounting; advertising; art; art education; athletic training/sports medicine; biology; broadcast journalism; business administration; business economics; communications; comparative literature; computer/information sciences; design/visual communications; education; elementary education; English; English composition; English education; equestrian studies; fine/studio arts; French language education; graphic design/commercial art/illustration; history; interdisciplinary studies; interior design; international business; international relations; management information systems/business data processing; mathematics; mathematics education; middle school education; paralegal/legal assistant; physical education; political science; psychology; public relations; radio/television broadcasting; science education; secondary education; sign language interpretation; social work; Spanish; special education; speech/theater education; theater arts/drama; theater design.

Academic Programs *Special study options:* academic remediation for entering students, accelerated degree program, adult/continuing education programs, advanced placement credit, double majors, English as a second language, honors programs, independent study, internships, off-campus study, part-time degree program, student-designed majors, study abroad, summer session for credit. *ROTC:* Army (c), Navy (c), Air Force (c).

Library Dulany Library with 93,917 titles, 26,773 audiovisual materials, an OPAC, a Web page.

Computers on Campus 105 computers available on campus for general student use. A campuswide network can be accessed from student residence rooms. Internet access, at least one staffed computer lab available.

Student Life *Housing:* on-campus residence required through senior year. *Options:* coed, men-only, women-only. *Activities and Organizations:* drama/theater group, Campus Crusade for Christ, Panhellenic Council, International Club, Little Brother/Little Sister, Student Assembly, national fraternities, national sororities. *Campus security:* 24-hour patrols, late-night transport/escort service, controlled dormitory access. *Student Services:* personal/psychological counseling.

Athletics Member NAIA. *Intercollegiate sports:* baseball M(s), basketball W(s), golf M(s)/W(s), soccer M(s)/W(s), softball W(s), volleyball M(s)/W(s). *Intramural sports:* badminton M/W, basketball M/W, bowling M/W, cross-country running M/W, football M/W, softball M/W, table tennis M/W, tennis M/W, volleyball M/W, weight lifting M/W.

Standardized Tests *Required:* SAT I or ACT (for admission).

Costs (2001–02) *Comprehensive fee:* $19,390 includes full-time tuition ($13,500), mandatory fees ($290), and room and board ($5600). Full-time tuition and fees vary according to program. Part-time tuition: $225 per credit. *Required fees:* $15 per term part-time. *Room and board:* Room and board charges vary according to board plan. *Payment plan:* installment. *Waivers:* children of alumni, senior citizens, and employees or children of employees.

Financial Aid Of all full-time matriculated undergraduates who enrolled in 2001, 577 applied for aid, 436 were judged to have need, 169 had their need fully met. 111 State and other part-time jobs (averaging $1281). In 2001, 40 non-need-based awards were made. *Average percent of need met:* 33%. *Average financial aid package:* $14,076. *Average need-based gift aid:* $2256. *Average non-need based aid:* $2256. *Average indebtedness upon graduation:* $20,290.

Applying *Options:* electronic application, early admission, deferred entrance. *Application fee:* $25. *Required:* high school transcript. *Required for some:* essay or personal statement, 2 letters of recommendation. *Recommended:* interview. *Application deadline:* rolling (freshmen), rolling (transfers).

Admissions Contact Ms. Laura Archuleta, Executive Director of Enrollment Services, William Woods University, One University Avenue, Fulton, MO 65251. *Phone:* 573-592-4221. *Toll-free phone:* 800-995-3159 Ext. 4221. *Fax:* 573-592-1146. *E-mail:* admissions@williamwoods.edu.

MONTANA

CARROLL COLLEGE
Helena, Montana

- **Independent Roman Catholic** 4-year, founded 1909
- **Calendar** semesters
- **Degrees** associate and bachelor's
- **Small-town** 64-acre campus
- **Endowment** $23.2 million
- **Coed,** 1,347 undergraduate students, 85% full-time, 61% women, 39% men
- **Moderately difficult** entrance level, 89% of applicants were admitted

Undergraduates 1,151 full-time, 196 part-time. Students come from 26 states and territories, 10 other countries, 32% are from out of state, 0.2% African American, 0.5% Asian American or Pacific Islander, 2% Hispanic American, 1% Native American, 2% international, 5% transferred in, 50% live on campus. *Retention:* 81% of 2001 full-time freshmen returned.

Freshmen *Admission:* 842 applied, 753 admitted, 344 enrolled. *Average high school GPA:* 3.46. *Test scores:* SAT verbal scores over 500: 78%; SAT math scores over 500: 76%; ACT scores over 18: 98%; SAT verbal scores over 600: 29%; SAT math scores over 600: 26%; ACT scores over 24: 55%; SAT verbal scores over 700: 5%; SAT math scores over 700: 4%; ACT scores over 30: 9%.

Faculty *Total:* 125, 63% full-time, 46% with terminal degrees. *Student/faculty ratio:* 14:1.

Majors Accounting; acting/directing; art; biology; biology education; business administration; business economics; chemistry; civil engineering; communications; computer science; education; elementary education; engineering; English; English education; environmental science; finance; French; general studies; history; history education; international relations; Latin (ancient and medieval); mathematics; mathematics education; medical records administration; medical technology; nursing; philosophy; physical education; political science; pre-dentistry; pre-law; pre-medicine; pre-pharmacy studies; pre-veterinary studies; psychology; public administration; public relations; religious education; religious studies; secondary education; social science education; social sciences; social work; sociology; Spanish; Spanish language education; sport/fitness administration; teaching English as a second language; technical/business writing; theater arts/drama; theater design; theology.

Academic Programs *Special study options:* accelerated degree program, adult/continuing education programs, advanced placement credit, cooperative education, double majors, English as a second language, freshman honors college,

Carroll College (continued)
honors programs, independent study, internships, part-time degree program, student-designed majors, study abroad, summer session for credit. *ROTC:* Army (b). *Unusual degree programs:* 3-2 engineering with Columbia University, University of Southern California, University of Notre Dame, Montana State University, Gonzaga University, Montana College of Mineral Science and Technology.

Library Corette Library plus 1 other with 89,003 titles, 2,721 serial subscriptions, 3,890 audiovisual materials, an OPAC, a Web page.

Computers on Campus 91 computers available on campus for general student use. A campuswide network can be accessed from student residence rooms and from off campus. Internet access, at least one staffed computer lab available.

Student Life *Housing:* on-campus residence required through sophomore year. *Options:* coed, men-only, women-only. *Activities and Organizations:* drama/theater group, student-run newspaper, radio station, choral group, student government, Drama Club, Into the Streets, Radio Club, Soccer Club. *Campus security:* late-night transport/escort service. *Student Services:* health clinic, personal/psychological counseling.

Athletics Member NAIA. *Intercollegiate sports:* basketball M(s)/W(s), football M(s), golf W(s), soccer W(s), swimming M/W, volleyball W(s). *Intramural sports:* badminton M/W, basketball M/W, bowling M/W, cross-country running M/W, football M/W, golf M/W, ice hockey M(c), racquetball M/W, rugby M(c), skiing (cross-country) M/W, skiing (downhill) M(c)/W(c), soccer M(c)/W(c), softball M/W, swimming M(c)/W(c), table tennis M/W, tennis M/W, track and field M/W, volleyball M/W, water polo M/W, weight lifting M/W, wrestling M.

Standardized Tests *Required:* SAT I or ACT (for admission). *Required for some:* SAT II: Subject Tests (for admission), SAT II: Writing Test (for admission).

Costs (2001–02) *Comprehensive fee:* $17,984 includes full-time tuition ($12,716), mandatory fees ($100), and room and board ($5168). Part-time tuition: $424 per semester hour. *Room and board:* College room only: $2390. Room and board charges vary according to board plan, housing facility, and student level. *Payment plan:* installment. *Waivers:* senior citizens and employees or children of employees.

Financial Aid Of all full-time matriculated undergraduates who enrolled in 2001, 1120 applied for aid, 745 were judged to have need, 153 had their need fully met. 497 Federal Work-Study jobs. In 2001, 352 non-need-based awards were made. *Average percent of need met:* 81%. *Average financial aid package:* $11,435. *Average need-based loan:* $5235. *Average need-based gift aid:* $6858. *Average indebtedness upon graduation:* $22,450.

Applying *Options:* common application, electronic application, deferred entrance. *Application fee:* $25. *Required:* essay or personal statement, high school transcript, minimum 2.0 GPA, 1 letter of recommendation. *Required for some:* interview. *Recommended:* minimum 3.0 GPA, interview. *Application deadlines:* 6/1 (freshmen), 6/1 (transfers). *Notification:* continuous (freshmen).

Admissions Contact Ms. Candace A. Cain, Director of Admission, Carroll College, 1601 North Benton Avenue, Helena, MT 59625-0002. *Phone:* 406-447-4384. *Toll-free phone:* 800-992-3648. *Fax:* 406-447-4533. *E-mail:* enroll@carroll.edu.

MONTANA STATE UNIVERSITY-BILLINGS
Billings, Montana

- **State-supported** comprehensive, founded 1927, part of Montana University System
- **Calendar** semesters
- **Degrees** certificates, associate, bachelor's, master's, post-master's, and postbachelor's certificates
- **Urban** 92-acre campus
- **Endowment** $8.2 million
- **Coed,** 3,840 undergraduate students, 78% full-time, 64% women, 36% men
- **Moderately difficult** entrance level, 100% of applicants were admitted

Undergraduates 2,985 full-time, 855 part-time. Students come from 35 states and territories, 18 other countries, 9% are from out of state, 0.6% African American, 1% Asian American or Pacific Islander, 3% Hispanic American, 7% Native American, 0.6% international, 10% transferred in, 12% live on campus. *Retention:* 53% of 2001 full-time freshmen returned.

Freshmen *Admission:* 1,017 applied, 1,012 admitted, 756 enrolled. *Average high school GPA:* 2.95. *Test scores:* SAT verbal scores over 500: 41%; SAT math scores over 500: 52%; ACT scores over 18: 67%; SAT verbal scores over 600: 7%; SAT math scores over 600: 10%; ACT scores over 24: 19%; SAT math scores over 700: 1%; ACT scores over 30: 2%.

Faculty *Total:* 249, 59% full-time. *Student/faculty ratio:* 21:1.

Majors Accounting; art; art education; auto mechanic/technician; biology; biology education; business; business administration; business economics; business marketing and marketing management; chemistry; chemistry education; computer/information sciences; data processing; data processing technology; diesel engine mechanic; drafting; early childhood education; education; elementary education; emergency medical technology; English; English education; environmental science; finance; fire protection/safety technology; health education; health services administration; heating/air conditioning/refrigeration; history; history education; legal administrative assistant; liberal arts and sciences/liberal studies; mass communications; mathematics; mathematics education; medical administrative assistant; medical records administration; music; music teacher education; petroleum technology; physical education; practical nurse; pre-engineering; psychology; public relations; rehabilitation therapy; science education; secondary education; secretarial science; social science education; sociology; Spanish; Spanish language education; special education; sport/fitness administration; theater arts/drama.

Academic Programs *Special study options:* academic remediation for entering students, accelerated degree program, adult/continuing education programs, advanced placement credit, cooperative education, distance learning, double majors, English as a second language, external degree program, honors programs, independent study, internships, off-campus study, part-time degree program, services for LD students, study abroad, summer session for credit.

Library Montana State University-Billings Library with 418,000 titles, 865 serial subscriptions, 1,907 audiovisual materials, an OPAC.

Computers on Campus 450 computers available on campus for general student use. A campuswide network can be accessed from student residence rooms and from off campus that provide access to on-line degree programs. Internet access, online (class) registration, at least one staffed computer lab available.

Student Life *Housing:* on-campus residence required for freshman year. *Options:* coed, men-only, women-only. *Activities and Organizations:* drama/theater group, student-run newspaper, radio station, choral group, Art Student League, Band Club, Inter-varsity Christian Fellowship, Residence Hall Association, Student Council for Exceptional Children. *Campus security:* 24-hour emergency response devices and patrols, late-night transport/escort service, controlled dormitory access. *Student Services:* health clinic, personal/psychological counseling, women's center, legal services.

Athletics Member NCAA. All Division II. *Intercollegiate sports:* basketball M(s)/W(s), cross-country running M(s)/W(s), soccer M(s)/W(s), softball W, tennis M(s)/W(s), volleyball W(s). *Intramural sports:* baseball M/W, basketball M/W, bowling M/W, cross-country running M/W, football M/W, golf M/W, racquetball M/W, skiing (cross-country) M/W, soccer M/W, softball M/W, swimming M/W, table tennis M/W, tennis M/W, track and field M/W, volleyball M/W.

Standardized Tests *Required:* SAT I or ACT (for admission).

Costs (2001–02) *Tuition:* state resident $3430 full-time, $95 per credit hour part-time; nonresident $9265 full-time, $257 per credit hour part-time. Full-time tuition and fees vary according to class time, course load, location, reciprocity agreements, and student level. Part-time tuition and fees vary according to class time, course load, location, reciprocity agreements, and student level. *Room and board:* $3000. Room and board charges vary according to board plan and housing facility. *Payment plan:* installment. *Waivers:* senior citizens and employees or children of employees.

Financial Aid Of all full-time matriculated undergraduates who enrolled in 2001, 2475 applied for aid, 1998 were judged to have need, 467 had their need fully met. 192 Federal Work-Study jobs (averaging $1514). 80 State and other part-time jobs (averaging $1104). In 2001, 125 non-need-based awards were made. *Average percent of need met:* 72%. *Average financial aid package:* $6415. *Average need-based loan:* $3134. *Average need-based gift aid:* $3301. *Average non-need based aid:* $7395. *Average indebtedness upon graduation:* $16,000.

Applying *Options:* common application, early admission, deferred entrance. *Application fee:* $30. *Required:* high school transcript, minimum 2.5 GPA. *Application deadline:* 7/1 (freshmen), rolling (transfers). *Notification:* continuous (freshmen).

Admissions Contact Ms. Shelly Beatty, Associate Director of Admissions, Montana State University-Billings, 1500 North 30th Street, Billings, MT 59101. *Phone:* 406-657-2158. *Toll-free phone:* 800-565-6782. *Fax:* 406-657-2302. *E-mail:* keverett@msubillings.edu.

MONTANA STATE UNIVERSITY-BOZEMAN
Bozeman, Montana

- **State-supported** university, founded 1893, part of Montana University System
- **Calendar** semesters
- **Degrees** bachelor's, master's, and doctoral
- **Small-town** 1170-acre campus
- **Endowment** $1.2 million

■ **Coed,** 10,462 undergraduate students, 87% full-time, 46% women, 54% men
■ **Moderately difficult** entrance level, 75% of applicants were admitted

Undergraduates 9,091 full-time, 1,371 part-time. Students come from 49 states and territories, 45 other countries, 24% are from out of state, 0.3% African American, 0.7% Asian American or Pacific Islander, 1% Hispanic American, 2% Native American, 1% international, 8% transferred in, 24% live on campus. *Retention:* 71% of 2001 full-time freshmen returned.

Freshmen *Admission:* 3,894 applied, 2,903 admitted, 2,069 enrolled. *Average high school GPA:* 3.28. *Test scores:* SAT verbal scores over 500: 69%; SAT math scores over 500: 75%; ACT scores over 18: 92%; SAT verbal scores over 600: 24%; SAT math scores over 600: 31%; ACT scores over 24: 42%; SAT verbal scores over 700: 2%; SAT math scores over 700: 5%; ACT scores over 30: 5%.

Faculty *Total:* 735, 75% full-time. *Student/faculty ratio:* 20:1.

Majors Agricultural business; agricultural education; agricultural mechanization; animal sciences; anthropology; architectural environmental design; art; biology; biotechnology research; business; chemical engineering; chemistry; civil engineering; computer engineering; computer science; construction technology; earth sciences; economics; electrical/electronic engineering technology; electrical engineering; elementary education; English; environmental science; film/video production; fine/studio arts; foreign languages/literatures; health/physical education; health services administration; history; home economics; horticulture science; industrial arts education; industrial/manufacturing engineering; mathematics; mechanical engineering; mechanical engineering technology; microbiology/bacteriology; music; music teacher education; natural resources conservation; nursing; philosophy; physics; plant sciences; political science; psychology; range management; secondary education; sociology; sport/fitness administration.

Academic Programs *Special study options:* academic remediation for entering students, adult/continuing education programs, advanced placement credit, distance learning, double majors, English as a second language, honors programs, independent study, internships, off-campus study, part-time degree program, services for LD students, student-designed majors, study abroad, summer session for credit. *ROTC:* Army (b), Air Force (b).

Library Renne Library plus 1 other with 574,634 titles, 3,790 serial subscriptions, 2,925 audiovisual materials, an OPAC, a Web page.

Computers on Campus 850 computers available on campus for general student use. A campuswide network can be accessed from student residence rooms and from off campus that provide access to e-mail. Internet access, online (class) registration, at least one staffed computer lab available.

Student Life *Housing:* on-campus residence required for freshman year. *Options:* coed, men-only, women-only, cooperative. *Activities and Organizations:* drama/theater group, student-run newspaper, radio and television station, choral group, marching band, Spurs, Intervarsity Christian Fellowship, Campus Crusade for Christ, Fangs, Mortar Board, national fraternities, national sororities. *Campus security:* 24-hour emergency response devices and patrols, student patrols, late-night transport/escort service, 24-hour residence hall monitoring. *Student Services:* health clinic, personal/psychological counseling, women's center, legal services.

Athletics Member NCAA. All Division I except football (Division I-AA). *Intercollegiate sports:* basketball M(s)/W(s), cross-country running M(s)/W(s), golf W(s), skiing (cross-country) W(s), skiing (downhill) W(s), tennis M(s)/W(s), track and field M(s)/W(s), volleyball W(s). *Intramural sports:* archery M/W, badminton M/W, baseball M, basketball M/W, bowling M/W, cross-country running M/W, fencing M/W, football M, golf M/W, gymnastics M/W, racquetball M/W, rugby M/W, skiing (cross-country) M/W, skiing (downhill) M/W, soccer M/W, softball M/W, swimming M/W, table tennis M/W, tennis M/W, track and field M/W, volleyball M/W, water polo M/W, weight lifting M/W, wrestling M.

Standardized Tests *Required:* SAT I or ACT (for admission).

Costs (2001–02) *Tuition:* state resident $3381 full-time; nonresident $10,147 full-time. Full-time tuition and fees vary according to course load. Part-time tuition and fees vary according to course load. *Room and board:* $5050. Room and board charges vary according to board plan and housing facility. *Payment plans:* installment, deferred payment. *Waivers:* minority students, senior citizens, and employees or children of employees.

Financial Aid Of all full-time matriculated undergraduates who enrolled in 2001, 6518 applied for aid, 4542 were judged to have need, 580 had their need fully met. In 2001, 574 non-need-based awards were made. *Average percent of need met:* 71%. *Average financial aid package:* $6454. *Average need-based loan:* $3967. *Average need-based gift aid:* $2978. *Average non-need based aid:* $3106. *Average indebtedness upon graduation:* $9905.

Applying *Options:* electronic application, early admission, deferred entrance. *Application fee:* $30. *Required:* high school transcript, minimum 2.5 GPA. *Application deadline:* rolling (freshmen), rolling (transfers). *Notification:* continuous (freshmen).

Admissions Contact Ms. Ronda Russell, Director of New Student Services, Montana State University-Bozeman, PO Box 172190, Bozeman, MT 59717-2190. *Phone:* 406-994-2452. *Toll-free phone:* 888-MSU-CATS. *Fax:* 406-994-1923. *E-mail:* admissions@montana.edu.

MONTANA STATE UNIVERSITY-NORTHERN
Havre, Montana

■ **State-supported** comprehensive, founded 1929, part of Montana University System
■ **Calendar** semesters
■ **Degrees** certificates, associate, bachelor's, and master's
■ **Small-town** 105-acre campus
■ **Endowment** $162,838
■ **Coed,** 1,428 undergraduate students, 74% full-time, 53% women, 47% men
■ **Moderately difficult** entrance level, 82% of applicants were admitted

Undergraduates 1,060 full-time, 368 part-time. Students come from 7 states and territories, 3 other countries, 1% are from out of state, 0.8% African American, 0.7% Asian American or Pacific Islander, 0.6% Hispanic American, 14% Native American, 1% international. *Retention:* 65% of 2001 full-time freshmen returned.

Freshmen *Admission:* 868 applied, 709 admitted, 234 enrolled.

Faculty *Total:* 103, 71% full-time. *Student/faculty ratio:* 15:1.

Majors Agricultural business; agricultural mechanization; auto mechanic/technician; biological/physical sciences; biology; business administration; business education; civil engineering technology; community services; drafting; education; electrical/electronic engineering technology; elementary education; graphic design/commercial art/illustration; heavy equipment maintenance; humanities; industrial technology; information sciences/systems; interdisciplinary studies; machine technology; mass communications; metallurgical technology; nursing; physical education; science education; secondary education; social sciences; water resources; welding technology.

Academic Programs *Special study options:* academic remediation for entering students, adult/continuing education programs, advanced placement credit, cooperative education, distance learning, double majors, English as a second language, honors programs, internships, part-time degree program, services for LD students, summer session for credit.

Library VandeBogart Libraries with 128,000 titles, 1,729 serial subscriptions, an OPAC, a Web page.

Computers on Campus 140 computers available on campus for general student use. A campuswide network can be accessed from student residence rooms and from off campus. Internet access, online (class) registration, at least one staffed computer lab available.

Student Life *Housing:* on-campus residence required for freshman year. *Options:* coed. *Activities and Organizations:* drama/theater group, student-run newspaper, radio station, Vocational and Industrial Clubs of America, Student Nurses Association of America, Student Education Association. *Student Services:* health clinic, personal/psychological counseling.

Athletics Member NAIA. *Intercollegiate sports:* basketball M(s)/W(s), football M(s), golf W(s), volleyball W(s), wrestling M(s). *Intramural sports:* basketball M/W, bowling M/W, football M/W, golf M/W, gymnastics M/W, racquetball M/W, skiing (cross-country) M/W, skiing (downhill) M/W, soccer M/W, softball M/W, swimming M/W, table tennis M/W, tennis M/W, track and field M/W, volleyball M/W, water polo M/W, weight lifting M/W.

Standardized Tests *Required:* ACT (for placement).

Costs (2001–02) *Tuition:* state resident $2436 full-time, $87 per credit part-time; nonresident $8586 full-time, $306 per credit part-time. Full-time tuition and fees vary according to class time, course load, degree level, location, reciprocity agreements, and student level. Part-time tuition and fees vary according to class time, course load, degree level, location, reciprocity agreements, and student level. *Required fees:* $778 full-time. *Room and board:* $4190; room only: $1500. Room and board charges vary according to board plan. *Payment plan:* deferred payment. *Waivers:* minority students, senior citizens, and employees or children of employees.

Financial Aid Of all full-time matriculated undergraduates who enrolled in 2001, 1003 applied for aid, 829 were judged to have need, 222 had their need fully met. In 2001, 37 non-need-based awards were made. *Average percent of need met:* 69%. *Average financial aid package:* $7432. *Average need-based loan:* $3330. *Average need-based gift aid:* $3931. *Average non-need based aid:* $2545. *Average indebtedness upon graduation:* $5551.

Applying *Options:* early admission, deferred entrance. *Application fee:* $30. *Required:* high school transcript. *Required for some:* minimum 2.0 GPA. *Application deadline:* rolling (freshmen), rolling (transfers). *Notification:* continuous (freshmen).

Montana State University-Northern (continued)

Admissions Contact Ms. Rosalie Spinler, Director of Admissions, Montana State University-Northern, PO Box 7751, Havre, MT 59501-7751. *Phone:* 406-265-3704. *Toll-free phone:* 800-662-6132. *Fax:* 406-265-3777. *E-mail:* msunadmit@nmc1.nmclites.edu.

MONTANA TECH OF THE UNIVERSITY OF MONTANA

Butte, Montana

- **State-supported** comprehensive, founded 1895, part of Montana University System
- **Calendar** semesters
- **Degrees** certificates, diplomas, associate, bachelor's, master's, and postbachelor's certificates
- **Small-town** 56-acre campus
- **Endowment** $14.0 million
- **Coed,** 2,005 undergraduate students, 82% full-time, 45% women, 55% men
- **Moderately difficult** entrance level, 96% of applicants were admitted

Undergraduates 1,654 full-time, 351 part-time. Students come from 33 states and territories, 13 other countries, 9% are from out of state, 0.3% African American, 0.6% Asian American or Pacific Islander, 2% Hispanic American, 1% Native American, 2% international, 9% transferred in, 15% live on campus. *Retention:* 71% of 2001 full-time freshmen returned.

Freshmen *Admission:* 563 applied, 542 admitted, 419 enrolled. *Average high school GPA:* 3.47. *Test scores:* SAT verbal scores over 500: 65%; SAT math scores over 500: 74%; ACT scores over 18: 79%; SAT verbal scores over 600: 27%; SAT math scores over 600: 39%; ACT scores over 24: 31%; SAT verbal scores over 700: 6%; SAT math scores over 700: 8%; ACT scores over 30: 6%.

Faculty *Total:* 150, 71% full-time, 41% with terminal degrees. *Student/faculty ratio:* 16:1.

Majors Accounting; applied mathematics; architectural drafting; auto body repair; auto mechanic/technician; biological/physical sciences; biology; business; business administration; chemistry; civil engineering; civil/structural drafting; communications; computer engineering; computer/information sciences; computer programming; computer science; computer systems analysis; data processing; data processing technology; drafting; engineering; engineering science; engineering technology; environmental engineering; executive assistant; finance; geological engineering; geophysical engineering; geotechnical engineering; health science; human resources management; information sciences/systems; legal administrative assistant; liberal arts and sciences/liberal studies; materials engineering; materials science; mathematics; mechanical drafting; mechanical engineering; medical administrative assistant; metallurgical engineering; mining/mineral engineering; nurse assistant/aide; nursing; occupational health/industrial hygiene; occupational safety/health technology; petroleum engineering; petroleum technology; robotics; secretarial science; systems engineering; technical/business writing; welding technology.

Academic Programs *Special study options:* academic remediation for entering students, adult/continuing education programs, advanced placement credit, cooperative education, distance learning, double majors, independent study, internships, part-time degree program, services for LD students, student-designed majors, summer session for credit.

Library Montana Tech Library plus 1 other with 161,187 titles, 495 serial subscriptions, 38 audiovisual materials, an OPAC, a Web page.

Computers on Campus 500 computers available on campus for general student use. A campuswide network can be accessed from student residence rooms and from off campus. Internet access, online (class) registration, at least one staffed computer lab available.

Student Life *Housing:* on-campus residence required for freshman year. *Options:* coed. *Activities and Organizations:* student-run newspaper, radio station, choral group, Environmental Engineering Club, SH/IH Club, Petroleum Club SPE, Marcus Daly Mining, Chemistry Club. *Campus security:* 24-hour patrols, controlled dormitory access. *Student Services:* health clinic, personal/psychological counseling.

Athletics Member NAIA. *Intercollegiate sports:* basketball M(s)/W(s), cross-country running M(c)/W(c), football M(s), golf M(s)/W(s), rugby M(c), soccer M(c)/W(c), swimming M(c)/W(c), volleyball W(s). *Intramural sports:* basketball M/W, football M/W, racquetball M/W, softball M/W, swimming M/W, tennis M/W, volleyball M/W, water polo M/W.

Standardized Tests *Required:* SAT I or ACT (for admission).

Costs (2001–02) *Tuition:* state resident $3404 full-time, $150 per credit part-time; nonresident $9724 full-time, $410 per credit part-time. Full-time tuition and fees vary according to class time, course load, degree level, location, reciprocity agreements, and student level. Part-time tuition and fees vary according to class time, course load, degree level, location, reciprocity agreements, and student level. *Room and board:* $4441. Room and board charges vary according to board plan and housing facility. *Payment plan:* deferred payment. *Waivers:* minority students, senior citizens, and employees or children of employees.

Financial Aid Of all full-time matriculated undergraduates who enrolled in 2001, 1500 applied for aid, 1300 were judged to have need, 700 had their need fully met. 200 Federal Work-Study jobs, 75 State and other part-time jobs (averaging $1800). In 2001, 100 non-need-based awards were made. *Average percent of need met:* 60%. *Average financial aid package:* $6000. *Average need-based loan:* $5000. *Average need-based gift aid:* $1000. *Average non-need based aid:* $4000. *Average indebtedness upon graduation:* $11,500.

Applying *Options:* common application, electronic application, early admission. *Application fee:* $30. *Required:* high school transcript, minimum 2.5 GPA, proof of immunization. *Application deadline:* rolling (freshmen), rolling (transfers). *Notification:* continuous (freshmen).

Admissions Contact Tony Campeau, Associate Director of Admissions, Montana Tech of The University of Montana, 1300 West Park Street, Butte, MT 59701-8997. *Phone:* 406-496-4178 Ext. 4632. *Toll-free phone:* 800-445-TECH Ext. 1. *Fax:* 406-496-4170. *E-mail:* admissions@mtech.edu.

ROCKY MOUNTAIN COLLEGE

Billings, Montana

- **Independent interdenominational** 4-year, founded 1878
- **Calendar** semesters
- **Degrees** certificates, diplomas, associate, and bachelor's
- **Urban** 60-acre campus
- **Endowment** $9.6 million
- **Coed,** 777 undergraduate students, 92% full-time, 53% women, 47% men
- **Moderately difficult** entrance level, 83% of applicants were admitted

Undergraduates 712 full-time, 65 part-time. Students come from 33 states and territories, 16 other countries, 26% are from out of state, 1% African American, 1% Asian American or Pacific Islander, 2% Hispanic American, 10% Native American, 3% international, 14% transferred in, 37% live on campus. *Retention:* 67% of 2001 full-time freshmen returned.

Freshmen *Admission:* 452 applied, 377 admitted, 226 enrolled. *Average high school GPA:* 3.18. *Test scores:* SAT verbal scores over 500: 50%; SAT math scores over 500: 59%; ACT scores over 18: 90%; SAT verbal scores over 600: 11%; SAT math scores over 600: 11%; ACT scores over 24: 41%; SAT math scores over 700: 2%; ACT scores over 30: 2%.

Faculty *Total:* 85, 53% full-time, 40% with terminal degrees. *Student/faculty ratio:* 13:1.

Majors Accounting; agricultural business; aircraft pilot (professional); art; art education; athletic training/sports medicine; aviation management; biological/physical sciences; biology; business administration; business economics; chemistry; chemistry education; communications; computer/information sciences; computer science; economics; education; education (K-12); elementary education; English; English education; environmental science; equestrian studies; exercise sciences; geology; health education; history; history education; information sciences/systems; interdisciplinary studies; international relations; liberal arts and sciences/liberal studies; management information systems/business data processing; mathematics; mathematics education; music; music teacher education; natural sciences; peace/conflict studies; philosophy; physical education; physician assistant; political science; pre-law; pre-medicine; pre-veterinary studies; psychology; religious studies; science education; secondary education; social science education; social studies education; sociology; theater arts/drama.

Academic Programs *Special study options:* academic remediation for entering students, accelerated degree program, adult/continuing education programs, advanced placement credit, cooperative education, distance learning, double majors, English as a second language, honors programs, independent study, internships, part-time degree program, services for LD students, student-designed majors, study abroad, summer session for credit. *Unusual degree programs:* 3-2 engineering with Montana State University-Bozeman, Montana Tech of the University of Montana; occupational therapy with Washington University in St. Louis.

Library Paul Adams Library with 86,449 titles, an OPAC, a Web page.

Computers on Campus 50 computers available on campus for general student use. A campuswide network can be accessed from student residence rooms and from off campus. Internet access, at least one staffed computer lab available.

Student Life *Housing:* on-campus residence required through sophomore year. *Options:* coed. *Activities and Organizations:* drama/theater group, student-run newspaper, choral group, marching band, Campus Ministry, STARs (theater), Aviation club, Indian club, Sojourners. *Campus security:* 24-hour emergency response devices, student patrols, controlled dormitory access, security cameras. *Student Services:* health clinic, personal/psychological counseling.

Athletics Member NAIA. *Intercollegiate sports:* basketball M(s)/W(s), football M(s), golf M(s)/W(s), skiing (downhill) M(s)/W(s), soccer W(s), volleyball W(s). *Intramural sports:* basketball M/W, bowling M(c)/W(c), equestrian sports M/W, field hockey M/W, football M/W, golf M(c)/W(c), ice hockey M(c), racquetball M(c)/W(c), skiing (cross-country) M(c)/W(c), skiing (downhill) M/W, soccer M(c)/W(c), softball M(c)/W(c), swimming M(c)/W(c), table tennis M(c)/W(c), tennis M(c)/W(c), track and field M(c)/W(c), volleyball M(c)/W, weight lifting M(c)/W(c).

Standardized Tests *Required:* SAT I or ACT (for admission). *Recommended:* ACT (for admission).

Costs (2001–02) *Comprehensive fee:* $18,113 includes full-time tuition ($12,680), mandatory fees ($155), and room and board ($5278). Full-time tuition and fees vary according to course load and program. Part-time tuition: $529 per credit. Part-time tuition and fees vary according to course load and program. *Required fees:* $35 per term part-time. *Room and board:* College room only: $2650. Room and board charges vary according to board plan and housing facility. *Payment plan:* installment. *Waivers:* employees or children of employees.

Financial Aid Of all full-time matriculated undergraduates who enrolled in 2001, 634 applied for aid, 555 were judged to have need, 98 had their need fully met. 266 Federal Work-Study jobs (averaging $514). 165 State and other part-time jobs (averaging $606). In 2001, 117 non-need-based awards were made. *Average percent of need met:* 72%. *Average financial aid package:* $10,330. *Average need-based loan:* $4132. *Average need-based gift aid:* $5682.

Applying *Options:* common application, electronic application, early admission, deferred entrance. *Application fee:* $25. *Required:* high school transcript, minimum 2.5 GPA. *Required for some:* essay or personal statement, interview. *Recommended:* 2 letters of recommendation. *Application deadline:* rolling (freshmen), rolling (transfers). *Notification:* continuous (freshmen).

Admissions Contact Ms. LynAnn Henderson, Director of Admissions, Rocky Mountain College, 1511 Poly Drive, Billings, MT 59102. *Phone:* 406-657-1026. *Toll-free phone:* 800-877-6259. *Fax:* 406-259-9751. *E-mail:* admissions@rocky.edu.

SALISH KOOTENAI COLLEGE
Pablo, Montana

- **Independent** primarily 2-year, founded 1977
- **Calendar** quarters
- **Degrees** certificates, associate, and bachelor's
- **Rural** 4-acre campus
- **Coed**
- **Noncompetitive** entrance level

Standardized Tests *Required:* ACT (for placement), TABE.

Financial Aid Of all full-time matriculated undergraduates who enrolled in 2001, 78 Federal Work-Study jobs (averaging $1277).

Applying *Options:* deferred entrance. *Required:* high school transcript, proof of immunization, tribal enrollment.

Admissions Contact Ms. Jackie Moran, Admissions Officer, Salish Kootenai College, PO 117, Highway 93, Pablo, MT 59855. *Phone:* 406-675-4800 Ext. 265. *Fax:* 406-675-4801. *E-mail:* jackie_moran@skc.edu.

UNIVERSITY OF GREAT FALLS
Great Falls, Montana

- **Independent Roman Catholic** comprehensive, founded 1932
- **Calendar** semesters
- **Degrees** certificates, associate, bachelor's, and master's
- **Urban** 40-acre campus
- **Endowment** $4.6 million
- **Coed,** 756 undergraduate students, 64% full-time, 69% women, 31% men
- **Noncompetitive** entrance level, 68% of applicants were admitted

Undergraduates 487 full-time, 269 part-time. Students come from 20 states and territories, 5 other countries, 7% are from out of state, 13% transferred in, 12% live on campus. *Retention:* 54% of 2001 full-time freshmen returned.

Freshmen *Admission:* 200 applied, 135 admitted, 197 enrolled. *Average high school GPA:* 3.00. *Test scores:* ACT scores over 18: 81%; ACT scores over 24: 28%.

Faculty *Total:* 100, 43% full-time, 31% with terminal degrees. *Student/faculty ratio:* 11:1.

Majors Accounting; alcohol/drug abuse counseling; art; art education; biology; botany; business administration; computer management; computer programming; computer science; counseling psychology; early childhood education; education of the gifted/talented; elementary education; fine/studio arts; health/physical education; health services administration; history; human services; law enforcement/police science; management science; marketing research; mathematics; mathematics education; microbiology/bacteriology; middle school education; paralegal/legal assistant; physiology; political science; psychology; reading education; religious studies; science education; secondary education; social science education; social sciences; sociology; special education; theology.

Academic Programs *Special study options:* academic remediation for entering students, accelerated degree program, adult/continuing education programs, advanced placement credit, cooperative education, distance learning, double majors, external degree program, independent study, internships, part-time degree program, services for LD students, summer session for credit. *Unusual degree programs:* 3-2 engineering with Montana State University-Bozeman; nursing with Montana State University-Bozeman.

Library University of Great Falls Library with 76,517 titles, 563 serial subscriptions, 4,069 audiovisual materials, an OPAC, a Web page.

Computers on Campus 75 computers available on campus for general student use. Internet access, at least one staffed computer lab available.

Student Life *Housing:* on-campus residence required for freshman year. *Options:* coed, disabled students. *Activities and Organizations:* drama/theater group, student-run newspaper, choral group, Student Montana Education Association, Student Senate, International Law and Justice Club, Students In Free Enterprise, Computer Science Club. *Campus security:* 24-hour emergency response devices and patrols, late-night transport/escort service. *Student Services:* personal/psychological counseling, women's center.

Athletics Member NAIA. *Intercollegiate sports:* basketball M(s)/W(s), volleyball W(s). *Intramural sports:* basketball M/W, football M/W, volleyball M/W.

Standardized Tests *Recommended:* SAT I or ACT (for placement).

Costs (2002–03) *Comprehensive fee:* $15,360 includes full-time tuition ($10,000), mandatory fees ($260), and room and board ($5100). Full-time tuition and fees vary according to course load, degree level, and reciprocity agreements. Part-time tuition: $280 per credit. Part-time tuition and fees vary according to course load, degree level, and reciprocity agreements. *Required fees:* $5 per credit, $70 per credit part-time. *Room and board:* Room and board charges vary according to board plan and housing facility. *Waivers:* senior citizens and employees or children of employees.

Financial Aid Of all full-time matriculated undergraduates who enrolled in 2001, 397 applied for aid, 381 were judged to have need, 65 had their need fully met. *Average percent of need met:* 73%. *Average financial aid package:* $9662. *Average need-based loan:* $3978. *Average need-based gift aid:* $3423. *Average indebtedness upon graduation:* $20,470.

Applying *Options:* early admission, early action, deferred entrance. *Application fee:* $25. *Required:* high school transcript. *Recommended:* interview. *Application deadlines:* 8/1 (freshmen), 8/1 (transfers).

Admissions Contact Mr. Michael Myers, Assistant Director of Admissions, University of Great Falls, 1301 Twentieth Street South, Great Falls, MT 59405. *Phone:* 406-791-5200. *Toll-free phone:* 800-856-9544. *Fax:* 406-791-5209. *E-mail:* adminrec@ugf.edu.

THE UNIVERSITY OF MONTANA-MISSOULA
Missoula, Montana

- **State-supported** university, founded 1893, part of Montana University System
- **Calendar** semesters
- **Degrees** certificates, associate, bachelor's, master's, doctoral, first professional, and post-master's certificates
- **Urban** 220-acre campus
- **Endowment** $78.3 million
- **Coed,** 10,828 undergraduate students, 87% full-time, 53% women, 47% men
- **Moderately difficult** entrance level, 88% of applicants were admitted

Undergraduates 9,458 full-time, 1,370 part-time. Students come from 52 states and territories, 61 other countries, 26% are from out of state, 0.5% African American, 1% Asian American or Pacific Islander, 1% Hispanic American, 3% Native American, 2% international, 27% transferred in, 23% live on campus. *Retention:* 70% of 2001 full-time freshmen returned.

Freshmen *Admission:* 3,560 applied, 3,142 admitted, 2,207 enrolled. *Average high school GPA:* 3.20. *Test scores:* SAT verbal scores over 500: 68%; SAT math scores over 500: 63%; ACT scores over 18: 89%; SAT verbal scores over 600: 26%; SAT math scores over 600: 22%; ACT scores over 24: 37%; SAT verbal scores over 700: 4%; SAT math scores over 700: 3%; ACT scores over 30: 4%.

The University of Montana-Missoula (continued)

Faculty *Total:* 728, 72% full-time, 75% with terminal degrees. *Student/faculty ratio:* 19:1.

Majors Accounting technician; African-American studies; American government; anthropology; apparel marketing; applied mathematics; area studies; art; art education; art history; Asian studies; astronomy; biochemistry; biology; botany; business; business education; business marketing and marketing management; chemistry; Chinese; city/community/regional planning; classics; communications; computer/information sciences; computer science; creative writing; culinary arts; curriculum and instruction; dance; drawing; East Asian studies; economics; education; electrical/electronic engineering technology; elementary education; English; environmental education; environmental science; executive assistant; fashion merchandising; foreign languages/literatures; forest management; forestry; French; geography; geology; German; health education; heavy equipment maintenance; history; industrial arts; information sciences/systems; interdisciplinary studies; international business; Japanese; journalism; Latin (ancient and medieval); legal administrative assistant; legal studies; liberal arts and sciences/liberal studies; linguistics; mathematical statistics; mathematics; mathematics education; medical administrative assistant; medical laboratory technician; medical pharmacology and pharmaceutical sciences; medical technology; microbiology/bacteriology; music; music (general performance); music teacher education; Native American studies; natural resources conservation; natural resources management; operating room technician; paralegal/legal assistant; pharmacy; pharmacy technician/assistant; philosophy; physical education; physical therapy; physics; practical nurse; pre-engineering; pre-law; pre-medicine; pre-pharmacy studies; psychology; radio/television broadcasting; reading education; receptionist; recreation/leisure studies; respiratory therapy; Russian; Russian/Slavic studies; science education; secondary education; secretarial science; small engine mechanic; social science education; social sciences; social work; sociology; Spanish; speech-language pathology/audiology; speech/rhetorical studies; teaching English as a second language; technical/business writing; theater arts/drama; vehicle/equipment operation; welding technology; wildlife management; women's studies; zoology.

Academic Programs *Special study options:* academic remediation for entering students, adult/continuing education programs, advanced placement credit, cooperative education, distance learning, double majors, English as a second language, freshman honors college, honors programs, independent study, internships, off-campus study, part-time degree program, services for LD students, study abroad, summer session for credit. *ROTC:* Army (b).

Library Maureen and Mike Mansfield Library plus 2 others with 570,287 titles, 6,248 serial subscriptions, 118,190 audiovisual materials, an OPAC, a Web page.

Computers on Campus 545 computers available on campus for general student use. A campuswide network can be accessed from student residence rooms and from off campus. Internet access, online (class) registration, at least one staffed computer lab available.

Student Life *Housing:* on-campus residence required for freshman year. *Options:* coed, men-only, women-only, disabled students. *Activities and Organizations:* drama/theater group, student-run newspaper, radio and television station, choral group, marching band, Forestry Club, Honors Student Association, Campus Outdoor Program, International Organization, Kyio Indian Club, national fraternities, national sororities. *Campus security:* 24-hour emergency response devices and patrols, student patrols, late-night transport/escort service, controlled dormitory access. *Student Services:* health clinic, personal/psychological counseling, women's center, legal services.

Athletics Member NCAA. All Division I except football (Division I-AA). *Intercollegiate sports:* baseball M, basketball M(s)/W(s), cross-country running M(s)/W(s), golf W, ice hockey M, lacrosse M, skiing (downhill) M/W, soccer W, tennis M(s)/W(s), track and field M(s)/W(s), volleyball W(s). *Intramural sports:* archery M/W, badminton M/W, baseball M, basketball M/W, bowling M/W, cross-country running M/W, football M/W, golf M, ice hockey M, racquetball M/W, rugby M/W, skiing (cross-country) M/W, soccer W, softball M/W, swimming M/W, table tennis M/W, tennis M/W, track and field M/W, volleyball M/W, water polo M/W, weight lifting M/W.

Standardized Tests *Required:* SAT I or ACT (for admission).

Costs (2001–02) *Tuition:* state resident $2543 full-time, $106 per credit part-time; nonresident $8742 full-time, $364 per credit part-time. Full-time tuition and fees vary according to program and student level. Part-time tuition and fees vary according to course load and program. *Required fees:* $1099 full-time, $69 per credit. *Room and board:* $4890; room only: $2236. Room and board charges vary according to board plan and housing facility. *Payment plan:* installment. *Waivers:* minority students and senior citizens.

Financial Aid Of all full-time matriculated undergraduates who enrolled in 2001, 6108 applied for aid, 4508 were judged to have need, 1664 had their need fully met. *Average percent of need met:* 88%. *Average financial aid package:* $5976. *Average need-based loan:* $4324. *Average need-based gift aid:* $2871. *Average indebtedness upon graduation:* $15,611.

Applying *Options:* common application, electronic application, early admission, deferred entrance. *Application fee:* $30. *Required:* high school transcript, minimum 2.5 GPA. *Application deadline:* 7/1 (freshmen), rolling (transfers). *Notification:* continuous (freshmen).

Admissions Contact Office of New Student Services, The University of Montana-Missoula, Missoula, MT 59812-0002. *Phone:* 406-243-6266. *Toll-free phone:* 800-462-8636. *Fax:* 406-243-5711. *E-mail:* admiss@selway.umt.edu.

THE UNIVERSITY OF MONTANA-WESTERN
Dillon, Montana

- **State-supported** 4-year, founded 1893, part of Montana University System
- **Calendar** semesters
- **Degrees** associate and bachelor's
- **Small-town** 36-acre campus
- **Endowment** $5.0 million
- **Coed,** 1,163 undergraduate students, 77% full-time, 60% women, 40% men
- **Moderately difficult** entrance level, 100% of applicants were admitted

Undergraduates 891 full-time, 272 part-time. Students come from 26 states and territories, 2 other countries, 14% are from out of state, 0.4% African American, 1% Asian American or Pacific Islander, 2% Hispanic American, 3% Native American, 0.2% international, 8% transferred in, 27% live on campus.

Freshmen *Admission:* 278 applied, 278 admitted, 192 enrolled. *Average high school GPA:* 2.94. *Test scores:* SAT verbal scores over 500: 33%; SAT math scores over 500: 33%; ACT scores over 18: 74%; SAT verbal scores over 600: 6%; SAT math scores over 600: 6%; ACT scores over 24: 18%; SAT verbal scores over 700: 3%; SAT math scores over 700: 3%.

Faculty *Total:* 60, 78% full-time, 53% with terminal degrees. *Student/faculty ratio:* 17:1.

Majors Applied art; applied mathematics; art; art education; biology; business; business administration; business communications; business education; chemistry; computer/information sciences; data processing; data processing technology; early childhood education; education; education (K-12); elementary education; English; English education; environmental science; geology; health education; history education; human resources management; industrial arts; information sciences/systems; liberal arts and sciences/liberal studies; library science; literature; mathematics; mathematics education; music; music teacher education; physical education; physical sciences; pre-dentistry; pre-law; pre-medicine; pre-veterinary studies; science education; secondary education; secretarial science; social sciences; special education; theater arts/drama; tourism/travel marketing; travel/tourism management; wildlife management.

Academic Programs *Special study options:* academic remediation for entering students, accelerated degree program, adult/continuing education programs, advanced placement credit, cooperative education, double majors, honors programs, independent study, internships, off-campus study, part-time degree program, services for LD students, student-designed majors, summer session for credit.

Library Lucy Carson Memorial Library with 63,000 titles, 550 serial subscriptions, 10,000 audiovisual materials, an OPAC, a Web page.

Computers on Campus 75 computers available on campus for general student use. A campuswide network can be accessed from student residence rooms and from off campus. Internet access, at least one staffed computer lab available.

Student Life *Housing:* on-campus residence required for freshman year. *Options:* coed, men-only, women-only, disabled students. *Activities and Organizations:* drama/theater group, student-run newspaper, radio station, choral group, soccer, IGNU-Poetry Club, admissions volunteers, Rodeo Club, Chi Alpha-Christian Fellowship. *Campus security:* 24-hour emergency response devices and patrols, late-night transport/escort service. *Student Services:* personal/psychological counseling, legal services.

Athletics Member NAIA. *Intercollegiate sports:* basketball M(s)/W(s), football M(s), golf M(s)/W(s), volleyball W(s). *Intramural sports:* archery M(c)/W(c), basketball M/W, bowling M/W, equestrian sports M/W, football M/W, golf M/W, racquetball M/W, skiing (cross-country) M/W, skiing (downhill) M/W, soccer M/W, softball M/W, table tennis M/W, tennis M/W, volleyball M/W, weight lifting M/W, wrestling M.

Standardized Tests *Required:* SAT I or ACT (for admission).

Costs (2001–02) *Tuition:* state resident $2268 full-time, $94 per credit part-time; nonresident $8012 full-time, $334 per credit part-time. Full-time tuition and fees vary according to class time, course load, and reciprocity agreements. Part-time tuition and fees vary according to class time, course load, and reciprocity agreements. *Required fees:* $748 full-time, $96 per credit, $99 per term part-time. *Room and board:* $4220; room only: $1710. Room and board charges vary according to board plan and housing facility. *Payment plan:* deferred payment. *Waivers:* minority students, senior citizens, and employees or children of employees.

Financial Aid Of all full-time matriculated undergraduates who enrolled in 2001, 669 applied for aid, 611 were judged to have need. 207 Federal Work-Study jobs (averaging $1374). In 2001, 137 non-need-based awards were made. *Average financial aid package:* $5960. *Average need-based loan:* $3298. *Average need-based gift aid:* $1860. *Average non-need based aid:* $3543. *Average indebtedness upon graduation:* $20,433.

Applying *Options:* common application, electronic application, early admission, deferred entrance. *Application fee:* $30. *Required:* high school transcript, minimum 2.5 GPA. *Application deadlines:* 7/1 (freshmen), 7/1 (transfers). *Notification:* continuous (freshmen).

Admissions Contact Ms. Arlene Williams, Director of Admissions, The University of Montana-Western, 710 South Atlantic, Dillon, MT 59725. *Phone:* 406-683-7331. *Toll-free phone:* 866-UMW-MONT (in-state); 866-UMW-MONT (out-of-state). *Fax:* 406-683-7493. *E-mail:* admissions@wmwestern.edu.

NEBRASKA

BELLEVUE UNIVERSITY
Bellevue, Nebraska

- **Independent** comprehensive, founded 1965
- **Calendar** semesters
- **Degrees** bachelor's and master's
- **Suburban** 19-acre campus with easy access to Omaha
- **Endowment** $18.0 million
- **Coed,** 3,205 undergraduate students, 66% full-time, 50% women, 50% men
- **Noncompetitive** entrance level, 96% of applicants were admitted

Undergraduates 2,122 full-time, 1,083 part-time. Students come from 6 states and territories, 49 other countries, 15% are from out of state, 6% African American, 1% Asian American or Pacific Islander, 3% Hispanic American, 0.5% Native American, 10% international.

Freshmen *Admission:* 142 applied, 137 admitted, 218 enrolled.

Faculty *Total:* 140, 44% full-time, 27% with terminal degrees. *Student/faculty ratio:* 17:1.

Majors Accounting; art; business administration; business marketing and marketing management; criminal justice/law enforcement administration; English; environmental science; geography; graphic design/commercial art/illustration; health services administration; history; management information systems/business data processing; mathematics; philosophy; physical education; political science; psychology; social sciences; sociology; Spanish; urban studies.

Academic Programs *Special study options:* academic remediation for entering students, accelerated degree program, adult/continuing education programs, advanced placement credit, cooperative education, distance learning, double majors, English as a second language, external degree program, independent study, internships, part-time degree program, summer session for credit. *ROTC:* Army (c), Air Force (c).

Library Freeman/Lozier Library plus 1 other with 131,400 titles, 2,858 serial subscriptions, 3,314 audiovisual materials, an OPAC, a Web page.

Computers on Campus 377 computers available on campus for general student use. A campuswide network can be accessed from off campus. Internet access, online (class) registration, at least one staffed computer lab available.

Student Life *Housing:* college housing not available. *Activities and Organizations:* student-run newspaper. *Campus security:* 24-hour emergency response devices. *Student Services:* personal/psychological counseling, women's center.

Athletics Member NAIA. *Intercollegiate sports:* baseball M(s), basketball M(s), soccer M(s)/W, softball W(s), volleyball W(s). *Intramural sports:* basketball M/W, football M/W, golf M/W, racquetball M/W, volleyball M.

Standardized Tests *Required for some:* SAT I or ACT (for placement).

Costs (2001–02) *Tuition:* $4050 full-time, $135 per credit hour part-time. Full-time tuition and fees vary according to program. Part-time tuition and fees vary according to program. *Required fees:* $35 full-time, $35 per term part-time. *Payment plans:* installment, deferred payment. *Waivers:* employees or children of employees.

Financial Aid Of all full-time matriculated undergraduates who enrolled in 2001, 1785 applied for aid, 1785 were judged to have need. 51 Federal Work-Study jobs (averaging $1300). *Average need-based loan:* $7563. *Average need-based gift aid:* $2268.

Applying *Options:* deferred entrance. *Application fee:* $25. *Required:* high school transcript, interview. *Required for some:* 3 letters of recommendation. *Application deadline:* rolling (freshmen), rolling (transfers).

Admissions Contact Kelley Dengel, Information Center Manager, Bellevue University, 1000 Galvin Road South, Bellevue, NE 68005-3098. *Phone:* 402-293-3769. *Toll-free phone:* 800-756-7920. *Fax:* 402-293-2020. *E-mail:* set@scholars.bellevue.edu.

CHADRON STATE COLLEGE
Chadron, Nebraska

- **State-supported** comprehensive, founded 1911, part of Nebraska State College System
- **Calendar** semesters
- **Degrees** bachelor's, master's, and post-master's certificates
- **Small-town** 281-acre campus
- **Endowment** $7.4 million
- **Coed,** 2,394 undergraduate students, 73% full-time, 59% women, 41% men
- **Noncompetitive** entrance level, 100% of applicants were admitted

When most people think of Nebraska, they think about the cornfields of the Great Plains or the metropolitan area of Omaha. Students at Chadron State College (CSC) know there is more. Located among the forest and hills of northwest Nebraska, CSC is known for outstanding academics and recreational activities.

Undergraduates 1,741 full-time, 653 part-time. Students come from 31 states and territories, 10 other countries, 26% are from out of state, 0.9% African American, 0.4% Asian American or Pacific Islander, 2% Hispanic American, 1% Native American, 0.8% international, 5% transferred in, 65% live on campus. *Retention:* 78% of 2001 full-time freshmen returned.

Freshmen *Admission:* 754 applied, 754 admitted, 399 enrolled. *Average high school GPA:* 3.19. *Test scores:* SAT verbal scores over 500: 33%; SAT math scores over 500: 50%; ACT scores over 18: 81%; SAT math scores over 600: 17%; ACT scores over 24: 35%; ACT scores over 30: 3%.

Faculty *Total:* 120, 83% full-time, 61% with terminal degrees. *Student/faculty ratio:* 18:1.

Majors Art; art education; biology; biology education; business administration; business education; chemistry; chemistry education; criminal justice/corrections related; drama/dance education; elementary education; English; English education; family/consumer studies; health/medical preparatory programs related; history; history education; home economics education; industrial arts education; industrial production technologies related; information sciences/systems; interdisciplinary studies; library science; mathematics; mathematics education; middle school education; music; music teacher education; parks, recreation, leisure and fitness studies related; physical education; physics; physics education; psychology; range management; science education; secondary education; social science education; social work; sociology; Spanish; Spanish language education; special education; speech education; speech/rhetorical studies; teacher education, specific programs related; theater arts/drama.

Academic Programs *Special study options:* adult/continuing education programs, advanced placement credit, cooperative education, distance learning, double majors, freshman honors college, honors programs, independent study, internships, part-time degree program, services for LD students, student-designed majors, study abroad, summer session for credit.

Library Reta King Library with 129,660 titles, 5,596 audiovisual materials, an OPAC.

Computers on Campus 200 computers available on campus for general student use. A campuswide network can be accessed from student residence rooms and from off campus. Internet access, online (class) registration, at least one staffed computer lab available.

Student Life *Housing:* on-campus residence required for freshman year. *Options:* coed, men-only, women-only. *Activities and Organizations:* drama/theater group, student-run newspaper, radio station, choral group. *Campus security:* 24-hour emergency response devices and patrols, student patrols, late-night transport/escort service. *Student Services:* health clinic, personal/psychological counseling.

Athletics Member NCAA. All Division II. *Intercollegiate sports:* basketball M(s)/W(s), equestrian sports M(c)/W(c), football M(s), golf W(s), track and field M(s)/W(s), volleyball W(s), wrestling M(s). *Intramural sports:* badminton M/W, basketball M/W, bowling M/W, golf M/W, racquetball M/W, rugby M(c), soccer M/W, softball M/W, track and field M/W, volleyball M/W, wrestling M.

Standardized Tests *Recommended:* SAT I or ACT (for admission).

Costs (2001–02) *Tuition:* state resident $2093 full-time, $70 per credit hour part-time; nonresident $4185 full-time, $140 per credit hour part-time. Full-time

Chadron State College (continued)
tuition and fees vary according to course load. Part-time tuition and fees vary according to course load. *Required fees:* $388 full-time, $11 per credit hour, $15 per term part-time. *Room and board:* $3828; room only: $1644. Room and board charges vary according to board plan and housing facility. *Payment plan:* installment. *Waivers:* senior citizens and employees or children of employees.

Financial Aid Of all full-time matriculated undergraduates who enrolled in 2001, 1281 applied for aid, 959 were judged to have need. *Average financial aid package:* $2171. *Average need-based loan:* $1109. *Average need-based gift aid:* $1824. *Average indebtedness upon graduation:* $11,000.

Applying *Options:* early admission. *Application fee:* $15. *Required:* high school transcript, health forms. *Application deadline:* rolling (freshmen), rolling (transfers). *Notification:* continuous (freshmen).

Admissions Contact Ms. Tena Cook Gould, Director of Admissions, Chadron State College, 1000 Main Street, Chadron, NE 69337-2690. *Phone:* 308-432-6263. *Toll-free phone:* 800-242-3766. *Fax:* 308-432-6229. *E-mail:* inquire@csc1.csc.edu.

CLARKSON COLLEGE
Omaha, Nebraska

- **Independent** comprehensive, founded 1888, part of Nebraska Health System
- **Calendar** semesters
- **Degrees** certificates, associate, bachelor's, master's, and post-master's certificates
- **Urban** 3-acre campus
- **Endowment** $2.2 million
- **Coed, primarily women,** 354 undergraduate students, 58% full-time, 92% women, 8% men
- **Moderately difficult** entrance level, 82% of applicants were admitted

Clarkson College focuses on student success, providing valuable services such as counseling, tutoring, academic skill development, and career planning. The College offers associate degrees in occupational therapy assistant studies, physical therapist assistant studies, radiologic technology, and patient information management; bachelor's degrees in nursing, medical imaging, and health-care-related business; a master's degree in nursing; and a post-master's certificate in family nurse practitioner studies. Distance education opportunities are available.

Undergraduates 204 full-time, 150 part-time. Students come from 35 states and territories, 33% are from out of state, 6% African American, 0.3% Asian American or Pacific Islander, 3% Hispanic American, 0.3% Native American, 2% international, 24% transferred in, 20% live on campus. *Retention:* 80% of 2001 full-time freshmen returned.

Freshmen *Admission:* 238 applied, 195 admitted, 152 enrolled. *Average high school GPA:* 3.39. *Test scores:* ACT scores over 18: 93%; ACT scores over 24: 28%; ACT scores over 30: 6%.

Faculty *Total:* 42, 95% full-time, 33% with terminal degrees. *Student/faculty ratio:* 12:1.

Majors Business administration; nursing; nursing administration; nursing science; occupational therapy; physical therapy; radiological science.

Academic Programs *Special study options:* accelerated degree program, adult/continuing education programs, advanced placement credit, cooperative education, distance learning, double majors, external degree program, independent study, internships, part-time degree program, study abroad, summer session for credit. *ROTC:* Army (c), Air Force (c).

Library Clarkson College Library with 8,807 titles, 262 serial subscriptions, 530 audiovisual materials, an OPAC, a Web page.

Computers on Campus 40 computers available on campus for general student use. A campuswide network can be accessed from off campus. Internet access, at least one staffed computer lab available.

Student Life *Housing Options:* coed. *Activities and Organizations:* Clarkson Student Nurses Association, Clarkson Radiology Student Association, Student Government Association, Student Ambassadors, Clarkson Fellows Program. *Campus security:* 24-hour emergency response devices and patrols, late-night transport/escort service, controlled dormitory access. *Student Services:* health clinic, personal/psychological counseling.

Standardized Tests *Required for some:* SAT I or ACT (for admission).

Costs (2001–02) *Tuition:* $8970 full-time, $299 per credit hour part-time. *Required fees:* $408 full-time, $25 per credit. *Room only:* $2800. Room and board charges vary according to housing facility and location. *Payment plans:* installment, deferred payment. *Waivers:* employees or children of employees.

Financial Aid Of all full-time matriculated undergraduates who enrolled in 2001, 111 applied for aid, 84 were judged to have need. 40 Federal Work-Study jobs (averaging $2500). 40 State and other part-time jobs (averaging $2500). In 2001, 24 non-need-based awards were made. *Average need-based loan:* $2600. *Average need-based gift aid:* $3600. *Average non-need based aid:* $6300. *Average indebtedness upon graduation:* $20,000.

Applying *Options:* electronic application, deferred entrance. *Application fee:* $15. *Required:* essay or personal statement, high school transcript, minimum 2.5 GPA. *Required for some:* 2 letters of recommendation. *Recommended:* minimum 3.0 GPA. *Application deadline:* rolling (freshmen), rolling (transfers). *Notification:* continuous (freshmen).

Admissions Contact Mr. Tony Damewood, Dean of Enrollment Services, Clarkson College, 101 South 42nd Street, Omaha, NE 68131-2739. *Phone:* 402-552-3100. *Toll-free phone:* 800-647-5500. *Fax:* 402-552-6057. *E-mail:* admiss@clarksoncollege.edu.

COLLEGE OF SAINT MARY
Omaha, Nebraska

- **Independent Roman Catholic** 4-year, founded 1923
- **Calendar** semesters
- **Degrees** certificates, associate, and bachelor's
- **Suburban** 25-acre campus
- **Endowment** $6.2 million
- **Women only,** 930 undergraduate students, 59% full-time
- **Minimally difficult** entrance level, 68% of applicants were admitted

Undergraduates 549 full-time, 381 part-time. Students come from 6 states and territories, 5 other countries, 13% are from out of state, 6% African American, 0.8% Asian American or Pacific Islander, 3% Hispanic American, 0.6% Native American, 0.6% international, 17% transferred in, 37% live on campus. *Retention:* 68% of 2001 full-time freshmen returned.

Freshmen *Admission:* 80 enrolled. *Average high school GPA:* 3.28. *Test scores:* ACT scores over 18: 89%; ACT scores over 24: 32%; ACT scores over 30: 3%.

Faculty *Total:* 56, 64% full-time, 23% with terminal degrees. *Student/faculty ratio:* 10:1.

Majors Biology; business administration; business communications; chemistry; computer management; early childhood education; education; education (K-12); elementary education; English; humanities; human services; information sciences/systems; liberal arts and sciences/liberal studies; mathematics; medical records administration; medical technology; natural sciences; nursing; occupational therapy; paralegal/legal assistant; pre-dentistry; pre-law; pre-medicine; pre-veterinary studies; psychology; science education; secondary education; social sciences; special education; telecommunications.

Academic Programs *Special study options:* academic remediation for entering students, accelerated degree program, adult/continuing education programs, advanced placement credit, independent study, internships, part-time degree program, services for LD students, summer session for credit. *ROTC:* Army (c), Air Force (c).

Library College of Saint Mary Library with 63,088 titles, 12,675 serial subscriptions, 1,371 audiovisual materials, an OPAC, a Web page.

Computers on Campus 105 computers available on campus for general student use. A campuswide network can be accessed from student residence rooms. Internet access, online (class) registration, at least one staffed computer lab available.

Student Life *Housing:* on-campus residence required through sophomore year. *Options:* women-only. *Activities and Organizations:* choral group, Student Senate, Campus Faith Council, Student Nurses Association, Student Occupational Therapy Club, Student Ambassadors. *Campus security:* 24-hour emergency response devices and patrols, late-night transport/escort service, controlled dormitory access, external cameras at residence hall entrances. *Student Services:* personal/psychological counseling.

Athletics Member NAIA. *Intercollegiate sports:* basketball W(s), cross-country running W(s), golf W(s), soccer W(s), softball W(s), volleyball W(s). *Intramural sports:* badminton W, basketball W, football W, racquetball W, soccer W, softball W, tennis W, volleyball W, water polo W.

Standardized Tests *Required:* SAT I or ACT (for admission).

Costs (2001–02) *One-time required fee:* $25. *Comprehensive fee:* $18,726 includes full-time tuition ($13,750) and room and board ($4976). Part-time tuition: $385 per credit hour. Part-time tuition and fees vary according to class time. *Room and board:* Room and board charges vary according to housing facility. *Payment plans:* installment, deferred payment. *Waivers:* senior citizens and employees or children of employees.

Financial Aid Of all full-time matriculated undergraduates who enrolled in 2001, 483 applied for aid, 415 were judged to have need, 86 had their need fully met. In 2001, 105 non-need-based awards were made. *Average percent of need*

met: 71%. *Average financial aid package:* $10,071. *Average need-based loan:* $3790. *Average need-based gift aid:* $6736. *Average non-need based aid:* $7239. *Average indebtedness upon graduation:* $13,326.

Applying *Options:* common application, electronic application. *Application fee:* $25. *Required:* high school transcript, minimum 2.0 GPA. *Required for some:* minimum 3.0 GPA, 2 letters of recommendation, interview. *Recommended:* essay or personal statement. *Application deadline:* rolling (freshmen), rolling (transfers). *Notification:* continuous until 8/24 (freshmen).

Admissions Contact Natalie Vrbka, Senior Admissions Counselor, College of Saint Mary, 1901 South 72nd Street, Omaha, NE 68124-2377. *Phone:* 402-399-2405. *Toll-free phone:* 800-926-5534. *Fax:* 402-399-2412. *E-mail:* enroll@csm.edu.

CONCORDIA UNIVERSITY
Seward, Nebraska

- **Independent** comprehensive, founded 1894, affiliated with Lutheran Church-Missouri Synod, part of Concordia University System
- **Calendar** 4-4-1
- **Degrees** bachelor's and master's
- **Small-town** 120-acre campus with easy access to Omaha
- **Endowment** $18.8 million
- **Coed,** 1,288 undergraduate students, 95% full-time, 56% women, 44% men
- **Moderately difficult** entrance level, 93% of applicants were admitted

Undergraduates 1,221 full-time, 67 part-time. Students come from 37 states and territories, 58% are from out of state, 2% African American, 0.6% Asian American or Pacific Islander, 0.7% Hispanic American, 0.2% Native American, 6% transferred in, 77% live on campus. *Retention:* 80% of 2001 full-time freshmen returned.

Freshmen *Admission:* 674 applied, 628 admitted, 286 enrolled. *Average high school GPA:* 3.50.

Faculty *Total:* 128, 51% full-time, 55% with terminal degrees. *Student/faculty ratio:* 14:1.

Majors Accounting; art; art education; athletic training/sports medicine; behavioral sciences; biology; biology education; business; business administration; business education; chemistry; chemistry education; communications; computer education; computer/information sciences; computer science; early childhood education; education; elementary education; English; English education; exercise sciences; fine/studio arts; geography; German; graphic design/commercial art/illustration; health education; health/physical education; health services administration; history; history education; home economics; home economics education; industrial arts education; literature; management information systems/business data processing; mass communications; mathematics; mathematics education; medical laboratory technician; middle school education; music; music (piano and organ performance); music teacher education; music (voice and choral/opera performance); natural sciences; operations management; pastoral counseling; physical education; physical sciences; physics education; psychology; religious education; religious music; science education; secondary education; social science education; social sciences; sociology; Spanish; Spanish language education; special education; speech education; speech/rhetorical studies; sport/fitness administration; theater arts/drama; theology.

Academic Programs *Special study options:* academic remediation for entering students, accelerated degree program, adult/continuing education programs, advanced placement credit, cooperative education, distance learning, double majors, English as a second language, honors programs, independent study, internships, off-campus study, part-time degree program, services for LD students, study abroad, summer session for credit.

Library Link Library with 171,688 titles, 575 serial subscriptions, 12,068 audiovisual materials, an OPAC, a Web page.

Computers on Campus 75 computers available on campus for general student use. A campuswide network can be accessed from student residence rooms and from off campus. At least one staffed computer lab available.

Student Life *Housing:* on-campus residence required through senior year. *Options:* men-only, women-only, disabled students. *Activities and Organizations:* drama/theater group, student-run newspaper, choral group, Student Activities Council, musical groups, Men's and Women's C-Club, Student Senate, Concordia Youth Ministry. *Campus security:* 24-hour emergency response devices and patrols, controlled dormitory access. *Student Services:* health clinic, personal/psychological counseling.

Athletics Member NAIA. *Intercollegiate sports:* baseball M(s), basketball M(s)/W(s), cross-country running M(s)/W(s), football M(s), golf M(s)/W(s), soccer M(s)/W(s), softball W(s), tennis M(s)/W(s), track and field M(s)/W(s), volleyball W(s). *Intramural sports:* badminton M/W, basketball M/W, bowling M(c)/W(c), cross-country running M/W, soccer M/W, softball M/W, table tennis M/W, tennis M/W, volleyball M/W.

Standardized Tests *Required:* SAT I or ACT (for admission).

Costs (2002–03) *Comprehensive fee:* $18,934 includes full-time tuition ($14,546) and room and board ($4388). Part-time tuition: $409 per credit. Part-time tuition and fees vary according to course load. *Room and board:* Room and board charges vary according to board plan. *Payment plans:* installment, deferred payment. *Waivers:* employees or children of employees.

Financial Aid Of all full-time matriculated undergraduates who enrolled in 2001, 1266 applied for aid, 1023 were judged to have need, 835 had their need fully met. 216 Federal Work-Study jobs (averaging $629). 13 State and other part-time jobs (averaging $923). In 2001, 62 non-need-based awards were made. *Average percent of need met:* 73%. *Average financial aid package:* $13,132. *Average need-based loan:* $3502. *Average need-based gift aid:* $3946. *Average non-need based aid:* $6842. *Average indebtedness upon graduation:* $13,139.

Applying *Options:* electronic application, deferred entrance. *Application fee:* $15. *Required:* high school transcript. *Required for some:* letters of recommendation. *Recommended:* minimum 2.0 GPA, interview. *Application deadlines:* 8/1 (freshmen), 8/1 (transfers).

Admissions Contact Mr. Pete Kenow, Director of Admissions, Concordia University, 800 North Columbia Avenue, Seward, NE 68434-1599. *Phone:* 402-643-7233. *Toll-free phone:* 800-535-5494. *Fax:* 402-643-4073. *E-mail:* admiss@seward.ccsn.edu.

CREIGHTON UNIVERSITY
Omaha, Nebraska

- **Independent Roman Catholic (Jesuit)** university, founded 1878
- **Calendar** semesters
- **Degrees** certificates, associate, bachelor's, master's, doctoral, and first professional
- **Urban** 90-acre campus
- **Endowment** $207.9 million
- **Coed,** 3,679 undergraduate students, 89% full-time, 58% women, 42% men
- **Moderately difficult** entrance level, 90% of applicants were admitted

Undergraduates 3,268 full-time, 411 part-time. Students come from 41 states and territories, 64 other countries, 46% are from out of state, 3% African American, 9% Asian American or Pacific Islander, 3% Hispanic American, 1% Native American, 3% international, 1% transferred in, 48% live on campus. *Retention:* 85% of 2001 full-time freshmen returned.

Freshmen *Admission:* 2,605 applied, 2,348 admitted, 746 enrolled. *Average high school GPA:* 3.61. *Test scores:* SAT verbal scores over 500: 84%; SAT math scores over 500: 83%; ACT scores over 18: 99%; SAT verbal scores over 600: 37%; SAT math scores over 600: 41%; ACT scores over 24: 68%; SAT verbal scores over 700: 4%; SAT math scores over 700: 9%; ACT scores over 30: 12%.

Faculty *Total:* 886, 73% full-time. *Student/faculty ratio:* 14:1.

Majors Accounting; American studies; art; art education; art history; atmospheric sciences; biology; business economics; business marketing and marketing management; chemistry; classics; computer science; economics; education; education (K-12); elementary education; emergency medical technology; English; environmental science; exercise sciences; finance; French; German; graphic design/commercial art/illustration; Greek (modern); health services administration; history; international business; international relations; journalism; Latin (ancient and medieval); management information systems/business data processing; mass communications; mathematics; modern languages; music; nursing; philosophy; physics; political science; psychology; social work; sociology; Spanish; special education; speech/rhetorical studies; theater arts/drama; theology.

Academic Programs *Special study options:* academic remediation for entering students, accelerated degree program, adult/continuing education programs, advanced placement credit, double majors, English as a second language, honors programs, independent study, internships, off-campus study, part-time degree program, services for LD students, study abroad, summer session for credit. *ROTC:* Army (b), Air Force (c). *Unusual degree programs:* 3-2 engineering with Marquette University.

Library Reinert Alumni Memorial Library plus 2 others with 481,848 titles, 1,666 serial subscriptions, 2,500 audiovisual materials, an OPAC, a Web page.

Computers on Campus A campuswide network can be accessed from student residence rooms and from off campus that provide access to on-line grade information. Internet access, online (class) registration, at least one staffed computer lab available.

Student Life *Housing:* on-campus residence required through sophomore year. *Options:* coed, women-only, disabled students. *Activities and Organizations:* drama/theater group, student-run newspaper, radio and television station, choral group, Alpha Phi Omega, Student Education Association of Nebraska, Alpha Kappa Psi, Occupational Therapy Association, Knights of Columbus, national

Creighton University (continued)
fraternities, national sororities. *Campus security:* 24-hour emergency response devices and patrols, student patrols, late-night transport/escort service, controlled dormitory access. *Student Services:* health clinic, personal/psychological counseling, women's center, legal services.

Athletics Member NCAA. All Division I. *Intercollegiate sports:* baseball M(s), basketball M(s)/W(s), crew W(s), cross-country running M(s)/W(s), golf M(s)/W(s), soccer M(s)/W(s), softball W(s), tennis M(s)/W(s), volleyball W(s). *Intramural sports:* basketball M/W, bowling M/W, crew M(c), fencing M(c)/W(c), football M/W, racquetball M/W, rugby M(c), soccer M/W, softball M/W, table tennis M/W, tennis M/W, volleyball M/W, weight lifting M(c)/W(c).

Standardized Tests *Required:* SAT I or ACT (for admission).

Costs (2001–02) *Comprehensive fee:* $23,326 includes full-time tuition ($16,500), mandatory fees ($636), and room and board ($6190). Part-time tuition: $516 per credit. Part-time tuition and fees vary according to course load. *Required fees:* $53 per term part-time. *Room and board:* College room only: $3150. Room and board charges vary according to board plan and housing facility. *Payment plan:* installment. *Waivers:* adult students and employees or children of employees.

Financial Aid Of all full-time matriculated undergraduates who enrolled in 2001, 1926 applied for aid, 1550 were judged to have need, 696 had their need fully met. In 2001, 959 non-need-based awards were made. *Average percent of need met:* 88%. *Average financial aid package:* $13,695. *Average need-based loan:* $5210. *Average need-based gift aid:* $5390. *Average non-need based aid:* $8447. *Average indebtedness upon graduation:* $20,072.

Applying *Options:* electronic application, deferred entrance. *Application fee:* $40. *Required:* high school transcript, minimum 2.75 GPA, 1 letter of recommendation. *Recommended:* essay or personal statement. *Application deadline:* 8/1 (freshmen), rolling (transfers). *Notification:* continuous (freshmen).

Admissions Contact Mr. Dennis J. O'Driscoll, Director of Admissions, Creighton University, 2500 California Plaza, Omaha, NE 68178-0001. *Phone:* 402-280-2703. *Toll-free phone:* 800-282-5835. *Fax:* 402-280-2685. *E-mail:* admissions@creighton.edu.

DANA COLLEGE
Blair, Nebraska

- **Independent** 4-year, founded 1884, affiliated with Evangelical Lutheran Church in America
- **Calendar** 4-1-4
- **Degree** bachelor's
- **Small-town** 150-acre campus with easy access to Omaha
- **Endowment** $7.6 million
- **Coed,** 565 undergraduate students, 98% full-time, 46% women, 54% men
- **Moderately difficult** entrance level, 89% of applicants were admitted

Undergraduates 553 full-time, 12 part-time. Students come from 30 states and territories, 7 other countries, 47% are from out of state, 5% African American, 3% Asian American or Pacific Islander, 2% Hispanic American, 0.5% Native American, 2% international, 5% transferred in, 72% live on campus. *Retention:* 66% of 2001 full-time freshmen returned.

Freshmen *Admission:* 601 applied, 533 admitted, 156 enrolled. *Average high school GPA:* 3.30. *Test scores:* SAT verbal scores over 500: 40%; SAT math scores over 500: 43%; ACT scores over 18: 89%; SAT verbal scores over 600: 17%; SAT math scores over 600: 10%; ACT scores over 24: 36%; SAT verbal scores over 700: 7%; ACT scores over 30: 3%.

Faculty *Total:* 71, 63% full-time, 37% with terminal degrees. *Student/faculty ratio:* 10:1.

Majors Art; art education; biology; business administration; business education; chemistry; communications; computer science; drama/dance education; education; elementary education; English; English education; environmental science; foreign languages education; German; health/physical education; history; history education; interdisciplinary studies; mathematics; mathematics education; music; music teacher education; physical education; psychology; religious studies; science education; secondary education; social science education; social sciences; social work; sociology; Spanish; special education; speech education.

Academic Programs *Special study options:* accelerated degree program, adult/continuing education programs, advanced placement credit, double majors, English as a second language, honors programs, independent study, internships, off-campus study, part-time degree program, services for LD students, student-designed majors, study abroad, summer session for credit. *ROTC:* Army (c), Air Force (c).

Library C. A. Dana-Life Library plus 1 other with 197,080 titles, 8,743 serial subscriptions, 3,757 audiovisual materials, an OPAC, a Web page.

Computers on Campus 110 computers available on campus for general student use. A campuswide network can be accessed from student residence rooms and from off campus that provide access to student schedules, campus events, e-mail. Internet access, at least one staffed computer lab available.

Student Life *Housing:* on-campus residence required through junior year. *Options:* coed, women-only. *Activities and Organizations:* drama/theater group, student-run newspaper, radio and television station, choral group, Residence Hall Association, Social Awareness Organization, Fellowship of Christian Athletes, Campus Ministry, HOPE (Helping Our People Expand). *Campus security:* 24-hour emergency response devices and patrols, late-night transport/escort service, controlled dormitory access. *Student Services:* health clinic, personal/psychological counseling.

Athletics Member NAIA. *Intercollegiate sports:* baseball M(s), basketball M(s)/W(s), cross-country running M(s)/W(s), football M(s), soccer M(c)/W(s), softball W(s), track and field M(s)/W(s), volleyball W(s), wrestling M(s). *Intramural sports:* basketball M/W, football M/W, softball M/W, swimming M/W, table tennis M/W, volleyball M/W, weight lifting M/W.

Standardized Tests *Required:* SAT I or ACT (for admission). *Recommended:* ACT (for admission).

Costs (2001–02) *Comprehensive fee:* $18,362 includes full-time tuition ($13,400), mandatory fees ($550), and room and board ($4412). Part-time tuition: $420 per semester hour. Part-time tuition and fees vary according to course load. *Required fees:* $30 per term part-time. *Room and board:* College room only: $1722. Room and board charges vary according to board plan and housing facility. *Payment plans:* installment, deferred payment.

Financial Aid Of all full-time matriculated undergraduates who enrolled in 2001, 547 applied for aid, 447 were judged to have need, 157 had their need fully met. In 2001, 100 non-need-based awards were made. *Average percent of need met:* 91%. *Average financial aid package:* $13,061. *Average need-based loan:* $4205. *Average need-based gift aid:* $4067. *Average non-need based aid:* $4797. *Average indebtedness upon graduation:* $14,330.

Applying *Options:* electronic application, deferred entrance. *Application fee:* $20. *Required:* essay or personal statement, high school transcript, minimum 2.0 GPA, class rank. *Required for some:* 1 letter of recommendation, interview. *Application deadline:* rolling (freshmen). *Notification:* continuous (freshmen).

Admissions Contact Ms. Judy Mathiesen, Office Manager, Dana College, 2848 College Drive, Blair, NE 68008-1099. *Phone:* 402-426-7337. *Toll-free phone:* 800-444-3262. *Fax:* 402-426-7386. *E-mail:* admissions@acad2.dana.edu.

DOANE COLLEGE
Crete, Nebraska

- **Independent** comprehensive, founded 1872, affiliated with United Church of Christ
- **Calendar** 4-1-4
- **Degrees** bachelor's and master's (nontraditional undergraduate programs and graduate programs offered at Lincoln campus)
- **Small-town** 300-acre campus with easy access to Omaha
- **Endowment** $66.0 million
- **Coed,** 971 undergraduate students, 99% full-time, 50% women, 50% men
- **Moderately difficult** entrance level, 84% of applicants were admitted

Undergraduates 962 full-time, 9 part-time. Students come from 23 states and territories, 7 other countries, 17% are from out of state, 0.9% transferred in, 74% live on campus. *Retention:* 82% of 2001 full-time freshmen returned.

Freshmen *Admission:* 1,079 applied, 910 admitted, 235 enrolled. *Average high school GPA:* 3.34. *Test scores:* ACT scores over 18: 89%; ACT scores over 24: 34%; ACT scores over 30: 4%.

Faculty *Total:* 128, 55% full-time, 35% with terminal degrees. *Student/faculty ratio:* 12:1.

Majors Accounting; art; biology; business administration; business education; chemistry; communications; computer/information sciences; computer science; economics; elementary education; English; environmental science; French; German; health/physical education; history; human services; international relations; mass communications; mathematics; music; natural sciences; philosophy; physical education; physical sciences; physics; political science; psychology; public administration; public relations; religious studies; secondary education; social sciences; sociology; Spanish; special education; speech/rhetorical studies; teaching English as a second language; theater arts/drama.

Academic Programs *Special study options:* academic remediation for entering students, accelerated degree program, adult/continuing education programs, advanced placement credit, cooperative education, double majors, English as a second language, honors programs, independent study, internships, off-campus study, part-time degree program, student-designed majors, study abroad, summer session for credit. *ROTC:* Army (c), Air Force (c). *Unusual degree programs:* 3-2 engineering with Columbia University, Washington University in St. Louis; forestry with Duke University; environmental studies with Duke University.

Library Perkins Library with 247,952 titles, 3,500 serial subscriptions, 1,313 audiovisual materials, an OPAC, a Web page.

Computers on Campus 200 computers available on campus for general student use. A campuswide network can be accessed from student residence rooms and from off campus. Internet access, online (class) registration, at least one staffed computer lab available.

Student Life *Housing:* on-campus residence required through senior year. *Options:* coed. *Activities and Organizations:* drama/theater group, student-run newspaper, radio and television station, choral group, marching band, Greek society, Student Activities Council, Hansen Leadership Program, band/choir, Doane Ambassadors. *Campus security:* student patrols, evening patrols by trained security personnel. *Student Services:* health clinic, personal/psychological counseling.

Athletics Member NAIA. *Intercollegiate sports:* baseball M(s), basketball M(s)/W(s), cross-country running M(s)/W(s), football M(s), golf M(s)/W(s), soccer M(s)/W(s), softball W(s), tennis M/W, track and field M(s)/W(s), volleyball W(s). *Intramural sports:* baseball M(c)/W(c), basketball M/W, bowling M/W, football M/W, golf M/W, ice hockey M, racquetball M(c)/W(c), softball M/W, swimming M/W, table tennis M(c)/W(c), tennis M/W, volleyball M/W, water polo M/W.

Standardized Tests *Required:* SAT I or ACT (for admission).

Costs (2001–02) *Comprehensive fee:* $17,600 includes full-time tuition ($13,150), mandatory fees ($320), and room and board ($4130). Full-time tuition and fees vary according to location. Part-time tuition: $438 per credit hour. Part-time tuition and fees vary according to course load and location. *Required fees:* $125 per credit hour. *Room and board:* College room only: $1600. Room and board charges vary according to board plan, housing facility, and location. *Payment plan:* installment. *Waivers:* senior citizens and employees or children of employees.

Financial Aid Of all full-time matriculated undergraduates who enrolled in 2001, 855 applied for aid, 726 were judged to have need, 314 had their need fully met. 364 Federal Work-Study jobs (averaging $771). 155 State and other part-time jobs (averaging $516). In 2001, 222 non-need-based awards were made. *Average percent of need met:* 97%. *Average financial aid package:* $12,039. *Average need-based loan:* $3886. *Average need-based gift aid:* $7485. *Average indebtedness upon graduation:* $14,009.

Applying *Options:* electronic application, early admission, deferred entrance. *Application fee:* $15. *Required:* high school transcript, 2 letters of recommendation. *Required for some:* interview. *Recommended:* minimum 2.0 GPA. *Application deadline:* rolling (freshmen), rolling (transfers). *Notification:* continuous (freshmen).

Admissions Contact Mr. Dan Kunzman, Dean of Admissions, Doane College, Crete, NE 68333. *Phone:* 402-826-8222. *Toll-free phone:* 800-333-6263. *Fax:* 402-826-8600. *E-mail:* admissions@doane.edu.

GRACE UNIVERSITY

Omaha, Nebraska

- **Independent interdenominational** comprehensive, founded 1943
- **Calendar** semesters
- **Degrees** certificates, associate, bachelor's, and master's
- **Urban** 15-acre campus
- **Endowment** $555,996
- **Coed,** 519 undergraduate students, 74% full-time, 55% women, 45% men
- **Moderately difficult** entrance level, 50% of applicants were admitted

Undergraduates 385 full-time, 134 part-time. Students come from 29 states and territories, 39% are from out of state, 4% African American, 0.2% Asian American or Pacific Islander, 1% Hispanic American, 1% international, 9% transferred in, 67% live on campus. *Retention:* 68% of 2001 full-time freshmen returned.

Freshmen *Admission:* 355 applied, 176 admitted, 100 enrolled.

Faculty *Total:* 56, 34% full-time, 27% with terminal degrees. *Student/faculty ratio:* 18:1.

Majors Accounting; aircraft pilot (professional); American studies; aviation technology; biblical studies; broadcast journalism; business administration; communications; computer science; divinity/ministry; education (K-12); elementary education; European studies; humanities; human resources management; journalism; liberal arts and sciences/liberal studies; marriage/family counseling; mass communications; mathematics; middle school education; missionary studies; music; music teacher education; nursing; pastoral counseling; pre-theology; psychology; radio/television broadcasting; religious education; religious music; secondary education.

Academic Programs *Special study options:* accelerated degree program, adult/continuing education programs, advanced placement credit, cooperative education, distance learning, double majors, external degree program, independent study, internships, off-campus study, part-time degree program, services for LD students, student-designed majors, study abroad, summer session for credit. *ROTC:* Air Force (c). *Unusual degree programs:* 3-2 nursing with Clarkson College; social work with University of Nebraska at Omaha.

Library Grace University Library with 43,900 titles, 2,777 serial subscriptions, 3,882 audiovisual materials, an OPAC, a Web page.

Computers on Campus 45 computers available on campus for general student use. At least one staffed computer lab available.

Student Life *Housing:* on-campus residence required through senior year. *Options:* men-only, women-only. *Activities and Organizations:* drama/theater group, student-run newspaper, radio station, choral group, yearbook, drama. *Campus security:* late-night transport/escort service, controlled dormitory access. *Student Services:* health clinic, personal/psychological counseling.

Athletics Member NCCAA. *Intercollegiate sports:* basketball M/W, soccer M, volleyball W. *Intramural sports:* basketball M/W, volleyball M/W.

Standardized Tests *Required:* SAT I or ACT (for admission). *Recommended:* ACT (for admission).

Costs (2001–02) *Comprehensive fee:* $13,175 includes full-time tuition ($8550), mandatory fees ($625), and room and board ($4000). Part-time tuition: $285 per credit hour. Part-time tuition and fees vary according to course load. No tuition increase for student's term of enrollment. *Required fees:* $310 per term part-time. *Room and board:* Room and board charges vary according to board plan and housing facility. *Payment plan:* installment. *Waivers:* children of alumni, senior citizens, and employees or children of employees.

Financial Aid Of all full-time matriculated undergraduates who enrolled in 2001, 353 applied for aid, 325 were judged to have need, 45 had their need fully met. 37 Federal Work-Study jobs (averaging $1674). In 2001, 45 non-need-based awards were made. *Average percent of need met:* 58%. *Average financial aid package:* $6440. *Average need-based loan:* $3458. *Average need-based gift aid:* $3993.

Applying *Options:* electronic application, early admission, deferred entrance. *Application fee:* $35. *Required:* essay or personal statement, high school transcript, minimum 2.0 GPA, 3 letters of recommendation. *Required for some:* interview. *Application deadline:* rolling (freshmen), rolling (transfers).

Admissions Contact Mrs. Terri L. Dingfield, Director of Admissions, Grace University, 1311 South Ninth Street, Omaha, NE 68108. *Phone:* 402-449-2831. *Toll-free phone:* 800-383-1422. *Fax:* 402-341-9587. *E-mail:* admissions@graceuniversity.edu.

HASTINGS COLLEGE

Hastings, Nebraska

- **Independent Presbyterian** comprehensive, founded 1882
- **Calendar** 4-1-4
- **Degrees** bachelor's and master's
- **Small-town** 88-acre campus
- **Endowment** $53.8 million
- **Coed,** 1,067 undergraduate students, 97% full-time, 51% women, 49% men
- **Moderately difficult** entrance level, 90% of applicants were admitted

Undergraduates 1,037 full-time, 30 part-time. Students come from 25 states and territories, 10 other countries, 24% are from out of state, 1% African American, 0.4% Asian American or Pacific Islander, 2% Hispanic American, 0.8% Native American, 1% international, 5% transferred in, 55% live on campus. *Retention:* 76% of 2001 full-time freshmen returned.

Freshmen *Admission:* 1,065 applied, 955 admitted, 255 enrolled. *Average high school GPA:* 3.30. *Test scores:* SAT verbal scores over 500: 60%; SAT math scores over 500: 66%; ACT scores over 18: 99%; SAT verbal scores over 600: 27%; SAT math scores over 600: 17%; ACT scores over 24: 48%; SAT verbal scores over 700: 8%; SAT math scores over 700: 3%; ACT scores over 30: 7%.

Faculty *Total:* 110, 67% full-time, 55% with terminal degrees. *Student/faculty ratio:* 13:1.

Majors Accounting; advertising; art; art education; art history; biology; biology education; business administration; business education; business marketing and marketing management; chemistry; chemistry education; communication equipment technology; communications; computer/information sciences; computer science; creative writing; drama/dance education; economics; education; education (K-12); elementary education; English; English education; foreign languages

Hastings College (continued)
education; foreign languages/literatures; German; health/physical education; health services administration; history; history education; human resources management; human services; interdisciplinary studies; international economics; international relations; journalism; liberal arts and sciences/liberal studies; literature; mass communications; mathematics; mathematics education; modern languages; music; music history; music (piano and organ performance); music teacher education; music (voice and choral/opera performance); philosophy; physical education; physics; physics education; political science; pre-dentistry; pre-law; pre-medicine; pre-veterinary studies; psychology; public relations; radio/television broadcasting; religious studies; science education; secondary education; social science education; social studies education; sociology; Spanish; special education; speech education; speech/rhetorical studies; speech/theater education; sport/fitness administration; stringed instruments; theater arts/drama.

Academic Programs *Special study options:* adult/continuing education programs, advanced placement credit, double majors, independent study, internships, off-campus study, part-time degree program, services for LD students, student-designed majors, study abroad, summer session for credit. *Unusual degree programs:* 3-2 engineering with Columbia University, Georgia Institute of Technology, Washington University in St. Louis, University of Colorado at Boulder, Colorado State University; occupational therapy with Washington University in St. Louis, Boston University.

Library Perkins Library with 101,000 titles, 607 serial subscriptions, 714 audiovisual materials, an OPAC, a Web page.

Computers on Campus 152 computers available on campus for general student use. A campuswide network can be accessed from student residence rooms and from off campus that provide access to e-mail. Internet access, at least one staffed computer lab available.

Student Life *Housing:* on-campus residence required through sophomore year. *Options:* coed, men-only, women-only. *Activities and Organizations:* drama/theater group, student-run newspaper, radio and television station, choral group, marching band, Student Association, Public Relations Council, Fellowship of Christian Athletes, Phi Mu Alpha Sinfonia, Hastings College Singers. *Campus security:* 24-hour emergency response devices, student patrols, late-night transport/escort service, controlled dormitory access. *Student Services:* health clinic, personal/psychological counseling.

Athletics Member NAIA. *Intercollegiate sports:* baseball M(s), basketball M(s)/W(s), cross-country running M(s)/W(s), football M(s), golf M(s)/W(s), soccer M(s)/W(s), softball W(s), tennis M(s)/W(s), track and field M(s)/W(s), volleyball W(s). *Intramural sports:* basketball M/W, bowling M/W, football M/W, racquetball M/W, softball M/W, table tennis M/W, volleyball M/W.

Standardized Tests *Required:* SAT I or ACT (for admission).

Costs (2001–02) *Comprehensive fee:* $17,854 includes full-time tuition ($13,116), mandatory fees ($550), and room and board ($4188). Full-time tuition and fees vary according to degree level and program. Part-time tuition: $543 per semester hour. Part-time tuition and fees vary according to course load, degree level, and program. *Required fees:* $145 per term part-time. *Room and board:* College room only: $1766. Room and board charges vary according to board plan. *Payment plans:* installment, deferred payment. *Waivers:* adult students and employees or children of employees.

Financial Aid Of all full-time matriculated undergraduates who enrolled in 2001, 867 applied for aid, 735 were judged to have need, 197 had their need fully met. In 2001, 281 non-need-based awards were made. *Average percent of need met:* 79%. *Average financial aid package:* $11,224. *Average need-based loan:* $4193. *Average need-based gift aid:* $7572. *Average indebtedness upon graduation:* $15,778. *Financial aid deadline:* 9/1.

Applying *Options:* common application. *Application fee:* $20. *Required:* high school transcript, minimum 2.0 GPA, counselor's recommendation. *Required for some:* essay or personal statement, 2 letters of recommendation, interview. *Application deadline:* 8/1 (freshmen), rolling (transfers). *Notification:* continuous (freshmen).

Admissions Contact Mr. Michael Karloff, Director of Admissions, Hastings College, 800 North Turner Avenue, Hastings, NE 68901-7696. *Phone:* 402-461-7316. *Toll-free phone:* 800-532-7642. *Fax:* 402-461-7490. *E-mail:* admissions@hastings.edu.

MIDLAND LUTHERAN COLLEGE
Fremont, Nebraska

- **Independent Lutheran** 4-year, founded 1883
- **Calendar** 4-1-4
- **Degrees** associate and bachelor's
- **Small-town** 27-acre campus with easy access to Omaha
- **Endowment** $28.9 million
- **Coed,** 991 undergraduate students, 95% full-time, 57% women, 43% men
- **Moderately difficult** entrance level, 87% of applicants were admitted

Undergraduates 941 full-time, 50 part-time. Students come from 24 states and territories, 8 other countries, 23% are from out of state, 3% African American, 2% Asian American or Pacific Islander, 2% Hispanic American, 0.1% Native American, 0.8% international, 6% transferred in, 60% live on campus. *Retention:* 76% of 2001 full-time freshmen returned.

Freshmen *Admission:* 848 applied, 738 admitted, 288 enrolled. *Average high school GPA:* 3.35. *Test scores:* ACT scores over 18: 98%; ACT scores over 24: 41%; ACT scores over 30: 10%.

Faculty *Total:* 82, 70% full-time, 59% with terminal degrees. *Student/faculty ratio:* 15:1.

Majors Accounting; art; art education; athletic training/sports medicine; behavioral sciences; biological/physical sciences; biology; broadcast journalism; business administration; business education; business marketing and marketing management; chemistry; community services; computer programming; computer science; criminal justice/law enforcement administration; criminology; early childhood education; economics; education; education (K-12); elementary education; English; environmental science; history; humanities; human services; journalism; legal administrative assistant; liberal arts and sciences/liberal studies; management information systems/business data processing; mass communications; mathematics; medical administrative assistant; middle school education; music; music teacher education; natural sciences; nursing; physical education; physical sciences; pre-dentistry; pre-law; pre-medicine; pre-veterinary studies; psychology; recreation/leisure studies; religious studies; respiratory therapy; science education; secondary education; secretarial science; social sciences; sociology; speech/theater education; theater arts/drama; travel/tourism management.

Academic Programs *Special study options:* academic remediation for entering students, accelerated degree program, advanced placement credit, cooperative education, double majors, English as a second language, honors programs, independent study, internships, off-campus study, part-time degree program, services for LD students, student-designed majors, study abroad, summer session for credit.

Library Luther Library with 110,000 titles, 900 serial subscriptions, an OPAC, a Web page.

Computers on Campus 180 computers available on campus for general student use. A campuswide network can be accessed from student residence rooms and from off campus. Internet access, at least one staffed computer lab available.

Student Life *Housing:* on-campus residence required through sophomore year. *Options:* coed, men-only, women-only. *Activities and Organizations:* drama/theater group, student-run newspaper, Student Nurses Association, Student Education Association, Phi Beta Lambda, Fellowship of Christian Athletics (FCA), Circle K. *Campus security:* 24-hour emergency response devices, student patrols, late-night transport/escort service, controlled dormitory access. *Student Services:* health clinic, personal/psychological counseling.

Athletics Member NAIA. *Intercollegiate sports:* baseball M(s), basketball M(s)/W(s), cross-country running M(s)/W(s), football M(s), golf M(s)/W(s), soccer M(s)/W(s), softball W(s), tennis M(s)/W(s), track and field M(s)/W(s), volleyball W(s). *Intramural sports:* basketball M/W, football M, golf M/W, gymnastics M/W, racquetball M/W, soccer M/W, swimming M/W, tennis M/W, track and field M/W, volleyball M/W, weight lifting M.

Standardized Tests *Required:* SAT I or ACT (for admission).

Costs (2002–03) *Comprehensive fee:* $19,710 includes full-time tuition ($15,400) and room and board ($4310). Full-time tuition and fees vary according to course load. Part-time tuition: $625 per credit hour. Part-time tuition and fees vary according to course load. *Room and board:* Room and board charges vary according to board plan. *Payment plan:* installment. *Waivers:* senior citizens and employees or children of employees.

Financial Aid Of all full-time matriculated undergraduates who enrolled in 2001, 941 applied for aid, 777 were judged to have need, 374 had their need fully met. 203 Federal Work-Study jobs (averaging $1072). 148 State and other part-time jobs (averaging $1479). In 2001, 146 non-need-based awards were made. *Average percent of need met:* 99%. *Average financial aid package:* $13,621. *Average need-based loan:* $4836. *Average need-based gift aid:* $8188. *Average indebtedness upon graduation:* $18,558.

Applying *Options:* electronic application, early admission. *Application fee:* $30. *Required:* high school transcript. *Required for some:* interview. *Recommended:* essay or personal statement, minimum 3.0 GPA, letters of recommendation. *Application deadline:* rolling (freshmen), rolling (transfers). *Notification:* continuous until 9/1 (freshmen).

Admissions Contact Mr. John W. Klockentager, Vice President for Enrollment Management, Midland Lutheran College, Admissions Office, Fremont, NE 68025-

4200. *Phone:* 402-941-6508. *Toll-free phone:* 800-642-8382 Ext. 6501. *Fax:* 402-941-6513. *E-mail:* admissions@admin.mlc.edu.

NEBRASKA CHRISTIAN COLLEGE
Norfolk, Nebraska

- **Independent** 4-year, founded 1944, affiliated with Christian Churches and Churches of Christ
- **Calendar** semesters
- **Degrees** associate and bachelor's
- **Small-town** 85-acre campus
- **Endowment** $300,000
- **Coed,** 150 undergraduate students, 88% full-time, 50% women, 50% men
- **Minimally difficult** entrance level, 57% of applicants were admitted

Undergraduates Students come from 17 states and territories, 2 other countries, 0.7% African American, 0.7% Asian American or Pacific Islander, 2% Hispanic American, 0.7% Native American, 1% international, 85% live on campus. *Retention:* 63% of 2001 full-time freshmen returned.

Freshmen *Admission:* 145 applied, 82 admitted. *Test scores:* ACT scores over 18: 88%; ACT scores over 24: 54%.

Faculty *Total:* 13, 77% with terminal degrees. *Student/faculty ratio:* 12:1.

Majors Divinity/ministry; elementary education; pastoral counseling; religious education; religious music; religious studies; secondary education; secretarial science; sign language interpretation; theology.

Academic Programs *Special study options:* internships, off-campus study, part-time degree program.

Library Swedberg Library with 250,000 titles, 149 serial subscriptions.

Computers on Campus 10 computers available on campus for general student use. Internet access, at least one staffed computer lab available.

Student Life *Housing:* on-campus residence required through junior year. *Activities and Organizations:* drama/theater group, student-run newspaper, choral group. *Student Services:* health clinic, personal/psychological counseling.

Athletics Member NCCAA. *Intercollegiate sports:* basketball M/W, soccer M, volleyball W. *Intramural sports:* basketball M/W, soccer M, volleyball M/W.

Standardized Tests *Required:* ACT (for admission).

Costs (2001–02) *Comprehensive fee:* $8760 includes full-time tuition ($4950), mandatory fees ($450), and room and board ($3360). Part-time tuition: $165 per credit. Part-time tuition and fees vary according to course load. *Required fees:* $123 per term part-time. *Payment plan:* installment. *Waivers:* employees or children of employees.

Financial Aid Of all full-time matriculated undergraduates who enrolled in 2001, 126 applied for aid, 126 were judged to have need. 14 Federal Work-Study jobs (averaging $1607). *Average need-based loan:* $3800.

Applying *Application fee:* $25. *Required:* high school transcript, 2 letters of recommendation. *Required for some:* interview. *Application deadline:* rolling (freshmen), rolling (transfers). *Notification:* continuous until 9/1 (freshmen).

Admissions Contact Mr. Jason Epperso, Associate Director of Admissions, Nebraska Christian College, 1800 Syracuse Avenue, Norfolk, NE 68701-2458. *Phone:* 402-378-5000 Ext. 413. *Fax:* 402-379-5100. *E-mail:* admissions@nechristian.edu.

NEBRASKA METHODIST COLLEGE
Omaha, Nebraska

- **Independent** comprehensive, founded 1891, affiliated with United Methodist Church
- **Calendar** semesters
- **Degrees** certificates, associate, bachelor's, master's, and post-master's certificates
- **Urban** 5-acre campus
- **Endowment** $30.2 million
- **Coed,** 347 undergraduate students, 62% full-time, 90% women, 10% men
- **Moderately difficult** entrance level, 93% of applicants were admitted

Undergraduates Students come from 7 states and territories, 1 other country, 20% are from out of state, 5% African American, 0.6% Asian American or Pacific Islander, 2% Hispanic American, 0.3% international, 20% live on campus. *Retention:* 72% of 2001 full-time freshmen returned.

Freshmen *Admission:* 30 applied, 28 admitted. *Average high school GPA:* 3.40. *Test scores:* ACT scores over 18: 90%; ACT scores over 24: 15%.

Faculty *Total:* 40, 70% full-time, 20% with terminal degrees. *Student/faculty ratio:* 10:1.

Majors Cardiovascular technology; diagnostic medical sonography; emergency medical technology; nursing; respiratory therapy.

Academic Programs *Special study options:* academic remediation for entering students, accelerated degree program, advanced placement credit, distance learning, independent study, internships, services for LD students, summer session for credit. *ROTC:* Army (c).

Library John Moritz Library plus 1 other with 8,656 titles, 468 serial subscriptions, 964 audiovisual materials.

Computers on Campus 45 computers available on campus for general student use. Internet access, at least one staffed computer lab available.

Student Life *Housing Options:* coed. *Activities and Organizations:* Student Senate, Student Nurses Association, Methodist Allied Health Student Association, Student Ambassadors, PRIDE. *Campus security:* 24-hour emergency response devices, late-night transport/escort service, controlled dormitory access. *Student Services:* health clinic, personal/psychological counseling.

Standardized Tests *Required:* SAT I or ACT (for admission).

Costs (2001–02) *Tuition:* $9000 full-time, $200 per credit hour part-time. *Required fees:* $600 full-time, $20 per credit hour. *Room only:* $1560. Room and board charges vary according to housing facility and location. *Payment plan:* installment. *Waivers:* employees or children of employees.

Financial Aid Of all full-time matriculated undergraduates who enrolled in 2001, 175 applied for aid, 144 were judged to have need, 37 had their need fully met. 1 State and other part-time jobs (averaging $1600). In 2001, 32 non-need-based awards were made. *Average percent of need met:* 74%. *Average financial aid package:* $7672. *Average need-based gift aid:* $4876. *Average indebtedness upon graduation:* $17,345.

Applying *Options:* deferred entrance. *Application fee:* $25. *Required:* essay or personal statement, high school transcript, minimum 2.0 GPA, 3 letters of recommendation, interview. *Application deadlines:* 4/1 (freshmen), 4/1 (transfers). *Notification:* 4/15 (freshmen).

Admissions Contact Ms. Deann Sterner, Director of Admissions, Nebraska Methodist College, Omaha, NE 68114. *Phone:* 402-354-4922. *Toll-free phone:* 800-335-5510. *Fax:* 402-354-8875. *E-mail:* dsterne@methodistcollege.edu.

NEBRASKA WESLEYAN UNIVERSITY
Lincoln, Nebraska

- **Independent United Methodist** comprehensive, founded 1887
- **Calendar** semesters
- **Degrees** certificates, bachelor's, and master's
- **Suburban** 50-acre campus with easy access to Omaha
- **Endowment** $32.6 million
- **Coed,** 1,621 undergraduate students, 91% full-time, 57% women, 43% men
- **Moderately difficult** entrance level, 93% of applicants were admitted

Undergraduates 1,474 full-time, 147 part-time. Students come from 22 states and territories, 6% are from out of state, 1% African American, 2% Asian American or Pacific Islander, 1% Hispanic American, 0.1% Native American, 3% transferred in, 52% live on campus. *Retention:* 84% of 2001 full-time freshmen returned.

Freshmen *Admission:* 1,128 applied, 1,045 admitted, 392 enrolled. *Test scores:* ACT scores over 18: 99%; ACT scores over 24: 57%; ACT scores over 30: 5%.

Faculty *Total:* 164, 60% full-time, 65% with terminal degrees. *Student/faculty ratio:* 13:1.

Majors Art; athletic training/sports medicine; biochemistry; biological/physical sciences; biology; biopsychology; business administration; business management/administrative services related; chemistry; communications; computer science; economics; elementary education; English; English related; exercise sciences; French; German; history; information sciences/systems; interdisciplinary studies; international business; international relations; mathematics; middle school education; music; music (general performance); music teacher education; nursing administration; organizational psychology; peace/conflict studies; philosophy; physical education; physics; political science; political science/government related; psychology; religious studies; science education; social sciences and history related; social work; sociology; Spanish; special education; speech/rhetorical studies; sport/fitness administration; theater arts/drama; theater arts/drama and stagecraft related; Web/multimedia management/webmaster; women's studies.

Academic Programs *Special study options:* adult/continuing education programs, advanced placement credit, double majors, independent study, internships, off-campus study, part-time degree program, services for LD students, study abroad, summer session for credit. *ROTC:* Army (c), Air Force (c). *Unusual degree programs:* 3-2 engineering with Washington University in St. Louis, Columbia University, University of Nebraska-Lincoln; physical therapy with University of Nebraska Medical Center, Mayo Medical School.

Nebraska Wesleyan University (continued)

Library Cochrane Woods Library with 178,531 titles, 743 serial subscriptions, 7,951 audiovisual materials, an OPAC, a Web page.

Computers on Campus 204 computers available on campus for general student use. A campuswide network can be accessed from student residence rooms and from off campus. Internet access, at least one staffed computer lab available.

Student Life *Housing:* on-campus residence required through sophomore year. *Options:* coed, women-only. *Activities and Organizations:* drama/theater group, student-run newspaper, choral group, Student Affairs Senate, Union programs, Ambassadors, FCA, national fraternities, national sororities. *Campus security:* 24-hour emergency response devices, late-night transport/escort service, controlled dormitory access. *Student Services:* health clinic, personal/psychological counseling, women's center.

Athletics Member NCAA, NAIA. All NCAA Division III. *Intercollegiate sports:* baseball M, basketball M/W, cross-country running M/W, football M, golf M/W, soccer M/W, softball W, tennis M/W, track and field M/W, volleyball W. *Intramural sports:* basketball M/W, bowling M/W, football M/W, soccer M/W, softball M/W, volleyball M/W.

Standardized Tests *Required:* SAT I or ACT (for admission).

Costs (2001–02) *One-time required fee:* $80. *Comprehensive fee:* $18,767 includes full-time tuition ($14,380), mandatory fees ($261), and room and board ($4126). Part-time tuition: $533 per hour. Part-time tuition and fees vary according to class time and course load. *Room and board:* Room and board charges vary according to board plan. *Payment plan:* installment. *Waivers:* adult students, senior citizens, and employees or children of employees.

Financial Aid Of all full-time matriculated undergraduates who enrolled in 2001, 1135 applied for aid, 1011 were judged to have need, 121 had their need fully met. In 2001, 363 non-need-based awards were made. *Average percent of need met:* 77%. *Average financial aid package:* $11,252. *Average need-based loan:* $4219. *Average need-based gift aid:* $7776. *Average indebtedness upon graduation:* $16,130.

Applying *Options:* common application, electronic application, early admission, early decision, deferred entrance. *Application fee:* $20. *Required:* high school transcript, minimum 2.0 GPA. *Required for some:* essay or personal statement, resume of activities. *Recommended:* interview. *Application deadline:* 5/1 (freshmen), rolling (transfers). *Early decision:* 11/15. *Notification:* continuous (freshmen), 12/15 (early decision).

Admissions Contact Mr. Kendal E. Sieg, Director of Admissions, Nebraska Wesleyan University, 5000 Saint Paul Avenue, Lincoln, NE 68504. *Phone:* 402-465-2218. *Toll-free phone:* 800-541-3818. *Fax:* 402-465-2179. *E-mail:* admissions@nebrwesleyan.edu.

PERU STATE COLLEGE
Peru, Nebraska

- **State-supported** comprehensive, founded 1867, part of Nebraska State College System
- **Calendar** semesters
- **Degrees** bachelor's and master's
- **Rural** 103-acre campus
- **Coed,** 1,450 undergraduate students, 61% full-time, 54% women, 46% men
- **Noncompetitive** entrance level, 73% of applicants were admitted

Undergraduates 878 full-time, 572 part-time. Students come from 28 states and territories, 3 other countries, 14% are from out of state, 2% African American, 1.0% Asian American or Pacific Islander, 2% Hispanic American, 0.3% Native American, 1.0% international, 12% transferred in. *Retention:* 53% of 2001 full-time freshmen returned.

Freshmen *Admission:* 497 applied, 365 admitted, 187 enrolled. *Average high school GPA:* 2.89. *Test scores:* ACT scores over 18: 64%; ACT scores over 24: 21%; ACT scores over 30: 1%.

Faculty *Total:* 120, 33% full-time. *Student/faculty ratio:* 16:1.

Majors Accounting; applied art; art; art education; biological/physical sciences; biology; business administration; business marketing and marketing management; chemistry; computer science; criminal justice/law enforcement administration; early childhood education; education; elementary education; English; graphic design/commercial art/illustration; health education; history; management information systems/business data processing; mathematics; medical technology; middle school education; music; music business management/merchandising; music teacher education; music (voice and choral/opera performance); natural resources conservation; natural sciences; nuclear medical technology; physical education; physical sciences; physician assistant; pre-dentistry; pre-law; premedicine; pre-veterinary studies; psychology; science education; secondary education; social sciences; sociology; special education; wildlife management; wind/percussion instruments.

Academic Programs *Special study options:* academic remediation for entering students, adult/continuing education programs, advanced placement credit, cooperative education, external degree program, freshman honors college, honors programs, internships, off-campus study, part-time degree program, services for LD students.

Library Peru State College Library with 177,373 titles, 232 serial subscriptions, a Web page.

Computers on Campus 120 computers available on campus for general student use. A campuswide network can be accessed from student residence rooms. Internet access, at least one staffed computer lab available.

Student Life *Housing:* on-campus residence required through sophomore year. *Options:* coed, men-only, women-only. *Activities and Organizations:* drama/theater group, student-run newspaper, choral group, marching band, Peru Chorus, Campus Activities Board, marching band, student government, Peru Players. *Campus security:* 24-hour patrols. *Student Services:* health clinic, personal/psychological counseling.

Athletics Member NAIA. *Intercollegiate sports:* baseball M(s), basketball M(s)/W(s), football M(s), softball W(s), volleyball W(s). *Intramural sports:* basketball M/W, bowling M/W, football M/W, softball M/W, swimming M/W, table tennis M/W, volleyball M/W, weight lifting M/W.

Standardized Tests *Required for some:* SAT I or ACT (for admission).

Costs (2001–02) *Tuition:* state resident $2093 full-time, $70 per semester hour part-time; nonresident $4185 full-time, $140 per semester hour part-time. Full-time tuition and fees vary according to course load, location, and reciprocity agreements. Part-time tuition and fees vary according to course load, location, and reciprocity agreements. *Required fees:* $453 full-time. *Room and board:* $3796; room only: $1910. Room and board charges vary according to board plan and housing facility. *Payment plan:* deferred payment. *Waivers:* employees or children of employees.

Financial Aid Of all full-time matriculated undergraduates who enrolled in 2001, 100 Federal Work-Study jobs (averaging $1260). *Average indebtedness upon graduation:* $16,251.

Applying *Options:* common application, early admission, deferred entrance. *Application fee:* $10. *Required:* high school transcript. *Required for some:* minimum 2.0 GPA, letters of recommendation. *Application deadline:* rolling (freshmen), rolling (transfers). *Notification:* continuous (freshmen).

Admissions Contact Ms. Janelle Moran, Director of Recruitment and Admissions, Peru State College, PO Box 10, Peru, NE 68421. *Phone:* 402-872-2221. *Toll-free phone:* 800-742-4412. *Fax:* 402-872-2296. *E-mail:* jmoran@oakmail.peru.edu.

UNION COLLEGE
Lincoln, Nebraska

- **Independent Seventh-day Adventist** 4-year, founded 1891
- **Calendar** semesters
- **Degrees** associate and bachelor's
- **Suburban** 26-acre campus with easy access to Omaha
- **Endowment** $6.4 million
- **Coed,** 992 undergraduate students, 78% full-time, 55% women, 45% men
- **Moderately difficult** entrance level, 58% of applicants were admitted

Undergraduates 778 full-time, 214 part-time. Students come from 44 states and territories, 34 other countries, 80% are from out of state, 2% African American, 2% Asian American or Pacific Islander, 4% Hispanic American, 1% Native American, 15% international, 7% transferred in, 69% live on campus. *Retention:* 69% of 2001 full-time freshmen returned.

Freshmen *Admission:* 555 applied, 321 admitted, 298 enrolled. *Average high school GPA:* 3.43. *Test scores:* ACT scores over 18: 89%; ACT scores over 24: 47%; ACT scores over 30: 8%.

Faculty *Total:* 100, 54% full-time, 28% with terminal degrees. *Student/faculty ratio:* 14:1.

Majors Accounting; art education; biochemistry; biology; biology education; business administration; business education; chemistry; chemistry education; computer education; computer science; education; elementary education; engineering; English; English education; enterprise management; fine/studio arts; French; German; graphic design/commercial art/illustration; health science; history; history education; information sciences/systems; international relations; journalism; mathematics; mathematics education; medical technology; music; music (general performance); music teacher education; nursing; office management; pastoral counseling; physical education; physician assistant; physics; physics education; psychology; public relations; religious education; religious studies; secondary education; social science education; social sciences; social work; Spanish; sport/fitness administration; theology.

Academic Programs *Special study options:* accelerated degree program, adult/continuing education programs, advanced placement credit, cooperative education, double majors, English as a second language, honors programs, independent study, internships, off-campus study, part-time degree program, services for LD students, student-designed majors, study abroad, summer session for credit.

Library Ella Johnson Crandall Library with 150,032 titles, 4,048 audiovisual materials, an OPAC, a Web page.

Computers on Campus 520 computers available on campus for general student use. A campuswide network can be accessed from student residence rooms and from off campus. At least one staffed computer lab available.

Student Life *Housing:* on-campus residence required through senior year. *Options:* men-only, women-only. *Activities and Organizations:* drama/theater group, student-run newspaper, choral group. *Campus security:* 24-hour emergency response devices, student patrols, late-night transport/escort service. *Student Services:* health clinic, personal/psychological counseling.

Athletics *Intercollegiate sports:* basketball M/W. *Intramural sports:* badminton M/W, baseball M/W, basketball M/W, football M/W, golf M/W, gymnastics M/W, racquetball M/W, sailing M/W, soccer M/W, softball M/W, swimming M/W, tennis M/W, volleyball M/W.

Standardized Tests *Required:* ACT (for admission).

Costs (2001–02) *Comprehensive fee:* $14,764 includes full-time tuition ($11,390), mandatory fees ($114), and room and board ($3260). Full-time tuition and fees vary according to course load. Part-time tuition: $475 per semester hour. *Room and board:* College room only: $2240. *Payment plans:* tuition prepayment, installment. *Waivers:* senior citizens and employees or children of employees.

Financial Aid Of all full-time matriculated undergraduates who enrolled in 2001, 523 applied for aid, 523 were judged to have need, 64 had their need fully met. 145 Federal Work-Study jobs (averaging $2000). In 2001, 308 non-need-based awards were made. *Average percent of need met:* 42%. *Average financial aid package:* $8015. *Average need-based loan:* $3701. *Average need-based gift aid:* $5170. *Average non-need based aid:* $3099. *Average indebtedness upon graduation:* $23,937.

Applying *Options:* common application, electronic application. *Required:* high school transcript, minimum 2.5 GPA, 3 letters of recommendation. *Required for some:* interview. *Recommended:* essay or personal statement. *Application deadline:* rolling (freshmen), rolling (transfers). *Notification:* continuous (freshmen).

Admissions Contact Huda McClelland, Director of Admissions, Union College, Lincoln, NE 68516. *Phone:* 402-486-2504. *Toll-free phone:* 800-228-4600. *Fax:* 402-486-2895. *E-mail:* ucenrol@ucollege.edu.

UNIVERSITY OF NEBRASKA AT KEARNEY
Kearney, Nebraska

- **State-supported** comprehensive, founded 1903, part of University of Nebraska System
- **Calendar** semesters
- **Degrees** bachelor's, master's, and post-master's certificates
- **Small-town** 235-acre campus
- **Coed,** 5,407 undergraduate students, 88% full-time, 55% women, 45% men
- **Moderately difficult** entrance level, 96% of applicants were admitted

Undergraduates 4,762 full-time, 645 part-time. Students come from 38 states and territories, 46 other countries, 6% are from out of state, 0.9% African American, 0.3% Asian American or Pacific Islander, 2% Hispanic American, 0.3% Native American, 5% international, 6% transferred in, 33% live on campus. *Retention:* 77% of 2001 full-time freshmen returned.

Freshmen *Admission:* 2,554 applied, 2,457 admitted, 1,197 enrolled. *Average high school GPA:* 3.36. *Test scores:* ACT scores over 18: 91%; ACT scores over 24: 34%; ACT scores over 30: 3%.

Faculty *Total:* 398, 78% full-time. *Student/faculty ratio:* 16:1.

Majors Adapted physical education; agricultural business; art; aviation management; biology; business administration; business education; chemistry; communication disorders; computer/information sciences; criminal justice studies; dietetics; economics; elementary education; English; family/consumer studies; French; general studies; geography; German; history; international relations; journalism; mass communications; mathematical statistics; mathematics; music; operations management; physical education; physics; political science; psychology; recreation/leisure studies; social work; sociology; Spanish; special education; speech/rhetorical studies; sport/fitness administration; technical education; theater arts/drama.

Academic Programs *Special study options:* academic remediation for entering students, advanced placement credit, cooperative education, distance learning, double majors, English as a second language, honors programs, independent study, internships, off-campus study, part-time degree program, services for LD students, study abroad, summer session for credit.

Library Calvin T. Ryan Library with 320,915 titles, 1,657 serial subscriptions, 75,881 audiovisual materials, an OPAC, a Web page.

Computers on Campus 277 computers available on campus for general student use. A campuswide network can be accessed from student residence rooms and from off campus that provide access to online grade reports. Internet access, online (class) registration, at least one staffed computer lab available.

Student Life *Housing:* on-campus residence required for freshman year. *Options:* coed, men-only, women-only. *Activities and Organizations:* drama/theater group, student-run newspaper, radio and television station, choral group, marching band, Student Activities Council, Intramurals Council, Residence Hall Association, International Student Association, Panhellenic/Interfraternity Council, national fraternities, national sororities. *Campus security:* 24-hour emergency response devices and patrols, late-night transport/escort service. *Student Services:* health clinic, personal/psychological counseling.

Athletics Member NCAA. All Division II except softball (Division III). *Intercollegiate sports:* baseball M(s), basketball M(s)/W(s), cross-country running M(s)/W(s), football M(s), golf M(s)/W(s), softball W(s), swimming W(s), tennis M(s)/W(s), track and field M(s)/W(s), volleyball W(s), wrestling M(s). *Intramural sports:* badminton M/W, basketball M/W, cross-country running M/W, football M/W, golf M/W, racquetball M/W, soccer M/W, softball M/W, tennis M/W, volleyball M/W, water polo M/W, wrestling M/W.

Standardized Tests *Required:* SAT I or ACT (for admission). *Recommended:* ACT (for admission).

Costs (2001–02) *Tuition:* state resident $2468 full-time, $82 per semester hour part-time; nonresident $4823 full-time, $161 per semester hour part-time. Full-time tuition and fees vary according to course load, reciprocity agreements, and student level. Part-time tuition and fees vary according to course load, reciprocity agreements, and student level. *Required fees:* $638 full-time, $6 per semester hour, $7 per term part-time. *Room and board:* $3902; room only: $2016. Room and board charges vary according to board plan and housing facility. *Payment plan:* installment. *Waivers:* employees or children of employees.

Financial Aid Of all full-time matriculated undergraduates who enrolled in 2001, 3380 applied for aid, 2708 were judged to have need, 1038 had their need fully met. *Average percent of need met:* 82%. *Average financial aid package:* $5075. *Average need-based loan:* $2945. *Average need-based gift aid:* $2389. *Average indebtedness upon graduation:* $14,775.

Applying *Options:* electronic application. *Application fee:* $25. *Required:* high school transcript. *Required for some:* 3 letters of recommendation. *Application deadlines:* 8/1 (freshmen), 8/1 (transfers). *Notification:* continuous (freshmen).

Admissions Contact Mr. John Kundel, Director of Admissions, University of Nebraska at Kearney, 905 West 25th Street, Kearney, NE 68849-0001. *Phone:* 308-865-8702. *Toll-free phone:* 800-532-7639. *Fax:* 308-865-8987. *E-mail:* admissionsug@unk.edu.

UNIVERSITY OF NEBRASKA AT OMAHA
Omaha, Nebraska

- **State-supported** university, founded 1908, part of University of Nebraska System
- **Calendar** semesters
- **Degrees** associate, bachelor's, master's, doctoral, post-master's, and postbachelor's certificates
- **Urban** 88-acre campus
- **Endowment** $6.3 million
- **Coed,** 11,138 undergraduate students, 71% full-time, 54% women, 46% men
- **Minimally difficult** entrance level, 86% of applicants were admitted

Undergraduates 7,906 full-time, 3,232 part-time. Students come from 45 states and territories, 72 other countries, 8% are from out of state, 6% African American, 2% Asian American or Pacific Islander, 3% Hispanic American, 0.4% Native American, 3% international, 10% transferred in, 5% live on campus. *Retention:* 72% of 2001 full-time freshmen returned.

Freshmen *Admission:* 4,121 applied, 3,527 admitted, 1,726 enrolled. *Average high school GPA:* 3.04. *Test scores:* ACT scores over 18: 89%; ACT scores over 24: 30%; ACT scores over 30: 4%.

Faculty *Total:* 871, 57% full-time, 55% with terminal degrees. *Student/faculty ratio:* 17:1.

Majors Accounting; advertising; African-American studies; art; art history; aviation management; banking; biological/physical sciences; biological technology; biology; biotechnology research; broadcast journalism; business economics; business marketing and marketing management; chemistry; communications; computer/information sciences; computer science; creative writing; criminal

University of Nebraska at Omaha (continued)
justice/law enforcement administration; criminal justice studies; drafting; earth sciences; economics; education; education administration; educational media design; education of the emotionally handicapped; education of the hearing impaired; elementary education; English; enterprise management; environmental biology; fashion merchandising; finance; fine/studio arts; French; general studies; geography; geology; German; gerontology; health education; history; human resources management; information sciences/systems; interdisciplinary studies; interior design; international relations; journalism; library science; management information systems/business data processing; marketing research; mass communications; mathematics; music; music teacher education; music (voice and choral/opera performance); operations management; paralegal/legal assistant; philosophy; physical education; physics; political science; pre-law; pre-medicine; psychology; public administration; public relations; radio/television broadcasting; real estate; recreation/leisure studies; religious studies; retail management; secondary education; social work; sociology; Spanish; special education; speech-language pathology; speech-language pathology/audiology; speech/rhetorical studies; theater arts/drama; trade/industrial education; urban studies.

Academic Programs *Special study options:* adult/continuing education programs, advanced placement credit, cooperative education, distance learning, double majors, English as a second language, honors programs, internships, off-campus study, part-time degree program, services for LD students, student-designed majors, study abroad, summer session for credit. *ROTC:* Army (c), Air Force (b).

Library University Library with 750,000 titles, 3,200 serial subscriptions, 7,000 audiovisual materials, a Web page.

Computers on Campus 64 computers available on campus for general student use. A campuswide network can be accessed from student residence rooms and from off campus. Internet access, online (class) registration, at least one staffed computer lab available.

Student Life *Housing Options:* coed. *Activities and Organizations:* drama/theater group, student-run newspaper, radio and television station, choral group, marching band, Student Programming Organization, fraternities/sororities, national fraternities, national sororities. *Campus security:* 24-hour emergency response devices and patrols, late-night transport/escort service, controlled dormitory access. *Student Services:* health clinic, personal/psychological counseling, women's center, legal services.

Athletics Member NCAA. All Division II except ice hockey (Division I). *Intercollegiate sports:* baseball M(s), basketball M(s)/W(s), cross-country running W(s), football M(s), ice hockey M(s), soccer W, softball W(s), swimming W, volleyball W(s), wrestling M(s). *Intramural sports:* basketball M/W, bowling M/W, football M, golf M/W, racquetball M/W, soccer M/W, softball M/W, squash M/W, swimming M/W, tennis M/W, volleyball M/W, wrestling M.

Standardized Tests *Required:* SAT I or ACT (for admission).

Costs (2001–02) *One-time required fee:* $50. *Tuition:* state resident $2226 full-time, $93 per semester hour part-time; nonresident $6264 full-time, $261 per semester hour part-time. Full-time tuition and fees vary according to course load and student level. Part-time tuition and fees vary according to course load and student level. *Required fees:* $412 full-time, $63 per credit hour. *Room and board:* room only: $2439. *Payment plans:* installment, deferred payment. *Waivers:* employees or children of employees.

Financial Aid Of all full-time matriculated undergraduates who enrolled in 2001, 4535 applied for aid, 3390 were judged to have need. 314 Federal Work-Study jobs (averaging $1692). *Average indebtedness upon graduation:* $16,900.

Applying *Options:* deferred entrance. *Application fee:* $25. *Required:* high school transcript, rank in upper 50% of high school class. *Application deadline:* rolling (freshmen), rolling (transfers). *Notification:* continuous (freshmen).

Admissions Contact Ms. Jolene Adams, Associate Director of Admissions, University of Nebraska at Omaha, 6001 Dodge Street, Omaha, NE 68182. *Phone:* 402-554-2416. *Toll-free phone:* 800-858-8648. *Fax:* 402-554-3472.

UNIVERSITY OF NEBRASKA-LINCOLN
Lincoln, Nebraska

- **State-supported** university, founded 1869, part of University of Nebraska System
- **Calendar** semesters
- **Degrees** associate, bachelor's, master's, doctoral, first professional, and post-master's certificates
- **Urban** 623-acre campus with easy access to Omaha
- **Endowment** $150.1 million
- **Coed,** 17,985 undergraduate students, 90% full-time, 47% women, 53% men
- **Moderately difficult** entrance level, 91% of applicants were admitted

Undergraduates 16,109 full-time, 1,876 part-time. Students come from 52 states and territories, 105 other countries, 14% are from out of state, 2% African American, 2% Asian American or Pacific Islander, 2% Hispanic American, 0.5% Native American, 3% international, 5% transferred in, 26% live on campus. *Retention:* 80% of 2001 full-time freshmen returned.

Freshmen *Admission:* 7,266 applied, 6,578 admitted, 3,532 enrolled. *Test scores:* SAT verbal scores over 500: 77%; SAT math scores over 500: 81%; ACT scores over 18: 96%; SAT verbal scores over 600: 38%; SAT math scores over 600: 46%; ACT scores over 24: 53%; SAT verbal scores over 700: 10%; SAT math scores over 700: 13%; ACT scores over 30: 12%.

Faculty *Total:* 1,072, 99% full-time, 93% with terminal degrees. *Student/faculty ratio:* 15:1.

Majors Accounting; actuarial science; advertising; agricultural business; agricultural business and production related; agricultural business related; agricultural economics; agricultural education; agricultural engineering; agricultural mechanization; agronomy/crop science; animal sciences; anthropology; architectural engineering; architecture; art education; art history; athletic training/sports medicine; atmospheric sciences; biochemistry; bioengineering; biological sciences/life sciences related; biology education; broadcast journalism; business administration; business economics; business education; business marketing and marketing management; business quantitative methods/management science related; chemical engineering; chemistry; chemistry education; civil engineering; classics; clothing/apparel/textile studies; communications; communications related; community health liaison; computer education; computer engineering; computer science; construction technology; dance; economics; education (multiple levels); education of the hearing impaired; electrical engineering; elementary education; engineering related; English; English education; environmental science; exercise sciences; family/consumer resource management related; film studies; finance; fine/studio arts; fire protection/safety technology; fishing sciences; food sciences; foreign languages education; French; French language education; geography; geology; German; German language education; Greek (ancient and medieval); health education; history; history education; horticulture science; industrial arts education; industrial/manufacturing engineering; industrial production technologies related; industrial technology; international business; international relations; journalism and mass communication related; Latin American studies; Latin (ancient and medieval); law and legal studies related; liberal arts and sciences/liberal studies; liberal arts and studies related; marketing/distribution education; mathematics; mathematics education; mechanical engineering; medieval/renaissance studies; middle school education; music; music teacher education; natural resources conservation; natural resources management; nutrition studies; office management; philosophy; physical education; physics; physics education; plant protection; political science; pre-dentistry; pre-medicine; pre-pharmacy studies; pre-veterinary studies; psychology; range management; Russian; science education; social science education; sociology; soil sciences; Spanish; Spanish language education; special education related; speech-language pathology; teacher education, specific programs related; teaching English as a second language; theater arts/drama; trade/industrial education; veterinarian assistant; Western European studies; women's studies.

Academic Programs *Special study options:* accelerated degree program, adult/continuing education programs, advanced placement credit, cooperative education, distance learning, double majors, English as a second language, honors programs, internships, off-campus study, part-time degree program, services for LD students, student-designed majors, study abroad, summer session for credit. *ROTC:* Army (b), Navy (b), Air Force (b).

Library Love Memorial Library plus 10 others with 1.2 million titles, 20,234 serial subscriptions, 46,995 audiovisual materials, an OPAC, a Web page.

Computers on Campus 500 computers available on campus for general student use. A campuswide network can be accessed from student residence rooms and from off campus. Internet access, at least one staffed computer lab available.

Student Life *Housing:* on-campus residence required for freshman year. *Options:* coed, men-only, women-only, cooperative. *Activities and Organizations:* drama/theater group, student-run newspaper, radio station, choral group, marching band, Student Alumni Association, University Ambassadors, University Program Council, Golden Key, national fraternities, national sororities. *Campus security:* 24-hour emergency response devices and patrols, student patrols, late-night transport/escort service, controlled dormitory access. *Student Services:* health clinic, personal/psychological counseling, women's center, legal services.

Athletics Member NCAA. All Division I except football (Division I-A). *Intercollegiate sports:* baseball M(s), basketball M(s)/W(s), crew M(c)/W(c), cross-country running M(s)/W(s), fencing M(c)/W(c), golf M(s)/W(s), gymnastics M(s)/W(s), riflery W(s), soccer W(s), softball W(s), swimming W(s), tennis M(s)/W(s), track and field M(s)/W(s), volleyball W(s), wrestling M(s). *Intramural sports:* archery M/W, badminton M/W, basketball M/W, bowling M/W, cross-country running M/W, football M/W, golf M/W, ice hockey M(c)/W(c), racquetball M/W, riflery M/W, rugby M(c)/W(c), soccer M/W, softball M/W, squash M/W, swimming W, table tennis M/W, tennis M/W, track and field M/W, volleyball M/W, water polo M/W, weight lifting M/W, wrestling M/W.

Standardized Tests *Required:* SAT I or ACT (for admission).

Costs (2001–02) *Tuition:* state resident $3037 full-time, $101 per credit hour part-time; nonresident $8640 full-time, $288 per credit hour part-time. Full-time tuition and fees vary according to course load. Part-time tuition and fees vary according to course load. *Required fees:* $722 full-time, $5 per credit hour, $140 per term part-time. *Room and board:* $4565; room only: $2110. Room and board charges vary according to board plan and housing facility. *Waivers:* employees or children of employees.

Financial Aid Of all full-time matriculated undergraduates who enrolled in 2001, 9656 applied for aid, 6833 were judged to have need, 2423 had their need fully met. 1022 Federal Work-Study jobs (averaging $1871). In 2001, 1026 non-need-based awards were made. *Average percent of need met:* 84%. *Average financial aid package:* $6006. *Average need-based loan:* $3502. *Average need-based gift aid:* $3482. *Average non-need based aid:* $2561. *Average indebtedness upon graduation:* $16,447.

Applying *Options:* electronic application. *Application fee:* $25. *Required:* high school transcript. *Required for some:* rank in upper 50% of high school class. *Application deadlines:* 6/30 (freshmen), 6/30 (transfers).

Admissions Contact Patrick McBride, Interim Director of Admissions, University of Nebraska-Lincoln, 1410 Q Street, Lincoln, NE 68588-0417. *Phone:* 402-472-2030. *Toll-free phone:* 800-742-8800. *Fax:* 402-472-0670. *E-mail:* nuhusker@unl.edu.

UNIVERSITY OF NEBRASKA MEDICAL CENTER
Omaha, Nebraska

- **State-supported** upper-level, founded 1869, part of University of Nebraska System
- **Calendar** semesters
- **Degrees** certificates, bachelor's, master's, doctoral, first professional, post-master's, postbachelor's, and first professional certificates
- **Urban** 51-acre campus
- **Endowment** $9.4 million
- **Coed,** 663 undergraduate students, 86% full-time, 92% women, 8% men
- **Moderately difficult** entrance level, 33% of applicants were admitted

Undergraduates 568 full-time, 95 part-time. 9% are from out of state, 0.6% African American, 1% Asian American or Pacific Islander, 3% Hispanic American, 0.2% international, 23% transferred in.

Freshmen *Admission:* 2,884 applied, 943 admitted.

Faculty *Total:* 786, 80% full-time.

Majors Dental hygiene; diagnostic medical sonography; medical radiologic technology; medical technology; nuclear medical technology; nursing.

Academic Programs *Special study options:* distance learning, honors programs, internships, off-campus study, part-time degree program, services for LD students, summer session for credit. *ROTC:* Army (c), Navy (c), Air Force (c).

Library McGoogan Medical Library plus 1 other with 247,434 titles, 1,741 serial subscriptions, 849 audiovisual materials, an OPAC, a Web page.

Computers on Campus 65 computers available on campus for general student use. A campuswide network can be accessed from off campus that provide access to various software packages. Internet access, at least one staffed computer lab available.

Student Life *Housing:* college housing not available. *Activities and Organizations:* student government, Toastmasters, Student Alliance for Global Health, Christian Medical Society, Student Research Group, national fraternities, national sororities. *Campus security:* 24-hour emergency response devices and patrols, late-night transport/escort service. *Student Services:* health clinic, personal/psychological counseling.

Costs (2001–02) *Tuition:* state resident $3855 full-time, $129 per semester hour part-time; nonresident $10,800 full-time, $360 per semester hour part-time. Full-time tuition and fees vary according to location and program. Part-time tuition and fees vary according to course load, location, and program. *Required fees:* $260 full-time.

Financial Aid Of all full-time matriculated undergraduates who enrolled in 2001, 663 applied for aid, 663 were judged to have need. 20 Federal Work-Study jobs (averaging $1479). *Average percent of need met:* 59%. *Average need-based loan:* $6752. *Average need-based gift aid:* $2863.

Applying *Application fee:* $25. *Application deadline:* rolling (transfers).

Admissions Contact Ms. Jo Wagner, Assistant Director of Academic Records, University of Nebraska Medical Center, 984230 Nebraska Medical Center, Omaha, NE 68198-4230. *Phone:* 402-559-6468. *Toll-free phone:* 800-626-8431. *Fax:* 402-559-6796.

WAYNE STATE COLLEGE
Wayne, Nebraska

- **State-supported** comprehensive, founded 1910, part of Nebraska State College System
- **Calendar** semesters
- **Degrees** bachelor's, master's, and post-master's certificates
- **Small-town** 128-acre campus
- **Coed,** 2,835 undergraduate students, 91% full-time, 58% women, 42% men
- **Noncompetitive** entrance level, 100% of applicants were admitted

Undergraduates 2,588 full-time, 247 part-time. Students come from 24 states and territories, 19 other countries, 14% are from out of state, 3% African American, 0.5% Asian American or Pacific Islander, 2% Hispanic American, 0.8% Native American, 1% international, 6% transferred in, 42% live on campus. *Retention:* 72% of 2001 full-time freshmen returned.

Freshmen *Admission:* 1,287 applied, 1,287 admitted, 597 enrolled. *Average high school GPA:* 3.05. *Test scores:* ACT scores over 18: 79%; ACT scores over 24: 26%; ACT scores over 30: 2%.

Faculty *Total:* 205, 62% full-time, 55% with terminal degrees. *Student/faculty ratio:* 19:1.

Majors Accounting; advertising; agricultural business; applied mathematics; art; biology; business administration; business economics; business education; chemistry; computer science; counselor education/guidance; creative writing; criminal justice/law enforcement administration; early childhood education; education; elementary education; English; exercise sciences; family/consumer studies; fashion merchandising; finance; food products retailing; French; geography; German; graphic design/commercial art/illustration; history; home economics; home economics education; information sciences/systems; interdisciplinary studies; interior design; international business; journalism; law enforcement/police science; literature; mass communications; mathematics; medical technology; modern languages; music; music teacher education; natural sciences; physical education; physical sciences; political science; pre-medicine; pre-veterinary studies; psychology; public administration; recreation/leisure studies; science education; social sciences; sociology; Spanish; special education; speech/rhetorical studies; sport/fitness administration; theater arts/drama.

Academic Programs *Special study options:* adult/continuing education programs, cooperative education, distance learning, double majors, honors programs, independent study, internships, off-campus study, part-time degree program, services for LD students, student-designed majors, summer session for credit. *ROTC:* Army (c).

Library U. S. Conn Library plus 1 other with 149,821 titles, 2,520 serial subscriptions, 5,437 audiovisual materials, an OPAC, a Web page.

Computers on Campus 200 computers available on campus for general student use. At least one staffed computer lab available.

Student Life *Housing:* on-campus residence required for freshman year. *Options:* coed, women-only. *Activities and Organizations:* drama/theater group, student-run newspaper, radio and television station, choral group, marching band, national fraternities, national sororities. *Campus security:* 24-hour patrols, student patrols, late-night transport/escort service, controlled dormitory access. *Student Services:* health clinic, personal/psychological counseling.

Athletics Member NCAA. All Division II. *Intercollegiate sports:* baseball M(s), basketball M(s)/W(s), cross-country running M(s)/W(s), football M(s), golf M/W, soccer M(c)/W(c), softball W(s), track and field M(s)/W(s), volleyball W(s). *Intramural sports:* archery M/W, badminton M/W, basketball M/W, bowling M/W, football M/W, golf M/W, racquetball M/W, softball M/W, swimming M/W, table tennis M/W, tennis M/W, track and field M/W, volleyball M/W, water polo M/W, weight lifting M/W, wrestling M.

Standardized Tests *Recommended:* SAT I or ACT (for placement).

Costs (2001–02) *Tuition:* state resident $2093 full-time, $70 per semester hour part-time; nonresident $4185 full-time, $140 per semester hour part-time. *Required fees:* $642 full-time, $321 per term part-time. *Room and board:* $3590; room only: $1680. Room and board charges vary according to board plan and housing facility. *Payment plan:* installment. *Waivers:* employees or children of employees.

Financial Aid Of all full-time matriculated undergraduates who enrolled in 2001, 2023 applied for aid, 1539 were judged to have need, 897 had their need fully met. *Average percent of need met:* 42%. *Average financial aid package:* $3381. *Average need-based loan:* $1458. *Average need-based gift aid:* $1281.

Applying *Options:* common application, deferred entrance. *Application fee:* $20. *Required:* high school transcript. *Required for some:* minimum 2.0 GPA. *Recommended:* minimum 3.0 GPA, interview. *Application deadline:* rolling (freshmen), rolling (transfers). *Notification:* continuous (freshmen).

Admissions Contact Ms. Teresa Moore, Director of Admissions, Wayne State College, 1111 Main Street, Wayne, NE 68787. *Phone:* 402-375-7234. *Toll-free phone:* 800-228-9972. *Fax:* 402-375-7204. *E-mail:* wscadmit@wscgate.wsc.edu.

Wayne State College (continued)

YORK COLLEGE
York, Nebraska

- **Independent** 4-year, founded 1890, affiliated with Church of Christ
- **Calendar** semesters
- **Degrees** associate and bachelor's
- **Small-town** 44-acre campus
- **Endowment** $3.9 million
- **Coed,** 455 undergraduate students, 94% full-time, 57% women, 43% men
- **Moderately difficult** entrance level, 61% of applicants were admitted

York College, founded in 1890, is a private, liberal arts college offering four bachelor's degrees in twenty-nine fields to a student body of more than 500. York is one of the most affordable Christian colleges in America and is accredited by North Central Association of Colleges and Schools (NCACS). The College offers NAIA sports and is located in one of the "top twenty best small towns in America."

Undergraduates 429 full-time, 26 part-time. Students come from 34 states and territories, 11 other countries, 65% are from out of state, 4% African American, 2% Asian American or Pacific Islander, 0.2% Hispanic American, 0.9% international, 6% transferred in, 64% live on campus. *Retention:* 84% of 2001 full-time freshmen returned.

Freshmen *Admission:* 325 applied, 199 admitted, 111 enrolled. *Average high school GPA:* 3.18. *Test scores:* ACT scores over 18: 81%; ACT scores over 24: 29%; ACT scores over 30: 4%.

Faculty *Total:* 56, 64% full-time, 25% with terminal degrees. *Student/faculty ratio:* 12:1.

Majors Accounting; biblical languages/literatures; biblical studies; biological/physical sciences; biology; business administration; education; education (multiple levels); education of the mentally handicapped; elementary education; English; finance; general studies; history; history education; human resources management; liberal arts and sciences/liberal studies; mathematics education; middle school education; music; music teacher education; natural sciences; physical education; physiological psychology/psychobiology; psychology; reading education; religious education; religious studies; science education; secondary education; speech/theater education.

Academic Programs *Special study options:* academic remediation for entering students, adult/continuing education programs, advanced placement credit, cooperative education, double majors, external degree program, honors programs, independent study, internships, part-time degree program, services for LD students, study abroad, summer session for credit. *ROTC:* Army (c), Navy (c), Air Force (c). *Unusual degree programs:* 3-2 engineering with Oklahoma Christian University; nursing with Harding University.

Library Levitt Library with 44,172 titles, 329 serial subscriptions, 2,560 audiovisual materials, a Web page.

Computers on Campus 36 computers available on campus for general student use. A campuswide network can be accessed from off campus. At least one staffed computer lab available.

Student Life *Housing:* on-campus residence required through sophomore year. *Options:* men-only, women-only. *Activities and Organizations:* drama/theater group, student-run newspaper, choral group, Concert Choir, Student Association, Promethians, social organizations, Marksmen. *Campus security:* 24-hour patrols, student patrols, controlled dormitory access. *Student Services:* personal/psychological counseling.

Athletics Member NAIA, NCCAA. *Intercollegiate sports:* baseball M(s), basketball M(s)/W(s), cross-country running M(s)/W(s), golf M(s)/W(s), soccer M(s)/W(s), softball W(s), track and field M(s)/W(s). *Intramural sports:* badminton M/W, basketball M/W, football M/W, soccer M/W, softball M/W, table tennis M/W, tennis M/W, volleyball M/W.

Standardized Tests *Required:* SAT I or ACT (for admission).

Costs (2001–02) *Comprehensive fee:* $13,500 includes full-time tuition ($9500), mandatory fees ($800), and room and board ($3200). Full-time tuition and fees vary according to course load. Part-time tuition: $300 per credit hour. Part-time tuition and fees vary according to course load. *Required fees:* $50 per hour. *Room and board:* College room only: $1200. Room and board charges vary according to board plan and housing facility. *Payment plan:* installment. *Waivers:* employees or children of employees.

Applying *Options:* common application, electronic application, early admission, deferred entrance. *Application fee:* $20. *Required:* high school transcript, 2 letters of recommendation. *Required for some:* minimum 2.0 GPA. *Recommended:* minimum 2.0 GPA. *Application deadline:* rolling (freshmen), rolling (transfers).

Admissions Contact Kristin Mathews, Admissions Counselor, York College, 1125 East 8th Street, York, NE 68467-2699. *Phone:* 402-363-5629. *Toll-free phone:* 800-950-9675. *Fax:* 402-363-5623. *E-mail:* enroll@york.edu.

NEVADA

GREAT BASIN COLLEGE
Elko, Nevada

- **State-supported** primarily 2-year, founded 1967, part of University and Community College System of Nevada
- **Calendar** semesters
- **Degrees** certificates, associate, and bachelor's
- **Rural** 58-acre campus
- **Endowment** $150,000
- **Coed**
- **Noncompetitive** entrance level

Student Life *Campus security:* evening patrols by trained security personnel.

Standardized Tests *Recommended:* SAT I or ACT (for placement).

Financial Aid Of all full-time matriculated undergraduates who enrolled in 2001, 35 Federal Work-Study jobs (averaging $1000).

Applying *Options:* common application, electronic application, early admission, deferred entrance. *Application fee:* $5. *Required:* high school transcript.

Admissions Contact Ms. Julie Burns, Admissions and Records Officer, Great Basin College, 1500 College Parkway, Elko, NV 89801-3348. *Phone:* 775-753-2361. *Fax:* 775-753-2311. *E-mail:* stdsvc@gbcnv.edu.

MORRISON UNIVERSITY
Reno, Nevada

Admissions Contact Ms. Teresa Sanders, Director of Admissions, Morrison University, 140 Washington Street, Reno, NV 89503-5600. *Phone:* 775-323-4145. *Toll-free phone:* 800-369-6144.

SIERRA NEVADA COLLEGE
Incline Village, Nevada

- **Independent** comprehensive, founded 1969
- **Calendar** semesters
- **Degrees** bachelor's and postbachelor's certificates
- **Small-town** 20-acre campus with easy access to Reno
- **Endowment** $3.5 million
- **Coed,** 345 undergraduate students, 93% full-time, 44% women, 56% men
- **Moderately difficult** entrance level, 89% of applicants were admitted

Undergraduates 320 full-time, 25 part-time. Students come from 32 states and territories, 9 other countries, 80% are from out of state, 0.9% African American, 0.3% Asian American or Pacific Islander, 1% Hispanic American, 0.6% Native American, 3% international, 14% transferred in, 43% live on campus. *Retention:* 54% of 2001 full-time freshmen returned.

Freshmen *Admission:* 246 applied, 220 admitted, 61 enrolled. *Average high school GPA:* 3.10. *Test scores:* SAT verbal scores over 500: 60%; SAT math scores over 500: 60%; ACT scores over 18: 80%; SAT verbal scores over 600: 10%; SAT math scores over 600: 10%; ACT scores over 24: 10%.

Faculty *Total:* 61, 34% full-time. *Student/faculty ratio:* 11:1.

Majors Art; biological/physical sciences; business administration; computer/information sciences; ecology; entrepreneurship; environmental science; fine/studio arts; hotel and restaurant management; humanities; music.

Academic Programs *Special study options:* academic remediation for entering students, accelerated degree program, adult/continuing education programs, advanced placement credit, cooperative education, double majors, honors programs, independent study, internships, part-time degree program, services for LD students, study abroad, summer session for credit. *ROTC:* Army (c).

Library MacLean Library with 18,500 titles, 175 serial subscriptions, an OPAC, a Web page.

Computers on Campus 50 computers available on campus for general student use. A campuswide network can be accessed from student residence rooms and from off campus. Internet access available.

Student Life *Housing:* on-campus residence required through sophomore year. *Options:* coed. *Activities and Organizations:* drama/theater group, student-run newspaper, choral group, Recycling Club, ski club (NASIS), enviroaction club, snowboard club, Rotaract. *Campus security:* 24-hour emergency response devices and patrols. *Student Services:* health clinic, personal/psychological counseling.

Athletics *Intercollegiate sports:* equestrian sports M/W, skiing (downhill) M(s)/W(s). *Intramural sports:* fencing M/W, skiing (downhill) M/W, soccer M/W, softball M/W, volleyball M/W.

Costs (2002–03) *Comprehensive fee:* $25,390 includes full-time tuition ($18,750), mandatory fees ($60), and room and board ($6580). Full-time tuition and fees vary according to course load, location, and program. Part-time tuition: $775 per hour. Part-time tuition and fees vary according to course load, location, and program. *Required fees:* $100 per term part-time. *Room and board:* Room and board charges vary according to housing facility. *Payment plans:* installment, deferred payment. *Waivers:* employees or children of employees.

Financial Aid Of all full-time matriculated undergraduates who enrolled in 2001, 145 applied for aid, 145 were judged to have need. 17 Federal Work-Study jobs (averaging $2000). 5 State and other part-time jobs (averaging $1000). *Average percent of need met:* 55%. *Average financial aid package:* $11,000. *Average need-based gift aid:* $5000. *Average indebtedness upon graduation:* $18,000.

Applying *Options:* common application, electronic application, early admission, deferred entrance. *Required:* essay or personal statement, high school transcript, minimum 2.0 GPA. *Required for some:* letters of recommendation, school report form for high school seniors. *Recommended:* interview. *Application deadline:* rolling (freshmen), rolling (transfers). *Notification:* continuous (freshmen).

Admissions Contact Mr. Brett Schraeder, Dean of Admission, Sierra Nevada College, 999 Tahoe Boulevard, David Hall II, Incline Village, NV 89451. *Phone:* 775-831-1314 Ext. 4047. *Toll-free phone:* 800-332-8666 Ext. 4046. *Fax:* 775-831-1347. *E-mail:* admissions@sierranevada.edu.

UNIVERSITY OF NEVADA, LAS VEGAS

Las Vegas, Nevada

- **State-supported** university, founded 1957, part of University and Community College System of Nevada
- **Calendar** semesters
- **Degrees** certificates, bachelor's, master's, doctoral, first professional, post-master's, postbachelor's, and first professional certificates
- **Urban** 335-acre campus
- **Endowment** $87.9 million
- **Coed,** 18,606 undergraduate students, 66% full-time, 55% women, 45% men
- **Moderately difficult** entrance level, 80% of applicants were admitted

UNLV is a doctoral, research-intensive university that offers 180 undergraduate, master's, and doctoral degree programs to 24,000 students. A premier, urban university, UNLV is located on a beautifully landscaped 335-acre enclosed campus that is just minutes from McCarren International Airport and the world-famous Las Vegas Strip.

Undergraduates 12,234 full-time, 6,372 part-time. Students come from 53 states and territories, 81 other countries, 20% are from out of state, 7% African American, 12% Asian American or Pacific Islander, 10% Hispanic American, 1% Native American, 5% international, 15% transferred in, 5% live on campus. *Retention:* 72% of 2001 full-time freshmen returned.

Freshmen *Admission:* 5,587 applied, 4,463 admitted, 2,541 enrolled. *Average high school GPA:* 3.20. *Test scores:* SAT verbal scores over 500: 51%; SAT math scores over 500: 56%; ACT scores over 18: 84%; SAT verbal scores over 600: 14%; SAT math scores over 600: 15%; ACT scores over 24: 29%; SAT verbal scores over 700: 1%; SAT math scores over 700: 2%; ACT scores over 30: 2%.

Faculty *Total:* 1,270, 56% full-time. *Student/faculty ratio:* 20:1.

Majors Accounting; adult/continuing education; African-American studies; anthropology; applied mathematics; architectural urban design; architecture; art; art history; athletic training/sports medicine; biochemistry; biology; business administration; business marketing and marketing management; chemistry; civil engineering; communications; comparative literature; computer engineering; computer science; construction engineering; criminal justice/law enforcement administration; culinary arts; cultural studies; dance; early childhood education; earth sciences; economics; education; electrical engineering; elementary education; English; environmental science; exercise sciences; film studies; finance; French; geological sciences related; geology; German; gerontology; health education; health physics/radiologic health; health science; health services administration; history; hospitality management; human resources management; human services; interdisciplinary studies; interior architecture; international business; jazz; landscape architecture; management information systems/business data processing; marriage/family counseling; mathematical statistics; mathematics; mechanical engineering; medical laboratory technology; medical radiologic technology; medical technology; music; music theory and composition; nuclear medical technology; nursing; nutritional sciences; philosophy; physical education; physics; physics related; political science; psychology; real estate; recreation/leisure studies; romance languages; secondary education; social sciences; social work; sociology; Spanish; special education; sport/fitness administration; theater arts/drama; theater arts/drama and stagecraft related; travel/tourism management; women's studies.

Academic Programs *Special study options:* academic remediation for entering students, adult/continuing education programs, advanced placement credit, cooperative education, distance learning, double majors, English as a second language, honors programs, independent study, internships, off-campus study, part-time degree program, services for LD students, student-designed majors, study abroad, summer session for credit.

Library James R. Dickinson Library with 1.2 million titles, 356,176 serial subscriptions, 119,593 audiovisual materials, an OPAC, a Web page.

Computers on Campus 1100 computers available on campus for general student use. A campuswide network can be accessed from student residence rooms and from off campus. Internet access, online (class) registration, at least one staffed computer lab available.

Student Life *Housing:* on-campus residence required for freshman year. *Options:* coed, women-only, disabled students. *Activities and Organizations:* drama/theater group, student-run newspaper, radio and television station, choral group, marching band, Inter-Varsity Christian Fellowship, Rebel Ski Club, Student Organization of Latinos, Latter Day Saints, Hawaii club, national fraternities, national sororities. *Campus security:* 24-hour emergency response devices and patrols, late-night transport/escort service, controlled dormitory access. *Student Services:* health clinic, personal/psychological counseling, women's center.

Athletics Member NCAA. All Division I except football (Division I-A). *Intercollegiate sports:* baseball M(s), basketball M(s)/W(s), cross-country running W(s), equestrian sports W, golf M(s), soccer M(s)/W(s), softball W(s), swimming M(s)/W(s), tennis M(s)/W(s), track and field W(s), volleyball W(s). *Intramural sports:* badminton M/W, basketball M/W, bowling M/W, cross-country running M/W, football M/W, golf M/W, racquetball M/W, soccer M/W, softball M/W, swimming M/W, tennis M/W, track and field W, volleyball M/W.

Standardized Tests *Required for some:* SAT I or ACT (for admission). *Recommended:* SAT I or ACT (for admission).

Costs (2001–02) *Tuition:* state resident $2415 full-time, $81 per credit hour part-time; nonresident $9630 full-time, $321 per credit hour part-time. Full-time tuition and fees vary according to course load. Part-time tuition and fees vary according to course load. *Required fees:* $66 full-time, $33 per term part-time. *Room and board:* $5800; room only: $3628. Room and board charges vary according to board plan. *Payment plan:* deferred payment. *Waivers:* children of alumni, senior citizens, and employees or children of employees.

Financial Aid Of all full-time matriculated undergraduates who enrolled in 2001, 8470 applied for aid, 4040 were judged to have need, 2180 had their need fully met. In 2001, 3310 non-need-based awards were made. *Average percent of need met:* 77%. *Average financial aid package:* $6915. *Average need-based loan:* $3210. *Average need-based gift aid:* $3035. *Average non-need based aid:* $1790. *Average indebtedness upon graduation:* $12,000.

Applying *Options:* deferred entrance. *Application fee:* $40. *Required:* high school transcript, minimum 2.5 GPA. *Required for some:* 2 letters of recommendation. *Application deadlines:* 7/15 (freshmen), 7/15 (transfers). *Notification:* continuous (freshmen).

Admissions Contact University of Nevada, Las Vegas, 4505 Maryland Parkway, Box 451021, Las Vegas, NV 89154-1021. *Phone:* 702-895-3443. *Fax:* 702-895-1118. *E-mail:* gounlv@ccmail.nevada.edu.

UNIVERSITY OF NEVADA, RENO

Reno, Nevada

- **State-supported** university, founded 1874, part of University and Community College System of Nevada
- **Calendar** semesters
- **Degrees** bachelor's, master's, doctoral, first professional, post-master's, and postbachelor's certificates
- **Urban** 200-acre campus
- **Endowment** $81.1 million
- **Coed,** 11,075 undergraduate students, 75% full-time, 55% women, 45% men
- **Moderately difficult** entrance level, 95% of applicants were admitted

Undergraduates 8,271 full-time, 2,804 part-time. Students come from 51 states and territories, 63 other countries, 18% are from out of state, 3% African American, 7% Asian American or Pacific Islander, 6% Hispanic American, 1%

University of Nevada, Reno (continued)
Native American, 4% international, 9% transferred in, 14% live on campus. *Retention:* 77% of 2001 full-time freshmen returned.

Freshmen *Admission:* 3,509 applied, 3,323 admitted, 1,992 enrolled. *Average high school GPA:* 3.26. *Test scores:* SAT verbal scores over 500: 61%; SAT math scores over 500: 65%; ACT scores over 18: 89%; SAT verbal scores over 600: 20%; SAT math scores over 600: 24%; ACT scores over 24: 36%; SAT verbal scores over 700: 3%; SAT math scores over 700: 3%; ACT scores over 30: 5%.

Faculty *Total:* 684, 80% full-time, 86% with terminal degrees. *Student/faculty ratio:* 18:1.

Majors Accounting; advertising; agricultural economics; agricultural education; animal sciences; anthropology; art; art education; art history; biochemistry; biology; botany; broadcast journalism; business; business economics; business education; business marketing and marketing management; chemical engineering; chemistry; civil engineering; communications; computer/information sciences; computer science; criminology; electrical engineering; elementary education; engineering physics; English; English composition; English education; enterprise management; environmental engineering; finance; foreign languages education; forestry; French; general studies; geography; geological engineering; geology; geophysics/seismology; German; health education; history; home economics education; hospitality management; human resources management; individual/family development; industrial arts education; interior design; international business; international relations; journalism; logistics/materials management; mathematics; mathematics education; mechanical engineering; medical technology; metallurgical engineering; mining/mineral engineering; music; music (general performance); music teacher education; natural resources conservation; natural resources management; nursing; nutrition studies; philosophy; physical education; physical therapy; physics; political science; pre-dentistry; pre-medicine; pre-pharmacy studies; pre-veterinary studies; psychology; public relations; range management; recreation/leisure studies; science education; science/technology and society; social psychology; social science education; social studies education; social work; sociology; Spanish; special education; speech-language pathology; speech-language pathology/audiology; theater arts/drama; trade/industrial education; water resources engineering; wildlife management; women's studies; zoology.

Academic Programs *Special study options:* academic remediation for entering students, adult/continuing education programs, advanced placement credit, distance learning, double majors, English as a second language, honors programs, independent study, internships, off-campus study, part-time degree program, services for LD students, study abroad, summer session for credit. *ROTC:* Army (b).

Library Getchell Library plus 5 others with 1.0 million titles, 10,499 serial subscriptions, 446,434 audiovisual materials, an OPAC, a Web page.

Computers on Campus 150 computers available on campus for general student use. A campuswide network can be accessed from student residence rooms and from off campus. At least one staffed computer lab available.

Student Life *Housing Options:* coed, men-only, women-only, disabled students. *Activities and Organizations:* drama/theater group, student-run newspaper, radio station, choral group, marching band, Asian-American Student Association, Ambassadors, Non-Traditional Student Union, The Alliance, Orvis Nursing Student Association, national fraternities, national sororities. *Campus security:* 24-hour emergency response devices and patrols, late-night transport/escort service, controlled dormitory access. *Student Services:* health clinic, personal/psychological counseling, women's center, legal services.

Athletics Member NCAA. All Division I except football (Division I-A). *Intercollegiate sports:* baseball M(s), basketball M(s)/W(s), cross-country running W(s), golf M(s)/W(s), riflery M(s)/W(s), skiing (cross-country) M(s)/W(s), skiing (downhill) M(s)/W(s), soccer W(s), swimming W(s), tennis M(s)/W(s), track and field W(s), volleyball W(s). *Intramural sports:* basketball M/W, cross-country running M/W, golf M/W, racquetball M/W, skiing (cross-country) M/W, skiing (downhill) M/W, soccer M/W, softball M/W, swimming M/W, table tennis M/W, tennis M/W, track and field M/W, volleyball M/W, water polo M/W.

Standardized Tests *Required:* SAT I or ACT (for placement).

Costs (2002–03) *Tuition:* state resident $2490 full-time, $83 per credit part-time; nonresident $9940 full-time, $170 per credit part-time. Full-time tuition and fees vary according to course load. Part-time tuition and fees vary according to course load. *Required fees:* $132 full-time. *Room and board:* $6190; room only: $3380. Room and board charges vary according to board plan and housing facility. *Payment plan:* deferred payment. *Waivers:* children of alumni, senior citizens, and employees or children of employees.

Financial Aid Of all full-time matriculated undergraduates who enrolled in 2001, 6285 applied for aid, 6000 were judged to have need, 3820 had their need fully met. 176 Federal Work-Study jobs (averaging $2085). 3067 State and other part-time jobs (averaging $2219). *Average percent of need met:* 75%. *Average financial aid package:* $8000. *Average need-based gift aid:* $1000. *Average non-need based aid:* $2500. *Average indebtedness upon graduation:* $14,000.

Applying *Options:* deferred entrance. *Application fee:* $40. *Required:* high school transcript, minimum 2.5 GPA. *Application deadline:* 3/1 (freshmen), rolling (transfers). *Notification:* continuous (freshmen).

Admissions Contact Dr. Melissa N. Choroszy, Associate Dean of Records and Enrollment Services, University of Nevada, Reno, Mail Stop 120, Reno, NV 89557. *Phone:* 775-784-6865. *Fax:* 775-784-4283. *E-mail:* asknevada@unr.edu.

UNIVERSITY OF PHOENIX-NEVADA CAMPUS
Las Vegas, Nevada

- **Proprietary** comprehensive, founded 1994
- **Calendar** continuous
- **Degrees** certificates, associate, bachelor's, master's, doctoral, post-master's, and postbachelor's certificates (courses conducted at 54 campuses and learning centers in 13 states)
- **Coed,** 1,488 undergraduate students, 100% full-time, 57% women, 43% men
- **Noncompetitive** entrance level

Undergraduates Students come from 25 states and territories, 3% are from out of state.

Freshmen *Admission:* 20 admitted.

Faculty *Total:* 207, 3% full-time, 30% with terminal degrees. *Student/faculty ratio:* 16:1.

Majors Business administration; computer/information sciences; enterprise management; public administration and services related.

Academic Programs *Special study options:* accelerated degree program, adult/continuing education programs, advanced placement credit, distance learning, external degree program, independent study.

Library University Library with 17.5 million titles, 9,000 serial subscriptions, an OPAC, a Web page.

Computers on Campus A campuswide network can be accessed from off campus. Internet access, at least one staffed computer lab available.

Student Life *Housing:* college housing not available.

Costs (2001–02) *Tuition:* $8160 full-time. Full-time tuition and fees vary according to location and program. *Payment plan:* deferred payment. *Waivers:* employees or children of employees.

Applying *Options:* deferred entrance. *Application fee:* $85. *Required:* 2 years of work experience. *Required for some:* high school transcript. *Application deadline:* rolling (freshmen), rolling (transfers).

Admissions Contact Ms. Beth Barilla, Director of Admissions, University of Phoenix-Nevada Campus, 4615 East Elwood Street, Phoenix, AZ 85040-1958. *Phone:* 480-927-0099 Ext. 1218. *Toll-free phone:* 800-228-7240. *Fax:* 480-594-1758. *E-mail:* beth.barilla@apollogrp.edu.

NEW HAMPSHIRE

COLBY-SAWYER COLLEGE
New London, New Hampshire

- **Independent** 4-year, founded 1837
- **Calendar** semesters
- **Degrees** associate and bachelor's
- **Small-town** 190-acre campus
- **Endowment** $15.6 million
- **Coed,** 901 undergraduate students, 97% full-time, 64% women, 36% men
- **Moderately difficult** entrance level, 87% of applicants were admitted

Undergraduates 871 full-time, 30 part-time. Students come from 27 states and territories, 9 other countries, 69% are from out of state, 0.2% African American, 0.4% Asian American or Pacific Islander, 0.4% Hispanic American, 0.3% Native American, 3% international, 3% transferred in, 88% live on campus. *Retention:* 81% of 2001 full-time freshmen returned.

Freshmen *Admission:* 1,246 applied, 1,083 admitted, 285 enrolled. *Average high school GPA:* 2.86. *Test scores:* SAT verbal scores over 500: 54%; SAT math scores over 500: 46%; ACT scores over 18: 80%; SAT verbal scores over 600: 10%; SAT math scores over 600: 11%; ACT scores over 24: 10%; SAT verbal scores over 700: 1%.

Faculty *Total:* 100, 49% full-time, 55% with terminal degrees. *Student/faculty ratio:* 12:1.

Majors Art; art education; athletic training/sports medicine; biology; biology education; business administration; communications; developmental/child psychology; elementary education; English; English education; environmental science; exercise sciences; graphic design/commercial art/illustration; liberal arts and sciences/liberal studies; nursing; psychology; social sciences and history related; social studies education; sport/fitness administration.

Academic Programs *Special study options:* accelerated degree program, advanced placement credit, double majors, English as a second language, honors programs, independent study, internships, off-campus study, part-time degree program, services for LD students, student-designed majors, study abroad. *ROTC:* Army (c), Air Force (c).

Library Susan Colgate Cleveland Library Learning Center with 78,389 titles, 1,409 serial subscriptions, 2,140 audiovisual materials, an OPAC.

Computers on Campus 74 computers available on campus for general student use. A campuswide network can be accessed from student residence rooms that provide access to e-mail. Internet access, at least one staffed computer lab available.

Student Life *Housing:* on-campus residence required for freshman year. *Options:* coed, women-only, disabled students. *Activities and Organizations:* drama/theater group, student-run newspaper, radio station, choral group, campus activities, Student Government Association, campus radio station, Alpha Chi Honor Society, outing club. *Campus security:* 24-hour emergency response devices and patrols, late-night transport/escort service, controlled dormitory access, awareness seminars. *Student Services:* health clinic, personal/psychological counseling.

Athletics Member NCAA. All Division III. *Intercollegiate sports:* baseball M, basketball M/W, cross-country running M(c)/W(c), equestrian sports M/W, golf M(c)/W(c), ice hockey M(c)/W(c), lacrosse M(c)/W, rugby M(c)/W(c), skiing (cross-country) M(c)/W(c), skiing (downhill) M/W, soccer M/W, softball W(c), swimming M/W, tennis M/W, track and field M/W, volleyball W. *Intramural sports:* basketball M/W, golf M/W, soccer M/W, volleyball M/W.

Standardized Tests *Required:* SAT I or ACT (for admission).

Costs (2002–03) *Comprehensive fee:* $29,250 includes full-time tuition ($21,140) and room and board ($8110). Part-time tuition: $705 per credit hour. Part-time tuition and fees vary according to course load. *Room and board:* College room only: $4510. *Payment plan:* installment. *Waivers:* employees or children of employees.

Applying *Options:* common application, early admission, early action, deferred entrance. *Application fee:* $40. *Required:* essay or personal statement, high school transcript, minimum 2.0 GPA, 2 letters of recommendation. *Recommended:* interview. *Application deadline:* rolling (freshmen), rolling (transfers). *Notification:* continuous (freshmen), 1/1 (early action).

Admissions Contact Ms. Wendy Beckemeyer, Vice President for Enrollment Management and Dean of Admissions, Colby-Sawyer College, New London, NH 03257. *Phone:* 603-526-3700. *Toll-free phone:* 800-272-1015. *Fax:* 603-526-3452. *E-mail:* csadmiss@colby-sawyer.edu.

DANIEL WEBSTER COLLEGE
Nashua, New Hampshire

- **Independent** 4-year, founded 1965
- **Calendar** semesters
- **Degrees** certificates, diplomas, associate, and bachelor's
- **Suburban** 50-acre campus with easy access to Boston
- **Endowment** $1.6 million
- **Coed,** 1,055 undergraduate students, 74% full-time, 28% women, 72% men
- **Moderately difficult** entrance level, 71% of applicants were admitted

Undergraduates 776 full-time, 279 part-time. Students come from 25 states and territories, 6 other countries, 2% African American, 0.7% Asian American or Pacific Islander, 2% Hispanic American, 0.1% Native American, 0.6% international, 80% live on campus. *Retention:* 56% of 2001 full-time freshmen returned.

Freshmen *Admission:* 784 applied, 560 admitted, 199 enrolled. *Average high school GPA:* 3.06. *Test scores:* SAT verbal scores over 500: 62%; SAT math scores over 500: 73%; ACT scores over 18: 78%; SAT verbal scores over 600: 21%; SAT math scores over 600: 21%; ACT scores over 24: 17%.

Faculty *Total:* 60, 55% full-time, 33% with terminal degrees. *Student/faculty ratio:* 13:1.

Majors Aerospace science; aircraft pilot (professional); air traffic control; aviation management; business administration; business marketing and marketing management; computer management; computer programming; computer science; engineering; engineering science; information sciences/systems; liberal arts and sciences/liberal studies; management information systems/business data processing; social sciences; sport/fitness administration.

Academic Programs *Special study options:* adult/continuing education programs, advanced placement credit, double majors, independent study, internships, off-campus study, part-time degree program, summer session for credit. *ROTC:* Army (c), Air Force (c).

Library Ann Bridge Baddour Library and Learning Center with 35,443 titles, 336 serial subscriptions, 970 audiovisual materials, an OPAC, a Web page.

Computers on Campus 137 computers available on campus for general student use. A campuswide network can be accessed from student residence rooms and from off campus. Internet access, at least one staffed computer lab available.

Student Life *Housing:* on-campus residence required through sophomore year. *Options:* coed, men-only, women-only, disabled students. *Activities and Organizations:* drama/theater group, student-run newspaper, choral group, Student Activities Board, Theatre Guild, Ice Hockey Club, student government, Jazz Band. *Campus security:* 24-hour emergency response devices and patrols, student patrols, late-night transport/escort service, controlled dormitory access. *Student Services:* health clinic, personal/psychological counseling.

Athletics Member NCAA. All Division III. *Intercollegiate sports:* baseball M, basketball M/W, cross-country running M/W, ice hockey M(c)/W(c), lacrosse M, soccer M/W, softball W, volleyball M(c)/W. *Intramural sports:* basketball M/W, cross-country running M/W, football M/W, golf M/W, skiing (downhill) M(c)/W(c), soccer M/W, softball M/W, tennis M/W, volleyball M/W, weight lifting M/W.

Standardized Tests *Required:* SAT I or ACT (for admission).

Costs (2001–02) *Comprehensive fee:* $24,870 includes full-time tuition ($17,300), mandatory fees ($570), and room and board ($7000). Full-time tuition and fees vary according to class time, course load, and program. Part-time tuition: $725 per credit. Part-time tuition and fees vary according to class time. *Room and board:* College room only: $3600. Room and board charges vary according to board plan and housing facility. *Payment plan:* installment. *Waivers:* senior citizens and employees or children of employees.

Financial Aid Of all full-time matriculated undergraduates who enrolled in 2001, 494 applied for aid, 458 were judged to have need. 299 Federal Work-Study jobs (averaging $2000). *Average percent of need met:* 80%. *Average financial aid package:* $13,000. *Average need-based loan:* $4100. *Average need-based gift aid:* $2860. *Average indebtedness upon graduation:* $36,958.

Applying *Options:* common application, electronic application, early admission, deferred entrance. *Application fee:* $35. *Required:* high school transcript. *Recommended:* 1 letter of recommendation, interview. *Application deadline:* rolling (freshmen), rolling (transfers). *Notification:* continuous (freshmen).

Admissions Contact Daniel Webster College, 20 University Drive, Nashua, NH 03063. *Phone:* 603-577-6604. *Toll-free phone:* 800-325-6876. *Fax:* 603-577-6001. *E-mail:* admissions@dwc.edu.

DARTMOUTH COLLEGE
Hanover, New Hampshire

- **Independent** university, founded 1769
- **Calendar** quarters
- **Degrees** bachelor's, master's, doctoral, and first professional
- **Rural** 265-acre campus
- **Endowment** $2.4 billion
- **Coed,** 4,118 undergraduate students, 99% full-time, 49% women, 51% men
- **Most difficult** entrance level, 23% of applicants were admitted

Undergraduates Students come from 52 states and territories, 64 other countries, 97% are from out of state, 6% African American, 11% Asian American or Pacific Islander, 6% Hispanic American, 3% Native American, 5% international, 87% live on campus. *Retention:* 97% of 2001 full-time freshmen returned.

Freshmen *Admission:* 9,719 applied, 2,220 admitted. *Test scores:* SAT verbal scores over 500: 99%; SAT math scores over 500: 100%; SAT verbal scores over 600: 92%; SAT math scores over 600: 96%; SAT verbal scores over 700: 59%; SAT math scores over 700: 66%.

Faculty *Total:* 640, 70% full-time, 88% with terminal degrees. *Student/faculty ratio:* 9:1.

Majors African-American studies; African studies; anthropology; Arabic; archaeology; art history; Asian studies; astronomy; biochemistry; biology; chemistry; chemistry related; Chinese; classics; cognitive psychology/psycholinguistics; comparative literature; computer science; creative writing; earth sciences; East and Southeast Asian languages related; ecology; economics; engineering; engineering physics; English; environmental science; evolutionary biology; film studies; fine/studio arts; French; genetics; geography; German; Greek (ancient and medieval); Hebrew; Hispanic-American studies; history; Italian; Japanese; Latin American studies; Latin (ancient and medieval); linguistics; mathematics; Middle Eastern studies; molecular biology; multi/interdisciplinary studies related;

Dartmouth College (continued)
music; Native American studies; philosophy; physics; political science; psychology; religious studies; romance languages; Russian; Russian/Slavic studies; sociology; Spanish; theater arts/drama; women's studies.

Academic Programs *Special study options:* accelerated degree program, advanced placement credit, double majors, honors programs, independent study, internships, off-campus study, services for LD students, student-designed majors, study abroad, summer session for credit. *ROTC:* Army (c).

Library Baker-Berry Library plus 10 others with 2.4 million titles, 20,679 serial subscriptions, 78,471 audiovisual materials, an OPAC, a Web page.

Computers on Campus 12000 computers available on campus for general student use. A campuswide network can be accessed from student residence rooms and from off campus. Internet access, online (class) registration, at least one staffed computer lab available.

Student Life *Housing:* on-campus residence required for freshman year. *Options:* coed. *Activities and Organizations:* drama/theater group, student-run newspaper, radio and television station, choral group, marching band, student government, Outing Club, intramural sports, community service, performing arts, national fraternities, national sororities. *Campus security:* 24-hour emergency response devices and patrols, student patrols, late-night transport/escort service, controlled dormitory access. *Student Services:* health clinic, personal/psychological counseling, women's center.

Athletics Member NCAA. All Division I except football (Division I-AA). *Intercollegiate sports:* badminton M(c)/W(c), baseball M, basketball M/W, crew M/W, cross-country running M/W, equestrian sports M/W, fencing M(c)/W(c), field hockey W, golf M/W, gymnastics M(c)/W(c), ice hockey M/W, lacrosse M/W, rugby M(c)/W(c), sailing M/W, skiing (cross-country) M/W, skiing (downhill) M/W, soccer M/W, softball W, squash M/W, swimming M/W, table tennis M(c)/W(c), tennis M/W, track and field M/W, volleyball M(c)/W, water polo M(c)/W(c), wrestling M(c). *Intramural sports:* baseball M, basketball M/W, cross-country running M/W, football M/W, golf M/W, ice hockey M/W, lacrosse M/W, racquetball M/W, riflery M/W, rugby M/W, skiing (cross-country) M/W, skiing (downhill) M/W, soccer M/W, softball M/W, squash M/W, swimming M/W, table tennis M/W, tennis M/W, track and field M/W, volleyball M/W, water polo M/W, weight lifting M/W, wrestling M.

Costs (2001–02) *One-time required fee:* $110. *Comprehensive fee:* $34,458 includes full-time tuition ($26,400), mandatory fees ($162), and room and board ($7896). *Room and board:* College room only: $4719. Room and board charges vary according to board plan and housing facility. *Payment plans:* tuition prepayment, installment.

Financial Aid Of all full-time matriculated undergraduates who enrolled in 2001, 2430 applied for aid, 1872 were judged to have need, 1872 had their need fully met. 1436 Federal Work-Study jobs (averaging $1901). 195 State and other part-time jobs (averaging $1899). In 2001, 204 non-need-based awards were made. *Average percent of need met:* 100%. *Average financial aid package:* $26,168. *Average need-based loan:* $5767. *Average need-based gift aid:* $18,845. *Average non-need based aid:* $2165. *Financial aid deadline:* 2/1.

Applying *Options:* common application, electronic application, early admission, early decision, deferred entrance. *Application fee:* $65. *Required:* essay or personal statement, high school transcript, 3 letters of recommendation. *Recommended:* interview. *Application deadlines:* 1/1 (freshmen), 3/1 (transfers). *Early decision:* 11/1. *Notification:* 4/10 (freshmen), 12/15 (early decision).

Admissions Contact Mr. Karl M. Furstenberg, Dean of Admissions and Financial Aid, Dartmouth College, 6016 McNutt Hall, Hanover, NH 03755. *Phone:* 603-646-2875. *E-mail:* admissions.office@dartmouth.edu.

FRANKLIN PIERCE COLLEGE
Rindge, New Hampshire

- **Independent** comprehensive, founded 1962
- **Calendar** semesters
- **Degrees** certificates, associate, bachelor's, and master's (profile does not reflect significant enrollment at 6 continuing education sites; master's degree is only offered at these sites)
- **Rural** 1000-acre campus
- **Endowment** $7.1 million
- **Coed,** 1,548 undergraduate students, 95% full-time, 52% women, 48% men
- **Moderately difficult** entrance level, 81% of applicants were admitted

Undergraduates Students come from 27 states and territories, 18 other countries, 86% are from out of state, 4% African American, 1% Asian American or Pacific Islander, 3% Hispanic American, 0.3% Native American, 2% international, 93% live on campus. *Retention:* 68% of 2001 full-time freshmen returned.

Freshmen *Admission:* 3,850 applied, 3,109 admitted. *Average high school GPA:* 2.81. *Test scores:* SAT verbal scores over 500: 43%; SAT math scores over 500: 36%; ACT scores over 18: 65%; SAT verbal scores over 600: 10%; SAT math scores over 600: 7%; ACT scores over 24: 14%; SAT math scores over 700: 1%.

Faculty *Total:* 141, 46% full-time, 45% with terminal degrees. *Student/faculty ratio:* 19:1.

Majors Accounting; adult/continuing education; advertising; American studies; anthropology; applied art; archaeology; art; art education; biology; business administration; business marketing and marketing management; ceramic arts; clinical psychology; computer programming; computer science; counselor education/guidance; creative writing; criminal justice/law enforcement administration; early childhood education; ecology; economics; education; elementary education; English; environmental biology; environmental science; finance; fine/studio arts; graphic design/commercial art/illustration; history; journalism; liberal arts and sciences/liberal studies; literature; mass communications; mathematics; music; political science; pre-dentistry; pre-law; pre-medicine; pre-veterinary studies; psychology; radio/television broadcasting; recreation/leisure facilities management; secondary education; social work; sociology; sport/fitness administration; theater arts/drama.

Academic Programs *Special study options:* academic remediation for entering students, adult/continuing education programs, advanced placement credit, double majors, English as a second language, external degree program, honors programs, independent study, internships, off-campus study, part-time degree program, services for LD students, student-designed majors, study abroad, summer session for credit. *ROTC:* Air Force (c).

Library Franklin Pierce College Library with 114,934 titles, 1,940 serial subscriptions, 3,742 audiovisual materials, an OPAC, a Web page.

Computers on Campus 171 computers available on campus for general student use. A campuswide network can be accessed from student residence rooms. At least one staffed computer lab available.

Student Life *Housing:* on-campus residence required through senior year. *Options:* coed, disabled students. *Activities and Organizations:* drama/theater group, student-run newspaper, radio and television station, choral group, Outing Club, WFPR-Radio, Student Senate, Law Club, Business Club. *Campus security:* 24-hour emergency response devices and patrols, student patrols, late-night transport/escort service, controlled dormitory access. *Student Services:* health clinic, personal/psychological counseling.

Athletics Member NCAA. All Division II. *Intercollegiate sports:* baseball M(s), basketball M(s)/W(s), crew M(c)/W(c), cross-country running M/W, field hockey W, golf M(s)/W, ice hockey M(c), sailing M(c)/W(c), soccer M(s)/W(s), softball W(s), tennis M(s)/W(s), volleyball W(s). *Intramural sports:* basketball M/W, field hockey W, football M, golf M/W, ice hockey M, lacrosse M, sailing M/W, soccer M/W, softball W, table tennis M/W, tennis M/W, volleyball M/W.

Standardized Tests *Required:* SAT I or ACT (for admission).

Costs (2002–03) *Comprehensive fee:* $27,455 includes full-time tuition ($19,560), mandatory fees ($965), and room and board ($6930). Part-time tuition: $652 per credit. *Room and board:* Room and board charges vary according to board plan. *Payment plan:* installment. *Waivers:* senior citizens and employees or children of employees.

Financial Aid Of all full-time matriculated undergraduates who enrolled in 2001, 1204 applied for aid, 1121 were judged to have need, 128 had their need fully met. In 2001, 280 non-need-based awards were made. *Average percent of need met:* 73%. *Average financial aid package:* $15,755. *Average need-based loan:* $4457. *Average need-based gift aid:* $10,907. *Average indebtedness upon graduation:* $19,308.

Applying *Options:* common application, electronic application, early admission, deferred entrance. *Required:* essay or personal statement, high school transcript, 1 letter of recommendation. *Recommended:* minimum 2.0 GPA, interview. *Application deadline:* rolling (freshmen), rolling (transfers). *Notification:* continuous until 9/1 (freshmen).

Admissions Contact Ms. Lucy C. Shonk, Dean of Admissions, Franklin Pierce College, 20 College Road, Franklin Pierce College, Rindge, NH 03461-0060. *Phone:* 603-899-4050. *Toll-free phone:* 800-437-0048. *Fax:* 603-899-4394. *E-mail:* admissions@fpc.edu.

HESSER COLLEGE
Manchester, New Hampshire

- **Proprietary** primarily 2-year, founded 1900, part of Quest Education Corporation
- **Calendar** semesters
- **Degrees** certificates, diplomas, associate, and bachelor's
- **Urban** 1-acre campus with easy access to Boston
- **Coed,** 2,766 undergraduate students, 49% full-time, 65% women, 35% men
- **Moderately difficult** entrance level, 90% of applicants were admitted

Undergraduates 1,363 full-time, 1,403 part-time. Students come from 12 states and territories, 2% African American, 0.9% Asian American or Pacific Islander, 4% Hispanic American, 0.1% Native American, 0.1% international, 50% live on campus.

Freshmen *Admission:* 1,800 applied, 1,620 admitted, 620 enrolled. *Average high school GPA:* 2.3.

Faculty *Total:* 164, 18% full-time, 2% with terminal degrees. *Student/faculty ratio:* 18:1.

Majors Accounting; broadcast journalism; business administration; business marketing and marketing management; business services marketing; child care/guidance; computer engineering technology; computer/information sciences; computer management; computer programming; computer science; computer systems analysis; computer typography/composition; corrections; criminal justice/law enforcement administration; criminal justice studies; early childhood education; entrepreneurship; fashion design/illustration; fashion merchandising; graphic design/commercial art/illustration; hotel and restaurant management; human services; information sciences/systems; interior design; law enforcement/police science; liberal arts and sciences/liberal studies; management information systems/business data processing; mass communications; medical administrative assistant; medical assistant; paralegal/legal assistant; physical therapy assistant; psychology; radio/television broadcasting; retail management; secretarial science; security; social work; sport/fitness administration; travel/tourism management.

Academic Programs *Special study options:* accelerated degree program, adult/continuing education programs, advanced placement credit, cooperative education, internships, part-time degree program, student-designed majors, summer session for credit.

Library Kenneth W. Galeucia Memorial Library with 38,000 titles, 200 serial subscriptions, an OPAC, a Web page.

Computers on Campus 60 computers available on campus for general student use. Internet access, at least one staffed computer lab available.

Student Life *Housing Options:* coed. *Activities and Organizations:* student-run radio and television station, student government, Ski Club, Amnesty International, yearbook, student ambassador. *Campus security:* 24-hour emergency response devices and patrols, student patrols, late-night transport/escort service, controlled dormitory access. *Student Services:* health clinic, personal/psychological counseling.

Athletics *Intercollegiate sports:* basketball M(s)/W(s), soccer M(s), softball W(s), volleyball M(s)/W(s). *Intramural sports:* basketball M/W, bowling M/W, skiing (downhill) M/W, softball M/W, table tennis M/W, volleyball M/W, weight lifting M/W.

Costs (2001–02) *Comprehensive fee:* $16,210 includes full-time tuition ($9800), mandatory fees ($410), and room and board ($6000). Full-time tuition and fees vary according to class time, course load, and program. Part-time tuition: $359 per credit. Part-time tuition and fees vary according to class time and program. *Required fees:* $205 per term part-time. *Room and board:* Room and board charges vary according to board plan. *Payment plans:* installment, deferred payment. *Waivers:* employees or children of employees.

Financial Aid Of all full-time matriculated undergraduates who enrolled in 2001, 700 Federal Work-Study jobs (averaging $1000).

Applying *Options:* common application, electronic application, deferred entrance. *Application fee:* $10. *Required:* high school transcript, interview. *Required for some:* letters of recommendation. *Recommended:* minimum 2.0 GPA. *Application deadline:* rolling (freshmen), rolling (transfers). *Notification:* continuous (freshmen).

Admissions Contact Hesser College, 3 Sundial Avenue, Manchester, NH 03103. *Phone:* 603-668-6660 Ext. 2101. *Toll-free phone:* 800-526-9231 Ext. 2110. *E-mail:* admissions@hesser.edu.

KEENE STATE COLLEGE

Keene, New Hampshire

- **State-supported** comprehensive, founded 1909, part of University System of New Hampshire
- **Calendar** semesters
- **Degrees** certificates, associate, bachelor's, master's, post-master's, and postbachelor's certificates
- **Small-town** 160-acre campus
- **Endowment** $8.4 million
- **Coed,** 4,400 undergraduate students, 86% full-time, 58% women, 42% men
- **Moderately difficult** entrance level, 78% of applicants were admitted

Keene State College, a public institution grounded in the liberal arts, offers programs in 35 academic areas. The campus, with 21st-century technology housed in traditional ivy-covered brick buildings, is located in the Monadnock Region of southwestern New Hampshire. KSC has an enrollment of 4,800 full- and part-time students.

Undergraduates Students come from 26 states and territories, 43% are from out of state, 0.3% African American, 0.7% Asian American or Pacific Islander, 0.8% Hispanic American, 0.3% Native American, 0.4% international, 56% live on campus. *Retention:* 77% of 2001 full-time freshmen returned.

Freshmen *Admission:* 3,428 applied, 2,682 admitted. *Average high school GPA:* 2.86. *Test scores:* SAT verbal scores over 500: 48%; SAT math scores over 500: 44%; ACT scores over 18: 68%; SAT verbal scores over 600: 10%; SAT math scores over 600: 10%; ACT scores over 24: 11%; SAT verbal scores over 700: 1%; SAT math scores over 700: 1%.

Faculty *Total:* 376, 51% full-time. *Student/faculty ratio:* 17:1.

Majors Alcohol/drug abuse counseling; American studies; art; athletic training/sports medicine; biology; business administration; chemistry; computer science; dietetics; drafting; early childhood education; ecology; economics; education; electrical/electronic engineering technology; elementary education; English; environmental science; film studies; French; geography; geology; graphic design/commercial art/illustration; health education; history; home economics; home economics education; industrial arts; industrial technology; interdisciplinary studies; journalism; liberal arts and sciences/liberal studies; mass communications; mathematics; music; music history; music teacher education; nutrition science; occupational safety/health technology; physical education; physics; political science; pre-engineering; psychology; safety/security technology; secondary education; social sciences; sociology; Spanish; special education; sport/fitness administration; theater arts/drama; trade/industrial education.

Academic Programs *Special study options:* advanced placement credit, cooperative education, double majors, English as a second language, honors programs, independent study, internships, off-campus study, part-time degree program, services for LD students, student-designed majors, study abroad, summer session for credit. *ROTC:* Air Force (c). *Unusual degree programs:* 3-2 engineering with Clarkson University, University of New Hampshire.

Library Mason Library with 958 serial subscriptions, an OPAC, a Web page.

Computers on Campus 285 computers available on campus for general student use. A campuswide network can be accessed from student residence rooms and from off campus that provide access to e-mail, personal web pages. Internet access, at least one staffed computer lab available.

Student Life *Housing Options:* coed, women-only, disabled students. *Activities and Organizations:* drama/theater group, student-run newspaper, radio and television station, choral group, Social Activities Council, Concerned Students Coalition, Pride, Habitat for Humanity, sports club, national fraternities, national sororities. *Campus security:* 24-hour emergency response devices and patrols, late-night transport/escort service, controlled dormitory access. *Student Services:* health clinic, personal/psychological counseling, women's center.

Athletics Member NCAA. All Division III. *Intercollegiate sports:* baseball M, basketball M/W, cross-country running M/W, field hockey W, lacrosse M/W, rugby M(c)/W(c), skiing (downhill) M(c)/W(c), soccer M/W, softball W, swimming M/W, track and field M/W, volleyball W. *Intramural sports:* badminton M/W, basketball M/W, football M/W, racquetball M/W, soccer W, softball M/W, squash M/W, tennis M/W, volleyball M/W, water polo M/W.

Standardized Tests *Required:* SAT I or ACT (for admission).

Costs (2001–02) *Tuition:* state resident $4220 full-time, $230 per credit hour part-time; nonresident $9720 full-time, $524 per credit hour part-time. Part-time tuition and fees vary according to course load. *Required fees:* $1334 full-time, $54 per credit, $10 per term part-time. *Room and board:* $5256; room only: $3580. Room and board charges vary according to board plan and housing facility. *Payment plan:* installment. *Waivers:* employees or children of employees.

Financial Aid Of all full-time matriculated undergraduates who enrolled in 2001, 2502 applied for aid, 1874 were judged to have need, 631 had their need fully met. 535 Federal Work-Study jobs (averaging $794). 438 State and other part-time jobs (averaging $862). In 2001, 331 non-need-based awards were made. *Average percent of need met:* 84%. *Average financial aid package:* $6814. *Average need-based loan:* $3601. *Average need-based gift aid:* $3759. *Average non-need based aid:* $2091. *Average indebtedness upon graduation:* $16,607. *Financial aid deadline:* 3/1.

Applying *Options:* deferred entrance. *Application fee:* $35 (non-residents). *Required:* essay or personal statement, high school transcript, 1 letter of recommendation. *Required for some:* interview. *Recommended:* interview. *Application deadlines:* 4/1 (freshmen), 5/1 (transfers). *Notification:* continuous (freshmen).

Admissions Contact Ms. Margaret Richmond, Director of Admissions, Keene State College, 229 Main Street, Keene, NH 03435-2604. *Phone:* 603-358-2273. *Toll-free phone:* 800-572-1909. *Fax:* 603-358-2767. *E-mail:* admissions@keene.edu.

MAGDALEN COLLEGE
Warner, New Hampshire

- **Independent Roman Catholic** 4-year, founded 1973
- **Calendar** semesters
- **Degree** bachelor's
- **Endowment** $1.0 million
- **Coed,** 85 undergraduate students, 100% full-time, 47% women, 53% men
- **Moderately difficult** entrance level, 66% of applicants were admitted

Undergraduates 85 full-time. Students come from 17 states and territories, 92% are from out of state, 100% live on campus. *Retention:* 81% of 2001 full-time freshmen returned.

Freshmen *Admission:* 53 applied, 35 admitted, 35 enrolled. *Average high school GPA:* 3.30. *Test scores:* SAT verbal scores over 500: 38%; SAT math scores over 500: 19%; ACT scores over 18: 60%; SAT verbal scores over 600: 13%; SAT math scores over 600: 6%; ACT scores over 24: 20%; SAT math scores over 700: 6%.

Faculty *Total:* 10, 80% full-time, 80% with terminal degrees. *Student/faculty ratio:* 9:1.

Majors Liberal arts and sciences/liberal studies.

Academic Programs *Special study options:* academic remediation for entering students, cooperative education, part-time degree program, summer session for credit.

Library St. Augustine Learning Center with 26,000 titles, 10 serial subscriptions.

Computers on Campus 6 computers available on campus for general student use. Internet access, at least one staffed computer lab available.

Student Life *Housing:* on-campus residence required through senior year. *Options:* men-only, women-only. *Activities and Organizations:* drama/theater group, student-run newspaper, choral group, Performance Choir, Polophony Choir, Drama Club, intramural sports, Leisure Activities Programs. *Campus security:* 24-hour emergency response devices, student patrols. *Student Services:* personal/psychological counseling.

Athletics *Intramural sports:* basketball M/W, skiing (cross-country) M/W, skiing (downhill) M/W, soccer M, softball M/W, table tennis M/W, tennis M/W, volleyball M/W, weight lifting M.

Standardized Tests *Required:* SAT I or ACT (for admission).

Costs (2001–02) *Comprehensive fee:* $12,750 includes full-time tuition ($7500) and room and board ($5250). Part-time tuition: $200 per credit. *Payment plan:* installment. *Waivers:* employees or children of employees.

Applying *Options:* early admission, early decision. *Application fee:* $35. *Required:* essay or personal statement, high school transcript, 2 letters of recommendation, interview, medical examination form. *Application deadline:* 5/1 (freshmen). *Early decision:* 1/1.

Admissions Contact Paul V. Sullivan, Director of Admissions, Magdalen College, 511 Kearsarge Mountain Road, Warner, NH 03278. *Phone:* 603-456-2656 Ext. 11. *Toll-free phone:* 877-498-1723. *Fax:* 603-456-2660. *E-mail:* admissions@magdalen.edu.

NEW ENGLAND COLLEGE
Henniker, New Hampshire

- **Independent** comprehensive, founded 1946
- **Calendar** semesters
- **Degrees** associate, bachelor's, and master's
- **Small-town** 225-acre campus with easy access to Boston
- **Endowment** $5.3 million
- **Coed,** 800 undergraduate students, 91% full-time, 49% women, 51% men
- **Moderately difficult** entrance level, 93% of applicants were admitted

Undergraduates 726 full-time, 74 part-time. Students come from 29 states and territories, 22 other countries, 68% are from out of state, 2% African American, 0.3% Asian American or Pacific Islander, 0.6% Hispanic American, 5% international, 5% transferred in. *Retention:* 71% of 2001 full-time freshmen returned.

Freshmen *Admission:* 1,031 applied, 963 admitted, 255 enrolled. *Average high school GPA:* 2.65. *Test scores:* SAT verbal scores over 500: 37%; SAT math scores over 500: 27%; ACT scores over 18: 50%; SAT verbal scores over 600: 5%; SAT math scores over 600: 4%; ACT scores over 24: 10%; SAT verbal scores over 700: 1%.

Faculty *Total:* 91, 57% full-time, 38% with terminal degrees. *Student/faculty ratio:* 13:1.

Majors Accounting; advertising; art; art history; athletic training/sports medicine; biology; business administration; business marketing and marketing management; computer management; criminal justice/law enforcement administration; drawing; ecology; education; education (K-12); elementary education; English; entrepreneurship; environmental science; fine/studio arts; health/physical education; history; journalism; mass communications; philosophy; photography; physical education; political science; pre-law; psychology; public relations; recreation/leisure facilities management; recreation/leisure studies; secondary education; sociology; special education; sport/fitness administration; theater arts/drama.

Academic Programs *Special study options:* adult/continuing education programs, advanced placement credit, cooperative education, double majors, English as a second language, external degree program, honors programs, independent study, internships, off-campus study, part-time degree program, services for LD students, student-designed majors, study abroad, summer session for credit. *ROTC:* Army (c).

Library Danforth Library with 107,200 titles, 400 serial subscriptions, 2,150 audiovisual materials, an OPAC.

Computers on Campus 57 computers available on campus for general student use. A campuswide network can be accessed from student residence rooms and from off campus. Internet access, online (class) registration, at least one staffed computer lab available.

Student Life *Housing:* on-campus residence required through sophomore year. *Options:* coed. *Activities and Organizations:* drama/theater group, student-run newspaper, radio station, choral group, Student Senate, Campus Activities Board, T.E.A.C.H. (Taking Education Across Children's Horizons), International Student Association, national sororities. *Campus security:* 24-hour emergency response devices and patrols, student patrols, late-night transport/escort service. *Student Services:* health clinic, personal/psychological counseling, women's center.

Athletics Member NCAA. All Division III. *Intercollegiate sports:* baseball M, basketball M/W, cross-country running M/W, field hockey W, ice hockey M/W, lacrosse M/W, skiing (downhill) M/W, soccer M/W, softball W. *Intramural sports:* badminton M/W, basketball M/W, bowling M/W, football M/W, golf M/W, ice hockey M/W, rugby M/W, skiing (cross-country) M/W, skiing (downhill) M/W, soccer M/W, softball M/W, tennis M/W, volleyball M/W.

Costs (2001–02) *One-time required fee:* $100. *Comprehensive fee:* $26,706 includes full-time tuition ($19,024), mandatory fees ($566), and room and board ($7116). Part-time tuition: $793 per credit. Part-time tuition and fees vary according to course load. *Required fees:* $168 per term part-time. *Room and board:* College room only: $3700. Room and board charges vary according to board plan. *Payment plan:* installment. *Waivers:* senior citizens and employees or children of employees.

Financial Aid Of all full-time matriculated undergraduates who enrolled in 2001, 517 applied for aid, 469 were judged to have need, 100 had their need fully met. 380 Federal Work-Study jobs (averaging $1369). 19 State and other part-time jobs (averaging $1783). *Average percent of need met:* 82%. *Average financial aid package:* $15,641. *Average need-based loan:* $3932. *Average need-based gift aid:* $11,389. *Average indebtedness upon graduation:* $22,519.

Applying *Options:* common application, electronic application, early action, deferred entrance. *Application fee:* $30. *Required:* essay or personal statement, high school transcript, 1 letter of recommendation. *Recommended:* interview. *Application deadline:* rolling (freshmen), rolling (transfers). *Notification:* continuous (freshmen), 12/20 (early action).

Admissions Contact Ms. Lisa M. Partridge, Director of Admission, New England College, 26 Bridge Street, Henniker, NH 03242. *Phone:* 603-428-2223. *Toll-free phone:* 800-521-7642. *Fax:* 603-428-3155. *E-mail:* admission@nec.edu.

NEW HAMPSHIRE INSTITUTE OF ART
Manchester, New Hampshire

Admissions Contact Admissions Department, New Hampshire Institute of Art, 148 Concort Street, Manchester, NH 03104-4858. *Phone:* 603-623-0313. *Toll-free phone:* 866-241-4918. *E-mail:* fmenard@nhia.edu or lsullivan@nhia.edu.

PLYMOUTH STATE COLLEGE
Plymouth, New Hampshire

- **State-supported** comprehensive, founded 1871, part of University System of New Hampshire
- **Calendar** semesters
- **Degrees** bachelor's, master's, post-master's, and postbachelor's certificates
- **Small-town** 170-acre campus
- **Endowment** $2.9 million
- **Coed,** 3,565 undergraduate students, 93% full-time, 52% women, 48% men
- **Moderately difficult** entrance level, 77% of applicants were admitted

Undergraduates 3,312 full-time, 253 part-time. Students come from 32 states and territories, 9 other countries, 43% are from out of state, 0.5% African American, 1.0% Asian American or Pacific Islander, 0.8% Hispanic American, 0.4% Native American, 0.3% international, 5% transferred in, 57% live on campus. *Retention:* 73% of 2001 full-time freshmen returned.

Freshmen *Admission:* 3,333 applied, 2,573 admitted, 879 enrolled. *Average high school GPA:* 2.76. *Test scores:* SAT verbal scores over 500: 41%; SAT math scores over 500: 38%; ACT scores over 18: 62%; SAT verbal scores over 600: 8%; SAT math scores over 600: 8%; ACT scores over 24: 13%.

Faculty *Total:* 301, 56% full-time, 59% with terminal degrees. *Student/faculty ratio:* 16:1.

Majors Accounting; applied economics; art; art education; athletic training/sports medicine; atmospheric sciences; biology; biotechnology research; business administration; business marketing and marketing management; chemistry; city/community/regional planning; communications; computer science; early childhood education; ecology; elementary education; English; fine/studio arts; French; geography; graphic design/commercial art/illustration; history; humanities; information sciences/systems; mathematics; mathematics education; medieval/renaissance studies; multi/interdisciplinary studies related; music; music teacher education; philosophy; physical education; political science; psychology; public administration; public health education/promotion; recreation/leisure studies; social science education; social sciences and history related; social work; Spanish; teacher education, specific programs related; theater arts/drama.

Academic Programs *Special study options:* accelerated degree program, advanced placement credit, double majors, honors programs, independent study, internships, off-campus study, part-time degree program, services for LD students, student-designed majors, study abroad, summer session for credit. *ROTC:* Army (c), Air Force (c).

Library Lamson Library with 243,717 titles, 1,065 serial subscriptions, 20,541 audiovisual materials, an OPAC, a Web page.

Computers on Campus 500 computers available on campus for general student use. A campuswide network can be accessed from student residence rooms and from off campus. Internet access, online (class) registration, at least one staffed computer lab available.

Student Life *Housing:* on-campus residence required through sophomore year. *Options:* coed. *Activities and Organizations:* drama/theater group, student-run newspaper, radio station, choral group, Programming Activities in College Environment, Student Senate, Alternative Spring Break, Leadership Effectiveness and Development Seminar, OSSIPEE—student wellness organization, national fraternities, national sororities. *Campus security:* 24-hour emergency response devices and patrols, student patrols, late-night transport/escort service, controlled dormitory access, shuttle bus service, crime prevention programs, self-defense education. *Student Services:* health clinic, personal/psychological counseling, women's center.

Athletics Member NCAA. All Division III. *Intercollegiate sports:* baseball M, basketball M/W, field hockey W, football M, ice hockey M, lacrosse M/W, rugby M(c)/W(c), skiing (downhill) M/W, soccer M/W, softball W, swimming W, tennis M/W, volleyball M(c)/W, wrestling M. *Intramural sports:* basketball M/W, football M/W, golf M/W, racquetball M/W, soccer M/W, softball M/W, tennis M/W, volleyball M/W.

Standardized Tests *Required:* SAT I or ACT (for admission).

Costs (2001–02) *Tuition:* state resident $4220 full-time, $176 per credit hour part-time; nonresident $9720 full-time, $486 per credit hour part-time. Full-time tuition and fees vary according to reciprocity agreements. Part-time tuition and fees vary according to course load. *Required fees:* $1330 full-time, $61 per credit hour. *Room and board:* $5474; room only: $3662. Room and board charges vary according to board plan and housing facility. *Payment plan:* installment. *Waivers:* senior citizens and employees or children of employees.

Financial Aid Of all full-time matriculated undergraduates who enrolled in 2001, 2530 applied for aid, 1883 were judged to have need, 333 had their need fully met. 991 Federal Work-Study jobs (averaging $1791). In 2001, 173 non-need-based awards were made. *Average percent of need met:* 80%. *Average financial aid package:* $7827. *Average need-based loan:* $3861. *Average need-based gift aid:* $3875. *Average non-need based aid:* $1850. *Average indebtedness upon graduation:* $17,232.

Applying *Options:* common application, electronic application. *Application fee:* $30. *Required:* essay or personal statement, high school transcript, 2 letters of recommendation. *Required for some:* interview. *Recommended:* minimum 2.0 GPA. *Application deadlines:* 4/1 (freshmen), 4/1 (transfers). *Notification:* continuous until 7/1 (freshmen).

Admissions Contact Mr. Eugene Fahey, Senior Associate Director of Admission, Plymouth State College, 17 High Street, MSC #52, Plymouth, NH 03264-1595. *Phone:* 800-842-6900. *Toll-free phone:* 800-842-6900. *Fax:* 603-535-2714. *E-mail:* pscadmit@mail.plymouth.edu.

RIVIER COLLEGE
Nashua, New Hampshire

- **Independent Roman Catholic** comprehensive, founded 1933
- **Calendar** semesters
- **Degrees** certificates, associate, bachelor's, master's, post-master's, and postbachelor's certificates
- **Suburban** 64-acre campus with easy access to Boston
- **Endowment** $13.9 million
- **Coed,** 852 undergraduate students
- **Moderately difficult** entrance level, 70% of applicants were admitted

Rivier's School of Undergraduate Studies enrolls approximately 800 day students and 500 evening students. Students pursue Rivier's commitment to social justice through service-learning experiences in the community, combining academic achievement in the liberal arts and professional studies with hands-on preparation for the future. Special opportunities, such as the Honors Program, offer added challenges and enrichment.

Undergraduates Students come from 10 states and territories, 6 other countries, 32% are from out of state, 0.5% African American, 3% Asian American or Pacific Islander, 2% Hispanic American, 0.3% Native American, 2% international, 46% live on campus. *Retention:* 78% of 2001 full-time freshmen returned.

Freshmen *Admission:* 900 applied, 630 admitted. *Average high school GPA:* 3.0.

Faculty *Total:* 209, 38% full-time. *Student/faculty ratio:* 13:1.

Majors American government; art; biology; biology education; business administration; chemistry; chemistry education; communications; computer science; drawing; early childhood education; education; elementary education; English; English education; fine/studio arts; foreign languages education; French; graphic design/commercial art/illustration; history; information sciences/systems; legal studies; liberal arts and sciences/liberal studies; mathematics; mathematics education; modern languages; nursing; painting; photography; pre-dentistry; pre-law; pre-medicine; pre-veterinary studies; psychology; secondary education; social science education; sociology; Spanish; special education.

Academic Programs *Special study options:* adult/continuing education programs, advanced placement credit, double majors, English as a second language, honors programs, independent study, internships, off-campus study, part-time degree program, services for LD students, summer session for credit. *ROTC:* Air Force (c).

Library Regina Library plus 1 other with 105,000 titles, 1,802 serial subscriptions, 29,094 audiovisual materials, an OPAC, a Web page.

Computers on Campus 93 computers available on campus for general student use. A campuswide network can be accessed from student residence rooms and from off campus. At least one staffed computer lab available.

Student Life *Housing Options:* coed. *Activities and Organizations:* drama/theater group, student-run newspaper, choral group, Student Government Association, Residence Hall Council, Student Business Organization, Student Admissions Committee, Behavioral Sciences Association. *Campus security:* 24-hour emergency response devices and patrols, late-night transport/escort service, controlled dormitory access. *Student Services:* health clinic, personal/psychological counseling.

Athletics Member NCAA. All Division III. *Intercollegiate sports:* baseball M, basketball M/W, cross-country running M/W, soccer M/W, softball W, volleyball M/W. *Intramural sports:* basketball M/W, skiing (cross-country) M/W, skiing (downhill) M/W, soccer M/W, softball M/W, table tennis M/W, tennis M/W, volleyball M/W, weight lifting M/W.

Standardized Tests *Required:* SAT I or ACT (for admission).

Costs (2001–02) *Comprehensive fee:* $21,620 includes full-time tuition ($15,210), mandatory fees ($310), and room and board ($6100). Part-time tuition: $563 per credit hour. Part-time tuition and fees vary according to class time. *Required fees:* $2 per credit hour, $25 per term part-time. *Payment plans:* installment, deferred payment. *Waivers:* senior citizens and employees or children of employees.

Financial Aid Of all full-time matriculated undergraduates who enrolled in 2001, 693 applied for aid, 681 were judged to have need, 115 had their need fully met. 315 Federal Work-Study jobs (averaging $2000). In 2001, 50 non-need-based awards were made. *Average percent of need met:* 68%. *Average financial aid package:* $9649. *Average need-based loan:* $3483. *Average need-based gift aid:* $5896. *Average non-need based aid:* $9649. *Average indebtedness upon graduation:* $16,555.

Applying *Options:* common application, early action, deferred entrance. *Application fee:* $25. *Required:* essay or personal statement, high school transcript, 1 letter of recommendation. *Required for some:* interview, portfolio for art program.

Rivier College (continued)
Recommended: minimum 2.3 GPA, interview. *Application deadline:* rolling (freshmen), rolling (transfers). *Notification:* continuous (freshmen), 12/1 (early action).

Admissions Contact Mr. David Boisvert, (Interim Director of Undergraduate Admissions) Executive Assistant to President for Enrollment Management, Rivier College, 420 Main Street, Nashua, NH 03060. *Phone:* 603-897-8502. *Toll-free phone:* 800-44RIVIER. *Fax:* 603-891-1799. *E-mail:* rivadmit@rivier.edu.

SAINT ANSELM COLLEGE
Manchester, New Hampshire

- **Independent Roman Catholic** 4-year, founded 1889
- **Calendar** semesters
- **Degree** certificates and bachelor's
- **Suburban** 450-acre campus with easy access to Boston
- **Endowment** $50.3 million
- **Coed,** 1,964 undergraduate students, 96% full-time, 55% women, 45% men
- **Moderately difficult** entrance level, 75% of applicants were admitted

Undergraduates 1,888 full-time, 76 part-time. Students come from 27 states and territories, 16 other countries, 0.3% African American, 0.7% Asian American or Pacific Islander, 0.9% Hispanic American, 0.2% Native American, 0.8% international, 1% transferred in, 88% live on campus. *Retention:* 80% of 2001 full-time freshmen returned.

Freshmen *Admission:* 2,553 applied, 1,912 admitted, 542 enrolled. *Average high school GPA:* 3.09. *Test scores:* SAT verbal scores over 500: 82%; SAT math scores over 500: 83%; ACT scores over 18: 98%; SAT verbal scores over 600: 28%; SAT math scores over 600: 26%; ACT scores over 24: 48%; SAT verbal scores over 700: 2%; SAT math scores over 700: 2%; ACT scores over 30: 4%.

Faculty *Total:* 164, 74% full-time, 84% with terminal degrees. *Student/faculty ratio:* 14:1.

Majors Accounting; art; biochemistry; biological/physical sciences; biology; business; chemistry related; classics; computer science; criminal justice studies; economics; engineering; English; environmental science; finance; French; history; liberal arts and studies related; mathematics; nursing related; philosophy; political science; pre-dentistry; pre-law; pre-medicine; psychology; secondary education; sociology; Spanish; theology.

Academic Programs *Special study options:* advanced placement credit, honors programs, independent study, internships, off-campus study, part-time degree program, services for LD students, study abroad, summer session for credit. *ROTC:* Army (c), Air Force (c). *Unusual degree programs:* 3-2 engineering with University of Massachusetts Lowell, Catholic University of America, University of Notre Dame, Manhattan College.

Library Geisel Library with 214,000 titles, 1,900 serial subscriptions, 6,800 audiovisual materials, an OPAC, a Web page.

Computers on Campus 400 computers available on campus for general student use. A campuswide network can be accessed from student residence rooms and from off campus. Internet access, at least one staffed computer lab available.

Student Life *Housing:* on-campus residence required for freshman year. *Options:* men-only, women-only, disabled students. *Activities and Organizations:* drama/theater group, student-run newspaper, choral group, Center for Volunteers, Anselmian Abbey Players, Knights of Columbus, Spring Break Alternative, International Relations Club. *Campus security:* 24-hour emergency response devices and patrols, late-night transport/escort service, controlled dormitory access. *Student Services:* health clinic, personal/psychological counseling.

Athletics Member NCAA. All Division II. *Intercollegiate sports:* baseball M, basketball M(s)/W(s), crew M(c)/W(c), cross-country running M/W, field hockey W, football M, golf M, ice hockey M, lacrosse M/W, rugby M(c)/W(c), skiing (downhill) M/W, soccer M/W, softball W, tennis M/W, volleyball W. *Intramural sports:* basketball M/W, field hockey W, ice hockey M/W, racquetball M/W, skiing (cross-country) M/W, soccer M/W, softball M/W, tennis M/W, volleyball M/W, weight lifting M/W.

Standardized Tests *Required:* SAT I or ACT (for admission). *Recommended:* SAT II: Subject Tests (for admission).

Costs (2001–02) *Comprehensive fee:* $27,475 includes full-time tuition ($19,460), mandatory fees ($665), and room and board ($7350). Part-time tuition: $1946 per course. *Room and board:* College room only: $4420. Room and board charges vary according to housing facility. *Payment plans:* installment, deferred payment. *Waivers:* senior citizens and employees or children of employees.

Financial Aid Of all full-time matriculated undergraduates who enrolled in 2001, 1610 applied for aid, 1586 were judged to have need, 301 had their need fully met. In 2001, 239 non-need-based awards were made. *Average percent of need met:* 72%. *Average financial aid package:* $17,455. *Average need-based loan:* $3622. *Average need-based gift aid:* $8146. *Average non-need based aid:* $7199. *Average indebtedness upon graduation:* $17,897.

Applying *Options:* common application, electronic application, early admission, early decision, deferred entrance. *Application fee:* $50. *Required:* essay or personal statement, high school transcript, minimum 2.0 GPA, 2 letters of recommendation. *Recommended:* interview. *Application deadline:* rolling (freshmen), rolling (transfers). *Early decision:* 12/1. *Notification:* continuous (freshmen), 12/15 (early decision).

Admissions Contact Ms. Alice Dunfey, Associate Director of Admissions, Saint Anselm College, 100 Saint Anselm Drive, Manchester, NH 03102-1310. *Phone:* 603-641-7500 Ext. 7171. *Toll-free phone:* 888-4ANSELM. *Fax:* 603-641-7550. *E-mail:* admissions@anselm.edu.

SOUTHERN NEW HAMPSHIRE UNIVERSITY
Manchester, New Hampshire

- **Independent** comprehensive, founded 1932
- **Calendar** semesters
- **Degrees** certificates, diplomas, associate, bachelor's, master's, doctoral, and postbachelor's certificates
- **Suburban** 280-acre campus with easy access to Boston
- **Endowment** $10.4 million
- **Coed,** 3,907 undergraduate students, 62% full-time, 55% women, 45% men
- **Moderately difficult** entrance level, 80% of applicants were admitted

Southern New Hampshire University, formerly New Hampshire College, is enhanced by growth in response to the changing times. The University is a private institution that offers more than thirty-five majors in business, education, hospitality, and liberal arts disciplines. Master's and doctoral degrees are also awarded. The students and faculty members at Southern New Hampshire University consider it to be a whole new "U."

Undergraduates 2,431 full-time, 1,476 part-time. Students come from 23 states and territories, 60 other countries, 51% are from out of state, 2% African American, 0.8% Asian American or Pacific Islander, 2% Hispanic American, 0.1% Native American, 5% international, 4% transferred in, 80% live on campus. *Retention:* 75% of 2001 full-time freshmen returned.

Freshmen *Admission:* 2,255 applied, 1,801 admitted, 806 enrolled. *Average high school GPA:* 2.75. *Test scores:* SAT verbal scores over 500: 35%; SAT math scores over 500: 41%; SAT verbal scores over 600: 7%; SAT math scores over 600: 9%.

Faculty *Total:* 265, 42% full-time, 28% with terminal degrees. *Student/faculty ratio:* 18:1.

Majors Accounting; advertising; American studies; baker/pastry chef; business administration; business economics; business education; business marketing and marketing management; business services marketing; communications; computer/information sciences; culinary arts; early childhood education; economics; education (K-12); English; English education; fashion merchandising; finance; hospitality management; hotel and restaurant management; humanities; information sciences/systems; international business; liberal arts and sciences/liberal studies; management information systems/business data processing; marketing/distribution education; marketing research; political science; psychology; retail management; secondary education; social sciences; special education; sport/fitness administration; travel/tourism management.

Academic Programs *Special study options:* academic remediation for entering students, accelerated degree program, adult/continuing education programs, advanced placement credit, cooperative education, distance learning, double majors, English as a second language, honors programs, independent study, internships, off-campus study, part-time degree program, services for LD students, study abroad, summer session for credit. *ROTC:* Army (c), Air Force (c).

Library Harry A. B. and Gertrude C. Shapiro Library with 1,943 audiovisual materials, an OPAC, a Web page.

Computers on Campus 250 computers available on campus for general student use. A campuswide network can be accessed from student residence rooms and from off campus. At least one staffed computer lab available.

Student Life *Housing:* on-campus residence required for freshman year. *Options:* coed, men-only, women-only, disabled students. *Activities and Organizations:* drama/theater group, student-run newspaper, radio station, Student Government Association, Intergreek Council, Student Programming Board, Association Cultural Exchange, Commuter Club, national fraternities, national sororities. *Campus security:* 24-hour emergency response devices and patrols, student patrols, late-night transport/escort service, controlled dormitory access. *Student Services:* health clinic, personal/psychological counseling.

Athletics Member NCAA. All Division II. *Intercollegiate sports:* baseball M, basketball M(s)/W(s), cross-country running M/W, golf M, ice hockey M, lacrosse M, soccer M(s)/W(s), softball W, tennis M/W, volleyball W. *Intramural sports:* basketball M/W, crew M(c)/W(c), football M, ice hockey M, racquetball M/W, skiing (downhill) M(c)/W(c), soccer M(c)/W(c), volleyball M/W.

Standardized Tests *Required:* SAT I or ACT (for admission).

Costs (2001–02) *Comprehensive fee:* $23,852 includes full-time tuition ($16,536), mandatory fees ($250), and room and board ($7066). Full-time tuition and fees vary according to class time. Part-time tuition: $689 per credit. Part-time tuition and fees vary according to class time. *Room and board:* College room only: $5946. Room and board charges vary according to board plan and housing facility. *Payment plans:* installment, deferred payment. *Waivers:* senior citizens and employees or children of employees.

Financial Aid Of all full-time matriculated undergraduates who enrolled in 2001, 510 Federal Work-Study jobs (averaging $1024).

Applying *Options:* common application, electronic application, early action, deferred entrance. *Application fee:* $25. *Required:* essay or personal statement, high school transcript, minimum 2.0 GPA, letters of recommendation, 1 letter of recommendation from guidance counselor. *Recommended:* interview. *Application deadline:* rolling (freshmen), rolling (transfers). *Notification:* continuous (freshmen), 12/15 (early action).

Admissions Contact Mr. Brad Poznanski, Director of Admission and Enrollment Planning, Southern New Hampshire University, 2500 North River Road, Belknap Hall, Manchester, NH 03106-1045. *Phone:* 603-645-9611 Ext. 9633. *Toll-free phone:* 800-642-4968. *Fax:* 603-645-9693. *E-mail:* admission@snhu.edu.

THOMAS MORE COLLEGE OF LIBERAL ARTS

Merrimack, New Hampshire

- **Independent** 4-year, founded 1978, affiliated with Roman Catholic Church
- **Calendar** semesters
- **Degree** bachelor's
- **Small-town** 14-acre campus with easy access to Boston
- **Coed,** 69 undergraduate students, 100% full-time, 46% women, 54% men
- **Moderately difficult** entrance level, 97% of applicants were admitted

Undergraduates 69 full-time. Students come from 21 states and territories, 88% are from out of state, 4% Hispanic American, 3% Native American, 3% international, 7% transferred in, 98% live on campus. *Retention:* 85% of 2001 full-time freshmen returned.

Freshmen *Admission:* 30 applied, 29 admitted, 15 enrolled. *Average high school GPA:* 3.1. *Test scores:* ACT scores over 18: 100%; ACT scores over 24: 100%.

Faculty *Total:* 10, 60% full-time, 60% with terminal degrees. *Student/faculty ratio:* 9:1.

Majors Biology; literature; philosophy; political science.

Academic Programs *Special study options:* independent study, study abroad.

Library Warren Memorial Library with 50,000 titles, 15 serial subscriptions, 1,000 audiovisual materials.

Computers on Campus 6 computers available on campus for general student use. Internet access, at least one staffed computer lab available.

Student Life *Housing:* on-campus residence required through senior year. *Options:* men-only, women-only. *Activities and Organizations:* choral group. *Campus security:* student patrols, late-night transport/escort service. *Student Services:* personal/psychological counseling.

Standardized Tests *Recommended:* SAT I or ACT (for admission).

Costs (2001–02) *Comprehensive fee:* $17,700 includes full-time tuition ($10,000) and room and board ($7700). Part-time tuition: $125 per credit hour. *Room and board:* College room only: $3850. *Payment plans:* installment, deferred payment. *Waivers:* employees or children of employees.

Financial Aid Of all full-time matriculated undergraduates who enrolled in 2001, 63 applied for aid, 63 were judged to have need, 5 had their need fully met. 36 State and other part-time jobs (averaging $1130). *Average percent of need met:* 80%. *Average financial aid package:* $9570. *Average need-based loan:* $3638. *Average need-based gift aid:* $7746. *Average indebtedness upon graduation:* $16,597.

Applying *Options:* early admission, deferred entrance. *Required:* essay or personal statement, high school transcript, 2 letters of recommendation. *Required for some:* interview. *Application deadline:* rolling (freshmen), rolling (transfers). *Notification:* continuous (freshmen).

Admissions Contact Ms. Catherine M. Alcarez, Director of Admissions, Thomas More College of Liberal Arts, 6 Manchester Street, Merrimack, NH 03054-4818. *Phone:* 603-880-8308. *Toll-free phone:* 800-880-8308. *Fax:* 603-880-9280. *E-mail:* admissions@thomasmorecollege.edu.

UNIVERSITY OF NEW HAMPSHIRE

Durham, New Hampshire

- **State-supported** university, founded 1866, part of University System of New Hampshire
- **Calendar** semesters
- **Degrees** associate, bachelor's, master's, doctoral, and post-master's certificates
- **Small-town** 200-acre campus with easy access to Boston
- **Endowment** $152.0 million
- **Coed,** 11,040 undergraduate students, 92% full-time, 57% women, 43% men
- **Moderately difficult** entrance level, 76% of applicants were admitted

Undergraduates 10,115 full-time, 925 part-time. Students come from 42 states and territories, 27 other countries, 40% are from out of state, 0.9% African American, 2% Asian American or Pacific Islander, 1.0% Hispanic American, 0.2% Native American, 0.7% international, 4% transferred in, 50% live on campus. *Retention:* 85% of 2001 full-time freshmen returned.

Freshmen *Admission:* 10,093 applied, 7,708 admitted, 2,555 enrolled. *Test scores:* SAT verbal scores over 500: 76%; SAT math scores over 500: 80%; SAT verbal scores over 600: 26%; SAT math scores over 600: 32%; SAT verbal scores over 700: 3%; SAT math scores over 700: 4%.

Faculty *Total:* 714, 82% full-time, 81% with terminal degrees. *Student/faculty ratio:* 14:1.

Majors Accounting; adult/continuing education; agricultural animal husbandry/production management; agricultural business; agricultural education; agricultural sciences; agronomy/crop science; American studies; animal sciences; anthropology; art; art education; art history; athletic training/sports medicine; biochemistry; biological/physical sciences; biology; biomedical technology; botany; business administration; cell biology; chemical engineering; chemistry; child care/development; city/community/regional planning; civil engineering; civil engineering technology; classics; community services; computer engineering; computer science; construction management; construction technology; culinary arts; dairy science; dietetics; early childhood education; earth sciences; ecology; economics; electrical/electronic engineering technology; electrical engineering; engineering technology; English; environmental engineering; environmental science; equestrian studies; evolutionary biology; exercise sciences; family/consumer studies; finance; fine/studio arts; food products retailing; forest harvesting production technology; forest products technology; forestry; French; geography; geology; German; Greek (modern); health services administration; history; home economics; horticulture science; hotel and restaurant management; humanities; interdisciplinary studies; international relations; journalism; landscape architecture; landscaping management; Latin (ancient and medieval); liberal arts and sciences/liberal studies; linguistics; literature; marine biology; marine science; mass communications; materials science; mathematical statistics; mathematics; mechanical engineering; mechanical engineering technology; medical laboratory technician; microbiology/bacteriology; modern languages; molecular biology; music; music history; music (piano and organ performance); music teacher education; music (voice and choral/opera performance); natural resources conservation; natural resources management; natural sciences; nursing; nutrition science; occupational therapy; ocean engineering; oceanography; ornamental horticulture; philosophy; physical education; physics; political science; pre-engineering; pre-medicine; pre-veterinary studies; psychology; recreational therapy; recreation/leisure studies; restaurant operations; romance languages; Russian; science education; social work; sociology; soil conservation; Spanish; speech-language pathology/audiology; speech therapy; stringed instruments; surveying; theater arts/drama; trade/industrial education; travel/tourism management; water resources; wildlife biology; wildlife management; wind/percussion instruments; women's studies; zoology.

Academic Programs *Special study options:* accelerated degree program, adult/continuing education programs, advanced placement credit, distance learning, double majors, English as a second language, external degree program, honors programs, independent study, internships, off-campus study, part-time degree program, services for LD students, student-designed majors, study abroad, summer session for credit. *ROTC:* Army (b), Air Force (b). *Unusual degree programs:* 3-2 liberal arts, French, botany.

Library Dimond Library plus 4 others with 856,939 titles, 9,200 serial subscriptions, 22,761 audiovisual materials, an OPAC, a Web page.

Computers on Campus 380 computers available on campus for general student use. A campuswide network can be accessed from student residence rooms and from off campus. Internet access, online (class) registration, at least one staffed computer lab available.

Student Life *Housing Options:* coed, women-only. *Activities and Organizations:* drama/theater group, student-run newspaper, radio station, choral group, marching band, Outing Club, student government, Diversity Support Coalition, Campus Activities Board, Memorial Union Student Organization (MUSO),

University of New Hampshire (continued)
national fraternities, national sororities. *Campus security:* 24-hour emergency response devices and patrols, student patrols, late-night transport/escort service, controlled dormitory access. *Student Services:* health clinic, personal/psychological counseling, women's center, legal services.

Athletics Member NCAA. All Division I except football (Division I-AA). *Intercollegiate sports:* baseball M(c), basketball M(s)/W(s), crew M(c)/W(s), cross-country running M/W(s), fencing M(c)/W(c), field hockey W(s), golf M(c)/W(c), gymnastics W(s), ice hockey M(s)/W(s), lacrosse M(c)/W(s), rugby W(c), sailing M(c)/W(c), skiing (cross-country) M(s)/W(s), skiing (downhill) M(s)/W(s), soccer M(s)/W(s), swimming M/W(s), tennis M/W(s), track and field M/W(s), volleyball M(c)/W(s), wrestling M(c). *Intramural sports:* archery M(c)/W(c), badminton M(c)/W(c), basketball M/W, field hockey W, football M/W, golf M/W, ice hockey M/W, racquetball M/W, skiing (cross-country) M(c)/W(c), soccer M/W, softball M/W, swimming M/W, table tennis M/W, tennis M/W, volleyball M/W, weight lifting W.

Standardized Tests *Required:* SAT I or ACT (for admission).

Costs (2002–03) *Tuition:* state resident $6340 full-time, $264 per credit part-time; nonresident $16,040 full-time, $668 per credit part-time. Part-time tuition and fees vary according to course load. *Required fees:* $1790 full-time. *Room and board:* $5882; room only: $3436. Room and board charges vary according to board plan and housing facility. *Payment plan:* installment. *Waivers:* minority students, senior citizens, and employees or children of employees.

Financial Aid Of all full-time matriculated undergraduates who enrolled in 2001, 6575 applied for aid, 5165 were judged to have need, 1104 had their need fully met. In 2001, 1948 non-need-based awards were made. *Average percent of need met:* 79%. *Average financial aid package:* $12,844. *Average need-based loan:* $3334. *Average need-based gift aid:* $2000. *Average non-need based aid:* $5221. *Average indebtedness upon graduation:* $19,515.

Applying *Options:* common application, electronic application, early action, deferred entrance. *Application fee:* $50 (non-residents). *Required:* essay or personal statement, high school transcript, 1 letter of recommendation. *Recommended:* minimum 3.0 GPA. *Application deadlines:* 2/1 (freshmen), 3/1 (transfers). *Notification:* 4/15 (freshmen), 1/15 (early action).

Admissions Contact Cecilia Leslie, Executive Director of Admissions, University of New Hampshire, Grant House, 4 Garrison Avenue, Durham, NH 03824. *Phone:* 603-862-1360. *Fax:* 603-862-0077. *E-mail:* admissions@unh.edu.

UNIVERSITY OF NEW HAMPSHIRE AT MANCHESTER

Manchester, New Hampshire

- **State-supported** comprehensive, founded 1967, part of University System of New Hampshire
- **Calendar** semesters
- **Degrees** certificates, associate, and bachelor's
- **Urban** 800-acre campus with easy access to Boston
- **Endowment** $18,851
- **Coed**
- **Moderately difficult** entrance level

Faculty *Student/faculty ratio:* 13:1.

Student Life *Campus security:* late-night transport/escort service.

Standardized Tests *Required for some:* SAT I (for admission). *Recommended:* ACT (for admission).

Financial Aid Of all full-time matriculated undergraduates who enrolled in 2001, 390 applied for aid, 282 were judged to have need, 39 had their need fully met. 98 Federal Work-Study jobs (averaging $1906). In 2001, 117. *Average percent of need met:* 67. *Average financial aid package:* $7330. *Average need-based loan:* $3355. *Average need-based gift aid:* $471. *Average indebtedness upon graduation:* $14,476.

Applying *Options:* deferred entrance. *Application fee:* $50 (non-residents). *Required:* essay or personal statement, high school transcript, 1 letter of recommendation. *Recommended:* interview.

Admissions Contact Ms. Susan Miller, Administrative Assistant, University of New Hampshire at Manchester, 400 Commercial Street, Manchester, NH 03101. *Phone:* 603-641-4150. *Toll-free phone:* 800-735-2964. *Fax:* 603-641-4125. *E-mail:* unhm@unh.edu.

UNIVERSITY SYSTEM COLLEGE FOR LIFELONG LEARNING

Concord, New Hampshire

- **State and locally supported** 4-year, founded 1972, part of University System of New Hampshire
- **Calendar** semesters
- **Degrees** certificates, associate, bachelor's, and postbachelor's certificates (offers primarily part-time degree programs; courses offered at 50 locations in New Hampshire)
- **Rural** campus
- **Coed,** 2,006 undergraduate students, 4% full-time, 80% women, 20% men
- **Noncompetitive** entrance level

Undergraduates 78 full-time, 1,928 part-time.

Faculty *Total:* 498, 22% with terminal degrees. *Student/faculty ratio:* 10:1.

Majors Behavioral sciences; business administration; computer management; criminal justice/law enforcement administration; early childhood education; general studies; health services administration; human resources management; liberal arts and sciences/liberal studies.

Academic Programs *Special study options:* academic remediation for entering students, accelerated degree program, adult/continuing education programs, advanced placement credit, cooperative education, distance learning, double majors, independent study, internships, off-campus study, part-time degree program, services for LD students, student-designed majors, summer session for credit.

Library a Web page.

Computers on Campus 128 computers available on campus for general student use. A campuswide network can be accessed from off campus. Internet access, at least one staffed computer lab available.

Student Life *Housing:* college housing not available. *Activities and Organizations:* Alumni Learner Association.

Costs (2001–02) *Tuition:* state resident $4152 full-time, $173 per credit part-time; nonresident $4632 full-time, $193 per credit part-time. Full-time tuition and fees vary according to course load. Part-time tuition and fees vary according to course load. *Required fees:* $150 full-time, $50 per term part-time. *Payment plan:* installment. *Waivers:* employees or children of employees.

Applying *Application fee:* $35. *Application deadline:* rolling (freshmen), rolling (transfers). *Notification:* continuous (freshmen).

Admissions Contact Ms. Teresa McDonnell, Associate Dean of Learner Services, University System College for Lifelong Learning, 125 North State Street, Concord, NH 03301. *Phone:* 603-228-3000 Ext. 308. *Toll-free phone:* 800-582-7248 Ext. 313. *Fax:* 603-229-0964. *E-mail:* n_dumont@unhf.unh.edu.

WHITE PINES COLLEGE

Chester, New Hampshire

- **Independent** 4-year, founded 1965
- **Calendar** semesters
- **Degrees** associate and bachelor's
- **Rural** 83-acre campus with easy access to Boston
- **Endowment** $4.0 million
- **Coed,** 140 undergraduate students, 74% full-time, 62% women, 38% men
- **Moderately difficult** entrance level, 85% of applicants were admitted

Undergraduates 103 full-time, 37 part-time. Students come from 10 states and territories, 1 other country, 30% are from out of state, 0.7% African American, 2% Asian American or Pacific Islander, 0.7% Hispanic American, 1% Native American, 0.7% international, 4% transferred in, 55% live on campus.

Freshmen *Admission:* 129 applied, 110 admitted, 58 enrolled. *Average high school GPA:* 2.62. *Test scores:* SAT verbal scores over 500: 47%; SAT math scores over 500: 30%; SAT verbal scores over 600: 23%; SAT math scores over 600: 3%.

Faculty *Total:* 26, 35% full-time, 54% with terminal degrees. *Student/faculty ratio:* 10:1.

Majors Art; creative writing; graphic design/commercial art/illustration; liberal arts and sciences/liberal studies; photography; technical/business writing.

Academic Programs *Special study options:* academic remediation for entering students, adult/continuing education programs, advanced placement credit, cooperative education, English as a second language, honors programs, independent study, internships, part-time degree program, services for LD students, student-designed majors, study abroad, summer session for credit.

Library Wadleigh Library plus 2 others with 28,000 titles, 100 serial subscriptions, an OPAC.
Computers on Campus 27 computers available on campus for general student use. A campuswide network can be accessed from student residence rooms. Internet access, at least one staffed computer lab available.
Student Life *Housing:* on-campus residence required for freshman year. *Options:* coed. *Activities and Organizations:* student government. *Campus security:* controlled dormitory access, regular patrols by trained security personnel. *Student Services:* personal/psychological counseling.
Athletics *Intramural sports:* badminton M/W, basketball M/W, football M/W, soccer M/W, softball M/W, table tennis M/W, tennis M/W, volleyball M/W.
Standardized Tests *Recommended:* SAT I and SAT II or ACT (for admission).
Costs (2002–03) *Comprehensive fee:* $20,100 includes full-time tuition ($12,100), mandatory fees ($1000), and room and board ($7000). Full-time tuition and fees vary according to course load. Part-time tuition: $405 per credit hour. Part-time tuition and fees vary according to course load. *Required fees:* $1000 per year part-time. *Waivers:* employees or children of employees.
Applying *Options:* common application, electronic application, early admission, deferred entrance. *Application fee:* $35. *Required:* essay or personal statement, high school transcript, 3 letters of recommendation, interview. *Recommended:* minimum 2.0 GPA, portfolio. *Application deadline:* rolling (freshmen), rolling (transfers).
Admissions Contact Ms. Jessie Girvin, Director of Admissions, White Pines College, 40 Chester Street, Chester, NH 03036. *Phone:* 603-887-7400. *Toll-free phone:* 877-818-0492. *Fax:* 603-887-1777. *E-mail:* admissions@whitepines.edu.

NEW JERSEY

BERKELEY COLLEGE
West Paterson, New Jersey

- **Proprietary** primarily 2-year, founded 1931
- **Calendar** quarters
- **Degrees** certificates, associate, and bachelor's
- **Suburban** 16-acre campus with easy access to New York City
- **Coed,** 2,144 undergraduate students, 84% full-time, 78% women, 22% men
- **Minimally difficult** entrance level

Undergraduates 1,811 full-time, 333 part-time. Students come from 6 states and territories, 18 other countries, 3% are from out of state, 17% African American, 3% Asian American or Pacific Islander, 33% Hispanic American, 0.4% Native American, 1% international, 12% transferred in, 1% live on campus.
Freshmen *Admission:* 736 enrolled. *Average high school GPA:* 2.7.
Faculty *Total:* 118, 50% full-time. *Student/faculty ratio:* 24:1.
Majors Accounting; business; business administration; business management/administrative services related; business marketing and marketing management; computer management; fashion merchandising; interior design; international business; marketing management and research related; paralegal/legal assistant; system administration; Web page, digital/multimedia and information resources design.
Academic Programs *Special study options:* academic remediation for entering students, adult/continuing education programs, advanced placement credit, cooperative education, English as a second language, internships, off-campus study, part-time degree program, study abroad, summer session for credit.
Library Walter A. Brower Library with 49,584 titles, 224 serial subscriptions, 2,659 audiovisual materials, an OPAC, a Web page.
Computers on Campus 300 computers available on campus for general student use. A campuswide network can be accessed from student residence rooms and from off campus. At least one staffed computer lab available.
Student Life *Housing Options:* coed. *Activities and Organizations:* student-run newspaper, Student Government Association, Athletics Club, Paralegal Student Association, International Club, Fashion and Marketing Club. *Campus security:* 24-hour emergency response devices, controlled dormitory access, security patrols. *Student Services:* personal/psychological counseling.
Athletics *Intramural sports:* basketball M/W, bowling M/W, football M/W, soccer M/W, softball M/W, tennis M/W, volleyball M/W.
Costs (2002–03) *One-time required fee:* $50. *Comprehensive fee:* $22,440 includes full-time tuition ($13,950), mandatory fees ($390), and room and board ($8100). Part-time tuition: $360 per credit. *Required fees:* $60 per term part-time. *Room and board:* Room and board charges vary according to housing facility. *Payment plan:* installment. *Waivers:* employees or children of employees.
Financial Aid Of all full-time matriculated undergraduates who enrolled in 2001, 150 Federal Work-Study jobs (averaging $1200).
Applying *Options:* electronic application, deferred entrance. *Application fee:* $40. *Required:* high school transcript. *Recommended:* interview. *Application deadline:* rolling (freshmen), rolling (transfers).
Admissions Contact Ms. Carol Allen, Director of High School Admissions, Berkeley College, 44 Rifle Camp Road, West Paterson, NJ 07424-3353. *Phone:* 973-278-5400 Ext. 210. *Toll-free phone:* 800-446-5400. *E-mail:* admissions@berkeleycollege.edu.

BETH MEDRASH GOVOHA
Lakewood, New Jersey

Admissions Contact Rabbi Yehuda Jacobs, Director of Admissions, Beth Medrash Govoha, 617 Sixth Street, Lakewood, NJ 08701-2797. *Phone:* 908-367-1060.

BLOOMFIELD COLLEGE
Bloomfield, New Jersey

- **Independent** 4-year, founded 1868, affiliated with Presbyterian Church (U.S.A.)
- **Calendar** semesters
- **Degree** certificates and bachelor's
- **Suburban** 12-acre campus with easy access to New York City
- **Endowment** $6.1 million
- **Coed,** 1,785 undergraduate students, 71% full-time, 69% women, 31% men
- **Minimally difficult** entrance level, 40% of applicants were admitted

Bloomfield College students come from a rich mixture of backgrounds and experiences. Reflecting the contemporary world, they learn together, share interests, build friendships to last a lifetime, and graduate fully prepared for careers and continued education. New programs include animation, allied health technology, and human resource management.

Undergraduates 1,263 full-time, 522 part-time. Students come from 16 states and territories, 2 other countries, 4% are from out of state, 49% African American, 4% Asian American or Pacific Islander, 17% Hispanic American, 0.2% Native American, 2% international, 39% transferred in, 15% live on campus. *Retention:* 70% of 2001 full-time freshmen returned.
Freshmen *Admission:* 1,331 applied, 533 admitted, 286 enrolled. *Average high school GPA:* 2.84. *Test scores:* SAT verbal scores over 500: 17%; SAT math scores over 500: 16%; SAT verbal scores over 600: 2%; SAT math scores over 600: 1%.
Faculty *Total:* 196, 31% full-time, 32% with terminal degrees. *Student/faculty ratio:* 14:1.
Majors Accounting; art; art education; biochemistry; biology; biology education; business administration; business marketing and marketing management; chemistry; computer graphics; creative writing; criminal justice/law enforcement administration; cytotechnology; economics; English; English education; environmental biology; film/video and photographic arts related; finance; history; human resources management; human resources management related; information sciences/systems; Internet; mathematics education; medical technology; musical instrument technology; nursing; philosophy; political science; pre-dentistry; pre-medicine; pre-veterinary studies; psychology; public administration; public policy analysis; purchasing/contracts management; religious studies; science education; social studies education; sociology; theater arts/drama; toxicology.
Academic Programs *Special study options:* academic remediation for entering students, accelerated degree program, advanced placement credit, cooperative education, distance learning, double majors, English as a second language, honors programs, independent study, internships, part-time degree program, services for LD students, student-designed majors, study abroad, summer session for credit. *ROTC:* Army (c). *Unusual degree programs:* 3-2 computer information systems with New Jersey Institute of Technology.
Library College Library plus 1 other with 65,000 titles, 5,200 serial subscriptions, 4,086 audiovisual materials, an OPAC, a Web page.
Computers on Campus 245 computers available on campus for general student use. A campuswide network can be accessed from student residence rooms. Internet access, at least one staffed computer lab available.
Student Life *Housing Options:* coed. *Activities and Organizations:* drama/theater group, student-run newspaper, Nursing Student Association, Team Infinite, Phi Beta Sigma, Roundtable Association, Sisters in Support, national fraternities, national sororities. *Campus security:* 24-hour emergency response devices and patrols, escort service, security cameras in high-traffic areas. *Student Services:* health clinic, personal/psychological counseling.
Athletics Member NCAA, NAIA. All NCAA Division II. *Intercollegiate sports:* baseball M(s), basketball M(s)/W(s), crew M(s), cross-country running

Bloomfield College (continued)
M(s), soccer M(s)/W(s), softball W(s), volleyball W(s). *Intramural sports:* basketball M/W, bowling M/W, soccer M/W, softball M/W, table tennis M/W, volleyball M/W.

Standardized Tests *Required:* SAT I or ACT (for admission).

Costs (2001–02) *Comprehensive fee:* $17,000 includes full-time tuition ($11,300), mandatory fees ($150), and room and board ($5550). Full-time tuition and fees vary according to program. Part-time tuition: $1140 per course. Part-time tuition and fees vary according to course load and program. *Required fees:* $25 per term part-time. *Room and board:* Room and board charges vary according to board plan. *Payment plans:* installment, deferred payment. *Waivers:* senior citizens and employees or children of employees.

Financial Aid Of all full-time matriculated undergraduates who enrolled in 2001, 1116 applied for aid, 1063 were judged to have need. 114 Federal Work-Study jobs (averaging $1393). 119 State and other part-time jobs (averaging $1598). In 2001, 25 non-need-based awards were made. *Average percent of need met:* 69%. *Average financial aid package:* $10,609. *Average need-based loan:* $2862. *Average need-based gift aid:* $8399. *Average non-need based aid:* $7514. *Average indebtedness upon graduation:* $12,967.

Applying *Options:* common application, electronic application, early admission, early action, deferred entrance. *Application fee:* $35. *Required:* high school transcript, minimum 2.40 GPA, 2 letters of recommendation. *Required for some:* essay or personal statement. *Recommended:* essay or personal statement, interview. *Application deadline:* 8/1 (freshmen), rolling (transfers). *Notification:* continuous (freshmen), 1/21 (early action).

Admissions Contact Mr. Michael Szarek, Associate Dean of Admission, Bloomfield College, Bloomfield, NJ 07003-9981. *Phone:* 973-748-9000 Ext. 390. *Toll-free phone:* 800-848-4555. *Fax:* 973-748-0916. *E-mail:* admission@bloomfield.edu.

CALDWELL COLLEGE
Caldwell, New Jersey

- **Independent Roman Catholic** comprehensive, founded 1939
- **Calendar** semesters
- **Degrees** bachelor's, master's, post-master's, and postbachelor's certificates
- **Suburban** 100-acre campus with easy access to New York City
- **Endowment** $2.9 million
- **Coed,** 1,923 undergraduate students, 52% full-time, 68% women, 32% men
- **Moderately difficult** entrance level, 77% of applicants were admitted

Caldwell College provides students with close, personal attention while enhancing technological facilities on campus. A recently completed, comprehensive roadway project has improved campus parking. In addition, an $8.2 million, 60,000-square-foot Student Activities and Recreation Center is near completion, meeting the social needs of a growing student population.

Undergraduates 995 full-time, 928 part-time. Students come from 12 states and territories, 29 other countries, 3% are from out of state, 14% African American, 3% Asian American or Pacific Islander, 9% Hispanic American, 0.2% Native American, 4% international, 8% transferred in, 22% live on campus. *Retention:* 73% of 2001 full-time freshmen returned.

Freshmen *Admission:* 1,150 applied, 887 admitted, 293 enrolled. *Average high school GPA:* 2.90. *Test scores:* SAT verbal scores over 500: 30%; SAT math scores over 500: 33%; SAT verbal scores over 600: 5%; SAT math scores over 600: 6%; SAT math scores over 700: 1%.

Faculty *Total:* 190, 39% full-time, 42% with terminal degrees. *Student/faculty ratio:* 13:1.

Majors Accounting; art; biology; business administration; business marketing and marketing management; chemistry; communications; computer/information sciences; computer science; criminal justice studies; elementary education; English; French; history; international business; management science; mathematics; medical technology; multi/interdisciplinary studies related; music; political science; psychology; social sciences; sociology; Spanish; theology.

Academic Programs *Special study options:* academic remediation for entering students, accelerated degree program, adult/continuing education programs, advanced placement credit, cooperative education, distance learning, double majors, English as a second language, external degree program, honors programs, independent study, internships, off-campus study, part-time degree program, services for LD students, student-designed majors, study abroad, summer session for credit. *ROTC:* Army (c).

Library Jennings Library with 132,204 titles, 765 serial subscriptions, 4,088 audiovisual materials, an OPAC, a Web page.

Computers on Campus 166 computers available on campus for general student use. A campuswide network can be accessed from student residence rooms. Internet access, at least one staffed computer lab available.

Student Life *Housing Options:* coed. *Activities and Organizations:* student-run newspaper, radio and television station, choral group, Student Government Association, International Students Organization, Caldwell College Education Association, Circle K, Black Student Cooperative Unit. *Campus security:* 24-hour patrols, late-night transport/escort service, controlled dormitory access, dusk-to-dawn patrols by trained security personnel. *Student Services:* health clinic, personal/psychological counseling.

Athletics Member NCAA, NAIA. All NCAA Division II. *Intercollegiate sports:* baseball M(s), basketball M(s)/W(s), golf M(s)/W(s), soccer M(s)/W(s), softball W(s), tennis M(s)/W(s). *Intramural sports:* basketball M/W, football M/W, soccer M/W, softball M/W, volleyball M/W.

Standardized Tests *Required:* SAT I or ACT (for admission).

Costs (2001–02) *Comprehensive fee:* $20,790 includes full-time tuition ($14,090), mandatory fees ($100), and room and board ($6600). Full-time tuition and fees vary according to program. Part-time tuition: $357 per credit. Part-time tuition and fees vary according to course load and program. *Payment plans:* installment, deferred payment. *Waivers:* senior citizens and employees or children of employees.

Financial Aid Of all full-time matriculated undergraduates who enrolled in 2001, 958 applied for aid, 749 were judged to have need, 23 had their need fully met. 12 State and other part-time jobs (averaging $5863). *Average percent of need met:* 71%. *Average financial aid package:* $8735. *Average need-based loan:* $3875. *Average need-based gift aid:* $5150. *Average indebtedness upon graduation:* $13,125.

Applying *Options:* common application, electronic application, early admission, early action, deferred entrance. *Application fee:* $40. *Required:* essay or personal statement, high school transcript, minimum 2.0 GPA, 1 letter of recommendation. *Required for some:* interview. *Application deadline:* rolling (transfers). *Notification:* continuous (freshmen), 1/15 (early action).

Admissions Contact Mr. Richard Ott, Vice President for Enrollment Management, Caldwell College, 9 Ryerson Avenue, Caldwell, NJ 07006. *Phone:* 973-618-3224. *Toll-free phone:* 888-864-9516. *Fax:* 973-618-3600. *E-mail:* admissions@caldwell.edu.

CENTENARY COLLEGE
Hackettstown, New Jersey

- **Independent** comprehensive, founded 1867, affiliated with United Methodist Church
- **Calendar** semesters
- **Degrees** associate, bachelor's, master's, and postbachelor's certificates
- **Suburban** 42-acre campus with easy access to New York City
- **Endowment** $2.0 million
- **Coed,** 1,448 undergraduate students, 50% full-time, 72% women, 28% men
- **Moderately difficult** entrance level, 83% of applicants were admitted

New majors are biology, criminal justice, sociology, and theater arts. New programs are sports management, and student-run television station. New services include waived fees for online applications, a renewable scholarship program, computers and printers in each dorm room, voice mail, Internet access, e-mail, cable television, and a library catalog system.

Undergraduates 719 full-time, 729 part-time. Students come from 21 states and territories, 16 other countries, 15% are from out of state, 3% African American, 0.1% Asian American or Pacific Islander, 2% Hispanic American, 0.3% Native American, 6% international, 14% transferred in, 55% live on campus. *Retention:* 61% of 2001 full-time freshmen returned.

Freshmen *Admission:* 528 applied, 439 admitted, 211 enrolled. *Average high school GPA:* 2.55. *Test scores:* SAT verbal scores over 500: 30%; SAT math scores over 500: 31%; ACT scores over 18: 75%; SAT verbal scores over 600: 8%; SAT math scores over 600: 4%; ACT scores over 24: 12%; SAT math scores over 700: 1%.

Faculty *Total:* 106, 44% full-time, 46% with terminal degrees. *Student/faculty ratio:* 15:1.

Majors Accounting; biology; business administration; business marketing and marketing management; criminology; education; elementary education; English; equestrian studies; fashion design/illustration; graphic design/commercial art/illustration; history; information sciences/systems; international relations; liberal arts and sciences/liberal studies; mass communications; mathematics; political science; psychology; secondary education; sociology; special education; sport/fitness administration; theater design.

Academic Programs *Special study options:* academic remediation for entering students, accelerated degree program, advanced placement credit, double majors, English as a second language, honors programs, independent study, internships, off-campus study, part-time degree program, services for LD students, student-designed majors, study abroad, summer session for credit.

Library Taylor Memorial Learning Resource Center with 67,272 titles, 211 serial subscriptions, 4,965 audiovisual materials, an OPAC.

Computers on Campus 30 computers available on campus for general student use. A campuswide network can be accessed from student residence rooms and from off campus that provide access to resident students have a computer and printer in their room. Internet access, at least one staffed computer lab available.

Student Life *Housing Options:* coed, women-only. *Activities and Organizations:* drama/theater group, student-run newspaper, radio and television station, Student Activities Council, equestrian teams, Quill, student government, Kappa Delta Epsilon. *Campus security:* late-night transport/escort service, controlled dormitory access, patrols by trained security personnel 4 p.m. to 8 a.m. *Student Services:* health clinic, personal/psychological counseling, women's center.

Athletics Member NCAA, NSCAA. All NCAA Division III. *Intercollegiate sports:* baseball M, basketball M/W, cross-country running M/W, equestrian sports M/W, golf M/W, lacrosse M/W, soccer M/W, softball W, volleyball W, wrestling M.

Standardized Tests *Required:* SAT I or ACT (for admission).

Costs (2001–02) *Comprehensive fee:* $22,430 includes full-time tuition ($15,100), mandatory fees ($930), and room and board ($6400). Full-time tuition and fees vary according to program. Part-time tuition: $305 per credit. Part-time tuition and fees vary according to course load, location, and program. *Required fees:* $20 per term part-time. *Payment plan:* installment. *Waivers:* senior citizens and employees or children of employees.

Financial Aid Of all full-time matriculated undergraduates who enrolled in 2001, 593 applied for aid, 507 were judged to have need, 103 had their need fully met. 45 Federal Work-Study jobs (averaging $1200). 81 State and other part-time jobs (averaging $1200). In 2001, 86 non-need-based awards were made. *Average percent of need met:* 74%. *Average financial aid package:* $11,218. *Average need-based loan:* $3844. *Average need-based gift aid:* $8502. *Average indebtedness upon graduation:* $7200.

Applying *Options:* common application, electronic application, deferred entrance. *Application fee:* $30. *Required:* essay or personal statement, high school transcript. *Required for some:* interview, portfolio. *Recommended:* minimum 2.0 GPA, letters of recommendation, interview. *Application deadline:* rolling (freshmen), rolling (transfers). *Notification:* continuous (freshmen).

Admissions Contact Centenary College, 400 Jefferson Street, Hackettstown, NJ 07840-2100. *Phone:* 908-852-1400 Ext. 2217. *Toll-free phone:* 800-236-8679. *Fax:* 908-852-3454. *E-mail:* admissions@centenarycollege.edu.

THE COLLEGE OF NEW JERSEY

Ewing, New Jersey

- **State-supported** comprehensive, founded 1855
- **Calendar** semesters
- **Degrees** certificates, bachelor's, and master's
- **Suburban** 255-acre campus with easy access to Philadelphia
- **Endowment** $4.5 million
- **Coed,** 5,973 undergraduate students, 94% full-time, 59% women, 41% men
- **Very difficult** entrance level, 51% of applicants were admitted

Highly competitive but not elitist, The College of New Jersey (TCNJ) is one of today's best buys in American higher education. College programs stress leadership skills, public service, and serious scholarship. Opportunities abound for study abroad, internships, undergraduate research, and artistic expression. Students who demonstrate curiosity, initiative, and enthusiasm find TCNJ eager to help them grow.

Undergraduates 5,627 full-time, 346 part-time. Students come from 22 states and territories, 12 other countries, 5% are from out of state, 6% African American, 5% Asian American or Pacific Islander, 5% Hispanic American, 0.1% Native American, 0.2% international, 4% transferred in, 60% live on campus. *Retention:* 96% of 2001 full-time freshmen returned.

Freshmen *Admission:* 5,988 applied, 3,069 admitted, 1,262 enrolled. *Test scores:* SAT verbal scores over 500: 98%; SAT math scores over 500: 99%; SAT verbal scores over 600: 64%; SAT math scores over 600: 79%; SAT verbal scores over 700: 13%; SAT math scores over 700: 20%.

Faculty *Total:* 658, 51% full-time. *Student/faculty ratio:* 12:1.

Majors Accounting; art; art education; biology; biology education; business administration; business economics; chemistry; chemistry education; computer science; criminal justice/law enforcement administration; early childhood education; economics; education; education of the hearing impaired; elementary education; engineering science; English; English education; finance; fine/studio arts; graphic design/commercial art/illustration; history; history education; industrial arts education; international business; international relations; management information systems/business data processing; mathematical statistics; mathematics; mathematics education; music; music teacher education; nursing; philosophy; physical education; physics; physics education; political science; pre-law; premedicine; psychology; secondary education; sociology; Spanish; Spanish language education; special education; speech/rhetorical studies; women's studies.

Academic Programs *Special study options:* academic remediation for entering students, advanced placement credit, double majors, honors programs, independent study, internships, off-campus study, part-time degree program, services for LD students, study abroad, summer session for credit. *ROTC:* Army (c), Air Force (c).

Library Roscoe L. West Library with 520,000 titles, 4,700 serial subscriptions, 2,500 audiovisual materials, an OPAC, a Web page.

Computers on Campus 800 computers available on campus for general student use. A campuswide network can be accessed from student residence rooms and from off campus. Internet access, online (class) registration, at least one staffed computer lab available.

Student Life *Housing Options:* coed. *Activities and Organizations:* drama/theater group, student-run newspaper, radio station, choral group, Student Government Association, College Union Board, The Signal, Intramurals, national fraternities, national sororities. *Campus security:* 24-hour emergency response devices and patrols, student patrols, late-night transport/escort service, controlled dormitory access. *Student Services:* health clinic, personal/psychological counseling, women's center, legal services.

Athletics Member NCAA. All Division III. *Intercollegiate sports:* baseball M, basketball M/W, cross-country running M/W, field hockey W, football M, golf M, lacrosse W, soccer M/W, softball W, swimming M/W, tennis M/W, track and field M/W, wrestling M. *Intramural sports:* basketball M/W, bowling M(c)/W(c), fencing M(c)/W(c), field hockey M/W, football M/W, ice hockey M(c), lacrosse M(c), racquetball M/W, rugby M/W, skiing (cross-country) M(c)/W(c), skiing (downhill) M(c)/W(c), soccer M/W, softball M/W, tennis M/W, volleyball M(c)/W(c), water polo M/W, weight lifting M(c)/W(c).

Standardized Tests *Required:* SAT I or ACT (for admission).

Costs (2001–02) *Tuition:* state resident $5022 full-time, $176 per semester hour part-time; nonresident $8770 full-time, $308 per semester hour part-time. *Required fees:* $1639 full-time, $54 per semester hour. *Room and board:* $6764; room only: $3806. Room and board charges vary according to board plan. *Payment plan:* installment. *Waivers:* minority students.

Financial Aid *Average indebtedness upon graduation:* $17,000. *Financial aid deadline:* 6/1.

Applying *Options:* electronic application, early admission, early decision, deferred entrance. *Application fee:* $50. *Required:* essay or personal statement, high school transcript, minimum 2.0 GPA. *Required for some:* interview, art portfolio or music audition. *Application deadlines:* 2/15 (freshmen), 2/15 (transfers). *Early decision:* 11/15. *Notification:* 4/1 (freshmen), 12/15 (early decision).

Admissions Contact Ms. Lisa Angeloni, Dean of Admissions, The College of New Jersey, PO Box 7718, Ewing, NJ 08628. *Phone:* 609-771-2131. *Toll-free phone:* 800-624-0967. *Fax:* 609-637-5174. *E-mail:* admiss@tcnj.edu.

COLLEGE OF SAINT ELIZABETH

Morristown, New Jersey

- **Independent Roman Catholic** comprehensive, founded 1899
- **Calendar** semesters
- **Degrees** certificates, bachelor's, master's, and postbachelor's certificates (also offers co-ed adult undergraduate degree program and co-ed graduate programs)
- **Suburban** 188-acre campus with easy access to New York City
- **Endowment** $18.6 million
- **Women only,** 1,251 undergraduate students, 48% full-time
- **Moderately difficult** entrance level, 80% of applicants were admitted

The College of Saint Elizabeth is a private women's college with a Catholic liberal arts tradition that also offers coeducational adult degree programs and graduate programs. The College is located in suburban Morristown, New Jersey. Students learn in an environment focused on women in which high-quality teaching is a primary goal, along with the development of leadership in the spirit of service and social responsibility.

Undergraduates 597 full-time, 654 part-time. Students come from 7 states and territories, 25 other countries, 3% are from out of state, 13% African American, 4% Asian American or Pacific Islander, 12% Hispanic American, 0.3% Native American, 5% international, 4% transferred in, 72% live on campus. *Retention:* 88% of 2001 full-time freshmen returned.

Freshmen *Admission:* 409 applied, 326 admitted, 149 enrolled. *Average high school GPA:* 3.06. *Test scores:* SAT verbal scores over 500: 44%; SAT math scores over 500: 44%; SAT verbal scores over 600: 10%; SAT math scores over 600: 11%; SAT verbal scores over 700: 2%; SAT math scores over 700: 4%.

College of Saint Elizabeth (continued)

Faculty *Total:* 166, 34% full-time, 52% with terminal degrees. *Student/faculty ratio:* 10:1.

Majors Accounting; American studies; art; biochemistry; biology; business administration; business marketing and marketing management; chemistry; communications; computer science; criminal justice studies; cytotechnology; dietetics; economics; education (multiple levels); English; history; human resources management; international relations; mathematics; medical technology; multi/interdisciplinary studies related; music; nursing science; philosophy; pre-dentistry; pre-law; pre-medicine; pre-veterinary studies; psychology; sociology; Spanish; special education; theology; toxicology.

Academic Programs *Special study options:* academic remediation for entering students, accelerated degree program, advanced placement credit, double majors, English as a second language, honors programs, independent study, internships, off-campus study, part-time degree program, services for LD students, student-designed majors, study abroad, summer session for credit.

Library Mahoney Library with 169,765 titles, 852 serial subscriptions, 1,563 audiovisual materials, an OPAC.

Computers on Campus 125 computers available on campus for general student use. A campuswide network can be accessed from student residence rooms and from off campus. Internet access, at least one staffed computer lab available.

Student Life *Housing Options:* women-only. *Activities and Organizations:* drama/theater group, student-run newspaper, choral group, Student Government Association, Students Take Action Committee, International/Intercultural Club, College Activities Board, campus ministry. *Campus security:* 24-hour emergency response devices and patrols, late-night transport/escort service, controlled dormitory access. *Student Services:* health clinic, personal/psychological counseling.

Athletics Member NCAA. All Division III. *Intercollegiate sports:* basketball W, cross-country running W, equestrian sports W, soccer W, softball W, swimming W, tennis W, volleyball W.

Standardized Tests *Required:* SAT I or ACT (for admission).

Costs (2001–02) *Comprehensive fee:* $22,510 includes full-time tuition ($14,700), mandatory fees ($610), and room and board ($7200). Part-time tuition: $445 per semester hour. Part-time tuition and fees vary according to course load. *Required fees:* $65 per course, $15 per term part-time. *Payment plan:* installment. *Waivers:* children of alumni, senior citizens, and employees or children of employees.

Financial Aid Of all full-time matriculated undergraduates who enrolled in 2001, 429 applied for aid, 381 were judged to have need, 109 had their need fully met. In 2001, 130 non-need-based awards were made. *Average percent of need met:* 85%. *Average financial aid package:* $16,756. *Average need-based loan:* $3185. *Average need-based gift aid:* $13,243. *Average non-need based aid:* $10,300. *Average indebtedness upon graduation:* $17,169.

Applying *Options:* electronic application, early admission, deferred entrance. *Application fee:* $35. *Required:* essay or personal statement, high school transcript, minimum 2.0 GPA, 2 letters of recommendation. *Recommended:* interview. *Application deadline:* 8/15 (freshmen), rolling (transfers). *Notification:* 11/15 (freshmen).

Admissions Contact Ms. Donna Tatarka, Dean of Admissions and Financial Aid, College of Saint Elizabeth, 2 Convent Road, Morristown, NJ 07960-6989. *Phone:* 973-290-4700. *Toll-free phone:* 800-210-7900. *Fax:* 973-290-4710. *E-mail:* apply@liza.st-elizabeth.edu.

DeVry College of Technology

North Brunswick, New Jersey

- **Proprietary** 4-year, founded 1969, part of DeVry, Inc
- **Calendar** semesters
- **Degrees** diplomas, associate, and bachelor's
- **Urban** 10-acre campus with easy access to New York City
- **Coed,** 3,912 undergraduate students, 61% full-time, 23% women, 77% men
- **Minimally difficult** entrance level, 82% of applicants were admitted

Undergraduates 2,377 full-time, 1,535 part-time. Students come from 22 states and territories, 25 other countries, 13% are from out of state, 24% African American, 9% Asian American or Pacific Islander, 17% Hispanic American, 0.3% Native American, 1% international, 0.0% transferred in. *Retention:* 52% of 2001 full-time freshmen returned.

Freshmen *Admission:* 2,015 applied, 1,650 admitted, 1,322 enrolled.

Faculty *Total:* 193, 36% full-time. *Student/faculty ratio:* 20:1.

Majors Business administration/management related; business systems networking/telecommunications; electrical/electronic engineering technology; information sciences/systems.

Academic Programs *Special study options:* adult/continuing education programs, advanced placement credit, part-time degree program, services for LD students, summer session for credit.

Library Learning Resource Center with 32,109 titles, 210 serial subscriptions, 1,870 audiovisual materials, an OPAC.

Computers on Campus 437 computers available on campus for general student use. A campuswide network can be accessed from off campus. Internet access, at least one staffed computer lab available.

Student Life *Housing:* college housing not available. *Activities and Organizations:* student-run newspaper, radio station, Phi Theta Kappa, Data Processing Management Association, Telecommunications Management Association, Institute of Electrical and Electronics Engineering. *Campus security:* 24-hour emergency response devices and patrols, late-night transport/escort service.

Standardized Tests *Recommended:* SAT I or ACT (for admission).

Costs (2001–02) *Tuition:* $8740 full-time, $345 per credit hour part-time. Full-time tuition and fees vary according to course load. Part-time tuition and fees vary according to course load. *Required fees:* $65 full-time. *Payment plans:* installment, deferred payment. *Waivers:* employees or children of employees.

Financial Aid Of all full-time matriculated undergraduates who enrolled in 2001, 3050 applied for aid, 2815 were judged to have need, 97 had their need fully met. *Average percent of need met:* 49%. *Average financial aid package:* $8323. *Average need-based loan:* $4961. *Average need-based gift aid:* $5688.

Applying *Options:* electronic application, deferred entrance. *Application fee:* $50. *Required:* high school transcript, interview. *Application deadline:* rolling (freshmen), rolling (transfers). *Notification:* continuous (freshmen).

Admissions Contact Ms. Norma Houze, New Student Coordinator, DeVry College of Technology, 630 US Highway One, North Brunswick, NJ 08902-3362. *Phone:* 732-435-4880. *Toll-free phone:* 800-333-3879.

Drew University

Madison, New Jersey

- **Independent** university, founded 1867, affiliated with United Methodist Church
- **Calendar** semesters
- **Degrees** bachelor's, master's, doctoral, first professional, and postbachelor's certificates
- **Suburban** 186-acre campus with easy access to New York City
- **Endowment** $211.0 million
- **Coed,** 1,536 undergraduate students, 97% full-time, 61% women, 39% men
- **Very difficult** entrance level, 72% of applicants were admitted

Drew is educating students to help shape the world of tomorrow. With its roots in the best traditions of the arts and sciences, Drew blends inspired teaching on a technologically integrated campus with numerous opportunities for academic internships in nearby corporate headquarters and research centers. Drew's innovative international seminars program and semesters in New York City on Wall Street and the United Nations, for example, provide students with an understanding of the issues that affect a global society.

Undergraduates 1,483 full-time, 53 part-time. Students come from 37 states and territories, 18 other countries, 42% are from out of state, 4% African American, 6% Asian American or Pacific Islander, 4% Hispanic American, 0.4% Native American, 2% international, 3% transferred in, 89% live on campus. *Retention:* 85% of 2001 full-time freshmen returned.

Freshmen *Admission:* 2,513 applied, 1,804 admitted, 397 enrolled. *Test scores:* SAT verbal scores over 500: 92%; SAT math scores over 500: 90%; SAT verbal scores over 600: 60%; SAT math scores over 600: 51%; SAT verbal scores over 700: 16%; SAT math scores over 700: 12%.

Faculty *Total:* 152, 79% full-time, 85% with terminal degrees. *Student/faculty ratio:* 11:1.

Majors Anthropology; art; behavioral sciences; biochemistry; biology; chemistry; classics; computer science; economics; English; French; German; history; interdisciplinary studies; Italian; mathematics; mathematics/computer science; music; neuroscience; philosophy; physics; political science; psychology; religious studies; Russian; sociology; Spanish; theater arts/drama; women's studies.

Academic Programs *Special study options:* academic remediation for entering students, accelerated degree program, adult/continuing education programs, advanced placement credit, double majors, independent study, internships, off-campus study, part-time degree program, services for LD students, student-designed majors, study abroad, summer session for credit. *ROTC:* Army (c), Air Force (c). *Unusual degree programs:* 3-2 engineering with Washington University in St. Louis, Stevens Institute of Technology, Columbia University; forestry with Duke University.

Library Drew University Library with 487,562 titles, 3,066 serial subscriptions.

Computers on Campus 200 computers available on campus for general student use. A campuswide network can be accessed from student residence rooms and from off campus. Internet access, online (class) registration, at least one staffed computer lab available.

Student Life *Housing:* on-campus residence required for freshman year. *Options:* coed, women-only, cooperative, disabled students. *Activities and Organizations:* drama/theater group, student-run newspaper, radio and television station, choral group, Drama Society, Student Government Association, Residence Hall Association, University Program Board. *Campus security:* 24-hour emergency response devices and patrols, late-night transport/escort service, controlled dormitory access. *Student Services:* health clinic, personal/psychological counseling.

Athletics Member NCAA. All Division III. *Intercollegiate sports:* baseball M, basketball M/W, cross-country running M/W, equestrian sports M/W, fencing M/W, field hockey W, lacrosse M/W, rugby M(c)/W(c), soccer M/W, softball W, swimming M/W, tennis M/W. *Intramural sports:* basketball M/W, bowling M/W, football M/W, racquetball M/W, soccer M/W, softball M/W, squash M/W, table tennis M/W, tennis M/W, volleyball M/W.

Standardized Tests *Required:* SAT I or ACT (for admission).

Costs (2001–02) *Comprehensive fee:* $32,152 includes full-time tuition ($24,576), mandatory fees ($546), and room and board ($7030). Part-time tuition: $1024 per credit. Part-time tuition and fees vary according to course load. *Required fees:* $23 per credit. *Room and board:* College room only: $4348. Room and board charges vary according to board plan and housing facility. *Payment plans:* tuition prepayment, installment. *Waivers:* senior citizens and employees or children of employees.

Financial Aid Of all full-time matriculated undergraduates who enrolled in 2001, 924 applied for aid, 749 were judged to have need, 248 had their need fully met. In 2001, 364 non-need-based awards were made. *Average percent of need met:* 83%. *Average financial aid package:* $18,093. *Average need-based loan:* $4278. *Average need-based gift aid:* $13,492. *Average non-need based aid:* $10,624. *Average indebtedness upon graduation:* $13,064. *Financial aid deadline:* 2/15.

Applying *Options:* common application, early admission, early decision, deferred entrance. *Application fee:* $40. *Required:* essay or personal statement, high school transcript, 1 letter of recommendation. *Recommended:* interview. *Application deadlines:* 2/15 (freshmen), 8/1 (transfers). *Early decision:* 12/1 (for plan 1), 1/15 (for plan 2). *Notification:* 3/15 (freshmen), 12/24 (early decision plan 1), 2/15 (early decision plan 2).

Admissions Contact Mr. Roberto Noya, Dean of Admissions and Financial Aid, Drew University, 36 Madison Avenue, Madison, NJ 07940. *Phone:* 973-408-3739. *Fax:* 973-408-3036. *E-mail:* cadm@drew.edu.

FAIRLEIGH DICKINSON UNIVERSITY, COLLEGE AT FLORHAM

Madison, New Jersey

- **Independent** comprehensive, founded 1942
- **Calendar** semesters
- **Degrees** associate, bachelor's, master's, and post-master's certificates
- **Suburban** 178-acre campus with easy access to New York City
- **Endowment** $27.9 million
- **Coed,** 2,427 undergraduate students, 82% full-time, 53% women, 47% men
- **Moderately difficult** entrance level, 69% of applicants were admitted

Undergraduates 1,989 full-time, 438 part-time. Students come from 23 states and territories, 33 other countries, 14% are from out of state, 6% African American, 3% Asian American or Pacific Islander, 7% Hispanic American, 0.1% Native American, 3% international, 6% transferred in, 53% live on campus. *Retention:* 78% of 2001 full-time freshmen returned.

Freshmen *Admission:* 2,524 applied, 1,752 admitted, 500 enrolled. *Test scores:* SAT verbal scores over 500: 52%; SAT math scores over 500: 58%; SAT verbal scores over 600: 12%; SAT math scores over 600: 13%; SAT math scores over 700: 1%.

Faculty *Total:* 245, 45% full-time. *Student/faculty ratio:* 17:1.

Majors Accounting; biology; business administration; business economics; business marketing and marketing management; chemistry; communications; computer/information sciences; economics; English; entrepreneurship; film/video production; French; health/medical diagnostic and treatment services related; history; hotel and restaurant management; humanities; marine biology; mathematics; medical basic sciences related; medical radiologic technology; medical technology; philosophy; physical therapy assistant; political science; psychology; sociology; Spanish; theater arts/drama; visual/performing arts.

Academic Programs *Special study options:* academic remediation for entering students, accelerated degree program, adult/continuing education programs, advanced placement credit, cooperative education, distance learning, English as a second language, honors programs, independent study, internships, off-campus study, part-time degree program, services for LD students, study abroad, summer session for credit. *ROTC:* Army (c). *Unusual degree programs:* 3-2 psychology, communications.

Library Friendship Library plus 1 other with 176,222 titles, 1,259 serial subscriptions, 591 audiovisual materials, an OPAC.

Computers on Campus 300 computers available on campus for general student use. A campuswide network can be accessed from student residence rooms and from off campus. At least one staffed computer lab available.

Student Life *Housing Options:* coed. *Activities and Organizations:* drama/theater group, student-run newspaper, radio station, choral group, marching band, student government, Student Activities Programming Board, Greek Council, Association of Black Collegians, "Metro" Newspaper, national fraternities, national sororities. *Campus security:* 24-hour emergency response devices and patrols, late-night transport/escort service, trained law enforcement personnel on staff. *Student Services:* health clinic, personal/psychological counseling, women's center.

Athletics Member NCAA. All Division III. *Intercollegiate sports:* baseball M, basketball M/W, cross-country running M/W, field hockey W, football M, golf M, lacrosse M/W, soccer M/W, softball W, swimming M/W, tennis M/W, volleyball W. *Intramural sports:* basketball M/W, bowling M/W, cross-country running M/W, football M/W, golf M, racquetball M/W, soccer M/W, softball M/W, table tennis M/W, tennis M/W, volleyball M/W.

Standardized Tests *Required:* SAT I or ACT (for admission). *Recommended:* SAT II: Subject Tests (for admission).

Costs (2002–03) *Comprehensive fee:* $26,978 includes full-time tuition ($18,654), mandatory fees ($420), and room and board ($7904). Part-time tuition: $599 per credit. Part-time tuition and fees vary according to course load and program. *Required fees:* $194 per year part-time. *Room and board:* Room and board charges vary according to board plan and housing facility. *Payment plans:* installment, deferred payment. *Waivers:* senior citizens and employees or children of employees.

Financial Aid Of all full-time matriculated undergraduates who enrolled in 2001, 1541 applied for aid, 1349 were judged to have need, 81 had their need fully met. 432 Federal Work-Study jobs (averaging $1116). In 2001, 256 non-need-based awards were made. *Average percent of need met:* 78%. *Average financial aid package:* $15,303. *Average need-based loan:* $3785. *Average need-based gift aid:* $6989. *Average non-need based aid:* $6076. *Average indebtedness upon graduation:* $15,968.

Applying *Options:* common application, early admission, deferred entrance. *Application fee:* $40. *Required:* essay or personal statement, high school transcript. *Application deadlines:* 3/1 (freshmen), 8/1 (transfers). *Notification:* continuous (freshmen).

Admissions Contact Mr. Gary Hamme, Vice President for Enrollment Services, Fairleigh Dickinson University, College at Florham, 285 Madison Avenue, M-MS1-03, Madison, NJ 07940. *Phone:* 201-692-7304. *Toll-free phone:* 800-338-8803. *Fax:* 973-443-8088. *E-mail:* globaleducation@fdu.edu.

FAIRLEIGH DICKINSON UNIVERSITY, METROPOLITAN CAMPUS

Teaneck, New Jersey

- **Independent** comprehensive, founded 1942
- **Calendar** semesters
- **Degrees** certificates, associate, bachelor's, master's, doctoral, and postbachelor's certificates
- **Suburban** 125-acre campus with easy access to New York City
- **Endowment** $27.9 million
- **Coed,** 4,113 undergraduate students, 45% full-time, 58% women, 42% men
- **Moderately difficult** entrance level, 70% of applicants were admitted

Undergraduates 1,860 full-time, 2,253 part-time. Students come from 23 states and territories, 53 other countries, 12% are from out of state, 21% African American, 6% Asian American or Pacific Islander, 14% Hispanic American, 0.4% Native American, 11% international, 9% transferred in, 29% live on campus. *Retention:* 74% of 2001 full-time freshmen returned.

Freshmen *Admission:* 2,343 applied, 1,630 admitted, 497 enrolled. *Test scores:* SAT verbal scores over 500: 35%; SAT math scores over 500: 40%; SAT verbal scores over 600: 6%; SAT math scores over 600: 7%; SAT math scores over 700: 1%.

Faculty *Total:* 433, 38% full-time. *Student/faculty ratio:* 15:1.

Majors Accounting; biochemistry; biological/physical sciences; biology; business administration; business economics; chemistry; civil engineering technol-

Fairleigh Dickinson University, Metropolitan Campus (continued)
ogy; communications; computer/information sciences; computer/information sciences related; construction technology; criminal justice studies; electrical/electronic engineering technology; electrical engineering; English; entrepreneurship; environmental science; French; general studies; health/medical diagnostic and treatment services related; history; hotel and restaurant management; humanities; international relations; liberal arts and sciences/liberal studies; marine biology; marketing research; mathematics; mechanical engineering technology; medical basic sciences related; medical radiologic technology; medical technology; multi/interdisciplinary studies related; nursing science; philosophy; political science; psychology; sociology; Spanish; theater arts/drama; visual/performing arts.

Academic Programs *Special study options:* academic remediation for entering students, accelerated degree program, adult/continuing education programs, advanced placement credit, cooperative education, distance learning, double majors, English as a second language, honors programs, independent study, internships, off-campus study, part-time degree program, services for LD students, study abroad, summer session for credit. *ROTC:* Army (c), Air Force (c). *Unusual degree programs:* 3-2 psychology.

Library Weiner Library plus 2 others with 435,718 titles, 15,508 serial subscriptions, 3,779 audiovisual materials, an OPAC.

Computers on Campus 210 computers available on campus for general student use. A campuswide network can be accessed from student residence rooms and from off campus. At least one staffed computer lab available.

Student Life *Housing Options:* coed, men-only, women-only. *Activities and Organizations:* drama/theater group, student-run newspaper, radio and television station, choral group, Indian Cultural Experience, Student Program Board, Student Government Association, InterGreek Council, Multicultural Council, national fraternities, national sororities. *Campus security:* 24-hour emergency response devices and patrols, late-night transport/escort service, controlled dormitory access, trained law enforcement personnel on staff. *Student Services:* health clinic, personal/psychological counseling, women's center.

Athletics Member NCAA. All Division I. *Intercollegiate sports:* baseball M(s), basketball M(s)/W(s), cross-country running M(s)/W(s), fencing W(s), golf M(s), lacrosse W(s), soccer M(s)/W(s), softball W(s), tennis M(s)/W(s), track and field M(s)/W(s), volleyball W(s). *Intramural sports:* basketball M/W, bowling M/W, cross-country running M/W, football M/W, racquetball M/W, skiing (cross-country) M/W, skiing (downhill) M/W, softball M/W, table tennis M/W, tennis M/W, track and field M/W, volleyball M/W, weight lifting M/W.

Standardized Tests *Required:* SAT I or ACT (for admission). *Recommended:* SAT II: Writing Test (for admission).

Costs (2002–03) *One-time required fee:* $280. *Comprehensive fee:* $26,978 includes full-time tuition ($18,654), mandatory fees ($420), and room and board ($7904). Full-time tuition and fees vary according to degree level and program. Part-time tuition: $599 per credit. Part-time tuition and fees vary according to program. *Required fees:* $194 per year part-time. *Room and board:* Room and board charges vary according to board plan and housing facility. *Payment plans:* installment, deferred payment. *Waivers:* senior citizens and employees or children of employees.

Financial Aid Of all full-time matriculated undergraduates who enrolled in 2001, 1237 applied for aid, 1136 were judged to have need, 54 had their need fully met. 335 Federal Work-Study jobs (averaging $1207). In 2001, 185 non-need-based awards were made. *Average percent of need met:* 78%. *Average financial aid package:* $15,776. *Average need-based loan:* $2345. *Average need-based gift aid:* $7824. *Average indebtedness upon graduation:* $18,493.

Applying *Options:* common application, early admission, deferred entrance. *Application fee:* $40. *Required:* high school transcript, 2 letters of recommendation. *Application deadlines:* 3/1 (freshmen), 8/1 (transfers). *Notification:* continuous (freshmen).

Admissions Contact Mr. Gary Hamme, Vice President of Enrollment Services, Fairleigh Dickinson University, Metropolitan Campus, 1000 River Road, Teaneck, NJ 07666. *Phone:* 201-692-7304. *Toll-free phone:* 800-338-8803. *Fax:* 201-692-2560. *E-mail:* globaleducation@fdu.edu.

FELICIAN COLLEGE
Lodi, New Jersey

- **Independent Roman Catholic** comprehensive, founded 1942
- **Calendar** semesters
- **Degrees** certificates, associate, bachelor's, master's, post-master's, and postbachelor's certificates
- **Suburban** 37-acre campus with easy access to New York City
- **Endowment** $2.2 million
- **Coed,** 1,618 undergraduate students, 59% full-time, 76% women, 24% men
- **Moderately difficult** entrance level, 63% of applicants were admitted

Undergraduates 959 full-time, 659 part-time. Students come from 10 states and territories, 5 other countries, 5% are from out of state, 13% African American, 4% Asian American or Pacific Islander, 15% Hispanic American, 0.1% Native American, 2% international, 16% transferred in, 20% live on campus. *Retention:* 92% of 2001 full-time freshmen returned.

Freshmen *Admission:* 947 applied, 596 admitted, 326 enrolled. *Average high school GPA:* 2.75. *Test scores:* SAT verbal scores over 500: 17%; SAT math scores over 500: 17%; SAT verbal scores over 600: 2%; SAT math scores over 600: 2%.

Faculty *Total:* 163, 44% full-time, 53% with terminal degrees. *Student/faculty ratio:* 15:1.

Majors Accounting; art; behavioral sciences; biochemistry; biology; business administration; business marketing and marketing management; computer science; cytotechnology; education; education (K-12); elementary education; English; environmental science; fine/studio arts; gerontology; graphic design/commercial art/illustration; history; humanities; interdisciplinary studies; liberal arts and sciences/liberal studies; mass communications; mathematics; mathematics education; medical laboratory technician; medical laboratory technology; medical technology; mental health/rehabilitation; natural sciences; nursing; philosophy; political science; pre-law; pre-medicine; psychology; religious studies; social sciences; sociology; special education; toxicology.

Academic Programs *Special study options:* academic remediation for entering students, accelerated degree program, adult/continuing education programs, advanced placement credit, distance learning, double majors, English as a second language, honors programs, independent study, internships, off-campus study, part-time degree program, services for LD students, student-designed majors, summer session for credit. *Unusual degree programs:* 3-2 clinical lab sciences with University of Medicine and Dentistry of New Jersey.

Library Felician College Library with 133,322 titles, 726 serial subscriptions, 14,845 audiovisual materials, an OPAC, a Web page.

Computers on Campus 100 computers available on campus for general student use. A campuswide network can be accessed from student residence rooms and from off campus. Internet access, at least one staffed computer lab available.

Student Life *Housing Options:* men-only, women-only. *Activities and Organizations:* drama/theater group, choral group, Student Nurses Association, Zeta Alpha Zeta teaching sorority, Campus Activity Board, Students In Free Enterprise, Student Government Association. *Campus security:* 24-hour patrols, student patrols, late-night transport/escort service. *Student Services:* health clinic, personal/psychological counseling.

Athletics Member NCAA, NAIA. All NCAA Division II. *Intercollegiate sports:* baseball M(s), basketball M(s)/W(s), cross-country running M(s)/W(s), soccer M(s)/W(s), softball W(s), track and field M(s)/W(s). *Intramural sports:* soccer M/W, softball W, volleyball M/W, weight lifting M/W.

Standardized Tests *Required:* SAT I (for admission).

Costs (2001–02) *Comprehensive fee:* $18,660 includes full-time tuition ($11,460), mandatory fees ($950), and room and board ($6250). Full-time tuition and fees vary according to class time, course load, degree level, and program. Part-time tuition: $382 per semester hour. Part-time tuition and fees vary according to class time, course load, degree level, and program. *Required fees:* $125 per term part-time. *Payment plans:* installment, deferred payment. *Waivers:* senior citizens and employees or children of employees.

Financial Aid Of all full-time matriculated undergraduates who enrolled in 2001, 710 applied for aid, 543 were judged to have need, 408 had their need fully met. 80 Federal Work-Study jobs (averaging $2200). *Average percent of need met:* 75%. *Average financial aid package:* $11,130. *Average need-based loan:* $5830. *Average indebtedness upon graduation:* $17,500.

Applying *Options:* deferred entrance. *Application fee:* $30. *Required:* high school transcript, minimum 2.0 GPA. *Required for some:* essay or personal statement, interview. *Application deadline:* rolling (freshmen), rolling (transfers).

Admissions Contact College Admissions Office, Felician College, 262 South Main Street, Lodi, NJ 07644. *Phone:* 201-559-6131. *Fax:* 201-559-6188. *E-mail:* admissions@inet.felician.edu.

GEORGIAN COURT COLLEGE
Lakewood, New Jersey

- **Independent Roman Catholic** comprehensive, founded 1908
- **Calendar** semesters
- **Degrees** certificates, bachelor's, master's, and postbachelor's certificates
- **Suburban** 150-acre campus with easy access to New York City and Philadelphia
- **Endowment** $33.3 million
- **Women only,** 1,767 undergraduate students, 67% full-time

■ **Moderately difficult** entrance level, 85% of applicants were admitted

Georgian Court College is a Catholic comprehensive college with a strong liberal arts core and special concern for women. Founded in 1908 and sponsored by the Sisters of Mercy, it offers 21 majors in the liberal arts and sciences and 3 professional studies majors. The Department of Art offers a BFA degree, with majors in general fine arts and graphic design/illustration. The Department of Business Administration, Accounting and Economics is accredited by the Association of Collegiate Business Schools and Programs. The Department of Social Work is accredited by the Council on Social Work Education.

Undergraduates 1,192 full-time, 575 part-time. Students come from 9 states and territories, 7% African American, 2% Asian American or Pacific Islander, 5% Hispanic American, 0.1% Native American, 1% international, 14% transferred in, 26% live on campus. *Retention:* 75% of 2001 full-time freshmen returned.

Freshmen *Admission:* 479 applied, 405 admitted, 199 enrolled. *Average high school GPA:* 2.96. *Test scores:* SAT verbal scores over 500: 30%; SAT math scores over 500: 30%; SAT verbal scores over 600: 5%; SAT math scores over 600: 4%; SAT verbal scores over 700: 1%.

Faculty *Total:* 213, 39% full-time, 30% with terminal degrees. *Student/faculty ratio:* 15:1.

Majors Accounting; art; art education; art history; biochemistry; biology; business administration; chemistry; computer/information sciences related; computer science; elementary education; English; French; graphic design/commercial art/illustration; health/medical diagnostic and treatment services related; history; humanities; mathematics; music; music teacher education; physics; pre-dentistry; pre-law; pre-medicine; psychology; religious studies; social work; sociology; Spanish; special education.

Academic Programs *Special study options:* academic remediation for entering students, adult/continuing education programs, advanced placement credit, honors programs, independent study, internships, part-time degree program, services for LD students, summer session for credit.

Library Georgian Court College Library with 121,724 titles, 1,076 serial subscriptions, an OPAC, a Web page.

Computers on Campus 131 computers available on campus for general student use. A campuswide network can be accessed from student residence rooms that provide access to intranet. Internet access, at least one staffed computer lab available.

Student Life *Housing Options:* women-only. *Activities and Organizations:* student-run newspaper, choral group, Social Work Club, Athletic Training Club, Re-Entry Women, Commuter Life, Phi Alpha Theta. *Campus security:* 24-hour emergency response devices and patrols, late-night transport/escort service, controlled dormitory access. *Student Services:* health clinic, personal/psychological counseling.

Athletics Member NAIA. *Intercollegiate sports:* basketball W(s), cross-country running W(s), soccer W(s), softball W(s), tennis W(s). *Intramural sports:* volleyball W.

Standardized Tests *Required:* SAT I or ACT (for admission).

Costs (2002–03) *Comprehensive fee:* $20,455 includes full-time tuition ($14,455), mandatory fees ($400), and room and board ($5600). Full-time tuition and fees vary according to program. Part-time tuition: $390 per credit. Part-time tuition and fees vary according to program. *Required fees:* $100 per term part-time. *Room and board:* Room and board charges vary according to board plan. *Payment plans:* installment, deferred payment. *Waivers:* senior citizens and employees or children of employees.

Applying *Options:* common application, early admission, early action. *Application fee:* $30. *Required:* essay or personal statement, high school transcript, minimum 2.0 GPA. *Recommended:* letters of recommendation, interview. *Application deadlines:* 8/1 (freshmen), 8/1 (transfers). *Notification:* 12/30 (early action).

Admissions Contact Mr. Michael Backes, Vice President for Enrollment, Georgian Court College, Office of Admissions, 900 Lakewood Avenue, Lakewood, NJ 08701-2697. *Phone:* 732-364-2200 Ext. 760. *Toll-free phone:* 800-458-8422. *Fax:* 732-364-4442. *E-mail:* admissions@georgian.edu.

KEAN UNIVERSITY
Union, New Jersey

■ **State-supported** comprehensive, founded 1855, part of New Jersey State College System
■ **Calendar** semesters
■ **Degrees** certificates, diplomas, bachelor's, master's, post-master's, and postbachelor's certificates
■ **Urban** 151-acre campus with easy access to New York City
■ **Endowment** $3.8 million
■ **Coed,** 9,467 undergraduate students, 71% full-time, 65% women, 35% men
■ **Moderately difficult** entrance level, 51% of applicants were admitted

Undergraduates 6,713 full-time, 2,754 part-time. Students come from 16 states and territories, 89 other countries, 1% are from out of state, 20% African American, 6% Asian American or Pacific Islander, 18% Hispanic American, 0.1% Native American, 4% international, 11% transferred in, 12% live on campus. *Retention:* 80% of 2001 full-time freshmen returned.

Freshmen *Admission:* 4,684 applied, 2,382 admitted, 1,195 enrolled. *Test scores:* SAT verbal scores over 500: 36%; SAT math scores over 500: 43%; SAT verbal scores over 600: 4%; SAT math scores over 600: 7%.

Faculty *Total:* 385, 98% full-time, 88% with terminal degrees. *Student/faculty ratio:* 20:1.

Majors Accounting; art; art history; biology; business administration; business marketing and marketing management; chemistry; communications; computer/information sciences; criminal justice/law enforcement administration; design/visual communications; early childhood education; earth sciences; economics; elementary education; English; finance; fine/studio arts; graphic/printing equipment; history; industrial arts education; industrial design; industrial technology; interior design; mathematics; medical records administration; medical technology; music; music teacher education; nursing science; occupational therapy; philosophy and religion related; physical education; physical therapy; political science; psychology; psychology related; public administration; recreation/leisure facilities management; social work; sociology; Spanish; special education; speech education; speech-language pathology/audiology; telecommunications; theater arts/drama.

Academic Programs *Special study options:* academic remediation for entering students, accelerated degree program, adult/continuing education programs, cooperative education, distance learning, double majors, English as a second language, external degree program, freshman honors college, honors programs, independent study, internships, off-campus study, part-time degree program, services for LD students, study abroad, summer session for credit. *ROTC:* Air Force (c).

Library Nancy Thompson Library plus 1 other with 272,000 titles, 14,500 serial subscriptions, an OPAC, a Web page.

Computers on Campus 600 computers available on campus for general student use. A campuswide network can be accessed from student residence rooms and from off campus. Internet access, online (class) registration, at least one staffed computer lab available.

Student Life *Housing Options:* coed. *Activities and Organizations:* drama/theater group, student-run newspaper, radio station, choral group, Student Organization, Greek Cooperative Council, national fraternities, national sororities. *Campus security:* 24-hour emergency response devices, student patrols, late-night transport/escort service, controlled dormitory access, 24-hour patrols by campus police. *Student Services:* health clinic, personal/psychological counseling, women's center, legal services.

Athletics Member NCAA, NAIA. All NCAA Division III. *Intercollegiate sports:* baseball M, basketball M/W, cross-country running M/W, field hockey W, football M, ice hockey M, lacrosse M/W, soccer M/W, softball W, swimming W, tennis M/W, track and field M/W, volleyball W. *Intramural sports:* basketball M/W, racquetball M/W, skiing (downhill) M/W, soccer M/W, swimming M/W, table tennis M/W, tennis M/W, track and field M/W, volleyball M/W, weight lifting M/W.

Standardized Tests *Required:* SAT I or ACT (for admission).

Costs (2001–02) *Tuition:* state resident $3750 full-time, $125 per credit part-time; nonresident $5670 full-time, $189 per credit part-time. *Required fees:* $1371 full-time, $45 per hour. *Room and board:* room only: $4840. Room and board charges vary according to board plan and housing facility. *Payment plans:* installment, deferred payment. *Waivers:* senior citizens and employees or children of employees.

Financial Aid Of all full-time matriculated undergraduates who enrolled in 2001, 4515 applied for aid, 3451 were judged to have need, 158 had their need fully met. In 2001, 911 non-need-based awards were made. *Average percent of need met:* 66%. *Average financial aid package:* $7768. *Average need-based loan:* $3399. *Average need-based gift aid:* $4338. *Average indebtedness upon graduation:* $13,685.

Applying *Options:* electronic application, early admission. *Application fee:* $35. *Required:* essay or personal statement, high school transcript, minimum 2.0 GPA. *Required for some:* interview. *Application deadlines:* 5/31 (freshmen), 7/15 (transfers). *Notification:* continuous until 8/1 (freshmen).

Admissions Contact Mr. Audley Bridges, Director of Admissions, Kean University, PO Box 411, Union, NJ 07083. *Phone:* 908-527-2195. *E-mail:* admitme@kean.edu.

MONMOUTH UNIVERSITY
West Long Branch, New Jersey

- **Independent** comprehensive, founded 1933
- **Calendar** semesters
- **Degrees** certificates, associate, bachelor's, master's, and post-master's certificates
- **Suburban** 147-acre campus with easy access to New York City and Philadelphia
- **Endowment** $32.9 million
- **Coed,** 4,179 undergraduate students, 87% full-time, 58% women, 42% men
- **Moderately difficult** entrance level, 82% of applicants were admitted

Undergraduates 3,635 full-time, 544 part-time. Students come from 23 states and territories, 6% are from out of state, 6% African American, 2% Asian American or Pacific Islander, 4% Hispanic American, 0.3% Native American, 0.3% international, 10% transferred in, 40% live on campus. *Retention:* 71% of 2001 full-time freshmen returned.

Freshmen *Admission:* 4,964 applied, 4,050 admitted, 886 enrolled. *Average high school GPA:* 3.00. *Test scores:* SAT verbal scores over 500: 58%; SAT math scores over 500: 64%; ACT scores over 18: 79%; SAT verbal scores over 600: 11%; SAT math scores over 600: 15%; ACT scores over 24: 16%; SAT verbal scores over 700: 1%; SAT math scores over 700: 1%.

Faculty *Total:* 463, 46% full-time, 46% with terminal degrees. *Student/faculty ratio:* 18:1.

Majors Accounting; anthropology; art; art history; biology; business administration; business marketing and marketing management; chemistry; communications; computer/information sciences; criminal justice studies; cytotechnology; economics; education; English; finance; fine/studio arts; foreign languages/ literatures; general studies; graphic design/commercial art/illustration; history; interdisciplinary studies; mathematics; medical technology; music; music business management/merchandising; nursing science; political science; psychology; secondary education; social work; special education; toxicology.

Academic Programs *Special study options:* academic remediation for entering students, accelerated degree program, adult/continuing education programs, advanced placement credit, cooperative education, honors programs, independent study, internships, part-time degree program, services for LD students, student-designed majors, study abroad, summer session for credit.

Library Murry and Leonie Guggenheim Memorial Library with 230,000 titles, 1,300 serial subscriptions, an OPAC, a Web page.

Computers on Campus 400 computers available on campus for general student use. A campuswide network can be accessed from student residence rooms and from off campus. At least one staffed computer lab available.

Student Life *Housing Options:* coed. *Activities and Organizations:* student-run newspaper, radio and television station, choral group, student-run radio station, Student Government Association, student newspaper, Student Activities Board, Shadows Yearbook, national fraternities, national sororities. *Campus security:* 24-hour emergency response devices and patrols, late-night transport/escort service, controlled dormitory access. *Student Services:* health clinic, personal/ psychological counseling.

Athletics Member NCAA. All Division I except football (Division I-AA). *Intercollegiate sports:* baseball M(s), basketball M(s)/W(s), cross-country running M(s)/W(s), field hockey W(s), golf M(s)/W(s), lacrosse W(s), soccer M(s)/W(s), softball W(s), tennis M(s)/W(s), track and field M(s)/W(s). *Intramural sports:* badminton M/W, basketball M/W, football M/W, soccer M/W, softball M/W, volleyball M/W.

Standardized Tests *Required:* SAT I or ACT (for admission). *Required for some:* SAT II: Subject Tests (for admission).

Costs (2001–02) *Comprehensive fee:* $24,150 includes full-time tuition ($16,506), mandatory fees ($568), and room and board ($7076). Part-time tuition: $478 per credit hour. *Required fees:* $142 per term part-time. *Room and board:* College room only: $3688. Room and board charges vary according to board plan and housing facility. *Payment plan:* installment. *Waivers:* senior citizens and employees or children of employees.

Financial Aid Of all full-time matriculated undergraduates who enrolled in 2001, 3366 applied for aid, 2309 were judged to have need, 406 had their need fully met. In 2001, 965 non-need-based awards were made. *Average percent of need met:* 70%. *Average financial aid package:* $12,769. *Average need-based loan:* $4475. *Average need-based gift aid:* $7182. *Average non-need based aid:* $4325. *Average indebtedness upon graduation:* $18,500.

Applying *Options:* early admission, early decision, early action, deferred entrance. *Application fee:* $35. *Required:* high school transcript. *Recommended:* essay or personal statement, minimum 2.25 GPA, interview. *Application deadlines:* 3/1 (freshmen), 1/1 (transfers). *Early decision:* 12/1. *Notification:* continuous until 4/1 (freshmen), 1/1 (early decision), 1/15 (early action).

Admissions Contact Ms. Christine Benol, Director of Undergraduate Admission, Monmouth University, 400 Cedar Avenue, West Long Branch, NJ 07764-1898. *Phone:* 732-571-3456. *Toll-free phone:* 800-543-9671. *Fax:* 732-263-5166. *E-mail:* cbenol@mondec.monmouth.edu.

MONTCLAIR STATE UNIVERSITY
Upper Montclair, New Jersey

- **State-supported** comprehensive, founded 1908
- **Calendar** semesters
- **Degrees** certificates, bachelor's, master's, doctoral, post-master's, and postbachelor's certificates
- **Suburban** 200-acre campus with easy access to New York City
- **Coed,** 10,404 undergraduate students, 77% full-time, 61% women, 39% men
- **Moderately difficult** entrance level, 23% of applicants were admitted

Undergraduates 7,986 full-time, 2,418 part-time. Students come from 32 states and territories, 75 other countries, 2% are from out of state, 11% African American, 5% Asian American or Pacific Islander, 15% Hispanic American, 0.2% Native American, 4% international, 9% transferred in, 21% live on campus. *Retention:* 85% of 2001 full-time freshmen returned.

Freshmen *Admission:* 7,073 applied, 1,596 admitted, 1,505 enrolled. *Test scores:* SAT verbal scores over 500: 59%; SAT math scores over 500: 68%; SAT verbal scores over 600: 15%; SAT math scores over 600: 20%; SAT verbal scores over 700: 1%; SAT math scores over 700: 1%.

Faculty *Total:* 962, 46% full-time, 44% with terminal degrees. *Student/faculty ratio:* 14:1.

Majors Accounting; anthropology; applied mathematics; art; art education; art history; biochemistry; biology; broadcast journalism; business administration; business economics; business education; business marketing and marketing management; chemistry; child care/development; classics; computer/information sciences; computer science; creative writing; dance; dietetics; early childhood education; earth sciences; economics; English; environmental science; exercise sciences; family/consumer studies; fashion merchandising; finance; fine/studio arts; food products retailing; French; geography; German; health education; health science; history; home economics; home economics education; humanities; industrial arts; industrial technology; international business; Italian; Latin (ancient and medieval); linguistics; management information systems/business data processing; mass communications; mathematics; molecular biology; music; music (piano and organ performance); music teacher education; music therapy; music (voice and choral/opera performance); nutrition science; philosophy; physical education; physics; political science; pre-dentistry; pre-law; pre-medicine; psychology; recreational therapy; recreation/leisure facilities management; recreation/ leisure studies; religious studies; retail management; secretarial science; sociology; Spanish; stringed instruments; theater arts/drama; travel/tourism management; urban studies; wind/percussion instruments.

Academic Programs *Special study options:* academic remediation for entering students, accelerated degree program, adult/continuing education programs, advanced placement credit, cooperative education, double majors, English as a second language, freshman honors college, honors programs, independent study, internships, off-campus study, part-time degree program, services for LD students, study abroad, summer session for credit. *Unusual degree programs:* 3-2 practical anthropology.

Library Sprague Library with 455,185 titles, 2,233 serial subscriptions, 47,939 audiovisual materials, an OPAC, a Web page.

Computers on Campus 650 computers available on campus for general student use. A campuswide network can be accessed from student residence rooms and from off campus. Internet access, at least one staffed computer lab available.

Student Life *Housing Options:* coed. *Activities and Organizations:* drama/ theater group, student-run newspaper, radio station, choral group, marching band, national fraternities, national sororities. *Campus security:* 24-hour emergency response devices and patrols, late-night transport/escort service, controlled dormitory access, video surveillance, student escorts. *Student Services:* health clinic, personal/psychological counseling, women's center, legal services.

Athletics Member NCAA. All Division III. *Intercollegiate sports:* baseball M, basketball M/W, cross-country running M/W, field hockey W, football M, golf M/W, lacrosse M/W, soccer M/W, softball W, swimming M/W, tennis M/W, track and field M/W, volleyball W, wrestling M. *Intramural sports:* baseball M, basketball M/W, bowling M/W, football M/W, ice hockey M(c), skiing (downhill) M(c), soccer M, softball M/W, tennis M/W, volleyball M/W.

Standardized Tests *Required:* SAT I or ACT (for admission).

Costs (2002–03) *Tuition:* state resident $4390 full-time, $146 per credit part-time; nonresident $7142 full-time, $238 per credit part-time. *Required fees:* $1351 full-time, $42 per credit, $25 per term part-time. *Room and board:* $6956;

room only: $4524. Room and board charges vary according to board plan and housing facility. *Payment plan:* installment. *Waivers:* senior citizens and employees or children of employees.

Financial Aid Of all full-time matriculated undergraduates who enrolled in 2001, 4989 applied for aid, 3855 were judged to have need, 2028 had their need fully met. 361 Federal Work-Study jobs (averaging $1080). 767 State and other part-time jobs (averaging $1817). In 2001, 366 non-need-based awards were made. *Average percent of need met:* 88%. *Average financial aid package:* $7149. *Average need-based loan:* $3154. *Average need-based gift aid:* $2530. *Average non-need based aid:* $2783. *Average indebtedness upon graduation:* $15,334.

Applying *Options:* electronic application, deferred entrance. *Application fee:* $40. *Required:* high school transcript. *Required for some:* essay or personal statement, interview. *Application deadlines:* 3/1 (freshmen), 5/1 (transfers). *Notification:* continuous (freshmen).

Admissions Contact Mr. Dennis Craig, Director of Admissions, Montclair State University, One Normal Avenue, Upper Montclair, NJ 07043-1624. *Phone:* 973-655-5116. *Toll-free phone:* 800-331-9205. *Fax:* 973-893-5455. *E-mail:* undergraduate.admissions@montclair.edu.

NEW JERSEY CITY UNIVERSITY

Jersey City, New Jersey

- **State-supported** comprehensive, founded 1927
- **Calendar** semesters
- **Degrees** bachelor's and master's
- **Urban** 46-acre campus with easy access to New York City
- **Endowment** $1.8 million
- **Coed,** 6,086 undergraduate students, 64% full-time, 61% women, 39% men
- **Moderately difficult** entrance level, 70% of applicants were admitted

New Jersey's only 4-year urban public university offers twenty-five undergraduate degree programs in the liberal arts, professional studies, and education. Cooperative education internships are available in all majors. The University is a center of cultural diversity and intellectual opportunity. The 47-acre campus is ideal for quiet study, although it is located just minutes from New York City.

Undergraduates 3,884 full-time, 2,202 part-time. Students come from 10 states and territories, 4% are from out of state, 20% African American, 10% Asian American or Pacific Islander, 32% Hispanic American, 0.3% Native American, 0.8% international, 10% transferred in, 4% live on campus.

Freshmen *Admission:* 2,588 applied, 1,818 admitted, 780 enrolled. *Average high school GPA:* 2.50. *Test scores:* SAT verbal scores over 500: 30%; SAT math scores over 500: 31%; SAT verbal scores over 600: 3%; SAT math scores over 600: 3%.

Faculty *Total:* 520, 46% full-time, 42% with terminal degrees. *Student/faculty ratio:* 15:1.

Majors Art; art education; biology; business administration; chemistry; communications; computer/information sciences; criminal justice studies; early childhood education; economics; elementary education; English; geology; health science; history; mathematics; music; music teacher education; nursing science; philosophy; physics; political science; psychology; sociology; Spanish; special education; urban studies.

Academic Programs *Special study options:* academic remediation for entering students, accelerated degree program, adult/continuing education programs, advanced placement credit, cooperative education, distance learning, double majors, English as a second language, honors programs, independent study, internships, off-campus study, part-time degree program, services for LD students, study abroad, summer session for credit. *ROTC:* Army (c), Navy (c), Air Force (c).

Library Congressman Frank J. Guarini Library with 710,875 titles, 11,260 serial subscriptions, 2,286 audiovisual materials, an OPAC.

Computers on Campus 1400 computers available on campus for general student use. At least one staffed computer lab available.

Student Life *Housing Options:* coed. *Activities and Organizations:* drama/theater group, student-run newspaper, radio station, choral group, International Student Association, Black Freedom Society, Latin Power Association, national fraternities. *Campus security:* 24-hour emergency response devices and patrols, late-night transport/escort service. *Student Services:* health clinic, personal/psychological counseling, women's center, legal services.

Athletics Member NCAA. All Division III. *Intercollegiate sports:* baseball M, basketball M/W, cross-country running W, football M, golf M, soccer M/W, softball W, tennis M, volleyball M/W. *Intramural sports:* basketball M/W, bowling M/W, football M/W, golf M/W, soccer M/W, softball M/W, swimming M/W, table tennis M/W, tennis M/W, volleyball M/W, weight lifting M/W.

Standardized Tests *Required:* SAT I or ACT (for admission). *Recommended:* SAT I (for admission).

Costs (2001–02) *Tuition:* state resident $3810 full-time, $127 per credit part-time; nonresident $7410 full-time, $247 per credit part-time. Part-time tuition and fees vary according to course load. *Required fees:* $1253 full-time. *Room and board:* $5800; room only: $3600. *Payment plan:* deferred payment. *Waivers:* senior citizens and employees or children of employees.

Applying *Options:* electronic application, deferred entrance. *Application fee:* $35. *Required:* essay or personal statement, high school transcript, minimum 2.0 GPA. *Required for some:* interview. *Recommended:* 1 letter of recommendation. *Application deadline:* 4/1 (freshmen), rolling (transfers).

Admissions Contact Ms. Drusilla Blackman, Director of Admissions, New Jersey City University, 2039 Kennedy Boulevard, Jersey City, NJ 07305-1597. *Phone:* 201-200-3234. *Toll-free phone:* 800-441-NJCU. *E-mail:* admissions@njcu.edu.

NEW JERSEY INSTITUTE OF TECHNOLOGY

Newark, New Jersey

- **State-supported** university, founded 1881
- **Calendar** semesters
- **Degrees** bachelor's, master's, and doctoral
- **Urban** 45-acre campus with easy access to New York City
- **Endowment** $36.8 million
- **Coed,** 5,698 undergraduate students, 72% full-time, 22% women, 78% men
- **Moderately difficult** entrance level, 65% of applicants were admitted

A part of one of the nation's most computing-intensive universities, NJIT's College of Computing Sciences offers one of the largest computing education programs in the nation. Undergraduate students can choose from an array of technology-rich majors and minors to design an educational program that matches their interests and career goals.

Undergraduates 4,123 full-time, 1,575 part-time. Students come from 25 states and territories, 69 other countries, 5% are from out of state, 11% African American, 23% Asian American or Pacific Islander, 11% Hispanic American, 0.2% Native American, 6% international, 8% transferred in, 33% live on campus. *Retention:* 80% of 2001 full-time freshmen returned.

Freshmen *Admission:* 2,227 applied, 1,457 admitted, 716 enrolled. *Test scores:* SAT verbal scores over 500: 72%; SAT math scores over 500: 94%; SAT verbal scores over 600: 23%; SAT math scores over 600: 51%; SAT verbal scores over 700: 3%; SAT math scores over 700: 10%.

Faculty *Total:* 651, 64% full-time, 95% with terminal degrees. *Student/faculty ratio:* 14:1.

Majors Actuarial science; applied mathematics; architecture; bioengineering; biology; business administration; chemical engineering; chemistry; civil engineering; computer engineering; computer/information sciences; computer/information sciences related; computer science; electrical engineering; engineering; engineering science; engineering technology; environmental engineering; environmental science; geophysical engineering; history; industrial/manufacturing engineering; information sciences/systems; mathematical statistics; mechanical engineering; nursing science; physics; science/technology and society; technical/business writing.

Academic Programs *Special study options:* academic remediation for entering students, accelerated degree program, adult/continuing education programs, advanced placement credit, cooperative education, distance learning, double majors, English as a second language, freshman honors college, honors programs, independent study, internships, off-campus study, part-time degree program, services for LD students, study abroad, summer session for credit. *ROTC:* Air Force (b). *Unusual degree programs:* 3-2 engineering with Seton Hall University, Lincoln University (PA), Stockton State College.

Library Van Houten Library plus 1 other with 160,000 titles, 1,100 serial subscriptions, an OPAC, a Web page.

Computers on Campus 4500 computers available on campus for general student use. A campuswide network can be accessed from student residence rooms and from off campus. At least one staffed computer lab available.

Student Life *Housing Options:* coed. *Activities and Organizations:* drama/theater group, student-run newspaper, radio station, Student Senate, Student Activities Council, Microcomputers Users Group, Chess Club, national fraternities, national sororities. *Campus security:* 24-hour emergency response devices and patrols, late-night transport/escort service, controlled dormitory access, bicycle patrols, sexual assault response team. *Student Services:* health clinic, personal/psychological counseling, women's center.

Athletics Member NCAA. All Division II except baseball (Division III), men's and women's basketball (Division III), men's and women's cross-country running

New Jersey Institute of Technology (continued)
(Division III), fencing (Division III), golf (Division III), soccer (Division III), softball (Division III), swimming (Division III), men's and women's tennis (Division III), track and field (Division III), men's and women's volleyball (Division III). *Intercollegiate sports:* baseball M, basketball M/W, cross-country running M/W, fencing M, golf M, soccer M, softball W, swimming W, tennis M/W, track and field W, volleyball M/W. *Intramural sports:* archery M/W, badminton M/W, basketball M/W, bowling M/W, football M, golf M/W, racquetball M/W, soccer M/W, softball M/W, swimming M/W, tennis M/W, track and field M/W, volleyball M/W, water polo M/W, weight lifting M/W.

Standardized Tests *Required:* SAT I or ACT (for admission). *Required for some:* SAT II: Subject Tests (for admission).

Costs (2001–02) *Tuition:* state resident $6158 full-time, $231 per credit part-time; nonresident $10,810 full-time, $464 per credit part-time. Full-time tuition and fees vary according to degree level. Part-time tuition and fees vary according to degree level. *Required fees:* $1042 full-time, $47 per credit, $76 per term part-time. *Room and board:* $7490. Room and board charges vary according to board plan and housing facility. *Payment plans:* installment, deferred payment. *Waivers:* employees or children of employees.

Financial Aid Of all full-time matriculated undergraduates who enrolled in 2001, 3963 applied for aid, 2240 were judged to have need, 1061 had their need fully met. In 2001, 514 non-need-based awards were made. *Average percent of need met:* 87%. *Average financial aid package:* $10,162. *Average need-based gift aid:* $7220. *Average non-need based aid:* $6500. *Average indebtedness upon graduation:* $7000. *Financial aid deadline:* 5/15.

Applying *Options:* electronic application, early admission, deferred entrance. *Application fee:* $35. *Required:* high school transcript. *Required for some:* essay or personal statement, interview. *Recommended:* 1 letter of recommendation. *Application deadlines:* 4/1 (freshmen), 6/1 (transfers). *Notification:* continuous (freshmen), 12/31 (early action).

Admissions Contact Ms. Kathy Kelly, Director of Admissions, New Jersey Institute of Technology, University Heights, Newark, NJ 07102-1982. *Phone:* 973-596-3300. *Toll-free phone:* 800-925-NJIT. *Fax:* 973-596-3461. *E-mail:* admissions@njit.edu.

PRINCETON UNIVERSITY
Princeton, New Jersey

- **Independent** university, founded 1746
- **Calendar** semesters
- **Degrees** bachelor's, master's, and doctoral
- **Suburban** 600-acre campus with easy access to New York City and Philadelphia
- **Endowment** $8.2 billion
- **Coed,** 4,744 undergraduate students, 97% full-time, 48% women, 52% men
- **Most difficult** entrance level, 12% of applicants were admitted

Undergraduates 4,613 full-time, 131 part-time. Students come from 53 states and territories, 66 other countries, 86% are from out of state, 8% African American, 12% Asian American or Pacific Islander, 6% Hispanic American, 0.5% Native American, 7% international, 97% live on campus. *Retention:* 97% of 2001 full-time freshmen returned.

Freshmen *Admission:* 14,288 applied, 1,677 admitted, 1,185 enrolled. *Average high school GPA:* 3.83. *Test scores:* SAT verbal scores over 500: 100%; SAT math scores over 500: 100%; SAT verbal scores over 600: 96%; SAT math scores over 600: 97%; SAT verbal scores over 700: 67%; SAT math scores over 700: 73%.

Faculty *Total:* 961, 81% full-time, 85% with terminal degrees. *Student/faculty ratio:* 6:1.

Majors Anthropology; architecture; art history; astrophysics; chemical engineering; chemistry; civil engineering; classics; comparative literature; computer engineering; East Asian studies; East European languages related; ecology; economics; electrical engineering; engineering/industrial management; English; geology; German; history; mathematics; mechanical engineering; Middle Eastern studies; molecular biology; multi/interdisciplinary studies related; music; philosophy; physics; political science; psychology; public administration; religious studies; romance languages; sociology.

Academic Programs *Special study options:* accelerated degree program, adult/continuing education programs, advanced placement credit, cooperative education, honors programs, independent study, internships, off-campus study, services for LD students, student-designed majors, study abroad. *ROTC:* Army (b), Air Force (c).

Library Harvey S. Firestone Memorial Library plus 22 others with 5.1 million titles, 34,348 serial subscriptions, 398,347 audiovisual materials, an OPAC, a Web page.

Computers on Campus 500 computers available on campus for general student use. A campuswide network can be accessed from student residence rooms and from off campus. At least one staffed computer lab available.

Student Life *Housing:* on-campus residence required through sophomore year. *Options:* coed, men-only, women-only, disabled students. *Activities and Organizations:* drama/theater group, student-run newspaper, radio station, choral group, marching band, Student Volunteer Council, Undergraduate Student Government, University Band, American Whig-Cliosophic Society, Players Club. *Campus security:* 24-hour emergency response devices and patrols, student patrols, late-night transport/escort service, controlled dormitory access. *Student Services:* health clinic, personal/psychological counseling, women's center, legal services.

Athletics Member NCAA. All Division I except football (Division I-AA). *Intercollegiate sports:* baseball M, basketball M/W, crew M/W, cross-country running M/W, fencing M/W, field hockey W, golf M/W, ice hockey M/W, lacrosse M/W, soccer M/W, softball W, squash M/W, swimming M/W, tennis M/W, track and field M/W, volleyball M/W, water polo M/W, wrestling M. *Intramural sports:* badminton M/W, basketball M/W, equestrian sports M(c)/W(c), ice hockey M/W, lacrosse M(c)/W(c), riflery M(c)/W(c), rugby M(c)/W(c), sailing M(c)/W(c), skiing (downhill) M(c)/W(c), soccer M(c)/W(c), softball M/W, table tennis M/W, tennis M/W, track and field M/W, volleyball M/W.

Standardized Tests *Required:* SAT I or ACT (for admission), SAT II: Subject Tests (for admission).

Costs (2001–02) *Comprehensive fee:* $33,613 includes full-time tuition ($26,160) and room and board ($7453). *Room and board:* College room only: $3596. *Payment plans:* installment, deferred payment. *Waivers:* employees or children of employees.

Financial Aid Of all full-time matriculated undergraduates who enrolled in 2001, 2212 applied for aid, 1812 were judged to have need, 1812 had their need fully met. 1034 Federal Work-Study jobs (averaging $1000). *Average percent of need met:* 100%. *Average financial aid package:* $21,909. *Average need-based loan:* $3546. *Average need-based gift aid:* $18,595. *Average indebtedness upon graduation:* $16,000.

Applying *Options:* early admission, early decision, deferred entrance. *Application fee:* $60. *Required:* essay or personal statement, high school transcript, 3 letters of recommendation. *Recommended:* interview. *Application deadline:* 1/1 (freshmen). *Early decision:* 11/1. *Notification:* 4/3 (freshmen), 12/15 (early decision).

Admissions Contact Mr. Fred A. Hargadon, Dean of Admission, Princeton University, PO Box 430, Princeton, NJ 08544. *Phone:* 609-258-3062. *Fax:* 609-258-6743.

RABBINICAL COLLEGE OF AMERICA
Morristown, New Jersey

- **Independent Jewish** 4-year, founded 1956
- **Calendar** semesters
- **Degree** bachelor's
- **Small-town** 81-acre campus with easy access to New York City
- **Men only,** 259 undergraduate students
- **Minimally difficult** entrance level, 100% of applicants were admitted

Undergraduates Students come from 24 states and territories, 10 other countries.

Freshmen *Admission:* 60 applied, 60 admitted.

Faculty *Total:* 13, 100% full-time.

Majors Religious studies.

Academic Programs *Special study options:* academic remediation for entering students, accelerated degree program, internships, off-campus study, study abroad, summer session for credit.

Library 10,000 titles.

Student Life *Housing:* on-campus residence required through senior year. *Student Services:* health clinic, personal/psychological counseling.

Applying *Required:* interview. *Required for some:* letters of recommendation. *Application deadline:* rolling (freshmen).

Admissions Contact Rabbi Israel Teitelbaum, Registrar, Rabbinical College of America, Box 1996, Morristown, NJ 07962. *Phone:* 973-267-9404.

RAMAPO COLLEGE OF NEW JERSEY
Mahwah, New Jersey

- **State-supported** comprehensive, founded 1969, part of New Jersey State College System
- **Calendar** semesters

- **Degrees** bachelor's and master's
- **Suburban** 315-acre campus with easy access to New York City
- **Endowment** $1.0 million
- **Coed,** 4,890 undergraduate students, 72% full-time, 60% women, 40% men
- **Moderately difficult** entrance level, 42% of applicants were admitted

As "the College of Choice for a Global Education," Ramapo College provides students with the opportunity to encounter the world beyond the campus through study-abroad and cooperative education programs and teleconferences. Undergraduate experiences through these programs have taken students to faraway countries such as China, Costa Rica, Czech Republic, England, Germany, Italy, and Kenya, and to corporate offices in the US and abroad.

Undergraduates 3,514 full-time, 1,376 part-time. Students come from 24 states and territories, 64 other countries, 16% are from out of state, 7% African American, 4% Asian American or Pacific Islander, 8% Hispanic American, 0.3% Native American, 4% international, 11% transferred in, 54% live on campus. *Retention:* 85% of 2001 full-time freshmen returned.

Freshmen *Admission:* 3,549 applied, 1,496 admitted, 633 enrolled. *Average high school GPA:* 3.20. *Test scores:* SAT verbal scores over 500: 68%; SAT math scores over 500: 70%; SAT verbal scores over 600: 20%; SAT math scores over 600: 22%; SAT verbal scores over 700: 2%; SAT math scores over 700: 3%.

Faculty *Total:* 339, 46% full-time. *Student/faculty ratio:* 16:1.

Majors Accounting; American studies; art; biochemistry; biology; business administration; chemistry; communications; comparative literature; computer/information sciences; economics; environmental science; fine/studio arts; history; information sciences/systems; interdisciplinary studies; international business; international relations; legal studies; literature; mathematics; nursing; physics; political science; psychology; social sciences; social work; sociology.

Academic Programs *Special study options:* academic remediation for entering students, accelerated degree program, adult/continuing education programs, advanced placement credit, cooperative education, distance learning, double majors, English as a second language, external degree program, freshman honors college, honors programs, independent study, internships, off-campus study, part-time degree program, services for LD students, student-designed majors, study abroad, summer session for credit. *Unusual degree programs:* 3-2 biology, chemistry with Rutgers, The State University of New Jersey.

Library George T. Potter Library plus 1 other with 145,413 titles, 719 serial subscriptions, 1,726 audiovisual materials, an OPAC.

Computers on Campus 350 computers available on campus for general student use. A campuswide network can be accessed from student residence rooms and from off campus. Internet access, online (class) registration, at least one staffed computer lab available.

Student Life *Housing Options:* coed, disabled students. *Activities and Organizations:* drama/theater group, student-run newspaper, radio and television station, choral group, Organization of African Unity, Student Activities Program Board, Ramapo News, International Student Organization, Student Activities Program Board, national fraternities, national sororities. *Campus security:* 24-hour emergency response devices and patrols, late-night transport/escort service, controlled dormitory access, surveillance cameras, patrols by trained security personnel. *Student Services:* health clinic, personal/psychological counseling, women's center.

Athletics Member NCAA. All Division III. *Intercollegiate sports:* baseball M, basketball M/W, cross-country running M/W, soccer M/W, softball W, tennis M/W, track and field M/W, volleyball M/W. *Intramural sports:* basketball M/W, golf M/W, skiing (cross-country) M/W, soccer M/W, softball W, swimming M/W, tennis M/W, track and field M/W, volleyball M/W.

Standardized Tests *Required:* SAT I (for admission). *Required for some:* ACT (for admission).

Costs (2001–02) *One-time required fee:* $200. *Tuition:* state resident $4416 full-time, $138 per credit part-time; nonresident $7802 full-time, $244 per credit part-time. Part-time tuition and fees vary according to course load. *Required fees:* $1762 full-time, $55 per credit. *Room and board:* $7372; room only: $4950. Room and board charges vary according to board plan and housing facility. *Payment plan:* installment. *Waivers:* senior citizens and employees or children of employees.

Financial Aid Of all full-time matriculated undergraduates who enrolled in 2001, 1907 applied for aid, 1429 were judged to have need, 227 had their need fully met. 187 Federal Work-Study jobs (averaging $1134). 486 State and other part-time jobs (averaging $1401). In 2001, 623 non-need-based awards were made. *Average percent of need met:* 82%. *Average financial aid package:* $8509. *Average need-based loan:* $3461. *Average need-based gift aid:* $5225. *Average indebtedness upon graduation:* $13,832.

Applying *Options:* early admission, deferred entrance. *Application fee:* $45. *Required:* essay or personal statement, high school transcript, 1 letter of recommendation. *Recommended:* minimum 3.0 GPA, interview. *Application deadlines:* 3/15 (freshmen), 5/1 (transfers). *Notification:* continuous until 5/1 (freshmen).

Admissions Contact Mr. Peter Goetz, Director of Recruitment and Retention, Ramapo College of New Jersey, Office of Admissions, 505 Ramapo Valley Road, Mahwah, NJ 07430-1680. *Phone:* 201-684-7307 Ext. 7307. *Toll-free phone:* 800-9RAMAPO. *Fax:* 201-684-7964. *E-mail:* admissions@ramapo.edu.

THE RICHARD STOCKTON COLLEGE OF NEW JERSEY

Pomona, New Jersey

- **State-supported** comprehensive, founded 1969, part of New Jersey State College System
- **Calendar** semesters
- **Degrees** bachelor's and master's
- **Suburban** 1600-acre campus with easy access to Philadelphia
- **Endowment** $3.3 million
- **Coed,** 6,138 undergraduate students, 82% full-time, 58% women, 42% men
- **Very difficult** entrance level, 45% of applicants were admitted

State-supported, 4-year coed college founded in 1969. Located 12 miles from Atlantic City, Stockton is primarily an undergraduate arts and sciences college within the New Jersey system. Special educational experiences are encouraged, including study abroad, internships, field studies, and independent study. Admission is selective.

Undergraduates 5,012 full-time, 1,126 part-time. Students come from 23 states and territories, 24 other countries, 2% are from out of state, 8% African American, 4% Asian American or Pacific Islander, 5% Hispanic American, 0.3% Native American, 0.7% international, 14% transferred in, 42% live on campus. *Retention:* 84% of 2001 full-time freshmen returned.

Freshmen *Admission:* 3,384 applied, 1,537 admitted, 784 enrolled. *Average high school GPA:* 3.2. *Test scores:* SAT verbal scores over 500: 75%; SAT math scores over 500: 79%; SAT verbal scores over 600: 19%; SAT math scores over 600: 22%; SAT verbal scores over 700: 2%; SAT math scores over 700: 2%.

Faculty *Total:* 359, 56% full-time, 58% with terminal degrees. *Student/faculty ratio:* 20:1.

Majors Biochemistry; biology; business administration; chemistry; communications; computer/information sciences; computer science; criminology; economics; education (multiple levels); English; environmental science; foreign languages/literatures; geology; history; information sciences/systems; interdisciplinary studies; liberal arts and sciences/liberal studies; marine biology; mathematics; nursing; nursing science; philosophy; physics; political science; psychology; public health; social work; sociology; speech-language pathology/audiology; visual/performing arts.

Academic Programs *Special study options:* academic remediation for entering students, accelerated degree program, adult/continuing education programs, advanced placement credit, distance learning, freshman honors college, honors programs, independent study, internships, off-campus study, part-time degree program, services for LD students, student-designed majors, study abroad, summer session for credit. *ROTC:* Army (c). *Unusual degree programs:* 3-2 engineering with New Jersey Institute of Technology; Rutgers, The State University of New Jersey; public administration with Rutgers, The State University of New Jersey.

Library The Richard Stockton College of New Jersey Library with 287,769 titles, 7,682 audiovisual materials, an OPAC, a Web page.

Computers on Campus 450 computers available on campus for general student use. A campuswide network can be accessed from student residence rooms and from off campus. Internet access, at least one staffed computer lab available.

Student Life *Housing Options:* coed. *Activities and Organizations:* drama/theater group, student-run newspaper, radio and television station, choral group, Stockton Action Volunteers for the Environment, Board of Activities, Los Latinos Unidos, Unified Black Student Society, Stockton Residents Association, national fraternities, national sororities. *Campus security:* 24-hour emergency response devices and patrols, late-night transport/escort service, on-campus police force. *Student Services:* health clinic, personal/psychological counseling, women's center.

Athletics Member NCAA. All Division III. *Intercollegiate sports:* baseball M, basketball M/W, crew W, cross-country running M/W, lacrosse M, soccer M/W, softball W, tennis W, track and field M/W, volleyball W. *Intramural sports:* baseball M(c), basketball M/W, bowling M(c)/W(c), crew M(c), fencing M(c)/W(c), football M/W, golf M(c)/W(c), skiing (downhill) M(c)/W(c), softball M/W, swimming M/W, table tennis M/W, tennis M/W, volleyball M/W, weight lifting M/W, wrestling M.

Standardized Tests *Required:* SAT I or ACT (for admission).

The Richard Stockton College of New Jersey (continued)

Costs (2001–02) *Tuition:* state resident $3952 full-time, $124 per credit part-time; nonresident $6400 full-time, $200 per credit part-time. *Required fees:* $1184 full-time, $37 per credit. *Room and board:* $5845; room only: $3700. Room and board charges vary according to board plan and housing facility. *Payment plan:* installment. *Waivers:* senior citizens and employees or children of employees.

Financial Aid Of all full-time matriculated undergraduates who enrolled in 2001, 3706 applied for aid, 2661 were judged to have need, 1813 had their need fully met. 244 Federal Work-Study jobs (averaging $1671). 778 State and other part-time jobs (averaging $848). In 2001, 393 non-need-based awards were made. *Average percent of need met:* 68%. *Average financial aid package:* $8087. *Average need-based loan:* $3495. *Average need-based gift aid:* $5018. *Average indebtedness upon graduation:* $14,388.

Applying *Options:* electronic application, early action. *Application fee:* $35. *Required:* essay or personal statement, high school transcript, minimum 2.0 GPA. *Recommended:* minimum 3.0 GPA, letters of recommendation. *Application deadlines:* 5/1 (freshmen), 6/1 (transfers). *Notification:* continuous until 5/15 (freshmen).

Admissions Contact Mr. Salvatore Catalfamo, Dean of Enrollment Management, The Richard Stockton College of New Jersey, PO Box 195, F-101, Pomona, NJ 08240. *Phone:* 609-652-4261. *Fax:* 609-748-5541. *E-mail:* admissions@pollux.stockton.edu.

RIDER UNIVERSITY
Lawrenceville, New Jersey

- **Independent** comprehensive, founded 1865
- **Calendar** semesters
- **Degrees** associate, bachelor's, master's, and post-master's certificates
- **Suburban** 340-acre campus with easy access to New York City and Philadelphia
- **Endowment** $46.4 million
- **Coed,** 4,306 undergraduate students, 80% full-time, 58% women, 42% men
- **Moderately difficult** entrance level, 74% of applicants were admitted

Rider University offers majors in business, education, liberal arts, sciences, and music. Rider's formula for career success includes a combination of small classes, personal advising, experiential learning, and use of modern facilities. Students enjoy activities ranging from social organizations to Division I athletics. Approximately 75 percent of the 3,000 full-time undergraduates receive financial assistance.

Undergraduates 3,448 full-time, 858 part-time. Students come from 30 states and territories, 8 other countries, 24% are from out of state, 8% African American, 3% Asian American or Pacific Islander, 4% Hispanic American, 0.5% Native American, 3% international, 5% transferred in, 50% live on campus. *Retention:* 77% of 2001 full-time freshmen returned.

Freshmen *Admission:* 4,348 applied, 3,199 admitted, 861 enrolled. *Average high school GPA:* 3.06. *Test scores:* SAT verbal scores over 500: 59%; SAT math scores over 500: 63%; SAT verbal scores over 600: 13%; SAT math scores over 600: 15%; SAT verbal scores over 700: 1%; SAT math scores over 700: 2%.

Faculty *Total:* 438, 51% full-time, 75% with terminal degrees. *Student/faculty ratio:* 13:1.

Majors Accounting; actuarial science; advertising; American studies; bilingual/bicultural education; biochemistry; biology; biopsychology; business administration; business economics; business education; business marketing and marketing management; chemistry; computer science; early childhood education; economics; education; elementary education; English; environmental science; finance; French; general studies; geology; German; history; human resources management; information sciences/systems; international business; journalism; management science; marine science; mathematics; music; music (piano and organ performance); music teacher education; music theory and composition; music (voice and choral/opera performance); oceanography; philosophy; physics; political science; psychology; public relations; radio/television broadcasting; religious music; Russian; science education; secondary education; sociology; Spanish; speech/rhetorical studies.

Academic Programs *Special study options:* academic remediation for entering students, adult/continuing education programs, advanced placement credit, cooperative education, double majors, English as a second language, honors programs, independent study, internships, part-time degree program, services for LD students, study abroad, summer session for credit. *ROTC:* Army (c).

Library Franklin F. Moore Library plus 1 other with 394,308 titles, 2,763 serial subscriptions, 24,457 audiovisual materials, an OPAC, a Web page.

Computers on Campus 403 computers available on campus for general student use. A campuswide network can be accessed from student residence rooms and from off campus. Internet access, at least one staffed computer lab available.

Student Life *Housing Options:* coed, men-only, women-only, disabled students. *Activities and Organizations:* drama/theater group, student-run newspaper, radio station, choral group, Student Government Association, Student Entertainment Council, Association of Commuter Students, Greek organizations, Latin American Student Organization, national fraternities, national sororities. *Campus security:* 24-hour emergency response devices and patrols, student patrols, late-night transport/escort service, controlled dormitory access. *Student Services:* health clinic, personal/psychological counseling, women's center.

Athletics Member NCAA. All Division I. *Intercollegiate sports:* baseball M(s), basketball M(s)/W(s), cross-country running M(s)/W(s), field hockey W(s), golf M(s), soccer M(s)/W(s), softball W(s), swimming M(s)/W(s), tennis M(s)/W(s), track and field M(s)/W(s), volleyball W(s), wrestling M(s). *Intramural sports:* basketball M/W, equestrian sports W(c), golf M, ice hockey M(c), lacrosse M(c)/W, soccer M/W, softball M/W, track and field M/W, volleyball M/W, water polo M/W.

Standardized Tests *Required:* SAT I or ACT (for admission).

Costs (2002–03) *Comprehensive fee:* $27,650 includes full-time tuition ($19,240), mandatory fees ($460), and room and board ($7950). Full-time tuition and fees vary according to course load. Part-time tuition: $640 per credit. Part-time tuition and fees vary according to course load. *Required fees:* $15 per course. *Room and board:* College room only: $4430. Room and board charges vary according to housing facility. *Payment plan:* installment. *Waivers:* employees or children of employees.

Financial Aid Of all full-time matriculated undergraduates who enrolled in 2001, 2841 applied for aid, 2151 were judged to have need, 502 had their need fully met. In 2001, 519 non-need-based awards were made. *Average percent of need met:* 90%. *Average financial aid package:* $16,457. *Average need-based loan:* $4496. *Average need-based gift aid:* $7859. *Average non-need based aid:* $6096. *Average indebtedness upon graduation:* $16,000.

Applying *Options:* common application, early admission, early action, deferred entrance. *Application fee:* $40. *Required:* essay or personal statement, high school transcript, minimum 2.0 GPA. *Required for some:* interview. *Recommended:* 2 letters of recommendation, interview. *Application deadline:* rolling (freshmen), rolling (transfers). *Notification:* continuous (freshmen), 12/15 (early action).

Admissions Contact Mrs. Susan C. Christian, Director, Office of Admissions, Rider University, 2083 Lawrenceville Road, Lawrenceville, NJ 08648-3099. *Phone:* 609-895-5768. *Toll-free phone:* 800-257-9026. *Fax:* 609-895-6645. *E-mail:* admissions@rider.edu.

ROWAN UNIVERSITY
Glassboro, New Jersey

- **State-supported** comprehensive, founded 1923, part of New Jersey State College System
- **Calendar** semesters
- **Degrees** bachelor's, master's, and doctoral
- **Small-town** 200-acre campus with easy access to Philadelphia
- **Endowment** $92.9 million
- **Coed,** 8,345 undergraduate students, 79% full-time, 58% women, 42% men
- **Moderately difficult** entrance level, 52% of applicants were admitted

Rowan University is a selective public university offering undergraduate majors plus graduate degrees and certificates. Included are nationally recognized programs in business, engineering, fine and performing arts, liberal arts and sciences, communications, and teacher education. The 200-acre campus hosts 6,200 full-time undergraduates in Glassboro, a southern New Jersey town.

Undergraduates 6,556 full-time, 1,789 part-time. Students come from 16 states and territories, 3% are from out of state, 9% African American, 4% Asian American or Pacific Islander, 6% Hispanic American, 0.4% Native American, 9% transferred in, 25% live on campus. *Retention:* 87% of 2001 full-time freshmen returned.

Freshmen *Admission:* 6,031 applied, 3,151 admitted, 1,282 enrolled. *Test scores:* SAT verbal scores over 500: 74%; SAT math scores over 500: 76%; SAT verbal scores over 600: 22%; SAT math scores over 600: 29%; SAT verbal scores over 700: 2%; SAT math scores over 700: 3%.

Faculty *Total:* 747, 52% full-time, 50% with terminal degrees. *Student/faculty ratio:* 14:1.

Majors Accounting; advertising; art; art education; biology; business administration; business marketing and marketing management; chemical engineering; chemistry; civil engineering; computer science; drawing; early childhood education; economics; electrical engineering; elementary education; engineering; English;

finance; fine/studio arts; geography; graphic design/commercial art/illustration; history; industrial technology; information sciences/systems; jazz; journalism; labor/personnel relations; law enforcement/police science; liberal arts and sciences/liberal studies; management information systems/business data processing; mass communications; mathematics; mechanical engineering; music; music teacher education; music (voice and choral/opera performance); physical education; physical sciences; political science; pre-law; pre-medicine; psychology; public relations; radio/television broadcasting; retail management; science education; secondary education; sociology; Spanish; special education; speech/rhetorical studies; theater arts/drama.

Academic Programs *Special study options:* academic remediation for entering students, accelerated degree program, adult/continuing education programs, advanced placement credit, cooperative education, double majors, English as a second language, honors programs, independent study, internships, part-time degree program, services for LD students, study abroad, summer session for credit. *ROTC:* Army (c). *Unusual degree programs:* 3-2 optometry with Pennsylvania College of Optometry, podiatry with Pennsylvania College of Podiatric Medicine, pharmacy with Philadelphia College of Pharmacy and Science.

Library Keith and Shirley Campbell Library plus 2 others with an OPAC, a Web page.

Computers on Campus 350 computers available on campus for general student use. A campuswide network can be accessed from student residence rooms and from off campus. Internet access, at least one staffed computer lab available.

Student Life *Housing:* on-campus residence required for freshman year. *Options:* coed, women-only, disabled students. *Activities and Organizations:* drama/theater group, student-run newspaper, radio station, choral group, marching band, Greek organizations, Student Government Association, Student Activities Board, national fraternities, national sororities. *Campus security:* 24-hour emergency response devices and patrols, late-night transport/escort service, controlled dormitory access. *Student Services:* health clinic, personal/psychological counseling, women's center, legal services.

Athletics Member NCAA. All Division III. *Intercollegiate sports:* baseball M, basketball M/W, cross-country running M/W, field hockey W, football M, golf M, lacrosse W, soccer M/W, softball W, swimming M/W, tennis M/W, track and field M/W. *Intramural sports:* baseball M, basketball M/W, cross-country running M/W, fencing M/W, football M/W, golf M/W, lacrosse M, softball W, swimming M/W, table tennis M/W, tennis M/W, volleyball M/W.

Standardized Tests *Required:* SAT I (for admission).

Costs (2001–02) *Tuition:* state resident $4500 full-time, $150 per semester hour part-time; nonresident $9000 full-time, $300 per semester hour part-time. *Required fees:* $1279 full-time, $42 per semester hour. *Room and board:* $6586; room only: $3986. Room and board charges vary according to board plan and housing facility. *Payment plan:* deferred payment. *Waivers:* employees or children of employees.

Financial Aid Of all full-time matriculated undergraduates who enrolled in 2001, 5175 applied for aid, 4156 were judged to have need, 1649 had their need fully met. In 2001, 496 non-need-based awards were made. *Average percent of need met:* 84%. *Average financial aid package:* $5624. *Average need-based loan:* $3423. *Average need-based gift aid:* $4374. *Average non-need based aid:* $1888. *Financial aid deadline:* 3/15.

Applying *Options:* deferred entrance. *Application fee:* $50. *Required:* essay or personal statement, high school transcript, minimum 2.0 GPA, 1 letter of recommendation. *Required for some:* interview. *Recommended:* minimum 3.0 GPA. *Application deadlines:* 3/15 (freshmen), 3/15 (transfers). *Notification:* 4/15 (freshmen).

Admissions Contact Mr. Marvin G. Sills, Director of Admissions, Rowan University, 201 Mullica Hill Road, Glassboro, NJ 08028. *Phone:* 856-256-4200. *Toll-free phone:* 800-447-1165. *Fax:* 856-256-4430. *E-mail:* admissions@rowan.edu.

RUTGERS, THE STATE UNIVERSITY OF NEW JERSEY, CAMDEN

Camden, New Jersey

- **State-supported** university, founded 1927, part of Rutgers, The State University of New Jersey
- **Calendar** semesters
- **Degrees** bachelor's, master's, and first professional
- **Endowment** $342.0 million
- **Coed,** 3,677 undergraduate students, 74% full-time, 60% women, 40% men
- 59% of applicants were admitted

Undergraduates 2,734 full-time, 943 part-time. 3% are from out of state, 15% African American, 7% Asian American or Pacific Islander, 6% Hispanic American, 0.3% Native American, 1.0% international, 10% transferred in.

Freshmen *Admission:* 6,205 applied, 3,662 admitted, 426 enrolled. *Test scores:* SAT verbal scores over 500: 62%; SAT math scores over 500: 68%; SAT verbal scores over 600: 19%; SAT math scores over 600: 21%; SAT verbal scores over 700: 2%; SAT math scores over 700: 1%.

Faculty *Total:* 380, 59% full-time, 98% with terminal degrees. *Student/faculty ratio:* 11:1.

Academic Programs *Special study options:* academic remediation for entering students, advanced placement credit, distance learning, double majors, English as a second language, freshman honors college, honors programs, independent study, internships, part-time degree program, services for LD students, student-designed majors, study abroad, summer session for credit. *ROTC:* Army (c), Air Force (c).

Library Paul Robeson Library plus 2 others with 3.8 million titles, 28,760 serial subscriptions.

Computers on Campus 184 computers available on campus for general student use. A campuswide network can be accessed from student residence rooms and from off campus that provide access to online grade reports. Internet access, at least one staffed computer lab available.

Student Life *Activities and Organizations:* drama/theater group, student-run newspaper, radio station.

Standardized Tests *Required:* SAT I or ACT (for admission). *Required for some:* SAT II: Subject Tests (for admission).

Costs (2001–02) *Tuition:* state resident $5250 full-time, $170 per credit part-time; nonresident $10,688 full-time, $347 per credit part-time. Full-time tuition and fees vary according to program. Part-time tuition and fees vary according to course load and program. *Required fees:* $1234 full-time, $225 per term part-time. *Room and board:* $6776; room only: $4376. Room and board charges vary according to board plan and housing facility. *Payment plans:* installment, deferred payment. *Waivers:* employees or children of employees.

Financial Aid Of all full-time matriculated undergraduates who enrolled in 2001, 2102 applied for aid, 1694 were judged to have need, 844 had their need fully met. 337 Federal Work-Study jobs (averaging $1905). In 2001, 86 non-need-based awards were made. *Average percent of need met:* 88%. *Average financial aid package:* $8282. *Average need-based loan:* $3210. *Average need-based gift aid:* $5859. *Average non-need based aid:* $3650. *Average indebtedness upon graduation:* $15,158.

Applying *Options:* electronic application, early admission. *Application fee:* $50. *Required:* high school transcript. *Application deadline:* rolling (freshmen). *Notification:* 2/28 (freshmen).

Admissions Contact Ms. Diane Williams Harris, Associate Director of University Undergraduate Admissions, Rutgers, The State University of New Jersey, Camden, 65 Davidson Road, Piscataway, NJ 08854-8097. *Phone:* 732-932-4636. *Fax:* 732-353-1440.

RUTGERS, THE STATE UNIVERSITY OF NEW JERSEY, NEWARK

Newark, New Jersey

- **State-supported** university, founded 1892, part of Rutgers, The State University of New Jersey
- **Calendar** semesters
- **Degrees** bachelor's, master's, doctoral, and first professional
- **Endowment** $342.0 million
- **Coed,** 6,108 undergraduate students, 72% full-time, 58% women, 42% men
- **Moderately difficult** entrance level, 52% of applicants were admitted

Undergraduates 4,425 full-time, 1,683 part-time. 5% are from out of state, 20% African American, 20% Asian American or Pacific Islander, 18% Hispanic American, 0.2% Native American, 4% international, 8% transferred in.

Freshmen *Admission:* 8,873 applied, 4,618 admitted, 895 enrolled. *Test scores:* SAT verbal scores over 500: 63%; SAT math scores over 500: 72%; SAT verbal scores over 600: 14%; SAT math scores over 600: 26%; SAT verbal scores over 700: 2%; SAT math scores over 700: 4%.

Faculty *Total:* 643, 70% full-time, 98% with terminal degrees. *Student/faculty ratio:* 10:1.

Academic Programs *Special study options:* academic remediation for entering students, accelerated degree program, adult/continuing education programs, advanced placement credit, distance learning, double majors, English as a second language, freshman honors college, honors programs, independent study, internships, off-campus study, part-time degree program, services for LD students, student-designed majors, study abroad, summer session for credit. *ROTC:* Army (b), Air Force (b). *Unusual degree programs:* 3-2 criminal justice.

Library John Cotton Dana Library plus 4 others with 3.8 million titles, 28,760 serial subscriptions.

Rutgers, The State University of New Jersey, Newark (continued)

Computers on Campus 708 computers available on campus for general student use. A campuswide network can be accessed from student residence rooms and from off campus that provide access to online grade reports. Internet access, at least one staffed computer lab available.

Student Life *Activities and Organizations:* drama/theater group, student-run newspaper, radio station, choral group.

Standardized Tests *Required:* SAT I or ACT (for admission). *Required for some:* SAT II: Subject Tests (for admission).

Costs (2001–02) *Tuition:* state resident $5250 full-time, $170 per credit part-time; nonresident $10,688 full-time, $347 per credit part-time. Full-time tuition and fees vary according to program. Part-time tuition and fees vary according to course load and program. *Required fees:* $1126 full-time, $138 per term part-time. *Room and board:* $7208; room only: $4364. Room and board charges vary according to board plan and housing facility. *Payment plans:* installment, deferred payment. *Waivers:* employees or children of employees.

Financial Aid Of all full-time matriculated undergraduates who enrolled in 2001, 3056 applied for aid, 2630 were judged to have need, 890 had their need fully met. In 2001, 81 non-need-based awards were made. *Average percent of need met:* 82%. *Average financial aid package:* $8368. *Average need-based loan:* $3077. *Average need-based gift aid:* $6412. *Average non-need based aid:* $3141. *Average indebtedness upon graduation:* $15,855.

Applying *Options:* electronic application, early admission. *Application fee:* $50. *Required:* high school transcript. *Application deadline:* rolling (freshmen). *Notification:* 2/28 (freshmen).

Admissions Contact Ms. Diane William Harris, Associate Director of University Undergraduate Admissions, Rutgers, The State University of New Jersey, Newark, 65 Davidson Road, Piscataway, NJ 08854-8097. *Phone:* 732-932-4636. *Fax:* 732-353-1440.

RUTGERS, THE STATE UNIVERSITY OF NEW JERSEY, NEW BRUNSWICK

New Brunswick, New Jersey

- **State-supported** university, founded 1766, part of Rutgers, The State University of New Jersey
- **Calendar** semesters
- **Degrees** bachelor's, master's, doctoral, and first professional
- **Endowment** $342.0 million
- **Coed,** 28,351 undergraduate students, 91% full-time, 53% women, 47% men
- **Moderately difficult** entrance level, 60% of applicants were admitted

Undergraduates 25,663 full-time, 2,688 part-time. Students come from 9 other countries, 8% are from out of state, 8% African American, 19% Asian American or Pacific Islander, 8% Hispanic American, 0.2% Native American, 3% international, 5% transferred in, 46% live on campus.

Freshmen *Admission:* 27,074 applied, 16,172 admitted, 5,465 enrolled. *Test scores:* SAT verbal scores over 500: 84%; SAT math scores over 500: 90%; SAT verbal scores over 600: 38%; SAT math scores over 600: 53%; SAT verbal scores over 700: 7%; SAT math scores over 700: 14%.

Faculty *Total:* 2,179, 69% full-time, 98% with terminal degrees. *Student/faculty ratio:* 15:1.

Majors Accounting; African studies; American studies; anthropology; art; art history; atmospheric sciences; biology; biomedical science; biometrics; biotechnology research; business administration; business marketing and marketing management; cell biology; ceramic arts; chemistry; Chinese; classics; communications; comparative literature; computer science; criminal justice/law enforcement administration; dance; drawing; East Asian studies; Eastern European area studies; ecology; economics; English; environmental science; evolutionary biology; exercise sciences; film studies; finance; food sciences; foreign languages/literatures; French; genetics; geography; geology; German; graphic design/commercial art/illustration; Greek (ancient and medieval); Hispanic-American studies; history; human ecology; interdisciplinary studies; Italian; jazz; journalism; Judaic studies; labor/personnel relations; Latin American studies; Latin (ancient and medieval); linguistics; management science; marine biology; mass communications; mathematical statistics; mathematics; medical technology; medieval/renaissance studies; microbiology/bacteriology; Middle Eastern studies; molecular biology; music; music teacher education; nutritional sciences; painting; pharmacy; philosophy; photography; physics; physiology; political science; Portuguese; pre-dentistry; pre-law; pre-medicine; printmaking; psychology; public health; religious studies; Russian; Russian/Slavic studies; sculpture; sociology; Spanish; theater arts/drama; urban studies; women's studies.

Academic Programs *Special study options:* academic remediation for entering students, accelerated degree program, advanced placement credit, cooperative education, distance learning, double majors, English as a second language, honors programs, independent study, student-designed majors, study abroad. *ROTC:* Army (b), Air Force (b). *Unusual degree programs:* 3-2 planning and public policy, education, criminal justice.

Library Archibald S. Alexander Library plus 14 others with 3.8 million titles, 28,760 serial subscriptions, an OPAC, a Web page.

Computers on Campus 1450 computers available on campus for general student use. A campuswide network can be accessed from student residence rooms and from off campus that provide access to online grade reports. Internet access, at least one staffed computer lab available.

Student Life *Housing Options:* coed, men-only, women-only, cooperative, disabled students. *Activities and Organizations:* drama/theater group, student-run newspaper, radio and television station, choral group, marching band, national fraternities, national sororities. *Student Services:* health clinic.

Athletics Member NCAA. All Division I except football (Division I-A). *Intercollegiate sports:* baseball M, basketball M/W, crew M/W, cross-country running M/W, fencing M/W, golf M/W, gymnastics W, lacrosse M/W, soccer M/W, softball W, swimming M/W, tennis M/W, track and field M/W, volleyball W, wrestling M. *Intramural sports:* badminton M/W, baseball M(c), basketball M/W, bowling M/W, cross-country running M/W, equestrian sports M(c)/W(c), field hockey W(c), football M, golf M/W, ice hockey M(c), lacrosse M/W, racquetball M/W, rugby M(c)/W(c), sailing M(c)/W(c), skiing (cross-country) M(c)/W(c), skiing (downhill) M(c)/W(c), soccer M/W, softball M/W, squash M(c)/W(c), swimming M/W, table tennis M(c)/W(c), tennis M/W, track and field M/W, volleyball M/W, water polo M/W, wrestling M.

Standardized Tests *Required:* SAT I or ACT (for admission). *Required for some:* SAT II: Writing Test (for admission).

Costs (2001–02) *Tuition:* state resident $5250 full-time, $170 per credit part-time; nonresident $10,688 full-time, $347 per credit part-time. Full-time tuition and fees vary according to program. Part-time tuition and fees vary according to class time and program. *Required fees:* $1370 full-time, $126 per term part-time. *Room and board:* $6676; room only: $4174. Room and board charges vary according to board plan and housing facility. *Payment plans:* installment, deferred payment. *Waivers:* employees or children of employees.

Financial Aid Of all full-time matriculated undergraduates who enrolled in 2001, 15621 applied for aid, 11935 were judged to have need, 4664 had their need fully met. In 2001, 2675 non-need-based awards were made. *Average percent of need met:* 86%. *Average financial aid package:* $9248. *Average need-based loan:* $3719. *Average need-based gift aid:* $6232. *Average non-need based aid:* $4556. *Average indebtedness upon graduation:* $15,311.

Applying *Options:* electronic application, early admission. *Application fee:* $50. *Required:* high school transcript. *Application deadline:* rolling (freshmen). *Notification:* 2/28 (freshmen).

Admissions Contact Ms. Diane Williams Harris, Associate Director of University Undergraduate Admissions, Rutgers, The State University of New Jersey, New Brunswick, 65 Davidson Road, Piscataway, NJ 08854-8097. *Phone:* 732-932-4636. *Fax:* 732-445-0237.

SAINT PETER'S COLLEGE

Jersey City, New Jersey

- **Independent Roman Catholic (Jesuit)** comprehensive, founded 1872
- **Calendar** semesters
- **Degrees** certificates, associate, bachelor's, and master's
- **Urban** 15-acre campus with easy access to New York City
- **Endowment** $20.0 million
- **Coed,** 2,586 undergraduate students, 81% full-time, 57% women, 43% men
- **Moderately difficult** entrance level, 73% of applicants were admitted

Undergraduates 2,098 full-time, 488 part-time. Students come from 28 states and territories, 9 other countries, 13% are from out of state, 19% African American, 7% Asian American or Pacific Islander, 27% Hispanic American, 0.5% Native American, 2% international, 3% transferred in, 27% live on campus. *Retention:* 69% of 2001 full-time freshmen returned.

Freshmen *Admission:* 2,460 applied, 1,791 admitted, 509 enrolled. *Average high school GPA:* 3.00. *Test scores:* SAT verbal scores over 500: 29%; SAT math scores over 500: 29%; SAT verbal scores over 600: 7%; SAT math scores over 600: 9%; SAT math scores over 700: 1%.

Faculty *Total:* 305, 37% full-time, 43% with terminal degrees. *Student/faculty ratio:* 20:1.

Majors Accounting; American studies; art; biochemistry; biological/physical sciences; biology; business administration; business economics; business marketing and marketing management; chemistry; classics; communications; computer/information sciences; computer programming; criminal justice studies; data processing technology; economics; elementary education; English; finance; fine/studio arts; foreign languages/literatures; health services administration; history; humanities; information sciences/systems; international business; liberal arts and sciences/liberal studies; mathematics; nursing science; philosophy; physics; political science; psychology; public policy analysis; religious studies; social sciences; sociology; Spanish; urban studies; visual/performing arts.

Academic Programs *Special study options:* academic remediation for entering students, accelerated degree program, adult/continuing education programs, advanced placement credit, cooperative education, distance learning, double majors, honors programs, independent study, internships, off-campus study, part-time degree program, services for LD students, student-designed majors, study abroad, summer session for credit. *ROTC:* Army (b), Air Force (c). *Unusual degree programs:* 3-2 medical technology, cytotechnology, toxicology with University of Medicine and Dentistry of New Jersey.

Library Theresa and Edward O'Toole Library plus 1 other with 178,587 titles, 1,741 serial subscriptions, 330 audiovisual materials, an OPAC, a Web page.

Computers on Campus 150 computers available on campus for general student use. A campuswide network can be accessed from student residence rooms and from off campus. Internet access, at least one staffed computer lab available.

Student Life *Housing Options:* coed, women-only. *Activities and Organizations:* drama/theater group, student-run newspaper, radio station, choral group, Caribbean Culture Club, Black Action Committee, Asian American Student Union, Argus Eyes Dramatic Society, Voices of Praise Gospel Choir. *Campus security:* 24-hour emergency response devices and patrols, late-night transport/escort service, controlled dormitory access, ID checks at residence halls and library. *Student Services:* health clinic, personal/psychological counseling.

Athletics Member NCAA. All Division I except football (Division I-AA). *Intercollegiate sports:* baseball M(s), basketball M(s)/W(s), bowling M/W, cross-country running M(s)/W(s), golf M(s), soccer M(s)/W(s), softball W(s), swimming M(s)/W(s), tennis M(s)/W(s), track and field M(s)/W(s), volleyball W(s). *Intramural sports:* badminton M/W, basketball M/W, bowling M/W, football M/W, golf M/W, racquetball M/W, soccer M/W, softball M/W, squash M/W, swimming M/W, table tennis M/W, tennis M/W, track and field M/W, volleyball M/W, water polo M/W, weight lifting M/W.

Standardized Tests *Required:* SAT I or ACT (for admission).

Costs (2001–02) *Comprehensive fee:* $23,605 includes full-time tuition ($16,102), mandatory fees ($450), and room and board ($7053). Full-time tuition and fees vary according to course load and location. Part-time tuition: $400 per credit. Part-time tuition and fees vary according to class time and course load. *Room and board:* College room only: $4390. Room and board charges vary according to board plan and housing facility. *Payment plans:* installment, deferred payment. *Waivers:* employees or children of employees.

Financial Aid Of all full-time matriculated undergraduates who enrolled in 2001, 1310 applied for aid, 1125 were judged to have need, 1036 had their need fully met. 214 Federal Work-Study jobs (averaging $1655). 219 State and other part-time jobs (averaging $2689). *Average percent of need met:* 70%. *Average financial aid package:* $8276. *Average need-based loan:* $3900. *Average need-based gift aid:* $4443. *Average non-need based aid:* $7939. *Average indebtedness upon graduation:* $16,500.

Applying *Options:* common application, early admission, deferred entrance. *Application fee:* $30. *Required:* essay or personal statement, high school transcript, minimum 2.0 GPA, 2 letters of recommendation. *Required for some:* interview. *Recommended:* interview. *Application deadlines:* rolling (freshmen), 6/1 (transfers). *Notification:* continuous (freshmen).

Admissions Contact Stephanie Decker, Director of Recruitment, Saint Peter's College, 2627 Kennedy Blvd., Jersey City, NJ 07306. *Phone:* 201-915-9213. *Toll-free phone:* 888-SPC-9933. *Fax:* 201-432-5860. *E-mail:* admissions@spcvxa.spc.edu.

SETON HALL UNIVERSITY
South Orange, New Jersey

- **Independent Roman Catholic** university, founded 1856
- **Calendar** semesters
- **Degrees** bachelor's, master's, doctoral, first professional, and post-master's certificates
- **Suburban** 58-acre campus with easy access to New York City
- **Endowment** $172.6 million
- **Coed,** 5,113 undergraduate students, 88% full-time, 52% women, 48% men
- **Moderately difficult** entrance level, 88% of applicants were admitted

Seton Hall University has been preparing students to assume leadership roles for nearly 150 years. A Catholic university founded with the purpose of "enriching the mind, the heart, and the spirit," Seton Hall offers more than 60 majors and concentrations, as well as honors and leadership programs. With a 14:1 student-faculty ratio and an average class size of 25, Seton Hall offers all the advantages of a big school but, with just 4,800 undergraduate students, the University also provides the personal attention of a small college. Seton Hall's mission of "preparing student leaders for a global society" is evidenced through its high academic standards, values-centered curriculum, and cutting-edge technology.

Undergraduates 4,518 full-time, 595 part-time. Students come from 46 states and territories, 49 other countries, 17% are from out of state, 11% African American, 8% Asian American or Pacific Islander, 9% Hispanic American, 0.1% Native American, 2% international, 6% transferred in, 42% live on campus. *Retention:* 79% of 2001 full-time freshmen returned.

Freshmen *Admission:* 4,887 applied, 4,304 admitted, 1,199 enrolled. *Average high school GPA:* 3.10. *Test scores:* SAT verbal scores over 500: 67%; SAT math scores over 500: 69%; ACT scores over 18: 60%; SAT verbal scores over 600: 19%; SAT math scores over 600: 24%; ACT scores over 24: 40%; SAT verbal scores over 700: 3%; SAT math scores over 700: 3%.

Faculty *Total:* 834, 45% full-time. *Student/faculty ratio:* 14:1.

Majors Accounting; African-American studies; anthropology; art education; art history; Asian studies; biochemistry; biology; business administration; business economics; business marketing and marketing management; chemistry; classics; communications; computer/information sciences; criminal justice studies; early childhood education; economics; elementary education; English; finance; foreign languages/literatures; French; graphic design/commercial art/illustration; history; humanities; international relations; Italian; labor/personnel relations; liberal arts and sciences/liberal studies; management information systems/business data processing; mathematics; music; music (general performance); music history; nursing; philosophy; physics; political science; psychology; religious education; religious studies; secondary education; social work; sociology; Spanish; special education; sport/fitness administration; visual/performing arts.

Academic Programs *Special study options:* academic remediation for entering students, accelerated degree program, advanced placement credit, cooperative education, distance learning, double majors, English as a second language, honors programs, independent study, internships, part-time degree program, services for LD students, study abroad, summer session for credit. *ROTC:* Army (b), Air Force (c). *Unusual degree programs:* 3-2 engineering with New Jersey Institute of Technology, Stevens Institute of Technology.

Library Walsh Library plus 1 other with 385,000 titles, 2,271 serial subscriptions, 3,558 audiovisual materials, an OPAC, a Web page.

Computers on Campus 500 computers available on campus for general student use. A campuswide network can be accessed from student residence rooms and from off campus. Internet access, online (class) registration, at least one staffed computer lab available.

Student Life *Housing Options:* coed. *Activities and Organizations:* drama/theater group, student-run newspaper, radio and television station, choral group, Martin Luther King Jr. Scholars Association, Adelante/Caribe, Black Student Union, National Council of Negro Women, national fraternities, national sororities. *Campus security:* 24-hour emergency response devices and patrols, late-night transport/escort service, controlled dormitory access. *Student Services:* health clinic, personal/psychological counseling, women's center.

Athletics Member NCAA. All Division I. *Intercollegiate sports:* baseball M(s), basketball M(s)/W(s), cross-country running M(s)/W(s), golf M(s), ice hockey M(c), lacrosse M(c), rugby M(c), soccer M(s)/W(s), softball W(s), swimming M(s)/W(s), tennis W(s), track and field M(s)/W(s), volleyball M(c)/W(s). *Intramural sports:* basketball M/W, football M/W, racquetball M/W, soccer M/W, softball M/W, tennis M/W, volleyball M/W.

Standardized Tests *Required:* SAT I or ACT (for admission).

Costs (2001–02) *Comprehensive fee:* $27,460 includes full-time tuition ($17,400), mandatory fees ($2000), and room and board ($8060). Full-time tuition and fees vary according to course load and student level. Part-time tuition: $580 per credit. Part-time tuition and fees vary according to course load and student level. *Required fees:* $185 per term part-time. *Room and board:* College room only: $5720. Room and board charges vary according to board plan and housing facility. *Payment plans:* installment, deferred payment. *Waivers:* senior citizens and employees or children of employees.

Applying *Options:* common application, electronic application, deferred entrance. *Application fee:* $45. *Required:* high school transcript, counselor report. *Required for some:* minimum 3.0 GPA, interview. *Recommended:* essay or personal statement, minimum 3.0 GPA, letters of recommendation, interview. *Application deadlines:* 3/1 (freshmen), 6/1 (transfers). *Notification:* continuous (freshmen).

Admissions Contact Ms. Alyssa McCloud, Acting Director of Admissions, Seton Hall University, Enrollment Services, Bayley Hall, South Orange, NJ 07079-2697. *Phone:* 973-275-2576. *Toll-free phone:* 800-THE HALL. *Fax:* 973-275-2040. *E-mail:* thehall@shu.edu.

STEVENS INSTITUTE OF TECHNOLOGY
Hoboken, New Jersey

- **Independent** university, founded 1870
- **Calendar** semesters
- **Degrees** bachelor's, master's, doctoral, and postbachelor's certificates
- **Urban** 55-acre campus with easy access to New York City
- **Endowment** $136.4 million
- **Coed,** 1,646 undergraduate students
- **Very difficult** entrance level, 49% of applicants were admitted

Stevens ranks in the top 5% of the nation's technological universities. A 9:1 student-faculty ratio and broad-based curricula in business, engineering, the sciences, and humanities fosters critical analysis and creativity, as well as hands-on research with world-renowned faculty. Students also combine their classroom and laboratory experience with cooperative education and summer internship opportunities. Plus, the residential campus is locate in Hoboken, just minutes from New York City and all of the excitement it offers.

Undergraduates Students come from 40 states and territories, 68 other countries, 35% are from out of state, 80% live on campus. *Retention:* 89% of 2001 full-time freshmen returned.

Freshmen *Admission:* 2,622 applied, 1,280 admitted. *Average high school GPA:* 3.80. *Test scores:* SAT verbal scores over 500: 92%; SAT math scores over 500: 100%; SAT verbal scores over 600: 56%; SAT math scores over 600: 93%; SAT verbal scores over 700: 12%; SAT math scores over 700: 36%.

Faculty *Total:* 212, 48% full-time, 100% with terminal degrees. *Student/faculty ratio:* 9:1.

Majors Biochemistry; bioengineering; chemical engineering; chemistry; civil engineering; computer engineering; computer science; electrical engineering; engineering/industrial management; English; environmental engineering; history; history of science and technology; humanities; mathematical statistics; mechanical engineering; philosophy; physics; pre-dentistry; pre-law; pre-medicine.

Academic Programs *Special study options:* accelerated degree program, advanced placement credit, cooperative education, distance learning, double majors, honors programs, independent study, internships, off-campus study, study abroad, summer session for credit. *ROTC:* Army (c), Air Force (c).

Library S. C. Williams Library with 59,489 titles, 162 serial subscriptions, an OPAC, a Web page.

Computers on Campus 1700 computers available on campus for general student use. A campuswide network can be accessed from student residence rooms and from off campus that provide access to online grade and account information. Internet access, online (class) registration, at least one staffed computer lab available.

Student Life *Housing Options:* coed, men-only, women-only. *Activities and Organizations:* drama/theater group, student-run newspaper, radio and television station, choral group, Drama Society, Student Council including Ethnic Student Council, foreign student clubs, Interdormitory Council, student newspaper, national fraternities, national sororities. *Campus security:* 24-hour emergency response devices and patrols, late-night transport/escort service, controlled dormitory access. *Student Services:* health clinic, personal/psychological counseling, women's center.

Athletics Member NCAA. All Division III. *Intercollegiate sports:* baseball M, basketball M/W, cross-country running M/W, fencing M/W, lacrosse M/W, soccer M/W, swimming W, tennis M/W, track and field M/W, volleyball M/W. *Intramural sports:* archery M/W, badminton M/W, baseball M, basketball M(c)/W(c), bowling M/W, equestrian sports M/W, golf M(c)/W(c), lacrosse M, racquetball M/W, skiing (cross-country) M(c)/W(c), soccer M/W, softball M/W, squash M/W, swimming M(c), table tennis M(c)/W(c), tennis M/W, volleyball M/W.

Standardized Tests *Required:* SAT I or ACT (for admission). *Required for some:* SAT I and SAT II or ACT (for admission), SAT II: Subject Tests (for admission), SAT II: Writing Test (for admission). *Recommended:* SAT II: Subject Tests (for admission), SAT II: Writing Test (for admission).

Costs (2001–02) *One-time required fee:* $325. *Comprehensive fee:* $30,880 includes full-time tuition ($22,900), mandatory fees ($250), and room and board ($7730). *Room and board:* Room and board charges vary according to board plan and housing facility. *Payment plan:* installment. *Waivers:* employees or children of employees.

Financial Aid Of all full-time matriculated undergraduates who enrolled in 2001, 1516 applied for aid, 1306 were judged to have need, 222 had their need fully met. In 2001, 183 non-need-based awards were made. *Average percent of need met:* 92%. *Average financial aid package:* $18,973. *Average need-based loan:* $4171. *Average need-based gift aid:* $10,810. *Average non-need based aid:* $9210. *Average indebtedness upon graduation:* $13,020.

Applying *Options:* common application, electronic application, early admission, early decision, deferred entrance. *Application fee:* $45. *Required:* high school transcript, interview. *Recommended:* essay or personal statement, letters of recommendation. *Application deadlines:* 2/15 (freshmen), 7/1 (transfers). *Early decision:* 11/15. *Notification:* continuous until 5/1 (freshmen), 12/15 (early decision).

Admissions Contact Mr. Daniel Gallagher, Dean of Undergraduate Admissions, Stevens Institute of Technology, Castle Point on Hudson, Hoboken, NJ 07030. *Phone:* 201-216-5197. *Toll-free phone:* 800-458-5323. *Fax:* 201-216-8348. *E-mail:* admissions@stevens-tech.edu.

TALMUDICAL ACADEMY OF NEW JERSEY
Adelphia, New Jersey

Admissions Contact Rabbi G. Finkel, Director of Admissions, Talmudical Academy of New Jersey, Route 524, Adelphia, NJ 07710. *Phone:* 201-431-1600.

THOMAS EDISON STATE COLLEGE
Trenton, New Jersey

- **State-supported** comprehensive, founded 1972
- **Calendar** continuous
- **Degrees** certificates, associate, bachelor's, and master's (offers only distance learning degree programs)
- **Coed,** 8,152 undergraduate students, 47% women, 53% men
- **Noncompetitive** entrance level

Undergraduates Students come from 50 states and territories, 80 other countries, 42% are from out of state, 10% African American, 2% Asian American or Pacific Islander, 4% Hispanic American, 0.9% Native American, 3% international.

Faculty *Total:* 613.

Majors Accounting; advertising; aircraft mechanic/powerplant; aircraft pilot (professional); air traffic control; anthropology; architectural engineering technology; art; banking; biology; biomedical engineering-related technology; business administration; business marketing and marketing management; chemistry; child guidance; civil engineering technology; communications; community services; computer/information sciences; computer science; construction technology; criminal justice/law enforcement administration; cytotechnology; dance; dental hygiene; drafting; economics; electrical/electronic engineering technology; English; entrepreneurship; environmental science; finance; fire protection/safety technology; foreign languages/literatures; forestry; gerontology; health services administration; history; horticulture science; hotel and restaurant management; humanities; human resources management; industrial technology; insurance/risk management; international business; journalism; laboratory animal medicine; labor/personnel relations; liberal arts and sciences/liberal studies; logistics/materials management; marine technology; mathematics; mechanical engineering technology; medical radiologic technology; mental health/rehabilitation; music; natural sciences; nuclear medical technology; nuclear technology; nursing science; operations management; organizational behavior; paralegal/legal assistant; perfusion technology; philosophy; photography; physics; political science; psychology; public administration; purchasing/contracts management; real estate; recreation/leisure studies; religious studies; respiratory therapy; retail management; social sciences; sociology; surveying; theater arts/drama.

Academic Programs *Special study options:* accelerated degree program, adult/continuing education programs, advanced placement credit, distance learning, double majors, external degree program, independent study, part-time degree program, services for LD students, student-designed majors, summer session for credit.

Computers on Campus A campuswide network can be accessed from off campus. Internet access, online (class) registration available.

Student Life *Housing:* college housing not available. *Campus security:* guard from 7 a.m. to 11 p.m., local police patrol.

Costs (2001–02) *Tuition:* state resident $2750 per year part-time; nonresident $3950 per year part-time. Part-time tuition and fees vary according to course load and program. *Required fees:* $87 per credit. *Payment plan:* installment. *Waivers:* senior citizens and employees or children of employees.

Applying *Options:* electronic application. *Application fee:* $75. *Required:* age 21 or over and a high school graduate. *Application deadline:* rolling (transfers).

Admissions Contact Mr. Gordon Holly, Director of Admissions Services, Thomas Edison State College, Trenton, NJ 08608-1176. *Phone:* 609-984-1150. *Toll-free phone:* 888-442-8372. *Fax:* 609-984-8447. *E-mail:* info@tesc.edu.

Westminster Choir College of Rider University

Princeton, New Jersey

- **Independent** comprehensive, founded 1926
- **Calendar** semesters
- **Degrees** bachelor's and master's
- **Small-town** 23-acre campus with easy access to New York City and Philadelphia
- **Coed,** 340 undergraduate students, 98% full-time, 60% women, 40% men
- **Moderately difficult** entrance level, 67% of applicants were admitted

Undergraduates 332 full-time, 8 part-time. Students come from 40 states and territories, 64% are from out of state, 4% transferred in, 58% live on campus. *Retention:* 84% of 2001 full-time freshmen returned.

Freshmen *Admission:* 193 applied, 129 admitted, 80 enrolled. *Average high school GPA:* 3.40. *Test scores:* SAT verbal scores over 500: 75%; SAT math scores over 500: 58%; SAT verbal scores over 600: 33%; SAT math scores over 600: 35%; SAT verbal scores over 700: 6%; SAT math scores over 700: 8%.

Faculty *Total:* 85, 41% full-time, 48% with terminal degrees. *Student/faculty ratio:* 7:1.

Majors Liberal arts and sciences/liberal studies; music; music conducting; music (piano and organ performance); music teacher education; music theory and composition; music (voice and choral/opera performance); religious music.

Academic Programs *Special study options:* academic remediation for entering students, adult/continuing education programs, advanced placement credit, double majors, English as a second language, honors programs, independent study, internships, off-campus study, part-time degree program, services for LD students, summer session for credit.

Library Talbott Library-Learning Center with 55,000 titles, 160 serial subscriptions.

Computers on Campus 60 computers available on campus for general student use. At least one staffed computer lab available.

Student Life *Housing:* on-campus residence required through sophomore year. *Options:* coed. *Activities and Organizations:* drama/theater group, student-run newspaper, radio station, choral group, Westminster Choir, Westminster Singers, Black and Hispanic Alliance, Westminster Handbell Choir, Student Activities Committee. *Campus security:* 24-hour emergency response devices and patrols, late-night transport/escort service. *Student Services:* health clinic, personal/psychological counseling.

Athletics *Intramural sports:* basketball M/W, volleyball M/W.

Standardized Tests *Required:* SAT I or ACT (for admission).

Costs (2002–03) *Comprehensive fee:* $27,370 includes full-time tuition ($19,240), mandatory fees ($240), and room and board ($7890). Part-time tuition: $745 per credit. *Room and board:* College room only: $3590. *Payment plan:* installment. *Waivers:* employees or children of employees.

Financial Aid Of all full-time matriculated undergraduates who enrolled in 2001, 277 applied for aid, 213 were judged to have need, 38 had their need fully met. 159 Federal Work-Study jobs (averaging $1765). In 2001, 63 non-need-based awards were made. *Average percent of need met:* 79%. *Average financial aid package:* $15,201. *Average need-based loan:* $4315. *Average need-based gift aid:* $7319. *Average indebtedness upon graduation:* $15,501.

Applying *Options:* deferred entrance. *Application fee:* $40. *Required:* essay or personal statement, high school transcript, 2 letters of recommendation, audition, music examination. *Recommended:* minimum 2.5 GPA, interview. *Application deadline:* rolling (freshmen), rolling (transfers). *Notification:* continuous (freshmen).

Admissions Contact Elizabeth S. Rush, Assistant Director of Admissions, Westminster Choir College of Rider University, 101 Walnut Lane, Princeton, NJ 08540-3899. *Phone:* 609-921-7144 Ext. 221. *Toll-free phone:* 800-96-CHOIR. *Fax:* 609-921-2538. *E-mail:* wccadmission@rider.edu.

William Paterson University of New Jersey

Wayne, New Jersey

- **State-supported** comprehensive, founded 1855, part of New Jersey State College System
- **Calendar** semesters
- **Degrees** bachelor's and master's
- **Suburban** 300-acre campus with easy access to New York City
- **Coed,** 8,862 undergraduate students, 77% full-time, 59% women, 41% men
- **Moderately difficult** entrance level, 67% of applicants were admitted

Committed to student success, William Paterson University seeks ambitious students who are up to its challenge. Small classes and a distinguished faculty; thirty majors; preprofessional programs in dentistry, engineering, medicine, law, physical therapy, and veterinary medicine; and seven distinctive honors programs provide a rewarding educational experience that far exceeds its cost.

Undergraduates 6,811 full-time, 2,051 part-time. Students come from 42 states and territories, 57 other countries, 2% are from out of state, 12% African American, 3% Asian American or Pacific Islander, 14% Hispanic American, 0.2% Native American, 1% international, 11% transferred in, 26% live on campus. *Retention:* 81% of 2001 full-time freshmen returned.

Freshmen *Admission:* 5,031 applied, 3,360 admitted, 1,401 enrolled. *Test scores:* SAT verbal scores over 500: 47%; SAT math scores over 500: 53%; SAT verbal scores over 600: 8%; SAT math scores over 600: 10%; SAT verbal scores over 700: 1%; SAT math scores over 700: 1%.

Faculty *Total:* 844, 42% full-time. *Student/faculty ratio:* 12:1.

Majors Accounting; African-American studies; African studies; anthropology; applied art; applied mathematics; art; art education; art history; behavioral sciences; biology; business administration; business economics; computer science; ecology; education; elementary education; English; environmental science; exercise sciences; fine/studio arts; geography; graphic design/commercial art/illustration; health education; health science; history; humanities; international business; jazz; literature; mass communications; mathematics; music; music business management/merchandising; music teacher education; music (voice and choral/opera performance); nursing; philosophy; physical education; physical sciences; political science; pre-dentistry; pre-law; pre-medicine; psychology; public health; recreation/leisure studies; secondary education; social sciences; sociology; Spanish; special education; theater arts/drama.

Academic Programs *Special study options:* academic remediation for entering students, accelerated degree program, adult/continuing education programs, advanced placement credit, distance learning, double majors, English as a second language, honors programs, independent study, internships, off-campus study, part-time degree program, services for LD students, study abroad, summer session for credit.

Library Sarah Byrd Askew Library with 291,852 titles, 1,950 serial subscriptions, 13,997 audiovisual materials, an OPAC, a Web page.

Computers on Campus 150 computers available on campus for general student use. A campuswide network can be accessed from student residence rooms. At least one staffed computer lab available.

Student Life *Housing Options:* coed. *Activities and Organizations:* drama/theater group, student-run newspaper, radio station, choral group, Greek Senate, Caribbean Student Association, Organization of Latin American Students (OLAS), Sisters of Awareness, Student Activities Committee, national fraternities, national sororities. *Campus security:* 24-hour emergency response devices and patrols, controlled dormitory access. *Student Services:* health clinic, personal/psychological counseling, women's center, legal services.

Athletics Member NCAA. All Division III. *Intercollegiate sports:* baseball M, basketball M/W, bowling M(c), cross-country running M/W, fencing M/W, field hockey W, football M, golf M, ice hockey M(c), skiing (downhill) M(c)/W(c), soccer M, softball W, swimming M/W, track and field M/W, volleyball W. *Intramural sports:* basketball M, equestrian sports M/W, football M, golf M, racquetball M/W, softball M/W, tennis M(c)/W(c), volleyball M/W, wrestling M.

Standardized Tests *Required:* SAT I or ACT (for admission).

Costs (2001–02) *Tuition:* state resident $5700 full-time, $183 per credit part-time; nonresident $8880 full-time, $287 per credit part-time. *Room and board:* $6680; room only: $4310. Room and board charges vary according to board plan and housing facility. *Payment plan:* installment.

Financial Aid Of all full-time matriculated undergraduates who enrolled in 2001, 4394 applied for aid, 3340 were judged to have need, 978 had their need fully met. 190 Federal Work-Study jobs (averaging $1474). 310 State and other part-time jobs (averaging $1403). In 2001, 234 non-need-based awards were made. *Average percent of need met:* 82%. *Average financial aid package:* $7487. *Average need-based loan:* $3305. *Average need-based gift aid:* $5127. *Average non-need based aid:* $3414. *Average indebtedness upon graduation:* $9431.

Applying *Options:* common application, electronic application, early action, deferred entrance. *Application fee:* $35. *Required:* essay or personal statement, high school transcript. *Required for some:* letters of recommendation, interview. *Recommended:* minimum 2.5 GPA. *Application deadlines:* 5/1 (freshmen), 5/1 (transfers).

Admissions Contact Mr. Jonathan McCoy, Director of Admissions, William Paterson University of New Jersey, 300 Pompton Road, Wayne, NJ 07470. *Phone:* 973-720-2906. *Toll-free phone:* 877-WPU-EXCEL. *Fax:* 973-720-2910. *E-mail:* admissions@wpunj.edu.

NEW MEXICO

COLLEGE OF SANTA FE
Santa Fe, New Mexico

- **Independent** comprehensive, founded 1947
- **Calendar** semesters
- **Degrees** associate, bachelor's, and master's
- **Suburban** 100-acre campus with easy access to Albuquerque
- **Endowment** $4.9 million
- **Coed,** 1,294 undergraduate students, 51% full-time, 62% women, 38% men
- **Moderately difficult** entrance level, 76% of applicants were admitted

Undergraduates 655 full-time, 639 part-time. Students come from 44 states and territories, 6 other countries, 68% are from out of state, 3% African American, 0.9% Asian American or Pacific Islander, 21% Hispanic American, 2% Native American, 0.4% international, 6% transferred in, 49% live on campus. *Retention:* 60% of 2001 full-time freshmen returned.

Freshmen *Admission:* 520 applied, 393 admitted, 214 enrolled. *Average high school GPA:* 3.15. *Test scores:* SAT verbal scores over 500: 83%; SAT math scores over 500: 73%; ACT scores over 18: 98%; SAT verbal scores over 600: 42%; SAT math scores over 600: 23%; ACT scores over 24: 51%; SAT verbal scores over 700: 7%; SAT math scores over 700: 2%; ACT scores over 30: 6%.

Faculty *Total:* 255, 24% full-time, 39% with terminal degrees. *Student/faculty ratio:* 8:1.

Majors Accounting; art history; arts management; art therapy; biological/physical sciences; biology; business administration; business education; computer science; creative writing; early childhood education; elementary education; English; English education; environmental science; film studies; film/video production; fine/studio arts; humanities; international business; management information systems/business data processing; mathematics; mathematics/computer science; music; natural resources conservation; painting; photography; political science; pre-dentistry; pre-law; pre-medicine; pre-theology; pre-veterinary studies; printmaking; psychology; religious studies; science education; sculpture; secondary education; social science education; technical/business writing; theater arts/drama; theater design.

Academic Programs *Special study options:* academic remediation for entering students, accelerated degree program, adult/continuing education programs, advanced placement credit, distance learning, double majors, external degree program, independent study, internships, off-campus study, part-time degree program, services for LD students, student-designed majors, study abroad, summer session for credit.

Library Fogelson Library Center with 106,920 titles, 465 serial subscriptions, 9,611 audiovisual materials, a Web page.

Computers on Campus 60 computers available on campus for general student use. A campuswide network can be accessed from student residence rooms and from off campus. At least one staffed computer lab available.

Student Life *Housing:* on-campus residence required for freshman year. *Options:* coed, men-only, women-only. *Activities and Organizations:* drama/theater group, student-run newspaper, Model UN Group, Renaissance club, Moving Image Student Council, social science club, Student Management Association. *Campus security:* 24-hour patrols, late-night transport/escort service. *Student Services:* health clinic, personal/psychological counseling.

Athletics *Intramural sports:* basketball M/W, football M/W, racquetball M/W, soccer M/W, softball M/W, tennis M/W, volleyball M/W.

Standardized Tests *Required:* SAT I or ACT (for admission).

Costs (2002–03) *One-time required fee:* $10. *Comprehensive fee:* $23,768 includes full-time tuition ($17,864), mandatory fees ($420), and room and board ($5484). Full-time tuition and fees vary according to program. Part-time tuition: $594 per credit hour. Part-time tuition and fees vary according to program. *Required fees:* $5 per credit hour. *Room and board:* College room only: $2620. Room and board charges vary according to board plan and housing facility. *Payment plan:* installment. *Waivers:* senior citizens and employees or children of employees.

Financial Aid Of all full-time matriculated undergraduates who enrolled in 2001, 531 applied for aid, 478 were judged to have need, 47 had their need fully met. In 2001, 128 non-need-based awards were made. *Average percent of need met:* 79%. *Average financial aid package:* $15,838. *Average need-based loan:* $4274. *Average need-based gift aid:* $8824. *Average non-need based aid:* $3583. *Average indebtedness upon graduation:* $20,720.

Applying *Options:* common application, electronic application, early admission, early decision, deferred entrance. *Application fee:* $35. *Required:* essay or personal statement, high school transcript, 2 letters of recommendation, interview, portfolio or audition for visual and performing arts programs. *Recommended:* minimum 3.0 GPA. *Application deadline:* rolling (freshmen), rolling (transfers). *Early decision:* 11/15. *Notification:* continuous (freshmen), 12/15 (early decision).

Admissions Contact Mr. Dale H. Reinhart, Director of Admissions and Enrollment Management, College of Santa Fe, Admissions Office, 1600 St. Michael's Drive, Santa Fe, NM 87505-7634. *Phone:* 505-473-6133. *Toll-free phone:* 800-456-2673. *Fax:* 505-473-6129. *E-mail:* admissions@csf.edu.

COLLEGE OF THE SOUTHWEST
Hobbs, New Mexico

- **Independent** comprehensive, founded 1962
- **Calendar** semesters
- **Degrees** bachelor's and master's
- **Small-town** 162-acre campus
- **Endowment** $480,646
- **Coed,** 613 undergraduate students, 65% full-time, 66% women, 34% men
- **Moderately difficult** entrance level, 64% of applicants were admitted

Undergraduates 400 full-time, 213 part-time. Students come from 8 states and territories, 5 other countries, 19% are from out of state, 3% African American, 0.5% Asian American or Pacific Islander, 22% Hispanic American, 0.3% Native American, 2% international, 21% transferred in, 12% live on campus. *Retention:* 55% of 2001 full-time freshmen returned.

Freshmen *Admission:* 69 applied, 44 admitted, 44 enrolled. *Average high school GPA:* 3.38. *Test scores:* SAT verbal scores over 500: 36%; SAT math scores over 500: 36%; ACT scores over 18: 85%; SAT verbal scores over 600: 14%; SAT math scores over 600: 14%; ACT scores over 24: 21%; ACT scores over 30: 3%.

Faculty *Total:* 104, 23% full-time, 15% with terminal degrees. *Student/faculty ratio:* 12:1.

Majors Accounting; athletic training/sports medicine; bilingual/bicultural education; biology; business administration; business education; business marketing and marketing management; criminal justice studies; education; elementary education; English; environmental science; history; mathematics; middle school education; natural sciences; physical education; psychology; science education; secondary education; social sciences; special education.

Academic Programs *Special study options:* accelerated degree program, adult/continuing education programs, advanced placement credit, internships, part-time degree program, summer session for credit.

Library Scarborough Memorial Library plus 1 other with 68,941 titles, 301 serial subscriptions, 1,166 audiovisual materials.

Computers on Campus 20 computers available on campus for general student use. At least one staffed computer lab available.

Student Life *Housing:* on-campus residence required through sophomore year. *Options:* coed. *Activities and Organizations:* drama/theater group, student-run newspaper, choral group, student government, Students in Free Enterprise, Southwest Association of Future Educators, Fellowship of Christian Athletes. *Campus security:* student patrols, night security.

Athletics Member NAIA. *Intercollegiate sports:* baseball M(s), soccer W(s), volleyball W(s). *Intramural sports:* badminton M/W, basketball M/W, football M, golf M, racquetball M/W, soccer M/W, volleyball M/W.

Standardized Tests *Required:* SAT I or ACT (for admission).

Costs (2001–02) *Comprehensive fee:* $8756 includes full-time tuition ($4800), mandatory fees ($190), and room and board ($3766). Part-time tuition: $150 per semester hour. *Required fees:* $95 per term part-time. *Room and board:* College room only: $1575. Room and board charges vary according to housing facility. *Payment plan:* deferred payment. *Waivers:* employees or children of employees.

Financial Aid Of all full-time matriculated undergraduates who enrolled in 2001, 360 applied for aid, 317 were judged to have need, 10 had their need fully met. 36 Federal Work-Study jobs (averaging $1988). 47 State and other part-time jobs (averaging $1921). In 2001, 98 non-need-based awards were made. *Average percent of need met:* 49%. *Average financial aid package:* $5220. *Average need-based loan:* $2936. *Average need-based gift aid:* $1896. *Average indebtedness upon graduation:* $15,927.

Applying *Options:* early admission, deferred entrance. *Application fee:* $25. *Required:* high school transcript, 2 letters of recommendation, medical history. *Application deadline:* rolling (freshmen), rolling (transfers). *Notification:* continuous (freshmen).

Admissions Contact Charlotte Smith, Director of Admissions, College of the Southwest, 6610 Lovington Highway, Hobbs, NM 88240. *Phone:* 505-392-6561 Ext. 1012. *Toll-free phone:* 800-530-4400 Ext. 1004. *Fax:* 505-392-6006. *E-mail:* csmith@csw.edu.

EASTERN NEW MEXICO UNIVERSITY
Portales, New Mexico

- **State-supported** comprehensive, founded 1934, part of Eastern New Mexico University System
- **Calendar** semesters
- **Degrees** associate, bachelor's, and master's
- **Rural** 240-acre campus
- **Endowment** $6.1 million
- **Coed,** 2,967 undergraduate students, 84% full-time, 59% women, 41% men
- **Minimally difficult** entrance level, 93% of applicants were admitted

Undergraduates 2,507 full-time, 460 part-time. Students come from 35 states and territories, 9 other countries, 19% are from out of state, 5% African American, 1% Asian American or Pacific Islander, 30% Hispanic American, 3% Native American, 0.5% international, 10% transferred in, 44% live on campus. *Retention:* 62% of 2001 full-time freshmen returned.

Freshmen *Admission:* 1,709 applied, 1,585 admitted, 557 enrolled. *Average high school GPA:* 3.18. *Test scores:* ACT scores over 18: 66%; ACT scores over 24: 13%.

Faculty *Total:* 192, 67% full-time, 61% with terminal degrees. *Student/faculty ratio:* 19:1.

Majors Accounting; agricultural business; agricultural education; anthropology; art; biology; business administration; business education; business marketing and marketing management; chemistry; child care/guidance; communications; computer/information sciences; criminal justice studies; early childhood education; elementary education; engineering-related technology; English; finance; general studies; geology; history; home economics; human resources management; liberal arts and sciences/liberal studies; management information systems/business data processing; marketing/distribution education; mathematical statistics; medical technology; multi/interdisciplinary studies related; music; music teacher education; nursing; physical education; physics; political science; psychology; religious studies; social sciences; sociology; Spanish; special education; speech-language pathology/audiology; theater arts/drama; wildlife management.

Academic Programs *Special study options:* academic remediation for entering students, accelerated degree program, adult/continuing education programs, advanced placement credit, cooperative education, distance learning, double majors, English as a second language, external degree program, honors programs, internships, part-time degree program, services for LD students, student-designed majors, study abroad, summer session for credit.

Library Golden Library with 506,751 titles, 8,795 serial subscriptions, 24,005 audiovisual materials, an OPAC, a Web page.

Computers on Campus 266 computers available on campus for general student use. A campuswide network can be accessed from student residence rooms and from off campus. Internet access, online (class) registration, at least one staffed computer lab available.

Student Life *Housing:* on-campus residence required for freshman year. *Options:* coed, women-only, disabled students. *Activities and Organizations:* drama/theater group, student-run newspaper, radio and television station, choral group, marching band, Student Government Association, Student Activities Board, Residence Hall Association, IFC, Panhellenic Council, national fraternities, national sororities. *Campus security:* 24-hour emergency response devices and patrols, late-night transport/escort service, controlled dormitory access. *Student Services:* health clinic, personal/psychological counseling.

Athletics Member NCAA. All Division II. *Intercollegiate sports:* baseball M(s), basketball M(s)/W(s), cross-country running M/W, football M(s), softball W(s), tennis W(s), volleyball W(s). *Intramural sports:* badminton M/W, basketball M/W, cross-country running M/W, football M/W, racquetball M/W, rugby M, soccer M/W, softball M/W, volleyball M/W, wrestling M(c).

Standardized Tests *Required:* SAT I or ACT (for admission).

Costs (2001–02) *Tuition:* state resident $1500 full-time, $63 per credit hour part-time; nonresident $7056 full-time, $294 per credit hour part-time. *Required fees:* $588 full-time. *Room and board:* $4160; room only: $1850. Room and board charges vary according to board plan and housing facility. *Payment plan:* installment. *Waivers:* employees or children of employees.

Financial Aid Of all full-time matriculated undergraduates who enrolled in 2001, 2748 applied for aid, 2550 were judged to have need, 372 had their need fully met. 667 Federal Work-Study jobs, 176 State and other part-time jobs. In 2001, 110 non-need-based awards were made. *Average percent of need met:* 17%. *Average financial aid package:* $5866. *Average need-based loan:* $3803. *Average need-based gift aid:* $3091. *Average non-need based aid:* $3515.

Applying *Options:* common application, electronic application, early admission, deferred entrance. *Required:* high school transcript, minimum 2.0 GPA. *Application deadline:* rolling (freshmen), rolling (transfers).

Admissions Contact Dr. Karyl C. Lyne, Assistant Vice President for Student Affairs, Eastern New Mexico University, Station #7 ENMU, Portales, NM 88130. *Phone:* 505-562-2178. *Toll-free phone:* 800-367-3668. *Fax:* 505-562-2118. *E-mail:* karyl.lyne@enmu.edu.

ITT TECHNICAL INSTITUTE
Albuquerque, New Mexico

- **Proprietary** primarily 2-year, founded 1989, part of ITT Educational Services, Inc
- **Calendar** quarters
- **Degrees** associate and bachelor's
- 392 undergraduate students
- **Minimally difficult** entrance level

Majors Computer/information sciences related; computer programming; drafting; electrical/electronic engineering technologies related; information technology.

Student Life *Housing:* college housing not available.

Costs (2001–02) *Tuition:* Full-time tuition and fees vary according to program. Part-time tuition and fees vary according to program. $260—$330 per credit hour.

Applying *Options:* deferred entrance. *Application fee:* $100. *Required:* high school transcript, interview. *Recommended:* letters of recommendation. *Application deadline:* rolling (freshmen), rolling (transfers). *Notification:* continuous (freshmen).

Admissions Contact Mr. John Crooks, Director of Recruitment, ITT Technical Institute, 5100 Masthead Street NE, Albuquerque, NM 87109-4366. *Phone:* 505-828-1114. *Toll-free phone:* 800-636-1114.

METROPOLITAN COLLEGE OF COURT REPORTING
Albuquerque, New Mexico

Admissions Contact 1717 Louisiana Boulevard NE, Suite 207, Albuquerque, NM 87110-7027.

NATIONAL AMERICAN UNIVERSITY
Albuquerque, New Mexico

- **Proprietary** 4-year, founded 1941, part of National College
- **Calendar** quarters
- **Degrees** associate and bachelor's
- **Suburban** campus
- **Coed,** 625 undergraduate students, 100% full-time, 49% women, 51% men
- **Noncompetitive** entrance level

Undergraduates Students come from 1 other state, 4 other countries, 0% are from out of state. *Retention:* 60% of 2001 full-time freshmen returned.

Faculty *Total:* 56, 9% with terminal degrees. *Student/faculty ratio:* 12:1.

Majors Accounting; applied art; business administration; hospitality management; hotel and restaurant management; information sciences/systems; management information systems/business data processing.

Academic Programs *Special study options:* accelerated degree program, adult/continuing education programs, cooperative education, distance learning, double majors, external degree program, independent study, internships, off-campus study, part-time degree program, summer session for credit.

Library a Web page.

Computers on Campus 70 computers available on campus for general student use. A campuswide network can be accessed from off campus. Internet access, online (class) registration, at least one staffed computer lab available.

Student Life *Housing:* college housing not available. *Campus security:* 24-hour patrols, late-night transport/escort service.

Costs (2001–02) *One-time required fee:* $100. *Tuition:* $9120 full-time, $190 per quarter hour part-time. Full-time tuition and fees vary according to location. Part-time tuition and fees vary according to location. *Required fees:* $315 full-time. *Payment plans:* installment, deferred payment.

Applying *Application fee:* $25. *Required:* high school transcript. *Application deadline:* rolling (freshmen), rolling (transfers).

Admissions Contact Ms. Karina Elliott-Long, Executive Admissions Representative, National American University, 4775 Indian School, NE, Albuquerque, NM 87110. *Phone:* 505-265-7517. *Toll-free phone:* 800-843-8892. *Fax:* 505-265-7542.

NEW MEXICO HIGHLANDS UNIVERSITY

Las Vegas, New Mexico

- **State-supported** comprehensive, founded 1893
- **Calendar** semesters
- **Degrees** associate, bachelor's, and master's
- **Small-town** 120-acre campus
- **Endowment** $3.9 million
- **Coed,** 1,881 undergraduate students, 68% full-time, 61% women, 39% men
- **Minimally difficult** entrance level, 85% of applicants were admitted

Undergraduates 1,274 full-time, 607 part-time. Students come from 40 states and territories, 7% are from out of state, 2% African American, 2% Asian American or Pacific Islander, 63% Hispanic American, 8% Native American, 0.9% international, 11% transferred in. *Retention:* 56% of 2001 full-time freshmen returned.

Freshmen *Admission:* 909 applied, 769 admitted, 258 enrolled. *Average high school GPA:* 2.95. *Test scores:* SAT verbal scores over 500: 23%; SAT math scores over 500: 38%; ACT scores over 18: 51%; SAT math scores over 600: 7%; ACT scores over 24: 8%.

Faculty *Total:* 136, 100% full-time, 77% with terminal degrees.

Majors Accounting; anthropology; art; art education; bilingual/bicultural education; biology; business administration; business marketing and marketing management; chemistry; computer programming; computer science; criminal justice studies; criminology; early childhood education; education; elementary education; engineering; English; environmental science; graphic design/commercial art/illustration; health education; health services administration; history; industrial arts; information sciences/systems; journalism; management information systems/business data processing; mass communications; mathematics; music; music teacher education; natural resources management; physical education; political science; pre-law; pre-medicine; psychology; science education; secondary education; social work; sociology; Spanish; special education; teacher assistant/aide; travel/tourism management.

Academic Programs *Special study options:* academic remediation for entering students, accelerated degree program, advanced placement credit, cooperative education, distance learning, double majors, honors programs, independent study, internships, off-campus study, part-time degree program, services for LD students, summer session for credit.

Library Donnelly Library with 429,978 titles, 47,100 serial subscriptions, 807 audiovisual materials, an OPAC, a Web page.

Computers on Campus 500 computers available on campus for general student use. A campuswide network can be accessed from student residence rooms ıd from off campus. Internet access, online (class) registration, at least one taffed computer lab available.

Student Life *Housing Options:* coed, women-only. *Activities and Organizations:* drama/theater group, student-run newspaper, radio station, choral group, marching band, BESO Club, Activities Board, Campus Crusade, AISES, Cowboy Cheerleaders. *Campus security:* 24-hour emergency response devices and patrols, late-night transport/escort service, controlled dormitory access. *Student Services:* health clinic, personal/psychological counseling.

Athletics Member NCAA. All Division II. *Intercollegiate sports:* baseball M(s), basketball M(s)/W(s), cross-country running M(s)/W(s), football M(s), soccer W(s), softball W(s), volleyball W(s). *Intramural sports:* badminton M/W, basketball M/W, bowling M/W, football M, golf M/W, racquetball M/W, rugby M, skiing (cross-country) M/W, skiing (downhill) M/W, softball W, swimming M/W, table tennis M/W, tennis M/W, volleyball M/W, weight lifting M/W.

Standardized Tests *Required:* ACT (for placement).

Costs (2001–02) *One-time required fee:* $5. *Tuition:* state resident $2094 full-time, $87 per hour part-time; nonresident $8814 full-time, $367 per hour part-time. Full-time tuition and fees vary according to degree level. Part-time tuition and fees vary according to course load. *Room and board:* $3998; room only: $1958. Room and board charges vary according to board plan and housing facility. *Payment plan:* deferred payment. *Waivers:* senior citizens and employees or children of employees.

Financial Aid Of all full-time matriculated undergraduates who enrolled in 2001, 887 applied for aid, 861 were judged to have need, 136 had their need fully met. In 2001, 150 non-need-based awards were made. *Average percent of need met:* 61%. *Average financial aid package:* $6220. *Average need-based loan:* $1910. *Average need-based gift aid:* $3140. *Average non-need based aid:* $2500.

Applying *Options:* common application, electronic application, early admission, deferred entrance. *Application fee:* $15. *Required:* high school transcript, minimum 2.0 GPA. *Required for some:* 2 letters of recommendation, interview. *Application deadline:* rolling (freshmen), rolling (transfers). *Notification:* continuous (freshmen).

Admissions Contact Dr. Dianne Brimmer, Vice President/Dean of Students, New Mexico Highlands University, Box 9000, Las Vegas, NM 87701. *Phone:* 505-454-3020. *Toll-free phone:* 800-338-6648. *Fax:* 505-454-3311. *E-mail:* admission@venus.nmnu.edu.

NEW MEXICO INSTITUTE OF MINING AND TECHNOLOGY

Socorro, New Mexico

- **State-supported** university, founded 1889
- **Calendar** semesters
- **Degrees** associate, bachelor's, master's, and doctoral
- **Small-town** 320-acre campus with easy access to Albuquerque
- **Endowment** $20.4 million
- **Coed,** 1,256 undergraduate students, 75% full-time, 38% women, 62% men
- **Moderately difficult** entrance level, 84% of applicants were admitted

Undergraduates 948 full-time, 308 part-time. Students come from 52 states and territories, 14 other countries, 17% are from out of state, 0.7% African American, 3% Asian American or Pacific Islander, 20% Hispanic American, 4% Native American, 3% international, 3% transferred in, 49% live on campus. *Retention:* 74% of 2001 full-time freshmen returned.

Freshmen *Admission:* 343 applied, 289 admitted, 218 enrolled. *Average high school GPA:* 3.50. *Test scores:* SAT verbal scores over 500: 88%; SAT math scores over 500: 86%; ACT scores over 18: 100%; SAT verbal scores over 600: 52%; SAT math scores over 600: 60%; ACT scores over 24: 72%; SAT verbal scores over 700: 12%; SAT math scores over 700: 17%; ACT scores over 30: 18%.

Faculty *Total:* 127, 87% full-time, 87% with terminal degrees. *Student/faculty ratio:* 12:1.

Majors Applied mathematics; astrophysics; atmospheric sciences; behavioral sciences; biological/physical sciences; biology; business administration; chemical engineering; chemistry; computer programming; computer science; electrical engineering; engineering; engineering mechanics; environmental biology; environmental engineering; environmental science; experimental psychology; geochemistry; geology; geophysics/seismology; information technology; interdisciplinary studies; liberal arts and sciences/liberal studies; materials engineering; mathematics; mechanical engineering; medical technology; metallurgical engineering; mining/mineral engineering; petroleum engineering; physics; predentistry; pre-medicine; pre-veterinary studies; psychology; science education; technical/business writing.

Academic Programs *Special study options:* accelerated degree program, adult/continuing education programs, advanced placement credit, cooperative education, distance learning, double majors, independent study, internships, part-time degree program, services for LD students, student-designed majors, study abroad, summer session for credit.

Library New Mexico Tech Library plus 1 other with 89,725 titles, 766 serial subscriptions, 2,065 audiovisual materials, a Web page.

Computers on Campus 225 computers available on campus for general student use. A campuswide network can be accessed from student residence rooms and from off campus. Internet access, at least one staffed computer lab available.

Student Life *Housing Options:* coed, men-only, women-only. *Activities and Organizations:* drama/theater group, student-run newspaper, radio station, choral group, Search and Rescue, Society for Creative Anachronism, Amateur Astronomers, Ski Club. *Campus security:* 24-hour emergency response devices and patrols, late-night transport/escort service. *Student Services:* health clinic, personal/psychological counseling.

Athletics *Intercollegiate sports:* golf M(c)/W(c), rugby M(c)/W(c), soccer M(c)/W(c). *Intramural sports:* basketball M/W, cross-country running M/W, fencing M/W, racquetball M/W, riflery M/W, skiing (downhill) M/W, softball M/W, squash M/W, table tennis M/W, tennis M/W, volleyball M/W, weight lifting M/W.

Standardized Tests *Required:* SAT I or ACT (for admission).

Costs (2001–02) *One-time required fee:* $16. *Tuition:* state resident $1884 full-time, $78 per credit hour part-time; nonresident $7581 full-time, $316 per credit hour part-time. Part-time tuition and fees vary according to course load. *Required fees:* $838 full-time, $26 per credit hour, $80 per term part-time. *Room and board:* $4430. Room and board charges vary according to board plan and housing facility. *Payment plan:* deferred payment. *Waivers:* senior citizens and employees or children of employees.

Financial Aid Of all full-time matriculated undergraduates who enrolled in 2001, 560 applied for aid, 558 were judged to have need, 114 had their need fully met. 208 Federal Work-Study jobs (averaging $1308). 685 State and other part-time jobs (averaging $1658). In 2001, 111 non-need-based awards were made. *Average percent of need met:* 90%. *Average financial aid package:* $5517.

Average need-based loan: $1122. *Average need-based gift aid:* $3587. *Average non-need based aid:* $3237. *Average indebtedness upon graduation:* $14,500.
Applying *Options:* electronic application, deferred entrance. *Application fee:* $15. *Required:* high school transcript, minimum 2.5 GPA. *Required for some:* 2 letters of recommendation. *Recommended:* interview. *Application deadlines:* 8/1 (freshmen), 8/1 (transfers). *Notification:* continuous (freshmen).
Admissions Contact Ms. Melissa Jaramillo-Fleming, Director of Admissions, New Mexico Institute of Mining and Technology, 801 Leroy Place, Socorro, NM 87801. *Phone:* 505-835-5424. *Toll-free phone:* 800-428-TECH. *Fax:* 505-835-5989. *E-mail:* admission@admin.nmt.edu.

NEW MEXICO STATE UNIVERSITY
Las Cruces, New Mexico

- **State-supported** university, founded 1888, part of New Mexico State University System
- **Calendar** semesters
- **Degrees** associate, bachelor's, master's, doctoral, and post-master's certificates
- **Suburban** 900-acre campus with easy access to El Paso
- **Endowment** $97.4 million
- **Coed,** 12,584 undergraduate students, 84% full-time, 54% women, 46% men
- **Moderately difficult** entrance level, 62% of applicants were admitted

Undergraduates 10,589 full-time, 1,995 part-time. Students come from 51 states and territories, 51 other countries, 20% are from out of state, 3% African American, 2% Asian American or Pacific Islander, 43% Hispanic American, 3% Native American, 1% international, 6% transferred in, 25% live on campus. *Retention:* 73% of 2001 full-time freshmen returned.
Freshmen *Admission:* 7,151 applied, 4,434 admitted, 2,103 enrolled. *Average high school GPA:* 3.30. *Test scores:* ACT scores over 18: 79%; ACT scores over 24: 24%; ACT scores over 30: 2%.
Faculty *Total:* 934, 70% full-time, 67% with terminal degrees. *Student/faculty ratio:* 19:1.
Majors Accounting; agricultural business; agricultural economics; agricultural education; agricultural sciences; agronomy/crop science; animal sciences; anthropology; art; athletic training/sports medicine; biochemistry; biology; business; business administration; business economics; business marketing and marketing management; chemical engineering; chemistry; city/community/regional planning; civil engineering; clothing/textiles; computer science; criminal justice/law enforcement administration; dance; early childhood education; economics; electrical engineering; elementary education; engineering-related technology; engineering technology; English; environmental health; environmental science; family/consumer studies; family resource management studies; fashion merchandising; finance; fine/studio arts; foreign languages/literatures; geography; geological engineering; geology; history; home economics education; horticulture science; hotel and restaurant management; industrial/manufacturing engineering; information sciences/systems; interdisciplinary studies; international business; journalism; liberal arts and sciences/liberal studies; mass communications; mathematics; mechanical engineering; microbiology/bacteriology; music; music teacher education; nursing; nutrition science; philosophy; physical education; physics; political science; psychology; public health; range management; secondary education; social work; sociology; soil sciences; special education; speech-language pathology/audiology; speech/rhetorical studies; surveying; teacher assistant/aide; theater arts/drama; tourism promotion operations; travel/tourism management; wildlife biology; wildlife management.
Academic Programs *Special study options:* academic remediation for entering students, accelerated degree program, adult/continuing education programs, advanced placement credit, cooperative education, distance learning, double majors, honors programs, independent study, internships, off-campus study, part-time degree program, services for LD students, student-designed majors, study abroad, summer session for credit. *ROTC:* Army (b), Air Force (b).
Library New Library plus 1 other with 11,784 serial subscriptions, 320 audiovisual materials, an OPAC, a Web page.
Computers on Campus 500 computers available on campus for general student use. A campuswide network can be accessed from student residence rooms and from off campus. Internet access, online (class) registration, at least one staffed computer lab available.
Student Life *Housing Options:* coed, men-only, women-only, disabled students. *Activities and Organizations:* drama/theater group, student-run newspaper, radio and television station, choral group, marching band, national fraternities, national sororities. *Campus security:* 24-hour emergency response devices and patrols, late-night transport/escort service, controlled dormitory access. *Student Services:* health clinic, personal/psychological counseling, women's center, legal services.
Athletics Member NCAA. All Division I except football (Division I-A). *Intercollegiate sports:* baseball M(s), basketball M(s)/W(s), cross-country running M(s)/W(s), equestrian sports M/W, golf M(s)/W(s), softball W(s), swimming W(s), tennis M(s)/W(s), track and field W(s), volleyball W(s). *Intramural sports:* archery M/W, badminton M/W, baseball M, basketball M/W, bowling M(c)/W(c), fencing M(c)/W(c), field hockey M(c)/W(c), football M/W, golf M/W, racquetball M/W, rugby M(c)/W(c), soccer M/W, softball M/W, tennis M/W, volleyball M/W, weight lifting M/W, wrestling M.
Standardized Tests *Required:* SAT I or ACT (for admission).
Costs (2001–02) *Tuition:* state resident $3006 full-time, $125 per credit part-time; nonresident $10,014 full-time, $417 per credit part-time. *Required fees:* $18 per term part-time. *Room and board:* $4296; room only: $2216. Room and board charges vary according to board plan and gender. *Payment plans:* installment, deferred payment. *Waivers:* senior citizens and employees or children of employees.
Financial Aid Of all full-time matriculated undergraduates who enrolled in 2001, 7268 applied for aid, 6446 were judged to have need, 448 had their need fully met. 606 Federal Work-Study jobs (averaging $1854). 560 State and other part-time jobs (averaging $2083). *Average percent of need met:* 69%. *Average financial aid package:* $6994. *Average need-based loan:* $2669. *Average need-based gift aid:* $5044.
Applying *Options:* electronic application, early admission, deferred entrance. *Application fee:* $15. *Required:* high school transcript, minimum 2.0 GPA. *Application deadlines:* 8/14 (freshmen), 8/14 (transfers). *Notification:* continuous (freshmen).
Admissions Contact Ms. Angela Mora-Riley, Director of Admissions, New Mexico State University, Box 30001, MSC, Las Cruces, NM 88003-8001. *Phone:* 505-646-3121. *Toll-free phone:* 800-662-6678. *Fax:* 505-646-6330. *E-mail:* admssions@nmsu.edu.

ST. JOHN'S COLLEGE
Santa Fe, New Mexico

- **Independent** comprehensive, founded 1964
- **Calendar** semesters
- **Degrees** bachelor's and master's
- **Small-town** 250-acre campus
- **Endowment** $21.7 million
- **Coed,** 445 undergraduate students
- **Very difficult** entrance level, 86% of applicants were admitted

Undergraduates Students come from 43 states and territories, 6 other countries, 92% are from out of state, 0.2% African American, 3% Asian American or Pacific Islander, 5% Hispanic American, 1% Native American, 0.9% international, 71% live on campus. *Retention:* 73% of 2001 full-time freshmen returned.
Freshmen *Admission:* 360 applied, 308 admitted. *Test scores:* SAT verbal scores over 500: 97%; SAT math scores over 500: 95%; ACT scores over 18: 100%; SAT verbal scores over 600: 82%; SAT math scores over 600: 59%; ACT scores over 24: 94%; SAT verbal scores over 700: 46%; SAT math scores over 700: 18%; ACT scores over 30: 38%.
Faculty *Total:* 68, 93% full-time, 84% with terminal degrees. *Student/faculty ratio:* 8:1.
Majors Classics; history of philosophy; liberal arts and sciences/liberal studies; literature; western civilization.
Academic Programs *Special study options:* off-campus study, summer session for credit.
Library Meem Library with 40,103 titles, 135 serial subscriptions, an OPAC, a Web page.
Computers on Campus 20 computers available on campus for general student use. At least one staffed computer lab available.
Student Life *Housing:* on-campus residence required through junior year. *Options:* coed, men-only, disabled students. *Activities and Organizations:* drama/theater group, student-run newspaper, choral group, student government, film society, Search and Rescue Team, student newspaper, theatre group. *Campus security:* 24-hour emergency response devices and patrols, student patrols, late-night transport/escort service. *Student Services:* health clinic, personal/psychological counseling.
Athletics *Intercollegiate sports:* fencing M/W. *Intramural sports:* badminton M/W, basketball M/W, cross-country running M/W, fencing M/W, football M/W, golf M/W, racquetball M/W, skiing (cross-country) M/W, skiing (downhill) M/W, soccer M/W, softball M/W, squash M/W, swimming M/W, table tennis M/W, tennis M/W, track and field M/W, volleyball M/W, water polo M/W, weight lifting M/W.
Standardized Tests *Required for some:* SAT I or ACT (for admission).

St. John's College (continued)

Costs (2001–02) *Comprehensive fee:* $32,760 includes full-time tuition ($25,790), mandatory fees ($200), and room and board ($6770). *Room and board:* Room and board charges vary according to board plan. *Payment plan:* installment. *Waivers:* employees or children of employees.

Financial Aid Of all full-time matriculated undergraduates who enrolled in 2001, 220 applied for aid, 196 were judged to have need, 188 had their need fully met. *Average percent of need met:* 99%. *Average financial aid package:* $21,734. *Average need-based loan:* $4565. *Average need-based gift aid:* $13,264. *Average indebtedness upon graduation:* $17,125.

Applying *Options:* common application, early admission, deferred entrance. *Required:* essay or personal statement, high school transcript, 2 letters of recommendation. *Required for some:* interview. *Recommended:* 3 letters of recommendation, interview. *Application deadline:* rolling (freshmen), rolling (transfers). *Notification:* continuous (freshmen).

Admissions Contact Mr. Larry Clendenin, Director of Admissions, St. John's College, 1160 Camino Cruz Blanca, Santa Fe, NM 87501. *Phone:* 505-984-6060. *Toll-free phone:* 800-331-5232. *Fax:* 505-984-6162. *E-mail:* admissions@mail.sjcsf.edu.

UNIVERSITY OF NEW MEXICO
Albuquerque, New Mexico

- **State-supported** university, founded 1889
- **Calendar** semesters
- **Degrees** associate, bachelor's, master's, doctoral, first professional, and post-master's certificates
- **Urban** 625-acre campus
- **Endowment** $313.9 million
- **Coed,** 16,441 undergraduate students, 77% full-time, 57% women, 43% men
- **Moderately difficult** entrance level, 75% of applicants were admitted

Undergraduates 12,690 full-time, 3,751 part-time. Students come from 51 states and territories, 90 other countries, 19% are from out of state, 3% African American, 3% Asian American or Pacific Islander, 33% Hispanic American, 6% Native American, 0.9% international, 5% transferred in, 11% live on campus. *Retention:* 73% of 2001 full-time freshmen returned.

Freshmen *Admission:* 5,750 applied, 4,306 admitted, 2,406 enrolled. *Average high school GPA:* 3.28. *Test scores:* SAT verbal scores over 500: 66%; SAT math scores over 500: 62%; ACT scores over 18: 86%; SAT verbal scores over 600: 28%; SAT math scores over 600: 23%; ACT scores over 24: 32%; SAT verbal scores over 700: 6%; SAT math scores over 700: 4%; ACT scores over 30: 3%.

Faculty *Total:* 875, 97% full-time, 88% with terminal degrees. *Student/faculty ratio:* 16:1.

Majors Accounting; African-American studies; American studies; anthropology; architectural environmental design; architecture; art; art education; art history; Asian studies; astrophysics; biochemistry; biology; business administration; business education; chemical engineering; chemistry; civil engineering; classics; community services; comparative literature; computer engineering; computer/information sciences; computer science; construction technology; corrections; creative writing; dance; dental hygiene; early childhood education; earth sciences; economics; education; electrical engineering; elementary education; engineering; engineering science; English; European studies; film studies; foreign languages/literatures; French; general studies; geography; geology; German; health education; history; home economics; home economics education; humanities; industrial arts education; industrial/manufacturing engineering; information sciences/systems; journalism; Latin American studies; liberal arts and sciences/liberal studies; linguistics; mass communications; mathematics; mechanical engineering; medical radiologic technology; music (general performance); music teacher education; nuclear engineering; nursing; nutrition studies; occupational therapy; pharmacy; philosophy; physical education; physical therapy; physician assistant; physics; political science; Portuguese; psychology; recreation/leisure studies; religious studies; robotics; Russian; Russian/Slavic studies; secondary education; sign language interpretation; sociology; Spanish; special education; speech-language pathology/audiology; speech/rhetorical studies; teacher assistant/aide; theater arts/drama; women's studies.

Academic Programs *Special study options:* academic remediation for entering students, accelerated degree program, adult/continuing education programs, advanced placement credit, cooperative education, distance learning, double majors, English as a second language, honors programs, independent study, internships, off-campus study, part-time degree program, services for LD students, student-designed majors, study abroad, summer session for credit. *ROTC:* Army (b), Air Force (b). *Unusual degree programs:* 3-2 Latin American studies, business.

Library Zimmerman Library plus 7 others with 2.3 million titles, 309,043 serial subscriptions, 3.8 million audiovisual materials, an OPAC, a Web page.

Computers on Campus 382 computers available on campus for general student use. A campuswide network can be accessed from student residence rooms and from off campus. Internet access, online (class) registration, at least one staffed computer lab available.

Student Life *Housing Options:* coed, women-only, disabled students. *Activities and Organizations:* drama/theater group, student-run newspaper, radio and television station, choral group, marching band, Golden Key National Honor Society, Associated Students of UNM, Graduate and Professional Students Association, national fraternities, national sororities. *Campus security:* 24-hour emergency response devices and patrols, student patrols, late-night transport/escort service, controlled dormitory access. *Student Services:* health clinic, personal/psychological counseling, women's center.

Athletics Member NCAA. All Division I except football (Division I-A). *Intercollegiate sports:* baseball M, basketball M(s)/W(s), cross-country running M(s)/W(s), golf M(s)/W(s), skiing (cross-country) M(s)/W(s), skiing (downhill) M(s)/W(s), soccer M(s)/W(s), softball W(s), swimming W(s), tennis M(s)/W(s), track and field M(s)/W(s), volleyball W(s). *Intramural sports:* archery M/W, badminton M/W, basketball M/W, bowling M/W, cross-country running M/W, fencing M/W, football M/W, golf M/W, ice hockey M(c), racquetball M/W, rugby M(c), skiing (downhill) M/W, soccer M/W, softball M/W, swimming W, table tennis M/W, tennis M/W, volleyball M/W, water polo M/W, weight lifting M/W.

Standardized Tests *Required:* SAT I or ACT (for admission). *Required for some:* SAT II: Subject Tests (for admission), SAT II: Writing Test (for admission).

Costs (2001–02) *Tuition:* state resident $3026 full-time, $126 per credit hour part-time; nonresident $11,424 full-time, $476 per credit hour part-time. Part-time tuition and fees vary according to course load. *Required fees:* $300 full-time, $150 per term part-time. *Room and board:* $5217; room only: $3604. Room and board charges vary according to board plan and housing facility. *Payment plan:* installment. *Waivers:* senior citizens and employees or children of employees.

Financial Aid Of all full-time matriculated undergraduates who enrolled in 2001, 1521 Federal Work-Study jobs, 865 State and other part-time jobs.

Applying *Options:* electronic application, early admission, deferred entrance. *Application fee:* $20. *Required:* high school transcript, minimum 2.25 GPA. *Required for some:* essay or personal statement, letters of recommendation. *Application deadline:* 6/15 (freshmen). *Notification:* continuous (freshmen).

Admissions Contact Ms. Robin Ryan, Associate Director of Admissions, University of New Mexico, Office of Admissions, Student Service Center Room 140, Albuquerque, NM 87131-2046. *Phone:* 505-277-2446. *Toll-free phone:* 800-CALLUNM. *Fax:* 505-277-6686. *E-mail:* apply@unm.edu.

UNIVERSITY OF NEW MEXICO-GALLUP
Gallup, New Mexico

- **State-supported** primarily 2-year, founded 1968, part of New Mexico Commission on Higher Education
- **Calendar** semesters
- **Degrees** certificates, diplomas, associate, and bachelor's
- **Small-town** 80-acre campus
- **Coed**
- **Noncompetitive** entrance level

Student Life *Campus security:* late-night transport/escort service.

Standardized Tests *Required for some:* SAT I (for admission), ACT (for admission).

Applying *Options:* early admission. *Application fee:* $15. *Required for some:* high school transcript.

Admissions Contact Ms. Pearl A. Morris, Admissions Representative, University of New Mexico-Gallup, 200 College Road, Gallup, NM 87301-5603. *Phone:* 505-863-7576. *Fax:* 505-863-7610. *E-mail:* pmorris@gallup.unm.edu.

UNIVERSITY OF PHOENIX-NEW MEXICO CAMPUS
Albuquerque, New Mexico

- **Proprietary** comprehensive
- **Calendar** continuous
- **Degrees** certificates, associate, bachelor's, master's, doctoral, post-master's, and postbachelor's certificates (courses conducted at 54 campuses and learning centers in 13 states)
- **Coed,** 2,822 undergraduate students, 100% full-time, 56% women, 44% men
- **Noncompetitive** entrance level

Undergraduates Students come from 27 states and territories, 55% are from out of state.

Freshmen *Admission:* 33 admitted.
Faculty *Total:* 451, 2% full-time, 16% with terminal degrees. *Student/faculty ratio:* 15:1.
Majors Accounting; business administration; criminal justice/law enforcement administration; information technology; management information systems/business data processing; management science; nursing; nursing science; public administration and services related.
Academic Programs *Special study options:* accelerated degree program, adult/continuing education programs, advanced placement credit, distance learning, external degree program, independent study.
Library University Library with 17.5 million titles, 9,000 serial subscriptions, an OPAC, a Web page.
Computers on Campus A campuswide network can be accessed from off campus. Internet access, at least one staffed computer lab available.
Student Life *Housing:* college housing not available.
Costs (2001–02) *Tuition:* $7860 full-time. Full-time tuition and fees vary according to location and program. *Payment plan:* deferred payment. *Waivers:* employees or children of employees.
Applying *Options:* deferred entrance. *Application fee:* $85. *Required:* 2 years of work experience. *Required for some:* high school transcript. *Application deadline:* rolling (freshmen), rolling (transfers).
Admissions Contact Ms. Beth Barilla, Director of Admissions, University of Phoenix-New Mexico Campus, 4615 East Elwood Street, Phoenix, AZ 85040-1958. *Phone:* 480-927-0099 Ext. 1218. *Toll-free phone:* 800-228-7240. *Fax:* 480-594-1758. *E-mail:* beth.barilla@apollogrp.edu.

WESTERN NEW MEXICO UNIVERSITY
Silver City, New Mexico

Admissions Contact Mr. Michael Alecksen, Director of Admissions, Western New Mexico University, College Avenue, Silver City, NM 88062-0680. *Phone:* 505-538-6106. *Toll-free phone:* 800-872-WNMU. *Fax:* 505-538-6155.

NEW YORK

ADELPHI UNIVERSITY
Garden City, New York

- **Independent** university, founded 1896
- **Calendar** semesters
- **Degrees** associate, bachelor's, master's, doctoral, post-master's, and postbachelor's certificates
- **Suburban** 75-acre campus with easy access to New York City
- **Endowment** $49.9 million
- **Coed,** 3,391 undergraduate students, 80% full-time, 71% women, 29% men
- **Moderately difficult** entrance level, 68% of applicants were admitted

Adelphi is a private, coeducational university offering degrees in the liberal arts and the professions at the bachelor's, master's, and doctoral levels. Undergraduate student-faculty ratio is 13:1. Entrance difficulty level is competitive and is highly competitive for the Honors College. Merit and talent scholarships as well as need-based aid are available.

Undergraduates 2,716 full-time, 675 part-time. Students come from 40 states and territories, 53 other countries, 11% are from out of state, 11% African American, 4% Asian American or Pacific Islander, 7% Hispanic American, 0.1% Native American, 4% international, 15% transferred in, 26% live on campus. *Retention:* 76% of 2001 full-time freshmen returned.
Freshmen *Admission:* 3,703 applied, 2,530 admitted, 690 enrolled. *Average high school GPA:* 3.30. *Test scores:* SAT verbal scores over 500: 68%; SAT math scores over 500: 69%; SAT verbal scores over 600: 21%; SAT math scores over 600: 24%; SAT verbal scores over 700: 1%; SAT math scores over 700: 2%.
Faculty *Total:* 565, 33% full-time. *Student/faculty ratio:* 14:1.
Majors Accounting; anthropology; art education; biochemistry; biological/physical sciences; biology; business administration; business management/administrative services related; chemistry; communications; computer/information sciences; dance; earth sciences; ecology; economics; elementary education; English; finance; foreign languages/literatures; French; history; humanities; Latin American studies; liberal arts and sciences/liberal studies; mathematics; music; music (general performance); music teacher education; nursing; nursing related; philosophy; physical education; physics; political science; psychology; social sciences; social work; sociology; Spanish; speech-language pathology/audiology; speech therapy; theater arts/drama.
Academic Programs *Special study options:* advanced placement credit, freshman honors college, honors programs, internships, off-campus study, part-time degree program, services for LD students, study abroad, summer session for credit. *ROTC:* Army (c), Air Force (c). *Unusual degree programs:* 3-2 engineering with Columbia University, Polytechnic University, Rensselaer Polytechnic Institute, Stevens Institute of Technology; physical therapy, New York Medical College.
Library Swirbul Library plus 1 other with 630,090 titles, 1,762 serial subscriptions, 43,298 audiovisual materials, an OPAC, a Web page.
Computers on Campus 450 computers available on campus for general student use. A campuswide network can be accessed from student residence rooms. Internet access, at least one staffed computer lab available.
Student Life *Housing Options:* coed, disabled students. *Activities and Organizations:* drama/theater group, student-run newspaper, radio station, choral group, Student Activities Board, Student Government Association, InterAct, Caribbean Cultural Awareness Club, African People's Organization, national fraternities, national sororities. *Campus security:* 24-hour emergency response devices and patrols, late-night transport/escort service, controlled dormitory access. *Student Services:* health clinic, personal/psychological counseling.
Athletics Member NCAA. All Division II except soccer (Division I). *Intercollegiate sports:* baseball M(s), basketball M(s)/W(s), cross-country running M(s)/W(s), golf M(s), lacrosse M(s)/W(s), soccer M(s)/W(s), softball W(s), swimming M(s)/W(s), tennis M(s)/W(s), track and field M(s), volleyball W(s). *Intramural sports:* badminton M/W, basketball M/W, bowling M/W, cross-country running M/W, football M/W, ice hockey M/W, soccer M/W, softball M/W, swimming M/W, table tennis M/W, tennis M/W, volleyball M/W, weight lifting M/W.
Standardized Tests *Required:* SAT I or ACT (for admission).
Costs (2001–02) *Comprehensive fee:* $23,320 includes full-time tuition ($16,100), mandatory fees ($170), and room and board ($7050). Full-time tuition and fees vary according to program. Part-time tuition: $500 per credit. Part-time tuition and fees vary according to program. *Required fees:* $209 per term part-time. *Room and board:* College room only: $4850. Room and board charges vary according to board plan and housing facility. *Payment plans:* tuition prepayment, installment, deferred payment. *Waivers:* employees or children of employees.
Financial Aid Of all full-time matriculated undergraduates who enrolled in 2001, 2329 applied for aid, 2329 were judged to have need. 2160 Federal Work-Study jobs (averaging $835). 489 State and other part-time jobs (averaging $1298). In 2001, 387 non-need-based awards were made. *Average financial aid package:* $12,500. *Average need-based loan:* $3864. *Average need-based gift aid:* $3763. *Average non-need based aid:* $6494. *Average indebtedness upon graduation:* $20,385.
Applying *Options:* common application, electronic application, early action, deferred entrance. *Application fee:* $35. *Required:* essay or personal statement, high school transcript. *Required for some:* interview, auditions/portfolios for performing and fine arts. *Recommended:* minimum 3.0 GPA, 1 letter of recommendation, interview. *Application deadline:* rolling (freshmen), rolling (transfers). *Notification:* continuous (freshmen), 12/31 (early action).
Admissions Contact Ms. Rory Shaffer-Walsh, Director of Admissions, Adelphi University, South Avenue, Garden City, NY 11530. *Phone:* 516-877-3056. *Toll-free phone:* 800-ADELPHI. *Fax:* 516-877-3039. *E-mail:* admissions@adelphi.edu.

ALBANY COLLEGE OF PHARMACY OF UNION UNIVERSITY
Albany, New York

- **Independent** comprehensive, founded 1881, part of Union University (Albany Law School, Albany Medical College, Union College, NY)
- **Calendar** semesters
- **Degrees** bachelor's and first professional
- **Urban** 1-acre campus
- **Endowment** $7.9 million
- **Coed,** 828 undergraduate students, 100% full-time, 56% women, 44% men
- **Moderately difficult** entrance level, 67% of applicants were admitted

Undergraduates 828 full-time. Students come from 11 states and territories, 6 other countries, 10% are from out of state, 7% transferred in, 30% live on campus. *Retention:* 72% of 2001 full-time freshmen returned.

Albany College of Pharmacy of Union University (continued)

Freshmen *Admission:* 403 applied, 271 admitted, 147 enrolled. *Average high school GPA:* 3.40. *Test scores:* SAT verbal scores over 500: 75%; SAT math scores over 500: 100%; SAT verbal scores over 600: 25%; SAT math scores over 600: 75%; SAT math scores over 700: 5%.

Faculty *Total:* 60, 78% full-time, 60% with terminal degrees. *Student/faculty ratio:* 15:1.

Majors Pharmacy; pharmacy related.

Academic Programs *Special study options:* accelerated degree program, advanced placement credit, internships, off-campus study, services for LD students, summer session for credit. *ROTC:* Army (c), Air Force (c).

Library George and Leona Lewis Library with 12,314 titles, 1,399 serial subscriptions, 2,676 audiovisual materials, an OPAC, a Web page.

Computers on Campus 100 computers available on campus for general student use. A campuswide network can be accessed from student residence rooms and from off campus. Internet access, at least one staffed computer lab available.

Student Life *Housing:* on-campus residence required through sophomore year. *Options:* coed. *Activities and Organizations:* student-run newspaper, choral group, national fraternities, national sororities. *Campus security:* 24-hour emergency response devices and patrols, controlled dormitory access. *Student Services:* health clinic, personal/psychological counseling.

Athletics *Intercollegiate sports:* basketball M/W, golf M/W, soccer M/W. *Intramural sports:* basketball M/W, bowling M/W, volleyball M/W.

Standardized Tests *Required:* SAT I or ACT (for admission).

Costs (2001–02) *Comprehensive fee:* $19,473 includes full-time tuition ($13,550), mandatory fees ($823), and room and board ($5100). Part-time tuition and fees vary according to course load. *Room and board:* College room only: $3500. Room and board charges vary according to board plan and student level. *Payment plan:* installment. *Waivers:* employees or children of employees.

Financial Aid Of all full-time matriculated undergraduates who enrolled in 2001, 560 applied for aid, 420 were judged to have need. 135 Federal Work-Study jobs (averaging $637). 50 State and other part-time jobs (averaging $1012). In 2001, 98 non-need-based awards were made. *Average percent of need met:* 75%. *Average financial aid package:* $7960. *Average need-based loan:* $4695. *Average need-based gift aid:* $4458. *Average non-need based aid:* $480. *Average indebtedness upon graduation:* $19,231.

Applying *Options:* electronic application. *Application fee:* $50. *Required:* high school transcript, 2 letters of recommendation. *Required for some:* interview. *Recommended:* minimum 2.0 GPA. *Application deadlines:* 2/1 (freshmen), 2/1 (transfers). *Notification:* continuous until 8/1 (freshmen).

Admissions Contact Mr. Robert Gould, Director of Admissions, Albany College of Pharmacy of Union University, 106 New Scotland Avenue, Albany, NY 12208-3425. *Phone:* 518-445-7221. *Toll-free phone:* 888-203-8010. *Fax:* 518-445-7202. *E-mail:* admissions@acp.edu.

ALFRED UNIVERSITY

Alfred, New York

- **Independent** university, founded 1836
- **Calendar** semesters
- **Degrees** bachelor's, master's, doctoral, and post-master's certificates
- **Rural** 232-acre campus with easy access to Rochester
- **Endowment** $79.9 million
- **Coed,** 2,115 undergraduate students, 95% full-time, 53% women, 47% men
- **Moderately difficult** entrance level, 75% of applicants were admitted

With more than 60 majors and programs of study, high-technology opportunities, and top-notch facilities, Alfred University provides and outstanding academic experience in a personal learning environment. All students are encouraged to value diversity, tolerance, interdisciplinary work, and active learning.

Undergraduates 2,012 full-time, 103 part-time. Students come from 38 states and territories, 12 other countries, 31% are from out of state, 4% African American, 2% Asian American or Pacific Islander, 4% Hispanic American, 0.5% Native American, 2% international, 4% transferred in, 65% live on campus. *Retention:* 77% of 2001 full-time freshmen returned.

Freshmen *Admission:* 2,048 applied, 1,538 admitted, 495 enrolled. *Test scores:* SAT verbal scores over 500: 76%; SAT math scores over 500: 82%; SAT verbal scores over 600: 32%; SAT math scores over 600: 34%; SAT verbal scores over 700: 5%; SAT math scores over 700: 4%.

Faculty *Total:* 206, 84% full-time, 84% with terminal degrees. *Student/faculty ratio:* 12:1.

Majors Accounting; applied art; art; art education; art history; athletic training/sports medicine; bilingual/bicultural education; biological/physical sciences; biology; biomedical technology; business administration; business economics; business education; business marketing and marketing management; ceramic arts; ceramic sciences/engineering; chemistry; clinical psychology; computer science; criminal justice studies; drawing; earth sciences; economics; education; electrical engineering; elementary education; English; environmental science; experimental psychology; finance; fine/studio arts; French; general studies; geology; German; gerontology; graphic design/commercial art/illustration; health services administration; history; information sciences/systems; interdisciplinary studies; international business; literature; mass communications; materials science; mathematics; mathematics/computer science; mechanical engineering; medical laboratory technician; modern languages; philosophy; photography; physics; political science; pre-dentistry; pre-law; pre-medicine; pre-veterinary studies; printmaking; psychology; public administration; science education; sculpture; secondary education; sociology; Spanish; theater arts/drama.

Academic Programs *Special study options:* academic remediation for entering students, accelerated degree program, adult/continuing education programs, advanced placement credit, cooperative education, double majors, honors programs, independent study, internships, off-campus study, part-time degree program, services for LD students, student-designed majors, study abroad, summer session for credit. *ROTC:* Army (c). *Unusual degree programs:* 3-2 engineering with Columbia University; forestry with Duke University.

Library Herrick Memorial Library plus 1 other with 317,832 titles, 1,507 serial subscriptions, 162,547 audiovisual materials, an OPAC, a Web page.

Computers on Campus 390 computers available on campus for general student use. A campuswide network can be accessed from student residence rooms and from off campus. Internet access, at least one staffed computer lab available.

Student Life *Housing:* on-campus residence required through sophomore year. *Options:* coed. *Activities and Organizations:* drama/theater group, student-run newspaper, radio and television station, choral group, Student Activities Board, Spectrum, WALF, Student Senate, Fiat Lux, national fraternities, national sororities. *Campus security:* 24-hour emergency response devices, student patrols, late-night transport/escort service. *Student Services:* health clinic, personal/psychological counseling, women's center.

Athletics Member NCAA. All Division III. *Intercollegiate sports:* basketball M/W, cross-country running M/W, equestrian sports M/W, football M, golf M/W, lacrosse M/W, skiing (cross-country) M(c)/W(c), skiing (downhill) M/W, soccer M/W, softball W, swimming M/W, tennis M/W, track and field M/W, volleyball W. *Intramural sports:* baseball M(c), basketball M/W, football M/W, ice hockey M(c), lacrosse M/W, racquetball M/W, rugby M(c)/W(c), soccer M/W, softball M/W, squash M/W, tennis M/W, volleyball M/W.

Standardized Tests *Required:* SAT I or ACT (for admission). *Recommended:* SAT II: Writing Test (for admission).

Costs (2001–02) *One-time required fee:* $300. *Comprehensive fee:* $27,212 includes full-time tuition ($18,498), mandatory fees ($698), and room and board ($8016). Full-time tuition and fees vary according to program and student level. Part-time tuition: $544 per credit hour. Part-time tuition and fees vary according to program. *Required fees:* $58 per term part-time. *Room and board:* College room only: $4174. Room and board charges vary according to board plan and housing facility. *Payment plans:* tuition prepayment, installment, deferred payment. *Waivers:* employees or children of employees.

Financial Aid Of all full-time matriculated undergraduates who enrolled in 2001, 1770 applied for aid, 1562 were judged to have need, 1327 had their need fully met. In 2001, 283 non-need-based awards were made. *Average percent of need met:* 92%. *Average financial aid package:* $18,239. *Average need-based loan:* $4816. *Average need-based gift aid:* $13,342. *Average non-need based aid:* $6122. *Average indebtedness upon graduation:* $17,500.

Applying *Options:* common application, electronic application, early admission, early decision, deferred entrance. *Application fee:* $40. *Required:* essay or personal statement, high school transcript, 1 letter of recommendation. *Required for some:* interview, portfolio. *Recommended:* interview. *Application deadlines:* 2/1 (freshmen), 8/1 (transfers). *Early decision:* 12/1. *Notification:* 3/15 (freshmen), 12/15 (early decision).

Admissions Contact Mr. Scott Hooker, Director of Admissions, Alfred University, Alumni Hall, Alfred, NY 14802-1205. *Phone:* 607-871-2115. *Toll-free phone:* 800-541-9229. *Fax:* 607-871-2198. *E-mail:* adm@alfred.edu.

AUDREY COHEN COLLEGE

New York, New York

- **Independent** comprehensive, founded 1964
- **Calendar** 3 15-week semesters
- **Degrees** certificates, associate, bachelor's, and master's
- **Urban** campus
- **Endowment** $4.6 million

- **Coed, primarily women,** 1,296 undergraduate students, 100% full-time, 82% women, 18% men
- **Moderately difficult** entrance level, 38% of applicants were admitted

Undergraduates 1,296 full-time. Students come from 5 states and territories, 2% are from out of state, 60% African American, 3% Asian American or Pacific Islander, 18% Hispanic American, 0.6% Native American, 8% transferred in. *Retention:* 70% of 2001 full-time freshmen returned.
Freshmen *Admission:* 405 applied, 153 admitted, 371 enrolled.
Faculty *Total:* 184, 15% full-time. *Student/faculty ratio:* 20:1.
Majors Business administration; human services.
Academic Programs *Special study options:* academic remediation for entering students, accelerated degree program, adult/continuing education programs, cooperative education, English as a second language, internships, study abroad, summer session for credit.
Library Main Library with 26,800 titles, 3,414 serial subscriptions, 45 audiovisual materials, an OPAC, a Web page.
Computers on Campus 130 computers available on campus for general student use. A campuswide network can be accessed from off campus. Internet access, at least one staffed computer lab available.
Student Life *Housing:* college housing not available. *Activities and Organizations:* student-run newspaper, student government, student newsletter, honor societies, Networking Club, Yearbook Committee. *Campus security:* 24-hour patrols. *Student Services:* personal/psychological counseling.
Standardized Tests *Recommended:* SAT I (for admission), SAT I or ACT (for admission).
Costs (2001–02) *Tuition:* $14,400 full-time, $310 per credit part-time. Full-time tuition and fees vary according to degree level, location, and program. No tuition increase for student's term of enrollment. *Required fees:* $105 full-time, $105 per term part-time. *Payment plan:* installment. *Waivers:* employees or children of employees.
Financial Aid Of all full-time matriculated undergraduates who enrolled in 2001, 1066 applied for aid, 1062 were judged to have need. 52 Federal Work-Study jobs (averaging $1969). 30 State and other part-time jobs (averaging $1920). *Average financial aid package:* $6337. *Average need-based loan:* $3377. *Average need-based gift aid:* $3650. *Average indebtedness upon graduation:* $20,130.
Applying *Options:* electronic application, deferred entrance. *Application fee:* $30. *Required:* essay or personal statement, high school transcript, 2 letters of recommendation, interview. *Required for some:* college entrance exam. *Recommended:* minimum 3.0 GPA. *Application deadlines:* 8/15 (freshmen), 8/15 (transfers). *Notification:* continuous until 8/31 (freshmen).
Admissions Contact Ms. Jennifer Gass, Admissions Counselor, Audrey Cohen College, 75 Varick Street, 12th Floor, New York, NY 10013. *Phone:* 212-343-1234 Ext. 2704. *Toll-free phone:* 800-33-THINK Ext. 5001. *Fax:* 212-343-8470.

BARD COLLEGE
Annandale-on-Hudson, New York

- **Independent** comprehensive, founded 1860
- **Calendar** 4-1-4
- **Degrees** bachelor's, master's, and doctoral
- **Rural** 600-acre campus
- **Endowment** $113.9 million
- **Coed,** 1,343 undergraduate students, 96% full-time, 56% women, 44% men
- **Very difficult** entrance level, 44% of applicants were admitted

Undergraduates 1,284 full-time, 59 part-time. Students come from 50 states and territories, 48 other countries, 74% are from out of state, 3% African American, 3% Asian American or Pacific Islander, 5% Hispanic American, 0.4% Native American, 6% international, 2% transferred in, 82% live on campus. *Retention:* 86% of 2001 full-time freshmen returned.
Freshmen *Admission:* 2,970 applied, 1,320 admitted, 358 enrolled. *Average high school GPA:* 3.60. *Test scores:* SAT verbal scores over 500: 100%; SAT math scores over 500: 98%; ACT scores over 18: 100%; SAT verbal scores over 600: 82%; SAT math scores over 600: 71%; ACT scores over 24: 94%; SAT verbal scores over 700: 32%; SAT math scores over 700: 22%; ACT scores over 30: 17%.
Faculty *Total:* 203, 56% full-time. *Student/faculty ratio:* 9:1.
Majors Acting/directing; African studies; American government; American history; American studies; anthropology; archaeology; area studies; art; art history; Asian studies; biochemistry; biological/physical sciences; biology; chemistry; Chinese; city/community/regional planning; classics; comparative literature; creative writing; cultural studies; dance; drama/theater literature; drawing; Eastern European area studies; ecology; economics; English; environmental biology; environmental science; European history; European studies; film studies; film/video production; fine/studio arts; French; German; Greek (ancient and medieval); Greek (modern); Hebrew; history; history of philosophy; history of science and technology; humanities; interdisciplinary studies; international economics; international relations; Italian; jazz; Judaic studies; Latin American studies; Latin (ancient and medieval); literature; mathematics; medieval/renaissance studies; modern languages; molecular biology; music; music (general performance); music history; music theory and composition; music (voice and choral/opera performance); natural sciences; painting; philosophy; photography; physical sciences; physics; play/screenwriting; political science; pre-dentistry; pre-law; pre-medicine; pre-veterinary studies; psychology; religious studies; romance languages; Russian; Russian/Slavic studies; sculpture; social sciences; sociology; Spanish; theater arts/drama; visual/performing arts; western civilization.
Academic Programs *Special study options:* accelerated degree program, adult/continuing education programs, advanced placement credit, double majors, English as a second language, independent study, internships, off-campus study, part-time degree program, student-designed majors, study abroad. *Unusual degree programs:* 3-2 business administration with University of Rochester; engineering with Columbia University, Washington University in St. Louis, Dartmouth College; forestry with Duke University; social work with Hunter College of the City University of New York, Adelphi University; public administration with Syracuse University, public health with Yale University.
Library Stevenson Library plus 3 others with 275,000 titles, 1,400 serial subscriptions, 5,800 audiovisual materials, an OPAC, a Web page.
Computers on Campus 150 computers available on campus for general student use. A campuswide network can be accessed from student residence rooms and from off campus. Internet access, at least one staffed computer lab available.
Student Life *Housing:* on-campus residence required for freshman year. *Options:* coed. *Activities and Organizations:* drama/theater group, student-run newspaper, radio station, choral group, student government, Social Action Workshop, Model United Nations, student newspaper, International Student Organization. *Campus security:* 24-hour emergency response devices and patrols, student patrols, late-night transport/escort service, controlled dormitory access. *Student Services:* health clinic, personal/psychological counseling, women's center, legal services.
Athletics Member NCAA, NAIA. All NCAA Division III. *Intercollegiate sports:* basketball M/W, cross-country running M/W, fencing M/W, rugby M/W, soccer M/W, squash M/W, tennis M/W, volleyball M/W. *Intramural sports:* badminton M/W, basketball M/W, fencing M/W, rugby M/W, skiing (cross-country) M/W, skiing (downhill) M/W, soccer M/W, softball M/W, squash M/W, swimming M/W, tennis M/W, volleyball M/W, water polo M/W, weight lifting M/W.
Standardized Tests *Recommended:* SAT I or ACT (for admission), SAT II: Subject Tests (for admission).
Costs (2001–02) *Comprehensive fee:* $33,912 includes full-time tuition ($25,620), mandatory fees ($550), and room and board ($7742). Part-time tuition: $801 per credit. Part-time tuition and fees vary according to course load. *Required fees:* $170 per term part-time. *Room and board:* College room only: $3880. Room and board charges vary according to board plan. *Payment plan:* installment. *Waivers:* employees or children of employees.
Financial Aid Of all full-time matriculated undergraduates who enrolled in 2001, 889 applied for aid, 789 were judged to have need, 473 had their need fully met. 492 Federal Work-Study jobs (averaging $1500). In 2001, 60 non-need-based awards were made. *Average percent of need met:* 87%. *Average financial aid package:* $20,092. *Average need-based loan:* $4116. *Average need-based gift aid:* $15,495. *Average non-need based aid:* $11,469. *Average indebtedness upon graduation:* $15,400. *Financial aid deadline:* 3/15.
Applying *Options:* common application, electronic application, early admission, early action, deferred entrance. *Application fee:* $50. *Required:* essay or personal statement, high school transcript, 3 letters of recommendation. *Required for some:* interview. *Recommended:* minimum 3.0 GPA, interview. *Application deadlines:* 1/15 (freshmen), 1/15 (transfers). *Notification:* 4/1 (freshmen), 1/1 (early action).
Admissions Contact Ms. Mary Inga Backlund, Director of Admissions, Bard College, Ravine Road, PO Box 5000, Annandale-on-Hudson, NY 12504. *Phone:* 845-758-7472. *Fax:* 845-758-5208. *E-mail:* admission@bard.edu.

BARNARD COLLEGE
New York, New York

- **Independent** 4-year, founded 1889, part of Columbia University
- **Calendar** semesters
- **Degree** bachelor's
- **Urban** 4-acre campus

Barnard College (continued)
- **Endowment** $138.4 million
- **Women only,** 2,261 undergraduate students, 98% full-time
- **Most difficult** entrance level, 33% of applicants were admitted

Undergraduates 2,213 full-time, 48 part-time. Students come from 51 states and territories, 27 other countries, 61% are from out of state, 5% African American, 21% Asian American or Pacific Islander, 6% Hispanic American, 0.5% Native American, 3% international, 3% transferred in, 88% live on campus. *Retention:* 93% of 2001 full-time freshmen returned.

Freshmen *Admission:* 541 enrolled. *Average high school GPA:* 3.83. *Test scores:* SAT verbal scores over 500: 99%; SAT math scores over 500: 98%; ACT scores over 18: 100%; SAT verbal scores over 600: 89%; SAT math scores over 600: 86%; ACT scores over 24: 91%; SAT verbal scores over 700: 37%; SAT math scores over 700: 29%; ACT scores over 30: 33%.

Faculty *Total:* 293, 62% full-time. *Student/faculty ratio:* 10:1.

Majors African studies; American studies; anthropology; applied mathematics; architecture; art history; Asian studies; astronomy; biochemistry; biology; biopsychology; chemistry; classics; comparative literature; computer science; dance; drama/theater literature; East Asian studies; Eastern European area studies; economics; English; environmental science; European studies; French; German; Greek (ancient and medieval); history; Italian; Latin American studies; Latin (ancient and medieval); mathematical statistics; mathematics; medieval/renaissance studies; Middle Eastern studies; music; philosophy; physics; physiological psychology/psychobiology; political science; pre-medicine; psychology; religious studies; Russian; Russian/Slavic studies; Slavic languages; sociology; South Asian studies; Spanish; theater arts/drama; urban studies; women's studies.

Academic Programs *Special study options:* accelerated degree program, advanced placement credit, double majors, honors programs, independent study, internships, off-campus study, services for LD students, student-designed majors, study abroad. *Unusual degree programs:* 3-2 engineering with Columbia University, The Fu Foundation School of Engineering and Applied Science; international affairs with Columbia University, School of International and Public Affairs.

Library Wollman Library with 198,020 titles, 900 serial subscriptions, 12,425 audiovisual materials, an OPAC, a Web page.

Computers on Campus 150 computers available on campus for general student use. A campuswide network can be accessed from student residence rooms and from off campus. Internet access, online (class) registration, at least one staffed computer lab available.

Student Life *Housing Options:* women-only, disabled students. *Activities and Organizations:* drama/theater group, student-run newspaper, radio and television station, choral group, marching band, Community Impact, Student Government Association, Student Activities Council, WBAR Radio, Asian-American Alliance. *Campus security:* 24-hour emergency response devices and patrols, late-night transport/escort service, 4 permanent security posts. *Student Services:* health clinic, personal/psychological counseling, women's center.

Athletics Member NCAA. All Division I. *Intercollegiate sports:* archery W, basketball W, crew W, cross-country running W, equestrian sports W(c), fencing W, field hockey W, ice hockey W(c), lacrosse W, rugby W(c), sailing W(c), skiing (downhill) W(c), soccer W, softball W, squash W(c), swimming W, tennis W, track and field W, volleyball W. *Intramural sports:* archery W, badminton W, basketball W, bowling W, equestrian sports W, fencing W, field hockey W, ice hockey W, lacrosse W, racquetball W, rugby W, sailing W, soccer W, squash W, tennis W, volleyball W.

Standardized Tests *Required:* SAT II: Writing Test (for admission).

Costs (2001–02) *Comprehensive fee:* $33,694 includes full-time tuition ($22,942), mandatory fees ($1094), and room and board ($9658). Part-time tuition: $765 per credit. *Room and board:* College room only: $5988. Room and board charges vary according to board plan and housing facility. *Payment plans:* tuition prepayment, installment, deferred payment. *Waivers:* employees or children of employees.

Financial Aid Of all full-time matriculated undergraduates who enrolled in 2001, 1100 applied for aid, 924 were judged to have need, 924 had their need fully met. 420 Federal Work-Study jobs (averaging $1214). 487 State and other part-time jobs (averaging $1410). In 2001, 125 non-need-based awards were made. *Average percent of need met:* 100%. *Average financial aid package:* $22,676. *Average need-based loan:* $4140. *Average need-based gift aid:* $18,802. *Average indebtedness upon graduation:* $13,421. *Financial aid deadline:* 2/1.

Applying *Options:* common application, early admission, early decision, deferred entrance. *Application fee:* $45. *Required:* essay or personal statement, high school transcript, 3 letters of recommendation. *Recommended:* interview. *Application deadlines:* 1/1 (freshmen), 4/1 (transfers). *Early decision:* 11/15. *Notification:* 4/1 (freshmen), 12/15 (early decision).

Admissions Contact Ms. Jennifer Gill Fondiller, Dean of Admissions, Barnard College, 3009 Broadway, New York, NY 10027. *Phone:* 212-854-2014. *Fax:* 212-854-6220. *E-mail:* admissions@barnard.edu.

BERKELEY COLLEGE
New York, New York

- **Proprietary** primarily 2-year, founded 1936
- **Calendar** quarters
- **Degrees** certificates, associate, and bachelor's
- **Urban** campus
- **Coed,** 1,666 undergraduate students, 91% full-time, 71% women, 29% men
- **Minimally difficult** entrance level, 87% of applicants were admitted

Undergraduates 1,512 full-time, 154 part-time. Students come from 10 states and territories, 58 other countries, 8% are from out of state, 30% African American, 6% Asian American or Pacific Islander, 31% Hispanic American, 0.2% Native American, 13% international, 13% transferred in.

Freshmen *Admission:* 1,295 applied, 1,123 admitted, 432 enrolled. *Average high school GPA:* 2.7.

Faculty *Total:* 110, 37% full-time. *Student/faculty ratio:* 24:1.

Majors Accounting; business; business administration; business management/administrative services related; business marketing and marketing management; fashion merchandising; international business; office management; paralegal/legal assistant.

Academic Programs *Special study options:* academic remediation for entering students, adult/continuing education programs, advanced placement credit, cooperative education, distance learning, English as a second language, internships, off-campus study, part-time degree program, study abroad, summer session for credit.

Library 13,164 titles, 138 serial subscriptions, 949 audiovisual materials, an OPAC, a Web page.

Computers on Campus 200 computers available on campus for general student use. A campuswide network can be accessed from off campus. Internet access, at least one staffed computer lab available.

Student Life *Housing:* college housing not available. *Activities and Organizations:* student-run newspaper, student government, International Club, Paralegal Club, Accounting Club. *Campus security:* 24-hour emergency response devices. *Student Services:* personal/psychological counseling.

Costs (2002–03) *One-time required fee:* $50. *Tuition:* $13,950 full-time, $360 per credit part-time. *Required fees:* $390 full-time, $60 per term part-time. *Payment plan:* installment. *Waivers:* employees or children of employees.

Financial Aid Of all full-time matriculated undergraduates who enrolled in 2001, 120 Federal Work-Study jobs (averaging $1500).

Applying *Options:* electronic application, deferred entrance. *Application fee:* $40. *Required:* high school transcript. *Recommended:* interview. *Application deadline:* rolling (freshmen), rolling (transfers).

Admissions Contact Mr. Stuart Siegman, Berkeley College, 3 East 43rd Street, New York, NY 10017. *Phone:* 212-986-4343 Ext. 123. *Toll-free phone:* 800-446-5400. *Fax:* 212-818-1079. *E-mail:* admissions@berkeleycollege.edu.

BERKELEY COLLEGE
White Plains, New York

- **Proprietary** primarily 2-year, founded 1945
- **Calendar** quarters
- **Degrees** certificates, associate, and bachelor's
- **Suburban** 10-acre campus with easy access to New York City
- **Coed,** 667 undergraduate students, 86% full-time, 71% women, 29% men
- **Minimally difficult** entrance level, 88% of applicants were admitted

Undergraduates 574 full-time, 93 part-time. Students come from 11 states and territories, 26 other countries, 15% are from out of state, 25% African American, 3% Asian American or Pacific Islander, 23% Hispanic American, 0.2% Native American, 5% international, 13% transferred in, 10% live on campus.

Freshmen *Admission:* 517 applied, 453 admitted, 247 enrolled. *Average high school GPA:* 2.7.

Faculty *Total:* 42, 40% full-time. *Student/faculty ratio:* 24:1.

Majors Accounting; business; business administration; business management/administrative services related; business marketing and marketing management; fashion merchandising; international business; office management; paralegal/legal assistant.

Academic Programs *Special study options:* academic remediation for entering students, adult/continuing education programs, advanced placement credit, cooperative education, distance learning, English as a second language, internships, off-campus study, part-time degree program, services for LD students, study abroad, summer session for credit.
Library 9,526 titles, 66 serial subscriptions, 777 audiovisual materials, an OPAC, a Web page.
Computers on Campus 175 computers available on campus for general student use. A campuswide network can be accessed from off campus. Internet access, at least one staffed computer lab available.
Student Life *Housing Options:* coed. *Activities and Organizations:* student-run newspaper, student government, Paralegal Club, Fashion Club, Phi Theta Kappa. *Campus security:* monitored entrance with front desk security guard. *Student Services:* personal/psychological counseling.
Costs (2002–03) *One-time required fee:* $50. *Tuition:* $13,950 full-time, $360 per credit part-time. *Required fees:* $390 full-time, $60 per term part-time. *Room only:* Room and board charges vary according to board plan. *Payment plan:* installment. *Waivers:* employees or children of employees.
Financial Aid Of all full-time matriculated undergraduates who enrolled in 2001, 40 Federal Work-Study jobs (averaging $1100).
Applying *Options:* electronic application, deferred entrance. *Application fee:* $40. *Required:* high school transcript. *Recommended:* interview. *Application deadline:* rolling (freshmen), rolling (transfers).
Admissions Contact Mr. David Bertrone, Director of High School Admissions, Berkeley College, 99 Church Street, White Plains, NY 10601. *Phone:* 914-694-1122 Ext. 3110. *Toll-free phone:* 800-446-5400. *Fax:* 914-328-9469. *E-mail:* wpcampus@berkeleycollege.edu.

BERNARD M. BARUCH COLLEGE OF THE CITY UNIVERSITY OF NEW YORK
New York, New York

- **State and locally supported** comprehensive, founded 1919, part of City University of New York System
- **Calendar** semesters
- **Degrees** bachelor's, master's, doctoral, and post-master's certificates
- **Urban** campus
- **Endowment** $25.2 million
- **Coed,** 13,086 undergraduate students, 68% full-time, 57% women, 43% men
- **Very difficult** entrance level, 33% of applicants were admitted

Undergraduates 8,955 full-time, 4,131 part-time. Students come from 7 states and territories, 144 other countries, 8% are from out of state, 19% African American, 25% Asian American or Pacific Islander, 19% Hispanic American, 0.1% Native American, 9% international, 8% transferred in. *Retention:* 92% of 2001 full-time freshmen returned.
Freshmen *Admission:* 15,337 applied, 5,045 admitted, 1,712 enrolled. *Average high school GPA:* 3.01. *Test scores:* SAT verbal scores over 500: 52%; SAT math scores over 500: 78%; SAT verbal scores over 600: 12%; SAT math scores over 600: 32%; SAT verbal scores over 700: 1%; SAT math scores over 700: 6%.
Faculty *Total:* 873, 46% full-time, 60% with terminal degrees. *Student/faculty ratio:* 22:1.
Majors Accounting; actuarial science; advertising; arts management; business administration; business economics; business marketing and marketing management; creative writing; economics; education; English; finance; history; human resources management; information sciences/systems; interdisciplinary studies; international business; journalism; literature; management information systems/ business data processing; mathematical statistics; mathematics; music; natural sciences; operations research; philosophy; political science; psychology; public administration; public policy analysis; romance languages; sociology; Spanish.
Academic Programs *Special study options:* adult/continuing education programs, advanced placement credit, English as a second language, honors programs, independent study, internships, part-time degree program, services for LD students, student-designed majors, study abroad, summer session for credit.
Library The William and Anita Newman Library plus 1 other with 248,909 titles, 4,167 serial subscriptions, 951 audiovisual materials.
Computers on Campus 1500 computers available on campus for general student use. A campuswide network can be accessed from off campus. Internet access, at least one staffed computer lab available.
Student Life *Housing:* college housing not available. *Activities and Organizations:* drama/theater group, student-run newspaper, radio station, choral group, Accounting Society, Asian Student Association, Caribbean Student Association, Golden Key International Society, Helpline, national fraternities, national sororities. *Campus security:* 24-hour emergency response devices and patrols, late-night transport/escort service, controlled access by ID card. *Student Services:* health clinic, personal/psychological counseling, legal services.
Athletics Member NCAA. All Division III. *Intercollegiate sports:* baseball M, basketball M/W, cross-country running W, soccer M, softball W, tennis M/W, volleyball M/W. *Intramural sports:* archery M/W, badminton M/W, basketball M/W, table tennis M/W, volleyball M/W, weight lifting M/W.
Standardized Tests *Required:* SAT I (for admission).
Costs (2001–02) *Tuition:* state resident $3200 full-time, $135 per credit part-time; nonresident $6800 full-time, $285 per credit part-time. Full-time tuition and fees vary according to class time. Part-time tuition and fees vary according to class time. *Required fees:* $150 full-time, $46 per term part-time. *Payment plans:* installment, deferred payment. *Waivers:* senior citizens and employees or children of employees.
Financial Aid Of all full-time matriculated undergraduates who enrolled in 2001, 7640 applied for aid, 7100 were judged to have need, 2600 had their need fully met. 520 Federal Work-Study jobs. In 2001, 482 non-need-based awards were made. *Average percent of need met:* 69%. *Average financial aid package:* $4650. *Average need-based loan:* $3650. *Average need-based gift aid:* $3450. *Average non-need based aid:* $1750. *Average indebtedness upon graduation:* $8100. *Financial aid deadline:* 4/30.
Applying *Options:* early decision, deferred entrance. *Application fee:* $40. *Required:* high school transcript, minimum 2.3 GPA, 14 academic units. *Required for some:* minimum 3.0 GPA, letters of recommendation. *Application deadlines:* 4/1 (freshmen), 5/1 (transfers). *Notification:* continuous until 6/30 (freshmen).
Admissions Contact Mr. James F. Murphy, Director of Undergraduate Admissions and Financial Aid, Bernard M. Baruch College of the City University of New York, Box H-0720, New York, NY 10010-5585. *Phone:* 212-802-2300. *E-mail:* admissions@baruch.cuny.edu.

BETH HAMEDRASH SHAAREI YOSHER INSTITUTE
Brooklyn, New York

Admissions Contact Mr. Menachem Steinberg, Director of Admissions, Beth HaMedrash Shaarei Yosher Institute, 4102-10 Sixteenth Avenue, Brooklyn, NY 11204. *Phone:* 718-854-2290.

BETH HATALMUD RABBINICAL COLLEGE
Brooklyn, New York

Admissions Contact Rabbi Osina, Director of Admissions, Beth Hatalmud Rabbinical College, 2127 Eighty-second Street, Brooklyn, NY 11214. *Phone:* 718-259-2525.

BORICUA COLLEGE
New York, New York

- **Independent** comprehensive, founded 1974
- **Calendar** 15-15-8
- **Degrees** associate, bachelor's, and master's
- **Urban** campus
- **Endowment** $50,000
- **Coed**
- **Moderately difficult** entrance level

Faculty *Student/faculty ratio:* 20:1.
Student Life *Campus security:* 24-hour emergency response devices.
Costs (2001–02) *Tuition:* $7350 full-time.
Financial Aid *Average percent of need met:* 80. *Average financial aid package:* $2650.
Applying *Options:* common application, deferred entrance. *Application fee:* $25. *Required:* high school transcript, 2 letters of recommendation, interview, proficiency in English and Spanish.
Admissions Contact Dr. Alicea Mercedes, Director of Registration and Assessment, Boricua College, 3755 Broadway, New York, NY 10032-1560. *Phone:* 212-694-1000 Ext. 525.

BRIARCLIFFE COLLEGE
Bethpage, New York

- **Proprietary** 4-year, founded 1966, part of Career Education Corporation
- **Calendar** semesters

Briarcliffe College (continued)

- **Degrees** diplomas, associate, and bachelor's
- **Suburban** 18-acre campus with easy access to New York City
- **Coed,** 2,608 undergraduate students, 81% full-time, 53% women, 47% men
- **Moderately difficult** entrance level, 65% of applicants were admitted

Undergraduates 2,108 full-time, 500 part-time. Students come from 10 states and territories, 7 other countries, 0% are from out of state, 6% African American, 1% Asian American or Pacific Islander, 7% Hispanic American, 1% Native American, 0.7% international, 10% transferred in. *Retention:* 75% of 2001 full-time freshmen returned.

Freshmen *Admission:* 1,334 applied, 867 admitted, 617 enrolled. *Average high school GPA:* 2.5.

Faculty *Total:* 160, 31% full-time, 22% with terminal degrees. *Student/faculty ratio:* 14:1.

Majors Business; business administration; computer programming; electrical/electronic engineering technology; fine/studio arts; graphic design/commercial art/illustration; information sciences/systems; paralegal/legal assistant; secretarial science; telecommunications.

Academic Programs *Special study options:* academic remediation for entering students, accelerated degree program, adult/continuing education programs, advanced placement credit, cooperative education, distance learning, external degree program, independent study, internships, part-time degree program, services for LD students, summer session for credit.

Library Briarcliffe Library with 11,834 titles, 191 serial subscriptions.

Computers on Campus 350 computers available on campus for general student use. Internet access, at least one staffed computer lab available.

Student Life *Housing:* college housing not available. *Activities and Organizations:* student-run newspaper, radio station, Student Government Association, Telecommunication Club, Graphic Design Club, Law Club. *Campus security:* late-night transport/escort service. *Student Services:* personal/psychological counseling.

Athletics Member NJCAA. *Intercollegiate sports:* baseball M(s), bowling M(s)/W(s), soccer W(s), softball W(s). *Intramural sports:* football M/W, tennis M/W, volleyball M/W.

Standardized Tests *Recommended:* SAT I and SAT II or ACT (for admission).

Costs (2001–02) *Tuition:* $10,800 full-time, $450 per credit part-time. Full-time tuition and fees vary according to course load. Part-time tuition and fees vary according to course load. *Required fees:* $600 full-time, $325 per term part-time. *Payment plans:* installment, deferred payment. *Waivers:* senior citizens and employees or children of employees.

Financial Aid Of all full-time matriculated undergraduates who enrolled in 2001, 54 Federal Work-Study jobs (averaging $1565).

Applying *Options:* electronic application, deferred entrance. *Application fee:* $35. *Required:* high school transcript, interview. *Application deadline:* rolling (freshmen), rolling (transfers). *Notification:* continuous (freshmen).

Admissions Contact Ms. Theresa Donohue, Dean of Marketing and Admissions, Briarcliffe College, Bethpage, NY 11714. *Phone:* 516-918-3705. *Toll-free phone:* 888-333-1150. *Fax:* 516-470-6020. *E-mail:* info@bcl.edu.

BROOKLYN COLLEGE OF THE CITY UNIVERSITY OF NEW YORK

Brooklyn, New York

- **State and locally supported** comprehensive, founded 1930, part of City University of New York System
- **Calendar** semesters
- **Degrees** bachelor's, master's, and post-master's certificates
- **Urban** 26-acre campus
- **Endowment** $27.2 million
- **Coed,** 10,112 undergraduate students, 66% full-time, 62% women, 38% men
- **Moderately difficult** entrance level, 49% of applicants were admitted

Undergraduates 6,717 full-time, 3,395 part-time. Students come from 20 states and territories, 65 other countries, 5% are from out of state, 29% African American, 9% Asian American or Pacific Islander, 10% Hispanic American, 0.0% Native American, 5% international, 11% transferred in. *Retention:* 82% of 2001 full-time freshmen returned.

Freshmen *Admission:* 4,546 applied, 2,249 admitted, 1,080 enrolled. *Average high school GPA:* 2.93. *Test scores:* SAT verbal scores over 500: 50%; SAT math scores over 500: 60%; SAT verbal scores over 600: 15%; SAT math scores over 600: 18%; SAT verbal scores over 700: 2%; SAT math scores over 700: 3%.

Faculty *Total:* 935, 53% full-time, 60% with terminal degrees. *Student/faculty ratio:* 13:1.

Majors Accounting; African studies; American studies; anthropology; art; art education; art history; bilingual/bicultural education; biology; broadcast journalism; business administration; chemistry; classics; comparative literature; computer/information sciences; computer science; creative writing; early childhood education; earth sciences; economics; education; elementary education; English; film studies; French; geology; German; Greek (modern); health science; history; interdisciplinary studies; Italian; journalism; Judaic studies; Latin (ancient and medieval); linguistics; mathematics; modern languages; music; music teacher education; nutrition science; philosophy; physical education; physics; political science; psychology; radio/television broadcasting; religious studies; Russian; secondary education; sociology; Spanish; speech-language pathology/audiology; speech/rhetorical studies; theater arts/drama; women's studies.

Academic Programs *Special study options:* adult/continuing education programs, advanced placement credit, distance learning, double majors, English as a second language, freshman honors college, honors programs, independent study, internships, off-campus study, part-time degree program, services for LD students, study abroad, summer session for credit. *ROTC:* Army (b), Navy (b), Air Force (b). *Unusual degree programs:* 3-2 engineering with City College of the City University of New York, Polytechnic University, College of Staten Island of the City University of New York.

Library Brooklyn College Library plus 1 other with 1.3 million titles, 13,500 serial subscriptions, 21,731 audiovisual materials, an OPAC, a Web page.

Computers on Campus 600 computers available on campus for general student use. A campuswide network can be accessed from off campus. Internet access, online (class) registration, at least one staffed computer lab available.

Student Life *Housing:* college housing not available. *Activities and Organizations:* drama/theater group, student-run newspaper, radio and television station, choral group, Academic Club Association, Kingsman and Excelsior Newspaper, NY Public Interest Group (NYPIRG), Student Government CIAS, SGS, and GSO, Student Forensics, national fraternities, national sororities. *Campus security:* 24-hour emergency response devices and patrols, late-night transport/escort service. *Student Services:* health clinic, personal/psychological counseling, women's center, legal services.

Athletics Member NCAA. All Division III. *Intercollegiate sports:* basketball M/W, cross-country running M/W, soccer M, softball W, swimming M/W, tennis M/W, track and field M/W, volleyball M/W. *Intramural sports:* basketball M/W, football M/W, racquetball M/W, softball M/W, swimming M/W, tennis M/W, volleyball M/W.

Standardized Tests *Required:* SAT I or ACT (for admission).

Costs (2001–02) *One-time required fee:* $55. *Tuition:* state resident $3200 full-time, $135 per credit part-time; nonresident $6800 full-time, $285 per credit part-time. Full-time tuition and fees vary according to class time and course load. Part-time tuition and fees vary according to class time and course load. *Required fees:* $193 full-time, $97 per term part-time. *Payment plan:* installment. *Waivers:* senior citizens.

Financial Aid Of all full-time matriculated undergraduates who enrolled in 2001, 5640 applied for aid, 5430 were judged to have need, 5319 had their need fully met. In 2001, 651 non-need-based awards were made. *Average percent of need met:* 99%. *Average financial aid package:* $4615. *Average need-based loan:* $2496. *Average need-based gift aid:* $2800. *Average non-need based aid:* $1700. *Average indebtedness upon graduation:* $13,000.

Applying *Options:* common application, early admission, deferred entrance. *Application fee:* $40. *Required:* high school transcript, minimum 3.0 GPA. *Required for some:* essay or personal statement, letters of recommendation, interview. *Application deadline:* rolling (freshmen), rolling (transfers). *Notification:* continuous (freshmen).

Admissions Contact Ms. Celia Adams, Admissions Counselor/Recruiter, Brooklyn College of the City University of New York, 2900 Bedford Avenue, 1203 Plaza, Brooklyn, NY 11210-2889. *Phone:* 718-951-5001. *Fax:* 718-951-4506. *E-mail:* admissions@brooklyn.cuny.edu.

CANISIUS COLLEGE

Buffalo, New York

- **Independent Roman Catholic (Jesuit)** comprehensive, founded 1870
- **Calendar** semesters
- **Degrees** certificates, associate, bachelor's, and master's
- **Urban** 26-acre campus
- **Endowment** $52.1 million
- **Coed,** 3,378 undergraduate students, 88% full-time, 53% women, 47% men
- **Moderately difficult** entrance level, 81% of applicants were admitted

Undergraduates 2,985 full-time, 393 part-time. Students come from 33 states and territories, 26 other countries, 7% are from out of state, 5% transferred in, 37% live on campus. *Retention:* 81% of 2001 full-time freshmen returned.

Freshmen *Admission:* 3,276 applied, 2,650 admitted, 719 enrolled. *Average high school GPA:* 3.38. *Test scores:* SAT verbal scores over 500: 69%; SAT math scores over 500: 74%; ACT scores over 18: 92%; SAT verbal scores over 600: 23%; SAT math scores over 600: 28%; ACT scores over 24: 46%; SAT verbal scores over 700: 2%; SAT math scores over 700: 3%; ACT scores over 30: 10%.

Faculty *Total:* 465, 45% full-time, 62% with terminal degrees. *Student/faculty ratio:* 16:1.

Majors Accounting; accounting related; anthropology; art history; athletic training/sports medicine; biochemistry; biological sciences/life sciences related; biology; biology education; business administration; business education; business marketing and marketing management; chemistry; chemistry education; computer science; criminal justice/law enforcement administration; design/visual communications; economics; education; elementary education; English; English education; entrepreneurship; environmental science; European studies; finance; French; French language education; German; German language education; history; humanities; international relations; liberal arts and sciences/liberal studies; management information systems/business data processing; mass communications; mathematics; mathematics education; medical technology; middle school education; philosophy; physical education; physics; physics education; political science; psychology; public administration; religious studies; science education; secondary education; social sciences; social studies education; sociology; Spanish; Spanish language education; special education; urban studies.

Academic Programs *Special study options:* academic remediation for entering students, advanced placement credit, English as a second language, external degree program, honors programs, independent study, internships, off-campus study, part-time degree program, services for LD students, student-designed majors, study abroad, summer session for credit. *ROTC:* Army (b). *Unusual degree programs:* 3-2 engineering with State University of New York at Buffalo, Cornell University, Clarkson University, Rensselaer Polytechnic Institute.

Library Andrew L. Bouwhuis Library plus 1 other with 318,789 titles, 9,637 serial subscriptions, 7,357 audiovisual materials, an OPAC, a Web page.

Computers on Campus 208 computers available on campus for general student use. A campuswide network can be accessed from student residence rooms and from off campus. Internet access, online (class) registration, at least one staffed computer lab available.

Student Life *Housing Options:* coed. *Activities and Organizations:* drama/theater group, student-run newspaper, radio station, choral group, Campus Programming Board, Undergraduate Student Association, Afro-American Society, Residence Hall Association, Student Association, national fraternities, national sororities. *Campus security:* 24-hour emergency response devices and patrols, late-night transport/escort service, controlled dormitory access, crime prevention programs, closed-circuit television monitors. *Student Services:* health clinic, personal/psychological counseling.

Athletics Member NCAA. All Division I except football (Division I-AA). *Intercollegiate sports:* baseball M(s), basketball M(s)/W(s), bowling M(c)/W(c), crew M(c)/W(c), cross-country running M(s)/W(s), golf M(s), ice hockey M(s), lacrosse M(s)/W, riflery M(s)/W(s), rugby M(c), soccer M(s)/W(s), softball W(s), swimming W(s), tennis M(s)/W(s), track and field M(s)/W(s), volleyball M(c)/W(s). *Intramural sports:* basketball M/W, field hockey W, racquetball M/W, soccer M/W, softball M(c)/W(c), tennis M/W, volleyball M/W.

Standardized Tests *Required:* SAT I or ACT (for admission).

Costs (2001–02) *Comprehensive fee:* $24,696 includes full-time tuition ($16,990), mandatory fees ($546), and room and board ($7160). Part-time tuition: $484 per credit. *Required fees:* $17 per credit, $18 per term part-time. *Room and board:* Room and board charges vary according to board plan, housing facility, and student level. *Payment plans:* installment, deferred payment. *Waivers:* employees or children of employees.

Financial Aid Of all full-time matriculated undergraduates who enrolled in 2001, 2454 applied for aid, 2120 were judged to have need, 732 had their need fully met. 530 Federal Work-Study jobs. In 2001, 542 non-need-based awards were made. *Average percent of need met:* 82%. *Average financial aid package:* $14,905. *Average need-based loan:* $3994. *Average need-based gift aid:* $10,179. *Average indebtedness upon graduation:* $19,782.

Applying *Options:* common application, electronic application, early admission, deferred entrance. *Application fee:* $25. *Required:* high school transcript. *Required for some:* interview. *Recommended:* essay or personal statement, letters of recommendation, interview. *Application deadline:* rolling (freshmen), rolling (transfers). *Notification:* continuous (freshmen).

Admissions Contact Miss Penelope H. Lips, Director of Admissions, Canisius College, 2001 Main Street, Buffalo, NY 14208-1098. *Phone:* 716-888-2200. *Toll-free phone:* 800-843-1517. *Fax:* 716-888-3230. *E-mail:* inquiry@canisius.edu.

CAZENOVIA COLLEGE
Cazenovia, New York

- **Independent** 4-year, founded 1824
- **Calendar** semesters
- **Degrees** associate and bachelor's
- **Small-town** 40-acre campus with easy access to Syracuse
- **Endowment** $46.5 million
- **Coed,** 913 undergraduate students, 81% full-time, 71% women, 29% men
- **Minimally difficult** entrance level, 86% of applicants were admitted

Campus improvements in 2001 included the creation of a new fitness center and major renovations to the college theater and Farber Residence Hall. A $4 million, 24,000-square-foot art and design center will be built in 2002-03. The College also announced an academic achievement scholarship program, with awards ranging from $8000 to full tuition.

Undergraduates 739 full-time, 174 part-time. Students come from 17 states and territories, 2 other countries, 14% are from out of state, 6% African American, 0.5% Asian American or Pacific Islander, 4% Hispanic American, 0.8% Native American, 0.5% international, 6% transferred in, 71% live on campus. *Retention:* 67% of 2001 full-time freshmen returned.

Freshmen *Admission:* 978 applied, 840 admitted, 244 enrolled. *Average high school GPA:* 2.80. *Test scores:* SAT verbal scores over 500: 29%; SAT math scores over 500: 26%; ACT scores over 18: 61%; SAT verbal scores over 600: 7%; SAT math scores over 600: 2%; ACT scores over 24: 6%; SAT verbal scores over 700: 1%.

Faculty *Total:* 85, 52% full-time, 74% with terminal degrees. *Student/faculty ratio:* 15:1.

Majors Accounting; business administration; community services; criminal justice studies; design/visual communications; early childhood education; English; equestrian studies; fashion design/illustration; fine/studio arts; human services; interior design; liberal arts and sciences/liberal studies; literature; photography; psychology; social sciences; sport/fitness administration; visual/performing arts.

Academic Programs *Special study options:* academic remediation for entering students, adult/continuing education programs, advanced placement credit, cooperative education, distance learning, honors programs, independent study, internships, off-campus study, part-time degree program, services for LD students, student-designed majors, study abroad, summer session for credit. *ROTC:* Army (c).

Library Witheral Library with 61,694 titles, 526 serial subscriptions, an OPAC, a Web page.

Computers on Campus 140 computers available on campus for general student use. A campuswide network can be accessed from student residence rooms and from off campus. Internet access, at least one staffed computer lab available.

Student Life *Housing:* on-campus residence required through sophomore year. *Options:* coed. *Activities and Organizations:* drama/theater group, student-run newspaper, radio station, Activities Board, Multicultural Student Group, performing arts, student radio station, yearbook. *Campus security:* 24-hour emergency response devices and patrols, late-night transport/escort service, controlled dormitory access. *Student Services:* health clinic, personal/psychological counseling, women's center.

Athletics Member NCAA. *Intercollegiate sports:* baseball M, basketball M/W, crew M/W, equestrian sports M/W, golf M, soccer W, softball W, volleyball W. *Intramural sports:* basketball M/W, bowling M/W, football M, racquetball M/W, soccer W, swimming M/W, volleyball M/W, weight lifting M/W.

Standardized Tests *Recommended:* SAT I and SAT II or ACT (for admission).

Costs (2001–02) *One-time required fee:* $110. *Comprehensive fee:* $19,895 includes full-time tuition ($13,150), mandatory fees ($245), and room and board ($6500). Part-time tuition: $318 per credit. Part-time tuition and fees vary according to class time and course load. *Room and board:* College room only: $3500. Room and board charges vary according to board plan. *Payment plan:* installment. *Waivers:* employees or children of employees.

Financial Aid Of all full-time matriculated undergraduates who enrolled in 2001, 701 applied for aid, 622 were judged to have need, 180 had their need fully met. 150 Federal Work-Study jobs (averaging $1000). In 2001, 103 non-need-based awards were made. *Average percent of need met:* 80%. *Average financial aid package:* $13,050. *Average need-based loan:* $2927. *Average need-based gift aid:* $9512. *Average non-need based aid:* $3145. *Average indebtedness upon graduation:* $14,808.

Applying *Options:* common application, early admission, deferred entrance. *Application fee:* $25. *Required:* high school transcript. *Application deadline:* rolling (freshmen), rolling (transfers). *Notification:* continuous (freshmen).

Cazenovia College (continued)

Admissions Contact Mr. Robert A. Croot, Dean for Enrollment Management, Cazenovia College, Cazenovia, NY 13035. *Phone:* 315-655-7208. *Toll-free phone:* 800-654-3210. *Fax:* 315-655-4860. *E-mail:* admission@cazcollege.edu.

CENTRAL YESHIVA TOMCHEI TMIMIM-LUBAVITCH

Brooklyn, New York

Admissions Contact Moses Gluckowsky, Director of Admissions, Central Yeshiva Tomchei Tmimim-Lubavitch, 841-853 Ocean Parkway, Brooklyn, NY 11230. *Phone:* 718-859-7600.

CITY COLLEGE OF THE CITY UNIVERSITY OF NEW YORK

New York, New York

- **State and locally supported** university, founded 1847, part of City University of New York System
- **Calendar** semesters
- **Degrees** bachelor's, master's, first professional, and post-master's certificates
- **Urban** 35-acre campus
- **Coed,** 8,408 undergraduate students, 60% full-time, 52% women, 48% men
- **Moderately difficult** entrance level, 42% of applicants were admitted

For more than 150 years, the City College of New York (CUNY) has provided an excellent higher education to generations of New Yorkers. City College offers degree programs in architecture, the arts, biomedical education, computer science, education, engineering, humanities, sciences, and social sciences. Conveniently located in New York City, students can take advantage of an environment that is diverse, politically and socially active, and artistically and intellectually stimulating. For more information, students can visit the Web site at http://www.ccny.cuny.edu.

Undergraduates 5,023 full-time, 3,385 part-time. Students come from 52 states and territories, 80 other countries, 28% African American, 12% Asian American or Pacific Islander, 26% Hispanic American, 0.3% Native American, 6% international. *Retention:* 80% of 2001 full-time freshmen returned.

Freshmen *Admission:* 3,651 applied, 1,536 admitted, 735 enrolled. *Test scores:* SAT verbal scores over 500: 41%; SAT math scores over 500: 57%; SAT verbal scores over 600: 14%; SAT math scores over 600: 24%; SAT verbal scores over 700: 2%; SAT math scores over 700: 7%.

Faculty *Total:* 902, 52% full-time. *Student/faculty ratio:* 15:1.

Majors African-American studies; anthropology; architecture; art; art education; art history; Asian studies; biochemistry; biology; biomedical science; business administration; chemical engineering; chemistry; civil engineering; computer science; creative writing; early childhood education; earth sciences; economics; education; electrical engineering; elementary education; English; film/video production; French; geography; geology; history; international relations; Italian; Judaic studies; landscape architecture; Latin American studies; linguistics; literature; mass communications; mathematics; mechanical engineering; music; music teacher education; philosophy; physician assistant; physics; political science; pre-dentistry; pre-law; pre-medicine; pre-veterinary studies; psychology; reading education; romance languages; secondary education; sociology; Spanish; special education; theater arts/drama; women's studies.

Academic Programs *Special study options:* academic remediation for entering students, accelerated degree program, adult/continuing education programs, advanced placement credit, cooperative education, English as a second language, freshman honors college, honors programs, independent study, internships, off-campus study, part-time degree program, services for LD students, student-designed majors, study abroad, summer session for credit. *ROTC:* Army (c), Air Force (c).

Library Morris Raphael Cohen Library plus 3 others with 1.4 million titles, 2,207 serial subscriptions, 19,586 audiovisual materials, an OPAC, a Web page.

Computers on Campus 3000 computers available on campus for general student use. A campuswide network can be accessed from off campus. Internet access, at least one staffed computer lab available.

Student Life *Housing:* college housing not available. *Activities and Organizations:* drama/theater group, student-run newspaper, radio station, national fraternities. *Campus security:* 24-hour patrols. *Student Services:* health clinic, personal/psychological counseling.

Athletics Member NCAA. All Division III. *Intercollegiate sports:* basketball M/W, cross-country running M/W, fencing W, lacrosse M, soccer M, softball W, tennis M/W, track and field M/W, volleyball W. *Intramural sports:* basketball M/W, fencing W, soccer M, softball W, tennis M/W, track and field M/W, volleyball M/W.

Standardized Tests *Required:* SAT I or ACT (for admission). *Required for some:* SAT I or ACT (for placement).

Costs (2001–02) *Tuition:* state resident $3200 full-time, $135 per credit part-time; nonresident $6800 full-time, $285 per credit part-time. Full-time tuition and fees vary according to class time and program. Part-time tuition and fees vary according to class time and program. *Required fees:* $38 per term part-time. *Payment plan:* deferred payment.

Financial Aid Of all full-time matriculated undergraduates who enrolled in 2001, 4213 applied for aid, 4002 were judged to have need, 406 had their need fully met. In 2001, 350 non-need-based awards were made. *Average percent of need met:* 75%. *Average financial aid package:* $5102. *Average need-based loan:* $1713. *Average need-based gift aid:* $4618. *Average non-need based aid:* $2400. *Average indebtedness upon graduation:* $16,800.

Applying *Options:* early admission, deferred entrance. *Application fee:* $40. *Required:* high school transcript. *Application deadline:* rolling (freshmen), rolling (transfers). *Notification:* continuous until 8/15 (freshmen).

Admissions Contact Mr. Thomas F. Sabia, Acting Director of Admissions, City College of the City University of New York, Convent Avenue at 138th Street, New York, NY 10031-9198. *Phone:* 212-650-6977. *Fax:* 212-650-6417. *E-mail:* admissions@ccny.cuny.edu.

CLARKSON UNIVERSITY

Potsdam, New York

- **Independent** university, founded 1896
- **Calendar** semesters
- **Degrees** bachelor's, master's, and doctoral
- **Small-town** 640-acre campus
- **Endowment** $93.4 million
- **Coed,** 2,610 undergraduate students, 99% full-time, 25% women, 75% men
- **Very difficult** entrance level, 81% of applicants were admitted

Undergraduates 2,579 full-time, 31 part-time. Students come from 41 states and territories, 35 other countries, 24% are from out of state, 2% African American, 3% Asian American or Pacific Islander, 1% Hispanic American, 0.8% Native American, 4% international, 3% transferred in, 70% live on campus. *Retention:* 87% of 2001 full-time freshmen returned.

Freshmen *Admission:* 2,584 applied, 2,082 admitted, 724 enrolled. *Average high school GPA:* 3.47. *Test scores:* SAT verbal scores over 500: 84%; SAT math scores over 500: 95%; SAT verbal scores over 600: 38%; SAT math scores over 600: 61%; SAT verbal scores over 700: 7%; SAT math scores over 700: 13%.

Faculty *Total:* 185, 89% full-time, 84% with terminal degrees. *Student/faculty ratio:* 17:1.

Majors Accounting; aerospace engineering; applied mathematics; biochemistry; biology; biophysics; biotechnology research; business administration; business economics; business marketing and marketing management; cell biology; chemical engineering; chemistry; civil engineering; communications; computer engineering; computer/information sciences; computer science; computer software engineering; economics; electrical engineering; engineering; entrepreneurship; environmental engineering; environmental health; environmental science; finance; history; humanities; human resources management; industrial/manufacturing engineering; interdisciplinary studies; liberal arts and sciences/liberal studies; management information systems/business data processing; materials engineering; materials science; mathematics; mechanical engineering; molecular biology; operations management; organizational psychology; physics; political science; pre-law; pre-medicine; pre-veterinary studies; psychology; social sciences; sociology; structural engineering; technical/business writing; toxicology.

Academic Programs *Special study options:* accelerated degree program, advanced placement credit, cooperative education, double majors, English as a second language, honors programs, independent study, internships, off-campus study, part-time degree program, services for LD students, student-designed majors, study abroad, summer session for credit. *ROTC:* Army (b), Air Force (b).

Library Andrew S. Schuler Educational Resources Center with 235,876 titles, 845 serial subscriptions, 3,730 audiovisual materials, an OPAC, a Web page.

Computers on Campus 250 computers available on campus for general student use. A campuswide network can be accessed from student residence rooms and from off campus. Internet access available.

Student Life *Housing:* on-campus residence required through senior year. *Options:* coed, men-only, women-only. *Activities and Organizations:* drama/theater group, student-run newspaper, radio and television station, Outing Club,

Auto Club, CUB, Pep Band, Men's Rugby, national fraternities, national sororities. *Campus security:* 24-hour emergency response devices and patrols, late-night transport/escort service, controlled dormitory access. *Student Services:* health clinic, personal/psychological counseling, legal services.

Athletics Member NCAA. All Division III except ice hockey (Division I). *Intercollegiate sports:* baseball M, basketball M/W, cross-country running M/W, golf M, ice hockey M(s)/W(c), lacrosse M/W, rugby M(c)/W(c), skiing (cross-country) M/W, skiing (downhill) M/W, soccer M/W, swimming M/W, tennis M/W, volleyball W. *Intramural sports:* basketball M/W, football M, ice hockey M/W, lacrosse M/W, racquetball M/W, soccer M/W, softball M/W, tennis M/W, volleyball M/W, water polo M/W.

Standardized Tests *Required:* SAT I or ACT (for admission). *Recommended:* SAT II: Subject Tests (for admission).

Costs (2002–03) *Comprehensive fee:* $31,033 includes full-time tuition ($22,235), mandatory fees ($400), and room and board ($8398). Full-time tuition and fees vary according to course load. Part-time tuition: $742 per credit. Part-time tuition and fees vary according to course load. *Room and board:* College room only: $4378. Room and board charges vary according to housing facility. *Payment plan:* installment. *Waivers:* employees or children of employees.

Financial Aid Of all full-time matriculated undergraduates who enrolled in 2001, 2299 applied for aid, 2184 were judged to have need, 546 had their need fully met. 678 Federal Work-Study jobs. In 2001, 255 non-need-based awards were made. *Average percent of need met:* 88%. *Average financial aid package:* $10,904. *Average need-based loan:* $7000. *Average need-based gift aid:* $10,095. *Average non-need based aid:* $5250. *Average indebtedness upon graduation:* $17,809.

Applying *Options:* common application, early admission, early decision, deferred entrance. *Application fee:* $30. *Required:* high school transcript, 1 letter of recommendation. *Recommended:* interview. *Application deadline:* 3/15 (freshmen), rolling (transfers). *Early decision:* 12/1 (for plan 1), 1/15 (for plan 2). *Notification:* continuous (freshmen), 12/15 (early decision plan 1), 2/1 (early decision plan 2).

Admissions Contact Mr. Brian T. Grant, Director of Enrollment Operations, Clarkson University, Holcroft House, Potsdam, NY 13699. *Phone:* 315-268-6479. *Toll-free phone:* 800-527-6577. *Fax:* 315-268-7647. *E-mail:* admission@clarkson.edu.

COLGATE UNIVERSITY
Hamilton, New York

- **Independent** comprehensive, founded 1819
- **Calendar** semesters
- **Degrees** bachelor's and master's
- **Rural** 515-acre campus
- **Endowment** $464.5 million
- **Coed,** 2,781 undergraduate students, 100% full-time, 51% women, 49% men
- **Very difficult** entrance level, 37% of applicants were admitted

Undergraduates 2,774 full-time, 7 part-time. Students come from 48 states and territories, 27 other countries, 69% are from out of state, 0.8% transferred in, 89% live on campus. *Retention:* 97% of 2001 full-time freshmen returned.

Freshmen *Admission:* 6,059 applied, 2,238 admitted, 740 enrolled. *Average high school GPA:* 3.61. *Test scores:* SAT verbal scores over 500: 97%; SAT math scores over 500: 98%; ACT scores over 18: 100%; SAT verbal scores over 600: 81%; SAT math scores over 600: 87%; ACT scores over 24: 93%; SAT verbal scores over 700: 28%; SAT math scores over 700: 32%; ACT scores over 30: 58%.

Faculty *Total:* 291, 81% full-time, 91% with terminal degrees. *Student/faculty ratio:* 11:1.

Majors African-American studies; African studies; anthropology; art; art history; Asian studies; astronomy; astrophysics; biochemistry; biology; chemistry; Chinese; classics; computer science; East Asian studies; economics; education; English; environmental biology; environmental science; French; geography; geology; German; Greek (modern); history; humanities; international relations; Japanese; Latin American studies; Latin (ancient and medieval); mathematics; molecular biology; music; Native American studies; natural sciences; neuroscience; peace/conflict studies; philosophy; physical sciences; physics; political science; psychology; religious studies; romance languages; Russian; Russian/Slavic studies; social sciences; sociology; Spanish; theater arts/drama; women's studies.

Academic Programs *Special study options:* advanced placement credit, double majors, honors programs, independent study, off-campus study, services for LD students, student-designed majors, study abroad. *ROTC:* Army (c). *Unusual degree programs:* 3-2 engineering with Rensselaer Polytechnic Institute, Columbia University, Washington University in St. Louis.

Library Everett Needham Case Library plus 1 other with 634,874 titles, 2,314 serial subscriptions, 8,091 audiovisual materials, an OPAC, a Web page.

Computers on Campus 577 computers available on campus for general student use. A campuswide network can be accessed from student residence rooms and from off campus that provide access to software applications. Internet access, online (class) registration, at least one staffed computer lab available.

Student Life *Housing:* on-campus residence required through sophomore year. *Options:* coed. *Activities and Organizations:* drama/theater group, student-run newspaper, radio and television station, choral group, marching band, Volunteer Colgate, student government, cultural/ethnic interest groups, student publications, performance groups, national fraternities, national sororities. *Campus security:* 24-hour emergency response devices and patrols, student patrols, late-night transport/escort service, controlled dormitory access. *Student Services:* health clinic, personal/psychological counseling, women's center, legal services.

Athletics Member NCAA. All Division I except football (Division I-AA). *Intercollegiate sports:* baseball M(c), basketball M/W, crew M/W, cross-country running M/W, equestrian sports M(c)/W(c), fencing M(c)/W(c), field hockey W, golf M/W(c), ice hockey M/W, lacrosse M/W, rugby M(c)/W(c), sailing M(c)/W(c), skiing (downhill) M(c)/W(c), soccer M/W, softball W, squash M(c)/W(c), swimming M/W, tennis M/W, track and field M/W, volleyball M(c)/W, water polo M(c)/W(c), wrestling M(c)/W(c). *Intramural sports:* basketball M/W, bowling M/W, football M/W, golf M/W, ice hockey M/W, racquetball M/W, riflery M/W, soccer M/W, softball M/W, squash M/W, tennis M/W, volleyball M/W.

Costs (2001–02) *Comprehensive fee:* $33,480 includes full-time tuition ($26,845), mandatory fees ($180), and room and board ($6455). Full-time tuition and fees vary according to course load. Part-time tuition: $3355 per course. Part-time tuition and fees vary according to course load. *Room and board:* College room only: $3115. Room and board charges vary according to board plan and housing facility. *Payment plans:* tuition prepayment, installment, deferred payment. *Waivers:* employees or children of employees.

Financial Aid Of all full-time matriculated undergraduates who enrolled in 2001, 1217 applied for aid, 1152 were judged to have need, 1152 had their need fully met. 743 Federal Work-Study jobs (averaging $1328). *Average percent of need met:* 100%. *Average financial aid package:* $22,950. *Average need-based loan:* $3348. *Average need-based gift aid:* $20,589. *Average indebtedness upon graduation:* $12,822. *Financial aid deadline:* 2/1.

Applying *Options:* common application, electronic application, early decision, deferred entrance. *Application fee:* $50. *Required:* essay or personal statement, high school transcript, 3 letters of recommendation. *Application deadlines:* 1/15 (freshmen), 3/1 (transfers). *Early decision:* 11/15 (for plan 1), 1/15 (for plan 2). *Notification:* 4/1 (freshmen), 12/15 (early decision plan 1), 2/15 (early decision plan 2).

Admissions Contact Mr. Gary L. Ross, Dean of Admission, Colgate University, 13 Oak Drive, Hamilton, NY 13346-1383. *Phone:* 315-228-7401. *Fax:* 315-228-7544. *E-mail:* admission@mail.colgate.edu.

COLLEGE OF AERONAUTICS
Flushing, New York

- **Independent** 4-year, founded 1932
- **Calendar** semesters
- **Degrees** associate and bachelor's
- **Urban** 6-acre campus
- **Endowment** $39.5 million
- **Coed, primarily men,** 1,384 undergraduate students, 75% full-time, 9% women, 91% men
- **Minimally difficult** entrance level, 57% of applicants were admitted

Undergraduates 1,036 full-time, 348 part-time. Students come from 10 states and territories, 15 other countries, 6% are from out of state, 20% African American, 13% Asian American or Pacific Islander, 36% Hispanic American, 5% international, 5% transferred in. *Retention:* 67% of 2001 full-time freshmen returned.

Freshmen *Admission:* 1,056 applied, 604 admitted, 341 enrolled. *Average high school GPA:* 2.8.

Faculty *Total:* 60, 87% full-time. *Student/faculty ratio:* 11:1.

Majors Aerospace science; aircraft mechanic/airframe; aircraft pilot (professional); aviation management; aviation technology; computer graphics; engineering technology; machine technology; pre-engineering.

Academic Programs *Special study options:* academic remediation for entering students, adult/continuing education programs, advanced placement credit, cooperative education, distance learning, internships, part-time degree program, services for LD students, summer session for credit. *ROTC:* Army (c), Air Force (c).

Library George A. Vaughn Memorial Library with 62,000 titles, 400 serial subscriptions, an OPAC.

College of Aeronautics (continued)

Computers on Campus 85 computers available on campus for general student use. At least one staffed computer lab available.

Student Life *Activities and Organizations:* student-run newspaper, Hispanic Society of Aeronautical Engineers, student government, Women in Aviation International, Society of Automotive Engineers, American Association of Airport Executives. *Campus security:* 24-hour emergency response devices and patrols. *Student Services:* personal/psychological counseling.

Athletics *Intramural sports:* basketball M/W, football M/W, soccer M/W, softball M/W, volleyball M/W, weight lifting M/W.

Standardized Tests *Required for some:* SAT I (for admission).

Costs (2002–03) *Tuition:* $9000 full-time, $325 per credit part-time. Full-time tuition and fees vary according to program. *Required fees:* $250 full-time, $125 per term part-time. *Payment plan:* installment.

Financial Aid Of all full-time matriculated undergraduates who enrolled in 2001, 941 applied for aid, 780 were judged to have need, 277 had their need fully met. In 2001, 157 non-need-based awards were made. *Average percent of need met:* 50%. *Average financial aid package:* $13,553. *Average need-based loan:* $2625. *Average need-based gift aid:* $500. *Average non-need based aid:* $1250. *Average indebtedness upon graduation:* $12,000.

Applying *Options:* deferred entrance. *Application fee:* $25. *Required:* high school transcript, minimum 2.0 GPA. *Required for some:* interview. *Recommended:* interview. *Application deadline:* rolling (freshmen), rolling (transfers).

Admissions Contact Thomas Bracken, Associate Director, Admissions, College of Aeronautics, La Guardia Airport, 86-01 23rd Avenue, Flushing, NY 11369. *Phone:* 718-429-6600 Ext. 167. *Toll-free phone:* 800-776-2376. *Fax:* 718-429-0256. *E-mail:* admissions@aero.edu.

COLLEGE OF MOUNT SAINT VINCENT

Riverdale, New York

- **Independent** comprehensive, founded 1911
- **Calendar** semesters
- **Degrees** certificates, associate, bachelor's, master's, and post-master's certificates
- **Suburban** 70-acre campus with easy access to New York City
- **Endowment** $3.4 million
- **Coed,** 1,161 undergraduate students, 80% full-time, 78% women, 22% men
- **Moderately difficult** entrance level, 70% of applicants were admitted

The College has 26 majors and 10 programs of study, including business, education, health sciences, and liberal arts. The Mount Saint Vincent internship program offers more than 500 opportunities annually within corporations in the New York metropolitan area. Internships are available in every major. World Wide Web: http://www.cmsv.edu.

Undergraduates 933 full-time, 228 part-time. Students come from 13 states and territories, 5 other countries, 4% are from out of state, 17% African American, 9% Asian American or Pacific Islander, 33% Hispanic American, 2% international, 3% transferred in, 53% live on campus. *Retention:* 82% of 2001 full-time freshmen returned.

Freshmen *Admission:* 1,181 applied, 825 admitted, 288 enrolled. *Test scores:* SAT verbal scores over 500: 41%; SAT math scores over 500: 41%; SAT verbal scores over 600: 9%; SAT math scores over 600: 5%; SAT verbal scores over 700: 1%.

Faculty *Total:* 146, 48% full-time, 54% with terminal degrees. *Student/faculty ratio:* 12:1.

Majors Biochemistry; biology; business administration; business economics; chemistry; computer science; economics; education; elementary education; English; exercise sciences; French; health education; health facilities administration; health science; history; interdisciplinary studies; liberal arts and sciences/liberal studies; mass communications; mathematics; middle school education; modern languages; nursing; philosophy; physical education; physics; pre-dentistry; pre-law; pre-medicine; psychology; religious studies; science education; secondary education; social sciences; sociology; Spanish; special education; urban studies.

Academic Programs *Special study options:* academic remediation for entering students, accelerated degree program, adult/continuing education programs, advanced placement credit, double majors, English as a second language, freshman honors college, honors programs, independent study, internships, off-campus study, part-time degree program, student-designed majors, study abroad, summer session for credit. *ROTC:* Army (c), Air Force (c). *Unusual degree programs:* 3-2 engineering with Manhattan College; occupational therapy with Columbia University, physical therapy with New York Medical College.

Library Elizabeth Seton Library with 169,529 titles, 616 serial subscriptions, 6,642 audiovisual materials, an OPAC, a Web page.

Computers on Campus 150 computers available on campus for general student use. A campuswide network can be accessed from student residence rooms and from off campus that provide access to e-mail. At least one staffed computer lab available.

Student Life *Housing Options:* coed, women-only. *Activities and Organizations:* drama/theater group, student-run newspaper, radio and television station, choral group, Latino Club, Players, Dance Club, Student Nurse Association, Black Student Union. *Campus security:* 24-hour emergency response devices and patrols, late-night transport/escort service, controlled dormitory access, emergency call boxes. *Student Services:* health clinic, personal/psychological counseling.

Athletics Member NCAA. All Division III. *Intercollegiate sports:* basketball M/W, cross-country running M/W, lacrosse M(c), soccer M/W, softball W, swimming W, tennis M/W, track and field W, volleyball M/W. *Intramural sports:* basketball M/W, soccer M/W, track and field M/W, volleyball M/W.

Standardized Tests *Required:* SAT I or ACT (for admission).

Costs (2001–02) *Comprehensive fee:* $24,330 includes full-time tuition ($17,030) and room and board ($7300). Part-time tuition: $495 per credit. *Required fees:* $50 per term part-time. *Payment plan:* installment. *Waivers:* senior citizens and employees or children of employees.

Applying *Options:* common application, electronic application, early admission, early decision, deferred entrance. *Application fee:* $35. *Required:* essay or personal statement, high school transcript, minimum 2.0 GPA, 1 letter of recommendation. *Required for some:* interview. *Recommended:* 2 letters of recommendation, interview. *Application deadline:* rolling (freshmen), rolling (transfers). *Early decision:* 11/15. *Notification:* continuous (freshmen), 12/15 (early decision).

Admissions Contact Mr. Timothy Nash, Dean of Admissions and Financial Aid, College of Mount Saint Vincent, 6301 Riverdale Avenue, Riverdale, NY 10471-1093. *Phone:* 718-405-3268. *Toll-free phone:* 800-665-CMSV. *Fax:* 718-549-7945. *E-mail:* admissns@cmsv.edu.

THE COLLEGE OF NEW ROCHELLE

New Rochelle, New York

- **Independent** comprehensive, founded 1904
- **Calendar** semesters
- **Degrees** bachelor's, master's, post-master's, and postbachelor's certificates (also offers a non-traditional adult program with significant enrollment not reflected in profile)
- **Suburban** 20-acre campus with easy access to New York City
- **Endowment** $16.9 million
- **Women only,** 908 undergraduate students, 64% full-time
- **Moderately difficult** entrance level, 60% of applicants were admitted

Undergraduates 585 full-time, 323 part-time. Students come from 21 states and territories, 6 other countries, 12% are from out of state, 27% African American, 3% Asian American or Pacific Islander, 12% Hispanic American, 0.2% Native American, 0.8% international, 5% transferred in, 58% live on campus. *Retention:* 73% of 2001 full-time freshmen returned.

Freshmen *Admission:* 804 applied, 479 admitted, 100 enrolled. *Average high school GPA:* 2.80. *Test scores:* SAT verbal scores over 500: 43%; SAT math scores over 500: 30%; ACT scores over 18: 50%; SAT verbal scores over 600: 7%; SAT math scores over 600: 5%; SAT verbal scores over 700: 1%.

Faculty *Total:* 160, 41% full-time. *Student/faculty ratio:* 8:1.

Majors Applied art; art education; art history; art therapy; biology; broadcast journalism; business administration; chemistry; classics; economics; education; elementary education; English; fine/studio arts; French; history; interdisciplinary studies; Latin (ancient and medieval); liberal arts and sciences/liberal studies; literature; mass communications; mathematics; modern languages; nursing; philosophy; physics; political science; pre-law; pre-medicine; psychology; religious studies; secondary education; social work; sociology; Spanish; special education; women's studies.

Academic Programs *Special study options:* academic remediation for entering students, accelerated degree program, adult/continuing education programs, advanced placement credit, cooperative education, English as a second language, honors programs, independent study, internships, off-campus study, part-time degree program, services for LD students, student-designed majors, study abroad, summer session for credit.

Library Gill Library plus 1 other with 200,000 titles, 1,441 serial subscriptions, 6,881 audiovisual materials, an OPAC.

Computers on Campus 120 computers available on campus for general student use. A campuswide network can be accessed from off campus. Internet access, online (class) registration, at least one staffed computer lab available.

Student Life *Housing Options:* women-only. *Activities and Organizations:* drama/theater group, student-run newspaper, Drama Club, Science and Math

Society, Business Board, Latin-American Women's Society, Karate Club. *Campus security:* 24-hour emergency response devices and patrols, late-night transport/escort service, controlled dormitory access, 24-hour monitored security cameras at residence hall entrances. *Student Services:* health clinic, personal/psychological counseling, women's center.

Athletics Member NCAA. All Division III. *Intercollegiate sports:* basketball W, softball W, swimming W, tennis W, volleyball W.

Standardized Tests *Required:* SAT I or ACT (for admission).

Costs (2002–03) *Comprehensive fee:* $20,100 includes full-time tuition ($13,000), mandatory fees ($250), and room and board ($6850). Full-time tuition and fees vary according to course load and program. Part-time tuition: $437 per credit. Part-time tuition and fees vary according to course load. *Required fees:* $15 per term part-time. *Room and board:* Room and board charges vary according to housing facility. *Payment plans:* tuition prepayment, installment. *Waivers:* senior citizens and employees or children of employees.

Financial Aid Of all full-time matriculated undergraduates who enrolled in 2001, 697 applied for aid, 697 were judged to have need, 697 had their need fully met. In 2001, 230 non-need-based awards were made. *Average percent of need met:* 100%. *Average financial aid package:* $13,655. *Average need-based loan:* $5182. *Average need-based gift aid:* $4883. *Average non-need based aid:* $5300. *Average indebtedness upon graduation:* $2000.

Applying *Options:* common application, early admission, deferred entrance. *Application fee:* $20. *Required:* high school transcript. *Recommended:* essay or personal statement, 2 letters of recommendation, interview. *Application deadline:* rolling (freshmen), rolling (transfers). *Notification:* continuous (freshmen).

Admissions Contact Ms. Stephany Decker, Director of Admission, The College of New Rochelle, 29 Castle Place, New Rochelle, NY 10805-2339. *Phone:* 914-654-5452. *Toll-free phone:* 800-933-5923. *Fax:* 914-654-5486.

THE COLLEGE OF SAINT ROSE
Albany, New York

- **Independent** comprehensive, founded 1920
- **Calendar** semesters
- **Degrees** bachelor's, master's, post-master's, and postbachelor's certificates
- **Urban** 22-acre campus
- **Endowment** $16.4 million
- **Coed,** 2,856 undergraduate students, 80% full-time, 72% women, 28% men
- **Moderately difficult** entrance level, 77% of applicants were admitted

Undergraduates Students come from 21 states and territories, 14 other countries, 5% are from out of state, 3% African American, 1.0% Asian American or Pacific Islander, 2% Hispanic American, 0.4% Native American, 0.4% international, 30% live on campus. *Retention:* 85% of 2001 full-time freshmen returned.

Freshmen *Admission:* 1,619 applied, 1,252 admitted. *Average high school GPA:* 3.50. *Test scores:* SAT verbal scores over 500: 68%; SAT math scores over 500: 70%; ACT scores over 18: 95%; SAT verbal scores over 600: 17%; SAT math scores over 600: 16%; ACT scores over 24: 32%; SAT verbal scores over 700: 3%; SAT math scores over 700: 1%; ACT scores over 30: 2%.

Faculty *Total:* 159. *Student/faculty ratio:* 14:1.

Majors Accounting; American studies; art education; biochemistry; biology; business administration; chemistry; communication disorders; communications; cytotechnology; education; elementary education; English; environmental science; fine/studio arts; graphic design/commercial art/illustration; history; information sciences/systems; interdisciplinary studies; mathematics; medical technology; music; music teacher education; psychology; religious studies; social work; sociology; Spanish; special education.

Academic Programs *Special study options:* academic remediation for entering students, accelerated degree program, adult/continuing education programs, advanced placement credit, double majors, external degree program, independent study, internships, off-campus study, part-time degree program, services for LD students, student-designed majors, study abroad, summer session for credit. *ROTC:* Army (c), Navy (c), Air Force (c). *Unusual degree programs:* 3-2 engineering with Alfred University, Clarkson University, Union College (NY), Rensselaer Polytechnic Institute.

Library Neil Hellman Library plus 1 other with 200,987 titles, 975 serial subscriptions, 1,089 audiovisual materials, an OPAC, a Web page.

Computers on Campus 322 computers available on campus for general student use. A campuswide network can be accessed from student residence rooms and from off campus. Internet access, online (class) registration, at least one staffed computer lab available.

Student Life *Housing Options:* coed, men-only, women-only. *Activities and Organizations:* drama/theater group, student-run newspaper, choral group, Student Association, Student Events Board, Circle K, Student Education Association, Student Speech, Hearing and Language Association. *Campus security:* 24-hour emergency response devices and patrols, student patrols, late-night transport/escort service, controlled dormitory access. *Student Services:* health clinic, personal/psychological counseling.

Athletics Member NCAA. All Division II. *Intercollegiate sports:* baseball M(s), basketball M(s)/W(s), cross-country running M(s)/W(s), soccer M(s)/W(s), softball W(s), swimming M(s)/W(s), volleyball W(s). *Intramural sports:* basketball M/W, soccer M/W, softball W, volleyball M/W.

Standardized Tests *Required:* SAT I or ACT (for admission).

Costs (2001–02) *Comprehensive fee:* $20,664 includes full-time tuition ($13,578), mandatory fees ($340), and room and board ($6746). Full-time tuition and fees vary according to course load and program. Part-time tuition: $450 per credit. Part-time tuition and fees vary according to class time. *Required fees:* $4 per credit, $15 per term part-time. *Room and board:* College room only: $3152. Room and board charges vary according to board plan. *Waivers:* senior citizens and employees or children of employees.

Financial Aid Of all full-time matriculated undergraduates who enrolled in 2001, 2107 applied for aid, 1827 were judged to have need, 356 had their need fully met. 406 Federal Work-Study jobs (averaging $815). 83 State and other part-time jobs (averaging $892). In 2001, 275 non-need-based awards were made. *Average percent of need met:* 73%. *Average financial aid package:* $10,698. *Average need-based loan:* $3729. *Average need-based gift aid:* $5232. *Average non-need based aid:* $3301. *Average indebtedness upon graduation:* $16,595.

Applying *Options:* electronic application, deferred entrance. *Application fee:* $30. *Required:* essay or personal statement, high school transcript, 1 letter of recommendation. *Required for some:* interview. *Recommended:* minimum 3.0 GPA, interview. *Application deadlines:* 2/1 (freshmen), 2/1 (transfers). *Notification:* continuous (freshmen).

Admissions Contact Ms. Mary Elizabeth Amico, Associate Dean of Admissions and Enrollment Services, The College of Saint Rose, 432 Western Avenue, Albany, NY 12203-1419. *Phone:* 518-454-5150. *Toll-free phone:* 800-637-8556. *Fax:* 518-454-2013. *E-mail:* admit@mail.strose.edu.

COLLEGE OF STATEN ISLAND OF THE CITY UNIVERSITY OF NEW YORK
Staten Island, New York

- **State and locally supported** comprehensive, founded 1955, part of City University of New York System
- **Calendar** semesters
- **Degrees** certificates, associate, bachelor's, master's, and post-master's certificates
- **Urban** 204-acre campus with easy access to New York City
- **Endowment** $4.3 million
- **Coed,** 9,876 undergraduate students, 63% full-time, 59% women, 41% men
- **Noncompetitive** entrance level, 100% of applicants were admitted

The College of Staten Island/CUNY, a senior college, offers 11,000 students a state-of-the-art, picturesque, 204-acre campus. In addition, SUNY has a comprehensive range of bachelor's degrees and selected associate and master's degree programs in liberal arts and sciences, engineering science and physics, and such professional areas as business, education, nursing, and social work. For more information, students should visit the Web site at http://www.csi.cuny.edu.

Undergraduates 6,263 full-time, 3,613 part-time. Students come from 12 states and territories, 1% are from out of state, 9% African American, 7% Asian American or Pacific Islander, 8% Hispanic American, 0.2% Native American, 5% transferred in. *Retention:* 83% of 2001 full-time freshmen returned.

Freshmen *Admission:* 4,031 applied, 4,031 admitted, 1,804 enrolled. *Average high school GPA:* 2.98. *Test scores:* SAT verbal scores over 500: 20%; SAT math scores over 500: 25%; SAT verbal scores over 600: 3%; SAT math scores over 600: 3%.

Faculty *Total:* 719, 46% full-time, 48% with terminal degrees. *Student/faculty ratio:* 17:1.

Majors Accounting; African-American studies; American studies; anthropology; applied art; architecture; biochemistry; biology; business; chemistry; civil engineering technology; communications; computer/information sciences related; computer programming; computer science; construction technology; economics; education; engineering; English; film/video production; fine arts and art studies related; history; information sciences/systems; international relations; liberal arts and sciences/liberal studies; mathematics; medical laboratory technician; medical technology; music; nursing; nursing related; philosophy; photography; physical therapy; physician assistant; physics; political science; psychology; social work; sociology; Spanish; theater arts/drama; women's studies.

College of Staten Island of the City University of New York (continued)

Academic Programs *Special study options:* accelerated degree program, adult/continuing education programs, advanced placement credit, cooperative education, double majors, English as a second language, freshman honors college, honors programs, independent study, internships, part-time degree program, services for LD students, study abroad, summer session for credit. *Unusual degree programs:* 3-2 physical therapy, physicians assistant, medical technology.

Library College of Staten Island Library with 203,368 titles, 11,074 serial subscriptions, 14,350 audiovisual materials, an OPAC, a Web page.

Computers on Campus 120 computers available on campus for general student use. A campuswide network can be accessed from off campus. Internet access, at least one staffed computer lab available.

Student Life *Housing:* college housing not available. *Activities and Organizations:* drama/theater group, student-run newspaper, radio station, choral group, Latin Club, Spanish Club, Southasian Cultural Club, Apostolic Christian Life Center. *Campus security:* 24-hour emergency response devices and patrols, late-night transport/escort service, emergency call boxes, blue light system, bicycle patrols, radar-controlled traffic monitoring. *Student Services:* health clinic, personal/psychological counseling, women's center.

Athletics Member NCAA. All Division III. *Intercollegiate sports:* baseball M, basketball M/W, soccer M, softball W, swimming M/W, tennis M/W, volleyball W. *Intramural sports:* badminton M/W, basketball M/W, bowling M(c)/W(c), football M/W, racquetball M/W, soccer M/W, softball M/W, table tennis M/W, tennis M/W, track and field M/W, volleyball M/W.

Standardized Tests *Required:* SAT I (for admission).

Costs (2002–03) *Tuition:* state resident $3200 full-time, $135 per semester hour part-time; nonresident $6800 full-time, $285 per semester hour part-time. Full-time tuition and fees vary according to course load. Part-time tuition and fees vary according to course load. *Required fees:* $158 full-time, $53 per term part-time. *Payment plan:* deferred payment. *Waivers:* senior citizens and employees or children of employees.

Financial Aid Of all full-time matriculated undergraduates who enrolled in 2001, 5440 applied for aid. In 2001, 127 non-need-based awards were made. *Average non-need based aid:* $1025.

Applying *Options:* deferred entrance. *Application fee:* $40. *Required:* high school transcript, minimum 2.0 GPA. *Application deadline:* rolling (freshmen), rolling (transfers).

Admissions Contact Ms. Mary-Beth Riley, Director of Admissions and Recruitment, College of Staten Island of the City University of New York, 2800 Victory Boulevard, Staten Island, NY 10314-6600. *Phone:* 718-982-2011. *Fax:* 718-982-2500.

COLUMBIA COLLEGE
New York, New York

- **Independent** 4-year, founded 1754, part of Columbia University
- **Calendar** semesters
- **Degree** bachelor's
- **Urban** 35-acre campus
- **Endowment** $3.4 billion
- **Coed,** 4,092 undergraduate students, 100% full-time, 51% women, 49% men
- **Most difficult** entrance level, 12% of applicants were admitted

Undergraduates 4,092 full-time. Students come from 54 states and territories, 72 other countries, 70% are from out of state, 9% African American, 13% Asian American or Pacific Islander, 8% Hispanic American, 0.2% Native American, 5% international, 1% transferred in, 98% live on campus. *Retention:* 98% of 2001 full-time freshmen returned.

Freshmen *Admission:* 14,094 applied, 1,729 admitted, 1,005 enrolled. *Average high school GPA:* 3.65. *Test scores:* SAT verbal scores over 500: 100%; SAT math scores over 500: 100%; ACT scores over 18: 100%; SAT verbal scores over 600: 90%; SAT math scores over 600: 92%; ACT scores over 24: 95%; SAT verbal scores over 700: 61%; SAT math scores over 700: 58%; ACT scores over 30: 55%.

Faculty *Total:* 632. *Student/faculty ratio:* 7:1.

Majors African-American studies; American studies; anthropology; archaeology; architecture; architecture related; art history; Asian-American studies; astronomy; astrophysics; biochemistry; biology; biophysics; biopsychology; chemical and atomic/molecular physics; chemistry; classics; comparative literature; computer science; dance; East Asian studies; economics; education (K-12); English; environmental biology; environmental science; film studies; French; geochemistry; geology; German; Greek (ancient and medieval); Greek (modern); Hispanic-American studies; history; Italian; Italian studies; Latin American studies; linguistics; mathematical statistics; mathematics; medieval/renaissance studies; Middle Eastern studies; music; philosophy; physics; political science; psychology; religious studies; Russian; Russian/Slavic studies; Slavic languages; sociology; Spanish; theater arts/drama; urban studies; visual/performing arts; women's studies.

Academic Programs *Special study options:* advanced placement credit, English as a second language, honors programs, internships, off-campus study, services for LD students, student-designed majors, study abroad, summer session for credit. *Unusual degree programs:* 3-2 engineering with Columbia University, The Fu Foundation School of Engineering and Applied Science; music with The Juilliard School.

Library Butler Library plus 20 others with 6.8 million titles, 66,000 serial subscriptions.

Computers on Campus 400 computers available on campus for general student use. A campuswide network can be accessed from student residence rooms. At least one staffed computer lab available.

Student Life *Housing:* on-campus residence required for freshman year. *Options:* coed, men-only, women-only, disabled students. *Activities and Organizations:* drama/theater group, student-run newspaper, radio and television station, choral group, marching band, community service, cultural organizations, performing arts, national fraternities, national sororities. *Campus security:* 24-hour emergency response devices and patrols, student patrols, late-night transport/escort service, 24-hour ID check at door. *Student Services:* health clinic, personal/psychological counseling, women's center.

Athletics Member NCAA. All Division I except football (Division I-AA). *Intercollegiate sports:* archery M(c)/W, badminton M(c)/W(c), baseball M, basketball M/W, crew M/W, cross-country running M/W, equestrian sports M(c)/W(c), fencing M/W, field hockey W, golf M, ice hockey M(c), lacrosse M(c)/W, racquetball M(c)/W(c), riflery M(c)/W(c), rugby M(c)/W(c), sailing M(c)/W(c), soccer M/W, softball W, squash M(c)/W(c), swimming M/W, table tennis M(c)/W(c), tennis M/W, track and field M/W, volleyball M(c)/W, water polo M(c)/W(c), wrestling M. *Intramural sports:* badminton M/W, basketball M/W, football M, racquetball M/W, soccer M/W, softball W, squash M/W, swimming M/W, tennis M/W, volleyball M/W.

Standardized Tests *Required:* SAT I or ACT (for admission), SAT II: Subject Tests (for admission), SAT II: Writing Test (for admission).

Costs (2001–02) *One-time required fee:* $45. *Comprehensive fee:* $35,188 includes full-time tuition ($25,970), mandatory fees ($938), and room and board ($8280). *Payment plans:* tuition prepayment, installment. *Waivers:* employees or children of employees.

Financial Aid Of all full-time matriculated undergraduates who enrolled in 2001, 1810 applied for aid, 1747 were judged to have need, 1747 had their need fully met. *Average percent of need met:* 100%. *Average financial aid package:* $23,266. *Average need-based loan:* $4605. *Average need-based gift aid:* $20,108. *Average indebtedness upon graduation:* $16,358. *Financial aid deadline:* 2/10.

Applying *Options:* electronic application, early admission, early decision, deferred entrance. *Required:* essay or personal statement, high school transcript, 3 letters of recommendation. *Application deadlines:* 1/2 (freshmen), 3/15 (transfers). *Early decision:* 11/1. *Notification:* 3/31 (freshmen), 12/15 (early decision).

Admissions Contact Mr. Eric Furda, Director of Undergraduate Admissions, Columbia College, 1130 Amsterdam Avenue MC 2807, New York, NY 10027. *Phone:* 212-854-2522. *Fax:* 212-854-1209. *E-mail:* ugrad-admiss@columbia.edu.

COLUMBIA UNIVERSITY, SCHOOL OF GENERAL STUDIES
New York, New York

- **Independent** 4-year, founded 1754, part of Columbia University
- **Calendar** semesters
- **Degrees** bachelor's and postbachelor's certificates
- **Urban** 36-acre campus
- **Endowment** $12.1 million
- **Coed,** 1,167 undergraduate students
- **Most difficult** entrance level, 45% of applicants were admitted

Undergraduates Students come from 36 states and territories, 38% are from out of state, 8% African American, 10% Asian American or Pacific Islander, 10% Hispanic American, 0.3% Native American. *Retention:* 90% of 2001 full-time freshmen returned.

Freshmen *Admission:* 904 applied, 404 admitted.

Faculty *Total:* 632, 100% full-time, 100% with terminal degrees. *Student/faculty ratio:* 7:1.

Majors African-American studies; anthropology; applied art; applied mathematics; architecture; art history; astronomy; biology; chemistry; classics; comparative literature; computer science; dance; East Asian studies; economics; English; film studies; French; geology; German; Hispanic-American studies; history; Italian; literature; mathematical statistics; mathematics; Middle Eastern studies; music; philosophy; physics; political science; psychology; religious studies; Russian; Slavic languages; sociology; Spanish; theater arts/drama; urban studies; women's studies.

Academic Programs *Special study options:* academic remediation for entering students, accelerated degree program, adult/continuing education programs, advanced placement credit, English as a second language, honors programs, internships, off-campus study, part-time degree program, services for LD students, student-designed majors, study abroad, summer session for credit. *Unusual degree programs:* 3-2 business administration with Columbia University, Graduate School of Business; engineering with Columbia University, School of Engineering and Applied Science; social work with Columbia University, School of Social Work; international affairs, public policy and administration with Columbia University, School of International and Public Affairs; public health with Columbia University, School of Public Health.

Library Butler Library plus 21 others with 5.6 million titles, 59,400 serial subscriptions, a Web page.

Computers on Campus 250 computers available on campus for general student use. A campuswide network can be accessed from student residence rooms.

Student Life *Housing Options:* coed. *Activities and Organizations:* drama/theater group, student-run newspaper, radio and television station, choral group, Columbia Dramatists, Writers Club, General Studies Student Council, The Observer, national fraternities, national sororities. *Campus security:* 24-hour emergency response devices and patrols, late-night transport/escort service. *Student Services:* health clinic, personal/psychological counseling, women's center.

Athletics Member NCAA. All Division I except football (Division I-AA). *Intercollegiate sports:* baseball M, basketball M/W, crew M/W, cross-country running M/W, fencing M/W, field hockey W(c), golf M, gymnastics W, soccer M/W, swimming M/W, tennis M/W, track and field M/W, volleyball W, wrestling M. *Intramural sports:* racquetball M/W, rugby M, softball W, squash M/W, volleyball M/W, weight lifting M/W.

Standardized Tests *Required for some:* SAT I or ACT (for admission).

Costs (2001–02) *Tuition:* $20,112 full-time, $838 per credit part-time. Full-time tuition and fees vary according to course load. Part-time tuition and fees vary according to course load. *Required fees:* $1543 full-time. *Room only:* $7980. Room and board charges vary according to housing facility. *Payment plans:* tuition prepayment, deferred payment. *Waivers:* employees or children of employees.

Financial Aid Of all full-time matriculated undergraduates who enrolled in 2001, 457 Federal Work-Study jobs (averaging $1975).

Applying *Options:* electronic application, deferred entrance. *Application fee:* $50. *Required:* essay or personal statement, high school transcript. *Required for some:* interview. *Application deadlines:* 7/1 (freshmen), 7/1 (transfers). *Notification:* continuous (freshmen).

Admissions Contact Mr. Carlos A. Porro, Director of Admissions, Columbia University, School of General Studies, Mail Code 4101, Lewisohn Hall, 2970 Broadway 10027-9829. *Phone:* 212-854-2772. *Toll-free phone:* 800-895-1169. *Fax:* 212-854-6316. *E-mail:* gsdegree@columbia.edu.

COLUMBIA UNIVERSITY, THE FU FOUNDATION SCHOOL OF ENGINEERING AND APPLIED SCIENCE

New York, New York

- **Independent** university, founded 1864, part of Columbia University
- **Calendar** semesters
- **Degrees** bachelor's, master's, and doctoral
- **Urban** campus
- **Endowment** $3.4 billion
- **Coed,** 1,264 undergraduate students, 100% full-time, 27% women, 73% men
- **Most difficult** entrance level, 26% of applicants were admitted

Undergraduates 1,264 full-time. Students come from 44 states and territories, 59 other countries, 75% are from out of state, 5% African American, 34% Asian American or Pacific Islander, 6% Hispanic American, 12% international, 2% transferred in, 99% live on campus. *Retention:* 97% of 2001 full-time freshmen returned.

Freshmen *Admission:* 2,466 applied, 649 admitted, 312 enrolled. *Average high school GPA:* 3.65. *Test scores:* SAT verbal scores over 500: 99%; SAT math scores over 500: 100%; SAT verbal scores over 600: 89%; SAT math scores over 600: 99%; ACT scores over 24: 100%; SAT verbal scores over 700: 41%; SAT math scores over 700: 83%; ACT scores over 30: 47%.

Faculty *Total:* 108. *Student/faculty ratio:* 7:1.

Majors Applied mathematics; bioengineering; chemical engineering; civil engineering; computer engineering; computer science; electrical engineering; engineering/industrial management; engineering mechanics; environmental engineering; industrial/manufacturing engineering; materials science; mechanical engineering; operations research; physics.

Academic Programs *Special study options:* academic remediation for entering students, accelerated degree program, adult/continuing education programs, advanced placement credit, English as a second language, honors programs, internships, services for LD students, study abroad, summer session for credit.

Library Butler Library plus 20 others with 6.8 million titles, 66,000 serial subscriptions.

Computers on Campus 400 computers available on campus for general student use. A campuswide network can be accessed from student residence rooms. Internet access, at least one staffed computer lab available.

Student Life *Housing:* on-campus residence required for freshman year. *Options:* coed, men-only, women-only, disabled students. *Activities and Organizations:* drama/theater group, student-run newspaper, radio and television station, choral group, marching band, community service, cultural organizations, performing arts, national fraternities, national sororities. *Campus security:* 24-hour emergency response devices and patrols, late-night transport/escort service, 24-hour ID check at door. *Student Services:* health clinic, personal/psychological counseling, women's center.

Athletics Member NCAA. All Division I except football (Division I-AA). *Intercollegiate sports:* archery M(c)/W, badminton M(c)/W(c), baseball M, basketball M/W, crew M/W, cross-country running M/W, equestrian sports M(c)/W(c), fencing M/W, field hockey W, golf M, ice hockey M(c), lacrosse M(c)/W, riflery M(c)/W(c), rugby M(c)/W(c), sailing M(c)/W(c), soccer M/W, softball W, squash M(c)/W(c), swimming M/W, table tennis M(c)/W(c), tennis M/W, track and field M/W, volleyball M(c)/W, water polo M(c)/W(c), wrestling M. *Intramural sports:* badminton M/W, basketball M/W, football M, racquetball M/W, soccer M/W, softball W, squash M/W, swimming M/W, tennis M/W, volleyball M/W.

Standardized Tests *Required:* SAT I or ACT (for admission), SAT II: Subject Tests (for admission), SAT II: Writing Test (for admission).

Costs (2001–02) *One-time required fee:* $45. *Comprehensive fee:* $35,188 includes full-time tuition ($25,970), mandatory fees ($938), and room and board ($8280). *Room and board:* College room only: $4840. *Payment plans:* tuition prepayment, installment, deferred payment. *Waivers:* minority students and employees or children of employees.

Financial Aid Of all full-time matriculated undergraduates who enrolled in 2001, 676 applied for aid, 651 were judged to have need, 651 had their need fully met. *Average percent of need met:* 100%. *Average financial aid package:* $23,337. *Average need-based loan:* $4666. *Average need-based gift aid:* $20,332. *Average indebtedness upon graduation:* $17,384. *Financial aid deadline:* 2/10.

Applying *Options:* electronic application, early admission, early decision, deferred entrance. *Application fee:* $65. *Required:* essay or personal statement, high school transcript, 3 letters of recommendation. *Recommended:* interview. *Application deadlines:* 1/1 (freshmen), 3/15 (transfers). *Early decision:* 11/1. *Notification:* 4/4 (freshmen), 12/15 (early decision).

Admissions Contact Mr. Eric J. Furda, Director of Undergraduate Admissions, Columbia University, The Fu Foundation School of Engineering and Applied Science, 1130 Amsterdam Avenue MC 2807, New York, NY 10027. *Phone:* 212-854-2522. *Fax:* 212-854-1209. *E-mail:* ugrad-admiss@columbia.edu.

CONCORDIA COLLEGE

Bronxville, New York

- **Independent Lutheran** 4-year, founded 1881, part of Concordia University System
- **Calendar** semesters
- **Degrees** associate and bachelor's
- **Suburban** 33-acre campus with easy access to New York City
- **Endowment** $6.4 million
- **Coed,** 662 undergraduate students, 82% full-time, 61% women, 39% men
- **Moderately difficult** entrance level, 72% of applicants were admitted

Undergraduates 542 full-time, 120 part-time. Students come from 23 states and territories, 36 other countries, 30% are from out of state, 7% transferred in, 68% live on campus. *Retention:* 72% of 2001 full-time freshmen returned.

Freshmen *Admission:* 502 applied, 361 admitted, 132 enrolled. *Average high school GPA:* 3.00. *Test scores:* SAT verbal scores over 500: 51%; SAT math scores

Concordia College (continued)
over 500: 46%; ACT scores over 18: 75%; SAT verbal scores over 600: 15%; SAT math scores over 600: 9%; ACT scores over 24: 35%; SAT verbal scores over 700: 2%.

Faculty *Total:* 57, 60% full-time. *Student/faculty ratio:* 12:1.

Majors Arts management; biology; business administration; business education; ecology; education; elementary education; English; history; international relations; liberal arts and sciences/liberal studies; mathematics; middle school education; music; music teacher education; pre-law; religious music; religious studies; science education; secondary education; secretarial science; social sciences; social work.

Academic Programs *Special study options:* academic remediation for entering students, accelerated degree program, adult/continuing education programs, advanced placement credit, distance learning, double majors, English as a second language, honors programs, independent study, internships, off-campus study, part-time degree program, services for LD students, student-designed majors, study abroad. *Unusual degree programs:* 3-2 physical therapy with New York Medical College.

Library Scheele Memorial Library with 71,500 titles, 467 serial subscriptions, 7,660 audiovisual materials, an OPAC, a Web page.

Computers on Campus 50 computers available on campus for general student use. A campuswide network can be accessed from student residence rooms and from off campus. Internet access, at least one staffed computer lab available.

Student Life *Housing Options:* men-only, women-only. *Activities and Organizations:* drama/theater group, student-run newspaper, choral group, Campus Christian Ministries, Drama Club, Student Government Association, International and Afro/Latin American Club, yearbook and newspaper, national fraternities, national sororities. *Campus security:* 24-hour emergency response devices and patrols, late-night transport/escort service, controlled dormitory access. *Student Services:* health clinic, personal/psychological counseling.

Athletics Member NCAA. All Division II except volleyball (Division I). *Intercollegiate sports:* baseball M(s), basketball M(s)/W(s), soccer M(s)/W(s), softball W(s), tennis M(s)/W(s), volleyball M(s)/W(s). *Intramural sports:* basketball M/W, racquetball M/W, squash M/W, table tennis M/W, tennis M/W, volleyball M/W.

Standardized Tests *Required:* SAT I or ACT (for admission).

Costs (2001–02) *Comprehensive fee:* $22,400 includes full-time tuition ($15,550) and room and board ($6850). Part-time tuition: $444 per credit hour. Part-time tuition and fees vary according to course load. *Room and board:* Room and board charges vary according to board plan. *Payment plan:* installment. *Waivers:* senior citizens and employees or children of employees.

Applying *Options:* electronic application, early admission, early decision, deferred entrance. *Application fee:* $30. *Required:* high school transcript, 1 letter of recommendation. *Required for some:* interview. *Recommended:* essay or personal statement, minimum 2.5 GPA. *Application deadlines:* 3/15 (freshmen), 7/15 (transfers). *Early decision:* 11/15. *Notification:* continuous until 6/15 (freshmen), 12/1 (early decision).

Admissions Contact Rebecca Hendricks, Director of Admission, Concordia College, Bronxville, NY 10708. *Phone:* 914-337-9300 Ext. 2149. *Toll-free phone:* 800-YES-COLLEGE. *Fax:* 914-395-4636. *E-mail:* admission@concordia-ny.edu.

COOPER UNION FOR THE ADVANCEMENT OF SCIENCE AND ART
New York, New York

- **Independent** 4-year, founded 1859
- **Calendar** semesters
- **Degree** certificates and bachelor's
- **Urban** campus
- **Endowment** $183.4 million
- **Coed,** 878 undergraduate students, 98% full-time, 36% women, 64% men
- **Most difficult** entrance level, 13% of applicants were admitted

Cooper Union awards full tuition scholarships to every registered student. The value of the scholarship is approximately $100,000 for four years. Cooper Union has been cited by *U.S. News & World Report* as one of the top three engineering schools of its kind and as one of the most selective colleges in the country.

Undergraduates 857 full-time, 21 part-time. Students come from 41 states and territories, 44% are from out of state, 5% African American, 28% Asian American or Pacific Islander, 7% Hispanic American, 0.5% Native American, 8% international, 4% transferred in, 19% live on campus. *Retention:* 92% of 2001 full-time freshmen returned.

Freshmen *Admission:* 2,210 applied, 297 admitted, 202 enrolled. *Average high school GPA:* 3.40. *Test scores:* SAT verbal scores over 500: 96%; SAT math scores over 500: 93%; SAT verbal scores over 600: 83%; SAT math scores over 600: 82%; SAT verbal scores over 700: 37%; SAT math scores over 700: 54%.

Faculty *Total:* 252, 22% full-time, 38% with terminal degrees. *Student/faculty ratio:* 7:1.

Majors Architecture; art; chemical engineering; civil engineering; electrical engineering; engineering; graphic design/commercial art/illustration; mechanical engineering.

Academic Programs *Special study options:* advanced placement credit, honors programs, independent study, internships, off-campus study, student-designed majors, study abroad, summer session for credit.

Library Cooper Union Library with 97,000 titles, 370 serial subscriptions, an OPAC, a Web page.

Computers on Campus 200 computers available on campus for general student use. A campuswide network can be accessed from student residence rooms and from off campus. Internet access, at least one staffed computer lab available.

Student Life *Housing Options:* coed. *Activities and Organizations:* drama/theater group, student-run newspaper, Campus Crusade for Christ, Chinese Students Association, Kesher, Athletic Association, Muslim Students Organization, national fraternities, national sororities. *Campus security:* 24-hour emergency response devices and patrols, security guards. *Student Services:* personal/psychological counseling.

Athletics *Intercollegiate sports:* basketball M, soccer M, table tennis M/W, tennis M/W, volleyball M/W. *Intramural sports:* basketball M/W, bowling M/W, soccer M, softball M/W, table tennis M/W, tennis M/W, volleyball M/W.

Standardized Tests *Required:* SAT I or ACT (for admission). *Required for some:* SAT II: Subject Tests (for admission).

Costs (2001–02) *Comprehensive fee:* includes mandatory fees ($600) and room and board ($11,400). All students are awarded full-tuition scholarships. Living expenses are subsidized by college-administered financial aid. *Room and board:* College room only: $8000.

Financial Aid Of all full-time matriculated undergraduates who enrolled in 2001, 398 applied for aid, 299 were judged to have need, 227 had their need fully met. 47 Federal Work-Study jobs (averaging $840). 560 State and other part-time jobs (averaging $1152). *Average percent of need met:* 92%. *Average financial aid package:* $5709. *Average need-based loan:* $2946. *Average need-based gift aid:* $3845. *Average indebtedness upon graduation:* $3570.

Applying *Options:* early admission, early decision, deferred entrance. *Application fee:* $35. *Required:* high school transcript, minimum 2.0 GPA. *Required for some:* essay or personal statement, 3 letters of recommendation, portfolio, home examination. *Recommended:* minimum 3.0 GPA. *Application deadlines:* 1/1 (freshmen), 1/1 (out-of-state freshmen), 1/1 (transfers). *Early decision:* 12/1.

Admissions Contact Mr. Richard Bory, Dean of Admissions and Records and Registrar, Cooper Union for the Advancement of Science and Art, 30 Cooper Square, New York, NY 10003. *Phone:* 212-353-4120. *Fax:* 212-353-4342. *E-mail:* admission@cooper.edu.

CORNELL UNIVERSITY
Ithaca, New York

- **Independent** university, founded 1865
- **Calendar** semesters
- **Degrees** bachelor's, master's, doctoral, and first professional
- **Small-town** 745-acre campus with easy access to Syracuse
- **Endowment** $2.7 billion
- **Coed,** 13,801 undergraduate students, 100% full-time, 48% women, 52% men
- **Most difficult** entrance level, 27% of applicants were admitted

Undergraduates 13,801 full-time. Students come from 55 states and territories, 82 other countries, 52% are from out of state, 5% African American, 16% Asian American or Pacific Islander, 5% Hispanic American, 0.5% Native American, 7% international, 4% transferred in, 54% live on campus. *Retention:* 93% of 2001 full-time freshmen returned.

Freshmen *Admission:* 21,519 applied, 5,861 admitted, 2,988 enrolled. *Test scores:* SAT verbal scores over 500: 98%; SAT math scores over 500: 100%; SAT verbal scores over 600: 85%; SAT math scores over 600: 92%; SAT verbal scores over 700: 37%; SAT math scores over 700: 56%.

Faculty *Total:* 1,777, 92% full-time, 88% with terminal degrees. *Student/faculty ratio:* 13:1.

Majors African-American studies; African studies; agribusiness; agricultural business; agricultural economics; agricultural education; agricultural engineering; agricultural mechanization; agricultural sciences; agronomy/crop science; American studies; anatomy; animal sciences; anthropology; applied art; applied economics; archaeology; architectural engineering technology; architectural environmental design; architecture; art; art history; Asian studies; astronomy; atmospheric sciences; behavioral sciences; biochemistry; bioengineering; biology; biometrics; biostatistics; botany; business administration; cell biology; chemical engineering; chemistry; child care/development; Chinese; city/community/regional planning; civil engineering; classical and ancient Near Eastern languages related; classics; clothing/textiles; communications; community services; comparative literature; computer science; consumer services; creative writing; crop production management; dairy science; dance; developmental/child psychology; dietetics; drawing; East Asian studies; Eastern European area studies; ecology; economics; education; electrical engineering; engineering; engineering physics; engineering science; English; entomology; environmental engineering; environmental science; European studies; family/community studies; family/consumer studies; family resource management studies; farm/ranch management; fine/studio arts; food sciences; French; genetics; geological engineering; geology; German; Greek (modern); Hebrew; Hispanic-American studies; history; history of science and technology; home economics education; horticulture science; hotel and restaurant management; human ecology; human services; individual/family development; industrial/manufacturing engineering; information sciences/systems; interdisciplinary studies; interior architecture; international agriculture; international relations; Italian; Japanese; Judaic studies; labor/personnel relations; landscape architecture; Latin American studies; Latin (ancient and medieval); liberal arts and sciences/liberal studies; linguistics; marine science; mass communications; materials engineering; materials science; mathematical statistics; mathematics; mechanical engineering; medieval/renaissance studies; microbiology/bacteriology; Middle Eastern studies; modern languages; molecular biology; music; Native American studies; natural resources management; neuroscience; nutritional sciences; nutrition science; operations research; ornamental horticulture; philosophy; photography; physics; physiology; plant breeding; plant pathology; plant sciences; political science; poultry science; pre-law; pre-medicine; pre-veterinary studies; psychology; public policy analysis; religious studies; romance languages; Russian; Russian/Slavic studies; science/technology and society; sculpture; Slavic languages; sociobiology; sociology; soil sciences; Southeast Asian studies; Spanish; textile arts; theater arts/drama; urban studies; women's studies; zoology.

Academic Programs *Special study options:* academic remediation for entering students, accelerated degree program, advanced placement credit, cooperative education, distance learning, double majors, English as a second language, honors programs, independent study, internships, off-campus study, services for LD students, student-designed majors, study abroad, summer session for credit. *ROTC:* Army (b), Air Force (b). *Unusual degree programs:* 3-2 law.

Library Olin Library plus 17 others with 6.3 million titles, 61,941 serial subscriptions, 140,443 audiovisual materials, an OPAC, a Web page.

Computers on Campus 700 computers available on campus for general student use. A campuswide network can be accessed from student residence rooms and from off campus. Internet access, at least one staffed computer lab available.

Student Life *Housing Options:* coed, men-only, women-only, cooperative, disabled students. *Activities and Organizations:* drama/theater group, student-run newspaper, radio station, choral group, marching band, Student Assembly, Residence Hall Association, Catholic Community, Hillel, Concert Commission, national fraternities, national sororities. *Campus security:* 24-hour emergency response devices and patrols, late-night transport/escort service, controlled dormitory access, escort service. *Student Services:* health clinic, personal/psychological counseling, women's center.

Athletics Member NCAA. All Division I except football (Division I-AA). *Intercollegiate sports:* baseball M, basketball M/W, crew M/W, cross-country running M/W, equestrian sports W, fencing W, field hockey W, golf M, gymnastics W, ice hockey M/W(c), lacrosse M/W, soccer M/W, softball W(c), squash M/W, swimming M/W, tennis M/W, track and field M/W, volleyball W, wrestling M. *Intramural sports:* badminton M/W, basketball M/W, bowling M/W, crew M(c)/W(c), cross-country running M/W, football M/W, golf M/W, ice hockey M/W, rugby M(c), skiing (downhill) M/W, soccer M/W, softball M/W, squash M/W, table tennis M/W, tennis M/W, track and field M/W, volleyball M/W, water polo M/W, wrestling M/W.

Standardized Tests *Required:* SAT I or ACT (for admission). *Required for some:* SAT II: Subject Tests (for admission), SAT II: Writing Test (for admission).

Costs (2001–02) *Comprehensive fee:* $34,614 includes full-time tuition ($25,970), mandatory fees ($92), and room and board ($8552). *Room and board:* College room only: $4972. Room and board charges vary according to board plan and housing facility. *Payment plans:* tuition prepayment, installment. *Waivers:* employees or children of employees.

Financial Aid Of all full-time matriculated undergraduates who enrolled in 2001, 7229 applied for aid, 6291 were judged to have need, 6291 had their need fully met. *Average percent of need met:* 100%. *Average financial aid package:* $21,390. *Average need-based loan:* $6316. *Average need-based gift aid:* $14,611. *Financial aid deadline:* 2/11.

Applying *Options:* electronic application, early admission, early decision, deferred entrance. *Application fee:* $65. *Required:* essay or personal statement, high school transcript, 1 letter of recommendation. *Required for some:* interview. *Application deadlines:* 1/1 (freshmen), 3/15 (transfers). *Early decision:* 11/10. *Notification:* 4/3 (freshmen), 12/15 (early decision).

Admissions Contact Ms. Wendy Schaerer, Director of Undergraduate Admissions, Cornell University, 410 Thurston Avenue, Ithaca, NY 14850. *Phone:* 607-255-5241. *Fax:* 607-255-0659. *E-mail:* admissions@cornell.edu.

THE CULINARY INSTITUTE OF AMERICA

Hyde Park, New York

- **Independent** 4-year, founded 1946
- **Calendar** semesters
- **Degrees** associate and bachelor's
- **Small-town** 150-acre campus
- **Coed,** 2,012 undergraduate students, 100% full-time, 32% women, 68% men
- **Moderately difficult** entrance level, 54% of applicants were admitted

Undergraduates 2,012 full-time. Students come from 45 states and territories, 30 other countries, 70% are from out of state, 2% African American, 3% Asian American or Pacific Islander, 5% Hispanic American, 0.2% Native American, 5% international, 70% live on campus.

Freshmen *Admission:* 1,084 applied, 587 admitted, 539 enrolled. *Average high school GPA:* 2.44.

Faculty *Total:* 120. *Student/faculty ratio:* 18:1.

Majors Culinary arts.

Academic Programs *Special study options:* academic remediation for entering students, adult/continuing education programs, cooperative education, internships, off-campus study, services for LD students.

Library Conrad N. Hilton Library with 61,000 titles, 310 serial subscriptions, 3,855 audiovisual materials, an OPAC.

Computers on Campus 170 computers available on campus for general student use. Internet access, at least one staffed computer lab available.

Student Life *Housing Options:* coed. *Activities and Organizations:* student-run newspaper, Epicures of Wine, Baker's Club, Food Art Club, Oye Me, Gourmet Society. *Campus security:* 24-hour emergency response devices and patrols, late-night transport/escort service, controlled dormitory access. *Student Services:* health clinic, personal/psychological counseling.

Athletics *Intercollegiate sports:* ice hockey M(c), soccer M(c). *Intramural sports:* basketball M/W, bowling M/W, fencing M/W, softball M/W, tennis M/W, volleyball M/W.

Standardized Tests *Recommended:* SAT I or ACT (for admission).

Costs (2001–02) *Tuition:* $18,620 full-time. Full-time tuition and fees vary according to class time, degree level, program, and student level. *Required fees:* $415 full-time. *Room only:* $3780. Room and board charges vary according to housing facility. *Payment plan:* installment. *Waivers:* minority students and employees or children of employees.

Financial Aid Of all full-time matriculated undergraduates who enrolled in 2001, 1800 applied for aid, 1773 were judged to have need, 10 had their need fully met. 677 Federal Work-Study jobs (averaging $638). In 2001, 100 non-need-based awards were made. *Average percent of need met:* 50%. *Average financial aid package:* $8500. *Average need-based loan:* $3000. *Average need-based gift aid:* $2000. *Average non-need based aid:* $2000. *Average indebtedness upon graduation:* $15,000.

Applying *Options:* common application, electronic application, early decision, deferred entrance. *Application fee:* $30. *Required:* essay or personal statement, high school transcript, 2 letters of recommendation. *Required for some:* interview, TOEFL and an Affidavit of Support. *Application deadline:* rolling (freshmen), rolling (transfers). *Early decision:* 12/1. *Notification:* continuous (freshmen), 1/15 (early decision).

Admissions Contact Mr. Larry Lopez, Interim Director of Admissions, The Culinary Institute of America, 1946 Campus Drive, Hyde Park, NY 12538. *Phone:* 845-451-1534. *Toll-free phone:* 800-CULINARY. *Fax:* 845-451-1068. *E-mail:* admissions@culinary.edu.

DAEMEN COLLEGE

Amherst, New York

- **Independent** comprehensive, founded 1947
- **Calendar** semesters
- **Degrees** certificates, bachelor's, master's, post-master's, and postbachelor's certificates

Daemen College (continued)
- **Suburban** 35-acre campus with easy access to Buffalo
- **Endowment** $2.0 million
- **Coed,** 1,875 undergraduate students, 76% full-time, 77% women, 23% men
- **Moderately difficult** entrance level, 77% of applicants were admitted

Undergraduates 1,423 full-time, 452 part-time. Students come from 24 states and territories, 9 other countries, 6% are from out of state, 13% African American, 2% Asian American or Pacific Islander, 2% Hispanic American, 1% Native American, 2% international, 10% transferred in, 33% live on campus. *Retention:* 68% of 2001 full-time freshmen returned.

Freshmen *Admission:* 1,792 applied, 1,375 admitted, 344 enrolled. *Average high school GPA:* 3.39. *Test scores:* SAT verbal scores over 500: 46%; SAT math scores over 500: 44%; ACT scores over 18: 79%; SAT verbal scores over 600: 8%; SAT math scores over 600: 9%; ACT scores over 24: 25%.

Faculty *Total:* 198, 35% full-time, 45% with terminal degrees. *Student/faculty ratio:* 14:1.

Majors Accounting; American government; applied art; art; art education; biochemistry; biology; biology education; business administration; business administration/management related; business education; early childhood education; elementary education; English; English education; fine/studio arts; French; French language education; graphic design/commercial art/illustration; history; humanities; mathematics; mathematics education; natural sciences; nursing science; physical therapy; physician assistant; political science; psychology; religious studies; science education; social studies education; social work; Spanish; Spanish language education; special education.

Academic Programs *Special study options:* academic remediation for entering students, adult/continuing education programs, advanced placement credit, cooperative education, double majors, independent study, internships, off-campus study, part-time degree program, services for LD students, student-designed majors, study abroad, summer session for credit. *ROTC:* Army (c).

Library Marian Library plus 1 other with 123,835 titles, 983 serial subscriptions, 14,533 audiovisual materials, an OPAC, a Web page.

Computers on Campus 154 computers available on campus for general student use. A campuswide network can be accessed from student residence rooms and from off campus. Internet access, at least one staffed computer lab available.

Student Life *Housing:* on-campus residence required for freshman year. *Options:* coed. *Activities and Organizations:* drama/theater group, student-run newspaper, choral group, Students Without Borders, Greek organizations, Student Association, Step Team, Resident Council. *Campus security:* 24-hour emergency response devices and patrols, late-night transport/escort service, 24-hour security cameras. *Student Services:* personal/psychological counseling.

Athletics Member NAIA. *Intercollegiate sports:* basketball M(s)/W(s), cross-country running M(s)/W(s), golf M(s), soccer M(s)/W(s), volleyball W(s). *Intramural sports:* basketball M/W, football M, ice hockey M(c), lacrosse M(c), skiing (downhill) M(c)/W(c), soccer M/W, softball M/W, volleyball M/W.

Standardized Tests *Required:* SAT I or ACT (for admission).

Costs (2001–02) *Comprehensive fee:* $20,620 includes full-time tuition ($13,200), mandatory fees ($420), and room and board ($7000). Part-time tuition: $440 per credit. Part-time tuition and fees vary according to course load. *Required fees:* $3 per credit, $68 per term part-time. *Room and board:* Room and board charges vary according to board plan. *Payment plans:* installment, deferred payment. *Waivers:* children of alumni, senior citizens, and employees or children of employees.

Financial Aid Of all full-time matriculated undergraduates who enrolled in 2001, 1205 applied for aid, 1049 were judged to have need, 160 had their need fully met. 39 State and other part-time jobs (averaging $465). In 2001, 88 non-need-based awards were made. *Average percent of need met:* 74%. *Average financial aid package:* $10,262. *Average need-based loan:* $3974. *Average need-based gift aid:* $4763. *Average non-need based aid:* $5969. *Average indebtedness upon graduation:* $11,527.

Applying *Options:* common application, electronic application, early admission, early action, deferred entrance. *Application fee:* $25. *Required:* high school transcript, minimum 2.0 GPA. *Required for some:* essay or personal statement, 3 letters of recommendation, interview, portfolio for art program, supplemental application for physician's assistant program. *Application deadline:* rolling (freshmen), rolling (transfers). *Notification:* continuous (freshmen), 9/1 (early action).

Admissions Contact Ms. Kimberly Pagano, Interim Director of Admissions, Daemen College, 4380 Main Street, Amherst, NY 14226-3592. *Phone:* 716-839-8225. *Toll-free phone:* 800-462-7652. *Fax:* 716-839-8370. *E-mail:* admissions@daemen.edu.

DARKEI NOAM RABBINICAL COLLEGE
Brooklyn, New York

Admissions Contact Rabbi Pinchas Horowitz, Director of Admissions, Darkei Noam Rabbinical College, 2822 Avenue J, Brooklyn, NY 11210. *Phone:* 718-338-6464.

DEVRY INSTITUTE OF TECHNOLOGY
Long Island City, New York

- **Proprietary** 4-year, founded 1998, part of DeVry, Inc
- **Calendar** semesters
- **Degrees** associate and bachelor's
- **Urban** campus
- **Coed,** 2,036 undergraduate students, 75% full-time, 21% women, 79% men
- **Minimally difficult** entrance level, 67% of applicants were admitted

Undergraduates 1,518 full-time, 518 part-time. Students come from 16 states and territories, 29 other countries, 4% are from out of state, 22% African American, 5% Asian American or Pacific Islander, 16% Hispanic American, 0.5% Native American, 5% international, 1% transferred in. *Retention:* 41% of 2001 full-time freshmen returned.

Freshmen *Admission:* 1,506 applied, 1,016 admitted, 794 enrolled.

Faculty *Total:* 125, 44% full-time. *Student/faculty ratio:* 20:1.

Majors Business administration/management related; business systems analysis/design; business systems networking/ telecommunications; computer engineering technology; electrical/electronic engineering technology; information sciences/systems.

Academic Programs *Special study options:* academic remediation for entering students, accelerated degree program, adult/continuing education programs, advanced placement credit, cooperative education, part-time degree program, summer session for credit.

Library Learning Resource Center with 120 serial subscriptions, 708 audiovisual materials, an OPAC.

Computers on Campus 250 computers available on campus for general student use. A campuswide network can be accessed from off campus. At least one staffed computer lab available.

Student Life *Housing:* college housing not available. *Activities and Organizations:* student-run newspaper, International Students Club, Video Games Club, DeVry Student Association, Chess Club, Muslim Student Association. *Campus security:* 24-hour emergency response devices and patrols, student patrols, late-night transport/escort service, lighted pathways/sidewalks.

Standardized Tests *Recommended:* SAT I or ACT (for admission).

Costs (2001–02) *Tuition:* $9800 full-time, $345 per credit hour part-time. Full-time tuition and fees vary according to course load. Part-time tuition and fees vary according to course load. *Payment plans:* installment, deferred payment. *Waivers:* employees or children of employees.

Financial Aid Of all full-time matriculated undergraduates who enrolled in 2001, 2058 applied for aid, 2012 were judged to have need, 16 had their need fully met. In 2001, 46 non-need-based awards were made. *Average percent of need met:* 50%. *Average financial aid package:* $10,321. *Average need-based loan:* $5393. *Average need-based gift aid:* $6162.

Applying *Options:* electronic application, deferred entrance. *Application fee:* $50. *Required:* high school transcript, interview. *Application deadline:* rolling (freshmen), rolling (transfers). *Notification:* continuous (freshmen).

Admissions Contact Ms. Edith Bolanos, New Student Coordinator, DeVry Institute of Technology, 30-20 Thomson Avenue, Long Island City, NY 11101. *Phone:* 718-472-2728. *Toll-free phone:* 888-71-Devry. *Fax:* 718-269-4288.

DOMINICAN COLLEGE
Orangeburg, New York

- **Independent** comprehensive, founded 1952
- **Calendar** semesters
- **Degrees** certificates, associate, bachelor's, and master's
- **Suburban** 14-acre campus with easy access to New York City
- **Coed,** 1,501 undergraduate students, 50% full-time, 69% women, 31% men
- **Moderately difficult** entrance level, 67% of applicants were admitted

Undergraduates 756 full-time, 745 part-time. Students come from 16 states and territories, 18% are from out of state, 18% African American, 5% Asian American or Pacific Islander, 12% Hispanic American, 10% transferred in. *Retention:* 68% of 2001 full-time freshmen returned.

Freshmen *Admission:* 430 applied, 287 admitted, 125 enrolled. *Test scores:* SAT verbal scores over 500: 25%; SAT math scores over 500: 28%; SAT verbal scores over 600: 6%; SAT math scores over 600: 7%.
Faculty *Total:* 154, 40% full-time, 31% with terminal degrees. *Student/faculty ratio:* 12:1.
Majors Accounting; actuarial science; American studies; athletic training/sports medicine; biology; biology education; business; business administration; business economics; economics; education; education of the visually handicapped; elementary education; English; English education; environmental science; finance; health services administration; history; history education; humanities; human resources management; information sciences/systems; international business; liberal arts and sciences/liberal studies; management information systems/business data processing; mathematics; mathematics education; nursing; nursing science; occupational therapy; political science; pre-law; psychology; public administration; science education; secondary education; social sciences; social work; Spanish; special education.
Academic Programs *Special study options:* academic remediation for entering students, accelerated degree program, adult/continuing education programs, advanced placement credit, cooperative education, English as a second language, honors programs, internships, part-time degree program, services for LD students, summer session for credit. *ROTC:* Army (c). *Unusual degree programs:* 3-2 engineering with Manhattan College.
Library Pius X Hall plus 1 other with 103,350 titles, 650 serial subscriptions, an OPAC.
Computers on Campus 38 computers available on campus for general student use. A campuswide network can be accessed from student residence rooms and from off campus. Internet access, at least one staffed computer lab available.
Student Life *Housing Options:* coed. *Activities and Organizations:* drama/theater group, student-run newspaper, choral group, Student Government Association, Student Ambassadors, Aquin Players, school newspaper, Teachers of Tomorrow. *Campus security:* 24-hour emergency response devices and patrols, student patrols, late-night transport/escort service, controlled dormitory access. *Student Services:* personal/psychological counseling.
Athletics Member NCAA, NAIA. All NCAA Division II. *Intercollegiate sports:* baseball M(s), basketball M(s)/W(s), cross-country running M(s)/W(s), golf M(s)/W(s), soccer M(s)/W(s), softball W(s), volleyball W(s). *Intramural sports:* football M/W, volleyball M/W.
Standardized Tests *Required:* SAT I or ACT (for admission).
Costs (2001–02) *Comprehensive fee:* $21,310 includes full-time tuition ($13,290), mandatory fees ($620), and room and board ($7400). Part-time tuition: $443 per credit. No tuition increase for student's term of enrollment. *Required fees:* $15 per credit, $35 per term part-time. *Payment plans:* installment, deferred payment.
Applying *Options:* common application, early admission, deferred entrance. *Application fee:* $35. *Required:* high school transcript, minimum 2.0 GPA. *Required for some:* interview. *Recommended:* 2 letters of recommendation. *Application deadline:* rolling (freshmen), rolling (transfers). *Notification:* continuous (freshmen).
Admissions Contact Joyce Elbe, Director of Admissions, Dominican College, 470 Western Highway, Orangeburg, NY 10962-1210. *Phone:* 914-359-7800 Ext. 271. *Fax:* 914-365-3150. *E-mail:* admissions@dc.edu.

DOWLING COLLEGE
Oakdale, New York

- **Independent** comprehensive, founded 1955
- **Calendar** semesters
- **Degrees** bachelor's, master's, doctoral, and post-master's certificates
- **Suburban** 156-acre campus with easy access to New York City
- **Endowment** $11.4 million
- **Coed,** 2,685 undergraduate students, 67% full-time, 61% women, 39% men
- **Moderately difficult** entrance level, 86% of applicants were admitted

Undergraduates 1,807 full-time, 878 part-time. Students come from 27 states and territories, 6% are from out of state, 10% African American, 3% Asian American or Pacific Islander, 9% Hispanic American, 0.3% Native American, 0.4% international, 16% transferred in, 86% live on campus. *Retention:* 69% of 2001 full-time freshmen returned.
Freshmen *Admission:* 1,628 applied, 1,403 admitted, 387 enrolled. *Average high school GPA:* 2.80. *Test scores:* SAT verbal scores over 500: 32%; SAT math scores over 500: 39%; SAT verbal scores over 600: 7%; SAT math scores over 600: 12%; SAT verbal scores over 700: 1%; SAT math scores over 700: 3%.
Faculty *Total:* 456, 24% full-time, 33% with terminal degrees. *Student/faculty ratio:* 17:1.
Majors Accounting; aerospace science; aircraft mechanic/airframe; anthropology; applied art; applied mathematics; art; aviation management; biological/physical sciences; biology; business administration; business marketing and marketing management; communications; computer science; economics; education; elementary education; English; finance; history; humanities; information sciences/systems; interdisciplinary studies; international business; liberal arts and sciences/liberal studies; marine science; mathematics; music; music teacher education; natural sciences; political science; psychology; romance languages; secondary education; social sciences; sociology; special education; speech/rhetorical studies; theater arts/drama; transportation engineering; transportation technology; travel/tourism management.
Academic Programs *Special study options:* academic remediation for entering students, accelerated degree program, advanced placement credit, cooperative education, double majors, English as a second language, honors programs, independent study, internships, off-campus study, part-time degree program, services for LD students, student-designed majors, summer session for credit. *ROTC:* Army (c), Navy (c), Air Force (c).
Library Dowling College Library with 118,830 titles, 3,131 serial subscriptions, an OPAC.
Computers on Campus 118 computers available on campus for general student use. Internet access, online (class) registration, at least one staffed computer lab available.
Student Life *Housing Options:* coed. *Activities and Organizations:* drama/theater group, student-run newspaper, radio station, choral group, Student Government Association, Residence Hall Council, Pan African-American Caribbean Club, Aeronautics Club, Lion's Voice: The Student Newspaper. *Campus security:* 24-hour emergency response devices and patrols, late-night transport/escort service. *Student Services:* health clinic, personal/psychological counseling.
Athletics Member NCAA. All Division II. *Intercollegiate sports:* baseball M(s), basketball M(s)/W(s), crew M(c)/W(c), equestrian sports W, lacrosse M, soccer M(s), softball W(s), tennis M(s)/W(s), volleyball W(s). *Intramural sports:* bowling M/W, cross-country running M/W, track and field M/W, weight lifting M/W.
Standardized Tests *Recommended:* SAT I or ACT (for admission).
Costs (2001–02) *Tuition:* $13,350 full-time, $445 per credit part-time. Part-time tuition and fees vary according to course load and degree level. No tuition increase for student's term of enrollment. *Required fees:* $740 full-time, $240 per term part-time. *Room only:* $4800. Room and board charges vary according to housing facility and location. *Payment plans:* installment, deferred payment. *Waivers:* minority students, children of alumni, adult students, senior citizens, and employees or children of employees.
Applying *Options:* common application, electronic application, deferred entrance. *Application fee:* $25. *Required:* high school transcript. *Recommended:* interview. *Application deadline:* rolling (freshmen), rolling (transfers). *Notification:* continuous (freshmen).
Admissions Contact Ms. Nancy Brewer, Director of Enrollment Services and Financial Aid, Dowling College, 150 Idle Hour Boulevard, Oakdale, NY 11769. *Phone:* 631-244-3385. *Toll-free phone:* 800-DOWLING. *Fax:* 631-563-3827. *E-mail:* brewern@dowling.edu.

D'YOUVILLE COLLEGE
Buffalo, New York

- **Independent** comprehensive, founded 1908
- **Calendar** semesters
- **Degrees** bachelor's, master's, post-master's, and postbachelor's certificates
- **Urban** 7-acre campus
- **Coed,** 961 undergraduate students, 77% full-time, 75% women, 25% men
- **Moderately difficult** entrance level, 71% of applicants were admitted

The College offers a new informational technology program (BS) and a combined 5-year informational technology (BS) and international business (MS) program. The 5-year combined bachelor's/master's degree is offered in occupational therapy, international business, nursing, education, and dietetics. All dual-degree students pay undergraduate full-time tuition all 5 years.

Undergraduates 737 full-time, 224 part-time. Students come from 23 states and territories, 26 other countries, 6% are from out of state, 10% African American, 3% Asian American or Pacific Islander, 4% Hispanic American, 1.0% Native American, 18% international, 45% transferred in, 20% live on campus. *Retention:* 70% of 2001 full-time freshmen returned.
Freshmen *Admission:* 652 applied, 464 admitted, 95 enrolled. *Average high school GPA:* 2.88. *Test scores:* SAT verbal scores over 500: 39%; SAT math scores over 500: 36%; ACT scores over 18: 91%; SAT verbal scores over 600: 5%; SAT math scores over 600: 6%; ACT scores over 24: 33%; SAT math scores over 700: 2%.

D'Youville College (continued)

Faculty *Total:* 196, 54% full-time, 34% with terminal degrees. *Student/faculty ratio:* 12:1.

Majors Accounting; biology; business administration; business education; business marketing and marketing management; dietetics; education; education (K-12); elementary education; English; health services administration; history; interdisciplinary studies; international business; liberal arts and sciences/liberal studies; nursing; occupational therapy; philosophy; physical therapy; physician assistant; pre-dentistry; pre-law; pre-medicine; pre-veterinary studies; science education; secondary education; social work; sociology; special education.

Academic Programs *Special study options:* academic remediation for entering students, accelerated degree program, adult/continuing education programs, distance learning, double majors, independent study, internships, off-campus study, part-time degree program, services for LD students, study abroad, summer session for credit. *ROTC:* Army (c). *Unusual degree programs:* 3-2 dietetics, international business, occupational therapy, physical therapy.

Library D'Youville College Library with 93,413 titles, 1,235 serial subscriptions, 3,280 audiovisual materials, an OPAC, a Web page.

Computers on Campus 70 computers available on campus for general student use. A campuswide network can be accessed from student residence rooms and from off campus. At least one staffed computer lab available.

Student Life *Housing:* on-campus residence required through sophomore year. *Options:* coed, men-only, women-only, disabled students. *Activities and Organizations:* drama/theater group, student-run newspaper, radio station, choral group, Student Association, Occupational Therapy Student Association, Physical Therapy Student Association, Student Nurses Association, Black Student Union. *Campus security:* 24-hour emergency response devices and patrols, late-night transport/escort service, controlled dormitory access. *Student Services:* health clinic, personal/psychological counseling.

Athletics Member NCAA, NSCAA. All NCAA Division III. *Intercollegiate sports:* baseball M, basketball M(s)/W(s), cross-country running M(s)/W(s), golf M/W, soccer M/W, softball W, volleyball M/W. *Intramural sports:* basketball M/W, cross-country running M/W, football M/W, golf M/W, ice hockey M, skiing (downhill) M/W, soccer M/W, table tennis M/W, tennis M/W, volleyball W.

Standardized Tests *Required:* SAT I or ACT (for admission).

Costs (2001–02) *Comprehensive fee:* $18,704 includes full-time tuition ($12,350), mandatory fees ($200), and room and board ($6154). Full-time tuition and fees vary according to program. Part-time tuition: $360 per credit. Part-time tuition and fees vary according to course load. No tuition increase for student's term of enrollment. *Required fees:* $100 per term part-time. *Payment plans:* tuition prepayment, installment, deferred payment. *Waivers:* minority students, children of alumni, adult students, senior citizens, and employees or children of employees.

Financial Aid Of all full-time matriculated undergraduates who enrolled in 2001, 620 applied for aid, 554 were judged to have need, 135 had their need fully met. 72 State and other part-time jobs (averaging $1500). In 2001, 145 non-need-based awards were made. *Average percent of need met:* 66%. *Average financial aid package:* $10,065. *Average need-based loan:* $4343. *Average need-based gift aid:* $6208. *Average non-need based aid:* $6050.

Applying *Options:* common application, electronic application, early action. *Application fee:* $25. *Required:* high school transcript, minimum 2.0 GPA. *Required for some:* essay or personal statement, minimum 3.0 GPA, letters of recommendation, interview. *Application deadline:* rolling (freshmen), rolling (transfers). *Notification:* continuous (freshmen).

Admissions Contact Mr. Ron Dannecker, Director of Admissions and Financial Aid, D'Youville College, 320 Porter Avenue, Buffalo, NY 14201-1084. *Phone:* 716-881-7600. *Toll-free phone:* 800-777-3921. *Fax:* 716-881-7790. *E-mail:* admiss@dyc.edu.

ELMIRA COLLEGE
Elmira, New York

- **Independent** 4-year, founded 1855
- **Calendar** 4-4-1
- **Degree** bachelor's
- **Small-town** 42-acre campus
- **Endowment** $37.0 million
- **Coed,** 1,584 undergraduate students, 78% full-time, 69% women, 31% men
- **Moderately difficult** entrance level, 80% of applicants were admitted

Undergraduates 1,229 full-time, 355 part-time. Students come from 35 states and territories, 18 other countries, 48% are from out of state, 2% African American, 0.7% Asian American or Pacific Islander, 2% Hispanic American, 0.2% Native American, 6% international, 4% transferred in, 95% live on campus. *Retention:* 79% of 2001 full-time freshmen returned.

Freshmen *Admission:* 1,691 applied, 1,345 admitted, 370 enrolled. *Average high school GPA:* 3.50. *Test scores:* SAT verbal scores over 500: 67%; SAT math scores over 500: 65%; ACT scores over 18: 93%; SAT verbal scores over 600: 22%; SAT math scores over 600: 17%; ACT scores over 24: 54%; SAT verbal scores over 700: 3%; SAT math scores over 700: 1%; ACT scores over 30: 2%.

Faculty *Total:* 110, 73% full-time, 81% with terminal degrees. *Student/faculty ratio:* 12:1.

Majors Accounting; American studies; anthropology; art; art education; biochemistry; biology; biology education; business administration; business economics; business marketing and marketing management; chemistry; chemistry education; classics; criminal justice/law enforcement administration; economics; education; elementary education; English; English education; environmental science; European studies; fine/studio arts; foreign languages education; foreign languages/literatures; French; French language education; Greek (ancient and medieval); history; history education; humanities; human services; information sciences/systems; interdisciplinary studies; international business; international relations; Latin (ancient and medieval); liberal arts and sciences/liberal studies; literature; mathematics; mathematics education; medical technology; mental health/rehabilitation; middle school education; modern languages; music; nursing; nursing science; philosophy; political science; pre-dentistry; pre-law; pre-medicine; pre-veterinary studies; psychology; religious studies; romance languages; science education; secondary education; social science education; social sciences; social studies education; social work; sociology; Spanish; Spanish language education; speech education; speech-language pathology/audiology; theater arts/drama.

Academic Programs *Special study options:* accelerated degree program, adult/continuing education programs, advanced placement credit, English as a second language, independent study, internships, off-campus study, part-time degree program, student-designed majors, study abroad, summer session for credit. *ROTC:* Army (c), Air Force (c). *Unusual degree programs:* 3-2 engineering with Clarkson University.

Library Gannet-Tripp Library with 389,036 titles, 855 serial subscriptions, 45,691 audiovisual materials, an OPAC, a Web page.

Computers on Campus 90 computers available on campus for general student use. A campuswide network can be accessed from student residence rooms. Internet access, at least one staffed computer lab available.

Student Life *Housing:* on-campus residence required through senior year. *Options:* coed, women-only. *Activities and Organizations:* drama/theater group, student-run newspaper, radio station, choral group, student radio station, Student Activities Board, Psychology Club, Ski Club, Pal Program. *Campus security:* 24-hour patrols, late-night transport/escort service, 24-hour locked residence hall entrances. *Student Services:* health clinic, personal/psychological counseling.

Athletics Member NCAA. All Division III. *Intercollegiate sports:* basketball M/W, field hockey W, golf M/W, ice hockey M/W, lacrosse M/W, soccer M/W, softball W, tennis M/W, volleyball W. *Intramural sports:* badminton M/W, basketball M/W, bowling M/W, football M, golf M/W, ice hockey M/W, lacrosse M/W, racquetball M/W, skiing (downhill) M/W, soccer M/W, softball M/W, squash M/W, swimming M/W, table tennis M/W, tennis M/W, volleyball M/W.

Standardized Tests *Required:* SAT I or ACT (for admission).

Costs (2002–03) *Comprehensive fee:* $32,410 includes full-time tuition ($23,980), mandatory fees ($580), and room and board ($7850). Part-time tuition: $240 per credit. *Payment plans:* tuition prepayment, installment. *Waivers:* employees or children of employees.

Financial Aid Of all full-time matriculated undergraduates who enrolled in 2001, 1008 applied for aid, 942 were judged to have need, 219 had their need fully met. 352 Federal Work-Study jobs (averaging $1300). 190 State and other part-time jobs (averaging $1300). In 2001, 239 non-need-based awards were made. *Average percent of need met:* 90%. *Average financial aid package:* $19,393. *Average need-based loan:* $5825. *Average need-based gift aid:* $14,129. *Average indebtedness upon graduation:* $17,137.

Applying *Options:* common application, electronic application, early admission, early decision, deferred entrance. *Application fee:* $40. *Required:* essay or personal statement, high school transcript, minimum 2.0 GPA, 2 letters of recommendation. *Required for some:* interview. *Recommended:* interview. *Application deadlines:* 5/15 (freshmen), 8/1 (transfers). *Early decision:* 11/15 (for plan 1), 1/15 (for plan 2). *Notification:* continuous until 5/30 (freshmen), 12/15 (early decision plan 1), 2/1 (early decision plan 2).

Admissions Contact Mr. William S. Neal, Dean of Admissions, Elmira College, Office of Admissions, Elmira, NY 14901. *Phone:* 607-735-1724. *Toll-free phone:* 800-935-6472. *Fax:* 607-735-1718. *E-mail:* admissions@elmira.edu.

EUGENE LANG COLLEGE, NEW SCHOOL UNIVERSITY
New York, New York

- **Independent** 4-year, founded 1978, part of New School University
- **Calendar** semesters
- **Degree** bachelor's
- **Urban** 5-acre campus
- **Endowment** $90.2 million
- **Coed,** 595 undergraduate students, 95% full-time, 68% women, 32% men
- **Moderately difficult** entrance level, 65% of applicants were admitted

Eugene Lang offers undergraduates a seminar style of learning that emphasizes interdisciplinary liberal arts courses in discussion-based classes of no more than 19 students. The internship program encourages students to extend their learning beyond the classroom. The Greenwich location means that all the cultural treasures of New York City—museums, theater, dance, and music—are at a student's doorstep.

Undergraduates 563 full-time, 32 part-time. Students come from 35 states and territories, 14 other countries, 53% are from out of state, 6% African American, 5% Asian American or Pacific Islander, 9% Hispanic American, 0.3% Native American, 3% international, 9% transferred in, 34% live on campus. *Retention:* 73% of 2001 full-time freshmen returned.

Freshmen *Admission:* 686 applied, 443 admitted, 155 enrolled. *Average high school GPA:* 3.09. *Test scores:* SAT verbal scores over 500: 94%; SAT math scores over 500: 77%; SAT verbal scores over 600: 66%; SAT math scores over 600: 37%; SAT verbal scores over 700: 22%; SAT math scores over 700: 3%.

Faculty *Total:* 102, 52% full-time. *Student/faculty ratio:* 10:1.

Majors Anthropology; creative writing; economics; education; English; history; humanities; interdisciplinary studies; international relations; liberal arts and sciences/liberal studies; literature; music history; philosophy; political science; psychology; religious studies; social sciences; sociology; theater arts/drama; urban studies; women's studies.

Academic Programs *Special study options:* accelerated degree program, adult/continuing education programs, independent study, internships, off-campus study, part-time degree program, study abroad, summer session for credit. *Unusual degree programs:* 3-2 media studies, education, social science, management and urban policy.

Library Fogelman Library plus 2 others with 368,390 titles, 1,155 serial subscriptions, 433,123 audiovisual materials.

Computers on Campus 705 computers available on campus for general student use. A campuswide network can be accessed from off campus. At least one staffed computer lab available.

Student Life *Housing Options:* coed, disabled students. *Activities and Organizations:* drama/theater group, student-run newspaper, choral group, Student Union, Theater Club, student newspaper, literary journal, ethnic organizations. *Campus security:* 24-hour emergency response devices, controlled dormitory access, 24-hour desk attendants in residence halls. *Student Services:* health clinic, personal/psychological counseling.

Costs (2001–02) *Comprehensive fee:* $31,592 includes full-time tuition ($21,530), mandatory fees ($450), and room and board ($9612). Part-time tuition: $790 per credit. Part-time tuition and fees vary according to course load. *Required fees:* $115 per term part-time. *Room and board:* College room only: $6984. Room and board charges vary according to board plan and housing facility. *Payment plan:* installment. *Waivers:* employees or children of employees.

Financial Aid Of all full-time matriculated undergraduates who enrolled in 2001, 385 applied for aid, 379 were judged to have need, 31 had their need fully met. 132 Federal Work-Study jobs (averaging $2453). In 2001, 4 non-need-based awards were made. *Average percent of need met:* 70%. *Average financial aid package:* $16,048. *Average need-based loan:* $3445. *Average need-based gift aid:* $12,178. *Average non-need based aid:* $4449. *Average indebtedness upon graduation:* $19,871.

Applying *Options:* common application, early admission, early decision, deferred entrance. *Application fee:* $40. *Required:* essay or personal statement, high school transcript, minimum 2.0 GPA, 2 letters of recommendation, interview. *Recommended:* minimum 3.0 GPA. *Application deadlines:* 2/1 (freshmen), 5/1 (transfers). *Early decision:* 11/15. *Notification:* 3/22 (freshmen), 12/15 (early decision).

Admissions Contact Mr. Terence Peavy, Director of Admissions, Eugene Lang College, New School University, 65 West 11th Street, New York, NY 10011-8601. *Phone:* 212-229-5665. *E-mail:* lang@newschool.edu.

EXCELSIOR COLLEGE
Albany, New York

- **Independent** comprehensive, founded 1970
- **Calendar** continuous
- **Degrees** associate, bachelor's, master's, and postbachelor's certificates (offers only external degree programs)
- **Urban** campus
- **Coed,** 18,860 undergraduate students, 62% women, 38% men
- **Noncompetitive** entrance level

Undergraduates Students come from 50 states and territories, 51 other countries, 85% are from out of state, 12% African American, 6% Asian American or Pacific Islander, 5% Hispanic American, 0.8% Native American, 0.9% international.

Majors Accounting; area studies; biology; business administration; business marketing and marketing management; chemical engineering technology; chemistry; computer engineering technology; computer science; economics; electrical/electronic engineering technology; electromechanical technology; finance; foreign languages/literatures; geography; geology; history; human resources management; industrial technology; information sciences/systems; insurance/risk management; international business; laser/optical technology; liberal arts and sciences/liberal studies; literature; management information systems/business data processing; mass communications; mathematics; mechanical engineering technology; music; nuclear technology; nursing; operations management; philosophy; physics; political science; psychology; sociology; welding technology.

Academic Programs *Special study options:* accelerated degree program, adult/continuing education programs, advanced placement credit, distance learning, external degree program, independent study, part-time degree program, student-designed majors.

Library Excelsior College Virtual Library with a Web page.

Computers on Campus A campuswide network can be accessed from off campus.

Student Life *Housing:* college housing not available.

Costs (2001–02) *Tuition:* $915 per year part-time. Part-time tuition and fees vary according to degree level. *Required fees:* $380 per year part-time. *Payment plan:* installment. *Waivers:* employees or children of employees.

Financial Aid *Average indebtedness upon graduation:* $4989.

Applying *Application deadline:* rolling (freshmen), rolling (transfers).

Admissions Contact Ms. Chari Leader, Vice President for Enrollment Management, Excelsior College, 7 Columbia Circle, Albany, NY 12203-5159. *Phone:* 518-464-8500. *Toll-free phone:* 888-647-2388. *Fax:* 518-464-8777. *E-mail:* info@excelsior.edu.

FASHION INSTITUTE OF TECHNOLOGY
New York, New York

- **State and locally supported** comprehensive, founded 1944, part of State University of New York System
- **Calendar** 4-1-4
- **Degrees** certificates, associate, bachelor's, and master's
- **Urban** 5-acre campus
- **Coed,** 10,680 undergraduate students, 60% full-time, 82% women, 18% men
- **Moderately difficult** entrance level, 36% of applicants were admitted

Undergraduates 6,367 full-time, 4,313 part-time. Students come from 52 states and territories, 80 other countries, 26% are from out of state, 7% African American, 11% Asian American or Pacific Islander, 10% Hispanic American, 0.2% Native American, 15% international, 8% transferred in, 17% live on campus. *Retention:* 73% of 2001 full-time freshmen returned.

Freshmen *Admission:* 4,469 applied, 1,588 admitted, 1,021 enrolled. *Average high school GPA:* 3.30.

Faculty *Total:* 928, 23% full-time. *Student/faculty ratio:* 13:1.

Majors Advertising; art; fashion design/illustration; fashion merchandising; graphic design/commercial art/illustration; industrial design.

Academic Programs *Special study options:* academic remediation for entering students, adult/continuing education programs, advanced placement credit, cooperative education, distance learning, English as a second language, honors programs, internships, part-time degree program, services for LD students, study abroad, summer session for credit.

Library Gladys Marcus Library with 154,015 titles, 1,770 audiovisual materials.

Computers on Campus 450 computers available on campus for general student use. A campuswide network can be accessed from student residence rooms and from off campus. Internet access, online (class) registration, at least one staffed computer lab available.

Fashion Institute of Technology (continued)

Student Life *Housing Options:* coed, women-only. *Activities and Organizations:* drama/theater group, student-run newspaper, radio station, choral group, American Marketing Association, Distributive Education Clubs of America, Merchandising Society, literary magazine. *Campus security:* 24-hour emergency response devices and patrols. *Student Services:* health clinic, personal/psychological counseling.

Athletics Member NJCAA. *Intercollegiate sports:* basketball M/W, tennis M/W, volleyball W. *Intramural sports:* basketball M/W, tennis M/W, volleyball M/W.

Standardized Tests *Recommended:* SAT I or ACT (for placement).

Costs (2001–02) *Tuition:* state resident $3156 full-time, $132 per credit part-time; nonresident $7684 full-time, $327 per credit part-time. Full-time tuition and fees vary according to degree level and program. Part-time tuition and fees vary according to degree level and program. *Required fees:* $210 full-time, $5 per term part-time. *Room and board:* $7535. Room and board charges vary according to board plan and housing facility. *Payment plan:* installment. *Waivers:* employees or children of employees.

Financial Aid Of all full-time matriculated undergraduates who enrolled in 2001, 3312 applied for aid, 2345 were judged to have need, 509 had their need fully met. In 2001, 91 non-need-based awards were made. *Average percent of need met:* 80%. *Average financial aid package:* $5997. *Average need-based loan:* $3323. *Average need-based gift aid:* $3429. *Average non-need based aid:* $1836. *Average indebtedness upon graduation:* $8568.

Applying *Options:* electronic application, deferred entrance. *Application fee:* $100. *Required:* essay or personal statement, high school transcript, portfolio for art and design programs. *Application deadlines:* 1/1 (freshmen), 1/1 (transfers). *Notification:* continuous (freshmen).

Admissions Contact Mr. Jim Pidgeon, Director of Admissions, Fashion Institute of Technology, Seventh Avenue at 27th Street, New York, NY 10001-5992. *Phone:* 212-217-7675. *Toll-free phone:* 800-GOTOFIT. *Fax:* 212-217-7481. *E-mail:* fitinfo@sfitva.cc.fitsuny.edu.

FIVE TOWNS COLLEGE
Dix Hills, New York

- **Independent** comprehensive, founded 1972
- **Calendar** semesters
- **Degrees** associate, bachelor's, and master's
- **Suburban** 40-acre campus with easy access to New York City
- **Coed,** 1,027 undergraduate students, 97% full-time, 33% women, 67% men
- 70% of applicants were admitted

Five Towns College offers associate, bachelor's, and master's degree programs. Students may select from nearly 40 different majors, including audio recording technology, broadcasting, music business, jazz/commercial music, music teacher education, elementary education, theater arts, and film/video. The College is accredited by the Middle States Association and the New York State Board of Regents.

Undergraduates 994 full-time, 33 part-time. Students come from 14 states and territories, 10 other countries, 20% African American, 2% Asian American or Pacific Islander, 14% Hispanic American, 0.1% Native American, 0.4% international, 10% live on campus. *Retention:* 74% of 2001 full-time freshmen returned.

Freshmen *Admission:* 532 applied, 375 admitted, 327 enrolled. *Average high school GPA:* 2.20. *Test scores:* SAT verbal scores over 500: 44%; SAT math scores over 500: 36%; SAT verbal scores over 600: 8%; SAT math scores over 600: 5%.

Faculty *Total:* 87, 47% full-time, 22% with terminal degrees. *Student/faculty ratio:* 13:1.

Majors Audio engineering; broadcast journalism; business administration; business marketing and marketing management; computer management; data processing technology; elementary education; film/video production; jazz; liberal arts and sciences/liberal studies; mass communications; music; music business management/merchandising; music (piano and organ performance); music teacher education; music (voice and choral/opera performance); stringed instruments; telecommunications; theater arts/drama; theater design; wind/percussion instruments.

Academic Programs *Special study options:* academic remediation for entering students, advanced placement credit, cooperative education, distance learning, independent study, internships, off-campus study, part-time degree program, summer session for credit.

Library Five Towns College Library with 32,000 titles, 550 serial subscriptions, 6,000 audiovisual materials, an OPAC.

Computers on Campus 84 computers available on campus for general student use. Internet access, at least one staffed computer lab available.

Student Life *Housing Options:* coed. *Activities and Organizations:* drama/theater group, student-run newspaper, choral group, Concert Choir, Live Audio Club, Dance Club, Musical Theatre, yearbook. *Campus security:* 24-hour emergency response devices and patrols, late-night transport/escort service, controlled dormitory access. *Student Services:* health clinic, personal/psychological counseling.

Athletics Member NAIA. *Intercollegiate sports:* basketball M(s)/W(s), cross-country running M(s)/W(s).

Costs (2001–02) *Comprehensive fee:* $18,800 includes full-time tuition ($10,500), mandatory fees ($500), and room and board ($7800). Full-time tuition and fees vary according to course load. Part-time tuition: $440 per credit. *Required fees:* $120 per term part-time. *Room and board:* Room and board charges vary according to board plan. *Payment plans:* installment, deferred payment. *Waivers:* senior citizens and employees or children of employees.

Financial Aid Of all full-time matriculated undergraduates who enrolled in 2001, 800 applied for aid, 760 were judged to have need, 75 had their need fully met. 50 Federal Work-Study jobs (averaging $1920). *Average percent of need met:* 50%. *Average financial aid package:* $5000. *Average need-based loan:* $4200. *Average need-based gift aid:* $2000. *Average indebtedness upon graduation:* $10,000.

Applying *Options:* early admission, deferred entrance. *Application fee:* $25. *Required:* essay or personal statement, high school transcript, minimum 2.3 GPA, letters of recommendation. *Required for some:* interview. *Application deadline:* rolling (freshmen), rolling (transfers). *Notification:* continuous (freshmen).

Admissions Contact Mr. Jerry Cohen, Enrollment Services, Five Towns College, 305 North Service Road, Dix Hills, NY 11746-6055. *Phone:* 631-424-7000 Ext. 2110. *Fax:* 631-424-7008.

FORDHAM UNIVERSITY
New York, New York

- **Independent Roman Catholic (Jesuit)** university, founded 1841
- **Calendar** semesters
- **Degrees** bachelor's, master's, doctoral, first professional, and post-master's certificates (branch locations: an 85-acre campus at Rose Hill and an 8-acre campus at Lincoln Center)
- **Urban** 85-acre campus
- **Endowment** $254.7 million
- **Coed,** 7,062 undergraduate students, 89% full-time, 60% women, 40% men
- **Very difficult** entrance level, 55% of applicants were admitted

Fordham, an independent institution offering an education based on the Jesuit tradition, has 2 major campuses in New York City. The Rose Hill campus is set on 85 acres and is the largest green campus in New York City. The Lincoln Center campus, with a new 20-story residence hall, is located in the heart of midtown Manhattan.

Undergraduates 6,283 full-time, 779 part-time. Students come from 53 states and territories, 40 other countries, 44% are from out of state, 5% African American, 5% Asian American or Pacific Islander, 11% Hispanic American, 0.2% Native American, 1% international, 4% transferred in, 60% live on campus. *Retention:* 89% of 2001 full-time freshmen returned.

Freshmen *Admission:* 10,663 applied, 5,901 admitted, 1,663 enrolled. *Average high school GPA:* 3.62. *Test scores:* SAT verbal scores over 500: 86%; SAT math scores over 500: 84%; ACT scores over 18: 96%; SAT verbal scores over 600: 43%; SAT math scores over 600: 39%; ACT scores over 24: 64%; SAT verbal scores over 700: 7%; SAT math scores over 700: 4%; ACT scores over 30: 11%.

Faculty *Total:* 1,125, 53% full-time. *Student/faculty ratio:* 10:1.

Majors Accounting; African-American studies; African studies; American studies; anthropology; art; art history; bilingual/bicultural education; biological/physical sciences; biology; broadcast journalism; business administration; business economics; business marketing and marketing management; chemistry; classics; comparative literature; computer/information sciences; computer management; computer science; creative writing; criminal justice/law enforcement administration; dance; Eastern European area studies; economics; education; elementary education; English; film studies; finance; fine/studio arts; French; German; graphic design/commercial art/illustration; Greek (modern); Hispanic-American studies; history; information sciences/systems; interdisciplinary studies; international business; international relations; Italian; journalism; Latin American studies; Latin (ancient and medieval); liberal arts and sciences/liberal studies; literature; management information systems/business data processing; mass communications; mathematics; medieval/renaissance studies; Middle Eastern studies; modern languages; music; music history; natural sciences; peace/conflict studies; philosophy; photography; physical sciences; physics; political science; pre-dentistry; pre-law; pre-medicine; pre-veterinary studies; psychology; public administration; radio/television broadcasting; religious studies; romance languages; Russian; Russian/Slavic studies; secondary education; social sciences; social work; sociology; Spanish; theater arts/drama; theology; urban studies; women's studies.

Academic Programs *Special study options:* accelerated degree program, adult/continuing education programs, advanced placement credit, double majors, English as a second language, honors programs, independent study, internships, off-campus study, part-time degree program, services for LD students, student-designed majors, study abroad, summer session for credit. *ROTC:* Army (b), Navy (c), Air Force (c). *Unusual degree programs:* 3-2 engineering with Columbia University, Case Western Reserve University.

Library Walsh Library plus 3 others with 1.8 million titles, 14,094 serial subscriptions, 13,318 audiovisual materials, an OPAC, a Web page.

Computers on Campus 617 computers available on campus for general student use. A campuswide network can be accessed from student residence rooms and from off campus. Internet access, online (class) registration, at least one staffed computer lab available.

Student Life *Housing Options:* coed. *Activities and Organizations:* drama/theater group, student-run newspaper, radio station, choral group, marching band, United Student Government, Commuting Student Association, Residence Hall Association, Ambassador Program. *Campus security:* 24-hour emergency response devices and patrols, student patrols, late-night transport/escort service, controlled dormitory access. *Student Services:* health clinic, personal/psychological counseling.

Athletics Member NCAA. All Division I except football (Division I-AA). *Intercollegiate sports:* baseball M(s), basketball M(s)/W(s), crew M(c)/W(s), cross-country running M(s)/W(s), equestrian sports M(c)/W(c), golf M, ice hockey M(c), lacrosse M(c)/W(c), rugby M(c)/W(c), soccer M(s)/W(s), softball W(s), squash M, swimming M(s)/W(s), tennis M(s)/W(s), track and field M(s)/W(s), volleyball W(s), water polo M(s). *Intramural sports:* badminton M/W, baseball M, basketball M/W, fencing M/W, field hockey M/W, football M, golf W, racquetball M/W, skiing (cross-country) M/W, skiing (downhill) M/W, softball M/W, squash M/W, swimming M/W, tennis M/W, volleyball W.

Standardized Tests *Required:* SAT I or ACT (for admission). *Recommended:* SAT II: Subject Tests (for admission).

Costs (2001–02) *Comprehensive fee:* $31,205 includes full-time tuition ($22,000), mandatory fees ($460), and room and board ($8745). Part-time tuition: $673 per credit. Part-time tuition and fees vary according to class time and course load. *Required fees:* $55 per term part-time. *Room and board:* College room only: $6375. Room and board charges vary according to housing facility. *Payment plans:* tuition prepayment, installment. *Waivers:* employees or children of employees.

Financial Aid Of all full-time matriculated undergraduates who enrolled in 2001, 4578 applied for aid, 4115 were judged to have need, 995 had their need fully met. In 2001, 455 non-need-based awards were made. *Average percent of need met:* 79%. *Average financial aid package:* $18,317. *Average need-based loan:* $4065. *Average need-based gift aid:* $11,565. *Average non-need based aid:* $7415. *Average indebtedness upon graduation:* $15,379.

Applying *Options:* common application, electronic application, early admission, early decision. *Application fee:* $50. *Required:* essay or personal statement, high school transcript, 1 letter of recommendation. *Required for some:* interview. *Recommended:* minimum 3.0 GPA, interview. *Application deadlines:* 2/1 (freshmen), 7/1 (transfers). *Early decision:* 11/1. *Notification:* 4/1 (freshmen), 12/15 (early decision).

Admissions Contact Mr. John W. Buckley, Dean of Admission, Fordham University, Theband Hall, 441 East Fordham Road, New York, NY 10458. *Phone:* 718-817-4000. *Toll-free phone:* 800-FORDHAM. *Fax:* 718-367-9404. *E-mail:* enroll@fordham.edu.

GLOBE INSTITUTE OF TECHNOLOGY
New York, New York

- **Proprietary** 4-year
- **Calendar** trimesters
- **Degrees** certificates, diplomas, associate, and bachelor's
- **Coed,** 620 undergraduate students, 85% full-time, 45% women, 55% men
- 80% of applicants were admitted

Undergraduates 528 full-time, 92 part-time. Students come from 4 states and territories, 58 other countries, 62% are from out of state, 17% African American, 18% Asian American or Pacific Islander, 8% Hispanic American, 17% international.

Freshmen *Admission:* 142 applied, 114 admitted, 114 enrolled.

Faculty *Total:* 36, 39% full-time, 33% with terminal degrees. *Student/faculty ratio:* 18:1.

Majors Computer programming; management information systems/business data processing.

Academic Programs *Special study options:* academic remediation for entering students, English as a second language, internships, part-time degree program, services for LD students.

Library Globe Institute of Technology's Library plus 1 other with 5,400 titles, 1,237 serial subscriptions, 60 audiovisual materials, a Web page.

Computers on Campus 140 computers available on campus for general student use. Internet access available.

Standardized Tests *Recommended:* SAT I (for placement), ACT (for placement).

Costs (2002–03) *Tuition:* $8950 full-time, $299 per credit part-time. No tuition increase for student's term of enrollment. *Required fees:* $120 full-time, $120 per term part-time. *Payment plan:* installment. *Waivers:* employees or children of employees.

Applying *Options:* common application, electronic application. *Application fee:* $50. *Required:* interview.

Admissions Contact Mr. Leon Rabinovich, President, Globe Institute of Technology, 291 Boradway, New York, NY 10007. *Phone:* 212-349-4330 Ext. 102.

HAMILTON COLLEGE
Clinton, New York

- **Independent** 4-year, founded 1812
- **Calendar** semesters
- **Degree** bachelor's
- **Rural** 1200-acre campus
- **Endowment** $482.9 million
- **Coed,** 1,770 undergraduate students, 98% full-time, 51% women, 49% men
- **Very difficult** entrance level, 35% of applicants were admitted

Undergraduates 1,732 full-time, 38 part-time. Students come from 43 states and territories, 29 other countries, 59% are from out of state, 4% African American, 4% Asian American or Pacific Islander, 4% Hispanic American, 0.2% Native American, 3% international, 1.0% transferred in, 97% live on campus. *Retention:* 92% of 2001 full-time freshmen returned.

Freshmen *Admission:* 4,601 applied, 1,615 admitted, 465 enrolled. *Test scores:* SAT verbal scores over 500: 93%; SAT math scores over 500: 98%; SAT verbal scores over 600: 74%; SAT math scores over 600: 84%; SAT verbal scores over 700: 20%; SAT math scores over 700: 23%.

Faculty *Total:* 198, 89% full-time, 92% with terminal degrees. *Student/faculty ratio:* 9:1.

Majors African studies; American studies; anthropology; art; art history; Asian studies; biochemistry; biology; chemistry; classics; comparative literature; computer science; creative writing; dance; East Asian studies; economics; English; fine/studio arts; French; geology; German; Greek (modern); history; international relations; Latin (ancient and medieval); literature; mass communications; mathematics; modern languages; molecular biology; music; neuroscience; philosophy; physics; physiological psychology/psychobiology; political science; psychology; public policy analysis; religious studies; Russian/Slavic studies; sociology; Spanish; theater arts/drama; women's studies.

Academic Programs *Special study options:* accelerated degree program, adult/continuing education programs, advanced placement credit, double majors, English as a second language, independent study, internships, off-campus study, part-time degree program, services for LD students, student-designed majors, study abroad. *ROTC:* Army (c), Air Force (c). *Unusual degree programs:* 3-2 engineering with Columbia University, Rensselaer Polytechnic Institute, Washington University in St. Louis; public policy analysis with University of Rochester.

Library Burke Library plus 3 others with 538,377 titles, 3,585 serial subscriptions, 52,051 audiovisual materials, an OPAC, a Web page.

Computers on Campus 475 computers available on campus for general student use. A campuswide network can be accessed from student residence rooms and from off campus. Internet access, at least one staffed computer lab available.

Student Life *Housing:* on-campus residence required through senior year. *Options:* coed, disabled students. *Activities and Organizations:* drama/theater group, student-run newspaper, radio station, choral group, community service groups, outing club, student newspaper, national fraternities. *Campus security:* 24-hour emergency response devices and patrols, late-night transport/escort service, controlled dormitory access, student safety program. *Student Services:* health clinic, personal/psychological counseling, women's center.

Athletics Member NCAA. All Division III. *Intercollegiate sports:* baseball M, basketball M/W, crew M/W, cross-country running M/W, fencing M(c)/W(c),

Hamilton College (continued)
field hockey W, football M, golf M/W(c), ice hockey M/W, lacrosse M/W, rugby M(c)/W(c), sailing M(c)/W(c), skiing (downhill) M(c)/W(c), soccer M/W, softball W, squash M/W, swimming M/W, tennis M/W, track and field M/W, volleyball M(c)/W, water polo M(c)/W(c). *Intramural sports:* basketball M/W, bowling M/W, cross-country running M/W, football M, golf M/W, ice hockey M/W, racquetball M/W, sailing M/W, skiing (cross-country) M/W, skiing (downhill) M/W, soccer M/W, softball M, squash M/W, swimming M/W, tennis M/W, track and field M/W, volleyball M/W, water polo M/W.

Costs (2001–02) *Comprehensive fee:* $34,150 includes full-time tuition ($27,250), mandatory fees ($100), and room and board ($6800). Part-time tuition: $2500 per unit. *Room and board:* College room only: $3500. Room and board charges vary according to board plan. *Payment plans:* installment, deferred payment. *Waivers:* adult students and employees or children of employees.

Financial Aid Of all full-time matriculated undergraduates who enrolled in 2001, 1123 applied for aid, 1012 were judged to have need, 1012 had their need fully met. In 2001, 42 non-need-based awards were made. *Average percent of need met:* 99%. *Average financial aid package:* $20,823. *Average need-based loan:* $3697. *Average need-based gift aid:* $17,334. *Average non-need based aid:* $8032. *Average indebtedness upon graduation:* $16,853. *Financial aid deadline:* 2/1.

Applying *Options:* common application, electronic application, early admission, early decision, deferred entrance. *Application fee:* $50. *Required:* essay or personal statement, high school transcript, 1 letter of recommendation, sample of expository prose. *Recommended:* interview. *Application deadlines:* 1/15 (freshmen), 3/15 (transfers). *Early decision:* 11/15. *Notification:* 4/1 (freshmen), 12/15 (early decision).

Admissions Contact Mr. Richard M. Fuller, Dean of Admission and Financial Aid, Hamilton College, 198 College Hill Road, Clinton, NY 13323-1296. *Phone:* 315-859-4421. *Toll-free phone:* 800-843-2655. *Fax:* 315-859-4457. *E-mail:* admission@hamilton.edu.

HARTWICK COLLEGE

Oneonta, New York

- **Independent** 4-year, founded 1797
- **Calendar** 4-1-4
- **Degree** bachelor's
- **Small-town** 425-acre campus with easy access to Albany
- **Endowment** $70.9 million
- **Coed,** 1,446 undergraduate students, 91% full-time, 56% women, 44% men
- **Moderately difficult** entrance level, 89% of applicants were admitted

Undergraduates 1,310 full-time, 136 part-time. Students come from 30 states and territories, 35 other countries, 36% are from out of state, 4% African American, 0.7% Asian American or Pacific Islander, 2% Hispanic American, 0.7% Native American, 4% international, 86% live on campus. *Retention:* 76% of 2001 full-time freshmen returned.

Freshmen *Admission:* 1,970 applied, 1,746 admitted, 431 enrolled. *Test scores:* SAT verbal scores over 500: 78%; SAT math scores over 500: 80%; ACT scores over 18: 97%; SAT verbal scores over 600: 30%; SAT math scores over 600: 28%; ACT scores over 24: 50%; SAT verbal scores over 700: 4%; SAT math scores over 700: 2%; ACT scores over 30: 5%.

Faculty *Total:* 152, 70% full-time. *Student/faculty ratio:* 11:1.

Majors Accounting; anthropology; art; art history; biochemistry; biology; business administration; chemistry; computer/information sciences; computer science; economics; English; French; geology; German; history; mathematics; medical technology; music; music teacher education; nursing; philosophy; physics; political science; pre-law; pre-medicine; pre-veterinary studies; psychology; religious studies; sociology; Spanish; theater arts/drama.

Academic Programs *Special study options:* accelerated degree program, advanced placement credit, double majors, honors programs, independent study, internships, off-campus study, part-time degree program, student-designed majors, study abroad. *Unusual degree programs:* 3-2 engineering with Clarkson University, Columbia University.

Library Stevens-German Library plus 1 other with 300,000 titles, 3,000 serial subscriptions, 6,000 audiovisual materials, an OPAC, a Web page.

Computers on Campus 80 computers available on campus for general student use. A campuswide network can be accessed from student residence rooms and from off campus that provide access to students receive notebook computer, printers and software. Internet access, at least one staffed computer lab available.

Student Life *Housing:* on-campus residence required through junior year. *Options:* coed, men-only, women-only. *Activities and Organizations:* drama/theater group, student-run newspaper, radio and television station, choral group, Student Union, student radio station, Student Senate, Hilltops, Cardboard Alley Players, national fraternities, national sororities. *Campus security:* 24-hour emergency response devices and patrols, late-night transport/escort service. *Student Services:* health clinic, personal/psychological counseling, women's center.

Athletics Member NCAA. All Division III except soccer (Division I). *Intercollegiate sports:* baseball M, basketball M/W, cross-country running M/W, equestrian sports W, field hockey W, football M, golf M/W, ice hockey M(c), lacrosse M/W, rugby M(c), soccer M(s)/W, softball W, swimming M/W, tennis M/W, track and field M/W, volleyball W, water polo M(c)/W(s). *Intramural sports:* archery M/W, badminton M/W, basketball M/W, cross-country running M/W, equestrian sports M/W, football M/W, golf M/W, racquetball M/W, soccer M/W, squash M/W, swimming M/W, table tennis M/W, tennis M/W, track and field M/W, volleyball M/W, water polo M/W.

Standardized Tests *Recommended:* SAT I or ACT (for admission).

Costs (2001–02) *Comprehensive fee:* $33,090 includes full-time tuition ($25,715), mandatory fees ($325), and room and board ($7050). Part-time tuition: $2824 per credit. *Room and board:* College room only: $3660. Room and board charges vary according to board plan and housing facility. *Payment plan:* installment. *Waivers:* employees or children of employees.

Financial Aid Of all full-time matriculated undergraduates who enrolled in 2001, 1194 applied for aid, 1079 were judged to have need, 809 had their need fully met. In 2001, 218 non-need-based awards were made. *Average percent of need met:* 82%. *Average financial aid package:* $20,000. *Average need-based loan:* $5113. *Average need-based gift aid:* $12,000. *Average non-need based aid:* $5791. *Average indebtedness upon graduation:* $19,364. *Financial aid deadline:* 2/1.

Applying *Options:* common application, electronic application, early admission, early decision, early action, deferred entrance. *Application fee:* $35. *Required:* essay or personal statement, high school transcript, 2 letters of recommendation, audition for music program. *Recommended:* minimum 3.0 GPA, interview. *Application deadlines:* 2/15 (freshmen), 8/1 (transfers). *Early decision:* 1/15. *Notification:* 3/5 (freshmen), 2/22 (early action).

Admissions Contact Ms. Susan Dileno, Dean of Admissions, Hartwick College, One Hartwick Drive, P.O. Box 4022, Oneonta, NY 13820-4022. *Phone:* 607-431-4150. *Toll-free phone:* 888-HARTWICK. *Fax:* 607-431-4138. *E-mail:* admissions@hartwick.edu.

HILBERT COLLEGE

Hamburg, New York

- **Independent** 4-year, founded 1957
- **Calendar** semesters
- **Degrees** associate and bachelor's
- **Small-town** 40-acre campus with easy access to Buffalo
- **Endowment** $2.6 million
- **Coed,** 964 undergraduate students, 68% full-time, 63% women, 37% men
- **Minimally difficult** entrance level, 86% of applicants were admitted

Hilbert College's pioneering Economic Crime Investigation degree is one of only two few baccalaureate programs in the country that offers students career education in the fields of computer investigation and forensic accounting. Through a new grant, Hilbert has the unique distinction of being the only western New York college to have a modern psychology computer lab dedicated exclusively to undergraduate research.

Undergraduates 651 full-time, 313 part-time. Students come from 5 states and territories, 3 other countries, 1% are from out of state, 4% African American, 0.3% Asian American or Pacific Islander, 1% Hispanic American, 0.8% Native American, 0.4% international, 13% transferred in, 10% live on campus. *Retention:* 81% of 2001 full-time freshmen returned.

Freshmen *Admission:* 319 applied, 275 admitted, 150 enrolled. *Average high school GPA:* 2.20. *Test scores:* SAT verbal scores over 500: 23%; SAT math scores over 500: 31%; ACT scores over 18: 85%; SAT verbal scores over 600: 7%; SAT math scores over 600: 6%; ACT scores over 24: 16%.

Faculty *Total:* 88, 39% full-time, 35% with terminal degrees. *Student/faculty ratio:* 16:1.

Majors Accounting; business administration; criminal justice/law enforcement administration; English; finance; human services; law enforcement/police science; legal studies; liberal arts and sciences/liberal studies; management information systems/business data processing; paralegal/legal assistant; psychology.

Academic Programs *Special study options:* academic remediation for entering students, advanced placement credit, cooperative education, honors programs, independent study, internships, part-time degree program, services for LD students, summer session for credit.

Library McGrath Library with 38,302 titles, 3,337 serial subscriptions, 724 audiovisual materials, an OPAC, a Web page.

Computers on Campus 82 computers available on campus for general student use. A campuswide network can be accessed from student residence rooms. At least one staffed computer lab available.

Student Life *Housing Options:* coed. *Activities and Organizations:* student-run newspaper, choral group, Student Government Association, Phi Beta Lambda, SADD, Students in Free Enterprise (SIFE), criminal justice association. *Campus security:* 24-hour emergency response devices and patrols, student patrols, late-night transport/escort service, controlled dormitory access. *Student Services:* personal/psychological counseling.

Athletics Member NCAA. All Division III. *Intercollegiate sports:* baseball M, basketball M/W, cross-country running W, golf M, lacrosse W, soccer M/W, softball W, volleyball M/W. *Intramural sports:* baseball M, basketball M/W, cross-country running W, golf M, lacrosse W, soccer M/W, softball W, volleyball M/W.

Standardized Tests *Recommended:* SAT I (for admission), ACT (for admission), SAT I or ACT (for admission).

Costs (2002–03) *Comprehensive fee:* $18,005 includes full-time tuition ($12,600), mandatory fees ($500), and room and board ($4905). Full-time tuition and fees vary according to course load. Part-time tuition: $287 per credit. *Required fees:* $287 per credit, $5 per credit part-time. *Room and board:* College room only: $1890. Room and board charges vary according to board plan and housing facility. *Payment plans:* installment, deferred payment. *Waivers:* children of alumni, senior citizens, and employees or children of employees.

Financial Aid Of all full-time matriculated undergraduates who enrolled in 2001, 588 applied for aid, 553 were judged to have need, 331 had their need fully met. 58 Federal Work-Study jobs (averaging $1877). In 2001, 14 non-need-based awards were made. *Average percent of need met:* 63%. *Average financial aid package:* $8188. *Average need-based loan:* $3550. *Average need-based gift aid:* $2016. *Average non-need based aid:* $3532. *Average indebtedness upon graduation:* $9910. *Financial aid deadline:* 5/1.

Applying *Options:* electronic application, early admission, deferred entrance. *Application fee:* $20. *Required:* high school transcript. *Required for some:* interview. *Recommended:* letters of recommendation, interview. *Application deadlines:* 9/1 (freshmen), 8/1 (transfers). *Notification:* continuous (freshmen).

Admissions Contact Admissions Counselor, Hilbert College, 5200 South Park Avenue, Hamburg, NY 14075-1597. *Phone:* 716-649-7900 Ext. 211. *Fax:* 716-649-0702.

HOBART AND WILLIAM SMITH COLLEGES
Geneva, New York

- **Independent** 4-year, founded 1822
- **Calendar** trimesters
- **Degree** bachelor's
- **Small-town** 200-acre campus with easy access to Rochester and Syracuse
- **Endowment** $120.0 million
- **Coed,** 1,892 undergraduate students, 99% full-time, 56% women, 44% men
- **Very difficult** entrance level, 69% of applicants were admitted

Hobart and William Smith Colleges are dedicated to providing a liberal arts education that is not merely informative but also transformative, by emphasizing ideals as well as knowledge. In other words, they are committed to nurturing the whole person, not just the academic student. To achieve this goal, HWS melds an interdisciplinary curriculum with a world view of learning, the highlights of which are an extensive and vibrant study-abroad program; local, national, and global internships; and a strong community service component.

Undergraduates 1,881 full-time, 11 part-time. Students come from 38 states and territories, 18 other countries, 50% are from out of state, 4% African American, 2% Asian American or Pacific Islander, 4% Hispanic American, 0.3% Native American, 1% international, 1% transferred in, 92% live on campus. *Retention:* 85% of 2001 full-time freshmen returned.

Freshmen *Admission:* 2,928 applied, 2,033 admitted, 548 enrolled. *Average high school GPA:* 3.21. *Test scores:* SAT verbal scores over 500: 87%; SAT math scores over 500: 88%; SAT verbal scores over 600: 37%; SAT math scores over 600: 36%; SAT verbal scores over 700: 4%; SAT math scores over 700: 3%.

Faculty *Total:* 166, 89% full-time, 91% with terminal degrees. *Student/faculty ratio:* 12:1.

Majors African-American studies; African studies; American studies; anthropology; architecture; art; art history; Asian studies; biochemistry; biology; chemistry; Chinese; classics; comparative literature; computer science; dance; economics; English; environmental science; European studies; fine/studio arts; French; geology; Greek (ancient and medieval); history; interdisciplinary studies; international relations; Japanese; Latin American studies; Latin (ancient and medieval); liberal arts and sciences/liberal studies; mass communications; mathematics; medieval/renaissance studies; modern languages; music; philosophy; physics; political science; pre-dentistry; pre-law; pre-medicine; pre-veterinary studies; psychology; public policy analysis; religious studies; Russian; Russian/Slavic studies; sociology; Spanish; theater arts/drama; urban studies; women's studies.

Academic Programs *Special study options:* accelerated degree program, adult/continuing education programs, advanced placement credit, double majors, English as a second language, honors programs, independent study, internships, off-campus study, services for LD students, student-designed majors, study abroad. *Unusual degree programs:* 3-2 business administration with Clarkson University, Rochester Institute of Technology; engineering with Columbia University, University of Rochester, Rensselaer Polytechnic Institute, Dartmouth College; architecture with Washington University in St. Louis.

Library Warren Hunting Smith Library plus 1 other with 359,742 titles, 3,289 serial subscriptions, 7,658 audiovisual materials, an OPAC, a Web page.

Computers on Campus 221 computers available on campus for general student use. A campuswide network can be accessed from student residence rooms and from off campus. Internet access, online (class) registration, at least one staffed computer lab available.

Student Life *Housing:* on-campus residence required through senior year. *Options:* coed, men-only, women-only, cooperative. *Activities and Organizations:* drama/theater group, student-run newspaper, radio station, choral group, Student Life and Leadership, student government, African-American Student Coalition, service network, sports clubs, national fraternities. *Campus security:* 24-hour emergency response devices and patrols, late-night transport/escort service, controlled dormitory access. *Student Services:* health clinic, personal/psychological counseling, women's center, legal services.

Athletics Member NCAA. All Division III except lacrosse (Division I). *Intercollegiate sports:* basketball M/W, crew M/W, cross-country running M/W, field hockey W, football M, golf M, ice hockey M/W(c), lacrosse M/W, rugby M(c)/W(c), sailing M/W, skiing (downhill) M(c)/W(c), soccer M/W, squash M/W, swimming W, tennis M/W. *Intramural sports:* archery M/W, badminton M/W, baseball M, basketball M/W, equestrian sports M/W, fencing M/W, football M, golf M/W, ice hockey M/W, lacrosse M/W, racquetball M/W, rugby M, sailing M(c)/W(c), skiing (cross-country) M/W, skiing (downhill) M/W, soccer M/W, softball M/W, squash M, swimming W, table tennis M/W, tennis W, track and field M, volleyball M/W, water polo M, weight lifting M/W.

Standardized Tests *Required:* SAT I or ACT (for admission). *Recommended:* SAT II: Subject Tests (for admission).

Costs (2001–02) *Comprehensive fee:* $33,195 includes full-time tuition ($25,664), mandatory fees ($513), and room and board ($7018). Part-time tuition: $3208 per course. Part-time tuition and fees vary according to course load. *Room and board:* College room only: $3700. Room and board charges vary according to board plan and housing facility. *Payment plans:* tuition prepayment, installment, deferred payment. *Waivers:* employees or children of employees.

Financial Aid Of all full-time matriculated undergraduates who enrolled in 2001, 1326 applied for aid, 1197 were judged to have need, 999 had their need fully met. 878 Federal Work-Study jobs (averaging $1013). 197 State and other part-time jobs (averaging $1785). In 2001, 217 non-need-based awards were made. *Average percent of need met:* 97%. *Average financial aid package:* $22,089. *Average need-based loan:* $3859. *Average need-based gift aid:* $18,025. *Average indebtedness upon graduation:* $17,294. *Financial aid deadline:* 3/15.

Applying *Options:* common application, electronic application, early admission, early decision, deferred entrance. *Application fee:* $45. *Required:* essay or personal statement, high school transcript, 2 letters of recommendation. *Recommended:* interview. *Application deadline:* 2/1 (freshmen), rolling (transfers). *Early decision:* 11/15 (for plan 1), 1/1 (for plan 2). *Notification:* 4/1 (freshmen), 12/15 (early decision plan 1), 2/1 (early decision plan 2).

Admissions Contact Ms. Mara O'Laughlin, Director of Admissions, Hobart and William Smith Colleges, 629 South Main Street, Geneva, NY 14456-3397. *Phone:* 315-781-3472. *Toll-free phone:* 800-245-0100. *Fax:* 315-781-5471. *E-mail:* admissions@hws.edu.

HOFSTRA UNIVERSITY
Hempstead, New York

- **Independent** university, founded 1935
- **Calendar** 4-1-4
- **Degrees** certificates, diplomas, associate, bachelor's, master's, doctoral, first professional, post-master's, and postbachelor's certificates
- **Suburban** 240-acre campus with easy access to New York City
- **Endowment** $112.4 million
- **Coed,** 9,645 undergraduate students, 87% full-time, 53% women, 47% men
- **Moderately difficult** entrance level, 77% of applicants were admitted

Hofstra University (continued)

Founded in 1935, Hofstra University has grown to be recognized both nationally and internationally for its resources, academic offerings, accreditations, conferences, and cultural events. Hofstra's undergraduate education places great emphasis on the role of the student in the life of the University. Hofstra also offers graduate programs in business, education, liberal arts, and law. Students have easy access to the theater and cultural life of New York City, yet have a learning environment on Long Island on a 240-acre campus that is also an accredited arboretum and museum.

Undergraduates 8,406 full-time, 1,239 part-time. Students come from 44 states and territories, 67 other countries, 21% are from out of state, 8% African American, 4% Asian American or Pacific Islander, 7% Hispanic American, 0.1% Native American, 2% international, 8% transferred in, 39% live on campus. *Retention:* 77% of 2001 full-time freshmen returned.

Freshmen *Admission:* 11,613 applied, 8,949 admitted, 2,004 enrolled. *Average high school GPA:* 2.90. *Test scores:* SAT verbal scores over 500: 79%; SAT math scores over 500: 82%; ACT scores over 18: 99%; SAT verbal scores over 600: 21%; SAT math scores over 600: 25%; ACT scores over 24: 37%; SAT verbal scores over 700: 2%; SAT math scores over 700: 2%; ACT scores over 30: 2%.

Faculty *Total:* 1,272, 39% full-time, 56% with terminal degrees. *Student/faculty ratio:* 16:1.

Majors Accounting; African-American studies; American studies; anthropology; applied mathematics; art education; art history; Asian studies; biochemistry; biological/physical sciences; biology; biology education; broadcast journalism; business administration; business marketing and marketing management; chemistry; chemistry education; classics; communications; communications technologies related; community health liaison; comparative literature; computer science; dance; early childhood education; economics; electrical engineering; elementary education; engineering science; English; English education; environmental science; exercise sciences; film studies; film/video production; finance; fine/studio arts; French; French language education; geography; geology; German; German language education; health education; health professions and related sciences; Hebrew; Hispanic-American studies; history; humanities; industrial/manufacturing engineering; interdisciplinary studies; international business; Italian; journalism; Judaic studies; labor/personnel relations; Latin American studies; liberal arts and sciences/liberal studies; marine biology; mass communications; mathematics; mathematics/computer science; mathematics education; mathematics related; mechanical engineering; music; music teacher education; natural sciences; philosophy; physical education; physics; physics education; political science; psychology; public relations; radio/television broadcasting technology; Russian; secondary education; social sciences; social studies education; sociology; Spanish; speech-language pathology/audiology; teacher education, specific programs related; theater arts/drama.

Academic Programs *Special study options:* academic remediation for entering students, accelerated degree program, adult/continuing education programs, advanced placement credit, double majors, English as a second language, honors programs, independent study, internships, part-time degree program, services for LD students, student-designed majors, study abroad, summer session for credit. *ROTC:* Army (b). *Unusual degree programs:* 3-2 engineering with Columbia University.

Library Axinn Library plus 1 other with 1.6 million titles, 7,017 serial subscriptions, 7,000 audiovisual materials, an OPAC, a Web page.

Computers on Campus 600 computers available on campus for general student use. A campuswide network can be accessed from student residence rooms. Internet access, at least one staffed computer lab available.

Student Life *Housing Options:* coed, women-only, disabled students. *Activities and Organizations:* drama/theater group, student-run newspaper, radio and television station, choral group, Student Government Association, Organization of Commuter Students, Interfraternity/Sorority Council, Entertainment Unlimited, Resident Students Association, national fraternities, national sororities. *Campus security:* 24-hour emergency response devices and patrols, student patrols, late-night transport/escort service, controlled dormitory access, security booths and cameras at each residence hall entrance. *Student Services:* health clinic, personal/psychological counseling.

Athletics Member NCAA. All Division I except football (Division I-AA). *Intercollegiate sports:* baseball M(s), basketball M(s)/W(s), cross-country running M(s)/W(s), field hockey W(s), golf M(s)/W(s), lacrosse M(s)/W(s), soccer M(s)/W(s), softball W(s), tennis M(s)/W(s), volleyball W(s), wrestling M(s). *Intramural sports:* badminton M/W, baseball M, basketball M/W, crew M/W, equestrian sports M/W, fencing M/W, football M, ice hockey M, lacrosse M/W, rugby M, soccer M/W, softball W, table tennis M/W, tennis M/W, volleyball M/W, water polo M/W, wrestling M.

Standardized Tests *Required:* SAT I or ACT (for admission).

Costs (2001–02) *Comprehensive fee:* $23,252 includes full-time tuition ($14,920), mandatory fees ($802), and room and board ($7530). Part-time tuition: $491 per semester hour. Part-time tuition and fees vary according to course load. *Required fees:* $118 per term part-time. *Room and board:* College room only: $5140. Room and board charges vary according to board plan and housing facility. *Payment plans:* installment, deferred payment. *Waivers:* senior citizens and employees or children of employees.

Financial Aid Of all full-time matriculated undergraduates who enrolled in 2001, 7019 applied for aid, 5212 were judged to have need. 453 Federal Work-Study jobs (averaging $2428). 83 State and other part-time jobs (averaging $1928). In 2001, 1116 non-need-based awards were made. *Average financial aid package:* $9992. *Average need-based loan:* $4263. *Average need-based gift aid:* $4917. *Average non-need based aid:* $3125. *Average indebtedness upon graduation:* $14,624.

Applying *Options:* common application, electronic application, early admission, early decision, deferred entrance. *Application fee:* $40. *Required:* high school transcript, 1 letter of recommendation. *Required for some:* essay or personal statement, interview. *Application deadline:* rolling (freshmen), rolling (transfers). *Early decision:* 12/1. *Notification:* continuous (freshmen), 12/15 (early decision).

Admissions Contact Ms. Mary Beth Carey, Vice President for Enrollment Services, Hofstra University, 100 Hofstra University, Hempstead, NY 11549. *Phone:* 516-463-6700. *Toll-free phone:* 800-HOFSTRA. *Fax:* 516-560-7660. *E-mail:* hofstra@hofstra.edu.

HOLY TRINITY ORTHODOX SEMINARY
Jordanville, New York

- **Independent Russian Orthodox** 5-year, founded 1948
- **Calendar** semesters
- **Degree** certificates and bachelor's
- **Rural** 900-acre campus
- **Men only,** 41 undergraduate students, 85% full-time
- **Noncompetitive** entrance level, 55% of applicants were admitted

Undergraduates 35 full-time, 6 part-time. Students come from 11 states and territories, 7 other countries, 30% are from out of state, 95% live on campus. *Retention:* 100% of 2001 full-time freshmen returned.

Freshmen *Admission:* 20 applied, 11 admitted, 9 enrolled.

Faculty *Total:* 19, 32% full-time. *Student/faculty ratio:* 4:1.

Majors Theology.

Academic Programs *Special study options:* accelerated degree program, English as a second language.

Library Holy Trinity Orthodox Seminary Library plus 1 other with 30,000 titles, 200 serial subscriptions.

Computers on Campus 5 computers available on campus for general student use. At least one staffed computer lab available.

Student Life *Housing:* on-campus residence required through senior year. *Options:* men-only. *Activities and Organizations:* student-run newspaper, choral group, Student Union. *Campus security:* 24-hour emergency response devices. *Student Services:* health clinic, personal/psychological counseling.

Costs (2001–02) *One-time required fee:* $25. *Comprehensive fee:* $4000 includes full-time tuition ($2000) and room and board ($2000).

Applying *Required:* essay or personal statement, high school transcript, letters of recommendation, special examination, proficiency in Russian, Eastern Orthodox baptism. *Recommended:* minimum 3.0 GPA. *Application deadlines:* 5/1 (freshmen), 5/1 (transfers).

Admissions Contact Fr. Vladimir Tsurikov, Assistant Dean, Holy Trinity Orthodox Seminary, PO Box 36, Jordanville, NY 13361. *Phone:* 315-858-0945. *Fax:* 315-858-0945. *E-mail:* info@hts.edu.

HOUGHTON COLLEGE
Houghton, New York

- **Independent Wesleyan** 4-year, founded 1883
- **Calendar** semesters
- **Degrees** associate and bachelor's
- **Rural** 1300-acre campus with easy access to Buffalo and Rochester
- **Endowment** $17.7 million
- **Coed,** 1,422 undergraduate students, 95% full-time, 64% women, 36% men
- **Moderately difficult** entrance level, 91% of applicants were admitted

Houghton College is a selective Christian liberal arts college of more than 1,300 undergraduates. Located on 1,300 acres in western New York, the College attracts talented students from around the world. Small classes in a traditional liberal arts curriculum of 49 majors and programs characterize

Houghton's academic life. More than 90 percent of students receive financial aid.

Undergraduates 1,356 full-time, 66 part-time. Students come from 39 states and territories, 24 other countries, 40% are from out of state, 2% African American, 1.0% Asian American or Pacific Islander, 1.0% Hispanic American, 0.4% Native American, 4% international, 4% transferred in, 79% live on campus. *Retention:* 88% of 2001 full-time freshmen returned.

Freshmen *Admission:* 1,025 applied, 935 admitted, 357 enrolled. *Average high school GPA:* 3.49. *Test scores:* SAT verbal scores over 500: 84%; SAT math scores over 500: 81%; ACT scores over 18: 96%; SAT verbal scores over 600: 46%; SAT math scores over 600: 39%; ACT scores over 24: 62%; SAT verbal scores over 700: 15%; SAT math scores over 700: 7%; ACT scores over 30: 20%.

Faculty *Total:* 100, 81% full-time, 68% with terminal degrees. *Student/faculty ratio:* 15:1.

Majors Accounting; art; art education; athletic training/sports medicine; biblical studies; biological/physical sciences; biology; business administration; chemistry; computer science; creative writing; cultural studies; elementary education; English; French; health/physical education; history; humanities; international relations; liberal arts and sciences/liberal studies; literature; mathematics; medical technology; music; music (piano and organ performance); music teacher education; music theory and composition; music (voice and choral/opera performance); pastoral counseling; philosophy; physical education; physics; political science; pre-dentistry; pre-law; pre-medicine; pre-veterinary studies; psychology; recreation/leisure studies; religious education; religious studies; secondary education; sociology; Spanish; stringed instruments; theology; wind/percussion instruments.

Academic Programs *Special study options:* adult/continuing education programs, advanced placement credit, double majors, honors programs, independent study, internships, off-campus study, part-time degree program, services for LD students, study abroad, summer session for credit. *ROTC:* Army (c). *Unusual degree programs:* 3-2 engineering with Clarkson University, Washington University in St. Louis.

Library Willard J. Houghton Library plus 1 other with 223,880 titles, 3,656 serial subscriptions, 1,944 audiovisual materials, an OPAC, a Web page.

Computers on Campus 50 computers available on campus for general student use. A campuswide network can be accessed from student residence rooms and from off campus. Internet access, at least one staffed computer lab available.

Student Life *Housing:* on-campus residence required through sophomore year. *Options:* men-only, women-only. *Activities and Organizations:* drama/theater group, student-run newspaper, radio station, choral group, student government, World Mission Fellowship, Allegany County Outreach, Youth for Christ, Climbing Club. *Campus security:* 24-hour patrols, late-night transport/escort service, controlled dormitory access, phone connection to security patrols. *Student Services:* health clinic, personal/psychological counseling.

Athletics Member NAIA. *Intercollegiate sports:* basketball M(s)/W(s), cross-country running M(s)/W(s), field hockey W(s), soccer M(s)/W(s), track and field M(s)/W(s), volleyball W(s). *Intramural sports:* basketball M/W, equestrian sports M/W, football M, golf M, lacrosse M, racquetball M/W, skiing (cross-country) M/W, skiing (downhill) M/W, soccer M/W, softball M/W, swimming M/W, table tennis M/W, tennis M/W, volleyball M/W, water polo M/W, weight lifting M/W.

Standardized Tests *Required:* SAT I or ACT (for admission).

Costs (2001–02) *Comprehensive fee:* $21,810 includes full-time tuition ($16,290) and room and board ($5520). Full-time tuition and fees vary according to course load and program. Part-time tuition: $680 per hour. *Room and board:* College room only: $2760. Room and board charges vary according to board plan and housing facility. *Payment plan:* installment. *Waivers:* senior citizens and employees or children of employees.

Financial Aid Of all full-time matriculated undergraduates who enrolled in 2001, 1111 applied for aid, 1009 were judged to have need, 371 had their need fully met. 393 Federal Work-Study jobs (averaging $1500). 266 State and other part-time jobs (averaging $1500). In 2001, 193 non-need-based awards were made. *Average percent of need met:* 75%. *Average financial aid package:* $13,026. *Average need-based loan:* $3300. *Average need-based gift aid:* $8740. *Average non-need based aid:* $6248. *Average indebtedness upon graduation:* $14,635.

Applying *Options:* electronic application, early admission, early action, deferred entrance. *Application fee:* $25. *Required:* essay or personal statement, high school transcript, 1 letter of recommendation, pastoral recommendation. *Recommended:* minimum 2.5 GPA, interview. *Application deadline:* rolling (freshmen), rolling (transfers). *Notification:* continuous (freshmen), 1/1 (early action).

Admissions Contact Mr. Bruce Campbell, Director of Admission, Houghton College, PO Box 128, Houghton, NY 14744. *Phone:* 585-567-9353. *Toll-free phone:* 800-777-2556. *Fax:* 585-567-9522. *E-mail:* admission@houghton.edu.

HUNTER COLLEGE OF THE CITY UNIVERSITY OF NEW YORK

New York, New York

- **State and locally supported** comprehensive, founded 1870, part of City University of New York System
- **Calendar** semesters
- **Degrees** bachelor's and master's
- **Urban** campus
- **Coed,** 15,703 undergraduate students, 64% full-time, 70% women, 30% men
- **Moderately difficult** entrance level, 47% of applicants were admitted

Undergraduates Students come from 29 states and territories, 3% are from out of state, 21% African American, 15% Asian American or Pacific Islander, 24% Hispanic American, 0.2% Native American, 7% international, 1% live on campus. *Retention:* 80% of 2001 full-time freshmen returned.

Freshmen *Admission:* 8,147 applied, 3,852 admitted. *Average high school GPA:* 2.79. *Test scores:* SAT verbal scores over 500: 45%; SAT math scores over 500: 47%; SAT verbal scores over 600: 11%; SAT math scores over 600: 10%; SAT verbal scores over 700: 2%; SAT math scores over 700: 1%.

Faculty *Total:* 1,298, 45% full-time, 49% with terminal degrees. *Student/faculty ratio:* 18:1.

Majors Accounting; African-American studies; anthropology; archaeology; art; art history; biology; chemistry; Chinese; classics; comparative literature; computer science; dance; early childhood education; economics; elementary education; English; film studies; fine/studio arts; French; geography; German; Greek (ancient and medieval); health education; Hebrew; Hispanic-American studies; history; Italian; Judaic studies; Latin American studies; Latin (ancient and medieval); literature; mathematical statistics; mathematics; medical laboratory technician; music; nursing; nutrition science; philosophy; physical education; physical therapy; physics; political science; psychology; public health; religious studies; romance languages; Russian; secondary education; sociology; Spanish; theater arts/drama; urban studies; women's studies.

Academic Programs *Special study options:* academic remediation for entering students, advanced placement credit, distance learning, double majors, English as a second language, freshman honors college, honors programs, independent study, internships, off-campus study, part-time degree program, services for LD students, student-designed majors, study abroad, summer session for credit. *Unusual degree programs:* 3-2 anthropology, economics, English, history, math, music, physics, sociology, biopharmacology.

Library Hunter College Library with 521,955 titles, 2,419 serial subscriptions, 12,515 audiovisual materials, an OPAC, a Web page.

Computers on Campus 600 computers available on campus for general student use. Internet access, at least one staffed computer lab available.

Student Life *Housing Options:* coed. *Activities and Organizations:* drama/theater group, student-run newspaper, radio station, choral group, Caribbean Student Union, Asian Students in Action, National Golden Key Honor Society. *Campus security:* 24-hour emergency response devices and patrols. *Student Services:* personal/psychological counseling, women's center, legal services.

Athletics Member NCAA. All Division III. *Intercollegiate sports:* basketball M/W, cross-country running M/W, fencing M/W, gymnastics W, soccer M, swimming W, tennis M/W, track and field M/W, volleyball M/W, wrestling M. *Intramural sports:* basketball M/W, cross-country running M/W, gymnastics M/W, racquetball M/W, rugby M, soccer M/W, swimming M/W, tennis M/W, volleyball M/W.

Standardized Tests *Required:* SAT I or ACT (for admission).

Costs (2001–02) *Tuition:* state resident $3200 full-time, $135 per credit part-time; nonresident $6800 full-time, $285 per credit part-time. *Required fees:* $143 full-time, $71 per term part-time. *Room and board:* room only: $1890. Room and board charges vary according to housing facility. *Payment plan:* deferred payment. *Waivers:* senior citizens.

Financial Aid Of all full-time matriculated undergraduates who enrolled in 2001, 6955 applied for aid, 6398 were judged to have need, 417 had their need fully met. *Average percent of need met:* 56%. *Average financial aid package:* $4809. *Average need-based loan:* $3145. *Average need-based gift aid:* $3829. *Average indebtedness upon graduation:* $7200.

Applying *Options:* early admission. *Application fee:* $40. *Required:* high school transcript. *Application deadlines:* 1/15 (freshmen), 3/1 (transfers). *Notification:* continuous (freshmen).

Admissions Contact Office of Admissions, Hunter College of the City University of New York, 695 Park Avenue, New York, NY 10021-5085. *Phone:* 212-772-4490.

IONA COLLEGE
New Rochelle, New York

- **Independent** comprehensive, founded 1940, affiliated with Roman Catholic Church
- **Calendar** 4-1-4
- **Degrees** associate, bachelor's, and master's
- **Suburban** 35-acre campus with easy access to New York City
- **Endowment** $15.8 million
- **Coed,** 3,417 undergraduate students, 85% full-time, 51% women, 49% men
- **Moderately difficult** entrance level, 80% of applicants were admitted

Founded in 1940, Iona College is dedicated to personal teaching in the tradition of American Catholic higher education and the Christian Brothers. The College endeavors to develop informed, critical, and responsible individuals who are equipped to participate actively in culture and society. At Iona College, students are the first priority.

Undergraduates 2,921 full-time, 496 part-time. Students come from 31 states and territories, 13 other countries, 16% are from out of state, 9% African American, 2% Asian American or Pacific Islander, 11% Hispanic American, 0.2% Native American, 0.6% international, 6% transferred in, 16% live on campus. *Retention:* 76% of 2001 full-time freshmen returned.

Freshmen *Admission:* 3,384 applied, 2,704 admitted, 842 enrolled. *Average high school GPA:* 2.70. *Test scores:* SAT verbal scores over 500: 53%; SAT math scores over 500: 53%; SAT verbal scores over 600: 12%; SAT math scores over 600: 13%; SAT verbal scores over 700: 1%; SAT math scores over 700: 1%.

Faculty *Total:* 339, 50% full-time. *Student/faculty ratio:* 15:1.

Majors Accounting; adult/continuing education; advertising; American studies; art; behavioral sciences; biochemistry; biology; broadcast journalism; business administration; business economics; business marketing and marketing management; chemistry; computer engineering; computer engineering technology; computer science; criminal justice/law enforcement administration; ecology; economics; education; elementary education; English; film studies; finance; French; gerontology; health services administration; history; information sciences/systems; interdisciplinary studies; international business; international relations; Italian; journalism; liberal arts and sciences/liberal studies; management information systems/business data processing; mass communications; mathematics; medical technology; modern languages; natural sciences; operations research; philosophy; physics; political science; psychology; public relations; religious studies; science education; secondary education; social sciences; social work; sociology; Spanish; special education; speech-language pathology/audiology; speech/rhetorical studies; speech therapy; theater arts/drama; urban studies.

Academic Programs *Special study options:* accelerated degree program, adult/continuing education programs, advanced placement credit, distance learning, double majors, honors programs, internships, off-campus study, part-time degree program, services for LD students, study abroad, summer session for credit. *ROTC:* Army (c).

Library Ryan Library plus 1 other with 264,917 titles, 803 serial subscriptions, 2,852 audiovisual materials, an OPAC, a Web page.

Computers on Campus 425 computers available on campus for general student use. A campuswide network can be accessed from student residence rooms and from off campus. Internet access, at least one staffed computer lab available.

Student Life *Housing Options:* coed. *Activities and Organizations:* drama/theater group, student-run newspaper, radio station, choral group, marching band, Council of Multicultural Leaders, student government, The Ionian, LASO, WICR, national fraternities, national sororities. *Campus security:* 24-hour emergency response devices and patrols, controlled dormitory access. *Student Services:* health clinic, personal/psychological counseling.

Athletics Member NCAA, NAIA. All NCAA Division I except football (Division I-AA). *Intercollegiate sports:* baseball M, basketball M(s)/W(s), crew M/W, cross-country running M/W, golf M, ice hockey M, soccer M/W, softball W, swimming M/W, tennis M(s)/W, track and field M(s)/W(s), volleyball W, water polo M/W. *Intramural sports:* basketball M/W(c), bowling M(c)/W(c), football M.

Standardized Tests *Required:* SAT I or ACT (for admission).

Costs (2001–02) *Comprehensive fee:* $26,456 includes full-time tuition ($16,500), mandatory fees ($540), and room and board ($9416). Full-time tuition and fees vary according to class time. Part-time tuition: $546 per credit. Part-time tuition and fees vary according to class time and course load. *Required fees:* $270 per term part-time. *Payment plans:* installment, deferred payment. *Waivers:* senior citizens and employees or children of employees.

Financial Aid Of all full-time matriculated undergraduates who enrolled in 2001, 2344 applied for aid, 1968 were judged to have need, 666 had their need fully met. In 2001, 574 non-need-based awards were made. *Average percent of need met:* 39%. *Average financial aid package:* $14,243. *Average need-based loan:* $2865. *Average need-based gift aid:* $4135. *Average non-need based aid:* $10,888. *Average indebtedness upon graduation:* $17,096.

Applying *Options:* common application, early admission, early action, deferred entrance. *Application fee:* $25. *Required:* essay or personal statement, high school transcript. *Recommended:* minimum 2.5 GPA, letters of recommendation, interview. *Application deadlines:* 3/15 (freshmen), 8/15 (transfers). *Notification:* continuous (freshmen), 12/20 (early action).

Admissions Contact Mr. Thomas Weede, Director of Undergraduate Admissions, Iona College, Admissions, 715 North Avenue, New Rochelle, NY 10801. *Phone:* 914-633-2502. *Toll-free phone:* 800-231-IONA (in-state); 914-633-2502 (out-of-state). *Fax:* 914-637-2778. *E-mail:* icad@iona.edu.

ITHACA COLLEGE
Ithaca, New York

- **Independent** comprehensive, founded 1892
- **Calendar** semesters
- **Degrees** certificates, bachelor's, and master's
- **Small-town** 757-acre campus with easy access to Syracuse
- **Endowment** $119.4 million
- **Coed,** 6,209 undergraduate students, 98% full-time, 55% women, 45% men
- **Moderately difficult** entrance level, 66% of applicants were admitted

Undergraduates 6,078 full-time, 131 part-time. Students come from 48 states and territories, 77 other countries, 51% are from out of state, 2% African American, 3% Asian American or Pacific Islander, 3% Hispanic American, 0.2% Native American, 2% international, 2% transferred in, 70% live on campus. *Retention:* 87% of 2001 full-time freshmen returned.

Freshmen *Admission:* 10,504 applied, 6,911 admitted, 1,755 enrolled. *Test scores:* SAT verbal scores over 500: 90%; SAT math scores over 500: 92%; SAT verbal scores over 600: 42%; SAT math scores over 600: 44%; SAT verbal scores over 700: 6%; SAT math scores over 700: 6%.

Faculty *Total:* 587, 71% full-time, 81% with terminal degrees. *Student/faculty ratio:* 13:1.

Majors Accounting; acting/directing; adapted physical education; anthropology; applied economics; applied mathematics; art; art history; arts management; athletic training/sports medicine; biochemistry; biology; biology education; broadcast journalism; business; business administration; business economics; business marketing and marketing management; chemistry; chemistry education; computer/information sciences; computer science; creative writing; dance; economics; educational media design; education (K-12); education (multiple levels); education of the speech impaired; English; English education; environmental science; exercise sciences; film studies; film/video production; finance; fine/studio arts; French; French language education; German; German language education; gerontology; health education; health facilities administration; health/medical preparatory programs related; health/physical education; health services administration; history; human resources management; interdisciplinary studies; international business; jazz; journalism; labor/personnel relations; liberal arts and sciences/liberal studies; marketing research; mass communications; mathematics; mathematics/computer science; mathematics education; middle school education; music; music (general performance); music (piano and organ performance); music teacher education; music theory and composition; music (voice and choral/opera performance); nutrition science; nutrition studies; occupational therapy; organizational psychology; philosophy; photography; physical education; physical therapy; physics; physics education; political science; pre-law; pre-medicine; psychology; public health education/promotion; public relations; radio/television broadcasting; recreational therapy; recreation/leisure studies; rehabilitation therapy; science education; secondary education; social sciences; social studies education; sociology; socio-psychological sports studies; Spanish; Spanish language education; speech-language pathology/audiology; speech/rhetorical studies; sport/fitness administration; telecommunications; theater arts/drama; theater design; visual/performing arts.

Academic Programs *Special study options:* accelerated degree program, adult/continuing education programs, advanced placement credit, double majors, freshman honors college, honors programs, independent study, internships, off-campus study, part-time degree program, services for LD students, student-designed majors, study abroad, summer session for credit. *ROTC:* Army (c), Air Force (c). *Unusual degree programs:* 3-2 engineering with Cornell University, Rensselaer Polytechnic Institute, Clarkson University, State University of New York at Binghamton.

Library Ithaca College Library with 238,613 titles, 2,400 serial subscriptions, 31,556 audiovisual materials, an OPAC, a Web page.

Computers on Campus 584 computers available on campus for general student use. A campuswide network can be accessed from student residence rooms and from off campus. Internet access, online (class) registration, at least one staffed computer lab available.

Student Life *Housing Options:* coed, women-only, disabled students. *Activities and Organizations:* drama/theater group, student-run newspaper, radio and television station, choral group, student government, Student Activities Board, African-Latino Society, Residence Hall Association, Community Service Network. *Campus security:* 24-hour emergency response devices, student patrols, late-night transport/escort service, patrols by trained security personnel 11 p.m. to 7 a.m. *Student Services:* health clinic, personal/psychological counseling.

Athletics Member NCAA. All Division III. *Intercollegiate sports:* baseball M, basketball M/W, crew M/W, cross-country running M/W, field hockey W, football M, gymnastics W, lacrosse M/W, soccer M/W, softball W, swimming M/W, tennis M/W, track and field M/W, volleyball W, wrestling M. *Intramural sports:* basketball M/W, bowling M(c)/W(c), crew M(c)/W(c), football M, golf M/W, ice hockey M(c), rugby W(c), skiing (downhill) M(c)/W(c), soccer M/W, softball M/W, tennis M/W, volleyball M/W.

Standardized Tests *Required:* SAT I or ACT (for admission).

Costs (2001–02) *Comprehensive fee:* $28,719 includes full-time tuition ($20,104) and room and board ($8615). Part-time tuition: $629 per credit hour. *Required fees:* $15 per term part-time. *Room and board:* College room only: $4304. Room and board charges vary according to housing facility. *Payment plan:* installment. *Waivers:* employees or children of employees.

Financial Aid Of all full-time matriculated undergraduates who enrolled in 2001, 4553 applied for aid, 4010 were judged to have need, 1816 had their need fully met. In 2001, 202 non-need-based awards were made. *Average percent of need met:* 87%. *Average financial aid package:* $18,960. *Average need-based loan:* $4645. *Average need-based gift aid:* $11,942. *Average non-need based aid:* $5581.

Applying *Options:* common application, electronic application, early admission, early decision, deferred entrance. *Application fee:* $55. *Required:* essay or personal statement, high school transcript, 1 letter of recommendation. *Required for some:* audition for music and theater programs. *Recommended:* minimum 3.0 GPA, interview. *Application deadlines:* 3/1 (freshmen), 7/15 (transfers). *Early decision:* 11/1. *Notification:* continuous until 4/15 (freshmen), 12/15 (early decision).

Admissions Contact Ms. Paula J. Mitchell, Director of Admission, Ithaca College, 100 Job Hall, Ithaca, NY 14850-7020. *Phone:* 607-274-3124. *Toll-free phone:* 800-429-4274. *Fax:* 607-274-1900. *E-mail:* admission@ithaca.edu.

JEWISH THEOLOGICAL SEMINARY OF AMERICA
New York, New York

- **Independent Jewish** university, founded 1886
- **Calendar** semesters
- **Degrees** bachelor's, master's, doctoral, and first professional (double bachelor's degree with Barnard College, Columbia University)
- **Urban** 1-acre campus
- **Coed,** 177 undergraduate students, 91% full-time, 50% women, 50% men
- **Very difficult** entrance level, 59% of applicants were admitted

The Albert A. List College of Jewish Studies, the undergraduate school of the Jewish Theological Seminary, offers students a unique opportunity to pursue 2 bachelor's degrees simultaneously. Students earn a degree from List in one of a dozen areas of Jewish study and a second degree in the liberal arts field of their choice from Columbia University or Barnard College. This exciting 4-year program enables students to experience an intimate and supportive Jewish community as well as a diverse and dynamic campus life.

Undergraduates 161 full-time, 16 part-time. Students come from 21 states and territories, 3 other countries, 65% are from out of state, 77% live on campus. *Retention:* 88% of 2001 full-time freshmen returned.

Freshmen *Admission:* 118 applied, 70 admitted, 51 enrolled. *Average high school GPA:* 3.80.

Faculty *Total:* 115. *Student/faculty ratio:* 5:1.

Majors Biblical studies; history; Judaic studies; literature; museum studies; music; philosophy; religious studies.

Academic Programs *Special study options:* academic remediation for entering students, adult/continuing education programs, advanced placement credit, distance learning, double majors, freshman honors college, honors programs, internships, off-campus study, part-time degree program, services for LD students, student-designed majors, study abroad, summer session for credit.

Library Library of the Jewish Theological Seminary with 271,000 titles, 720 serial subscriptions, an OPAC, a Web page.

Computers on Campus 20 computers available on campus for general student use. A campuswide network can be accessed from student residence rooms and from off campus. Internet access available.

Student Life *Housing Options:* coed. *Activities and Organizations:* drama/theater group, student-run newspaper, radio station, choral group. *Campus security:* 24-hour emergency response devices and patrols, late-night transport/escort service, controlled dormitory access. *Student Services:* health clinic, personal/psychological counseling, women's center.

Athletics *Intramural sports:* basketball M, softball M/W.

Standardized Tests *Required:* SAT II: Writing Test (for admission).

Costs (2001–02) *Tuition:* $9440 full-time, $500 per credit part-time. Full-time tuition and fees vary according to program. Part-time tuition and fees vary according to program. *Required fees:* $500 full-time, $225 per term part-time. *Room only:* $6470. Room and board charges vary according to housing facility. *Payment plan:* installment. *Waivers:* senior citizens and employees or children of employees.

Financial Aid Of all full-time matriculated undergraduates who enrolled in 2001, 97 applied for aid, 91 were judged to have need, 81 had their need fully met. In 2001, 38 non-need-based awards were made. *Average percent of need met:* 75%. *Average non-need based aid:* $2411. *Average indebtedness upon graduation:* $12,325. *Financial aid deadline:* 3/1.

Applying *Options:* early admission, early decision, deferred entrance. *Application fee:* $60. *Required:* essay or personal statement, high school transcript, 2 letters of recommendation. *Recommended:* minimum 3.0 GPA, interview. *Application deadlines:* 2/15 (freshmen), 5/1 (transfers). *Early decision:* 11/15 (for plan 1), 1/15 (for plan 2). *Notification:* continuous until 4/15 (freshmen), 12/15 (early decision plan 1), 2/15 (early decision plan 2).

Admissions Contact Ms. Reena Kamins, Assistant Director of Admissions, Jewish Theological Seminary of America, Room 614 Schiff, 3080 Broadway, New York, NY 10027-4649. *Phone:* 212-678-8832. *Fax:* 212-678-8947. *E-mail:* rekamins@jtsa.edu.

JOHN JAY COLLEGE OF CRIMINAL JUSTICE OF THE CITY UNIVERSITY OF NEW YORK
New York, New York

- **State and locally supported** comprehensive, founded 1964, part of City University of New York System
- **Calendar** semesters
- **Degrees** associate, bachelor's, and master's
- **Urban** campus
- **Endowment** $221,000
- **Coed,** 10,202 undergraduate students, 100% full-time, 60% women, 40% men
- **Moderately difficult** entrance level, 73% of applicants were admitted

Undergraduates 10,202 full-time. Students come from 10 states and territories, 12 other countries. *Retention:* 72% of 2001 full-time freshmen returned.

Freshmen *Admission:* 3,144 applied, 2,299 admitted, 4,038 enrolled.

Faculty *Total:* 628, 44% full-time, 61% with terminal degrees. *Student/faculty ratio:* 20:1.

Majors Behavioral sciences; corrections; criminal justice/law enforcement administration; fire science; forensic technology; information sciences/systems; law enforcement/police science; legal studies; pre-law; psychology; public administration; safety/security technology.

Academic Programs *Special study options:* academic remediation for entering students, advanced placement credit, cooperative education, English as a second language, honors programs, internships, off-campus study, part-time degree program, services for LD students, summer session for credit. *ROTC:* Navy (c), Air Force (c).

Library Lloyd George Sealy Library with 310,000 titles, 1,325 serial subscriptions, an OPAC.

Computers on Campus 250 computers available on campus for general student use. A campuswide network can be accessed from off campus. Internet access, at least one staffed computer lab available.

Student Life *Housing:* college housing not available. *Activities and Organizations:* drama/theater group, student-run newspaper, radio station, Organization of Black Students, Latino Diversity Club, Lex Review, Women's Awareness Club, Forensic Psychology Society. *Campus security:* 24-hour emergency response devices and patrols. *Student Services:* personal/psychological counseling, women's center, legal services.

Athletics Member NCAA. All Division III. *Intercollegiate sports:* basketball M/W, cross-country running M/W, tennis M/W, volleyball W. *Intramural sports:* basketball M/W, bowling M/W, football M/W, golf M/W, riflery M/W, swimming M/W, tennis M/W, track and field M/W, volleyball M/W, weight lifting M/W, wrestling M/W.

Costs (2002–03) *Tuition:* state resident $3200 full-time, $135 per credit part-time; nonresident $3400 full-time, $285 per credit part-time. Full-time tuition

John Jay College of Criminal Justice of the City University of New York (continued)

and fees vary according to class time and course load. Part-time tuition and fees vary according to class time. *Required fees:* $259 full-time, $137 per term part-time.

Financial Aid Of all full-time matriculated undergraduates who enrolled in 2001, 6736 applied for aid, 6736 were judged to have need. 318 Federal Work-Study jobs (averaging $1238). 190 State and other part-time jobs (averaging $10000). In 2001, 14 non-need-based awards were made. *Average percent of need met:* 70%. *Average financial aid package:* $5100. *Average need-based loan:* $2400. *Average non-need based aid:* $500. *Average indebtedness upon graduation:* $10,000.

Applying *Options:* early admission, deferred entrance. *Application fee:* $40. *Required:* high school transcript. *Application deadline:* rolling (freshmen), rolling (transfers). *Notification:* continuous (freshmen).

Admissions Contact Mr. Richard Saulnier, Acting Dean for Admissions and Registration, John Jay College of Criminal Justice of the City University of New York, 899 Tenth Avenue, New York, NY 10019-1093. *Phone:* 212-237-8878.

THE JUILLIARD SCHOOL
New York, New York

- **Independent** comprehensive, founded 1905
- **Calendar** semesters
- **Degrees** bachelor's, master's, and doctoral
- **Urban** campus
- **Endowment** $467.6 million
- **Coed,** 506 undergraduate students, 100% full-time, 51% women, 49% men
- **Most difficult** entrance level, 9% of applicants were admitted

Undergraduates 505 full-time, 1 part-time. Students come from 38 states and territories, 24 other countries, 78% are from out of state, 10% African American, 14% Asian American or Pacific Islander, 5% Hispanic American, 23% international, 5% transferred in, 48% live on campus. *Retention:* 95% of 2001 full-time freshmen returned.

Freshmen *Admission:* 1,624 applied, 143 admitted, 119 enrolled.

Faculty *Total:* 259, 46% full-time. *Student/faculty ratio:* 4:1.

Majors Dance; music; music (piano and organ performance); music (voice and choral/opera performance); stringed instruments; theater arts/drama; wind/percussion instruments.

Academic Programs *Special study options:* accelerated degree program, adult/continuing education programs, double majors, English as a second language, off-campus study, student-designed majors. *Unusual degree programs:* 3-2 music/liberal arts with Columbia University.

Library Lila Acheson Wallace Library with 80,793 titles, 220 serial subscriptions, 21,867 audiovisual materials, an OPAC, a Web page.

Computers on Campus 34 computers available on campus for general student use. A campuswide network can be accessed from off campus. Internet access, at least one staffed computer lab available.

Student Life *Housing:* on-campus residence required for freshman year. *Options:* coed. *Activities and Organizations:* drama/theater group, choral group, Christian Fellowship, Korean Crusade for Christ, Raw Dog Films, Greens, Gay Student Organization. *Campus security:* 24-hour emergency response devices and patrols, controlled dormitory access, electronically operated main building entrances. *Student Services:* health clinic, personal/psychological counseling, legal services.

Costs (2001–02) *Comprehensive fee:* $26,500 includes full-time tuition ($18,400), mandatory fees ($600), and room and board ($7500). *Room and board:* Room and board charges vary according to housing facility. *Payment plan:* installment. *Waivers:* employees or children of employees.

Financial Aid Of all full-time matriculated undergraduates who enrolled in 2001, 462 applied for aid, 377 were judged to have need, 149 had their need fully met. 232 Federal Work-Study jobs (averaging $1168). In 2001, 41 non-need-based awards were made. *Average percent of need met:* 83%. *Average financial aid package:* $18,843. *Average need-based loan:* $4829. *Average need-based gift aid:* $14,785. *Average non-need based aid:* $7603. *Average indebtedness upon graduation:* $19,679. *Financial aid deadline:* 3/1.

Applying *Options:* early admission. *Application fee:* $100. *Required:* essay or personal statement, high school transcript, audition. *Application deadlines:* 12/1 (freshmen), 12/1 (transfers). *Notification:* 4/1 (freshmen).

Admissions Contact Ms. Mary K. Gray, Associate Dean for Admissions, The Juilliard School, 60 Lincoln Center Plaza, New York, NY 10023-6588. *Phone:* 212-799-5000 Ext. 527. *Fax:* 212-724-0263. *E-mail:* webmaster@juilliard.edu.

KEHILATH YAKOV RABBINICAL SEMINARY
Brooklyn, New York

Admissions Contact Rabbi Zalman Gombo, Admissions Officer, Kehilath Yakov Rabbinical Seminary, 206 Wilson Street, Brooklyn, NY 11211-7207. *Phone:* 718-963-1212.

KEUKA COLLEGE
Keuka Park, New York

- **Independent** 4-year, founded 1890, affiliated with American Baptist Churches in the U.S.A.
- **Calendar** 4-1-4
- **Degrees** bachelor's and master's
- **Rural** 173-acre campus with easy access to Rochester
- **Endowment** $5.0 million
- **Coed,** 1,063 undergraduate students, 97% full-time, 73% women, 27% men
- **Moderately difficult** entrance level, 96% of applicants were admitted

Undergraduates 1,032 full-time, 31 part-time. Students come from 23 states and territories, 8% are from out of state, 6% transferred in, 68% live on campus. *Retention:* 71% of 2001 full-time freshmen returned.

Freshmen *Admission:* 980 applied, 938 admitted, 254 enrolled. *Average high school GPA:* 3.00. *Test scores:* SAT verbal scores over 500: 40%; SAT math scores over 500: 47%; ACT scores over 18: 77%; SAT verbal scores over 600: 10%; SAT math scores over 600: 6%; ACT scores over 24: 18%; SAT verbal scores over 700: 1%.

Faculty *Total:* 53, 94% full-time, 58% with terminal degrees. *Student/faculty ratio:* 15:1.

Majors Accounting; biochemistry; biology; biology education; business administration; business marketing and marketing management; communications; criminal justice/law enforcement administration; elementary education; English; English education; history; hotel and restaurant management; interdisciplinary studies; liberal arts and sciences/liberal studies; mathematics; mathematics education; medical technology; nursing; occupational therapy; psychology; social sciences; social studies education; social work; sociology; special education.

Academic Programs *Special study options:* academic remediation for entering students, accelerated degree program, adult/continuing education programs, advanced placement credit, cooperative education, double majors, independent study, internships, off-campus study, part-time degree program, services for LD students, student-designed majors, study abroad, summer session for credit.

Library Lightner Library with 83,108 titles, 16,886 serial subscriptions, 819 audiovisual materials, an OPAC.

Computers on Campus 62 computers available on campus for general student use. A campuswide network can be accessed from student residence rooms and from off campus. Internet access, at least one staffed computer lab available.

Student Life *Housing:* on-campus residence required through senior year. *Options:* coed, women-only, cooperative. *Activities and Organizations:* drama/theater group, student-run newspaper, radio station, choral group, Student Senate, Campus Activities Board, OTTERS (occupational therapy club), Education Club, BAKU. *Campus security:* 24-hour emergency response devices and patrols, late-night transport/escort service. *Student Services:* health clinic, personal/psychological counseling.

Athletics Member NCAA. All Division III. *Intercollegiate sports:* baseball M, basketball M/W, cross-country running M/W, lacrosse M/W, soccer M/W, softball W, swimming W, volleyball W. *Intramural sports:* badminton M/W, basketball M/W, crew M/W, skiing (cross-country) M/W, skiing (downhill) M/W, soccer M/W, softball M/W, table tennis M/W, tennis M/W, volleyball M/W, water polo M/W.

Standardized Tests *Required:* SAT I or ACT (for admission).

Costs (2001–02) *Comprehensive fee:* $21,170 includes full-time tuition ($14,050), mandatory fees ($240), and room and board ($6880). Full-time tuition and fees vary according to program. Part-time tuition: $470 per credit hour. Part-time tuition and fees vary according to program. *Room and board:* College room only: $3260. Room and board charges vary according to board plan and housing facility. *Payment plan:* installment. *Waivers:* employees or children of employees.

Financial Aid Of all full-time matriculated undergraduates who enrolled in 2001, 819 applied for aid, 819 were judged to have need. 555 Federal Work-Study jobs (averaging $815). *Average percent of need met:* 82%. *Average financial aid package:* $9521.

Applying *Options:* common application, electronic application, early admission, deferred entrance. *Application fee:* $30. *Required:* essay or personal statement, high school transcript, letters of recommendation. *Required for some:* interview. *Recommended:* minimum 2.75 GPA, interview. *Application deadline:* rolling (freshmen), rolling (transfers).

Admissions Contact Mr. Robert Callahan, Dean of Enrollment Management, Keuka College, Office of Admissions, Keuka Park, NY 14478-0098. *Phone:* 315-279-4411 Ext. 5254. *Toll-free phone:* 800-33-KEUKA. *Fax:* 315-279-5386. *E-mail:* admissions@mail.keuka.edu.

KOL YAAKOV TORAH CENTER
Monsey, New York

Admissions Contact Assistant Director of Admissions, Kol Yaakov Torah Center, 29 West Maple Avenue, Monsey, NY 10952-2954. *Phone:* 914-425-3871. *E-mail:* horizonss@aol.com.

LABORATORY INSTITUTE OF MERCHANDISING
New York, New York

- **Proprietary** 4-year, founded 1939
- **Calendar** semesters
- **Degrees** associate and bachelor's
- **Urban** campus
- **Coed, primarily women,** 340 undergraduate students, 99% full-time, 95% women, 5% men
- **Moderately difficult** entrance level, 74% of applicants were admitted

A private, Middle States-accredited 4-year college offering bachelor's and associate degrees in fashion merchandising, marketing, and visual merchandising. Distinctive educational opportunity through a combination of academics and industry work-study/co-ops. Prepares students for careers in fashion marketing, buying, product development, retail management, production, cosmetics, magazines, and more. Experience broadened by weekly field trips and guest lectures. Campus setting is in the finest area of New York City near business, fashion, and cultural centers. Summer sessions available for high school and college students.

Undergraduates 338 full-time, 2 part-time. Students come from 17 states and territories, 4 other countries, 47% are from out of state, 9% African American, 7% Asian American or Pacific Islander, 17% Hispanic American, 0.6% Native American, 1% international, 15% transferred in.

Freshmen *Admission:* 261 applied, 194 admitted, 81 enrolled. *Test scores:* SAT verbal scores over 500: 40%; SAT math scores over 500: 32%; SAT verbal scores over 600: 4%; SAT math scores over 600: 1%.

Faculty *Total:* 44, 20% full-time, 16% with terminal degrees. *Student/faculty ratio:* 8:1.

Majors Business marketing and marketing management; fashion merchandising.

Academic Programs *Special study options:* academic remediation for entering students, advanced placement credit, internships, study abroad, summer session for credit.

Library LIM Library with 11,000 titles, 80 serial subscriptions, 420 audiovisual materials.

Computers on Campus 65 computers available on campus for general student use. Internet access, at least one staffed computer lab available.

Student Life *Housing:* college housing not available. *Activities and Organizations:* student government, LIMlight Club (yearbook), Fashion Club, Latin Cultures Club, Marketing club/SIFE. *Student Services:* personal/psychological counseling.

Standardized Tests *Required:* SAT I or ACT (for admission).

Costs (2001–02) *Tuition:* $13,400 full-time, $425 per credit part-time. *Required fees:* $350 full-time, $100 per term part-time. *Payment plan:* installment.

Financial Aid Of all full-time matriculated undergraduates who enrolled in 2001, 225 applied for aid, 200 were judged to have need. In 2001, 7 non-need-based awards were made. *Average percent of need met:* 85%. *Average financial aid package:* $10,000. *Average need-based loan:* $3500. *Average need-based gift aid:* $1000. *Average non-need based aid:* $1000. *Average indebtedness upon graduation:* $14,000.

Applying *Options:* deferred entrance. *Application fee:* $35. *Required:* essay or personal statement, high school transcript, interview. *Recommended:* minimum 2.5 GPA, letters of recommendation. *Application deadline:* rolling (freshmen), rolling (transfers). *Notification:* continuous (freshmen).

Admissions Contact Ms. Karen Hammil Iglio, Director of Admissions, Laboratory Institute of Merchandising, 12 East 53rd Street, New York, NY 10022-5268. *Phone:* 212-752-1530 Ext. 17. *Toll-free phone:* 800-677-1323. *Fax:* 212-421-4341. *E-mail:* admissions@limcollege.edu.

LEHMAN COLLEGE OF THE CITY UNIVERSITY OF NEW YORK
Bronx, New York

- **State and locally supported** comprehensive, founded 1931, part of City University of New York System
- **Calendar** semesters
- **Degrees** bachelor's and master's
- **Urban** 37-acre campus
- **Coed,** 7,060 undergraduate students, 55% full-time, 72% women, 28% men
- **Moderately difficult** entrance level, 48% of applicants were admitted

Undergraduates 3,885 full-time, 3,175 part-time. Students come from 5 states and territories, 0% are from out of state, 26% African American, 3% Asian American or Pacific Islander, 36% Hispanic American, 0.1% Native American, 2% international, 11% transferred in. *Retention:* 69% of 2001 full-time freshmen returned.

Freshmen *Admission:* 1,673 applied, 810 admitted, 664 enrolled. *Average high school GPA:* 2.60. *Test scores:* SAT verbal scores over 500: 25%; SAT math scores over 500: 25%; SAT verbal scores over 600: 5%; SAT math scores over 600: 4%.

Faculty *Total:* 634, 50% full-time, 39% with terminal degrees. *Student/faculty ratio:* 23:1.

Majors Accounting; African-American studies; American studies; anthropology; art; art history; biochemistry; biology; business administration; business education; chemistry; classics; computer management; computer science; creative writing; dance; dietetics; economics; English; French; geography; geology; Greek (modern); health education; health services administration; Hebrew; history; interdisciplinary studies; Italian; Judaic studies; Latin American studies; Latin (ancient and medieval); linguistics; mass communications; mathematics; music; nursing; nutrition science; philosophy; physics; political science; psychology; recreation/leisure studies; Russian; social work; sociology; Spanish; speech-language pathology/audiology; speech/rhetorical studies; theater arts/drama.

Academic Programs *Special study options:* academic remediation for entering students, adult/continuing education programs, advanced placement credit, cooperative education, double majors, English as a second language, freshman honors college, honors programs, independent study, internships, off-campus study, part-time degree program, services for LD students, student-designed majors, summer session for credit. *ROTC:* Army (c). *Unusual degree programs:* 3-2 math.

Library Lehman College Library plus 1 other with 541,944 titles, 1,350 serial subscriptions, an OPAC, a Web page.

Computers on Campus 600 computers available on campus for general student use. Internet access, at least one staffed computer lab available.

Student Life *Housing:* college housing not available. *Activities and Organizations:* drama/theater group, student-run newspaper, radio station, choral group, Club Mac, Central and South American Club, Dominican Student Association, Health Services Association, academic society, national sororities. *Campus security:* 24-hour emergency response devices and patrols, student patrols. *Student Services:* health clinic.

Athletics Member NCAA. All Division III. *Intercollegiate sports:* baseball M, basketball M/W, cross-country running M/W, soccer M, softball W, swimming M/W, tennis M/W, track and field M/W, volleyball M/W, water polo M, wrestling M. *Intramural sports:* baseball M/W, basketball M, racquetball M/W, soccer M, softball M/W, tennis M/W, volleyball M/W, wrestling M.

Standardized Tests *Recommended:* SAT I (for admission), ACT (for admission).

Costs (2001–02) *Tuition:* state resident $1600 full-time, $135 per credit part-time; nonresident $3400 full-time, $285 per credit part-time. Full-time tuition and fees vary according to course load and program. Part-time tuition and fees vary according to course load and program. *Required fees:* $110 full-time, $35 per term part-time. *Payment plan:* installment. *Waivers:* senior citizens.

Financial Aid Of all full-time matriculated undergraduates who enrolled in 2001, 5991 applied for aid, 5770 were judged to have need. 1850 Federal Work-Study jobs. *Average percent of need met:* 70%. *Average financial aid package:* $5300. *Average need-based loan:* $3400. *Average need-based gift aid:* $3800. *Average indebtedness upon graduation:* $7200.

Applying *Options:* deferred entrance. *Application fee:* $40. *Required:* high school transcript, minimum 3.0 GPA. *Required for some:* letters of recommendation, interview. *Application deadline:* rolling (freshmen), rolling (transfers). *Notification:* continuous (freshmen).

Admissions Contact Ms. Gloria Ortiz, Assistant Director of Undergraduate Admissions, Lehman College of the City University of New York, 250 Bedford

Lehman College of the City University of New York (continued)
Park Boulevard West, Bronx, NY 10468. *Phone:* 718-960-8096. *Toll-free phone:* 877-Lehman1. *Fax:* 718-960-8712. *E-mail:* cawic@cunyum.cunx.edu.

LE MOYNE COLLEGE
Syracuse, New York

- **Independent Roman Catholic (Jesuit)** comprehensive, founded 1946
- **Calendar** semesters
- **Degrees** bachelor's, master's, and postbachelor's certificates
- **Suburban** 151-acre campus
- **Endowment** $31.5 million
- **Coed,** 2,445 undergraduate students, 88% full-time, 59% women, 41% men
- **Moderately difficult** entrance level, 77% of applicants were admitted

Le Moyne is a coeducational, residential college founded in the Jesuit tradition of academic excellence. Offering a comprehensive program rooted in the liberal arts and sciences, Le Moyne's shared mission of learning and services stresses education of the whole person. Strong academic programs, committed faculty, a reassuring Jesuit presence, an career advisement/internship opportunities prepare Le Moyne students for leadership and service in their personal and professional lives. Le Moyne is consistently recognized for outstanding value in *U.S. News & World Report's* annual college rankings.

Undergraduates 2,150 full-time, 295 part-time. Students come from 22 states and territories, 5% are from out of state, 4% African American, 1% Asian American or Pacific Islander, 3% Hispanic American, 0.8% Native American, 0.0% international, 7% transferred in, 64% live on campus. *Retention:* 84% of 2001 full-time freshmen returned.

Freshmen *Admission:* 2,443 applied, 1,881 admitted, 502 enrolled. *Average high school GPA:* 3.33. *Test scores:* SAT verbal scores over 500: 77%; SAT math scores over 500: 82%; ACT scores over 18: 98%; SAT verbal scores over 600: 24%; SAT math scores over 600: 25%; ACT scores over 24: 39%; SAT verbal scores over 700: 5%; SAT math scores over 700: 2%; ACT scores over 30: 4%.

Faculty *Total:* 253, 55% full-time, 63% with terminal degrees. *Student/faculty ratio:* 13:1.

Majors Accounting; applied mathematics; biochemistry; biological/physical sciences; biology; business administration; chemistry; communications; creative writing; criminology; economics; elementary education; English; English education; foreign languages education; French; history; information sciences/systems; international relations; labor/personnel relations; mathematics; mathematics education; philosophy; physician assistant; physics; political science; pre-dentistry; pre-law; pre-medicine; pre-pharmacy studies; pre-veterinary studies; psychology; religious studies; science education; secondary education; social studies education; sociology; Spanish; theater arts/drama.

Academic Programs *Special study options:* academic remediation for entering students, accelerated degree program, adult/continuing education programs, advanced placement credit, double majors, honors programs, independent study, internships, off-campus study, part-time degree program, services for LD students, study abroad, summer session for credit. *ROTC:* Army (c), Air Force (c). *Unusual degree programs:* 3-2 engineering with Manhattan College, Clarkson University, University of Detroit Mercy; forestry with State University of New York College of Environmental Science and Forestry.

Library Noreen Reale Falcone Library with 159,323 titles, 1,308 serial subscriptions, 10,129 audiovisual materials, an OPAC, a Web page.

Computers on Campus 225 computers available on campus for general student use. A campuswide network can be accessed from student residence rooms and from off campus. Internet access, at least one staffed computer lab available.

Student Life *Housing:* on-campus residence required through senior year. *Options:* coed, men-only, women-only, disabled students. *Activities and Organizations:* drama/theater group, student-run newspaper, radio station, choral group, Student Programming Board, Outing Club, theater group, Student Dancers, New Student Orientation Committee. *Campus security:* 24-hour emergency response devices and patrols, late-night transport/escort service, controlled dormitory access, campus watch program, self-defense education, lighted pathways, closed circuit TV monitors, security phones. *Student Services:* health clinic, personal/psychological counseling.

Athletics Member NCAA. All Division II except baseball (Division I), lacrosse (Division I). *Intercollegiate sports:* baseball M(s), basketball M(s)/W(s), cross-country running M(s)/W(s), golf M(s), lacrosse M(s)/W(s), soccer M(s)/W(s), softball W(s), swimming M/W, tennis M(s)/W(s), volleyball W(s). *Intramural sports:* basketball M/W, cross-country running M/W, football M, ice hockey M(c), racquetball M/W, rugby M(c), soccer M/W, softball M/W, volleyball M/W.

Standardized Tests *Required:* SAT I or ACT (for admission).

Costs (2001–02) *Comprehensive fee:* $23,840 includes full-time tuition ($16,350), mandatory fees ($500), and room and board ($6990). Part-time tuition: $359 per credit hour. Part-time tuition and fees vary according to class time. *Room and board:* College room only: $4320. Room and board charges vary according to board plan and housing facility. *Payment plans:* installment, deferred payment. *Waivers:* employees or children of employees.

Financial Aid Of all full-time matriculated undergraduates who enrolled in 2001, 1804 applied for aid, 1647 were judged to have need, 1230 had their need fully met. 521 Federal Work-Study jobs (averaging $790). In 2001, 157 non-need-based awards were made. *Average percent of need met:* 85%. *Average financial aid package:* $12,413. *Average need-based loan:* $3408. *Average need-based gift aid:* $10,599. *Average non-need based aid:* $4971. *Average indebtedness upon graduation:* $17,000.

Applying *Options:* common application, electronic application, early admission, early decision, deferred entrance. *Application fee:* $35. *Required:* essay or personal statement, high school transcript, 2 letters of recommendation. *Recommended:* interview. *Application deadlines:* 3/1 (freshmen), 6/1 (transfers). *Early decision:* 12/1. *Notification:* continuous until 5/1 (freshmen), 12/15 (early decision).

Admissions Contact Mr. Dennis J. Nicholson, Director of Admission, Le Moyne College, 1419 Salt Spring Road, Syracuse, NY 13214-1399. *Phone:* 315-445-4300. *Toll-free phone:* 800-333-4733. *Fax:* 315-445-4711. *E-mail:* admission@lemoyne.edu.

LONG ISLAND UNIVERSITY, BRENTWOOD CAMPUS
Brentwood, New York

- **Independent** upper-level, founded 1959, part of Long Island University
- **Degrees** certificates, bachelor's, master's, and post-master's certificates
- **Coed,** 88 undergraduate students, 32% full-time, 66% women, 34% men
- 100% of applicants were admitted

Undergraduates 28 full-time, 60 part-time. Students come from 1 other state, 1% are from out of state, 6% African American, 1% Asian American or Pacific Islander, 11% Hispanic American, 1% Native American, 132% transferred in.

Freshmen *Admission:* 25 applied, 25 admitted.

Faculty *Total:* 110, 18% full-time, 86% with terminal degrees. *Student/faculty ratio:* 7:1.

Majors Accounting; business administration; business marketing and marketing management; criminal justice studies; finance.

Student Life *Campus security:* evening security guard. *Student Services:* health clinic, personal/psychological counseling.

Costs (2001–02) *Tuition:* $17,220 full-time, $537 per credit part-time. *Required fees:* $740 full-time, $160 per term part-time.

Applying *Application deadline:* 9/14 (transfers).

Admissions Contact Mr. John P. Metcalfe, Director of Admissions, Long Island University, Brentwood Campus, 100 Second Avenue, Brentwood, NY 11717. *Phone:* 631-273-5112 Ext. 26. *E-mail:* brentwd@raptor.liu.edu.

LONG ISLAND UNIVERSITY, BROOKLYN CAMPUS
Brooklyn, New York

- **Independent** university, founded 1926, part of Long Island University
- **Calendar** semesters
- **Degrees** certificates, associate, bachelor's, master's, doctoral, first professional, post-master's, postbachelor's, and first professional certificates
- **Urban** 10-acre campus
- **Endowment** $41.4 million
- **Coed,** 5,509 undergraduate students, 80% full-time, 71% women, 29% men
- **Minimally difficult** entrance level, 74% of applicants were admitted

Undergraduates 4,424 full-time, 1,085 part-time. Students come from 37 states and territories, 15 other countries, 9% are from out of state, 48% African American, 11% Asian American or Pacific Islander, 16% Hispanic American, 0.2% Native American, 2% international, 13% transferred in, 5% live on campus.

Freshmen *Admission:* 3,157 applied, 2,343 admitted, 999 enrolled. *Average high school GPA:* 3.0.

Faculty *Total:* 1,028, 28% full-time. *Student/faculty ratio:* 19:1.

Majors Accounting; anthropology; art; art education; athletic training/sports medicine; biological/physical sciences; biology; business administration; business marketing and marketing management; chemistry; clinical psychology; computer/information sciences; computer science; cytotechnology; dance; early childhood education; economics; education; education administration; elementary education; English; finance; health science; history; humanities; information sciences/systems; interdisciplinary studies; jazz; journalism; liberal arts and sciences/liberal studies; mass communications; mathematics; medical technology; modern languages; molecular biology; music; nuclear medical technology; nursing; paralegal/legal assistant; pharmacy; philosophy; physical education; physical therapy; physician assistant; physics; political science; pre-law; premedicine; psychology; public administration; radio/television broadcasting; respiratory therapy; secondary education; social sciences; social work; sociology; special education; speech/rhetorical studies.

Academic Programs *Special study options:* academic remediation for entering students, adult/continuing education programs, advanced placement credit, cooperative education, double majors, English as a second language, honors programs, internships, part-time degree program, services for LD students, student-designed majors, summer session for credit. *Unusual degree programs:* 3-2 physical therapy, pharmacy.

Library Selena Library with 149,455 titles, 1,667 serial subscriptions, 23,794 audiovisual materials, an OPAC.

Computers on Campus 345 computers available on campus for general student use. A campuswide network can be accessed from student residence rooms and from off campus. At least one staffed computer lab available.

Student Life *Housing Options:* coed. *Activities and Organizations:* student-run newspaper, radio and television station, Caribbean Students Movement, Asian Students Association, African Students United, Speech and Hearing Society, Hillel, national fraternities. *Campus security:* 24-hour emergency response devices and patrols. *Student Services:* health clinic, personal/psychological counseling.

Athletics Member NCAA. All Division I. *Intercollegiate sports:* baseball M(s), basketball M(s)/W(s), cross-country running M/W(s), golf M(s), soccer M(s)/W(s), softball W, tennis W, track and field M/W(s), volleyball W(s). *Intramural sports:* baseball M, basketball M, football M, softball W, tennis M/W, volleyball W, weight lifting M/W, wrestling M/W.

Standardized Tests *Required for some:* SAT I or ACT (for admission).

Costs (2002–03) *Tuition:* $15,938 full-time, $570 per credit part-time. Part-time tuition and fees vary according to course load. *Required fees:* $203 per term. *Room only:* Room and board charges vary according to board plan. *Payment plan:* deferred payment. *Waivers:* employees or children of employees.

Financial Aid Of all full-time matriculated undergraduates who enrolled in 2001, 4247 applied for aid, 4120 were judged to have need, 2225 had their need fully met. 445 Federal Work-Study jobs (averaging $3529). In 2001, 177 non-need-based awards were made. *Average percent of need met:* 90%. *Average financial aid package:* $16,300. *Average need-based loan:* $9854. *Average need-based gift aid:* $12,218. *Average non-need based aid:* $8099. *Average indebtedness upon graduation:* $21,366.

Applying *Options:* common application, electronic application, early action, deferred entrance. *Application fee:* $30. *Required:* high school transcript, minimum 2.0 GPA. *Required for some:* 2 letters of recommendation, interview. *Recommended:* essay or personal statement. *Application deadline:* rolling (freshmen), rolling (transfers). *Notification:* 1/2 (early action).

Admissions Contact Mr. Alan B. Chaves, Dean of Admissions, Long Island University, Brooklyn Campus, One University Plaza, Brooklyn, NY 11201-8423. *Phone:* 718-488-1011. *Toll-free phone:* 800-LIU-PLAN. *Fax:* 718-797-2399. *E-mail:* admissions@brooklyn.liu.edu.

LONG ISLAND UNIVERSITY, C.W. POST CAMPUS

Brookville, New York

- **Independent** comprehensive, founded 1954, part of Long Island University
- **Calendar** semesters
- **Degrees** certificates, associate, bachelor's, master's, and doctoral
- **Suburban** 308-acre campus with easy access to New York City
- **Endowment** $41.4 million
- **Coed,** 6,496 undergraduate students, 60% full-time, 58% women, 42% men
- **Moderately difficult** entrance level, 84% of applicants were admitted

Undergraduates 3,868 full-time, 2,628 part-time. Students come from 32 states and territories, 46 other countries, 9% are from out of state, 10% transferred in, 41% live on campus. *Retention:* 87% of 2001 full-time freshmen returned.

Freshmen *Admission:* 4,417 applied, 3,701 admitted, 876 enrolled. *Average high school GPA:* 2.88. *Test scores:* SAT verbal scores over 500: 46%; SAT math scores over 500: 45%; SAT verbal scores over 600: 11%; SAT math scores over 600: 10%; SAT verbal scores over 700: 1%.

Faculty *Total:* 1,139, 27% full-time, 26% with terminal degrees. *Student/faculty ratio:* 15:1.

Majors Accounting; applied art; applied mathematics; art; art education; art history; arts management; art therapy; biology; biology education; broadcast journalism; business administration; business marketing and marketing management; chemistry; chemistry education; communications; computer graphics; computer/information sciences; computer science; criminal justice/law enforcement administration; curriculum and instruction; cytotechnology; dance; early childhood education; earth sciences; economics; education; elementary education; English; English education; environmental science; film studies; film/video production; finance; fine/studio arts; foreign languages education; French; French language education; geography; geology; German; graphic design/commercial art/illustration; health education; health facilities administration; health services administration; history; information sciences/systems; interdisciplinary studies; international business; international relations; Italian; journalism; liberal arts and sciences/liberal studies; management information systems/business data processing; mathematics; mathematics/computer science; mathematics education; medical laboratory technician; medical radiologic technology; medical records administration; medical technology; molecular biology; multimedia; music; music (general performance); music teacher education; nuclear medical technology; nursing science; nutrition science; philosophy; photography; physical education; physics; political science; pre-dentistry; pre-law; pre-medicine; pre-pharmacy studies; pre-veterinary studies; psychology; public administration; public relations; radio/television broadcasting; secondary education; social studies education; social work; sociology; Spanish; Spanish language education; speech-language pathology/audiology; theater arts/drama; visual and performing arts related; visual/performing arts.

Academic Programs *Special study options:* academic remediation for entering students, accelerated degree program, adult/continuing education programs, advanced placement credit, cooperative education, double majors, English as a second language, honors programs, independent study, internships, off-campus study, part-time degree program, services for LD students, student-designed majors, study abroad, summer session for credit. *ROTC:* Army (c), Air Force (c). *Unusual degree programs:* 3-2 engineering with Polytechnic University, Arizona State University, Stevens Institute of Technology; respiratory therapy and pharmacy with Long Island University, Brooklyn Campus.

Library B. Davis Schwartz Memorial Library with 859,212 titles, 11,446 serial subscriptions, 34,530 audiovisual materials, an OPAC, a Web page.

Computers on Campus 357 computers available on campus for general student use. A campuswide network can be accessed from student residence rooms and from off campus. Internet access, at least one staffed computer lab available.

Student Life *Housing Options:* coed. *Activities and Organizations:* drama/theater group, student-run newspaper, radio and television station, choral group, Student Government Association, Association for Campus Programming, Newman Club, Council of Latin American Studies, Ski and Snowboard Club, national fraternities, national sororities. *Campus security:* 24-hour emergency response devices and patrols, student patrols, late-night transport/escort service, controlled dormitory access, closed campus after hours. *Student Services:* health clinic, personal/psychological counseling, women's center, legal services.

Athletics Member NCAA. All Division II except baseball (Division I). *Intercollegiate sports:* baseball M(s), basketball M(s)/W(s), crew M(c)/W(c), cross-country running M(s)/W(s), equestrian sports M(c)/W(c), field hockey W(s), football M, ice hockey M(c), lacrosse M(s)/W(s), soccer M(s)/W(s), softball W(s), tennis W(s), track and field M(s)/W(s), volleyball W(s). *Intramural sports:* basketball M/W, cross-country running M, football M, softball M, tennis W, track and field M/W, volleyball M/W.

Standardized Tests *Required:* SAT I or ACT (for admission).

Costs (2001–02) *Comprehensive fee:* $25,380 includes full-time tuition ($17,220), mandatory fees ($870), and room and board ($7290). Full-time tuition and fees vary according to degree level. Part-time tuition: $537 per credit. Part-time tuition and fees vary according to course load and degree level. *Required fees:* $330 per year part-time. *Room and board:* College room only: $4640. Room and board charges vary according to board plan and housing facility. *Payment plans:* installment, deferred payment. *Waivers:* senior citizens and employees or children of employees.

Financial Aid Of all full-time matriculated undergraduates who enrolled in 2001, 2628 applied for aid, 2233 were judged to have need. 565 Federal Work-Study jobs (averaging $1739). *Average percent of need met:* 75%. *Average financial aid package:* $13,000. *Average need-based loan:* $4800. *Average need-based gift aid:* $5300. *Financial aid deadline:* 5/15.

Applying *Options:* common application, electronic application, deferred entrance. *Application fee:* $30. *Required:* high school transcript, minimum 2.5 GPA. *Recommended:* essay or personal statement, minimum 3.0 GPA, 2 letters of recommendation, interview. *Application deadline:* rolling (freshmen), rolling (transfers). *Notification:* continuous (freshmen).

Admissions Contact Ms. Jacqueline Reyes, Associate Director of Admissions, Long Island University, C.W. Post Campus, 720 Northern Boulevard, Brookville,

Long Island University, C.W. Post Campus (continued)
NY 11548-1300. *Phone:* 516-299-2900. *Toll-free phone:* 800-LIU-PLAN. *Fax:* 516-299-2137. *E-mail:* enroll@cwpost.liu.edu.

LONG ISLAND UNIVERSITY, SOUTHAMPTON COLLEGE
Southampton, New York

- **Independent** comprehensive, founded 1963, part of Long Island University
- **Calendar** semesters
- **Degrees** certificates, bachelor's, and master's
- **Rural** 110-acre campus
- **Endowment** $41.4 million
- **Coed,** 1,298 undergraduate students, 91% full-time, 70% women, 30% men
- **Moderately difficult** entrance level, 67% of applicants were admitted

Undergraduates 1,181 full-time, 117 part-time. Students come from 49 states and territories, 20 other countries, 39% are from out of state, 5% African American, 2% Asian American or Pacific Islander, 4% Hispanic American, 0.6% Native American, 3% international, 13% transferred in, 54% live on campus. *Retention:* 58% of 2001 full-time freshmen returned.

Freshmen *Admission:* 1,298 applied, 866 admitted, 257 enrolled. *Average high school GPA:* 3.20. *Test scores:* SAT verbal scores over 500: 72%; SAT math scores over 500: 71%; ACT scores over 18: 91%; SAT verbal scores over 600: 29%; SAT math scores over 600: 24%; ACT scores over 24: 46%; SAT verbal scores over 700: 5%; SAT math scores over 700: 3%; ACT scores over 30: 3%.

Faculty *Total:* 206, 33% full-time, 46% with terminal degrees. *Student/faculty ratio:* 17:1.

Majors Accounting; art; art education; behavioral sciences; biology; business administration; chemistry; creative writing; elementary education; English; environmental biology; environmental education; environmental science; fine/studio arts; graphic design/commercial art/illustration; history; liberal arts and sciences/liberal studies; literature; marine biology; mass communications; natural sciences; physiological psychology/psychobiology; political science; pre-law; psychology; social sciences; sociology.

Academic Programs *Special study options:* academic remediation for entering students, adult/continuing education programs, advanced placement credit, cooperative education, distance learning, double majors, English as a second language, external degree program, honors programs, independent study, internships, off-campus study, part-time degree program, student-designed majors, study abroad, summer session for credit.

Library Southampton Campus Library plus 1 other with 147,496 titles, 678 serial subscriptions, 903 audiovisual materials, an OPAC, a Web page.

Computers on Campus 150 computers available on campus for general student use. A campuswide network can be accessed from student residence rooms and from off campus that provide access to online degree audit. Internet access, at least one staffed computer lab available.

Student Life *Housing:* on-campus residence required through sophomore year. *Options:* coed, women-only. *Activities and Organizations:* drama/theater group, student-run newspaper, radio and television station, choral group, Student Government Association, Marine Science Club, Submersibles, PEACE environmental club, women's issues collective. *Campus security:* 24-hour emergency response devices and patrols, student patrols, late-night transport/escort service, controlled dormitory access, bicycle patrol. *Student Services:* health clinic, personal/psychological counseling, women's center.

Athletics Member NCAA. All Division II. *Intercollegiate sports:* basketball M(s)/W(s), lacrosse M(s), soccer M(s)/W(s), softball W(s), tennis M/W, volleyball M(s)/W(s). *Intramural sports:* badminton M(c)/W(c), basketball M/W, football M(c)/W(c), golf M(c)/W(c), ice hockey M(c), lacrosse M/W(c), sailing M(c)/W(c), soccer M/W, softball M/W, tennis M/W, volleyball M/W, weight lifting M.

Standardized Tests *Required:* SAT I or ACT (for admission).

Costs (2001–02) *Comprehensive fee:* $26,270 includes full-time tuition ($17,220), mandatory fees ($900), and room and board ($8150). Full-time tuition and fees vary according to degree level and location. Part-time tuition: $537 per credit. Part-time tuition and fees vary according to course load, degree level, and location. *Required fees:* $200 per term part-time. *Room and board:* College room only: $4560. Room and board charges vary according to board plan and housing facility. *Payment plans:* installment, deferred payment. *Waivers:* children of alumni, senior citizens, and employees or children of employees.

Financial Aid Of all full-time matriculated undergraduates who enrolled in 2001, 978 applied for aid, 864 were judged to have need, 223 had their need fully met. 246 Federal Work-Study jobs (averaging $1250). In 2001, 200 non-need-based awards were made. *Average financial aid package:* $12,185. *Average need-based loan:* $4643. *Average need-based gift aid:* $7579. *Average non-need based aid:* $5828. *Average indebtedness upon graduation:* $14,566.

Applying *Options:* common application, electronic application, deferred entrance. *Application fee:* $30. *Required:* high school transcript. *Recommended:* essay or personal statement, minimum 2.5 GPA, 2 letters of recommendation, interview. *Application deadline:* rolling (freshmen), rolling (transfers). *Notification:* continuous (freshmen).

Admissions Contact Long Island University, Southampton College, 239 Montauk Highway, Southampton, NY 11968-9822. *Phone:* 631-287-8200 Ext. 8342. *Toll-free phone:* 800-LIU PLAN Ext. 2. *Fax:* 631-287-8130. *E-mail:* admissions@southampton.liu.edu.

LONG ISLAND UNIVERSITY, SOUTHAMPTON COLLEGE, FRIENDS WORLD PROGRAM
Southampton, New York

- **Independent** 4-year, founded 1965, part of Long Island University
- **Calendar** semesters
- **Degree** bachelor's
- **Rural** 110-acre campus
- **Endowment** $42.7 million
- **Coed,** 192 undergraduate students, 90% full-time, 72% women, 28% men
- **Noncompetitive** entrance level, 85% of applicants were admitted

Friends World is committed to a uniquely international education with an emphasis on deeper understanding of current world issues. Dedicated family members serve at all international centers and programs, assisting students with individual study programs and core curriculum. In 1991, the academic programs of Friends World College were affiliated with Long Island University and became Friends World Program. See Long Island University, Friends World Program, in the In-Depth Descriptions section of this guide.

Undergraduates 173 full-time, 19 part-time. Students come from 38 states and territories, 6 other countries, 82% are from out of state, 17% transferred in, 20% live on campus. *Retention:* 53% of 2001 full-time freshmen returned.

Freshmen *Admission:* 101 applied, 86 admitted, 27 enrolled. *Average high school GPA:* 3.35.

Faculty *Total:* 31, 32% full-time, 61% with terminal degrees. *Student/faculty ratio:* 9:1.

Majors Adult/continuing education; African-American studies; African languages; African studies; American studies; anthropology; applied art; Arabic; archaeology; art; art education; art history; arts management; art therapy; Asian studies; behavioral sciences; biblical languages/literatures; biblical studies; bilingual/bicultural education; Canadian studies; ceramic arts; child care/development; Chinese; city/community/regional planning; clothing/textiles; community services; comparative literature; creative writing; cultural studies; dance; dance therapy; developmental/child psychology; drama therapy; drawing; early childhood education; East Asian studies; Eastern European area studies; ecology; education; elementary education; English; environmental education; environmental science; European studies; family/community studies; fashion design/illustration; film studies; film/video production; fine/studio arts; folklore; French; geography; geology; German; gerontology; Greek (modern); Hebrew; Hispanic-American studies; history; human ecology; humanities; interdisciplinary studies; international business; international economics; international relations; Islamic studies; Italian; Japanese; jazz; journalism; Latin American studies; liberal arts and sciences/liberal studies; linguistics; literature; mass communications; medieval/renaissance studies; metal/jewelry arts; Mexican-American studies; Middle Eastern studies; middle school education; modern languages; museum studies; music; music history; music teacher education; music therapy; Native American studies; natural resources conservation; natural resources management; natural sciences; nutrition science; ornamental horticulture; paleontology; peace/conflict studies; philosophy; photography; physiological psychology/psychobiology; political science; Portuguese; printmaking; psychology; public policy analysis; public relations; recreational therapy; recreation/leisure facilities management; recreation/leisure studies; religious studies; romance languages; Russian; Russian/Slavic studies; Scandinavian languages; sculpture; secondary education; sign language interpretation; Slavic languages; social sciences; social work; sociobiology; sociology; South Asian studies; Southeast Asian studies; Spanish; special education; teacher assistant/aide; teaching English as a second language; textile arts; theater arts/drama; travel/tourism management; urban studies; western civilization; wildlife management; women's studies.

Academic Programs *Special study options:* advanced placement credit, cooperative education, external degree program, independent study, internships, off-campus study, student-designed majors, study abroad.

Student Life *Housing:* on-campus residence required for freshman year. *Options:* coed. *Activities and Organizations:* student-run newspaper, Activist

Club, P.E.A.C.E., LaFuenza Latina, Caribbean Student Association, Women's Issues Collective. *Student Services:* health clinic, personal/psychological counseling.

Costs (2001–02) *One-time required fee:* $100. *Comprehensive fee:* $26,240 includes full-time tuition ($17,220), mandatory fees ($740), and room and board ($8280). Part-time tuition: $537 per credit. Part-time tuition and fees vary according to course load. *Required fees:* $160 per term part-time. *Room and board:* Room and board charges vary according to board plan, housing facility, and location. *Payment plan:* installment. *Waivers:* senior citizens and employees or children of employees.

Applying *Options:* electronic application, early admission, deferred entrance. *Application fee:* $30. *Required:* essay or personal statement, high school transcript, interview. *Recommended:* minimum 3.0 GPA, 2 letters of recommendation. *Application deadline:* rolling (freshmen), rolling (transfers). *Notification:* continuous (freshmen).

Admissions Contact Trish Maginsky, Admissions Secretary, Long Island University, Southampton College, Friends World Program, 239 Montauk Highway, Southampton, NY 11968. *Phone:* 631-287-8474. *Toll-free phone:* 800-LIU PLAN. *Fax:* 631-287-8463. *E-mail:* fw@southampton.liu.edu.

MACHZIKEI HADATH RABBINICAL COLLEGE
Brooklyn, New York

Admissions Contact Rabbi Abraham M. Lezerowitz, Director of Admissions, Machzikei Hadath Rabbinical College, 5407 Sixteenth Avenue, Brooklyn, NY 11204-1805. *Phone:* 718-854-8777.

MANHATTAN COLLEGE
Riverdale, New York

- **Independent** comprehensive, founded 1853, affiliated with Roman Catholic Church
- **Calendar** semesters
- **Degrees** bachelor's, master's, and post-master's certificates
- **Urban** 31-acre campus with easy access to New York City
- **Endowment** $27.0 million
- **Coed,** 2,608 undergraduate students, 94% full-time, 48% women, 52% men
- **Moderately difficult** entrance level, 63% of applicants were admitted

Radiation therapy is commonly used in hospitals to help cancer patients and ease pain in others. The program at Manhattan College includes 24 credits of clinical internship courses, equal to about 275 days in a Radiation Therapy Department in 1 of 8 hospitals, such as New York University Hospital, St. Vincent's Hospital, and Westchester Medical Center.

Undergraduates 2,447 full-time, 161 part-time. Students come from 34 states and territories, 10 other countries, 36% are from out of state, 6% African American, 6% Asian American or Pacific Islander, 14% Hispanic American, 0.1% Native American, 2% international, 5% transferred in, 54% live on campus. *Retention:* 83% of 2001 full-time freshmen returned.

Freshmen *Admission:* 3,947 applied, 2,491 admitted, 593 enrolled. *Average high school GPA:* 3.20. *Test scores:* SAT verbal scores over 500: 73%; SAT math scores over 500: 77%; SAT verbal scores over 600: 18%; SAT math scores over 600: 27%; SAT verbal scores over 700: 2%; SAT math scores over 700: 3%.

Faculty *Total:* 253, 61% full-time, 71% with terminal degrees. *Student/faculty ratio:* 13:1.

Majors Accounting; biochemistry; biology; biotechnology research; business marketing and marketing management; chemical engineering; chemistry; civil engineering; classics; computer engineering; computer science; economics; education; education (multiple levels); electrical engineering; elementary education; engineering; English; environmental engineering; finance; French; history; international relations; liberal arts and sciences/liberal studies; management science; mathematics; mechanical engineering; middle school education; nuclear medical technology; organizational behavior; philosophy; physical education; physics; political science; psychology; radiological science; religious studies; sociology; Spanish; special education; urban studies.

Academic Programs *Special study options:* academic remediation for entering students, accelerated degree program, adult/continuing education programs, advanced placement credit, cooperative education, double majors, English as a second language, honors programs, independent study, internships, off-campus study, part-time degree program, services for LD students, study abroad, summer session for credit. *ROTC:* Army (c), Air Force (b).

Library Cardinal Hayes Library plus 1 other with 193,100 titles, 1,527 serial subscriptions, 3,680 audiovisual materials, an OPAC.

Computers on Campus 375 computers available on campus for general student use. A campuswide network can be accessed from student residence rooms and from off campus. Internet access, at least one staffed computer lab available.

Student Life *Housing Options:* coed. *Activities and Organizations:* drama/theater group, student-run newspaper, radio station, choral group, marching band, Minority Student Union, student government, student radio station, Manhattan College Singers, Resident/Commuter Student Association, national fraternities, national sororities. *Campus security:* 24-hour patrols, late-night transport/escort service, controlled dormitory access. *Student Services:* health clinic, personal/psychological counseling.

Athletics Member NCAA. All Division I. *Intercollegiate sports:* baseball M(s), basketball M(s)/W(s), crew M(c)/W(c), cross-country running M(s)/W(s), golf M(s), lacrosse M(s)/W(s), rugby M(c), soccer M(s)/W(s), softball W(s), swimming W(s), tennis M(s)/W(s), track and field M(s)/W(s), volleyball M/W(s). *Intramural sports:* baseball M, basketball M/W, cross-country running M/W, equestrian sports M/W, soccer M/W, softball M/W, swimming W, track and field M/W, volleyball M/W.

Standardized Tests *Required:* SAT I or ACT (for admission).

Costs (2001–02) *One-time required fee:* $200. *Comprehensive fee:* $26,900 includes full-time tuition ($17,700), mandatory fees ($1500), and room and board ($7700). Full-time tuition and fees vary according to program. Part-time tuition: $450 per credit. *Required fees:* $100 per term part-time. *Room and board:* Room and board charges vary according to board plan. *Payment plan:* installment. *Waivers:* employees or children of employees.

Financial Aid Of all full-time matriculated undergraduates who enrolled in 2001, 2064 applied for aid, 1730 were judged to have need, 259 had their need fully met. In 2001, 327 non-need-based awards were made. *Average percent of need met:* 65%. *Average financial aid package:* $11,846. *Average need-based loan:* $4025. *Average need-based gift aid:* $6385. *Average non-need based aid:* $6758. *Average indebtedness upon graduation:* $15,715.

Applying *Options:* common application, early admission, early decision, deferred entrance. *Application fee:* $35. *Required:* essay or personal statement, high school transcript, 1 letter of recommendation. *Required for some:* interview. *Recommended:* interview. *Application deadlines:* 3/1 (freshmen), 7/1 (transfers). *Early decision:* 11/15. *Notification:* continuous until 8/15 (freshmen), 12/1 (early decision).

Admissions Contact Mr. William J. Bisset Jr., Assistant Vice President for Enrollment Management, Manhattan College, 4513 Manhattan College Parkway, Riverdale, NY 10471. *Phone:* 718-862-7200. *Toll-free phone:* 800-622-9235. *Fax:* 718-862-8019. *E-mail:* admit@manhattan.edu.

MANHATTAN SCHOOL OF MUSIC
New York, New York

- **Independent** comprehensive, founded 1917
- **Calendar** semesters
- **Degrees** diplomas, bachelor's, master's, doctoral, post-master's, and postbachelor's certificates
- **Urban** 1-acre campus
- **Endowment** $12.0 million
- **Coed,** 395 undergraduate students, 94% full-time, 52% women, 48% men
- **Very difficult** entrance level, 40% of applicants were admitted

Undergraduates 372 full-time, 23 part-time. Students come from 35 states and territories, 30 other countries, 62% are from out of state, 4% African American, 10% Asian American or Pacific Islander, 6% Hispanic American, 0.8% Native American, 29% international, 15% transferred in, 28% live on campus. *Retention:* 79% of 2001 full-time freshmen returned.

Freshmen *Admission:* 699 applied, 281 admitted, 87 enrolled.

Faculty *Total:* 270, 15% full-time, 33% with terminal degrees. *Student/faculty ratio:* 8:1.

Majors Jazz; music; music (piano and organ performance); music (voice and choral/opera performance); stringed instruments; wind/percussion instruments.

Academic Programs *Special study options:* academic remediation for entering students, advanced placement credit, English as a second language, off-campus study, services for LD students.

Library Francis Hall Ballard Library with 71,400 titles, 93 serial subscriptions, 19,600 audiovisual materials, an OPAC.

Computers on Campus 10 computers available on campus for general student use. Internet access, at least one staffed computer lab available.

Student Life *Housing:* on-campus residence required through sophomore year. *Options:* coed. *Activities and Organizations:* choral group, Pan-African Student Union, Composers Now, Chinese Student Association, Korean Student Association, Gay/Lesbian/Bisexual Students Association. *Campus security:* 24-hour patrols. *Student Services:* personal/psychological counseling.

Manhattan School of Music (continued)

Standardized Tests *Recommended:* SAT I or ACT (for admission).

Costs (2001–02) *Tuition:* $21,100 full-time, $450 per credit part-time. Full-time tuition and fees vary according to course load and program. Part-time tuition and fees vary according to course load and program. *Required fees:* $400 full-time. *Room only:* $7200. Room and board charges vary according to housing facility. *Payment plan:* installment. *Waivers:* employees or children of employees.

Financial Aid Of all full-time matriculated undergraduates who enrolled in 2001, 203 applied for aid, 170 were judged to have need, 9 had their need fully met. 60 Federal Work-Study jobs (averaging $1703). *Average percent of need met:* 47%. *Average financial aid package:* $12,599. *Average need-based loan:* $4246. *Average need-based gift aid:* $10,480. *Average indebtedness upon graduation:* $17,125.

Applying *Application fee:* $100. *Required:* essay or personal statement, high school transcript, minimum 2.0 GPA, 1 letter of recommendation, audition. *Recommended:* minimum 3.0 GPA, interview. *Application deadlines:* 12/1 (freshmen), 12/1 (transfers). *Notification:* 4/1 (freshmen).

Admissions Contact Manhattan School of Music, 120 Claremont Avenue, New York, NY 10027. *Phone:* 212-749-2802 Ext. 4449. *Fax:* 212-749-3025. *E-mail:* admission@msmnyc.edu.

MANHATTANVILLE COLLEGE

Purchase, New York

- **Independent** comprehensive, founded 1841
- **Calendar** semesters
- **Degrees** bachelor's and master's
- **Suburban** 100-acre campus with easy access to New York City
- **Coed,** 1,578 undergraduate students, 89% full-time, 69% women, 31% men
- **Moderately difficult** entrance level, 58% of applicants were admitted

Manhattanville College, founded in 1841, is a private, coeducational, 4-year, comprehensive liberal arts institution. Located in scenic Westchester County, NY, approximately 30 minutes northeast of New York City. The College offers more than 40 academic areas of concentration. An active social life involves nearly 50 student organizations, 19 Division III varsity teams, intramurals, and sports clubs to choose from.

Undergraduates 1,408 full-time, 170 part-time. Students come from 33 states and territories, 48 other countries, 29% are from out of state, 6% African American, 2% Asian American or Pacific Islander, 13% Hispanic American, 0.1% Native American, 8% international, 5% transferred in, 70% live on campus. *Retention:* 72% of 2001 full-time freshmen returned.

Freshmen *Admission:* 2,328 applied, 1,347 admitted, 404 enrolled. *Average high school GPA:* 3. *Test scores:* SAT verbal scores over 500: 63%; SAT math scores over 500: 61%; ACT scores over 18: 83%; SAT verbal scores over 600: 19%; SAT math scores over 600: 15%; ACT scores over 24: 40%; SAT verbal scores over 700: 2%; SAT math scores over 700: 2%; ACT scores over 30: 6%.

Faculty *Total:* 201, 37% full-time, 35% with terminal degrees. *Student/faculty ratio:* 13:1.

Majors American studies; art; art education; art history; Asian studies; biochemistry; biology; biology education; business administration; chemistry; chemistry education; classics; computer science; dance; economics; education; elementary education; English; English education; finance; fine/studio arts; French; French language education; history; international business; international relations; legal studies; mathematics; mathematics education; music; music business management/merchandising; music teacher education; neuroscience; philosophy; political science; pre-dentistry; pre-law; pre-medicine; psychology; religious studies; romance languages; secondary education; social studies education; sociology; Spanish; Spanish language education; theater arts/drama.

Academic Programs *Special study options:* academic remediation for entering students, accelerated degree program, adult/continuing education programs, advanced placement credit, English as a second language, freshman honors college, honors programs, internships, off-campus study, part-time degree program, services for LD students, student-designed majors, study abroad, summer session for credit. *Unusual degree programs:* 3-2 business administration with New York University; education.

Library Manhattanville College Library plus 1 other with 182,789 titles, 912 serial subscriptions, 3,096 audiovisual materials, an OPAC, a Web page.

Computers on Campus 83 computers available on campus for general student use. A campuswide network can be accessed from student residence rooms and from off campus. Internet access, at least one staffed computer lab available.

Student Life *Housing Options:* coed, women-only, disabled students. *Activities and Organizations:* drama/theater group, student-run newspaper, radio and television station, choral group, student government, International Student Organization, Touchstone (newspaper), WMVL (radio station), Philosophy Club. *Campus security:* 24-hour emergency response devices and patrols, late-night transport/escort service, controlled dormitory access. *Student Services:* health clinic, personal/psychological counseling, women's center.

Athletics Member NCAA. All Division III. *Intercollegiate sports:* baseball M, basketball M/W, equestrian sports M/W, field hockey W, golf M/W, ice hockey M/W, lacrosse M/W, soccer M/W, softball W, swimming M/W, tennis M/W, volleyball W. *Intramural sports:* basketball M/W, football M.

Standardized Tests *Required:* SAT I or ACT (for admission). *Required for some:* SAT I (for admission), ACT (for admission), SAT I and SAT II or ACT (for admission), SAT II: Subject Tests (for admission), SAT II: Writing Test (for admission).

Costs (2002–03) *Comprehensive fee:* $30,160 includes full-time tuition ($20,600), mandatory fees ($830), and room and board ($8730). Part-time tuition: $470 per credit. Part-time tuition and fees vary according to program. *Required fees:* $35 per term part-time. *Room and board:* College room only: $5090. Room and board charges vary according to board plan. *Payment plans:* installment, deferred payment. *Waivers:* senior citizens and employees or children of employees.

Financial Aid Of all full-time matriculated undergraduates who enrolled in 2001, 1120 applied for aid, 979 were judged to have need, 541 had their need fully met. 250 Federal Work-Study jobs (averaging $865). In 2001, 166 non-need-based awards were made. *Average percent of need met:* 90%. *Average financial aid package:* $18,668. *Average need-based loan:* $4267. *Average need-based gift aid:* $7426. *Average non-need based aid:* $11,100.

Applying *Options:* common application, early admission, early decision. *Application fee:* $50. *Required:* essay or personal statement, high school transcript, minimum 2.0 GPA, 2 letters of recommendation. *Recommended:* minimum 3.0 GPA, interview. *Application deadlines:* 3/1 (freshmen), 3/1 (transfers). *Early decision:* 12/1. *Notification:* continuous (freshmen), 12/31 (early decision).

Admissions Contact Mr. Jose Flores, Director of Admissions, Manhattanville College, 2900 Purchase Street, Purchase, NY 10577-2132. *Phone:* 914-323-5124. *Toll-free phone:* 800-328-4553. *Fax:* 914-694-1732. *E-mail:* admissions@mville.edu.

MANNES COLLEGE OF MUSIC, NEW SCHOOL UNIVERSITY

New York, New York

- **Independent** comprehensive, founded 1916, part of New School University
- **Calendar** semesters
- **Degrees** diplomas, bachelor's, master's, and post-master's certificates
- **Urban** campus
- **Endowment** $90.4 million
- **Coed,** 127 undergraduate students, 100% full-time, 65% women, 35% men
- **Very difficult** entrance level, 37% of applicants were admitted

A small, distinguished conservatory in the heart of New York City, Mannes College of Music features faculty who are members of New York City's most prominent and internationally know ensembles. Students receive rigorous professional training as members of a friendly, supportive community dedicated to the highest artistic achievement.

Undergraduates 127 full-time. Students come from 17 states and territories, 33 other countries, 53% are from out of state, 4% African American, 7% Asian American or Pacific Islander, 4% Hispanic American, 42% international, 14% transferred in, 52% live on campus. *Retention:* 75% of 2001 full-time freshmen returned.

Freshmen *Admission:* 268 applied, 98 admitted, 43 enrolled.

Faculty *Total:* 133, 3% full-time. *Student/faculty ratio:* 2:1.

Majors Music; music conducting; music (piano and organ performance); music theory and composition; music (voice and choral/opera performance); stringed instruments; wind/percussion instruments.

Academic Programs *Special study options:* academic remediation for entering students, accelerated degree program, adult/continuing education programs, advanced placement credit, double majors, English as a second language, summer session for credit.

Library Fogelman Library plus 2 others with 368,390 titles, 1,155 serial subscriptions, 433,123 audiovisual materials.

Computers on Campus 475 computers available on campus for general student use. At least one staffed computer lab available.

Student Life *Housing Options:* coed, disabled students. *Activities and Organizations:* drama/theater group, choral group. *Campus security:* 24-hour emergency response devices, controlled dormitory access. *Student Services:* health clinic, personal/psychological counseling.

Costs (2001–02) *Comprehensive fee:* $29,858 includes full-time tuition ($19,800), mandatory fees ($446), and room and board ($9612). Full-time tuition and fees vary according to degree level. Part-time tuition: $650 per credit. *Required fees:* $115 per term part-time. *Room and board:* College room only: $6984. *Payment plan:* installment. *Waivers:* employees or children of employees.

Financial Aid Of all full-time matriculated undergraduates who enrolled in 2001, 114 applied for aid, 105 were judged to have need, 9 had their need fully met. 19 Federal Work-Study jobs (averaging $1911). In 2001, 14 non-need-based awards were made. *Average percent of need met:* 57%. *Average financial aid package:* $10,815. *Average need-based loan:* $3180. *Average need-based gift aid:* $7983. *Average non-need based aid:* $6119. *Average indebtedness upon graduation:* $22,834.

Applying *Options:* deferred entrance. *Application fee:* $100. *Required:* high school transcript, minimum 2.5 GPA, 1 letter of recommendation, audition. *Application deadline:* 12/15 (freshmen), rolling (transfers). *Notification:* continuous (freshmen).

Admissions Contact Ms. Allison Scola, Director of Enrollment, Mannes College of Music, New School University, 150 West 85th Street, New York, NY 10024-4402. *Phone:* 212-580-0210 Ext. 247. *Toll-free phone:* 800-292-3040. *Fax:* 212-580-1738. *E-mail:* mannasadmissions@newschool.edu.

MARIST COLLEGE
Poughkeepsie, New York

- **Independent** comprehensive, founded 1929
- **Calendar** semesters
- **Degrees** certificates, bachelor's, and master's
- **Small-town** 135-acre campus with easy access to Albany and New York City
- **Endowment** $15.2 million
- **Coed,** 4,713 undergraduate students, 87% full-time, 57% women, 43% men
- **Moderately difficult** entrance level, 52% of applicants were admitted

Undergraduates 4,079 full-time, 634 part-time. Students come from 36 states and territories, 19 other countries, 39% are from out of state, 3% African American, 1% Asian American or Pacific Islander, 4% Hispanic American, 0.1% Native American, 0.5% international, 3% transferred in, 70% live on campus. *Retention:* 88% of 2001 full-time freshmen returned.

Freshmen *Admission:* 6,254 applied, 3,236 admitted, 983 enrolled. *Average high school GPA:* 3.2. *Test scores:* SAT verbal scores over 500: 91%; SAT math scores over 500: 92%; SAT verbal scores over 600: 32%; SAT math scores over 600: 38%; SAT verbal scores over 700: 3%; SAT math scores over 700: 2%.

Faculty *Total:* 489, 36% full-time. *Student/faculty ratio:* 14:1.

Majors Accounting; advertising; American studies; art; athletic training/sports medicine; behavioral sciences; biochemistry; biology; broadcast journalism; business administration; chemistry; communications; computer engineering technology; computer science; criminal justice/law enforcement administration; economics; elementary education; English; environmental biology; environmental science; fashion design/illustration; fashion merchandising; fine/studio arts; French; history; humanities; information sciences/systems; journalism; literature; mass communications; mathematics; medical technology; paralegal/legal assistant; political science; pre-dentistry; pre-law; pre-medicine; pre-veterinary studies; psychology; public administration; public relations; radio/television broadcasting; secondary education; social work; Spanish; special education; theater arts/drama.

Academic Programs *Special study options:* academic remediation for entering students, accelerated degree program, adult/continuing education programs, advanced placement credit, cooperative education, distance learning, double majors, English as a second language, honors programs, independent study, internships, off-campus study, part-time degree program, services for LD students, study abroad, summer session for credit. *Unusual degree programs:* 3-2 psychology, computer science.

Library Marist College Library with 283,941 titles, 115,661 serial subscriptions, 5,646 audiovisual materials, an OPAC, a Web page.

Computers on Campus 450 computers available on campus for general student use. A campuswide network can be accessed from student residence rooms and from off campus. Internet access, at least one staffed computer lab available.

Student Life *Housing Options:* coed. *Activities and Organizations:* drama/theater group, student-run newspaper, radio station, choral group, marching band, Outback Club, student newspaper, student government, Theater Club, community service and campus ministry, national fraternities. *Campus security:* 24-hour emergency response devices and patrols, student patrols, late-night transport/escort service, controlled dormitory access, night residence hall monitors. *Student Services:* health clinic, personal/psychological counseling.

Athletics Member NCAA. All Division I except football (Division I-AA). *Intercollegiate sports:* baseball M(s), basketball M(s)/W(s), crew M/W, cross-country running M(s)/W(s), equestrian sports M(c)/W(c), field hockey W(c), ice hockey M(c), lacrosse M/W, rugby M(c)/W(c), sailing M(c)/W(c), skiing (cross-country) M(c)/W(c), skiing (downhill) M(c)/W(c), soccer M(s)/W(s), softball W(s), swimming M(s)/W(s), tennis M(s)/W(s), track and field M(s)/W(s), volleyball M(c)/W(s), water polo W(s). *Intramural sports:* baseball M, basketball M/W, bowling M/W, football M, golf M/W, ice hockey M, lacrosse M, racquetball M/W, skiing (downhill) M/W, soccer M/W, softball W, swimming M/W, table tennis M/W, tennis M/W, track and field M/W, volleyball M/W, water polo M/W.

Standardized Tests *Required:* SAT I or ACT (for admission).

Costs (2001–02) *One-time required fee:* $25. *Comprehensive fee:* $24,756 includes full-time tuition ($16,364), mandatory fees ($428), and room and board ($7964). Part-time tuition: $381 per credit. *Required fees:* $65 per term part-time. *Room and board:* Room and board charges vary according to board plan and housing facility. *Payment plan:* installment. *Waivers:* employees or children of employees.

Financial Aid Of all full-time matriculated undergraduates who enrolled in 2001, 3431 applied for aid, 3057 were judged to have need, 224 had their need fully met. In 2001, 435 non-need-based awards were made. *Average percent of need met:* 76%. *Average financial aid package:* $10,287. *Average need-based loan:* $4345. *Average need-based gift aid:* $8943. *Average non-need based aid:* $4536.

Applying *Options:* common application, electronic application, early admission, early action, deferred entrance. *Application fee:* $40. *Required:* high school transcript, 1 letter of recommendation. *Recommended:* essay or personal statement. *Application deadlines:* 2/15 (freshmen), 6/1 (transfers). *Notification:* continuous (freshmen), 1/1 (early action).

Admissions Contact Mr. Jay Murray, Director of Admissions, Marist College, 3399 North Road. *Phone:* 845-575-3226 Ext. 2190. *Toll-free phone:* 800-436-5483. *E-mail:* admissions@marist.edu.

MARYMOUNT COLLEGE OF FORDHAM UNIVERSITY
Tarrytown, New York

- **Independent** 4-year, founded 1907
- **Calendar** semesters
- **Degrees** associate and bachelor's
- **Suburban** 25-acre campus with easy access to New York City
- **Women only,** 1,001 undergraduate students, 83% full-time
- **Moderately difficult** entrance level, 81% of applicants were admitted

Marymount College will consolidate with Fordham University on July 1, 2002, to create a new model of a Catholic women's college—with the academic and administrative resources of a major university and the character of a small, liberal arts college. The new school will be known as Marymount College of Fordham University.

Undergraduates 827 full-time, 174 part-time. Students come from 32 states and territories, 20 other countries, 33% are from out of state, 15% African American, 5% Asian American or Pacific Islander, 15% Hispanic American, 0.1% Native American, 8% international, 10% transferred in, 48% live on campus. *Retention:* 69% of 2001 full-time freshmen returned.

Freshmen *Admission:* 226 enrolled. *Average high school GPA:* 2.7. *Test scores:* SAT verbal scores over 500: 43%; SAT math scores over 500: 36%; SAT verbal scores over 600: 11%; SAT math scores over 600: 5%; SAT verbal scores over 700: 1%.

Faculty *Total:* 57. *Student/faculty ratio:* 9:1.

Majors Accounting; American studies; area studies; art; art education; art history; art therapy; biological/physical sciences; biology; biology education; business; business administration; business economics; business marketing and marketing management; chemistry; chemistry education; clothing/textiles; community health liaison; computer/information sciences; creative writing; dietetics; economics; education; elementary education; English; fashion design/illustration; fashion merchandising; finance; fine/studio arts; food sciences; French; French language education; history; home economics; home economics education; human ecology; information sciences/systems; interdisciplinary studies; interior design; international business; international relations; journalism; legal studies; liberal arts and sciences/liberal studies; literature; mass communications; mathematics; mathematics education; medical technology; middle school education; modern languages; nutrition science; political science; pre-law; pre-medicine; psychology; science education; secondary education; social studies education; social work; sociology; Spanish; Spanish language education; special education; speech/rhetorical studies; theater arts/drama.

Academic Programs *Special study options:* academic remediation for entering students, adult/continuing education programs, advanced placement credit, dis-

Marymount College of Fordham University (continued)
tance learning, double majors, English as a second language, honors programs, independent study, internships, off-campus study, part-time degree program, services for LD students, student-designed majors, study abroad, summer session for credit. *Unusual degree programs:* 3-2 business administration with Fordham University, Pace University, St. Thomas Aquinas College, Richmond University in London; social work with Fordham University; education with Fordham University, physical therapy with New York Medical College, optometry with State University of New York State College of Optometry, physical therapy, occupational therapy, physician assistant with Touro Collge.

Library Gloria Gaines Memorial Library plus 1 other with 80,601 titles, 349 serial subscriptions, 219 audiovisual materials, an OPAC, a Web page.

Computers on Campus 135 computers available on campus for general student use. A campuswide network can be accessed from student residence rooms and from off campus. Internet access, at least one staffed computer lab available.

Student Life *Housing Options:* women-only. *Activities and Organizations:* drama/theater group, student-run newspaper, television station, choral group, Campus Activities Board, Student Government Association, Latin Unity, Black Student Union, Residence Hall Association. *Campus security:* 24-hour emergency response devices and patrols, late-night transport/escort service, controlled dormitory access. *Student Services:* health clinic, personal/psychological counseling.

Athletics *Intercollegiate sports:* basketball W, equestrian sports W, softball W, swimming W, tennis W, volleyball W. *Intramural sports:* badminton W, basketball W, soccer W, table tennis W, tennis W.

Standardized Tests *Required:* SAT I or ACT (for admission).

Costs (2002–03) *Comprehensive fee:* $25,905 includes full-time tuition ($16,680), mandatory fees ($530), and room and board ($8695). Part-time tuition: $540 per credit hour. Tuition for continuing students is $16,065. *Required fees:* $190 per term part-time. *Payment plans:* installment, deferred payment. *Waivers:* employees or children of employees.

Financial Aid Of all full-time matriculated undergraduates who enrolled in 2001, 723 applied for aid, 723 were judged to have need, 37 had their need fully met. 219 Federal Work-Study jobs (averaging $1289). In 2001, 43 non-need-based awards were made. *Average percent of need met:* 67%. *Average financial aid package:* $14,441. *Average need-based loan:* $4202. *Average need-based gift aid:* $10,231. *Average indebtedness upon graduation:* $11,793.

Applying *Options:* common application, early action, deferred entrance. *Application fee:* $30. *Required:* essay or personal statement, high school transcript, minimum 2.0 GPA. *Recommended:* minimum 3.0 GPA, 1 letter of recommendation, interview. *Application deadline:* rolling (transfers). *Notification:* continuous (freshmen), 11/30 (early action).

Admissions Contact Daniela Esposito, Director of Admissions, Marymount College of Fordham University, 100 Marymount Avenue, Tarrytown, NY 10591-3796. *Phone:* 914-332-8295. *Toll-free phone:* 800-724-4312. *Fax:* 914-332-7442. *E-mail:* admiss@mmc.marymt.edu.

MARYMOUNT MANHATTAN COLLEGE
New York, New York

- **Independent** 4-year, founded 1936
- **Calendar** semesters
- **Degree** certificates and bachelor's
- **Urban** 1-acre campus
- **Endowment** $8.3 million
- **Coed,** 2,707 undergraduate students, 68% full-time, 79% women, 21% men
- **Moderately difficult** entrance level, 57% of applicants were admitted

Undergraduates 1,828 full-time, 879 part-time. Students come from 48 states and territories, 62 other countries, 35% are from out of state, 20% African American, 4% Asian American or Pacific Islander, 16% Hispanic American, 0.3% Native American, 6% international, 4% transferred in, 21% live on campus. *Retention:* 78% of 2001 full-time freshmen returned.

Freshmen *Admission:* 1,804 applied, 1,028 admitted, 509 enrolled. *Average high school GPA:* 3.40. *Test scores:* SAT verbal scores over 500: 68%; SAT math scores over 500: 45%; ACT scores over 18: 92%; SAT verbal scores over 600: 30%; SAT math scores over 600: 12%; ACT scores over 24: 42%; SAT verbal scores over 700: 5%; SAT math scores over 700: 2%; ACT scores over 30: 12%.

Faculty *Total:* 352, 18% full-time, 62% with terminal degrees. *Student/faculty ratio:* 20:1.

Majors Accounting; acting/directing; art; art history; biology; business administration; dance; drama/theater literature; English; fine/studio arts; history; international relations; liberal arts and sciences/liberal studies; mass communications; political science; psychology; sociology; speech-language pathology/audiology; theater arts/drama.

Academic Programs *Special study options:* academic remediation for entering students, accelerated degree program, adult/continuing education programs, advanced placement credit, double majors, English as a second language, honors programs, independent study, internships, off-campus study, part-time degree program, services for LD students, study abroad, summer session for credit. *Unusual degree programs:* 3-2 computer science with Polytechnic University.

Library Shanahan Library with 100,535 titles, 600 serial subscriptions, 13,285 audiovisual materials, an OPAC, a Web page.

Computers on Campus 150 computers available on campus for general student use. A campuswide network can be accessed from off campus. Internet access, at least one staffed computer lab available.

Student Life *Housing Options:* coed. *Activities and Organizations:* drama/theater group, student-run newspaper, radio station, Education Club, African-American Heritage Club, Asian-American Heritage Club, Latino Heritage Club, Business Club. *Campus security:* 24-hour emergency response devices and patrols, student patrols, 24-hour security in residence halls. *Student Services:* personal/psychological counseling.

Standardized Tests *Required:* SAT I or ACT (for admission).

Costs (2001–02) *Tuition:* $14,200 full-time, $395 per credit part-time. Full-time tuition and fees vary according to course load. Part-time tuition and fees vary according to course load. *Required fees:* $495 full-time, $220 per term part-time. *Room only:* $8500. Room and board charges vary according to housing facility. *Payment plan:* installment. *Waivers:* children of alumni, adult students, senior citizens, and employees or children of employees.

Financial Aid Of all full-time matriculated undergraduates who enrolled in 2001, 1359 applied for aid, 1111 were judged to have need, 114 had their need fully met. 183 Federal Work-Study jobs (averaging $1491). In 2001, 211 non-need-based awards were made. *Average percent of need met:* 85%. *Average financial aid package:* $11,718. *Average need-based loan:* $3447. *Average need-based gift aid:* $6834. *Average non-need based aid:* $3910.

Applying *Options:* electronic application, early decision, deferred entrance. *Application fee:* $50. *Required:* high school transcript, 2 letters of recommendation, audition for dance and theater programs. *Required for some:* interview. *Recommended:* essay or personal statement. *Application deadline:* rolling (freshmen), rolling (transfers). *Early decision:* 11/1. *Notification:* continuous (freshmen), 12/15 (early decision).

Admissions Contact Mr. Thomas Friebel, Associate Vice President for Enrollment Services, Marymount Manhattan College, 221 East 71st Street, New York, NY 10021. *Phone:* 212-517-0430. *Toll-free phone:* 800-MARYMOUNT. *Fax:* 212-517-0448. *E-mail:* admissions@mmm.edu.

MEDAILLE COLLEGE
Buffalo, New York

- **Independent** comprehensive, founded 1875
- **Calendar** semesters
- **Degrees** certificates, associate, bachelor's, and master's
- **Urban** 13-acre campus
- **Endowment** $669,736
- **Coed,** 1,512 undergraduate students, 86% full-time, 71% women, 29% men
- **Moderately difficult** entrance level, 63% of applicants were admitted

Undergraduates 1,306 full-time, 206 part-time. Students come from 4 states and territories, 2 other countries, 1% are from out of state, 13% African American, 0.5% Asian American or Pacific Islander, 3% Hispanic American, 0.6% Native American, 11% international, 23% transferred in, 10% live on campus. *Retention:* 70% of 2001 full-time freshmen returned.

Freshmen *Admission:* 579 applied, 364 admitted, 215 enrolled. *Average high school GPA:* 2.70. *Test scores:* SAT verbal scores over 500: 30%; SAT math scores over 500: 20%; SAT verbal scores over 600: 5%; SAT math scores over 600: 2%.

Faculty *Total:* 117, 52% full-time, 62% with terminal degrees. *Student/faculty ratio:* 19:1.

Majors Accounting; biology; business administration; business marketing and marketing management; child care/development; computer/information sciences; criminal justice studies; early childhood education; education; elementary education; financial planning; humanities; human resources management; human services; information sciences/systems; liberal arts and sciences/liberal studies; mass communications; middle school education; political science; pre-law; psychology; social sciences; sport/fitness administration; veterinary technology.

Academic Programs *Special study options:* academic remediation for entering students, accelerated degree program, adult/continuing education programs, advanced placement credit, double majors, independent study, internships, off-campus study, part-time degree program, services for LD students, student-designed majors, summer session for credit. *ROTC:* Army (c).

Library Medaille College Library with 53,848 titles, 240 serial subscriptions, 2,063 audiovisual materials, an OPAC, a Web page.

Computers on Campus 105 computers available on campus for general student use. A campuswide network can be accessed from student residence rooms and from off campus. Internet access, at least one staffed computer lab available.

Student Life *Housing Options:* coed, men-only, women-only, disabled students. *Activities and Organizations:* drama/theater group, student-run newspaper, radio and television station, student government, radio station, ASRA (Admissions Club), Student Activities Board, Teach. *Campus security:* 24-hour emergency response devices, late-night transport/escort service, controlled dormitory access. *Student Services:* health clinic, personal/psychological counseling.

Athletics Member NCAA, NSCAA. All NCAA Division III. *Intercollegiate sports:* baseball M, basketball M/W, cross-country running M/W, lacrosse M/W, soccer M/W, softball W, volleyball M/W. *Intramural sports:* basketball M/W, skiing (downhill) M/W, soccer M/W, softball M/W, table tennis M/W, tennis M/W, volleyball M/W, weight lifting M/W.

Standardized Tests *Required:* SAT I or ACT (for admission).

Costs (2001–02) *Comprehensive fee:* $18,320 includes full-time tuition ($12,240), mandatory fees ($280), and room and board ($5800). Full-time tuition and fees vary according to location. Part-time tuition: $408 per credit hour. Part-time tuition and fees vary according to course load. *Required fees:* $88 per term part-time. *Room and board:* Room and board charges vary according to board plan and housing facility. *Payment plan:* installment. *Waivers:* adult students, senior citizens, and employees or children of employees.

Financial Aid Of all full-time matriculated undergraduates who enrolled in 2001, 926 applied for aid, 896 were judged to have need, 75 had their need fully met. 140 Federal Work-Study jobs (averaging $1500). In 2001, 29 non-need-based awards were made. *Average percent of need met:* 60%. *Average financial aid package:* $10,000. *Average need-based loan:* $4100. *Average need-based gift aid:* $4200. *Average non-need based aid:* $1000. *Average indebtedness upon graduation:* $18,000.

Applying *Options:* common application, electronic application, early admission, deferred entrance. *Application fee:* $25. *Required:* high school transcript, interview. *Required for some:* essay or personal statement, 2.5 high school GPA for veterinary technology and elementary teacher education majors. *Recommended:* essay or personal statement, minimum 2.0 GPA, 1 letter of recommendation. *Application deadline:* 8/1 (freshmen), rolling (transfers). *Notification:* continuous (freshmen).

Admissions Contact Mrs. Jacqueline S. Matheny, Director of Enrollment Management, Medaille College, Medaille College, Office of Admissions, Buffalo, NY 14214. *Phone:* 716-884-3281 Ext. 203. *Toll-free phone:* 800-292-1582. *Fax:* 716-884-0291. *E-mail:* jmatheny@medaille.edu.

MEDGAR EVERS COLLEGE OF THE CITY UNIVERSITY OF NEW YORK

Brooklyn, New York

- **State and locally supported** 4-year, founded 1969, part of City University of New York System
- **Calendar** semesters
- **Degrees** certificates, associate, and bachelor's
- **Urban** 1-acre campus
- **Coed,** 4,716 undergraduate students, 55% full-time, 78% women, 22% men
- **Noncompetitive** entrance level

Undergraduates 2,574 full-time, 2,142 part-time. Students come from 3 states and territories, 50 other countries, 1% are from out of state, 87% African American, 0.7% Asian American or Pacific Islander, 4% Hispanic American, 0.2% Native American, 5% international, 7% transferred in.

Freshmen *Admission:* 651 admitted, 651 enrolled. *Average high school GPA:* 2.87.

Faculty *Total:* 424, 33% full-time, 39% with terminal degrees. *Student/faculty ratio:* 18:1.

Majors Accounting; applied mathematics; biological/physical sciences; biology; business administration; business computer facilities operation; computer science; education; environmental science; information sciences/systems; liberal arts and sciences/liberal studies; natural sciences; nursing; practical nurse; pre-engineering; pre-medicine; psychology; public administration; special education.

Academic Programs *Special study options:* academic remediation for entering students, adult/continuing education programs, advanced placement credit, cooperative education, English as a second language, external degree program, honors programs, independent study, internships, off-campus study, part-time degree program, services for LD students, study abroad, summer session for credit.

Library Charles Innis Memorial Library with 74,826 titles, 585 serial subscriptions.

Computers on Campus 300 computers available on campus for general student use. A campuswide network can be accessed from off campus. Internet access, at least one staffed computer lab available.

Student Life *Housing:* college housing not available. *Activities and Organizations:* drama/theater group, student-run newspaper, radio station, choral group, Caribbean American Student Association, African Heritage, Phi Beta Sigma, Black Social Worker, Latino Club. *Campus security:* 24-hour patrols. *Student Services:* women's center, legal services.

Athletics Member NCAA. All Division III. *Intercollegiate sports:* basketball M, cross-country running M/W, soccer M, track and field M/W, volleyball W. *Intramural sports:* basketball M, bowling M/W, swimming M/W, table tennis M/W, tennis M/W, volleyball M/W.

Standardized Tests *Recommended:* SAT I or ACT (for admission).

Costs (2001–02) *Tuition:* state resident $3200 full-time, $135 per credit part-time; nonresident $6800 full-time, $285 per credit part-time. *Required fees:* $82 full-time, $41 per term part-time. *Payment plans:* installment, deferred payment.

Applying *Options:* common application, deferred entrance. *Application fee:* $40. *Required:* high school transcript, GED. *Application deadline:* rolling (freshmen), rolling (transfers). *Notification:* continuous (freshmen).

Admissions Contact Mr. Gregory Thomas, Acting Director of Admissions, Medgar Evers College of the City University of New York, Brooklyn, NY 11225. *Phone:* 718-270-6025. *Fax:* 718-270-6198.

MERCY COLLEGE

Dobbs Ferry, New York

- **Independent** comprehensive, founded 1951
- **Calendar** semesters
- **Degrees** certificates, associate, bachelor's, and master's
- **Suburban** 60-acre campus with easy access to New York City
- **Endowment** $24.0 million
- **Coed,** 6,833 undergraduate students, 64% full-time, 71% women, 29% men
- **Noncompetitive** entrance level

Undergraduates Students come from 6 states and territories, 49 other countries.

Freshmen *Admission:* 2,708 applied.

Faculty *Total:* 665, 25% full-time. *Student/faculty ratio:* 13:1.

Majors Accounting; actuarial science; art; behavioral sciences; bilingual/bicultural education; biology; business administration; business economics; business marketing and marketing management; child care provider; computer science; criminal justice/law enforcement administration; early childhood education; education; elementary education; English; finance; fire science; French; gerontology; graphic design/commercial art/illustration; health services administration; history; human services; information sciences/systems; interdisciplinary studies; Italian; journalism; liberal arts and sciences/liberal studies; mathematics; medical technology; music; music teacher education; nursing; occupational safety/health technology; operations research; paralegal/legal assistant; political science; pre-dentistry; pre-law; pre-medicine; psychology; radio/television broadcasting; safety/security technology; secondary education; social work; sociology; Spanish; special education; speech-language pathology/audiology; speech/rhetorical studies; teaching English as a second language; veterinary sciences; veterinary technology.

Academic Programs *Special study options:* academic remediation for entering students, accelerated degree program, adult/continuing education programs, advanced placement credit, cooperative education, distance learning, double majors, English as a second language, honors programs, independent study, internships, off-campus study, part-time degree program, services for LD students, student-designed majors, study abroad, summer session for credit. *ROTC:* Air Force (c). *Unusual degree programs:* 3-2 pharmacy.

Library Mercy College Library with 322,610 titles, 1,765 serial subscriptions, an OPAC, a Web page.

Computers on Campus 138 computers available on campus for general student use. A campuswide network can be accessed from off campus. Internet access, at least one staffed computer lab available.

Student Life *Housing Options:* coed. *Activities and Organizations:* student-run newspaper, Latin American Student Association, African Descendants of One Mind, Veterinarian Technology, The Reporters Impact, Resident Student Association. *Campus security:* 24-hour patrols. *Student Services:* personal/psychological counseling.

Athletics Member NCAA. All Division II. *Intercollegiate sports:* badminton M(s), baseball M(s), basketball M(s)/W(s), cross-country running M(s)/W(s), equestrian sports M(c)/W(c), golf M(s), soccer M(s)/W(s), softball W(s), tennis M(s), volleyball W(s). *Intramural sports:* basketball M/W, volleyball M/W.

Mercy College (continued)

Standardized Tests *Recommended:* SAT I (for admission).

Costs (2002–03) *Comprehensive fee:* $18,000 includes full-time tuition ($10,000) and room and board ($8000). Full-time tuition and fees vary according to course load and degree level. Part-time tuition: $420 per credit. *Room and board:* Room and board charges vary according to board plan and housing facility. *Payment plans:* installment, deferred payment. *Waivers:* children of alumni, senior citizens, and employees or children of employees.

Financial Aid Of all full-time matriculated undergraduates who enrolled in 2001, 8950 applied for aid, 5513 were judged to have need.

Applying *Options:* electronic application, early admission, deferred entrance. *Application fee:* $35. *Required:* high school transcript, 1 letter of recommendation. *Recommended:* interview. *Application deadline:* rolling (freshmen), rolling (transfers). *Notification:* continuous (freshmen).

Admissions Contact Mrs. Sharon Handelson, Director of Admissions and Recruitment, Mercy College, 555 Broadway, Dobbs Ferry, NY 10522-1189. *Phone:* 800-Mercy-NY Ext. 7499. *Toll-free phone:* 800-MERCY-NY. *Fax:* 914-674-7382. *E-mail:* admissions@mercy.edu.

MESIVTA OF EASTERN PARKWAY RABBINICAL SEMINARY
Brooklyn, New York

Admissions Contact Rabbi Joseph Halberstadt, Dean, Mesivta of Eastern Parkway Rabbinical Seminary, 510 Dahill Road, Brooklyn, NY 11218-5559. *Phone:* 718-438-1002.

MESIVTA TIFERETH JERUSALEM OF AMERICA
New York, New York

Admissions Contact Rabbi Fishellis, Director of Admissions, Mesivta Tifereth Jerusalem of America, 141 East Broadway, New York, NY 10002-6301. *Phone:* 212-964-2830.

MESIVTA TORAH VODAATH RABBINICAL SEMINARY
Brooklyn, New York

Admissions Contact Rabbi Issac Braun, Administrator, Mesivta Torah Vodaath Rabbinical Seminary, 425 East Ninth Street, Brooklyn, NY 11218-5209. *Phone:* 718-941-8000. *Fax:* 718-941-8032.

MIRRER YESHIVA
Brooklyn, New York

Admissions Contact Director of Admissions, Mirrer Yeshiva, 1795 Ocean Parkway, Brooklyn, NY 11223-2010. *Phone:* 718-645-0536.

MOLLOY COLLEGE
Rockville Centre, New York

- **Independent** comprehensive, founded 1955
- **Calendar** 4-1-4
- **Degrees** associate, bachelor's, master's, and post-master's certificates
- **Suburban** 25-acre campus with easy access to New York City
- **Coed,** 2,010 undergraduate students, 72% full-time, 77% women, 23% men
- **Moderately difficult** entrance level, 86% of applicants were admitted

Undergraduates 1,449 full-time, 561 part-time. Students come from 4 states and territories, 7 other countries, 17% African American, 3% Asian American or Pacific Islander, 7% Hispanic American, 0.2% Native American, 0.2% international, 19% transferred in. *Retention:* 82% of 2001 full-time freshmen returned.

Freshmen *Admission:* 607 applied, 523 admitted, 223 enrolled. *Average high school GPA:* 3.0. *Test scores:* SAT verbal scores over 500: 36%; SAT math scores over 500: 45%; SAT verbal scores over 600: 10%; SAT math scores over 600: 4%.

Faculty *Total:* 324, 40% full-time, 36% with terminal degrees. *Student/faculty ratio:* 9:1.

Majors Accounting; art; biology; biology education; business administration; cardiovascular technology; communications; computer science; criminal justice studies; education; elementary education; English; English education; environmental science; French; French language education; history; interdisciplinary studies; liberal arts and sciences/liberal studies; mathematics; mathematics education; medical records technology; music; music therapy; nuclear medical technology; nursing; peace/conflict studies; philosophy; political science; predentistry; pre-law; pre-medicine; pre-veterinary studies; psychology; religious studies; respiratory therapy; secondary education; social studies education; social work; sociology; Spanish; Spanish language education; special education; speech-language pathology/audiology.

Academic Programs *Special study options:* academic remediation for entering students, adult/continuing education programs, advanced placement credit, cooperative education, double majors, English as a second language, honors programs, internships, part-time degree program, services for LD students, student-designed majors, study abroad, summer session for credit. *ROTC:* Army (c), Navy (c), Air Force (c).

Library James Edward Tobin Library with 135,000 titles, 9,675 audiovisual materials, an OPAC.

Computers on Campus 246 computers available on campus for general student use. Internet access, at least one staffed computer lab available.

Student Life *Housing:* college housing not available. *Activities and Organizations:* drama/theater group, student-run newspaper, choral group, Nursing Student Association, African-American Caribbean Organization, Gaelic Society, Education Club, International Society. *Campus security:* 24-hour emergency response devices and patrols, late-night transport/escort service. *Student Services:* health clinic, personal/psychological counseling, women's center.

Athletics Member NCAA. All Division II. *Intercollegiate sports:* baseball M(s), basketball M(s)/W(s), cross-country running M(s)/W(s), equestrian sports M(s)/W(s), lacrosse M(s)/W, soccer M(s)/W(s), softball W(s), tennis W(s), volleyball W(s).

Standardized Tests *Required:* SAT I or ACT (for admission).

Costs (2001–02) *Tuition:* $13,190 full-time, $440 per credit part-time. Part-time tuition and fees vary according to course load. *Required fees:* $750 full-time. *Payment plan:* installment. *Waivers:* minority students, children of alumni, senior citizens, and employees or children of employees.

Applying *Options:* common application, early admission, early decision, deferred entrance. *Application fee:* $30. *Required:* essay or personal statement, high school transcript. *Required for some:* 1 letter of recommendation. *Recommended:* interview. *Application deadline:* rolling (freshmen), rolling (transfers). *Early decision:* 11/1. *Notification:* 12/1 (early decision).

Admissions Contact Molloy College, 1000 Hempstead Avenue, PO Box 5002, Rockville Centre, NY 11571-5002. *Phone:* 516-678-5000 Ext. 6240. *Toll-free phone:* 888-4MOLLOY. *Fax:* 516-256-2247. *E-mail:* lucieline@molloy.edu.

MONROE COLLEGE
Bronx, New York

- **Proprietary** primarily 2-year, founded 1933
- **Calendar** trimesters
- **Degrees** associate and bachelor's
- **Urban** campus
- **Coed,** 3,449 undergraduate students, 86% full-time, 72% women, 28% men
- **Moderately difficult** entrance level, 69% of applicants were admitted

Undergraduates 2,974 full-time, 475 part-time. Students come from 4 states and territories, 8 other countries, 1% are from out of state, 46% African American, 2% Asian American or Pacific Islander, 45% Hispanic American, 0.1% Native American, 0.9% international, 4% transferred in. *Retention:* 45% of 2001 full-time freshmen returned.

Freshmen *Admission:* 1,281 applied, 885 admitted, 672 enrolled.

Faculty *Total:* 149, 44% full-time, 17% with terminal degrees. *Student/faculty ratio:* 29:1.

Majors Accounting; business; business administration; computer science; computer typography/composition; hospitality management; information sciences/systems; medical records administration; medical records technology; secretarial science.

Academic Programs *Special study options:* academic remediation for entering students, adult/continuing education programs, cooperative education, English as a second language, internships, part-time degree program, summer session for credit.

Library Main Library plus 1 other with 28,000 titles, 301 serial subscriptions, an OPAC, a Web page.

Computers on Campus 541 computers available on campus for general student use. Internet access, at least one staffed computer lab available.

Student Life *Activities and Organizations:* drama/theater group, student-run newspaper. *Campus security:* late-night transport/escort service. *Student Services:* personal/psychological counseling.

Athletics Member NJCAA. *Intercollegiate sports:* basketball M/W, soccer M/W. *Intramural sports:* basketball M/W, bowling M/W, soccer M/W, volleyball M/W.

Standardized Tests *Required:* ACT ASSET.

Costs (2001–02) *Comprehensive fee:* $16,640 includes full-time tuition ($7440), mandatory fees ($400), and room and board ($8800). Part-time tuition: $930 per course. *Required fees:* $100 per term part-time. *Room and board:* College room only: $4480. *Payment plans:* installment, deferred payment.

Financial Aid Of all full-time matriculated undergraduates who enrolled in 2001, 125 Federal Work-Study jobs (averaging $4000).

Applying *Options:* early admission, deferred entrance. *Application fee:* $25. *Required:* high school transcript, interview. *Application deadlines:* 8/26 (freshmen), 8/26 (transfers). *Notification:* continuous until 9/3 (freshmen).

Admissions Contact Lauren Rosenthal, Director of Admissions, Monroe College, Monroe College Way, 2501 Jerome Avenue, Bronx, NY 10468. *Phone:* 718-933-6700 Ext. 536. *Toll-free phone:* 800-55MONROE.

MONROE COLLEGE
New Rochelle, New York

- **Proprietary** primarily 2-year, founded 1983
- **Calendar** trimesters
- **Degrees** associate and bachelor's
- **Urban** campus with easy access to New York City
- **Coed,** 1,156 undergraduate students, 82% full-time, 67% women, 33% men
- **Moderately difficult** entrance level, 69% of applicants were admitted

Undergraduates 948 full-time, 208 part-time. Students come from 4 states and territories, 8 other countries, 1% are from out of state, 56% African American, 1% Asian American or Pacific Islander, 17% Hispanic American, 0.1% Native American, 7% international, 7% transferred in, 5% live on campus. *Retention:* 60% of 2001 full-time freshmen returned.

Freshmen *Admission:* 689 applied, 476 admitted, 343 enrolled.

Faculty *Total:* 54, 39% full-time, 9% with terminal degrees. *Student/faculty ratio:* 32:1.

Majors Accounting; business; business administration; computer science; computer typography/composition; hospitality management; information sciences/systems; medical records technology; secretarial science.

Academic Programs *Special study options:* academic remediation for entering students, adult/continuing education programs, cooperative education, English as a second language, internships, part-time degree program, summer session for credit.

Library Main Library plus 1 other with 8,400 titles, 211 serial subscriptions.

Computers on Campus 214 computers available on campus for general student use. At least one staffed computer lab available.

Student Life *Housing Options:* coed. *Activities and Organizations:* drama/theater group, student-run newspaper. *Campus security:* late-night transport/escort service. *Student Services:* personal/psychological counseling.

Athletics Member NJCAA. *Intercollegiate sports:* basketball M/W, soccer M/W. *Intramural sports:* basketball M/W, bowling M/W, soccer M/W, volleyball M/W.

Standardized Tests *Required:* ACT ASSET.

Costs (2001–02) *Comprehensive fee:* $16,640 includes full-time tuition ($7440), mandatory fees ($400), and room and board ($8800). Part-time tuition: $930 per course. *Required fees:* $100 per term part-time. *Room and board:* College room only: $4480. Room and board charges vary according to board plan. *Payment plans:* installment, deferred payment.

Financial Aid Of all full-time matriculated undergraduates who enrolled in 2001, 50 Federal Work-Study jobs (averaging $4000).

Applying *Options:* common application, electronic application, early admission, deferred entrance. *Application fee:* $25. *Required:* high school transcript, interview. *Application deadlines:* 8/26 (freshmen), 8/26 (transfers). *Notification:* continuous until 9/3 (freshmen).

Admissions Contact Ms. Lisa Scorca, High School Admissions, Monroe College, Monroe College Way, 2468 Jerome Avenue, Bronx, NY 10468. *Phone:* 914-632-5400 Ext. 407. *Toll-free phone:* 800-55-monroe.

MOUNT SAINT MARY COLLEGE
Newburgh, New York

- **Independent** comprehensive, founded 1960
- **Calendar** semesters
- **Degrees** certificates, bachelor's, and master's
- **Suburban** 72-acre campus with easy access to New York City
- **Endowment** $5.4 million
- **Coed,** 1,915 undergraduate students, 76% full-time, 70% women, 30% men
- **Moderately difficult** entrance level, 82% of applicants were admitted

Undergraduates 1,458 full-time, 457 part-time. Students come from 14 states and territories, 12% are from out of state, 10% African American, 2% Asian American or Pacific Islander, 7% Hispanic American, 7% transferred in, 39% live on campus. *Retention:* 70% of 2001 full-time freshmen returned.

Freshmen *Admission:* 1,346 applied, 1,109 admitted, 341 enrolled. *Average high school GPA:* 3.10. *Test scores:* SAT verbal scores over 500: 55%; SAT math scores over 500: 48%; SAT verbal scores over 600: 10%; SAT math scores over 600: 9%; SAT verbal scores over 700: 1%; SAT math scores over 700: 1%.

Faculty *Total:* 178, 33% full-time, 38% with terminal degrees. *Student/faculty ratio:* 17:1.

Majors Accounting; biology; business administration; chemistry; computer/information sciences; computer science; criminal justice studies; education; education (K-12); elementary education; English; Hispanic-American studies; history; human services; interdisciplinary studies; international business; international relations; liberal arts and sciences/liberal studies; mass communications; mathematics; medical laboratory technician; medical technology; nursing; physical therapy; political science; pre-law; psychology; public relations; secondary education; social sciences; sociology; special education.

Academic Programs *Special study options:* academic remediation for entering students, accelerated degree program, adult/continuing education programs, advanced placement credit, cooperative education, double majors, freshman honors college, honors programs, independent study, internships, off-campus study, part-time degree program, study abroad, summer session for credit. *ROTC:* Army (c). *Unusual degree programs:* 3-2 engineering with The Catholic University of America; physical therapy with New York Medical College.

Library Curtin Memorial Library plus 1 other with 119,146 titles, 1,117 serial subscriptions.

Computers on Campus 150 computers available on campus for general student use. A campuswide network can be accessed from student residence rooms and from off campus that provide access to intranet. Internet access, at least one staffed computer lab available.

Student Life *Housing Options:* men-only, women-only. *Activities and Organizations:* drama/theater group, student-run newspaper, choral group, Student Government Association, Different Stages, Peer Educators, Black and Latin Student Unions, CARE. *Campus security:* 24-hour emergency response devices and patrols, student patrols, late-night transport/escort service, controlled dormitory access, monitored surveillance cameras in all residence halls. *Student Services:* health clinic, personal/psychological counseling.

Athletics Member NCAA. All Division III. *Intercollegiate sports:* baseball M, basketball M/W, soccer M/W, softball W, swimming M/W, tennis M/W, volleyball W. *Intramural sports:* baseball M, basketball M/W, football M, skiing (cross-country) M(c)/W(c), soccer M/W, softball W, swimming M/W, table tennis M/W, tennis M/W, volleyball W.

Standardized Tests *Required:* SAT I or ACT (for admission).

Costs (2001–02) *One-time required fee:* $15. *Comprehensive fee:* $18,695 includes full-time tuition ($12,270), mandatory fees ($405), and room and board ($6020). Part-time tuition: $409 per credit hour. *Required fees:* $15 per term part-time. *Room and board:* College room only: $3470. Room and board charges vary according to board plan and student level. *Payment plan:* installment. *Waivers:* minority students and employees or children of employees.

Financial Aid Of all full-time matriculated undergraduates who enrolled in 2001, 182 Federal Work-Study jobs (averaging $1250). 34 State and other part-time jobs (averaging $1500). *Average financial aid package:* $8200. *Average indebtedness upon graduation:* $15,000.

Applying *Options:* common application, deferred entrance. *Application fee:* $30. *Required:* high school transcript. *Required for some:* essay or personal statement, 3 letters of recommendation, interview. *Recommended:* 3 letters of recommendation, interview. *Application deadline:* rolling (freshmen), rolling (transfers). *Notification:* continuous (freshmen).

Mount Saint Mary College (continued)

Admissions Contact Mr. J. Randall Ognibene, Director of Admissions, Mount Saint Mary College, Newburgh, NY 12550. *Phone:* 845-569-3248. *Toll-free phone:* 888-937-6762. *Fax:* 845-562-6762. *E-mail:* admissions@msmc.edu.

NAZARETH COLLEGE OF ROCHESTER

Rochester, New York

- **Independent** comprehensive, founded 1924
- **Calendar** semesters
- **Degrees** bachelor's and master's
- **Suburban** 75-acre campus
- **Endowment** $44.1 million
- **Coed,** 1,898 undergraduate students, 86% full-time, 76% women, 24% men
- **Moderately difficult** entrance level, 76% of applicants were admitted

Undergraduates 1,638 full-time, 260 part-time. Students come from 20 states and territories, 12 other countries, 5% are from out of state, 3% African American, 2% Asian American or Pacific Islander, 2% Hispanic American, 0.2% Native American, 0.2% international, 7% transferred in, 62% live on campus. *Retention:* 84% of 2001 full-time freshmen returned.

Freshmen *Admission:* 1,750 applied, 1,328 admitted, 361 enrolled. *Average high school GPA:* 3.40. *Test scores:* SAT verbal scores over 500: 87%; SAT math scores over 500: 86%; ACT scores over 18: 99%; SAT verbal scores over 600: 34%; SAT math scores over 600: 32%; ACT scores over 24: 62%; SAT verbal scores over 700: 3%; SAT math scores over 700: 5%; ACT scores over 30: 6%.

Faculty *Total:* 204, 66% full-time. *Student/faculty ratio:* 12:1.

Majors Accounting; American studies; art; art education; art history; art therapy; biochemistry; biology; biology education; business administration; business education; business marketing and marketing management; ceramic arts; chemistry; chemistry education; creative writing; drawing; economics; education; elementary education; English; English education; environmental science; fine/studio arts; foreign languages education; French; German; gerontology; graphic design/commercial art/illustration; history; history education; human resources management; information sciences/systems; information technology; interdisciplinary studies; international relations; Italian; literature; management information systems/business data processing; mathematics; mathematics education; modern languages; music; music history; music teacher education; music therapy; nursing; philosophy; photography; physical therapy; political science; pre-dentistry; pre-law; pre-medicine; pre-veterinary studies; psychology; religious studies; science education; secondary education; social sciences; social studies education; social work; sociology; Spanish; special education; speech-language pathology/audiology; theater arts/drama; women's studies.

Academic Programs *Special study options:* academic remediation for entering students, adult/continuing education programs, advanced placement credit, cooperative education, double majors, honors programs, independent study, internships, off-campus study, part-time degree program, services for LD students, study abroad, summer session for credit. *ROTC:* Air Force (c).

Library Lorette Wilmot Library with 283,810 titles, 1,959 serial subscriptions, 18,503 audiovisual materials, an OPAC, a Web page.

Computers on Campus 190 computers available on campus for general student use. A campuswide network can be accessed from student residence rooms and from off campus. Internet access, at least one staffed computer lab available.

Student Life *Housing Options:* coed, women-only, disabled students. *Activities and Organizations:* drama/theater group, student-run newspaper, radio station, choral group, Student Activities Council, French club, theater club, Campus Ministry Council, Coffeehouse, Arts, Lecture, Entertainment Board (CALEB). *Campus security:* 24-hour emergency response devices and patrols, student patrols, late-night transport/escort service, controlled dormitory access, alarm system, security beeper, lighted pathways. *Student Services:* health clinic, personal/psychological counseling.

Athletics Member NCAA. All Division III. *Intercollegiate sports:* basketball M/W, equestrian sports M/W, field hockey W, golf M/W, lacrosse M/W, soccer M/W, swimming M/W, tennis M/W, volleyball W. *Intramural sports:* basketball M/W, golf M/W, soccer M/W, swimming M/W, tennis M/W, volleyball M/W.

Standardized Tests *Required:* SAT I or ACT (for admission).

Costs (2001–02) *Comprehensive fee:* $22,044 includes full-time tuition ($14,940), mandatory fees ($444), and room and board ($6660). Full-time tuition and fees vary according to course load. Part-time tuition: $388 per credit hour. *Required fees:* $20 per term part-time. *Room and board:* College room only: $3880. Room and board charges vary according to board plan and housing facility. *Payment plan:* installment. *Waivers:* children of alumni and employees or children of employees.

Financial Aid Of all full-time matriculated undergraduates who enrolled in 2001, 1457 applied for aid, 1280 were judged to have need. 605 Federal Work-Study jobs (averaging $1586). In 2001, 183 non-need-based awards were made. *Average percent of need met:* 90%. *Average financial aid package:* $14,539. *Average need-based loan:* $4533. *Average need-based gift aid:* $8635. *Average non-need based aid:* $4878. *Average indebtedness upon graduation:* $21,118.

Applying *Options:* common application, electronic application, early admission, early decision, deferred entrance. *Application fee:* $40. *Required:* essay or personal statement, high school transcript, 1 letter of recommendation. *Recommended:* 2 letters of recommendation, interview. *Application deadlines:* 2/15 (freshmen), 3/15 (transfers). *Early decision:* 12/1. *Notification:* continuous (freshmen), 1/1 (early decision).

Admissions Contact Mr. Thomas K. DaRin, Vice President for Enrollment Management, Nazareth College of Rochester, 4245 East Avenue, Rochester, NY 14618-3790. *Phone:* 585-389-2860. *Toll-free phone:* 800-462-3944. *Fax:* 585-389-2826. *E-mail:* admissions@naz.edu.

NEW SCHOOL BACHELOR OF ARTS, NEW SCHOOL UNIVERSITY

New York, New York

- **Independent** upper-level, founded 1919, part of New School University
- **Calendar** semesters
- **Degrees** bachelor's, master's, and doctoral
- **Urban** campus
- **Endowment** $93.4 million
- **Coed,** 530 undergraduate students, 47% full-time, 65% women, 35% men
- **Moderately difficult** entrance level

The New School offers an individualized undergraduate program in the liberal arts designed for adults. Students select their curriculum from nearly 1,000 courses offered each semester. Special features include the New School OnLine University, which offers courses at a distance via computer conferencing; accelerated bachelor's/master's options, which enable undergraduates to begin graduate study; and credit for prior experiential learning through portfolio assessment.

Undergraduates 250 full-time, 280 part-time. Students come from 19 states and territories, 23 other countries, 20% are from out of state, 11% African American, 2% Asian American or Pacific Islander, 7% Hispanic American, 0.2% Native American, 5% international, 27% transferred in.

Faculty *Total:* 442. *Student/faculty ratio:* 11:1.

Majors Liberal arts and sciences/liberal studies.

Academic Programs *Special study options:* accelerated degree program, adult/continuing education programs, advanced placement credit, distance learning, English as a second language, independent study, internships, part-time degree program, student-designed majors, summer session for credit.

Library Raymond Fogelman Library plus 2 others with 368,890 titles, 1,155 serial subscriptions, 433,123 audiovisual materials.

Computers on Campus 705 computers available on campus for general student use. A campuswide network can be accessed from off campus. Internet access, at least one staffed computer lab available.

Student Life *Housing Options:* coed. *Activities and Organizations:* university committees, B.A. program committees, student advisory committees, publications. *Campus security:* 24-hour emergency response devices, controlled dormitory access, trained security personnel in central buildings. *Student Services:* health clinic, personal/psychological counseling.

Costs (2001–02) *Comprehensive fee:* $24,170 includes full-time tuition ($14,112), mandatory fees ($446), and room and board ($9612). Part-time tuition: $588 per credit. *Required fees:* $115 per term part-time. *Room and board:* College room only: $6984. *Payment plan:* installment. *Waivers:* employees or children of employees.

Financial Aid Of all full-time matriculated undergraduates who enrolled in 2001, 189 applied for aid, 177 were judged to have need, 16 had their need fully met. 29 Federal Work-Study jobs (averaging $2167). In 2001, 2 non-need-based awards were made. *Average percent of need met:* 67%. *Average financial aid package:* $10,260. *Average need-based loan:* $4563. *Average need-based gift aid:* $5781. *Average non-need based aid:* $3337. *Average indebtedness upon graduation:* $15,370.

Applying *Options:* deferred entrance. *Application fee:* $30. *Application deadline:* 8/1 (transfers).

Admissions Contact Ms. Gerianne Brusati, Director of Educational Advising and Admissions, New School Bachelor of Arts, New School University, 66 West 12th Street, New York, NY 10011-8603. *Phone:* 212-229-5630. *E-mail:* admissions@dialnsa.edu.

NEW YORK CITY TECHNICAL COLLEGE OF THE CITY UNIVERSITY OF NEW YORK

Brooklyn, New York

Admissions Contact Mr. Joseph Lento, Director of Admissions, New York City Technical College of the City University of New York, 300 Jay Street, Brooklyn, NY 11201-2983. *Phone:* 718-260-5500. *E-mail:* jlento@nyctc.cuny.edu.

THE NEW YORK COLLEGE OF HEALTH PROFESSIONS

Syosset, New York

- **Independent** founded 1981
- **Calendar** trimesters
- **Degrees** diplomas, associate, incidental bachelor's, and master's
- **Suburban** campus with easy access to New York City
- **Coed**
- **Moderately difficult** entrance level

Faculty *Student/faculty ratio:* 10:1.
Student Life *Campus security:* 24-hour patrols, security guard during certain evening and weekend hours.
Financial Aid Of all full-time matriculated undergraduates who enrolled in 2001, 15 Federal Work-Study jobs.
Applying *Options:* common application, deferred entrance. *Application fee:* $85. *Required:* essay or personal statement, high school transcript, minimum 2.0 GPA, 3 letters of recommendation, interview.
Admissions Contact Mr. Paul Goodman, Dean of Admissions and Financial Aid, The New York College of Health Professions, 6801 Jericho Turnpike, Syosset, NY 11791. *Phone:* 516-364-0808 Ext. 285. *Toll-free phone:* 800-922-7337.

NEW YORK INSTITUTE OF TECHNOLOGY

Old Westbury, New York

- **Independent** comprehensive, founded 1955
- **Calendar** semesters
- **Degrees** associate, bachelor's, master's, first professional, post-master's, and postbachelor's certificates
- **Suburban** 1050-acre campus with easy access to New York City
- **Endowment** $29.4 million
- **Coed,** 5,549 undergraduate students, 71% full-time, 38% women, 62% men
- **Moderately difficult** entrance level, 79% of applicants were admitted

Undergraduates 3,918 full-time, 1,631 part-time. Students come from 32 states and territories, 92 other countries, 9% are from out of state, 13% African American, 11% Asian American or Pacific Islander, 10% Hispanic American, 0.4% Native American, 9% international, 11% transferred in, 9% live on campus. *Retention:* 67% of 2001 full-time freshmen returned.
Freshmen *Admission:* 3,251 applied, 2,568 admitted, 868 enrolled. *Average high school GPA:* 3.10. *Test scores:* SAT verbal scores over 500: 66%; SAT math scores over 500: 87%; SAT verbal scores over 600: 20%; SAT math scores over 600: 40%; SAT verbal scores over 700: 2%; SAT math scores over 700: 5%.
Faculty *Total:* 784, 34% full-time. *Student/faculty ratio:* 16:1.
Majors Accounting; accounting technician; advertising; aerospace engineering technology; architecture; architecture related; art education; biology; biology education; biomedical engineering-related technology; business administration; business education; business marketing and marketing management; chemistry; chemistry education; community psychology; computer/information sciences; criminal justice/law enforcement administration; culinary arts and services related; data processing technology; design/applied arts related; economics; education; electrical/electronic engineering technologies related; electrical/electronic engineering technology; electrical engineering; elementary education; English; English education; environmental control technologies related; environmental technology; finance; fine/studio arts; graphic design/commercial art/illustration; health occupations education; hotel and restaurant management; human resources management; industrial arts education; industrial/manufacturing engineering; information sciences/systems; interior design; international business; management information systems/business data processing; marketing/distribution education; mathematics education; mechanical engineering; mechanical engineering technologies related; mechanical engineering technology; multi/interdisciplinary studies related; nursing; nursing related; nutritional sciences; occupational therapy; physical therapy; physician assistant; physics; physics education; political science; pre-medicine; psychology; radio/television broadcasting; radio/television broadcasting technology; secretarial science; social sciences; social studies education; sociology; technical/business writing; technical education; telecommunications; trade/industrial education.
Academic Programs *Special study options:* academic remediation for entering students, accelerated degree program, adult/continuing education programs, advanced placement credit, cooperative education, distance learning, double majors, English as a second language, external degree program, honors programs, independent study, internships, off-campus study, part-time degree program, services for LD students, student-designed majors, study abroad, summer session for credit. *ROTC:* Army (b), Air Force (b). *Unusual degree programs:* 3-2 business administration with architectural technology/MBA; engineering with mechanical engineering/energy management; occupational therapy, physical therapy, communication arts (BFA/MA), architectural technology/energy management.
Library George and Gertrude Wisser Memorial Library plus 4 others with 213,646 titles, 2,971 serial subscriptions, 44,448 audiovisual materials, an OPAC, a Web page.
Computers on Campus 634 computers available on campus for general student use. A campuswide network can be accessed from student residence rooms and from off campus that provide access to e-mail. Internet access, at least one staffed computer lab available.
Student Life *Housing Options:* coed. *Activities and Organizations:* drama/theater group, student-run newspaper, radio and television station, choral group, Physical Therapy Society, Occupational Therapy Association, ASHRAM, Bio-Medical Society, National Society of Black Engineers, national fraternities, national sororities. *Campus security:* 24-hour emergency response devices and patrols, late-night transport/escort service, controlled dormitory access. *Student Services:* health clinic, personal/psychological counseling, women's center.
Athletics Member NCAA. All Division II except baseball (Division I). *Intercollegiate sports:* baseball M(s), basketball M(s), cross-country running M(s)/W(s), lacrosse M(s), soccer M(s)/W(s), softball W(s), track and field M(s)/W(s), volleyball W(s). *Intramural sports:* basketball M, football M/W, golf M/W, swimming M/W, tennis M/W, volleyball M/W, weight lifting M/W.
Standardized Tests *Required:* SAT I or ACT (for admission).
Costs (2001–02) *Comprehensive fee:* $22,456 includes full-time tuition ($14,876) and room and board ($7580). Full-time tuition and fees vary according to course load and program. Part-time tuition: $470 per credit. Part-time tuition and fees vary according to course load. *Required fees:* $100 per term part-time. *Room and board:* College room only: $3830. Room and board charges vary according to board plan, housing facility, and location. *Payment plan:* installment. *Waivers:* senior citizens and employees or children of employees.
Financial Aid Of all full-time matriculated undergraduates who enrolled in 2001, 3624 applied for aid, 2790 were judged to have need. *Average financial aid package:* $9014. *Average need-based gift aid:* $4443. *Average indebtedness upon graduation:* $17,125.
Applying *Options:* electronic application, deferred entrance. *Application fee:* $50. *Required:* essay or personal statement, high school transcript. *Required for some:* minimum X GPA, letters of recommendation, interview, proof of volunteer or work experience required for physical therapy, physician assistant and occupational therapy programs; portfolio for fine arts programs. *Application deadline:* rolling (freshmen), rolling (transfers). *Notification:* continuous (freshmen).
Admissions Contact Mr. James Newell, Director of Financial Aid, New York Institute of Technology, PO Box 8000, Old Westbury, NY 11568. *Phone:* 516-686-7680. *Toll-free phone:* 800-345-NYIT. *Fax:* 516-686-7613. *E-mail:* admissions@nyit.edu.

NEW YORK SCHOOL OF INTERIOR DESIGN

New York, New York

- **Independent** comprehensive, founded 1916
- **Calendar** semesters
- **Degrees** certificates, associate, bachelor's, and master's
- **Urban** campus
- **Coed,** 631 undergraduate students, 29% full-time, 87% women, 13% men
- **Moderately difficult** entrance level, 81% of applicants were admitted

The New York School of Interior Design is an NASAD-accredited private college devoted to interior design education. The Bachelor of Fine Arts degree is FIDER-accredited. Located on Manhattan's Upper East Side, the School is surrounded by world-famous museums, showrooms, and architectural landmarks.

New York School of Interior Design (continued)

Undergraduates 183 full-time, 448 part-time. Students come from 15 states and territories, 30 other countries, 17% are from out of state, 7% transferred in. *Retention:* 50% of 2001 full-time freshmen returned.

Freshmen *Admission:* 204 applied, 166 admitted, 166 enrolled. *Average high school GPA:* 3.00. *Test scores:* SAT verbal scores over 500: 50%; SAT math scores over 500: 52%; SAT verbal scores over 600: 3%; SAT math scores over 600: 2%.

Faculty *Student/faculty ratio:* 8:1.

Majors Interior design.

Academic Programs *Special study options:* advanced placement credit, English as a second language, independent study, internships, part-time degree program, services for LD students, summer session for credit.

Library NYSID Library with 10,000 titles, 88 serial subscriptions, 100 audiovisual materials, an OPAC, a Web page.

Computers on Campus 50 computers available on campus for general student use. A campuswide network can be accessed from off campus. Internet access, at least one staffed computer lab available.

Student Life *Housing:* college housing not available. *Activities and Organizations:* ASID. *Campus security:* security during school hours.

Standardized Tests *Required:* SAT I or ACT (for admission).

Costs (2002–03) *Tuition:* $17,920 full-time, $560 per credit part-time. *Required fees:* $150 full-time, $75 per term part-time.

Financial Aid Of all full-time matriculated undergraduates who enrolled in 2001, 74 applied for aid, 58 were judged to have need. 15 Federal Work-Study jobs (averaging $3000). *Average percent of need met:* 50%. *Average financial aid package:* $3500. *Average need-based gift aid:* $4000. *Average indebtedness upon graduation:* $7500.

Applying *Options:* common application, deferred entrance. *Application fee:* $50. *Required:* essay or personal statement, high school transcript, minimum 2.5 GPA, 2 letters of recommendation, portfolio. *Required for some:* interview. *Recommended:* interview. *Application deadline:* rolling (freshmen), rolling (transfers). *Notification:* continuous (freshmen).

Admissions Contact Mr. Douglas Robbins, Admissions Associate, New York School of Interior Design, 170 East 70th Street, New York, NY 10021-5110. *Phone:* 212-472-1500 Ext. 204. *Toll-free phone:* 800-336-9743. *Fax:* 212-472-1867. *E-mail:* admissions@nysid.edu.

NEW YORK UNIVERSITY
New York, New York

- **Independent** university, founded 1831
- **Calendar** semesters
- **Degrees** certificates, diplomas, associate, bachelor's, master's, doctoral, first professional, post-master's, postbachelor's, and first professional certificates
- **Urban** 28-acre campus
- **Endowment** $1.1 billion
- **Coed,** 19,028 undergraduate students, 89% full-time, 60% women, 40% men
- **Most difficult** entrance level, 28% of applicants were admitted

Undergraduates 16,962 full-time, 2,066 part-time. Students come from 52 states and territories, 137 other countries, 52% are from out of state, 6% African American, 14% Asian American or Pacific Islander, 7% Hispanic American, 0.1% Native American, 5% international, 4% transferred in, 55% live on campus. *Retention:* 91% of 2001 full-time freshmen returned.

Freshmen *Admission:* 30,533 applied, 8,701 admitted, 4,009 enrolled. *Average high school GPA:* 3.70. *Test scores:* SAT verbal scores over 500: 100%; SAT math scores over 500: 99%; ACT scores over 18: 100%; SAT verbal scores over 600: 88%; SAT math scores over 600: 87%; ACT scores over 24: 96%; SAT verbal scores over 700: 35%; SAT math scores over 700: 37%; ACT scores over 30: 51%.

Faculty *Total:* 3,742, 46% full-time. *Student/faculty ratio:* 12:1.

Majors Accounting; actuarial science; African-American studies; anthropology; archaeology; art; art history; biochemistry; biology; biology education; business administration; business economics; business marketing and marketing management; chemical engineering; chemistry; chemistry education; city/community/regional planning; civil engineering; classics; communications; comparative literature; computer engineering; computer/information sciences; computer programming; computer science; dance; dental hygiene; diagnostic medical sonography; drama/dance education; drawing; early childhood education; East Asian studies; economics; education; education of the speech impaired; electrical engineering; elementary education; engineering; engineering physics; English; English education; European studies; film studies; film/video production; finance; fine/studio arts; foreign languages education; French; French language education; German; graphic design/commercial art/illustration; Greek (modern); health services administration; Hebrew; history; hotel and restaurant management; humanities; human services; information sciences/systems; interdisciplinary studies; international business; international relations; Italian; jazz; journalism; Judaic studies; Latin American studies; Latin (ancient and medieval); liberal arts and sciences/liberal studies; linguistics; management information systems/business data processing; marketing operations; mass communications; materials engineering; mathematical statistics; mathematics; mathematics education; mechanical engineering; medical radiologic technology; medical records technology; medieval/renaissance studies; Middle Eastern studies; middle school education; music; musical instrument technology; music business management/merchandising; music (general performance); music (piano and organ performance); music teacher education; music theory and composition; music (voice and choral/opera performance); neuroscience; nursing; nutrition science; operations research; philosophy; photography; physical therapy assistant; physics; physics education; play/screenwriting; political science; Portuguese; pre-dentistry; pre-law; pre-medicine; psychology; radio/television broadcasting; real estate; religious studies; respiratory therapy; romance languages; Russian; science education; sculpture; secondary education; social sciences; social studies education; social work; sociology; Spanish; special education; sport/fitness administration; theater arts/drama; theater design; travel/tourism management; urban studies; women's studies.

Academic Programs *Special study options:* accelerated degree program, adult/continuing education programs, advanced placement credit, distance learning, double majors, English as a second language, freshman honors college, honors programs, independent study, internships, off-campus study, part-time degree program, services for LD students, student-designed majors, study abroad, summer session for credit. *Unusual degree programs:* 3-2 engineering with Stevens Institute of Technology.

Library Elmer H. Bobst Library plus 11 others with 4.5 million titles, 32,766 serial subscriptions, 58,500 audiovisual materials, an OPAC, a Web page.

Computers on Campus 1400 computers available on campus for general student use. A campuswide network can be accessed from student residence rooms and from off campus. Internet access, online (class) registration, at least one staffed computer lab available.

Student Life *Housing Options:* coed, disabled students. *Activities and Organizations:* drama/theater group, student-run newspaper, radio and television station, choral group, national fraternities, national sororities. *Campus security:* 24-hour emergency response devices and patrols, student patrols, late-night transport/escort service, controlled dormitory access, 24-hour security in residence halls. *Student Services:* health clinic, personal/psychological counseling, women's center.

Athletics Member NCAA. All Division III. *Intercollegiate sports:* badminton M(c)/W(c), baseball M(c), basketball M/W, crew M(c)/W(c), cross-country running M/W, equestrian sports M(c)/W(c), fencing M/W, golf M, ice hockey M(c), lacrosse M(c)/W(c), racquetball M(c)/W(c), soccer M/W, softball W(c), swimming M/W, tennis M/W, track and field M/W, volleyball M/W, water polo M(c)/W(c), wrestling M. *Intramural sports:* badminton M/W, basketball M/W, bowling M/W, cross-country running M/W, football M/W, soccer M/W, softball M/W, squash M(c)/W(c), swimming M/W, tennis M/W, volleyball M/W, weight lifting M/W.

Standardized Tests *Required:* SAT I or ACT (for admission). *Required for some:* SAT II: Subject Tests (for admission). *Recommended:* SAT II: Subject Tests (for admission), SAT II: Writing Test (for admission).

Costs (2001–02) *Comprehensive fee:* $35,200 includes full-time tuition ($23,986), mandatory fees ($1394), and room and board ($9820). Full-time tuition and fees vary according to program. Part-time tuition: $694 per credit. Part-time tuition and fees vary according to program. *Room and board:* Room and board charges vary according to board plan and housing facility. *Payment plans:* tuition prepayment, installment, deferred payment. *Waivers:* employees or children of employees.

Financial Aid Of all full-time matriculated undergraduates who enrolled in 2001, 10718 applied for aid, 9073 were judged to have need. 2967 Federal Work-Study jobs (averaging $2191). In 2001, 2487 non-need-based awards were made. *Average percent of need met:* 73%. *Average financial aid package:* $17,413. *Average need-based loan:* $4847. *Average need-based gift aid:* $11,368. *Average indebtedness upon graduation:* $20,079.

Applying *Options:* common application, electronic application, early decision, deferred entrance. *Application fee:* $55. *Required:* essay or personal statement, high school transcript, minimum 3.0 GPA, 2 letters of recommendation. *Required for some:* interview, audition, portfolio. *Application deadlines:* 1/15 (freshmen), 4/1 (transfers). *Early decision:* 11/15. *Notification:* 4/1 (freshmen), 1/15 (early decision).

Admissions Contact New York University, 22 Washington Square North, New York, NY 10011. *Phone:* 212-998-4500. *Fax:* 212-995-4902.

NIAGARA UNIVERSITY
Niagara Falls, New York

- **Independent** comprehensive, founded 1856, affiliated with Roman Catholic Church
- **Calendar** semesters
- **Degrees** associate, bachelor's, master's, and post-master's certificates
- **Suburban** 160-acre campus with easy access to Buffalo and Toronto
- **Endowment** $38.0 million
- **Coed,** 2,460 undergraduate students, 92% full-time, 60% women, 40% men
- **Moderately difficult** entrance level, 83% of applicants were admitted

Niagara University offers an extensive merit scholarship and grant program. Students, regardless of need, may be eligible to receive an academic award ranging from $4500 up to full tuition. These merit-based grants, awards, and scholarships are renewable. To be considered, students must meet certain academic criteria and other NU guidelines.

Undergraduates 2,268 full-time, 192 part-time. Students come from 31 states and territories, 16 other countries, 8% are from out of state, 4% African American, 0.7% Asian American or Pacific Islander, 2% Hispanic American, 0.7% Native American, 5% international, 6% transferred in, 59% live on campus. *Retention:* 81% of 2001 full-time freshmen returned.

Freshmen *Admission:* 2,483 applied, 2,065 admitted, 598 enrolled. *Average high school GPA:* 3.0. *Test scores:* SAT verbal scores over 500: 60%; SAT math scores over 500: 63%; ACT scores over 18: 91%; SAT verbal scores over 600: 15%; SAT math scores over 600: 17%; ACT scores over 24: 33%; SAT verbal scores over 700: 1%; SAT math scores over 700: 1%; ACT scores over 30: 4%.

Faculty *Total:* 280, 46% full-time. *Student/faculty ratio:* 16:1.

Majors Accounting; biochemistry; biological technology; biology; biology education; business administration; business economics; business education; business marketing and marketing management; chemistry; chemistry education; computer science; criminal justice/law enforcement administration; criminology; economics; education; elementary education; English; French; French language education; history; hotel and restaurant management; human resources management; information sciences/systems; international business; international relations; liberal arts and sciences/liberal studies; mass communications; mathematics; mathematics education; nursing; philosophy; political science; pre-dentistry; pre-engineering; pre-law; pre-medicine; pre-veterinary studies; psychology; religious studies; science education; secondary education; social sciences; social studies education; social work; sociology; Spanish; Spanish language education; special education; theater arts/drama; transportation technology; travel/tourism management.

Academic Programs *Special study options:* academic remediation for entering students, accelerated degree program, adult/continuing education programs, advanced placement credit, cooperative education, double majors, English as a second language, freshman honors college, honors programs, internships, off-campus study, part-time degree program, services for LD students, study abroad, summer session for credit. *ROTC:* Army (b).

Library Our Lady of Angels Library with 313,895 titles, 4,500 serial subscriptions, an OPAC.

Computers on Campus 150 computers available on campus for general student use. A campuswide network can be accessed from student residence rooms. At least one staffed computer lab available.

Student Life *Housing:* on-campus residence required through sophomore year. *Options:* coed, women-only. *Activities and Organizations:* drama/theater group, student-run newspaper, radio station, choral group, Niagara University Community Action Program, student government, Programming Board, national fraternities. *Campus security:* 24-hour emergency response devices and patrols, late-night transport/escort service, controlled dormitory access, 24-hour escort service. *Student Services:* health clinic, personal/psychological counseling.

Athletics Member NCAA. All Division I. *Intercollegiate sports:* baseball M(s), basketball M(s)/W(s), cross-country running M(s)/W(s), golf M(s), ice hockey M(s)/W(s), lacrosse M/W(s), soccer M(s)/W(s), softball W(s), swimming M(s)/W(s), tennis M(s)/W(s), volleyball W(s). *Intramural sports:* basketball M/W, ice hockey M/W, lacrosse M/W, racquetball M/W, rugby M(c)/W(c), skiing (downhill) M(c)/W(c), soccer M/W, softball M/W, volleyball M/W, water polo M/W.

Standardized Tests *Required:* SAT I or ACT (for admission).

Costs (2001–02) *Comprehensive fee:* $22,250 includes full-time tuition ($14,700), mandatory fees ($600), and room and board ($6950). Part-time tuition: $450 per credit hour. Part-time tuition and fees vary according to program. *Required fees:* $10 per term part-time. *Room and board:* Room and board charges vary according to board plan. *Payment plans:* installment, deferred payment. *Waivers:* employees or children of employees.

Financial Aid Of all full-time matriculated undergraduates who enrolled in 2001, 2199 applied for aid, 1831 were judged to have need, 423 had their need fully met. 404 Federal Work-Study jobs (averaging $2101). 36 State and other part-time jobs (averaging $2603). In 2001, 213 non-need-based awards were made. *Average percent of need met:* 92%. *Average financial aid package:* $12,902. *Average need-based loan:* $3818. *Average need-based gift aid:* $9678. *Average non-need based aid:* $5880. *Average indebtedness upon graduation:* $17,390.

Applying *Options:* electronic application, early admission, deferred entrance. *Application fee:* $30. *Required:* high school transcript. *Recommended:* minimum 3.0 GPA, 3 letters of recommendation, interview. *Application deadlines:* 8/1 (freshmen), 8/15 (transfers).

Admissions Contact Ms. Christine M. McDermott, Associate Director of Admissions, Niagara University, Office of Admissions, Niagara, NY 14109. *Phone:* 716-286-8700 Ext. 8715. *Toll-free phone:* 800-462-2111. *Fax:* 716-286-8733. *E-mail:* admissions@niagara.edu.

NYACK COLLEGE
Nyack, New York

- **Independent** 4-year, founded 1882, affiliated with The Christian and Missionary Alliance
- **Calendar** semesters
- **Degrees** associate and bachelor's (Nyack College's graduate programs are listed separately under Alliance Theological Seminary)
- **Suburban** 102-acre campus with easy access to New York City
- **Endowment** $3.7 million
- **Coed,** 1,897 undergraduate students, 91% full-time, 60% women, 40% men
- **Moderately difficult** entrance level, 67% of applicants were admitted

Undergraduates 1,717 full-time, 180 part-time. Students come from 45 states and territories, 46 other countries, 33% are from out of state, 27% African American, 7% Asian American or Pacific Islander, 23% Hispanic American, 0.1% Native American, 5% international, 18% transferred in, 42% live on campus. *Retention:* 64% of 2001 full-time freshmen returned.

Freshmen *Admission:* 1,023 applied, 688 admitted, 338 enrolled. *Average high school GPA:* 2.80. *Test scores:* SAT verbal scores over 500: 47%; SAT math scores over 500: 37%; ACT scores over 18: 84%; SAT verbal scores over 600: 13%; SAT math scores over 600: 9%; ACT scores over 24: 36%; SAT verbal scores over 700: 2%; ACT scores over 30: 7%.

Faculty *Total:* 192, 44% full-time, 52% with terminal degrees. *Student/faculty ratio:* 16:1.

Majors Accounting; biblical studies; business administration; communications; computer science; elementary education; English; general studies; history; interdisciplinary studies; liberal arts and sciences/liberal studies; mathematics; missionary studies; music; music (piano and organ performance); music teacher education; music theory and composition; music (voice and choral/opera performance); pastoral counseling; philosophy; psychology; religious education; religious music; religious studies; secondary education; social sciences; social work; teaching English as a second language; theology.

Academic Programs *Special study options:* academic remediation for entering students, accelerated degree program, adult/continuing education programs, advanced placement credit, distance learning, double majors, English as a second language, honors programs, independent study, internships, off-campus study, part-time degree program, study abroad, summer session for credit.

Library The Bailey Library plus 1 other with 66,616 titles, 564 serial subscriptions, 2,411 audiovisual materials, an OPAC, a Web page.

Computers on Campus 100 computers available on campus for general student use. Internet access, at least one staffed computer lab available.

Student Life *Housing Options:* men-only, women-only. *Activities and Organizations:* drama/theater group, student-run newspaper, radio station, choral group, gospel Teams, Drama Club, Student Government Association. *Campus security:* 24-hour emergency response devices and patrols, student patrols, late-night transport/escort service. *Student Services:* health clinic, personal/psychological counseling.

Athletics Member NAIA, NCCAA. *Intercollegiate sports:* baseball M, basketball M(s)/W(s), cross-country running M/W, soccer M(s)/W(s), softball W, volleyball M/W(s). *Intramural sports:* basketball M, football M, volleyball M/W.

Standardized Tests *Required:* SAT I or ACT (for admission).

Costs (2001–02) *Comprehensive fee:* $19,480 includes full-time tuition ($12,480), mandatory fees ($800), and room and board ($6200). Full-time tuition and fees vary according to program. Part-time tuition: $520 per credit. Part-time tuition and fees vary according to course load and program. *Required fees:* $150 per term part-time. *Room and board:* Room and board charges vary according to housing facility. *Payment plan:* installment. *Waivers:* employees or children of employees.

Nyack College (continued)

Financial Aid Of all full-time matriculated undergraduates who enrolled in 2001, 1062 applied for aid, 1006 were judged to have need, 160 had their need fully met. 260 Federal Work-Study jobs (averaging $1009). 40 State and other part-time jobs (averaging $1974). In 2001, 174 non-need-based awards were made. *Average percent of need met:* 67%. *Average financial aid package:* $12,383. *Average need-based loan:* $3750. *Average need-based gift aid:* $8439. *Average indebtedness upon graduation:* $17,000.

Applying *Options:* electronic application, early admission, deferred entrance. *Application fee:* $15. *Required:* essay or personal statement, high school transcript, minimum 2.0 GPA, 2 letters of recommendation. *Required for some:* interview. *Application deadline:* rolling (freshmen), rolling (transfers). *Notification:* continuous (freshmen).

Admissions Contact Mr. Miguel Sanchez, Director of Admissions, Nyack College, 1 South Boulevard, Nyack, NY 10960-3698. *Phone:* 845-358-1710 Ext. 350. *Toll-free phone:* 800-33-NYACK. *Fax:* 845-358-3047. *E-mail:* enroll@nyack.edu.

OHR HAMEIR THEOLOGICAL SEMINARY
Peekskill, New York

Admissions Contact Rabbi M. Z. Weisverg, Director of Admissions, Ohr Hameir Theological Seminary, Furnace Woods Road, Peekskill, NY 10566. *Phone:* 914-736-1500.

OHR SOMAYACH/JOSEPH TANENBAUM EDUCATIONAL CENTER
Monsey, New York

Admissions Contact Rabbi Avrohom Braun, Dean of Students, Ohr Somayach/Joseph Tanenbaum Educational Center, PO Box 334, Monsey, NY 10952-0334. *Phone:* 914-425-1370 Ext. 22.

PACE UNIVERSITY
New York, New York

- **Independent** university, founded 1906
- **Calendar** semesters
- **Degrees** certificates, diplomas, associate, bachelor's, master's, doctoral, first professional, post-master's, and postbachelor's certificates
- **Endowment** $90.1 million
- **Coed,** 8,913 undergraduate students, 77% full-time, 60% women, 40% men
- **Moderately difficult** entrance level, 76% of applicants were admitted

Pace offers a variety of scholarships and grants that range from $1000 to $10,000 per year. Candidates are encouraged to apply early. Pace's nationally recognized co-op education program also helps qualified students finance and enhance their education through paid career-related work experiences in the public and private sectors.

Undergraduates 6,831 full-time, 2,082 part-time. Students come from 46 states and territories, 58 other countries, 12% are from out of state, 5% transferred in, 23% live on campus. *Retention:* 76% of 2001 full-time freshmen returned.

Freshmen *Admission:* 7,072 applied, 5,362 admitted, 1,647 enrolled. *Average high school GPA:* 3.00. *Test scores:* SAT verbal scores over 500: 53%; SAT math scores over 500: 61%; ACT scores over 18: 78%; SAT verbal scores over 600: 11%; SAT math scores over 600: 19%; ACT scores over 24: 24%; SAT verbal scores over 700: 1%; SAT math scores over 700: 2%; ACT scores over 30: 1%.

Faculty *Total:* 1,282, 33% full-time, 51% with terminal degrees. *Student/faculty ratio:* 15:1.

Majors Accounting; accounting technician; advertising; art; art education; art history; banking; biochemistry; biology; biology education; business administration; business economics; business education; business marketing and marketing management; chemistry; chemistry education; child guidance; computer/information sciences; criminal justice/law enforcement administration; data processing; design/visual communications; ecology; economics; education of the specific learning disabled; elementary education; English; English education; finance; fine/studio arts; foreign languages/literatures; French language education; graphic design/commercial art/illustration; history; hotel and restaurant management; human resources management; information sciences/systems; interdisciplinary studies; international business; international business marketing; journalism; labor/personnel relations; liberal arts and sciences/liberal studies; literature; management information systems/business data processing; mathematics; mathematics education; medical records administration; medical technology; modern languages; nursing; physician assistant; physics; physics education; political science; psychology; respiratory therapy; retailing operations; science education; social science education; social sciences; social studies education; Spanish; Spanish language education; special education; speech education; speech-language pathology; speech/rhetorical studies.

Academic Programs *Special study options:* academic remediation for entering students, accelerated degree program, adult/continuing education programs, advanced placement credit, cooperative education, distance learning, double majors, English as a second language, freshman honors college, honors programs, independent study, internships, part-time degree program, study abroad, summer session for credit. *ROTC:* Air Force (c). *Unusual degree programs:* 3-2 engineering with Manhattan College, Rensselaer Polytechnic Institute; physical therapy with New York Medical College.

Library Henry Birnbaum Library plus 3 others with 786,132 titles, 2,637 serial subscriptions, an OPAC, a Web page.

Computers on Campus 155 computers available on campus for general student use. A campuswide network can be accessed from student residence rooms and from off campus. At least one staffed computer lab available.

Student Life *Housing Options:* coed. *Activities and Organizations:* drama/theater group, student-run newspaper, radio and television station, choral group, student government, Pace Press Newspaper, United Chinese Students Association, Alianza Latina, National Association of Black Accountants, national fraternities, national sororities. *Campus security:* 24-hour emergency response devices and patrols, late-night transport/escort service, controlled dormitory access. *Student Services:* health clinic, personal/psychological counseling.

Athletics Member NCAA. All Division II except baseball (Division I). *Intercollegiate sports:* baseball M(s), basketball M(s)/W(s), cross-country running M(s)/W(s), equestrian sports M/W, football M, golf M(s)/W(s), lacrosse M(s), soccer W(s), softball W(s), tennis M(s)/W(s), track and field M(s)/W(s), volleyball W(s). *Intramural sports:* basketball M/W, football M/W, soccer M/W, volleyball M/W.

Standardized Tests *Required:* SAT I or ACT (for admission).

Costs (2001–02) *Comprehensive fee:* $24,200 includes full-time tuition ($16,650), mandatory fees ($380), and room and board ($7170). Part-time tuition: $520 per credit. Part-time tuition and fees vary according to course load. *Required fees:* $126 per term part-time. *Room and board:* Room and board charges vary according to board plan and housing facility. *Payment plan:* installment. *Waivers:* senior citizens and employees or children of employees.

Applying *Options:* common application, electronic application, early action, deferred entrance. *Application fee:* $45. *Required:* high school transcript. *Recommended:* essay or personal statement, minimum 3.0 GPA, 2 letters of recommendation, interview. *Application deadline:* rolling (freshmen), rolling (transfers). *Notification:* continuous (freshmen), 12/15 (early action).

Admissions Contact Ms. Joanna Broda, Director of Admission, NY and Westchester, Pace University, One Pace Plaza, New York, NY 10038. *Phone:* 212-346-1323. *Toll-free phone:* 800-874-7223. *Fax:* 212-346-1040. *E-mail:* infoctr@pace.edu.

PARSONS SCHOOL OF DESIGN, NEW SCHOOL UNIVERSITY
New York, New York

- **Independent** comprehensive, founded 1896, part of New School University
- **Calendar** semesters
- **Degrees** associate, bachelor's, and master's
- **Urban** 2-acre campus
- **Endowment** $90.2 million
- **Coed,** 2,311 undergraduate students, 92% full-time, 75% women, 25% men
- **Very difficult** entrance level, 44% of applicants were admitted

Undergraduates 2,124 full-time, 187 part-time. Students come from 42 states and territories, 57 other countries, 47% are from out of state, 4% African American, 20% Asian American or Pacific Islander, 7% Hispanic American, 0.2% Native American, 29% international, 18% transferred in, 24% live on campus. *Retention:* 80% of 2001 full-time freshmen returned.

Freshmen *Admission:* 1,690 applied, 738 admitted, 361 enrolled. *Test scores:* SAT verbal scores over 500: 57%; SAT math scores over 500: 68%; SAT verbal scores over 600: 25%; SAT math scores over 600: 28%; SAT verbal scores over 700: 6%; SAT math scores over 700: 6%.

Faculty *Total:* 643, 9% full-time. *Student/faculty ratio:* 11:1.

Majors Architectural environmental design; architecture; art; art education; drawing; fashion design/illustration; fashion merchandising; graphic design/commercial art/illustration; industrial design; interior design; photography; sculpture.

Academic Programs *Special study options:* accelerated degree program, adult/continuing education programs, advanced placement credit, distance learning, English as a second language, honors programs, independent study, internships, off-campus study, services for LD students, study abroad, summer session for credit.

Library Raymond Fogelman Library plus 2 others with 368,390 titles, 1,155 serial subscriptions, 433,123 audiovisual materials, an OPAC, a Web page.

Computers on Campus 705 computers available on campus for general student use. A campuswide network can be accessed from off campus that provide access to e-mail. Internet access, at least one staffed computer lab available.

Student Life *Housing Options:* coed, disabled students. *Activities and Organizations:* gallery committees, Latino/Latina Student Group, Chinese Student Association, American Institute of Architectural Students. *Campus security:* 24-hour emergency response devices, controlled dormitory access. *Student Services:* health clinic, personal/psychological counseling.

Standardized Tests *Required:* SAT I or ACT (for admission).

Costs (2001–02) *Comprehensive fee:* $32,738 includes full-time tuition ($22,630), mandatory fees ($496), and room and board ($9612). Part-time tuition: $770 per credit. *Required fees:* $140 per term part-time. *Room and board:* College room only: $6984. Room and board charges vary according to board plan and student level. *Payment plan:* installment.

Financial Aid Of all full-time matriculated undergraduates who enrolled in 2001, 1824 applied for aid, 1251 were judged to have need, 95 had their need fully met. 213 Federal Work-Study jobs (averaging $1722). In 2001, 154 non-need-based awards were made. *Average percent of need met:* 66%. *Average financial aid package:* $13,129. *Average need-based loan:* $4516. *Average need-based gift aid:* $10,305. *Average indebtedness upon graduation:* $23,450.

Applying *Application fee:* $40. *Required:* high school transcript, minimum 2.0 GPA, portfolio, home examination. *Required for some:* essay or personal statement, interview. *Recommended:* minimum 3.0 GPA. *Application deadline:* rolling (freshmen), rolling (transfers). *Notification:* continuous (freshmen).

Admissions Contact Ms. Nadine M. Bourgeois, Director of Admissions and Associate Dean of Enrollment Management, Parsons School of Design, New School University, 66 Fifth Avenue, New York, NY 10011-8878. *Phone:* 212-229-8910. *Toll-free phone:* 800-252-0852. *E-mail:* parsadm@newschool.edu.

PAUL SMITH'S COLLEGE OF ARTS AND SCIENCES

Paul Smiths, New York

- **Independent** 4-year, founded 1937
- **Calendar** semesters
- **Degrees** certificates, associate, and bachelor's
- **Rural** 14,200-acre campus
- **Endowment** $11.8 million
- **Coed,** 817 undergraduate students, 97% full-time, 30% women, 70% men
- **Minimally difficult** entrance level, 80% of applicants were admitted

Undergraduates 794 full-time, 23 part-time. Students come from 29 states and territories, 11 other countries, 40% are from out of state, 4% African American, 0.6% Asian American or Pacific Islander, 2% Hispanic American, 1% Native American, 1% international, 9% transferred in, 95% live on campus. *Retention:* 63% of 2001 full-time freshmen returned.

Freshmen *Admission:* 1,173 applied, 933 admitted, 330 enrolled. *Test scores:* SAT verbal scores over 500: 39%; SAT math scores over 500: 33%; ACT scores over 18: 59%; SAT verbal scores over 600: 6%; SAT math scores over 600: 8%; ACT scores over 24: 7%; SAT verbal scores over 700: 1%.

Faculty *Total:* 65, 98% full-time, 18% with terminal degrees. *Student/faculty ratio:* 13:1.

Majors American studies; business administration; culinary arts; ecology; environmental science; forest harvesting production technology; forestry; hospitality management; hotel and restaurant management; liberal arts and sciences/liberal studies; natural resources management; recreation/leisure facilities management; surveying; technical/business writing; travel/tourism management.

Academic Programs *Special study options:* academic remediation for entering students, adult/continuing education programs, advanced placement credit, cooperative education, double majors, English as a second language, honors programs, internships, services for LD students, student-designed majors, study abroad, summer session for credit.

Library Frank C. Cubley Library with 56,000 titles, 504 serial subscriptions, an OPAC, a Web page.

Computers on Campus 65 computers available on campus for general student use. A campuswide network can be accessed from student residence rooms and from off campus. Internet access, at least one staffed computer lab available.

Student Life *Housing:* on-campus residence required through sophomore year. *Options:* coed. *Activities and Organizations:* drama/theater group, student-run newspaper, radio station, Forestry Club, Adirondack Experience Club, student radio station, Emergency Wilderness Response Team, Junior American Culinary. *Campus security:* 24-hour emergency response devices and patrols, late-night transport/escort service. *Student Services:* health clinic, personal/psychological counseling.

Athletics Member NJCAA. *Intercollegiate sports:* basketball M(s)/W(s), ice hockey M(s), skiing (downhill) M(s)/W(s), soccer M(s)/W(s). *Intramural sports:* basketball M/W, cross-country running M(c)/W(c), football M, golf M, ice hockey M(c), riflery M(c)/W(c), rugby M(c), soccer M/W, softball M/W, swimming M/W, table tennis M/W, tennis M/W, volleyball M/W.

Standardized Tests *Required:* SAT I or ACT (for admission).

Costs (2002–03) *Comprehensive fee:* $21,060 includes full-time tuition ($14,200), mandatory fees ($700), and room and board ($6160). Full-time tuition and fees vary according to program. Part-time tuition: $320 per credit hour. Part-time tuition and fees vary according to course load and program. No tuition increase for student's term of enrollment. *Room and board:* College room only: $3080. Room and board charges vary according to board plan. *Payment plan:* installment. *Waivers:* employees or children of employees.

Applying *Options:* common application, electronic application, early admission, deferred entrance. *Application fee:* $30. *Required:* essay or personal statement, high school transcript, 1 letter of recommendation. *Required for some:* interview. *Application deadline:* rolling (freshmen), rolling (transfers).

Admissions Contact Mr. Douglas Zander, Vice President for Enrollment and Campus Life, Paul Smith's College of Arts and Sciences, PO Box 265, Paul Smiths, NY 12970-0265. *Phone:* 518-327-6227 Ext. 6230. *Toll-free phone:* 800-421-2605. *Fax:* 518-327-6016.

PLATTSBURGH STATE UNIVERSITY OF NEW YORK

Plattsburgh, New York

- **State-supported** comprehensive, founded 1889, part of State University of New York System
- **Calendar** plus 2 5-week summer sessions and 1 winter session
- **Degrees** bachelor's, master's, and post-master's certificates
- **Small-town** 265-acre campus with easy access to Montreal
- **Endowment** $11.3 million
- **Coed,** 5,382 undergraduate students, 93% full-time, 57% women, 43% men
- **Moderately difficult** entrance level, 63% of applicants were admitted

Plattsburgh State offers students an exceptional education in one of America's best college locations. The curriculum's traditional liberal arts foundation supports programs that focus on preparing students for successful professional careers. Majors span liberal arts and science, business and economics, and professional studies. Internships and study-abroad programs are available.

Undergraduates 4,999 full-time, 383 part-time. Students come from 25 states and territories, 61 other countries, 3% are from out of state, 3% African American, 2% Asian American or Pacific Islander, 3% Hispanic American, 0.4% Native American, 6% international, 11% transferred in, 59% live on campus. *Retention:* 79% of 2001 full-time freshmen returned.

Freshmen *Admission:* 5,211 applied, 3,266 admitted, 1,016 enrolled. *Average high school GPA:* 3.50. *Test scores:* SAT verbal scores over 500: 66%; SAT math scores over 500: 69%; ACT scores over 18: 93%; SAT verbal scores over 600: 16%; SAT math scores over 600: 17%; ACT scores over 24: 25%; SAT verbal scores over 700: 2%; SAT math scores over 700: 1%; ACT scores over 30: 1%.

Faculty *Total:* 437, 61% full-time, 62% with terminal degrees. *Student/faculty ratio:* 17:1.

Majors Accounting; anthropology; art history; biochemistry; biology; broadcast journalism; business administration; business economics; business marketing and marketing management; Canadian studies; chemistry; child care/development; communication disorders; communications; computer science; criminology; economics; education; elementary education; English; environmental science; fine/studio arts; French; geography; geology; history; hotel and restaurant management; interdisciplinary studies; international business; Latin American studies; mass communications; mathematics; medical technology; music; nursing; nutrition science; philosophy; physics; political science; psychology; secondary education; social work; sociology; Spanish; special education; speech-language pathology/audiology; theater arts/drama.

Academic Programs *Special study options:* academic remediation for entering students, accelerated degree program, adult/continuing education programs,

Plattsburgh State University of New York (continued)
advanced placement credit, cooperative education, distance learning, double majors, English as a second language, honors programs, independent study, internships, off-campus study, part-time degree program, services for LD students, student-designed majors, study abroad, summer session for credit. *Unusual degree programs:* 3-2 engineering with Clarkson University, State University of New York at Stony Brook, Syracuse University, University of Vermont, McGill University, State University of New York at Binghamton; international policy studies with Monterey Institute of International Studies in French and Spanish.

Library Feinberg Library with 754,096 titles, 1,466 serial subscriptions, 23,329 audiovisual materials, an OPAC, a Web page.

Computers on Campus 366 computers available on campus for general student use. A campuswide network can be accessed from student residence rooms and from off campus. Internet access, online (class) registration, at least one staffed computer lab available.

Student Life *Housing:* on-campus residence required through sophomore year. *Options:* coed, disabled students. *Activities and Organizations:* drama/theater group, student-run newspaper, radio and television station, choral group, Student Association, honor societies, student media organizations, service/leadership organizations, intramural and recreational sports, national fraternities, national sororities. *Campus security:* 24-hour emergency response devices and patrols, late-night transport/escort service, controlled dormitory access, enhanced 911 system. *Student Services:* health clinic, personal/psychological counseling, women's center, legal services.

Athletics Member NCAA. All Division III. *Intercollegiate sports:* basketball M/W, cross-country running M/W, golf M/W, ice hockey M, lacrosse M, soccer M/W, softball W, swimming M/W, tennis W, track and field M/W, volleyball W. *Intramural sports:* basketball M/W, football M, golf M/W, ice hockey M(c), lacrosse M, racquetball M(c)/W(c), rugby M(c)/W(c), soccer M/W, softball W, tennis W, volleyball M/W, weight lifting M(c)/W(c).

Standardized Tests *Required:* SAT I or ACT (for admission).

Costs (2001–02) *Tuition:* state resident $3400 full-time, $137 per credit hour part-time; nonresident $8300 full-time, $346 per credit hour part-time. Part-time tuition and fees vary according to course load. *Required fees:* $749 full-time, $16 per credit hour. *Room and board:* $5580; room only: $3300. Room and board charges vary according to board plan. *Payment plans:* installment, deferred payment. *Waivers:* minority students, adult students, senior citizens, and employees or children of employees.

Financial Aid Of all full-time matriculated undergraduates who enrolled in 2001, 3713 applied for aid, 2839 were judged to have need, 1298 had their need fully met. In 2001, 1178 non-need-based awards were made. *Average percent of need met:* 92%. *Average financial aid package:* $7497. *Average need-based loan:* $4852. *Average need-based gift aid:* $3622. *Average indebtedness upon graduation:* $15,274.

Applying *Options:* electronic application, early admission, early decision, deferred entrance. *Application fee:* $30. *Required:* high school transcript, minimum 2.5 GPA. *Recommended:* essay or personal statement, minimum 3.4 GPA, letters of recommendation, interview. *Application deadline:* rolling (freshmen), rolling (transfers). *Early decision:* 11/1. *Notification:* continuous (freshmen), 12/15 (early decision).

Admissions Contact Mr. Richard Higgins, Director of Admissions, Plattsburgh State University of New York, 101 Broad Street, Plattsburgh, NY 12901-2681. *Phone:* 518-564-2040. *Toll-free phone:* 888-673-0012. *Fax:* 518-564-2045. *E-mail:* admissions@plattsburgh.edu.

POLYTECHNIC UNIVERSITY, BROOKLYN CAMPUS

Brooklyn, New York

- **Independent** university, founded 1854
- **Calendar** semesters
- **Degrees** certificates, bachelor's, master's, and doctoral (all information given is for both Brooklyn and Farmingdale campuses)
- **Urban** 3-acre campus
- **Endowment** $167.9 million
- **Coed,** 1,709 undergraduate students, 93% full-time, 20% women, 80% men
- **Very difficult** entrance level, 69% of applicants were admitted

Undergraduates 1,582 full-time, 127 part-time. Students come from 10 states and territories, 6 other countries, 3% are from out of state, 10% African American, 40% Asian American or Pacific Islander, 6% Hispanic American, 0.2% Native American, 6% international, 3% transferred in, 3% live on campus. *Retention:* 81% of 2001 full-time freshmen returned.

Freshmen *Admission:* 1,573 applied, 1,079 admitted, 454 enrolled. *Average high school GPA:* 3.40. *Test scores:* SAT verbal scores over 500: 96%; SAT math scores over 500: 100%; SAT verbal scores over 600: 39%; SAT math scores over 600: 87%; SAT verbal scores over 700: 4%; SAT math scores over 700: 25%.

Faculty *Total:* 333, 51% full-time. *Student/faculty ratio:* 12:1.

Majors Chemical engineering; chemistry; civil engineering; computer engineering; computer science; electrical engineering; information sciences/systems; liberal arts and sciences/liberal studies; mathematics; mechanical engineering; physics; pre-law; pre-medicine; technical/business writing.

Academic Programs *Special study options:* academic remediation for entering students, accelerated degree program, advanced placement credit, cooperative education, double majors, English as a second language, honors programs, internships, part-time degree program, summer session for credit. *ROTC:* Air Force (c).

Library Bern Dibner Library with 148,000 titles, 613 serial subscriptions, 235 audiovisual materials, an OPAC, a Web page.

Computers on Campus 350 computers available on campus for general student use. A campuswide network can be accessed from off campus. Internet access, at least one staffed computer lab available.

Student Life *Housing Options:* coed. *Activities and Organizations:* student-run newspaper, radio station, National Society of Black Engineers, Society of Hispanic Professional Engineers, Association for Computing Machinery, Alpha Phi Omega, Chinese Student Society, national fraternities, national sororities. *Campus security:* 24-hour patrols. *Student Services:* personal/psychological counseling, women's center.

Athletics Member NCAA. All Division III. *Intercollegiate sports:* baseball M, basketball M/W, cross-country running M/W, soccer M, softball W, tennis M/W, track and field M/W, volleyball M/W. *Intramural sports:* baseball M, basketball M/W, bowling M/W, football M(c)/W(c), golf M(c)/W(c), soccer M(c)/W(c), table tennis M(c)/W(c), track and field M(c)/W(c), volleyball M/W, weight lifting M(c)/W(c).

Standardized Tests *Required:* SAT I or ACT (for admission). *Recommended:* SAT II: Subject Tests (for admission), SAT II: Writing Test (for admission).

Costs (2001–02) *Comprehensive fee:* $28,190 includes full-time tuition ($22,280), mandatory fees ($660), and room and board ($5250). Full-time tuition and fees vary according to course load. Part-time tuition: $708 per credit. Part-time tuition and fees vary according to course load. *Required fees:* $225 per term part-time. *Room and board:* Room and board charges vary according to board plan. *Payment plans:* tuition prepayment, deferred payment. *Waivers:* minority students and employees or children of employees.

Financial Aid Of all full-time matriculated undergraduates who enrolled in 2001, 1627 applied for aid, 1335 were judged to have need, 336 had their need fully met. 235 Federal Work-Study jobs (averaging $1883). In 2001, 227 non-need-based awards were made. *Average percent of need met:* 86%. *Average financial aid package:* $18,024. *Average need-based loan:* $4542. *Average need-based gift aid:* $7635. *Average non-need based aid:* $13,059. *Average indebtedness upon graduation:* $18,491.

Applying *Options:* common application, electronic application, deferred entrance. *Application fee:* $40. *Required:* essay or personal statement, high school transcript, 2 letters of recommendation. *Recommended:* interview. *Application deadline:* rolling (freshmen), rolling (transfers).

Admissions Contact Mr. John S. Kerge, Dean of Admissions, Polytechnic University, Brooklyn Campus, Six Metrotech Center, Brooklyn, NY 11201-2990. *Phone:* 718-260-3100. *Toll-free phone:* 800-POLYTECH. *Fax:* 718-260-3446. *E-mail:* admitme@poly.edu.

PRACTICAL BIBLE COLLEGE

Bible School Park, New York

- **Independent nondenominational** 4-year, founded 1900
- **Calendar** semesters
- **Degrees** certificates, diplomas, associate, and bachelor's
- **Suburban** 22-acre campus with easy access to Syracuse
- **Coed,** 245 undergraduate students, 86% full-time, 44% women, 56% men
- **Minimally difficult** entrance level, 53% of applicants were admitted

Undergraduates 211 full-time, 34 part-time. Students come from 13 states and territories, 4 other countries, 23% are from out of state, 2% African American, 0.4% Asian American or Pacific Islander, 2% Hispanic American, 3% international, 13% transferred in, 61% live on campus. *Retention:* 84% of 2001 full-time freshmen returned.

Freshmen *Admission:* 98 applied, 52 admitted, 54 enrolled. *Average high school GPA:* 3.38. *Test scores:* ACT scores over 18: 62%; ACT scores over 24: 26%; ACT scores over 30: 5%.

Faculty *Total:* 24, 29% full-time, 42% with terminal degrees. *Student/faculty ratio:* 17:1.

Majors Biblical studies.
Academic Programs *Special study options:* academic remediation for entering students, adult/continuing education programs, advanced placement credit, cooperative education, English as a second language, independent study, internships, part-time degree program, services for LD students, summer session for credit.
Library Alice E. Chatlos Library with 77,000 titles, 644 serial subscriptions, 8,500 audiovisual materials, an OPAC, a Web page.
Computers on Campus 12 computers available on campus for general student use. Internet access, at least one staffed computer lab available.
Student Life *Housing:* on-campus residence required through senior year. *Options:* men-only, women-only. *Activities and Organizations:* drama/theater group, choral group, Student Missionary Fellowship, Student Wives Fellowship, Student Life Committee, Married Couples Fellowship. *Campus security:* 24-hour emergency response devices and patrols, student patrols, late-night transport/escort service. *Student Services:* health clinic, personal/psychological counseling.
Athletics Member NCCAA. *Intercollegiate sports:* basketball M/W, soccer M, volleyball W. *Intramural sports:* skiing (downhill) M/W, soccer M/W, table tennis M/W, volleyball M/W, weight lifting M/W.
Standardized Tests *Required:* SAT I or ACT (for admission). *Recommended:* ACT (for admission).
Costs (2001–02) *Comprehensive fee:* $11,445 includes full-time tuition ($6340), mandatory fees ($685), and room and board ($4420). Part-time tuition: $264 per credit. Part-time tuition and fees vary according to class time and course load. *Required fees:* $215 per term part-time. *Room and board:* Room and board charges vary according to housing facility. *Payment plan:* installment. *Waivers:* children of alumni and employees or children of employees.
Financial Aid Of all full-time matriculated undergraduates who enrolled in 2001, 182 applied for aid, 175 were judged to have need, 27 had their need fully met. 77 Federal Work-Study jobs (averaging $898). In 2001, 10 non-need-based awards were made. *Average percent of need met:* 37%. *Average financial aid package:* $5120. *Average need-based loan:* $4893. *Average need-based gift aid:* $4360. *Average non-need based aid:* $610. *Average indebtedness upon graduation:* $5360.
Applying *Options:* common application, electronic application, deferred entrance. *Application fee:* $25. *Required:* high school transcript, 2 letters of recommendation, references. *Required for some:* essay or personal statement. *Recommended:* minimum 2.0 GPA, interview. *Application deadline:* rolling (freshmen), rolling (transfers). *Notification:* continuous (freshmen).
Admissions Contact Mr. Brian J. Murphy, Director of Admissions, Practical Bible College, PO Box 601, Bible School Park, NY 13737-0601. *Phone:* 607-729-1581 Ext. 406. *Toll-free phone:* 800-331-4137 Ext. 406. *Fax:* 607-729-2962. *E-mail:* admissions@practical.edu.

PRATT INSTITUTE
Brooklyn, New York

- **Independent** comprehensive, founded 1887
- **Calendar** semesters
- **Degrees** associate, bachelor's, master's, and first professional
- **Urban** 25-acre campus
- **Endowment** $27.0 million
- **Coed,** 2,922 undergraduate students, 88% full-time, 51% women, 49% men
- **Very difficult** entrance level, 43% of applicants were admitted

Pratt Institute, one of the premier art, design, writing, and architecture schools nationwide, is located in the historic Clinton Hill section of Brooklyn, just 25 minutes from downtown Manhattan. The majority of Pratt's freshmen live on the Institute's 25-acre tree-lined campus. Pratt offers 4-year bachelor's, 2-year associate, and combined bachelor's and master's degrees.

Undergraduates 2,580 full-time, 342 part-time. Students come from 41 states and territories, 38 other countries, 7% African American, 10% Asian American or Pacific Islander, 8% Hispanic American, 0.1% Native American, 15% international, 7% transferred in, 55% live on campus. *Retention:* 90% of 2001 full-time freshmen returned.
Freshmen *Admission:* 3,592 applied, 1,550 admitted, 596 enrolled. *Average high school GPA:* 3.4. *Test scores:* SAT verbal scores over 500: 84%; SAT math scores over 500: 86%; SAT verbal scores over 600: 30%; SAT math scores over 600: 38%; SAT verbal scores over 700: 5%; SAT math scores over 700: 8%.
Faculty *Total:* 756, 13% full-time. *Student/faculty ratio:* 9:1.
Majors Adult/continuing education; applied art; architecture; area, ethnic, and cultural studies related; art; art education; art history; ceramic arts; city/community/regional planning; computer graphics; construction management; creative writing; drawing; fashion design/illustration; film/video production; fine/studio arts; graphic design/commercial art/illustration; industrial design; interior design; metal/jewelry arts; photography; printmaking; sculpture.
Academic Programs *Special study options:* advanced placement credit, English as a second language, independent study, internships, off-campus study, part-time degree program, services for LD students, study abroad, summer session for credit. *ROTC:* Army (c).
Library Pratt Institute Library with 172,000 titles, 540 serial subscriptions, 2,851 audiovisual materials, an OPAC, a Web page.
Computers on Campus 250 computers available on campus for general student use. A campuswide network can be accessed from student residence rooms and from off campus. Internet access, online (class) registration, at least one staffed computer lab available.
Student Life *Housing Options:* coed. *Activities and Organizations:* drama/theater group, student-run newspaper, radio and television station, Travel and Recreation, student newspaper, athletic clubs, Performing Arts Committee, national fraternities. *Campus security:* 24-hour emergency response devices and patrols, late-night transport/escort service. *Student Services:* health clinic, personal/psychological counseling.
Athletics Member NCAA. All Division III. *Intercollegiate sports:* basketball M, cross-country running M/W, soccer M/W, tennis M/W, track and field M/W, volleyball W. *Intramural sports:* badminton M/W, basketball M, field hockey M, football M, golf M, lacrosse M/W, volleyball M, weight lifting M/W.
Standardized Tests *Required:* SAT I (for admission), SAT I or ACT (for admission). *Required for some:* SAT II: Subject Tests (for admission), SAT II: Writing Test (for admission).
Costs (2001–02) *Comprehensive fee:* $29,294 includes full-time tuition ($20,744), mandatory fees ($610), and room and board ($7940). Part-time tuition: $659 per credit. *Required fees:* $305 per term part-time. *Room and board:* College room only: $4840. Room and board charges vary according to board plan, housing facility, and student level. *Payment plans:* installment, deferred payment. *Waivers:* employees or children of employees.
Financial Aid Of all full-time matriculated undergraduates who enrolled in 2001, 2204 applied for aid, 1896 were judged to have need. 408 Federal Work-Study jobs (averaging $1240). In 2001, 308 non-need-based awards were made. *Average percent of need met:* 66%. *Average financial aid package:* $12,960. *Average need-based loan:* $4180. *Average need-based gift aid:* $6130.
Applying *Options:* common application, electronic application, early decision. *Application fee:* $40. *Required:* essay or personal statement, high school transcript, 1 letter of recommendation. *Required for some:* interview, portfolio. *Recommended:* minimum 3.0 GPA. *Application deadlines:* 2/1 (freshmen), 2/11 (transfers). *Early decision:* 11/15. *Notification:* continuous until 4/11 (freshmen), 12/15 (early decision).
Admissions Contact Ms. Erica Wilson, Visit Coordinator, Pratt Institute, DeKalb Hall, 200 Willoughby Avenue, Brooklyn, NY 11205-3899. *Phone:* 718-636-3669 Ext. 3779. *Toll-free phone:* 800-331-0834. *Fax:* 718-636-3670. *E-mail:* admissions@pratt.edu.

PURCHASE COLLEGE, STATE UNIVERSITY OF NEW YORK
Purchase, New York

- **State-supported** comprehensive, founded 1967, part of State University of New York System
- **Calendar** semesters
- **Degrees** certificates, bachelor's, master's, and postbachelor's certificates
- **Small-town** 500-acre campus with easy access to New York City
- **Endowment** $28.3 million
- **Coed,** 3,866 undergraduate students, 79% full-time, 57% women, 43% men
- **Moderately difficult** entrance level, 33% of applicants were admitted

Purchase College combines selective liberal arts and sciences programs with professional conservatory programs in the visual and performing arts. Purchase offers undergraduate degree programs in music, film, acting, dramatic writing, stage design/technology (including costume design), dance, visual arts, humanities, social sciences, and natural sciences. New programs in cinema studies, new media, creative writing, arts management, and journalism are very successful. Purchase is a small college community that offers students the opportunity to enter into apprentice relationships with artists, performers, scholars, and scientists who are making significant contributions to their fields. Purchase is committed to fostering educational creativity in a climate of artistic and intellectual freedom.

Undergraduates 3,039 full-time, 827 part-time. Students come from 46 states and territories, 30 other countries, 19% are from out of state, 9% African

Purchase College, State University of New York (continued)
American, 4% Asian American or Pacific Islander, 9% Hispanic American, 0.3% Native American, 3% international, 10% transferred in, 58% live on campus. *Retention:* 77% of 2001 full-time freshmen returned.

Freshmen *Admission:* 6,427 applied, 2,115 admitted, 679 enrolled. *Average high school GPA:* 2.90. *Test scores:* SAT verbal scores over 500: 78%; SAT math scores over 500: 68%; SAT verbal scores over 600: 33%; SAT math scores over 600: 19%; SAT verbal scores over 700: 5%; SAT math scores over 700: 2%.

Faculty *Total:* 341, 40% full-time. *Student/faculty ratio:* 14:1.

Majors Anthropology; art; art history; biology; chemistry; communications; creative writing; dance; economics; environmental science; film studies; film/video production; French; history; journalism; liberal arts and sciences/liberal studies; literature; mathematics; modern languages; music; philosophy; play/screenwriting; political science; psychology; sociology; Spanish; theater arts/drama; theater design; women's studies.

Academic Programs *Special study options:* academic remediation for entering students, adult/continuing education programs, advanced placement credit, distance learning, double majors, English as a second language, independent study, internships, off-campus study, part-time degree program, student-designed majors, study abroad, summer session for credit.

Library Purchase College Library with 178,365 titles, 1,400 serial subscriptions, 102,302 audiovisual materials, an OPAC, a Web page.

Computers on Campus 350 computers available on campus for general student use. A campuswide network can be accessed from student residence rooms and from off campus that provide access to e-mail. Internet access, at least one staffed computer lab available.

Student Life *Housing Options:* coed. *Activities and Organizations:* drama/theater group, student-run newspaper, radio and television station, choral group, Student Union, WPUR radio station, Latinos Unidos, Gay/Lesbian/Bi-Sexual/Transgender Union, Organization of African People in America. *Campus security:* 24-hour emergency response devices and patrols, late-night transport/escort service, controlled dormitory access, 24-hour patrols by police officers. *Student Services:* health clinic, personal/psychological counseling, women's center, legal services.

Athletics *Intercollegiate sports:* basketball M/W, cross-country running M/W, soccer M, volleyball W. *Intramural sports:* badminton M/W, basketball M/W, bowling M/W, cross-country running M/W, fencing M/W, football M/W, golf M/W, racquetball M/W, skiing (cross-country) M/W, skiing (downhill) M/W, soccer M/W, softball M/W, squash M/W, swimming M/W, table tennis M/W, tennis M/W, volleyball M/W, water polo M/W, weight lifting M/W.

Standardized Tests *Required:* SAT I (for admission).

Costs (2002–03) *Tuition:* state resident $3400 full-time, $137 per credit part-time; nonresident $8300 full-time, $346 per credit part-time. *Required fees:* $800 full-time, $1 per credit, $29 per term part-time. *Room and board:* $6500; room only: $4000. Room and board charges vary according to board plan and housing facility. *Payment plan:* installment. *Waivers:* senior citizens and employees or children of employees.

Financial Aid Of all full-time matriculated undergraduates who enrolled in 2001, 1886 applied for aid, 1498 were judged to have need, 211 had their need fully met. 210 Federal Work-Study jobs (averaging $1150). In 2001, 377 non-need-based awards were made. *Average percent of need met:* 70%. *Average financial aid package:* $7413. *Average need-based loan:* $3711. *Average need-based gift aid:* $3926. *Average non-need based aid:* $1628. *Average indebtedness upon graduation:* $13,510.

Applying *Options:* early admission, early decision, deferred entrance. *Application fee:* $30. *Required:* high school transcript, minimum 3.0 GPA. *Required for some:* essay or personal statement, 1 letter of recommendation, interview, audition, portfolio. *Application deadline:* 7/1 (freshmen), rolling (transfers). *Early decision:* 11/1. *Notification:* 5/1 (freshmen), 12/15 (early decision).

Admissions Contact Ms. Betsy Immergut, Director of Admissions, Purchase College, State University of New York, 735 Anderson Hill Road, Purchase, NY 10577-1400. *Phone:* 914-251-6300. *Fax:* 914-251-6314. *E-mail:* admissn@purchase.edu.

QUEENS COLLEGE OF THE CITY UNIVERSITY OF NEW YORK

Flushing, New York

- **State and locally supported** comprehensive, founded 1937, part of City University of New York System
- **Calendar** semesters
- **Degrees** bachelor's and master's
- **Urban** 76-acre campus
- **Endowment** $15,000
- **Coed,** 11,213 undergraduate students, 64% full-time, 63% women, 37% men
- **Very difficult** entrance level, 46% of applicants were admitted

College years are a time to discover and dream, a time to broaden horizons. Queens College offers sophisticated technology, distinguished professors teaching innovative programs, and a stimulating environment. Students come from around the globe and around the corner and help fellow students travel the world without leaving New York. Discover Queens College and get more than a degree—get an education for a lifetime.

Undergraduates 7,183 full-time, 4,030 part-time. Students come from 18 states and territories, 118 other countries, 1% are from out of state, 10% African American, 19% Asian American or Pacific Islander, 15% Hispanic American, 0.1% Native American, 5% international, 12% transferred in. *Retention:* 85% of 2001 full-time freshmen returned.

Freshmen *Admission:* 5,086 applied, 2,350 admitted, 1,271 enrolled. *Average high school GPA:* 3.09. *Test scores:* SAT verbal scores over 500: 53%; SAT math scores over 500: 69%; SAT verbal scores over 600: 15%; SAT math scores over 600: 24%; SAT verbal scores over 700: 2%; SAT math scores over 700: 3%.

Faculty *Total:* 1,065, 48% full-time, 52% with terminal degrees. *Student/faculty ratio:* 17:1.

Majors Accounting; African studies; American studies; anthropology; applied mathematics; area, ethnic, and cultural studies related; art; art education; art history; Asian studies; biochemistry; biology; chemistry; classics; clothing/textiles; communications; comparative literature; computer science; dance; dietetics; early childhood education; earth sciences; East Asian studies; economics; education; education (K-12); elementary education; English; environmental science; film studies; fine/studio arts; French; geology; German; Greek (modern); Hebrew; history; home economics; home economics education; interdisciplinary studies; Italian; Judaic studies; labor/personnel relations; Latin American studies; Latin (ancient and medieval); linguistics; mathematics; Middle Eastern studies; modern languages; music; music teacher education; nutrition science; philosophy; physical education; physics; political science; pre-dentistry; pre-medicine; psychology; religious studies; romance languages; Russian; secondary education; social sciences and history related; sociology; Spanish; speech-language pathology/audiology; speech therapy; teaching English as a second language; theater arts/drama; urban studies; women's studies.

Academic Programs *Special study options:* accelerated degree program, adult/continuing education programs, advanced placement credit, cooperative education, double majors, English as a second language, freshman honors college, honors programs, independent study, internships, off-campus study, part-time degree program, services for LD students, student-designed majors, study abroad, summer session for credit. *ROTC:* Army (c). *Unusual degree programs:* 3-2 engineering with Columbia University, City College of the City University of New York.

Library Benjamin S. Rosenthal Library plus 1 other with 3,439 serial subscriptions, 94,631 audiovisual materials, an OPAC, a Web page.

Computers on Campus 500 computers available on campus for general student use. A campuswide network can be accessed from off campus. Internet access, at least one staffed computer lab available.

Student Life *Housing:* college housing not available. *Activities and Organizations:* drama/theater group, student-run newspaper, choral group, Alliance of Latin American Students, Black Student Union, Caribbean Student Association, Hillel-Jewish Student Organization, India Cultural Exchange, national fraternities, national sororities. *Campus security:* 24-hour emergency response devices and patrols. *Student Services:* health clinic, personal/psychological counseling, women's center, legal services.

Athletics Member NCAA. All Division II. *Intercollegiate sports:* baseball M(s), basketball M(s)/W(s), bowling W, cross-country running M/W, fencing W(s), golf M(s), soccer W(s), softball M(s), swimming M(s)/W(s), tennis M(s)/W(s), track and field M(s)/W(s), volleyball M(s)/W(s), water polo M(s)/W(s). *Intramural sports:* basketball M/W, cross-country running M/W, fencing M, ice hockey M, racquetball M/W, soccer M/W, softball M/W, tennis M/W, volleyball M/W, water polo M/W.

Standardized Tests *Required:* SAT I (for admission). *Required for some:* SAT II: Subject Tests (for admission). *Recommended:* SAT II: Subject Tests (for admission).

Costs (2001–02) *Tuition:* state resident $3200 full-time, $135 per credit part-time; nonresident $6800 full-time, $285 per credit part-time. Full-time tuition and fees vary according to program. Part-time tuition and fees vary according to program. *Required fees:* $203 full-time, $71 per term part-time. *Payment plan:* installment. *Waivers:* senior citizens.

Financial Aid Of all full-time matriculated undergraduates who enrolled in 2001, 4993 applied for aid, 3744 were judged to have need, 2700 had their need fully met. 1253 Federal Work-Study jobs (averaging $1300). In 2001, 292 non-need-based awards were made. *Average percent of need met:* 90%. *Average* *financial aid package:* $5000. *Average need-based gift aid:* $3400. *Average indebtedness upon graduation:* $12,000.

Applying *Options:* electronic application, early admission, deferred entrance. *Application fee:* $40. *Required:* high school transcript, minimum 3.0 GPA. *Required for some:* essay or personal statement, 2 letters of recommendation, interview. *Application deadline:* rolling (freshmen), rolling (transfers). *Notification:* continuous (freshmen).

Admissions Contact Undergraduate Admissions Office, Queens College of the City University of New York, Undergraduate Admissions, Kiely Hall 217, 65-30 Kissena Boulevard, Flushing, NY 11367. *Phone:* 718-997-5600. *Fax:* 718-997-5617. *E-mail:* admissions@qc.edu.

RABBINICAL ACADEMY MESIVTA RABBI CHAIM BERLIN
Brooklyn, New York

Admissions Contact Mr. Mayer Weinberger, Executive Administrator, Office of Admissions, Rabbinical Academy Mesivta Rabbi Chaim Berlin, 1605 Coney Island Avenue, Brooklyn, NY 11230-4715. *Phone:* 718-377-0777.

RABBINICAL COLLEGE BETH SHRAGA
Monsey, New York

Admissions Contact Rabbi Schiff, Director of Admissions, Rabbinical College Beth Shraga, 28 Saddle River Road, Monsey, NY 10952-3035.

RABBINICAL COLLEGE BOBOVER YESHIVA B'NEI ZION
Brooklyn, New York

Admissions Contact Mr. Israel Licht, Director of Admissions, Rabbinical College Bobover Yeshiva B'nei Zion, 1577 Forty-eighth Street, Brooklyn, NY 11219. *Phone:* 718-438-2018.

RABBINICAL COLLEGE CH'SAN SOFER
Brooklyn, New York

Admissions Contact Director of Admissions, Rabbinical College Ch'san Sofer, 1876 Fiftieth Street, Brooklyn, NY 11204. *Phone:* 718-236-1171.

RABBINICAL COLLEGE OF LONG ISLAND
Long Beach, New York

Admissions Contact Director of Admissions, Rabbinical College of Long Island, 201 Magnolia Boulevard, Long Beach, NY 11561-3305. *Phone:* 516-431-7414.

RABBINICAL SEMINARY ADAS YEREIM
Brooklyn, New York

Admissions Contact Mr. Hersch Greenschweig, Director of Admissions, Rabbinical Seminary Adas Yereim, 185 Wilson Street, Brooklyn, NY 11211-7206. *Phone:* 718-388-1751.

RABBINICAL SEMINARY M'KOR CHAIM
Brooklyn, New York

Admissions Contact Rabbi Benjamin Paler, Director of Admissions, Rabbinical Seminary M'kor Chaim, 1571 Fifty-fifth Street, Brooklyn, NY 11219. *Phone:* 718-851-0183.

RABBINICAL SEMINARY OF AMERICA
Forest Hills, New York

Admissions Contact Rabbi Abraham Semmel, Director of Admissions, Rabbinical Seminary of America, 92-15 Sixty-ninth Avenue, Forest Hills, NY 11375. *Phone:* 718-268-4700.

RENSSELAER POLYTECHNIC INSTITUTE
Troy, New York

- **Independent** university, founded 1824
- **Calendar** semesters
- **Degrees** bachelor's, master's, and doctoral
- **Suburban** 260-acre campus with easy access to Albany
- **Endowment** $626.4 million
- **Coed,** 5,272 undergraduate students, 98% full-time, 24% women, 76% men
- **Very difficult** entrance level, 68% of applicants were admitted

Hands-on programs emphasize the practical and responsible application of technology and prepare students for meaningful careers in a global society. Tomorrow's leaders are educated in the fields of architecture, engineering, humanities and social sciences, information technology, management, and science. The 5,100 undergraduate students come from all 50 states and 83 countries.

Undergraduates 5,186 full-time, 86 part-time. Students come from 53 states and territories, 81 other countries, 49% are from out of state, 4% African American, 12% Asian American or Pacific Islander, 5% Hispanic American, 0.4% Native American, 5% international, 3% transferred in, 55% live on campus. *Retention:* 91% of 2001 full-time freshmen returned.

Freshmen *Admission:* 5,542 applied, 3,748 admitted, 1,112 enrolled. *Test scores:* SAT verbal scores over 500: 96%; SAT math scores over 500: 100%; ACT scores over 18: 98%; SAT verbal scores over 600: 67%; SAT math scores over 600: 93%; ACT scores over 24: 76%; SAT verbal scores over 700: 17%; SAT math scores over 700: 43%; ACT scores over 30: 11%.

Faculty *Total:* 465, 77% full-time, 90% with terminal degrees. *Student/faculty ratio:* 16:1.

Majors Aerospace engineering; Air Force R.O.T.C./air science; applied mathematics; architecture; Army R.O.T.C./military science; biochemistry; bioengineering; biological/physical sciences; biology; biophysics; business administration; chemical engineering; chemistry; civil engineering; computer engineering; computer/information sciences; computer science; economics; electrical engineering; engineering; engineering/industrial management; engineering physics; engineering science; environmental engineering; environmental science; geology; German; industrial/manufacturing engineering; information sciences/systems; interdisciplinary studies; management information systems/business data processing; mass communications; materials engineering; mathematics; mechanical engineering; natural sciences; Navy/Marine Corps R.O.T.C./naval science; nuclear engineering; philosophy; physical sciences; physics; pre-dentistry; pre-law; premedicine; psychology; science education; science/technology and society; speech/rhetorical studies; systems engineering; technical/business writing; transportation engineering; water resources.

Academic Programs *Special study options:* accelerated degree program, adult/continuing education programs, advanced placement credit, cooperative education, distance learning, double majors, English as a second language, honors programs, independent study, internships, off-campus study, part-time degree program, services for LD students, student-designed majors, study abroad, summer session for credit. *ROTC:* Army (b), Navy (b), Air Force (b).

Library Folsom Library plus 1 other with 309,171 titles, 10,210 serial subscriptions, 91,435 audiovisual materials, an OPAC, a Web page.

Computers on Campus 500 computers available on campus for general student use. A campuswide network can be accessed from student residence rooms and from off campus. Internet access, online (class) registration, at least one staffed computer lab available.

Student Life *Housing:* on-campus residence required for freshman year. *Options:* coed, men-only, disabled students. *Activities and Organizations:* drama/theater group, student-run newspaper, radio station, choral group, Ski Club, musical organizations, weightlifting, ballroom dance, campus radio station, national fraternities, national sororities. *Campus security:* 24-hour emergency response devices and patrols, late-night transport/escort service, controlled dormitory access, campus foot patrols at night. *Student Services:* health clinic, personal/psychological counseling, legal services.

Athletics Member NCAA. All Division III except ice hockey (Division I). *Intercollegiate sports:* archery M(c)/W(c), badminton M(c)/W(c), baseball M, basketball M/W, crew M(c)/W(c), cross-country running M/W, equestrian sports M(c)/W(c), fencing M(c)/W(c), field hockey W, football M, golf M, gymnastics M(c)/W(c), ice hockey M/W, lacrosse M/W, racquetball M(c)/W(c), riflery M(c)/W(c), rugby M(c)/W(c), sailing M(c)/W(c), skiing (cross-country) M(c)/W(c), skiing (downhill) M(c)/W(c), soccer M/W, softball W, squash M(c)/W(c), swimming M/W, table tennis M(c)/W(c), tennis M/W, track and field M/W, volleyball M(c)/W, water polo M(c)/W(c), weight lifting M(c)/W(c). *Intramural sports:* badminton M/W, basketball M/W, bowling M/W, football M/W, golf M/W,

Rensselaer Polytechnic Institute (continued)
ice hockey M/W, soccer M/W, softball M/W, swimming M/W, table tennis M/W, tennis M/W, track and field M/W, volleyball M/W, water polo M/W, wrestling M.

Standardized Tests *Required:* SAT I or ACT (for admission). *Required for some:* SAT II: Subject Tests (for admission).

Costs (2001–02) *Comprehensive fee:* $33,863 includes full-time tuition ($24,820), mandatory fees ($735), and room and board ($8308). Part-time tuition: $735 per credit hour. *Room and board:* College room only: $4496. Room and board charges vary according to board plan and housing facility. *Payment plan:* installment. *Waivers:* employees or children of employees.

Financial Aid Of all full-time matriculated undergraduates who enrolled in 2001, 4296 applied for aid, 3607 were judged to have need, 2230 had their need fully met. In 2001, 732 non-need-based awards were made. *Average percent of need met:* 90%. *Average financial aid package:* $22,727. *Average need-based loan:* $5809. *Average need-based gift aid:* $15,216. *Average non-need based aid:* $10,396. *Average indebtedness upon graduation:* $25,100.

Applying *Options:* common application, electronic application, early admission, early decision, deferred entrance. *Application fee:* $50. *Required:* essay or personal statement, high school transcript, 1 letter of recommendation. *Required for some:* portfolio for architecture and electronic arts programs. *Application deadlines:* 1/1 (freshmen), 7/1 (transfers). *Early decision:* 11/15. *Notification:* 3/15 (freshmen), 12/19 (early decision).

Admissions Contact Ms. Teresa Duffy, Dean of Enrollment Management, Rensselaer Polytechnic Institute, 110 8th Street, Troy, NY 12180-3590. *Phone:* 518-276-6216. *Toll-free phone:* 800-448-6562. *Fax:* 518-276-4072. *E-mail:* admissions@rpi.edu.

ROBERTS WESLEYAN COLLEGE
Rochester, New York

- **Independent** comprehensive, founded 1866, affiliated with Free Methodist Church of North America
- **Calendar** semesters
- **Degrees** associate, bachelor's, and master's
- **Suburban** 75-acre campus
- **Endowment** $11.9 million
- **Coed,** 1,235 undergraduate students, 91% full-time, 66% women, 34% men
- **Moderately difficult** entrance level, 84% of applicants were admitted

William Crothers concludes 21 years as Roberts Wesleyan president in May 2002. According to President-elect John Martin, the College is in a very solid position. Enrollment is higher than ever at 1,800 students; a $31 million capital campaign got a $5 million boost from Paychex CEO Tom Golisano; and the College is debt free.

Undergraduates 1,122 full-time, 113 part-time. Students come from 29 states and territories, 13 other countries, 14% are from out of state, 5% African American, 0.6% Asian American or Pacific Islander, 3% Hispanic American, 0.5% Native American, 4% international, 21% transferred in, 69% live on campus. *Retention:* 81% of 2001 full-time freshmen returned.

Freshmen *Admission:* 651 applied, 549 admitted, 252 enrolled. *Test scores:* SAT verbal scores over 500: 75%; SAT math scores over 500: 70%; ACT scores over 18: 95%; SAT verbal scores over 600: 25%; SAT math scores over 600: 20%; ACT scores over 24: 38%; SAT verbal scores over 700: 4%; SAT math scores over 700: 1%; ACT scores over 30: 5%.

Faculty *Total:* 151, 53% full-time. *Student/faculty ratio:* 14:1.

Majors Accounting; art; art education; biochemistry; biological/physical sciences; biology; business administration; business marketing and marketing management; chemistry; communications; computer science; criminal justice/law enforcement administration; divinity/ministry; education; elementary education; English; fine/studio arts; graphic design/commercial art/illustration; history; humanities; human resources management; information sciences/systems; management information systems/business data processing; mathematics; medical technology; music; music (piano and organ performance); music teacher education; music (voice and choral/opera performance); natural sciences; nursing; pastoral counseling; philosophy; physical sciences; physics; pre-dentistry; pre-engineering; pre-law; pre-medicine; pre-pharmacy studies; pre-veterinary studies; psychology; religious studies; secondary education; social sciences; social work; sociology.

Academic Programs *Special study options:* academic remediation for entering students, adult/continuing education programs, advanced placement credit, cooperative education, double majors, English as a second language, freshman honors college, honors programs, independent study, internships, off-campus study, services for LD students, study abroad, summer session for credit. *ROTC:* Army (c), Air Force (c). *Unusual degree programs:* 3-2 engineering with Clarkson University, Rensselaer Polytechnic Institute, Rochester Institute of Technology.

Library Ora A. Sprague Library with 111,548 titles, 906 serial subscriptions, 3,559 audiovisual materials, an OPAC, a Web page.

Computers on Campus 160 computers available on campus for general student use. A campuswide network can be accessed from student residence rooms and from off campus. At least one staffed computer lab available.

Student Life *Housing:* on-campus residence required through senior year. *Options:* men-only, women-only. *Activities and Organizations:* drama/theater group, student-run newspaper, radio station, choral group, Habitat for Humanity, Foot of the Cross, Radiant Light, nursing club, drama club. *Campus security:* 24-hour emergency response devices and patrols, late-night transport/escort service, controlled dormitory access, 24-hour Resident Life staff on-call. *Student Services:* health clinic, personal/psychological counseling.

Athletics Member NCAA, NAIA, NCCAA. All NCAA Division II. *Intercollegiate sports:* basketball M(s)/W(s), bowling W, cross-country running M(s)/W(s), golf M(s)/W(s), soccer M(s)/W(s), tennis M(s)/W(s), track and field M(s)/W(s), volleyball W(s). *Intramural sports:* basketball M/W, racquetball M/W, soccer M/W, softball M/W, table tennis M/W, tennis M/W, volleyball M/W.

Standardized Tests *Required:* SAT I or ACT (for admission).

Costs (2001–02) *One-time required fee:* $225. *Comprehensive fee:* $20,160 includes full-time tuition ($14,366), mandatory fees ($550), and room and board ($5244). Part-time tuition: $300 per credit. Part-time tuition and fees vary according to course load. *Room and board:* College room only: $3746. Room and board charges vary according to board plan. *Payment plan:* installment. *Waivers:* employees or children of employees.

Financial Aid Of all full-time matriculated undergraduates who enrolled in 2001, 791 applied for aid, 744 were judged to have need, 159 had their need fully met. 46 State and other part-time jobs (averaging $1592). In 2001, 114 non-need-based awards were made. *Average percent of need met:* 82%. *Average financial aid package:* $12,866. *Average need-based loan:* $4584. *Average need-based gift aid:* $7855. *Average indebtedness upon graduation:* $6585.

Applying *Options:* electronic application, early admission, deferred entrance. *Application fee:* $35. *Required:* essay or personal statement, high school transcript, 2 letters of recommendation. *Recommended:* minimum 2.5 GPA, interview. *Application deadline:* 2/1 (freshmen), rolling (transfers).

Admissions Contact Ms. Linda Kurtz, Dean of Admissions, Roberts Wesleyan College, 2301 Westside Drive, Rochester, NY 14624. *Phone:* 585-594-6400. *Toll-free phone:* 800-777-4RWC. *Fax:* 585-594-6371. *E-mail:* admissions@roberts.edu.

ROCHESTER INSTITUTE OF TECHNOLOGY
Rochester, New York

- **Independent** comprehensive, founded 1829
- **Calendar** quarters
- **Degrees** certificates, diplomas, associate, bachelor's, master's, doctoral, post-master's, and postbachelor's certificates
- **Suburban** 1300-acre campus with easy access to Buffalo
- **Endowment** $490.4 million
- **Coed,** 12,029 undergraduate students, 83% full-time, 32% women, 68% men
- **Moderately difficult** entrance level, 70% of applicants were admitted

Undergraduates 9,967 full-time, 2,062 part-time. Students come from 50 states and territories, 85 other countries, 43% are from out of state, 5% African American, 6% Asian American or Pacific Islander, 3% Hispanic American, 0.4% Native American, 5% international, 8% transferred in, 60% live on campus. *Retention:* 87% of 2001 full-time freshmen returned.

Freshmen *Admission:* 8,493 applied, 5,950 admitted, 2,245 enrolled. *Average high school GPA:* 3.70. *Test scores:* SAT verbal scores over 500: 88%; SAT math scores over 500: 96%; ACT scores over 18: 100%; SAT verbal scores over 600: 45%; SAT math scores over 600: 63%; ACT scores over 24: 74%; SAT verbal scores over 700: 8%; SAT math scores over 700: 15%; ACT scores over 30: 17%.

Faculty *Total:* 1,139, 58% full-time, 67% with terminal degrees. *Student/faculty ratio:* 14:1.

Majors Accounting; advertising; aerospace engineering; applied art; applied mathematics; art; automotive engineering technology; biochemistry; biological/physical sciences; biological sciences/life sciences related; biology; biotechnology research; business administration; business marketing and marketing management; ceramic arts; chemistry; civil engineering technology; commercial photography; communications; computer engineering; computer engineering technology; computer graphics; computer/information sciences; computer/information sciences related; computer programming; computer science; craft/folk art; criminal justice/law enforcement administration; criminal justice studies; design/visual communications; diagnostic medical sonography; dietetics; economics; electrical/electronic engineering technology; electrical engineering; electromechanical technology; engineering; engineering related; engineering-related technology; engineering science; engineering technology; environmental science; film/video production; finance; fine/studio arts; food products retailing; food sales operations; furniture design; general studies; genetics; graphic design/commercial art/illustration; graphic/printing equipment; hospitality management; hospitality/recreation marketing; hotel and restaurant management; industrial design; industrial/manufacturing engineering; industrial technology; information sciences/systems; interdisciplinary studies; interior design; international business; international finance; management information systems/business data processing; marketing operations; marketing research; mathematical statistics; mathematics; mathematics/computer science; mechanical engineering; mechanical engineering technology; medical illustrating; medical technology; metal/jewelry arts; natural resources management; nuclear medical technology; occupational safety/health technology; optometric/ophthalmic laboratory technician; photographic technology; photography; physician assistant; physics; political science/government related; polymer chemistry; pre-dentistry; pre-law; pre-medicine; pre-veterinary studies; psychology; public policy analysis; publishing; sculpture; sign language interpretation; social work; telecommunications; tourism/travel marketing; travel/tourism management.

Academic Programs *Special study options:* accelerated degree program, adult/continuing education programs, advanced placement credit, cooperative education, distance learning, English as a second language, honors programs, independent study, internships, off-campus study, part-time degree program, services for LD students, student-designed majors, study abroad, summer session for credit. *ROTC:* Army (b), Navy (c), Air Force (b).

Library Wallace Memorial Library with 350,000 titles, 4,305 serial subscriptions, 8,215 audiovisual materials, an OPAC, a Web page.

Computers on Campus 2500 computers available on campus for general student use. A campuswide network can be accessed from student residence rooms and from off campus that provide access to student account information. Internet access, online (class) registration, at least one staffed computer lab available.

Student Life *Housing:* on-campus residence required for freshman year. *Options:* coed, men-only, women-only, disabled students. *Activities and Organizations:* drama/theater group, student-run newspaper, radio station, choral group, campus radio station, Campus Weekly Magazine, student government, Off-Campus Student Association, national fraternities, national sororities. *Campus security:* 24-hour emergency response devices and patrols, student patrols, late-night transport/escort service. *Student Services:* health clinic, personal/psychological counseling, women's center, legal services.

Athletics Member NCAA. All Division III. *Intercollegiate sports:* baseball M, basketball M/W, bowling M(c)/W(c), crew M/W, cross-country running M/W, equestrian sports M(c)/W(c), field hockey W(c), ice hockey M/W, lacrosse M/W, rugby M(c)/W(c), skiing (downhill) M(c)/W(c), soccer M/W, softball W, swimming M/W, tennis M/W, track and field M/W, volleyball M(c)/W, water polo M(c), wrestling M. *Intramural sports:* badminton M/W, basketball M/W, bowling M/W, football M, golf M/W, ice hockey M/W, lacrosse M(c), racquetball M/W, soccer M/W, softball M/W, table tennis M/W, tennis M/W, volleyball M/W.

Standardized Tests *Required:* SAT I or ACT (for admission).

Costs (2001–02) *Comprehensive fee:* $26,232 includes full-time tuition ($18,633), mandatory fees ($333), and room and board ($7266). Full-time tuition and fees vary according to course load and program. Part-time tuition: $446 per credit hour. Part-time tuition and fees vary according to class time, class time, course load, and program. *Required fees:* $27 per term part-time. *Room and board:* College room only: $4095. Room and board charges vary according to board plan and housing facility. *Payment plans:* tuition prepayment, installment, deferred payment. *Waivers:* employees or children of employees.

Financial Aid Of all full-time matriculated undergraduates who enrolled in 2001, 7250 applied for aid, 6380 were judged to have need, 6030 had their need fully met. 2100 Federal Work-Study jobs (averaging $1066). 2600 State and other part-time jobs (averaging $2223). In 2001, 850 non-need-based awards were made. *Average percent of need met:* 90%. *Average financial aid package:* $14,800. *Average need-based loan:* $4000. *Average need-based gift aid:* $9000. *Average non-need based aid:* $5100.

Applying *Options:* common application, electronic application, early admission, early decision, deferred entrance. *Application fee:* $50. *Required:* essay or personal statement, high school transcript. *Required for some:* portfolio for art program. *Recommended:* minimum 3.0 GPA, 1 letter of recommendation, interview. *Application deadline:* 3/15 (freshmen), rolling (transfers). *Early decision:* 12/15. *Notification:* continuous (freshmen), 1/15 (early decision).

Admissions Contact Mr. Daniel Shelley, Director of Admissions, Rochester Institute of Technology, 60 Lomb Memorial Drive, Rochester, NY 14623-5604. *Phone:* 585-475-6631. *Fax:* 585-475-7424. *E-mail:* admissons@rit.edu.

RUSSELL SAGE COLLEGE

Troy, New York

- **Independent** 4-year, founded 1916, part of The Sage Colleges
- **Calendar** semesters
- **Degree** bachelor's
- **Urban** 8-acre campus
- **Endowment** $30.1 million
- **Women only,** 797 undergraduate students, 93% full-time
- **Moderately difficult** entrance level, 90% of applicants were admitted

Russell Sage College, located in the Capital Region of New York State, is a small college for women where individuals count and are consistently challenged. The College offers liberal arts and professional degree programs in fields such as the health sciences, humanities, natural sciences and mathematics, and social and professional sciences. To schedule a campus visit, students should call 518-244-2217 or 888-VERY-SAGE (toll-free). E-mail: rscadmi@sage.edu; Web site: http://www.sage.edu/rsc.

Undergraduates 742 full-time, 55 part-time. Students come from 16 states and territories, 11% are from out of state, 6% African American, 3% Asian American or Pacific Islander, 3% Hispanic American, 0.5% Native American, 15% transferred in, 49% live on campus. *Retention:* 88% of 2001 full-time freshmen returned.

Freshmen *Admission:* 133 enrolled. *Average high school GPA:* 3.40. *Test scores:* SAT verbal scores over 500: 69%; SAT math scores over 500: 61%; ACT scores over 18: 87%; SAT verbal scores over 600: 16%; SAT math scores over 600: 18%; ACT scores over 24: 47%; SAT verbal scores over 700: 1%; ACT scores over 30: 7%.

Faculty *Total:* 103, 63% full-time, 66% with terminal degrees. *Student/faculty ratio:* 11:1.

Majors Art therapy; athletic training/sports medicine; biochemistry; biology; biopsychology; business administration; chemistry; computer science; criminal justice/law enforcement administration; economics; elementary education; engineering; English; history; information sciences/systems; interdisciplinary studies; international relations; mass communications; mathematics; nursing; nutritional sciences; occupational therapy; physical therapy; political science; psychology; sociology; Spanish; special education; theater arts/drama.

Academic Programs *Special study options:* academic remediation for entering students, accelerated degree program, adult/continuing education programs, advanced placement credit, cooperative education, double majors, English as a second language, freshman honors college, honors programs, independent study, internships, off-campus study, part-time degree program, services for LD students, student-designed majors, study abroad, summer session for credit. *ROTC:* Army (c), Air Force (c). *Unusual degree programs:* 3-2 business administration with Sage Graduate School; engineering with Rensselaer Polytechnic Institute; nursing with Sage Graduate School; occupational therapy, physical therapy, public administration with Sage Graduate School.

Library James Wheelock Clark Library plus 1 other with 350,466 titles, 8,022 serial subscriptions, 34,672 audiovisual materials, an OPAC.

Computers on Campus 117 computers available on campus for general student use. A campuswide network can be accessed from student residence rooms and from off campus. Internet access, at least one staffed computer lab available.

Student Life *Housing:* on-campus residence required through senior year. *Options:* women-only. *Activities and Organizations:* drama/theater group, student-run newspaper, choral group, student government, Sage Recreation Association, physical therapy club, crew club, Black-Latin Student Alliance. *Campus security:* 24-hour emergency response devices and patrols, late-night transport/escort service, controlled dormitory access. *Student Services:* health clinic, personal/psychological counseling, women's center.

Athletics Member NCAA. All Division III. *Intercollegiate sports:* basketball W, soccer W, softball W, tennis W, volleyball W. *Intramural sports:* basketball W, crew W(c), equestrian sports W(c), field hockey W(c), ice hockey W(c), lacrosse W(c), skiing (cross-country) W(c), skiing (downhill) W(c), soccer W, tennis W, volleyball W, water polo W, weight lifting W(c).

Standardized Tests *Required:* SAT I or ACT (for admission).

Costs (2002–03) *Comprehensive fee:* $25,346 includes full-time tuition ($18,200), mandatory fees ($620), and room and board ($6526). Part-time tuition: $610 per credit hour. *Room and board:* College room only: $3150.

Financial Aid Of all full-time matriculated undergraduates who enrolled in 2001, 734 applied for aid, 670 were judged to have need. 328 Federal Work-Study jobs. In 2001, 59 non-need-based awards were made. *Average non-need based aid:* $12,531. *Average indebtedness upon graduation:* $19,200.

Applying *Options:* common application, electronic application, early admission, early decision, deferred entrance. *Application fee:* $30. *Required:* essay or personal statement, high school transcript, minimum 2.0 GPA, 2 letters of

Russell Sage College (continued)
recommendation. *Recommended:* interview. *Application deadline:* 8/1 (freshmen), rolling (transfers). *Early decision:* 12/1. *Notification:* continuous (freshmen), 12/15 (early decision).

Admissions Contact Ms. Beth Robertson, Senior Associate Director of Admissions, Russell Sage College, 45 Ferry Street, Troy, NY 12180. *Phone:* 518-244-2217. *Toll-free phone:* 888-VERY-SAGE (in-state); 888-VERY SAGE (out-of-state). *Fax:* 518-244-6880. *E-mail:* rscadm@sage.edu.

SAGE COLLEGE OF ALBANY
Albany, New York

- **Independent** 4-year, founded 1957, part of The Sage Colleges
- **Calendar** semesters
- **Degrees** certificates, associate, and bachelor's
- **Urban** 15-acre campus
- **Endowment** $30.1 million
- **Coed,** 1,271 undergraduate students, 51% full-time, 71% women, 29% men
- **Minimally difficult** entrance level, 70% of applicants were admitted

Sage College of Albany, a member of The Sage Colleges, has innovative higher education options, offering associate and bachelor's degrees in applied studies in a 2+2 model and bachelor degree completion programs for adults who want flexible schedules and formats. Design your own future at Sage College of Albany!

Undergraduates 653 full-time, 618 part-time. Students come from 10 states and territories, 2% are from out of state, 12% African American, 1% Asian American or Pacific Islander, 3% Hispanic American, 0.4% Native American, 7% transferred in, 33% live on campus. *Retention:* 65% of 2001 full-time freshmen returned.

Freshmen *Admission:* 600 applied, 417 admitted, 279 enrolled. *Test scores:* SAT verbal scores over 500: 29%; SAT math scores over 500: 24%; ACT scores over 18: 47%; SAT verbal scores over 600: 6%; SAT math scores over 600: 2%; ACT scores over 24: 6%; SAT math scores over 700: 1%.

Faculty *Total:* 65, 55% full-time, 37% with terminal degrees. *Student/faculty ratio:* 11:1.

Majors Accounting; business administration; business marketing and marketing management; communications; computer/information sciences; computer systems networking/telecommunications; criminal justice/law enforcement administration; elementary education; fine/studio arts; graphic design/commercial art/illustration; humanities; interior design; legal studies; liberal arts and sciences/liberal studies; paralegal/legal assistant; photography; psychology; social sciences.

Academic Programs *Special study options:* academic remediation for entering students, adult/continuing education programs, advanced placement credit, cooperative education, English as a second language, external degree program, freshman honors college, honors programs, independent study, internships, off-campus study, part-time degree program, services for LD students, student-designed majors, summer session for credit.

Library Troy and Albany Campus Libraries with 204,667 titles, 8,022 serial subscriptions, 34,672 audiovisual materials, an OPAC.

Computers on Campus 127 computers available on campus for general student use. A campuswide network can be accessed from student residence rooms and from off campus. At least one staffed computer lab available.

Student Life *Housing Options:* coed, women-only. *Activities and Organizations:* student-run newspaper, student government, Phi Theta Kappa, Psychology Club, Ski Club, "Vernacular" (art and literary publication). *Campus security:* 24-hour emergency response devices and patrols, late-night transport/escort service, controlled dormitory access, 24-hour security cameras. *Student Services:* health clinic, personal/psychological counseling.

Athletics Member NJCAA. *Intercollegiate sports:* basketball M(s)/W(s), volleyball W(s). *Intramural sports:* basketball M/W, skiing (downhill) M(c)/W(c), volleyball W.

Standardized Tests *Required:* SAT I or ACT (for admission).

Costs (2002–03) *Comprehensive fee:* $20,946 includes full-time tuition ($13,750), mandatory fees ($570), and room and board ($6626). Part-time tuition: $460 per credit hour. *Room and board:* College room only: $3250. *Payment plans:* installment, deferred payment. *Waivers:* employees or children of employees.

Financial Aid Of all full-time matriculated undergraduates who enrolled in 2001, 624 applied for aid, 553 were judged to have need. In 2001, 71 non-need-based awards were made. *Average non-need based aid:* $3321. *Average indebtedness upon graduation:* $17,125.

Applying *Options:* common application, electronic application, deferred entrance. *Application fee:* $30. *Required:* high school transcript, 1 letter of recommendation, portfolio for fine arts program. *Recommended:* essay or personal statement, interview. *Application deadlines:* 8/1 (freshmen), 8/1 (transfers). *Notification:* continuous until 8/15 (freshmen).

Admissions Contact Sage College of Albany, 140 New Scotland Avenue, Albany, NY 12208. *Phone:* 518-292-1730. *Toll-free phone:* 888-VERY-SAGE. *Fax:* 518-292-1912. *E-mail:* scaadm@sage.edu.

ST. BONAVENTURE UNIVERSITY
St. Bonaventure, New York

- **Independent** comprehensive, founded 1858, affiliated with Roman Catholic Church
- **Calendar** semesters
- **Degrees** bachelor's, master's, post-master's, and postbachelor's certificates
- **Small-town** 600-acre campus
- **Endowment** $36.4 million
- **Coed,** 2,164 undergraduate students, 96% full-time, 53% women, 47% men
- **Moderately difficult** entrance level, 94% of applicants were admitted

Offering more than 30 majors and Division I athletics, St. Bonaventure University attracts exceptional undergraduates from 34 states and 13 countries. Adding to the Bonaventure experience are a broadcast journalism laboratory, an expanded fiber-optic computer network, an endowed visiting professorship, a modern language laboratory, a regional arts center, and a dynamic intramural program. *U.S. News & World Report* repeatedly ranks St. Bonaventure in its "top tier" of regional universities.

Undergraduates 2,076 full-time, 88 part-time. Students come from 34 states and territories, 8 other countries, 22% are from out of state, 1% African American, 0.3% Asian American or Pacific Islander, 1.0% Hispanic American, 0.1% Native American, 1% international, 3% transferred in, 77% live on campus. *Retention:* 85% of 2001 full-time freshmen returned.

Freshmen *Admission:* 1,579 applied, 1,487 admitted, 520 enrolled. *Average high school GPA:* 3.00. *Test scores:* SAT verbal scores over 500: 62%; SAT math scores over 500: 68%; ACT scores over 18: 89%; SAT verbal scores over 600: 18%; SAT math scores over 600: 18%; ACT scores over 24: 28%; SAT verbal scores over 700: 1%; SAT math scores over 700: 2%; ACT scores over 30: 2%.

Faculty *Total:* 207, 73% full-time. *Student/faculty ratio:* 15:1.

Majors Accounting; art education; biochemistry; biology; biophysics; business administration; business economics; business education; business marketing and marketing management; chemistry; classics; computer science; ecology; elementary education; engineering physics; English; environmental science; finance; French; history; interdisciplinary studies; international business; journalism; Latin (ancient and medieval); mass communications; mathematics; medical technology; modern languages; philosophy; physical education; physics; political science; pre-dentistry; pre-law; pre-medicine; pre-veterinary studies; psychology; religious education; secondary education; social sciences; sociology; Spanish; visual/performing arts.

Academic Programs *Special study options:* advanced placement credit, double majors, freshman honors college, honors programs, independent study, internships, off-campus study, part-time degree program, services for LD students, student-designed majors, study abroad, summer session for credit. *ROTC:* Army (b). *Unusual degree programs:* 3-2 English, physics, psychology.

Library Friedsam Library with 372,090 titles, 1,621 serial subscriptions, 6,186 audiovisual materials, an OPAC, a Web page.

Computers on Campus 200 computers available on campus for general student use. A campuswide network can be accessed from student residence rooms and from off campus. Internet access, online (class) registration, at least one staffed computer lab available.

Student Life *Housing:* on-campus residence required through junior year. *Options:* coed, men-only, women-only, disabled students. *Activities and Organizations:* drama/theater group, student-run newspaper, radio and television station, choral group, student government, Student Programming Board, campus media, Bonaventure Business Association, Student Ambassadors. *Campus security:* 24-hour emergency response devices and patrols, student patrols, late-night transport/escort service. *Student Services:* health clinic, personal/psychological counseling.

Athletics Member NCAA. All Division I. *Intercollegiate sports:* baseball M(s), basketball M(s)/W(s), cross-country running M(s)/W(s), golf M(s), lacrosse M(c)/W, rugby M(c)/W(c), soccer M(s)/W(s), softball W(s), swimming M(s)/W(s), tennis M(s)/W(s), volleyball M(c)/W(s). *Intramural sports:* basketball M/W, bowling M/W, football M/W, racquetball M/W, skiing (cross-country) M/W, skiing (downhill) M/W, soccer M/W, softball M/W, squash M/W, swimming M/W, table tennis M/W, tennis M/W, volleyball M/W, water polo M/W, weight lifting M/W.

Standardized Tests *Required:* SAT I or ACT (for admission).
Costs (2001–02) *Comprehensive fee:* $22,106 includes full-time tuition ($15,526), mandatory fees ($630), and room and board ($5950). *Room and board:* College room only: $3020. Room and board charges vary according to board plan and housing facility. *Payment plans:* installment, deferred payment. *Waivers:* senior citizens and employees or children of employees.
Financial Aid Of all full-time matriculated undergraduates who enrolled in 2001, 1688 applied for aid, 1469 were judged to have need, 1149 had their need fully met. In 2001, 437 non-need-based awards were made. *Average percent of need met:* 94%. *Average financial aid package:* $15,629. *Average need-based loan:* $4068. *Average non-need based aid:* $5625. *Average indebtedness upon graduation:* $16,843.
Applying *Options:* common application, early admission, deferred entrance. *Application fee:* $30. *Required:* high school transcript, 1 letter of recommendation. *Required for some:* essay or personal statement. *Recommended:* essay or personal statement, minimum 3.0 GPA, 3 letters of recommendation, interview. *Application deadlines:* 4/15 (freshmen), 8/15 (transfers). *Notification:* continuous (freshmen).
Admissions Contact Mr. James Dirisio, Director of Admissions, St. Bonaventure University, PO Box D. *Phone:* 716-375-2400. *Toll-free phone:* 800-462-5050. *Fax:* 716-375-4005. *E-mail:* admissions@sbu.edu.

St. Francis College
Brooklyn Heights, New York

- **Independent Roman Catholic** 4-year, founded 1884
- **Calendar** semesters
- **Degrees** associate and bachelor's
- **Urban** 1-acre campus with easy access to New York City
- **Endowment** $39.1 million
- **Coed,** 2,451 undergraduate students, 82% full-time, 58% women, 42% men
- **Moderately difficult** entrance level, 81% of applicants were admitted

St. Francis College offers an exceptional value in private college education in the New York area, offering low tuition and an emphasis on the values of the Franciscan tradition. Small, urban, friendly, and caring, St. Francis provides students with a college experience that translates into development of the whole person, as well as academic achievement. Bachelor's and associate degrees in arts and science are offered in a wide array of disciplines. Proximity to Manhattan extends the classroom to offer students diverse cultural and career opportunities.

Undergraduates 2,009 full-time, 442 part-time. Students come from 38 states and territories, 50 other countries, 1% are from out of state, 17% African American, 2% Asian American or Pacific Islander, 14% Hispanic American, 0.2% Native American, 15% international, 6% transferred in. *Retention:* 76% of 2001 full-time freshmen returned.
Freshmen *Admission:* 1,558 applied, 1,263 admitted, 499 enrolled. *Test scores:* SAT verbal scores over 500: 52%; SAT math scores over 500: 50%; SAT verbal scores over 600: 11%; SAT math scores over 600: 16%; SAT verbal scores over 700: 1%; SAT math scores over 700: 1%.
Faculty *Total:* 227, 29% full-time. *Student/faculty ratio:* 20:1.
Majors Accounting; aviation management; biology; biomedical science; broadcast journalism; business administration; business education; communications; computer science; criminal justice/law enforcement administration; economics; elementary education; English; health services administration; Hispanic-American studies; history; information sciences/systems; interdisciplinary studies; liberal arts and sciences/liberal studies; mathematics; medical technology; philosophy; physical education; political science; pre-dentistry; pre-law; pre-medicine; psychology; public health education/promotion; radiological science; secondary education; social sciences; social work; sociology; Western European studies.
Academic Programs *Special study options:* academic remediation for entering students, accelerated degree program, adult/continuing education programs, advanced placement credit, double majors, English as a second language, external degree program, honors programs, independent study, internships, part-time degree program, study abroad, summer session for credit. *ROTC:* Army (c), Air Force (c). *Unusual degree programs:* 3-2 podiatric medicine with New York College of Podiatric Medicine.
Library McGarry Library with 139,725 titles, 571 serial subscriptions, 2,000 audiovisual materials.
Computers on Campus 83 computers available on campus for general student use. Internet access, at least one staffed computer lab available.
Student Life *Housing:* college housing not available. *Activities and Organizations:* drama/theater group, student-run newspaper, choral group, Troupers Drama Club, psychology club, Latin American Society, Caribbean Student Association, Black Student Association, national fraternities. *Campus security:* ID checks, crime awareness workshops. *Student Services:* personal/psychological counseling.
Athletics Member NCAA. All Division I. *Intercollegiate sports:* baseball M(s), basketball M(s)/W(s), cross-country running M(s)/W(s), soccer M(s), softball W(s), swimming M(s)/W(s), tennis M(s)/W(s), track and field M(s)/W(s), volleyball W(s), water polo M(s)/W(s). *Intramural sports:* basketball M/W, football M, soccer M/W, softball M/W, volleyball M/W.
Standardized Tests *Required:* SAT I or ACT (for admission).
Costs (2001–02) *One-time required fee:* $25. *Tuition:* $9450 full-time, $325 per credit part-time. Full-time tuition and fees vary according to course load. Part-time tuition and fees vary according to course load. *Required fees:* $100 full-time, $20 per term part-time. *Payment plan:* installment. *Waivers:* employees or children of employees.
Financial Aid Of all full-time matriculated undergraduates who enrolled in 2001, 1613 applied for aid, 1564 were judged to have need, 32 had their need fully met. *Average percent of need met:* 69%. *Average financial aid package:* $8040. *Average need-based loan:* $4000. *Average need-based gift aid:* $2240.
Applying *Options:* electronic application, deferred entrance. *Application fee:* $20. *Required:* essay or personal statement, high school transcript, 1 letter of recommendation. *Required for some:* interview. *Recommended:* interview. *Application deadline:* rolling (freshmen), rolling (transfers). *Notification:* continuous (freshmen).
Admissions Contact Br. George Larkin OSF, Dean of Admissions, St. Francis College, 180 Remsen Street, Brooklyn Heights, NY 11201-4398. *Phone:* 718-489-5200. *Fax:* 718-522-1274.

St. John Fisher College
Rochester, New York

- **Independent** comprehensive, founded 1948, affiliated with Roman Catholic Church
- **Calendar** semesters
- **Degrees** bachelor's and master's
- **Suburban** 136-acre campus
- **Endowment** $33.9 million
- **Coed,** 2,350 undergraduate students, 82% full-time, 60% women, 40% men
- **Moderately difficult** entrance level, 72% of applicants were admitted

With record enrollment and an increasing number of students choosing to live on campus, St. John Fisher College opened its newest residence, Founders Hall, in fall 2002. Designed as an upper-class residence facility, Founders Hall houses nearly 200 students. Amenities include laundry facilities, kitchenettes, and study lounges in each of the six wings of the building. Founders Hall is dedicated to the priests of the Congregation of St. Basil, the founding order of St. John Fisher College.

Undergraduates 1,924 full-time, 426 part-time. Students come from 8 states and territories, 9 other countries, 2% are from out of state, 5% African American, 1% Asian American or Pacific Islander, 2% Hispanic American, 0.6% Native American, 0.4% international, 11% transferred in. *Retention:* 82% of 2001 full-time freshmen returned.
Freshmen *Admission:* 1,949 applied, 1,397 admitted, 544 enrolled. *Average high school GPA:* 3.33. *Test scores:* SAT verbal scores over 500: 66%; SAT math scores over 500: 69%; ACT scores over 18: 94%; SAT verbal scores over 600: 17%; SAT math scores over 600: 21%; ACT scores over 24: 38%; SAT verbal scores over 700: 1%; SAT math scores over 700: 1%; ACT scores over 30: 2%.
Faculty *Total:* 283, 43% full-time. *Student/faculty ratio:* 16:1.
Majors Accounting; American studies; anthropology; biochemistry; biology; business administration; business marketing and marketing management; chemistry; computer science; economics; elementary education; English; finance; French; German; history; human resources management; industrial arts; interdisciplinary studies; international business; international relations; Italian; management information systems/business data processing; mass communications; mathematics; mathematics education; nursing; philosophy; physics; political science; psychology; religious studies; science education; sociology; socio-psychological sports studies; Spanish; special education.
Academic Programs *Special study options:* academic remediation for entering students, accelerated degree program, adult/continuing education programs, advanced placement credit, double majors, honors programs, independent study, internships, off-campus study, part-time degree program, student-designed majors, study abroad, summer session for credit. *ROTC:* Army (c), Air Force (c). *Unusual degree programs:* 3-2 engineering with Clarkson University, Manhattan College, State University of New York at Buffalo, Columbia University, University of Detroit Mercy; public policy analysis with University of Rochester.

St. John Fisher College (continued)

Library Charles V. Lavery Library plus 1 other with 195,000 titles, 1,330 serial subscriptions, 27,666 audiovisual materials, an OPAC, a Web page.

Computers on Campus 133 computers available on campus for general student use. A campuswide network can be accessed from student residence rooms and from off campus. Internet access, online (class) registration, at least one staffed computer lab available.

Student Life *Housing Options:* coed, women-only. *Activities and Organizations:* drama/theater group, student-run newspaper, radio station, choral group, student government, Student Activities Board, Commuter Council, resident student association. *Campus security:* 24-hour emergency response devices and patrols, late-night transport/escort service. *Student Services:* health clinic, personal/psychological counseling.

Athletics Member NCAA. All Division III. *Intercollegiate sports:* baseball M, basketball M/W, bowling M(c)/W(c), cross-country running M/W, football M, golf M, lacrosse M(c)/W, soccer M/W, softball W, tennis M/W, volleyball W. *Intramural sports:* basketball M/W, football M, golf M/W, racquetball M/W, rugby M/W, skiing (cross-country) M/W, skiing (downhill) M(c)/W(c), soccer M/W, softball M/W, tennis M/W, volleyball M/W.

Standardized Tests *Required:* SAT I or ACT (for admission).

Costs (2002–03) *One-time required fee:* $300. *Comprehensive fee:* $23,450 includes full-time tuition ($16,100), mandatory fees ($350), and room and board ($7000). Part-time tuition: $450 per credit hour. *Room and board:* College room only: $4600. *Payment plans:* installment, deferred payment. *Waivers:* senior citizens and employees or children of employees.

Financial Aid Of all full-time matriculated undergraduates who enrolled in 2001, 1747 applied for aid, 1560 were judged to have need, 763 had their need fully met. 287 Federal Work-Study jobs (averaging $1150). In 2001, 99 non-need-based awards were made. *Average percent of need met:* 83%. *Average financial aid package:* $12,237. *Average need-based loan:* $4331. *Average non-need based aid:* $5415. *Average indebtedness upon graduation:* $18,400.

Applying *Options:* common application, electronic application, early admission, early decision, deferred entrance. *Application fee:* $25. *Required:* high school transcript. *Recommended:* 1 letter of recommendation, interview. *Application deadline:* rolling (freshmen), rolling (transfers). *Early decision:* 12/1. *Notification:* continuous until 9/1 (freshmen), 12/15 (early decision).

Admissions Contact Ms. Stacy A. Ledermann, Director of Freshmen Admissions, St. John Fisher College, Rochester, NY 14610. *Phone:* 585-385-8064. *Toll-free phone:* 800-444-4640. *Fax:* 585-385-8386. *E-mail:* admissions@sjfc.edu.

St. John's University
Jamaica, New York

- **Independent** university, founded 1870, affiliated with Roman Catholic Church
- **Calendar** semesters
- **Degrees** certificates, diplomas, associate, bachelor's, master's, doctoral, first professional, post-master's, and postbachelor's certificates
- **Urban** 95-acre campus with easy access to New York City
- **Endowment** $120.9 million
- **Coed,** 14,485 undergraduate students, 80% full-time, 57% women, 43% men
- **Moderately difficult** entrance level, 80% of applicants were admitted

Founded in 1870, St. John's University prepares students for personal and professional success. St. John's combines a rigorous academic program, a close-knit campus environment, and nationally renowned athletic teams with the vast business and cultural opportunities of New York City. With magnificent new residence halls and the latest academic technologies, a St. John's education is the right step toward a bright future.

Undergraduates 11,602 full-time, 2,883 part-time. Students come from 43 states and territories, 106 other countries, 7% are from out of state, 14% African American, 13% Asian American or Pacific Islander, 15% Hispanic American, 0.2% Native American, 3% international, 4% transferred in, 12% live on campus. *Retention:* 80% of 2001 full-time freshmen returned.

Freshmen *Admission:* 10,254 applied, 8,186 admitted, 2,689 enrolled. *Average high school GPA:* 3.00. *Test scores:* SAT verbal scores over 500: 48%; SAT math scores over 500: 55%; SAT verbal scores over 600: 11%; SAT math scores over 600: 17%; SAT verbal scores over 700: 1%; SAT math scores over 700: 2%.

Faculty *Total:* 1,167, 46% full-time. *Student/faculty ratio:* 18:1.

Majors Accounting; actuarial science; American studies; anthropology; art education; Asian studies; biology; biology education; business administration; business economics; chemistry; chemistry education; communications; community services; computer/information sciences; criminal justice/law enforcement administration; cytotechnology; data processing technology; ecology; economics; education of the speech impaired; elementary education; English; English education; finance; fine/studio arts; foreign languages education; French; French language education; graphic design/commercial art/illustration; health facilities administration; history; hotel and restaurant management; information sciences/systems; insurance/risk management; Italian; journalism; liberal arts and sciences/liberal studies; logistics/materials management; mathematics; mathematics education; medical technology; middle school education; mortuary science; paralegal/legal assistant; pharmacy; philosophy; photography; physical sciences; physician assistant; physics; physics education; political science; psychology; public administration; real estate; science education; secondary education; social sciences; social studies education; sociology; Spanish; Spanish language education; special education; speech-language pathology/audiology; speech/rhetorical studies; sport/fitness administration; teacher assistant/aide; telecommunications; theology; toxicology.

Academic Programs *Special study options:* accelerated degree program, adult/continuing education programs, advanced placement credit, distance learning, double majors, English as a second language, honors programs, independent study, internships, off-campus study, part-time degree program, services for LD students, study abroad, summer session for credit. *ROTC:* Army (b). *Unusual degree programs:* 3-2 engineering with Manhattan College.

Library St. John's University Library plus 2 others with 5.0 million titles, 15,974 serial subscriptions, 22,095 audiovisual materials, an OPAC, a Web page.

Computers on Campus 950 computers available on campus for general student use. A campuswide network can be accessed from student residence rooms and from off campus that provide access to various software packages. Internet access, online (class) registration, at least one staffed computer lab available.

Student Life *Housing Options:* coed. *Activities and Organizations:* drama/theater group, student-run newspaper, radio and television station, choral group, Student Government, Incorporated, Student Programming Board, Community and University Services in Education, Haraya, American Pharmaceutical Association, national fraternities, national sororities. *Campus security:* 24-hour emergency response devices and patrols, student patrols, late-night transport/escort service, controlled dormitory access. *Student Services:* health clinic, personal/psychological counseling.

Athletics Member NCAA. All Division I except football (Division I-AA). *Intercollegiate sports:* baseball M(s), basketball M(s)/W(s), cross-country running M(s)/W(s), fencing M(s)/W(s), golf M(s), soccer M(s)/W(s), softball W(s), swimming M(s)/W(s), tennis M(s)/W(s), track and field M(s)/W(s), volleyball W(s). *Intramural sports:* basketball M/W, bowling M(c)/W(c), equestrian sports M/W(c), football M(c), racquetball M/W, softball M/W, table tennis M(c)/W(c), volleyball M/W, weight lifting M/W.

Standardized Tests *Required:* SAT I or ACT (for admission).

Costs (2001–02) *Comprehensive fee:* $26,660 includes full-time tuition ($16,900), mandatory fees ($430), and room and board ($9330). Full-time tuition and fees vary according to class time, class time, course load, program, and student level. Part-time tuition: $563 per credit. Part-time tuition and fees vary according to class time, class time, course load, program, and student level. No tuition increase for student's term of enrollment. *Required fees:* $70 per term part-time. *Room and board:* Room and board charges vary according to board plan and housing facility. *Payment plans:* installment, deferred payment. *Waivers:* senior citizens and employees or children of employees.

Financial Aid Of all full-time matriculated undergraduates who enrolled in 2001, 9166 applied for aid, 8189 were judged to have need, 1192 had their need fully met. 905 Federal Work-Study jobs (averaging $3111). In 2001, 1059 non-need-based awards were made. *Average percent of need met:* 70%. *Average financial aid package:* $13,283. *Average need-based loan:* $8317. *Average need-based gift aid:* $8762. *Average non-need based aid:* $6327. *Average indebtedness upon graduation:* $16,947.

Applying *Options:* common application, electronic application, deferred entrance. *Application fee:* $30. *Required:* essay or personal statement, high school transcript, letters of recommendation. *Application deadline:* rolling (freshmen), rolling (transfers). *Notification:* continuous (freshmen).

Admissions Contact Mr. Glenn Sklarin, Vice President, Enrollment Management, St. John's University, 8000 Utopia Parkway, Jamaica, NY 11439. *Phone:* 718-990-2000. *Toll-free phone:* 888-9STJOHNS (in-state); 888-9ST JOHNS (out-of-state). *Fax:* 718-990-1677. *E-mail:* admissions@stjohns.edu.

St. Joseph's College, New York
Brooklyn, New York

- **Independent** 4-year, founded 1916
- **Calendar** semesters
- **Degrees** bachelor's and master's

- **Urban** campus
- **Endowment** $23.4 million
- **Coed,** 1,123 undergraduate students, 46% full-time, 78% women, 22% men
- **Moderately difficult** entrance level, 51% of applicants were admitted

For more than eighty years, St. Joseph's has provided a high-quality liberal arts education to a diverse group of students. Students can take advantage of small classes and individualized academic and career counseling. Preprofessional programs in law and medicine and career-oriented majors, such as education and accounting, afford students the opportunity to prepare for a successful career while obtaining a traditional liberal arts education.

Undergraduates 515 full-time, 608 part-time. Students come from 1 other state, 1% are from out of state, 42% African American, 4% Asian American or Pacific Islander, 9% Hispanic American, 0.4% international, 18% transferred in. *Retention:* 86% of 2001 full-time freshmen returned.

Freshmen *Admission:* 425 applied, 217 admitted, 82 enrolled. *Average high school GPA:* 3.0. *Test scores:* SAT verbal scores over 500: 59%; SAT math scores over 500: 18%; SAT verbal scores over 600: 10%; SAT math scores over 600: 1%; SAT verbal scores over 700: 2%.

Faculty *Total:* 139, 37% full-time. *Student/faculty ratio:* 16:1.

Majors Accounting; biology; business administration; chemistry; child guidance; developmental/child psychology; education; English; general studies; health services administration; history; human resources management; human services; mathematics; mathematics/computer science; nursing; pre-law; psychology; public health; social sciences; Spanish; speech/rhetorical studies.

Academic Programs *Special study options:* adult/continuing education programs, advanced placement credit, honors programs, internships, part-time degree program, summer session for credit. *Unusual degree programs:* 3-2 podiatry with New York College of Podiatric Medicine.

Library McEntegart Hall Library with 100,000 titles, 432 serial subscriptions, 4,482 audiovisual materials.

Computers on Campus 71 computers available on campus for general student use. At least one staffed computer lab available.

Student Life *Housing:* college housing not available. *Activities and Organizations:* drama/theater group, student-run newspaper, choral group, Admissions Club, Science Club, dramatics, Child Study Club, dance team. *Campus security:* late-night transport/escort service. *Student Services:* personal/psychological counseling.

Athletics *Intercollegiate sports:* basketball M/W, cross-country running M/W, softball W, volleyball M/W. *Intramural sports:* basketball M/W, bowling M/W, table tennis M/W, volleyball M/W.

Standardized Tests *Required:* SAT I (for admission).

Costs (2002–03) *Tuition:* $10,050 full-time, $325 per credit part-time. Part-time tuition and fees vary according to course load. *Required fees:* $350 full-time, $11 per credit. *Payment plans:* installment, deferred payment. *Waivers:* employees or children of employees.

Financial Aid Of all full-time matriculated undergraduates who enrolled in 2001, 435 applied for aid, 350 were judged to have need, 300 had their need fully met. 31 Federal Work-Study jobs (averaging $1350). 7 State and other part-time jobs (averaging $1400). *Average percent of need met:* 60%. *Average financial aid package:* $7000. *Average need-based loan:* $4400. *Average need-based gift aid:* $3500. *Average indebtedness upon graduation:* $14,250.

Applying *Options:* early admission, deferred entrance. *Application fee:* $25. *Required:* high school transcript, minimum 3.0 GPA. *Required for some:* interview. *Recommended:* essay or personal statement, 2 letters of recommendation. *Application deadlines:* 8/15 (freshmen), 8/15 (transfers). *Notification:* continuous until 8/30 (freshmen).

Admissions Contact Mr. Michael Learmond, Director of Admissions, St. Joseph's College, New York, 245 Clinton Avenue, Brooklyn, NY 11205-3688. *Phone:* 718-636-6868. *E-mail:* asinfob@sjcny.edu.

St. Joseph's College, Suffolk Campus

Patchogue, New York

- **Independent** comprehensive, founded 1916
- **Calendar** 4-1-4
- **Degrees** certificates, bachelor's, and master's (master's degree in education only)
- **Small-town** 28-acre campus with easy access to New York City
- **Coed,** 3,316 undergraduate students, 70% full-time, 78% women, 22% men
- **Moderately difficult** entrance level, 74% of applicants were admitted

Undergraduates 2,333 full-time, 983 part-time. 6% are from out of state, 3% African American, 2% Asian American or Pacific Islander, 4% Hispanic American, 0.2% Native American, 14% transferred in. *Retention:* 98% of 2001 full-time freshmen returned.

Freshmen *Admission:* 796 applied, 588 admitted, 324 enrolled. *Average high school GPA:* 3.50. *Test scores:* SAT verbal scores over 500: 62%; SAT math scores over 500: 69%; ACT scores over 18: 100%; SAT verbal scores over 600: 16%; SAT math scores over 600: 19%; ACT scores over 24: 33%; SAT verbal scores over 700: 1%; SAT math scores over 700: 1%.

Faculty *Total:* 318, 28% full-time, 27% with terminal degrees. *Student/faculty ratio:* 15:1.

Majors Accounting; adult/continuing education; behavioral sciences; biology; business administration; computer science; developmental/child psychology; early childhood education; education; elementary education; English; health services administration; history; human resources management; liberal arts and sciences/liberal studies; mathematics; nursing; pre-dentistry; pre-law; pre-medicine; pre-veterinary studies; psychology; recreational therapy; recreation/leisure studies; secondary education; social sciences; sociology; special education; speech/rhetorical studies.

Academic Programs *Special study options:* adult/continuing education programs, advanced placement credit, off-campus study, part-time degree program, services for LD students, summer session for credit. *ROTC:* Army (c), Air Force (c). *Unusual degree programs:* 3-2 biology with New York College of Podiatric Medicine; BA/BS and MS Program computer science with Polytechnic University, Farmingdale Campus.

Library Callahan Library with 65,530 titles, 514 serial subscriptions, 727 audiovisual materials, an OPAC.

Computers on Campus 85 computers available on campus for general student use. A campuswide network can be accessed from off campus. Internet access, at least one staffed computer lab available.

Student Life *Housing:* college housing not available. *Activities and Organizations:* drama/theater group, student-run newspaper, choral group, Campus Activities Board, Child Study Club, Circle K, STARS (Students Taking an Active Role in Society), business/accounting club, national fraternities. *Campus security:* 24-hour patrols, late-night transport/escort service. *Student Services:* personal/psychological counseling.

Athletics Member NCAA. All Division III. *Intercollegiate sports:* baseball M, basketball M/W, cross-country running M/W, equestrian sports M/W, soccer M/W, softball W, tennis M/W, volleyball W.

Standardized Tests *Required:* SAT I or ACT (for admission).

Costs (2001–02) *Tuition:* $9750 full-time, $315 per credit part-time. Part-time tuition and fees vary according to course load. *Required fees:* $332 full-time, $96 per term part-time. *Payment plan:* installment. *Waivers:* employees or children of employees.

Financial Aid Of all full-time matriculated undergraduates who enrolled in 2001, 1878 applied for aid, 1567 were judged to have need, 979 had their need fully met. 58 Federal Work-Study jobs (averaging $2051). 59 State and other part-time jobs (averaging $2068). In 2001, 396 non-need-based awards were made. *Average percent of need met:* 80%. *Average financial aid package:* $9120. *Average need-based loan:* $4026. *Average need-based gift aid:* $3490. *Average non-need based aid:* $4419. *Average indebtedness upon graduation:* $16,800.

Applying *Options:* early admission, deferred entrance. *Application fee:* $25. *Required:* high school transcript, minimum 3.0 GPA. *Required for some:* 2 letters of recommendation. *Recommended:* essay or personal statement, interview. *Application deadline:* rolling (freshmen), rolling (transfers). *Notification:* continuous (freshmen).

Admissions Contact Mrs. Marion E. Salgado, Director of Admissions, St. Joseph's College, Suffolk Campus, 155 West Roe Boulevard, Patchogue, NY 11772. *Phone:* 631-447-3219. *Toll-free phone:* 866-AT ST JOE. *Fax:* 631-447-1734. *E-mail:* admissions_patchogue@sjcny.edu.

St. Lawrence University

Canton, New York

- **Independent** comprehensive, founded 1856
- **Calendar** semesters
- **Degrees** bachelor's, master's, and post-master's certificates
- **Small-town** 1000-acre campus with easy access to Ottawa
- **Endowment** $200.1 million
- **Coed,** 1,968 undergraduate students, 99% full-time, 53% women, 47% men
- **Very difficult** entrance level, 61% of applicants were admitted

Undergraduates 1,943 full-time, 25 part-time. Students come from 37 states and territories, 19 other countries, 46% are from out of state, 2% African

St. Lawrence University (continued)
American, 0.7% Asian American or Pacific Islander, 2% Hispanic American, 0.4% Native American, 4% international, 1% transferred in, 96% live on campus. *Retention:* 84% of 2001 full-time freshmen returned.

Freshmen *Admission:* 2,745 applied, 1,674 admitted, 510 enrolled. *Average high school GPA:* 3.35. *Test scores:* SAT verbal scores over 500: 83%; SAT math scores over 500: 84%; ACT scores over 18: 97%; SAT verbal scores over 600: 37%; SAT math scores over 600: 38%; ACT scores over 24: 65%; SAT verbal scores over 700: 6%; SAT math scores over 700: 4%; ACT scores over 30: 12%.

Faculty *Total:* 192, 83% full-time, 87% with terminal degrees. *Student/faculty ratio:* 11:1.

Majors African studies; anthropology; art; art history; Asian studies; biochemistry; biology; biophysics; Canadian studies; chemistry; computer science; creative writing; ecology; economics; English; environmental science; foreign languages/literatures; French; geology; geophysics/seismology; German; history; mathematics; modern languages; music; neuroscience; philosophy; physics; political science; psychology; religious studies; sociology; Spanish; theater arts/drama.

Academic Programs *Special study options:* advanced placement credit, double majors, independent study, internships, off-campus study, part-time degree program, services for LD students, student-designed majors, study abroad, summer session for credit. *ROTC:* Army (c), Air Force (c). *Unusual degree programs:* 3-2 business administration with Clarkson University; engineering with Columbia University, Clarkson University, Rensselaer Polytechnic Institute, University of Rochester, University of Southern California, Washington University in St. Louis, Worcester Polytechnic Institute.

Library Owen D. Young Library plus 1 other with 509,348 titles, 2,014 serial subscriptions, an OPAC, a Web page.

Computers on Campus 600 computers available on campus for general student use. A campuswide network can be accessed from student residence rooms and from off campus that provide access to internships, shadowing programs. Internet access, at least one staffed computer lab available.

Student Life *Housing:* on-campus residence required through senior year. *Options:* coed. *Activities and Organizations:* drama/theater group, student-run newspaper, radio and television station, choral group, Outing Club, student newspaper, Student Government, Environmental Action, Habitat for Humanity, national fraternities, national sororities. *Campus security:* 24-hour emergency response devices and patrols, student patrols, late-night transport/escort service, controlled dormitory access. *Student Services:* health clinic, personal/psychological counseling, women's center.

Athletics Member NCAA. All Division III except men's and women's ice hockey (Division I). *Intercollegiate sports:* baseball M, basketball M/W, crew M/W, cross-country running M/W, equestrian sports M/W, field hockey W, football M, golf M/W, ice hockey M(s)/W(s), lacrosse M/W, skiing (cross-country) M/W, skiing (downhill) M/W, soccer M/W, softball W, squash M/W, swimming M/W, tennis M/W, track and field M/W, volleyball W. *Intramural sports:* basketball M/W, crew M/W, football M, ice hockey M/W, rugby M/W, soccer M/W, softball W, volleyball M/W.

Standardized Tests *Required:* SAT I or ACT (for admission). *Recommended:* SAT II: Subject Tests (for admission).

Costs (2001–02) *Comprehensive fee:* $32,605 includes full-time tuition ($24,655), mandatory fees ($195), and room and board ($7755). Part-time tuition: $3080 per course. *Required fees:* $93 per term part-time. *Room and board:* College room only: $4170. Room and board charges vary according to board plan. *Payment plans:* installment, deferred payment. *Waivers:* employees or children of employees.

Financial Aid Of all full-time matriculated undergraduates who enrolled in 2001, 1503 applied for aid, 1364 were judged to have need, 613 had their need fully met. 747 Federal Work-Study jobs (averaging $1370). 562 State and other part-time jobs (averaging $1320). In 2001, 247 non-need-based awards were made. *Average percent of need met:* 92%. *Average financial aid package:* $24,726. *Average need-based loan:* $5416. *Average need-based gift aid:* $17,619. *Average indebtedness upon graduation:* $19,648.

Applying *Options:* common application, electronic application, early decision, deferred entrance. *Application fee:* $50. *Required:* essay or personal statement, high school transcript, 2 letters of recommendation. *Recommended:* minimum 2.0 GPA, interview. *Application deadlines:* 2/15 (freshmen), 4/1 (transfers). *Early decision:* 11/15 (for plan 1), 1/15 (for plan 2). *Notification:* 3/31 (freshmen), 12/15 (early decision plan 1), 2/15 (early decision plan 2).

Admissions Contact Ms. Terry Cowdrey, Dean of Admissions and Financial Aid, St. Lawrence University, Canton, NY 13617-1455. *Phone:* 315-229-5261. *Toll-free phone:* 800-285-1856. *Fax:* 315-229-5818. *E-mail:* admissions@stlawu.edu.

ST. THOMAS AQUINAS COLLEGE
Sparkill, New York

- **Independent** comprehensive, founded 1952
- **Calendar** 4-1-4
- **Degrees** associate, bachelor's, master's, post-master's, and postbachelor's certificates
- **Suburban** 46-acre campus with easy access to New York City
- **Endowment** $8.4 million
- **Coed,** 1,944 undergraduate students, 65% full-time, 55% women, 45% men
- **Moderately difficult** entrance level, 75% of applicants were admitted

Undergraduates 1,262 full-time, 682 part-time. Students come from 17 states and territories, 10 other countries, 37% are from out of state, 6% African American, 3% Asian American or Pacific Islander, 11% Hispanic American, 0.1% Native American, 2% international, 9% transferred in, 34% live on campus. *Retention:* 74% of 2001 full-time freshmen returned.

Freshmen *Admission:* 1,080 applied, 809 admitted, 306 enrolled. *Average high school GPA:* 2.8. *Test scores:* SAT verbal scores over 500: 32%; SAT math scores over 500: 31%; SAT verbal scores over 600: 8%; SAT math scores over 600: 7%; SAT verbal scores over 700: 1%; SAT math scores over 700: 1%.

Faculty *Total:* 150, 43% full-time, 75% with terminal degrees. *Student/faculty ratio:* 17:1.

Majors Accounting; applied art; applied mathematics; art; art education; art therapy; biology; business administration; business marketing and marketing management; criminal justice/law enforcement administration; early childhood education; education; elementary education; engineering science; English; finance; fine/studio arts; graphic design/commercial art/illustration; history; humanities; information sciences/systems; journalism; mass communications; mathematics; medical laboratory technician; medical technology; modern languages; natural sciences; philosophy; pre-medicine; psychology; recreation/leisure studies; religious studies; romance languages; secondary education; social sciences; Spanish; special education.

Academic Programs *Special study options:* academic remediation for entering students, accelerated degree program, adult/continuing education programs, advanced placement credit, English as a second language, freshman honors college, honors programs, internships, off-campus study, part-time degree program, services for LD students, summer session for credit. *ROTC:* Air Force (c). *Unusual degree programs:* 3-2 engineering with George Washington University, Manhattan College; physical therapy with New York Medical College.

Library Lougheed Library plus 1 other with 176,000 titles, 940 serial subscriptions, an OPAC.

Computers on Campus 200 computers available on campus for general student use. A campuswide network can be accessed from student residence rooms and from off campus. Internet access, at least one staffed computer lab available.

Student Life *Housing Options:* coed. *Activities and Organizations:* drama/theater group, student-run newspaper, radio station. *Campus security:* 24-hour emergency response devices and patrols, late-night transport/escort service, controlled dormitory access. *Student Services:* personal/psychological counseling.

Athletics Member NAIA. *Intercollegiate sports:* baseball M(s), basketball M(s)/W(s), cross-country running M(s)/W(s), golf M/W, soccer M(s)/W(s), softball W(s), volleyball W(s). *Intramural sports:* basketball M/W, volleyball M/W.

Standardized Tests *Required:* SAT I or ACT (for admission).

Costs (2002–03) *Comprehensive fee:* $22,080 includes full-time tuition ($13,780), mandatory fees ($320), and room and board ($7980). Part-time tuition: $460 per credit. *Required fees:* $75 per term part-time.

Applying *Options:* common application, electronic application, early admission, early decision, early action, deferred entrance. *Application fee:* $30. *Required:* high school transcript, minimum 2.0 GPA. *Required for some:* 3 letters of recommendation. *Recommended:* essay or personal statement, interview. *Application deadline:* rolling (freshmen), rolling (transfers). *Early decision:* 12/1. *Notification:* continuous (freshmen), 1/15 (early decision), 1/15 (early action).

Admissions Contact Mr. John Edel, Dean of Enrollment Management, St. Thomas Aquinas College, 125 Route 340, Sparkill, NY 10976. *Phone:* 914-398-4100. *Toll-free phone:* 800-999-STAC.

SARAH LAWRENCE COLLEGE
Bronxville, New York

- **Independent** comprehensive, founded 1926
- **Calendar** semesters
- **Degrees** bachelor's and master's

- **Suburban** 40-acre campus with easy access to New York City
- **Endowment** $46.5 million
- **Coed,** 1,214 undergraduate students, 94% full-time, 73% women, 27% men
- **Very difficult** entrance level, 37% of applicants were admitted

At the heart of the Sarah Lawrence learning experience is the seminar and conference system. Every course has 2 parts: a seminar limited to 15 students and an individual meeting held every 2 weeks between student and teacher, during which they create a project that extends the seminar material and connects it to the student's academic goals and aspirations. Through dialogue, reading, and research, students work with their teachers to create an individualized education.

Undergraduates 1,143 full-time, 71 part-time. Students come from 50 states and territories, 27 other countries, 78% are from out of state, 5% African American, 5% Asian American or Pacific Islander, 4% Hispanic American, 0.4% Native American, 4% international, 2% transferred in, 87% live on campus. *Retention:* 94% of 2001 full-time freshmen returned.

Freshmen *Admission:* 2,782 applied, 1,027 admitted, 323 enrolled. *Average high school GPA:* 3.60. *Test scores:* SAT verbal scores over 500: 97%; SAT math scores over 500: 93%; ACT scores over 18: 100%; SAT verbal scores over 600: 79%; SAT math scores over 600: 50%; ACT scores over 24: 83%; SAT verbal scores over 700: 31%; SAT math scores over 700: 7%; ACT scores over 30: 30%.

Faculty *Total:* 222, 79% full-time. *Student/faculty ratio:* 6:1.

Majors African-American studies; American studies; anthropology; art; art history; Asian studies; biological/physical sciences; biology; chemistry; classics; comparative literature; computer science; creative writing; dance; developmental/child psychology; drawing; early childhood education; Eastern European area studies; ecology; economics; education; English; environmental science; European studies; film studies; film/video production; fine/studio arts; French; genetics; geology; German; history; humanities; individual/family development; interdisciplinary studies; international relations; Italian; Latin American studies; Latin (ancient and medieval); liberal arts and sciences/liberal studies; literature; marine biology; mathematics; modern languages; music; music history; music (piano and organ performance); music (voice and choral/opera performance); natural sciences; philosophy; photography; physics; political science; pre-dentistry; pre-law; pre-medicine; psychology; public policy analysis; religious studies; romance languages; Russian; sculpture; social sciences; sociology; Spanish; stringed instruments; theater arts/drama; urban studies; western civilization; wind/percussion instruments; women's studies.

Academic Programs *Special study options:* adult/continuing education programs, advanced placement credit, double majors, independent study, internships, off-campus study, part-time degree program, student-designed majors, study abroad. *Unusual degree programs:* art of teaching.

Library Esther Rauschenbush Library plus 2 others with 194,090 titles, 877 serial subscriptions, 7,564 audiovisual materials, an OPAC, a Web page.

Computers on Campus 110 computers available on campus for general student use. A campuswide network can be accessed from student residence rooms and from off campus. Internet access, at least one staffed computer lab available.

Student Life *Housing:* on-campus residence required for freshman year. *Options:* coed, men-only, women-only, cooperative. *Activities and Organizations:* drama/theater group, student-run newspaper, radio station, choral group, Student Senate, APICAD, UNIDAD, Harambe, Amnesty International. *Campus security:* 24-hour emergency response devices and patrols, student patrols, late-night transport/escort service, controlled dormitory access. *Student Services:* health clinic, personal/psychological counseling.

Athletics *Intercollegiate sports:* basketball M, crew M/W, cross-country running M/W, equestrian sports M/W, swimming W, tennis M/W, volleyball W. *Intramural sports:* basketball M/W, bowling M/W, fencing M/W, soccer M/W, softball M/W, squash M/W, swimming M/W, tennis M/W, volleyball M/W.

Costs (2001–02) *Comprehensive fee:* $37,516 includes full-time tuition ($27,330), mandatory fees ($652), and room and board ($9534). Full-time tuition and fees vary according to course load. Part-time tuition: $911 per credit. Part-time tuition and fees vary according to course load. *Required fees:* $248 per term part-time. *Room and board:* College room only: $6216. Room and board charges vary according to board plan. *Payment plan:* installment. *Waivers:* employees or children of employees.

Financial Aid Of all full-time matriculated undergraduates who enrolled in 2001, 747 applied for aid, 656 were judged to have need, 343 had their need fully met. 432 Federal Work-Study jobs (averaging $1768). 39 State and other part-time jobs (averaging $1661). *Average percent of need met:* 92%. *Average financial aid package:* $24,803. *Average need-based loan:* $3137. *Average need-based gift aid:* $18,239. *Average indebtedness upon graduation:* $13,042. *Financial aid deadline:* 2/1.

Applying *Options:* common application, electronic application, early admission, early decision, deferred entrance. *Application fee:* $50. *Required:* essay or personal statement, high school transcript, 3 letters of recommendation. *Recommended:* minimum 3.0 GPA, interview. *Application deadlines:* 1/15 (freshmen), 3/1 (transfers). *Early decision:* 11/15 (for plan 1), 1/1 (for plan 2). *Notification:* 4/1 (freshmen), 12/15 (early decision plan 1), 2/15 (early decision plan 2).

Admissions Contact Ms. Thyra L. Briggs, Dean of Admission, Sarah Lawrence College, 1 Mead Way, Bronxville, NY 10708-5999. *Phone:* 914-395-2510. *Toll-free phone:* 800-888-2858. *Fax:* 914-395-2515. *E-mail:* slcadmit@slc.edu.

SCHOOL OF VISUAL ARTS
New York, New York

- **Proprietary** comprehensive, founded 1947
- **Calendar** semesters
- **Degrees** bachelor's and master's
- **Urban** 1-acre campus
- **Coed,** 4,849 undergraduate students, 62% full-time, 52% women, 48% men
- **Moderately difficult** entrance level, 62% of applicants were admitted

Undergraduates 3,005 full-time, 1,844 part-time. Students come from 45 states and territories, 19 other countries, 40% are from out of state, 4% African American, 11% Asian American or Pacific Islander, 9% Hispanic American, 0.4% Native American, 11% international, 7% transferred in, 25% live on campus. *Retention:* 86% of 2001 full-time freshmen returned.

Freshmen *Admission:* 1,822 applied, 1,127 admitted, 423 enrolled. *Average high school GPA:* 3.00. *Test scores:* SAT verbal scores over 500: 64%; SAT math scores over 500: 56%; ACT scores over 18: 88%; SAT verbal scores over 600: 20%; SAT math scores over 600: 15%; ACT scores over 24: 26%; SAT verbal scores over 700: 4%; SAT math scores over 700: 2%; ACT scores over 30: 3%.

Faculty *Total:* 848, 17% full-time, 27% with terminal degrees. *Student/faculty ratio:* 8:1.

Majors Advertising; applied art; art; art education; art therapy; computer graphics; drawing; film studies; film/video production; fine/studio arts; graphic design/commercial art/illustration; interior design; painting; photography; sculpture.

Academic Programs *Special study options:* academic remediation for entering students, adult/continuing education programs, double majors, English as a second language, independent study, internships, part-time degree program, services for LD students, study abroad, summer session for credit.

Library School of Visual Arts Library with 70,680 titles, 306 serial subscriptions, 1,600 audiovisual materials, an OPAC.

Computers on Campus 600 computers available on campus for general student use. A campuswide network can be accessed from off campus. At least one staffed computer lab available.

Student Life *Housing Options:* coed, women-only. *Activities and Organizations:* drama/theater group, student-run newspaper, radio station, Visual Arts Student Association, Film Club, Korean Christian, Asian Association, Bible Study. *Campus security:* 24-hour patrols. *Student Services:* health clinic.

Athletics *Intramural sports:* basketball M/W, softball M/W.

Standardized Tests *Required:* SAT I or ACT (for admission).

Costs (2001–02) *Tuition:* $16,500 full-time, $700 per credit part-time. Full-time tuition and fees vary according to program. *Required fees:* $500 full-time. *Room only:* $6700. Room and board charges vary according to gender and housing facility. *Payment plan:* installment. *Waivers:* employees or children of employees.

Financial Aid Of all full-time matriculated undergraduates who enrolled in 2001, 1708 applied for aid, 1534 were judged to have need, 3 had their need fully met. 120 Federal Work-Study jobs (averaging $2056). In 2001, 147 non-need-based awards were made. *Average percent of need met:* 50%. *Average financial aid package:* $10,753. *Average need-based gift aid:* $4923. *Average non-need based aid:* $1297. *Average indebtedness upon graduation:* $15,000.

Applying *Options:* early decision, deferred entrance. *Application fee:* $45. *Required:* essay or personal statement, high school transcript, minimum 2.3 GPA, portfolio. *Required for some:* 1 letter of recommendation. *Recommended:* interview. *Application deadline:* rolling (freshmen), rolling (transfers). *Early decision:* 12/1. *Notification:* 1/16 (early decision).

Admissions Contact Mr. Richard M. Longo, Executive Director of Admissions, School of Visual Arts, 209 East 23rd Street, New York, NY 10010-3994.

School of Visual Arts (continued)
Phone: 212-592-2100. *Toll-free phone:* 800-436-4204. *Fax:* 212-592-2116. *E-mail:* admissions@adm.schoolofvisualarts.edu.

SH'OR YOSHUV RABBINICAL COLLEGE
Far Rockaway, New York

Admissions Contact Rabbi Avrohom Halpern, Executive Director, Sh'or Yoshuv Rabbinical College, 1284 Central Avenue, Far Rockaway, NY 11691-4002. *Phone:* 718-327-7244.

SIENA COLLEGE
Loudonville, New York

- **Independent Roman Catholic** 4-year, founded 1937
- **Calendar** semesters
- **Degrees** bachelor's and master's
- **Suburban** 155-acre campus
- **Endowment** $39.5 million
- **Coed,** 3,379 undergraduate students, 86% full-time, 54% women, 46% men
- **Moderately difficult** entrance level, 69% of applicants were admitted

Located in Loudonville, New York, Siena is a community of about 2,700 men and women that offers degrees in the liberal arts, business, and science. Student-focused professors are the heart of a supportive and challenging learning environment that prepares students for careers, for active roles in their communities, and for the real world. Founded by the Franciscans, Siena provides a personal, values-oriented education 1 student at a time.

Undergraduates 2,918 full-time, 461 part-time. Students come from 27 states and territories, 15% are from out of state, 2% African American, 2% Asian American or Pacific Islander, 2% Hispanic American, 0.2% Native American, 0.3% international, 4% transferred in, 74% live on campus. *Retention:* 88% of 2001 full-time freshmen returned.

Freshmen *Admission:* 3,346 applied, 2,294 admitted, 712 enrolled. *Test scores:* SAT verbal scores over 500: 79%; SAT math scores over 500: 84%; ACT scores over 18: 96%; SAT verbal scores over 600: 22%; SAT math scores over 600: 29%; ACT scores over 24: 50%; SAT verbal scores over 700: 1%; SAT math scores over 700: 2%; ACT scores over 30: 4%.

Faculty *Total:* 272, 60% full-time, 62% with terminal degrees. *Student/faculty ratio:* 14:1.

Majors Accounting; American studies; biology; business economics; business marketing and marketing management; chemistry; classics; computer science; economics; English; environmental science; finance; French; history; mathematics; philosophy; physics; political science; pre-dentistry; pre-law; pre-medicine; psychology; religious studies; secondary education; social work; sociology; Spanish.

Academic Programs *Special study options:* academic remediation for entering students, adult/continuing education programs, advanced placement credit, double majors, honors programs, independent study, internships, off-campus study, part-time degree program, services for LD students, study abroad, summer session for credit. *ROTC:* Army (b), Air Force (c). *Unusual degree programs:* 3-2 engineering with Clarkson University, Manhattan College, Catholic University of America, Western New England College, Rensselaer Polytechnic Institute, State University of New York at Binghamton; forestry with State University of New York College of Environmental Science and Forestry; Pace University Law School, Western New England College of Law.

Library J. Spencer and Patricia Standish Library with 299,918 titles, 1,243 serial subscriptions, 4,101 audiovisual materials, an OPAC, a Web page.

Computers on Campus 650 computers available on campus for general student use. A campuswide network can be accessed from student residence rooms and from off campus. Internet access, at least one staffed computer lab available.

Student Life *Housing:* on-campus residence required for freshman year. *Options:* coed. *Activities and Organizations:* drama/theater group, student-run newspaper, radio station, choral group, Student Senate, Student Events Board, Big Brothers/Big Sisters, Gaelic Society, outing club. *Campus security:* 24-hour emergency response devices and patrols, late-night transport/escort service, controlled dormitory access, call boxes in parking lots and on roadways. *Student Services:* health clinic, personal/psychological counseling, legal services.

Athletics Member NCAA. All Division I except football (Division I-AA). *Intercollegiate sports:* baseball M(s), basketball M(s)/W(s), cross-country running M/W, equestrian sports M(c)/W(c), field hockey W, golf M/W, ice hockey M(c), lacrosse M/W, rugby M(c), soccer M(s)/W(s), softball W(s), swimming W, tennis M/W, track and field M(c)/W(c), volleyball W. *Intramural sports:* basketball M/W, bowling M/W, football M/W, golf M/W, racquetball M/W, soccer M/W, softball M/W, volleyball M/W.

Standardized Tests *Required:* SAT I or ACT (for admission).

Costs (2001–02) *Comprehensive fee:* $22,685 includes full-time tuition ($15,330), mandatory fees ($540), and room and board ($6815). Part-time tuition: $265 per credit hour. *Required fees:* $25 per term part-time. *Room and board:* Room and board charges vary according to board plan and housing facility. *Payment plan:* installment. *Waivers:* senior citizens and employees or children of employees.

Financial Aid Of all full-time matriculated undergraduates who enrolled in 2001, 2346 applied for aid, 1951 were judged to have need, 319 had their need fully met. 411 Federal Work-Study jobs (averaging $776). In 2001, 339 non-need-based awards were made. *Average percent of need met:* 75%. *Average financial aid package:* $10,501. *Average need-based loan:* $3890. *Average need-based gift aid:* $7317. *Average non-need based aid:* $5382. *Average indebtedness upon graduation:* $14,000.

Applying *Options:* electronic application, early admission, early decision, early action, deferred entrance. *Application fee:* $40. *Required:* essay or personal statement, high school transcript, 1 letter of recommendation. *Required for some:* interview. *Application deadlines:* 3/1 (freshmen), 6/1 (transfers). *Early decision:* 12/1. *Notification:* 3/15 (freshmen), 12/15 (early decision), 12/1 (early action).

Admissions Contact Mr. Edward Jones, Director of Admissions, Siena College, 515 Loudon Road, Loudonville, NY 12211-1462. *Phone:* 518-783-2423. *Toll-free phone:* 888-ATSIENA. *Fax:* 518-783-2436. *E-mail:* admit@siena.edu.

SKIDMORE COLLEGE
Saratoga Springs, New York

- **Independent** comprehensive, founded 1903
- **Calendar** semesters
- **Degrees** bachelor's and master's
- **Small-town** 800-acre campus with easy access to Albany
- **Endowment** $156.0 million
- **Coed,** 2,488 undergraduate students, 90% full-time, 60% women, 40% men
- **Very difficult** entrance level, 42% of applicants were admitted

Undergraduates 2,249 full-time, 239 part-time. Students come from 46 states and territories, 19 other countries, 71% are from out of state, 2% African American, 4% Asian American or Pacific Islander, 5% Hispanic American, 0.4% Native American, 1% international, 1% transferred in, 77% live on campus. *Retention:* 93% of 2001 full-time freshmen returned.

Freshmen *Admission:* 5,633 applied, 2,383 admitted, 599 enrolled. *Average high school GPA:* 3.40. *Test scores:* SAT verbal scores over 500: 96%; SAT math scores over 500: 96%; ACT scores over 18: 97%; SAT verbal scores over 600: 63%; SAT math scores over 600: 63%; ACT scores over 24: 81%; SAT verbal scores over 700: 13%; SAT math scores over 700: 9%; ACT scores over 30: 11%.

Faculty *Total:* 206, 95% full-time, 82% with terminal degrees. *Student/faculty ratio:* 11:1.

Majors American studies; anthropology; area, ethnic, and cultural studies related; art history; Asian studies; biochemistry; biological sciences/life sciences related; biology; business; business management/administrative services related; chemistry; classics; computer/information sciences; dance; economics; elementary education; English related; exercise sciences; fine arts and art studies related; French; geology; German; history; liberal arts and sciences/liberal studies; literature; mathematics; music history; philosophy; physics; political science; psychology; psychology related; religious studies; social sciences and history related; social work; sociology; Spanish; theater arts/drama; women's studies.

Academic Programs *Special study options:* accelerated degree program, adult/continuing education programs, advanced placement credit, double majors, external degree program, honors programs, independent study, internships, off-campus study, student-designed majors, study abroad, summer session for credit. *ROTC:* Army (c), Air Force (c). *Unusual degree programs:* 3-2 business administration with Rensselaer Polytechnic Institute; engineering with Dartmouth College, Clarkson University.

Library Scribner Library with 477,658 titles, 2,164 serial subscriptions, 130,040 audiovisual materials, an OPAC, a Web page.

Computers on Campus 173 computers available on campus for general student use. A campuswide network can be accessed from student residence rooms and from off campus. Internet access, at least one staffed computer lab available.

Student Life *Housing:* on-campus residence required through sophomore year. *Options:* coed, women-only. *Activities and Organizations:* drama/theater group, student-run newspaper, radio and television station, choral group, Student Government Association, student radio station, Student Volunteer Bureau, outing club,

Skidmore News. *Campus security:* 24-hour emergency response devices and patrols, late-night transport/escort service, controlled dormitory access, well-lit campus. *Student Services:* health clinic, personal/psychological counseling.

Athletics Member NCAA. All Division III. *Intercollegiate sports:* baseball M, basketball M/W, crew M/W, equestrian sports M/W, field hockey W, golf M, ice hockey M/W(c), lacrosse M/W, skiing (downhill) M(c)/W(c), soccer M/W, softball W, swimming M/W, tennis M/W, volleyball W. *Intramural sports:* basketball M/W, football M/W, racquetball M/W, soccer M/W, softball W, swimming M/W, tennis M/W, volleyball M/W.

Standardized Tests *Required:* SAT I or ACT (for admission).

Costs (2001–02) *Comprehensive fee:* $34,201 includes full-time tuition ($26,400), mandatory fees ($276), and room and board ($7525). Full-time tuition and fees vary according to course load. Part-time tuition: $880 per semester hour. Part-time tuition and fees vary according to course load. *Required fees:* $25 per year part-time. *Room and board:* College room only: $4170. Room and board charges vary according to board plan and housing facility. *Payment plans:* tuition prepayment, installment. *Waivers:* employees or children of employees.

Financial Aid Of all full-time matriculated undergraduates who enrolled in 2001, 943 applied for aid, 893 were judged to have need, 761 had their need fully met. 500 Federal Work-Study jobs (averaging $1000). 700 State and other part-time jobs (averaging $642). In 2001, 20 non-need-based awards were made. *Average percent of need met:* 97%. *Average financial aid package:* $22,095. *Average need-based loan:* $3526. *Average need-based gift aid:* $16,644. *Average non-need based aid:* $9350. *Average indebtedness upon graduation:* $15,400. *Financial aid deadline:* 1/15.

Applying *Options:* common application, early admission, early decision, deferred entrance. *Application fee:* $50. *Required:* essay or personal statement, high school transcript, 2 letters of recommendation. *Recommended:* interview. *Application deadlines:* 1/15 (freshmen), 4/1 (transfers). *Early decision:* 12/1 (for plan 1), 1/15 (for plan 2). *Notification:* 4/1 (freshmen), 1/1 (early decision plan 1), 2/15 (early decision plan 2).

Admissions Contact Skidmore College, 815 North Broadway, Saratoga Springs, NY 12866-1632. *Phone:* 518-580-5570. *Toll-free phone:* 800-867-6007. *Fax:* 518-580-5584. *E-mail:* admissions@skidmore.edu.

STATE UNIVERSITY OF NEW YORK AT ALBANY

Albany, New York

- **State-supported** university, founded 1844, part of State University of New York System
- **Calendar** semesters
- **Degrees** bachelor's, master's, doctoral, and post-master's certificates
- **Suburban** 560-acre campus
- **Endowment** $13.3 million
- **Coed,** 11,780 undergraduate students, 91% full-time, 49% women, 51% men
- **Moderately difficult** entrance level, 58% of applicants were admitted

Undergraduates 10,667 full-time, 1,113 part-time. Students come from 38 states and territories, 36 other countries, 3% are from out of state, 9% African American, 7% Asian American or Pacific Islander, 7% Hispanic American, 0.2% Native American, 1% international, 10% transferred in, 54% live on campus. *Retention:* 83% of 2001 full-time freshmen returned.

Freshmen *Admission:* 17,019 applied, 9,853 admitted, 2,216 enrolled. *Average high school GPA:* 3.53. *Test scores:* SAT verbal scores over 500: 81%; SAT math scores over 500: 87%; SAT verbal scores over 600: 32%; SAT math scores over 600: 36%; SAT verbal scores over 700: 4%; SAT math scores over 700: 4%.

Faculty *Total:* 886, 63% full-time. *Student/faculty ratio:* 19:1.

Majors Accounting; actuarial science; African-American studies; anthropology; applied mathematics; art; art history; Asian studies; atmospheric sciences; biochemistry; biology; biology education; business administration; chemistry; chemistry education; Chinese; classics; computer/information sciences; computer science; criminal justice/law enforcement administration; earth sciences; East Asian studies; Eastern European area studies; economics; English; English education; foreign languages education; French; French language education; geography; geology; Hispanic-American studies; history; information sciences/systems; interdisciplinary studies; Italian; Judaic studies; Latin American studies; Latin (ancient and medieval); linguistics; mass communications; mathematics; mathematics/computer science; mathematics education; medical technology; medieval/renaissance studies; molecular biology; music; philosophy; physics; political science; psychology; public administration; public policy analysis; religious studies; romance languages; Russian; Russian/Slavic studies; science education; Slavic languages; social science education; social work; sociology; Spanish; Spanish language education; speech/rhetorical studies; theater arts/drama; urban studies; women's studies.

Academic Programs *Special study options:* advanced placement credit, double majors, English as a second language, freshman honors college, honors programs, independent study, internships, off-campus study, services for LD students, student-designed majors, study abroad, summer session for credit. *ROTC:* Army (c), Air Force (c). *Unusual degree programs:* 3-2 engineering with Rensselaer Polytechnic Institute, State University of New York at Binghamton, State University of New York at New Paltz, Clarkson University; library science, law.

Library University Library plus 2 others with 1.1 million titles, 16,103 serial subscriptions, an OPAC, a Web page.

Computers on Campus 500 computers available on campus for general student use. A campuswide network can be accessed from student residence rooms and from off campus. At least one staffed computer lab available.

Student Life *Housing:* on-campus residence required through sophomore year. *Options:* coed, men-only, women-only. *Activities and Organizations:* drama/theater group, student-run newspaper, radio station, choral group, intramural athletics, cultural organizations, political organizations, national fraternities, national sororities. *Campus security:* 24-hour emergency response devices and patrols, late-night transport/escort service, controlled dormitory access. *Student Services:* health clinic, personal/psychological counseling, legal services.

Athletics Member NCAA. All Division I. *Intercollegiate sports:* baseball M(s), basketball M(s)/W(s), crew M/W, cross-country running M(s)/W(s), field hockey W(s), football M(s), golf W(s), lacrosse M(s)/W(s), rugby M/W, soccer M(s)/W(s), softball W(s), tennis W(s), track and field M(s)/W(s), volleyball W(s). *Intramural sports:* basketball M/W, equestrian sports M/W, fencing M/W, ice hockey M, racquetball M/W, skiing (cross-country) M/W, skiing (downhill) M/W, soccer M/W, softball M/W, squash M/W, track and field M/W, volleyball M/W, water polo M/W, wrestling M.

Standardized Tests *Required:* SAT I or ACT (for admission).

Costs (2001–02) *Tuition:* state resident $3400 full-time, $137 per credit part-time; nonresident $8300 full-time, $346 per credit part-time. Part-time tuition and fees vary according to course load. *Required fees:* $1320 full-time. *Room and board:* $6635; room only: $4085. Room and board charges vary according to board plan and housing facility. *Payment plan:* installment. *Waivers:* senior citizens.

Financial Aid Of all full-time matriculated undergraduates who enrolled in 2001, 7360 applied for aid, 5674 were judged to have need, 1164 had their need fully met. 1249 Federal Work-Study jobs (averaging $1626). In 2001, 497 non-need-based awards were made. *Average percent of need met:* 70%. *Average financial aid package:* $7540. *Average need-based loan:* $4003. *Average need-based gift aid:* $3874. *Average non-need based aid:* $2919. *Average indebtedness upon graduation:* $15,439.

Applying *Options:* electronic application, early admission, early action, deferred entrance. *Application fee:* $40. *Required:* high school transcript. *Required for some:* portfolio, audition. *Recommended:* essay or personal statement, letters of recommendation. *Application deadlines:* 3/1 (freshmen), 4/1 (transfers). *Notification:* continuous (freshmen), 1/1 (early action).

Admissions Contact Mr. Harry Wood, Director of Undergraduate Admissions, State University of New York at Albany, 1400 Washington Avenue, University Administration Building 101, Albany, NY 12222. *Phone:* 518-442-5435. *Toll-free phone:* 800-293-7869. *E-mail:* ugadmissions@albany.edu.

STATE UNIVERSITY OF NEW YORK AT BINGHAMTON

Binghamton, New York

- **State-supported** university, founded 1946, part of State University of New York System
- **Calendar** semesters
- **Degrees** bachelor's, master's, doctoral, and post-master's certificates
- **Suburban** 606-acre campus
- **Endowment** $37.8 million
- **Coed,** 10,167 undergraduate students, 97% full-time, 54% women, 46% men
- **Very difficult** entrance level, 45% of applicants were admitted

Undergraduates 9,837 full-time, 330 part-time. Students come from 32 states and territories, 48 other countries, 4% are from out of state, 6% African American, 17% Asian American or Pacific Islander, 5% Hispanic American, 0.2% Native American, 2% international, 7% transferred in, 57% live on campus. *Retention:* 91% of 2001 full-time freshmen returned.

Freshmen *Admission:* 17,381 applied, 7,791 admitted, 2,227 enrolled. *Average high school GPA:* 3.63. *Test scores:* SAT verbal scores over 500: 91%; SAT math scores over 500: 97%; ACT scores over 18: 99%; SAT verbal scores over 600: 48%; SAT math scores over 600: 66%; ACT scores over 24: 79%; SAT verbal scores over 700: 7%; SAT math scores over 700: 16%; ACT scores over 30: 17%.

Faculty *Total:* 758, 66% full-time. *Student/faculty ratio:* 19:1.

Majors Accounting; African-American studies; African studies; anthropology; Arabic; art; art history; biochemistry; biology; chemistry; classics; comparative

State University of New York at Binghamton (continued)
literature; computer engineering; computer science; drawing; economics; electrical engineering; English; environmental science; film studies; fine/studio arts; French; geography; geology; German; Hebrew; history; industrial/manufacturing engineering; information sciences/systems; interdisciplinary studies; Italian; Judaic studies; Latin American studies; linguistics; literature; management science; mathematics; mathematics/computer science; mechanical engineering; medieval/renaissance studies; music; music (general performance); nursing; philosophy; physics; physiological psychology/psychobiology; political science; pre-law; psychology; sociology; Spanish; theater arts/drama.

Academic Programs *Special study options:* academic remediation for entering students, accelerated degree program, adult/continuing education programs, advanced placement credit, distance learning, double majors, English as a second language, honors programs, independent study, internships, off-campus study, part-time degree program, services for LD students, student-designed majors, study abroad, summer session for credit. *ROTC:* Air Force (c). *Unusual degree programs:* 3-2 management, engineering and physics with Columbia University, Clarkson University, Rochester Institute of Technology, State University of New York at Buffalo, State University of New York at Stony Brook, University of Rochester.

Library Glenn G. Bartle Library plus 1 other with 1.7 million titles, 9,196 serial subscriptions, 120,191 audiovisual materials, an OPAC, a Web page.

Computers on Campus 5300 computers available on campus for general student use. A campuswide network can be accessed from student residence rooms and from off campus. Internet access, online (class) registration, at least one staffed computer lab available.

Student Life *Housing:* on-campus residence required for freshman year. *Options:* coed, disabled students. *Activities and Organizations:* drama/theater group, student-run newspaper, radio and television station, choral group, student radio station, student association, student newspaper, cultural organizations, peer counseling/mentoring/volunteering program, national fraternities, national sororities. *Campus security:* 24-hour emergency response devices and patrols, student patrols, late-night transport/escort service, controlled dormitory access, safety awareness programs, well-lit campus, self-defense education, secured campus entrance 12 a.m. to 5 a.m., emergency telephones. *Student Services:* health clinic, personal/psychological counseling, women's center, legal services.

Athletics Member NCAA. All Division I. *Intercollegiate sports:* badminton M(c)/W(c), baseball M(s), basketball M(s)/W(s), bowling M(c)/W(c), crew M(c)/W(c), cross-country running M(s)/W(s), equestrian sports M(c)/W(c), fencing M(c)/W(c), golf M(s), ice hockey M(c), lacrosse M(s)/W(s), racquetball M(c)/W(c), rugby M(c)/W(c), skiing (downhill) M(c)/W(c), soccer M(s)/W(s), softball W(s), swimming M(s)/W(s), table tennis M(c)/W(c), tennis M(s)/W(s), track and field M(s)/W(s), volleyball M(c)/W(s), wrestling M(s). *Intramural sports:* badminton M/W, basketball M/W, bowling M/W, cross-country running M/W, football M/W, golf M/W, racquetball M/W, soccer M/W, squash M/W, table tennis M/W, tennis M/W, volleyball M/W, water polo M/W, wrestling M.

Standardized Tests *Required:* SAT I or ACT (for admission).

Costs (2001–02) *Tuition:* state resident $3400 full-time, $137 per credit part-time; nonresident $8300 full-time, $346 per credit part-time. *Required fees:* $1151 full-time. *Room and board:* $6102; room only: $3800. Room and board charges vary according to board plan and housing facility. *Payment plan:* installment. *Waivers:* employees or children of employees.

Financial Aid Of all full-time matriculated undergraduates who enrolled in 2001, 6911 applied for aid, 4871 were judged to have need, 2406 had their need fully met. 1471 Federal Work-Study jobs (averaging $1411). In 2001, 665 non-need-based awards were made. *Average percent of need met:* 100%. *Average financial aid package:* $9814. *Average need-based loan:* $3627. *Average need-based gift aid:* $4288. *Average non-need based aid:* $2226. *Average indebtedness upon graduation:* $13,957.

Applying *Options:* common application, electronic application, early admission, early action, deferred entrance. *Application fee:* $30. *Required:* essay or personal statement, high school transcript. *Required for some:* 1 letter of recommendation, portfolio, audition. *Application deadline:* rolling (freshmen), rolling (transfers). *Notification:* continuous (freshmen), 12/22 (early action).

Admissions Contact Cheryl S. Brown, Acting Director of Admissions, State University of New York at Binghamton, PO Box 6001, Binghamton, NY 13902-6001. *Phone:* 607-777-2171. *Fax:* 607-777-4445. *E-mail:* admit@binghamton.edu.

STATE UNIVERSITY OF NEW YORK AT FARMINGDALE

Farmingdale, New York

- **State-supported** 4-year, founded 1912, part of State University of New York System
- **Calendar** semesters
- **Degrees** certificates, associate, and bachelor's (one bachelor's degree program is upper level)
- **Small-town** 380-acre campus with easy access to New York City
- **Endowment** $444,187
- **Coed,** 5,449 undergraduate students, 61% full-time, 44% women, 56% men
- **Moderately difficult** entrance level, 70% of applicants were admitted

Undergraduates 3,350 full-time, 2,099 part-time. Students come from 8 states and territories, 1% are from out of state, 14% African American, 4% Asian American or Pacific Islander, 10% Hispanic American, 0.1% Native American, 0.5% international, 8% transferred in, 12% live on campus. *Retention:* 74% of 2001 full-time freshmen returned.

Freshmen *Admission:* 2,949 applied, 2,057 admitted, 1,092 enrolled. *Average high school GPA:* 2.50. *Test scores:* SAT verbal scores over 500: 25%; SAT math scores over 500: 34%; SAT verbal scores over 600: 5%; SAT math scores over 600: 7%; SAT math scores over 700: 1%.

Faculty *Total:* 322, 52% full-time, 27% with terminal degrees. *Student/faculty ratio:* 20:1.

Majors Aircraft mechanic/airframe; aircraft mechanic/powerplant; aircraft pilot (professional); applied mathematics; architectural engineering technology; aviation management; biomedical engineering-related technology; business administration; communication equipment technology; computer engineering technology; computer programming; computer science; construction management; construction technology; criminal justice/law enforcement administration; data processing technology; dental hygiene; electrical/electronic engineering technology; graphic design/commercial art/illustration; industrial/manufacturing engineering; industrial technology; information sciences/systems; landscape architecture; liberal arts and sciences/liberal studies; mechanical engineering technology; medical laboratory technician; nursing; nutrition science; ornamental horticulture; safety/security technology; transportation technology.

Academic Programs *Special study options:* academic remediation for entering students, advanced placement credit, distance learning, double majors, internships, part-time degree program, services for LD students, study abroad, summer session for credit. *ROTC:* Army (c), Air Force (c).

Library Greenley Hall with 132,049 titles, 1,185 serial subscriptions, 18,021 audiovisual materials, an OPAC, a Web page.

Computers on Campus 305 computers available on campus for general student use. A campuswide network can be accessed from off campus. Internet access, online (class) registration, at least one staffed computer lab available.

Student Life *Housing Options:* coed. *Activities and Organizations:* drama/theater group, student-run newspaper, radio station, choral group, Liberal Arts Club, Campus Activities Board, Student Government Association, student radio station, Rambler Newspaper. *Campus security:* 24-hour emergency response devices and patrols. *Student Services:* health clinic, personal/psychological counseling.

Athletics Member NJCAA. *Intercollegiate sports:* baseball M, basketball M/W, cross-country running M/W, golf M, lacrosse M, soccer M/W, softball W, track and field M/W, volleyball W. *Intramural sports:* basketball M/W, football M, golf M/W, racquetball M/W, soccer M/W, softball M/W, squash M/W, swimming M/W, tennis M/W, volleyball M/W, weight lifting M/W.

Standardized Tests *Required:* SAT I or ACT (for admission).

Costs (2002–03) *Tuition:* state resident $3400 full-time, $137 per credit part-time; nonresident $8300 full-time, $346 per credit part-time. *Required fees:* $840 full-time, $22 per credit. *Room and board:* $7250; room only: $3825.

Financial Aid Of all full-time matriculated undergraduates who enrolled in 2001, 1872 applied for aid, 1480 were judged to have need, 257 had their need fully met. 134 Federal Work-Study jobs, 78 State and other part-time jobs. In 2001, 213 non-need-based awards were made. *Average percent of need met:* 63%. *Average financial aid package:* $5127. *Average need-based gift aid:* $3786. *Average non-need based aid:* $3198.

Applying *Options:* electronic application, early admission. *Application fee:* $30. *Required:* high school transcript, minimum 2.0 GPA. *Required for some:* portfolio. *Application deadline:* rolling (freshmen), rolling (transfers). *Notification:* continuous (freshmen).

Admissions Contact Ms. Kathleen Fitzwilliam, Assistant Dean for Enrollment Services, State University of New York at Farmingdale, Route 110, Farmingdale, NY 11735-1021. *Phone:* 631-420-2457. *Toll-free phone:* 877-4-FARMINGDALE. *Fax:* 631-420-2633. *E-mail:* admissions@farmingdale.edu.

STATE UNIVERSITY OF NEW YORK AT NEW PALTZ

New Paltz, New York

- **State-supported** comprehensive, founded 1828, part of State University of New York System
- **Calendar** semesters
- **Degrees** bachelor's, master's, and post-master's certificates
- **Small-town** 216-acre campus
- **Endowment** $9.0 million
- **Coed,** 6,082 undergraduate students, 85% full-time, 63% women, 37% men
- **Moderately difficult** entrance level, 35% of applicants were admitted

Undergraduates 5,172 full-time, 910 part-time. Students come from 25 states and territories, 30 other countries, 5% are from out of state, 8% African American, 4% Asian American or Pacific Islander, 9% Hispanic American, 0.2% Native American, 3% international, 12% transferred in, 52% live on campus. *Retention:* 83% of 2001 full-time freshmen returned.

Freshmen *Admission:* 9,617 applied, 3,406 admitted, 916 enrolled. *Average high school GPA:* 3.30. *Test scores:* SAT verbal scores over 500: 83%; SAT math scores over 500: 87%; SAT verbal scores over 600: 27%; SAT math scores over 600: 27%; SAT verbal scores over 700: 3%; SAT math scores over 700: 2%.

Faculty *Total:* 558, 52% full-time, 55% with terminal degrees. *Student/faculty ratio:* 17:1.

Majors Accounting; African-American studies; anthropology; applied mathematics; art; art education; art history; biochemistry; biology; broadcast journalism; business administration; business economics; business marketing and marketing management; ceramic arts; chemistry; city/community/regional planning; comparative literature; computer engineering; computer science; creative writing; drawing; early childhood education; earth sciences; economics; education; electrical engineering; elementary education; engineering physics; English; environmental science; finance; fine/studio arts; French; geography; geology; German; graphic design/commercial art/illustration; history; international business; international economics; international relations; jazz; journalism; Judaic studies; Latin American studies; mass communications; mathematics; metal/jewelry arts; music; music history; music therapy; nursing; ophthalmic/optometric services; philosophy; photography; physics; physiological psychology/psychobiology; political science; pre-dentistry; pre-law; pre-medicine; psychology; radio/television broadcasting; science education; sculpture; secondary education; social work; sociology; Spanish; special education; speech-language pathology/audiology; speech/rhetorical studies; speech therapy; theater arts/drama; women's studies.

Academic Programs *Special study options:* academic remediation for entering students, adult/continuing education programs, advanced placement credit, distance learning, double majors, English as a second language, honors programs, independent study, internships, off-campus study, part-time degree program, services for LD students, study abroad, summer session for credit. *Unusual degree programs:* 3-2 forestry with State University of New York College of Environmental Science and Forestry.

Library Sojourner Truth Library with 524,000 titles, 4,950 serial subscriptions, 764 audiovisual materials, an OPAC, a Web page.

Computers on Campus 600 computers available on campus for general student use. A campuswide network can be accessed from student residence rooms and from off campus that provide access to e-mail. Internet access, online (class) registration, at least one staffed computer lab available.

Student Life *Housing:* on-campus residence required for freshman year. *Options:* coed, disabled students. *Activities and Organizations:* drama/theater group, student-run newspaper, radio and television station, choral group, Outing Club, Greek letter organizations, Intramurals, Residence Hall Student Association, Student Art Alliance, national fraternities, national sororities. *Campus security:* 24-hour emergency response devices and patrols, late-night transport/escort service, controlled dormitory access, safety seminars. *Student Services:* health clinic, personal/psychological counseling, women's center, legal services.

Athletics Member NCAA. All Division III. *Intercollegiate sports:* baseball M, basketball M/W, cross-country running M/W, equestrian sports W(c), field hockey W, ice hockey M(c), lacrosse M(c)/W, rugby M(c)/W(c), soccer M/W, softball W, swimming M/W, tennis M/W, track and field M/W, volleyball M/W. *Intramural sports:* badminton M/W, basketball M/W, football M, golf M/W, racquetball M/W, softball M/W, track and field M/W, volleyball M/W.

Standardized Tests *Required:* SAT I or ACT (for admission).

Costs (2002–03) *Tuition:* state resident $3400 full-time, $137 per credit part-time; nonresident $8300 full-time, $346 per credit part-time. *Required fees:* $600 full-time, $19 per credit, $60 per term part-time. *Room and board:* $5600. Room and board charges vary according to board plan. *Payment plan:* installment.

Financial Aid Of all full-time matriculated undergraduates who enrolled in 2001, 5100 applied for aid, 3570 were judged to have need, 800 had their need fully met. In 2001, 500 non-need-based awards were made. *Average percent of need met:* 75%. *Average financial aid package:* $7000. *Average need-based loan:* $3500. *Average need-based gift aid:* $3000. *Average non-need based aid:* $900. *Average indebtedness upon graduation:* $15,000.

Applying *Options:* electronic application, early admission, early action, deferred entrance. *Application fee:* $40. *Required:* high school transcript, portfolio for art program, audition for music and theater programs. *Required for some:* essay or personal statement, letters of recommendation, interview. *Recommended:* minimum 3.0 GPA. *Application deadlines:* 3/30 (freshmen), 6/1 (transfers). *Notification:* continuous (freshmen), 12/15 (early action).

Admissions Contact Ms. Kimberly A. Lavoie, Director of Freshmen and International Admissions, State University of New York at New Paltz, 75 South Manheim Boulevard, Suite 1, New Paltz, NY 12561-2499. *Phone:* 845-257-3200. *Toll-free phone:* 888-639-7589. *Fax:* 845-257-3209. *E-mail:* admissions@newpaltz.edu.

STATE UNIVERSITY OF NEW YORK AT OSWEGO

Oswego, New York

- **State-supported** comprehensive, founded 1861, part of State University of New York System
- **Calendar** semesters
- **Degrees** bachelor's, master's, and post-master's certificates
- **Small-town** 696-acre campus with easy access to Syracuse
- **Endowment** $4.2 million
- **Coed,** 7,062 undergraduate students, 90% full-time, 54% women, 46% men
- **Moderately difficult** entrance level, 58% of applicants were admitted

Undergraduates 6,376 full-time, 686 part-time. Students come from 28 states and territories, 26 other countries, 2% are from out of state, 4% African American, 2% Asian American or Pacific Islander, 3% Hispanic American, 0.5% Native American, 0.7% international, 11% transferred in, 53% live on campus. *Retention:* 75% of 2001 full-time freshmen returned.

Freshmen *Admission:* 7,697 applied, 4,446 admitted, 1,353 enrolled. *Average high school GPA:* 3.21. *Test scores:* SAT verbal scores over 500: 75%; SAT math scores over 500: 76%; ACT scores over 18: 99%; SAT verbal scores over 600: 18%; SAT math scores over 600: 20%; ACT scores over 24: 41%; SAT verbal scores over 700: 1%; SAT math scores over 700: 1%; ACT scores over 30: 2%.

Faculty *Total:* 421, 72% full-time, 79% with terminal degrees. *Student/faculty ratio:* 20:1.

Majors Accounting; accounting related; American studies; anthropology; applied mathematics; art; atmospheric sciences; biology; business administration; business marketing and marketing management; chemistry; cognitive psychology/psycholinguistics; computer science; creative writing; criminal justice/law enforcement administration; economics; education; elementary education; English; finance; French; geochemistry; geology; German; graphic design/commercial art/illustration; history; human resources management; individual/family development; industrial arts; information sciences/systems; international economics; international relations; journalism; linguistics; management science; mass communications; mathematics; music; philosophy; philosophy and religion related; physics; political science; pre-dentistry; pre-law; pre-medicine; pre-veterinary studies; psychology; psychology related; public relations; quantitative economics; science education; secondary education; sociology; Spanish; theater arts/drama; trade/industrial education; women's studies; zoology.

Academic Programs *Special study options:* academic remediation for entering students, accelerated degree program, adult/continuing education programs, advanced placement credit, cooperative education, distance learning, double majors, English as a second language, freshman honors college, honors programs, independent study, internships, part-time degree program, services for LD students, student-designed majors, study abroad, summer session for credit. *Unusual degree programs:* 3-2 engineering with Clarkson University, Case Western Reserve University, State University of New York at Binghamton.

Library Penfield Library plus 1 other with 453,390 titles, 1,802 serial subscriptions, 36,749 audiovisual materials, an OPAC, a Web page.

Computers on Campus 600 computers available on campus for general student use. A campuswide network can be accessed from student residence rooms and from off campus. Internet access, online (class) registration, at least one staffed computer lab available.

Student Life *Housing:* on-campus residence required through sophomore year. *Options:* coed, disabled students. *Activities and Organizations:* drama/theater group, student-run newspaper, radio and television station, choral group, club/intramural sports, student radio/television stations, outing/recreation club, student government, ski club, national fraternities, national sororities. *Campus security:*

State University of New York at Oswego (continued)
24-hour emergency response devices and patrols, student patrols, controlled dormitory access. *Student Services:* health clinic, personal/psychological counseling, women's center, legal services.

Athletics Member NCAA. All Division III. *Intercollegiate sports:* baseball M, basketball M/W, crew M(c)/W(c), cross-country running M/W, field hockey W, golf M/W, ice hockey M, lacrosse M/W, soccer M/W, softball W, swimming M/W, tennis M/W, track and field M/W, volleyball W, weight lifting M(c), wrestling M. *Intramural sports:* basketball M/W, equestrian sports M(c)/W(c), fencing M(c)/W(c), football M/W, golf M/W, ice hockey M, lacrosse M/W, racquetball M/W, rugby M(c)/W(c), sailing M(c)/W(c), skiing (cross-country) M/W, skiing (downhill) M/W, soccer M/W, softball M/W, swimming M/W, tennis M/W, volleyball M(c)/W, wrestling M.

Standardized Tests *Required:* SAT I or ACT (for admission).

Costs (2001–02) *Tuition:* state resident $3400 full-time, $137 per credit hour part-time; nonresident $8300 full-time, $346 per credit hour part-time. Part-time tuition and fees vary according to class time and location. *Required fees:* $760 full-time, $25 per credit hour. *Room and board:* $6696; room only: $3980. Room and board charges vary according to board plan and housing facility. *Payment plans:* installment, deferred payment.

Financial Aid Of all full-time matriculated undergraduates who enrolled in 2001, 5062 applied for aid, 3986 were judged to have need, 1458 had their need fully met. 441 Federal Work-Study jobs (averaging $833). In 2001, 964 non-need-based awards were made. *Average percent of need met:* 89%. *Average financial aid package:* $7337. *Average need-based loan:* $4273. *Average need-based gift aid:* $3016. *Average indebtedness upon graduation:* $16,468.

Applying *Options:* electronic application, early admission, early decision, deferred entrance. *Application fee:* $30. *Required:* high school transcript. *Required for some:* letters of recommendation. *Recommended:* essay or personal statement, interview. *Application deadline:* rolling (freshmen), rolling (transfers). *Early decision:* 11/15. *Notification:* 1/15 (freshmen), 12/15 (early decision).

Admissions Contact State University of New York at Oswego, 7060 State Route 104, Oswego, NY 13126. *Phone:* 315-312-2250. *Fax:* 315-312-3260. *E-mail:* admiss@oswego.edu.

STATE UNIVERSITY OF NEW YORK COLLEGE AT BROCKPORT

Brockport, New York

- **State-supported** comprehensive, founded 1867, part of State University of New York System
- **Calendar** semesters
- **Degrees** bachelor's, master's, and postbachelor's certificates
- **Small-town** 435-acre campus with easy access to Rochester
- **Endowment** $2.8 million
- **Coed,** 6,764 undergraduate students, 85% full-time, 58% women, 42% men
- **Moderately difficult** entrance level, 54% of applicants were admitted

Undergraduates 5,777 full-time, 987 part-time. Students come from 35 states and territories, 21 other countries, 2% are from out of state, 6% African American, 1% Asian American or Pacific Islander, 2% Hispanic American, 0.4% Native American, 0.7% international, 14% transferred in, 37% live on campus. *Retention:* 76% of 2001 full-time freshmen returned.

Freshmen *Admission:* 6,947 applied, 3,782 admitted, 1,086 enrolled. *Average high school GPA:* 2.8. *Test scores:* SAT verbal scores over 500: 61%; SAT math scores over 500: 66%; ACT scores over 18: 94%; SAT verbal scores over 600: 13%; SAT math scores over 600: 17%; ACT scores over 24: 34%; SAT verbal scores over 700: 1%; SAT math scores over 700: 1%; ACT scores over 30: 2%.

Faculty *Total:* 620, 52% full-time, 46% with terminal degrees. *Student/faculty ratio:* 19:1.

Majors Accounting; African-American studies; African studies; alcohol/drug abuse counseling; anthropology; art; arts management; Asian studies; astronomy; athletic training/sports medicine; atmospheric sciences; biochemistry; biological technology; biology; broadcast journalism; business administration; business marketing and marketing management; Canadian studies; cell biology; ceramic arts; chemistry; computer science; corrections; creative writing; criminal justice/law enforcement administration; criminology; dance; drawing; earth sciences; education; elementary education; English; environmental biology; environmental science; European studies; exercise sciences; film studies; finance; fine/studio arts; French; geology; gerontology; health education; health science; history; interdisciplinary studies; international business; international relations; journalism; Judaic studies; Latin American studies; literature; mass communications; mathematics; medical technology; metal/jewelry arts; molecular biology; nursing; painting; philosophy; physical education; physics; political science; pre-dentistry; pre-law; pre-medicine; pre-veterinary studies; psychology; public relations; radio/television broadcasting; recreation/leisure studies; sculpture; secondary education; social work; sociology; Spanish; speech/rhetorical studies; sport/fitness administration; theater arts/drama; water resources; women's studies.

Academic Programs *Special study options:* academic remediation for entering students, accelerated degree program, advanced placement credit, cooperative education, distance learning, double majors, freshman honors college, honors programs, independent study, internships, off-campus study, part-time degree program, services for LD students, student-designed majors, study abroad, summer session for credit. *ROTC:* Army (b), Navy (c), Air Force (c). *Unusual degree programs:* 3-2 engineering with State University of New York at Buffalo, Clarkson University, Syracuse University, Case Western Reserve University, State University of New York at Binghamton; environmental science with State University of New York College of Environmental Science and Forestry.

Library Drake Memorial Library with 551,072 titles, 1,485 serial subscriptions, 37,292 audiovisual materials, an OPAC, a Web page.

Computers on Campus 700 computers available on campus for general student use. A campuswide network can be accessed from student residence rooms and from off campus. Internet access, at least one staffed computer lab available.

Student Life *Housing:* on-campus residence required for freshman year. *Options:* coed, disabled students. *Activities and Organizations:* drama/theater group, student-run newspaper, radio and television station, choral group, fine arts clubs, criminal justice club, communication club, student radio station, sports clubs, national fraternities, national sororities. *Campus security:* 24-hour emergency response devices and patrols, student patrols, late-night transport/escort service, controlled dormitory access. *Student Services:* health clinic, personal/psychological counseling, women's center, legal services.

Athletics Member NCAA. All Division III. *Intercollegiate sports:* baseball M, basketball M/W, cross-country running M/W, field hockey W, football M, golf W, gymnastics W, ice hockey M, lacrosse M/W, soccer M/W, softball W, swimming M/W, tennis W, track and field M/W, volleyball W, wrestling M. *Intramural sports:* badminton M/W, basketball M/W, cross-country running M/W, football M, golf M, ice hockey M/W, lacrosse M/W, racquetball M/W, rugby M/W, skiing (downhill) M/W, soccer M/W, softball M/W, squash M/W, swimming M/W, tennis M/W, track and field M/W, volleyball M/W, water polo M/W, weight lifting M/W, wrestling M/W.

Standardized Tests *Required:* SAT I or ACT (for admission).

Costs (2001–02) *Tuition:* state resident $3400 full-time, $137 per credit hour part-time; nonresident $8300 full-time, $346 per credit hour part-time. Full-time tuition and fees vary according to course load. Part-time tuition and fees vary according to course load. *Required fees:* $727 full-time, $31 per credit hour. *Room and board:* $6140; room only: $3740. Room and board charges vary according to board plan and housing facility. *Payment plans:* installment, deferred payment. *Waivers:* senior citizens and employees or children of employees.

Financial Aid Of all full-time matriculated undergraduates who enrolled in 2001, 4643 applied for aid, 3692 were judged to have need, 1743 had their need fully met. 1842 State and other part-time jobs. In 2001, 2003 non-need-based awards were made. *Average percent of need met:* 85%. *Average financial aid package:* $7228. *Average need-based loan:* $3380. *Average need-based gift aid:* $2725. *Average indebtedness upon graduation:* $16,451.

Applying *Options:* electronic application, deferred entrance. *Application fee:* $40. *Required:* high school transcript. *Required for some:* essay or personal statement, letters of recommendation, interview. *Recommended:* minimum 2.5 GPA, letters of recommendation. *Application deadline:* rolling (freshmen), rolling (transfers). *Notification:* continuous (freshmen).

Admissions Contact Mr. Bernard S. Valento, Associate Director of Undergraduate Admissions, State University of New York College at Brockport, 350 New Campus Drive, Brockport, NY 14420-2997. *Phone:* 585-395-5059 Ext. 5059. *Toll-free phone:* 800-382-8447. *Fax:* 585-395-5452. *E-mail:* admit@brockport.edu.

STATE UNIVERSITY OF NEW YORK COLLEGE AT BUFFALO

Buffalo, New York

- **State-supported** comprehensive, founded 1867, part of State University of New York System
- **Calendar** semesters
- **Degrees** bachelor's, master's, and post-master's certificates
- **Urban** 115-acre campus
- **Endowment** $8.7 million
- **Coed,** 9,590 undergraduate students, 82% full-time, 60% women, 40% men
- **Moderately difficult** entrance level, 57% of applicants were admitted

Undergraduates 7,848 full-time, 1,742 part-time. Students come from 4 states and territories, 8 other countries, 1% are from out of state, 11% African American, 1% Asian American or Pacific Islander, 4% Hispanic American, 0.6% Native American, 0.6% international, 10% transferred in, 17% live on campus. *Retention:* 77% of 2001 full-time freshmen returned.

Freshmen *Admission:* 7,089 applied, 4,018 admitted, 1,354 enrolled. *Average high school GPA:* 2.95. *Test scores:* SAT verbal scores over 500: 45%; SAT math scores over 500: 40%; SAT verbal scores over 600: 8%; SAT math scores over 600: 5%; SAT verbal scores over 700: 1%.

Faculty *Total:* 716, 57% full-time. *Student/faculty ratio:* 18:1.

Majors Anthropology; applied art; art; art education; art history; biology; broadcast journalism; business administration; business education; chemistry; city/community/regional planning; criminal justice/law enforcement administration; dietetics; drawing; early childhood education; earth sciences; economics; electrical/electronic engineering technology; elementary education; engineering; engineering technology; English; exercise sciences; fashion design/illustration; fashion merchandising; fine/studio arts; food products retailing; forensic technology; French; geography; geology; graphic design/commercial art/illustration; history; hotel and restaurant management; humanities; industrial arts; industrial technology; information sciences/systems; journalism; mass communications; mathematics; mechanical engineering technology; music; philosophy; photography; physics; political science; pre-dentistry; pre-law; pre-medicine; pre-veterinary studies; printmaking; psychology; public relations; radio/television broadcasting; science education; sculpture; secondary education; social work; sociology; Spanish; special education; speech-language pathology/audiology; theater arts/drama; trade/industrial education; urban studies.

Academic Programs *Special study options:* academic remediation for entering students, adult/continuing education programs, advanced placement credit, distance learning, double majors, English as a second language, freshman honors college, honors programs, independent study, internships, off-campus study, part-time degree program, services for LD students, study abroad, summer session for credit. *ROTC:* Army (c). *Unusual degree programs:* 3-2 engineering with State University of New York at Binghamton, Clarkson University, State University of New York at Buffalo.

Library E. H. Butler Library with 359,433 titles, 3,033 serial subscriptions, 17,824 audiovisual materials, an OPAC, a Web page.

Computers on Campus 900 computers available on campus for general student use. A campuswide network can be accessed from student residence rooms and from off campus. Internet access, at least one staffed computer lab available.

Student Life *Housing:* on-campus residence required through sophomore year. *Options:* coed. *Activities and Organizations:* drama/theater group, student-run newspaper, radio station, choral group, United Student Government, African-American Student Organization, Caribbean Student Organization, The Record, WBNY Radio, national fraternities, national sororities. *Campus security:* 24-hour emergency response devices and patrols, student patrols, late-night transport/escort service, controlled dormitory access. *Student Services:* health clinic, personal/psychological counseling, women's center, legal services.

Athletics Member NCAA. All Division III. *Intercollegiate sports:* baseball M(c), basketball M/W, bowling M(c)/W(c), cross-country running M/W, fencing M(c), football M, ice hockey M/W, lacrosse M(c)/W, rugby M(c), skiing (cross-country) M(c)/W(c), skiing (downhill) M(c)/W(c), soccer M/W, softball W, swimming M/W, tennis W, track and field M/W, volleyball M(c)/W. *Intramural sports:* basketball M, football M, racquetball M/W, softball M/W, volleyball M/W.

Standardized Tests *Required:* SAT I or ACT (for admission).

Costs (2001–02) *Tuition:* state resident $3400 full-time, $137 per semester hour part-time; nonresident $8300 full-time, $346 per semester hour part-time. *Required fees:* $629 full-time, $25 per credit hour. *Room and board:* $5484; room only: $3486. Room and board charges vary according to board plan, housing facility, and student level. *Payment plan:* installment. *Waivers:* employees or children of employees.

Financial Aid Of all full-time matriculated undergraduates who enrolled in 2001, 6439 applied for aid, 5241 were judged to have need, 903 had their need fully met. *Average percent of need met:* 62%. *Average financial aid package:* $3037. *Average need-based loan:* $1558. *Average need-based gift aid:* $889. *Average indebtedness upon graduation:* $13,430.

Applying *Options:* early admission, early decision, deferred entrance. *Application fee:* $30. *Required:* high school transcript, minimum 3.0 GPA. *Required for some:* essay or personal statement, letters of recommendation, interview. *Application deadline:* rolling (freshmen), rolling (transfers). *Early decision:* 11/15. *Notification:* continuous (freshmen), 12/15 (early decision).

Admissions Contact Ms. Lesa Loritts, Director of Admissions, State University of New York College at Buffalo, 1300 Elmwood Avenue, Buffalo, NY 14222-1095. *Phone:* 716-878-5519. *Fax:* 716-878-6100. *E-mail:* admissio@buffalostate.edu.

State University of New York College at Cortland

Cortland, New York

- **State-supported** comprehensive, founded 1868, part of State University of New York System
- **Calendar** semesters
- **Degrees** bachelor's, master's, post-master's, and postbachelor's certificates
- **Small-town** 191-acre campus with easy access to Syracuse
- **Coed,** 5,850 undergraduate students, 95% full-time, 59% women, 41% men
- **Moderately difficult** entrance level, 55% of applicants were admitted

Undergraduates 5,567 full-time, 283 part-time. 2% are from out of state, 2% African American, 0.8% Asian American or Pacific Islander, 3% Hispanic American, 0.3% Native American, 0.1% international, 11% transferred in, 55% live on campus.

Freshmen *Admission:* 8,341 applied, 4,613 admitted, 1,194 enrolled. *Average high school GPA:* 3.20. *Test scores:* SAT verbal scores over 500: 61%; SAT math scores over 500: 72%; ACT scores over 18: 98%; SAT verbal scores over 600: 9%; SAT math scores over 600: 13%; ACT scores over 24: 40%; ACT scores over 30: 1%.

Faculty *Total:* 479, 52% full-time. *Student/faculty ratio:* 16:1.

Majors African-American studies; anthropology; art history; athletic training/sports medicine; biology; chemistry; communications; early childhood education; earth sciences; economics; education of the speech impaired; elementary education; English; environmental biology; film studies; fine/studio arts; French; geochemistry; geography; geology; German; health education; health science; history; international relations; liberal arts and sciences/liberal studies; mathematics; middle school education; philosophy; physical education; physics; political science; pre-dentistry; pre-law; pre-medicine; psychology; reading education; recreational therapy; recreation/leisure facilities management; recreation/leisure studies; science education; secondary education; social work; sociology; Spanish; speech-language pathology/audiology; speech/rhetorical studies.

Academic Programs *Special study options:* academic remediation for entering students, adult/continuing education programs, advanced placement credit, cooperative education, distance learning, double majors, honors programs, independent study, internships, off-campus study, part-time degree program, services for LD students, student-designed majors, study abroad, summer session for credit. *ROTC:* Army (c), Air Force (c). *Unusual degree programs:* 3-2 engineering with State University of New York at Buffalo, State University of New York at Stony Brook, Alfred University, Clarkson University, State University of New York at Binghamton, Case Western Reserve University; forestry with Duke University, State University of New York College of Environmental Science and Forestry.

Library Memorial Library with 396,222 titles, 2,744 serial subscriptions, 4,557 audiovisual materials, an OPAC, a Web page.

Computers on Campus 832 computers available on campus for general student use. A campuswide network can be accessed from student residence rooms and from off campus. At least one staffed computer lab available.

Student Life *Housing:* on-campus residence required through sophomore year. *Options:* coed. *Activities and Organizations:* drama/theater group, student-run newspaper, radio and television station, choral group, national fraternities, national sororities. *Campus security:* 24-hour emergency response devices and patrols, late-night transport/escort service. *Student Services:* health clinic, personal/psychological counseling, women's center, legal services.

Athletics Member NCAA. All Division III. *Intercollegiate sports:* baseball M, basketball M/W, cross-country running M/W, field hockey W, football M/W(c), golf W, gymnastics W, ice hockey M/W(c), lacrosse M/W, racquetball M(c)/W(c), rugby M(c)/W(c), soccer M/W, softball W, swimming M/W, tennis W, track and field M/W, volleyball M(c)/W, wrestling M. *Intramural sports:* archery M/W, badminton M/W, baseball M, basketball M/W, bowling M/W, cross-country running M/W, fencing M/W, field hockey W, football M/W, golf M/W, gymnastics W, ice hockey M, lacrosse M/W, racquetball M/W, rugby M/W, skiing (cross-country) M/W, skiing (downhill) M/W, soccer M/W, softball M/W, squash M/W, swimming M/W, table tennis M/W, tennis M/W, track and field M/W, volleyball M/W, weight lifting M/W, wrestling M.

Standardized Tests *Required:* SAT I or ACT (for admission).

Costs (2001–02) *Tuition:* state resident $3400 full-time, $168 per credit part-time; nonresident $8300 full-time, $377 per credit part-time. Part-time tuition and fees vary according to course load. *Required fees:* $774 full-time, $14 per credit. *Room and board:* $6390. Room and board charges vary according to board plan. *Payment plan:* installment. *Waivers:* employees or children of employees.

Financial Aid Of all full-time matriculated undergraduates who enrolled in 2001, 4500 applied for aid, 3335 were judged to have need, 772 had their need fully met. In 2001, 1079 non-need-based awards were made. *Average percent of*

State University of New York College at Cortland (continued)
need met: 77%. *Average financial aid package:* $7329. *Average need-based loan:* $3378. *Average need-based gift aid:* $3329. *Financial aid deadline:* 4/1.

Applying *Options:* electronic application, early admission, early decision, deferred entrance. *Application fee:* $30. *Required:* essay or personal statement, high school transcript, minimum 2.3 GPA, 1 letter of recommendation. *Recommended:* minimum 3.0 GPA, 3 letters of recommendation, interview. *Early decision:* 11/15. *Notification:* 12/15 (early decision).

Admissions Contact Mr. Gradon Avery, Director of Admission, State University of New York College at Cortland, PO Box 2000, Cortland, NY 13045. *Phone:* 607-753-4711. *Fax:* 607-753-5998. *E-mail:* admssn_info@snycorva.cortland.edu.

STATE UNIVERSITY OF NEW YORK COLLEGE AT FREDONIA

Fredonia, New York

- **State-supported** comprehensive, founded 1826, part of State University of New York System
- **Calendar** semesters
- **Degrees** bachelor's and master's
- **Small-town** 266-acre campus with easy access to Buffalo
- **Endowment** $10.0 million
- **Coed,** 4,907 undergraduate students, 94% full-time, 59% women, 41% men
- **Moderately difficult** entrance level, 60% of applicants were admitted

Undergraduates 4,634 full-time, 273 part-time. Students come from 27 states and territories, 9 other countries, 2% are from out of state, 1% African American, 1% Asian American or Pacific Islander, 2% Hispanic American, 0.8% Native American, 0.4% international, 8% transferred in, 53% live on campus. *Retention:* 81% of 2001 full-time freshmen returned.

Freshmen *Admission:* 5,412 applied, 3,227 admitted, 926 enrolled. *Average high school GPA:* 3.32. *Test scores:* SAT verbal scores over 500: 83%; SAT math scores over 500: 83%; ACT scores over 18: 100%; SAT verbal scores over 600: 25%; SAT math scores over 600: 22%; ACT scores over 24: 46%; SAT verbal scores over 700: 4%; SAT math scores over 700: 2%; ACT scores over 30: 5%.

Faculty *Total:* 428, 61% full-time, 56% with terminal degrees. *Student/faculty ratio:* 19:1.

Majors Accounting; American studies; applied art; art; art history; arts management; audio engineering; biochemistry; biological/physical sciences; biological technology; biology; biomedical science; broadcast journalism; business administration; business marketing and marketing management; chemistry; communication disorders; computer graphics; computer science; criminal justice/law enforcement administration; dance; drawing; early childhood education; earth sciences; economics; education; elementary education; English; environmental science; film studies; finance; fine/studio arts; French; geochemistry; geology; geophysics/seismology; gerontology; graphic design/commercial art/illustration; health services administration; history; information sciences/systems; interdisciplinary studies; labor/personnel relations; legal studies; liberal arts and sciences/liberal studies; mass communications; mathematics; medical technology; multimedia; music; music business management/merchandising; music history; music (piano and organ performance); music teacher education; music therapy; music (voice and choral/opera performance); philosophy; physics; political science; pre-law; pre-medicine; pre-veterinary studies; psychology; radio/television broadcasting; science education; secondary education; social work; sociology; Spanish; speech-language pathology/audiology; speech therapy; stringed instruments; theater arts/drama; wind/percussion instruments; women's studies.

Academic Programs *Special study options:* accelerated degree program, adult/continuing education programs, advanced placement credit, distance learning, double majors, honors programs, independent study, internships, off-campus study, part-time degree program, services for LD students, student-designed majors, study abroad, summer session for credit. *ROTC:* Army (c). *Unusual degree programs:* 3-2 business administration with Clarkson University, State University of New York at Binghamton, State University of New York at Buffalo, University of Pittsburgh; engineering with Clarkson University, State University of New York at Buffalo; agriculture with Cornell University.

Library Reed Library with 396,000 titles, 2,270 serial subscriptions, 17,607 audiovisual materials, an OPAC, a Web page.

Computers on Campus 500 computers available on campus for general student use. A campuswide network can be accessed from student residence rooms and from off campus. At least one staffed computer lab available.

Student Life *Housing:* on-campus residence required through sophomore year. *Options:* coed, men-only, women-only. *Activities and Organizations:* drama/theater group, student-run newspaper, radio and television station, choral group, Student Association, Undergraduate Alumni Council, communication club, Greek organizations, ethnic organizations, national fraternities, national sororities. *Campus security:* 24-hour emergency response devices and patrols, late-night transport/escort service, controlled dormitory access. *Student Services:* health clinic, personal/psychological counseling, legal services.

Athletics Member NCAA. All Division III. *Intercollegiate sports:* baseball M, basketball M/W, cross-country running M/W, ice hockey M, lacrosse W, soccer M/W, softball W, tennis M/W, track and field M/W, volleyball W. *Intramural sports:* basketball M/W, cross-country running M/W, field hockey W, football M, golf M, lacrosse M, racquetball M/W, rugby M/W, skiing (cross-country) M/W, skiing (downhill) M/W, soccer M/W, softball W, squash M/W, table tennis M/W, tennis M/W, volleyball M/W.

Standardized Tests *Required:* SAT I or ACT (for admission).

Costs (2002–03) *Tuition:* state resident $3400 full-time, $137 per credit hour part-time; nonresident $9300 full-time, $346 per credit hour part-time. *Required fees:* $975 full-time, $40 per credit hour. *Room and board:* $5900; room only: $3800. Room and board charges vary according to board plan and housing facility. *Payment plan:* installment.

Financial Aid Of all full-time matriculated undergraduates who enrolled in 2001, 3723 applied for aid, 2864 were judged to have need, 2517 had their need fully met. 315 Federal Work-Study jobs (averaging $1320). *Average percent of need met:* 78%. *Average financial aid package:* $6464. *Average need-based loan:* $3851. *Average need-based gift aid:* $2703. *Average indebtedness upon graduation:* $12,139.

Applying *Options:* electronic application, early admission, early decision, deferred entrance. *Application fee:* $30. *Required:* high school transcript, minimum 2.5 GPA. *Required for some:* essay or personal statement, interview, audition for music and theater programs, portfolio for art programs, essay for media arts program. *Recommended:* letters of recommendation. *Application deadline:* rolling (freshmen), rolling (transfers). *Early decision:* 11/1. *Notification:* continuous (freshmen), 12/15 (early decision).

Admissions Contact Mr. J. Denis Bolton, Director of Admissions, State University of New York College at Fredonia, Fredonia, NY 14063-1136. *Phone:* 716-673-3251. *Toll-free phone:* 800-252-1212. *Fax:* 716-673-3249. *E-mail:* admissionsinq@fredonia.edu.

STATE UNIVERSITY OF NEW YORK COLLEGE AT GENESEO

Geneseo, New York

- **State-supported** comprehensive, founded 1871, part of State University of New York System
- **Calendar** semesters
- **Degrees** bachelor's and master's
- **Small-town** 220-acre campus with easy access to Rochester
- **Endowment** $5.6 million
- **Coed,** 5,371 undergraduate students, 98% full-time, 65% women, 35% men
- **Very difficult** entrance level, 52% of applicants were admitted

Undergraduates 5,245 full-time, 126 part-time. Students come from 19 states and territories, 19 other countries, 1% are from out of state, 2% African American, 5% Asian American or Pacific Islander, 3% Hispanic American, 0.2% Native American, 0.8% international, 6% transferred in, 54% live on campus. *Retention:* 91% of 2001 full-time freshmen returned.

Freshmen *Admission:* 7,794 applied, 4,044 admitted, 1,145 enrolled. *Average high school GPA:* 3.62. *Test scores:* SAT verbal scores over 500: 96%; SAT math scores over 500: 97%; ACT scores over 18: 100%; SAT verbal scores over 600: 55%; SAT math scores over 600: 60%; ACT scores over 24: 81%; SAT verbal scores over 700: 7%; SAT math scores over 700: 7%; ACT scores over 30: 10%.

Faculty *Total:* 340, 74% full-time, 74% with terminal degrees. *Student/faculty ratio:* 19:1.

Majors Accounting; African-American studies; American studies; anthropology; art; art history; biochemistry; biology; biophysics; business administration; chemistry; communications; comparative literature; computer science; early childhood education; economics; education; elementary education; English; fine/studio arts; French; geochemistry; geography; geology; geophysics/seismology; history; international relations; mathematics; music; natural sciences; philosophy; physics; political science; pre-dentistry; pre-law; pre-medicine; pre-veterinary studies; psychology; sociology; Spanish; special education; speech-language pathology/audiology; speech therapy; theater arts/drama; visual and performing arts related.

Academic Programs *Special study options:* academic remediation for entering students, advanced placement credit, double majors, English as a second language, honors programs, independent study, internships, off-campus study, part-time degree program, services for LD students, study abroad, summer session for credit. *ROTC:* Army (c), Air Force (c). *Unusual degree programs:* 3-2 business administration with Pace University, Syracuse University, State University of New York at Buffalo; engineering with 9 schools including Columbia University, Case Western Reserve University, Alfred University, Clarkson University, Syracuse University; forestry with State University of New York College of Environmental Science and Forestry.

Library Milne Library plus 1 other with 502,537 titles, 2,284 serial subscriptions, 22,641 audiovisual materials, an OPAC, a Web page.

Computers on Campus 800 computers available on campus for general student use. A campuswide network can be accessed from student residence rooms and from off campus. Internet access, online (class) registration, at least one staffed computer lab available.

Student Life *Housing:* on-campus residence required for freshman year. *Options:* coed. *Activities and Organizations:* drama/theater group, student-run newspaper, radio and television station, choral group, national fraternities, national sororities. *Campus security:* 24-hour emergency response devices and patrols, student patrols, late-night transport/escort service, controlled dormitory access. *Student Services:* health clinic, personal/psychological counseling, women's center, legal services.

Athletics Member NCAA. All Division III. *Intercollegiate sports:* basketball M/W, crew M(c)/W(c), cross-country running M/W, equestrian sports M(c)/W(c), field hockey W, ice hockey M, lacrosse M/W, racquetball M(c)/W(c), rugby M(c)/W(c), sailing M(c)/W(c), soccer M/W, softball W, squash M(c)/W(c), swimming M/W, tennis W, track and field M/W, volleyball M/W. *Intramural sports:* badminton M/W, basketball M/W, cross-country running M/W, football M/W, golf M/W, ice hockey M/W, racquetball M/W, rugby M/W, skiing (cross-country) M/W, skiing (downhill) M/W, soccer M/W, softball M/W, squash M/W, table tennis M/W, tennis M/W, volleyball M/W, water polo M/W.

Standardized Tests *Required:* SAT I or ACT (for admission).

Costs (2001–02) *Tuition:* state resident $3400 full-time, $137 per credit hour part-time; nonresident $8300 full-time, $346 per credit hour part-time. Part-time tuition and fees vary according to course load. *Required fees:* $910 full-time, $38 per credit hour. *Room and board:* $5660; room only: $3260. Room and board charges vary according to board plan and housing facility. *Payment plans:* installment, deferred payment. *Waivers:* senior citizens.

Financial Aid Of all full-time matriculated undergraduates who enrolled in 2001, 3875 applied for aid, 2464 were judged to have need, 2095 had their need fully met. 430 Federal Work-Study jobs (averaging $1177). In 2001, 1059 non-need-based awards were made. *Average percent of need met:* 85%. *Average financial aid package:* $7421. *Average need-based loan:* $3495. *Average need-based gift aid:* $994. *Average indebtedness upon graduation:* $15,000.

Applying *Options:* electronic application, early admission, early decision, deferred entrance. *Application fee:* $30. *Required:* essay or personal statement, high school transcript. *Recommended:* letters of recommendation, interview. *Application deadlines:* 2/15 (freshmen), 1/15 (transfers). *Early decision:* 11/15. *Notification:* continuous until 3/15 (freshmen), 12/15 (early decision).

Admissions Contact Kris Shay, Associate Director of Admissions, State University of New York College at Geneseo, 1 College Circle, Geneseo, NY 14454-1401. *Phone:* 585-245-5571. *Toll-free phone:* 866-245-5211. *Fax:* 585-245-5550. *E-mail:* admissions@geneseo.edu.

STATE UNIVERSITY OF NEW YORK COLLEGE AT OLD WESTBURY

Old Westbury, New York

- **State-supported** comprehensive, founded 1965, part of State University of New York System
- **Calendar** semesters
- **Degree** certificates and bachelor's
- **Suburban** 605-acre campus with easy access to New York City
- **Coed,** 3,076 undergraduate students, 76% full-time, 60% women, 40% men
- **Minimally difficult** entrance level, 50% of applicants were admitted

SUNY Old Westbury has exchange programs with colleges and universities in the Far East, South Africa, and Europe. SUNY tuition, room and board costs, and fees are paid to the College at Old Westbury. Travel is the only additional expense. Exchange faculty members from China and Korea are regularly on campus.

Undergraduates Students come from 6 states and territories, 17 other countries, 1% are from out of state, 30% African American, 8% Asian American or Pacific Islander, 15% Hispanic American, 0.2% Native American, 1% international, 25% live on campus. *Retention:* 70% of 2001 full-time freshmen returned.

Freshmen *Admission:* 2,783 applied, 1,402 admitted. *Test scores:* SAT verbal scores over 500: 16%; SAT math scores over 500: 23%; SAT verbal scores over 600: 2%; SAT math scores over 600: 4%.

Faculty *Total:* 228, 53% full-time. *Student/faculty ratio:* 22:1.

Majors Accounting; American studies; art; bilingual/bicultural education; biology; business administration; business marketing and marketing management; chemistry; communications; criminology; elementary education; finance; humanities; information sciences/systems; labor/personnel relations; literature; mathematics; middle school education; philosophy; psychology; religious studies; science education; secondary education; social sciences; sociology; Spanish; special education.

Academic Programs *Special study options:* academic remediation for entering students, advanced placement credit, double majors, English as a second language, independent study, internships, off-campus study, part-time degree program, services for LD students, study abroad, summer session for credit. *ROTC:* Army (c), Air Force (c). *Unusual degree programs:* engineering with State University of New York at Stony Brook.

Library SUNY College at Old Westbury Library with 216,289 titles, 850 serial subscriptions, an OPAC, a Web page.

Computers on Campus 245 computers available on campus for general student use. Internet access, at least one staffed computer lab available.

Student Life *Housing Options:* coed. *Activities and Organizations:* student-run newspaper, radio station, choral group, Alianza Latina, Caribbean Student Association, Asian Club, Finance/Accounting Society, national fraternities, national sororities. *Campus security:* 24-hour emergency response devices and patrols, student patrols, late-night transport/escort service, controlled dormitory access. *Student Services:* health clinic, personal/psychological counseling, women's center.

Athletics Member NCAA. All Division III. *Intercollegiate sports:* baseball M, basketball M/W, cross-country running M/W, soccer M, softball W, tennis M/W, volleyball W.

Standardized Tests *Required:* SAT I or ACT (for admission).

Costs (2001–02) *One-time required fee:* $100. *Tuition:* state resident $3400 full-time, $138 per credit part-time; nonresident $8300 full-time, $346 per credit part-time. Part-time tuition and fees vary according to course load. *Required fees:* $585 full-time. *Room and board:* $5769; room only: $3547. Room and board charges vary according to board plan and housing facility. *Payment plan:* installment. *Waivers:* senior citizens.

Financial Aid Of all full-time matriculated undergraduates who enrolled in 2001, 1650 applied for aid, 1510 were judged to have need, 333 had their need fully met. 251 Federal Work-Study jobs (averaging $931). 82 State and other part-time jobs (averaging $973). In 2001, 7 non-need-based awards were made. *Average percent of need met:* 55%. *Average financial aid package:* $6072. *Average need-based loan:* $2368. *Average need-based gift aid:* $4270. *Average non-need based aid:* $4764. *Average indebtedness upon graduation:* $11,051.

Applying *Options:* electronic application, early admission, early action, deferred entrance. *Application fee:* $30. *Required:* high school transcript. *Required for some:* essay or personal statement, 2 letters of recommendation, interview. *Application deadlines:* rolling (freshmen), 12/15 (transfers). *Notification:* continuous (freshmen), 12/15 (early action).

Admissions Contact Ms. Mary Marquez Bell, Vice President, State University of New York College at Old Westbury, PO Box 307, Old Westbury, NY 11568. *Phone:* 516-876-3073. *Fax:* 516-876-3307.

STATE UNIVERSITY OF NEW YORK COLLEGE AT ONEONTA

Oneonta, New York

- **State-supported** comprehensive, founded 1889, part of State University of New York System
- **Calendar** semesters
- **Degrees** bachelor's, master's, and post-master's certificates
- **Small-town** 250-acre campus
- **Endowment** $15.9 million
- **Coed,** 5,458 undergraduate students, 96% full-time, 60% women, 40% men
- **Moderately difficult** entrance level, 52% of applicants were admitted

The College at Oneonta is a comprehensive college with studies that include the arts and sciences, elementary and secondary education, business, accounting, computer science, music industry, computer art, and prelaw as well as premedicine. An exceptional library, outstanding campuswide computing facilities, and a distinctive student center for volunteering enhance students' intellectual and personal development in a safe, scenic, and convenient campus environment.

State University of New York College at Oneonta (continued)

Undergraduates 5,241 full-time, 217 part-time. Students come from 27 states and territories, 23 other countries, 3% are from out of state, 3% African American, 2% Asian American or Pacific Islander, 4% Hispanic American, 0.2% Native American, 1% international, 11% transferred in, 58% live on campus. *Retention:* 72% of 2001 full-time freshmen returned.

Freshmen *Admission:* 9,286 applied, 4,826 admitted, 1,144 enrolled. *Average high school GPA:* 3.08. *Test scores:* SAT verbal scores over 500: 69%; SAT math scores over 500: 74%; ACT scores over 18: 96%; SAT verbal scores over 600: 13%; SAT math scores over 600: 14%; ACT scores over 24: 30%; SAT verbal scores over 700: 1%; SAT math scores over 700: 1%.

Faculty *Total:* 415, 61% full-time, 52% with terminal degrees. *Student/faculty ratio:* 18:1.

Majors Accounting; African-American studies; anthropology; art; art history; atmospheric sciences; biological technology; biology; business economics; cartography; chemistry; child care/development; computer graphics; computer science; consumer services; dietetics; earth sciences; economics; education; elementary education; engineering science; English; environmental science; fashion merchandising; fine/studio arts; French; geography; geology; gerontology; Hispanic-American studies; history; home economics; home economics education; human ecology; institutional food services; interdisciplinary studies; international relations; liberal arts and sciences/liberal studies; mass communications; mathematical statistics; mathematics; music; music business management/merchandising; ophthalmic/optometric services; philosophy; physics; political science; pre-dentistry; pre-law; pre-medicine; pre-veterinary studies; psychology; science education; secondary education; sociology; Spanish; speech/rhetorical studies; theater arts/drama; water resources.

Academic Programs *Special study options:* academic remediation for entering students, adult/continuing education programs, advanced placement credit, distance learning, double majors, English as a second language, honors programs, independent study, internships, off-campus study, part-time degree program, services for LD students, study abroad, summer session for credit. *Unusual degree programs:* 3-2 business administration with State University of New York at Binghamton, University of Rochester; engineering with Georgia Institute of Technology, State University of New York at Buffalo, Clarkson University; forestry with State University of New York College of Environmental Science and Forestry; nursing with Johns Hopkins University; accounting with State University of New York at Binghamton, fashion with American Intercontinental University in London.

Library Milne Library with 546,770 titles, 2,221 serial subscriptions, 33,865 audiovisual materials, an OPAC, a Web page.

Computers on Campus 525 computers available on campus for general student use. A campuswide network can be accessed from student residence rooms and from off campus. Internet access, online (class) registration, at least one staffed computer lab available.

Student Life *Housing:* on-campus residence required through sophomore year. *Options:* coed. *Activities and Organizations:* drama/theater group, student-run newspaper, radio and television station, choral group, Center for Social Responsibility and Community, Mask and Hammer, Terpsichorean, student government, WONY Radio Station, national sororities. *Campus security:* 24-hour emergency response devices and patrols, late-night transport/escort service, controlled dormitory access. *Student Services:* health clinic, personal/psychological counseling, women's center.

Athletics Member NCAA. All Division III except soccer (Division I). *Intercollegiate sports:* baseball M, basketball M/W, cross-country running M/W, field hockey W, lacrosse M/W, rugby M(c)/W(c), soccer M/W, softball W, swimming M/W, tennis M/W, volleyball W, wrestling M. *Intramural sports:* badminton M/W, basketball M/W, fencing M/W, football M, golf M/W, lacrosse M, racquetball M/W, skiing (cross-country) M/W, skiing (downhill) M/W, soccer M/W, softball M, swimming M/W, tennis M/W, track and field M/W, volleyball M/W, weight lifting M/W.

Standardized Tests *Required:* SAT I or ACT (for admission).

Costs (2001–02) *Tuition:* state resident $3400 full-time, $137 per semester hour part-time; nonresident $8300 full-time, $346 per semester hour part-time. Part-time tuition and fees vary according to course load. *Required fees:* $831 full-time, $17 per semester hour. *Room and board:* $5750; room only: $3400. Room and board charges vary according to board plan and housing facility. *Payment plan:* installment. *Waivers:* employees or children of employees.

Financial Aid Of all full-time matriculated undergraduates who enrolled in 2001, 4123 applied for aid, 3189 were judged to have need, 560 had their need fully met. 380 Federal Work-Study jobs (averaging $662). 395 State and other part-time jobs (averaging $1675). *Average percent of need met:* 67%. *Average financial aid package:* $7623. *Average need-based loan:* $3914. *Average need-based gift aid:* $3213. *Average indebtedness upon graduation:* $7902.

Applying *Options:* electronic application, early admission, early decision, deferred entrance. *Application fee:* $30. *Required:* essay or personal statement, high school transcript. *Recommended:* minimum 3.0 GPA, 3 letters of recommendation. *Application deadline:* rolling (freshmen), rolling (transfers). *Early decision:* 11/1 (for plan 1), 12/1 (for plan 2). *Notification:* continuous (freshmen), 11/15 (early decision plan 1), 12/15 (early decision plan 2).

Admissions Contact Ms. Karen A. Brown, Director of Admissions, State University of New York College at Oneonta, Alumni Hall 116, Oneonta, NY 13820-4015. *Phone:* 607-436-2524. *Toll-free phone:* 800-SUNY-123. *Fax:* 607-436-3074. *E-mail:* admissions@oneonta.edu.

STATE UNIVERSITY OF NEW YORK COLLEGE AT POTSDAM

Potsdam, New York

- **State-supported** comprehensive, founded 1816, part of State University of New York System
- **Calendar** semesters
- **Degrees** bachelor's and master's
- **Small-town** 240-acre campus
- **Endowment** $10.8 million
- **Coed,** 3,475 undergraduate students, 95% full-time, 59% women, 41% men
- **Moderately difficult** entrance level, 67% of applicants were admitted

Potsdam, the oldest liberal arts college of SUNY, has strong programs in the arts and sciences, teacher education, and the Crane School of Music. With more than 344 faculty members, the student-faculty ratio is 18:1. Within the Crane School of Music, the ratio is 10:1. Potsdam is within an easy drive of Interstates 81 and 87, Lake Placid, Ottawa, Syracuse, and Montreal. Potsdam offers more than 41 majors, including new programs in archeological studies, business administration, community health, computer and information science, criminal justice, and the business of music.

Undergraduates 3,307 full-time, 168 part-time. Students come from 17 states and territories, 10 other countries, 3% are from out of state, 2% African American, 0.7% Asian American or Pacific Islander, 2% Hispanic American, 2% Native American, 2% international, 9% transferred in, 50% live on campus. *Retention:* 75% of 2001 full-time freshmen returned.

Freshmen *Admission:* 3,397 applied, 2,291 admitted, 645 enrolled. *Average high school GPA:* 3.00. *Test scores:* SAT verbal scores over 500: 66%; SAT math scores over 500: 67%; ACT scores over 18: 98%; SAT verbal scores over 600: 23%; SAT math scores over 600: 19%; ACT scores over 24: 41%; SAT verbal scores over 700: 3%; SAT math scores over 700: 2%; ACT scores over 30: 8%.

Faculty *Total:* 346, 69% full-time, 53% with terminal degrees. *Student/faculty ratio:* 18:1.

Majors Anthropology; archaeology; art; art history; biology; biology education; business administration; business economics; ceramic arts; chemistry; chemistry education; computer/information sciences; criminal justice studies; dance; economics; education related; elementary education; English; English education; foreign languages education; French; French language education; geography; geology; history; labor/personnel relations; mathematics; mathematics education; multi/interdisciplinary studies related; music; music business management/merchandising; music (general performance); music history; music related; music teacher education; music theory and composition; painting; philosophy; photography; physical education; physics; physics education; political science; printmaking; psychology; science education; sculpture; social studies education; sociology; Spanish; Spanish language education; speech/rhetorical studies; theater arts/drama.

Academic Programs *Special study options:* adult/continuing education programs, advanced placement credit, cooperative education, distance learning, double majors, freshman honors college, honors programs, independent study, internships, off-campus study, part-time degree program, services for LD students, student-designed majors, study abroad, summer session for credit. *ROTC:* Army (c), Air Force (c). *Unusual degree programs:* 3-2 engineering with Clarkson University, State University of New York at Binghamton; management, accounting with State University of New York Institute of Technology at Utica/Rome, applied science with State University of New York College of Technology at Canton.

Library F. W. Crumb Memorial Library plus 1 other with 325,079 titles, 1,309 serial subscriptions, 19,134 audiovisual materials, an OPAC, a Web page.

Computers on Campus 400 computers available on campus for general student use. A campuswide network can be accessed from student residence rooms and from off campus that provide access to Appletalk network. Internet access, online (class) registration, at least one staffed computer lab available.

Student Life *Housing:* on-campus residence required through sophomore year. *Options:* coed, women-only, disabled students. *Activities and Organizations:* drama/theater group, student-run newspaper, radio station, choral group, national fraternities, national sororities. *Campus security:* 24-hour emergency response devices and patrols, late-night transport/escort service, controlled dormitory access, self defense education, pamphlets/posters/films. *Student Services:* health clinic, personal/psychological counseling, women's center, legal services.

Athletics Member NCAA. All Division III. *Intercollegiate sports:* basketball M/W, cross-country running M/W, equestrian sports W(c), golf M, ice hockey M, lacrosse M/W, rugby M(c)/W(c), soccer M/W, softball W, swimming M/W, tennis W, track and field M(c)/W(c), volleyball W. *Intramural sports:* badminton M/W, basketball M/W, equestrian sports M/W, racquetball M/W, skiing (cross-country) M/W, skiing (downhill) M/W, squash M/W, tennis M/W, volleyball M/W, water polo M/W.

Standardized Tests *Required:* SAT I or ACT (for admission).

Costs (2001–02) *Tuition:* state resident $3400 full-time, $137 per credit hour part-time; nonresident $8300 full-time, $346 per credit hour part-time. *Required fees:* $729 full-time, $30 per credit hour. *Room and board:* $6390; room only: $3720. Room and board charges vary according to board plan and housing facility. *Payment plan:* installment.

Financial Aid Of all full-time matriculated undergraduates who enrolled in 2001, 2799 applied for aid, 2277 were judged to have need, 1946 had their need fully met. 341 Federal Work-Study jobs (averaging $1000). In 2001, 350 non-need-based awards were made. *Average percent of need met:* 86%. *Average financial aid package:* $10,063. *Average need-based loan:* $3988. *Average need-based gift aid:* $3816. *Average non-need based aid:* $5232. *Average indebtedness upon graduation:* $19,084.

Applying *Options:* common application, electronic application, early admission, deferred entrance. *Application fee:* $30. *Required:* high school transcript, minimum 3.0 GPA. *Required for some:* essay or personal statement, audition for music program. *Recommended:* interview. *Application deadline:* rolling (freshmen), rolling (transfers). *Notification:* continuous (freshmen).

Admissions Contact Mr. Thomas Nesbitt, Director of Admissions, State University of New York College at Potsdam, Potsdam, NY 13676. *Phone:* 315-267-2180. *Toll-free phone:* 877-POTSDAM. *Fax:* 315-267-2163. *E-mail:* admissions@potsdam.edu.

STATE UNIVERSITY OF NEW YORK COLLEGE OF AGRICULTURE AND TECHNOLOGY AT COBLESKILL

Cobleskill, New York

- **State-supported** 4-year, founded 1916, part of State University of New York System
- **Calendar** semesters
- **Degrees** certificates, associate, and bachelor's
- **Rural** 750-acre campus
- **Endowment** $1.7 million
- **Coed,** 2,450 undergraduate students, 93% full-time, 44% women, 56% men
- **Moderately difficult** entrance level, 84% of applicants were admitted

Undergraduates 2,274 full-time, 176 part-time. Students come from 16 states and territories, 8 other countries, 8% are from out of state, 6% African American, 1% Asian American or Pacific Islander, 4% Hispanic American, 0.4% Native American, 2% international, 12% transferred in, 62% live on campus. *Retention:* 80% of 2001 full-time freshmen returned.

Freshmen *Admission:* 3,384 applied, 2,851 admitted, 1,034 enrolled. *Average high school GPA:* 2.37. *Test scores:* SAT verbal scores over 500: 25%; SAT math scores over 500: 30%; ACT scores over 18: 60%; SAT verbal scores over 600: 4%; SAT math scores over 600: 4%; ACT scores over 24: 9%; SAT verbal scores over 700: 1%; SAT math scores over 700: 1%.

Faculty *Total:* 169, 67% full-time, 30% with terminal degrees. *Student/faculty ratio:* 17:1.

Majors Accounting; agricultural business; agricultural engineering; agricultural mechanization; agricultural sciences; agronomy/crop science; animal sciences; biological/physical sciences; biological technology; business administration; business communications; chemical technology; computer maintenance technology; computer programming; computer science; culinary arts; dairy science; data processing technology; early childhood education; engineering technology; environmental science; equestrian studies; family/community studies; fish/game management; fishing sciences; food services technology; horticulture science; hotel and restaurant management; information sciences/systems; institutional food workers; international business; landscape architecture; landscaping management; liberal arts and sciences/liberal studies; medical laboratory technician; nursery management; ornamental horticulture; plant sciences; pre-medicine; recreation/leisure facilities management; telecommunications; tourism/travel marketing; turf management; wildlife management.

Academic Programs *Special study options:* academic remediation for entering students, adult/continuing education programs, advanced placement credit, freshman honors college, honors programs, internships, off-campus study, part-time degree program, services for LD students, study abroad, summer session for credit.

Library Jared van Wagenen Library with 86,735 titles, 313 serial subscriptions, 20,083 audiovisual materials, an OPAC, a Web page.

Computers on Campus 200 computers available on campus for general student use. A campuswide network can be accessed from student residence rooms and from off campus. Internet access, at least one staffed computer lab available.

Student Life *Housing:* on-campus residence required for freshman year. *Options:* coed, men-only, women-only. *Activities and Organizations:* drama/theater group, student-run newspaper, choral group, Orange Key, American Animal Producers Club (AAPC), Outing Club, Phi Theta Kappa, Little Theater. *Campus security:* 24-hour emergency response devices and patrols, late-night transport/escort service, controlled dormitory access, bicycle patrols. *Student Services:* health clinic, personal/psychological counseling.

Athletics Member NJCAA. *Intercollegiate sports:* baseball M, basketball M/W, cross-country running M/W, golf M/W, lacrosse M, soccer M/W, softball W, swimming M/W, tennis M/W, track and field M/W, volleyball W, wrestling M. *Intramural sports:* archery M/W, badminton M/W, basketball M/W, bowling M/W, football M/W, racquetball M/W, soccer M/W, softball M/W, table tennis M/W, tennis M/W, volleyball M/W, weight lifting M/W.

Standardized Tests *Required for some:* SAT I or ACT (for admission). *Recommended:* SAT I or ACT (for admission).

Costs (2001–02) *Tuition:* state resident $3200 full-time, $128 per credit part-time; nonresident $5000 full-time, $346 per credit part-time. Full-time tuition and fees vary according to class time and degree level. Part-time tuition and fees vary according to class time and degree level. *Required fees:* $1540 full-time, $30 per credit, $18 per term part-time. *Room and board:* $6460; room only: $3700. Room and board charges vary according to board plan and housing facility. *Payment plan:* installment. *Waivers:* employees or children of employees.

Financial Aid Of all full-time matriculated undergraduates who enrolled in 2001, 1758 applied for aid, 1375 were judged to have need, 164 had their need fully met. 160 Federal Work-Study jobs (averaging $750). *Average percent of need met:* 87%. *Average financial aid package:* $5338. *Average need-based loan:* $2563. *Average need-based gift aid:* $3394. *Average indebtedness upon graduation:* $5810. *Financial aid deadline:* 3/15.

Applying *Options:* electronic application, early admission, deferred entrance. *Application fee:* $30. *Required:* high school transcript, minimum 2.0 GPA. *Required for some:* interview. *Application deadline:* rolling (freshmen), rolling (transfers). *Notification:* continuous (freshmen).

Admissions Contact Mr. Clayton Smith, Director of Admissions, State University of New York College of Agriculture and Technology at Cobleskill, Cobleskill, NY 12043. *Phone:* 518-255-5525. *Toll-free phone:* 800-295-8988. *Fax:* 518-255-6769. *E-mail:* admwpc@cobleskill.edu.

STATE UNIVERSITY OF NEW YORK COLLEGE OF AGRICULTURE AND TECHNOLOGY AT MORRISVILLE

Morrisville, New York

- **State-supported** primarily 2-year, founded 1908, part of State University of New York System
- **Calendar** semesters
- **Degrees** certificates, associate, and bachelor's
- **Rural** 740-acre campus with easy access to Syracuse
- **Endowment** $363,621
- **Coed**
- **Minimally difficult** entrance level

Faculty *Student/faculty ratio:* 14:1.

Student Life *Campus security:* 24-hour emergency response devices and patrols, late-night transport/escort service, controlled dormitory access.

Athletics Member NJCAA.

Standardized Tests *Recommended:* SAT I and SAT II or ACT (for admission).

Costs (2001–02) *Tuition:* state resident $3200 full-time, $128 per credit hour part-time; nonresident $5000 full-time, $208 per credit hour part-time. Full-time tuition and fees vary according to degree level and student level. Part-time tuition and fees vary according to course load. *Required fees:* $1100 full-time, $25 per

State University of New York College of Agriculture and Technology at Morrisville (continued)

credit hour. *Room and board:* $6030; room only: $3270. Room and board charges vary according to board plan and housing facility.

Financial Aid Of all full-time matriculated undergraduates who enrolled in 2001, 300 Federal Work-Study jobs (averaging $1500).

Applying *Options:* electronic application, early admission, deferred entrance. *Application fee:* $30. *Required:* high school transcript. *Required for some:* essay or personal statement, letters of recommendation. *Recommended:* minimum 2.0 GPA, letters of recommendation, interview.

Admissions Contact Mr. Paul Rose, Associate Dean of Enrollment Management, State University of New York College of Agriculture and Technology at Morrisville, Box 901, Morrisville, NY 13408. *Phone:* 315-684-6046. *Toll-free phone:* 800-258-0111. *Fax:* 315-684-6116. *E-mail:* admissions@morrisville.edu.

STATE UNIVERSITY OF NEW YORK COLLEGE OF ENVIRONMENTAL SCIENCE AND FORESTRY

Syracuse, New York

- **State-supported** university, founded 1911, part of State University of New York System
- **Calendar** semesters
- **Degrees** associate, bachelor's, master's, and doctoral
- **Urban** 12-acre campus
- **Endowment** $7.0 million
- **Coed,** 1,263 undergraduate students, 88% full-time, 39% women, 61% men
- **Very difficult** entrance level, 57% of applicants were admitted

Undergraduates 1,114 full-time, 149 part-time. Students come from 23 states and territories, 2 other countries, 10% are from out of state, 3% African American, 2% Asian American or Pacific Islander, 3% Hispanic American, 0.4% Native American, 0.6% international, 18% transferred in, 40% live on campus. *Retention:* 81% of 2001 full-time freshmen returned.

Freshmen *Admission:* 694 applied, 397 admitted, 202 enrolled. *Average high school GPA:* 3.50. *Test scores:* SAT verbal scores over 500: 82%; SAT math scores over 500: 85%; ACT scores over 18: 95%; SAT verbal scores over 600: 33%; SAT math scores over 600: 36%; ACT scores over 24: 55%; SAT verbal scores over 700: 4%; SAT math scores over 700: 4%; ACT scores over 30: 2%.

Faculty *Total:* 125, 98% full-time, 79% with terminal degrees. *Student/faculty ratio:* 12:1.

Majors Architectural environmental design; biochemistry; biological/physical sciences; biology; biology education; biotechnology research; botany; chemical engineering; chemistry; chemistry education; city/community/regional planning; construction engineering; ecology; entomology; environmental biology; environmental education; environmental engineering; environmental science; fish/game management; fishing sciences; forest engineering; forest management; forestry; landscape architecture; land use management; natural resources conservation; natural resources management; plant pathology; plant physiology; plant protection; plant sciences; polymer chemistry; pre-dentistry; pre-law; pre-medicine; pre-veterinary studies; recreation/leisure studies; science education; water resources; water resources engineering; wildlife biology; wildlife management; wood science/paper technology; zoology.

Academic Programs *Special study options:* academic remediation for entering students, accelerated degree program, adult/continuing education programs, advanced placement credit, cooperative education, distance learning, double majors, English as a second language, freshman honors college, honors programs, independent study, internships, off-campus study, part-time degree program, services for LD students, study abroad. *ROTC:* Army (c), Air Force (c). *Unusual degree programs:* 3-2 landscape architecture.

Library F. Franklin Moon Library plus 1 other with 130,305 titles, 2,001 serial subscriptions, 732 audiovisual materials, an OPAC.

Computers on Campus 150 computers available on campus for general student use. A campuswide network can be accessed from student residence rooms and from off campus. Internet access, online (class) registration, at least one staffed computer lab available.

Student Life *Housing:* on-campus residence required for freshman year. *Options:* coed, men-only, women-only, disabled students. *Activities and Organizations:* drama/theater group, student-run newspaper, radio station, choral group, marching band, Bob Marshall/Outing Club, Forestry Club, Student Environmental Action Coalition, national fraternities, national sororities. *Campus security:* 24-hour emergency response devices and patrols, late-night transport/escort service, controlled dormitory access. *Student Services:* health clinic, personal/psychological counseling, women's center, legal services.

Athletics *Intramural sports:* archery M/W, badminton M/W, baseball M/W, basketball M/W, bowling M/W, cross-country running M/W, equestrian sports M/W, fencing M/W, field hockey W, football M, golf M/W, gymnastics M/W, ice hockey M/W, lacrosse M/W, racquetball M/W, riflery M, rugby M/W, sailing M/W, skiing (cross-country) M/W, skiing (downhill) M/W, soccer M/W, softball M/W, squash M/W, swimming M/W, table tennis M/W, tennis M/W, track and field M/W, volleyball M/W, weight lifting M/W.

Standardized Tests *Required:* SAT I or ACT (for admission).

Costs (2001–02) *Tuition:* state resident $3400 full-time, $137 per credit hour part-time; nonresident $8300 full-time, $346 per credit hour part-time. Full-time tuition and fees vary according to location. Part-time tuition and fees vary according to course load and location. *Required fees:* $376 full-time, $12 per credit hour. *Room and board:* $8670; room only: $4340. Room and board charges vary according to board plan, housing facility, and location. *Payment plans:* installment, deferred payment.

Financial Aid Of all full-time matriculated undergraduates who enrolled in 2001, 687 applied for aid, 612 were judged to have need. 290 Federal Work-Study jobs (averaging $1100). 118 State and other part-time jobs. In 2001, 15 non-need-based awards were made. *Average percent of need met:* 85%. *Average financial aid package:* $8500. *Average need-based loan:* $5500. *Average need-based gift aid:* $1620. *Average non-need based aid:* $3300. *Average indebtedness upon graduation:* $16,000.

Applying *Options:* electronic application, early admission, early decision, deferred entrance. *Application fee:* $30. *Required:* essay or personal statement, high school transcript, minimum 3.3 GPA, inventory of courses-in-progress form. *Recommended:* 3 letters of recommendation, interview. *Application deadline:* rolling (freshmen), rolling (transfers). *Early decision:* 11/15. *Notification:* continuous (freshmen), 12/15 (early decision).

Admissions Contact Ms. Susan Sanford, Director of Admissions, State University of New York College of Environmental Science and Forestry, 1 Forestry Drive, Syracuse, NY 13210-2779. *Phone:* 315-470-6600. *Toll-free phone:* 800-777-7373. *Fax:* 315-470-6933. *E-mail:* esfinfo@esf.edu.

STATE UNIVERSITY OF NEW YORK COLLEGE OF TECHNOLOGY AT ALFRED

Alfred, New York

- **State-supported** primarily 2-year, founded 1908, part of State University of New York System
- **Calendar** semesters
- **Degrees** certificates, associate, and bachelor's
- **Rural** 175-acre campus
- **Endowment** $3.2 million
- **Coed,** 3,041 undergraduate students, 90% full-time, 33% women, 67% men
- **Moderately difficult** entrance level, 71% of applicants were admitted

Undergraduates Students come from 6 states and territories, 4 other countries, 1% are from out of state, 6% African American, 1% Asian American or Pacific Islander, 2% Hispanic American, 0.8% Native American, 1.0% international, 70% live on campus. *Retention:* 96% of 2001 full-time freshmen returned.

Freshmen *Admission:* 3,979 applied, 2,843 admitted. *Average high school GPA:* 3.10.

Faculty *Total:* 184, 72% full-time, 10% with terminal degrees. *Student/faculty ratio:* 20:1.

Majors Accounting; agricultural business; agricultural sciences; animal sciences; architectural engineering technology; auto body repair; auto mechanic/technician; biological/physical sciences; biological technology; business administration; business marketing and marketing management; carpentry; civil engineering technology; computer engineering technology; computer graphics; computer/information sciences; computer science; computer typography/composition; construction engineering; construction technology; court reporting; culinary arts; dairy science; data processing technology; drafting; electrical/electronic engineering technology; electromechanical technology; engineering science; entrepreneurship; environmental science; finance; heating/air conditioning/refrigeration; heavy equipment maintenance; horticulture science; humanities; human services; landscaping management; liberal arts and sciences/liberal studies; machine technology; masonry/tile setting; mathematics; mechanical design technology; mechanical engineering technology; medical assistant; medical records administration; nursing; ornamental horticulture; plumbing; social sciences; sport/fitness administration; surveying; veterinary sciences; welding technology.

Academic Programs *Special study options:* academic remediation for entering students, adult/continuing education programs, advanced placement credit, distance learning, external degree program, honors programs, independent study, off-campus study, part-time degree program, services for LD students, student-designed majors, summer session for credit. *ROTC:* Army (c).

Library Walter C. Hinkle Memorial Library plus 1 other with 72,295 titles, 729 serial subscriptions, an OPAC.

Computers on Campus 1600 computers available on campus for general student use. A campuswide network can be accessed from student residence rooms and from off campus. Internet access, online (class) registration, at least one staffed computer lab available.

Student Life *Housing Options:* coed, disabled students. *Activities and Organizations:* drama/theater group, student-run newspaper, radio station, choral group, Outdoor Activity Club, BACCHUS, Sondai Society, Drama Club, choir. *Campus security:* 24-hour emergency response devices and patrols, late-night transport/escort service, residence hall entrance guards. *Student Services:* health clinic, personal/psychological counseling.

Athletics Member NJCAA. *Intercollegiate sports:* baseball M, basketball M(s)/W(s), cross-country running M(s)/W(s), football M(s), lacrosse M(s), soccer M(s)/W(s), softball W(s), swimming M/W, track and field M(s)/W(s), volleyball W, wrestling M. *Intramural sports:* basketball M/W, bowling M/W, cross-country running M/W, football M, golf M/W, lacrosse M/W, racquetball M/W, rugby M/W, skiing (cross-country) M/W, soccer M/W, softball M/W, table tennis M/W, tennis M/W, volleyball M/W, water polo M/W.

Standardized Tests *Recommended:* SAT I or ACT (for admission).

Costs (2001–02) *Tuition:* state resident $3200 full-time, $137 per credit hour part-time; nonresident $5000 full-time, $346 per credit hour part-time. Full-time tuition and fees vary according to degree level and program. Part-time tuition and fees vary according to course load, degree level, and program. *Required fees:* $790 full-time. *Room and board:* $5358. Room and board charges vary according to board plan and housing facility. *Payment plan:* installment. *Waivers:* employees or children of employees.

Financial Aid Of all full-time matriculated undergraduates who enrolled in 2001, 350 Federal Work-Study jobs (averaging $1000).

Applying *Options:* common application, electronic application, deferred entrance. *Application fee:* $30. *Required:* high school transcript. *Required for some:* minimum 2.0 GPA. *Recommended:* essay or personal statement, letters of recommendation, interview, SAT and ACT scores recommended for all. *Application deadline:* rolling (freshmen), rolling (transfers). *Notification:* continuous (freshmen).

Admissions Contact Ms. Deborah J. Goodrich, Director of Admissions, State University of New York College of Technology at Alfred, Huntington Administration Building, Alfred, NY 14802. *Phone:* 607-587-4215. *Toll-free phone:* 800-4-ALFRED. *Fax:* 607-587-4299. *E-mail:* admissions@alfredstate.edu.

STATE UNIVERSITY OF NEW YORK COLLEGE OF TECHNOLOGY AT CANTON

Canton, New York

- **State-supported** primarily 2-year, founded 1906, part of State University of New York System
- **Calendar** semesters
- **Degrees** certificates, associate, and bachelor's
- **Small-town** 555-acre campus
- **Endowment** $5.0 million
- **Coed,** 2,223 undergraduate students, 79% full-time, 48% women, 52% men
- **Minimally difficult** entrance level, 91% of applicants were admitted

Undergraduates 1,749 full-time, 474 part-time. Students come from 18 states and territories, 5 other countries, 3% are from out of state, 9% African American, 0.5% Asian American or Pacific Islander, 3% Hispanic American, 2% Native American, 0.4% international, 8% transferred in, 48% live on campus.

Freshmen *Admission:* 1,778 applied, 1,611 admitted, 746 enrolled.

Faculty *Total:* 114, 73% full-time, 15% with terminal degrees. *Student/faculty ratio:* 20:1.

Majors Accounting; auto mechanic/technician; biological/physical sciences; business administration; business economics; carpentry; civil engineering technology; construction technology; corrections; criminal justice/law enforcement administration; early childhood education; electrical/electronic engineering technology; engineering science; engineering technology; environmental science; forest harvesting production technology; heating/air conditioning/refrigeration; humanities; industrial technology; information sciences/systems; interdisciplinary studies; landscape architecture; law enforcement/police science; liberal arts and sciences/liberal studies; mechanical engineering technology; medical laboratory technician; mortuary science; nursing; occupational therapy assistant; office management; physical therapy assistant; plumbing; recreational therapy; social sciences; veterinary technology; wood science/paper technology.

Academic Programs *Special study options:* academic remediation for entering students, adult/continuing education programs, advanced placement credit, distance learning, internships, off-campus study, part-time degree program, services for LD students, student-designed majors, summer session for credit. *ROTC:* Army (c), Air Force (c).

Library Southworth Library with 71,200 titles, 397 serial subscriptions, 2,042 audiovisual materials, an OPAC, a Web page.

Computers on Campus 300 computers available on campus for general student use. Internet access, at least one staffed computer lab available.

Student Life *Housing:* on-campus residence required through sophomore year. *Options:* coed, men-only, women-only. *Activities and Organizations:* drama/theater group, student-run newspaper, radio station, choral group, Karate Club, Automotive Club, Outing Club, WATC-Radio, Afro-Latin Society, national fraternities, national sororities. *Campus security:* 24-hour emergency response devices and patrols, late-night transport/escort service, controlled dormitory access. *Student Services:* health clinic, personal/psychological counseling.

Athletics Member NJCAA. *Intercollegiate sports:* basketball M/W, bowling M/W, football M, golf M/W, ice hockey M, lacrosse M, soccer M/W, softball W, volleyball W. *Intramural sports:* badminton M/W, basketball M/W, golf M/W, skiing (cross-country) M/W, soccer M/W, softball M/W, tennis M/W, volleyball M/W.

Costs (2002–03) *Tuition:* $128 per credit hour part-time; state resident $3200 full-time, $210 per credit hour part-time; nonresident $5000 full-time. Full-time tuition and fees vary according to degree level, location, and program. Part-time tuition and fees vary according to degree level, location, and program. *Required fees:* $805 full-time, $33 per credit hour. *Room and board:* $6490. Room and board charges vary according to housing facility. *Payment plans:* installment, deferred payment. *Waivers:* employees or children of employees.

Applying *Options:* electronic application, early admission, deferred entrance. *Application fee:* $30. *Required:* high school transcript. *Required for some:* interview. *Recommended:* minimum 2.0 GPA. *Application deadline:* rolling (freshmen), rolling (transfers). *Notification:* continuous (freshmen).

Admissions Contact Mr. David M. Gerlach, Dean of Enrollment Management, State University of New York College of Technology at Canton, Canton, NY 13617. *Phone:* 315-386-7123. *Toll-free phone:* 800-388-7123. *Fax:* 315-386-7929. *E-mail:* williama@scanva.canton.edu.

STATE UNIVERSITY OF NEW YORK COLLEGE OF TECHNOLOGY AT DELHI

Delhi, New York

- **State-supported** primarily 2-year, founded 1913, part of State University of New York System
- **Calendar** semesters
- **Degrees** certificates, associate, and bachelor's
- **Small-town** 1100-acre campus
- **Endowment** $1.2 million
- **Coed,** 2,013 undergraduate students, 92% full-time, 43% women, 57% men
- **Moderately difficult** entrance level

Undergraduates 1,857 full-time, 156 part-time. Students come from 7 states and territories, 3 other countries, 2% are from out of state, 10% African American, 1% Asian American or Pacific Islander, 6% Hispanic American, 0.7% Native American, 0.2% international, 8% transferred in, 61% live on campus.

Freshmen *Admission:* 3,126 applied, 2,013 enrolled. *Average high school GPA:* 2.8.

Faculty *Total:* 140, 73% full-time. *Student/faculty ratio:* 16:1.

Majors Accounting; architectural engineering technology; business administration; business marketing and marketing management; carpentry; computer/information technology services administration and management related; construction management; construction technology; culinary arts; drafting; drafting/design technology; electrical/power transmission installation; engineering-related technology; engineering science; forestry; general studies; health/physical education; heating/air conditioning/refrigeration; heating/air conditioning/refrigeration technology; horticulture science; hotel and restaurant management; hotel/motel services marketing operations; humanities; information sciences/systems; laboratory animal medicine; landscape architecture; landscaping management; masonry/tile setting; mathematics; nursing; physical education; plumbing; recreation/leisure facilities management; recreation/leisure studies; restaurant operations; social sciences; travel/tourism management; turf management; veterinary technology; Web page, digital/multimedia and information resources design; welding technology; woodworking.

Academic Programs *Special study options:* academic remediation for entering students, adult/continuing education programs, advanced placement credit, distance learning, English as a second language, honors programs, internships, part-time degree program, services for LD students, student-designed majors, summer session for credit.

Library Resnick Library with 47,909 titles, 384 serial subscriptions, an OPAC.

State University of New York College of Technology at Delhi (continued)

Computers on Campus 350 computers available on campus for general student use. A campuswide network can be accessed from off campus. Internet access, online (class) registration, at least one staffed computer lab available.

Student Life *Housing:* on-campus residence required through sophomore year. *Options:* coed. *Activities and Organizations:* drama/theater group, student-run newspaper, radio station, Latin American Student Organization, Hotel Sales Management Association, student radio station, Phi Theta Kappa, Student Programming Board, national fraternities. *Campus security:* 24-hour emergency response devices and patrols. *Student Services:* health clinic, personal/psychological counseling, legal services.

Athletics Member NAIA, NJCAA. *Intercollegiate sports:* basketball M/W, cross-country running M/W, golf M/W, lacrosse M, soccer M/W, softball W, swimming M/W, tennis M/W, track and field M/W, volleyball W, wrestling M. *Intramural sports:* basketball M/W, bowling M/W, cross-country running M/W, football M/W, golf M/W, racquetball M/W, skiing (cross-country) M/W, skiing (downhill) M/W, swimming M/W, tennis M/W, volleyball M/W, weight lifting M/W.

Costs (2001–02) *Tuition:* state resident $3200 full-time, $137 per credit hour part-time; nonresident $5000 full-time, $210 per credit hour part-time. Full-time tuition and fees vary according to degree level. Part-time tuition and fees vary according to degree level. *Required fees:* $735 full-time, $29 per credit hour. *Room and board:* $5790; room only: $3190. Room and board charges vary according to board plan and location. *Payment plan:* installment.

Financial Aid Of all full-time matriculated undergraduates who enrolled in 2001, 150 Federal Work-Study jobs (averaging $1050).

Applying *Options:* electronic application, early admission, deferred entrance. *Application fee:* $30. *Required:* high school transcript. *Required for some:* minimum 2.0 GPA. *Application deadline:* rolling (freshmen), rolling (transfers). *Notification:* continuous (freshmen).

Admissions Contact State University of New York College of Technology at Delhi, Delhi, NY 13753. *Phone:* 607-746-4558. *Toll-free phone:* 800-96-DELHI. *Fax:* 607-746-4104.

STATE UNIVERSITY OF NEW YORK EMPIRE STATE COLLEGE

Saratoga Springs, New York

- **State-supported** comprehensive, founded 1971, part of State University of New York System
- **Calendar** continuous
- **Degrees** associate, bachelor's, and master's (branch locations at 7 regional centers with 38 auxiliary units)
- **Small-town** campus
- **Coed,** 8,060 undergraduate students, 28% full-time, 55% women, 45% men
- **Minimally difficult** entrance level, 43% of applicants were admitted

SUNY Empire State College is an international leader in adult higher education. Students design their own individualized associate, bachelor's, and master's degree programs based on their academic and professional goals. Students benefit from flexible, guided independent study, credit earned for learning gained in work and life, and low SUNY tuition. Empire State College, accredited by the Middle States Association of Colleges and Schools, has more than 40 locations throughout New York State as well as distance learning options.

Undergraduates 2,285 full-time, 5,775 part-time. Students come from 13 states and territories, 25 other countries, 1% are from out of state, 13% African American, 1% Asian American or Pacific Islander, 7% Hispanic American, 0.6% Native American, 5% international, 24% transferred in. *Retention:* 35% of 2001 full-time freshmen returned.

Freshmen *Admission:* 478 applied, 204 admitted, 704 enrolled.

Faculty *Total:* 419, 33% full-time. *Student/faculty ratio:* 30:1.

Majors Art; biological/physical sciences; business administration; community services; economics; education; history; humanities; human services; individual/family development; interdisciplinary studies; labor/personnel relations; mathematics; social sciences.

Academic Programs *Special study options:* adult/continuing education programs, advanced placement credit, cooperative education, external degree program, off-campus study, part-time degree program, services for LD students, student-designed majors, study abroad.

Library 5,300 titles, 209 serial subscriptions.

Computers on Campus 100 computers available on campus for general student use. A campuswide network can be accessed from off campus. Internet access, online (class) registration, at least one staffed computer lab available.

Student Life *Housing:* college housing not available.

Costs (2002–03) *Tuition:* state resident $3400 full-time, $137 per credit part-time; nonresident $8300 full-time, $346 per credit part-time. *Required fees:* $155 full-time, $5 per credit, $50 per term part-time.

Applying *Options:* electronic application, early admission. *Required:* essay or personal statement. *Required for some:* interview. *Application deadline:* rolling (freshmen), rolling (transfers).

Admissions Contact Ms. Jennifer Riley, Assistant Director of Admissions, State University of New York Empire State College, 2 Union Avenue, Saratoga Springs, NY 12866-4397. *Phone:* 518-587-2100 Ext. 214. *Toll-free phone:* 800-847-3000. *Fax:* 518-580-0105.

STATE UNIVERSITY OF NEW YORK HEALTH SCIENCE CENTER AT BROOKLYN

Brooklyn, New York

- **State-supported** upper-level, founded 1858, part of State University of New York System
- **Calendar** semesters
- **Degrees** bachelor's, master's, doctoral, first professional, post-master's, and postbachelor's certificates
- **Urban** campus
- **Coed,** 329 undergraduate students, 50% full-time, 87% women, 13% men
- **Moderately difficult** entrance level

Undergraduates 166 full-time, 163 part-time. 2% are from out of state, 47% African American, 6% Asian American or Pacific Islander, 7% Hispanic American, 45% transferred in.

Majors Nursing; occupational therapy; physical therapy; physician assistant.

Academic Programs *Special study options:* academic remediation for entering students, accelerated degree program, adult/continuing education programs, advanced placement credit, distance learning, independent study, internships, off-campus study, part-time degree program, services for LD students, study abroad, summer session for credit. *Unusual degree programs:* physical therapy.

Library The Medical Research Library of Brooklyn with 357,209 titles, 2,104 serial subscriptions, 812 audiovisual materials, an OPAC, a Web page.

Computers on Campus 183 computers available on campus for general student use. A campuswide network can be accessed from student residence rooms and from off campus. Internet access, at least one staffed computer lab available.

Student Life *Housing Options:* coed. *Campus security:* late-night transport/escort service. *Student Services:* health clinic, personal/psychological counseling, women's center.

Athletics *Intramural sports:* basketball M/W, rugby M, soccer M, swimming M/W, volleyball M/W.

Standardized Tests *Recommended:* SAT I (for admission).

Costs (2001–02) *Tuition:* state resident $3400 full-time, $137 per credit hour part-time; nonresident $8300 full-time, $346 per credit hour part-time. Full-time tuition and fees vary according to degree level and program. Part-time tuition and fees vary according to degree level and program. *Required fees:* $603 full-time, $23 per term part-time. *Room and board:* $9041. Room and board charges vary according to housing facility. *Waivers:* employees or children of employees.

Financial Aid *Financial aid deadline:* 2/15.

Applying *Application fee:* $30. *Application deadline:* 5/1 (transfers). *Notification:* continuous until 8/31 (transfers).

Admissions Contact Ms. Lorraine Terracina, Associate Vice President of Student Affairs and Dean of Students, State University of New York Health Science Center at Brooklyn, 450 Clarkson Avenue, Box 60, Brooklyn, NY 11203. *Phone:* 718-270-2446. *Toll-free phone:* 718-270-2446. *Fax:* 718-270-7592.

STATE UNIVERSITY OF NEW YORK INSTITUTE OF TECHNOLOGY AT UTICA/ROME

Utica, New York

- **State-supported** upper-level, founded 1966, part of State University of New York System
- **Calendar** semesters
- **Degrees** bachelor's, master's, and post-master's certificates
- **Suburban** 800-acre campus
- **Endowment** $1.2 million
- **Coed,** 2,046 undergraduate students, 58% full-time, 49% women, 51% men

SUNY Institute of Technology (SUNYIT) primarily serves 2-year college transfer and graduate students. In fall 2003, freshmen are admitted to select programs. Residence halls feature town house-style suites. Distinctive pro-

grams include computer science, engineering technologies, health information management, health services management, professional and technical communications, and telecommunications. A variety of scholarships are available to reward academic excellence.

Undergraduates 1,183 full-time, 863 part-time. Students come from 10 states and territories, 14 other countries, 1% are from out of state, 6% African American, 4% Asian American or Pacific Islander, 3% Hispanic American, 0.6% Native American, 3% international, 26% transferred in, 18% live on campus.

Faculty *Total:* 172, 49% full-time. *Student/faculty ratio:* 19:1.

Majors Accounting; applied mathematics; business administration; civil engineering technology; communications related; computer engineering technology; computer/information sciences; computer science; electrical/electronic engineering technology; finance; general studies; health services administration; industrial technology; information sciences/systems; mechanical engineering technology; medical records administration; nursing; psychology; sociology.

Academic Programs *Special study options:* academic remediation for entering students, accelerated degree program, adult/continuing education programs, advanced placement credit, distance learning, double majors, English as a second language, independent study, internships, part-time degree program, services for LD students, summer session for credit. *ROTC:* Army (c), Air Force (c). *Unusual degree programs:* 3-2 computer information science.

Library SUNY Institute of Technology at Utica/Rome Library with 193,682 titles, 1,090 serial subscriptions, 11,818 audiovisual materials, an OPAC, a Web page.

Computers on Campus 250 computers available on campus for general student use. A campuswide network can be accessed from student residence rooms and from off campus that provide access to various other software applications. Internet access, online (class) registration, at least one staffed computer lab available.

Student Life *Housing Options:* coed. *Activities and Organizations:* student-run newspaper, radio station, Telecommunications Club, Snowmobile Club, Phi Beta Lambda, Black Student Union, American Society of Mechanical Engineers. *Campus security:* 24-hour emergency response devices and patrols, late-night transport/escort service, controlled dormitory access, closed circuit TV monitors. *Student Services:* health clinic, personal/psychological counseling, legal services.

Athletics Member NCAA. All Division III. *Intercollegiate sports:* baseball M, basketball M/W, bowling M/W, cross-country running W, golf M/W, lacrosse M, soccer M/W, softball W, volleyball W. *Intramural sports:* badminton M/W, basketball M/W, bowling M/W, golf M/W, racquetball M/W, soccer M/W, softball M/W, tennis M/W, volleyball M/W.

Costs (2001–02) *Tuition:* state resident $3400 full-time, $137 per credit hour part-time; nonresident $8300 full-time, $346 per credit hour part-time. Part-time tuition and fees vary according to course load. *Required fees:* $655 full-time, $25 per credit hour. *Room and board:* $6240; room only: $3820. Room and board charges vary according to board plan and housing facility. *Payment plans:* installment, deferred payment. *Waivers:* employees or children of employees.

Financial Aid Of all full-time matriculated undergraduates who enrolled in 2001, 1353 applied for aid, 1205 were judged to have need. *Average percent of need met:* 85%. *Average financial aid package:* $7474. *Average need-based loan:* $3580. *Average need-based gift aid:* $1327.

Applying *Options:* electronic application, deferred entrance. *Application fee:* $30. *Application deadline:* rolling (transfers). *Notification:* continuous (transfers).

Admissions Contact Ms. Marybeth Lyons, Director of Admissions, State University of New York Institute of Technology at Utica/Rome, PO Box 3050, Utica, NY 13504-3050. *Phone:* 315-792-7500. *Toll-free phone:* 800-SUNYTEC. *Fax:* 315-792-7837. *E-mail:* admissions@sunyit.edu.

State University of New York Maritime College

Throggs Neck, New York

- **State-supported** comprehensive, founded 1874, part of State University of New York System
- **Calendar** semesters
- **Degrees** associate, bachelor's, and master's
- **Suburban** 56-acre campus
- **Endowment** $1.0 million
- **Coed, primarily men,** 631 undergraduate students, 92% full-time, 13% women, 87% men
- **Moderately difficult** entrance level, 84% of applicants were admitted

Undergraduates 581 full-time, 50 part-time. Students come from 15 states and territories, 28 other countries, 29% are from out of state, 6% African American, 4% Asian American or Pacific Islander, 8% Hispanic American, 0.2% Native American, 3% international, 3% transferred in, 98% live on campus. *Retention:* 79% of 2001 full-time freshmen returned.

Freshmen *Admission:* 612 applied, 515 admitted, 184 enrolled. *Average high school GPA:* 2.85. *Test scores:* SAT verbal scores over 500: 53%; SAT math scores over 500: 64%; SAT verbal scores over 600: 13%; SAT math scores over 600: 18%; SAT verbal scores over 700: 1%; SAT math scores over 700: 1%.

Faculty *Total:* 82, 71% full-time, 43% with terminal degrees. *Student/faculty ratio:* 8:1.

Majors Atmospheric sciences; business administration; electrical engineering; engineering related; environmental science; humanities; marine science; maritime science; mechanical engineering; naval architecture/marine engineering; Navy/Marine Corps R.O.T.C./naval science; oceanography.

Academic Programs *Special study options:* adult/continuing education programs, advanced placement credit, cooperative education, independent study, internships, services for LD students, student-designed majors, study abroad, summer session for credit. *ROTC:* Navy (b), Air Force (c).

Library Stephen Luce Library with 69,637 titles, 1,087 serial subscriptions, 6,280 audiovisual materials, an OPAC, a Web page.

Computers on Campus 110 computers available on campus for general student use. A campuswide network can be accessed from student residence rooms and from off campus. Internet access, at least one staffed computer lab available.

Student Life *Housing:* on-campus residence required through senior year. *Options:* coed. *Activities and Organizations:* student-run newspaper, marching band, Propeller Club, Eagle Scout Fraternity, Society of Naval Architects and Marine Engineers, Culture Club, Society for Professional Hispanic Engineers. *Campus security:* 24-hour emergency response devices and patrols, student patrols, late-night transport/escort service. *Student Services:* health clinic, personal/psychological counseling.

Athletics Member NCAA. All Division III. *Intercollegiate sports:* baseball M, basketball M/W, crew M/W, cross-country running M/W, ice hockey M(c), lacrosse M, riflery M/W, sailing M/W, soccer M, softball W, swimming M/W, tennis M/W, volleyball W, wrestling M. *Intramural sports:* basketball M/W, crew M/W, racquetball M/W, sailing M/W, skiing (downhill) M/W, soccer M, softball W, squash M/W, swimming M/W, tennis M/W, water polo M/W, weight lifting M/W.

Standardized Tests *Required:* SAT I or ACT (for admission). *Recommended:* SAT II: Subject Tests (for admission).

Costs (2001–02) *One-time required fee:* $2000. *Tuition:* state resident $3400 full-time, $137 per credit part-time; nonresident $8300 full-time, $346 per credit part-time. Full-time tuition and fees vary according to reciprocity agreements. Part-time tuition and fees vary according to reciprocity agreements. *Required fees:* $2500 full-time, $18 per credit, $170 per term part-time. *Room and board:* $5900. Room and board charges vary according to board plan. *Payment plan:* installment. *Waivers:* employees or children of employees.

Applying *Options:* electronic application, early admission, early decision, deferred entrance. *Application fee:* $30. *Required:* high school transcript, minimum 2.5 GPA, medical history. *Recommended:* essay or personal statement, 1 letter of recommendation, interview. *Application deadline:* rolling (freshmen), rolling (transfers). *Early decision:* 12/1. *Notification:* continuous (freshmen), 12/15 (early decision).

Admissions Contact Ms. Deirdre Whitman, Vice President of Enrollment and Campus Life, State University of New York Maritime College, 6 Pennyfield Avenue, Throggs Neck, NY 10465-4198. *Phone:* 718-409-7220 Ext. 7222. *Toll-free phone:* 800-654-1874 (in-state); 800-642-1874 (out-of-state). *Fax:* 718-409-7465. *E-mail:* admissions@sunymaritime.edu.

State University of New York Upstate Medical University

Syracuse, New York

- **State-supported** upper-level, founded 1950, part of State University of New York System
- **Calendar** semesters
- **Degrees** bachelor's, master's, doctoral, and first professional
- **Urban** 25-acre campus
- **Coed,** 241 undergraduate students, 50% full-time, 80% women, 20% men
- **Moderately difficult** entrance level, 49% of applicants were admitted

Undergraduates 120 full-time, 121 part-time. Students come from 4 states and territories, 2 other countries, 2% are from out of state, 4% African American, 4% Asian American or Pacific Islander, 0.4% Hispanic American, 0.8% Native American, 1% international, 45% transferred in, 50% live on campus.

Freshmen *Admission:* 475 applied, 235 admitted.

State University of New York Upstate Medical University (continued)

Faculty *Total:* 695, 69% full-time. *Student/faculty ratio:* 10:1.

Majors Cardiovascular technology; cytotechnology; medical radiologic technology; medical technology; nursing science; perfusion technology; physical therapy; radiological science; respiratory therapy.

Academic Programs *Special study options:* advanced placement credit, internships, off-campus study, part-time degree program, services for LD students, summer session for credit. *Unusual degree programs:* 3-2 physical therapy.

Library Weiskotten Library with 132,500 titles, 1,800 serial subscriptions, 29,515 audiovisual materials, an OPAC, a Web page.

Computers on Campus 130 computers available on campus for general student use. A campuswide network can be accessed from student residence rooms and from off campus. Internet access, at least one staffed computer lab available.

Student Life *Housing Options:* coed. *Activities and Organizations:* Undergraduate Student Council, Diversity in Allied Health. *Campus security:* late-night transport/escort service, controlled dormitory access. *Student Services:* health clinic, personal/psychological counseling.

Athletics *Intramural sports:* basketball M/W, football M, golf M/W, racquetball M/W, skiing (cross-country) M/W, skiing (downhill) M/W, softball M, squash M/W, swimming M/W, table tennis M/W, tennis M/W, volleyball M/W, water polo M/W, weight lifting M/W.

Standardized Tests *Recommended:* SAT I or ACT (for admission).

Costs (2001–02) *Tuition:* state resident $3400 full-time, $137 per credit part-time; nonresident $8300 full-time, $346 per credit part-time. Full-time tuition and fees vary according to degree level. Part-time tuition and fees vary according to course load and degree level. *Required fees:* $460 full-time, $9 per credit, $33 per term part-time. *Room and board:* $6665; room only: $4245. Room and board charges vary according to housing facility. *Payment plan:* installment.

Financial Aid Of all full-time matriculated undergraduates who enrolled in 2001, 200 applied for aid, 200 were judged to have need, 24 had their need fully met. 43 Federal Work-Study jobs (averaging $1210). In 2001, 24 non-need-based awards were made. *Average percent of need met:* 100%. *Average financial aid package:* $7226. *Average need-based loan:* $8165. *Average need-based gift aid:* $1691. *Average non-need based aid:* $350. *Financial aid deadline:* 4/1.

Applying *Options:* early admission, deferred entrance. *Application fee:* $30. *Application deadline:* rolling (transfers).

Admissions Contact Ms. Donna L. Vavonese, Associate Director of Admissions, State University of New York Upstate Medical University, Weiskotten Hall, 766 Irving Avenue, Syracuse, NY 13210. *Phone:* 315-464-4570. *Toll-free phone:* 800-736-2171. *Fax:* 315-464-8867. *E-mail:* stuadmis@upstate.edu.

STONY BROOK UNIVERSITY, STATE UNIVERSITY OF NEW YORK

Stony Brook, New York

- **State-supported** university, founded 1957, part of State University of New York System
- **Calendar** semesters
- **Degrees** bachelor's, master's, doctoral, first professional, post-master's, and first professional certificates
- **Small-town** 1100-acre campus with easy access to New York City
- **Endowment** $40.5 million
- **Coed,** 13,646 undergraduate students, 90% full-time, 48% women, 52% men
- **Very difficult** entrance level, 50% of applicants were admitted

Since its founding in 1957, Stony Brook University has grown tremendously and is now recognized as one of the nation's leading centers of learning and scholarship, as demonstrated by its recent invitation to join the Association of American Universities. Stony Brook is at the forefront of integrating research and education at the undergraduate level and prides itself on the quality of its academic programs and outstanding faculty.

Undergraduates 12,339 full-time, 1,307 part-time. Students come from 38 states and territories, 74 other countries, 2% are from out of state, 10% African American, 23% Asian American or Pacific Islander, 8% Hispanic American, 0.1% Native American, 4% international, 12% transferred in. *Retention:* 85% of 2001 full-time freshmen returned.

Freshmen *Admission:* 17,065 applied, 8,580 admitted, 2,212 enrolled. *Average high school GPA:* 3.40. *Test scores:* SAT verbal scores over 500: 73%; SAT math scores over 500: 92%; SAT verbal scores over 600: 25%; SAT math scores over 600: 45%; SAT verbal scores over 700: 3%; SAT math scores over 700: 9%.

Faculty *Total:* 1,264, 67% full-time. *Student/faculty ratio:* 18:1.

Majors African studies; American studies; anthropology; applied mathematics; art history; astronomy; atmospheric sciences; biochemistry; bioengineering; biology; business administration; chemical engineering; chemistry; comparative literature; computer engineering; computer science; cytotechnology; earth sciences; economics; engineering science; English; environmental science; film studies; fine/studio arts; French; geology; German; health science; history; humanities; information sciences/systems; interdisciplinary studies; Italian; linguistics; mathematics; mechanical engineering; medical laboratory technology; music; nursing; pharmacology; philosophy; physician assistant; physics; political science; psychology; religious studies; respiratory therapy; Russian; secondary education; social sciences; social work; sociology; Spanish; theater arts/drama; women's studies.

Academic Programs *Special study options:* academic remediation for entering students, adult/continuing education programs, advanced placement credit, distance learning, double majors, English as a second language, freshman honors college, honors programs, independent study, internships, off-campus study, part-time degree program, services for LD students, student-designed majors, study abroad, summer session for credit.

Library Frank Melville, Jr. Building Library plus 7 others with 1.9 million titles, 14,024 serial subscriptions, an OPAC, a Web page.

Computers on Campus 500 computers available on campus for general student use. A campuswide network can be accessed from student residence rooms and from off campus. Internet access, online (class) registration, at least one staffed computer lab available.

Student Life *Housing Options:* coed. *Activities and Organizations:* drama/theater group, student-run newspaper, radio station, choral group, national fraternities, national sororities. *Campus security:* 24-hour emergency response devices and patrols, late-night transport/escort service, controlled dormitory access. *Student Services:* health clinic, personal/psychological counseling, women's center, legal services.

Athletics Member NCAA, NAIA. All NCAA Division I. *Intercollegiate sports:* baseball M(s), basketball M/W, cross-country running M/W, equestrian sports M/W, football M(s), golf M, lacrosse M(s), soccer M(s)/W(s), softball W(s), squash M, swimming M(s)/W(s), tennis M(s)/W(s), track and field M(s)/W(s), volleyball W(s). *Intramural sports:* badminton M/W, basketball M/W, bowling M/W, cross-country running M/W, football M, golf M, racquetball M/W, soccer M/W, softball M/W, squash M/W, swimming M/W, table tennis M/W, tennis M/W, track and field M/W, volleyball M/W, weight lifting M/W.

Standardized Tests *Required:* SAT I or ACT (for admission). *Recommended:* SAT II: Subject Tests (for admission), SAT II: Writing Test (for admission).

Costs (2001–02) *Tuition:* state resident $3400 full-time, $137 per credit part-time; nonresident $8300 full-time, $346 per credit part-time. *Required fees:* $868 full-time. *Room and board:* $6730; room only: $4350. Room and board charges vary according to board plan and housing facility. *Payment plans:* installment, deferred payment. *Waivers:* minority students.

Applying *Options:* common application, early admission, early action, deferred entrance. *Application fee:* $30. *Required:* high school transcript, minimum 3.0 GPA. *Recommended:* 2 letters of recommendation, interview. *Application deadline:* rolling (freshmen), rolling (transfers).

Admissions Contact Ms. Gigi Lamens, Director of Admissions and Enrollment Planning, Stony Brook University, State University of New York, Stony Brook, NY 11794. *Phone:* 631-632-6868. *Toll-free phone:* 800-USB-SUNY. *E-mail:* admiss@mail.upsa.sunysb.edu.

SYRACUSE UNIVERSITY

Syracuse, New York

- **Independent** university, founded 1870
- **Calendar** semesters
- **Degrees** bachelor's, master's, doctoral, first professional, and post-master's certificates
- **Urban** 200-acre campus
- **Endowment** $675.4 million
- **Coed,** 10,702 undergraduate students, 99% full-time, 55% women, 45% men
- **Very difficult** entrance level, 64% of applicants were admitted

Undergraduates 10,581 full-time, 121 part-time. Students come from 52 states and territories, 61 other countries, 55% are from out of state, 7% African American, 5% Asian American or Pacific Islander, 4% Hispanic American, 0.2% Native American, 3% international, 3% transferred in, 73% live on campus. *Retention:* 92% of 2001 full-time freshmen returned.

Freshmen *Admission:* 14,514 applied, 9,221 admitted, 2,627 enrolled. *Average high school GPA:* 3.50. *Test scores:* SAT verbal scores over 500: 91%; SAT math scores over 500: 95%; SAT verbal scores over 600: 50%; SAT math scores over 600: 61%; SAT verbal scores over 700: 9%; SAT math scores over 700: 13%.

Faculty *Total:* 1,404, 59% full-time. *Student/faculty ratio:* 12:1.

Majors Accounting; advertising; aerospace engineering; African-American studies; American studies; anthropology; applied art; architecture; art; art education; art history; behavioral sciences; biochemistry; bioengineering; biology; broadcast journalism; business administration; business marketing and marketing management; ceramic arts; chemical engineering; chemistry; child care/development; civil engineering; classics; clothing/textiles; communication disorders; computer engineering; computer graphics; computer/information sciences; computer science; consumer services; design/visual communications; dietetics; early childhood education; economics; education; education (K-12); electrical engineering; elementary education; engineering physics; English; English education; enterprise management; entrepreneurship; environmental engineering; environmental science; exercise sciences; family/community studies; family studies; fashion design/illustration; film studies; film/video production; finance; fine/studio arts; food products retailing; foreign languages/literatures; French; geography; geology; German; graphic design/commercial art/illustration; Greek (modern); health education; health science; history; hospitality management; individual/family development; industrial design; information sciences/systems; interdisciplinary studies; interior design; interior environments; international relations; Italian; journalism; Latin American studies; Latin (ancient and medieval); linguistics; literature; mathematics; mathematics education; mechanical engineering; medieval/renaissance studies; metal/jewelry arts; middle school education; modern languages; music; music business management/merchandising; music (general performance); music (piano and organ performance); music teacher education; music theory and composition; music (voice and choral/opera performance); natural sciences; nursing; nutrition science; nutrition studies; painting; philosophy; photography; physical education; physics; political science; pre-dentistry; pre-law; pre-medicine; pre-veterinary studies; printmaking; psychology; public policy analysis; public relations; radio/television broadcasting; religious studies; retail management; Russian; Russian/Slavic studies; science education; sculpture; secondary education; social sciences; social studies education; social work; sociology; Spanish; special education; speech-language pathology/audiology; speech/rhetorical studies; stringed instruments; telecommunications; textile arts; theater arts/drama; theater design; wind/percussion instruments; women's studies.

Academic Programs *Special study options:* accelerated degree program, adult/continuing education programs, advanced placement credit, cooperative education, distance learning, double majors, English as a second language, external degree program, honors programs, independent study, internships, off-campus study, part-time degree program, services for LD students, student-designed majors, study abroad, summer session for credit. *ROTC:* Army (b), Air Force (b). *Unusual degree programs:* 3-2 public administration, computer science.

Library E. S. Bird Library plus 6 others with 3.0 million titles, 12,000 serial subscriptions, 763,000 audiovisual materials, an OPAC, a Web page.

Computers on Campus 1200 computers available on campus for general student use. A campuswide network can be accessed from student residence rooms and from off campus that provide access to online services, networked client and server computing. Internet access, online (class) registration, at least one staffed computer lab available.

Student Life *Housing:* on-campus residence required through sophomore year. *Options:* coed. *Activities and Organizations:* drama/theater group, student-run newspaper, radio and television station, choral group, marching band, Student Government Association, Programming Council, First Year Players, Student African-American Society, national fraternities, national sororities. *Campus security:* 24-hour emergency response devices and patrols, late-night transport/escort service, controlled dormitory access, crime prevention and neighborhood outreach programs. *Student Services:* health clinic, personal/psychological counseling, women's center, legal services.

Athletics Member NCAA. All Division I except football (Division I-A). *Intercollegiate sports:* archery M(c)/W(c), badminton M(c)/W(c), baseball M(c), basketball M(s)/W(s), bowling M(c)/W(c), crew M(s)/W(s), cross-country running M(s)/W(s), equestrian sports M(c)/W(c), fencing M(c)/W(c), field hockey W(s), gymnastics M(c)/W(c), ice hockey M(c)/W(c), lacrosse M(s)/W(s), racquetball M(c)/W(c), riflery M(c)/W(c), rugby M(c)/W(c), sailing M(c)/W(c), skiing (downhill) M(c)/W(c), soccer M(s)/W(s), softball M(c)/W(s), squash M(c)/W(c), swimming M(s)/W(s), table tennis M(c)/W(c), tennis M(c)/W(s), track and field M(s)/W(s), volleyball M(c)/W(s), water polo M(c)/W(c), weight lifting M(c)/W(c). *Intramural sports:* badminton M/W, basketball M/W, cross-country running M/W, football M/W, golf M/W, lacrosse M(c)/W(c), racquetball M/W, soccer M/W, softball M/W, squash M/W, swimming M/W, table tennis M/W, tennis M/W, track and field M/W, volleyball M/W.

Standardized Tests *Required:* SAT I or ACT (for admission).

Costs (2002–03) *Comprehensive fee:* $32,934 includes full-time tuition ($22,800), mandatory fees ($624), and room and board ($9510). Part-time tuition: $993 per credit hour. Part-time tuition and fees vary according to course load, location, and program. *Room and board:* College room only: $4990. Room and board charges vary according to board plan and housing facility. *Payment plan:* installment. *Waivers:* employees or children of employees.

Financial Aid Of all full-time matriculated undergraduates who enrolled in 2001, 6996 applied for aid, 5794 were judged to have need. In 2001, 2046 non-need-based awards were made. *Average percent of need met:* 80%. *Average financial aid package:* $17,000. *Average need-based loan:* $5500. *Average need-based gift aid:* $11,300. *Average non-need based aid:* $6440. *Average indebtedness upon graduation:* $18,925.

Applying *Options:* common application, early admission, early decision, deferred entrance. *Application fee:* $50. *Required:* essay or personal statement, high school transcript, 2 letters of recommendation. *Required for some:* audition for drama and music programs, portfolio for art and architecture programs. *Recommended:* interview. *Application deadlines:* 1/1 (freshmen), 1/1 (transfers). *Early decision:* 11/15. *Notification:* 3/15 (freshmen), 12/31 (early decision).

Admissions Contact Office of Admissions, Syracuse University, 201 Tolley Administration Building, Syracuse, NY 13244-1100. *Phone:* 315-443-3611. *E-mail:* orange@syr.edu.

TALMUDICAL INSTITUTE OF UPSTATE NEW YORK

Rochester, New York

- **Independent Jewish** 5-year, founded 1974
- **Calendar** semesters
- **Degrees** bachelor's (also offers some graduate courses)
- **Urban** 1-acre campus
- **Men only**
- **Noncompetitive** entrance level

Student Life *Campus security:* student patrols.

Financial Aid Of all full-time matriculated undergraduates who enrolled in 2001, 5 Federal Work-Study jobs.

Applying *Options:* common application, early admission. *Required:* high school transcript. *Required for some:* interview.

Admissions Contact Director of Admissions, Talmudical Institute of Upstate New York, 769 Park Avenue, Rochester, NY 14607-3046. *Phone:* 716-473-2810.

TALMUDICAL SEMINARY OHOLEI TORAH

Brooklyn, New York

Admissions Contact Rabbi E. Piekarski, Director of Academic Affairs, Talmudical Seminary Oholei Torah, 667 Eastern Parkway, Brooklyn, NY 11213-3310. *Phone:* 718-363-2034.

TORAH TEMIMAH TALMUDICAL SEMINARY

Brooklyn, New York

Admissions Contact Rabbi I. Hisiger, Principal, Torah Temimah Talmudical Seminary, 555 Ocean Parkway, Brooklyn, NY 11218-5913. *Phone:* 718-853-8500.

TOURO COLLEGE

New York, New York

- **Independent** comprehensive, founded 1971
- **Calendar** semesters
- **Degrees** certificates, diplomas, associate, bachelor's, master's, doctoral, first professional, and post-master's certificates
- **Urban** campus
- **Coed,** 6,119 undergraduate students, 88% full-time, 69% women, 31% men
- **Moderately difficult** entrance level, 69% of applicants were admitted

Undergraduates 5,364 full-time, 755 part-time. Students come from 25 states and territories, 30 other countries, 5% are from out of state.

Freshmen *Admission:* 3,575 applied, 2,470 admitted, 1,340 enrolled. *Test scores:* SAT verbal scores over 500: 78%; SAT math scores over 500: 73%; ACT scores over 18: 89%; SAT verbal scores over 600: 40%; SAT math scores over 600: 33%; ACT scores over 24: 34%; SAT verbal scores over 700: 8%; SAT math scores over 700: 6%; ACT scores over 30: 17%.

Faculty *Total:* 889, 33% full-time. *Student/faculty ratio:* 21:1.

Touro College (continued)

Majors Accounting; area, ethnic, and cultural studies related; banking; biblical studies; biology; business administration; business marketing and marketing management; chemistry; community services; computer science; desktop publishing equipment operation; early childhood education; economics; education; English; finance; health professions and related sciences; health science; Hebrew; history; humanities; human services; information sciences/systems; interdisciplinary studies; international business; Judaic studies; liberal arts and sciences/liberal studies; literature; mathematics; medical records administration; occupational therapy; philosophy; physical therapy; physician assistant; political science; pre-dentistry; pre-law; pre-medicine; psychology; social sciences; sociology; special education; speech-language pathology/audiology.

Academic Programs *Special study options:* academic remediation for entering students, accelerated degree program, advanced placement credit, English as a second language, external degree program, honors programs, internships, part-time degree program, student-designed majors, study abroad, summer session for credit. *Unusual degree programs:* 3-2 physical therapy, occupational therapy.

Library 534,280 titles, 4,715 serial subscriptions.

Computers on Campus 350 computers available on campus for general student use. At least one staffed computer lab available.

Student Life *Activities and Organizations:* drama/theater group, student-run newspaper. *Campus security:* 24-hour emergency response devices and patrols. *Student Services:* personal/psychological counseling.

Standardized Tests *Recommended:* SAT I or ACT (for admission).

Costs (2001–02) *Tuition:* $9950 full-time, $410 per credit part-time. Full-time tuition and fees vary according to program. Part-time tuition and fees vary according to program. *Required fees:* $300 full-time, $150 per term part-time. *Room only:* $4700. Room and board charges vary according to gender. *Waivers:* employees or children of employees.

Applying *Options:* early admission, deferred entrance. *Application fee:* $50. *Required:* high school transcript. *Required for some:* 2 letters of recommendation, interview. *Recommended:* essay or personal statement, 1 letter of recommendation. *Application deadline:* rolling (freshmen), rolling (transfers). *Notification:* continuous (freshmen).

Admissions Contact Mr. Andre Baron, Director of Admissions, Touro College, 27-33 West 23rd Street, New York, NY 10010. *Phone:* 212-463-0400 Ext. 665.

UNION COLLEGE
Schenectady, New York

- **Independent** comprehensive, founded 1795
- **Calendar** trimesters
- **Degrees** bachelor's and master's
- **Suburban** 100-acre campus
- **Endowment** $268.9 million
- **Coed,** 2,118 undergraduate students, 98% full-time, 48% women, 52% men
- **Very difficult** entrance level, 41% of applicants were admitted

Recent major additions to the Union College campus are the F. W. Olin Center, a $9-million high-technology classroom and laboratory building funded by the F. W. Olin Foundation; the $17.6-million renovated and expanded College library; and a $10-million community revitalization project in which the College renovated neighboring old houses into apartment-style residences for 160 students.

Undergraduates 2,082 full-time, 36 part-time. Students come from 33 states and territories, 22 other countries, 53% are from out of state, 4% African American, 5% Asian American or Pacific Islander, 4% Hispanic American, 0.1% Native American, 3% international, 1% transferred in, 81% live on campus. *Retention:* 92% of 2001 full-time freshmen returned.

Freshmen *Admission:* 3,910 applied, 1,616 admitted, 522 enrolled. *Average high school GPA:* 3.40. *Test scores:* SAT verbal scores over 500: 95%; SAT math scores over 500: 98%; SAT verbal scores over 600: 52%; SAT math scores over 600: 68%; SAT verbal scores over 700: 7%; SAT math scores over 700: 15%.

Faculty *Total:* 224, 87% full-time. *Student/faculty ratio:* 11:1.

Majors American studies; anthropology; biochemistry; biological/physical sciences; biology; chemistry; classics; computer/information sciences; economics; electrical engineering; English; fine/studio arts; foreign languages/literatures; geology; history; humanities; liberal arts and sciences/liberal studies; mathematics; mechanical engineering; philosophy; physics; political science; psychology; social sciences; sociology.

Academic Programs *Special study options:* accelerated degree program, advanced placement credit, cooperative education, double majors, English as a second language, honors programs, independent study, internships, off-campus study, part-time degree program, student-designed majors, study abroad, summer session for credit. *ROTC:* Army (c), Navy (c), Air Force (c).

Library Schaffer Library with 287,293 titles, 6,826 serial subscriptions, 7,429 audiovisual materials, an OPAC, a Web page.

Computers on Campus 320 computers available on campus for general student use. A campuswide network can be accessed from student residence rooms and from off campus. Internet access, at least one staffed computer lab available.

Student Life *Housing:* on-campus residence required through senior year. *Options:* coed, men-only, women-only, cooperative. *Activities and Organizations:* drama/theater group, student-run newspaper, radio station, choral group, Big Brothers/Big Sisters, We Care About U Schenectady, student radio station, student newspaper, African and Latino Alliance of Students, national fraternities, national sororities. *Campus security:* 24-hour emergency response devices and patrols, student patrols, late-night transport/escort service, controlled dormitory access, awareness programs, bicycle patrol, shuttle service. *Student Services:* health clinic, personal/psychological counseling, women's center.

Athletics Member NCAA. All Division III except ice hockey (Division I). *Intercollegiate sports:* baseball M, basketball M/W, crew M/W, cross-country running M/W, fencing M(c)/W(c), field hockey W, football M, ice hockey M/W, lacrosse M/W, rugby M(c)/W(c), skiing (cross-country) M(c)/W(c), skiing (downhill) M(c)/W(c), soccer M/W, softball W, swimming M/W, tennis M/W, track and field M/W, volleyball W, water polo M(c)/W(c). *Intramural sports:* basketball M/W, football M/W, ice hockey M/W, lacrosse M/W, soccer M/W, softball M/W, volleyball M/W.

Costs (2001–02) *Comprehensive fee:* $32,646 includes full-time tuition ($25,788), mandatory fees ($219), and room and board ($6639). Part-time tuition: $2865 per course. *Room and board:* College room only: $3597. Room and board charges vary according to board plan. *Payment plan:* installment. *Waivers:* employees or children of employees.

Financial Aid Of all full-time matriculated undergraduates who enrolled in 2001, 1134 applied for aid, 1046 were judged to have need, 985 had their need fully met. 644 Federal Work-Study jobs (averaging $1110). 51 State and other part-time jobs (averaging $1544). In 2001, 17 non-need-based awards were made. *Average percent of need met:* 97%. *Average financial aid package:* $21,580. *Average need-based loan:* $4235. *Average need-based gift aid:* $17,785. *Average non-need based aid:* $1073. *Average indebtedness upon graduation:* $16,930.

Applying *Options:* common application, electronic application, early admission, early decision, deferred entrance. *Application fee:* $50. *Required:* essay or personal statement, high school transcript, 2 letters of recommendation. *Recommended:* interview. *Application deadlines:* 1/15 (freshmen), 6/1 (transfers). *Early decision:* 11/15 (for plan 1), 1/15 (for plan 2). *Notification:* 4/1 (freshmen), 12/15 (early decision plan 1), 2/1 (early decision plan 2).

Admissions Contact Mr. Daniel Lundquist, Vice President for Admissions and Financial Aid, Union College, Grant Hall, Schenectady, NY 12308. *Phone:* 518-388-6112. *Toll-free phone:* 888-843-6688. *Fax:* 518-388-6986. *E-mail:* admissions@union.edu.

UNITED STATES MERCHANT MARINE ACADEMY
Kings Point, New York

- **Federally supported** 4-year, founded 1943
- **Calendar** quarters
- **Degree** bachelor's
- **Suburban** 80-acre campus with easy access to New York City
- **Coed,** 931 undergraduate students, 100% full-time, 10% women, 90% men
- **Very difficult** entrance level, 18% of applicants were admitted

Undergraduates Students come from 53 states and territories, 4 other countries, 100% live on campus. *Retention:* 92% of 2001 full-time freshmen returned.

Freshmen *Admission:* 1,586 applied, 283 admitted. *Average high school GPA:* 3.50. *Test scores:* SAT verbal scores over 500: 100%; SAT math scores over 500: 100%; SAT verbal scores over 600: 47%; SAT math scores over 600: 59%; SAT verbal scores over 700: 10%; SAT math scores over 700: 5%.

Faculty *Total:* 90, 89% full-time. *Student/faculty ratio:* 12:1.

Majors Engineering/industrial management; maritime science; naval architecture/marine engineering.

Academic Programs *Special study options:* cooperative education, honors programs, internships.

Library Schuyler Otis Bland Memorial Library with 232,576 titles, 985 serial subscriptions.

Computers on Campus 1200 computers available on campus for general student use. A campuswide network can be accessed from student residence rooms that provide access to engineering and economics software. At least one staffed computer lab available.

Student Life *Housing:* on-campus residence required through senior year. *Options:* coed. *Activities and Organizations:* drama/theater group, student-run newspaper, choral group, marching band. *Campus security:* 24-hour patrols. *Student Services:* health clinic, personal/psychological counseling.

Athletics Member NCAA. All Division III. *Intercollegiate sports:* baseball M, basketball M/W, crew M/W, cross-country running M/W, football M, golf M/W, ice hockey M(c), lacrosse M, riflery M/W, rugby M(c), sailing M/W, soccer M, softball W, swimming M/W, tennis M/W, track and field M/W, volleyball M/W, water polo M, wrestling M. *Intramural sports:* basketball M/W, bowling M/W, crew M/W, cross-country running M/W, football M, golf M/W, ice hockey M, lacrosse M, racquetball M/W, riflery M/W, rugby M, sailing M/W, skiing (cross-country) M/W, skiing (downhill) M/W, soccer M/W, softball M/W, swimming M/W, tennis M/W, track and field M/W, volleyball M/W, water polo M, wrestling M.

Standardized Tests *Required:* SAT I or ACT (for admission).

Costs (2001–02) *Tuition:* Tuition, room and board, and medical and dental care provided by the U.S. government. Each midshipman receives a monthly salary while assigned aboard ship for training. Entering freshmen are required to deposit $5800 to defray the initial cost of computer equipment and activities fees.

Applying *Options:* electronic application, early decision. *Required:* essay or personal statement, high school transcript, 3 letters of recommendation. *Recommended:* interview. *Application deadlines:* 3/1 (freshmen), 3/1 (transfers). *Early decision:* 11/1. *Notification:* continuous until 4/1 (freshmen), 12/1 (early decision).

Admissions Contact Capt. James M. Skinner, Director of Admissions, United States Merchant Marine Academy, 300 Steamboat Road, Wiley Hall, Kings Point, NY 11024-1699. *Phone:* 516-773-5391. *Toll-free phone:* 800-732-6267. *Fax:* 516-773-5390. *E-mail:* admissions@usmma.edu.

UNITED STATES MILITARY ACADEMY

West Point, New York

- **Federally supported** 4-year, founded 1802
- **Calendar** semesters
- **Degree** bachelor's
- **Small-town** 16,080-acre campus with easy access to New York City
- **Coed, primarily men,** 4,394 undergraduate students, 100% full-time, 20% women, 80% men
- **Most difficult** entrance level, 15% of applicants were admitted

Become a leader who can make a difference for the nation in the 21st century. West Point offers this opportunity, challenging outstanding young men and women in academics, leadership, and physical development. The West Point experience builds a foundation for career success as an Army officer; it is tough but rewarding. Graduates earn a Bachelor of Science degree and a commission as a second lieutenant in the U.S. Army.

Undergraduates Students come from 53 states and territories, 18 other countries, 92% are from out of state, 8% African American, 6% Asian American or Pacific Islander, 6% Hispanic American, 0.7% Native American, 0.7% international, 100% live on campus. *Retention:* 92% of 2001 full-time freshmen returned.

Freshmen *Admission:* 9,893 applied, 1,495 admitted. *Test scores:* SAT verbal scores over 500: 98%; SAT math scores over 500: 99%; ACT scores over 18: 100%; SAT verbal scores over 600: 65%; SAT math scores over 600: 76%; ACT scores over 24: 96%; SAT verbal scores over 700: 18%; SAT math scores over 700: 22%; ACT scores over 30: 34%.

Faculty *Total:* 588, 100% full-time, 56% with terminal degrees. *Student/faculty ratio:* 7:1.

Majors Aerospace engineering; American studies; applied mathematics; Arabic; Army R.O.T.C./military science; behavioral sciences; biological/physical sciences; biology; business administration; chemical engineering; chemistry; Chinese; civil engineering; computer engineering; computer science; East Asian studies; Eastern European area studies; economics; electrical engineering; engineering; engineering/industrial management; engineering physics; environmental engineering; environmental science; European studies; French; geography; German; history; humanities; information sciences/systems; interdisciplinary studies; Latin American studies; literature; mathematics; mechanical engineering; Middle Eastern studies; modern languages; nuclear engineering; operations research; philosophy; physics; political science; Portuguese; pre-law; pre-medicine; psychology; public policy analysis; Russian; Spanish; systems engineering.

Academic Programs *Special study options:* academic remediation for entering students, advanced placement credit, double majors, off-campus study, summer session for credit.

Library United States Military Academy Library plus 1 other with 457,340 titles, 2,220 serial subscriptions, 8,000 audiovisual materials, an OPAC, a Web page.

Computers on Campus 5500 computers available on campus for general student use. A campuswide network can be accessed from student residence rooms and from off campus. At least one staffed computer lab available.

Student Life *Housing:* on-campus residence required through senior year. *Options:* coed. *Activities and Organizations:* drama/theater group, student-run radio station, choral group, Rugby Club, chapel choirs, Big Brothers/Big Sisters, Orienteering Team, Spirit Support Group. *Campus security:* 24-hour emergency response devices and patrols, student patrols, late-night transport/escort service. *Student Services:* health clinic, personal/psychological counseling, legal services.

Athletics Member NCAA. All Division I except football (Division I-A). *Intercollegiate sports:* baseball M, basketball M/W, bowling M(c)/W(c), crew M(c)/W(c), cross-country running M/W, equestrian sports M(c)/W(c), fencing M(c)/W(c), golf M, gymnastics M, ice hockey M, lacrosse M/W(c), racquetball M(c)/W(c), riflery M(c)/W(c), rugby M(c), sailing M(c)/W(c), skiing (cross-country) M(c)/W(c), skiing (downhill) M(c)/W(c), soccer M/W, softball W, squash M(c)/W(c), swimming M/W, tennis M/W, track and field M/W, volleyball M(c)/W, water polo M(c), weight lifting M(c)/W(c), wrestling M. *Intramural sports:* basketball M/W, cross-country running M/W, football M, lacrosse M, soccer M/W, softball M/W, swimming M/W.

Standardized Tests *Required:* SAT I or ACT (for admission).

Costs (2001–02) *Tuition:* Tuition, room and board, and medical and dental care are provided by the U.S. government. Each cadet receives a salary from which to pay for personal computer, uniforms, activities, books, services, and personal expenses. Entering freshmen are required to deposit $2400 to defray the initial cost of uniforms, books, supplies, equipment and fees.

Applying *Options:* early action. *Required:* essay or personal statement, high school transcript, 4 letters of recommendation, medical examination, authorized nomination. *Recommended:* interview. *Application deadlines:* 3/21 (freshmen), 3/21 (transfers). *Notification:* continuous until 6/1 (freshmen), 1/5 (early action).

Admissions Contact Col. Michael C. Jones, Director of Admissions, United States Military Academy, United States Military Academy, West Point, NY 10996. *Phone:* 845-938-4041. *E-mail:* 8dad@sunams.usma.army.mil.

UNITED TALMUDICAL SEMINARY

Brooklyn, New York

Admissions Contact Director of Admissions, United Talmudical Seminary, 82 Lee Avenue, Brooklyn, NY 11211-7900. *Phone:* 719-963-9770.

UNIVERSITY AT BUFFALO, THE STATE UNIVERSITY OF NEW YORK

Buffalo, New York

- **State-supported** university, founded 1846, part of State University of New York System
- **Calendar** semesters
- **Degrees** bachelor's, master's, doctoral, first professional, post-master's, and first professional certificates
- **Suburban** 1350-acre campus
- **Endowment** $450.0 million
- **Coed,** 17,290 undergraduate students, 89% full-time, 46% women, 54% men
- **Moderately difficult** entrance level, 63% of applicants were admitted

UB attracts highly qualified students with its honors program—the largest in the SUNY system—and an expanded merit scholarship program. UB offers a growing number of combined bachelor's and master's programs. The University is dedicated to providing educational technology and assistance, exposing students to computer-enhanced classwork and training them for the 21st century. UB is also committed to enhancing students' life quality by offering new on-campus apartment housing options, NCAA Division I men's and women's athletics, and recreational, intramural, and club sports.

Undergraduates 15,321 full-time, 1,969 part-time. Students come from 44 states and territories, 71 other countries, 2% are from out of state, 8% African American, 9% Asian American or Pacific Islander, 4% Hispanic American, 0.4% Native American, 5% international, 9% transferred in, 41% live on campus. *Retention:* 85% of 2001 full-time freshmen returned.

Freshmen *Admission:* 16,016 applied, 10,051 admitted, 3,020 enrolled. *Average high school GPA:* 3.70. *Test scores:* SAT verbal scores over 500: 76%; SAT math scores over 500: 86%; ACT scores over 18: 96%; SAT verbal scores over 600: 28%; SAT math scores over 600: 40%; ACT scores over 24: 57%; SAT verbal scores over 700: 4%; SAT math scores over 700: 7%; ACT scores over 30: 10%.

Faculty *Total:* 1,932, 64% full-time, 98% with terminal degrees. *Student/faculty ratio:* 14:1.

University at Buffalo, The State University of New York (continued)

Majors Accounting; aerospace engineering; African-American studies; American studies; anthropology; architectural environmental design; architecture; art; art history; biochemical technology; biochemistry; biology; biophysics; biotechnology research; business administration; chemical engineering; chemistry; civil engineering; classics; communication disorders; computer engineering technology; computer science; dance; economics; electrical engineering; engineering physics; English; environmental engineering; exercise sciences; film studies; fine/studio arts; French; geography; geology; German; history; industrial/manufacturing engineering; Italian; linguistics; mass communications; mathematics; mechanical engineering; medical technology; medicinal/pharmaceutical chemistry; music; music (general performance); Native American studies; nuclear medical technology; nursing; occupational therapy; pharmacy administration/pharmaceutics; philosophy; physics; political science; psychology; social sciences; sociology; Spanish; speech-language pathology/audiology; theater arts/drama; women's studies.

Academic Programs *Special study options:* academic remediation for entering students, adult/continuing education programs, advanced placement credit, distance learning, double majors, English as a second language, freshman honors college, honors programs, independent study, internships, off-campus study, part-time degree program, services for LD students, student-designed majors, study abroad, summer session for credit. *ROTC:* Army (c). *Unusual degree programs:* 3-2 law.

Library Lockwood Library plus 7 others with 3.2 million titles, 26,444 serial subscriptions, 157,596 audiovisual materials, an OPAC, a Web page.

Computers on Campus 1800 computers available on campus for general student use. A campuswide network can be accessed from student residence rooms and from off campus. Internet access, online (class) registration, at least one staffed computer lab available.

Student Life *Housing Options:* coed. *Activities and Organizations:* drama/theater group, student-run newspaper, radio and television station, choral group, marching band, Schussmeisters Ski Club, student association, Black Student Union, national fraternities, national sororities. *Campus security:* 24-hour emergency response devices and patrols, student patrols, late-night transport/escort service, controlled dormitory access, self-defense and awareness programs. *Student Services:* health clinic, personal/psychological counseling, women's center, legal services.

Athletics Member NCAA. All Division I except football (Division I-AA). *Intercollegiate sports:* baseball M(s), basketball M(s)/W(s), crew W(s), cross-country running M(s)/W(s), soccer M(s)/W(s), softball W(s), swimming M(s)/W(s), tennis M(s)/W(s), track and field M(s)/W(s), volleyball W(s), wrestling M(s). *Intramural sports:* badminton M/W, basketball M/W, crew M(c), cross-country running M/W, field hockey W(c), football M, gymnastics M(c)/W(c), ice hockey M(c)/W(c), lacrosse M(c)/W(c), racquetball M/W, rugby M(c)/W(c), skiing (cross-country) M(c)/W(c), skiing (downhill) M(c)/W(c), soccer M/W, softball M/W, squash M/W, tennis M/W, volleyball M/W, weight lifting M(c)/W(c), wrestling M(c)/W(c).

Standardized Tests *Required:* SAT I or ACT (for admission).

Costs (2001–02) *Tuition:* state resident $3400 full-time, $137 per credit hour part-time; nonresident $8300 full-time, $346 per credit hour part-time. *Required fees:* $1390 full-time, $58 per credit hour. *Room and board:* $6318; room only: $3718. Room and board charges vary according to board plan and housing facility. *Payment plan:* installment.

Financial Aid Of all full-time matriculated undergraduates who enrolled in 2001, 10940 applied for aid, 9961 were judged to have need, 6004 had their need fully met. 913 State and other part-time jobs (averaging $5428). In 2001, 605 non-need-based awards were made. *Average percent of need met:* 70%. *Average financial aid package:* $7491. *Average need-based loan:* $2942. *Average need-based gift aid:* $3426. *Average indebtedness upon graduation:* $16,189.

Applying *Options:* common application, electronic application, early admission, early decision. *Application fee:* $30. *Required:* high school transcript. *Required for some:* letters of recommendation, portfolio, audition. *Application deadline:* rolling (freshmen), rolling (transfers). *Early decision:* 11/1. *Notification:* 12/10 (early decision).

Admissions Contact Ms. Regina Toomey, Director of Admissions, University at Buffalo, The State University of New York, Capen Hall, Room 17, North Campus, Buffalo, NY 14260-1660. *Phone:* 716-645-6900. *Toll-free phone:* 888-UB-ADMIT. *Fax:* 716-645-6411. *E-mail:* ubadmissions@admissions.buffalo.edu.

UNIVERSITY OF ROCHESTER
Rochester, New York

- **Independent** university, founded 1850
- **Calendar** semesters
- **Degrees** bachelor's, master's, doctoral, and first professional
- **Suburban** 534-acre campus
- **Endowment** $1.2 billion
- **Coed,** 3,715 undergraduate students
- **Very difficult** entrance level, 50% of applicants were admitted

Rochester is a leading private university with a rich diversity of programs and personal attention that allows close contact with faculty members. Distinctive opportunities include the nationally recognized Take Five program for a tuition-free 5th year, the management certificate, and, for selected students, simultaneous admission to the undergraduate and medical schools.

Undergraduates Students come from 52 states and territories, 45 other countries, 85% live on campus. *Retention:* 93% of 2001 full-time freshmen returned.

Freshmen *Admission:* 10,080 applied, 5,086 admitted. *Average high school GPA:* 3.63. *Test scores:* SAT verbal scores over 500: 97%; SAT math scores over 500: 98%; ACT scores over 18: 99%; SAT verbal scores over 600: 79%; SAT math scores over 600: 87%; ACT scores over 24: 87%; SAT verbal scores over 700: 25%; SAT math scores over 700: 35%; ACT scores over 30: 36%.

Faculty *Total:* 1,010. *Student/faculty ratio:* 12:1.

Majors Anthropology; applied mathematics; art history; astronomy; biochemistry; bioengineering; biological/physical sciences; biology; cell biology; chemical engineering; chemistry; classics; cognitive psychology/psycholinguistics; comparative literature; computer engineering technology; computer science; earth sciences; economics; electrical engineering; engineering; engineering science; English; environmental science; evolutionary biology; film studies; fine/studio arts; French; genetics; geology; German; health science; history; interdisciplinary studies; Japanese; jazz; linguistics; mathematical statistics; mathematics; mechanical engineering; microbiology/bacteriology; music; music history; music teacher education; music theory and composition; natural sciences; neuroscience; optics; philosophy; physics; political science; psychology; religious studies; Russian; Russian/Slavic studies; sign language interpretation; Spanish; women's studies.

Academic Programs *Special study options:* advanced placement credit, double majors, English as a second language, independent study, internships, off-campus study, part-time degree program, services for LD students, student-designed majors, study abroad, summer session for credit. *ROTC:* Army (c), Navy (b), Air Force (c). *Unusual degree programs:* 3-2 public health, optics, public policy, human development, computer science, medical statistics, applied mathematics, elementary teacher education, music education, materials science.

Library Rush Rhees Library plus 5 others with 3.0 million titles, 11,254 serial subscriptions, 78,600 audiovisual materials, an OPAC, a Web page.

Computers on Campus 260 computers available on campus for general student use. A campuswide network can be accessed from student residence rooms and from off campus. At least one staffed computer lab available.

Student Life *Housing:* on-campus residence required through sophomore year. *Options:* coed, men-only, women-only. *Activities and Organizations:* drama/theater group, student-run newspaper, radio station, choral group, student radio station, Cinema Group, Debate Union, Campus Board Program, national fraternities, national sororities. *Campus security:* 24-hour emergency response devices and patrols, late-night transport/escort service, controlled dormitory access. *Student Services:* health clinic, personal/psychological counseling, women's center, legal services.

Athletics Member NCAA. All Division III. *Intercollegiate sports:* baseball M, basketball M/W, crew M(c)/W(c), cross-country running M/W, equestrian sports M(c)/W(c), field hockey W, football M, golf M/W, ice hockey M(c), lacrosse M(c)/W, rugby M(c), skiing (cross-country) M(c)/W(c), skiing (downhill) M(c)/W(c), soccer M/W, softball W, squash M, swimming M/W, tennis M/W, track and field M/W, volleyball M(c)/W. *Intramural sports:* badminton M(c)/W(c), basketball M/W, fencing M(c)/W(c), football M/W, gymnastics M(c)/W(c), racquetball M/W, sailing M(c)/W(c), soccer M/W, softball M/W, tennis M/W, volleyball M/W, water polo M/W.

Standardized Tests *Required:* SAT I or ACT (for admission). *Recommended:* SAT II: Subject Tests (for admission).

Costs (2001–02) *Comprehensive fee:* $33,339 includes full-time tuition ($24,150), mandatory fees ($604), and room and board ($8585). *Room and board:* College room only: $3700. Room and board charges vary according to board plan. *Payment plans:* tuition prepayment, installment. *Waivers:* children of alumni and employees or children of employees.

Financial Aid Of all full-time matriculated undergraduates who enrolled in 2001, 2553 applied for aid, 2209 were judged to have need, 2209 had their need fully met. 1150 Federal Work-Study jobs (averaging $1979). In 2001, 1350 non-need-based awards were made. *Average percent of need met:* 100%. *Average financial aid package:* $21,627. *Average need-based loan:* $3821. *Average need-based gift aid:* $16,984.

Applying *Options:* common application, electronic application, early admission, early decision, deferred entrance. *Application fee:* $50. *Required:* essay or personal statement, high school transcript, 1 letter of recommendation. *Required for some:* audition, portfolio. *Recommended:* 2 letters of recommendation. *Application deadline:* 1/15 (freshmen), rolling (transfers). *Early decision:* 11/1. *Notification:* 4/15 (freshmen), 12/15 (early decision).

Admissions Contact Mr. Jamie Hobba, Director of Admissions, University of Rochester, PO Box 270251, Rochester, NY 14627. *Phone:* 585-275-3221. *Toll-free phone:* 888-822-2256. *Fax:* 585-461-4595. *E-mail:* admit@admissions.rochester.edu.

UTICA COLLEGE OF SYRACUSE UNIVERSITY
Utica, New York

- **Independent** comprehensive, founded 1946, part of Syracuse University
- **Calendar** semesters
- **Degrees** bachelor's and master's
- **Suburban** 138-acre campus
- **Endowment** $13.9 million
- **Coed,** 2,143 undergraduate students, 85% full-time, 60% women, 40% men
- **Moderately difficult** entrance level, 77% of applicants were admitted

Utica College offers a warm, friendly atmosphere with small classes and a dedicated faculty. Students choose from 33 majors in both the liberal arts and professional career programs. Extensive cooperative education and internship opportunities provide students with valuable experience in the workplace. Upon graduation, Utica College students receive the internationally recognized Syracuse University degree.

Undergraduates 1,815 full-time, 328 part-time. Students come from 34 states and territories, 19 other countries, 10% are from out of state, 8% African American, 2% Asian American or Pacific Islander, 4% Hispanic American, 0.7% Native American, 2% international, 10% transferred in, 48% live on campus. *Retention:* 68% of 2001 full-time freshmen returned.

Freshmen *Admission:* 2,109 applied, 1,628 admitted, 473 enrolled. *Average high school GPA:* 3.2. *Test scores:* SAT verbal scores over 500: 48%; SAT math scores over 500: 54%; ACT scores over 18: 67%; SAT verbal scores over 600: 10%; SAT math scores over 600: 11%; ACT scores over 24: 17%; SAT verbal scores over 700: 1%; SAT math scores over 700: 1%; ACT scores over 30: 9%.

Faculty *Total:* 213, 49% full-time, 45% with terminal degrees. *Student/faculty ratio:* 17:1.

Majors Accounting; biology; biology education; business administration; business economics; business education; business management/administrative services related; chemistry; chemistry education; communications; computer education; computer/information sciences; construction management; criminal justice/law enforcement administration; developmental/child psychology; economics; elementary education; English; English education; fine/studio arts; health/medical preparatory programs related; history; history education; international business; international relations; journalism; liberal arts and sciences/liberal studies; mathematics; mathematics education; nursing; occupational therapy; philosophy; physical therapy; physics; physics education; political science; pre-dentistry; pre-law; pre-medicine; pre-veterinary studies; psychology; public relations; recreational therapy; secondary education; social science education; social sciences; social studies education; sociology; theater arts/drama.

Academic Programs *Special study options:* academic remediation for entering students, accelerated degree program, adult/continuing education programs, advanced placement credit, cooperative education, distance learning, double majors, English as a second language, freshman honors college, honors programs, independent study, internships, off-campus study, part-time degree program, services for LD students, study abroad, summer session for credit. *ROTC:* Army (c), Air Force (c). *Unusual degree programs:* 3-2 engineering with Syracuse University.

Library Gannett Memorial Library with 179,672 titles, 1,311 serial subscriptions, 1,131 audiovisual materials, an OPAC.

Computers on Campus 191 computers available on campus for general student use. A campuswide network can be accessed from student residence rooms and from off campus. Internet access, at least one staffed computer lab available.

Student Life *Housing:* on-campus residence required through sophomore year. *Options:* coed. *Activities and Organizations:* drama/theater group, student-run newspaper, radio station, choral group, Honor Association, Latin American Student Union, theatre ensemble, Student Nurses, Young Scholars Liberty Partnership Program, national fraternities, national sororities. *Campus security:* 24-hour emergency response devices and patrols, late-night transport/escort service, controlled dormitory access. *Student Services:* health clinic, personal/psychological counseling, women's center.

Athletics Member NCAA. All Division III. *Intercollegiate sports:* baseball M, basketball M/W, field hockey W, football M, golf M/W, ice hockey M/W, lacrosse M/W, soccer M/W, softball W, swimming M/W, tennis M/W, volleyball W, water polo W. *Intramural sports:* badminton M/W, baseball M, basketball M/W, bowling M/W, cross-country running M(c)/W(c), fencing M(c)/W(c), golf M/W, racquetball M/W, soccer M/W, softball W, swimming M/W, table tennis M/W, tennis M/W, volleyball M/W.

Standardized Tests *Required for some:* SAT I or ACT (for admission). *Recommended:* SAT I or ACT (for admission).

Costs (2001–02) *Comprehensive fee:* $25,120 includes full-time tuition ($17,790), mandatory fees ($260), and room and board ($7070). Part-time tuition: $600 per credit hour. Part-time tuition and fees vary according to class time. *Room and board:* College room only: $3600. Room and board charges vary according to board plan and housing facility. *Payment plan:* deferred payment. *Waivers:* senior citizens and employees or children of employees.

Financial Aid Of all full-time matriculated undergraduates who enrolled in 2001, 1757 applied for aid, 1618 were judged to have need, 332 had their need fully met. 654 Federal Work-Study jobs (averaging $1377). 361 State and other part-time jobs (averaging $1756). In 2001, 37 non-need-based awards were made. *Average need-based loan:* $3875. *Average need-based gift aid:* $11,271. *Average non-need based aid:* $6182.

Applying *Options:* common application. *Application fee:* $35. *Required:* essay or personal statement, high school transcript, minimum 2.0 GPA. *Required for some:* minimum 3.0 GPA. *Recommended:* letters of recommendation, interview. *Application deadline:* rolling (freshmen), rolling (transfers).

Admissions Contact Mr. Patrick Quinn, Vice President for Enrollment Management, Utica College of Syracuse University, 160 Burrstone Road, Utica, NY 13502. *Phone:* 315-792-3006. *Toll-free phone:* 800-782-8884. *Fax:* 315-792-3003. *E-mail:* admiss@utica.ucsu.edu.

VASSAR COLLEGE
Poughkeepsie, New York

- **Independent** comprehensive, founded 1861
- **Calendar** semesters
- **Degrees** bachelor's and master's
- **Suburban** 1000-acre campus with easy access to New York City
- **Endowment** $616.2 million
- **Coed,** 2,439 undergraduate students, 97% full-time, 61% women, 39% men
- **Very difficult** entrance level, 34% of applicants were admitted

Undergraduates 2,377 full-time, 62 part-time. Students come from 52 states and territories, 43 other countries, 67% are from out of state, 5% African American, 9% Asian American or Pacific Islander, 5% Hispanic American, 0.4% Native American, 4% international, 0.4% transferred in, 98% live on campus. *Retention:* 94% of 2001 full-time freshmen returned.

Freshmen *Admission:* 5,690 applied, 1,921 admitted, 696 enrolled. *Average high school GPA:* 3.60. *Test scores:* SAT verbal scores over 500: 100%; SAT math scores over 500: 100%; SAT verbal scores over 600: 93%; SAT math scores over 600: 87%; SAT verbal scores over 700: 44%; SAT math scores over 700: 27%.

Faculty *Total:* 286, 86% full-time, 92% with terminal degrees. *Student/faculty ratio:* 9:1.

Majors African studies; American studies; anthropology; art history; Asian studies; astronomy; biochemistry; biology; chemistry; classics; cognitive psychology/psycholinguistics; computer science; economics; elementary education; English; environmental science; film studies; fine/studio arts; French; geography; geology; German; Hispanic-American studies; history; interdisciplinary studies; international relations; Italian; Judaic studies; Latin American studies; Latin (ancient and medieval); mathematics; medieval/renaissance studies; music; philosophy; physics; physiological psychology/psychobiology; political science; psychology; religious studies; Russian; science/technology and society; sociology; theater arts/drama; urban studies; women's studies.

Academic Programs *Special study options:* academic remediation for entering students, advanced placement credit, double majors, independent study, internships, off-campus study, part-time degree program, services for LD students, student-designed majors, study abroad. *Unusual degree programs:* 3-2 engineering with Dartmouth College.

Library Vassar College Libraries with 803,021 titles, 5,887 serial subscriptions, 16,635 audiovisual materials, an OPAC, a Web page.

Computers on Campus 300 computers available on campus for general student use. A campuswide network can be accessed from student residence rooms and from off campus that provide access to Ethernet. Internet access, online (class) registration, at least one staffed computer lab available.

Student Life *Housing:* on-campus residence required for freshman year. *Options:* coed, women-only, cooperative. *Activities and Organizations:* drama/theater group, student-run newspaper, radio station, choral group, Student Asso-

Vassar College (continued)
ciation, Black Students Union, VICE (Programming Social Events), Student Activists' Union, Poder Latino. *Campus security:* 24-hour emergency response devices and patrols, student patrols, late-night transport/escort service, controlled dormitory access. *Student Services:* health clinic, personal/psychological counseling, women's center.

Athletics Member NCAA. All Division III. *Intercollegiate sports:* baseball M, basketball M/W, crew M/W, cross-country running M/W, fencing M/W, field hockey W, golf M(c)/W(c), lacrosse M/W, rugby M(c)/W(c), sailing M(c)/W(c), soccer M/W, squash M/W, swimming M/W, tennis M/W, volleyball M/W. *Intramural sports:* badminton M(c)/W(c), basketball M/W, equestrian sports M(c)/W(c), fencing M(c)/W(c), skiing (cross-country) M(c)/W(c), skiing (downhill) M(c)/W(c), soccer M/W, softball M/W, squash M/W, swimming M/W, tennis M/W, volleyball M/W, water polo M/W, weight lifting M(c)/W(c).

Costs (2001–02) *Comprehensive fee:* $33,450 includes full-time tuition ($25,890), mandatory fees ($400), and room and board ($7160). Part-time tuition and fees vary according to course load. *Room and board:* College room only: $3800. Room and board charges vary according to board plan. *Payment plan:* installment. *Waivers:* employees or children of employees.

Financial Aid Of all full-time matriculated undergraduates who enrolled in 2001, 1511 applied for aid, 1247 were judged to have need, 1247 had their need fully met. 901 Federal Work-Study jobs (averaging $1424). 200 State and other part-time jobs. In 2001, 73 non-need-based awards were made. *Average percent of need met:* 100%. *Average financial aid package:* $20,835. *Average need-based loan:* $4182. *Average need-based gift aid:* $16,318. *Average non-need based aid:* $2673. *Average indebtedness upon graduation:* $16,150. *Financial aid deadline:* 1/10.

Applying *Options:* common application, electronic application, early decision, deferred entrance. *Application fee:* $60. *Required:* essay or personal statement, high school transcript, 2 letters of recommendation. *Recommended:* interview. *Application deadlines:* 1/1 (freshmen), 4/1 (transfers). *Early decision:* 11/15 (for plan 1), 1/1 (for plan 2). *Notification:* 4/1 (freshmen), 12/15 (early decision plan 1), 2/1 (early decision plan 2).

Admissions Contact Dr. David M. Borus, Dean of Admission and Financial Aid, Vassar College, 124 Raymond Avenue, Poughkeepsie, NY 12604. *Phone:* 845-437-7300. *Toll-free phone:* 800-827-7270. *Fax:* 914-437-7063. *E-mail:* admissions@vassar.edu.

WADHAMS HALL SEMINARY-COLLEGE
Ogdensburg, New York

- **Independent Roman Catholic** 4-year, founded 1924
- **Calendar** semesters
- **Degrees** bachelor's and postbachelor's certificates
- **Rural** 208-acre campus with easy access to Ottawa
- **Endowment** $3.8 million
- **Men only,** 21 undergraduate students, 100% full-time
- **Moderately difficult** entrance level, 100% of applicants were admitted

Undergraduates 21 full-time. Students come from 4 states and territories, 2 other countries, 19% are from out of state, 11% Asian American or Pacific Islander, 11% international, 10% transferred in, 100% live on campus. *Retention:* 33% of 2001 full-time freshmen returned.

Freshmen *Admission:* 6 applied, 6 admitted, 6 enrolled. *Average high school GPA:* 3.50. *Test scores:* SAT verbal scores over 500: 50%; SAT math scores over 500: 50%; SAT verbal scores over 600: 50%.

Faculty *Total:* 13, 69% full-time, 38% with terminal degrees. *Student/faculty ratio:* 2:1.

Majors Philosophy; religious studies.

Academic Programs *Special study options:* academic remediation for entering students, adult/continuing education programs, advanced placement credit, part-time degree program, services for LD students.

Library Reverend Richard S. Sturtz Library with 100,387 titles, 209 serial subscriptions, 5,204 audiovisual materials.

Computers on Campus 7 computers available on campus for general student use. A campuswide network can be accessed from student residence rooms. Internet access, at least one staffed computer lab available.

Student Life *Housing:* on-campus residence required through senior year. *Options:* men-only. *Activities and Organizations:* choral group, Community Service Program. *Campus security:* 24-hour emergency response devices. *Student Services:* health clinic, personal/psychological counseling.

Athletics *Intramural sports:* baseball M, basketball M, football M, golf M, racquetball M, skiing (cross-country) M, skiing (downhill) M, soccer M, softball M, swimming M, table tennis M, track and field M, volleyball M, weight lifting M.

Standardized Tests *Recommended:* SAT I or ACT (for admission), SAT II: Subject Tests (for admission).

Costs (2001–02) *One-time required fee:* $100. *Comprehensive fee:* $12,445 includes full-time tuition ($6000), mandatory fees ($445), and room and board ($6000). Part-time tuition: $170 per credit hour. *Room and board:* College room only: $2800. *Payment plans:* installment, deferred payment. *Waivers:* employees or children of employees.

Financial Aid Of all full-time matriculated undergraduates who enrolled in 2001, 17 applied for aid, 14 were judged to have need, 12 had their need fully met. 7 Federal Work-Study jobs (averaging $848). In 2001, 4 non-need-based awards were made. *Average percent of need met:* 98%. *Average financial aid package:* $9686. *Average need-based loan:* $3207. *Average need-based gift aid:* $6764. *Average non-need based aid:* $9706. *Average indebtedness upon graduation:* $10,579.

Applying *Options:* common application. *Application fee:* $15. *Required:* essay or personal statement, high school transcript, 3 letters of recommendation, interview. *Application deadlines:* 8/15 (freshmen), 8/15 (transfers).

Admissions Contact Rev. Edward J. Sheedy, Director of Admissions, Wadhams Hall Seminary-College, 6866 State Highway 37, Ogdensburg, NY 13669. *Phone:* 315-393-4231 Ext. 224. *Fax:* 315-393-4249. *E-mail:* admissions@wadhams.edu.

WAGNER COLLEGE
Staten Island, New York

- **Independent** comprehensive, founded 1883
- **Calendar** semesters
- **Degrees** bachelor's and master's
- **Urban** 105-acre campus with easy access to New York City
- **Endowment** $7.0 million
- **Coed,** 1,743 undergraduate students, 96% full-time, 61% women, 39% men
- **Moderately difficult** entrance level, 67% of applicants were admitted

Undergraduates 1,671 full-time, 72 part-time. Students come from 37 states and territories, 14 other countries, 44% are from out of state, 5% African American, 3% Asian American or Pacific Islander, 5% Hispanic American, 0.2% Native American, 2% international, 2% transferred in, 70% live on campus. *Retention:* 84% of 2001 full-time freshmen returned.

Freshmen *Admission:* 2,416 applied, 1,630 admitted, 534 enrolled. *Average high school GPA:* 3.20. *Test scores:* SAT verbal scores over 500: 76%; SAT math scores over 500: 73%; ACT scores over 18: 99%; SAT verbal scores over 600: 21%; SAT math scores over 600: 21%; ACT scores over 24: 55%; SAT verbal scores over 700: 1%; SAT math scores over 700: 2%; ACT scores over 30: 2%.

Faculty *Total:* 95. *Student/faculty ratio:* 16:1.

Majors Accounting; anthropology; art; arts management; biology; business administration; chemistry; computer science; early childhood education; education; elementary education; English; finance; gerontology; history; mathematics; microbiology/bacteriology; middle school education; music; nursing; physician assistant; physics; physiological psychology/psychobiology; political science; pre-dentistry; pre-law; pre-medicine; psychology; public administration; secondary education; sociology; Spanish; theater arts/drama; veterinary sciences.

Academic Programs *Special study options:* academic remediation for entering students, accelerated degree program, advanced placement credit, double majors, English as a second language, honors programs, internships, off-campus study, part-time degree program, services for LD students, student-designed majors, study abroad, summer session for credit. *ROTC:* Army (c), Air Force (c).

Library August Hormann Library with 310,000 titles, 1,000 serial subscriptions, a Web page.

Computers on Campus 150 computers available on campus for general student use. A campuswide network can be accessed from student residence rooms and from off campus. Internet access, at least one staffed computer lab available.

Student Life *Housing Options:* coed. *Activities and Organizations:* drama/theater group, student-run newspaper, radio station, choral group, Student Government Association, Student Activities Board, Wagner College Theatre, Wagner College Choir, student newspaper, national fraternities, national sororities. *Campus security:* 24-hour emergency response devices and patrols, late-night transport/escort service, controlled dormitory access. *Student Services:* health clinic, personal/psychological counseling.

Athletics Member NCAA. All Division I except football (Division I-AA). *Intercollegiate sports:* baseball M(s), basketball M(s)/W(s), cross-country running M(s)/W(s), golf M(s)/W(s), ice hockey M(c), lacrosse M(s)/W(s), soccer W(s), softball W(s), swimming W(s), tennis M(s)/W(s), track and field M(s)/W(s), volleyball W(s), water polo W(s), wrestling M(s). *Intramural sports:* basketball M/W, bowling M/W, football M, racquetball M/W, rugby M, soccer M/W, softball M/W, tennis M/W, volleyball M/W.

Standardized Tests *Required:* SAT I or ACT (for admission). *Required for some:* SAT II: Subject Tests (for admission). *Recommended:* SAT II: Subject Tests (for admission), SAT II: Writing Test (for admission).

Costs (2001–02) *Comprehensive fee:* $27,500 includes full-time tuition ($20,500) and room and board ($7000). Part-time tuition: $1950 per course. Part-time tuition and fees vary according to course load. *Payment plan:* installment. *Waivers:* senior citizens and employees or children of employees.

Financial Aid Of all full-time matriculated undergraduates who enrolled in 2001, 1302 applied for aid, 1108 were judged to have need. In 2001, 401 non-need-based awards were made. *Average need-based loan:* $3998. *Average need-based gift aid:* $8152. *Average non-need based aid:* $6705. *Average indebtedness upon graduation:* $15,308.

Applying *Options:* common application, electronic application, early admission, early decision, deferred entrance. *Application fee:* $45. *Required:* essay or personal statement, high school transcript, minimum 2.7 GPA, 2 letters of recommendation. *Required for some:* interview. *Recommended:* minimum 3.0 GPA, interview. *Application deadline:* 2/15 (freshmen), rolling (transfers). *Early decision:* 12/1. *Notification:* 3/1 (freshmen), 1/1 (early decision).

Admissions Contact Mr. Angelo Araimo, Dean of Admissions, Wagner College, One Campus Road, Staten Island, NY 10301. *Phone:* 718-390-3411. *Toll-free phone:* 800-221-1010. *Fax:* 718-390-3105. *E-mail:* admissions@wagner.edu.

WEBB INSTITUTE
Glen Cove, New York

- **Independent** 4-year, founded 1889
- **Calendar** semesters
- **Degree** bachelor's
- **Suburban** 26-acre campus with easy access to New York City
- **Endowment** $59.6 million
- **Coed,** 73 undergraduate students, 100% full-time, 22% women, 78% men
- **Most difficult** entrance level, 42% of applicants were admitted

Webb Institute is a private engineering college, where all undergraduate students receive a full-tuition scholarship. BS degrees in naval architecture and marine engineering are offered. There is a cooperative work term in each year and a 100% employment record. Competitive selection of students is based on academic record, standardized test scores, and motivation for program. The Institute's programs are fully accredited.

Undergraduates 73 full-time. Students come from 23 states and territories, 2 other countries, 70% are from out of state, 3% Asian American or Pacific Islander, 1% transferred in, 100% live on campus. *Retention:* 90% of 2001 full-time freshmen returned.

Freshmen *Admission:* 69 applied, 29 admitted, 20 enrolled. *Average high school GPA:* 3.60. *Test scores:* SAT verbal scores over 500: 100%; SAT math scores over 500: 100%; SAT verbal scores over 600: 80%; SAT math scores over 600: 100%; SAT verbal scores over 700: 35%; SAT math scores over 700: 55%.

Faculty *Total:* 16, 50% full-time, 75% with terminal degrees. *Student/faculty ratio:* 5:1.

Majors Naval architecture/marine engineering.

Academic Programs *Special study options:* cooperative education, double majors, independent study, internships, off-campus study.

Library Livingston Library with 40,545 titles, 256 serial subscriptions, 1,851 audiovisual materials, an OPAC, a Web page.

Computers on Campus 75 computers available on campus for general student use. A campuswide network can be accessed from student residence rooms and from off campus. Internet access, at least one staffed computer lab available.

Student Life *Housing:* on-campus residence required through senior year. *Options:* coed, men-only, women-only. *Activities and Organizations:* choral group, Student Organization, Society of Naval Architects and Marine Engineers, American Society of Naval Engineers, Society of Women Engineers. *Campus security:* 24-hour emergency response devices and patrols, controlled dormitory access. *Student Services:* personal/psychological counseling.

Athletics *Intercollegiate sports:* basketball M/W, cross-country running M/W, sailing M/W, soccer M/W, tennis M/W, volleyball M/W. *Intramural sports:* baseball M/W, volleyball M/W.

Standardized Tests *Required:* SAT I (for admission), SAT II: Writing Test (for admission).

Financial Aid Of all full-time matriculated undergraduates who enrolled in 2001, 13 applied for aid, 13 were judged to have need. *Average percent of need met:* 38%. *Average financial aid package:* $2360. *Average indebtedness upon graduation:* $11,000.

Applying *Options:* early decision. *Application fee:* $25. *Required:* high school transcript, minimum 3.5 GPA, 2 letters of recommendation, interview, proof of U.S. citizenship. *Application deadlines:* 2/15 (freshmen), 2/15 (transfers). *Early decision:* 10/15. *Notification:* continuous until 4/30 (freshmen), 12/15 (early decision).

Admissions Contact Mr. William G. Murray, Executive Director of Student Administrative Services, Webb Institute, Crescent Beach Road, Glen Cove, NY 11542-1398. *Phone:* 516-671-2213. *Fax:* 516-674-9838. *E-mail:* admissions@webb-institute.edu.

WELLS COLLEGE
Aurora, New York

- **Independent** 4-year, founded 1868
- **Calendar** semesters
- **Degree** bachelor's
- **Rural** 365-acre campus with easy access to Syracuse
- **Endowment** $46.5 million
- **Women only,** 443 undergraduate students, 96% full-time
- **Moderately difficult** entrance level, 88% of applicants were admitted

Wells College believes that the 21st century will be a time of unprecedented opportunity for women. Women who are prepared for leadership roles will have a distinct advantage. Wells College has an integrative liberal arts curriculum designed to prepare women for the leadership roles they will assume in all areas of life in the next century. Wells women are being prepared to become the leaders in a variety of fields: business, government, the arts, sciences, medicine, and education. The liberal arts curriculum, combined with a wide array of internships, outstanding study-abroad opportunities, leadership programs, and a wealth of cocurricular activities, helps Wells women realize their potential and career goals.

Undergraduates 427 full-time, 16 part-time. Students come from 30 states and territories, 8 other countries, 24% are from out of state, 5% African American, 4% Asian American or Pacific Islander, 4% Hispanic American, 0.2% Native American, 2% international, 10% transferred in, 97% live on campus. *Retention:* 69% of 2001 full-time freshmen returned.

Freshmen *Admission:* 417 applied, 369 admitted, 100 enrolled. *Average high school GPA:* 3.4. *Test scores:* SAT verbal scores over 500: 85%; SAT math scores over 500: 73%; ACT scores over 18: 93%; SAT verbal scores over 600: 36%; SAT math scores over 600: 23%; ACT scores over 24: 60%; SAT verbal scores over 700: 6%; SAT math scores over 700: 1%; ACT scores over 30: 7%.

Faculty *Total:* 66, 74% full-time, 100% with terminal degrees. *Student/faculty ratio:* 9:1.

Majors African-American studies; American studies; anthropology; art; art history; biochemistry; biology; business administration; chemistry; computer science; creative writing; dance; economics; education; elementary education; engineering; English; environmental science; fine/studio arts; French; German; history; international relations; mathematics; molecular biology; music; philosophy; physics; political science; pre-dentistry; pre-law; pre-medicine; pre-veterinary studies; psychology; public policy analysis; religious studies; secondary education; sociology; Spanish; theater arts/drama; women's studies.

Academic Programs *Special study options:* accelerated degree program, adult/continuing education programs, advanced placement credit, double majors, independent study, internships, off-campus study, part-time degree program, student-designed majors, study abroad. *ROTC:* Air Force (c). *Unusual degree programs:* 3-2 business administration with University of Rochester; engineering with Washington University in St. Louis, Columbia University, Clarkson University, Cornell University, Case Western Reserve University; community health with University of Rochester.

Library Louis Jefferson Long Library with 248,390 titles, 384 serial subscriptions, 897 audiovisual materials, an OPAC, a Web page.

Computers on Campus 98 computers available on campus for general student use. A campuswide network can be accessed from student residence rooms and from off campus. Internet access, at least one staffed computer lab available.

Student Life *Housing:* on-campus residence required through senior year. *Options:* women-only. *Activities and Organizations:* drama/theater group, student-run newspaper, choral group, creative and performing arts groups, POWER, Amnesty International, Athletic Association, choral groups. *Campus security:* 24-hour emergency response devices and patrols, late-night transport/escort service, controlled dormitory access. *Student Services:* health clinic, personal/psychological counseling, women's center.

Athletics Member NCAA. All Division III. *Intercollegiate sports:* field hockey W, lacrosse W, soccer W, softball W, swimming W, tennis W. *Intramural sports:*

Wells College (continued)
basketball W, field hockey W, football W, golf W, lacrosse W, sailing W, skiing (cross-country) W, skiing (downhill) W, soccer W, swimming W, tennis W, volleyball W.
Standardized Tests *Required:* SAT I or ACT (for admission).
Costs (2001–02) *Comprehensive fee:* $19,350 includes full-time tuition ($12,570), mandatory fees ($480), and room and board ($6300). Part-time tuition: $275 per semester hour. *Payment plan:* installment. *Waivers:* senior citizens and employees or children of employees.
Financial Aid Of all full-time matriculated undergraduates who enrolled in 2001, 397 applied for aid, 349 were judged to have need, 71 had their need fully met. 105 Federal Work-Study jobs (averaging $1053). 260 State and other part-time jobs (averaging $823). In 2001, 62 non-need-based awards were made. *Average percent of need met:* 90%. *Average financial aid package:* $12,905. *Average need-based loan:* $3934. *Average need-based gift aid:* $8954. *Average non-need based aid:* $5130. *Average indebtedness upon graduation:* $17,125.
Applying *Options:* common application, electronic application, early admission, early decision, early action, deferred entrance. *Application fee:* $40. *Required:* essay or personal statement, high school transcript, 2 letters of recommendation. *Recommended:* interview. *Application deadline:* 3/1 (freshmen), rolling (transfers). *Early decision:* 12/15. *Notification:* 4/1 (freshmen), 1/15 (early decision), 2/1 (early action).
Admissions Contact Ms. Susan Raith Sloan, Director of Admissions, Wells College, MacMillan Hall, Aurora, NY 13026. *Phone:* 315-364-3264. *Toll-free phone:* 800-952-9355. *Fax:* 315-364-3227. *E-mail:* admissions@wells.edu.

YESHIVA DERECH CHAIM
Brooklyn, New York

Admissions Contact Mr. Y. Borchardt, Administrator, Yeshiva Derech Chaim, 4907 18th Avenue, Brooklyn, NY 11218. *Phone:* 718-438-5476.

YESHIVA KARLIN STOLIN RABBINICAL INSTITUTE
Brooklyn, New York

- **Independent Jewish** comprehensive, founded 1948
- **Calendar** semesters
- **Degrees** bachelor's and master's
- **Urban** campus
- **Men only**
- **Very difficult** entrance level

Student Life *Campus security:* 24-hour emergency response devices.
Applying *Required:* high school transcript, interview.
Admissions Contact Mr. Aryeh L. Wolpin, Director of Admissions, Yeshiva Karlin Stolin Rabbinical Institute, 1818 Fifty-fourth Street, Brooklyn, NY 11204. *Phone:* 718-232-7800 Ext. 26. *Fax:* 718-331-4833.

YESHIVA OF NITRA RABBINICAL COLLEGE
Mount Kisco, New York

Admissions Contact Mr. Ernest Schwartz, Administrator, Yeshiva of Nitra Rabbinical College, Pines Bridge Road, Mount Kisco, NY 10549. *Phone:* 718-384-5460.

YESHIVA SHAAR HATORAH TALMUDIC RESEARCH INSTITUTE
Kew Gardens, New York

Admissions Contact Rabbi Kalman Epstein, Assistant Dean, Yeshiva Shaar Hatorah Talmudic Research Institute, 83-96 117th Street, Kew Gardens, NY 11418-1469. *Phone:* 718-846-1940.

YESHIVATH VIZNITZ
Monsey, New York

Admissions Contact Rabbi Bernard Rosenfeld, Registrar, Yeshivath Viznitz, Phyllis Terrace, PO Box 446, Monsey, NY 10952. *Phone:* 914-356-1010.

YESHIVATH ZICHRON MOSHE
South Fallsburg, New York

Admissions Contact Yeshivath Zichron Moshe, Laurel Park Road, South Fallsburg, NY 12779. *Phone:* 914-434-5240.

YESHIVAT MIKDASH MELECH
Brooklyn, New York

Admissions Contact Rabbi S. Churba, Director of Admissions, Yeshivat Mikdash Melech, 1326 Ocean Parkway, Brooklyn, NY 11230-5601. *Phone:* 718-339-1090.

YESHIVA UNIVERSITY
New York, New York

- **Independent** university, founded 1886
- **Calendar** semesters
- **Degrees** bachelor's, master's, doctoral, and first professional (Yeshiva College and Stern College for Women are coordinate undergraduate colleges of arts and sciences for men and women, respectively. Sy Syms School of Business offers programs at both campuses)
- **Urban** campus
- **Endowment** $493.0 million
- **Coed,** 2,819 undergraduate students, 99% full-time, 44% women, 56% men
- **Moderately difficult** entrance level, 78% of applicants were admitted

Undergraduates 2,778 full-time, 41 part-time. Students come from 31 states and territories, 30 other countries, 0.8% transferred in. *Retention:* 85% of 2001 full-time freshmen returned.
Freshmen *Admission:* 1,768 applied, 1,372 admitted, 755 enrolled. *Average high school GPA:* 3.4.
Faculty *Total:* 235.
Majors Accounting; biology; business administration; business marketing and marketing management; chemistry; classics; computer science; early childhood education; economics; education; elementary education; English; finance; French; Hebrew; history; interdisciplinary studies; Judaic studies; management information systems/business data processing; mass communications; mathematics; music; philosophy; physics; political science; pre-dentistry; pre-law; pre-medicine; psychology; sociology; speech-language pathology; speech-language pathology/audiology; speech/rhetorical studies; theater arts/drama.
Academic Programs *Special study options:* advanced placement credit, double majors, English as a second language, honors programs, internships, off-campus study, student-designed majors, study abroad, summer session for credit. *Unusual degree programs:* 3-2 engineering with Columbia University; nursing with New York University; Jewish studies, Jewish education, occupational therapy with Columbia University, New York University; podiatry with New York College of Podiatric Medicine; optometry with State University of New York College of Optometry; dentistry with New York University College of Dentistry.
Library Mendel Gottesman Library plus 6 others with 995,312 titles, 9,760 serial subscriptions.
Computers on Campus 142 computers available on campus for general student use. Internet access, at least one staffed computer lab available.
Student Life *Activities and Organizations:* drama/theater group, student-run newspaper, radio station, choral group, dramatics societies, student newspapers, social action groups. *Campus security:* 24-hour emergency response devices and patrols, late-night transport/escort service. *Student Services:* personal/psychological counseling.
Athletics Member NCAA. All Division III. *Intercollegiate sports:* basketball M/W, cross-country running M, fencing M, tennis M/W, volleyball M, wrestling M. *Intramural sports:* basketball M/W, fencing M/W, swimming M/W, table tennis M, volleyball M/W.
Standardized Tests *Required:* SAT I or ACT (for admission). *Recommended:* SAT II: Subject Tests (for admission).
Costs (2002–03) *Comprehensive fee:* $25,936 includes full-time tuition ($19,065), mandatory fees ($445), and room and board ($6426). Full-time tuition and fees vary according to student level. Part-time tuition: $715 per credit. *Required fees:* $25 per term part-time. *Room and board:* College room only: $4645. *Payment plan:* installment. *Waivers:* employees or children of employees.
Financial Aid Of all full-time matriculated undergraduates who enrolled in 2001, 1606 applied for aid, 1228 were judged to have need, 168 had their need fully met. In 2001, 183 non-need-based awards were made. *Average percent of*

need met: 73%. *Average financial aid package:* $14,088. *Average need-based loan:* $4757. *Average need-based gift aid:* $11,682. *Average non-need based aid:* $4712.

Applying *Options:* early admission, deferred entrance. *Application fee:* $40. *Required:* essay or personal statement, high school transcript, 2 letters of recommendation, interview. *Application deadlines:* 2/15 (freshmen), 2/15 (transfers). *Notification:* continuous (freshmen).

Admissions Contact Mr. Michael Kranzler, Director of Undergraduate Admissions, Yeshiva University, 500 West 185th Street, New York, NY 10033-3201. *Phone:* 212-960-5277. *Fax:* 212-960-0086. *E-mail:* yuadmit@ymail.yu.edu.

YORK COLLEGE OF THE CITY UNIVERSITY OF NEW YORK

Jamaica, New York

- **State and locally supported** 4-year, founded 1967, part of City University of New York System
- **Calendar** semesters
- **Degree** bachelor's
- **Urban** 50-acre campus with easy access to New York City
- **Coed,** 5,253 undergraduate students, 54% full-time, 71% women, 29% men
- **Noncompetitive** entrance level

Undergraduates 2,850 full-time, 2,403 part-time. Students come from 4 states and territories, 100 other countries, 0% are from out of state, 44% African American, 7% Asian American or Pacific Islander, 15% Hispanic American, 0.2% Native American, 8% international, 11% transferred in. *Retention:* 88% of 2001 full-time freshmen returned.

Freshmen *Admission:* 507 enrolled.

Faculty *Total:* 433, 39% full-time, 47% with terminal degrees.

Majors Accounting; African-American studies; anthropology; art; biological technology; biology; business administration; business marketing and marketing management; chemistry; computer management; economics; English; environmental health; French; geology; gerontology; health education; history; information sciences/systems; Italian; liberal arts and sciences/liberal studies; mathematics; medical technology; music; nursing; occupational therapy; philosophy; physical education; physics; political science; psychology; social work; sociology; Spanish; speech/rhetorical studies; theater arts/drama.

Academic Programs *Special study options:* adult/continuing education programs, advanced placement credit, cooperative education, double majors, English as a second language, honors programs, independent study, internships, off-campus study, part-time degree program, services for LD students, student-designed majors, study abroad, summer session for credit. *ROTC:* Army (c), Navy (c), Air Force (c).

Library 176,299 titles, 1,121 serial subscriptions, an OPAC, a Web page.

Computers on Campus 530 computers available on campus for general student use. A campuswide network can be accessed from off campus. At least one staffed computer lab available.

Student Life *Housing:* college housing not available. *Activities and Organizations:* drama/theater group, student-run newspaper, television station, choral group, Haitian Students Association, Caribbean Students Association, Haitian Cultural Association, Latin Caucus. *Campus security:* 24-hour emergency response devices and patrols, late-night transport/escort service. *Student Services:* health clinic, personal/psychological counseling, women's center.

Athletics Member NCAA. All Division III. *Intercollegiate sports:* basketball M/W, cross-country running M/W, soccer M/W, softball W, swimming M/W, tennis M/W, track and field M/W, volleyball M/W, weight lifting M/W. *Intramural sports:* badminton M/W, basketball M/W, soccer M/W, softball W, swimming M/W, table tennis M/W, tennis M/W, track and field M/W, volleyball M/W, weight lifting M/W.

Standardized Tests *Required:* SAT I or ACT (for admission).

Costs (2002–03) *Tuition:* state resident $3200 full-time, $135 per credit part-time; nonresident $6800 full-time, $285 per credit part-time. *Required fees:* $90 full-time, $26 per term part-time. *Payment plan:* deferred payment. *Waivers:* senior citizens and employees or children of employees.

Applying *Options:* early admission, deferred entrance. *Application fee:* $40. *Required:* high school transcript, minimum 2.0 GPA. *Required for some:* minimum 2.5 GPA. *Recommended:* minimum 3.0 GPA. *Application deadline:* rolling (freshmen), rolling (transfers). *Notification:* continuous (freshmen).

Admissions Contact Ms. Sally Nelson, Director of Admissions, York College of the City University of New York, 94-20 Guy R. Brewer Boulevard, Jamaica, NY 11451. *Phone:* 718-262-2165. *Fax:* 718-262-2601.

NORTH CAROLINA

APPALACHIAN STATE UNIVERSITY

Boone, North Carolina

- **State-supported** comprehensive, founded 1899, part of University of North Carolina System
- **Calendar** semesters
- **Degrees** bachelor's, master's, doctoral, and post-master's certificates
- **Small-town** 255-acre campus
- **Endowment** $50.0 million
- **Coed,** 12,560 undergraduate students, 90% full-time, 51% women, 49% men
- **Moderately difficult** entrance level, 65% of applicants were admitted

Undergraduates 11,343 full-time, 1,217 part-time. Students come from 44 states and territories, 12% are from out of state, 3% African American, 0.9% Asian American or Pacific Islander, 0.9% Hispanic American, 0.4% Native American, 0.4% international, 7% transferred in, 41% live on campus.

Freshmen *Admission:* 8,853 applied, 5,770 admitted, 2,312 enrolled. *Average high school GPA:* 3.55. *Test scores:* SAT verbal scores over 500: 75%; SAT math scores over 500: 80%; ACT scores over 18: 85%; SAT verbal scores over 600: 25%; SAT math scores over 600: 27%; ACT scores over 24: 28%; SAT verbal scores over 700: 3%; SAT math scores over 700: 2%; ACT scores over 30: 2%.

Faculty *Total:* 921, 67% full-time, 60% with terminal degrees. *Student/faculty ratio:* 17:1.

Majors Accounting; advertising; anthropology; archaeology; art; art education; art history; arts management; athletic training/sports medicine; biology; business administration; business education; business marketing and marketing management; cartography; chemistry; chemistry education; city/community/regional planning; clothing/apparel/textile studies; clothing/textiles; computer science; criminal justice/law enforcement administration; criminal justice studies; developmental/child psychology; drama/dance education; early childhood education; ecology; economics; education of the specific learning disabled; electrical/electronic engineering technology; engineering science; English; English education; finance; fine/studio arts; French; geography; geology; graphic design/commercial art/illustration; graphic/printing equipment; health education; health services administration; history; history education; home economics; home economics education; hotel and restaurant management; industrial arts; industrial design; insurance/risk management; interior design; international business; journalism; liberal arts and sciences/liberal studies; library science; marketing/distribution education; mathematical statistics; mathematics; mathematics education; medical technology; middle school education; music; music business management/merchandising; music (general performance); music history; music (piano and organ performance); music teacher education; music theory and composition; music therapy; music (voice and choral/opera performance); natural sciences; nutrition science; nutrition studies; operations management; physical education; physics; physics education; political science; pre-medicine; psychology; public health education/promotion; public relations; radio/television broadcasting; real estate; recreation/leisure facilities management; recreation/leisure studies; religious music; religious studies; science education; secretarial science; social sciences; social studies education; social work; sociology; Spanish; speech-language pathology/audiology; speech/rhetorical studies; stringed instruments; theater arts/drama; wind/percussion instruments.

Academic Programs *Special study options:* academic remediation for entering students, accelerated degree program, adult/continuing education programs, advanced placement credit, distance learning, double majors, English as a second language, honors programs, independent study, internships, off-campus study, part-time degree program, services for LD students, student-designed majors, study abroad, summer session for credit. *ROTC:* Army (b). *Unusual degree programs:* 3-2 engineering with Auburn University; forestry with North Carolina State University.

Library Carol Grotnes Belk Library plus 1 other with 780,111 titles, 4,998 serial subscriptions, 36,228 audiovisual materials, an OPAC, a Web page.

Computers on Campus 500 computers available on campus for general student use. A campuswide network can be accessed from student residence rooms. Internet access, at least one staffed computer lab available.

Student Life *Housing:* on-campus residence required for freshman year. *Options:* coed. *Activities and Organizations:* drama/theater group, student-run newspaper, radio station, choral group, marching band, Baptist Student Union, Inter-University Christian Fellowship, Campus Crusade for Christ, Circle K, Criminal Justice Association, national fraternities, national sororities. *Campus security:* 24-hour emergency response devices and patrols, late-night transport/escort service, controlled dormitory access. *Student Services:* health clinic, personal/psychological counseling, legal services.

Appalachian State University (continued)

Athletics Member NCAA. All Division I except football (Division I-AA). *Intercollegiate sports:* baseball M(s), basketball M(s)/W(s), cross-country running M(s)/W(s), field hockey W(s), golf M(s)/W(s), soccer M(s)/W(s), tennis M(s)/W(s), track and field M(s)/W(s), volleyball W(s), wrestling M(s). *Intramural sports:* archery M/W, badminton M/W, basketball M/W, bowling M/W, cross-country running M/W, fencing M/W, field hockey W, football M/W, golf M/W, gymnastics M/W, racquetball M/W, rugby M, skiing (cross-country) M/W, skiing (downhill) M/W, soccer M/W, squash M/W, swimming M/W, table tennis M/W, tennis M/W, track and field M/W, volleyball M/W, water polo M/W, weight lifting M/W, wrestling M.

Standardized Tests *Required:* SAT I or ACT (for admission).

Costs (2001–02) *Tuition:* state resident $1222 full-time, $318 per term part-time; nonresident $9144 full-time, $1227 per term part-time. Part-time tuition and fees vary according to course load. *Required fees:* $1086 full-time. *Room and board:* $4045; room only: $2285. Room and board charges vary according to board plan and housing facility. *Payment plan:* installment. *Waivers:* employees or children of employees.

Financial Aid Of all full-time matriculated undergraduates who enrolled in 2001, 6746 applied for aid, 3588 were judged to have need, 1294 had their need fully met. 2450 State and other part-time jobs (averaging $1250). In 2001, 1335 non-need-based awards were made. *Average percent of need met:* 82%. *Average financial aid package:* $5107. *Average need-based loan:* $3042. *Average need-based gift aid:* $3004. *Average non-need based aid:* $2513. *Average indebtedness upon graduation:* $13,000.

Applying *Options:* common application, early admission, deferred entrance. *Application fee:* $45. *Required:* high school transcript. *Application deadline:* rolling (freshmen), rolling (transfers). *Notification:* continuous (freshmen).

Admissions Contact Mr. Joe Watts, Associate Vice Chancellor, Appalachian State University, John Thomas Hall. *Phone:* 828-262-2120. *Fax:* 828-262-3296. *E-mail:* admissions@appstate.edu.

BARBER-SCOTIA COLLEGE
Concord, North Carolina

- **Independent** 4-year, founded 1867, affiliated with Presbyterian Church (U.S.A.)
- **Calendar** semesters
- **Degree** bachelor's
- **Small-town** 23-acre campus with easy access to Charlotte
- **Endowment** $4.3 million
- **Coed,** 566 undergraduate students, 98% full-time, 49% women, 51% men
- **Minimally difficult** entrance level, 69% of applicants were admitted

Undergraduates 554 full-time, 12 part-time. Students come from 20 states and territories, 32% are from out of state, 97% African American, 0.2% Asian American or Pacific Islander, 0.9% Hispanic American, 13% transferred in, 90% live on campus. *Retention:* 77% of 2001 full-time freshmen returned.

Freshmen *Admission:* 1,003 applied, 690 admitted, 177 enrolled. *Average high school GPA:* 2.12.

Faculty *Total:* 35, 71% full-time, 49% with terminal degrees. *Student/faculty ratio:* 18:1.

Majors Accounting; biology; business administration; business marketing and marketing management; computer science; criminal justice/law enforcement administration; elementary education; English; finance; hotel and restaurant management; mass communications; mathematics; political science; pre-law; sociology; sport/fitness administration.

Academic Programs *Special study options:* academic remediation for entering students, advanced placement credit, cooperative education, double majors, honors programs, internships, off-campus study, summer session for credit. *ROTC:* Army (c), Air Force (b). *Unusual degree programs:* 3-2 nursing with University of North Carolina at Charlotte; law with St. John's University.

Library Sage Memorial Library with 24,270 titles, 193 serial subscriptions.

Computers on Campus 125 computers available on campus for general student use. A campuswide network can be accessed from off campus. Internet access, at least one staffed computer lab available.

Student Life *Housing:* on-campus residence required through senior year. *Activities and Organizations:* drama/theater group, student-run newspaper, choral group, SGA (Student Government Association), Student Christian Association, Pre-Alumni Council, Scotia Express, yearbook, national fraternities, national sororities. *Campus security:* 24-hour emergency response devices and patrols. *Student Services:* health clinic, personal/psychological counseling.

Athletics Member NAIA. *Intercollegiate sports:* basketball M(s)/W(s), cross-country running M(s)/W(s), softball W(s), tennis M(s), track and field M(s)/W(s), volleyball W(s). *Intramural sports:* basketball M/W, football M, golf M, tennis M.

Standardized Tests *Required:* SAT I or ACT (for admission).

Costs (2001–02) *Comprehensive fee:* $13,000 includes full-time tuition ($7800), mandatory fees ($1248), and room and board ($3952). Full-time tuition and fees vary according to course load. Part-time tuition: $310 per semester hour. Part-time tuition and fees vary according to course load. *Required fees:* $44 per year part-time. *Room and board:* College room only: $2080. *Payment plan:* installment. *Waivers:* employees or children of employees.

Applying *Options:* common application, electronic application, early admission. *Application fee:* $15. *Required:* high school transcript, letters of recommendation. *Required for some:* minimum 2.0 GPA. *Recommended:* essay or personal statement, minimum 3.0 GPA, interview. *Application deadline:* rolling (freshmen), rolling (transfers). *Notification:* continuous (freshmen).

Admissions Contact Dr. Alexander Erwin, Academic Dean, Barber-Scotia College, 145 Cabarrus Avenue, West, Concord, NC 28025-5187. *Phone:* 704-789-2948. *Toll-free phone:* 800-610-0778. *Fax:* 704-784-3817.

BARTON COLLEGE
Wilson, North Carolina

- **Independent** 4-year, founded 1902, affiliated with Christian Church (Disciples of Christ)
- **Calendar** 4-1-4
- **Degree** bachelor's
- **Small-town** 62-acre campus
- **Endowment** $19.0 million
- **Coed,** 1,229 undergraduate students, 78% full-time, 69% women, 31% men
- **Minimally difficult** entrance level, 87% of applicants were admitted

Undergraduates 960 full-time, 269 part-time. Students come from 29 states and territories, 16 other countries, 29% are from out of state, 19% African American, 0.4% Asian American or Pacific Islander, 2% Hispanic American, 0.3% Native American, 2% international, 6% transferred in, 40% live on campus. *Retention:* 59% of 2001 full-time freshmen returned.

Freshmen *Admission:* 893 applied, 779 admitted, 272 enrolled. *Average high school GPA:* 2.60. *Test scores:* SAT verbal scores over 500: 28%; SAT math scores over 500: 31%; SAT verbal scores over 600: 2%; SAT math scores over 600: 3%.

Faculty *Total:* 100, 77% full-time, 100% with terminal degrees. *Student/faculty ratio:* 13:1.

Majors Accounting; art education; athletic training/sports medicine; biology; broadcast journalism; business administration; ceramic arts; chemistry; criminal justice studies; education; education of the hearing impaired; elementary education; English; environmental science; finance; fine/studio arts; graphic design/commercial art/illustration; Hispanic-American studies; history; human resources management; mass communications; mathematics; middle school education; musical instrument technology; nursing; painting; philosophy; photography; physical education; political science; pre-dentistry; pre-law; pre-medicine; pre-pharmacy studies; pre-veterinary studies; psychology; religious studies; science education; secondary education; social sciences; social work; special education; sport/fitness administration; theater arts/drama.

Academic Programs *Special study options:* academic remediation for entering students, adult/continuing education programs, advanced placement credit, cooperative education, double majors, independent study, internships, part-time degree program, services for LD students, study abroad, summer session for credit. *Unusual degree programs:* 3-2 engineering with North Carolina State University, North Carolina Agricultural and Technical State University.

Library Willis N. Hackney Library with 179,758 titles, 725 serial subscriptions, 4,656 audiovisual materials, an OPAC, a Web page.

Computers on Campus 250 computers available on campus for general student use. A campuswide network can be accessed from student residence rooms and from off campus. Internet access, at least one staffed computer lab available.

Student Life *Housing:* on-campus residence required through sophomore year. *Options:* coed, women-only. *Activities and Organizations:* drama/theater group, student-run newspaper, television station, choral group, Barton College Association of Nurses, Black Student Awareness, Stage and Script, Campus Activities Board, national fraternities, national sororities. *Campus security:* 24-hour emergency response devices and patrols, student patrols, late-night transport/escort service, controlled dormitory access. *Student Services:* health clinic, personal/psychological counseling.

Athletics Member NCAA. All Division II. *Intercollegiate sports:* baseball M(s), basketball M(s)/W(s), cross-country running M(s)/W(s), golf M(s), soccer M(s)/W(s), softball W(s), tennis M(s)/W(s), volleyball W(s). *Intramural sports:* badminton M/W, basketball M/W, bowling M/W, football M/W, golf M/W, racquetball M/W, soccer M/W, softball M/W, table tennis M/W, tennis M/W, volleyball M/W.

Standardized Tests *Required:* SAT I or ACT (for admission).

Costs (2002–03) *Comprehensive fee:* $17,838 includes full-time tuition ($12,378), mandatory fees ($706), and room and board ($4754). Full-time tuition and fees vary according to course load. Part-time tuition: $526 per hour. Part-time tuition and fees vary according to course load and program. *Required fees:* $30 per hour. *Room and board:* College room only: $2276. Room and board charges vary according to board plan and housing facility. *Payment plan:* installment. *Waivers:* adult students and employees or children of employees.

Financial Aid Of all full-time matriculated undergraduates who enrolled in 2001, 805 applied for aid, 652 were judged to have need, 404 had their need fully met. In 2001, 268 non-need-based awards were made. *Average percent of need met:* 82%. *Average financial aid package:* $9282. *Average need-based loan:* $3800. *Average need-based gift aid:* $2258. *Average non-need based aid:* $6510. *Average indebtedness upon graduation:* $11,500.

Applying *Options:* electronic application, deferred entrance. *Application fee:* $25. *Required:* high school transcript. *Recommended:* essay or personal statement, minimum 2.5 GPA, 2 letters of recommendation, interview. *Application deadline:* rolling (freshmen), rolling (transfers).

Admissions Contact Ms. Amy Denton, Director of In-State Admissions, Barton College, Box 500, College Station, Hardy Center, Wilson, NC 27893. *Phone:* 252-399-6314. *Toll-free phone:* 800-345-4973. *Fax:* 252-399-6572. *E-mail:* enroll@barton.edu.

BELMONT ABBEY COLLEGE

Belmont, North Carolina

- **Independent Roman Catholic** 4-year, founded 1876
- **Calendar** semesters
- **Degree** bachelor's
- **Small-town** 650-acre campus with easy access to Charlotte
- **Endowment** $19.4 million
- **Coed,** 873 undergraduate students, 86% full-time, 56% women, 44% men
- **Moderately difficult** entrance level, 79% of applicants were admitted

Undergraduates 752 full-time, 121 part-time. Students come from 37 states and territories, 15 other countries, 34% are from out of state, 9% African American, 0.8% Asian American or Pacific Islander, 3% Hispanic American, 0.4% Native American, 3% international, 11% transferred in, 51% live on campus. *Retention:* 68% of 2001 full-time freshmen returned.

Freshmen *Admission:* 616 applied, 487 admitted, 144 enrolled. *Average high school GPA:* 3.03. *Test scores:* SAT verbal scores over 500: 59%; SAT math scores over 500: 54%; ACT scores over 18: 75%; SAT verbal scores over 600: 17%; SAT math scores over 600: 14%; ACT scores over 24: 25%; SAT verbal scores over 700: 1%.

Faculty *Total:* 83, 52% full-time, 55% with terminal degrees. *Student/faculty ratio:* 15:1.

Majors Accounting; biology; business administration; economics; education; elementary education; English; history; information sciences/systems; international business; medical technology; philosophy; political science; pre-dentistry; pre-law; pre-medicine; pre-pharmacy studies; pre-veterinary studies; psychology; recreational therapy; secondary education; sociology; theology.

Academic Programs *Special study options:* accelerated degree program, adult/continuing education programs, advanced placement credit, cooperative education, double majors, external degree program, freshman honors college, honors programs, independent study, internships, off-campus study, part-time degree program, services for LD students, summer session for credit. *ROTC:* Army (c), Air Force (c).

Library Abbot Vincent Taylor Library plus 1 other with 110,050 titles, 630 serial subscriptions, an OPAC.

Computers on Campus 125 computers available on campus for general student use. A campuswide network can be accessed from student residence rooms. At least one staffed computer lab available.

Student Life *Housing:* on-campus residence required through senior year. *Options:* coed, men-only. *Activities and Organizations:* drama/theater group, student-run newspaper, radio station, choral group, Greek system, College Union, WABY (student radio station), Abbey Players, national fraternities, national sororities. *Campus security:* 24-hour emergency response devices and patrols, late-night transport/escort service. *Student Services:* health clinic, personal/psychological counseling.

Athletics Member NCAA. All Division II. *Intercollegiate sports:* baseball M(s), basketball M(s)/W(s), cross-country running M(s)/W(s), golf M(s), soccer M(s)/W(s), softball W(s), tennis M(s)/W(s). *Intramural sports:* basketball M/W, cross-country running M/W, football M/W, rugby M(c), soccer M/W, softball M/W, tennis M/W, weight lifting M, wrestling M.

Standardized Tests *Required:* SAT I or ACT (for admission).

Costs (2002–03) *One-time required fee:* $624. *Comprehensive fee:* $20,830 includes full-time tuition ($12,722), mandatory fees ($1252), and room and board ($6856). Full-time tuition and fees vary according to class time, class time, course load, location, program, reciprocity agreements, and student level. Part-time tuition: $398 per credit. Part-time tuition and fees vary according to class time, class time, course load, location, reciprocity agreements, and student level. *Room and board:* College room only: $3860. Room and board charges vary according to board plan, housing facility, location, and student level. *Payment plans:* installment, deferred payment. *Waivers:* senior citizens and employees or children of employees.

Financial Aid Of all full-time matriculated undergraduates who enrolled in 2001, 681 applied for aid, 507 were judged to have need, 32 had their need fully met. 175 Federal Work-Study jobs (averaging $1600). In 2001, 103 non-need-based awards were made. *Average percent of need met:* 73%. *Average financial aid package:* $14,500. *Average need-based loan:* $4500. *Average need-based gift aid:* $6500. *Average non-need based aid:* $2500. *Average indebtedness upon graduation:* $14,000.

Applying *Options:* common application, electronic application. *Application fee:* $25. *Required:* high school transcript, minimum 2.0 GPA. *Required for some:* essay or personal statement, 2 letters of recommendation. *Recommended:* interview. *Application deadlines:* 8/1 (freshmen), 8/15 (transfers). *Notification:* continuous (freshmen).

Admissions Contact Mr. R. Lawton Blandford, Director of Administration, Belmont Abbey College, 100 Belmont-Mt. Holly Road, Belmont, NC 28012-1802. *Phone:* 704-825-6665. *Toll-free phone:* 888-BAC-0110. *Fax:* 704-825-6220. *E-mail:* admissions@bac.edu.

BENNETT COLLEGE

Greensboro, North Carolina

- **Independent United Methodist** 4-year, founded 1873
- **Calendar** semesters
- **Degree** bachelor's
- **Urban** 55-acre campus
- **Women only,** 521 undergraduate students, 98% full-time
- **Moderately difficult** entrance level, 62% of applicants were admitted

Undergraduates 513 full-time, 8 part-time. Students come from 30 states and territories, 5 other countries, 72% are from out of state, 98% African American, 2% international, 2% transferred in, 76% live on campus. *Retention:* 63% of 2001 full-time freshmen returned.

Freshmen *Admission:* 1,050 applied, 655 admitted, 137 enrolled. *Average high school GPA:* 2.80. *Test scores:* SAT verbal scores over 500: 15%; SAT math scores over 500: 10%; SAT verbal scores over 600: 1%.

Faculty *Total:* 64, 92% full-time, 67% with terminal degrees. *Student/faculty ratio:* 8:1.

Majors Accounting; art; arts management; biology; business administration; chemistry; computer science; dietetics; early childhood education; elementary education; English; fashion merchandising; home economics; interdisciplinary studies; mass communications; mathematics; middle school education; music; music teacher education; political science; psychology; science education; social work; sociology; special education.

Academic Programs *Special study options:* academic remediation for entering students, adult/continuing education programs, cooperative education, freshman honors college, honors programs, internships, off-campus study, part-time degree program, services for LD students, student-designed majors, summer session for credit. *ROTC:* Army (c), Air Force (c). *Unusual degree programs:* 3-2 engineering with North Carolina Agricultural and Technical State University.

Library Holgate Library with 105,000 titles, 310 serial subscriptions, an OPAC.

Computers on Campus 115 computers available on campus for general student use. Internet access, at least one staffed computer lab available.

Student Life *Housing:* on-campus residence required through sophomore year. *Activities and Organizations:* drama/theater group, student-run newspaper, choral group, Christian Fellowship, Pre-Alumnae Council, Belles of Harmony, NAACP, National Council of Negro Women, national sororities. *Campus security:* 24-hour patrols, late-night transport/escort service. *Student Services:* health clinic, personal/psychological counseling, women's center, legal services.

Athletics Member NCAA. All Division III. *Intercollegiate sports:* basketball W, cross-country running W, softball W, tennis W, track and field W, volleyball W. *Intramural sports:* basketball W, softball W, swimming W, tennis W, track and field W, volleyball W.

Standardized Tests *Required:* SAT I or ACT (for admission).

Costs (2001–02) *Comprehensive fee:* $14,297 includes full-time tuition ($7911), mandatory fees ($2095), and room and board ($4291). Part-time tuition: $331 per

Bennett College (continued)
semester hour. *Required fees:* $905 per term part-time. *Room and board:* College room only: $2137. *Payment plan:* deferred payment. *Waivers:* employees or children of employees.

Financial Aid Of all full-time matriculated undergraduates who enrolled in 2001, 362 applied for aid, 362 were judged to have need, 50 had their need fully met. In 2001, 19 non-need-based awards were made. *Average percent of need met:* 76%. *Average financial aid package:* $10,000. *Average need-based gift aid:* $4000. *Average non-need based aid:* $5000.

Applying *Options:* deferred entrance. *Application fee:* $20. *Required:* essay or personal statement, high school transcript, minimum 2.0 GPA, letters of recommendation. *Required for some:* interview. *Application deadline:* rolling (freshmen), rolling (transfers). *Notification:* continuous (freshmen).

Admissions Contact Ms. Linda K. Torrence, Director of Admissions, Bennett College, Campus Box H, Greensboro, NC 27401. *Phone:* 336-517-2167. *E-mail:* admiss@bennett.edu.

BREVARD COLLEGE
Brevard, North Carolina

- **Independent United Methodist** 4-year, founded 1853
- **Calendar** semesters
- **Degrees** diplomas, associate, and bachelor's
- **Small-town** 120-acre campus
- **Endowment** $17.4 million
- **Coed,** 701 undergraduate students, 93% full-time, 47% women, 53% men
- **Minimally difficult** entrance level, 89% of applicants were admitted

Undergraduates 654 full-time, 47 part-time. Students come from 40 states and territories, 52% are from out of state, 8% African American, 0.3% Asian American or Pacific Islander, 2% Hispanic American, 0.4% Native American, 3% international, 9% transferred in, 64% live on campus. *Retention:* 52% of 2001 full-time freshmen returned.

Freshmen *Admission:* 515 applied, 456 admitted, 176 enrolled. *Average high school GPA:* 2.83. *Test scores:* SAT verbal scores over 500: 42%; SAT math scores over 500: 49%; ACT scores over 18: 65%; SAT verbal scores over 600: 12%; SAT math scores over 600: 10%; ACT scores over 24: 14%; SAT verbal scores over 700: 1%; SAT math scores over 700: 2%; ACT scores over 30: 2%.

Faculty *Total:* 102, 62% full-time, 40% with terminal degrees. *Student/faculty ratio:* 9:1.

Majors Art; business; ecology; English; environmental science; exercise sciences; history; interdisciplinary studies; liberal arts and sciences/liberal studies; mathematics; music; pre-dentistry; pre-medicine; pre-pharmacy studies; pre-veterinary studies; recreation/leisure studies; religious studies.

Academic Programs *Special study options:* academic remediation for entering students, adult/continuing education programs, advanced placement credit, double majors, English as a second language, honors programs, independent study, internships, part-time degree program, services for LD students, student-designed majors, study abroad.

Library Jones Library plus 1 other with 51,086 titles, 325 serial subscriptions, 3,134 audiovisual materials, an OPAC, a Web page.

Computers on Campus 70 computers available on campus for general student use. A campuswide network can be accessed from student residence rooms and from off campus. Internet access, at least one staffed computer lab available.

Student Life *Housing:* on-campus residence required through sophomore year. *Options:* coed, men-only, women-only. *Activities and Organizations:* drama/theater group, student-run newspaper, choral group, fine arts organizations, Omicron Delta Kappa, Fellowship of Christian Athletes, Student Ambassadors, Coalition for Service for Learning. *Campus security:* 24-hour emergency response devices and patrols. *Student Services:* health clinic, personal/psychological counseling.

Athletics Member NAIA. *Intercollegiate sports:* baseball M(s), basketball M(s)/W(s), cross-country running M(s)/W(s), golf M(s), soccer M(s)/W(s), softball W(s), tennis W(s), track and field M(s)/W(s), volleyball W(s). *Intramural sports:* archery M/W, badminton M/W, basketball M/W, bowling M/W, cross-country running M/W, equestrian sports M/W, football M/W, golf W, skiing (cross-country) M/W, skiing (downhill) M/W, soccer M/W, softball M/W, swimming M/W, tennis M/W, track and field M/W, volleyball M/W, weight lifting M/W.

Standardized Tests *Required:* SAT I or ACT (for admission).

Costs (2001–02) *Comprehensive fee:* $17,230 includes full-time tuition ($11,280), mandatory fees ($890), and room and board ($5060). Part-time tuition: $340 per semester hour. Part-time tuition and fees vary according to course load. *Required fees:* $445 per term. *Room and board:* College room only: $2000. Room and board charges vary according to housing facility. *Payment plan:* installment. *Waivers:* employees or children of employees.

Financial Aid Of all full-time matriculated undergraduates who enrolled in 2001, 463 applied for aid, 401 were judged to have need, 148 had their need fully met. 74 Federal Work-Study jobs (averaging $1080). 36 State and other part-time jobs (averaging $1150). In 2001, 201 non-need-based awards were made. *Average percent of need met:* 85%. *Average financial aid package:* $12,168. *Average need-based loan:* $3729. *Average need-based gift aid:* $9341. *Average non-need based aid:* $3365. *Average indebtedness upon graduation:* $14,795.

Applying *Options:* common application, electronic application, early admission, deferred entrance. *Application fee:* $30. *Required:* essay or personal statement, high school transcript, minimum 2.0 GPA. *Required for some:* 3 letters of recommendation, interview. *Application deadline:* rolling (freshmen), rolling (transfers). *Notification:* continuous (freshmen).

Admissions Contact Ms. Bridgett N. Golman, Dean of Admissions and Financial Aid, Brevard College, 400 North Broad Street, Brevard, NC 28712-3306. *Phone:* 828-884-8300. *Toll-free phone:* 800-527-9090. *Fax:* 828-884-3790. *E-mail:* admissions@brevard.edu.

CABARRUS COLLEGE OF HEALTH SCIENCES
Concord, North Carolina

- **Independent** primarily 2-year, founded 1942
- **Calendar** semesters
- **Degrees** certificates, diplomas, associate, and bachelor's
- **Small-town** 5-acre campus with easy access to Charlotte
- **Endowment** $568,924
- **Coed, primarily women,** 258 undergraduate students, 55% full-time, 93% women, 7% men
- **Moderately difficult** entrance level, 88% of applicants were admitted

Undergraduates 141 full-time, 117 part-time. Students come from 2 states and territories, 2% are from out of state, 14% African American, 1% Hispanic American, 25% transferred in.

Freshmen *Admission:* 40 applied, 35 admitted, 26 enrolled. *Average high school GPA:* 3.53. *Test scores:* SAT verbal scores over 500: 35%; SAT math scores over 500: 48%; ACT scores over 18: 50%; SAT verbal scores over 600: 5%; ACT scores over 24: 17%.

Faculty *Total:* 31, 52% full-time, 13% with terminal degrees. *Student/faculty ratio:* 9:1.

Majors Medical assistant; nurse assistant/aide; nursing; occupational therapy assistant; operating room technician.

Academic Programs *Special study options:* advanced placement credit, distance learning, double majors, independent study, part-time degree program.

Library Northeast Medical Center Library with 7,676 titles, 2,127 serial subscriptions, 923 audiovisual materials.

Computers on Campus 30 computers available on campus for general student use. A campuswide network can be accessed from off campus. Internet access, at least one staffed computer lab available.

Student Life *Housing:* college housing not available. *Activities and Organizations:* student-run newspaper, Student Nurse Association, Christian Student Union, student government, Honor Society, Allied Health Student Association. *Campus security:* 24-hour emergency response devices and patrols. *Student Services:* health clinic, personal/psychological counseling.

Standardized Tests *Required:* SAT I or ACT (for admission).

Financial Aid Of all full-time matriculated undergraduates who enrolled in 2001, 20 Federal Work-Study jobs.

Applying *Application fee:* $35. *Required:* essay or personal statement, high school transcript, minimum 2.0 GPA, 2 letters of recommendation, interview. *Recommended:* minimum 3.0 GPA. *Application deadlines:* 3/1 (freshmen), 3/1 (transfers). *Notification:* 4/15 (freshmen).

Admissions Contact Ms. Diane Blackwelder, Admissions Coordinator, Cabarrus College of Health Sciences, 431 Copperfield Boulevard, NE, Concord, NC 28025-2405. *Phone:* 704-783-1616. *Fax:* 704-783-1764. *E-mail:* cchsadm@northeastmedical.org.

CAMPBELL UNIVERSITY
Buies Creek, North Carolina

- **Independent Baptist** university, founded 1887
- **Calendar** semesters
- **Degrees** associate, bachelor's, master's, doctoral, and first professional
- **Rural** 850-acre campus with easy access to Raleigh

- **Endowment** $83.7 million
- **Coed,** 2,453 undergraduate students, 97% full-time, 54% women, 46% men
- **Moderately difficult** entrance level, 70% of applicants were admitted

Undergraduates 2,391 full-time, 62 part-time. Students come from 50 states and territories, 56 other countries, 37% are from out of state, 10% African American, 2% Hispanic American, 0.5% Native American, 3% international, 9% transferred in, 70% live on campus. *Retention:* 87% of 2001 full-time freshmen returned.

Freshmen *Admission:* 2,365 applied, 1,647 admitted, 688 enrolled. *Average high school GPA:* 2.90. *Test scores:* SAT verbal scores over 500: 58%; SAT math scores over 500: 58%; SAT verbal scores over 600: 17%; SAT math scores over 600: 20%; SAT verbal scores over 700: 4%; SAT math scores over 700: 3%.

Faculty *Total:* 288, 70% full-time, 64% with terminal degrees. *Student/faculty ratio:* 13:1.

Majors Accounting; advertising; Army R.O.T.C./military science; art; athletic training/sports medicine; biochemistry; biology; biology education; business; chemistry; communications; computer/information sciences; criminal justice/law enforcement administration; economics; education; education administration; education (K-12); elementary education; elementary/middle/secondary education administration; English; finance; fine/studio arts; French; graphic design/commercial art/illustration; health aide; health/physical education; health science; history; home economics; home economics education; industrial design; international business; international relations; journalism; liberal arts and sciences/liberal studies; mathematics; medical pharmacology and pharmaceutical sciences; middle school education; music; music (piano and organ performance); music teacher education; music theory and composition; pharmacy; physical education; political science; pre-dentistry; pre-engineering; pre-law; pre-medicine; pre-veterinary studies; psychology; public administration; public relations; radio/television broadcasting; religious studies; secondary education; social sciences; social work; Spanish; sport/fitness administration; theater arts/drama.

Academic Programs *Special study options:* academic remediation for entering students, accelerated degree program, adult/continuing education programs, advanced placement credit, cooperative education, distance learning, double majors, freshman honors college, honors programs, independent study, internships, part-time degree program, study abroad, summer session for credit. *ROTC:* Army (b).

Library Carrie Rich Memorial Library plus 3 others with 196,000 titles, 6,700 serial subscriptions, 3,500 audiovisual materials, an OPAC, a Web page.

Computers on Campus 250 computers available on campus for general student use. Internet access, at least one staffed computer lab available.

Student Life *Housing:* on-campus residence required through sophomore year. *Options:* men-only, women-only. *Activities and Organizations:* drama/theater group, student-run newspaper, radio station, choral group, Student Government Association, Baptist Student Union, Campbell Catholic Community, Presidential Scholars Club, Pre-Pharmacy Club. *Campus security:* 24-hour emergency response devices and patrols, late-night transport/escort service, controlled dormitory access. *Student Services:* health clinic, personal/psychological counseling.

Athletics Member NCAA. All Division I. *Intercollegiate sports:* baseball M(s), basketball M(s)/W(s), cross-country running M(s)/W(s), golf M(s)/W(s), soccer M(s)/W(s), softball W(s), tennis M(s)/W(s), track and field M(s)/W(s), volleyball W(s), wrestling M(s). *Intramural sports:* basketball M/W, football M/W, golf M/W, soccer M/W, softball M/W, swimming M/W, table tennis M/W, tennis M/W, track and field M/W, volleyball W, wrestling M.

Standardized Tests *Required:* SAT I or ACT (for admission).

Costs (2002–03) *Comprehensive fee:* $17,399 includes full-time tuition ($12,600), mandatory fees ($249), and room and board ($4550). Full-time tuition and fees vary according to course load and location. Part-time tuition: $196 per semester hour. Part-time tuition and fees vary according to location and program. *Room and board:* Room and board charges vary according to board plan and housing facility. *Payment plan:* installment. *Waivers:* employees or children of employees.

Financial Aid Of all full-time matriculated undergraduates who enrolled in 2001, 3793 applied for aid, 1851 were judged to have need. 1030 Federal Work-Study jobs (averaging $1219). In 2001, 1858 non-need-based awards were made. *Average percent of need met:* 100%. *Average financial aid package:* $16,491. *Average need-based loan:* $3207. *Average need-based gift aid:* $4584. *Average non-need based aid:* $2771. *Average indebtedness upon graduation:* $9341.

Applying *Options:* common application, electronic application, early admission, deferred entrance. *Application fee:* $25. *Required:* high school transcript, minimum 2.5 GPA. *Required for some:* 3 letters of recommendation. *Recommended:* interview. *Application deadline:* rolling (freshmen), rolling (transfers). *Notification:* continuous (freshmen).

Admissions Contact Ms. Peggy Mason, Director of Admissions, Campbell University, PO Box 546, Buies Creek, NC 27506. *Phone:* 910-893-1300. *Toll-free phone:* 800-334-4111. *Fax:* 910-893-1288. *E-mail:* adm@mailcenter.campbell.edu.

CATAWBA COLLEGE
Salisbury, North Carolina

- **Independent** comprehensive, founded 1851, affiliated with United Church of Christ
- **Calendar** semesters
- **Degrees** bachelor's and master's
- **Small-town** 210-acre campus with easy access to Charlotte
- **Endowment** $38.6 million
- **Coed,** 1,435 undergraduate students, 96% full-time, 51% women, 49% men
- **Moderately difficult** entrance level, 82% of applicants were admitted

Undergraduates 1,384 full-time, 51 part-time. Students come from 35 states and territories, 9 other countries, 33% are from out of state, 16% African American, 0.6% Asian American or Pacific Islander, 2% Hispanic American, 0.3% Native American, 1% international, 13% transferred in, 49% live on campus. *Retention:* 57% of 2001 full-time freshmen returned.

Freshmen *Admission:* 1,107 applied, 910 admitted, 353 enrolled. *Average high school GPA:* 3.13. *Test scores:* SAT verbal scores over 500: 48%; SAT math scores over 500: 48%; SAT verbal scores over 600: 8%; SAT math scores over 600: 8%.

Faculty *Total:* 126, 58% full-time, 50% with terminal degrees. *Student/faculty ratio:* 17:1.

Majors Athletic training/sports medicine; biology; business administration; business economics; business marketing and marketing management; chemistry; computer science; education; elementary education; English; environmental science; French; history; humanities; information sciences/systems; interdisciplinary studies; international relations; mass communications; mathematics; medical technology; middle school education; music; music (piano and organ performance); music teacher education; music (voice and choral/opera performance); philosophy; physical education; physician assistant; political science; pre-dentistry; pre-law; pre-medicine; pre-veterinary studies; psychology; reading education; recreational therapy; recreation/leisure studies; religious studies; secondary education; sociology; Spanish; theater arts/drama.

Academic Programs *Special study options:* adult/continuing education programs, advanced placement credit, double majors, honors programs, independent study, internships, part-time degree program, services for LD students, student-designed majors, study abroad, summer session for credit. *ROTC:* Army (c).

Library Corriher-Linn-Black Memorial Library plus 1 other with 144,788 titles, 3,661 serial subscriptions, 24,281 audiovisual materials, an OPAC.

Computers on Campus 80 computers available on campus for general student use. A campuswide network can be accessed from student residence rooms. Internet access, at least one staffed computer lab available.

Student Life *Housing:* on-campus residence required through sophomore year. *Options:* coed, men-only, women-only. *Activities and Organizations:* drama/theater group, student-run newspaper, choral group, United In Service, Catawba Guides, Blue Masque (drama), L'il Chiefs, Wigwam Productions. *Campus security:* 24-hour emergency response devices and patrols, late-night transport/escort service, controlled dormitory access. *Student Services:* health clinic, personal/psychological counseling.

Athletics Member NCAA. All Division II. *Intercollegiate sports:* baseball M(s), basketball M(s)/W(s), cross-country running M(s)/W(s), field hockey W(s), football M(s), golf M(s), lacrosse M, soccer M(s)/W(s), softball W(s), swimming W(s), tennis M(s)/W(s), volleyball W(s). *Intramural sports:* archery M/W, basketball M/W, football M/W, golf M/W, ice hockey M, lacrosse M, racquetball M/W, skiing (downhill) M/W, soccer M/W, swimming M/W, table tennis M/W, tennis M/W, volleyball M/W, weight lifting M/W, wrestling M.

Standardized Tests *Required:* SAT I or ACT (for admission).

Costs (2001–02) *Comprehensive fee:* $19,620 includes full-time tuition ($14,540) and room and board ($5080). Part-time tuition: $420 per semester hour. *Payment plan:* installment. *Waivers:* employees or children of employees.

Financial Aid Of all full-time matriculated undergraduates who enrolled in 2001, 933 applied for aid, 809 were judged to have need, 199 had their need fully met. 273 Federal Work-Study jobs (averaging $1608). 176 State and other part-time jobs (averaging $1238). In 2001, 117 non-need-based awards were made. *Average percent of need met:* 72%. *Average financial aid package:* $11,959. *Average need-based loan:* $3092. *Average need-based gift aid:* $3072. *Average non-need based aid:* $4053. *Average indebtedness upon graduation:* $25,000.

Applying *Options:* common application, electronic application, early admission, deferred entrance. *Application fee:* $25. *Required:* high school transcript,

Catawba College (continued)
minimum 2.0 GPA. *Recommended:* essay or personal statement, letters of recommendation, interview. *Application deadline:* rolling (freshmen), rolling (transfers). *Notification:* continuous (freshmen).

Admissions Contact Mr. Brian Best, Chief Enrollment Officer, Catawba College, 2300 West Innes Street, Salisbury, NC 28144-2488. *Phone:* 800-CATAWBA. *Toll-free phone:* 800-CATAWBA. *Fax:* 704-637-4222. *E-mail:* bdbest@catawba.edu.

CHOWAN COLLEGE
Murfreesboro, North Carolina

- **Independent Baptist** 4-year, founded 1848
- **Calendar** semesters
- **Degree** bachelor's
- **Rural** 300-acre campus with easy access to Norfolk
- **Endowment** $13.0 million
- **Coed,** 795 undergraduate students, 97% full-time, 47% women, 53% men
- **Minimally difficult** entrance level, 82% of applicants were admitted

Undergraduates 775 full-time, 20 part-time. Students come from 23 states and territories, 6 other countries, 60% are from out of state, 26% African American, 2% Asian American or Pacific Islander, 2% Hispanic American, 0.8% Native American, 1% international, 7% transferred in, 79% live on campus. *Retention:* 58% of 2001 full-time freshmen returned.

Freshmen *Admission:* 1,101 applied, 899 admitted, 277 enrolled. *Average high school GPA:* 2.67. *Test scores:* SAT verbal scores over 500: 26%; SAT math scores over 500: 23%; ACT scores over 18: 39%; SAT verbal scores over 600: 3%; SAT math scores over 600: 3%; SAT verbal scores over 700: 1%; SAT math scores over 700: 1%.

Faculty *Total:* 82, 85% full-time, 35% with terminal degrees. *Student/faculty ratio:* 10:1.

Majors Accounting; art; athletic training/sports medicine; biological/physical sciences; biology; business administration; business marketing and marketing management; criminal justice studies; elementary education; English; English education; environmental biology; exercise sciences; fine/studio arts; graphic design/commercial art/illustration; graphic/printing equipment; history; information sciences/systems; liberal arts and sciences/liberal studies; mathematics; mathematics education; music; music business management/merchandising; music teacher education; physical education; physical sciences; pre-dentistry; pre-law; pre-medicine; pre-veterinary studies; psychology; religious studies; sport/fitness administration.

Academic Programs *Special study options:* advanced placement credit, double majors, internships, part-time degree program, student-designed majors, study abroad, summer session for credit.

Library Whitaker Library plus 1 other with 96,994 titles, 925 serial subscriptions, 3,991 audiovisual materials, an OPAC.

Computers on Campus A campuswide network can be accessed from student residence rooms and from off campus. At least one staffed computer lab available.

Student Life *Housing:* on-campus residence required through sophomore year. *Options:* men-only, women-only. *Activities and Organizations:* drama/theater group, student-run newspaper, choral group, marching band, Christian Student Union, Student Government Association, Habitat for Humanity, Phi Kappa Tau, SNCAE (Students of North Carolina Association of Educators), national fraternities. *Campus security:* 24-hour emergency response devices and patrols, late-night transport/escort service, controlled dormitory access. *Student Services:* health clinic, personal/psychological counseling.

Athletics Member NCAA. All Division III. *Intercollegiate sports:* baseball M, basketball M/W, football M, golf M/W, soccer M/W, softball W, tennis M/W, volleyball W. *Intramural sports:* basketball M/W, football M/W, racquetball M/W, soccer M/W, softball M/W, table tennis M/W, tennis M/W, volleyball M/W.

Standardized Tests *Required:* SAT I or ACT (for admission).

Costs (2001–02) *Comprehensive fee:* $17,540 includes full-time tuition ($12,400), mandatory fees ($100), and room and board ($5040). Part-time tuition: $185 per course. Part-time tuition and fees vary according to course load and program. *Room and board:* College room only: $2360. Room and board charges vary according to board plan. *Payment plans:* installment, deferred payment. *Waivers:* senior citizens and employees or children of employees.

Financial Aid Of all full-time matriculated undergraduates who enrolled in 2001, 674 applied for aid, 598 were judged to have need, 99 had their need fully met. 338 Federal Work-Study jobs (averaging $678). 83 State and other part-time jobs (averaging $1197). In 2001, 122 non-need-based awards were made. *Average percent of need met:* 81%. *Average financial aid package:* $10,362. *Average need-based loan:* $3233. *Average need-based gift aid:* $7225. *Average indebtedness upon graduation:* $9282.

Applying *Options:* electronic application, early admission, deferred entrance. *Application fee:* $20. *Required:* high school transcript. *Required for some:* essay or personal statement, interview. *Recommended:* minimum 2.0 GPA, 2 letters of recommendation. *Application deadline:* rolling (freshmen), rolling (transfers). *Notification:* continuous (freshmen).

Admissions Contact Mr. Don Williams, Associate Vice President for Enrollment Management, Chowan College, 200 Jones Drive, Murfreesboro, NC 27855. *Phone:* 252-398-6314. *Toll-free phone:* 800-488-4101. *Fax:* 252-398-1190. *E-mail:* admissions@chowan.edu.

DAVIDSON COLLEGE
Davidson, North Carolina

- **Independent Presbyterian** 4-year, founded 1837
- **Calendar** semesters
- **Degree** bachelor's
- **Small-town** 464-acre campus with easy access to Charlotte
- **Endowment** $317.9 million
- **Coed,** 1,673 undergraduate students, 100% full-time, 51% women, 49% men
- **Very difficult** entrance level, 35% of applicants were admitted

Undergraduates 1,672 full-time, 1 part-time. Students come from 44 states and territories, 32 other countries, 81% are from out of state, 5% African American, 3% Asian American or Pacific Islander, 3% Hispanic American, 0.4% Native American, 3% international, 0.6% transferred in, 91% live on campus. *Retention:* 96% of 2001 full-time freshmen returned.

Freshmen *Admission:* 3,363 applied, 1,164 admitted, 465 enrolled. *Test scores:* SAT verbal scores over 500: 99%; SAT math scores over 500: 99%; ACT scores over 18: 99%; SAT verbal scores over 600: 83%; SAT math scores over 600: 85%; ACT scores over 24: 90%; SAT verbal scores over 700: 31%; SAT math scores over 700: 30%; ACT scores over 30: 40%.

Faculty *Total:* 164, 94% full-time. *Student/faculty ratio:* 11:1.

Majors Anthropology; art; biology; chemistry; classics; economics; English; French; German; history; mathematics; multi/interdisciplinary studies related; music; philosophy; physics; political science; psychology; religious studies; sociology; Spanish; theater arts/drama.

Academic Programs *Special study options:* accelerated degree program, advanced placement credit, double majors, honors programs, independent study, off-campus study, services for LD students, student-designed majors, study abroad. *ROTC:* Army (b), Air Force (c). *Unusual degree programs:* 3-2 engineering with Columbia University, Washington University in St. Louis, North Carolina State University, Georgia Institute of Technology, Duke University.

Library E. H. Little Library plus 1 other with 569,981 titles, 2,566 serial subscriptions, 8,256 audiovisual materials, an OPAC, a Web page.

Computers on Campus 118 computers available on campus for general student use. A campuswide network can be accessed from student residence rooms and from off campus. Internet access, at least one staffed computer lab available.

Student Life *Housing:* on-campus residence required through senior year. *Options:* coed, men-only, women-only. *Activities and Organizations:* drama/theater group, student-run newspaper, radio station, choral group, Intervarsity Christian Fellowship, Dean Rusk Program Student Advisory Council, music organizations, Community Service Council, Student Government Association, national fraternities. *Campus security:* 24-hour emergency response devices and patrols, late-night transport/escort service, controlled dormitory access. *Student Services:* health clinic, personal/psychological counseling, women's center.

Athletics Member NCAA. All Division I except football (Division I-AA). *Intercollegiate sports:* baseball M(s), basketball M(s)/W(s), crew M(c)/W(c), cross-country running M(s)/W(s), fencing M(c)/W(c), field hockey W(s), golf M(s), lacrosse M(c)/W(s), rugby M(c), sailing M(c)/W(c), soccer M(s)/W(s), swimming M(s)/W(s), tennis M(s)/W(s), track and field M(s)/W(s), volleyball W(s), weight lifting M(c), wrestling M(s). *Intramural sports:* basketball M/W, field hockey M(c)/W(c), football M/W, soccer M/W, tennis M(c)/W(c).

Standardized Tests *Required:* SAT I or ACT (for admission). *Recommended:* SAT II: Subject Tests (for admission), SAT II: Writing Test (for admission).

Costs (2001–02) *Comprehensive fee:* $30,823 includes full-time tuition ($23,739), mandatory fees ($256), and room and board ($6828). *Room and board:* College room only: $3605. Room and board charges vary according to board plan and housing facility. *Payment plan:* installment. *Waivers:* employees or children of employees.

Financial Aid Of all full-time matriculated undergraduates who enrolled in 2001, 701 applied for aid, 553 were judged to have need, 553 had their need fully met. 217 Federal Work-Study jobs (averaging $1657). 183 State and other part-time jobs (averaging $1458). In 2001, 375 non-need-based awards were made. *Average percent of need met:* 100%. *Average financial aid package:*

$14,947. *Average need-based loan:* $3180. *Average need-based gift aid:* $12,613. *Average non-need based aid:* $5761. *Average indebtedness upon graduation:* $13,876.

Applying *Options:* common application, early admission, early decision, deferred entrance. *Application fee:* $50. *Required:* essay or personal statement, high school transcript, 4 letters of recommendation. *Recommended:* interview. *Application deadlines:* 1/2 (freshmen), 3/15 (transfers). *Early decision:* 11/15 (for plan 1), 1/2 (for plan 2). *Notification:* 4/1 (freshmen), 12/15 (early decision plan 1), 2/1 (early decision plan 2).

Admissions Contact Dr. Nancy J. Cable, Dean of Admission and Financial Aid, Davidson College, Box 7156, Davidson, NC 28035-7156. *Phone:* 704-894-2230. *Toll-free phone:* 800-768-0380. *Fax:* 704-894-2016. *E-mail:* admission@davidson.edu.

DUKE UNIVERSITY
Durham, North Carolina

- **Independent** university, founded 1838, affiliated with United Methodist Church
- **Calendar** semesters
- **Degrees** bachelor's, master's, doctoral, first professional, and post-master's certificates
- **Suburban** 8500-acre campus
- **Endowment** $2.6 billion
- **Coed,** 6,071 undergraduate students, 100% full-time, 48% women, 52% men
- **Most difficult** entrance level, 26% of applicants were admitted

Undergraduates 6,043 full-time, 28 part-time. Students come from 52 states and territories, 85 other countries, 85% are from out of state, 10% African American, 12% Asian American or Pacific Islander, 6% Hispanic American, 0.4% Native American, 4% international, 0.4% transferred in, 82% live on campus. *Retention:* 96% of 2001 full-time freshmen returned.

Freshmen *Admission:* 13,976 applied, 3,673 admitted, 1,615 enrolled. *Average high school GPA:* 3.85. *Test scores:* SAT verbal scores over 500: 99%; SAT math scores over 500: 100%; ACT scores over 18: 100%; SAT verbal scores over 600: 91%; SAT math scores over 600: 94%; ACT scores over 24: 98%; SAT verbal scores over 700: 50%; SAT math scores over 700: 63%; ACT scores over 30: 58%.

Faculty *Total:* 2,299. *Student/faculty ratio:* 11:1.

Majors African-American studies; anatomy; anthropology; art; art history; Asian studies; bioengineering; biology; chemistry; civil engineering; classics; computer science; economics; electrical engineering; English; environmental science; French; geology; German; Greek (ancient and medieval); history; international relations; Italian; Latin (ancient and medieval); linguistics; literature; materials science; mathematics; mechanical engineering; medieval/renaissance studies; music; philosophy; physics; political science; psychology; public policy analysis; religious studies; Russian; Russian/Slavic studies; Slavic languages; sociology; Spanish; theater arts/drama; women's studies.

Academic Programs *Special study options:* accelerated degree program, adult/continuing education programs, advanced placement credit, distance learning, English as a second language, honors programs, independent study, internships, off-campus study, part-time degree program, services for LD students, student-designed majors, study abroad, summer session for credit. *ROTC:* Army (b), Navy (b), Air Force (b). *Unusual degree programs:* 3-2 law.

Library Perkins Library plus 11 others with 5.0 million titles, 31,941 serial subscriptions, 232,106 audiovisual materials, an OPAC, a Web page.

Computers on Campus 600 computers available on campus for general student use. A campuswide network can be accessed from student residence rooms and from off campus. Internet access, online (class) registration, at least one staffed computer lab available.

Student Life *Housing:* on-campus residence required through junior year. *Options:* coed, men-only, women-only. *Activities and Organizations:* drama/theater group, student-run newspaper, radio and television station, choral group, marching band, national fraternities, national sororities. *Campus security:* 24-hour emergency response devices and patrols, late-night transport/escort service, controlled dormitory access. *Student Services:* health clinic, personal/psychological counseling, women's center, legal services.

Athletics Member NCAA. All Division I except football (Division I-A). *Intercollegiate sports:* baseball M(s), basketball M(s)/W(s), crew M(c)/W(s), cross-country running M/W, equestrian sports M(c)/W(c), fencing M/W, field hockey M(c)/W(s), football M(s)/W(c), golf M(s)/W(s), ice hockey M(c)/W(c), lacrosse M(s)/W(s), racquetball M(c)/W(c), rugby M(c)/W(c), sailing M(c)/W(c), skiing (cross-country) M(c)/W(c), skiing (downhill) M(c)/W(c), soccer M(s)/W(s), softball M(c)/W(c), swimming M/W, tennis M(s)/W(s), track and field M/W, volleyball M(c)/W(s), water polo M(c)/W(c), wrestling M. *Intramural sports:* badminton M/W, baseball M/W, basketball M/W, football M, golf M/W, soccer M/W, softball M/W, squash M/W, swimming M/W, table tennis M/W, tennis M/W, volleyball M/W.

Standardized Tests *Required:* SAT I or ACT (for admission). *Required for some:* SAT II: Subject Tests (for admission), SAT II: Writing Test (for admission).

Costs (2001–02) *Comprehensive fee:* $34,396 includes full-time tuition ($26,000), mandatory fees ($768), and room and board ($7628). Full-time tuition and fees vary according to program. Part-time tuition: $3250 per course. Part-time tuition and fees vary according to program. *Required fees:* $2222 per term part-time. *Room and board:* College room only: $4108. Room and board charges vary according to board plan and housing facility. *Payment plans:* tuition prepayment, installment, deferred payment. *Waivers:* employees or children of employees.

Financial Aid Of all full-time matriculated undergraduates who enrolled in 2001, 2621 applied for aid, 2298 were judged to have need, 2298 had their need fully met. 1779 Federal Work-Study jobs (averaging $1781). In 2001, 149 non-need-based awards were made. *Average percent of need met:* 100%. *Average financial aid package:* $22,687. *Average need-based loan:* $4530. *Average need-based gift aid:* $18,318. *Average non-need based aid:* $30,166. *Average indebtedness upon graduation:* $16,502. *Financial aid deadline:* 2/1.

Applying *Options:* common application, electronic application, early admission, early decision, deferred entrance. *Application fee:* $65. *Required:* essay or personal statement, high school transcript, 3 letters of recommendation. *Recommended:* minimum 3.0 GPA, interview, audition tape for applicants with outstanding dance, dramatic, or musical talent; slides of artwork. *Application deadlines:* 1/2 (freshmen), 3/15 (transfers). *Early decision:* 11/1. *Notification:* 4/15 (freshmen), 12/15 (early decision).

Admissions Contact Mr. Christoph Guttentag, Director of Admissions, Duke University, 2138 Campus Drive, Durham, NC 27708. *Phone:* 919-684-3214. *Fax:* 919-684-8941. *E-mail:* askduke@admiss.duke.edu.

EAST CAROLINA UNIVERSITY
Greenville, North Carolina

- **State-supported** university, founded 1907, part of The University of North Carolina
- **Calendar** semesters
- **Degrees** bachelor's, master's, doctoral, first professional, and post-master's certificates
- **Urban** 465-acre campus
- **Endowment** $10.3 million
- **Coed,** 15,460 undergraduate students, 92% full-time, 58% women, 42% men
- **Moderately difficult** entrance level, 78% of applicants were admitted

Undergraduates 14,279 full-time, 1,181 part-time. Students come from 48 states and territories, 53 other countries, 14% are from out of state, 14% African American, 2% Asian American or Pacific Islander, 2% Hispanic American, 0.7% Native American, 0.4% international, 7% transferred in, 32% live on campus. *Retention:* 78% of 2001 full-time freshmen returned.

Freshmen *Admission:* 10,433 applied, 8,155 admitted, 3,197 enrolled. *Average high school GPA:* 3.08. *Test scores:* SAT verbal scores over 500: 57%; SAT math scores over 500: 62%; ACT scores over 18: 80%; SAT verbal scores over 600: 11%; SAT math scores over 600: 12%; ACT scores over 24: 12%; SAT verbal scores over 700: 1%; SAT math scores over 700: 1%; ACT scores over 30: 1%.

Faculty *Total:* 1,096, 83% full-time, 61% with terminal degrees.

Majors Accounting; accounting related; anthropology; applied history; art; art education; art history; athletic training/sports medicine; biochemistry; biology; broadcast journalism; business administration; business education; business marketing and marketing management; chemistry; child care/development; city/community/regional planning; clothing/apparel/textile studies; communications; computer engineering technology; computer science; criminal justice studies; dance; data processing; dietetics; drama/dance education; early childhood education; economics; education of the emotionally handicapped; education of the mentally handicapped; education of the specific learning disabled; elementary education; engineering technologies related; English; English education; environmental health; environmental technology; exercise sciences; finance; fine/studio arts; French; French language education; geography; geology; German; German language education; health education; health/physical education/fitness related; history; home economics education; hotel and restaurant management; individual/family development; industrial production technologies related; industrial technology; interior design; liberal arts and sciences/liberal studies; management information systems/business data processing; marketing/distribution education; mathematics; mathematics education; medical records administration; medical technology; middle school education; music (general performance); music teacher education; music theory and composition; music therapy; nursing; occupational

East Carolina University (continued)
therapy; philosophy; physical education; physician assistant; physics; political science; psychology; public health education/promotion; recreational therapy; recreation/leisure facilities management; science education; social studies education; social work; sociology; Spanish; Spanish language education; speech-language pathology/audiology; theater arts/drama; vocational rehabilitation counseling; women's studies.

Academic Programs *Special study options:* academic remediation for entering students, accelerated degree program, adult/continuing education programs, advanced placement credit, cooperative education, distance learning, double majors, honors programs, independent study, internships, off-campus study, part-time degree program, services for LD students, study abroad, summer session for credit. *ROTC:* Army (b), Air Force (b). *Unusual degree programs:* 3-2 accounting.

Library Joyner Library plus 1 other with 1.2 million titles, 7,788 serial subscriptions, an OPAC, a Web page.

Computers on Campus 1465 computers available on campus for general student use. A campuswide network can be accessed from student residence rooms and from off campus. Internet access, online (class) registration, at least one staffed computer lab available.

Student Life *Housing Options:* coed, men-only, women-only, disabled students. *Activities and Organizations:* drama/theater group, student-run newspaper, radio station, choral group, marching band, Student Government Association, Pan Hellenic Association, Student Union, Interfraternity Council, Residence Hall Association, national fraternities, national sororities. *Campus security:* 24-hour emergency response devices and patrols, student patrols, late-night transport/escort service, controlled dormitory access, Operation ID. *Student Services:* health clinic, personal/psychological counseling, legal services.

Athletics Member NCAA. All Division I except football (Division I-A). *Intercollegiate sports:* baseball M(s), basketball M(s)/W(s), cross-country running M(s)/W(s), golf M(s)/W(s), soccer M(s)/W(s), softball W(s), swimming M(s)/W(s), tennis M(s)/W(s), track and field M(s)/W(s), volleyball W(s). *Intramural sports:* badminton M(c)/W(c), basketball M/W, bowling M(c)/W(c), crew M(c)/W(c), cross-country running M/W, field hockey W(c), football M/W, golf M/W, lacrosse M(c)/W(c), racquetball M(c)/W(c), rugby M(c), soccer M(c)/W, softball M/W, squash M/W(c), swimming M(c)/W(c), table tennis M/W, tennis M/W, volleyball M(c)/W(c), water polo M(c)/W(c).

Standardized Tests *Required:* SAT I or ACT (for admission).

Costs (2001–02) *Tuition:* state resident $1453 full-time; nonresident $10,022 full-time. Part-time tuition and fees vary according to course load. *Required fees:* $1113 full-time. *Room and board:* $5200; room only: $2860. Room and board charges vary according to board plan and housing facility. *Payment plans:* installment, deferred payment. *Waivers:* senior citizens and employees or children of employees.

Financial Aid Of all full-time matriculated undergraduates who enrolled in 2001, 9181 applied for aid, 4474 were judged to have need, 1662 had their need fully met. 516 Federal Work-Study jobs (averaging $1517). 130 State and other part-time jobs (averaging $4877). In 2001, 3232 non-need-based awards were made. *Average need-based loan:* $3298. *Average need-based gift aid:* $2040. *Average indebtedness upon graduation:* $16,895.

Applying *Options:* electronic application, early admission, deferred entrance. *Application fee:* $45. *Required:* high school transcript, minimum 2.0 GPA. *Application deadlines:* 3/15 (freshmen), 4/15 (transfers). *Notification:* continuous (freshmen).

Admissions Contact Dr. Thomas Powell Jr., Director of Admissions, East Carolina University, East Fifth Street, Whichard Building 106, Greenville, NC 27858-4353. *Phone:* 252-328-6640. *Fax:* 252-328-6945. *E-mail:* admis@mail.ecu.edu.

ELIZABETH CITY STATE UNIVERSITY
Elizabeth City, North Carolina

- **State-supported** 4-year, founded 1891, part of University of North Carolina System
- **Calendar** semesters
- **Degrees** bachelor's and master's
- **Small-town** 125-acre campus with easy access to Norfolk
- **Coed,** 1,976 undergraduate students
- **Moderately difficult** entrance level, 71% of applicants were admitted

Undergraduates Students come from 23 states and territories, 8 other countries, 12% are from out of state, 78% African American, 0.4% Asian American or Pacific Islander, 0.6% Hispanic American, 0.3% Native American, 54% live on campus. *Retention:* 75% of 2001 full-time freshmen returned.

Freshmen *Admission:* 1,305 applied, 930 admitted. *Average high school GPA:* 2.74.

Faculty *Total:* 183, 62% full-time.

Majors Accounting; applied art; applied mathematics; art; aviation technology; biology; broadcast journalism; business administration; business education; chemistry; computer science; criminal justice/law enforcement administration; early childhood education; education; electrical/electronic engineering technology; elementary education; English; geology; history; industrial arts; industrial technology; information sciences/systems; mathematics; music; music business management/merchandising; music teacher education; physical education; physics; political science; psychology; secondary education; secretarial science; social sciences; social work; sociology; special education.

Academic Programs *Special study options:* academic remediation for entering students, adult/continuing education programs, advanced placement credit, double majors, honors programs, independent study, internships, off-campus study, part-time degree program, services for LD students, summer session for credit. *ROTC:* Army (b).

Library G. R. Little Library with 147,479 titles, 1,665 serial subscriptions.

Computers on Campus 300 computers available on campus for general student use. A campuswide network can be accessed from student residence rooms. Internet access, at least one staffed computer lab available.

Student Life *Housing Options:* men-only, women-only. *Activities and Organizations:* drama/theater group, student-run newspaper, radio and television station, choral group, marching band, national fraternities, national sororities. *Campus security:* 24-hour emergency response devices and patrols. *Student Services:* health clinic.

Athletics Member NCAA. All Division II. *Intercollegiate sports:* basketball M(s)/W(s), football M(s), tennis M/W, track and field M/W, volleyball M/W. *Intramural sports:* basketball M/W, football M, golf M/W, gymnastics M/W, tennis M/W, volleyball M/W.

Standardized Tests *Required:* SAT I or ACT (for admission).

Costs (2001–02) *Tuition:* state resident $896 full-time, $225 per term part-time; nonresident $7892 full-time, $1973 per term part-time. Part-time tuition and fees vary according to course load. *Required fees:* $944 full-time, $235 per term part-time. *Room and board:* $4172; room only: $2498. *Waivers:* senior citizens.

Applying *Options:* electronic application, deferred entrance. *Application fee:* $30. *Required:* high school transcript, minimum 2.0 GPA. *Application deadline:* rolling (freshmen), rolling (transfers). *Notification:* continuous (freshmen).

Admissions Contact Mr. Grady Deese, Director of Admissions, Elizabeth City State University, Campus Box 901, Elizabeth City, NC 27909-7806. *Phone:* 252-335-3305. *Toll-free phone:* 800-347-3278. *Fax:* 252-335-3537. *E-mail:* admissions@mail.ecsu.edu.

ELON UNIVERSITY
Elon, North Carolina

- **Independent** comprehensive, founded 1889, affiliated with United Church of Christ
- **Calendar** 4-1-4
- **Degrees** bachelor's and master's
- **Suburban** 500-acre campus with easy access to Raleigh
- **Endowment** $56.6 million
- **Coed,** 4,160 undergraduate students, 98% full-time, 61% women, 39% men
- **Moderately difficult** entrance level, 65% of applicants were admitted

Elon is a small, selective, private university located in central North Carolina. Elon specializes in the undergraduate student experience, offering 46 majors as well as exceptional programs in study abroad, undergraduate research, career preparation, service learning, and leadership. Outstanding facilities and a campus well-known for its friendly atmosphere characterize Elon.

Undergraduates 4,064 full-time, 96 part-time. Students come from 46 states and territories, 30 other countries, 72% are from out of state, 6% African American, 0.7% Asian American or Pacific Islander, 1% Hispanic American, 0.2% Native American, 1% international, 2% transferred in, 63% live on campus. *Retention:* 83% of 2001 full-time freshmen returned.

Freshmen *Admission:* 5,328 applied, 3,468 admitted, 1,214 enrolled. *Average high school GPA:* 3.50. *Test scores:* SAT verbal scores over 500: 85%; SAT math scores over 500: 87%; SAT verbal scores over 600: 29%; SAT math scores over 600: 30%; SAT verbal scores over 700: 3%; SAT math scores over 700: 3%.

Faculty *Total:* 287, 73% full-time, 73% with terminal degrees. *Student/faculty ratio:* 16:1.

Majors Accounting; art; athletic training/sports medicine; biology; broadcast journalism; business administration; business communications; chemistry; communications; computer science; economics; education; elementary education; engineering; English; environmental science; foreign languages/literatures; French; health education; history; human services; international relations; journalism; mathematics; medical technology; middle school education; music; music (general performance); music teacher education; philosophy; physical education; physics; political science; pre-dentistry; pre-law; pre-medicine; pre-veterinary studies; psychology; public administration; recreation/leisure studies; religious studies; science education; secondary education; social science education; social studies education; sociology; Spanish; special education; sport/fitness administration; theater arts/drama.

Academic Programs *Special study options:* accelerated degree program, advanced placement credit, cooperative education, double majors, English as a second language, honors programs, independent study, internships, off-campus study, part-time degree program, services for LD students, student-designed majors, study abroad, summer session for credit. *ROTC:* Army (b). *Unusual degree programs:* 3-2 engineering with North Carolina State University.

Library Carol Grotnes Belk with 145,056 titles, 4,858 serial subscriptions, 8,164 audiovisual materials, an OPAC, a Web page.

Computers on Campus 500 computers available on campus for general student use. A campuswide network can be accessed from student residence rooms and from off campus that provide access to e-mail. Internet access, at least one staffed computer lab available.

Student Life *Housing:* on-campus residence required through sophomore year. *Options:* coed, men-only, women-only. *Activities and Organizations:* drama/theater group, student-run newspaper, radio station, choral group, marching band, Elon Volunteers, Student Media, Greek Affairs, intramural athletics, Religious Life, national fraternities, national sororities. *Campus security:* 24-hour emergency response devices and patrols, student patrols, late-night transport/escort service, controlled dormitory access, residence hall entrances locked at dusk with combination locks. *Student Services:* health clinic, personal/psychological counseling, women's center.

Athletics Member NCAA. All Division I except football (Division I-AA). *Intercollegiate sports:* baseball M(s), basketball M(s)/W(s), cross-country running M(s)/W(s), golf M(s), lacrosse M(c), rugby M(c)/W(c), soccer M(s)/W(s), softball W(s), swimming M(c)/W(c), tennis M(s)/W(s), track and field W, volleyball W(s). *Intramural sports:* basketball M/W, bowling M/W, equestrian sports M/W, field hockey W(c), football M, golf M/W, racquetball M/W, skiing (downhill) M/W, soccer M/W, softball M/W, squash M/W, table tennis M/W, tennis M/W, volleyball M/W, water polo M/W, weight lifting M/W.

Standardized Tests *Required:* SAT I or ACT (for admission).

Costs (2001–02) *Comprehensive fee:* $18,992 includes full-time tuition ($14,335), mandatory fees ($225), and room and board ($4432). Part-time tuition: $450 per hour. Part-time tuition and fees vary according to course load. *Room and board:* College room only: $2654. Room and board charges vary according to board plan and housing facility. *Payment plan:* installment. *Waivers:* employees or children of employees.

Financial Aid Of all full-time matriculated undergraduates who enrolled in 2001, 1909 applied for aid, 1402 were judged to have need. In 2001, 1104 non-need-based awards were made. *Average percent of need met:* 75%. *Average financial aid package:* $9815. *Average need-based loan:* $3206. *Average need-based gift aid:* $5351. *Average indebtedness upon graduation:* $14,580.

Applying *Options:* common application, early admission, early decision, deferred entrance. *Application fee:* $35. *Required:* essay or personal statement, high school transcript, minimum 2.5 GPA, 1 letter of recommendation. *Application deadline:* rolling (freshmen), rolling (transfers). *Early decision:* 11/15. *Notification:* continuous (freshmen).

Admissions Contact Director of Admissions Records, Elon University, 2700 Campus Box, Elon, NC 27244. *Phone:* 336-278-3566. *Toll-free phone:* 800-334-8448. *Fax:* 336-278-7699. *E-mail:* admissions@elon.edu.

FAYETTEVILLE STATE UNIVERSITY
Fayetteville, North Carolina

- **State-supported** comprehensive, founded 1867, part of University of North Carolina System
- **Calendar** semesters
- **Degrees** associate, bachelor's, master's, and doctoral
- **Urban** 156-acre campus
- **Endowment** $4.0 million
- **Coed,** 4,091 undergraduate students, 78% full-time, 63% women, 37% men
- **Minimally difficult** entrance level, 85% of applicants were admitted

Undergraduates 3,174 full-time, 917 part-time. Students come from 35 states and territories, 77% African American, 1% Asian American or Pacific Islander, 4% Hispanic American, 1% Native American, 0.5% international, 30% live on campus. *Retention:* 70% of 2001 full-time freshmen returned.

Freshmen *Admission:* 1,570 applied, 1,333 admitted, 776 enrolled. *Average high school GPA:* 2.80. *Test scores:* SAT verbal scores over 500: 19%; SAT math scores over 500: 14%; SAT verbal scores over 600: 3%; SAT math scores over 600: 2%.

Faculty *Total:* 231, 87% full-time, 64% with terminal degrees. *Student/faculty ratio:* 20:1.

Majors Accounting; art; biology; business administration; business education; business marketing and marketing management; chemistry; computer science; criminal justice/law enforcement administration; early childhood education; economics; education; elementary education; English; finance; geography; German; health education; history; law enforcement/police science; liberal arts and sciences/liberal studies; literature; mathematics; music; music teacher education; nursing; physical education; physiological psychology/psychobiology; political science; psychology; secretarial science; social sciences; sociology; Spanish; theater arts/drama.

Academic Programs *Special study options:* academic remediation for entering students, accelerated degree program, adult/continuing education programs, cooperative education, honors programs, part-time degree program, summer session for credit. *ROTC:* Air Force (b). *Unusual degree programs:* 3-2 engineering with North Carolina State University.

Library Charles W. Chestnut Library with 197,814 titles, 2,769 serial subscriptions, an OPAC, a Web page.

Computers on Campus 300 computers available on campus for general student use. A campuswide network can be accessed from student residence rooms and from off campus. Internet access, at least one staffed computer lab available.

Student Life *Activities and Organizations:* drama/theater group, student-run newspaper, choral group, marching band, national fraternities, national sororities. *Campus security:* 24-hour patrols, late-night transport/escort service. *Student Services:* health clinic, personal/psychological counseling.

Athletics Member NCAA. All Division II. *Intercollegiate sports:* basketball M(s)/W, cross-country running M/W, football M(s), golf M/W, tennis M/W, track and field M/W, volleyball W. *Intramural sports:* basketball M/W, golf M/W, gymnastics M/W, tennis M/W, volleyball M/W.

Standardized Tests *Required:* SAT I (for placement).

Costs (2001–02) *Tuition:* state resident $1072 full-time; nonresident $8994 full-time. *Required fees:* $698 full-time. *Room and board:* $3820; room only: $2120.

Applying *Options:* early admission, deferred entrance. *Application fee:* $15. *Required:* high school transcript. *Application deadline:* rolling (freshmen), rolling (transfers). *Notification:* continuous (freshmen).

Admissions Contact Mr. Charles Darlington, Director of Enrollment Management and Admissions, Fayetteville State University, 1200 Murchison Road, Fayetteville, NC 28301-4298. *Phone:* 910-486-1371. *Toll-free phone:* 800-222-2594.

GARDNER-WEBB UNIVERSITY
Boiling Springs, North Carolina

- **Independent Baptist** comprehensive, founded 1905
- **Calendar** semesters
- **Degrees** associate, bachelor's, master's, doctoral, and first professional
- **Small-town** 200-acre campus with easy access to Charlotte
- **Endowment** $27.5 million
- **Coed,** 2,578 undergraduate students, 82% full-time, 65% women, 35% men
- **Moderately difficult** entrance level, 73% of applicants were admitted

Undergraduates 2,125 full-time, 453 part-time. Students come from 36 states and territories, 34 other countries, 26% are from out of state, 13% African American, 1.0% Asian American or Pacific Islander, 1% Hispanic American, 0.2% Native American, 0.1% international, 16% transferred in, 42% live on campus. *Retention:* 80% of 2001 full-time freshmen returned.

Freshmen *Admission:* 1,756 applied, 1,286 admitted, 378 enrolled. *Average high school GPA:* 3.41. *Test scores:* SAT verbal scores over 500: 59%; SAT math scores over 500: 56%; ACT scores over 18: 80%; SAT verbal scores over 600: 18%; SAT math scores over 600: 17%; ACT scores over 24: 28%; SAT verbal scores over 700: 3%; SAT math scores over 700: 1%.

Faculty *Total:* 132, 93% full-time, 74% with terminal degrees. *Student/faculty ratio:* 16:1.

Majors Accounting; art; athletic training/sports medicine; biology; business administration; chemistry; computer science; criminal justice/law enforcement administration; data processing technology; early childhood education; education; elementary education; English; French; health education; history; liberal arts and sciences/liberal studies; management information systems/business data processing; mass communications; mathematics; medical laboratory technician;

Gardner-Webb University (continued)
medical technology; music; music teacher education; nursing; physical education; physician assistant; political science; pre-law; pre-medicine; pre-veterinary studies; psychology; religious education; religious music; religious studies; secondary education; sign language interpretation; social sciences; sociology; Spanish; sport/fitness administration.

Academic Programs *Special study options:* academic remediation for entering students, accelerated degree program, adult/continuing education programs, advanced placement credit, English as a second language, honors programs, internships, off-campus study, part-time degree program, services for LD students, study abroad, summer session for credit. *Unusual degree programs:* 3-2 engineering with Auburn University, University of North Carolina at Charlotte.

Library Dover Memorial Library with 210,000 titles, 5,600 serial subscriptions, 9,065 audiovisual materials, an OPAC.

Computers on Campus 150 computers available on campus for general student use. A campuswide network can be accessed from student residence rooms and from off campus. Internet access, online (class) registration, at least one staffed computer lab available.

Student Life *Housing:* on-campus residence required through senior year. *Options:* men-only, women-only, disabled students. *Activities and Organizations:* drama/theater group, student-run newspaper, radio station, choral group, Student Volunteer Corps, GAP (God and People), Fellowship of Christian Athletes, Gospel Choir, Outdoor Explorers Club. *Campus security:* 24-hour patrols. *Student Services:* personal/psychological counseling.

Athletics Member NCAA. All Division I except football (Division I-AA). *Intercollegiate sports:* baseball M(s), basketball M(s)/W(s), cross-country running M(s)/W, golf M(s), soccer M(s)/W, softball W(s), swimming W(s), tennis M(s)/W(s), volleyball W(s), wrestling M(s). *Intramural sports:* basketball M/W, football M/W, racquetball M/W, table tennis M/W, tennis M/W, volleyball M/W.

Standardized Tests *Required:* SAT I or ACT (for admission).

Costs (2001–02) *Comprehensive fee:* $17,750 includes full-time tuition ($12,520), mandatory fees ($350), and room and board ($4880). Part-time tuition: $250 per credit hour. Part-time tuition and fees vary according to course load. *Room and board:* College room only: $2440. Room and board charges vary according to board plan and housing facility. *Payment plan:* installment. *Waivers:* senior citizens and employees or children of employees.

Financial Aid Of all full-time matriculated undergraduates who enrolled in 2001, 1520 applied for aid, 1329 were judged to have need, 474 had their need fully met. 165 Federal Work-Study jobs (averaging $1413). 493 State and other part-time jobs (averaging $1307). In 2001, 572 non-need-based awards were made. *Average percent of need met:* 82%. *Average financial aid package:* $9191. *Average need-based loan:* $3533. *Average need-based gift aid:* $5438.

Applying *Options:* common application, electronic application, early admission, deferred entrance. *Application fee:* $25. *Required:* essay or personal statement, high school transcript, minimum 2.4 GPA. *Required for some:* letters of recommendation. *Application deadline:* rolling (freshmen), rolling (transfers).

Admissions Contact Mr. Nathan Alexander, Director of Admissions and Enrollment Management, Gardner-Webb University, PO Box 817, Boiling Springs, NC 28017. *Phone:* 704-406-4491. *Toll-free phone:* 800-253-6472. *Fax:* 810-253-6477. *E-mail:* admissions@gardner-webb.edu.

GREENSBORO COLLEGE
Greensboro, North Carolina

- **Independent United Methodist** 4-year, founded 1838
- **Calendar** semesters
- **Degree** certificates and bachelor's
- **Urban** 40-acre campus
- **Endowment** $31.3 million
- **Coed,** 1,139 undergraduate students, 78% full-time, 54% women, 46% men
- **Moderately difficult** entrance level, 78% of applicants were admitted

Undergraduates 889 full-time, 250 part-time. Students come from 34 states and territories, 33% are from out of state, 16% African American, 0.7% Asian American or Pacific Islander, 2% Hispanic American, 0.4% Native American, 0.6% international, 7% transferred in, 48% live on campus. *Retention:* 66% of 2001 full-time freshmen returned.

Freshmen *Admission:* 735 applied, 570 admitted, 246 enrolled. *Average high school GPA:* 2.93. *Test scores:* SAT verbal scores over 500: 36%; SAT math scores over 500: 40%; ACT scores over 18: 58%; SAT verbal scores over 600: 9%; SAT math scores over 600: 10%; ACT scores over 24: 20%; SAT verbal scores over 700: 2%; SAT math scores over 700: 2%.

Faculty *Total:* 112, 48% full-time, 52% with terminal degrees. *Student/faculty ratio:* 13:1.

Majors Accounting; acting/directing; art; art education; athletic training/sports medicine; biology; biology education; business economics; chemistry; drama/dance education; early childhood education; education; education of the emotionally handicapped; education of the mentally handicapped; education of the specific learning disabled; elementary education; English; English education; French; history; interdisciplinary studies; mathematics; mathematics education; medical technology; middle school education; music; music teacher education; physical education; political science; psychology; religious studies; science education; secondary education; social studies education; sociology; socio-psychological sports studies; Spanish; Spanish language education; special education; sport/fitness administration; theater arts/drama; theater design.

Academic Programs *Special study options:* academic remediation for entering students, accelerated degree program, adult/continuing education programs, advanced placement credit, double majors, freshman honors college, honors programs, independent study, internships, off-campus study, part-time degree program, services for LD students, student-designed majors, study abroad, summer session for credit. *ROTC:* Army (c), Air Force (c).

Library James Addison Jones Library with 69,472 titles, 5,800 serial subscriptions, 2,294 audiovisual materials, an OPAC, a Web page.

Computers on Campus 60 computers available on campus for general student use. A campuswide network can be accessed from student residence rooms and from off campus that provide access to online course support. Internet access, at least one staffed computer lab available.

Student Life *Housing:* on-campus residence required through sophomore year. *Options:* coed, men-only, women-only. *Activities and Organizations:* drama/theater group, student-run newspaper, choral group, marching band, Student Christian Fellowship, Campus Activities Board, student government, Peer Awareness With Students, United African American Society. *Campus security:* 24-hour patrols, late-night transport/escort service, controlled dormitory access. *Student Services:* health clinic, personal/psychological counseling.

Athletics Member NCAA. All Division III. *Intercollegiate sports:* baseball M, basketball M/W, cross-country running M/W, football M, golf M, lacrosse M/W, soccer M/W, softball W, swimming W, tennis M/W, volleyball W. *Intramural sports:* basketball M/W, bowling M/W, football M/W, golf M/W, skiing (downhill) M/W.

Standardized Tests *Required:* SAT I or ACT (for admission).

Costs (2001–02) *Comprehensive fee:* $19,080 includes full-time tuition ($13,500), mandatory fees ($200), and room and board ($5380). Full-time tuition and fees vary according to course load. Part-time tuition: $350 per semester hour. Part-time tuition and fees vary according to course load. *Room and board:* Room and board charges vary according to board plan and housing facility. *Payment plan:* installment. *Waivers:* employees or children of employees.

Financial Aid Of all full-time matriculated undergraduates who enrolled in 2001, 621 applied for aid, 510 were judged to have need, 273 had their need fully met. 205 Federal Work-Study jobs (averaging $1100). 17 State and other part-time jobs (averaging $1200). In 2001, 111 non-need-based awards were made. *Average percent of need met:* 90%. *Average financial aid package:* $8603. *Average need-based loan:* $4904. *Average need-based gift aid:* $3654. *Average non-need based aid:* $5193. *Average indebtedness upon graduation:* $13,774.

Applying *Options:* common application, electronic application, early admission, early action, deferred entrance. *Application fee:* $35. *Required:* essay or personal statement, high school transcript. *Required for some:* 2 letters of recommendation, interview. *Recommended:* interview. *Application deadline:* rolling (freshmen), rolling (transfers). *Notification:* continuous (freshmen), 1/15 (early action).

Admissions Contact Mr. Timothy L. Jackson, Director of Admissions, Greensboro College, Greensboro, NC 27401-1875. *Phone:* 336-272-7102 Ext. 211. *Toll-free phone:* 800-346-8226. *Fax:* 336-378-0154. *E-mail:* admissions@gborocollege.edu.

GUILFORD COLLEGE
Greensboro, North Carolina

- **Independent** 4-year, founded 1837, affiliated with Society of Friends
- **Calendar** semesters
- **Degree** certificates and bachelor's
- **Suburban** 340-acre campus
- **Endowment** $59.8 million
- **Coed,** 1,490 undergraduate students, 88% full-time, 53% women, 47% men
- **Moderately difficult** entrance level, 79% of applicants were admitted

Undergraduates 1,307 full-time, 183 part-time. Students come from 43 states and territories, 22 other countries, 51% are from out of state, 11% African American, 1% Asian American or Pacific Islander, 2% Hispanic American, 1%

Native American, 3% international, 3% transferred in, 78% live on campus. *Retention:* 77% of 2001 full-time freshmen returned.

Freshmen *Admission:* 1,355 applied, 1,077 admitted, 336 enrolled. *Average high school GPA:* 3.02. *Test scores:* SAT verbal scores over 500: 83%; SAT math scores over 500: 77%; ACT scores over 18: 94%; SAT verbal scores over 600: 45%; SAT math scores over 600: 30%; ACT scores over 24: 61%; SAT verbal scores over 700: 8%; SAT math scores over 700: 4%.

Faculty *Total:* 136, 51% full-time, 56% with terminal degrees. *Student/faculty ratio:* 15:1.

Majors Accounting; African-American studies; art; athletic training/sports medicine; biological sciences/life sciences related; biology; business administration; chemistry; computer/information sciences; criminal justice studies; earth sciences; economics; elementary education; English; environmental science; exercise sciences; French; geology; German; health/medical preparatory programs related; history; information sciences/systems; interdisciplinary studies; international relations; mathematics; music; peace/conflict studies; philosophy; physics; political science; psychology; religious studies; secondary education; sociology; Spanish; sport/fitness administration; theater arts/drama; women's studies.

Academic Programs *Special study options:* academic remediation for entering students, accelerated degree program, adult/continuing education programs, advanced placement credit, double majors, English as a second language, honors programs, independent study, internships, off-campus study, part-time degree program, student-designed majors, study abroad, summer session for credit. *ROTC:* Army (c), Air Force (c). *Unusual degree programs:* 3-2 forestry with Duke University; physician's assistant program with Bowman-Gray School of Medicine at Wake Forest University.

Library Hege Library with 250,000 titles, 2,000 serial subscriptions, 9,660 audiovisual materials, an OPAC, a Web page.

Computers on Campus 150 computers available on campus for general student use. A campuswide network can be accessed from student residence rooms and from off campus. Internet access, online (class) registration, at least one staffed computer lab available.

Student Life *Housing:* on-campus residence required through junior year. *Options:* coed, men-only, women-only, cooperative. *Activities and Organizations:* drama/theater group, student-run newspaper, radio station, choral group, student government, student radio station, student newspaper, Project Community, African-American Cultural Society. *Campus security:* 24-hour emergency response devices and patrols, student patrols, late-night transport/escort service, controlled dormitory access. *Student Services:* health clinic, personal/psychological counseling, women's center.

Athletics Member NCAA. All Division III. *Intercollegiate sports:* baseball M, basketball M/W, bowling M(c)/W(c), football M, golf M, lacrosse M/W, rugby M(c)/W(c), soccer M/W, softball W, tennis M/W, track and field M(c)/W(c), volleyball W. *Intramural sports:* basketball M(c)/W(c), table tennis M/W, tennis M/W.

Standardized Tests *Required:* SAT I or ACT (for admission).

Costs (2002–03) *Comprehensive fee:* $23,980 includes full-time tuition ($17,900), mandatory fees ($300), and room and board ($5780). Part-time tuition: $550 per credit hour. Part-time tuition and fees vary according to course load. *Required fees:* $300 per year part-time. *Room and board:* College room only: $2990. Room and board charges vary according to board plan, housing facility, and location. *Payment plan:* installment. *Waivers:* employees or children of employees.

Financial Aid Of all full-time matriculated undergraduates who enrolled in 2001, 170 Federal Work-Study jobs (averaging $1260). 172 State and other part-time jobs (averaging $1161).

Applying *Options:* common application, electronic application, early admission, early decision, early action, deferred entrance. *Application fee:* $25. *Required:* essay or personal statement, high school transcript, minimum 2.0 GPA, 2 letters of recommendation. *Recommended:* minimum 3.0 GPA, interview. *Application deadlines:* 2/15 (freshmen), 4/1 (transfers). *Early decision:* 11/15. *Notification:* 4/1 (freshmen), 12/15 (early decision), 2/15 (early action).

Admissions Contact Mr. Randy Doss, Vice President of Enrollment, Guilford College, Greensboro, NC 27410. *Phone:* 336-316-2100. *Toll-free phone:* 800-992-7759. *Fax:* 336-316-2954. *E-mail:* admission@guilford.edu.

HERITAGE BIBLE COLLEGE

Dunn, North Carolina

- **Independent Pentecostal Free Will Baptist** 4-year, founded 1971
- **Calendar** semesters
- **Degrees** associate and bachelor's
- **Small-town** 82-acre campus with easy access to Raleigh-Durham
- **Coed,** 50 undergraduate students, 74% full-time, 26% women, 74% men
- **Minimally difficult** entrance level, 100% of applicants were admitted

Undergraduates 37 full-time, 13 part-time. Students come from 1 other state, 4% are from out of state, 34% African American, 6% Hispanic American, 6% transferred in, 2% live on campus. *Retention:* 62% of 2001 full-time freshmen returned.

Freshmen *Admission:* 10 applied, 10 admitted, 6 enrolled.

Faculty *Total:* 15, 27% full-time, 13% with terminal degrees. *Student/faculty ratio:* 3:1.

Majors Theology.

Academic Programs *Special study options:* adult/continuing education programs, external degree program, independent study, internships, off-campus study, summer session for credit.

Library Alphin Learning Center with 16,997 titles, 108 serial subscriptions, 1,183 audiovisual materials, an OPAC.

Computers on Campus 6 computers available on campus for general student use. Internet access available.

Student Life *Housing Options:* coed. *Activities and Organizations:* drama/theater group, choral group.

Standardized Tests *Required:* ACT ASSET.

Costs (2002–03) *One-time required fee:* $25. *Comprehensive fee:* $6640 includes full-time tuition ($3600), mandatory fees ($600), and room and board ($2440). Full-time tuition and fees vary according to class time. Part-time tuition: $150 per credit. Part-time tuition and fees vary according to class time. *Required fees:* $150 per term part-time. *Room and board:* College room only: $1440. Room and board charges vary according to board plan and housing facility. *Payment plans:* installment, deferred payment. *Waivers:* employees or children of employees.

Financial Aid Of all full-time matriculated undergraduates who enrolled in 2001, 41 applied for aid, 41 were judged to have need. 3 Federal Work-Study jobs (averaging $5616). *Average financial aid package:* $4330. *Average need-based loan:* $3500. *Average indebtedness upon graduation:* $15,152.

Applying *Options:* common application. *Application fee:* $25. *Required:* essay or personal statement, high school transcript, letters of recommendation. *Application deadline:* rolling (freshmen), rolling (transfers).

Admissions Contact Heritage Bible College, PO Box 1628, Dunn, NC 28335. *Phone:* 910-892-3178. *Fax:* 910-892-1809. *E-mail:* hbchead@intrstar.net.

HIGH POINT UNIVERSITY

High Point, North Carolina

- **Independent United Methodist** comprehensive, founded 1924
- **Calendar** semesters
- **Degrees** bachelor's, master's, and post-master's certificates
- **Suburban** 77-acre campus with easy access to Charlotte
- **Endowment** $44.8 million
- **Coed,** 2,590 undergraduate students, 89% full-time, 63% women, 37% men
- **Moderately difficult** entrance level, 88% of applicants were admitted

Undergraduates 2,315 full-time, 275 part-time. Students come from 38 states and territories, 55% are from out of state, 18% African American, 0.8% Asian American or Pacific Islander, 1% Hispanic American, 0.2% Native American, 0.9% international, 9% transferred in, 60% live on campus. *Retention:* 74% of 2001 full-time freshmen returned.

Freshmen *Admission:* 1,571 applied, 1,384 admitted, 489 enrolled. *Average high school GPA:* 2.80. *Test scores:* SAT verbal scores over 500: 52%; SAT math scores over 500: 54%; SAT verbal scores over 600: 13%; SAT math scores over 600: 16%; SAT verbal scores over 700: 2%; SAT math scores over 700: 2%.

Faculty *Total:* 209, 56% full-time, 47% with terminal degrees. *Student/faculty ratio:* 16:1.

Majors Accounting; American studies; art education; athletic training/sports medicine; biology; business administration; business marketing and marketing management; chemistry; community services; computer/information sciences; computer science; creative writing; criminal justice studies; early childhood education; education; elementary education; English; exercise sciences; fine/studio arts; French; history; human services; information sciences/systems; interior design; international business; international relations; literature; mass communications; mathematics; medical technology; middle school education; philosophy; physical education; physician assistant; political science; pre-dentistry; pre-law; pre-medicine; pre-veterinary studies; psychology; recreation/leisure facilities management; recreation/leisure studies; religious studies; secondary education; sociology; Spanish; special education; sport/fitness administration; theater arts/drama.

High Point University (continued)

Academic Programs *Special study options:* academic remediation for entering students, accelerated degree program, adult/continuing education programs, advanced placement credit, cooperative education, double majors, English as a second language, honors programs, independent study, internships, off-campus study, part-time degree program, student-designed majors, study abroad, summer session for credit. *ROTC:* Army (c), Air Force (c). *Unusual degree programs:* 3-2 forestry with Duke University; medical technology with Wake Forest University.

Library Herman and Louise Smith Library with 105,040 titles, 7,081 serial subscriptions, 11,000 audiovisual materials, an OPAC, a Web page.

Computers on Campus 176 computers available on campus for general student use. A campuswide network can be accessed from student residence rooms and from off campus. Internet access, at least one staffed computer lab available.

Student Life *Housing Options:* coed, men-only, women-only, disabled students. *Activities and Organizations:* drama/theater group, student-run newspaper, radio station, choral group, student government, Habitat for Humanity, International Club, Student Activities Board, Honors Club, national fraternities, national sororities. *Campus security:* 24-hour emergency response devices and patrols, student patrols, late-night transport/escort service, controlled dormitory access. *Student Services:* health clinic, personal/psychological counseling.

Athletics Member NCAA. All Division I. *Intercollegiate sports:* baseball M(s), basketball M(s)/W(s), cross-country running M(s)/W(s), golf M(s), soccer M(s)/W(s), tennis M(s)/W(s), track and field M/W(s), volleyball W(s). *Intramural sports:* basketball M/W, bowling M/W, football M/W, racquetball M/W, soccer M/W, softball M/W, swimming M/W, table tennis M/W, tennis M/W, track and field M/W, volleyball M/W.

Standardized Tests *Required:* SAT I or ACT (for admission). *Recommended:* SAT II: Subject Tests (for admission), SAT II: Writing Test (for admission).

Costs (2001–02) *Comprehensive fee:* $20,220 includes full-time tuition ($12,620), mandatory fees ($1280), and room and board ($6320). Full-time tuition and fees vary according to class time. Part-time tuition: $217 per credit hour. *Room and board:* College room only: $2690. Room and board charges vary according to board plan. *Waivers:* employees or children of employees.

Financial Aid Of all full-time matriculated undergraduates who enrolled in 2001, 2515 applied for aid, 2515 were judged to have need, 57 had their need fully met. *Average percent of need met:* 87%. *Average financial aid package:* $9200. *Average need-based loan:* $4500. *Average need-based gift aid:* $4000. *Average non-need based aid:* $3000. *Average indebtedness upon graduation:* $14,000.

Applying *Options:* common application, electronic application, deferred entrance. *Application fee:* $25. *Required:* high school transcript, minimum 2.0 GPA, 2 letters of recommendation. *Recommended:* essay or personal statement, minimum 3.0 GPA, interview. *Application deadlines:* 8/15 (freshmen), 8/15 (transfers). *Notification:* continuous until 8/15 (freshmen).

Admissions Contact Mr. James L. Schlimmer, Dean of Enrollment Management, High Point University, University Station 3188, 833 Montlieu Avenue, High Point, NC 2726-3598. *Phone:* 336-841-9216. *Toll-free phone:* 800-345-6993. *Fax:* 336-841-5123. *E-mail:* admiss@highpoint.edu.

JOHNSON C. SMITH UNIVERSITY
Charlotte, North Carolina

- **Independent** 4-year, founded 1867
- **Calendar** semesters
- **Degree** bachelor's
- **Urban** 105-acre campus
- **Endowment** $27.6 million
- **Coed,** 1,595 undergraduate students, 94% full-time, 58% women, 42% men
- **Minimally difficult** entrance level, 44% of applicants were admitted

Johnson C. Smith University is committed to maintaining its rich liberal arts heritage while concurrently developing new programs that are responsive to the needs of society, including infusing technology into the curriculum through the IBM ThinkPad Initiative and developing programs that focus on banking and finance, computer science, and computer engineering.

Undergraduates 1,493 full-time, 102 part-time. Students come from 35 states and territories, 73% are from out of state, 100% African American, 0.1% Asian American or Pacific Islander, 1% transferred in, 80% live on campus. *Retention:* 69% of 2001 full-time freshmen returned.

Freshmen *Admission:* 4,542 applied, 2,019 admitted, 462 enrolled. *Average high school GPA:* 2.72. *Test scores:* SAT verbal scores over 500: 25%; SAT math scores over 500: 35%; SAT verbal scores over 600: 15%; SAT math scores over 600: 15%; SAT verbal scores over 700: 4%; SAT math scores over 700: 2%.

Faculty *Total:* 116, 79% full-time, 72% with terminal degrees. *Student/faculty ratio:* 16:1.

Majors Accounting; applied mathematics; biological/physical sciences; biology; business administration; business marketing and marketing management; chemistry; computer engineering; computer science; criminal justice/law enforcement administration; early childhood education; economics; education; elementary education; English; finance; health education; history; information sciences/systems; mass communications; mathematics; physical education; political science; pre-law; pre-medicine; psychology; science education; secondary education; social sciences; social work; sociology.

Academic Programs *Special study options:* accelerated degree program, adult/continuing education programs, advanced placement credit, cooperative education, double majors, freshman honors college, honors programs, independent study, internships, off-campus study, part-time degree program, services for LD students, study abroad, summer session for credit. *ROTC:* Army (b), Air Force (b). *Unusual degree programs:* 3-2 engineering with University of North Carolina at Charlotte, Florida Agricultural and Mechanical University.

Library James B. Duke Library plus 1 other with 112,477 titles, 800 serial subscriptions, 1,993 audiovisual materials, an OPAC, a Web page.

Computers on Campus 250 computers available on campus for general student use. A campuswide network can be accessed from off campus. Internet access, at least one staffed computer lab available.

Student Life *Housing:* on-campus residence required for freshman year. *Options:* coed, men-only, women-only. *Activities and Organizations:* drama/theater group, student-run newspaper, radio station, choral group, marching band, Union Program Board, Royal Golden Bull Pep Squad, health and physical education club, Delta Sigma Theta, Alpha Kappa Alpha, national fraternities, national sororities. *Campus security:* 24-hour emergency response devices and patrols, late-night transport/escort service, controlled dormitory access. *Student Services:* health clinic, personal/psychological counseling.

Athletics Member NCAA. All Division II. *Intercollegiate sports:* basketball M(s)/W(s), cross-country running M/W, football M(s), golf M(s), tennis M(s)/W, track and field M(s)/W(s), volleyball W. *Intramural sports:* badminton M/W, basketball M/W, track and field M/W, volleyball M/W.

Costs (2001–02) *Comprehensive fee:* $16,560 includes full-time tuition ($10,066), mandatory fees ($1905), and room and board ($4589). Part-time tuition: $221 per credit hour. Part-time tuition and fees vary according to course load. *Room and board:* College room only: $2608. Room and board charges vary according to board plan, housing facility, and location. *Payment plan:* installment. *Waivers:* employees or children of employees.

Financial Aid Of all full-time matriculated undergraduates who enrolled in 2001, 1501 applied for aid, 1361 were judged to have need, 36 had their need fully met. In 2001, 170 non-need-based awards were made. *Average percent of need met:* 100%. *Average financial aid package:* $6200. *Average need-based gift aid:* $2000. *Average indebtedness upon graduation:* $22,000.

Applying *Options:* common application, electronic application, early admission, deferred entrance. *Application fee:* $25. *Required:* high school transcript. *Required for some:* letters of recommendation. *Recommended:* essay or personal statement, interview. *Application deadlines:* 8/1 (freshmen), 8/1 (transfers). *Notification:* continuous (freshmen).

Admissions Contact Mr. Jeffrey Smith, Director of Admissions, Johnson C. Smith University, 100 Beatties Ford Road, Charlotte, NC 28216. *Phone:* 704-378-1010. *Toll-free phone:* 800-782-7303.

JOHN WESLEY COLLEGE
High Point, North Carolina

- **Independent interdenominational** 4-year, founded 1932
- **Calendar** semesters
- **Degrees** associate and bachelor's
- **Urban** 24-acre campus
- **Coed,** 179 undergraduate students, 78% full-time, 43% women, 57% men
- **Minimally difficult** entrance level, 79% of applicants were admitted

Undergraduates 139 full-time, 40 part-time. Students come from 8 states and territories, 5% are from out of state, 23% African American, 1% Asian American or Pacific Islander, 0.6% Hispanic American, 1% Native American, 27% transferred in, 15% live on campus. *Retention:* 80% of 2001 full-time freshmen returned.

Freshmen *Admission:* 19 applied, 15 admitted, 19 enrolled. *Average high school GPA:* 2.5.

Faculty *Total:* 18, 61% full-time, 44% with terminal degrees. *Student/faculty ratio:* 12:1.

Majors Biblical studies; business administration; divinity/ministry; elementary education; liberal arts and sciences/liberal studies; pastoral counseling; psychology; religious education; religious studies; theology.

Academic Programs *Special study options:* academic remediation for entering students, adult/continuing education programs, advanced placement credit, internships, off-campus study, part-time degree program, summer session for credit.
Library Temple Library with 43,305 titles, 146 serial subscriptions, 2,886 audiovisual materials.
Computers on Campus 5 computers available on campus for general student use. Internet access, at least one staffed computer lab available.
Student Life *Housing:* on-campus residence required through senior year. *Activities and Organizations:* student-run newspaper, choral group.
Standardized Tests *Recommended:* SAT I and SAT II or ACT (for placement), SAT II: Writing Test (for placement).
Costs (2001–02) *Tuition:* $6378 full-time, $263 per semester hour part-time. Part-time tuition and fees vary according to course load. *Required fees:* $334 full-time, $167 per term part-time. *Room only:* $1990. Room and board charges vary according to housing facility. *Payment plan:* installment. *Waivers:* employees or children of employees.
Financial Aid Of all full-time matriculated undergraduates who enrolled in 2001, 103 applied for aid, 103 were judged to have need. 5 Federal Work-Study jobs (averaging $2500). *Average percent of need met:* 75%. *Average financial aid package:* $6900. *Average need-based loan:* $3500. *Average need-based gift aid:* $1500. *Average indebtedness upon graduation:* $12,000.
Applying *Options:* early admission, deferred entrance. *Application fee:* $30. *Required:* high school transcript, 2 letters of recommendation, interview. *Recommended:* minimum 2.0 GPA. *Application deadlines:* 8/1 (freshmen), 8/1 (transfers). *Notification:* continuous until 8/10 (freshmen).
Admissions Contact Mr. Greg Workman, Admissions Officer, John Wesley College, 2314 North Centennial Street, High Point, NC 27265-3197. *Phone:* 336-889-2262 Ext. 127. *Fax:* 336-889-2261. *E-mail:* gworkman@johnwesley.edu.

LEES-MCRAE COLLEGE
Banner Elk, North Carolina

- **Independent** 4-year, founded 1900, affiliated with Presbyterian Church (U.S.A.)
- **Calendar** semesters
- **Degree** bachelor's
- **Rural** 400-acre campus
- **Endowment** $15.4 million
- **Coed,** 792 undergraduate students, 96% full-time, 57% women, 43% men
- **Minimally difficult** entrance level, 95% of applicants were admitted

Undergraduates 762 full-time, 30 part-time. Students come from 31 states and territories, 20 other countries, 38% are from out of state, 6% African American, 0.5% Asian American or Pacific Islander, 1% Hispanic American, 0.4% Native American, 5% international, 16% transferred in, 70% live on campus. *Retention:* 58% of 2001 full-time freshmen returned.
Freshmen *Admission:* 536 applied, 511 admitted, 199 enrolled. *Average high school GPA:* 2.94. *Test scores:* SAT verbal scores over 500: 43%; SAT math scores over 500: 35%; SAT verbal scores over 600: 5%; SAT math scores over 600: 10%.
Faculty *Total:* 83, 83% full-time, 51% with terminal degrees. *Student/faculty ratio:* 14:1.
Majors Athletic training/sports medicine; biological/physical sciences; biology; business administration; criminal justice/law enforcement administration; education; elementary education; English; environmental science; forestry; history; humanities; information sciences/systems; interdisciplinary studies; international relations; liberal arts and sciences/liberal studies; mass communications; mathematics; natural sciences; physical education; pre-law; pre-medicine; preveterinary studies; psychology; religious studies; social sciences; sociology; theater arts/drama.
Academic Programs *Special study options:* academic remediation for entering students, adult/continuing education programs, advanced placement credit, double majors, external degree program, honors programs, independent study, internships, off-campus study, part-time degree program, services for LD students, student-designed majors, study abroad, summer session for credit. *ROTC:* Army (c). *Unusual degree programs:* 3-2 forestry with Duke University.
Library James H. Carson Library with 88,756 titles, 429 serial subscriptions.
Computers on Campus 60 computers available on campus for general student use. A campuswide network can be accessed from student residence rooms and from off campus. Internet access, at least one staffed computer lab available.
Student Life *Housing:* on-campus residence required through sophomore year. *Options:* coed, men-only, women-only. *Activities and Organizations:* drama/theater group, student-run newspaper, choral group, Student Government Association, Students Against a Vanishing Environment, CATCH, Order of the Tower, Student Ambassadors. *Campus security:* 24-hour patrols. *Student Services:* health clinic, personal/psychological counseling.
Athletics Member NCAA. All Division II. *Intercollegiate sports:* basketball M(s)/W(s), cross-country running M(s)/W(s), golf M(s), lacrosse M(s)/W(s), skiing (downhill) M(s)/W(s), soccer M(s)/W(s), softball W(s), tennis M(s)/W(s), track and field M(s)/W(s), volleyball M(s)/W(s). *Intramural sports:* basketball M/W, cross-country running M/W, fencing M/W, football M, golf M, lacrosse M(c), skiing (downhill) M/W, soccer M/W, softball M/W, swimming M/W, table tennis M/W, tennis M/W, track and field M/W, volleyball M/W, weight lifting M.
Standardized Tests *Required:* SAT I or ACT (for admission).
Costs (2001–02) *Comprehensive fee:* $17,106 includes full-time tuition ($12,292), mandatory fees ($150), and room and board ($4664). Part-time tuition: $370 per semester hour. *Room and board:* College room only: $2190. Room and board charges vary according to board plan. *Payment plan:* installment. *Waivers:* employees or children of employees.
Financial Aid Of all full-time matriculated undergraduates who enrolled in 2001, 733 applied for aid, 478 were judged to have need, 148 had their need fully met. 100 Federal Work-Study jobs (averaging $1400). In 2001, 269 non-need-based awards were made. *Average percent of need met:* 90%. *Average financial aid package:* $10,600. *Average need-based loan:* $2806. *Average need-based gift aid:* $5607. *Average non-need based aid:* $4821. *Average indebtedness upon graduation:* $6414.
Applying *Options:* common application, electronic application, early admission, deferred entrance. *Application fee:* $25. *Required:* high school transcript, minimum 2.0 GPA. *Required for some:* letters of recommendation, interview. *Recommended:* essay or personal statement. *Application deadlines:* 8/15 (freshmen), 8/15 (transfers). *Notification:* continuous until 8/30 (freshmen).
Admissions Contact Mr. Bart Walker, Director of Admissions, Lees-McRae College, PO Box 128, Banner Elk, NC 28604-0128. *Phone:* 828-898-8702. *Toll-free phone:* 800-280-4562. *Fax:* 828-898-8707. *E-mail:* admissions@lmc.edu.

LENOIR-RHYNE COLLEGE
Hickory, North Carolina

- **Independent Lutheran** comprehensive, founded 1891
- **Calendar** semesters
- **Degrees** bachelor's and master's
- **Small-town** 100-acre campus with easy access to Charlotte
- **Endowment** $40.6 million
- **Coed,** 1,316 undergraduate students, 88% full-time, 64% women, 36% men
- **Moderately difficult** entrance level, 85% of applicants were admitted

Undergraduates 1,160 full-time, 156 part-time. Students come from 29 states and territories, 29% are from out of state, 8% African American, 2% Asian American or Pacific Islander, 1% Hispanic American, 0.3% Native American, 0.1% international, 11% transferred in, 60% live on campus. *Retention:* 77% of 2001 full-time freshmen returned.
Freshmen *Admission:* 1,121 applied, 948 admitted, 273 enrolled. *Average high school GPA:* 3.37. *Test scores:* SAT verbal scores over 500: 49%; SAT math scores over 500: 51%; ACT scores over 18: 73%; SAT verbal scores over 600: 14%; SAT math scores over 600: 17%; ACT scores over 24: 27%; SAT verbal scores over 700: 1%; SAT math scores over 700: 2%; ACT scores over 30: 3%.
Faculty *Total:* 158, 60% full-time. *Student/faculty ratio:* 11:1.
Majors Accounting; adult/continuing education; art education; athletic training/sports medicine; biology; business administration; business education; chemistry; classics; computer science; early childhood education; ecology; economics; education; elementary education; English; environmental science; exercise sciences; French; German; history; human services; international business; international relations; Latin (ancient and medieval); mass communications; mathematics; medical technology; modern languages; music; music teacher education; nursing; occupational therapy; pastoral counseling; philosophy; physical education; physical sciences; physician assistant; physics; political science; pre-dentistry; pre-law; pre-medicine; pre-veterinary studies; psychology; religious education; religious music; religious studies; science education; secondary education; sociology; Spanish; theater arts/drama; theology.
Academic Programs *Special study options:* academic remediation for entering students, accelerated degree program, adult/continuing education programs, advanced placement credit, double majors, English as a second language, honors programs, independent study, internships, part-time degree program, services for LD students, student-designed majors, study abroad, summer session for credit. *ROTC:* Army (c), Air Force (c). *Unusual degree programs:* 3-2 engineering with North Carolina State University, University of North Carolina at Charlotte, Clemson University, North Carolina Agricultural and Technical State University; forestry with Duke University.

Lenoir-Rhyne College (continued)

Library Carl Rudisill Library plus 3 others with 139,726 titles, 2,335 serial subscriptions, 36,728 audiovisual materials, an OPAC, a Web page.

Computers on Campus 94 computers available on campus for general student use. A campuswide network can be accessed from student residence rooms and from off campus. Internet access, at least one staffed computer lab available.

Student Life *Housing:* on-campus residence required through junior year. *Options:* coed, men-only, women-only, disabled students. *Activities and Organizations:* drama/theater group, student-run newspaper, radio and television station, choral group, Student Government Association, Religious Clubs, Outdoors and Service Club, Playmakers, Bear Trackers (Student Recruitment Organization), national fraternities, national sororities. *Campus security:* 24-hour emergency response devices and patrols, late-night transport/escort service, controlled dormitory access. *Student Services:* health clinic, personal/psychological counseling, women's center.

Athletics Member NCAA. All Division II. *Intercollegiate sports:* baseball M(s), basketball M(s)/W(s), cross-country running M(s)/W(s), football M(s), golf M(s)/W(s), soccer M(s)/W(s), softball W(s), volleyball W(s). *Intramural sports:* badminton M/W, basketball M/W, football M/W, golf M/W, racquetball M/W, skiing (downhill) M/W, soccer M/W, softball M/W, swimming M/W, tennis M/W, volleyball M/W, weight lifting M/W.

Standardized Tests *Required:* SAT I or ACT (for admission).

Costs (2002–03) *Comprehensive fee:* $20,294 includes full-time tuition ($14,358), mandatory fees ($636), and room and board ($5300). Part-time tuition: $360 per credit. Part-time tuition and fees vary according to class time. *Room and board:* Room and board charges vary according to board plan. *Payment plans:* installment, deferred payment. *Waivers:* employees or children of employees.

Applying *Options:* common application, electronic application, early admission, deferred entrance. *Application fee:* $25. *Required:* high school transcript, minimum 2.5 GPA. *Recommended:* interview. *Application deadline:* rolling (freshmen), rolling (transfers). *Notification:* continuous (freshmen).

Admissions Contact Mrs. Rachel Nichols, Director of Admissions and Financial Aid, Lenoir-Rhyne College, PO Box 7227, Hickory, NC 28603. *Phone:* 828-328-7300. *Toll-free phone:* 800-277-5721. *Fax:* 828-328-7338. *E-mail:* admission@lrc.edu.

LIVINGSTONE COLLEGE
Salisbury, North Carolina

- **Independent** 4-year, founded 1879, affiliated with African Methodist Episcopal Zion Church
- **Calendar** semesters
- **Degree** certificates and bachelor's
- **Small-town** 272-acre campus
- **Endowment** $4.3 million
- **Coed**
- **Minimally difficult** entrance level

Faculty *Student/faculty ratio:* 17:1.

Student Life *Campus security:* 24-hour patrols.

Athletics Member NCAA. All Division II.

Standardized Tests *Required:* SAT I or ACT (for admission).

Applying *Options:* deferred entrance. *Application fee:* $15. *Required:* high school transcript, 2 letters of recommendation. *Recommended:* essay or personal statement.

Admissions Contact Ms. Marjorie Kinard, Director of Enrollment Management, Livingstone College, 701 West Monroe Street, Salisbury, NC 28144. *Phone:* 704-216-6183. *Toll-free phone:* 800-835-3435. *Fax:* 704-216-6215. *E-mail:* admissions@livingstone.edu.

MARS HILL COLLEGE
Mars Hill, North Carolina

- **Independent Baptist** 4-year, founded 1856
- **Calendar** semesters
- **Degree** bachelor's
- **Small-town** 194-acre campus
- **Endowment** $34.0 million
- **Coed,** 1,242 undergraduate students, 89% full-time, 57% women, 43% men
- **Moderately difficult** entrance level, 85% of applicants were admitted

Undergraduates 1,101 full-time, 141 part-time. Students come from 29 states and territories, 16 other countries, 33% are from out of state, 11% African American, 0.4% Asian American or Pacific Islander, 1% Hispanic American, 1.0% Native American, 2% international, 11% transferred in, 56% live on campus. *Retention:* 73% of 2001 full-time freshmen returned.

Freshmen *Admission:* 1,006 applied, 856 admitted, 267 enrolled. *Average high school GPA:* 3.4. *Test scores:* SAT verbal scores over 500: 47%; SAT math scores over 500: 46%; ACT scores over 18: 100%; SAT verbal scores over 600: 13%; SAT math scores over 600: 11%; ACT scores over 24: 35%; SAT verbal scores over 700: 1%; SAT math scores over 700: 2%; ACT scores over 30: 6%.

Faculty *Total:* 84. *Student/faculty ratio:* 12:1.

Majors Accounting; adult/continuing education; art; art education; art history; athletic training/sports medicine; behavioral sciences; biological/physical sciences; biology; botany; business administration; business economics; business marketing and marketing management; chemistry; computer science; criminal justice/law enforcement administration; dental hygiene; early childhood education; education; elementary education; English; fashion merchandising; finance; gerontology; history; industrial radiologic technology; interdisciplinary studies; international business; international relations; journalism; liberal arts and sciences/liberal studies; mass communications; mathematics; music; music teacher education; music (voice and choral/opera performance); nursing; physical education; physician assistant; political science; pre-dentistry; pre-law; pre-medicine; pre-veterinary studies; psychology; recreational therapy; recreation/leisure studies; religious education; religious music; religious studies; science education; secondary education; social sciences; social work; sociology; Spanish; sport/fitness administration; stringed instruments; theater arts/drama; wind/percussion instruments; zoology.

Academic Programs *Special study options:* academic remediation for entering students, accelerated degree program, adult/continuing education programs, advanced placement credit, cooperative education, double majors, English as a second language, honors programs, independent study, internships, part-time degree program, services for LD students, student-designed majors, study abroad, summer session for credit. *Unusual degree programs:* 3-2 physician's assistant, medical technology with Wake Forest University.

Library Renfro Library plus 1 other with 98,150 titles, 650 serial subscriptions, an OPAC, a Web page.

Computers on Campus 188 computers available on campus for general student use. A campuswide network can be accessed from student residence rooms and from off campus. Internet access, at least one staffed computer lab available.

Student Life *Housing:* on-campus residence required through sophomore year. *Options:* men-only, women-only. *Activities and Organizations:* drama/theater group, student-run newspaper, radio station, choral group, marching band, Student Government Association, Fellowship of Christian Athletes, Christian Student Movement, Student Union Board, Inter-Greek Council, national fraternities, national sororities. *Campus security:* 24-hour emergency response devices and patrols, late-night transport/escort service, controlled dormitory access. *Student Services:* health clinic, personal/psychological counseling.

Athletics Member NCAA. All Division II. *Intercollegiate sports:* basketball M(s)/W(s), cross-country running M(s)/W(s), football M(s), golf M(s), lacrosse M(s), soccer M(s)/W(s), softball W(s), tennis M(s)/W(s), volleyball W(s). *Intramural sports:* basketball M/W, football M/W, skiing (downhill) M(c)/W(c), soccer M/W, track and field M(c)/W(c), volleyball M/W, water polo M/W.

Standardized Tests *Required:* SAT I or ACT (for admission).

Costs (2001–02) *Comprehensive fee:* $18,600 includes full-time tuition ($13,800) and room and board ($4800). Full-time tuition and fees vary according to student level. Part-time tuition: $450 per credit hour. Part-time tuition and fees vary according to student level. *Room and board:* College room only: $2500. Room and board charges vary according to board plan and housing facility. *Payment plan:* installment. *Waivers:* employees or children of employees.

Financial Aid Available in 2001, 51 State and other part-time jobs (averaging $1300).

Applying *Options:* early admission, deferred entrance. *Application fee:* $25. *Required:* high school transcript, minimum 2.0 GPA. *Required for some:* interview. *Recommended:* minimum 3.0 GPA. *Application deadline:* rolling (freshmen), rolling (transfers).

Admissions Contact Ms. Ophelia H. DeGroot, Dean of Enrollment Services, Mars Hill College, PO Box 370, Mars Hill, NC 28754. *Phone:* 828-689-1201. *Toll-free phone:* 800-543-1514. *Fax:* 828-689-1473. *E-mail:* admissions@mhc.edu.

MEREDITH COLLEGE
Raleigh, North Carolina

- **Independent** comprehensive, founded 1891
- **Calendar** semesters
- **Degrees** bachelor's, master's, and postbachelor's certificates

- **Urban** 225-acre campus
- **Endowment** $55.8 million
- **Women only,** 2,307 undergraduate students, 78% full-time
- **Moderately difficult** entrance level, 83% of applicants were admitted

Undergraduates 1,792 full-time, 515 part-time. Students come from 25 states and territories, 24 other countries, 9% are from out of state, 6% African American, 1% Asian American or Pacific Islander, 2% Hispanic American, 0.2% Native American, 0.9% international, 4% transferred in, 48% live on campus. *Retention:* 79% of 2001 full-time freshmen returned.

Freshmen *Admission:* 389 enrolled. *Average high school GPA:* 3.05. *Test scores:* SAT verbal scores over 500: 66%; SAT math scores over 500: 62%; ACT scores over 18: 91%; SAT verbal scores over 600: 17%; SAT math scores over 600: 15%; ACT scores over 24: 29%; SAT verbal scores over 700: 2%; SAT math scores over 700: 1%; ACT scores over 30: 3%.

Faculty *Total:* 282, 50% full-time, 50% with terminal degrees. *Student/faculty ratio:* 10:1.

Majors Accounting; American studies; applied history; art education; art history; biology; business administration; business economics; business marketing and marketing management; chemistry; child care/development; communications; computer/information sciences; computer science; dance; dietetics; drama/dance education; economics; English; environmental science; exercise sciences; fashion design/illustration; fashion merchandising; finance; fine/studio arts; French; graphic design/commercial art/illustration; history; home economics; human resources management; interior design; international business; international relations; mass communications; mathematics; molecular biology; music; music (piano and organ performance); music teacher education; music theory and composition; music (voice and choral/opera performance); physical education; political science; pre-dentistry; pre-medicine; pre-pharmacy studies; pre-veterinary studies; psychology; religious studies; social work; sociology; Spanish; sport/fitness administration; stringed instruments; theater arts/drama; wind/percussion instruments.

Academic Programs *Special study options:* academic remediation for entering students, accelerated degree program, adult/continuing education programs, advanced placement credit, cooperative education, double majors, honors programs, independent study, internships, off-campus study, part-time degree program, services for LD students, student-designed majors, study abroad, summer session for credit. *ROTC:* Army (c), Air Force (c).

Library Carlyle Campbell Library plus 1 other with 113,179 titles, 4,952 serial subscriptions, 11,751 audiovisual materials, an OPAC, a Web page.

Computers on Campus 150 computers available on campus for general student use. A campuswide network can be accessed from student residence rooms. Internet access, at least one staffed computer lab available.

Student Life *Housing:* on-campus residence required through sophomore year. *Options:* women-only. *Activities and Organizations:* drama/theater group, student-run newspaper, choral group, Student Government Association, Entertainment Association, Recreation Association, Christian Association, choral groups. *Campus security:* 24-hour emergency response devices and patrols, late-night transport/escort service, controlled dormitory access. *Student Services:* health clinic, personal/psychological counseling.

Athletics Member NCAA. All Division III. *Intercollegiate sports:* basketball W, soccer W, softball W, tennis W, volleyball W.

Standardized Tests *Required:* SAT I or ACT (for admission). *Required for some:* SAT II: Subject Tests (for admission).

Costs (2002–03) *Comprehensive fee:* $18,900 includes full-time tuition ($14,300) and room and board ($4600). Part-time tuition: $440 per credit hour. additional freshman technology fee of $2165 (includes lap top computer and software); $800 technology fee for returning students.

Financial Aid Of all full-time matriculated undergraduates who enrolled in 2001, 1202 applied for aid, 953 were judged to have need, 145 had their need fully met. 347 Federal Work-Study jobs. In 2001, 243 non-need-based awards were made. *Average percent of need met:* 85%. *Average financial aid package:* $11,086. *Average need-based loan:* $2891. *Average need-based gift aid:* $8218. *Average non-need based aid:* $4575. *Average indebtedness upon graduation:* $9167.

Applying *Options:* common application, electronic application, early admission, early decision, deferred entrance. *Application fee:* $35. *Required:* high school transcript, minimum 2.0 GPA, 2 letters of recommendation. *Required for some:* essay or personal statement, interview. *Application deadlines:* 2/15 (freshmen), 2/15 (transfers). *Early decision:* 10/15. *Notification:* continuous (freshmen), 11/1 (early decision).

Admissions Contact Ms. Carol R. Kercheval, Director of Admissions, Meredith College, 3800 Hillsborough Street, Raleigh, NC 27607-5298. *Phone:* 919-760-8581. *Toll-free phone:* 800-MEREDITH. *Fax:* 919-760-2348. *E-mail:* admissions@meredith.edu.

METHODIST COLLEGE
Fayetteville, North Carolina

- **Independent United Methodist** comprehensive, founded 1956
- **Calendar** semesters
- **Degrees** associate, bachelor's, and master's
- **Suburban** 600-acre campus with easy access to Raleigh-Durham
- **Endowment** $8.9 million
- **Coed,** 2,133 undergraduate students, 77% full-time, 43% women, 57% men
- **Moderately difficult** entrance level, 73% of applicants were admitted

Undergraduates 1,641 full-time, 492 part-time. Students come from 48 states and territories, 37 other countries, 51% are from out of state, 22% African American, 1% Asian American or Pacific Islander, 5% Hispanic American, 1.0% Native American, 3% international, 9% transferred in, 50% live on campus. *Retention:* 68% of 2001 full-time freshmen returned.

Freshmen *Admission:* 1,487 applied, 1,085 admitted, 435 enrolled. *Average high school GPA:* 3.09. *Test scores:* SAT verbal scores over 500: 45%; SAT math scores over 500: 50%; ACT scores over 18: 74%; SAT verbal scores over 600: 9%; SAT math scores over 600: 15%; ACT scores over 24: 20%; SAT verbal scores over 700: 1%; SAT math scores over 700: 1%; ACT scores over 30: 3%.

Faculty *Total:* 211, 45% full-time, 55% with terminal degrees. *Student/faculty ratio:* 14:1.

Majors Accounting; Army R.O.T.C./military science; art; art education; athletic training/sports medicine; behavioral sciences; biblical studies; biological/physical sciences; biology; business administration; chemistry; computer science; creative writing; criminal justice/law enforcement administration; early childhood education; economics; education; education (K-12); elementary education; English; finance; French; German; health services administration; history; hospitality/recreation marketing operations; international relations; legal studies; liberal arts and sciences/liberal studies; marketing research; mass communications; mathematics; music; music business management/merchandising; music teacher education; philosophy; physical education; physician assistant; political science; pre-dentistry; pre-engineering; pre-law; pre-medicine; pre-veterinary studies; psychology; recreation/leisure facilities management; religious education; religious studies; science education; secondary education; social work; sociology; Spanish; special education; sport/fitness administration; theater arts/drama.

Academic Programs *Special study options:* academic remediation for entering students, accelerated degree program, adult/continuing education programs, advanced placement credit, cooperative education, double majors, English as a second language, honors programs, independent study, internships, part-time degree program, services for LD students, study abroad, summer session for credit. *ROTC:* Army (b), Air Force (c). *Unusual degree programs:* 3-2 engineering with North Carolina State University, Georgia Institute of Technology.

Library Davis Memorial Library plus 1 other with 93,773 titles, 620 serial subscriptions, an OPAC, a Web page.

Computers on Campus 175 computers available on campus for general student use. A campuswide network can be accessed from student residence rooms and from off campus. Internet access, at least one staffed computer lab available.

Student Life *Housing:* on-campus residence required for freshman year. *Options:* coed, men-only, women-only. *Activities and Organizations:* drama/theater group, student-run newspaper, choral group, Student Activities Committee, Student Government Association, Student Education Association, Fellowship of Christian Athletes, Residence Hall Association, national sororities. *Campus security:* 24-hour emergency response devices and patrols, late-night transport/escort service, controlled dormitory access, campus police station. *Student Services:* health clinic, personal/psychological counseling.

Athletics Member NCAA. All Division III. *Intercollegiate sports:* baseball M, basketball M/W, cross-country running M/W, football M, golf M/W, lacrosse W, soccer M/W, softball W, tennis M/W, track and field M/W, volleyball W. *Intramural sports:* basketball M/W, bowling M/W, football M/W, golf M/W, racquetball M/W, soccer M/W, softball M/W, table tennis M/W, tennis M/W, volleyball M/W, weight lifting M/W.

Standardized Tests *Required:* SAT I or ACT (for admission).

Costs (2001–02) *Comprehensive fee:* $19,526 includes full-time tuition ($14,070), mandatory fees ($126), and room and board ($5330). Full-time tuition and fees vary according to class time and program. Part-time tuition: $460 per semester hour. Part-time tuition and fees vary according to class time and program. *Room and board:* Room and board charges vary according to board plan and housing facility. *Payment plans:* installment, deferred payment. *Waivers:* senior citizens and employees or children of employees.

Financial Aid Of all full-time matriculated undergraduates who enrolled in 2001, 1405 applied for aid, 1044 were judged to have need. 791 Federal Work-Study jobs (averaging $1200). 350 State and other part-time jobs (averaging $1200). In 2001, 91 non-need-based awards were made. *Average percent of*

Methodist College (continued)
need met: 84%. *Average financial aid package:* $11,300. *Average need-based loan:* $4500. *Average non-need based aid:* $5200. *Average indebtedness upon graduation:* $19,703.

Applying *Options:* common application, deferred entrance. *Application fee:* $25. *Required:* high school transcript. *Required for some:* essay or personal statement, 2 letters of recommendation, interview. *Recommended:* 2 letters of recommendation, interview. *Application deadline:* rolling (freshmen), rolling (transfers). *Notification:* continuous until 8/15 (freshmen).

Admissions Contact Ms. Jamie Legg, Director of Admissions, Methodist College, Admissions Office, 5400 Ramsey Street, Fayetteville, NC 28311. *Phone:* 910-630-7027. *Toll-free phone:* 800-488-7110 Ext. 7027. *Fax:* 910-630-7285. *E-mail:* admissions@methodist.edu.

MONTREAT COLLEGE
Montreat, North Carolina

- **Independent Presbyterian** comprehensive, founded 1916
- **Calendar** semesters
- **Degrees** associate, bachelor's, and master's
- **Small-town** 100-acre campus
- **Endowment** $12.0 million
- **Coed,** 1,109 undergraduate students, 98% full-time, 61% women, 39% men
- **Moderately difficult** entrance level, 86% of applicants were admitted

Undergraduates 1,084 full-time, 25 part-time. Students come from 30 states and territories, 9 other countries, 19% are from out of state, 4% transferred in.

Freshmen *Admission:* 450 applied, 388 admitted, 298 enrolled. *Average high school GPA:* 3.13. *Test scores:* SAT verbal scores over 500: 50%; SAT math scores over 500: 52%; SAT verbal scores over 600: 15%; SAT math scores over 600: 13%; SAT verbal scores over 700: 3%; SAT math scores over 700: 1%.

Faculty *Total:* 57, 58% full-time.

Majors Accounting; American studies; art; biblical studies; business administration; business economics; business marketing and marketing management; child care/development; ecology; economics; education; elementary education; English; environmental science; history; human services; liberal arts and sciences/liberal studies; literature; management information systems/business data processing; mass communications; mathematics; music; music business management/merchandising; music (piano and organ performance); music teacher education; music (voice and choral/opera performance); physical education; pre-dentistry; pre-engineering; pre-law; pre-medicine; religious studies; secondary education; social sciences; Spanish; sport/fitness administration.

Academic Programs *Special study options:* adult/continuing education programs, advanced placement credit, cooperative education, double majors, independent study, internships, off-campus study, part-time degree program, study abroad.

Library L. Nelson Bell Library with 67,378 titles, 426 serial subscriptions, an OPAC.

Computers on Campus 60 computers available on campus for general student use. A campuswide network can be accessed from student residence rooms and from off campus. Internet access, at least one staffed computer lab available.

Student Life *Housing:* on-campus residence required through sophomore year. *Activities and Organizations:* drama/theater group, student-run newspaper, choral group, student government, Student Christian Association, Intervarsity Missions Fellowship, Paint Ball Club, Business Club. *Campus security:* 24-hour emergency response devices and patrols, controlled dormitory access. *Student Services:* health clinic, personal/psychological counseling.

Athletics Member NAIA. *Intercollegiate sports:* baseball M(s), basketball M(s)/W(s), cross-country running M(s)/W(s), golf M(s), soccer M(s)/W(s), softball W(s), tennis M(s)/W(s), volleyball W(s). *Intramural sports:* badminton M/W, basketball M/W, bowling M/W, football M, skiing (cross-country) M/W, skiing (downhill) M/W, softball M/W, table tennis M/W, tennis M/W, volleyball M/W.

Standardized Tests *Required:* SAT I or ACT (for admission).

Costs (2001–02) *Comprehensive fee:* $17,164 includes full-time tuition ($12,318) and room and board ($4846). *Payment plan:* installment. *Waivers:* senior citizens and employees or children of employees.

Financial Aid Of all full-time matriculated undergraduates who enrolled in 2001, 1038 applied for aid, 758 were judged to have need. 128 Federal Work-Study jobs (averaging $1044). 23 State and other part-time jobs (averaging $824). In 2001, 280 non-need-based awards were made. *Average financial aid package:* $9263. *Average need-based loan:* $5542. *Average need-based gift aid:* $4483. *Average indebtedness upon graduation:* $16,876.

Applying *Options:* early admission, deferred entrance. *Application fee:* $15. *Required:* essay or personal statement, high school transcript, minimum 2.25 GPA, 1 letter of recommendation. *Required for some:* interview. *Application deadlines:* 8/15 (freshmen), 8/15 (transfers). *Notification:* continuous (freshmen).

Admissions Contact Ms. Anita Darby, Director of Admissions, Montreat College, PO Box 1267, 310 Gaither Circle, Montreat, NC 28757-1267. *Phone:* 828-669-8012 Ext. 3784. *Toll-free phone:* 800-622-6968. *Fax:* 828-669-0120. *E-mail:* admissions@montreat.edu.

MOUNT OLIVE COLLEGE
Mount Olive, North Carolina

- **Independent Free Will Baptist** 4-year, founded 1951
- **Calendar** semester or continuous accelerated programs
- **Degrees** associate and bachelor's
- **Small-town** 123-acre campus with easy access to Raleigh
- **Coed,** 1,775 undergraduate students, 81% full-time, 55% women, 45% men
- **Minimally difficult** entrance level, 89% of applicants were admitted

Undergraduates 1,432 full-time, 343 part-time. Students come from 21 states and territories, 14% are from out of state, 25% African American, 0.2% Asian American or Pacific Islander, 2% Hispanic American, 7% transferred in, 22% live on campus. *Retention:* 54% of 2001 full-time freshmen returned.

Freshmen *Admission:* 401 applied, 357 admitted, 224 enrolled. *Average high school GPA:* 3.00. *Test scores:* SAT verbal scores over 500: 29%; SAT math scores over 500: 33%; ACT scores over 18: 38%; SAT verbal scores over 600: 4%; SAT math scores over 600: 5%; ACT scores over 24: 3%; SAT verbal scores over 700: 1%.

Faculty *Total:* 176, 25% full-time, 36% with terminal degrees. *Student/faculty ratio:* 18:1.

Majors Accounting; art; athletic training/sports medicine; biological/physical sciences; biology; business administration; criminal justice/law enforcement administration; divinity/ministry; English; environmental science; graphic design/commercial art/illustration; health science; history; human services; information sciences/systems; liberal arts and sciences/liberal studies; mathematics; middle school education; music; psychology; recreation/leisure studies; religious studies.

Academic Programs *Special study options:* academic remediation for entering students, accelerated degree program, adult/continuing education programs, advanced placement credit, cooperative education, double majors, external degree program, freshman honors college, honors programs, independent study, internships, off-campus study, part-time degree program, summer session for credit.

Library Moye Library plus 1 other with 79,620 titles, 5,732 serial subscriptions, 1,958 audiovisual materials, an OPAC, a Web page.

Computers on Campus 50 computers available on campus for general student use. A campuswide network can be accessed from student residence rooms and from off campus that provide access to Web site. Internet access, at least one staffed computer lab available.

Student Life *Housing:* on-campus residence required for freshman year. *Options:* men-only, women-only. *Activities and Organizations:* student-run newspaper, choral group, Student Government Association, Phi Beta Lambda, commuters organization, Christian Student Fellowship, English Society. *Campus security:* overnight security patrols; weekend patrols. *Student Services:* health clinic, personal/psychological counseling.

Athletics Member NCAA. All Division II. *Intercollegiate sports:* baseball M(s), basketball M(s)/W(s), cross-country running M(s)/W(s), golf M(s), soccer M(s)/W(s), softball W(s), tennis M(s)/W(s), volleyball W(s). *Intramural sports:* basketball M/W, football M/W, racquetball M/W, soccer M/W, softball W, table tennis M/W, tennis M/W, volleyball M/W.

Standardized Tests *Required:* SAT I or ACT (for admission). *Recommended:* SAT I (for admission).

Costs (2002–03) *Comprehensive fee:* $14,410 includes full-time tuition ($9900), mandatory fees ($110), and room and board ($4400). Full-time tuition and fees vary according to location. Part-time tuition: $260 per semester hour. Part-time tuition and fees vary according to course load and location. *Required fees:* $110 per term part-time. *Room and board:* College room only: $1950. Room and board charges vary according to board plan and housing facility. *Payment plan:* installment. *Waivers:* senior citizens and employees or children of employees.

Financial Aid Of all full-time matriculated undergraduates who enrolled in 2001, 890 applied for aid, 799 were judged to have need, 215 had their need fully met. 120 Federal Work-Study jobs (averaging $719). In 2001, 230 non-need-based awards were made. *Average percent of need met:* 61%. *Average financial aid package:* $6285. *Average need-based loan:* $2622. *Average need-based gift aid:* $4742. *Average non-need based aid:* $4183. *Average indebtedness upon graduation:* $6730.

Applying *Options:* common application, early admission, deferred entrance. *Application fee:* $20. *Required:* high school transcript, minimum 2.0 GPA.

Recommended: 2 letters of recommendation, interview. *Application deadline:* rolling (freshmen), rolling (transfers). *Notification:* continuous (freshmen).

Admissions Contact Mr. Tim Woodard, Director of Admissions, Mount Olive College, Mount Olive, NC 28365. *Phone:* 919-658-2502 Ext. 3009. *Toll-free phone:* 800-653-0854. *Fax:* 919-658-8934. *E-mail:* twppdard@moc.edu.

NORTH CAROLINA AGRICULTURAL AND TECHNICAL STATE UNIVERSITY

Greensboro, North Carolina

- **State-supported** university, founded 1891, part of University of North Carolina System
- **Calendar** semesters
- **Degrees** bachelor's, master's, and doctoral
- **Urban** 191-acre campus
- **Endowment** $10.4 million
- **Coed,** 6,850 undergraduate students, 89% full-time, 53% women, 47% men
- **Moderately difficult** entrance level, 93% of applicants were admitted

Undergraduates 6,094 full-time, 756 part-time. Students come from 42 states and territories, 18% are from out of state, 93% African American, 0.6% Asian American or Pacific Islander, 0.4% Hispanic American, 0.3% Native American, 0.7% international, 5% transferred in, 42% live on campus. *Retention:* 75% of 2001 full-time freshmen returned.

Freshmen *Admission:* 3,655 applied, 3,403 admitted, 1,672 enrolled. *Average high school GPA:* 2.78. *Test scores:* SAT verbal scores over 500: 20%; SAT math scores over 500: 23%; ACT scores over 18: 11%; SAT verbal scores over 600: 3%; SAT math scores over 600: 4%; ACT scores over 24: 2%; SAT verbal scores over 700: 1%; SAT math scores over 700: 1%.

Faculty *Student/faculty ratio:* 17:1.

Majors Accounting; agricultural business; agricultural economics; agricultural education; agricultural mechanization; agricultural sciences; animal sciences; applied mathematics; architectural engineering; art education; biology; business administration; business education; chemical engineering; chemistry; child care/development; civil engineering; clothing/textiles; computer science; construction management; dietetics; early childhood education; economics; education; electrical engineering; elementary education; engineering physics; English; food sciences; French; health education; history; home economics; home economics education; industrial arts; industrial/manufacturing engineering; industrial technology; laboratory animal medicine; landscape architecture; mass communications; mathematics; mechanical engineering; music teacher education; nursing; nutrition science; occupational safety/health technology; physical education; physics; political science; psychology; recreation/leisure studies; secretarial science; social sciences; social work; sociology; special education; speech/rhetorical studies; theater arts/drama; trade/industrial education; transportation technology.

Academic Programs *Special study options:* academic remediation for entering students, adult/continuing education programs, advanced placement credit, cooperative education, honors programs, internships, off-campus study, part-time degree program, services for LD students, study abroad, summer session for credit. *ROTC:* Army (b), Air Force (b).

Library F. D. Bluford Library plus 1 other with 449,766 titles, 4,004 serial subscriptions.

Computers on Campus 250 computers available on campus for general student use. A campuswide network can be accessed from off campus. Internet access, online (class) registration, at least one staffed computer lab available.

Student Life *Housing Options:* men-only, women-only. *Activities and Organizations:* drama/theater group, student-run newspaper, radio station, choral group, marching band, student government, national fraternities, national sororities. *Campus security:* 24-hour emergency response devices and patrols, late-night transport/escort service, controlled dormitory access. *Student Services:* health clinic, personal/psychological counseling.

Athletics Member NCAA. All Division I except football (Division I-AA). *Intercollegiate sports:* baseball M(s), basketball M(s)/W(s), cross-country running M(s)/W(s), softball W, swimming W(s), tennis M(s)/W(s), track and field M(s)/W(s), volleyball W(s). *Intramural sports:* baseball M/W, basketball M/W, bowling W, cross-country running M/W, football M, golf M/W, racquetball M/W, soccer M/W, softball M/W, swimming M/W, table tennis M/W, tennis M/W, track and field M/W, volleyball M/W, weight lifting M/W.

Standardized Tests *Required:* SAT I or ACT (for admission).

Costs (2002–03) *Tuition:* state resident $1172 full-time, $91 per credit hour part-time; nonresident $8442 full-time, $349 per credit hour part-time. *Required fees:* $1017 full-time. *Room and board:* room only: $2595.

Financial Aid Of all full-time matriculated undergraduates who enrolled in 2001, 5538 applied for aid, 4597 were judged to have need, 243 had their need fully met. In 2001, 278 non-need-based awards were made. *Average percent of need met:* 53%. *Average financial aid package:* $5098. *Average need-based loan:* $5579. *Average need-based gift aid:* $1265. *Average non-need based aid:* $3873. *Average indebtedness upon graduation:* $15,008.

Applying *Options:* early admission, deferred entrance. *Application fee:* $35. *Required:* high school transcript, minimum 2.0 GPA. *Application deadlines:* 6/1 (freshmen), 6/1 (transfers). *Notification:* continuous (freshmen).

Admissions Contact Mr. John Smith, Director of Admissions, North Carolina Agricultural and Technical State University, 1601 East Market Street, Webb Hall, Greensboro, NC 27411. *Phone:* 336-334-7946. *Toll-free phone:* 800-443-8964. *Fax:* 336-334-7478.

NORTH CAROLINA CENTRAL UNIVERSITY

Durham, North Carolina

- **State-supported** comprehensive, founded 1910, part of University of North Carolina System
- **Calendar** semesters
- **Degrees** bachelor's, master's, and first professional
- **Urban** 103-acre campus
- **Coed,** 4,232 undergraduate students, 80% full-time, 64% women, 36% men
- **Minimally difficult** entrance level, 77% of applicants were admitted

A historically black constituent institution of the UNC System, NCCU is located in Durham, near Research Triangle, NC. Raleigh, Durham, and Chapel Hill are a hotbed of academic institutions. Both major private grant and federal funding support opportunities for undergraduate involvement in meaningful research activity under the guidance of a faculty mentor.

Undergraduates 3,393 full-time, 839 part-time. Students come from 34 states and territories, 17 other countries, 12% are from out of state, 90% African American, 0.7% Asian American or Pacific Islander, 0.6% Hispanic American, 0.3% Native American, 1% international, 8% transferred in.

Freshmen *Admission:* 2,167 applied, 1,674 admitted, 798 enrolled. *Average high school GPA:* 2.55. *Test scores:* SAT verbal scores over 500: 17%; SAT math scores over 500: 15%; ACT scores over 18: 32%; SAT verbal scores over 600: 2%; SAT math scores over 600: 1%; ACT scores over 24: 2%.

Faculty *Total:* 349, 74% full-time, 64% with terminal degrees. *Student/faculty ratio:* 13:1.

Majors Accounting; art; art education; athletic training/sports medicine; biology; biology education; business administration; chemistry; chemistry education; computer science; criminal justice/law enforcement administration; early childhood education; elementary education; English; English education; environmental science; family/consumer studies; fine/studio arts; French; French language education; geography; health education; health/physical education; history; history education; home economics; home economics education; hospitality management; information sciences/systems; jazz; mathematics; mathematics education; middle school education; music; music teacher education; nursing; physical education; physics; physics education; political science; psychology; public health education/promotion; recreation/leisure facilities management; religious music; social work; sociology; Spanish; Spanish language education; theater arts/drama.

Academic Programs *Special study options:* academic remediation for entering students, adult/continuing education programs, advanced placement credit, cooperative education, double majors, honors programs, independent study, internships, off-campus study, part-time degree program, services for LD students, summer session for credit. *ROTC:* Army (c), Navy (c), Air Force (c). *Unusual degree programs:* 3-2 engineering with Georgia Institute of Technology, North Carolina State University.

Library Shepherd Library plus 1 other with an OPAC.

Computers on Campus 400 computers available on campus for general student use. At least one staffed computer lab available.

Student Life *Housing Options:* coed. *Activities and Organizations:* drama/theater group, student-run newspaper, national fraternities, national sororities. *Campus security:* 24-hour emergency response devices and patrols, controlled dormitory access. *Student Services:* health clinic, personal/psychological counseling.

Athletics Member NCAA, NAIA. All NCAA Division II. *Intercollegiate sports:* basketball M(s)/W(s), bowling M/W, cross-country running M, football M(s), softball W, tennis M/W, track and field M/W, volleyball W.

Standardized Tests *Required:* SAT I or ACT (for admission).

Costs (2001–02) *Tuition:* state resident $1272 full-time, $153 per course part-time; nonresident $9194 full-time, $1062 per course part-time. Part-time tuition and fees vary according to course load. *Required fees:* $1078 full-time, $45 per credit. *Room and board:* $3284; room only: $1742. *Waivers:* employees or children of employees.

North Carolina Central University (continued)

Financial Aid Of all full-time matriculated undergraduates who enrolled in 2001, 2894 applied for aid, 2429 were judged to have need, 862 had their need fully met. In 2001, 410 non-need-based awards were made. *Average percent of need met:* 72%. *Average financial aid package:* $6621. *Average need-based loan:* $3487. *Average need-based gift aid:* $3348. *Average non-need based aid:* $7144.

Applying *Application fee:* $30. *Required:* high school transcript. *Application deadlines:* 7/1 (freshmen), 7/1 (transfers). *Notification:* continuous (freshmen).

Admissions Contact Ms. Jocelyn L. Foy, Undergraduate Director of Admissions, North Carolina Central University, 1801 Fayetteville Street, Durham, NC 27707-3129. *Phone:* 919-560-6298. *Fax:* 919-530-7625. *E-mail:* ebridges@wpo.nccu.edu.

NORTH CAROLINA SCHOOL OF THE ARTS
Winston-Salem, North Carolina

- **State-supported** comprehensive, founded 1963, part of University of North Carolina System
- **Calendar** trimesters
- **Degrees** diplomas, bachelor's, and master's
- **Urban** 57-acre campus
- **Endowment** $16.8 million
- **Coed,** 708 undergraduate students, 97% full-time, 43% women, 57% men
- **Very difficult** entrance level, 45% of applicants were admitted

Undergraduates 687 full-time, 21 part-time. Students come from 40 states and territories, 21 other countries, 52% are from out of state, 10% African American, 2% Asian American or Pacific Islander, 2% Hispanic American, 0.4% Native American, 2% international, 9% transferred in, 55% live on campus. *Retention:* 74% of 2001 full-time freshmen returned.

Freshmen *Admission:* 698 applied, 316 admitted, 187 enrolled. *Average high school GPA:* 3.48. *Test scores:* SAT verbal scores over 500: 82%; SAT math scores over 500: 74%; ACT scores over 18: 99%; SAT verbal scores over 600: 38%; SAT math scores over 600: 27%; ACT scores over 24: 51%; SAT verbal scores over 700: 8%; SAT math scores over 700: 3%; ACT scores over 30: 7%.

Faculty *Total:* 138, 91% full-time, 70% with terminal degrees. *Student/faculty ratio:* 8:1.

Majors Dance; film studies; film/video production; music; music (piano and organ performance); music (voice and choral/opera performance); theater arts/drama.

Academic Programs *Special study options:* academic remediation for entering students, services for LD students.

Library Semans Library plus 1 other with 85,672 titles, 48,546 serial subscriptions, 12,597 audiovisual materials.

Computers on Campus 20 computers available on campus for general student use. At least one staffed computer lab available.

Student Life *Housing:* on-campus residence required through sophomore year. *Options:* coed. *Activities and Organizations:* drama/theater group, choral group, Pride (gay/lesbian organization), Appreciation of Black Artists. *Campus security:* 24-hour emergency response devices and patrols, controlled dormitory access. *Student Services:* health clinic, personal/psychological counseling.

Standardized Tests *Required:* SAT I or ACT (for admission).

Costs (2001–02) *Tuition:* state resident $1662 full-time; nonresident $11,067 full-time. Full-time tuition and fees vary according to program. Part-time tuition and fees vary according to course load. *Required fees:* $1215 full-time. *Room and board:* $4920; room only: $2550. Room and board charges vary according to board plan and housing facility.

Financial Aid Of all full-time matriculated undergraduates who enrolled in 2001, 410 applied for aid, 320 were judged to have need, 49 had their need fully met. 111 Federal Work-Study jobs (averaging $394). *Average percent of need met:* 79%. *Average financial aid package:* $7851. *Average need-based loan:* $3541. *Average need-based gift aid:* $4568. *Average indebtedness upon graduation:* $15,566.

Applying *Options:* electronic application. *Application fee:* $45. *Required:* high school transcript, 2 letters of recommendation, audition. *Required for some:* essay or personal statement, interview. *Application deadline:* rolling (freshmen), rolling (transfers). *Notification:* continuous (freshmen).

Admissions Contact Ms. Sheeler Lawson, Director of Admissions, North Carolina School of the Arts, 1533 South Main Street, PO Box 12189, Winston-Salem, NC 27127-2188. *Phone:* 336-770-3290. *Fax:* 336-770-3370. *E-mail:* admissions@ncarts.edu.

NORTH CAROLINA STATE UNIVERSITY
Raleigh, North Carolina

- **State-supported** university, founded 1887, part of University of North Carolina System
- **Calendar** semesters
- **Degrees** associate, bachelor's, master's, doctoral, first professional, and first professional certificates
- **Suburban** 1623-acre campus
- **Endowment** $314.3 million
- **Coed,** 22,418 undergraduate students, 82% full-time, 42% women, 58% men
- **Very difficult** entrance level, 66% of applicants were admitted

Undergraduates 18,345 full-time, 4,073 part-time. Students come from 51 states and territories, 65 other countries, 8% are from out of state, 10% African American, 5% Asian American or Pacific Islander, 2% Hispanic American, 0.7% Native American, 1% international, 5% transferred in, 35% live on campus. *Retention:* 89% of 2001 full-time freshmen returned.

Freshmen *Admission:* 11,835 applied, 7,789 admitted, 3,893 enrolled. *Average high school GPA:* 3.94. *Test scores:* SAT verbal scores over 500: 85%; SAT math scores over 500: 91%; ACT scores over 18: 99%; SAT verbal scores over 600: 37%; SAT math scores over 600: 53%; ACT scores over 24: 71%; SAT verbal scores over 700: 6%; SAT math scores over 700: 12%; ACT scores over 30: 14%.

Faculty *Total:* 1,684, 95% full-time, 91% with terminal degrees. *Student/faculty ratio:* 13:1.

Majors Accounting; aerospace engineering; agribusiness; agricultural business; agricultural education; agricultural engineering; agricultural/food products processing; agricultural sciences; agronomy/crop science; animal sciences; applied mathematics; architecture; arts management; atmospheric sciences; biochemistry; biology; biology education; botany; business administration; business marketing and marketing management; chemical engineering; chemistry; chemistry education; civil engineering; communications; computer engineering; computer science; construction engineering; creative writing; criminal justice/law enforcement administration; design/visual communications; economics; education; electrical engineering; engineering; English; English education; environmental engineering; environmental science; food sciences; forest management; French; French language education; geology; German; graphic design/commercial art/illustration; health occupations education; history; horticulture science; human resources management; industrial design; industrial/manufacturing engineering; landscape architecture; landscaping management; liberal arts and sciences/liberal studies; marketing/distribution education; materials engineering; mathematical statistics; mathematics; mathematics education; mechanical engineering; microbiology/bacteriology; natural resources conservation; natural resources management; nuclear engineering; oceanography; philosophy; physics; plant protection; political science; poultry science; psychology; public policy analysis; recreation/leisure facilities management; religious studies; science education; secondary education; social studies education; social work; sociology; Spanish; Spanish language education; textile sciences/engineering; travel/tourism management; turf management; wood science/paper technology; zoology.

Academic Programs *Special study options:* academic remediation for entering students, accelerated degree program, adult/continuing education programs, advanced placement credit, cooperative education, distance learning, double majors, freshman honors college, honors programs, independent study, internships, off-campus study, part-time degree program, services for LD students, student-designed majors, study abroad, summer session for credit. *ROTC:* Army (b), Navy (b), Air Force (b).

Library D. H. Hill Library plus 4 others with 951,788 titles, 35,882 serial subscriptions, 142,831 audiovisual materials, an OPAC, a Web page.

Computers on Campus 4600 computers available on campus for general student use. A campuswide network can be accessed from student residence rooms and from off campus. Internet access, at least one staffed computer lab available.

Student Life *Housing Options:* coed, men-only, women-only, disabled students. *Activities and Organizations:* drama/theater group, student-run newspaper, radio and television station, choral group, marching band, student government, student media, student musical groups, intramural sports, national fraternities, national sororities. *Campus security:* 24-hour emergency response devices and patrols, student patrols, late-night transport/escort service, controlled dormitory access. *Student Services:* health clinic, personal/psychological counseling, women's center, legal services.

Athletics Member NCAA. All Division I except football (Division I-A). *Intercollegiate sports:* baseball M(s), basketball M(s)/W(s), cross-country running M(s)/W(s), fencing M/W, golf M(s)/W, gymnastics M/W(s), ice hockey M(c), lacrosse M(c), racquetball M(c)/W(c), riflery M/W, rugby M(c)/W(c), sailing M(c)/W(c), skiing (downhill) M(c)/W(c), soccer M(s)/W(s), swimming M(s)/W(s), tennis M(s)/W(s), track and field M(s)/W(s), volleyball M(c)/W(s), water polo M(c)/W(c), weight lifting M(c)/W(c), wrestling M(s). *Intramural* *sports:* archery M/W, badminton M/W, baseball M, basketball M/W, bowling M/W, crew M/W, cross-country running M/W, equestrian sports M/W, fencing M/W, field hockey W, football M/W, golf M/W, gymnastics M/W, ice hockey M, lacrosse M/W, racquetball M/W, riflery M/W, rugby M/W, sailing M/W, skiing (downhill) M/W, soccer M/W, softball M/W, squash M/W, swimming M/W, table tennis M/W, tennis M/W, track and field M/W, volleyball M/W, water polo M/W, weight lifting M, wrestling M.

Standardized Tests *Required:* SAT I or ACT (for admission).

Costs (2002–03) *Tuition:* state resident $2440 full-time; nonresident $12,432 full-time. Full-time tuition and fees vary according to program. Part-time tuition and fees vary according to course load and program. *Required fees:* $1012 full-time. *Room and board:* $5796; room only: $3296. Room and board charges vary according to board plan and housing facility. *Payment plan:* deferred payment. *Waivers:* senior citizens and employees or children of employees.

Financial Aid Of all full-time matriculated undergraduates who enrolled in 2001, 8098 applied for aid, 5714 were judged to have need, 783 had their need fully met. 591 Federal Work-Study jobs (averaging $1041). 202 State and other part-time jobs (averaging $5110). In 2001, 4269 non-need-based awards were made. *Average percent of need met:* 85%. *Average financial aid package:* $6725. *Average need-based loan:* $2655. *Average need-based gift aid:* $4305. *Average indebtedness upon graduation:* $15,999.

Applying *Options:* electronic application, early admission, early action, deferred entrance. *Application fee:* $55. *Required:* high school transcript. *Required for some:* 1 letter of recommendation, interview. *Recommended:* essay or personal statement, minimum 3.0 GPA. *Application deadlines:* 2/1 (freshmen), 4/1 (transfers). *Notification:* continuous (freshmen), 1/1 (early action).

Admissions Contact Dr. George R. Dixon, Vice Provost and Director of Admissions, North Carolina State University, Box 7103, 112 Peele Hall, Raleigh, NC 27695. *Phone:* 919-515-2434. *E-mail:* undergrad_admissions@ncsu.edu.

NORTH CAROLINA WESLEYAN COLLEGE

Rocky Mount, North Carolina

- **Independent** 4-year, founded 1956, affiliated with United Methodist Church
- **Calendar** 4-1-4
- **Degrees** bachelor's (also offers adult part-time degree program with significant enrollment not reflected in profile)
- **Suburban** 200-acre campus
- **Endowment** $4.1 million
- **Coed,** 1,886 undergraduate students, 50% full-time, 58% women, 42% men
- **Moderately difficult** entrance level, 69% of applicants were admitted

North Carolina Wesleyan, a private liberal arts college affiliated with the Methodist Church, educates men and women for productive and fulfilling lives, rewarding careers, and service to their community. The curriculum, both in traditional and preprofessional fields, emphasizes critical thinking, reading and writing, listening and speaking, and making informed decisions. The College focuses on personal attention and student self-development.

Undergraduates Students come from 22 states and territories, 17% are from out of state, 35% African American, 0.8% Asian American or Pacific Islander, 2% Hispanic American, 0.4% Native American, 2% international, 28% live on campus. *Retention:* 57% of 2001 full-time freshmen returned.

Freshmen *Admission:* 1,284 applied, 889 admitted. *Average high school GPA:* 2.51. *Test scores:* SAT verbal scores over 500: 27%; SAT math scores over 500: 25%; SAT verbal scores over 600: 3%; SAT math scores over 600: 2%.

Faculty *Total:* 192, 21% full-time, 35% with terminal degrees. *Student/faculty ratio:* 16:1.

Majors Accounting; anthropology; biology; business administration; chemistry; criminal justice/law enforcement administration; education; elementary education; English; environmental science; food products retailing; history; hotel and restaurant management; information sciences/systems; legal studies; mathematics; middle school education; philosophy; physical education; political science; pre-medicine; psychology; religious studies; secondary education; sociology; theater arts/drama.

Academic Programs *Special study options:* academic remediation for entering students, adult/continuing education programs, advanced placement credit, cooperative education, honors programs, internships, part-time degree program, services for LD students, study abroad, summer session for credit.

Library Elizabeth Braswell Pearsall Library with 62,000 titles, 5,225 serial subscriptions, 2,100 audiovisual materials, an OPAC, a Web page.

Computers on Campus 43 computers available on campus for general student use. At least one staffed computer lab available.

Student Life *Housing:* on-campus residence required through sophomore year. *Options:* coed, men-only, women-only. *Activities and Organizations:* drama/theater group, student-run newspaper, choral group, Club Dramatica, Student Government Association, Gospel Choir, Wesleyan Singers, Pep Band, national fraternities, national sororities. *Campus security:* 24-hour emergency response devices and patrols, student patrols, late-night transport/escort service, controlled dormitory access. *Student Services:* health clinic, personal/psychological counseling.

Athletics Member NCAA. All Division III. *Intercollegiate sports:* baseball M, basketball M/W, golf M, soccer M/W, softball W, tennis M/W, volleyball W. *Intramural sports:* basketball M/W, football M/W, lacrosse M/W, softball M/W, table tennis M/W, tennis M/W, volleyball M/W.

Standardized Tests *Required:* SAT I or ACT (for admission).

Costs (2002–03) *Comprehensive fee:* $15,650 includes full-time tuition ($8832), mandatory fees ($936), and room and board ($5882). Part-time tuition: $190 per credit hour. *Room and board:* College room only: $2688.

Financial Aid Of all full-time matriculated undergraduates who enrolled in 2001, 1187 applied for aid, 831 were judged to have need, 349 had their need fully met. In 2001, 566 non-need-based awards were made. *Average percent of need met:* 85%. *Average financial aid package:* $9725. *Average need-based loan:* $4800. *Average need-based gift aid:* $6500. *Average non-need based aid:* $2000. *Average indebtedness upon graduation:* $14,271.

Applying *Options:* common application, electronic application, early admission, deferred entrance. *Application fee:* $25. *Required:* high school transcript. *Recommended:* minimum 2.0 GPA, 2 letters of recommendation, interview. *Application deadlines:* 7/15 (freshmen), 7/15 (transfers). *Notification:* continuous (freshmen).

Admissions Contact Cecelia Summers, Associate Director of Admissions, North Carolina Wesleyan College, 3400 N Wesleyan Boulevard, Rocky Mount, NC 27804. *Phone:* 800-488-6292 Ext. 5202. *Toll-free phone:* 800-488-6292. *Fax:* 252-985-5295. *E-mail:* adm@ncwc.edu.

PEACE COLLEGE

Raleigh, North Carolina

- **Independent** 4-year, founded 1857, affiliated with Presbyterian Church (U.S.A.)
- **Calendar** semesters
- **Degrees** diplomas, associate, and bachelor's
- **Urban** 16-acre campus
- **Endowment** $43.3 million
- **Women only,** 634 undergraduate students, 93% full-time
- **Moderately difficult** entrance level, 87% of applicants were admitted

Undergraduates 588 full-time, 46 part-time. 63% are from out of state, 8% African American, 2% Asian American or Pacific Islander, 1% Hispanic American, 0.6% Native American, 0.5% international, 2% transferred in, 82% live on campus. *Retention:* 71% of 2001 full-time freshmen returned.

Freshmen *Admission:* 173 enrolled. *Average high school GPA:* 2.92.

Faculty *Total:* 71, 56% full-time, 56% with terminal degrees. *Student/faculty ratio:* 14:1.

Majors Biology; business administration; communications; design/visual communications; English; human resources management; liberal arts and sciences/liberal studies; music; music (general performance); psychology; Spanish.

Academic Programs *Special study options:* academic remediation for entering students, adult/continuing education programs, advanced placement credit, double majors, English as a second language, freshman honors college, honors programs, independent study, internships, off-campus study, services for LD students, study abroad. *ROTC:* Army (c), Navy (c), Air Force (c).

Library Lucy Cooper Finch Library with 51,118 titles, 3,900 serial subscriptions, 1,200 audiovisual materials, an OPAC, a Web page.

Computers on Campus 45 computers available on campus for general student use. Internet access, at least one staffed computer lab available.

Student Life *Housing:* on-campus residence required through sophomore year. *Options:* women-only. *Activities and Organizations:* drama/theater group, student-run newspaper, choral group, Student Government Association, Peace Student Christian Association, Recreation Association, Human Resources Society, psychology club. *Campus security:* 24-hour emergency response devices and patrols, late-night transport/escort service, controlled dormitory access. *Student Services:* health clinic, personal/psychological counseling.

Athletics Member NCAA. All Division III. *Intercollegiate sports:* basketball W, tennis W, volleyball W. *Intramural sports:* badminton W, basketball W, equestrian sports W, soccer W, softball W, swimming W, table tennis W, tennis W, volleyball W.

Standardized Tests *Required:* SAT I or ACT (for admission).

Peace College (continued)

Costs (2002–03) *Comprehensive fee:* $18,100 includes full-time tuition ($12,450) and room and board ($5650). Part-time tuition: $400 per credit hour. *Payment plans:* installment, deferred payment. *Waivers:* employees or children of employees.

Financial Aid Of all full-time matriculated undergraduates who enrolled in 2001, 382 applied for aid, 282 were judged to have need, 38 had their need fully met. 89 Federal Work-Study jobs, 178 State and other part-time jobs. In 2001, 327 non-need-based awards were made. *Average percent of need met:* 75%. *Average financial aid package:* $9013. *Average need-based loan:* $2794. *Average need-based gift aid:* $6542. *Average indebtedness upon graduation:* $12,466.

Applying *Options:* early admission, deferred entrance. *Application fee:* $25. *Required:* essay or personal statement, high school transcript, minimum 2.0 GPA, 2 letters of recommendation. *Recommended:* interview. *Application deadline:* rolling (freshmen), rolling (transfers). *Notification:* continuous (freshmen).

Admissions Contact Dr. E. Carole Tyler, Dean of Admissions and Financial Aid, Peace College, Admissions and Financial Aid, Raleigh, NC 27604. *Phone:* 919-508-2000 Ext. 2202. *Toll-free phone:* 800-PEACE-47. *Fax:* 919-508-2306. *E-mail:* chill@peace.edu.

PFEIFFER UNIVERSITY
Misenheimer, North Carolina

- **Independent United Methodist** comprehensive, founded 1885
- **Calendar** semesters
- **Degrees** bachelor's and master's
- **Rural** 300-acre campus with easy access to Charlotte
- **Endowment** $11.0 million
- **Coed,** 1,076 undergraduate students, 83% full-time, 58% women, 42% men
- **Moderately difficult** entrance level, 72% of applicants were admitted

Undergraduates 898 full-time, 178 part-time. Students come from 27 states and territories, 20% African American, 0.9% Asian American or Pacific Islander, 2% Hispanic American, 0.1% Native American, 4% international, 7% transferred in, 65% live on campus. *Retention:* 68% of 2001 full-time freshmen returned.

Freshmen *Admission:* 615 applied, 443 admitted, 146 enrolled. *Average high school GPA:* 3.20. *Test scores:* SAT verbal scores over 500: 42%; SAT math scores over 500: 43%; ACT scores over 18: 72%; SAT verbal scores over 600: 5%; SAT math scores over 600: 7%; ACT scores over 24: 12%; SAT verbal scores over 700: 1%.

Faculty *Total:* 124, 44% full-time, 69% with terminal degrees. *Student/faculty ratio:* 13:1.

Majors Accounting; American studies; arts management; athletic training/sports medicine; biology; business administration; chemistry; criminal justice/law enforcement administration; education; elementary education; engineering science; English; environmental science; history; humanities; information sciences/systems; mass communications; mathematics; music; music teacher education; physical education; political science; pre-law; pre-medicine; psychology; religious education; religious music; religious studies; social sciences; sociology; special education; sport/fitness administration; theater arts/drama.

Academic Programs *Special study options:* academic remediation for entering students, accelerated degree program, advanced placement credit, cooperative education, double majors, English as a second language, honors programs, independent study, internships, part-time degree program, services for LD students, study abroad, summer session for credit. *ROTC:* Army (c). *Unusual degree programs:* 3-2 engineering with Auburn University.

Library Gustavus A. Pfeiffer Library with 116,200 titles, 415 serial subscriptions, 2,349 audiovisual materials, an OPAC, a Web page.

Computers on Campus 64 computers available on campus for general student use. Internet access, at least one staffed computer lab available.

Student Life *Housing:* on-campus residence required through senior year. *Options:* coed, men-only, women-only. *Activities and Organizations:* drama/theater group, student-run newspaper, choral group, Student Government Association, Religious Life Council, Commuter Student Association, Programming Activities Council, Residence Hall Association. *Campus security:* 24-hour emergency response devices and patrols, late-night transport/escort service, controlled dormitory access. *Student Services:* health clinic, personal/psychological counseling, women's center.

Athletics Member NCAA. All Division II. *Intercollegiate sports:* baseball M(s), basketball M(s)/W(s), cross-country running M(s)/W(s), golf M(s), lacrosse M(s)/W(s), soccer M(s)/W(s), softball W(s), swimming W(s), tennis M(s)/W(s), volleyball W(s). *Intramural sports:* basketball M/W, bowling M/W, soccer M/W, softball M/W, table tennis M/W, tennis M/W, volleyball M/W.

Standardized Tests *Required:* SAT I or ACT (for admission).

Costs (2001–02) *Comprehensive fee:* $15,940 includes full-time tuition ($12,066) and room and board ($3874). Part-time tuition: $275 per credit hour. Part-time tuition and fees vary according to course load. *Room and board:* Room and board charges vary according to board plan and housing facility. *Payment plans:* installment, deferred payment. *Waivers:* employees or children of employees.

Financial Aid Of all full-time matriculated undergraduates who enrolled in 2001, 704 applied for aid, 610 were judged to have need, 152 had their need fully met. 197 Federal Work-Study jobs (averaging $765). In 2001, 50 non-need-based awards were made. *Average percent of need met:* 87%. *Average financial aid package:* $9750. *Average need-based loan:* $3246. *Average need-based gift aid:* $7309. *Average non-need based aid:* $5569. *Average indebtedness upon graduation:* $14,650.

Applying *Options:* common application, early admission, deferred entrance. *Application fee:* $25. *Required:* high school transcript. *Required for some:* 2 letters of recommendation. *Recommended:* minimum 2.0 GPA, interview. *Application deadline:* rolling (freshmen), rolling (transfers). *Notification:* continuous (freshmen).

Admissions Contact Mr. Steve Cumming, Director of Admissions, Pfeiffer University, PO Box 960, Highway 52 North, Misenheimer, NC 28109. *Phone:* 704-463-1360 Ext. 2079. *Toll-free phone:* 800-338-2060. *Fax:* 704-463-1363. *E-mail:* admiss@pfeiffer.edu.

PIEDMONT BAPTIST COLLEGE
Winston-Salem, North Carolina

- **Independent Baptist** comprehensive, founded 1947
- **Calendar** semesters
- **Degrees** certificates, associate, bachelor's, and master's
- **Urban** 12-acre campus
- **Coed**
- **Noncompetitive** entrance level

Faculty *Student/faculty ratio:* 11:1.

Student Life *Campus security:* student patrols, late-night transport/escort service, controlled dormitory access, security guards on duty during evening hours.

Athletics Member NCCAA.

Standardized Tests *Required:* ACT (for admission), SAT I or ACT (for placement). *Recommended:* SAT II: Subject Tests (for placement).

Applying *Options:* common application, electronic application, early admission, early action, deferred entrance. *Application fee:* $50. *Required:* essay or personal statement, high school transcript, 2 letters of recommendation, medical history, proof of immunization. *Recommended:* minimum 2.0 GPA, interview.

Admissions Contact Mrs. Carole Beverly, Director of Admissions, Piedmont Baptist College, 716 Franklin Street, Winston-Salem, NC 27101-5197. *Phone:* 336-725-8344 Ext. 2327. *Toll-free phone:* 800-937-5097. *Fax:* 336-725-5522. *E-mail:* admissions@pbc.edu.

QUEENS COLLEGE
Charlotte, North Carolina

- **Independent Presbyterian** comprehensive, founded 1857
- **Calendar** semesters
- **Degrees** bachelor's, master's, and postbachelor's certificates
- **Suburban** 25-acre campus
- **Endowment** $38.0 million
- **Coed,** 1,199 undergraduate students, 62% full-time, 78% women, 22% men
- **Moderately difficult** entrance level, 79% of applicants were admitted

Undergraduates 743 full-time, 456 part-time. Students come from 33 states and territories, 22 other countries, 33% are from out of state, 17% African American, 2% Asian American or Pacific Islander, 2% Hispanic American, 0.5% Native American, 3% international, 6% transferred in, 75% live on campus. *Retention:* 77% of 2001 full-time freshmen returned.

Freshmen *Admission:* 677 applied, 538 admitted, 211 enrolled. *Average high school GPA:* 3.30. *Test scores:* SAT verbal scores over 500: 66%; SAT math scores over 500: 64%; ACT scores over 18: 94%; SAT verbal scores over 600: 18%; SAT math scores over 600: 14%; ACT scores over 24: 36%; SAT verbal scores over 700: 2%; ACT scores over 30: 2%.

Faculty *Total:* 91, 65% full-time, 68% with terminal degrees. *Student/faculty ratio:* 12:1.

Majors Accounting; American literature; American studies; applied mathematics; art; art history; biochemistry; biology; business administration; early childhood education; education; elementary education; English; English education; environmental biology; fine/studio arts; French; history; information sciences/ systems; international relations; journalism; mass communications; mathematics; mathematics education; music; music (piano and organ performance); music therapy; music (voice and choral/opera performance); nursing; nursing science; philosophy; political science; pre-law; pre-medicine; pre-veterinary studies; psychology; public relations; religious studies; secondary education; Spanish; theater arts/drama.

Academic Programs *Special study options:* adult/continuing education programs, advanced placement credit, double majors, honors programs, independent study, internships, off-campus study, part-time degree program, student-designed majors, study abroad, summer session for credit. *ROTC:* Army (c), Air Force (c).

Library Everett Library plus 1 other with 129,061 titles, 459 serial subscriptions, 1,365 audiovisual materials, an OPAC, a Web page.

Computers on Campus 125 computers available on campus for general student use. A campuswide network can be accessed from student residence rooms. Internet access, online (class) registration, at least one staffed computer lab available.

Student Life *Housing:* on-campus residence required for freshman year. *Options:* coed, women-only. *Activities and Organizations:* drama/theater group, student-run newspaper, choral group, Senate, College Union Board, Admissions Ambassadors, Students for Black Awareness, International Club, national fraternities, national sororities. *Campus security:* 24-hour emergency response devices and patrols, late-night transport/escort service, controlled dormitory access. *Student Services:* health clinic, personal/psychological counseling.

Athletics Member NCAA. All Division II. *Intercollegiate sports:* basketball M(s)/W(s), cross-country running M(s)/W(s), golf M(s)/W(s), soccer M(s)/W(s), softball W(s), tennis M(s)/W(s), volleyball W(s). *Intramural sports:* basketball M/W, sailing M/W, soccer M/W, softball M/W, table tennis M/W, tennis M/W, volleyball M/W.

Standardized Tests *Required:* SAT I or ACT (for admission).

Costs (2002–03) *Comprehensive fee:* $18,300 includes full-time tuition ($12,290) and room and board ($6010). Part-time tuition: $235 per credit hour. *Payment plan:* installment. *Waivers:* employees or children of employees.

Financial Aid Of all full-time matriculated undergraduates who enrolled in 2001, 476 applied for aid, 383 were judged to have need, 123 had their need fully met. 125 Federal Work-Study jobs (averaging $1500). 10 State and other part-time jobs (averaging $1500). *Average percent of need met:* 79%. *Average financial aid package:* $9828. *Average need-based loan:* $3123. *Average need-based gift aid:* $6992. *Average indebtedness upon graduation:* $14,069.

Applying *Options:* common application, early admission, deferred entrance. *Application fee:* $35. *Required:* essay or personal statement, high school transcript, minimum 2.0 GPA, 2 letters of recommendation. *Recommended:* interview. *Application deadline:* rolling (freshmen), rolling (transfers). *Notification:* continuous (freshmen).

Admissions Contact Ms. Eileen T. Dills, Dean of Admissions and Financial Aid, Queens College, Charlotte, NC 28274. *Phone:* 704-337-2212. *Toll-free phone:* 800-849-0202. *Fax:* 704-337-2403. *E-mail:* case@rex.queens.edu.

Roanoke Bible College

Elizabeth City, North Carolina

- **Independent Christian** 4-year, founded 1948
- **Calendar** semesters
- **Degrees** certificates, associate, and bachelor's
- **Small-town** 19-acre campus with easy access to Norfolk
- **Endowment** $1.0 million
- **Coed,** 170 undergraduate students, 85% full-time, 48% women, 52% men
- **Minimally difficult** entrance level, 39% of applicants were admitted

Undergraduates 145 full-time, 25 part-time. Students come from 11 states and territories, 1 other country, 65% are from out of state, 6% African American, 6% Asian American or Pacific Islander, 1% Hispanic American, 1% Native American, 9% transferred in, 65% live on campus. *Retention:* 54% of 2001 full-time freshmen returned.

Freshmen *Admission:* 106 applied, 41 admitted, 41 enrolled. *Average high school GPA:* 2.76. *Test scores:* SAT verbal scores over 500: 67%; SAT math scores over 500: 47%; SAT verbal scores over 600: 17%; SAT math scores over 600: 10%; SAT math scores over 700: 3%.

Faculty *Total:* 16, 63% full-time, 25% with terminal degrees. *Student/faculty ratio:* 13:1.

Majors Biblical studies; religious studies; sign language interpretation; theology.

Academic Programs *Special study options:* academic remediation for entering students, advanced placement credit, internships, part-time degree program.

Library Watson-Griffith Library with 26,911 titles, 210 serial subscriptions, 6,695 audiovisual materials, an OPAC.

Computers on Campus 24 computers available on campus for general student use. A campuswide network can be accessed from student residence rooms. Internet access, at least one staffed computer lab available.

Student Life *Housing:* on-campus residence required through senior year. *Options:* men-only, women-only. *Activities and Organizations:* choral group, Student Advisory Council, counseling club, drama club, choral group. *Campus security:* 24-hour emergency response devices, controlled dormitory access. *Student Services:* personal/psychological counseling.

Athletics *Intercollegiate sports:* basketball M/W. *Intramural sports:* basketball M/W, golf M/W, softball M/W, table tennis M/W, tennis M/W, volleyball M/W, weight lifting M.

Standardized Tests *Required:* SAT I or ACT (for admission), SAT I or ACT (for placement).

Costs (2002–03) *Comprehensive fee:* $11,266 includes full-time tuition ($5664), mandatory fees ($760), and room and board ($4842). Part-time tuition: $165 per semester hour. *Required fees:* $48 per term part-time. *Room and board:* College room only: $2785.

Financial Aid Of all full-time matriculated undergraduates who enrolled in 2001, 137 applied for aid, 121 were judged to have need, 31 had their need fully met. 20 Federal Work-Study jobs (averaging $707). In 2001, 28 non-need-based awards were made. *Average percent of need met:* 67%. *Average financial aid package:* $5974. *Average need-based loan:* $3231. *Average need-based gift aid:* $3466. *Average non-need based aid:* $2428. *Average indebtedness upon graduation:* $16,480.

Applying *Options:* electronic application, early admission, deferred entrance. *Application fee:* $25. *Required:* essay or personal statement, high school transcript, reference from church. *Required for some:* interview. *Application deadlines:* 8/1 (freshmen), 8/1 (transfers). *Notification:* continuous (freshmen).

Admissions Contact Roanoke Bible College, 715 North Poindexter Street, Elizabeth City, NC 27909-4054. *Phone:* 252-334-2019. *Toll-free phone:* 800-RBC-8980. *Fax:* 252-334-2071. *E-mail:* admissions@roanokebible.edu.

St. Andrews Presbyterian College

Laurinburg, North Carolina

- **Independent Presbyterian** 4-year, founded 1958
- **Calendar** semesters
- **Degree** bachelor's
- **Small-town** 600-acre campus
- **Endowment** $11.0 million
- **Coed,** 704 undergraduate students, 86% full-time, 60% women, 40% men
- **Moderately difficult** entrance level, 87% of applicants were admitted

Undergraduates 607 full-time, 97 part-time. Students come from 42 states and territories, 15 other countries, 56% are from out of state, 10% African American, 3% Asian American or Pacific Islander, 2% Hispanic American, 1% Native American, 4% international, 6% transferred in, 83% live on campus. *Retention:* 40% of 2001 full-time freshmen returned.

Freshmen *Admission:* 491 applied, 427 admitted, 178 enrolled. *Average high school GPA:* 2.88. *Test scores:* SAT verbal scores over 500: 50%; SAT math scores over 500: 44%; SAT verbal scores over 600: 15%; SAT math scores over 600: 12%; SAT verbal scores over 700: 4%.

Faculty *Total:* 83, 42% full-time, 45% with terminal degrees. *Student/faculty ratio:* 10:1.

Majors Art; Asian studies; biology; business administration; chemistry; creative writing; elementary education; English; equestrian studies; fine/studio arts; history; interdisciplinary studies; international business; liberal arts and sciences/ liberal studies; mass communications; mathematics; philosophy; physical education; political science; pre-law; pre-medicine; pre-veterinary studies; psychology; religious studies; sport/fitness administration.

Academic Programs *Special study options:* accelerated degree program, adult/continuing education programs, advanced placement credit, double majors, honors programs, independent study, internships, part-time degree program, services for LD students, student-designed majors, study abroad, summer session for credit. *Unusual degree programs:* 3-2 engineering with North Carolina State University; accounting with University of Georgia.

Library DeTamble Library with 108,734 titles, 436 serial subscriptions, 4,405 audiovisual materials, an OPAC, a Web page.

Computers on Campus 100 computers available on campus for general student use. A campuswide network can be accessed from student residence rooms and from off campus. Internet access, at least one staffed computer lab available.

Student Life *Housing:* on-campus residence required through senior year. *Options:* coed, men-only, women-only, disabled students. *Activities and Organi-*

St. Andrews Presbyterian College (continued)

zations: drama/theater group, choral group, Business Club, Breaking the Mirror (women's group), Writer's Forum, Student Activities Union, Eco-Action. *Campus security:* 24-hour emergency response devices and patrols, late-night transport/escort service. *Student Services:* health clinic, personal/psychological counseling.

Athletics Member NCAA. All Division II. *Intercollegiate sports:* baseball M(s), basketball M(s)/W(s), cross-country running M(s)/W(s), equestrian sports M(s)/W(s), golf M(s), lacrosse M(s), rugby M(c)/W(c), soccer M(s)/W(s), softball W(s), tennis M/W, volleyball W(s). *Intramural sports:* basketball M/W, equestrian sports M/W, football M/W, golf M/W, racquetball M/W, rugby M(c)/W(c), softball M/W, table tennis M/W, tennis M/W, volleyball M/W.

Standardized Tests *Required:* SAT I or ACT (for admission).

Costs (2001–02) *Comprehensive fee:* $19,720 includes full-time tuition ($14,090), mandatory fees ($220), and room and board ($5410). Full-time tuition and fees vary according to location. Part-time tuition: $410 per credit. Part-time tuition and fees vary according to location. *Room and board:* College room only: $2220. *Payment plan:* installment. *Waivers:* adult students, senior citizens, and employees or children of employees.

Financial Aid Of all full-time matriculated undergraduates who enrolled in 2001, 480 applied for aid, 388 were judged to have need, 112 had their need fully met. 159 Federal Work-Study jobs (averaging $1245). 28 State and other part-time jobs (averaging $1460). In 2001, 198 non-need-based awards were made. *Average percent of need met:* 78%. *Average financial aid package:* $12,504. *Average need-based loan:* $3294. *Average need-based gift aid:* $9402. *Average indebtedness upon graduation:* $20,000.

Applying *Options:* common application, electronic application, early admission, early decision, deferred entrance. *Application fee:* $30. *Required:* high school transcript, 1 letter of recommendation. *Required for some:* essay or personal statement, interview. *Recommended:* minimum 2.0 GPA. *Application deadline:* rolling (freshmen), rolling (transfers). *Early decision:* 12/1. *Notification:* continuous (freshmen), 1/1 (early decision).

Admissions Contact Rev. Glenn Batten, Dean for Student Affairs and Enrollment, St. Andrews Presbyterian College, Laurinburg, NC 28352. *Phone:* 910-277-5555. *Toll-free phone:* 800-763-0198. *Fax:* 910-277-5087. *E-mail:* admission@sapc.edu.

SAINT AUGUSTINE'S COLLEGE
Raleigh, North Carolina

- **Independent Episcopal** 4-year, founded 1867
- **Calendar** semesters
- **Degree** bachelor's
- **Urban** 110-acre campus
- **Endowment** $20.0 million
- **Coed,** 1,360 undergraduate students, 91% full-time, 59% women, 41% men
- **Minimally difficult** entrance level, 24% of applicants were admitted

Undergraduates 1,235 full-time, 125 part-time. Students come from 29 states and territories, 26 other countries, 43% are from out of state, 1% transferred in, 59% live on campus. *Retention:* 58% of 2001 full-time freshmen returned.

Freshmen *Admission:* 2,181 applied, 523 admitted, 324 enrolled. *Average high school GPA:* 2.29. *Test scores:* SAT verbal scores over 500: 10%; SAT math scores over 500: 7%; ACT scores over 18: 100%; SAT verbal scores over 600: 2%; SAT math scores over 600: 1%; ACT scores over 24: 84%; SAT math scores over 700: 1%; ACT scores over 30: 33%.

Faculty *Total:* 129, 69% full-time, 43% with terminal degrees. *Student/faculty ratio:* 13:1.

Majors Accounting; African-American studies; biology; biology education; business administration; business education; chemistry; communications; computer/information sciences; computer science; criminology; education (K-12); elementary education; English; English education; French; history; international relations; mathematics; mathematics education; medical technology; music business management/merchandising; music (general performance); music teacher education; occupational health/industrial hygiene; occupational safety/health technology; physical education; political science; pre-medicine; psychology; social studies education; sociology; Spanish; special education; visual/performing arts.

Academic Programs *Special study options:* academic remediation for entering students, accelerated degree program, adult/continuing education programs, cooperative education, honors programs, independent study, internships, off-campus study, part-time degree program, study abroad, summer session for credit. *ROTC:* Army (b), Air Force (c). *Unusual degree programs:* 3-2 engineering with North Carolina State University.

Library Prezell R. Robinson Library with 500 serial subscriptions, 300 audiovisual materials.

Computers on Campus 130 computers available on campus for general student use. A campuswide network can be accessed from student residence rooms and from off campus. Internet access, at least one staffed computer lab available.

Student Life *Housing:* on-campus residence required for freshman year. *Options:* men-only, women-only. *Activities and Organizations:* drama/theater group, student-run newspaper, radio and television station, choral group, chorale group, jazz band, International Student Organization, Pershing Rifles, national fraternities, national sororities. *Campus security:* 24-hour emergency response devices and patrols. *Student Services:* health clinic, personal/psychological counseling.

Athletics Member NCAA. All Division II. *Intercollegiate sports:* baseball M(s), basketball M(s)/W(s), bowling W, cross-country running M(s)/W(s), golf M(s), softball W(s), tennis M(s)/W, track and field M(s)/W(s), volleyball W(s). *Intramural sports:* baseball M, basketball M/W, football M, softball W, volleyball M/W.

Standardized Tests *Required:* SAT I or ACT (for admission).

Costs (2001–02) *Comprehensive fee:* $12,990 includes full-time tuition ($5780), mandatory fees ($2250), and room and board ($4960). Full-time tuition and fees vary according to course load, program, and student level. Part-time tuition: $230 per credit hour. Part-time tuition and fees vary according to course load, program, reciprocity agreements, and student level. *Room and board:* Room and board charges vary according to housing facility and location. *Payment plan:* installment. *Waivers:* employees or children of employees.

Applying *Options:* electronic application, deferred entrance. *Application fee:* $25. *Required:* essay or personal statement, high school transcript, 3 letters of recommendation, medical history. *Recommended:* minimum 2.0 GPA. *Application deadline:* 7/1 (freshmen), rolling (transfers). *Notification:* continuous (freshmen).

Admissions Contact Mr. Tim Chapman, Interim Director of Admissions, Saint Augustine's College, 1315 Oakwood Avenue, Raleigh, NC 27610-2298. *Phone:* 919-516-4011. *Toll-free phone:* 800-948-1126. *Fax:* 919-516-4415. *E-mail:* admissions@es.st-aug.edu.

SALEM COLLEGE
Winston-Salem, North Carolina

- **Independent Moravian** comprehensive, founded 1772
- **Calendar** 4-1-4
- **Degrees** bachelor's and master's (only students 23 or over are eligible to enroll part-time; men may attend evening program only)
- **Urban** 57-acre campus
- **Endowment** $47.4 million
- **Women only,** 926 undergraduate students, 71% full-time
- **Moderately difficult** entrance level, 76% of applicants were admitted

Undergraduates 662 full-time, 264 part-time. Students come from 24 states and territories, 16 other countries, 48% are from out of state, 18% African American, 2% Asian American or Pacific Islander, 2% Hispanic American, 0.9% Native American, 4% international, 1% transferred in, 89% live on campus. *Retention:* 79% of 2001 full-time freshmen returned.

Freshmen *Admission:* 193 enrolled. *Average high school GPA:* 3.57. *Test scores:* SAT verbal scores over 500: 82%; SAT math scores over 500: 66%; ACT scores over 18: 91%; SAT verbal scores over 600: 39%; SAT math scores over 600: 18%; ACT scores over 24: 62%; SAT verbal scores over 700: 6%; SAT math scores over 700: 1%; ACT scores over 30: 9%.

Faculty *Total:* 92, 57% full-time, 64% with terminal degrees. *Student/faculty ratio:* 13:1.

Majors Accounting; American studies; art history; arts management; biology; business administration; chemistry; economics; education; English; fine/studio arts; French; German; history; interdisciplinary studies; interior design; international business; international relations; mass communications; mathematics; medical technology; music; music (general performance); philosophy; physician assistant; psychology; religious studies; sociology; Spanish.

Academic Programs *Special study options:* adult/continuing education programs, advanced placement credit, double majors, external degree program, honors programs, independent study, internships, off-campus study, part-time degree program, student-designed majors, study abroad, summer session for credit. *ROTC:* Army (c). *Unusual degree programs:* 3-2 engineering with Duke University, Vanderbilt University.

Library Gramley Library plus 1 other with 125,858 titles, 3,607 serial subscriptions, 13,147 audiovisual materials, an OPAC, a Web page.

Computers on Campus 54 computers available on campus for general student use. A campuswide network can be accessed from student residence rooms that provide access to e-mail. Internet access, at least one staffed computer lab available.

Student Life *Housing:* on-campus residence required through senior year. *Activities and Organizations:* drama/theater group, student-run newspaper, choral group, marching band, Student Government Association, Onua, Campus Activities Council, International Club, Ambassadors. *Campus security:* 24-hour emergency response devices and patrols, late-night transport/escort service, controlled dormitory access. *Student Services:* health clinic, personal/psychological counseling.

Athletics *Intercollegiate sports:* cross-country running W, equestrian sports W, field hockey W, soccer W, softball W, swimming W, tennis W, volleyball W. *Intramural sports:* badminton W, basketball W, fencing W, football W, golf W, softball W, volleyball W, water polo W.

Standardized Tests *Required:* SAT I or ACT (for admission).

Costs (2001–02) *Comprehensive fee:* $23,065 includes full-time tuition ($14,280), mandatory fees ($215), and room and board ($8570). Full-time tuition and fees vary according to program. Part-time tuition: $780 per course. Part-time tuition and fees vary according to program. *Payment plan:* installment. *Waivers:* employees or children of employees.

Financial Aid *Average financial aid package:* $12,300.

Applying *Options:* common application, electronic application, early admission, deferred entrance. *Application fee:* $25. *Required:* essay or personal statement, high school transcript, 2 letters of recommendation. *Recommended:* interview. *Application deadline:* rolling (freshmen), rolling (transfers). *Notification:* continuous (freshmen), 1/1 (early action).

Admissions Contact Ms. Dana E. Evans, Dean of Admissions and Financial Aid, Salem College, PO Box 10548, Shober House, Winston-Salem, NC 27108. *Phone:* 336-721-2621. *Toll-free phone:* 800-327-2536. *Fax:* 336-724-7102. *E-mail:* admissions@salem.edu.

SHAW UNIVERSITY

Raleigh, North Carolina

- **Independent Baptist** comprehensive, founded 1865
- **Calendar** semesters
- **Degrees** certificates, associate, bachelor's, and first professional
- **Urban** 18-acre campus
- **Coed,** 2,372 undergraduate students, 82% full-time, 67% women, 33% men
- **Minimally difficult** entrance level, 64% of applicants were admitted

Undergraduates 1,955 full-time, 417 part-time. Students come from 34 states and territories, 23% are from out of state, 85% African American, 0.0% Asian American or Pacific Islander, 0.4% Hispanic American, 0.3% Native American, 3% international, 12% transferred in, 38% live on campus. *Retention:* 60% of 2001 full-time freshmen returned.

Freshmen *Admission:* 2,908 applied, 1,855 admitted, 475 enrolled. *Average high school GPA:* 2.39. *Test scores:* SAT verbal scores over 500: 10%; SAT math scores over 500: 7%; SAT verbal scores over 600: 2%; SAT math scores over 600: 2%.

Faculty *Total:* 298, 32% full-time, 42% with terminal degrees. *Student/faculty ratio:* 15:1.

Majors Accounting; adapted physical education; African studies; biology; biology education; business administration; chemistry; computer/information sciences; computer science; criminal justice studies; education of the mentally handicapped; elementary education; English; English education; environmental science; gerontology; international business; international relations; liberal arts and sciences/liberal studies; mass communications; mathematics; mathematics education; music; philosophy; physics; political science; psychology; public administration; recreation/leisure studies; religious studies; social studies education; social work; sociology; speech-language pathology/audiology; theater arts/drama.

Academic Programs *Special study options:* academic remediation for entering students, accelerated degree program, adult/continuing education programs, advanced placement credit, distance learning, double majors, English as a second language, honors programs, independent study, internships, off-campus study, part-time degree program, student-designed majors, summer session for credit. *ROTC:* Army (c), Air Force (c). *Unusual degree programs:* 3-2 engineering with North Carolina State University, North Carolina Agricultural and Technical State University.

Library James E. Cheek Learning Resources Center with 137,349 titles, 5,002 serial subscriptions, 435 audiovisual materials, an OPAC, a Web page.

Computers on Campus 150 computers available on campus for general student use. Internet access, online (class) registration, at least one staffed computer lab available.

Student Life *Housing:* on-campus residence required for freshman year. *Options:* men-only, women-only. *Activities and Organizations:* drama/theater group, student-run newspaper, radio station, choral group, Student Government Association, choir, university band, Shaw Players, academic clubs, national fraternities, national sororities. *Campus security:* 24-hour emergency response devices and patrols, late-night transport/escort service, 24-hour electronic surveillance cameras. *Student Services:* health clinic, personal/psychological counseling.

Athletics Member NCAA. All Division II. *Intercollegiate sports:* baseball M(s), basketball M(s)/W(s), bowling W, cross-country running M/W, softball W(s), tennis M(s)/W(s), track and field M(s)/W(s), volleyball W(s). *Intramural sports:* basketball M/W, football M, tennis M/W, volleyball M/W.

Standardized Tests *Required:* SAT I or ACT (for admission).

Costs (2001–02) *Comprehensive fee:* $12,810 includes full-time tuition ($7056), mandatory fees ($874), and room and board ($4880). Part-time tuition: $294 per credit hour. *Required fees:* $151 per term part-time. *Payment plan:* installment. *Waivers:* employees or children of employees.

Financial Aid Of all full-time matriculated undergraduates who enrolled in 2001, 2055 applied for aid, 1862 were judged to have need. 508 Federal Work-Study jobs (averaging $1110). In 2001, 12 non-need-based awards were made. *Average financial aid package:* $7758. *Average need-based gift aid:* $4959. *Average non-need based aid:* $12,004. *Average indebtedness upon graduation:* $8781.

Applying *Options:* common application, electronic application, early admission, deferred entrance. *Application fee:* $25. *Required:* essay or personal statement, high school transcript, minimum 2.0 GPA. *Application deadlines:* 7/30 (freshmen), 7/30 (transfers). *Notification:* continuous until 8/25 (freshmen).

Admissions Contact Mr. Paul Vandergrift, Director of Admissions and Recruitment, Shaw University, 118 East South Street, Raleigh, NC 27601-2399. *Phone:* 919-546-8275. *Toll-free phone:* 800-214-6683. *Fax:* 919-546-8271. *E-mail:* paulv@shawu.edu.

THE UNIVERSITY OF NORTH CAROLINA AT ASHEVILLE

Asheville, North Carolina

- **State-supported** comprehensive, founded 1927, part of University of North Carolina System
- **Calendar** semesters
- **Degrees** certificates, bachelor's, and master's
- **Suburban** 265-acre campus
- **Endowment** $14.7 million
- **Coed,** 3,211 undergraduate students, 77% full-time, 58% women, 42% men
- **Moderately difficult** entrance level, 59% of applicants were admitted

Undergraduates 2,485 full-time, 726 part-time. Students come from 37 states and territories, 20 other countries, 11% are from out of state, 3% African American, 1% Asian American or Pacific Islander, 1% Hispanic American, 0.5% Native American, 1% international, 10% transferred in, 35% live on campus. *Retention:* 80% of 2001 full-time freshmen returned.

Freshmen *Admission:* 2,020 applied, 1,189 admitted, 455 enrolled. *Average high school GPA:* 3.77. *Test scores:* SAT verbal scores over 500: 89%; SAT math scores over 500: 88%; ACT scores over 18: 92%; SAT verbal scores over 600: 41%; SAT math scores over 600: 39%; ACT scores over 24: 47%; SAT verbal scores over 700: 8%; SAT math scores over 700: 5%; ACT scores over 30: 3%.

Faculty *Total:* 300, 58% full-time, 62% with terminal degrees. *Student/faculty ratio:* 13:1.

Majors Accounting; art; atmospheric sciences; biology; business administration; chemistry; classics; computer science; economics; English; environmental science; fine/studio arts; French; German; history; journalism and mass communication related; liberal arts and sciences/liberal studies; mathematics; music; music related; operations management; philosophy; physics; political science; psychology; sociology; Spanish; theater arts/drama.

Academic Programs *Special study options:* academic remediation for entering students, adult/continuing education programs, advanced placement credit, distance learning, double majors, honors programs, independent study, internships, off-campus study, part-time degree program, student-designed majors, study abroad, summer session for credit.

Library D. Hidden Ramsey Library with 252,601 titles, 2,313 serial subscriptions, 8,855 audiovisual materials, an OPAC, a Web page.

Computers on Campus 300 computers available on campus for general student use. A campuswide network can be accessed from student residence rooms and from off campus that provide access to online grade reports. Internet access, online (class) registration, at least one staffed computer lab available.

Student Life *Housing:* on-campus residence required for freshman year. *Options:* coed, men-only, women-only, disabled students. *Activities and Organi-*

The University of North Carolina at Asheville (continued)

zations: drama/theater group, student-run newspaper, choral group, Student Government Association, Underdog Productions, Residence Hall Association, African-American Association, International Student Association, national fraternities, national sororities. *Campus security:* 24-hour patrols, late-night transport/escort service, dorm entrances secured at night. *Student Services:* health clinic, personal/psychological counseling, women's center.

Athletics Member NCAA. All Division I. *Intercollegiate sports:* baseball M(s), basketball M(s)/W(s), cross-country running M(s)/W(s), soccer M(s)/W(s), tennis M(s)/W(s), track and field M(s)/W(s), volleyball W(s). *Intramural sports:* basketball M/W, football M, golf M/W, racquetball M/W, soccer M/W, softball M/W, tennis M/W, volleyball W.

Standardized Tests *Required:* SAT I or ACT (for admission).

Costs (2001–02) *Tuition:* state resident $1196 full-time, $311 per term part-time; nonresident $8658 full-time, $1244 per term part-time. Part-time tuition and fees vary according to course load. *Required fees:* $1300 full-time. *Room and board:* $4400; room only: $2160. Room and board charges vary according to board plan and housing facility. *Payment plan:* installment. *Waivers:* senior citizens and employees or children of employees.

Financial Aid Of all full-time matriculated undergraduates who enrolled in 2001, 1686 applied for aid, 830 were judged to have need, 422 had their need fully met. 143 Federal Work-Study jobs (averaging $1108). 625 State and other part-time jobs (averaging $1292). In 2001, 548 non-need-based awards were made. *Average percent of need met:* 85%. *Average financial aid package:* $6796. *Average need-based loan:* $3292. *Average need-based gift aid:* $2830. *Average indebtedness upon graduation:* $14,305.

Applying *Options:* common application, early action, deferred entrance. *Application fee:* $50. *Required:* high school transcript. *Required for some:* interview. *Recommended:* essay or personal statement, minimum 3.0 GPA. *Application deadlines:* 3/15 (freshmen), 6/1 (transfers). *Notification:* continuous (freshmen), 12/5 (early action).

Admissions Contact Ms. Fran Barrett, Director of Admissions, The University of North Carolina at Asheville, 117 Lipinsky Hall, CPO 2210, One University Heights, Asheville, NC 28804-8510. *Phone:* 828-251-6481. *Toll-free phone:* 800-531-9842. *Fax:* 828-251-6482. *E-mail:* admissions@unca.edu.

THE UNIVERSITY OF NORTH CAROLINA AT CHAPEL HILL

Chapel Hill, North Carolina

- **State-supported** university, founded 1789, part of University of North Carolina System
- **Calendar** semesters
- **Degrees** certificates, diplomas, bachelor's, master's, doctoral, first professional, and post-master's certificates
- **Suburban** 789-acre campus with easy access to Raleigh-Durham
- **Endowment** $1.1 billion
- **Coed,** 15,844 undergraduate students, 95% full-time, 60% women, 40% men
- **Very difficult** entrance level, 40% of applicants were admitted

Undergraduates 15,060 full-time, 784 part-time. Students come from 52 states and territories, 100 other countries, 18% are from out of state, 11% African American, 5% Asian American or Pacific Islander, 2% Hispanic American, 0.8% Native American, 1% international, 5% transferred in, 59% live on campus. *Retention:* 95% of 2001 full-time freshmen returned.

Freshmen *Admission:* 15,947 applied, 6,339 admitted, 3,687 enrolled. *Average high school GPA:* 4.00. *Test scores:* SAT verbal scores over 500: 95%; SAT math scores over 500: 96%; ACT scores over 18: 98%; SAT verbal scores over 600: 65%; SAT math scores over 600: 70%; ACT scores over 24: 78%; SAT verbal scores over 700: 18%; SAT math scores over 700: 22%; ACT scores over 30: 26%.

Faculty *Total:* 2,690, 88% full-time. *Student/faculty ratio:* 14:1.

Majors African-American studies; American studies; anthropology; applied mathematics; area, ethnic, and cultural studies related; art history; Asian studies; biology; business administration; chemistry; classics; communications; comparative literature; dental hygiene; early childhood education; East European languages related; economics; elementary education; English; environmental health; environmental science; fine/studio arts; geography; geology; German; health/medical biostatistics; health/physical education; health services administration; history; human resources management; Latin American studies; liberal arts and sciences/liberal studies; linguistics; mass communications; mathematics; medical radiologic technology; medical technology; middle school education; music; music (general performance); nursing; nutrition studies; peace/conflict studies; philosophy; physics; political science; psychology; public policy analysis; recreation/leisure facilities management; religious studies; romance languages; Russian; Russian/Slavic studies; sociology; theater arts/drama; women's studies.

Academic Programs *Special study options:* advanced placement credit, distance learning, double majors, freshman honors college, honors programs, independent study, internships, off-campus study, services for LD students, student-designed majors, study abroad, summer session for credit. *ROTC:* Army (b), Navy (b), Air Force (b).

Library Davis Library plus 14 others with 4.9 million titles, 44,023 serial subscriptions, 176,445 audiovisual materials, an OPAC, a Web page.

Computers on Campus 540 computers available on campus for general student use. A campuswide network can be accessed from student residence rooms and from off campus that provide access to on-line grade reports. Internet access, online (class) registration, at least one staffed computer lab available.

Student Life *Housing Options:* coed, men-only, women-only, disabled students. *Activities and Organizations:* drama/theater group, student-run newspaper, radio and television station, choral group, marching band, Campus Y, Black Student Movement, Carolina Athletic Association, Residence Hall Association, Campus Crusade for Christ, national fraternities, national sororities. *Campus security:* 24-hour emergency response devices and patrols, student patrols, late-night transport/escort service, controlled dormitory access, crime prevention programs. *Student Services:* health clinic, personal/psychological counseling, women's center, legal services.

Athletics Member NCAA. All Division I except football (Division I-A). *Intercollegiate sports:* baseball M(s), basketball M(s)/W(s), crew W(s), cross-country running M(s)/W(s), fencing M/W, field hockey W(s), golf M(s)/W(s), gymnastics W(s), lacrosse M(s)/W(s), soccer M(s)/W(s), softball W(s), swimming M(s)/W(s), tennis M(s)/W(s), track and field M(s)/W(s), volleyball W(s), wrestling M(s). *Intramural sports:* badminton M/W, basketball M/W, bowling M/W, crew M/W, cross-country running M/W, fencing M/W, field hockey M/W, football M/W, golf M/W, gymnastics M/W, ice hockey M/W, lacrosse M/W, racquetball M/W, rugby M, sailing M/W, skiing (cross-country) M/W, skiing (downhill) M/W, soccer M/W, softball M/W, squash M/W, swimming M/W, tennis M/W, track and field M/W, volleyball M/W, water polo M/W, weight lifting M, wrestling M.

Standardized Tests *Required:* SAT I or ACT (for admission).

Costs (2001–02) *Tuition:* state resident $2328 full-time; nonresident $12,320 full-time. Full-time tuition and fees vary according to program. Part-time tuition and fees vary according to course load, program, and student level. *Required fees:* $949 full-time. *Room and board:* $5570; room only: $2800. Room and board charges vary according to board plan, housing facility, and location. *Payment plan:* deferred payment. *Waivers:* senior citizens and employees or children of employees.

Financial Aid Of all full-time matriculated undergraduates who enrolled in 2001, 7652 applied for aid, 3855 were judged to have need, 1249 had their need fully met. In 2001, 3328 non-need-based awards were made. *Average percent of need met:* 86%. *Average financial aid package:* $7129. *Average need-based loan:* $3490. *Average need-based gift aid:* $4632.

Applying *Options:* electronic application, early action, deferred entrance. *Application fee:* $55. *Required:* essay or personal statement, high school transcript, letters of recommendation. *Application deadlines:* 1/15 (freshmen), 3/1 (transfers). *Early decision:* 10/15. *Notification:* 3/31 (freshmen), 12/1 (early decision), 1/30 (early action).

Admissions Contact Mr. Jerome A. Lucido, Vice Provost and Director of Undergraduate Admissions, The University of North Carolina at Chapel Hill, Office of Undergraduate Admissions, Jackson Hall 153A, Campus Box 2200, Chapel Hill, NC 27599-2200. *Phone:* 919-966-3621. *Fax:* 919-962-3045. *E-mail:* uadm@email.unc.edu.

THE UNIVERSITY OF NORTH CAROLINA AT CHARLOTTE

Charlotte, North Carolina

- **State-supported** university, founded 1946, part of University of North Carolina System
- **Calendar** semesters
- **Degrees** bachelor's, master's, doctoral, and post-master's certificates
- **Suburban** 1000-acre campus
- **Endowment** $79.3 million
- **Coed,** 15,135 undergraduate students, 75% full-time, 54% women, 46% men
- **Moderately difficult** entrance level, 73% of applicants were admitted

Undergraduates 11,340 full-time, 3,795 part-time. Students come from 51 states and territories, 69 other countries, 10% are from out of state, 17% African American, 5% Asian American or Pacific Islander, 2% Hispanic American, 0.4% Native American, 3% international, 11% transferred in, 22% live on campus. *Retention:* 78% of 2001 full-time freshmen returned.

Freshmen *Admission:* 7,731 applied, 5,656 admitted, 2,351 enrolled. *Average high school GPA:* 3.50. *Test scores:* SAT verbal scores over 500: 61%; SAT math scores over 500: 67%; ACT scores over 18: 81%; SAT verbal scores over 600: 15%; SAT math scores over 600: 20%; ACT scores over 24: 23%; SAT verbal scores over 700: 1%; SAT math scores over 700: 1%; ACT scores over 30: 1%.

Faculty *Total:* 1,020, 66% full-time, 67% with terminal degrees. *Student/faculty ratio:* 16:1.

Majors Accounting; African-American studies; anthropology; architecture; area, ethnic, and cultural studies related; art; art education; biology; business administration; business economics; business marketing and marketing management; chemistry; chemistry education; civil engineering; civil engineering technology; communications; computer engineering; computer science; criminal justice studies; dance; drama/dance education; early childhood education; earth sciences; economics; education of the mentally handicapped; electrical/electronic engineering technology; electrical engineering; elementary education; English; English education; finance; fine/studio arts; fire services administration; French; French language education; geography; geology; German; German language education; health/physical education; history; history education; individual/family development; industrial technology; international business; management information systems/business data processing; mathematics; mathematics education; mechanical engineering; mechanical engineering technology; medical technology; middle school education; music (general performance); music teacher education; nursing; operations management; philosophy; physics; political science; psychology; religious studies; social work; sociology; Spanish; Spanish language education; theater arts/drama.

Academic Programs *Special study options:* adult/continuing education programs, advanced placement credit, cooperative education, distance learning, double majors, English as a second language, freshman honors college, honors programs, internships, off-campus study, part-time degree program, services for LD students, study abroad, summer session for credit. *ROTC:* Army (b), Air Force (b).

Library J. Murrey Atkins Library with 874,834 titles, 39,918 audiovisual materials, an OPAC, a Web page.

Computers on Campus 750 computers available on campus for general student use. A campuswide network can be accessed from student residence rooms and from off campus. Internet access, online (class) registration, at least one staffed computer lab available.

Student Life *Housing Options:* coed, women-only, disabled students. *Activities and Organizations:* drama/theater group, student-run newspaper, choral group, University Program Board, Student Government Association, Resident Student Association, Black Student Union, Greek Council, national fraternities, national sororities. *Campus security:* 24-hour emergency response devices and patrols, late-night transport/escort service, controlled dormitory access. *Student Services:* health clinic, personal/psychological counseling.

Athletics Member NCAA. All Division I. *Intercollegiate sports:* baseball M(s), basketball M(s)/W(s), cross-country running M(s)/W(s), golf M(s), soccer M(s)/W(s), softball W(s), tennis M(s)/W(s), track and field M(s)/W(s), volleyball W(s). *Intramural sports:* badminton M(c)/W(c), baseball M(c)/W(c), basketball M/W, bowling M/W, fencing M(c)/W(c), football M/W, golf M/W, lacrosse M(c)/W(c), racquetball M/W, rugby M(c)/W(c), soccer M(c)/W(c), softball M/W, swimming M(c)/W(c), table tennis M/W, tennis M(c)/W(c), track and field M/W, volleyball M(c)/W(c), water polo M/W, wrestling M(c)/W(c).

Standardized Tests *Required:* SAT I or ACT (for admission).

Costs (2001–02) *Tuition:* state resident $1417 full-time, $354 per term part-time; nonresident $9637 full-time, $2410 per term part-time. Full-time tuition and fees vary according to course load. Part-time tuition and fees vary according to course load. *Required fees:* $1043 full-time, $277 per term part-time. *Room and board:* $4798; room only: $2398. Room and board charges vary according to board plan and housing facility. *Waivers:* senior citizens.

Financial Aid Of all full-time matriculated undergraduates who enrolled in 2001, 6053 applied for aid, 4549 were judged to have need, 1467 had their need fully met. In 2001, 1252 non-need-based awards were made. *Average percent of need met:* 82%. *Average financial aid package:* $7189. *Average need-based loan:* $3705. *Average need-based gift aid:* $2888. *Average indebtedness upon graduation:* $11,800.

Applying *Options:* common application, electronic application, early admission, deferred entrance. *Application fee:* $35. *Required:* high school transcript, minimum 2.0 GPA, 1 letter of recommendation, medical history. *Required for some:* interview. *Application deadlines:* 7/1 (freshmen), 7/1 (transfers).

Admissions Contact Mr. Craig Fulton, Director of Admissions, The University of North Carolina at Charlotte, 9201 University City Boulevard, Charlotte, NC 28223-0001. *Phone:* 704-687-2213. *Fax:* 704-687-6483. *E-mail:* unccadm@email.uncc.edu.

THE UNIVERSITY OF NORTH CAROLINA AT GREENSBORO

Greensboro, North Carolina

- **State-supported** university, founded 1891, part of University of North Carolina System
- **Calendar** semesters
- **Degrees** bachelor's, master's, and doctoral
- **Urban** 200-acre campus
- **Endowment** $112.3 million
- **Coed,** 10,376 undergraduate students, 84% full-time, 68% women, 32% men
- **Moderately difficult** entrance level, 75% of applicants were admitted

Undergraduates 8,671 full-time, 1,705 part-time. Students come from 41 states and territories, 55 other countries, 9% are from out of state, 20% African American, 3% Asian American or Pacific Islander, 2% Hispanic American, 0.4% Native American, 1% international, 10% transferred in. *Retention:* 75% of 2001 full-time freshmen returned.

Freshmen *Admission:* 6,619 applied, 4,964 admitted, 1,915 enrolled. *Average high school GPA:* 3.43. *Test scores:* SAT verbal scores over 500: 59%; SAT math scores over 500: 55%; SAT verbal scores over 600: 18%; SAT math scores over 600: 15%; SAT verbal scores over 700: 3%; SAT math scores over 700: 1%.

Faculty *Total:* 886, 77% full-time, 77% with terminal degrees. *Student/faculty ratio:* 15:1.

Majors Accounting; African-American studies; anthropology; applied mathematics; archaeology; art; art education; art history; biology; business administration; business education; business marketing and marketing management; chemistry; classics; clothing/textiles; computer/information sciences; dance; dietetics; economics; education of the hearing impaired; elementary education; English; European studies; family/community studies; film/video production; finance; fine/studio arts; French; geography; German; gerontology; health education; history; home economics; individual/family development; interdisciplinary studies; interior design; Latin American studies; Latin (ancient and medieval); liberal arts and sciences/liberal studies; linguistics; management information systems/business data processing; marriage/family counseling; mass communications; mathematical statistics; mathematics; medical technology; middle school education; museum studies; music history; music (piano and organ performance); music teacher education; music (voice and choral/opera performance); nursing; nutrition studies; philosophy; physical education; physics; political science; pre-dentistry; pre-law; pre-medicine; pre-veterinary studies; psychology; radio/television broadcasting; recreation/leisure facilities management; religious studies; Russian; sculpture; sign language interpretation; social work; sociology; Spanish; speech-language pathology/audiology; speech/rhetorical studies; theater arts/drama; urban studies; women's studies.

Academic Programs *Special study options:* academic remediation for entering students, accelerated degree program, adult/continuing education programs, advanced placement credit, distance learning, double majors, English as a second language, freshman honors college, honors programs, independent study, internships, off-campus study, part-time degree program, services for LD students, student-designed majors, study abroad, summer session for credit. *ROTC:* Army (c), Air Force (c). *Unusual degree programs:* 3-2 business administration with North Carolina State University, University of North Carolina at Charlotte.

Library Jackson Library plus 1 other with 914,914 titles, 5,317 serial subscriptions, an OPAC, a Web page.

Computers on Campus 400 computers available on campus for general student use. A campuswide network can be accessed from student residence rooms and from off campus. Internet access, online (class) registration, at least one staffed computer lab available.

Student Life *Housing Options:* coed, men-only, women-only. *Activities and Organizations:* drama/theater group, student-run newspaper, radio station, choral group, Campus Activities Board, Neo-Black Society, religious organizations, International Students Association, national fraternities, national sororities. *Campus security:* 24-hour emergency response devices and patrols, late-night transport/escort service, controlled dormitory access. *Student Services:* health clinic, personal/psychological counseling.

Athletics Member NCAA. All Division I. *Intercollegiate sports:* baseball M(s), basketball M(s)/W(s), cross-country running M(s)/W(s), golf M(s)/W(s), soccer M(s)/W(s), softball W(s), tennis M(s)/W(s), volleyball W(s), wrestling M(s). *Intramural sports:* badminton M/W, basketball M/W, bowling M/W, equestrian sports M(c)/W(c), fencing M(c)/W(c), football M/W, golf M/W, ice hockey M(c), lacrosse M(c)/W(c), racquetball M/W, rugby M(c)/W(c), soccer M/W, softball M/W, swimming M/W, table tennis M/W, tennis M/W, track and field M/W, volleyball M/W.

Standardized Tests *Required:* SAT I or ACT (for admission). *Recommended:* SAT II: Subject Tests (for admission).

The University of North Carolina at Greensboro (continued)

Costs (2001–02) *Tuition:* state resident $1302 full-time; nonresident $9752 full-time. Part-time tuition and fees vary according to course load. *Required fees:* $1243 full-time. *Room and board:* $4313; room only: $2313. Room and board charges vary according to board plan and housing facility. *Waivers:* employees or children of employees.

Financial Aid Of all full-time matriculated undergraduates who enrolled in 2001, 5852 applied for aid, 3665 were judged to have need, 2067 had their need fully met. In 2001, 783 non-need-based awards were made. *Average percent of need met:* 87%. *Average financial aid package:* $8415. *Average need-based gift aid:* $2352. *Average non-need based aid:* $2631. *Average indebtedness upon graduation:* $10,856.

Applying *Options:* early admission. *Application fee:* $35. *Required:* high school transcript, minimum 2.0 GPA. *Application deadlines:* 8/1 (freshmen), 8/1 (transfers). *Notification:* continuous (freshmen).

Admissions Contact Mr. Jerry Harrelson, Associate Director of Admissions, The University of North Carolina at Greensboro, 1000 Spring Garden Street, Greensboro, NC 27412-5001. *Phone:* 336-334-5243. *Fax:* 336-334-4180. *E-mail:* undergrad_admissions@uncg.edu.

THE UNIVERSITY OF NORTH CAROLINA AT PEMBROKE
Pembroke, North Carolina

- **State-supported** comprehensive, founded 1887, part of University of North Carolina System
- **Calendar** semesters
- **Degrees** bachelor's and master's
- **Rural** 126-acre campus
- **Endowment** $4.7 million
- **Coed,** 3,506 undergraduate students, 77% full-time, 62% women, 38% men
- **Moderately difficult** entrance level, 51% of applicants were admitted

Undergraduates 2,692 full-time, 814 part-time. Students come from 32 states and territories, 13 other countries, 4% are from out of state, 21% African American, 1% Asian American or Pacific Islander, 2% Hispanic American, 22% Native American, 0.5% international, 11% transferred in, 22% live on campus. *Retention:* 69% of 2001 full-time freshmen returned.

Freshmen *Admission:* 1,384 applied, 700 admitted, 700 enrolled. *Average high school GPA:* 3.00. *Test scores:* SAT verbal scores over 500: 29%; SAT math scores over 500: 31%; ACT scores over 18: 42%; SAT verbal scores over 600: 5%; SAT math scores over 600: 4%; ACT scores over 24: 7%; SAT verbal scores over 700: 1%.

Faculty *Total:* 247, 67% full-time, 100% with terminal degrees. *Student/faculty ratio:* 17:1.

Majors Accounting; art; art education; biology; biomedical science; broadcast journalism; business administration; chemistry; computer science; criminal justice/law enforcement administration; early childhood education; economics; education; elementary education; English; health education; history; journalism; literature; mass communications; mathematics; medical laboratory technician; medical technology; music; music teacher education; Native American studies; nursing; philosophy; physical education; political science; pre-law; psychology; public administration; public relations; recreation/leisure studies; religious studies; science education; secondary education; secretarial science; social work; sociology; special education; theater arts/drama.

Academic Programs *Special study options:* academic remediation for entering students, accelerated degree program, adult/continuing education programs, advanced placement credit, cooperative education, distance learning, double majors, English as a second language, honors programs, independent study, internships, off-campus study, part-time degree program, services for LD students, summer session for credit. *ROTC:* Army (b), Air Force (b).

Library Sampson-Livermore Library with 296,080 titles, 1,471 serial subscriptions, 1,806 audiovisual materials, an OPAC, a Web page.

Computers on Campus 367 computers available on campus for general student use. A campuswide network can be accessed from student residence rooms and from off campus. Internet access, at least one staffed computer lab available.

Student Life *Housing Options:* coed, men-only, women-only. *Activities and Organizations:* drama/theater group, student-run newspaper, television station, choral group, Phi Kappa Tau, Zeta Tau Alpha, Tau Kappa Epsilon, Sigma Sigma Sigma, Pi Lambda Upsilon, national fraternities, national sororities. *Campus security:* 24-hour emergency response devices and patrols, late-night transport/escort service, controlled dormitory access. *Student Services:* health clinic, personal/psychological counseling.

Athletics Member NCAA. All Division II. *Intercollegiate sports:* baseball M(s), basketball M(s)/W(s), cross-country running M(s)/W(s), golf M(s), soccer M(s)/W(s), softball W(s), tennis W(s), track and field M(s), volleyball W(s), wrestling M(s). *Intramural sports:* basketball M/W, bowling M/W, football M/W, golf M/W, racquetball M/W, soccer M/W, softball M/W, tennis M/W, track and field M/W, volleyball M/W, water polo M/W, weight lifting M/W, wrestling M/W.

Standardized Tests *Required:* SAT I or ACT (for admission).

Costs (2001–02) *Tuition:* state resident $1152 full-time, $432 per term part-time; nonresident $9074 full-time, $3403 per term part-time. Part-time tuition and fees vary according to course load. *Required fees:* $917 full-time, $344 per term part-time. *Room and board:* $3845; room only: $2120. Room and board charges vary according to board plan and housing facility. *Payment plan:* installment. *Waivers:* senior citizens.

Financial Aid Of all full-time matriculated undergraduates who enrolled in 2001, 1895 applied for aid, 1538 were judged to have need, 514 had their need fully met. 202 Federal Work-Study jobs (averaging $1500). 48 State and other part-time jobs (averaging $1500). In 2001, 198 non-need-based awards were made. *Average percent of need met:* 79%. *Average financial aid package:* $5752. *Average need-based loan:* $3006. *Average need-based gift aid:* $3663. *Average non-need based aid:* $1334.

Applying *Options:* common application, early admission, deferred entrance. *Application fee:* $40. *Required:* high school transcript. *Required for some:* letters of recommendation, interview. *Recommended:* essay or personal statement, minimum 2.0 GPA. *Application deadline:* rolling (freshmen), rolling (transfers). *Notification:* continuous (freshmen).

Admissions Contact John Kelly Brookins III, Associate Director of Admissions, The University of North Carolina at Pembroke, PO Box 1510, Pembroke, NC 28372-1510. *Phone:* 910-521-6262. *Toll-free phone:* 800-949-UNCP (in-state); 800-949-uncp (out-of-state). *Fax:* 910-521-6497.

THE UNIVERSITY OF NORTH CAROLINA AT WILMINGTON
Wilmington, North Carolina

- **State-supported** comprehensive, founded 1947, part of University of North Carolina System
- **Calendar** semesters
- **Degrees** bachelor's and master's
- **Urban** 650-acre campus
- **Endowment** $23.4 million
- **Coed,** 9,792 undergraduate students, 89% full-time, 60% women, 40% men
- **Moderately difficult** entrance level, 80% of applicants were admitted

Undergraduates 8,666 full-time, 1,126 part-time. Students come from 47 states and territories, 38 other countries, 14% are from out of state, 4% African American, 1% Asian American or Pacific Islander, 1% Hispanic American, 0.5% Native American, 0.7% international, 10% transferred in, 23% live on campus. *Retention:* 82% of 2001 full-time freshmen returned.

Freshmen *Admission:* 5,373 applied, 4,301 admitted, 1,996 enrolled. *Average high school GPA:* 3.40. *Test scores:* SAT verbal scores over 500: 70%; SAT math scores over 500: 76%; ACT scores over 18: 94%; SAT verbal scores over 600: 17%; SAT math scores over 600: 18%; ACT scores over 24: 31%; SAT verbal scores over 700: 1%; SAT math scores over 700: 1%; ACT scores over 30: 3%.

Faculty *Total:* 641, 68% full-time, 71% with terminal degrees. *Student/faculty ratio:* 16:1.

Majors Accounting; anthropology; art history; athletic training/sports medicine; biology; biology education; business administration; business economics; business marketing and marketing management; chemistry; chemistry education; computer/information sciences; creative writing; criminal justice studies; early childhood education; economics; education of the emotionally handicapped; education of the mentally handicapped; education of the specific learning disabled; elementary education; English; English education; environmental science; film/video production; finance; fine/studio arts; French; French language education; geography; geology; health/physical education; history; history education; management information systems/business data processing; marine biology; mathematics; mathematics education; medical technology; middle school education; music; music (general performance); music teacher education; nursing; philosophy and religion related; physical education; physics; physics education; political science; psychology; recreation/leisure facilities management; social work; sociology; Spanish; Spanish language education; speech/rhetorical studies; teacher education, specific programs related; theater arts/drama.

Academic Programs *Special study options:* academic remediation for entering students, accelerated degree program, adult/continuing education programs, advanced placement credit, cooperative education, distance learning, double majors, English as a second language, freshman honors college, honors programs, independent study, internships, part-time degree program, services for LD students, study abroad, summer session for credit.

Library William M. Randall Library with 852,937 titles, 4,304 serial subscriptions, 51,202 audiovisual materials, an OPAC, a Web page.

Computers on Campus 778 computers available on campus for general student use. A campuswide network can be accessed from student residence rooms and from off campus. Internet access, online (class) registration, at least one staffed computer lab available.

Student Life *Housing Options:* coed, women-only. *Activities and Organizations:* drama/theater group, student-run newspaper, radio and television station, choral group, Student Government Association, Association of Campus Entertainment, Residence Hall Association, Greek governing bodies, sailing club, national fraternities, national sororities. *Campus security:* 24-hour emergency response devices and patrols, late-night transport/escort service, controlled dormitory access, escort service. *Student Services:* health clinic, personal/psychological counseling, legal services.

Athletics Member NCAA. All Division I. *Intercollegiate sports:* baseball M(s), basketball M(s)/W(s), cross-country running M(s)/W(s), golf M(s)/W(s), soccer M(s)/W(s), softball W(s), swimming M(s)/W(s), tennis M(s)/W(s), track and field M(s)/W(s), volleyball W(s). *Intramural sports:* badminton M/W, baseball M(c), basketball M/W, field hockey W(c), golf M(c)/W(c), gymnastics M(c)/W(c), lacrosse M(c)/W(c), rugby M(c), sailing M(c)/W(c), soccer M(c)/W(c), softball M/W, table tennis M(c)/W(c), tennis M/W, volleyball W(c).

Standardized Tests *Required:* SAT I or ACT (for admission).

Costs (2001–02) *Tuition:* state resident $1317 full-time; nonresident $9412 full-time. Part-time tuition and fees vary according to course load and program. *Required fees:* $1310 full-time. *Room and board:* $5142. Room and board charges vary according to board plan and housing facility. *Payment plan:* installment. *Waivers:* senior citizens and employees or children of employees.

Financial Aid Of all full-time matriculated undergraduates who enrolled in 2001, 4102 applied for aid, 2963 were judged to have need, 892 had their need fully met. 523 Federal Work-Study jobs (averaging $2783). *Average percent of need met:* 72%. *Average financial aid package:* $5864. *Average need-based loan:* $3757. *Average need-based gift aid:* $3033. *Average indebtedness upon graduation:* $12,726.

Applying *Options:* common application, electronic application, deferred entrance. *Application fee:* $45. *Required:* essay or personal statement, high school transcript. *Application deadline:* 2/1 (freshmen), rolling (transfers).

Admissions Contact Dr. Roxie Shabazz, Assistant Vice Chancellor for Admissions, The University of North Carolina at Wilmington, 601 South College Road, Wilmington, NC 28403-3297. *Phone:* 910-962-4198. *Toll-free phone:* 800-228-5571. *Fax:* 910-962-3038. *E-mail:* admissions@uncwil.edu.

WAKE FOREST UNIVERSITY
Winston-Salem, North Carolina

- **Independent** university, founded 1834, affiliated with North Carolina Baptist State Convention
- **Calendar** semesters
- **Degrees** certificates, bachelor's, master's, doctoral, and first professional
- **Suburban** 340-acre campus
- **Endowment** $812.4 million
- **Coed,** 3,987 undergraduate students, 94% full-time, 51% women, 49% men
- **Very difficult** entrance level, 46% of applicants were admitted

Undergraduates 3,745 full-time, 242 part-time. Students come from 50 states and territories, 23 other countries, 74% are from out of state, 7% African American, 3% Asian American or Pacific Islander, 1% Hispanic American, 0.2% Native American, 0.8% international, 2% transferred in, 75% live on campus. *Retention:* 93% of 2001 full-time freshmen returned.

Freshmen *Admission:* 5,271 applied, 2,421 admitted, 983 enrolled. *Test scores:* SAT verbal scores over 500: 97%; SAT math scores over 500: 98%; SAT verbal scores over 600: 80%; SAT math scores over 600: 85%; SAT verbal scores over 700: 20%; SAT math scores over 700: 28%.

Faculty *Total:* 550, 78% full-time, 82% with terminal degrees. *Student/faculty ratio:* 10:1.

Majors Accounting; anthropology; applied mathematics; art; art history; biology; business; chemistry; classics; communications; computer/information sciences; economics; education; elementary education; English; exercise sciences; finance; French; German; Greek (ancient and medieval); history; Latin (ancient and medieval); management science; mathematics; music; philosophy; physician assistant; physics; political science; psychology; religious studies; Russian; sociology; Spanish; theater arts/drama.

Academic Programs *Special study options:* academic remediation for entering students, accelerated degree program, advanced placement credit, double majors, honors programs, independent study, internships, off-campus study, part-time degree program, services for LD students, student-designed majors, study abroad, summer session for credit. *ROTC:* Army (b). *Unusual degree programs:* 3-2 engineering with North Carolina State University; forestry with Duke University; dentistry with University of North Carolina at Chapel Hill; physician's assistant, accounting, medical technology, Latin American studies with Georgetown University.

Library Z. Smith Reynolds Library plus 3 others with 923,123 titles, 16,448 serial subscriptions, 21,055 audiovisual materials, an OPAC, a Web page.

Computers on Campus 150 computers available on campus for general student use. A campuswide network can be accessed from student residence rooms and from off campus that provide access to personal computer. Internet access, online (class) registration, at least one staffed computer lab available.

Student Life *Housing:* on-campus residence required for freshman year. *Options:* coed, women-only. *Activities and Organizations:* drama/theater group, student-run newspaper, radio and television station, choral group, marching band, Student Union Network, Volunteer Service Corps, Intervarsity Christian Fellowship, student government, national fraternities, national sororities. *Campus security:* 24-hour emergency response devices and patrols, late-night transport/escort service, controlled dormitory access. *Student Services:* health clinic, personal/psychological counseling.

Athletics Member NCAA. All Division I except football (Division I-A). *Intercollegiate sports:* baseball M(s), basketball M(s)/W(s), cross-country running M(s)/W(s), field hockey W(s), golf M(s)/W(s), soccer M(s)/W(s), tennis M(s)/W(s), track and field M(s)/W(s), volleyball W(s). *Intramural sports:* baseball M(c), basketball M/W, bowling M/W, crew M(c)/W(c), cross-country running M/W, equestrian sports M(c)/W(c), fencing M(c)/W(c), field hockey W(c), football M/W, golf M/W, ice hockey M(c), lacrosse M(c)/W(c), racquetball M/W, rugby M(c), soccer M(c)/W(c), softball M/W, swimming M(c)/W(c), tennis M/W, volleyball M/W, water polo M(c), wrestling M(c).

Standardized Tests *Required:* SAT I (for admission). *Recommended:* SAT II: Subject Tests (for admission).

Costs (2001–02) *Comprehensive fee:* $30,290 includes full-time tuition ($23,530) and room and board ($6760). Part-time tuition: $910 per credit hour. *Room and board:* College room only: $3960. Room and board charges vary according to board plan and housing facility. *Payment plan:* installment. *Waivers:* employees or children of employees.

Financial Aid Of all full-time matriculated undergraduates who enrolled in 2001, 1452 applied for aid, 1149 were judged to have need, 461 had their need fully met. 855 Federal Work-Study jobs (averaging $1802). In 2001, 1114 non-need-based awards were made. *Average percent of need met:* 91%. *Average financial aid package:* $18,976. *Average need-based loan:* $5028. *Average need-based gift aid:* $14,514. *Average indebtedness upon graduation:* $20,339.

Applying *Options:* common application, electronic application, early admission, early decision, deferred entrance. *Application fee:* $40. *Required:* essay or personal statement, high school transcript, 1 letter of recommendation. *Application deadlines:* 1/15 (freshmen), 2/15 (transfers). *Early decision:* 11/15. *Notification:* 4/1 (freshmen), 12/15 (early decision).

Admissions Contact Martha Allman, Director of Admissions, Wake Forest University, PO Box 7305, Winston-Salem, NC 27109. *Phone:* 336-758-5201. *Fax:* 336-758-6074. *E-mail:* admissions@wfu.edu.

WARREN WILSON COLLEGE
Asheville, North Carolina

- **Independent** comprehensive, founded 1894, affiliated with Presbyterian Church (U.S.A.)
- **Calendar** semesters
- **Degrees** bachelor's and master's
- **Small-town** 1100-acre campus
- **Endowment** $30.7 million
- **Coed,** 781 undergraduate students, 99% full-time, 61% women, 39% men
- **Moderately difficult** entrance level, 82% of applicants were admitted

Warren Wilson isn't for everyone. Some colleges treat prospective students as if they're all alike. There are very few alike students at Warren Wilson. Balancing academics, working on campus, and performing community service may not be the experience many are looking for. But that's the point—Warren Wilson is not for everyone. Solid academic students who want to make a difference in the world and who are environmentally aware may want to consider applying to Warren Wilson.

Undergraduates 773 full-time, 8 part-time. Students come from 41 states and territories, 24 other countries, 69% are from out of state, 1% African American, 0.5% Asian American or Pacific Islander, 2% Hispanic American, 0.3% Native American, 4% international, 8% transferred in, 88% live on campus. *Retention:* 67% of 2001 full-time freshmen returned.

Warren Wilson College (continued)

Freshmen *Admission:* 661 applied, 539 admitted, 212 enrolled. *Average high school GPA:* 3.23. *Test scores:* SAT verbal scores over 500: 87%; SAT math scores over 500: 74%; ACT scores over 18: 100%; SAT verbal scores over 600: 57%; SAT math scores over 600: 34%; ACT scores over 24: 88%; SAT verbal scores over 700: 17%; SAT math scores over 700: 4%; ACT scores over 30: 17%.

Faculty *Total:* 75, 83% full-time, 73% with terminal degrees. *Student/faculty ratio:* 11:1.

Majors Agricultural sciences; American studies; anthropology; art; biochemistry; biology; business administration; chemistry; creative writing; economics; education; elementary education; English; English education; environmental science; fashion merchandising; forest management; history; humanities; interdisciplinary studies; international business; Latin American studies; mathematics; natural resources management; nonprofit/public management; political science; pre-medicine; pre-veterinary studies; psychology; recreation/leisure studies; secondary education; social work; sociology; theater arts/drama; wildlife management; women's studies.

Academic Programs *Special study options:* advanced placement credit, cooperative education, double majors, English as a second language, honors programs, independent study, internships, off-campus study, part-time degree program, services for LD students, student-designed majors, study abroad. *Unusual degree programs:* 3-2 engineering with Washington University in St. Louis; forestry with Duke University.

Library Pew Learning Center and Ellison Library with 99,000 titles, 4,060 serial subscriptions, 1,731 audiovisual materials, an OPAC, a Web page.

Computers on Campus 68 computers available on campus for general student use. A campuswide network can be accessed from student residence rooms and from off campus that provide access to word processing, software. Internet access, at least one staffed computer lab available.

Student Life *Housing:* on-campus residence required for freshman year. *Options:* coed, men-only, women-only. *Activities and Organizations:* drama/theater group, student-run newspaper, radio station, choral group, Collective Conscience/Social Justice, Student Caucus, wellness activities; yoga, martial arts, meditation, outing club, community service SOA.R. (Students Organized for Active Resistance). *Campus security:* 24-hour emergency response devices and patrols, student patrols, late-night transport/escort service, controlled dormitory access. *Student Services:* health clinic, personal/psychological counseling.

Athletics Member NSCAA. *Intercollegiate sports:* basketball M/W, cross-country running M/W, soccer M/W, swimming M/W. *Intramural sports:* fencing M/W, lacrosse M/W, soccer M/W.

Standardized Tests *Required:* SAT I or ACT (for admission).

Costs (2002–03) *Comprehensive fee:* $20,842 includes full-time tuition ($15,848) and room and board ($4994). Full-time tuition and fees vary according to course load. Part-time tuition: $400 per credit hour. Part-time tuition and fees vary according to course load. *Room and board:* Room and board charges vary according to board plan. *Payment plan:* installment. *Waivers:* employees or children of employees.

Financial Aid Of all full-time matriculated undergraduates who enrolled in 2001, 596 applied for aid, 389 were judged to have need, 60 had their need fully met. 304 Federal Work-Study jobs (averaging $2190). 380 State and other part-time jobs (averaging $1912). In 2001, 151 non-need-based awards were made. *Average percent of need met:* 75%. *Average financial aid package:* $12,018. *Average need-based loan:* $2937. *Average need-based gift aid:* $6624. *Average non-need based aid:* $4195. *Average indebtedness upon graduation:* $15,075.

Applying *Options:* common application, electronic application, early admission, early decision, deferred entrance. *Required:* essay or personal statement, high school transcript, minimum 2.5 GPA, 2 letters of recommendation. *Recommended:* interview. *Application deadlines:* 3/15 (freshmen), 3/15 (transfers). *Early decision:* 11/15. *Notification:* continuous (freshmen), 12/1 (early decision).

Admissions Contact Warren Wilson College, PO Box 9000, Asheville, NC 28815-9000. *Phone:* 800-934-3536. *Toll-free phone:* 800-934-3536. *Fax:* 828-298-1440. *E-mail:* admit@warren-wilson.edu.

WESTERN CAROLINA UNIVERSITY
Cullowhee, North Carolina

- **State-supported** comprehensive, founded 1889, part of University of North Carolina System
- **Calendar** semesters
- **Degrees** bachelor's, master's, doctoral, and post-master's certificates
- **Rural** 260-acre campus
- **Endowment** $21.1 million
- **Coed,** 5,665 undergraduate students, 86% full-time, 52% women, 48% men
- **Moderately difficult** entrance level, 73% of applicants were admitted

Undergraduates 4,872 full-time, 793 part-time. Students come from 42 states and territories, 34 other countries, 9% are from out of state, 5% African American, 0.7% Asian American or Pacific Islander, 0.9% Hispanic American, 2% Native American, 3% international, 10% transferred in, 43% live on campus. *Retention:* 69% of 2001 full-time freshmen returned.

Freshmen *Admission:* 3,979 applied, 2,903 admitted, 1,180 enrolled. *Average high school GPA:* 3.17. *Test scores:* SAT verbal scores over 500: 50%; SAT math scores over 500: 52%; SAT verbal scores over 600: 12%; SAT math scores over 600: 12%; SAT verbal scores over 700: 2%; SAT math scores over 700: 1%.

Faculty *Total:* 513, 61% full-time, 61% with terminal degrees. *Student/faculty ratio:* 15:1.

Majors Accounting; anthropology; art; art education; biology; business administration; business marketing and marketing management; chemistry; communication disorders; communications; computer science; criminal justice studies; dietetics; early childhood education; electrical/electronic engineering technology; elementary education; emergency medical technology; English; English education; entrepreneurship; environmental health; finance; fine/studio arts; French language education; German; German language education; history; hospitality management; industrial technology; interior design; international business; liberal arts and sciences/liberal studies; management information systems/business data processing; mathematics; mathematics education; medical records administration; medical technology; middle school education; music; music teacher education; natural resources management; nursing; philosophy; physical education; political science; psychology; recreational therapy; recreation/leisure facilities management; science education; social sciences; social studies education; social work; sociology; Spanish; Spanish language education; special education; sport/fitness administration; theater arts/drama.

Academic Programs *Special study options:* academic remediation for entering students, accelerated degree program, adult/continuing education programs, advanced placement credit, cooperative education, distance learning, double majors, English as a second language, honors programs, independent study, internships, part-time degree program, services for LD students, student-designed majors, study abroad, summer session for credit.

Library Hunter Library with 527,866 titles, 2,926 serial subscriptions, 22,598 audiovisual materials, an OPAC, a Web page.

Computers on Campus 351 computers available on campus for general student use. A campuswide network can be accessed from student residence rooms and from off campus that provide access to e-mail. Internet access, online (class) registration, at least one staffed computer lab available.

Student Life *Housing:* on-campus residence required for freshman year. *Options:* coed, men-only, women-only. *Activities and Organizations:* drama/theater group, student-run newspaper, radio station, choral group, marching band, Inter-Fraternity Council, Student Government Association, Panhellenic Council, Organization of Ebony Students, Resident Student Association, national fraternities, national sororities. *Campus security:* 24-hour emergency response devices and patrols, controlled dormitory access. *Student Services:* health clinic, personal/psychological counseling, women's center.

Athletics Member NCAA. All Division I except football (Division I-AA). *Intercollegiate sports:* baseball M(s), basketball M(s)/W(s), cross-country running M(s)/W(s), golf M(s)/W(s), soccer W(s), tennis W(s), track and field M(s)/W(s), volleyball W(s). *Intramural sports:* archery M/W, badminton M/W, basketball M/W, bowling M/W, cross-country running M/W, football M/W, racquetball M/W, rugby M, soccer M/W, softball M/W, swimming M/W, table tennis M/W, tennis M/W, track and field M/W, volleyball M/W, water polo M/W, weight lifting M/W, wrestling M.

Standardized Tests *Required:* SAT I (for admission).

Costs (2001–02) *Tuition:* state resident $1072 full-time; nonresident $8704 full-time. Part-time tuition and fees vary according to course load. *Required fees:* $1171 full-time. *Room and board:* $3424; room only: $1780. Room and board charges vary according to board plan and housing facility. *Payment plan:* installment. *Waivers:* senior citizens.

Financial Aid Of all full-time matriculated undergraduates who enrolled in 2001, 3341 applied for aid, 2000 were judged to have need, 1615 had their need fully met. 571 Federal Work-Study jobs (averaging $1328). In 2001, 503 non-need-based awards were made. *Average percent of need met:* 82%. *Average financial aid package:* $5715. *Average need-based loan:* $3131. *Average need-based gift aid:* $3121. *Average non-need based aid:* $2125. *Average indebtedness upon graduation:* $15,118.

Applying *Options:* electronic application, early admission. *Application fee:* $35. *Required:* high school transcript, minimum 2.5 GPA. *Application deadlines:* 8/1 (freshmen), 7/1 (transfers). *Notification:* continuous (freshmen).

Admissions Contact Mr. Philip Cauley, Director of Admissions, Western Carolina University, Cullowhee, NC 28723. *Phone:* 828-227-7317. *Toll-free phone:* 877-WCU4YOU. *Fax:* 828-277-7319. *E-mail:* admiss@email.wcu.edu.

WINGATE UNIVERSITY
Wingate, North Carolina

- **Independent Baptist** comprehensive, founded 1896
- **Calendar** semesters
- **Degrees** bachelor's and master's
- **Small-town** 330-acre campus with easy access to Charlotte
- **Coed,** 1,255 undergraduate students, 97% full-time, 53% women, 47% men
- **Moderately difficult** entrance level, 80% of applicants were admitted

Undergraduates 1,213 full-time, 42 part-time. Students come from 35 states and territories, 17 other countries, 41% are from out of state, 11% African American, 0.6% Asian American or Pacific Islander, 2% Hispanic American, 0.4% Native American, 2% international, 4% transferred in, 81% live on campus. *Retention:* 72% of 2001 full-time freshmen returned.

Freshmen *Admission:* 1,245 applied, 991 admitted, 396 enrolled. *Average high school GPA:* 3.22. *Test scores:* SAT verbal scores over 500: 58%; SAT math scores over 500: 61%; ACT scores over 18: 90%; SAT verbal scores over 600: 13%; SAT math scores over 600: 18%; ACT scores over 24: 29%; SAT verbal scores over 700: 2%; SAT math scores over 700: 2%; ACT scores over 30: 7%.

Faculty *Total:* 119, 67% full-time, 66% with terminal degrees. *Student/faculty ratio:* 13:1.

Majors Accounting; American studies; art; art education; athletic training/sports medicine; biology; business administration; business economics; business marketing and marketing management; chemistry; computer graphics; drawing; early childhood education; economics; education; elementary education; English; environmental biology; finance; fine/studio arts; history; human services; information sciences/systems; interdisciplinary studies; journalism; liberal arts and sciences/liberal studies; management information systems/business data processing; mass communications; mathematics; middle school education; music; music business management/merchandising; music (piano and organ performance); music teacher education; music (voice and choral/opera performance); philosophy; physical education; pre-law; pre-medicine; pre-veterinary studies; psychology; public relations; reading education; recreation/leisure studies; religious studies; science education; secondary education; social sciences; sociology; Spanish; speech/rhetorical studies; sport/fitness administration; telecommunications.

Academic Programs *Special study options:* accelerated degree program, adult/continuing education programs, advanced placement credit, double majors, honors programs, independent study, internships, off-campus study, part-time degree program, services for LD students, study abroad, summer session for credit. *ROTC:* Army (c), Air Force (c).

Library Ethel K. Smith Library plus 2 others with 110,000 titles, 600 serial subscriptions, 8,011 audiovisual materials, an OPAC, a Web page.

Computers on Campus 75 computers available on campus for general student use. A campuswide network can be accessed from student residence rooms and from off campus. Internet access, at least one staffed computer lab available.

Student Life *Housing:* on-campus residence required through senior year. *Options:* men-only, women-only. *Activities and Organizations:* drama/theater group, student-run newspaper, television station, choral group, Student Community Service Organization, Fellowship of Christian Athletes, Student Government Association, Christian Student Union, national fraternities, national sororities. *Campus security:* 24-hour emergency response devices and patrols, late-night transport/escort service, controlled dormitory access. *Student Services:* health clinic, personal/psychological counseling.

Athletics Member NCAA. All Division II. *Intercollegiate sports:* baseball M(s), basketball M(s)/W(s), cross-country running M(s)/W, football M(s), golf M(s)/W(s), lacrosse M(s), soccer M(s)/W, softball W(s), swimming W(s), tennis M(s)/W(s), volleyball W(s). *Intramural sports:* basketball M/W, bowling M/W, cross-country running M, football M/W, golf M/W, racquetball M/W, swimming M/W, table tennis M/W, tennis M/W, track and field M/W, volleyball M/W, water polo M/W, weight lifting M/W.

Standardized Tests *Required:* SAT I or ACT (for admission).

Costs (2001–02) *Comprehensive fee:* $19,140 includes full-time tuition ($12,900), mandatory fees ($780), and room and board ($5460). Part-time tuition: $430 per credit hour. *Payment plan:* installment. *Waivers:* employees or children of employees.

Financial Aid Of all full-time matriculated undergraduates who enrolled in 2001, 1043 applied for aid, 688 were judged to have need, 5 had their need fully met. 373 State and other part-time jobs (averaging $560). In 2001, 525 non-need-based awards were made. *Average percent of need met:* 56%. *Average financial aid package:* $10,818. *Average need-based gift aid:* $6150. *Average non-need based aid:* $3820. *Average indebtedness upon graduation:* $24,000.

Applying *Options:* common application, electronic application, early admission, early decision, deferred entrance. *Application fee:* $25. *Required:* high school transcript, minimum 2.0 GPA. *Required for some:* letters of recommendation, interview. *Recommended:* essay or personal statement, minimum 3.0 GPA. *Application deadline:* rolling (freshmen), rolling (transfers). *Early decision:* 12/1. *Notification:* continuous (freshmen), 12/15 (early decision).

Admissions Contact Mr. Walter P. Crutchfield III, Dean of Admissions, Wingate University, PO Box 159, Wingate, NC 28174. *Phone:* 704-233-8000. *Toll-free phone:* 800-755-5550. *Fax:* 704-233-8110. *E-mail:* admit@wingate.edu.

WINSTON-SALEM STATE UNIVERSITY
Winston-Salem, North Carolina

- **State-supported** comprehensive, founded 1892, part of University of North Carolina System
- **Calendar** semesters
- **Degrees** certificates, bachelor's, and master's
- **Urban** 94-acre campus
- **Endowment** $13.7 million
- **Coed,** 2,962 undergraduate students, 82% full-time, 68% women, 32% men
- **Minimally difficult** entrance level, 76% of applicants were admitted

Undergraduates 2,426 full-time, 536 part-time. Students come from 30 states and territories, 8% are from out of state, 85% African American, 0.9% Asian American or Pacific Islander, 0.5% Hispanic American, 0.2% Native American, 0.0% international, 8% transferred in, 40% live on campus. *Retention:* 73% of 2001 full-time freshmen returned.

Freshmen *Admission:* 1,914 applied, 1,451 admitted, 624 enrolled. *Average high school GPA:* 2.86. *Test scores:* SAT math scores over 500: 15%; SAT math scores over 600: 1%.

Faculty *Total:* 263, 62% full-time, 46% with terminal degrees. *Student/faculty ratio:* 15:1.

Majors Accounting; art; art education; biology; business administration; chemistry; computer science; early childhood education; economics; education; education of the specific learning disabled; elementary education; English; English education; general studies; gerontology; history; management information systems/business data processing; mass communications; mathematics; mathematics education; medical technology; middle school education; molecular biology; music teacher education; nursing; occupational therapy; physical education; political science; psychology; recreational therapy; social sciences; social studies education; sociology; Spanish; Spanish language education; special education; sport/fitness administration.

Academic Programs *Special study options:* academic remediation for entering students, accelerated degree program, adult/continuing education programs, advanced placement credit, cooperative education, double majors, freshman honors college, honors programs, independent study, internships, part-time degree program, services for LD students, summer session for credit. *ROTC:* Army (b).

Library O'Kelly Library with 175,982 titles, 1,694 serial subscriptions, an OPAC, a Web page.

Computers on Campus 66 computers available on campus for general student use. At least one staffed computer lab available.

Student Life *Housing Options:* coed, men-only, women-only. *Activities and Organizations:* drama/theater group, student-run newspaper, radio station, choral group, marching band, national fraternities, national sororities. *Campus security:* 24-hour emergency response devices and patrols. *Student Services:* health clinic, personal/psychological counseling.

Athletics Member NCAA. All Division II. *Intercollegiate sports:* basketball M(s)/W(s), bowling M(s)/W(s), cross-country running M(s)/W(s), football M(s), softball W(s), tennis M(s)/W(s), volleyball W(s). *Intramural sports:* basketball M/W, softball M/W, swimming M/W, table tennis M/W, tennis M/W, track and field M/W, volleyball W, weight lifting M/W.

Standardized Tests *Required:* SAT I or ACT (for admission).

Costs (2001–02) *Tuition:* state resident $896 full-time, $498 per term part-time; nonresident $7892 full-time, $2103 per term part-time. Full-time tuition and fees vary according to course load. Part-time tuition and fees vary according to course load. *Required fees:* $1167 full-time. *Room and board:* $3864; room only: $2058. Room and board charges vary according to board plan and housing facility. *Payment plan:* installment. *Waivers:* senior citizens and employees or children of employees.

Financial Aid Of all full-time matriculated undergraduates who enrolled in 2001, 1910 applied for aid, 1774 were judged to have need, 450 had their need fully met. 14 State and other part-time jobs (averaging $940). In 2001, 205

Winston-Salem State University (continued)

non-need-based awards were made. *Average percent of need met:* 81%. *Average financial aid package:* $4177. *Average need-based loan:* $3600. *Average need-based gift aid:* $3703. *Average non-need based aid:* $2465. *Average indebtedness upon graduation:* $10,900. *Financial aid deadline:* 4/1.

Applying *Options:* early admission, deferred entrance. *Application fee:* $30. *Required:* high school transcript. *Recommended:* 1 letter of recommendation. *Application deadline:* rolling (freshmen), rolling (transfers).

Admissions Contact Mr. Van C. Wilson, Director of Admissions, Winston-Salem State University, 601 Martin Luther King Jr Drive, Winston-Salem, NC 27110-0003. *Phone:* 336-750-2070. *Toll-free phone:* 800-257-4052. *Fax:* 336-750-2079. *E-mail:* wilsonv@wssu1adp.wssu.edu.

NORTH DAKOTA

DICKINSON STATE UNIVERSITY
Dickinson, North Dakota

- **State-supported** 4-year, founded 1918, part of North Dakota University System
- **Calendar** semesters
- **Degrees** certificates, associate, and bachelor's
- **Small-town** 100-acre campus
- **Endowment** $5.1 million
- **Coed,** 2,101 undergraduate students, 72% full-time, 57% women, 43% men
- **Noncompetitive** entrance level, 100% of applicants were admitted

Dickinson State, with an enrollment of approximately 2,000 students, offers Bachelor of Arts and Bachelor of Science degrees. Programs include liberal arts and specialized programs in education, business, nursing, agriculture, and computer science. There is opportunity for preprofessional study and vocational training in selected areas as well.

Undergraduates 1,520 full-time, 581 part-time. Students come from 30 states and territories, 15 other countries, 26% are from out of state, 0.5% African American, 0.1% Asian American or Pacific Islander, 0.7% Hispanic American, 2% Native American, 2% international, 9% transferred in, 30% live on campus. *Retention:* 56% of 2001 full-time freshmen returned.

Freshmen *Admission:* 585 applied, 585 admitted, 422 enrolled. *Average high school GPA:* 3.13. *Test scores:* ACT scores over 18: 76%; ACT scores over 24: 21%; ACT scores over 30: 2%.

Faculty *Total:* 146, 51% full-time, 42% with terminal degrees. *Student/faculty ratio:* 19:1.

Majors Accounting; agricultural business; art; art education; biology; business administration; business education; business marketing and marketing management; chemistry; computer science; earth sciences; education; education (K-12); elementary education; English; environmental science; finance; geography; history; international business; liberal arts and sciences/liberal studies; mathematics; medical administrative assistant; music; music teacher education; nursing; physical education; political science; practical nurse; pre-dentistry; pre-law; pre-medicine; pre-veterinary studies; psychology; science education; secondary education; secretarial science; social sciences; social work; Spanish; speech/rhetorical studies; speech/theater education; theater arts/drama.

Academic Programs *Special study options:* academic remediation for entering students, accelerated degree program, adult/continuing education programs, advanced placement credit, cooperative education, distance learning, double majors, external degree program, independent study, internships, part-time degree program, services for LD students, student-designed majors, study abroad, summer session for credit.

Library Matilda Stoxen Library with 166,755 titles, 674 serial subscriptions, 4,477 audiovisual materials, an OPAC, a Web page.

Computers on Campus 201 computers available on campus for general student use. A campuswide network can be accessed from student residence rooms and from off campus. Internet access, at least one staffed computer lab available.

Student Life *Housing:* on-campus residence required through sophomore year. *Options:* coed. *Activities and Organizations:* drama/theater group, student-run newspaper, choral group, marching band, Rodeo Club, Blue Hawk Brigade, Chorale, Business Club, Navigators, national sororities. *Campus security:* late-night transport/escort service. *Student Services:* health clinic.

Athletics Member NAIA. *Intercollegiate sports:* baseball M(s), basketball M(s)/W(s), cross-country running M(s)/W(s), football M(s), golf M/W, softball W(s), track and field M(s)/W(s), volleyball W(s), wrestling M(s). *Intramural sports:* basketball M/W, football M, soccer M/W, softball W, volleyball M/W, water polo M/W.

Standardized Tests *Required:* SAT I or ACT (for admission).

Costs (2001–02) *Tuition:* state resident $2067 full-time, $86 per semester hour part-time; nonresident $5519 full-time, $230 per semester hour part-time. Full-time tuition and fees vary according to reciprocity agreements. Part-time tuition and fees vary according to reciprocity agreements. *Required fees:* $396 full-time, $17 per semester hour. *Room and board:* $3032. Room and board charges vary according to board plan. *Waivers:* minority students, senior citizens, and employees or children of employees.

Financial Aid Of all full-time matriculated undergraduates who enrolled in 2001, 1366 applied for aid, 1084 were judged to have need, 814 had their need fully met. 126 State and other part-time jobs (averaging $1030). *Average financial aid package:* $5847. *Average need-based loan:* $3044. *Average need-based gift aid:* $2266. *Average indebtedness upon graduation:* $9849.

Applying *Options:* electronic application, early admission. *Application fee:* $25. *Required:* high school transcript, minimum 2.0 GPA, medical history, proof of measles-rubella shot. *Application deadline:* rolling (freshmen), rolling (transfers). *Notification:* continuous (freshmen).

Admissions Contact Deb Dazell, Director of Student Recruitment, Dickinson State University, ND 58601. *Phone:* 701-483-2175. *Toll-free phone:* 800-279-4295. *Fax:* 701-483-2409. *E-mail:* dsu_hawks@dsu.nodak.edu.

JAMESTOWN COLLEGE
Jamestown, North Dakota

- **Independent Presbyterian** 4-year, founded 1883
- **Calendar** semesters
- **Degree** bachelor's
- **Small-town** 107-acre campus
- **Endowment** $16.8 million
- **Coed,** 1,136 undergraduate students, 93% full-time, 56% women, 44% men
- **Minimally difficult** entrance level, 99% of applicants were admitted

Undergraduates 1,058 full-time, 78 part-time. Students come from 29 states and territories, 16 other countries, 31% are from out of state, 1% African American, 0.2% Asian American or Pacific Islander, 0.9% Hispanic American, 1.0% Native American, 3% international, 4% transferred in, 70% live on campus. *Retention:* 69% of 2001 full-time freshmen returned.

Freshmen *Admission:* 1,094 applied, 1,085 admitted, 308 enrolled. *Average high school GPA:* 3.36. *Test scores:* ACT scores over 18: 90%; ACT scores over 24: 38%; ACT scores over 30: 6%.

Faculty *Total:* 72, 76% full-time, 43% with terminal degrees. *Student/faculty ratio:* 18:1.

Majors Accounting; actuarial science; art; biochemistry; biology; business administration; business economics; chemistry; communications; computer science; criminal justice studies; education (K-12); elementary education; English; history; industrial radiologic technology; management information systems/business data processing; mathematics; medical technology; music; nursing; philosophy; physical education; political science; psychology; religious studies; theater arts/drama.

Academic Programs *Special study options:* academic remediation for entering students, advanced placement credit, cooperative education, double majors, honors programs, independent study, internships, part-time degree program, services for LD students, student-designed majors, summer session for credit. *Unusual degree programs:* 3-2 engineering with North Dakota State University, University of North Dakota, South Dakota State University, Washington University in St. Louis.

Library Raugust Library with 124,678 titles, 558 serial subscriptions, 4,696 audiovisual materials, an OPAC, a Web page.

Computers on Campus 440 computers available on campus for general student use. A campuswide network can be accessed from student residence rooms and from off campus. Internet access, online (class) registration, at least one staffed computer lab available.

Student Life *Housing:* on-campus residence required through sophomore year. *Options:* coed, disabled students. *Activities and Organizations:* drama/theater group, student-run newspaper, choral group, All-Campus Christian Fellowship, Student Education Association, International Students Association, Spurs, Jimmie Janes. *Campus security:* late-night transport/escort service, controlled dormitory access. *Student Services:* personal/psychological counseling.

Athletics Member NAIA. *Intercollegiate sports:* baseball M(s), basketball M(s)/W(s), cross-country running M(s)/W(s), football M(s), golf M(s)/W(s), soccer W(s), softball W(s), track and field M(s)/W(s), volleyball W(s), wrestling M(s). *Intramural sports:* basketball M/W, bowling M/W, racquetball M/W, soccer M/W, softball M/W, volleyball M/W.

Standardized Tests *Required for some:* SAT I or ACT (for admission). *Recommended:* SAT I or ACT (for admission).

Costs (2002–03) *Comprehensive fee:* $11,900 includes full-time tuition ($8350) and room and board ($3550). Part-time tuition: $250 per credit hour. Part-time tuition and fees vary according to course load. *Room and board:* College room only: $1600. Room and board charges vary according to board plan and housing facility. *Payment plan:* installment. *Waivers:* employees or children of employees.

Financial Aid Of all full-time matriculated undergraduates who enrolled in 2001, 1052 applied for aid, 933 were judged to have need, 133 had their need fully met. 292 Federal Work-Study jobs (averaging $706). 109 State and other part-time jobs (averaging $812). In 2001, 122 non-need-based awards were made. *Average percent of need met:* 68%. *Average financial aid package:* $7457. *Average need-based loan:* $3535. *Average need-based gift aid:* $4249. *Average indebtedness upon graduation:* $17,675.

Applying *Options:* common application, electronic application, deferred entrance. *Application fee:* $20. *Required:* high school transcript. *Required for some:* letters of recommendation. *Recommended:* minimum 2.5 GPA. *Application deadline:* rolling (freshmen), rolling (transfers).

Admissions Contact Judy Erickson, Director of Admissions, Jamestown College, 6081 College Lane, Jamestown, ND 58405. *Phone:* 701-252-3467 Ext. 2548. *Toll-free phone:* 800-336-2554. *Fax:* 701-253-4318. *E-mail:* admissions@jc.edu.

MAYVILLE STATE UNIVERSITY
Mayville, North Dakota

- **State-supported** 4-year, founded 1889, part of North Dakota University System
- **Calendar** semesters
- **Degrees** associate and bachelor's
- **Rural** 60-acre campus
- **Endowment** $1.7 million
- **Coed,** 755 undergraduate students, 77% full-time, 54% women, 46% men
- **Noncompetitive** entrance level, 100% of applicants were admitted

Undergraduates 579 full-time, 176 part-time. Students come from 17 states and territories, 2 other countries, 27% are from out of state, 2% African American, 0.3% Asian American or Pacific Islander, 0.9% Hispanic American, 1% Native American, 3% international, 7% transferred in, 30% live on campus. *Retention:* 60% of 2001 full-time freshmen returned.

Freshmen *Admission:* 202 applied, 201 admitted, 144 enrolled. *Average high school GPA:* 2.96. *Test scores:* ACT scores over 18: 74%; ACT scores over 24: 17%; ACT scores over 30: 1%.

Faculty *Total:* 61, 52% full-time, 30% with terminal degrees. *Student/faculty ratio:* 15:1.

Majors Biology; biology education; business administration; business education; chemistry; chemistry education; child care provider; computer/information sciences; education; elementary education; English; English education; health education; health/physical education; health/physical education/fitness related; liberal arts and sciences/liberal studies; mathematics; mathematics education; office management; physical education; physical sciences; pre-dentistry; pre-law; pre-medicine; pre-pharmacy studies; pre-veterinary studies; science education; secretarial science; social science education; social sciences.

Academic Programs *Special study options:* academic remediation for entering students, accelerated degree program, adult/continuing education programs, advanced placement credit, cooperative education, distance learning, double majors, internships, part-time degree program, services for LD students, student-designed majors, study abroad, summer session for credit. *ROTC:* Army (c).

Library Byrnes-Quanbeck Library plus 1 other with 70,482 titles, 614 serial subscriptions, 20,549 audiovisual materials, an OPAC.

Computers on Campus A campuswide network can be accessed from student residence rooms and from off campus that provide access to laptop for each student. Internet access, online (class) registration, at least one staffed computer lab available.

Student Life *Housing:* on-campus residence required through sophomore year. *Options:* coed, men-only, women-only. *Activities and Organizations:* drama/theater group, choral group, Student Activities Council, Student Education Association, Health and Physical Education Club, Campus Crusade, Student Ambassadors. *Campus security:* controlled dormitory access. *Student Services:* health clinic, personal/psychological counseling.

Athletics Member NAIA. *Intercollegiate sports:* baseball M(s), basketball M(s)/W(s), football M(s), softball W(s), volleyball W(s). *Intramural sports:* basketball M/W, bowling M/W, football M/W, golf M/W, ice hockey M, racquetball M/W, softball M/W, tennis M/W, track and field M/W, volleyball M/W.

Standardized Tests *Required:* SAT I or ACT (for admission).

Costs (2001–02) *Tuition:* state resident $2067 full-time, $86 per credit hour part-time; nonresident $5519 full-time, $230 per credit hour part-time. Full-time tuition and fees vary according to reciprocity agreements. Part-time tuition and fees vary according to reciprocity agreements. *Required fees:* $1247 full-time, $52 per credit hour. *Room and board:* $3126; room only: $1304. Room and board charges vary according to board plan and housing facility. *Waivers:* minority students and senior citizens.

Financial Aid Of all full-time matriculated undergraduates who enrolled in 2001, 606 applied for aid, 432 were judged to have need, 232 had their need fully met. 71 Federal Work-Study jobs (averaging $1226). 224 State and other part-time jobs (averaging $874). In 2001, 71 non-need-based awards were made. *Average percent of need met:* 86%. *Average financial aid package:* $5823. *Average need-based loan:* $3368. *Average need-based gift aid:* $2328. *Average non-need based aid:* $1001. *Average indebtedness upon graduation:* $17,679.

Applying *Options:* electronic application, deferred entrance. *Application fee:* $25. *Required:* high school transcript. *Recommended:* interview. *Application deadline:* rolling (freshmen), rolling (transfers). *Notification:* 1/1 (freshmen).

Admissions Contact Brian Larson, Director of Enrollment Services, Mayville State University, 330 3rd Street, NE, Mayville, ND 58257-1299. *Phone:* 701-786-4768 Ext. 34768. *Toll-free phone:* 800-437-4104. *Fax:* 701-786-4748. *E-mail:* admit@mail.masu.nodak.edu.

MEDCENTER ONE COLLEGE OF NURSING
Bismarck, North Dakota

- **Independent** upper-level, founded 1988
- **Calendar** semesters
- **Degree** bachelor's
- **Small-town** 15-acre campus
- **Endowment** $100,000
- **Coed, primarily women,** 91 undergraduate students, 89% full-time, 91% women, 9% men
- **Moderately difficult** entrance level, 48% of applicants were admitted

Undergraduates 81 full-time, 10 part-time. Students come from 3 states and territories, 3% are from out of state, 1% Asian American or Pacific Islander, 1% Hispanic American, 1% Native American, 55% transferred in, 4% live on campus.

Freshmen *Admission:* 106 applied, 51 admitted.

Faculty *Total:* 11, 82% full-time. *Student/faculty ratio:* 9:1.

Majors Nursing.

Academic Programs *Special study options:* honors programs, independent study, internships, summer session for credit.

Library Q & R/Medcenter One Health Sciences Library plus 1 other with 26,700 titles, 312 serial subscriptions, 1,424 audiovisual materials, an OPAC, a Web page.

Computers on Campus 13 computers available on campus for general student use. Internet access available.

Student Life *Housing Options:* coed. *Activities and Organizations:* student-run newspaper, Student Body Organization, Student Nurses Association. *Campus security:* late-night transport/escort service. *Student Services:* health clinic, personal/psychological counseling, women's center.

Costs (2001–02) *One-time required fee:* $100. *Tuition:* $3258 full-time, $136 per credit part-time. Part-time tuition and fees vary according to course load. *Required fees:* $320 full-time, $5 per credit, $120 per term part-time. *Room only:* $900. Room and board charges vary according to housing facility.

Financial Aid Of all full-time matriculated undergraduates who enrolled in 2001, 64 applied for aid, 44 were judged to have need, 34 had their need fully met. 7 Federal Work-Study jobs (averaging $1005). In 2001, 7 non-need-based awards were made. *Average percent of need met:* 95%. *Average financial aid package:* $6387. *Average need-based loan:* $3167. *Average need-based gift aid:* $3966. *Average non-need based aid:* $442. *Average indebtedness upon graduation:* $9077.

Applying *Application fee:* $40. *Application deadline:* 11/7 (transfers). *Notification:* continuous (transfers).

Admissions Contact Mary Smith, Director of Student Services, Medcenter One College of Nursing, 512 North 7th Street, Bismarck, ND 58501-4494. *Phone:* 701-323-6271. *Fax:* 701-323-6967.

MINOT STATE UNIVERSITY
Minot, North Dakota

- **State-supported** comprehensive, founded 1913, part of North Dakota University System

Minot State University (continued)

- **Calendar** semesters
- **Degrees** bachelor's, master's, and post-master's certificates
- **Small-town** 103-acre campus
- **Endowment** $9.5 million
- **Coed,** 3,326 undergraduate students, 75% full-time, 62% women, 38% men
- **Minimally difficult** entrance level, 97% of applicants were admitted

Undergraduates 2,496 full-time, 830 part-time. Students come from 43 states and territories, 15 other countries, 15% are from out of state, 3% African American, 1% Asian American or Pacific Islander, 1% Hispanic American, 4% Native American, 5% international, 13% transferred in, 15% live on campus. *Retention:* 62% of 2001 full-time freshmen returned.

Freshmen *Admission:* 757 applied, 732 admitted, 520 enrolled. *Average high school GPA:* 3.15. *Test scores:* ACT scores over 18: 84%; ACT scores over 24: 29%; ACT scores over 30: 2%.

Faculty *Total:* 236, 67% full-time, 41% with terminal degrees. *Student/faculty ratio:* 15:1.

Majors Accounting; alcohol/drug abuse counseling; art; art education; biology; biology education; business administration; business education; business marketing and marketing management; chemistry; chemistry education; communication disorders; computer science; criminal justice studies; economics; education of the hearing impaired; education of the mentally handicapped; education of the speech impaired; elementary education; English; English education; finance; French; French language education; general studies; geology; German; German language education; history; history education; international business; management information systems/business data processing; mathematics; mathematics education; medical radiologic technology; medical technology; music; music teacher education; nursing; physical education; physical sciences; physics; physics education; psychology; radio/television broadcasting; science education; social science education; social sciences; social work; sociology; Spanish; Spanish language education; special education related; speech/rhetorical studies; sport/fitness administration; teacher education, specific programs related.

Academic Programs *Special study options:* academic remediation for entering students, accelerated degree program, adult/continuing education programs, advanced placement credit, cooperative education, distance learning, double majors, honors programs, independent study, internships, part-time degree program, services for LD students, student-designed majors, study abroad, summer session for credit.

Library Gordon B. Olson Library with 240,395 titles, 928 serial subscriptions, 13,172 audiovisual materials, an OPAC, a Web page.

Computers on Campus 300 computers available on campus for general student use. A campuswide network can be accessed from student residence rooms and from off campus. Internet access, online (class) registration, at least one staffed computer lab available.

Student Life *Housing Options:* coed, men-only, women-only. *Activities and Organizations:* drama/theater group, student-run newspaper, radio and television station, choral group, Student ND Education Association, Minot State Club of Physical Education, Inter-Varsity Christian Fellowship, Residence Hall Association, National Student Speech and Hearing Association. *Campus security:* controlled dormitory access, patrols by trained security personnel. *Student Services:* health clinic, personal/psychological counseling, women's center.

Athletics Member NAIA. *Intercollegiate sports:* baseball M(s), basketball M(s)/W(s), cross-country running M(s)/W(s), football M(s), golf M/W, ice hockey M(c), softball W(s), track and field M(s)/W(s), volleyball W(s). *Intramural sports:* basketball M/W, racquetball M/W, softball M/W, volleyball M/W.

Standardized Tests *Required:* SAT I or ACT (for admission).

Costs (2001–02) *Tuition:* state resident $2244 full-time, $94 per semester hour part-time; nonresident $5991 full-time, $250 per semester hour part-time. Full-time tuition and fees vary according to program and reciprocity agreements. Part-time tuition and fees vary according to course load, program, and reciprocity agreements. *Required fees:* $310 full-time, $13 per semester hour. *Room and board:* $3100; room only: $1100. Room and board charges vary according to board plan, housing facility, and student level. *Waivers:* minority students.

Financial Aid Of all full-time matriculated undergraduates who enrolled in 2001, 2459 applied for aid, 2048 were judged to have need, 2048 had their need fully met. 171 Federal Work-Study jobs (averaging $1594). In 2001, 432 non-need-based awards were made. *Average percent of need met:* 99%. *Average financial aid package:* $5411. *Average need-based loan:* $2847. *Average need-based gift aid:* $2708. *Average non-need based aid:* $2651. *Average indebtedness upon graduation:* $11,388.

Applying *Options:* electronic application, deferred entrance. *Application fee:* $35. *Required:* high school transcript, Core Curriculum. *Required for some:* minimum 2.75 GPA. *Application deadline:* rolling (freshmen), rolling (transfers). *Notification:* continuous (freshmen).

Admissions Contact Ms. Ann Hendrick, Admissions Specialist, Minot State University, 500 University Avenue West, Minot, ND 58707-0002. *Phone:* 701-858-3346. *Toll-free phone:* 800-777-0750 Ext. 3350. *Fax:* 701-839-6933. *E-mail:* askmsu@misu.nodak.edu.

NORTH DAKOTA STATE UNIVERSITY

Fargo, North Dakota

- **State-supported** university, founded 1890, part of North Dakota University System
- **Calendar** semesters
- **Degrees** bachelor's, master's, doctoral, and first professional
- **Urban** 2100-acre campus
- **Endowment** $49.5 million
- **Coed,** 9,429 undergraduate students, 90% full-time, 42% women, 58% men
- **Moderately difficult** entrance level, 66% of applicants were admitted

Undergraduates 8,478 full-time, 951 part-time. Students come from 44 states and territories, 54 other countries, 39% are from out of state, 1% African American, 1% Asian American or Pacific Islander, 0.4% Hispanic American, 1% Native American, 0.9% international, 8% transferred in, 32% live on campus. *Retention:* 71% of 2001 full-time freshmen returned.

Freshmen *Admission:* 3,353 applied, 2,221 admitted, 1,953 enrolled. *Average high school GPA:* 3.35. *Test scores:* ACT scores over 18: 94%; ACT scores over 24: 43%; ACT scores over 30: 6%.

Faculty *Total:* 595, 84% full-time, 70% with terminal degrees. *Student/faculty ratio:* 19:1.

Majors Accounting; actuarial science; aerospace engineering; agribusiness; agricultural animal husbandry/production management; agricultural economics; agricultural education; agricultural engineering; agricultural mechanization; agricultural production; agricultural sciences; agronomy/crop science; animal sciences; anthropology; architectural environmental design; architecture; art; athletic training/sports medicine; biochemistry; bioengineering; biology; biology education; biotechnology research; botany; business administration; chemistry; chemistry education; child care/development; civil engineering; clothing/apparel/textile studies; clothing/textiles; computer engineering; computer science; construction engineering; construction management; criminal justice/law enforcement administration; dietetics; earth sciences; economics; education; electrical engineering; elementary education; engineering; engineering/industrial management; engineering physics; English; English education; equestrian studies; family/consumer studies; farm/ranch management; fashion design/illustration; fashion merchandising; fish/game management; food sciences; forestry; French; French language education; genetics; geology; health/physical education; history; history education; home economics education; horticulture science; hotel and restaurant management; humanities; industrial/manufacturing engineering; interior design; international relations; landscape architecture; management information systems/business data processing; mass communications; mathematics; mathematics education; mechanical engineering; medical technology; microbiology/bacteriology; music; music teacher education; natural resources management; nursing; nutrition science; pharmacy; physical education; physics; physics education; plant breeding; plant protection; plastics engineering; political science; polymer chemistry; pre-dentistry; pre-law; pre-medicine; pre-veterinary studies; psychology; range management; recreation/leisure studies; respiratory therapy; science education; secondary education; social science education; social sciences; sociology; soil sciences; Spanish; Spanish language education; speech education; speech/rhetorical studies; theater arts/drama; veterinary technology; zoology.

Academic Programs *Special study options:* academic remediation for entering students, accelerated degree program, advanced placement credit, cooperative education, distance learning, double majors, English as a second language, honors programs, independent study, internships, off-campus study, part-time degree program, services for LD students, student-designed majors, study abroad, summer session for credit. *ROTC:* Army (b), Air Force (b).

Library North Dakota State University Library plus 3 others with 400,000 titles, 4,500 serial subscriptions, 3,200 audiovisual materials, an OPAC, a Web page.

Computers on Campus 500 computers available on campus for general student use. A campuswide network can be accessed from student residence rooms and from off campus. Internet access, at least one staffed computer lab available.

Student Life *Housing:* on-campus residence required for freshman year. *Options:* coed, men-only, women-only, disabled students. *Activities and Organizations:* drama/theater group, student-run newspaper, radio station, choral group, marching band, Saddle and Sirloin, Habitat for Humanity, Residence Hall Association, Juggling Club, national fraternities, national sororities. *Campus security:* 24-hour emergency response devices and patrols, student patrols, late-night transport/escort service, controlled dormitory access. *Student Services:* health clinic, personal/psychological counseling, legal services.

Athletics Member NCAA. All Division II. *Intercollegiate sports:* archery M(c)/W(c), baseball M(s), basketball M(s)/W(s), bowling M(c)/W(c), cross-country running M(s)/W(s), football M(s), golf M/W, ice hockey M(c), riflery M(c)/W(c), rugby M(c)/W(c), soccer M(c)/W(s), softball W(s), swimming M(c)/W(c), track and field M(s)/W(s), volleyball M(c)/W(s), wrestling M(s). *Intramural sports:* basketball M/W, football M/W, softball M/W, volleyball M/W, wrestling M.

Standardized Tests *Required:* SAT I or ACT (for admission).

Costs (2001–02) *One-time required fee:* $45. *Tuition:* state resident $2754 full-time, $115 per credit part-time; nonresident $7363 full-time, $306 per credit part-time. Full-time tuition and fees vary according to reciprocity agreements. Part-time tuition and fees vary according to course load and reciprocity agreements. *Required fees:* $518 full-time, $22 per credit. *Room and board:* $3732; room only: $1414. Room and board charges vary according to board plan and housing facility. *Payment plan:* installment. *Waivers:* minority students, children of alumni, senior citizens, and employees or children of employees.

Financial Aid Of all full-time matriculated undergraduates who enrolled in 2001, 5970 applied for aid, 4445 were judged to have need, 2628 had their need fully met. In 2001, 841 non-need-based awards were made. *Average percent of need met:* 72%. *Average financial aid package:* $4441. *Average need-based loan:* $3544. *Average need-based gift aid:* $2551. *Average non-need based aid:* $1623. *Average indebtedness upon graduation:* $20,107.

Applying *Options:* electronic application. *Application fee:* $25. *Required:* high school transcript, minimum 2.5 GPA. *Application deadlines:* 8/15 (freshmen), 8/15 (transfers). *Notification:* continuous (freshmen).

Admissions Contact Dr. Kate Haugen, Director of Admission, North Dakota State University, PO Box 5454, Fargo, ND 58105-5454. *Phone:* 701-231-8643. *Toll-free phone:* 800-488-NDSU. *Fax:* 701-231-8802. *E-mail:* ndsu.admission@ndsu.nodak.edu.

TRINITY BIBLE COLLEGE

Ellendale, North Dakota

- **Independent** 4-year, founded 1948, affiliated with Assemblies of God
- **Calendar** semesters
- **Degrees** associate and bachelor's
- **Rural** 28-acre campus
- **Endowment** $203,119
- **Coed,** 272 undergraduate students, 94% full-time, 50% women, 50% men
- **Noncompetitive** entrance level, 46% of applicants were admitted

Undergraduates 255 full-time, 17 part-time. Students come from 27 states and territories, 1 other country, 67% are from out of state, 1% African American, 2% Hispanic American, 2% Native American, 0.7% international, 3% transferred in, 56% live on campus. *Retention:* 67% of 2001 full-time freshmen returned.

Freshmen *Admission:* 202 applied, 93 admitted, 54 enrolled. *Average high school GPA:* 2.88. *Test scores:* ACT scores over 18: 69%; ACT scores over 24: 16%; ACT scores over 30: 1%.

Faculty *Total:* 35, 60% full-time, 17% with terminal degrees. *Student/faculty ratio:* 11:1.

Majors Biblical studies; business administration; elementary education; liberal arts and sciences/liberal studies; music; pastoral counseling; psychology; religious education; secretarial science; theater arts/drama; theology.

Academic Programs *Special study options:* academic remediation for entering students, accelerated degree program, advanced placement credit, distance learning, double majors, internships, part-time degree program, summer session for credit.

Library Graham Library with 67,868 titles, 227 serial subscriptions, 2,258 audiovisual materials.

Computers on Campus 40 computers available on campus for general student use. At least one staffed computer lab available.

Student Life *Housing:* on-campus residence required through junior year. *Options:* men-only, women-only. *Activities and Organizations:* drama/theater group, student-run radio station, choral group, GAP, Youth Ministry, Inner City Ministry, fine arts club, Children's Ministry. *Campus security:* 24-hour emergency response devices, student patrols, late-night transport/escort service. *Student Services:* personal/psychological counseling.

Athletics Member NCCAA. *Intercollegiate sports:* baseball M, basketball M/W, cross-country running M(c)/W(c), football M, track and field M(c)/W(c), volleyball W, wrestling M(c). *Intramural sports:* basketball M/W, football M, golf M/W, softball M/W, tennis M/W, volleyball W, weight lifting M(c)/W(c).

Standardized Tests *Required:* ACT (for admission). *Required for some:* SAT I (for admission).

Costs (2002–03) *Comprehensive fee:* $13,248 includes full-time tuition ($7080), mandatory fees ($2178), and room and board ($3990). Full-time tuition and fees vary according to course load. Part-time tuition: $295 per credit. Part-time tuition and fees vary according to course load. *Required fees:* $350 per term part-time. *Room and board:* Room and board charges vary according to gender and housing facility. *Payment plans:* installment, deferred payment. *Waivers:* employees or children of employees.

Financial Aid Of all full-time matriculated undergraduates who enrolled in 2001, 291 applied for aid, 268 were judged to have need, 29 had their need fully met. 148 Federal Work-Study jobs (averaging $1196). In 2001, 14 non-need-based awards were made. *Average percent of need met:* 69%. *Average financial aid package:* $7236. *Average need-based loan:* $3631. *Average need-based gift aid:* $2799. *Average non-need based aid:* $2541. *Financial aid deadline:* 9/1.

Applying *Options:* common application, deferred entrance. *Application fee:* $25. *Required:* essay or personal statement, high school transcript, minimum 2.0 GPA, 2 letters of recommendation, health form, evidence of Christian conversion. *Required for some:* interview. *Application deadline:* rolling (freshmen), rolling (transfers). *Notification:* continuous (freshmen).

Admissions Contact Rev. Steve Tvedt, Vice President of College Relations, Trinity Bible College, 50 South Sixth Avenue, Ellendale, ND 58436. *Phone:* 701-349-3621 Ext. 2045. *Toll-free phone:* 800-TBC-2DAY. *Fax:* 701-349-5443. *E-mail:* TBC@DAY.edu.

UNIVERSITY OF MARY

Bismarck, North Dakota

- **Independent Roman Catholic** comprehensive, founded 1959
- **Calendar** 4-4-1
- **Degrees** associate, bachelor's, and master's
- **Suburban** 107-acre campus
- **Endowment** $6.3 million
- **Coed,** 2,051 undergraduate students, 96% full-time, 61% women, 39% men
- **Moderately difficult** entrance level, 83% of applicants were admitted

Undergraduates 1,969 full-time, 82 part-time. Students come from 32 states and territories, 4 other countries, 26% are from out of state, 1% African American, 0.6% Asian American or Pacific Islander, 1% Hispanic American, 4% Native American, 0.4% international, 10% transferred in, 46% live on campus. *Retention:* 72% of 2001 full-time freshmen returned.

Freshmen *Admission:* 672 applied, 560 admitted, 370 enrolled. *Average high school GPA:* 3.40. *Test scores:* ACT scores over 18: 93%; ACT scores over 24: 34%; ACT scores over 30: 3%.

Faculty *Total:* 198, 46% full-time, 36% with terminal degrees. *Student/faculty ratio:* 16:1.

Majors Accounting; alcohol/drug abuse counseling; athletic training/sports medicine; behavioral sciences; biological/physical sciences; biology; biology education; business administration; business communications; divinity/ministry; early childhood education; education; elementary education; English; English education; exercise sciences; information sciences/systems; interdisciplinary studies; liberal arts and sciences/liberal studies; mass communications; mathematics; mathematics education; medical laboratory technician; medical technology; music; music teacher education; natural sciences; nursing; physical education; psychology; radiological science; religious studies; respiratory therapy; social science education; social sciences; social work; special education.

Academic Programs *Special study options:* academic remediation for entering students, accelerated degree program, adult/continuing education programs, advanced placement credit, cooperative education, distance learning, double majors, external degree program, independent study, internships, off-campus study, part-time degree program, services for LD students, study abroad, summer session for credit.

Library University of Mary Library with 55,000 titles, 550 serial subscriptions.

Computers on Campus Internet access, at least one staffed computer lab available.

Student Life *Housing:* on-campus residence required through sophomore year. *Options:* men-only, women-only. *Activities and Organizations:* drama/theater group, student-run newspaper, radio station, choral group, Student Senate, Student Social Workers Association, Nursing Student Organization, student newspaper. *Student Services:* health clinic, personal/psychological counseling.

Athletics Member NAIA. *Intercollegiate sports:* baseball M(s), basketball M(s)/W(s), cross-country running M(s)/W(s), football M(s), golf M(s), soccer M(s)/W(s), softball W(s), tennis M(s)/W(s), track and field M(s)/W(s), volleyball W(s), wrestling M(s). *Intramural sports:* badminton M/W, basketball M/W, bowling M/W, football M/W, golf M/W, racquetball M/W, soccer M/W, softball M/W, swimming M/W, table tennis M/W, tennis M/W, volleyball M/W, weight lifting M/W.

Standardized Tests *Required:* ACT (for admission).

University of Mary (continued)

Costs (2002–03) *Comprehensive fee:* $13,135 includes full-time tuition ($9200), mandatory fees ($200), and room and board ($3735). Full-time tuition and fees vary according to course load and program. Part-time tuition: $290 per credit hour. *Required fees:* $5 per credit hour. *Room and board:* College room only: $1735. Room and board charges vary according to board plan, housing facility, and location. *Payment plan:* installment. *Waivers:* senior citizens and employees or children of employees.

Financial Aid Of all full-time matriculated undergraduates who enrolled in 2001, 1598 applied for aid, 1408 were judged to have need, 315 had their need fully met. 305 Federal Work-Study jobs. *Average percent of need met:* 75%. *Average financial aid package:* $7447. *Average need-based loan:* $3606. *Average need-based gift aid:* $4406. *Average indebtedness upon graduation:* $15,671.

Applying *Options:* common application, electronic application, early admission, deferred entrance. *Application fee:* $15. *Required:* high school transcript, 1 letter of recommendation. *Required for some:* essay or personal statement, interview. *Application deadline:* rolling (freshmen), rolling (transfers).

Admissions Contact Dr. Dave Hebinger, Vice President for Enrollment Services, University of Mary, 7500 University Drive, Bismarck, ND 58504-9652. *Phone:* 701-255-7500 Ext. 598. *Toll-free phone:* 800-288-6279. *Fax:* 701-255-7687. *E-mail:* marauder@umary.edu.

UNIVERSITY OF NORTH DAKOTA
Grand Forks, North Dakota

- **State-supported** university, founded 1883, part of North Dakota University System
- **Calendar** semesters
- **Degrees** bachelor's, master's, doctoral, first professional, and post-master's certificates
- **Small-town** 570-acre campus
- **Endowment** $17.8 million
- **Coed,** 9,785 undergraduate students, 90% full-time, 47% women, 53% men
- **Minimally difficult** entrance level, 68% of applicants were admitted

Undergraduates 8,836 full-time, 949 part-time. Students come from 58 states and territories, 48 other countries, 42% are from out of state, 0.8% African American, 1% Asian American or Pacific Islander, 0.7% Hispanic American, 3% Native American, 3% international, 9% transferred in, 32% live on campus. *Retention:* 12% of 2001 full-time freshmen returned.

Freshmen *Admission:* 3,471 applied, 2,346 admitted, 1,995 enrolled. *Average high school GPA:* 3.34. *Test scores:* SAT verbal scores over 500: 64%; SAT math scores over 500: 79%; ACT scores over 18: 95%; SAT verbal scores over 600: 21%; SAT math scores over 600: 24%; ACT scores over 24: 44%; SAT verbal scores over 700: 2%; SAT math scores over 700: 1%; ACT scores over 30: 5%.

Faculty *Total:* 593, 79% full-time. *Student/faculty ratio:* 18:1.

Majors Accounting; aerospace engineering; aircraft pilot (professional); air traffic control; anthropology; art; athletic training/sports medicine; atmospheric sciences; aviation/airway science; aviation management; biology; business; business economics; business education; business marketing and marketing management; chemical engineering; chemistry; civil engineering; communications; computer/information sciences; criminal justice studies; cytotechnology; dietetics; early childhood education; economics; electrical engineering; elementary education; English; environmental engineering; environmental technology; finance; foreign languages/literatures; French; geography; geological engineering; geology; German; history; humanities; industrial technology; management science; marketing/distribution education; mathematics; mechanical engineering; medical technology; middle school education; music; music (general performance); music teacher education; Native American studies; nursing; occupational safety/health technology; occupational therapy; office management; philosophy; physical education; physical therapy; physics; political science; psychology; public administration; recreation/leisure studies; religious studies; Scandinavian languages; science education; social sciences; social work; sociology; Spanish; speech-language pathology/audiology; theater arts/drama; trade/industrial education.

Academic Programs *Special study options:* accelerated degree program, adult/continuing education programs, advanced placement credit, cooperative education, distance learning, double majors, honors programs, independent study, internships, off-campus study, part-time degree program, services for LD students, student-designed majors, study abroad, summer session for credit. *ROTC:* Army (b), Air Force (b).

Library Chester Fritz Library plus 2 others with 658,957 titles, 10,438 serial subscriptions, 14,306 audiovisual materials, an OPAC, a Web page.

Computers on Campus 951 computers available on campus for general student use. A campuswide network can be accessed from student residence rooms and from off campus. Internet access, at least one staffed computer lab available.

Student Life *Housing Options:* coed, men-only, women-only, disabled students. *Activities and Organizations:* drama/theater group, student-run newspaper, radio and television station, choral group, marching band, Student Government, Association of Residence Halls, Mortar Board, Indian Association, Telesis, national fraternities, national sororities. *Campus security:* 24-hour emergency response devices and patrols, student patrols, late-night transport/escort service, controlled dormitory access, emergency telephones. *Student Services:* health clinic, personal/psychological counseling, women's center, legal services.

Athletics Member NCAA. All Division II except ice hockey (Division I). *Intercollegiate sports:* baseball M(s), basketball M(s)/W(s), cross-country running M/W, football M(s), golf M/W, ice hockey M(s)/W(c), soccer W, softball W(s), swimming M/W(s), tennis W, track and field M(s)/W(s), volleyball W(s). *Intramural sports:* badminton M/W, basketball M/W, cross-country running M/W, football M, golf M/W, ice hockey M, racquetball M/W, soccer M/W, softball M/W, swimming M/W, table tennis M/W, tennis M/W, track and field M/W, volleyball M/W, weight lifting M/W.

Standardized Tests *Required:* SAT I or ACT (for admission).

Costs (2001–02) *Tuition:* state resident $3262 full-time, $162 per credit hour part-time; nonresident $7862 full-time, $354 per credit hour part-time. Part-time tuition and fees vary according to course load. *Required fees:* $508 full-time, $47 per credit hour, $254 per term part-time. *Room and board:* $3805; room only: $1505. Room and board charges vary according to board plan and housing facility. *Waivers:* senior citizens and employees or children of employees.

Financial Aid Of all full-time matriculated undergraduates who enrolled in 2001, 7143 applied for aid, 4951 were judged to have need, 2678 had their need fully met. 940 Federal Work-Study jobs (averaging $1245). In 2001, 1164 non-need-based awards were made. *Average percent of need met:* 89%. *Average financial aid package:* $7139. *Average need-based loan:* $3624. *Average need-based gift aid:* $2571. *Average indebtedness upon graduation:* $21,199.

Applying *Options:* electronic application, early admission, deferred entrance. *Application fee:* $25. *Required:* high school transcript. *Recommended:* minimum 2.5 GPA. *Application deadline:* 7/1 (freshmen), rolling (transfers). *Notification:* continuous (freshmen).

Admissions Contact Ms. Heidi Kippenhan, Assistant Director of Admissions, University of North Dakota, Box 8382, Grand Forks, ND 58202. *Phone:* 701-777-3821. *Toll-free phone:* 800-CALL UND. *Fax:* 701-777-2696. *E-mail:* enrolser@sage.und.nodak.edu.

VALLEY CITY STATE UNIVERSITY
Valley City, North Dakota

- **State-supported** 4-year, founded 1890, part of North Dakota University System
- **Calendar** semesters
- **Degree** bachelor's
- **Small-town** 55-acre campus
- **Endowment** $610,363
- **Coed,** 1,005 undergraduate students, 74% full-time, 57% women, 43% men
- **Noncompetitive** entrance level, 95% of applicants were admitted

Undergraduates 741 full-time, 264 part-time. Students come from 24 states and territories, 8 other countries, 19% are from out of state, 1% African American, 0.3% Asian American or Pacific Islander, 0.9% Hispanic American, 2% Native American, 5% international, 10% transferred in, 32% live on campus. *Retention:* 57% of 2001 full-time freshmen returned.

Freshmen *Admission:* 275 applied, 262 admitted, 160 enrolled. *Average high school GPA:* 3.11. *Test scores:* ACT scores over 18: 88%; ACT scores over 24: 24%; ACT scores over 30: 1%.

Faculty *Total:* 79, 73% full-time, 34% with terminal degrees. *Student/faculty ratio:* 15:1.

Majors Art; art education; biology; biology education; business administration; business education; chemistry; chemistry education; computer/information sciences; computer/information sciences related; education; elementary education; English; English education; health education; history; history education; human resources management; industrial arts education; mathematics; mathematics education; music; music teacher education; office management; physical education; pre-dentistry; pre-engineering; pre-law; pre-medicine; pre-pharmacy studies; pre-veterinary studies; science education; secondary education; social science education; social sciences; Spanish; Spanish language education; technical education.

Academic Programs *Special study options:* academic remediation for entering students, cooperative education, distance learning, double majors, English as a second language, internships, off-campus study, part-time degree program, services for LD students, student-designed majors, summer session for credit.

Library Allen Memorial Library with 92,362 titles, 1,937 serial subscriptions, 15,624 audiovisual materials, an OPAC, a Web page.

Computers on Campus 925 computers available on campus for general student use. A campuswide network can be accessed from student residence rooms and from off campus. Internet access, online (class) registration, at least one staffed computer lab available.

Student Life *Housing:* on-campus residence required through sophomore year. *Options:* coed, men-only, women-only. *Activities and Organizations:* drama/theater group, student-run newspaper, choral group, departmental clubs, Greek Organizations. *Campus security:* controlled dormitory access. *Student Services:* health clinic, personal/psychological counseling.

Athletics Member NAIA. *Intercollegiate sports:* baseball M(s), basketball M(s)/W(s), cross-country running M(s)/W(s), football M(s), softball W(s), track and field M(s)/W(s), volleyball W(s). *Intramural sports:* basketball M/W, bowling M/W, cross-country running M/W, football M, golf M/W, racquetball M/W, skiing (cross-country) M/W, softball M/W, track and field M/W, volleyball M/W.

Standardized Tests *Required:* SAT I or ACT (for placement).

Costs (2001–02) *Tuition:* state resident $2067 full-time, $86 per semester hour part-time; nonresident $5519 full-time, $230 per semester hour part-time. Full-time tuition and fees vary according to reciprocity agreements. Part-time tuition and fees vary according to course load and reciprocity agreements. *Required fees:* $1239 full-time, $52 per semester hour. *Room and board:* $3010; room only: $1120. Room and board charges vary according to board plan and housing facility. *Waivers:* children of alumni.

Financial Aid Of all full-time matriculated undergraduates who enrolled in 2001, 773 applied for aid, 550 were judged to have need, 328 had their need fully met. In 2001, 129 non-need-based awards were made. *Average percent of need met:* 93%. *Average financial aid package:* $6133. *Average need-based loan:* $3320. *Average need-based gift aid:* $2979. *Average non-need based aid:* $1476. *Average indebtedness upon graduation:* $16,626.

Applying *Options:* electronic application, early admission, deferred entrance. *Application fee:* $35. *Required:* high school transcript. *Application deadline:* rolling (freshmen), rolling (transfers). *Notification:* continuous (freshmen).

Admissions Contact Mr. Monte Johnson, Director of Admissions, Valley City State University, 101 College Street Southwest, Valley City, ND 58072. *Phone:* 701-845-7101 Ext. 37297. *Toll-free phone:* 800-532-8641 Ext. 37101. *Fax:* 701-845-7299. *E-mail:* enrollment_services@mail.vcsu.nodak.edu.

OHIO

ANTIOCH COLLEGE
Yellow Springs, Ohio

- **Independent** 4-year, founded 1852, part of Antioch University
- **Calendar** trimesters
- **Degree** bachelor's
- **Small-town** 100-acre campus with easy access to Dayton
- **Endowment** $14.9 million
- **Coed**
- **Moderately difficult** entrance level

Faculty *Student/faculty ratio:* 9:1.

Student Life *Campus security:* 24-hour emergency response devices and patrols, late-night transport/escort service.

Financial Aid Of all full-time matriculated undergraduates who enrolled in 2001, 381 Federal Work-Study jobs (averaging $1966). *Average percent of need met:* 92. *Average financial aid package:* $17,496. *Average non-need based aid:* $8997. *Average indebtedness upon graduation:* $13,927.

Applying *Options:* common application, early action, deferred entrance. *Application fee:* $35. *Required:* essay or personal statement, high school transcript, minimum 2.5 GPA, 2.0 letters of recommendation. *Recommended:* interview.

Admissions Contact Ms. Cathy Paige, Information Manager, Antioch College, 795 Livermore Street, Yellow Springs, OH 45387-1697. *Phone:* 937-767-6400 Ext. 6559. *Toll-free phone:* 800-543-9436. *Fax:* 937-767-6473. *E-mail:* admissions@antioch-college.edu.

ANTIOCH UNIVERSITY MCGREGOR
Yellow Springs, Ohio

- **Independent** upper-level, founded 1988, part of Antioch University
- **Calendar** quarters
- **Degrees** certificates, bachelor's, and master's
- **Small-town** 100-acre campus with easy access to Dayton
- **Coed,** 131 undergraduate students, 37% full-time, 74% women, 26% men
- **Noncompetitive** entrance level

Undergraduates 48 full-time, 83 part-time. Students come from 1 other state, 0% are from out of state, 17% African American, 31% transferred in.

Faculty *Total:* 107, 19% full-time, 61% with terminal degrees. *Student/faculty ratio:* 7:1.

Majors Business administration; humanities; human resources management; human services; individual/family development; liberal arts and sciences/liberal studies.

Academic Programs *Special study options:* accelerated degree program, adult/continuing education programs, advanced placement credit, cooperative education, distance learning, double majors, independent study, internships, part-time degree program, summer session for credit.

Library Olive Kettering Library with 285,000 titles, 1,000 serial subscriptions, a Web page.

Computers on Campus 49 computers available on campus for general student use. A campuswide network can be accessed from off campus. Internet access, at least one staffed computer lab available.

Student Life *Housing:* college housing not available. *Campus security:* 24-hour emergency response devices and patrols. *Student Services:* personal/psychological counseling.

Costs (2001–02) *Tuition:* $8100 full-time, $225 per credit part-time. *Required fees:* $225 full-time, $75 per term part-time. *Payment plan:* installment.

Financial Aid Of all full-time matriculated undergraduates who enrolled in 2001, 89 applied for aid, 89 were judged to have need. 1 Federal Work-Study jobs (averaging $1095). In 2001, 5 non-need-based awards were made. *Average percent of need met:* 45%. *Average financial aid package:* $10,500. *Average need-based loan:* $4248. *Average need-based gift aid:* $1489. *Average non-need based aid:* $10,500. *Average indebtedness upon graduation:* $18,000.

Applying *Options:* deferred entrance. *Application fee:* $45. *Application deadline:* rolling (transfers).

Admissions Contact Oscar Robinson, Enrollment Services Manager, Antioch University McGregor, Student and Alumni Services Division, Enrollment Services, 800 Livermore Street, Yellow Springs, OH 45387. *Phone:* 937-769-1823. *Toll-free phone:* 937-769-1818. *Fax:* 937-769-1805. *E-mail:* sas@mcgregor.edu.

ART ACADEMY OF CINCINNATI
Cincinnati, Ohio

- **Independent** comprehensive, founded 1887
- **Calendar** semesters
- **Degrees** associate, bachelor's, and master's
- **Urban** 184-acre campus
- **Endowment** $14.0 million
- **Coed,** 218 undergraduate students, 98% full-time, 54% women, 46% men
- **Moderately difficult** entrance level, 73% of applicants were admitted

Undergraduates 214 full-time, 4 part-time. Students come from 13 states and territories, 6 other countries, 47% are from out of state, 1% African American, 0.9% Asian American or Pacific Islander, 3% international, 14% transferred in. *Retention:* 84% of 2001 full-time freshmen returned.

Freshmen *Admission:* 164 applied, 120 admitted, 33 enrolled. *Average high school GPA:* 3.10. *Test scores:* SAT verbal scores over 500: 58%; SAT math scores over 500: 86%; ACT scores over 18: 79%; SAT verbal scores over 600: 58%; SAT math scores over 600: 57%; ACT scores over 24: 32%; SAT verbal scores over 700: 29%; SAT math scores over 700: 14%.

Faculty *Total:* 51, 33% full-time, 84% with terminal degrees. *Student/faculty ratio:* 12:1.

Majors Art; art history; drawing; fine/studio arts; graphic design/commercial art/illustration; photography; sculpture.

Academic Programs *Special study options:* academic remediation for entering students, adult/continuing education programs, advanced placement credit, double majors, independent study, internships, off-campus study, part-time degree program, services for LD students, student-designed majors, study abroad, summer session for credit.

Library Mary Schiff Library with 50,000 titles, 75 serial subscriptions.

Computers on Campus 40 computers available on campus for general student use. Internet access, at least one staffed computer lab available.

Student Life *Housing:* college housing not available. *Campus security:* 24-hour emergency response devices and patrols. *Student Services:* health clinic, personal/psychological counseling.

Art Academy of Cincinnati (continued)

Standardized Tests *Required:* SAT I or ACT (for admission).

Costs (2002–03) *Tuition:* $16,250 full-time, $680 per credit hour part-time. Part-time tuition and fees vary according to course load. *Required fees:* $300 full-time, $150 per term part-time. *Payment plan:* installment. *Waivers:* employees or children of employees.

Financial Aid Of all full-time matriculated undergraduates who enrolled in 2001, 153 applied for aid, 122 were judged to have need, 24 had their need fully met. 22 Federal Work-Study jobs. In 2001, 58 non-need-based awards were made. *Average percent of need met:* 65%. *Average financial aid package:* $8359. *Average need-based loan:* $4537. *Average need-based gift aid:* $4635. *Average indebtedness upon graduation:* $11,290.

Applying *Options:* common application, deferred entrance. *Application fee:* $25. *Required:* essay or personal statement, high school transcript, minimum 2.5 GPA, letters of recommendation, interview, portfolio. *Application deadlines:* 6/30 (freshmen), 6/30 (transfers). *Notification:* continuous (freshmen).

Admissions Contact Ms. Mary Jane Zumwalde, Director of Admissions, Art Academy of Cincinnati, 1125 Saint Gregory Street, Cincinnati, OH 45202. *Phone:* 513-562-8744. *Toll-free phone:* 800-323-5692. *Fax:* 513-562-8778. *E-mail:* admissions@artacademy.edu.

ASHLAND UNIVERSITY

Ashland, Ohio

- **Independent** comprehensive, founded 1878, affiliated with Brethren Church
- **Calendar** semesters
- **Degrees** associate, bachelor's, master's, doctoral, and first professional
- **Small-town** 98-acre campus with easy access to Cleveland
- **Endowment** $36.3 million
- **Coed,** 2,760 undergraduate students, 79% full-time, 56% women, 44% men
- **Moderately difficult** entrance level, 87% of applicants were admitted

Ashland University provides a liberal arts and science curriculum that prepares students for various professions and careers with such distinctive programs as environmental science and toxicology. AU's philosophy of "Accent on the Individual" is evident both in and out of the classroom. The 55,000-square-foot student center and a new technology center are examples of AU's commitment to the future.

Undergraduates 2,194 full-time, 566 part-time. Students come from 27 states and territories, 10 other countries, 9% are from out of state, 9% African American, 0.4% Asian American or Pacific Islander, 1% Hispanic American, 0.2% Native American, 2% international, 4% transferred in, 72% live on campus. *Retention:* 74% of 2001 full-time freshmen returned.

Freshmen *Admission:* 1,893 applied, 1,648 admitted, 497 enrolled. *Average high school GPA:* 3.22. *Test scores:* SAT verbal scores over 500: 58%; SAT math scores over 500: 57%; ACT scores over 18: 87%; SAT verbal scores over 600: 16%; SAT math scores over 600: 19%; ACT scores over 24: 38%; SAT verbal scores over 700: 1%; SAT math scores over 700: 3%; ACT scores over 30: 4%.

Faculty *Total:* 222, 97% full-time, 79% with terminal degrees. *Student/faculty ratio:* 16:1.

Majors Accounting; American studies; art; art education; athletic training/sports medicine; biology; business administration; business marketing and marketing management; chemistry; child care/development; computer science; creative writing; criminal justice/law enforcement administration; dietetics; early childhood education; economics; education; elementary education; English; environmental science; family/consumer studies; fashion merchandising; finance; fine/studio arts; French; geology; graphic design/commercial art/illustration; health education; history; home economics; home economics education; hotel and restaurant management; individual/family development; information sciences/systems; international relations; journalism; liberal arts and sciences/liberal studies; marketing research; mass communications; mathematics; middle school education; music; music teacher education; nutrition science; philosophy; physical education; physics; political science; pre-dentistry; pre-law; pre-medicine; pre-pharmacy studies; pre-theology; pre-veterinary studies; psychology; radio/television broadcasting; recreational therapy; recreation/leisure studies; religious education; religious studies; science education; secondary education; social sciences; social work; sociology; Spanish; special education; speech/rhetorical studies; theater arts/drama; toxicology.

Academic Programs *Special study options:* academic remediation for entering students, accelerated degree program, adult/continuing education programs, advanced placement credit, double majors, English as a second language, external degree program, freshman honors college, honors programs, independent study, internships, off-campus study, part-time degree program, services for LD students, study abroad, summer session for credit. *ROTC:* Air Force (c). *Unusual degree programs:* 3-2 engineering with Washington University in St. Louis, University of Detroit Mercy, University of Toledo, Akron University.

Library Ashland Library plus 2 others with 265,229 titles, 950 serial subscriptions, an OPAC, a Web page.

Computers on Campus 90 computers available on campus for general student use. A campuswide network can be accessed from student residence rooms and from off campus. At least one staffed computer lab available.

Student Life *Housing:* on-campus residence required through senior year. *Options:* coed, men-only, women-only. *Activities and Organizations:* drama/theater group, student-run newspaper, radio and television station, choral group, marching band, Campus Activity Board, Fellowship of Christian Athletes, Hope Fellowship, Intramurals, Community Care, national fraternities, national sororities. *Campus security:* 24-hour emergency response devices and patrols, student patrols, late-night transport/escort service, controlled dormitory access. *Student Services:* health clinic, personal/psychological counseling.

Athletics Member NCAA. All Division II. *Intercollegiate sports:* baseball M(s), basketball M(s)/W(s), cross-country running M(s)/W(s), football M(s), golf M(s)/W(s), soccer M(s)/W(s), softball M/W(s), swimming M(s)/W(s), tennis M/W, track and field M(s)/W(s), volleyball W(s), wrestling M(s). *Intramural sports:* badminton M/W, baseball M(c), basketball M/W, bowling M/W, cross-country running M/W, football M, golf M/W, racquetball M/W, skiing (downhill) M(c)/W(c), soccer M/W, softball M(c)/W(c), swimming M/W, table tennis M/W, tennis M/W, track and field M/W, volleyball M(c)/W(c), wrestling M.

Standardized Tests *Required:* SAT I or ACT (for admission).

Costs (2001–02) *Comprehensive fee:* $22,182 includes full-time tuition ($15,814), mandatory fees ($506), and room and board ($5862). Full-time tuition and fees vary according to class time, course load, and program. Part-time tuition: $486 per credit hour. Part-time tuition and fees vary according to class time and program. *Room and board:* College room only: $2772. Room and board charges vary according to board plan and housing facility. *Payment plan:* installment. *Waivers:* senior citizens and employees or children of employees.

Financial Aid Of all full-time matriculated undergraduates who enrolled in 2001, 1964 applied for aid, 1495 were judged to have need. 43 State and other part-time jobs (averaging $5410). In 2001, 322 non-need-based awards were made. *Average percent of need met:* 90%. *Average financial aid package:* $14,545. *Average need-based loan:* $4232. *Average need-based gift aid:* $8878. *Average non-need based aid:* $4358. *Average indebtedness upon graduation:* $18,250. *Financial aid deadline:* 3/15.

Applying *Options:* common application, electronic application, deferred entrance. *Application fee:* $25. *Required:* essay or personal statement, high school transcript, minimum 2.5 GPA. *Required for some:* letters of recommendation, interview. *Recommended:* interview. *Application deadline:* 8/30 (freshmen), rolling (transfers). *Notification:* continuous (freshmen).

Admissions Contact Carolyn O'Lenic, Admission Representative, Ashland University, 401 College Avenue, Ashland, OH 44805. *Phone:* 419-289-5943. *Toll-free phone:* 800-882-1548. *Fax:* 419-289-5999. *E-mail:* auadmsn@ashland.edu.

BALDWIN-WALLACE COLLEGE

Berea, Ohio

- **Independent Methodist** comprehensive, founded 1845
- **Calendar** semesters
- **Degrees** bachelor's and master's
- **Suburban** 92-acre campus with easy access to Cleveland
- **Endowment** $123.2 million
- **Coed,** 3,993 undergraduate students, 76% full-time, 62% women, 38% men
- **Moderately difficult** entrance level, 85% of applicants were admitted

Undergraduates 3,042 full-time, 951 part-time. Students come from 29 states and territories, 23 other countries, 9% are from out of state, 4% African American, 1% Asian American or Pacific Islander, 1% Hispanic American, 0.2% Native American, 1% international, 4% transferred in, 62% live on campus. *Retention:* 84% of 2001 full-time freshmen returned.

Freshmen *Admission:* 2,090 applied, 1,785 admitted, 701 enrolled. *Average high school GPA:* 3.50. *Test scores:* SAT verbal scores over 500: 84%; SAT math scores over 500: 83%; ACT scores over 18: 97%; SAT verbal scores over 600: 39%; SAT math scores over 600: 43%; ACT scores over 24: 50%; SAT verbal scores over 700: 6%; SAT math scores over 700: 8%; ACT scores over 30: 6%.

Faculty *Total:* 365, 44% full-time, 46% with terminal degrees. *Student/faculty ratio:* 15:1.

Majors Accounting; art; art education; art history; arts management; athletic training/sports medicine; biology; broadcast journalism; business administration; business education; business marketing and marketing management; chemistry;

computer science; criminal justice/law enforcement administration; dance; economics; education; elementary education; engineering science; English; environmental science; family/consumer studies; finance; fine/studio arts; French; geology; German; health education; history; home economics; home economics education; human services; information sciences/systems; interdisciplinary studies; international relations; mass communications; mathematics; medical technology; middle school education; music; music business management/merchandising; music history; music (piano and organ performance); music teacher education; music therapy; music (voice and choral/opera performance); neuroscience; philosophy; physical education; physical therapy; physics; political science; pre-dentistry; pre-law; pre-medicine; pre-veterinary studies; psychology; religious studies; science education; secondary education; social work; sociology; Spanish; special education; speech-language pathology/audiology; sport/fitness administration; stringed instruments; theater arts/drama; wind/percussion instruments.

Academic Programs *Special study options:* academic remediation for entering students, accelerated degree program, adult/continuing education programs, advanced placement credit, distance learning, double majors, English as a second language, honors programs, independent study, internships, off-campus study, part-time degree program, services for LD students, student-designed majors, study abroad, summer session for credit. *ROTC:* Army (c), Air Force (c). *Unusual degree programs:* 3-2 engineering with Case Western Reserve University, Columbia University, Washington University in St. Louis; forestry with Duke University; social work with Case Western Reserve University; biology with Case Western Reserve University, ecology/environmental studies with Duke University.

Library Ritter Library plus 2 others with 200,000 titles, 12,960 serial subscriptions, an OPAC, a Web page.

Computers on Campus 386 computers available on campus for general student use. A campuswide network can be accessed from student residence rooms. Internet access, at least one staffed computer lab available.

Student Life *Housing Options:* coed, men-only, women-only, disabled students. *Activities and Organizations:* drama/theater group, student-run newspaper, radio station, choral group, campus entertainment productions, Student Senate, Commuter Activity Board, Campus Crusade, Black Student Alliance, national fraternities, national sororities. *Campus security:* 24-hour emergency response devices and patrols, student patrols, late-night transport/escort service, controlled dormitory access. *Student Services:* health clinic, personal/psychological counseling, women's center.

Athletics Member NCAA. All Division III. *Intercollegiate sports:* baseball M, basketball M/W, cross-country running M/W, football M, golf M/W, soccer M/W, softball W, swimming M/W, tennis M/W, track and field M/W, volleyball W, wrestling M. *Intramural sports:* badminton M, basketball M/W, bowling M/W, football M/W, golf M/W, ice hockey M(c), lacrosse M(c)/W(c), racquetball M(c)/W(c), rugby M(c), skiing (cross-country) M(c)/W(c), skiing (downhill) M(c)/W(c), softball M/W, swimming M/W, table tennis M, tennis M/W, track and field M/W, volleyball M(c)/W, weight lifting M(c)/W(c), wrestling M.

Standardized Tests *Required:* SAT I or ACT (for admission).

Costs (2001–02) *Comprehensive fee:* $22,010 includes full-time tuition ($16,330) and room and board ($5680). Part-time tuition: $520 per hour. Part-time tuition and fees vary according to class time. *Room and board:* College room only: $2870. *Payment plans:* installment, deferred payment. *Waivers:* children of alumni and employees or children of employees.

Financial Aid Of all full-time matriculated undergraduates who enrolled in 2001, 2474 applied for aid, 2434 were judged to have need. 1467 Federal Work-Study jobs (averaging $1690). 798 State and other part-time jobs (averaging $1439). In 2001, 298 non-need-based awards were made. *Average percent of need met:* 97%. *Average financial aid package:* $13,822. *Average need-based loan:* $4224. *Average need-based gift aid:* $7908. *Average non-need based aid:* $5858. *Average indebtedness upon graduation:* $16,125. *Financial aid deadline:* 9/1.

Applying *Options:* common application, electronic application, deferred entrance. *Application fee:* $15. *Required:* essay or personal statement, high school transcript, minimum 2.6 GPA, 1 letter of recommendation. *Recommended:* minimum 3.2 GPA, interview. *Application deadline:* rolling (freshmen), rolling (transfers). *Notification:* continuous until 5/1 (freshmen).

Admissions Contact Mrs. Julie Baker, Director of Undergraduate Admission, Baldwin-Wallace College, 275 Eastland Road, Berea, OH 44017-2088. *Phone:* 440-826-2222. *Toll-free phone:* 877-BWAPPLY. *Fax:* 440-826-3830. *E-mail:* admit@bw.edu.

BLUFFTON COLLEGE
Bluffton, Ohio

- **Independent Mennonite** comprehensive, founded 1899
- **Calendar** semesters
- **Degrees** bachelor's and master's
- **Small-town** 65-acre campus with easy access to Toledo
- **Endowment** $19.1 million
- **Coed,** 976 undergraduate students, 93% full-time, 58% women, 42% men
- **Moderately difficult** entrance level, 75% of applicants were admitted

Undergraduates 910 full-time, 66 part-time. Students come from 14 states and territories, 11 other countries, 8% are from out of state, 2% African American, 0.5% Asian American or Pacific Islander, 0.9% Hispanic American, 0.2% Native American, 2% international, 4% transferred in, 80% live on campus. *Retention:* 79% of 2001 full-time freshmen returned.

Freshmen *Admission:* 813 applied, 613 admitted, 239 enrolled. *Average high school GPA:* 3.28. *Test scores:* SAT verbal scores over 500: 68%; SAT math scores over 500: 60%; ACT scores over 18: 91%; SAT verbal scores over 600: 26%; SAT math scores over 600: 13%; ACT scores over 24: 41%; SAT verbal scores over 700: 2%; SAT math scores over 700: 2%; ACT scores over 30: 3%.

Faculty *Total:* 106, 70% full-time, 52% with terminal degrees. *Student/faculty ratio:* 14:1.

Majors Accounting; art; art education; biology; business administration; business economics; business education; chemistry; child care/development; clothing/textiles; computer science; criminal justice/law enforcement administration; developmental/child psychology; dietetics; divinity/ministry; early childhood education; economics; education; elementary education; English; exercise sciences; fashion design/illustration; fashion merchandising; graphic design/commercial art/illustration; health education; history; home economics; home economics education; humanities; liberal arts and sciences/liberal studies; mass communications; mathematics; medical technology; music; music teacher education; nutrition science; peace/conflict studies; philosophy; physical education; physics; political science; pre-law; pre-medicine; psychology; recreation/leisure studies; religious studies; retail management; secondary education; social sciences; social work; sociology; Spanish; special education; speech/rhetorical studies; sport/fitness administration.

Academic Programs *Special study options:* academic remediation for entering students, accelerated degree program, adult/continuing education programs, advanced placement credit, English as a second language, freshman honors college, honors programs, internships, off-campus study, part-time degree program, student-designed majors, study abroad, summer session for credit.

Library Musselman Library with 150,060 titles, 1,000 serial subscriptions, an OPAC.

Computers on Campus 123 computers available on campus for general student use. A campuswide network can be accessed from student residence rooms and from off campus. At least one staffed computer lab available.

Student Life *Housing:* on-campus residence required through senior year. *Options:* men-only, women-only. *Activities and Organizations:* drama/theater group, student-run newspaper, radio station, choral group, Brothers and Sisters in Christ, campus government, Student Union Board, music groups/chorale, chapel service. *Campus security:* late-night transport/escort service, controlled dormitory access, night security guards. *Student Services:* health clinic, personal/psychological counseling, women's center.

Athletics Member NCAA. All Division III. *Intercollegiate sports:* baseball M, basketball M/W, cross-country running M/W, football M, golf M, soccer M/W, softball W, tennis M/W, track and field M/W, volleyball W. *Intramural sports:* basketball M/W, bowling M/W, football M/W, golf M, racquetball M/W, softball M/W, volleyball M/W.

Standardized Tests *Required:* SAT I or ACT (for admission).

Costs (2002–03) *Comprehensive fee:* $22,066 includes full-time tuition ($16,130), mandatory fees ($300), and room and board ($5636). Part-time tuition and fees vary according to course load. *Payment plan:* installment. *Waivers:* employees or children of employees.

Financial Aid Of all full-time matriculated undergraduates who enrolled in 2001, 703 applied for aid, 628 were judged to have need, 344 had their need fully met. 413 Federal Work-Study jobs (averaging $1478). 386 State and other part-time jobs (averaging $1557). In 2001, 144 non-need-based awards were made. *Average percent of need met:* 94%. *Average financial aid package:* $14,283. *Average need-based loan:* $4360. *Average need-based gift aid:* $8958. *Average non-need based aid:* $6965. *Financial aid deadline:* 10/1.

Applying *Options:* early admission, deferred entrance. *Application fee:* $20. *Required:* high school transcript, 2 letters of recommendation, rank in upper 50% of high school class or 2.3 high school GPA. *Required for some:* essay or personal statement. *Recommended:* interview. *Application deadline:* 5/31 (freshmen), rolling (transfers).

Admissions Contact Mr. Eric Fulcomer, Director of Admissions, Associate Dean for Enrollment Management, Bluffton College, 280 West College Avenue, Bluffton, OH 45817. *Phone:* 419-358-3254. *Toll-free phone:* 800-488-3257. *Fax:* 419-358-3232. *E-mail:* admissions@bluffton.edu.

BOWLING GREEN STATE UNIVERSITY

Bowling Green, Ohio

- **State-supported** university, founded 1910
- **Calendar** semesters
- **Degrees** bachelor's, master's, doctoral, and post-master's certificates
- **Small-town** 1230-acre campus with easy access to Toledo
- **Endowment** $88.3 million
- **Coed,** 15,868 undergraduate students, 93% full-time, 56% women, 44% men
- **Moderately difficult** entrance level, 92% of applicants were admitted

BGSU offers the ultimate university experience—a small college atmosphere and a major university opportunity. A residential campus, BGSU emphasizes values education and character development, first-year student programs, leadership development, cocurricular activities, and an appreciation for diversity. Award-winning career services and a nationally ranked cooperative education program are part of BGSU's distinctive environment. Sixty-five percent of students receive financial aid.

Undergraduates 14,725 full-time, 1,143 part-time. Students come from 50 states and territories, 50 other countries, 6% are from out of state, 5% African American, 0.8% Asian American or Pacific Islander, 2% Hispanic American, 0.3% Native American, 1.0% international, 4% transferred in, 48% live on campus. *Retention:* 78% of 2001 full-time freshmen returned.

Freshmen *Admission:* 9,941 applied, 9,105 admitted, 3,624 enrolled. *Average high school GPA:* 3.14. *Test scores:* SAT verbal scores over 500: 57%; SAT math scores over 500: 56%; ACT scores over 18: 92%; SAT verbal scores over 600: 13%; SAT math scores over 600: 16%; ACT scores over 24: 22%; SAT verbal scores over 700: 2%; SAT math scores over 700: 2%; ACT scores over 30: 1%.

Faculty *Total:* 1,082, 73% full-time. *Student/faculty ratio:* 19:1.

Majors Accounting; African studies; aircraft pilot (professional); American studies; architectural environmental design; art; art education; art history; art therapy; Asian studies; athletic training/sports medicine; aviation management; biochemistry; biology; biology education; broadcast journalism; business; business administration; business education; business marketing and marketing management; ceramic arts; chemistry; chemistry education; child care/development; classics; clothing/textiles; college/postsecondary student counseling; communication disorders; communications; computer education; computer/information sciences; construction technology; counselor education/guidance; craft/folk art; creative writing; dance; design/visual communications; dietetics; drama/dance education; drawing; early childhood education; economics; education; education of the hearing impaired; education of the mentally handicapped; education of the multiple handicapped; education of the specific learning disabled; electrical/electronic engineering technology; elementary education; English; English education; environmental health; exercise sciences; family/community studies; fashion design/illustration; fashion merchandising; film studies; finance; foreign languages education; French; French language education; geography; geology; geophysics/seismology; German; gerontological services; gerontology; health education; health services administration; higher education administration; history; history education; home economics education; hospitality management; humanities; human resources management; individual/family development; industrial technology; international business; international relations; jazz; journalism; labor/personnel relations; Latin (ancient and medieval); liberal arts and sciences/liberal studies; logistics/materials management; management information systems/business data processing; marketing/distribution education; marketing research; mass communications; mathematical statistics; mathematics; mechanical design technology; medical technology; metal/jewelry arts; microbiology/bacteriology; middle school education; music; music conducting; music (general performance); music history; music (piano and organ performance); music teacher education; music theory and composition; music (voice and choral/opera performance); natural resources management; neuroscience; nursing; nutrition science; office management; operations management; painting; paleontology; philosophy; photography; physical education; physical therapy; physics; physics education; political science; pre-law; printmaking; psychology; public administration; public relations; radio/television broadcasting; reading education; recreation/leisure studies; Russian; school psychology; science education; sculpture; secondary education; social science education; social sciences; social studies education; social work; sociology; Spanish; Spanish language education; special education; speech education; speech/rhetorical studies; sport/fitness administration; technical/business writing; technical education; telecommunications; textile arts; theater arts/drama; wind/percussion instruments; women's studies.

Academic Programs *Special study options:* academic remediation for entering students, accelerated degree program, adult/continuing education programs, advanced placement credit, cooperative education, distance learning, double majors, English as a second language, honors programs, independent study, internships, off-campus study, part-time degree program, services for LD students, student-designed majors, study abroad, summer session for credit. *ROTC:* Army (b), Air Force (b).

Library Jerome Library plus 7 others with 2.3 million titles, 4,520 serial subscriptions, 672,745 audiovisual materials, an OPAC, a Web page.

Computers on Campus 1800 computers available on campus for general student use. A campuswide network can be accessed from student residence rooms and from off campus. Internet access, online (class) registration, at least one staffed computer lab available.

Student Life *Housing:* on-campus residence required through sophomore year. *Options:* coed, disabled students. *Activities and Organizations:* drama/theater group, student-run newspaper, radio station, choral group, marching band, University Activities Organization, undergraduate student government, Latino Student Union, H20 (Religious/Spiritual Group), national fraternities, national sororities. *Campus security:* 24-hour emergency response devices and patrols, student patrols, late-night transport/escort service, controlled dormitory access. *Student Services:* health clinic, personal/psychological counseling, women's center, legal services.

Athletics Member NCAA. All Division I except football (Division I-A). *Intercollegiate sports:* baseball M(s), basketball M(s)/W(s), crew M(c), cross-country running M(s)/W(s), golf M(s)/W(s), gymnastics W(s), ice hockey M(s), soccer M(s), softball W(s), swimming M(s)/W(s), tennis M(s)/W(s), track and field M(s)/W(s), volleyball M(c)/W(s), water polo M(c)/W(c), weight lifting M(c)/W(c). *Intramural sports:* basketball M/W, bowling M/W, cross-country running M/W, football M/W, golf M/W, ice hockey M/W, lacrosse M(c)/W(c), racquetball M/W, rugby M(c)/W(c), skiing (cross-country) M(c)/W(c), skiing (downhill) M(c)/W(c), soccer M/W, softball M/W, tennis M/W, track and field M/W, volleyball M/W, water polo M(c)/W(c).

Standardized Tests *Required:* SAT I or ACT (for admission).

Costs (2001–02) *Tuition:* state resident $4660 full-time, $229 per credit hour part-time; nonresident $10,912 full-time, $527 per credit hour part-time. Part-time tuition and fees vary according to course load. *Required fees:* $944 full-time, $47 per credit hour. *Room and board:* $5190; room only: $3288. Room and board charges vary according to board plan and housing facility. *Payment plan:* installment. *Waivers:* senior citizens and employees or children of employees.

Financial Aid Of all full-time matriculated undergraduates who enrolled in 2001, 9844 applied for aid, 7509 were judged to have need, 2767 had their need fully met. 953 Federal Work-Study jobs (averaging $1056). In 2001, 1838 non-need-based awards were made. *Average percent of need met:* 70%. *Average financial aid package:* $5701. *Average need-based loan:* $3582. *Average need-based gift aid:* $2659. *Average non-need based aid:* $4412. *Average indebtedness upon graduation:* $17,027.

Applying *Options:* electronic application, deferred entrance. *Application fee:* $35. *Required:* high school transcript, minimum 2.5 GPA. *Recommended:* interview. *Application deadlines:* 7/15 (freshmen), 7/15 (transfers). *Notification:* continuous (freshmen).

Admissions Contact Mr. Gary Swegan, Director of Admissions, Bowling Green State University, 110 McFall, Bowling Green, OH 43403. *Phone:* 419-372-2086. *Fax:* 419-372-6955. *E-mail:* admissions@bgnet.bgsu.edu.

BRYANT AND STRATTON COLLEGE

Cleveland, Ohio

- **Proprietary** 4-year, founded 1929, part of Bryant and Stratton Business Institute, Inc
- **Calendar** semesters
- **Degrees** associate and bachelor's
- **Urban** campus
- **Coed**
- **Minimally difficult** entrance level

Faculty *Student/faculty ratio:* 10:1.

Student Life *Campus security:* controlled dormitory access.

Standardized Tests *Recommended:* SAT I or ACT (for admission).

Financial Aid Of all full-time matriculated undergraduates who enrolled in 2001, 110 applied for aid, 108 were judged to have need, 90 had their need fully met. 8 Federal Work-Study jobs (averaging $3000). *Average percent of need met:* 89. *Average financial aid package:* $6200. *Average need-based loan:* $3065. *Average need-based gift aid:* $1500. *Average non-need based aid:* $4025. *Average indebtedness upon graduation:* $12,000.

Applying *Options:* deferred entrance. *Application fee:* $25. *Required:* essay or personal statement, high school transcript, interview.

Admissions Contact Kerry Burton, Director of Admissions, Bryant and Stratton College, 1700 East 13th Street, Cleveland, OH 44114-3203. *Phone:* 216-771-1700. *Fax:* 216-771-7787.

CAPITAL UNIVERSITY
Columbus, Ohio

- **Independent comprehensive, founded 1830, affiliated with Evangelical Lutheran Church in America**
- **Calendar semesters**
- **Degrees bachelor's, master's, and first professional**
- **Suburban 48-acre campus**
- **Endowment $38.5 million**
- **Coed, 2,671 undergraduate students, 73% full-time, 64% women, 36% men**
- **Moderately difficult entrance level, 81% of applicants were admitted**

Recognition as one of the top universities-master's in *U.S. News & World Report*, a Center for Academic Achievement to help each student succeed academically, and the construction of the new Capital Center, a 126,000-square-foot recreational, educational, and athletic complex, are just a few reasons Capital University is a leader in the Midwest.

Undergraduates 1,949 full-time, 722 part-time. Students come from 24 states and territories, 14 other countries, 8% are from out of state, 16% African American, 1% Asian American or Pacific Islander, 2% Hispanic American, 0.4% Native American, 0.5% international, 3% transferred in, 65% live on campus. *Retention:* 79% of 2001 full-time freshmen returned.

Freshmen *Admission:* 2,223 applied, 1,792 admitted, 559 enrolled. *Average high school GPA:* 3.40. *Test scores:* SAT verbal scores over 500: 72%; SAT math scores over 500: 67%; ACT scores over 18: 97%; SAT verbal scores over 600: 25%; SAT math scores over 600: 21%; ACT scores over 24: 42%; SAT verbal scores over 700: 3%; SAT math scores over 700: 2%; ACT scores over 30: 5%.

Faculty *Total:* 444, 41% full-time, 58% with terminal degrees. *Student/faculty ratio:* 11:1.

Majors Accounting; agricultural business; art; art education; art therapy; athletic training/sports medicine; biology; business administration; business marketing and marketing management; computer science; criminology; economics; education; elementary education; English; environmental science; finance; fine/studio arts; French; health education; history; interdisciplinary studies; international relations; jazz; liberal arts and sciences/liberal studies; literature; mathematics; music; music business management/merchandising; music (general performance); music (piano and organ performance); music teacher education; music (voice and choral/opera performance); nursing; philosophy; physical education; political science; pre-dentistry; pre-medicine; pre-veterinary studies; public relations; religious studies; science education; secondary education; social work; sociology; Spanish; speech/rhetorical studies; stringed instruments; wind/percussion instruments.

Academic Programs *Special study options:* adult/continuing education programs, advanced placement credit, double majors, English as a second language, freshman honors college, independent study, internships, off-campus study, part-time degree program, services for LD students, student-designed majors, study abroad, summer session for credit. *ROTC:* Army (b), Air Force (c). *Unusual degree programs:* 3-2 engineering with Washington University in St. Louis, Case Western Reserve University; occupational therapy with Washington University in St. Louis, University of Indianapolis.

Library Blackmore Library with 187,281 titles, 3,741 serial subscriptions, 6,048 audiovisual materials, an OPAC.

Computers on Campus 100 computers available on campus for general student use. A campuswide network can be accessed from student residence rooms and from off campus. Internet access, at least one staffed computer lab available.

Student Life *Housing:* on-campus residence required through sophomore year. *Options:* coed. *Activities and Organizations:* drama/theater group, student-run newspaper, radio and television station, choral group, student government, University Programming, ROTC, Chapel Choir, national fraternities, national sororities. *Campus security:* 24-hour patrols, late-night transport/escort service, controlled dormitory access. *Student Services:* health clinic, personal/psychological counseling.

Athletics Member NCAA. All Division III. *Intercollegiate sports:* baseball M, basketball M/W, cross-country running M/W, football M, golf M/W, soccer M/W, softball W, tennis M/W, track and field M/W, volleyball W, wrestling M. *Intramural sports:* basketball M/W, bowling M/W, football M/W, soccer M/W, softball M/W, table tennis M/W, tennis M/W, track and field M/W, volleyball M/W.

Standardized Tests *Required:* SAT I or ACT (for admission).

Costs (2001–02) *One-time required fee:* $175. *Comprehensive fee:* $23,630 includes full-time tuition ($17,990) and room and board ($5640). Full-time tuition and fees vary according to program. Part-time tuition: $600 per semester hour. *Room and board:* College room only: $3230. Room and board charges vary according to board plan and housing facility. *Payment plan:* installment. *Waivers:* senior citizens and employees or children of employees.

Financial Aid Of all full-time matriculated undergraduates who enrolled in 2001, 1677 applied for aid, 1533 were judged to have need, 1059 had their need fully met. In 2001, 144 non-need-based awards were made. *Average financial aid package:* $16,854. *Average need-based loan:* $6025. *Average need-based gift aid:* $10,893. *Average non-need based aid:* $7379. *Average indebtedness upon graduation:* $19,555.

Applying *Options:* common application, deferred entrance. *Application fee:* $25. *Required:* high school transcript, minimum 2.6 GPA. *Required for some:* essay or personal statement, 1 letter of recommendation, audition. *Recommended:* interview. *Application deadline:* 4/15 (freshmen), rolling (transfers).

Admissions Contact Mrs. Kimberly V. Ebbrecht, Director of Admission, Capital University, 2199 East Main Street, Columbus, OH 43209. *Phone:* 614-236-6101. *Toll-free phone:* 800-289-6289. *Fax:* 614-236-6926. *E-mail:* admissions@capital.edu.

CASE WESTERN RESERVE UNIVERSITY
Cleveland, Ohio

- **Independent** university, founded 1826
- **Calendar** semesters
- **Degrees** bachelor's, master's, doctoral, first professional, and postbachelor's certificates
- **Urban** 128-acre campus
- **Endowment** $1.4 billion
- **Coed,** 3,381 undergraduate students, 92% full-time, 39% women, 61% men
- **Very difficult** entrance level, 74% of applicants were admitted

College-bound students most often list diversity of academic programs as the most important factor in choosing a college. They understand that their academic interests are not fully tested in high school and that a high-quality college education should offer them the opportunity to explore more varied academic offerings. CWRU has long recognized the importance of academic diversity. At CWRU, regardless of their tentative interest in engineering, liberal arts, management, sciences, or nursing, students apply through a single admission process; admission is not based on academic interest. Once enrolled, students can choose from more than 60 available majors and can double major across disciplinary lines (engineering and music is a popular combination).

Undergraduates 3,117 full-time, 264 part-time. Students come from 51 states and territories, 29 other countries, 38% are from out of state, 4% African American, 14% Asian American or Pacific Islander, 2% Hispanic American, 0.2% Native American, 3% international, 2% transferred in, 78% live on campus. *Retention:* 90% of 2001 full-time freshmen returned.

Freshmen *Admission:* 4,663 applied, 3,429 admitted, 738 enrolled. *Test scores:* SAT verbal scores over 500: 98%; SAT math scores over 500: 99%; ACT scores over 18: 100%; SAT verbal scores over 600: 78%; SAT math scores over 600: 88%; ACT scores over 24: 93%; SAT verbal scores over 700: 32%; SAT math scores over 700: 47%; ACT scores over 30: 51%.

Faculty *Total:* 562, 100% full-time, 95% with terminal degrees. *Student/faculty ratio:* 8:1.

Majors Accounting; aerospace engineering; American studies; anthropology; applied mathematics; art education; art history; Asian studies; astronomy; biochemistry; bioengineering; biological/physical sciences; biology; business administration; chemical engineering; chemistry; civil engineering; classics; communication disorders; comparative literature; computer engineering; computer science; dietetics; economics; electrical engineering; engineering; engineering physics; engineering science; English; environmental science; European studies; evolutionary biology; French; geology; German; gerontology; history; history of science and technology; international relations; materials engineering; materials science; mathematical statistics; mathematics; mechanical engineering; music; music teacher education; nursing; nutrition science; philosophy; physics; plastics engineering; political science; psychology; religious studies; sociology; Spanish; systems engineering; theater arts/drama; women's studies.

Academic Programs *Special study options:* accelerated degree program, adult/continuing education programs, advanced placement credit, cooperative education, double majors, English as a second language, honors programs, independent study, internships, off-campus study, part-time degree program, services for LD students, student-designed majors, study abroad, summer session for credit. *ROTC:* Army (c), Air Force (c). *Unusual degree programs:* 3-2 astronomy, biochemistry.

Library University Library plus 6 others with 14,520 serial subscriptions, 106,307 audiovisual materials, an OPAC, a Web page.

Case Western Reserve University (continued)

Computers on Campus 100 computers available on campus for general student use. A campuswide network can be accessed from student residence rooms and from off campus that provide access to software library, CD-ROM databases. Internet access, online (class) registration, at least one staffed computer lab available.

Student Life *Housing:* on-campus residence required through senior year. *Options:* coed, women-only. *Activities and Organizations:* drama/theater group, student-run newspaper, radio station, choral group, marching band, student radio station, Habitat for Humanity, international student groups, music/dance groups, national fraternities, national sororities. *Campus security:* 24-hour emergency response devices and patrols, student patrols, late-night transport/escort service, controlled dormitory access, crime prevention programs. *Student Services:* health clinic, personal/psychological counseling, women's center, legal services.

Athletics Member NCAA. All Division III. *Intercollegiate sports:* archery M(c)/W(c), badminton M(c)/W(c), baseball M, basketball M/W, crew M(c)/W(c), cross-country running M/W, fencing M/W, football M, golf M, ice hockey M(c)/W(c), skiing (downhill) M(c)/W(c), soccer M/W, softball W, swimming M/W, tennis M/W, track and field M/W, volleyball M(c)/W, wrestling M. *Intramural sports:* badminton M/W, basketball M/W, bowling M/W, cross-country running M/W, football M/W, golf M/W, racquetball M/W, soccer M/W, softball M/W, squash M/W, swimming M/W, table tennis M/W, tennis M/W, track and field M/W, volleyball M/W, water polo M/W, weight lifting M/W, wrestling M.

Standardized Tests *Required:* SAT I or ACT (for admission). *Recommended:* SAT II: Subject Tests (for admission).

Costs (2001–02) *Comprehensive fee:* $27,418 includes full-time tuition ($21,000), mandatory fees ($168), and room and board ($6250). Part-time tuition: $875 per credit. Part-time tuition and fees vary according to course load. *Room and board:* College room only: $3850. Room and board charges vary according to board plan and housing facility. *Payment plans:* tuition prepayment, installment. *Waivers:* employees or children of employees.

Financial Aid Of all full-time matriculated undergraduates who enrolled in 2001, 1894 applied for aid, 1526 were judged to have need, 1290 had their need fully met. In 2001, 1269 non-need-based awards were made. *Average percent of need met:* 99%. *Average financial aid package:* $20,418. *Average need-based loan:* $6412. *Average need-based gift aid:* $13,580. *Average non-need based aid:* $11,172. *Average indebtedness upon graduation:* $21,418.

Applying *Options:* common application, electronic application, early admission, early decision, deferred entrance. *Required:* essay or personal statement, high school transcript, 1 letter of recommendation. *Recommended:* interview. *Application deadlines:* 2/1 (freshmen), 6/30 (transfers). *Early decision:* 1/1. *Notification:* 4/1 (freshmen), 1/15 (early decision).

Admissions Contact Mr. William T. Conley, Dean of Undergraduate Admission, Case Western Reserve University, 10900 Euclid Avenue, Cleveland, OH 44106. *Phone:* 216-368-4450. *E-mail:* admission@po.cwru.edu.

CEDARVILLE UNIVERSITY
Cedarville, Ohio

- **Independent Baptist** comprehensive, founded 1887
- **Calendar** quarters
- **Degrees** associate, bachelor's, and master's
- **Rural** 300-acre campus with easy access to Columbus and Dayton
- **Endowment** $8.2 million
- **Coed,** 2,943 undergraduate students, 96% full-time, 54% women, 46% men
- **Moderately difficult** entrance level, 73% of applicants were admitted

Undergraduates 2,831 full-time, 112 part-time. Students come from 43 states and territories, 10 other countries, 67% are from out of state, 0.6% African American, 1% Asian American or Pacific Islander, 0.7% Hispanic American, 0.2% Native American, 0.3% international, 5% transferred in, 89% live on campus. *Retention:* 86% of 2001 full-time freshmen returned.

Freshmen *Admission:* 2,103 applied, 1,544 admitted, 833 enrolled. *Average high school GPA:* 3.60. *Test scores:* SAT verbal scores over 500: 92%; SAT math scores over 500: 89%; ACT scores over 18: 100%; SAT verbal scores over 600: 48%; SAT math scores over 600: 45%; ACT scores over 24: 73%; SAT verbal scores over 700: 14%; SAT math scores over 700: 9%; ACT scores over 30: 15%.

Faculty *Total:* 221, 83% full-time, 52% with terminal degrees. *Student/faculty ratio:* 16:1.

Majors Accounting; American studies; athletic training/sports medicine; biblical studies; biological/physical sciences; biology; biology education; broadcast journalism; business administration; business marketing and marketing management; chemistry; communication equipment technology; communications; computer science; criminal justice/law enforcement administration; early childhood education; education; electrical engineering; elementary education; English; English education; environmental biology; finance; health education; health/physical education; history; information sciences/systems; international business; international relations; mathematics; mathematics education; mechanical engineering; medical technology; missionary studies; music; music (piano and organ performance); music teacher education; music (voice and choral/opera performance); nursing; pastoral counseling; philosophy; physical education; political science; pre-dentistry; pre-law; pre-medicine; pre-veterinary studies; psychology; public administration; radio/television broadcasting; religious music; science education; secondary education; secretarial science; social sciences; social studies education; social work; sociology; Spanish; Spanish language education; special education; speech education; speech/rhetorical studies; technical/business writing; theater arts/drama; theology.

Academic Programs *Special study options:* academic remediation for entering students, accelerated degree program, advanced placement credit, distance learning, double majors, honors programs, independent study, internships, off-campus study, part-time degree program, services for LD students, study abroad, summer session for credit. *ROTC:* Army (c), Air Force (c).

Library Centennial Library with 139,026 titles, 4,112 serial subscriptions, 14,717 audiovisual materials, an OPAC, a Web page.

Computers on Campus 1850 computers available on campus for general student use. A campuswide network can be accessed from student residence rooms and from off campus that provide access to software packages. At least one staffed computer lab available.

Student Life *Housing:* on-campus residence required through senior year. *Options:* men-only, women-only. *Activities and Organizations:* drama/theater group, student-run newspaper, radio station, choral group, Student Government Association, Commuter Crossroads, Mu Kappa, Chi Delta Nu, Society of Automotive Engineers. *Campus security:* 24-hour emergency response devices and patrols, student patrols, late-night transport/escort service, controlled dormitory access. *Student Services:* health clinic, personal/psychological counseling.

Athletics Member NAIA, NCCAA. *Intercollegiate sports:* baseball M(s), basketball M(s)/W(s), cross-country running M(s)/W(s), golf M(s), soccer M(s)/W(s), softball W(s), tennis M(s)/W(s), track and field M(s)/W(s), volleyball W(s). *Intramural sports:* badminton M/W, basketball M/W, bowling M/W, football M/W, golf M/W, racquetball M/W, skiing (downhill) M/W, soccer M/W, softball M/W, table tennis M/W, tennis M/W, volleyball M/W.

Standardized Tests *Required:* SAT I or ACT (for admission).

Costs (2001–02) *Comprehensive fee:* $17,553 includes full-time tuition ($12,624) and room and board ($4929). Part-time tuition: $263 per quarter hour. Part-time tuition and fees vary according to course load. *Room and board:* Room and board charges vary according to board plan. *Payment plan:* installment. *Waivers:* senior citizens and employees or children of employees.

Financial Aid Of all full-time matriculated undergraduates who enrolled in 2001, 1887 applied for aid, 1588 were judged to have need, 598 had their need fully met. 502 Federal Work-Study jobs (averaging $1035). 1056 State and other part-time jobs (averaging $960). In 2001, 531 non-need-based awards were made. *Average percent of need met:* 41%. *Average financial aid package:* $9761. *Average need-based loan:* $4543. *Average need-based gift aid:* $1339. *Average non-need based aid:* $4543. *Average indebtedness upon graduation:* $16,168.

Applying *Options:* electronic application, early admission, deferred entrance. *Application fee:* $30. *Required:* essay or personal statement, high school transcript, minimum 3.0 GPA, 2 letters of recommendation. *Required for some:* interview. *Application deadline:* rolling (freshmen), rolling (transfers). *Notification:* continuous (freshmen).

Admissions Contact Mr. Roscoe Smith, Director of Admissions, Cedarville University, 251 North Main Street, Cedarville, OH 45314-0601. *Phone:* 937-766-7700. *Toll-free phone:* 800-CEDARVILLE. *Fax:* 937-766-7575. *E-mail:* admiss@cedarville.edu.

CENTRAL STATE UNIVERSITY
Wilberforce, Ohio

- **State-supported** comprehensive, founded 1887, part of Ohio Board of Regents
- **Calendar** quarters
- **Degrees** bachelor's, master's, and postbachelor's certificates
- **Rural** 60-acre campus with easy access to Dayton
- **Endowment** $1.9 million
- **Coed,** 1,320 undergraduate students, 91% full-time, 54% women, 46% men
- **Minimally difficult** entrance level, 49% of applicants were admitted

Undergraduates 1,202 full-time, 118 part-time. Students come from 24 states and territories, 2 other countries, 23% are from out of state, 89% African

American, 0.2% Asian American or Pacific Islander, 0.2% Native American, 0.6% international, 10% transferred in, 50% live on campus. *Retention:* 58% of 2001 full-time freshmen returned.

Freshmen *Admission:* 2,567 applied, 1,270 admitted, 391 enrolled. *Average high school GPA:* 2.30. *Test scores:* ACT scores over 18: 24%; ACT scores over 24: 2%.

Faculty *Total:* 127, 61% full-time, 46% with terminal degrees. *Student/faculty ratio:* 13:1.

Majors Accounting; art; art education; biology; business administration; business marketing and marketing management; chemistry; computer/information sciences; early childhood education; economics; English; English education; finance; health education; history; hotel and restaurant management; industrial/manufacturing engineering; industrial technology; jazz; journalism and mass communication related; management information systems/business data processing; mathematics; mathematics education; middle school education; music; music teacher education; physical education; political science; psychology; radio/television broadcasting; recreation/leisure studies; science education; social studies education; social work; sociology; special education; water resources engineering.

Academic Programs *Special study options:* adult/continuing education programs, cooperative education, double majors, honors programs, independent study, internships, off-campus study, part-time degree program, services for LD students, study abroad, summer session for credit. *ROTC:* Army (b).

Library Hallie Q. Brown Memorial Library plus 1 other with 280,470 titles, 26,066 serial subscriptions, 497 audiovisual materials, an OPAC.

Computers on Campus 338 computers available on campus for general student use. Internet access, at least one staffed computer lab available.

Student Life *Housing:* on-campus residence required for freshman year. *Options:* men-only, women-only. *Activities and Organizations:* drama/theater group, student-run radio station, choral group, marching band, Student Ambassadors, student government, national fraternities, national sororities. *Campus security:* 24-hour emergency response devices and patrols, controlled dormitory access. *Student Services:* health clinic, personal/psychological counseling.

Athletics Member NAIA. *Intercollegiate sports:* basketball M(s)/W(s), golf M(s)/W(s), track and field M(s)/W(s), volleyball W(s). *Intramural sports:* basketball M/W, football M, tennis M/W.

Standardized Tests *Required:* SAT I or ACT (for admission). *Recommended:* ACT (for admission).

Costs (2001–02) *Tuition:* state resident $2064 full-time, $100 per quarter hour part-time; nonresident $6468 full-time, $234 per quarter hour part-time. Full-time tuition and fees vary according to course load. *Required fees:* $1650 full-time. *Room and board:* $5208; room only: $2676. *Payment plan:* installment. *Waivers:* senior citizens and employees or children of employees.

Applying *Options:* common application. *Application fee:* $15. *Required:* high school transcript. *Required for some:* minimum 2.0 GPA, 2.5 high school GPA for nonresidents. *Recommended:* interview. *Application deadlines:* 6/15 (freshmen), 6/15 (transfers). *Notification:* continuous (freshmen).

Admissions Contact Mr. Thandabantu Maceo, Director, Admissions, Central State University, PO Box 1004, 1400 Blush Row Road, Wilberforce, OH 45384. *Phone:* 937-376-6348. *Toll-free phone:* 800-388-CSU1. *Fax:* 937-376-6648. *E-mail:* admissions@csu.ces.edu.

CINCINNATI BIBLE COLLEGE AND SEMINARY
Cincinnati, Ohio

- **Independent** comprehensive, founded 1924, affiliated with Church of Christ
- **Calendar** semesters
- **Degrees** associate, bachelor's, and master's
- **Urban** 40-acre campus
- **Endowment** $988,063
- **Coed,** 662 undergraduate students
- **Minimally difficult** entrance level, 99% of applicants were admitted

Undergraduates Students come from 33 states and territories, 6 other countries, 33% are from out of state. *Retention:* 62% of 2001 full-time freshmen returned.

Freshmen *Admission:* 227 applied, 224 admitted. *Average high school GPA:* 2.88. *Test scores:* SAT verbal scores over 500: 92%; SAT math scores over 500: 91%; ACT scores over 18: 95%; SAT verbal scores over 600: 45%; SAT math scores over 600: 42%; ACT scores over 24: 50%; SAT verbal scores over 700: 6%; SAT math scores over 700: 4%; ACT scores over 30: 8%.

Faculty *Total:* 63, 48% full-time. *Student/faculty ratio:* 16:1.

Majors Biblical studies; divinity/ministry; early childhood education; education; journalism; music (piano and organ performance); music (voice and choral/opera performance); psychology; religious education; religious music; sign language interpretation; trade/industrial education.

Academic Programs *Special study options:* academic remediation for entering students, adult/continuing education programs, advanced placement credit, double majors, independent study, internships, off-campus study, part-time degree program, summer session for credit. *Unusual degree programs:* 3-2 business administration with Xavier University; engineering with University of Cincinnati; nursing with Thomas More College; social work with Northern Kentucky University.

Library Cincinnati Bible College Library with 93,000 titles, 656 serial subscriptions, an OPAC.

Computers on Campus 32 computers available on campus for general student use. A campuswide network can be accessed from student residence rooms and from off campus. Internet access, at least one staffed computer lab available.

Student Life *Housing:* on-campus residence required through sophomore year. *Options:* men-only, women-only. *Activities and Organizations:* drama/theater group, student-run newspaper, choral group. *Campus security:* 24-hour emergency response devices and patrols, student patrols. *Student Services:* health clinic, personal/psychological counseling.

Athletics Member NCCAA. *Intercollegiate sports:* basketball M/W, golf M, soccer M/W, volleyball W. *Intramural sports:* baseball M, basketball M, football M, tennis M/W, volleyball M/W.

Standardized Tests *Required:* SAT I or ACT (for admission).

Costs (2002–03) *Comprehensive fee:* $12,970 includes full-time tuition ($8000), mandatory fees ($230), and room and board ($4740). Part-time tuition: $250 per credit hour. *Required fees:* $10 per credit hour. *Room and board:* College room only: $2350. Room and board charges vary according to board plan. *Payment plans:* installment, deferred payment. *Waivers:* employees or children of employees.

Financial Aid Of all full-time matriculated undergraduates who enrolled in 2001, 479 applied for aid, 415 were judged to have need, 60 had their need fully met. 90 Federal Work-Study jobs (averaging $905). In 2001, 50 non-need-based awards were made. *Average percent of need met:* 65%. *Average financial aid package:* $6648. *Average need-based loan:* $3147. *Average need-based gift aid:* $3625. *Average non-need based aid:* $3715. *Average indebtedness upon graduation:* $14,589.

Applying *Options:* early admission, deferred entrance. *Application fee:* $35. *Required:* essay or personal statement, high school transcript, 3 letters of recommendation. *Recommended:* minimum 2.0 GPA, interview. *Application deadlines:* 8/10 (freshmen), 8/10 (transfers). *Notification:* continuous (freshmen).

Admissions Contact Mr. Alex Eady, Director of Undergraduate Admissions, Cincinnati Bible College and Seminary, 2700 Glenway Avenue, Cincinnati, OH 45204-1799. *Phone:* 800-949-4222 Ext. 8610. *Toll-free phone:* 800-949-4CBC. *Fax:* 513-244-8140. *E-mail:* admissions@cincybible.edu.

CINCINNATI COLLEGE OF MORTUARY SCIENCE
Cincinnati, Ohio

- **Independent** primarily 2-year, founded 1882
- **Calendar** quarters
- **Degrees** associate and bachelor's
- **Urban** 10-acre campus
- **Coed,** 131 undergraduate students, 100% full-time, 37% women, 63% men
- **Minimally difficult** entrance level, 100% of applicants were admitted

Undergraduates 131 full-time. Students come from 15 states and territories, 10% African American, 56% transferred in.

Freshmen *Admission:* 8 applied, 8 admitted, 12 enrolled.

Faculty *Total:* 12, 58% full-time. *Student/faculty ratio:* 5:1.

Majors Mortuary science.

Academic Programs *Special study options:* academic remediation for entering students, adult/continuing education programs, advanced placement credit, summer session for credit.

Library 5,000 titles, 30 serial subscriptions, a Web page.

Computers on Campus 16 computers available on campus for general student use. At least one staffed computer lab available.

Student Life *Housing:* college housing not available.

Athletics *Intramural sports:* basketball M/W, bowling M/W, football M/W, softball M/W.

Costs (2001–02) *Tuition:* $12,780 full-time, $142 per credit part-time. Full-time tuition and fees vary according to course load. *Required fees:* $25 full-time. *Waivers:* employees or children of employees.

Cincinnati College of Mortuary Science (continued)

Applying *Options:* deferred entrance. *Application fee:* $25. *Required:* high school transcript. *Recommended:* letters of recommendation. *Application deadline:* rolling (freshmen), rolling (transfers).

Admissions Contact Ms. Pat Leon, Director of Financial Aid, Cincinnati College of Mortuary Science, 645 West North Bend Road, Cincinnati, OH 45224-1462. *Phone:* 513-761-2020. *Fax:* 513-761-3333.

CIRCLEVILLE BIBLE COLLEGE
Circleville, Ohio

- **Independent** 4-year, founded 1948, affiliated with Churches of Christ in Christian Union
- **Calendar** semesters
- **Degrees** associate and bachelor's
- **Small-town** 40-acre campus with easy access to Columbus
- **Coed,** 308 undergraduate students, 90% full-time, 46% women, 54% men
- **Minimally difficult** entrance level, 61% of applicants were admitted

Undergraduates 276 full-time, 32 part-time. Students come from 11 states and territories, 26% are from out of state, 7% African American, 0.7% Asian American or Pacific Islander, 1% Hispanic American, 0.7% Native American, 7% transferred in, 55% live on campus. *Retention:* 71% of 2001 full-time freshmen returned.

Freshmen *Admission:* 135 applied, 83 admitted, 45 enrolled. *Average high school GPA:* 2.9. *Test scores:* ACT scores over 18: 70%; ACT scores over 24: 18%.

Faculty *Total:* 38, 26% full-time. *Student/faculty ratio:* 13:1.

Majors Behavioral sciences; biblical studies; business; counselor education/guidance; education; elementary education; missionary studies; pre-theology; religious education; religious music; religious studies; theology.

Academic Programs *Special study options:* academic remediation for entering students, adult/continuing education programs, advanced placement credit, double majors, honors programs, independent study, internships, off-campus study, part-time degree program, services for LD students, student-designed majors, summer session for credit.

Library Melvin Maxwell Memorial Library with 37,521 titles, 111 serial subscriptions, 1,995 audiovisual materials, an OPAC.

Computers on Campus 25 computers available on campus for general student use. A campuswide network can be accessed from student residence rooms. Internet access, at least one staffed computer lab available.

Student Life *Housing:* on-campus residence required through senior year. *Options:* men-only, women-only. *Activities and Organizations:* drama/theater group, choral group, Student Council, S.I., SHINE, prison ministries, choir. *Campus security:* security checks after midnight. *Student Services:* personal/psychological counseling, legal services.

Athletics Member NCCAA. *Intercollegiate sports:* baseball M, basketball M/W, volleyball W. *Intramural sports:* basketball M/W, soccer M/W, table tennis M/W, volleyball M/W.

Standardized Tests *Required for some:* ACT (for admission). *Recommended:* SAT I (for admission).

Costs (2001–02) *Comprehensive fee:* $12,345 includes full-time tuition ($6614), mandatory fees ($800), and room and board ($4931). Full-time tuition and fees vary according to course load, program, and reciprocity agreements. Part-time tuition: $286 per semester hour. Part-time tuition and fees vary according to course load, program, and reciprocity agreements. *Required fees:* $243 per term part-time. *Room and board:* College room only: $2075. Room and board charges vary according to board plan. *Payment plan:* installment. *Waivers:* senior citizens and employees or children of employees.

Financial Aid Of all full-time matriculated undergraduates who enrolled in 2001, 287 applied for aid, 263 were judged to have need, 47 had their need fully met. 40 Federal Work-Study jobs (averaging $2500). *Average percent of need met:* 85%. *Average financial aid package:* $8000. *Average need-based loan:* $4000. *Average need-based gift aid:* $500. *Average indebtedness upon graduation:* $15,000.

Applying *Options:* common application, electronic application, early admission. *Application fee:* $25. *Required:* essay or personal statement, high school transcript, 4 letters of recommendation, medical form. *Required for some:* interview. *Application deadline:* rolling (freshmen), rolling (transfers). *Notification:* continuous (freshmen).

Admissions Contact Rev. Matt Taylor, Director of Enrollment, Circleville Bible College, PO Box 458, Circleville, OH 43113-9487. *Phone:* 740-477-7701. *Toll-free phone:* 800-701-0222. *Fax:* 740-477-7755. *E-mail:* enroll@biblecollege.edu.

THE CLEVELAND INSTITUTE OF ART
Cleveland, Ohio

- **Independent** 5-year, founded 1882
- **Calendar** semesters
- **Degrees** bachelor's and master's
- **Urban** 488-acre campus
- **Endowment** $19.5 million
- **Coed,** 614 undergraduate students, 93% full-time, 52% women, 48% men
- **Moderately difficult** entrance level, 91% of applicants were admitted

Undergraduates 573 full-time, 41 part-time. Students come from 29 states and territories, 12 other countries, 30% are from out of state, 4% African American, 2% Asian American or Pacific Islander, 2% Hispanic American, 0.3% Native American, 3% international, 9% transferred in, 21% live on campus. *Retention:* 82% of 2001 full-time freshmen returned.

Freshmen *Admission:* 444 applied, 405 admitted, 105 enrolled. *Average high school GPA:* 3.14. *Test scores:* SAT verbal scores over 500: 79%; SAT math scores over 500: 62%; ACT scores over 18: 83%; SAT verbal scores over 600: 30%; SAT math scores over 600: 19%; ACT scores over 24: 33%; ACT scores over 30: 1%.

Faculty *Total:* 84, 54% full-time, 65% with terminal degrees. *Student/faculty ratio:* 10:1.

Majors Ceramic arts; craft/folk art; drawing; graphic design/commercial art/illustration; industrial design; interior design; medical illustrating; metal/jewelry arts; painting; photography; printmaking; sculpture; textile arts; Web page, digital/multimedia and information resources design.

Academic Programs *Special study options:* academic remediation for entering students, advanced placement credit, double majors, independent study, internships, off-campus study, part-time degree program, services for LD students, study abroad.

Library Jessica R. Gund Memorial Library with 42,000 titles, 262 serial subscriptions, 90,000 audiovisual materials.

Computers on Campus 80 computers available on campus for general student use. A campuswide network can be accessed from off campus. At least one staffed computer lab available.

Student Life *Housing:* on-campus residence required for freshman year. *Options:* coed. *Activities and Organizations:* student-run newspaper, Nature and Hiking club, Student Artist Association, Student Programming Board. *Campus security:* 24-hour emergency response devices and patrols, late-night transport/escort service, controlled dormitory access. *Student Services:* health clinic, personal/psychological counseling.

Athletics *Intramural sports:* basketball M/W, cross-country running M/W, football M/W, golf M/W, racquetball M/W, soccer M/W, softball M/W, swimming M/W, tennis M/W, track and field M/W, volleyball M/W, wrestling M.

Standardized Tests *Required:* SAT I or ACT (for admission).

Costs (2001–02) *Comprehensive fee:* $23,194 includes full-time tuition ($16,546), mandatory fees ($1052), and room and board ($5596). Part-time tuition: $615 per credit. Part-time tuition and fees vary according to course load. *Required fees:* $50 per credit. *Room and board:* College room only: $3196. Room and board charges vary according to housing facility. *Payment plan:* installment. *Waivers:* employees or children of employees.

Financial Aid Of all full-time matriculated undergraduates who enrolled in 2001, 460 applied for aid, 393 were judged to have need, 52 had their need fully met. In 2001, 152 non-need-based awards were made. *Average percent of need met:* 70%. *Average financial aid package:* $11,739. *Average need-based loan:* $4064. *Average need-based gift aid:* $6801. *Average indebtedness upon graduation:* $22,778.

Applying *Options:* electronic application, deferred entrance. *Application fee:* $30. *Required:* essay or personal statement, high school transcript, minimum 2.0 GPA, 2 letters of recommendation, portfolio. *Recommended:* interview. *Application deadline:* rolling (freshmen), rolling (transfers). *Notification:* continuous (freshmen).

Admissions Contact Office of Admissions, The Cleveland Institute of Art, 11141 East Boulevard, Cleveland, OH 44106. *Phone:* 216-421-7418. *Toll-free phone:* 800-223-4700. *Fax:* 216-754-3634. *E-mail:* admiss@gate.cia.edu.

CLEVELAND INSTITUTE OF MUSIC
Cleveland, Ohio

- **Independent** comprehensive, founded 1920
- **Calendar** semesters
- **Degrees** bachelor's, master's, and doctoral
- **Urban** 488-acre campus
- **Endowment** $30.0 million

- **Coed,** 224 undergraduate students
- **Very difficult** entrance level, 29% of applicants were admitted

Ranked as one of the foremost schools of music in the US, CIM's curriculum is based upon solid, traditional musical values while incorporating liberal arts instruction and new technologies that equip students to meet the challenges of the 21st century. Graduates are admitted routinely to leading graduate schools, are winners of major competitions, and occupy important performance and teaching positions throughout the world.

Undergraduates Students come from 37 states and territories, 13 other countries, 83% are from out of state, 0.9% African American, 12% Asian American or Pacific Islander, 3% Hispanic American, 13% international. *Retention:* 86% of 2001 full-time freshmen returned.

Freshmen *Admission:* 355 applied, 103 admitted.

Faculty *Total:* 98, 32% full-time. *Student/faculty ratio:* 7:1.

Majors Audio engineering; music; music (piano and organ performance); music teacher education; music (voice and choral/opera performance); stringed instruments; wind/percussion instruments.

Academic Programs *Special study options:* academic remediation for entering students, accelerated degree program, advanced placement credit, English as a second language, internships, off-campus study, summer session for credit. *ROTC:* Army (c), Air Force (c).

Library 47,500 titles, 110 serial subscriptions, an OPAC, a Web page.

Computers on Campus 25 computers available on campus for general student use. A campuswide network can be accessed from student residence rooms and from off campus. Internet access, at least one staffed computer lab available.

Student Life *Housing:* on-campus residence required through sophomore year. *Options:* coed. *Activities and Organizations:* choral group. *Campus security:* 24-hour emergency response devices and patrols, late-night transport/escort service, controlled dormitory access. *Student Services:* health clinic, personal/psychological counseling.

Standardized Tests *Required:* SAT I or ACT (for placement).

Costs (2001–02) *Comprehensive fee:* $26,512 includes full-time tuition ($19,550), mandatory fees ($762), and room and board ($6200). Part-time tuition: $875 per credit hour. *Required fees:* $762 per year part-time. *Room and board:* College room only: $3800.

Financial Aid Of all full-time matriculated undergraduates who enrolled in 2001, 191 applied for aid, 138 were judged to have need, 24 had their need fully met. 89 Federal Work-Study jobs (averaging $984). 28 State and other part-time jobs (averaging $920). In 2001, 86 non-need-based awards were made. *Average percent of need met:* 80%. *Average financial aid package:* $13,885. *Average need-based loan:* $5434. *Average need-based gift aid:* $9121. *Average indebtedness upon graduation:* $7333. *Financial aid deadline:* 2/15.

Applying *Options:* early admission, deferred entrance. *Application fee:* $70. *Required:* essay or personal statement, high school transcript, 2 letters of recommendation, audition. *Recommended:* interview. *Application deadlines:* 12/1 (freshmen), 12/1 (transfers). *Notification:* 4/1 (freshmen).

Admissions Contact Mr. William Fay, Director of Admission, Cleveland Institute of Music, 11021 East Boulevard, Cleveland, OH 44106-1776. *Phone:* 216-795-3107. *Fax:* 216-791-1530. *E-mail:* cimadmission@po.cwru.edu.

CLEVELAND STATE UNIVERSITY
Cleveland, Ohio

- **State-supported** university, founded 1964
- **Calendar** semesters
- **Degrees** certificates, bachelor's, master's, doctoral, and first professional
- **Urban** 70-acre campus
- **Endowment** $2.4 million
- **Coed,** 10,414 undergraduate students, 65% full-time, 55% women, 45% men
- **Noncompetitive** entrance level, 86% of applicants were admitted

Undergraduates 6,798 full-time, 3,616 part-time. Students come from 37 states and territories, 93 other countries, 0% are from out of state, 20% African American, 3% Asian American or Pacific Islander, 3% Hispanic American, 0.3% Native American, 3% international, 10% transferred in, 4% live on campus. *Retention:* 68% of 2001 full-time freshmen returned.

Freshmen *Admission:* 2,531 applied, 2,165 admitted, 1,121 enrolled. *Average high school GPA:* 2.60. *Test scores:* SAT verbal scores over 500: 40%; SAT math scores over 500: 43%; ACT scores over 18: 65%; SAT verbal scores over 600: 10%; SAT math scores over 600: 10%; ACT scores over 24: 18%; SAT math scores over 700: 1%; ACT scores over 30: 1%.

Faculty *Total:* 917, 54% full-time, 67% with terminal degrees. *Student/faculty ratio:* 17:1.

Majors Accounting; anthropology; applied art; art; art education; art history; biology; biomedical technology; biotechnology research; business economics; business marketing and marketing management; chemical engineering; chemistry; civil engineering; computer/information sciences; computer science; early childhood education; economics; education; electrical/electronic engineering technology; electrical engineering; elementary education; English; environmental science; finance; French; geology; German; history; industrial/manufacturing engineering; information sciences/systems; interdisciplinary studies; international relations; labor/personnel relations; liberal arts and sciences/liberal studies; linguistics; mass communications; mathematical statistics; mathematics; mechanical engineering; mechanical engineering technology; medieval/renaissance studies; music; nursing; occupational therapy; philosophy; physical education; physical therapy; physics; political science; pre-medicine; pre-veterinary studies; psychology; public relations; religious studies; social sciences; social work; sociology; Spanish; special education; speech-language pathology/audiology; theater arts/drama; urban studies.

Academic Programs *Special study options:* academic remediation for entering students, accelerated degree program, adult/continuing education programs, advanced placement credit, cooperative education, English as a second language, freshman honors college, internships, off-campus study, part-time degree program, student-designed majors, study abroad, summer session for credit. *ROTC:* Army (b), Air Force (c).

Library University Library plus 1 other with 470,659 titles, 6,503 serial subscriptions, 159,934 audiovisual materials, an OPAC, a Web page.

Computers on Campus 600 computers available on campus for general student use. At least one staffed computer lab available.

Student Life *Housing Options:* coed. *Activities and Organizations:* drama/theater group, student-run newspaper, radio station, choral group, honor societies, sororities, fraternities, International Student Association, Chinese Student Association, national fraternities, national sororities. *Campus security:* 24-hour emergency response devices and patrols, student patrols, late-night transport/escort service, controlled dormitory access. *Student Services:* health clinic, personal/psychological counseling, women's center.

Athletics Member NCAA. All Division I. *Intercollegiate sports:* baseball M(s), basketball M(s)/W(s), cross-country running W(s), fencing M(s)/W(s), golf M(s), soccer M(s), softball W(s), swimming M(s)/W(s), tennis W(s), track and field W(s), volleyball W(s), wrestling M(s). *Intramural sports:* badminton M/W, basketball M/W, bowling M/W, cross-country running M/W, fencing M/W, field hockey M/W, football M, golf M/W, racquetball M/W, sailing M/W, soccer M/W, swimming M/W, tennis M/W, track and field M/W, volleyball M/W, water polo M/W, weight lifting M(c)/W(c), wrestling M.

Standardized Tests *Required for some:* SAT I (for placement). *Recommended:* ACT (for placement).

Costs (2001–02) *Tuition:* state resident $4728 full-time, $197 per semester hour part-time; nonresident $9318 full-time, $388 per semester hour part-time. Full-time tuition and fees vary according to program. Part-time tuition and fees vary according to program. *Room and board:* $5550; room only: $3336. Room and board charges vary according to board plan and housing facility. *Payment plan:* installment. *Waivers:* senior citizens and employees or children of employees.

Financial Aid Of all full-time matriculated undergraduates who enrolled in 2001, 4206 applied for aid, 3665 were judged to have need, 646 had their need fully met. In 2001, 749 non-need-based awards were made. *Average percent of need met:* 68%. *Average financial aid package:* $6812. *Average need-based loan:* $3257. *Average need-based gift aid:* $4334.

Applying *Options:* early admission, deferred entrance. *Application fee:* $30. *Required:* high school transcript. *Application deadlines:* 7/15 (freshmen), 7/15 (transfers). *Notification:* continuous until 9/15 (freshmen).

Admissions Contact Office of Admissions, Cleveland State University, 1983 East 24th Street, Rhodes Tower West, Room 204, Cleveland, OH 44115. *Phone:* 216-687-3754. *Toll-free phone:* 800-CSU-OHIO. *Fax:* 216-687-9210.

COLLEGE OF MOUNT ST. JOSEPH
Cincinnati, Ohio

- **Independent Roman Catholic** comprehensive, founded 1920
- **Calendar** semesters
- **Degrees** certificates, associate, bachelor's, master's, and postbachelor's certificates
- **Suburban** 75-acre campus
- **Endowment** $18.0 million
- **Coed,** 2,071 undergraduate students, 62% full-time, 71% women, 29% men
- **Moderately difficult** entrance level, 81% of applicants were admitted

College of Mount St. Joseph (continued)

Undergraduates 1,294 full-time, 777 part-time. Students come from 14 states and territories, 18 other countries, 15% are from out of state, 8% African American, 1% Asian American or Pacific Islander, 0.5% Hispanic American, 0.2% Native American, 2% international, 7% transferred in, 18% live on campus. *Retention:* 86% of 2001 full-time freshmen returned.

Freshmen *Admission:* 675 applied, 544 admitted, 326 enrolled. *Average high school GPA:* 3.25. *Test scores:* SAT verbal scores over 500: 46%; SAT math scores over 500: 50%; ACT scores over 18: 88%; SAT verbal scores over 600: 12%; SAT math scores over 600: 11%; ACT scores over 24: 32%; SAT verbal scores over 700: 1%; SAT math scores over 700: 2%; ACT scores over 30: 2%.

Faculty *Total:* 205, 60% full-time, 42% with terminal degrees. *Student/faculty ratio:* 15:1.

Majors Accounting; art; art education; biochemistry; biology; business administration; chemistry; communications; computer science; early childhood education; English; fine/studio arts; general studies; gerontology; graphic design/commercial art/illustration; health services administration; history; humanities; information sciences/systems; interior design; liberal arts and sciences/liberal studies; mathematics; medical technology; middle school education; music; natural sciences; nursing; paralegal/legal assistant; pastoral counseling; physical education; physical therapy; psychology; recreational therapy; religious education; religious studies; social work; sociology; special education.

Academic Programs *Special study options:* academic remediation for entering students, accelerated degree program, adult/continuing education programs, advanced placement credit, cooperative education, distance learning, double majors, English as a second language, external degree program, freshman honors college, honors programs, independent study, internships, off-campus study, part-time degree program, services for LD students, study abroad, summer session for credit. *ROTC:* Army (c), Air Force (c).

Library Archbishop Alter Library with 97,637 titles, 4,960 serial subscriptions, 1,305 audiovisual materials, an OPAC, a Web page.

Computers on Campus 227 computers available on campus for general student use. A campuswide network can be accessed from student residence rooms and from off campus that provide access to computer-aided instruction. Internet access, online (class) registration, at least one staffed computer lab available.

Student Life *Housing Options:* coed. *Activities and Organizations:* drama/theater group, student-run newspaper, choral group, marching band, Student Government Association, Student Physical Therapy Association, Peer Educators, Alpha Chi Honors Program, Campus Ambassadors. *Campus security:* 24-hour emergency response devices and patrols, late-night transport/escort service. *Student Services:* health clinic, personal/psychological counseling, women's center.

Athletics Member NCAA. All Division III. *Intercollegiate sports:* baseball M, basketball M/W, cross-country running W, football M, soccer W, softball W, tennis M/W, volleyball W, wrestling M. *Intramural sports:* basketball M/W, racquetball M/W, soccer M(c), softball M/W, table tennis M/W, tennis M/W, volleyball M/W.

Standardized Tests *Required:* SAT I or ACT (for admission).

Costs (2001–02) *Comprehensive fee:* $20,560 includes full-time tuition ($14,200), mandatory fees ($840), and room and board ($5520). Full-time tuition and fees vary according to course load and program. Part-time tuition: $363 per semester hour. Part-time tuition and fees vary according to course load and location. *Required fees:* $15 per term part-time. *Room and board:* Room and board charges vary according to board plan and housing facility. *Payment plan:* installment. *Waivers:* senior citizens and employees or children of employees.

Financial Aid Of all full-time matriculated undergraduates who enrolled in 2001, 1206 applied for aid, 837 were judged to have need, 300 had their need fully met. 96 Federal Work-Study jobs (averaging $1531). 20 State and other part-time jobs (averaging $1000). In 2001, 362 non-need-based awards were made. *Average percent of need met:* 90%. *Average financial aid package:* $11,200. *Average need-based loan:* $3212. *Average need-based gift aid:* $7900. *Average non-need based aid:* $3754.

Applying *Options:* common application, electronic application. *Application fee:* $25. *Required:* high school transcript, minimum 2.25 GPA, minimum SAT score of 960 or ACT score of 19. *Required for some:* essay or personal statement, 1 letter of recommendation, interview. *Recommended:* minimum 3.0 GPA. *Application deadlines:* 8/15 (freshmen), 8/15 (transfers). *Notification:* continuous (freshmen).

Admissions Contact Ms. Peggy Minnich, Director of Admission, College of Mount St. Joseph, 5701 Delhi Road, Cincinnati, OH 45233-1672. *Phone:* 513-244-4814. *Toll-free phone:* 800-654-9314. *Fax:* 513-244-4629. *E-mail:* peggy_minnich@mail.msj.edu.

THE COLLEGE OF WOOSTER
Wooster, Ohio

- **Independent** 4-year, founded 1866, affiliated with Presbyterian Church (U.S.A.)
- **Calendar** semesters
- **Degree** bachelor's
- **Small-town** 320-acre campus with easy access to Cleveland
- **Endowment** $201.5 million
- **Coed,** 1,823 undergraduate students, 98% full-time, 53% women, 47% men
- **Moderately difficult** entrance level, 72% of applicants were admitted

Wooster encourages students to be active participants in their education. First-year seminars; small classes; internships; a required Independent Study (IS) program, which enables each student to work with a faculty mentor on a student-designed research project and which is supported by an IS library with computer-ready study carrels for each senior; and the Copeland Fund, which allows students to travel or purchase relevant research materials, are central to the curriculum. Wooster also encourages students to be active in areas such as music, theater, student government, athletics, and community service organizations.

Undergraduates 1,790 full-time, 33 part-time. Students come from 45 states and territories, 35 other countries, 43% are from out of state, 5% African American, 1% Asian American or Pacific Islander, 0.9% Hispanic American, 0.2% Native American, 7% international, 0.7% transferred in, 95% live on campus. *Retention:* 88% of 2001 full-time freshmen returned.

Freshmen *Admission:* 2,357 applied, 1,704 admitted, 532 enrolled. *Average high school GPA:* 3.50. *Test scores:* SAT verbal scores over 500: 89%; SAT math scores over 500: 86%; ACT scores over 18: 99%; SAT verbal scores over 600: 52%; SAT math scores over 600: 47%; ACT scores over 24: 66%; SAT verbal scores over 700: 13%; SAT math scores over 700: 7%; ACT scores over 30: 13%.

Faculty *Total:* 169, 80% full-time, 91% with terminal degrees. *Student/faculty ratio:* 12:1.

Majors African-American studies; African studies; archaeology; art; art history; Asian studies; biochemistry; biology; business economics; chemical and atomic/molecular physics; chemistry; classics; communications; comparative literature; computer science; economics; English; European studies; fine/studio arts; French; geology; German; Greek (modern); history; interdisciplinary studies; international relations; Latin American studies; Latin (ancient and medieval); mass communications; mathematics; music; music history; music teacher education; music therapy; music (voice and choral/opera performance); philosophy; physics; political science; pre-dentistry; pre-law; pre-medicine; pre-veterinary studies; psychology; religious studies; Russian; sociology; South Asian studies; Spanish; speech-language pathology/audiology; speech/rhetorical studies; theater arts/drama; urban studies; women's studies.

Academic Programs *Special study options:* advanced placement credit, double majors, independent study, internships, off-campus study, services for LD students, student-designed majors, study abroad, summer session for credit. *Unusual degree programs:* 3-2 engineering with Case Western Reserve University, Washington University in St. Louis, University of Michigan; forestry with Duke University; nursing with Case Western Reserve University; social work with Case Western Reserve University; dentistry with Case Western Reserve University, architecture with Washington University in St. Louis.

Library The College of Wooster Libraries plus 3 others with 448,348 titles, 5,039 serial subscriptions, 10,650 audiovisual materials, an OPAC, a Web page.

Computers on Campus 230 computers available on campus for general student use. A campuswide network can be accessed from student residence rooms and from off campus. Internet access, at least one staffed computer lab available.

Student Life *Housing:* on-campus residence required through senior year. *Options:* coed, men-only, women-only. *Activities and Organizations:* drama/theater group, student-run newspaper, radio station, choral group, marching band, Volunteer Network, Christian Fellowship, National Student Speech, Hearing, and Language Association, Gay, Lesbian, Bisexual, Transgendered and Allies, Let's Dance. *Campus security:* 24-hour emergency response devices and patrols, student patrols, late-night transport/escort service, controlled dormitory access. *Student Services:* health clinic, personal/psychological counseling, women's center.

Athletics Member NCAA. All Division III. *Intercollegiate sports:* badminton M(c)/W(c), baseball M, basketball M/W, cross-country running M/W, field hockey W, football M, golf M, ice hockey M(c), lacrosse M/W, rugby M(c)/W(c), soccer M/W, softball W, swimming M/W, tennis M/W, track and field M/W, volleyball M(c)/W. *Intramural sports:* badminton M/W, basketball M/W, bowling M/W, football M, golf M/W, soccer M/W, table tennis M/W, tennis M/W, track and field M/W, volleyball M/W.

Standardized Tests *Required:* SAT I or ACT (for admission).

Costs (2001–02) *Comprehensive fee:* $28,350 includes full-time tuition ($22,282), mandatory fees ($148), and room and board ($5920). Full-time tuition and fees vary according to course load and reciprocity agreements. Part-time tuition and fees vary according to course load. *Room and board:* College room only: $2700. *Payment plan:* installment. *Waivers:* employees or children of employees.

Financial Aid Of all full-time matriculated undergraduates who enrolled in 2001, 1266 applied for aid, 1125 were judged to have need, 897 had their need fully met. 633 Federal Work-Study jobs (averaging $1280). 109 State and other part-time jobs (averaging $1900). In 2001, 679 non-need-based awards were made. *Average percent of need met:* 100%. *Average financial aid package:* $19,821. *Average need-based loan:* $4232. *Average need-based gift aid:* $14,910. *Average non-need based aid:* $8904. *Average indebtedness upon graduation:* $13,296.

Applying *Options:* common application, electronic application, early admission, early decision, deferred entrance. *Application fee:* $35. *Required:* essay or personal statement, high school transcript, 2 letters of recommendation. *Recommended:* interview. *Application deadlines:* 2/15 (freshmen), 6/1 (transfers). *Early decision:* 12/1 (for plan 1), 1/15 (for plan 2). *Notification:* 4/1 (freshmen), 12/15 (early decision plan 1), 2/1 (early decision plan 2).

Admissions Contact Ms. Carol D. Wheatley, Director of Admissions, The College of Wooster, 1189 Beall Avenue, Wooster, OH 44691. *Phone:* 330-263-2270 Ext. 2118. *Toll-free phone:* 800-877-9905. *Fax:* 330-263-2621. *E-mail:* admissions@wooster.edu.

COLUMBUS COLLEGE OF ART AND DESIGN

Columbus, Ohio

- **Independent** 4-year, founded 1879
- **Calendar** semesters
- **Degree** bachelor's
- **Urban** 7-acre campus
- **Endowment** $5.4 million
- **Coed,** 1,737 undergraduate students, 77% full-time, 51% women, 49% men
- **Moderately difficult** entrance level, 79% of applicants were admitted

The Joseph V. Canzani Center, opened in 1993, is the focal point of the seventeen-building campus and houses a large exhibition hall, an auditorium, and a library and resource center. In addition, a student recreation center opened in 1996.

Undergraduates 1,338 full-time, 399 part-time. Students come from 30 states and territories, 30% are from out of state, 6% African American, 6% Asian American or Pacific Islander, 2% Hispanic American, 0.5% Native American, 6% transferred in, 18% live on campus. *Retention:* 85% of 2001 full-time freshmen returned.

Freshmen *Admission:* 646 applied, 511 admitted, 310 enrolled. *Average high school GPA:* 2.94. *Test scores:* SAT verbal scores over 500: 73%; ACT scores over 18: 83%; SAT verbal scores over 600: 26%; ACT scores over 24: 24%; SAT verbal scores over 700: 4%; ACT scores over 30: 2%.

Faculty *Total:* 165, 42% full-time, 38% with terminal degrees. *Student/faculty ratio:* 11:1.

Majors Advertising; applied art; art; ceramic arts; drafting; drawing; fashion design/illustration; fine/studio arts; graphic design/commercial art/illustration; industrial design; interior design; multimedia; painting; photography; printmaking; sculpture.

Academic Programs *Special study options:* academic remediation for entering students, advanced placement credit, double majors, English as a second language, independent study, internships, off-campus study, part-time degree program, services for LD students, summer session for credit.

Library Packard Library with 43,783 titles, 268 serial subscriptions, 122,868 audiovisual materials, an OPAC, a Web page.

Computers on Campus 150 computers available on campus for general student use. Internet access, at least one staffed computer lab available.

Student Life *Housing:* on-campus residence required for freshman year. *Options:* coed. *Activities and Organizations:* Student Government Interest Group, International Student Group, Student Art Critique, Anime Club, Environmental Awareness Society. *Campus security:* 24-hour emergency response devices and patrols, late-night transport/escort service, controlled dormitory access. *Student Services:* personal/psychological counseling, legal services.

Athletics *Intramural sports:* basketball M/W, soccer M/W, volleyball M/W.

Standardized Tests *Required:* SAT I or ACT (for admission).

Costs (2001–02) *Comprehensive fee:* $22,530 includes full-time tuition ($15,840), mandatory fees ($490), and room and board ($6200). Part-time tuition: $660 per credit. Part-time tuition and fees vary according to class time and course load. *Required fees:* $100 per term part-time. *Room and board:* Room and board charges vary according to board plan. *Payment plan:* installment. *Waivers:* senior citizens and employees or children of employees.

Financial Aid Available in 2001, 150 State and other part-time jobs (averaging $3100). *Average percent of need met:* 71%. *Average financial aid package:* $13,100. *Average indebtedness upon graduation:* $16,500.

Applying *Options:* deferred entrance. *Application fee:* $25. *Required:* essay or personal statement, high school transcript, minimum 2.0 GPA, portfolio. *Required for some:* letters of recommendation. *Recommended:* interview. *Application deadline:* rolling (freshmen), rolling (transfers). *Notification:* continuous (freshmen).

Admissions Contact Mr. Thomas E. Green, Director of Admissions, Columbus College of Art and Design, 107 North Ninth Street, Columbus, OH 43215-1758. *Phone:* 614-224-9101. *Fax:* 614-232-8344. *E-mail:* brooke@ccad.edu.

DAVID N. MYERS UNIVERSITY

Cleveland, Ohio

- **Independent** comprehensive, founded 1848
- **Calendar** semesters
- **Degrees** certificates, associate, bachelor's, and master's
- **Urban** 1-acre campus
- **Endowment** $631,558
- **Coed,** 1,096 undergraduate students, 52% full-time, 71% women, 29% men
- **Minimally difficult** entrance level, 65% of applicants were admitted

Undergraduates 573 full-time, 523 part-time. Students come from 1 other state, 0% are from out of state, 45% African American, 0.3% Asian American or Pacific Islander, 3% Hispanic American, 13% transferred in.

Freshmen *Admission:* 382 applied, 250 admitted, 115 enrolled. *Average high school GPA:* 2.6.

Faculty *Total:* 165, 10% full-time, 23% with terminal degrees. *Student/faculty ratio:* 12:1.

Majors Accounting; business administration; business marketing and marketing management; computer typography/composition; economics; finance; health services administration; legal administrative assistant; paralegal/legal assistant; public administration; real estate; retail management; secretarial science; social sciences.

Academic Programs *Special study options:* academic remediation for entering students, accelerated degree program, adult/continuing education programs, advanced placement credit, cooperative education, distance learning, double majors, external degree program, independent study, internships, off-campus study, part-time degree program, student-designed majors, summer session for credit.

Library Library Resource Center with 15,027 titles, 140 serial subscriptions, 377 audiovisual materials, a Web page.

Computers on Campus 70 computers available on campus for general student use. A campuswide network can be accessed from off campus. Internet access, at least one staffed computer lab available.

Student Life *Housing:* college housing not available. *Activities and Organizations:* student-run newspaper, Students in Free Enterprise, Accounting Association, Mock Trial Association, Delta Club. *Campus security:* 24-hour patrols, late-night transport/escort service. *Student Services:* personal/psychological counseling.

Standardized Tests *Required:* SAT I or ACT (for admission).

Costs (2001–02) *Tuition:* $9450 full-time, $315 per credit part-time. *Payment plans:* installment, deferred payment. *Waivers:* employees or children of employees.

Financial Aid Of all full-time matriculated undergraduates who enrolled in 2001, 31 Federal Work-Study jobs (averaging $1730).

Applying *Options:* common application, early admission, deferred entrance. *Application fee:* $25. *Required:* high school transcript. *Required for some:* essay or personal statement, interview. *Recommended:* letters of recommendation. *Application deadline:* rolling (freshmen), rolling (transfers). *Notification:* continuous (freshmen).

Admissions Contact Ms. Tiffiney Payton, Interim Director of Admissions, David N. Myers University, 112 Prospect Avenue, Cleveland, OH 44115. *Phone:* 216-523-3806 Ext. 805. *Toll-free phone:* 800-424-3953. *Fax:* 216-696-6430. *E-mail:* tpayton@dnmyers.edu.

DEFIANCE COLLEGE
Defiance, Ohio

- **Independent** comprehensive, founded 1850, affiliated with United Church of Christ
- **Calendar** semesters
- **Degrees** associate, bachelor's, and master's
- **Small-town** 150-acre campus with easy access to Toledo
- **Coed,** 906 undergraduate students, 77% full-time, 56% women, 44% men
- **Moderately difficult** entrance level, 79% of applicants were admitted

Undergraduates 698 full-time, 208 part-time. Students come from 9 states and territories, 5 other countries, 4% African American, 0.3% Asian American or Pacific Islander, 3% Hispanic American, 0.3% Native American, 0.6% international, 7% transferred in, 50% live on campus. *Retention:* 69% of 2001 full-time freshmen returned.

Freshmen *Admission:* 656 applied, 521 admitted, 207 enrolled. *Average high school GPA:* 3.13. *Test scores:* SAT verbal scores over 500: 47%; SAT math scores over 500: 53%; ACT scores over 18: 87%; SAT verbal scores over 600: 16%; SAT math scores over 600: 15%; ACT scores over 24: 29%; ACT scores over 30: 4%.

Faculty *Total:* 78, 53% full-time, 31% with terminal degrees. *Student/faculty ratio:* 14:1.

Majors Accounting; art; art education; athletic training/sports medicine; biology; business administration; business education; business marketing and marketing management; chemistry; computer science; criminal justice/law enforcement administration; ecology; education; elementary education; English; environmental science; exercise sciences; finance; health education; history; law enforcement/police science; liberal arts and sciences/liberal studies; literature; mass communications; mathematics; medical technology; natural sciences; physical education; physical sciences; pre-dentistry; pre-law; pre-medicine; preveterinary studies; psychology; public relations; religious education; religious studies; science education; secondary education; social sciences; social work; special education; speech/rhetorical studies; sport/fitness administration.

Academic Programs *Special study options:* academic remediation for entering students, adult/continuing education programs, advanced placement credit, cooperative education, distance learning, double majors, external degree program, honors programs, independent study, internships, off-campus study, part-time degree program, student-designed majors, study abroad, summer session for credit.

Library Pilgrim Library with 88,000 titles, 424 serial subscriptions, 25,000 audiovisual materials, an OPAC.

Computers on Campus 100 computers available on campus for general student use. A campuswide network can be accessed from student residence rooms and from off campus. Internet access, at least one staffed computer lab available.

Student Life *Housing:* on-campus residence required through junior year. *Options:* coed, men-only, women-only. *Activities and Organizations:* drama/theater group, student-run newspaper, choral group, Campus Activities Board, Criminal Justice Society, Greek Life, Student Senate, Marketing Association, national fraternities, national sororities. *Campus security:* late-night transport/escort service, controlled dormitory access. *Student Services:* health clinic, personal/psychological counseling.

Athletics Member NCAA. All Division III. *Intercollegiate sports:* baseball M, basketball M/W, cross-country running M/W, football M, golf M/W, soccer M/W, softball W, tennis M/W, track and field M/W, volleyball W. *Intramural sports:* baseball M, basketball M/W, bowling M/W, field hockey M/W, football M/W, racquetball M/W, soccer M/W, softball M/W, table tennis M/W, volleyball M/W, weight lifting M.

Standardized Tests *Required:* SAT I or ACT (for admission).

Costs (2001–02) *Comprehensive fee:* $20,555 includes full-time tuition ($15,580), mandatory fees ($275), and room and board ($4700). Part-time tuition: $290 per semester hour. *Required fees:* $25 per term. *Room and board:* Room and board charges vary according to board plan and housing facility. *Payment plan:* installment. *Waivers:* senior citizens and employees or children of employees.

Financial Aid Of all full-time matriculated undergraduates who enrolled in 2001, 688 applied for aid, 587 were judged to have need. 127 Federal Work-Study jobs (averaging $599). 186 State and other part-time jobs (averaging $758). In 2001, 51 non-need-based awards were made. *Average non-need based aid:* $9003. *Average indebtedness upon graduation:* $14,399.

Applying *Options:* common application, electronic application, early admission, deferred entrance. *Application fee:* $25. *Required:* high school transcript, minimum 2.0 GPA. *Required for some:* essay or personal statement, letters of recommendation, interview. *Recommended:* interview. *Application deadlines:* 8/15 (freshmen), 8/15 (transfers). *Notification:* continuous (freshmen).

Admissions Contact Mr. Brad M. Harsha, Acting Director of Admissions, Defiance College, 701 North Clinton Street, Defiance, OH 43512-1610. *Phone:* 419-783-2365. *Toll-free phone:* 800-520-4632 Ext. 2359. *Fax:* 419-783-2468. *E-mail:* admissions@defiance.edu.

DENISON UNIVERSITY
Granville, Ohio

- **Independent** 4-year, founded 1831
- **Calendar** semesters
- **Degree** bachelor's
- **Small-town** 1200-acre campus with easy access to Columbus
- **Endowment** $430.6 million
- **Coed,** 2,107 undergraduate students, 99% full-time, 57% women, 43% men
- **Moderately difficult** entrance level, 58% of applicants were admitted

Denison University attracts intellectually serious, well-rounded students from throughout the US and 38 other countries. Its Environmental Studies Center, model Honors Program, exceptional collaborative research opportunities with faculty members, state-of-the-art science facilities, and leadership training through more than 120 campus organizations provide its students with a challenging and enriching college experience.

Undergraduates 2,089 full-time, 18 part-time. Students come from 50 states and territories, 29 other countries, 54% are from out of state, 5% African American, 3% Asian American or Pacific Islander, 2% Hispanic American, 0.1% Native American, 5% international, 1% transferred in, 98% live on campus. *Retention:* 87% of 2001 full-time freshmen returned.

Freshmen *Admission:* 3,336 applied, 1,947 admitted, 553 enrolled. *Average high school GPA:* 3.5. *Test scores:* SAT verbal scores over 500: 95%; SAT math scores over 500: 96%; ACT scores over 18: 99%; SAT verbal scores over 600: 51%; SAT math scores over 600: 55%; ACT scores over 24: 82%; SAT verbal scores over 700: 12%; SAT math scores over 700: 10%; ACT scores over 30: 20%.

Faculty *Total:* 187, 96% full-time, 95% with terminal degrees. *Student/faculty ratio:* 11:1.

Majors African-American studies; anthropology; area studies; art; art history; biochemistry; biology; chemistry; classics; computer science; creative writing; dance; East Asian studies; economics; English; environmental science; film studies; fine/studio arts; French; geology; German; history; international relations; Latin American studies; mass communications; mathematics; music; organizational behavior; philosophy; physical education; physics; political science; psychology; religious studies; sociology; Spanish; speech/rhetorical studies; theater arts/drama; women's studies.

Academic Programs *Special study options:* advanced placement credit, cooperative education, double majors, honors programs, independent study, internships, off-campus study, part-time degree program, services for LD students, student-designed majors, study abroad. *ROTC:* Army (c). *Unusual degree programs:* 3-2 engineering with Case Western Reserve University, Columbia University, Rensselaer Polytechnic Institute, Washington University in St. Louis; forestry with Duke University; natural resources with University of Michigan; occupational therapy with Washington University in St. Louis; environmental management, dentistry with Case Western Reserve University; medical technology with Rochester General Hospital.

Library William Howard Doane Library with 687,933 titles, 1,212 serial subscriptions, 23,083 audiovisual materials, an OPAC, a Web page.

Computers on Campus 410 computers available on campus for general student use. A campuswide network can be accessed from student residence rooms and from off campus. Internet access, at least one staffed computer lab available.

Student Life *Housing:* on-campus residence required through senior year. *Options:* coed, men-only, women-only. *Activities and Organizations:* drama/theater group, student-run newspaper, radio and television station, choral group, Community Association, Black Student Union, International Student Association, Student Activities Committee, national fraternities, national sororities. *Campus security:* 24-hour emergency response devices and patrols, student patrols, late-night transport/escort service, controlled dormitory access, security lighting, escort service. *Student Services:* health clinic, personal/psychological counseling, women's center.

Athletics Member NCAA. All Division III. *Intercollegiate sports:* baseball M, basketball M/W, crew M(c), cross-country running M/W, equestrian sports M(c)/W(c), field hockey W, football M, golf M, ice hockey M(c), lacrosse M/W, riflery M(c)/W(c), rugby M(c)/W(c), sailing M(c)/W(c), skiing (downhill) M(c)/W(c), soccer M/W, softball W, squash M(c)/W(c), swimming M/W, tennis M/W, track and field M/W, volleyball W. *Intramural sports:* badminton M(c)/W(c), basketball M/W, crew W(c), fencing M(c)/W(c), football M/W, golf M/W, lacrosse M(c), racquetball M/W, soccer M/W, softball M/W, squash M/W, table tennis M/W, tennis M/W, volleyball M(c)/W, water polo M/W, weight lifting M/W.

Standardized Tests *Required:* SAT I or ACT (for admission). *Recommended:* SAT II: Subject Tests (for admission).

Costs (2001–02) *Comprehensive fee:* $29,640 includes full-time tuition ($22,550), mandatory fees ($540), and room and board ($6550). Part-time tuition: $700 per credit hour. Part-time tuition and fees vary according to course load. *Room and board:* College room only: $3580. Room and board charges vary according to housing facility. *Payment plans:* tuition prepayment, installment. *Waivers:* employees or children of employees.

Financial Aid Of all full-time matriculated undergraduates who enrolled in 2001, 1151 applied for aid, 971 were judged to have need, 663 had their need fully met. 494 Federal Work-Study jobs (averaging $1806). In 2001, 1083 non-need-based awards were made. *Average percent of need met:* 98%. *Average financial aid package:* $20,593. *Average need-based loan:* $3954. *Average need-based gift aid:* $15,272. *Average non-need based aid:* $9258. *Average indebtedness upon graduation:* $13,250.

Applying *Options:* common application, early admission, early decision, deferred entrance. *Application fee:* $40. *Required:* essay or personal statement, high school transcript, 2 letters of recommendation. *Recommended:* interview. *Application deadlines:* 2/1 (freshmen), 5/1 (transfers). *Early decision:* 11/15 (for plan 1), 1/15 (for plan 2). *Notification:* 4/1 (freshmen), 12/1 (early decision plan 1), 2/1 (early decision plan 2).

Admissions Contact Ms. Mollie Rodenbeck, Campus Visit Coordinator, Denison University, Box H, Granville, OH 43023. *Phone:* 740-587-6276. *Toll-free phone:* 800-DENISON. *E-mail:* admissions@denison.edu.

DeVry University
Columbus, Ohio

- **Proprietary** 4-year, founded 1952, part of DeVry, Inc
- **Calendar** semesters
- **Degrees** diplomas, associate, and bachelor's
- **Urban** 21-acre campus
- **Coed,** 3,793 undergraduate students, 76% full-time, 24% women, 76% men
- **Minimally difficult** entrance level, 88% of applicants were admitted

Undergraduates 2,892 full-time, 901 part-time. Students come from 32 states and territories, 4 other countries, 17% are from out of state, 19% African American, 3% Asian American or Pacific Islander, 1% Hispanic American, 0.2% Native American, 0.8% international, 12% transferred in. *Retention:* 45% of 2001 full-time freshmen returned.

Freshmen *Admission:* 1,712 applied, 1,503 admitted, 1,116 enrolled.

Faculty *Total:* 157, 53% full-time. *Student/faculty ratio:* 24:1.

Majors Business administration/management related; business systems analysis/design; computer engineering technology; electrical/electronic engineering technology; information sciences/systems; operations management.

Academic Programs *Special study options:* academic remediation for entering students, accelerated degree program, adult/continuing education programs, advanced placement credit, cooperative education, part-time degree program, services for LD students, summer session for credit. *ROTC:* Army (c).

Library Learning Resource Center with 19,066 titles, 73 serial subscriptions, 1,603 audiovisual materials.

Computers on Campus 321 computers available on campus for general student use. A campuswide network can be accessed from off campus. At least one staffed computer lab available.

Student Life *Housing:* college housing not available. *Activities and Organizations:* student-run newspaper, Institute for Electrical and Electronic Engineers, American Production and Inventory Control Society, Association of Information Technology Professionals, Tau Alpha Pi, Asian American Association or Prism. *Campus security:* late-night transport/escort service, security at evening activities.

Athletics *Intramural sports:* basketball M/W, football M/W, soccer M, volleyball M/W.

Standardized Tests *Recommended:* SAT I or ACT (for admission).

Costs (2001–02) *Tuition:* $8740 full-time, $310 per credit hour part-time. Full-time tuition and fees vary according to course load. Part-time tuition and fees vary according to course load. *Required fees:* $65 full-time. *Payment plans:* installment, deferred payment. *Waivers:* employees or children of employees.

Financial Aid Of all full-time matriculated undergraduates who enrolled in 2001, 3914 applied for aid, 3694 were judged to have need, 171 had their need fully met. In 2001, 310 non-need-based awards were made. *Average percent of need met:* 47%. *Average financial aid package:* $7947. *Average need-based loan:* $5439. *Average need-based gift aid:* $3696.

Applying *Options:* electronic application, deferred entrance. *Application fee:* $50. *Required:* high school transcript, interview. *Application deadline:* rolling (freshmen), rolling (transfers). *Notification:* continuous (freshmen).

Admissions Contact Ms. Shelia Brown, New Student Coordinator, DeVry University, 1350 Alum Creek Drive, Columbus, OH 43209-2705. *Phone:* 614-253-1850. *Toll-free phone:* 800-426-3916 (in-state); 800-426-3090 (out-of-state). *E-mail:* admissions@devrycol5.edu.

Franciscan University of Steubenville
Steubenville, Ohio

- **Independent Roman Catholic** comprehensive, founded 1946
- **Calendar** semesters
- **Degrees** associate, bachelor's, and master's
- **Suburban** 116-acre campus with easy access to Pittsburgh
- **Endowment** $16.2 million
- **Coed,** 1,733 undergraduate students, 92% full-time, 59% women, 41% men
- **Moderately difficult** entrance level, 90% of applicants were admitted

Ever mindful of the spirit of St. Francis of Assisi, Franciscan University of Steubenville takes to heart the divine directive to "rebuild my Church" by integrating strong academics with lively faith environment. This "faith and reason" combination has been hailed by graduates, Church leaders, and educators for providing an invigorating, Catholic, liberal arts experience.

Undergraduates 1,586 full-time, 147 part-time. Students come from 52 states and territories, 24 other countries, 78% are from out of state, 1% African American, 1% Asian American or Pacific Islander, 4% Hispanic American, 0.2% Native American, 3% international, 10% transferred in, 62% live on campus. *Retention:* 82% of 2001 full-time freshmen returned.

Freshmen *Admission:* 777 applied, 697 admitted, 325 enrolled. *Average high school GPA:* 3.41. *Test scores:* SAT verbal scores over 500: 82%; SAT math scores over 500: 78%; ACT scores over 18: 95%; SAT verbal scores over 600: 39%; SAT math scores over 600: 27%; ACT scores over 24: 49%; SAT verbal scores over 700: 6%; SAT math scores over 700: 3%; ACT scores over 30: 8%.

Faculty *Total:* 169, 60% full-time, 43% with terminal degrees. *Student/faculty ratio:* 17:1.

Majors Accounting; anthropology; biology; business administration; chemistry; child care/development; classics; communications; computer/information sciences; computer science; economics; elementary education; engineering science; English; French; general studies; history; humanities; legal studies; mathematics; nursing; philosophy; political science; psychiatric/mental health services; psychology; social work; sociology; Spanish; theology.

Academic Programs *Special study options:* accelerated degree program, adult/continuing education programs, advanced placement credit, distance learning, double majors, honors programs, independent study, internships, part-time degree program, services for LD students, study abroad, summer session for credit.

Library John Paul II Library with 222,425 titles, 737 serial subscriptions, 896 audiovisual materials, an OPAC, a Web page.

Computers on Campus 126 computers available on campus for general student use. Internet access, at least one staffed computer lab available.

Student Life *Housing:* on-campus residence required through junior year. *Options:* men-only, women-only. *Activities and Organizations:* drama/theater group, student-run newspaper, radio station, choral group, Franciscan University Student Association, Student Activities Board, Human Life Concerns, Works of Mercy, Troubadour, national fraternities, national sororities. *Campus security:* 24-hour emergency response devices and patrols, student patrols, late-night transport/escort service. *Student Services:* health clinic, personal/psychological counseling.

Athletics *Intramural sports:* baseball M(c), basketball M/W, racquetball M/W, rugby M(c), soccer M(c)/W(c), softball W(c), tennis M/W, volleyball M/W, weight lifting M/W, wrestling M.

Standardized Tests *Required:* SAT I or ACT (for admission).

Costs (2001–02) *Comprehensive fee:* $19,100 includes full-time tuition ($13,520), mandatory fees ($380), and room and board ($5200). Part-time tuition: $450 per credit. Part-time tuition and fees vary according to class time. *Required fees:* $10 per credit. *Room and board:* Room and board charges vary according to board plan. *Payment plan:* installment. *Waivers:* employees or children of employees.

Financial Aid Of all full-time matriculated undergraduates who enrolled in 2001, 1413 applied for aid, 1155 were judged to have need, 309 had their need fully met. 248 Federal Work-Study jobs (averaging $857). 460 State and other part-time jobs (averaging $1678). In 2001, 191 non-need-based awards were made. *Average percent of need met:* 75%. *Average financial aid package:* $9691.

Franciscan University of Steubenville (continued)
Average need-based loan: $4235. *Average need-based gift aid:* $5031. *Average non-need based aid:* $1732. *Average indebtedness upon graduation:* $22,940.

Applying *Options:* common application, early admission, deferred entrance. *Application fee:* $20. *Required:* essay or personal statement, high school transcript, minimum 2.4 GPA, letters of recommendation. *Recommended:* interview. *Application deadlines:* 5/1 (freshmen), 5/1 (transfers). *Notification:* 8/30 (freshmen).

Admissions Contact Mrs. Margaret Weber, Director of Admissions, Franciscan University of Steubenville, 1235 University Boulevard, Steubenville, OH 43952-1763. *Phone:* 740-283-6226. *Toll-free phone:* 800-783-6220. *Fax:* 740-284-5456. *E-mail:* admissions@franuniv.edu.

FRANKLIN UNIVERSITY
Columbus, Ohio

- **Independent** comprehensive, founded 1902
- **Calendar** trimesters
- **Degrees** associate, bachelor's, and master's
- **Urban** 14-acre campus
- **Endowment** $22.3 million
- **Coed,** 4,650 undergraduate students, 31% full-time, 57% women, 43% men
- **Noncompetitive** entrance level, 100% of applicants were admitted

Undergraduates 1,444 full-time, 3,206 part-time. Students come from 26 states and territories, 66 other countries, 8% are from out of state, 15% African American, 3% Asian American or Pacific Islander, 1% Hispanic American, 0.3% Native American, 10% international, 24% transferred in.

Freshmen *Admission:* 304 applied, 304 admitted, 107 enrolled.

Faculty *Total:* 350, 11% full-time, 19% with terminal degrees. *Student/faculty ratio:* 15:1.

Majors Accounting; business; business marketing and marketing management; computer/information sciences; finance; health services administration; human resources management; interdisciplinary studies; Internet; management information systems/business data processing; management science; nursing; operations management; protective services related.

Academic Programs *Special study options:* academic remediation for entering students, accelerated degree program, adult/continuing education programs, advanced placement credit, cooperative education, distance learning, English as a second language, independent study, internships, off-campus study, part-time degree program, services for LD students, student-designed majors, study abroad, summer session for credit. *ROTC:* Army (c), Air Force (c).

Library Franklin University Library with 95,291 titles, 3,878 serial subscriptions, 289 audiovisual materials, an OPAC.

Computers on Campus 194 computers available on campus for general student use. Internet access, online (class) registration, at least one staffed computer lab available.

Student Life *Housing:* college housing not available. *Activities and Organizations:* American Marketing Association, International Student Association, Human Resources Society, Accounting Association. *Campus security:* security personnel during operating hours.

Costs (2001–02) *One-time required fee:* $25. *Tuition:* $6324 full-time, $204 per credit hour part-time. Full-time tuition and fees vary according to program. Part-time tuition and fees vary according to program. *Payment plans:* installment, deferred payment. *Waivers:* employees or children of employees.

Financial Aid Of all full-time matriculated undergraduates who enrolled in 2001, 864 applied for aid, 627 were judged to have need. 12 Federal Work-Study jobs (averaging $4667). In 2001, 197 non-need-based awards were made. *Average need-based loan:* $4164. *Average need-based gift aid:* $3372. *Average non-need based aid:* $2285.

Applying *Options:* deferred entrance. *Required for some:* high school transcript. *Application deadline:* rolling (freshmen), rolling (transfers).

Admissions Contact Ms. Evelyn Levino, Vice President for Students, Franklin University, 201 South Grant Avenue, Columbus, OH 43215. *Phone:* 614-341-6256. *Toll-free phone:* 877-341-6300. *Fax:* 614-224-8027. *E-mail:* info@franklin.edu.

GOD'S BIBLE SCHOOL AND COLLEGE
Cincinnati, Ohio

- **Independent interdenominational** 4-year, founded 1900
- **Calendar** semesters
- **Degrees** associate and bachelor's
- **Urban** 14-acre campus
- **Coed,** 259 undergraduate students, 85% full-time, 45% women, 55% men
- **Minimally difficult** entrance level, 74% of applicants were admitted

Undergraduates 219 full-time, 40 part-time. Students come from 24 states and territories, 12 other countries, 3% African American, 6% international. *Retention:* 62% of 2001 full-time freshmen returned.

Freshmen *Admission:* 77 applied, 57 admitted, 57 enrolled.

Faculty *Student/faculty ratio:* 15:1.

Majors Biblical studies; missionary studies; music teacher education; music (voice and choral/opera performance); pastoral counseling; religious education; religious music; secretarial science.

Academic Programs *Special study options:* academic remediation for entering students, advanced placement credit, independent study, internships, part-time degree program, summer session for credit.

Library R. G. Flexon Memorial Library with 28,452 titles, 240 serial subscriptions.

Computers on Campus 14 computers available on campus for general student use. At least one staffed computer lab available.

Student Life *Housing:* on-campus residence required through senior year. *Activities and Organizations:* student-run newspaper, choral group. *Campus security:* 24-hour patrols. *Student Services:* health clinic.

Standardized Tests *Required:* SAT I or ACT (for placement).

Costs (2001–02) *Comprehensive fee:* $7060 includes full-time tuition ($3780), mandatory fees ($480), and room and board ($2800). Part-time tuition: $145 per credit hour. *Room and board:* College room only: $1100.

Applying *Options:* common application. *Application fee:* $50. *Required:* high school transcript, 3 letters of recommendation, interview. *Application deadline:* rolling (freshmen), rolling (transfers).

Admissions Contact Ms. Laura Ellison, Director of Admissions, God's Bible School and College, 1810 Young Street, Cincinnati, OH 45210-1599. *Phone:* 513-721-7944 Ext. 204. *Toll-free phone:* 800-486-4637. *Fax:* 513-721-3971. *E-mail:* admissions@gbs.edu.

HEIDELBERG COLLEGE
Tiffin, Ohio

- **Independent** comprehensive, founded 1850, affiliated with United Church of Christ
- **Calendar** semesters
- **Degrees** bachelor's and master's
- **Small-town** 110-acre campus with easy access to Toledo
- **Endowment** $29.0 million
- **Coed,** 1,288 undergraduate students, 77% full-time, 54% women, 46% men
- **Moderately difficult** entrance level, 89% of applicants were admitted

Undergraduates 990 full-time, 298 part-time. Students come from 25 states and territories, 7 other countries, 13% are from out of state, 3% African American, 0.5% Asian American or Pacific Islander, 1% Hispanic American, 0.5% Native American, 0.8% international, 3% transferred in, 83% live on campus. *Retention:* 79% of 2001 full-time freshmen returned.

Freshmen *Admission:* 1,424 applied, 1,267 admitted, 294 enrolled. *Average high school GPA:* 3.2. *Test scores:* SAT verbal scores over 500: 65%; SAT math scores over 500: 80%; ACT scores over 18: 91%; SAT verbal scores over 600: 23%; SAT math scores over 600: 20%; ACT scores over 24: 33%; SAT verbal scores over 700: 1%; ACT scores over 30: 4%.

Faculty *Total:* 122, 61% full-time, 54% with terminal degrees. *Student/faculty ratio:* 13:1.

Majors Accounting; anthropology; athletic training/sports medicine; biology; business administration; chemistry; computer science; economics; education; elementary education; English; environmental biology; German; health education; health services administration; history; information sciences/systems; international relations; mass communications; mathematics; music; music business management/merchandising; music (piano and organ performance); music teacher education; music (voice and choral/opera performance); philosophy; physical education; physics; political science; pre-dentistry; pre-law; pre-medicine; pre-veterinary studies; psychology; public administration; public relations; religious studies; science education; secondary education; Spanish; special education; stringed instruments; theater arts/drama; water resources.

Academic Programs *Special study options:* academic remediation for entering students, accelerated degree program, adult/continuing education programs, advanced placement credit, double majors, English as a second language, honors programs, internships, off-campus study, part-time degree program, services for LD students, study abroad, summer session for credit. *ROTC:* Army (c), Air Force (c). *Unusual degree programs:* 3-2 engineering with Case Western Reserve University; nursing with Case Western Reserve University; environmental management with Duke University.

Library Beeghly Library plus 1 other with 260,055 titles, 829 serial subscriptions, an OPAC, a Web page.

Computers on Campus 125 computers available on campus for general student use. A campuswide network can be accessed from student residence rooms and from off campus. Internet access, online (class) registration, at least one staffed computer lab available.

Student Life *Housing:* on-campus residence required through senior year. *Options:* coed. *Activities and Organizations:* drama/theater group, student-run newspaper, radio station, choral group, Concert Choir, yearbook, World Student Union, Alpha Phi Omega. *Campus security:* 24-hour emergency response devices, student patrols, late-night transport/escort service, controlled dormitory access. *Student Services:* health clinic, personal/psychological counseling.

Athletics Member NCAA. All Division III. *Intercollegiate sports:* baseball M, basketball M/W, cross-country running M/W, football M, golf M/W, soccer M/W, softball W, tennis M/W, track and field M/W, volleyball W, wrestling M. *Intramural sports:* archery M/W, badminton M/W, basketball M/W, bowling M/W, football M, golf M/W, racquetball M/W, soccer M/W, softball M/W, tennis M/W, volleyball M/W.

Standardized Tests *Required:* SAT I or ACT (for admission).

Costs (2002–03) *Comprehensive fee:* $19,121 includes full-time tuition ($12,850), mandatory fees ($293), and room and board ($5978). Part-time tuition: $405 per semester hour. Part-time tuition and fees vary according to location. *Required fees:* $50 per term part-time. *Room and board:* College room only: $2717. Room and board charges vary according to housing facility. *Payment plans:* installment, deferred payment. *Waivers:* employees or children of employees.

Financial Aid Of all full-time matriculated undergraduates who enrolled in 2001, 894 applied for aid, 826 were judged to have need, 229 had their need fully met. 501 Federal Work-Study jobs (averaging $846). 47 State and other part-time jobs (averaging $1998). In 2001, 144 non-need-based awards were made. *Average percent of need met:* 91%. *Average financial aid package:* $16,011. *Average need-based loan:* $4172. *Average need-based gift aid:* $11,719. *Average non-need based aid:* $6369. *Average indebtedness upon graduation:* $20,489.

Applying *Options:* common application, electronic application, deferred entrance. *Application fee:* $25. *Required:* high school transcript, minimum 2.4 GPA. *Recommended:* 1 letter of recommendation, interview. *Application deadlines:* 8/1 (freshmen), 8/1 (transfers). *Notification:* continuous until 8/1 (freshmen), 9/15 (early action).

Admissions Contact Ms. Sharon Pugh, Director of Admission, Heidelberg College, 310 East Market Street, Tiffin, OH 44883. *Phone:* 419-448-2330. *Toll-free phone:* 800-434-3352. *Fax:* 419-448-2334. *E-mail:* adminfo@heidelberg.edu.

HIRAM COLLEGE
Hiram, Ohio

- **Independent** 4-year, founded 1850, affiliated with Christian Church (Disciples of Christ)
- **Calendar** semesters
- **Degree** bachelor's
- **Rural** 110-acre campus with easy access to Cleveland
- **Endowment** $71.6 million
- **Coed,** 1,190 undergraduate students, 81% full-time, 57% women, 43% men
- **Very difficult** entrance level, 79% of applicants were admitted

Each of Hiram's 15-week semesters is divided into 12- and 3-week terms. During the 3-week terms, students take only 1 course. Hiram supplements classroom study through an extensive study-abroad program. More than 50 percent of students participate, with all courses taught by Hiram faculty members. Hiram opened a $7.2-million library in 1995, and the $6.2-million Esther and Carl Gerstacker Science Hall opened in January 2000.

Undergraduates 964 full-time, 226 part-time. Students come from 23 states and territories, 19 other countries, 21% are from out of state, 8% African American, 1% Asian American or Pacific Islander, 1% Hispanic American, 0.3% Native American, 3% international, 1% transferred in, 95% live on campus. *Retention:* 77% of 2001 full-time freshmen returned.

Freshmen *Admission:* 1,022 applied, 806 admitted, 275 enrolled. *Average high school GPA:* 3.42. *Test scores:* SAT verbal scores over 500: 78%; SAT math scores over 500: 76%; ACT scores over 18: 94%; SAT verbal scores over 600: 41%; SAT math scores over 600: 33%; ACT scores over 24: 49%; SAT verbal scores over 700: 10%; SAT math scores over 700: 4%; ACT scores over 30: 6%.

Faculty *Total:* 110, 66% full-time, 64% with terminal degrees. *Student/faculty ratio:* 11:1.

Majors Art; art history; biology; business administration; chemistry; classics; computer science; economics; elementary education; English; environmental science; fine/studio arts; French; German; health science; history; international business; international economics; mass communications; mathematics; music; philosophy; physics; physiological psychology/psychobiology; political science; pre-dentistry; pre-law; pre-medicine; pre-veterinary studies; psychology; religious studies; secondary education; sociology; Spanish; theater arts/drama.

Academic Programs *Special study options:* accelerated degree program, adult/continuing education programs, advanced placement credit, double majors, English as a second language, independent study, internships, off-campus study, part-time degree program, services for LD students, student-designed majors, study abroad, summer session for credit. *Unusual degree programs:* 3-2 engineering with Case Western Reserve University, Washington University in St. Louis.

Library Hiram College Library with 185,153 titles, 4,191 serial subscriptions, 10,351 audiovisual materials, an OPAC, a Web page.

Computers on Campus A campuswide network can be accessed from student residence rooms and from off campus. Internet access, at least one staffed computer lab available.

Student Life *Housing:* on-campus residence required through junior year. *Options:* coed, women-only, disabled students. *Activities and Organizations:* drama/theater group, student-run newspaper, radio and television station, choral group, Student Senate, African American Students United, Outdoors Club, Resident Student Association, Christian Outreach. *Campus security:* 24-hour emergency response devices and patrols, late-night transport/escort service, controlled dormitory access. *Student Services:* health clinic, personal/psychological counseling.

Athletics Member NCAA. All Division III. *Intercollegiate sports:* baseball M, basketball M/W, cross-country running M/W, equestrian sports M(c)/W(c), football M, golf M/W, rugby M(c)/W(c), sailing M(c)/W(c), soccer M/W, softball W, swimming M/W, table tennis M(c)/W(c), tennis M/W, track and field M/W, volleyball W. *Intramural sports:* basketball M/W, football M/W, racquetball M/W, soccer M/W, softball M/W, tennis M/W, volleyball M/W.

Standardized Tests *Required:* SAT I or ACT (for admission).

Costs (2001–02) *Comprehensive fee:* $25,906 includes full-time tuition ($18,720), mandatory fees ($672), and room and board ($6514). Part-time tuition: $624 per credit hour. Part-time tuition and fees vary according to class time. *Room and board:* College room only: $2894. Room and board charges vary according to board plan and housing facility. *Payment plan:* installment. *Waivers:* employees or children of employees.

Financial Aid Of all full-time matriculated undergraduates who enrolled in 2001, 798 applied for aid, 732 were judged to have need, 508 had their need fully met. 69 State and other part-time jobs (averaging $1449). In 2001, 116 non-need-based awards were made. *Average percent of need met:* 84%. *Average financial aid package:* $16,455. *Average need-based loan:* $3448. *Average need-based gift aid:* $8155. *Average indebtedness upon graduation:* $16,455.

Applying *Options:* common application, electronic application, early admission, early decision, deferred entrance. *Application fee:* $35. *Required:* essay or personal statement, high school transcript, 2 letters of recommendation. *Required for some:* interview. *Recommended:* 3 letters of recommendation, interview. *Application deadlines:* 2/1 (freshmen), 7/15 (transfers). *Early decision:* 12/1. *Notification:* continuous (freshmen), 1/1 (early decision)..

Admissions Contact Mr. Ed Frato Sweeney, Director of Admission, Hiram College, Box 96, Hiram, OH 44234-0067. *Phone:* 330-569-5169. *Toll-free phone:* 800-362-5280. *Fax:* 330-569-5944. *E-mail:* admission@hiram.edu.

JOHN CARROLL UNIVERSITY
University Heights, Ohio

- **Independent Roman Catholic (Jesuit)** comprehensive, founded 1886
- **Calendar** semesters
- **Degrees** bachelor's and master's
- **Suburban** 60-acre campus with easy access to Cleveland
- **Endowment** $139.8 million
- **Coed,** 3,508 undergraduate students, 95% full-time, 55% women, 45% men
- **Moderately difficult** entrance level, 86% of applicants were admitted

The beautiful front lawn of John Carroll University will soon become a new academic quad. Construction continues on the new Bolan Center for Science and Technology, which is scheduled to open for classes in fall 2003. The biology, chemistry, computer science, mathematics, physics, and psychology departments will relocate to the Bolan Center.

Undergraduates 3,331 full-time, 177 part-time. Students come from 35 states and territories, 27% are from out of state, 4% African American, 3% Asian

John Carroll University (continued)
American or Pacific Islander, 2% Hispanic American, 0.2% Native American, 0.1% international, 5% transferred in, 59% live on campus. *Retention:* 86% of 2001 full-time freshmen returned.

Freshmen *Admission:* 2,764 applied, 2,387 admitted, 792 enrolled. *Average high school GPA:* 3.27. *Test scores:* SAT verbal scores over 500: 84%; SAT math scores over 500: 88%; ACT scores over 18: 96%; SAT verbal scores over 600: 32%; SAT math scores over 600: 43%; ACT scores over 24: 48%; SAT verbal scores over 700: 6%; SAT math scores over 700: 4%; ACT scores over 30: 6%.

Faculty *Total:* 417, 59% full-time. *Student/faculty ratio:* 15:1.

Majors Accounting; art history; Asian studies; biological/physical sciences; biology; business administration; business marketing and marketing management; chemistry; classics; computer science; early childhood education; East Asian studies; economics; education; education (K-12); elementary education; engineering physics; English; environmental science; finance; French; German; gerontology; Greek (modern); history; humanities; interdisciplinary studies; international economics; international relations; Latin (ancient and medieval); literature; mass communications; mathematics; neuroscience; philosophy; physical education; physics; political science; pre-dentistry; pre-law; pre-medicine; pre-veterinary studies; psychology; public administration; religious education; religious studies; secondary education; sociology; Spanish; special education.

Academic Programs *Special study options:* accelerated degree program, adult/continuing education programs, advanced placement credit, cooperative education, double majors, honors programs, independent study, internships, off-campus study, part-time degree program, student-designed majors, study abroad, summer session for credit. *ROTC:* Army (b). *Unusual degree programs:* 3-2 engineering with Case Western Reserve University, University of Detroit Mercy; nursing with Case Western Reserve University.

Library Grasselli Library with 620,000 titles, 2,198 serial subscriptions, 5,820 audiovisual materials, an OPAC, a Web page.

Computers on Campus 210 computers available on campus for general student use. A campuswide network can be accessed from student residence rooms and from off campus. Internet access, online (class) registration, at least one staffed computer lab available.

Student Life *Housing:* on-campus residence required for freshman year. *Options:* coed, men-only, women-only. *Activities and Organizations:* drama/theater group, student-run newspaper, radio station, choral group, Volunteer Service Organization, Student Union, Carroll News, band, University Concert Choir, national fraternities, national sororities. *Campus security:* 24-hour emergency response devices and patrols, late-night transport/escort service. *Student Services:* health clinic, personal/psychological counseling.

Athletics Member NCAA. All Division III. *Intercollegiate sports:* baseball M, basketball M/W, crew M(c)/W(c), cross-country running M/W, football M, golf M/W, ice hockey M(c), lacrosse M(c)/W(c), rugby M(c)/W(c), sailing M(c)/W(c), skiing (downhill) M(c)/W(c), soccer M/W, softball W, swimming M/W, tennis M/W, track and field M/W, volleyball M(c)/W, wrestling M. *Intramural sports:* basketball M/W, football M/W, racquetball M/W, softball M/W, swimming M/W, tennis M/W, volleyball M/W, water polo M/W.

Standardized Tests *Required:* SAT I or ACT (for admission).

Costs (2002–03) *Comprehensive fee:* $25,756 includes full-time tuition ($18,842), mandatory fees ($350), and room and board ($6564). Part-time tuition: $544 per credit hour. Part-time tuition and fees vary according to course load. *Required fees:* $10 per credit hour. *Room and board:* Room and board charges vary according to board plan. *Payment plan:* installment. *Waivers:* employees or children of employees.

Financial Aid Of all full-time matriculated undergraduates who enrolled in 2001, 3129 applied for aid, 2161 were judged to have need, 1010 had their need fully met. 774 Federal Work-Study jobs (averaging $1822). 297 State and other part-time jobs (averaging $1756). In 2001, 853 non-need-based awards were made. *Average percent of need met:* 88%. *Average financial aid package:* $14,104. *Average need-based loan:* $3883. *Average need-based gift aid:* $7128. *Average non-need based aid:* $2954. *Average indebtedness upon graduation:* $12,695.

Applying *Options:* early admission, deferred entrance. *Application fee:* $25. *Required:* high school transcript, 1 letter of recommendation. *Required for some:* interview. *Recommended:* essay or personal statement, interview. *Application deadline:* 2/1 (freshmen), rolling (transfers). *Notification:* continuous (freshmen).

Admissions Contact Mr. Thomas P. Fanning, Director of Admission, John Carroll University, 20700 North Park Boulevard, University Heights, OH 44118-4581. *Phone:* 216-397-4294. *Fax:* 216-397-4981. *E-mail:* admission@jcu.edu.

KENT STATE UNIVERSITY
Kent, Ohio

- **State-supported** university, founded 1910, part of Kent State University System
- **Calendar** semesters
- **Degrees** associate, bachelor's, master's, and doctoral
- **Small-town** 1200-acre campus with easy access to Cleveland
- **Endowment** $42.8 million
- **Coed,** 18,382 undergraduate students, 84% full-time, 60% women, 40% men
- **Moderately difficult** entrance level, 90% of applicants were admitted

Undergraduates 15,450 full-time, 2,932 part-time. Students come from 48 states and territories, 24 other countries, 7% are from out of state, 6% transferred in, 31% live on campus. *Retention:* 72% of 2001 full-time freshmen returned.

Freshmen *Admission:* 9,694 applied, 8,745 admitted, 3,654 enrolled. *Average high school GPA:* 3.09. *Test scores:* SAT verbal scores over 500: 55%; SAT math scores over 500: 52%; ACT scores over 18: 86%; SAT verbal scores over 600: 14%; SAT math scores over 600: 14%; ACT scores over 24: 27%; SAT verbal scores over 700: 2%; SAT math scores over 700: 1%; ACT scores over 30: 2%.

Faculty *Total:* 1,263, 51% full-time. *Student/faculty ratio:* 20:1.

Majors Accounting; accounting technician; advertising; African-American studies; American studies; anthropology; applied mathematics; archaeology; architecture; art education; art history; athletic training/sports medicine; aviation/airway science; banking; biological sciences/life sciences related; biological specializations related; biology; botany; business; business administration; business computer programming; business economics; business education; business marketing and marketing management; business systems analysis/design; chemistry; classics; computer systems analysis; craft/folk art; criminal justice studies; criminology; cultural studies; dance; early childhood education; earth sciences; Eastern European area studies; economics; education; education related; engineering technologies related; English; exercise sciences; fashion design/illustration; fashion merchandising; finance; fine/studio arts; French; general studies; geography; geology; German; graphic design/commercial art/illustration; health education; health/medical administrative services related; health/medical diagnostic and treatment services related; history; home economics; horticulture services; human services; individual/family development; industrial arts education; industrial/manufacturing engineering; industrial production technologies related; industrial technology; interior architecture; interior design; international relations; journalism and mass communication related; landscape architecture; Latin American studies; Latin (ancient and medieval); liberal arts and sciences/liberal studies; marketing/distribution education; mathematics; mechanical engineering technology; medical radiologic technology; medical technology; middle school education; multi/interdisciplinary studies related; music; music teacher education; natural resources conservation; nuclear medical technology; nursing; nutrition studies; occupational therapy assistant; paralegal/legal assistant; peace/conflict studies; philosophy; photographic technology; physical education; physical therapy assistant; physics; plastics engineering; plastics technology; political science; pre-dentistry; professional studies; psychology; public relations; radio/television broadcasting; real estate; recreation/leisure facilities management; Russian; Russian/Slavic studies; science education; secretarial science; social sciences; social studies education; sociology; Spanish; special education; speech-language pathology/audiology; speech/rhetorical studies; theater arts/drama; trade/industrial education; zoology.

Academic Programs *Special study options:* academic remediation for entering students, adult/continuing education programs, advanced placement credit, cooperative education, distance learning, double majors, English as a second language, freshman honors college, honors programs, independent study, internships, off-campus study, part-time degree program, services for LD students, student-designed majors, study abroad, summer session for credit. *ROTC:* Army (b), Air Force (b). *Unusual degree programs:* 3-2 international relations.

Library Kent Library plus 5 others with 1.1 million titles, 14,895 serial subscriptions, 41,614 audiovisual materials, an OPAC, a Web page.

Computers on Campus 800 computers available on campus for general student use. A campuswide network can be accessed from student residence rooms and from off campus. Internet access, at least one staffed computer lab available.

Student Life *Housing:* on-campus residence required through sophomore year. *Options:* coed, men-only, women-only. *Activities and Organizations:* drama/theater group, student-run newspaper, radio and television station, choral group, marching band, Kent Student Education Association, Black United Students, May 4th Task Force, Student Recreation Council, Late Night Christian Fellowship, national fraternities, national sororities. *Campus security:* 24-hour emergency response devices, late-night transport/escort service, controlled dormitory access, on campus police and fire department. *Student Services:* health clinic, personal/psychological counseling, women's center, legal services.

Athletics Member NCAA. All Division I except football (Division I-A). *Intercollegiate sports:* baseball M(s), basketball M(s)/W(s), cross-country running M(s)/W(s), field hockey W(s), golf M(s)/W(s), gymnastics W(s), soccer W(s), softball W(s), track and field M(s)/W(s), volleyball W(s), wrestling M(s). *Intramural sports:* badminton M(c)/W(c), basketball M/W, bowling M(c)/W(c), crew M(c)/W(c), equestrian sports M(c)/W(c), fencing M(c)/W(c), football M/W, golf M/W, gymnastics M(c)/W(c), ice hockey M(c), lacrosse M(c), racquetball M(c)/W(c), rugby M(c)/W(c), sailing M(c)/W(c), skiing (downhill) M(c)/W(c), soccer M(c)/W(c), softball M/W, swimming M(c)/W(c), tennis M/W, track and field M/W, volleyball M(c)/W(c), water polo M/W, wrestling M.

Standardized Tests *Required for some:* SAT I or ACT (for admission). *Recommended:* SAT I or ACT (for admission).

Costs (2001–02) *Tuition:* state resident $4846 full-time, $250 per hour part-time; nonresident $10,333 full-time, $500 per hour part-time. Full-time tuition and fees vary according to course load and program. Part-time tuition and fees vary according to course load and program. *Required fees:* $1108 full-time, $45 per hour, $55 per term part-time. *Room and board:* $5150; room only: $3080. Room and board charges vary according to board plan and housing facility. *Payment plan:* installment. *Waivers:* employees or children of employees.

Financial Aid Of all full-time matriculated undergraduates who enrolled in 2001, 13585 applied for aid, 11120 were judged to have need, 2181 had their need fully met. 744 Federal Work-Study jobs (averaging $2375). In 2001, 2465 non-need-based awards were made. *Average percent of need met:* 67%. *Average financial aid package:* $6715. *Average need-based loan:* $3592. *Average need-based gift aid:* $3712. *Average non-need based aid:* $2280. *Average indebtedness upon graduation:* $14,277.

Applying *Options:* electronic application, early admission. *Application fee:* $30. *Required:* high school transcript, minimum 2.5 GPA, rank in upper 50% of high school class for nonresidents. *Application deadlines:* 6/1 (freshmen), 10/1 (transfers).

Admissions Contact Mr. Christopher Buttenschon, Assistant Director of Admissions, Kent State University, 161 Michael Schwartz Center, Kent, OH 44242-0001. *Phone:* 330-672-2444. *Toll-free phone:* 800-988-KENT. *Fax:* 330-672-2499. *E-mail:* kentadm@admissions.kent.edu.

KENT STATE UNIVERSITY, GEAUGA CAMPUS
Burton, Ohio

- **State-supported** founded 1964, part of Kent State University System
- **Calendar** semesters
- **Degrees** associate, bachelor's, and master's
- **Rural** 87-acre campus with easy access to Cleveland
- **Coed,** 670 undergraduate students, 41% full-time, 54% women, 46% men
- **Noncompetitive** entrance level, 100% of applicants were admitted

Undergraduates 274 full-time, 396 part-time. Students come from 3 states and territories, 2 other countries, 0% are from out of state, 4% African American, 0.5% Asian American or Pacific Islander, 0.5% Hispanic American, 0.5% international, 0.3% transferred in. *Retention:* 53% of 2001 full-time freshmen returned.

Freshmen *Admission:* 274 applied, 274 admitted, 192 enrolled.

Faculty *Total:* 55, 13% full-time, 7% with terminal degrees. *Student/faculty ratio:* 16:1.

Majors Accounting; business administration; computer engineering technology; computer programming; horticulture services; industrial technology; liberal arts and sciences/liberal studies.

Academic Programs *Special study options:* academic remediation for entering students, adult/continuing education programs, advanced placement credit, distance learning, double majors, internships, part-time degree program, services for LD students, student-designed majors, summer session for credit. *ROTC:* Army (c), Air Force (c).

Library Kent State University Library with 8,300 titles, 6,600 serial subscriptions, an OPAC, a Web page.

Computers on Campus 50 computers available on campus for general student use. Internet access, at least one staffed computer lab available.

Student Life *Housing:* college housing not available. *Activities and Organizations:* student-run newspaper, Computer Club, Student Senate, Accounting Club, student newspaper. *Campus security:* 24-hour emergency response devices.

Athletics *Intramural sports:* basketball M/W, skiing (downhill) M/W, table tennis M/W, volleyball M/W.

Standardized Tests *Recommended:* ACT (for placement).

Costs (2001–02) *Tuition:* state resident $3052 full-time, $139 per hour part-time; nonresident $8540 full-time, $389 per hour part-time. *Required fees:* $216 full-time. *Payment plan:* installment. *Waivers:* senior citizens and employees or children of employees.

Applying *Options:* early admission, deferred entrance. *Application fee:* $30. *Required:* high school transcript, interview. *Recommended:* minimum 2.0 GPA. *Application deadline:* rolling (freshmen), rolling (transfers).

Admissions Contact Ms. Betty Landrus, Admissions and Records Secretary, Kent State University, Geauga Campus, 14111 Clandon Stroy Road, Burton, OH 44021. *Phone:* 440-834-4187. *Fax:* 440-834-8846. *E-mail:* cbaker@geauga.kent.edu.

KENT STATE UNIVERSITY, STARK CAMPUS
Canton, Ohio

- **State-supported** primarily 2-year, founded 1967, part of Kent State University System
- **Calendar** semesters
- **Degrees** associate and bachelor's (also offers some graduate courses)
- **Suburban** 200-acre campus with easy access to Cleveland
- **Coed,** 3,449 undergraduate students
- **Noncompetitive** entrance level, 100% of applicants were admitted

Undergraduates Students come from 2 states and territories.

Freshmen *Admission:* 631 applied, 631 admitted. *Average high school GPA:* 2.70.

Majors Art; biological/physical sciences; business administration; education; interdisciplinary studies; liberal arts and sciences/liberal studies.

Academic Programs *Special study options:* academic remediation for entering students, adult/continuing education programs, advanced placement credit, English as a second language, freshman honors college, honors programs, internships, off-campus study, part-time degree program, services for LD students, student-designed majors, summer session for credit. *ROTC:* Army (c), Air Force (c).

Library Kent State University Library with 72,807 titles, 313 serial subscriptions, an OPAC, a Web page.

Computers on Campus 76 computers available on campus for general student use. A campuswide network can be accessed from off campus. Internet access, at least one staffed computer lab available.

Student Life *Housing:* college housing not available. *Activities and Organizations:* drama/theater group, choral group, Psychology Club, Pan African Student Alliance, Criminal Justice Society, Women's Studies, History Club. *Campus security:* 24-hour emergency response devices, late-night transport/escort service.

Standardized Tests *Required for some:* SAT I or ACT (for admission).

Costs (2001–02) *Tuition:* state resident $3344 full-time, $157 per credit part-time; nonresident $8832 full-time, $402 per credit part-time. No tuition increase for student's term of enrollment. *Payment plan:* installment. *Waivers:* senior citizens and employees or children of employees.

Financial Aid Of all full-time matriculated undergraduates who enrolled in 2001, 50 Federal Work-Study jobs (averaging $2000).

Applying *Options:* early admission, deferred entrance. *Application fee:* $30. *Required:* high school transcript. *Required for some:* interview. *Application deadline:* rolling (freshmen), rolling (transfers).

Admissions Contact Ms. Deborah Ann Phillipp, Acting Director of Admissions, Kent State University, Stark Campus, 6000 Frank Avenue NW, Canton, OH 44720-7599. *Phone:* 330-499-9600 Ext. 53259. *Fax:* 330-499-0301. *E-mail:* dphillipp@stark.kent.edu.

KENT STATE UNIVERSITY, TUSCARAWAS CAMPUS
New Philadelphia, Ohio

- **State-supported** primarily 2-year, founded 1962, part of Kent State University System
- **Calendar** semesters
- **Degrees** certificates, diplomas, associate, and bachelor's (also offers some upper-level and graduate courses)
- **Small-town** 172-acre campus with easy access to Cleveland
- **Endowment** $3.0 million
- **Coed,** 1,845 undergraduate students, 51% full-time, 63% women, 37% men
- **Noncompetitive** entrance level

Undergraduates Students come from 2 states and territories, 1 other country, 1% African American, 0.5% Asian American or Pacific Islander, 0.3% Hispanic American, 0.3% Native American, 0.3% international.

Kent State University, Tuscarawas Campus (continued)

Freshmen *Average high school GPA:* 2.76.

Faculty *Total:* 147, 29% full-time, 21% with terminal degrees. *Student/faculty ratio:* 17:1.

Majors Accounting; business administration; computer engineering technology; electrical/electronic engineering technology; engineering technology; environmental science; industrial technology; law enforcement/police science; liberal arts and sciences/liberal studies; mechanical engineering technology; nursing; secretarial science.

Academic Programs *Special study options:* academic remediation for entering students, accelerated degree program, adult/continuing education programs, advanced placement credit, distance learning, double majors, freshman honors college, honors programs, internships, part-time degree program, services for LD students, student-designed majors, summer session for credit. *ROTC:* Army (c), Air Force (c).

Library Tuscarawas Campus Library with 58,946 titles, 400 serial subscriptions, 520 audiovisual materials, an OPAC, a Web page.

Computers on Campus 161 computers available on campus for general student use. A campuswide network can be accessed from off campus. Internet access, online (class) registration, at least one staffed computer lab available.

Student Life *Housing:* college housing not available. *Activities and Organizations:* choral group, Society of Mechanical Engineers, IEEE, Imagineers, Criminal Justice Club, The Way.

Athletics *Intramural sports:* basketball M/W, volleyball M/W.

Standardized Tests *Required for some:* SAT I or ACT (for placement).

Costs (2001–02) *Tuition:* state resident $3184 full-time, $145 per semester hour part-time; nonresident $8672 full-time. Full-time tuition and fees vary according to class time. Part-time tuition and fees vary according to class time. *Payment plan:* installment. *Waivers:* employees or children of employees.

Applying *Options:* common application, early admission, deferred entrance. *Application fee:* $30. *Required:* high school transcript. *Application deadlines:* 9/1 (freshmen), 9/1 (transfers). *Notification:* continuous (freshmen).

Admissions Contact Ms. Denise L. Testa, Director of Admissions, Kent State University, Tuscarawas Campus, 330 University Drive, NE, New Philadelphia, OH 44663-9403. *Phone:* 330-339-3391 Ext. 47425. *Fax:* 330-339-3321.

KENYON COLLEGE
Gambier, Ohio

- **Independent** 4-year, founded 1824
- **Calendar** semesters
- **Degree** bachelor's
- **Rural** 800-acre campus with easy access to Columbus
- **Endowment** $136.5 million
- **Coed,** 1,587 undergraduate students, 98% full-time, 55% women, 45% men
- **Very difficult** entrance level, 66% of applicants were admitted

Undergraduates 1,558 full-time, 29 part-time. Students come from 49 states and territories, 28 other countries, 75% are from out of state, 4% African American, 2% Asian American or Pacific Islander, 3% Hispanic American, 3% international, 0.6% transferred in, 99% live on campus. *Retention:* 92% of 2001 full-time freshmen returned.

Freshmen *Admission:* 2,001 applied, 1,329 admitted, 425 enrolled. *Average high school GPA:* 3.68. *Test scores:* SAT verbal scores over 500: 99%; SAT math scores over 500: 98%; ACT scores over 18: 100%; SAT verbal scores over 600: 79%; SAT math scores over 600: 71%; ACT scores over 24: 95%; SAT verbal scores over 700: 30%; SAT math scores over 700: 17%; ACT scores over 30: 42%.

Faculty *Total:* 165, 86% full-time, 93% with terminal degrees. *Student/faculty ratio:* 10:1.

Majors African-American studies; American studies; anthropology; art; art history; Asian studies; biochemistry; biology; chemistry; classics; computer science related; creative writing; dance; economics; English; environmental science; fine/studio arts; French; German; Greek (modern); history; humanities; interdisciplinary studies; international relations; Latin (ancient and medieval); legal studies; literature; mathematics; modern languages; molecular biology; music; natural sciences; neuroscience; philosophy; physics; political science; psychology; public policy analysis; religious studies; romance languages; sociology; Spanish; theater arts/drama; women's studies.

Academic Programs *Special study options:* accelerated degree program, advanced placement credit, double majors, honors programs, independent study, internships, off-campus study, services for LD students, student-designed majors, study abroad. *Unusual degree programs:* 3-2 engineering with Washington University in St. Louis, Case Western Reserve University, Rensselaer Polytechnic Institute; environmental science with Duke University.

Library Olin Library plus 1 other with 858,000 titles, 4,500 serial subscriptions, 166,000 audiovisual materials, an OPAC, a Web page.

Computers on Campus 225 computers available on campus for general student use. A campuswide network can be accessed from student residence rooms and from off campus that provide access to commercial databases. Internet access, at least one staffed computer lab available.

Student Life *Housing:* on-campus residence required through senior year. *Options:* coed, women-only, cooperative, disabled students. *Activities and Organizations:* drama/theater group, student-run newspaper, radio station, choral group, music groups, Student Theater Organization, writing organizations, student radio station, Ballroom Dance Club, national fraternities, national sororities. *Campus security:* 24-hour emergency response devices and patrols, student patrols, late-night transport/escort service. *Student Services:* health clinic, personal/psychological counseling, women's center.

Athletics Member NCAA. All Division III. *Intercollegiate sports:* baseball M, basketball M/W, cross-country running M/W, field hockey W, football M, golf M, lacrosse M/W, soccer M/W, softball W, swimming M/W, tennis M/W, track and field M/W, volleyball W. *Intramural sports:* basketball M/W, crew M(c)/W(c), equestrian sports M(c)/W(c), fencing M(c)/W(c), football M, ice hockey M(c), racquetball M/W, rugby M(c)/W(c), sailing M(c)/W(c), soccer M(c)/W(c), softball M/W, squash M(c)/W(c), tennis M/W, volleyball M(c)/W(c), water polo M(c)/W(c).

Standardized Tests *Required:* SAT I or ACT (for admission).

Costs (2001–02) *Comprehensive fee:* $32,130 includes full-time tuition ($26,800), mandatory fees ($750), and room and board ($4580). Part-time tuition: $3350 per course. *Room and board:* College room only: $2040. Room and board charges vary according to housing facility. *Payment plan:* installment. *Waivers:* employees or children of employees.

Financial Aid Of all full-time matriculated undergraduates who enrolled in 2001, 833 applied for aid, 691 were judged to have need, 691 had their need fully met. 246 Federal Work-Study jobs (averaging $938). In 2001, 263 non-need-based awards were made. *Average percent of need met:* 98%. *Average financial aid package:* $18,941. *Average need-based loan:* $3356. *Average need-based gift aid:* $16,029. *Average non-need based aid:* $8270. *Average indebtedness upon graduation:* $20,800.

Applying *Options:* common application, early admission, early decision, deferred entrance. *Application fee:* $45. *Required:* essay or personal statement, high school transcript, minimum 2.0 GPA, 1 letter of recommendation. *Recommended:* minimum 3.0 GPA, 2 letters of recommendation, interview. *Application deadlines:* 1/15 (freshmen), 4/1 (transfers). *Early decision:* 12/1 (for plan 1), 1/15 (for plan 2). *Notification:* 4/1 (freshmen), 12/15 (early decision plan 1), 2/1 (early decision plan 2).

Admissions Contact Mr. John W. Anderson, Dean of Admissions, Kenyon College, Office of Admissions, Gambier, OH 43022-9623. *Phone:* 740-427-5776. *Toll-free phone:* 800-848-2468. *Fax:* 740-427-5770. *E-mail:* admissions@kenyon.edu.

KETTERING COLLEGE OF MEDICAL ARTS
Kettering, Ohio

Admissions Contact Mr. David Lofthouse, Director of Enrollment Services, Kettering College of Medical Arts, 3737 Southern Boulevard, Kettering, OH 45429-1299. *Phone:* 937-296-7228. *Toll-free phone:* 800-433-5262. *Fax:* 937-296-4238.

LAKE ERIE COLLEGE
Painesville, Ohio

- **Independent** comprehensive, founded 1856
- **Calendar** semesters
- **Degrees** bachelor's and master's
- **Small-town** 57-acre campus with easy access to Cleveland
- **Endowment** $9.1 million
- **Coed,** 607 undergraduate students, 83% full-time, 78% women, 22% men
- **Minimally difficult** entrance level, 83% of applicants were admitted

Undergraduates 501 full-time, 106 part-time. Students come from 31 states and territories, 8 other countries, 15% are from out of state, 5% African American, 0.6% Asian American or Pacific Islander, 2% Hispanic American, 0.4% Native American, 3% international, 15% transferred in, 40% live on campus. *Retention:* 70% of 2001 full-time freshmen returned.

Freshmen *Admission:* 461 applied, 383 admitted, 127 enrolled. *Average high school GPA:* 3.02. *Test scores:* SAT verbal scores over 500: 67%; SAT math scores

over 500: 64%; ACT scores over 18: 88%; SAT verbal scores over 600: 33%; SAT math scores over 600: 23%; ACT scores over 24: 31%; SAT verbal scores over 700: 7%; SAT math scores over 700: 4%; ACT scores over 30: 7%.

Faculty *Total:* 89, 35% full-time, 51% with terminal degrees. *Student/faculty ratio:* 13:1.

Majors Accounting; aquaculture operations/production management; art; biology; business administration; buying operations; chemistry; dance; education (K-12); elementary education; English; environmental science; equestrian studies; fine/studio arts; French; German; hotel/motel services marketing operations; human services; international business; Italian; Italian studies; marketing operations; mass communications; mathematics; modern languages; music; paralegal/legal assistant; personal services marketing operations; pre-dentistry; pre-law; pre-medicine; pre-veterinary studies; professional studies; psychology; retailing operations; sales operations; social sciences; sociology; Spanish; theater arts/drama.

Academic Programs *Special study options:* academic remediation for entering students, accelerated degree program, adult/continuing education programs, advanced placement credit, cooperative education, double majors, independent study, internships, off-campus study, part-time degree program, services for LD students, student-designed majors, study abroad, summer session for credit.

Library Lincoln Library plus 2 others with 85,978 titles, 767 serial subscriptions, an OPAC, a Web page.

Computers on Campus A campuswide network can be accessed from student residence rooms and from off campus. Internet access, at least one staffed computer lab available.

Student Life *Housing:* on-campus residence required through senior year. *Options:* coed, men-only, women-only. *Activities and Organizations:* drama/theater group, choral group, Riding Club, Student Government Association, Mortar Board, Pre-Veterinary Medicine Association, Activities Council. *Campus security:* 24-hour emergency response devices and patrols, late-night transport/escort service. *Student Services:* personal/psychological counseling, legal services.

Athletics Member NCAA. All Division III. *Intercollegiate sports:* basketball M/W, cross-country running M, equestrian sports M/W, golf M, soccer M/W, softball W, tennis M/W, volleyball W. *Intramural sports:* basketball M/W, cross-country running W, equestrian sports M/W, soccer M/W, softball M/W, tennis M/W, volleyball M/W.

Standardized Tests *Required:* SAT I or ACT (for admission).

Costs (2001–02) *Comprehensive fee:* $22,910 includes full-time tuition ($16,370), mandatory fees ($840), and room and board ($5700). Full-time tuition and fees vary according to course load and program. Part-time tuition: $435 per credit hour. *Required fees:* $50 per credit hour. *Room and board:* College room only: $3000. Room and board charges vary according to board plan. *Payment plan:* installment. *Waivers:* senior citizens and employees or children of employees.

Financial Aid Of all full-time matriculated undergraduates who enrolled in 2001, 430 applied for aid, 331 were judged to have need. 57 Federal Work-Study jobs (averaging $1164). 110 State and other part-time jobs (averaging $1034). *Average percent of need met:* 85%. *Average indebtedness upon graduation:* $17,125.

Applying *Options:* electronic application, early admission, deferred entrance. *Application fee:* $25. *Required:* high school transcript, minimum 2.0 GPA, 1 letter of recommendation. *Required for some:* interview. *Recommended:* interview. *Notification:* continuous (freshmen).

Admissions Contact Kevin Coughlin, Dean of Admissions and Financial Aid, Lake Erie College, 391 West Washington Street, Painesville, OH 44077-3389. *Phone:* 440-639-7879. *Toll-free phone:* 800-916-0904. *Fax:* 440-352-3533. *E-mail:* lecadmit@lakeerie.edu.

LAURA AND ALVIN SIEGAL COLLEGE OF JUDAIC STUDIES

Beachwood, Ohio

- **Independent** comprehensive, founded 1963
- **Calendar** semesters
- **Degrees** certificates, bachelor's, and master's
- **Suburban** 2-acre campus with easy access to Cleveland
- **Coed,** 17 undergraduate students, 12% full-time, 88% women, 12% men
- **Noncompetitive** entrance level, 71% of applicants were admitted

Undergraduates 2 full-time, 15 part-time. Students come from 1 other country, 0% are from out of state, 27% international. *Retention:* 100% of 2001 full-time freshmen returned.

Freshmen *Admission:* 7 applied, 5 admitted, 5 enrolled.

Faculty *Total:* 35, 37% full-time, 49% with terminal degrees. *Student/faculty ratio:* 8:1.

Majors Biblical languages/literatures; biblical studies; education; education administration; Hebrew; history; Judaic studies; religious education; religious studies; theology.

Academic Programs *Special study options:* adult/continuing education programs, cooperative education, distance learning, double majors, external degree program, independent study, internships, off-campus study, part-time degree program, summer session for credit.

Library Aaron Garber Library with 28,000 titles, 100 serial subscriptions, an OPAC.

Computers on Campus 5 computers available on campus for general student use.

Student Life *Housing:* college housing not available. *Activities and Organizations:* "YES"-Young Educators and Scholars. *Campus security:* 24-hour emergency response devices.

Costs (2001–02) *Tuition:* $6750 full-time, $225 per credit part-time. *Required fees:* $25 full-time, $25 per year part-time. *Payment plan:* installment. *Waivers:* senior citizens and employees or children of employees.

Applying *Options:* common application, deferred entrance. *Application fee:* $50. *Required:* essay or personal statement, high school transcript, 2 letters of recommendation, interview. *Application deadline:* rolling (freshmen), rolling (transfers). *Notification:* continuous (freshmen).

Admissions Contact Ms. Linda L. Rosen, Director of Student Services, Laura and Alvin Siegal College of Judaic Studies, 26500 Shaker Boulevard, Beachwood, OH 44122-7116. *Phone:* 216-464-4050 Ext. 101. *Toll-free phone:* 888-336-2257. *Fax:* 216-464-5827. *E-mail:* admissions@ccjs.edu.

LOURDES COLLEGE

Sylvania, Ohio

- **Independent Roman Catholic** 4-year, founded 1958
- **Calendar** semesters
- **Degrees** certificates, associate, and bachelor's
- **Suburban** 90-acre campus with easy access to Toledo
- **Endowment** $3.1 million
- **Coed,** 1,219 undergraduate students, 37% full-time, 81% women, 19% men
- **Moderately difficult** entrance level, 49% of applicants were admitted

Undergraduates 451 full-time, 768 part-time. Students come from 2 states and territories, 2 other countries, 7% are from out of state, 10% African American, 0.3% Asian American or Pacific Islander, 2% Hispanic American, 0.3% Native American, 0.2% international, 14% transferred in. *Retention:* 56% of 2001 full-time freshmen returned.

Freshmen *Admission:* 201 applied, 98 admitted, 71 enrolled. *Average high school GPA:* 2.90. *Test scores:* SAT verbal scores over 500: 50%; SAT math scores over 500: 50%; ACT scores over 18: 77%; ACT scores over 24: 17%; ACT scores over 30: 2%.

Faculty *Total:* 127, 45% full-time, 24% with terminal degrees. *Student/faculty ratio:* 12:1.

Majors Accounting; art; art history; biology; business administration; chemistry; criminal justice/law enforcement administration; early childhood education; English; gerontology; history; liberal arts and sciences/liberal studies; management science; middle school education; music; natural sciences; nursing; occupational therapy; pre-medicine; psychology; religious studies; social work; sociology.

Academic Programs *Special study options:* academic remediation for entering students, accelerated degree program, adult/continuing education programs, advanced placement credit, cooperative education, double majors, independent study, internships, part-time degree program, services for LD students, student-designed majors, study abroad, summer session for credit. *ROTC:* Army (c).

Library Duns Scotus Library plus 1 other with 59,057 titles, 451 serial subscriptions, 1,800 audiovisual materials, an OPAC.

Computers on Campus 86 computers available on campus for general student use. Internet access, at least one staffed computer lab available.

Student Life *Housing:* college housing not available. *Activities and Organizations:* drama/theater group, student-run newspaper, choral group, Future Educators Association, Student Leader Advisory Council, Lourdes College Chorus, Student Nurse Association, Campus Ministry Organization. *Campus security:* 24-hour emergency response devices, late-night transport/escort service, evening patrols by trained security personnel. *Student Services:* personal/psychological counseling.

Athletics *Intramural sports:* badminton M, baseball M/W, basketball M/W, bowling M/W, football M, golf M/W, soccer M/W, table tennis M/W, tennis M/W, volleyball M/W.

Lourdes College (continued)

Standardized Tests *Required:* SAT I or ACT (for admission).

Costs (2001–02) *Tuition:* $12,200 full-time, $300 per credit hour part-time. Full-time tuition and fees vary according to course load and program. Part-time tuition and fees vary according to course load and program. *Required fees:* $900 full-time, $40 per credit hour. *Payment plans:* installment, deferred payment. *Waivers:* senior citizens and employees or children of employees.

Applying *Options:* common application, early admission, deferred entrance. *Application fee:* $25. *Required:* high school transcript. *Required for some:* interview. *Application deadline:* rolling (freshmen), rolling (transfers). *Notification:* continuous (freshmen).

Admissions Contact Office of Admissions, Lourdes College, 6832 Convent Boulevard, Sylvania, OH 43560. *Phone:* 419-885-5291. *Toll-free phone:* 800-878-3210 Ext. 1299. *Fax:* 419-882-3987. *E-mail:* lcadmits@lourdes.edu.

MALONE COLLEGE
Canton, Ohio

- **Independent** comprehensive, founded 1892, affiliated with Evangelical Friends Church-Eastern Region
- **Calendar** semesters
- **Degrees** bachelor's and master's
- **Suburban** 78-acre campus with easy access to Cleveland
- **Endowment** $5.4 million
- **Coed,** 1,900 undergraduate students, 89% full-time, 60% women, 40% men
- **Moderately difficult** entrance level, 86% of applicants were admitted

Malone College is a Christian college committed to offering an education of the highest quality in a setting that encourages a solid devotion to God. The combination of strong academics, great location, and spiritual development makes Malone an attractive and challenging opportunity for students.

Undergraduates 1,690 full-time, 210 part-time. Students come from 24 states and territories, 11 other countries, 9% are from out of state, 5% African American, 0.3% Asian American or Pacific Islander, 0.8% Hispanic American, 0.2% Native American, 1.0% international, 4% transferred in, 50% live on campus. *Retention:* 74% of 2001 full-time freshmen returned.

Freshmen *Admission:* 902 applied, 773 admitted, 357 enrolled. *Average high school GPA:* 3.29. *Test scores:* SAT verbal scores over 500: 79%; SAT math scores over 500: 71%; ACT scores over 18: 94%; SAT verbal scores over 600: 24%; SAT math scores over 600: 31%; ACT scores over 24: 43%; SAT verbal scores over 700: 3%; SAT math scores over 700: 5%; ACT scores over 30: 6%.

Faculty *Total:* 195, 53% full-time, 35% with terminal degrees. *Student/faculty ratio:* 14:1.

Majors Accounting; art; art education; biblical studies; biology; biology education; broadcast journalism; business administration; business management/ administrative services related; chemistry; chemistry education; communications; computer science; early childhood education; education of the specific learning disabled; English; English education; exercise sciences; health education; health/ physical education; history; journalism; liberal arts and sciences/liberal studies; mathematics; medical technology; middle school education; music; musical instrument technology; music teacher education; nursing related; pastoral counseling; physical education; physics education; political science; psychology; public health education/promotion; public relations; recreation/leisure studies; religious music; science education; social studies education; social work; Spanish; Spanish language education; speech education; sport/fitness administration; theater arts/drama; theology/ministry related.

Academic Programs *Special study options:* academic remediation for entering students, accelerated degree program, adult/continuing education programs, advanced placement credit, cooperative education, distance learning, double majors, honors programs, independent study, internships, off-campus study, part-time degree program, services for LD students, student-designed majors, study abroad, summer session for credit.

Library Everett L. Cattell Library with 154,226 titles, 1,850 serial subscriptions, 13,511 audiovisual materials, an OPAC.

Computers on Campus 145 computers available on campus for general student use. A campuswide network can be accessed from student residence rooms and from off campus. Internet access, at least one staffed computer lab available.

Student Life *Housing:* on-campus residence required through junior year. *Options:* men-only, women-only. *Activities and Organizations:* drama/theater group, student-run newspaper, radio station, choral group, marching band, Spiritual Life Committee, student activities committee, student senate, Woolman-Whittier-Fox hall council, intramural athletics. *Campus security:* 24-hour emergency response devices and patrols, late-night transport/escort service. *Student Services:* health clinic, personal/psychological counseling.

Athletics Member NAIA, NCCAA. *Intercollegiate sports:* baseball M(s), basketball M(s)/W(s), cross-country running M(s)/W(s), football M(s), golf M(s)/W(s), soccer M(s)/W(s), softball W(s), tennis M(s)/W(s), track and field M(s)/W(s), volleyball W(s). *Intramural sports:* badminton M/W, basketball M/W, bowling M/W, cross-country running M/W, football M, racquetball M/W, skiing (cross-country) M/W, soccer M/W, softball M/W, table tennis M/W, tennis M/W, volleyball M/W, weight lifting M/W.

Standardized Tests *Required:* SAT I or ACT (for admission).

Costs (2001–02) *Comprehensive fee:* $19,190 includes full-time tuition ($13,310), mandatory fees ($240), and room and board ($5640). Part-time tuition: $300 per semester hour. Part-time tuition and fees vary according to course load. *Required fees:* $60 per term part-time. *Room and board:* College room only: $3100. Room and board charges vary according to board plan. *Payment plan:* installment. *Waivers:* senior citizens and employees or children of employees.

Financial Aid Of all full-time matriculated undergraduates who enrolled in 2001, 1513 applied for aid, 1124 were judged to have need, 216 had their need fully met. 351 Federal Work-Study jobs (averaging $1616). 104 State and other part-time jobs (averaging $1561). In 2001, 353 non-need-based awards were made. *Average percent of need met:* 84%. *Average financial aid package:* $10,979. *Average need-based loan:* $3295. *Average need-based gift aid:* $7375. *Average non-need based aid:* $3485. *Average indebtedness upon graduation:* $16,072. *Financial aid deadline:* 7/31.

Applying *Options:* common application, electronic application, early admission, deferred entrance. *Application fee:* $20. *Required:* essay or personal statement, high school transcript, minimum 2.5 GPA. *Required for some:* interview. *Application deadlines:* 7/1 (freshmen), 7/1 (transfers). *Notification:* continuous (freshmen).

Admissions Contact Mr. John Chopka, Vice President of Enrollment Management, Malone College, 515 25th Street, NW, Canton, OH 44709-3897. *Phone:* 330-471-8145. *Toll-free phone:* 800-521-1146. *Fax:* 330-471-8149. *E-mail:* admissions@malone.edu.

MARIETTA COLLEGE
Marietta, Ohio

- **Independent** comprehensive, founded 1835
- **Calendar** semesters
- **Degrees** associate, bachelor's, and master's
- **Small-town** 120-acre campus
- **Endowment** $52.7 million
- **Coed,** 1,205 undergraduate students, 93% full-time, 50% women, 50% men
- **Moderately difficult** entrance level, 94% of applicants were admitted

Founded in 1788, the city of Marietta, Ohio, has the distinction of being the first permanent settlement of America's Northwest Territory. The College traces its beginning to 1797. Both the city and the College are rich in history and lined with stately homes, brick-paved streets, and antiques stores. In 1860, Marietta College became only the sixteenth college in America to be awarded a chapter of Phi Beta Kappa. Students' academic life is enriched by the McDonough Leadership Program, which is one of the most comprehensive programs in leadership studies in the country. In the program, students may earn a minor, be actively involved in volunteer work, and participate in internships throughout the world.

Undergraduates 1,115 full-time, 90 part-time. Students come from 37 states and territories, 9 other countries, 38% are from out of state, 2% African American, 1% Asian American or Pacific Islander, 1% Hispanic American, 0.3% Native American, 5% international, 4% transferred in, 85% live on campus. *Retention:* 76% of 2001 full-time freshmen returned.

Freshmen *Admission:* 1,152 applied, 1,079 admitted, 367 enrolled. *Average high school GPA:* 3.25. *Test scores:* SAT verbal scores over 500: 66%; SAT math scores over 500: 73%; ACT scores over 18: 91%; SAT verbal scores over 600: 25%; SAT math scores over 600: 31%; ACT scores over 24: 43%; SAT verbal scores over 700: 3%; SAT math scores over 700: 3%; ACT scores over 30: 7%.

Faculty *Total:* 128. *Student/faculty ratio:* 12:1.

Majors Accounting; art; athletic training/sports medicine; biochemistry; biology; business administration; business communications; business marketing and marketing management; chemistry; communications; computer science; economics; education; elementary education; English; environmental science; fine/studio arts; geology; graphic design/commercial art/illustration; history; human resources management; information sciences/systems; international business; journalism; liberal arts and sciences/liberal studies; mathematics; music; petroleum engineering; philosophy; physics; political science; psychology; public relations; radio/ television broadcasting; secondary education; Spanish; speech/rhetorical studies; theater arts/drama.

Academic Programs *Special study options:* academic remediation for entering students, accelerated degree program, adult/continuing education programs, advanced placement credit, double majors, English as a second language, honors programs, independent study, internships, off-campus study, part-time degree program, services for LD students, student-designed majors, study abroad, summer session for credit. *Unusual degree programs:* 3-2 engineering with University of Pennsylvania, Columbia University, Case Western Reserve University, Washington University in St. Louis.

Library Dawes Memorial Library with 250,000 titles, 1,300 serial subscriptions, 7,300 audiovisual materials, an OPAC, a Web page.

Computers on Campus 200 computers available on campus for general student use. A campuswide network can be accessed from student residence rooms and from off campus. Internet access, at least one staffed computer lab available.

Student Life *Housing:* on-campus residence required through senior year. *Options:* coed, men-only, women-only. *Activities and Organizations:* drama/theater group, student-run newspaper, radio and television station, choral group, Student Programming Board, student government, Great Outdoors Club, Inter-Varsity Christian Fellowship, Arts and Humanities Council, national fraternities, national sororities. *Campus security:* 24-hour emergency response devices and patrols, student patrols, late-night transport/escort service, controlled dormitory access. *Student Services:* health clinic, personal/psychological counseling.

Athletics Member NCAA. All Division III. *Intercollegiate sports:* baseball M, basketball M/W, crew M/W, cross-country running M/W, football M, golf M/W, lacrosse M, soccer M/W, softball W, tennis M/W, track and field M/W, volleyball W. *Intramural sports:* badminton W, basketball M/W, bowling M/W, cross-country running M/W, football M/W, golf M/W, ice hockey M, racquetball M/W, rugby M(c)/W(c), soccer M/W, softball M/W, swimming M/W, tennis M/W, volleyball M/W, weight lifting M.

Standardized Tests *Required:* SAT I or ACT (for admission). *Recommended:* SAT II: Subject Tests (for admission).

Costs (2001–02) *Comprehensive fee:* $24,580 includes full-time tuition ($18,838), mandatory fees ($238), and room and board ($5504). Part-time tuition: $625 per hour. Part-time tuition and fees vary according to class time. *Room and board:* College room only: $2564. *Payment plan:* installment. *Waivers:* employees or children of employees.

Financial Aid Of all full-time matriculated undergraduates who enrolled in 2001, 928 applied for aid, 837 were judged to have need, 328 had their need fully met. 607 Federal Work-Study jobs (averaging $955). In 2001, 103 non-need-based awards were made. *Average percent of need met:* 90%. *Average financial aid package:* $16,520. *Average need-based loan:* $4153. *Average need-based gift aid:* $7993. *Average non-need based aid:* $7322. *Average indebtedness upon graduation:* $16,461.

Applying *Options:* common application, electronic application, early admission, deferred entrance. *Application fee:* $25. *Required:* essay or personal statement, high school transcript, minimum 2.0 GPA, 2 letters of recommendation. *Recommended:* minimum 3.0 GPA, interview. *Application deadline:* 4/15 (freshmen), rolling (transfers). *Notification:* continuous until 5/1 (freshmen).

Admissions Contact Ms. Marke Vickers, Director of Admission, Marietta College, 215 Fifth Street, Marietta, OH 45750-4000. *Phone:* 740-376-4600. *Toll-free phone:* 800-331-7896. *Fax:* 740-376-8888. *E-mail:* admit@marietta.edu.

Mercy College of Northwest Ohio
Toledo, Ohio

- **Independent** primarily 2-year, founded 1993, affiliated with Roman Catholic Church
- **Calendar** semesters
- **Degrees** certificates, associate, and bachelor's
- **Urban** campus with easy access to Detroit
- **Endowment** $2.5 million
- **Coed, primarily women**
- **Moderately difficult** entrance level

Faculty *Student/faculty ratio:* 6:1.

Student Life *Campus security:* 24-hour emergency response devices and patrols, late-night transport/escort service, controlled dormitory access.

Standardized Tests *Required for some:* SAT I or ACT (for admission).

Costs (2001–02) *One-time required fee:* $60. *Tuition:* $5668 full-time, $218 per semester hour part-time. Full-time tuition and fees vary according to course load and program. Part-time tuition and fees vary according to course load. *Required fees:* $147 full-time, $50 per term part-time. *Room only:* $1740. Room and board charges vary according to location. *Payment plans:* installment, deferred payment.

Financial Aid Of all full-time matriculated undergraduates who enrolled in 2001, 18 Federal Work-Study jobs (averaging $21560).

Applying *Application fee:* $25. *Required:* high school transcript. *Required for some:* minimum 2.3 GPA.

Admissions Contact Diana Hernandez, Data Research Coordinator, Mercy College of Northwest Ohio, 2221 Madison Avenue, Toledo, OH 43624-1197. *Phone:* 419-251-1313. *Toll-free phone:* 888-80-Mercy. *Fax:* 419-251-1462.

Miami University
Oxford, Ohio

- **State-related** university, founded 1809, part of Miami University System
- **Calendar** semesters
- **Degrees** bachelor's, master's, doctoral, and post-master's certificates
- **Small-town** 2000-acre campus with easy access to Cincinnati
- **Endowment** $236.3 million
- **Coed,** 15,153 undergraduate students, 97% full-time, 55% women, 45% men
- **Moderately difficult** entrance level, 74% of applicants were admitted

Undergraduates 14,720 full-time, 433 part-time. Students come from 49 states and territories, 70 other countries, 27% are from out of state, 4% African American, 2% Asian American or Pacific Islander, 2% Hispanic American, 0.5% Native American, 0.5% international, 2% transferred in, 45% live on campus. *Retention:* 90% of 2001 full-time freshmen returned.

Freshmen *Admission:* 12,500 applied, 9,293 admitted, 3,385 enrolled. *Test scores:* SAT verbal scores over 500: 94%; SAT math scores over 500: 95%; ACT scores over 18: 99%; SAT verbal scores over 600: 50%; SAT math scores over 600: 66%; ACT scores over 24: 84%; SAT verbal scores over 700: 7%; SAT math scores over 700: 12%; ACT scores over 30: 15%.

Faculty *Total:* 1,035, 79% full-time, 75% with terminal degrees. *Student/faculty ratio:* 17:1.

Majors Accounting; aerospace engineering; African-American studies; American studies; anthropology; architectural environmental design; architecture; art; art education; art history; athletic training/sports medicine; biochemistry; biology; biology education; botany; business; business administration; business economics; business marketing and marketing management; chemistry; child care/development; city/community/regional planning; classics; computer/information sciences; computer systems analysis; creative writing; dietetics; early childhood education; earth sciences; economics; elementary education; engineering/industrial management; engineering physics; engineering technology; English; English education; exercise sciences; family/consumer studies; finance; fine/studio arts; French; geography; geology; German; Greek (ancient and medieval); health education; health/physical education; history; home economics; home economics education; human resources management; individual/family development; industrial/manufacturing engineering; interdisciplinary studies; interior design; international relations; journalism; Latin (ancient and medieval); linguistics; management information systems/business data processing; management science; mass communications; mathematical statistics; mathematics; mechanical engineering; medical technology; microbiology/bacteriology; middle school education; music; music (general performance); music teacher education; nursing; operations management; operations research; organizational behavior; philosophy; physical education; physics; political science; pre-dentistry; pre-law; pre-medicine; pre-veterinary studies; psychology; public administration; purchasing/contracts management; religious studies; Russian; science education; secondary education; social studies education; social work; sociology; Spanish; special education; speech-language pathology; speech-language pathology/audiology; speech/rhetorical studies; sport/fitness administration; systems science/theory; technical/business writing; theater arts/drama; wood science/paper technology; zoology.

Academic Programs *Special study options:* adult/continuing education programs, advanced placement credit, cooperative education, double majors, honors programs, independent study, internships, off-campus study, services for LD students, student-designed majors, study abroad, summer session for credit. *ROTC:* Army (c), Navy (b), Air Force (b). *Unusual degree programs:* 3-2 engineering with Case Western Reserve University, Columbia University; forestry with Duke University.

Library King Library plus 3 others with 2.7 million titles, 12,234 serial subscriptions, 134,404 audiovisual materials, an OPAC, a Web page.

Computers on Campus 1000 computers available on campus for general student use. A campuswide network can be accessed from student residence rooms and from off campus. Internet access, online (class) registration, at least one staffed computer lab available.

Student Life *Housing:* on-campus residence required for freshman year. *Options:* coed, men-only, women-only, disabled students. *Activities and Organizations:* drama/theater group, student-run newspaper, radio and television station, choral group, marching band, student government, Alpha Phi Omega, Miami Marketing Enterprises, Campus Crusade for Christ, national fraternities, national sororities. *Campus security:* 24-hour emergency response devices and patrols,

Miami University (continued)
student patrols, late-night transport/escort service, controlled dormitory access. *Student Services:* health clinic, personal/psychological counseling, women's center.

Athletics Member NCAA. All Division I except football (Division I-A). *Intercollegiate sports:* archery M(c)/W(c), baseball M(s), basketball M(s)/W(s), cross-country running M(s)/W(s), equestrian sports M(c)/W(c), fencing M(c)/W(c), field hockey W(s), golf M(s), gymnastics M(c)/W(c), ice hockey M(s), lacrosse M(c), racquetball M(c)/W(c), rugby M(c), sailing M(c)/W(c), soccer M(c)/W(s), softball W(s), swimming M(s)/W(s), tennis M(c)/W(s), track and field M(s)/W(s), volleyball M(c)/W(s), wrestling M(c). *Intramural sports:* archery M/W, badminton M(c)/W(c), basketball M/W, crew M(c)/W(c), cross-country running M(c)/W(c), equestrian sports M(c)/W(c), fencing M(c)/W(c), field hockey W, football M/W, golf M(c)/W(c), gymnastics M(c)/W(c), ice hockey M(c)/W(c), lacrosse M(c)/W(c), racquetball M(c)/W(c), rugby M(c), sailing M/W, skiing (cross-country) M/W, skiing (downhill) M(c)/W(c), soccer M(c)/W(c), softball M/W, squash M(c)/W(c), swimming M/W, table tennis M(c)/W(c), tennis M(c)/W(c), track and field M/W, volleyball M(c)/W(c), water polo M(c)/W(c), weight lifting M(c)/W(c), wrestling M(c).

Standardized Tests *Required:* SAT I or ACT (for admission).

Costs (2001–02) *Tuition:* state resident $5796 full-time, $288 per credit hour part-time; nonresident $13,470 full-time, $607 per credit hour part-time. Full-time tuition and fees vary according to course load. Part-time tuition and fees vary according to course load. *Required fees:* $1119 full-time, $47 per credit hour, $18 per term part-time. *Room and board:* $5970; room only: $2910. Room and board charges vary according to board plan and housing facility. *Payment plan:* installment. *Waivers:* senior citizens and employees or children of employees.

Financial Aid Of all full-time matriculated undergraduates who enrolled in 2001, 9469 applied for aid, 5484 were judged to have need, 1461 had their need fully met. 1349 Federal Work-Study jobs. In 2001, 2686 non-need-based awards were made. *Average percent of need met:* 72%. *Average financial aid package:* $6636. *Average need-based loan:* $3321. *Average need-based gift aid:* $3988. *Average non-need based aid:* $3108. *Average indebtedness upon graduation:* $16,379.

Applying *Options:* electronic application, early decision, early action. *Application fee:* $45. *Required:* high school transcript. *Recommended:* essay or personal statement, 1 letter of recommendation. *Application deadlines:* 1/31 (freshmen), 5/1 (transfers). *Early decision:* 11/1. *Notification:* 3/15 (freshmen), 12/15 (early decision), 2/1 (early action).

Admissions Contact Michael E. Mills, Miami University, 301 South Campus Avenue, Campus Avenue Building, Oxford, OH 45056. *Phone:* 513-529-5040. *Fax:* 513-529-1550. *E-mail:* admission@muohio.edu.

MIAMI UNIVERSITY-HAMILTON CAMPUS
Hamilton, Ohio

- **State-supported** founded 1968, part of Miami University System
- **Calendar** semesters
- **Degrees** certificates, associate, bachelor's, and master's (degrees awarded by Miami University main campus)
- **Suburban** 78-acre campus with easy access to Cincinnati
- **Coed,** 2,900 undergraduate students, 44% full-time, 57% women, 43% men
- **Noncompetitive** entrance level

Undergraduates 5% African American, 1% Asian American or Pacific Islander, 0.8% Hispanic American, 0.4% Native American, 1% international.

Faculty *Total:* 207, 40% full-time. *Student/faculty ratio:* 16:1.

Majors Accounting technician; computer engineering technology; data processing technology; early childhood education; electrical/electronic engineering technology; engineering technology; liberal arts and sciences/liberal studies; mechanical engineering technology; nursing.

Academic Programs *Special study options:* academic remediation for entering students, adult/continuing education programs, advanced placement credit, cooperative education, internships, part-time degree program, services for LD students, student-designed majors, study abroad, summer session for credit. *ROTC:* Navy (c), Air Force (c).

Library Rentschler Library with 68,000 titles, 400 serial subscriptions, an OPAC, a Web page.

Computers on Campus 150 computers available on campus for general student use. A campuswide network can be accessed from off campus. Internet access, online (class) registration, at least one staffed computer lab available.

Student Life *Housing:* college housing not available. *Activities and Organizations:* drama/theater group, student-run newspaper, choral group, student government, Campus Activities Committee, Organization for Wiser Learners, Community Empowerment Committee, Minority Action Committee. *Campus security:* 24-hour emergency response devices and patrols, late-night transport/escort service. *Student Services:* personal/psychological counseling.

Athletics *Intercollegiate sports:* baseball M, basketball M/W, golf M, tennis M/W, volleyball W. *Intramural sports:* basketball M/W, bowling M/W, skiing (cross-country) M/W, soccer M/W, softball M/W, tennis M/W, volleyball M/W, weight lifting M/W.

Standardized Tests *Required for some:* SAT I or ACT (for placement).

Costs (2001–02) *Tuition:* state resident $2812 full-time, $117 per credit part-time; nonresident $10,486 full-time, $437 per credit part-time. Full-time tuition and fees vary according to class time. Part-time tuition and fees vary according to class time. *Required fees:* $328 full-time, $12 per credit, $15 per term part-time. *Payment plan:* installment. *Waivers:* employees or children of employees.

Applying *Application fee:* $25. *Required:* high school transcript. *Application deadline:* rolling (freshmen), rolling (transfers). *Notification:* continuous (freshmen).

Admissions Contact Ms. Triana Adlon, Director of Admission and Financial Aid, Miami University-Hamilton Campus, 1601 Peck Boulevard, Hamilton, OH 45011-3399. *Phone:* 513-785-3111.

MIAMI UNIVERSITY-MIDDLETOWN CAMPUS
Middletown, Ohio

- **State-supported** primarily 2-year, founded 1966, part of Miami University System
- **Calendar** semesters
- **Degrees** certificates, diplomas, associate, and bachelor's (also offers up to 2 years of most bachelor's degree programs offered at Miami University main campus)
- **Small-town** 141-acre campus with easy access to Cincinnati and Dayton
- **Endowment** $779,742
- **Coed**
- **Noncompetitive** entrance level

Faculty *Student/faculty ratio:* 20:1.

Student Life *Campus security:* 24-hour patrols, late-night transport/escort service.

Standardized Tests *Recommended:* SAT I or ACT (for placement).

Applying *Options:* electronic application, early admission, deferred entrance. *Application fee:* $25. *Required:* high school transcript.

Admissions Contact Mrs. Mary Lu Flynn, Director of Enrollment Services, Miami University-Middletown Campus, 4200 East University Boulevard, Middletown, OH 45042. *Phone:* 513-727-3216. *Toll-free phone:* 800-622-2262. *Fax:* 513-727-3223. *E-mail:* flynnml@muohio.edu.

MOUNT CARMEL COLLEGE OF NURSING
Columbus, Ohio

- **Independent** 4-year
- **Degree** bachelor's
- 375 undergraduate students
- 50% of applicants were admitted

Undergraduates 7% African American, 1% Asian American or Pacific Islander, 1% Hispanic American. *Retention:* 80% of 2001 full-time freshmen returned.

Freshmen *Admission:* 260 applied, 130 admitted. *Average high school GPA:* 2.60.

Faculty *Total:* 31, 74% full-time. *Student/faculty ratio:* 8:1.

Costs (2002–03) *Tuition:* $9167 full-time, $260 per credit hour part-time. Full-time tuition and fees vary according to student level. Part-time tuition and fees vary according to student level. *Required fees:* $300 full-time, $150 per term part-time. *Room only:* $2592.

Financial Aid Of all full-time matriculated undergraduates who enrolled in 2001, 245 applied for aid, 200 were judged to have need, 50 had their need fully met. 27 State and other part-time jobs (averaging $1388). In 2001, 20 non-need-based awards were made. *Average percent of need met:* 70%. *Average financial aid package:* $8562. *Average non-need based aid:* $2000. *Average indebtedness upon graduation:* $25,000.

Admissions Contact Ms. Merschel Menefield, Director of Admissions, Mount Carmel College of Nursing, 127 South Davis Avenue, Columbus, OH 43222. *Phone:* 614-234-5800.

MOUNT UNION COLLEGE
Alliance, Ohio

- **Independent United Methodist** 4-year, founded 1846
- **Calendar** semesters
- **Degree** bachelor's
- **Suburban** 105-acre campus with easy access to Cleveland
- **Endowment** $126.2 million
- **Coed,** 2,368 undergraduate students, 87% full-time, 58% women, 42% men
- **Moderately difficult** entrance level, 81% of applicants were admitted

There are numerous international education opportunities at Mount Union College. In addition to the cultural interaction with students from approximately fifteen countries who study at the College, many students take advantage of the study-abroad program. The College makes grants available for study overseas, regardless of the student's major.

Undergraduates 2,060 full-time, 308 part-time. Students come from 20 states and territories, 15 other countries, 8% are from out of state, 4% African American, 0.3% Asian American or Pacific Islander, 0.6% Hispanic American, 0.3% Native American, 1% international, 8% transferred in, 78% live on campus. *Retention:* 74% of 2001 full-time freshmen returned.

Freshmen *Admission:* 2,026 applied, 1,639 admitted, 608 enrolled. *Average high school GPA:* 3.23. *Test scores:* ACT scores over 18: 91%; ACT scores over 24: 33%; ACT scores over 30: 2%.

Faculty *Total:* 231, 51% full-time, 42% with terminal degrees. *Student/faculty ratio:* 14:1.

Majors Accounting; American studies; art; Asian studies; astronomy; athletic training/sports medicine; biology; business administration; chemistry; communications; computer science; design/visual communications; early childhood education; economics; English; English composition; environmental biology; exercise sciences; French; geology; German; history; information sciences/systems; interdisciplinary studies; international business; Japanese; mass communications; mathematics; middle school education; music; music (general performance); music teacher education; philosophy; physical education; physics; political science; psychology; religious studies; sociology; Spanish; sport/fitness administration; theater arts/drama.

Academic Programs *Special study options:* accelerated degree program, adult/continuing education programs, advanced placement credit, cooperative education, double majors, English as a second language, honors programs, independent study, internships, off-campus study, part-time degree program, services for LD students, student-designed majors, study abroad, summer session for credit. *ROTC:* Army (c), Air Force (c).

Library Mount Union College Library plus 2 others with 228,850 titles, 972 serial subscriptions, 500 audiovisual materials, an OPAC, a Web page.

Computers on Campus 200 computers available on campus for general student use. A campuswide network can be accessed from student residence rooms and from off campus. Internet access, online (class) registration, at least one staffed computer lab available.

Student Life *Housing:* on-campus residence required through sophomore year. *Options:* coed, men-only, women-only, disabled students. *Activities and Organizations:* drama/theater group, student-run newspaper, radio station, choral group, marching band, Association of Women Students, Student Senate, Black Student Union, Student Activities Council, Association of International Students, national fraternities, national sororities. *Campus security:* 24-hour emergency response devices and patrols, 24-hour locked residence hall entrances, outside phones. *Student Services:* health clinic, personal/psychological counseling.

Athletics Member NCAA. All Division III. *Intercollegiate sports:* baseball M, basketball M/W, cross-country running M/W, football M, golf M/W, soccer M/W, swimming M/W, tennis M/W, track and field M/W, volleyball W, wrestling M. *Intramural sports:* archery M/W, badminton M/W, basketball M/W, bowling M/W, football M, golf M/W, gymnastics M/W, racquetball M/W, soccer M/W, softball M/W, swimming M/W, tennis M/W, track and field M/W, volleyball M/W, weight lifting M/W.

Standardized Tests *Required:* SAT I or ACT (for admission).

Costs (2001–02) *Comprehensive fee:* $21,120 includes full-time tuition ($15,440), mandatory fees ($870), and room and board ($4810). Part-time tuition: $650 per semester hour. *Room and board:* College room only: $2870. Room and board charges vary according to housing facility. *Payment plans:* tuition prepayment, installment. *Waivers:* children of alumni, adult students, senior citizens, and employees or children of employees.

Financial Aid Of all full-time matriculated undergraduates who enrolled in 2001, 1744 applied for aid, 1573 were judged to have need, 329 had their need fully met. 235 State and other part-time jobs (averaging $1336). In 2001, 401 non-need-based awards were made. *Average percent of need met:* 85%. *Average financial aid package:* $13,422. *Average need-based loan:* $3647. *Average need-based gift aid:* $9660. *Average indebtedness upon graduation:* $14,762.

Applying *Options:* electronic application, early admission, deferred entrance. *Application fee:* $2. *Required:* essay or personal statement, high school transcript, minimum 2.0 GPA, 1 letter of recommendation. *Recommended:* interview. *Application deadline:* rolling (freshmen), rolling (transfers). *Notification:* continuous (freshmen).

Admissions Contact Ms. Amy Tomko, Vice President of Enrollment Services, Mount Union College, 1972 Clark Avenue, Alliance, OH 44601. *Phone:* 330-823-2590. *Toll-free phone:* 800-334-6682 (in-state); 800-992-6682 (out-of-state). *Fax:* 330-823-3487. *E-mail:* admissn@muc.edu.

MOUNT VERNON NAZARENE UNIVERSITY
Mount Vernon, Ohio

- **Independent Nazarene** comprehensive, founded 1964
- **Calendar** 4-1-4
- **Degrees** associate, bachelor's, and master's
- **Small-town** 210-acre campus with easy access to Columbus
- **Endowment** $7.6 million
- **Coed,** 2,106 undergraduate students, 91% full-time, 56% women, 44% men
- **Moderately difficult** entrance level, 83% of applicants were admitted

Undergraduates 1,907 full-time, 199 part-time. Students come from 21 states and territories, 12% are from out of state, 2% African American, 0.8% Asian American or Pacific Islander, 0.7% Hispanic American, 0.3% Native American, 0.3% international, 4% transferred in, 75% live on campus. *Retention:* 77% of 2001 full-time freshmen returned.

Freshmen *Admission:* 813 applied, 671 admitted, 360 enrolled. *Average high school GPA:* 3.18. *Test scores:* SAT verbal scores over 500: 61%; SAT math scores over 500: 78%; ACT scores over 18: 91%; SAT verbal scores over 600: 30%; SAT math scores over 600: 25%; ACT scores over 24: 35%; SAT verbal scores over 700: 7%; SAT math scores over 700: 7%; ACT scores over 30: 4%.

Faculty *Total:* 182, 39% full-time, 39% with terminal degrees. *Student/faculty ratio:* 18:1.

Majors Accounting; applied art; art; art education; athletic training/sports medicine; audio engineering; biblical studies; biological/physical sciences; biology; broadcast journalism; business administration; business education; business marketing and marketing management; chemistry; child care services management; communications; computer science; criminal justice/law enforcement administration; data processing technology; design/visual communications; early childhood education; education; elementary education; English; English education; exercise sciences; health education; history; home economics; home economics education; human services; journalism; liberal arts and sciences/liberal studies; literature; mass communications; mathematics; mathematics education; medical technology; middle school education; music; music (piano and organ performance); music teacher education; music (voice and choral/opera performance); natural resources conservation; philosophy; physical education; physical therapy; pre-dentistry; pre-law; pre-medicine; pre-pharmacy studies; pre-veterinary studies; psychology; religious education; religious music; religious studies; science education; secondary education; secretarial science; social sciences; social studies education; social work; sociology; Spanish; special education; sport/fitness administration; theater arts/drama; theology; wind/percussion instruments.

Academic Programs *Special study options:* academic remediation for entering students, adult/continuing education programs, advanced placement credit, double majors, freshman honors college, honors programs, independent study, internships, off-campus study, part-time degree program, services for LD students, study abroad, summer session for credit.

Library Thorne Library/Learning Resource Center with 93,743 titles, 560 serial subscriptions, 3,382 audiovisual materials, an OPAC, a Web page.

Computers on Campus 212 computers available on campus for general student use. A campuswide network can be accessed from student residence rooms and from off campus. Internet access, at least one staffed computer lab available.

Student Life *Housing:* on-campus residence required through senior year. *Options:* men-only, women-only, disabled students. *Activities and Organizations:* drama/theater group, student-run newspaper, radio station, choral group, campus ministry groups, Student Government Association, Student Education Association, Drama Club, Music Department Ensembles. *Campus security:* 24-hour emergency response devices and patrols, late-night transport/escort service, controlled dormitory access. *Student Services:* health clinic, personal/psychological counseling.

Athletics Member NAIA, NCCAA. *Intercollegiate sports:* baseball M(s), basketball M(s)/W(s), golf M(s), soccer M(s)/W(s), softball W(s), volleyball W(s). *Intramural sports:* basketball M/W, bowling M/W, football M/W, skiing (downhill) M/W, soccer M/W, softball M/W, table tennis M/W, volleyball M/W.

Mount Vernon Nazarene University (continued)

Standardized Tests *Required:* ACT (for admission).

Costs (2002–03) *One-time required fee:* $146. *Comprehensive fee:* $17,815 includes full-time tuition ($12,810), mandatory fees ($478), and room and board ($4527). Full-time tuition and fees vary according to course load, program, reciprocity agreements, and student level. Part-time tuition: $458 per credit hour. Part-time tuition and fees vary according to course load, program, and reciprocity agreements. *Required fees:* $17 per credit hour. *Room and board:* College room only: $2511. Room and board charges vary according to board plan and housing facility. *Payment plan:* installment. *Waivers:* senior citizens and employees or children of employees.

Financial Aid Of all full-time matriculated undergraduates who enrolled in 2001, 1286 applied for aid, 1124 were judged to have need, 209 had their need fully met. 199 Federal Work-Study jobs (averaging $1445). 350 State and other part-time jobs (averaging $1462). *Average financial aid package:* $8025. *Average need-based loan:* $4997. *Average need-based gift aid:* $3939. *Average indebtedness upon graduation:* $16,700.

Applying *Options:* electronic application, early admission, deferred entrance. *Application fee:* $25. *Required:* essay or personal statement, high school transcript, minimum 2.5 GPA, 2 letters of recommendation. *Recommended:* interview. *Application deadlines:* 5/31 (freshmen), 5/31 (transfers). *Notification:* continuous until 8/1 (freshmen).

Admissions Contact Mount Vernon Nazarene University, 800 Martinsburg Road, Mount Vernon, OH 43050-9500. *Phone:* 740-397-6862 Ext. 4510. *Toll-free phone:* 800-782-2435. *Fax:* 740-393-0511. *E-mail:* admissions@mvnc.edu.

MUSKINGUM COLLEGE

New Concord, Ohio

- **Independent** comprehensive, founded 1837, affiliated with Presbyterian Church (U.S.A.)
- **Calendar** semesters
- **Degrees** bachelor's and master's
- **Small-town** 215-acre campus with easy access to Columbus
- **Endowment** $55.7 million
- **Coed,** 1,660 undergraduate students, 95% full-time, 51% women, 49% men
- **Moderately difficult** entrance level, 86% of applicants were admitted

Undergraduates 1,579 full-time, 81 part-time. 90% live on campus.

Freshmen *Admission:* 1,636 applied, 1,403 admitted, 440 enrolled. *Average high school GPA:* 3.2. *Test scores:* SAT verbal scores over 500: 61%; SAT math scores over 500: 65%; ACT scores over 18: 84%; SAT verbal scores over 600: 22%; SAT math scores over 600: 26%; ACT scores over 24: 31%; SAT verbal scores over 700: 3%; SAT math scores over 700: 4%; ACT scores over 30: 4%.

Faculty *Total:* 140, 62% full-time, 77% with terminal degrees. *Student/faculty ratio:* 16:1.

Majors Accounting; American studies; applied art; art; art education; biology; business administration; business education; chemistry; computer science; early childhood education; earth sciences; economics; education; elementary education; English; environmental science; French; geology; German; health education; history; humanities; interdisciplinary studies; international business; international relations; journalism; mass communications; mathematics; medical technology; molecular biology; music; music teacher education; natural resources conservation; neuroscience; philosophy; physical education; physics; political science; pre-dentistry; pre-law; pre-medicine; pre-veterinary studies; psychology; public policy analysis; radio/television broadcasting; religious studies; science education; secondary education; social sciences; sociology; Spanish; special education; theater arts/drama.

Academic Programs *Special study options:* accelerated degree program, advanced placement credit, double majors, English as a second language, external degree program, independent study, internships, off-campus study, part-time degree program, services for LD students, student-designed majors, study abroad, summer session for credit. *Unusual degree programs:* 3-2 engineering with Case Western Reserve University; nursing with Case Western Reserve University.

Library College Library with 233,000 titles, 900 serial subscriptions, 6,000 audiovisual materials, a Web page.

Computers on Campus 76 computers available on campus for general student use. A campuswide network can be accessed from student residence rooms and from off campus. Internet access, at least one staffed computer lab available.

Student Life *Housing:* on-campus residence required through sophomore year. *Options:* coed, men-only, women-only. *Activities and Organizations:* drama/theater group, student-run newspaper, radio and television station, choral group, marching band, Centerboard, student radio station, BACCHUS, Cable TV 8, Fellowship of Christian Students, national fraternities, national sororities. *Campus security:* 24-hour emergency response devices and patrols, student patrols, late-night transport/escort service. *Student Services:* health clinic, personal/psychological counseling, women's center.

Athletics Member NCAA. All Division III. *Intercollegiate sports:* baseball M, basketball M/W, cross-country running M/W, football M/W, golf M/W, soccer M/W, softball W, tennis M/W, track and field M/W, volleyball W, wrestling M. *Intramural sports:* badminton M/W, basketball M/W, bowling M/W, cross-country running M/W, football M/W, golf M/W, lacrosse M/W, racquetball M/W, rugby M/W, softball M/W, swimming M/W, table tennis M/W, tennis M/W, track and field M/W, volleyball M/W, weight lifting M/W, wrestling M.

Standardized Tests *Required:* SAT I or ACT (for admission).

Costs (2002–03) *One-time required fee:* $150. *Comprehensive fee:* $19,675 includes full-time tuition ($13,500), mandatory fees ($575), and room and board ($5600). Part-time tuition: $228 per hour. Part-time tuition and fees vary according to course load. *Room and board:* College room only: $2800. Room and board charges vary according to board plan and housing facility. *Payment plan:* installment. *Waivers:* senior citizens and employees or children of employees.

Financial Aid Of all full-time matriculated undergraduates who enrolled in 2001, 1283 applied for aid, 1151 were judged to have need, 567 had their need fully met. In 2001, 380 non-need-based awards were made. *Average percent of need met:* 91%. *Average financial aid package:* $12,271. *Average need-based loan:* $3780. *Average need-based gift aid:* $8787. *Average non-need based aid:* $4698. *Average indebtedness upon graduation:* $17,118.

Applying *Options:* electronic application, early admission, deferred entrance. *Required:* high school transcript, minimum 2.0 GPA, 1 letter of recommendation. *Recommended:* essay or personal statement, minimum 3.0 GPA, interview. *Application deadlines:* 6/1 (freshmen), 8/1 (transfers). *Notification:* continuous (freshmen).

Admissions Contact Mrs. Beth DaLonzo, Director of Admission, Muskingum College, 163 Stormont Street, New Concord, OH 43762. *Phone:* 740-826-8137. *Toll-free phone:* 800-752-6082. *Fax:* 740-826-8100. *E-mail:* adminfo@muskingum.edu.

NOTRE DAME COLLEGE

South Euclid, Ohio

- **Independent Roman Catholic** comprehensive, founded 1922
- **Calendar** semesters
- **Degrees** certificates, associate, bachelor's, and master's
- **Suburban** 53-acre campus with easy access to Cleveland
- **Endowment** $10.3 million
- **Coed,** 800 undergraduate students, 38% full-time, 90% women, 10% men
- **Moderately difficult** entrance level, 37% of applicants were admitted

NDC is a special place. The focus is on helping students of all ages develop confidence and build self-esteem through a rigorous yet supportive, career-oriented liberal arts environment. NDC is large enough to provide many of the opportunities of a large college, yet small enough to give students the individual attention important to their development.

Undergraduates Students come from 7 states and territories, 1 other country, 2% are from out of state, 30% African American, 0.9% Asian American or Pacific Islander, 1% Hispanic American, 0.2% Native American, 0.6% international, 21% live on campus. *Retention:* 62% of 2001 full-time freshmen returned.

Freshmen *Admission:* 401 applied, 148 admitted. *Average high school GPA:* 3.20. *Test scores:* SAT verbal scores over 500: 50%; SAT math scores over 500: 50%; ACT scores over 18: 88%; SAT verbal scores over 600: 25%; SAT math scores over 600: 25%; ACT scores over 24: 19%.

Faculty *Total:* 80, 36% full-time. *Student/faculty ratio:* 12:1.

Majors Accounting; art; art history; biochemistry; biology; business administration; business marketing and marketing management; chemistry; communications; dietetics; early childhood education; elementary education; English; environmental science; finance; fine/studio arts; history; human resources management; information sciences/systems; international business; mathematics; medical technology; nutrition science; paralegal/legal assistant; pastoral counseling; political science; pre-dentistry; pre-law; pre-medicine; psychology; secondary education; Spanish; theology.

Academic Programs *Special study options:* academic remediation for entering students, accelerated degree program, adult/continuing education programs, advanced placement credit, cooperative education, double majors, independent study, internships, off-campus study, part-time degree program, student-designed majors, study abroad, summer session for credit.

Library Clara Fritzsche Library with 9,983 audiovisual materials, an OPAC.

Computers on Campus Internet access, at least one staffed computer lab available.

Student Life *Housing:* on-campus residence required through junior year. *Options:* women-only. *Activities and Organizations:* drama/theater group, student-run newspaper, choral group, Undergraduate Student Senate, Resident Association Board, Masquers, Commuter Board, Gospel Choir. *Campus security:* 24-hour emergency response devices, late-night transport/escort service, controlled dormitory access, residence hall desk attendants. *Student Services:* health clinic, personal/psychological counseling.

Athletics Member NAIA. *Intercollegiate sports:* basketball W, soccer W, softball W, volleyball W. *Intramural sports:* basketball W, cross-country running W, football W, soccer W, softball W, swimming W, tennis W, volleyball W.

Standardized Tests *Required:* SAT I or ACT (for admission).

Costs (2002–03) *Comprehensive fee:* $21,958 includes full-time tuition ($15,552), mandatory fees ($500), and room and board ($5906). Full-time tuition and fees vary according to class time. Part-time tuition: $405 per credit. Part-time tuition and fees vary according to class time. *Room and board:* College room only: $2940. Room and board charges vary according to board plan. *Payment plan:* installment. *Waivers:* employees or children of employees.

Applying *Options:* deferred entrance. *Application fee:* $30. *Required:* high school transcript, minimum 2.0 GPA. *Recommended:* minimum 2.5 GPA, interview. *Application deadline:* rolling (freshmen), rolling (transfers). *Notification:* continuous (freshmen).

Admissions Contact Director of Admissions, Notre Dame College, South Euclid, OH 44121-4293. *Phone:* 216-381-1680 Ext. 355. *Toll-free phone:* 800-NDC-1680. *Fax:* 216-381-3802. *E-mail:* admissions@ndc.edu.

OBERLIN COLLEGE
Oberlin, Ohio

- **Independent** comprehensive, founded 1833
- **Calendar** 4-1-4
- **Degrees** diplomas, bachelor's, master's, and postbachelor's certificates
- **Small-town** 440-acre campus with easy access to Cleveland
- **Endowment** $631.2 million
- **Coed,** 2,840 undergraduate students, 97% full-time, 57% women, 43% men
- **Very difficult** entrance level, 36% of applicants were admitted

Oberlin College is an independent, coeducational liberal arts college of approximately 2,900 students. It comprises 2 divisions, the College of Arts and Sciences and the Conservatory of Music. Oberlin has a history of progressive thinking, a supportive academic community, and a diverse, active student body.

Undergraduates 2,753 full-time, 87 part-time. Students come from 55 states and territories, 26 other countries, 89% are from out of state, 8% African American, 6% Asian American or Pacific Islander, 4% Hispanic American, 0.7% Native American, 6% international, 3% transferred in, 70% live on campus. *Retention:* 90% of 2001 full-time freshmen returned.

Freshmen *Admission:* 5,548 applied, 1,972 admitted, 767 enrolled. *Average high school GPA:* 3.50. *Test scores:* SAT verbal scores over 500: 96%; SAT math scores over 500: 98%; ACT scores over 18: 100%; SAT verbal scores over 600: 84%; SAT math scores over 600: 79%; ACT scores over 24: 91%; SAT verbal scores over 700: 45%; SAT math scores over 700: 27%; ACT scores over 30: 48%.

Faculty *Total:* 273, 96% full-time. *Student/faculty ratio:* 10:1.

Majors African-American studies; anthropology; archaeology; art; art history; biochemistry; biology; chemistry; classics; comparative literature; computer science; creative writing; dance; East Asian studies; ecology; economics; English; environmental science; fine/studio arts; French; geology; German; Greek (modern); history; interdisciplinary studies; jazz; Judaic studies; Latin American studies; Latin (ancient and medieval); legal studies; mathematics; Middle Eastern studies; music; music history; music (piano and organ performance); music teacher education; music (voice and choral/opera performance); neuroscience; philosophy; physics; physiological psychology/psychobiology; political science; psychology; religious studies; romance languages; Russian; Russian/Slavic studies; sociology; Spanish; stringed instruments; theater arts/drama; wind/percussion instruments; women's studies.

Academic Programs *Special study options:* academic remediation for entering students, accelerated degree program, advanced placement credit, double majors, English as a second language, honors programs, independent study, internships, off-campus study, part-time degree program, services for LD students, student-designed majors, study abroad. *Unusual degree programs:* 3-2 engineering with Washington University in St. Louis, Case Western Reserve University, University of Pennsylvania.

Library Mudd Center Library plus 3 others with 1.5 million titles, 4,560 serial subscriptions, 59,186 audiovisual materials, an OPAC.

Computers on Campus 275 computers available on campus for general student use. A campuswide network can be accessed from student residence rooms and from off campus. At least one staffed computer lab available.

Student Life *Housing:* on-campus residence required through sophomore year. *Options:* coed, men-only, women-only, cooperative. *Activities and Organizations:* drama/theater group, student-run newspaper, radio station, choral group, Experimental College, Community Outreach, Black Students Organization, Students Cooperative Association, student radio station. *Campus security:* 24-hour emergency response devices and patrols, late-night transport/escort service, controlled dormitory access, crime prevention programs. *Student Services:* health clinic, personal/psychological counseling, women's center.

Athletics Member NCAA. All Division III. *Intercollegiate sports:* baseball M, basketball M/W, cross-country running M/W, equestrian sports M(c)/W(c), fencing M(c)/W(c), field hockey W, football M, golf M, ice hockey M(c)/W(c), lacrosse M/W, racquetball M(c)/W(c), rugby M(c)/W(c), soccer M/W, softball W(c), squash M(c)/W(c), swimming M/W, tennis M/W, track and field M/W, volleyball M(c)/W, water polo M(c). *Intramural sports:* basketball M/W, bowling M/W, cross-country running M/W, football M, golf M, racquetball M/W, soccer M/W, softball M/W, squash M/W, table tennis M/W, tennis M/W, track and field M/W, volleyball M/W, water polo M/W, weight lifting M/W.

Standardized Tests *Required:* SAT I or ACT (for admission). *Recommended:* SAT II: Subject Tests (for admission).

Costs (2001–02) *Comprehensive fee:* $33,140 includes full-time tuition ($26,580) and room and board ($6560). Part-time tuition: $1100 per credit. Part-time tuition and fees vary according to course load. *Room and board:* College room only: $3430. Room and board charges vary according to housing facility. *Payment plan:* installment. *Waivers:* employees or children of employees.

Financial Aid Of all full-time matriculated undergraduates who enrolled in 2001, 2166 applied for aid, 1513 were judged to have need, 1513 had their need fully met. *Average percent of need met:* 100%. *Average financial aid package:* $23,851. *Average indebtedness upon graduation:* $13,926. *Financial aid deadline:* 1/15.

Applying *Options:* common application, electronic application, early admission, early decision, deferred entrance. *Application fee:* $30. *Required:* essay or personal statement, high school transcript, 2 letters of recommendation. *Required for some:* interview. *Application deadlines:* 1/15 (freshmen), 5/1 (transfers). *Early decision:* 11/15 (for plan 1), 1/2 (for plan 2). *Notification:* 4/1 (freshmen), 12/1 (early decision plan 1), 1/18 (early decision plan 2).

Admissions Contact Ms. Debra Chermonte, Dean of Admissions and Financial Aid, Oberlin College, Admissions Office, Carnegie Building, Oberlin, OH 44074-1090. *Phone:* 440-775-8411. *Toll-free phone:* 800-622-OBIE. *Fax:* 440-775-6905. *E-mail:* ad_mail@oberlin.edu.

OHIO DOMINICAN COLLEGE
Columbus, Ohio

- **Independent Roman Catholic** 4-year, founded 1911
- **Calendar** semesters
- **Degrees** certificates, associate, and bachelor's
- **Urban** 62-acre campus
- **Endowment** $12.9 million
- **Coed,** 2,197 undergraduate students, 70% full-time, 69% women, 31% men
- **Moderately difficult** entrance level, 60% of applicants were admitted

Undergraduates 1,536 full-time, 661 part-time. Students come from 18 states and territories, 29 other countries, 1% are from out of state, 26% African American, 2% Asian American or Pacific Islander, 2% Hispanic American, 0.3% Native American, 2% international, 10% transferred in, 17% live on campus. *Retention:* 68% of 2001 full-time freshmen returned.

Freshmen *Admission:* 893 applied, 535 admitted, 198 enrolled. *Average high school GPA:* 2.98. *Test scores:* ACT scores over 18: 78%; ACT scores over 24: 18%.

Faculty *Total:* 131, 46% full-time, 56% with terminal degrees. *Student/faculty ratio:* 18:1.

Majors Accounting; art education; biology; business administration; business communications; chemistry; communications; computer science; criminal justice/law enforcement administration; design/visual communications; early childhood education; economics; education; education (K-12); English; fine/studio arts; gerontology; history; information sciences/systems; interdisciplinary studies; international business; legal studies; library science; mathematics; middle school education; peace/conflict studies; philosophy; political science; psychology; public relations; science education; secondary education; social sciences; social work; sociology; special education; teaching English as a second language; theology.

Academic Programs *Special study options:* academic remediation for entering students, adult/continuing education programs, advanced placement credit, English as a second language, honors programs, independent study, internships, off-

Ohio Dominican College (continued)
campus study, part-time degree program, student-designed majors, study abroad, summer session for credit. *ROTC:* Army (c), Air Force (c).

Library Spangler Library with 110,953 titles, 553 serial subscriptions, 4,302 audiovisual materials, an OPAC, a Web page.

Computers on Campus 150 computers available on campus for general student use. A campuswide network can be accessed from student residence rooms and from off campus that provide access to laptop for each student, intranet. Internet access, at least one staffed computer lab available.

Student Life *Housing:* on-campus residence required through junior year. *Options:* coed, women-only. *Activities and Organizations:* drama/theater group, student-run newspaper, radio station, choral group, Campus Ministry, honors program, College Choir, Black Student Union, American-International Membership. *Campus security:* 24-hour emergency response devices and patrols, late-night transport/escort service, controlled dormitory access. *Student Services:* health clinic, personal/psychological counseling.

Athletics Member NAIA. *Intercollegiate sports:* baseball M(s), basketball M(s)/W(s), soccer M(s)/W, softball W(s), tennis M/W, volleyball W(s). *Intramural sports:* badminton M/W, basketball M/W, football M/W, golf M/W, soccer M/W, softball M/W, table tennis M/W, tennis M/W, volleyball M/W.

Standardized Tests *Required for some:* SAT I and SAT II or ACT (for admission).

Costs (2001–02) *Comprehensive fee:* $18,100 includes full-time tuition ($12,530), mandatory fees ($200), and room and board ($5370). Part-time tuition: $360 per credit hour. *Required fees:* $100 per term part-time. *Room and board:* Room and board charges vary according to housing facility. *Payment plan:* installment. *Waivers:* senior citizens and employees or children of employees.

Applying *Options:* deferred entrance. *Required:* essay or personal statement, high school transcript, minimum 2.0 GPA, interview. *Required for some:* letters of recommendation. *Application deadline:* rolling (freshmen), rolling (transfers). *Notification:* continuous (freshmen).

Admissions Contact Ms. Vicki Thompson-Campbell, Director of Admissions, Ohio Dominican College, 1216 Sunbury Road, Columbus, OH 43219-2099. *Phone:* 614-251-4500. *Toll-free phone:* 800-854-2670. *Fax:* 614-251-0156. *E-mail:* admissions@odc.edu.

OHIO NORTHERN UNIVERSITY
Ada, Ohio

- **Independent United Methodist** comprehensive, founded 1871
- **Calendar** quarters
- **Degrees** bachelor's and first professional
- **Small-town** 260-acre campus
- **Endowment** $124.3 million
- **Coed,** 2,366 undergraduate students, 95% full-time, 47% women, 53% men
- **Moderately difficult** entrance level, 91% of applicants were admitted

Undergraduates 2,236 full-time, 130 part-time. Students come from 42 states and territories, 17 other countries, 14% are from out of state, 4% transferred in, 64% live on campus. *Retention:* 82% of 2001 full-time freshmen returned.

Freshmen *Admission:* 2,358 applied, 2,140 admitted, 483 enrolled. *Average high school GPA:* 3.74. *Test scores:* SAT verbal scores over 500: 80%; SAT math scores over 500: 83%; ACT scores over 18: 96%; SAT verbal scores over 600: 36%; SAT math scores over 600: 44%; ACT scores over 24: 61%; SAT verbal scores over 700: 5%; SAT math scores over 700: 7%; ACT scores over 30: 11%.

Faculty *Total:* 315, 59% full-time. *Student/faculty ratio:* 13:1.

Majors Accounting; art; art education; athletic training/sports medicine; biochemistry; biology; broadcast journalism; business administration; ceramic arts; chemistry; civil engineering; computer engineering; computer science; creative writing; criminal justice/law enforcement administration; early childhood education; electrical engineering; elementary education; English; environmental science; French; graphic design/commercial art/illustration; health education; history; industrial arts; industrial technology; international business; international relations; mass communications; mathematical statistics; mathematics; mechanical engineering; medical technology; medicinal/pharmaceutical chemistry; middle school education; molecular biology; music; music business management/merchandising; music teacher education; pharmacy; philosophy; physical education; physics; political science; psychology; public relations; religious studies; sociology; Spanish; speech/rhetorical studies; sport/fitness administration; theater arts/drama.

Academic Programs *Special study options:* academic remediation for entering students, advanced placement credit, cooperative education, distance learning, double majors, honors programs, internships, part-time degree program, services for LD students, study abroad, summer session for credit. *ROTC:* Army (c), Air Force (c).

Library Heterick Memorial Library plus 1 other with 246,103 titles, 1,038 serial subscriptions, 8,655 audiovisual materials, an OPAC, a Web page.

Computers on Campus 461 computers available on campus for general student use. A campuswide network can be accessed from student residence rooms and from off campus. Internet access, online (class) registration, at least one staffed computer lab available.

Student Life *Housing:* on-campus residence required through junior year. *Options:* coed, men-only, women-only. *Activities and Organizations:* drama/theater group, student-run newspaper, radio and television station, choral group, marching band, Good News Bears, Student Planning Committee, Student Senate, national fraternities, national sororities. *Campus security:* 24-hour emergency response devices and patrols, late-night transport/escort service, controlled dormitory access. *Student Services:* health clinic, personal/psychological counseling, legal services.

Athletics Member NCAA. All Division III. *Intercollegiate sports:* baseball M, basketball M/W, cross-country running M/W, football M, golf M/W, soccer M/W, softball W, swimming M/W, tennis M/W, track and field M/W, volleyball W, wrestling M. *Intramural sports:* badminton M/W, basketball M/W, bowling M/W, football M, golf M, racquetball M/W, rugby M(c)/W(c), skiing (downhill) M(c)/W(c), soccer M/W, softball M/W, swimming M/W, table tennis M/W, tennis M/W, volleyball M(c)/W, water polo M(c)/W(c), wrestling M.

Standardized Tests *Required:* SAT I or ACT (for admission).

Costs (2001–02) *Comprehensive fee:* $27,765 includes full-time tuition ($22,275) and room and board ($5490). Full-time tuition and fees vary according to program. Part-time tuition: $619 per quarter hour. Part-time tuition and fees vary according to program. *Room and board:* College room only: $2625. Room and board charges vary according to board plan and housing facility. *Payment plan:* installment. *Waivers:* employees or children of employees.

Financial Aid Of all full-time matriculated undergraduates who enrolled in 2001, 2426 applied for aid, 2249 were judged to have need, 636 had their need fully met. 1775 Federal Work-Study jobs (averaging $807). In 2001, 447 non-need-based awards were made. *Average percent of need met:* 90%. *Average financial aid package:* $19,130. *Average need-based loan:* $4563. *Average need-based gift aid:* $8650. *Average non-need based aid:* $11,924. *Financial aid deadline:* 6/1.

Applying *Options:* common application, electronic application, early admission, deferred entrance. *Application fee:* $30. *Required:* high school transcript. *Recommended:* essay or personal statement, minimum 2.5 GPA, interview. *Application deadlines:* 8/15 (freshmen), 8/15 (transfers). *Notification:* continuous until 8/31 (freshmen).

Admissions Contact Ms. Karen Condeni, Vice President of Admissions and Financial Aid, Ohio Northern University, 525 South Main, Ada, OH 45810-1599. *Phone:* 419-772-2260. *Toll-free phone:* 888-408-4ONU. *Fax:* 419-772-2313. *E-mail:* admissions-ug@onu.edu.

THE OHIO STATE UNIVERSITY
Columbus, Ohio

- **State-supported** university, founded 1870
- **Calendar** quarters
- **Degrees** bachelor's, master's, doctoral, first professional, and post-master's certificates
- **Urban** campus
- **Coed,** 36,049 undergraduate students, 87% full-time, 48% women, 52% men
- **Moderately difficult** entrance level, 73% of applicants were admitted

Undergraduates 31,240 full-time, 4,809 part-time. Students come from 53 states and territories, 89 other countries, 11% are from out of state, 8% African American, 5% Asian American or Pacific Islander, 2% Hispanic American, 0.4% Native American, 4% international, 6% transferred in, 24% live on campus. *Retention:* 86% of 2001 full-time freshmen returned.

Freshmen *Admission:* 19,968 applied, 14,501 admitted, 5,996 enrolled. *Test scores:* SAT verbal scores over 500: 83%; SAT math scores over 500: 87%; ACT scores over 18: 97%; SAT verbal scores over 600: 41%; SAT math scores over 600: 50%; ACT scores over 24: 69%; SAT verbal scores over 700: 9%; SAT math scores over 700: 12%; ACT scores over 30: 13%.

Faculty *Total:* 3,526, 77% full-time. *Student/faculty ratio:* 13:1.

Majors Accounting; actuarial science; aerospace engineering; African-American studies; African studies; agricultural business; agricultural economics; agricultural education; agricultural engineering; agricultural/food products processing; agricultural plant pathology; agronomy/crop science; animal sciences; anthropology; Arabic; architecture; art; art education; art history; Asian-American studies; astronomy; athletic training/sports medicine; aviation management; aviation technology; biochemistry; biology; biotechnology research; botany; business administration; business economics; business home economics; business marketing and marketing management; ceramic arts; ceramic sciences/engineering; chemical engineering; chemistry; Chinese; city/community/regional planning; civil engineering; classics; clothing/apparel/textile studies; clothing/textiles; communications; communications related; comparative literature; computer engineering; computer/information sciences; computer science; creative writing; criminal justice studies; criminology; cultural studies; dance; dental hygiene; design/visual communications; development economics; dietetics; drama/dance education; drawing; East Asian studies; economics; electrical engineering; engineering physics; English; entomology; environmental education; environmental science; exercise sciences; family resource management studies; finance; fine/studio arts; fishing sciences; folklore; food sciences; forestry; French; genetics; geography; geology; German; graphic design/commercial art/illustration; Greek (modern); health professions and related sciences; Hebrew; history; history related; horticulture science; hospitality management; humanities; human resources management; individual/family development; industrial arts education; industrial design; industrial/manufacturing engineering; information sciences/systems; insurance/risk management; interior design; international business; international relations; Islamic studies; Italian; Japanese; jazz; journalism; Judaic studies; landscape architecture; Latin American studies; linguistics; logistics/materials management; management information systems/business data processing; materials engineering; materials science; mathematics; mathematics related; mechanical engineering; medical dietician; medical radiologic technology; medical records administration; medical technology; metallurgical engineering; microbiology/bacteriology; Middle Eastern studies; music; music (general performance); music history; music (piano and organ performance); music teacher education; music theory and composition; music (voice and choral/opera performance); natural resources management; natural resources protective services; nursing; nursing science; nutrition studies; occupational therapy; operations management; painting; peace/conflict studies; pharmacy; philosophy; physical education; physical therapy; physics; plant sciences; political science; Portuguese; printmaking; psychology; radiological science; real estate; religious studies; respiratory therapy; Russian; Russian/Slavic studies; sculpture; social sciences; social work; sociology; soil conservation; Spanish; special education; speech-language pathology/audiology; surveying; systems engineering; technical education; theater arts/drama; turf management; Western European studies; wildlife management; women's studies; zoology.

Academic Programs *Special study options:* academic remediation for entering students, accelerated degree program, adult/continuing education programs, advanced placement credit, cooperative education, distance learning, double majors, English as a second language, freshman honors college, honors programs, independent study, internships, off-campus study, part-time degree program, services for LD students, student-designed majors, study abroad, summer session for credit. *ROTC:* Army (b), Air Force (b).

Library Main Library plus 12 others with 5.4 million titles, 42,707 serial subscriptions, 38,138 audiovisual materials, an OPAC, a Web page.

Computers on Campus 1000 computers available on campus for general student use. A campuswide network can be accessed from student residence rooms and from off campus. Internet access, online (class) registration, at least one staffed computer lab available.

Student Life *Housing:* on-campus residence required for freshman year. *Options:* coed, women-only, cooperative, disabled students. *Activities and Organizations:* drama/theater group, student-run newspaper, radio and television station, choral group, marching band, Afrikan Student Union, Bisexual, Gay and Lesbian Alliance, Campus Crusade for Christ, University Wide Council of Hispanic Organizations, Asian American Association, national fraternities, national sororities. *Campus security:* 24-hour emergency response devices and patrols, student patrols, late-night transport/escort service, controlled dormitory access, dorm entrances locked after 9 p.m. *Student Services:* health clinic, personal/psychological counseling, women's center, legal services.

Athletics Member NCAA. All Division I except football (Division I-A). *Intercollegiate sports:* baseball M(s), basketball M(s)/W(s), cross-country running M(s)/W(s), fencing M(s)/W(s), field hockey W(s), golf M(s)/W(s), gymnastics M(s)/W(s), ice hockey M(s)/W(s), lacrosse M(s)/W(s), riflery M/W, soccer M(s)/W(s), softball W(s), swimming M(s)/W(s), tennis M(s)/W(s), track and field M(s)/W(s), volleyball M(s)/W(s), wrestling M(s). *Intramural sports:* badminton M(c)/W(c), baseball M(c), basketball M/W, bowling M(c)/W(c), crew M(c)/W, cross-country running M/W, equestrian sports M(c)/W(c), fencing M(c)/W(c), field hockey W, football M/W, golf M/W, gymnastics M(c)/W(c), ice hockey M(c)/W(c), lacrosse M(c)/W(c), racquetball M(c)/W(c), riflery M(c)/W(c), rugby M(c)/W(c), sailing M(c)/W(c), skiing (downhill) M(c)/W(c), soccer M(c)/W(c), softball W(c), squash M(c)/W(c), swimming M(c)/W(c), table tennis M/W, tennis M/W, track and field M(c)/W(c), volleyball M(c)/W(c), water polo M(c)/W(c), weight lifting M(c), wrestling M/W.

Standardized Tests *Required:* SAT I or ACT (for admission).

Costs (2001–02) *Tuition:* state resident $4788 full-time; nonresident $13,554 full-time. Full-time tuition and fees vary according to course load, location, program, and reciprocity agreements. Part-time tuition and fees vary according to course load, location, program, and reciprocity agreements. *Room and board:* $6031. Room and board charges vary according to board plan and housing facility. *Payment plan:* installment. *Waivers:* senior citizens and employees or children of employees.

Financial Aid Of all full-time matriculated undergraduates who enrolled in 2001, 18574 applied for aid, 14110 were judged to have need, 4125 had their need fully met. 3021 Federal Work-Study jobs (averaging $3321). In 2001, 2822 non-need-based awards were made. *Average percent of need met:* 76%. *Average financial aid package:* $7747. *Average need-based loan:* $3993. *Average need-based gift aid:* $3946. *Average non-need based aid:* $2660. *Average indebtedness upon graduation:* $15,482.

Applying *Options:* common application, electronic application. *Application fee:* $30. *Required:* high school transcript. *Application deadlines:* 2/15 (freshmen), 6/25 (transfers). *Notification:* continuous (freshmen).

Admissions Contact Dr. Mabel G. Freeman, Director of Undergraduate Admissions and Vice President for First-Year Experience, The Ohio State University, 3rd Floor, Lincoln Tower, 1800 Cannon Drive, Columbus, OH 43210. *Phone:* 614-292-3974. *Fax:* 614-292-4818. *E-mail:* askabuckeye@osu.edu.

THE OHIO STATE UNIVERSITY AT LIMA
Lima, Ohio

- **State-supported** 4-year, founded 1960, part of Ohio State University
- **Calendar** quarters
- **Degrees** associate and bachelor's (also offers some graduate courses)
- **Small-town** 565-acre campus
- **Coed,** 1,213 undergraduate students, 80% full-time, 59% women, 41% men
- **Noncompetitive** entrance level, 72% of applicants were admitted

Undergraduates 968 full-time, 245 part-time. Students come from 1 other state, 1 other country, 2% African American, 1% Asian American or Pacific Islander, 0.5% Hispanic American, 0.2% Native American, 0.1% international. *Retention:* 57% of 2001 full-time freshmen returned.

Freshmen *Admission:* 507 applied, 365 admitted, 405 enrolled. *Test scores:* SAT verbal scores over 500: 55%; SAT math scores over 500: 45%; SAT verbal scores over 600: 15%; SAT math scores over 600: 25%; SAT verbal scores over 700: 5%.

Faculty *Total:* 91, 62% full-time. *Student/faculty ratio:* 13:1.

Majors Elementary education; English; financial planning; hospitality management; liberal arts and sciences/liberal studies; psychology.

Academic Programs *Special study options:* academic remediation for entering students, accelerated degree program, adult/continuing education programs, advanced placement credit, English as a second language, honors programs, part-time degree program, services for LD students, summer session for credit. *ROTC:* Army (c), Navy (c), Air Force (c).

Library Ohio State University-Lima Campus Library with 74,619 titles, 592 serial subscriptions, an OPAC.

Computers on Campus 104 computers available on campus for general student use.

Student Life *Housing:* college housing not available. *Activities and Organizations:* drama/theater group, student-run newspaper, radio station, choral group, Chorus, Psychology Club, Buckeye Scholars, Bucks for Buckeyes, Theatre. *Campus security:* 24-hour emergency response devices and patrols, late-night transport/escort service.

Athletics *Intercollegiate sports:* basketball M/W, golf M. *Intramural sports:* baseball M, basketball M/W, football M/W, softball M/W, table tennis M/W, volleyball M/W.

Standardized Tests *Required:* ACT (for admission).

Costs (2001–02) *Tuition:* state resident $3606 full-time; nonresident $12,372 full-time. Part-time tuition and fees vary according to course load. *Payment plan:* installment. *Waivers:* senior citizens and employees or children of employees.

Applying *Options:* early admission. *Application fee:* $30. *Required:* high school transcript. *Application deadlines:* 7/1 (freshmen), 7/1 (transfers). *Notification:* continuous until 9/1 (freshmen).

Admissions Contact Ms. Marissa Christoff Snyder, Admissions Counselor, The Ohio State University at Lima, 4240 Campus Drive, Lima, OH 45804. *Phone:* 419-995-8220. *E-mail:* admissions@lima.ohio-state.edu.

THE OHIO STATE UNIVERSITY AT MARION
Marion, Ohio

- **State-supported** 4-year, founded 1958, part of Ohio State University
- **Calendar** quarters
- **Degrees** associate and bachelor's (also offers some graduate courses)
- **Small-town** 180-acre campus with easy access to Columbus
- **Coed,** 1,295 undergraduate students, 71% full-time, 59% women, 41% men
- **Noncompetitive** entrance level, 98% of applicants were admitted

Undergraduates 921 full-time, 374 part-time. Students come from 6 states and territories, 2% African American, 1% Asian American or Pacific Islander, 0.8% Hispanic American, 0.1% Native American, 0.2% international. *Retention:* 66% of 2001 full-time freshmen returned.

Freshmen *Admission:* 463 applied, 452 admitted, 368 enrolled. *Test scores:* SAT verbal scores over 500: 44%; SAT math scores over 500: 33%; SAT verbal scores over 600: 11%; SAT math scores over 600: 11%.

Faculty *Total:* 95, 35% full-time. *Student/faculty ratio:* 12:1.

Majors Elementary education; liberal arts and sciences/liberal studies.

Academic Programs *Special study options:* academic remediation for entering students, accelerated degree program, adult/continuing education programs, advanced placement credit, English as a second language, honors programs, part-time degree program, services for LD students, summer session for credit. *ROTC:* Army (c), Navy (c), Air Force (c).

Library Ohio State University-Marion Campus Library with 38,858 titles, 413 serial subscriptions, an OPAC.

Computers on Campus 174 computers available on campus for general student use.

Student Life *Housing:* college housing not available. *Activities and Organizations:* student-run newspaper, choral group. *Campus security:* 24-hour emergency response devices. *Student Services:* personal/psychological counseling.

Athletics *Intramural sports:* basketball M/W, football M/W, golf M/W, table tennis M/W, volleyball M/W, weight lifting M/W.

Standardized Tests *Recommended:* SAT I or ACT (for placement).

Costs (2001–02) *Tuition:* state resident $3606 full-time; nonresident $12,372 full-time.

Applying *Options:* early admission. *Application fee:* $30. *Required:* high school transcript. *Application deadlines:* 7/1 (freshmen), 7/1 (transfers). *Notification:* continuous until 9/1 (freshmen).

Admissions Contact Mr. Mathrey Moreau, Admissions Coordinator, The Ohio State University at Marion, 1465 Mount Vernon Avenue, Marion, OH 43302-5695. *Phone:* 740-389-6786 Ext. 6337.

THE OHIO STATE UNIVERSITY-MANSFIELD CAMPUS
Mansfield, Ohio

- **State-supported** 4-year, founded 1958, part of Ohio State University
- **Calendar** quarters
- **Degrees** associate and bachelor's (also offers some graduate courses)
- **Small-town** 593-acre campus with easy access to Columbus and Cleveland
- **Coed,** 1,399 undergraduate students, 71% full-time, 62% women, 38% men
- **Noncompetitive** entrance level, 94% of applicants were admitted

Undergraduates 995 full-time, 404 part-time. Students come from 10 states and territories, 1 other country, 4% African American, 2% Asian American or Pacific Islander, 0.8% Hispanic American, 0.4% Native American. *Retention:* 55% of 2001 full-time freshmen returned.

Freshmen *Admission:* 621 applied, 581 admitted, 433 enrolled. *Test scores:* SAT verbal scores over 500: 75%; SAT math scores over 500: 50%; SAT verbal scores over 600: 25%; SAT math scores over 600: 19%; SAT verbal scores over 700: 6%; SAT math scores over 700: 6%.

Faculty *Total:* 64, 66% full-time.

Majors Elementary education; liberal arts and sciences/liberal studies.

Academic Programs *Special study options:* academic remediation for entering students, accelerated degree program, adult/continuing education programs, advanced placement credit, English as a second language, honors programs, part-time degree program, services for LD students, summer session for credit. *ROTC:* Army (c), Navy (c), Air Force (c).

Library Ohio State University-Mansfield Campus Library with 45,977 titles, 453 serial subscriptions, an OPAC.

Computers on Campus 103 computers available on campus for general student use.

Student Life *Housing:* college housing not available. *Activities and Organizations:* drama/theater group, student-run newspaper, choral group. *Campus security:* 24-hour emergency response devices and patrols, late-night transport/escort service. *Student Services:* personal/psychological counseling.

Athletics *Intramural sports:* basketball M/W, bowling M/W, football M/W, golf M/W, softball M/W, table tennis M/W, tennis M/W, volleyball M/W.

Standardized Tests *Recommended:* SAT I or ACT (for placement).

Costs (2001–02) *Tuition:* state resident $3606 full-time; nonresident $12,372 full-time.

Applying *Options:* early admission. *Application fee:* $30. *Required:* high school transcript. *Application deadlines:* 7/1 (freshmen), 7/1 (transfers). *Notification:* continuous until 9/1 (freshmen).

Admissions Contact Mr. Henry D. Thomas, Coordinator of Admissions and Financial Aid, The Ohio State University-Mansfield Campus, 1680 University Drive, Mansfield, OH 44906-1599. *Phone:* 419-755-4226.

THE OHIO STATE UNIVERSITY-NEWARK CAMPUS
Newark, Ohio

- **State-supported** 4-year, founded 1957, part of Ohio State University
- **Calendar** quarters
- **Degrees** associate and bachelor's (also offers some graduate courses)
- **Small-town** 101-acre campus with easy access to Columbus
- **Coed,** 1,918 undergraduate students, 76% full-time, 58% women, 42% men
- **Noncompetitive** entrance level, 97% of applicants were admitted

Undergraduates 1,466 full-time, 452 part-time. Students come from 14 states and territories, 1 other country, 4% African American, 2% Asian American or Pacific Islander, 0.6% Hispanic American, 0.7% Native American, 0.2% international. *Retention:* 57% of 2001 full-time freshmen returned.

Freshmen *Admission:* 1,291 applied, 1,250 admitted, 653 enrolled. *Test scores:* SAT verbal scores over 500: 46%; SAT math scores over 500: 17%; SAT verbal scores over 600: 15%; SAT math scores over 600: 4%; SAT verbal scores over 700: 1%.

Faculty *Total:* 89, 47% full-time. *Student/faculty ratio:* 23:1.

Majors Elementary education; liberal arts and sciences/liberal studies.

Academic Programs *Special study options:* academic remediation for entering students, accelerated degree program, adult/continuing education programs, advanced placement credit, English as a second language, honors programs, part-time degree program, services for LD students, summer session for credit. *ROTC:* Army (c), Navy (c), Air Force (c).

Library Ohio State University Newark Campus Library with 49,232 titles, 423 serial subscriptions, an OPAC.

Computers on Campus 36 computers available on campus for general student use.

Student Life *Housing:* college housing not available. *Activities and Organizations:* drama/theater group, choral group. *Campus security:* 24-hour emergency response devices and patrols, late-night transport/escort service, self-defense education. *Student Services:* personal/psychological counseling.

Athletics *Intramural sports:* badminton M/W, baseball M(c), basketball M/W, football M, golf M, soccer M/W, softball M/W(c), table tennis M/W, tennis M/W, volleyball M/W, weight lifting M/W.

Standardized Tests *Recommended:* SAT I or ACT (for placement).

Costs (2001–02) *Tuition:* state resident $3606 full-time; nonresident $12,372 full-time. Part-time tuition and fees vary according to course load and student level. *Room and board:* Room and board charges vary according to housing facility.

Applying *Options:* early admission. *Application fee:* $30. *Required:* high school transcript. *Application deadlines:* 7/1 (freshmen), 7/1 (transfers). *Notification:* continuous until 9/1 (freshmen).

Admissions Contact Ms. Ann Donahue, Director of Enrollment, The Ohio State University-Newark Campus, 1179 University Drive, Newark, OH 43055-1797. *Phone:* 614-366-9333.

OHIO UNIVERSITY
Athens, Ohio

- **State-supported** university, founded 1804, part of Ohio Board of Regents
- **Calendar** quarters
- **Degrees** associate, bachelor's, master's, doctoral, and first professional
- **Small-town** 1700-acre campus

- **Endowment** $195.8 million
- **Coed,** 17,178 undergraduate students, 93% full-time, 55% women, 45% men
- **Moderately difficult** entrance level, 78% of applicants were admitted

Undergraduates 15,977 full-time, 1,201 part-time. Students come from 52 states and territories, 51 other countries, 9% are from out of state, 3% African American, 0.8% Asian American or Pacific Islander, 1% Hispanic American, 0.3% Native American, 3% international, 3% transferred in, 44% live on campus. *Retention:* 85% of 2001 full-time freshmen returned.

Freshmen *Admission:* 12,433 applied, 9,747 admitted, 3,771 enrolled. *Average high school GPA:* 3.37. *Test scores:* SAT verbal scores over 500: 76%; SAT math scores over 500: 76%; ACT scores over 18: 98%; SAT verbal scores over 600: 25%; SAT math scores over 600: 27%; ACT scores over 24: 49%; SAT verbal scores over 700: 4%; SAT math scores over 700: 4%; ACT scores over 30: 6%.

Faculty *Total:* 1,143, 72% full-time, 80% with terminal degrees. *Student/faculty ratio:* 21:1.

Majors Accounting; accounting technician; acting/directing; actuarial science; adapted physical education; advertising; aerospace engineering technology; African-American studies; African languages; African studies; Air Force R.O.T.C./air science; anthropology; applied mathematics; Army R.O.T.C./military science; art; art education; art history; arts management; art therapy; Asian studies; astrophysics; athletic training/sports medicine; atmospheric sciences; aviation/airway science; aviation management; biochemistry; biological/physical sciences; biology education; botany; broadcast journalism; business; business administration; business management/administrative services related; business marketing and marketing management; cell biology; ceramic arts; chemical and atomic/molecular physics; chemical engineering; chemistry; child care/development; civil engineering; classics; clothing/apparel/textile studies; commercial photography; communication disorders sciences/services related; communications; communications related; community health liaison; computer science; counselor education/guidance; creative writing; criminal justice/law enforcement administration; criminal justice studies; criminology; curriculum and instruction; dance; design/applied arts related; design/visual communications; dietetics; drama/theater literature; drawing; early childhood education; economics; education; education administration; educational media design; educational statistics/research methods; electrical engineering; elementary education; elementary/middle/secondary education administration; engineering; engineering related; engineering technologies related; English; entrepreneurship; environmental biology; environmental engineering; environmental health; equestrian studies; European studies; exercise sciences; family resource management studies; film/video production; finance; fine/studio arts; French; French language education; general studies; geography; geological sciences related; geology; German; German language education; gerontological services; graphic design/commercial art/illustration; Greek (ancient and medieval); health facilities administration; health/physical education; health professions and related sciences; health science; health services administration; hearing sciences; history; history related; home economics; housing studies; humanities; human resources management; human services; individual/family development; industrial/manufacturing engineering; industrial technology; interdisciplinary studies; interior architecture; interior environments; international business; international economics; international relations; journalism; journalism and mass communication related; Latin American studies; Latin (ancient and medieval); law enforcement/police science; liberal arts and sciences/liberal studies; liberal arts and studies related; linguistics; management information systems/business data processing; mathematics; mathematics education; mathematics related; mechanical engineering; medical administrative assistant; medical assistant; microbiology/bacteriology; multi/interdisciplinary studies related; music; music business management/merchandising; music conducting; music (general performance); music history; music (piano and organ performance); music teacher education; music theory and composition; music (voice and choral/opera performance); nursing; nutrition studies; painting; philosophy; photographic technology; photography; physical education; physical sciences related; physics; physics related; play/screenwriting; political science; pre-dentistry; pre-law; pre-medicine; pre-pharmacy studies; pre-veterinary studies; printmaking; protective services related; psychology; public administration and services related; public relations; radio/television broadcasting; radio/television broadcasting technology; reading education; recreational therapy; recreation/leisure facilities management; recreation/leisure studies; Russian; safety/security technology; science education; sculpture; secondary education; secretarial science; security; social/philosophical foundations of education; social sciences; social studies education; social work; sociology; Spanish; Spanish language education; special education; speech-language pathology/audiology; speech/rhetorical studies; speech therapy; sport/fitness administration; systems engineering; teacher education, specific programs related; teaching English as a second language; telecommunications; theater arts/drama; theater arts/drama and stagecraft related; theater design; tourism/travel marketing; travel/tourism management; visual/performing arts; wildlife biology; women's studies; zoology.

Academic Programs *Special study options:* academic remediation for entering students, accelerated degree program, adult/continuing education programs, advanced placement credit, cooperative education, distance learning, double majors, English as a second language, external degree program, honors programs, independent study, internships, off-campus study, part-time degree program, services for LD students, student-designed majors, study abroad, summer session for credit. *ROTC:* Army (b), Air Force (b). *Unusual degree programs:* 3-2 forestry with Duke University, North Carolina State University, University of Michigan; natural resources with University of Michigan.

Library Alden Library with 2.3 million titles, 20,808 serial subscriptions, 368,484 audiovisual materials, an OPAC, a Web page.

Computers on Campus 1500 computers available on campus for general student use. A campuswide network can be accessed from student residence rooms and from off campus. At least one staffed computer lab available.

Student Life *Housing:* on-campus residence required through sophomore year. *Options:* coed, men-only, women-only, cooperative, disabled students. *Activities and Organizations:* drama/theater group, student-run newspaper, radio and television station, choral group, marching band, Gamma Pi Delta, Golden Key, International Student Union, Chinese students and visiting scholars club, Campus Crusade for Christ, national fraternities, national sororities. *Campus security:* 24-hour emergency response devices and patrols, late-night transport/escort service, controlled dormitory access, security lighting. *Student Services:* health clinic, personal/psychological counseling, legal services.

Athletics Member NCAA. All Division I except football (Division I-A). *Intercollegiate sports:* baseball M(s), basketball M(s)/W(s), cross-country running M(s)/W(s), equestrian sports M(c)/W(c), field hockey W(s), golf M(s)/W(s), ice hockey M(c), lacrosse M(c)/W(c), rugby M(c)/W(c), soccer M(c)/W(s), softball W(s), swimming M(s)/W(s), track and field M(s)/W(s), volleyball M(c)/W(s), water polo M(c)/W(c), weight lifting M(c), wrestling M(s). *Intramural sports:* baseball M, basketball M/W, bowling M/W, cross-country running M/W, football M, racquetball M/W, soccer M/W, softball M/W, swimming M/W, tennis M/W, track and field M/W, volleyball M/W.

Standardized Tests *Required:* SAT I or ACT (for admission).

Costs (2001–02) *Tuition:* state resident $5493 full-time, $176 per quarter hour part-time; nonresident $11,562 full-time, $376 per quarter hour part-time. *Room and board:* $6276; room only: $3087. Room and board charges vary according to board plan. *Payment plan:* installment. *Waivers:* employees or children of employees.

Financial Aid Of all full-time matriculated undergraduates who enrolled in 2001, 11130 applied for aid, 6980 were judged to have need, 1073 had their need fully met. In 2001, 2045 non-need-based awards were made. *Average percent of need met:* 71%. *Average financial aid package:* $6221. *Average need-based loan:* $3691. *Average need-based gift aid:* $3412. *Average non-need based aid:* $2338. *Average indebtedness upon graduation:* $13,996.

Applying *Options:* early admission, deferred entrance. *Application fee:* $40. *Required:* high school transcript. *Required for some:* essay or personal statement, interview. *Recommended:* 2 letters of recommendation. *Application deadlines:* 2/1 (freshmen), 5/15 (transfers). *Notification:* continuous (freshmen).

Admissions Contact Mr. N. Kip Howard Jr., Director of Admissions, Ohio University, Athens, OH 45701-2979. *Phone:* 740-593-4100. *E-mail:* admissions.freshmen@ohiou.edu.

OHIO UNIVERSITY-CHILLICOTHE
Chillicothe, Ohio

- **State-supported** 4-year, founded 1946, part of Ohio Board of Regents
- **Calendar** quarters
- **Degrees** certificates, associate, bachelor's, and master's (offers first 2 years of most bachelor's degree programs available at the main campus in Athens; also offers several bachelor's degree programs that can be completed at this campus and several programs exclusive to this campus; also offers some graduate programs)
- **Small-town** 124-acre campus with easy access to Columbus
- **Coed,** 1,510 undergraduate students
- **Noncompetitive** entrance level

Undergraduates Students come from 2 states and territories. *Retention:* 55% of 2001 full-time freshmen returned.

Freshmen *Admission:* 350 admitted.

Faculty *Total:* 101, 41% full-time.

Majors Biological/physical sciences; business administration; criminal justice/law enforcement administration; education of the hearing impaired; elementary education; environmental engineering; environmental science; human services; law enforcement/police science; liberal arts and sciences/liberal studies; nursing; paralegal/legal assistant; safety/security technology; secretarial science.

Ohio University-Chillicothe (continued)

Academic Programs *Special study options:* academic remediation for entering students, accelerated degree program, adult/continuing education programs, advanced placement credit, distance learning, double majors, independent study, internships, part-time degree program, services for LD students, student-designed majors, summer session for credit. *ROTC:* Army (c), Air Force (c).

Library Quinn Library with 47,900 titles, 418 serial subscriptions.

Computers on Campus 215 computers available on campus for general student use. A campuswide network can be accessed from off campus. Internet access, online (class) registration, at least one staffed computer lab available.

Student Life *Housing:* college housing not available. *Activities and Organizations:* drama/theater group, Nursing Student Association, Students In Free Enterprise Club, drama club, Phi Theta Kappa, Gamma Phi Delta. *Campus security:* 24-hour emergency response devices, patrols by city police. *Student Services:* personal/psychological counseling.

Athletics *Intercollegiate sports:* baseball M(c), basketball M(c)/W(c), golf M/W, volleyball W(c).

Standardized Tests *Required:* SAT I or ACT (for placement).

Costs (2001–02) *Tuition:* state resident $3246 full-time, $99 per quarter hour part-time; nonresident $8328 full-time, $268 per quarter hour part-time. *Payment plan:* installment. *Waivers:* senior citizens and employees or children of employees.

Financial Aid Of all full-time matriculated undergraduates who enrolled in 2001, 668 applied for aid, 544 were judged to have need, 44 had their need fully met. In 2001, 59 non-need-based awards were made. *Average percent of need met:* 62%. *Average financial aid package:* $6602. *Average need-based loan:* $3212. *Average need-based gift aid:* $3895. *Average non-need based aid:* $1911.

Applying *Options:* early admission. *Application fee:* $20. *Required:* high school transcript. *Application deadlines:* 9/1 (freshmen), 9/1 (transfers). *Notification:* continuous (freshmen).

Admissions Contact Mr. Richard R. Whitney, Director of Student Services, Ohio University-Chillicothe, 571 West Fifth Street, Chillicothe, OH 45601. *Phone:* 740-774-7200 Ext. 242. *Toll-free phone:* 877-462-6824. *Fax:* 740-774-7295.

OHIO UNIVERSITY-EASTERN

St. Clairsville, Ohio

- **State-supported** 4-year, founded 1957, part of Ohio Board of Regents
- **Calendar** quarters
- **Degrees** associate and bachelor's (also offers some graduate courses)
- **Rural** 300-acre campus
- **Coed**
- **Noncompetitive** entrance level

Faculty *Student/faculty ratio:* 23:1.

Standardized Tests *Required:* SAT I or ACT (for placement).

Financial Aid Of all full-time matriculated undergraduates who enrolled in 2001, 532 applied for aid, 458 were judged to have need, 51 had their need fully met. In 2001, 37. *Average percent of need met:* 62. *Average financial aid package:* $5856. *Average need-based loan:* $3397. *Average need-based gift aid:* $3611. *Average non-need based aid:* $2179.

Applying *Options:* early admission, deferred entrance. *Application fee:* $15. *Required:* high school transcript.

Admissions Contact Mr. Kevin Chenoweth, Student Services Manager, Ohio University-Eastern, 45425 National Road, St. Clairsville, OH 43950-9724. *Phone:* 614-695-1720 Ext. 209. *Toll-free phone:* 800-648-3331. *E-mail:* chenowet@ohio.edu.

OHIO UNIVERSITY-LANCASTER

Lancaster, Ohio

- **State-supported** comprehensive, founded 1968, part of Ohio Board of Regents
- **Calendar** quarters
- **Degrees** associate, bachelor's, and master's
- **Small-town** 360-acre campus with easy access to Columbus
- **Coed,** 1,537 undergraduate students, 58% full-time, 59% women, 41% men
- **Noncompetitive** entrance level, 100% of applicants were admitted

Undergraduates 891 full-time, 646 part-time. Students come from 12 states and territories, 1 other country, 0.9% African American, 0.7% Asian American or Pacific Islander, 0.5% Hispanic American, 0.5% Native American, 0.1% international.

Freshmen *Admission:* 486 applied, 486 admitted, 306 enrolled. *Average high school GPA:* 2.72.

Faculty *Total:* 101, 31% full-time.

Majors Accounting; art; biological/physical sciences; business administration; business education; child care/development; computer engineering technology; computer science; criminal justice/law enforcement administration; drafting; education; electrical/electronic engineering technology; elementary education; industrial design; industrial technology; law enforcement/police science; legal administrative assistant; liberal arts and sciences/liberal studies; medical administrative assistant; secretarial science.

Academic Programs *Special study options:* academic remediation for entering students, accelerated degree program, adult/continuing education programs, advanced placement credit, external degree program, part-time degree program, student-designed majors, summer session for credit. *ROTC:* Army (c), Air Force (c).

Library Ohio University-Lancaster Library with 69,978 titles, 393 serial subscriptions.

Computers on Campus 150 computers available on campus for general student use. A campuswide network can be accessed from off campus. Internet access, at least one staffed computer lab available.

Student Life *Housing:* college housing not available. *Activities and Organizations:* drama/theater group, Student Activities Association.

Athletics *Intercollegiate sports:* basketball M/W, tennis M/W. *Intramural sports:* basketball M/W, fencing M/W, tennis M/W, volleyball M/W.

Standardized Tests *Required:* SAT I or ACT (for placement).

Costs (2001–02) *Tuition:* state resident $3246 full-time, $99 per credit hour part-time; nonresident $8328 full-time, $268 per credit hour part-time. Full-time tuition and fees vary according to student level. Part-time tuition and fees vary according to student level.

Financial Aid Of all full-time matriculated undergraduates who enrolled in 2001, 634 applied for aid, 485 were judged to have need, 54 had their need fully met. In 2001, 74 non-need-based awards were made. *Average percent of need met:* 59%. *Average financial aid package:* $5161. *Average need-based loan:* $3294. *Average need-based gift aid:* $3645. *Average non-need based aid:* $1904.

Applying *Options:* common application, early admission, deferred entrance. *Application fee:* $15. *Required:* high school transcript. *Recommended:* interview. *Application deadline:* rolling (freshmen), rolling (transfers). *Notification:* continuous (freshmen).

Admissions Contact Dr. Scott Shepherd, Director of Student Services, Ohio University-Lancaster, 1570 Granville Pike, Lancaster, OH 43130-1097. *Phone:* 740-654-6711 Ext. 209. *Toll-free phone:* 888-446-4468. *E-mail:* shepherd@ouvaxa.cats.ohiou.edu.

OHIO UNIVERSITY-SOUTHERN CAMPUS

Ironton, Ohio

- **State-supported** comprehensive, founded 1956, part of Ohio Board of Regents
- **Calendar** quarters
- **Degrees** associate, bachelor's, and master's
- **Small-town** 9-acre campus
- **Coed,** 1,782 undergraduate students, 60% full-time, 66% women, 34% men
- **Noncompetitive** entrance level, 100% of applicants were admitted

Undergraduates 1,075 full-time, 707 part-time. Students come from 4 states and territories, 2% African American, 0.4% Asian American or Pacific Islander, 0.3% Hispanic American, 0.7% Native American, 0.1% international.

Freshmen *Admission:* 600 applied, 600 admitted, 349 enrolled.

Faculty *Total:* 120, 13% full-time.

Majors Biological/physical sciences; business administration; computer science; criminal justice/law enforcement administration; early childhood education; education; interdisciplinary studies; liberal arts and sciences/liberal studies.

Academic Programs *Special study options:* academic remediation for entering students, adult/continuing education programs, part-time degree program, student-designed majors, summer session for credit.

Library Ohio University-Southern Campus Library with 16,300 titles, 230 serial subscriptions, an OPAC, a Web page.

Computers on Campus 66 computers available on campus for general student use. A campuswide network can be accessed from off campus. Internet access, at least one staffed computer lab available.

Student Life *Housing:* college housing not available. *Activities and Organizations:* choral group. *Student Services:* legal services.

Athletics *Intercollegiate sports:* basketball M/W. *Intramural sports:* archery M/W, skiing (downhill) M/W, tennis M/W, volleyball M/W.

Standardized Tests *Recommended:* SAT I or ACT (for placement).

Costs (2001–02) *Tuition:* state resident $2988 full-time, $91 per hour part-time; nonresident $3648 full-time, $111 per hour part-time. Full-time tuition and fees vary according to student level. Part-time tuition and fees vary according to student level. *Waivers:* senior citizens and employees or children of employees.

Financial Aid Of all full-time matriculated undergraduates who enrolled in 2001, 825 applied for aid, 743 were judged to have need, 49 had their need fully met. In 2001, 34 non-need-based awards were made. *Average percent of need met:* 62%. *Average financial aid package:* $6655. *Average need-based loan:* $3465. *Average need-based gift aid:* $3805. *Average non-need based aid:* $1123.

Applying *Options:* early admission, deferred entrance. *Application fee:* $20. *Required for some:* high school transcript. *Application deadline:* rolling (freshmen), rolling (transfers).

Admissions Contact Dr. Kim K. Lawson, Coordinator of Admissions, Ohio University-Southern Campus, 1804 Liberty Avenue, Ironton, OH 45638-2214. *Phone:* 740-533-4612.

OHIO UNIVERSITY-ZANESVILLE

Zanesville, Ohio

- **State-supported** comprehensive, founded 1946, part of Ohio Board of Regents
- **Calendar** quarters
- **Degrees** associate, bachelor's, and master's (offers first 2 years of most bachelor's degree programs available at the main campus in Athens; also offers several bachelor's degree programs that can be completed at this campus; also offers some graduate courses)
- **Rural** 179-acre campus with easy access to Columbus
- **Coed,** 1,543 undergraduate students, 58% full-time, 72% women, 28% men
- **Noncompetitive** entrance level, 100% of applicants were admitted

Undergraduates Students come from 4 states and territories, 1% are from out of state. *Retention:* 60% of 2001 full-time freshmen returned.

Freshmen *Admission:* 546 applied, 546 admitted. *Average high school GPA:* 3.15.

Faculty *Total:* 96, 30% full-time, 31% with terminal degrees. *Student/faculty ratio:* 17:1.

Majors Biological/physical sciences; broadcast journalism; criminal justice/law enforcement administration; elementary education; liberal arts and sciences/liberal studies; nursing; public relations; radio/television broadcasting; social sciences.

Academic Programs *Special study options:* academic remediation for entering students, adult/continuing education programs, advanced placement credit, external degree program, off-campus study, part-time degree program, services for LD students, student-designed majors, summer session for credit.

Library Zanesville Campus Library plus 1 other with 64,227 titles, 489 serial subscriptions, an OPAC.

Computers on Campus 42 computers available on campus for general student use. A campuswide network can be accessed from off campus. Internet access, at least one staffed computer lab available.

Student Life *Housing:* college housing not available. *Activities and Organizations:* drama/theater group, student-run newspaper, radio station, Student Senate, Student Nurses Association, Drama Club, Chess Club. *Campus security:* night security.

Athletics *Intercollegiate sports:* baseball M, basketball M/W, golf M/W, softball W, tennis M/W, volleyball W. *Intramural sports:* basketball M/W, bowling M/W, football M, golf M/W, skiing (downhill) M/W, soccer M/W, softball M/W, table tennis M/W, tennis M/W, volleyball M/W.

Standardized Tests *Required for some:* SAT I or ACT (for placement), nursing examination.

Costs (2001–02) *Tuition:* state resident $3246 full-time, $99 per credit hour part-time; nonresident $8328 full-time, $268 per credit hour part-time. *Waivers:* senior citizens and employees or children of employees.

Financial Aid Of all full-time matriculated undergraduates who enrolled in 2001, 737 applied for aid, 587 were judged to have need, 96 had their need fully met. In 2001, 99 non-need-based awards were made. *Average percent of need met:* 64%. *Average financial aid package:* $5862. *Average need-based loan:* $3179. *Average need-based gift aid:* $3488. *Average non-need based aid:* $2620.

Applying *Options:* common application, early admission, deferred entrance. *Application fee:* $20. *Required:* high school transcript. *Application deadline:* rolling (freshmen), rolling (transfers).

Admissions Contact Mrs. Karen Ragsdale, Student Services Secretary, Ohio University-Zanesville, 1425 Newark Road, Zanesville, OH 43701-2695. *Phone:* 740-588-1440. *Fax:* 740-453-6161.

OHIO WESLEYAN UNIVERSITY

Delaware, Ohio

- **Independent United Methodist** 4-year, founded 1842
- **Calendar** semesters
- **Degree** bachelor's
- **Small-town** 200-acre campus with easy access to Columbus
- **Endowment** $123.5 million
- **Coed,** 1,886 undergraduate students, 98% full-time, 52% women, 48% men
- **Very difficult** entrance level, 78% of applicants were admitted

Personalized honors study offers unusual opportunities to talented students as early as freshman year. Internships and research are encouraged. The University's distinctive commitment to public service and civic involvement is reflected in annual student work trips to South America and other states in the U.S., the acclaimed Sagan National Colloquium, and extensive volunteer and community service opportunities.

Undergraduates 1,845 full-time, 41 part-time. Students come from 42 states and territories, 52 other countries, 47% are from out of state, 5% African American, 2% Asian American or Pacific Islander, 2% Hispanic American, 0.2% Native American, 12% international, 1% transferred in, 84% live on campus. *Retention:* 79% of 2001 full-time freshmen returned.

Freshmen *Admission:* 2,227 applied, 1,743 admitted, 582 enrolled. *Average high school GPA:* 3.35. *Test scores:* SAT verbal scores over 500: 90%; SAT math scores over 500: 91%; ACT scores over 18: 100%; SAT verbal scores over 600: 57%; SAT math scores over 600: 59%; ACT scores over 24: 73%; SAT verbal scores over 700: 12%; SAT math scores over 700: 14%; ACT scores over 30: 23%.

Faculty *Total:* 177, 72% full-time, 81% with terminal degrees. *Student/faculty ratio:* 13:1.

Majors Accounting; African-American studies; anthropology; art education; art history; art therapy; astronomy; biology; botany; broadcast journalism; business administration; business economics; chemistry; classics; computer science; creative writing; cultural studies; earth sciences; East Asian studies; economics; education; education (K-12); elementary education; engineering related; engineering science; English; environmental science; fine/studio arts; French; general studies; genetics; geography; geology; German; health education; history; humanities; international business; international relations; journalism; literature; mathematical statistics; mathematics; medieval/renaissance studies; microbiology/bacteriology; multi/interdisciplinary studies related; music; music teacher education; neuroscience; philosophy; physical education; physics; political science; pre-dentistry; pre-law; pre-medicine; pre-theology; pre-veterinary studies; psychology; public administration; religious studies; secondary education; sociology; Spanish; theater arts/drama; urban studies; women's studies; zoology.

Academic Programs *Special study options:* advanced placement credit, double majors, freshman honors college, honors programs, independent study, internships, off-campus study, part-time degree program, services for LD students, student-designed majors, study abroad, summer session for credit. *ROTC:* Army (c). *Unusual degree programs:* 3-2 engineering with Rensselaer Polytechnic Institute, California Institute of Technology, Case Western Reserve University, New York State College of Ceramics at Alfred University, Polytechnic Institute of New York, Washington University in St. Louis; medical technology, optometry, physical therapy.

Library L. A. Beeghly Library plus 3 others with 348,952 titles, 2,829 serial subscriptions, 2,542 audiovisual materials, an OPAC, a Web page.

Computers on Campus 275 computers available on campus for general student use. A campuswide network can be accessed from student residence rooms and from off campus. Internet access, at least one staffed computer lab available.

Student Life *Housing:* on-campus residence required through senior year. *Options:* coed, men-only, women-only. *Activities and Organizations:* drama/theater group, student-run newspaper, radio station, choral group, community services, student government, Campus Programming Board, religious organizations, ethnic organizations, national fraternities, national sororities. *Campus security:* 24-hour emergency response devices and patrols, late-night transport/escort service, controlled dormitory access. *Student Services:* health clinic, personal/psychological counseling, women's center.

Athletics Member NCAA. All Division III. *Intercollegiate sports:* baseball M, basketball M/W, cross-country running M/W, equestrian sports M(c)/W(c), field hockey W, football M, golf M, ice hockey M(c), lacrosse M/W, rugby M(c)/W(c), sailing M(c)/W(c), soccer M/W, softball W, swimming M/W, tennis M/W, track and field M/W, volleyball M(c)/W. *Intramural sports:* badminton M/W, basketball M/W, cross-country running M/W, football M/W, golf M/W, lacrosse M/W, racquetball M/W, skiing (cross-country) M/W, skiing (downhill) M/W, soccer M/W, softball M/W, squash M/W, swimming M/W, tennis M/W, track and field M/W, volleyball M/W, water polo M/W.

Ohio Wesleyan University (continued)

Standardized Tests *Required:* SAT I or ACT (for admission). *Recommended:* SAT II: Subject Tests (for admission).

Costs (2001–02) *Comprehensive fee:* $29,670 includes full-time tuition ($22,860) and room and board ($6810). Part-time tuition: $2490 per course. *Room and board:* College room only: $3430. Room and board charges vary according to board plan. *Payment plan:* installment. *Waivers:* children of alumni, senior citizens, and employees or children of employees.

Financial Aid Of all full-time matriculated undergraduates who enrolled in 2001, 1126 applied for aid, 1070 were judged to have need, 154 had their need fully met. 703 Federal Work-Study jobs (averaging $1382). In 2001, 729 non-need-based awards were made. *Average percent of need met:* 91%. *Average financial aid package:* $20,422. *Average need-based loan:* $3070. *Average need-based gift aid:* $13,803. *Average non-need based aid:* $10,851. *Average indebtedness upon graduation:* $19,520.

Applying *Options:* common application, electronic application, early admission, early decision, early action, deferred entrance. *Application fee:* $35. *Required:* essay or personal statement, high school transcript, 2 letters of recommendation. *Recommended:* minimum 2.5 GPA, interview. *Application deadlines:* 3/15 (freshmen), 5/15 (transfers). *Early decision:* 12/1. *Notification:* continuous (freshmen), 12/30 (early decision), 1/15 (early action).

Admissions Contact Ohio Wesleyan University, 61 South Sandusky Street, Delaware, OH 43015. *Phone:* 740-368-3020. *Toll-free phone:* 800-922-8953. *Fax:* 740-368-3314. *E-mail:* owuadmit@owu.edu.

OTTERBEIN COLLEGE
Westerville, Ohio

- **Independent United Methodist** comprehensive, founded 1847
- **Calendar** quarters
- **Degrees** bachelor's and master's
- **Suburban** 140-acre campus with easy access to Columbus
- **Coed,** 2,551 undergraduate students, 75% full-time, 65% women, 35% men
- **Moderately difficult** entrance level, 85% of applicants were admitted

Otterbein continues to offer an excellent combination of a broad-based liberal arts education with professional/career preparation. Its campus in Westerville provides access to Ohio's capital city, Columbus, for internships as well as cultural and social activities. A student-faculty ratio of 14:1 ensures individual attention for students pursuing one of 38 majors offered. More than $9 million in grants and scholarships was awarded last year. Students graduate in 4 years.

Undergraduates Students come from 29 states and territories, 28 other countries, 9% are from out of state, 7% African American, 1% Asian American or Pacific Islander, 1% Hispanic American, 0.2% Native American, 52% live on campus. *Retention:* 90% of 2001 full-time freshmen returned.

Freshmen *Admission:* 2,231 applied, 1,891 admitted. *Average high school GPA:* 3.30. *Test scores:* SAT verbal scores over 500: 73%; SAT math scores over 500: 68%; ACT scores over 18: 92%; SAT verbal scores over 600: 28%; SAT math scores over 600: 27%; ACT scores over 24: 40%; SAT verbal scores over 700: 3%; SAT math scores over 700: 1%; ACT scores over 30: 6%.

Faculty *Total:* 246, 58% full-time. *Student/faculty ratio:* 14:1.

Majors Accounting; art; art education; athletic training/sports medicine; biochemistry; biology; business administration; business economics; business marketing and marketing management; chemistry; computer science; dance; economics; education; elementary education; English; environmental biology; equestrian studies; finance; French; health education; history; international business; international relations; journalism; literature; mathematics; middle school education; molecular biology; multi/interdisciplinary studies related; music; music business management/merchandising; music (general performance); music history; music (piano and organ performance); music teacher education; music (voice and choral/opera performance); nursing; philosophy; physical education; physical sciences; physics; political science; pre-dentistry; pre-law; pre-medicine; pre-veterinary studies; psychology; public relations; radio/television broadcasting; religious studies; science education; secondary education; sociology; Spanish; speech-language pathology/audiology; sport/fitness administration; stringed instruments; theater arts/drama; wind/percussion instruments.

Academic Programs *Special study options:* academic remediation for entering students, adult/continuing education programs, advanced placement credit, double majors, English as a second language, freshman honors college, honors programs, internships, off-campus study, part-time degree program, services for LD students, student-designed majors, study abroad, summer session for credit. *ROTC:* Army (c), Air Force (c). *Unusual degree programs:* 3-2 engineering with Case Western Reserve University, Washington University in St. Louis.

Library Courtright Memorial Library with 182,629 titles, 1,012 serial subscriptions, 8,971 audiovisual materials, an OPAC, a Web page.

Computers on Campus 146 computers available on campus for general student use. A campuswide network can be accessed from student residence rooms and from off campus. Internet access, at least one staffed computer lab available.

Student Life *Housing:* on-campus residence required through sophomore year. *Options:* men-only, women-only. *Activities and Organizations:* drama/theater group, student-run newspaper, radio and television station, choral group, marching band, musical groups, Greek organizations, honoraries, academic interest clubs, Governance, national fraternities. *Campus security:* 24-hour emergency response devices and patrols, student patrols, late-night transport/escort service, controlled dormitory access, 24-hour locked residence hall entrances. *Student Services:* health clinic, personal/psychological counseling.

Athletics Member NCAA. All Division III. *Intercollegiate sports:* baseball M, basketball M/W, cross-country running M/W, equestrian sports M/W, football M, golf M/W, soccer M/W, softball W, tennis M/W, track and field M/W, volleyball W. *Intramural sports:* badminton M/W, basketball M/W, football M, racquetball M/W, softball M/W, volleyball M/W.

Standardized Tests *Required:* SAT I or ACT (for admission).

Costs (2001–02) *Comprehensive fee:* $23,439 includes full-time tuition ($17,928) and room and board ($5511). Full-time tuition and fees vary according to course load and program. Part-time tuition: $215 per credit hour. Part-time tuition and fees vary according to course load and program. *Room and board:* College room only: $2460. Room and board charges vary according to housing facility. *Payment plan:* installment. *Waivers:* employees or children of employees.

Applying *Options:* common application, electronic application, deferred entrance. *Application fee:* $25. *Required:* high school transcript. *Recommended:* minimum 2.5 GPA, interview. *Application deadline:* 3/1 (freshmen), rolling (transfers). *Notification:* continuous (freshmen).

Admissions Contact Cass Johnson PhD, Director of Admissions, Otterbein College, One Otterbein College, Westerville, OH 43081-9924. *Phone:* 614-823-1500. *Toll-free phone:* 800-488-8144. *Fax:* 614-823-1200. *E-mail:* uotterb@otterbein.edu.

PONTIFICAL COLLEGE JOSEPHINUM
Columbus, Ohio

- **Independent Roman Catholic** comprehensive, founded 1888
- **Calendar** semesters
- **Degrees** bachelor's, master's, and first professional
- **Suburban** 100-acre campus
- **Endowment** $27.9 million
- **Coed, primarily men,** 61 undergraduate students, 100% full-time, 100% men
- **Minimally difficult** entrance level, 100% of applicants were admitted

Undergraduates 61 full-time. Students come from 8 states and territories, 3 other countries, 7% Asian American or Pacific Islander, 2% Hispanic American, 5% international. *Retention:* 50% of 2001 full-time freshmen returned.

Freshmen *Admission:* 9 enrolled.

Faculty *Total:* 16, 50% full-time. *Student/faculty ratio:* 4:1.

Majors English; Latin American studies; philosophy.

Academic Programs *Special study options:* academic remediation for entering students, advanced placement credit, English as a second language, internships, off-campus study, services for LD students.

Library Wehrle Memorial Library with 124,742 titles, 520 serial subscriptions.

Computers on Campus 10 computers available on campus for general student use. At least one staffed computer lab available.

Student Life *Housing:* on-campus residence required through senior year. *Activities and Organizations:* drama/theater group, choral group. *Campus security:* 24-hour emergency response devices, controlled dormitory access. *Student Services:* health clinic, personal/psychological counseling.

Athletics Member NSCAA. *Intramural sports:* basketball M, bowling M, football M, golf M, gymnastics M, racquetball M, skiing (cross-country) M, skiing (downhill) M, soccer M, softball M, swimming M, table tennis M, tennis M, track and field M, volleyball M, weight lifting M.

Standardized Tests *Recommended:* SAT I and SAT II or ACT (for admission).

Costs (2001–02) *Comprehensive fee:* $14,400 includes full-time tuition ($8854), mandatory fees ($50), and room and board ($5496). Part-time tuition: $370 per credit. *Room and board:* College room only: $2748. *Payment plans:* installment, deferred payment.

Financial Aid Of all full-time matriculated undergraduates who enrolled in 2001, 32 applied for aid, 25 were judged to have need, 6 had their need fully met. 10 Federal Work-Study jobs (averaging $507). In 2001, 17 non-need-based awards were made. *Average percent of need met:* 66%. *Average financial aid* *package:* $13,513. *Average need-based loan:* $4613. *Average need-based gift aid:* $3447. *Average non-need based aid:* $11,456. *Average indebtedness upon graduation:* $15,000.

Applying *Options:* deferred entrance. *Application fee:* $25. *Required:* essay or personal statement, high school transcript, 3 letters of recommendation. *Required for some:* interview. *Application deadline:* rolling (freshmen), rolling (transfers).

Admissions Contact Arminda Crawford, Secretary for Admissions, Pontifical College Josephinum, 7625 North High Street, Columbus, OH 43235-1498. *Phone:* 614-985-2241 Ext. 436.

SHAWNEE STATE UNIVERSITY

Portsmouth, Ohio

- **State-supported** 4-year, founded 1986, part of Ohio Board of Regents
- **Calendar** quarters
- **Degrees** certificates, associate, and bachelor's
- **Small-town** campus
- **Endowment** $9.6 million
- **Coed,** 3,364 undergraduate students, 80% full-time, 62% women, 38% men
- **Noncompetitive** entrance level, 100% of applicants were admitted

Shawnee State University offers baccalaureate and associate degrees through the College of Arts and Sciences and the College of Professional Studies. Programs are available in business, health sciences, engineering technologies, arts and sciences, and teacher education. With distinctive student housing and a beautiful new campus, SSU offers a high-quality education with individualized attention.

Undergraduates 2,678 full-time, 686 part-time. Students come from 9 states and territories, 7 other countries, 9% are from out of state, 2% African American, 0.2% Asian American or Pacific Islander, 0.7% Hispanic American, 0.9% Native American, 0.4% international, 5% transferred in, 5% live on campus. *Retention:* 56% of 2001 full-time freshmen returned.

Freshmen *Admission:* 2,184 applied, 2,184 admitted, 683 enrolled. *Test scores:* ACT scores over 18: 68%; ACT scores over 24: 15%.

Faculty *Total:* 257, 48% full-time. *Student/faculty ratio:* 17:1.

Majors Accounting; applied mathematics; art; athletic training/sports medicine; biological/physical sciences; biology; business administration; chemistry; computer engineering technology; data processing technology; dental hygiene; drafting; drawing; education; electromechanical technology; elementary education; emergency medical technology; English; environmental technology; fine/studio arts; history; humanities; industrial radiologic technology; information sciences/systems; instrumentation technology; international relations; legal administrative assistant; management information systems/business data processing; mathematics; medical laboratory technician; medical radiologic technology; natural sciences; nursing; occupational therapy; painting; paralegal/legal assistant; physical sciences; physical therapy; plastics technology; pre-engineering; pre-law; premedicine; pre-veterinary studies; respiratory therapy; science education; secondary education; secretarial science; social sciences; sport/fitness administration.

Academic Programs *Special study options:* academic remediation for entering students, adult/continuing education programs, advanced placement credit, distance learning, double majors, honors programs, independent study, internships, off-campus study, part-time degree program, services for LD students, study abroad, summer session for credit.

Library Shawnee State University Library with 125,257 titles, 2,773 serial subscriptions, 2,141 audiovisual materials, an OPAC, a Web page.

Computers on Campus 400 computers available on campus for general student use. A campuswide network can be accessed from off campus. Internet access, online (class) registration, at least one staffed computer lab available.

Student Life *Housing:* on-campus residence required through sophomore year. *Options:* coed. *Activities and Organizations:* drama/theater group, student-run newspaper, choral group, Campus Ministry, Health Executives and Administrators Learning Society, Greek sororities and fraternities, Student Programming Board, SGA, national fraternities. *Campus security:* 24-hour emergency response devices and patrols. *Student Services:* personal/psychological counseling, women's center.

Athletics Member NAIA. *Intercollegiate sports:* baseball M, basketball M/W, cross-country running M/W, golf M, soccer M/W, softball W, tennis W, volleyball W. *Intramural sports:* basketball M/W, bowling M/W, golf M/W, racquetball M/W, softball M, swimming M/W, table tennis M/W, tennis M/W, volleyball M/W.

Standardized Tests *Recommended:* ACT (for placement).

Costs (2001–02) *Tuition:* state resident $2808 full-time, $78 per quarter hour part-time; nonresident $5400 full-time, $150 per quarter hour part-time. Full-time tuition and fees vary according to reciprocity agreements. Part-time tuition and fees vary according to reciprocity agreements. *Required fees:* $594 full-time, $17 per quarter hour. *Room and board:* $5232; room only: $3213. Room and board charges vary according to board plan and housing facility. *Payment plan:* installment. *Waivers:* senior citizens and employees or children of employees.

Financial Aid Of all full-time matriculated undergraduates who enrolled in 2001, 2591 applied for aid, 1806 were judged to have need, 1751 had their need fully met. 104 Federal Work-Study jobs (averaging $2018). *Average percent of need met:* 70%. *Average financial aid package:* $3972. *Average need-based gift aid:* $2620. *Average indebtedness upon graduation:* $10,944.

Applying *Options:* electronic application, deferred entrance. *Required:* high school transcript. *Required for some:* letters of recommendation, interview. *Application deadline:* rolling (freshmen), rolling (transfers). *Notification:* continuous (freshmen).

Admissions Contact Mr. Bob Trusz, Director of Admission, Shawnee State University, 940 Second Street, Commons Building, Portsmouth, OH 45662. *Phone:* 740-351-3610 Ext. 610. *Toll-free phone:* 800-959-2SSU. *Fax:* 740-351-3111. *E-mail:* to_ssu@shawnee.edu.

TIFFIN UNIVERSITY

Tiffin, Ohio

- **Independent** comprehensive, founded 1888
- **Calendar** semesters
- **Degrees** certificates, associate, bachelor's, and master's
- **Small-town** 108-acre campus with easy access to Toledo
- **Endowment** $2.8 million
- **Coed,** 1,307 undergraduate students, 78% full-time, 54% women, 46% men
- **Minimally difficult** entrance level, 78% of applicants were admitted

Undergraduates 1,019 full-time, 288 part-time. Students come from 22 states and territories, 19 other countries, 8% are from out of state, 12% African American, 2% Asian American or Pacific Islander, 2% Hispanic American, 2% international, 8% transferred in, 40% live on campus. *Retention:* 61% of 2001 full-time freshmen returned.

Freshmen *Admission:* 1,354 applied, 1,052 admitted, 281 enrolled. *Average high school GPA:* 2.91. *Test scores:* SAT verbal scores over 500: 21%; SAT math scores over 500: 22%; ACT scores over 18: 76%; SAT verbal scores over 600: 6%; SAT math scores over 600: 9%; ACT scores over 24: 14%.

Faculty *Total:* 98, 44% full-time, 37% with terminal degrees. *Student/faculty ratio:* 21:1.

Majors Accounting; business administration; business marketing and marketing management; communications; computer management; computer programming; corrections; criminal justice/law enforcement administration; economics; finance; hospitality management; humanities; human resources management; information sciences/systems; international business; international relations; law enforcement/police science; liberal arts and sciences/liberal studies; management information systems/business data processing; psychology; social sciences; sport/fitness administration.

Academic Programs *Special study options:* accelerated degree program, adult/continuing education programs, advanced placement credit, distance learning, double majors, independent study, internships, part-time degree program, study abroad, summer session for credit. *ROTC:* Army (c).

Library Pfeiffer Library with 28,042 titles, 250 serial subscriptions, 497 audiovisual materials, an OPAC.

Computers on Campus 60 computers available on campus for general student use. A campuswide network can be accessed from student residence rooms and from off campus. Internet access, online (class) registration, at least one staffed computer lab available.

Student Life *Housing:* on-campus residence required through sophomore year. *Options:* coed, men-only, disabled students. *Activities and Organizations:* drama/theater group, student-run newspaper, choral group, marching band, Hospitality Management Club, Student Government Association, Greek organizations, Black United Students, International Student Association, national fraternities, national sororities. *Campus security:* student patrols, late-night transport/escort service. *Student Services:* personal/psychological counseling.

Athletics Member NCAA, NAIA. All NCAA Division II. *Intercollegiate sports:* baseball M(s), basketball M(s)/W(s), cross-country running M(s)/W(s), football M(s), golf M(s)/W(s), soccer M(s)/W(s), softball W(s), tennis M(s)/W(s), track and field M(s)/W(s), volleyball W(s). *Intramural sports:* basketball M/W, bowling M/W, football M/W, soccer M/W, softball M/W, table tennis M/W, tennis M/W, volleyball M/W, weight lifting M/W.

Standardized Tests *Required:* SAT I or ACT (for admission).

Costs (2001–02) *Comprehensive fee:* $17,250 includes full-time tuition ($11,850) and room and board ($5400). Full-time tuition and fees vary according

Tiffin University (continued)
to course load. Part-time tuition: $1185 per course. Part-time tuition and fees vary according to course load. *Room and board:* College room only: $2850. Room and board charges vary according to board plan and housing facility. *Payment plan:* installment. *Waivers:* employees or children of employees.

Financial Aid Of all full-time matriculated undergraduates who enrolled in 2001, 926 applied for aid, 801 were judged to have need, 56 had their need fully met. 277 Federal Work-Study jobs (averaging $1026). 185 State and other part-time jobs (averaging $1026). In 2001, 99 non-need-based awards were made. *Average percent of need met:* 61%. *Average financial aid package:* $3888. *Average need-based loan:* $1993. *Average need-based gift aid:* $1802. *Average non-need based aid:* $2112. *Average indebtedness upon graduation:* $17,125.

Applying *Options:* electronic application, early admission, deferred entrance. *Application fee:* $20. *Required:* essay or personal statement, high school transcript. *Required for some:* letters of recommendation, interview. *Recommended:* minimum 2.50 GPA, interview. *Application deadline:* rolling (freshmen), rolling (transfers). *Notification:* continuous until 8/1 (freshmen).

Admissions Contact Mr. Darby Roggow, Director of Admissions, Tiffin University, 155 Miami Street, Tiffin, OH 44883-2161. *Phone:* 419-448-3425. *Toll-free phone:* 800-968-6446. *Fax:* 419-443-5006. *E-mail:* admiss@tiffin.edu.

UNION INSTITUTE & UNIVERSITY
Cincinnati, Ohio

- **Independent** university, founded 1969
- **Calendar** semesters
- **Degrees** bachelor's, master's, doctoral, and post-master's certificates
- **Urban** 5-acre campus
- **Endowment** $3.5 million
- **Coed,** 652 undergraduate students, 57% full-time, 66% women, 34% men
- **Moderately difficult** entrance level, 85% of applicants were admitted

Undergraduates 371 full-time, 281 part-time. Students come from 27 states and territories, 2 other countries, 9% are from out of state, 36% African American, 1% Asian American or Pacific Islander, 9% Hispanic American, 0.5% Native American, 0.2% international, 17% transferred in. *Retention:* 62% of 2001 full-time freshmen returned.

Freshmen *Admission:* 146 applied, 124 admitted, 15 enrolled.

Faculty *Total:* 222, 50% full-time, 84% with terminal degrees. *Student/faculty ratio:* 16:1.

Majors Business; communications; criminal justice/law enforcement administration; education; health science; history; humanities; liberal arts and sciences/liberal studies; psychology; public administration; social sciences; social work.

Academic Programs *Special study options:* accelerated degree program, adult/continuing education programs, advanced placement credit, distance learning, double majors, external degree program, independent study, part-time degree program, student-designed majors, summer session for credit.

Library 4,500 titles, 18 audiovisual materials, an OPAC, a Web page.

Computers on Campus 18 computers available on campus for general student use. A campuswide network can be accessed from off campus. Internet access, at least one staffed computer lab available.

Student Life *Housing:* college housing not available. *Campus security:* late-night transport/escort service, security during class hours.

Costs (2001–02) *Tuition:* $6912 full-time, $288 per semester hour part-time. *Payment plan:* installment. *Waivers:* employees or children of employees.

Financial Aid Of all full-time matriculated undergraduates who enrolled in 2001, 587 applied for aid, 507 were judged to have need, 75 had their need fully met. 14 Federal Work-Study jobs (averaging $4500). *Average percent of need met:* 70%. *Average need-based loan:* $8000. *Average indebtedness upon graduation:* $26,250.

Applying *Options:* electronic application, deferred entrance. *Application fee:* $50. *Required:* essay or personal statement, high school transcript, 2 letters of recommendation, interview. *Application deadlines:* 10/1 (freshmen), 10/1 (transfers).

Admissions Contact Ms. Lisa Schrenger, Director, Admissions, Union Institute & University, 440 East McMillan Street, Cincinnati, OH 45206-1925. *Phone:* 513-861-6400. *Toll-free phone:* 800-486-3116. *E-mail:* admissions@tui.edu.

THE UNIVERSITY OF AKRON
Akron, Ohio

- **State-supported** university, founded 1870
- **Calendar** semesters
- **Degrees** certificates, associate, bachelor's, master's, doctoral, and first professional
- **Urban** 170-acre campus with easy access to Cleveland
- **Endowment** $180.0 million
- **Coed,** 20,180 undergraduate students, 66% full-time, 52% women, 48% men
- **Noncompetitive** entrance level, 85% of applicants were admitted

The University of Akron is northern Ohio's oldest public university. A major metropolitan research and teaching institution, UA has the only science/engineering program in Ohio ranked among the nation's top 5 by *U.S. News & World Report.* UA offers more than 320 associate, bachelor's, master's, doctoral, and law degree programs. In 1999, UA began a $200-million building plan that is adding 6 new buildings and 30 acres of green space to the campus.

Undergraduates 13,384 full-time, 6,796 part-time. Students come from 33 states and territories, 79 other countries, 1% are from out of state, 14% African American, 2% Asian American or Pacific Islander, 0.8% Hispanic American, 0.5% Native American, 1% international, 5% transferred in, 9% live on campus. *Retention:* 67% of 2001 full-time freshmen returned.

Freshmen *Admission:* 7,057 applied, 5,986 admitted, 3,638 enrolled. *Average high school GPA:* 2.88. *Test scores:* SAT verbal scores over 500: 49%; SAT math scores over 500: 52%; ACT scores over 18: 69%; SAT verbal scores over 600: 14%; SAT math scores over 600: 19%; ACT scores over 24: 19%; SAT verbal scores over 700: 4%; SAT math scores over 700: 1%; ACT scores over 30: 2%.

Faculty *Total:* 1,634, 48% full-time, 64% with terminal degrees. *Student/faculty ratio:* 15:1.

Majors Accounting; accounting related; accounting technician; acting/directing; administrative/secretarial services; alcohol/drug abuse counseling; applied art; applied mathematics; art; art education; art history; athletic training/sports medicine; banking; behavioral sciences; bioengineering; biological/physical sciences; biology; botany; broadcast journalism; business; business administration; business education; business management/administrative services related; business marketing and marketing management; buying operations; cartography; ceramic arts; chemical engineering; chemical engineering technology; chemistry; child care/development; civil engineering; classics; clothing/textiles; communication disorders; communications related; computer education; computer engineering; computer science; construction technology; corrections; criminal justice/law enforcement administration; criminal justice studies; culinary arts; cytotechnology; dance; data processing; design/applied arts related; developmental/child psychology; dietetics; drafting; drama/dance education; drawing; early childhood education; economics; economics related; education; education of the multiple handicapped; education of the specific learning disabled; education of the speech impaired; electrical engineering; elementary education; engineering; engineering-related technology; English; enterprise management; environmental health; executive assistant; family/consumer studies; family studies; fashion merchandising; finance; financial management and services related; fine arts and art studies related; fine/studio arts; fire protection related; fire protection/safety technology; food sciences; foreign languages education; French; general retailing/wholesaling related; geography; geological engineering; geological sciences related; geology; geophysics/seismology; German; German language education; gerontology; graphic design/commercial art/illustration; health education; health/medical laboratory technologies related; health/medical preparatory programs related; health/physical education/fitness related; history; history education; home economics; home economics education; hospitality management; hospitality/recreation marketing operations; hotel and restaurant management; humanities; human resources management; industrial production technologies related; industrial technology; interdisciplinary studies; interior design; interior environments; international business; law enforcement/police science; liberal arts and sciences/liberal studies; liberal arts and studies related; literature; logistics/materials management; management information systems/business data processing; mass communications; mathematical statistics; mathematics; mathematics/computer science; mathematics related; mechanical engineering; mechanical engineering technology; medical administrative assistant; medical assistant; medical office management; medical radiologic technology; medical technology; metal/jewelry arts; microbiology/bacteriology; middle school education; multi/interdisciplinary studies related; music; music (general performance); music history; musicology; music (piano and organ performance); music teacher education; music theory and composition; music (voice and choral/opera performance); natural sciences; nursing; nursing related; nursing science; nutrition studies; operating room technician; opticianry; paralegal/legal assistant; philosophy; photography; physical education; physical science technologies related; physics; physiology; plastics engineering; political science; political science/government related; polymer chemistry; pre-dentistry; pre-law; pre-medicine; pre-pharmacy studies; pre-veterinary studies; printmaking; psychology; public administration and services related; respiratory therapy; retailing operations; sales operations; science education; sculpture; secondary education; social science education; social sciences; social studies education; social work; sociology; Spanish; special education related; speech education;

speech-language pathology/audiology; speech/rhetorical studies; stringed instruments; surveying; teacher education, specific programs related; technical education; theater arts/drama; theater arts/drama and stagecraft related; visual and performing arts related; wind/percussion instruments; zoology.

Academic Programs *Special study options:* academic remediation for entering students, accelerated degree program, adult/continuing education programs, advanced placement credit, cooperative education, distance learning, double majors, English as a second language, honors programs, independent study, internships, part-time degree program, services for LD students, student-designed majors, study abroad, summer session for credit. *ROTC:* Army (b), Air Force (b).

Library Bierce Library plus 3 others with 742,213 titles, 6,087 serial subscriptions, 39,773 audiovisual materials, an OPAC, a Web page.

Computers on Campus 1200 computers available on campus for general student use. A campuswide network can be accessed from student residence rooms and from off campus. Internet access, online (class) registration, at least one staffed computer lab available.

Student Life *Housing:* on-campus residence required for freshman year. *Options:* coed, men-only, women-only. *Activities and Organizations:* drama/theater group, student-run newspaper, radio station, choral group, marching band, Inter-Fraternity Council, Panhellenic Council, Associated Student Government, Residence Hall Program Board, American Society of Mechanical Engineers, national fraternities, national sororities. *Campus security:* 24-hour emergency response devices and patrols, student patrols, late-night transport/escort service, controlled dormitory access. *Student Services:* health clinic, personal/psychological counseling, women's center, legal services.

Athletics Member NCAA. All Division I except football (Division I-A). *Intercollegiate sports:* baseball M(s), basketball M(s)/W(s), cross-country running M(s)/W(s), golf M(s), riflery M/W, soccer M(s), softball W(s), tennis M(s)/W(s), track and field M(s)/W(s), volleyball W(s). *Intramural sports:* archery M/W, basketball M/W, bowling M/W, cross-country running M/W, football M, golf M/W, lacrosse M/W, racquetball M/W, riflery M(c)/W(c), skiing (cross-country) M(c)/W(c), skiing (downhill) M(c)/W(c), soccer M/W, softball M/W, swimming W, table tennis M/W, tennis M/W, track and field M/W, volleyball M/W, weight lifting M, wrestling M.

Standardized Tests *Required:* SAT I or ACT (for admission).

Costs (2001–02) *One-time required fee:* $100. *Tuition:* state resident $4350 full-time, $181 per credit part-time; nonresident $10,552 full-time, $388 per credit part-time. Full-time tuition and fees vary according to class time, degree level, and location. Part-time tuition and fees vary according to class time, degree level, and location. *Required fees:* $580 full-time, $15 per credit. *Room and board:* $5600; room only: $3550. Room and board charges vary according to board plan and housing facility. *Payment plan:* installment. *Waivers:* senior citizens and employees or children of employees.

Financial Aid Of all full-time matriculated undergraduates who enrolled in 2001, 8848 applied for aid, 7431 were judged to have need, 1486 had their need fully met. 415 Federal Work-Study jobs (averaging $2853). 2444 State and other part-time jobs (averaging $1598). In 2001, 534 non-need-based awards were made. *Average financial aid package:* $5296. *Average need-based loan:* $3988. *Average need-based gift aid:* $3655. *Average non-need based aid:* $2649. *Average indebtedness upon graduation:* $14,632.

Applying *Options:* electronic application, early admission, early action, deferred entrance. *Application fee:* $30. *Required:* high school transcript. *Required for some:* essay or personal statement, 3 letters of recommendation, interview. *Application deadlines:* 8/15 (freshmen), 8/15 (transfers). *Notification:* continuous (freshmen), 3/15 (early action).

Admissions Contact Ms. Kim Gentile, Interim Director of Admissions, The University of Akron, 381 Buchtel Common, Akron, OH 44325-2001. *Phone:* 330-972-6428. *Toll-free phone:* 800-655-4884. *Fax:* 330-972-7676. *E-mail:* admissions@uakron.edu.

UNIVERSITY OF CINCINNATI

Cincinnati, Ohio

- **State-supported** university, founded 1819, part of University of Cincinnati System
- **Calendar** quarters
- **Degrees** certificates, associate, bachelor's, master's, doctoral, first professional, and postbachelor's certificates
- **Urban** 137-acre campus
- **Endowment** $960.3 million
- **Coed,** 19,841 undergraduate students, 75% full-time, 49% women, 51% men
- **Moderately difficult** entrance level, 82% of applicants were admitted

At the University of Cincinnati, students receive an outstanding education and select from 325 academic programs, exceptional co-op opportunities with 1,400 employers, and 275 student organizations. Rich with opportunity and fascinatingly diverse, the University of Cincinnati prepares students for their future job, graduate school, and life. Campus tours and information sessions are available daily. For more information, students may telephone 513-556-1100 or send an e-mail to admissions@uc.edu.

Undergraduates 14,905 full-time, 4,936 part-time. Students come from 46 states and territories, 50 other countries, 14% African American, 3% Asian American or Pacific Islander, 1% Hispanic American, 0.3% Native American, 0.2% international, 6% transferred in, 18% live on campus. *Retention:* 70% of 2001 full-time freshmen returned.

Freshmen *Admission:* 8,189 applied, 6,724 admitted, 3,040 enrolled. *Test scores:* SAT verbal scores over 500: 63%; SAT math scores over 500: 65%; ACT scores over 18: 83%; SAT verbal scores over 600: 24%; SAT math scores over 600: 30%; ACT scores over 24: 39%; SAT verbal scores over 700: 4%; SAT math scores over 700: 5%; ACT scores over 30: 6%.

Faculty *Total:* 1,160, 100% full-time, 69% with terminal degrees. *Student/faculty ratio:* 18:1.

Majors Accounting; aerospace engineering; African-American studies; anthropology; architectural engineering; architectural engineering technology; architecture; art; art education; art history; Asian studies; biochemistry; biological/physical sciences; biology; broadcast journalism; business administration; business marketing and marketing management; chemical engineering; chemical engineering technology; chemistry; child care/development; city/community/regional planning; civil engineering; civil engineering technology; classics; comparative literature; computer engineering; computer engineering technology; computer/information sciences; computer management; computer programming; computer science; construction engineering; construction management; construction technology; court reporting; criminal justice/law enforcement administration; dance; data processing technology; drafting; early childhood education; economics; education; electrical/electronic engineering technology; electrical engineering; elementary education; energy management technology; engineering; engineering mechanics; engineering science; English; environmental science; environmental technology; fashion design/illustration; finance; fire protection/safety technology; fire science; French; geography; geology; German; graphic design/commercial art/illustration; health education; health services administration; heating/air conditioning/refrigeration; history; humanities; human services; industrial arts; industrial design; industrial/manufacturing engineering; industrial radiologic technology; industrial technology; information sciences/systems; insurance/risk management; interior design; international relations; jazz; Judaic studies; Latin American studies; law enforcement/police science; legal administrative assistant; liberal arts and sciences/liberal studies; linguistics; literature; management information systems/business data processing; mass communications; mathematics; mechanical engineering; mechanical engineering technology; medical administrative assistant; medical laboratory technician; medical laboratory technology; medical technology; metallurgical engineering; metallurgical technology; microbiology/bacteriology; music; music history; music (piano and organ performance); music teacher education; music (voice and choral/opera performance); natural sciences; nuclear engineering; nuclear medical technology; nursing; nutrition science; occupational safety/health technology; operations research; paralegal/legal assistant; pharmacology; pharmacy; philosophy; physical education; physical therapy; physics; political science; pre-law; pre-medicine; pre-veterinary studies; psychology; public health; public policy analysis; quality control technology; radio/television broadcasting; real estate; robotics; romance languages; safety/security technology; science education; secondary education; secretarial science; social sciences; social work; sociology; Spanish; special education; speech-language pathology/audiology; stringed instruments; theater arts/drama; transportation technology; urban studies; wind/percussion instruments.

Academic Programs *Special study options:* academic remediation for entering students, accelerated degree program, adult/continuing education programs, advanced placement credit, cooperative education, distance learning, double majors, English as a second language, honors programs, independent study, internships, off-campus study, part-time degree program, services for LD students, student-designed majors, study abroad, summer session for credit. *ROTC:* Army (b), Air Force (b).

Library Langsam Library plus 7 others with 16,363 serial subscriptions, 48,757 audiovisual materials, an OPAC, a Web page.

Computers on Campus 325 computers available on campus for general student use. A campuswide network can be accessed from student residence rooms and from off campus. At least one staffed computer lab available.

Student Life *Housing:* on-campus residence required for freshman year. *Options:* coed, men-only, women-only. *Activities and Organizations:* drama/theater group, student-run newspaper, radio station, choral group, marching band, national fraternities, national sororities. *Campus security:* 24-hour emergency response devices and patrols, late-night transport/escort service, controlled dormitory access. *Student Services:* health clinic, personal/psychological counseling, women's center, legal services.

University of Cincinnati (continued)

Athletics Member NCAA. All Division I except football (Division I-A). *Intercollegiate sports:* basketball M(s)/W(s), crew M(c)/W(c), cross-country running M(s)/W(s), golf M(s), rugby M(c), soccer M(s)/W(s), swimming M(s)/W(s), tennis M(s)/W(s), track and field M(s)/W, volleyball W(s). *Intramural sports:* archery W, badminton M/W, basketball M/W, bowling M/W, crew M(c)/W(c), football M, golf M/W, gymnastics W, racquetball M/W, soccer M/W, squash M/W, swimming M/W, tennis M/W, track and field M/W, volleyball M/W, weight lifting M, wrestling M.

Standardized Tests *Required:* SAT I or ACT (for admission). *Recommended:* ACT (for admission).

Costs (2001–02) *Tuition:* state resident $4869 full-time, $162 per credit hour part-time; nonresident $13,806 full-time, $410 per credit hour part-time. Full-time tuition and fees vary according to location. Part-time tuition and fees vary according to location. *Required fees:* $954 full-time. *Room and board:* $6498. *Payment plan:* installment. *Waivers:* employees or children of employees.

Financial Aid Of all full-time matriculated undergraduates who enrolled in 2001, 8657 applied for aid, 6839 were judged to have need, 720 had their need fully met. 1893 Federal Work-Study jobs (averaging $1427). In 2001, 635 non-need-based awards were made. *Average percent of need met:* 61%. *Average financial aid package:* $6681. *Average need-based loan:* $2593. *Average need-based gift aid:* $3815. *Average non-need based aid:* $3511.

Applying *Options:* electronic application. *Application fee:* $35. *Required:* high school transcript. *Required for some:* 2 letters of recommendation, audition. *Recommended:* interview. *Application deadline:* rolling (freshmen), rolling (transfers). *Notification:* continuous (freshmen).

Admissions Contact Terry Davis, Director of Admissions, University of Cincinnati, Cincinnati, OH 45221-0091. *Phone:* 513-556-1100. *Fax:* 513-556-1105. *E-mail:* admissions@uc.edu.

UNIVERSITY OF DAYTON

Dayton, Ohio

- **Independent Roman Catholic** university, founded 1850
- **Calendar** semesters
- **Degrees** bachelor's, master's, doctoral, and first professional
- **Suburban** 110-acre campus with easy access to Cincinnati
- **Endowment** $274.4 million
- **Coed,** 7,156 undergraduate students, 92% full-time, 51% women, 49% men
- **Moderately difficult** entrance level, 80% of applicants were admitted

Recognized as one of the nation's leading Catholic universities, the University of Dayton offers the resources and diversity of a comprehensive university and the attention and accessibility of a small college. The impressive campus, challenging academic programs, advanced research facilities, NCAA Division I athletic programs, wired campus, and access to the Dayton metropolitan community are big-school advantages. Small classes, undergraduate emphasis, student-centered faculty and staff, residential campus, and friendliness are small-school qualities.

Undergraduates 6,617 full-time, 539 part-time. Students come from 47 states and territories, 23 other countries, 35% are from out of state, 3% African American, 1% Asian American or Pacific Islander, 2% Hispanic American, 0.1% Native American, 0.8% international, 2% transferred in, 87% live on campus. *Retention:* 89% of 2001 full-time freshmen returned.

Freshmen *Admission:* 7,339 applied, 5,844 admitted, 1,738 enrolled. *Test scores:* SAT verbal scores over 500: 82%; SAT math scores over 500: 87%; ACT scores over 18: 99%; SAT verbal scores over 600: 39%; SAT math scores over 600: 46%; ACT scores over 24: 64%; SAT verbal scores over 700: 7%; SAT math scores over 700: 11%; ACT scores over 30: 14%.

Faculty *Total:* 815, 48% full-time. *Student/faculty ratio:* 15:1.

Majors Accounting; American studies; applied art; applied mathematics related; art; art education; art history; biochemistry; biology; broadcast journalism; business administration; business economics; business marketing and marketing management; chemical engineering; chemistry; civil engineering; computer engineering; computer engineering technology; computer science; criminal justice/law enforcement administration; dietetics; early childhood education; economics; education; electrical/electronic engineering technology; electrical engineering; elementary education; English; environmental biology; environmental science; exercise sciences; finance; fine/studio arts; French; general studies; geology; German; graphic design/commercial art/illustration; health education; history; industrial technology; information sciences/systems; international business; international relations; journalism; management information systems/business data processing; mass communications; mathematics; mechanical engineering; mechanical engineering technology; music; music teacher education; music therapy; nutrition science; philosophy; photography; physical education; physical sciences; physics; political science; pre-dentistry; pre-law; pre-medicine; psychology; public relations; radio/television broadcasting; religious education; religious studies; science education; secondary education; sociology; Spanish; special education; sport/fitness administration; theater arts/drama.

Academic Programs *Special study options:* academic remediation for entering students, accelerated degree program, adult/continuing education programs, advanced placement credit, cooperative education, double majors, English as a second language, honors programs, independent study, internships, off-campus study, part-time degree program, services for LD students, study abroad, summer session for credit. *ROTC:* Army (b), Air Force (c).

Library Roesch Library plus 1 other with 948,677 titles, 4,196 serial subscriptions, 2,108 audiovisual materials, an OPAC, a Web page.

Computers on Campus 550 computers available on campus for general student use. A campuswide network can be accessed from student residence rooms and from off campus. Internet access, online (class) registration, at least one staffed computer lab available.

Student Life *Housing:* on-campus residence required through sophomore year. *Options:* coed, men-only, women-only, disabled students. *Activities and Organizations:* drama/theater group, student-run newspaper, radio and television station, choral group, marching band, Student Government Association, marching band, Red Scare (basketball student cheering section), Campus Connection, Chi Omega, national fraternities, national sororities. *Campus security:* 24-hour emergency response devices and patrols, student patrols, late-night transport/escort service, controlled dormitory access. *Student Services:* health clinic, personal/psychological counseling.

Athletics Member NCAA. All Division I except football (Division I-AA). *Intercollegiate sports:* baseball M(s), basketball M(s)/W(s), crew W, cross-country running M(s)/W(s), golf M(s)/W(s), soccer M(s)/W(s), softball W(s), tennis M(s)/W(s), track and field W(s), volleyball W(s). *Intramural sports:* archery M(c)/W(c), baseball M(c), basketball M/W, bowling M/W, crew M(c), cross-country running M/W, football M/W, golf M/W, ice hockey M(c), lacrosse M(c)/W(c), racquetball M/W, rugby M(c)/W(c), skiing (downhill) M(c)/W(c), soccer M(c)/W(c), softball M/W, squash M/W, table tennis M/W, tennis M/W, track and field M(c)/W(c), volleyball M(c)/W(c), water polo M(c)/W.

Standardized Tests *Required:* SAT I or ACT (for admission).

Costs (2002–03) *One-time required fee:* $90. *Comprehensive fee:* $23,600 includes full-time tuition ($17,450), mandatory fees ($550), and room and board ($5600). Full-time tuition and fees vary according to program. Part-time tuition: $582 per credit hour. Part-time tuition and fees vary according to course load and program. *Required fees:* $25 per term part-time. *Room and board:* College room only: $3100. Room and board charges vary according to board plan, housing facility, and student level. *Payment plan:* deferred payment. *Waivers:* adult students, senior citizens, and employees or children of employees.

Financial Aid Of all full-time matriculated undergraduates who enrolled in 2001, 4416 applied for aid, 3374 were judged to have need, 2509 had their need fully met. 910 Federal Work-Study jobs (averaging $1080). 3168 State and other part-time jobs (averaging $1280). *Average percent of need met:* 75%. *Average financial aid package:* $13,776. *Average need-based loan:* $4321. *Average need-based gift aid:* $7558. *Average indebtedness upon graduation:* $18,200.

Applying *Options:* electronic application, early admission, deferred entrance. *Required:* high school transcript, 1 letter of recommendation. *Required for some:* essay or personal statement. *Recommended:* interview. *Application deadline:* 6/15 (transfers). *Notification:* continuous (freshmen).

Admissions Contact Mr. Robert F. Durkle, Director of Admission, University of Dayton, 300 College Park, Dayton, OH 45469-1300. *Phone:* 937-229-4411. *Toll-free phone:* 800-837-7433. *Fax:* 937-229-4729. *E-mail:* admission@udayton.edu.

THE UNIVERSITY OF FINDLAY

Findlay, Ohio

- **Independent** comprehensive, founded 1882, affiliated with Church of God
- **Calendar** semesters
- **Degrees** certificates, associate, bachelor's, and master's
- **Small-town** 160-acre campus with easy access to Toledo
- **Endowment** $19.6 million
- **Coed,** 3,381 undergraduate students, 77% full-time, 57% women, 43% men
- **Moderately difficult** entrance level, 84% of applicants were admitted

Eleven pre-health profession tracks are offered leading to current and proposed degree programs, including athletic training, nuclear medicine, occupational therapy, physical therapy, and physician assistant studies. Environmental, safety, and occupational health management programs prepare students for these fields. Equestrian studies (English, Western, and equine management),

pre-veterinary medicine, and bilingual studies in Spanish and Japanese are other programs that earn Findlay recognition.

Undergraduates 2,615 full-time, 766 part-time. Students come from 43 states and territories, 13% are from out of state, 4% African American, 4% Asian American or Pacific Islander, 2% Hispanic American, 0.3% Native American, 0.8% international, 5% transferred in, 38% live on campus. *Retention:* 72% of 2001 full-time freshmen returned.

Freshmen *Admission:* 2,404 applied, 2,025 admitted, 858 enrolled. *Average high school GPA:* 3.20. *Test scores:* SAT verbal scores over 500: 54%; SAT math scores over 500: 58%; ACT scores over 18: 80%; SAT verbal scores over 600: 22%; SAT math scores over 600: 11%; ACT scores over 24: 31%; SAT math scores over 700: 1%; ACT scores over 30: 1%.

Faculty *Total:* 350, 46% full-time. *Student/faculty ratio:* 16:1.

Majors Accounting; art; art education; athletic training/sports medicine; bilingual/bicultural education; biological/physical sciences; biology; broadcast journalism; business administration; business communications; business education; business marketing and marketing management; business systems networking/ telecommunications; community services; computer science; creative writing; criminal justice/law enforcement administration; economics; education; elementary education; English; entrepreneurship; environmental science; equestrian studies; farm/ranch management; history; hotel and restaurant management; humanities; human resources management; international business; Japanese; journalism; logistics/materials management; mathematics; medical technology; natural sciences; nuclear medical technology; occupational therapy; philosophy; physical education; physical therapy; physician assistant; political science; pre-law; premedicine; pre-veterinary studies; psychology; public relations; radiological science; recreational therapy; religious studies; science education; secondary education; secretarial science; social sciences; social work; sociology; Spanish; special education; teaching English as a second language; theater arts/drama.

Academic Programs *Special study options:* academic remediation for entering students, accelerated degree program, adult/continuing education programs, advanced placement credit, cooperative education, distance learning, double majors, English as a second language, honors programs, independent study, internships, part-time degree program, services for LD students, student-designed majors, study abroad, summer session for credit. *ROTC:* Army (c), Air Force (c). *Unusual degree programs:* 3-2 engineering with University of Toledo, Washington University in St. Louis, Ohio Northern University; nursing with Mt.Carmel College of Nursing.

Library Shafer Library with 135,000 titles, 1,050 serial subscriptions, 2,000 audiovisual materials, an OPAC.

Computers on Campus 200 computers available on campus for general student use. A campuswide network can be accessed from student residence rooms and from off campus. Internet access, at least one staffed computer lab available.

Student Life *Housing:* on-campus residence required through junior year. *Options:* coed, men-only, women-only, disabled students. *Activities and Organizations:* drama/theater group, student-run newspaper, radio and television station, choral group, marching band, Campus Program Board, prevet club, horse club, Circle K, International Club, national fraternities, national sororities. *Campus security:* 24-hour emergency response devices and patrols, late-night transport/escort service. *Student Services:* health clinic, personal/psychological counseling, women's center.

Athletics Member NCAA. All Division II. *Intercollegiate sports:* baseball M(s), basketball M(s)/W(s), cross-country running M(s)/W(s), football M(s), golf M(s)/W(s), ice hockey M(s)/W(s), soccer M(s)/W(s), softball W(s), swimming M(s)/W(s), tennis M(s)/W(s), track and field M(s)/W(s), volleyball M(s)/W(s), water polo M(c)/W(c), wrestling M(s). *Intramural sports:* basketball M/W, volleyball M/W.

Standardized Tests *Required:* SAT I or ACT (for admission).

Costs (2001–02) *Comprehensive fee:* $23,962 includes full-time tuition ($17,088), mandatory fees ($440), and room and board ($6434). Full-time tuition and fees vary according to location and program. Part-time tuition: $372 per semester hour. Part-time tuition and fees vary according to location and program. *Required fees:* $50 per term part-time. *Room and board:* College room only: $3130. Room and board charges vary according to board plan and housing facility. *Payment plan:* installment. *Waivers:* children of alumni, senior citizens, and employees or children of employees.

Financial Aid Of all full-time matriculated undergraduates who enrolled in 2001, 2048 applied for aid, 1678 were judged to have need, 410 had their need fully met. 300 Federal Work-Study jobs (averaging $830). In 2001, 150 non-need-based awards were made. *Average percent of need met:* 88%. *Average financial aid package:* $13,450. *Average need-based loan:* $4000. *Average need-based gift aid:* $8950. *Average non-need based aid:* $6500. *Average indebtedness upon graduation:* $16,500.

Applying *Options:* common application, electronic application, deferred entrance. *Required:* high school transcript, minimum 2.3 GPA. *Required for some:* essay or personal statement, letters of recommendation, interview. *Application deadlines:* 7/1 (freshmen), 8/1 (transfers). *Notification:* continuous (freshmen).

Admissions Contact Curtis Davidson, Director, Undergraduate Admissions, The University of Findlay, 1000 North Main Street, Findlay, OH 45840-3653. *Phone:* 419-434-4638. *Toll-free phone:* 800-548-0932. *Fax:* 419-434-4898. *E-mail:* admissions@findlay.edu.

UNIVERSITY OF NORTHWESTERN OHIO
Lima, Ohio

- **Independent** primarily 2-year, founded 1920
- **Calendar** quarters
- **Degrees** diplomas, associate, and bachelor's
- **Small-town** 35-acre campus with easy access to Dayton and Toledo
- **Coed,** 2,125 undergraduate students, 84% full-time, 29% women, 71% men
- **Noncompetitive** entrance level, 97% of applicants were admitted

Undergraduates 1,784 full-time, 341 part-time. Students come from 23 states and territories, 15% are from out of state, 1% African American, 0.1% Hispanic American, 3% transferred in, 45% live on campus.

Freshmen *Admission:* 3,000 applied, 2,900 admitted, 1,481 enrolled. *Average high school GPA:* 2.5.

Faculty *Total:* 92, 71% full-time, 10% with terminal degrees. *Student/faculty ratio:* 25:1.

Majors Accounting; agricultural business; auto mechanic/technician; business administration; business marketing and marketing management; computer programming; diesel engine mechanic; health services administration; heating/air conditioning/refrigeration; legal administrative assistant; medical administrative assistant; medical assistant; paralegal/legal assistant; pharmacy technician/assistant; secretarial science; travel/tourism management.

Academic Programs *Special study options:* academic remediation for entering students, adult/continuing education programs, advanced placement credit, cooperative education, distance learning, double majors, part-time degree program, summer session for credit.

Library Northwestern College Library with 8,857 titles, 117 serial subscriptions, 10 audiovisual materials.

Computers on Campus 86 computers available on campus for general student use. A campuswide network can be accessed from off campus. Internet access, at least one staffed computer lab available.

Student Life *Housing Options:* men-only, women-only, disabled students. *Activities and Organizations:* student-run newspaper, Students in Free Enterprise. *Campus security:* 24-hour emergency response devices and patrols, late-night transport/escort service. *Student Services:* personal/psychological counseling.

Athletics *Intramural sports:* basketball M, bowling M/W, volleyball M/W.

Costs (2001–02) *Tuition:* $8880 full-time, $160 per credit part-time. Full-time tuition and fees vary according to course load and program. Part-time tuition and fees vary according to course load and program. No tuition increase for student's term of enrollment. *Room only:* $3040. *Payment plan:* installment. *Waivers:* employees or children of employees.

Financial Aid Of all full-time matriculated undergraduates who enrolled in 2001, 31 Federal Work-Study jobs (averaging $1405).

Applying *Options:* electronic application, early admission, deferred entrance. *Application fee:* $50. *Required:* high school transcript. *Application deadline:* rolling (freshmen), rolling (transfers).

Admissions Contact Mr. Dan Klopp, Vice President for Enrollment Management, University of Northwestern Ohio, 1441 North Cable Road, Lima, OH 45805-1498. *Phone:* 419-227-3141. *Fax:* 419-229-6926. *E-mail:* info@nc.edu.

UNIVERSITY OF PHOENIX-OHIO CAMPUS
Independence, Ohio

- **Proprietary** comprehensive
- **Calendar** continuous
- **Degrees** certificates, associate, bachelor's, master's, doctoral, post-master's, and postbachelor's certificates (courses conducted at 54 campuses and learning centers in 13 states)
- **Coed,** 232 undergraduate students, 100% full-time, 56% women, 44% men
- **Noncompetitive** entrance level

Undergraduates Students come from 1 other state, 0% are from out of state.

Freshmen *Admission:* 6 admitted.

Faculty *Total:* 113, 4% full-time, 4% with terminal degrees. *Student/faculty ratio:* 11:1.

University of Phoenix-Ohio Campus (continued)

Majors Business administration; business marketing and marketing management; computer/information sciences; management information systems/business data processing.

Academic Programs *Special study options:* accelerated degree program, adult/continuing education programs, advanced placement credit, distance learning, external degree program, independent study.

Library University Library with 17.5 million titles, 9,000 serial subscriptions, an OPAC, a Web page.

Computers on Campus A campuswide network can be accessed from off campus. Internet access, at least one staffed computer lab available.

Student Life *Housing:* college housing not available.

Costs (2001–02) *Tuition:* $10,500 full-time. Full-time tuition and fees vary according to location and program. *Payment plan:* deferred payment. *Waivers:* employees or children of employees.

Applying *Options:* deferred entrance. *Application fee:* $85. *Required:* 2 years of work experience. *Required for some:* high school transcript. *Application deadline:* rolling (freshmen), rolling (transfers).

Admissions Contact Ms. Beth Barilla, Director of Admissions, University of Phoenix-Ohio Campus, 4615 East Elwood Street, Phoenix, AZ 85040-1958. *Phone:* 480-927-0099 Ext. 1218. *Fax:* 480-594-1758. *E-mail:* beth.barilla@apollogrp.edu.

UNIVERSITY OF RIO GRANDE

Rio Grande, Ohio

- **Independent** comprehensive, founded 1876
- **Calendar** quarters
- **Degrees** associate, bachelor's, and master's
- **Rural** 170-acre campus
- **Endowment** $22.6 million
- **Coed,** 1,932 undergraduate students, 80% full-time, 59% women, 41% men
- **Noncompetitive** entrance level, 100% of applicants were admitted

Undergraduates 1,546 full-time, 386 part-time. Students come from 11 states and territories, 15 other countries, 5% are from out of state, 4% transferred in, 27% live on campus. *Retention:* 60% of 2001 full-time freshmen returned.

Freshmen *Admission:* 597 applied, 597 admitted, 343 enrolled. *Test scores:* ACT scores over 18: 65%; ACT scores over 24: 15%; ACT scores over 30: 1%.

Faculty *Total:* 146, 58% full-time. *Student/faculty ratio:* 18:1.

Majors Accounting; accounting technician; American studies; art; art education; biology; biology education; business administration; business communications; business education; business marketing and marketing management; chemistry; communications; computer science; data processing; drafting; early childhood education; ecology; economics; education; education (multiple levels); education of the mentally handicapped; education of the specific learning disabled; elementary education; English; English education; general studies; health education; health/physical education; history; history education; humanities; industrial technology; international business; legal administrative assistant; mass communications; mathematics; mathematics education; mechanical engineering technology; medical administrative assistant; medical laboratory technician; medical technology; music; music teacher education; nursing; physical education; physical sciences; physics education; political science; pre-dentistry; pre-law; pre-medicine; pre-theology; pre-veterinary studies; psychology; public relations; robotics technology; science education; secondary education; secretarial science; social science education; social sciences; social work; sociology; speech education; theater design; visual/performing arts.

Academic Programs *Special study options:* academic remediation for entering students, accelerated degree program, adult/continuing education programs, advanced placement credit, cooperative education, English as a second language, freshman honors college, honors programs, independent study, internships, part-time degree program, services for LD students, student-designed majors, summer session for credit. *ROTC:* Army (c).

Library Jeanette Albiez Davis Library plus 2 others with 96,731 titles, 850 serial subscriptions, an OPAC, a Web page.

Computers on Campus 225 computers available on campus for general student use. A campuswide network can be accessed from student residence rooms and from off campus. Internet access, at least one staffed computer lab available.

Student Life *Housing:* on-campus residence required through senior year. *Options:* coed, men-only, women-only. *Activities and Organizations:* drama/theater group, student-run newspaper, radio and television station, choral group, Greek organizations, student government, Honoraries, Bible Studies, Students in Free Enterprise, national fraternities. *Campus security:* 24-hour emergency response devices and patrols, late-night transport/escort service, controlled dormitory access. *Student Services:* health clinic, personal/psychological counseling.

Athletics Member NAIA. *Intercollegiate sports:* baseball M(s), basketball M(s)/W(s), cross-country running M(s)/W(s), soccer M(s), softball W(s), track and field M(s)/W(s), volleyball W(s). *Intramural sports:* basketball M/W, football M, golf M, gymnastics W, racquetball M/W, soccer M/W, table tennis M/W, tennis M/W, volleyball M/W.

Standardized Tests *Required:* ACT (for placement).

Costs (2001–02) *Tuition:* area resident $8544 full-time, $79 per credit hour part-time; state resident $8736 full-time, $94 per credit hour part-time; nonresident $9456 full-time, $263 per credit hour part-time. Full-time tuition and fees vary according to reciprocity agreements and student level. Part-time tuition and fees vary according to reciprocity agreements and student level. *Required fees:* $440 full-time, $80 per year part-time. *Room and board:* $5362. *Payment plans:* installment, deferred payment. *Waivers:* employees or children of employees.

Financial Aid Of all full-time matriculated undergraduates who enrolled in 2001, 1108 applied for aid, 1039 were judged to have need, 507 had their need fully met. 155 Federal Work-Study jobs (averaging $1268). *Average percent of need met:* 65%. *Average financial aid package:* $7406. *Average need-based loan:* $4281. *Average need-based gift aid:* $3755. *Average indebtedness upon graduation:* $13,750.

Applying *Options:* common application. *Application fee:* $15. *Required:* high school transcript, medical history. *Application deadline:* rolling (freshmen), rolling (transfers). *Notification:* continuous (freshmen).

Admissions Contact Mr. Mark F. Abell, Executive Director of Admissions, University of Rio Grande, PO Box 500, Rio Grande, OH 45674. *Phone:* 740-245-5353 Ext. 7206. *Toll-free phone:* 800-288-2746 (in-state); 800-282-7204 (out-of-state). *Fax:* 740-245-7260. *E-mail:* mabell@urgrgcc.edu.

UNIVERSITY OF TOLEDO

Toledo, Ohio

- **State-supported** university, founded 1872
- **Calendar** semesters
- **Degrees** certificates, associate, bachelor's, master's, doctoral, first professional, post-master's, and postbachelor's certificates
- **Suburban** 407-acre campus with easy access to Detroit
- **Endowment** $36.5 million
- **Coed,** 16,754 undergraduate students, 75% full-time, 52% women, 48% men
- **Noncompetitive** entrance level, 99% of applicants were admitted

Undergraduates 12,626 full-time, 4,128 part-time. Students come from 42 states and territories, 82 other countries, 9% are from out of state, 6% transferred in, 18% live on campus. *Retention:* 72% of 2001 full-time freshmen returned.

Freshmen *Admission:* 7,174 applied, 7,110 admitted, 3,633 enrolled. *Average high school GPA:* 3.02. *Test scores:* SAT verbal scores over 500: 55%; SAT math scores over 500: 61%; ACT scores over 18: 83%; SAT verbal scores over 600: 17%; SAT math scores over 600: 24%; ACT scores over 24: 34%; SAT verbal scores over 700: 2%; SAT math scores over 700: 4%; ACT scores over 30: 3%.

Faculty *Total:* 1,049, 64% full-time, 56% with terminal degrees. *Student/faculty ratio:* 18:1.

Majors Accounting; adapted physical education; adult/continuing education; alcohol/drug abuse counseling; American studies; anthropology; applied art; architectural drafting; art; art education; art history; Asian studies; bioengineering; biological/physical sciences; biology; business administration; business computer programming; business economics; business education; business marketing and marketing management; business systems analysis/design; cardiovascular technology; chemical engineering; chemical engineering technology; chemical technology; chemistry; civil engineering; civil engineering technology; communications; community services; computer engineering; computer programming; computer science; computer typography/composition; construction technology; corrections; criminal justice studies; data processing technology; developmental/child psychology; diagnostic medical sonography; drafting; drawing; early childhood education; economics; education; educational media design; education of the speech impaired; electrical/electronic engineering technology; electrical engineering; electromechanical technology; elementary education; emergency medical technology; English; English education; environmental science; environmental technology; European studies; exercise sciences; experimental psychology; film studies; finance; fine/studio arts; fire protection/safety technology; French; French language education; geography; geology; German; gerontological services; gerontology; health education; health facilities administration; health/medical diagnostic and treatment services related; history; humanities; human resources management; individual/family development related; industrial/manufacturing engineering; industrial technology; information sciences/systems; international business; international relations; journalism; Latin American studies; law enforcement/police science; legal administrative assistant; liberal arts and sciences/liberal studies; linguistics; literature; mass communications; mathematics; mathematics education; mechanical engineering; mechanical engineering technology; medical assistant; medical technology; medieval/renaissance studies; mental health/rehabilitation; Middle Eastern studies; multi/interdisciplinary studies related; music; music teacher education; natural sciences; nursing; paralegal/legal assistant; pharmacy; philosophy; physical education; physical sciences; physical therapy; physics; political science; pre-dentistry; pre-law; pre-medicine; psychiatric/mental health services; psychology; public health education/promotion; public policy analysis; real estate; recreational therapy; recreation/leisure studies; respiratory therapy; retail management; sales operations; science education; secondary education; secretarial science; social sciences; social studies education; social work; sociology; Spanish; Spanish language education; special education; speech-language pathology; speech therapy; teacher education, specific programs related; theater arts/drama; trade/industrial education; transportation technology; urban studies; welding technology; women's studies.

Academic Programs *Special study options:* academic remediation for entering students, adult/continuing education programs, advanced placement credit, cooperative education, distance learning, double majors, honors programs, independent study, internships, off-campus study, part-time degree program, services for LD students, student-designed majors, study abroad, summer session for credit. *ROTC:* Army (b), Air Force (c).

Library Carlson Library plus 3 others with 1.3 million titles, 4,527 serial subscriptions, 7,224 audiovisual materials, an OPAC, a Web page.

Computers on Campus 1700 computers available on campus for general student use. A campuswide network can be accessed from student residence rooms and from off campus that provide access to online transcripts, student account and grade information. Internet access, online (class) registration, at least one staffed computer lab available.

Student Life *Housing:* on-campus residence required for freshman year. *Options:* coed, women-only, disabled students. *Activities and Organizations:* drama/theater group, student-run newspaper, radio station, choral group, marching band, student government, University YMCA, Newman Club, International Student Association, Campus Activities and Programming, national fraternities, national sororities. *Campus security:* 24-hour emergency response devices and patrols, student patrols, late-night transport/escort service, controlled dormitory access, bicycle patrols by security staff, crime prevention officer. *Student Services:* health clinic, personal/psychological counseling, women's center, legal services.

Athletics Member NCAA. All Division I except football (Division I-A). *Intercollegiate sports:* baseball M(s), basketball M(s)/W(s), cross-country running M(s)/W(s), golf M(s)/W(s), soccer W(s), softball W(s), swimming M(s)/W(s), tennis M(s)/W(s), track and field M(s)/W(s), volleyball W(s). *Intramural sports:* badminton M/W, basketball M/W, bowling M/W, crew M(c)/W(c), fencing M(c)/W(c), football M/W, golf M/W, lacrosse M/W, racquetball M/W, sailing M(c)/W(c), skiing (cross-country) M(c)/W(c), skiing (downhill) M(c)/W(c), soccer M(c)/W(c), softball M/W, swimming M/W, table tennis M/W, tennis M/W, track and field M/W, volleyball M/W, water polo M/W, weight lifting M/W.

Standardized Tests *Required for some:* SAT I or ACT (for admission).

Costs (2001–02) *Tuition:* state resident $4172 full-time, $213 per semester hour part-time; nonresident $11,532 full-time, $519 per semester hour part-time. *Required fees:* $930 full-time. *Room and board:* $6104.

Financial Aid Of all full-time matriculated undergraduates who enrolled in 2001, 10017 applied for aid, 6437 were judged to have need, 809 had their need fully met. *Average percent of need met:* 62%. *Average financial aid package:* $6053. *Average need-based loan:* $3625. *Average need-based gift aid:* $4000. *Average indebtedness upon graduation:* $16,870.

Applying *Options:* electronic application, deferred entrance. *Application fee:* $30. *Required:* high school transcript. *Required for some:* minimum 2.0 GPA. *Application deadline:* rolling (freshmen), rolling (transfers). *Notification:* continuous (freshmen).

Admissions Contact Ms. Nancy Hintz, Assistant Director, University of Toledo, 2801 West Bancroft, Toledo, OH 43606-3398. *Phone:* 419-530-5728. *Toll-free phone:* 800-5TOLEDO. *Fax:* 419-530-5872. *E-mail:* enroll@utnet.utoledo.edu.

URBANA UNIVERSITY
Urbana, Ohio

- **Independent** comprehensive, founded 1850, affiliated with Church of the New Jerusalem
- **Calendar** semesters
- **Degrees** associate, bachelor's, and master's
- **Small-town** 128-acre campus with easy access to Columbus and Dayton
- **Coed,** 1,358 undergraduate students, 63% full-time, 55% women, 45% men
- **Moderately difficult** entrance level, 59% of applicants were admitted

The mission of Urbana University is to offer an exemplary liberal arts education in a small college environment emphasizing individual attention, excellence in instruction, career-oriented programs, and affirmation of moral and ethical values. Urbana University operates on the principle that all policies, practices, and decisions must be made in the best interest of the students served.

Undergraduates 860 full-time, 498 part-time. Students come from 8 states and territories, 2 other countries, 1% are from out of state, 15% transferred in. *Retention:* 76% of 2001 full-time freshmen returned.

Freshmen *Admission:* 543 applied, 320 admitted, 220 enrolled. *Average high school GPA:* 2.8.

Faculty *Total:* 92, 53% full-time, 43% with terminal degrees. *Student/faculty ratio:* 18:1.

Majors Accounting; adult/continuing education; athletic training/sports medicine; biology; business administration; business economics; business marketing and marketing management; chemistry; criminal justice/law enforcement administration; education; elementary education; English; health education; history; human resources management; liberal arts and sciences/liberal studies; mass communications; middle school education; philosophy; pre-dentistry; pre-law; pre-medicine; pre-veterinary studies; psychology; religious studies; science education; secondary education; sociology.

Academic Programs *Special study options:* academic remediation for entering students, accelerated degree program, adult/continuing education programs, advanced placement credit, cooperative education, distance learning, double majors, English as a second language, independent study, internships, off-campus study, part-time degree program, services for LD students, student-designed majors, summer session for credit.

Library Swedenborg Memorial Library with 61,600 titles, 800 serial subscriptions, 22,036 audiovisual materials, an OPAC, a Web page.

Computers on Campus 69 computers available on campus for general student use. Internet access, at least one staffed computer lab available.

Student Life *Housing:* on-campus residence required through junior year. *Options:* coed, men-only, women-only. *Activities and Organizations:* drama/theater group, student-run newspaper, radio station, choral group, Student Government Association, business club, education club, drama club, Student Activities Planning Committee. *Campus security:* 24-hour patrols, late-night transport/escort service. *Student Services:* health clinic, personal/psychological counseling.

Athletics Member NAIA. *Intercollegiate sports:* baseball M(s), basketball M(s)/W(s), football M(s), golf M(s)/W, soccer M(s)/W(s), softball W(s), volleyball W(s). *Intramural sports:* basketball M/W, football M, racquetball M/W, soccer M/W, softball M/W, tennis M/W, track and field M/W, volleyball M/W, weight lifting M.

Standardized Tests *Required:* SAT I or ACT (for admission).

Costs (2001–02) *Comprehensive fee:* $17,004 includes full-time tuition ($11,844), mandatory fees ($160), and room and board ($5000). Full-time tuition and fees vary according to location. Part-time tuition: $250 per credit hour. Part-time tuition and fees vary according to location. *Required fees:* $40 per term part-time. *Room and board:* College room only: $1900. Room and board charges vary according to board plan, housing facility, location, and student level. *Payment plans:* installment, deferred payment. *Waivers:* children of alumni, senior citizens, and employees or children of employees.

Applying *Options:* electronic application, early admission, deferred entrance. *Application fee:* $25. *Required:* essay or personal statement, high school transcript, minimum 2.0 GPA. *Required for some:* 2 letters of recommendation. *Recommended:* interview. *Application deadline:* rolling (freshmen), rolling (transfers). *Notification:* 8/15 (freshmen).

Admissions Contact Ms. Mona Newcomer, Admissions Office Manager, Urbana University, 579 College Way, Urbana, OH 43078-2091. *Phone:* 937-484-1356. *Toll-free phone:* 800-787-2262. *Fax:* 937-484-1389. *E-mail:* admiss@urbana.edu.

URSULINE COLLEGE
Pepper Pike, Ohio

- **Independent Roman Catholic** comprehensive, founded 1871
- **Calendar** semesters
- **Degrees** bachelor's, master's, and postbachelor's certificates
- **Suburban** 112-acre campus with easy access to Cleveland
- **Endowment** $19.4 million
- **Coed, primarily women,** 1,019 undergraduate students, 52% full-time, 92% women, 8% men
- **Minimally difficult** entrance level, 65% of applicants were admitted

Undergraduates 532 full-time, 487 part-time. Students come from 8 states and territories, 6 other countries, 20% are from out of state, 21% African American,

Ursuline College (continued)
1% Asian American or Pacific Islander, 3% Hispanic American, 0.2% Native American, 0.9% international, 13% transferred in, 11% live on campus. *Retention:* 64% of 2001 full-time freshmen returned.

Freshmen *Admission:* 308 applied, 200 admitted, 100 enrolled. *Average high school GPA:* 3.15. *Test scores:* SAT verbal scores over 500: 47%; SAT math scores over 500: 44%; ACT scores over 18: 87%; SAT verbal scores over 600: 13%; SAT math scores over 600: 3%; ACT scores over 24: 26%; ACT scores over 30: 3%.

Faculty *Total:* 167, 33% full-time, 38% with terminal degrees. *Student/faculty ratio:* 9:1.

Majors Accounting; American studies; architectural history; art; art education; art history; biological sciences/life sciences related; biology; business administration; business marketing and marketing management; design/visual communications; education; English; English education; environmental biology; family/community studies; fashion design/illustration; fashion merchandising; health/medical administrative services related; health science; health services administration; health unit management; history; humanities; human resources management; interior design; management information systems/business data processing; mathematics; mathematics education; middle school education; multi/interdisciplinary studies related; nursing; philosophy; pre-law; pre-medicine; psychology; public relations; religious studies; science education; social studies education; social work; sociology; special education.

Academic Programs *Special study options:* academic remediation for entering students, adult/continuing education programs, advanced placement credit, cooperative education, double majors, independent study, internships, off-campus study, part-time degree program, services for LD students, student-designed majors, summer session for credit. *ROTC:* Army (c).

Library Ralph M. Besse Library with 92,525 titles, 3,654 serial subscriptions, 7,495 audiovisual materials, an OPAC, a Web page.

Computers on Campus 66 computers available on campus for general student use. A campuswide network can be accessed from student residence rooms. Internet access, at least one staffed computer lab available.

Student Life *Activities and Organizations:* drama/theater group, student-run newspaper, Student Government Association, Student Nurses of Ursuline College, Fashion Focus, Students United for Black Awareness, drama club. *Campus security:* 24-hour emergency response devices and patrols. *Student Services:* health clinic, personal/psychological counseling.

Athletics Member NAIA. *Intercollegiate sports:* basketball W(s), golf W(s), soccer W(s), softball W(s), volleyball W(s). *Intramural sports:* volleyball W.

Standardized Tests *Required:* SAT I or ACT (for admission).

Costs (2001–02) *Comprehensive fee:* $19,730 includes full-time tuition ($14,730) and room and board ($5000). Part-time tuition: $491 per credit hour. *Room and board:* Room and board charges vary according to board plan. *Payment plan:* installment. *Waivers:* employees or children of employees.

Financial Aid Of all full-time matriculated undergraduates who enrolled in 2001, 286 applied for aid, 268 were judged to have need. 126 Federal Work-Study jobs (averaging $662). *Average financial aid package:* $12,885. *Average indebtedness upon graduation:* $19,750.

Applying *Options:* early admission, deferred entrance. *Application fee:* $25. *Required:* high school transcript. *Recommended:* essay or personal statement, minimum 2.0 GPA, letters of recommendation, interview. *Application deadline:* rolling (freshmen), rolling (transfers). *Notification:* continuous (freshmen).

Admissions Contact Ms. Jill Oakley-Jeppe, Director of Admissions, Ursuline College, 2550 Lander Road, Pepper Pike, OH 44124. *Phone:* 440-449-4203. *Toll-free phone:* 888-URSULINE. *Fax:* 440-684-6138. *E-mail:* admission@ursuline.edu.

WALSH UNIVERSITY

North Canton, Ohio

- **Independent Roman Catholic** comprehensive, founded 1958
- **Calendar** semesters
- **Degrees** associate, bachelor's, and master's
- **Small-town** 100-acre campus with easy access to Cleveland
- **Endowment** $2.1 million
- **Coed,** 1,401 undergraduate students, 75% full-time, 59% women, 41% men
- **Moderately difficult** entrance level, 80% of applicants were admitted

Undergraduates 1,055 full-time, 346 part-time. Students come from 10 states and territories, 2% are from out of state, 6% African American, 0.8% Asian American or Pacific Islander, 1% Hispanic American, 0.4% Native American, 0.5% international, 15% transferred in, 50% live on campus.

Freshmen *Admission:* 968 applied, 772 admitted, 269 enrolled. *Test scores:* ACT scores over 18: 89%; ACT scores over 24: 29%; ACT scores over 30: 1%.

Faculty *Total:* 62. *Student/faculty ratio:* 12:1.

Majors Accounting; athletic training/sports medicine; behavioral sciences; biological/physical sciences; biology; business administration; business education; business marketing and marketing management; chemistry; computer science; early childhood education; education; elementary education; English; finance; French; history; human services; international relations; Latin American studies; liberal arts and sciences/liberal studies; mass communications; mathematics; modern languages; natural sciences; nursing; pastoral counseling; philosophy; physical education; physical sciences; political science; pre-dentistry; pre-law; pre-medicine; pre-veterinary studies; psychology; reading education; religious studies; romance languages; science education; secondary education; sociology; Spanish; special education; theology.

Academic Programs *Special study options:* academic remediation for entering students, accelerated degree program, adult/continuing education programs, advanced placement credit, English as a second language, freshman honors college, honors programs, internships, off-campus study, part-time degree program, services for LD students, student-designed majors, summer session for credit. *Unusual degree programs:* 3-2 forestry with University of Michigan.

Library Walsh University Library with 130,000 titles, 683 serial subscriptions, an OPAC.

Computers on Campus 90 computers available on campus for general student use. A campuswide network can be accessed from student residence rooms and from off campus. At least one staffed computer lab available.

Student Life *Housing:* on-campus residence required through senior year. *Options:* coed, men-only, women-only. *Activities and Organizations:* drama/theater group, student-run newspaper, radio station, choral group, BACCHUS, Circle K, business club, Student Activities, student government. *Campus security:* 24-hour emergency response devices and patrols, controlled dormitory access. *Student Services:* health clinic, personal/psychological counseling.

Athletics Member NAIA. *Intercollegiate sports:* baseball M(s), basketball M(s)/W(s), cross-country running M(s)/W(s), football M(s), golf M(s), soccer M(s)/W(s), softball W(s), swimming W(s), tennis M(s)/W(s), track and field M(s)/W(s), volleyball W(s). *Intramural sports:* basketball M/W, bowling M/W, football M/W, soccer M/W, softball M/W, table tennis M/W, volleyball M/W.

Standardized Tests *Required:* SAT I or ACT (for admission).

Costs (2002–03) *Comprehensive fee:* $22,140 includes full-time tuition ($13,450), mandatory fees ($420), and room and board ($8270). Full-time tuition and fees vary according to course load. Part-time tuition: $450 per credit hour. *Room and board:* College room only: $5300. *Payment plans:* installment, deferred payment.

Financial Aid Of all full-time matriculated undergraduates who enrolled in 2001, 917 applied for aid, 798 were judged to have need, 351 had their need fully met. 233 Federal Work-Study jobs (averaging $1473). 19 State and other part-time jobs (averaging $1063). In 2001, 119 non-need-based awards were made. *Average percent of need met:* 87%. *Average financial aid package:* $9996. *Average need-based loan:* $2764. *Average need-based gift aid:* $5698. *Average non-need based aid:* $3313. *Average indebtedness upon graduation:* $17,120.

Applying *Options:* common application, electronic application, early admission, deferred entrance. *Application fee:* $25. *Required:* high school transcript, minimum 2.0 GPA. *Required for some:* essay or personal statement, minimum 3.0 GPA, 2 letters of recommendation. *Recommended:* interview. *Application deadline:* rolling (freshmen), rolling (transfers). *Notification:* continuous (freshmen).

Admissions Contact Mr. Brett Freshour, Director of Admissions, Walsh University, 2020 Easton Street, NW, North Canton, OH 44720-3396. *Phone:* 330-490-7171. *Toll-free phone:* 800-362-9846 (in-state); 800-362-8846 (out-of-state). *Fax:* 330-490-7165. *E-mail:* admissions@alex.walsh.edu.

WILBERFORCE UNIVERSITY

Wilberforce, Ohio

- **Independent** 4-year, founded 1856, affiliated with African Methodist Episcopal Church
- **Calendar** semesters
- **Degree** bachelor's
- **Rural** 125-acre campus with easy access to Dayton
- **Endowment** $10.7 million
- **Coed,** 908 undergraduate students, 100% full-time, 59% women, 41% men
- **Minimally difficult** entrance level, 22% of applicants were admitted

For 146 years, Wilberforce University, the nation's oldest historically African-American private college, has provided academically excellent education opportunities. A rigorous curriculum; mandatory cooperative education; study abroad in England, Egypt, and Israel; cultural and extracurricular programming; and intercollegiate athletic programs are provided to prepare students for careers and graduate and professional studies.

Undergraduates 908 full-time. Students come from 34 states and territories, 8 other countries, 54% are from out of state, 91% African American, 0.2% Asian American or Pacific Islander, 0.4% Hispanic American, 2% international, 6% transferred in, 85% live on campus.

Freshmen *Admission:* 2,495 applied, 538 admitted, 184 enrolled. *Average high school GPA:* 2.5.

Faculty *Total:* 72, 79% full-time, 53% with terminal degrees. *Student/faculty ratio:* 12:1.

Majors Accounting; biology; business administration; business economics; business marketing and marketing management; chemistry; computer engineering; computer science; economics; electrical engineering; engineering physics; finance; fine/studio arts; health services administration; information sciences/systems; liberal arts and sciences/liberal studies; literature; mass communications; mathematics; music theory and composition; music (voice and choral/opera performance); political science; psychology; rehabilitation therapy; sociology.

Academic Programs *Special study options:* academic remediation for entering students, advanced placement credit, cooperative education, external degree program, freshman honors college, honors programs, off-campus study, study abroad. *ROTC:* Army (c), Air Force (c). *Unusual degree programs:* 3-2 engineering with University of Dayton, University of Cincinnati; computer science with University of Dayton.

Library Rembert E. Stokes Library with 63,000 titles, 650 serial subscriptions, 500 audiovisual materials, an OPAC, a Web page.

Computers on Campus 77 computers available on campus for general student use. A campuswide network can be accessed from student residence rooms and from off campus. Internet access, at least one staffed computer lab available.

Student Life *Housing:* on-campus residence required through junior year. *Options:* men-only, women-only. *Activities and Organizations:* drama/theater group, student-run newspaper, radio station, choral group, yearbook staff, campus radio station, National Student Business Leagu, Student Government Association, national fraternities, national sororities. *Campus security:* 24-hour emergency response devices and patrols, controlled dormitory access. *Student Services:* health clinic, personal/psychological counseling.

Athletics Member NAIA. *Intercollegiate sports:* basketball M/W, cross-country running M/W, golf M/W, track and field M/W, volleyball W. *Intramural sports:* basketball M/W, soccer M/W, softball M/W, tennis M/W, volleyball M/W.

Standardized Tests *Required:* SAT I or ACT (for admission).

Costs (2001–02) *One-time required fee:* $30. *Comprehensive fee:* $15,416 includes full-time tuition ($9152), mandatory fees ($1014), and room and board ($5250). *Room and board:* College room only: $2850. *Payment plans:* installment, deferred payment. *Waivers:* employees or children of employees.

Financial Aid *Financial aid deadline:* 6/1.

Applying *Options:* common application, electronic application, early admission, deferred entrance. *Application fee:* $20. *Required:* essay or personal statement, high school transcript, minimum 2.0 GPA, 2 letters of recommendation. *Recommended:* interview. *Application deadlines:* 7/1 (freshmen), 7/1 (transfers). *Notification:* continuous until 8/1 (freshmen).

Admissions Contact Mr. Kenneth C. Christmon, Director of Admissions, Wilberforce University, PO Box 1001, Wilberforce, OH 45384-1001. *Phone:* 937-708-5789. *Toll-free phone:* 800-367-8568. *Fax:* 937-376-4751. *E-mail:* kchristm@wilberforce.edu.

WILMINGTON COLLEGE
Wilmington, Ohio

- **Independent Friends** 4-year, founded 1870
- **Calendar** semesters
- **Degree** bachelor's
- **Small-town** 1465-acre campus with easy access to Cincinnati and Columbus
- **Endowment** $19.0 million
- **Coed,** 1,243 undergraduate students, 99% full-time, 55% women, 45% men
- **Moderately difficult** entrance level, 80% of applicants were admitted

Undergraduates 1,227 full-time, 16 part-time. Students come from 15 states and territories, 6 other countries, 5% are from out of state, 11% African American, 0.2% Asian American or Pacific Islander, 0.3% Hispanic American, 0.1% Native American, 1% international, 6% transferred in, 68% live on campus. *Retention:* 73% of 2001 full-time freshmen returned.

Freshmen *Admission:* 1,151 applied, 924 admitted, 368 enrolled. *Average high school GPA:* 3.10. *Test scores:* ACT scores over 18: 80%; ACT scores over 24: 25%; ACT scores over 30: 3%.

Faculty *Total:* 77, 91% full-time, 69% with terminal degrees. *Student/faculty ratio:* 16:1.

Majors Accounting; agricultural business; agricultural education; agricultural sciences; art education; athletic training/sports medicine; biological/physical sciences; biology; business administration; business economics; business education; business marketing and marketing management; chemistry; computer science; criminal justice/law enforcement administration; economics; education; elementary education; English; health education; history; liberal arts and sciences/liberal studies; mass communications; mathematics; modern languages; music teacher education; philosophy; physical education; political science; pre-dentistry; pre-law; pre-medicine; pre-veterinary studies; psychology; religious studies; science education; secondary education; social sciences; social work; Spanish; sport/fitness administration; theater arts/drama.

Academic Programs *Special study options:* academic remediation for entering students, adult/continuing education programs, advanced placement credit, double majors, honors programs, independent study, internships, off-campus study, part-time degree program, services for LD students, student-designed majors, study abroad, summer session for credit.

Library Watson Library plus 1 other with 103,706 titles, 408 serial subscriptions, 1,280 audiovisual materials, an OPAC.

Computers on Campus 80 computers available on campus for general student use. A campuswide network can be accessed from student residence rooms and from off campus that provide access to OhioLink. Internet access, online (class) registration, at least one staffed computer lab available.

Student Life *Housing:* on-campus residence required through senior year. *Options:* coed, men-only, women-only. *Activities and Organizations:* drama/theater group, student-run newspaper, choral group, Greek organizations, Aggie Club, Quest, student publications, Commuter Concerns, national fraternities. *Campus security:* 24-hour emergency response devices and patrols, late-night transport/escort service, controlled dormitory access. *Student Services:* health clinic, personal/psychological counseling.

Athletics Member NCAA. All Division III. *Intercollegiate sports:* baseball M, basketball M/W, cross-country running M/W, football M, golf M/W, soccer M/W, softball W, swimming M/W, tennis M/W, track and field M/W, volleyball W, wrestling M. *Intramural sports:* basketball M/W, football M, racquetball M/W, soccer M/W, softball M/W, squash M/W, swimming M/W, table tennis M/W, volleyball M/W.

Standardized Tests *Required:* SAT I or ACT (for admission).

Costs (2001–02) *Comprehensive fee:* $22,765 includes full-time tuition ($16,128), mandatory fees ($386), and room and board ($6251). Part-time tuition: $310 per hour. Part-time tuition and fees vary according to course load. *Room and board:* Room and board charges vary according to board plan and housing facility. *Payment plan:* installment. *Waivers:* employees or children of employees.

Financial Aid Of all full-time matriculated undergraduates who enrolled in 2001, 1060 applied for aid, 987 were judged to have need, 364 had their need fully met. *Average percent of need met:* 90%. *Average financial aid package:* $14,869. *Average need-based loan:* $4340. *Average need-based gift aid:* $5856. *Average non-need based aid:* $1038. *Average indebtedness upon graduation:* $18,645. *Financial aid deadline:* 6/1.

Applying *Options:* deferred entrance. *Application fee:* $25. *Required:* high school transcript. *Recommended:* minimum 2.5 GPA, 1 letter of recommendation, interview. *Application deadline:* rolling (freshmen), rolling (transfers).

Admissions Contact Tina Garland, Interim Director of Admission and Financial Aid, Wilmington College, Pyle Center Box 1325, 251 Ludovic Street, Wilmington, OH 45177. *Phone:* 937-382-6661 Ext. 260. *Toll-free phone:* 800-341-9318 Ext. 260. *Fax:* 937-382-7077. *E-mail:* admission@wilmington.edu.

WITTENBERG UNIVERSITY
Springfield, Ohio

- **Independent** comprehensive, founded 1845, affiliated with Evangelical Lutheran Church
- **Calendar** semesters
- **Degrees** bachelor's and master's
- **Suburban** 71-acre campus with easy access to Columbus and Dayton
- **Endowment** $115.0 million
- **Coed,** 2,216 undergraduate students, 93% full-time, 55% women, 45% men
- **Moderately difficult** entrance level, 85% of applicants were admitted

Undergraduates 2,061 full-time, 155 part-time. Students come from 41 states and territories, 27 other countries, 40% are from out of state, 6% African American, 0.7% Asian American or Pacific Islander, 0.7% Hispanic American, 0.1% Native American, 2% international, 1% transferred in, 98% live on campus. *Retention:* 85% of 2001 full-time freshmen returned.

Freshmen *Admission:* 2,415 applied, 2,056 admitted, 580 enrolled. *Average high school GPA:* 3.50. *Test scores:* SAT verbal scores over 500: 85%; SAT math scores over 500: 82%; ACT scores over 18: 99%; SAT verbal scores over 600: 37%; SAT math scores over 600: 39%; ACT scores over 24: 63%; SAT verbal scores over 700: 2%; SAT math scores over 700: 5%; ACT scores over 30: 13%.

Wittenberg University (continued)

Faculty *Total:* 154. *Student/faculty ratio:* 14:1.

Majors American studies; art; art education; art history; Asian studies; behavioral sciences; biochemistry; biological/physical sciences; biology; botany; business administration; business economics; business marketing and marketing management; cartography; cell biology; ceramic arts; chemistry; communications; comparative literature; computer graphics; computer science; creative writing; developmental/child psychology; drawing; earth sciences; East Asian studies; economics; education; elementary education; English; environmental biology; environmental science; finance; fine/studio arts; French; geography; geology; German; graphic design/commercial art/illustration; history; humanities; interdisciplinary studies; international business; international relations; liberal arts and sciences/liberal studies; literature; marine biology; mathematics; microbiology/bacteriology; middle school education; modern languages; music; music (piano and organ performance); music teacher education; music (voice and choral/opera performance); natural sciences; philosophy; physical sciences; physics; physiological psychology/psychobiology; political science; pre-dentistry; pre-law; pre-medicine; pre-veterinary studies; psychology; religious studies; Russian/Slavic studies; science education; sculpture; secondary education; social sciences; sociology; Spanish; special education; technical/business writing; theater arts/drama; theology; urban studies.

Academic Programs *Special study options:* academic remediation for entering students, accelerated degree program, adult/continuing education programs, advanced placement credit, cooperative education, double majors, English as a second language, external degree program, freshman honors college, honors programs, independent study, internships, off-campus study, part-time degree program, student-designed majors, study abroad, summer session for credit. *ROTC:* Army (c), Air Force (c). *Unusual degree programs:* 3-2 engineering with Georgia Institute of Technology, Washington University in St. Louis, Case Western Reserve University; forestry with Duke University; nursing with Case Western Reserve University, Johns Hopkins University; occupational therapy with Washington University in St. Louis.

Library Thomas Library plus 2 others with 350,000 titles, 1,300 serial subscriptions, an OPAC, a Web page.

Computers on Campus 500 computers available on campus for general student use. A campuswide network can be accessed from student residence rooms and from off campus. Internet access, online (class) registration, at least one staffed computer lab available.

Student Life *Housing:* on-campus residence required through junior year. *Options:* coed, women-only. *Activities and Organizations:* drama/theater group, student-run newspaper, radio station, choral group, American International Association, East Asian Studies Program, Caving Club, Union Board, music groups, national fraternities, national sororities. *Campus security:* 24-hour emergency response devices and patrols, student patrols, late-night transport/escort service, controlled dormitory access, crime prevention programs. *Student Services:* health clinic, personal/psychological counseling, women's center.

Athletics Member NCAA. All Division III. *Intercollegiate sports:* baseball M, basketball M/W, crew W(c), cross-country running M/W, field hockey W, football M, golf M/W(c), ice hockey M(c), lacrosse M/W, rugby M(c)/W(c), soccer M/W, softball W, swimming M/W, tennis M/W, track and field M/W, volleyball M(c)/W. *Intramural sports:* archery M/W, badminton M/W, basketball M/W, fencing M/W, football M/W, golf M/W, racquetball M/W, sailing M/W, skiing (downhill) M/W, soccer M/W, softball M/W, swimming M/W, table tennis M/W, tennis M/W, track and field M/W, volleyball M/W, water polo M/W, weight lifting M/W.

Standardized Tests *Required:* SAT I or ACT (for admission). *Recommended:* SAT II: Subject Tests (for admission).

Costs (2001–02) *Comprehensive fee:* $28,616 includes full-time tuition ($22,530), mandatory fees ($310), and room and board ($5776). Part-time tuition and fees vary according to course load. *Room and board:* College room only: $2984. Room and board charges vary according to board plan. *Payment plans:* installment, deferred payment. *Waivers:* children of alumni, adult students, senior citizens, and employees or children of employees.

Financial Aid *Financial aid deadline:* 3/15.

Applying *Options:* common application, electronic application, early admission, early decision, early action, deferred entrance. *Application fee:* $40. *Required:* essay or personal statement, high school transcript, 1 letter of recommendation. *Required for some:* interview. *Recommended:* interview. *Application deadline:* 3/15 (freshmen), rolling (transfers). *Early decision:* 11/15. *Notification:* continuous (freshmen), 1/1 (early decision), 1/1 (early action).

Admissions Contact Mr. Kenneth G. Benne, Dean of Admissions and Financial Aid, Wittenberg University, PO Box 720, Springfield, OH 45501-0720. *Phone:* 937-327-6314 Ext. 6366. *Toll-free phone:* 800-677-7558 Ext. 6314. *Fax:* 937-327-6379. *E-mail:* admission@wittenberg.edu.

WRIGHT STATE UNIVERSITY
Dayton, Ohio

- **State-supported** university, founded 1964
- **Calendar** quarters
- **Degrees** associate, bachelor's, master's, doctoral, first professional, and postbachelor's certificates
- **Suburban** 557-acre campus with easy access to Cincinnati and Columbus
- **Endowment** $6.3 million
- **Coed,** 12,220 undergraduate students, 80% full-time, 56% women, 44% men
- **Minimally difficult** entrance level, 92% of applicants were admitted

Undergraduates 9,781 full-time, 2,439 part-time. Students come from 49 states and territories, 69 other countries, 3% are from out of state, 11% African American, 2% Asian American or Pacific Islander, 0.8% Hispanic American, 0.4% Native American, 1% international, 7% transferred in, 16% live on campus. *Retention:* 71% of 2001 full-time freshmen returned.

Freshmen *Admission:* 4,488 applied, 4,129 admitted, 2,503 enrolled. *Average high school GPA:* 2.97. *Test scores:* ACT scores over 18: 82%; ACT scores over 24: 27%; ACT scores over 30: 3%.

Faculty *Total:* 801, 58% full-time, 54% with terminal degrees. *Student/faculty ratio:* 20:1.

Majors Accounting; anthropology; art; art education; art history; bioengineering; biology; business administration; business economics; business education; business marketing and marketing management; chemistry; city/community/regional planning; classics; computer engineering; computer science; dance; data processing technology; drafting; drawing; early childhood education; economics; education; electrical engineering; elementary education; engineering physics; English; environmental health; film studies; finance; French; geography; geology; German; Greek (modern); health education; history; industrial technology; international relations; law enforcement/police science; legal administrative assistant; management information systems/business data processing; mass communications; materials engineering; mathematics; mechanical engineering; medical administrative assistant; medical technology; mental health/rehabilitation; modern languages; music; music history; music teacher education; nursing; philosophy; photography; physical education; physics; political science; psychology; reading education; religious studies; science education; secondary education; secretarial science; social work; sociology; Spanish; theater arts/drama; urban studies; water resources.

Academic Programs *Special study options:* academic remediation for entering students, adult/continuing education programs, advanced placement credit, cooperative education, English as a second language, honors programs, internships, off-campus study, part-time degree program, services for LD students, student-designed majors, study abroad, summer session for credit. *ROTC:* Army (b), Air Force (b).

Library Paul Laurence Dunbar Library plus 2 others with 695,805 titles, 5,312 serial subscriptions, an OPAC, a Web page.

Computers on Campus 450 computers available on campus for general student use. A campuswide network can be accessed from student residence rooms and from off campus. At least one staffed computer lab available.

Student Life *Housing Options:* coed. *Activities and Organizations:* drama/theater group, student-run newspaper, radio station, choral group, national fraternities, national sororities. *Campus security:* 24-hour emergency response devices and patrols, student patrols, late-night transport/escort service, controlled dormitory access. *Student Services:* health clinic, personal/psychological counseling, women's center, legal services.

Athletics Member NCAA. All Division I. *Intercollegiate sports:* baseball M(s), basketball M(s)/W(s), cross-country running M(s)/W(s), golf M(s), soccer M(s)/W(s), softball W(s), swimming M(s)/W(s), tennis M(s)/W(s), track and field W(s), volleyball W(s). *Intramural sports:* baseball M, basketball M/W, cross-country running M/W, football M/W, golf M/W, racquetball M(c)/W(c), rugby M(c)/W(c), soccer M/W, softball M/W, squash M/W, table tennis M(c)/W(c), tennis M/W, volleyball M(c)/W.

Standardized Tests *Required:* SAT I or ACT (for admission).

Costs (2001–02) *Tuition:* state resident $4596 full-time, $142 per hour part-time; nonresident $9192 full-time, $284 per hour part-time. *Room and board:* $5400. Room and board charges vary according to board plan and housing facility. *Payment plans:* tuition prepayment, installment. *Waivers:* senior citizens and employees or children of employees.

Applying *Options:* electronic application, early admission, deferred entrance. *Application fee:* $30. *Required:* high school transcript. *Recommended:* minimum 2.0 GPA. *Application deadline:* rolling (freshmen), rolling (transfers). *Notification:* continuous (freshmen).

Admissions Contact Ms. Cathy Davis, Director of Undergraduate Admissions, Wright State University, 3640 Colonel Glenn Highway, Dayton, OH 45435. *Phone:* 937-775-5700. *Toll-free phone:* 800-247-1770. *Fax:* 937-775-5795. *E-mail:* admissions@wright.edu.

XAVIER UNIVERSITY
Cincinnati, Ohio

- **Independent Roman Catholic** comprehensive, founded 1831
- **Calendar** semesters
- **Degrees** certificates, associate, bachelor's, master's, doctoral, post-master's, and postbachelor's certificates
- **Suburban** 100-acre campus
- **Endowment** $92.8 million
- **Coed,** 4,006 undergraduate students, 84% full-time, 58% women, 42% men
- **Moderately difficult** entrance level, 83% of applicants were admitted

Founded in 1831, Xavier University is a Jesuit university that seeks to educate the whole person. The Jesuit tradition is evident in Xavier's love of ideas and rigorous intellectual inquiry, respect for life, passion for justice, sense of community, and working together for the common good. With sixty-eight majors and thirty-eight minors, numerous scholarships, and opportunities for leadership and service, Xavier is more than a degree—it's an education for life.

Undergraduates 3,356 full-time, 650 part-time. Students come from 45 states and territories, 43 other countries, 65% are from out of state, 9% African American, 2% Asian American or Pacific Islander, 1% Hispanic American, 0.1% Native American, 3% international, 2% transferred in, 42% live on campus. *Retention:* 88% of 2001 full-time freshmen returned.

Freshmen *Admission:* 3,534 applied, 2,950 admitted, 797 enrolled. *Average high school GPA:* 3.53. *Test scores:* SAT verbal scores over 500: 88%; SAT math scores over 500: 84%; ACT scores over 18: 99%; SAT verbal scores over 600: 46%; SAT math scores over 600: 43%; ACT scores over 24: 68%; SAT verbal scores over 700: 8%; SAT math scores over 700: 8%; ACT scores over 30: 14%.

Faculty *Total:* 547, 48% full-time, 49% with terminal degrees. *Student/faculty ratio:* 17:1.

Majors Accounting; advertising; art; athletic training/sports medicine; biological/physical sciences; biology; biology education; business; business administration; business economics; business marketing and marketing management; chemical engineering; chemistry; chemistry education; classics; computer science; corrections; criminal justice studies; early childhood education; economics; education; elementary education; English; entrepreneurship; environmental science; finance; fine/studio arts; French; German; history; human resources management; industrial radiologic technology; international relations; liberal arts and sciences/liberal studies; management information systems/business data processing; mathematics; medical technology; middle school education; music; music teacher education; nursing science; occupational therapy; philosophy; physics; physics education; political science; psychology; public relations; radio/television broadcasting; science education; social work; sociology; Spanish; special education; sport/fitness administration; teacher education related; theology.

Academic Programs *Special study options:* academic remediation for entering students, adult/continuing education programs, advanced placement credit, cooperative education, double majors, English as a second language, honors programs, independent study, internships, off-campus study, part-time degree program, services for LD students, study abroad, summer session for credit. *ROTC:* Army (b), Air Force (c). *Unusual degree programs:* 3-2 engineering with University of Cincinnati; forestry with Duke University; environmental management, accounting.

Library McDonald Library plus 1 other with 200,044 titles, 1,586 serial subscriptions, 4,292 audiovisual materials, an OPAC, a Web page.

Computers on Campus 200 computers available on campus for general student use. A campuswide network can be accessed from student residence rooms and from off campus. Internet access, at least one staffed computer lab available.

Student Life *Housing:* on-campus residence required through sophomore year. *Options:* coed. *Activities and Organizations:* drama/theater group, student-run newspaper, radio station, choral group, Student Government Association, Student Activities Council, Performing Arts Group, Xavier Action (service organization), Residence Hall Association. *Campus security:* 24-hour emergency response devices and patrols, late-night transport/escort service, campus-wide shuttle service. *Student Services:* health clinic, personal/psychological counseling.

Athletics Member NCAA. All Division I. *Intercollegiate sports:* baseball M(s), basketball M(s)/W(s), crew M(c)/W(c), cross-country running M(s)/W(s), fencing M(c)/W(c), golf M(s)/W(s), lacrosse M(c)/W(c), riflery M(s)/W(s), rugby M(c)/W(c), sailing M(c)/W(c), skiing (downhill) M(c)/W(c), soccer M(s)/W(s), swimming M(s)/W(s), tennis M(s)/W(s), volleyball M(c)/W(s), wrestling M(c). *Intramural sports:* basketball M/W, fencing M/W, racquetball M/W, soccer M/W, softball M/W, table tennis M/W, tennis M/W, volleyball M/W.

Standardized Tests *Required:* SAT I or ACT (for admission).

Costs (2001–02) *Comprehensive fee:* $24,010 includes full-time tuition ($16,540), mandatory fees ($240), and room and board ($7230). Full-time tuition and fees vary according to program. Part-time tuition: $375 per credit hour. Part-time tuition and fees vary according to course load. *Room and board:* College room only: $3990. Room and board charges vary according to board plan and housing facility. *Payment plans:* installment, deferred payment. *Waivers:* senior citizens and employees or children of employees.

Financial Aid Of all full-time matriculated undergraduates who enrolled in 2001, 1929 applied for aid, 1509 were judged to have need, 453 had their need fully met. 308 Federal Work-Study jobs (averaging $2070). 161 State and other part-time jobs (averaging $1780). In 2001, 1251 non-need-based awards were made. *Average percent of need met:* 80%. *Average financial aid package:* $12,325. *Average need-based loan:* $4065. *Average need-based gift aid:* $8567. *Average indebtedness upon graduation:* $9828.

Applying *Options:* common application, electronic application, early admission, deferred entrance. *Application fee:* $30. *Required:* essay or personal statement, high school transcript, 1 letter of recommendation. *Recommended:* interview. *Application deadline:* 2/1 (freshmen), rolling (transfers).

Admissions Contact Mr. Marc Camille, Dean of Admission, Xavier University, 3800 Victory Parkway, Cincinnati, OH 45207-5311. *Phone:* 513-745-3301. *Toll-free phone:* 800-344-4698. *Fax:* 513-745-4319. *E-mail:* xuadmit@xu.edu.

YOUNGSTOWN STATE UNIVERSITY
Youngstown, Ohio

- **State-supported** comprehensive, founded 1908
- **Calendar** semesters
- **Degrees** certificates, diplomas, associate, bachelor's, master's, doctoral, and postbachelor's certificates
- **Urban** 150-acre campus with easy access to Cleveland and Pittsburgh
- **Endowment** $4.1 million
- **Coed,** 11,036 undergraduate students, 78% full-time, 53% women, 47% men
- **Noncompetitive** entrance level, 88% of applicants were admitted

Located on a beautiful campus in northeast Ohio, YSU offers more than 100 major programs at 2-year, 4-year, and graduate levels. A 19:1 student-faculty ratio, flexible curriculum planning, simplified transfer options, and an expanding honors program characterize YSU's academics. A comprehensive scholarship and financial aid program is available. Prospective students are invited to tour the campus and meet with professors in their major.

Undergraduates 8,652 full-time, 2,384 part-time. Students come from 42 states and territories, 50 other countries, 9% are from out of state, 9% African American, 0.7% Asian American or Pacific Islander, 2% Hispanic American, 0.3% Native American, 0.9% international, 5% transferred in, 9% live on campus. *Retention:* 71% of 2001 full-time freshmen returned.

Freshmen *Admission:* 3,989 applied, 3,506 admitted, 2,133 enrolled. *Test scores:* ACT scores over 18: 73%; ACT scores over 24: 25%; ACT scores over 30: 3%.

Faculty *Total:* 831, 47% full-time, 50% with terminal degrees. *Student/faculty ratio:* 19:1.

Majors Accounting; accounting technician; acting/directing; advertising; African-American studies; African studies; American studies; anthropology; apparel marketing; art; art education; art history; astronomy; athletic training/sports medicine; banking; biological/physical sciences; biology; biology education; business; business administration; business economics; business education; business marketing and marketing management; buying operations; chemical engineering; chemistry; chemistry education; child care/development; child care/guidance; civil engineering; civil engineering technology; clothing/apparel/textile studies; communications; community health liaison; computer education; computer/information sciences; computer programming; computer science; corrections; criminal justice/law enforcement administration; criminal justice studies; data processing; data processing technology; dental hygiene; dietetics; dietician assistant; distribution operations; drafting; drafting/design technology; drama/dance education; early childhood education; earth sciences; economics; education; education (multiple levels); education of the specific learning disabled; electrical/electronic engineering technology; electrical engineering; elementary education; emergency medical technology; engineering; engineering-related technology; engineering technology; English; English education; environmental engineering; environmental science; executive assistant; exercise sciences; family/community studies; fashion merchandising; finance; fine/studio arts; foreign languages education; foreign languages/literatures; French; French language education; general

Youngstown State University (continued)
office/clerical; geography; geology; German language education; graphic design/commercial art/illustration; health education; health/physical education; health science; history; history education; home economics; home economics education; hospitality management; hotel and restaurant management; individual/family development; industrial/manufacturing engineering; information sciences/systems; international economics; Italian; journalism; labor/personnel relations; law enforcement/police science; legal administrative assistant; management information systems/business data processing; marketing operations; mathematics; mathematics education; mechanical engineering; mechanical engineering technology; medical administrative assistant; medical assistant; medical laboratory assistant; medical laboratory technician; medical office management; medical technology; middle school education; music; music (general performance); music history; music (piano and organ performance); music teacher education; music theory and composition; music (voice and choral/opera performance); nursing; nutrition studies; office management; operations management; painting; philosophy; photography; physical education; physics; physics education; political science; predentistry; pre-law; pre-medicine; pre-pharmacy studies; pre-veterinary studies; printmaking; psychology; public administration; public relations; quantitative economics; radio/television broadcasting; religious studies; respiratory therapy; retailing operations; retail management; sales operations; science education; secondary education; secretarial science; security; social science education; social sciences; social studies education; social work; sociology; Spanish; Spanish language education; special education; speech education; speech/rhetorical studies; sport/fitness administration; stringed instruments; technical/business writing; telecommunications; theater arts/drama; theater design; travel/tourism management.

Academic Programs *Special study options:* academic remediation for entering students, accelerated degree program, adult/continuing education programs, advanced placement credit, cooperative education, distance learning, double majors, English as a second language, honors programs, internships, off-campus study, part-time degree program, services for LD students, student-designed majors, study abroad, summer session for credit. *ROTC:* Army (b), Air Force (c). *Unusual degree programs:* 3-2 chemistry, physical therapy.

Library Maag Library with 993,314 titles, 6,518 serial subscriptions, 16,573 audiovisual materials, an OPAC, a Web page.

Computers on Campus 1250 computers available on campus for general student use. A campuswide network can be accessed from student residence rooms and from off campus that provide access to online registration. Internet access, at least one staffed computer lab available.

Student Life *Housing Options:* coed, women-only. *Activities and Organizations:* drama/theater group, student-run newspaper, choral group, marching band, student government, Panhellenic Council, Interfraternity Council, Omicron Delta Kappa, golden key, national fraternities, national sororities. *Campus security:* 24-hour emergency response devices and patrols, student patrols, late-night transport/escort service, controlled dormitory access, residence hall patrols. *Student Services:* health clinic, personal/psychological counseling, women's center.

Athletics Member NCAA. All Division I except football (Division I-AA). *Intercollegiate sports:* baseball M(s), basketball M(s)/W(s), cross-country running M(s)/W(s), golf M(s)/W, soccer W, softball W(s), swimming W, tennis M(s)/W(s), track and field M(s)/W(s), volleyball W(s). *Intramural sports:* badminton M/W, basketball M/W, bowling M/W, golf M/W, racquetball M/W, soccer M/W, softball M/W, swimming M/W, table tennis M/W, tennis M/W, volleyball M/W, water polo M/W.

Standardized Tests *Required:* SAT I or ACT (for admission).

Costs (2001–02) *Tuition:* state resident $3576 full-time, $149 per credit part-time; nonresident $7944 full-time, $331 per credit part-time. Part-time tuition and fees vary according to course load. *Required fees:* $1012 full-time, $35 per credit. *Room and board:* $4970. Room and board charges vary according to board plan and housing facility. *Payment plan:* installment. *Waivers:* senior citizens and employees or children of employees.

Financial Aid Of all full-time matriculated undergraduates who enrolled in 2001, 319 Federal Work-Study jobs (averaging $1667). 630 State and other part-time jobs (averaging $4387).

Applying *Options:* common application, early admission, early action, deferred entrance. *Application fee:* $30. *Required:* high school transcript. *Required for some:* interview. *Application deadlines:* 8/15 (freshmen), 8/15 (transfers). *Notification:* continuous (freshmen), 2/15 (early action).

Admissions Contact Ms. Sue Davis, Interim Director of Undergraduate Admissions, Youngstown State University, One University Plaza, Youngstown, OH 44555-0001. *Phone:* 330-742-2000. *Toll-free phone:* 877-468-6978. *Fax:* 330-742-3674. *E-mail:* enroll@ysu.edu.

OKLAHOMA

American Christian College and Seminary
Oklahoma City, Oklahoma

- **Independent interdenominational** comprehensive, founded 1976
- **Calendar** semesters
- **Degrees** associate, bachelor's, master's, doctoral, and first professional
- **Small-town** 1-acre campus with easy access to Oklahoma City
- **Endowment** $742.4 million
- **Coed,** 292 undergraduate students, 38% full-time, 45% women, 55% men
- **Noncompetitive** entrance level

Undergraduates 111 full-time, 181 part-time. 36% African American, 10% Asian American or Pacific Islander, 22% Hispanic American.

Freshmen *Admission:* 109 admitted, 292 enrolled.

Faculty *Total:* 35, 31% full-time, 60% with terminal degrees. *Student/faculty ratio:* 8:1.

Majors Biblical languages/literatures; business administration; English; pastoral counseling.

Academic Programs *Special study options:* adult/continuing education programs, advanced placement credit, cooperative education, distance learning, independent study, internships, part-time degree program, summer session for credit.

Library Corvin Library with 14,652 titles, 47 serial subscriptions, 554 audiovisual materials.

Computers on Campus 1 computer available on campus for general student use. .

Student Life *Housing:* college housing not available. *Student Services:* personal/psychological counseling.

Costs (2001–02) *Tuition:* $3360 full-time, $420 per course part-time. *Required fees:* $156 full-time, $140 per credit. *Payment plan:* installment. *Waivers:* employees or children of employees.

Applying *Options:* common application, electronic application. *Application fee:* $50. *Required:* high school transcript.

Admissions Contact American Christian College and Seminary, 4300 Highline Boulevard #202, Oklahoma City, OK 73108. *Phone:* 405-945-0100 Ext. 120. *Toll-free phone:* 800-488-2528. *Fax:* 405-945-0311. *E-mail:* info@accs.edu.

Cameron University
Lawton, Oklahoma

- **State-supported** comprehensive, founded 1908, part of Oklahoma State Regents for Higher Education
- **Calendar** semesters
- **Degrees** associate, bachelor's, and master's
- **Suburban** 160-acre campus
- **Endowment** $4.6 million
- **Coed,** 4,772 undergraduate students, 59% full-time, 57% women, 43% men
- **Minimally difficult** entrance level, 89% of applicants were admitted

Undergraduates 2,807 full-time, 1,965 part-time. Students come from 22 states and territories, 21 other countries, 2% are from out of state, 22% African American, 3% Asian American or Pacific Islander, 7% Hispanic American, 5% Native American, 1% international, 6% transferred in, 1% live on campus. *Retention:* 37% of 2001 full-time freshmen returned.

Freshmen *Admission:* 1,459 applied, 1,295 admitted, 911 enrolled. *Average high school GPA:* 3.09. *Test scores:* ACT scores over 18: 68%; ACT scores over 24: 13%; ACT scores over 30: 1%.

Faculty *Total:* 289, 64% full-time, 21% with terminal degrees. *Student/faculty ratio:* 20:1.

Majors Accounting; agricultural business; agricultural mechanization; agricultural sciences; agronomy/crop science; animal sciences; art; art education; biological/physical sciences; biology; business; business administration; business economics; business marketing and marketing management; business systems analysis/design; chemistry; child care/development; computer/information sciences; computer science; criminal justice/law enforcement administration; data processing technology; drafting; education; electrical/electronic engineering technology; elementary education; engineering design; English; environmental science; finance; health/physical education; history; horticulture science; human ecology; individual/family development; information sciences/systems; interdisciplinary studies; journalism; mass communications; mathematics; medical technology; music; music (general performance); music (piano and organ performance); music teacher education; music theory and composition; music (voice and choral/opera performance); natural sciences; physical education; physics; political science; psychology; public relations; radio/television broadcasting; romance languages; sociology; speech/rhetorical studies; telecommunications; theater arts/drama.

Academic Programs *Special study options:* academic remediation for entering students, accelerated degree program, adult/continuing education programs, advanced placement credit, distance learning, double majors, honors programs, independent study, off-campus study, part-time degree program, services for LD students, summer session for credit. *ROTC:* Army (b).

Library Cameron University Library with 258,000 titles, 3,840 serial subscriptions, 7,053 audiovisual materials.

Computers on Campus 350 computers available on campus for general student use. At least one staffed computer lab available.

Student Life *Housing Options:* men-only, women-only. *Activities and Organizations:* drama/theater group, student-run newspaper, radio and television station, choral group, Student Government Association, Aggie Club, Intramural Club, Baptist Student Union, Sociology Club, national fraternities, national sororities. *Campus security:* 24-hour emergency response devices and patrols, student patrols, late-night transport/escort service. *Student Services:* personal/psychological counseling.

Athletics Member NCAA. All Division II. *Intercollegiate sports:* baseball M(s), basketball M(s)/W(s), golf M(s), softball W(s), tennis M(s)/W(s), volleyball W(s). *Intramural sports:* badminton M/W, basketball M/W, bowling M/W, racquetball M/W, table tennis M/W, volleyball M/W, water polo M/W.

Standardized Tests *Required:* SAT I or ACT (for admission).

Costs (2002–03) *Tuition:* state resident $2180 full-time, $1090 per term part-time; nonresident $5220 full-time, $2610 per term part-time. Full-time tuition and fees vary according to class time, course load, degree level, and student level. Part-time tuition and fees vary according to class time, course load, degree level, and student level. *Required fees:* $120 full-time, $60 per term part-time. *Room and board:* $2830. Room and board charges vary according to board plan. *Payment plan:* installment. *Waivers:* senior citizens and employees or children of employees.

Financial Aid Available in 2001, 180 State and other part-time jobs (averaging $1843). *Average indebtedness upon graduation:* $6300.

Applying *Options:* common application, electronic application, early admission, deferred entrance. *Application fee:* $15. *Required:* high school transcript. *Application deadline:* rolling (freshmen), rolling (transfers). *Notification:* continuous until 8/10 (freshmen).

Admissions Contact Ms. Brenda Dally, Coordinator of Student Recruitment, Cameron University, Cameron University, Attention: Admissions, 2800 West Gore Boulevard, Lawton, OK 73505. *Phone:* 580-581-2837. *Toll-free phone:* 888-454-7600. *Fax:* 580-581-5514. *E-mail:* admiss@cua.cameron.edu.

EAST CENTRAL UNIVERSITY
Ada, Oklahoma

- **State-supported** comprehensive, founded 1909, part of Oklahoma State Regents for Higher Education
- **Calendar** semesters
- **Degrees** bachelor's and master's
- **Small-town** 140-acre campus with easy access to Oklahoma City
- **Endowment** $847,022
- **Coed,** 3,423 undergraduate students, 85% full-time, 59% women, 41% men
- **Moderately difficult** entrance level

Undergraduates 2,893 full-time, 530 part-time. Students come from 20 states and territories, 25 other countries, 3% are from out of state, 4% African American, 1% Asian American or Pacific Islander, 2% Hispanic American, 15% Native American, 3% international, 11% transferred in, 17% live on campus. *Retention:* 62% of 2001 full-time freshmen returned.

Freshmen *Admission:* 591 admitted, 1,197 enrolled. *Average high school GPA:* 3.41. *Test scores:* ACT scores over 18: 50%; ACT scores over 24: 13%; ACT scores over 30: 2%.

Faculty *Total:* 265, 72% full-time. *Student/faculty ratio:* 19:1.

Majors Accounting; art; art education; biology; business administration; business economics; business education; business marketing and marketing management; cartography; chemistry; computer science; counselor education/guidance; criminal justice/law enforcement administration; drafting; early childhood education; ecology; education; electrical/electronic engineering technology; elementary education; English; environmental health; environmental science; fashion merchandising; finance; history; home economics; human resources management; law enforcement/police science; legal studies; literature; mass communications; mathematics; medical laboratory technician; medical records administration; music; music teacher education; nursing; physical education; physics; political science; pre-dentistry; pre-law; pre-medicine; pre-veterinary studies; psychology; radio/television broadcasting; secondary education; secretarial science; social work; sociology; special education; speech/rhetorical studies; water resources.

Academic Programs *Special study options:* academic remediation for entering students, accelerated degree program, adult/continuing education programs, advanced placement credit, distance learning, double majors, honors programs, internships, off-campus study, part-time degree program, services for LD students, summer session for credit.

Library Linscheid Library with 213,000 titles, 800 serial subscriptions, an OPAC, a Web page.

Computers on Campus 40 computers available on campus for general student use. At least one staffed computer lab available.

Student Life *Housing Options:* coed. *Activities and Organizations:* drama/theater group, student-run newspaper, choral group, marching band, Panhellenic Council, Interfraternity Council, BACCHUS, Fellowship of Christian Athletes, national fraternities, national sororities. *Campus security:* 24-hour patrols, controlled dormitory access. *Student Services:* health clinic, personal/psychological counseling.

Athletics Member NCAA, NAIA. All NCAA Division II. *Intercollegiate sports:* baseball M(s), basketball M(s)/W(s), cross-country running M(s)/W(s), football M(s), golf M(s), soccer W(s), softball W(s), tennis M(s)/W(s). *Intramural sports:* basketball M/W, football M/W, racquetball M/W, soccer M/W, softball M/W, tennis M/W, volleyball M/W.

Standardized Tests *Required:* SAT I or ACT (for admission). *Recommended:* ACT (for admission).

Costs (2001–02) *One-time required fee:* $22. *Tuition:* state resident $2129 full-time, $71 per semester hour part-time; nonresident $5169 full-time, $172 per semester hour part-time. Full-time tuition and fees vary according to class time, course load, and student level. Part-time tuition and fees vary according to class time, course load, and student level. *Required fees:* $43 full-time, $18 per term part-time. *Room and board:* $2452; room only: $800. Room and board charges vary according to board plan and housing facility. *Waivers:* senior citizens and employees or children of employees.

Financial Aid Of all full-time matriculated undergraduates who enrolled in 2001, 1774 applied for aid, 1556 were judged to have need, 652 had their need fully met. 180 Federal Work-Study jobs (averaging $1758). 322 State and other part-time jobs (averaging $2234). In 2001, 194 non-need-based awards were made. *Average percent of need met:* 63%. *Average financial aid package:* $6760. *Average need-based loan:* $3136. *Average need-based gift aid:* $3488. *Average non-need based aid:* $2323. *Average indebtedness upon graduation:* $10,904.

Applying *Options:* early admission. *Required:* high school transcript. *Required for some:* minimum 2.7 GPA, rank in upper 50% of high school class. *Application deadlines:* 9/1 (freshmen), 9/1 (transfers).

Admissions Contact Ms. Pamela Armstrong, Registrar, East Central University, PMBJ8, 1100 East 14th Street, Ada, OK 74820-6999. *Phone:* 580-332-8000 Ext. 239. *Fax:* 580-310-5432. *E-mail:* parmstro@mailclerk.ecok.edu.

HILLSDALE FREE WILL BAPTIST COLLEGE
Moore, Oklahoma

- **Independent Free Will Baptist** 4-year, founded 1959
- **Calendar** semesters
- **Degrees** certificates, associate, and bachelor's
- **Suburban** 40-acre campus with easy access to Oklahoma City
- **Endowment** $277,141
- **Coed,** 287 undergraduate students, 85% full-time, 41% women, 59% men
- **Noncompetitive** entrance level

Undergraduates 244 full-time, 43 part-time. Students come from 15 states and territories, 13 other countries, 19% are from out of state, 7% African American, 0.4% Asian American or Pacific Islander, 3% Hispanic American, 8% Native American, 11% international, 12% transferred in, 45% live on campus. *Retention:* 58% of 2001 full-time freshmen returned.

Freshmen *Admission:* 75 admitted, 79 enrolled. *Average high school GPA:* 3.03. *Test scores:* ACT scores over 18: 55%; ACT scores over 24: 9%.

Faculty *Total:* 42, 43% full-time, 43% with terminal degrees. *Student/faculty ratio:* 15:1.

Majors Biblical studies; business; elementary education; English; general studies; interdisciplinary studies; liberal arts and sciences/liberal studies; mathematics; missionary studies; music; nursing; physical education; psychology; religious education; religious music; theology.

Hillsdale Free Will Baptist College (continued)

Academic Programs *Special study options:* academic remediation for entering students, accelerated degree program, adult/continuing education programs, advanced placement credit, double majors, English as a second language, independent study, internships, part-time degree program, summer session for credit.

Library Geri Ann Hull Learning Resource Center with 20,102 titles, 363 serial subscriptions, 1,800 audiovisual materials, an OPAC.

Computers on Campus 22 computers available on campus for general student use. Internet access, at least one staffed computer lab available.

Student Life *Housing:* on-campus residence required through sophomore year. *Options:* men-only, women-only. *Activities and Organizations:* drama/theater group, choral group, Student Mission Fellowship, Ironmen Fellowship, society organizations, Fellowship of Christian Athletes. *Campus security:* 24-hour emergency response devices, controlled dormitory access. *Student Services:* personal/psychological counseling.

Athletics Member NCCAA. *Intercollegiate sports:* baseball M, basketball M/W, golf M, softball W, volleyball W. *Intramural sports:* baseball M/W, football M, table tennis M/W.

Standardized Tests *Required:* SAT I or ACT (for placement).

Costs (2002–03) *One-time required fee:* $20. *Comprehensive fee:* $11,130 includes full-time tuition ($6150), mandatory fees ($740), and room and board ($4240). Full-time tuition and fees vary according to course load. Part-time tuition: $205 per credit hour. Part-time tuition and fees vary according to course load. *Required fees:* $130 per term part-time. *Room and board:* College room only: $1950. Room and board charges vary according to board plan and housing facility. *Payment plan:* deferred payment. *Waivers:* children of alumni, adult students, senior citizens, and employees or children of employees.

Applying *Options:* common application, early admission, deferred entrance. *Application fee:* $20. *Required:* essay or personal statement, high school transcript, 1 letter of recommendation, Biblical foundation statement, student conduct pledge; medical form required for some. *Required for some:* 1 letter of recommendation, interview. *Recommended:* minimum 2.0 GPA, 2 letters of recommendation. *Application deadline:* rolling (freshmen), rolling (transfers).

Admissions Contact Ms. Sue Chaffin, Registrar/Assistant Director of Admissions, Hillsdale Free Will Baptist College, PO Box 7208, Moore, OK 73153-1208. *Phone:* 405-912-9005. *Fax:* 405-912-9050. *E-mail:* hillsdale@hc.edu.

LANGSTON UNIVERSITY
Langston, Oklahoma

- **State-supported** comprehensive, founded 1897, part of Oklahoma State Regents for Higher Education
- **Calendar** semesters
- **Degrees** associate, bachelor's, and master's
- **Rural** 40-acre campus with easy access to Oklahoma City
- **Coed**
- **Minimally difficult** entrance level

Athletics Member NAIA.

Standardized Tests *Required:* SAT I or ACT (for placement).

Financial Aid Of all full-time matriculated undergraduates who enrolled in 2001, 2499 applied for aid, 1885 were judged to have need, 1335 had their need fully met. In 2001, 1045. *Average percent of need met:* 77. *Average financial aid package:* $6391. *Average need-based loan:* $3845. *Average need-based gift aid:* $2791. *Average non-need based aid:* $1431.

Applying *Options:* electronic application, early admission, deferred entrance. *Required:* high school transcript. *Required for some:* letters of recommendation.

Admissions Contact Ms. Vickie Alexander, Langston University, Langston, OK 73050. *Phone:* 405-466-3231. *Fax:* 405-466-3381.

METROPOLITAN COLLEGE
Oklahoma City, Oklahoma

- **Proprietary** 4-year
- **Calendar** trimesters
- **Degree** certificates and bachelor's
- **Coed, primarily women**
- **Minimally difficult** entrance level

Costs (2001–02) *Tuition:* $6593 full-time, $4275 per year part-time. $50.00 one-time program registration fee.

Admissions Contact Mr. Keith Wells, Admissions Director, Metropolitan College, 2901 North Classen Boulevard, Suite 200, Oklahoma City, OK 73106. *Phone:* 405-528-5000.

METROPOLITAN COLLEGE
Tulsa, Oklahoma

- **Proprietary** 4-year
- **Calendar** trimesters
- **Degrees** diplomas, associate, and bachelor's
- **Urban** campus
- **Coed, primarily women,** 112 undergraduate students, 100% full-time, 96% women, 4% men
- **Minimally difficult** entrance level, 78% of applicants were admitted

Undergraduates 112 full-time. Students come from 3 states and territories, 1% are from out of state, 21% African American, 0.9% Hispanic American, 12% Native American, 8% transferred in. *Retention:* 70% of 2001 full-time freshmen returned.

Freshmen *Admission:* 45 applied, 35 admitted, 35 enrolled. *Average high school GPA:* 3.00.

Faculty *Total:* 22, 18% full-time, 100% with terminal degrees. *Student/faculty ratio:* 15:1.

Majors Court reporting; paralegal/legal assistant.

Academic Programs *Special study options:* academic remediation for entering students, accelerated degree program, adult/continuing education programs, internships, part-time degree program.

Library Learning Resource Center.

Computers on Campus 25 computers available on campus for general student use. Internet access, at least one staffed computer lab available.

Student Life *Housing:* college housing not available. *Activities and Organizations:* student-run newspaper.

Costs (2002–03) *Tuition:* $6535 full-time, $200 per credit hour part-time. Full-time tuition and fees vary according to course load and program. *Payment plan:* installment.

Applying *Application fee:* $50. *Required:* high school transcript, interview.

Admissions Contact Ms. Lee Griffith, Admission Representative, Metropolitan College, 4528 South Sheridan Road, Suite 105, Tulsa, OK 74145-1011. *Phone:* 918-627-9300.

MID-AMERICA BIBLE COLLEGE
Oklahoma City, Oklahoma

- **Independent** 4-year, founded 1953, affiliated with Church of God
- **Calendar** semesters
- **Degrees** associate and bachelor's
- **Suburban** 145-acre campus
- **Endowment** $421,051
- **Coed**
- **Noncompetitive** entrance level

Faculty *Student/faculty ratio:* 19:1.

Student Life *Campus security:* 24-hour patrols, student patrols.

Athletics Member NCCAA.

Standardized Tests *Required:* SAT I or ACT (for placement).

Financial Aid Of all full-time matriculated undergraduates who enrolled in 2001, 566 applied for aid, 522 were judged to have need. In 2001, 20. *Average percent of need met:* 75. *Average financial aid package:* $6729. *Average need-based loan:* $3497. *Average need-based gift aid:* $2717. *Average non-need based aid:* $3462.

Applying *Options:* common application, early admission. *Application fee:* $20. *Required:* high school transcript. *Required for some:* 2 letters of recommendation, interview.

Admissions Contact Ms. Dianna Rea, Director of College Relations, Mid-America Bible College, 3500 Southwest 119th Street, Oklahoma City, OK 73170. *Phone:* 405-692-3180. *Fax:* 405-692-3165. *E-mail:* mbcinfo@mabc.edu.

NORTHEASTERN STATE UNIVERSITY
Tahlequah, Oklahoma

- **State-supported** comprehensive, founded 1846, part of Oklahoma State Regents for Higher Education
- **Calendar** semesters
- **Degrees** bachelor's, master's, and first professional
- **Small-town** 160-acre campus with easy access to Tulsa
- **Endowment** $522,002
- **Coed,** 7,611 undergraduate students, 76% full-time, 59% women, 41% men

■ **Moderately difficult** entrance level, 97% of applicants were admitted

Undergraduates 5,782 full-time, 1,829 part-time. Students come from 30 states and territories, 37 other countries, 0% are from out of state, 5% African American, 0.5% Asian American or Pacific Islander, 1.0% Hispanic American, 28% Native American, 1% international, 17% transferred in. *Retention:* 60% of 2001 full-time freshmen returned.

Freshmen *Admission:* 1,751 applied, 1,693 admitted, 1,067 enrolled. *Average high school GPA:* 2.74.

Faculty *Total:* 446. *Student/faculty ratio:* 17:1.

Majors Accounting; art; art education; biology; business administration; business education; business marketing and marketing management; cell biology; chemistry; computer science; criminal justice/law enforcement administration; early childhood education; education; electrical/electronic engineering technology; elementary education; engineering physics; English; fashion merchandising; finance; fine/studio arts; French; geography; German; graphic design/commercial art/illustration; health education; health services administration; history; home economics; home economics education; human resources management; industrial arts; industrial technology; journalism; law enforcement/police science; library science; mathematics; medical technology; microbiology/bacteriology; music; music (piano and organ performance); music teacher education; music (voice and choral/opera performance); Native American studies; nursing; nutrition science; ophthalmic/optometric services; physical education; physics; political science; pre-dentistry; pre-law; pre-medicine; pre-veterinary studies; psychology; reading education; religious music; secondary education; social work; sociology; Spanish; special education; speech-language pathology/audiology; speech therapy; theater arts/drama; trade/industrial education; travel/tourism management; wildlife biology; zoology.

Academic Programs *Special study options:* academic remediation for entering students, adult/continuing education programs, advanced placement credit, distance learning, double majors, honors programs, internships, part-time degree program, services for LD students, summer session for credit.

Library John Vaughn Library with 379,173 titles, 3,442 serial subscriptions, an OPAC, a Web page.

Computers on Campus 300 computers available on campus for general student use. A campuswide network can be accessed from student residence rooms and from off campus. Internet access, at least one staffed computer lab available.

Student Life *Housing:* on-campus residence required through sophomore year. *Options:* coed. *Activities and Organizations:* drama/theater group, student-run newspaper, television station, choral group, marching band, national fraternities, national sororities. *Campus security:* 24-hour emergency response devices and patrols, late-night transport/escort service, controlled dormitory access. *Student Services:* health clinic, personal/psychological counseling.

Athletics Member NCAA, NAIA. All NCAA Division II. *Intercollegiate sports:* baseball M(s), basketball M(s)/W(s), football M(s), golf M(s)/W(s), soccer M(s)/W(s), softball W(s), tennis M(s)/W(s). *Intramural sports:* basketball M/W, bowling M/W, football M, golf M/W, racquetball M/W, soccer M/W, softball M/W, swimming M/W, tennis M/W, track and field M, volleyball M/W, water polo M/W, weight lifting M, wrestling M.

Standardized Tests *Required:* ACT (for admission).

Costs (2001–02) *Tuition:* state resident $1980 full-time, $52 per credit hour part-time; nonresident $4500 full-time, $144 per credit hour part-time. Full-time tuition and fees vary according to class time, course load, location, and student level. Part-time tuition and fees vary according to class time, course load, and student level. *Required fees:* $150 full-time, $17 per credit hour. *Room and board:* $2724. Room and board charges vary according to board plan and housing facility. *Waivers:* senior citizens and employees or children of employees.

Financial Aid Of all full-time matriculated undergraduates who enrolled in 2001, 4915 applied for aid, 4618 were judged to have need, 3516 had their need fully met. In 2001, 780 non-need-based awards were made. *Average percent of need met:* 65%. *Average financial aid package:* $6500. *Average need-based loan:* $4500. *Average need-based gift aid:* $3250.

Applying *Options:* early admission. *Required:* high school transcript. *Required for some:* letters of recommendation, interview. *Application deadlines:* 8/5 (freshmen), 8/5 (transfers). *Notification:* continuous (freshmen).

Admissions Contact William E. Nowlin, Registrar, Department of Admissions and Records, Northeastern State University, 601 North Grand, Tahlequah, OK 74464. *Phone:* 918-456-5511 Ext. 2200. *Toll-free phone:* 800-722-9614. *Fax:* 918-458-2342. *E-mail:* nsuadmis@nsuok.edu.

NORTHWESTERN OKLAHOMA STATE UNIVERSITY

Alva, Oklahoma

- **State-supported** comprehensive, founded 1897, part of Oklahoma State Regents for Higher Education
- **Calendar** semesters
- **Degrees** bachelor's, master's, post-master's, and postbachelor's certificates
- **Small-town** 70-acre campus
- **Endowment** $11.0 million
- **Coed,** 1,781 undergraduate students, 75% full-time, 54% women, 46% men
- **Moderately difficult** entrance level, 100% of applicants were admitted

Undergraduates 1,328 full-time, 453 part-time. Students come from 25 states and territories, 15% are from out of state, 4% African American, 0.3% Asian American or Pacific Islander, 2% Hispanic American, 4% Native American, 1.0% international, 14% transferred in, 26% live on campus. *Retention:* 64% of 2001 full-time freshmen returned.

Freshmen *Admission:* 513 applied, 511 admitted, 331 enrolled. *Average high school GPA:* 3.24. *Test scores:* ACT scores over 18: 77%; ACT scores over 24: 22%; ACT scores over 30: 2%.

Faculty *Total:* 149, 60% full-time, 37% with terminal degrees. *Student/faculty ratio:* 14:1.

Majors Accounting; agricultural business; agricultural sciences; biology; business administration; business education; business systems networking/ telecommunications; chemistry; computer science; early childhood education; education (K-12); elementary education; English; health education; history; information sciences/systems; law enforcement/police science; mass communications; mathematics; medical laboratory technician; music; music teacher education; nursing; physical education; political science; pre-dentistry; pre-law; pre-medicine; protective services related; psychology; public relations; science education; secondary education; social sciences; social work; sociology; Spanish; special education; speech/rhetorical studies; speech/theater education.

Academic Programs *Special study options:* academic remediation for entering students, adult/continuing education programs, advanced placement credit, off-campus study, part-time degree program, services for LD students, summer session for credit.

Library J. W. Martin Library plus 1 other with 225,000 titles, 1,411 serial subscriptions, an OPAC, a Web page.

Computers on Campus 100 computers available on campus for general student use. Internet access, at least one staffed computer lab available.

Student Life *Activities and Organizations:* drama/theater group, student-run newspaper, radio and television station, choral group, marching band, Student Government Association, Aggie Club, Phi Beta Lambda, Baptist Student Union. *Campus security:* 24-hour emergency response devices and patrols. *Student Services:* health clinic, personal/psychological counseling.

Athletics Member NAIA. *Intercollegiate sports:* baseball M(s), basketball M(s)/W(s), football M(s), soccer W(s), softball M(s)/W(s). *Intramural sports:* basketball M/W, football M, softball M/W, volleyball M/W.

Standardized Tests *Required:* SAT I or ACT (for admission).

Costs (2001–02) *Tuition:* state resident $1976 full-time, $66 per credit hour part-time; nonresident $4869 full-time, $157 per credit hour part-time. Full-time tuition and fees vary according to course load, location, and student level. Part-time tuition and fees vary according to course load, location, and student level. *Required fees:* $56 full-time, $16 per term part-time. *Room and board:* $2550; room only: $860. Room and board charges vary according to board plan. *Waivers:* senior citizens and employees or children of employees.

Financial Aid Of all full-time matriculated undergraduates who enrolled in 2001, 1090 applied for aid, 680 were judged to have need, 279 had their need fully met. 141 Federal Work-Study jobs (averaging $1100). 153 State and other part-time jobs (averaging $970). *Average percent of need met:* 86%. *Average financial aid package:* $4800. *Average need-based loan:* $4100. *Average need-based gift aid:* $3700. *Average indebtedness upon graduation:* $10,200.

Applying *Options:* early admission. *Application fee:* $15. *Required:* high school transcript. *Required for some:* essay or personal statement, minimum 2.0 GPA, 3 letters of recommendation. *Application deadline:* rolling (freshmen), rolling (transfers). *Notification:* continuous (freshmen).

Northwestern Oklahoma State University (continued)
Admissions Contact Mrs. Shirley Murrow, Registrar, Northwestern Oklahoma State University, 709 Oklahoma Boulevard, Alva, OK 73717-2799. *Phone:* 580-327-8550. *Fax:* 580-327-8699. *E-mail:* smmurrow@nwosu.edu.

OKLAHOMA BAPTIST UNIVERSITY
Shawnee, Oklahoma

- **Independent Southern Baptist** comprehensive, founded 1910
- **Calendar** 4-1-4
- **Degrees** bachelor's and master's
- **Small-town** 125-acre campus with easy access to Oklahoma City
- **Endowment** $68.2 million
- **Coed,** 1,911 undergraduate students, 81% full-time, 56% women, 44% men
- **Moderately difficult** entrance level, 86% of applicants were admitted

Undergraduates 1,543 full-time, 368 part-time. Students come from 42 states and territories, 19 other countries, 39% are from out of state, 5% transferred in, 72% live on campus. *Retention:* 74% of 2001 full-time freshmen returned.

Freshmen *Admission:* 958 applied, 820 admitted, 435 enrolled. *Average high school GPA:* 3.65. *Test scores:* SAT verbal scores over 500: 84%; SAT math scores over 500: 79%; ACT scores over 18: 96%; SAT verbal scores over 600: 48%; SAT math scores over 600: 38%; ACT scores over 24: 55%; SAT verbal scores over 700: 12%; SAT math scores over 700: 9%; ACT scores over 30: 10%.

Faculty *Total:* 153, 75% full-time, 61% with terminal degrees. *Student/faculty ratio:* 14:1.

Majors Accounting; advertising; applied art; art; art education; athletic training/sports medicine; biblical languages/literatures; biblical studies; biological/physical sciences; biology; biology education; broadcast journalism; business administration; business computer programming; business marketing and marketing management; chemistry; chemistry education; child care/development; child guidance; computer/information sciences; computer management; computer science; computer systems analysis; developmental/child psychology; divinity/ministry; drama/dance education; early childhood education; education; education of the emotionally handicapped; education of the mentally handicapped; education of the specific learning disabled; elementary education; English; English composition; English education; exercise sciences; finance; fine/studio arts; French; French language education; German; German language education; health/physical education; history; history education; humanities; human resources management; information sciences/systems; interdisciplinary studies; international business; international business marketing; journalism; management information systems/business data processing; marriage/family counseling; mass communications; mathematics; mathematics education; missionary studies; museum studies; music; music (piano and organ performance); music teacher education; music theory and composition; music (voice and choral/opera performance); natural sciences; nursing; pastoral counseling; philosophy; physical education; physical sciences; physics; political science; pre-dentistry; pre-law; pre-medicine; pre-pharmacy studies; pre-veterinary studies; psychology; public relations; radio/television broadcasting; recreation/leisure studies; religious education; religious music; religious studies; science education; secondary education; social science education; social sciences; social studies education; social work; sociology; Spanish; Spanish language education; special education; speech education; speech/rhetorical studies; telecommunications; theater arts/drama; theology; wind/percussion instruments.

Academic Programs *Special study options:* academic remediation for entering students, advanced placement credit, cooperative education, double majors, honors programs, independent study, internships, off-campus study, part-time degree program, services for LD students, student-designed majors, study abroad, summer session for credit. *ROTC:* Air Force (c).

Library Mabee Learning Center with 230,000 titles, 1,800 serial subscriptions, 1,600 audiovisual materials, an OPAC, a Web page.

Computers on Campus 170 computers available on campus for general student use. A campuswide network can be accessed from student residence rooms. Internet access, at least one staffed computer lab available.

Student Life *Housing:* on-campus residence required through junior year. *Options:* men-only, women-only. *Activities and Organizations:* drama/theater group, student-run newspaper, television station, choral group, Campus Activities Board, Student Ambassadors, Student Government Association, Baptist Student Union, University Concert Series. *Campus security:* 24-hour emergency response devices and patrols, late-night transport/escort service, controlled dormitory access. *Student Services:* health clinic, personal/psychological counseling.

Athletics Member NAIA. *Intercollegiate sports:* baseball M(s), basketball M(s)/W(s), cross-country running M(s)/W(s), golf M(s)/W(s), softball W(s), tennis M(s)/W(s), track and field M(s)/W(s). *Intramural sports:* badminton M/W, basketball M/W, bowling M/W, football M/W, racquetball M/W, soccer M/W, softball M/W, swimming M/W, table tennis M/W, tennis M/W, volleyball M/W.

Standardized Tests *Required:* SAT I or ACT (for admission).

Costs (2002–03) *Comprehensive fee:* $14,790 includes full-time tuition ($10,300), mandatory fees ($740), and room and board ($3750). Full-time tuition and fees vary according to course load. Part-time tuition: $325 per credit hour. Part-time tuition and fees vary according to course load. *Room and board:* College room only: $1650. Room and board charges vary according to board plan and housing facility. *Payment plan:* installment. *Waivers:* senior citizens and employees or children of employees.

Financial Aid Of all full-time matriculated undergraduates who enrolled in 2001, 1404 applied for aid, 969 were judged to have need, 333 had their need fully met. 220 Federal Work-Study jobs (averaging $890). In 2001, 435 non-need-based awards were made. *Average percent of need met:* 59%. *Average financial aid package:* $10,428. *Average need-based loan:* $3609. *Average need-based gift aid:* $3002. *Average non-need based aid:* $5142. *Average indebtedness upon graduation:* $14,260.

Applying *Options:* early admission, deferred entrance. *Application fee:* $25. *Required:* high school transcript, minimum 2.5 GPA. *Required for some:* essay or personal statement, letters of recommendation, interview. *Application deadlines:* 8/1 (freshmen), 8/1 (transfers). *Notification:* continuous until 9/1 (freshmen).

Admissions Contact Mr. Michael Cappo, Dean of Admissions, Oklahoma Baptist University, Box 61174, Shawnee, OK 74804. *Phone:* 405-878-2033. *Toll-free phone:* 800-654-3285. *Fax:* 405-878-2046. *E-mail:* admissions@mail.okbu.edu.

OKLAHOMA CHRISTIAN UNIVERSITY
Oklahoma City, Oklahoma

- **Independent** comprehensive, founded 1950, affiliated with Church of Christ
- **Calendar** trimesters
- **Degrees** bachelor's and master's
- **Suburban** 200-acre campus
- **Endowment** $21.3 million
- **Coed,** 1,714 undergraduate students, 91% full-time, 50% women, 50% men
- **Noncompetitive** entrance level, 82% of applicants were admitted

Undergraduates Students come from 59 states and territories, 53% are from out of state, 5% African American, 2% Asian American or Pacific Islander, 3% Hispanic American, 3% Native American, 71% live on campus. *Retention:* 67% of 2001 full-time freshmen returned.

Freshmen *Admission:* 1,350 applied, 1,105 admitted. *Test scores:* SAT verbal scores over 500: 67%; SAT math scores over 500: 71%; ACT scores over 18: 87%; SAT verbal scores over 600: 28%; SAT math scores over 600: 39%; ACT scores over 24: 51%; SAT verbal scores over 700: 1%; SAT math scores over 700: 8%; ACT scores over 30: 12%.

Faculty *Total:* 165, 53% full-time, 45% with terminal degrees. *Student/faculty ratio:* 16:1.

Majors Accounting; advertising; American government; art; art education; biblical studies; biochemistry; biological/physical sciences; biology; broadcast journalism; business; business administration; business marketing and marketing management; chemistry; child care/development; community services; computer engineering; computer science; creative writing; divinity/ministry; early childhood education; electrical engineering; elementary education; engineering; engineering physics; English; English education; family/community studies; graphic design/commercial art/illustration; history; information sciences/systems; interior design; journalism; liberal arts and sciences/liberal studies; mass communications; mathematics; mathematics education; mechanical engineering; medical technology; missionary studies; music; music teacher education; music (voice and choral/opera performance); pastoral counseling; physical education; pre-law; psychology; public relations; radio/television broadcasting; religious education; religious studies; science education; secondary education; social studies education; Spanish; special education; speech/rhetorical studies; teaching English as a second language; theater arts/drama; wind/percussion instruments.

Academic Programs *Special study options:* academic remediation for entering students, accelerated degree program, adult/continuing education programs, advanced placement credit, English as a second language, honors programs, internships, off-campus study, services for LD students, study abroad, summer session for credit. *ROTC:* Army (c), Air Force (c).

Library Mabee Learning Center with 95,789 titles, 415 serial subscriptions, an OPAC.

Computers on Campus 135 computers available on campus for general student use. A campuswide network can be accessed from student residence rooms and from off campus. Internet access, at least one staffed computer lab available.

Student Life *Housing:* on-campus residence required through senior year. *Options:* men-only, women-only, disabled students. *Activities and Organizations:*

drama/theater group, student-run newspaper, radio station, choral group, Outreach, College Women for Christ. *Campus security:* 24-hour emergency response devices and patrols, late-night transport/escort service. *Student Services:* health clinic, personal/psychological counseling.

Athletics Member NAIA. *Intercollegiate sports:* basketball M(s)/W(s), cross-country running M(s)/W(s), golf M(s), soccer M(s)/W(s), softball W(s), tennis M(s)/W(s), track and field M(s)/W(s). *Intramural sports:* basketball M/W, bowling M/W, cross-country running M/W, football M/W, soccer M/W, softball M/W, swimming M/W, table tennis M/W, tennis M/W, track and field M/W, volleyball M/W.

Standardized Tests *Required:* SAT I or ACT (for admission).

Costs (2001–02) *Comprehensive fee:* $16,500 includes full-time tuition ($10,500), mandatory fees ($1600), and room and board ($4400). Part-time tuition: $440 per credit hour. *Required fees:* $800 per term part-time. *Payment plan:* tuition prepayment. *Waivers:* employees or children of employees.

Financial Aid Of all full-time matriculated undergraduates who enrolled in 2001, 1643 applied for aid, 1115 were judged to have need, 472 had their need fully met. 230 Federal Work-Study jobs (averaging $1500). In 2001, 375 non-need-based awards were made. *Average percent of need met:* 88%. *Average need-based loan:* $1340. *Average need-based gift aid:* $1568. *Average non-need based aid:* $1889. *Average indebtedness upon graduation:* $17,237. *Financial aid deadline:* 8/31.

Applying *Options:* early admission, deferred entrance. *Application fee:* $25. *Required:* high school transcript. *Application deadline:* rolling (freshmen), rolling (transfers). *Notification:* continuous (freshmen).

Admissions Contact Mr. Kyle Ray, Director of Admissions, Oklahoma Christian University, Box 11000, Oklahoma City, OK 73136-1100. *Phone:* 405-425-5050. *Toll-free phone:* 800-877-5010. *Fax:* 405-425-5208. *E-mail:* info@oc.edu.

OKLAHOMA CITY UNIVERSITY

Oklahoma City, Oklahoma

- **Independent United Methodist** comprehensive, founded 1904
- **Calendar** semesters
- **Degrees** bachelor's, master's, and first professional
- **Urban** 68-acre campus
- **Endowment** $45.0 million
- **Coed,** 1,861 undergraduate students, 79% full-time, 59% women, 41% men
- **Moderately difficult** entrance level, 70% of applicants were admitted

Undergraduates 1,473 full-time, 388 part-time. Students come from 49 states and territories, 75 other countries, 17% are from out of state, 5% African American, 2% Asian American or Pacific Islander, 3% Hispanic American, 4% Native American, 25% international, 8% transferred in, 36% live on campus. *Retention:* 70% of 2001 full-time freshmen returned.

Freshmen *Admission:* 1,381 applied, 970 admitted, 291 enrolled. *Average high school GPA:* 3.52. *Test scores:* SAT verbal scores over 500: 74%; SAT math scores over 500: 78%; ACT scores over 18: 93%; SAT verbal scores over 600: 26%; SAT math scores over 600: 26%; ACT scores over 24: 43%; SAT verbal scores over 700: 3%; SAT math scores over 700: 5%; ACT scores over 30: 2%.

Faculty *Total:* 304, 52% full-time, 51% with terminal degrees. *Student/faculty ratio:* 14:1.

Majors Accounting; advertising; American studies; art; art education; art history; arts management; biochemistry; biological/physical sciences; biology; broadcast journalism; business; business administration; business economics; business marketing and marketing management; chemistry; computer science; corrections; criminal justice/law enforcement administration; dance; early childhood education; education; elementary education; English; film/video production; finance; fine/studio arts; French; German; graphic design/commercial art/illustration; history; humanities; international business; journalism; law enforcement/police science; liberal arts and sciences/liberal studies; management information systems/business data processing; mass communications; mathematics; music; music business management/merchandising; music (piano and organ performance); music teacher education; music theory and composition; music (voice and choral/opera performance); nursing; philosophy; physical education; physics; political science; pre-dentistry; pre-law; pre-medicine; pre-veterinary studies; psychology; public relations; radio/television broadcasting; religious education; religious music; religious studies; science education; secondary education; sociology; Spanish; speech/rhetorical studies; speech/theater education; stringed instruments; theater arts/drama; theater design; wind/percussion instruments.

Academic Programs *Special study options:* academic remediation for entering students, accelerated degree program, adult/continuing education programs, advanced placement credit, cooperative education, double majors, English as a second language, external degree program, honors programs, independent study, internships, off-campus study, part-time degree program, student-designed majors, study abroad, summer session for credit. *ROTC:* Army (c), Air Force (c).

Library Dulaney Browne Library plus 1 other with 280,457 titles, 5,699 serial subscriptions, 10,605 audiovisual materials, an OPAC, a Web page.

Computers on Campus 264 computers available on campus for general student use. A campuswide network can be accessed from student residence rooms and from off campus. Internet access, at least one staffed computer lab available.

Student Life *Housing:* on-campus residence required through senior year. *Options:* men-only, women-only. *Activities and Organizations:* drama/theater group, student-run newspaper, television station, choral group, national fraternities, national sororities. *Campus security:* 24-hour emergency response devices and patrols, student patrols, late-night transport/escort service, Operation ID. *Student Services:* health clinic, personal/psychological counseling.

Athletics Member NAIA. *Intercollegiate sports:* baseball M(s), basketball M(s)/W(s), golf M(s)/W(s), soccer M(s)/W(s), softball W(s), tennis M(s)/W(s). *Intramural sports:* badminton M/W, basketball M/W, bowling M/W, crew M/W, football M, golf M/W, softball M/W, table tennis M/W, volleyball M/W.

Standardized Tests *Required:* SAT I or ACT (for admission).

Costs (2002–03) *Comprehensive fee:* $17,200 includes full-time tuition ($11,600), mandatory fees ($400), and room and board ($5200). Full-time tuition and fees vary according to program. Part-time tuition: $395 per semester hour. Part-time tuition and fees vary according to program. *Required fees:* $100 per term part-time. *Room and board:* Room and board charges vary according to board plan and housing facility. *Payment plans:* installment, deferred payment. *Waivers:* employees or children of employees.

Financial Aid Of all full-time matriculated undergraduates who enrolled in 2001, 898 applied for aid, 764 were judged to have need. 269 Federal Work-Study jobs (averaging $1662). 89 State and other part-time jobs (averaging $1718). In 2001, 115 non-need-based awards were made. *Average financial aid package:* $7591. *Average need-based loan:* $2754. *Average need-based gift aid:* $2867. *Average non-need based aid:* $3839. *Average indebtedness upon graduation:* $19,832.

Applying *Options:* common application, deferred entrance. *Application fee:* $20. *Required:* high school transcript, minimum 2.5 GPA. *Required for some:* interview, audition for music and dance programs. *Application deadline:* 8/22 (freshmen), rolling (transfers).

Admissions Contact Ms. Stacy Messinger, Director of Admissions, Oklahoma City University, 2501 North Blackwelder, Oklahoma City, OK 73106. *Phone:* 405-521-5050. *Toll-free phone:* 800-633-7242. *Fax:* 405-521-5916. *E-mail:* uadmissions@okcu.edu.

OKLAHOMA PANHANDLE STATE UNIVERSITY

Goodwell, Oklahoma

- **State-supported** 4-year, founded 1909, part of Oklahoma State Regents for Higher Education
- **Calendar** semesters
- **Degrees** associate and bachelor's
- **Rural** 40-acre campus
- **Endowment** $4.0 million
- **Coed,** 1,226 undergraduate students, 81% full-time, 54% women, 46% men
- **Noncompetitive** entrance level, 54% of applicants were admitted

Undergraduates 993 full-time, 233 part-time. Students come from 36 states and territories, 25 other countries, 53% are from out of state, 13% transferred in, 17% live on campus. *Retention:* 50% of 2001 full-time freshmen returned.

Freshmen *Admission:* 435 applied, 233 admitted, 233 enrolled. *Test scores:* ACT scores over 18: 65%; ACT scores over 24: 15%; ACT scores over 30: 3%.

Faculty *Total:* 67, 82% full-time, 30% with terminal degrees. *Student/faculty ratio:* 24:1.

Majors Accounting; agricultural business; agricultural education; agricultural sciences; agronomy/crop science; animal sciences; biological/physical sciences; biology; business administration; business education; chemistry; computer/information sciences; elementary education; English; farm/ranch management; general studies; history; humanities; industrial arts; industrial arts education; industrial technology; information sciences/systems; mathematics; medical technology; natural sciences; nursing; physical education; psychology; recreation/leisure studies; science education; secondary education; social sciences.

Academic Programs *Special study options:* academic remediation for entering students, accelerated degree program, adult/continuing education programs, advanced placement credit, cooperative education, distance learning, double majors, English as a second language, internships, part-time degree program, summer session for credit.

Library McKee Library with 106,000 titles, 308 serial subscriptions, 2,079 audiovisual materials, an OPAC.

Oklahoma Panhandle State University (continued)

Computers on Campus 50 computers available on campus for general student use. A campuswide network can be accessed from off campus. Internet access, at least one staffed computer lab available.

Student Life *Housing:* on-campus residence required for freshman year. *Options:* coed. *Activities and Organizations:* drama/theater group, student-run newspaper, radio station, choral group, marching band. *Campus security:* 24-hour emergency response devices and patrols, student patrols, safety bars over door latches. *Student Services:* health clinic, personal/psychological counseling.

Athletics Member NCAA. except football (Division II) *Intercollegiate sports:* baseball M(s), basketball M(s)/W(s), cross-country running W(s), equestrian sports M(s)/W(s), football M(s), golf M(s), softball W(s). *Intramural sports:* basketball M/W, bowling M/W, equestrian sports M/W, football M/W, softball M/W, volleyball M/W.

Standardized Tests *Required:* SAT I or ACT (for placement).

Costs (2001–02) *One-time required fee:* $441. *Tuition:* state resident $1470 full-time, $45 per credit hour part-time; nonresident $2356 full-time, $76 per credit hour part-time. Full-time tuition and fees vary according to class time. Part-time tuition and fees vary according to class time. *Required fees:* $441 full-time, $50 per credit hour, $33 per term part-time. *Room and board:* $2580; room only: $850. Room and board charges vary according to board plan, housing facility, and student level. *Waivers:* employees or children of employees.

Financial Aid Of all full-time matriculated undergraduates who enrolled in 2001, 1002 applied for aid, 1002 were judged to have need. 20 Federal Work-Study jobs (averaging $1749). 300 State and other part-time jobs (averaging $3296). *Average percent of need met:* 70%. *Average financial aid package:* $8830. *Average need-based loan:* $4281. *Average need-based gift aid:* $3639. *Average indebtedness upon graduation:* $4281.

Applying *Options:* common application. *Required:* high school transcript. *Application deadline:* rolling (freshmen), rolling (transfers).

Admissions Contact Oklahoma Panhandle State University, PO Box 430, 323 Eagle Boulevard, Goodwell, OK 73939-0430. *Phone:* 580-349-1376. *Toll-free phone:* 800-664-6778. *Fax:* 580-349-2302. *E-mail:* opsu@opsu.edu.

OKLAHOMA STATE UNIVERSITY
Stillwater, Oklahoma

- **State-supported** university, founded 1890, part of Oklahoma State University
- **Calendar** semesters
- **Degrees** bachelor's, master's, doctoral, and first professional
- **Small-town** 840-acre campus with easy access to Oklahoma City and Tulsa
- **Endowment** $157.1 million
- **Coed,** 17,211 undergraduate students, 90% full-time, 48% women, 52% men
- **Moderately difficult** entrance level, 91% of applicants were admitted

Undergraduates 15,532 full-time, 1,679 part-time. Students come from 50 states and territories, 114 other countries, 12% are from out of state, 3% African American, 2% Asian American or Pacific Islander, 2% Hispanic American, 8% Native American, 5% international, 9% transferred in, 39% live on campus. *Retention:* 82% of 2001 full-time freshmen returned.

Freshmen *Admission:* 5,591 applied, 5,083 admitted, 3,165 enrolled. *Average high school GPA:* 3.50. *Test scores:* SAT verbal scores over 500: 75%; SAT math scores over 500: 77%; ACT scores over 18: 96%; SAT verbal scores over 600: 32%; SAT math scores over 600: 39%; ACT scores over 24: 49%; SAT verbal scores over 700: 5%; SAT math scores over 700: 8%; ACT scores over 30: 9%.

Faculty *Total:* 1,111, 85% full-time, 83% with terminal degrees. *Student/faculty ratio:* 18:1.

Majors Accounting; advertising; aerospace engineering; agricultural business; agricultural economics; agricultural education; agricultural sciences; aircraft pilot (professional); American studies; animal sciences; architectural engineering; architecture; art; athletic training/sports medicine; aviation management; aviation technology; biochemistry; bioengineering; biology; botany; broadcast journalism; business; business economics; business marketing and marketing management; cell biology; chemical engineering; chemistry; child care/development; civil engineering; clothing/textiles; communication disorders; communications related; computer engineering; computer/information sciences; computer management; computer science; construction management; construction technology; economics; education; electrical/electronic engineering technology; electrical engineering; elementary education; engineering; engineering technology; English; entomology; environmental science; family/community studies; family/consumer studies; fashion merchandising; finance; fine/studio arts; fire protection/safety technology; forestry; French; geography; geology; German; graphic design/commercial art/illustration; health/physical education; health science; history; home economics; horticulture science; hotel and restaurant management; human resources management; industrial arts; industrial/manufacturing engineering; industrial technology; information sciences/systems; interior design; international business; journalism; landscape architecture; landscaping management; management information systems/business data processing; management science; mathematical statistics; mathematics; mechanical engineering; mechanical engineering technology; medical technology; microbiology/bacteriology; music; music business management/merchandising; music teacher education; nutrition science; philosophy; physical education; physics; plant sciences; political science; pre-dentistry; pre-law; pre-medicine; pre-veterinary studies; psychology; Russian; secondary education; sociology; Spanish; speech/rhetorical studies; technical/business writing; theater arts/drama; trade/industrial education; wildlife management; zoology.

Academic Programs *Special study options:* academic remediation for entering students, accelerated degree program, adult/continuing education programs, advanced placement credit, cooperative education, distance learning, double majors, English as a second language, freshman honors college, honors programs, independent study, internships, off-campus study, part-time degree program, services for LD students, student-designed majors, study abroad, summer session for credit. *ROTC:* Army (b), Air Force (b). *Unusual degree programs:* 3-2 accounting.

Library Edmon Low Library plus 4 others with 2.1 million titles, 35,698 serial subscriptions, 6,529 audiovisual materials, an OPAC, a Web page.

Computers on Campus 2000 computers available on campus for general student use. A campuswide network can be accessed from student residence rooms and from off campus. Internet access, online (class) registration, at least one staffed computer lab available.

Student Life *Housing:* on-campus residence required for freshman year. *Options:* coed, men-only, women-only. *Activities and Organizations:* drama/theater group, student-run newspaper, radio and television station, choral group, marching band, Student Government Association, Campus Crusade for Christ, Flying Aggies, Block and Bridle Club, OSU Ski Club, national fraternities, national sororities. *Campus security:* 24-hour emergency response devices and patrols, student patrols, controlled dormitory access. *Student Services:* health clinic, personal/psychological counseling, women's center, legal services.

Athletics Member NCAA. All Division I except football (Division I-A). *Intercollegiate sports:* baseball M(s), basketball M(s)/W(s), cross-country running M(s)/W(s), equestrian sports W(s), golf M(s)/W(s), soccer W, softball W(s), tennis M(s)/W(s), track and field M(s)/W(s), wrestling M(s). *Intramural sports:* archery M/W, badminton M/W, basketball M/W, bowling M/W, crew M(c)/W(c), cross-country running M/W, football M/W, golf M/W, ice hockey M(c)/W(c), lacrosse M(c), racquetball M/W, riflery M(c)/W(c), rugby M(c)/W(c), sailing M(c)/W(c), soccer M/W, softball M/W, squash M/W, swimming M/W, table tennis M/W, tennis M/W, track and field M/W, volleyball M/W, water polo M/W, weight lifting M/W, wrestling M.

Standardized Tests *Required:* SAT I or ACT (for admission). *Recommended:* ACT (for admission).

Costs (2001–02) *One-time required fee:* $20. *Tuition:* state resident $2022 full-time, $65 per credit hour part-time; nonresident $6746 full-time, $213 per credit hour part-time. Full-time tuition and fees vary according to class time, program, and reciprocity agreements. Part-time tuition and fees vary according to class time, course load, program, and reciprocity agreements. *Required fees:* $772 full-time, $22 per credit hour, $68 per term part-time. *Room and board:* $4856; room only: $2286. Room and board charges vary according to board plan and housing facility. *Payment plan:* installment. *Waivers:* children of alumni, senior citizens, and employees or children of employees.

Financial Aid Of all full-time matriculated undergraduates who enrolled in 2001, 11770 applied for aid, 7141 were judged to have need, 2013 had their need fully met. 600 Federal Work-Study jobs (averaging $1500). In 2001, 3937 non-need-based awards were made. *Average percent of need met:* 80%. *Average financial aid package:* $7208. *Average need-based loan:* $3695. *Average need-based gift aid:* $2940. *Average indebtedness upon graduation:* $18,100.

Applying *Options:* early admission. *Application fee:* $25. *Required:* high school transcript, minimum 3.0 GPA, class rank. *Required for some:* interview. *Application deadline:* rolling (freshmen), rolling (transfers). *Notification:* continuous (freshmen).

Admissions Contact Ms. Paulette Cundiff, Coordinator of Admissions Processing, Oklahoma State University, 324 Student Union, Stillwater, OK 74078. *Phone:* 405-744-6858. *Toll-free phone:* 800-233-5019 (in-state); 800-852-1255 (out-of-state). *Fax:* 405-744-5285. *E-mail:* admit@okstate.edu.

OKLAHOMA WESLEYAN UNIVERSITY
Bartlesville, Oklahoma

- **Independent** comprehensive, founded 1909, affiliated with Wesleyan Church
- **Calendar** semesters

- **Degrees** certificates, diplomas, associate, bachelor's, and master's
- **Small-town** 127-acre campus with easy access to Tulsa
- **Coed,** 834 undergraduate students
- **Minimally difficult** entrance level, 60% of applicants were admitted

Undergraduates Students come from 26 states and territories, 8 other countries, 46% are from out of state, 6% African American, 2% Asian American or Pacific Islander, 2% Hispanic American, 7% Native American, 3% international, 48% live on campus. *Retention:* 70% of 2001 full-time freshmen returned.

Freshmen *Admission:* 427 applied, 257 admitted. *Average high school GPA:* 3.37. *Test scores:* SAT verbal scores over 500: 67%; SAT math scores over 500: 54%; SAT verbal scores over 600: 32%; SAT math scores over 600: 19%; SAT verbal scores over 700: 2%; SAT math scores over 700: 4%.

Faculty *Total:* 37. *Student/faculty ratio:* 14:1.

Majors Accounting; athletic training/sports medicine; behavioral sciences; biological/physical sciences; biology; business administration; business education; chemistry; divinity/ministry; education; elementary education; English; exercise sciences; history; information sciences/systems; liberal arts and sciences/liberal studies; linguistics; mass communications; mathematics; music; music (general performance); natural sciences; nursing; physical education; physical therapy; political science; pre-dentistry; pre-law; pre-medicine; pre-veterinary studies; religious studies; science education; secondary education; secretarial science; social sciences; teaching English as a second language; theology.

Academic Programs *Special study options:* academic remediation for entering students, adult/continuing education programs, advanced placement credit, cooperative education, distance learning, English as a second language, independent study, internships, off-campus study, part-time degree program, student-designed majors, summer session for credit.

Library Bartlesville Wesleyan College Library with 124,722 titles, 300 serial subscriptions.

Computers on Campus 30 computers available on campus for general student use. A campuswide network can be accessed from student residence rooms and from off campus. At least one staffed computer lab available.

Student Life *Housing:* on-campus residence required through junior year. *Activities and Organizations:* student-run newspaper, choral group, Forensics Club, Fellowship of Christian Athletes, Teachers Association, Theology Club, Education Club. *Campus security:* 24-hour emergency response devices and patrols, controlled dormitory access. *Student Services:* health clinic, personal/psychological counseling.

Athletics Member NAIA, NCCAA. *Intercollegiate sports:* baseball M(s), basketball M(s)/W(s), golf M(s), soccer M(s)/W(s), softball W(s), volleyball W(s). *Intramural sports:* basketball M/W, football M/W, golf M/W, racquetball M/W, soccer M/W, softball M/W, swimming M/W, table tennis M/W, tennis M/W, track and field M/W, volleyball M/W, weight lifting M/W.

Standardized Tests *Required:* SAT I or ACT (for admission).

Costs (2002–03) *Comprehensive fee:* $14,500 includes full-time tuition ($9800), mandatory fees ($600), and room and board ($4100). Part-time tuition: $360 per semester hour. *Required fees:* $40 per semester hour. *Room and board:* College room only: $2000. Room and board charges vary according to board plan and housing facility. *Payment plans:* installment, deferred payment. *Waivers:* senior citizens and employees or children of employees.

Financial Aid Of all full-time matriculated undergraduates who enrolled in 2001, 640 applied for aid, 568 were judged to have need, 131 had their need fully met. 130 Federal Work-Study jobs (averaging $1596). 13 State and other part-time jobs (averaging $1550). In 2001, 41 non-need-based awards were made. *Average percent of need met:* 58%. *Average financial aid package:* $6466. *Average need-based loan:* $4286. *Average need-based gift aid:* $3917. *Average non-need based aid:* $2184. *Average indebtedness upon graduation:* $13,486.

Applying *Options:* early admission, deferred entrance. *Application fee:* $25. *Required:* high school transcript, letters of recommendation, ACT/SAT. Min. ACT of 18 or SAT 860. *Recommended:* minimum 2.0 GPA. *Application deadline:* rolling (freshmen), rolling (transfers).

Admissions Contact Mr. Marty Carver, Director of Enrollment Services, Oklahoma Wesleyan University, 2201 Silver Lake Road, Bartlesville, OK 74006-6299. *Phone:* 918-335-6219. *Toll-free phone:* 800-468-6292. *Fax:* 918-335-6229. *E-mail:* admissions@okwu.edu.

ORAL ROBERTS UNIVERSITY

Tulsa, Oklahoma

- **Independent interdenominational** comprehensive, founded 1963
- **Calendar** semesters
- **Degrees** bachelor's, master's, doctoral, and first professional
- **Urban** 263-acre campus
- **Endowment** $66.4 million
- **Coed,** 3,087 undergraduate students, 91% full-time, 58% women, 42% men
- **Moderately difficult** entrance level, 72% of applicants were admitted

Undergraduates 2,821 full-time, 266 part-time. Students come from 52 states and territories, 41 other countries, 64% are from out of state, 16% African American, 3% Asian American or Pacific Islander, 5% Hispanic American, 2% Native American, 3% international, 6% transferred in, 71% live on campus. *Retention:* 78% of 2001 full-time freshmen returned.

Freshmen *Admission:* 1,303 applied, 936 admitted, 628 enrolled. *Average high school GPA:* 3.62. *Test scores:* SAT verbal scores over 500: 69%; SAT math scores over 500: 63%; ACT scores over 18: 89%; SAT verbal scores over 600: 27%; SAT math scores over 600: 26%; ACT scores over 24: 38%; SAT verbal scores over 700: 4%; SAT math scores over 700: 5%; ACT scores over 30: 5%.

Faculty *Total:* 289, 68% full-time, 46% with terminal degrees. *Student/faculty ratio:* 17:1.

Majors Accounting; art education; biblical studies; biochemistry; bioengineering; biology; biomedical engineering-related technology; British literature; business administration; business marketing and marketing management; chemistry; communications; computer engineering; computer science; early childhood education; education; education administration; education (multiple levels); electrical engineering; elementary education; engineering mechanics; English education; exercise sciences; finance; fine/studio arts; French; French language education; German; German language education; graphic design/commercial art/illustration; history; international relations; journalism; liberal arts and sciences/liberal studies; management information systems/business data processing; management science; mathematics; mathematics education; mechanical engineering; missionary studies; music; music (general performance); music teacher education; music theory and composition; nursing; pastoral counseling; philosophy; physical education; physics; political science; pre-dentistry; pre-medicine; psychology; public relations; radio/television broadcasting; religious music; religious studies; science education; social studies education; social work; Spanish; Spanish language education; special education; teaching English as a second language; theater arts/drama; theology.

Academic Programs *Special study options:* academic remediation for entering students, adult/continuing education programs, advanced placement credit, distance learning, double majors, English as a second language, external degree program, freshman honors college, honors programs, independent study, internships, off-campus study, part-time degree program, services for LD students, student-designed majors, study abroad, summer session for credit. *ROTC:* Air Force (c). *Unusual degree programs:* 3-2 education.

Library John D. Messick Resources Center plus 1 other with 210,625 titles, 5,613 serial subscriptions, 23,149 audiovisual materials, an OPAC, a Web page.

Computers on Campus 253 computers available on campus for general student use. A campuswide network can be accessed from student residence rooms and from off campus. Internet access, at least one staffed computer lab available.

Student Life *Housing:* on-campus residence required through senior year. *Options:* men-only, women-only. *Activities and Organizations:* drama/theater group, student-run newspaper, radio and television station, choral group, missions, Student Nurse Association, American Management Society, Accounting Society. *Campus security:* 24-hour emergency response devices and patrols, late-night transport/escort service. *Student Services:* health clinic, personal/psychological counseling.

Athletics Member NCAA. All Division I. *Intercollegiate sports:* baseball M(s), basketball M(s)/W(s), cross-country running M(s)/W(s), golf M(s)/W(s), soccer M(s)/W(s), tennis M(s)/W(s), track and field M(s)/W(s), volleyball W(s). *Intramural sports:* badminton M/W, basketball M/W, bowling M/W, football M/W, racquetball M/W, soccer M/W, softball M/W, table tennis M/W, tennis M/W, volleyball M/W.

Standardized Tests *Required:* SAT I or ACT (for admission).

Costs (2002–03) *Comprehensive fee:* $18,550 includes full-time tuition ($12,600), mandatory fees ($380), and room and board ($5570). Part-time tuition: $525 per credit hour. *Required fees:* $90 per term part-time. *Room and board:* College room only: $2720. Room and board charges vary according to board plan. *Payment plan:* installment. *Waivers:* children of alumni and employees or children of employees.

Financial Aid Of all full-time matriculated undergraduates who enrolled in 2001, 2143 applied for aid, 1916 were judged to have need, 885 had their need fully met. 313 Federal Work-Study jobs (averaging $1590). 750 State and other part-time jobs (averaging $1500). In 2001, 655 non-need-based awards were made. *Average percent of need met:* 90%. *Average financial aid package:* $12,448. *Average need-based loan:* $6316. *Average need-based gift aid:* $6501. *Average non-need based aid:* $5858. *Average indebtedness upon graduation:* $23,075.

Applying *Options:* common application, early admission, early action, deferred entrance. *Application fee:* $35. *Required:* essay or personal statement, high school

Oral Roberts University (continued)
transcript, minimum 2.6 GPA, 1 letter of recommendation, proof of immunization. *Required for some:* interview. *Application deadline:* rolling (freshmen), rolling (transfers). *Notification:* continuous (freshmen).

Admissions Contact Chris Miller, Director of Undergraduate Admissions, Oral Roberts University, Tulsa, OK 74171. *Phone:* 918-495-6518. *Toll-free phone:* 800-678-8876. *Fax:* 918-495-6222. *E-mail:* admissions@oru.edu.

ROGERS STATE UNIVERSITY
Claremore, Oklahoma

- **State-supported** 4-year, founded 1909, part of Oklahoma State Regents for Higher Education
- **Calendar** semesters
- **Degrees** certificates, diplomas, associate, and bachelor's
- **Small-town** campus with easy access to Tulsa
- **Endowment** $3.5 million
- **Coed,** 2,852 undergraduate students, 50% full-time, 64% women, 36% men
- **Noncompetitive** entrance level, 79% of applicants were admitted

Undergraduates 1,427 full-time, 1,425 part-time. Students come from 36 states and territories, 15 other countries, 5% are from out of state, 2% African American, 0.5% Asian American or Pacific Islander, 2% Hispanic American, 24% Native American, 1% international, 27% transferred in, 10% live on campus. *Retention:* 51% of 2001 full-time freshmen returned.

Freshmen *Admission:* 1,091 applied, 859 admitted, 669 enrolled. *Average high school GPA:* 2.96. *Test scores:* ACT scores over 18: 68%; ACT scores over 24: 12%.

Faculty *Total:* 122, 63% full-time, 42% with terminal degrees. *Student/faculty ratio:* 21:1.

Majors Accounting; agricultural business; alcohol/drug abuse counseling; art; biology; broadcast journalism; business administration; business information/data processing related; chemistry; computer engineering technology; computer programming; computer science; criminal justice/law enforcement administration; elementary education; emergency medical technology; engineering technologies related; equestrian studies; farm/ranch management; graphic design/commercial art/illustration; history; information sciences/systems; law enforcement/police science; legal administrative assistant; liberal arts and sciences/liberal studies; mathematics; Native American studies; nursing; nursing related; paralegal/legal assistant; physical sciences; political science; radio/television broadcasting; secondary education; secretarial science; social sciences.

Academic Programs *Special study options:* academic remediation for entering students, adult/continuing education programs, advanced placement credit, cooperative education, distance learning, double majors, external degree program, independent study, internships, off-campus study, part-time degree program, services for LD students, summer session for credit. *ROTC:* Air Force (c).

Library Thunderbird Library with 48,194 titles, 506 serial subscriptions, 4,911 audiovisual materials, an OPAC, a Web page.

Computers on Campus 314 computers available on campus for general student use. A campuswide network can be accessed from student residence rooms and from off campus that provide access to software to support courses. Internet access, online (class) registration, at least one staffed computer lab available.

Student Life *Housing Options:* coed. *Activities and Organizations:* student-run newspaper, radio and television station, Phi Theta Kappa, Adult Students Aspiring to Prosper, Horse and Ag Student Association, Native American Student Association, Criminal Justice Student Association. *Campus security:* 24-hour patrols, late-night transport/escort service. *Student Services:* personal/psychological counseling, women's center.

Athletics *Intramural sports:* basketball M/W, bowling M/W, football M/W, riflery M(c), soccer M/W, softball M/W, table tennis M/W, volleyball M/W.

Standardized Tests *Required for some:* ACT (for admission).

Costs (2001–02) *One-time required fee:* $20. *Tuition:* state resident $1700 full-time, $69 per credit part-time; nonresident $3898 full-time, $161 per credit part-time. Full-time tuition and fees vary according to class time and course load. Part-time tuition and fees vary according to class time and course load. *Required fees:* $30 full-time, $2 per credit, $15 per term part-time. *Room and board:* room only: $3070. Room and board charges vary according to board plan. *Payment plan:* installment. *Waivers:* minority students, senior citizens, and employees or children of employees.

Financial Aid Of all full-time matriculated undergraduates who enrolled in 2001, 891 applied for aid, 891 were judged to have need, 891 had their need fully met. *Average percent of need met:* 76%. *Average financial aid package:* $7425. *Average need-based loan:* $3063. *Average need-based gift aid:* $4800. *Average indebtedness upon graduation:* $12,250.

Applying *Options:* electronic application. *Required:* high school transcript. *Required for some:* minimum 2.7 GPA. *Application deadline:* rolling (freshmen), rolling (transfers).

Admissions Contact Rogers State University, Roger's State University, Office of Admissions, 1701 West Will Rogers Boulevard, Claremore, OK 74017. *Phone:* 918-343-7546. *Toll-free phone:* 800-256-7511. *Fax:* 918-343-7595. *E-mail:* shunter@rsu.edu.

ST. GREGORY'S UNIVERSITY
Shawnee, Oklahoma

- **Independent Roman Catholic** 4-year, founded 1875
- **Calendar** semesters
- **Degrees** associate and bachelor's
- **Small-town** 640-acre campus with easy access to Oklahoma City
- **Endowment** $5.8 million
- **Coed,** 843 undergraduate students, 73% full-time, 56% women, 44% men
- **Minimally difficult** entrance level, 77% of applicants were admitted

Undergraduates 618 full-time, 225 part-time. Students come from 20 states and territories, 17 other countries, 9% are from out of state, 5% African American, 1% Asian American or Pacific Islander, 5% Hispanic American, 7% Native American, 10% international, 3% transferred in, 70% live on campus. *Retention:* 65% of 2001 full-time freshmen returned.

Freshmen *Admission:* 475 applied, 365 admitted, 186 enrolled. *Average high school GPA:* 3.21. *Test scores:* ACT scores over 18: 82%; ACT scores over 24: 31%.

Faculty *Total:* 87, 40% full-time, 26% with terminal degrees. *Student/faculty ratio:* 18:1.

Majors Business administration; criminal justice studies; humanities; liberal arts and sciences/liberal studies; natural sciences; pre-engineering; social sciences; theology.

Academic Programs *Special study options:* academic remediation for entering students, adult/continuing education programs, advanced placement credit, double majors, English as a second language, external degree program, honors programs, independent study, internships, off-campus study, part-time degree program, services for LD students, student-designed majors, study abroad, summer session for credit. *ROTC:* Army (c), Navy (c), Air Force (c).

Library James J. Kelly Library plus 1 other with 55,500 titles, 284 serial subscriptions.

Computers on Campus 60 computers available on campus for general student use. A campuswide network can be accessed from student residence rooms and from off campus. Online (class) registration, at least one staffed computer lab available.

Student Life *Housing:* on-campus residence required through junior year. *Options:* men-only, women-only, disabled students. *Activities and Organizations:* drama/theater group, student-run newspaper, choral group, Residence Halls Association, Phi Theta Kappa, Campus Ministry, This Is My Environment (TIME). *Campus security:* 24-hour emergency response devices and patrols, late-night transport/escort service, controlled dormitory access. *Student Services:* health clinic, personal/psychological counseling.

Athletics Member NAIA. *Intercollegiate sports:* baseball M(s), basketball M(s)/W(s), cross-country running M(s)/W(s), golf M(s)/W(s), soccer M(s)/W(s), softball W(s), tennis W(s), volleyball W(s). *Intramural sports:* basketball M/W, football M, racquetball M/W, soccer M/W, softball M/W, swimming M/W, tennis M/W, volleyball M/W, weight lifting M/W.

Standardized Tests *Required:* SAT I or ACT (for admission).

Costs (2001–02) *Comprehensive fee:* $13,980 includes full-time tuition ($8762), mandatory fees ($740), and room and board ($4478). Full-time tuition and fees vary according to course load and reciprocity agreements. Part-time tuition: $292 per credit hour. Part-time tuition and fees vary according to course load and reciprocity agreements. *Required fees:* $30 per credit hour. *Room and board:* College room only: $2570. Room and board charges vary according to board plan and housing facility. *Payment plans:* installment, deferred payment. *Waivers:* adult students, senior citizens, and employees or children of employees.

Financial Aid Of all full-time matriculated undergraduates who enrolled in 2001, 517 applied for aid, 347 were judged to have need, 33 had their need fully met. 49 Federal Work-Study jobs (averaging $924). 23 State and other part-time jobs (averaging $2477). In 2001, 103 non-need-based awards were made. *Average percent of need met:* 56%. *Average financial aid package:* $8244. *Average need-based loan:* $2740. *Average need-based gift aid:* $7612. *Average non-need based aid:* $1875. *Average indebtedness upon graduation:* $12,576.

Applying *Options:* common application, electronic application, deferred entrance. *Application fee:* $25. *Required:* high school transcript, minimum 2.0 GPA.

Required for some: essay or personal statement, letters of recommendation, interview. *Application deadline:* rolling (freshmen), rolling (transfers). *Notification:* continuous (freshmen).

Admissions Contact Mr. Dan Rutledge, Director of Admissions, St. Gregory's University, 1900 West MacArthur Drive, Shawnee, OK 74804. *Phone:* 405-878-5444 Ext. 447. *Toll-free phone:* 888-STGREGS. *Fax:* 405-878-5198. *E-mail:* admissions@sgc.edu.

SOUTHEASTERN OKLAHOMA STATE UNIVERSITY

Durant, Oklahoma

- **State-supported** comprehensive, founded 1909, part of Oklahoma State Regents for Higher Education
- **Calendar** semesters
- **Degrees** bachelor's, master's, and post-master's certificates
- **Small-town** 176-acre campus
- **Endowment** $8.2 million
- **Coed,** 3,639 undergraduate students, 79% full-time, 53% women, 47% men
- **Moderately difficult** entrance level, 72% of applicants were admitted

Undergraduates 2,884 full-time, 755 part-time. Students come from 36 states and territories, 16 other countries, 22% are from out of state, 5% African American, 0.6% Asian American or Pacific Islander, 1% Hispanic American, 30% Native American, 2% international, 13% transferred in, 15% live on campus. *Retention:* 52% of 2001 full-time freshmen returned.

Freshmen *Admission:* 1,089 applied, 785 admitted, 646 enrolled. *Average high school GPA:* 3.27. *Test scores:* ACT scores over 18: 42%; ACT scores over 24: 19%; ACT scores over 30: 3%.

Faculty *Total:* 225, 63% full-time, 52% with terminal degrees. *Student/faculty ratio:* 18:1.

Majors Accounting; aircraft pilot (professional); art; art education; aviation management; biology; botany; business administration; business economics; business education; business marketing and marketing management; chemistry; communications; computer/information sciences; criminal justice studies; early childhood education; education; electrical/electronic engineering technology; elementary education; English; English education; environmental science; finance; fish/game management; gerontology; health education; history; industrial technology; information sciences/systems; management science; mathematics; mathematics education; medical laboratory technology; medical technology; music; music (general performance); music teacher education; natural resources conservation; occupational safety/health technology; office management; physical education; physics; political science; psychology; recreation/leisure studies; science education; secondary education; social studies education; sociology; Spanish language education; special education; speech education; theater arts/drama; wildlife management; zoology.

Academic Programs *Special study options:* academic remediation for entering students, accelerated degree program, adult/continuing education programs, advanced placement credit, distance learning, double majors, honors programs, independent study, internships, off-campus study, part-time degree program, services for LD students, summer session for credit.

Library Henry G. Bennett Memorial Library with 192,471 titles, 1,322 serial subscriptions, 1,543 audiovisual materials, an OPAC, a Web page.

Computers on Campus 118 computers available on campus for general student use. Internet access, at least one staffed computer lab available.

Student Life *Housing Options:* coed, men-only, women-only. *Activities and Organizations:* drama/theater group, student-run newspaper, radio station, choral group, marching band, Baptist Collegiate Ministries, Wesley Student Center, Sigma Tau Gamma, Kappa Sigma, Panhellenic, national fraternities, national sororities. *Campus security:* 24-hour patrols, late-night transport/escort service. *Student Services:* health clinic, personal/psychological counseling.

Athletics Member NCAA. All Division II. *Intercollegiate sports:* baseball M(s), basketball M(s)/W(s), cross-country running W(s), football M(s), softball W(s), tennis M(s)/W(s), volleyball W(s). *Intramural sports:* basketball M/W, football M, softball M/W, volleyball M/W.

Standardized Tests *Required for some:* SAT I (for admission), ACT (for admission), SAT II: Subject Tests (for admission).

Costs (2002–03) *Tuition:* state resident $1572 full-time, $52 per credit hour part-time; nonresident $4319 full-time, $144 per credit hour part-time. Full-time tuition and fees vary according to class time. Part-time tuition and fees vary according to class time and course load. *Required fees:* $692 full-time, $20 per semester hour, $51 per term part-time. *Room and board:* $2542; room only: $872. Room and board charges vary according to board plan and housing facility. *Waivers:* minority students, children of alumni, senior citizens, and employees or children of employees.

Financial Aid Of all full-time matriculated undergraduates who enrolled in 2001, 2207 applied for aid, 1424 were judged to have need, 93 had their need fully met. In 2001, 23 non-need-based awards were made. *Average percent of need met:* 68%. *Average financial aid package:* $5015. *Average need-based loan:* $1454. *Average need-based gift aid:* $6402. *Average non-need based aid:* $803. *Average indebtedness upon graduation:* $10,646.

Applying *Options:* deferred entrance. *Application fee:* $20. *Required:* high school transcript. *Application deadline:* 8/15 (transfers).

Admissions Contact Mr. Rudy Manley, Director of Enrollment Management, Southeastern Oklahoma State University, Box 4225, Durant, OK 74701-0609. *Phone:* 580-745-2050. *Toll-free phone:* 800-435-1327 Ext. 2307. *Fax:* 580-920-7472.

SOUTHERN NAZARENE UNIVERSITY

Bethany, Oklahoma

- **Independent Nazarene** comprehensive, founded 1899
- **Calendar** semesters
- **Degrees** associate, bachelor's, and master's
- **Suburban** 40-acre campus with easy access to Oklahoma City
- **Endowment** $7.9 million
- **Coed,** 1,757 undergraduate students, 94% full-time, 54% women, 46% men
- **Noncompetitive** entrance level, 100% of applicants were admitted

Undergraduates 1,654 full-time, 103 part-time. 47% are from out of state, 6% African American, 1% Asian American or Pacific Islander, 3% Hispanic American, 3% Native American, 1% international, 5% transferred in, 65% live on campus. *Retention:* 77% of 2001 full-time freshmen returned.

Freshmen *Admission:* 348 applied, 348 admitted, 358 enrolled. *Average high school GPA:* 3.4. *Test scores:* ACT scores over 18: 83%; ACT scores over 24: 38%; ACT scores over 30: 6%.

Faculty *Total:* 203, 36% full-time. *Student/faculty ratio:* 21:1.

Majors Accounting; American studies; art education; athletic training/sports medicine; aviation management; biblical studies; biological/physical sciences; biology; biology education; broadcast journalism; business; business administration; business education; business marketing and marketing management; chemistry; chemistry education; communications; computer science; criminal justice studies; early childhood education; education; elementary education; English; English education; environmental science; exercise sciences; family/community studies; family studies; finance; general studies; health education; history; information sciences/systems; interdisciplinary studies; international relations; journalism; literature; management information systems/business data processing; management science; mass communications; mathematics; mathematics education; missionary studies; music business management/merchandising; music (general performance); music (piano and organ performance); music teacher education; music (voice and choral/opera performance); natural sciences; nursing; philosophy; physical education; physics; political science; pre-dentistry; pre-law; pre-medicine; pre-pharmacy studies; psychology; religious education; religious music; religious studies; secondary education; social science education; social work; sociology; Spanish; Spanish language education; speech education; speech/rhetorical studies; sport/fitness administration.

Academic Programs *Special study options:* academic remediation for entering students, accelerated degree program, adult/continuing education programs, advanced placement credit, double majors, external degree program, honors programs, internships, off-campus study, part-time degree program, services for LD students, student-designed majors, study abroad, summer session for credit. *ROTC:* Army (c), Air Force (c).

Library R. T. Williams Learning Resources Center with 115,564 titles, 2,748 audiovisual materials, an OPAC, a Web page.

Computers on Campus 55 computers available on campus for general student use. A campuswide network can be accessed from student residence rooms and from off campus. Internet access, at least one staffed computer lab available.

Student Life *Housing:* on-campus residence required through senior year. *Options:* men-only, women-only. *Activities and Organizations:* drama/theater group, student-run newspaper, television station, choral group, Business Gaming Team, Campus Social Life Committee, Intramural Sports Societies, Choral Society, Inter Club. *Campus security:* 24-hour emergency response devices, controlled dormitory access. *Student Services:* health clinic, personal/psychological counseling.

Athletics Member NAIA. *Intercollegiate sports:* baseball M(s), basketball M(s)/W(s), cross-country running M(s)/W(s), golf M(s)/W(s), soccer M(s)/W(s), softball W(s), tennis M(s)/W(s), track and field M(s)/W(s), volleyball W(s). *Intramural sports:* basketball M/W, football M/W, golf M/W, racquetball M/W, skiing (downhill) M/W, soccer M/W, softball M/W, swimming M/W, table tennis M/W, tennis M/W, volleyball M/W, weight lifting M/W.

Southern Nazarene University (continued)

Standardized Tests *Required:* SAT I or ACT (for placement).

Costs (2001–02) *Comprehensive fee:* $12,400 includes full-time tuition ($9870), mandatory fees ($216), and room and board ($2314). Part-time tuition: $329 per credit hour. *Required fees:* $15 per credit hour. *Room and board:* College room only: $1113.

Financial Aid Of all full-time matriculated undergraduates who enrolled in 2001, 1521 applied for aid, 1437 were judged to have need.

Applying *Options:* deferred entrance. *Application fee:* $25. *Required:* high school transcript. *Recommended:* interview. *Application deadlines:* 8/15 (freshmen), 8/15 (transfers). *Notification:* continuous (freshmen).

Admissions Contact Mr. Larry Hess, Director of Admissions, Southern Nazarene University, 6729 Northwest 39th Expressway, Bethany, OK 73008. *Phone:* 405-491-6324. *Toll-free phone:* 800-648-9899. *Fax:* 405-491-6320. *E-mail:* admiss@snu.edu.

SOUTHWESTERN CHRISTIAN UNIVERSITY
Bethany, Oklahoma

- **Independent** comprehensive, founded 1946, affiliated with Pentecostal Holiness Church
- **Calendar** semesters
- **Degrees** certificates, associate, bachelor's, and master's
- **Suburban** 7-acre campus with easy access to Oklahoma City
- **Coed**
- **Minimally difficult** entrance level

Faculty *Student/faculty ratio:* 15:1.

Student Life *Campus security:* 24-hour emergency response devices.

Athletics Member NCCAA.

Standardized Tests *Required:* ACT (for admission).

Financial Aid Of all full-time matriculated undergraduates who enrolled in 2001, 120 applied for aid, 120 were judged to have need, 48 had their need fully met. 45 Federal Work-Study jobs (averaging $1500). 6 State and other part-time jobs (averaging $1500). In 2001, 5. *Average percent of need met:* 68. *Average financial aid package:* $6850. *Average need-based loan:* $4000. *Average need-based gift aid:* $2000. *Average non-need based aid:* $4200. *Average indebtedness upon graduation:* $16,500.

Applying *Options:* common application, early admission, deferred entrance. *Application fee:* $25. *Required:* essay or personal statement, high school transcript, minimum 2.0 GPA, letters of recommendation, minimum ACT score of 19 or SAT score of 910. *Recommended:* interview.

Admissions Contact Mr. Johnny Lipton, Director of Admissions, Southwestern Christian University, PO Box 340, Bethany, OK 73008-0340. *Phone:* 405-789-7661 Ext. 3449. *E-mail:* admissions@sccm.edu.

SOUTHWESTERN OKLAHOMA STATE UNIVERSITY
Weatherford, Oklahoma

- **State-supported** comprehensive, founded 1901, part of Southwestern Oklahoma State University
- **Calendar** semesters
- **Degrees** bachelor's, master's, and first professional
- **Small-town** 73-acre campus with easy access to Oklahoma City
- **Endowment** $9.1 million
- **Coed,** 3,858 undergraduate students, 89% full-time, 56% women, 44% men
- **Moderately difficult** entrance level, 94% of applicants were admitted

Undergraduates Students come from 37 states and territories, 10% are from out of state, 3% African American, 2% Asian American or Pacific Islander, 3% Hispanic American, 5% Native American, 0.3% international, 27% live on campus. *Retention:* 65% of 2001 full-time freshmen returned.

Freshmen *Admission:* 1,247 applied, 1,167 admitted. *Average high school GPA:* 3.34. *Test scores:* ACT scores over 18: 78%; ACT scores over 24: 26%; ACT scores over 30: 3%.

Faculty *Total:* 223, 85% full-time, 60% with terminal degrees. *Student/faculty ratio:* 19:1.

Majors Accounting; art education; biology; biophysics; business administration; business marketing and marketing management; chemistry; computer/information sciences; computer science; criminal justice/law enforcement administration; education; elementary education; engineering physics; engineering technology; English; English education; finance; graphic design/commercial art/illustration; health services administration; history; history education; industrial arts; industrial arts education; industrial technology; mass communications; mathematics; medical records administration; medical technology; music; music business management/merchandising; music (piano and organ performance); music teacher education; music therapy; music (voice and choral/opera performance); nursing; pharmacy; physical education; physics; political science; pre-dentistry; pre-law; pre-medicine; pre-veterinary studies; psychology; recreational therapy; recreation/leisure studies; religious music; science education; secondary education; social science education; social work; special education; wind/percussion instruments.

Academic Programs *Special study options:* academic remediation for entering students, accelerated degree program, adult/continuing education programs, advanced placement credit, cooperative education, distance learning, double majors, independent study, internships, off-campus study, part-time degree program, services for LD students, summer session for credit.

Library Al Harris Library with 280,000 titles, 1,200 serial subscriptions, 872 audiovisual materials, an OPAC, a Web page.

Computers on Campus 270 computers available on campus for general student use. A campuswide network can be accessed from off campus. Internet access, at least one staffed computer lab available.

Student Life *Housing Options:* men-only, women-only. *Activities and Organizations:* drama/theater group, student-run newspaper, choral group, marching band, Student Education Association, Baptist Student Union, Southwestern Pharmaceutical Association, Gamma Delta Kappa, Bible Chair Student Union, national fraternities. *Campus security:* late-night transport/escort service, controlled dormitory access, 20-hour campus emergency security. *Student Services:* health clinic, personal/psychological counseling.

Athletics Member NCAA. All Division II. *Intercollegiate sports:* baseball M(s), basketball M(s)/W(s), cross-country running W(s), equestrian sports M(s)/W(s), football M(s), golf M(s)/W(s), soccer M(s)/W(s), softball W(s). *Intramural sports:* basketball M/W, bowling M/W, football M/W, softball M/W, volleyball M/W, weight lifting M.

Standardized Tests *Required:* ACT (for admission).

Costs (2001–02) *Tuition:* state resident $1589 full-time, $52 per credit hour part-time; nonresident $4482 full-time, $144 per credit hour part-time. Full-time tuition and fees vary according to class time and program. Part-time tuition and fees vary according to class time and program. *Required fees:* $549 full-time, $17 per credit hour, $47 per term part-time. *Room and board:* $2550. Room and board charges vary according to board plan and housing facility. *Payment plan:* installment. *Waivers:* children of alumni, senior citizens, and employees or children of employees.

Financial Aid Of all full-time matriculated undergraduates who enrolled in 2001, 2483 applied for aid, 2084 were judged to have need, 481 had their need fully met. In 2001, 467 non-need-based awards were made. *Average percent of need met:* 91%. *Average financial aid package:* $967. *Average need-based loan:* $1250. *Average need-based gift aid:* $927. *Average non-need based aid:* $647. *Average indebtedness upon graduation:* $9822. *Financial aid deadline:* 3/1.

Applying *Options:* deferred entrance. *Application fee:* $15. *Required:* high school transcript, minimum 2.0 GPA. *Notification:* continuous (freshmen).

Admissions Contact Ms. Connie Phillips, Admission Counselor, Southwestern Oklahoma State University, 100 Campus Drive, Weatherford, OK 73096. *Phone:* 580-774-3009. *Fax:* 580-774-3795. *E-mail:* phillic@swosu.edu.

SPARTAN SCHOOL OF AERONAUTICS
Tulsa, Oklahoma

Admissions Contact Mr. John Buck, Vice President of Marketing, Spartan School of Aeronautics, 8820 East Pine Street, PO Box 582833, Tulsa, OK 74158-2833. *Phone:* 918-836-6886.

UNIVERSITY OF CENTRAL OKLAHOMA
Edmond, Oklahoma

- **State-supported** comprehensive, founded 1890, part of Oklahoma State Regents for Higher Education
- **Calendar** semesters
- **Degrees** certificates, bachelor's, and master's
- **Suburban** 200-acre campus with easy access to Oklahoma City
- **Endowment** $453,079
- **Coed,** 11,790 undergraduate students, 68% full-time, 57% women, 43% men
- **Minimally difficult** entrance level, 96% of applicants were admitted

Undergraduates 8,044 full-time, 3,746 part-time. Students come from 38 states and territories, 108 other countries, 2% are from out of state, 7% African

American, 3% Asian American or Pacific Islander, 3% Hispanic American, 4% Native American, 10% international, 11% transferred in, 9% live on campus. *Retention:* 57% of 2001 full-time freshmen returned.

Freshmen *Admission:* 6,701 applied, 6,429 admitted, 2,045 enrolled. *Average high school GPA:* 3.17. *Test scores:* ACT scores over 18: 88%; ACT scores over 24: 28%; ACT scores over 30: 3%.

Faculty *Total:* 713, 53% full-time, 52% with terminal degrees. *Student/faculty ratio:* 20:1.

Majors Accounting; actuarial science; adult/continuing education; advertising; applied mathematics; art; art education; bioengineering; biology; broadcast journalism; business; business administration; business economics; business education; business marketing and marketing management; chemistry; child care/development; child guidance; clothing/textiles; communications; computer science; counselor education/guidance; criminal justice/law enforcement administration; criminal justice studies; dance; dietetics; early childhood education; economics; education administration; educational media design; elementary education; English; English education; fashion merchandising; finance; forensic technology; French; geography; German; graphic design/commercial art/illustration; health occupations education; health/physical education/fitness related; history; history education; home economics; home economics education; hotel and restaurant management; human resources management; interior design; journalism; liberal arts and sciences/liberal studies; marketing operations; mathematics; mathematics education; medical technology; mortuary science; music; music (piano and organ performance); music teacher education; music (voice and choral/opera performance); nursing; nutrition science; occupational safety/health technology; philosophy; photography; physical education; physics; political science; psychology; public relations; radio/television broadcasting; reading education; real estate; retailing operations; retail management; safety/security technology; science education; secondary education; social studies education; sociology; Spanish; special education; speech-language pathology/audiology; stringed instruments; teacher education, specific programs related; theater arts/drama; trade/industrial education; wind/percussion instruments.

Academic Programs *Special study options:* accelerated degree program, adult/continuing education programs, advanced placement credit, distance learning, double majors, English as a second language, honors programs, independent study, internships, part-time degree program, services for LD students, summer session for credit. *ROTC:* Army (b).

Library Max Chambers Library with 254,478 titles, 3,707 serial subscriptions, 37,484 audiovisual materials, an OPAC, a Web page.

Computers on Campus 250 computers available on campus for general student use. A campuswide network can be accessed from student residence rooms and from off campus. Internet access, at least one staffed computer lab available.

Student Life *Housing Options:* coed, men-only, women-only. *Activities and Organizations:* drama/theater group, student-run newspaper, radio and television station, choral group, marching band, Malaysian Student Association, Baptist Student Union, student government association, Association of Women Students, University Center Activities Board, national fraternities, national sororities. *Campus security:* 24-hour emergency response devices and patrols, late-night transport/escort service. *Student Services:* health clinic, personal/psychological counseling.

Athletics Member NCAA. All Division II. *Intercollegiate sports:* baseball M(s), basketball M(s)/W(s), cross-country running M(s)/W(s), football M(s), golf M(s), soccer W, softball W(s), tennis M(s)/W(s), volleyball W(s), wrestling M(s). *Intramural sports:* baseball M, basketball M/W, bowling M/W, football M/W, golf M/W, soccer M/W, softball M/W, swimming M/W, table tennis M/W, tennis M/W, track and field M/W, volleyball M/W, wrestling M.

Standardized Tests *Required:* SAT I or ACT (for admission).

Costs (2001–02) *Tuition:* state resident $1572 full-time, $52 per credit hour part-time; nonresident $4318 full-time, $144 per credit hour part-time. Full-time tuition and fees vary according to class time, course load, program, and student level. Part-time tuition and fees vary according to class time, course load, program, and student level. *Required fees:* $495 full-time, $17 per credit hour. *Room and board:* $3138. Room and board charges vary according to board plan and housing facility. *Waivers:* employees or children of employees.

Financial Aid Of all full-time matriculated undergraduates who enrolled in 2001, 4906 applied for aid, 4121 were judged to have need, 1833 had their need fully met. In 2001, 1809 non-need-based awards were made. *Average percent of need met:* 75%. *Average financial aid package:* $5000. *Average need-based loan:* $3500. *Average need-based gift aid:* $1350. *Average indebtedness upon graduation:* $10,500.

Applying *Options:* deferred entrance. *Application fee:* $15. *Required:* high school transcript, minimum 2.7 GPA, rank in upper 50% of high school class. *Application deadline:* rolling (freshmen), rolling (transfers). *Notification:* continuous until 8/1 (freshmen).

Admissions Contact Ms. Linda Lofton, Director, Admissions and Records Processing, University of Central Oklahoma, Office of Enrollment Services, 100 North University Drive, Box 151, Edmond, OK 73034. *Phone:* 405-974-2338 Ext. 2338. *Toll-free phone:* 800-254-4215. *Fax:* 405-341-4964. *E-mail:* admituco@ucok.edu.

UNIVERSITY OF OKLAHOMA
Norman, Oklahoma

- **State-supported** university, founded 1890
- **Calendar** semesters
- **Degrees** certificates, bachelor's, master's, doctoral, first professional, and post-master's certificates
- **Suburban** 3500-acre campus with easy access to Oklahoma City
- **Endowment** $428.4 million
- **Coed,** 18,660 undergraduate students, 86% full-time, 49% women, 51% men
- **Moderately difficult** entrance level, 93% of applicants were admitted

Undergraduates 16,127 full-time, 2,533 part-time. Students come from 48 states and territories, 87 other countries, 18% are from out of state, 7% African American, 5% Asian American or Pacific Islander, 4% Hispanic American, 8% Native American, 3% international, 8% transferred in, 21% live on campus. *Retention:* 83% of 2001 full-time freshmen returned.

Freshmen *Admission:* 6,943 applied, 6,459 admitted, 3,748 enrolled. *Average high school GPA:* 3.57. *Test scores:* ACT scores over 18: 98%; ACT scores over 24: 66%; ACT scores over 30: 14%.

Faculty *Total:* 1,171, 80% full-time, 78% with terminal degrees. *Student/faculty ratio:* 19:1.

Majors Accounting; advertising; aerospace engineering; African-American studies; aircraft pilot (professional); anthropology; architectural environmental design; architecture; area studies; art; art history; astronomy; astrophysics; atmospheric sciences; biochemistry; botany; broadcast journalism; business administration; business economics; business marketing and marketing management; ceramic arts; chemical engineering; chemistry; civil engineering; classics; communications; computer engineering; computer science; construction technology; criminology; dance; early childhood education; economics; electrical engineering; elementary education; energy management technology; engineering; engineering physics; English; English education; environmental engineering; environmental science; film/video production; finance; fine/studio arts; foreign languages education; French; geography; geological engineering; geology; geophysics/seismology; German; health/physical education; history; industrial/manufacturing engineering; interior architecture; international business; journalism; liberal arts and studies related; library science; linguistics; management information systems/business data processing; mathematics; mathematics education; mechanical engineering; medical laboratory technology; microbiology/bacteriology; music; music (piano and organ performance); music teacher education; music theory and composition; music (voice and choral/opera performance); Native American studies; petroleum engineering; philosophy; philosophy and religion related; physics; political science; pre-dentistry; pre-medicine; pre-veterinary studies; printmaking; professional studies; psychology; public administration; public relations; radio/television broadcasting; real estate; religious studies; Russian; science education; sculpture; social studies education; social work; sociology; Spanish; special education; stringed instruments; theater arts/drama; visual and performing arts related; wind/percussion instruments; women's studies; zoology.

Academic Programs *Special study options;* academic remediation for entering students, accelerated degree program, adult/continuing education programs, advanced placement credit, cooperative education, distance learning, double majors, English as a second language, external degree program, freshman honors college, honors programs, independent study, internships, off-campus study, part-time degree program, services for LD students, student-designed majors, study abroad, summer session for credit. *ROTC:* Army (b), Navy (b), Air Force (b).

Library Bizzell Memorial Library plus 7 others with 3.7 million titles, 15,833 serial subscriptions, 4,388 audiovisual materials, an OPAC, a Web page.

Computers on Campus 600 computers available on campus for general student use. A campuswide network can be accessed from student residence rooms and from off campus. Internet access, online (class) registration, at least one staffed computer lab available.

Student Life *Housing:* on-campus residence required for freshman year. *Options:* coed, men-only, women-only, disabled students. *Activities and Organizations:* drama/theater group, student-run newspaper, radio and television station, choral group, marching band, intramural sports, international student organizations, OU Cousins, American Indian Student Associations, Black Student Association, national fraternities, national sororities. *Campus security:* 24-hour

University of Oklahoma (continued)

emergency response devices and patrols, student patrols, late-night transport/escort service, controlled dormitory access, crime prevention programs, police bicycle patrols, self-defense classes. *Student Services:* health clinic, personal/psychological counseling, women's center, legal services.

Athletics Member NCAA. All Division I except football (Division I-A). *Intercollegiate sports:* baseball M(s), basketball M(s)/W(s), cross-country running M(s)/W(s), golf M(s)/W(s), gymnastics M(s)/W(s), soccer W(s), softball W(s), tennis M(s)/W(s), track and field M(s)/W(s), volleyball W(s), wrestling M(s). *Intramural sports:* badminton M/W, basketball M/W, bowling M/W, crew M(c)/W(c), cross-country running M/W, fencing M/W, football M, golf M/W, lacrosse M, racquetball M/W, rugby M(c)/W(c), sailing M(c)/W(c), soccer M/W, softball M/W, squash M/W, swimming M/W, table tennis M/W, tennis M/W, track and field M/W, volleyball M/W, water polo M/W.

Standardized Tests *Required:* SAT I or ACT (for admission).

Costs (2001–02) *Tuition:* state resident $2022 full-time, $67 per credit hour part-time; nonresident $6746 full-time, $225 per credit hour part-time. Full-time tuition and fees vary according to class time, course load, location, program, and reciprocity agreements. Part-time tuition and fees vary according to class time, course load, location, program, and reciprocity agreements. *Required fees:* $691 full-time, $18 per credit, $74 per term part-time. *Room and board:* $4903. Room and board charges vary according to board plan and housing facility. *Payment plan:* installment. *Waivers:* children of alumni, senior citizens, and employees or children of employees.

Financial Aid Of all full-time matriculated undergraduates who enrolled in 2001, 7946 applied for aid, 7358 were judged to have need, 6695 had their need fully met. 551 Federal Work-Study jobs (averaging $1785). In 2001, 2036 non-need-based awards were made. *Average percent of need met:* 91%. *Average financial aid package:* $7354. *Average need-based loan:* $4054. *Average need-based gift aid:* $3204. *Average non-need based aid:* $3738. *Average indebtedness upon graduation:* $17,560.

Applying *Options:* electronic application. *Application fee:* $25. *Required:* high school transcript, minimum 3.0 GPA. *Required for some:* essay or personal statement. *Application deadline:* 6/1 (freshmen), rolling (transfers). *Notification:* continuous (freshmen).

Admissions Contact Karen Renfroe, Executive Director of Recruitment Services, University of Oklahoma, 1000 Asp Avenue, Norman, OK 73019. *Phone:* 405-325-2151. *Toll-free phone:* 800-234-6868. *Fax:* 405-325-7124. *E-mail:* admrec@ou.edu.

University of Oklahoma Health Sciences Center

Oklahoma City, Oklahoma

- **State-supported** upper-level, founded 1890, part of University of Oklahoma
- **Calendar** semesters
- **Degrees** bachelor's, master's, doctoral, and first professional
- **Urban** 200-acre campus
- **Endowment** $97.0 million
- **Coed,** 582 undergraduate students, 85% full-time, 89% women, 11% men
- **Moderately difficult** entrance level, 62% of applicants were admitted

Undergraduates Students come from 30 states and territories, 5 other countries, 12% are from out of state, 5% African American, 3% Asian American or Pacific Islander, 4% Hispanic American, 9% Native American, 3% international.

Freshmen *Admission:* 545 applied, 336 admitted.

Faculty *Total:* 347, 65% full-time, 95% with terminal degrees.

Majors Dental hygiene; dietetics; industrial radiologic technology; nuclear medical technology; nursing; nutrition science; speech-language pathology/audiology; speech therapy.

Academic Programs *Special study options:* advanced placement credit, distance learning, honors programs, internships, part-time degree program, summer session for credit. *ROTC:* Army (c), Navy (c), Air Force (c).

Library Robert M. Bird Health Sciences Library with 234,000 titles, 2,658 serial subscriptions.

Computers on Campus 120 computers available on campus for general student use. A campuswide network can be accessed from off campus. Internet access, at least one staffed computer lab available.

Student Life *Housing:* college housing not available. *Activities and Organizations:* student-run newspaper, Student Government Association, Public Health Student Association, Student National Medical Association, Graduate Student Council, Student Medical Association. *Campus security:* 24-hour emergency response devices and patrols, late-night transport/escort service. *Student Services:* health clinic, personal/psychological counseling.

Costs (2001–02) *One-time required fee:* $40. *Tuition:* state resident $2340 full-time, $65 per credit part-time; nonresident $7848 full-time, $218 per credit part-time. Full-time tuition and fees vary according to student level. Part-time tuition and fees vary according to student level. *Required fees:* $638 full-time, $11 per credit hour, $61 per term part-time. *Payment plan:* installment. *Waivers:* children of alumni, senior citizens, and employees or children of employees.

Applying *Options:* deferred entrance. *Application fee:* $25. *Application deadline:* 10/1 (transfers).

Admissions Contact Dr. Willie V. Bryan, Vice Provost for Educational Services and Registrar, University of Oklahoma Health Sciences Center, PO Box 26901, Oklahoma City, OK 73190. *Phone:* 405-271-2655. *Fax:* 405-271-2480. *E-mail:* sophie-mack@ouhsc.edu.

University of Phoenix-Oklahoma City Campus

Oklahoma City, Oklahoma

- **Proprietary** comprehensive, founded 1976
- **Calendar** continuous
- **Degrees** certificates, associate, bachelor's, master's, doctoral, post-master's, and postbachelor's certificates (courses conducted at 54 campuses and learning centers in 13 states)
- **Coed,** 555 undergraduate students, 100% full-time, 56% women, 44% men
- **Noncompetitive** entrance level

Undergraduates Students come from 11 states and territories, 2% are from out of state.

Freshmen *Admission:* 6 admitted.

Faculty *Total:* 116, 3% full-time, 16% with terminal degrees. *Student/faculty ratio:* 14:1.

Majors Business administration; information technology; management information systems/business data processing; management science.

Academic Programs *Special study options:* accelerated degree program, adult/continuing education programs, advanced placement credit, distance learning, external degree program, independent study.

Library University Library with 17.5 million titles, 9,000 serial subscriptions, an OPAC, a Web page.

Computers on Campus A campuswide network can be accessed from off campus. Internet access, at least one staffed computer lab available.

Student Life *Housing:* college housing not available.

Costs (2001–02) *Tuition:* $7950 full-time. Full-time tuition and fees vary according to location and program. *Payment plan:* deferred payment. *Waivers:* employees or children of employees.

Applying *Options:* deferred entrance. *Application fee:* $85. *Required:* 2 years of work experience. *Required for some:* high school transcript. *Application deadline:* rolling (freshmen), rolling (transfers).

Admissions Contact Ms. Beth Barilla, Director of Admissions, University of Phoenix-Oklahoma City Campus, 4615 East Elwood Street, Phoenix, AZ 85040-1958. *Phone:* 480-927-0099 Ext. 1218. *Toll-free phone:* 800-228-7240. *Fax:* 480-594-1758. *E-mail:* beth.barilla@apollogrp.edu.

University of Phoenix-Tulsa Campus

Tulsa, Oklahoma

- **Proprietary** comprehensive
- **Calendar** continuous
- **Degrees** certificates, associate, bachelor's, master's, doctoral, post-master's, and postbachelor's certificates (courses conducted at 54 campuses and learning centers in 13 states)
- **Coed,** 305 undergraduate students, 198% full-time, 109% women, 89% men
- **Noncompetitive** entrance level

Undergraduates Students come from 10 states and territories, 2% are from out of state.

Freshmen *Admission:* 5 admitted.

Faculty *Total:* 167, 2% full-time, 13% with terminal degrees. *Student/faculty ratio:* 13:1.

Majors Accounting; business administration; computer/information sciences; criminal justice/law enforcement administration; enterprise management; management information systems/business data processing; management science; nursing; nursing science.

Academic Programs *Special study options:* accelerated degree program, adult/continuing education programs, advanced placement credit, distance learning, external degree program, independent study.

Library University Library with 17.5 million titles, 9,000 serial subscriptions, an OPAC, a Web page.
Computers on Campus A campuswide network can be accessed from off campus. Internet access, at least one staffed computer lab available.
Student Life *Housing:* college housing not available.
Costs (2001–02) *Tuition:* $7950 full-time. Full-time tuition and fees vary according to location and program. *Payment plan:* deferred payment. *Waivers:* employees or children of employees.
Applying *Options:* deferred entrance. *Application fee:* $85. *Required:* 2 years of work experience. *Required for some:* high school transcript. *Application deadline:* rolling (freshmen), rolling (transfers).
Admissions Contact Ms. Beth Barilla, Director of Admissions, University of Phoenix-Tulsa Campus, 4615 East Elwood Street, Phoenix, AZ 85040-1958. *Phone:* 480-927-0099 Ext. 1218. *Toll-free phone:* 800-228-7240. *Fax:* 480-594-1758. *E-mail:* beth.barilla@apollogrp.edu.

University of Science and Arts of Oklahoma
Chickasha, Oklahoma

- **State-supported** 4-year, founded 1908, part of Oklahoma State Regents for Higher Education
- **Calendar** trimesters
- **Degree** bachelor's
- **Small-town** 75-acre campus with easy access to Oklahoma City
- **Endowment** $271,130
- **Coed,** 1,452 undergraduate students, 72% full-time, 62% women, 38% men
- **Moderately difficult** entrance level, 84% of applicants were admitted

Undergraduates 1,041 full-time, 411 part-time. 4% are from out of state, 5% African American, 1% Asian American or Pacific Islander, 2% Hispanic American, 13% Native American, 3% international, 7% transferred in, 29% live on campus. *Retention:* 59% of 2001 full-time freshmen returned.
Freshmen *Admission:* 411 applied, 346 admitted, 241 enrolled. *Average high school GPA:* 3.33. *Test scores:* ACT scores over 18: 70%; ACT scores over 24: 21%; ACT scores over 30: 2%.
Faculty *Total:* 94, 55% full-time, 56% with terminal degrees. *Student/faculty ratio:* 18:1.
Majors Accounting; art; biology; business; business administration; chemistry; communications; computer science; early childhood education; economics; education of the hearing impaired; elementary education; English; health/physical education; history; mathematics; medical laboratory technician; music; Native American studies; natural sciences; physics; political science; psychology; sociology; speech-language pathology; theater arts/drama.
Academic Programs *Special study options:* academic remediation for entering students, accelerated degree program, adult/continuing education programs, advanced placement credit, cooperative education, distance learning, double majors, English as a second language, honors programs, internships, off-campus study, part-time degree program, services for LD students, student-designed majors, summer session for credit.
Library Nash Library with 81,197 titles, 3,500 serial subscriptions, 12,231 audiovisual materials, an OPAC, a Web page.
Computers on Campus 125 computers available on campus for general student use. A campuswide network can be accessed from student residence rooms and from off campus. Internet access, at least one staffed computer lab available.
Student Life *Housing Options:* men-only, women-only. *Activities and Organizations:* drama/theater group, student-run newspaper, television station, choral group, Student Activities Council, Chi Alpha, Baptist Student Union, Intertribal Heritage Club, Volunteer Action Council. *Campus security:* 24-hour emergency response devices and patrols, controlled dormitory access. *Student Services:* health clinic, personal/psychological counseling.
Athletics Member NAIA. *Intercollegiate sports:* baseball M(s), basketball M(s)/W(s), soccer M(s)/W(s), softball W(s), tennis M(s)/W(s). *Intramural sports:* basketball M/W, bowling M/W, fencing M/W, football M, golf M/W, softball M/W, swimming M/W, tennis M/W, volleyball M/W.
Standardized Tests *Required:* SAT I or ACT (for admission).
Costs (2002–03) *Tuition:* state resident $1698 full-time, $57 per hour part-time; nonresident $4794 full-time, $160 per hour part-time. Full-time tuition and fees vary according to course load. Part-time tuition and fees vary according to course load. *Required fees:* $610 full-time, $20 per hour. *Room and board:* $2790; room only: $1250. Room and board charges vary according to board plan and housing facility. *Payment plan:* installment. *Waivers:* senior citizens and employees or children of employees.
Financial Aid Of all full-time matriculated undergraduates who enrolled in 2001, 937 applied for aid, 745 were judged to have need, 184 had their need fully met. 175 Federal Work-Study jobs (averaging $1793). In 2001, 141 non-need-based awards were made. *Average percent of need met:* 76%. *Average financial aid package:* $5517. *Average need-based loan:* $2425. *Average need-based gift aid:* $3981. *Average non-need based aid:* $2104. *Average indebtedness upon graduation:* $12,573.
Applying *Options:* common application, electronic application. *Required:* high school transcript. *Recommended:* minimum 2.7 GPA. *Application deadline:* 9/10 (freshmen), rolling (transfers). *Notification:* 2/10 (freshmen).
Admissions Contact Mr. Joseph Evans, Registrar and Director of Admissions and Records, University of Science and Arts of Oklahoma, 1727 West Alabama, Chickasha, OK 73018-5322. *Phone:* 405-574-1204. *Toll-free phone:* 800-933-8726 Ext. 1204. *Fax:* 405-574-1220. *E-mail:* jwevans@usao.edu.

University of Tulsa
Tulsa, Oklahoma

- **Independent** university, founded 1894, affiliated with Presbyterian Church
- **Calendar** semesters
- **Degrees** bachelor's, master's, doctoral, first professional, and first professional certificates
- **Urban** 160-acre campus
- **Endowment** $730.0 million
- **Coed,** 2,769 undergraduate students, 91% full-time, 52% women, 48% men
- **Moderately difficult** entrance level, 67% of applicants were admitted

Undergraduates 2,533 full-time, 236 part-time. Students come from 39 states and territories, 57 other countries, 23% are from out of state, 8% African American, 2% Asian American or Pacific Islander, 3% Hispanic American, 5% Native American, 11% international, 7% transferred in, 52% live on campus. *Retention:* 77% of 2001 full-time freshmen returned.
Freshmen *Admission:* 2,235 applied, 1,505 admitted, 498 enrolled. *Average high school GPA:* 3.70. *Test scores:* SAT verbal scores over 500: 96%; SAT math scores over 500: 93%; ACT scores over 18: 100%; SAT verbal scores over 600: 62%; SAT math scores over 600: 60%; ACT scores over 24: 75%; SAT verbal scores over 700: 21%; SAT math scores over 700: 20%; ACT scores over 30: 23%.
Faculty *Total:* 410, 73% full-time, 96% with terminal degrees. *Student/faculty ratio:* 11:1.
Majors Accounting; anthropology; applied mathematics; art; art history; arts management; athletic training/sports medicine; biochemistry; biology; broadcast journalism; business administration; business marketing and marketing management; chemical engineering; chemistry; communications; computer science; economics; education; electrical engineering; elementary education; engineering; engineering physics; English; environmental science; exercise sciences; finance; French; geology; geophysics/seismology; German; history; information sciences/systems; international business; legal studies; management information systems/business data processing; mathematics; mechanical engineering; music; music (piano and organ performance); music teacher education; music (voice and choral/opera performance); nursing; petroleum engineering; philosophy; physics; political science; psychology; religious studies; sociology; Spanish; special education; speech-language pathology/audiology; sport/fitness administration.
Academic Programs *Special study options:* accelerated degree program, adult/continuing education programs, advanced placement credit, double majors, English as a second language, external degree program, honors programs, independent study, internships, part-time degree program, services for LD students, student-designed majors, study abroad, summer session for credit. *ROTC:* Air Force (c). *Unusual degree programs:* 3-2 law.
Library McFarlin Library plus 1 other with 900,000 titles, 9,100 serial subscriptions, 13,300 audiovisual materials, an OPAC, a Web page.
Computers on Campus 718 computers available on campus for general student use. A campuswide network can be accessed from student residence rooms and from off campus. Internet access, at least one staffed computer lab available.
Student Life *Housing:* on-campus residence required through sophomore year. *Options:* coed, men-only, women-only, disabled students. *Activities and Organizations:* drama/theater group, student-run newspaper, radio and television station, choral group, marching band, Student Association, Residence Hall Association, honor societies, intramural sports, pre-professional clubs, national fraternities, national sororities. *Campus security:* 24-hour emergency response devices and patrols, late-night transport/escort service, controlled dormitory access. *Student Services:* health clinic, personal/psychological counseling, women's center.
Athletics Member NCAA. All Division I except football (Division I-A). *Intercollegiate sports:* basketball M(s)/W(s), crew W(s), cross-country running M(s)/W(s), golf M(s)/W(s), soccer M(s)/W(s), softball W(s), tennis M(s)/W(s), track and field M(s)/W(s), volleyball W(s). *Intramural sports:* badminton M/W,

University of Tulsa (continued)
basketball M/W, bowling M/W, crew M(c), cross-country running M/W, fencing M(c)/W(c), football M/W, golf M/W, racquetball M/W, rugby M(c), soccer M/W, softball M/W, squash M/W, swimming M/W, table tennis M/W, tennis M/W, track and field M/W, volleyball M/W, water polo M/W, weight lifting M/W.

Standardized Tests *Required:* SAT I or ACT (for admission).

Costs (2001–02) *One-time required fee:* $275. *Comprehensive fee:* $19,090 includes full-time tuition ($14,200), mandatory fees ($80), and room and board ($4810). Part-time tuition: $509 per credit hour. *Required fees:* $3 per credit hour. *Room and board:* College room only: $2560. Room and board charges vary according to board plan and housing facility. *Payment plans:* tuition prepayment, installment. *Waivers:* employees or children of employees.

Financial Aid Of all full-time matriculated undergraduates who enrolled in 2001, 2256 applied for aid, 1406 were judged to have need, 434 had their need fully met. In 2001, 568 non-need-based awards were made. *Average percent of need met:* 80%. *Average financial aid package:* $13,275. *Average need-based loan:* $4116. *Average need-based gift aid:* $4536. *Average non-need based aid:* $7167. *Average indebtedness upon graduation:* $17,670.

Applying *Options:* common application, electronic application, early admission, early decision, deferred entrance. *Application fee:* $35. *Required:* high school transcript, 1 letter of recommendation. *Recommended:* essay or personal statement, minimum 3.0 GPA, interview. *Application deadline:* rolling (transfers). *Early decision:* 11/15. *Notification:* continuous (freshmen), 12/15 (early decision).

Admissions Contact Mr. John C. Corso, Associate Vice President for Administration/Dean of Admission, University of Tulsa, 600 South College Avenue, Tulsa, OK 74104. *Phone:* 918-631-2307. *Toll-free phone:* 800-331-3050. *Fax:* 918-631-5003. *E-mail:* admission@utulsa.edu.

OREGON

THE ART INSTITUTE OF PORTLAND
Portland, Oregon

- **Proprietary** 4-year, founded 1963, part of Education Management Corporation
- **Calendar** quarters
- **Degrees** associate and bachelor's
- **Urban** 1-acre campus
- **Coed,** 903 undergraduate students, 79% full-time, 53% women, 47% men
- **Minimally difficult** entrance level, 98% of applicants were admitted

Undergraduates 714 full-time, 189 part-time. 31% are from out of state, 2% African American, 5% Asian American or Pacific Islander, 5% Hispanic American, 1% Native American, 3% international, 15% transferred in, 5% live on campus. *Retention:* 56% of 2001 full-time freshmen returned.

Freshmen *Admission:* 240 applied, 236 admitted, 161 enrolled.

Faculty *Total:* 95, 26% full-time, 29% with terminal degrees. *Student/faculty ratio:* 16:1.

Majors Computer graphics; fashion design/illustration; graphic design/commercial art/illustration; interior design; multimedia.

Academic Programs *Special study options:* academic remediation for entering students, advanced placement credit, independent study, internships, part-time degree program, summer session for credit.

Library AIPD Learning Resource Center with 19,831 titles, 200 serial subscriptions, 400 audiovisual materials.

Computers on Campus 100 computers available on campus for general student use. Internet access, at least one staffed computer lab available.

Student Life *Housing Options:* coed. *Activities and Organizations:* student-run newspaper, Fashion Group International, Interior Design Student Chapter. *Campus security:* 24-hour emergency response devices, security patrol from 4 p.m. to midnight, electronically operated building entrances. *Student Services:* personal/psychological counseling.

Costs (2001–02) *Tuition:* $13,725 full-time, $305 per credit part-time. No tuition increase for student's term of enrollment. *Room only:* $5250. *Payment plan:* installment. *Waivers:* employees or children of employees.

Financial Aid Of all full-time matriculated undergraduates who enrolled in 2001, 513 applied for aid, 455 were judged to have need, 7 had their need fully met. 26 Federal Work-Study jobs (averaging $1905). In 2001, 82 non-need-based awards were made. *Average percent of need met:* 1%. *Average financial aid package:* $2747. *Average need-based loan:* $1346. *Average need-based gift aid:* $1441. *Average non-need based aid:* $2587. *Average indebtedness upon graduation:* $15,600.

Applying *Options:* electronic application, deferred entrance. *Application fee:* $50. *Required:* essay or personal statement, high school transcript, interview. *Required for some:* portfolio. *Recommended:* letters of recommendation. *Application deadline:* rolling (freshmen), rolling (transfers). *Notification:* continuous (freshmen).

Admissions Contact Ms. Kelly Alston, Director of Admissions, The Art Institute of Portland, 2000 Southwest Fifth Avenue, Portland, OR 97201-4907. *Phone:* 503-228-6528 Ext. 139. *Toll-free phone:* 888-228-6528. *Fax:* 503-525-8331. *E-mail:* aipdadm@aii.edu.

CASCADE COLLEGE
Portland, Oregon

- **Independent** 4-year, founded 1994, affiliated with Church of Christ, part of Oklahoma Christian University of Science and Arts
- **Calendar** trimesters
- **Degree** bachelor's
- **Urban** 13-acre campus
- **Endowment** $358,467
- **Coed,** 330 undergraduate students, 92% full-time, 49% women, 51% men
- **Noncompetitive** entrance level, 100% of applicants were admitted

Undergraduates 303 full-time, 27 part-time. Students come from 19 states and territories, 7 other countries, 52% are from out of state, 8% African American, 2% Asian American or Pacific Islander, 3% Hispanic American, 1% Native American, 6% international, 15% transferred in, 68% live on campus. *Retention:* 60% of 2001 full-time freshmen returned.

Freshmen *Admission:* 254 applied, 254 admitted, 76 enrolled. *Test scores:* SAT verbal scores over 500: 62%; SAT math scores over 500: 45%; ACT scores over 18: 85%; SAT verbal scores over 600: 28%; SAT math scores over 600: 9%; ACT scores over 24: 25%; SAT verbal scores over 700: 20%.

Faculty *Total:* 37, 32% full-time, 22% with terminal degrees. *Student/faculty ratio:* 16:1.

Majors Biblical studies; business administration; liberal arts and sciences/liberal studies; missionary studies; psychology.

Academic Programs *Special study options:* academic remediation for entering students, accelerated degree program, advanced placement credit, double majors, independent study, internships, off-campus study, part-time degree program, services for LD students, study abroad, summer session for credit. *ROTC:* Army (c), Air Force (c).

Library E.W. McMillan Library with 28,050 titles, 104 serial subscriptions, an OPAC, a Web page.

Computers on Campus 26 computers available on campus for general student use. A campuswide network can be accessed from student residence rooms and from off campus. Internet access, at least one staffed computer lab available.

Student Life *Housing:* on-campus residence required through senior year. *Options:* coed, men-only, women-only. *Activities and Organizations:* drama/theater group, choral group, choir, service clubs, Student Government. *Campus security:* student patrols, late-night transport/escort service, controlled dormitory access, 8-hour patrols by trained security personnel. *Student Services:* health clinic, personal/psychological counseling.

Athletics Member NAIA, NCCAA. *Intercollegiate sports:* basketball M/W, cross-country running M/W, soccer M/W, track and field M/W, volleyball W. *Intramural sports:* basketball M/W, football M/W, soccer M/W, softball M/W, table tennis M/W, tennis M/W, volleyball M/W.

Standardized Tests *Required:* SAT I or ACT (for placement).

Costs (2001–02) *Comprehensive fee:* $14,800 includes full-time tuition ($9400), mandatory fees ($200), and room and board ($5200). Full-time tuition and fees vary according to course load. Part-time tuition: $392 per semester hour. *Room and board:* Room and board charges vary according to board plan. *Payment plan:* installment. *Waivers:* employees or children of employees.

Financial Aid Of all full-time matriculated undergraduates who enrolled in 2001, 253 applied for aid, 128 were judged to have need, 5 had their need fully met. 42 Federal Work-Study jobs (averaging $1300). In 2001, 74 non-need-based awards were made. *Average percent of need met:* 69%. *Average financial aid package:* $10,819. *Average need-based loan:* $3593. *Average need-based gift aid:* $2965. *Average non-need based aid:* $7179. *Average indebtedness upon graduation:* $19,549. *Financial aid deadline:* 8/1.

Applying *Options:* common application, early admission, deferred entrance. *Application fee:* $25. *Required:* high school transcript. *Recommended:* essay or personal statement, 1 letter of recommendation. *Application deadline:* rolling (freshmen), rolling (transfers).

Admissions Contact Mr. Clint La Rue, Director of Admissions, Cascade College, 9101 East Burnside, Portland, OR 97216-1515. *Phone:* 503-257-1202. *Toll-free phone:* 800-550-7678. *E-mail:* admissions@cascade.edu.

CONCORDIA UNIVERSITY
Portland, Oregon

- **Independent** comprehensive, founded 1905, affiliated with Lutheran Church-Missouri Synod, part of Concordia University System
- **Calendar** semesters
- **Degrees** certificates, associate, bachelor's, master's, post-master's, and postbachelor's certificates
- **Urban** 13-acre campus
- **Endowment** $6.3 million
- **Coed,** 889 undergraduate students, 85% full-time, 63% women, 37% men
- **Moderately difficult** entrance level, 61% of applicants were admitted

Concordia University, Portland, Oregon, an accredited 4-year Lutheran university, is committed to enlightening students to become competent, experienced, and ethical leaders in society. Degree programs in business, health and social services, theological studies, education, and arts and sciences offer the insights and skills that employers and graduate schools seek. Situated in the beautiful Pacific Northwest, Concordia University utilizes the educational, cultural, and recreational resources of this pristine and progressive region.

Undergraduates 756 full-time, 133 part-time. Students come from 30 states and territories, 8 other countries, 42% are from out of state, 5% African American, 3% Asian American or Pacific Islander, 3% Hispanic American, 1% Native American, 6% international, 16% transferred in. *Retention:* 60% of 2001 full-time freshmen returned.

Freshmen *Admission:* 704 applied, 432 admitted, 129 enrolled. *Average high school GPA:* 3.36. *Test scores:* SAT verbal scores over 500: 61%; SAT math scores over 500: 49%; ACT scores over 18: 86%; SAT verbal scores over 600: 16%; SAT math scores over 600: 15%; ACT scores over 24: 19%; SAT verbal scores over 700: 6%; SAT math scores over 700: 1%.

Faculty *Total:* 107, 37% full-time, 44% with terminal degrees. *Student/faculty ratio:* 13:1.

Majors Biological/physical sciences; biology; business administration; chemistry; early childhood education; education; elementary education; English; English education; environmental science; health services administration; humanities; interdisciplinary studies; liberal arts and sciences/liberal studies; mathematics education; natural sciences; physical education; physical sciences; premedicine; pre-theology; psychology; religious education; religious studies; science education; secondary education; social sciences; social studies education; social work; sport/fitness administration; theater arts/drama; theology.

Academic Programs *Special study options:* academic remediation for entering students, accelerated degree program, adult/continuing education programs, advanced placement credit, double majors, English as a second language, internships, off-campus study, part-time degree program, student-designed majors, study abroad, summer session for credit. *ROTC:* Air Force (c).

Library Concordia Library plus 1 other with 56,040 titles, 418 serial subscriptions, 7,764 audiovisual materials, an OPAC.

Computers on Campus 60 computers available on campus for general student use. A campuswide network can be accessed from student residence rooms and from off campus. Internet access, at least one staffed computer lab available.

Student Life *Housing:* on-campus residence required through sophomore year. *Options:* coed. *Activities and Organizations:* drama/theater group, student-run newspaper, choral group, Drama Club, Business Club, Christian Life Ministry, service organization, The Promethean. *Campus security:* 24-hour emergency response devices and patrols, student patrols, late-night transport/escort service, controlled dormitory access. *Student Services:* health clinic, personal/psychological counseling.

Athletics Member NAIA. *Intercollegiate sports:* baseball M(s), basketball M(s)/W(s), soccer M(s)/W(s), softball W(s), volleyball W(s). *Intramural sports:* basketball M/W, volleyball M/W.

Standardized Tests *Required:* SAT I or ACT (for admission).

Costs (2002–03) *Comprehensive fee:* $21,300 includes full-time tuition ($16,900) and room and board ($4400). Full-time tuition and fees vary according to program. Part-time tuition: $517 per credit. Part-time tuition and fees vary according to course load and program. *Room and board:* Room and board charges vary according to housing facility. *Payment plan:* installment. *Waivers:* employees or children of employees.

Financial Aid Of all full-time matriculated undergraduates who enrolled in 2001, 625 applied for aid, 495 were judged to have need, 320 had their need fully met. 75 Federal Work-Study jobs (averaging $1150). 150 State and other part-time jobs (averaging $2050). In 2001, 60 non-need-based awards were made. *Average percent of need met:* 85%. *Average financial aid package:* $12,000. *Average need-based loan:* $5000. *Average need-based gift aid:* $7900. *Average non-need based aid:* $4600. *Average indebtedness upon graduation:* $10,500.

Applying *Options:* electronic application, deferred entrance. *Application fee:* $20. *Required:* essay or personal statement, high school transcript, minimum 2.5 GPA, 1 letter of recommendation. *Required for some:* interview. *Recommended:* interview. *Application deadline:* rolling (freshmen), rolling (transfers). *Notification:* continuous (freshmen).

Admissions Contact Mr. Peter D. Johnson, Director of Admission, Concordia University, 2811 Northeast Holman, Portland, OR 97211-6099. *Phone:* 503-493-6521. *Toll-free phone:* 800-321-9371. *Fax:* 503-280-8531. *E-mail:* admissions@portland.edu.

EASTERN OREGON UNIVERSITY
La Grande, Oregon

- **State-supported** comprehensive, founded 1929, part of Oregon University System
- **Calendar** quarters
- **Degrees** associate, bachelor's, and master's
- **Rural** 121-acre campus
- **Endowment** $1.6 million
- **Coed,** 2,820 undergraduate students, 72% full-time, 58% women, 42% men
- **Moderately difficult** entrance level, 55% of applicants were admitted

Located in the northeast Oregon mountains, this 4-year liberal arts university charges in-state tuition to all undergraduates. Eastern offers twenty-three baccalaureate degree programs; groundbreaking faculty-student research; teacher preparation; preparatory programs for professional school study; BA, BS, and master's degrees; regional and global internships; and study abroad. Eastern emphasizes faculty-student interaction and research.

Undergraduates 2,029 full-time, 791 part-time. Students come from 40 states and territories, 27 other countries, 28% are from out of state, 1% African American, 2% Asian American or Pacific Islander, 3% Hispanic American, 2% Native American, 5% international, 14% transferred in, 15% live on campus. *Retention:* 65% of 2001 full-time freshmen returned.

Freshmen *Admission:* 747 applied, 409 admitted, 365 enrolled. *Average high school GPA:* 3.28. *Test scores:* SAT verbal scores over 500: 44%; ACT scores over 18: 81%; SAT verbal scores over 600: 10%; ACT scores over 24: 24%; SAT verbal scores over 700: 1%; ACT scores over 30: 2%.

Faculty *Total:* 129, 67% full-time, 72% with terminal degrees. *Student/faculty ratio:* 14:1.

Majors Accounting; agricultural business; agricultural economics; agronomy/crop science; anthropology; art; biological/physical sciences; biology; business economics; chemistry; city/community/regional planning; computer science; economics; education; English; fire science; history; liberal arts and sciences/liberal studies; mathematics; music; natural resources management; physical education; physics; pre-dentistry; pre-law; pre-medicine; pre-veterinary studies; psychology; secretarial science; sociology; special education; theater arts/drama.

Academic Programs *Special study options:* academic remediation for entering students, adult/continuing education programs, advanced placement credit, cooperative education, distance learning, double majors, English as a second language, external degree program, independent study, internships, off-campus study, part-time degree program, services for LD students, student-designed majors, study abroad, summer session for credit. *ROTC:* Army (b). *Unusual degree programs:* 3-2 engineering with Oregon State University; nursing with Oregon Health Sciences University; agriculture with Oregon State University.

Library Pierce Library plus 1 other with 329,942 titles, 998 serial subscriptions, 35,556 audiovisual materials, an OPAC, a Web page.

Computers on Campus 125 computers available on campus for general student use. A campuswide network can be accessed from student residence rooms and from off campus. Internet access, online (class) registration, at least one staffed computer lab available.

Student Life *Housing:* on-campus residence required for freshman year. *Options:* coed, men-only, women-only. *Activities and Organizations:* drama/theater group, student-run newspaper, radio station, choral group, Outdoor Club, Island Magic, student radio station, Intramurals, Student government. *Campus security:* 24-hour emergency response devices and patrols, late-night transport/escort service, controlled dormitory access. *Student Services:* health clinic, personal/psychological counseling.

Athletics Member NCAA, NAIA. All NCAA Division III. *Intercollegiate sports:* baseball M, basketball M/W, cross-country running M/W, football M, golf M(c)/W(c), rugby M(c), skiing (cross-country) M(c)/W(c), skiing (downhill)

Eastern Oregon University (continued)

M(c)/W(c), softball W, tennis M(c)/W(c), track and field M/W, volleyball M(c)/W. *Intramural sports:* badminton M/W, basketball M/W, football M/W, golf M/W, racquetball M/W, softball M/W, tennis M/W, volleyball M/W, weight lifting M.

Standardized Tests *Required:* SAT I or ACT (for admission).

Costs (2001–02) *Tuition:* $173 per credit hour part-time; state resident $2409 full-time; nonresident $2409 full-time. Full-time tuition and fees vary according to location. Part-time tuition and fees vary according to course load and location. *Required fees:* $1212 full-time. *Room and board:* $5151. Room and board charges vary according to board plan and housing facility. *Payment plan:* installment. *Waivers:* employees or children of employees.

Financial Aid Of all full-time matriculated undergraduates who enrolled in 2001, 1578 applied for aid, 1244 were judged to have need, 339 had their need fully met. In 2001, 285 non-need-based awards were made. *Average percent of need met:* 73%. *Average financial aid package:* $8732. *Average need-based loan:* $3329. *Average need-based gift aid:* $2172. *Average indebtedness upon graduation:* $14,147.

Applying *Options:* early admission, early action, deferred entrance. *Application fee:* $50. *Required:* high school transcript, minimum 3.0 GPA. *Required for some:* essay or personal statement, 2 letters of recommendation. *Application deadline:* 9/27 (freshmen). *Notification:* continuous (freshmen), 1/15 (early action).

Admissions Contact Ms. Christian Steinmetz, Director, Admissions, Eastern Oregon University, One University Boulevard, La Grande, OR 97850. *Phone:* 541-962-3393. *Toll-free phone:* 800-452-8639. *Fax:* 541-962-3418. *E-mail:* admissions@eou.edu.

EUGENE BIBLE COLLEGE
Eugene, Oregon

- **Independent** 4-year, founded 1925, affiliated with Open Bible Standard Churches
- **Calendar** quarters
- **Degree** certificates and bachelor's
- **Suburban** 40-acre campus
- **Endowment** $546,055
- **Coed,** 179 undergraduate students, 72% full-time, 47% women, 53% men
- **Minimally difficult** entrance level, 56% of applicants were admitted

Since 1925, Eugene Bible College has been fulfilling the Great Commission by equipping students for spirit-empowered leadership and ministry. In addition to the bachelor degree programs, Eugene Bible College offers students opportunities for community ministry, music, drama, athletics, and other activities that open doors to spiritual growth, fellowship, and lifelong friendships.

Undergraduates 128 full-time, 51 part-time. Students come from 18 states and territories, 4 other countries, 49% are from out of state, 0.8% African American, 0.8% Asian American or Pacific Islander, 0.8% Hispanic American, 0.8% Native American, 11% transferred in, 53% live on campus. *Retention:* 51% of 2001 full-time freshmen returned.

Freshmen *Admission:* 91 applied, 51 admitted, 51 enrolled. *Average high school GPA:* 2.85. *Test scores:* SAT verbal scores over 500: 28%; SAT math scores over 500: 40%; ACT scores over 18: 65%; SAT verbal scores over 600: 5%; SAT math scores over 600: 5%; ACT scores over 24: 26%; SAT verbal scores over 700: 1%; SAT math scores over 700: 1%.

Faculty *Total:* 23, 39% full-time, 26% with terminal degrees. *Student/faculty ratio:* 15:1.

Majors Biblical studies; divinity/ministry; missionary studies; pastoral counseling; religious education; religious music.

Academic Programs *Special study options:* academic remediation for entering students, advanced placement credit, distance learning, double majors, independent study, internships, part-time degree program, summer session for credit.

Library Flint Memorial Library with 34,000 titles, 260 serial subscriptions, 288 audiovisual materials.

Computers on Campus 10 computers available on campus for general student use. A campuswide network can be accessed from that provide access to e-mail. At least one staffed computer lab available.

Student Life *Housing:* on-campus residence required through junior year. *Options:* men-only, women-only. *Activities and Organizations:* drama/theater group, choral group, Harvesters, Lights of the World, Element X. *Campus security:* 24-hour emergency response devices, student patrols, controlled dormitory access. *Student Services:* personal/psychological counseling.

Athletics Member NCCAA. *Intercollegiate sports:* basketball M. *Intramural sports:* basketball M/W, football M, golf M, soccer M, volleyball M/W.

Standardized Tests *Required:* SAT I or ACT (for admission).

Costs (2001–02) *Comprehensive fee:* $10,575 includes full-time tuition ($5985), mandatory fees ($645), and room and board ($3945). Part-time tuition: $175 per credit. Part-time tuition and fees vary according to class time and course load. *Required fees:* $136 per term part-time. *Room and board:* Room and board charges vary according to housing facility. *Payment plans:* tuition prepayment, installment. *Waivers:* senior citizens and employees or children of employees.

Financial Aid Of all full-time matriculated undergraduates who enrolled in 2001, 95 applied for aid, 84 were judged to have need, 30 had their need fully met. 10 Federal Work-Study jobs (averaging $2000). 27 State and other part-time jobs (averaging $1700). In 2001, 10 non-need-based awards were made. *Average financial aid package:* $5000. *Average need-based loan:* $3600. *Average need-based gift aid:* $3000. *Average non-need based aid:* $600. *Average indebtedness upon graduation:* $14,464. *Financial aid deadline:* 9/1.

Applying *Application fee:* $30. *Required:* essay or personal statement, high school transcript, minimum 2.0 GPA, 2 letters of recommendation. *Application deadlines:* 9/1 (freshmen), 9/1 (transfers). *Notification:* continuous until 9/1 (freshmen).

Admissions Contact Mr. Trent Combs, Director of Admissions, Eugene Bible College, 2155 Bailey Hill Road, Eugene, OR 97405. *Phone:* 541-485-1780 Ext. 135. *Toll-free phone:* 800-322-2638. *Fax:* 541-343-5801. *E-mail:* admissions@ebc.edu.

GEORGE FOX UNIVERSITY
Newberg, Oregon

- **Independent Friends** university, founded 1891
- **Calendar** semesters
- **Degrees** bachelor's, master's, doctoral, and first professional
- **Small-town** 73-acre campus with easy access to Portland
- **Endowment** $16.9 million
- **Coed,** 1,665 undergraduate students, 79% full-time, 59% women, 41% men
- **Moderately difficult** entrance level, 91% of applicants were admitted

Undergraduates 1,314 full-time, 351 part-time. Students come from 25 states and territories, 16 other countries, 39% are from out of state, 1.0% African American, 2% Asian American or Pacific Islander, 3% Hispanic American, 1.0% Native American, 3% international, 4% transferred in, 59% live on campus. *Retention:* 83% of 2001 full-time freshmen returned.

Freshmen *Admission:* 824 applied, 748 admitted, 318 enrolled. *Average high school GPA:* 3.59. *Test scores:* SAT verbal scores over 500: 82%; SAT math scores over 500: 77%; ACT scores over 18: 94%; SAT verbal scores over 600: 37%; SAT math scores over 600: 33%; ACT scores over 24: 47%; SAT verbal scores over 700: 8%; SAT math scores over 700: 5%; ACT scores over 30: 9%.

Faculty *Total:* 134, 53% full-time, 41% with terminal degrees. *Student/faculty ratio:* 15:1.

Majors Art; athletic training/sports medicine; biblical studies; biology; biology education; business administration; business economics; chemistry; chemistry education; clinical psychology; cognitive psychology/psycholinguistics; communications; computer/information sciences; education (multiple levels); elementary education; engineering; English; English education; family resource management studies; fashion merchandising; health education; history; home economics; home economics education; human resources management; interdisciplinary studies; international relations; management information systems/business data processing; mathematics; mathematics education; missionary studies; music; music teacher education; nursing related; pastoral counseling; physical education; psychology; public relations; radio/television broadcasting; religious education; religious studies; social studies education; social work; sociology; Spanish; sport/fitness administration.

Academic Programs *Special study options:* academic remediation for entering students, accelerated degree program, adult/continuing education programs, advanced placement credit, cooperative education, distance learning, double majors, English as a second language, external degree program, honors programs, independent study, internships, off-campus study, part-time degree program, services for LD students, student-designed majors, study abroad. *ROTC:* Air Force (c). *Unusual degree programs:* 3-2 engineering with University of Portland, Washington University in St. Louis, Oregon State University.

Library Murdock Learning Resource Center plus 1 other with 123,734 titles, 1,323 serial subscriptions, 2,687 audiovisual materials, an OPAC, a Web page.

Computers on Campus 1300 computers available on campus for general student use. A campuswide network can be accessed from student residence rooms and from off campus. Internet access, online (class) registration, at least one staffed computer lab available.

Student Life *Housing:* on-campus residence required through junior year. *Options:* men-only, women-only. *Activities and Organizations:* drama/theater group, student-run newspaper, radio station, choral group, student government, student activities, Christian Ministries, Orientation Committee, Chaplain's Committee. *Campus security:* 24-hour emergency response devices and patrols, student patrols, late-night transport/escort service, controlled dormitory access. *Student Services:* health clinic, personal/psychological counseling.

Athletics Member NAIA. *Intercollegiate sports:* baseball M, basketball M/W, cross-country running M/W, soccer M/W, softball W, tennis M/W, track and field M/W, volleyball W. *Intramural sports:* badminton M/W, basketball M/W, football M/W, golf M/W, racquetball M/W, soccer M/W, table tennis M/W, tennis W, volleyball M/W, weight lifting M/W.

Standardized Tests *Required:* SAT I or ACT (for admission).

Costs (2001–02) *Comprehensive fee:* $24,095 includes full-time tuition ($18,000), mandatory fees ($325), and room and board ($5770). Full-time tuition and fees vary according to program. Part-time tuition: $557 per semester hour. Part-time tuition and fees vary according to course load. *Required fees:* $100 per term part-time. *Room and board:* College room only: $2940. Room and board charges vary according to housing facility and location. *Payment plan:* installment. *Waivers:* minority students, senior citizens, and employees or children of employees.

Financial Aid Of all full-time matriculated undergraduates who enrolled in 2001, 1247 applied for aid, 995 were judged to have need, 284 had their need fully met. 788 Federal Work-Study jobs (averaging $1907). 19 State and other part-time jobs (averaging $1503). *Average percent of need met:* 82%. *Average financial aid package:* $12,162. *Average need-based loan:* $4062. *Average need-based gift aid:* $19,877. *Average indebtedness upon graduation:* $16,912.

Applying *Options:* common application, electronic application, early admission, deferred entrance. *Application fee:* $40. *Required:* essay or personal statement, high school transcript, 2 letters of recommendation. *Required for some:* interview. *Recommended:* interview. *Application deadlines:* 6/1 (freshmen), 6/1 (transfers). *Notification:* continuous until 9/1 (freshmen).

Admissions Contact Mr. Dale Seipp, Director of Admissions, George Fox University, 414 North Meridian, Newberg, CT 97132. *Phone:* 503-554-2240. *Toll-free phone:* 800-765-4369. *Fax:* 503-554-3110. *E-mail:* admissions@georgefox.edu.

ITT Technical Institute
Portland, Oregon

- **Proprietary** primarily 2-year, founded 1971, part of ITT Educational Services, Inc
- **Calendar** quarters
- **Degrees** associate and bachelor's
- **Urban** 4-acre campus
- **Coed,** 499 undergraduate students
- **Minimally difficult** entrance level

Majors Computer/information sciences related; computer programming; design/applied arts related; drafting; electrical/electronic engineering technologies related; information technology; robotics technology.

Student Life *Housing:* college housing not available. *Activities and Organizations:* student-run newspaper.

Costs (2001–02) *Tuition:* Full-time tuition and fees vary according to program. Part-time tuition and fees vary according to program. $260—$330 per credit hour.

Applying *Options:* deferred entrance. *Application fee:* $100. *Required:* high school transcript, interview. *Recommended:* letters of recommendation. *Application deadline:* rolling (freshmen), rolling (transfers). *Notification:* continuous (freshmen).

Admissions Contact Mr. Cliff Custer, Director of Recruitment, ITT Technical Institute, 6035 Northeast 78th Court, Portland, OR 97218-2854. *Phone:* 503-255-6500 Ext. 314. *Toll-free phone:* 800-234-5488.

Lewis & Clark College
Portland, Oregon

- **Independent** comprehensive, founded 1867
- **Calendar** semesters
- **Degrees** bachelor's, master's, first professional, and first professional certificates
- **Suburban** 115-acre campus
- **Endowment** $138.0 million
- **Coed,** 1,682 undergraduate students, 98% full-time, 60% women, 40% men
- **Very difficult** entrance level, 67% of applicants were admitted

Lewis & Clark combines a solid foundation in the liberal arts and sciences with a reputation as a national college with a global reach. Students come from 50 states and 34 countries. More than 62% participate in overseas and off-campus study programs. Portland provides many internship and community service opportunities. Lewis & Clark also offers one of the top-rated outdoors programs in the country.

Undergraduates 1,644 full-time, 38 part-time. Students come from 51 states and territories, 26 other countries, 77% are from out of state, 1% African American, 6% Asian American or Pacific Islander, 3% Hispanic American, 1% Native American, 5% international, 4% transferred in, 57% live on campus. *Retention:* 82% of 2001 full-time freshmen returned.

Freshmen *Admission:* 3,040 applied, 2,025 admitted, 416 enrolled. *Average high school GPA:* 3.60. *Test scores:* SAT verbal scores over 500: 98%; SAT math scores over 500: 97%; ACT scores over 18: 99%; SAT verbal scores over 600: 80%; SAT math scores over 600: 61%; ACT scores over 24: 70%; SAT verbal scores over 700: 22%; SAT math scores over 700: 13%; ACT scores over 30: 26%.

Faculty *Total:* 334, 57% full-time, 77% with terminal degrees. *Student/faculty ratio:* 12:1.

Majors Anthropology; art; biochemistry; biology; chemistry; computer science; East Asian studies; economics; English; environmental science; French; German; Hispanic-American studies; history; international relations; mass communications; mathematics; modern languages; music; philosophy; physics; political science; pre-dentistry; pre-engineering; pre-law; pre-medicine; pre-veterinary studies; psychology; religious studies; sociology; Spanish; theater arts/drama.

Academic Programs *Special study options:* accelerated degree program, advanced placement credit, double majors, English as a second language, honors programs, independent study, internships, off-campus study, part-time degree program, services for LD students, student-designed majors, study abroad, summer session for credit. *Unusual degree programs:* 3-2 engineering with Columbia University, Washington University in St. Louis, University of Southern California, Oregon Health Sciences University.

Library Aubrey Watzek Library plus 1 other with 442,265 titles, 8,326 serial subscriptions, 9,046 audiovisual materials, an OPAC, a Web page.

Computers on Campus 150 computers available on campus for general student use. A campuswide network can be accessed from student residence rooms and from off campus. Internet access, at least one staffed computer lab available.

Student Life *Housing:* on-campus residence required through sophomore year. *Options:* coed. *Activities and Organizations:* drama/theater group, student-run newspaper, radio and television station, choral group, College Outdoors, Associated Students, Center for Service and Work, musical groups, student radio station. *Campus security:* 24-hour emergency response devices and patrols, student patrols, late-night transport/escort service, controlled dormitory access. *Student Services:* health clinic, personal/psychological counseling, women's center.

Athletics Member NCAA, NAIA. All NCAA Division III. *Intercollegiate sports:* baseball M, basketball M/W, crew M/W, cross-country running M/W, football M, golf M/W, lacrosse M(c)/W(c), rugby M(c)/W(c), soccer M(c)/W(c), softball W, swimming M/W, tennis M/W, track and field M/W, volleyball W. *Intramural sports:* badminton M/W, basketball M/W, cross-country running M/W, football M/W, softball M/W, swimming M/W, table tennis M/W, tennis M/W, volleyball M/W, water polo M/W.

Costs (2001–02) *Comprehensive fee:* $29,460 includes full-time tuition ($22,610), mandatory fees ($200), and room and board ($6650). Part-time tuition: $1131 per semester hour. Part-time tuition and fees vary according to course load. *Room and board:* College room only: $3450. Room and board charges vary according to board plan and student level. *Payment plan:* installment. *Waivers:* employees or children of employees.

Financial Aid Of all full-time matriculated undergraduates who enrolled in 2001, 1014 applied for aid, 889 were judged to have need, 445 had their need fully met. 664 Federal Work-Study jobs (averaging $1634). In 2001, 243 non-need-based awards were made. *Average percent of need met:* 88%. *Average financial aid package:* $18,957. *Average need-based loan:* $4561. *Average need-based gift aid:* $13,288. *Average non-need based aid:* $8454. *Average indebtedness upon graduation:* $15,845.

Applying *Options:* common application, electronic application, early admission, early action, deferred entrance. *Application fee:* $45. *Required:* essay or personal statement, high school transcript, minimum 2.0 GPA, 2 letters of recommendation. *Required for some:* 4 letters of recommendation, portfolio applicants must submit samples of graded work. *Recommended:* minimum 3.0 GPA, interview. *Application deadline:* 2/1 (freshmen). *Notification:* 4/1 (freshmen), 1/15 (early action).

Admissions Contact Mr. Michael Sexton, Dean of Admissions, Lewis & Clark College, 0615 SW Palatine Hill Road, Portland, OR 97219-7899. *Phone:* 503-768-7040. *Toll-free phone:* 800-444-4111. *Fax:* 503-768-7055. *E-mail:* admissions@lclark.edu.

Linfield College
McMinnville, Oregon

- **Independent American Baptist Churches in the USA** 4-year, founded 1849
- **Calendar** 4-1-4
- **Degree** bachelor's
- **Small-town** 95-acre campus with easy access to Portland
- **Endowment** $57.0 million
- **Coed,** 1,602 undergraduate students, 98% full-time, 55% women, 45% men
- **Moderately difficult** entrance level, 80% of applicants were admitted

Linfield College, tracing its roots back to 1849, is an independent, 4-year institution nationally recognized for its strong teaching faculty, outstanding science programs, and extensive study-abroad opportunities. Nearly 50 percent of graduating students have spent a January term, a semester, or an academic year in another country. Linfield is located in the heart of the Willamette Valley.

Undergraduates 1,571 full-time, 31 part-time. Students come from 33 states and territories, 24 other countries, 41% are from out of state, 2% African American, 6% Asian American or Pacific Islander, 3% Hispanic American, 0.6% Native American, 2% international, 3% transferred in, 74% live on campus. *Retention:* 84% of 2001 full-time freshmen returned.

Freshmen *Admission:* 1,693 applied, 1,356 admitted, 422 enrolled. *Average high school GPA:* 3.50. *Test scores:* SAT verbal scores over 500: 74%; SAT math scores over 500: 77%; ACT scores over 18: 94%; SAT verbal scores over 600: 26%; SAT math scores over 600: 26%; ACT scores over 24: 48%; SAT verbal scores over 700: 4%; SAT math scores over 700: 2%; ACT scores over 30: 5%.

Faculty *Total:* 158, 63% full-time, 75% with terminal degrees. *Student/faculty ratio:* 12:1.

Majors Accounting; anthropology; area, ethnic, and cultural studies related; art; athletic training/sports medicine; biology; business; chemistry; communications; computer science; creative writing; economics; elementary education; English; exercise sciences; finance; French; German; health/physical education; history; international business; mathematics; music; philosophy; physical sciences; physics; political science; psychology; religious studies; sociology; Spanish; theater arts/drama.

Academic Programs *Special study options:* accelerated degree program, adult/continuing education programs, advanced placement credit, cooperative education, distance learning, double majors, English as a second language, external degree program, honors programs, independent study, internships, off-campus study, part-time degree program, services for LD students, student-designed majors, study abroad, summer session for credit. *ROTC:* Army (c), Air Force (c). *Unusual degree programs:* 3-2 engineering with Washington State University, Oregon State University, University of Southern California.

Library Emanuel Northup Library with 160,227 titles, 1,309 serial subscriptions, 12,228 audiovisual materials, an OPAC, a Web page.

Computers on Campus 189 computers available on campus for general student use. A campuswide network can be accessed from student residence rooms and from off campus. Internet access, at least one staffed computer lab available.

Student Life *Housing:* on-campus residence required through junior year. *Options:* coed, men-only, women-only. *Activities and Organizations:* drama/theater group, student-run newspaper, radio station, choral group, Campus Crusade for Christ, club sports, Hawaiian Club, Ski Club, Habitat for Humanity, national fraternities, national sororities. *Campus security:* 24-hour emergency response devices and patrols, student patrols, late-night transport/escort service. *Student Services:* health clinic, personal/psychological counseling, women's center.

Athletics Member NCAA. All Division III. *Intercollegiate sports:* baseball M, basketball M/W, cross-country running M/W, football M, golf M/W, lacrosse W, soccer M/W, softball W, swimming M/W, tennis M/W, track and field M/W, volleyball W. *Intramural sports:* basketball M/W, bowling M/W, football M/W, lacrosse M, soccer M/W, softball M/W, volleyball M/W, water polo M/W.

Standardized Tests *Required:* SAT I or ACT (for admission).

Costs (2001–02) *One-time required fee:* $300. *Comprehensive fee:* $25,840 includes full-time tuition ($19,380), mandatory fees ($170), and room and board ($6290). Part-time tuition: $605 per credit hour. Part-time tuition and fees vary according to course load. *Required fees:* $45 per term part-time. *Room and board:* College room only: $3130. Room and board charges vary according to housing facility. *Payment plan:* installment. *Waivers:* senior citizens and employees or children of employees.

Financial Aid Of all full-time matriculated undergraduates who enrolled in 2001, 1451 applied for aid, 1047 were judged to have need, 620 had their need fully met. 705 Federal Work-Study jobs (averaging $1523). In 2001, 437 non-need-based awards were made. *Average percent of need met:* 88%. *Average financial aid package:* $15,566. *Average need-based loan:* $4492. *Average need-based gift aid:* $4917. *Average non-need based aid:* $6094. *Average indebtedness upon graduation:* $17,000.

Applying *Options:* common application, electronic application, early action, deferred entrance. *Application fee:* $40. *Required:* essay or personal statement, high school transcript, 2 letters of recommendation. *Recommended:* interview. *Application deadlines:* 2/15 (freshmen), 4/15 (transfers). *Notification:* 4/1 (freshmen), 1/15 (early action).

Admissions Contact Ms. Lisa Knodle-Bragiel, Director of Admissions, Linfield College, McMinnville, OR 97128-6894. *Phone:* 503-434-2489. *Toll-free phone:* 800-640-2287. *Fax:* 503-434-2472. *E-mail:* admissions@linfield.edu.

Marylhurst University
Marylhurst, Oregon

- **Independent Roman Catholic** comprehensive, founded 1893
- **Calendar** quarters
- **Degrees** bachelor's, master's, post-master's, and postbachelor's certificates
- **Suburban** 73-acre campus with easy access to Portland
- **Endowment** $10.0 million
- **Coed,** 672 undergraduate students, 30% full-time, 78% women, 22% men
- **Noncompetitive** entrance level, 100% of applicants were admitted

Undergraduates 204 full-time, 468 part-time. Students come from 9 states and territories, 22 other countries, 12% are from out of state, 1% African American, 2% Asian American or Pacific Islander, 0.6% Hispanic American, 11% international, 81% transferred in, 3% live on campus. *Retention:* 50% of 2001 full-time freshmen returned.

Freshmen *Admission:* 7 applied, 7 admitted, 14 enrolled.

Faculty *Total:* 192, 16% full-time, 32% with terminal degrees. *Student/faculty ratio:* 7:1.

Majors Art; biological/physical sciences; British literature; business administration; creative writing; divinity/ministry; education related; environmental science; ethnic/cultural studies related; history related; interdisciplinary studies; interior design; mass communications; music; music related; pastoral counseling; psychology; public relations; real estate; religious studies; social sciences.

Academic Programs *Special study options:* accelerated degree program, adult/continuing education programs, advanced placement credit, distance learning, double majors, English as a second language, independent study, internships, off-campus study, part-time degree program, services for LD students, student-designed majors, summer session for credit.

Library Shoen Library with 1,449 audiovisual materials, an OPAC, a Web page.

Computers on Campus 40 computers available on campus for general student use. Internet access, online (class) registration, at least one staffed computer lab available.

Student Life *Housing Options:* coed. *Activities and Organizations:* choral group, Toastmasters, Environmental Science Club, Student Ambassadors, Bahia Club, Student Government. *Campus security:* 24-hour emergency response devices and patrols, late-night transport/escort service, controlled dormitory access. *Student Services:* personal/psychological counseling.

Costs (2001–02) *Tuition:* $11,655 full-time, $259 per credit hour part-time. Full-time tuition and fees vary according to course load. Part-time tuition and fees vary according to course load. *Required fees:* $195 full-time, $42 per term part-time. *Room only:* Room and board charges vary according to housing facility. *Payment plans:* installment, deferred payment. *Waivers:* employees or children of employees.

Financial Aid Of all full-time matriculated undergraduates who enrolled in 2001, 128 applied for aid, 101 were judged to have need, 12 had their need fully met. In 2001, 27 non-need-based awards were made. *Average percent of need met:* 63%. *Average financial aid package:* $9011. *Average need-based loan:* $3558. *Average need-based gift aid:* $5935. *Average non-need based aid:* $3960. *Average indebtedness upon graduation:* $9055.

Applying *Options:* deferred entrance. *Application fee:* $20. *Required:* high school transcript. *Application deadline:* rolling (freshmen), rolling (transfers). *Notification:* continuous (freshmen).

Admissions Contact Mr. John French, Academic Advising Specialist, Marylhurst University, 17600 Pacific Highway (Hwy 43), PO Box 261, Marylhurst, OR 97036. *Phone:* 503-699-6268 Ext. 3325. *Toll-free phone:* 800-634-9982 Ext. 6268. *Fax:* 503-635-6585. *E-mail:* admissions@marylhurst.edu.

Mount Angel Seminary
Saint Benedict, Oregon

Admissions Contact Registrar/Admissions Officer, Mount Angel Seminary, Saint Benedict, OR 97373. *Phone:* 503-845-3951 Ext. 14.

MULTNOMAH BIBLE COLLEGE AND BIBLICAL SEMINARY
Portland, Oregon

- **Independent interdenominational** comprehensive, founded 1936
- **Calendar** early semesters
- **Degrees** bachelor's, master's, and first professional
- **Urban** 22-acre campus
- **Endowment** $5.6 million
- **Coed,** 587 undergraduate students, 89% full-time, 48% women, 52% men
- **Moderately difficult** entrance level, 79% of applicants were admitted

Undergraduates 520 full-time, 67 part-time. Students come from 39 states and territories, 6 other countries, 47% are from out of state, 0.7% African American, 4% Asian American or Pacific Islander, 2% Hispanic American, 0.2% Native American, 0.9% international, 18% transferred in, 53% live on campus. *Retention:* 66% of 2001 full-time freshmen returned.

Freshmen *Admission:* 176 applied, 139 admitted, 83 enrolled. *Test scores:* SAT verbal scores over 500: 74%; SAT math scores over 500: 53%; ACT scores over 18: 83%; SAT verbal scores over 600: 29%; SAT math scores over 600: 22%; ACT scores over 24: 44%; SAT verbal scores over 700: 2%; SAT math scores over 700: 2%.

Faculty *Total:* 39, 46% full-time, 33% with terminal degrees. *Student/faculty ratio:* 19:1.

Majors Biblical languages/literatures; biblical studies; communications; divinity/ministry; Greek (ancient and medieval); history; journalism; missionary studies; music; pastoral counseling; religious education; theology.

Academic Programs *Special study options:* academic remediation for entering students, adult/continuing education programs, advanced placement credit, double majors, internships, part-time degree program, services for LD students, summer session for credit.

Library John Mitchell Library with 55,427 titles, 377 serial subscriptions, 940 audiovisual materials, an OPAC.

Computers on Campus 39 computers available on campus for general student use. A campuswide network can be accessed from student residence rooms and from off campus. Internet access, at least one staffed computer lab available.

Student Life *Housing:* on-campus residence required through senior year. *Options:* men-only, women-only. *Activities and Organizations:* drama/theater group, student-run newspaper, choral group. *Campus security:* 24-hour emergency response devices and patrols, late-night transport/escort service, controlled dormitory access. *Student Services:* health clinic, personal/psychological counseling.

Athletics Member NCCAA. *Intercollegiate sports:* basketball M/W, soccer M(c), tennis M(c)/W(c), volleyball W. *Intramural sports:* basketball M/W, football M, tennis M/W, volleyball M/W.

Standardized Tests *Required:* SAT I or ACT (for admission).

Costs (2001–02) *One-time required fee:* $60. *Comprehensive fee:* $13,630 includes full-time tuition ($9350), mandatory fees ($190), and room and board ($4090). Part-time tuition: $390 per semester hour. Part-time tuition and fees vary according to course load. *Room and board:* College room only: $1990. Room and board charges vary according to board plan and housing facility. *Payment plan:* installment. *Waivers:* employees or children of employees.

Financial Aid Of all full-time matriculated undergraduates who enrolled in 2001, 439 applied for aid, 391 were judged to have need, 12 had their need fully met. 85 Federal Work-Study jobs (averaging $1660). *Average percent of need met:* 60%. *Average financial aid package:* $7361. *Average need-based loan:* $3703. *Average need-based gift aid:* $3790. *Average indebtedness upon graduation:* $17,000.

Applying *Options:* deferred entrance. *Application fee:* $40. *Required:* essay or personal statement, high school transcript, minimum 2.5 GPA, 4 letters of recommendation. *Application deadlines:* 7/15 (freshmen), 7/15 (transfers). *Notification:* 8/15 (freshmen).

Admissions Contact Ms. Nancy Gerecz, Admissions Assistant, Multnomah Bible College and Biblical Seminary, 8435 Northeast Glisan Street, Portland, OR 97220-5898. *Phone:* 503-255-0332 Ext. 373. *Toll-free phone:* 800-275-4672. *Fax:* 503-254-1268. *E-mail:* admiss@multnomah.edu.

NORTHWEST CHRISTIAN COLLEGE
Eugene, Oregon

- **Independent interdenominational** comprehensive, founded 1895
- **Calendar** quarters
- **Degrees** certificates, associate, bachelor's, and master's
- **Urban** 8-acre campus with easy access to Portland
- **Endowment** $5.3 million
- **Coed,** 409 undergraduate students, 93% full-time, 62% women, 38% men
- **Moderately difficult** entrance level, 99% of applicants were admitted

Undergraduates 382 full-time, 27 part-time. Students come from 14 states and territories, 15% are from out of state, 4% African American, 1.0% Asian American or Pacific Islander, 2% Hispanic American, 1% Native American, 24% transferred in, 38% live on campus. *Retention:* 49% of 2001 full-time freshmen returned.

Freshmen *Admission:* 141 applied, 140 admitted, 53 enrolled. *Average high school GPA:* 3.20. *Test scores:* SAT verbal scores over 500: 48%; SAT math scores over 500: 53%; ACT scores over 18: 86%; SAT verbal scores over 600: 12%; SAT math scores over 600: 5%; ACT scores over 24: 14%; SAT verbal scores over 700: 5%; ACT scores over 30: 14%.

Faculty *Total:* 57, 35% full-time, 54% with terminal degrees. *Student/faculty ratio:* 13:1.

Majors Biblical studies; business administration; business communications; business marketing and marketing management; elementary education; general studies; humanities; information sciences/systems; interdisciplinary studies; missionary studies; music; pre-theology; psychology; social sciences; speech/rhetorical studies.

Academic Programs *Special study options:* academic remediation for entering students, accelerated degree program, adult/continuing education programs, advanced placement credit, cooperative education, double majors, independent study, internships, off-campus study, part-time degree program, services for LD students, student-designed majors, study abroad. *ROTC:* Army (c).

Library Kellenberger Library with 60,247 titles, 261 serial subscriptions, an OPAC.

Computers on Campus 40 computers available on campus for general student use. Internet access, at least one staffed computer lab available.

Student Life *Housing:* on-campus residence required through sophomore year. *Options:* coed, men-only, women-only. *Activities and Organizations:* drama/theater group, student-run newspaper, choral group, Praise Gathering, Spirit Club, Teachers for Tomorrow, Environmental Club, Drama Club. *Campus security:* 24-hour emergency response devices, late-night transport/escort service, controlled dormitory access, late-night patrols by trained security personnel. *Student Services:* personal/psychological counseling.

Athletics Member NCCAA, NSCAA. *Intercollegiate sports:* basketball M(s), softball W(s). *Intramural sports:* basketball W.

Standardized Tests *Required:* SAT I or ACT (for admission). *Required for some:* SAT II: Subject Tests (for admission).

Costs (2001–02) *Comprehensive fee:* $19,827 includes full-time tuition ($14,580) and room and board ($5247). Part-time tuition: $324 per credit. *Room and board:* College room only: $2130. Room and board charges vary according to board plan and housing facility. *Payment plans:* installment, deferred payment. *Waivers:* employees or children of employees.

Financial Aid Of all full-time matriculated undergraduates who enrolled in 2001, 49 Federal Work-Study jobs (averaging $2550). 88 State and other part-time jobs (averaging $2550). *Average indebtedness upon graduation:* $18,687.

Applying *Options:* common application, electronic application, deferred entrance. *Required:* essay or personal statement, high school transcript, minimum 2.5 GPA, 2 letters of recommendation. *Recommended:* interview. *Application deadline:* rolling (freshmen), rolling (transfers). *Notification:* continuous (freshmen).

Admissions Contact Mr. Bill Stenberg, Director of Admissions, Northwest Christian College, 828 East 11th Avenue, Eugene, OR 97401-3745. *Phone:* 541-684-7209. *Toll-free phone:* 877-463-6622. *Fax:* 541-684-7317. *E-mail:* admissions@nwcc.edu.

OREGON COLLEGE OF ART & CRAFT
Portland, Oregon

- **Independent** 4-year, founded 1907
- **Calendar** semesters
- **Degrees** certificates, bachelor's, and postbachelor's certificates
- **Urban** 7-acre campus
- **Endowment** $5.2 million
- **Coed,** 92 undergraduate students, 60% full-time, 73% women, 27% men
- **Minimally difficult** entrance level, 29% of applicants were admitted

Undergraduates 55 full-time, 37 part-time. Students come from 21 states and territories, 51% are from out of state, 3% Asian American or Pacific Islander, 1% Hispanic American, 1% international, 37% transferred in. *Retention:* 100% of 2001 full-time freshmen returned.

Freshmen *Admission:* 7 applied, 2 admitted, 1 enrolled. *Average high school GPA:* 2.83.

Oregon College of Art & Craft (continued)

Faculty *Total:* 17, 35% full-time, 76% with terminal degrees. *Student/faculty ratio:* 6:1.

Majors Craft/folk art; fine arts and art studies related.

Academic Programs *Special study options:* adult/continuing education programs, advanced placement credit, double majors, independent study, internships, off-campus study, part-time degree program.

Library Oregon College of Art and Craft Library plus 1 other with 6,500 titles, 90 serial subscriptions, 24,000 audiovisual materials, an OPAC.

Computers on Campus 4 computers available on campus for general student use. Internet access, at least one staffed computer lab available.

Student Life *Housing:* college housing not available. *Activities and Organizations:* Student Life Committee. *Campus security:* 24-hour emergency response devices, late-night transport/escort service. *Student Services:* personal/psychological counseling.

Costs (2001–02) *Tuition:* $12,442 full-time, $540 per credit part-time. Part-time tuition and fees vary according to course load. *Required fees:* $200 full-time. *Payment plans:* installment, deferred payment.

Financial Aid Of all full-time matriculated undergraduates who enrolled in 2001, 29 applied for aid, 27 were judged to have need, 1 had their need fully met. 14 Federal Work-Study jobs (averaging $750). 28 State and other part-time jobs (averaging $715). In 2001, 1 non-need-based awards were made. *Average percent of need met:* 49%. *Average financial aid package:* $11,500. *Average need-based loan:* $3500. *Average need-based gift aid:* $7152. *Average non-need based aid:* $4000.

Applying *Options:* deferred entrance. *Application fee:* $35. *Required:* essay or personal statement, high school transcript, minimum 2.5 GPA, 2 letters of recommendation, interview, portfolio. *Application deadline:* rolling (freshmen), rolling (transfers). *Notification:* continuous (freshmen).

Admissions Contact Ms. Sarah Turner, Admissions Officer, Oregon College of Art & Craft, 8245 Southwest Barnes Road, Portland, OR 97225. *Phone:* 503-297-5544 Ext. 141. *Toll-free phone:* 800-390-0632. *Fax:* 503-297-9651. *E-mail:* admissions@ocac.edu.

OREGON HEALTH & SCIENCE UNIVERSITY

Portland, Oregon

- **State-related** upper-level, founded 1974
- **Calendar** quarters
- **Degrees** certificates, bachelor's, master's, doctoral, first professional, post-master's, postbachelor's, and first professional certificates
- **Urban** 116-acre campus
- **Endowment** $13.9 million
- **Coed,** 657 undergraduate students, 78% full-time, 84% women, 16% men
- **Moderately difficult** entrance level

Undergraduates 510 full-time, 147 part-time. Students come from 31 states and territories, 3 other countries, 6% are from out of state, 0.3% African American, 5% Asian American or Pacific Islander, 3% Hispanic American, 2% Native American, 0.6% international.

Faculty *Total:* 836, 60% full-time.

Majors Dental hygiene; medical radiologic technology; medical technology; nursing; physician assistant.

Academic Programs *Special study options:* advanced placement credit, off-campus study, part-time degree program, summer session for credit. *ROTC:* Army (c).

Library Bic Bio-Informational Center plus 2 others with 200,771 titles, 2,110 serial subscriptions, an OPAC, a Web page.

Computers on Campus 49 computers available on campus for general student use. A campuswide network can be accessed from student residence rooms and from off campus. Internet access, at least one staffed computer lab available.

Student Life *Housing Options:* coed. *Campus security:* 24-hour patrols. *Student Services:* health clinic, personal/psychological counseling.

Athletics *Intramural sports:* basketball M/W, racquetball M/W, squash M/W, swimming M/W, tennis M/W, volleyball M/W.

Standardized Tests *Required for some:* SAT I (for admission).

Costs (2001–02) *Tuition:* state resident $6005 full-time; nonresident $12,383 full-time. Full-time tuition and fees vary according to program. Part-time tuition and fees vary according to program.

Financial Aid Of all full-time matriculated undergraduates who enrolled in 2001, 419 applied for aid, 390 were judged to have need, 12 had their need fully met. 34 Federal Work-Study jobs (averaging $2640). In 2001, 15 non-need-based awards were made. *Average percent of need met:* 47%. *Average financial aid package:* $9454. *Average need-based loan:* $5576. *Average need-based gift aid:* $4178. *Average non-need based aid:* $3312. *Average indebtedness upon graduation:* $21,337.

Applying *Application fee:* $60.

Admissions Contact Ms. Cherie Honnell, Registrar and Director of Financial Aid, Oregon Health & Science University, 3181 Southwest Sam Jackson Park Road, Portland, OR 97201-3098. *Phone:* 503-494-7800.

OREGON INSTITUTE OF TECHNOLOGY

Klamath Falls, Oregon

- **State-supported** 4-year, founded 1947, part of Oregon University System
- **Calendar** quarters
- **Degrees** associate, bachelor's, and master's
- **Small-town** 173-acre campus
- **Endowment** $13.1 million
- **Coed,** 3,086 undergraduate students, 63% full-time, 45% women, 55% men
- **Moderately difficult** entrance level, 61% of applicants were admitted

Undergraduates 1,945 full-time, 1,141 part-time. Students come from 12 states and territories, 16 other countries, 14% are from out of state, 1% African American, 6% Asian American or Pacific Islander, 4% Hispanic American, 2% Native American, 0.8% international, 8% transferred in, 17% live on campus. *Retention:* 73% of 2001 full-time freshmen returned.

Freshmen *Admission:* 792 applied, 482 admitted, 382 enrolled. *Average high school GPA:* 3.29. *Test scores:* SAT verbal scores over 500: 57%; SAT math scores over 500: 60%; ACT scores over 18: 82%; SAT verbal scores over 600: 20%; SAT math scores over 600: 20%; ACT scores over 24: 31%; SAT verbal scores over 700: 3%; SAT math scores over 700: 4%; ACT scores over 30: 4%.

Faculty *Total:* 214, 57% full-time, 27% with terminal degrees. *Student/faculty ratio:* 14:1.

Majors Accounting; business administration; civil engineering; communications; computer engineering technology; computer/information sciences; computer programming; counseling psychology; dental hygiene; electrical/electronic engineering technology; environmental science; industrial radiologic technology; industrial technology; laser/optical technology; legal administrative assistant; liberal arts and sciences/liberal studies; management information systems/business data processing; mechanical engineering technology; medical administrative assistant; pre-medicine; radiological science; secretarial science; surveying.

Academic Programs *Special study options:* academic remediation for entering students, adult/continuing education programs, advanced placement credit, cooperative education, distance learning, double majors, English as a second language, internships, off-campus study, part-time degree program, services for LD students, study abroad, summer session for credit.

Library Center for Learning and Teaching plus 2 others with 83,553 titles, 1,855 serial subscriptions, 2,797 audiovisual materials, an OPAC, a Web page.

Computers on Campus 700 computers available on campus for general student use. A campuswide network can be accessed from off campus that provide access to online grade information. Internet access, online (class) registration, at least one staffed computer lab available.

Student Life *Housing Options:* coed. *Activities and Organizations:* student-run newspaper, Phi Delta Theta, Christian Fellowship, International Club, Society of Women Engineers, CELSA, national fraternities. *Campus security:* 24-hour emergency response devices and patrols, late-night transport/escort service. *Student Services:* health clinic, personal/psychological counseling.

Athletics Member NAIA. *Intercollegiate sports:* baseball M, basketball M(s)/W, cross-country running M(s)/W(s), soccer M/W, softball W(s), track and field M(s)/W(s), volleyball W(s). *Intramural sports:* basketball M/W, bowling M/W, cross-country running M/W, football M/W, golf M/W, soccer M/W, softball W, track and field M/W, volleyball M/W.

Standardized Tests *Required:* SAT I or ACT (for admission).

Costs (2001–02) *One-time required fee:* $25. *Tuition:* state resident $2697 full-time, $75 per credit part-time; nonresident $11,655 full-time, $75 per credit part-time. Full-time tuition and fees vary according to course load. Part-time tuition and fees vary according to course load. *Required fees:* $945 full-time, $114 per term part-time. *Room and board:* $5154. Room and board charges vary according to board plan. *Payment plans:* installment, deferred payment. *Waivers:* senior citizens.

Financial Aid Of all full-time matriculated undergraduates who enrolled in 2001, 1591 applied for aid, 1184 were judged to have need, 68 had their need fully met. *Average percent of need met:* 45%. *Average financial aid package:* $6676. *Average need-based loan:* $3892. *Average need-based gift aid:* $3728. *Average indebtedness upon graduation:* $22,629.

Applying *Options:* common application, electronic application, deferred entrance. *Application fee:* $50. *Required:* high school transcript, minimum 2.5 GPA.

Required for some: letters of recommendation. *Application deadlines:* 6/1 (freshmen), 6/1 (transfers). *Notification:* continuous until 9/1 (freshmen).

Admissions Contact Palmer Muntz, Director of Admissions, Oregon Institute of Technology, 3201 Campus Drive, Klamath Falls, OR 97601-8801. *Phone:* 541-885-1150. *Toll-free phone:* 800-422-2017 (in-state); 800-343-6653 (out-of-state). *Fax:* 541-885-1115. *E-mail:* oit@oit.edu.

OREGON STATE UNIVERSITY
Corvallis, Oregon

- **State-supported** university, founded 1868, part of Oregon University System
- **Calendar** quarters
- **Degrees** bachelor's, master's, doctoral, and first professional
- **Small-town** 422-acre campus with easy access to Portland
- **Endowment** $266.3 million
- **Coed,** 14,877 undergraduate students, 90% full-time, 47% women, 53% men
- **Moderately difficult** entrance level, 51% of applicants were admitted

Small classes, motivated students, honors-level instruction, and close interaction with some of Oregon State University's finest faculty members create an exciting, challenging University Honors College atmosphere. In honors classes, colloquia, and other innovative ways, Honors College students explore their majors with an interdisciplinary approach. Students also work with faculty mentors to prepare honors theses. Graduates receive an honors baccalaureate degree in their major, conferred jointly by the Honors College and their academic college.

Undergraduates 13,417 full-time, 1,460 part-time. Students come from 50 states and territories, 90 other countries, 15% are from out of state, 1% African American, 8% Asian American or Pacific Islander, 3% Hispanic American, 1% Native American, 2% international, 8% transferred in, 29% live on campus. *Retention:* 80% of 2001 full-time freshmen returned.

Freshmen *Admission:* 6,645 applied, 3,402 admitted, 3,115 enrolled. *Average high school GPA:* 3.43. *Test scores:* SAT verbal scores over 500: 65%; SAT math scores over 500: 71%; ACT scores over 18: 88%; SAT verbal scores over 600: 24%; SAT math scores over 600: 30%; ACT scores over 24: 43%; SAT verbal scores over 700: 2%; SAT math scores over 700: 4%; ACT scores over 30: 5%.

Faculty *Total:* 1,386, 98% full-time, 72% with terminal degrees. *Student/faculty ratio:* 12:1.

Majors Accounting; actuarial science; agricultural business; agricultural economics; agricultural sciences; agronomy/crop science; American studies; animal sciences; anthropology; applied art; applied mathematics; archaeology; art; art history; athletic training/sports medicine; biochemistry; biological/physical sciences; biology; biophysics; botany; business administration; business marketing and marketing management; cell biology; chemical engineering; chemistry; child care/development; civil engineering; clothing/textiles; comparative literature; computer engineering; computer science; construction engineering; construction management; cultural studies; dairy science; dietetics; early childhood education; economics; electrical engineering; engineering; engineering physics; English; entomology; environmental biology; environmental engineering; environmental health; environmental science; equestrian studies; evolutionary biology; exercise sciences; family/community studies; family/consumer studies; fashion design/illustration; fashion merchandising; finance; fine/studio arts; fish/game management; food products retailing; food sciences; forest engineering; forestry; French; geography; geological engineering; geology; geophysics/seismology; German; health science; health services administration; history; history of science and technology; home economics; horticulture science; individual/family development; industrial/manufacturing engineering; information sciences/systems; interdisciplinary studies; interior design; international business; international relations; landscaping management; liberal arts and sciences/liberal studies; literature; management information systems/business data processing; marine science; mass communications; materials science; mathematics; mechanical engineering; medical technology; metallurgical engineering; microbiology/bacteriology; mining/mineral engineering; music; natural resources management; nuclear engineering; nutrition science; occupational safety/health technology; pharmacy; philosophy; physical education; physical sciences; physics; political science; pre-dentistry; pre-medicine; pre-veterinary studies; psychology; public health; range management; recreation/leisure facilities management; recreation/leisure studies; sociology; Spanish; speech/rhetorical studies; technical/business writing; textile arts; theater arts/drama; wildlife management; wood science/paper technology; zoology.

Academic Programs *Special study options:* academic remediation for entering students, advanced placement credit, cooperative education, distance learning, double majors, English as a second language, freshman honors college, honors programs, internships, off-campus study, part-time degree program, services for LD students, student-designed majors, study abroad, summer session for credit. *ROTC:* Army (b), Air Force (b).

Library Valley Library with 689,119 titles, 12,254 serial subscriptions, 6,225 audiovisual materials, an OPAC, a Web page.

Computers on Campus 2251 computers available on campus for general student use. A campuswide network can be accessed from student residence rooms and from off campus. At least one staffed computer lab available.

Student Life *Housing Options:* coed, cooperative, disabled students. *Activities and Organizations:* drama/theater group, student-run newspaper, radio and television station, choral group, marching band, Associated Students of OSU, International Students of OSU, graduate students organization, Campus Crusade, MECHA, national fraternities, national sororities. *Campus security:* 24-hour emergency response devices and patrols, student patrols, late-night transport/escort service, controlled dormitory access, crime prevention office. *Student Services:* health clinic, personal/psychological counseling, women's center, legal services.

Athletics Member NCAA. All Division I except football (Division I-A). *Intercollegiate sports:* baseball M(s), basketball M(s)/W(s), crew M/W, golf M(s)/W(s), gymnastics W(s), soccer M(s)/W(s), softball W(s), swimming W(s), volleyball W(s), wrestling M(s). *Intramural sports:* archery M/W, badminton M/W, basketball M/W, bowling M/W, crew M/W, cross-country running M/W, equestrian sports M(c)/W(c), fencing M(c)/W(c), football M, golf M/W, lacrosse M(c)/W(c), racquetball M/W, riflery M(c)/W(c), rugby M(c)/W(c), sailing M(c)/W(c), skiing (cross-country) M(c)/W(c), skiing (downhill) M(c)/W(c), soccer M/W, softball M/W, squash M(c), swimming M/W, table tennis M(c)/W(c), tennis M/W, track and field M/W, volleyball M/W, water polo M/W, wrestling M.

Standardized Tests *Required:* SAT I or ACT (for admission). *Required for some:* SAT II: Subject Tests (for admission).

Costs (2001–02) *One-time required fee:* $50. *Tuition:* state resident $2802 full-time, $78 per credit part-time; nonresident $12,750 full-time, $354 per credit part-time. Part-time tuition and fees vary according to course load. *Required fees:* $1185 full-time. *Room and board:* $5625. Room and board charges vary according to board plan and housing facility. *Payment plan:* deferred payment.

Financial Aid *Financial aid deadline:* 5/1.

Applying *Options:* common application, electronic application, early admission, early action, deferred entrance. *Application fee:* $50. *Required:* high school transcript, minimum 3.0 GPA. *Application deadlines:* 3/1 (freshmen), 5/1 (transfers). *Notification:* continuous (freshmen).

Admissions Contact Ms. Michele Sandlin, Director of Admissions, Oregon State University, Corvallis, OR 97331. *Phone:* 541-737-4411. *Toll-free phone:* 800-291-4192. *E-mail:* osuadmit@orst.edu.

PACIFIC NORTHWEST COLLEGE OF ART
Portland, Oregon

- **Independent** 4-year, founded 1909
- **Calendar** semesters
- **Degree** certificates and bachelor's
- **Urban** campus
- **Endowment** $3.0 million
- **Coed,** 293 undergraduate students, 90% full-time, 60% women, 40% men
- **Moderately difficult** entrance level, 92% of applicants were admitted

Undergraduates 263 full-time, 30 part-time. Students come from 20 states and territories, 3 other countries, 16% are from out of state, 2% African American, 4% Asian American or Pacific Islander, 5% Hispanic American, 3% Native American, 2% international, 24% transferred in, 2% live on campus. *Retention:* 60% of 2001 full-time freshmen returned.

Freshmen *Admission:* 65 applied, 60 admitted, 35 enrolled. *Average high school GPA:* 3.00.

Faculty *Total:* 50, 24% full-time, 66% with terminal degrees. *Student/faculty ratio:* 11:1.

Majors Art; ceramic arts; drawing; fine/studio arts; graphic design/commercial art/illustration; painting; photography; printmaking; sculpture.

Academic Programs *Special study options:* academic remediation for entering students, adult/continuing education programs, advanced placement credit, cooperative education, double majors, independent study, internships, off-campus study, part-time degree program, services for LD students, student-designed majors, study abroad, summer session for credit.

Library Charles Vorhies Fine Arts Library plus 1 other with 25,000 titles, 82 serial subscriptions, an OPAC, a Web page.

Computers on Campus 60 computers available on campus for general student use. Internet access, online (class) registration, at least one staffed computer lab available.

Pacific Northwest College of Art (continued)

Student Life *Housing Options:* coed, cooperative. *Activities and Organizations:* student-run newspaper. *Campus security:* entrance security guards during open hours. *Student Services:* personal/psychological counseling.

Costs (2001–02) *Tuition:* $12,856 full-time, $555 per semester hour part-time. Part-time tuition and fees vary according to course load. *Required fees:* $114 full-time. *Room only:* $3537. *Payment plan:* installment. *Waivers:* employees or children of employees.

Financial Aid Of all full-time matriculated undergraduates who enrolled in 2001, 257 applied for aid, 257 were judged to have need, 23 had their need fully met. 26 Federal Work-Study jobs (averaging $1200). 21 State and other part-time jobs (averaging $1200). In 2001, 7 non-need-based awards were made. *Average percent of need met:* 72%. *Average financial aid package:* $6240. *Average need-based loan:* $5320. *Average need-based gift aid:* $3856. *Average non-need based aid:* $1245. *Average indebtedness upon graduation:* $18,917.

Applying *Options:* common application, electronic application, early action, deferred entrance. *Application fee:* $30. *Required:* essay or personal statement, high school transcript, minimum 2.5 GPA, 2 letters of recommendation, portfolio of artwork. *Recommended:* interview. *Application deadlines:* 8/1 (freshmen), 8/1 (transfers). *Notification:* 12/15 (early action).

Admissions Contact Mr. Clarence Goodman, Enrollment Counselor, Pacific Northwest College of Art, 1241 NW Johnson Street, Portland, OR 97209. *Phone:* 503-821-8975. *Toll-free phone:* 800-818-PNCA. *Fax:* 503-821-8978. *E-mail:* admissions@pnca.edu.

PACIFIC UNIVERSITY
Forest Grove, Oregon

- **Independent** comprehensive, founded 1849
- **Calendar** 4-1-4
- **Degrees** bachelor's, master's, doctoral, and first professional
- **Small-town** 55-acre campus with easy access to Portland
- **Endowment** $24.2 million
- **Coed,** 1,169 undergraduate students, 93% full-time, 63% women, 37% men
- **Moderately difficult** entrance level, 82% of applicants were admitted

Undergraduates 1,093 full-time, 76 part-time. Students come from 19 states and territories, 3 other countries, 55% are from out of state, 0.4% African American, 18% Asian American or Pacific Islander, 2% Hispanic American, 2% Native American, 0.7% international, 6% transferred in, 63% live on campus. *Retention:* 78% of 2001 full-time freshmen returned.

Freshmen *Admission:* 1,176 applied, 969 admitted, 315 enrolled. *Average high school GPA:* 3.52. *Test scores:* SAT verbal scores over 500: 75%; SAT math scores over 500: 82%; ACT scores over 18: 99%; SAT verbal scores over 600: 30%; SAT math scores over 600: 29%; ACT scores over 24: 53%; SAT verbal scores over 700: 6%; SAT math scores over 700: 4%; ACT scores over 30: 9%.

Faculty *Total:* 259, 61% full-time. *Student/faculty ratio:* 11:1.

Majors Accounting; art; art education; athletic training/sports medicine; biology; broadcast journalism; business administration; business marketing and marketing management; chemistry; Chinese; computer science; creative writing; early childhood education; economics; education; elementary education; English; environmental science; exercise sciences; finance; French; German; health science; history; humanities; international relations; Japanese; journalism; liberal arts and sciences/liberal studies; literature; mass communications; mathematics; modern languages; music; music teacher education; philosophy; physics; political science; pre-dentistry; pre-medicine; psychology; radio/television broadcasting; secondary education; social work; sociology; Spanish; telecommunications; theater arts/drama.

Academic Programs *Special study options:* accelerated degree program, advanced placement credit, cooperative education, double majors, English as a second language, honors programs, independent study, internships, off-campus study, services for LD students, study abroad, summer session for credit. *ROTC:* Army (c), Air Force (c). *Unusual degree programs:* 3-2 engineering with Washington State University, Washington University in St. Louis, Oregon Graduate Institute of Science and Technology, Oregon State University; medical technology, computer science, environmental science with Oregon Graduate Institute of Science and Technology.

Library Scott Memorial Library with 1,052 serial subscriptions, 1,026 audiovisual materials, an OPAC, a Web page.

Computers on Campus 150 computers available on campus for general student use. A campuswide network can be accessed from student residence rooms and from off campus. Internet access, at least one staffed computer lab available.

Student Life *Housing:* on-campus residence required through sophomore year. *Options:* coed, disabled students. *Activities and Organizations:* drama/theater group, student-run newspaper, radio station, choral group, Pacific Outback Activities, Hawaiian Club, Big Buddy Program, Business and Economics Club, Exercise Science Club. *Campus security:* 24-hour emergency response devices and patrols, late-night transport/escort service. *Student Services:* health clinic, personal/psychological counseling.

Athletics Member NCAA. All Division III. *Intercollegiate sports:* baseball M, basketball M/W, cross-country running M/W, golf M/W, soccer M/W, softball W, swimming M(c), tennis M/W, track and field M/W, volleyball M(c)/W, wrestling M/W(c). *Intramural sports:* basketball M/W, golf M/W, racquetball M/W, soccer M/W, softball M/W, tennis M/W, volleyball M/W.

Standardized Tests *Required:* SAT I or ACT (for admission).

Costs (2002–03) *Comprehensive fee:* $24,671 includes full-time tuition ($18,720), mandatory fees ($572), and room and board ($5379). Full-time tuition and fees vary according to program. Part-time tuition: $750 per credit hour. Part-time tuition and fees vary according to course load and program. *Room and board:* Room and board charges vary according to board plan and housing facility. *Payment plans:* installment, deferred payment. *Waivers:* employees or children of employees.

Financial Aid Of all full-time matriculated undergraduates who enrolled in 2001, 1086 applied for aid, 906 were judged to have need, 349 had their need fully met. 590 Federal Work-Study jobs (averaging $1683). 167 State and other part-time jobs (averaging $1736). In 2001, 182 non-need-based awards were made. *Average percent of need met:* 86%. *Average financial aid package:* $15,949. *Average need-based loan:* $4303. *Average need-based gift aid:* $11,074. *Average non-need based aid:* $7801.

Applying *Options:* common application, electronic application, deferred entrance. *Application fee:* $30. *Required:* essay or personal statement, high school transcript, minimum 3.0 GPA, 1 letter of recommendation. *Recommended:* interview. *Application deadlines:* 8/15 (freshmen), 8/15 (transfers). *Notification:* continuous (freshmen).

Admissions Contact Mr. Ian Symmonds, Executive Director of Admissions, Pacific University, 2043 College Way, Forest Grove, OR 97116-1797. *Phone:* 503-359-2218. *Toll-free phone:* 800-677-6712. *Fax:* 503-359-2975. *E-mail:* admissions@pacificu.edu.

PORTLAND STATE UNIVERSITY
Portland, Oregon

- **State-supported** university, founded 1946, part of Oregon University System
- **Calendar** quarters
- **Degrees** certificates, bachelor's, master's, doctoral, and postbachelor's certificates
- **Urban** 36-acre campus
- **Endowment** $9.5 million
- **Coed,** 14,575 undergraduate students, 58% full-time, 55% women, 45% men
- **Minimally difficult** entrance level, 85% of applicants were admitted

Undergraduates 8,436 full-time, 6,139 part-time. Students come from 51 states and territories, 66 other countries, 11% are from out of state, 3% African American, 10% Asian American or Pacific Islander, 4% Hispanic American, 1% Native American, 4% international, 18% transferred in, 9% live on campus. *Retention:* 69% of 2001 full-time freshmen returned.

Freshmen *Admission:* 2,786 applied, 2,358 admitted, 1,293 enrolled. *Average high school GPA:* 3.17. *Test scores:* SAT verbal scores over 500: 53%; SAT math scores over 500: 56%; ACT scores over 18: 87%; SAT verbal scores over 600: 22%; SAT math scores over 600: 18%; ACT scores over 24: 34%; SAT verbal scores over 700: 3%; SAT math scores over 700: 2%; ACT scores over 30: 3%.

Faculty *Total:* 998, 63% full-time. *Student/faculty ratio:* 18:1.

Majors Accounting; advertising; African studies; anthropology; applied art; architecture; art; art history; biochemistry; biological/physical sciences; biology; business administration; business marketing and marketing management; chemistry; child care/development; Chinese; city/community/regional planning; civil engineering; computer engineering; computer/information sciences; computer science; criminal justice/law enforcement administration; drawing; East Asian studies; Eastern European area studies; economics; electrical engineering; English; environmental science; finance; French; geography; geology; German; graphic design/commercial art/illustration; health education; history; humanities; human resources management; international relations; Japanese; Latin American studies; liberal arts and sciences/liberal studies; linguistics; logistics/materials management; mathematics; mechanical engineering; Middle Eastern studies; music; philosophy; physics; political science; psychology; Russian; sculpture; social sciences; sociology; Spanish; speech/rhetorical studies; theater arts/drama; urban studies; women's studies.

Academic Programs *Special study options:* academic remediation for entering students, accelerated degree program, adult/continuing education programs,

advanced placement credit, cooperative education, distance learning, double majors, English as a second language, honors programs, independent study, internships, off-campus study, part-time degree program, services for LD students, student-designed majors, study abroad, summer session for credit. *ROTC:* Army (b), Air Force (c).

Library Branford P. Millar Library with 1.8 million titles, 10,230 serial subscriptions, 127,925 audiovisual materials, an OPAC, a Web page.

Computers on Campus 340 computers available on campus for general student use. A campuswide network can be accessed from student residence rooms and from off campus. Internet access, online (class) registration, at least one staffed computer lab available.

Student Life *Housing Options:* coed, disabled students. *Activities and Organizations:* drama/theater group, student-run newspaper, radio station, choral group, radio station, Women's Union, Association of African Students, Queers and Allies, OSPERG, national fraternities, national sororities. *Campus security:* 24-hour emergency response devices and patrols, late-night transport/escort service, controlled dormitory access, self-defense education. *Student Services:* health clinic, personal/psychological counseling, women's center, legal services.

Athletics Member NCAA. All Division I except football (Division I-AA). *Intercollegiate sports:* baseball M(s), basketball M(s)/W(s), cross-country running M(s)/W(s), golf M(s)/W(s), soccer W(s), softball W(s), tennis M(s)/W(s), track and field M(s)/W(s), volleyball W(s), wrestling M(s). *Intramural sports:* archery M/W, basketball M/W, bowling M(c)/W(c), crew M(c)/W(c), fencing M(c)/W(c), football M, golf M/W, racquetball M/W, sailing M(c)/W(c), skiing (downhill) M(c)/W(c), soccer M(c)/W, softball M/W, table tennis M(c)/W(c), tennis M(c)/W(c), volleyball M/W, water polo M(c)/W(c).

Standardized Tests *Required:* SAT I or ACT (for admission).

Costs (2001–02) *Tuition:* state resident $2808 full-time, $78 per credit part-time; nonresident $11,916 full-time, $78 per credit part-time. Part-time tuition and fees vary according to course load. *Required fees:* $912 full-time, $17 per credit, $21 per term part-time. *Room and board:* $7500; room only: $5400. Room and board charges vary according to board plan and housing facility. *Payment plans:* installment, deferred payment. *Waivers:* minority students, senior citizens, and employees or children of employees.

Financial Aid In 2001, 385 non-need-based awards were made. *Average percent of need met:* 64%. *Average financial aid package:* $6229. *Average non-need based aid:* $6025.

Applying *Options:* electronic application, early admission, deferred entrance. *Application fee:* $50. *Required:* high school transcript, minimum 2.5 GPA. *Application deadline:* rolling (freshmen), rolling (transfers). *Notification:* continuous (freshmen).

Admissions Contact Ms. Agnes A. Hoffman, Director of Admissions and Records, Portland State University, PO Box 751, Portland, OR 97207-0751. *Phone:* 503-725-3511. *Toll-free phone:* 800-547-8887. *Fax:* 503-725-5525. *E-mail:* askadm@ess.pdx.edu.

REED COLLEGE
Portland, Oregon

- **Independent** comprehensive, founded 1908
- **Calendar** semesters
- **Degrees** bachelor's and master's
- **Suburban** 98-acre campus
- **Endowment** $324.8 million
- **Coed,** 1,396 undergraduate students, 97% full-time, 54% women, 46% men
- **Very difficult** entrance level, 71% of applicants were admitted

Undergraduates 1,348 full-time, 48 part-time. Students come from 52 states and territories, 31 other countries, 85% are from out of state, 0.8% African American, 5% Asian American or Pacific Islander, 3% Hispanic American, 1% Native American, 4% international, 3% transferred in, 65% live on campus. *Retention:* 87% of 2001 full-time freshmen returned.

Freshmen *Admission:* 1,731 applied, 1,235 admitted, 352 enrolled. *Average high school GPA:* 3.7. *Test scores:* SAT verbal scores over 500: 99%; SAT math scores over 500: 100%; ACT scores over 18: 100%; SAT verbal scores over 600: 91%; SAT math scores over 600: 83%; ACT scores over 24: 98%; SAT verbal scores over 700: 49%; SAT math scores over 700: 24%; ACT scores over 30: 55%.

Faculty *Total:* 124, 93% full-time, 84% with terminal degrees. *Student/faculty ratio:* 10:1.

Majors American studies; anthropology; art; biochemistry; biology; chemistry; Chinese; classics; dance; economics; English; fine/studio arts; French; German; history; international relations; linguistics; literature; mathematics; music; philosophy; physics; political science; psychology; religious studies; Russian; sociology; Spanish; theater arts/drama.

Academic Programs *Special study options:* accelerated degree program, advanced placement credit, double majors, independent study, off-campus study, part-time degree program, services for LD students, student-designed majors, study abroad. *ROTC:* Army (c). *Unusual degree programs:* 3-2 business administration with University of Oregon; engineering with California Institute of Technology, Rensselaer Polytechnic Institute, Columbia University; forestry with Duke University; computer science with University of Washington; studio art with Pacific Northwest College of Art; applied physics, electronic science with Oregon Graduate Institute.

Library Hauser Library plus 1 other with 470,000 titles, 1,858 serial subscriptions, 15,485 audiovisual materials, an OPAC, a Web page.

Computers on Campus 190 computers available on campus for general student use. A campuswide network can be accessed from student residence rooms and from off campus. Internet access, online (class) registration, at least one staffed computer lab available.

Student Life *Housing:* on-campus residence required for freshman year. *Options:* coed, women-only, disabled students. *Activities and Organizations:* drama/theater group, student-run newspaper, radio station, choral group, Reed Recycling, Movie Board, Outdoor Club. *Campus security:* 24-hour emergency response devices and patrols, student patrols, late-night transport/escort service, controlled dormitory access, 24-hour emergency dispatch. *Student Services:* health clinic, personal/psychological counseling, women's center.

Athletics *Intercollegiate sports:* basketball M(c), crew M(c)/W(c), fencing M(c)/W(c), rugby M(c)/W(c), sailing M(c)/W(c), soccer M(c)/W(c), squash M(c)/W(c). *Intramural sports:* archery M/W, badminton M/W, basketball M/W, equestrian sports M/W, racquetball M/W, skiing (downhill) M/W, soccer M/W, softball M/W, squash M/W, swimming M/W, tennis M/W, volleyball M/W, weight lifting M/W.

Standardized Tests *Required:* SAT I or ACT (for admission). *Recommended:* SAT II: Subject Tests (for admission), SAT II: Writing Test (for admission).

Costs (2001–02) *Comprehensive fee:* $33,350 includes full-time tuition ($26,060), mandatory fees ($200), and room and board ($7090). Part-time tuition: $4480 per course. Part-time tuition and fees vary according to course load. *Room and board:* College room only: $3680. Room and board charges vary according to board plan. *Payment plan:* installment. *Waivers:* employees or children of employees.

Financial Aid Of all full-time matriculated undergraduates who enrolled in 2001, 812 applied for aid, 700 were judged to have need, 572 had their need fully met. 386 Federal Work-Study jobs (averaging $651). 54 State and other part-time jobs (averaging $609). *Average percent of need met:* 100%. *Average financial aid package:* $18,740. *Average need-based loan:* $2556. *Average need-based gift aid:* $15,517. *Average indebtedness upon graduation:* $14,570. *Financial aid deadline:* 1/15.

Applying *Options:* common application, electronic application, early admission, early decision, deferred entrance. *Application fee:* $40. *Required:* essay or personal statement, high school transcript, 2 letters of recommendation. *Recommended:* minimum 3.0 GPA, interview. *Application deadlines:* 1/15 (freshmen), 3/1 (transfers). *Early decision:* 11/15 (for plan 1), 1/2 (for plan 2). *Notification:* 4/1 (freshmen), 12/15 (early decision plan 1), 2/1 (early decision plan 2).

Admissions Contact Mr. Paul Marthers, Dean of Admission, Reed College, 3203 Southeast Woodstock Boulevard, Portland, OR 97202-8199. *Phone:* 503-777-7511. *Toll-free phone:* 800-547-4750. *Fax:* 503-777-7553. *E-mail:* admission@reed.edu.

SOUTHERN OREGON UNIVERSITY
Ashland, Oregon

- **State-supported** comprehensive, founded 1926, part of Oregon University System
- **Calendar** quarters
- **Degrees** bachelor's, master's, and postbachelor's certificates
- **Small-town** 175-acre campus
- **Endowment** $9.8 million
- **Coed,** 4,890 undergraduate students, 75% full-time, 56% women, 44% men
- **Moderately difficult** entrance level, 92% of applicants were admitted

Undergraduates 3,653 full-time, 1,237 part-time. Students come from 45 states and territories, 33 other countries, 20% are from out of state, 0.9% African American, 4% Asian American or Pacific Islander, 4% Hispanic American, 2% Native American, 2% international, 10% transferred in, 25% live on campus. *Retention:* 67% of 2001 full-time freshmen returned.

Freshmen *Admission:* 1,872 applied, 1,717 admitted, 815 enrolled. *Average high school GPA:* 3.2. *Test scores:* SAT verbal scores over 500: 61%; SAT math scores over 500: 60%; ACT scores over 18: 89%; SAT verbal scores over 600:

Southern Oregon University (continued)
21%; SAT math scores over 600: 16%; ACT scores over 24: 33%; SAT verbal scores over 700: 2%; SAT math scores over 700: 1%; ACT scores over 30: 1%.

Faculty *Total:* 327, 58% full-time, 59% with terminal degrees. *Student/faculty ratio:* 17:1.

Majors Accounting; anthropology; art; biochemistry; biology; business administration; business marketing and marketing management; business statistics; chemistry; communications; computer science; criminology; economics; English; environmental science; geography; geology; health education; history; hotel and restaurant management; interdisciplinary studies; international relations; liberal arts and sciences/liberal studies; mathematics; mathematics/computer science; music; music business management/merchandising; nursing; physical education; physics; political science; pre-law; pre-medicine; psychology; social sciences; sociology; Spanish; theater arts/drama.

Academic Programs *Special study options:* academic remediation for entering students, accelerated degree program, adult/continuing education programs, advanced placement credit, cooperative education, double majors, honors programs, off-campus study, part-time degree program, services for LD students, student-designed majors, study abroad, summer session for credit.

Library Southern Oregon University Library with 260,662 titles, 2,076 serial subscriptions, 38,483 audiovisual materials, an OPAC, a Web page.

Computers on Campus 400 computers available on campus for general student use. At least one staffed computer lab available.

Student Life *Housing:* on-campus residence required for freshman year. *Options:* coed. *Activities and Organizations:* drama/theater group, student-run newspaper, radio and television station, choral group, Native American Student Union, International Student Association, Impact (religious club), Ho'opa'a Hawaii Club, Omicron Delta Kappa. *Campus security:* 24-hour emergency response devices and patrols, student patrols, late-night transport/escort service. *Student Services:* health clinic, personal/psychological counseling, women's center, legal services.

Athletics Member NAIA. *Intercollegiate sports:* baseball M, basketball M(s)/W(s), cross-country running M(s)/W(s), football M(s), skiing (downhill) M/W, soccer W(s), softball W(s), tennis W(s), track and field M(s)/W(s), volleyball W(s), wrestling M(s). *Intramural sports:* basketball M/W, bowling M/W, football M/W, golf M/W, racquetball M/W, rugby M/W, sailing M/W, skiing (cross-country) M/W, soccer M/W, softball M/W, swimming M/W, table tennis M/W, tennis M/W, track and field M/W, volleyball M/W, water polo M/W.

Standardized Tests *Required:* SAT I or ACT (for admission). *Required for some:* SAT II: Subject Tests (for admission).

Costs (2001–02) *Tuition:* state resident $2628 full-time, $73 per credit part-time; nonresident $10,044 full-time, $279 per credit part-time. Full-time tuition and fees vary according to course load, location, and reciprocity agreements. Part-time tuition and fees vary according to course load, location, and reciprocity agreements. *Required fees:* $927 full-time. *Room and board:* $5445. Room and board charges vary according to board plan and housing facility. *Payment plan:* deferred payment. *Waivers:* senior citizens and employees or children of employees.

Financial Aid Of all full-time matriculated undergraduates who enrolled in 2001, 2510 applied for aid, 2196 were judged to have need, 253 had their need fully met. 627 Federal Work-Study jobs (averaging $1049). In 2001, 465 non-need-based awards were made. *Average percent of need met:* 58%. *Average financial aid package:* $6041. *Average need-based loan:* $3696. *Average need-based gift aid:* $3678. *Average indebtedness upon graduation:* $16,672.

Applying *Options:* common application, early admission, deferred entrance. *Application fee:* $50. *Required:* high school transcript, 2.75 high school GPA or minimum SAT score of 1010. *Application deadline:* rolling (freshmen), rolling (transfers). *Notification:* continuous (freshmen).

Admissions Contact Ms. Mara A. Affre, Director of Admissions, Southern Oregon University, 1250 Siskiyou Boulevard, Ashland, OR 97520. *Phone:* 541-552-6411. *Toll-free phone:* 800-482-7672. *Fax:* 541-552-6614. *E-mail:* admissions@sou.edu.

UNIVERSITY OF OREGON
Eugene, Oregon

- **State-supported** university, founded 1872, part of Oregon University System
- **Calendar** quarters
- **Degrees** bachelor's, master's, doctoral, and first professional
- **Urban** 280-acre campus
- **Endowment** $246.5 million
- **Coed,** 15,113 undergraduate students, 90% full-time, 53% women, 47% men
- **Moderately difficult** entrance level, 90% of applicants were admitted

Undergraduates 13,638 full-time, 1,475 part-time. Students come from 54 states and territories, 79 other countries, 26% are from out of state, 2% African American, 6% Asian American or Pacific Islander, 3% Hispanic American, 1.0% Native American, 6% international, 9% transferred in, 21% live on campus. *Retention:* 82% of 2001 full-time freshmen returned.

Freshmen *Admission:* 8,686 applied, 7,819 admitted, 3,107 enrolled. *Average high school GPA:* 3.43. *Test scores:* SAT verbal scores over 500: 75%; SAT math scores over 500: 74%; SAT verbal scores over 600: 33%; SAT math scores over 600: 31%; SAT verbal scores over 700: 6%; SAT math scores over 700: 4%.

Faculty *Total:* 1,078, 72% full-time, 94% with terminal degrees. *Student/faculty ratio:* 18:1.

Majors Accounting; advertising; anthropology; applied art; architecture; art; art history; Asian studies; biochemistry; biological/physical sciences; biology; broadcast journalism; business administration; business marketing and marketing management; ceramic arts; chemistry; Chinese; city/community/regional planning; classics; community services; comparative literature; computer science; cultural studies; dance; drawing; East Asian studies; Eastern European area studies; economics; education; education administration; English; environmental science; exercise sciences; finance; folklore; French; geography; geology; German; graphic design/commercial art/illustration; Greek (modern); Hebrew; history; human services; interior design; international business; international relations; Italian; Japanese; journalism; Judaic studies; landscape architecture; Latin (ancient and medieval); liberal arts and sciences/liberal studies; linguistics; mass communications; mathematical statistics; mathematics; mathematics/computer science; metal/jewelry arts; music; musicology; music teacher education; music (voice and choral/opera performance); philosophy; physics; political science; pre-dentistry; pre-medicine; printmaking; psychology; public administration; public policy analysis; public relations; radio/television broadcasting; religious studies; romance languages; Russian; sculpture; sociology; Spanish; speech-language pathology/audiology; textile arts; theater arts/drama; women's studies.

Academic Programs *Special study options:* academic remediation for entering students, accelerated degree program, adult/continuing education programs, advanced placement credit, distance learning, double majors, English as a second language, freshman honors college, honors programs, independent study, internships, off-campus study, part-time degree program, services for LD students, student-designed majors, study abroad, summer session for credit. *ROTC:* Army (b), Air Force (c). *Unusual degree programs:* 3-2 engineering with Oregon State University; nursing with Oregon Health Sciences University.

Library Knight Library plus 5 others with 2.4 million titles, 15,898 serial subscriptions, 65,560 audiovisual materials, an OPAC, a Web page.

Computers on Campus 1250 computers available on campus for general student use. A campuswide network can be accessed from student residence rooms and from off campus. Internet access, online (class) registration, at least one staffed computer lab available.

Student Life *Housing Options:* coed, men-only, women-only, disabled students. *Activities and Organizations:* drama/theater group, student-run newspaper, radio station, choral group, marching band, Political and Environment Action, cultural organizations, student newspaper, Frat Council/Panhellenic, club sports, national fraternities, national sororities. *Campus security:* 24-hour emergency response devices and patrols, student patrols, late-night transport/escort service, controlled dormitory access. *Student Services:* health clinic, personal/psychological counseling, women's center, legal services.

Athletics Member NCAA. All Division I except football (Division I-A). *Intercollegiate sports:* badminton M(c)/W(c), basketball M(s)/W(s), bowling M(c)/W(c), crew M(c)/W(c), cross-country running M(s)/W(s), fencing M(c)/W(c), field hockey W(c), golf M(s)/W(s), ice hockey M(c)/W(c), lacrosse M(c)/W(c), racquetball M(c)/W(c), rugby M(c), sailing M(c)/W(c), skiing (cross-country) M(c)/W(c), skiing (downhill) M(c)/W(c), soccer M(c)/W(s), softball W(s), squash M(c)/W(c), swimming M(c)/W(c), table tennis M(c)/W(c), tennis M(s)/W(s), track and field M(s)/W(s), volleyball M(c)/W(s), water polo M(c)/W(c), wrestling M(s). *Intramural sports:* badminton M/W, basketball M/W, bowling M/W, crew M/W, cross-country running M/W, fencing M/W, field hockey W, football M, golf M/W, gymnastics M/W, ice hockey M/W, lacrosse M/W, racquetball M/W, rugby M, sailing M/W, skiing (cross-country) M/W, skiing (downhill) M/W, soccer M/W, softball W, squash M/W, swimming M/W, tennis M/W, track and field M/W, volleyball M/W, water polo M/W, weight lifting M/W, wrestling M.

Standardized Tests *Required:* SAT I or ACT (for admission).

Costs (2001–02) *Tuition:* state resident $2802 full-time, $78 per credit hour part-time; nonresident $13,224 full-time, $367 per credit hour part-time. Part-time tuition and fees vary according to course load. *Required fees:* $1269 full-time, $278 per credit hour part-time. *Room and board:* $5898. Room and board charges vary according to housing facility. *Payment plan:* installment. *Waivers:* minority students and employees or children of employees.

Financial Aid Of all full-time matriculated undergraduates who enrolled in 2001, 8721 applied for aid, 5796 were judged to have need, 2268 had their need fully met. In 2001, 1347 non-need-based awards were made. *Average percent of need met:* 74%. *Average financial aid package:* $7559. *Average need-based gift aid:* $3789. *Average non-need based aid:* $2460. *Average indebtedness upon graduation:* $19,916.

Applying *Options:* electronic application, early admission. *Application fee:* $50. *Required:* high school transcript, minimum 3.0 GPA. *Required for some:* essay or personal statement, 2 letters of recommendation. *Application deadlines:* 2/1 (freshmen), 5/15 (transfers). *Notification:* 3/15 (freshmen).

Admissions Contact Ms. Martha Pitts, Director of Admissions, University of Oregon, Eugene, OR 97403. *Phone:* 541-346-3201. *Toll-free phone:* 800-232-3825. *Fax:* 541-346-5815. *E-mail:* uoadmit@oregon.uoregon.edu.

UNIVERSITY OF PHOENIX-OREGON CAMPUS

Portland, Oregon

- **Proprietary** comprehensive, founded 1976
- **Calendar** continuous
- **Degrees** certificates, associate, bachelor's, master's, doctoral, post-master's, and postbachelor's certificates (courses conducted at 54 campuses and learning centers in 13 states)
- **Coed,** 1,078 undergraduate students, 100% full-time, 42% women, 58% men
- **Noncompetitive** entrance level

Undergraduates Students come from 17 states and territories, 11% are from out of state.

Freshmen *Admission:* 8 admitted.

Faculty *Total:* 237, 2% full-time, 17% with terminal degrees. *Student/faculty ratio:* 12:1.

Majors Business administration; business marketing and marketing management; information technology; management information systems/business data processing; management science.

Academic Programs *Special study options:* accelerated degree program, adult/continuing education programs, advanced placement credit, distance learning, external degree program, independent study.

Library University Library with 17.5 million titles, 9,000 serial subscriptions, an OPAC, a Web page.

Computers on Campus A campuswide network can be accessed from off campus. Internet access, at least one staffed computer lab available.

Student Life *Housing:* college housing not available.

Costs (2001–02) *Tuition:* $8880 full-time. Full-time tuition and fees vary according to location and program. *Payment plan:* deferred payment. *Waivers:* employees or children of employees.

Applying *Options:* deferred entrance. *Application fee:* $85. *Required:* 2 years of work experience. *Required for some:* high school transcript. *Application deadline:* rolling (freshmen), rolling (transfers).

Admissions Contact Ms. Beth Barilla, Director of Admissions, University of Phoenix-Oregon Campus, 4615 East Elwood Street, Phoenix, AZ 85040-1958. *Phone:* 480-927-0099 Ext. 1218. *Toll-free phone:* 800-228-7240. *Fax:* 480-594-1758. *E-mail:* beth.barilla@apollogrp.edu.

UNIVERSITY OF PORTLAND

Portland, Oregon

- **Independent Roman Catholic** comprehensive, founded 1901
- **Calendar** semesters
- **Degrees** bachelor's, master's, and post-master's certificates
- **Suburban** 125-acre campus
- **Endowment** $89.0 million
- **Coed,** 2,573 undergraduate students, 95% full-time, 58% women, 42% men
- **Moderately difficult** entrance level, 87% of applicants were admitted

Undergraduates 2,447 full-time, 126 part-time. Students come from 42 states and territories, 31 other countries, 52% are from out of state, 1% African American, 9% Asian American or Pacific Islander, 4% Hispanic American, 0.6% Native American, 4% international, 6% transferred in, 57% live on campus. *Retention:* 84% of 2001 full-time freshmen returned.

Freshmen *Admission:* 2,242 applied, 1,960 admitted, 611 enrolled. *Average high school GPA:* 3.58. *Test scores:* SAT verbal scores over 500: 83%; SAT math scores over 500: 85%; SAT verbal scores over 600: 35%; SAT math scores over 600: 40%; SAT verbal scores over 700: 4%; SAT math scores over 700: 5%.

Faculty *Total:* 263, 63% full-time. *Student/faculty ratio:* 13:1.

Majors Accounting; arts management; biology; business administration; business marketing and marketing management; chemistry; civil engineering; computer engineering; computer science; criminal justice studies; education; electrical engineering; elementary education; engineering; engineering/industrial management; engineering science; English; environmental science; finance; history; interdisciplinary studies; international business; journalism; mass communications; mathematics; mechanical engineering; music; music teacher education; nursing; philosophy; physics; political science; pre-dentistry; pre-law; premedicine; psychology; secondary education; social work; sociology; Spanish; theater arts/drama; theology.

Academic Programs *Special study options:* accelerated degree program, adult/continuing education programs, advanced placement credit, cooperative education, double majors, English as a second language, honors programs, internships, part-time degree program, services for LD students, student-designed majors, study abroad, summer session for credit. *ROTC:* Army (b), Air Force (b).

Library Wilson M. Clark Library plus 1 other with 1,446 serial subscriptions, 7,827 audiovisual materials, an OPAC, a Web page.

Computers on Campus 200 computers available on campus for general student use. A campuswide network can be accessed from student residence rooms and from off campus. Internet access, at least one staffed computer lab available.

Student Life *Housing Options:* coed, men-only, women-only. *Activities and Organizations:* drama/theater group, student-run newspaper, radio station, choral group, English Society, international club, Hawaiian club, rugby club, social science club. *Campus security:* 24-hour patrols, student patrols, late-night transport/escort service, controlled dormitory access. *Student Services:* health clinic, personal/psychological counseling.

Athletics Member NCAA. All Division I. *Intercollegiate sports:* baseball M(s), basketball M(s)/W(s), cross-country running M(s)/W(s), golf M(s)/W(s), rugby M(c), soccer M(s)/W(s), tennis M(s)/W(s), track and field M(s)/W(s), volleyball W(s). *Intramural sports:* basketball M/W, crew M/W, cross-country running M/W, football M/W, rugby M, skiing (cross-country) M/W, skiing (downhill) M/W, soccer M(c)/W, softball M/W, swimming M/W, tennis M/W, track and field M/W, volleyball M/W, water polo M/W, weight lifting M/W.

Standardized Tests *Required:* SAT I or ACT (for admission).

Costs (2001–02) *Comprehensive fee:* $25,522 includes full-time tuition ($18,930), mandatory fees ($720), and room and board ($5872). Full-time tuition and fees vary according to program. Part-time tuition: $600 per credit hour. Part-time tuition and fees vary according to program. *Room and board:* Room and board charges vary according to board plan and housing facility. *Payment plans:* installment, deferred payment. *Waivers:* employees or children of employees.

Financial Aid Of all full-time matriculated undergraduates who enrolled in 2001, 1752 applied for aid, 1386 were judged to have need, 587 had their need fully met. 718 Federal Work-Study jobs (averaging $1744). 183 State and other part-time jobs (averaging $1911). In 2001, 819 non-need-based awards were made. *Average percent of need met:* 88%. *Average financial aid package:* $16,971. *Average need-based loan:* $5229. *Average need-based gift aid:* $10,096. *Average non-need based aid:* $13,203. *Average indebtedness upon graduation:* $18,595.

Applying *Options:* common application, electronic application, early decision, deferred entrance. *Application fee:* $45. *Required:* essay or personal statement, high school transcript, 1 letter of recommendation. *Application deadlines:* 6/1 (freshmen), 6/1 (transfers). *Early decision:* 11/15. *Notification:* continuous (freshmen), 1/15 (early decision).

Admissions Contact Mr. James C. Lyons, Dean of Admissions, University of Portland, 5000 North Willamette Boulevard, Portland, OR 97203-5798. *Phone:* 503-943-7147. *Toll-free phone:* 888-627-5601. *Fax:* 503-943-7315. *E-mail:* admissio@up.edu.

WARNER PACIFIC COLLEGE

Portland, Oregon

- **Independent** comprehensive, founded 1937, affiliated with Church of God
- **Calendar** semesters
- **Degrees** associate, bachelor's, master's, and postbachelor's certificates
- **Urban** 15-acre campus
- **Endowment** $1.2 million
- **Coed,** 59 undergraduate students, 100% full-time, 63% women, 37% men
- **Moderately difficult** entrance level, 73% of applicants were admitted

Undergraduates 59 full-time. Students come from 16 states and territories, 5 other countries, 26% are from out of state, 3% African American, 3% Asian American or Pacific Islander, 2% Hispanic American, 0.9% Native American, 1% international, 95% transferred in, 32% live on campus. *Retention:* 76% of 2001 full-time freshmen returned.

Warner Pacific College (continued)

Freshmen *Admission:* 189 applied, 138 admitted, 59 enrolled. *Average high school GPA:* 3.30. *Test scores:* SAT verbal scores over 500: 59%; SAT math scores over 500: 49%; ACT scores over 18: 92%; SAT verbal scores over 600: 17%; SAT math scores over 600: 19%; ACT scores over 24: 31%; SAT verbal scores over 700: 4%; SAT math scores over 700: 2%.

Faculty *Total:* 41, 100% full-time. *Student/faculty ratio:* 14:1.

Majors American studies; biblical studies; biological/physical sciences; biology; business administration; divinity/ministry; early childhood education; education; elementary education; English; exercise sciences; health science; history; individual/family development; liberal arts and sciences/liberal studies; mathematics; middle school education; music; music business management/merchandising; music teacher education; nursing; pastoral counseling; physical education; physical sciences; pre-law; pre-medicine; pre-veterinary studies; psychology; religious education; religious studies; science education; secondary education; social sciences; social work; theology.

Academic Programs *Special study options:* academic remediation for entering students, adult/continuing education programs, advanced placement credit, cooperative education, double majors, external degree program, honors programs, independent study, internships, off-campus study, part-time degree program, services for LD students, student-designed majors, study abroad, summer session for credit. *ROTC:* Army (c), Air Force (c).

Library Otto F. Linn Library with 54,000 titles, 400 serial subscriptions, an OPAC.

Computers on Campus 15 computers available on campus for general student use. A campuswide network can be accessed from student residence rooms and from off campus. Internet access, at least one staffed computer lab available.

Student Life *Housing:* on-campus residence required through sophomore year. *Options:* men-only, women-only. *Activities and Organizations:* drama/theater group, student-run newspaper, choral group, Associated Students of Warner Pacific College, yearbook, College Activities Board, Fellowship of Christian Athletes. *Campus security:* 24-hour emergency response devices, student patrols, late-night transport/escort service, controlled dormitory access, 14-hour patrols by trained security personnel. *Student Services:* health clinic, personal/psychological counseling.

Athletics Member NCCAA. *Intercollegiate sports:* basketball M(s)/W(s), cross-country running M(s)/W(s), soccer M(s), volleyball W(s). *Intramural sports:* basketball M/W, football M/W, skiing (cross-country) M/W, skiing (downhill) M/W, soccer M/W, softball M/W, table tennis M/W, volleyball M/W.

Standardized Tests *Required:* SAT I or ACT (for admission). *Recommended:* SAT II: Subject Tests (for admission), SAT II: Writing Test (for admission).

Costs (2002–03) *Comprehensive fee:* $20,880 includes full-time tuition ($15,950) and room and board ($4930). Part-time tuition: $350 per credit. Part-time tuition and fees vary according to course load. *Room and board:* Room and board charges vary according to board plan and housing facility. *Payment plan:* installment. *Waivers:* children of alumni and employees or children of employees.

Financial Aid Of all full-time matriculated undergraduates who enrolled in 2001, 446 applied for aid, 410 were judged to have need, 70 had their need fully met. 143 Federal Work-Study jobs (averaging $1491). In 2001, 56 non-need-based awards were made. *Average percent of need met:* 69%. *Average financial aid package:* $11,273. *Average need-based loan:* $4151. *Average need-based gift aid:* $4413. *Average non-need based aid:* $6843.

Applying *Application fee:* $25. *Required:* essay or personal statement, high school transcript, minimum 2.5 GPA, 2 letters of recommendation. *Required for some:* interview. *Recommended:* minimum 3.0 GPA, interview. *Application deadline:* rolling (freshmen), rolling (transfers). *Notification:* continuous (freshmen).

Admissions Contact Dawna A. Williams, Chief Admissions and Financial Aid Officer, Warner Pacific College, 2219 Southeast 68th Avenue, Portland, OR 97215. *Phone:* 503-517-1020. *Toll-free phone:* 800-582-7885 (in-state); 800-804-1510 (out-of-state). *Fax:* 503-517-1352. *E-mail:* admiss@warnerpacific.edu.

WESTERN BAPTIST COLLEGE
Salem, Oregon

- **Independent religious** 4-year, founded 1935
- **Calendar** semesters
- **Degrees** associate and bachelor's
- **Suburban** 107-acre campus with easy access to Portland
- **Endowment** $1.7 million
- **Coed,** 725 undergraduate students, 91% full-time, 60% women, 40% men
- **Moderately difficult** entrance level, 76% of applicants were admitted

Undergraduates 659 full-time, 66 part-time. Students come from 19 states and territories, 5 other countries, 34% are from out of state, 0.6% African American, 1% Asian American or Pacific Islander, 2% Hispanic American, 0.6% Native American, 1% international, 14% transferred in, 51% live on campus. *Retention:* 78% of 2001 full-time freshmen returned.

Freshmen *Admission:* 408 applied, 312 admitted, 151 enrolled. *Average high school GPA:* 3.52. *Test scores:* SAT verbal scores over 500: 77%; SAT math scores over 500: 69%; ACT scores over 18: 85%; SAT verbal scores over 600: 29%; SAT math scores over 600: 27%; ACT scores over 24: 46%; SAT verbal scores over 700: 2%; SAT math scores over 700: 5%.

Faculty *Total:* 54, 57% full-time, 24% with terminal degrees. *Student/faculty ratio:* 18:1.

Majors Accounting; biblical studies; business administration; community services; computer science; divinity/ministry; education; elementary education; English; finance; health science; humanities; interdisciplinary studies; liberal arts and sciences/liberal studies; mathematics; music; music teacher education; pastoral counseling; pre-law; psychology; religious education; religious studies; secondary education; social sciences; sport/fitness administration; theology.

Academic Programs *Special study options:* accelerated degree program, adult/continuing education programs, advanced placement credit, distance learning, double majors, freshman honors college, honors programs, internships, off-campus study, services for LD students, study abroad, summer session for credit. *ROTC:* Army (c), Air Force (c).

Library 80,712 titles, 575 serial subscriptions, 4,370 audiovisual materials, an OPAC, a Web page.

Computers on Campus 34 computers available on campus for general student use. A campuswide network can be accessed from student residence rooms and from off campus. Internet access, at least one staffed computer lab available.

Student Life *Housing:* on-campus residence required through sophomore year. *Options:* men-only, women-only. *Activities and Organizations:* drama/theater group, student-run newspaper, choral group. *Campus security:* 24-hour emergency response devices, student patrols, late-night transport/escort service. *Student Services:* health clinic, personal/psychological counseling.

Athletics Member NAIA, NCCAA. *Intercollegiate sports:* baseball M(s), basketball M(s)/W(s), soccer M(s)/W(s), softball W(c), volleyball W(s). *Intramural sports:* baseball W, basketball M/W, football M, soccer M/W, volleyball M/W.

Standardized Tests *Required:* SAT I or ACT (for admission).

Costs (2001–02) *Comprehensive fee:* $19,700 includes full-time tuition ($14,160), mandatory fees ($200), and room and board ($5340). Part-time tuition: $590 per credit hour. Part-time tuition and fees vary according to course load. *Required fees:* $30 per term part-time. *Room and board:* Room and board charges vary according to board plan. *Payment plan:* installment. *Waivers:* employees or children of employees.

Financial Aid Of all full-time matriculated undergraduates who enrolled in 2001, 538 applied for aid, 476 were judged to have need, 108 had their need fully met. 106 Federal Work-Study jobs (averaging $1500). In 2001, 97 non-need-based awards were made. *Average percent of need met:* 69%. *Average financial aid package:* $11,158. *Average need-based gift aid:* $7420. *Average indebtedness upon graduation:* $14,000.

Applying *Options:* early admission. *Application fee:* $35. *Required:* essay or personal statement, high school transcript, minimum 2.5 GPA, 3 letters of recommendation. *Application deadlines:* 8/1 (freshmen), 8/1 (transfers).

Admissions Contact Western Baptist College, 5000 Deer Park Drive, SE, Salem, OR 97301-9392. *Phone:* 503-375-7115. *Toll-free phone:* 800-845-3005. *E-mail:* admissions@wbc.edu.

WESTERN OREGON UNIVERSITY
Monmouth, Oregon

- **State-supported** comprehensive, founded 1856, part of Oregon University System
- **Calendar** quarters
- **Degrees** associate, bachelor's, and master's
- **Rural** 157-acre campus with easy access to Portland
- **Endowment** $2.8 million
- **Coed,** 4,339 undergraduate students, 92% full-time, 60% women, 40% men
- **Moderately difficult** entrance level, 92% of applicants were admitted

Undergraduates 3,978 full-time, 361 part-time. Students come from 24 states and territories, 18 other countries, 10% are from out of state, 2% African American, 3% Asian American or Pacific Islander, 5% Hispanic American, 1% Native American, 1% international, 12% transferred in, 20% live on campus. *Retention:* 69% of 2001 full-time freshmen returned.

Freshmen *Admission:* 1,585 applied, 1,453 admitted, 827 enrolled. *Average high school GPA:* 3.26. *Test scores:* SAT verbal scores over 500: 43%; SAT math scores over 500: 46%; ACT scores over 18: 76%; SAT verbal scores over 600: 11%; SAT math scores over 600: 10%; ACT scores over 24: 21%; SAT verbal scores over 700: 1%; SAT math scores over 700: 1%; ACT scores over 30: 2%.

Faculty *Total:* 313, 71% full-time, 57% with terminal degrees. *Student/faculty ratio:* 20:1.

Majors Anthropology; art; biology; business; chemistry; computer science; corrections; criminal justice/law enforcement administration; dance; economics; educational media design; English; fire services administration; geography; history; humanities; interdisciplinary studies; international relations; law enforcement/police science; liberal arts and sciences/liberal studies; mathematics; music; natural sciences; philosophy; political science; psychology; public administration; secondary education; sign language interpretation; social sciences; sociology; Spanish; theater arts/drama.

Academic Programs *Special study options:* academic remediation for entering students, adult/continuing education programs, advanced placement credit, distance learning, double majors, English as a second language, freshman honors college, honors programs, independent study, internships, off-campus study, part-time degree program, services for LD students, student-designed majors, study abroad, summer session for credit. *ROTC:* Army (b), Air Force (c).

Library Wayne Lynn Hamersly Library with 257,194 titles, 1,700 serial subscriptions, 2,562 audiovisual materials, an OPAC, a Web page.

Computers on Campus 277 computers available on campus for general student use. A campuswide network can be accessed from student residence rooms and from off campus. Internet access, at least one staffed computer lab available.

Student Life *Housing:* on-campus residence required for freshman year. *Options:* coed. *Activities and Organizations:* drama/theater group, student-run newspaper, television station, choral group, Model United Nations, Multicultural Student Union, Oregon Student Association. *Campus security:* 24-hour emergency response devices and patrols, student patrols, late-night transport/escort service, controlled dormitory access. *Student Services:* health clinic, personal/psychological counseling, women's center.

Athletics Member NCAA. All Division II. *Intercollegiate sports:* baseball M, basketball M/W, cross-country running M/W, football M, soccer W, softball W, track and field M/W, volleyball W. *Intramural sports:* badminton M/W, basketball M/W, bowling M/W, cross-country running M(c)/W(c), football M/W, golf M/W, racquetball M(c)/W(c), riflery M/W, skiing (downhill) M/W, soccer M(c)/W(c), softball M/W, table tennis M/W, tennis M/W, track and field M/W, volleyball M(c)/W(c), water polo M(c)/W(c), weight lifting M/W, wrestling M.

Standardized Tests *Required:* SAT I or ACT (for admission). *Recommended:* SAT I and SAT II or ACT (for admission).

Costs (2001–02) *Tuition:* state resident $2622 full-time, $73 per credit part-time; nonresident $10,440 full-time, $290 per credit part-time. Part-time tuition and fees vary according to course load. *Required fees:* $1038 full-time. *Room and board:* $5169; room only: $3900. Room and board charges vary according to board plan and housing facility. *Payment plans:* installment, deferred payment. *Waivers:* minority students, senior citizens, and employees or children of employees.

Financial Aid Of all full-time matriculated undergraduates who enrolled in 2001, 2811 applied for aid, 2214 were judged to have need, 452 had their need fully met. In 2001, 706 non-need-based awards were made. *Average percent of need met:* 76%. *Average financial aid package:* $6225. *Average need-based loan:* $3304. *Average need-based gift aid:* $3978. *Average indebtedness upon graduation:* $16,205.

Applying *Options:* electronic application, deferred entrance. *Application fee:* $50. *Required:* high school transcript, minimum 2.75 GPA. *Application deadline:* rolling (freshmen), rolling (transfers).

Admissions Contact Mr. Rob Kvidt, Director of Admissions, Western Oregon University, 345 North Monmouth Avenue, Monmouth, OR 97361. *Phone:* 503-838-8211. *Toll-free phone:* 877-877-1593. *Fax:* 503-838-8067. *E-mail:* wolfgram@wou.edu.

WESTERN STATES CHIROPRACTIC COLLEGE
Portland, Oregon

- **Independent** upper-level, founded 1904
- **Calendar** quarters
- **Degrees** diplomas, incidental bachelor's, and first professional
- **Suburban** 22-acre campus
- **Endowment** $1.2 million
- **Coed**
- **Moderately difficult** entrance level, 53% of applicants were admitted

Undergraduates Students come from 40 states and territories, 9 other countries.

Freshmen *Admission:* 145 applied, 77 admitted.

Faculty *Total:* 68, 53% full-time, 100% with terminal degrees. *Student/faculty ratio:* 7:1.

Majors Biology.

Academic Programs *Special study options:* off-campus study, services for LD students, summer session for credit.

Library W. A. Buden Library plus 1 other with 14,700 titles, 365 serial subscriptions, an OPAC.

Computers on Campus 15 computers available on campus for general student use.

Student Life *Housing:* college housing not available. *Activities and Organizations:* student-run newspaper, American Chiropractic Association, Canadian Chiropractic Club, Sports Medicine Club, Gonstead Club, LDS (Latter Day Saints) Club. *Campus security:* student patrols, late-night transport/escort service. *Student Services:* health clinic, personal/psychological counseling.

Athletics *Intramural sports:* basketball M, football M/W, golf M/W, soccer M, softball M/W, table tennis M/W, volleyball M/W.

Costs (2002–03) *Tuition:* $16,614 full-time.

Applying *Options:* common application. *Application fee:* $50. *Application deadline:* rolling (transfers).

Admissions Contact Dr. Lee Smith, Director of Admissions, Western States Chiropractic College, 2900 Northeast 132nd Avenue, Portland, OR 97230-3099. *Phone:* 503-251-2812. *Toll-free phone:* 800-641-5641. *Fax:* 503-251-5723.

WILLAMETTE UNIVERSITY
Salem, Oregon

- **Independent United Methodist** comprehensive, founded 1842
- **Calendar** semesters
- **Degrees** bachelor's, master's, and first professional
- **Urban** 72-acre campus with easy access to Portland
- **Endowment** $203.6 million
- **Coed**, 1,773 undergraduate students, 94% full-time, 56% women, 44% men
- **Very difficult** entrance level, 84% of applicants were admitted

Undergraduates 1,659 full-time, 114 part-time. Students come from 39 states and territories, 14 other countries, 58% are from out of state, 2% African American, 7% Asian American or Pacific Islander, 5% Hispanic American, 2% Native American, 1% international, 2% transferred in, 73% live on campus. *Retention:* 87% of 2001 full-time freshmen returned.

Freshmen *Admission:* 1,634 applied, 1,366 admitted, 476 enrolled. *Average high school GPA:* 3.71. *Test scores:* SAT verbal scores over 500: 94%; SAT math scores over 500: 95%; ACT scores over 18: 99%; SAT verbal scores over 600: 62%; SAT math scores over 600: 63%; ACT scores over 24: 83%; SAT verbal scores over 700: 14%; SAT math scores over 700: 14%; ACT scores over 30: 22%.

Faculty *Total:* 235, 78% full-time, 83% with terminal degrees. *Student/faculty ratio:* 10:1.

Majors American studies; art; art history; Asian studies; biology; chemistry; classics; comparative literature; computer science; economics; English; environmental science; exercise sciences; fine/studio arts; French; German; Hispanic-American studies; history; humanities; international relations; mathematics; music; music teacher education; music therapy; philosophy; physical education; physics; political science; pre-dentistry; pre-law; pre-medicine; pre-veterinary studies; psychology; religious studies; sociology; Spanish; speech/rhetorical studies; theater arts/drama.

Academic Programs *Special study options:* accelerated degree program, advanced placement credit, cooperative education, double majors, honors programs, independent study, internships, off-campus study, part-time degree program, services for LD students, student-designed majors, study abroad. *ROTC:* Air Force (c). *Unusual degree programs:* 3-2 engineering with University of Southern California, Washington University in St. Louis, Columbia University; forestry with Duke University; computer science with University of Oregon, Oregon Graduate Institute of Science and Technology.

Library Mark O. Hatfield Library plus 1 other with 279,574 titles, 1,569 serial subscriptions, 8,456 audiovisual materials, an OPAC, a Web page.

Computers on Campus 200 computers available on campus for general student use. A campuswide network can be accessed from student residence rooms and from off campus. At least one staffed computer lab available.

Student Life *Housing:* on-campus residence required through sophomore year. *Options:* coed. *Activities and Organizations:* drama/theater group, student-run newspaper, radio station, choral group, Hawaii club, Bush Mentor Program, outdoors club, Campus Ambassadors, Associated Students, national fraternities, national sororities. *Campus security:* 24-hour emergency response devices and

Willamette University (continued)
patrols, student patrols, late-night transport/escort service, controlled dormitory access. *Student Services:* health clinic, personal/psychological counseling, women's center.

Athletics Member NCAA. All Division III. *Intercollegiate sports:* baseball M, basketball M/W, crew M/W, cross-country running M/W, football M, golf M/W, lacrosse M(c), rugby M(c)/W(c), soccer M/W, softball W, swimming M/W, tennis M/W, track and field M/W, volleyball W. *Intramural sports:* badminton M/W, basketball M/W, bowling M/W, cross-country running M/W, fencing M(c)/W(c), football M/W, golf M/W, racquetball M/W, skiing (cross-country) M(c)/W(c), skiing (downhill) M(c)/W(c), soccer M/W, softball M/W, table tennis M/W, tennis M/W, volleyball M/W, water polo M/W, weight lifting M/W.

Standardized Tests *Required:* SAT I or ACT (for admission).

Costs (2001–02) *Comprehensive fee:* $29,422 includes full-time tuition ($23,150), mandatory fees ($122), and room and board ($6150). Full-time tuition and fees vary according to course load. Part-time tuition: $2894 per course. Part-time tuition and fees vary according to course load. *Room and board:* Room and board charges vary according to board plan and housing facility. *Payment plans:* tuition prepayment, installment. *Waivers:* employees or children of employees.

Financial Aid Of all full-time matriculated undergraduates who enrolled in 2001, 1281 applied for aid, 1074 were judged to have need, 371 had their need fully met. 642 Federal Work-Study jobs. In 2001, 457 non-need-based awards were made. *Average percent of need met:* 90%. *Average financial aid package:* $19,792. *Average need-based loan:* $3406. *Average need-based gift aid:* $15,819. *Average non-need based aid:* $10,419. *Average indebtedness upon graduation:* $17,762.

Applying *Options:* common application, electronic application, early admission, early action, deferred entrance. *Application fee:* $50. *Required:* essay or personal statement, high school transcript, minimum 2.0 GPA, 1 letter of recommendation. *Required for some:* interview. *Recommended:* interview. *Application deadlines:* 2/1 (freshmen), 2/1 (transfers). *Notification:* 4/1 (freshmen), 1/15 (early action).

Admissions Contact Dr. Robin Brown, Vice President for Enrollment, Willamette University, 900 State Street, Salem, OR 97301-3931. *Phone:* 503-370-6303. *Toll-free phone:* 877-542-2787. *Fax:* 503-375-5363. *E-mail:* undergrad-admission@willamette.edu.

PENNSYLVANIA

ALBRIGHT COLLEGE
Reading, Pennsylvania

- **Independent** 4-year, founded 1856, affiliated with United Methodist Church
- **Calendar** 4-1-4
- **Degree** certificates and bachelor's
- **Suburban** 110-acre campus with easy access to Philadelphia
- **Endowment** $36.5 million
- **Coed,** 1,809 undergraduate students, 95% full-time, 57% women, 43% men
- **Moderately difficult** entrance level, 73% of applicants were admitted

Albright College's motto could well be "excellence without attitude." Students achieve their goals in an open, flexible, and creative academic environment. For 146 years, it has been a place where students have a real impact, realize their dreams, and go on to make their mark in the real world.

Undergraduates 1,717 full-time, 92 part-time. Students come from 25 states and territories, 20 other countries, 27% are from out of state, 7% African American, 2% Asian American or Pacific Islander, 3% Hispanic American, 0.5% Native American, 4% international, 2% transferred in, 69% live on campus. *Retention:* 74% of 2001 full-time freshmen returned.

Freshmen *Admission:* 2,502 applied, 1,828 admitted, 402 enrolled. *Average high school GPA:* 3.2. *Test scores:* SAT verbal scores over 500: 57%; SAT math scores over 500: 56%; ACT scores over 18: 85%; SAT verbal scores over 600: 16%; SAT math scores over 600: 15%; ACT scores over 24: 29%; SAT verbal scores over 700: 2%; SAT math scores over 700: 1%; ACT scores over 30: 3%.

Faculty *Total:* 128, 69% full-time, 68% with terminal degrees. *Student/faculty ratio:* 14:1.

Majors Accounting; American studies; art; art education; biochemistry; biology; business administration; business marketing and marketing management; chemistry; clothing/apparel/textile studies; communications; computer science; criminology; early childhood education; economics; elementary education; English; environmental science; finance; forestry; French; history; information sciences/systems; interdisciplinary studies; international business; Latin American studies; mathematics; music; natural resources management; optics; organizational psychology; philosophy; physics; physiological psychology/psychobiology; political science; pre-dentistry; pre-law; pre-medicine; pre-veterinary studies; psychology; religious studies; secondary education; sociology; Spanish; special education; theater arts/drama; women's studies.

Academic Programs *Special study options:* academic remediation for entering students, accelerated degree program, advanced placement credit, double majors, English as a second language, honors programs, independent study, internships, off-campus study, part-time degree program, services for LD students, student-designed majors, study abroad, summer session for credit. *Unusual degree programs:* 3-2 forestry with Duke University; natural resource management with University of Michigan.

Library Gingrich Library plus 1 other with 208,457 titles, 2,280 serial subscriptions, 8,188 audiovisual materials, an OPAC, a Web page.

Computers on Campus 271 computers available on campus for general student use. A campuswide network can be accessed from student residence rooms and from off campus. Internet access, at least one staffed computer lab available.

Student Life *Housing:* on-campus residence required for freshman year. *Options:* coed, women-only. *Activities and Organizations:* drama/theater group, student-run newspaper, radio station, choral group, Campus Center Board, Student Government Association, yearbook, newspaper, radio station, national fraternities, national sororities. *Campus security:* 24-hour emergency response devices and patrols, student patrols, late-night transport/escort service, controlled dormitory access. *Student Services:* health clinic, personal/psychological counseling, women's center.

Athletics Member NCAA. All Division III. *Intercollegiate sports:* badminton W, baseball M, basketball M/W, cross-country running M/W, field hockey W, football M, golf M, lacrosse M(c)/W(c), rugby M(c)/W(c), soccer M/W, softball W, swimming M/W, tennis M/W, track and field M/W, volleyball W, wrestling M. *Intramural sports:* basketball M/W, football M, racquetball M/W, softball M/W, volleyball M/W, water polo M/W.

Standardized Tests *Required:* SAT I or ACT (for admission).

Costs (2001–02) *Comprehensive fee:* $27,642 includes full-time tuition ($20,750), mandatory fees ($550), and room and board ($6342). Full-time tuition and fees vary according to program. Part-time tuition: $2594 per course. Part-time tuition and fees vary according to class time. *Room and board:* College room only: $3549. Room and board charges vary according to board plan and housing facility. *Payment plan:* installment. *Waivers:* children of alumni, senior citizens, and employees or children of employees.

Financial Aid Of all full-time matriculated undergraduates who enrolled in 2001, 1252 applied for aid, 1135 were judged to have need, 271 had their need fully met. In 2001, 187 non-need-based awards were made. *Average percent of need met:* 82%. *Average financial aid package:* $16,749. *Average need-based loan:* $4190. *Average need-based gift aid:* $12,798. *Average indebtedness upon graduation:* $23,000.

Applying *Options:* common application, electronic application, early admission, deferred entrance. *Application fee:* $25. *Required:* essay or personal statement, high school transcript, 1 letter of recommendation, secondary school report (guidance department). *Recommended:* interview. *Application deadlines:* rolling (freshmen), 8/15 (transfers). *Notification:* continuous (freshmen).

Admissions Contact Mr. Gregory E. Eichhorn, Vice President for Enrollment Management, Albright College, P.O. Box 15234, 13th and Bern Streets, Reading, PA 19612-5234. *Phone:* 610-921-7260. *Toll-free phone:* 800-252-1856. *Fax:* 610-921-7294. *E-mail:* admission@alb.edu.

ALLEGHENY COLLEGE
Meadville, Pennsylvania

- **Independent** 4-year, founded 1815, affiliated with United Methodist Church
- **Calendar** semesters
- **Degree** bachelor's
- **Small-town** 254-acre campus
- **Endowment** $114.3 million
- **Coed,** 1,879 undergraduate students, 98% full-time, 53% women, 47% men
- **Very difficult** entrance level, 79% of applicants were admitted

The Allegheny College Center for Experiential Learning (ACCEL) is a vivid symbol of the College's commitment to preparing students for the working world and graduate and professional school. ACCEL gives students one-stop shopping for internships, off-campus study in the US and abroad, service learning opportunities, and leadership development programs.

Undergraduates 1,838 full-time, 41 part-time. Students come from 35 states and territories, 14 other countries, 33% are from out of state, 2% African

American, 2% Asian American or Pacific Islander, 1% Hispanic American, 0.3% Native American, 1% international, 1% transferred in, 75% live on campus. *Retention:* 88% of 2001 full-time freshmen returned.

Freshmen *Admission:* 2,530 applied, 1,994 admitted, 489 enrolled. *Average high school GPA:* 3.69. *Test scores:* SAT verbal scores over 500: 91%; SAT math scores over 500: 91%; ACT scores over 18: 98%; SAT verbal scores over 600: 51%; SAT math scores over 600: 50%; ACT scores over 24: 66%; SAT verbal scores over 700: 11%; SAT math scores over 700: 7%; ACT scores over 30: 13%.

Faculty *Total:* 161, 84% full-time, 81% with terminal degrees. *Student/faculty ratio:* 13:1.

Majors Art history; biology; chemistry; communications; computer/information sciences; computer science related; economics; English; environmental science; fine arts and art studies related; fine/studio arts; French; geology; German; history; international relations; mathematics; multi/interdisciplinary studies related; music; neuroscience; philosophy; physics; political science; psychology; religious studies; Spanish; theater arts/drama; women's studies.

Academic Programs *Special study options:* accelerated degree program, advanced placement credit, double majors, independent study, internships, off-campus study, part-time degree program, services for LD students, student-designed majors, study abroad. *ROTC:* Army (c). *Unusual degree programs:* 3-2 engineering with Columbia University, Case Western Reserve University, Duke University, Washington University, University of Pittsburgh; nursing with Case Western Reserve University.

Library Lawrence Lee Pelletier Library with 266,096 titles, 3,100 serial subscriptions, 6,095 audiovisual materials, an OPAC, a Web page.

Computers on Campus 245 computers available on campus for general student use. A campuswide network can be accessed from student residence rooms and from off campus. Internet access, at least one staffed computer lab available.

Student Life *Housing:* on-campus residence required through sophomore year. *Options:* coed, men-only, women-only, disabled students. *Activities and Organizations:* drama/theater group, student-run newspaper, radio and television station, choral group, student government, gators activity programming, Orchesis Dance Company, Service Network, Christian Outreach, national fraternities, national sororities. *Campus security:* 24-hour emergency response devices and patrols, student patrols, late-night transport/escort service, local police patrol. *Student Services:* health clinic, personal/psychological counseling.

Athletics Member NCAA. All Division III. *Intercollegiate sports:* baseball M, basketball M/W, cross-country running M/W, equestrian sports M(c)/W(c), fencing M(c)/W(c), football M, golf M, ice hockey M(c), lacrosse M(c)/W, rugby M(c)/W(c), soccer M/W, softball W, swimming M/W, tennis M/W, track and field M/W, volleyball M(c)/W. *Intramural sports:* basketball M/W, cross-country running M/W, football M/W, golf M/W, soccer M/W, softball M/W, tennis M/W, track and field M/W, volleyball M/W.

Standardized Tests *Required:* SAT I or ACT (for admission). *Recommended:* SAT II: Subject Tests (for admission), SAT II: Writing Test (for admission).

Costs (2001–02) *One-time required fee:* $300. *Comprehensive fee:* $27,780 includes full-time tuition ($22,210), mandatory fees ($280), and room and board ($5290). Part-time tuition: $925 per credit hour. Part-time tuition and fees vary according to course load. *Required fees:* $140 per term part-time. *Room and board:* College room only: $2660. Room and board charges vary according to board plan and housing facility. *Payment plans:* tuition prepayment, installment. *Waivers:* employees or children of employees.

Financial Aid Of all full-time matriculated undergraduates who enrolled in 2001, 1515 applied for aid, 1338 were judged to have need, 733 had their need fully met. 1091 Federal Work-Study jobs (averaging $1394). 330 State and other part-time jobs (averaging $1390). In 2001, 421 non-need-based awards were made. *Average percent of need met:* 95%. *Average financial aid package:* $18,348. *Average need-based loan:* $4378. *Average need-based gift aid:* $12,873. *Average non-need based aid:* $7873. *Average indebtedness upon graduation:* $21,324. *Financial aid deadline:* 2/15.

Applying *Options:* common application, electronic application, early admission, early decision, deferred entrance. *Application fee:* $35. *Required:* essay or personal statement, high school transcript, 2 letters of recommendation. *Recommended:* interview. *Application deadlines:* 2/15 (freshmen), 7/1 (transfers). *Early decision:* 1/15. *Notification:* 4/1 (freshmen), 10/15 (early decision).

Admissions Contact Ms. Megan K. Murphy, Dean of Admissions and Enrollment Management, Allegheny College, 520 North Main Street, Box 5, Meadville, PA 16335. *Phone:* 814-332-4351. *Toll-free phone:* 800-521-5293. *Fax:* 814-337-0431. *E-mail:* admiss@allegheny.edu.

ALVERNIA COLLEGE
Reading, Pennsylvania

- **Independent Roman Catholic** comprehensive, founded 1958
- **Calendar** semesters
- **Degrees** associate, bachelor's, and master's
- **Suburban** 85-acre campus with easy access to Philadelphia
- **Endowment** $10.6 million
- **Coed,** 1,582 undergraduate students, 71% full-time, 66% women, 34% men
- **Moderately difficult** entrance level, 78% of applicants were admitted

Alvernia College, a private Catholic college, blends traditional liberal arts with professional programs. Alvernia offers twenty-seven bachelor's degree programs geared to meet the needs of students and the community. Programs include athletic training, forensic science, and sports management. A 25,000-square-foot campus center and new residence hall opened in summer 1999.

Undergraduates 1,130 full-time, 452 part-time. Students come from 11 states and territories, 16 other countries, 8% are from out of state, 9% African American, 2% Asian American or Pacific Islander, 3% Hispanic American, 0.3% Native American, 0.7% international, 11% transferred in, 25% live on campus. *Retention:* 69% of 2001 full-time freshmen returned.

Freshmen *Admission:* 755 applied, 592 admitted, 248 enrolled. *Average high school GPA:* 2.92. *Test scores:* SAT verbal scores over 500: 39%; SAT math scores over 500: 33%; ACT scores over 18: 55%; SAT verbal scores over 600: 7%; SAT math scores over 600: 4%; ACT scores over 24: 11%; SAT verbal scores over 700: 1%.

Faculty *Total:* 184, 32% full-time, 31% with terminal degrees. *Student/faculty ratio:* 14:1.

Majors Accounting; alcohol/drug abuse counseling; biochemistry; biological/physical sciences; biology; biology education; biomedical technology; business administration; business marketing and marketing management; chemistry; chemistry education; communications; criminal justice/law enforcement administration; early childhood education; education; elementary education; English; English education; forensic technology; health services administration; history; information sciences/systems; liberal arts and sciences/liberal studies; mathematics; mathematics education; medical technology; nursing; occupational therapy; philosophy; physical therapy; political science; pre-law; pre-medicine; psychology; religious studies; science education; social sciences; social work; sport/fitness administration; theology.

Academic Programs *Special study options:* academic remediation for entering students, accelerated degree program, adult/continuing education programs, advanced placement credit, double majors, honors programs, independent study, internships, off-campus study, part-time degree program, services for LD students, summer session for credit. *ROTC:* Army (c). *Unusual degree programs:* occupational therapy.

Library Franco Library with 86,000 titles, 400 serial subscriptions, 7,600 audiovisual materials, an OPAC, a Web page.

Computers on Campus 60 computers available on campus for general student use. A campuswide network can be accessed from student residence rooms. At least one staffed computer lab available.

Student Life *Housing Options:* coed. *Activities and Organizations:* drama/theater group, student-run newspaper, choral group, Student Government Association, Phi Beta Lambda, Criminal Justice Association, Education Association, Society for Human Resource Management. *Campus security:* 24-hour patrols, late-night transport/escort service, controlled dormitory access. *Student Services:* health clinic, personal/psychological counseling.

Athletics Member NCAA. All Division III. *Intercollegiate sports:* baseball M, basketball M/W, cross-country running M/W, field hockey W, golf M, lacrosse W, soccer M/W, softball W, tennis M/W, volleyball W. *Intramural sports:* basketball M/W, lacrosse M(c), skiing (downhill) M(c)/W(c), volleyball M(c).

Standardized Tests *Required:* SAT I or ACT (for admission).

Costs (2001–02) *Comprehensive fee:* $20,790 includes full-time tuition ($14,140) and room and board ($6650). Part-time tuition: $435 per credit. Part-time tuition and fees vary according to class time and course load. *Room and board:* College room only: $3500. Room and board charges vary according to board plan and housing facility. *Payment plans:* installment, deferred payment. *Waivers:* senior citizens and employees or children of employees.

Financial Aid Available in 2001, 56 State and other part-time jobs. *Average need-based loan:* $5000. *Average indebtedness upon graduation:* $12,000.

Applying *Options:* common application, electronic application, early admission, deferred entrance. *Application fee:* $25. *Required:* essay or personal statement, high school transcript. *Required for some:* 2 letters of recommendation, interview. *Recommended:* minimum 2.0 GPA, 1 letter of recommendation. *Application deadline:* rolling (freshmen), rolling (transfers).

Admissions Contact Betsy Stiles, Assistant Dean of Enrollment Management, Alvernia College, 400 Saint Bernardine Street, Reading, PA 19607. *Phone:* 610-796-8220. *Toll-free phone:* 888-ALVERNIA. *Fax:* 610-796-8336.

ARCADIA UNIVERSITY
Glenside, Pennsylvania

- **Independent** comprehensive, founded 1853, affiliated with Presbyterian Church (U.S.A.)
- **Calendar** semesters
- **Degrees** bachelor's, master's, and doctoral
- **Suburban** 60-acre campus with easy access to Philadelphia
- **Endowment** $23.1 million
- **Coed,** 1,636 undergraduate students, 81% full-time, 73% women, 27% men
- **Moderately difficult** entrance level, 84% of applicants were admitted

Undergraduates 1,320 full-time, 316 part-time. Students come from 22 states and territories, 9 other countries, 27% are from out of state, 11% African American, 3% Asian American or Pacific Islander, 2% Hispanic American, 0.1% Native American, 2% international, 6% transferred in, 60% live on campus. *Retention:* 82% of 2001 full-time freshmen returned.

Freshmen *Admission:* 1,642 applied, 1,374 admitted, 357 enrolled. *Average high school GPA:* 2.9. *Test scores:* SAT verbal scores over 500: 73%; SAT math scores over 500: 64%; SAT verbal scores over 600: 27%; SAT math scores over 600: 18%; SAT verbal scores over 700: 3%; SAT math scores over 700: 1%.

Faculty *Total:* 289, 36% full-time, 85% with terminal degrees. *Student/faculty ratio:* 12:1.

Majors Accounting; art; art education; art history; art therapy; biology; business administration; business marketing and marketing management; ceramic arts; chemistry; community services; computer programming; computer science; drawing; early childhood education; education; elementary education; English; environmental biology; finance; fine/studio arts; graphic design/commercial art/illustration; health services administration; history; human resources management; human services; interior design; international business; liberal arts and sciences/liberal studies; literature; management information systems/business data processing; mass communications; mathematics; medical illustrating; metal/jewelry arts; natural sciences; philosophy; photography; physiological psychology/psychobiology; political science; pre-dentistry; pre-law; pre-medicine; pre-veterinary studies; psychology; secondary education; sociology; Spanish; special education; theater arts/drama.

Academic Programs *Special study options:* adult/continuing education programs, advanced placement credit, cooperative education, distance learning, double majors, English as a second language, honors programs, independent study, internships, off-campus study, part-time degree program, services for LD students, student-designed majors, study abroad, summer session for credit. *ROTC:* Army (c). *Unusual degree programs:* 3-2 engineering with Columbia University; environmental studies; optometry with Pennsylvania College of Optometry.

Library Eugenia Fuller Atwood Library with 139,903 titles, 798 serial subscriptions, 2,861 audiovisual materials, an OPAC, a Web page.

Computers on Campus 110 computers available on campus for general student use. A campuswide network can be accessed from student residence rooms and from off campus. Internet access, at least one staffed computer lab available.

Student Life *Housing Options:* coed, women-only. *Activities and Organizations:* drama/theater group, student-run newspaper, radio station, choral group, Student Program Board, Residence Hall Council, student government, Beaver College Christian Fellowship, Student Alumni Association. *Campus security:* 24-hour emergency response devices and patrols, student patrols, late-night transport/escort service, controlled dormitory access. *Student Services:* health clinic, personal/psychological counseling.

Athletics Member NCAA. All Division III. *Intercollegiate sports:* baseball M, basketball M/W, cross-country running M/W, equestrian sports M/W, field hockey W, golf M/W, lacrosse W, soccer M/W, softball W, swimming M/W, tennis M/W, volleyball W. *Intramural sports:* basketball M/W, equestrian sports M/W, field hockey W, soccer M/W, swimming M, tennis M/W, volleyball M/W, weight lifting M/W.

Standardized Tests *Required:* SAT I or ACT (for admission).

Costs (2001–02) *Comprehensive fee:* $26,650 includes full-time tuition ($18,390), mandatory fees ($280), and room and board ($7980). Full-time tuition and fees vary according to program. Part-time tuition: $330 per credit. *Room and board:* Room and board charges vary according to board plan. *Payment plans:* installment, deferred payment. *Waivers:* employees or children of employees.

Financial Aid Of all full-time matriculated undergraduates who enrolled in 2001, 1289 applied for aid, 1261 were judged to have need, 402 had their need fully met. 612 Federal Work-Study jobs (averaging $1294). 182 State and other part-time jobs (averaging $1081). *Average percent of need met:* 91%. *Average financial aid package:* $12,637. *Average need-based loan:* $3136. *Average need-based gift aid:* $5809. *Average non-need based aid:* $5376. *Average indebtedness upon graduation:* $20,727.

Applying *Options:* common application, electronic application, early admission, early decision, deferred entrance. *Application fee:* $30. *Required:* essay or personal statement, high school transcript, 2 letters of recommendation. *Required for some:* portfolio. *Recommended:* interview. *Application deadline:* rolling (freshmen), rolling (transfers). *Early decision:* 11/1. *Notification:* continuous until 9/1 (freshmen), 12/1 (early decision).

Admissions Contact Mr. Dennis L. Nostrand, Director of Enrollment Management, Arcadia University, 450 South Easton Road, Glenside, PA 19038. *Phone:* 215-572-2910. *Toll-free phone:* 877-ARCADIA. *Fax:* 215-572-4049. *E-mail:* admiss@arcadia.edu.

THE ART INSTITUTE OF PHILADELPHIA
Philadelphia, Pennsylvania

- **Proprietary** primarily 2-year, founded 1966, part of The Art Institutes
- **Calendar** quarters
- **Degrees** associate and bachelor's
- **Urban** campus
- **Coed,** 2,807 undergraduate students, 70% full-time, 41% women, 59% men
- **Minimally difficult** entrance level, 56% of applicants were admitted

Undergraduates 1,975 full-time, 832 part-time. Students come from 30 states and territories, 25 other countries, 23% African American, 6% Asian American or Pacific Islander, 7% Hispanic American, 1% Native American, 2% international, 0.4% transferred in, 26% live on campus.

Freshmen *Admission:* 2,065 applied, 1,158 admitted, 778 enrolled. *Average high school GPA:* 2.7. *Test scores:* SAT verbal scores over 500: 54%; SAT math scores over 500: 54%; ACT scores over 18: 3%; SAT verbal scores over 600: 24%; SAT math scores over 600: 24%; ACT scores over 24: 1%; SAT verbal scores over 700: 1%; SAT math scores over 700: 1%.

Faculty *Total:* 230, 33% full-time. *Student/faculty ratio:* 20:1.

Majors Applied art; art; culinary arts; fashion design/illustration; fashion merchandising; film/video and photographic arts related; film/video production; graphic design/commercial art/illustration; industrial design; interior design; multimedia; photography; visual and performing arts related.

Academic Programs *Special study options:* academic remediation for entering students, adult/continuing education programs, advanced placement credit, cooperative education, internships, off-campus study, part-time degree program, services for LD students, summer session for credit.

Library The Art Institute of Philadelphia Library with 19,200 titles, 150 serial subscriptions, 2,000 audiovisual materials, an OPAC.

Computers on Campus 368 computers available on campus for general student use. Internet access, at least one staffed computer lab available.

Student Life *Housing Options:* coed, disabled students. *Activities and Organizations:* student-run newspaper. *Campus security:* controlled dormitory access. *Student Services:* personal/psychological counseling.

Standardized Tests *Recommended:* SAT I or ACT (for placement).

Costs (2001–02) *One-time required fee:* $100. *Tuition:* $19,500 full-time, $325 per credit hour part-time. Full-time tuition and fees vary according to course load and program. Part-time tuition and fees vary according to course load and program. No tuition increase for student's term of enrollment. *Room only:* $7472. Room and board charges vary according to housing facility. *Payment plans:* installment, deferred payment. *Waivers:* employees or children of employees.

Applying *Options:* common application, deferred entrance. *Application fee:* $50. *Required:* essay or personal statement, high school transcript, interview. *Recommended:* minimum 2.0 GPA, letters of recommendation. *Application deadline:* rolling (freshmen), rolling (transfers). *Notification:* continuous (freshmen).

Admissions Contact Mr. Tim Howard, Director of Admissions, The Art Institute of Philadelphia, 1622 Chestnut Street, Philadelphia, PA 19103. *Phone:* 215-567-7080 Ext. 6337. *Toll-free phone:* 800-275-2474. *Fax:* 215-405-6399.

THE ART INSTITUTE OF PITTSBURGH
Pittsburgh, Pennsylvania

- **Proprietary** primarily 2-year, founded 1921, part of The Art Institutes International
- **Calendar** quarters
- **Degrees** diplomas, associate, and bachelor's
- **Urban** campus
- **Coed**
- **Minimally difficult** entrance level

Faculty *Student/faculty ratio:* 20:1.

Student Life *Campus security:* 24-hour emergency response devices and patrols, controlled dormitory access.

Standardized Tests *Required:* ACT ASSET. *Recommended:* SAT I or ACT (for placement).

Applying *Options:* common application, deferred entrance. *Application fee:* $50. *Required:* essay or personal statement, high school transcript, minimum 2.0 GPA. *Recommended:* interview.

Admissions Contact Ms. Elaine Cook-Bartoli, Director of Admissions, The Art Institute of Pittsburgh, 420 Boulevard of the Allies, Pittsburgh, PA 15219. *Phone:* 412-291-6220. *Toll-free phone:* 800-275-2470. *Fax:* 412-263-6667. *E-mail:* admissions@aii.edu.

BAPTIST BIBLE COLLEGE OF PENNSYLVANIA
Clarks Summit, Pennsylvania

- **Independent Baptist** comprehensive, founded 1932
- **Calendar** semesters
- **Degrees** certificates, associate, bachelor's, master's, doctoral, and first professional
- **Suburban** 124-acre campus
- **Endowment** $1.3 million
- **Coed,** 734 undergraduate students, 93% full-time, 56% women, 44% men
- **Minimally difficult** entrance level, 87% of applicants were admitted

Undergraduates 683 full-time, 51 part-time. Students come from 30 states and territories, 4 other countries, 51% are from out of state, 0.3% African American, 0.7% Asian American or Pacific Islander, 0.5% Hispanic American, 0.4% Native American, 0.3% international, 10% transferred in, 80% live on campus. *Retention:* 74% of 2001 full-time freshmen returned.

Freshmen *Admission:* 352 applied, 306 admitted, 153 enrolled. *Average high school GPA:* 3.11. *Test scores:* SAT verbal scores over 500: 55%; SAT math scores over 500: 45%; ACT scores over 18: 72%; SAT verbal scores over 600: 20%; SAT math scores over 600: 14%; ACT scores over 24: 31%; SAT verbal scores over 700: 5%; SAT math scores over 700: 1%; ACT scores over 30: 3%.

Faculty *Total:* 32, 88% full-time, 28% with terminal degrees. *Student/faculty ratio:* 25:1.

Majors Biblical studies; divinity/ministry; education; elementary education; music; music (piano and organ performance); music teacher education; pastoral counseling; psychology; religious education; religious music; secondary education; secretarial science; speech/theater education.

Academic Programs *Special study options:* academic remediation for entering students, advanced placement credit, internships, part-time degree program, study abroad, summer session for credit. *ROTC:* Army (c).

Library Murphy Memorial Library plus 1 other with 104,534 titles, 502 serial subscriptions, 27,088 audiovisual materials.

Computers on Campus 25 computers available on campus for general student use. A campuswide network can be accessed from student residence rooms. Internet access, at least one staffed computer lab available.

Student Life *Housing:* on-campus residence required through senior year. *Options:* men-only, women-only. *Activities and Organizations:* drama/theater group, choral group. *Campus security:* 24-hour patrols, student patrols. *Student Services:* health clinic, personal/psychological counseling.

Athletics Member NCCAA. *Intercollegiate sports:* basketball M/W, cross-country running M/W, soccer M/W, track and field M/W, volleyball M/W, wrestling M. *Intramural sports:* basketball M/W, football M, soccer M/W, softball M/W, table tennis M/W, tennis M/W, volleyball M/W.

Standardized Tests *Required:* SAT I or ACT (for admission).

Costs (2002–03) *Comprehensive fee:* $15,492 includes full-time tuition ($9700), mandatory fees ($900), and room and board ($4892). Part-time tuition: $270 per hour. Part-time tuition and fees vary according to course load. *Required fees:* $30 per hour. *Room and board:* College room only: $1922. *Payment plan:* installment. *Waivers:* employees or children of employees.

Financial Aid Of all full-time matriculated undergraduates who enrolled in 2001, 508 applied for aid, 437 were judged to have need, 6 had their need fully met. In 2001, 30 non-need-based awards were made. *Average percent of need met:* 60%. *Average financial aid package:* $5451. *Average need-based loan:* $1856. *Average need-based gift aid:* $1471. *Average non-need based aid:* $4238. *Average indebtedness upon graduation:* $14,500.

Applying *Options:* early admission, deferred entrance. *Application fee:* $30. *Required:* essay or personal statement, high school transcript, 3 letters of recommendation, Christian testimony. *Required for some:* interview. *Application deadline:* 8/15 (freshmen), rolling (transfers).

Admissions Contact Ms. Chris Hansen, Applications Coordinator, Baptist Bible College of Pennsylvania, PO Box 800, Clarks Summit, PA 18411-1297. *Phone:* 570-586-2400 Ext. 9370. *Toll-free phone:* 800-451-7664. *Fax:* 570-585-9400. *E-mail:* gamos@bbc.edu.

BLOOMSBURG UNIVERSITY OF PENNSYLVANIA
Bloomsburg, Pennsylvania

- **State-supported** comprehensive, founded 1839, part of Pennsylvania State System of Higher Education
- **Calendar** semesters
- **Degrees** associate, bachelor's, master's, and postbachelor's certificates
- **Small-town** 282-acre campus
- **Endowment** $9.8 million
- **Coed,** 7,222 undergraduate students, 92% full-time, 61% women, 39% men
- **Moderately difficult** entrance level, 79% of applicants were admitted

Undergraduates 6,657 full-time, 565 part-time. Students come from 26 states and territories, 28 other countries, 10% are from out of state, 3% African American, 0.8% Asian American or Pacific Islander, 2% Hispanic American, 0.2% Native American, 0.5% international, 5% transferred in, 43% live on campus. *Retention:* 80% of 2001 full-time freshmen returned.

Freshmen *Admission:* 6,413 applied, 5,083 admitted, 1,692 enrolled. *Average high school GPA:* 3.00. *Test scores:* SAT verbal scores over 500: 55%; SAT math scores over 500: 58%; SAT verbal scores over 600: 10%; SAT math scores over 600: 12%.

Faculty *Total:* 394, 91% full-time, 73% with terminal degrees. *Student/faculty ratio:* 20:1.

Majors Accounting; anthropology; art history; biology; business administration; business economics; business education; chemistry; communications; computer/information sciences; criminal justice studies; early childhood education; earth sciences; economics; economics related; education of the speech impaired; electrical engineering; elementary education; English; exercise sciences; fine/studio arts; French; geography; geology; German; health physics/radiologic health; health science; history; humanities; interdisciplinary studies; mass communications; mathematics; medical laboratory technician; medical radiologic technology; medical technology; music; nursing; philosophy; physics; political science; psychology; science education; secondary education; sign language interpretation; social sciences; social studies education; social work; sociology; Spanish; special education; speech/rhetorical studies; theater arts/drama.

Academic Programs *Special study options:* academic remediation for entering students, adult/continuing education programs, advanced placement credit, cooperative education, distance learning, double majors, freshman honors college, honors programs, independent study, internships, off-campus study, part-time degree program, services for LD students, study abroad, summer session for credit. *ROTC:* Army (b), Air Force (c). *Unusual degree programs:* 3-2 engineering with Pennsylvania State University, Wilkes University.

Library Andruss Library with 278,835 titles, 2,372 serial subscriptions, 6,118 audiovisual materials, an OPAC.

Computers on Campus 700 computers available on campus for general student use. A campuswide network can be accessed from student residence rooms and from off campus. Internet access, online (class) registration, at least one staffed computer lab available.

Student Life *Housing:* on-campus residence required for freshman year. *Options:* coed, men-only, women-only. *Activities and Organizations:* drama/theater group, student-run newspaper, radio and television station, choral group, marching band, national fraternities, national sororities. *Campus security:* 24-hour emergency response devices and patrols, late-night transport/escort service, monitored surveillance cameras. *Student Services:* health clinic, personal/psychological counseling, women's center, legal services.

Athletics Member NCAA. All Division II except wrestling (Division I). *Intercollegiate sports:* baseball M, basketball M(s)/W(s), bowling M(c)/W(c), cross-country running M/W(s), field hockey W(s), football M(s), lacrosse W, soccer M/W(s), softball W(s), swimming M(s)/W(s), tennis M(s)/W(s), track and field M(s)/W(s), wrestling M(s). *Intramural sports:* badminton W, baseball M, basketball M/W, bowling M(c)/W, cross-country running M, fencing M(c)/W(c), field hockey W, football M/W, golf M/W, gymnastics M/W, ice hockey M(c), lacrosse M(c), racquetball M/W, rugby M(c)/W(c), skiing (downhill) M(c)/W(c), soccer M, softball M/W, table tennis M(c)/W(c), tennis M/W, track and field M, volleyball M/W, water polo M(c)/W(c), weight lifting M, wrestling M.

Standardized Tests *Required:* SAT I or ACT (for admission).

Costs (2001–02) *Tuition:* state resident $4016 full-time, $167 per credit part-time; nonresident $10,040 full-time, $418 per credit part-time. Full-time tuition and fees vary according to course load. Part-time tuition and fees vary

Bloomsburg University of Pennsylvania (continued)
according to course load. *Required fees:* $976 full-time. *Room and board:* $4442. Room and board charges vary according to board plan and housing facility. *Waivers:* minority students and employees or children of employees.

Financial Aid Of all full-time matriculated undergraduates who enrolled in 2001, 5301 applied for aid, 4241 were judged to have need, 3626 had their need fully met. 739 Federal Work-Study jobs (averaging $1053). 962 State and other part-time jobs (averaging $1319). *Average percent of need met:* 65%. *Average financial aid package:* $7203. *Average need-based gift aid:* $2899. *Average indebtedness upon graduation:* $14,911.

Applying *Options:* common application, electronic application, early admission, early decision, deferred entrance. *Application fee:* $30. *Required:* high school transcript, letters of recommendation. *Application deadline:* rolling (freshmen), rolling (transfers). *Early decision:* 11/15. *Notification:* 10/1 (freshmen), 12/1 (early decision).

Admissions Contact Mr. Christopher Keller, Director of Admissions, Bloomsburg University of Pennsylvania, 104 Student Services Center, Bloomsburg, PA 17815-1905. *Phone:* 570-389-4316. *E-mail:* buadmiss@bloomu.edu.

BRYN ATHYN COLLEGE OF THE NEW CHURCH
Bryn Athyn, Pennsylvania

- **Independent Swedenborgian** comprehensive, founded 1876
- **Calendar** 3 12-week terms
- **Degrees** associate, bachelor's, master's, and first professional
- **Small-town** 130-acre campus with easy access to Philadelphia
- **Coed,** 138 undergraduate students, 94% full-time, 63% women, 37% men
- **Minimally difficult** entrance level, 99% of applicants were admitted

Undergraduates 130 full-time, 8 part-time. Students come from 17 states and territories, 14 other countries, 26% are from out of state, 0.9% African American, 2% Asian American or Pacific Islander, 18% international, 3% transferred in, 62% live on campus. *Retention:* 71% of 2001 full-time freshmen returned.

Freshmen *Admission:* 145 applied, 144 admitted, 59 enrolled. *Test scores:* SAT verbal scores over 500: 87%; SAT math scores over 500: 67%; SAT verbal scores over 600: 44%; SAT math scores over 600: 39%; SAT verbal scores over 700: 13%.

Faculty *Total:* 53, 68% full-time, 45% with terminal degrees. *Student/faculty ratio:* 6:1.

Majors Biological/physical sciences; biology; chemistry; elementary education; English; history; humanities; interdisciplinary studies; religious studies; social sciences.

Academic Programs *Special study options:* academic remediation for entering students, accelerated degree program, advanced placement credit, cooperative education, double majors, independent study, internships, part-time degree program, services for LD students, student-designed majors.

Library Swedenborg Library plus 2 others with 91,591 titles, 180 serial subscriptions, 559 audiovisual materials, an OPAC.

Computers on Campus 40 computers available on campus for general student use. A campuswide network can be accessed from student residence rooms. Internet access, at least one staffed computer lab available.

Student Life *Housing:* on-campus residence required for freshman year. *Options:* men-only, women-only. *Activities and Organizations:* drama/theater group, student-run newspaper, choral group, Outing Club, community interest activities, Drama Club. *Campus security:* 24-hour patrols, controlled dormitory access. *Student Services:* health clinic, personal/psychological counseling.

Athletics *Intercollegiate sports:* badminton W, ice hockey M, lacrosse M, soccer M, volleyball W. *Intramural sports:* basketball M, lacrosse W, soccer M, volleyball M/W.

Standardized Tests *Required:* SAT I or ACT (for admission).

Costs (2001–02) *Comprehensive fee:* $10,590 includes full-time tuition ($5100), mandatory fees ($909), and room and board ($4581). Part-time tuition: $199 per credit. *Required fees:* $33 per credit. *Payment plan:* installment. *Waivers:* senior citizens and employees or children of employees.

Financial Aid Of all full-time matriculated undergraduates who enrolled in 2001, 71 applied for aid, 63 were judged to have need, 8 had their need fully met. In 2001, 11 non-need-based awards were made. *Average financial aid package:* $5784. *Average need-based loan:* $2000. *Average non-need based aid:* $761. *Financial aid deadline:* 6/1.

Applying *Options:* common application, electronic application, deferred entrance. *Application fee:* $30. *Required:* essay or personal statement, high school transcript, 2 letters of recommendation. *Required for some:* interview. *Application deadline:* 7/1 (freshmen), rolling (transfers).

Admissions Contact Dr. Dan Synnestvedt, Director of Admissions, Bryn Athyn College of the New Church, PO Box 717, Bryn Athyn, PA 19009-0717. *Phone:* 215-938-2503. *Fax:* 215-938-2658.

BRYN MAWR COLLEGE
Bryn Mawr, Pennsylvania

- **Independent** university, founded 1885
- **Calendar** semesters
- **Degrees** bachelor's, master's, and doctoral
- **Suburban** 135-acre campus with easy access to Philadelphia
- **Endowment** $437.2 million
- **Women only,** 1,333 undergraduate students, 96% full-time
- **Most difficult** entrance level, 60% of applicants were admitted

Bryn Mawr students enjoy a demanding liberal arts education in a small university setting 10 miles from one of the largest cities in the United States—Philadelphia. Distinctive cooperative agreements with nearby Haverford College, Swarthmore College, and the University of Pennsylvania allow for extensive and varied academic, social, and residential exchange. A $22-million chemistry complex and science library opened in 1993, and the Rhys Carpenter Library for Art, Archaeology and Cities was opened to the public in 1997.

Undergraduates 1,279 full-time, 54 part-time. Students come from 48 states and territories, 44 other countries, 80% are from out of state, 4% African American, 15% Asian American or Pacific Islander, 3% Hispanic American, 8% international, 1% transferred in, 98% live on campus. *Retention:* 89% of 2001 full-time freshmen returned.

Freshmen *Admission:* 338 enrolled. *Test scores:* SAT verbal scores over 500: 98%; SAT math scores over 500: 97%; SAT verbal scores over 600: 81%; SAT math scores over 600: 71%; SAT verbal scores over 700: 31%; SAT math scores over 700: 14%.

Faculty *Total:* 184, 79% full-time, 93% with terminal degrees. *Student/faculty ratio:* 9:1.

Majors Anthropology; archaeology; art; art history; astronomy; biology; chemistry; classics; comparative literature; East Asian studies; economics; English; French; geology; German; Greek (ancient and medieval); history; Italian; Latin (ancient and medieval); mathematics; music; philosophy; physics; political science; psychology; religious studies; romance languages; Russian; sociology; Spanish; urban studies.

Academic Programs *Special study options:* academic remediation for entering students, accelerated degree program, adult/continuing education programs, advanced placement credit, double majors, honors programs, independent study, off-campus study, services for LD students, student-designed majors, study abroad, summer session for credit. *ROTC:* Air Force (c). *Unusual degree programs:* 3-2 engineering with University of Pennsylvania; city and regional planning with University of Pennsylvania.

Library Miriam Coffin Canaday Library plus 2 others with 932,423 titles, 4,045 serial subscriptions, 1,380 audiovisual materials, an OPAC, a Web page.

Computers on Campus 200 computers available on campus for general student use. A campuswide network can be accessed from student residence rooms and from off campus. Internet access, at least one staffed computer lab available.

Student Life *Housing:* on-campus residence required for freshman year. *Options:* women-only. *Activities and Organizations:* drama/theater group, student-run newspaper, choral group, musical and theater groups, community service, Student Government Association, International Students Association, cultural groups. *Campus security:* 24-hour emergency response devices and patrols, late-night transport/escort service, controlled dormitory access, shuttle bus service, awareness programs, bicycle registration, security Website. *Student Services:* health clinic, personal/psychological counseling, women's center.

Athletics Member NCAA. All Division III. *Intercollegiate sports:* badminton W, basketball W, crew W, cross-country running W, field hockey W, lacrosse W, rugby W(c), soccer W, swimming W, tennis W, track and field W, volleyball W. *Intramural sports:* archery W, badminton W, cross-country running W, equestrian sports W, field hockey W, lacrosse W, rugby W, soccer W, softball W, swimming W, tennis W, track and field W, volleyball W, weight lifting W.

Costs (2001–02) *Comprehensive fee:* $33,580 includes full-time tuition ($24,340), mandatory fees ($650), and room and board ($8590). Part-time tuition: $3050 per course. Part-time tuition and fees vary according to course load. *Room and board:* College room only: $4960. Room and board charges vary according to board plan. *Payment plans:* tuition prepayment, installment. *Waivers:* senior citizens and employees or children of employees.

Financial Aid Of all full-time matriculated undergraduates who enrolled in 2001, 849 applied for aid, 761 were judged to have need, 579 had their need fully

met. 466 Federal Work-Study jobs (averaging $1580). 113 State and other part-time jobs (averaging $1400). *Average percent of need met:* 96%. *Average financial aid package:* $22,848. *Average need-based loan:* $6497. *Average need-based gift aid:* $18,324. *Financial aid deadline:* 1/15.

Applying *Options:* common application, electronic application, early admission, early decision, deferred entrance. *Application fee:* $50. *Required:* essay or personal statement, high school transcript, 3 letters of recommendation. *Recommended:* interview. *Application deadlines:* 1/15 (freshmen), 3/15 (transfers). *Early decision:* 11/15 (for plan 1), 1/1 (for plan 2). *Notification:* 4/1 (freshmen), 12/15 (early decision plan 1), 2/1 (early decision plan 2).

Admissions Contact Ms. Elizabeth Mosier, Acting Director of Admissions, Bryn Mawr College, 101 North Merion Avenue, Bryn Mawr, PA 19010. *Phone:* 610-526-5152. *Toll-free phone:* 800-BMC-1885. *E-mail:* admissions@brynmawr.edu.

BUCKNELL UNIVERSITY
Lewisburg, Pennsylvania

- **Independent** comprehensive, founded 1846
- **Calendar** semesters
- **Degrees** bachelor's and master's
- **Small-town** 393-acre campus
- **Endowment** $428.9 million
- **Coed,** 3,430 undergraduate students, 99% full-time, 49% women, 51% men
- **Very difficult** entrance level, 39% of applicants were admitted

Bucknell University is a top-ranked university that gives students broad choices of academic programs and activities and the intense personal support of faculty members who help students make the most of their college education. The University's 3,350 undergraduates and 200 graduate students are high achievers who enjoy becoming active members of a close-knit Bucknell community.

Undergraduates 3,399 full-time, 31 part-time. Students come from 48 states and territories, 33 other countries, 67% are from out of state, 3% African American, 5% Asian American or Pacific Islander, 3% Hispanic American, 0.4% Native American, 2% international, 0.8% transferred in, 87% live on campus. *Retention:* 94% of 2001 full-time freshmen returned.

Freshmen *Admission:* 8,033 applied, 3,123 admitted, 913 enrolled. *Test scores:* SAT verbal scores over 500: 97%; SAT math scores over 500: 99%; ACT scores over 18: 100%; SAT verbal scores over 600: 72%; SAT math scores over 600: 85%; ACT scores over 24: 89%; SAT verbal scores over 700: 15%; SAT math scores over 700: 25%; ACT scores over 30: 32%.

Faculty *Total:* 314, 92% full-time, 84% with terminal degrees. *Student/faculty ratio:* 12:1.

Majors Accounting; anthropology; area studies; art; art history; biology; biopsychology; business administration; cell biology; chemical engineering; chemistry; civil engineering; classics; computer engineering; computer/information sciences; early childhood education; East Asian studies; economics; education; educational statistics/research methods; electrical engineering; elementary education; English; environmental science; fine/studio arts; French; geography; geology; German; history; humanities; interdisciplinary studies; international relations; Latin American studies; mathematics; mechanical engineering; music; music (general performance); music history; music teacher education; music theory and composition; philosophy; physics; political science; psychology; religious studies; Russian; secondary education; sociology; Spanish; theater arts/drama; women's studies.

Academic Programs *Special study options:* advanced placement credit, double majors, honors programs, independent study, internships, off-campus study, part-time degree program, services for LD students, student-designed majors, study abroad, summer session for credit. *ROTC:* Army (b). *Unusual degree programs:* 3-2 chemistry, biology, mathematics.

Library Ellen Clarke Bertrand Library with 432,730 titles, 2,789 serial subscriptions, 5,946 audiovisual materials, an OPAC, a Web page.

Computers on Campus 350 computers available on campus for general student use. A campuswide network can be accessed from student residence rooms and from off campus. Internet access, at least one staffed computer lab available.

Student Life *Housing:* on-campus residence required through senior year. *Options:* coed, men-only, women-only, disabled students. *Activities and Organizations:* drama/theater group, student-run newspaper, radio station, choral group, Alpha Phi Omega, Outing Club, C.A.L.V.I.N. & H.O.B.B.E.S., International Spectrum, Activities Council, national fraternities, national sororities. *Campus security:* 24-hour emergency response devices and patrols, student patrols, late-night transport/escort service, well-lit pathways, self-defense education, safety/security orientation. *Student Services:* health clinic, personal/psychological counseling, women's center.

Athletics Member NCAA. All Division I except football (Division I-AA). *Intercollegiate sports:* baseball M, basketball M/W, crew M/W, cross-country running M/W, equestrian sports M(c)/W(c), field hockey W, golf M/W, ice hockey M(c), lacrosse M/W, rugby M(c)/W(c), skiing (downhill) M(c)/W(c), soccer M/W, softball W, swimming M/W, tennis M/W, track and field M/W, volleyball M(c)/W, water polo M/W, wrestling M. *Intramural sports:* basketball M/W, bowling M/W, cross-country running M/W, racquetball M/W, soccer M/W, softball M/W, squash M/W, tennis M/W, volleyball M/W.

Standardized Tests *Required:* SAT I or ACT (for admission).

Costs (2001–02) *Comprehensive fee:* $31,096 includes full-time tuition ($25,144), mandatory fees ($191), and room and board ($5761). Part-time tuition: $719 per credit. *Room and board:* College room only: $3078. Room and board charges vary according to board plan and housing facility. *Payment plans:* tuition prepayment, installment. *Waivers:* employees or children of employees.

Financial Aid Of all full-time matriculated undergraduates who enrolled in 2001, 1900 applied for aid, 1750 were judged to have need, 1500 had their need fully met. 700 Federal Work-Study jobs (averaging $1500). 30 State and other part-time jobs (averaging $1500). *Average percent of need met:* 100%. *Average financial aid package:* $18,072. *Average need-based loan:* $4200. *Average need-based gift aid:* $17,000. *Average indebtedness upon graduation:* $15,000. *Financial aid deadline:* 1/1.

Applying *Options:* common application, electronic application, early decision, deferred entrance. *Application fee:* $50. *Required:* essay or personal statement, high school transcript, 2 letters of recommendation. *Recommended:* interview. *Application deadlines:* 1/1 (freshmen), 4/1 (transfers). *Early decision:* 11/15 (for plan 1), 1/1 (for plan 2). *Notification:* 4/1 (freshmen), 12/15 (early decision plan 1), 2/1 (early decision plan 2).

Admissions Contact Mr. Mark D. Davies, Dean of Admissions, Bucknell University, Lewisburg, PA 17837. *Phone:* 570-577-1101. *Fax:* 570-577-3538. *E-mail:* admissions@bucknell.edu.

CABRINI COLLEGE
Radnor, Pennsylvania

- **Independent Roman Catholic** comprehensive, founded 1957
- **Calendar** semesters
- **Degrees** certificates, bachelor's, and master's
- **Suburban** 112-acre campus with easy access to Philadelphia
- **Endowment** $12.0 million
- **Coed,** 1,639 undergraduate students, 80% full-time, 64% women, 36% men
- **Minimally difficult** entrance level, 86% of applicants were admitted

Undergraduates 1,315 full-time, 324 part-time. Students come from 22 states and territories, 27% are from out of state, 7% African American, 2% Asian American or Pacific Islander, 2% Hispanic American, 0.3% Native American, 2% international, 5% transferred in, 95% live on campus. *Retention:* 68% of 2001 full-time freshmen returned.

Freshmen *Admission:* 1,827 applied, 1,578 admitted, 388 enrolled. *Average high school GPA:* 2.97. *Test scores:* SAT verbal scores over 500: 41%; SAT math scores over 500: 36%; SAT verbal scores over 600: 7%; SAT math scores over 600: 7%; SAT verbal scores over 700: 1%.

Faculty *Total:* 198, 27% full-time, 41% with terminal degrees. *Student/faculty ratio:* 14:1.

Majors Accounting; American studies; biology; biology education; biotechnology research; business administration; business marketing and marketing management; chemistry; chemistry education; communications; computer/information sciences; early childhood education; education; elementary education; English; English education; environmental science; exercise sciences; finance; fine/studio arts; French; graphic design/commercial art/illustration; history; human resources management; liberal arts and sciences/liberal studies; management information systems/business data processing; mathematics; mathematics education; medical technology; philosophy; political science; psychology; religious studies; social studies education; social work; sociology; Spanish; special education.

Academic Programs *Special study options:* academic remediation for entering students, accelerated degree program, adult/continuing education programs, advanced placement credit, cooperative education, distance learning, double majors, honors programs, independent study, internships, off-campus study, part-time degree program, services for LD students, student-designed majors, study abroad, summer session for credit. *ROTC:* Army (c). *Unusual degree programs:* 3-2 physical therapy, occupational therapy with Thomas Jefferson University.

Library Holy Spirit Library with 178,499 titles, 545 serial subscriptions, 991 audiovisual materials, an OPAC, a Web page.

Cabrini College (continued)

Computers on Campus 195 computers available on campus for general student use. A campuswide network can be accessed from student residence rooms. Internet access, at least one staffed computer lab available.

Student Life *Housing Options:* coed, women-only, disabled students. *Activities and Organizations:* drama/theater group, student-run newspaper, radio station, choral group, Student Government Association, student newspaper, International Club, campus radio station, Council for Exceptional Children. *Campus security:* 24-hour emergency response devices and patrols, student patrols, late-night transport/escort service, controlled dormitory access, resident assistants and directors on nightly duty. *Student Services:* health clinic, personal/psychological counseling.

Athletics Member NCAA. All Division III. *Intercollegiate sports:* basketball M/W, cross-country running M/W, field hockey W, golf M, lacrosse M/W, soccer M/W, softball W, tennis M/W, track and field M/W, volleyball W. *Intramural sports:* basketball M/W, football M/W, racquetball M/W, soccer M/W, softball M/W, squash M/W, swimming M/W, tennis M/W, volleyball M/W.

Standardized Tests *Required:* SAT I or ACT (for admission). *Recommended:* SAT I (for admission).

Costs (2001–02) *Comprehensive fee:* $25,950 includes full-time tuition ($17,340), mandatory fees ($750), and room and board ($7860). Part-time tuition: $330 per credit. Part-time tuition and fees vary according to course load. *Room and board:* Room and board charges vary according to housing facility. *Payment plan:* installment. *Waivers:* children of alumni, senior citizens, and employees or children of employees.

Financial Aid Of all full-time matriculated undergraduates who enrolled in 2001, 1173 applied for aid, 893 were judged to have need, 115 had their need fully met. 188 Federal Work-Study jobs. In 2001, 256 non-need-based awards were made. *Average percent of need met:* 50%. *Average financial aid package:* $13,423. *Average need-based loan:* $4034. *Average need-based gift aid:* $9838. *Average non-need based aid:* $4911. *Average indebtedness upon graduation:* $17,050.

Applying *Options:* common application, electronic application, early admission, deferred entrance. *Application fee:* $25. *Required:* high school transcript, minimum 2.0 GPA. *Recommended:* essay or personal statement, minimum 3.0 GPA, 3 letters of recommendation, interview. *Application deadline:* rolling (freshmen), rolling (transfers).

Admissions Contact Mr. Mark Osborn, Director of Admissions, Cabrini College, 610 King of Prussia Road, Radnor, PA 19087-3698. *Phone:* 610-902-8552. *Toll-free phone:* 800-848-1003. *Fax:* 610-902-8508. *E-mail:* admit@cabrini.edu.

CALIFORNIA UNIVERSITY OF PENNSYLVANIA
California, Pennsylvania

- **State-supported** comprehensive, founded 1852, part of Pennsylvania State System of Higher Education
- **Calendar** semesters
- **Degrees** associate, bachelor's, and master's
- **Small-town** 148-acre campus with easy access to Pittsburgh
- **Endowment** $328,585
- **Coed,** 5,076 undergraduate students, 87% full-time, 53% women, 47% men
- **Moderately difficult** entrance level, 77% of applicants were admitted

Cal U offers more than 100 programs. Offerings in science and technology are the University's special mission. Education and human services programs hold a long tradition of excellence. Liberal arts programs offer outstanding opportunities while providing the general education curriculum. With about 5,000 undergraduate students and a student-faculty ratio of 19:1, education is economical and personal.

Undergraduates 4,416 full-time, 660 part-time. Students come from 23 states and territories, 16 other countries, 3% are from out of state, 5% African American, 0.3% Asian American or Pacific Islander, 0.4% Hispanic American, 0.4% Native American, 1.0% international, 10% transferred in, 25% live on campus. *Retention:* 73% of 2001 full-time freshmen returned.

Freshmen *Admission:* 2,571 applied, 1,974 admitted, 839 enrolled. *Average high school GPA:* 2.90. *Test scores:* SAT verbal scores over 500: 36%; SAT math scores over 500: 33%; SAT verbal scores over 600: 8%; SAT math scores over 600: 6%; SAT verbal scores over 700: 2%; SAT math scores over 700: 2%.

Faculty *Total:* 334, 80% full-time, 43% with terminal degrees. *Student/faculty ratio:* 19:1.

Majors Accounting; anthropology; art; biological/physical sciences; biology; business; business administration; chemistry; communications; computer programming; drafting; early childhood education; earth sciences; economics; education; electrical/electronic engineering technology; elementary education; English; environmental science; French; geography; geology; German; gerontology; history; industrial technology; liberal arts and sciences/liberal studies; mathematics; medical laboratory technician; nursing; occupational therapy assistant; philosophy; physics; political science; psychology; recreation/leisure facilities management; social sciences; social work; sociology; Spanish; special education; theater arts/drama.

Academic Programs *Special study options:* academic remediation for entering students, accelerated degree program, adult/continuing education programs, advanced placement credit, cooperative education, distance learning, double majors, honors programs, internships, off-campus study, part-time degree program, services for LD students, study abroad, summer session for credit. *Unusual degree programs:* 3-2 engineering with University of Pittsburgh, Pennsylvania State University University Park Campus.

Library Manderino Library with 437,160 titles, 881 serial subscriptions, 59,703 audiovisual materials, an OPAC, a Web page.

Computers on Campus 720 computers available on campus for general student use. A campuswide network can be accessed from student residence rooms and from off campus. Internet access, at least one staffed computer lab available.

Student Life *Housing Options:* men-only, women-only. *Activities and Organizations:* drama/theater group, student-run newspaper, radio and television station, choral group, marching band, student government, In-Res Hall Council, Graduate Student Association, Black Student Union, sports recreation, national fraternities, national sororities. *Campus security:* 24-hour emergency response devices and patrols, student patrols, late-night transport/escort service. *Student Services:* health clinic, personal/psychological counseling, women's center, legal services.

Athletics Member NCAA. All Division II. *Intercollegiate sports:* basketball M(s)/W(s), cross-country running M(s)/W(s), fencing M/W, football M(s), golf M(s), rugby M/W, soccer M(s)/W, tennis W(s), track and field M(s)/W(s), volleyball W(s). *Intramural sports:* basketball M/W, cross-country running M/W, fencing M/W, football M/W, golf M/W, racquetball M/W, rugby M/W, skiing (cross-country) M/W, skiing (downhill) M/W, soccer M/W, swimming M/W, table tennis M/W, tennis M/W, track and field M/W, volleyball M/W.

Standardized Tests *Required:* SAT I (for admission). *Recommended:* SAT II: Subject Tests (for admission).

Costs (2001–02) *Tuition:* state resident $4016 full-time, $167 per credit part-time; nonresident $10,400 full-time, $418 per credit part-time. Full-time tuition and fees vary according to location. Part-time tuition and fees vary according to location. *Required fees:* $1188 full-time, $198 per course. *Room and board:* $5134; room only: $2598. Room and board charges vary according to board plan. *Payment plan:* installment. *Waivers:* employees or children of employees.

Financial Aid Of all full-time matriculated undergraduates who enrolled in 2001, 3700 applied for aid, 3050 were judged to have need, 2900 had their need fully met. 450 Federal Work-Study jobs (averaging $1050). In 2001, 277 non-need-based awards were made. *Average percent of need met:* 95%. *Average financial aid package:* $7025. *Average need-based loan:* $3600. *Average need-based gift aid:* $3900. *Average non-need based aid:* $1900.

Applying *Options:* common application, electronic application, early admission, deferred entrance. *Application fee:* $25. *Required:* high school transcript, minimum 2.0 GPA. *Required for some:* letters of recommendation, interview. *Recommended:* essay or personal statement, minimum 3.0 GPA. *Application deadlines:* 7/30 (freshmen), 7/30 (transfers). *Notification:* continuous (freshmen).

Admissions Contact Mr. William A. Edmonds, Dean of Enrollment Management and Academic Services, California University of Pennsylvania, 250 University Avenue, California, PA 15419. *Phone:* 724-938-4404. *Fax:* 724-938-4564. *E-mail:* inquiry@cup.edu.

CARLOW COLLEGE
Pittsburgh, Pennsylvania

- **Independent Roman Catholic** comprehensive, founded 1929
- **Calendar** semesters
- **Degrees** bachelor's and master's
- **Urban** 13-acre campus
- **Endowment** $3.4 million
- **Coed, primarily women,** 1,623 undergraduate students, 59% full-time, 94% women, 6% men
- **Moderately difficult** entrance level, 67% of applicants were admitted

Undergraduates 964 full-time, 659 part-time. Students come from 11 states and territories, 10 other countries, 4% are from out of state, 19% African American, 0.8% Asian American or Pacific Islander, 0.7% Hispanic American, 0.5% Native American, 0.8% international, 12% transferred in, 17% live on campus. *Retention:* 78% of 2001 full-time freshmen returned.

Freshmen *Admission:* 837 applied, 560 admitted, 188 enrolled. *Average high school GPA:* 3.20. *Test scores:* SAT verbal scores over 500: 53%; SAT math scores over 500: 39%; ACT scores over 18: 89%; SAT verbal scores over 600: 11%; SAT math scores over 600: 8%; ACT scores over 24: 31%; SAT math scores over 700: 1%; ACT scores over 30: 5%.

Faculty *Total:* 217, 31% full-time, 51% with terminal degrees. *Student/faculty ratio:* 12:1.

Majors Accounting; art; art education; art history; biology; business; chemical engineering; chemistry; communications; computer science; creative writing; design/visual communications; early childhood education; ecology; elementary education; English; environmental biology; health products/services marketing; health science; history; information sciences/systems; liberal arts and sciences/ liberal studies; mathematics; mathematics/computer science; nursing; philosophy; psychology; social studies education; social work; sociology; special education; technical/business writing; theology.

Academic Programs *Special study options:* academic remediation for entering students, accelerated degree program, adult/continuing education programs, advanced placement credit, distance learning, double majors, English as a second language, external degree program, honors programs, independent study, internships, off-campus study, part-time degree program, services for LD students, student-designed majors, summer session for credit. *ROTC:* Army (c), Navy (c), Air Force (c). *Unusual degree programs:* engineering with Carnegie Mellon University; social work with Duquesne University.

Library Grace Library with 79,690 titles, 434 serial subscriptions, 4,542 audiovisual materials, an OPAC, a Web page.

Computers on Campus 660 computers available on campus for general student use. A campuswide network can be accessed from student residence rooms and from off campus that provide access to applications software, e-mail. Internet access, online (class) registration, at least one staffed computer lab available.

Student Life *Housing Options:* women-only. *Activities and Organizations:* drama/theater group, student-run newspaper, choral group, Commuter Student Association, Resident Student Association, Student Athletic Association, Gospel Choir "Blessed", Student Government Association. *Campus security:* 24-hour emergency response devices and patrols, late-night transport/escort service, controlled dormitory access. *Student Services:* health clinic, personal/psychological counseling, women's center.

Athletics Member NAIA. *Intercollegiate sports:* basketball W(s), crew W(c), soccer W(s), softball W(s), tennis W(s), volleyball W(s).

Standardized Tests *Required:* SAT I or ACT (for admission).

Costs (2001–02) *Comprehensive fee:* $19,366 includes full-time tuition ($13,468), mandatory fees ($408), and room and board ($5490). Full-time tuition and fees vary according to course load and program. Part-time tuition: $412 per credit. Part-time tuition and fees vary according to course load and program. *Required fees:* $26 per credit. *Room and board:* Room and board charges vary according to board plan. *Payment plans:* installment, deferred payment. *Waivers:* adult students and employees or children of employees.

Financial Aid Of all full-time matriculated undergraduates who enrolled in 2001, 792 applied for aid, 631 were judged to have need, 476 had their need fully met. 332 Federal Work-Study jobs (averaging $697). In 2001, 31 non-need-based awards were made. *Average percent of need met:* 87%. *Average financial aid package:* $11,487. *Average need-based loan:* $4210. *Average need-based gift aid:* $6344. *Average non-need based aid:* $3945. *Average indebtedness upon graduation:* $11,131.

Applying *Options:* common application, electronic application, early admission, early action, deferred entrance. *Application fee:* $20. *Required:* high school transcript. *Recommended:* essay or personal statement, minimum 3.0 GPA, 2 letters of recommendation, interview, rank in upper two-fifths of high school class. *Application deadline:* rolling (freshmen), rolling (transfers). *Notification:* continuous (freshmen), 10/30 (early action).

Admissions Contact Ms. Susan Winstel, Assistant Director of Admissions, Carlow College, Pittsburgh, PA 15213. *Phone:* 412-578-6330. *Toll-free phone:* 800-333-CARLOW. *Fax:* 412-578-6668. *E-mail:* admissions@carlow.edu.

CARNEGIE MELLON UNIVERSITY
Pittsburgh, Pennsylvania

- **Independent** university, founded 1900
- **Calendar** semesters
- **Degrees** bachelor's, master's, doctoral, and post-master's certificates
- **Urban** 103-acre campus
- **Coed,** 5,310 undergraduate students, 96% full-time, 38% women, 62% men
- **Very difficult** entrance level, 31% of applicants were admitted

Undergraduates 5,085 full-time, 225 part-time. Students come from 52 states and territories, 61 other countries, 76% are from out of state, 4% African American, 22% Asian American or Pacific Islander, 5% Hispanic American, 0.4% Native American, 11% international, 0.8% transferred in, 72% live on campus. *Retention:* 93% of 2001 full-time freshmen returned.

Freshmen *Admission:* 16,696 applied, 5,211 admitted, 1,318 enrolled. *Average high school GPA:* 3.61. *Test scores:* SAT verbal scores over 500: 96%; SAT math scores over 500: 100%; ACT scores over 18: 100%; SAT verbal scores over 600: 77%; SAT math scores over 600: 96%; ACT scores over 24: 97%; SAT verbal scores over 700: 27%; SAT math scores over 700: 67%; ACT scores over 30: 50%.

Faculty *Total:* 874, 89% full-time, 98% with terminal degrees. *Student/faculty ratio:* 10:1.

Majors Applied mathematics; architecture; art; biochemistry; bioengineering; biology; biophysics; business administration; business economics; ceramic arts; chemical engineering; chemistry; civil engineering; cognitive psychology/ psycholinguistics; computer engineering; computer/information sciences; computer science; creative writing; economics; electrical engineering; engineering; engineering design; English; environmental engineering; European studies; fine/ studio arts; French; German; graphic design/commercial art/illustration; history; humanities; industrial design; information sciences/systems; interdisciplinary studies; Japanese; liberal arts and sciences/liberal studies; literature; mass communications; materials engineering; materials science; mathematical statistics; mathematics; mechanical engineering; modern languages; music; music (general performance); music theory and composition; philosophy; physics; political science; polymer chemistry; psychology; Russian; sculpture; social sciences; Spanish; technical/business writing; theater arts/drama; western civilization.

Academic Programs *Special study options:* accelerated degree program, adult/continuing education programs, advanced placement credit, cooperative education, double majors, English as a second language, freshman honors college, honors programs, independent study, internships, off-campus study, part-time degree program, services for LD students, student-designed majors, study abroad, summer session for credit. *ROTC:* Army (b), Navy (b), Air Force (b). *Unusual degree programs:* 3-2 public management and policy.

Library Hunt Library plus 2 others with 961,507 titles, 5,714 serial subscriptions, 218,779 audiovisual materials, an OPAC, a Web page.

Computers on Campus 450 computers available on campus for general student use. A campuswide network can be accessed from student residence rooms and from off campus. Internet access, online (class) registration, at least one staffed computer lab available.

Student Life *Housing:* on-campus residence required for freshman year. *Options:* coed, men-only, women-only, disabled students. *Activities and Organizations:* drama/theater group, student-run newspaper, radio station, choral group, marching band, Student Senate, Alpha Phi Omega, Tartan Club, Spirit Club, national fraternities, national sororities. *Campus security:* 24-hour emergency response devices and patrols, late-night transport/escort service, controlled dormitory access. *Student Services:* health clinic, personal/psychological counseling, women's center, legal services.

Athletics Member NCAA. All Division III. *Intercollegiate sports:* baseball M(c), basketball M/W, crew M(c)/W(c), cross-country running M/W, fencing M(c)/W(c), football M, golf M, ice hockey M(c), lacrosse M(c)/W(c), riflery M, rugby M(c), skiing (cross-country) M(c)/W(c), soccer M/W, swimming M/W, tennis M/W, track and field M/W, volleyball M/W. *Intramural sports:* badminton M/W, basketball M/W, bowling M/W, cross-country running M/W, fencing M/W, football M/W, golf M/W, racquetball M/W, soccer M/W, softball M/W, swimming M/W, table tennis M/W, tennis M/W, track and field M/W, volleyball M/W, water polo M/W, weight lifting M, wrestling M.

Standardized Tests *Required:* SAT I or ACT (for admission), SAT II: Subject Tests (for admission). *Required for some:* SAT II: Writing Test (for admission).

Costs (2001–02) *Comprehensive fee:* $33,136 includes full-time tuition ($25,670), mandatory fees ($202), and room and board ($7264). Full-time tuition and fees vary according to student level. Part-time tuition: $356 per unit. Part-time tuition and fees vary according to student level. *Room and board:* College room only: $4354. Room and board charges vary according to board plan, housing facility, and student level. *Payment plan:* installment. *Waivers:* employees or children of employees.

Financial Aid Of all full-time matriculated undergraduates who enrolled in 2001, 2978 applied for aid, 2476 were judged to have need, 1053 had their need fully met. 1250 State and other part-time jobs (averaging $102). In 2001, 768 non-need-based awards were made. *Average percent of need met:* 82%. *Average financial aid package:* $18,069. *Average need-based loan:* $4569. *Average need-based gift aid:* $12,874. *Average non-need based aid:* $10,552. *Average indebtedness upon graduation:* $18,280.

Applying *Options:* common application, electronic application, early admission, early decision, deferred entrance. *Application fee:* $55. *Required:* essay or personal statement, high school transcript, 1 letter of recommendation. *Required for some:* portfolio, audition. *Recommended:* interview. *Application deadlines:*

Carnegie Mellon University (continued)
1/1 (freshmen), 3/15 (transfers). *Early decision:* 11/1 (for plan 1), 11/15 (for plan 2). *Notification:* 4/15 (freshmen), 1/15 (early decision plan 1), 1/15 (early decision plan 2).

Admissions Contact Mr. Michael Steidel, Director of Admissions, Carnegie Mellon University, 5000 Forbes Avenue, Warner Hall, Room 101, Pittsburgh, PA 15213. *Phone:* 412-268-2082. *Fax:* 412-268-7838. *E-mail:* undergraduate-admissions@andrew.cmu.edu.

CEDAR CREST COLLEGE
Allentown, Pennsylvania

- **Independent** 4-year, founded 1867, affiliated with United Church of Christ
- **Calendar** semesters
- **Degrees** associate, bachelor's, and postbachelor's certificates
- **Suburban** 84-acre campus with easy access to Philadelphia
- **Endowment** $13.5 million
- **Women only,** 1,593 undergraduate students, 49% full-time
- **Moderately difficult** entrance level, 76% of applicants were admitted

For the last ten years, *U.S. News & World Report* has named Cedar Crest a top-tier regional liberal arts college. New programs include bioinformatics, dance, forensic science, and information systems. Qualified students may participate in internships, the freshmen research and honors program, cross-registration at five colleges, academic scholarships, and may have free-tuition senior year.

Undergraduates 783 full-time, 810 part-time. Students come from 31 states and territories, 18% are from out of state, 5% African American, 2% Asian American or Pacific Islander, 5% Hispanic American, 0.2% Native American, 2% international, 2% transferred in, 92% live on campus. *Retention:* 83% of 2001 full-time freshmen returned.

Freshmen *Admission:* 1,083 applied, 818 admitted, 168 enrolled. *Average high school GPA:* 3.16. *Test scores:* SAT verbal scores over 500: 70%; SAT math scores over 500: 63%; ACT scores over 18: 100%; SAT verbal scores over 600: 30%; SAT math scores over 600: 25%; ACT scores over 24: 62%; SAT verbal scores over 700: 3%; SAT math scores over 700: 2%; ACT scores over 30: 10%.

Faculty *Total:* 86, 80% full-time, 70% with terminal degrees. *Student/faculty ratio:* 11:1.

Majors Accounting; alcohol/drug abuse counseling; art; behavioral sciences; biochemistry; bioengineering; biological/physical sciences; biology; biomedical science; biomedical technology; business administration; business economics; chemistry; communications; comparative literature; computer/information sciences; dance; education; elementary education; engineering related; English; environmental biology; environmental science; experimental psychology; fine/studio arts; French; genetics; gerontology; health science; health services administration; history; information sciences/systems; international relations; liberal arts and sciences/liberal studies; mathematics; medical technology; middle school education; molecular biology; music; natural sciences; neuroscience; nuclear medical technology; nursing science; nutrition science; paralegal/legal assistant; philosophy; political science; pre-dentistry; pre-law; pre-medicine; pre-veterinary studies; psychology; science education; secondary education; social work; sociology; Spanish; theater arts/drama.

Academic Programs *Special study options:* academic remediation for entering students, accelerated degree program, adult/continuing education programs, advanced placement credit, distance learning, double majors, English as a second language, freshman honors college, honors programs, independent study, internships, off-campus study, part-time degree program, services for LD students, student-designed majors, study abroad, summer session for credit. *ROTC:* Army (c). *Unusual degree programs:* 3-2 engineering with Georgia Institute of Technology.

Library Cressman Library with 133,763 titles, 6,191 serial subscriptions, 15,836 audiovisual materials, an OPAC, a Web page.

Computers on Campus 227 computers available on campus for general student use. A campuswide network can be accessed from student residence rooms and from off campus that provide access to intranet. Internet access, at least one staffed computer lab available.

Student Life *Housing:* on-campus residence required through junior year. *Options:* women-only, disabled students. *Activities and Organizations:* drama/theater group, student-run newspaper, radio and television station, choral group, Alpha Phi Omega, Out there, Athletes Club, Student Activities Board, Student Government Association. *Campus security:* 24-hour emergency response devices and patrols, late-night transport/escort service, controlled dormitory access, crime prevention programs. *Student Services:* health clinic, personal/psychological counseling.

Athletics Member NCAA. All Division III. *Intercollegiate sports:* basketball W, cross-country running W, equestrian sports W(c), field hockey W, lacrosse W, soccer W, softball W, tennis W, track and field W(c), volleyball W. *Intramural sports:* badminton M/W, basketball M/W, soccer M/W, softball M/W, tennis M/W, volleyball M/W.

Standardized Tests *Required:* SAT I or ACT (for admission).

Costs (2001–02) *Comprehensive fee:* $25,145 includes full-time tuition ($18,680) and room and board ($6465). Full-time tuition and fees vary according to course load. Part-time tuition: $520 per credit. Part-time tuition and fees vary according to class time. *Room and board:* College room only: $3622. Room and board charges vary according to board plan. *Payment plan:* installment. *Waivers:* children of alumni and employees or children of employees.

Financial Aid Of all full-time matriculated undergraduates who enrolled in 2001, 723 applied for aid, 674 were judged to have need, 131 had their need fully met. 104 Federal Work-Study jobs (averaging $1550). 260 State and other part-time jobs (averaging $1798). In 2001, 76 non-need-based awards were made. *Average percent of need met:* 82%. *Average financial aid package:* $15,721. *Average need-based loan:* $4035. *Average need-based gift aid:* $11,861. *Average non-need based aid:* $12,191. *Average indebtedness upon graduation:* $20,514.

Applying *Options:* common application, electronic application, early admission, deferred entrance. *Application fee:* $30. *Required:* essay or personal statement, high school transcript. *Required for some:* 2 letters of recommendation. *Recommended:* minimum 2.0 GPA, interview. *Application deadline:* rolling (freshmen), rolling (transfers).

Admissions Contact Ms. Judith A. Neyhart, Vice President for Enrollment and Advancement, Cedar Crest College, 100 College Drive, Allentown, PA 18104-6196. *Phone:* 610-740-3780. *Toll-free phone:* 800-360-1222. *Fax:* 610-606-4647. *E-mail:* cccadmis@cedarcrest.edu.

CENTRAL PENNSYLVANIA COLLEGE
Summerdale, Pennsylvania

- **Proprietary** primarily 2-year, founded 1922
- **Calendar** quarters
- **Degrees** associate and bachelor's
- **Small-town** 30-acre campus
- **Coed,** 604 undergraduate students, 84% full-time, 67% women, 33% men
- **Noncompetitive** entrance level, 34% of applicants were admitted

Undergraduates 506 full-time, 98 part-time. Students come from 7 states and territories, 1% are from out of state, 5% African American, 2% Asian American or Pacific Islander, 2% Hispanic American, 1% Native American, 6% transferred in, 51% live on campus.

Freshmen *Admission:* 696 applied, 235 admitted, 188 enrolled.

Faculty *Total:* 58, 43% full-time, 14% with terminal degrees. *Student/faculty ratio:* 14:1.

Majors Accounting; accounting related; business administration; business marketing and marketing management; child care/development; computer programming related; criminal justice/law enforcement administration; entrepreneurship; executive assistant; finance; hotel and restaurant management; information sciences/systems; legal administrative assistant; management science; mass communications; medical administrative assistant; medical assistant; optometric/ophthalmic laboratory technician; paralegal/legal assistant; physical therapy assistant; retail management; travel/tourism management; Web/multimedia management/webmaster.

Academic Programs *Special study options:* academic remediation for entering students, advanced placement credit, double majors, independent study, internships, part-time degree program, summer session for credit.

Library Learning Resource Center with 6,122 titles, 94 serial subscriptions, 1,404 audiovisual materials, an OPAC.

Computers on Campus 120 computers available on campus for general student use. Internet access, at least one staffed computer lab available.

Student Life *Housing Options:* coed. *Activities and Organizations:* student-run newspaper, choral group, Campus Christian Fellowship, College Council, Student Ambassadors, Phi Beta Lambda, Travel Club. *Campus security:* 24-hour emergency response devices and patrols. *Student Services:* personal/psychological counseling.

Athletics *Intercollegiate sports:* basketball M, cross-country running M/W, golf M/W, volleyball W. *Intramural sports:* volleyball M/W.

Costs (2002–03) *One-time required fee:* $75. *Tuition:* $9330 full-time, $249 per credit part-time. Full-time tuition and fees vary according to program. Part-time tuition and fees vary according to course load and program. *Required fees:* $525 full-time, $175 per term part-time. *Room only:* $4550. Room and board charges vary according to housing facility. *Payment plan:* deferred payment. *Waivers:* employees or children of employees.

Financial Aid Of all full-time matriculated undergraduates who enrolled in 2001, 50 Federal Work-Study jobs (averaging $500).

Applying *Options:* electronic application. *Required:* high school transcript, interview. *Required for some:* minimum 2.0 GPA. *Application deadlines:* 9/20 (freshmen), 9/20 (transfers). *Notification:* continuous (freshmen).

Admissions Contact Jennifer Verhagen, Director of Admissions, Central Pennsylvania College, Central Pennsylvania College, Summerdale, PA 17093. *Phone:* 717-728-2213. *Toll-free phone:* 800-759-2727. *Fax:* 717-732-5254.

CHATHAM COLLEGE
Pittsburgh, Pennsylvania

- **Independent** comprehensive, founded 1869
- **Calendar** 4-1-4
- **Degrees** bachelor's, master's, doctoral, and postbachelor's certificates
- **Urban** 34-acre campus
- **Endowment** $59.4 million
- **Women only,** 589 undergraduate students, 90% full-time
- **Moderately difficult** entrance level, 78% of applicants were admitted

Chatham College, founded in 1869, is the oldest college for women west of the Alleghenies. Chatham offers a distinctive undergraduate education, preparing students for a lifetime of personal and professional achievement. Chatham is dedicated to enabling its graduates to have an impact on and be ready for the world around them.

Undergraduates 529 full-time, 60 part-time. Students come from 36 states and territories, 24 other countries, 24% are from out of state, 11% African American, 2% Asian American or Pacific Islander, 2% Hispanic American, 0.7% Native American, 7% international, 9% transferred in, 64% live on campus. *Retention:* 71% of 2001 full-time freshmen returned.

Freshmen *Admission:* 534 applied, 415 admitted, 134 enrolled. *Average high school GPA:* 3.28. *Test scores:* SAT verbal scores over 500: 78%; SAT math scores over 500: 57%; ACT scores over 18: 92%; SAT verbal scores over 600: 29%; SAT math scores over 600: 16%; ACT scores over 24: 52%; SAT verbal scores over 700: 2%; ACT scores over 30: 9%.

Faculty *Total:* 80, 89% full-time, 85% with terminal degrees. *Student/faculty ratio:* 13:1.

Majors Accounting; area, ethnic, and cultural studies related; art history; arts management; biochemistry; biology; business administration; business marketing and marketing management; chemistry; communications; computer/information sciences; economics; engineering; English; English related; enterprise management; environmental science; fine/studio arts; French; graphic design/commercial art/illustration; history; international business; international relations; management information systems/business data processing; mathematics; music; neuroscience; philosophy; physics; physiological psychology/psychobiology; political science; psychology; public policy analysis; social work; Spanish; theater arts/drama; women's studies.

Academic Programs *Special study options:* accelerated degree program, adult/continuing education programs, advanced placement credit, cooperative education, double majors, English as a second language, independent study, internships, off-campus study, part-time degree program, services for LD students, student-designed majors, study abroad, summer session for credit. *ROTC:* Army (c), Navy (c), Air Force (c). *Unusual degree programs:* 3-2 engineering with Carnegie Mellon University, Washington University in St. Louis, Pennsylvania State University University Park Campus, University of Pittsburgh; physical therapy, occupational therapy, physician assistant studies (Chatham).

Library Jennie King Mellon Library with 95,625 titles, 1,240 serial subscriptions, 321 audiovisual materials, an OPAC, a Web page.

Computers on Campus 312 computers available on campus for general student use. A campuswide network can be accessed from student residence rooms and from off campus that provide access to computer-aided instruction. Internet access, at least one staffed computer lab available.

Student Life *Housing Options:* women-only. *Activities and Organizations:* drama/theater group, student-run newspaper, choral group, Chatham Student Government, choir, Chatham Feminist Collective, Students of Community Service, Activities Board. *Campus security:* 24-hour emergency response devices and patrols, late-night transport/escort service, controlled dormitory access. *Student Services:* health clinic, personal/psychological counseling.

Athletics Member NCAA. All Division III. *Intercollegiate sports:* basketball W, ice hockey W, soccer W, softball W, tennis W, volleyball W. *Intramural sports:* archery W, badminton W, basketball W, crew W(c), golf W, skiing (cross-country) W, skiing (downhill) W, soccer W, softball W, swimming W, tennis W, volleyball W, weight lifting W.

Standardized Tests *Required:* SAT I or ACT (for admission).

Costs (2001–02) *Comprehensive fee:* $25,454 includes full-time tuition ($18,804), mandatory fees ($156), and room and board ($6494). Full-time tuition and fees vary according to course load and degree level. Part-time tuition: $458 per credit. Part-time tuition and fees vary according to course load. *Required fees:* $39 per term part-time. *Room and board:* College room only: $3344. Room and board charges vary according to board plan and housing facility. *Payment plan:* installment. *Waivers:* employees or children of employees.

Financial Aid Of all full-time matriculated undergraduates who enrolled in 2001, 434 applied for aid, 391 were judged to have need, 2 had their need fully met. 242 Federal Work-Study jobs (averaging $1932). In 2001, 104 non-need-based awards were made. *Average percent of need met:* 68%. *Average financial aid package:* $18,859. *Average need-based loan:* $3509. *Average need-based gift aid:* $6799. *Average non-need based aid:* $6027. *Average indebtedness upon graduation:* $18,655. *Financial aid deadline:* 5/1.

Applying *Options:* common application, electronic application, early admission, deferred entrance. *Application fee:* $25. *Required:* high school transcript, minimum 2.5 GPA. *Recommended:* essay or personal statement, minimum 3.0 GPA, interview. *Application deadline:* rolling (freshmen), rolling (transfers). *Notification:* continuous (freshmen).

Admissions Contact Dean of Admissions and Financial Aid, Chatham College, Woodland Road, Pittsburgh, PA 15232. *Phone:* 412-365-1290. *Toll-free phone:* 800-837-1290. *Fax:* 412-365-1609. *E-mail:* admissions@chatham.edu.

CHESTNUT HILL COLLEGE
Philadelphia, Pennsylvania

- **Independent Roman Catholic** comprehensive, founded 1924
- **Calendar** semesters
- **Degrees** certificates, associate, bachelor's, master's, doctoral, post-master's, and postbachelor's certificates (profile includes figures from both traditional and accelerated (part-time) programs)
- **Suburban** 45-acre campus
- **Endowment** $12.4 million
- **Coed,** 922 undergraduate students, 63% full-time, 86% women, 14% men
- **Moderately difficult** entrance level, 92% of applicants were admitted

Undergraduates 578 full-time, 344 part-time. Students come from 12 states and territories, 22% are from out of state, 41% African American, 2% Asian American or Pacific Islander, 5% Hispanic American, 0.4% Native American, 0.7% international, 4% transferred in, 26% live on campus. *Retention:* 66% of 2001 full-time freshmen returned.

Freshmen *Admission:* 335 applied, 308 admitted, 108 enrolled. *Average high school GPA:* 3.04. *Test scores:* SAT verbal scores over 500: 45%; SAT math scores over 500: 25%; SAT verbal scores over 600: 15%; SAT math scores over 600: 5%.

Faculty *Total:* 258, 21% full-time, 52% with terminal degrees. *Student/faculty ratio:* 10:1.

Majors Accounting; accounting related; art history; biochemistry; biology; business administration; business administration/management related; business communications; business marketing and marketing management; chemistry; child care services management; communications technologies related; computer/information sciences; computer science; criminal justice/law enforcement administration; early childhood education; economics; education (multiple levels); elementary education; English; environmental science; fine arts and art studies related; fine/studio arts; French; gerontology; health services administration; history; human resources management; mathematics/computer science; mathematics related; molecular biology; music; music related; music teacher education; political science; psychology; social sciences; sociology; Spanish.

Academic Programs *Special study options:* academic remediation for entering students, adult/continuing education programs, advanced placement credit, cooperative education, double majors, English as a second language, honors programs, independent study, internships, off-campus study, part-time degree program, student-designed majors, study abroad, summer session for credit. *ROTC:* Army (c). *Unusual degree programs:* 3-2 biology, chemistry with the College of Podiatric Medicine of Temple University; biology, chemistry and medical technology with the College of Health Professions of Thomas Jefferson University; Education, Psychology, Computer/Applied Technology Chestnut Hill College.

Library Logue Library with 141,430 titles, 596 serial subscriptions, 2,026 audiovisual materials, an OPAC, a Web page.

Computers on Campus 185 computers available on campus for general student use. Internet access, at least one staffed computer lab available.

Student Life *Housing Options:* men-only, women-only. *Activities and Organizations:* drama/theater group, student-run newspaper, choral group, student government, Hispanics in Action, African American Awareness Society, campus ministry community service group, Phi Beta Lambda. *Campus security:* 24-hour

Chestnut Hill College (continued)
emergency response devices and patrols, late-night transport/escort service, controlled dormitory access. *Student Services:* health clinic, personal/psychological counseling.

Athletics Member NCAA. All Division III. *Intercollegiate sports:* basketball W, field hockey W, lacrosse W, softball W, tennis W, volleyball W.

Standardized Tests *Required:* SAT I or ACT (for admission).

Costs (2001–02) *Comprehensive fee:* $24,790 includes full-time tuition ($16,990), mandatory fees ($630), and room and board ($7170). Full-time tuition and fees vary according to course load. Part-time tuition: $330 per hour. *Required fees:* $50 per term part-time. *Room and board:* Room and board charges vary according to housing facility. *Payment plans:* installment, deferred payment. *Waivers:* senior citizens and employees or children of employees.

Financial Aid Of all full-time matriculated undergraduates who enrolled in 2001, 369 applied for aid, 369 were judged to have need, 69 had their need fully met. 106 Federal Work-Study jobs (averaging $750). *Average percent of need met:* 87%. *Average financial aid package:* $7824. *Average non-need based aid:* $11,353.

Applying *Options:* common application, early admission, early decision, deferred entrance. *Application fee:* $35. *Required:* essay or personal statement, high school transcript, 1 letter of recommendation. *Required for some:* interview. *Recommended:* minimum 2.0 GPA, interview. *Application deadline:* rolling (freshmen), rolling (transfers). *Early decision:* 12/1. *Notification:* 1/10 (early decision).

Admissions Contact Ms. Jodie King, Associate Director of Admissions, Chestnut Hill College, 9601 Germantown Avenue, Philadelphia, PA 19118-2693. *Phone:* 215-248-7001. *Toll-free phone:* 800-248-0052. *Fax:* 215-248-7082. *E-mail:* chcapply@chc.edu.

CHEYNEY UNIVERSITY OF PENNSYLVANIA
Cheyney, Pennsylvania

- **State-supported** comprehensive, founded 1837, part of Pennsylvania State System of Higher Education
- **Calendar** 4-1-4
- **Degrees** bachelor's and master's
- **Suburban** 275-acre campus with easy access to Philadelphia
- **Endowment** $8.8 million
- **Coed,** 1,195 undergraduate students, 89% full-time, 55% women, 45% men
- **Minimally difficult** entrance level, 70% of applicants were admitted

Cheyney University of Pennsylvania, established in 1837, is America's oldest historically black educational institution. Cheyney strives to develop scholars who are not only well educated but also willing to set priorities that enable them to reach their highest potential in their personal and professional lives. Cheyney graduates are well-prepared to assume leadership roles through which they work for the greater public good.

Undergraduates 1,058 full-time, 137 part-time. Students come from 15 states and territories, 6 other countries, 17% are from out of state, 97% African American, 0.1% Asian American or Pacific Islander, 0.9% Hispanic American, 0.1% Native American, 1% international, 4% transferred in, 66% live on campus.

Freshmen *Admission:* 1,249 applied, 874 admitted, 302 enrolled.

Faculty *Total:* 129, 68% full-time, 50% with terminal degrees. *Student/faculty ratio:* 11:1.

Majors Art; biological/physical sciences; biology; business administration; chemistry; clothing/textiles; communication equipment technology; computer science; early childhood education; economics; education; elementary education; English; French; geography; home economics education; hotel and restaurant management; industrial technology; mass communications; mathematics; medical technology; music; political science; psychology; recreation/leisure studies; secondary education; social sciences; sociology; Spanish; special education; theater arts/drama.

Academic Programs *Special study options:* academic remediation for entering students, adult/continuing education programs, cooperative education, internships, off-campus study, part-time degree program, services for LD students, summer session for credit. *ROTC:* Army (b), Air Force (c).

Library Leslie Pickney Hill Library plus 1 other with 85,533 titles, 1,526 serial subscriptions, 1,379 audiovisual materials, a Web page.

Computers on Campus 150 computers available on campus for general student use. A campuswide network can be accessed from student residence rooms and from off campus that provide access to various software packages. Internet access, online (class) registration, at least one staffed computer lab available.

Student Life *Housing Options:* coed. *Activities and Organizations:* drama/theater group, student-run newspaper, radio station, choral group, marching band, national fraternities, national sororities. *Campus security:* 24-hour emergency response devices and patrols. *Student Services:* health clinic, personal/psychological counseling, women's center.

Athletics Member NCAA. All Division II. *Intercollegiate sports:* basketball M(s)/W(s), bowling W, cross-country running M(s)/W(s), football M(s), tennis M(s)/W(s), track and field M(s)/W(s), volleyball W(s), wrestling M(s). *Intramural sports:* basketball M, football M, tennis M/W, volleyball M/W.

Standardized Tests *Required:* SAT I or ACT (for admission). *Recommended:* SAT II: Subject Tests (for admission).

Costs (2001–02) *Tuition:* state resident $4016 full-time, $167 per credit hour part-time; nonresident $10,040 full-time, $418 per credit hour part-time. Full-time tuition and fees vary according to reciprocity agreements. Part-time tuition and fees vary according to reciprocity agreements. *Required fees:* $655 full-time, $164 per term part-time. *Room and board:* $5322. Room and board charges vary according to board plan. *Payment plan:* deferred payment. *Waivers:* senior citizens and employees or children of employees.

Financial Aid Of all full-time matriculated undergraduates who enrolled in 2001, 901 applied for aid, 792 were judged to have need, 274 had their need fully met. 352 Federal Work-Study jobs (averaging $1047). In 2001, 61 non-need-based awards were made. *Average percent of need met:* 80%. *Average financial aid package:* $7200. *Average need-based loan:* $3800. *Average non-need based aid:* $4700. *Average indebtedness upon graduation:* $20,000.

Applying *Application fee:* $20. *Required:* essay or personal statement, high school transcript. *Required for some:* 3 letters of recommendation. *Recommended:* interview. *Application deadline:* rolling (freshmen), rolling (transfers).

Admissions Contact Mr. William Bickley, Interim Director of Admissions, Cheyney University of Pennsylvania, Cheyney, PA 19319. *Phone:* 610-399-2275. *Toll-free phone:* 800-CHEYNEY. *Fax:* 610-399-2099.

CLARION UNIVERSITY OF PENNSYLVANIA
Clarion, Pennsylvania

- **State-supported** comprehensive, founded 1867, part of Pennsylvania State System of Higher Education
- **Calendar** semesters
- **Degrees** associate, bachelor's, master's, and post-master's certificates
- **Rural** 100-acre campus
- **Coed,** 5,812 undergraduate students, 90% full-time, 62% women, 38% men
- **Minimally difficult** entrance level, 81% of applicants were admitted

Clarion University is located in an inviting environment in central western Pennsylvania. People—students and faculty—are its most valuable resource; students from about 30 states and more than 20 countries specialize in more than 90 different degree programs. Committed to excellence, Clarion's faculty members are outstanding in their respective disciplines and sensitive to the aspirations and needs of students.

Undergraduates 5,244 full-time, 568 part-time. Students come from 29 states and territories, 40 other countries, 4% are from out of state, 5% African American, 0.5% Asian American or Pacific Islander, 0.7% Hispanic American, 0.2% Native American, 2% international, 6% transferred in, 34% live on campus. *Retention:* 72% of 2001 full-time freshmen returned.

Freshmen *Admission:* 3,412 applied, 2,748 admitted, 1,688 enrolled. *Average high school GPA:* 3.10. *Test scores:* SAT verbal scores over 500: 34%; SAT math scores over 500: 33%; SAT verbal scores over 600: 6%; SAT math scores over 600: 6%.

Faculty *Total:* 292, 100% full-time, 60% with terminal degrees. *Student/faculty ratio:* 18:1.

Majors Accounting; anthropology; art; biological/physical sciences; biology; business administration; business economics; business marketing and marketing management; chemistry; communications; computer/information sciences; early childhood education; earth sciences; economics; education; elementary education; English; environmental science; finance; French; geography; geology; history; humanities; information sciences/systems; international business; labor/personnel relations; legal administrative assistant; liberal arts and sciences/liberal studies; library science; management science; mathematics; medical technology; molecular biology; music business management/merchandising; music (general performance); music teacher education; nursing; occupational therapy assistant; philosophy; physics; political science; psychology; radiological science; reading education; real estate; science education; social psychology; social sciences; social studies education; sociology; Spanish; special education; speech-language pathology/audiology; speech/rhetorical studies; theater arts/drama.

Academic Programs *Special study options:* academic remediation for entering students, accelerated degree program, adult/continuing education programs, advanced placement credit, distance learning, double majors, honors programs, independent study, internships, part-time degree program, services for LD students, study abroad, summer session for credit. *Unusual degree programs:* 3-2 engineering with University of Pittsburgh, Case Western Reserve University.

Library Carlson Library with 2.2 million titles, 12,198 serial subscriptions, 223,570 audiovisual materials, an OPAC, a Web page.

Computers on Campus 400 computers available on campus for general student use. A campuswide network can be accessed from student residence rooms and from off campus. Internet access, online (class) registration, at least one staffed computer lab available.

Student Life *Housing Options:* coed, men-only, women-only. *Activities and Organizations:* drama/theater group, student-run newspaper, radio station, choral group, marching band, national fraternities, national sororities. *Campus security:* 24-hour emergency response devices and patrols, student patrols. *Student Services:* health clinic, personal/psychological counseling, women's center.

Athletics Member NCAA. All Division II except wrestling (Division I). *Intercollegiate sports:* baseball M(s), basketball M(s)/W(s), cross-country running M(s)/W(s), football M(s), golf M(s), softball W(s), swimming M(s)/W(s), tennis W(s), track and field M(s)/W(s), volleyball W(s), wrestling M(s). *Intramural sports:* badminton M/W, basketball M/W, bowling M/W, cross-country running M/W, football M, golf M/W, racquetball M/W, soccer M/W, swimming M/W, tennis M/W, track and field M/W, volleyball M(c)/W, weight lifting M/W, wrestling M.

Standardized Tests *Required:* SAT I or ACT (for admission).

Costs (2001–02) *Tuition:* Full-time tuition and fees vary according to course load and location. Part-time tuition and fees vary according to course load and location. *Room and board:* Room and board charges vary according to board plan and housing facility. *Payment plan:* installment. *Waivers:* senior citizens and employees or children of employees.

Financial Aid Of all full-time matriculated undergraduates who enrolled in 2001, 4187 applied for aid, 3408 were judged to have need. 300 Federal Work-Study jobs (averaging $1540). *Average indebtedness upon graduation:* $12,858.

Applying *Options:* early admission, deferred entrance. *Application fee:* $30. *Required:* high school transcript. *Required for some:* essay or personal statement, interview. *Recommended:* essay or personal statement, letters of recommendation, interview. *Application deadline:* rolling (freshmen), rolling (transfers).

Admissions Contact Ms. Sue McMillen, Interim Director of Admissions, Clarion University of Pennsylvania, Clarion, PA 16214. *Phone:* 814-393-2306. *Toll-free phone:* 800-672-7171. *Fax:* 814-393-2030. *E-mail:* smcmille@clarion.edu.

COLLEGE MISERICORDIA
Dallas, Pennsylvania

- **Independent Roman Catholic** comprehensive, founded 1924
- **Calendar** semesters
- **Degrees** bachelor's and master's
- **Small-town** 100-acre campus
- **Endowment** $9.5 million
- **Coed,** 1,640 undergraduate students, 70% full-time, 73% women, 27% men
- **Moderately difficult** entrance level, 84% of applicants were admitted

Misericordia's Guaranteed Placement Program integrates academics, cocurricular activities, and internships to fully prepare students for employment. The College guarantees that if a student fulfills the requirements of the program and is not employed in his or her field or enrolled in graduate or professional school within 6 months of graduation, he or she is assured a paid internship.

Undergraduates 1,153 full-time, 487 part-time. Students come from 17 states and territories, 20% are from out of state, 6% transferred in, 55% live on campus. *Retention:* 93% of 2001 full-time freshmen returned.

Freshmen *Admission:* 923 applied, 772 admitted, 286 enrolled. *Average high school GPA:* 3.20. *Test scores:* SAT verbal scores over 500: 49%; SAT math scores over 500: 51%; ACT scores over 18: 94%; SAT verbal scores over 600: 8%; SAT math scores over 600: 9%; ACT scores over 24: 50%.

Faculty *Total:* 161, 52% full-time. *Student/faculty ratio:* 14:1.

Majors Accounting; biochemistry; biology; business administration; business marketing and marketing management; chemistry; communications; computer science; early childhood education; elementary education; English; health science; history; information sciences/systems; interdisciplinary studies; liberal arts and sciences/liberal studies; management information systems/business data processing; mathematics; medical radiologic technology; medical technology; nursing; philosophy; pre-dentistry; pre-law; pre-medicine; pre-veterinary studies; psychology; secondary education; social work; special education; sport/fitness administration.

Academic Programs *Special study options:* academic remediation for entering students, accelerated degree program, adult/continuing education programs, advanced placement credit, cooperative education, distance learning, double majors, honors programs, independent study, internships, off-campus study, part-time degree program, services for LD students, student-designed majors, study abroad, summer session for credit. *ROTC:* Army (c), Air Force (c). *Unusual degree programs:* 3-2 occupational therapy, physical therapy, speech therapy, language theory.

Library Mary Kintz Bevevina Library with 72,836 titles, 782 serial subscriptions, 2,240 audiovisual materials, an OPAC, a Web page.

Computers on Campus 50 computers available on campus for general student use. A campuswide network can be accessed from student residence rooms and from off campus. Internet access, at least one staffed computer lab available.

Student Life *Housing Options:* coed. *Activities and Organizations:* drama/theater group, student-run newspaper, radio station, choral group, Circle K, International Club, BACCHUS, Student Nurses Association of Pennsylvania, Commuter Council. *Campus security:* 24-hour emergency response devices and patrols, late-night transport/escort service, controlled dormitory access. *Student Services:* health clinic, personal/psychological counseling, women's center.

Athletics Member NCAA. All Division III. *Intercollegiate sports:* baseball M, basketball M/W, cross-country running M/W, field hockey W, golf M, lacrosse M/W, soccer M/W, softball W, swimming M/W, track and field M/W, volleyball W. *Intramural sports:* basketball M/W, cross-country running M/W, football M/W, golf M/W, lacrosse M/W, racquetball M/W, soccer M/W, softball M/W, tennis M/W, volleyball M/W, weight lifting M/W.

Standardized Tests *Required:* SAT I or ACT (for admission).

Costs (2002–03) *Comprehensive fee:* $24,430 includes full-time tuition ($16,420), mandatory fees ($880), and room and board ($7130). Full-time tuition and fees vary according to class time and reciprocity agreements. Part-time tuition: $395 per credit. Part-time tuition and fees vary according to reciprocity agreements. *Room and board:* College room only: $4060. Room and board charges vary according to board plan and housing facility. *Payment plans:* installment, deferred payment. *Waivers:* employees or children of employees.

Financial Aid Of all full-time matriculated undergraduates who enrolled in 2001, 1071 applied for aid, 969 were judged to have need, 471 had their need fully met. 236 Federal Work-Study jobs (averaging $1100). 62 State and other part-time jobs (averaging $1100). In 2001, 102 non-need-based awards were made. *Average percent of need met:* 68%. *Average financial aid package:* $11,158. *Average need-based loan:* $2530. *Average need-based gift aid:* $5628. *Average non-need based aid:* $5224. *Average indebtedness upon graduation:* $16,850.

Applying *Options:* common application, electronic application, deferred entrance. *Application fee:* $25. *Required:* high school transcript. *Required for some:* essay or personal statement, 2 letters of recommendation, interview. *Recommended:* interview. *Application deadline:* rolling (freshmen), rolling (transfers).

Admissions Contact Ms. Jane Dessoye, Executive Director of Admissions and Financial Aid, College Misericordia, 301 Lake Street, Dallas, PA 18612. *Phone:* 570-675-4449 Ext. 6168. *Toll-free phone:* 800-852-7675. *Fax:* 570-675-2441. *E-mail:* admiss@miseri.edu.

THE CURTIS INSTITUTE OF MUSIC
Philadelphia, Pennsylvania

- **Independent** comprehensive, founded 1924
- **Calendar** semesters
- **Degrees** bachelor's and master's
- **Urban** campus
- **Coed,** 148 undergraduate students
- **Most difficult** entrance level, 7% of applicants were admitted

Undergraduates Students come from 24 states and territories, 22 other countries.

Freshmen *Admission:* 671 applied, 48 admitted.

Faculty *Total:* 80.

Majors Music; music (piano and organ performance); music (voice and choral/opera performance); stringed instruments; wind/percussion instruments.

Academic Programs *Special study options:* accelerated degree program, advanced placement credit, English as a second language, off-campus study.

Library Curtis Institute of Music Library with 70,000 titles.

Student Life *Housing:* college housing not available. *Campus security:* 24-hour patrols. *Student Services:* personal/psychological counseling.

Standardized Tests *Required:* SAT I (for placement).

Costs (2001–02) *One-time required fee:* $85. *Tuition:* $0 full-time. *Required fees:* $695 full-time.

Financial Aid Of all full-time matriculated undergraduates who enrolled in 2001, 64 applied for aid, 64 were judged to have need, 27 had their need fully met.

The Curtis Institute of Music (continued)
60 State and other part-time jobs (averaging $2026). *Average percent of need met:* 80%. *Average financial aid package:* $9500. *Average need-based loan:* $3470. *Average need-based gift aid:* $2820. *Average indebtedness upon graduation:* $17,000. *Financial aid deadline:* 3/1.

Applying *Options:* common application, early admission. *Application fee:* $60. *Required:* essay or personal statement, high school transcript, letters of recommendation, audition. *Application deadlines:* 1/15 (freshmen), 1/15 (transfers). *Notification:* continuous (freshmen).

Admissions Contact Mr. Christopher Hodges, Admissions Officer, The Curtis Institute of Music, 1726 Locust Street, Philadelphia, PA 19103-6107. *Phone:* 215-893-5262. *Fax:* 215-893-7900.

DELAWARE VALLEY COLLEGE
Doylestown, Pennsylvania

- **Independent** comprehensive, founded 1896
- **Calendar** semesters
- **Degrees** associate, bachelor's, and master's
- **Suburban** 600-acre campus with easy access to Philadelphia
- **Endowment** $13.3 million
- **Coed,** 1,926 undergraduate students, 68% full-time, 53% women, 47% men
- **Moderately difficult** entrance level, 86% of applicants were admitted

The distinctive DVC Employment Program gets results. All students complete 24 weeks of hands-on work in jobs related to their academic programs. This on-the-job learning expands resumes, exposes students to real-life work experience in their chosen fields, and allows employers to recognize students' skills and abilities—all before graduation.

Undergraduates 1,309 full-time, 617 part-time. Students come from 21 states and territories, 2 other countries, 28% are from out of state, 3% African American, 0.5% Asian American or Pacific Islander, 2% Hispanic American, 0.3% Native American, 0.5% international, 4% transferred in, 66% live on campus. *Retention:* 66% of 2001 full-time freshmen returned.

Freshmen *Admission:* 1,172 applied, 1,007 admitted, 362 enrolled. *Average high school GPA:* 3.08. *Test scores:* SAT verbal scores over 500: 47%; SAT math scores over 500: 52%; ACT scores over 18: 88%; SAT verbal scores over 600: 11%; SAT math scores over 600: 12%; ACT scores over 24: 25%; SAT verbal scores over 700: 1%; SAT math scores over 700: 1%.

Faculty *Total:* 135, 51% full-time, 51% with terminal degrees. *Student/faculty ratio:* 16:1.

Majors Accounting; adult/continuing education; agricultural business; agronomy/crop science; animal sciences; biology; business administration; business marketing and marketing management; chemistry; communications; criminal justice/law enforcement administration; dairy science; English; environmental science; equestrian studies; food products retailing; food sciences; food services technology; horticulture science; information sciences/systems; landscape architecture; ornamental horticulture; pre-veterinary studies; secondary education; sport/fitness administration.

Academic Programs *Special study options:* academic remediation for entering students, adult/continuing education programs, advanced placement credit, cooperative education, honors programs, internships, part-time degree program, services for LD students, study abroad, summer session for credit.

Library Joseph Krauskopf Memorial Library with 58,020 titles, 734 serial subscriptions, an OPAC, a Web page.

Computers on Campus 210 computers available on campus for general student use. At least one staffed computer lab available.

Student Life *Housing Options:* coed. *Activities and Organizations:* drama/theater group, student-run newspaper, radio station, choral group, Block and Bridle Club, Community Service Corps, student government, Halloween Haunting. *Campus security:* 24-hour patrols, late-night transport/escort service, controlled dormitory access. *Student Services:* health clinic, personal/psychological counseling.

Athletics Member NCAA. All Division III. *Intercollegiate sports:* baseball M, basketball M/W, cross-country running M/W, equestrian sports M/W, field hockey W, football M, golf M, soccer M/W, softball W, track and field M/W, volleyball W, wrestling M. *Intramural sports:* basketball M/W, bowling M/W, cross-country running M/W, football M, golf M/W, lacrosse M, racquetball M/W, soccer M, softball M/W, tennis M/W, volleyball M/W, weight lifting M.

Standardized Tests *Required:* SAT I or ACT (for admission).

Costs (2001–02) *One-time required fee:* $150. *Comprehensive fee:* $23,918 includes full-time tuition ($16,874), mandatory fees ($500), and room and board ($6544). Part-time tuition: $420 per credit. Part-time tuition and fees vary according to class time. *Required fees:* $50 per term part-time. *Room and board:* College room only: $2888. Room and board charges vary according to board plan. *Payment plan:* installment. *Waivers:* employees or children of employees.

Financial Aid Of all full-time matriculated undergraduates who enrolled in 2001, 1109 applied for aid, 891 were judged to have need, 337 had their need fully met. 182 Federal Work-Study jobs (averaging $1589). 160 State and other part-time jobs. In 2001, 264 non-need-based awards were made. *Average percent of need met:* 87%. *Average financial aid package:* $15,086. *Average need-based loan:* $3938. *Average need-based gift aid:* $10,711. *Average non-need based aid:* $7490. *Average indebtedness upon graduation:* $15,700.

Applying *Options:* common application, electronic application, early admission, deferred entrance. *Application fee:* $35. *Required:* high school transcript, 1 letter of recommendation. *Recommended:* interview. *Application deadline:* rolling (freshmen), rolling (transfers). *Notification:* continuous (freshmen).

Admissions Contact Mr. Stephen Zenko, Director of Admissions, Delaware Valley College, 18901. *Phone:* 215-489-2211 Ext. 2211. *Toll-free phone:* 800-2DELVAL. *Fax:* 215-230-2968. *E-mail:* admitme@devalcol.edu.

DESALES UNIVERSITY
Center Valley, Pennsylvania

- **Independent Roman Catholic** comprehensive, founded 1964
- **Calendar** semesters
- **Degrees** bachelor's and master's (also offers adult program with significant enrollment not reflected in profile)
- **Suburban** 300-acre campus with easy access to Philadelphia
- **Endowment** $23.2 million
- **Coed,** 2,013 undergraduate students, 76% full-time, 55% women, 45% men
- **Moderately difficult** entrance level, 73% of applicants were admitted

Undergraduates 1,522 full-time, 491 part-time. Students come from 12 states and territories, 26% are from out of state, 1.0% African American, 1.0% Asian American or Pacific Islander, 2% Hispanic American, 0.1% Native American, 0.1% international, 2% transferred in, 80% live on campus. *Retention:* 81% of 2001 full-time freshmen returned.

Freshmen *Admission:* 1,418 applied, 1,029 admitted, 357 enrolled. *Test scores:* SAT math scores over 500: 67%; SAT math scores over 600: 24%; SAT math scores over 700: 3%.

Faculty *Total:* 124, 63% full-time, 56% with terminal degrees. *Student/faculty ratio:* 18:1.

Majors Accounting; biology; business administration; business marketing and marketing management; chemistry; computer science; criminal justice/law enforcement administration; criminal justice studies; dance; elementary education; English; environmental science; film/video production; finance; history; human resources management; liberal arts and sciences/liberal studies; management information systems/business data processing; mass communications; mathematics; medical technology; nursing; pharmacy administration/pharmaceutics; political science; pre-dentistry; pre-medicine; pre-veterinary studies; psychology; secondary education; social work; Spanish; sport/fitness administration; theater arts/drama; theology.

Academic Programs *Special study options:* accelerated degree program, adult/continuing education programs, advanced placement credit, distance learning, double majors, independent study, internships, off-campus study, part-time degree program, services for LD students, study abroad, summer session for credit. *ROTC:* Army (c).

Library Trexler Library with 100,325 titles, 1,710 serial subscriptions, 2,614 audiovisual materials, an OPAC, a Web page.

Computers on Campus 270 computers available on campus for general student use. A campuswide network can be accessed from student residence rooms and from off campus. Internet access, at least one staffed computer lab available.

Student Life *Housing Options:* coed, men-only, women-only. *Activities and Organizations:* drama/theater group, student-run newspaper, radio and television station, choral group, Sigma Alpha Omega, social outreach, Student Nursing Organization, Student Government Association, business club. *Campus security:* 24-hour emergency response devices and patrols, late-night transport/escort service, controlled dormitory access, desk security in residence halls 24 hours per day. *Student Services:* health clinic, personal/psychological counseling.

Athletics Member NCAA. All Division III. *Intercollegiate sports:* baseball M, basketball M/W, cross-country running M/W, equestrian sports W(c), golf M, ice hockey M(c), lacrosse M, soccer M/W, softball W, tennis M/W, track and field M/W, volleyball W. *Intramural sports:* badminton M/W, basketball M/W, football M/W, golf M, soccer M/W, softball M/W, volleyball M/W, weight lifting M/W.

Standardized Tests *Required:* SAT I or ACT (for admission).

Costs (2001–02) *Comprehensive fee:* $22,610 includes full-time tuition ($16,000), mandatory fees ($340), and room and board ($6270). Full-time tuition and fees vary according to class time and course load. Part-time tuition: $660 per credit. Part-time tuition and fees vary according to class time and course load. *Room and board:* College room only: $3300. Room and board charges vary according to housing facility. *Payment plans:* installment, deferred payment. *Waivers:* employees or children of employees.

Financial Aid Of all full-time matriculated undergraduates who enrolled in 2001, 1282 applied for aid, 923 were judged to have need, 404 had their need fully met. 233 State and other part-time jobs (averaging $875). In 2001, 359 non-need-based awards were made. *Average percent of need met:* 79%. *Average financial aid package:* $12,545. *Average need-based loan:* $2624. *Average need-based gift aid:* $9424. *Average indebtedness upon graduation:* $13,977.

Applying *Options:* common application, electronic application, early admission, deferred entrance. *Application fee:* $30. *Required:* high school transcript, 2 letters of recommendation. *Recommended:* essay or personal statement, interview. *Application deadlines:* 8/1 (freshmen), 8/1 (transfers). *Notification:* continuous (freshmen).

Admissions Contact Mr. Peter Rautzhan, Director of Admissions and Financial Aid, DeSales University, 2755 Station Avenue, Center Valley, PA 18034-9568. *Phone:* 610-282-1100 Ext. 1332. *Toll-free phone:* 877-433-72537 (in-state); 800-228-5114 (out-of-state). *Fax:* 610-282-2254. *E-mail:* admiss@desales.edu.

DICKINSON COLLEGE
Carlisle, Pennsylvania

- **Independent** 4-year, founded 1773
- **Calendar** semesters
- **Degree** bachelor's
- **Suburban** 103-acre campus with easy access to Harrisburg
- **Endowment** $168.3 million
- **Coed,** 2,208 undergraduate students, 98% full-time, 58% women, 42% men
- **Very difficult** entrance level, 64% of applicants were admitted

Undergraduates 2,172 full-time, 36 part-time. Students come from 48 states and territories, 18 other countries, 59% are from out of state, 2% African American, 2% Asian American or Pacific Islander, 2% Hispanic American, 0.2% Native American, 1% international, 0.4% transferred in, 92% live on campus. *Retention:* 89% of 2001 full-time freshmen returned.

Freshmen *Admission:* 3,820 applied, 2,453 admitted, 611 enrolled. *Test scores:* SAT verbal scores over 500: 99%; SAT math scores over 500: 97%; SAT verbal scores over 600: 66%; SAT math scores over 600: 62%; SAT verbal scores over 700: 15%; SAT math scores over 700: 8%.

Faculty *Total:* 203, 80% full-time, 77% with terminal degrees. *Student/faculty ratio:* 12:1.

Majors American studies; anthropology; biochemistry; biology; chemistry; classics; computer science; dance; East Asian studies; economics; English; environmental science; fine/studio arts; French; geology; German; Greek (ancient and medieval); history; international business; international relations; Italian; Judaic studies; Latin (ancient and medieval); mathematics; medieval/renaissance studies; molecular biology; music; philosophy; physics; political science; pre-dentistry; pre-law; pre-medicine; psychology; public policy analysis; religious studies; Russian; Russian/Slavic studies; sociology; Spanish; theater arts/drama; theater design; women's studies.

Academic Programs *Special study options:* accelerated degree program, adult/continuing education programs, advanced placement credit, double majors, independent study, internships, off-campus study, part-time degree program, services for LD students, student-designed majors, study abroad, summer session for credit. *ROTC:* Army (b). *Unusual degree programs:* 3-2 engineering with Case Western Reserve University, University of Pennsylvania, Rensselaer Polytechnic Institute.

Library Waidner-Spahr Library plus 6 others with 305,272 titles, 6,163 serial subscriptions, 12,247 audiovisual materials, an OPAC, a Web page.

Computers on Campus 472 computers available on campus for general student use. A campuswide network can be accessed from student residence rooms and from off campus. Internet access, online (class) registration, at least one staffed computer lab available.

Student Life *Housing:* on-campus residence required for freshman year. *Options:* coed, men-only, women-only, disabled students. *Activities and Organizations:* drama/theater group, student-run newspaper, radio station, choral group, Campus Activities Board, Student Senate, volunteer/community service groups, Arts House, national fraternities, national sororities. *Campus security:* 24-hour emergency response devices and patrols, student patrols, late-night transport/escort service, controlled dormitory access. *Student Services:* health clinic, personal/psychological counseling, women's center.

Athletics Member NCAA. All Division III. *Intercollegiate sports:* baseball M, basketball M/W, cross-country running M/W, equestrian sports M(c)/W(c), fencing M(c)/W(c), field hockey W, football M, golf M/W, ice hockey M(c), lacrosse M/W, skiing (downhill) M(c)/W(c), soccer M/W, softball W, squash M(c)/W(c), swimming M/W, tennis M/W, track and field M/W, volleyball M(c)/W, wrestling M(c). *Intramural sports:* badminton M/W, basketball M, bowling M/W, field hockey W, football M, golf M/W, racquetball M/W, soccer M/W, softball M/W, squash M/W, table tennis M/W, tennis M/W, volleyball M.

Standardized Tests *Recommended:* SAT I and SAT II or ACT (for admission).

Costs (2001–02) *One-time required fee:* $25. *Comprehensive fee:* $32,210 includes full-time tuition ($25,250), mandatory fees ($235), and room and board ($6725). Part-time tuition: $4135 per course. *Required fees:* $40 per course. *Room and board:* College room only: $3450. Room and board charges vary according to housing facility. *Payment plan:* installment. *Waivers:* employees or children of employees.

Financial Aid Of all full-time matriculated undergraduates who enrolled in 2001, 1446 applied for aid, 1274 were judged to have need, 1026 had their need fully met. 887 Federal Work-Study jobs (averaging $1540). 80 State and other part-time jobs (averaging $3267). In 2001, 324 non-need-based awards were made. *Average percent of need met:* 98%. *Average financial aid package:* $21,229. *Average need-based loan:* $4475. *Average need-based gift aid:* $16,432. *Average non-need based aid:* $11,982. *Average indebtedness upon graduation:* $16,945.

Applying *Options:* common application, electronic application, early decision, early action, deferred entrance. *Application fee:* $40. *Required:* essay or personal statement, high school transcript, 2 letters of recommendation. *Recommended:* minimum 3.0 GPA, interview. *Application deadlines:* 2/1 (freshmen), 4/1 (transfers). *Early decision:* 11/15 (for plan 1), 1/15 (for plan 2). *Notification:* 3/31 (freshmen), 12/15 (early decision plan 1), 2/15 (early decision plan 2), 1/15 (early action).

Admissions Contact Mr. Christopher Seth Allen, Director of Admissions, Dickinson College, PO Box 1773, Carlisle, PA 17013-2896. *Phone:* 717-245-1231. *Toll-free phone:* 800-644-1773. *Fax:* 717-245-1231. *E-mail:* admit@dickinson.edu.

DREXEL UNIVERSITY
Philadelphia, Pennsylvania

- **Independent** university, founded 1891
- **Calendar** quarters
- **Degrees** bachelor's, master's, doctoral, and post-master's certificates
- **Urban** 42-acre campus
- **Endowment** $248.3 million
- **Coed,** 11,019 undergraduate students, 83% full-time, 38% women, 62% men
- **Moderately difficult** entrance level, 73% of applicants were admitted

Drexel is a national leader in curricular innovation and cooperative education. Through Drexel Co-op-The Ultimate Internship, students alternate between periods of classroom study and paid professional employment. By the time they graduate, Drexel students have gained the experience needed to pursue the graduate school or career of their choice.

Undergraduates 9,103 full-time, 1,916 part-time. Students come from 44 states and territories, 96 other countries, 40% are from out of state, 8% African American, 14% Asian American or Pacific Islander, 2% Hispanic American, 0.2% Native American, 6% international, 5% transferred in, 26% live on campus. *Retention:* 86% of 2001 full-time freshmen returned.

Freshmen *Admission:* 9,888 applied, 7,193 admitted, 2,049 enrolled. *Average high school GPA:* 3.12. *Test scores:* SAT verbal scores over 500: 83%; SAT math scores over 500: 91%; SAT verbal scores over 600: 33%; SAT math scores over 600: 50%; SAT verbal scores over 700: 4%; SAT math scores over 700: 8%.

Faculty *Total:* 889, 56% full-time. *Student/faculty ratio:* 14:1.

Majors Accounting; architectural engineering; architecture; area studies related; bioengineering; biological/physical sciences; biology; business; business economics; business management/administrative services related; business marketing and marketing management; chemical engineering; chemistry; civil engineering; civil engineering related; communications related; computer engineering; computer science; culinary arts; design/applied arts related; electrical engineering; engineering; English related; environmental engineering; environmental science; fashion design/illustration; film/video production; finance; general studies; graphic design/commercial art/illustration; health services administration; history; hospitality services management related; humanities; human resources management; industrial/manufacturing engineering; information sciences/systems; interior design; international business; Internet; management information systems/business data processing; materials engineering; mathematics; mechanical engineering; music; nutritional sciences; photography; physics related; play/screenwriting; psychology; social sciences; sociology; taxation; teacher education, specific programs related; technical/business writing.

Drexel University (continued)

Academic Programs *Special study options:* academic remediation for entering students, accelerated degree program, adult/continuing education programs, advanced placement credit, cooperative education, distance learning, double majors, English as a second language, freshman honors college, honors programs, independent study, internships, part-time degree program, services for LD students, study abroad, summer session for credit. *ROTC:* Army (b), Navy (c), Air Force (c).

Library W. W. Hagerty Library with 258,243 titles, 7,048 serial subscriptions, 5,561 audiovisual materials, an OPAC, a Web page.

Computers on Campus 6500 computers available on campus for general student use. A campuswide network can be accessed from student residence rooms and from off campus that provide access to campuswide wireless network. Internet access, online (class) registration, at least one staffed computer lab available.

Student Life *Housing:* on-campus residence required for freshman year. *Options:* coed, disabled students. *Activities and Organizations:* drama/theater group, student-run newspaper, radio and television station, choral group, student government, Black Student Union, Society of Hispanic Professional Engineers, Society of Minority Engineers and Scientists, Campus Activities Board, national fraternities, national sororities. *Campus security:* 24-hour emergency response devices and patrols, late-night transport/escort service, controlled dormitory access. *Student Services:* health clinic, personal/psychological counseling.

Athletics Member NCAA. All Division I. *Intercollegiate sports:* baseball M(s), basketball M(s)/W(s), crew M(s)/W(s), field hockey W(s), golf M(s), lacrosse M(s)/W(s), soccer M(s)/W(s), softball W(s), swimming M(s)/W(s), tennis M(s)/W(s), volleyball W(s), wrestling M(s). *Intramural sports:* badminton M/W, basketball M/W, fencing M/W, football M, ice hockey M, riflery M/W, rugby M/W, sailing M/W, softball M, squash M/W, table tennis M/W, tennis M/W, volleyball M/W, water polo M/W.

Standardized Tests *Required:* SAT I or ACT (for admission). *Recommended:* SAT I (for admission).

Costs (2002–03) *Comprehensive fee:* $27,503 includes full-time tuition ($17,393), mandatory fees ($1020), and room and board ($9090). Full-time tuition and fees vary according to student level. Part-time tuition: $440 per quarter hour. *Required fees:* $78 per term part-time. *Room and board:* College room only: $5490. *Waivers:* employees or children of employees.

Financial Aid Of all full-time matriculated undergraduates who enrolled in 2001, 6976 applied for aid, 6179 were judged to have need, 1311 had their need fully met. 749 Federal Work-Study jobs (averaging $1400). In 2001, 1475 non-need-based awards were made. *Average percent of need met:* 78%. *Average financial aid package:* $12,900. *Average need-based loan:* $3770. *Average need-based gift aid:* $6600. *Financial aid deadline:* 2/15.

Applying *Options:* common application, electronic application, early admission, deferred entrance. *Application fee:* $50. *Required:* essay or personal statement, high school transcript, minimum 2.0 GPA. *Recommended:* 2 letters of recommendation, interview. *Application deadline:* 3/1 (freshmen), rolling (transfers). *Notification:* continuous (freshmen).

Admissions Contact Mr. David Eddy, Director of Undergraduate Admissions, Drexel University, 3141 Chestnut Street, Room 220, Philadelphia, PA 19104-2875. *Phone:* 215-895-2400. *Toll-free phone:* 800-2-DREXEL. *Fax:* 215-895-5939. *E-mail:* enroll@drexel.edu.

DUQUESNE UNIVERSITY
Pittsburgh, Pennsylvania

- **Independent Roman Catholic** university, founded 1878
- **Calendar** semesters
- **Degrees** bachelor's, master's, doctoral, first professional, post-master's, and postbachelor's certificates
- **Urban** 43-acre campus
- **Endowment** $107.3 million
- **Coed,** 5,404 undergraduate students, 92% full-time, 58% women, 42% men
- **Moderately difficult** entrance level, 96% of applicants were admitted

Undergraduates 4,953 full-time, 451 part-time. Students come from 48 states and territories, 83 other countries, 18% are from out of state, 4% African American, 1% Asian American or Pacific Islander, 2% Hispanic American, 0.1% Native American, 3% international, 3% transferred in, 45% live on campus. *Retention:* 85% of 2001 full-time freshmen returned.

Freshmen *Admission:* 3,139 applied, 3,018 admitted, 1,191 enrolled. *Average high school GPA:* 3.40. *Test scores:* SAT verbal scores over 500: 71%; SAT math scores over 500: 72%; ACT scores over 18: 93%; SAT verbal scores over 600: 23%; SAT math scores over 600: 25%; ACT scores over 24: 41%; SAT verbal scores over 700: 2%; SAT math scores over 700: 3%; ACT scores over 30: 4%.

Faculty *Total:* 885, 46% full-time. *Student/faculty ratio:* 14:1.

Majors Accounting; accounting related; art history; athletic training/sports medicine; biochemistry; biology; biology education; business; business management/administrative services related; business marketing and marketing management; chemistry; chemistry education; chemistry related; classics; communications; computer science; early childhood education; education; educational media technology; elementary education; English; English education; English related; environmental science; finance; fine/studio arts; foreign languages education; foreign languages/literatures; French language education; German language education; Greek (ancient and medieval); health/medical preparatory programs related; health services administration; history; international business; international relations; investments and securities; journalism; journalism and mass communication related; Latin (ancient and medieval); liberal arts and studies related; logistics/materials management; management information systems/business data processing; management science; marketing management and research related; mathematics; mathematics education; medical pharmacology and pharmaceutical sciences; microbiology/bacteriology; music (general performance); music related; music teacher education; music therapy; nursing; occupational therapy; philosophy; physical therapy; physician assistant; physics; physics education; political science; psychology; science education; secondary education; social sciences; social studies education; sociology; Spanish; Spanish language education; speech-language pathology; teacher education, specific programs related; theater arts/drama; theology.

Academic Programs *Special study options:* academic remediation for entering students, accelerated degree program, adult/continuing education programs, advanced placement credit, cooperative education, distance learning, double majors, English as a second language, freshman honors college, honors programs, independent study, internships, off-campus study, part-time degree program, services for LD students, student-designed majors, study abroad, summer session for credit. *ROTC:* Army (c), Navy (c), Air Force (c). *Unusual degree programs:* 3-2 engineering with Case Western Reserve University, University of Pittsburgh.

Library Gumberg Library plus 1 other with 325,377 titles, 4,135 serial subscriptions, 32,677 audiovisual materials, an OPAC, a Web page.

Computers on Campus 650 computers available on campus for general student use. A campuswide network can be accessed from student residence rooms and from off campus. Internet access, at least one staffed computer lab available.

Student Life *Housing:* on-campus residence required for freshman year. *Options:* coed, men-only, women-only, disabled students. *Activities and Organizations:* drama/theater group, student-run newspaper, radio and television station, choral group, marching band, Student Government Association, University Volunteers, Program Council, Commuter Council, Black Student Union, national fraternities, national sororities. *Campus security:* 24-hour emergency response devices and patrols, late-night transport/escort service, controlled dormitory access, 24-hour front desk personnel, 24-hour video monitors at residence hall entrances, surveillance cameras throughout the campus. *Student Services:* health clinic, personal/psychological counseling.

Athletics Member NCAA. All Division I except football (Division I-AA). *Intercollegiate sports:* baseball M(s), basketball M(s)/W(s), crew M(c)/W(s), cross-country running M(s)/W(s), golf M(s), ice hockey M(c), lacrosse M(c)/W(s), riflery M(s)/W(s), soccer M(s)/W(s), swimming M(s)/W(s), tennis M(s)/W(s), track and field M(c)/W(s), volleyball W(s), wrestling M(s). *Intramural sports:* badminton M/W, basketball M/W, bowling M/W, football M/W, racquetball M/W, skiing (cross-country) M/W, soccer M/W, softball M/W, squash M/W, table tennis M/W, tennis M/W, volleyball M/W, water polo M/W.

Standardized Tests *Required:* SAT I or ACT (for admission).

Costs (2001–02) *Comprehensive fee:* $24,242 includes full-time tuition ($16,049), mandatory fees ($1429), and room and board ($6764). Full-time tuition and fees vary according to program. Part-time tuition: $542 per credit. Part-time tuition and fees vary according to program. *Required fees:* $56 per credit. *Room and board:* College room only: $3690. Room and board charges vary according to board plan. *Payment plans:* installment, deferred payment. *Waivers:* senior citizens and employees or children of employees.

Financial Aid Of all full-time matriculated undergraduates who enrolled in 2001, 4567 applied for aid, 3095 were judged to have need, 1256 had their need fully met. 1190 Federal Work-Study jobs (averaging $2126). *Average percent of need met:* 82%. *Average financial aid package:* $13,444. *Average need-based loan:* $4255. *Average need-based gift aid:* $8351. *Average indebtedness upon graduation:* $16,461. *Financial aid deadline:* 5/1.

Applying *Options:* common application, electronic application, early admission, early decision, early action, deferred entrance. *Application fee:* $50. *Required:* essay or personal statement, high school transcript. *Required for some:* minimum 2.75 GPA, interview. *Recommended:* 1 letter of recommendation. *Application deadlines:* 7/1 (freshmen), 7/1 (transfers). *Early decision:* 11/1. *Notification:* continuous (freshmen), 12/15 (early decision), 1/15 (early action).

Admissions Contact Office of Admissions, Duquesne University, 600 Forbes Avenue, Pittsburgh, PA 15282-0201. *Phone:* 412-396-5000. *Toll-free phone:* 800-456-0590. *Fax:* 412-396-5644. *E-mail:* admissions@duq.edu.

EASTERN UNIVERSITY
St. Davids, Pennsylvania

- **Independent American Baptist Churches in the USA** comprehensive, founded 1952
- **Calendar** semesters
- **Degrees** associate, bachelor's, and master's
- **Small-town** 107-acre campus with easy access to Philadelphia
- **Coed,** 2,075 undergraduate students, 86% full-time, 64% women, 36% men
- **Moderately difficult** entrance level, 81% of applicants were admitted

Eastern University is a Christian university of the arts and sciences committed to the integration of faith, reason, and justice, which equip students with the knowledge and skills to make a difference in all areas of society. Eastern enrolls 3,000 students to its undergraduate, graduate, professional, and international programs. The curriculum is firmly rooted in a Christian worldview. With dramatic growth over the past decade, Eastern has increased its faculty, raised the percentage of faculty members with Ph.D. degrees to 84 percent, improved facilities, built three new residence halls, and raised the standards of admission. Eastern is located near Philadelphia, Pennsylvania, one of America's educational centers, and is only 2 hours from Washington, D.C., and New York City.

Undergraduates 1,780 full-time, 295 part-time. Students come from 38 states and territories, 26 other countries, 40% are from out of state, 13% African American, 1% Asian American or Pacific Islander, 4% Hispanic American, 0.1% Native American, 2% international, 3% transferred in, 47% live on campus. *Retention:* 79% of 2001 full-time freshmen returned.

Freshmen *Admission:* 1,032 applied, 839 admitted, 413 enrolled. *Average high school GPA:* 3.36. *Test scores:* SAT verbal scores over 500: 78%; SAT math scores over 500: 70%; ACT scores over 18: 94%; SAT verbal scores over 600: 32%; SAT math scores over 600: 26%; ACT scores over 24: 41%; SAT verbal scores over 700: 8%; SAT math scores over 700: 2%.

Faculty *Total:* 278, 29% full-time, 39% with terminal degrees. *Student/faculty ratio:* 13:1.

Majors Accounting; art history; astronomy; biblical studies; biochemistry; biology; business marketing and marketing management; chemistry; communications; creative writing; elementary education; English; English education; environmental science; finance; French; health facilities administration; health/physical education; history; liberal arts and sciences/liberal studies; management information systems/business data processing; management science; mathematics; missionary studies; multimedia; music; nursing; philosophy; political science; psychology; secondary education; social work; sociology; Spanish; theology; urban studies.

Academic Programs *Special study options:* academic remediation for entering students, accelerated degree program, adult/continuing education programs, advanced placement credit, English as a second language, honors programs, independent study, internships, off-campus study, part-time degree program, student-designed majors, summer session for credit. *ROTC:* Army (c), Air Force (c).

Library Warner Library plus 1 other with 143,815 titles, 1,215 serial subscriptions, 11,673 audiovisual materials, an OPAC, a Web page.

Computers on Campus 60 computers available on campus for general student use. A campuswide network can be accessed from student residence rooms and from off campus. Internet access, at least one staffed computer lab available.

Student Life *Housing:* on-campus residence required through senior year. *Options:* coed. *Activities and Organizations:* drama/theater group, student-run newspaper, radio station, choral group, Habitat for Humanity, Y.A.C.H.T. club, Angels of Harmony, Black Student League, Fellowship of Christian Athletes. *Campus security:* 24-hour emergency response devices and patrols, late-night transport/escort service, controlled dormitory access, emergency call boxes. *Student Services:* health clinic, personal/psychological counseling, women's center.

Athletics Member NCAA. All Division III. *Intercollegiate sports:* baseball M, basketball M/W, field hockey W, lacrosse M/W, soccer M/W, softball W, volleyball W. *Intramural sports:* basketball M/W, soccer M/W, volleyball W.

Standardized Tests *Required:* SAT I or ACT (for admission).

Costs (2002–03) *One-time required fee:* $40. *Comprehensive fee:* $22,616 includes full-time tuition ($15,832) and room and board ($6784). Part-time tuition: $360 per credit. *Room and board:* College room only: $3640.

Financial Aid Of all full-time matriculated undergraduates who enrolled in 2001, 1338 applied for aid, 1138 were judged to have need, 225 had their need fully met. 359 Federal Work-Study jobs (averaging $792). 364 State and other part-time jobs (averaging $956). In 2001, 211 non-need-based awards were made. *Average percent of need met:* 77%. *Average financial aid package:* $10,845. *Average need-based gift aid:* $8821. *Average non-need based aid:* $12,444. *Average indebtedness upon graduation:* $16,413.

Applying *Options:* electronic application, early admission, deferred entrance. *Application fee:* $25. *Required:* essay or personal statement, high school transcript, minimum 2.0 GPA, 1 letter of recommendation. *Recommended:* minimum 3.0 GPA, 3 letters of recommendation, interview. *Application deadline:* rolling (freshmen), rolling (transfers). *Notification:* continuous (freshmen).

Admissions Contact Mr. David Urban, Director of Undergraduate Admissions, Eastern University, 1300 Eagle Road, St. Davids, PA 19087-3696. *Phone:* 610-225-5005. *Toll-free phone:* 800-452-0996. *Fax:* 610-341-1723. *E-mail:* ugadm@eastern.edu.

EAST STROUDSBURG UNIVERSITY OF PENNSYLVANIA
East Stroudsburg, Pennsylvania

- **State-supported** comprehensive, founded 1893, part of Pennsylvania State System of Higher Education
- **Calendar** semesters
- **Degrees** associate, bachelor's, and master's
- **Small-town** 184-acre campus
- **Endowment** $5.2 million
- **Coed,** 4,967 undergraduate students, 88% full-time, 58% women, 42% men
- **Moderately difficult** entrance level, 73% of applicants were admitted

Undergraduates 4,392 full-time, 575 part-time. Students come from 21 states and territories, 23 other countries, 18% are from out of state, 4% African American, 1% Asian American or Pacific Islander, 3% Hispanic American, 0.1% Native American, 0.8% international, 7% transferred in, 45% live on campus. *Retention:* 75% of 2001 full-time freshmen returned.

Freshmen *Admission:* 4,173 applied, 3,062 admitted, 983 enrolled. *Test scores:* SAT verbal scores over 500: 39%; SAT math scores over 500: 61%; SAT verbal scores over 600: 4%; SAT math scores over 600: 11%; SAT math scores over 700: 1%.

Faculty *Total:* 292, 84% full-time, 66% with terminal degrees. *Student/faculty ratio:* 19:1.

Majors Athletic training/sports medicine; biochemistry; biology; biotechnology research; business administration; chemistry; communications; computer/information sciences; computer/information sciences related; early childhood education; earth sciences; ecology; economics; elementary education; English; exercise sciences; French; geography; health education; history; hotel and restaurant management; marine biology; mathematics; medical laboratory technician; nursing; philosophy; physical education; physical sciences; physics; political science; psychology; radio/television broadcasting technology; recreation/leisure studies; rehabilitation therapy; secondary education; social science education; sociology; Spanish; special education; speech-language pathology/audiology; speech/rhetorical studies; theater arts/drama; visual/performing arts.

Academic Programs *Special study options:* academic remediation for entering students, adult/continuing education programs, advanced placement credit, double majors, honors programs, independent study, internships, off-campus study, part-time degree program, services for LD students, student-designed majors, summer session for credit. *ROTC:* Army (c), Air Force (c). *Unusual degree programs:* 3-2 engineering with Pennsylvania State University University Park Campus, University of Pittsburgh; podiatric medicine with Pennsylvania College of Podiatric Medicine.

Library Kemp Library with 1,758 serial subscriptions, 12,506 audiovisual materials, an OPAC, a Web page.

Computers on Campus 164 computers available on campus for general student use. A campuswide network can be accessed from off campus. Internet access, at least one staffed computer lab available.

Student Life *Housing:* on-campus residence required through sophomore year. *Options:* coed, men-only, women-only. *Activities and Organizations:* drama/theater group, student-run newspaper, radio station, choral group, Student Senate, Stage II, Council for Exceptional Children, United Campus Ministry/ESU Christian Fellowship, University Band/Vocal Performing Choirs, national fraternities, national sororities. *Campus security:* 24-hour emergency response devices and patrols, student patrols, late-night transport/escort service, controlled dormitory access. *Student Services:* health clinic, personal/psychological counseling, women's center.

Athletics Member NCAA. All Division II except wrestling (Division I). *Intercollegiate sports:* baseball M, basketball M(s)/W(s), cross-country running

East Stroudsburg University of Pennsylvania (continued)
M(s)/W(s), field hockey W(s), football M(s), lacrosse W(s), soccer M(s)/W(s), softball W(s), swimming W(s), tennis M/W, track and field M(s)/W(s), volleyball M/W, wrestling M(s). *Intramural sports:* badminton M/W, basketball M/W, bowling M/W, equestrian sports M/W, football M, golf M/W, ice hockey M, lacrosse M, racquetball M/W, rugby M/W, soccer M/W, softball W, swimming M/W, tennis M/W, track and field M/W, volleyball M/W, water polo M/W, weight lifting M/W.

Standardized Tests *Required:* SAT I or ACT (for admission).

Costs (2001–02) *Tuition:* state resident $4016 full-time, $167 per credit part-time; nonresident $10,040 full-time, $418 per credit part-time. Part-time tuition and fees vary according to course load. *Required fees:* $968 full-time, $40 per credit. *Room and board:* $4224; room only: $2682. Room and board charges vary according to board plan and housing facility. *Waivers:* senior citizens and employees or children of employees.

Financial Aid Of all full-time matriculated undergraduates who enrolled in 2001, 3212 applied for aid, 2353 were judged to have need, 1909 had their need fully met. 340 Federal Work-Study jobs, 813 State and other part-time jobs. In 2001, 749 non-need-based awards were made. *Average percent of need met:* 91%. *Average financial aid package:* $4974. *Average need-based loan:* $3545. *Average need-based gift aid:* $2817. *Average indebtedness upon graduation:* $15,079. *Financial aid deadline:* 3/1.

Applying *Options:* electronic application. *Application fee:* $25. *Required:* high school transcript. *Recommended:* 1 letter of recommendation. *Application deadlines:* 4/1 (freshmen), 6/1 (transfers). *Notification:* continuous until 5/1 (freshmen).

Admissions Contact Mr. Alan T. Chesterton, Director of Admissions, East Stroudsburg University of Pennsylvania, 200 Prospect Street, East Stroudsburg, PA 18301. *Phone:* 570-422-3542. *Toll-free phone:* 877-230-5547. *Fax:* 570-422-3933. *E-mail:* undergrads@po-box.esu.edu.

EDINBORO UNIVERSITY OF PENNSYLVANIA
Edinboro, Pennsylvania

- **State-supported** comprehensive, founded 1857, part of Pennsylvania State System of Higher Education
- **Calendar** semesters
- **Degrees** associate, bachelor's, master's, post-master's, and postbachelor's certificates
- **Small-town** 585-acre campus
- **Endowment** $7.3 million
- **Coed,** 6,684 undergraduate students, 91% full-time, 57% women, 43% men
- **Moderately difficult** entrance level, 81% of applicants were admitted

Undergraduates 6,096 full-time, 588 part-time. Students come from 37 states and territories, 48 other countries, 10% are from out of state, 6% African American, 0.7% Asian American or Pacific Islander, 1% Hispanic American, 0.2% Native American, 3% international, 7% transferred in, 31% live on campus. *Retention:* 75% of 2001 full-time freshmen returned.

Freshmen *Admission:* 3,575 applied, 2,882 admitted, 1,451 enrolled. *Test scores:* SAT verbal scores over 500: 39%; SAT math scores over 500: 36%; ACT scores over 18: 62%; SAT verbal scores over 600: 9%; SAT math scores over 600: 6%; ACT scores over 24: 14%; SAT verbal scores over 700: 1%; ACT scores over 30: 1%.

Faculty *Total:* 376, 93% full-time, 65% with terminal degrees. *Student/faculty ratio:* 18:1.

Majors Anthropology; art education; art history; biochemistry; biological/physical sciences; biology; biomedical engineering-related technology; broadcast journalism; business administration; chemistry; chemistry related; communication disorders; communications; computer/information sciences; criminal justice studies; early childhood education; earth sciences; economics; electrical/electronic engineering technology; elementary education; English; environmental science; fine/studio arts; geography; geology; German; health/physical education; history; humanities; industrial technology; journalism; law enforcement/police science; liberal arts and sciences/liberal studies; mathematics; medical laboratory technician; medical nutrition; music; nursing; operations management; philosophy; physical education; physics; political science; psychology; social sciences; social studies education; social work; sociology; Spanish; special education; sport/fitness administration; theater arts/drama.

Academic Programs *Special study options:* academic remediation for entering students, accelerated degree program, adult/continuing education programs, advanced placement credit, distance learning, double majors, freshman honors college, honors programs, independent study, internships, off-campus study, part-time degree program, services for LD students, student-designed majors, study abroad, summer session for credit. *ROTC:* Army (b). *Unusual degree programs:* 3-2 engineering with Pennsylvania State University University Park Campus, University of Pittsburgh, Case Western Reserve University, Pennsylvania State University at Erie, The Behrend College.

Library Baron-Forness Library plus 1 other with 468,977 titles, 1,829 serial subscriptions, 12,796 audiovisual materials, an OPAC, a Web page.

Computers on Campus 700 computers available on campus for general student use. A campuswide network can be accessed from student residence rooms and from off campus that provide access to e-mail. Internet access, online (class) registration, at least one staffed computer lab available.

Student Life *Housing:* on-campus residence required for freshman year. *Options:* coed, men-only, women-only, disabled students. *Activities and Organizations:* drama/theater group, student-run newspaper, radio and television station, choral group, marching band, Student Government Association, Sigma Tau Gamma, Phi Mu Alpha, Gamma Sigma Sigma, Health and Physical Education Majors Club, national fraternities, national sororities. *Campus security:* 24-hour emergency response devices and patrols, self-defense education. *Student Services:* health clinic, personal/psychological counseling, legal services.

Athletics Member NCAA. All Division II except wrestling (Division I). *Intercollegiate sports:* baseball M(s), basketball M(s)/W(s), cross-country running M(s)/W(s), football M(s), ice hockey M(c), soccer W(s), softball W(s), swimming M(s)/W(s), tennis M(s)/W(s), track and field M(s)/W(s), volleyball W(s), wrestling M(s). *Intramural sports:* badminton M/W, basketball M/W, football M/W, racquetball M/W, soccer M/W, softball M/W, table tennis M/W, volleyball M/W, wrestling M.

Standardized Tests *Required:* SAT I or ACT (for admission).

Costs (2001–02) *Tuition:* area resident $4016 full-time, $167 per credit part-time; nonresident $6024 full-time, $251 per credit part-time. Part-time tuition and fees vary according to course load. *Required fees:* $928 full-time, $39 per credit. *Room and board:* $4384. Room and board charges vary according to board plan. *Payment plan:* installment. *Waivers:* senior citizens and employees or children of employees.

Financial Aid Of all full-time matriculated undergraduates who enrolled in 2001, 4946 applied for aid, 3993 were judged to have need, 888 had their need fully met. In 2001, 808 non-need-based awards were made. *Average percent of need met:* 95%. *Average financial aid package:* $5490. *Average need-based loan:* $3750. *Average need-based gift aid:* $1500. *Average indebtedness upon graduation:* $13,717.

Applying *Options:* electronic application, early admission, deferred entrance. *Application fee:* $25. *Required:* high school transcript. *Required for some:* interview. *Recommended:* minimum 2.0 GPA. *Application deadline:* rolling (freshmen), rolling (transfers). *Notification:* continuous (freshmen).

Admissions Contact Mr. Terrence Carlin, Assistant Vice President for Admissions, Edinboro University of Pennsylvania, Biggers House, Edinboro, PA 16444. *Phone:* 814-732-2761. *Toll-free phone:* 888-846-2676 (in-state); 800-626-2203 (out-of-state). *Fax:* 814-732-2420. *E-mail:* eup_admissions@edinboro.edu.

ELIZABETHTOWN COLLEGE
Elizabethtown, Pennsylvania

- **Independent** comprehensive, founded 1899, affiliated with Church of the Brethren
- **Calendar** semesters
- **Degrees** certificates, associate, bachelor's, master's, and postbachelor's certificates
- **Small-town** 185-acre campus with easy access to Baltimore and Philadelphia
- **Endowment** $35.5 million
- **Coed,** 1,901 undergraduate students, 91% full-time, 62% women, 38% men
- **Moderately difficult** entrance level, 69% of applicants were admitted

The College, founded in 1899, emphasizes the importance of a strong liberal arts background combined with preprofessional study. A dedicated faculty and a 12:1 student-faculty ratio promote mentoring relationships among students and the faculty. The 19 academic departments collectively offer 40 majors and more than 50 minors and concentrations. The campus community is made up of 1,730 students from 30 states and 40 other countries. Elizabethtown College emphasizes personal attenton and experiential learning. Elizabethtown encourages all interested students to visit the campus.

Undergraduates 1,735 full-time, 166 part-time. Students come from 30 states and territories, 30 other countries, 31% are from out of state, 1% African American, 1% Asian American or Pacific Islander, 1% Hispanic American, 0.2% Native American, 3% international, 2% transferred in, 85% live on campus. *Retention:* 84% of 2001 full-time freshmen returned.

Freshmen *Admission:* 2,763 applied, 1,900 admitted, 542 enrolled. *Test scores:* SAT verbal scores over 500: 79%; SAT math scores over 500: 76%; ACT scores over 18: 81%; SAT verbal scores over 600: 30%; SAT math scores over 600: 30%; ACT scores over 24: 40%; SAT verbal scores over 700: 3%; SAT math scores over 700: 3%; ACT scores over 30: 9%.

Faculty *Total:* 198, 56% full-time, 55% with terminal degrees. *Student/faculty ratio:* 12:1.

Majors Accounting; anthropology; art; biochemistry; biology; biotechnology research; business administration; chemistry; communications; computer engineering; computer science; criminal justice studies; early childhood education; economics; education; elementary education; engineering; engineering physics; English; environmental science; French; German; history; industrial/manufacturing engineering; international business; mathematics; modern languages; music; music teacher education; music therapy; occupational therapy; peace/conflict studies; philosophy; physics; political science; pre-dentistry; pre-law; pre-medicine; pre-veterinary studies; psychology; religious studies; science education; secondary education; social sciences; social work; sociology; Spanish.

Academic Programs *Special study options:* adult/continuing education programs, advanced placement credit, double majors, English as a second language, external degree program, honors programs, independent study, internships, off-campus study, part-time degree program, study abroad, summer session for credit. *Unusual degree programs:* 3-2 engineering with Pennsylvania State University University Park Campus; forestry with Duke University; nursing with Thomas Jefferson University; allied health programs with Thomas Jefferson University, Widener University, University of Maryland at Baltimore.

Library High Library plus 1 other with 184,052 titles, 1,090 serial subscriptions, 31,195 audiovisual materials, an OPAC, a Web page.

Computers on Campus 175 computers available on campus for general student use. A campuswide network can be accessed from student residence rooms and from off campus that provide access to e-mail, file space, personal Web page. Internet access, at least one staffed computer lab available.

Student Life *Housing:* on-campus residence required through senior year. *Options:* coed, women-only. *Activities and Organizations:* drama/theater group, student-run newspaper, radio and television station, choral group, Activities Planning Board, Student Senate, Residence Hall Association, student newspaper, Habitat for Humanity. *Campus security:* 24-hour emergency response devices and patrols, student patrols, late-night transport/escort service, self-defense workshops, crime prevention program. *Student Services:* health clinic, personal/psychological counseling.

Athletics Member NCAA. All Division III. *Intercollegiate sports:* baseball M, basketball M/W, cross-country running M/W, field hockey W, golf M, lacrosse M/W, soccer M/W, softball W, swimming M/W, tennis M/W, track and field M/W, volleyball M(c)/W, wrestling M. *Intramural sports:* basketball M/W, racquetball M/W, soccer M/W, softball M/W, tennis M/W, volleyball M/W.

Standardized Tests *Required:* SAT I or ACT (for admission).

Costs (2001–02) *Comprehensive fee:* $27,350 includes full-time tuition ($21,350) and room and board ($6000). Part-time tuition: $525 per credit hour. Part-time tuition and fees vary according to class time, course load, and program. *Room and board:* College room only: $3050. Room and board charges vary according to board plan and housing facility. *Payment plan:* installment. *Waivers:* employees or children of employees.

Financial Aid Of all full-time matriculated undergraduates who enrolled in 2001, 1397 applied for aid, 1253 were judged to have need, 376 had their need fully met. 746 Federal Work-Study jobs (averaging $1284). 39 State and other part-time jobs. In 2001, 367 non-need-based awards were made. *Average percent of need met:* 89%. *Average financial aid package:* $15,714. *Average need-based loan:* $3740. *Average need-based gift aid:* $11,724. *Average indebtedness upon graduation:* $20,273.

Applying *Options:* common application, electronic application, early admission, deferred entrance. *Application fee:* $20. *Required:* essay or personal statement, high school transcript, minimum 2.0 GPA, 2 letters of recommendation. *Required for some:* interview. *Recommended:* minimum 3.0 GPA, interview. *Application deadline:* rolling (freshmen), rolling (transfers).

Admissions Contact W. Kent Barnds, Director of Admissions, Elizabethtown College, 1 Alpha Drive, Elizabethtown, PA 17022-2298. *Phone:* 717-361-1400. *Fax:* 717-361-1365. *E-mail:* admissions@acad.etown.edu.

FRANKLIN AND MARSHALL COLLEGE
Lancaster, Pennsylvania

- **Independent** 4-year, founded 1787
- **Calendar** semesters
- **Degree** bachelor's
- **Suburban** 125-acre campus with easy access to Philadelphia
- **Endowment** $301.0 million
- **Coed,** 1,887 undergraduate students, 98% full-time, 50% women, 50% men
- **Very difficult** entrance level, 55% of applicants were admitted

Undergraduates 1,847 full-time, 40 part-time. Students come from 43 states and territories, 62 other countries, 64% are from out of state, 2% African American, 3% Asian American or Pacific Islander, 3% Hispanic American, 0.1% Native American, 8% international, 0.7% transferred in, 67% live on campus. *Retention:* 87% of 2001 full-time freshmen returned.

Freshmen *Admission:* 3,702 applied, 2,024 admitted, 511 enrolled. *Test scores:* SAT verbal scores over 500: 96%; SAT math scores over 500: 98%; SAT verbal scores over 600: 64%; SAT math scores over 600: 73%; SAT verbal scores over 700: 18%; SAT math scores over 700: 21%.

Faculty *Total:* 185, 86% full-time, 91% with terminal degrees. *Student/faculty ratio:* 11:1.

Majors African studies; American studies; anthropology; art; biochemistry; biology; business administration; chemistry; classics; economics; English; finance; French; geology; German; Greek (ancient and medieval); history; Latin (ancient and medieval); mathematics; music; neuroscience; philosophy; physics; political science; psychology; religious studies; sociology; Spanish; theater arts/drama.

Academic Programs *Special study options:* accelerated degree program, advanced placement credit, double majors, honors programs, independent study, internships, off-campus study, student-designed majors, study abroad, summer session for credit. *Unusual degree programs:* 3-2 engineering with Rensselaer Polytechnic Institute, Washington University in St. Louis, University of Pennsylvania, Columbia University, Case Western Reserve University, Georgia Institute of Technology; forestry with Duke University; environmental studies with Duke University.

Library Shadek-Fackenthal Library plus 1 other with 437,789 titles, 2,135 serial subscriptions, 11,219 audiovisual materials, an OPAC, a Web page.

Computers on Campus 139 computers available on campus for general student use. A campuswide network can be accessed from student residence rooms and from off campus. Internet access, online (class) registration, at least one staffed computer lab available.

Student Life *Housing:* on-campus residence required through sophomore year. *Options:* coed, men-only, women-only, disabled students. *Activities and Organizations:* drama/theater group, student-run newspaper, radio and television station, choral group, Women's Center, campus radio station, College Reporter, Ben's Underground, Ice Hockey Club. *Campus security:* 24-hour emergency response devices and patrols, late-night transport/escort service, controlled dormitory access, residence hall security, campus security connected to city police and fire company. *Student Services:* health clinic, personal/psychological counseling, women's center.

Athletics Member NCAA. All Division III except wrestling (Division I). *Intercollegiate sports:* baseball M, basketball M/W, crew M(c)/W(c), cross-country running M/W, fencing M(c)/W(c), field hockey W, football M, golf M/W, ice hockey M(c), lacrosse M/W, rugby M(c)/W(c), soccer M/W, softball W, squash M/W, swimming M/W, tennis M/W, track and field M/W, volleyball M(c)/W, wrestling M. *Intramural sports:* archery M/W, badminton M/W, basketball M/W, bowling M/W, football M, soccer M/W, softball M/W, squash M/W, table tennis M/W, tennis M/W, volleyball M/W, wrestling M.

Standardized Tests *Required:* SAT II: Writing Test (for admission).

Costs (2001–02) *Comprehensive fee:* $32,410 includes full-time tuition ($26,060), mandatory fees ($50), and room and board ($6300). Full-time tuition and fees vary according to reciprocity agreements. Part-time tuition: $3260 per course. Part-time tuition and fees vary according to course load. *Room and board:* Room and board charges vary according to board plan and housing facility. *Payment plans:* installment, deferred payment. *Waivers:* employees or children of employees.

Financial Aid Of all full-time matriculated undergraduates who enrolled in 2001, 950 applied for aid, 820 were judged to have need, 820 had their need fully met. In 2001, 351 non-need-based awards were made. *Average percent of need met:* 100%. *Average financial aid package:* $18,107. *Average need-based loan:* $3942. *Average need-based gift aid:* $14,765. *Average indebtedness upon graduation:* $17,774. *Financial aid deadline:* 2/1.

Applying *Options:* common application, electronic application, early admission, early decision, deferred entrance. *Application fee:* $50. *Required:* essay or personal statement, high school transcript, 2 letters of recommendation. *Recommended:* interview. *Application deadlines:* 2/1 (freshmen), 5/1 (transfers). *Early decision:* 11/15 (for plan 1), 1/15 (for plan 2). *Notification:* 4/1 (freshmen), 12/15 (early decision plan 1), 2/15 (early decision plan 2).

Admissions Contact Ms. Penny Johnston, Acting Director of Admissions, Franklin and Marshall College, PO Box 3003, Lancaster, PA 17604-3003. *Phone:* 717-291-3953. *Fax:* 717-291-4389. *E-mail:* admission@fandm.edu.

GANNON UNIVERSITY
Erie, Pennsylvania

- **Independent Roman Catholic** comprehensive, founded 1925
- **Calendar** semesters
- **Degrees** certificates, associate, bachelor's, master's, doctoral, post-master's, and postbachelor's certificates
- **Urban** 13-acre campus with easy access to Cleveland
- **Endowment** $28.7 million
- **Coed,** 2,463 undergraduate students, 87% full-time, 58% women, 42% men
- **Moderately difficult** entrance level, 90% of applicants were admitted

At Gannon, students can custom-tailor their education to meet their specific personal, educational, and spiritual goals. Students explore internships, co-ops, study-abroad opportunities, service learning projects, honors courses, and campus ministry activities while developing a values-centered, liberal arts education in one of more than 70 undergraduate majors.

Undergraduates Students come from 29 states and territories, 20 other countries, 19% are from out of state, 4% African American, 0.9% Asian American or Pacific Islander, 0.9% Hispanic American, 0.4% Native American, 3% international, 38% live on campus. *Retention:* 80% of 2001 full-time freshmen returned.

Freshmen *Admission:* 1,951 applied, 1,762 admitted. *Average high school GPA:* 3.18. *Test scores:* SAT verbal scores over 500: 64%; SAT math scores over 500: 62%; ACT scores over 18: 78%; SAT verbal scores over 600: 14%; SAT math scores over 600: 17%; ACT scores over 24: 35%; SAT verbal scores over 700: 1%; SAT math scores over 700: 1%; ACT scores over 30: 4%.

Faculty *Total:* 264, 61% full-time. *Student/faculty ratio:* 14:1.

Majors Accounting; accounting technician; advertising; biological/physical sciences; biology; British literature; business; business administration; business marketing and marketing management; chemistry; communications; computer/information sciences; criminal justice studies; dietetics; early childhood education; earth sciences; electrical engineering; elementary education; engineering; enterprise management; environmental engineering; finance; foreign languages education; foreign languages/literatures; health aide; health science; history; humanities; international business; international relations; legal studies; liberal arts and sciences/liberal studies; management information systems/business data processing; mathematics; mechanical engineering; medical radiologic technology; medical technology; modern languages; mortuary science; nursing; occupational therapy; ophthalmic/optometric services; paralegal/legal assistant; philosophy; physician assistant; political science; pre-dentistry; pre-law; pre-medicine; pre-veterinary studies; psychology; radio/television broadcasting; respiratory therapy; secondary education; social work; special education; technical/business writing; theater arts/drama; theology.

Academic Programs *Special study options:* academic remediation for entering students, accelerated degree program, adult/continuing education programs, advanced placement credit, cooperative education, distance learning, double majors, English as a second language, external degree program, honors programs, independent study, internships, off-campus study, part-time degree program, services for LD students, study abroad, summer session for credit. *ROTC:* Army (b). *Unusual degree programs:* 3-2 engineering with University of Akron, University of Pittsburgh, University of Detroit Mercy; law with Duquesne University.

Library Nash Library plus 1 other with 257,670 titles, 9,389 serial subscriptions, 2,274 audiovisual materials, an OPAC, a Web page.

Computers on Campus 229 computers available on campus for general student use. A campuswide network can be accessed from student residence rooms and from off campus. Internet access, at least one staffed computer lab available.

Student Life *Housing:* on-campus residence required through sophomore year. *Options:* coed. *Activities and Organizations:* drama/theater group, student-run newspaper, radio station, Model United Nations, Vitality Through Exercise, Gannon University Residence Union, Interfraternity Council, Panhellenic Council, national fraternities, national sororities. *Campus security:* 24-hour emergency response devices and patrols, student patrols, late-night transport/escort service, controlled dormitory access, security cameras. *Student Services:* health clinic, personal/psychological counseling.

Athletics Member NCAA. All Division II. *Intercollegiate sports:* baseball M(s), basketball M(s)/W(s), cross-country running M(s)/W(s), football M, golf M(s)/W(s), lacrosse W(s), soccer M(s)/W(s), softball W(s), swimming M(s)/W(s), tennis M(s)/W(s), volleyball W(s), wrestling M(s). *Intramural sports:* badminton M/W, basketball M/W, bowling M/W, cross-country running M/W, football M, golf M/W, racquetball M/W, soccer M/W, softball M/W, swimming M/W, tennis M/W, volleyball M(c)/W, water polo M, weight lifting M, wrestling M.

Standardized Tests *Required:* SAT I or ACT (for admission).

Costs (2002–03) *Comprehensive fee:* $21,770 includes full-time tuition ($15,330), mandatory fees ($450), and room and board ($5990). Full-time tuition and fees vary according to class time and program. Part-time tuition: $475 per credit. Part-time tuition and fees vary according to class time and program. *Required fees:* $14 per credit. *Room and board:* College room only: $3150. Room and board charges vary according to board plan and housing facility. *Payment plans:* installment, deferred payment. *Waivers:* senior citizens and employees or children of employees.

Financial Aid Of all full-time matriculated undergraduates who enrolled in 2001, 2024 applied for aid, 1708 were judged to have need, 918 had their need fully met. 467 Federal Work-Study jobs (averaging $1170). 181 State and other part-time jobs (averaging $1700). In 2001, 205 non-need-based awards were made. *Average percent of need met:* 80%. *Average financial aid package:* $12,950. *Average need-based loan:* $4350. *Average need-based gift aid:* $7800. *Average non-need based aid:* $4000. *Average indebtedness upon graduation:* $18,900.

Applying *Options:* common application, electronic application, early admission, deferred entrance. *Application fee:* $25. *Required:* high school transcript, minimum 2.0 GPA, counselor's recommendation. *Required for some:* minimum 3.0 GPA, 3 letters of recommendation, interview. *Recommended:* essay or personal statement. *Application deadline:* rolling (freshmen), rolling (transfers).

Admissions Contact Ms. Beth Nemenz, Director of Admissions, Gannon University, University Square, Erie, PA 16541. *Phone:* 814-871-7240. *Toll-free phone:* 800-GANNONU. *Fax:* 814-871-5803. *E-mail:* admissions@gannon.edu.

GENEVA COLLEGE
Beaver Falls, Pennsylvania

- **Independent** comprehensive, founded 1848, affiliated with Reformed Presbyterian Church of North America
- **Calendar** semesters
- **Degrees** associate, bachelor's, and master's
- **Small-town** 55-acre campus with easy access to Pittsburgh
- **Endowment** $31.7 million
- **Coed,** 1,829 undergraduate students, 85% full-time, 58% women, 42% men
- **Moderately difficult** entrance level, 80% of applicants were admitted

Geneva College is a Christian coeducational liberal arts college whose purpose is to develop servant-leaders. Geneva offers more than thirty undergraduate majors. Innovative offerings include Master of Arts degree programs in professional psychology, higher education, and business; a Master of Science degree in organizational leadership; and an accelerated adult degree-completion program in which students who qualify can transfer two years of credit and can earn a bachelor's degree in only fifteen months. Cultural diversity in the student body, faculty, and staff members is a priority; applications from members of minority groups are especially welcome.

Undergraduates Students come from 37 states and territories, 25 other countries, 26% are from out of state, 5% African American, 0.4% Asian American or Pacific Islander, 0.7% Hispanic American, 0.1% Native American, 2% international, 75% live on campus. *Retention:* 80% of 2001 full-time freshmen returned.

Freshmen *Admission:* 984 applied, 787 admitted. *Average high school GPA:* 3.20. *Test scores:* SAT verbal scores over 500: 69%; SAT math scores over 500: 60%; ACT scores over 18: 93%; SAT verbal scores over 600: 25%; SAT math scores over 600: 22%; ACT scores over 24: 47%; SAT verbal scores over 700: 5%; SAT math scores over 700: 2%; ACT scores over 30: 2%.

Faculty *Total:* 142, 51% full-time, 42% with terminal degrees. *Student/faculty ratio:* 18:1.

Majors Accounting; applied mathematics; aviation management; biblical studies; biology; business administration; business education; chemical engineering; chemistry; communications; computer science; creative writing; elementary education; engineering; English; history; human services; individual/family development; mathematics education; music; music business management/merchandising; music (general performance); music teacher education; philosophy; physics; political science; pre-theology; psychology; radio/television broadcasting; secondary education; sociology; Spanish; special education; speech-language pathology/audiology; speech/rhetorical studies.

Academic Programs *Special study options:* academic remediation for entering students, accelerated degree program, adult/continuing education programs, advanced placement credit, cooperative education, double majors, English as a second language, honors programs, independent study, internships, off-campus study, services for LD students, student-designed majors, study abroad, summer session for credit. *ROTC:* Army (c). *Unusual degree programs:* 3-2 nursing with University of Rochester.

Library McCartney Library plus 5 others with 160,000 titles, 916 serial subscriptions, 23,403 audiovisual materials, an OPAC, a Web page.

Computers on Campus 150 computers available on campus for general student use. A campuswide network can be accessed from off campus. At least one staffed computer lab available.

Student Life *Housing:* on-campus residence required through senior year. *Options:* men-only, women-only. *Activities and Organizations:* drama/theater group, student-run newspaper, radio and television station, choral group, marching band, marching band, Genevans A Capella Choir, ministry groups, International Student Organization, discipleship. *Campus security:* 24-hour emergency response devices and patrols, late-night transport/escort service, controlled dormitory access. *Student Services:* health clinic, personal/psychological counseling.

Athletics Member NAIA, NCCAA. *Intercollegiate sports:* baseball M(s), basketball M(s)/W(s), cross-country running M(s)/W(s), football M(s), soccer M(s)/W(s), softball W(s), tennis M(s)/W(s), track and field M(s)/W(s), volleyball M(c)/W(s). *Intramural sports:* basketball M/W, football M, ice hockey M(c), racquetball M/W, rugby M(c)/W(c), skiing (downhill) M(c)/W(c), soccer M/W, softball M/W, volleyball M/W.

Standardized Tests *Required:* SAT I or ACT (for admission).

Costs (2001–02) *Comprehensive fee:* $19,990 includes full-time tuition ($13,600), mandatory fees ($450), and room and board ($5940). Part-time tuition: $450 per credit hour. *Room and board:* College room only: $3080.

Financial Aid Of all full-time matriculated undergraduates who enrolled in 2001, 1107 applied for aid, 1024 were judged to have need, 244 had their need fully met. In 2001, 139 non-need-based awards were made. *Average percent of need met:* 82%. *Average financial aid package:* $12,572. *Average need-based loan:* $3700. *Average need-based gift aid:* $8833. *Average indebtedness upon graduation:* $20,000.

Applying *Options:* common application, electronic application, early admission, deferred entrance. *Application fee:* $25. *Required:* essay or personal statement, high school transcript, minimum 2.0 GPA, letters of recommendation. *Required for some:* interview. *Recommended:* minimum 3.0 GPA, interview. *Application deadline:* rolling (freshmen), rolling (transfers). *Notification:* continuous (freshmen).

Admissions Contact Mr. David Layton, Director of Admissions, Geneva College, Beaver Falls, PA 15010. *Phone:* 724-847-6500. *Toll-free phone:* 800-847-8255. *Fax:* 724-847-6776. *E-mail:* admissions@geneva.edu.

GETTYSBURG COLLEGE

Gettysburg, Pennsylvania

- **Independent** 4-year, founded 1832, affiliated with Evangelical Lutheran Church in America
- **Calendar** semesters
- **Degree** bachelor's
- **Small-town** 200-acre campus with easy access to Baltimore and Washington, DC
- **Endowment** $205.2 million
- **Coed,** 2,258 undergraduate students, 100% full-time, 52% women, 48% men
- **Very difficult** entrance level, 53% of applicants were admitted

Undergraduates 2,248 full-time, 10 part-time. Students come from 35 other countries, 72% are from out of state, 2% African American, 1% Asian American or Pacific Islander, 1% Hispanic American, 0.2% Native American, 2% international, 93% live on campus. *Retention:* 88% of 2001 full-time freshmen returned.

Freshmen *Admission:* 4,364 applied, 2,293 admitted, 659 enrolled. *Test scores:* SAT verbal scores over 500: 94%; SAT math scores over 500: 97%; SAT verbal scores over 600: 47%; SAT math scores over 600: 52%; SAT verbal scores over 700: 5%; SAT math scores over 700: 6%.

Faculty *Total:* 246, 71% full-time. *Student/faculty ratio:* 11:1.

Majors Accounting; African-American studies; American studies; anthropology; area studies; art; art history; biochemistry; biological/physical sciences; biology; business administration; chemistry; classics; computer science; economics; education; elementary education; English; environmental science; fine/studio arts; French; German; Greek (modern); health science; history; interdisciplinary studies; international business; international economics; international relations; Latin American studies; Latin (ancient and medieval); liberal arts and sciences/liberal studies; literature; marine biology; mathematics; modern languages; music; music teacher education; philosophy; physical education; physics; political science; pre-dentistry; pre-law; pre-medicine; pre-veterinary studies; psychology; religious studies; romance languages; science education; secondary education; social sciences; sociology; South Asian studies; Spanish; theater arts/drama; western civilization; women's studies.

Academic Programs *Special study options:* accelerated degree program, adult/continuing education programs, advanced placement credit, double majors, independent study, internships, off-campus study, student-designed majors, study abroad. *Unusual degree programs:* 3-2 engineering with Rensselaer Polytechnic Institute, Washington University , Columbia University; forestry with Duke University; nursing with Johns Hopkins University.

Library Mussleman Library with 328,503 titles, 2,331 serial subscriptions, 20,148 audiovisual materials, an OPAC, a Web page.

Computers on Campus 620 computers available on campus for general student use. A campuswide network can be accessed from student residence rooms and from off campus. Internet access, online (class) registration, at least one staffed computer lab available.

Student Life *Housing:* on-campus residence required for freshman year. *Options:* coed, women-only. *Activities and Organizations:* drama/theater group, student-run newspaper, radio and television station, choral group, marching band, national fraternities, national sororities. *Campus security:* 24-hour emergency response devices and patrols, late-night transport/escort service, controlled dormitory access. *Student Services:* health clinic, personal/psychological counseling, women's center.

Athletics Member NCAA. All Division III. *Intercollegiate sports:* baseball M, basketball M/W, cross-country running M/W, field hockey W, football M, golf M/W, ice hockey M(c), lacrosse M/W, rugby M(c), soccer M/W, softball W, swimming M/W, tennis M/W, track and field M/W, volleyball W, wrestling M. *Intramural sports:* archery M/W, badminton M/W, basketball M/W, cross-country running M/W, equestrian sports M/W, field hockey W, football M, golf M/W, gymnastics M/W, ice hockey M, lacrosse M/W, riflery M/W, rugby M, skiing (cross-country) M/W, skiing (downhill) M/W, soccer M/W, softball M/W, swimming M/W, tennis M/W, track and field M/W, volleyball M/W, wrestling M.

Standardized Tests *Required:* SAT I or ACT (for admission).

Costs (2001–02) *Comprehensive fee:* $32,070 includes full-time tuition ($25,630), mandatory fees ($118), and room and board ($6322). Part-time tuition: $814 per credit hour. *Room and board:* College room only: $3352. Room and board charges vary according to board plan and housing facility. *Payment plans:* tuition prepayment, installment.

Financial Aid Of all full-time matriculated undergraduates who enrolled in 2001, 1471 applied for aid, 1380 were judged to have need, 1376 had their need fully met. In 2001, 60 non-need-based awards were made. *Average percent of need met:* 100%. *Average financial aid package:* $21,100. *Average need-based loan:* $3600. *Average need-based gift aid:* $16,100. *Average non-need based aid:* $7000. *Average indebtedness upon graduation:* $14,800. *Financial aid deadline:* 3/15.

Applying *Options:* common application, electronic application, early admission, early decision, deferred entrance. *Application fee:* $45. *Required:* essay or personal statement, high school transcript, 2 letters of recommendation. *Recommended:* minimum 3.0 GPA, interview. *Application deadline:* 2/15 (freshmen), rolling (transfers). *Early decision:* 11/15. *Notification:* 4/1 (freshmen), 2/15 (early decision).

Admissions Contact Ms. Gail Sweezey, Director of Admissions, Gettysburg College, 300 North Washington Street, Gettysburg, PA 17325. *Phone:* 717-337-6100. *Toll-free phone:* 800-431-0803. *Fax:* 717-337-6145. *E-mail:* admiss@gettysburg.edu.

GRATZ COLLEGE

Melrose Park, Pennsylvania

- **Independent Jewish** comprehensive, founded 1895
- **Calendar** semesters
- **Degrees** certificates, bachelor's, master's, and post-master's certificates
- **Suburban** 28-acre campus with easy access to Philadelphia
- **Coed,** 21 undergraduate students, 14% full-time, 90% women, 10% men
- **Moderately difficult** entrance level, 67% of applicants were admitted

Undergraduates 3 full-time, 18 part-time. Students come from 4 states and territories, 10% are from out of state. *Retention:* 100% of 2001 full-time freshmen returned.

Freshmen *Admission:* 15 applied, 10 admitted, 10 enrolled.

Faculty *Total:* 14, 57% full-time, 100% with terminal degrees. *Student/faculty ratio:* 12:1.

Majors Judaic studies.

Academic Programs *Special study options:* adult/continuing education programs, double majors, independent study, internships, part-time degree program, study abroad, summer session for credit.

Library Tuttleman Library with 100,000 titles, 175 serial subscriptions, 380 audiovisual materials, an OPAC.

Computers on Campus 2 computers available on campus for general student use. A campuswide network can be accessed from off campus.

Student Life *Housing:* college housing not available. *Activities and Organizations:* choral group. *Campus security:* 24-hour patrols.

Gratz College (continued)
Costs (2001–02) *Tuition:* $7950 full-time, $382 per credit part-time. *Payment plan:* installment. *Waivers:* employees or children of employees.
Applying *Options:* early admission, deferred entrance. *Application fee:* $50. *Required:* essay or personal statement, high school transcript, letters of recommendation. *Required for some:* interview. *Application deadline:* rolling (freshmen), rolling (transfers). *Notification:* continuous (freshmen).
Admissions Contact Ms. Adena E. Johnston, Director of Admissions, Gratz College, 7605 Old York Road, Melrose Park, PA 19027. *Phone:* 215-635-7300 Ext. 140. *Toll-free phone:* 800-475-4635 Ext. 140. *Fax:* 215-635-7320 Ext. 140. *E-mail:* admissions@gratz.edu.

GROVE CITY COLLEGE
Grove City, Pennsylvania

- **Independent Presbyterian** 4-year, founded 1876
- **Calendar** semesters
- **Degree** bachelor's
- **Small-town** 150-acre campus with easy access to Pittsburgh
- **Coed,** 2,331 undergraduate students, 98% full-time, 50% women, 50% men
- **Very difficult** entrance level, 43% of applicants were admitted

Grove City College has won national acclaim for strong academics, Christian values, and a surprising tuition. Its humanities and social sciences emphasize classic books and great thinkers proved across the ages to be of value in the quest for knowledge; its excellent professional studies programs include mechanical and electrical/computer engineering programs, which are accredited by the engineering accreditation commission of the Accreditation Board for Engineering and Technology, Inc. Included in its cost of education, the Grove City College Information Technology Initiative distributes color notebook computers and printers to every freshman.

Undergraduates 2,293 full-time, 38 part-time. Students come from 46 states and territories, 11 other countries, 46% are from out of state, 0.3% African American, 0.7% Asian American or Pacific Islander, 0.2% Hispanic American, 0.2% Native American, 0.9% international, 1% transferred in, 90% live on campus. *Retention:* 90% of 2001 full-time freshmen returned.
Freshmen *Admission:* 2,188 applied, 930 admitted, 586 enrolled. *Average high school GPA:* 3.70. *Test scores:* SAT verbal scores over 500: 96%; SAT math scores over 500: 97%; ACT scores over 18: 100%; SAT verbal scores over 600: 71%; SAT math scores over 600: 73%; ACT scores over 24: 88%; SAT verbal scores over 700: 22%; SAT math scores over 700: 20%; ACT scores over 30: 26%.
Faculty *Total:* 165, 73% full-time, 58% with terminal degrees. *Student/faculty ratio:* 19:1.
Majors Accounting; biochemistry; biology; business administration; business communications; business economics; business marketing and marketing management; chemistry; computer management; divinity/ministry; early childhood education; economics; electrical engineering; elementary education; English; finance; French; history; international business; literature; mass communications; mathematics; mechanical engineering; modern languages; molecular biology; music business management/merchandising; music teacher education; philosophy; physics; political science; pre-dentistry; pre-law; pre-medicine; pre-veterinary studies; psychology; religious studies; science education; secondary education; sociology; Spanish.
Academic Programs *Special study options:* advanced placement credit, double majors, independent study, internships, student-designed majors, study abroad, summer session for credit. *ROTC:* Army (c).
Library Henry Buhl Library with 158,467 titles, 976 serial subscriptions, 431 audiovisual materials, an OPAC.
Computers on Campus 50 computers available on campus for general student use. A campuswide network can be accessed from student residence rooms and from off campus. Internet access, at least one staffed computer lab available.
Student Life *Housing:* on-campus residence required through senior year. *Options:* men-only, women-only. *Activities and Organizations:* drama/theater group, student-run newspaper, radio station, choral group, marching band, Salt Company, Warriors for Christ, Orientation Board, Orchesis, Touring Choir. *Campus security:* 24-hour emergency response devices and patrols, student patrols, late-night transport/escort service, controlled dormitory access, monitored women's residence hall entrances. *Student Services:* health clinic, personal/psychological counseling.
Athletics Member NCAA. All Division III. *Intercollegiate sports:* baseball M, basketball M/W, cross-country running M/W, football M, golf M/W, soccer M/W, softball W, swimming M/W, tennis M/W, track and field M/W, volleyball W, water polo M/W. *Intramural sports:* basketball M/W, bowling M/W, football M, golf M/W, racquetball M/W, soccer M, softball M, swimming M/W, table tennis W, tennis M/W, volleyball M/W, weight lifting M.
Standardized Tests *Required:* SAT I or ACT (for admission).
Costs (2001–02) *One-time required fee:* $150. *Comprehensive fee:* $12,280 includes full-time tuition ($7870) and room and board ($4410). Full-time tuition and fees vary according to course load and program. Part-time tuition: $265 per credit. *Waivers:* employees or children of employees.
Financial Aid Of all full-time matriculated undergraduates who enrolled in 2001, 1636 applied for aid, 808 were judged to have need, 166 had their need fully met. 900 State and other part-time jobs (averaging $844). In 2001, 451 non-need-based awards were made. *Average percent of need met:* 66%. *Average financial aid package:* $5348. *Average need-based loan:* $3302. *Average need-based gift aid:* $4942. *Average non-need based aid:* $2319. *Average indebtedness upon graduation:* $20,950. *Financial aid deadline:* 4/15.
Applying *Options:* electronic application, early admission, early decision, deferred entrance. *Application fee:* $30. *Required:* essay or personal statement, high school transcript, 2 letters of recommendation. *Recommended:* interview. *Application deadline:* 2/15 (freshmen), rolling (transfers). *Early decision:* 11/15. *Notification:* 3/15 (freshmen), 12/15 (early decision).
Admissions Contact Mr. Jeffrey C. Mincey, Director of Admissions, Grove City College, 100 Campus Drive, Grove City, PA 16127-2104. *Phone:* 724-458-2100. *Fax:* 724-458-3395. *E-mail:* admissions@gcc.edu.

GWYNEDD-MERCY COLLEGE
Gwynedd Valley, Pennsylvania

- **Independent Roman Catholic** comprehensive, founded 1948
- **Calendar** semesters
- **Degrees** certificates, associate, bachelor's, master's, post-master's, and postbachelor's certificates
- **Suburban** 170-acre campus with easy access to Philadelphia
- **Endowment** $5.9 million
- **Coed,** 1,900 undergraduate students, 54% full-time, 76% women, 24% men
- **Moderately difficult** entrance level, 70% of applicants were admitted

Gwynedd-Mercy combines strong academic programs with extensive opportunities for students to gain practical experience through internships, co-ops, and clinicals. With pass rates on national examinations of more than 95%, students are prepared to enter the workforce of the 21st century. The College has affiliations with more than 200 health-care organizations, businesses, and school districts.

Undergraduates 1,020 full-time, 880 part-time. 4% are from out of state, 11% African American, 3% Asian American or Pacific Islander, 2% Hispanic American, 0.1% Native American, 2% international, 20% transferred in, 21% live on campus. *Retention:* 88% of 2001 full-time freshmen returned.
Freshmen *Admission:* 998 applied, 698 admitted, 192 enrolled. *Test scores:* SAT verbal scores over 500: 47%; SAT math scores over 500: 43%; SAT verbal scores over 600: 9%; SAT math scores over 600: 8%; SAT verbal scores over 700: 1%.
Faculty *Total:* 218, 30% full-time, 33% with terminal degrees. *Student/faculty ratio:* 19:1.
Majors Accounting; behavioral sciences; biology; business administration; business education; business marketing and marketing management; computer programming; early childhood education; education; education (K-12); elementary education; English; finance; gerontology; health education; health science; health services administration; history; human resources management; industrial radiologic technology; information sciences/systems; liberal arts and sciences/liberal studies; mathematics; medical records administration; medical technology; natural sciences; nursing; pre-dentistry; pre-law; pre-medicine; pre-veterinary studies; psychology; public relations; religious music; respiratory therapy; science education; secondary education; social work; sociology; special education.
Academic Programs *Special study options:* academic remediation for entering students, accelerated degree program, adult/continuing education programs, advanced placement credit, cooperative education, double majors, English as a second language, external degree program, freshman honors college, honors programs, independent study, internships, part-time degree program, summer session for credit.
Library Lourdes Library plus 1 other with 83,953 titles, 825 serial subscriptions, 52,722 audiovisual materials, an OPAC, a Web page.
Computers on Campus 97 computers available on campus for general student use. A campuswide network can be accessed from student residence rooms and from off campus. Internet access, at least one staffed computer lab available.
Student Life *Housing Options:* coed. *Activities and Organizations:* drama/theater group, student-run newspaper, choral group, Voices of Gwynedd, Athletic Association, student government, Program Board, Peer Mentors. *Campus security:* 24-hour emergency response devices and patrols, late-night transport/escort service. *Student Services:* health clinic, personal/psychological counseling.

Athletics Member NCAA. All Division III. *Intercollegiate sports:* basketball M/W, field hockey W, lacrosse W, soccer M, softball W(c), tennis M/W, volleyball W.

Standardized Tests *Required:* SAT I (for admission), SAT I or ACT (for admission). *Required for some:* ACT (for admission).

Costs (2001–02) *Comprehensive fee:* $22,350 includes full-time tuition ($15,100), mandatory fees ($250), and room and board ($7000). Full-time tuition and fees vary according to program. Part-time tuition: $310 per credit. Part-time tuition and fees vary according to program. *Required fees:* $10 per credit. *Room and board:* Room and board charges vary according to board plan. *Payment plan:* installment. *Waivers:* employees or children of employees.

Financial Aid Of all full-time matriculated undergraduates who enrolled in 2001, 831 applied for aid, 741 were judged to have need, 600 had their need fully met. 272 Federal Work-Study jobs (averaging $1278). 15 State and other part-time jobs (averaging $1266). In 2001, 105 non-need-based awards were made. *Average percent of need met:* 80%. *Average financial aid package:* $12,112. *Average need-based loan:* $3839. *Average need-based gift aid:* $6229. *Average non-need based aid:* $6750. *Average indebtedness upon graduation:* $15,310.

Applying *Options:* common application, electronic application, early admission, deferred entrance. *Application fee:* $25. *Required:* high school transcript, 1 letter of recommendation. *Required for some:* interview. *Recommended:* interview. *Application deadlines:* rolling (freshmen), 8/1 (transfers). *Notification:* continuous (freshmen).

Admissions Contact Mr. Dennis Murphy, Vice President of Enrollment Management, Gwynedd-Mercy College, 1325 Sunneytown Pike, Gwynedd Valley, PA 19437-0901. *Phone:* 215-646-7300. *Toll-free phone:* 800-DIAL-GMC. *E-mail:* admissions@gmc.edu.

HAVERFORD COLLEGE
Haverford, Pennsylvania

- **Independent** 4-year, founded 1833
- **Calendar** semesters
- **Degree** bachelor's
- **Suburban** 200-acre campus with easy access to Philadelphia
- **Endowment** $311.2 million
- **Coed,** 1,138 undergraduate students, 100% full-time, 52% women, 48% men
- **Most difficult** entrance level, 33% of applicants were admitted

Undergraduates 1,138 full-time. Students come from 45 states and territories, 27 other countries, 79% are from out of state, 6% African American, 13% Asian American or Pacific Islander, 5% Hispanic American, 0.4% Native American, 3% international, 0.2% transferred in, 98% live on campus. *Retention:* 96% of 2001 full-time freshmen returned.

Freshmen *Admission:* 2,574 applied, 839 admitted, 296 enrolled. *Test scores:* SAT verbal scores over 500: 99%; SAT math scores over 500: 99%; SAT verbal scores over 600: 88%; SAT math scores over 600: 88%; SAT verbal scores over 700: 52%; SAT math scores over 700: 44%.

Faculty *Total:* 111, 93% full-time, 95% with terminal degrees. *Student/faculty ratio:* 9:1.

Majors African studies; anthropology; archaeology; art; art history; astronomy; biochemistry; biology; biophysics; chemistry; classics; comparative literature; computer science; East Asian studies; economics; education; English; French; geology; German; Greek (modern); history; Italian; Latin American studies; Latin (ancient and medieval); mathematics; music; neuroscience; peace/conflict studies; philosophy; physics; political science; pre-law; pre-medicine; pre-veterinary studies; psychology; quantitative economics; religious studies; romance languages; Russian; sociology; Spanish; urban studies; women's studies.

Academic Programs *Special study options:* accelerated degree program, advanced placement credit, double majors, independent study, internships, off-campus study, services for LD students, student-designed majors, study abroad. *Unusual degree programs:* 3-2 engineering with University of Pennsylvania.

Library Magill Library plus 5 others with 395,799 titles, 3,240 serial subscriptions, 10,716 audiovisual materials, an OPAC, a Web page.

Computers on Campus 196 computers available on campus for general student use. A campuswide network can be accessed from student residence rooms and from off campus. At least one staffed computer lab available.

Student Life *Housing:* on-campus residence required for freshman year. *Options:* coed, men-only, women-only, disabled students. *Activities and Organizations:* drama/theater group, student-run newspaper, radio station, choral group, volunteer programs, student government, Choral Groups, Multicultural Groups, orientation team/residential life leaders. *Campus security:* 24-hour emergency response devices and patrols, late-night transport/escort service. *Student Services:* health clinic, personal/psychological counseling, women's center.

Athletics Member NCAA. All Division III. *Intercollegiate sports:* baseball M, basketball M/W, crew M(c)/W(c), cross-country running M/W, fencing M/W, field hockey W, golf M(c)/W(c), lacrosse M/W, soccer M/W, softball W, squash M/W, tennis M/W, track and field M/W, volleyball W, wrestling M(c). *Intramural sports:* basketball M/W, ice hockey M(c)/W(c), rugby M(c)/W(c), sailing M(c)/W(c), soccer M/W, softball M/W, tennis M/W, volleyball M/W.

Standardized Tests *Required:* SAT I or ACT (for admission), SAT II: Subject Tests (for admission), SAT II: Writing Test (for admission).

Costs (2001–02) *Comprehensive fee:* $34,300 includes full-time tuition ($25,826), mandatory fees ($244), and room and board ($8230). *Room and board:* College room only: $4600. Room and board charges vary according to board plan. *Payment plan:* installment. *Waivers:* employees or children of employees.

Financial Aid Of all full-time matriculated undergraduates who enrolled in 2001, 548 applied for aid, 486 were judged to have need, 486 had their need fully met. 227 Federal Work-Study jobs (averaging $1162). 392 State and other part-time jobs (averaging $1164). *Average percent of need met:* 100%. *Average financial aid package:* $22,646. *Average need-based loan:* $4246. *Average need-based gift aid:* $20,074. *Average indebtedness upon graduation:* $14,685. *Financial aid deadline:* 1/31.

Applying *Options:* common application, electronic application, early admission, early decision, deferred entrance. *Application fee:* $50. *Required:* high school transcript, 2 letters of recommendation. *Recommended:* interview. *Application deadlines:* 1/15 (freshmen), 3/31 (transfers). *Early decision:* 11/15. *Notification:* continuous until 4/15 (freshmen), 12/15 (early decision).

Admissions Contact Ms. Delsie Z. Phillips, Director of Admission, Haverford College, 370 Lancaster Avenue, Haverford, PA 19041-1392. *Phone:* 610-896-1350. *Fax:* 610-896-1338. *E-mail:* admitme@haverford.edu.

HOLY FAMILY COLLEGE
Philadelphia, Pennsylvania

- **Independent Roman Catholic** comprehensive, founded 1954
- **Calendar** semesters
- **Degrees** certificates, associate, bachelor's, master's, and postbachelor's certificates
- **Suburban** 47-acre campus
- **Endowment** $5.7 million
- **Coed,** 1,849 undergraduate students, 58% full-time, 77% women, 23% men
- **Moderately difficult** entrance level, 84% of applicants were admitted

Undergraduates 1,072 full-time, 777 part-time. Students come from 7 states and territories, 17 other countries, 10% are from out of state, 3% African American, 2% Asian American or Pacific Islander, 2% Hispanic American, 0.1% Native American, 2% international, 7% transferred in. *Retention:* 82% of 2001 full-time freshmen returned.

Freshmen *Admission:* 527 applied, 441 admitted, 210 enrolled. *Average high school GPA:* 2.90. *Test scores:* SAT verbal scores over 500: 35%; SAT math scores over 500: 26%; SAT verbal scores over 600: 3%; SAT math scores over 600: 4%.

Faculty *Total:* 276, 29% full-time, 42% with terminal degrees. *Student/faculty ratio:* 11:1.

Majors Accounting; art; biochemistry; biology; business administration; business marketing and marketing management; chemistry; communications; computer/information sciences; computer management; criminal justice/law enforcement administration; early childhood education; economics; education; elementary education; English; fire science; French; history; humanities; international business; liberal arts and sciences/liberal studies; literature; mathematics; medical laboratory technician; medical radiologic technology; nursing science; organizational psychology; physiological psychology/psychobiology; pre-dentistry; pre-law; pre-medicine; pre-pharmacy studies; pre-veterinary studies; psychology; radiological science; religious education; religious studies; secondary education; social sciences; social studies education; social work; sociology; Spanish; special education; sport/fitness administration.

Academic Programs *Special study options:* academic remediation for entering students, accelerated degree program, adult/continuing education programs, advanced placement credit, cooperative education, double majors, freshman honors college, honors programs, independent study, internships, part-time degree program, services for LD students, study abroad, summer session for credit.

Library Holy Family College Library plus 1 other with 115,000 titles, 840 serial subscriptions, 1,556 audiovisual materials, an OPAC.

Computers on Campus 148 computers available on campus for general student use. Internet access, at least one staffed computer lab available.

Student Life *Housing:* college housing not available. *Activities and Organizations:* drama/theater group, student-run newspaper, Students at Your Service (S.A.Y.S.), Rainbow Connections, Campus Ministry Team, Folio, Tri-lite. *Cam-*

Holy Family College (continued)
pus security: 24-hour emergency response devices and patrols, student patrols, late-night transport/escort service. *Student Services:* health clinic, personal/psychological counseling.

Athletics Member NAIA. *Intercollegiate sports:* basketball M(s)/W(s), cross-country running W(s), golf M(s), soccer M(s)/W(s). *Intramural sports:* basketball M/W, racquetball M/W, volleyball M/W.

Standardized Tests *Required:* SAT I or ACT (for admission).

Costs (2001–02) *Tuition:* $13,250 full-time, $290 per credit part-time. Full-time tuition and fees vary according to course load and program. Part-time tuition and fees vary according to program. *Required fees:* $460 full-time. *Payment plans:* installment, deferred payment. *Waivers:* employees or children of employees.

Financial Aid Of all full-time matriculated undergraduates who enrolled in 2001, 217 Federal Work-Study jobs (averaging $1113). *Average indebtedness upon graduation:* $17,125.

Applying *Options:* common application, deferred entrance. *Application fee:* $25. *Required:* essay or personal statement, high school transcript, 1 letter of recommendation. *Recommended:* interview. *Application deadline:* rolling (freshmen), rolling (transfers).

Admissions Contact Mrs. Roberta Nolan, Director of Admissions, Holy Family College, Grant and Frankford Avenues, Philadelphia, PA 19114-2094. *Phone:* 215-637-3050. *Toll-free phone:* 800-637-1191. *Fax:* 215-281-1022. *E-mail:* rnolan@hfc.edu.

IMMACULATA COLLEGE
Immaculata, Pennsylvania

- **Independent Roman Catholic** comprehensive, founded 1920
- **Calendar** semesters
- **Degrees** associate, bachelor's, master's, and doctoral
- **Suburban** 400-acre campus with easy access to Philadelphia
- **Endowment** $9.0 million
- **Women only,** 2,349 undergraduate students, 27% full-time
- **Moderately difficult** entrance level, 85% of applicants were admitted

Immaculata College, The University Within a College, is a Catholic, comprehensive, liberal arts college dedicated to educating women of all faiths. Founded in 1920, Immaculata has grown to more than 3,400. Immaculata is composed of three areas: the Women's College, the College of Lifelong Learning, and the Graduate Division. Approximately 400 women attend the Women's College; 85% live in campus housing. A fixed tuition rate is offered to all full-time students entering the Women's College. The evening division includes graduate and undergraduate programs that are open to both men and women. The College is located 20 miles west of Philadelphia.

Undergraduates 630 full-time, 1,719 part-time. Students come from 15 states and territories, 23 other countries, 15% are from out of state, 8% African American, 2% Asian American or Pacific Islander, 2% Hispanic American, 0.1% Native American, 1% international, 1% transferred in, 80% live on campus. *Retention:* 81% of 2001 full-time freshmen returned.

Freshmen *Admission:* 117 enrolled. *Average high school GPA:* 3.10. *Test scores:* SAT verbal scores over 500: 54%; SAT math scores over 500: 40%; SAT verbal scores over 600: 19%; SAT math scores over 600: 12%; SAT verbal scores over 700: 2%.

Faculty *Total:* 234, 32% full-time, 46% with terminal degrees. *Student/faculty ratio:* 13:1.

Majors Accounting; adult/continuing education; art; art education; biochemistry; biology; biomedical science; business administration; business economics; business marketing and marketing management; chemistry; computer/information sciences; computer science; dietetics; early childhood education; economics; education; elementary education; English; fashion merchandising; food products retailing; food sales operations; French; German; history; home economics; home economics education; humanities; international business; international relations; Italian; liberal arts and sciences/liberal studies; literature; mathematics; modern languages; music; music teacher education; music therapy; music (voice and choral/opera performance); nursing science; nutrition science; physics; pre-dentistry; pre-law; pre-medicine; pre-veterinary studies; psychology; religious music; secondary education; social work; sociology; Spanish; theology.

Academic Programs *Special study options:* academic remediation for entering students, accelerated degree program, adult/continuing education programs, advanced placement credit, double majors, English as a second language, freshman honors college, honors programs, independent study, internships, part-time degree program, services for LD students, student-designed majors, study abroad, summer session for credit.

Library Gabriele Library with 1.1 million titles, 982 serial subscriptions, 1,749 audiovisual materials, an OPAC, a Web page.

Computers on Campus 150 computers available on campus for general student use. A campuswide network can be accessed from student residence rooms and from off campus. Internet access, at least one staffed computer lab available.

Student Life *Housing Options:* women-only. *Activities and Organizations:* drama/theater group, student-run newspaper, choral group, Campus Ministry, Student Association, chorale, Honor Society, Cue and Curtain. *Campus security:* 24-hour emergency response devices and patrols, late-night transport/escort service, controlled dormitory access. *Student Services:* health clinic, personal/psychological counseling.

Athletics Member NCAA. All Division III. *Intercollegiate sports:* basketball W, cross-country running W, field hockey W, soccer W, softball W, tennis W, volleyball W. *Intramural sports:* archery W, badminton W, equestrian sports W, fencing W, lacrosse W, swimming W.

Standardized Tests *Required:* SAT I or ACT (for admission).

Costs (2001–02) *Comprehensive fee:* $22,400 includes full-time tuition ($14,900), mandatory fees ($300), and room and board ($7200). Part-time tuition: $280 per credit. Part-time tuition and fees vary according to class time. No tuition increase for student's term of enrollment. *Required fees:* $50 per term part-time. *Room and board:* College room only: $3800. Room and board charges vary according to board plan. *Payment plan:* installment. *Waivers:* senior citizens and employees or children of employees.

Financial Aid Of all full-time matriculated undergraduates who enrolled in 2001, 406 applied for aid, 309 were judged to have need, 92 had their need fully met. 165 Federal Work-Study jobs (averaging $938). 150 State and other part-time jobs (averaging $900). In 2001, 31 non-need-based awards were made. *Average percent of need met:* 50%. *Average financial aid package:* $14,712. *Average need-based loan:* $5074. *Average need-based gift aid:* $2053. *Average non-need based aid:* $5653. *Average indebtedness upon graduation:* $17,125. *Financial aid deadline:* 4/15.

Applying *Options:* early admission, deferred entrance. *Application fee:* $25. *Required:* high school transcript, minimum 2.0 GPA, 1 letter of recommendation. *Recommended:* essay or personal statement, minimum 3.0 GPA, interview. *Application deadline:* 8/15 (freshmen), rolling (transfers). *Notification:* 9/1 (freshmen).

Admissions Contact Ms. Sandra Zerby, Executive Director of Admission, Immaculata College, PO Box 642, Immaculata, PA 19345-0642. *Phone:* 610-647-4400 Ext. 3015. *Toll-free phone:* 877-428-6328. *Fax:* 610-640-0836. *E-mail:* admiss@immaculata.edu.

INDIANA UNIVERSITY OF PENNSYLVANIA
Indiana, Pennsylvania

- **State-supported** university, founded 1875, part of Pennsylvania State System of Higher Education
- **Calendar** semesters
- **Degrees** certificates, diplomas, associate, bachelor's, master's, and doctoral
- **Small-town** 350-acre campus with easy access to Pittsburgh
- **Endowment** $27.5 million
- **Coed,** 11,763 undergraduate students, 93% full-time, 56% women, 44% men
- **Moderately difficult** entrance level, 57% of applicants were admitted

IUP has one of the largest student internship programs in Pennsylvania. More than 50% of its students participate in experiential and cooperative education and student teaching programs prior to graduation. Many graduates are offered a selection of positions by the companies that sponsor their internships. Employers are becoming more interested in graduates who have completed a supervised experience.

Undergraduates 10,923 full-time, 840 part-time. Students come from 39 states and territories, 42 other countries, 3% are from out of state, 6% African American, 0.8% Asian American or Pacific Islander, 0.8% Hispanic American, 0.3% Native American, 2% international, 6% transferred in, 33% live on campus. *Retention:* 74% of 2001 full-time freshmen returned.

Freshmen *Admission:* 7,459 applied, 4,271 admitted, 2,593 enrolled. *Test scores:* SAT verbal scores over 500: 66%; SAT math scores over 500: 60%; SAT verbal scores over 600: 17%; SAT math scores over 600: 13%; SAT verbal scores over 700: 2%; SAT math scores over 700: 1%.

Faculty *Total:* 758, 89% full-time. *Student/faculty ratio:* 17:1.

Majors Accounting; anthropology; applied mathematics; art; art education; biochemistry; biological/physical sciences; biology; business administration; business education; business marketing and marketing management; chemistry; city/community/regional planning; communications; computer/information sciences; consumer economics; criminology; dietetics; early childhood education;

earth sciences; economics; education of the hearing impaired; education of the physically handicapped; education of the speech impaired; elementary education; English; English education; environmental health; environmental science; fashion merchandising; finance; French; general studies; geography; geology; German; health/physical education; history; home economics education; hotel and restaurant management; human resources management; individual/family development; interior architecture; international business; international relations; journalism; management information systems/business data processing; mathematics; mathematics education; medical technology; multimedia; music; music (general performance); music teacher education; nuclear medical technology; nursing; nutrition studies; occupational safety/health technology; office management; philosophy; physical education; physics; political science; psychology; religious studies; respiratory therapy; Russian; science education; secondary education; social studies education; sociology; Spanish; special education; theater arts/drama; trade/industrial education.

Academic Programs *Special study options:* academic remediation for entering students, accelerated degree program, adult/continuing education programs, advanced placement credit, cooperative education, distance learning, double majors, English as a second language, freshman honors college, honors programs, independent study, internships, off-campus study, part-time degree program, services for LD students, study abroad, summer session for credit. *ROTC:* Army (b). *Unusual degree programs:* 3-2 engineering with Drexel University, University of Pittsburgh; forestry with Duke University.

Library Stapleton Library with 542,832 titles, 3,611 serial subscriptions, 224,613 audiovisual materials, an OPAC, a Web page.

Computers on Campus 3200 computers available on campus for general student use. A campuswide network can be accessed from student residence rooms and from off campus. At least one staffed computer lab available.

Student Life *Housing:* on-campus residence required for freshman year. *Options:* coed. *Activities and Organizations:* drama/theater group, student-run newspaper, radio and television station, choral group, marching band, NAACP, Interfraternity Council, Panhellenic Association, Student Congress, Alpha Phi Omega, national fraternities, national sororities. *Campus security:* 24-hour emergency response devices and patrols, late-night transport/escort service, controlled dormitory access. *Student Services:* health clinic, personal/psychological counseling, women's center, legal services.

Athletics Member NCAA. All Division II. *Intercollegiate sports:* baseball M(s), basketball M(s)/W(s), cross-country running M(s)/W(s), field hockey W(s), football M(s), golf M(s), lacrosse W(s), soccer W(s), softball W(s), swimming M/W(s), tennis W(s), track and field M(s)/W(s), volleyball W(s). *Intramural sports:* archery M/W, badminton M/W, basketball M/W, bowling M/W, cross-country running M(c)/W(c), equestrian sports M(c)/W(c), fencing M(c), football M/W, golf M/W, ice hockey M(c), racquetball M/W, riflery M(c)/W(c), sailing M(c)/W(c), skiing (downhill) M(c)/W(c), soccer M(c)/W(c), softball M(c)/W(c), swimming M/W, table tennis M/W, tennis M/W, track and field M/W, volleyball M/W, water polo M/W, weight lifting M/W, wrestling M.

Standardized Tests *Required:* SAT I or ACT (for admission).

Costs (2001–02) *Tuition:* state resident $4016 full-time, $167 per semester hour part-time; nonresident $10,040 full-time, $418 per semester hour part-time. Full-time tuition and fees vary according to course load and location. Part-time tuition and fees vary according to course load and location. *Required fees:* $859 full-time, $255 per term part-time. *Room and board:* $4258; room only: $2492. Room and board charges vary according to board plan and housing facility. *Payment plans:* installment, deferred payment. *Waivers:* minority students and employees or children of employees.

Financial Aid Of all full-time matriculated undergraduates who enrolled in 2001, 9831 applied for aid, 7691 were judged to have need, 4726 had their need fully met. 1600 Federal Work-Study jobs. In 2001, 265 non-need-based awards were made. *Average percent of need met:* 92%. *Average financial aid package:* $7512. *Average need-based loan:* $3408. *Average need-based gift aid:* $3256. *Average non-need based aid:* $4139. *Average indebtedness upon graduation:* $14,250. *Financial aid deadline:* 4/15.

Applying *Options:* common application, electronic application, early admission, deferred entrance. *Application fee:* $30. *Required:* high school transcript, letters of recommendation. *Application deadline:* rolling (freshmen), rolling (transfers). *Notification:* 9/1 (freshmen).

Admissions Contact Mr. William Nunn, Dean of Admissions, Indiana University of Pennsylvania, 216 Pratt Hall, Indiana, PA 15705. *Phone:* 724-357-2230. *Toll-free phone:* 800-442-6830. *E-mail:* admissions_inquiry@grove.iup.edu.

JUNIATA COLLEGE
Huntingdon, Pennsylvania

- **Independent** 4-year, founded 1876, affiliated with Church of the Brethren
- **Calendar** semesters
- **Degree** bachelor's
- **Small-town** 110-acre campus
- **Endowment** $63.9 million
- **Coed,** 1,302 undergraduate students, 97% full-time, 58% women, 42% men
- **Moderately difficult** entrance level, 79% of applicants were admitted

Students who welcome academic challenges and are ready to discover who they are and what they are capable of should consider Juniata College. The College's traditions include excellence in academics, small classes, a close-knit community, and many surprises, like Mountain Day.

Undergraduates 1,260 full-time, 42 part-time. Students come from 36 states and territories, 22 other countries, 24% are from out of state, 0.6% African American, 0.4% Asian American or Pacific Islander, 1.0% Hispanic American, 0.1% Native American, 3% international, 2% transferred in, 81% live on campus. *Retention:* 90% of 2001 full-time freshmen returned.

Freshmen *Admission:* 1,402 applied, 1,108 admitted, 342 enrolled. *Average high school GPA:* 3.70. *Test scores:* SAT verbal scores over 500: 87%; SAT math scores over 500: 89%; SAT verbal scores over 600: 41%; SAT math scores over 600: 45%; SAT verbal scores over 700: 6%; SAT math scores over 700: 6%.

Faculty *Total:* 112, 74% full-time, 81% with terminal degrees. *Student/faculty ratio:* 14:1.

Majors Accounting; anthropology; art history; biochemistry; biological/physical sciences; biology; biology education; botany; business administration; business marketing and marketing management; cell biology; chemistry; chemistry education; communications; communications related; computer/information sciences; criminal justice studies; early childhood education; ecology; economics; education; elementary education; engineering; engineering physics; English; English education; environmental science; finance; fine/studio arts; foreign languages education; foreign languages/literatures; French; French language education; geology; German; German language education; health/medical preparatory programs related; history; humanities; human resources management; interdisciplinary studies; international business; international relations; liberal arts and sciences/liberal studies; management information systems/business data processing; marine biology; mathematics; mathematics education; microbiology/bacteriology; molecular biology; museum studies; natural sciences; peace/conflict studies; physical sciences; physics; physics education; political science; pre-dentistry; pre-law; pre-medicine; pre-pharmacy studies; pre-theology; pre-veterinary studies; professional studies; psychology; public administration; Russian; science education; secondary education; social sciences; social studies education; social work; sociology; Spanish; Spanish language education; special education; teacher education, specific programs related; zoology.

Academic Programs *Special study options:* adult/continuing education programs, advanced placement credit, distance learning, double majors, English as a second language, freshman honors college, honors programs, independent study, internships, off-campus study, part-time degree program, services for LD students, student-designed majors, study abroad, summer session for credit. *Unusual degree programs:* 3-2 engineering with Pennsylvania State University University Park Campus, Columbia University, Washington University in St. Louis, Clarkson University; forestry with Duke University; nursing with Thomas Jefferson University, Johns Hopkins University, Case Western Reserve University; biotechnology; cytogenetics; diagnostic imaging; medical technology; occupational therapy, physical therapy with Thomas Jefferson University; Widener University; Allegheny University of Health Sciences.

Library Beeghly Library with 208,000 titles, 3,500 serial subscriptions, 1,300 audiovisual materials, an OPAC, a Web page.

Computers on Campus 250 computers available on campus for general student use. A campuswide network can be accessed from student residence rooms and from off campus. Internet access, online (class) registration, at least one staffed computer lab available.

Student Life *Housing:* on-campus residence required through senior year. *Options:* coed, women-only. *Activities and Organizations:* drama/theater group, student-run newspaper, radio station, choral group, student government, Activities Board, HOSA, International Club, Habitat for Humanity. *Campus security:* 24-hour emergency response devices and patrols, student patrols, late-night transport/escort service. *Student Services:* health clinic, personal/psychological counseling, women's center.

Athletics Member NCAA. All Division III. *Intercollegiate sports:* baseball M, basketball M/W, cross-country running M/W, equestrian sports M(c)/W(c), field hockey W, football M, golf M(c)/W(c), lacrosse M(c)/W(c), rugby M(c)/W(c), skiing (downhill) M(c)/W(c), soccer M/W, softball W, swimming W, tennis W, track and field M/W, volleyball M/W, wrestling M(c)/W(c). *Intramural sports:* badminton M/W, baseball M(c), basketball M/W, racquetball M/W, skiing (cross-country) M/W, soccer M/W, softball M/W, swimming M/W, table tennis M/W, tennis M/W, volleyball M/W, weight lifting M/W.

Standardized Tests *Required:* SAT I or ACT (for admission).

Juniata College (continued)

Costs (2002–03) *Comprehensive fee:* $27,510 includes full-time tuition ($21,160), mandatory fees ($420), and room and board ($5930). Part-time tuition: $890 per credit hour. *Room and board:* College room only: $3110. *Payment plan:* installment. *Waivers:* adult students and employees or children of employees.

Financial Aid Of all full-time matriculated undergraduates who enrolled in 2001, 1097 applied for aid, 1004 were judged to have need, 596 had their need fully met. 696 Federal Work-Study jobs (averaging $1154). 510 State and other part-time jobs (averaging $1392). In 2001, 256 non-need-based awards were made. *Average percent of need met:* 90%. *Average financial aid package:* $17,273. *Average need-based loan:* $3968. *Average need-based gift aid:* $12,915. *Average non-need based aid:* $8944. *Average indebtedness upon graduation:* $16,500.

Applying *Options:* common application, electronic application, early admission, early decision, deferred entrance. *Application fee:* $30. *Required:* essay or personal statement, high school transcript, minimum 3.0 GPA, 1 letter of recommendation. *Recommended:* interview. *Application deadlines:* 3/15 (freshmen), 6/15 (transfers). *Early decision:* 11/15. *Notification:* continuous (freshmen), 12/30 (early decision).

Admissions Contact Terry Bollman, Director of Admissions, Juniata College, 1700 Moore Street, Huntingdon, PA 16652-2119. *Phone:* 814-641-3424. *Toll-free phone:* 877-JUNIATA. *Fax:* 814-641-3100. *E-mail:* info@juniata.edu.

KEYSTONE COLLEGE
La Plume, Pennsylvania

- **Independent** primarily 2-year, founded 1868
- **Calendar** semesters
- **Degrees** certificates, associate, and bachelor's
- **Rural** 270-acre campus
- **Endowment** $12.0 million
- **Coed,** 1,373 undergraduate students, 71% full-time, 60% women, 40% men
- **Minimally difficult** entrance level, 80% of applicants were admitted

Undergraduates 968 full-time, 405 part-time. Students come from 14 states and territories, 11 other countries, 13% are from out of state, 5% African American, 0.2% Asian American or Pacific Islander, 2% Hispanic American, 0.3% Native American, 1% international, 10% transferred in, 48% live on campus.

Freshmen *Admission:* 1,030 applied, 822 admitted, 398 enrolled. *Test scores:* SAT verbal scores over 500: 24%; SAT math scores over 500: 17%; SAT verbal scores over 600: 4%; SAT math scores over 600: 3%; SAT math scores over 700: 1%.

Faculty *Total:* 179, 31% full-time, 18% with terminal degrees. *Student/faculty ratio:* 11:1.

Majors Accounting; art; biology; business; business administration; business computer programming; business systems networking/ telecommunications; communications; computer programming; criminal justice/law enforcement administration; criminal justice studies; culinary arts; data processing technology; early childhood education; education (K-12); environmental science; forestry; hotel and restaurant management; human resources management; human services; landscape architecture; liberal arts and sciences/liberal studies; medical radiologic technology; occupational therapy; physical therapy; physical therapy assistant; recreation/leisure facilities management; restaurant operations; sport/fitness administration; wildlife biology; wildlife management.

Academic Programs *Special study options:* academic remediation for entering students, adult/continuing education programs, advanced placement credit, cooperative education, English as a second language, independent study, internships, part-time degree program, services for LD students, student-designed majors, summer session for credit. *ROTC:* Army (c), Air Force (c).

Library Miller Library with 47,900 titles, 292 serial subscriptions, 37,395 audiovisual materials, an OPAC, a Web page.

Computers on Campus 80 computers available on campus for general student use. A campuswide network can be accessed from student residence rooms. Internet access, at least one staffed computer lab available.

Student Life *Housing Options:* coed, women-only, disabled students. *Activities and Organizations:* drama/theater group, student-run newspaper, radio station, choral group, Campus Activity Board, Student Senate, Art Society, Inter-Hall Council, Commuter Council. *Campus security:* 24-hour emergency response devices and patrols, student patrols, late-night transport/escort service, controlled dormitory access. *Student Services:* health clinic, personal/psychological counseling, women's center.

Athletics Member NJCAA. *Intercollegiate sports:* baseball M, basketball M/W, cross-country running M/W, golf M/W, soccer M/W, softball W, tennis M/W, volleyball W. *Intramural sports:* badminton M/W, basketball M/W, bowling M/W, football M/W, lacrosse M/W, soccer M/W, softball M/W, table tennis M/W, tennis M/W, volleyball M/W, weight lifting M/W.

Standardized Tests *Required for some:* SAT I or ACT (for admission). *Recommended:* SAT I or ACT (for admission).

Costs (2001–02) *One-time required fee:* $175. *Comprehensive fee:* $19,021 includes full-time tuition ($11,820), mandatory fees ($801), and room and board ($6400). Part-time tuition: $285 per credit. *Required fees:* $40 per term part-time. *Payment plans:* installment, deferred payment. *Waivers:* children of alumni and employees or children of employees.

Financial Aid Of all full-time matriculated undergraduates who enrolled in 2001, 310 Federal Work-Study jobs (averaging $1165). 481 State and other part-time jobs (averaging $1146).

Applying *Options:* common application, electronic application, early admission, deferred entrance. *Application fee:* $25. *Required:* high school transcript. *Required for some:* interview, physical therapist assistant program. *Recommended:* essay or personal statement, minimum 2.0 GPA, 2 letters of recommendation, interview. *Application deadline:* rolling (freshmen), rolling (transfers).

Admissions Contact Ms. Sarah Keating, Director of Admissions, Keystone College, One College Green, La Plume, PA 18440-1099. *Phone:* 570-945-5141 Ext. 2403. *Toll-free phone:* 877-4COLLEGE Ext. 1. *Fax:* 570-945-7916. *E-mail:* admissns@keystone.edu.

KING'S COLLEGE
Wilkes-Barre, Pennsylvania

- **Independent Roman Catholic** comprehensive, founded 1946
- **Calendar** semesters
- **Degrees** associate, bachelor's, and master's
- **Suburban** 48-acre campus
- **Endowment** $39.4 million
- **Coed,** 2,068 undergraduate students, 83% full-time, 52% women, 48% men
- **Moderately difficult** entrance level, 83% of applicants were admitted

King's College is a Catholic liberal arts college founded more than 50 years ago by the Holy Cross Fathers and Brothers of the University of Notre Dame. There are 36 undergraduate majors in the arts and sciences and in the William G. McGowan School of Business. Graduate programs in education, finance, and health-care administration and a 5-year physician assistant program are also available. Of King's alumni, 99% are employed or attend graduate school within 6 months after graduation, and more than 85% of King's students receive financial aid.

Undergraduates 1,720 full-time, 348 part-time. Students come from 26 states and territories, 8 other countries, 25% are from out of state, 3% African American, 0.8% Asian American or Pacific Islander, 2% Hispanic American, 0.3% Native American, 0.7% international, 3% transferred in, 35% live on campus. *Retention:* 81% of 2001 full-time freshmen returned.

Freshmen *Admission:* 1,502 applied, 1,245 admitted, 443 enrolled. *Test scores:* SAT verbal scores over 500: 60%; SAT math scores over 500: 59%; SAT verbal scores over 600: 16%; SAT math scores over 600: 18%; SAT verbal scores over 700: 1%; SAT math scores over 700: 1%.

Faculty *Total:* 189, 59% full-time. *Student/faculty ratio:* 13:1.

Majors Accounting; athletic training/sports medicine; biological/physical sciences; biology; business administration; business marketing and marketing management; chemistry; communications; computer/information sciences; computer science; criminal justice studies; early childhood education; economics; elementary education; English; environmental science; finance; French; gerontology; health professions and related sciences; health services administration; history; human resources management; human resources management related; international business; mathematics; medical technology; neuroscience; philosophy; political science; pre-dentistry; pre-law; pre-medicine; pre-pharmacy studies; pre-veterinary studies; psychology; secondary education; sociology; Spanish; special education; theater arts/drama; theology.

Academic Programs *Special study options:* accelerated degree program, adult/continuing education programs, advanced placement credit, distance learning, double majors, English as a second language, honors programs, independent study, internships, off-campus study, part-time degree program, services for LD students, student-designed majors, study abroad, summer session for credit. *ROTC:* Army (b), Air Force (b).

Library D. Leonard Corgan Library with 163,239 titles, 839 serial subscriptions, 4,740 audiovisual materials, an OPAC, a Web page.

Computers on Campus 273 computers available on campus for general student use. A campuswide network can be accessed from student residence rooms and from off campus. Internet access, at least one staffed computer lab available.

Student Life *Housing:* on-campus residence required through sophomore year. *Options:* men-only, women-only. *Activities and Organizations:* drama/theater group, student-run newspaper, radio station, choral group, Association of Campus Events, Student Government Association, Accounting Association, international/multicultural club, Biology Club. *Campus security:* 24-hour emergency response devices and patrols, student patrols, late-night transport/escort service, bicycle patrols. *Student Services:* health clinic, personal/psychological counseling, women's center.

Athletics Member NCAA. All Division III. *Intercollegiate sports:* baseball M, basketball M/W, cross-country running M/W, field hockey W, football M, golf M, lacrosse M/W, riflery M/W, soccer M/W, softball W, swimming M/W, tennis M/W, volleyball W, wrestling M. *Intramural sports:* basketball M/W, bowling M/W, ice hockey M(c), racquetball M/W, riflery M/W, softball M/W, track and field M(c)/W(c), volleyball M/W.

Standardized Tests *Required:* SAT I or ACT (for admission).

Costs (2001–02) *Comprehensive fee:* $24,680 includes full-time tuition ($16,720), mandatory fees ($730), and room and board ($7230). Part-time tuition: $411 per credit hour. *Room and board:* College room only: $3420. Room and board charges vary according to board plan and housing facility. *Payment plans:* installment, deferred payment. *Waivers:* senior citizens and employees or children of employees.

Financial Aid Of all full-time matriculated undergraduates who enrolled in 2001, 1490 applied for aid, 1305 were judged to have need, 272 had their need fully met. 261 Federal Work-Study jobs (averaging $1293). 186 State and other part-time jobs (averaging $900). In 2001, 195 non-need-based awards were made. *Average percent of need met:* 69%. *Average financial aid package:* $12,187. *Average need-based loan:* $3978. *Average need-based gift aid:* $6713. *Average non-need based aid:* $7334. *Average indebtedness upon graduation:* $14,900.

Applying *Options:* common application, early admission, deferred entrance. *Application fee:* $30. *Required:* essay or personal statement, high school transcript. *Recommended:* 2 letters of recommendation, interview. *Application deadline:* rolling (freshmen), rolling (transfers). *Notification:* continuous (freshmen).

Admissions Contact Ms. Susan McGarry-Hannon, Director of Admissions, King's College, 133 North River Street, Wilkes-Barre, PA 18711-0801. *Phone:* 570-208-5858. *Toll-free phone:* 888-KINGSPA. *Fax:* 570-208-5971. *E-mail:* admissions@kings.edu.

KUTZTOWN UNIVERSITY OF PENNSYLVANIA
Kutztown, Pennsylvania

- **State-supported** comprehensive, founded 1866, part of Pennsylvania State System of Higher Education
- **Calendar** semesters
- **Degrees** bachelor's and master's
- **Rural** 326-acre campus with easy access to Philadelphia
- **Endowment** $9.1 million
- **Coed,** 7,293 undergraduate students, 90% full-time, 60% women, 40% men
- **Moderately difficult** entrance level, 69% of applicants were admitted

Kutztown University has completed the following projects recently to enhance the quality of student life: the University dining hall has a new, modern addition, and the student union has been expanded and modernized; a new addition doubles the size of Rohrbach Library and provides more modern, functional, and comfortable areas and more than 500 personal computer links; all residence hall rooms are now wired for Internet usage, and new multistation computer labs have been opened in buildings across the campus.

Undergraduates 6,579 full-time, 714 part-time. Students come from 19 states and territories, 34 other countries, 9% are from out of state, 4% African American, 1.0% Asian American or Pacific Islander, 2% Hispanic American, 0.2% Native American, 1% international, 7% transferred in, 35% live on campus. *Retention:* 74% of 2001 full-time freshmen returned.

Freshmen *Admission:* 6,252 applied, 4,302 admitted, 1,660 enrolled. *Test scores:* SAT verbal scores over 500: 46%; SAT math scores over 500: 44%; SAT verbal scores over 600: 9%; SAT math scores over 600: 8%; SAT verbal scores over 700: 1%.

Faculty *Total:* 384, 94% full-time, 73% with terminal degrees. *Student/faculty ratio:* 19:1.

Majors Accounting; anthropology; art education; biological/physical sciences; biology; business marketing and marketing management; chemistry; computer/information sciences; craft/folk art; criminal justice studies; earth sciences; education; education of the speech impaired; elementary education; English; environmental science; finance; fine/studio arts; French; geography; geology; graphic design/commercial art/illustration; history; human resources management; international business; liberal arts and sciences/liberal studies; library science; mathematics; medical technology; music; nursing science; oceanography; philosophy; physical sciences; physics; political science; psychology; public administration; secondary education; social work; sociology; Spanish; special education; speech/rhetorical studies; telecommunications; theater arts/drama; visual/performing arts.

Academic Programs *Special study options:* academic remediation for entering students, accelerated degree program, adult/continuing education programs, advanced placement credit, distance learning, double majors, external degree program, honors programs, independent study, internships, off-campus study, part-time degree program, services for LD students, student-designed majors, study abroad, summer session for credit. *ROTC:* Army (c), Air Force (c). *Unusual degree programs:* 3-2 engineering with Pennsylvania State University University Park Campus.

Library Rohrbach Library with 492,117 titles, 1,308 serial subscriptions, 15,981 audiovisual materials, an OPAC, a Web page.

Computers on Campus 650 computers available on campus for general student use. A campuswide network can be accessed from student residence rooms and from off campus. Internet access, at least one staffed computer lab available.

Student Life *Housing Options:* coed, women-only, cooperative. *Activities and Organizations:* drama/theater group, student-run newspaper, radio and television station, choral group, marching band, Student Government Board, Student Pennsylvania State Education Association (PSEA), National Art Education Association, Greek Organizations, Residence Hall Association, national fraternities, national sororities. *Campus security:* 24-hour emergency response devices and patrols, student patrols, late-night transport/escort service, secondary door electronic alarm system in residence halls, 24-hour student desk personnel at main entrance of residence halls. *Student Services:* health clinic, personal/psychological counseling, women's center.

Athletics Member NCAA. All Division II. *Intercollegiate sports:* baseball M(s), basketball M(s)/W(s), cross-country running M(s)/W(s), equestrian sports M(c)/W(c), field hockey W(s), football M(s), golf W(s), riflery M(c)/W(c), rugby M(c)/W(c), skiing (downhill) M(c)/W(c), soccer M(s)/W(s), softball W(s), swimming M(s)/W(s), tennis M(s)/W(s), track and field M(s)/W(s), volleyball W(s), wrestling M(s). *Intramural sports:* basketball M/W, equestrian sports M/W, football M/W, golf M/W, ice hockey M, lacrosse M/W, riflery M/W, rugby M/W, skiing (cross-country) M/W, skiing (downhill) M/W, soccer M/W, softball M/W, tennis M/W, volleyball M/W.

Standardized Tests *Required:* SAT I or ACT (for admission). *Required for some:* SAT II: Subject Tests (for admission).

Costs (2001–02) *One-time required fee:* $135. *Tuition:* state resident $4016 full-time, $167 per credit part-time; nonresident $10,040 full-time, $418 per credit part-time. Part-time tuition and fees vary according to course load. *Required fees:* $931 full-time, $167 per credit. *Room and board:* $4426; room only: $3088. Room and board charges vary according to board plan. *Payment plans:* tuition prepayment, installment, deferred payment. *Waivers:* senior citizens and employees or children of employees.

Financial Aid Of all full-time matriculated undergraduates who enrolled in 2001, 5031 applied for aid, 3382 were judged to have need, 2622 had their need fully met. 326 Federal Work-Study jobs (averaging $953). In 2001, 216 non-need-based awards were made. *Average percent of need met:* 71%. *Average financial aid package:* $5543. *Average need-based loan:* $3120. *Average need-based gift aid:* $2957. *Average non-need based aid:* $1497. *Average indebtedness upon graduation:* $13,922.

Applying *Options:* electronic application, early admission, deferred entrance. *Application fee:* $30. *Required:* high school transcript, minimum 2.0 GPA. *Required for some:* Music Art-Audition required for music program; portfolio and/or art test required for art education, communication design, crafts, and fine arts programs. *Application deadline:* rolling (freshmen), rolling (transfers). *Notification:* continuous (freshmen).

Admissions Contact Dr. Valerie Reidout, Acting Director of Admissions, Kutztown University of Pennsylvania, 15200 Kutztown Road, Kutztown, PA 19530-0730. *Phone:* 610-683-4060 Ext. 4053. *Toll-free phone:* 877-628-1915. *Fax:* 610-683-1375. *E-mail:* admission@kutztown.edu.

LAFAYETTE COLLEGE
Easton, Pennsylvania

- **Independent** 4-year, founded 1826, affiliated with Presbyterian Church (U.S.A.)
- **Calendar** semesters
- **Degree** bachelor's
- **Suburban** 110-acre campus with easy access to New York City and Philadelphia
- **Endowment** $537.0 million

Lafayette College (continued)

- **Coed,** 2,330 undergraduate students, 95% full-time, 49% women, 51% men
- **Very difficult** entrance level, 39% of applicants were admitted

Undergraduates 2,223 full-time, 107 part-time. Students come from 42 states and territories, 53 other countries, 71% are from out of state, 4% African American, 2% Asian American or Pacific Islander, 2% Hispanic American, 0.3% Native American, 4% international, 0.3% transferred in, 98% live on campus. *Retention:* 95% of 2001 full-time freshmen returned.

Freshmen *Admission:* 5,195 applied, 2,028 admitted, 576 enrolled. *Average high school GPA:* 3.90. *Test scores:* SAT verbal scores over 500: 97%; SAT math scores over 500: 98%; ACT scores over 18: 99%; SAT verbal scores over 600: 58%; SAT math scores over 600: 76%; ACT scores over 24: 82%; SAT verbal scores over 700: 11%; SAT math scores over 700: 19%; ACT scores over 30: 16%.

Faculty *Total:* 226, 81% full-time, 97% with terminal degrees. *Student/faculty ratio:* 11:1.

Majors American studies; anthropology; art; art history; biochemistry; biology; business economics; chemical engineering; chemistry; civil engineering; computer science; economics; electrical engineering; engineering; English; environmental engineering; fine/studio arts; French; geology; German; history; international relations; mathematics; mechanical engineering; music; music history; philosophy; physics; political science; psychology; religious studies; Russian/Slavic studies; sociology; Spanish.

Academic Programs *Special study options:* academic remediation for entering students, accelerated degree program, adult/continuing education programs, advanced placement credit, honors programs, internships, off-campus study, part-time degree program, services for LD students, student-designed majors, study abroad, summer session for credit. *ROTC:* Army (c).

Library Skillman Library plus 1 other with 500,000 titles, 2,630 serial subscriptions, an OPAC, a Web page.

Computers on Campus 600 computers available on campus for general student use. A campuswide network can be accessed from student residence rooms and from off campus. Internet access, online (class) registration, at least one staffed computer lab available.

Student Life *Housing:* on-campus residence required through senior year. *Options:* coed. *Activities and Organizations:* drama/theater group, student-run newspaper, radio station, choral group, Association of Biscer Collegians, International Student Association, Activities Forum, national fraternities, national sororities. *Campus security:* 24-hour emergency response devices and patrols, student patrols, late-night transport/escort service, controlled dormitory access. *Student Services:* health clinic, personal/psychological counseling, women's center.

Athletics Member NCAA. All Division I except football (Division I-AA). *Intercollegiate sports:* baseball M, basketball M/W, crew M(c)/W(c), cross-country running M/W, equestrian sports M(c)/W(c), fencing M/W, field hockey W, golf M, ice hockey M(c), lacrosse M/W, rugby M(c)/W(c), skiing (downhill) M(c)/W(c), soccer M/W, softball W, squash M(c), swimming M/W, tennis M/W, track and field M/W, volleyball W, weight lifting M(c)/W(c), wrestling M(c). *Intramural sports:* badminton M/W, baseball M, basketball M/W, bowling M/W, cross-country running M/W, fencing M/W, field hockey W, football M, golf M/W, lacrosse M/W, racquetball M/W, sailing M(c)/W(c), skiing (cross-country) M(c)/W(c), soccer M/W, softball M/W, squash M/W, swimming M/W, table tennis M/W, tennis M/W, track and field M/W, volleyball M/W, weight lifting M/W, wrestling M.

Standardized Tests *Required:* SAT I (for admission), SAT II: Subject Tests (for admission). *Recommended:* SAT II: Writing Test (for admission).

Costs (2002–03) *Comprehensive fee:* $32,655 includes full-time tuition ($24,828), mandatory fees ($93), and room and board ($7734). *Room and board:* College room only: $4300.

Financial Aid Of all full-time matriculated undergraduates who enrolled in 2001, 1388 applied for aid, 1064 were judged to have need, 1016 had their need fully met. 159 Federal Work-Study jobs (averaging $948). 140 State and other part-time jobs (averaging $3773). In 2001, 131 non-need-based awards were made. *Average percent of need met:* 96%. *Average financial aid package:* $20,593. *Average need-based loan:* $3873. *Average need-based gift aid:* $17,982. *Average non-need based aid:* $10,935. *Average indebtedness upon graduation:* $15,393. *Financial aid deadline:* 2/1.

Applying *Options:* common application, electronic application, early admission, early decision, deferred entrance. *Application fee:* $50. *Required:* essay or personal statement, high school transcript, 1 letter of recommendation. *Recommended:* interview. *Application deadlines:* 1/1 (freshmen), 6/1 (transfers). *Early decision:* 12/1. *Notification:* continuous until 4/1 (freshmen), 3/15 (early decision).

Admissions Contact Ms. Carol Rowlands, Director of Admissions, Lafayette College, Easton, PA 18042-1798. *Phone:* 610-330-5100. *Fax:* 610-330-5355. *E-mail:* admissions@lafayette.edu.

LANCASTER BIBLE COLLEGE
Lancaster, Pennsylvania

- **Independent nondenominational** comprehensive, founded 1933
- **Calendar** semesters
- **Degrees** certificates, associate, bachelor's, master's, and postbachelor's certificates
- **Suburban** 100-acre campus with easy access to Philadelphia
- **Endowment** $2.4 million
- **Coed,** 714 undergraduate students, 76% full-time, 54% women, 46% men
- **Minimally difficult** entrance level, 76% of applicants were admitted

LBC is a nondenominational Bible college offering BS or AS degrees. Programs prepare students for Christian careers in Christian education, computer ministries, counseling, Bible education, Bible music, early childhood and elementary education, missions, music, pastoral studies, secretarial studies, vocational technology, and youth ministry. New programs include women's ministries, guidance counseling/Bible, and health/physical/Bible education. Two 1-year certificate programs are available. Graduate study is also available.

Undergraduates 543 full-time, 171 part-time. Students come from 25 states and territories, 10 other countries, 26% are from out of state, 3% African American, 0.8% Asian American or Pacific Islander, 1% Hispanic American, 0.8% Native American, 2% international, 10% transferred in, 49% live on campus. *Retention:* 83% of 2001 full-time freshmen returned.

Freshmen *Admission:* 243 applied, 184 admitted, 114 enrolled. *Average high school GPA:* 3.03. *Test scores:* SAT verbal scores over 500: 52%; SAT math scores over 500: 50%; ACT scores over 18: 67%; SAT verbal scores over 600: 13%; SAT math scores over 600: 12%; ACT scores over 24: 19%; SAT verbal scores over 700: 1%; SAT math scores over 700: 1%.

Faculty *Total:* 60, 45% full-time, 43% with terminal degrees. *Student/faculty ratio:* 15:1.

Majors Biblical studies; education; secretarial science.

Academic Programs *Special study options:* academic remediation for entering students, adult/continuing education programs, advanced placement credit, double majors, independent study, internships, part-time degree program, services for LD students, study abroad, summer session for credit.

Library Lancaster Bible College Library with 118,519 titles, 1,273 serial subscriptions, 3,943 audiovisual materials, an OPAC.

Computers on Campus 20 computers available on campus for general student use. A campuswide network can be accessed from student residence rooms. Internet access, at least one staffed computer lab available.

Student Life *Housing:* on-campus residence required through senior year. *Options:* men-only, women-only. *Activities and Organizations:* drama/theater group, student-run newspaper, choral group, Student Government Association, Student Missionary Fellowship, International Student Fellowship, Resident Affairs Council, Student Intramural Association. *Campus security:* student patrols, late-night transport/escort service, controlled dormitory access. *Student Services:* health clinic, personal/psychological counseling.

Athletics Member NCCAA. *Intercollegiate sports:* baseball M, basketball M/W, soccer M, softball W, volleyball M/W. *Intramural sports:* basketball M/W, football M, soccer M/W, softball M/W, table tennis M/W, tennis M/W.

Standardized Tests *Required:* SAT I or ACT (for admission).

Costs (2001–02) *Comprehensive fee:* $15,340 includes full-time tuition ($10,110), mandatory fees ($430), and room and board ($4800). Full-time tuition and fees vary according to course load and program. Part-time tuition: $337 per credit hour. Part-time tuition and fees vary according to program. *Required fees:* $10 per credit hour. *Room and board:* College room only: $2000. Room and board charges vary according to board plan. *Payment plan:* installment. *Waivers:* children of alumni, adult students, senior citizens, and employees or children of employees.

Financial Aid Of all full-time matriculated undergraduates who enrolled in 2001, 436 applied for aid, 409 were judged to have need, 51 had their need fully met. In 2001, 8 non-need-based awards were made. *Average percent of need met:* 44%. *Average financial aid package:* $8010. *Average need-based loan:* $2589. *Average need-based gift aid:* $5872. *Average non-need based aid:* $2358. *Average indebtedness upon graduation:* $13,014.

Applying *Options:* early admission, deferred entrance. *Application fee:* $25. *Required:* essay or personal statement, high school transcript, minimum 2.0 GPA, 3 letters of recommendation. *Required for some:* interview. *Application deadline:* rolling (freshmen), rolling (transfers). *Notification:* continuous (freshmen).

Admissions Contact Mrs. Joanne M. Roper, Director of Admissions, Lancaster Bible College, 901 Eden Road, Lancaster, PA 17601-5036. *Phone:* 717-560-8271. *Toll-free phone:* 888-866-LBC-4-YOU. *Fax:* 717-560-8213. *E-mail:* admissions@lbc.edu.

LA ROCHE COLLEGE

Pittsburgh, Pennsylvania

- **Independent** comprehensive, founded 1963, affiliated with Roman Catholic Church
- **Calendar** semesters
- **Degrees** certificates, associate, bachelor's, and master's
- **Suburban** 80-acre campus
- **Endowment** $6.2 million
- **Coed,** 1,661 undergraduate students, 75% full-time, 61% women, 39% men
- **Minimally difficult** entrance level, 79% of applicants were admitted

Undergraduates 1,240 full-time, 421 part-time. Students come from 16 states and territories, 28 other countries, 6% are from out of state, 4% African American, 0.6% Asian American or Pacific Islander, 0.7% Hispanic American, 0.2% Native American, 17% international, 10% transferred in, 38% live on campus. *Retention:* 83% of 2001 full-time freshmen returned.

Freshmen *Admission:* 559 applied, 444 admitted, 215 enrolled. *Average high school GPA:* 3.06.

Faculty *Total:* 207, 27% full-time, 46% with terminal degrees. *Student/faculty ratio:* 18:1.

Majors Accounting; applied mathematics; biology; biology education; business administration; chemistry; chemistry education; communications; computer/information sciences; criminal justice studies; dance; early childhood education; elementary education; English; English education; finance; general studies; graphic design/commercial art/illustration; history; human services; interior design; international business; international relations; liberal arts and sciences/liberal studies; marketing management and research related; mathematics education; medical radiologic technology; nursing science; psychology; religious education; religious studies; respiratory therapy; sociology; Spanish language education; technical/business writing.

Academic Programs *Special study options:* academic remediation for entering students, adult/continuing education programs, advanced placement credit, cooperative education, double majors, English as a second language, freshman honors college, honors programs, independent study, internships, part-time degree program, services for LD students, summer session for credit. *ROTC:* Army (c), Air Force (c).

Library John J. Wright Library with 62,361 titles, 2,220 serial subscriptions, 935 audiovisual materials, an OPAC.

Computers on Campus 95 computers available on campus for general student use. A campuswide network can be accessed from student residence rooms and from off campus. Internet access, online (class) registration, at least one staffed computer lab available.

Student Life *Housing Options:* coed. *Activities and Organizations:* student-run newspaper, radio station, choral group, American Society of Interior Design, Student Government, Visions (environmental club), Helping Hands, Project Achievement. *Campus security:* 24-hour emergency response devices and patrols, student patrols, late-night transport/escort service, controlled dormitory access. *Student Services:* health clinic, personal/psychological counseling.

Athletics Member NCAA. All Division III. *Intercollegiate sports:* baseball M, basketball M/W, cross-country running M/W, golf M, soccer M/W, softball W, tennis W, volleyball W. *Intramural sports:* basketball M/W, football M/W, golf M/W, racquetball M/W, soccer M/W, table tennis M/W, volleyball M/W, weight lifting M/W.

Standardized Tests *Required:* SAT I or ACT (for admission).

Costs (2001–02) *Comprehensive fee:* $18,854 includes full-time tuition ($12,180), mandatory fees ($200), and room and board ($6474). Full-time tuition and fees vary according to program. Part-time tuition: $440 per credit. Part-time tuition and fees vary according to program. *Required fees:* $7 per credit, $50 per term part-time. *Room and board:* College room only: $4010. *Payment plan:* installment. *Waivers:* senior citizens and employees or children of employees.

Financial Aid Of all full-time matriculated undergraduates who enrolled in 2001, 847 applied for aid, 729 were judged to have need, 361 had their need fully met. In 2001, 81 non-need-based awards were made. *Average percent of need met:* 90%. *Average financial aid package:* $16,000. *Average need-based loan:* $4500. *Average need-based gift aid:* $2000. *Average non-need based aid:* $2000. *Average indebtedness upon graduation:* $15,000. *Financial aid deadline:* 5/1.

Applying *Options:* electronic application, early admission, deferred entrance. *Application fee:* $35. *Required:* high school transcript, minimum 2.0 GPA, letters of recommendation. *Recommended:* essay or personal statement, minimum 3.0 GPA, interview. *Application deadline:* rolling (freshmen), rolling (transfers).

Admissions Contact Ms. Dayna R. McNally, Director of Enrollment Services, La Roche College, Pittsburgh, PA 15237. *Phone:* 412-536-1049. *Toll-free phone:* 800-838-4LRC. *Fax:* 412-536-1048. *E-mail:* admsns@laroche.edu.

LA SALLE UNIVERSITY

Philadelphia, Pennsylvania

- **Independent Roman Catholic** comprehensive, founded 1863
- **Calendar** semesters
- **Degrees** associate, bachelor's, master's, and doctoral
- **Urban** 100-acre campus
- **Endowment** $43.9 million
- **Coed,** 3,905 undergraduate students, 81% full-time, 57% women, 43% men
- **Moderately difficult** entrance level, 80% of applicants were admitted

Undergraduates 3,178 full-time, 727 part-time. Students come from 30 states and territories, 35 other countries, 34% are from out of state, 11% African American, 3% Asian American or Pacific Islander, 5% Hispanic American, 0.1% Native American, 1% international, 3% transferred in, 61% live on campus. *Retention:* 88% of 2001 full-time freshmen returned.

Freshmen *Admission:* 3,942 applied, 3,168 admitted, 849 enrolled. *Test scores:* SAT verbal scores over 500: 74%; SAT math scores over 500: 71%; SAT verbal scores over 600: 27%; SAT math scores over 600: 25%; SAT verbal scores over 700: 3%; SAT math scores over 700: 4%.

Faculty *Total:* 463, 42% full-time. *Student/faculty ratio:* 16:1.

Majors Accounting; Air Force R.O.T.C./air science; applied mathematics; Army R.O.T.C./military science; art; art history; biochemistry; biology; broadcast journalism; business administration; business economics; business education; business marketing and marketing management; chemistry; classics; computer/information sciences; computer programming; computer science; creative writing; criminal justice studies; economics; education; elementary education; English; environmental science; film studies; finance; French; geology; German; graphic design/commercial art/illustration; Greek (modern); history; human resources management; information sciences/systems; Italian; journalism; Latin (ancient and medieval); liberal arts and sciences/liberal studies; literature; management information systems/business data processing; mass communications; mathematics; modern languages; music; music history; nursing; nutritional sciences; occupational therapy; philosophy; physical therapy; political science; pre-dentistry; pre-medicine; pre-veterinary studies; psychology; public administration; public relations; radio/television broadcasting; religious education; religious studies; Russian; Russian/Slavic studies; science education; secondary education; social sciences; social work; sociology; Spanish; special education; speech-language pathology/audiology; speech/rhetorical studies.

Academic Programs *Special study options:* accelerated degree program, adult/continuing education programs, advanced placement credit, cooperative education, double majors, freshman honors college, honors programs, independent study, internships, off-campus study, part-time degree program, services for LD students, student-designed majors, summer session for credit. *ROTC:* Army (c), Air Force (c). *Unusual degree programs:* 3-2 physical therapy with Thomas Jefferson University.

Library Connelly Library with 365,000 titles, 1,700 serial subscriptions, 5,200 audiovisual materials, an OPAC, a Web page.

Computers on Campus 350 computers available on campus for general student use. A campuswide network can be accessed from student residence rooms and from off campus. Internet access, online (class) registration, at least one staffed computer lab available.

Student Life *Housing Options:* coed. *Activities and Organizations:* drama/theater group, student-run newspaper, radio and television station, choral group, Student Government Association, Community Service Organization, La Salle Entertainment Organization, The Explorer (yearbook), The Masque (theater group), national fraternities, national sororities. *Campus security:* 24-hour emergency response devices and patrols, student patrols, late-night transport/escort service, controlled dormitory access. *Student Services:* health clinic, personal/psychological counseling, women's center.

Athletics Member NCAA, NAIA. All NCAA Division I except football (Division I-AA). *Intercollegiate sports:* baseball M(s), basketball M(s)/W(s), crew M(s)/W(s), cross-country running M(s)/W(s), field hockey W(s), golf M(s)/W(s), lacrosse W(s), soccer M(s)/W(s), softball W(s), swimming M(s)/W(s), tennis M(s)/W(s), track and field M(s)/W(s), volleyball W(s). *Intramural sports:* baseball M, basketball M/W, crew M/W, fencing M/W, field hockey W, football M/W, golf M/W, ice hockey M(c), racquetball M/W, riflery M/W, rugby M(c), skiing (cross-country) M/W, skiing (downhill) M/W, soccer M/W, softball W, squash M/W, swimming M/W, table tennis M/W, tennis M/W, track and field M/W, volleyball M/W, water polo M/W, weight lifting M/W.

Standardized Tests *Required:* SAT I or ACT (for admission).

Costs (2001–02) *Comprehensive fee:* $26,900 includes full-time tuition ($19,740), mandatory fees ($150), and room and board ($7010). Full-time tuition and fees vary according to program. Part-time tuition: $350 per credit hour. Part-time tuition and fees vary according to class time and course load. *Required*

La Salle University (continued)
fees: $50 per term part-time. *Room and board:* Room and board charges vary according to board plan, housing facility, and location. *Payment plans:* installment, deferred payment. *Waivers:* employees or children of employees.

Financial Aid Of all full-time matriculated undergraduates who enrolled in 2001, 2987 applied for aid, 2325 were judged to have need, 592 had their need fully met. 875 Federal Work-Study jobs (averaging $770). In 2001, 440 non-need-based awards were made. *Average percent of need met:* 81%. *Average financial aid package:* $14,462. *Average need-based loan:* $4329. *Average need-based gift aid:* $6627. *Average non-need based aid:* $7544.

Applying *Options:* electronic application, early admission, early action, deferred entrance. *Application fee:* $35. *Required:* essay or personal statement, high school transcript, 1 letter of recommendation. *Recommended:* interview. *Application deadlines:* 4/1 (freshmen), 8/1 (transfers). *Notification:* continuous (freshmen), 12/15 (early action).

Admissions Contact Mr. Robert G. Voss, Dean of Admission and Financial Aid, La Salle University, 1900 West Olney Avenue, Philadelphia, PA 19141-1199. *Phone:* 215-951-1500. *Toll-free phone:* 800-328-1910. *Fax:* 215-951-1656. *E-mail:* admiss@lasalle.edu.

LEBANON VALLEY COLLEGE
Annville, Pennsylvania

- **Independent United Methodist** comprehensive, founded 1866
- **Calendar** semesters
- **Degrees** certificates, associate, bachelor's, master's, and postbachelor's certificates (offers master of business administration degree on a part-time basis only)
- **Small-town** 275-acre campus
- **Endowment** $33.5 million
- **Coed,** 1,920 undergraduate students, 79% full-time, 60% women, 40% men
- **Moderately difficult** entrance level, 79% of applicants were admitted

Undergraduates 1,517 full-time, 403 part-time. Students come from 21 states and territories, 10 other countries, 21% are from out of state, 2% African American, 1% Asian American or Pacific Islander, 2% Hispanic American, 0.1% Native American, 0.8% international, 2% transferred in, 72% live on campus. *Retention:* 81% of 2001 full-time freshmen returned.

Freshmen *Admission:* 1,864 applied, 1,468 admitted, 422 enrolled. *Test scores:* SAT verbal scores over 500: 74%; SAT math scores over 500: 73%; SAT verbal scores over 600: 25%; SAT math scores over 600: 31%; SAT verbal scores over 700: 2%; SAT math scores over 700: 5%.

Faculty *Total:* 179, 50% full-time, 50% with terminal degrees. *Student/faculty ratio:* 14:1.

Majors Accounting; actuarial science; biochemistry; biology; business administration; chemistry; communications technologies related; computer science; economics; elementary education; English; French; German; health professions and related sciences; history; international business; liberal arts and sciences/liberal studies; mathematics; medical technology; music; music business management/merchandising; music related; music teacher education; nuclear medical technology; philosophy; physics; physiological psychology/psychobiology; political science; pre-dentistry; pre-law; pre-medicine; pre-veterinary studies; psychology; religious studies; secondary education; social sciences; Spanish.

Academic Programs *Special study options:* academic remediation for entering students, adult/continuing education programs, advanced placement credit, double majors, independent study, internships, part-time degree program, student-designed majors, study abroad, summer session for credit. *ROTC:* Army (b). *Unusual degree programs:* 3-2 engineering with University of Pennsylvania, Case Western Reserve University, Widener University; forestry with Duke University.

Library Bishop Library with 165,642 titles, 6,160 serial subscriptions, 3,346 audiovisual materials, an OPAC, a Web page.

Computers on Campus 194 computers available on campus for general student use. A campuswide network can be accessed from student residence rooms and from off campus. Internet access, at least one staffed computer lab available.

Student Life *Housing:* on-campus residence required through senior year. *Options:* coed, men-only, women-only. *Activities and Organizations:* drama/theater group, student-run newspaper, radio station, choral group, marching band, LVC PSEA, Council of Christian Organization, Kwon Do Club, Phi Beta Lambda, Wig and Buckle (theatrical group), national fraternities, national sororities. *Campus security:* 24-hour emergency response devices and patrols, late-night transport/escort service, dormitory entrances locked at midnight. *Student Services:* health clinic, personal/psychological counseling.

Athletics Member NCAA. All Division III. *Intercollegiate sports:* baseball M, basketball M/W, cross-country running M/W, field hockey W, football M, golf M/W, ice hockey M, soccer M/W, softball W, swimming M/W, tennis M/W, track and field M/W, volleyball W. *Intramural sports:* basketball M/W, football M, racquetball M/W, softball M/W, tennis M/W, volleyball M(c)/W(c).

Standardized Tests *Required:* SAT I or ACT (for admission).

Costs (2001–02) *Comprehensive fee:* $25,700 includes full-time tuition ($19,210), mandatory fees ($600), and room and board ($5890). Part-time tuition: $360 per credit. Part-time tuition and fees vary according to class time. *Room and board:* College room only: $2860. Room and board charges vary according to board plan and housing facility. *Payment plans:* tuition prepayment, installment. *Waivers:* senior citizens and employees or children of employees.

Financial Aid Of all full-time matriculated undergraduates who enrolled in 2001, 1280 applied for aid, 1153 were judged to have need, 456 had their need fully met. In 2001, 173 non-need-based awards were made. *Average percent of need met:* 85%. *Average financial aid package:* $14,762. *Average need-based loan:* $4060. *Average need-based gift aid:* $5967. *Average non-need based aid:* $8035. *Average indebtedness upon graduation:* $17,483.

Applying *Options:* electronic application, early admission, deferred entrance. *Application fee:* $25. *Required:* high school transcript. *Required for some:* essay or personal statement, audition for music majors; interview for physical therapy program. *Recommended:* 2 letters of recommendation, interview. *Application deadline:* rolling (freshmen), rolling (transfers). *Notification:* continuous (freshmen).

Admissions Contact William J. Brown Jr., Dean of Admission and Financial Aid, Lebanon Valley College, 101 N. College Avenue, Annville, PA 17003-1400. *Phone:* 717-867-6181. *Toll-free phone:* 866-582-4236. *Fax:* 717-867-6026. *E-mail:* admission@lvc.edu.

LEHIGH UNIVERSITY
Bethlehem, Pennsylvania

- **Independent** university, founded 1865
- **Calendar** semesters
- **Degrees** bachelor's, master's, doctoral, and post-master's certificates
- **Suburban** 1600-acre campus with easy access to Philadelphia
- **Endowment** $731.8 million
- **Coed,** 4,650 undergraduate students, 99% full-time, 41% women, 59% men
- **Most difficult** entrance level, 47% of applicants were admitted

Lehigh is among the nation's most highly ranked private research universities. Located on the East coast, the University is close to New York City and Philadelphia, located in historic Bethlehem, Pennsylvania. Lehigh offers the broad academic programs of a leading research university and the personal attention of a small college, with a student-faculty ratio of 12:1. Four colleges offer more than 110 majors in the liberal arts, business, education, engineering, and the sciences. Students can customize their college experience and work with renowned faculty members on hands-on projects, internships, and innovative studies that cross disciplines. With a culture that encourages diversity and involvement, it's no wonder that Lehigh is widely known as a place where students emerge as leaders in careers and life.

Undergraduates 4,595 full-time, 55 part-time. Students come from 52 states and territories, 46 other countries, 68% are from out of state, 3% African American, 6% Asian American or Pacific Islander, 3% Hispanic American, 0.1% Native American, 3% international, 2% transferred in, 69% live on campus. *Retention:* 94% of 2001 full-time freshmen returned.

Freshmen *Admission:* 8,088 applied, 3,776 admitted, 1,112 enrolled. *Average high school GPA:* 3.75. *Test scores:* SAT verbal scores over 500: 96%; SAT math scores over 500: 99%; SAT verbal scores over 600: 63%; SAT math scores over 600: 83%; SAT verbal scores over 700: 12%; SAT math scores over 700: 31%.

Faculty *Total:* 457, 86% full-time, 99% with terminal degrees. *Student/faculty ratio:* 11:1.

Majors Accounting; African studies; American studies; anthropology; architecture; art; Asian studies; biochemistry; biology; business administration; business economics; business marketing and marketing management; chemical engineering; chemistry; civil engineering; classics; cognitive psychology/psycholinguistics; computer engineering; computer science; economics; electrical engineering; engineering; engineering mechanics; engineering physics; English; environmental science; finance; French; German; history; industrial/manufacturing engineering; information sciences/systems; international business; international relations; journalism; materials engineering; mathematical statistics; mathematics; mechanical engineering; molecular biology; music; natural sciences; neuroscience; philosophy; physics; political science; pre-dentistry; pre-medicine; psychology; religious studies; Russian/Slavic studies; science/technology and society; sociology; Spanish; theater arts/drama; urban studies.

Academic Programs *Special study options:* accelerated degree program, adult/continuing education programs, advanced placement credit, cooperative education, distance learning, double majors, English as a second language, honors programs, independent study, internships, off-campus study, services for LD students, study abroad, summer session for credit. *ROTC:* Army (b). *Unusual degree programs:* 3-2 education.

Library E. W. Fairchild-Martindale Library plus 1 other with 1.2 million titles, 6,271 serial subscriptions, 8,415 audiovisual materials, an OPAC, a Web page.

Computers on Campus 516 computers available on campus for general student use. A campuswide network can be accessed from student residence rooms and from off campus. Internet access, online (class) registration, at least one staffed computer lab available.

Student Life *Housing Options:* coed, disabled students. *Activities and Organizations:* drama/theater group, student-run newspaper, radio station, choral group, marching band, Student Senate, University Productions, Graduate Student Council, Residence Hall Association, Global Union, national fraternities, national sororities. *Campus security:* 24-hour emergency response devices and patrols, student patrols, late-night transport/escort service, controlled dormitory access. *Student Services:* health clinic, personal/psychological counseling, women's center.

Athletics Member NCAA. All Division I except football (Division I-AA). *Intercollegiate sports:* baseball M(s), basketball M(s)/W, bowling M(c)/W(c), crew M(c)/W(c), cross-country running M(s)/W(s), equestrian sports M(c)/W(c), field hockey W(s), football M(s)/W(c), golf M(s), ice hockey M(c), lacrosse M(s)/W(s), riflery M/W, rugby M(c), skiing (downhill) M(c)/W(c), soccer M(s)/W(s), softball W(s), squash M(c), swimming M(s)/W(s), tennis M(s)/W(s), track and field M(s)/W(s), volleyball M(c)/W(s), wrestling M(s). *Intramural sports:* badminton M/W, basketball M/W, bowling M(c)/W(c), cross-country running M/W, fencing M(c)/W(c), field hockey W(c), football M, golf M/W, gymnastics M(c)/W(c), ice hockey M(c), lacrosse M(c), racquetball M/W, rugby W(c), skiing (cross-country) M/W, skiing (downhill) M/W, soccer M/W, softball M/W, squash M/W, swimming M/W, table tennis M/W, tennis M/W, track and field M/W, volleyball M/W, weight lifting M, wrestling M.

Standardized Tests *Required:* SAT I or ACT (for admission). *Recommended:* SAT II: Subject Tests (for admission).

Costs (2001–02) *Comprehensive fee:* $32,290 includes full-time tuition ($24,940), mandatory fees ($200), and room and board ($7150). Full-time tuition and fees vary according to program. Part-time tuition: $1040 per credit hour. Part-time tuition and fees vary according to program. *Room and board:* College room only: $3150. *Payment plans:* tuition prepayment, installment, deferred payment. *Waivers:* senior citizens and employees or children of employees.

Financial Aid Of all full-time matriculated undergraduates who enrolled in 2001, 2665 applied for aid, 2127 were judged to have need, 1522 had their need fully met. In 2001, 335 non-need-based awards were made. *Average percent of need met:* 98%. *Average financial aid package:* $19,697. *Average need-based loan:* $4026. *Average need-based gift aid:* $15,146. *Average non-need based aid:* $7692. *Financial aid deadline:* 1/15.

Applying *Options:* common application, electronic application, early admission, early decision, deferred entrance. *Application fee:* $50. *Required:* high school transcript, 1 letter of recommendation, graded writing sample. *Recommended:* essay or personal statement, interview. *Application deadlines:* 1/1 (freshmen), 4/1 (transfers). *Early decision:* 11/15. *Notification:* 4/1 (freshmen), 12/23 (early decision).

Admissions Contact Mr. J. Bruce Gardiner, Interim Dean of Admissions and Financial Aid, Lehigh University, 27 Memorial Drive West, Bethlehem, PA 18015. *Phone:* 610-758-3100. *Fax:* 610-758-4361. *E-mail:* admissions@lehigh.edu.

LINCOLN UNIVERSITY
Lincoln University, Pennsylvania

- **State-related** comprehensive, founded 1854
- **Calendar** semesters
- **Degrees** bachelor's and master's
- **Rural** 442-acre campus with easy access to Philadelphia
- **Endowment** $17.0 million
- **Coed,** 1,438 undergraduate students, 96% full-time, 60% women, 40% men
- **Moderately difficult** entrance level, 53% of applicants were admitted

Undergraduates 1,385 full-time, 53 part-time. Students come from 20 states and territories, 14 other countries, 49% are from out of state, 93% African American, 0.1% Asian American or Pacific Islander, 0.2% Hispanic American, 6% international, 3% transferred in, 92% live on campus. *Retention:* 64% of 2001 full-time freshmen returned.

Freshmen *Admission:* 2,631 applied, 1,382 admitted, 479 enrolled. *Average high school GPA:* 2.75.

Faculty *Total:* 159, 59% full-time. *Student/faculty ratio:* 14:1.

Majors Accounting; actuarial science; African-American studies; African languages; anthropology; art education; behavioral sciences; biology; business administration; chemistry; computer science; criminal justice/law enforcement administration; early childhood education; economics; education; elementary education; English; English education; finance; foreign languages education; French; health education; history; human resources management; human services; international relations; journalism; mathematics; mathematics education; music; organizational psychology; philosophy; physical education; physical sciences; physics; physiological psychology/psychobiology; political science; psychology; public policy analysis; recreation/leisure studies; religious studies; Russian; science education; social studies education; social work; sociology; Spanish.

Academic Programs *Special study options:* academic remediation for entering students, accelerated degree program, adult/continuing education programs, advanced placement credit, cooperative education, double majors, honors programs, independent study, internships, off-campus study, part-time degree program, student-designed majors, study abroad, summer session for credit. *ROTC:* Army (c), Air Force (c). *Unusual degree programs:* 3-2 engineering with Drexel University, Pennsylvania State University University Park Campus, Lafayette College, New Jersey Institute of Technology, University of Delaware, Howard University, Rensselaer Polytechnic Institute.

Library Langston Hughes Memorial Library with 178,750 titles, 580 serial subscriptions, 2,633 audiovisual materials.

Computers on Campus 200 computers available on campus for general student use. A campuswide network can be accessed from student residence rooms and from off campus. Internet access, at least one staffed computer lab available.

Student Life *Housing:* on-campus residence required for freshman year. *Options:* coed, men-only, women-only. *Activities and Organizations:* drama/theater group, student-run newspaper, radio and television station, choral group, The Gospel Ensemble, Ziana Fashion Club, drill team, Militants for Christ, Greek organizations, national fraternities, national sororities. *Campus security:* 24-hour emergency response devices and patrols, late-night transport/escort service. *Student Services:* health clinic, personal/psychological counseling.

Athletics Member NCAA. All Division III. *Intercollegiate sports:* baseball M, basketball M/W, cross-country running M/W, soccer M/W, tennis M/W, track and field M/W, volleyball W. *Intramural sports:* bowling M/W, football M, softball M/W, swimming M/W.

Standardized Tests *Required for some:* SAT I or ACT (for placement), MAPS.

Costs (2001–02) *Tuition:* state resident $5786 full-time, $168 per credit hour part-time; nonresident $9050 full-time, $286 per credit hour part-time. Full-time tuition and fees vary according to course load. *Room and board:* $5412. Room and board charges vary according to board plan. *Payment plans:* installment, deferred payment. *Waivers:* employees or children of employees.

Applying *Options:* early admission, deferred entrance. *Application fee:* $20. *Required:* essay or personal statement, high school transcript, minimum 2.5 GPA, 2 letters of recommendation, interview. *Application deadline:* rolling (freshmen), rolling (transfers).

Admissions Contact Dr. Robert Laney Jr., Director of Admissions, Lincoln University, MSC 147, Lincoln University, PO Box 179, Lincoln University, PA 19352-0999. *Phone:* 610-932-8300 Ext. 3206. *Toll-free phone:* 800-215-4858. *Fax:* 610-932-1209. *E-mail:* admiss@lu.lincoln.edu.

LOCK HAVEN UNIVERSITY OF PENNSYLVANIA
Lock Haven, Pennsylvania

- **State-supported** comprehensive, founded 1870, part of Pennsylvania State System of Higher Education
- **Calendar** semesters
- **Degrees** associate, bachelor's, and master's
- **Small-town** 165-acre campus
- **Endowment** $5.8 million
- **Coed,** 4,081 undergraduate students, 93% full-time, 59% women, 41% men
- **Moderately difficult** entrance level, 81% of applicants were admitted

Lock Haven University pursues a special mission in international education that features diverse student-faculty exchanges and overseas student teaching. Students from all majors have an opportunity to participate in an exchange program during any year of study in Australia, Canada, China, Costa Rica, Croatia, England, Finland, France, Germany, Italy, Japan, Mexico, Morocco, Poland, Russia, Scotland, Spain, Taiwan, Tunisia, or Ukraine.

Undergraduates 3,782 full-time, 299 part-time. Students come from 24 states and territories, 35 other countries, 9% are from out of state, 3% African American, 0.7% Asian American or Pacific Islander, 1% Hispanic American, 0.3% Native American, 1% international, 4% transferred in, 55% live on campus. *Retention:* 74% of 2001 full-time freshmen returned.

Lock Haven University of Pennsylvania (continued)

Freshmen *Admission:* 3,451 applied, 2,800 admitted, 1,021 enrolled. *Test scores:* SAT verbal scores over 500: 40%; SAT math scores over 500: 44%; ACT scores over 18: 63%; SAT verbal scores over 600: 6%; SAT math scores over 600: 8%; ACT scores over 24: 20%.

Faculty *Total:* 231, 87% full-time, 47% with terminal degrees. *Student/faculty ratio:* 18:1.

Majors Accounting; advertising; anthropology; art; athletic training/sports medicine; biological/physical sciences; biology; broadcast journalism; business administration; business economics; cell biology; chemistry; computer science; criminal justice/law enforcement administration; early childhood education; earth sciences; ecology; economics; education; elementary education; engineering; engineering science; English; environmental biology; French; geography; geology; German; health education; health professions and related sciences; health science; history; humanities; information sciences/systems; international relations; journalism; Latin American studies; liberal arts and sciences/liberal studies; management information systems/business data processing; mass communications; mathematics; medical technology; music; natural sciences; nursing; philosophy; physical education; physical sciences; physics; political science; pre-dentistry; pre-law; pre-medicine; pre-veterinary studies; psychology; public relations; radio/television broadcasting; recreational therapy; recreation/leisure facilities management; recreation/leisure studies; science education; secondary education; social sciences; social work; sociology; Spanish; special education; speech/rhetorical studies; sport/fitness administration; theater arts/drama.

Academic Programs *Special study options:* academic remediation for entering students, accelerated degree program, adult/continuing education programs, advanced placement credit, cooperative education, distance learning, double majors, honors programs, independent study, internships, off-campus study, part-time degree program, services for LD students, student-designed majors, study abroad, summer session for credit. *ROTC:* Army (b). *Unusual degree programs:* 3-2 engineering with Pennsylvania State University University Park Campus.

Library Stevenson Library with 366,342 titles, 1,510 serial subscriptions, 8,158 audiovisual materials, an OPAC, a Web page.

Computers on Campus 270 computers available on campus for general student use. A campuswide network can be accessed from student residence rooms and from off campus. At least one staffed computer lab available.

Student Life *Housing:* on-campus residence required through sophomore year. *Options:* coed, women-only. *Activities and Organizations:* drama/theater group, student-run newspaper, radio and television station, choral group, marching band, student government, Residence Hall Association, fraternities, sororities, national fraternities, national sororities. *Campus security:* 24-hour emergency response devices and patrols. *Student Services:* health clinic, personal/psychological counseling.

Athletics Member NCAA. All Division II except wrestling (Division I). *Intercollegiate sports:* baseball M(s), basketball M(s)/W(s), cross-country running M(s)/W(s), field hockey W(s), football M(s), lacrosse W(s), soccer M(s)/W(s), softball W(s), swimming W(s), track and field M(s)/W(s), volleyball W(s), wrestling M(s). *Intramural sports:* badminton M/W, basketball M/W, cross-country running M/W, field hockey W, football M, golf M/W, ice hockey M, lacrosse M/W, racquetball M/W, rugby M/W, skiing (cross-country) M/W, skiing (downhill) M/W, soccer M/W, softball M/W, swimming M/W, tennis M/W, track and field M/W, volleyball M/W, water polo M, weight lifting M/W, wrestling M.

Standardized Tests *Required:* SAT I or ACT (for admission).

Costs (2001–02) *Tuition:* state resident $4016 full-time, $167 per credit part-time; nonresident $8040 full-time, $335 per credit part-time. Full-time tuition and fees vary according to location. Part-time tuition and fees vary according to course load and location. *Required fees:* $868 full-time, $45 per credit. *Room and board:* $4776; room only: $2624. Room and board charges vary according to board plan and housing facility. *Payment plans:* installment, deferred payment. *Waivers:* minority students, senior citizens, and employees or children of employees.

Financial Aid Of all full-time matriculated undergraduates who enrolled in 2001, 3345 applied for aid, 2853 were judged to have need, 1483 had their need fully met. 235 Federal Work-Study jobs (averaging $923). 1050 State and other part-time jobs (averaging $643). In 2001, 190 non-need-based awards were made. *Average percent of need met:* 78%. *Average financial aid package:* $6860. *Average need-based loan:* $4400. *Average need-based gift aid:* $3350. *Average non-need based aid:* $3500. *Average indebtedness upon graduation:* $16,472.

Applying *Options:* electronic application, deferred entrance. *Application fee:* $25. *Required:* high school transcript. *Required for some:* letters of recommendation, interview. *Recommended:* essay or personal statement, minimum 3.0 GPA. *Application deadline:* rolling (freshmen), rolling (transfers). *Notification:* continuous (freshmen).

Admissions Contact Mr. Steven Lee, Director of Admissions, Lock Haven University of Pennsylvania, Office of Admission, Akeley Hall, Lock Haven, PA 17745. *Phone:* 570-893-2027. *Toll-free phone:* 800-332-8900 (in-state); 800-233-8978 (out-of-state). *Fax:* 570-893-2201. *E-mail:* admissions@lhup.edu.

LYCOMING COLLEGE
Williamsport, Pennsylvania

- **Independent United Methodist** 4-year, founded 1812
- **Calendar** semesters
- **Degree** bachelor's
- **Small-town** 35-acre campus
- **Endowment** $84.0 million
- **Coed,** 1,429 undergraduate students, 97% full-time, 55% women, 45% men
- **Moderately difficult** entrance level, 80% of applicants were admitted

Undergraduates 1,386 full-time, 43 part-time. Students come from 21 states and territories, 9 other countries, 21% are from out of state, 2% African American, 0.6% Asian American or Pacific Islander, 0.7% Hispanic American, 0.4% Native American, 0.8% international, 3% transferred in, 83% live on campus. *Retention:* 81% of 2001 full-time freshmen returned.

Freshmen *Admission:* 1,431 applied, 1,144 admitted, 408 enrolled. *Average high school GPA:* 3.20. *Test scores:* SAT verbal scores over 500: 68%; SAT math scores over 500: 65%; SAT verbal scores over 600: 23%; SAT math scores over 600: 20%; SAT verbal scores over 700: 2%; SAT math scores over 700: 2%.

Faculty *Total:* 103, 85% full-time, 83% with terminal degrees. *Student/faculty ratio:* 13:1.

Majors Accounting; actuarial science; American studies; anthropology; archaeology; art; art education; art history; astronomy; biology; business administration; business marketing and marketing management; chemistry; computer science; creative writing; criminal justice/law enforcement administration; economics; education; elementary education; English; finance; fine/studio arts; French; German; graphic design/commercial art/illustration; history; interdisciplinary studies; international business; international relations; literature; mass communications; mathematics; medical technology; music; music teacher education; philosophy; physics; political science; pre-dentistry; pre-law; pre-medicine; pre-veterinary studies; psychology; religious studies; secondary education; sociology; Spanish; theater arts/drama.

Academic Programs *Special study options:* accelerated degree program, advanced placement credit, double majors, honors programs, independent study, internships, off-campus study, part-time degree program, services for LD students, student-designed majors, study abroad, summer session for credit. *ROTC:* Army (c). *Unusual degree programs:* 3-2 engineering with Pennsylvania State University University Park Campus,; forestry with Duke University; environmental management with Duke University.

Library Snowden Library plus 1 other with 165,000 titles, 950 serial subscriptions, an OPAC, a Web page.

Computers on Campus 140 computers available on campus for general student use. A campuswide network can be accessed from student residence rooms and from off campus. Internet access, online (class) registration, at least one staffed computer lab available.

Student Life *Housing:* on-campus residence required through senior year. *Options:* coed, women-only. *Activities and Organizations:* drama/theater group, student-run newspaper, radio and television station, choral group, Radio Club (WRLC), Wilderness Club, student newspaper, Campus Ministry, Habitat for Humanity, national fraternities, national sororities. *Campus security:* 24-hour emergency response devices and patrols, student patrols, late-night transport/escort service, controlled dormitory access. *Student Services:* health clinic, personal/psychological counseling.

Athletics Member NCAA. All Division III. *Intercollegiate sports:* basketball M/W, crew M(c)/W(c), cross-country running M/W, football M, golf M, lacrosse M/W, soccer M/W, softball W, swimming M/W, tennis M/W, track and field M/W, volleyball W, water polo M(c)/W(c), wrestling M. *Intramural sports:* basketball M/W, football M/W, soccer M/W, softball M/W, volleyball M/W.

Standardized Tests *Required:* SAT I or ACT (for admission).

Costs (2001–02) *Comprehensive fee:* $24,780 includes full-time tuition ($19,104), mandatory fees ($300), and room and board ($5376). Part-time tuition: $597 per credit. *Room and board:* Room and board charges vary according to housing facility. *Payment plan:* installment. *Waivers:* employees or children of employees.

Financial Aid Of all full-time matriculated undergraduates who enrolled in 2001, 1302 applied for aid, 1123 were judged to have need, 313 had their need fully met. 497 Federal Work-Study jobs (averaging $1281). In 2001, 121 non-need-based awards were made. *Average percent of need met:* 86%. *Average* *financial aid package:* $16,232. *Average need-based loan:* $3437. *Average need-based gift aid:* $12,114. *Average non-need based aid:* $7194. *Average indebtedness upon graduation:* $15,100.

Applying *Options:* common application, electronic application, early admission, deferred entrance. *Application fee:* $35. *Required:* essay or personal statement, high school transcript, 2 letters of recommendation. *Recommended:* minimum 2.3 GPA, interview. *Application deadlines:* 4/1 (freshmen), 6/1 (transfers). *Notification:* continuous (freshmen).

Admissions Contact Mr. James Spencer, Dean of Admissions and Financial Aid, Lycoming College, Admissions House, 700 College Place, Williamsport, PA 17701. *Phone:* 570-321-4026. *Toll-free phone:* 800-345-3920 Ext. 4026. *Fax:* 570-321-4317. *E-mail:* admissions@lycoming.edu.

MANSFIELD UNIVERSITY OF PENNSYLVANIA

Mansfield, Pennsylvania

- **State-supported** comprehensive, founded 1857, part of Pennsylvania State System of Higher Education
- **Calendar** semesters
- **Degrees** associate, bachelor's, master's, and postbachelor's certificates
- **Small-town** 205-acre campus
- **Endowment** $5.3 million
- **Coed,** 3,018 undergraduate students, 89% full-time, 59% women, 41% men
- **Moderately difficult** entrance level, 73% of applicants were admitted

Mansfield University students enjoy a private school environment at a public school price. A small university in the scenic mountains of north-central Pennsylvania, Mansfield prepares students seeking their first employment or graduate school. Mansfield offers more than 80 high-quality programs of study in the liberal arts tradition. Classes are small, and the learning experience is personalized. A new, technologically advanced library, fitness center, and student union provide students with many experiences outside the classroom.

Undergraduates 2,690 full-time, 328 part-time. Students come from 14 states and territories, 13 other countries, 22% are from out of state, 3% African American, 0.5% Asian American or Pacific Islander, 0.9% Hispanic American, 0.8% Native American, 1% international, 9% transferred in, 60% live on campus. *Retention:* 67% of 2001 full-time freshmen returned.

Freshmen *Admission:* 2,314 applied, 1,699 admitted, 650 enrolled. *Average high school GPA:* 3.20. *Test scores:* SAT verbal scores over 500: 46%; SAT math scores over 500: 43%; ACT scores over 18: 81%; SAT verbal scores over 600: 10%; SAT math scores over 600: 7%; ACT scores over 24: 17%; SAT verbal scores over 700: 1%; SAT math scores over 700: 1%.

Faculty *Total:* 191, 81% full-time. *Student/faculty ratio:* 16:1.

Majors Accounting; actuarial science; anthropology; applied art; art; art education; art history; biochemistry; biological/physical sciences; biology; biology education; broadcast journalism; business administration; business marketing and marketing management; cartography; cell biology; chemistry; chemistry education; city/community/regional planning; clinical psychology; computer/information sciences; computer science; criminal justice/law enforcement administration; dietetics; early childhood education; earth sciences; economics; education; elementary education; English; English education; environmental biology; environmental science; fine/studio arts; fishing sciences; food services technology; French; French language education; geography; German; German language education; history; human resources management; human services; information sciences/systems; international business; international relations; journalism; liberal arts and sciences/liberal studies; mass communications; mathematics; mathematics education; medical technology; music; music business management/merchandising; music (general performance); music (piano and organ performance); music teacher education; music therapy; music (voice and choral/opera performance); nursing; philosophy; physical sciences; physics; physics education; political science; pre-law; pre-medicine; psychology; public relations; radiological science; radio/television broadcasting; respiratory therapy; science education; secondary education; social science education; social sciences; social studies education; social work; sociology; Spanish; Spanish language education; special education; speech/rhetorical studies; technical/business writing; theater arts/drama; travel/tourism management.

Academic Programs *Special study options:* academic remediation for entering students, accelerated degree program, adult/continuing education programs, advanced placement credit, distance learning, double majors, freshman honors college, honors programs, independent study, internships, off-campus study, part-time degree program, services for LD students, student-designed majors, study abroad, summer session for credit.

Library North Hill Library with 237,911 titles, 3,110 serial subscriptions, 2,693 audiovisual materials, an OPAC, a Web page.

Computers on Campus 371 computers available on campus for general student use. A campuswide network can be accessed from student residence rooms and from off campus. Internet access, at least one staffed computer lab available.

Student Life *Housing:* on-campus residence required through senior year. *Options:* coed, women-only. *Activities and Organizations:* drama/theater group, student-run newspaper, radio station, choral group, marching band, Mansfield International Student Organization, P.R. Society, PSEA, Ski Club, activities council, national fraternities, national sororities. *Campus security:* 24-hour emergency response devices and patrols, student patrols, late-night transport/escort service, controlled dormitory access. *Student Services:* health clinic, personal/psychological counseling, women's center.

Athletics Member NCAA. All Division II. *Intercollegiate sports:* baseball M(s), basketball M(s)/W(s), cross-country running M/W, field hockey W(s), football M(s), soccer W(s), softball W(s), swimming W, track and field M/W. *Intramural sports:* badminton M/W, basketball M/W, bowling M/W, cross-country running M/W, equestrian sports M/W, football M/W, golf M/W, racquetball M/W, skiing (cross-country) M/W, skiing (downhill) M/W, soccer M/W, softball M/W, swimming M/W, tennis M/W, track and field M/W, volleyball M/W, water polo M/W, weight lifting M/W.

Standardized Tests *Required:* SAT I or ACT (for admission).

Costs (2001–02) *One-time required fee:* $50. *Tuition:* state resident $4016 full-time, $167 per credit part-time; nonresident $10,040 full-time, $418 per credit part-time. Part-time tuition and fees vary according to course load. *Required fees:* $1080 full-time, $17 per credit, $153 per term part-time. *Room and board:* $4552. Room and board charges vary according to board plan. *Payment plans:* installment, deferred payment. *Waivers:* senior citizens and employees or children of employees.

Financial Aid Of all full-time matriculated undergraduates who enrolled in 2001, 1923 applied for aid, 1755 were judged to have need, 225 had their need fully met. 268 Federal Work-Study jobs (averaging $1490). 256 State and other part-time jobs. *Average financial aid package:* $1920. *Average non-need based aid:* $1334. *Average indebtedness upon graduation:* $20,862.

Applying *Options:* electronic application, early admission, deferred entrance. *Application fee:* $25. *Required:* high school transcript. *Required for some:* interview. *Recommended:* essay or personal statement, minimum 2.5 GPA, letters of recommendation. *Application deadline:* rolling (freshmen), rolling (transfers). *Notification:* continuous (freshmen).

Admissions Contact Mr. Brian D. Barden, Director of Admissions, Mansfield University of Pennsylvania, Alumni Hall, Mansfield, PA 16933. *Phone:* 570-662-4813. *Toll-free phone:* 800-577-6826. *Fax:* 570-662-4121. *E-mail:* admissions@mnsfld.edu.

MARYWOOD UNIVERSITY

Scranton, Pennsylvania

- **Independent Roman Catholic** comprehensive, founded 1915
- **Calendar** semesters
- **Degrees** certificates, associate, bachelor's, master's, doctoral, post-master's, and postbachelor's certificates
- **Suburban** 115-acre campus
- **Endowment** $25.1 million
- **Coed,** 1,668 undergraduate students, 86% full-time, 72% women, 28% men
- **Moderately difficult** entrance level, 81% of applicants were admitted

Building on its tradition of preparing students from around the world to be successful in professional life and to contribute to the welfare and happiness of others, Marywood continues to strengthen and expand its undergraduate and graduate programs in the arts and sciences. Using its attractive 115-acre campus in northeastern Pennsylvania creatively, Marywood continues to expand its facilities with a new Studio Arts Center and Center for Healthy Families. Marywood is committed to a remarkable scholarship/grant program.

Undergraduates 1,442 full-time, 226 part-time. Students come from 18 states and territories, 20 other countries, 20% are from out of state, 0.9% African American, 0.7% Asian American or Pacific Islander, 2% Hispanic American, 0.2% Native American, 1% international, 12% transferred in, 32% live on campus. *Retention:* 81% of 2001 full-time freshmen returned.

Freshmen *Admission:* 1,206 applied, 981 admitted, 291 enrolled. *Average high school GPA:* 3.17. *Test scores:* SAT verbal scores over 500: 61%; SAT math scores over 500: 51%; ACT scores over 18: 90%; SAT verbal scores over 600: 16%; SAT math scores over 600: 13%; ACT scores over 24: 30%; SAT verbal scores over 700: 3%; SAT math scores over 700: 3%.

Faculty *Total:* 302, 43% full-time, 36% with terminal degrees. *Student/faculty ratio:* 12:1.

Marywood University (continued)

Majors Accounting; applied art; art education; arts management; art therapy; athletic training/sports medicine; aviation management; biological specializations related; biology; business administration; business marketing and marketing management; computer/information sciences; design/visual communications; dietetics; drama/dance education; education; education related; elementary education; English; environmental science; financial planning; fine/studio arts; French; health education; health/physical education; health services administration; home economics education; hospitality management; interdisciplinary studies; liberal arts and sciences/liberal studies; mathematics; medical technology; music; music teacher education; music therapy; nursing; paralegal/legal assistant; physical education; physician assistant; psychology; public relations; radio/television broadcasting; religious education; religious music; religious studies; retail management; science education; secondary education; social sciences; social sciences and history related; social work; Spanish; special education; speech-language pathology/audiology; telecommunications; theater arts/drama; visual/performing arts.

Academic Programs *Special study options:* academic remediation for entering students, accelerated degree program, adult/continuing education programs, advanced placement credit, distance learning, double majors, English as a second language, external degree program, honors programs, independent study, internships, off-campus study, part-time degree program, services for LD students, student-designed majors, study abroad, summer session for credit. *ROTC:* Army (c), Air Force (c).

Library Learning Resources Center with 219,852 titles, 984 serial subscriptions, 43,717 audiovisual materials, an OPAC, a Web page.

Computers on Campus 350 computers available on campus for general student use. A campuswide network can be accessed from student residence rooms and from off campus. Internet access, online (class) registration, at least one staffed computer lab available.

Student Life *Housing:* on-campus residence required through sophomore year. *Options:* coed, men-only, women-only, disabled students. *Activities and Organizations:* drama/theater group, student-run newspaper, radio and television station, choral group, Outdoor Adventure Club, Psi Chi, International Club, Peer Mediators, Speech and Hearing. *Campus security:* 24-hour emergency response devices and patrols, late-night transport/escort service, controlled dormitory access, apartments with deadbolts, self-defense education, lighted pathways, seminars on safety. *Student Services:* health clinic, personal/psychological counseling.

Athletics Member NCAA. All Division III. *Intercollegiate sports:* baseball M, basketball M/W, cross-country running M/W, field hockey W, soccer M/W, softball W, tennis M/W, volleyball W. *Intramural sports:* badminton M/W, baseball M, basketball M/W, field hockey W, football M, golf M/W, lacrosse M(c)/W, racquetball M/W, soccer M(c)/W(c), softball M/W, swimming M/W, table tennis M/W, tennis M/W, volleyball M/W.

Standardized Tests *Required:* SAT I or ACT (for admission).

Costs (2001–02) *Comprehensive fee:* $24,739 includes full-time tuition ($16,640), mandatory fees ($789), and room and board ($7310). Part-time tuition: $520 per credit. Part-time tuition and fees vary according to course load. *Required fees:* $125 per term part-time. *Room and board:* College room only: $3950. Room and board charges vary according to board plan and housing facility. *Payment plans:* installment, deferred payment. *Waivers:* senior citizens and employees or children of employees.

Financial Aid Of all full-time matriculated undergraduates who enrolled in 2001, 1416 applied for aid, 1191 were judged to have need, 295 had their need fully met. In 2001, 248 non-need-based awards were made. *Average percent of need met:* 72%. *Average financial aid package:* $14,448. *Average need-based gift aid:* $9677. *Average non-need based aid:* $6523. *Average indebtedness upon graduation:* $17,125.

Applying *Options:* common application, electronic application, early admission, deferred entrance. *Application fee:* $25. *Required:* high school transcript, 1 letter of recommendation. *Required for some:* essay or personal statement, interview. *Recommended:* essay or personal statement, interview. *Application deadline:* rolling (freshmen), rolling (transfers). *Notification:* continuous (freshmen).

Admissions Contact Mr. Robert W. Reese, Director of Admissions, Marywood University, 2300 Adams Avenue, Scranton, PA 18509-1598. *Phone:* 570-348-6234. *Toll-free phone:* 800-346-5014. *Fax:* 570-961-4763. *E-mail:* ugadm@ac.marywood.edu.

MCP Hahnemann University
Philadelphia, Pennsylvania

- **Independent** university, founded 1848
- **Calendar** semesters
- **Degrees** certificates, associate, bachelor's, master's, doctoral, first professional, post-master's, and postbachelor's certificates
- **Urban** campus
- **Endowment** $55.2 million
- **Coed,** 672 undergraduate students, 60% full-time, 66% women, 34% men
- **Moderately difficult** entrance level, 72% of applicants were admitted

Undergraduates 403 full-time, 269 part-time. Students come from 25 states and territories, 37% are from out of state, 21% African American, 4% Asian American or Pacific Islander, 3% Hispanic American, 0.6% Native American, 3% international, 35% transferred in, 2% live on campus.

Freshmen *Admission:* 83 applied, 60 admitted, 37 enrolled.

Faculty *Total:* 187, 95% full-time, 86% with terminal degrees. *Student/faculty ratio:* 9:1.

Majors Alcohol/drug abuse counseling; biomedical science; emergency medical technology; health science; medical radiologic technology; nursing; perfusion technology; physician assistant; psychiatric/mental health services.

Academic Programs *Special study options:* adult/continuing education programs, cooperative education, distance learning, internships, part-time degree program, summer session for credit.

Library University Library plus 4 others with 83,743 titles, 3,238 serial subscriptions, 2,468 audiovisual materials, an OPAC, a Web page.

Computers on Campus 130 computers available on campus for general student use. A campuswide network can be accessed from student residence rooms and from off campus. At least one staffed computer lab available.

Student Life *Activities and Organizations:* Homeless Clinics Project, student government, Minority Student Association, Pre-Med Society, Physician Assistant Club. *Campus security:* 24-hour emergency response devices and patrols, late-night transport/escort service, controlled dormitory access. *Student Services:* health clinic, personal/psychological counseling.

Athletics *Intercollegiate sports:* volleyball M/W. *Intramural sports:* basketball M/W, racquetball M/W, soccer M/W, softball M/W.

Standardized Tests *Required:* SAT I or ACT (for admission).

Costs (2001–02) *Comprehensive fee:* $18,510 includes full-time tuition ($10,280), mandatory fees ($130), and room and board ($8100). Full-time tuition and fees vary according to program. Part-time tuition: $500 per credit. Part-time tuition and fees vary according to course load and program. *Required fees:* $68 per term part-time. *Room and board:* Room and board charges vary according to housing facility. *Payment plan:* installment. *Waivers:* employees or children of employees.

Financial Aid Of all full-time matriculated undergraduates who enrolled in 2001, 340 applied for aid, 311 were judged to have need, 9 had their need fully met. In 2001, 20 non-need-based awards were made. *Average percent of need met:* 33%. *Average financial aid package:* $7930. *Average need-based gift aid:* $5751. *Average non-need based aid:* $920. *Average indebtedness upon graduation:* $36,797. *Financial aid deadline:* 5/1.

Applying *Options:* deferred entrance. *Application fee:* $35. *Required:* essay or personal statement, high school transcript. *Required for some:* minimum 2.0 GPA, letters of recommendation, interview, class rank, community/work experience. *Application deadlines:* 6/1 (freshmen), 6/1 (transfers). *Notification:* continuous (freshmen).

Admissions Contact Ms. Jarmila H. Force, Associate Director of Enrollment Management, MCP Hahnemann University, 245 North 15th Street, Mail Stop 472, Philadelphia, PA 19102-1192. *Phone:* 215-762-4671. *Toll-free phone:* 800-2-DREXEL Ext. 6333. *Fax:* 215-762-6194. *E-mail:* enroll@mcphu.edu.

Mercyhurst College
Erie, Pennsylvania

- **Independent Roman Catholic** comprehensive, founded 1926
- **Calendar** 4-3-3
- **Degrees** certificates, associate, bachelor's, master's, and postbachelor's certificates
- **Suburban** 88-acre campus with easy access to Buffalo
- **Endowment** $9.9 million
- **Coed,** 3,209 undergraduate students, 85% full-time, 62% women, 38% men
- **Moderately difficult** entrance level, 77% of applicants were admitted

Mercyhurst emphasizes the role of the liberal arts as a basis for sound career preparation and many other life objectives. With this balance in mind, the College supports a wide range of programs. Mercyhurst College strives constantly to remain distinctive in the choice of its academic offerings. For additional information, students should call 814-824-2202 or 800-825-1926 (toll-free) or visit the Web site (www.mercyhurst.edu).

Undergraduates 2,738 full-time, 471 part-time. Students come from 41 states and territories, 12 other countries, 45% are from out of state, 4% African American, 0.7% Asian American or Pacific Islander, 1.0% Hispanic American, 0.2% Native American, 3% international, 2% transferred in, 70% live on campus. *Retention:* 80% of 2001 full-time freshmen returned.

Freshmen *Admission:* 2,220 applied, 1,709 admitted, 996 enrolled. *Average high school GPA:* 3.40. *Test scores:* SAT verbal scores over 500: 66%; SAT math scores over 500: 65%; ACT scores over 18: 93%; SAT verbal scores over 600: 21%; SAT math scores over 600: 18%; ACT scores over 24: 29%; SAT verbal scores over 700: 2%; SAT math scores over 700: 1%; ACT scores over 30: 2%.

Faculty *Total:* 224, 63% full-time, 42% with terminal degrees. *Student/faculty ratio:* 19:1.

Majors Accounting; actuarial science; advertising; anthropology; archaeology; art; art education; arts management; art therapy; athletic training/sports medicine; biology; broadcast journalism; business administration; business education; business marketing and marketing management; chemistry; clothing/textiles; computer science; corrections; creative writing; criminal justice/law enforcement administration; culinary arts; dance; dance therapy; dietetics; early childhood education; earth sciences; education; elementary education; English; fashion merchandising; finance; fine/studio arts; French; geology; German; history; home economics; home economics education; hospitality management; hotel and restaurant management; human ecology; humanities; human resources management; information sciences/systems; insurance/risk management; interior design; journalism; law enforcement/police science; liberal arts and sciences/liberal studies; mass communications; materials engineering; mathematical statistics; mathematics; medical technology; music; music teacher education; music therapy; music (voice and choral/opera performance); nursing; paleontology; pastoral counseling; petroleum technology; philosophy; physical therapy; physics; political science; pre-dentistry; pre-law; pre-medicine; pre-veterinary studies; psychology; public administration; public relations; purchasing/contracts management; radio/television broadcasting; recreation/leisure facilities management; recreation/leisure studies; religious education; religious studies; science education; sculpture; secondary education; secretarial science; social sciences; social work; sociology; Spanish; special education; sport/fitness administration; technical/business writing; textile arts; wind/percussion instruments.

Academic Programs *Special study options:* academic remediation for entering students, accelerated degree program, adult/continuing education programs, advanced placement credit, cooperative education, double majors, external degree program, freshman honors college, honors programs, independent study, internships, off-campus study, part-time degree program, services for LD students, student-designed majors, study abroad, summer session for credit. *ROTC:* Army (c). *Unusual degree programs:* 3-2 nursing with University of Rochester, Catholic University of America, Case Western Reserve University; Law with Duquesene University.

Library Hammermill Library plus 1 other with 123,467 titles, 849 serial subscriptions, 8,051 audiovisual materials, an OPAC, a Web page.

Computers on Campus 350 computers available on campus for general student use. A campuswide network can be accessed from student residence rooms and from off campus. Internet access, at least one staffed computer lab available.

Student Life *Housing:* on-campus residence required through sophomore year. *Options:* men-only, women-only. *Activities and Organizations:* drama/theater group, student-run newspaper, radio and television station, choral group, student government, chorus, Admission Ambassadors, Amnesty International, The Merciad. *Campus security:* 24-hour emergency response devices and patrols, campus-wide camera system. *Student Services:* health clinic, personal/psychological counseling.

Athletics Member NCAA. All Division II except men's and women's ice hockey (Division I), lacrosse (Division I). *Intercollegiate sports:* baseball M(s), basketball M(s)/W(s), crew M(s)/W(s), cross-country running M(s)/W(s), field hockey W(s), football M, golf M(s)/W(s), ice hockey M(s)/W(s), lacrosse M(s)/W(s), soccer M(s)/W(s), softball W(s), tennis M(s)/W(s), volleyball M(s)/W(s), water polo M(s)/W(s), wrestling M(s). *Intramural sports:* basketball M/W, football M, skiing (cross-country) M/W, skiing (downhill) M/W, tennis M/W, volleyball M/W.

Standardized Tests *Required:* SAT I or ACT (for admission).

Costs (2002–03) *Comprehensive fee:* $21,849 includes full-time tuition ($14,820), mandatory fees ($1050), and room and board ($5979). Part-time tuition: $494 per credit. Part-time tuition and fees vary according to course load and location. *Required fees:* $350 per term part-time. *Room and board:* College room only: $2989. Room and board charges vary according to board plan and housing facility. *Payment plan:* installment. *Waivers:* adult students and employees or children of employees.

Financial Aid Of all full-time matriculated undergraduates who enrolled in 2001, 2591 applied for aid. 230 Federal Work-Study jobs (averaging $1100). In 2001, 264 non-need-based awards were made. *Average non-need based aid:* $1841. *Average indebtedness upon graduation:* $17,100.

Applying *Options:* common application, electronic application, early admission, deferred entrance. *Application fee:* $30. *Required:* high school transcript, minimum 2.75 GPA. *Required for some:* essay or personal statement, interview. *Recommended:* 2 letters of recommendation. *Application deadline:* rolling (freshmen), rolling (transfers). *Notification:* continuous (freshmen).

Admissions Contact Mr. Robin Engel, Director of Undergraduate Admissions, Mercyhurst College, 501 East 38th Street, Erie, PA 16546-0001. *Phone:* 814-824-2573. *Toll-free phone:* 800-825-1926. *Fax:* 814-824-2071. *E-mail:* admug@mercyhurst.edu.

MESSIAH COLLEGE
Grantham, Pennsylvania

- **Independent interdenominational** 4-year, founded 1909
- **Calendar** semesters
- **Degree** bachelor's
- **Small-town** 400-acre campus
- **Endowment** $106.3 million
- **Coed,** 2,858 undergraduate students, 98% full-time, 61% women, 39% men
- **Moderately difficult** entrance level, 78% of applicants were admitted

Undergraduates 2,797 full-time, 61 part-time. Students come from 38 states and territories, 25 other countries, 48% are from out of state, 2% African American, 1% Asian American or Pacific Islander, 2% Hispanic American, 0.2% Native American, 2% international, 3% transferred in, 86% live on campus. *Retention:* 85% of 2001 full-time freshmen returned.

Freshmen *Admission:* 2,231 applied, 1,742 admitted, 702 enrolled. *Average high school GPA:* 3.69. *Test scores:* SAT verbal scores over 500: 90%; SAT math scores over 500: 92%; ACT scores over 18: 98%; SAT verbal scores over 600: 46%; SAT math scores over 600: 47%; ACT scores over 24: 70%; SAT verbal scores over 700: 11%; SAT math scores over 700: 8%; ACT scores over 30: 17%.

Faculty *Total:* 262, 60% full-time. *Student/faculty ratio:* 13:1.

Majors Accounting; adapted physical education; art education; art history; athletic training/sports medicine; biblical studies; biochemistry; biology; biology education; business administration; business economics; business management/administrative services related; business marketing and marketing management; chemistry; chemistry education; civil engineering; communications; computer science; dietetics; early childhood education; economics; elementary education; engineering; English; English education; environmental science; exercise sciences; family/community studies; fine/studio arts; French; French language education; German; German language education; history; humanities; human resources management; information sciences/systems; international business; journalism; mathematics; mathematics education; music; music teacher education; nursing; philosophy; physical education; physics; political science; psychology; radio/television broadcasting; recreation/leisure studies; religious education; religious studies; social studies education; social work; sociology; Spanish; Spanish language education; theater arts/drama.

Academic Programs *Special study options:* academic remediation for entering students, accelerated degree program, adult/continuing education programs, advanced placement credit, double majors, freshman honors college, honors programs, independent study, internships, off-campus study, part-time degree program, services for LD students, student-designed majors, study abroad, summer session for credit.

Library Murray Library with 247,627 titles, 1,260 serial subscriptions, 12,930 audiovisual materials, an OPAC, a Web page.

Computers on Campus 479 computers available on campus for general student use. A campuswide network can be accessed from student residence rooms. Internet access, online (class) registration, at least one staffed computer lab available.

Student Life *Housing:* on-campus residence required through senior year. *Options:* coed, men-only, women-only, disabled students. *Activities and Organizations:* drama/theater group, student-run newspaper, radio station, choral group, outreach teams, student government, music ensembles, Small Group Program, Outdoors Club. *Campus security:* 24-hour emergency response devices and patrols, student patrols, late-night transport/escort service, controlled dormitory access, bicycle patrols, security lighting, self-defense classes, prevention/awareness programs. *Student Services:* health clinic, personal/psychological counseling.

Athletics Member NCAA. All Division III. *Intercollegiate sports:* baseball M, basketball M/W, cross-country running M/W, field hockey W, golf M, lacrosse M/W, soccer M/W, softball W, tennis M/W, track and field M/W, volleyball W, wrestling M. *Intramural sports:* basketball M/W, racquetball M/W, soccer M/W, track and field M(c)/W(c), volleyball M/W.

Messiah College (continued)

Standardized Tests *Required for some:* SAT I or ACT (for admission).

Costs (2001–02) *Comprehensive fee:* $23,180 includes full-time tuition ($16,860), mandatory fees ($350), and room and board ($5970). Part-time tuition: $705 per credit. *Required fees:* $15 per credit. *Room and board:* College room only: $3080. Room and board charges vary according to board plan. *Payment plan:* installment. *Waivers:* minority students, children of alumni, adult students, senior citizens, and employees or children of employees.

Financial Aid Of all full-time matriculated undergraduates who enrolled in 2001, 2231 applied for aid, 1955 were judged to have need, 420 had their need fully met. 755 Federal Work-Study jobs (averaging $1912). 604 State and other part-time jobs (averaging $2339). In 2001, 576 non-need-based awards were made. *Average percent of need met:* 72%. *Average financial aid package:* $12,387. *Average need-based loan:* $3698. *Average need-based gift aid:* $5392. *Average non-need based aid:* $4206. *Average indebtedness upon graduation:* $17,183.

Applying *Options:* common application, electronic application, early admission, early decision, early action, deferred entrance. *Application fee:* $30. *Required:* essay or personal statement, high school transcript, 2 letters of recommendation. *Recommended:* minimum 3.0 GPA, interview. *Application deadline:* rolling (freshmen), rolling (transfers). *Early decision:* 10/15. *Notification:* continuous (freshmen), 11/1 (early decision), 12/1 (early action).

Admissions Contact Mr. William G. Strausbaugh, Dean for Enrollment Management, Messiah College, One College Avenue, Grantham, PA 17027. *Phone:* 717-691-6000. *Toll-free phone:* 800-382-1349 (in-state); 800-233-4220 (out-of-state). *Fax:* 717-796-5374. *E-mail:* admiss@messiah.edu.

MILLERSVILLE UNIVERSITY OF PENNSYLVANIA
Millersville, Pennsylvania

- **State-supported** comprehensive, founded 1855, part of Pennsylvania State System of Higher Education
- **Calendar** 4-1-4
- **Degrees** associate, bachelor's, master's, post-master's, and postbachelor's certificates
- **Suburban** 190-acre campus
- **Endowment** $794,254
- **Coed,** 6,597 undergraduate students, 87% full-time, 58% women, 42% men
- **Moderately difficult** entrance level, 67% of applicants were admitted

Undergraduates 5,727 full-time, 870 part-time. Students come from 20 states and territories, 4% are from out of state, 6% African American, 1% Asian American or Pacific Islander, 2% Hispanic American, 0.2% Native American, 0.5% international, 5% transferred in, 39% live on campus. *Retention:* 81% of 2001 full-time freshmen returned.

Freshmen *Admission:* 5,462 applied, 3,684 admitted, 1,271 enrolled. *Test scores:* SAT verbal scores over 500: 68%; SAT math scores over 500: 73%; ACT scores over 18: 84%; SAT verbal scores over 600: 19%; SAT math scores over 600: 23%; ACT scores over 24: 25%; SAT verbal scores over 700: 2%; SAT math scores over 700: 2%.

Faculty *Total:* 447, 73% full-time, 71% with terminal degrees. *Student/faculty ratio:* 18:1.

Majors Anthropology; area studies; art; art education; atmospheric sciences; biology; business administration; chemistry; communications; computer science; early childhood education; earth sciences; economics; elementary education; English; English education; foreign languages education; French; geography; geology; German; gerontology; history; industrial arts; industrial arts education; industrial technology; liberal arts and sciences/liberal studies; mathematics; mathematics education; music; music teacher education; nursing science; occupational safety/health technology; oceanography; philosophy; physical science technologies related; physics; political science; psychology; reading education; science education; social studies education; social work; sociology; Spanish; special education.

Academic Programs *Special study options:* academic remediation for entering students, adult/continuing education programs, advanced placement credit, cooperative education, distance learning, double majors, English as a second language, honors programs, independent study, internships, off-campus study, part-time degree program, services for LD students, study abroad, summer session for credit. *ROTC:* Army (b). *Unusual degree programs:* 3-2 engineering with Pennsylvania State University University Park Campus, University of Pennsylvania.

Library Helen A. Ganser Library with 496,162 titles, 2,557 serial subscriptions, 30,163 audiovisual materials, an OPAC, a Web page.

Computers on Campus 425 computers available on campus for general student use. A campuswide network can be accessed from student residence rooms and from off campus. At least one staffed computer lab available.

Student Life *Housing:* on-campus residence required through sophomore year. *Options:* coed, women-only. *Activities and Organizations:* drama/theater group, student-run newspaper, radio and television station, choral group, marching band, Black Student Union, John Newman Association, Student Ambassadors, Resident Student Association, University Activities Board, national fraternities, national sororities. *Campus security:* 24-hour emergency response devices and patrols, student patrols, late-night transport/escort service, controlled dormitory access. *Student Services:* health clinic, personal/psychological counseling, women's center.

Athletics Member NCAA. All Division II except wrestling (Division I). *Intercollegiate sports:* baseball M(s), basketball M(s)/W(s), cross-country running M(s)/W(s), field hockey W(s), football M(s), golf M(s), lacrosse W(s), soccer M(s)/W(s), softball W(s), swimming W(s), tennis M(s)/W(s), track and field M(s)/W(s), volleyball W(s), wrestling M(s). *Intramural sports:* archery M(c)/W(c), badminton M/W, basketball M/W, bowling M(c)/W(c), fencing M(c)/W(c), ice hockey M(c), lacrosse M(c), racquetball M/W, rugby M(c)/W(c), soccer M/W, softball M/W, tennis M/W, volleyball M(c)/W, water polo M(c)/W(c).

Standardized Tests *Required:* SAT I or ACT (for admission).

Costs (2001–02) *Tuition:* state resident $4016 full-time, $167 per credit part-time; nonresident $10,040 full-time, $418 per credit part-time. Part-time tuition and fees vary according to course load. *Required fees:* $1037 full-time, $44 per credit. *Room and board:* $5100. Room and board charges vary according to board plan. *Payment plan:* installment. *Waivers:* employees or children of employees.

Financial Aid Of all full-time matriculated undergraduates who enrolled in 2001, 4039 applied for aid, 2778 were judged to have need, 769 had their need fully met. 515 Federal Work-Study jobs (averaging $1180). 1976 State and other part-time jobs (averaging $1188). In 2001, 1244 non-need-based awards were made. *Average percent of need met:* 93%. *Average financial aid package:* $5573. *Average need-based loan:* $3054. *Average need-based gift aid:* $4586. *Financial aid deadline:* 3/15.

Applying *Options:* common application, electronic application, early admission, deferred entrance. *Application fee:* $30. *Required:* high school transcript, minimum 2.8 GPA. *Required for some:* letters of recommendation. *Recommended:* letters of recommendation. *Application deadline:* rolling (freshmen), rolling (transfers). *Notification:* continuous (freshmen).

Admissions Contact Mr. Darrell Davis, Director of Admissions, Millersville University of Pennsylvania, PO Box 1002, Millersville, PA 17551-0302. *Phone:* 717-872-3371. *Toll-free phone:* 800-MU-ADMIT. *Fax:* 717-871-2147. *E-mail:* admissions@millersville.edu.

MOORE COLLEGE OF ART AND DESIGN
Philadelphia, Pennsylvania

- **Independent** 4-year, founded 1848
- **Calendar** semesters
- **Degree** certificates and bachelor's
- **Urban** 3-acre campus
- **Endowment** $8.6 million
- **Women only,** 613 undergraduate students, 75% full-time
- **Moderately difficult** entrance level, 54% of applicants were admitted

Moore College of Art and Design, the only fully accredited visual arts college for women in the country, grants BFA degrees in nine fine and professional arts disciplines. Moore offers small classes taught by practicing artists, designers, and liberal arts scholars, with an emphasis on preparing women for careers in the visual arts.

Undergraduates 457 full-time, 156 part-time. Students come from 27 states and territories, 8 other countries, 40% are from out of state, 10% African American, 6% Asian American or Pacific Islander, 6% Hispanic American, 0.8% Native American, 3% international, 26% transferred in, 55% live on campus. *Retention:* 87% of 2001 full-time freshmen returned.

Freshmen *Admission:* 398 applied, 214 admitted, 105 enrolled. *Average high school GPA:* 3.08. *Test scores:* SAT verbal scores over 500: 55%; SAT math scores over 500: 40%; SAT verbal scores over 600: 18%; SAT math scores over 600: 9%; SAT verbal scores over 700: 2%.

Faculty *Total:* 104, 34% full-time, 45% with terminal degrees. *Student/faculty ratio:* 8:1.

Majors Art; art education; art history; fashion design/illustration; fine/studio arts; graphic design/commercial art/illustration; interior design; sculpture; textile arts.

Academic Programs *Special study options:* academic remediation for entering students, accelerated degree program, adult/continuing education programs, advanced placement credit, double majors, independent study, internships, part-time degree program, services for LD students, study abroad, summer session for credit.
Library Moore College Library with 33,114 titles, 181 serial subscriptions, 722 audiovisual materials.
Computers on Campus 125 computers available on campus for general student use. Internet access, at least one staffed computer lab available.
Student Life *Housing Options:* women-only. *Activities and Organizations:* student-run newspaper, Student Government Association, Into the Streets, Moore Environment Action Now, Black Student Union, Asian Student Union. *Campus security:* 24-hour patrols, late-night transport/escort service. *Student Services:* health clinic, personal/psychological counseling, women's center.
Athletics *Intramural sports:* volleyball W.
Standardized Tests *Required:* SAT I or ACT (for admission).
Costs (2001–02) *Comprehensive fee:* $23,125 includes full-time tuition ($16,250), mandatory fees ($545), and room and board ($6330). Part-time tuition: $677 per credit. Part-time tuition and fees vary according to course load. *Required fees:* $274 per term part-time. *Room and board:* College room only: $3810. Room and board charges vary according to housing facility. *Payment plan:* installment. *Waivers:* employees or children of employees.
Financial Aid Of all full-time matriculated undergraduates who enrolled in 2001, 389 applied for aid, 353 were judged to have need, 66 had their need fully met. 105 Federal Work-Study jobs (averaging $1071). In 2001, 108 non-need-based awards were made. *Average percent of need met:* 71%. *Average financial aid package:* $13,609. *Average need-based loan:* $5023. *Average need-based gift aid:* $8199. *Average indebtedness upon graduation:* $10,000.
Applying *Options:* common application, early admission, early decision, deferred entrance. *Application fee:* $35. *Required:* high school transcript, minimum 2.5 GPA, 1 letter of recommendation, portfolio. *Required for some:* minimum 3.0 GPA. *Recommended:* essay or personal statement, interview. *Application deadline:* 8/15 (freshmen), rolling (transfers). *Early decision:* 11/15. *Notification:* continuous (freshmen), 11/30 (early decision).
Admissions Contact Wendy Elliott Pyle, Director of Admissions, Moore College of Art and Design, 20th and the Parkway, Philadelphia, PA 19103. *Phone:* 215-568-4515 Ext. 1108. *Toll-free phone:* 800-523-2025. *Fax:* 215-965-8544. *E-mail:* admiss@moore.edu.

MORAVIAN COLLEGE
Bethlehem, Pennsylvania

- **Independent** comprehensive, founded 1742, affiliated with Moravian Church
- **Calendar** semesters
- **Degrees** certificates, bachelor's, master's, and first professional
- **Suburban** 70-acre campus with easy access to Philadelphia
- **Endowment** $63.5 million
- **Coed,** 1,723 undergraduate students, 79% full-time, 60% women, 40% men
- **Moderately difficult** entrance level, 68% of applicants were admitted

Undergraduates 1,357 full-time, 366 part-time. Students come from 19 states and territories, 18 other countries, 37% are from out of state, 2% African American, 1% Asian American or Pacific Islander, 2% Hispanic American, 0.3% Native American, 1% international, 4% transferred in, 73% live on campus. *Retention:* 81% of 2001 full-time freshmen returned.
Freshmen *Admission:* 1,502 applied, 1,014 admitted, 378 enrolled. *Test scores:* SAT verbal scores over 500: 81%; SAT math scores over 500: 81%; SAT verbal scores over 600: 30%; SAT math scores over 600: 27%; SAT verbal scores over 700: 6%; SAT math scores over 700: 5%.
Faculty *Total:* 177, 58% full-time. *Student/faculty ratio:* 13:1.
Majors Accounting; art; art education; art history; biology; business administration; chemistry; classics; clinical psychology; computer science; criminal justice/law enforcement administration; economics; education; elementary education; English; English related; experimental psychology; fine/studio arts; French; geology; German; graphic design/commercial art/illustration; history; international business; journalism; mathematics; medical technology; music; music teacher education; nursing; organizational psychology; philosophy; physics; political science; psychology; religious studies; science education; secondary education; social sciences; sociology; Spanish.
Academic Programs *Special study options:* accelerated degree program, adult/continuing education programs, advanced placement credit, cooperative education, double majors, honors programs, independent study, internships, off-campus study, part-time degree program, services for LD students, student-designed majors, study abroad, summer session for credit. *ROTC:* Army (c). *Unusual degree programs:* 3-2 engineering with Washington University in St. Louis, University of Pennsylvania, Lehigh University; forestry with Duke University; natural resource management with Duke University, occupational therapy with Washington University in St. Louis, allied health with Thomas Jefferson University.
Library Reeves Library with 247,841 titles, 1,268 serial subscriptions, 1,462 audiovisual materials, an OPAC, a Web page.
Computers on Campus 150 computers available on campus for general student use. A campuswide network can be accessed from student residence rooms and from off campus. Internet access, at least one staffed computer lab available.
Student Life *Housing:* on-campus residence required for freshman year. *Options:* coed, men-only, women-only, disabled students. *Activities and Organizations:* drama/theater group, student-run newspaper, radio station, choral group, marching band, Student Alumni Association, United Student Government, Moravian College Choir, Twenty-Six Points (Student Ambassador Group), International Club, national fraternities, national sororities. *Campus security:* 24-hour emergency response devices and patrols, late-night transport/escort service, controlled dormitory access. *Student Services:* health clinic, personal/psychological counseling.
Athletics Member NCAA. All Division III. *Intercollegiate sports:* baseball M, basketball M/W, cross-country running M/W, equestrian sports W(c), field hockey W, football M, golf M, ice hockey M(c), lacrosse M(c), soccer M/W, softball W, tennis M/W, track and field M/W, volleyball W. *Intramural sports:* badminton M/W, basketball M/W, football M/W, racquetball M/W, skiing (downhill) M(c)/W(c), soccer M/W, softball M/W, table tennis M/W, tennis M/W, volleyball M/W.
Standardized Tests *Required:* SAT I or ACT (for admission).
Costs (2001–02) *Comprehensive fee:* $27,065 includes full-time tuition ($20,115), mandatory fees ($380), and room and board ($6570). Part-time tuition: $629 per credit. Part-time tuition and fees vary according to class time. *Room and board:* Room and board charges vary according to board plan and housing facility. *Payment plan:* installment. *Waivers:* minority students, children of alumni, and employees or children of employees.
Financial Aid Of all full-time matriculated undergraduates who enrolled in 2001, 1123 applied for aid, 995 were judged to have need, 235 had their need fully met. *Average percent of need met:* 83%. *Average financial aid package:* $14,913. *Average need-based loan:* $3795. *Average need-based gift aid:* $10,574.
Applying *Options:* common application, electronic application, early admission, early decision, deferred entrance. *Application fee:* $30. *Required:* essay or personal statement, high school transcript, minimum 2.5 GPA, 3 letters of recommendation. *Recommended:* interview. *Application deadlines:* 3/1 (freshmen), 3/1 (transfers). *Early decision:* 2/1. *Notification:* 3/15 (freshmen), 2/15 (early decision).
Admissions Contact Moravian College, 1200 Main Street, Bethlehem, PA 18018. *Phone:* 610-861-1320. *Toll-free phone:* 800-441-3191. *Fax:* 610-625-7930. *E-mail:* admissions@moravian.edu.

MOUNT ALOYSIUS COLLEGE
Cresson, Pennsylvania

- **Independent Roman Catholic** 4-year, founded 1939
- **Calendar** semesters
- **Degrees** diplomas, associate, and bachelor's
- **Rural** 125-acre campus
- **Endowment** $6.3 million
- **Coed,** 1,153 undergraduate students, 75% full-time, 75% women, 25% men
- **Minimally difficult** entrance level, 48% of applicants were admitted

Mount Aloysius College offers merit scholarships that are renewable annually and valued up to $5000. Baccalaureate and associate degrees are offered. All students at Mount Aloysius College receive a broad-based liberal arts education. Committed to excellence, the faculty and staff provide personalized attention.

Undergraduates 860 full-time, 293 part-time. Students come from 7 states and territories, 7 other countries, 2% are from out of state, 16% transferred in, 20% live on campus.
Freshmen *Admission:* 908 applied, 439 admitted, 153 enrolled. *Average high school GPA:* 3.20. *Test scores:* SAT verbal scores over 500: 27%; SAT math scores over 500: 20%; ACT scores over 18: 100%; SAT verbal scores over 600: 3%; SAT math scores over 600: 2%; ACT scores over 24: 8%.
Faculty *Total:* 123, 41% full-time, 18% with terminal degrees. *Student/faculty ratio:* 14:1.
Majors Accounting; behavioral sciences; business administration; child care services management; computer science; criminal justice studies; early childhood education; English; general studies; humanities; human services; information

Mount Aloysius College (continued)
sciences/systems; liberal arts and sciences/liberal studies; medical assistant; nursing; nursing science; occupational therapy; occupational therapy assistant; operating room technician; paralegal/legal assistant; pharmacy technician/ assistant; physical therapy assistant; pre-law; professional studies; psychology; radiological science; sign language interpretation.

Academic Programs *Special study options:* academic remediation for entering students, adult/continuing education programs, advanced placement credit, distance learning, independent study, internships, part-time degree program, services for LD students, summer session for credit.

Library Mount Aloysius College Library plus 1 other with 70,000 titles, 350 serial subscriptions.

Computers on Campus 175 computers available on campus for general student use. A campuswide network can be accessed from student residence rooms. Internet access, at least one staffed computer lab available.

Student Life *Housing Options:* men-only, women-only, disabled students. *Activities and Organizations:* drama/theater group, student-run newspaper, choral group, Phi Theta Kappa, Student Nursing Association, Student Occupational Therapy Association, Criminology Club, campus ministry. *Campus security:* 24-hour emergency response devices and patrols, late-night transport/escort service, controlled dormitory access. *Student Services:* health clinic, personal/ psychological counseling.

Athletics Member NAIA. *Intercollegiate sports:* baseball M(s), basketball M(s)/W(s), golf M(s)/W, soccer M(s)/W(s), softball M/W(s), volleyball W(s). *Intramural sports:* basketball M/W, football M/W, skiing (cross-country) M/W, skiing (downhill) M/W, soccer M/W, softball M/W, table tennis M/W, tennis M/W, volleyball M/W, weight lifting M/W.

Standardized Tests *Required for some:* SAT I or ACT (for admission). *Recommended:* SAT I or ACT (for admission).

Costs (2001–02) *Comprehensive fee:* $19,126 includes full-time tuition ($13,676), mandatory fees ($260), and room and board ($5190). Full-time tuition and fees vary according to program. Part-time tuition: $425 per credit. Part-time tuition and fees vary according to class time, class time, course load, program, and student level. *Required fees:* $65 per term part-time. *Room and board:* College room only: $2450. Room and board charges vary according to board plan and housing facility. *Payment plan:* installment. *Waivers:* employees or children of employees.

Financial Aid Of all full-time matriculated undergraduates who enrolled in 2001, 850 applied for aid, 840 were judged to have need. 132 Federal Work-Study jobs (averaging $1520). *Average percent of need met:* 80%. *Average financial aid package:* $8500. *Average need-based gift aid:* $2000. *Average indebtedness upon graduation:* $17,000. *Financial aid deadline:* 5/1.

Applying *Options:* early admission, deferred entrance. *Application fee:* $25. *Required:* high school transcript, minimum 2.0 GPA. *Required for some:* essay or personal statement, 3 letters of recommendation, interview. *Recommended:* interview. *Application deadline:* rolling (freshmen), rolling (transfers). *Notification:* continuous (freshmen).

Admissions Contact Mr. Francis Crouse, Dean of Enrollment Management, Mount Aloysius College, 7373 Admiral Peary Highway, Cresson, PA 16630. *Phone:* 814-886-6383. *Toll-free phone:* 888-823-2220. *Fax:* 814-886-6441. *E-mail:* admissions@mtaloy.edu.

MUHLENBERG COLLEGE
Allentown, Pennsylvania

- **Independent** 4-year, founded 1848, affiliated with Lutheran Church
- **Calendar** semesters
- **Degree** bachelor's
- **Suburban** 75-acre campus with easy access to Philadelphia
- **Endowment** $80.7 million
- **Coed,** 2,629 undergraduate students, 88% full-time, 57% women, 43% men
- **Very difficult** entrance level, 35% of applicants were admitted

"Friendly" and "challenging" are the words that students use most often to describe Muhlenberg. The educational experience is active and hands-on, with small classes, a caring environment, and easy access to faculty members. Internships, field study, study abroad, and a Washington semester supplement traditional classroom experiences. Students are able to analyze and think critically as well as effectively express themselves in person and in writing—the most prized outcomes of a Muhlenberg education.

Undergraduates 2,311 full-time, 318 part-time. Students come from 34 states and territories, 6 other countries, 66% are from out of state, 2% African American, 3% Asian American or Pacific Islander, 3% Hispanic American, 0.3% Native American, 0.3% transferred in, 90% live on campus. *Retention:* 93% of 2001 full-time freshmen returned.

Freshmen *Admission:* 3,892 applied, 1,374 admitted, 573 enrolled. *Average high school GPA:* 3.69. *Test scores:* SAT verbal scores over 500: 93%; SAT math scores over 500: 94%; SAT verbal scores over 600: 50%; SAT math scores over 600: 54%; SAT verbal scores over 700: 8%; SAT math scores over 700: 9%.

Faculty *Total:* 235, 62% full-time. *Student/faculty ratio:* 13:1.

Majors Accounting; American studies; anthropology; art; art history; biochemistry; biology; business administration; chemistry; communications; computer science; dance; economics; elementary education; English; environmental science; fine/studio arts; French; German; history; human resources management; international economics; international relations; mathematics; music; natural sciences; philosophy; physical sciences; physics; political science; pre-dentistry; pre-law; pre-medicine; pre-veterinary studies; psychology; religious studies; Russian/Slavic studies; secondary education; social sciences; sociology; Spanish; theater arts/drama.

Academic Programs *Special study options:* accelerated degree program, adult/continuing education programs, advanced placement credit, distance learning, double majors, honors programs, independent study, internships, off-campus study, part-time degree program, services for LD students, student-designed majors, study abroad, summer session for credit. *ROTC:* Army (c). *Unusual degree programs:* 3-2 engineering with Columbia University, Washington University in St. Louis; forestry with Duke University.

Library Trexler Library with 270,700 titles, 1,700 serial subscriptions, 4,400 audiovisual materials, an OPAC, a Web page.

Computers on Campus 150 computers available on campus for general student use. A campuswide network can be accessed from student residence rooms and from off campus. Internet access, at least one staffed computer lab available.

Student Life *Housing:* on-campus residence required for freshman year. *Options:* coed, women-only, disabled students. *Activities and Organizations:* drama/theater group, student-run newspaper, radio and television station, choral group, Theater Association, Environmental Action Team, Jefferson School Partnership, Select Choir, Habitat for Humanity, national fraternities, national sororities. *Campus security:* 24-hour emergency response devices and patrols, late-night transport/escort service, controlled dormitory access. *Student Services:* health clinic, personal/psychological counseling.

Athletics Member NCAA. All Division III. *Intercollegiate sports:* baseball M, basketball M/W, cross-country running M/W, field hockey W, football M, golf M/W, lacrosse M/W, soccer M/W, softball W, tennis M/W, track and field M/W, volleyball W, wrestling M. *Intramural sports:* basketball M/W, cross-country running M/W, football M/W, ice hockey M, racquetball M/W, rugby M/W, skiing (downhill) M/W, soccer M/W, softball M, squash M/W, swimming M/W, tennis M/W, track and field M/W, volleyball M/W, weight lifting M/W.

Standardized Tests *Required for some:* SAT I or ACT (for admission).

Costs (2001–02) *Comprehensive fee:* $28,170 includes full-time tuition ($22,025), mandatory fees ($185), and room and board ($5960). Part-time tuition: $1555 per course. *Room and board:* Room and board charges vary according to board plan, housing facility, and location. *Payment plans:* tuition prepayment, installment. *Waivers:* employees or children of employees.

Financial Aid *Financial aid deadline:* 2/15.

Applying *Options:* common application, electronic application, early admission, early decision, deferred entrance. *Application fee:* $40. *Required:* essay or personal statement, high school transcript, 2 letters of recommendation. *Required for some:* interview. *Recommended:* interview. *Application deadlines:* 2/15 (freshmen), 6/1 (transfers). *Early decision:* 1/15. *Notification:* 4/1 (freshmen), 2/1 (early decision).

Admissions Contact Mr. Christopher Hooker-Haring, Dean of Admissions, Muhlenberg College, 2400 Chew Street, Allentown, PA 18104-5586. *Phone:* 484-664-3245. *Fax:* 484-664-3234. *E-mail:* adm@muhlenberg.edu.

NEUMANN COLLEGE
Aston, Pennsylvania

- **Independent Roman Catholic** comprehensive, founded 1965
- **Calendar** semesters
- **Degrees** certificates, associate, bachelor's, and master's
- **Suburban** 28-acre campus with easy access to Philadelphia
- **Endowment** $43.2 million
- **Coed,** 1,741 undergraduate students, 77% full-time, 65% women, 35% men
- **Moderately difficult** entrance level, 97% of applicants were admitted

Undergraduates 1,332 full-time, 409 part-time. Students come from 19 states and territories, 4 other countries, 27% are from out of state, 12% African American, 0.9% Asian American or Pacific Islander, 0.9% Hispanic American, 0.1% Native American, 0.2% international, 4% transferred in, 45% live on campus. *Retention:* 76% of 2001 full-time freshmen returned.

Freshmen *Admission:* 1,131 applied, 1,092 admitted, 379 enrolled. *Average high school GPA:* 2.88. *Test scores:* SAT verbal scores over 500: 26%; SAT math scores over 500: 20%; SAT verbal scores over 600: 3%; SAT math scores over 600: 3%.

Faculty *Total:* 192, 30% full-time, 30% with terminal degrees. *Student/faculty ratio:* 16:1.

Majors Accounting; biology; business administration; business marketing and marketing management; communications; computer/information sciences; early childhood education; elementary education; English; environmental education; international business; liberal arts and sciences/liberal studies; nursing; political science; psychology; sport/fitness administration.

Academic Programs *Special study options:* academic remediation for entering students, accelerated degree program, adult/continuing education programs, advanced placement credit, cooperative education, distance learning, double majors, freshman honors college, honors programs, independent study, internships, off-campus study, part-time degree program, services for LD students, student-designed majors, study abroad, summer session for credit. *ROTC:* Army (c).

Library Neumann College Library with 95,216 titles, 1,702 serial subscriptions, 52,305 audiovisual materials, an OPAC.

Computers on Campus 121 computers available on campus for general student use. A campuswide network can be accessed from student residence rooms and from off campus that provide access to e-mail. Internet access, at least one staffed computer lab available.

Student Life *Housing Options:* coed. *Activities and Organizations:* drama/theater group, student-run newspaper, choral group, Professional Education Society, Student Nurses Association, theater ensemble, environmental club, community chorus. *Campus security:* 24-hour emergency response devices and patrols, late-night transport/escort service, controlled dormitory access. *Student Services:* health clinic, personal/psychological counseling.

Athletics Member NCAA. All Division III. *Intercollegiate sports:* baseball M, basketball M/W, cross-country running M/W, field hockey W, golf M, ice hockey M/W, lacrosse M/W, soccer M/W, softball W, tennis M/W, volleyball W. *Intramural sports:* basketball M/W, lacrosse M, softball W, tennis M/W, volleyball M/W.

Standardized Tests *Required:* SAT I or ACT (for admission).

Costs (2001–02) *Comprehensive fee:* $22,040 includes full-time tuition ($14,460), mandatory fees ($570), and room and board ($7010). Full-time tuition and fees vary according to program. Part-time tuition: $350 per credit. Part-time tuition and fees vary according to program. *Room and board:* College room only: $3990. Room and board charges vary according to board plan. *Payment plans:* installment, deferred payment. *Waivers:* employees or children of employees.

Financial Aid Of all full-time matriculated undergraduates who enrolled in 2001, 1190 applied for aid, 1190 were judged to have need. 35 Federal Work-Study jobs (averaging $1200). In 2001, 128 non-need-based awards were made. *Average financial aid package:* $15,000. *Average need-based gift aid:* $5000. *Average non-need based aid:* $5000. *Average indebtedness upon graduation:* $15,000.

Applying *Options:* early admission, deferred entrance. *Application fee:* $35. *Required:* high school transcript, minimum 2.00 GPA. *Recommended:* interview. *Application deadline:* rolling (freshmen), rolling (transfers). *Notification:* continuous (freshmen).

Admissions Contact Mr. Scott Bogard, Director of Admissions, Neumann College, One Neumann Drive, Aston, PA 19014-1298. *Phone:* 610-558-5612. *Toll-free phone:* 800-963-8626. *Fax:* 610-558-5652. *E-mail:* neumann@neumann.edu.

PEIRCE COLLEGE
Philadelphia, Pennsylvania

- **Independent** 4-year, founded 1865
- **Calendar** continuous
- **Degrees** certificates, associate, and bachelor's
- **Urban** 1-acre campus
- **Endowment** $6.6 million
- **Coed, primarily women,** 2,837 undergraduate students, 24% full-time, 77% women, 23% men
- **Minimally difficult** entrance level, 57% of applicants were admitted

Founded in 1865, Peirce College has a long-standing reputation for providing a leading-edge, high-quality, business-related education that reflects current hiring trends. New information technology programs include networking, business information systems, and technology management. The College is located off the Avenue of the Arts at Broad and Pine streets in Philadelphia.

Undergraduates 686 full-time, 2,151 part-time. Students come from 23 states and territories, 16 other countries, 12% are from out of state, 60% African American, 2% Asian American or Pacific Islander, 4% Hispanic American, 0.2% Native American, 2% international, 32% transferred in. *Retention:* 70% of 2001 full-time freshmen returned.

Freshmen *Admission:* 814 applied, 461 admitted, 358 enrolled.

Faculty *Total:* 148, 20% full-time, 82% with terminal degrees. *Student/faculty ratio:* 16:1.

Majors Accounting technician; building maintenance/management; business; business administration; business systems networking/ telecommunications; computer engineering technology; computer maintenance technology; data processing; data processing technology; general studies; health services administration; hotel and restaurant management; information sciences/systems; legal administrative assistant; medical administrative assistant; office management; paralegal/legal assistant; secretarial science.

Academic Programs *Special study options:* academic remediation for entering students, accelerated degree program, advanced placement credit, cooperative education, distance learning, double majors, external degree program, freshman honors college, independent study, internships, off-campus study, part-time degree program, services for LD students, summer session for credit.

Library Peirce College Library with 36,900 titles, 159 serial subscriptions, 4,578 audiovisual materials, an OPAC, a Web page.

Computers on Campus 350 computers available on campus for general student use. A campuswide network can be accessed from off campus. Internet access, online (class) registration, at least one staffed computer lab available.

Student Life *Housing:* college housing not available. *Activities and Organizations:* Chi Alpha Epsilon. *Campus security:* 24-hour emergency response devices and patrols, late-night transport/escort service, 24-hour security cameras.

Costs (2001–02) *Tuition:* $9750 full-time, $325 per credit part-time. Full-time tuition and fees vary according to course load. Part-time tuition and fees vary according to course load. *Required fees:* $900 full-time, $90 per course. *Payment plan:* installment. *Waivers:* minority students and employees or children of employees.

Financial Aid Of all full-time matriculated undergraduates who enrolled in 2001, 595 applied for aid, 550 were judged to have need, 125 had their need fully met. 108 Federal Work-Study jobs (averaging $1000). In 2001, 110 non-need-based awards were made. *Average percent of need met:* 45%. *Average financial aid package:* $3500. *Average need-based loan:* $4000. *Average need-based gift aid:* $1000. *Average non-need based aid:* $700. *Average indebtedness upon graduation:* $12,500.

Applying *Options:* common application, electronic application. *Application fee:* $50. *Required:* high school transcript. *Recommended:* essay or personal statement, minimum 2.0 GPA, letters of recommendation, interview. *Application deadline:* rolling (freshmen), rolling (transfers). *Notification:* continuous (freshmen).

Admissions Contact Mr. Steve W. Bird, College Representative, Peirce College, 1420 Pine Street, Philadelphia, PA 19102. *Phone:* 215-670-9375. *Toll-free phone:* 877-670-9190 Ext. 9314 (in-state); 877-670-9190 Ext. 9214 (out-of-state). *Fax:* 215-545-3683. *E-mail:* info@peirce.edu.

PENNSYLVANIA COLLEGE OF TECHNOLOGY
Williamsport, Pennsylvania

- **State-related** 4-year, founded 1965
- **Calendar** semesters
- **Degrees** certificates, associate, and bachelor's
- **Small-town** 927-acre campus
- **Endowment** $597,980
- **Coed,** 5,538 undergraduate students, 80% full-time, 34% women, 66% men
- **Noncompetitive** entrance level, 59% of applicants were admitted

Pennsylvania College of Technology is a special-mission affiliate of The Pennsylvania State University and Pennsylvania's premier technical college. Committed to applied technology education, Penn College offers partnerships with business and industry that are a key ingredient of its success in placing graduates (90 percent overall, 100 percent in many majors). Unique bachelor and associate degrees focus on applied technology and combine hands-on experience with theory and management education related to the student's field of study.

Undergraduates 4,449 full-time, 1,089 part-time. Students come from 32 states and territories, 16 other countries, 6% are from out of state, 2% African American, 0.9% Asian American or Pacific Islander, 0.7% Hispanic American, 0.5% Native American, 0.6% international, 2% transferred in, 19% live on campus.

Pennsylvania College of Technology (continued)

Freshmen *Admission:* 4,351 applied, 2,567 admitted, 1,571 enrolled.

Faculty *Total:* 411, 64% full-time. *Student/faculty ratio:* 18:1.

Majors Accounting; accounting technician; aerospace engineering technology; aircraft mechanic/powerplant; architectural engineering technology; auto body repair; automotive engineering technology; baker/pastry chef; banking; biology; biomedical engineering-related technology; broadcast journalism; business administration; business administration/management related; business computer programming; business systems analysis/design; business systems networking/telecommunications; child care/guidance; civil engineering technology; computer/information sciences; computer/information sciences related; computer maintenance technology; construction technology; culinary arts; data processing; dental hygiene; diesel engine mechanic; dietician assistant; drafting; drafting related; electrical/electronic engineering technologies related; electrical/electronic engineering technology; emergency medical technology; engineering science; environmental control technologies related; environmental technology; forest harvesting production technology; general studies; graphic design/commercial art/illustration; graphic/printing equipment; health/medical administrative services related; health/medical diagnostic and treatment services related; health/physical education/fitness related; health professions and related sciences; heating/air conditioning/refrigeration technology; heavy equipment maintenance; industrial electronics installation/repair; industrial machinery maintenance/repair; industrial production technologies related; industrial technology; institutional food workers; instrumentation technology; laser/optical technology; law and legal studies related; legal studies; liberal arts and sciences/liberal studies; lithography; masonry/tile setting; mass communications; mechanical drafting; medical administrative assistant; medical radiologic technology; mental health services related; nursery management; nursing; nursing (adult health); occupational therapy assistant; ornamental horticulture; paralegal/legal assistant; physical sciences; plastics technology; practical nurse; psychiatric/mental health services; quality control technology; secretarial science; surveying; teacher education, specific programs related; technical/business writing; tool/die making; travel/tourism management; vehicle/mobile equipment mechanics and repair related.

Academic Programs *Special study options:* academic remediation for entering students, advanced placement credit, cooperative education, distance learning, double majors, English as a second language, independent study, internships, off-campus study, part-time degree program, services for LD students, student-designed majors, summer session for credit. *ROTC:* Army (c).

Library Penn College Library plus 1 other with 64,462 titles, 6,985 audiovisual materials, an OPAC, a Web page.

Computers on Campus A campuswide network can be accessed from student residence rooms and from off campus. At least one staffed computer lab available.

Student Life *Housing Options:* coed. *Activities and Organizations:* student-run newspaper, radio station, Student Government Association, Resident Hall Association (RHA), Wildcats Event Board (WEB), Phi Beta Lambda, Early Educators. *Campus security:* 24-hour emergency response devices and patrols, late-night transport/escort service. *Student Services:* personal/psychological counseling, women's center.

Athletics *Intercollegiate sports:* archery M/W, baseball M, basketball M/W, bowling M/W, cross-country running M/W, golf M/W, soccer M/W, softball W, tennis M/W, volleyball W. *Intramural sports:* archery M/W, badminton M/W, basketball M/W, bowling M/W, football M/W, golf M/W, lacrosse M/W, racquetball M/W, soccer M/W, softball M/W, table tennis M/W, tennis M/W, volleyball M/W, weight lifting M/W, wrestling M.

Costs (2001–02) *Tuition:* state resident $7860 full-time, $262 per credit part-time; nonresident $9960 full-time, $332 per credit part-time. Full-time tuition and fees vary according to course load. Part-time tuition and fees vary according to course load. *Required fees:* $750 full-time. *Room and board:* $5000; room only: $3600. Room and board charges vary according to board plan and location. *Payment plan:* deferred payment. *Waivers:* employees or children of employees.

Financial Aid Of all full-time matriculated undergraduates who enrolled in 2001, 335 Federal Work-Study jobs (averaging $1305).

Applying *Options:* electronic application, early admission, deferred entrance. *Application fee:* $50. *Required:* high school transcript. *Application deadline:* rolling (freshmen), rolling (transfers).

Admissions Contact Mr. Chester D. Schuman, Director of Admissions, Pennsylvania College of Technology, One College Avenue, DIF #119, Williamsport, PA 17701. *Phone:* 570-327-4761. *Toll-free phone:* 800-367-9222. *Fax:* 570-321-5551. *E-mail:* cschuman@pct.edu.

PENNSYLVANIA SCHOOL OF ART & DESIGN
Lancaster, Pennsylvania

- **Independent** 4-year, founded 1982
- **Calendar** semesters
- **Degree** certificates and bachelor's
- **Coed,** 201 undergraduate students, 78% full-time, 53% women, 47% men
- **Moderately difficult** entrance level, 60% of applicants were admitted

Undergraduates 156 full-time, 45 part-time. 2% African American, 1% Asian American or Pacific Islander, 3% Hispanic American, 0.5% Native American.

Freshmen *Admission:* 167 applied, 100 admitted, 60 enrolled. *Average high school GPA:* 2.87.

Majors Fine/studio arts; graphic design/commercial art/illustration.

Academic Programs *Special study options:* advanced placement credit, cooperative education, internships, part-time degree program.

Library 7,000 titles, 35 serial subscriptions, 42 audiovisual materials.

Computers on Campus 38 computers available on campus for general student use. Internet access, at least one staffed computer lab available.

Student Life *Housing:* college housing not available. *Activities and Organizations:* student-run newspaper, Student Council, yearbook. *Campus security:* trained evening/weekend security personnel.

Costs (2001–02) *Tuition:* $10,500 full-time, $438 per credit part-time. *Required fees:* $375 full-time, $65 per term part-time. *Payment plan:* installment.

Financial Aid Of all full-time matriculated undergraduates who enrolled in 2001, 19 Federal Work-Study jobs (averaging $743).

Applying *Options:* deferred entrance. *Application fee:* $35. *Required:* essay or personal statement, high school transcript, interview, portfolio. *Required for some:* 2 letters of recommendation. *Recommended:* minimum 2.0 GPA, 2 letters of recommendation. *Application deadlines:* 5/1 (freshmen), 5/1 (transfers).

Admissions Contact Ms. Wendy Sweigart, Director of Admissions, Pennsylvania School of Art & Design, Admissions Office, PO Box 59, Lancaster, PA 17608-0059. *Phone:* 717-396-7833 Ext. 19. *Fax:* 717-396-1339. *E-mail:* admissions@psad.edu.

THE PENNSYLVANIA STATE UNIVERSITY ABINGTON COLLEGE
Abington, Pennsylvania

- **State-related** 4-year, founded 1950, part of Pennsylvania State University
- **Calendar** semesters
- **Degrees** associate and bachelor's
- **Small-town** 45-acre campus with easy access to Philadelphia
- **Coed,** 3,177 undergraduate students, 76% full-time, 50% women, 50% men
- **Moderately difficult** entrance level, 83% of applicants were admitted

Undergraduates 2,416 full-time, 761 part-time. 3% are from out of state, 10% African American, 11% Asian American or Pacific Islander, 4% Hispanic American, 0.1% Native American, 0.1% international, 3% transferred in. *Retention:* 75% of 2001 full-time freshmen returned.

Freshmen *Admission:* 2,611 applied, 2,174 admitted, 797 enrolled. *Average high school GPA:* 3.00. *Test scores:* SAT verbal scores over 500: 39%; SAT math scores over 500: 44%; SAT verbal scores over 600: 9%; SAT math scores over 600: 11%; SAT math scores over 700: 1%.

Faculty *Total:* 211, 45% full-time, 43% with terminal degrees. *Student/faculty ratio:* 20:1.

Majors Agricultural business related; American studies; biological/physical sciences; business; criminal justice studies; English; history; information sciences/systems; liberal arts and sciences/liberal studies; visual/performing arts.

Academic Programs *Special study options:* academic remediation for entering students, adult/continuing education programs, advanced placement credit, cooperative education, distance learning, double majors, English as a second language, external degree program, honors programs, independent study, internships, services for LD students, student-designed majors, study abroad, summer session for credit. *ROTC:* Army (b), Air Force (c).

Library 58,227 titles, 378 serial subscriptions, 3,727 audiovisual materials.

Computers on Campus 286 computers available on campus for general student use. A campuswide network can be accessed from off campus. Internet access, online (class) registration, at least one staffed computer lab available.

Student Life *Housing:* college housing not available. *Activities and Organizations:* drama/theater group, student-run newspaper. *Campus security:* 24-hour patrols. *Student Services:* personal/psychological counseling.

Athletics Member NJCAA. *Intercollegiate sports:* baseball M, basketball M/W, cross-country running M(c)/W(c), equestrian sports M(c)/W(c), golf M, soccer M/W, softball W, tennis M/W, volleyball M(c)/W. *Intramural sports:* basketball M, cross-country running M, football M, soccer M/W, softball M/W, table tennis M/W, tennis M/W, volleyball M/W, weight lifting M/W.

Standardized Tests *Required:* SAT I or ACT (for admission).

Costs (2001–02) *Tuition:* state resident $6936 full-time, $278 per credit part-time; nonresident $10,774 full-time, $450 per credit part-time. Full-time tuition and fees vary according to class time, location, program, and student level. Part-time tuition and fees vary according to class time, course load, location, program, and student level. *Required fees:* $322 full-time, $54 per credit. *Payment plan:* deferred payment. *Waivers:* senior citizens and employees or children of employees.

Financial Aid Of all full-time matriculated undergraduates who enrolled in 2001, 1626 applied for aid, 1249 were judged to have need, 63 had their need fully met. 81 Federal Work-Study jobs (averaging $999). In 2001, 399 non-need-based awards were made. *Average percent of need met:* 62%. *Average financial aid package:* $7296. *Average need-based loan:* $3048. *Average need-based gift aid:* $3790. *Average indebtedness upon graduation:* $17,453.

Applying *Options:* electronic application, early admission, deferred entrance. *Application fee:* $50. *Required:* high school transcript. *Application deadline:* rolling (freshmen), rolling (transfers). *Notification:* continuous (freshmen).

Admissions Contact Undergraduate Admissions Office, The Pennsylvania State University Abington College, 1600 Woodland Road, Abington, PA 19001. *Phone:* 814-865-5471. *Fax:* 215-881-7317. *E-mail:* admissions@psu.edu.

THE PENNSYLVANIA STATE UNIVERSITY ALTOONA COLLEGE

Altoona, Pennsylvania

- **State-related** 4-year, founded 1939, part of Pennsylvania State University
- **Calendar** semesters
- **Degrees** associate and bachelor's
- **Suburban** 115-acre campus
- **Coed,** 3,813 undergraduate students, 91% full-time, 50% women, 50% men
- **Moderately difficult** entrance level, 87% of applicants were admitted

Undergraduates 3,459 full-time, 354 part-time. 12% are from out of state, 5% African American, 2% Asian American or Pacific Islander, 2% Hispanic American, 0.1% Native American, 0.8% international, 2% transferred in, 24% live on campus. *Retention:* 84% of 2001 full-time freshmen returned.

Freshmen *Admission:* 4,140 applied, 3,591 admitted, 1,357 enrolled. *Average high school GPA:* 3.02. *Test scores:* SAT verbal scores over 500: 52%; SAT math scores over 500: 58%; SAT verbal scores over 600: 10%; SAT math scores over 600: 17%; SAT verbal scores over 700: 1%; SAT math scores over 700: 2%.

Faculty *Total:* 258, 47% full-time, 43% with terminal degrees. *Student/faculty ratio:* 21:1.

Majors Agricultural business; biological/physical sciences; business; criminal justice studies; electrical engineering; English; environmental science; individual/family development; information sciences/systems; liberal arts and sciences/liberal studies; nursing; visual/performing arts.

Academic Programs *Special study options:* academic remediation for entering students, adult/continuing education programs, advanced placement credit, distance learning, double majors, English as a second language, honors programs, independent study, internships, services for LD students, student-designed majors, study abroad, summer session for credit. *ROTC:* Army (b).

Library 55,703 titles, 308 serial subscriptions, 34 audiovisual materials.

Computers on Campus 167 computers available on campus for general student use. A campuswide network can be accessed from student residence rooms and from off campus. Internet access, online (class) registration, at least one staffed computer lab available.

Student Life *Housing Options:* coed. *Activities and Organizations:* drama/theater group, student-run newspaper, choral group, national fraternities, national sororities. *Campus security:* 24-hour emergency response devices and patrols, student patrols, late-night transport/escort service, controlled dormitory access.

Athletics Member NCAA. All Division III. *Intercollegiate sports:* baseball M, basketball M/W, golf M, rugby M(c)/W(c), soccer M/W, softball W, swimming M/W, tennis M/W, volleyball M(c)/W. *Intramural sports:* badminton M/W, baseball M/W, basketball M/W, cross-country running M/W, football M/W, golf M/W, ice hockey M/W, racquetball M/W, skiing (downhill) M/W, soccer M(c)/W(c), softball M/W, swimming M/W, table tennis M/W, tennis M/W, track and field M/W, volleyball M/W, weight lifting M/W.

Standardized Tests *Required:* SAT I or ACT (for admission).

Costs (2001–02) *Tuition:* state resident $6936 full-time, $278 per credit part-time; nonresident $10,774 full-time, $450 per credit part-time. Full-time tuition and fees vary according to class time, location, program, and student level. Part-time tuition and fees vary according to class time, course load, location, program, and student level. *Required fees:* $342 full-time, $57 per credit. *Room and board:* $5300; room only: $2680. Room and board charges vary according to board plan and housing facility. *Payment plan:* deferred payment. *Waivers:* senior citizens and employees or children of employees.

Financial Aid Of all full-time matriculated undergraduates who enrolled in 2001, 2633 applied for aid, 2155 were judged to have need, 120 had their need fully met. 345 Federal Work-Study jobs (averaging $1472). In 2001, 489 non-need-based awards were made. *Average percent of need met:* 66%. *Average financial aid package:* $9192. *Average need-based loan:* $3269. *Average need-based gift aid:* $3669. *Average indebtedness upon graduation:* $17,453.

Applying *Options:* electronic application, early admission, deferred entrance. *Application fee:* $50. *Required:* high school transcript. *Application deadline:* rolling (freshmen), rolling (transfers). *Notification:* continuous (freshmen).

Admissions Contact Mr. Richard Shaffer, Director of Admissions and Enrollment Services, The Pennsylvania State University Altoona College, E108 Smith Building, 3000 Ivyside Park, Altoona, PA 16601-3760. *Phone:* 814-949-5466. *Fax:* 814-949-5564. *E-mail:* admissions@psu.edu.

THE PENNSYLVANIA STATE UNIVERSITY AT ERIE, THE BEHREND COLLEGE

Erie, Pennsylvania

- **State-related** comprehensive, founded 1948, part of Pennsylvania State University
- **Calendar** semesters
- **Degrees** associate, bachelor's, and master's
- **Suburban** 727-acre campus
- **Coed,** 3,550 undergraduate students, 92% full-time, 37% women, 63% men
- **Very difficult** entrance level, 81% of applicants were admitted

New majors in computer science and software engineering complement the physical growth of the campus. New facilities include an athletics and recreation center, a multifaith chapel, residence halls, an observatory, and a high-tech business park. Students benefit from small classes and participate in undergraduate research as they earn an internationally recognized Penn State degree.

Undergraduates 3,256 full-time, 294 part-time. 7% are from out of state, 3% African American, 2% Asian American or Pacific Islander, 1% Hispanic American, 0.0% Native American, 1% international, 2% transferred in, 42% live on campus. *Retention:* 85% of 2001 full-time freshmen returned.

Freshmen *Admission:* 2,832 applied, 2,296 admitted, 836 enrolled. *Average high school GPA:* 3.23. *Test scores:* SAT verbal scores over 500: 64%; SAT math scores over 500: 73%; SAT verbal scores over 600: 15%; SAT math scores over 600: 26%; SAT verbal scores over 700: 1%; SAT math scores over 700: 2%.

Faculty *Total:* 255, 73% full-time, 47% with terminal degrees. *Student/faculty ratio:* 16:1.

Majors Accounting; agribusiness; biology; business; business administration; business economics; business marketing and marketing management; chemistry; communications; computer engineering; computer/information sciences; economics; electrical engineering; English; finance; history; industrial technology; international business; liberal arts and sciences/liberal studies; management information systems/business data processing; mathematics; mechanical engineering; multi/interdisciplinary studies related; physical sciences; physics; plastics engineering; political science; psychology.

Academic Programs *Special study options:* academic remediation for entering students, adult/continuing education programs, advanced placement credit, cooperative education, distance learning, double majors, honors programs, independent study, internships, services for LD students, study abroad, summer session for credit. *ROTC:* Army (b).

Library 89,907 titles, 835 serial subscriptions, 2,838 audiovisual materials.

Computers on Campus 448 computers available on campus for general student use. A campuswide network can be accessed from student residence rooms and from off campus. Internet access, online (class) registration, at least one staffed computer lab available.

Student Life *Housing Options:* coed, men-only, women-only, disabled students. *Activities and Organizations:* drama/theater group, student-run newspaper, radio station, choral group, Student Government Association, national fraternities, national sororities. *Campus security:* 24-hour emergency response devices and patrols, student patrols, late-night transport/escort service, controlled dormitory access.

Athletics Member NCAA. All Division III. *Intercollegiate sports:* badminton M(c)/W(c), baseball M, basketball M/W, bowling M(c)/W(c), cross-country running M/W, football M(c)/W(c), golf M/W, ice hockey M(c), lacrosse M(c), skiing (downhill) M(c)/W(c), soccer M/W, softball W, swimming M/W, tennis M/W, track and field M/W, volleyball M(c)/W, water polo M/W. *Intramural sports:* badminton M/W, basketball M/W, bowling M/W, cross-country running M/W, football M, golf M/W, racquetball M/W, soccer M/W, softball M/W, swimming M/W, table tennis M/W, tennis M/W, volleyball M.

The Pennsylvania State University at Erie, The Behrend College (continued)

Standardized Tests *Required:* SAT I or ACT (for admission).

Costs (2001–02) *Tuition:* state resident $7054 full-time, $295 per credit part-time; nonresident $13,534 full-time, $564 per credit part-time. Full-time tuition and fees vary according to class time, location, program, and student level. Part-time tuition and fees vary according to class time, course load, location, program, and student level. *Required fees:* $342 full-time, $57 per credit. *Room and board:* $5300; room only: $2680. Room and board charges vary according to board plan and housing facility. *Payment plan:* deferred payment. *Waivers:* senior citizens and employees or children of employees.

Financial Aid Of all full-time matriculated undergraduates who enrolled in 2001, 2591 applied for aid, 2160 were judged to have need, 140 had their need fully met. 358 Federal Work-Study jobs (averaging $1103). In 2001, 473 non-need-based awards were made. *Average percent of need met:* 67%. *Average financial aid package:* $9060. *Average need-based loan:* $3613. *Average need-based gift aid:* $3486. *Average indebtedness upon graduation:* $17,453.

Applying *Options:* electronic application, early admission, deferred entrance. *Application fee:* $50. *Required:* high school transcript. *Application deadline:* rolling (freshmen), rolling (transfers). *Notification:* continuous (freshmen).

Admissions Contact Undergraduate Admissions Office, The Pennsylvania State University at Erie, The Behrend College, 5091 Station Road, Erie, PA 16563. *Phone:* 814-865-5471. *Fax:* 814-898-6044. *E-mail:* behrend.admissions@psu.edu.

The Pennsylvania State University Beaver Campus of the Commonwealth College

Monaca, Pennsylvania

- **State-related** primarily 2-year, founded 1964, part of Pennsylvania State University
- **Calendar** semesters
- **Degrees** associate and bachelor's (also offers up to 2 years of most bachelor's degree programs offered at University Park campus)
- **Small-town** 90-acre campus with easy access to Pittsburgh
- **Coed,** 752 undergraduate students, 91% full-time, 35% women, 65% men
- **Moderately difficult** entrance level, 93% of applicants were admitted

Undergraduates 687 full-time, 65 part-time. 6% are from out of state, 5% African American, 1% Asian American or Pacific Islander, 1% Hispanic American, 3% transferred in, 35% live on campus. *Retention:* 71% of 2001 full-time freshmen returned.

Freshmen *Admission:* 581 applied, 541 admitted, 283 enrolled. *Average high school GPA:* 2.92. *Test scores:* SAT verbal scores over 500: 50%; SAT math scores over 500: 50%; SAT verbal scores over 600: 8%; SAT math scores over 600: 12%; SAT math scores over 700: 2%.

Faculty *Total:* 69, 52% full-time. *Student/faculty ratio:* 15:1.

Majors Agricultural business; biological/physical sciences; biomedical engineering-related technology; business; business administration; electrical/electronic engineering technology; hotel and restaurant management; information sciences/systems; liberal arts and sciences/liberal studies; mechanical engineering technology.

Academic Programs *Special study options:* academic remediation for entering students, adult/continuing education programs, advanced placement credit, distance learning, double majors, English as a second language, honors programs, independent study, internships, services for LD students, student-designed majors, summer session for credit.

Library 38,493 titles, 245 serial subscriptions, 6,587 audiovisual materials.

Computers on Campus 106 computers available on campus for general student use. A campuswide network can be accessed from student residence rooms and from off campus. Internet access, online (class) registration, at least one staffed computer lab available.

Student Life *Housing Options:* coed. *Activities and Organizations:* drama/theater group, student-run newspaper, radio station. *Campus security:* 24-hour patrols, controlled dormitory access.

Athletics Member NJCAA. *Intercollegiate sports:* baseball M, golf M/W, softball W, volleyball W. *Intramural sports:* basketball M/W, bowling M/W, fencing M/W, golf M/W, ice hockey M/W, racquetball M/W, skiing (downhill) M/W, tennis M/W, track and field M/W, volleyball M/W.

Standardized Tests *Required:* SAT I or ACT (for admission).

Costs (2001–02) *Tuition:* state resident $6832 full-time, $276 per credit part-time; nonresident $10,574 full-time, $442 per credit part-time. Full-time tuition and fees vary according to class time, location, program, and student level. Part-time tuition and fees vary according to class time, course load, location, program, and student level. *Required fees:* $342 full-time, $57 per credit. *Room and board:* $5300; room only: $2680. Room and board charges vary according to board plan and housing facility. *Payment plan:* deferred payment. *Waivers:* senior citizens and employees or children of employees.

Financial Aid Of all full-time matriculated undergraduates who enrolled in 2001, 41 Federal Work-Study jobs (averaging $868).

Applying *Options:* electronic application, early admission, deferred entrance. *Application fee:* $50. *Required:* high school transcript. *Application deadline:* rolling (freshmen), rolling (transfers). *Notification:* continuous (freshmen).

Admissions Contact Ms. Trish Head, The Pennsylvania State University Beaver Campus of the Commonwealth College, 100 University Drive, Monaca, PA 15061-2799. *Phone:* 724-773-3800. *Fax:* 724-773-3658. *E-mail:* admissions@psu.edu.

The Pennsylvania State University Berks Campus of the Berks-Lehigh Valley College

Reading, Pennsylvania

- **State-related** 4-year, founded 1924, part of Pennsylvania State University
- **Calendar** semesters
- **Degrees** associate and bachelor's
- **Suburban** 240-acre campus with easy access to Philadelphia
- **Coed,** 2,316 undergraduate students, 89% full-time, 40% women, 60% men
- **Moderately difficult** entrance level, 85% of applicants were admitted

Undergraduates 2,059 full-time, 257 part-time. 8% are from out of state, 6% African American, 4% Asian American or Pacific Islander, 3% Hispanic American, 0.1% Native American, 0.4% international, 2% transferred in, 29% live on campus. *Retention:* 79% of 2001 full-time freshmen returned.

Freshmen *Admission:* 2,342 applied, 1,997 admitted, 820 enrolled. *Average high school GPA:* 2.85. *Test scores:* SAT verbal scores over 500: 45%; SAT math scores over 500: 53%; SAT verbal scores over 600: 9%; SAT math scores over 600: 16%; SAT verbal scores over 700: 1%; SAT math scores over 700: 1%.

Faculty *Total:* 150, 55% full-time, 45% with terminal degrees. *Student/faculty ratio:* 20:1.

Majors Agricultural business; biological/physical sciences; biomedical engineering-related technology; business; business administration; electrical/electronic engineering technology; electromechanical technology; English composition; environmental engineering; hotel and restaurant management; information sciences/systems; liberal arts and studies related; mechanical engineering technology; multi/interdisciplinary studies related; occupational therapy; structural engineering.

Academic Programs *Special study options:* academic remediation for entering students, adult/continuing education programs, advanced placement credit, distance learning, honors programs, independent study, internships, services for LD students, study abroad, summer session for credit. *ROTC:* Army (b).

Library 44,544 titles, 287 serial subscriptions, 2,471 audiovisual materials.

Computers on Campus 156 computers available on campus for general student use. A campuswide network can be accessed from student residence rooms and from off campus. Internet access, online (class) registration, at least one staffed computer lab available.

Student Life *Housing Options:* coed. *Activities and Organizations:* drama/theater group, student-run newspaper, radio station. *Campus security:* 24-hour emergency response devices and patrols, controlled dormitory access.

Athletics Member NJCAA. *Intercollegiate sports:* baseball M, basketball M/W, bowling M(c)/W(c), cross-country running M/W, golf M, ice hockey M(c)/W(c), soccer M/W, tennis M/W, volleyball M(c)/W. *Intramural sports:* badminton M/W, basketball M/W, bowling M/W, cross-country running M/W, football M/W, golf M/W, soccer M/W, softball W, tennis M/W, volleyball M/W.

Standardized Tests *Required:* SAT I or ACT (for admission).

Costs (2001–02) *Tuition:* state resident $6936 full-time, $278 per credit part-time; nonresident $10,774 full-time, $450 per credit part-time. Full-time tuition and fees vary according to class time, location, program, and student level. Part-time tuition and fees vary according to class time, course load, location, program, and student level. *Required fees:* $342 full-time, $57 per credit. *Room and board:* $5300; room only: $2680. Room and board charges vary according to board plan and housing facility. *Payment plan:* deferred payment. *Waivers:* senior citizens and employees or children of employees.

Financial Aid Of all full-time matriculated undergraduates who enrolled in 2001, 1258 applied for aid, 912 were judged to have need, 41 had their need fully met. 71 Federal Work-Study jobs (averaging $804). In 2001, 382 non-need-based awards were made. *Average percent of need met:* 64%. *Average financial aid* *package:* $8549. *Average need-based loan:* $3023. *Average need-based gift aid:* $3507. *Average indebtedness upon graduation:* $17,453.

Applying *Options:* electronic application, early admission, deferred entrance. *Application fee:* $50. *Required:* high school transcript. *Application deadline:* rolling (freshmen), rolling (transfers). *Notification:* continuous (freshmen).

Admissions Contact Ms. Jennifer Peters, Admissions Counselor, The Pennsylvania State University Berks Campus of the Berks-Lehigh Valley College, 14 Perkins Student Center, PO Box 7009, Reading, PA 19610-6009. *Phone:* 610-396-6066. *Fax:* 610-396-6077. *E-mail:* admissions@psu.edu.

The Pennsylvania State University Delaware County Campus of the Commonwealth College

Media, Pennsylvania

- **State-related** primarily 2-year, founded 1966, part of Pennsylvania State University
- **Calendar** semesters
- **Degrees** associate and bachelor's (also offers up to 2 years of most bachelor's degree programs offered at University Park campus)
- **Small-town** 87-acre campus with easy access to Philadelphia
- **Coed,** 1,646 undergraduate students, 82% full-time, 48% women, 52% men
- **Moderately difficult** entrance level, 85% of applicants were admitted

Undergraduates 1,345 full-time, 301 part-time. 4% are from out of state, 11% African American, 7% Asian American or Pacific Islander, 2% Hispanic American, 0.9% international, 4% transferred in. *Retention:* 70% of 2001 full-time freshmen returned.

Freshmen *Admission:* 1,298 applied, 1,100 admitted, 439 enrolled. *Average high school GPA:* 2.85. *Test scores:* SAT verbal scores over 500: 34%; SAT math scores over 500: 38%; SAT verbal scores over 600: 8%; SAT math scores over 600: 12%; SAT verbal scores over 700: 1%; SAT math scores over 700: 1%.

Faculty *Total:* 119, 55% full-time. *Student/faculty ratio:* 17:1.

Majors Agricultural business; American studies; business; business administration; elementary education; English; individual/family development; information sciences/systems; liberal arts and sciences/liberal studies; speech/rhetorical studies.

Academic Programs *Special study options:* academic remediation for entering students, adult/continuing education programs, advanced placement credit, distance learning, double majors, English as a second language, honors programs, independent study, internships, services for LD students, student-designed majors, study abroad, summer session for credit. *ROTC:* Army (c).

Library 51,495 titles, 176 serial subscriptions, 3,226 audiovisual materials.

Computers on Campus 180 computers available on campus for general student use. A campuswide network can be accessed from off campus. Internet access, online (class) registration, at least one staffed computer lab available.

Student Life *Housing:* college housing not available. *Activities and Organizations:* drama/theater group, student-run newspaper. *Campus security:* late-night transport/escort service, part-time trained security personnel.

Athletics Member NJCAA. *Intercollegiate sports:* baseball M, basketball M/W, soccer M, tennis M/W, volleyball W. *Intramural sports:* basketball M/W, bowling M/W, golf M/W, ice hockey M/W, racquetball M/W, riflery M/W, skiing (downhill) M/W, soccer M/W, softball W, tennis M/W, volleyball M/W.

Standardized Tests *Required:* SAT I or ACT (for admission).

Costs (2001–02) *Tuition:* state resident $6832 full-time, $276 per credit part-time; nonresident $10,574 full-time, $442 per credit part-time. Full-time tuition and fees vary according to class time, location, program, and student level. Part-time tuition and fees vary according to class time, course load, location, program, and student level. *Required fees:* $332 full-time, $56 per credit. *Waivers:* senior citizens and employees or children of employees.

Financial Aid Of all full-time matriculated undergraduates who enrolled in 2001, 26 Federal Work-Study jobs (averaging $997).

Applying *Options:* electronic application, early admission, deferred entrance. *Application fee:* $50. *Application deadline:* rolling (freshmen), rolling (transfers). *Notification:* continuous (freshmen).

Admissions Contact Ms. Deborah Erie, The Pennsylvania State University Delaware County Campus of the Commonwealth College, 25 Yearsley Mill Road, Media, PA 19063-5596. *Phone:* 610-892-1200. *Fax:* 610-892-1200. *E-mail:* admissions@psu.edu.

The Pennsylvania State University DuBois Campus of the Commonwealth College

DuBois, Pennsylvania

- **State-related** primarily 2-year, founded 1935, part of Pennsylvania State University
- **Calendar** semesters
- **Degrees** associate and bachelor's (also offers up to 2 years of most bachelor's degree programs offered at University Park campus)
- **Small-town** 13-acre campus
- **Coed,** 997 undergraduate students, 77% full-time, 50% women, 50% men
- **Moderately difficult** entrance level, 95% of applicants were admitted

Undergraduates 769 full-time, 228 part-time. 7% are from out of state, 0.7% African American, 0.5% Asian American or Pacific Islander, 0.1% Hispanic American, 0.1% Native American, 0.1% international, 2% transferred in. *Retention:* 70% of 2001 full-time freshmen returned.

Freshmen *Admission:* 396 applied, 377 admitted, 252 enrolled. *Average high school GPA:* 2.77. *Test scores:* SAT verbal scores over 500: 37%; SAT math scores over 500: 45%; SAT verbal scores over 600: 11%; SAT math scores over 600: 8%.

Faculty *Total:* 89, 55% full-time, 40% with terminal degrees. *Student/faculty ratio:* 14:1.

Majors Agricultural business; biological/physical sciences; business; business administration; electrical/electronic engineering technology; individual/family development; industrial technology; information sciences/systems; liberal arts and sciences/liberal studies; mechanical engineering technology; occupational therapy assistant; physical therapy assistant; wildlife management.

Academic Programs *Special study options:* academic remediation for entering students, adult/continuing education programs, advanced placement credit, distance learning, double majors, honors programs, independent study, internships, services for LD students, student-designed majors, summer session for credit. *ROTC:* Army (c), Navy (c), Air Force (c).

Library 38,966 titles, 1,146 serial subscriptions.

Computers on Campus 126 computers available on campus for general student use. A campuswide network can be accessed from off campus. Internet access, online (class) registration, at least one staffed computer lab available.

Student Life *Housing:* college housing not available. *Activities and Organizations:* student-run newspaper, choral group.

Athletics Member NJCAA. *Intercollegiate sports:* cross-country running M/W, golf M/W, volleyball W. *Intramural sports:* badminton M/W, basketball M, football M, tennis M/W, volleyball M/W.

Standardized Tests *Required:* SAT I or ACT (for admission).

Costs (2001–02) *Tuition:* state resident $6832 full-time, $276 per credit part-time; nonresident $10,574 full-time, $442 per credit part-time. Full-time tuition and fees vary according to class time, location, program, and student level. Part-time tuition and fees vary according to class time, course load, location, program, and student level. *Required fees:* $322 full-time, $54 per credit. *Payment plan:* installment. *Waivers:* employees or children of employees.

Financial Aid Of all full-time matriculated undergraduates who enrolled in 2001, 65 Federal Work-Study jobs (averaging $1048). 1 State and other part-time jobs (averaging $986).

Applying *Options:* electronic application, early admission, deferred entrance. *Application fee:* $50. *Required:* high school transcript. *Application deadline:* rolling (freshmen), rolling (transfers). *Notification:* continuous (freshmen).

Admissions Contact Undergraduate Admissions Offfice, The Pennsylvania State University DuBois Campus of the Commonwealth College, 101 Hiller, College Place, DuBois, PA 15801. *Phone:* 814-865-5471. *Fax:* 814-375-4784. *E-mail:* smc200@psu.edu.

The Pennsylvania State University Fayette Campus of the Commonwealth College

Uniontown, Pennsylvania

- **State-related** primarily 2-year, founded 1934, part of Pennsylvania State University
- **Calendar** semesters
- **Degrees** associate and bachelor's (also offers up to 2 years of most bachelor's degree programs offered at University Park campus)
- **Small-town** 193-acre campus
- **Coed,** 1,128 undergraduate students, 75% full-time, 55% women, 45% men

The Pennsylvania State University Fayette Campus of the Commonwealth College (continued)

■ **Moderately difficult** entrance level, 91% of applicants were admitted

Undergraduates 842 full-time, 286 part-time. 1% are from out of state, 4% African American, 0.5% Asian American or Pacific Islander, 0.4% Hispanic American, 0.4% Native American, 3% transferred in. *Retention:* 80% of 2001 full-time freshmen returned.

Freshmen *Admission:* 313 applied, 286 admitted, 190 enrolled. *Average high school GPA:* 2.93. *Test scores:* SAT verbal scores over 500: 38%; SAT math scores over 500: 35%; SAT verbal scores over 600: 6%; SAT math scores over 600: 9%; SAT verbal scores over 700: 1%; SAT math scores over 700: 1%.

Faculty *Total:* 93, 57% full-time. *Student/faculty ratio:* 14:1.

Majors Agricultural business; architectural engineering technology; business; business administration; criminal justice studies; electrical/electronic engineering technology; individual/family development; information sciences/systems; liberal arts and sciences/liberal studies; nursing.

Academic Programs *Special study options:* academic remediation for entering students, adult/continuing education programs, advanced placement credit, distance learning, double majors, honors programs, independent study, internships, services for LD students, student-designed majors, summer session for credit.

Library 49,620 titles, 170 serial subscriptions, 5,912 audiovisual materials.

Computers on Campus 103 computers available on campus for general student use. A campuswide network can be accessed from off campus. Internet access, online (class) registration, at least one staffed computer lab available.

Student Life *Housing:* college housing not available. *Activities and Organizations:* drama/theater group, student-run newspaper. *Campus security:* student patrols, 8-hour patrols by trained security personnel.

Athletics Member NJCAA. *Intercollegiate sports:* baseball M, basketball M, softball W, volleyball W. *Intramural sports:* badminton M/W, basketball M/W, fencing M/W, football M/W, racquetball M/W, skiing (downhill) M/W, soccer M/W, tennis M/W, track and field M/W, volleyball M/W.

Standardized Tests *Required:* SAT I or ACT (for admission).

Costs (2001–02) *Tuition:* state resident $6832 full-time, $276 per credit part-time; nonresident $10,574 full-time, $442 per credit part-time. Full-time tuition and fees vary according to class time, location, program, and student level. Part-time tuition and fees vary according to class time, course load, location, program, and student level. *Required fees:* $322 full-time, $54 per credit. *Payment plan:* deferred payment. *Waivers:* senior citizens and employees or children of employees.

Financial Aid Of all full-time matriculated undergraduates who enrolled in 2001, 60 Federal Work-Study jobs (averaging $1239).

Applying *Options:* electronic application, early admission, deferred entrance. *Application fee:* $50. *Required:* high school transcript. *Application deadline:* rolling (freshmen), rolling (transfers). *Notification:* continuous (freshmen).

Admissions Contact Undergraduate Admissions Office, The Pennsylvania State University Fayette Campus of the Commonwealth College, 108 Williams Building, Uniontown, PA 15401. *Phone:* 814-865-5471. *Fax:* 724-430-4175. *E-mail:* admissions@psu.edu.

THE PENNSYLVANIA STATE UNIVERSITY HARRISBURG CAMPUS OF THE CAPITAL COLLEGE

Middletown, Pennsylvania

■ **State-related** comprehensive, founded 1966, part of Pennsylvania State University
■ **Calendar** semesters
■ **Degrees** certificates, associate, bachelor's, master's, doctoral, and postbachelor's certificates
■ **Small-town** 218-acre campus
■ **Coed,** 1,762 undergraduate students, 63% full-time, 51% women, 49% men
■ **Moderately difficult** entrance level, 85% of applicants were admitted

Penn State Harrisburg, Capital College, is an undergraduate transfer college and graduate school of The Pennsylvania State University. At the undergraduate level, the College accepts applications from students who have successfully completed most of their freshman- and sophomore-level course work. Penn State Harrisburg also accepts applications for freshmen for the major in information sciences and technology. The College offers twenty-seven baccalaureate, nineteen master's, and two doctoral programs. At the College, there are all the resources of a major research university in a smaller, more intimate setting. For more information, students can visit the Web site at http://www.hbg.psu.edu.

Undergraduates 1,106 full-time, 656 part-time. 4% are from out of state, 5% African American, 5% Asian American or Pacific Islander, 2% Hispanic American, 0.2% Native American, 1% international, 10% transferred in, 16% live on campus.

Freshmen *Admission:* 20 applied, 17 admitted, 10 enrolled. *Average high school GPA:* 3.10. *Test scores:* SAT verbal scores over 500: 89%; SAT math scores over 500: 89%; SAT verbal scores over 600: 56%; SAT math scores over 600: 45%; SAT verbal scores over 700: 11%.

Faculty *Total:* 256, 59% full-time, 59% with terminal degrees. *Student/faculty ratio:* 10:1.

Majors Accounting; applied mathematics; business; business administration; business marketing and marketing management; computer/information sciences; criminal justice studies; electrical/electronic engineering technology; electrical engineering; environmental engineering; finance; liberal arts and sciences/liberal studies; management information systems/business data processing; mechanical engineering technology; nursing science; organizational behavior; psychology; public policy analysis; sociology; structural engineering.

Academic Programs *Special study options:* academic remediation for entering students, adult/continuing education programs, advanced placement credit, distance learning, double majors, honors programs, independent study, internships, part-time degree program, services for LD students, study abroad, summer session for credit. *ROTC:* Army (c).

Library 246,143 titles, 2,447 serial subscriptions, 5,373 audiovisual materials.

Computers on Campus 132 computers available on campus for general student use. A campuswide network can be accessed from student residence rooms and from off campus. Internet access, online (class) registration, at least one staffed computer lab available.

Student Life *Activities and Organizations:* student-run newspaper, radio station. *Campus security:* 24-hour patrols, student patrols, late-night transport/escort service.

Athletics *Intercollegiate sports:* volleyball M(c)/W(c). *Intramural sports:* badminton M/W, basketball M/W, bowling M/W, football M, racquetball M/W, softball M/W, table tennis M/W, volleyball M/W.

Standardized Tests *Required:* SAT I or ACT (for admission).

Costs (2001–02) *Tuition:* state resident $7054 full-time, $295 per credit part-time; nonresident $13,534 full-time, $564 per credit part-time. Full-time tuition and fees vary according to class time, location, program, and student level. Part-time tuition and fees vary according to class time, course load, location, program, and student level. *Required fees:* $322 full-time, $54 per credit. *Room and board:* $5980; room only: $3360. Room and board charges vary according to board plan and housing facility. *Payment plan:* deferred payment. *Waivers:* senior citizens and employees or children of employees.

Financial Aid Of all full-time matriculated undergraduates who enrolled in 2001, 949 applied for aid, 828 were judged to have need, 87 had their need fully met. 63 Federal Work-Study jobs (averaging $1036). In 2001, 135 non-need-based awards were made. *Average percent of need met:* 75%. *Average financial aid package:* $10,225. *Average need-based loan:* $4482. *Average need-based gift aid:* $3775. *Average indebtedness upon graduation:* $17,453.

Applying *Options:* electronic application, early admission, deferred entrance. *Application fee:* $50. *Required:* high school transcript. *Application deadline:* rolling (freshmen), rolling (transfers). *Notification:* continuous (freshmen).

Admissions Contact Undergraduate Admissions Office, The Pennsylvania State University Harrisburg Campus of the Capital College, 777 West Harrisburg Pike, Middletown, PA 17057-4898. *Phone:* 814-865-5471. *Fax:* 717-948-6325. *E-mail:* admissions@psu.edu.

THE PENNSYLVANIA STATE UNIVERSITY HAZLETON CAMPUS OF THE COMMONWEALTH COLLEGE

Hazleton, Pennsylvania

■ **State-related** primarily 2-year, founded 1934, part of Pennsylvania State University
■ **Calendar** semesters
■ **Degrees** associate and bachelor's (also offers up to 2 years of most bachelor's degree programs offered at University Park campus)
■ **Small-town** 92-acre campus
■ **Coed,** 1,342 undergraduate students, 93% full-time, 43% women, 57% men
■ **Moderately difficult** entrance level, 93% of applicants were admitted

Undergraduates 1,247 full-time, 95 part-time. 14% are from out of state, 2% African American, 4% Asian American or Pacific Islander, 3% Hispanic American, 0.6% international, 3% transferred in, 34% live on campus. *Retention:* 84% of 2001 full-time freshmen returned.

Freshmen *Admission:* 1,211 applied, 1,122 admitted, 535 enrolled. *Average high school GPA:* 2.92. *Test scores:* SAT verbal scores over 500: 43%; SAT math scores over 500: 50%; SAT verbal scores over 600: 7%; SAT math scores over 600: 10%.

Faculty *Total:* 98, 56% full-time. *Student/faculty ratio:* 19:1.

Majors Agricultural business; business; business administration; electrical/electronic engineering technology; industrial technology; information sciences/systems; liberal arts and sciences/liberal studies; mechanical engineering technology; medical laboratory technician; physical therapy assistant.

Academic Programs *Special study options:* academic remediation for entering students, adult/continuing education programs, advanced placement credit, distance learning, double majors, honors programs, independent study, internships, services for LD students, student-designed majors, summer session for credit. *ROTC:* Army (b).

Library 77,995 titles, 283 serial subscriptions, 6,590 audiovisual materials.

Computers on Campus 131 computers available on campus for general student use. A campuswide network can be accessed from student residence rooms and from off campus. Internet access, online (class) registration, at least one staffed computer lab available.

Student Life *Housing Options:* coed. *Activities and Organizations:* drama/theater group, student-run newspaper, radio station, choral group. *Campus security:* 24-hour patrols, late-night transport/escort service, controlled dormitory access.

Athletics Member NJCAA. *Intercollegiate sports:* baseball M, basketball M, soccer M, softball W, tennis M/W, volleyball M/W. *Intramural sports:* basketball M/W, soccer M/W, volleyball M/W.

Standardized Tests *Required:* SAT I or ACT (for admission).

Costs (2001–02) *Tuition:* state resident $6832 full-time, $276 per credit part-time; nonresident $10,574 full-time, $442 per credit part-time. Full-time tuition and fees vary according to class time, location, program, and student level. Part-time tuition and fees vary according to class time, course load, location, program, and student level. *Required fees:* $332 full-time, $56 per credit. *Room and board:* $5300; room only: $2680. Room and board charges vary according to board plan and housing facility. *Payment plan:* deferred payment. *Waivers:* senior citizens and employees or children of employees.

Financial Aid Of all full-time matriculated undergraduates who enrolled in 2001, 115 Federal Work-Study jobs (averaging $1220).

Applying *Options:* common application, electronic application, early admission, deferred entrance. *Application fee:* $50. *Required:* high school transcript. *Application deadline:* rolling (freshmen), rolling (transfers). *Notification:* continuous (freshmen).

Admissions Contact Undergraduate Admissions Office, The Pennsylvania State University Hazleton Campus of the Commonwealth College, 101 Administration Building, Hazleton, PA 18201. *Phone:* 814-865-5471. *Fax:* 570-450-3182. *E-mail:* admissions@psu.edu.

The Pennsylvania State University Lehigh Valley Campus of the Berks-Lehigh Valley College

Fogelsville, Pennsylvania

- **State-related** 4-year, founded 1912, part of Pennsylvania State University
- **Calendar** semesters
- **Degrees** associate and bachelor's
- **Small-town** 42-acre campus
- **Coed,** 685 undergraduate students, 74% full-time, 38% women, 62% men
- **Moderately difficult** entrance level, 87% of applicants were admitted

Undergraduates 508 full-time, 177 part-time. 3% are from out of state, 1% African American, 9% Asian American or Pacific Islander, 4% Hispanic American, 0.9% international, 6% transferred in. *Retention:* 74% of 2001 full-time freshmen returned.

Freshmen *Admission:* 490 applied, 428 admitted, 189 enrolled. *Average high school GPA:* 2.90. *Test scores:* SAT verbal scores over 500: 43%; SAT math scores over 500: 57%; SAT verbal scores over 600: 14%; SAT math scores over 600: 19%; SAT verbal scores over 700: 1%; SAT math scores over 700: 3%.

Faculty *Total:* 59, 41% full-time, 37% with terminal degrees. *Student/faculty ratio:* 16:1.

Majors Agribusiness; business; information sciences/systems; liberal arts and sciences/liberal studies; psychology.

Academic Programs *Special study options:* academic remediation for entering students, adult/continuing education programs, advanced placement credit, honors programs, independent study, internships, services for LD students, study abroad, summer session for credit. *ROTC:* Army (c).

Library 34,453 titles, 163 serial subscriptions, 6,459 audiovisual materials.

Computers on Campus 62 computers available on campus for general student use. A campuswide network can be accessed from off campus. Internet access, online (class) registration, at least one staffed computer lab available.

Student Life *Housing:* college housing not available. *Activities and Organizations:* drama/theater group.

Athletics *Intercollegiate sports:* basketball M(c)/W(c), bowling M(c)/W(c), cross-country running M, football M(c)/W(c), golf M/W, ice hockey M(c), skiing (downhill) M(c)/W(c), soccer M(c)/W(c), tennis M(c)/W(c), volleyball M(c)/W(c), weight lifting M(c)/W(c). *Intramural sports:* basketball M/W, bowling M, football M/W, golf M/W, racquetball M/W, soccer M, tennis M/W, volleyball M/W.

Standardized Tests *Required:* SAT I or ACT (for admission).

Costs (2001–02) *Tuition:* state resident $6832 full-time, $276 per credit part-time; nonresident $10,574 full-time, $442 per credit part-time. Full-time tuition and fees vary according to class time, location, program, and student level. Part-time tuition and fees vary according to class time, course load, location, program, and student level. *Required fees:* $342 full-time, $57 per credit. *Payment plan:* deferred payment. *Waivers:* senior citizens and employees or children of employees.

Financial Aid Of all full-time matriculated undergraduates who enrolled in 2001, 346 applied for aid, 268 were judged to have need, 18 had their need fully met. 16 Federal Work-Study jobs (averaging $1456). In 2001, 81 non-need-based awards were made. *Average percent of need met:* 65%. *Average financial aid package:* $7196. *Average need-based loan:* $2916. *Average need-based gift aid:* $3347. *Average indebtedness upon graduation:* $17,453.

Applying *Options:* electronic application, early admission, deferred entrance. *Application fee:* $50. *Required:* high school transcript. *Application deadline:* rolling (freshmen), rolling (transfers). *Notification:* continuous (freshmen).

Admissions Contact Admissions Coordinator, The Pennsylvania State University Lehigh Valley Campus of the Berks-Lehigh Valley College, Fogelsville, PA 18051. *Phone:* 610-821-6577. *Fax:* 610-285-5220. *E-mail:* admissions@psu.edu.

The Pennsylvania State University McKeesport Campus of the Commonwealth College

McKeesport, Pennsylvania

- **State-related** primarily 2-year, founded 1947, part of Pennsylvania State University
- **Calendar** semesters
- **Degrees** associate and bachelor's (also offers up to 2 years of most bachelor's degree programs offered at University Park campus)
- **Small-town** 40-acre campus with easy access to Pittsburgh
- **Coed,** 941 undergraduate students, 87% full-time, 39% women, 61% men
- **Moderately difficult** entrance level, 94% of applicants were admitted

Undergraduates 822 full-time, 119 part-time. 7% are from out of state, 13% African American, 2% Asian American or Pacific Islander, 1% Hispanic American, 0.1% Native American, 0.4% international, 4% transferred in, 19% live on campus. *Retention:* 83% of 2001 full-time freshmen returned.

Freshmen *Admission:* 678 applied, 640 admitted, 342 enrolled. *Average high school GPA:* 2.82. *Test scores:* SAT verbal scores over 500: 35%; SAT math scores over 500: 42%; SAT verbal scores over 600: 5%; SAT math scores over 600: 10%; SAT verbal scores over 700: 1%; SAT math scores over 700: 1%.

Faculty *Total:* 79, 46% full-time. *Student/faculty ratio:* 17:1.

Majors Agricultural business; biological/physical sciences; business; business administration; information sciences/systems; liberal arts and sciences/liberal studies; mechanical engineering technologies related; mechanical engineering technology.

Academic Programs *Special study options:* academic remediation for entering students, adult/continuing education programs, advanced placement credit, distance learning, double majors, honors programs, independent study, internships, services for LD students, student-designed majors, summer session for credit. *ROTC:* Air Force (c).

Library 38,254 titles, 213 serial subscriptions, 4,046 audiovisual materials.

Computers on Campus 167 computers available on campus for general student use. A campuswide network can be accessed from student residence rooms and from off campus. Internet access, online (class) registration, at least one staffed computer lab available.

Student Life *Housing Options:* coed. *Activities and Organizations:* drama/theater group, student-run newspaper, radio station. *Campus security:* 24-hour patrols, controlled dormitory access.

The Pennsylvania State University McKeesport Campus of the Commonwealth College (continued)

Athletics Member NJCAA. *Intercollegiate sports:* baseball M, basketball M, softball W, volleyball W. *Intramural sports:* basketball M/W, bowling M/W, fencing M/W, football M/W, golf M/W, ice hockey M, racquetball M/W, skiing (downhill) M/W, soccer M, softball M/W, swimming M/W, tennis M/W, track and field M/W, volleyball M/W.

Standardized Tests *Required:* SAT I or ACT (for admission).

Costs (2001–02) *Tuition:* state resident $6832 full-time, $276 per credit part-time; nonresident $10,574 full-time, $442 per credit part-time. Full-time tuition and fees vary according to class time, location, program, and student level. Part-time tuition and fees vary according to class time, course load, location, program, and student level. *Required fees:* $322 full-time, $54 per credit. *Room and board:* $5300; room only: $2680. Room and board charges vary according to board plan and housing facility. *Payment plan:* deferred payment. *Waivers:* senior citizens and employees or children of employees.

Financial Aid Of all full-time matriculated undergraduates who enrolled in 2001, 45 Federal Work-Study jobs (averaging $1180).

Applying *Options:* electronic application, early admission, deferred entrance. *Application fee:* $50. *Required:* high school transcript. *Application deadline:* rolling (freshmen), rolling (transfers). *Notification:* continuous (freshmen).

Admissions Contact Undergraduate Admissions Office, The Pennsylvania State University McKeesport Campus of the Commonwealth College, 400 University Drive, McKeesport, PA 15132-7698. *Phone:* 814-865-5471. *Toll-free phone:* 800-248-5466. *Fax:* 412-675-9056. *E-mail:* dam7@psu.edu.

The Pennsylvania State University Mont Alto Campus of the Commonwealth College

Mont Alto, Pennsylvania

- **State-related** primarily 2-year, founded 1929, part of Pennsylvania State University
- **Calendar** semesters
- **Degrees** associate and bachelor's (also offers up to 2 years of most bachelor's degree programs offered at University Park campus)
- **Small-town** 62-acre campus
- **Coed,** 1,105 undergraduate students, 75% full-time, 55% women, 45% men
- **Moderately difficult** entrance level, 85% of applicants were admitted

Undergraduates 825 full-time, 280 part-time. 15% are from out of state, 9% African American, 4% Asian American or Pacific Islander, 3% Hispanic American, 0.1% Native American, 0.2% international, 4% transferred in, 40% live on campus. *Retention:* 74% of 2001 full-time freshmen returned.

Freshmen *Admission:* 697 applied, 590 admitted, 348 enrolled. *Average high school GPA:* 2.77. *Test scores:* SAT verbal scores over 500: 37%; SAT math scores over 500: 40%; SAT verbal scores over 600: 9%; SAT math scores over 600: 11%; SAT verbal scores over 700: 1%.

Faculty *Total:* 95, 61% full-time. *Student/faculty ratio:* 13:1.

Majors Agricultural business; business; business administration; forest harvesting production technology; individual/family development; information sciences/systems; liberal arts and sciences/liberal studies; nursing; occupational therapy; physical therapy assistant.

Academic Programs *Special study options:* academic remediation for entering students, adult/continuing education programs, advanced placement credit, distance learning, double majors, honors programs, independent study, internships, services for LD students, student-designed majors, summer session for credit. *ROTC:* Army (c).

Library 34,596 titles, 252 serial subscriptions, 1,947 audiovisual materials.

Computers on Campus 182 computers available on campus for general student use. A campuswide network can be accessed from student residence rooms and from off campus. Internet access, online (class) registration, at least one staffed computer lab available.

Student Life *Housing Options:* coed. *Activities and Organizations:* student-run radio station. *Campus security:* 24-hour patrols, controlled dormitory access.

Athletics Member NJCAA. *Intercollegiate sports:* baseball M, basketball M/W, cross-country running M/W, golf M/W, soccer M/W, softball W, tennis M/W, volleyball W. *Intramural sports:* badminton M/W, basketball M/W, racquetball M/W, skiing (downhill) M/W, soccer M/W, softball W, volleyball M/W.

Standardized Tests *Required:* SAT I or ACT (for admission).

Costs (2001–02) *Tuition:* state resident $6832 full-time, $276 per credit part-time; nonresident $10,574 full-time, $442 per credit part-time. Full-time tuition and fees vary according to class time, location, and program. Part-time tuition and fees vary according to class time, course load, location, and program. *Required fees:* $332 full-time, $56 per credit. *Room and board:* $5300; room only: $2680. Room and board charges vary according to board plan and housing facility. *Payment plan:* deferred payment. *Waivers:* senior citizens and employees or children of employees.

Financial Aid Of all full-time matriculated undergraduates who enrolled in 2001, 69 Federal Work-Study jobs (averaging $966).

Applying *Options:* electronic application, early admission. *Application fee:* $50. *Required:* high school transcript. *Application deadline:* rolling (freshmen), rolling (transfers). *Notification:* continuous (freshmen).

Admissions Contact Ms. Shawn Wiley, The Pennsylvania State University Mont Alto Campus of the Commonwealth College, 1 Campus Drive, Mont Alto, PA 17237-9703. *Phone:* 717-749-6130. *Fax:* 717-749-6132. *E-mail:* admissions@psu.edu.

The Pennsylvania State University New Kensington Campus of the Commonwealth College

New Kensington, Pennsylvania

- **State-related** primarily 2-year, founded 1958, part of Pennsylvania State University
- **Calendar** semesters
- **Degrees** associate and bachelor's (also offers up to 2 years of most bachelor's degree programs offered at University Park campus)
- **Small-town** 71-acre campus with easy access to Pittsburgh
- **Coed,** 979 undergraduate students, 72% full-time, 38% women, 62% men
- **Moderately difficult** entrance level, 93% of applicants were admitted

Undergraduates 708 full-time, 271 part-time. 2% are from out of state, 3% African American, 1% Asian American or Pacific Islander, 0.4% Hispanic American, 4% transferred in. *Retention:* 78% of 2001 full-time freshmen returned.

Freshmen *Admission:* 437 applied, 408 admitted, 244 enrolled. *Average high school GPA:* 2.87. *Test scores:* SAT verbal scores over 500: 50%; SAT math scores over 500: 66%; SAT verbal scores over 600: 11%; SAT math scores over 600: 32%; SAT math scores over 700: 19%.

Faculty *Total:* 98, 39% full-time. *Student/faculty ratio:* 14:1.

Majors Agricultural business; biological/physical sciences; biomedical engineering-related technology; business; business administration; computer engineering technology; electrical/electronic engineering technology; electromechanical technology; individual/family development; information sciences/systems; liberal arts and sciences/liberal studies; mechanical engineering technology; medical laboratory technician; nursing.

Academic Programs *Special study options:* academic remediation for entering students, adult/continuing education programs, advanced placement credit, distance learning, double majors, honors programs, independent study, internships, services for LD students, student-designed majors, summer session for credit.

Library 27,427 titles, 195 serial subscriptions, 4,086 audiovisual materials.

Computers on Campus 264 computers available on campus for general student use. A campuswide network can be accessed from off campus. Internet access, online (class) registration, at least one staffed computer lab available.

Student Life *Housing:* college housing not available. *Activities and Organizations:* drama/theater group, student-run newspaper, choral group. *Campus security:* part-time trained security personnel.

Athletics Member NJCAA. *Intercollegiate sports:* baseball M, basketball M, cross-country running M/W, golf M/W, softball W, volleyball W. *Intramural sports:* badminton M/W, basketball M/W, football M/W, racquetball M/W, soccer M/W, softball W, volleyball M/W.

Standardized Tests *Required:* SAT I or ACT (for admission).

Costs (2001–02) *Tuition:* state resident $6832 full-time, $276 per credit part-time; nonresident $10,574 full-time, $442 per credit part-time. Full-time tuition and fees vary according to class time, location, program, and student level. Part-time tuition and fees vary according to class time, course load, location, program, and student level. *Required fees:* $332 full-time, $56 per credit. *Payment plan:* deferred payment. *Waivers:* senior citizens and employees or children of employees.

Financial Aid Of all full-time matriculated undergraduates who enrolled in 2001, 38 Federal Work-Study jobs (averaging $1191).

Applying *Options:* electronic application, early admission, deferred entrance. *Application fee:* $50. *Required:* high school transcript. *Application deadline:* rolling (freshmen), rolling (transfers). *Notification:* continuous (freshmen).

Admissions Contact Undergraduate Admissions Office, The Pennsylvania State University New Kensington Campus of the Commonwealth College, 3550

7th Street Road, New Kensington, PA 15068-1798. *Phone:* 814-865-7641. *Toll-free phone:* 888-968-PAWS. *Fax:* 724-334-6111. *E-mail:* nkadmissions@psu.edu.

THE PENNSYLVANIA STATE UNIVERSITY SCHUYLKILL CAMPUS OF THE CAPITAL COLLEGE

Schuylkill Haven, Pennsylvania

- **State-related** 4-year, founded 1934, part of Pennsylvania State University
- **Calendar** semesters
- **Degrees** associate and bachelor's (bachelor's degree programs completed at the Harrisburg campus)
- **Small-town** 42-acre campus
- **Coed,** 1,052 undergraduate students, 80% full-time, 57% women, 43% men
- **Moderately difficult** entrance level, 88% of applicants were admitted

Undergraduates 844 full-time, 208 part-time. 11% are from out of state, 13% African American, 4% Asian American or Pacific Islander, 3% Hispanic American, 0.1% Native American, 0.1% international, 3% transferred in, 24% live on campus. *Retention:* 85% of 2001 full-time freshmen returned.

Freshmen *Admission:* 674 applied, 591 admitted, 281 enrolled. *Average high school GPA:* 2.80. *Test scores:* SAT verbal scores over 500: 43%; SAT math scores over 500: 44%; SAT verbal scores over 600: 7%; SAT math scores over 600: 10%; SAT verbal scores over 700: 1%; SAT math scores over 700: 1%.

Faculty *Total:* 83, 63% full-time, 49% with terminal degrees. *Student/faculty ratio:* 15:1.

Majors Agricultural business related; biological/physical sciences; business; computer/information sciences; criminal justice studies; individual/family development; information sciences/systems; liberal arts and sciences/liberal studies; psychology.

Academic Programs *Special study options:* academic remediation for entering students, adult/continuing education programs, advanced placement credit, distance learning, double majors, independent study, internships, services for LD students, study abroad, summer session for credit.

Library 35,224 titles, 227 serial subscriptions, 633 audiovisual materials.

Computers on Campus 146 computers available on campus for general student use. A campuswide network can be accessed from student residence rooms and from off campus. Internet access, online (class) registration, at least one staffed computer lab available.

Student Life *Activities and Organizations:* drama/theater group, student-run newspaper, choral group. *Campus security:* 24-hour patrols, controlled dormitory access.

Athletics Member NJCAA. *Intercollegiate sports:* basketball M, cross-country running M/W, soccer M, softball W, volleyball W. *Intramural sports:* basketball M/W, football M, racquetball M/W, soccer M/W, softball M/W, swimming M/W, table tennis M/W, tennis M/W, track and field M/W, volleyball M/W.

Standardized Tests *Required:* SAT I or ACT (for admission).

Costs (2001–02) *Tuition:* state resident $6832 full-time, $276 per credit hour part-time; nonresident $10,574 full-time, $442 per credit hour part-time. Full-time tuition and fees vary according to class time, location, program, and student level. Part-time tuition and fees vary according to class time, course load, location, program, and student level. *Required fees:* $322 full-time, $54 per credit. *Room and board:* $5300; room only: $3700. Room and board charges vary according to board plan and housing facility. *Payment plan:* deferred payment. *Waivers:* senior citizens and employees or children of employees.

Financial Aid Of all full-time matriculated undergraduates who enrolled in 2001, 638 applied for aid, 565 were judged to have need, 29 had their need fully met. 69 Federal Work-Study jobs (averaging $941). In 2001, 94 non-need-based awards were made. *Average percent of need met:* 64%. *Average financial aid package:* $8903. *Average need-based loan:* $3254. *Average need-based gift aid:* $4120. *Average indebtedness upon graduation:* $17,453.

Applying *Options:* electronic application, early admission, deferred entrance. *Application fee:* $50. *Required:* high school transcript. *Application deadline:* rolling (freshmen), rolling (transfers). *Notification:* continuous (freshmen).

Admissions Contact Undergraduate Admissions Office, The Pennsylvania State University Schuylkill Campus of the Capital College, 200 University Dirve, Schuylkill Haven, PA 17972-2208. *Phone:* 814-865-5471. *Fax:* 570-385-3672. *E-mail:* admissions@psu.edu.

THE PENNSYLVANIA STATE UNIVERSITY SHENANGO CAMPUS OF THE COMMONWEALTH COLLEGE

Sharon, Pennsylvania

- **State-related** primarily 2-year, founded 1965, part of Pennsylvania State University
- **Calendar** semesters
- **Degrees** associate and bachelor's (also offers up to 2 years of most bachelor's degree programs offered at University Park campus)
- **Small-town** 14-acre campus
- **Coed,** 984 undergraduate students, 59% full-time, 60% women, 40% men
- **Moderately difficult** entrance level, 94% of applicants were admitted

Undergraduates 577 full-time, 407 part-time. 11% are from out of state, 6% African American, 0.4% Asian American or Pacific Islander, 2% Hispanic American, 0.3% Native American, 2% transferred in. *Retention:* 64% of 2001 full-time freshmen returned.

Freshmen *Admission:* 280 applied, 263 admitted, 170 enrolled. *Average high school GPA:* 2.79. *Test scores:* SAT verbal scores over 500: 27%; SAT math scores over 500: 36%; SAT verbal scores over 600: 5%; SAT math scores over 600: 5%; SAT verbal scores over 700: 1%.

Faculty *Total:* 94, 34% full-time. *Student/faculty ratio:* 14:1.

Majors Agricultural business; biological/physical sciences; business; business administration; individual/family development; information sciences/systems; liberal arts and sciences/liberal studies; mechanical engineering technology; nursing; occupational therapy; physical therapy assistant.

Academic Programs *Special study options:* academic remediation for entering students, adult/continuing education programs, advanced placement credit, distance learning, double majors, honors programs, independent study, internships, services for LD students, student-designed majors, summer session for credit.

Library 23,263 titles, 168 serial subscriptions, 1,953 audiovisual materials.

Computers on Campus 102 computers available on campus for general student use. A campuswide network can be accessed from off campus. Internet access, online (class) registration, at least one staffed computer lab available.

Student Life *Housing:* college housing not available. *Campus security:* part-time trained security personnel.

Athletics *Intramural sports:* basketball M/W, bowling M/W, golf M/W, racquetball M/W, tennis M/W, volleyball M/W.

Standardized Tests *Required:* SAT I or ACT (for admission).

Costs (2001–02) *Tuition:* state resident $6832 full-time, $276 per credit part-time; nonresident $10,574 full-time, $442 per credit part-time. Full-time tuition and fees vary according to class time, location, program, and student level. Part-time tuition and fees vary according to class time, course load, location, program, and student level. *Required fees:* $332 full-time, $56 per credit. *Payment plan:* deferred payment. *Waivers:* senior citizens and employees or children of employees.

Financial Aid Of all full-time matriculated undergraduates who enrolled in 2001, 24 Federal Work-Study jobs (averaging $1166).

Applying *Options:* electronic application, early admission, deferred entrance. *Application fee:* $50. *Required:* high school transcript. *Application deadline:* rolling (freshmen), rolling (transfers). *Notification:* continuous (freshmen).

Admissions Contact Undergraduate Admissions Office, The Pennsylvania State University Shenango Campus of the Commonwealth College, 147 Shenango Avenue, Sharon, PA 16146. *Phone:* 814-865-5471. *E-mail:* admissions@psu.edu.

THE PENNSYLVANIA STATE UNIVERSITY UNIVERSITY PARK CAMPUS

State College, Pennsylvania

- **State-related** university, founded 1855, part of Pennsylvania State University
- **Calendar** semesters
- **Degrees** certificates, associate, bachelor's, master's, doctoral, and postbachelor's certificates
- **Small-town** 5617-acre campus
- **Coed,** 34,539 undergraduate students, 95% full-time, 47% women, 53% men
- **Very difficult** entrance level, 57% of applicants were admitted

The Pennsylvania State University University Park Campus (continued)

Undergraduates 32,870 full-time, 1,669 part-time. Students come from 54 states and territories, 23% are from out of state, 4% African American, 5% Asian American or Pacific Islander, 3% Hispanic American, 0.1% Native American, 2% international, 1% transferred in, 36% live on campus. *Retention:* 92% of 2001 full-time freshmen returned.

Freshmen *Admission:* 27,899 applied, 15,966 admitted, 6,122 enrolled. *Average high school GPA:* 3.57. *Test scores:* SAT verbal scores over 500: 86%; SAT math scores over 500: 92%; SAT verbal scores over 600: 42%; SAT math scores over 600: 59%; SAT verbal scores over 700: 8%; SAT math scores over 700: 15%.

Faculty *Total:* 2,407, 87% full-time, 70% with terminal degrees. *Student/faculty ratio:* 18:1.

Majors Accounting; acting/directing; actuarial science; adult/continuing education administration; advertising; aerospace engineering; African-American studies; agribusiness; agricultural business; agricultural business related; agricultural engineering; agricultural mechanization; agricultural sciences; agronomy/crop science; American studies; animal sciences; anthropology; applied economics; applied mathematics; architectural engineering; architecture; art; art education; art history; astronomy; astrophysics; atmospheric sciences; biochemistry; bioengineering; biological/physical sciences; biological technology; biology; business; business administration; business economics; business marketing and marketing management; chemical engineering; chemistry; civil engineering; classics; communications; comparative literature; computer engineering; computer/information sciences; criminal justice/law enforcement administration; criminal justice studies; cultural studies; earth sciences; East Asian studies; economics; electrical engineering; elementary education; engineering science; English; environmental engineering; film studies; finance; fishing sciences; food sciences; forest products technology; forestry sciences; French; geography; geology; German; graphic design/commercial art/illustration; health services administration; history; horticulture science; hospitality management; hotel and restaurant management; individual/family development; industrial/manufacturing engineering; information sciences/systems; insurance/risk management; interdisciplinary studies; international business; international relations; Italian; Japanese; journalism; Judaic studies; labor/personnel relations; landscape architecture; landscaping management; Latin American studies; liberal arts and sciences/liberal studies; logistics/materials management; management information systems/business data processing; mathematical statistics; mathematics; mechanical engineering; medieval/renaissance studies; metallurgical engineering; microbiology/bacteriology; mining/mineral engineering; molecular biology; music; music (general performance); music teacher education; natural resources conservation; nuclear engineering; nursing; nutrition studies; petroleum engineering; philosophy; physics; political science; pre-medicine; psychology; real estate; recreation/leisure facilities management; religious studies; Russian; secondary education; sociology; soil sciences; Spanish; special education; speech-language pathology/audiology; speech/rhetorical studies; telecommunications; theater design; turf management; visual/performing arts; wildlife biology; women's studies.

Academic Programs *Special study options:* academic remediation for entering students, adult/continuing education programs, advanced placement credit, cooperative education, distance learning, double majors, English as a second language, external degree program, freshman honors college, honors programs, independent study, internships, part-time degree program, services for LD students, student-designed majors, study abroad, summer session for credit. *ROTC:* Army (b), Navy (b), Air Force (b). *Unusual degree programs:* 3-2 nursing with Lincoln University (PA); earth science, mineral science.

Library Pattee Library plus 7 others with 2.8 million titles, 22,879 serial subscriptions, 684,067 audiovisual materials, an OPAC, a Web page.

Computers on Campus 3589 computers available on campus for general student use. A campuswide network can be accessed from student residence rooms and from off campus. Internet access, online (class) registration, at least one staffed computer lab available.

Student Life *Housing:* on-campus residence required for freshman year. *Options:* coed, men-only, women-only, disabled students. *Activities and Organizations:* drama/theater group, student-run newspaper, radio and television station, choral group, marching band, national fraternities, national sororities. *Campus security:* 24-hour emergency response devices and patrols, student patrols, late-night transport/escort service, controlled dormitory access. *Student Services:* health clinic, personal/psychological counseling, women's center, legal services.

Athletics Member NCAA. All Division I except football (Division I-A). *Intercollegiate sports:* baseball M(s), basketball M(s)/W(s), bowling M(c), cross-country running M(s)/W(s), equestrian sports M(c)/W(c), fencing M(s)/W(s), field hockey W(s), golf M(s)/W(s), gymnastics M(s)/W(s), ice hockey M(c)/W(c), lacrosse M(s)/W(s), rugby M(c)/W(c), skiing (downhill) M(c)/W(c), soccer M(s)/W(s), softball W(s), swimming M(s)/W(s), table tennis M(c), tennis M(s)/W(s), track and field M(s)/W(s), volleyball M(s)/W(s), water polo M(c)/W(c), weight lifting M(c)/W(c), wrestling M(s). *Intramural sports:* archery M(c)/W(c), badminton M/W, basketball M/W, bowling M/W, crew M(c)/W(c), cross-country running M/W, fencing M(c)/W(c), field hockey W, football M, golf M/W, gymnastics M(c)/W(c), lacrosse M(c)/W(c), racquetball M/W, riflery M(c)/W(c), sailing M(c)/W(c), soccer M/W, softball M/W, squash M/W, swimming M/W, tennis M/W, track and field M/W, volleyball M/W, wrestling M.

Standardized Tests *Required:* SAT I or ACT (for admission).

Costs (2001–02) *Tuition:* state resident $7054 full-time, $295 per credit part-time; nonresident $15,180 full-time, $634 per credit part-time. Full-time tuition and fees vary according to class time, course load, location, program, and student level. Part-time tuition and fees vary according to class time, course load, location, program, and student level. *Required fees:* $342 full-time, $57 per credit. *Room and board:* $5310; room only: $2628. Room and board charges vary according to board plan. *Payment plan:* deferred payment. *Waivers:* senior citizens and employees or children of employees.

Financial Aid Of all full-time matriculated undergraduates who enrolled in 2001, 20931 applied for aid, 15925 were judged to have need, 1490 had their need fully met. 1875 Federal Work-Study jobs (averaging $1126). In 2001, 7046 non-need-based awards were made. *Average percent of need met:* 69%. *Average financial aid package:* $10,032. *Average need-based loan:* $3978. *Average need-based gift aid:* $3728. *Average indebtedness upon graduation:* $17,453.

Applying *Options:* electronic application, early admission, deferred entrance. *Application fee:* $50. *Required:* high school transcript, minimum 2.0 GPA. *Required for some:* 1 letter of recommendation, interview. *Recommended:* essay or personal statement. *Application deadline:* rolling (freshmen), rolling (transfers). *Notification:* continuous (freshmen).

Admissions Contact Undergraduate Admissions Office, The Pennsylvania State University University Park Campus, 201 Old Main, University Park, PA 16802. *Phone:* 814-865-5471. *Fax:* 814-863-7590. *E-mail:* admissions@psu.edu.

THE PENNSYLVANIA STATE UNIVERSITY WILKES-BARRE CAMPUS OF THE COMMONWEALTH COLLEGE

Lehman, Pennsylvania

- **State-related** primarily 2-year, founded 1916, part of Pennsylvania State University
- **Calendar** semesters
- **Degrees** associate and bachelor's (also offers up to 2 years of most bachelor's degree programs offered at University Park campus)
- **Rural** 58-acre campus
- **Coed,** 832 undergraduate students, 78% full-time, 35% women, 65% men
- **Moderately difficult** entrance level, 92% of applicants were admitted

Undergraduates 651 full-time, 181 part-time. 4% are from out of state, 1% African American, 3% Asian American or Pacific Islander, 0.6% Hispanic American, 0.3% international, 4% transferred in. *Retention:* 85% of 2001 full-time freshmen returned.

Freshmen *Admission:* 550 applied, 506 admitted, 244 enrolled. *Average high school GPA:* 2.88. *Test scores:* SAT verbal scores over 500: 45%; SAT math scores over 500: 49%; SAT verbal scores over 600: 7%; SAT math scores over 600: 11%.

Faculty *Total:* 94, 39% full-time. *Student/faculty ratio:* 13:1.

Majors Agricultural business; biomedical engineering-related technology; business; business administration; electrical/electronic engineering technology; information sciences/systems; liberal arts and sciences/liberal studies; mechanical engineering technologies related; surveying.

Academic Programs *Special study options:* academic remediation for entering students, adult/continuing education programs, advanced placement credit, distance learning, double majors, honors programs, independent study, internships, services for LD students, student-designed majors, summer session for credit. *ROTC:* Air Force (c).

Library 32,882 titles, 205 serial subscriptions, 1,963 audiovisual materials.

Computers on Campus 137 computers available on campus for general student use. A campuswide network can be accessed from off campus. Internet access, online (class) registration, at least one staffed computer lab available.

Student Life *Housing:* college housing not available. *Activities and Organizations:* student-run newspaper, radio station. *Campus security:* part-time trained security personnel.

Athletics Member NJCAA. *Intercollegiate sports:* baseball M, basketball M, cross-country running M/W, golf M/W, soccer M/W, softball W, volleyball W. *Intramural sports:* basketball M/W, skiing (downhill) M/W, volleyball M/W.

Standardized Tests *Required:* SAT I or ACT (for admission).

Costs (2001–02) *Tuition:* state resident $6832 full-time, $276 per credit part-time; nonresident $10,574 full-time, $442 per credit part-time. Full-time tuition and fees vary according to class time, location, program, and student level.

Part-time tuition and fees vary according to class time, course load, location, program, and student level. *Required fees:* $342 full-time, $57 per credit. *Payment plan:* deferred payment. *Waivers:* senior citizens and employees or children of employees.

Financial Aid Of all full-time matriculated undergraduates who enrolled in 2001, 28 Federal Work-Study jobs (averaging $953).

Applying *Options:* electronic application, early admission, deferred entrance. *Application fee:* $50. *Required:* high school transcript. *Application deadline:* rolling (freshmen), rolling (transfers). *Notification:* continuous (freshmen).

Admissions Contact Undergraduate Admissions Office, The Pennsylvania State University Wilkes-Barre Campus of the Commonwealth College, PO Box PSU, Lehman, PA 18627-0217. *Phone:* 814-865-5471. *Fax:* 570-675-8308. *E-mail:* admissions@psu.edu.

The Pennsylvania State University Worthington Scranton Campus of the Commonwealth College

Dunmore, Pennsylvania

- **State-related** primarily 2-year, founded 1923, part of Pennsylvania State University
- **Calendar** semesters
- **Degrees** associate and bachelor's (also offers up to 2 years of most bachelor's degree programs offered at University Park campus)
- **Small-town** 43-acre campus
- **Coed,** 1,520 undergraduate students, 77% full-time, 49% women, 51% men
- **Moderately difficult** entrance level, 85% of applicants were admitted

Undergraduates 1,175 full-time, 345 part-time. 2% are from out of state, 1% African American, 1% Asian American or Pacific Islander, 1% Hispanic American, 0.1% international, 5% transferred in. *Retention:* 73% of 2001 full-time freshmen returned.

Freshmen *Admission:* 657 applied, 557 admitted, 285 enrolled. *Average high school GPA:* 2.82. *Test scores:* SAT verbal scores over 500: 35%; SAT math scores over 500: 40%; SAT verbal scores over 600: 9%; SAT math scores over 600: 6%.

Faculty *Total:* 117, 55% full-time. *Student/faculty ratio:* 16:1.

Majors Agricultural business; architectural engineering technology; business; business administration; individual/family development; information sciences/systems; liberal arts and sciences/liberal studies; nursing; occupational therapy.

Academic Programs *Special study options:* academic remediation for entering students, adult/continuing education programs, advanced placement credit, distance learning, double majors, honors programs, independent study, internships, services for LD students, student-designed majors, summer session for credit.

Library 47,563 titles, 204 serial subscriptions, 2,985 audiovisual materials.

Computers on Campus 104 computers available on campus for general student use. A campuswide network can be accessed from off campus. Internet access, online (class) registration, at least one staffed computer lab available.

Student Life *Housing:* college housing not available. *Activities and Organizations:* drama/theater group, student-run newspaper. *Campus security:* part-time trained security personnel.

Athletics Member NJCAA. *Intercollegiate sports:* baseball M, basketball M, cross-country running M/W, soccer M, softball W, volleyball W. *Intramural sports:* basketball M/W, soccer M/W, softball W, tennis M/W, volleyball M/W.

Standardized Tests *Required:* SAT I or ACT (for admission).

Costs (2001–02) *Tuition:* state resident $6832 full-time, $276 per credit part-time; nonresident $10,574 full-time, $442 per credit part-time. Full-time tuition and fees vary according to class time, location, program, and student level. Part-time tuition and fees vary according to class time, course load, location, program, and student level. *Required fees:* $322 full-time, $54 per credit. *Payment plan:* deferred payment. *Waivers:* senior citizens and employees or children of employees.

Financial Aid Of all full-time matriculated undergraduates who enrolled in 2001, 24 Federal Work-Study jobs (averaging $957).

Applying *Options:* electronic application, early admission, deferred entrance. *Application fee:* $50. *Required:* high school transcript. *Application deadline:* rolling (freshmen), rolling (transfers). *Notification:* continuous (freshmen).

Admissions Contact Undergraduate Admissions Office, The Pennsylvania State University Worthington Scranton Campus of the Commonwealth College, 120 Ridge View Drive, Dunmore, PA 18512-1699. *Phone:* 814-865-5471. *Fax:* 570-963-2535. *E-mail:* admissions@psu.edu.

The Pennsylvania State University York Campus of the Commonwealth College

York, Pennsylvania

- **State-related** primarily 2-year, founded 1926, part of Pennsylvania State University
- **Calendar** semesters
- **Degrees** associate and bachelor's (also offers up to 2 years of most bachelor's degree programs offered at University Park campus)
- **Suburban** 52-acre campus
- **Coed,** 1,729 undergraduate students, 53% full-time, 44% women, 56% men
- **Moderately difficult** entrance level, 91% of applicants were admitted

Undergraduates 909 full-time, 820 part-time. 3% are from out of state, 3% African American, 6% Asian American or Pacific Islander, 3% Hispanic American, 0.2% Native American, 0.3% international, 3% transferred in. *Retention:* 69% of 2001 full-time freshmen returned.

Freshmen *Admission:* 672 applied, 609 admitted, 312 enrolled. *Average high school GPA:* 2.78. *Test scores:* SAT verbal scores over 500: 43%; SAT math scores over 500: 47%; SAT verbal scores over 600: 11%; SAT math scores over 600: 14%; SAT verbal scores over 700: 1%; SAT math scores over 700: 2%.

Faculty *Total:* 130, 48% full-time. *Student/faculty ratio:* 15:1.

Majors Agricultural business; business; business administration; electrical/electronic engineering technology; engineering; industrial technology; information sciences/systems; liberal arts and sciences/liberal studies; mechanical engineering technology.

Academic Programs *Special study options:* academic remediation for entering students, adult/continuing education programs, advanced placement credit, distance learning, double majors, English as a second language, honors programs, independent study, internships, services for LD students, student-designed majors, study abroad, summer session for credit.

Library 44,007 titles, 245 serial subscriptions, 2,977 audiovisual materials.

Computers on Campus 155 computers available on campus for general student use. A campuswide network can be accessed from off campus. Internet access, online (class) registration, at least one staffed computer lab available.

Student Life *Housing:* college housing not available. *Activities and Organizations:* student-run newspaper. *Campus security:* part-time trained security personnel.

Athletics Member NJCAA. *Intercollegiate sports:* basketball M/W, cross-country running M/W, soccer M, tennis M/W, volleyball W. *Intramural sports:* archery M/W, basketball M/W, football M, soccer M/W, softball M/W, table tennis M/W, tennis M/W, volleyball M/W.

Standardized Tests *Required:* SAT I or ACT (for admission).

Costs (2001–02) *Tuition:* state resident $6832 full-time, $276 per credit part-time; nonresident $10,574 full-time, $442 per credit part-time. Full-time tuition and fees vary according to class time, location, program, and student level. Part-time tuition and fees vary according to class time, course load, location, program, and student level. *Required fees:* $322 full-time, $54 per credit. *Payment plan:* deferred payment. *Waivers:* senior citizens and employees or children of employees.

Financial Aid Of all full-time matriculated undergraduates who enrolled in 2001, 39 Federal Work-Study jobs (averaging $960).

Applying *Options:* electronic application, early admission, deferred entrance. *Application fee:* $50. *Required:* high school transcript. *Application deadline:* rolling (freshmen), rolling (transfers). *Notification:* continuous (freshmen).

Admissions Contact Undergraduate Admissions Office, The Pennsylvania State University York Campus of the Commonwealth College, 18 Student Center, York, PA 17403. *Phone:* 814-865-5471. *Fax:* 717-771-4062. *E-mail:* admissions@psu.edu.

Philadelphia Biblical University

Langhorne, Pennsylvania

- **Independent nondenominational** comprehensive, founded 1913
- **Calendar** semesters
- **Degrees** certificates, associate, bachelor's, and master's
- **Suburban** 105-acre campus with easy access to Philadelphia
- **Endowment** $5.3 million
- **Coed,** 1,060 undergraduate students, 89% full-time, 55% women, 45% men
- **Moderately difficult** entrance level, 95% of applicants were admitted

Philadelphia Biblical University is a conservative, evangelical, nondenominational, selective Christian university. PBU is dedicated to developing leaders for the church and related ministries who possess a foundational knowledge

Philadelphia Biblical University (continued)

of scripture and a biblical world/life view. Each student graduates from PBU with a bachelor's degree in Bible. In addition to a major in bible, the dual-degree program offers each student the opportunity to select a second major in business, education, music, or social work.

Undergraduates 942 full-time, 118 part-time. Students come from 39 states and territories, 32 other countries, 53% are from out of state, 10% African American, 2% Asian American or Pacific Islander, 1% Hispanic American, 0.1% Native American, 3% international, 8% transferred in, 53% live on campus. *Retention:* 72% of 2001 full-time freshmen returned.

Freshmen *Admission:* 515 applied, 487 admitted, 204 enrolled. *Test scores:* SAT verbal scores over 500: 73%; SAT math scores over 500: 69%; ACT scores over 18: 100%; SAT verbal scores over 600: 31%; SAT math scores over 600: 23%; ACT scores over 24: 52%; SAT verbal scores over 700: 5%; SAT math scores over 700: 1%; ACT scores over 30: 13%.

Faculty *Total:* 133, 46% full-time, 43% with terminal degrees. *Student/faculty ratio:* 15:1.

Majors Biblical studies; business administration; early childhood education; elementary education; English education; mathematics education; music; physical education; religious studies; social studies education; social work.

Academic Programs *Special study options:* academic remediation for entering students, accelerated degree program, adult/continuing education programs, advanced placement credit, double majors, honors programs, independent study, internships, off-campus study, part-time degree program, services for LD students, study abroad, summer session for credit.

Library Masland Learning Resource Center with 89,743 titles, 680 serial subscriptions, 13,272 audiovisual materials, an OPAC.

Computers on Campus 90 computers available on campus for general student use. A campuswide network can be accessed from student residence rooms and from off campus. Internet access, at least one staffed computer lab available.

Student Life *Housing:* on-campus residence required through senior year. *Options:* men-only, women-only, disabled students. *Activities and Organizations:* drama/theater group, student-run newspaper, choral group, Student Theological Society, Student Missionary Fellowship, Cultural Awareness Association, All College Social Committee, Student Senate. *Campus security:* 24-hour emergency response devices and patrols, student patrols, late-night transport/escort service, controlled dormitory access. *Student Services:* health clinic, personal/psychological counseling.

Athletics Member NCAA, NCCAA. All NCAA Division III. *Intercollegiate sports:* baseball M, basketball M/W, cross-country running M/W, field hockey W, soccer M/W, tennis M/W, volleyball M/W. *Intramural sports:* archery M, basketball M/W, soccer M/W, tennis M/W, volleyball M/W.

Standardized Tests *Required:* SAT I or ACT (for admission).

Costs (2002–03) *Comprehensive fee:* $17,390 includes full-time tuition ($11,700), mandatory fees ($285), and room and board ($5405). Full-time tuition and fees vary according to course load, location, and program. Part-time tuition and fees vary according to course load, location, and program. *Room and board:* College room only: $2635. Room and board charges vary according to board plan, housing facility, and location. *Payment plan:* installment. *Waivers:* children of alumni and employees or children of employees.

Financial Aid Of all full-time matriculated undergraduates who enrolled in 2001, 797 applied for aid, 704 were judged to have need, 124 had their need fully met. 106 Federal Work-Study jobs (averaging $1043). *Average percent of need met:* 61%. *Average financial aid package:* $7680. *Average need-based loan:* $3406. *Average need-based gift aid:* $5571. *Average indebtedness upon graduation:* $12,000.

Applying *Options:* common application, electronic application, early admission, deferred entrance. *Application fee:* $25. *Required:* essay or personal statement, high school transcript, 1 letter of recommendation. *Required for some:* minimum 2.0 GPA, interview. *Recommended:* minimum 3.0 GPA, interview. *Application deadline:* rolling (freshmen), rolling (transfers).

Admissions Contact Ms. Lisa Fuller, Director of Admissions, Philadelphia Biblical University, 200 Manor Avenue, Langhorne, PA 19047. *Phone:* 215-702-4550. *Toll-free phone:* 800-366-0049. *Fax:* 215-752-4248. *E-mail:* admissions@pbu.edu.

PHILADELPHIA UNIVERSITY
Philadelphia, Pennsylvania

- **Independent** comprehensive, founded 1884
- **Calendar** semesters
- **Degrees** certificates, associate, bachelor's, and master's
- **Suburban** 100-acre campus
- **Endowment** $19.5 million
- **Coed,** 2,756 undergraduate students, 83% full-time, 66% women, 34% men
- **Moderately difficult** entrance level, 75% of applicants were admitted

Undergraduates 2,276 full-time, 480 part-time. Students come from 42 states and territories, 33 other countries, 41% are from out of state, 10% African American, 3% Asian American or Pacific Islander, 3% Hispanic American, 3% international, 4% transferred in, 53% live on campus. *Retention:* 69% of 2001 full-time freshmen returned.

Freshmen *Admission:* 3,177 applied, 2,389 admitted, 648 enrolled. *Average high school GPA:* 3.36. *Test scores:* SAT verbal scores over 500: 65%; SAT math scores over 500: 70%; SAT verbal scores over 600: 16%; SAT math scores over 600: 20%; SAT verbal scores over 700: 2%; SAT math scores over 700: 1%.

Faculty *Total:* 374, 27% full-time. *Student/faculty ratio:* 12:1.

Majors Accounting; apparel marketing; architecture; biochemistry; biology; biopsychology; business administration; business marketing and marketing management; chemistry; clothing/textiles; computer/information sciences; computer science; fashion design/illustration; fashion merchandising; finance; graphic design/commercial art/illustration; industrial design; information sciences/systems; interior architecture; interior design; international business; management information systems/business data processing; physician assistant; premedicine; psychology; textile arts; textile sciences/engineering.

Academic Programs *Special study options:* academic remediation for entering students, accelerated degree program, adult/continuing education programs, advanced placement credit, cooperative education, English as a second language, freshman honors college, honors programs, independent study, internships, off-campus study, part-time degree program, services for LD students, study abroad, summer session for credit.

Library Paul J. Gutman Library with 104,000 titles, 1,600 serial subscriptions, 37,650 audiovisual materials, an OPAC, a Web page.

Computers on Campus 400 computers available on campus for general student use. A campuswide network can be accessed from student residence rooms and from off campus that provide access to on-line registration for advanced workshops and seminars. Internet access, at least one staffed computer lab available.

Student Life *Housing Options:* coed, women-only. *Activities and Organizations:* drama/theater group, student-run newspaper, choral group, Gemini Theatre, Black Student Union, Cornerstone, Phila'cappella, Global Friends, national fraternities, national sororities. *Campus security:* 24-hour emergency response devices and patrols, late-night transport/escort service, controlled dormitory access. *Student Services:* health clinic, personal/psychological counseling.

Athletics Member NCAA. All Division II except soccer (Division I). *Intercollegiate sports:* baseball M(s), basketball M(s)/W(s), field hockey W(s), golf M(s), lacrosse W(s), soccer M(s)/W(s), softball W(s), tennis M(s)/W(s), volleyball W(s). *Intramural sports:* basketball M/W, cross-country running M/W, football M, skiing (downhill) M(c)/W(c), soccer M/W, softball M/W, swimming M/W, table tennis M/W, tennis M/W, volleyball M/W, weight lifting M/W.

Standardized Tests *Required:* SAT I or ACT (for admission).

Costs (2001–02) *Comprehensive fee:* $24,722 includes full-time tuition ($17,600) and room and board ($7122). Full-time tuition and fees vary according to program. Part-time tuition: $568 per credit. Part-time tuition and fees vary according to class time and program. *Room and board:* College room only: $3508. Room and board charges vary according to board plan and housing facility. *Payment plans:* installment, deferred payment. *Waivers:* employees or children of employees.

Financial Aid Of all full-time matriculated undergraduates who enrolled in 2001, 1822 applied for aid, 1586 were judged to have need, 210 had their need fully met. 42 State and other part-time jobs (averaging $5000). In 2001, 525 non-need-based awards were made. *Average percent of need met:* 69%. *Average financial aid package:* $12,998. *Average need-based loan:* $3774. *Average need-based gift aid:* $7894. *Average non-need based aid:* $4334. *Average indebtedness upon graduation:* $22,432. *Financial aid deadline:* 4/15.

Applying *Options:* common application, electronic application, early admission, deferred entrance. *Application fee:* $35. *Required:* high school transcript. *Recommended:* essay or personal statement, 2 letters of recommendation, interview. *Application deadline:* rolling (freshmen), rolling (transfers).

Admissions Contact Ms. Christine Greb, Acting Director of Admissions, Philadelphia University, School House Lane and Henry Avenue, Philadelphia, PA 19144-5497. *Phone:* 215-951-2800. *Fax:* 215-951-2907. *E-mail:* admissions@philau.edu.

POINT PARK COLLEGE
Pittsburgh, Pennsylvania

- **Independent** comprehensive, founded 1960
- **Calendar** semesters
- **Degrees** certificates, associate, bachelor's, master's, post-master's, and postbachelor's certificates
- **Urban** campus
- **Endowment** $6.0 million
- **Coed,** 2,644 undergraduate students, 65% full-time, 55% women, 45% men
- **Moderately difficult** entrance level, 77% of applicants were admitted

Point Park College offers students the opportunity to attend small, intimate classes in a facility located in the midst of vibrant downtown Pittsburgh. Recognized for providing a liberal arts education with career preparation, Point Park's location gives students access to important internships that provide valuable professional-level experience to complement classroom activities.

Undergraduates 1,730 full-time, 914 part-time. Students come from 42 states and territories, 32 other countries, 15% are from out of state, 12% African American, 1.0% Asian American or Pacific Islander, 1% Hispanic American, 0.3% Native American, 3% international, 7% transferred in, 21% live on campus. *Retention:* 68% of 2001 full-time freshmen returned.

Freshmen *Admission:* 1,397 applied, 1,077 admitted, 335 enrolled. *Average high school GPA:* 3.10. *Test scores:* SAT verbal scores over 500: 61%; SAT math scores over 500: 52%; ACT scores over 18: 90%; SAT verbal scores over 600: 16%; SAT math scores over 600: 11%; ACT scores over 24: 34%; SAT verbal scores over 700: 5%; SAT math scores over 700: 1%; ACT scores over 30: 3%.

Faculty *Total:* 266, 29% full-time. *Student/faculty ratio:* 16:1.

Majors Accounting; advertising; applied art; arts management; behavioral sciences; biological/physical sciences; biology; biology education; broadcast journalism; business administration; business communications; civil engineering technology; computer science; criminal justice studies; dance; drama/dance education; early childhood education; education; electrical/electronic engineering technology; elementary education; engineering technologies related; English; English education; environmental science; film/video production; general studies; health services administration; history; human resources management; international relations; journalism; legal studies; liberal arts and sciences/liberal studies; mass communications; mathematics education; mechanical engineering technology; mortuary science; photography; political science; pre-law; psychology; psychology related; public administration; public relations; radio/television broadcasting; respiratory therapy; secondary education; social science education; social sciences; theater arts/drama.

Academic Programs *Special study options:* academic remediation for entering students, accelerated degree program, adult/continuing education programs, advanced placement credit, distance learning, English as a second language, independent study, internships, off-campus study, part-time degree program, services for LD students, student-designed majors, summer session for credit. *ROTC:* Army (c), Air Force (c).

Library The Library Center with 269,192 titles, 681 serial subscriptions, an OPAC.

Computers on Campus 200 computers available on campus for general student use. A campuswide network can be accessed from student residence rooms and from off campus. Internet access, at least one staffed computer lab available.

Student Life *Housing Options:* coed. *Activities and Organizations:* drama/theater group, student-run newspaper, radio and television station, Dance Club, student radio station, Alpha Phi Omega, BASICS, Gamma Phi Omega. *Campus security:* 24-hour emergency response devices and patrols, late-night transport/escort service, 24-hour security desk, video security. *Student Services:* health clinic, personal/psychological counseling.

Athletics Member NAIA. *Intercollegiate sports:* baseball M(s), basketball M(s)/W(s), soccer M(s), softball W(s), volleyball W(s). *Intramural sports:* basketball M, football M, golf M, tennis M/W, volleyball M/W, weight lifting M/W.

Standardized Tests *Required:* SAT I or ACT (for admission).

Costs (2001–02) *Comprehensive fee:* $19,634 includes full-time tuition ($13,226), mandatory fees ($460), and room and board ($5948). Full-time tuition and fees vary according to course load and program. Part-time tuition: $352 per credit. Part-time tuition and fees vary according to course load and program. *Required fees:* $10 per credit. *Room and board:* College room only: $2964. Room and board charges vary according to board plan. *Payment plans:* installment, deferred payment. *Waivers:* senior citizens and employees or children of employees.

Financial Aid Of all full-time matriculated undergraduates who enrolled in 2001, 1670 applied for aid, 1513 were judged to have need, 337 had their need fully met. In 2001, 417 non-need-based awards were made. *Average percent of need met:* 75%. *Average financial aid package:* $10,862. *Average need-based loan:* $4333. *Average need-based gift aid:* $6190.

Applying *Options:* common application, electronic application, early admission, deferred entrance. *Application fee:* $20. *Required:* high school transcript. *Required for some:* 2 letters of recommendation, interview, audition. *Recommended:* essay or personal statement, minimum 2.0 GPA. *Application deadline:* rolling (freshmen), rolling (transfers).

Admissions Contact Point Park College, Point Park College, 201 Wood Street, Pittsburgh, PA 15222. *Phone:* 412-392-3430. *Toll-free phone:* 800-321-0129. *Fax:* 412-391-1980. *E-mail:* enroll@ppc.edu.

THE RESTAURANT SCHOOL
Philadelphia, Pennsylvania

- **Proprietary** primarily 2-year, founded 1974
- **Calendar** semesters
- **Degrees** associate and bachelor's
- **Urban** 2-acre campus
- **Coed,** 585 undergraduate students

Undergraduates Students come from 10 states and territories, 5 other countries, 57% are from out of state, 20% live on campus.

Freshmen *Average high school GPA:* 2.65.

Faculty *Total:* 27, 78% full-time, 37% with terminal degrees. *Student/faculty ratio:* 25:1.

Majors Baker/pastry chef; culinary arts; hotel and restaurant management.

Academic Programs *Special study options:* academic remediation for entering students, internships, part-time degree program.

Library Alumni Resource Center with 5,000 titles, 200 serial subscriptions.

Student Life *Housing Options:* coed. *Activities and Organizations:* student-run newspaper, Community Action Society, Les Gastronome, Culinary Salon, Tastevin, Pastry Club.

Standardized Tests *Recommended:* SAT I or ACT (for admission).

Applying *Options:* common application, early admission, early decision, deferred entrance. *Application fee:* $50. *Required:* essay or personal statement, high school transcript, 2 letters of recommendation, interview. *Recommended:* minimum 2.0 GPA. *Require for some:* entrance exam. *Application deadline:* rolling (freshmen).

Admissions Contact Mr. Karl Becker, Director of Admissions, The Restaurant School, 4207 Walnut Street, Philadelphia, PA 19104. *Phone:* 215-222-4200 Ext. 3007. *Toll-free phone:* 877-925-6884 Ext. 3011. *Fax:* 215-222-4219. *E-mail:* info@therestaurantschool.com.

ROBERT MORRIS UNIVERSITY
Moon Township, Pennsylvania

- **Independent** comprehensive, founded 1921
- **Calendar** semesters
- **Degrees** certificates, associate, bachelor's, master's, doctoral, and postbachelor's certificates
- **Suburban** 230-acre campus with easy access to Pittsburgh
- **Endowment** $14.7 million
- **Coed,** 3,813 undergraduate students, 70% full-time, 49% women, 51% men
- **Moderately difficult** entrance level, 71% of applicants were admitted

Robert Morris College, consistently a leading institution of higher learning in the Pittsburgh region, offers more than 30 undergraduate degree programs. A broad range of business majors lead to a degree in business administration, while excellent programs are offered in communications, elementary education, engineering, sport management, actuarial science, and visual communications.

Undergraduates 2,686 full-time, 1,127 part-time. Students come from 27 states and territories, 28 other countries, 8% are from out of state, 8% African American, 1% Asian American or Pacific Islander, 0.6% Hispanic American, 0.2% Native American, 2% international, 12% transferred in, 33% live on campus. *Retention:* 74% of 2001 full-time freshmen returned.

Freshmen *Admission:* 2,129 applied, 1,512 admitted, 541 enrolled. *Average high school GPA:* 3.01. *Test scores:* SAT verbal scores over 500: 42%; SAT math scores over 500: 47%; SAT verbal scores over 600: 9%; SAT math scores over 600: 12%; SAT verbal scores over 700: 1%; SAT math scores over 700: 1%.

Faculty *Total:* 312, 34% full-time, 37% with terminal degrees. *Student/faculty ratio:* 19:1.

Majors Accounting; applied mathematics; aviation management; business administration; business economics; business education; business marketing and mar-

Robert Morris University (continued)
keting management; communications; computer engineering; economics; elementary education; engineering; engineering/industrial management; English; finance; health/medical administrative services related; health services administration; hospitality management; human resources management; industrial/manufacturing engineering; information sciences/systems; liberal arts and sciences/liberal studies; logistics/materials management; management information systems/business data processing; mass communications; medical radiologic technology; operations management; secretarial science; social sciences; sport/fitness administration; travel/tourism management.

Academic Programs *Special study options:* academic remediation for entering students, accelerated degree program, adult/continuing education programs, advanced placement credit, cooperative education, distance learning, double majors, honors programs, independent study, internships, off-campus study, part-time degree program, services for LD students, study abroad, summer session for credit. *ROTC:* Army (c), Air Force (c).

Library Robert Morris College Library with 212,950 titles, 853 serial subscriptions, 3,165 audiovisual materials, an OPAC.

Computers on Campus 300 computers available on campus for general student use. A campuswide network can be accessed from off campus. Internet access, online (class) registration, at least one staffed computer lab available.

Student Life *Housing Options:* coed, men-only, women-only, disabled students. *Activities and Organizations:* drama/theater group, student-run television station, marching band, Student Government Association, Residence Hall Association, Interfraternity Council/Panhellenic Council, R-MOVE, National Society of Collegiate Scholars, national fraternities, national sororities. *Campus security:* 24-hour emergency response devices and patrols, late-night transport/escort service, controlled dormitory access. *Student Services:* health clinic, personal/psychological counseling.

Athletics Member NCAA. All Division I except football (Division I-AA). *Intercollegiate sports:* basketball M(s)/W(s), crew W(s), cross-country running M(s)/W(s), golf M(s), soccer M(s)/W(s), softball W(s), tennis M(s)/W(s), track and field M(s)/W(s), volleyball W(s). *Intramural sports:* basketball M/W, bowling M(c)/W(c), crew M(c), football M/W, ice hockey M(c), softball M/W, table tennis M/W, volleyball M(c)/W.

Standardized Tests *Required:* SAT I or ACT (for admission).

Costs (2001–02) *One-time required fee:* $150. *Comprehensive fee:* $18,580 includes full-time tuition ($12,000) and room and board ($6580). Full-time tuition and fees vary according to student level. Part-time tuition: $360 per credit. Part-time tuition and fees vary according to program. *Room and board:* College room only: $3900. Room and board charges vary according to board plan and housing facility. *Payment plans:* installment, deferred payment. *Waivers:* senior citizens and employees or children of employees.

Financial Aid Of all full-time matriculated undergraduates who enrolled in 2001, 2428 applied for aid, 2145 were judged to have need, 721 had their need fully met. In 2001, 263 non-need-based awards were made. *Average percent of need met:* 70%. *Average financial aid package:* $9500. *Average need-based loan:* $4700. *Average need-based gift aid:* $3800. *Average non-need based aid:* $2500.

Applying *Options:* common application, electronic application, deferred entrance. *Application fee:* $30. *Required:* high school transcript, minimum 2.5 GPA. *Required for some:* interview. *Recommended:* minimum 3.0 GPA, letters of recommendation, interview. *Application deadline:* rolling (freshmen), rolling (transfers). *Notification:* continuous (freshmen).

Admissions Contact Keith A. Paylo, Assistant Dean of Enrollment Services, Robert Morris University, Enrollment Services Department, 881 Narrows Run Road, Moon Township, PA 15108-1189. *Phone:* 412-262-8402. *Toll-free phone:* 800-762-0097. *Fax:* 412-299-2425. *E-mail:* enrollmentoffice@rmu.edu.

ROSEMONT COLLEGE
Rosemont, Pennsylvania

- **Independent Roman Catholic** comprehensive, founded 1921
- **Calendar** semesters
- **Degrees** certificates, bachelor's, master's, and postbachelor's certificates
- **Suburban** 56-acre campus with easy access to Philadelphia
- **Endowment** $7.8 million
- **Women only,** 797 undergraduate students, 54% full-time
- **Moderately difficult** entrance level, 81% of applicants were admitted

Founded in 1921, Rosemont College has been ranked by *U.S. News & World Report* for consecutive years as one of the top regional liberal arts colleges in the North. In addition, Rosemont was selected for the John Templeton Foundation's Honor Roll for Character Building Colleges and is listed among Barron's "best buys."

Undergraduates 427 full-time, 370 part-time. Students come from 18 states and territories, 33% are from out of state, 19% African American, 4% Asian American or Pacific Islander, 3% Hispanic American, 1% international, 3% transferred in, 68% live on campus. *Retention:* 72% of 2001 full-time freshmen returned.

Freshmen *Admission:* 58 enrolled. *Average high school GPA:* 3.10. *Test scores:* SAT verbal scores over 500: 76%; SAT math scores over 500: 62%; SAT verbal scores over 600: 32%; SAT math scores over 600: 17%; SAT verbal scores over 700: 4%; SAT math scores over 700: 4%.

Faculty *Total:* 167, 26% full-time, 96% with terminal degrees. *Student/faculty ratio:* 8:1.

Majors Accounting; art history; biochemistry; biology; business administration; chemistry; communications; economics; English; fine/studio arts; French; German; history; humanities; Italian; mathematics; philosophy; political science; psychology; religious studies; social sciences; sociology; Spanish; women's studies.

Academic Programs *Special study options:* accelerated degree program, adult/continuing education programs, advanced placement credit, double majors, English as a second language, honors programs, independent study, internships, off-campus study, part-time degree program, services for LD students, student-designed majors, study abroad, summer session for credit. *ROTC:* Army (c). *Unusual degree programs:* 3-2 engineering with Villanova University; counseling psychology, dentistry.

Library Kistler Library with 154,000 titles, 736 serial subscriptions, 2,600 audiovisual materials, an OPAC, a Web page.

Computers on Campus 90 computers available on campus for general student use. A campuswide network can be accessed from student residence rooms and from off campus. Internet access, at least one staffed computer lab available.

Student Life *Housing:* on-campus residence required through junior year. *Options:* women-only. *Activities and Organizations:* drama/theater group, student-run newspaper, choral group, marching band, student government, Triad, Jest and Gesture, Best Buddies, political science club. *Campus security:* 24-hour emergency response devices and patrols, late-night transport/escort service, controlled dormitory access. *Student Services:* health clinic, personal/psychological counseling, women's center, legal services.

Athletics Member NCAA. All Division III. *Intercollegiate sports:* basketball W, field hockey W, softball W, tennis W, volleyball W.

Standardized Tests *Required:* SAT I or ACT (for admission).

Costs (2001–02) *Comprehensive fee:* $24,060 includes full-time tuition ($16,000), mandatory fees ($750), and room and board ($7310). Part-time tuition: $675 per credit. *Required fees:* $70 per course. *Payment plan:* installment. *Waivers:* senior citizens and employees or children of employees.

Financial Aid Of all full-time matriculated undergraduates who enrolled in 2001, 352 applied for aid, 350 were judged to have need. In 2001, 10 non-need-based awards were made. *Average percent of need met:* 93%. *Average financial aid package:* $16,600. *Average need-based loan:* $5500. *Average need-based gift aid:* $9600. *Average non-need based aid:* $9600. *Average indebtedness upon graduation:* $16,500.

Applying *Options:* common application, electronic application, early admission, deferred entrance. *Application fee:* $35. *Required:* essay or personal statement, high school transcript, 2 letters of recommendation. *Recommended:* minimum 3.0 GPA, interview. *Application deadline:* rolling (freshmen), rolling (transfers). *Notification:* continuous until 8/1 (freshmen).

Admissions Contact Rosemont College, 1400 Montgomery Avenue, Rosemont, PA 19010. *Phone:* 610-527-0200 Ext. 2952. *Toll-free phone:* 800-331-0708. *Fax:* 610-520-4399. *E-mail:* admissions@rosemont.edu.

ST. CHARLES BORROMEO SEMINARY, OVERBROOK
Wynnewood, Pennsylvania

- **Independent Roman Catholic** comprehensive, founded 1832
- **Calendar** semesters
- **Degrees** certificates, bachelor's, master's, and first professional (also offers co-ed part-time programs)
- **Suburban** 77-acre campus with easy access to Philadelphia
- **Men only,** 320 undergraduate students, 28% full-time
- **Moderately difficult** entrance level, 100% of applicants were admitted

Undergraduates 88 full-time, 232 part-time. Students come from 8 states and territories, 2 other countries, 34% are from out of state, 2% African American, 15% Asian American or Pacific Islander, 6% Hispanic American, 5% international, 4% transferred in. *Retention:* 100% of 2001 full-time freshmen returned.

Freshmen *Admission:* 12 applied, 12 admitted, 12 enrolled. *Test scores:* SAT verbal scores over 500: 91%; SAT math scores over 500: 82%; SAT verbal scores over 600: 36%; SAT math scores over 600: 18%; SAT verbal scores over 700: 9%.
Faculty *Total:* 40, 33% full-time, 38% with terminal degrees. *Student/faculty ratio:* 8:1.
Majors Philosophy.
Academic Programs *Special study options:* academic remediation for entering students, accelerated degree program, adult/continuing education programs, advanced placement credit, English as a second language, independent study, summer session for credit.
Library Ryan Memorial Library with 130,485 titles, 564 serial subscriptions, 8,838 audiovisual materials, a Web page.
Computers on Campus 48 computers available on campus for general student use. Internet access, at least one staffed computer lab available.
Student Life *Housing:* on-campus residence required through senior year. *Options:* men-only. *Activities and Organizations:* drama/theater group, student-run newspaper, choral group, Seminarians for Life, student council. *Campus security:* 24-hour emergency response devices and patrols. *Student Services:* health clinic, personal/psychological counseling.
Athletics *Intramural sports:* basketball M, soccer M, volleyball M.
Standardized Tests *Recommended:* SAT I or ACT (for admission).
Costs (2001–02) *Comprehensive fee:* $14,820 includes full-time tuition ($8800) and room and board ($6020). Part-time tuition: $90 per credit. *Payment plan:* installment. *Waivers:* employees or children of employees.
Applying *Options:* deferred entrance. *Required:* essay or personal statement, high school transcript, 3 letters of recommendation, interview, sponsorship by diocese or religious community. *Application deadlines:* 7/15 (freshmen), 7/15 (transfers). *Notification:* continuous (freshmen).
Admissions Contact Rev. Christopher J. Schreck, Vice Rector, St. Charles Borromeo Seminary, Overbrook, 100 East Wynnewood Road, Wynnewood, PA 19096. *Phone:* 610-785-6271 Ext. 271. *E-mail:* vicerectorscs@adphila.org.

SAINT FRANCIS UNIVERSITY
Loretto, Pennsylvania

- **Independent Roman Catholic** comprehensive, founded 1847
- **Calendar** semesters
- **Degrees** certificates, associate, bachelor's, and master's
- **Rural** 600-acre campus
- **Endowment** $11.4 million
- **Coed,** 1,416 undergraduate students, 84% full-time, 61% women, 39% men
- **Moderately difficult** entrance level, 86% of applicants were admitted

Saint Francis University's physical therapy program has received full accrediation by the Commission on Accrediation in Physical Therapy Programs. Saint Francis University continues to improve technological capabilities with the addition of several multimedia facilities. Also, all incoming freshman at Saint Francis University will receive a laptop computer.

Undergraduates 1,196 full-time, 220 part-time. Students come from 22 states and territories, 12 other countries, 15% are from out of state, 5% African American, 0.4% Asian American or Pacific Islander, 0.7% Hispanic American, 0.3% Native American, 0.9% international, 4% transferred in, 83% live on campus. *Retention:* 75% of 2001 full-time freshmen returned.
Freshmen *Admission:* 1,251 applied, 1,081 admitted, 342 enrolled. *Average high school GPA:* 3.38. *Test scores:* SAT verbal scores over 500: 58%; SAT math scores over 500: 57%; ACT scores over 18: 94%; SAT verbal scores over 600: 12%; SAT math scores over 600: 13%; ACT scores over 24: 34%; SAT verbal scores over 700: 1%; SAT math scores over 700: 1%; ACT scores over 30: 3%.
Faculty *Total:* 117, 74% full-time, 58% with terminal degrees. *Student/faculty ratio:* 11:1.
Majors Accounting; American studies; anthropology; biology; business administration; business marketing and marketing management; chemistry; computer programming; computer science; criminal justice/law enforcement administration; culinary arts; data processing technology; drafting; economics; education; elementary education; emergency medical technology; English; environmental science; finance; French; history; human resources management; international business; international relations; journalism; labor/personnel relations; literature; management information systems/business data processing; marine biology; mass communications; mathematics; medical technology; modern languages; nursing; occupational therapy; pastoral counseling; philosophy; physical therapy; physician assistant; political science; pre-dentistry; pre-law; pre-medicine; pre-veterinary studies; psychology; public administration; public relations; real estate; religious studies; science education; secondary education; social work; sociology; Spanish.
Academic Programs *Special study options:* academic remediation for entering students, accelerated degree program, adult/continuing education programs, advanced placement credit, distance learning, double majors, freshman honors college, honors programs, internships, off-campus study, part-time degree program, student-designed majors, study abroad, summer session for credit. *ROTC:* Army (c). *Unusual degree programs:* 3-2 engineering with Pennsylvania State University University Park Campus, University of Pittsburgh, Clarkson University; forestry with Duke University.
Library Pasquerella Library with 155,143 titles, 975 serial subscriptions, 1,957 audiovisual materials, an OPAC, a Web page.
Computers on Campus 60 computers available on campus for general student use. A campuswide network can be accessed from student residence rooms. At least one staffed computer lab available.
Student Life *Housing:* on-campus residence required through junior year. *Options:* men-only, women-only. *Activities and Organizations:* drama/theater group, student-run newspaper, radio and television station, choral group, Student Activities Organization, New Theatre, Student Government Association, national fraternities, national sororities. *Campus security:* 24-hour emergency response devices and patrols, late-night transport/escort service, controlled dormitory access. *Student Services:* health clinic, personal/psychological counseling.
Athletics Member NCAA. All Division I except football (Division I-AA). *Intercollegiate sports:* basketball M(s)/W(s), cross-country running M(s)/W(s), golf M(s)/W(s), soccer M(s)/W(s), softball W(s), swimming W(s), tennis M(s)/W(s), track and field M(s)/W(s), volleyball M(s)/W(s). *Intramural sports:* basketball M/W, bowling M/W, cross-country running M/W, football M, golf M/W, ice hockey M/W, racquetball M/W, skiing (cross-country) M/W, skiing (downhill) M/W, soccer M/W, softball W, swimming M/W, table tennis M/W, tennis M/W, track and field M/W, volleyball M/W, weight lifting M/W.
Standardized Tests *Required:* SAT I or ACT (for admission).
Costs (2001–02) *Comprehensive fee:* $24,486 includes full-time tuition ($17,512) and room and board ($6974). Part-time tuition: $516 per hour. Part-time tuition and fees vary according to course load. *Room and board:* College room only: $3266. Room and board charges vary according to board plan, housing facility, and location. *Payment plans:* installment, deferred payment. *Waivers:* children of alumni and employees or children of employees.
Financial Aid Of all full-time matriculated undergraduates who enrolled in 2001, 1065 applied for aid, 978 were judged to have need, 300 had their need fully met. In 2001, 54 non-need-based awards were made. *Average percent of need met:* 82%. *Average financial aid package:* $15,098. *Average need-based loan:* $3707. *Average need-based gift aid:* $11,248. *Average non-need based aid:* $4630. *Average indebtedness upon graduation:* $14,100.
Applying *Options:* electronic application, deferred entrance. *Application fee:* $30. *Required:* high school transcript, 1 letter of recommendation. *Required for some:* 3 letters of recommendation, interview. *Recommended:* essay or personal statement, interview. *Application deadline:* rolling (freshmen), rolling (transfers).
Admissions Contact Evan E. Lipp, Dean for Enrollment Management, Saint Francis University, PO Box 600, Loretto, PA 15940-0600. *Phone:* 814-472-3100. *Toll-free phone:* 800-342-5732. *Fax:* 814-472-3335. *E-mail:* admission@sfcpa.edu.

SAINT JOSEPH'S UNIVERSITY
Philadelphia, Pennsylvania

- **Independent Roman Catholic (Jesuit)** comprehensive, founded 1851
- **Calendar** semesters
- **Degrees** certificates, associate, bachelor's, master's, doctoral, and post-master's certificates
- **Suburban** 60-acre campus
- **Endowment** $73.7 million
- **Coed,** 4,590 undergraduate students, 80% full-time, 54% women, 46% men
- **Very difficult** entrance level, 57% of applicants were admitted

Saint Joseph's is celebrating 150 years of scholarship and service. The Haub School of Business is part of an elite group of colleges accredited by the AACSB. The College of Arts and Sciences houses a chapter of Phi Beta Kappa, the country's oldest and most prestigious honors organization.

Undergraduates 3,665 full-time, 925 part-time. 49% are from out of state, 7% African American, 2% Asian American or Pacific Islander, 2% Hispanic American, 0.1% Native American, 2% international, 53% live on campus. *Retention:* 86% of 2001 full-time freshmen returned.
Freshmen *Admission:* 5,866 applied, 3,343 admitted, 960 enrolled. *Average high school GPA:* 3.14.
Faculty *Total:* 454, 50% full-time. *Student/faculty ratio:* 13:1.
Majors Accounting; art; biology; business administration; business marketing and marketing management; chemistry; computer programming; computer sci-

Saint Joseph's University (continued)
ence; criminal justice/law enforcement administration; economics; education; elementary education; English; environmental science; finance; food sales operations; French; German; health services administration; history; humanities; human services; interdisciplinary studies; international relations; labor/personnel relations; liberal arts and sciences/liberal studies; management information systems/ business data processing; mathematics; philosophy; physics; political science; psychology; public administration; purchasing/contracts management; secondary education; social sciences; sociology; Spanish; theology.

Academic Programs *Special study options:* academic remediation for entering students, accelerated degree program, adult/continuing education programs, advanced placement credit, cooperative education, double majors, English as a second language, honors programs, independent study, internships, off-campus study, part-time degree program, services for LD students, student-designed majors, study abroad, summer session for credit. *ROTC:* Army (c), Air Force (b). *Unusual degree programs:* 3-2 psychology.

Library Francis A. Drexel Library plus 1 other with 197,788 titles, 4,900 serial subscriptions, 3,457 audiovisual materials, an OPAC, a Web page.

Computers on Campus 180 computers available on campus for general student use. A campuswide network can be accessed from student residence rooms and from off campus. Internet access, online (class) registration, at least one staffed computer lab available.

Student Life *Housing Options:* coed, men-only, women-only, disabled students. *Activities and Organizations:* drama/theater group, student-run newspaper, radio station, choral group, Student Government Association, Student Union Board, Cap and Bells Dramatic Arts Society, national fraternities, national sororities. *Campus security:* 24-hour emergency response devices and patrols, late-night transport/escort service, controlled dormitory access, 24-hour shuttle/ escort service, bicycle patrols. *Student Services:* health clinic, personal/ psychological counseling, women's center.

Athletics Member NCAA. All Division I. *Intercollegiate sports:* baseball M(s), basketball M(s)/W(s), crew M(c)/W(c), cross-country running M(s)/W(s), field hockey W, golf M(s), lacrosse M(s)/W(s), soccer M(s)/W(s), softball W(s), tennis M(s)/W(s), track and field M(s)/W(s). *Intramural sports:* basketball M/W, football M/W, golf M, ice hockey M, racquetball M/W, rugby M, tennis M/W, volleyball M/W, weight lifting M/W.

Standardized Tests *Required:* SAT I or ACT (for admission). *Recommended:* SAT II: Subject Tests (for admission).

Costs (2001–02) *Comprehensive fee:* $29,715 includes full-time tuition ($21,270) and room and board ($8445). Full-time tuition and fees vary according to program. Part-time tuition: $709 per credit. Part-time tuition and fees vary according to class time. *Room and board:* College room only: $5385. Room and board charges vary according to board plan and housing facility. *Payment plans:* installment, deferred payment. *Waivers:* employees or children of employees.

Financial Aid Of all full-time matriculated undergraduates who enrolled in 2001, 2540 applied for aid, 2044 were judged to have need, 1021 had their need fully met. In 2001, 544 non-need-based awards were made. *Average percent of need met:* 80%. *Average financial aid package:* $11,270. *Average need-based loan:* $4261. *Average need-based gift aid:* $6296. *Average non-need based aid:* $6296.

Applying *Options:* common application, electronic application, early admission, deferred entrance. *Application fee:* $45. *Required:* essay or personal statement, high school transcript, 1 letter of recommendation. *Recommended:* minimum 3.0 GPA. *Application deadline:* 3/1 (transfers).

Admissions Contact Mr. David Conway, Assistant Vice President of Enrollment Management, Saint Joseph's University, 5600 City Avenue, Philadelphia, PA 19131-1395. *Phone:* 610-660-1300. *Toll-free phone:* 888-BEAHAWK. *Fax:* 610-660-1314. *E-mail:* admi@sju.edu.

SAINT VINCENT COLLEGE
Latrobe, Pennsylvania

- **Independent Roman Catholic** 4-year, founded 1846
- **Calendar** semesters
- **Degree** certificates and bachelor's
- **Suburban** 200-acre campus with easy access to Pittsburgh
- **Endowment** $34.4 million
- **Coed,** 1,222 undergraduate students, 91% full-time, 49% women, 51% men
- **Moderately difficult** entrance level, 84% of applicants were admitted

Undergraduates 1,107 full-time, 115 part-time. Students come from 25 states and territories, 15 other countries, 12% are from out of state, 3% African American, 0.7% Asian American or Pacific Islander, 0.7% Hispanic American, 0.1% Native American, 2% international, 5% transferred in, 67% live on campus. *Retention:* 85% of 2001 full-time freshmen returned.

Freshmen *Admission:* 687 applied, 579 admitted, 262 enrolled. *Average high school GPA:* 3.41. *Test scores:* SAT verbal scores over 500: 69%; SAT math scores over 500: 66%; ACT scores over 18: 86%; SAT verbal scores over 600: 26%; SAT math scores over 600: 26%; ACT scores over 24: 48%; SAT verbal scores over 700: 6%; SAT math scores over 700: 4%; ACT scores over 30: 5%.

Faculty *Total:* 112, 64% full-time. *Student/faculty ratio:* 14:1.

Majors Accounting; anthropology; art education; art history; biochemistry; biology; business administration; business education; business management/ administrative services related; business marketing and marketing management; chemistry; communications; computer/information sciences; economics; engineering; English; environmental science; finance; fine/studio arts; history; international business; liberal arts and sciences/liberal studies; mathematics; music; music (general performance); music teacher education; occupational therapy; pharmacy; philosophy; physical therapy; physician assistant; physics; physics education; political science; psychology; public policy analysis; religious education; sociology; Spanish; theater arts/drama; theology.

Academic Programs *Special study options:* academic remediation for entering students, accelerated degree program, adult/continuing education programs, advanced placement credit, cooperative education, honors programs, independent study, internships, off-campus study, part-time degree program, study abroad, summer session for credit. *ROTC:* Air Force (c). *Unusual degree programs:* 3-2 engineering with University of Pittsburgh, Pennsylvania State University, Boston University, The Catholic University of America.

Library Saint Vincent College Library with 259,919 titles, 811 serial subscriptions, 2,747 audiovisual materials, an OPAC.

Computers on Campus 167 computers available on campus for general student use. A campuswide network can be accessed from student residence rooms and from off campus. At least one staffed computer lab available.

Student Life *Housing Options:* coed. *Activities and Organizations:* drama/ theater group, student-run newspaper, radio and television station, choral group, Campus Ministry, prelaw club, The Review (Newspaper), Student Government, SVC Student Education Association. *Campus security:* 24-hour emergency response devices and patrols, late-night transport/escort service, controlled dormitory access, limited access to residence halls on weekends. *Student Services:* health clinic, personal/psychological counseling.

Athletics Member NAIA. *Intercollegiate sports:* baseball M(s), basketball M(s)/W(s), cross-country running M(s)/W(s), lacrosse M(s)/W(s), soccer M(s)/ W(s), softball W(s), tennis M(s), volleyball W(s). *Intramural sports:* archery M/W, basketball M/W, football M/W, golf M/W, skiing (cross-country) M/W, skiing (downhill) M/W, soccer M, softball M/W, swimming M/W, table tennis M/W, tennis M/W, volleyball M/W, weight lifting M/W.

Standardized Tests *Required:* SAT I or ACT (for admission).

Costs (2001–02) *Comprehensive fee:* $22,814 includes full-time tuition ($17,120), mandatory fees ($260), and room and board ($5434). Full-time tuition and fees vary according to course load. Part-time tuition: $535 per credit hour. Part-time tuition and fees vary according to course load. *Required fees:* $40 per term part-time. *Room and board:* College room only: $2762. Room and board charges vary according to board plan and housing facility. *Payment plans:* installment, deferred payment. *Waivers:* senior citizens and employees or children of employees.

Financial Aid Of all full-time matriculated undergraduates who enrolled in 2001, 963 applied for aid, 782 were judged to have need, 289 had their need fully met. 101 Federal Work-Study jobs (averaging $1875). 312 State and other part-time jobs (averaging $1917). In 2001, 157 non-need-based awards were made. *Average percent of need met:* 83%. *Average financial aid package:* $13,280. *Average need-based loan:* $4076. *Average need-based gift aid:* $9947. *Average non-need based aid:* $4789.

Applying *Options:* early admission, deferred entrance. *Application fee:* $25. *Required:* essay or personal statement, high school transcript, minimum 2.5 GPA. *Required for some:* interview. *Recommended:* minimum 3.2 GPA, 3 letters of recommendation, interview. *Application deadlines:* 5/1 (freshmen), 7/1 (transfers). *Notification:* continuous (freshmen).

Admissions Contact Mr. David A. Collins, Director of Admission, Saint Vincent College, 300 Fraser Purchase Road, Latrobe, PA 15650. *Phone:* 724-532-5089. *Toll-free phone:* 800-782-5549. *Fax:* 724-532-5069. *E-mail:* admission@ stvincent.edu.

SETON HILL COLLEGE
Greensburg, Pennsylvania

- **Independent Roman Catholic** comprehensive, founded 1883
- **Calendar** semesters
- **Degrees** bachelor's, master's, and post-master's certificates
- **Small-town** 200-acre campus with easy access to Pittsburgh

- **Endowment** $7.5 million
- **Coed, primarily women,** 1,128 undergraduate students, 72% full-time, 82% women, 18% men
- **Moderately difficult** entrance level, 78% of applicants were admitted

***U.S. News & World Report* ranks Seton Hill College as a top regional liberal arts college in the northern U.S. Seton Hill offers 30 undergraduate majors, including physician assistant studies, dietetics, and teacher training, and master's degrees in education, art therapy, management, writing, counseling psychology, and technologies enhanced learning.**

Undergraduates 809 full-time, 319 part-time. Students come from 22 states and territories, 12 other countries, 17% are from out of state, 7% African American, 1% Asian American or Pacific Islander, 2% Hispanic American, 0.4% Native American, 2% international, 12% transferred in, 60% live on campus. *Retention:* 71% of 2001 full-time freshmen returned.

Freshmen *Admission:* 940 applied, 731 admitted, 156 enrolled. *Average high school GPA:* 3.25. *Test scores:* SAT verbal scores over 500: 59%; SAT math scores over 500: 45%; SAT verbal scores over 600: 12%; SAT math scores over 600: 11%; SAT verbal scores over 700: 3%.

Faculty *Total:* 128, 40% full-time, 51% with terminal degrees. *Student/faculty ratio:* 13:1.

Majors Accounting; acting/directing; actuarial science; applied art; art; art education; art history; arts management; art therapy; biochemistry; biology; biology education; business administration; business economics; business marketing and marketing management; ceramic arts; chemistry; chemistry education; child care/development; child care services management; communications; computer science; creative writing; criminal justice studies; dietetics; drawing; early childhood education; economics; education; educational media technology; elementary education; engineering; English; English education; entrepreneurship; family/community studies; family/consumer studies; finance; fine/studio arts; foreign languages education; general studies; graphic design/commercial art/illustration; history; history education; home economics; home economics education; human resources management; human services; individual/family development; interdisciplinary studies; international business; international relations; journalism; liberal arts and sciences/liberal studies; literature; management information systems/business data processing; mass communications; mathematics; mathematics education; medical technology; metal/jewelry arts; modern languages; music; music (general performance); music (piano and organ performance); music teacher education; music theory and composition; music (voice and choral/opera performance); nursing; nutrition science; painting; physician assistant; physics; physics education; political science; pre-dentistry; pre-law; pre-medicine; pre-veterinary studies; printmaking; psychology; public administration; public relations; religious music; religious studies; science education; sculpture; secondary education; social studies education; social work; sociology; Spanish; Spanish language education; special education; stringed instruments; theater arts/drama; theater arts/drama and stagecraft related; theater design; theology; visual/performing arts; wind/percussion instruments.

Academic Programs *Special study options:* academic remediation for entering students, accelerated degree program, adult/continuing education programs, advanced placement credit, distance learning, double majors, English as a second language, honors programs, independent study, internships, off-campus study, part-time degree program, student-designed majors, study abroad, summer session for credit. *ROTC:* Army (c). *Unusual degree programs:* 3-2 engineering with University of Pittsburgh, Pennsylvania State University University Park Campus, Georgia Institute of Technology; nursing with Catholic University of America.

Library Reeves Memorial Library with 83,354 titles, 501 serial subscriptions, 6,000 audiovisual materials, an OPAC.

Computers on Campus 260 computers available on campus for general student use. A campuswide network can be accessed from student residence rooms and from off campus that provide access to e-mail. Internet access, at least one staffed computer lab available.

Student Life *Housing Options:* coed, men-only, women-only. *Activities and Organizations:* drama/theater group, student-run newspaper, television station, choral group, Intercultural Student Organization, biology/environmental club, Association of Black Collegians, chemistry club, Pennsylvania Student Education Association. *Campus security:* 24-hour emergency response devices and patrols, late-night transport/escort service, controlled dormitory access, student personnel at entrances during evening hours, 15-hour overnight patrols by trained police officers. *Student Services:* health clinic, personal/psychological counseling.

Athletics Member NAIA. *Intercollegiate sports:* basketball W(s), cross-country running M/W(s), equestrian sports M/W, golf M(s)/W(s), soccer M(s)/W(s), softball W(s), tennis W(s), volleyball W(s). *Intramural sports:* basketball W, skiing (cross-country) M(c)/W(c), skiing (downhill) M(c)/W(c).

Standardized Tests *Recommended:* SAT I or ACT (for admission).

Costs (2001–02) *Comprehensive fee:* $21,875 includes full-time tuition ($16,425) and room and board ($5450). Part-time tuition: $400 per credit. *Required fees:* $40 per term part-time. *Room and board:* Room and board charges vary according to board plan. *Payment plans:* installment, deferred payment. *Waivers:* employees or children of employees.

Financial Aid Of all full-time matriculated undergraduates who enrolled in 2001, 734 applied for aid, 655 were judged to have need, 400 had their need fully met. 294 Federal Work-Study jobs (averaging $1320). 62 State and other part-time jobs (averaging $1205). In 2001, 65 non-need-based awards were made. *Average percent of need met:* 85%. *Average financial aid package:* $15,600. *Average need-based loan:* $4300. *Average need-based gift aid:* $12,130. *Average indebtedness upon graduation:* $20,140.

Applying *Options:* common application, electronic application, early admission, deferred entrance. *Application fee:* $30. *Required:* high school transcript, minimum 2.0 GPA, portfolio for art program, audition for music and theater programs, separate application process required for physician assistant program. *Recommended:* essay or personal statement, letters of recommendation, interview. *Application deadline:* rolling (freshmen), rolling (transfers). *Notification:* continuous (freshmen).

Admissions Contact Ms. Mary Kay Cooper, Director of Admissions, Seton Hill College, Seton Hill Drive, Greensburg, PA 15601. *Phone:* 724-838-4255. *Toll-free phone:* 800-826-6234. *Fax:* 724-830-1294. *E-mail:* admit@setonhill.edu.

SHIPPENSBURG UNIVERSITY OF PENNSYLVANIA

Shippensburg, Pennsylvania

- **State-supported** comprehensive, founded 1871, part of Pennsylvania State System of Higher Education
- **Calendar** semesters
- **Degrees** bachelor's and master's
- **Rural** 200-acre campus
- **Endowment** $16.8 million
- **Coed,** 6,238 undergraduate students, 96% full-time, 54% women, 46% men
- **Moderately difficult** entrance level, 62% of applicants were admitted

Recognized for its academic excellence, Shippensburg University has a national reputation for providing students with opportunities for student-faculty research, volunteer community service projects, and internships. The talented, dedicated faculty offers a personalized education. Renovation of several academic buildings are in progress and will further complement the academic quality.

Undergraduates 5,962 full-time, 276 part-time. Students come from 23 states and territories, 33 other countries, 6% are from out of state, 4% African American, 1% Asian American or Pacific Islander, 1% Hispanic American, 0.3% Native American, 1.0% international, 6% transferred in, 39% live on campus. *Retention:* 80% of 2001 full-time freshmen returned.

Freshmen *Admission:* 6,424 applied, 4,001 admitted, 1,486 enrolled. *Average high school GPA:* 3.20. *Test scores:* SAT verbal scores over 500: 68%; SAT math scores over 500: 70%; SAT verbal scores over 600: 16%; SAT math scores over 600: 21%; SAT verbal scores over 700: 1%; SAT math scores over 700: 1%.

Faculty *Total:* 351, 85% full-time, 78% with terminal degrees. *Student/faculty ratio:* 19:1.

Majors Accounting; art; biology; business administration; business education; business marketing and marketing management; business systems analysis/design; chemistry; computer/information sciences; criminal justice studies; earth sciences; economics; elementary education; English; environmental science; finance; French; geography; history; journalism; management science; mathematics; multi/interdisciplinary studies related; physics; political science; psychology; public administration; social work; sociology; Spanish; speech/rhetorical studies.

Academic Programs *Special study options:* academic remediation for entering students, accelerated degree program, advanced placement credit, cooperative education, distance learning, double majors, honors programs, independent study, internships, off-campus study, part-time degree program, services for LD students, study abroad, summer session for credit. *ROTC:* Army (b). *Unusual degree programs:* 3-2 engineering with Pennsylvania State University University Park and Harrisburg Campus, University of Maryland College Park.

Library Ezra Lehman Memorial Library plus 1 other with 445,631 titles, 1,443 serial subscriptions, 15,383 audiovisual materials, an OPAC, a Web page.

Computers on Campus 527 computers available on campus for general student use. A campuswide network can be accessed from student residence rooms and from off campus that provide access to personal Web pages. Internet access, at least one staffed computer lab available.

Student Life *Housing:* on-campus residence required for freshman year. *Options:* coed, men-only, women-only. *Activities and Organizations:* drama/

Shippensburg University of Pennsylvania (continued)
theater group, student-run newspaper, radio and television station, choral group, marching band, TOUCH, Big Brother/Big Sister, band, Christian Fellowship, Concert Committee, national fraternities, national sororities. *Campus security:* 24-hour emergency response devices and patrols, student patrols, late-night transport/escort service, controlled dormitory access, surveillance cameras in certain parking lots and buildings, foot, vehicular and bicycle patrols by security officers. *Student Services:* health clinic, personal/psychological counseling, women's center.

Athletics Member NCAA. All Division II. *Intercollegiate sports:* baseball M(s), basketball M(s)/W(s), cross-country running M(s)/W(s), field hockey W(s), football M(s), lacrosse W(s), soccer M(s)/W(s), softball W(s), swimming M(s)/W(s), tennis W(s), track and field M(s)/W(s), volleyball W(s), wrestling M(s). *Intramural sports:* basketball M/W, bowling M/W, cross-country running M/W, golf M/W, ice hockey M(c)/W(c), lacrosse M(c), racquetball M/W, rugby M(c)/W(c), soccer M/W, softball M/W, swimming M/W, table tennis M/W, tennis M/W, volleyball M/W, water polo M(c)/W(c), weight lifting M(c)/W(c), wrestling M.

Standardized Tests *Required:* SAT I or ACT (for admission).

Costs (2001–02) *Tuition:* state resident $4016 full-time, $167 per credit hour part-time; nonresident $10,040 full-time, $418 per credit hour part-time. Part-time tuition and fees vary according to course load. *Required fees:* $988 full-time, $16 per credit hour, $118 per term part-time. *Room and board:* $4864; room only: $2736. Room and board charges vary according to board plan. *Waivers:* senior citizens and employees or children of employees.

Financial Aid Of all full-time matriculated undergraduates who enrolled in 2001, 4312 applied for aid, 2813 were judged to have need, 1001 had their need fully met. 327 Federal Work-Study jobs (averaging $1449). 471 State and other part-time jobs (averaging $1849). In 2001, 2110 non-need-based awards were made. *Average percent of need met:* 69%. *Average financial aid package:* $5631. *Average need-based loan:* $3152. *Average need-based gift aid:* $3345. *Average indebtedness upon graduation:* $14,956. *Financial aid deadline:* 5/1.

Applying *Options:* common application, electronic application, early admission, deferred entrance. *Application fee:* $30. *Required:* high school transcript. *Recommended:* letters of recommendation. *Application deadline:* rolling (freshmen), rolling (transfers).

Admissions Contact Mr. Joseph Cretella, Dean of Undergraduate and Graduate Admissions, Shippensburg University of Pennsylvania, 1871 Old Main Drive, Shippensburg, PA 17257-2299. *Phone:* 717-477-1231. *Toll-free phone:* 800-822-8028. *Fax:* 717-477-4016. *E-mail:* admiss@ship.edu.

SLIPPERY ROCK UNIVERSITY OF PENNSYLVANIA

Slippery Rock, Pennsylvania

- **State-supported** comprehensive, founded 1889, part of Pennsylvania State System of Higher Education
- **Calendar** semesters
- **Degrees** bachelor's, master's, and doctoral
- **Rural** 611-acre campus with easy access to Pittsburgh
- **Endowment** $11.4 million
- **Coed,** 6,500 undergraduate students, 91% full-time, 58% women, 42% men
- **Moderately difficult** entrance level, 81% of applicants were admitted

Slippery Rock University's students benefit from more than 100 programs in the Colleges of Education; Humanities, Fine, and Performing Arts; Business, Information, and Behavioral Sciences; and Health, Environment, and Science; twenty-eight study-abroad programs; more than 160 student organizations; athletics; and an online environment linking every student residence hall room to the electronic world. A flexible admission policy and attractive financial aid packages draw 7,000 students from forty states and more than seventy countries.

Undergraduates 5,923 full-time, 577 part-time. Students come from 34 states and territories, 59 other countries, 4% are from out of state, 3% African American, 0.4% Asian American or Pacific Islander, 0.6% Hispanic American, 0.2% Native American, 3% international, 9% transferred in, 40% live on campus. *Retention:* 71% of 2001 full-time freshmen returned.

Freshmen *Admission:* 3,429 applied, 2,766 admitted, 1,330 enrolled. *Average high school GPA:* 3.03. *Test scores:* SAT verbal scores over 500: 43%; SAT math scores over 500: 40%; ACT scores over 18: 74%; SAT verbal scores over 600: 8%; SAT math scores over 600: 8%; ACT scores over 24: 17%; SAT verbal scores over 700: 1%; SAT math scores over 700: 1%; ACT scores over 30: 1%.

Faculty *Total:* 400, 90% full-time, 73% with terminal degrees. *Student/faculty ratio:* 18:1.

Majors Accounting; anthropology; art; athletic training/sports medicine; biology; business administration; business marketing and marketing management; chemistry; computer science; cytotechnology; dance; early childhood education; earth sciences; ecology; economics; education; elementary education; English; environmental education; environmental science; exercise sciences; finance; French; geography; geology; health education; health services administration; history; information sciences/systems; international business; journalism; mass communications; mathematics; medical technology; modern languages; music; music (general performance); music teacher education; music therapy; nursing; philosophy; physical education; physical sciences; physics; political science; pre-dentistry; pre-medicine; pre-veterinary studies; psychology; public administration; public health; recreational therapy; recreation/leisure facilities management; recreation/leisure studies; science education; science/technology and society; secondary education; social work; sociology; Spanish; special education; sport/fitness administration; theater arts/drama; travel/tourism management.

Academic Programs *Special study options:* academic remediation for entering students, accelerated degree program, adult/continuing education programs, advanced placement credit, distance learning, double majors, honors programs, independent study, internships, off-campus study, part-time degree program, services for LD students, study abroad, summer session for credit. *ROTC:* Army (b). *Unusual degree programs:* 3-2 engineering with Pennsylvania State University, University Park Campus.

Library Bailey Library with 774,723 titles, 14,101 serial subscriptions, 86,686 audiovisual materials, an OPAC, a Web page.

Computers on Campus 545 computers available on campus for general student use. A campuswide network can be accessed from student residence rooms and from off campus. Internet access, online (class) registration, at least one staffed computer lab available.

Student Life *Housing:* on-campus residence required for freshman year. *Options:* coed, men-only, women-only. *Activities and Organizations:* drama/theater group, student-run newspaper, radio and television station, choral group, marching band, Association of Residence Hall Students, University Program Board, Black Action Society, internations club, Student Government Association, national fraternities, national sororities. *Campus security:* 24-hour emergency response devices and patrols, late-night transport/escort service, controlled dormitory access. *Student Services:* health clinic, personal/psychological counseling, women's center, legal services.

Athletics Member NCAA. All Division II except wrestling (Division I). *Intercollegiate sports:* baseball M(s), basketball M(s)/W(s), cross-country running M(s)/W(s), field hockey W(s), football M(s), golf M(s)/W(s), soccer M(s)/W(s), softball W(s), swimming M(s)/W(s), tennis M(s)/W(s), track and field M(s)/W(s), volleyball W(s), water polo M/W, wrestling M(s). *Intramural sports:* basketball M/W, equestrian sports M/W, football M, ice hockey M, racquetball M/W, rugby M, soccer M/W, softball M/W, tennis M/W, volleyball M/W, wrestling M.

Standardized Tests *Required:* SAT I or ACT (for admission).

Costs (2001–02) *Tuition:* state resident $4016 full-time, $167 per credit part-time; nonresident $10,040 full-time, $418 per credit part-time. Full-time tuition and fees vary according to course load. *Required fees:* $926 full-time, $40 per credit. *Room and board:* $4210; room only: $2254. Room and board charges vary according to board plan, housing facility, and location. *Payment plan:* installment. *Waivers:* minority students, senior citizens, and employees or children of employees.

Financial Aid Of all full-time matriculated undergraduates who enrolled in 2001, 5255 applied for aid, 3639 were judged to have need, 2745 had their need fully met. 582 Federal Work-Study jobs (averaging $643). 789 State and other part-time jobs (averaging $1701). In 2001, 1421 non-need-based awards were made. *Average percent of need met:* 89%. *Average financial aid package:* $5966. *Average need-based loan:* $2783. *Average need-based gift aid:* $2417. *Average indebtedness upon graduation:* $21,021.

Applying *Options:* common application, electronic application, early admission, deferred entrance. *Application fee:* $25. *Required:* essay or personal statement, high school transcript. *Required for some:* interview. *Recommended:* letters of recommendation, interview. *Application deadlines:* 5/1 (freshmen), 5/1 (transfers). *Notification:* continuous (freshmen).

Admissions Contact Ms. Marian Hargrave, Director of Undergraduate Admissions, Slippery Rock University of Pennsylvania, Maltby Center, Slippery Rock, PA 16057. *Phone:* 724-738-2111. *Toll-free phone:* 800-SRU-9111. *Fax:* 724-738-2913. *E-mail:* apply@sru.edu.

SUSQUEHANNA UNIVERSITY

Selinsgrove, Pennsylvania

- **Independent** 4-year, founded 1858, affiliated with Lutheran Church
- **Calendar** semesters

- **Degrees** bachelor's (also offers associate degree through evening program to local students)
- **Small-town** 210-acre campus with easy access to Harrisburg
- **Endowment** $89.9 million
- **Coed,** 1,949 undergraduate students, 94% full-time, 57% women, 43% men
- **Moderately difficult** entrance level, 76% of applicants were admitted

Undergraduates 1,840 full-time, 109 part-time. Students come from 26 states and territories, 13 other countries, 36% are from out of state, 2% African American, 2% Asian American or Pacific Islander, 2% Hispanic American, 0.3% Native American, 0.6% international, 2% transferred in, 80% live on campus. *Retention:* 90% of 2001 full-time freshmen returned.

Freshmen *Admission:* 2,299 applied, 1,757 admitted, 574 enrolled. *Test scores:* SAT verbal scores over 500: 88%; SAT math scores over 500: 88%; SAT verbal scores over 600: 32%; SAT math scores over 600: 38%; SAT verbal scores over 700: 4%; SAT math scores over 700: 4%.

Faculty *Total:* 163, 65% full-time, 69% with terminal degrees. *Student/faculty ratio:* 14:1.

Majors Accounting; art; art history; biochemistry; biology; business administration; business economics; business marketing and marketing management; chemistry; communications; computer science; creative writing; early childhood education; economics; elementary education; English; finance; French; geology; German; history; human resources management; information sciences/systems; international relations; journalism; mass communications; mathematics; music; music (piano and organ performance); music teacher education; music (voice and choral/opera performance); philosophy; physics; political science; pre-dentistry; pre-law; pre-medicine; pre-veterinary studies; psychology; public relations; radio/television broadcasting; religious music; religious studies; secondary education; sociology; Spanish; speech/rhetorical studies; stringed instruments; theater arts/drama; wind/percussion instruments.

Academic Programs *Special study options:* accelerated degree program, adult/continuing education programs, advanced placement credit, double majors, honors programs, independent study, internships, off-campus study, part-time degree program, student-designed majors, study abroad, summer session for credit. *ROTC:* Army (c). *Unusual degree programs:* 3-2 engineering with University of Pennsylvania, Pennsylvania State University University Park Campus; forestry with Duke University; environmental management with Duke University, allied health programs with Thomas Jefferson University, dentistry with Temple University.

Library Blough-Weis Library with 243,937 titles, 2,408 serial subscriptions, 19,487 audiovisual materials, an OPAC, a Web page.

Computers on Campus 287 computers available on campus for general student use. A campuswide network can be accessed from student residence rooms and from off campus that provide access to e-mail, online class listings and course assignments. Internet access, at least one staffed computer lab available.

Student Life *Housing:* on-campus residence required through junior year. *Options:* coed, women-only. *Activities and Organizations:* drama/theater group, student-run newspaper, radio station, choral group, Student Government Association, community service organizations, music performance groups, theater performance groups, Intramurals and outdoor recreation, national fraternities, national sororities. *Campus security:* 24-hour patrols, late-night transport/escort service, controlled dormitory access. *Student Services:* health clinic, personal/psychological counseling, women's center.

Athletics Member NCAA. All Division III. *Intercollegiate sports:* baseball M, basketball M/W, crew M(c)/W(c), cross-country running M/W, field hockey W, football M, golf M, lacrosse M/W, rugby M(c)/W(c), soccer M/W, softball W, swimming M/W, tennis M/W, track and field M/W, volleyball M(c)/W. *Intramural sports:* basketball M/W, football M/W, soccer M/W, softball M/W, tennis M/W, volleyball M/W.

Standardized Tests *Required for some:* SAT I or ACT (for admission). *Recommended:* SAT II: Subject Tests (for admission), SAT II: Writing Test (for admission).

Costs (2001–02) *Comprehensive fee:* $27,270 includes full-time tuition ($20,960), mandatory fees ($310), and room and board ($6000). Part-time tuition: $675 per semester hour. *Room and board:* College room only: $3190. *Payment plans:* tuition prepayment, installment, deferred payment. *Waivers:* employees or children of employees.

Financial Aid Of all full-time matriculated undergraduates who enrolled in 2001, 1321 applied for aid, 1145 were judged to have need, 278 had their need fully met. 804 Federal Work-Study jobs (averaging $1551). In 2001, 437 non-need-based awards were made. *Average percent of need met:* 84%. *Average financial aid package:* $15,535. *Average need-based loan:* $3809. *Average need-based gift aid:* $11,621. *Average indebtedness upon graduation:* $13,587.

Applying *Options:* common application, electronic application, early admission, early decision, deferred entrance. *Application fee:* $35. *Required:* essay or personal statement, high school transcript, minimum 2.5 GPA, 1 letter of recommendation. *Required for some:* writing portfolio, auditions for music programs. *Recommended:* minimum 3.0 GPA, interview. *Application deadlines:* 3/1 (freshmen), 7/1 (transfers). *Early decision:* 12/15. *Notification:* 4/15 (freshmen), 1/15 (early decision).

Admissions Contact Mr. Chris Markle, Director of Admissions, Susquehanna University, 514 University Avenue, Selinsgrove, PA 17870-1040. *Phone:* 570-372-4260. *Toll-free phone:* 800-326-9672. *Fax:* 570-372-2722. *E-mail:* suadmiss@susqu.edu.

SWARTHMORE COLLEGE
Swarthmore, Pennsylvania

- **Independent** 4-year, founded 1864
- **Calendar** semesters
- **Degree** bachelor's
- **Suburban** 330-acre campus with easy access to Philadelphia
- **Endowment** $949.9 million
- **Coed,** 1,473 undergraduate students, 99% full-time, 53% women, 47% men
- **Most difficult** entrance level, 26% of applicants were admitted

Consistently ranked among the top 3 small liberal arts colleges, Swarthmore is a coeducational institution located 11 miles southwest of Philadelphia. It has a student-faculty ratio of 8:1, an engineering department, and need-blind admission. The student body includes more than 30% students of color and 8% international students.

Undergraduates 1,461 full-time, 12 part-time. Students come from 47 states and territories, 42 other countries, 82% are from out of state, 8% African American, 16% Asian American or Pacific Islander, 8% Hispanic American, 0.8% Native American, 6% international, 1% transferred in, 93% live on campus. *Retention:* 95% of 2001 full-time freshmen returned.

Freshmen *Admission:* 3,504 applied, 909 admitted, 381 enrolled. *Test scores:* SAT verbal scores over 500: 100%; SAT math scores over 500: 100%; SAT verbal scores over 600: 94%; SAT math scores over 600: 95%; SAT verbal scores over 700: 72%; SAT math scores over 700: 67%.

Faculty *Total:* 193, 83% full-time, 92% with terminal degrees. *Student/faculty ratio:* 8:1.

Majors Anthropology; area studies related; art history; Asian studies; astronomy; astrophysics; biochemistry; biological sciences/life sciences related; biology; chemical and atomic/molecular physics; chemistry; Chinese; classics; comparative literature; computer/information sciences; dance; economics; education related; engineering; English; fine/studio arts; French; German; Greek (ancient and medieval); history; Latin (ancient and medieval); linguistics; mathematics; medieval/renaissance studies; music; philosophy; physics; physiological psychology/psychobiology; political science; psychology; religious studies; Russian; sociology; Spanish; theater arts/drama; visual and performing arts related.

Academic Programs *Special study options:* advanced placement credit, double majors, honors programs, independent study, internships, off-campus study, services for LD students, student-designed majors, study abroad. *ROTC:* Army (c), Navy (c), Air Force (c).

Library McCabe Library plus 3 others with 558,508 titles, 8,202 serial subscriptions, 17,987 audiovisual materials, an OPAC, a Web page.

Computers on Campus 125 computers available on campus for general student use. A campuswide network can be accessed from student residence rooms and from off campus. Internet access, online (class) registration, at least one staffed computer lab available.

Student Life *Housing:* on-campus residence required for freshman year. *Options:* coed, men-only, women-only. *Activities and Organizations:* drama/theater group, student-run newspaper, radio station, choral group, community service and activist groups, Drama Board, music/acapella groups, social/cultural clubs, club sports, national fraternities. *Campus security:* 24-hour emergency response devices and patrols, student patrols, late-night transport/escort service. *Student Services:* health clinic, personal/psychological counseling, women's center.

Athletics Member NCAA. All Division III. *Intercollegiate sports:* badminton M(c)/W, baseball M, basketball M/W, cross-country running M/W, field hockey W, golf M, ice hockey M(c)/W(c), lacrosse M/W, rugby M(c)/W(c), soccer M/W, softball W, squash M(c)/W(c), swimming M/W, tennis M/W, track and field M/W, volleyball M(c)/W. *Intramural sports:* basketball M/W, soccer M/W, softball M/W, tennis M/W, volleyball M/W.

Standardized Tests *Required:* SAT I or ACT (for admission), SAT II: Subject Tests (for admission), SAT II: Writing Test (for admission).

Costs (2001–02) *Comprehensive fee:* $34,538 includes full-time tuition ($26,098), mandatory fees ($278), and room and board ($8162). *Room and board:* College room only: $4188. Room and board charges vary according to board plan. *Payment plan:* installment. *Waivers:* employees or children of employees.

Swarthmore College (continued)

Financial Aid Of all full-time matriculated undergraduates who enrolled in 2001, 794 applied for aid, 705 were judged to have need, 705 had their need fully met. 576 Federal Work-Study jobs (averaging $1449). In 2001, 11 non-need-based awards were made. *Average percent of need met:* 100%. *Average financial aid package:* $24,474. *Average need-based loan:* $2056. *Average need-based gift aid:* $20,974. *Average non-need based aid:* $26,098. *Average indebtedness upon graduation:* $12,726.

Applying *Options:* common application, early admission, early decision, deferred entrance. *Application fee:* $60. *Required:* essay or personal statement, high school transcript, 2 letters of recommendation. *Recommended:* interview. *Application deadlines:* 1/1 (freshmen), 4/1 (transfers). *Early decision:* 11/15 (for plan 1), 1/1 (for plan 2). *Notification:* 4/1 (freshmen), 12/15 (early decision plan 1), 2/1 (early decision plan 2).

Admissions Contact Office of Admissions, Swarthmore College, Swarthmore, PA 19081. *Phone:* 610-328-8300. *Toll-free phone:* 800-667-3110. *Fax:* 610-328-8580. *E-mail:* admissions@swarthmore.edu.

TALMUDICAL YESHIVA OF PHILADELPHIA

Philadelphia, Pennsylvania

- **Independent Jewish** 4-year, founded 1953
- **Calendar** trimesters
- **Degrees** bachelor's (also offers some graduate courses)
- **Urban** 3-acre campus
- **Men only,** 114 undergraduate students, 100% full-time
- **Moderately difficult** entrance level, 78% of applicants were admitted

Undergraduates 114 full-time. Students come from 13 states and territories, 5 other countries, 94% are from out of state, 24% international, 100% live on campus. *Retention:* 87% of 2001 full-time freshmen returned.

Freshmen *Admission:* 30 enrolled. *Average high school GPA:* 3.8.

Faculty *Total:* 5, 60% full-time. *Student/faculty ratio:* 29:1.

Majors Rabbinical/Talmudic studies; theology.

Academic Programs *Special study options:* academic remediation for entering students, honors programs, internships, study abroad.

Library 4,800 titles, 300 serial subscriptions.

Student Life *Housing:* on-campus residence required through senior year. *Options:* men-only. *Activities and Organizations:* Pirchei, Mishmar, Bikur Cholim. *Campus security:* controlled dormitory access, Night Security Patrol. *Student Services:* health clinic, personal/psychological counseling.

Costs (2001–02) *Comprehensive fee:* $9900 includes full-time tuition ($5200), mandatory fees ($100), and room and board ($4600). *Payment plans:* installment, deferred payment. *Waivers:* employees or children of employees.

Financial Aid Of all full-time matriculated undergraduates who enrolled in 2001, 71 applied for aid, 71 were judged to have need, 71 had their need fully met. 28 Federal Work-Study jobs (averaging $1000). *Average percent of need met:* 100%. *Average financial aid package:* $4870.

Applying *Options:* common application, early admission, deferred entrance. *Required:* high school transcript, 1 letter of recommendation, interview, oral examination. *Application deadlines:* 7/15 (freshmen), 7/15 (transfers). *Notification:* 8/5 (freshmen).

Admissions Contact Rabbi Shmuel Kamenetsky, Co-Dean, Talmudical Yeshiva of Philadelphia, 6063 Drexel Road, Philadelphia, PA 19131-1296. *Phone:* 215-473-1212.

TEMPLE UNIVERSITY

Philadelphia, Pennsylvania

- **State-related** university, founded 1884
- **Calendar** semesters
- **Degrees** associate, bachelor's, master's, doctoral, first professional, post-master's, and first professional certificates
- **Urban** 76-acre campus
- **Endowment** $140.3 million
- **Coed,** 19,606 undergraduate students, 82% full-time, 58% women, 42% men
- **Moderately difficult** entrance level, 65% of applicants were admitted

Temple University is a major teaching and research university with a faculty of men and women who are nationally and internationally recognized in their fields. Taking full advantage of its location in Philadelphia, Temple actively promotes programs that help students bridge the worlds of academia and work.

Undergraduates 16,125 full-time, 3,481 part-time. Students come from 41 states and territories, 79 other countries, 22% are from out of state, 26% African American, 8% Asian American or Pacific Islander, 3% Hispanic American, 0.2% Native American, 4% international, 13% transferred in, 26% live on campus. *Retention:* 78% of 2001 full-time freshmen returned.

Freshmen *Admission:* 12,010 applied, 7,794 admitted, 3,189 enrolled. *Average high school GPA:* 3.05. *Test scores:* SAT verbal scores over 500: 64%; SAT math scores over 500: 63%; ACT scores over 18: 84%; SAT verbal scores over 600: 20%; SAT math scores over 600: 19%; ACT scores over 24: 24%; SAT verbal scores over 700: 3%; SAT math scores over 700: 3%; ACT scores over 30: 3%.

Faculty *Total:* 2,046, 60% full-time. *Student/faculty ratio:* 14:1.

Majors Accounting; actuarial science; advertising; African-American studies; American studies; anthropology; architecture; art; art education; art history; Asian studies; athletic training/sports medicine; biochemistry; biology; broadcast journalism; business administration; business economics; business education; business marketing and marketing management; ceramic arts; chemistry; civil engineering; civil engineering technology; classics; computer science; construction engineering; criminal justice/law enforcement administration; dance; drawing; early childhood education; economics; education; electrical/electronic engineering technology; electrical engineering; elementary education; engineering technology; English; film studies; film/video production; finance; French; geography; geology; German; graphic design/commercial art/illustration; health education; Hebrew; history; human resources management; information sciences/systems; insurance/risk management; interdisciplinary studies; international business; Italian; jazz; journalism; Judaic studies; landscape architecture; Latin American studies; linguistics; mass communications; mathematical statistics; mathematics; mechanical engineering; mechanical engineering technology; medical records administration; metal/jewelry arts; music; music history; music (piano and organ performance); music teacher education; music therapy; music (voice and choral/opera performance); nursing; occupational therapy; philosophy; photography; physical education; physics; political science; psychology; public relations; radio/television broadcasting; real estate; recreation/leisure studies; religious studies; Russian; science education; sculpture; secondary education; social work; sociology; Spanish; special education; speech-language pathology/audiology; speech/rhetorical studies; speech therapy; sport/fitness administration; stringed instruments; theater arts/drama; trade/industrial education; urban studies; wind/percussion instruments; women's studies.

Academic Programs *Special study options:* academic remediation for entering students, adult/continuing education programs, advanced placement credit, cooperative education, distance learning, double majors, English as a second language, honors programs, independent study, internships, off-campus study, part-time degree program, services for LD students, student-designed majors, study abroad, summer session for credit. *ROTC:* Army (b), Navy (c), Air Force (c). *Unusual degree programs:* 3-2 physical therapy, pharmacy.

Library Paley Library plus 11 others with 5.1 million titles, 16,755 serial subscriptions, 10.1 million audiovisual materials, an OPAC, a Web page.

Computers on Campus 2000 computers available on campus for general student use. A campuswide network can be accessed from student residence rooms and from off campus that provide access to student account and grade information. Internet access, online (class) registration, at least one staffed computer lab available.

Student Life *Housing Options:* coed. *Activities and Organizations:* drama/theater group, student-run newspaper, radio station, choral group, marching band, African Student Union, India Student Association at Temple, Student Organization for Caribbean Awareness, national fraternities, national sororities. *Campus security:* 24-hour emergency response devices and patrols, late-night transport/escort service, controlled dormitory access. *Student Services:* health clinic, personal/psychological counseling, legal services.

Athletics Member NCAA. All Division I except football (Division I-A). *Intercollegiate sports:* baseball M(s), basketball M(s)/W(s), crew M(s)/W(s), fencing W(s), field hockey W(s), golf M(s), gymnastics M(s)/W(s), lacrosse W(s), soccer M(s)/W(s), softball M(s)/W(s), tennis M(s), track and field M(s)/W(s), volleyball W(s). *Intramural sports:* basketball M/W, bowling M/W, football M/W, golf M/W, lacrosse M, racquetball M/W, rugby M, soccer M/W, softball M, tennis M/W, volleyball M/W, water polo M/W.

Standardized Tests *Required:* SAT I or ACT (for admission).

Costs (2001–02) *Tuition:* state resident $6974 full-time, $265 per credit hour part-time; nonresident $12,712 full-time, $438 per credit hour part-time. Full-time tuition and fees vary according to course load, program, and reciprocity agreements. Part-time tuition and fees vary according to course load, location, program, and reciprocity agreements. *Required fees:* $350 full-time. *Room and board:* $6800. Room and board charges vary according to board plan and housing facility. *Payment plan:* installment. *Waivers:* employees or children of employees.

Financial Aid Of all full-time matriculated undergraduates who enrolled in 2001, 13280 applied for aid, 10709 were judged to have need, 3139 had their need

fully met. In 2001, 2569 non-need-based awards were made. *Average percent of need met:* 83%. *Average financial aid package:* $10,265. *Average need-based loan:* $3294. *Average need-based gift aid:* $3836. *Average non-need based aid:* $2500. *Average indebtedness upon graduation:* $15,070.

Applying *Options:* electronic application, early admission, deferred entrance. *Application fee:* $35. *Required:* high school transcript, minimum 2.0 GPA. *Required for some:* letters of recommendation, interview, portfolio, audition. *Recommended:* essay or personal statement. *Application deadlines:* 4/1 (freshmen), 6/15 (transfers). *Notification:* continuous (freshmen).

Admissions Contact Dr. Timm Rinehart, Acting Director of Admissions, Temple University, 1801 North Broad Street, Philadelphia, PA 19122-6096. *Phone:* 215-204-8556. *Toll-free phone:* 888-340-2222. *Fax:* 215-204-5694. *E-mail:* tuadm@vm.temple.edu.

THIEL COLLEGE
Greenville, Pennsylvania

- **Independent** 4-year, founded 1866, affiliated with Evangelical Lutheran Church in America
- **Calendar** semesters
- **Degrees** associate and bachelor's
- **Rural** 135-acre campus with easy access to Cleveland and Pittsburgh
- **Endowment** $18.1 million
- **Coed,** 1,189 undergraduate students, 91% full-time, 50% women, 50% men
- **Moderately difficult** entrance level, 77% of applicants were admitted

Undergraduates 1,081 full-time, 108 part-time. Students come from 15 states and territories, 14 other countries, 21% are from out of state, 8% African American, 0.5% Asian American or Pacific Islander, 0.6% Hispanic American, 0.3% Native American, 4% international, 5% transferred in, 78% live on campus. *Retention:* 72% of 2001 full-time freshmen returned.

Freshmen *Admission:* 1,507 applied, 1,154 admitted, 388 enrolled. *Average high school GPA:* 2.90. *Test scores:* SAT verbal scores over 500: 40%; SAT math scores over 500: 41%; ACT scores over 18: 65%; SAT verbal scores over 600: 12%; SAT math scores over 600: 7%; ACT scores over 24: 19%.

Faculty *Total:* 105, 54% full-time, 43% with terminal degrees. *Student/faculty ratio:* 14:1.

Majors Accounting; actuarial science; art; biology; business administration; chemical engineering; chemistry; communications; computer science; criminal justice studies; cytotechnology; elementary education; engineering physics; English; environmental science; French; history; information sciences/systems; international business; liberal arts and sciences/liberal studies; management information systems/business data processing; mathematics; medical technology; mortuary science; philosophy; physics; political science; pre-dentistry; pre-law; pre-medicine; pre-veterinary studies; psychology; religious education; religious studies; secondary education; sociology; Spanish; speech-language pathology/audiology.

Academic Programs *Special study options:* academic remediation for entering students, adult/continuing education programs, advanced placement credit, cooperative education, double majors, English as a second language, freshman honors college, honors programs, independent study, internships, off-campus study, part-time degree program, services for LD students, study abroad, summer session for credit. *Unusual degree programs:* 3-2 engineering with Case Western Reserve University, Point Park College, University of Pittsburgh; forestry with Duke University.

Library Langenheim Library with 650,506 titles, 532 serial subscriptions, 7,085 audiovisual materials, an OPAC, a Web page.

Computers on Campus 146 computers available on campus for general student use. A campuswide network can be accessed from student residence rooms. Internet access, at least one staffed computer lab available.

Student Life *Housing Options:* coed, men-only, women-only, disabled students. *Activities and Organizations:* drama/theater group, student-run newspaper, radio station, choral group, Thiel Players Theatre Group, Greek organizations, student government, Thiel Choir, national fraternities, national sororities. *Campus security:* 24-hour emergency response devices and patrols, student patrols, late-night transport/escort service, controlled dormitory access. *Student Services:* health clinic, personal/psychological counseling, women's center.

Athletics Member NCAA. All Division III. *Intercollegiate sports:* baseball M, basketball M/W, cross-country running M/W, football M, golf M/W, lacrosse M/W, soccer M/W, softball W, tennis M/W, track and field M/W, volleyball W, wrestling M. *Intramural sports:* badminton M/W, basketball M/W, football M, soccer M, softball M/W, volleyball M/W.

Standardized Tests *Required:* SAT I or ACT (for admission).

Costs (2001–02) *Comprehensive fee:* $18,419 includes full-time tuition ($11,688), mandatory fees ($757), and room and board ($5974). Part-time tuition: $539 per credit. Part-time tuition and fees vary according to course load. *Required fees:* $20 per credit. *Room and board:* College room only: $3094. Room and board charges vary according to board plan and housing facility. *Payment plan:* installment. *Waivers:* senior citizens and employees or children of employees.

Financial Aid Of all full-time matriculated undergraduates who enrolled in 2001, 1016 applied for aid, 890 were judged to have need. 149 Federal Work-Study jobs (averaging $1224). In 2001, 128 non-need-based awards were made. *Average percent of need met:* 80%. *Average financial aid package:* $13,153. *Average need-based gift aid:* $9342. *Average indebtedness upon graduation:* $18,426.

Applying *Options:* common application, electronic application, early admission, deferred entrance. *Application fee:* $25. *Required:* high school transcript, minimum 2.0 GPA. *Required for some:* essay or personal statement, letters of recommendation, interview. *Recommended:* essay or personal statement, letters of recommendation, interview. *Application deadline:* 8/15 (freshmen), rolling (transfers). *Notification:* continuous (freshmen).

Admissions Contact Mr. Mark Thompson, Director of Admissions, Thiel College, 75 College Avenue, Greenville, PA 16125-2181. *Phone:* 724-589-2176. *Toll-free phone:* 800-24THIEL. *Fax:* 724-589-2013. *E-mail:* admission@thiel.edu.

THOMAS JEFFERSON UNIVERSITY
Philadelphia, Pennsylvania

- **Independent** upper-level, founded 1824
- **Calendar** semesters
- **Degrees** bachelor's, master's, and postbachelor's certificates
- **Urban** 13-acre campus
- **Endowment** $21.0 million
- **Coed,** 776 undergraduate students, 46% full-time, 81% women, 19% men
- **Moderately difficult** entrance level

Jefferson gives its students the small-college advantage of a 9:1 student-faculty ratio for the entire college plus the resources of one of the nation's leading academic health centers. The University is composed of a medical school, a graduate school, and the College of Health Professions and shares its campus with a 620-bed hospital.

Undergraduates 360 full-time, 416 part-time. Students come from 18 states and territories, 33% are from out of state, 14% African American, 10% Asian American or Pacific Islander, 2% Hispanic American, 0.7% Native American, 37% transferred in, 30% live on campus.

Faculty *Total:* 152, 30% full-time, 29% with terminal degrees. *Student/faculty ratio:* 11:1.

Majors Biotechnology research; cardiovascular technology; cytotechnology; industrial radiologic technology; medical technology; nursing; occupational therapy; physical therapy.

Academic Programs *Special study options:* adult/continuing education programs, advanced placement credit, part-time degree program, services for LD students, study abroad. *ROTC:* Air Force (c).

Library Scott Memorial Library plus 1 other with 170,000 titles, 2,290 serial subscriptions, a Web page.

Computers on Campus 100 computers available on campus for general student use. A campuswide network can be accessed from off campus. At least one staffed computer lab available.

Student Life *Housing Options:* coed. *Activities and Organizations:* choral group, Commons Board, student government, choir, Admission Ambassadors, Student Nurses Association of Pennsylvania. *Campus security:* 24-hour emergency response devices and patrols, late-night transport/escort service, controlled dormitory access. *Student Services:* health clinic, personal/psychological counseling.

Athletics *Intercollegiate sports:* rugby M(c). *Intramural sports:* basketball M/W, fencing M(c)/W(c), racquetball M(c)/W(c), soccer M(c)/W(c), softball M/W, swimming M/W, tennis W, volleyball M/W, water polo M(c)/W(c).

Standardized Tests *Recommended:* SAT I or ACT (for admission).

Costs (2001–02) *Comprehensive fee:* $24,663 includes full-time tuition ($18,200) and room and board ($6463). Full-time tuition and fees vary according to class time. Part-time tuition: $630 per credit. Part-time tuition and fees vary according to class time. *Room and board:* College room only: $2565. Room and board charges vary according to housing facility. *Payment plan:* installment. *Waivers:* employees or children of employees.

Financial Aid Of all full-time matriculated undergraduates who enrolled in 2001, 380 applied for aid, 358 were judged to have need. 114 Federal Work-Study jobs (averaging $1476). *Average need-based loan:* $10,479.

Thomas Jefferson University (continued)

Applying *Options:* deferred entrance. *Application fee:* $45. *Application deadline:* rolling (transfers). *Notification:* continuous (transfers).

Admissions Contact Assistant Director of Admissions, Thomas Jefferson University, Edison Building, Suite 1610, 130 South Ninth Street, Philadelphia, PA 19107. *Phone:* 215-503-8890. *Toll-free phone:* 877-533-3247. *Fax:* 215-503-7241. *E-mail:* chp.admissions@mail.tju.edu.

UNIVERSITY OF PENNSYLVANIA
Philadelphia, Pennsylvania

- **Independent** university, founded 1740
- **Calendar** semesters
- **Degrees** associate, bachelor's, master's, doctoral, first professional, and post-master's certificates (also offers evening program with significant enrollment not reflected in profile)
- **Urban** 260-acre campus
- **Endowment** $3.4 billion
- **Coed,** 9,730 undergraduate students, 96% full-time, 48% women, 52% men
- **Most difficult** entrance level, 22% of applicants were admitted

Undergraduates 9,344 full-time, 386 part-time. Students come from 54 states and territories, 81% are from out of state, 6% African American, 20% Asian American or Pacific Islander, 5% Hispanic American, 0.2% Native American, 8% international, 2% transferred in, 62% live on campus. *Retention:* 96% of 2001 full-time freshmen returned.

Freshmen *Admission:* 19,153 applied, 4,132 admitted, 2,362 enrolled. *Average high school GPA:* 3.85. *Test scores:* SAT verbal scores over 500: 99%; SAT math scores over 500: 100%; ACT scores over 18: 100%; SAT verbal scores over 600: 90%; SAT math scores over 600: 96%; ACT scores over 24: 98%; SAT verbal scores over 700: 47%; SAT math scores over 700: 63%; ACT scores over 30: 62%.

Faculty *Total:* 1,770, 73% full-time, 100% with terminal degrees. *Student/faculty ratio:* 7:1.

Majors Accounting; actuarial science; African-American studies; African studies; American studies; anthropology; architectural environmental design; architecture; art; art history; biochemistry; bioengineering; biology; biophysics; business administration; business marketing and marketing management; business quantitative methods/management science related; chemical engineering; chemistry; civil engineering; classics; communications; comparative literature; computer engineering; computer/information sciences; East Asian studies; economics; electrical engineering; elementary education; English; entrepreneurship; finance; folklore; French; geology; German; health facilities administration; health professions and related sciences; history; history of science and technology; humanities; human resources management; insurance/risk management; interdisciplinary studies; international relations; Italian; Judaic studies; Latin American studies; legal studies; liberal arts and sciences/liberal studies; liberal arts and studies related; linguistics; management information systems/business data processing; management science; materials engineering; mathematical statistics; mathematics; mechanical engineering; multi/interdisciplinary studies related; music; nursing; nursing related; operations management; organizational behavior; philosophy; physics; physiological psychology/psychobiology; political science; pre-dentistry; psychology; public policy analysis; real estate; religious studies; romance languages; Russian; sociology; South Asian studies; Spanish; systems engineering; theater arts/drama; transportation engineering; urban studies; women's studies.

Academic Programs *Special study options:* academic remediation for entering students, accelerated degree program, adult/continuing education programs, advanced placement credit, distance learning, double majors, English as a second language, honors programs, independent study, internships, off-campus study, part-time degree program, services for LD students, student-designed majors, study abroad, summer session for credit. *ROTC:* Army (b), Navy (b), Air Force (c). *Unusual degree programs:* 3-2 education.

Library Van Pelt-Dietrich Library plus 13 others with 4.9 million titles, 35,543 serial subscriptions, an OPAC, a Web page.

Computers on Campus 1000 computers available on campus for general student use. A campuswide network can be accessed from student residence rooms and from off campus. Internet access, online (class) registration, at least one staffed computer lab available.

Student Life *Housing Options:* coed, disabled students. *Activities and Organizations:* drama/theater group, student-run newspaper, radio station, choral group, marching band, Kite and Key Club, Daily Pennsylvania newspaper, band, national fraternities, national sororities. *Campus security:* 24-hour emergency response devices and patrols, student patrols, late-night transport/escort service. *Student Services:* health clinic, personal/psychological counseling, women's center.

Athletics Member NCAA. All Division I except football (Division I-AA). *Intercollegiate sports:* baseball M, basketball M/W, crew M/W, cross-country running M/W, fencing M/W, field hockey W, golf M, gymnastics W, lacrosse M/W, soccer M/W, softball W, squash M/W, swimming M/W, tennis M/W, track and field M/W, volleyball W, wrestling M. *Intramural sports:* badminton M(c)/W(c), baseball M(c), basketball M/W, equestrian sports M(c)/W(c), football M/W, gymnastics M(c), ice hockey M(c)/W(c), rugby M(c)/W(c), sailing M(c)/W(c), skiing (downhill) M(c)/W(c), softball M/W, swimming M/W, table tennis M(c)/W(c), tennis M(c)/W(c), track and field M/W, volleyball M/W, water polo M(c)/W(c), wrestling M.

Standardized Tests *Required:* SAT II: Writing Test (for admission).

Costs (2001–02) *Comprehensive fee:* $34,614 includes full-time tuition ($23,998), mandatory fees ($2632), and room and board ($7984). Part-time tuition: $3065 per course. Part-time tuition and fees vary according to course load. *Required fees:* $329 per course. *Room and board:* College room only: $4850. Room and board charges vary according to board plan and housing facility. *Payment plans:* tuition prepayment, installment. *Waivers:* senior citizens and employees or children of employees.

Financial Aid Of all full-time matriculated undergraduates who enrolled in 2001, 4975 applied for aid, 3944 were judged to have need, 3944 had their need fully met. 4569 Federal Work-Study jobs (averaging $2392). *Average percent of need met:* 100%. *Average financial aid package:* $23,984. *Average need-based loan:* $4505. *Average need-based gift aid:* $18,397. *Average indebtedness upon graduation:* $21,556.

Applying *Options:* early admission, early decision, deferred entrance. *Required:* essay or personal statement, high school transcript, 2 letters of recommendation. *Recommended:* interview. *Application deadlines:* 1/1 (freshmen), 4/1 (transfers). *Early decision:* 11/1. *Notification:* 4/1 (freshmen), 12/15 (early decision).

Admissions Contact Mr. Willis J. Stetson Jr., Dean of Admissions, University of Pennsylvania, 1 College Hall, Levy Park, Philadelphia, PA 19104. *Phone:* 215-898-7507.

UNIVERSITY OF PHOENIX-PHILADELPHIA CAMPUS
Wayne, Pennsylvania

- **Proprietary** comprehensive
- **Calendar** continuous
- **Degrees** certificates, associate, bachelor's, master's, doctoral, post-master's, and postbachelor's certificates (courses conducted at 54 campuses and learning centers in 13 states)
- **Coed,** 592 undergraduate students, 100% full-time, 43% women, 57% men
- **Noncompetitive** entrance level

Undergraduates Students come from 8 states and territories, 15% are from out of state.

Freshmen *Admission:* 5 admitted.

Faculty *Total:* 59, 8% full-time, 20% with terminal degrees. *Student/faculty ratio:* 13:1.

Majors Business administration; information technology; management science.

Academic Programs *Special study options:* accelerated degree program, adult/continuing education programs, advanced placement credit, distance learning, external degree program, independent study.

Library University Library with 17.5 million titles, 9,000 serial subscriptions, an OPAC, a Web page.

Computers on Campus A campuswide network can be accessed from off campus. Internet access, at least one staffed computer lab available.

Student Life *Housing:* college housing not available.

Costs (2001–02) *Tuition:* $10,350 full-time. Full-time tuition and fees vary according to location and program. *Payment plan:* deferred payment. *Waivers:* employees or children of employees.

Applying *Options:* deferred entrance. *Application fee:* $85. *Required:* 2 years of work experience. *Required for some:* high school transcript. *Application deadline:* rolling (freshmen), rolling (transfers).

Admissions Contact Ms. Beth Barilla, Director of Admissions, University of Phoenix-Philadelphia Campus, 4615 East Elwood Street, Phoenix, AZ 85040-1958. *Phone:* 480-927-0099 Ext. 1218. *Toll-free phone:* 800-228-7240. *Fax:* 480-594-1758. *E-mail:* beth.barilla@apollogrp.edu.

UNIVERSITY OF PHOENIX-PITTSBURGH CAMPUS
Pittsburgh, Pennsylvania

- **Proprietary** comprehensive
- **Calendar** continuous

- **Degrees** certificates, associate, bachelor's, master's, doctoral, post-master's, and postbachelor's certificates (courses conducted at 54 campuses and learning centers in 13 states)
- **Coed,** 179 undergraduate students, 100% full-time, 51% women, 49% men
- **Noncompetitive** entrance level

Undergraduates Students come from 3 states and territories, 3% are from out of state.
Freshmen *Admission:* 7 admitted.
Faculty *Total:* 73, 7% full-time, 29% with terminal degrees. *Student/faculty ratio:* 10:1.
Majors Business administration; information technology.
Academic Programs *Special study options:* accelerated degree program, adult/continuing education programs, cooperative education, external degree program, independent study.
Library University Library with 17.5 million titles, 9,000 serial subscriptions, an OPAC, a Web page.
Computers on Campus A campuswide network can be accessed from off campus. Internet access, at least one staffed computer lab available.
Student Life *Housing:* college housing not available.
Costs (2001–02) *Tuition:* $10,350 full-time. Full-time tuition and fees vary according to location and program. *Payment plan:* deferred payment. *Waivers:* employees or children of employees.
Applying *Options:* deferred entrance. *Application fee:* $85. *Required:* 2 years of work experience. *Required for some:* high school transcript. *Application deadline:* rolling (freshmen), rolling (transfers).
Admissions Contact Ms. Beth Barilla, Director of Admissions, University of Phoenix-Pittsburgh Campus, 4615 East Elwood Street, Phoenix, AZ 85040-1958. *Phone:* 480-927-0099 Ext. 1218. *Toll-free phone:* 800-228-7240. *Fax:* 480-594-1758. *E-mail:* beth.barilla@apollogrp.edu.

UNIVERSITY OF PITTSBURGH
Pittsburgh, Pennsylvania

- **State-related** university, part of Commonwealth System of Higher Education
- **Calendar** semesters
- **Degrees** certificates, bachelor's, master's, doctoral, first professional, post-master's, and postbachelor's certificates
- **Urban** 132-acre campus
- **Endowment** $1.1 billion
- **Coed,** 17,798 undergraduate students, 86% full-time, 53% women, 47% men
- **Moderately difficult** entrance level, 60% of applicants were admitted

Undergraduates 15,367 full-time, 2,431 part-time. Students come from 53 states and territories, 54 other countries, 13% are from out of state, 9% African American, 4% Asian American or Pacific Islander, 1% Hispanic American, 0.2% Native American, 0.9% international, 3% transferred in, 43% live on campus. *Retention:* 88% of 2001 full-time freshmen returned.
Freshmen *Admission:* 15,438 applied, 9,224 admitted, 3,296 enrolled. *Test scores:* SAT verbal scores over 500: 88%; SAT math scores over 500: 90%; ACT scores over 18: 98%; SAT verbal scores over 600: 41%; SAT math scores over 600: 47%; ACT scores over 24: 66%; SAT verbal scores over 700: 8%; SAT math scores over 700: 8%; ACT scores over 30: 14%.
Faculty *Total:* 1,828, 70% full-time. *Student/faculty ratio:* 17:1.
Majors Accounting; African-American studies; anthropology; applied mathematics; art history; bioengineering; biological/physical sciences; biology; British literature; business; business marketing and marketing management; chemical engineering; chemistry; child care/development; Chinese; civil engineering; classics; communications; computer engineering; computer science; corrections; creative writing; dental hygiene; dietetics; ecology; economics; electrical engineering; engineering physics; English; ethnic/cultural studies related; film studies; finance; fine/studio arts; French; geological sciences related; geology; German; health professions and related sciences; history; history of science and technology; humanities; industrial/manufacturing engineering; interdisciplinary studies; Italian; Japanese; legal studies; liberal arts and sciences/liberal studies; linguistics; materials engineering; mathematical statistics; mathematics; mathematics related; mechanical engineering; medical records administration; medical technology; metallurgical engineering; microbiology/bacteriology; molecular biology; music; neuroscience; nursing; occupational therapy; pharmacy; philosophy; physical education; physical sciences; physics; political science; psychology; public administration; rehabilitation/therapeutic services related; religious studies; Russian; Slavic languages; social sciences; social work; sociology; Spanish; speech-language pathology/audiology; speech/rhetorical studies; theater arts/drama; urban studies.
Academic Programs *Special study options:* academic remediation for entering students, adult/continuing education programs, advanced placement credit, cooperative education, distance learning, double majors, English as a second language, external degree program, freshman honors college, honors programs, independent study, internships, off-campus study, part-time degree program, services for LD students, student-designed majors, study abroad, summer session for credit. *ROTC:* Army (b), Navy (c), Air Force (b). *Unusual degree programs:* 3-2 statistics.
Library Hillman Library plus 26 others with 3.6 million titles, 22,058 serial subscriptions, 926,142 audiovisual materials, an OPAC, a Web page.
Computers on Campus 600 computers available on campus for general student use. A campuswide network can be accessed from student residence rooms and from off campus that provide access to on-line class listings. Internet access, online (class) registration, at least one staffed computer lab available.
Student Life *Housing Options:* coed, women-only. *Activities and Organizations:* drama/theater group, student-run newspaper, radio and television station, choral group, marching band, Pitt Program Council, Quo Vadis, Black Action Society, crew team, Blue and Gold Society, national fraternities, national sororities. *Campus security:* 24-hour emergency response devices and patrols, late-night transport/escort service, controlled dormitory access, on-call van transportation. *Student Services:* health clinic, personal/psychological counseling, women's center.
Athletics Member NCAA. All Division I except football (Division I-A). *Intercollegiate sports:* baseball M(s), basketball M(s)/W(s), cross-country running M(s)/W(s), gymnastics W(s), soccer M(s)/W(s), softball W(s), swimming M(s)/W(s), tennis W(s), track and field M(s)/W(s), volleyball W(s), wrestling M(s). *Intramural sports:* basketball M/W, crew M(c)/W(c), equestrian sports M(c)/W(c), football M, golf M(c)/W(c), ice hockey M(c)/W(c), lacrosse M(c)/W(c), racquetball M/W, riflery M(c)/W(c), rugby M(c)/W(c), skiing (downhill) M(c)/W(c), soccer M/W, squash M/W, swimming M/W, volleyball M/W, wrestling M.
Standardized Tests *Required:* SAT I or ACT (for admission). *Recommended:* SAT I (for admission).
Costs (2001–02) *Tuition:* state resident $6902 full-time, $238 per credit part-time; nonresident $15,160 full-time, $517 per credit part-time. Full-time tuition and fees vary according to degree level and program. Part-time tuition and fees vary according to degree level and program. *Required fees:* $580 full-time, $90 per term part-time. *Room and board:* $6110; room only: $3560. Room and board charges vary according to board plan and housing facility. *Payment plans:* installment, deferred payment. *Waivers:* senior citizens and employees or children of employees.
Financial Aid Of all full-time matriculated undergraduates who enrolled in 2001, 10813 applied for aid, 8440 were judged to have need, 2477 had their need fully met. In 2001, 1958 non-need-based awards were made. *Average percent of need met:* 66%. *Average financial aid package:* $8816. *Average need-based loan:* $4186. *Average need-based gift aid:* $4180. *Average non-need based aid:* $5420. *Average indebtedness upon graduation:* $16,000.
Applying *Options:* common application, early admission, deferred entrance. *Application fee:* $35. *Required:* high school transcript. *Recommended:* essay or personal statement, letters of recommendation, interview. *Application deadline:* rolling (freshmen), rolling (transfers). *Notification:* continuous (freshmen).
Admissions Contact Dr. Betsy A. Porter, Director of Office of Admissions and Financial Aid, University of Pittsburgh, 4227 Fifth Avenue, First Floor, Masonic Temple, Pittsburgh, PA 15213. *Phone:* 412-624-7488. *Fax:* 412-648-8815. *E-mail:* oafa+@pitt.edu.

UNIVERSITY OF PITTSBURGH AT BRADFORD
Bradford, Pennsylvania

- **State-related** 4-year, founded 1963, part of University of Pittsburgh System
- **Calendar** semesters
- **Degrees** associate and bachelor's
- **Small-town** 145-acre campus with easy access to Buffalo
- **Endowment** $17.5 million
- **Coed,** 1,465 undergraduate students, 64% full-time, 61% women, 39% men
- **Moderately difficult** entrance level, 82% of applicants were admitted

Undergraduates 935 full-time, 530 part-time. Students come from 20 states and territories, 6 other countries, 16% are from out of state, 2% African American, 1% Asian American or Pacific Islander, 0.5% Hispanic American, 0.8% Native American, 0.5% international, 6% transferred in. *Retention:* 70% of 2001 full-time freshmen returned.

University of Pittsburgh at Bradford (continued)

Freshmen *Admission:* 633 applied, 516 admitted, 245 enrolled. *Average high school GPA:* 3.02. *Test scores:* SAT verbal scores over 500: 50%; SAT math scores over 500: 52%; SAT verbal scores over 600: 12%; SAT math scores over 600: 12%; SAT math scores over 700: 2%.

Faculty *Total:* 114, 60% full-time, 51% with terminal degrees. *Student/faculty ratio:* 13:1.

Majors American studies; applied mathematics; athletic training/sports medicine; biology; business administration; chemistry; computer science; creative writing; criminal justice/law enforcement administration; economics; English; environmental science; geology; history; information sciences/systems; mass communications; nursing; physical sciences; political science; psychology; public relations; radiological science; social sciences; social sciences and history related; sociology; sport/fitness administration.

Academic Programs *Special study options:* academic remediation for entering students, accelerated degree program, adult/continuing education programs, advanced placement credit, distance learning, double majors, internships, off-campus study, part-time degree program, services for LD students, summer session for credit. *ROTC:* Air Force (c).

Library T. Edward and Tullah Hanley Library with 96,364 titles, 14,842 serial subscriptions, 2,797 audiovisual materials, an OPAC, a Web page.

Computers on Campus 90 computers available on campus for general student use. A campuswide network can be accessed from student residence rooms and from off campus. Internet access, at least one staffed computer lab available.

Student Life *Housing:* on-campus residence required through sophomore year. *Options:* coed. *Activities and Organizations:* drama/theater group, student-run newspaper, radio station, choral group, Student Government Association, Student Activities Board, The Source (student newspaper), Alpha Phi Omega (national service fraternity), WDRQ (student radio station). *Campus security:* 24-hour emergency response devices and patrols, late-night transport/escort service. *Student Services:* health clinic, personal/psychological counseling.

Athletics Member NCAA. All Division III. *Intercollegiate sports:* baseball M, basketball M/W, cross-country running M/W, golf M/W, soccer M/W, softball W, volleyball W. *Intramural sports:* basketball M/W, bowling M/W, cross-country running M/W, equestrian sports M/W, football M/W, golf M/W, racquetball M/W, rugby M/W, skiing (cross-country) M/W, skiing (downhill) M/W, soccer M/W, softball M/W, table tennis M/W, tennis M/W, volleyball M/W, weight lifting M/W.

Standardized Tests *Required:* SAT I or ACT (for admission).

Costs (2001–02) *Tuition:* state resident $6902 full-time, $238 per credit part-time; nonresident $15,160 full-time, $517 per credit part-time. Full-time tuition and fees vary according to course load and program. Part-time tuition and fees vary according to course load and program. *Required fees:* $484 full-time, $45 per term part-time. *Room and board:* $5310; room only: $2750. Room and board charges vary according to board plan and housing facility. *Payment plan:* installment. *Waivers:* employees or children of employees.

Financial Aid Of all full-time matriculated undergraduates who enrolled in 2001, 859 applied for aid, 721 were judged to have need. 150 Federal Work-Study jobs (averaging $1150). 12 State and other part-time jobs (averaging $1000). *Average indebtedness upon graduation:* $15,500.

Applying *Options:* common application, deferred entrance. *Application fee:* $35. *Required:* high school transcript, minimum 2.0 GPA. *Required for some:* minimum 3.0 GPA. *Recommended:* essay or personal statement, letters of recommendation, interview. *Application deadline:* rolling (freshmen), rolling (transfers).

Admissions Contact Janet Shade, Administrative Secretary, University of Pittsburgh at Bradford, 300 Campus Drive, Bradford, PA 16701. *Phone:* 814-362-7555. *Toll-free phone:* 800-872-1787. *E-mail:* shade@imap.pitt.edu.

UNIVERSITY OF PITTSBURGH AT GREENSBURG

Greensburg, Pennsylvania

- **State-related** 4-year, founded 1963, part of University of Pittsburgh System
- **Calendar** semesters
- **Degree** bachelor's
- **Small-town** 217-acre campus with easy access to Pittsburgh
- **Endowment** $523,014
- **Coed,** 1,758 undergraduate students, 87% full-time, 56% women, 44% men
- **Moderately difficult** entrance level, 78% of applicants were admitted

Many people who visit the University of Pittsburgh at Greensburg wonder why the campus buildings look so new. All of the buildings on the Greensburg campus have been built or totally renovated since 1989. Students can experience the Greensburg campus by scheduling a tour. Tours twice daily: Monday thru Friday.

Undergraduates 1,525 full-time, 233 part-time. Students come from 10 states and territories, 1 other country, 2% are from out of state, 2% African American, 1% Asian American or Pacific Islander, 0.5% Hispanic American, 0.6% Native American, 0.2% international, 6% transferred in, 35% live on campus. *Retention:* 75% of 2001 full-time freshmen returned.

Freshmen *Admission:* 1,247 applied, 971 admitted, 550 enrolled. *Average high school GPA:* 3.20. *Test scores:* SAT verbal scores over 500: 54%; SAT math scores over 500: 56%; SAT verbal scores over 600: 11%; SAT math scores over 600: 12%.

Faculty *Total:* 126, 54% full-time. *Student/faculty ratio:* 18:1.

Majors Accounting; American studies; anthropology; applied mathematics; biology; business administration; computer/information sciences; creative writing; criminal justice/law enforcement administration; education; English; environmental biology; humanities; journalism; law enforcement/police science; literature; mass communications; natural sciences; political science; pre-law; psychology; social sciences.

Academic Programs *Special study options:* academic remediation for entering students, accelerated degree program, adult/continuing education programs, advanced placement credit, distance learning, double majors, independent study, internships, off-campus study, part-time degree program, services for LD students, student-designed majors, summer session for credit. *ROTC:* Air Force (c).

Library Millstein Library with 75,000 titles, 418 serial subscriptions, an OPAC, a Web page.

Computers on Campus 400 computers available on campus for general student use. A campuswide network can be accessed from student residence rooms and from off campus. Internet access, at least one staffed computer lab available.

Student Life *Housing Options:* coed. *Activities and Organizations:* drama/theater group, student-run newspaper, choral group, Ski Club, Activities Board, Prelaw Club. *Campus security:* 24-hour emergency response devices and patrols, late-night transport/escort service, controlled dormitory access. *Student Services:* health clinic, personal/psychological counseling.

Athletics *Intercollegiate sports:* baseball M, basketball M/W, golf M/W, soccer M/W, softball W, tennis M/W, volleyball W. *Intramural sports:* baseball M, basketball M/W, bowling M/W, football M/W, golf M/W, racquetball M/W, skiing (cross-country) M/W, skiing (downhill) M/W, soccer M/W, softball M/W, table tennis M/W, tennis M/W, volleyball M/W, weight lifting M/W.

Standardized Tests *Required:* SAT I or ACT (for admission).

Costs (2001–02) *Tuition:* state resident $6902 full-time, $238 per credit part-time; nonresident $15,160 full-time, $517 per credit part-time. *Required fees:* $540 full-time, $72 per term part-time. *Room and board:* $5930; room only: $3500. Room and board charges vary according to board plan and housing facility. *Payment plan:* installment. *Waivers:* senior citizens and employees or children of employees.

Financial Aid Of all full-time matriculated undergraduates who enrolled in 2001, 160 Federal Work-Study jobs (averaging $1408). *Average indebtedness upon graduation:* $15,200.

Applying *Options:* common application, electronic application, early admission, deferred entrance. *Application fee:* $35. *Required:* high school transcript, minimum 2.5 GPA. *Required for some:* letters of recommendation. *Recommended:* essay or personal statement, interview. *Application deadlines:* 8/1 (freshmen), 8/1 (transfers). *Notification:* continuous (freshmen).

Admissions Contact Mr. John R. Sparks, Director of Admissions and Financial Aid, University of Pittsburgh at Greensburg, 1150 Mount Pleasant Road, Greensburg, PA 15601-5860. *Phone:* 724-836-9880. *Fax:* 724-836-7160. *E-mail:* upgadmit@pitt.edu.

UNIVERSITY OF PITTSBURGH AT JOHNSTOWN

Johnstown, Pennsylvania

- **State-related** 4-year, founded 1927, part of University of Pittsburgh System
- **Calendar** semesters
- **Degrees** certificates, associate, and bachelor's
- **Suburban** 650-acre campus with easy access to Pittsburgh
- **Coed,** 3,096 undergraduate students, 89% full-time, 53% women, 47% men
- **Moderately difficult** entrance level, 85% of applicants were admitted

Undergraduates 2,765 full-time, 331 part-time. Students come from 11 states and territories, 1 other country, 1% African American, 0.7% Asian American or Pacific Islander, 0.5% Hispanic American, 0.2% Native American, 0.0% international, 3% transferred in, 63% live on campus. *Retention:* 77% of 2001 full-time freshmen returned.

Freshmen *Admission:* 2,156 applied, 1,836 admitted, 878 enrolled. *Average high school GPA:* 3.20. *Test scores:* SAT verbal scores over 500: 54%; SAT math scores over 500: 59%; ACT scores over 18: 80%; SAT verbal scores over 600:

11%; SAT math scores over 600: 13%; ACT scores over 24: 25%; SAT verbal scores over 700: 1%; SAT math scores over 700: 1%.

Faculty *Total:* 188, 68% full-time. *Student/faculty ratio:* 19:1.

Majors Accounting; American studies; biology; biopsychology; business administration; business economics; chemistry; civil engineering technology; computer science; creative writing; ecology; economics; education; electrical/electronic engineering technology; elementary education; emergency medical technology; engineering technology; English; environmental biology; environmental science; finance; geography; geology; history; humanities; journalism; literature; mass communications; mathematics; mechanical engineering technology; medical technology; natural sciences; operating room technician; political science; pre-dentistry; pre-law; pre-medicine; pre-veterinary studies; psychology; respiratory therapy; science education; secondary education; social sciences; social studies education; sociology; theater arts/drama.

Academic Programs *Special study options:* accelerated degree program, adult/continuing education programs, advanced placement credit, cooperative education, distance learning, double majors, independent study, internships, off-campus study, part-time degree program, services for LD students, student-designed majors, study abroad, summer session for credit.

Library Owen Library with 136,790 titles, 1,290 serial subscriptions, 1,675 audiovisual materials.

Computers on Campus 150 computers available on campus for general student use. A campuswide network can be accessed from off campus. At least one staffed computer lab available.

Student Life *Housing Options:* coed, women-only. *Activities and Organizations:* drama/theater group, student-run newspaper, radio and television station, choral group, student radio station, Student Senate, programming board, dance ensemble, Greek organizations, national fraternities, national sororities. *Campus security:* 24-hour patrols, late-night transport/escort service. *Student Services:* health clinic, personal/psychological counseling.

Athletics Member NCAA. All Division II. *Intercollegiate sports:* baseball M, basketball M(s)/W(s), cross-country running W, soccer M, track and field W, volleyball W, wrestling M(s). *Intramural sports:* archery M(c)/W(c), basketball M/W, bowling M/W, cross-country running M/W, football M, golf M/W, ice hockey M(c), rugby M(c), skiing (cross-country) M/W, skiing (downhill) M(c)/W(c), soccer M/W(c), softball M/W, swimming M/W, table tennis M/W, tennis M/W, track and field M/W, volleyball M/W, weight lifting M/W, wrestling M.

Standardized Tests *Required:* SAT I or ACT (for admission).

Costs (2001–02) *Tuition:* state resident $6902 full-time, $238 per credit part-time; nonresident $15,160 full-time, $517 per credit part-time. Full-time tuition and fees vary according to program. Part-time tuition and fees vary according to program. *Required fees:* $562 full-time. *Room and board:* $5510; room only: $3320. Room and board charges vary according to board plan and housing facility. *Payment plans:* installment, deferred payment. *Waivers:* employees or children of employees.

Financial Aid Of all full-time matriculated undergraduates who enrolled in 2001, 2273 applied for aid, 1922 were judged to have need, 382 had their need fully met. 312 State and other part-time jobs. In 2001, 52 non-need-based awards were made. *Average percent of need met:* 80%. *Average financial aid package:* $6632. *Average need-based loan:* $2674. *Average need-based gift aid:* $8173. *Average non-need based aid:* $5473. *Average indebtedness upon graduation:* $18,756.

Applying *Options:* electronic application, early admission, deferred entrance. *Application fee:* $35. *Required:* essay or personal statement, high school transcript, minimum 2.0 GPA. *Required for some:* interview. *Application deadline:* rolling (freshmen), rolling (transfers). *Notification:* continuous (freshmen).

Admissions Contact Mr. James F. Gyure, Director of Admissions, University of Pittsburgh at Johnstown, 157 Blackington Hall, Johnstown, PA 15904-2990. *Phone:* 814-269-7050. *Toll-free phone:* 800-765-4875. *Fax:* 814-269-7044.

THE UNIVERSITY OF SCRANTON

Scranton, Pennsylvania

- **Independent Roman Catholic (Jesuit)** comprehensive, founded 1888
- **Calendar** 4-1-4
- **Degrees** certificates, associate, bachelor's, master's, post-master's, and postbachelor's certificates
- **Urban** 50-acre campus
- **Endowment** $88.5 million
- **Coed,** 4,060 undergraduate students, 91% full-time, 57% women, 43% men
- **Moderately difficult** entrance level, 88% of applicants were admitted

Undergraduates 3,687 full-time, 373 part-time. Students come from 30 states and territories, 12 other countries, 48% are from out of state, 1.0% African American, 2% Asian American or Pacific Islander, 2% Hispanic American, 0.2% Native American, 0.6% international, 2% transferred in, 48% live on campus. *Retention:* 90% of 2001 full-time freshmen returned.

Freshmen *Admission:* 3,820 applied, 3,362 admitted, 1,028 enrolled. *Average high school GPA:* 3.27. *Test scores:* SAT verbal scores over 500: 79%; SAT math scores over 500: 79%; SAT verbal scores over 600: 28%; SAT math scores over 600: 32%; SAT verbal scores over 700: 4%; SAT math scores over 700: 4%.

Faculty *Total:* 377, 65% full-time, 63% with terminal degrees. *Student/faculty ratio:* 13:1.

Majors Accounting; biology; biophysics; business administration; business administration/management related; business marketing and marketing management; chemistry; chemistry related; communications; computer engineering; computer science; criminal justice studies; early childhood education; economics; electrical engineering; elementary education; English; enterprise management; entomology; environmental science; exercise sciences; finance; foreign languages/literatures; French; German; gerontology; Greek (ancient and medieval); health services administration; history; human resources management; human services; information sciences/systems; information technology; international business; international relations; Italian; Japanese; Latin (ancient and medieval); management science; mathematics; mathematics related; medical technology; neuroscience; nursing; occupational therapy; operations management; philosophy; physical therapy; physics; political science; Portuguese; psychology; religious studies; Russian; secondary education; Slavic languages; sociology; Spanish; special education; theater arts/drama.

Academic Programs *Special study options:* academic remediation for entering students, adult/continuing education programs, advanced placement credit, distance learning, double majors, external degree program, freshman honors college, honors programs, independent study, internships, off-campus study, part-time degree program, services for LD students, student-designed majors, summer session for credit. *ROTC:* Army (b), Air Force (c). *Unusual degree programs:* 3-2 engineering with University of Detroit Mercy, Widener University.

Library Harry and Jeanette Weinberg Memorial Library plus 1 other with 433,900 titles, 7,553 serial subscriptions, 12,460 audiovisual materials, an OPAC, a Web page.

Computers on Campus 777 computers available on campus for general student use. A campuswide network can be accessed from student residence rooms and from off campus. Internet access, online (class) registration, at least one staffed computer lab available.

Student Life *Housing:* on-campus residence required through sophomore year. *Options:* coed, men-only, women-only, disabled students. *Activities and Organizations:* drama/theater group, student-run newspaper, radio station, choral group, Service-Oriented Students Club, United Colors, Retreat Program, biology/pre-medicine club, pre-law society. *Campus security:* 24-hour emergency response devices and patrols, student patrols, late-night transport/escort service, controlled dormitory access. *Student Services:* health clinic, personal/psychological counseling, women's center.

Athletics Member NCAA. All Division III. *Intercollegiate sports:* baseball M, basketball M/W, bowling M(c)/W(c), crew M(c)/W(c), cross-country running M/W, equestrian sports M(c)/W(c), field hockey W, golf M, ice hockey M, lacrosse M/W(c), rugby M(c)/W(c), skiing (downhill) M(c)/W(c), soccer M/W, softball W, swimming M/W, tennis M/W, track and field M(c)/W(c), volleyball M(c)/W, wrestling M. *Intramural sports:* badminton M/W, baseball M, basketball M/W, bowling M/W, cross-country running M/W, football M, golf M/W, racquetball M/W, soccer M/W, softball M/W, swimming M/W, table tennis M/W, tennis M/W, volleyball M/W, water polo M/W, weight lifting M/W, wrestling M.

Standardized Tests *Required:* SAT I or ACT (for admission).

Costs (2001–02) *Comprehensive fee:* $27,964 includes full-time tuition ($19,330), mandatory fees ($200), and room and board ($8434). Full-time tuition and fees vary according to degree level, program, and student level. Part-time tuition: $539 per credit. Part-time tuition and fees vary according to degree level and student level. *Room and board:* College room only: $4912. Room and board charges vary according to board plan and housing facility. *Payment plan:* installment. *Waivers:* senior citizens and employees or children of employees.

Financial Aid Of all full-time matriculated undergraduates who enrolled in 2001, 2791 applied for aid, 2363 were judged to have need, 432 had their need fully met. 645 Federal Work-Study jobs (averaging $2200). In 2001, 243 non-need-based awards were made. *Average percent of need met:* 75%. *Average financial aid package:* $13,781. *Average need-based loan:* $4068. *Average need-based gift aid:* $9825. *Average non-need based aid:* $7258. *Average indebtedness upon graduation:* $14,900.

Applying *Options:* common application, electronic application, early admission, early action, deferred entrance. *Application fee:* $40. *Required:* high school transcript. *Required for some:* 2 letters of recommendation, interview. *Recommended:* essay or personal statement. *Application deadline:* 3/1 (freshmen). *Notification:* continuous until 5/1 (freshmen), 12/15 (early action).

The University of Scranton (continued)

Admissions Contact Mr. Joseph Roback, Director of Admissions, The University of Scranton, Scranton, PA 18510-4622. *Phone:* 570-941-7540. *Toll-free phone:* 888-SCRANTON. *Fax:* 570-941-4370. *E-mail:* admissions@uofs.edu.

THE UNIVERSITY OF THE ARTS

Philadelphia, Pennsylvania

- **Independent** comprehensive, founded 1870
- **Calendar** semesters
- **Degrees** certificates, diplomas, bachelor's, master's, and postbachelor's certificates
- **Urban** 18-acre campus
- **Endowment** $20.6 million
- **Coed,** 1,938 undergraduate students, 97% full-time, 54% women, 46% men
- **Moderately difficult** entrance level, 51% of applicants were admitted

In addition to many degree programs in the fine arts, performing arts, and visual arts, recent developments include a BFA degree in writing for film and television, a BFA in multimedia, and a BS in communication (with a choice of marketing, documentary media production, and cyber journalism).

Undergraduates 1,881 full-time, 57 part-time. Students come from 40 states and territories, 41 other countries, 59% are from out of state, 8% African American, 4% Asian American or Pacific Islander, 4% Hispanic American, 0.2% Native American, 2% international, 7% transferred in, 23% live on campus. *Retention:* 80% of 2001 full-time freshmen returned.

Freshmen *Admission:* 2,147 applied, 1,091 admitted, 439 enrolled. *Average high school GPA:* 2.98. *Test scores:* SAT verbal scores over 500: 70%; SAT math scores over 500: 57%; SAT verbal scores over 600: 23%; SAT math scores over 600: 14%; SAT verbal scores over 700: 1%; SAT math scores over 700: 1%.

Faculty *Total:* 420, 26% full-time, 47% with terminal degrees. *Student/faculty ratio:* 10:1.

Majors Communications; communications related; craft/folk art; dance; education related; film/video and photographic arts related; film/video production; graphic design/commercial art/illustration; industrial design; multi/interdisciplinary studies related; music (general performance); music theory and composition; painting; photography; printmaking; sculpture; theater arts/drama; visual and performing arts related.

Academic Programs *Special study options:* academic remediation for entering students, adult/continuing education programs, advanced placement credit, double majors, English as a second language, independent study, internships, off-campus study, part-time degree program, services for LD students, study abroad.

Library Albert M. Greenfield Library plus 2 others with 118,496 titles, 534 serial subscriptions, 307,149 audiovisual materials, an OPAC, a Web page.

Computers on Campus 365 computers available on campus for general student use. Internet access, at least one staffed computer lab available.

Student Life *Housing Options:* coed. *Activities and Organizations:* drama/theater group, choral group, African-American Student Union, Gaming Society, Outreach, Multimedia Artist Society, Student Council. *Campus security:* 24-hour emergency response devices and patrols, late-night transport/escort service, crime prevention workshops and seminars. *Student Services:* health clinic, personal/psychological counseling.

Standardized Tests *Required:* SAT I or ACT (for admission).

Costs (2001–02) *Tuition:* $18,630 full-time, $870 per credit part-time. Part-time tuition and fees vary according to course load. *Required fees:* $600 full-time. *Room only:* $4800. Room and board charges vary according to housing facility. *Payment plan:* installment. *Waivers:* children of alumni and employees or children of employees.

Financial Aid Of all full-time matriculated undergraduates who enrolled in 2001, 1480 applied for aid, 1184 were judged to have need, 355 had their need fully met. In 2001, 550 non-need-based awards were made. *Average financial aid package:* $16,500. *Average need-based loan:* $4000. *Average need-based gift aid:* $3000. *Average non-need based aid:* $6500.

Applying *Options:* common application, electronic application, early admission, deferred entrance. *Application fee:* $40. *Required:* essay or personal statement, high school transcript, minimum 2.0 GPA, 1 letter of recommendation, portfolio or audition. *Required for some:* interview. *Recommended:* interview. *Application deadline:* rolling (freshmen), rolling (transfers). *Notification:* continuous (freshmen).

Admissions Contact Barbara Elliott, Director of Admissions, The University of the Arts, 320 South Broad Street, Philadelphia, PA 19102-4944. *Phone:* 215-717-6030. *Toll-free phone:* 800-616-ARTS. *Fax:* 215-717-6045. *E-mail:* admissions@uarts.edu.

UNIVERSITY OF THE SCIENCES IN PHILADELPHIA

Philadelphia, Pennsylvania

- **Independent** university, founded 1821
- **Calendar** semesters
- **Degrees** bachelor's, master's, doctoral, and first professional
- **Urban** 35-acre campus
- **Endowment** $86.3 million
- **Coed,** 957 undergraduate students, 97% full-time, 69% women, 31% men
- **Moderately difficult** entrance level, 74% of applicants were admitted

The University of the Sciences in Philadelphia, formerly known as the Philadelphia College of Pharmacy and Science, is a private university of more than 2,100 students. USP offers 19 majors in 3 colleges: Philadelphia College of Pharmacy, College of Health Sciences, and Misher College of Arts and Sciences. All students are admitted directly into their major of choice for the entire program length and are not required to reapply for admission at a later date. Contact the Admission Office at 888-996-8747.

Undergraduates 932 full-time, 25 part-time. Students come from 35 states and territories, 28 other countries, 47% are from out of state, 7% African American, 29% Asian American or Pacific Islander, 3% Hispanic American, 0.3% Native American, 2% international, 21% transferred in, 40% live on campus. *Retention:* 87% of 2001 full-time freshmen returned.

Freshmen *Admission:* 1,301 applied, 958 admitted, 304 enrolled. *Average high school GPA:* 3.40. *Test scores:* SAT verbal scores over 500: 74%; SAT math scores over 500: 85%; ACT scores over 18: 99%; SAT verbal scores over 600: 24%; SAT math scores over 600: 29%; ACT scores over 24: 82%; SAT verbal scores over 700: 2%; SAT math scores over 700: 3%; ACT scores over 30: 21%.

Faculty *Total:* 236, 57% full-time, 88% with terminal degrees. *Student/faculty ratio:* 15:1.

Majors Biochemistry; biology; chemistry; computer/information sciences; computer science; environmental science; health science; medical pharmacology and pharmaceutical sciences; medical technology; microbiology/bacteriology; occupational therapy; pharmacology; pharmacy; pharmacy administration/pharmaceutics; pharmacy related; physical therapy; physician assistant; pre-dentistry; pre-medicine; pre-veterinary studies; psychology; science education; toxicology.

Academic Programs *Special study options:* academic remediation for entering students, adult/continuing education programs, advanced placement credit, cooperative education, distance learning, double majors, English as a second language, honors programs, internships, off-campus study, part-time degree program, services for LD students, summer session for credit. *ROTC:* Army (c).

Library Joseph W. England Library with 76,000 titles, 809 serial subscriptions, an OPAC, a Web page.

Computers on Campus 105 computers available on campus for general student use. A campuswide network can be accessed from student residence rooms and from off campus. Internet access, at least one staffed computer lab available.

Student Life *Housing:* on-campus residence required through sophomore year. *Options:* coed. *Activities and Organizations:* drama/theater group, student-run newspaper, choral group, student government, Bharat, Academy of Students of Pharmacy, Student Physical Therapy Association, Asian Student Association, national fraternities, national sororities. *Campus security:* 24-hour emergency response devices and patrols, late-night transport/escort service, controlled dormitory access. *Student Services:* health clinic, personal/psychological counseling.

Athletics Member NCAA. All Division II. *Intercollegiate sports:* baseball M(s), basketball M(s)/W(s), cross-country running M/W, golf M/W, riflery M/W, softball W(s), tennis M/W, volleyball W(s). *Intramural sports:* archery M/W, basketball M/W, bowling M/W, riflery M/W, softball M/W, table tennis M/W, volleyball M/W.

Standardized Tests *Required:* SAT I or ACT (for admission). *Recommended:* SAT I (for admission).

Costs (2001–02) *Comprehensive fee:* $25,512 includes full-time tuition ($17,122), mandatory fees ($940), and room and board ($7450). Full-time tuition and fees vary according to course load and student level. Part-time tuition: $713 per credit hour. Part-time tuition and fees vary according to course load. *Required fees:* $24 per credit hour. *Room and board:* Room and board charges vary according to board plan and housing facility. *Payment plans:* installment, deferred payment. *Waivers:* employees or children of employees.

Applying *Options:* electronic application, early admission, deferred entrance. *Application fee:* $45. *Required:* high school transcript. *Recommended:* minimum 3.0 GPA. *Application deadline:* rolling (freshmen), rolling (transfers). *Notification:* continuous (freshmen).

Admissions Contact Mr. Louis L. Hegyes, Director of Admission, University of the Sciences in Philadelphia, 600 South 43rd Street, Philadelphia, PA 19104-4495. *Phone:* 215-596-8810. *Toll-free phone:* 888-996-8747. *Fax:* 215-596-8821. *E-mail:* admit@usip.edu.

URSINUS COLLEGE
Collegeville, Pennsylvania

- **Independent** 4-year, founded 1869, affiliated with United Church of Christ
- **Calendar** semesters
- **Degree** bachelor's
- **Suburban** 140-acre campus with easy access to Philadelphia
- **Endowment** $110.0 million
- **Coed,** 1,340 undergraduate students, 99% full-time, 57% women, 43% men
- **Very difficult** entrance level, 78% of applicants were admitted

Ursinus College, founded in 1869, is selective and coeducational and offers a high-quality liberal arts curriculum that prepares students for professional and graduate schools. Ursinus, known for its excellent placement of graduates in advanced schools of medicine, science, law, education, and business, provides each incoming freshman with a laptop computer. Ursinus holds a distinguished campus chapter of Phi Beta Kappa.

Undergraduates Students come from 25 states and territories, 19 other countries, 28% are from out of state, 7% African American, 3% Asian American or Pacific Islander, 2% Hispanic American, 0.1% Native American, 3% international, 90% live on campus. *Retention:* 94% of 2001 full-time freshmen returned.

Freshmen *Admission:* 1,562 applied, 1,225 admitted. *Average high school GPA:* 3.5. *Test scores:* SAT verbal scores over 500: 93%; SAT math scores over 500: 91%; SAT verbal scores over 600: 53%; SAT math scores over 600: 57%; SAT verbal scores over 700: 13%; SAT math scores over 700: 7%.

Faculty *Total:* 147, 66% full-time, 64% with terminal degrees. *Student/faculty ratio:* 11:1.

Majors Accounting; anthropology; applied mathematics; art; athletic training/sports medicine; biochemistry; biology; business administration; chemistry; classics; computer science; creative writing; East Asian studies; ecology; economics; education; English; environmental science; French; German; Greek (modern); health education; health science; history; international relations; Japanese; Latin (ancient and medieval); liberal arts and sciences/liberal studies; mass communications; mathematics; modern languages; music; philosophy; physical education; physical therapy; physics; political science; pre-dentistry; pre-law; pre-medicine; pre-veterinary studies; psychology; religious studies; romance languages; secondary education; sociology; South Asian studies; Spanish.

Academic Programs *Special study options:* adult/continuing education programs, advanced placement credit, double majors, English as a second language, honors programs, independent study, internships, off-campus study, part-time degree program, student-designed majors, study abroad. *Unusual degree programs:* 3-2 engineering with University of Pennsylvania, Georgia Institute of Technology, University of Southern California.

Library Myrin Library plus 2 others with 200,000 titles, 900 serial subscriptions, 17,500 audiovisual materials, an OPAC, a Web page.

Computers on Campus 350 computers available on campus for general student use. A campuswide network can be accessed from student residence rooms and from off campus that provide access to class of 2004, all freshmen receive a laptop computer. Internet access, at least one staffed computer lab available.

Student Life *Housing Options:* coed, men-only, women-only. *Activities and Organizations:* drama/theater group, student-run newspaper, radio and television station, choral group, Environmental Action Committee, Habitat for Humanity, Campus Activities Board, Christian Fellowship, Multicultural Student Union, national fraternities. *Campus security:* 24-hour emergency response devices and patrols, late-night transport/escort service. *Student Services:* health clinic, personal/psychological counseling.

Athletics Member NCAA. All Division III. *Intercollegiate sports:* baseball M, basketball M/W, cross-country running M/W, field hockey W, football M, golf M/W, gymnastics W, lacrosse M/W, rugby M(c)/W(c), soccer M/W, softball W, swimming M/W, tennis M/W, track and field M/W, volleyball W, wrestling M. *Intramural sports:* basketball M/W, cross-country running W, fencing M/W, field hockey W, football M/W, lacrosse M, racquetball M/W, sailing M/W, skiing (cross-country) M/W, skiing (downhill) M/W, softball M/W, squash M/W, swimming M/W, tennis M/W, volleyball M/W, water polo M/W.

Standardized Tests *Required:* SAT I or ACT (for admission). *Recommended:* SAT II: Subject Tests (for admission).

Costs (2001–02) *Comprehensive fee:* $31,350 includes full-time tuition ($24,850) and room and board ($6500). Part-time tuition: $828 per credit. *Payment plan:* installment. *Waivers:* senior citizens and employees or children of employees.

Financial Aid Of all full-time matriculated undergraduates who enrolled in 2001, 1260 applied for aid, 982 were judged to have need, 737 had their need fully met. 646 Federal Work-Study jobs (averaging $1250). In 2001, 60 non-need-based awards were made. *Average percent of need met:* 90%. *Average financial aid package:* $21,080. *Average need-based loan:* $3800. *Average need-based gift aid:* $16,230. *Average non-need based aid:* $7500. *Average indebtedness upon graduation:* $16,400.

Applying *Options:* common application, electronic application, early admission, early decision, deferred entrance. *Application fee:* $40. *Required:* essay or personal statement, high school transcript, 2 letters of recommendation, graded paper. *Recommended:* interview. *Application deadlines:* 2/15 (freshmen), 8/1 (transfers). *Early decision:* 1/15. *Notification:* 4/1 (freshmen), 2/1 (early decision).

Admissions Contact Mr. Paul M. Cramer, Director of Admissions, Ursinus College, Box 1000, Collegeville, PA 19426. *Phone:* 610-409-3200. *Fax:* 610-409-3662. *E-mail:* admissions@ursinus.edu.

VALLEY FORGE CHRISTIAN COLLEGE
Phoenixville, Pennsylvania

- **Independent** 4-year, founded 1938, affiliated with Assemblies of God
- **Calendar** semesters
- **Degrees** certificates, associate, and bachelor's
- **Small-town** 77-acre campus with easy access to Philadelphia
- **Endowment** $548,572
- **Coed,** 722 undergraduate students, 88% full-time, 50% women, 50% men
- **Minimally difficult** entrance level, 48% of applicants were admitted

Undergraduates Students come from 23 states and territories, 2 other countries, 40% are from out of state, 4% African American, 2% Asian American or Pacific Islander, 8% Hispanic American, 0.3% Native American, 0.6% international.

Freshmen *Admission:* 341 applied, 165 admitted.

Faculty *Total:* 50, 56% full-time, 22% with terminal degrees. *Student/faculty ratio:* 19:1.

Majors Biblical studies; early childhood education; elementary education; religious education; religious music; theology.

Academic Programs *Special study options:* academic remediation for entering students, adult/continuing education programs, advanced placement credit, double majors, English as a second language, independent study, internships, summer session for credit.

Library Valley Forge Christian College Library with 52,577 titles, 199 serial subscriptions, an OPAC.

Computers on Campus 30 computers available on campus for general student use. A campuswide network can be accessed from student residence rooms and from off campus. Internet access, at least one staffed computer lab available.

Student Life *Housing:* on-campus residence required through senior year. *Options:* men-only, women-only. *Activities and Organizations:* drama/theater group, student-run newspaper, choral group, Prison Ministries Organization, Homeless Outreach Ministry, J.C. Powerhouse. *Campus security:* late-night transport/escort service, 16-hour patrols by trained security personnel. *Student Services:* health clinic, personal/psychological counseling.

Athletics Member NCCAA. *Intercollegiate sports:* baseball M, basketball M/W, cross-country running M, soccer M, volleyball W. *Intramural sports:* basketball M/W, softball M/W, volleyball M/W, weight lifting M/W.

Standardized Tests *Required:* SAT I or ACT (for admission).

Costs (2001–02) *Comprehensive fee:* $12,661 includes full-time tuition ($7550), mandatory fees ($711), and room and board ($4400). Part-time tuition: $290 per credit. *Room and board:* College room only: $1800. Room and board charges vary according to board plan and housing facility. *Payment plan:* installment. *Waivers:* adult students, senior citizens, and employees or children of employees.

Financial Aid Of all full-time matriculated undergraduates who enrolled in 2001, 75 Federal Work-Study jobs (averaging $878). *Average indebtedness upon graduation:* $17,010.

Applying *Options:* common application, electronic application, early admission, deferred entrance. *Application fee:* $25. *Required:* high school transcript, 2 letters of recommendation. *Required for some:* interview. *Recommended:* essay or personal statement. *Application deadlines:* 8/15 (freshmen), 8/15 (transfers). *Notification:* continuous (freshmen).

Admissions Contact Rev. William Chenco, Director of Admissions, Valley Forge Christian College, 1401 Charlestown Road, Phoenixville, PA 19460. *Phone:* 610-935-0450 Ext. 1430. *Toll-free phone:* 800-432-8322. *Fax:* 610-935-9353. *E-mail:* admissions@vfcc.edu.

VILLANOVA UNIVERSITY
Villanova, Pennsylvania

- **Independent Roman Catholic** comprehensive, founded 1842
- **Calendar** semesters
- **Degrees** certificates, associate, bachelor's, master's, doctoral, and first professional
- **Suburban** 222-acre campus with easy access to Philadelphia
- **Endowment** $172.4 million
- **Coed,** 7,314 undergraduate students, 90% full-time, 51% women, 49% men
- **Very difficult** entrance level, 50% of applicants were admitted

Undergraduates 6,594 full-time, 720 part-time. Students come from 50 states and territories, 30 other countries, 68% are from out of state, 3% African American, 4% Asian American or Pacific Islander, 5% Hispanic American, 0.1% Native American, 2% international, 2% transferred in, 65% live on campus. *Retention:* 94% of 2001 full-time freshmen returned.

Freshmen *Admission:* 10,291 applied, 5,139 admitted, 1,743 enrolled. *Average high school GPA:* 3.64. *Test scores:* SAT verbal scores over 500: 94%; SAT math scores over 500: 97%; SAT verbal scores over 600: 56%; SAT math scores over 600: 73%; SAT verbal scores over 700: 7%; SAT math scores over 700: 14%.

Faculty *Total:* 840, 60% full-time, 73% with terminal degrees. *Student/faculty ratio:* 13:1.

Majors Accounting; art history; astronomy; astrophysics; biology; business administration; business economics; business marketing and marketing management; chemical engineering; chemistry; civil engineering; classics; computer engineering; computer science; criminal justice/law enforcement administration; economics; education; electrical engineering; elementary education; English; finance; French; geography; German; history; human services; information sciences/systems; international business; liberal arts and sciences/liberal studies; management information systems/business data processing; mass communications; mathematics; mechanical engineering; natural sciences; nursing; philosophy; physics; political science; pre-dentistry; pre-law; pre-medicine; pre-veterinary studies; psychology; religious studies; secondary education; sociology; Spanish.

Academic Programs *Special study options:* accelerated degree program, adult/continuing education programs, advanced placement credit, distance learning, double majors, English as a second language, honors programs, independent study, internships, off-campus study, part-time degree program, services for LD students, study abroad, summer session for credit. *ROTC:* Army (c), Navy (b), Air Force (c). *Unusual degree programs:* 3-2 allied health programs with Thomas Jefferson University, MCP Hannemann, University of Pennsylvania, Philadelphia College of Optometry.

Library Falvey Library plus 2 others with 1.0 million titles, 5,338 serial subscriptions, 8,000 audiovisual materials, an OPAC, a Web page.

Computers on Campus 800 computers available on campus for general student use. A campuswide network can be accessed from student residence rooms and from off campus. Internet access, online (class) registration, at least one staffed computer lab available.

Student Life *Housing Options:* coed, men-only, women-only, disabled students. *Activities and Organizations:* drama/theater group, student-run newspaper, radio and television station, choral group, marching band, Blue Key Society, orientation counselor program, Special Olympics, campus activities team, national fraternities, national sororities. *Campus security:* 24-hour emergency response devices and patrols, student patrols, late-night transport/escort service, controlled dormitory access. *Student Services:* health clinic, personal/psychological counseling, legal services.

Athletics Member NCAA. All Division I except football (Division I-A). *Intercollegiate sports:* baseball M(s), basketball M(s)/W(s), crew M(c)/W(s), cross-country running M(s)/W(s), field hockey W(s), golf M, ice hockey M(c), lacrosse M/W, rugby M(c), sailing M(c)/W(c), soccer M(s)/W(s), softball W(s), swimming M/W(s), tennis M/W, track and field M(s)/W(s), volleyball M(c)/W(s), water polo M(c)/W, weight lifting M(c)/W(c). *Intramural sports:* basketball M/W, football M/W, soccer M/W, softball M/W, tennis M/W, track and field M/W, volleyball M/W.

Standardized Tests *Required:* SAT I or ACT (for admission).

Costs (2001–02) *Comprehensive fee:* $31,997 includes full-time tuition ($23,312), mandatory fees ($415), and room and board ($8270). Full-time tuition and fees vary according to program and student level. Part-time tuition: $495 per credit hour. Part-time tuition and fees vary according to class time and program. *Required fees:* $150 per term part-time. *Room and board:* College room only: $4180. Room and board charges vary according to board plan and housing facility. *Payment plan:* installment. *Waivers:* employees or children of employees.

Financial Aid Of all full-time matriculated undergraduates who enrolled in 2001, 3836 applied for aid, 3061 were judged to have need, 540 had their need fully met. 868 Federal Work-Study jobs (averaging $1803). In 2001, 912 non-need-based awards were made. *Average percent of need met:* 78%. *Average financial aid package:* $16,390. *Average need-based loan:* $4522. *Average need-based gift aid:* $10,241. *Average non-need based aid:* $9952.

Applying *Options:* electronic application, early admission, early action, deferred entrance. *Application fee:* $55. *Required:* essay or personal statement, high school transcript, activities resume. *Application deadlines:* 1/7 (freshmen), 7/15 (transfers). *Notification:* 4/1 (freshmen), 1/7 (early action).

Admissions Contact Mr. Michael M. Gaynor, Director of University Admission, Villanova University, 800 Lancaster Avenue, Villanova, PA 19085-1672. *Phone:* 610-519-4000. *Fax:* 610-519-6450. *E-mail:* gotovu@villanova.edu.

WASHINGTON & JEFFERSON COLLEGE
Washington, Pennsylvania

- **Independent** 4-year, founded 1781
- **Calendar** 4-1-4
- **Degrees** certificates, associate, and bachelor's
- **Small-town** 40-acre campus with easy access to Pittsburgh
- **Endowment** $6.6 million
- **Coed,** 1,240 undergraduate students, 95% full-time, 49% women, 51% men
- **Moderately difficult** entrance level, 85% of applicants were admitted

Now in its 3rd century, Washington & Jefferson College continues to be one of America's premier liberal arts colleges. High-quality academic programs and a student-centered approach characterize a W&J education. Programs in pre-health and prelaw are nationally recognized, with medical and law school acceptance rates among the highest in the country.

Undergraduates 1,176 full-time, 64 part-time. Students come from 23 states and territories, 5 other countries, 23% are from out of state, 3% African American, 2% Asian American or Pacific Islander, 0.9% Hispanic American, 0.2% Native American, 1% international, 2% transferred in, 88% live on campus. *Retention:* 82% of 2001 full-time freshmen returned.

Freshmen *Admission:* 1,110 applied, 948 admitted, 322 enrolled. *Average high school GPA:* 3.4. *Test scores:* SAT verbal scores over 500: 76%; SAT math scores over 500: 78%; ACT scores over 18: 98%; SAT verbal scores over 600: 25%; SAT math scores over 600: 33%; ACT scores over 24: 76%; SAT verbal scores over 700: 1%; SAT math scores over 700: 2%; ACT scores over 30: 7%.

Faculty *Total:* 108, 82% full-time, 82% with terminal degrees. *Student/faculty ratio:* 12:1.

Majors Accounting; art; art education; biology; business administration; chemistry; child care/development; economics; English; French; German; history; international business; mathematics; music; philosophy; physics; political science; psychology; sociology; Spanish; theater arts/drama.

Academic Programs *Special study options:* academic remediation for entering students, accelerated degree program, advanced placement credit, distance learning, double majors, honors programs, independent study, internships, off-campus study, part-time degree program, student-designed majors, study abroad, summer session for credit. *ROTC:* Army (c). *Unusual degree programs:* 3-2 engineering with Case Western Reserve University, Washington University in St. Louis.

Library U. Grant Miller Library with 178,590 titles, 1,539 serial subscriptions, 7,823 audiovisual materials, an OPAC, a Web page.

Computers on Campus 145 computers available on campus for general student use. A campuswide network can be accessed from student residence rooms and from off campus. Internet access, at least one staffed computer lab available.

Student Life *Housing:* on-campus residence required through senior year. *Options:* coed, men-only, women-only. *Activities and Organizations:* drama/theater group, student-run newspaper, radio station, choral group, student government, Saturday Nite Life, George and Tom's, pre-health, pre-law, national fraternities, national sororities. *Campus security:* 24-hour emergency response devices and patrols, late-night transport/escort service, controlled dormitory access. *Student Services:* health clinic, personal/psychological counseling.

Athletics Member NCAA. All Division III. *Intercollegiate sports:* baseball M, basketball M/W, cross-country running M/W, field hockey W, football M, golf M/W, ice hockey M(c), lacrosse M, soccer M/W, softball W, swimming M/W, tennis M/W, track and field M/W, volleyball W, water polo M/W, wrestling M. *Intramural sports:* basketball M/W, football M, ice hockey M, racquetball M/W, softball W, swimming M/W, tennis M/W, track and field M/W, volleyball W, wrestling M.

Standardized Tests *Required:* SAT I or ACT (for admission).

Costs (2001–02) *One-time required fee:* $30. *Comprehensive fee:* $26,255 includes full-time tuition ($20,150), mandatory fees ($400), and room and board ($5705). Part-time tuition: $2000 per course. *Room and board:* College room only: $3110. Room and board charges vary according to board plan. *Payment plans:* installment, deferred payment. *Waivers:* employees or children of employees.

Financial Aid Of all full-time matriculated undergraduates who enrolled in 2001, 1039 applied for aid, 921 were judged to have need, 111 had their need fully met. 261 Federal Work-Study jobs (averaging $1149). 125 State and other part-time jobs (averaging $800). In 2001, 135 non-need-based awards were made. *Average percent of need met:* 74%. *Average financial aid package:* $15,229. *Average need-based loan:* $2306. *Average need-based gift aid:* $14,573. *Average non-need based aid:* $8313.

Applying *Options:* electronic application, early admission, early decision, early action, deferred entrance. *Application fee:* $25. *Required:* essay or personal statement, high school transcript. *Recommended:* 3 letters of recommendation, interview. *Application deadline:* 3/1 (freshmen), rolling (transfers). *Early decision:* 11/1. *Notification:* 12/1 (early decision).

Admissions Contact Mr. Alton E. Newell, Dean of Enrollment, Washington & Jefferson College, 60 South Lincoln Street, Washington, PA 15301-4601. *Phone:* 724-223-6510. *Toll-free phone:* 888-WANDJAY. *Fax:* 724-223-6534. *E-mail:* admission@washjeff.edu.

WAYNESBURG COLLEGE

Waynesburg, Pennsylvania

- **Independent** comprehensive, founded 1849, affiliated with Presbyterian Church (U.S.A.)
- **Calendar** semesters
- **Degrees** associate, bachelor's, and master's
- **Small-town** 30-acre campus with easy access to Pittsburgh
- **Endowment** $31.4 million
- **Coed,** 1,456 undergraduate students, 90% full-time, 56% women, 44% men
- **Moderately difficult** entrance level, 80% of applicants were admitted

Undergraduates 1,314 full-time, 142 part-time. Students come from 20 states and territories, 7 other countries, 18% are from out of state, 4% African American, 0.4% Hispanic American, 0.1% Native American, 0.9% international, 4% transferred in, 55% live on campus. *Retention:* 72% of 2001 full-time freshmen returned.

Freshmen *Admission:* 1,308 applied, 1,045 admitted, 313 enrolled. *Average high school GPA:* 3.15.

Faculty *Total:* 97, 63% full-time, 34% with terminal degrees. *Student/faculty ratio:* 16:1.

Majors Accounting; advertising; art; arts management; athletic training/sports medicine; biology; business administration; business marketing and marketing management; chemistry; communications; computer/information sciences; computer science; criminal justice/law enforcement administration; elementary education; English; environmental science; exercise sciences; finance; forensic technology; graphic design/commercial art/illustration; health services administration; history; international business; journalism; liberal arts and sciences/liberal studies; marine biology; mathematics; medical technology; nursing; political science; pre-dentistry; pre-engineering; pre-law; pre-medicine; pre-theology; pre-veterinary studies; psychology; public administration; radio/television broadcasting; secondary education; social sciences; sociology; special education.

Academic Programs *Special study options:* academic remediation for entering students, accelerated degree program, adult/continuing education programs, advanced placement credit, distance learning, double majors, English as a second language, honors programs, independent study, internships, part-time degree program, study abroad. *ROTC:* Army (c). *Unusual degree programs:* 3-2 engineering with Case Western Reserve University, Washington University in St. Louis, Pennsylvania State University University Park Campus.

Library Waynesburg College Library with 100,000 titles, 450 serial subscriptions, an OPAC, a Web page.

Computers on Campus 150 computers available on campus for general student use. A campuswide network can be accessed from student residence rooms and from off campus. Internet access, at least one staffed computer lab available.

Student Life *Housing:* on-campus residence required through junior year. *Options:* men-only, women-only. *Activities and Organizations:* drama/theater group, student-run newspaper, radio and television station, choral group, marching band, Student Senate, Student Activities Board (SAB), Student Nurses Association, Christian Fellowship. *Campus security:* 24-hour emergency response devices and patrols, late-night transport/escort service, controlled dormitory access. *Student Services:* health clinic, personal/psychological counseling.

Athletics Member NCAA. All Division III. *Intercollegiate sports:* baseball M, basketball M/W, cross-country running W, football M, golf M/W, soccer M/W, softball W, tennis M/W, volleyball W, wrestling M. *Intramural sports:* basketball M/W, bowling M/W, football M, racquetball M/W, softball M/W, volleyball M/W.

Standardized Tests *Required:* SAT I or ACT (for admission).

Costs (2001–02) *Comprehensive fee:* $17,610 includes full-time tuition ($12,250), mandatory fees ($310), and room and board ($5050). Full-time tuition and fees vary according to class time. Part-time tuition: $510 per credit. Part-time tuition and fees vary according to class time, course load, and location. *Required fees:* $12 per credit. *Room and board:* College room only: $2570. Room and board charges vary according to board plan. *Waivers:* employees or children of employees.

Financial Aid Of all full-time matriculated undergraduates who enrolled in 2001, 1222 applied for aid, 1111 were judged to have need, 310 had their need fully met. 300 Federal Work-Study jobs (averaging $650). In 2001, 31 non-need-based awards were made. *Average percent of need met:* 86%. *Average financial aid package:* $11,786. *Average need-based loan:* $4374. *Average need-based gift aid:* $7975. *Average non-need based aid:* $3995. *Average indebtedness upon graduation:* $18,000.

Applying *Options:* common application, early admission. *Application fee:* $20. *Required:* high school transcript, minimum 2.0 GPA. *Required for some:* essay or personal statement, letters of recommendation. *Recommended:* minimum 3.0 GPA, interview. *Application deadline:* rolling (freshmen), rolling (transfers). *Notification:* continuous (freshmen).

Admissions Contact Ms. Robin L. King, Dean of Admissions, Waynesburg College, 51 West College Street, Waynesburg, PA 15070. *Phone:* 724-852-3333. *Toll-free phone:* 800-225-7393. *Fax:* 724-627-8124. *E-mail:* admissions@waynesburg.edu.

WEST CHESTER UNIVERSITY OF PENNSYLVANIA

West Chester, Pennsylvania

- **State-supported** comprehensive, founded 1871, part of Pennsylvania State System of Higher Education
- **Calendar** semesters
- **Degrees** associate, bachelor's, and master's
- **Suburban** 547-acre campus with easy access to Philadelphia
- **Endowment** $8.7 million
- **Coed,** 10,220 undergraduate students, 86% full-time, 60% women, 40% men
- **Moderately difficult** entrance level, 48% of applicants were admitted

Undergraduates 8,769 full-time, 1,451 part-time. Students come from 34 states and territories, 11% are from out of state, 8% African American, 2% Asian American or Pacific Islander, 2% Hispanic American, 0.2% Native American, 9% transferred in, 35% live on campus. *Retention:* 83% of 2001 full-time freshmen returned.

Freshmen *Admission:* 8,851 applied, 4,245 admitted, 1,632 enrolled. *Average high school GPA:* 3.23. *Test scores:* SAT verbal scores over 500: 67%; SAT math scores over 500: 66%; SAT verbal scores over 600: 13%; SAT math scores over 600: 13%; SAT verbal scores over 700: 1%; SAT math scores over 700: 1%.

Faculty *Total:* 757, 76% full-time, 65% with terminal degrees. *Student/faculty ratio:* 17:1.

Majors Accounting; American studies; anthropology; art; athletic training/sports medicine; biochemistry; biological/physical sciences; biology; business administration; business economics; business marketing and marketing management; cell biology; chemistry; comparative literature; computer management; computer programming; computer science; criminal justice/law enforcement administration; early childhood education; earth sciences; ecology; economics; education; elementary education; English; environmental health; environmental science; exercise sciences; fine/studio arts; forensic technology; French; geochemistry; geography; geology; German; health education; health science; history; information sciences/systems; international relations; Latin (ancient and medieval); law enforcement/police science; liberal arts and sciences/liberal studies; literature; mass communications; mathematics; microbiology/bacteriology; modern languages; molecular biology; music; music history; music (piano and organ performance); music teacher education; music (voice and choral/opera performance); natural sciences; nursing; philosophy; physical education; physics; political science; pre-dentistry; pre-law; pre-medicine; pre-veterinary studies; psychology; public administration; public health; religious studies; romance languages; Russian; science education; secondary education; social sciences; social work; sociology; Spanish; special education; speech-language pathology/audiology; speech/rhetorical studies; speech therapy; stringed instruments; theater arts/drama.

Academic Programs *Special study options:* academic remediation for entering students, adult/continuing education programs, advanced placement credit, distance learning, double majors, English as a second language, honors programs, independent study, internships, off-campus study, part-time degree program, services for LD students, student-designed majors, study abroad, summer session for credit. *ROTC:* Army (c), Air Force (c).

Library Francis Harvey Green Library plus 1 other with 524,976 titles, 2,800 serial subscriptions, an OPAC, a Web page.

West Chester University of Pennsylvania (continued)

Computers on Campus 1000 computers available on campus for general student use. A campuswide network can be accessed from student residence rooms and from off campus. Internet access, online (class) registration, at least one staffed computer lab available.

Student Life *Housing Options:* coed, women-only. *Activities and Organizations:* drama/theater group, student-run newspaper, radio station, choral group, marching band, Abbess Club, Friars Club, University Ambassadors, Inter-Greek Council, Student Government Association, national fraternities, national sororities. *Campus security:* 24-hour emergency response devices and patrols, late-night transport/escort service. *Student Services:* health clinic, personal/psychological counseling, women's center, legal services.

Athletics Member NCAA. All Division II except field hockey (Division I). *Intercollegiate sports:* baseball M(s), basketball M(s)/W(s), cross-country running M/W, equestrian sports M(c)/W(c), field hockey W(s), football M(s), golf M(s), gymnastics W(s), ice hockey M(c)/W(c), lacrosse M(s)/W(s), rugby M(c)/W(c), skiing (downhill) M(c)/W(c), soccer M(s)/W(s), softball W(s), swimming M(s)/W(s), tennis M(s)/W(s), track and field M(s)/W(s), volleyball W(s), water polo M(c)/W(c). *Intramural sports:* badminton M/W, basketball M/W, fencing M/W, football M/W, soccer M/W, softball M/W, tennis M/W, volleyball M/W.

Standardized Tests *Required:* SAT I or ACT (for admission).

Costs (2001–02) *Tuition:* state resident $4016 full-time, $167 per credit part-time; nonresident $10,040 full-time, $418 per credit part-time. *Required fees:* $908 full-time, $38 per credit. *Room and board:* $4990; room only: $3220. Room and board charges vary according to board plan, housing facility, and location. *Payment plans:* tuition prepayment, installment, deferred payment. *Waivers:* senior citizens and employees or children of employees.

Financial Aid Of all full-time matriculated undergraduates who enrolled in 2001, 6130 applied for aid, 5672 were judged to have need, 1648 had their need fully met. 439 Federal Work-Study jobs (averaging $908). 838 State and other part-time jobs (averaging $2176). In 2001, 1533 non-need-based awards were made. *Average percent of need met:* 74%. *Average financial aid package:* $5686. *Average need-based loan:* $2357. *Average need-based gift aid:* $3171. *Average indebtedness upon graduation:* $17,000.

Applying *Options:* early admission, deferred entrance. *Application fee:* $30. *Required:* essay or personal statement, high school transcript, minimum 2.0 GPA. *Required for some:* minimum 3.0 GPA, letters of recommendation, interview. *Recommended:* minimum 3.0 GPA. *Application deadline:* rolling (freshmen), rolling (transfers). *Notification:* continuous (freshmen).

Admissions Contact Ms. Marsha Haug, Director of Admissions, West Chester University of Pennsylvania, Messikomer Hall, Rosedale Avenue, West Chester, PA 19383. *Phone:* 610-436-3411. *Toll-free phone:* 877-315-2165. *Fax:* 610-436-2907. *E-mail:* ugadmiss@wcupa.edu.

WESTMINSTER COLLEGE
New Wilmington, Pennsylvania

- **Independent** comprehensive, founded 1852, affiliated with Presbyterian Church (U.S.A.)
- **Calendar** semesters
- **Degrees** bachelor's and master's
- **Small-town** 300-acre campus with easy access to Pittsburgh
- **Endowment** $85.0 million
- **Coed,** 1,490 undergraduate students, 95% full-time, 61% women, 39% men
- **Moderately difficult** entrance level, 86% of applicants were admitted

Westminster College, an independent, coeducational liberal arts college affiliated with the Presbyterian Church (USA), was founded in 1852. Westminster's liberal arts foundation thrives in a caring environment supported by an integrative curriculum featuring state-of-the-art technology and opportunities for involvement to prepare students for a diverse world while choosing from 40 different majors.

Undergraduates 1,416 full-time, 74 part-time. Students come from 22 states and territories, 2 other countries, 19% are from out of state, 0.6% African American, 0.5% Asian American or Pacific Islander, 0.5% Hispanic American, 0.1% international, 1% transferred in. *Retention:* 89% of 2001 full-time freshmen returned.

Freshmen *Admission:* 1,111 applied, 954 admitted, 402 enrolled. *Average high school GPA:* 3.30. *Test scores:* SAT verbal scores over 500: 69%; SAT math scores over 500: 74%; ACT scores over 18: 93%; SAT verbal scores over 600: 23%; SAT math scores over 600: 22%; ACT scores over 24: 42%; SAT verbal scores over 700: 3%; SAT math scores over 700: 4%; ACT scores over 30: 3%.

Faculty *Total:* 138, 66% full-time. *Student/faculty ratio:* 13:1.

Majors Accounting; art; behavioral sciences; biological technology; biology; broadcast journalism; business administration; chemistry; classics; computer science; creative writing; criminal justice/law enforcement administration; economics; education; elementary education; English; environmental science; French; German; history; information sciences/systems; interdisciplinary studies; international business; international economics; international relations; labor/personnel relations; Latin (ancient and medieval); mass communications; mathematics; modern languages; molecular biology; music; music teacher education; music (voice and choral/opera performance); philosophy; physics; physiological psychology/psychobiology; political science; pre-dentistry; pre-law; pre-medicine; pre-veterinary studies; psychology; public relations; radio/television broadcasting; religious education; religious music; religious studies; sociology; Spanish; telecommunications; theater arts/drama.

Academic Programs *Special study options:* accelerated degree program, adult/continuing education programs, advanced placement credit, double majors, honors programs, independent study, internships, off-campus study, part-time degree program, student-designed majors, summer session for credit. *ROTC:* Army (c). *Unusual degree programs:* 3-2 engineering with Pennsylvania State University University Park Campus, Washington University in St. Louis, Case Western Reserve University.

Library McGill Memorial Library plus 1 other with 230,000 titles, 827 serial subscriptions, an OPAC, a Web page.

Computers on Campus 158 computers available on campus for general student use. A campuswide network can be accessed from student residence rooms and from off campus. Internet access, at least one staffed computer lab available.

Student Life *Housing:* on-campus residence required through junior year. *Options:* men-only, women-only. *Activities and Organizations:* drama/theater group, student-run newspaper, radio station, choral group, marching band, student government, Greek life, Habitat for Humanity, established service teams, national fraternities, national sororities. *Campus security:* 24-hour patrols, late-night transport/escort service. *Student Services:* health clinic, personal/psychological counseling.

Athletics Member NCAA. All Division II. *Intercollegiate sports:* baseball M, basketball M/W, cross-country running M/W, equestrian sports M(c)/W(c), football M(s), golf M/W, soccer M/W, softball W, swimming M/W, tennis M/W, track and field M/W, volleyball W. *Intramural sports:* archery M/W, badminton M/W, basketball M/W, cross-country running M/W, football M, golf M/W, racquetball M/W, skiing (cross-country) M/W, skiing (downhill) M/W, swimming M/W, tennis M/W, track and field W, volleyball W, weight lifting M/W.

Standardized Tests *Required:* SAT I or ACT (for admission). *Recommended:* SAT II: Subject Tests (for admission).

Costs (2001–02) *Comprehensive fee:* $22,960 includes full-time tuition ($16,920), mandatory fees ($830), and room and board ($5210). Part-time tuition: $525 per hour. *Room and board:* College room only: $2600. Room and board charges vary according to board plan. *Payment plan:* installment.

Financial Aid Of all full-time matriculated undergraduates who enrolled in 2001, 1188 applied for aid, 1080 were judged to have need, 526 had their need fully met. 357 Federal Work-Study jobs (averaging $1539). 251 State and other part-time jobs (averaging $1732). In 2001, 266 non-need-based awards were made. *Average percent of need met:* 97%. *Average financial aid package:* $15,605. *Average need-based loan:* $4009. *Average need-based gift aid:* $8082. *Average non-need based aid:* $6841. *Average indebtedness upon graduation:* $18,125.

Applying *Options:* early admission, deferred entrance. *Application fee:* $20. *Required:* essay or personal statement, high school transcript, minimum 2.0 GPA, 2 letters of recommendation. *Recommended:* minimum 3.0 GPA, interview. *Application deadline:* rolling (freshmen), rolling (transfers). *Notification:* continuous (freshmen).

Admissions Contact Mr. Doug Swartz, Director of Admissions, Westminster College, 319 South Market Street, New Wilmington, PA 16172-0001. *Phone:* 724-946-7100. *Toll-free phone:* 800-942-8033. *Fax:* 724-946-7171. *E-mail:* swartzdl@westminster.edu.

WIDENER UNIVERSITY
Chester, Pennsylvania

- **Independent** comprehensive, founded 1821
- **Calendar** semesters
- **Degrees** bachelor's, master's, doctoral, and first professional
- **Suburban** 110-acre campus with easy access to Philadelphia
- **Endowment** $37.0 million
- **Coed,** 2,272 undergraduate students, 94% full-time, 44% women, 56% men
- **Moderately difficult** entrance level, 74% of applicants were admitted

Widener University, located just 10 miles from historic and culturally rich Philadelphia, provides the advantages of a small-college environment with the benefits of a large university. A distinguished and friendly faculty, a low

11:1 student-faculty ratio, 60 undergraduate programs, and internship, co-op, and research opportunities give students the support and options they need to succeed.

Undergraduates 2,127 full-time, 145 part-time. Students come from 21 states and territories, 35% are from out of state, 9% African American, 3% Asian American or Pacific Islander, 1% Hispanic American, 0.3% Native American, 0.9% international, 6% transferred in, 60% live on campus. *Retention:* 85% of 2001 full-time freshmen returned.

Freshmen *Admission:* 2,340 applied, 1,729 admitted, 535 enrolled. *Average high school GPA:* 3.25. *Test scores:* SAT verbal scores over 500: 66%; SAT math scores over 500: 68%; SAT verbal scores over 600: 13%; SAT math scores over 600: 18%; SAT verbal scores over 700: 1%; SAT math scores over 700: 3%.

Faculty *Total:* 391, 54% full-time. *Student/faculty ratio:* 12:1.

Majors Accounting; advertising; anthropology; behavioral sciences; biology; business administration; business economics; chemical engineering; chemistry; civil engineering; computer/information sciences; computer science; criminal justice/law enforcement administration; early childhood education; economics; educational media design; electrical engineering; elementary education; engineering/industrial management; English; environmental science; foreign languages/literatures; French; history; hotel and restaurant management; humanities; industrial radiologic technology; information sciences/systems; international business; international relations; mass communications; mathematics; mechanical engineering; modern languages; nursing; paralegal/legal assistant; physics; political science; pre-medicine; psychology; science education; social sciences; social work; sociology; Spanish; special education; sport/fitness administration.

Academic Programs *Special study options:* academic remediation for entering students, accelerated degree program, adult/continuing education programs, advanced placement credit, cooperative education, distance learning, double majors, English as a second language, external degree program, honors programs, independent study, internships, off-campus study, part-time degree program, services for LD students, student-designed majors, study abroad, summer session for credit. *ROTC:* Army (b), Air Force (c). *Unusual degree programs:* 3-2 physical therapy.

Library Wolfgram Memorial Library with 161,632 titles, 2,286 serial subscriptions, 12,663 audiovisual materials, an OPAC, a Web page.

Computers on Campus 310 computers available on campus for general student use. A campuswide network can be accessed from student residence rooms and from off campus. Internet access, at least one staffed computer lab available.

Student Life *Housing:* on-campus residence required through senior year. *Options:* coed, men-only, women-only. *Activities and Organizations:* drama/theater group, student-run newspaper, radio and television station, choral group, WDNR Radio, Black Student Union, volunteer services, rugby club, Theatre Widener, national fraternities, national sororities. *Campus security:* 24-hour emergency response devices and patrols, late-night transport/escort service, controlled dormitory access. *Student Services:* health clinic, personal/psychological counseling.

Athletics Member NCAA. All Division III. *Intercollegiate sports:* baseball M, basketball M/W, cross-country running M/W, field hockey W, football M, golf M, lacrosse M/W, soccer M/W, softball W, swimming M/W, tennis M/W, track and field M/W, volleyball W. *Intramural sports:* basketball M/W, ice hockey M(c), rugby M(c)/W(c), softball M/W, tennis M/W, volleyball M(c).

Standardized Tests *Required:* SAT I or ACT (for admission). *Required for some:* SAT II: Writing Test (for admission). *Recommended:* SAT II: Subject Tests (for admission).

Costs (2001–02) *Comprehensive fee:* $26,920 includes full-time tuition ($19,300) and room and board ($7620). Full-time tuition and fees vary according to class time, course load, program, and student level. Part-time tuition: $600 per credit. Part-time tuition and fees vary according to class time, class time, program, and student level. *Room and board:* Room and board charges vary according to housing facility. *Waivers:* employees or children of employees.

Financial Aid Of all full-time matriculated undergraduates who enrolled in 2001, 1732 applied for aid, 1550 were judged to have need, 344 had their need fully met. In 2001, 344 non-need-based awards were made. *Average percent of need met:* 87%. *Average financial aid package:* $16,604. *Average need-based loan:* $4791. *Average need-based gift aid:* $10,387. *Average non-need based aid:* $8791. *Average indebtedness upon graduation:* $19,821.

Applying *Options:* common application, electronic application, early admission, early decision, deferred entrance. *Application fee:* $35. *Required:* essay or personal statement, high school transcript, letters of recommendation, interview. *Required for some:* minimum 2.5 GPA. *Recommended:* minimum 3.0 GPA. *Application deadline:* rolling (freshmen), rolling (transfers). *Early decision:* 12/1. *Notification:* continuous (freshmen), 12/15 (early decision).

Admissions Contact Michael Hendricks, Dean of Admissions, Widener University, One University Place, Chester, PA 19013. *Phone:* 610-499-4126. *Toll-free phone:* 888-WIDENER. *Fax:* 610-499-4676. *E-mail:* admissions.office@widener.edu.

WILKES UNIVERSITY
Wilkes-Barre, Pennsylvania

- **Independent** comprehensive, founded 1933
- **Calendar** semesters
- **Degrees** bachelor's, master's, and first professional
- **Urban** 25-acre campus
- **Endowment** $28.9 million
- **Coed,** 1,771 undergraduate students, 85% full-time, 50% women, 50% men
- **Moderately difficult** entrance level, 87% of applicants were admitted

A comprehensive private university of intimate size, Wilkes University offers high-quality academic programs in business, engineering, sciences, and liberal arts; preprofessional programs in dentistry, medicine, optometry, and law; and a 6-year Doctor of Pharmacy degree. Students have unparalleled access to faculty members and research opportunities, and 99 percent gain employment or attend graduate/professional school within 6 months of graduation.

Undergraduates 1,500 full-time, 271 part-time. Students come from 21 states and territories, 4 other countries, 13% are from out of state, 2% African American, 2% Asian American or Pacific Islander, 1% Hispanic American, 0.3% Native American, 1% international, 7% transferred in, 34% live on campus. *Retention:* 75% of 2001 full-time freshmen returned.

Freshmen *Admission:* 1,786 applied, 1,557 admitted, 439 enrolled. *Test scores:* SAT verbal scores over 500: 60%; SAT math scores over 500: 61%; SAT verbal scores over 600: 17%; SAT math scores over 600: 24%; SAT verbal scores over 700: 2%; SAT math scores over 700: 4%.

Faculty *Total:* 106. *Student/faculty ratio:* 13:1.

Majors Accounting; biochemistry; biology; business administration; chemistry; communications; computer/information sciences; criminal justice studies; earth sciences; education; electrical engineering; elementary education; engineering; engineering/industrial management; English; environmental engineering; French; history; information sciences/systems; international relations; liberal arts and sciences/liberal studies; mathematics; mechanical engineering; medical technology; multi/interdisciplinary studies related; music (general performance); music teacher education; nursing; philosophy; political science; pre-dentistry; pre-law; pre-medicine; pre-veterinary studies; psychology; sociology; Spanish; theater arts/drama.

Academic Programs *Special study options:* academic remediation for entering students, accelerated degree program, adult/continuing education programs, advanced placement credit, cooperative education, distance learning, double majors, honors programs, independent study, internships, part-time degree program, student-designed majors, study abroad, summer session for credit. *ROTC:* Army (c), Air Force (b).

Library Eugene S. Farley Library with 175,249 titles, 4,831 serial subscriptions, 10,973 audiovisual materials, an OPAC.

Computers on Campus 700 computers available on campus for general student use. A campuswide network can be accessed from student residence rooms and from off campus. Internet access, online (class) registration, at least one staffed computer lab available.

Student Life *Housing:* on-campus residence required through sophomore year. *Options:* coed, men-only, women-only. *Activities and Organizations:* drama/theater group, student-run newspaper, radio and television station, choral group. *Campus security:* 24-hour emergency response devices and patrols, late-night transport/escort service, controlled dormitory access. *Student Services:* health clinic, personal/psychological counseling.

Athletics Member NCAA. All Division III. *Intercollegiate sports:* baseball M, basketball M/W, field hockey W, football M, golf M, lacrosse W, soccer M/W, softball W, tennis M/W, volleyball W, wrestling M. *Intramural sports:* basketball M/W, football M, volleyball M/W, weight lifting M/W.

Standardized Tests *Required:* SAT I or ACT (for admission).

Costs (2001–02) *Comprehensive fee:* $25,800 includes full-time tuition ($17,142), mandatory fees ($878), and room and board ($7780). Part-time tuition: $476 per credit. Part-time tuition and fees vary according to program. *Required fees:* $13 per credit. *Room and board:* College room only: $4694. Room and board charges vary according to board plan and housing facility. *Payment plan:* installment. *Waivers:* children of alumni, senior citizens, and employees or children of employees.

Financial Aid Of all full-time matriculated undergraduates who enrolled in 2001, 1359 applied for aid, 1214 were judged to have need, 326 had their need

Wilkes University (continued)
fully met. 30 State and other part-time jobs (averaging $1576). In 2001, 133 non-need-based awards were made. *Average percent of need met:* 67%. *Average financial aid package:* $12,286. *Average need-based loan:* $2299. *Average need-based gift aid:* $9192. *Average non-need based aid:* $6810. *Average indebtedness upon graduation:* $18,473.

Applying *Options:* electronic application, early admission, deferred entrance. *Application fee:* $30. *Required:* high school transcript. *Required for some:* letters of recommendation. *Recommended:* interview. *Application deadline:* rolling (freshmen), rolling (transfers). *Notification:* continuous until 8/30 (freshmen).

Admissions Contact Wilkes University, PO Box 111, Wilkes-Barre, PA 18766. *Phone:* 570-408-4400. *Toll-free phone:* 800-945-5378 Ext. 4400. *Fax:* 570-408-4904. *E-mail:* admissions@wilkes.edu.

WILSON COLLEGE
Chambersburg, Pennsylvania

- **Independent** 4-year, founded 1869, affiliated with Presbyterian Church (U.S.A.)
- **Calendar** 4-1-4
- **Degrees** associate and bachelor's
- **Small-town** 262-acre campus
- **Endowment** $29.4 million
- **Women only,** 710 undergraduate students, 49% full-time
- **Moderately difficult** entrance level, 90% of applicants were admitted

For more than 130 years, Wilson has been educating women in a rich tradition of liberal arts. The College offers rigorous and timely courses of study grounded in the liberal arts and sciences, engaging students in intercultural and environmental studies and a wide range of majors in promising professional fields.

Undergraduates 346 full-time, 364 part-time. Students come from 20 states and territories, 12 other countries, 27% are from out of state, 2% transferred in, 87% live on campus. *Retention:* 72% of 2001 full-time freshmen returned.

Freshmen *Admission:* 75 enrolled. *Average high school GPA:* 3.50. *Test scores:* SAT verbal scores over 500: 52%; SAT math scores over 500: 51%; ACT scores over 18: 75%; SAT verbal scores over 600: 13%; SAT math scores over 600: 10%; ACT scores over 24: 25%.

Faculty *Total:* 103, 37% full-time, 59% with terminal degrees. *Student/faculty ratio:* 10:1.

Majors Accounting; animal sciences related; art; behavioral sciences; biological specializations related; biology; business administration; business marketing and marketing management; chemistry; elementary education; English; environmental science; exercise sciences; foreign languages/literatures; international relations; law and legal studies related; liberal arts and sciences/liberal studies; management information systems/business data processing; mass communications; mathematics; physiological psychology/psychobiology; social sciences; theological studies/religious vocations related; veterinarian assistant.

Academic Programs *Special study options:* academic remediation for entering students, accelerated degree program, adult/continuing education programs, advanced placement credit, cooperative education, double majors, English as a second language, external degree program, independent study, internships, off-campus study, part-time degree program, student-designed majors, summer session for credit. *ROTC:* Army (c).

Library Stewart Library with 171,699 titles, 370 serial subscriptions, 1,663 audiovisual materials, an OPAC, a Web page.

Computers on Campus 80 computers available on campus for general student use. A campuswide network can be accessed from student residence rooms and from off campus. Internet access, at least one staffed computer lab available.

Student Life *Housing:* on-campus residence required through junior year. *Options:* women-only. *Activities and Organizations:* drama/theater group, student-run newspaper, radio station, choral group, Muhibbah Club, Orchesis Club, student newspaper, student government, Black Student Union. *Campus security:* 24-hour emergency response devices and patrols, late-night transport/escort service, controlled dormitory access. *Student Services:* health clinic, personal/psychological counseling, women's center.

Athletics Member NCAA. All Division III. *Intercollegiate sports:* basketball W, equestrian sports W, field hockey W, gymnastics W, soccer W, softball W, tennis W, volleyball W. *Intramural sports:* archery W, badminton W, bowling W, equestrian sports W, gymnastics W, volleyball W.

Standardized Tests *Required:* SAT I or ACT (for admission).

Costs (2001–02) *Comprehensive fee:* $21,237 includes full-time tuition ($14,250), mandatory fees ($425), and room and board ($6562). Full-time tuition and fees vary according to program. Part-time tuition: $564 per course. Part-time tuition and fees vary according to program. *Required fees:* $30 per course. *Room and board:* Room and board charges vary according to board plan. *Payment plans:* tuition prepayment, installment. *Waivers:* children of alumni and employees or children of employees.

Financial Aid Of all full-time matriculated undergraduates who enrolled in 2001, 287 applied for aid, 258 were judged to have need, 64 had their need fully met. 63 Federal Work-Study jobs (averaging $1339). In 2001, 64 non-need-based awards were made. *Average percent of need met:* 85%. *Average financial aid package:* $12,304. *Average need-based loan:* $4000. *Average need-based gift aid:* $8922. *Average non-need based aid:* $10,900. *Average indebtedness upon graduation:* $10,800.

Applying *Options:* electronic application, early admission, deferred entrance. *Application fee:* $20. *Required:* essay or personal statement, high school transcript. *Required for some:* letters of recommendation. *Recommended:* minimum 2.7 GPA, interview. *Application deadline:* rolling (freshmen), rolling (transfers). *Notification:* continuous (freshmen).

Admissions Contact Deborah Arthur, Admissions Administrator, Wilson College, 1015 Philadelphia Avenue, Chambersburg, PA 17201. *Phone:* 717-262-2002. *Toll-free phone:* 800-421-8402. *Fax:* 717-264-1578. *E-mail:* admissions@wilson.edu.

YESHIVA BETH MOSHE
Scranton, Pennsylvania

Admissions Contact Rabbi I. Bressler, Dean, Yeshiva Beth Moshe, 930 Hickory Street, PO Box 1141, Scranton, PA 18505-2124. *Phone:* 717-346-1747.

YORK COLLEGE OF PENNSYLVANIA
York, Pennsylvania

- **Independent** comprehensive, founded 1787
- **Calendar** semesters
- **Degrees** associate, bachelor's, and master's
- **Suburban** 80-acre campus with easy access to Baltimore
- **Endowment** $54.0 million
- **Coed,** 5,119 undergraduate students, 78% full-time, 60% women, 40% men
- **Moderately difficult** entrance level, 71% of applicants were admitted

Undergraduates 4,017 full-time, 1,102 part-time. Students come from 30 states and territories, 53% are from out of state, 1% African American, 1% Asian American or Pacific Islander, 1% Hispanic American, 0.2% Native American, 0.7% international, 5% transferred in, 42% live on campus. *Retention:* 82% of 2001 full-time freshmen returned.

Freshmen *Admission:* 3,723 applied, 2,640 admitted, 979 enrolled. *Average high school GPA:* 3.00. *Test scores:* SAT verbal scores over 500: 83%; SAT math scores over 500: 81%; SAT verbal scores over 600: 27%; SAT math scores over 600: 22%; SAT verbal scores over 700: 4%; SAT math scores over 700: 2%.

Faculty *Total:* 377, 36% full-time, 78% with terminal degrees. *Student/faculty ratio:* 15:1.

Majors Accounting; art; behavioral sciences; biology; business administration; business economics; business marketing and marketing management; chemistry; computer programming; corrections; criminal justice/law enforcement administration; economics; education; elementary education; engineering/industrial management; English; finance; graphic design/commercial art/illustration; health services administration; history; humanities; information sciences/systems; international business; international relations; law enforcement/police science; liberal arts and sciences/liberal studies; mass communications; mathematics; mechanical engineering; medical technology; modern languages; music; music teacher education; nuclear medical technology; nursing; philosophy; physical sciences; physics; political science; pre-dentistry; pre-law; pre-medicine; pre-veterinary studies; psychology; public administration; public relations; radio/television broadcasting; recreational therapy; recreation/leisure studies; respiratory therapy; retail management; safety/security technology; science education; secondary education; sociology; Spanish; special education; speech/rhetorical studies; sport/fitness administration.

Academic Programs *Special study options:* academic remediation for entering students, accelerated degree program, adult/continuing education programs, advanced placement credit, internships, part-time degree program, student-designed majors, study abroad, summer session for credit.

Library Schmidt Library plus 1 other with 300,000 titles, 1,400 serial subscriptions, 11,000 audiovisual materials, an OPAC, a Web page.

Computers on Campus 250 computers available on campus for general student use. A campuswide network can be accessed from student residence rooms and from off campus. Internet access, online (class) registration, at least one staffed computer lab available.

Student Life *Housing:* on-campus residence required for freshman year. *Options:* coed, women-only. *Activities and Organizations:* drama/theater group, student-run newspaper, radio station, choral group, Student Senate, Theater Company, ski and outdoor club, marketing club, Student Education Association, national fraternities, national sororities. *Campus security:* 24-hour emergency response devices and patrols, late-night transport/escort service. *Student Services:* health clinic, personal/psychological counseling.

Athletics Member NCAA. All Division III. *Intercollegiate sports:* baseball M, basketball M/W, cross-country running M/W, field hockey W, golf M, ice hockey M(c), lacrosse M, soccer M/W, softball W, swimming M/W, tennis M/W, track and field M/W, volleyball M(c)/W, wrestling M. *Intramural sports:* badminton M/W, basketball M/W, football M/W, lacrosse M(c), rugby M(c)/W(c), skiing (downhill) M(c)/W(c), soccer M/W, softball M/W, swimming M/W, table tennis M, tennis M/W, track and field M/W, volleyball M/W, water polo M/W, weight lifting M(c)/W(c), wrestling M.

Standardized Tests *Required:* SAT I or ACT (for admission).

Costs (2001–02) *Comprehensive fee:* $12,550 includes full-time tuition ($7000), mandatory fees ($422), and room and board ($5128). Part-time tuition: $220 per credit hour. *Required fees:* $86 per term part-time. *Room and board:* College room only: $2578. Room and board charges vary according to housing facility. *Payment plan:* installment. *Waivers:* employees or children of employees.

Financial Aid Of all full-time matriculated undergraduates who enrolled in 2001, 3010 applied for aid, 1891 were judged to have need, 611 had their need fully met. 273 Federal Work-Study jobs (averaging $1308). 93 State and other part-time jobs (averaging $1153). In 2001, 152 non-need-based awards were made. *Average percent of need met:* 75%. *Average financial aid package:* $6339. *Average need-based loan:* $3360. *Average need-based gift aid:* $3494. *Average non-need based aid:* $2273. *Average indebtedness upon graduation:* $15,198.

Applying *Options:* common application, electronic application, early admission, deferred entrance. *Application fee:* $30. *Required:* essay or personal statement, high school transcript. *Required for some:* interview. *Recommended:* 1 letter of recommendation. *Application deadline:* rolling (freshmen), rolling (transfers). *Notification:* continuous (freshmen).

Admissions Contact Mrs. Nancy L. Spataro, Director of Admissions, York College of Pennsylvania, York, PA 17405-7199. *Phone:* 717-849-1600. *Toll-free phone:* 800-455-8018. *Fax:* 717-849-1607. *E-mail:* admissions@ycp.edu.

RHODE ISLAND

BROWN UNIVERSITY

Providence, Rhode Island

- **Independent** university, founded 1764
- **Calendar** semesters
- **Degrees** bachelor's, master's, doctoral, and first professional
- **Urban** 140-acre campus with easy access to Boston
- **Coed,** 5,999 undergraduate students, 95% full-time, 54% women, 46% men
- **Most difficult** entrance level, 16% of applicants were admitted

Undergraduates 5,677 full-time, 322 part-time. Students come from 52 states and territories, 72 other countries, 96% are from out of state, 6% African American, 14% Asian American or Pacific Islander, 7% Hispanic American, 0.5% Native American, 6% international, 0.4% transferred in, 85% live on campus. *Retention:* 97% of 2001 full-time freshmen returned.

Freshmen *Admission:* 16,606 applied, 2,729 admitted, 1,401 enrolled. *Test scores:* SAT verbal scores over 500: 98%; SAT math scores over 500: 99%; ACT scores over 18: 100%; SAT verbal scores over 600: 86%; SAT math scores over 600: 91%; ACT scores over 24: 94%; SAT verbal scores over 700: 51%; SAT math scores over 700: 55%; ACT scores over 30: 61%.

Faculty *Total:* 758, 98% full-time, 98% with terminal degrees. *Student/faculty ratio:* 8:1.

Majors African-American studies; American studies; anthropology; applied mathematics; archaeology; architecture; art; art history; behavioral sciences; biochemistry; bioengineering; biology; biomedical science; biophysics; chemical engineering; chemistry; civil engineering; classics; cognitive psychology/psycholinguistics; comparative literature; computer engineering; computer science; creative writing; development economics; East Asian studies; economics; education; electrical engineering; engineering; engineering physics; English; environmental science; film studies; fine/studio arts; French; geochemistry; geology; geophysics/seismology; German; Hispanic-American studies; history; international relations; Italian; Italian studies; Judaic studies; Latin American studies; linguistics; literature; marine biology; materials engineering; mathematics; mathematics/computer science; mechanical engineering; medieval/renaissance studies; Middle Eastern studies; molecular biology; music; musicology; music related; neuroscience; organizational behavior; philosophy; physics; political science; psychology; religious studies; Russian/Slavic studies; sociology; South Asian studies; Spanish; theater arts/drama; urban studies; visual/performing arts; women's studies.

Academic Programs *Special study options:* accelerated degree program, adult/continuing education programs, advanced placement credit, double majors, honors programs, independent study, internships, off-campus study, part-time degree program, services for LD students, student-designed majors, study abroad, summer session for credit. *ROTC:* Army (c).

Library John D. Rockefeller Library plus 6 others with 3.0 million titles, 17,000 serial subscriptions, an OPAC, a Web page.

Computers on Campus 400 computers available on campus for general student use. A campuswide network can be accessed from student residence rooms and from off campus. Internet access, online (class) registration, at least one staffed computer lab available.

Student Life *Housing:* on-campus residence required through junior year. *Options:* coed, women-only, cooperative. *Activities and Organizations:* drama/theater group, student-run newspaper, radio and television station, choral group, marching band, Community Outreach, Bruin Club, Undergraduate Council of Students, orchestra and chorus, Daily Herald, national fraternities, national sororities. *Campus security:* 24-hour emergency response devices and patrols, late-night transport/escort service, controlled dormitory access. *Student Services:* health clinic, personal/psychological counseling, women's center, legal services.

Athletics Member NCAA. All Division I except football (Division I-AA). *Intercollegiate sports:* badminton M(c)/W(c), baseball M, basketball M/W, crew M/W, cross-country running M/W, equestrian sports W, fencing M/W, field hockey W, golf M/W, gymnastics W, ice hockey M/W, lacrosse M/W, rugby M(c)/W(c), sailing M(c)/W(c), skiing (cross-country) M(c)/W(c), skiing (downhill) M(c)/W, soccer M/W, softball W, squash M/W, swimming M/W, tennis M/W, track and field M/W, volleyball M(c)/W, water polo M/W, wrestling M. *Intramural sports:* archery M/W, badminton M/W, basketball M/W, fencing M/W, field hockey W, football M, ice hockey M/W, lacrosse M/W, racquetball M/W, rugby M/W, sailing W, skiing (downhill) M/W, soccer M/W, softball M/W, squash M/W, swimming M/W, table tennis M(c)/W(c), tennis M/W, volleyball M/W, water polo M/W.

Standardized Tests *Recommended:* SAT II: Writing Test (for admission).

Costs (2001–02) *One-time required fee:* $223. *Comprehensive fee:* $34,750 includes full-time tuition ($26,568), mandatory fees ($604), and room and board ($7578). Part-time tuition: $3321 per course. *Room and board:* College room only: $4698. Room and board charges vary according to board plan. *Payment plans:* tuition prepayment, installment, deferred payment. *Waivers:* employees or children of employees.

Financial Aid Of all full-time matriculated undergraduates who enrolled in 2001, 2936 applied for aid, 2269 were judged to have need, 2269 had their need fully met. 1652 Federal Work-Study jobs, 111 State and other part-time jobs (averaging $1978). In 2001, 448 non-need-based awards were made. *Average percent of need met:* 100%. *Average financial aid package:* $22,093. *Average need-based loan:* $4331. *Average need-based gift aid:* $17,536. *Average non-need based aid:* $2894. *Average indebtedness upon graduation:* $22,530. *Financial aid deadline:* 2/1.

Applying *Options:* early admission, early decision, early action, deferred entrance. *Application fee:* $70. *Required:* essay or personal statement, high school transcript, 2 letters of recommendation. *Application deadlines:* 1/1 (freshmen), 4/1 (transfers). *Early decision:* 11/1. *Notification:* 4/1 (freshmen), 12/15 (early decision).

Admissions Contact Mr. Michael Goldberger, Director of Admission, Brown University, Box 1876, Providence, RI 02912. *Phone:* 401-863-2378. *Fax:* 401-863-9300. *E-mail:* admission_undergraduate@brown.edu.

BRYANT COLLEGE

Smithfield, Rhode Island

- **Independent** comprehensive, founded 1863
- **Calendar** semesters
- **Degrees** bachelor's, master's, and post-master's certificates
- **Suburban** 387-acre campus with easy access to Boston
- **Endowment** $134.7 million
- **Coed,** 3,007 undergraduate students, 90% full-time, 39% women, 61% men
- **Moderately difficult** entrance level, 72% of applicants were admitted

Undergraduates 2,699 full-time, 308 part-time. Students come from 32 states and territories, 39 other countries, 73% are from out of state, 3% African American, 2% Asian American or Pacific Islander, 3% Hispanic American, 0.2% Native American, 5% international, 4% transferred in, 75% live on campus. *Retention:* 86% of 2001 full-time freshmen returned.

Bryant College (continued)

Freshmen *Admission:* 3,013 applied, 2,155 admitted, 712 enrolled. *Average high school GPA:* 3.04. *Test scores:* SAT verbal scores over 500: 65%; SAT math scores over 500: 84%; ACT scores over 18: 92%; SAT verbal scores over 600: 13%; SAT math scores over 600: 30%; ACT scores over 24: 39%; SAT math scores over 700: 2%; ACT scores over 30: 4%.

Faculty *Total:* 208, 63% full-time, 65% with terminal degrees. *Student/faculty ratio:* 19:1.

Majors Accounting; accounting technician; actuarial science; business administration; business marketing and marketing management; communications; computer/information sciences; economics; English; finance; financial management and services related; history; information sciences/systems; international relations; psychology.

Academic Programs *Special study options:* academic remediation for entering students, adult/continuing education programs, advanced placement credit, double majors, English as a second language, honors programs, independent study, internships, part-time degree program, services for LD students, study abroad, summer session for credit. *ROTC:* Army (b).

Library Edith M. Hodgson Memorial Library with 127,000 titles, 4,000 serial subscriptions, 810 audiovisual materials, an OPAC, a Web page.

Computers on Campus 365 computers available on campus for general student use. A campuswide network can be accessed from student residence rooms and from off campus that provide access to e-mail. Internet access, at least one staffed computer lab available.

Student Life *Housing Options:* coed, women-only, disabled students. *Activities and Organizations:* drama/theater group, student-run newspaper, radio station, choral group, Bryant Outdoor Activities Club, Student Programming Board, Bryant Environmental Society, radio station, Bryant Players (drama club), national fraternities, national sororities. *Campus security:* 24-hour emergency response devices and patrols, late-night transport/escort service, bicycle patrols, video cameras. *Student Services:* health clinic, personal/psychological counseling.

Athletics Member NCAA. All Division II. *Intercollegiate sports:* baseball M, basketball M(s)/W(s), bowling M(c)/W(c), cross-country running M/W, field hockey W, football M, golf M/W, ice hockey M(c), lacrosse M/W, racquetball M(c)/W(c), rugby M(c)/W(c), soccer M/W, softball W, squash M(c)/W(c), tennis M/W, track and field M/W, volleyball W, wrestling M(c). *Intramural sports:* basketball M/W, football M, soccer M/W, softball M/W.

Standardized Tests *Required:* SAT I or ACT (for admission).

Costs (2002–03) *Comprehensive fee:* $27,552 includes full-time tuition ($19,776) and room and board ($7776). Full-time tuition and fees vary according to course load and program. Part-time tuition: $756 per course. Part-time tuition and fees vary according to course load and program. *Room and board:* College room only: $4560. Room and board charges vary according to board plan and housing facility. *Payment plans:* tuition prepayment, installment. *Waivers:* employees or children of employees.

Financial Aid Of all full-time matriculated undergraduates who enrolled in 2001, 2372 applied for aid, 1661 were judged to have need, 249 had their need fully met. 163 Federal Work-Study jobs (averaging $1511). 949 State and other part-time jobs (averaging $1511). In 2001, 380 non-need-based awards were made. *Average percent of need met:* 76%. *Average financial aid package:* $12,631. *Average need-based loan:* $4341. *Average need-based gift aid:* $8483. *Average non-need based aid:* $7453. *Average indebtedness upon graduation:* $20,479.

Applying *Options:* common application, electronic application, early admission, early decision, early action, deferred entrance. *Application fee:* $50. *Required:* essay or personal statement, high school transcript, 1 letter of recommendation, senior year first-quarter grades. *Recommended:* minimum 3.0 GPA, interview. *Application deadlines:* 3/15 (freshmen), 8/15 (transfers). *Early decision:* 11/1. *Notification:* continuous (freshmen), 12/15 (early decision), 12/15 (early action).

Admissions Contact Ms. Cynthia Bonn, Director of Admission, Bryant College, 1150 Douglas Pike, Smithfield, RI 02917. *Phone:* 401-232-6100. *Toll-free phone:* 800-622-7001. *Fax:* 401-232-6741. *E-mail:* admissions@bryant.edu.

JOHNSON & WALES UNIVERSITY
Providence, Rhode Island

- **Independent** comprehensive, founded 1914
- **Calendar** quarters
- **Degrees** certificates, diplomas, associate, bachelor's, master's, and doctoral (branch locations: Charleston, SC; Denver, CO; North Miami, FL; Norfolk, VA; Gothenberg, Sweden)
- **Urban** 47-acre campus with easy access to Boston
- **Endowment** $178.8 million
- **Coed,** 8,635 undergraduate students, 87% full-time, 48% women, 52% men
- **Minimally difficult** entrance level, 82% of applicants were admitted

Undergraduates 7,527 full-time, 1,108 part-time. Students come from 50 states and territories, 92 other countries, 12% African American, 3% Asian American or Pacific Islander, 6% Hispanic American, 0.2% Native American, 9% international, 4% transferred in, 36% live on campus. *Retention:* 68% of 2001 full-time freshmen returned.

Freshmen *Admission:* 13,153 applied, 10,731 admitted, 2,351 enrolled. *Average high school GPA:* 2.67. *Test scores:* SAT verbal scores over 500: 33%; SAT math scores over 500: 35%; SAT verbal scores over 600: 6%; SAT math scores over 600: 6%; SAT verbal scores over 700: 1%; SAT math scores over 700: 1%.

Faculty *Total:* 440, 61% full-time. *Student/faculty ratio:* 30:1.

Majors Accounting; advertising; baker/pastry chef; business administration; business marketing and marketing management; computer engineering; computer engineering technology; computer/information sciences; computer programming; computer science; court reporting; criminal justice/law enforcement administration; culinary arts; electrical/electronic engineering technology; electrical/electronics drafting; electrical engineering; entrepreneurship; equestrian studies; farm/ranch management; fashion merchandising; finance; food products retailing; food sales operations; food services technology; health services administration; hospitality management; hotel and restaurant management; information sciences/systems; institutional food services; interdisciplinary studies; international business; legal administrative assistant; mass communications; mechanical engineering; mechanical engineering technology; paralegal/legal assistant; public relations; recreational therapy; recreation/leisure facilities management; recreation/leisure studies; restaurant operations; retailing operations; retail management; secretarial science; structural engineering; tourism/travel marketing; travel/tourism management.

Academic Programs *Special study options:* academic remediation for entering students, accelerated degree program, adult/continuing education programs, advanced placement credit, cooperative education, double majors, English as a second language, freshman honors college, honors programs, independent study, internships, part-time degree program, services for LD students, study abroad, summer session for credit.

Library Johnson & Wales University Library plus 2 others with 85,523 titles, 1,921 serial subscriptions, 531 audiovisual materials, an OPAC, a Web page.

Computers on Campus 340 computers available on campus for general student use. A campuswide network can be accessed from student residence rooms and from off campus. Internet access, at least one staffed computer lab available.

Student Life *Housing:* on-campus residence required for freshman year. *Options:* coed. *Activities and Organizations:* drama/theater group, student-run newspaper, choral group, Delta Epsilon Chi, Vocational Industrial Clubs of America, Phi Beta Lambda, FHA/HERO, FFA, national fraternities, national sororities. *Campus security:* 24-hour emergency response devices and patrols, student patrols, late-night transport/escort service. *Student Services:* health clinic, personal/psychological counseling, women's center.

Athletics Member NCAA. All Division III. *Intercollegiate sports:* baseball M(c), basketball M/W, cross-country running M/W, equestrian sports M(c)/W(c), golf M/W, ice hockey M(c), soccer M/W, tennis M/W, volleyball M/W. *Intramural sports:* basketball M/W, bowling M(c)/W(c), football M/W, golf M(c)/W(c), gymnastics M(c), skiing (downhill) M(c)/W(c), tennis M(c)/W(c), volleyball M/W.

Standardized Tests *Required for some:* SAT I or ACT (for admission). *Recommended:* SAT I or ACT (for admission).

Costs (2002–03) *Comprehensive fee:* $21,558 includes full-time tuition ($14,562), mandatory fees ($630), and room and board ($6366). Full-time tuition and fees vary according to program. No tuition increase for student's term of enrollment. *Room and board:* Room and board charges vary according to housing facility. *Waivers:* employees or children of employees.

Financial Aid Of all full-time matriculated undergraduates who enrolled in 2001, 6255 applied for aid, 5327 were judged to have need, 285 had their need fully met. In 2001, 406 non-need-based awards were made. *Average percent of need met:* 70%. *Average financial aid package:* $10,673. *Average need-based loan:* $5355. *Average need-based gift aid:* $3583. *Average non-need based aid:* $2860. *Average indebtedness upon graduation:* $19,008.

Applying *Options:* common application, early admission, deferred entrance. *Required:* high school transcript. *Required for some:* minimum 3.0 GPA, 1 letter of recommendation. *Recommended:* minimum 2.0 GPA, interview. *Application deadline:* rolling (freshmen), rolling (transfers). *Notification:* continuous (freshmen).

Admissions Contact Ms. Maureen Dumas, Dean of Admissions, Johnson & Wales University, 8 Abbott Park Place, Providence, RI 02903-3703. *Phone:* 401-598-2310. *Toll-free phone:* 800-342-5598. *Fax:* 401-598-2948. *E-mail:* admissions@jwu.edu.

New England Institute of Technology
Warwick, Rhode Island

- **Independent** primarily 2-year, founded 1940
- **Calendar** quarters
- **Degrees** associate and bachelor's
- **Suburban** 10-acre campus with easy access to Boston
- **Coed**
- **Noncompetitive** entrance level

Faculty *Student/faculty ratio:* 15:1.
Student Life *Campus security:* security personnel during open hours.
Applying *Options:* early admission, deferred entrance. *Application fee:* $25. *Required:* high school transcript, interview.
Admissions Contact Mr. Michael Kwiatkowski, Director of Admissions, New England Institute of Technology, 2500 Post Road, Warwick, RI 02886-2266. *Phone:* 401-739-5000. *E-mail:* neit@ids.net.

Providence College
Providence, Rhode Island

- **Independent Roman Catholic** comprehensive, founded 1917
- **Calendar** semesters
- **Degrees** associate, bachelor's, and master's
- **Suburban** 105-acre campus with easy access to Boston
- **Endowment** $104.0 million
- **Coed,** 4,389 undergraduate students, 87% full-time, 57% women, 43% men
- **Very difficult** entrance level, 57% of applicants were admitted

Providence College is the only liberal arts college in the US that was founded and administered by the Dominican Friars, a Catholic teaching order whose heritage spans nearly 800 years. The College is not only concerned with the rigors of intellectual life but also recognizes the importance of students' experiences outside the classroom, including service to others. Scholarship, service, and the exuberant PC spirit—these are the qualities that shape the character of Providence College.

Undergraduates 3,814 full-time, 575 part-time. Students come from 43 states and territories, 16 other countries, 75% are from out of state, 2% African American, 1% Asian American or Pacific Islander, 4% Hispanic American, 0.0% Native American, 1% international, 2% transferred in, 74% live on campus. *Retention:* 92% of 2001 full-time freshmen returned.
Freshmen *Admission:* 5,440 applied, 3,100 admitted, 934 enrolled. *Average high school GPA:* 3.37. *Test scores:* SAT verbal scores over 500: 93%; SAT math scores over 500: 93%; ACT scores over 18: 99%; SAT verbal scores over 600: 45%; SAT math scores over 600: 48%; ACT scores over 24: 65%; SAT verbal scores over 700: 8%; SAT math scores over 700: 5%; ACT scores over 30: 9%.
Faculty *Total:* 329, 79% full-time, 67% with terminal degrees. *Student/faculty ratio:* 13:1.
Majors Accounting; American studies; art history; biology; business administration; business economics; business marketing and marketing management; chemistry; community services; computer science; economics; English; environmental science; finance; fine/studio arts; fire science; French; health services administration; history; humanities; instrumentation technology; Italian; labor/personnel relations; liberal arts and sciences/liberal studies; mathematics; music; paralegal/legal assistant; pastoral counseling; philosophy; political science; psychology; secondary education; social sciences; social work; sociology; Spanish; special education; systems science/theory; theology; visual/performing arts.
Academic Programs *Special study options:* adult/continuing education programs, advanced placement credit, cooperative education, distance learning, double majors, honors programs, independent study, internships, part-time degree program, services for LD students, student-designed majors, study abroad, summer session for credit. *ROTC:* Army (b). *Unusual degree programs:* 3-2 engineering with Columbia University, Washington University in St. Louis.
Library Phillips Memorial Library with 383,396 titles, 1,812 serial subscriptions, 981 audiovisual materials, an OPAC, a Web page.
Computers on Campus 150 computers available on campus for general student use. A campuswide network can be accessed from student residence rooms and from off campus. Internet access, at least one staffed computer lab available.
Student Life *Housing:* on-campus residence required through sophomore year. *Options:* coed, men-only, women-only, disabled students. *Activities and Organizations:* drama/theater group, student-run newspaper, radio and television station, choral group, Board of Programmers, Student Congress, student newspaper, Big Brothers/Big Sisters, Pastoral Council. *Campus security:* 24-hour emergency response devices and patrols, student patrols, late-night transport/escort service, controlled dormitory access. *Student Services:* health clinic, personal/psychological counseling, legal services.
Athletics Member NCAA. All Division I. *Intercollegiate sports:* basketball M(s)/W(s), cross-country running M(s)/W(s), field hockey W(s), ice hockey M(s)/W(s), lacrosse M, racquetball M(c)/W(c), rugby M(c)/W(c), soccer M(s)/W(s), softball W(s), swimming M/W, tennis W(s), track and field M(s)/W(s), volleyball W(s). *Intramural sports:* baseball M, basketball M/W, bowling M(c)/W(c), cross-country running M/W, football M/W, golf M/W, ice hockey M/W, racquetball M/W, sailing M/W, skiing (cross-country) M(c)/W(c), skiing (downhill) M(c)/W(c), softball M/W, squash M/W, swimming M/W, tennis M/W, volleyball M/W, water polo M/W, weight lifting M/W.
Standardized Tests *Required:* SAT I or ACT (for admission). *Recommended:* SAT II: Subject Tests (for admission), SAT II: Writing Test (for admission).
Costs (2001–02) *Comprehensive fee:* $27,620 includes full-time tuition ($19,375), mandatory fees ($320), and room and board ($7925). Part-time tuition: $197 per credit. Part-time tuition and fees vary according to course load. *Room and board:* College room only: $3935. Room and board charges vary according to board plan, housing facility, and student level. *Payment plan:* installment. *Waivers:* employees or children of employees.
Financial Aid Of all full-time matriculated undergraduates who enrolled in 2001, 2453 applied for aid, 2085 were judged to have need, 521 had their need fully met. In 2001, 445 non-need-based awards were made. *Average percent of need met:* 85%. *Average financial aid package:* $15,500. *Average need-based loan:* $5850. *Average need-based gift aid:* $8500. *Average non-need based aid:* $6100. *Average indebtedness upon graduation:* $19,625. *Financial aid deadline:* 2/1.
Applying *Options:* electronic application, early admission, early action, deferred entrance. *Application fee:* $55. *Required:* essay or personal statement, high school transcript, 2 letters of recommendation. *Recommended:* minimum 3.25 GPA, interview. *Application deadlines:* 1/15 (freshmen), 4/15 (transfers). *Notification:* 4/1 (freshmen), 1/1 (early action).
Admissions Contact Mr. Christopher Lydon, Dean of Enrollment Management, Providence College, River Avenue and Eaton Street, Providence, RI 02918. *Phone:* 401-865-2535. *Toll-free phone:* 800-721-6444. *Fax:* 401-865-2826. *E-mail:* pcadmiss@providence.edu.

Rhode Island College
Providence, Rhode Island

- **State-supported** comprehensive, founded 1854
- **Calendar** semesters
- **Degrees** bachelor's, master's, doctoral, and post-master's certificates
- **Suburban** 170-acre campus with easy access to Boston
- **Coed,** 6,917 undergraduate students, 64% full-time, 68% women, 32% men
- **Moderately difficult** entrance level, 69% of applicants were admitted

Undergraduates 4,443 full-time, 2,474 part-time. Students come from 10 states and territories, 8% are from out of state, 4% African American, 3% Asian American or Pacific Islander, 4% Hispanic American, 0.3% Native American, 9% transferred in, 14% live on campus. *Retention:* 74% of 2001 full-time freshmen returned.
Freshmen *Admission:* 2,414 applied, 1,657 admitted, 953 enrolled. *Test scores:* SAT verbal scores over 500: 49%; SAT math scores over 500: 29%; SAT verbal scores over 600: 10%; SAT math scores over 600: 9%; SAT verbal scores over 700: 1%.
Faculty *Total:* 646, 49% full-time. *Student/faculty ratio:* 14:1.
Majors Accounting; African-American studies; anthropology; Army R.O.T.C./military science; art; art education; art history; behavioral sciences; biological/physical sciences; biology; business administration; business marketing and marketing management; chemistry; computer science; criminal justice studies; dance; early childhood education; economics; education; elementary education; English; film studies; finance; fine/studio arts; French; geography; health education; health/medical preparatory programs related; history; industrial arts; industrial technology; information sciences/systems; labor/personnel relations; liberal arts and sciences/liberal studies; management information systems/business data processing; mass communications; mathematics; medical technology; middle school education; music; music teacher education; nursing; philosophy; physical education; physical sciences; physics; political science; pre-dentistry; pre-law; pre-medicine; pre-veterinary studies; psychology; public administration; science education; secondary education; social sciences; social work; sociology; Spanish; special education; speech/rhetorical studies; theater arts/drama.
Academic Programs *Special study options:* academic remediation for entering students, adult/continuing education programs, advanced placement credit, double majors, freshman honors college, honors programs, independent study, intern-

Rhode Island College (continued)
ships, off-campus study, part-time degree program, services for LD students, student-designed majors, study abroad, summer session for credit. *ROTC:* Army (c). *Unusual degree programs:* 3-2 engineering with University of Rhode Island; occupational therapy with Washington University in St. Louis.

Library Adams Library with 368,891 titles, 1,766 serial subscriptions, 3,982 audiovisual materials, an OPAC, a Web page.

Computers on Campus 350 computers available on campus for general student use. A campuswide network can be accessed from off campus. At least one staffed computer lab available.

Student Life *Housing Options:* coed, women-only, disabled students. *Activities and Organizations:* drama/theater group, student-run newspaper, radio and television station, choral group, student government, newspaper, campus radio station (WXIN), OASPA (Organization of African Students and Professionals in the Americas), Asian Student Association. *Campus security:* 24-hour patrols, late-night transport/escort service. *Student Services:* health clinic, personal/psychological counseling, women's center.

Athletics Member NCAA. All Division III. *Intercollegiate sports:* baseball M, basketball M/W, cross-country running M/W, gymnastics W, soccer M/W, softball W, tennis M/W, track and field M/W, volleyball W, wrestling M. *Intramural sports:* basketball M/W, football M, golf M, tennis M/W, volleyball M/W.

Standardized Tests *Required:* SAT I or ACT (for admission). *Recommended:* SAT II: Writing Test (for admission).

Costs (2001–02) *Tuition:* state resident $2860 full-time, $128 per credit part-time; nonresident $8250 full-time, $345 per credit part-time. Full-time tuition and fees vary according to reciprocity agreements. Part-time tuition and fees vary according to course load and reciprocity agreements. *Required fees:* $661 full-time, $21 per credit. *Room and board:* $5760; room only: $2940. Room and board charges vary according to board plan and housing facility. *Payment plan:* installment. *Waivers:* senior citizens and employees or children of employees.

Applying *Options:* common application, early admission, deferred entrance. *Application fee:* $25. *Required:* essay or personal statement, high school transcript, letters of recommendation. *Required for some:* interview. *Application deadlines:* 5/1 (freshmen), 6/1 (transfers). *Notification:* continuous (freshmen).

Admissions Contact Dr. Holly Shadoian, Director of Admissions, Rhode Island College, 600 Mount Pleasant Avenue, Providence, RI 02908-1924. *Phone:* 401-456-8234. *Toll-free phone:* 800-669-5760. *Fax:* 401-456-8817. *E-mail:* admissions@ric.edu.

RHODE ISLAND SCHOOL OF DESIGN
Providence, Rhode Island

- **Independent** comprehensive, founded 1877
- **Calendar** 4-1-4
- **Degrees** bachelor's, master's, and first professional
- **Urban** 13-acre campus with easy access to Boston
- **Endowment** $213.1 million
- **Coed,** 1,845 undergraduate students, 100% full-time, 63% women, 37% men
- **Very difficult** entrance level, 41% of applicants were admitted

Undergraduates 1,845 full-time. Students come from 51 states and territories, 53 other countries, 94% are from out of state, 3% African American, 11% Asian American or Pacific Islander, 5% Hispanic American, 0.2% Native American, 12% international, 6% transferred in, 38% live on campus. *Retention:* 96% of 2001 full-time freshmen returned.

Freshmen *Admission:* 2,004 applied, 813 admitted, 418 enrolled. *Average high school GPA:* 3.30. *Test scores:* SAT verbal scores over 500: 87%; SAT math scores over 500: 93%; SAT verbal scores over 600: 51%; SAT math scores over 600: 53%; SAT verbal scores over 700: 15%; SAT math scores over 700: 10%.

Faculty *Total:* 399, 35% full-time. *Student/faculty ratio:* 11:1.

Majors Architecture; art; ceramic arts; clothing/textiles; drawing; fashion design/illustration; film studies; graphic design/commercial art/illustration; industrial design; interior design; metal/jewelry arts; photography; printmaking; sculpture; textile arts; theater arts/drama.

Academic Programs *Special study options:* academic remediation for entering students, adult/continuing education programs, advanced placement credit, English as a second language, internships, off-campus study, study abroad.

Library RISD Library with 95,161 titles, 423 serial subscriptions, 158,325 audiovisual materials, an OPAC.

Computers on Campus 300 computers available on campus for general student use. A campuswide network can be accessed from student residence rooms and from off campus. Internet access, at least one staffed computer lab available.

Student Life *Housing:* on-campus residence required for freshman year. *Options:* coed. *Activities and Organizations:* drama/theater group, student-run newspaper, athletic clubs, industrial design club, Korean Students Association, Lesbian/Gay/Bisexual Alliance. *Campus security:* 24-hour emergency response devices and patrols, late-night transport/escort service, controlled dormitory access. *Student Services:* health clinic, personal/psychological counseling, legal services.

Athletics *Intramural sports:* baseball M/W, basketball M/W, bowling M(c)/W(c), ice hockey M/W, sailing M(c)/W(c), skiing (downhill) M(c)/W(c), soccer M/W, softball M/W, table tennis M/W, volleyball M/W, weight lifting M/W.

Standardized Tests *Required:* SAT I or ACT (for admission).

Costs (2001–02) *Comprehensive fee:* $30,227 includes full-time tuition ($22,952), mandatory fees ($445), and room and board ($6830). *Room and board:* College room only: $3630. Room and board charges vary according to board plan and housing facility. *Payment plan:* installment. *Waivers:* employees or children of employees.

Financial Aid Of all full-time matriculated undergraduates who enrolled in 2001, 973 applied for aid, 881 were judged to have need, 84 had their need fully met. In 2001, 36 non-need-based awards were made. *Average percent of need met:* 70%. *Average financial aid package:* $14,900. *Average need-based loan:* $5450. *Average need-based gift aid:* $7642. *Average non-need based aid:* $1250. *Average indebtedness upon graduation:* $21,000.

Applying *Options:* early admission, early action, deferred entrance. *Application fee:* $45. *Required:* essay or personal statement, high school transcript, portfolio, drawing assignments. *Recommended:* 3 letters of recommendation. *Application deadlines:* 2/15 (freshmen), 3/31 (transfers). *Notification:* 4/2 (freshmen), 1/25 (early action).

Admissions Contact Mr. Edward Newhall, Director of Admissions, Rhode Island School of Design, 2 College Street, Providence, RI 02905-2791. *Phone:* 401-454-6300. *Toll-free phone:* 800-364-RISD. *Fax:* 401-454-6309. *E-mail:* admissions@risd.edu.

ROGER WILLIAMS UNIVERSITY
Bristol, Rhode Island

- **Independent** comprehensive, founded 1956
- **Calendar** semesters
- **Degrees** associate, bachelor's, master's, and first professional
- **Small-town** 140-acre campus with easy access to Boston
- **Endowment** $26.2 million
- **Coed,** 4,031 undergraduate students, 76% full-time, 51% women, 49% men
- **Moderately difficult** entrance level, 90% of applicants were admitted

Thinking about where you'll apply to college? Take a few minutes and check out Roger Williams University in Bristol, Rhode Island. In addition to enjoying a beautiful bayside campus, it's easy to make friends while you learn. Dedicated faculty members teach students the liberal arts and professional career courses. For more information, students may visit the University's Web site at http://www.rwu.edu.

Undergraduates 3,062 full-time, 969 part-time. Students come from 26 states and territories, 31 other countries, 88% are from out of state, 2% African American, 1% Asian American or Pacific Islander, 2% Hispanic American, 0.4% Native American, 2% international, 3% transferred in, 81% live on campus. *Retention:* 81% of 2001 full-time freshmen returned.

Freshmen *Admission:* 4,221 applied, 3,817 admitted, 1,097 enrolled. *Average high school GPA:* 3.03. *Test scores:* SAT verbal scores over 500: 65%; SAT math scores over 500: 70%; SAT verbal scores over 600: 17%; SAT math scores over 600: 22%; SAT verbal scores over 700: 1%; SAT math scores over 700: 2%.

Faculty *Total:* 337, 40% full-time, 43% with terminal degrees. *Student/faculty ratio:* 17:1.

Majors Accounting; American studies; architectural history; architecture; art history; biology; business; business administration; business marketing and marketing management; chemistry; communications; computer science; construction management; creative writing; criminal justice/law enforcement administration; dance; elementary education; engineering; English; environmental engineering; environmental science; financial planning; foreign languages/literatures; history; industrial technology; information sciences/systems; international business; liberal arts and sciences/liberal studies; marine biology; mathematics; paralegal/legal assistant; philosophy; political science; pre-dentistry; pre-medicine; pre-veterinary studies; psychology; public administration; secondary education; social sciences; theater arts/drama; visual/performing arts.

Academic Programs *Special study options:* adult/continuing education programs, advanced placement credit, cooperative education, double majors, English as a second language, external degree program, freshman honors college, honors programs, independent study, internships, part-time degree program, services for LD students, student-designed majors, study abroad, summer session for credit. *ROTC:* Army (b).

Library Roger Williams University Library plus 2 others with 168,460 titles, 1,225 serial subscriptions, 60,694 audiovisual materials, an OPAC, a Web page.
Computers on Campus 425 computers available on campus for general student use. A campuswide network can be accessed from student residence rooms and from off campus that provide access to telephone registration. Internet access, at least one staffed computer lab available.
Student Life *Housing:* on-campus residence required through sophomore year. *Options:* coed, disabled students. *Activities and Organizations:* drama/theater group, student-run newspaper, radio station, choral group, Entertainment Network, Student Senate, American Institute of Architects, John Jay Society, residence hall councils. *Campus security:* 24-hour emergency response devices and patrols, student patrols, late-night transport/escort service, controlled dormitory access. *Student Services:* health clinic, personal/psychological counseling, women's center.
Athletics Member NCAA. All Division III. *Intercollegiate sports:* baseball M, basketball M/W, crew M(c)/W(c), cross-country running M/W, equestrian sports M/W, golf M/W, rugby M(c), sailing M/W, soccer M/W, softball W, tennis M/W, track and field M(c)/W(c), volleyball M/W, wrestling M. *Intramural sports:* basketball M/W, golf M/W, soccer M/W, softball M/W, tennis M/W, volleyball M/W.
Standardized Tests *Required:* SAT I or ACT (for admission).
Costs (2001–02) *Comprehensive fee:* $29,010 includes full-time tuition ($19,280), mandatory fees ($795), and room and board ($8935). Full-time tuition and fees vary according to class time, course load, and program. Part-time tuition: $800 per credit. Part-time tuition and fees vary according to class time. *Room and board:* College room only: $4670. Room and board charges vary according to board plan and housing facility. *Payment plans:* installment, deferred payment. *Waivers:* employees or children of employees.
Financial Aid Of all full-time matriculated undergraduates who enrolled in 2001, 1971 applied for aid, 1717 were judged to have need, 966 had their need fully met. In 2001, 150 non-need-based awards were made. *Average percent of need met:* 87%. *Average financial aid package:* $14,415. *Average need-based loan:* $4142. *Average need-based gift aid:* $7460. *Average non-need based aid:* $6247. *Average indebtedness upon graduation:* $19,002.
Applying *Options:* common application, electronic application, early admission, early decision, deferred entrance. *Application fee:* $35. *Required:* essay or personal statement, high school transcript, minimum 2.0 GPA, letters of recommendation. *Recommended:* 2.0 letters of recommendation, interview. *Application deadline:* rolling (freshmen), rolling (transfers). *Early decision:* 12/1. *Notification:* continuous (freshmen), 12/15 (early decision).
Admissions Contact Ms. Julie H. Cairns, Director of Freshman Admission, Roger Williams University, 1 Old Ferry Road, Bristol, RI 02809. *Phone:* 401-254-3500. *Toll-free phone:* 800-458-7144. *Fax:* 401-254-3557. *E-mail:* admit@rwu.edu.

SALVE REGINA UNIVERSITY
Newport, Rhode Island

- **Independent Roman Catholic** comprehensive, founded 1934
- **Calendar** semesters
- **Degrees** associate, bachelor's, master's, doctoral, and post-master's certificates
- **Suburban** 65-acre campus with easy access to Boston
- **Endowment** $16.1 million
- **Coed,** 1,894 undergraduate students, 94% full-time, 68% women, 32% men
- **Moderately difficult** entrance level, 65% of applicants were admitted

Undergraduates 1,773 full-time, 121 part-time. Students come from 40 states and territories, 10 other countries, 80% are from out of state, 1% African American, 0.9% Asian American or Pacific Islander, 2% Hispanic American, 0.4% Native American, 1.0% international, 3% transferred in, 60% live on campus. *Retention:* 77% of 2001 full-time freshmen returned.
Freshmen *Admission:* 3,329 applied, 2,157 admitted, 554 enrolled. *Average high school GPA:* 3.15. *Test scores:* SAT verbal scores over 500: 63%; SAT math scores over 500: 61%; SAT verbal scores over 600: 16%; SAT math scores over 600: 11%; SAT verbal scores over 700: 1%.
Faculty *Total:* 269, 39% full-time, 41% with terminal degrees. *Student/faculty ratio:* 12:1.
Majors Accounting; American studies; anthropology; architectural history; art history; biology; biology education; business administration; chemistry; chemistry education; criminal justice/law enforcement administration; cytotechnology; drama/dance education; early childhood education; economics; educational media technology; elementary education; English; English education; fine/studio arts; French; French language education; history; history education; information sciences/systems; liberal arts and sciences/liberal studies; mathematics; mathematics education; medical technology; music; nursing; philosophy; political science; psychology; religious studies; secondary education; social work; sociology; Spanish; Spanish language education; special education; theater arts/drama.
Academic Programs *Special study options:* accelerated degree program, adult/continuing education programs, advanced placement credit, distance learning, double majors, English as a second language, freshman honors college, honors programs, independent study, internships, part-time degree program, services for LD students, study abroad, summer session for credit. *ROTC:* Army (c).
Library McKillop Library with 105,262 titles, 783 serial subscriptions, 18,785 audiovisual materials, an OPAC, a Web page.
Computers on Campus 163 computers available on campus for general student use. A campuswide network can be accessed from student residence rooms and from off campus. Internet access, at least one staffed computer lab available.
Student Life *Housing:* on-campus residence required through sophomore year. *Options:* coed, men-only, women-only, disabled students. *Activities and Organizations:* drama/theater group, student-run newspaper, radio station, choral group, Orpheus Musical Society, Student Government Association, Student Outdoor Adventures, Student Nurse Organization, Stagefright Theatre Company. *Campus security:* 24-hour emergency response devices and patrols, late-night transport/escort service, controlled dormitory access. *Student Services:* health clinic, personal/psychological counseling.
Athletics Member NCAA. All Division III. *Intercollegiate sports:* baseball M, basketball M/W, cross-country running W, equestrian sports M(c)/W(c), field hockey W, football M, golf M(c)/W, ice hockey M/W, lacrosse M/W, rugby M(c), sailing M/W, soccer M/W, softball W, tennis W, track and field W, volleyball W. *Intramural sports:* basketball M/W, field hockey W, football M/W, soccer M/W, softball M/W, tennis M/W, track and field W, volleyball M/W, weight lifting M/W.
Standardized Tests *Required:* SAT I or ACT (for admission).
Costs (2001–02) *Comprehensive fee:* $26,460 includes full-time tuition ($17,950), mandatory fees ($410), and room and board ($8100). Part-time tuition: $600 per credit. Part-time tuition and fees vary according to course load. *Required fees:* $35 per term part-time. *Room and board:* Room and board charges vary according to board plan. *Payment plan:* installment. *Waivers:* employees or children of employees.
Financial Aid Of all full-time matriculated undergraduates who enrolled in 2001, 1317 applied for aid, 1129 were judged to have need, 195 had their need fully met. 308 Federal Work-Study jobs (averaging $1257). 239 State and other part-time jobs (averaging $1106). *Average percent of need met:* 76%. *Average financial aid package:* $13,931. *Average need-based loan:* $4589. *Average need-based gift aid:* $9165. *Average indebtedness upon graduation:* $18,875.
Applying *Options:* common application, electronic application, early action, deferred entrance. *Application fee:* $40. *Required:* essay or personal statement, high school transcript, 2 letters of recommendation. *Recommended:* minimum 2.5 GPA. *Application deadline:* 3/1 (freshmen), rolling (transfers). *Notification:* continuous (freshmen), 12/15 (early action).
Admissions Contact Colleen Emerson, Director of Admissions, Salve Regina University, 100 Ochre Point Avenue, Newport, RI 02840-4192. *Phone:* 401-341-2109. *Toll-free phone:* 888-GO SALVE. *Fax:* 401-848-2823. *E-mail:* sruadmis@salve.edu.

UNIVERSITY OF RHODE ISLAND
Kingston, Rhode Island

- **State-supported** university, founded 1892, part of Rhode Island State System of Higher Education
- **Calendar** semesters
- **Degrees** bachelor's, master's, doctoral, first professional, and postbachelor's certificates
- **Small-town** 1200-acre campus
- **Endowment** $39.6 million
- **Coed,** 10,579 undergraduate students, 83% full-time, 56% women, 44% men
- **Moderately difficult** entrance level, 67% of applicants were admitted

Undergraduates 8,780 full-time, 1,799 part-time. Students come from 38 states and territories, 47 other countries, 38% are from out of state, 4% African American, 3% Asian American or Pacific Islander, 4% Hispanic American, 0.4% Native American, 0.4% international, 5% transferred in, 32% live on campus. *Retention:* 79% of 2001 full-time freshmen returned.
Freshmen *Admission:* 10,794 applied, 7,203 admitted, 2,129 enrolled. *Average high school GPA:* 3.40. *Test scores:* SAT verbal scores over 500: 74%; SAT math scores over 500: 77%; SAT verbal scores over 600: 25%; SAT math scores over 600: 29%; SAT verbal scores over 700: 3%; SAT math scores over 700: 3%.

University of Rhode Island (continued)
Faculty *Total:* 682, 98% full-time, 90% with terminal degrees. *Student/faculty ratio:* 18:1.
Majors Accounting; animal sciences; anthropology; apparel marketing; applied economics; art; art history; bioengineering; biology; business administration; business marketing and marketing management; chemical engineering; chemistry; civil engineering; classics; clothing/apparel/textile studies; communication disorders; communications; comparative literature; computer engineering; computer/information sciences; consumer economics; dental hygiene; dietetics; economics; electrical engineering; elementary education; English; environmental science; finance; fishing sciences; French; geology; German; health services administration; history; human services; individual/family development; industrial/manufacturing engineering; interdisciplinary studies; international business; Italian; journalism; landscape architecture; Latin American studies; liberal arts and sciences/liberal studies; management information systems/business data processing; marine biology; mathematics; mechanical engineering; medical technology; microbiology/bacteriology; music; music (general performance); music teacher education; music theory and composition; natural resources conservation; natural resources management; nursing; nutrition studies; ocean engineering; pharmacy; philosophy; physical education; physics; political science; psychology; public policy analysis; quantitative economics; secondary education; sociology; Spanish; turf management; wildlife management; women's studies; zoology.
Academic Programs *Special study options:* academic remediation for entering students, accelerated degree program, adult/continuing education programs, advanced placement credit, cooperative education, distance learning, double majors, honors programs, independent study, internships, off-campus study, part-time degree program, services for LD students, student-designed majors, study abroad, summer session for credit. *ROTC:* Army (b). *Unusual degree programs:* 3-2 physical therapy, speech pathology, audiology.
Library University Library plus 1 other with 783,237 titles, 7,966 serial subscriptions, 9,510 audiovisual materials, an OPAC, a Web page.
Computers on Campus 552 computers available on campus for general student use. A campuswide network can be accessed from off campus. At least one staffed computer lab available.
Student Life *Housing Options:* coed. *Activities and Organizations:* drama/theater group, student-run newspaper, radio station, choral group, marching band, Student Entertainment Committee, student radio station, intramural sport clubs, Student Alumni Association, student newspaper, national fraternities, national sororities. *Campus security:* 24-hour emergency response devices and patrols, student patrols, late-night transport/escort service, controlled dormitory access. *Student Services:* health clinic, personal/psychological counseling, women's center.
Athletics Member NCAA. All Division I except football (Division I-AA). *Intercollegiate sports:* baseball M(s), basketball M(s)/W(s), crew M(c)/W, cross-country running M(s)/W(s), equestrian sports M(c)/W(c), fencing M(c)/W(c), field hockey W(s), golf M(s), gymnastics W(s), ice hockey M(c), lacrosse M(c)/W(c), rugby M(c)/W(c), sailing M(c)/W(c), skiing (downhill) M(c)/W(c), soccer M(s)/W(s), softball W(s), swimming M(s)/W(s), tennis M/W(s), track and field M(s)/W(s), volleyball M(c)/W(s), water polo M(c). *Intramural sports:* badminton M/W, basketball M/W, football M/W, golf M/W, soccer M/W, softball M/W, swimming M/W, tennis M/W, volleyball M/W, water polo M/W.
Standardized Tests *Required:* SAT I or ACT (for admission).
Costs (2001–02) *Tuition:* state resident $3580 full-time, $149 per credit part-time; nonresident $12,358 full-time, $515 per credit part-time. Part-time tuition and fees vary according to reciprocity agreements. *Required fees:* $1806 full-time, $51 per credit, $43 per term part-time. *Room and board:* $7028; room only: $4028. Room and board charges vary according to board plan and housing facility. *Payment plan:* installment. *Waivers:* minority students, senior citizens, and employees or children of employees.
Financial Aid Of all full-time matriculated undergraduates who enrolled in 2001, 8018 applied for aid, 6481 were judged to have need, 5067 had their need fully met. In 2001, 822 non-need-based awards were made. *Average percent of need met:* 84%. *Average financial aid package:* $8940. *Average need-based loan:* $5319. *Average need-based gift aid:* $4244. *Average indebtedness upon graduation:* $12,500.
Applying *Options:* electronic application, early admission, early action. *Application fee:* $45 (non-residents). *Required:* high school transcript. *Required for some:* minimum 3.0 GPA. *Recommended:* minimum 3.0 GPA, letters of recommendation, interview. *Application deadlines:* 3/1 (freshmen), 5/1 (transfers). *Notification:* continuous (freshmen), 1/15 (early action).
Admissions Contact Ms. Catherine Zeiser, Assistant Dean of Admissions, University of Rhode Island, 8 Ranger Road, Suite 1, Kingston, RI 02881-2020. *Phone:* 401-874-7100. *Fax:* 401-874-5523. *E-mail:* uriadmit@uri.edu.

SOUTH CAROLINA

ALLEN UNIVERSITY
Columbia, South Carolina

- **Independent African Methodist Episcopal** 4-year, founded 1870
- **Calendar** semesters
- **Degree** bachelor's
- **Suburban** campus
- **Coed**
- **Minimally difficult** entrance level

Faculty *Student/faculty ratio:* 10:1.
Student Life *Campus security:* 24-hour patrols.
Athletics Member NAIA.
Standardized Tests *Recommended:* SAT I (for placement).
Costs (2001–02) *Comprehensive fee:* $8960 includes full-time tuition ($4650), mandatory fees ($100), and room and board ($4210). Part-time tuition: $132 per credit.
Financial Aid *Financial aid deadline:* 6/30.
Applying *Options:* common application. *Application fee:* $15. *Required:* high school transcript, 2 letters of recommendation.
Admissions Contact Admissions Office, Allen University, 1530 Harden Street, Columbia, SC 29204-1085. *Phone:* 803-376-5741. *Fax:* 803-376-5731. *E-mail:* auniv@mindspring.com.

ANDERSON COLLEGE
Anderson, South Carolina

- **Independent Baptist** 4-year, founded 1911
- **Calendar** semesters
- **Degrees** associate and bachelor's
- **Suburban** 44-acre campus
- **Endowment** $15.0 million
- **Coed,** 1,450 undergraduate students, 78% full-time, 64% women, 36% men
- **Moderately difficult** entrance level, 70% of applicants were admitted

Undergraduates 1,132 full-time, 318 part-time. Students come from 24 states and territories, 13% are from out of state, 11% African American, 0.8% Asian American or Pacific Islander, 0.9% Hispanic American, 0.4% Native American, 0.7% international, 5% transferred in, 50% live on campus. *Retention:* 62% of 2001 full-time freshmen returned.
Freshmen *Admission:* 958 applied, 669 admitted, 332 enrolled. *Average high school GPA:* 3.34. *Test scores:* SAT verbal scores over 500: 51%; SAT math scores over 500: 52%; ACT scores over 18: 80%; SAT verbal scores over 600: 14%; SAT math scores over 600: 11%; ACT scores over 24: 13%; SAT math scores over 700: 2%.
Faculty *Total:* 109, 50% full-time, 43% with terminal degrees. *Student/faculty ratio:* 14:1.
Majors Accounting; art; art education; biology; biology education; business administration; business information/data processing related; business marketing and marketing management; creative writing; cytotechnology; drawing; early childhood education; education; elementary education; English; English education; finance; fine/studio arts; graphic design/commercial art/illustration; history; history education; human resources management; human services; interior design; journalism; liberal arts and sciences/liberal studies; mass communications; mathematics; mathematics education; music; music teacher education; physical education; psychology; religious studies; secondary education; Spanish; Spanish language education; special education; speech/rhetorical studies; sport/fitness administration; theater arts/drama.
Academic Programs *Special study options:* academic remediation for entering students, adult/continuing education programs, advanced placement credit, freshman honors college, honors programs, independent study, internships, part-time degree program, study abroad, summer session for credit. *ROTC:* Army (c), Air Force (c).
Library Olin D. Johnston Library with 55,000 titles, 425 serial subscriptions, an OPAC.
Computers on Campus 60 computers available on campus for general student use. Internet access, at least one staffed computer lab available.
Student Life *Housing:* on-campus residence required through sophomore year. *Options:* men-only, women-only. *Activities and Organizations:* drama/theater group, student-run newspaper, choral group, Baptist Campus Ministries, Fellowship of Christian Athletes, Student Government Association, Minorities Involved

in Change, Student Alumni Council. *Campus security:* 24-hour emergency response devices and patrols, late-night transport/escort service, controlled dormitory access. *Student Services:* health clinic, personal/psychological counseling.

Athletics Member NCAA. All Division II. *Intercollegiate sports:* baseball M(s), basketball M(s)/W(s), cross-country running M(s)/W(s), equestrian sports M/W, golf M(s)/W(s), soccer M(s)/W(s), softball W(s), tennis M(s)/W(s), track and field M(s)/W(s), volleyball W(s), wrestling M(s). *Intramural sports:* basketball M/W, football M/W, racquetball M/W, softball M/W, tennis M/W, volleyball M/W.

Standardized Tests *Required:* SAT I or ACT (for admission).

Costs (2001–02) *Comprehensive fee:* $16,435 includes full-time tuition ($10,600), mandatory fees ($795), and room and board ($5040). Part-time tuition: $272 per credit hour. *Room and board:* College room only: $2590. Room and board charges vary according to board plan. *Payment plan:* installment. *Waivers:* adult students, senior citizens, and employees or children of employees.

Financial Aid Of all full-time matriculated undergraduates who enrolled in 2001, 912 applied for aid, 912 were judged to have need, 87 had their need fully met. *Average percent of need met:* 57%. *Average financial aid package:* $11,243. *Average need-based gift aid:* $5300. *Average indebtedness upon graduation:* $14,360. *Financial aid deadline:* 7/31.

Applying *Options:* common application, electronic application, early admission, early decision, deferred entrance. *Application fee:* $35. *Required:* high school transcript. *Required for some:* essay or personal statement, 2 letters of recommendation, interview. *Recommended:* minimum 2.5 GPA. *Application deadlines:* 6/30 (freshmen), 8/1 (transfers). *Early decision:* 11/15. *Notification:* continuous (freshmen), 12/1 (early decision).

Admissions Contact Ms. Pam Bryant, Director of Admissions, Anderson College, 316 Boulevard, Anderson, SC 29621. *Phone:* 864-231-5607. *Toll-free phone:* 800-542-3594. *Fax:* 864-231-3033. *E-mail:* admissions@ac.edu.

BENEDICT COLLEGE
Columbia, South Carolina

- **Independent Baptist** 4-year, founded 1870
- **Calendar** semesters
- **Degree** bachelor's
- **Urban** 20-acre campus
- **Endowment** $17.9 million
- **Coed,** 2,936 undergraduate students, 96% full-time, 50% women, 50% men
- **Noncompetitive** entrance level, 68% of applicants were admitted

Undergraduates 2,833 full-time, 103 part-time. Students come from 34 states and territories, 19% are from out of state, 99% African American, 0.3% Hispanic American, 0.1% Native American, 5% transferred in, 66% live on campus.

Freshmen *Admission:* 4,042 applied, 2,767 admitted, 636 enrolled. *Average high school GPA:* 2.30.

Faculty *Total:* 169, 75% full-time, 43% with terminal degrees. *Student/faculty ratio:* 19:1.

Majors Accounting; art; art education; biology; broadcast journalism; business administration; business marketing and marketing management; chemistry; child care/development; computer/information sciences; computer science; criminal justice/law enforcement administration; early childhood education; elementary education; English; environmental health; finance; graphic design/commercial art/illustration; history; journalism; mathematics; music; philosophy; physics; political science; pre-dentistry; pre-law; pre-medicine; recreation/leisure studies; religious studies; secretarial science; social work; sociology.

Academic Programs *Special study options:* adult/continuing education programs, advanced placement credit, honors programs, internships, part-time degree program, summer session for credit. *ROTC:* Army (b), Air Force (c). *Unusual degree programs:* 3-2 engineering with Georgia Institute of Technology, Southern College of Technology, Clemson University, South Carolina State University, Rensselaer Polytechnic Institute.

Library Benjamin Payton Learning Resource Center with 160,000 titles, 220 serial subscriptions, a Web page.

Computers on Campus 392 computers available on campus for general student use. A campuswide network can be accessed from student residence rooms and from off campus. Internet access, at least one staffed computer lab available.

Student Life *Housing Options:* coed. *Activities and Organizations:* drama/theater group, student-run newspaper, choral group, NAACP, Student Education Association, African Awareness Student Union, national fraternities, national sororities. *Campus security:* 24-hour emergency response devices and patrols. *Student Services:* personal/psychological counseling.

Athletics Member NAIA. *Intercollegiate sports:* baseball M, basketball M(s)/W(s), cross-country running M/W, football M, golf M, softball W, tennis M, track and field M(s), volleyball W. *Intramural sports:* baseball M, basketball M/W, golf M, tennis M/W, track and field W, volleyball W.

Standardized Tests *Recommended:* SAT I or ACT (for placement).

Costs (2001–02) *Comprehensive fee:* $14,814 includes full-time tuition ($9002), mandatory fees ($762), and room and board ($5050). Part-time tuition: $300 per credit hour. *Required fees:* $85 per credit hour.

Applying *Options:* common application, early admission, deferred entrance. *Application fee:* $25. *Required:* high school transcript. *Application deadline:* rolling (freshmen), rolling (transfers). *Notification:* continuous until 7/31 (freshmen).

Admissions Contact Mr. Gary Knight, Interim Vice President, Institutional Effectiveness, Benedict College, PO Box 98, Columbia, SC 29204. *Phone:* 803-253-5275. *Toll-free phone:* 800-868-6598. *Fax:* 803-253-5167.

CHARLESTON SOUTHERN UNIVERSITY
Charleston, South Carolina

- **Independent Baptist** comprehensive, founded 1964
- **Calendar** 4-1-4
- **Degrees** associate, bachelor's, and master's
- **Suburban** 500-acre campus
- **Endowment** $9.2 million
- **Coed,** 2,444 undergraduate students, 80% full-time, 61% women, 39% men
- **Moderately difficult** entrance level, 77% of applicants were admitted

Located in one of the Southeast's most beautiful regions, Charleston Southern University (CSU) is the second-largest accredited, private university in South Carolina. CSU's enrollment has grown to 2,700 students and offers both a traditional liberal arts curriculum and a comprehensive professional program. CSU encourages interested students to schedule a campus visit.

Undergraduates 1,966 full-time, 478 part-time. Students come from 45 states and territories, 29 other countries, 19% are from out of state, 27% African American, 1% Asian American or Pacific Islander, 5% Hispanic American, 0.1% Native American, 3% international, 8% transferred in, 44% live on campus. *Retention:* 72% of 2001 full-time freshmen returned.

Freshmen *Admission:* 1,569 applied, 1,212 admitted, 439 enrolled. *Average high school GPA:* 3.25. *Test scores:* SAT verbal scores over 500: 72%; SAT math scores over 500: 73%; ACT scores over 18: 93%; SAT verbal scores over 600: 17%; SAT math scores over 600: 14%; ACT scores over 24: 27%; SAT verbal scores over 700: 2%; ACT scores over 30: 1%.

Faculty *Total:* 202, 46% full-time, 38% with terminal degrees. *Student/faculty ratio:* 17:1.

Majors Accounting; applied mathematics; biochemistry; biology; business administration; business economics; business marketing and marketing management; chemistry; computer programming; computer science; criminal justice/law enforcement administration; early childhood education; education; education (K-12); elementary education; engineering-related technology; English; environmental science; history; humanities; liberal arts and sciences/liberal studies; management information systems/business data processing; mathematics; music; music teacher education; music therapy; music (voice and choral/opera performance); natural sciences; nursing; physical education; political science; pre-dentistry; pre-engineering; pre-law; pre-medicine; psychology; religious music; religious studies; science education; secondary education; social sciences; sociology; Spanish; speech/rhetorical studies.

Academic Programs *Special study options:* academic remediation for entering students, accelerated degree program, advanced placement credit, double majors, internships, off-campus study, part-time degree program, services for LD students, summer session for credit. *ROTC:* Air Force (b). *Unusual degree programs:* 3-2 engineering with University of South Carolina.

Library L. Mendel Rivers Library with 195,563 titles, 1,267 serial subscriptions, 7,745 audiovisual materials, an OPAC.

Computers on Campus 150 computers available on campus for general student use. Internet access, at least one staffed computer lab available.

Student Life *Housing:* on-campus residence required through sophomore year. *Options:* men-only, women-only. *Activities and Organizations:* drama/theater group, student-run newspaper, choral group, marching band, student government, Baptist Student Union, Fellowship of Christian Athletics. *Campus security:* 24-hour emergency response devices and patrols, late-night transport/escort service. *Student Services:* personal/psychological counseling.

Athletics Member NCAA. All Division I except football (Division I-AA). *Intercollegiate sports:* baseball M(s), basketball M(s)/W(s), cross-country running M(s)/W(s), golf M(s)/W(s), soccer M(s)/W(s), softball W(s), tennis M(s)/W(s), track and field M(s)/W(s), volleyball W(s). *Intramural sports:* basketball M/W, football M/W, soccer M/W, softball M/W, volleyball M/W.

Standardized Tests *Required:* SAT I or ACT (for admission).

Charleston Southern University (continued)

Costs (2001–02) *Comprehensive fee:* $17,122 includes full-time tuition ($12,368) and room and board ($4754). Part-time tuition: $200 per credit. Part-time tuition and fees vary according to course load. *Room and board:* Room and board charges vary according to housing facility. *Waivers:* employees or children of employees.

Financial Aid Of all full-time matriculated undergraduates who enrolled in 2001, 1495 applied for aid, 1363 were judged to have need, 246 had their need fully met. 442 Federal Work-Study jobs (averaging $1005). In 2001, 200 non-need-based awards were made. *Average percent of need met:* 65%. *Average financial aid package:* $8489. *Average need-based loan:* $3269. *Average need-based gift aid:* $5781. *Average non-need based aid:* $6220. *Average indebtedness upon graduation:* $17,125.

Applying *Options:* early admission, deferred entrance. *Application fee:* $25. *Required:* high school transcript. *Required for some:* essay or personal statement, 1 letter of recommendation, interview. *Application deadline:* rolling (freshmen), rolling (transfers). *Notification:* continuous (freshmen).

Admissions Contact Ms. Cheryl Burton, Director of Enrollment Management, Charleston Southern University, PO Box 118087, Charleston, SC 29423-8087. *Phone:* 843-863-7050. *Toll-free phone:* 800-947-7474. *E-mail:* enroll@csuniv.edu.

THE CITADEL, THE MILITARY COLLEGE OF SOUTH CAROLINA
Charleston, South Carolina

- **State-supported** comprehensive, founded 1842
- **Calendar** semesters
- **Degrees** bachelor's, master's, and post-master's certificates
- **Urban** 130-acre campus
- **Endowment** $38.0 million
- **Coed, primarily men,** 2,100 undergraduate students, 96% full-time, 6% women, 94% men
- **Moderately difficult** entrance level, 83% of applicants were admitted

The Citadel, a comprehensive military college, prepares students for leadership through a challenging curriculum of 20 majors. Graduates participate in all walks of life, from graduate study to private sector and military careers. New barracks and a first-class campuswide computer network are new features. The college actively seeks qualified students regardless of gender or ethnicity.

Undergraduates 2,013 full-time, 87 part-time. Students come from 46 states and territories, 29 other countries, 52% are from out of state, 8% African American, 3% Asian American or Pacific Islander, 5% Hispanic American, 0.3% Native American, 3% international, 4% transferred in, 100% live on campus. *Retention:* 81% of 2001 full-time freshmen returned.

Freshmen *Admission:* 1,678 applied, 1,390 admitted, 570 enrolled. *Average high school GPA:* 3.08. *Test scores:* SAT verbal scores over 500: 67%; SAT math scores over 500: 69%; ACT scores over 18: 99%; SAT verbal scores over 600: 22%; SAT math scores over 600: 21%; ACT scores over 24: 34%; SAT verbal scores over 700: 2%; SAT math scores over 700: 3%; ACT scores over 30: 1%.

Faculty *Total:* 196, 73% full-time, 83% with terminal degrees. *Student/faculty ratio:* 15:1.

Majors Biology; biology education; business administration; chemistry; civil engineering; computer science; criminal justice/law enforcement administration; electrical engineering; English; English education; French; German; history; history education; mathematics; mathematics education; physical education; physics; political science; psychology; science education; social studies education; Spanish.

Academic Programs *Special study options:* adult/continuing education programs, advanced placement credit, double majors, English as a second language, honors programs, independent study, internships, off-campus study, part-time degree program, services for LD students, summer session for credit. *ROTC:* Army (b), Navy (b), Air Force (b).

Library Daniel Library with 173,765 titles, 1,318 serial subscriptions, 1,426 audiovisual materials, an OPAC, a Web page.

Computers on Campus 350 computers available on campus for general student use. A campuswide network can be accessed from student residence rooms and from off campus. Internet access, online (class) registration, at least one staffed computer lab available.

Student Life *Housing:* on-campus residence required through senior year. *Options:* coed. *Activities and Organizations:* drama/theater group, student-run newspaper, choral group, marching band. *Campus security:* 24-hour patrols, student patrols, late-night transport/escort service. *Student Services:* health clinic, personal/psychological counseling.

Athletics Member NCAA. All Division I except football (Division I-AA). *Intercollegiate sports:* baseball M(s), basketball M(s), crew M(c)/W(c), cross-country running M(s)/W(s), golf M(s)/W(s), lacrosse M(c)/W(c), riflery M(c)/W(c), rugby M(c)/W(c), sailing M(c)/W(c), soccer M(s)/W(s), tennis M(s), track and field M(s)/W(s), volleyball M(c)/W(s), wrestling M(s). *Intramural sports:* badminton M/W, basketball M/W, football M/W, racquetball M/W, softball M/W, swimming M/W, table tennis M/W, tennis M/W, track and field M/W, volleyball M/W, weight lifting M/W, wrestling M/W.

Standardized Tests *Required:* SAT I or ACT (for admission).

Costs (2001–02) *One-time required fee:* $4680. *Tuition:* state resident $3727 full-time, $141 per credit hour part-time; nonresident $10,402 full-time, $285 per credit hour part-time. *Required fees:* $874 full-time. *Room and board:* $4525. *Payment plan:* installment. *Waivers:* senior citizens.

Financial Aid Of all full-time matriculated undergraduates who enrolled in 2001, 1224 applied for aid, 862 were judged to have need, 462 had their need fully met. In 2001, 110 non-need-based awards were made. *Average percent of need met:* 72%. *Average financial aid package:* $5097. *Average need-based loan:* $3302. *Average need-based gift aid:* $6565. *Average non-need based aid:* $13,500. *Average indebtedness upon graduation:* $11,843.

Applying *Options:* electronic application. *Application fee:* $35. *Required:* high school transcript, minimum 2.0 GPA. *Recommended:* interview. *Application deadline:* rolling (freshmen), rolling (transfers). *Notification:* 9/1 (freshmen).

Admissions Contact Lt. Col. John Powell, Acting Dean of Enrollment Management, The Citadel, The Military College of South Carolina, 171 Moultrie Street, Charleston, SC 29409. *Phone:* 843-953-5230. *Toll-free phone:* 800-868-1842. *Fax:* 843-953-7036. *E-mail:* admissions@citadel.edu.

CLAFLIN UNIVERSITY
Orangeburg, South Carolina

- **Independent United Methodist** 4-year, founded 1869
- **Calendar** semesters
- **Degree** bachelor's
- **Small-town** 32-acre campus with easy access to Columbia
- **Endowment** $12.0 million
- **Coed,** 1,460 undergraduate students, 92% full-time, 65% women, 35% men
- **Minimally difficult** entrance level, 45% of applicants were admitted

Undergraduates 1,350 full-time, 110 part-time. Students come from 24 states and territories, 14 other countries, 17% are from out of state, 94% African American, 0.2% Hispanic American, 4% international, 4% transferred in, 61% live on campus. *Retention:* 79% of 2001 full-time freshmen returned.

Freshmen *Admission:* 2,025 applied, 903 admitted, 335 enrolled. *Average high school GPA:* 2.98.

Faculty *Total:* 96, 75% full-time. *Student/faculty ratio:* 14:1.

Majors African-American studies; art; art education; biology; business administration; chemistry; computer science; elementary education; English; history; information sciences/systems; mass communications; mathematics; music; music teacher education; physical education; pre-medicine; religious studies; sociology.

Academic Programs *Special study options:* academic remediation for entering students, adult/continuing education programs, advanced placement credit, cooperative education, freshman honors college, honors programs, independent study, internships, off-campus study, part-time degree program, study abroad, summer session for credit. *ROTC:* Army (c). *Unusual degree programs:* 3-2 engineering with South Carolina State College; cytotechnology, medical technology, occupational therapy, physical therapy, radiological technology and medical records service with the Medical University of South Carolina.

Library H. V. Manning Library with 148,584 titles, 334 serial subscriptions, 469 audiovisual materials, an OPAC.

Computers on Campus 144 computers available on campus for general student use. A campuswide network can be accessed from student residence rooms and from off campus. Internet access, at least one staffed computer lab available.

Student Life *Housing Options:* men-only, women-only. *Activities and Organizations:* drama/theater group, student-run newspaper, radio and television station, choral group, national fraternities, national sororities. *Campus security:* 24-hour emergency response devices and patrols, student patrols. *Student Services:* health clinic, personal/psychological counseling.

Athletics Member NAIA. *Intercollegiate sports:* basketball M(s)/W(s), softball W, tennis M/W, track and field M/W, volleyball W. *Intramural sports:* basketball M/W, table tennis M/W, tennis M/W, volleyball M/W.

Standardized Tests *Required:* SAT I or ACT (for admission). *Recommended:* SAT II: Subject Tests (for admission).

Costs (2001–02) *Comprehensive fee:* $12,735 includes full-time tuition ($8140), mandatory fees ($150), and room and board ($4445). Full-time tuition and fees vary according to student level. Part-time tuition: $250 per credit hour. *Required fees:* $15 per term part-time. *Room and board:* College room only: $2013. Room and board charges vary according to gender and housing facility. *Payment plans:* installment, deferred payment. *Waivers:* employees or children of employees.

Financial Aid Of all full-time matriculated undergraduates who enrolled in 2001, 1229 applied for aid, 1191 were judged to have need. *Average percent of need met:* 74%. *Average need-based loan:* $5202. *Average need-based gift aid:* $6750. *Average indebtedness upon graduation:* $16,100.

Applying *Options:* common application, early admission, deferred entrance. *Application fee:* $20. *Required:* essay or personal statement, high school transcript, interview. *Recommended:* letters of recommendation. *Application deadline:* rolling (freshmen), rolling (transfers). *Notification:* continuous (freshmen).

Admissions Contact Mr. Michael Zeigler, Director of Admissions, Claflin University, 400 Magnolia Street, Orangeburg, SC 29115. *Phone:* 803-535-5340. *Toll-free phone:* 800-922-1276. *Fax:* 803-535-5387. *E-mail:* zeiglerm@claf1.claflin.edu.

CLEMSON UNIVERSITY

Clemson, South Carolina

- **State-supported** university, founded 1889
- **Calendar** semesters
- **Degrees** bachelor's, master's, and doctoral
- **Small-town** 1400-acre campus
- **Endowment** $249.1 million
- **Coed,** 13,975 undergraduate students, 94% full-time, 45% women, 55% men
- **Moderately difficult** entrance level, 51% of applicants were admitted

Undergraduates 13,140 full-time, 835 part-time. Students come from 52 states and territories, 62 other countries, 30% are from out of state, 8% African American, 2% Asian American or Pacific Islander, 0.9% Hispanic American, 0.2% Native American, 0.6% international, 4% transferred in, 49% live on campus. *Retention:* 88% of 2001 full-time freshmen returned.

Freshmen *Admission:* 11,432 applied, 5,877 admitted, 2,543 enrolled. *Average high school GPA:* 3.64. *Test scores:* SAT verbal scores over 500: 85%; SAT math scores over 500: 91%; ACT scores over 18: 98%; SAT verbal scores over 600: 37%; SAT math scores over 600: 51%; ACT scores over 24: 59%; SAT verbal scores over 700: 6%; SAT math scores over 700: 10%; ACT scores over 30: 15%.

Faculty *Total:* 1,126, 86% full-time, 81% with terminal degrees. *Student/faculty ratio:* 16:1.

Majors Accounting; agricultural business; agricultural economics; agricultural education; agricultural engineering; animal sciences; aquaculture operations/production management; architecture; architecture related; art; biochemistry; biology; business administration; business management/administrative services related; business marketing and marketing management; ceramic sciences/engineering; chemical engineering; chemistry; chemistry related; civil engineering; computer engineering; computer/information sciences; early childhood education; economics; electrical engineering; elementary education; English; finance; food sciences; foreign languages/literatures; foreign languages/literatures related; forest management; geology; health professions and related sciences; history; horticulture science; industrial arts education; industrial design; industrial/manufacturing engineering; information sciences/systems; landscape architecture; mathematics; mathematics education; mechanical engineering; medical technology; nursing; operations management; philosophy; physics; political science; polymer chemistry; pre-medicine; pre-pharmacy studies; pre-veterinary studies; psychology; recreation/leisure facilities management; science education; science technologies related; secondary education; sociology; special education; speech/rhetorical studies; visual and performing arts related.

Academic Programs *Special study options:* academic remediation for entering students, accelerated degree program, advanced placement credit, cooperative education, distance learning, double majors, honors programs, internships, part-time degree program, services for LD students, study abroad, summer session for credit. *ROTC:* Army (b), Air Force (b).

Library Robert Muldrow Cooper Library plus 1 other with 1.6 million titles, 5,978 serial subscriptions, 94,641 audiovisual materials, an OPAC, a Web page.

Computers on Campus 1000 computers available on campus for general student use. A campuswide network can be accessed from student residence rooms and from off campus. At least one staffed computer lab available.

Student Life *Housing:* on-campus residence required for freshman year. *Options:* coed, men-only, women-only. *Activities and Organizations:* drama/theater group, student-run newspaper, radio and television station, choral group, marching band, student government, Fellowship of Christian Athletes, Tiger Band, national fraternities, national sororities. *Campus security:* 24-hour emergency response devices and patrols, late-night transport/escort service, controlled dormitory access. *Student Services:* health clinic, personal/psychological counseling, legal services.

Athletics Member NCAA. All Division I except football (Division I-A). *Intercollegiate sports:* baseball M, basketball M(s)/W(s), bowling M(c)/W(c), crew M(c)/W(s), cross-country running M(s)/W(s), equestrian sports M(c)/W(c), fencing M(c)/W(c), field hockey M(c)/W(c), golf M(s), ice hockey M(c)/W(c), lacrosse M(c)/W(c), riflery M(c)/W(c), rugby M(c)/W(c), sailing M(c)/W(c), soccer M(s)/W(s), softball W(c), swimming M(s)/W(s), tennis M(s)/W(s), track and field M(s)/W(s), volleyball M(c)/W(s), weight lifting M(c)/W(c), wrestling M(c). *Intramural sports:* basketball M/W, golf M/W, racquetball M/W, soccer M/W, softball M/W, swimming M(c)/W(c), table tennis M/W, tennis M(c)/W(c), volleyball M/W, water polo M/W.

Standardized Tests *Required:* SAT I or ACT (for admission).

Costs (2001–02) *Tuition:* state resident $5090 full-time, $206 per hour part-time; nonresident $11,284 full-time, $466 per hour part-time. *Required fees:* $5 per term part-time. *Room and board:* $4532; room only: $2510. Room and board charges vary according to board plan and housing facility. *Payment plan:* installment.

Financial Aid Of all full-time matriculated undergraduates who enrolled in 2001, 6465 applied for aid, 4572 were judged to have need, 1577 had their need fully met. 700 Federal Work-Study jobs (averaging $2520). 3752 State and other part-time jobs (averaging $2168). In 2001, 4057 non-need-based awards were made. *Average percent of need met:* 72%. *Average financial aid package:* $7244. *Average need-based loan:* $3839. *Average need-based gift aid:* $3171. *Average non-need based aid:* $4933. *Average indebtedness upon graduation:* $13,970.

Applying *Options:* electronic application, early admission, deferred entrance. *Application fee:* $40. *Required:* high school transcript. *Recommended:* essay or personal statement, letters of recommendation, interview. *Application deadlines:* 5/1 (freshmen), 8/1 (transfers). *Notification:* continuous (freshmen).

Admissions Contact Ms. Audrey Bodell, Assistant Director of Undergraduate Admissions, Clemson University, 105 Sikes Hall, PO Box 345124, Clemson, SC 29634. *Phone:* 864-656-5460. *Fax:* 864-656-2464. *E-mail:* cuadmissions@clemson.edu.

COASTAL CAROLINA UNIVERSITY

Conway, South Carolina

- **State-supported** comprehensive, founded 1954
- **Calendar** semesters
- **Degrees** bachelor's, master's, and postbachelor's certificates
- **Suburban** 244-acre campus
- **Endowment** $9.6 million
- **Coed,** 4,771 undergraduate students, 84% full-time, 56% women, 44% men
- **Moderately difficult** entrance level, 74% of applicants were admitted

Undergraduates 4,007 full-time, 764 part-time. Students come from 48 states and territories, 49 other countries, 41% are from out of state, 8% African American, 1% Asian American or Pacific Islander, 1% Hispanic American, 0.4% Native American, 3% international, 11% transferred in, 28% live on campus. *Retention:* 68% of 2001 full-time freshmen returned.

Freshmen *Admission:* 3,095 applied, 2,296 admitted, 941 enrolled. *Average high school GPA:* 3.21. *Test scores:* SAT verbal scores over 500: 58%; SAT math scores over 500: 64%; ACT scores over 18: 98%; SAT verbal scores over 600: 12%; SAT math scores over 600: 17%; ACT scores over 24: 24%; SAT verbal scores over 700: 1%; SAT math scores over 700: 1%; ACT scores over 30: 1%.

Faculty *Total:* 309, 58% full-time, 58% with terminal degrees. *Student/faculty ratio:* 19:1.

Majors Accounting; applied mathematics; art; art education; biology; business administration; business marketing and marketing management; chemistry; computer science; early childhood education; elementary education; English; finance; history; liberal arts and sciences/liberal studies; marine biology; middle school education; music; philosophy; physical education; political science; psychology; public health education/promotion; secondary education; sociology; Spanish; special education; theater arts/drama; theater arts/drama and stagecraft related; travel/tourism management.

Academic Programs *Special study options:* accelerated degree program, adult/continuing education programs, advanced placement credit, distance learning, double majors, honors programs, independent study, internships, part-time degree program, student-designed majors, study abroad, summer session for credit. *Unusual degree programs:* 3-2 engineering with Clemson University.

Library Kimbel Library with 189,468 titles, 1,736 serial subscriptions, 11,636 audiovisual materials, an OPAC, a Web page.

Coastal Carolina University (continued)

Computers on Campus 220 computers available on campus for general student use. A campuswide network can be accessed from student residence rooms and from off campus that provide access to on-line grades. Internet access, at least one staffed computer lab available.

Student Life *Housing Options:* coed. *Activities and Organizations:* drama/theater group, student-run newspaper, choral group, Student Government Association, Coastal Productions Board, STAR (Students Taking Active Responsibility), FCA (Fellowship of Christian Athletes), Diversity of Programming, national fraternities, national sororities. *Campus security:* 24-hour emergency response devices and patrols, late-night transport/escort service. *Student Services:* health clinic, personal/psychological counseling, women's center.

Athletics Member NCAA. All Division I. *Intercollegiate sports:* baseball M(s), basketball M(s)/W(s), cross-country running M(s)/W(s), golf M(s)/W(s), soccer M(s)/W(s), softball W(s), tennis M(s)/W(s), track and field M(s)/W(s), volleyball W(s). *Intramural sports:* badminton M/W, basketball M/W, bowling M/W, football M/W, golf M/W, lacrosse M/W, racquetball M/W, rugby M, soccer M/W, softball M/W, swimming M/W, table tennis M/W, tennis M/W, track and field M/W, volleyball M/W, water polo M/W, weight lifting M/W.

Standardized Tests *Required:* SAT I or ACT (for admission).

Costs (2001–02) *Tuition:* state resident $3770 full-time, $159 per credit hour part-time; nonresident $10,680 full-time, $445 per credit hour part-time. Full-time tuition and fees vary according to course load. Part-time tuition and fees vary according to course load. *Room and board:* $5450. Room and board charges vary according to board plan. *Payment plans:* installment, deferred payment. *Waivers:* senior citizens and employees or children of employees.

Financial Aid Of all full-time matriculated undergraduates who enrolled in 2001, 1253 applied for aid, 1025 were judged to have need, 219 had their need fully met. 203 Federal Work-Study jobs (averaging $1141). In 2001, 430 non-need-based awards were made. *Average percent of need met:* 65%. *Average financial aid package:* $6730. *Average need-based loan:* $6271. *Average need-based gift aid:* $2480. *Average non-need based aid:* $4106. *Average indebtedness upon graduation:* $13,000.

Applying *Options:* common application, electronic application, deferred entrance. *Application fee:* $35. *Required:* high school transcript, minimum 2.0 GPA. *Recommended:* essay or personal statement, 1 letter of recommendation, interview. *Application deadlines:* 8/15 (freshmen), 8/15 (transfers). *Notification:* continuous until 8/15 (freshmen).

Admissions Contact Dr. Judy Vogt, Associate Vice President, Enrollment Services, Coastal Carolina University, PO Box 261954, Admissions and Financial Aid Offices, Conway, SC 29528. *Phone:* 843-349-2037. *Toll-free phone:* 800-277-7000. *Fax:* 843-349-2127. *E-mail:* admis@coastal.edu.

COKER COLLEGE

Hartsville, South Carolina

- **Independent** 4-year, founded 1908
- **Calendar** semesters
- **Degrees** bachelor's (also offers evening program with significant enrollment not reflected in profile)
- **Small-town** 30-acre campus with easy access to Charlotte
- **Endowment** $36.2 million
- **Coed,** 449 undergraduate students, 97% full-time, 63% women, 37% men
- **Moderately difficult** entrance level, 90% of applicants were admitted

Undergraduates 435 full-time, 14 part-time. Students come from 26 states and territories, 10 other countries, 20% are from out of state, 20% African American, 0.4% Asian American or Pacific Islander, 2% Hispanic American, 0.4% Native American, 3% international, 6% transferred in, 31% live on campus. *Retention:* 63% of 2001 full-time freshmen returned.

Freshmen *Admission:* 134 applied, 121 admitted, 116 enrolled. *Average high school GPA:* 3.22. *Test scores:* SAT verbal scores over 500: 51%; SAT math scores over 500: 44%; ACT scores over 18: 75%; SAT verbal scores over 600: 11%; SAT math scores over 600: 9%; ACT scores over 24: 25%; SAT verbal scores over 700: 1%; ACT scores over 30: 5%.

Faculty *Total:* 55, 100% full-time. *Student/faculty ratio:* 8:1.

Majors Accounting; art; art education; athletic training/sports medicine; behavioral sciences; biology; business administration; business marketing and marketing management; chemistry; computer science; criminal justice/law enforcement administration; dance; early childhood education; education; elementary education; English; exercise sciences; finance; fine/studio arts; French; graphic design/commercial art/illustration; history; mass communications; mathematics; medical technology; middle school education; music; music business management/merchandising; music (piano and organ performance); music teacher education; music (voice and choral/opera performance); photography; physical education; political science; psychology; religious studies; secondary education; social work; sociology; Spanish; theater arts/drama.

Academic Programs *Special study options:* academic remediation for entering students, accelerated degree program, adult/continuing education programs, advanced placement credit, cooperative education, double majors, English as a second language, honors programs, independent study, internships, part-time degree program, student-designed majors, study abroad, summer session for credit.

Library James Lide Coker III Memorial Library plus 1 other with 82,000 titles, 590 serial subscriptions, 3,400 audiovisual materials, an OPAC, a Web page.

Computers on Campus 40 computers available on campus for general student use. A campuswide network can be accessed from student residence rooms and from off campus. Internet access, at least one staffed computer lab available.

Student Life *Housing:* on-campus residence required through junior year. *Options:* coed, men-only, women-only. *Activities and Organizations:* drama/theater group, student-run newspaper, choral group, Coker College Union, student government, African-American Sisterhood, Sigma Alpha Chi, Commissioners. *Campus security:* 24-hour patrols, late-night transport/escort service, controlled dormitory access. *Student Services:* health clinic, personal/psychological counseling.

Athletics Member NCAA. All Division II. *Intercollegiate sports:* baseball M(s), basketball M(s)/W(s), cross-country running M(s)/W(s), golf M(s), soccer M(s)/W(s), softball W(s), tennis M(s)/W(s), volleyball W(s). *Intramural sports:* badminton M/W, basketball M/W, bowling M/W, crew W, cross-country running M/W, fencing M/W, football M/W, racquetball M/W, sailing M/W, soccer M/W, softball M/W, swimming M/W, table tennis M/W, tennis M/W, track and field M/W, volleyball M/W, water polo M/W, weight lifting M/W.

Standardized Tests *Required:* SAT I or ACT (for admission).

Costs (2001–02) *Comprehensive fee:* $20,181 includes full-time tuition ($15,072), mandatory fees ($289), and room and board ($4820). Full-time tuition and fees vary according to location. Part-time tuition: $628 per semester hour. Part-time tuition and fees vary according to location. *Required fees:* $3 per semester hour. *Room and board:* College room only: $2720. Room and board charges vary according to housing facility. *Payment plan:* installment. *Waivers:* employees or children of employees.

Financial Aid Of all full-time matriculated undergraduates who enrolled in 2001, 433 applied for aid, 352 were judged to have need, 156 had their need fully met. 127 Federal Work-Study jobs (averaging $1061). In 2001, 36 non-need-based awards were made. *Average percent of need met:* 96%. *Average financial aid package:* $15,078. *Average need-based loan:* $3652. *Average need-based gift aid:* $5777. *Average non-need based aid:* $8991. *Average indebtedness upon graduation:* $20,265.

Applying *Options:* common application, electronic application, deferred entrance. *Application fee:* $15. *Required:* high school transcript, 1 letter of recommendation. *Required for some:* essay or personal statement, minimum 2.2 GPA, 2 letters of recommendation. *Recommended:* minimum 2.2 GPA, interview. *Application deadline:* rolling (freshmen), rolling (transfers). *Notification:* continuous until 8/1 (freshmen).

Admissions Contact Mr. David Anthony, Director of Admissions and Student Financial Planning, Coker College, Hartsville, SC 29550. *Phone:* 843-383-8050. *Toll-free phone:* 800-950-1908. *Fax:* 843-383-8056. *E-mail:* admissions@coker.edu.

COLLEGE OF CHARLESTON

Charleston, South Carolina

- **State-supported** 4-year, founded 1770
- **Calendar** semesters
- **Degrees** bachelor's and master's (also offers graduate degree programs through University of Charleston, South Carolina)
- **Urban** 52-acre campus
- **Endowment** $28.9 million
- **Coed,** 9,934 undergraduate students, 90% full-time, 63% women, 37% men
- **Moderately difficult** entrance level, 65% of applicants were admitted

Undergraduates 8,960 full-time, 974 part-time. Students come from 50 states and territories, 73 other countries, 37% are from out of state, 9% African American, 1% Asian American or Pacific Islander, 1% Hispanic American, 0.2% Native American, 3% international, 6% transferred in, 23% live on campus. *Retention:* 80% of 2001 full-time freshmen returned.

Freshmen *Admission:* 8,356 applied, 5,471 admitted, 1,974 enrolled. *Average high school GPA:* 3.56. *Test scores:* SAT verbal scores over 500: 94%; SAT math scores over 500: 93%; ACT scores over 18: 97%; SAT verbal scores over 600:

40%; SAT math scores over 600: 36%; ACT scores over 24: 47%; SAT verbal scores over 700: 5%; SAT math scores over 700: 3%; ACT scores over 30: 5%.

Faculty *Total:* 794, 65% full-time, 60% with terminal degrees. *Student/faculty ratio:* 15:1.

Majors Accounting; anthropology; architectural history; art history; arts management; biochemistry; biology; business administration; chemistry; classics; communications; computer/information sciences; economics; elementary education; English; fine/studio arts; French; geology; German; history; information sciences/systems; international business; marine biology; mathematics; music; philosophy; physical education; physics; political science; pre-dentistry; pre-medicine; psychology; religious studies; sociology; Spanish; special education; theater arts/drama; urban studies.

Academic Programs *Special study options:* accelerated degree program, adult/continuing education programs, advanced placement credit, cooperative education, double majors, English as a second language, honors programs, independent study, internships, off-campus study, part-time degree program, services for LD students, study abroad, summer session for credit. *ROTC:* Air Force (c). *Unusual degree programs:* 3-2 engineering with Case Western Reserve University, Clemson University, Georgia Institute of Technology, University of South Carolina; biometry with Medical University of South Carolina, marine engineering with University of Michigan.

Library Robert Scott Small Library plus 1 other with 375,442 titles, 3,194 serial subscriptions, 4,901 audiovisual materials, an OPAC, a Web page.

Computers on Campus 2500 computers available on campus for general student use. A campuswide network can be accessed from off campus. Internet access, online (class) registration, at least one staffed computer lab available.

Student Life *Housing Options:* coed, men-only, women-only. *Activities and Organizations:* drama/theater group, student-run newspaper, choral group, Student Government Association, College Activities Board, Black Student Union, Panhellenic Council, Inter-Fraternity Council, national fraternities, national sororities. *Campus security:* 24-hour emergency response devices and patrols, student patrols, late-night transport/escort service. *Student Services:* health clinic, personal/psychological counseling.

Athletics Member NCAA. All Division I. *Intercollegiate sports:* baseball M(s), basketball M(s)/W(s), cross-country running M(s)/W(s), equestrian sports M/W, golf M(s)/W(s), sailing M/W, soccer M(s)/W(s), softball W(s), swimming M(s)/W(s), tennis M(s)/W(s), volleyball W(s). *Intramural sports:* badminton M/W, basketball M/W, crew M/W, equestrian sports M/W, fencing M/W, football M/W, racquetball M/W, rugby W, soccer M/W, softball M/W, tennis M/W, volleyball M/W, weight lifting M/W.

Standardized Tests *Required:* SAT I or ACT (for admission).

Costs (2001–02) *Tuition:* state resident $3780 full-time, $157 per semester hour part-time; nonresident $8540 full-time, $356 per semester hour part-time. Part-time tuition and fees vary according to course load. *Required fees:* $15 per term part-time. *Room and board:* $4570; room only: $2950. Room and board charges vary according to board plan. *Payment plan:* installment. *Waivers:* senior citizens.

Financial Aid Of all full-time matriculated undergraduates who enrolled in 2001, 4212 applied for aid, 3294 were judged to have need, 508 had their need fully met. In 2001, 365 non-need-based awards were made. *Average percent of need met:* 64%. *Average financial aid package:* $5644. *Average need-based loan:* $5261. *Average need-based gift aid:* $3474. *Average non-need based aid:* $4103. *Average indebtedness upon graduation:* $11,511.

Applying *Options:* common application, electronic application, early admission, deferred entrance. *Application fee:* $35. *Required:* high school transcript. *Recommended:* essay or personal statement, letters of recommendation. *Application deadlines:* 6/1 (freshmen), 5/1 (out-of-state freshmen), 6/1 (transfers). *Notification:* continuous (freshmen), continuous (out-of-state freshmen).

Admissions Contact Mr. Donald Burkard, Dean of Admissions, College of Charleston, 66 George Street, Charleston, SC 29424-0001. *Phone:* 843-953-5670. *Fax:* 843-953-6322. *E-mail:* admissions@cofc.edu.

COLUMBIA COLLEGE

Columbia, South Carolina

- **Independent United Methodist** comprehensive, founded 1854
- **Calendar** semesters
- **Degrees** bachelor's and master's
- **Suburban** 33-acre campus
- **Women only,** 1,234 undergraduate students, 85% full-time
- **Moderately difficult** entrance level, 79% of applicants were admitted

Undergraduates 1,052 full-time, 182 part-time. Students come from 19 states and territories, 14 other countries, 4% are from out of state, 43% African American, 0.7% Asian American or Pacific Islander, 2% Hispanic American, 0.2% Native American, 0.7% international, 11% transferred in. *Retention:* 67% of 2001 full-time freshmen returned.

Freshmen *Admission:* 907 applied, 720 admitted, 252 enrolled. *Average high school GPA:* 3.23. *Test scores:* SAT verbal scores over 500: 56%; SAT math scores over 500: 49%; SAT verbal scores over 600: 25%; SAT math scores over 600: 11%; SAT verbal scores over 700: 4%; SAT math scores over 700: 2%.

Faculty *Total:* 171, 54% full-time, 52% with terminal degrees. *Student/faculty ratio:* 14:1.

Majors Accounting; applied art; art; art education; art history; arts management; biology; business administration; business marketing and marketing management; chemistry; creative writing; dance; early childhood education; education; elementary education; English; entrepreneurship; fine/studio arts; French; graphic design/commercial art/illustration; history; literature; mathematics; medical technology; music; music (piano and organ performance); music teacher education; music (voice and choral/opera performance); physical sciences; political science; pre-dentistry; pre-law; pre-medicine; pre-veterinary studies; psychology; public policy analysis; religious education; religious music; religious studies; science education; science/technology and society; secondary education; social work; sociology; Spanish; special education; speech-language pathology/audiology; speech therapy.

Academic Programs *Special study options:* academic remediation for entering students, accelerated degree program, adult/continuing education programs, advanced placement credit, freshman honors college, honors programs, internships, part-time degree program, student-designed majors, study abroad, summer session for credit. *ROTC:* Army (c).

Library Edens Library with 645 serial subscriptions, 8,123 audiovisual materials, an OPAC, a Web page.

Computers on Campus 182 computers available on campus for general student use. A campuswide network can be accessed from student residence rooms and from off campus. At least one staffed computer lab available.

Student Life *Housing Options:* women-only. *Activities and Organizations:* drama/theater group, student-run newspaper, choral group. *Campus security:* 24-hour emergency response devices and patrols, late-night transport/escort service, controlled dormitory access. *Student Services:* health clinic, personal/psychological counseling, women's center.

Athletics Member NAIA. *Intercollegiate sports:* cross-country running W(s), soccer W(s), tennis W(s), volleyball W(s). *Intramural sports:* crew W, equestrian sports W, football W, golf W, soccer W, swimming W, weight lifting W.

Standardized Tests *Required:* SAT I or ACT (for admission).

Costs (2002–03) *Comprehensive fee:* $21,860 includes full-time tuition ($16,270), mandatory fees ($350), and room and board ($5240). Part-time tuition: $434 per credit. Part-time tuition and fees vary according to course load. *Room and board:* Room and board charges vary according to board plan. *Payment plan:* installment. *Waivers:* employees or children of employees.

Financial Aid Of all full-time matriculated undergraduates who enrolled in 2001, 1032 applied for aid, 850 were judged to have need, 284 had their need fully met. 235 State and other part-time jobs. In 2001, 163 non-need-based awards were made. *Average percent of need met:* 86%. *Average financial aid package:* $16,209. *Average need-based loan:* $3880. *Average need-based gift aid:* $6381. *Average non-need based aid:* $3166.

Applying *Options:* common application, early admission, deferred entrance. *Application fee:* $25. *Required:* high school transcript, 1 letter of recommendation. *Required for some:* interview. *Recommended:* minimum 3.0 GPA. *Application deadline:* rolling (freshmen), rolling (transfers). *Notification:* continuous (freshmen).

Admissions Contact Ms. Julie King, Director of Enrollment Management, Columbia College, 1301 Columbia College Drive, Columbia, SC 29203. *Phone:* 803-786-3871. *Toll-free phone:* 800-277-1301. *Fax:* 803-786-3674. *E-mail:* admissions@colacoll.edu.

COLUMBIA INTERNATIONAL UNIVERSITY

Columbia, South Carolina

- **Independent nondenominational** comprehensive, founded 1923
- **Calendar** semesters
- **Degrees** certificates, associate, bachelor's, master's, doctoral, and first professional
- **Suburban** 450-acre campus
- **Endowment** $8.2 million
- **Coed,** 635 undergraduate students, 86% full-time, 54% women, 46% men
- **Minimally difficult** entrance level, 59% of applicants were admitted

Undergraduates 549 full-time, 86 part-time. Students come from 38 states and territories, 13 other countries, 56% are from out of state, 5% African American,

Columbia International University (continued)
0.9% Asian American or Pacific Islander, 0.8% Hispanic American, 0.2% Native American, 3% international, 16% transferred in, 44% live on campus. *Retention:* 78% of 2001 full-time freshmen returned.

Freshmen *Admission:* 363 applied, 213 admitted, 137 enrolled. *Average high school GPA:* 3.23.

Faculty *Total:* 49, 49% full-time. *Student/faculty ratio:* 19:1.

Majors Biblical languages/literatures; biblical studies; communications; cultural studies; early childhood education; elementary education; general studies; humanities; Middle Eastern studies; music; pastoral counseling; pre-theology; psychology; religious education.

Academic Programs *Special study options:* academic remediation for entering students, accelerated degree program, advanced placement credit, cooperative education, distance learning, double majors, independent study, internships, off-campus study, part-time degree program, study abroad, summer session for credit.

Library G. Allen Fleece Library with 99,052 titles, 425 serial subscriptions, 6,781 audiovisual materials, an OPAC.

Computers on Campus 42 computers available on campus for general student use. A campuswide network can be accessed from student residence rooms. At least one staffed computer lab available.

Student Life *Housing Options:* men-only, women-only, disabled students. *Activities and Organizations:* drama/theater group, student-run newspaper, radio station, choral group, Student Union, Student Senate, Student Missions Connection. *Campus security:* 24-hour emergency response devices and patrols, late-night transport/escort service. *Student Services:* health clinic, personal/psychological counseling.

Athletics *Intramural sports:* basketball M/W, football M/W, soccer M/W, softball M/W, table tennis M/W, tennis M/W, volleyball M/W.

Standardized Tests *Required:* SAT I or ACT (for admission).

Costs (2002–03) *Comprehensive fee:* $15,628 includes full-time tuition ($10,398), mandatory fees ($290), and room and board ($4940). Full-time tuition and fees vary according to course load. Part-time tuition: $435 per semester hour. Part-time tuition and fees vary according to course load. *Room and board:* Room and board charges vary according to board plan. *Payment plan:* installment. *Waivers:* employees or children of employees.

Financial Aid Of all full-time matriculated undergraduates who enrolled in 2001, 399 applied for aid, 381 were judged to have need, 1 had their need fully met. 72 Federal Work-Study jobs (averaging $2000). In 2001, 18 non-need-based awards were made. *Average percent of need met:* 55%. *Average financial aid package:* $7807. *Average need-based loan:* $4050. *Average need-based gift aid:* $8437. *Average non-need based aid:* $3200. *Average indebtedness upon graduation:* $13,350. *Financial aid deadline:* 3/18.

Applying *Options:* common application, electronic application, deferred entrance. *Application fee:* $25. *Required:* essay or personal statement, high school transcript, minimum 2.0 GPA, 4 letters of recommendation. *Required for some:* interview. *Application deadline:* rolling (freshmen), rolling (transfers).

Admissions Contact Columbia International University, P.O. Box 3122, Columbia, SC 29230-3122. *Phone:* 803-754-4100 Ext. 3024. *Toll-free phone:* 800-777-2227 Ext. 3024. *Fax:* 803-786-4041. *E-mail:* yesciu@ciu.edu.

CONVERSE COLLEGE
Spartanburg, South Carolina

- **Independent** comprehensive, founded 1889
- **Calendar** 4-2-4
- **Degrees** bachelor's, master's, and post-master's certificates
- **Urban** 70-acre campus
- **Endowment** $59.8 million
- **Women only,** 732 undergraduate students, 90% full-time
- **Moderately difficult** entrance level, 79% of applicants were admitted

Undergraduates 657 full-time, 75 part-time. Students come from 17 states and territories, 10 other countries, 35% are from out of state, 9% African American, 2% Asian American or Pacific Islander, 1% Hispanic American, 2% international, 2% transferred in, 90% live on campus. *Retention:* 73% of 2001 full-time freshmen returned.

Freshmen *Admission:* 164 enrolled. *Average high school GPA:* 3.60. *Test scores:* SAT verbal scores over 500: 77%; SAT math scores over 500: 76%; ACT scores over 18: 85%; SAT verbal scores over 600: 37%; SAT math scores over 600: 28%; ACT scores over 24: 43%; SAT verbal scores over 700: 6%; SAT math scores over 700: 3%; ACT scores over 30: 8%.

Faculty *Total:* 86, 83% full-time, 74% with terminal degrees. *Student/faculty ratio:* 13:1.

Majors Accounting; applied art; art; art education; art history; art therapy; biochemistry; biology; business administration; business marketing and marketing management; chemistry; computer science; early childhood education; economics; education; elementary education; English; fine/studio arts; French; history; interior design; international business; mathematics; modern languages; music; music history; music (piano and organ performance); music teacher education; music (voice and choral/opera performance); political science; pre-dentistry; pre-law; pre-medicine; pre-veterinary studies; psychology; religious studies; secondary education; sign language interpretation; sociology; Spanish; special education; stringed instruments; theater arts/drama.

Academic Programs *Special study options:* accelerated degree program, adult/continuing education programs, advanced placement credit, distance learning, double majors, English as a second language, honors programs, independent study, internships, off-campus study, part-time degree program, study abroad, summer session for credit. *ROTC:* Army (c).

Library Mickel Library with 129,411 titles, 1,467 serial subscriptions, 30,132 audiovisual materials, an OPAC, a Web page.

Computers on Campus 65 computers available on campus for general student use. A campuswide network can be accessed from student residence rooms and from off campus. Internet access, at least one staffed computer lab available.

Student Life *Housing:* on-campus residence required through senior year. *Options:* women-only. *Activities and Organizations:* drama/theater group, student-run newspaper, choral group, student government, student volunteer services, Student Christian Organization, Student Activities Committee, Athletic Association. *Campus security:* 24-hour emergency response devices and patrols, late-night transport/escort service, controlled dormitory access. *Student Services:* health clinic, personal/psychological counseling, women's center.

Athletics Member NCAA. All Division II. *Intercollegiate sports:* basketball W(s), cross-country running W(s), soccer W(s), tennis W(s), volleyball W(s). *Intramural sports:* archery W, basketball W, bowling W, equestrian sports W, fencing W, field hockey W, gymnastics W, soccer W, softball W, swimming W, tennis W, volleyball W, weight lifting W.

Standardized Tests *Required:* SAT I or ACT (for admission).

Costs (2001–02) *Comprehensive fee:* $21,990 includes full-time tuition ($16,850) and room and board ($5140). Full-time tuition and fees vary according to program. Part-time tuition: $540 per credit hour. Part-time tuition and fees vary according to program. *Payment plan:* installment. *Waivers:* adult students, senior citizens, and employees or children of employees.

Financial Aid Of all full-time matriculated undergraduates who enrolled in 2001, 482 applied for aid, 430 were judged to have need, 199 had their need fully met. 130 Federal Work-Study jobs (averaging $1403). 85 State and other part-time jobs (averaging $1250). In 2001, 166 non-need-based awards were made. *Average percent of need met:* 89%. *Average financial aid package:* $13,994. *Average need-based loan:* $3790. *Average need-based gift aid:* $11,934. *Average non-need based aid:* $12,932. *Average indebtedness upon graduation:* $18,380.

Applying *Options:* electronic application, early admission, early decision, early action, deferred entrance. *Application fee:* $35. *Required:* essay or personal statement, high school transcript, minimum 2.00 GPA. *Required for some:* 1 letter of recommendation. *Recommended:* minimum 2.50 GPA, interview. *Application deadlines:* 3/1 (freshmen), 7/1 (transfers). *Early decision:* 11/15. *Notification:* continuous until 8/15 (freshmen), 1/1 (early decision), 7/1 (early action).

Admissions Contact Ms. Wanda McDowell, Director of Admissions, Converse College, 580 East Main Street, Spartanburg, SC 29302-0006. *Phone:* 864-596-9040 Ext. 9746. *Toll-free phone:* 800-766-1125. *Fax:* 864-596-9158. *E-mail:* admissions@converse.edu.

ERSKINE COLLEGE
Due West, South Carolina

- **Independent** 4-year, founded 1839, affiliated with Associate Reformed Presbyterian Church
- **Calendar** 4-1-4
- **Degree** bachelor's
- **Rural** 85-acre campus
- **Coed,** 588 undergraduate students, 97% full-time, 60% women, 40% men
- **Moderately difficult** entrance level, 72% of applicants were admitted

Undergraduates 573 full-time, 15 part-time. Students come from 20 states and territories, 3 other countries, 21% are from out of state, 5% African American, 0.2% Asian American or Pacific Islander, 0.7% Hispanic American, 0.2% Native American, 1% international, 1% transferred in, 91% live on campus. *Retention:* 82% of 2001 full-time freshmen returned.

Freshmen *Admission:* 773 applied, 556 admitted, 217 enrolled. *Test scores:* SAT verbal scores over 500: 80%; SAT math scores over 500: 79%; ACT scores over 18: 96%; SAT verbal scores over 600: 37%; SAT math scores over 600: 34%; ACT scores over 24: 66%; SAT verbal scores over 700: 5%; SAT math scores over 700: 3%; ACT scores over 30: 7%.

Faculty *Total:* 66, 64% full-time, 74% with terminal degrees. *Student/faculty ratio:* 14:1.

Majors American studies; athletic training/sports medicine; behavioral sciences; biblical studies; biological/physical sciences; biology; business administration; chemistry; early childhood education; elementary education; English; French; health science; history; mathematics; medical technology; music; music business management/merchandising; music (piano and organ performance); music teacher education; music (voice and choral/opera performance); natural sciences; philosophy; physical education; physics; psychology; religious education; religious music; religious studies; social studies education; Spanish; special education; sport/fitness administration.

Academic Programs *Special study options:* accelerated degree program, advanced placement credit, double majors, independent study, internships, off-campus study, part-time degree program, study abroad, summer session for credit. *Unusual degree programs:* 3-2 engineering with Clemson University, University of Tennessee, Knoxville; allied health programs with Medical University of South Carolina.

Library McCain Library with 229,150 titles, 693 serial subscriptions, 1,130 audiovisual materials, an OPAC, a Web page.

Computers on Campus 100 computers available on campus for general student use. A campuswide network can be accessed from student residence rooms and from off campus. Internet access, at least one staffed computer lab available.

Student Life *Housing:* on-campus residence required through senior year. *Options:* men-only, women-only. *Activities and Organizations:* drama/theater group, student-run newspaper, radio station, choral group, literary societies, religious organizations, Student Government Organization, publications, honor societies. *Campus security:* 24-hour patrols, late-night transport/escort service, controlled dormitory access. *Student Services:* health clinic, personal/psychological counseling.

Athletics Member NCAA. All Division II. *Intercollegiate sports:* baseball M(s), basketball M(s)/W(s), cross-country running M(s)/W(s), equestrian sports M(c)/W(c), soccer M(s)/W(s), softball W(s), tennis M(s)/W(s). *Intramural sports:* basketball M/W, football M/W, racquetball M/W, soccer M/W, softball M/W, tennis M/W, volleyball M/W.

Standardized Tests *Required:* SAT I or ACT (for admission). *Required for some:* SAT II: Subject Tests (for admission).

Costs (2001–02) *Comprehensive fee:* $21,399 includes full-time tuition ($15,138), mandatory fees ($1015), and room and board ($5246). Part-time tuition: $255 per semester hour. *Room and board:* Room and board charges vary according to board plan and housing facility. *Payment plan:* installment. *Waivers:* children of alumni and employees or children of employees.

Financial Aid Of all full-time matriculated undergraduates who enrolled in 2001, 543 applied for aid, 430 were judged to have need, 220 had their need fully met. 120 Federal Work-Study jobs (averaging $1000). 60 State and other part-time jobs (averaging $1000). In 2001, 104 non-need-based awards were made. *Average percent of need met:* 65%. *Average financial aid package:* $14,500. *Average need-based loan:* $3500. *Average need-based gift aid:* $4000. *Average non-need based aid:* $8000. *Average indebtedness upon graduation:* $12,425. *Financial aid deadline:* 5/1.

Applying *Options:* electronic application. *Application fee:* $15. *Required:* high school transcript, 1 letter of recommendation. *Required for some:* essay or personal statement, interview. *Recommended:* interview. *Application deadline:* rolling (freshmen), rolling (transfers). *Notification:* continuous (freshmen).

Admissions Contact Mr. Jeff Craft, Director of Admissions, Erskine College, PO Box 176, Due West, SC 29639. *Phone:* 864-379-8830. *Toll-free phone:* 800-241-8721. *Fax:* 864-379-8759. *E-mail:* admissions@erskine.edu.

FRANCIS MARION UNIVERSITY
Florence, South Carolina

- **State-supported** comprehensive, founded 1970
- **Calendar** semesters
- **Degrees** bachelor's and master's
- **Rural** 309-acre campus
- **Endowment** $200,000
- **Coed,** 2,822 undergraduate students, 92% full-time, 61% women, 39% men
- **Moderately difficult** entrance level, 77% of applicants were admitted

Undergraduates 2,586 full-time, 236 part-time. Students come from 30 states and territories, 27 other countries, 7% are from out of state, 31% African American, 0.9% Asian American or Pacific Islander, 0.5% Hispanic American, 0.7% Native American, 2% international, 9% transferred in, 38% live on campus. *Retention:* 67% of 2001 full-time freshmen returned.

Freshmen *Admission:* 1,657 applied, 1,281 admitted, 637 enrolled. *Average high school GPA:* 3.13. *Test scores:* SAT verbal scores over 500: 40%; SAT math scores over 500: 41%; SAT verbal scores over 600: 10%; SAT math scores over 600: 9%; SAT verbal scores over 700: 1%; SAT math scores over 700: 1%.

Faculty *Total:* 199, 80% full-time, 66% with terminal degrees. *Student/faculty ratio:* 14:1.

Majors Accounting; art; art education; biology; business administration; business economics; business marketing and marketing management; chemistry; civil engineering technology; computer science; early childhood education; economics; electrical/electronic engineering technology; elementary education; English; finance; French; geography; German; history; industrial radiologic technology; information sciences/systems; international relations; liberal arts and sciences/liberal studies; management information systems/business data processing; mass communications; mathematics; medical technology; physics; political science; pre-dentistry; pre-law; pre-medicine; pre-veterinary studies; psychology; sociology; Spanish; theater arts/drama.

Academic Programs *Special study options:* academic remediation for entering students, accelerated degree program, adult/continuing education programs, advanced placement credit, cooperative education, double majors, honors programs, internships, off-campus study, part-time degree program, services for LD students, summer session for credit. *Unusual degree programs:* 3-2 engineering with Clemson University; forestry with Clemson University.

Library James A. Rogers Library plus 1 other with 305,352 titles, 1,691 serial subscriptions, an OPAC, a Web page.

Computers on Campus 170 computers available on campus for general student use. At least one staffed computer lab available.

Student Life *Housing Options:* coed. *Activities and Organizations:* drama/theater group, student-run newspaper, choral group, Baptist Student Union, Education Club, University Ambassadors, Psychology Club, Crossroads, national fraternities, national sororities. *Campus security:* 24-hour emergency response devices and patrols, late-night transport/escort service, controlled dormitory access. *Student Services:* health clinic, personal/psychological counseling.

Athletics Member NCAA. All Division II. *Intercollegiate sports:* baseball M(s), basketball M(s)/W(s), cross-country running M(s)/W(s), golf M(s), soccer M(s)/W(s), softball W(s), tennis M(s)/W(s), track and field M(s)/W(s), volleyball W(s). *Intramural sports:* basketball M/W, bowling M/W, football M/W, golf M/W, racquetball M/W, soccer M, softball M/W, table tennis M/W, tennis M/W, track and field M/W, volleyball M/W, water polo M/W.

Standardized Tests *Required:* SAT I or ACT (for admission).

Costs (2001–02) *Tuition:* state resident $3620 full-time, $181 per credit hour part-time; nonresident $7240 full-time, $362 per credit hour part-time. Full-time tuition and fees vary according to course load. Part-time tuition and fees vary according to course load. *Required fees:* $170 full-time, $4 per credit hour. *Room and board:* $3892; room only: $1902. Room and board charges vary according to board plan and housing facility. *Waivers:* senior citizens and employees or children of employees.

Financial Aid *Average indebtedness upon graduation:* $18,841.

Applying *Options:* common application, electronic application, early admission, deferred entrance. *Application fee:* $30. *Required:* high school transcript. *Recommended:* letters of recommendation. *Application deadline:* rolling (freshmen), rolling (transfers).

Admissions Contact Ms. Drucilla P. Russell, Director of Admissions, Francis Marion University, Francis Mellon University, PO Box 100547, Florence, SC 29501-0547. *Phone:* 843-661-1231. *Toll-free phone:* 800-368-7551. *Fax:* 843-661-4635. *E-mail:* admission@fmarion.edu.

FURMAN UNIVERSITY
Greenville, South Carolina

- **Independent** comprehensive, founded 1826
- **Calendar** 3-2-3
- **Degrees** bachelor's, master's, and postbachelor's certificates
- **Suburban** 750-acre campus
- **Endowment** $247.7 million
- **Coed,** 2,767 undergraduate students, 95% full-time, 56% women, 44% men
- **Very difficult** entrance level, 61% of applicants were admitted

Undergraduates 2,626 full-time, 141 part-time. Students come from 48 states and territories, 20 other countries, 70% are from out of state, 6% African American, 1% Asian American or Pacific Islander, 1% Hispanic American, 0.1% Native American, 1% international, 1% transferred in, 95% live on campus. *Retention:* 92% of 2001 full-time freshmen returned.

Furman University (continued)

Freshmen *Admission:* 3,564 applied, 2,167 admitted, 736 enrolled. *Average high school GPA:* 3.52. *Test scores:* SAT verbal scores over 500: 96%; SAT math scores over 500: 97%; ACT scores over 18: 100%; SAT verbal scores over 600: 68%; SAT math scores over 600: 68%; ACT scores over 24: 86%; SAT verbal scores over 700: 19%; SAT math scores over 700: 17%; ACT scores over 30: 28%.

Faculty *Total:* 273, 73% full-time, 78% with terminal degrees. *Student/faculty ratio:* 12:1.

Majors Accounting; art; art history; Asian studies; biochemistry; biology; business administration; chemistry; communications; computer science; early childhood education; economics; education; elementary education; English; environmental science; exercise sciences; fine/studio arts; French; geology; German; Greek (modern); history; Latin (ancient and medieval); mathematics; music; music (piano and organ performance); music teacher education; music (voice and choral/opera performance); philosophy; physics; political science; pre-dentistry; pre-law; pre-medicine; pre-veterinary studies; psychology; religious music; religious studies; secondary education; sociology; Spanish; special education; theater arts/drama; urban studies.

Academic Programs *Special study options:* accelerated degree program, adult/continuing education programs, advanced placement credit, double majors, independent study, internships, part-time degree program, services for LD students, student-designed majors, study abroad, summer session for credit. *ROTC:* Army (b). *Unusual degree programs:* 3-2 engineering with Georgia Institute of Technology, Clemson University, Auburn University, North Carolina State University, Washington University in St. Louis; forestry with Duke University.

Library James Buchanan Duke Library plus 2 others with 445,900 titles, 3,347 serial subscriptions, 4,200 audiovisual materials, an OPAC, a Web page.

Computers on Campus 340 computers available on campus for general student use. A campuswide network can be accessed from student residence rooms and from off campus. Internet access, online (class) registration, at least one staffed computer lab available.

Student Life *Housing:* on-campus residence required through senior year. *Options:* coed, men-only, women-only. *Activities and Organizations:* drama/theater group, student-run newspaper, radio station, choral group, marching band, Collegiate Educational Service Corps, Fellowship of Christian Athletes, Baptist Student Union, Student Activities Board, Furman Singers, national fraternities, national sororities. *Campus security:* 24-hour emergency response devices and patrols, student patrols, late-night transport/escort service, controlled dormitory access. *Student Services:* health clinic, personal/psychological counseling.

Athletics Member NCAA. All Division I except football (Division I-AA). *Intercollegiate sports:* baseball M(s), basketball M(s)/W(s), crew M(c)/W(c), cross-country running M(s)/W(s), fencing M(c)/W(c), golf M(s)/W(s), ice hockey M(c), lacrosse M(c), rugby M(c)/W(c), soccer M(s)/W(s), softball W(s), swimming M(c)/W(c), tennis M(s)/W(s), track and field M(s)/W(s), volleyball M(c)/W(s), weight lifting M(c)/W(c). *Intramural sports:* basketball M/W, bowling M/W, cross-country running M/W, football M/W, golf M/W, racquetball M/W, soccer M/W, softball M/W, swimming M/W, tennis M/W, track and field M/W, volleyball M/W.

Standardized Tests *Required:* SAT I or ACT (for admission). *Required for some:* SAT II: Subject Tests (for admission), SAT II: Writing Test (for admission).

Costs (2001–02) *Comprehensive fee:* $25,492 includes full-time tuition ($19,680), mandatory fees ($396), and room and board ($5416). Part-time tuition: $615 per credit hour. Part-time tuition and fees vary according to course load. *Room and board:* College room only: $2944. Room and board charges vary according to board plan and housing facility. *Payment plan:* installment. *Waivers:* employees or children of employees.

Financial Aid Of all full-time matriculated undergraduates who enrolled in 2001, 2157 applied for aid, 1026 were judged to have need, 796 had their need fully met. In 2001, 979 non-need-based awards were made. *Average percent of need met:* 89%. *Average financial aid package:* $16,500. *Average need-based loan:* $4512. *Average need-based gift aid:* $12,547. *Average non-need based aid:* $8847. *Average indebtedness upon graduation:* $15,711. *Financial aid deadline:* 1/15.

Applying *Options:* common application, electronic application, early admission, early decision. *Application fee:* $40. *Required:* essay or personal statement, high school transcript. *Recommended:* minimum 3.0 GPA, 2 letters of recommendation. *Application deadlines:* 1/15 (freshmen), 6/1 (transfers). *Early decision:* 11/15. *Notification:* 3/15 (freshmen), 12/15 (early decision).

Admissions Contact Mr. David R. O'Cain, Director of Admissions, Furman University, 3300 Poinsett Highway, Greenville, SC 29613. *Phone:* 864-294-2034. *Fax:* 864-294-3127. *E-mail:* admissions@furman.edu.

JOHNSON & WALES UNIVERSITY
Charleston, South Carolina

Admissions Contact Ms. Deborah Langenstein, Director of Admissions, Johnson & Wales University, 701 East Bay Street, Charleston, SC 29403. *Phone:* 843-727-3000. *Toll-free phone:* 800-868-1522. *Fax:* 843-763-0318. *E-mail:* admissions@jwu.edu.

LANDER UNIVERSITY
Greenwood, South Carolina

- **State-supported** comprehensive, founded 1872, part of South Carolina Commission on Higher Education
- **Calendar** semesters
- **Degrees** bachelor's and master's
- **Small-town** 100-acre campus
- **Coed,** 2,505 undergraduate students, 88% full-time, 62% women, 38% men
- **Moderately difficult** entrance level, 87% of applicants were admitted

Undergraduates 2,198 full-time, 307 part-time. Students come from 20 states and territories, 28 other countries, 3% are from out of state, 19% African American, 0.4% Asian American or Pacific Islander, 0.8% Hispanic American, 0.1% Native American, 2% international, 8% transferred in, 40% live on campus. *Retention:* 67% of 2001 full-time freshmen returned.

Freshmen *Admission:* 1,453 applied, 1,259 admitted, 491 enrolled. *Average high school GPA:* 3.18. *Test scores:* SAT verbal scores over 500: 44%; SAT math scores over 500: 50%; ACT scores over 18: 81%; SAT verbal scores over 600: 10%; SAT math scores over 600: 10%; ACT scores over 24: 14%; SAT verbal scores over 700: 1%; SAT math scores over 700: 1%.

Faculty *Total:* 175, 73% full-time, 54% with terminal degrees. *Student/faculty ratio:* 16:1.

Majors Accounting; art; biology; business administration; business economics; chemistry; computer science; early childhood education; education; elementary education; English; environmental science; exercise sciences; health/medical preparatory programs related; health services administration; history; interdisciplinary studies; mass communications; mathematics; medical technology; music; music teacher education; nursing; physical education; political science; pre-dentistry; pre-law; pre-medicine; pre-pharmacy studies; pre-veterinary studies; psychology; sociology; Spanish; special education; theater arts/drama.

Academic Programs *Special study options:* academic remediation for entering students, accelerated degree program, adult/continuing education programs, advanced placement credit, cooperative education, distance learning, double majors, honors programs, independent study, internships, off-campus study, part-time degree program, services for LD students, student-designed majors, study abroad, summer session for credit. *ROTC:* Army (b). *Unusual degree programs:* 3-2 engineering with Clemson University.

Library Jackson Library with 169,919 titles, 692 serial subscriptions, 2,089 audiovisual materials, an OPAC, a Web page.

Computers on Campus 150 computers available on campus for general student use. A campuswide network can be accessed from student residence rooms and from off campus. Internet access, online (class) registration, at least one staffed computer lab available.

Student Life *Housing Options:* coed, women-only. *Activities and Organizations:* drama/theater group, student-run newspaper, choral group, Students Promoting Intelligent Choices and Experiences (S.P.I.C.E.), Lander Association of Biological Science, national fraternities, national sororities. *Campus security:* 24-hour emergency response devices and patrols, late-night transport/escort service, controlled dormitory access. *Student Services:* health clinic, personal/psychological counseling.

Athletics Member NCAA. All Division II. *Intercollegiate sports:* baseball M, basketball M(s)/W(s), cross-country running W(s), soccer M(s)/W(s), softball W(s), tennis M(s), volleyball W(s). *Intramural sports:* basketball M/W, bowling M/W, football M/W, racquetball M/W, soccer M/W, softball M/W, swimming M/W, table tennis M/W, tennis M/W, track and field M/W, volleyball M/W.

Standardized Tests *Required:* SAT I or ACT (for admission).

Costs (2001–02) *One-time required fee:* $75. *Tuition:* state resident $4152 full-time, $173 per semester hour part-time; nonresident $8520 full-time, $355 per semester hour part-time. Full-time tuition and fees vary according to degree level. Part-time tuition and fees vary according to degree level. *Required fees:* $90 full-time. *Room and board:* $4376. Room and board charges vary according to board plan, gender, and housing facility. *Payment plan:* installment. *Waivers:* senior citizens.

Financial Aid Of all full-time matriculated undergraduates who enrolled in 2001, 1548 applied for aid, 929 were judged to have need, 481 had their need fully met. 189 Federal Work-Study jobs (averaging $1529). 348 State and other part-time jobs (averaging $2021). In 2001, 419 non-need-based awards were made. *Average percent of need met:* 68%. *Average financial aid package:* $5105. *Average need-based loan:* $3870. *Average need-based gift aid:* $1903. *Average non-need based aid:* $3417. *Average indebtedness upon graduation:* $16,450.

Applying *Options:* common application, early admission, deferred entrance. *Application fee:* $25. *Required:* high school transcript, 1 letter of recommendation. *Recommended:* interview. *Application deadline:* rolling (freshmen), rolling (transfers). *Notification:* continuous (freshmen).

Admissions Contact Mr. Jeffrey A. Constant, Assistant Director of Admissions, Lander University, Greenwood, SC 29649. *Phone:* 864-388-8307. *Toll-free phone:* 888-452-6337. *Fax:* 864-388-8125. *E-mail:* admissions@lander.edu.

LIMESTONE COLLEGE

Gaffney, South Carolina

- **Independent** 4-year, founded 1845
- **Calendar** semesters
- **Degrees** associate and bachelor's
- **Small-town** 115-acre campus with easy access to Charlotte
- **Endowment** $5.8 million
- **Coed,** 516 undergraduate students, 98% full-time, 50% women, 50% men
- **Minimally difficult** entrance level, 66% of applicants were admitted

Founded in 1845, Limestone is a private, coeducational liberal arts college that maintains a small student body and a well-qualified faculty, creating an atmosphere that assures intellectual, social, ethical, and physical development of students. With a student-faculty ratio of 10:1, Limestone provides the individual attention often lacking in larger institutions.

Undergraduates 504 full-time, 12 part-time. Students come from 25 states and territories, 10 other countries, 37% are from out of state, 17% African American, 0.8% Asian American or Pacific Islander, 1% Hispanic American, 0.2% Native American, 0.6% international, 11% transferred in, 45% live on campus. *Retention:* 50% of 2001 full-time freshmen returned.

Freshmen *Admission:* 501 applied, 333 admitted, 121 enrolled. *Average high school GPA:* 2.88. *Test scores:* SAT verbal scores over 500: 35%; SAT math scores over 500: 43%; ACT scores over 18: 58%; SAT verbal scores over 600: 8%; SAT math scores over 600: 9%; ACT scores over 24: 8%; SAT math scores over 700: 1%; ACT scores over 30: 2%.

Faculty *Total:* 58, 67% full-time, 66% with terminal degrees. *Student/faculty ratio:* 9:1.

Majors Accounting; applied mathematics; art education; athletic training/sports medicine; biology; biology education; business; business administration; business computer programming; business economics; business marketing and marketing management; chemistry; computer programming; computer science; counseling psychology; criminal justice studies; education; elementary education; English; English education; fine/studio arts; graphic design/commercial art/illustration; history; human resources management related; information sciences/systems; liberal arts and sciences/liberal studies; mathematics education; music; music teacher education; physical education; pre-law; psychology; social studies education; social work; sport/fitness administration.

Academic Programs *Special study options:* academic remediation for entering students, accelerated degree program, adult/continuing education programs, advanced placement credit, distance learning, double majors, English as a second language, honors programs, independent study, internships, part-time degree program, services for LD students, student-designed majors, summer session for credit. *ROTC:* Army (c).

Library A. J. Eastwood Library with 60,626 titles, 252 serial subscriptions, 2,140 audiovisual materials, an OPAC, a Web page.

Computers on Campus 53 computers available on campus for general student use. A campuswide network can be accessed from student residence rooms and from off campus that provide access to online (class) registration for internet classes only. Internet access, at least one staffed computer lab available.

Student Life *Housing:* on-campus residence required through junior year. *Options:* men-only, women-only. *Activities and Organizations:* drama/theater group, choral group, Fellowship of Christian Athletes, Student Government Association, Delta Chi Sigma, KDK, Student Ambassadors. *Campus security:* 24-hour emergency response devices and patrols, late-night transport/escort service, controlled dormitory access. *Student Services:* health clinic, personal/psychological counseling.

Athletics Member NCAA. All Division II. *Intercollegiate sports:* baseball M(s), basketball M(s)/W(s), cross-country running M(s)/W(s), golf M(s), lacrosse M(s)/W(s), soccer M(s)/W(s), softball W(s), swimming W(s), tennis M(s)/W(s), volleyball W(s). *Intramural sports:* badminton M/W, basketball M/W, bowling M/W, football M, lacrosse M, soccer M/W, softball M/W, swimming M/W, table tennis M/W, tennis M/W, volleyball M/W.

Standardized Tests *Required:* SAT I or ACT (for admission).

Costs (2002–03) *Comprehensive fee:* $16,900 includes full-time tuition ($11,500) and room and board ($5400). Full-time tuition and fees vary according to class time, course load, location, and program. Part-time tuition: $480 per semester hour. Part-time tuition and fees vary according to class time, location, and program. *Payment plan:* installment. *Waivers:* employees or children of employees.

Financial Aid Of all full-time matriculated undergraduates who enrolled in 2001, 437 applied for aid, 378 were judged to have need, 88 had their need fully met. 78 Federal Work-Study jobs (averaging $1223). 32 State and other part-time jobs (averaging $1223). In 2001, 61 non-need-based awards were made. *Average percent of need met:* 69%. *Average financial aid package:* $8470. *Average need-based loan:* $3186. *Average need-based gift aid:* $5703. *Average indebtedness upon graduation:* $7698.

Applying *Options:* common application, electronic application. *Application fee:* $25. *Required:* high school transcript, minimum 2.0 GPA. *Recommended:* 2 letters of recommendation, interview. *Application deadline:* rolling (freshmen), rolling (transfers). *Notification:* continuous (freshmen).

Admissions Contact Ms. Debbie Borders, Office Manager of Admissions, Limestone College, Limestone College, 1115 College Drive, Gaffney, SC 29340-3799. *Phone:* 864-489-7151 Ext. 554. *Toll-free phone:* 800-795-7151 Ext. 554 (in-state); 800-795-7151 Ext. 553 (out-of-state). *Fax:* 864-487-8706. *E-mail:* cphenicie@limestone.edu.

MEDICAL UNIVERSITY OF SOUTH CAROLINA

Charleston, South Carolina

- **State-supported** upper-level, founded 1824
- **Calendar** semesters
- **Degrees** bachelor's, master's, doctoral, first professional, post-master's, and postbachelor's certificates
- **Urban** 61-acre campus
- **Endowment** $67.9 million
- **Coed,** 400 undergraduate students, 74% full-time, 83% women, 17% men
- **Very difficult** entrance level, 42% of applicants were admitted

Undergraduates 294 full-time, 106 part-time. Students come from 17 states and territories, 9% are from out of state, 15% African American, 2% Asian American or Pacific Islander, 1% Hispanic American, 1% Native American, 0.3% international, 44% transferred in.

Freshmen *Admission:* 640 applied, 267 admitted.

Faculty *Total:* 1,209, 89% full-time, 82% with terminal degrees. *Student/faculty ratio:* 12:1.

Majors Health science; nursing; perfusion technology; physician assistant.

Academic Programs *Special study options:* advanced placement credit, distance learning, independent study, internships, off-campus study, part-time degree program.

Library Medical University of South Carolina Library plus 1 other with 217,841 titles, 2,180 serial subscriptions, 6,596 audiovisual materials, an OPAC, a Web page.

Computers on Campus 189 computers available on campus for general student use. A campuswide network can be accessed from off campus. Internet access, at least one staffed computer lab available.

Student Life *Housing:* college housing not available. *Activities and Organizations:* national fraternities, national sororities. *Campus security:* 24-hour emergency response devices and patrols, late-night transport/escort service. *Student Services:* health clinic, personal/psychological counseling.

Athletics *Intramural sports:* basketball M/W, softball M/W, volleyball M/W.

Standardized Tests *Required for some:* SAT I or ACT (for admission). *Recommended:* SAT I or ACT (for admission).

Costs (2002–03) *Tuition:* state resident $6230 full-time, $270 per hour part-time; nonresident $17,227 full-time, $756 per hour part-time. Full-time tuition and fees vary according to program. Part-time tuition and fees vary according to program. *Required fees:* $448 per term part-time. *Payment plan:* installment. *Waivers:* senior citizens and employees or children of employees.

Financial Aid Of all full-time matriculated undergraduates who enrolled in 2001, 260 applied for aid, 240 were judged to have need. *Average percent of need met:* 83%. *Average financial aid package:* $11,633. *Average need-based loan:* $8500. *Average need-based gift aid:* $3782. *Average indebtedness upon graduation:* $20,532.

Applying *Options:* electronic application, deferred entrance. *Application fee:* $55. *Application deadline:* rolling (transfers).

Medical University of South Carolina (continued)

Admissions Contact Mr. James F. Menzel, Executive Director, Office of Enrollment Services, Medical University of South Carolina, 171 Ashley Avenue, Charleston, SC 29425-0002. *Phone:* 843-792-5396. *Fax:* 843-792-3764. *E-mail:* smithman@musc.edu.

MORRIS COLLEGE
Sumter, South Carolina

- **Independent** 4-year, founded 1908, affiliated with Baptist Educational and Missionary Convention of South Carolina
- **Calendar** semesters
- **Degree** bachelor's
- **Small-town** 34-acre campus
- **Endowment** $4.2 million
- **Coed,** 986 undergraduate students, 97% full-time, 64% women, 36% men
- **Minimally difficult** entrance level, 94% of applicants were admitted

Undergraduates 958 full-time, 28 part-time. Students come from 20 states and territories, 14% are from out of state, 100% African American, 0.1% Hispanic American, 2% transferred in, 72% live on campus. *Retention:* 50% of 2001 full-time freshmen returned.

Freshmen *Admission:* 1,220 applied, 1,144 admitted, 272 enrolled. *Average high school GPA:* 2.42. *Test scores:* SAT verbal scores over 500: 6%; SAT math scores over 500: 8%.

Faculty *Total:* 60, 78% full-time, 57% with terminal degrees. *Student/faculty ratio:* 16:1.

Majors Biology; broadcast journalism; business administration; criminal justice/law enforcement administration; early childhood education; elementary education; English; enterprise management; health science; history; journalism; liberal arts and sciences/liberal studies; mathematics; political science; recreation/leisure studies; religious education; secondary education; social sciences; sociology; theology.

Academic Programs *Special study options:* academic remediation for entering students, accelerated degree program, adult/continuing education programs, cooperative education, double majors, honors programs, internships, summer session for credit. *ROTC:* Army (b).

Library Richardson-Johnson Learning Resources Center with 99,462 titles, 415 serial subscriptions, 3,391 audiovisual materials, an OPAC.

Computers on Campus 149 computers available on campus for general student use. A campuswide network can be accessed from student residence rooms. Internet access, at least one staffed computer lab available.

Student Life *Housing Options:* men-only, women-only. *Activities and Organizations:* drama/theater group, student-run newspaper, radio station, choral group, Student Government Association, New Emphasis on Nontraditional Students, Block ""M" Club, Students of South Carolina Educational Association, Baptist Student Union, national fraternities, national sororities. *Campus security:* 24-hour patrols, controlled dormitory access. *Student Services:* health clinic, personal/psychological counseling.

Athletics Member NAIA. *Intercollegiate sports:* baseball M(s), basketball M(s)/W(s), cross-country running M(s)/W(s), golf M(s), softball W(s), tennis M(s)/W(s), track and field M(s)/W(s), volleyball W(s). *Intramural sports:* basketball M/W, football M/W, golf M/W, softball M/W, table tennis M/W, tennis M/W, volleyball M/W.

Standardized Tests *Required for some:* SAT I or ACT (for admission).

Costs (2001–02) *Comprehensive fee:* $9995 includes full-time tuition ($6483), mandatory fees ($202), and room and board ($3310). Part-time tuition: $270 per credit hour. *Required fees:* $38 per term part-time. *Room and board:* College room only: $1392. *Payment plan:* installment.

Financial Aid Of all full-time matriculated undergraduates who enrolled in 2001, 900 applied for aid, 900 were judged to have need, 5 had their need fully met. 352 Federal Work-Study jobs (averaging $1000). *Average percent of need met:* 85%. *Average financial aid package:* $9400. *Average need-based loan:* $3500. *Average need-based gift aid:* $5290.

Applying *Options:* deferred entrance. *Application fee:* $10. *Required:* high school transcript, medical examination. *Application deadline:* rolling (freshmen), rolling (transfers).

Admissions Contact Ms. Deborah Calhoun, Director of Admissions and Records, Morris College, 100 West College Street, Sumter, SC 29150-3599. *Phone:* 803-934-3225. *Toll-free phone:* 888-853-1345. *Fax:* 803-773-3687.

NEWBERRY COLLEGE
Newberry, South Carolina

- **Independent Lutheran** 4-year, founded 1856
- **Calendar** semesters
- **Degree** bachelor's
- **Small-town** 60-acre campus
- **Endowment** $12.4 million
- **Coed,** 726 undergraduate students, 93% full-time, 46% women, 54% men
- **Moderately difficult** entrance level, 76% of applicants were admitted

Newberry College has the only bachelor's-level veterinary technology program in the southeastern US, an innovative general honors program, a communications program with a television studio and Internet radio studio, a major in sports management, a professional writing and editing minor, exceptional teacher education and music programs, a beautiful campus, small classes, strong athletic programs, and a family-like environment.

Undergraduates 675 full-time, 51 part-time. Students come from 19 states and territories, 4 other countries, 12% are from out of state, 21% African American, 0.3% Asian American or Pacific Islander, 1% Hispanic American, 0.1% Native American, 1.0% international, 6% transferred in, 78% live on campus. *Retention:* 66% of 2001 full-time freshmen returned.

Freshmen *Admission:* 806 applied, 616 admitted, 184 enrolled. *Average high school GPA:* 3.19. *Test scores:* SAT verbal scores over 500: 35%; SAT math scores over 500: 34%; ACT scores over 18: 53%; SAT verbal scores over 600: 7%; SAT math scores over 600: 5%; ACT scores over 24: 10%; ACT scores over 30: 1%.

Faculty *Total:* 69, 70% full-time, 59% with terminal degrees. *Student/faculty ratio:* 12:1.

Majors Accounting; art; arts management; athletic training/sports medicine; biology; business administration; business economics; chemistry; computer science; early childhood education; economics; education; elementary education; English; French; German; history; mass communications; mathematics; music; music (piano and organ performance); music teacher education; music (voice and choral/opera performance); philosophy; physical education; political science; pre-dentistry; pre-law; pre-medicine; pre-veterinary studies; psychology; religious music; religious studies; secondary education; sociology; Spanish; special education; speech/rhetorical studies; theater arts/drama; veterinary technology.

Academic Programs *Special study options:* adult/continuing education programs, advanced placement credit, cooperative education, double majors, honors programs, independent study, internships, part-time degree program, student-designed majors, study abroad, summer session for credit. *ROTC:* Army (c). *Unusual degree programs:* 3-2 engineering with Clemson University; forestry with Duke University.

Library Wessels Library with 61,857 titles, 399 serial subscriptions, 565 audiovisual materials, an OPAC, a Web page.

Computers on Campus 75 computers available on campus for general student use. A campuswide network can be accessed from student residence rooms and from off campus. Internet access, at least one staffed computer lab available.

Student Life *Housing:* on-campus residence required through sophomore year. *Options:* coed, men-only, women-only. *Activities and Organizations:* drama/theater group, student-run newspaper, radio and television station, choral group, marching band, Fellowship of Christian Athletes (FCA), Metoka Galeda (gospel choir and service group), Lutheran Student Movement (LSM), Baptist Student Union (BSU), Students Organized for Community Service (SOCS), national fraternities, national sororities. *Campus security:* 24-hour patrols. *Student Services:* health clinic, personal/psychological counseling.

Athletics Member NCAA. All Division II. *Intercollegiate sports:* baseball M(s), basketball M(s)/W(s), cross-country running M(s)/W(s), football M(s), golf M(s)/W(s), soccer M(s)/W(s), softball W(s), tennis M(s)/W(s), volleyball W(s). *Intramural sports:* basketball M/W, football M.

Standardized Tests *Required:* SAT I or ACT (for admission).

Costs (2002–03) *Comprehensive fee:* $20,688 includes full-time tuition ($15,700), mandatory fees ($400), and room and board ($4588). Part-time tuition: $205 per credit hour. *Required fees:* $70 per year part-time. *Room and board:* College room only: $2100. Room and board charges vary according to board plan and housing facility. *Payment plan:* installment. *Waivers:* employees or children of employees.

Financial Aid Of all full-time matriculated undergraduates who enrolled in 2001, 577 applied for aid, 519 were judged to have need, 159 had their need fully met. 76 Federal Work-Study jobs (averaging $990). *Average percent of need met:* 79%. *Average financial aid package:* $11,807. *Average need-based loan:* $3296.

Average need-based gift aid: $9388. *Average non-need based aid:* $7874. *Average indebtedness upon graduation:* $5300.

Applying *Options:* common application, electronic application, early admission, deferred entrance. *Application fee:* $30. *Required:* high school transcript, minimum 2.0 GPA. *Required for some:* essay or personal statement. *Recommended:* 2 letters of recommendation, interview. *Application deadline:* rolling (freshmen), rolling (transfers). *Notification:* continuous (freshmen).

Admissions Contact Mr. Jonathan Reece, Director of Admissions, Newberry College, 2100 College Street, Smeltzer Hall, Newberry, SC 29108. *Phone:* 803-321-5127. *Toll-free phone:* 800-845-4955 Ext. 5127. *Fax:* 803-321-5138. *E-mail:* admissions@newberry.edu.

NORTH GREENVILLE COLLEGE

Tigerville, South Carolina

- **Independent Southern Baptist** 4-year, founded 1892
- **Calendar** semesters
- **Degrees** associate and bachelor's
- **Rural** 500-acre campus with easy access to Greenville
- **Coed,** 1,380 undergraduate students, 91% full-time, 48% women, 52% men
- **Minimally difficult** entrance level, 93% of applicants were admitted

Undergraduates Students come from 25 states and territories, 17 other countries, 16% are from out of state, 10% African American, 0.7% Asian American or Pacific Islander, 0.5% Hispanic American, 0.1% Native American, 2% international, 65% live on campus. *Retention:* 65% of 2001 full-time freshmen returned.

Freshmen *Admission:* 845 applied, 782 admitted. *Average high school GPA:* 3.25. *Test scores:* SAT verbal scores over 500: 59%; SAT math scores over 500: 54%; ACT scores over 18: 75%; SAT verbal scores over 600: 12%; SAT math scores over 600: 14%; ACT scores over 24: 18%; SAT verbal scores over 700: 1%; SAT math scores over 700: 1%.

Faculty *Total:* 120, 49% full-time, 39% with terminal degrees. *Student/faculty ratio:* 12:1.

Majors Art; biblical languages/literatures; biblical studies; business administration; business economics; early childhood education; elementary education; humanities; interdisciplinary studies; journalism; liberal arts and sciences/liberal studies; mass communications; music; music history; music (piano and organ performance); music teacher education; music (voice and choral/opera performance); pastoral counseling; religious education; religious music; religious studies; sport/fitness administration; theater arts/drama; theology.

Academic Programs *Special study options:* academic remediation for entering students, accelerated degree program, advanced placement credit, double majors, English as a second language, external degree program, freshman honors college, honors programs, independent study, internships, part-time degree program, services for LD students, student-designed majors, summer session for credit. *ROTC:* Army (c).

Library Hester Memorial Library with 47,000 titles, 536 serial subscriptions, 4,170 audiovisual materials, an OPAC, a Web page.

Computers on Campus 40 computers available on campus for general student use. A campuswide network can be accessed from student residence rooms and from off campus. Internet access, at least one staffed computer lab available.

Student Life *Housing:* on-campus residence required through sophomore year. *Options:* men-only, women-only. *Activities and Organizations:* drama/theater group, student-run newspaper, radio station, choral group, Baptist Student Union, Fellowship of Christians in Service, Fellowship of Christian Athletes, Black Student Fellowship, Education Club. *Campus security:* 24-hour emergency response devices and patrols, controlled dormitory access. *Student Services:* health clinic, personal/psychological counseling.

Athletics Member NAIA. *Intercollegiate sports:* baseball M(s), basketball M(s)/W(s), cross-country running M(s)/W(s), football M(s), golf M(s), soccer M(s)/W(s), softball W(s), tennis M(s)/W(s), volleyball W(s). *Intramural sports:* basketball M/W, bowling M/W, football M, golf M/W, skiing (downhill) M/W, softball M/W, table tennis M/W, tennis M/W, volleyball W, weight lifting M/W.

Standardized Tests *Required:* SAT I or ACT (for admission).

Costs (2001–02) *Comprehensive fee:* $13,240 includes full-time tuition ($8200), mandatory fees ($250), and room and board ($4790). Part-time tuition: $150 per hour. Part-time tuition and fees vary according to course load. *Required fees:* $75 per term part-time. *Payment plan:* installment. *Waivers:* employees or children of employees.

Financial Aid Of all full-time matriculated undergraduates who enrolled in 2001, 173 Federal Work-Study jobs (averaging $1000). 76 State and other part-time jobs (averaging $1000).

Applying *Options:* electronic application, early admission, deferred entrance. *Application fee:* $20. *Required:* high school transcript. *Recommended:* minimum 2.0 GPA. *Application deadlines:* 8/21 (freshmen), 8/21 (transfers). *Notification:* continuous until 8/21 (freshmen).

Admissions Contact Mr. Buddy Freeman, Executive Director of Admissions, North Greenville College, Admissions, PO Box 1872, Tigerville, SC 29688. *Phone:* 864-977-7052. *Toll-free phone:* 800-468-6642 Ext. 7001. *Fax:* 864-977-7177. *E-mail:* bfreeman@ngc.edu.

PRESBYTERIAN COLLEGE

Clinton, South Carolina

- **Independent Presbyterian** 4-year, founded 1880
- **Calendar** semesters
- **Degree** bachelor's
- **Small-town** 215-acre campus with easy access to Greenville—Spartanburg
- **Endowment** $79.6 million
- **Coed,** 1,202 undergraduate students, 96% full-time, 56% women, 44% men
- **Very difficult** entrance level, 78% of applicants were admitted

Undergraduates 1,151 full-time, 51 part-time. Students come from 26 states and territories, 7 other countries, 40% are from out of state, 5% African American, 0.8% Asian American or Pacific Islander, 0.9% Hispanic American, 1% transferred in, 90% live on campus. *Retention:* 86% of 2001 full-time freshmen returned.

Freshmen *Admission:* 951 applied, 743 admitted, 322 enrolled. *Average high school GPA:* 3.3. *Test scores:* SAT verbal scores over 500: 84%; SAT math scores over 500: 86%; ACT scores over 18: 95%; SAT verbal scores over 600: 30%; SAT math scores over 600: 37%; ACT scores over 24: 44%; SAT verbal scores over 700: 4%; SAT math scores over 700: 5%; ACT scores over 30: 6%.

Faculty *Total:* 110, 72% full-time, 70% with terminal degrees. *Student/faculty ratio:* 13:1.

Majors Accounting; art; biology; business administration; chemistry; computer science; early childhood education; economics; education; elementary education; English; French; German; history; mathematics; modern languages; music; music teacher education; philosophy; physics; political science; pre-dentistry; pre-law; pre-medicine; pre-veterinary studies; psychology; religious studies; social sciences; sociology; Spanish; special education; theater arts/drama.

Academic Programs *Special study options:* advanced placement credit, double majors, freshman honors college, honors programs, independent study, internships, off-campus study, part-time degree program, services for LD students, study abroad, summer session for credit. *ROTC:* Army (b). *Unusual degree programs:* 3-2 engineering with Auburn University, Clemson University, Mercer University, Vanderbilt University; forestry with Duke University.

Library James H. Thomason Library with 149,273 titles, 797 serial subscriptions, 7,204 audiovisual materials, an OPAC, a Web page.

Computers on Campus 130 computers available on campus for general student use. A campuswide network can be accessed from student residence rooms and from off campus. Internet access, online (class) registration, at least one staffed computer lab available.

Student Life *Housing:* on-campus residence required through senior year. *Options:* men-only, women-only. *Activities and Organizations:* drama/theater group, student-run newspaper, radio station, choral group, Student Volunteer Services, Intramurals, Student Union Board, Fellowship of Christian Athletes, national fraternities, national sororities. *Campus security:* 24-hour emergency response devices and patrols, late-night transport/escort service, controlled dormitory access. *Student Services:* health clinic, personal/psychological counseling.

Athletics Member NCAA. All Division II. *Intercollegiate sports:* baseball M(s), basketball M(s)/W(s), cross-country running M(s)/W(s), football M(s), golf M(s), riflery M/W, soccer M(s)/W(s), softball W(s), tennis M(s)/W(s), volleyball W(s). *Intramural sports:* basketball M/W, cross-country running M/W, football M/W, golf M/W, racquetball M/W, soccer M/W, softball M/W, swimming M/W, table tennis M/W, tennis M/W, volleyball M/W.

Standardized Tests *Required:* SAT I or ACT (for admission).

Costs (2001–02) *Comprehensive fee:* $23,356 includes full-time tuition ($16,656), mandatory fees ($1544), and room and board ($5156). Full-time tuition and fees vary according to course load. Part-time tuition: $694 per semester hour. Part-time tuition and fees vary according to course load. *Required fees:* $9 per semester hour, $15 per term part-time. *Room and board:* College room only: $2440. Room and board charges vary according to board plan. *Payment plans:* tuition prepayment, installment. *Waivers:* senior citizens and employees or children of employees.

Financial Aid Of all full-time matriculated undergraduates who enrolled in 2001, 1086 applied for aid, 688 were judged to have need, 336 had their need fully

Presbyterian College (continued)
met. In 2001, 392 non-need-based awards were made. *Average percent of need met:* 83%. *Average financial aid package:* $17,359. *Average need-based loan:* $3494. *Average need-based gift aid:* $14,976. *Average non-need based aid:* $8487. *Average indebtedness upon graduation:* $14,018.

Applying *Options:* electronic application, early action, deferred entrance. *Application fee:* $30. *Required:* essay or personal statement, high school transcript, 1 letter of recommendation. *Recommended:* interview. *Application deadlines:* 4/1 (freshmen), 7/1 (transfers). *Notification:* continuous until 6/1 (freshmen), 1/31 (early action).

Admissions Contact Mr. Richard Dana Paul, Vice President of Enrollment and Dean of Admissions, Presbyterian College, South Broad Street, Clinton, SC 29325. *Phone:* 864-833-8229. *Toll-free phone:* 800-476-7272. *Fax:* 864-833-8481. *E-mail:* rdpaul@admin.presby.edu.

SOUTH CAROLINA STATE UNIVERSITY
Orangeburg, South Carolina

- **State-supported** comprehensive, founded 1896, part of South Carolina Commission on Higher Education
- **Calendar** semesters
- **Degrees** bachelor's, master's, and doctoral
- **Small-town** 160-acre campus
- **Endowment** $651,061
- **Coed,** 3,487 undergraduate students, 90% full-time, 58% women, 42% men
- **Minimally difficult** entrance level, 53% of applicants were admitted

Undergraduates 3,149 full-time, 338 part-time. Students come from 36 states and territories, 21 other countries, 97% African American, 0.2% Asian American or Pacific Islander, 0.2% Hispanic American, 0.1% Native American, 0.1% international, 47% live on campus. *Retention:* 80% of 2001 full-time freshmen returned.

Freshmen *Admission:* 3,535 applied, 1,873 admitted, 615 enrolled. *Average high school GPA:* 2.80. *Test scores:* SAT verbal scores over 500: 13%; SAT math scores over 500: 17%; ACT scores over 18: 50%; SAT verbal scores over 600: 2%; SAT math scores over 600: 3%; ACT scores over 24: 2%; SAT math scores over 700: 1%.

Faculty *Total:* 271, 97% full-time, 64% with terminal degrees. *Student/faculty ratio:* 17:1.

Majors Accounting; agricultural business; art education; biology; business administration; business economics; business education; business marketing and marketing management; chemistry; civil engineering technology; computer science; criminal justice/law enforcement administration; early childhood education; economics; education; electrical/electronic engineering technology; elementary education; English; fashion merchandising; French; health education; history; home economics; home economics education; industrial arts; industrial technology; mathematics; mechanical engineering technology; music business management/merchandising; music teacher education; nursing; nutrition science; physical education; physics; political science; pre-dentistry; pre-law; pre-medicine; pre-veterinary studies; psychology; secretarial science; social work; sociology; Spanish; special education; speech-language pathology/audiology; theater arts/drama; trade/industrial education.

Academic Programs *Special study options:* academic remediation for entering students, adult/continuing education programs, advanced placement credit, cooperative education, distance learning, honors programs, independent study, internships, off-campus study, part-time degree program, study abroad, summer session for credit. *ROTC:* Army (b), Air Force (c).

Library Miller F. Whittaker Library plus 1 other with 273,264 titles, 1,346 serial subscriptions, a Web page.

Computers on Campus 300 computers available on campus for general student use. Internet access, at least one staffed computer lab available.

Student Life *Housing Options:* men-only, women-only. *Activities and Organizations:* drama/theater group, student-run newspaper, choral group, marching band, student government, Student Union Board, NAACP, national fraternities, national sororities. *Campus security:* 24-hour emergency response devices and patrols, late-night transport/escort service, controlled dormitory access. *Student Services:* health clinic, personal/psychological counseling.

Athletics Member NCAA. All Division I except football (Division I-AA). *Intercollegiate sports:* basketball M(s)/W(s), cross-country running M(s)/W(s), golf M(s), softball W(s), tennis M(s)/W(s), track and field M(s)/W(s), volleyball W(s).

Standardized Tests *Required:* SAT I or ACT (for admission). *Recommended:* SAT II: Subject Tests (for admission).

Costs (2001–02) *Tuition:* state resident $4096 full-time, $171 per credit hour part-time; nonresident $7092 full-time, $329 per credit hour part-time. *Room and board:* $1792; room only: $905. Room and board charges vary according to board plan and housing facility. *Payment plan:* deferred payment. *Waivers:* senior citizens and employees or children of employees.

Applying *Options:* common application, deferred entrance. *Application fee:* $25. *Required:* high school transcript, minimum 2.0 GPA. *Application deadlines:* 7/31 (freshmen), 7/31 (transfers). *Notification:* continuous (freshmen).

Admissions Contact Ms. Lillian Adderson, Director of Admissions, South Carolina State University, 300 College Street Northeast, Orangeburg, SC 29117-0001. *Phone:* 803-536-8408. *Toll-free phone:* 800-260-5956. *Fax:* 803-536-8990. *E-mail:* carolyn-free@scsu.scsu.edu.

SOUTHERN METHODIST COLLEGE
Orangeburg, South Carolina

- **Independent religious** 4-year, founded 1956
- **Degrees** certificates, associate, and bachelor's
- **Coed,** 92 undergraduate students, 79% full-time, 60% women, 40% men
- **Moderately difficult** entrance level

Undergraduates 73 full-time, 19 part-time. Students come from 6 states and territories, 3 other countries, 17% African American, 1% Asian American or Pacific Islander, 2% Hispanic American, 4% international.

Freshmen *Admission:* 14 enrolled.

Faculty *Total:* 12.

Majors Biblical studies; missionary studies.

Costs (2001–02) *Comprehensive fee:* $8720 includes full-time tuition ($4200), mandatory fees ($300), and room and board ($4220). Part-time tuition: $175 per semester hour. *Required fees:* $75 per term part-time.

Financial Aid Of all full-time matriculated undergraduates who enrolled in 2001, 41 applied for aid, 41 were judged to have need. 7 Federal Work-Study jobs (averaging $141). 21 State and other part-time jobs (averaging $404). *Average percent of need met:* 24%. *Average financial aid package:* $2809. *Average need-based gift aid:* $2435.

Applying *Application fee:* $25. *Required:* essay or personal statement, high school transcript, interview, health certificate.

Admissions Contact Mr. John Hucks, Director of Admissions, Southern Methodist College, 541 Broughton Stret, PO Box 1027, Orangeburg, SC 29116-1027. *Phone:* 803-534-7826.

SOUTHERN WESLEYAN UNIVERSITY
Central, South Carolina

- **Independent** comprehensive, founded 1906, affiliated with Wesleyan Church
- **Calendar** semesters
- **Degrees** associate, bachelor's, and master's
- **Small-town** 230-acre campus
- **Endowment** $2.0 million
- **Coed,** 1,996 undergraduate students, 94% full-time, 63% women, 37% men
- **Minimally difficult** entrance level, 65% of applicants were admitted

Undergraduates 1,879 full-time, 117 part-time. Students come from 25 states and territories, 8 other countries, 13% are from out of state, 26% African American, 0.3% Asian American or Pacific Islander, 1% Hispanic American, 0.8% Native American, 0.6% international, 2% transferred in, 32% live on campus. *Retention:* 75% of 2001 full-time freshmen returned.

Freshmen *Admission:* 303 applied, 196 admitted, 103 enrolled. *Average high school GPA:* 3.38. *Test scores:* SAT verbal scores over 500: 61%; SAT math scores over 500: 53%; ACT scores over 18: 72%; SAT verbal scores over 600: 11%; SAT math scores over 600: 13%; ACT scores over 24: 19%; SAT math scores over 700: 1%.

Faculty *Total:* 149, 18% full-time, 38% with terminal degrees. *Student/faculty ratio:* 14:1.

Majors Accounting; biology; business administration; chemistry; computer/information sciences; divinity/ministry; early childhood education; education; elementary education; English; Greek (modern); history; mathematics; medical technology; music; music teacher education; physical education; psychology; recreation/leisure studies; religious studies; social sciences; special education.

Academic Programs *Special study options:* academic remediation for entering students, accelerated degree program, adult/continuing education programs, advanced placement credit, distance learning, double majors, honors programs, independent study, internships, off-campus study, part-time degree program, services for LD students, study abroad, summer session for credit. *ROTC:* Army (c), Air Force (c).

Library Rickman Library with 79,628 titles, 520 serial subscriptions, 3,100 audiovisual materials, an OPAC.

Computers on Campus 60 computers available on campus for general student use. A campuswide network can be accessed from student residence rooms and from off campus. Internet access, at least one staffed computer lab available.

Student Life *Housing:* on-campus residence required through senior year. *Options:* men-only, women-only. *Activities and Organizations:* drama/theater group, choral group, Christian Service Organization, Student Missions Fellowship, Rotaract, Minority Awareness Association, Council for Exceptional Children. *Campus security:* 24-hour emergency response devices, late night security patrols. *Student Services:* health clinic, personal/psychological counseling.

Athletics Member NAIA, NCCAA. *Intercollegiate sports:* baseball M(s), basketball M(s)/W(s), cross-country running M(s)/W(s), golf M(s), soccer M(s)/W(s), softball W(s), volleyball W(s). *Intramural sports:* archery M, badminton M/W, basketball M/W, football M/W, soccer M, softball M, table tennis M/W, tennis M/W, volleyball M/W, weight lifting M/W.

Standardized Tests *Required:* SAT I or ACT (for admission).

Costs (2001–02) *Comprehensive fee:* $17,280 includes full-time tuition ($12,400), mandatory fees ($400), and room and board ($4480). Full-time tuition and fees vary according to course load, degree level, and program. Part-time tuition: $420 per credit hour. Part-time tuition and fees vary according to course load and degree level. *Required fees:* $100 per term part-time. *Room and board:* Room and board charges vary according to board plan and housing facility. *Payment plan:* installment. *Waivers:* senior citizens and employees or children of employees.

Financial Aid Of all full-time matriculated undergraduates who enrolled in 2001, 995 applied for aid, 899 were judged to have need, 135 had their need fully met. 137 Federal Work-Study jobs (averaging $1000). In 2001, 139 non-need-based awards were made. *Average percent of need met:* 58%. *Average financial aid package:* $7482. *Average need-based loan:* $3393. *Average need-based gift aid:* $4928. *Average indebtedness upon graduation:* $5191.

Applying *Options:* early admission, deferred entrance. *Application fee:* $25. *Required:* high school transcript, minimum 2.0 GPA, 2 letters of recommendation, lifestyle statement. *Required for some:* interview. *Application deadlines:* 8/10 (freshmen), 8/10 (transfers). *Notification:* continuous (freshmen).

Admissions Contact Mrs. Joy Bryant, Director of Admissions, Southern Wesleyan University, 907 Wesleyan Drive, PO Box 1020, Central, SC 29630-1020. *Phone:* 864-644-5550. *Toll-free phone:* 800-289-1292. *Fax:* 864-644-5972. *E-mail:* admissions@swu.edu.

UNIVERSITY OF SOUTH CAROLINA

Columbia, South Carolina

- **State-supported** university, founded 1801, part of University of South Carolina System
- **Calendar** semesters
- **Degrees** associate, bachelor's, master's, doctoral, first professional, post-master's, and postbachelor's certificates
- **Urban** 315-acre campus
- **Endowment** $267.7 million
- **Coed,** 15,506 undergraduate students, 84% full-time, 54% women, 46% men
- **Moderately difficult** entrance level, 70% of applicants were admitted

Undergraduates 13,092 full-time, 2,414 part-time. Students come from 51 states and territories, 84 other countries, 13% are from out of state, 18% African American, 3% Asian American or Pacific Islander, 1% Hispanic American, 0.3% Native American, 2% international, 6% transferred in, 46% live on campus. *Retention:* 81% of 2001 full-time freshmen returned.

Freshmen *Admission:* 11,176 applied, 7,788 admitted, 3,287 enrolled. *Average high school GPA:* 3.59. *Test scores:* SAT verbal scores over 500: 73%; SAT math scores over 500: 78%; ACT scores over 18: 96%; SAT verbal scores over 600: 26%; SAT math scores over 600: 30%; ACT scores over 24: 40%; SAT verbal scores over 700: 5%; SAT math scores over 700: 6%; ACT scores over 30: 8%.

Faculty *Total:* 1,023, 98% full-time, 88% with terminal degrees. *Student/faculty ratio:* 14:1.

Majors Accounting; advertising; African-American studies; anthropology; art education; art history; biology; broadcast journalism; business administration; business economics; business marketing and marketing management; chemical engineering; chemistry; civil engineering; classics; computer engineering; computer/information sciences; criminal justice/law enforcement administration; economics; electrical engineering; English; European studies; exercise sciences; experimental psychology; finance; fine/studio arts; French; general retailing/wholesaling; geography; geology; geophysics/seismology; German; history; hospitality management; insurance/risk management; international relations; Italian; journalism; Latin American studies; liberal arts and sciences/liberal studies; management science; marine biology; mathematical statistics; mathematics; mechanical engineering; music; music teacher education; nursing; office management; philosophy; physical education; physics; political science; public relations; real estate; religious studies; sociology; Spanish; sport/fitness administration; theater arts/drama; women's studies.

Academic Programs *Special study options:* accelerated degree program, adult/continuing education programs, advanced placement credit, cooperative education, distance learning, double majors, English as a second language, external degree program, freshman honors college, honors programs, independent study, internships, part-time degree program, services for LD students, student-designed majors, study abroad, summer session for credit. *ROTC:* Army (b), Navy (b), Air Force (b).

Library Thomas Cooper Library plus 7 others with 3.2 million titles, 20,468 serial subscriptions, 44,089 audiovisual materials, an OPAC, a Web page.

Computers on Campus 11000 computers available on campus for general student use. A campuswide network can be accessed from student residence rooms and from off campus. Internet access, online (class) registration, at least one staffed computer lab available.

Student Life *Housing:* on-campus residence required for freshman year. *Options:* coed, men-only, women-only, disabled students. *Activities and Organizations:* drama/theater group, student-run newspaper, radio station, choral group, marching band, Fellowship of Christian Athletes, Association of African-American Students, Baptist Student Union, Garnet Circle/Student Alumni, national fraternities, national sororities. *Campus security:* 24-hour emergency response devices and patrols, student patrols, late-night transport/escort service, controlled dormitory access, Division of Law Enforcement and Safety. *Student Services:* health clinic, personal/psychological counseling, women's center.

Athletics Member NCAA. All Division I except football (Division I-A). *Intercollegiate sports:* baseball M(s), basketball M(s)/W(s), cross-country running W(s), equestrian sports W(s), golf M(s)/W(s), soccer M(s)/W(s), softball W(s), swimming M(s)/W(s), tennis M(s)/W(s), track and field M(s)/W(s), volleyball W(s). *Intramural sports:* badminton M/W, basketball M/W, bowling M/W, football M/W, golf M/W, racquetball M/W, soccer M/W, softball M/W, swimming M/W, table tennis M/W, tennis M/W, track and field M/W, volleyball M/W, weight lifting M(c)/W(c), wrestling M(c).

Standardized Tests *Required:* SAT I or ACT (for admission).

Costs (2001–02) *Tuition:* state resident $3964 full-time, $187 per credit hour part-time; nonresident $10,904 full-time, $496 per credit hour part-time. Full-time tuition and fees vary according to program and reciprocity agreements. Part-time tuition and fees vary according to course load. *Required fees:* $100 full-time, $4 per credit hour. *Room and board:* $4684; room only: $2680. Room and board charges vary according to board plan, housing facility, and location. *Payment plans:* installment, deferred payment. *Waivers:* senior citizens and employees or children of employees.

Financial Aid Of all full-time matriculated undergraduates who enrolled in 2001, 7445 applied for aid, 5725 were judged to have need, 1548 had their need fully met. 934 Federal Work-Study jobs (averaging $1243). 2700 State and other part-time jobs (averaging $3316). In 2001, 1456 non-need-based awards were made. *Average percent of need met:* 65%. *Average financial aid package:* $3200. *Average need-based loan:* $2300. *Average need-based gift aid:* $1100. *Average non-need based aid:* $2900. *Average indebtedness upon graduation:* $16,200.

Applying *Options:* electronic application. *Application fee:* $40. *Required:* high school transcript. *Application deadlines:* 5/15 (freshmen), 5/15 (transfers). *Notification:* continuous until 10/1 (freshmen).

Admissions Contact Ms. Terry L. Davis, Director of Undergraduate Admissions, University of South Carolina, Columbia, SC 29208. *Phone:* 803-777-7700. *Toll-free phone:* 800-868-5872. *Fax:* 803-777-0101. *E-mail:* admissions-ugrad@sc.edu.

UNIVERSITY OF SOUTH CAROLINA AIKEN

Aiken, South Carolina

- **State-supported** comprehensive, founded 1961, part of University of South Carolina System
- **Calendar** semesters
- **Degrees** associate, bachelor's, and master's
- **Suburban** 453-acre campus with easy access to Columbia
- **Endowment** $11.9 million
- **Coed,** 3,139 undergraduate students, 69% full-time, 66% women, 34% men
- **Minimally difficult** entrance level, 59% of applicants were admitted

Undergraduates 2,157 full-time, 982 part-time. Students come from 38 states and territories, 23 other countries, 14% are from out of state, 23% African American, 1% Asian American or Pacific Islander, 1% Hispanic American, 0.2%

University of South Carolina Aiken (continued)
Native American, 1% international, 7% transferred in, 12% live on campus. *Retention:* 70% of 2001 full-time freshmen returned.

Freshmen *Admission:* 1,207 applied, 708 admitted, 458 enrolled. *Average high school GPA:* 3.18. *Test scores:* SAT verbal scores over 500: 47%; SAT math scores over 500: 41%; ACT scores over 18: 79%; SAT verbal scores over 600: 10%; SAT math scores over 600: 9%; ACT scores over 24: 26%; SAT verbal scores over 700: 1%; SAT math scores over 700: 1%; ACT scores over 30: 3%.

Faculty *Total:* 222, 56% full-time. *Student/faculty ratio:* 16:1.

Majors Applied mathematics; biology; business administration; chemistry; communications; early childhood education; elementary education; English; exercise sciences; fine/studio arts; history; liberal arts and sciences/liberal studies; nursing; political science; psychology; secondary education; sociology.

Academic Programs *Special study options:* accelerated degree program, adult/continuing education programs, advanced placement credit, cooperative education, double majors, English as a second language, honors programs, independent study, internships, off-campus study, part-time degree program, services for LD students, student-designed majors, study abroad, summer session for credit.

Library Gregg-Graniteville Library with 138,077 titles, 853 serial subscriptions, an OPAC, a Web page.

Computers on Campus 350 computers available on campus for general student use. At least one staffed computer lab available.

Student Life *Housing Options:* coed. *Activities and Organizations:* drama/theater group, student-run newspaper, choral group, student government, Pacesetters, Student Alumni Ambassadors, African-American Student Alliance, Pacer Union Board, national fraternities, national sororities. *Campus security:* 24-hour emergency response devices and patrols, late-night transport/escort service. *Student Services:* health clinic, personal/psychological counseling.

Athletics Member NCAA. All Division II. *Intercollegiate sports:* baseball M(s), basketball M(s)/W(s), cross-country running M(s)/W(s), golf M(s), soccer M(s)/W(s), softball W(s), tennis M(s)/W(s), volleyball W(s). *Intramural sports:* basketball M/W, football M/W, softball M/W, table tennis M/W, tennis M/W, weight lifting M.

Standardized Tests *Required:* SAT I or ACT (for admission).

Costs (2001–02) *One-time required fee:* $50. *Tuition:* state resident $3638 full-time, $159 per semester hour part-time; nonresident $8164 full-time, $358 per semester hour part-time. Part-time tuition and fees vary according to course load. *Required fees:* $140 full-time, $5 per semester hour, $10 per term part-time. *Room and board:* $4050; room only: $2450. Room and board charges vary according to board plan. *Payment plan:* deferred payment. *Waivers:* senior citizens and employees or children of employees.

Applying *Options:* electronic application, early admission, deferred entrance. *Application fee:* $35. *Required:* high school transcript. *Recommended:* essay or personal statement, letters of recommendation, interview. *Application deadline:* 8/1 (freshmen), rolling (transfers). *Notification:* continuous (freshmen).

Admissions Contact Mr. Andrew Hendrix, Director of Admissions, University of South Carolina Aiken, 471 University Parkway, Aiken, SC 29801-6309. *Phone:* 803-648-6851 Ext. 3366. *Toll-free phone:* 888-WOW-USCA. *Fax:* 803-641-3727. *E-mail:* admit@sc.edu.

UNIVERSITY OF SOUTH CAROLINA SPARTANBURG
Spartanburg, South Carolina

- **State-supported** comprehensive, founded 1967, part of University of South Carolina System
- **Calendar** semesters
- **Degrees** associate, bachelor's, and master's
- **Urban** 298-acre campus with easy access to Charlotte
- **Endowment** $2.2 million
- **Coed,** 3,899 undergraduate students, 75% full-time, 64% women, 36% men
- **Moderately difficult** entrance level, 62% of applicants were admitted

Undergraduates 2,911 full-time, 988 part-time. Students come from 34 states and territories, 33 other countries, 5% are from out of state, 25% African American, 2% Asian American or Pacific Islander, 2% Hispanic American, 0.2% Native American, 2% international, 12% transferred in, 10% live on campus. *Retention:* 61% of 2001 full-time freshmen returned.

Freshmen *Admission:* 1,356 applied, 834 admitted, 616 enrolled. *Average high school GPA:* 3.24. *Test scores:* SAT verbal scores over 500: 42%; SAT math scores over 500: 37%; ACT scores over 18: 75%; SAT verbal scores over 600: 8%; SAT math scores over 600: 9%; ACT scores over 24: 17%; SAT verbal scores over 700: 1%; SAT math scores over 700: 1%.

Faculty *Total:* 268, 56% full-time, 43% with terminal degrees. *Student/faculty ratio:* 17:1.

Majors Biology; business administration; chemistry; communications; computer/information sciences; criminal justice/law enforcement administration; early childhood education; elementary education; English; French; history; interdisciplinary studies; mathematics; nursing; physical education; political science; psychology; secondary education; sociology; Spanish.

Academic Programs *Special study options:* academic remediation for entering students, accelerated degree program, adult/continuing education programs, advanced placement credit, cooperative education, distance learning, double majors, independent study, internships, off-campus study, part-time degree program, services for LD students, student-designed majors, study abroad, summer session for credit. *ROTC:* Army (c).

Library University of South Carolina Spartanburg Library with 156,558 titles, 3,151 serial subscriptions, 11,119 audiovisual materials, an OPAC, a Web page.

Computers on Campus 254 computers available on campus for general student use. A campuswide network can be accessed from student residence rooms and from off campus. Internet access, online (class) registration, at least one staffed computer lab available.

Student Life *Housing Options:* coed. *Activities and Organizations:* drama/theater group, student-run newspaper, choral group, African-American Association, Campus Activity Board, Student Nurses Association, Student Government Association, Association for the Education of Young Children, national fraternities, national sororities. *Campus security:* 24-hour emergency response devices and patrols, late-night transport/escort service, campus security cameras. *Student Services:* health clinic, personal/psychological counseling, women's center.

Athletics Member NCAA. All Division II. *Intercollegiate sports:* baseball M(s), basketball M(s)/W(s), cross-country running M(s)/W(s), soccer M(s)/W(s), softball W(s), tennis M(s)/W(s), volleyball W(s). *Intramural sports:* basketball M/W, football M/W, golf M/W, soccer M/W, softball M/W, table tennis M/W, tennis M/W, track and field M/W, volleyball M/W.

Standardized Tests *Required:* SAT I or ACT (for admission).

Costs (2001–02) *One-time required fee:* $50. *Tuition:* state resident $3844 full-time, $169 per hour part-time; nonresident $8736 full-time, $385 per hour part-time. *Required fees:* $170 full-time, $7 per hour. *Room and board:* $3360; room only: $2460.

Financial Aid Of all full-time matriculated undergraduates who enrolled in 2001, 1817 applied for aid, 1528 were judged to have need, 70 had their need fully met. 121 Federal Work-Study jobs (averaging $933). In 2001, 66 non-need-based awards were made. *Average percent of need met:* 57%. *Average financial aid package:* $5267. *Average need-based loan:* $3218. *Average need-based gift aid:* $2698. *Average non-need based aid:* $3459. *Average indebtedness upon graduation:* $15,460.

Applying *Options:* electronic application, deferred entrance. *Application fee:* $25. *Required:* high school transcript, minimum 2.0 GPA. *Notification:* continuous (freshmen).

Admissions Contact Ms. Donette Stewart, Director of Admissions, University of South Carolina Spartanburg, 800 University Way, Spartanburg, SC 29303. *Phone:* 864-503-5280. *Toll-free phone:* 800-277-8727. *Fax:* 864-503-5727. *E-mail:* dstawart@uscs.edu.

VOORHEES COLLEGE
Denmark, South Carolina

- **Independent Episcopal** 4-year, founded 1897
- **Calendar** semesters
- **Degree** bachelor's
- **Rural** 350-acre campus
- **Coed,** 756 undergraduate students
- **Minimally difficult** entrance level, 80% of applicants were admitted

Founded in 1897, Voorhees was the first historically black institution in South Carolina to achieve full accreditation by the Southern Association of Colleges and Schools. It is a small liberal arts college with a family-like atmosphere and a caring faculty, 70 percent of which hold doctorate degrees.

Undergraduates Students come from 18 states and territories, 3 other countries, 98% African American, 1% Hispanic American, 85% live on campus. *Retention:* 58% of 2001 full-time freshmen returned.

Freshmen *Admission:* 1,586 applied, 1,266 admitted. *Average high school GPA:* 2.5. *Test scores:* SAT verbal scores over 500: 15%; SAT math scores over 500: 11%; SAT math scores over 600: 2%.

Faculty *Total:* 49, 63% full-time. *Student/faculty ratio:* 17:1.

Majors Accounting; biology; business administration; chemistry; computer science; criminal justice/law enforcement administration; early childhood education; education; elementary education; English; exercise sciences; mathematics; physical education; political science; recreational therapy; sociology.

Academic Programs *Special study options:* academic remediation for entering students, adult/continuing education programs, advanced placement credit, cooperative education, honors programs, internships, part-time degree program, summer session for credit. *ROTC:* Army (c).

Library Wright-Potts Library with 86,261 titles, 408 serial subscriptions, an OPAC, a Web page.

Computers on Campus 150 computers available on campus for general student use. Internet access, at least one staffed computer lab available.

Student Life *Housing:* on-campus residence required through sophomore year. *Activities and Organizations:* drama/theater group, student-run newspaper, choral group, White Rose, Elizabeth Evelyn Wright Culture Club, Panhellenic Council, national fraternities, national sororities. *Campus security:* 24-hour emergency response devices and patrols, student patrols, late-night transport/escort service. *Student Services:* health clinic, personal/psychological counseling.

Athletics Member NAIA. *Intercollegiate sports:* baseball M, basketball M(s)/W(s), cross-country running M/W, softball W, track and field M(s)/W, volleyball W. *Intramural sports:* basketball M/W, swimming M/W, table tennis M/W, tennis M/W, volleyball M/W, weight lifting M/W.

Standardized Tests *Required:* SAT I or ACT (for admission).

Costs (2001–02) *Comprehensive fee:* $9976 includes full-time tuition ($6460) and room and board ($3516). Part-time tuition: $220 per credit hour. *Room and board:* College room only: $1464. *Payment plans:* installment, deferred payment. *Waivers:* employees or children of employees.

Financial Aid Of all full-time matriculated undergraduates who enrolled in 2001, 696 applied for aid, 675 were judged to have need, 18 had their need fully met. 225 Federal Work-Study jobs (averaging $1252). 3 State and other part-time jobs (averaging $1010). *Average percent of need met:* 51%. *Average financial aid package:* $7056. *Average need-based loan:* $2903. *Average need-based gift aid:* $4438. *Average indebtedness upon graduation:* $8939.

Applying *Options:* common application, electronic application, deferred entrance. *Application fee:* $25. *Required:* high school transcript, letters of recommendation. *Required for some:* essay or personal statement, interview. *Recommended:* minimum 2.0 GPA. *Application deadline:* rolling (freshmen), rolling (transfers).

Admissions Contact Carolyn White, Dean of Enrollment Management, Voorhees College, Massachusetts Hall, PO Box 678, Denmark, SC 29042. *Phone:* 800-446-6250. *Toll-free phone:* 800-446-6250. *Fax:* 803-793-1117. *E-mail:* elfphi@voorhees.edu.

WINTHROP UNIVERSITY
Rock Hill, South Carolina

- **State-supported** comprehensive, founded 1886, part of South Carolina Commission on Higher Education
- **Calendar** semesters
- **Degrees** bachelor's, master's, and postbachelor's certificates
- **Suburban** 418-acre campus with easy access to Charlotte
- **Endowment** $693,815
- **Coed,** 4,838 undergraduate students, 87% full-time, 69% women, 31% men
- **Moderately difficult** entrance level, 74% of applicants were admitted

Undergraduates 4,201 full-time, 637 part-time. Students come from 40 states and territories, 32 other countries, 12% are from out of state, 27% African American, 1% Asian American or Pacific Islander, 1% Hispanic American, 0.4% Native American, 2% international, 7% transferred in, 52% live on campus. *Retention:* 75% of 2001 full-time freshmen returned.

Freshmen *Admission:* 3,207 applied, 2,389 admitted, 946 enrolled. *Average high school GPA:* 3.51. *Test scores:* SAT verbal scores over 500: 64%; SAT math scores over 500: 65%; ACT scores over 18: 97%; SAT verbal scores over 600: 20%; SAT math scores over 600: 16%; ACT scores over 24: 31%; SAT verbal scores over 700: 3%; SAT math scores over 700: 2%; ACT scores over 30: 2%.

Faculty *Total:* 405, 63% full-time, 63% with terminal degrees. *Student/faculty ratio:* 15:1.

Majors Art; art history; biology; business administration; business education; chemistry; communication disorders; computer science; dance; early childhood education; elementary education; English; history; home economics education; mass communications; mathematics; medical technology; modern languages; music; music teacher education; nutrition science; philosophy; physical education; political science; psychology; religious studies; social work; sociology; special education; sport/fitness administration; technical/business writing; theater arts/drama.

Academic Programs *Special study options:* adult/continuing education programs, advanced placement credit, cooperative education, distance learning, double majors, honors programs, independent study, internships, off-campus study, part-time degree program, services for LD students, study abroad, summer session for credit.

Library Dacus Library with 638,454 titles, 2,706 serial subscriptions, 1,826 audiovisual materials, an OPAC, a Web page.

Computers on Campus 250 computers available on campus for general student use. A campuswide network can be accessed from student residence rooms and from off campus. Internet access, at least one staffed computer lab available.

Student Life *Housing Options:* coed, men-only, women-only. *Activities and Organizations:* drama/theater group, student-run newspaper, radio station, choral group, Ebonites, Greek organizations, Campus Ministries, student government association, Dinkins Student Union, national fraternities, national sororities. *Campus security:* 24-hour emergency response devices and patrols, late-night transport/escort service. *Student Services:* health clinic, personal/psychological counseling.

Athletics Member NCAA. All Division I. *Intercollegiate sports:* baseball M(s), basketball M(s)/W(s), cross-country running M(s)/W(s), golf M(s)/W(s), soccer M(s), softball W(s), tennis M(s)/W(s), track and field M(s)/W(s), volleyball W(s). *Intramural sports:* badminton M/W, basketball M/W, cross-country running M/W, football M/W, golf M/W, racquetball M/W, soccer M/W, softball M/W, swimming M/W, table tennis M/W, tennis M/W, volleyball M/W, water polo M/W, weight lifting M/W.

Standardized Tests *Required:* SAT I or ACT (for admission).

Costs (2001–02) *Tuition:* state resident $4668 full-time, $194 per semester hour part-time; nonresident $8756 full-time, $364 per semester hour part-time. *Required fees:* $20 full-time, $10 per term part-time. *Room and board:* $4418. Room and board charges vary according to board plan and housing facility. *Payment plan:* installment. *Waivers:* senior citizens and employees or children of employees.

Financial Aid Of all full-time matriculated undergraduates who enrolled in 2001, 2836 applied for aid, 2188 were judged to have need, 686 had their need fully met. 225 Federal Work-Study jobs (averaging $1200). In 2001, 642 non-need-based awards were made. *Average percent of need met:* 72%. *Average financial aid package:* $5639. *Average need-based loan:* $3472. *Average need-based gift aid:* $3194. *Average non-need based aid:* $3400. *Average indebtedness upon graduation:* $16,000.

Applying *Options:* deferred entrance. *Application fee:* $35. *Required:* high school transcript, 1 letter of recommendation. *Recommended:* essay or personal statement. *Application deadlines:* 6/1 (freshmen), 7/1 (transfers). *Notification:* continuous until 6/21 (freshmen).

Admissions Contact Ms. Deborah Barber, Director of Admissions, Winthrop University, Stewart House, Rock Hill, SC 29733. *Phone:* 803-323-2191. *Toll-free phone:* 800-763-0230. *Fax:* 803-323-2137. *E-mail:* admissions@winthrop.edu.

WOFFORD COLLEGE
Spartanburg, South Carolina

- **Independent** 4-year, founded 1854, affiliated with United Methodist Church
- **Calendar** 4-1-4
- **Degree** bachelor's
- **Urban** 140-acre campus with easy access to Charlotte
- **Endowment** $101.4 million
- **Coed,** 1,107 undergraduate students, 99% full-time, 48% women, 52% men
- **Very difficult** entrance level, 82% of applicants were admitted

Each year, a rising senior is named the Wofford Presidential International Scholar. He or she travels around the developing world, studying a specific issue of global importance, and shares the experience with the College community. Some scholars develop illustrated lectures, others have published journals, and others have reported back through an Internet link (http://www.wofford.edu).

Undergraduates 1,097 full-time, 10 part-time. Students come from 30 states and territories, 1 other country, 33% are from out of state, 9% African American, 2% Asian American or Pacific Islander, 0.5% Hispanic American, 0.2% Native American, 0.1% international, 1% transferred in, 88% live on campus. *Retention:* 90% of 2001 full-time freshmen returned.

Freshmen *Admission:* 1,209 applied, 991 admitted, 303 enrolled. *Average high school GPA:* 3.83. *Test scores:* SAT verbal scores over 500: 89%; SAT math scores over 500: 92%; ACT scores over 18: 100%; SAT verbal scores over 600: 46%; SAT math scores over 600: 52%; ACT scores over 24: 57%; SAT verbal scores over 700: 7%; SAT math scores over 700: 9%; ACT scores over 30: 8%.

Faculty *Total:* 109, 69% full-time, 72% with terminal degrees. *Student/faculty ratio:* 13:1.

Majors Accounting; art history; biology; business economics; chemistry; computer science; economics; English; finance; French; German; history; humanities;

Wofford College (continued)
international business; international relations; mathematics; philosophy; physics; political science; pre-dentistry; pre-law; pre-medicine; pre-veterinary studies; psychology; religious studies; sociology; Spanish.

Academic Programs *Special study options:* accelerated degree program, advanced placement credit, double majors, independent study, internships, off-campus study, part-time degree program, student-designed majors, study abroad, summer session for credit. *ROTC:* Army (b). *Unusual degree programs:* 3-2 engineering with Clemson University.

Library Sandor Teszler Library with 194,569 titles, 642 serial subscriptions, 2,717 audiovisual materials, an OPAC.

Computers on Campus 225 computers available on campus for general student use. A campuswide network can be accessed from student residence rooms and from off campus. Internet access, at least one staffed computer lab available.

Student Life *Housing:* on-campus residence required through senior year. *Options:* coed, men-only, women-only. *Activities and Organizations:* drama/theater group, student-run newspaper, choral group, performing arts groups, Twin Towers Student Volunteers, Fellowship of Christian Athletes, national fraternities, national sororities. *Campus security:* 24-hour emergency response devices and patrols, late-night transport/escort service, controlled dormitory access. *Student Services:* health clinic, personal/psychological counseling.

Athletics Member NCAA. All Division I except football (Division I-AA). *Intercollegiate sports:* baseball M(s), basketball M(s)/W(s), cross-country running M(s)/W(s), fencing M(c)/W(c), golf M(s)/W(s), soccer M(s)/W(s), tennis M(s)/W(s), track and field M/W(s), volleyball W(s). *Intramural sports:* basketball M/W, bowling M/W, football M/W, racquetball M/W, soccer M/W, softball M/W, tennis M/W, volleyball M/W, weight lifting M/W.

Standardized Tests *Required:* SAT I or ACT (for admission). *Recommended:* SAT II: Writing Test (for admission).

Costs (2001–02) *Comprehensive fee:* $23,995 includes full-time tuition ($17,760), mandatory fees ($755), and room and board ($5480). Part-time tuition: $660 per semester hour. *Payment plan:* installment. *Waivers:* employees or children of employees.

Financial Aid Of all full-time matriculated undergraduates who enrolled in 2001, 753 applied for aid, 577 were judged to have need, 237 had their need fully met. In 2001, 354 non-need-based awards were made. *Average percent of need met:* 84%. *Average financial aid package:* $13,717. *Average need-based loan:* $3586. *Average need-based gift aid:* $11,804. *Average non-need based aid:* $9030. *Average indebtedness upon graduation:* $15,302.

Applying *Options:* common application, electronic application, early admission, early action, deferred entrance. *Application fee:* $40. *Required:* essay or personal statement, high school transcript. *Recommended:* 2 letters of recommendation, interview. *Application deadline:* 2/1 (freshmen), rolling (transfers). *Notification:* 3/15 (freshmen), 12/1 (early action).

Admissions Contact Mr. Brand Stille, Director of Admissions, Wofford College, 429 North Church Street, Spartanburg, SC 29303-3663. *Phone:* 864-597-4130. *Fax:* 864-597-4147. *E-mail:* admissions@wofford.edu.

SOUTH DAKOTA

AUGUSTANA COLLEGE
Sioux Falls, South Dakota

- **Independent** comprehensive, founded 1860, affiliated with Evangelical Lutheran Church in America
- **Calendar** 4-1-4
- **Degrees** bachelor's and master's
- **Urban** 100-acre campus
- **Endowment** $27.2 million
- **Coed,** 1,774 undergraduate students, 93% full-time, 65% women, 35% men
- **Moderately difficult** entrance level, 85% of applicants were admitted

Undergraduates 1,653 full-time, 121 part-time. Students come from 28 states and territories, 9 other countries, 52% are from out of state, 0.7% African American, 0.5% Asian American or Pacific Islander, 0.3% Hispanic American, 0.3% Native American, 2% international, 5% transferred in, 68% live on campus. *Retention:* 76% of 2001 full-time freshmen returned.

Freshmen *Admission:* 1,389 applied, 1,176 admitted, 426 enrolled. *Average high school GPA:* 3.55. *Test scores:* SAT verbal scores over 500: 81%; SAT math scores over 500: 84%; ACT scores over 18: 97%; SAT verbal scores over 600: 39%; SAT math scores over 600: 48%; ACT scores over 24: 56%; SAT verbal scores over 700: 7%; SAT math scores over 700: 6%; ACT scores over 30: 9%.

Faculty *Total:* 170, 66% full-time, 64% with terminal degrees. *Student/faculty ratio:* 12:1.

Majors Accounting; art; art education; athletic training/sports medicine; biology; business administration; business communications; chemistry; computer science; economics; education (K-12); education of the hearing impaired; elementary education; engineering physics; English; exercise sciences; foreign languages/literatures; French; German; health services administration; history; international relations; journalism; liberal arts and sciences/liberal studies; management information systems/business data processing; mass communications; mathematics; medical technology; music; music teacher education; nursing; philosophy; physical education; physics; political science; pre-dentistry; pre-law; pre-medicine; pre-veterinary studies; psychology; religious studies; secondary education; social studies education; social work; sociology; Spanish; special education; speech-language pathology/audiology; speech/theater education; sport/fitness administration; theater arts/drama.

Academic Programs *Special study options:* academic remediation for entering students, accelerated degree program, adult/continuing education programs, advanced placement credit, cooperative education, double majors, honors programs, independent study, internships, off-campus study, part-time degree program, services for LD students, student-designed majors, study abroad, summer session for credit. *Unusual degree programs:* 3-2 engineering with Columbia University, Washington University in St. Louis, South Dakota State University, University of Minnesota; occupational therapy with Washington University in St. Louis.

Library Mikkelsen Library plus 1 other with 234,515 titles, 1,085 serial subscriptions, 6,147 audiovisual materials, an OPAC, a Web page.

Computers on Campus 360 computers available on campus for general student use. A campuswide network can be accessed from student residence rooms and from off campus. Internet access, at least one staffed computer lab available.

Student Life *Housing:* on-campus residence required through sophomore year. *Options:* coed. *Activities and Organizations:* drama/theater group, student-run newspaper, radio station, choral group, Community Service Day, Fellowship of Christian Athletes, Union Board of Governors, Student Association, hall councils. *Campus security:* 24-hour emergency response devices and patrols, late-night transport/escort service, controlled dormitory access. *Student Services:* health clinic, personal/psychological counseling, legal services.

Athletics Member NCAA. All Division II. *Intercollegiate sports:* baseball M, basketball M(s)/W(s), cross-country running M(s)/W(s), football M(s), golf M/W, soccer W(s), softball W(s), tennis M/W, track and field M(s)/W(s), volleyball W(s), wrestling M(s). *Intramural sports:* basketball M/W, bowling M/W, cross-country running M/W, football M, golf M, racquetball M/W, soccer M/W, swimming M/W, tennis M/W, volleyball M/W.

Standardized Tests *Required:* SAT I or ACT (for admission).

Costs (2001–02) *Comprehensive fee:* $19,938 includes full-time tuition ($15,280), mandatory fees ($180), and room and board ($4478). Part-time tuition and fees vary according to course load. No tuition increase for student's term of enrollment. *Required fees:* $200 per hour. *Room and board:* Room and board charges vary according to board plan and housing facility. *Payment plan:* installment. *Waivers:* adult students, senior citizens, and employees or children of employees.

Financial Aid Of all full-time matriculated undergraduates who enrolled in 2001, 1344 applied for aid, 1133 were judged to have need, 234 had their need fully met. 469 Federal Work-Study jobs (averaging $1382). In 2001, 497 non-need-based awards were made. *Average percent of need met:* 91%. *Average financial aid package:* $13,343. *Average need-based loan:* $4750. *Average need-based gift aid:* $9011. *Average non-need based aid:* $6200. *Average indebtedness upon graduation:* $17,255.

Applying *Options:* common application, early admission, deferred entrance. *Application fee:* $25. *Required:* high school transcript, minimum 2.5 GPA, 1 letter of recommendation, minimum ACT score of 20. *Required for some:* essay or personal statement. *Recommended:* interview. *Application deadline:* 8/1 (freshmen), rolling (transfers). *Notification:* continuous (freshmen).

Admissions Contact Robert Preloger, Vice President for Enrollment, Augustana College, 2001 South Summit Avenue, Sioux Falls, SD 57197. *Phone:* 605-274-5516 Ext. 5504. *Toll-free phone:* 800-727-2844 Ext. 5516 (in-state); 800-727-2844 (out-of-state). *Fax:* 605-274-5518. *E-mail:* info@inst.augie.edu.

BLACK HILLS STATE UNIVERSITY
Spearfish, South Dakota

- **State-supported** comprehensive, founded 1883, part of South Dakota University System
- **Calendar** semesters
- **Degrees** certificates, diplomas, associate, bachelor's, master's, post-master's, and postbachelor's certificates

- **Small-town** 123-acre campus
- **Endowment** $7.5 million
- **Coed,** 3,431 undergraduate students, 74% full-time, 63% women, 37% men
- **Minimally difficult** entrance level, 94% of applicants were admitted

BHSU is a coeducational, 4-year undergraduate institution with an enrollment of 4,068 students. Students looking for a small, but growing public university located in one of the most scenic parts of the United States should consider Black Hills State. BHSU's liberal arts philosophy and state-of-the-art technology provide the tools necessary for success.

Undergraduates 2,533 full-time, 898 part-time. Students come from 36 states and territories, 6 other countries, 19% are from out of state, 0.6% African American, 0.4% Asian American or Pacific Islander, 1% Hispanic American, 3% Native American, 0.3% international, 1% transferred in, 20% live on campus. *Retention:* 54% of 2001 full-time freshmen returned.

Freshmen *Admission:* 1,288 applied, 1,214 admitted, 626 enrolled. *Average high school GPA:* 3.06. *Test scores:* ACT scores over 18: 83%; ACT scores over 24: 20%; ACT scores over 30: 2%.

Faculty *Total:* 113. *Student/faculty ratio:* 24:1.

Majors Accounting; art; biology; business administration; business education; business marketing and marketing management; chemistry; computer science; drafting; early childhood education; elementary education; English; entrepreneurship; environmental science; general studies; graphic design/commercial art/illustration; health/physical education; health services administration; history; human resources management; human services; industrial arts education; industrial technology; mass communications; mathematics; middle school education; music; music (general performance); music (voice and choral/opera performance); Native American studies; physical sciences; political science; psychology; recreation/leisure studies; secretarial science; social sciences; sociology; Spanish; special education; speech/rhetorical studies; sport/fitness administration; travel/tourism management.

Academic Programs *Special study options:* academic remediation for entering students, accelerated degree program, advanced placement credit, cooperative education, distance learning, double majors, independent study, internships, off-campus study, part-time degree program, services for LD students, summer session for credit. *ROTC:* Army (b).

Library E. Y. Berry Library-Learning Center with 209,738 titles, 4,481 serial subscriptions, 23,901 audiovisual materials, an OPAC.

Computers on Campus 220 computers available on campus for general student use. A campuswide network can be accessed from student residence rooms and from off campus. Internet access available.

Student Life *Housing:* on-campus residence required through sophomore year. *Options:* coed, men-only, women-only, disabled students. *Activities and Organizations:* drama/theater group, student-run newspaper, radio station, choral group, Student Activities Committee, student government, national fraternities, national sororities. *Campus security:* 24-hour patrols, late-night transport/escort service, controlled dormitory access. *Student Services:* health clinic, personal/psychological counseling.

Athletics Member NAIA. *Intercollegiate sports:* basketball M(s)/W(s), cross-country running M(s)/W(s), football M(s), track and field M(s)/W(s), volleyball W(s). *Intramural sports:* archery M/W, badminton M/W, basketball M/W, bowling M/W, football M, golf M/W, racquetball M/W, skiing (cross-country) M/W, skiing (downhill) M/W, soccer M/W, softball M/W, tennis M/W, volleyball M/W, weight lifting M/W.

Standardized Tests *Required:* SAT I or ACT (for admission).

Costs (2001–02) *Tuition:* state resident $1997 full-time, $62 per credit part-time; nonresident $6352 full-time, $200 per credit part-time. Full-time tuition and fees vary according to course load and reciprocity agreements. Part-time tuition and fees vary according to course load and reciprocity agreements. *Required fees:* $1874 full-time, $59 per credit. *Room and board:* $3024; room only: $1624. Room and board charges vary according to board plan and housing facility. *Payment plan:* installment. *Waivers:* senior citizens and employees or children of employees.

Financial Aid Of all full-time matriculated undergraduates who enrolled in 2001, 267 Federal Work-Study jobs (averaging $1200). 644 State and other part-time jobs (averaging $970). *Average financial aid package:* $5117. *Average indebtedness upon graduation:* $18,444.

Applying *Options:* electronic application. *Application fee:* $15. *Required:* high school transcript, minimum 2.0 high school GPA in core curriculum. *Application deadline:* rolling (freshmen), rolling (transfers).

Admissions Contact Ms. Judy Berry, Assistant Director of Admissions, Black Hills State University, University Street Box 9502, Spearfish, SD 57799-9502. *Phone:* 605-642-6343. *Toll-free phone:* 800-255-2478. *E-mail:* jberry@mystic.bhsu.edu.

COLORADO TECHNICAL UNIVERSITY SIOUX FALLS CAMPUS

Sioux Falls, South Dakota

- **Proprietary** comprehensive, founded 1965, part of Colorado Technical University—Main Campus Colorado Springs, CO
- **Calendar** quarters
- **Degrees** certificates, associate, bachelor's, and master's
- **Coed,** 754 undergraduate students, 41% full-time, 55% women, 45% men
- **Minimally difficult** entrance level, 95% of applicants were admitted

Undergraduates 307 full-time, 447 part-time. Students come from 3 states and territories, 5% are from out of state, 2% African American, 0.9% Asian American or Pacific Islander, 0.5% Hispanic American, 1% Native American, 8% transferred in.

Freshmen *Admission:* 229 applied, 217 admitted, 117 enrolled.

Faculty *Total:* 61, 15% full-time, 13% with terminal degrees. *Student/faculty ratio:* 16:1.

Majors Accounting; business administration; business marketing and marketing management; computer science; criminal justice studies; finance; human resources management; information sciences/systems; management information systems/business data processing; marketing operations; medical assistant.

Academic Programs *Special study options:* accelerated degree program, adult/continuing education programs, cooperative education, distance learning, double majors, internships, part-time degree program, summer session for credit. *ROTC:* Army (c).

Library Resource Center with an OPAC, a Web page.

Computers on Campus 55 computers available on campus for general student use. A campuswide network can be accessed from off campus. Internet access, at least one staffed computer lab available.

Student Life *Housing:* college housing not available. *Activities and Organizations:* Phi Beta Lambda, AITP, CJ Honor Society.

Standardized Tests *Recommended:* ACT (for admission).

Costs (2002–03) *Tuition:* $8775 full-time, $195 per credit hour part-time. Full-time tuition and fees vary according to course load. Part-time tuition and fees vary according to course load. *Required fees:* $513 full-time, $50 per term part-time. *Payment plans:* installment, deferred payment. *Waivers:* employees or children of employees.

Applying *Options:* early admission, deferred entrance. *Application fee:* $25. *Required:* high school transcript, interview. *Application deadline:* rolling (freshmen), rolling (transfers). *Notification:* continuous (freshmen).

Admissions Contact Ms. Angela Haley, Admissions Advisor/Mentor, Colorado Technical University Sioux Falls Campus, 3901 West 59th Street, Sioux Falls, SD 57108. *Phone:* 605-361-0200 Ext. 113. *Fax:* 605-361-5954. *E-mail:* callen@sf.coloradotech.edu.

DAKOTA STATE UNIVERSITY

Madison, South Dakota

- **State-supported** comprehensive, founded 1881
- **Calendar** semesters
- **Degrees** certificates, associate, bachelor's, and master's
- **Rural** 40-acre campus with easy access to Sioux Falls
- **Endowment** $3.8 million
- **Coed,** 1,843 undergraduate students, 74% full-time, 49% women, 51% men
- **Minimally difficult** entrance level

Undergraduates 1,364 full-time, 479 part-time. Students come from 22 states and territories, 10 other countries, 16% are from out of state, 0.6% African American, 0.9% Asian American or Pacific Islander, 0.7% Hispanic American, 0.8% Native American, 1% international, 4% transferred in, 37% live on campus. *Retention:* 70% of 2001 full-time freshmen returned.

Freshmen *Admission:* 599 admitted, 364 enrolled. *Test scores:* ACT scores over 18: 89%; ACT scores over 24: 28%; ACT scores over 30: 2%.

Faculty *Total:* 100, 76% full-time, 53% with terminal degrees. *Student/faculty ratio:* 19:1.

Majors Accounting; art education; arts management; biology; business administration; business education; business marketing and marketing management; chemistry; computer graphics; computer programming; computer science; education; elementary education; English; exercise sciences; finance; information sciences/systems; liberal arts and sciences/liberal studies; mathematics; medical laboratory technician; medical records administration; music teacher education; physical education; physics; pre-dentistry; pre-law; pre-medicine; pre-veterinary

Dakota State University (continued)
studies; respiratory therapy; secondary education; secretarial science; special education; trade/industrial education; Web page, digital/multimedia and information resources design.

Academic Programs *Special study options:* academic remediation for entering students, adult/continuing education programs, advanced placement credit, cooperative education, distance learning, double majors, English as a second language, external degree program, honors programs, independent study, internships, off-campus study, part-time degree program, services for LD students, study abroad, summer session for credit. *ROTC:* Air Force (c).

Library Karl E. Mundt Library plus 1 other with 4.6 million titles, 7,456 serial subscriptions, 2,738 audiovisual materials, an OPAC, a Web page.

Computers on Campus 391 computers available on campus for general student use. A campuswide network can be accessed from student residence rooms and from off campus. Internet access, online (class) registration, at least one staffed computer lab available.

Student Life *Housing:* on-campus residence required through sophomore year. *Options:* coed, men-only, women-only, disabled students. *Activities and Organizations:* drama/theater group, student-run newspaper, choral group, marching band, Business Club, Band, Computer Club. *Campus security:* controlled dormitory access, night watchman. *Student Services:* health clinic, personal/psychological counseling.

Athletics Member NAIA. *Intercollegiate sports:* baseball M, basketball M(s)/W(s), cross-country running M(s)/W(s), football M(s), golf M/W, softball W, tennis M/W, track and field M(s)/W(s), volleyball W(s). *Intramural sports:* archery M/W, badminton M/W, basketball M/W, bowling M/W, softball M/W, tennis M/W, volleyball M/W, weight lifting M/W.

Standardized Tests *Required:* ACT (for admission).

Costs (2001–02) *Tuition:* state resident $4026 full-time, $126 per credit hour part-time; nonresident $8381 full-time, $262 per credit hour part-time. Full-time tuition and fees vary according to reciprocity agreements. Part-time tuition and fees vary according to reciprocity agreements. *Room and board:* $2924. *Payment plan:* deferred payment. *Waivers:* senior citizens and employees or children of employees.

Financial Aid Of all full-time matriculated undergraduates who enrolled in 2001, 1082 applied for aid, 860 were judged to have need. 172 Federal Work-Study jobs (averaging $1650). 194 State and other part-time jobs (averaging $1400). In 2001, 180 non-need-based awards were made. *Average financial aid package:* $4731. *Average non-need based aid:* $1824. *Average indebtedness upon graduation:* $16,588.

Applying *Options:* electronic application, early admission. *Application fee:* $20. *Required:* high school transcript, rank in upper two-thirds of high school class. *Application deadline:* rolling (freshmen), rolling (transfers). *Notification:* continuous (freshmen).

Admissions Contact Ms. Katy O'Hara, Admissions Secretary, Dakota State University, 820 North Washington, Madison, SD 57042-1799. *Phone:* 605-256-5139. *Toll-free phone:* 888-DSU-9988. *Fax:* 605-256-5316. *E-mail:* yourfuture@dsu.edu.

DAKOTA WESLEYAN UNIVERSITY
Mitchell, South Dakota

- **Independent United Methodist** 4-year, founded 1885
- **Calendar** semesters
- **Degrees** associate and bachelor's
- **Small-town** 40-acre campus
- **Endowment** $18.8 million
- **Coed,** 687 undergraduate students, 89% full-time, 60% women, 40% men
- **Moderately difficult** entrance level, 84% of applicants were admitted

Undergraduates 613 full-time, 74 part-time. Students come from 32 states and territories, 28% are from out of state, 5% African American, 0.7% Asian American or Pacific Islander, 2% Hispanic American, 4% Native American, 0.7% international, 12% transferred in, 40% live on campus. *Retention:* 63% of 2001 full-time freshmen returned.

Freshmen *Admission:* 438 applied, 369 admitted, 149 enrolled. *Average high school GPA:* 3.03. *Test scores:* ACT scores over 18: 71%; ACT scores over 24: 17%; ACT scores over 30: 1%.

Faculty *Total:* 61, 69% full-time, 38% with terminal degrees. *Student/faculty ratio:* 13:1.

Majors Accounting; adult/continuing education; art; art education; athletic training/sports medicine; behavioral sciences; biology; biology education; business administration; business education; business marketing and marketing management; computer software and media applications related; criminal justice/law enforcement administration; elementary education; English; English education; finance; history; history education; human services; liberal arts and sciences/liberal studies; mathematics; mathematics education; music teacher education; nursing; philosophy; physical education; psychology; religious studies; social studies education; sociology; special education; theater arts/drama; theology.

Academic Programs *Special study options:* academic remediation for entering students, adult/continuing education programs, double majors, English as a second language, honors programs, independent study, internships, part-time degree program, services for LD students, student-designed majors, study abroad, summer session for credit.

Library Layne Library with 61,000 titles, 404 serial subscriptions, 7,600 audiovisual materials, an OPAC, a Web page.

Computers on Campus 65 computers available on campus for general student use. A campuswide network can be accessed from student residence rooms and from off campus. Internet access, at least one staffed computer lab available.

Student Life *Housing:* on-campus residence required through sophomore year. *Options:* coed, men-only, women-only. *Activities and Organizations:* drama/theater group, student-run newspaper, choral group, DWU Future Teachers Organization, Student Nurses Association, Culture Club, Human Services Club, Student Ministry Council. *Campus security:* 24-hour emergency response devices, student patrols, late-night transport/escort service, controlled dormitory access, do not have campus patrol from 2am to 6am; will patrol during those hours if called to do so. *Student Services:* health clinic, personal/psychological counseling.

Athletics Member NAIA. *Intercollegiate sports:* baseball M(s), basketball M(s)/W(s), cross-country running M(s)/W(s), football M(s), golf M(s)/W(s), softball W(s), track and field M(s)/W(s), volleyball W(s), wrestling M(s). *Intramural sports:* basketball M/W, softball M/W, volleyball M/W, weight lifting M/W.

Standardized Tests *Required:* SAT I or ACT (for admission).

Costs (2002–03) *Comprehensive fee:* $16,525 includes full-time tuition ($12,035), mandatory fees ($400), and room and board ($4090). Full-time tuition and fees vary according to program. Part-time tuition: $251 per credit. Part-time tuition and fees vary according to course load and program. *Required fees:* $15 per credit. *Room and board:* College room only: $1768. Room and board charges vary according to board plan and student level. *Payment plan:* installment. *Waivers:* children of alumni, senior citizens, and employees or children of employees.

Financial Aid Of all full-time matriculated undergraduates who enrolled in 2001, 523 applied for aid, 445 were judged to have need, 89 had their need fully met. 265 Federal Work-Study jobs (averaging $1339). *Average percent of need met:* 74%. *Average financial aid package:* $11,430. *Average need-based gift aid:* $4210. *Average non-need based aid:* $2331. *Average indebtedness upon graduation:* $13,675.

Applying *Options:* electronic application, early admission. *Application fee:* $25. *Required:* high school transcript. *Recommended:* minimum 2.0 GPA. *Application deadlines:* 8/31 (freshmen), 8/31 (transfers). *Notification:* continuous (freshmen).

Admissions Contact Ms. Laura Miller, Director of Admissions Operations and Outreach Programming, Dakota Wesleyan University, 1200 West University Avenue, Mitchell, SD 57301-4398. *Phone:* 605-995-2650. *Toll-free phone:* 800-333-8506. *Fax:* 605-995-2699. *E-mail:* admissions@dwu.edu.

HURON UNIVERSITY
Huron, South Dakota

- **Proprietary** 4-year, founded 1883
- **Calendar** quarters
- **Degrees** associate and bachelor's
- **Small-town** 15-acre campus
- **Coed,** 528 undergraduate students, 84% full-time, 45% women, 55% men
- **Minimally difficult** entrance level, 39% of applicants were admitted

Undergraduates 442 full-time, 86 part-time. Students come from 27 states and territories, 38% are from out of state, 10% African American, 1% Asian American or Pacific Islander, 9% Hispanic American, 12% Native American, 15% transferred in, 50% live on campus. *Retention:* 41% of 2001 full-time freshmen returned.

Freshmen *Admission:* 622 applied, 242 admitted, 175 enrolled. *Average high school GPA:* 2.90. *Test scores:* ACT scores over 18: 60%; ACT scores over 24: 3%.

Faculty *Total:* 45, 64% full-time, 20% with terminal degrees. *Student/faculty ratio:* 15:1.

Majors Accounting; business administration; computer science; criminal justice/law enforcement administration; elementary education; finance; general studies; history education; information sciences/systems; nursing; physical education; science education; secondary education.

Academic Programs *Special study options:* accelerated degree program, adult/continuing education programs, advanced placement credit, cooperative education, double majors, freshman honors college, honors programs, independent study, part-time degree program, summer session for credit.

Library Ella McIntire Library with 50,000 titles, 240 serial subscriptions, 1,300 audiovisual materials.

Computers on Campus 75 computers available on campus for general student use. A campuswide network can be accessed from student residence rooms. Internet access, at least one staffed computer lab available.

Student Life *Housing:* on-campus residence required for freshman year. *Options:* coed, men-only, women-only. *Activities and Organizations:* drama/theater group, student-run newspaper, choral group, marching band, Phi Beta Lambda, International Club, Computer Science Club, student government, Fellowship of Christian Athletes. *Campus security:* 24-hour emergency response devices, student patrols, controlled dormitory access. *Student Services:* health clinic, personal/psychological counseling, legal services.

Athletics Member NAIA. *Intercollegiate sports:* baseball M(s), basketball M(s)/W(s), football M(s), soccer M(s)/W(s), softball W(s), track and field M(s)/W(s), volleyball W(s), wrestling M(s). *Intramural sports:* baseball M/W, basketball M/W, bowling M/W, football M, golf M/W, racquetball M/W, soccer M/W, softball W, table tennis M/W, tennis M/W, track and field M/W, volleyball M/W.

Standardized Tests *Recommended:* SAT I or ACT (for admission).

Costs (2002–03) *Comprehensive fee:* $11,650 includes full-time tuition ($8400), mandatory fees ($300), and room and board ($2950). Part-time tuition: $300 per credit.

Financial Aid Of all full-time matriculated undergraduates who enrolled in 2001, 448 applied for aid, 348 were judged to have need, 94 had their need fully met. 85 Federal Work-Study jobs (averaging $1068). In 2001, 76 non-need-based awards were made. *Average percent of need met:* 55%. *Average financial aid package:* $10,425. *Average need-based loan:* $2787. *Average need-based gift aid:* $2265. *Average non-need based aid:* $2175. *Average indebtedness upon graduation:* $22,547.

Applying *Options:* common application, early admission, deferred entrance. *Application fee:* $35. *Required:* high school transcript, minimum 2.0 GPA, applicants for athletic scholarship programs must meet approved ACT requirement. *Recommended:* interview. *Application deadline:* rolling (freshmen), rolling (transfers). *Notification:* continuous until 8/30 (freshmen).

Admissions Contact Mr. Tyler Fisher, Director of Admissions, Huron University, 333 9th Street Southwest, Huron, SD 57350. *Phone:* 605-352-8721 Ext. 41. *Toll-free phone:* 800-710-7159. *Fax:* 605-352-7421.

MOUNT MARTY COLLEGE
Yankton, South Dakota

- **Independent Roman Catholic** comprehensive, founded 1936
- **Calendar** semesters
- **Degrees** certificates, associate, bachelor's, and master's
- **Small-town** 80-acre campus
- **Endowment** $8.1 million
- **Coed,** 1,069 undergraduate students, 64% full-time, 67% women, 33% men
- **Moderately difficult** entrance level

Undergraduates 681 full-time, 388 part-time. Students come from 14 states and territories, 2 other countries, 22% are from out of state, 1% African American, 0.8% Asian American or Pacific Islander, 2% Hispanic American, 0.9% Native American, 0.2% international, 9% transferred in. *Retention:* 74% of 2001 full-time freshmen returned.

Freshmen *Admission:* 166 enrolled. *Average high school GPA:* 3.20. *Test scores:* ACT scores over 18: 77%; ACT scores over 24: 26%; ACT scores over 30: 2%.

Faculty *Total:* 104, 34% full-time, 21% with terminal degrees. *Student/faculty ratio:* 14:1.

Majors Accounting; athletic training/sports medicine; behavioral sciences; biology; business administration; chemistry; chemistry education; computer science; criminal justice studies; education; elementary education; English; English education; environmental science; general studies; history; history education; liberal arts and sciences/liberal studies; mathematics; mathematics education; medical radiologic technology; medical technology; music; music teacher education; nursing; nutrition science; physical education; recreation/leisure facilities management; religious studies; secondary education; special education.

Academic Programs *Special study options:* academic remediation for entering students, accelerated degree program, adult/continuing education programs, advanced placement credit, cooperative education, double majors, honors programs, independent study, internships, off-campus study, part-time degree program, services for LD students, student-designed majors, summer session for credit. *ROTC:* Army (c).

Library Mount Marty College Library with 78,684 titles, 446 serial subscriptions, 8,336 audiovisual materials, an OPAC.

Computers on Campus 53 computers available on campus for general student use. A campuswide network can be accessed from student residence rooms. Internet access, at least one staffed computer lab available.

Student Life *Housing:* on-campus residence required through senior year. *Options:* coed. *Activities and Organizations:* drama/theater group, student-run newspaper, radio station, choral group, Campus Ministry, Student Government Association, Nursing Club, Education Club, Theater Club or SIFE (Students in Free Enterprise). *Campus security:* 24-hour emergency response devices and patrols, controlled dormitory access. *Student Services:* health clinic, personal/psychological counseling.

Athletics Member NAIA. *Intercollegiate sports:* baseball M(s), basketball M(s)/W(s), cross-country running M(s)/W(s), golf M(s)/W(s), soccer M(s), softball W(s), track and field M(s)/W(s), volleyball W(s). *Intramural sports:* basketball M/W, soccer M, softball W, tennis M/W, volleyball M/W.

Standardized Tests *Required:* ACT (for admission).

Costs (2001–02) *Comprehensive fee:* $15,656 includes full-time tuition ($9942), mandatory fees ($1442), and room and board ($4272). Part-time tuition: $186 per credit. Part-time tuition and fees vary according to course load. No tuition increase for student's term of enrollment. *Payment plan:* installment. *Waivers:* employees or children of employees.

Financial Aid Of all full-time matriculated undergraduates who enrolled in 2001, 463 applied for aid, 397 were judged to have need, 101 had their need fully met. 222 Federal Work-Study jobs (averaging $1000). 57 State and other part-time jobs (averaging $1000). In 2001, 59 non-need-based awards were made. *Average percent of need met:* 83%. *Average financial aid package:* $11,637. *Average need-based loan:* $4419. *Average need-based gift aid:* $4765. *Average indebtedness upon graduation:* $17,407.

Applying *Options:* electronic application, early admission, deferred entrance. *Application fee:* $35. *Required:* high school transcript. *Required for some:* letters of recommendation. *Recommended:* interview. *Application deadline:* rolling (freshmen), rolling (transfers). *Notification:* continuous (freshmen).

Admissions Contact Office of Admissions, Mount Marty College, 1105 West 8th Street, Yankton, SD 57078. *Phone:* 605-668-1545. *Toll-free phone:* 800-658-4552. *Fax:* 605-668-1607. *E-mail:* mmcadmit@mtmc.edu.

NATIONAL AMERICAN UNIVERSITY
Rapid City, South Dakota

- **Proprietary** comprehensive, founded 1941, part of National College
- **Calendar** quarters
- **Degrees** certificates, diplomas, associate, bachelor's, and master's
- **Urban** 8-acre campus
- **Endowment** $30,000
- **Coed,** 852 undergraduate students, 66% full-time, 46% women, 54% men
- **Noncompetitive** entrance level

Undergraduates 562 full-time, 290 part-time. Students come from 25 states and territories, 16 other countries, 21% are from out of state, 21% live on campus.

Freshmen *Admission:* 284 enrolled.

Majors Accounting; athletic training/sports medicine; business administration; computer engineering technology; computer management; computer programming; equestrian studies; information sciences/systems; liberal arts and sciences/liberal studies; management information systems/business data processing; paralegal/legal assistant; sport/fitness administration; veterinary technology.

Academic Programs *Special study options:* academic remediation for entering students, accelerated degree program, adult/continuing education programs, advanced placement credit, cooperative education, distance learning, English as a second language, external degree program, independent study, internships, part-time degree program, services for LD students, summer session for credit. *ROTC:* Army (c).

Library Jefferson Library with 31,018 titles, 268 serial subscriptions, a Web page.

Computers on Campus 50 computers available on campus for general student use. Internet access, at least one staffed computer lab available.

Student Life *Housing:* on-campus residence required through sophomore year. *Options:* coed. *Activities and Organizations:* Student Senate, Phi Beta Lambda, Dormitory Council, Student Association of Legal Assistants, President's Advisory Council. *Campus security:* part-time security personnel. *Student Services:* personal/psychological counseling.

National American University (continued)

Athletics Member NAIA. *Intercollegiate sports:* baseball M, equestrian sports M(s)/W(s), soccer M(s)/W, volleyball W(s). *Intramural sports:* basketball M/W, bowling M/W, skiing (cross-country) M/W, skiing (downhill) M(c)/W(c), softball M/W, volleyball M/W.

Standardized Tests *Recommended:* ACT (for admission).

Costs (2002–03) *One-time required fee:* $50. *Comprehensive fee:* $13,740 includes full-time tuition ($9840), mandatory fees ($315), and room and board ($3585). *Room and board:* College room only: $1605. Room and board charges vary according to board plan. *Payment plan:* installment. *Waivers:* employees or children of employees.

Applying *Options:* common application, electronic application, early admission, deferred entrance. *Application fee:* $25. *Required:* high school transcript. *Recommended:* interview. *Application deadline:* rolling (freshmen), rolling (transfers). *Notification:* continuous (freshmen).

Admissions Contact Mr. Tom Shea, Vice President of Enrollment Management, National American University, 321 Kansas City Street, Rapid City, SD 57701. *Phone:* 605-394-4902. *Toll-free phone:* 800-843-8892. *Fax:* 605-394-4871. *E-mail:* apply@server1.natcol-rcy.edu.

NATIONAL AMERICAN UNIVERSITY-SIOUX FALLS BRANCH

Sioux Falls, South Dakota

- **Proprietary** 4-year, founded 1941, part of National College
- **Calendar** quarters
- **Degrees** certificates, diplomas, associate, and bachelor's
- **Urban** campus
- **Coed,** 350 undergraduate students
- **Noncompetitive** entrance level, 100% of applicants were admitted

Undergraduates Students come from 5 states and territories, 6 other countries, 0.6% African American, 0.6% Native American. *Retention:* 70% of 2001 full-time freshmen returned.

Freshmen *Admission:* 9 applied, 9 admitted.

Faculty *Total:* 35.

Majors Accounting; business administration; computer programming; hotel and restaurant management; information sciences/systems; management information systems/business data processing; medical assistant; paralegal/legal assistant; travel/tourism management.

Academic Programs *Special study options:* academic remediation for entering students, accelerated degree program, adult/continuing education programs, advanced placement credit, cooperative education, English as a second language, internships, part-time degree program, summer session for credit.

Library 1,580 titles, 57 serial subscriptions, a Web page.

Computers on Campus 30 computers available on campus for general student use. Internet access, at least one staffed computer lab available.

Student Life *Housing:* college housing not available. *Campus security:* 24-hour emergency response devices.

Costs (2001–02) *Tuition:* $8500 full-time, $195 per credit part-time. *Required fees:* $300 full-time, $75 per term part-time. *Payment plan:* installment. *Waivers:* employees or children of employees.

Applying *Options:* common application, electronic application, deferred entrance. *Application fee:* $25. *Required:* high school transcript, interview. *Application deadline:* rolling (freshmen), rolling (transfers). *Notification:* continuous (freshmen).

Admissions Contact Ms. Lisa Houtsma, Director of Admissions, National American University-Sioux Falls Branch, 2801 South Kiwanis Avenue, Suite 100, Sioux Falls, SD 57105. *Phone:* 605-334-5430. *E-mail:* lhautsma@national.edu.

NORTHERN STATE UNIVERSITY

Aberdeen, South Dakota

- **State-supported** comprehensive, founded 1901, part of South Dakota Board of Regents
- **Calendar** semesters
- **Degrees** certificates, diplomas, associate, bachelor's, master's, and postbachelor's certificates
- **Small-town** 52-acre campus
- **Endowment** $8.4 million
- **Coed,** 2,649 undergraduate students, 64% full-time, 58% women, 42% men
- **Minimally difficult** entrance level, 92% of applicants were admitted

Northern State University offers the personalized academic atmosphere of a private college at a public school price. Northern has 38 nationally accredited majors in business, education, fine arts, and arts and sciences. Current technology, with superior access, numerous social opportunities, and an almost perfect placement rate are some of the benefits that Northern's 3,200 students enjoy. Telephone: 800-NSU-5330 (toll-free).

Undergraduates 1,685 full-time, 964 part-time. Students come from 29 states and territories, 10 other countries, 13% are from out of state, 5% transferred in. *Retention:* 65% of 2001 full-time freshmen returned.

Freshmen *Admission:* 919 applied, 846 admitted, 443 enrolled. *Average high school GPA:* 3.28. *Test scores:* ACT scores over 18: 83%; ACT scores over 24: 27%; ACT scores over 30: 2%.

Faculty *Total:* 109, 100% full-time, 76% with terminal degrees. *Student/faculty ratio:* 21:1.

Majors Accounting; art; art education; biological/physical sciences; biology; business administration; business economics; business education; business marketing and marketing management; chemistry; community services; data processing technology; drafting; economics; education; electrical/electronic engineering technology; elementary education; English; environmental science; finance; French; German; graphic design/commercial art/illustration; health education; history; industrial arts; international business; law enforcement/police science; liberal arts and sciences/liberal studies; management information systems/business data processing; mathematics; medical laboratory technician; medical technology; music; music teacher education; music (voice and choral/opera performance); physical education; political science; pre-dentistry; pre-engineering; pre-law; pre-medicine; psychology; public administration; secondary education; secretarial science; social work; sociology; Spanish; special education; speech-language pathology/audiology; speech/rhetorical studies; theater arts/drama.

Academic Programs *Special study options:* academic remediation for entering students, accelerated degree program, adult/continuing education programs, advanced placement credit, cooperative education, distance learning, English as a second language, honors programs, internships, off-campus study, part-time degree program, services for LD students, student-designed majors, study abroad, summer session for credit.

Library Beulah Williams Library with 187,961 titles, 1,084 serial subscriptions, an OPAC, a Web page.

Computers on Campus 800 computers available on campus for general student use. A campuswide network can be accessed from student residence rooms and from off campus. Internet access, online (class) registration, at least one staffed computer lab available.

Student Life *Housing:* on-campus residence required through sophomore year. *Options:* coed. *Activities and Organizations:* drama/theater group, student-run newspaper, choral group, marching band, Student Ambassadors, Choices, Honor Society, Native American Student Association. *Campus security:* 24-hour emergency response devices, controlled dormitory access, evening patrols. *Student Services:* health clinic, personal/psychological counseling.

Athletics Member NCAA. All Division II. *Intercollegiate sports:* baseball M, basketball M(s)/W(s), cross-country running M(s)/W(s), football M(s), golf M/W(s), soccer W(s), softball W(s), tennis M/W(s), track and field M(s)/W(s), volleyball W(s), wrestling M(s). *Intramural sports:* archery M/W, badminton M/W, basketball M/W, cross-country running M/W, football M, golf M/W, ice hockey M(c), racquetball M/W, softball M/W, swimming M/W, table tennis M/W, tennis M/W, track and field M/W, volleyball M/W, weight lifting M/W, wrestling M.

Standardized Tests *Required:* SAT I or ACT (for admission).

Costs (2001–02) *Tuition:* state resident $1872 full-time, $62 per credit hour part-time; nonresident $5955 full-time, $199 per credit hour part-time. Full-time tuition and fees vary according to class time, course load, and reciprocity agreements. Part-time tuition and fees vary according to class time, course load, and reciprocity agreements. *Required fees:* $1667 full-time, $56 per credit hour. *Room and board:* $2740; room only: $1398. Room and board charges vary according to board plan. *Payment plan:* installment.

Applying *Options:* common application, early admission, deferred entrance. *Application fee:* $15. *Required:* high school transcript, minimum X GPA. *Required for some:* letters of recommendation. *Application deadlines:* 9/1 (freshmen), 9/1 (transfers). *Notification:* continuous (freshmen).

Admissions Contact Mr. Mike Mutzinger, Director of Admissions, Northern State University, 1200 South Jay Street, Aberdeen, SD 57401. *Phone:* 605-626-2544. *Toll-free phone:* 800-678-5330. *Fax:* 605-626-2587. *E-mail:* admissions1@northern.edu.

OGLALA LAKOTA COLLEGE
Kyle, South Dakota

Admissions Contact Miss Billi K. Hornbeck, Registrar, Oglala Lakota College, 490 Piya Wiconi Road, Kyle, SD 57752-0490. *Phone:* 605-455-2321 Ext. 236.

PRESENTATION COLLEGE
Aberdeen, South Dakota

- **Independent Roman Catholic** 4-year, founded 1951
- **Calendar** semesters
- **Degrees** certificates, associate, and bachelor's
- **Small-town** 100-acre campus
- **Coed,** 615 undergraduate students, 61% full-time, 85% women, 15% men
- **Noncompetitive** entrance level, 100% of applicants were admitted

Undergraduates Students come from 4 states and territories, 17% are from out of state, 2% African American, 0.7% Hispanic American, 7% Native American, 15% live on campus.

Freshmen *Admission:* 228 applied, 228 admitted. *Average high school GPA:* 2.88.

Faculty *Total:* 73, 44% full-time, 10% with terminal degrees. *Student/faculty ratio:* 12:1.

Majors Accounting; biology; business administration; English; health services administration; hotel and restaurant management; legal administrative assistant; liberal arts and sciences/liberal studies; mass communications; medical administrative assistant; medical assistant; medical laboratory technician; medical radiologic technology; medical records administration; nursing; operating room technician; religious studies; secretarial science; social work.

Academic Programs *Special study options:* academic remediation for entering students, accelerated degree program, adult/continuing education programs, advanced placement credit, cooperative education, distance learning, double majors, external degree program, internships, part-time degree program, summer session for credit.

Library Presentation College Library plus 1 other with 40,000 titles, 430 serial subscriptions, 2,900 audiovisual materials, an OPAC.

Computers on Campus 30 computers available on campus for general student use. A campuswide network can be accessed from student residence rooms. Internet access, at least one staffed computer lab available.

Student Life *Housing:* on-campus residence required for freshman year. *Options:* coed. *Activities and Organizations:* drama/theater group, choral group, Wellness, National Student Nursing Association, Social Work Organization, Theatre Production. *Campus security:* 24-hour emergency response devices and patrols, late-night transport/escort service, controlled dormitory access. *Student Services:* personal/psychological counseling.

Athletics Member NAIA, NSCAA. *Intercollegiate sports:* basketball M/W, volleyball W. *Intramural sports:* bowling M/W, softball M/W, volleyball M/W.

Standardized Tests *Required for some:* ACT (for admission). *Recommended:* ACT (for admission).

Costs (2001–02) *Comprehensive fee:* $14,114 includes full-time tuition ($8508), mandatory fees ($250), and room and board ($5356). Full-time tuition and fees vary according to course load, location, and program. Part-time tuition and fees vary according to course load, location, and program. *Room and board:* College room only: $3811. Room and board charges vary according to board plan, housing facility, and student level. *Payment plan:* installment. *Waivers:* senior citizens and employees or children of employees.

Financial Aid Of all full-time matriculated undergraduates who enrolled in 2001, 366 applied for aid, 366 were judged to have need, 240 had their need fully met. 43 Federal Work-Study jobs (averaging $1500). 22 State and other part-time jobs (averaging $1500). *Average percent of need met:* 98%. *Average financial aid package:* $7706. *Average need-based loan:* $3042. *Average need-based gift aid:* $4599. *Average indebtedness upon graduation:* $21,349.

Applying *Options:* electronic application. *Application fee:* $20. *Required:* high school transcript. *Required for some:* minimum 2.0 GPA. *Application deadline:* rolling (freshmen), rolling (transfers).

Admissions Contact Mr. Joddy Meidinger, Director of Admissions, Presentation College, 1500 North Main Street, Aberdeen, SC 57401. *Phone:* 605-229-8493 Ext. 492. *Toll-free phone:* 800-437-6060. *E-mail:* admit@presentation.edu.

SINTE GLESKA UNIVERSITY
Rosebud, South Dakota

- **Independent** comprehensive, founded 1970
- **Calendar** semesters
- **Degrees** certificates, associate, bachelor's, and master's
- **Rural** 52-acre campus
- **Coed,** 1,020 undergraduate students
- **Noncompetitive** entrance level, 100% of applicants were admitted

Freshmen *Admission:* 168 applied, 168 admitted.

Majors Accounting; art; business administration; business education; criminal justice/law enforcement administration; data processing technology; early childhood education; education; elementary education; human services; liberal arts and sciences/liberal studies; Native American studies; natural resources management; trade/industrial education.

Academic Programs *Special study options:* academic remediation for entering students, adult/continuing education programs, distance learning, double majors, honors programs, internships, off-campus study, part-time degree program, summer session for credit.

Library Sinte Gleska University Library with 25,000 titles, 80 serial subscriptions, an OPAC.

Computers on Campus 35 computers available on campus for general student use. Internet access, at least one staffed computer lab available.

Student Life *Housing:* college housing not available. *Activities and Organizations:* Student Association, Lakota Club. *Campus security:* late-night transport/escort service. *Student Services:* personal/psychological counseling, women's center.

Athletics *Intramural sports:* basketball M/W, cross-country running M/W, volleyball M/W, weight lifting M/W.

Costs (2001–02) *Tuition:* $2448 full-time, $68 per credit part-time. *Required fees:* $138 full-time, $3 per credit, $45 per term part-time. *Payment plan:* installment. *Waivers:* employees or children of employees.

Applying *Required:* high school transcript. *Application deadlines:* 8/20 (freshmen), 8/20 (transfers). *Notification:* continuous until 8/30 (freshmen).

Admissions Contact Mr. Jack Herman, Registrar and Director of Admissions, Sinte Gleska University, PO Box 490, Rosebud, SD 57570-0490. *Phone:* 605-747-2263 Ext. 224. *Fax:* 605-747-2098.

SOUTH DAKOTA SCHOOL OF MINES AND TECHNOLOGY
Rapid City, South Dakota

- **State-supported** university, founded 1885
- **Calendar** semesters
- **Degrees** bachelor's, master's, and doctoral
- **Suburban** 120-acre campus
- **Endowment** $19.2 million
- **Coed,** 2,075 undergraduate students, 80% full-time, 32% women, 68% men
- **Moderately difficult** entrance level, 93% of applicants were admitted

Undergraduates 1,664 full-time, 411 part-time. Students come from 31 states and territories, 10 other countries, 25% are from out of state, 0.5% African American, 0.5% Asian American or Pacific Islander, 0.9% Hispanic American, 2% Native American, 2% international, 6% transferred in, 28% live on campus.

Freshmen *Admission:* 843 applied, 786 admitted, 422 enrolled. *Average high school GPA:* 3.37. *Test scores:* ACT scores over 18: 96%; ACT scores over 24: 54%; ACT scores over 30: 9%.

Faculty *Total:* 130, 79% full-time, 75% with terminal degrees. *Student/faculty ratio:* 18:1.

Majors Chemical engineering; chemistry; civil engineering; computer engineering; computer science; electrical engineering; environmental engineering; general studies; geological engineering; geology; industrial/manufacturing engineering; interdisciplinary studies; mathematics; mechanical engineering; metallurgical engineering; mining/mineral engineering; physics.

Academic Programs *Special study options:* academic remediation for entering students, adult/continuing education programs, advanced placement credit, cooperative education, distance learning, double majors, English as a second language, independent study, internships, part-time degree program, services for LD students, study abroad, summer session for credit. *ROTC:* Army (b).

Library Devereaux Library with 246,438 titles, 496 serial subscriptions, 2,209 audiovisual materials, an OPAC, a Web page.

South Dakota School of Mines and Technology (continued)

Computers on Campus 205 computers available on campus for general student use. A campuswide network can be accessed from student residence rooms and from off campus. Internet access, online (class) registration, at least one staffed computer lab available.

Student Life *Housing:* on-campus residence required through sophomore year. *Options:* coed, men-only, women-only. *Activities and Organizations:* drama/theater group, student-run newspaper, radio station, choral group, TONITE (Techs Outrageous New Initiative for Total Entertainment), SADD (Students Against Drunk Driving), ASCE (American Society of Civil Engineers), ASME (American Society of Mechanical Engineers), ski club, national fraternities, national sororities. *Campus security:* 24-hour emergency response devices and patrols, student patrols, late-night transport/escort service, controlled dormitory access. *Student Services:* health clinic, personal/psychological counseling.

Athletics Member NAIA. *Intercollegiate sports:* basketball M(s)/W(s), cross-country running M(s)/W(s), football M(s), golf M/W, tennis M, track and field M(s)/W(s), volleyball W(s). *Intramural sports:* basketball M/W, bowling M/W, football M/W, racquetball M/W, skiing (cross-country) M/W, soccer M/W, softball M/W, squash M/W, swimming M/W, tennis M/W, track and field M/W, volleyball M/W, weight lifting M/W.

Standardized Tests *Required:* SAT I or ACT (for admission). *Required for some:* ACT (for placement).

Costs (2001–02) *Tuition:* state resident $1997 full-time, $62 per semester hour part-time; nonresident $6352 full-time, $199 per semester hour part-time. Full-time tuition and fees vary according to course load, program, and reciprocity agreements. Part-time tuition and fees vary according to course load, program, and reciprocity agreements. *Required fees:* $1852 full-time, $58 per semester hour. *Room and board:* $3370; room only: $1538. Room and board charges vary according to board plan and housing facility. *Payment plan:* installment. *Waivers:* senior citizens.

Financial Aid Of all full-time matriculated undergraduates who enrolled in 2001, 1410 applied for aid, 1188 were judged to have need, 337 had their need fully met. 173 Federal Work-Study jobs (averaging $1300). In 2001, 144 non-need-based awards were made. *Average percent of need met:* 74%. *Average financial aid package:* $5181. *Average need-based loan:* $4613. *Average need-based gift aid:* $954. *Average non-need based aid:* $2362.

Applying *Options:* electronic application. *Application fee:* $20. *Required:* high school transcript. *Recommended:* minimum 2.6 GPA. *Application deadline:* rolling (freshmen), rolling (transfers). *Notification:* continuous (freshmen).

Admissions Contact Leonard C. Colombe, Director of Admissions-Acting, South Dakota School of Mines and Technology, 501 East Saint Joseph, Rapid City, SD 57701-3995. *Phone:* 605-394-2414 Ext. 1266. *Toll-free phone:* 800-544-8162 Ext. 2414. *Fax:* 605-394-1268. *E-mail:* admissions@sdsmt.edu.

SOUTH DAKOTA STATE UNIVERSITY

Brookings, South Dakota

- **State-supported** university, founded 1881
- **Calendar** semesters
- **Degrees** associate, bachelor's, master's, doctoral, and first professional
- **Small-town** 260-acre campus
- **Endowment** $41.3 million
- **Coed,** 7,793 undergraduate students, 82% full-time, 52% women, 48% men
- **Moderately difficult** entrance level, 94% of applicants were admitted

SDSU is a 4-year, comprehensive university ranked by *U.S. News & World Report* as the most efficient university in the Midwest and a best-value university. SDSU offers the largest selection of academic programs within the state. Majors are available in agriculture and biological sciences, arts and science, education, engineering, family and consumer sciences, nursing, and pharmacy.

Undergraduates 6,357 full-time, 1,436 part-time. Students come from 39 states and territories, 19 other countries, 26% are from out of state, 0.4% African American, 0.8% Asian American or Pacific Islander, 0.4% Hispanic American, 1% Native American, 0.7% international, 8% transferred in, 32% live on campus.

Freshmen *Admission:* 3,004 applied, 2,836 admitted, 2,166 enrolled. *Average high school GPA:* 3.26. *Test scores:* ACT scores over 18: 86%; ACT scores over 24: 29%.

Faculty *Total:* 517, 97% full-time. *Student/faculty ratio:* 16:1.

Majors Agribusiness; agricultural economics; agricultural education; agricultural engineering; agricultural mechanization; agricultural sciences; agronomy/crop science; animal sciences; art; art education; athletic training/sports medicine; biochemistry; biology; chemistry; child care/development; civil engineering; computer education; computer graphics; computer/information sciences; construction technology; consumer services; dairy science; dietetics; early childhood education; economics; education; electrical/electronic engineering technology; electrical engineering; engineering physics; English; environmental engineering; fashion merchandising; fish/game management; food sciences; French; geography; German; health/physical education; history; home economics education; horticulture services; hotel and restaurant management; individual/family development; industrial technology; information sciences/systems; interior design; journalism; landscaping management; mass communications; mathematics; mechanical engineering; medical technology; microbiology/bacteriology; music; music business management/merchandising; music teacher education; nursing; nutrition science; pharmacy; physical education; physics; political science; pre-dentistry; pre-law; pre-medicine; pre-veterinary studies; psychology; range management; recreation/leisure facilities management; recreation/leisure studies; secondary education; sociology; Spanish; speech/rhetorical studies; theater arts/drama; visual/performing arts; wildlife management.

Academic Programs *Special study options:* academic remediation for entering students, accelerated degree program, adult/continuing education programs, advanced placement credit, cooperative education, distance learning, double majors, English as a second language, freshman honors college, honors programs, independent study, internships, off-campus study, part-time degree program, services for LD students, study abroad, summer session for credit. *ROTC:* Army (b), Air Force (b).

Library H. M. Briggs Library with 555,523 titles, 6,023 serial subscriptions, 2,504 audiovisual materials, an OPAC, a Web page.

Computers on Campus 278 computers available on campus for general student use. A campuswide network can be accessed from student residence rooms and from off campus. Internet access, at least one staffed computer lab available.

Student Life *Housing:* on-campus residence required through sophomore year. *Options:* coed. *Activities and Organizations:* drama/theater group, student-run newspaper, radio station, choral group, marching band, Student Association, University Programming Council, Block and Bridle club, national fraternities, national sororities. *Campus security:* 24-hour emergency response devices and patrols, student patrols, late-night transport/escort service. *Student Services:* health clinic, personal/psychological counseling, women's center, legal services.

Athletics Member NCAA. All Division II. *Intercollegiate sports:* baseball M(s), basketball M(s)/W(s), cross-country running M(s)/W(s), football M(s), golf M/W, soccer W(s), softball W(s), swimming M(s)/W(s), tennis M/W, track and field M(s)/W(s), volleyball W(s), wrestling M(s). *Intramural sports:* archery M(c)/W(c), badminton M/W, baseball M, basketball M/W, fencing M(c)/W(c), football M/W, golf M/W, ice hockey M(c)/W, racquetball M/W, riflery M(c)/W(c), rugby M(c)/W(c), soccer M(c), softball M/W, swimming M/W, table tennis M/W, tennis M/W, track and field M/W, volleyball M/W, water polo M(c)/W(c), weight lifting M(c)/W(c), wrestling M.

Standardized Tests *Required:* ACT (for admission).

Costs (2001–02) *Tuition:* state resident $1996 full-time, $62 per credit part-time; nonresident $6352 full-time, $199 per credit part-time. Full-time tuition and fees vary according to course load and program. Part-time tuition and fees vary according to course load and program. *Required fees:* $1812 full-time, $58 per credit. *Room and board:* $3040; room only: $1478. Room and board charges vary according to board plan and housing facility. *Payment plans:* installment, deferred payment. *Waivers:* senior citizens and employees or children of employees.

Financial Aid Of all full-time matriculated undergraduates who enrolled in 2001, 5401 applied for aid, 4890 were judged to have need, 3816 had their need fully met. 514 Federal Work-Study jobs (averaging $1180). 2016 State and other part-time jobs (averaging $1258). In 2001, 536 non-need-based awards were made. *Average percent of need met:* 84%. *Average financial aid package:* $6582. *Average need-based loan:* $4074. *Average need-based gift aid:* $2820. *Average non-need based aid:* $680. *Average indebtedness upon graduation:* $16,193.

Applying *Options:* electronic application, deferred entrance. *Application fee:* $20. *Required:* high school transcript, minimum 2.6 GPA, minimum ACT score of 18. *Application deadline:* rolling (freshmen), rolling (transfers).

Admissions Contact Ms. Michelle Kuebler, Assistant Director of Admissions, South Dakota State University, PO Box 2201, Brookings, SD 57007. *Phone:* 605-688-4121. *Toll-free phone:* 800-952-3541. *Fax:* 605-688-6891. *E-mail:* sdsu_admissions@sdstate.edu.

UNIVERSITY OF SIOUX FALLS

Sioux Falls, South Dakota

- **Independent American Baptist Churches in the USA** comprehensive, founded 1883
- **Calendar** 4-1-4
- **Degrees** associate, bachelor's, and master's

- **Suburban** 22-acre campus
- **Endowment** $9.6 million
- **Coed,** 1,122 undergraduate students, 81% full-time, 54% women, 46% men
- **Moderately difficult** entrance level, 96% of applicants were admitted

Undergraduates 906 full-time, 216 part-time. Students come from 28 states and territories, 5 other countries, 32% are from out of state, 1% African American, 0.4% Asian American or Pacific Islander, 1% Hispanic American, 0.6% Native American, 0.9% international, 8% transferred in, 28% live on campus. *Retention:* 66% of 2001 full-time freshmen returned.

Freshmen *Admission:* 691 applied, 660 admitted, 223 enrolled. *Average high school GPA:* 3.2. *Test scores:* ACT scores over 18: 83%; ACT scores over 24: 25%; ACT scores over 30: 2%.

Faculty *Total:* 96, 47% full-time, 33% with terminal degrees. *Student/faculty ratio:* 17:1.

Majors Accounting; applied art; applied mathematics; art education; behavioral sciences; biology; business administration; business marketing and marketing management; chemistry; computer science; developmental/child psychology; early childhood education; economics; education; elementary education; English; exercise sciences; graphic design/commercial art/illustration; health education; history; humanities; industrial radiologic technology; information sciences/systems; interdisciplinary studies; liberal arts and sciences/liberal studies; management information systems/business data processing; mass communications; mathematics; medical technology; middle school education; music; music business management/merchandising; music (piano and organ performance); music teacher education; music (voice and choral/opera performance); pastoral counseling; philosophy; physical education; political science; pre-dentistry; pre-engineering; pre-law; pre-medicine; pre-veterinary studies; psychology; public relations; radio/television broadcasting; religious studies; science education; secondary education; secretarial science; social sciences; social work; sociology; speech/rhetorical studies; theater arts/drama; wind/percussion instruments.

Academic Programs *Special study options:* academic remediation for entering students, accelerated degree program, adult/continuing education programs, advanced placement credit, cooperative education, distance learning, double majors, external degree program, honors programs, independent study, internships, off-campus study, part-time degree program, services for LD students, student-designed majors, study abroad, summer session for credit. *Unusual degree programs:* 3-2 engineering with South Dakota State University; religious studies with North American Baptist Seminary.

Library Norman B. Mears Library plus 1 other with 57,399 titles, 364 serial subscriptions, 4,500 audiovisual materials, an OPAC, a Web page.

Computers on Campus 120 computers available on campus for general student use. A campuswide network can be accessed from student residence rooms and from off campus. Internet access, at least one staffed computer lab available.

Student Life *Housing:* on-campus residence required through sophomore year. *Options:* coed, men-only, women-only. *Activities and Organizations:* drama/theater group, student-run newspaper, radio and television station, choral group, Fellowship of Christian Athletes, Campus Ministry Outreach. *Campus security:* late-night transport/escort service, controlled dormitory access. *Student Services:* health clinic, personal/psychological counseling, women's center.

Athletics Member NAIA. *Intercollegiate sports:* baseball M(s), basketball M(s)/W(s), cross-country running M(s)/W(s), football M(s), soccer M(s)/W(s), softball W(s), tennis M(s)/W(s), track and field M(s)/W(s), volleyball W(s). *Intramural sports:* basketball M/W, football M/W, racquetball M/W, table tennis M/W, tennis M/W, volleyball M/W.

Costs (2002–03) *Comprehensive fee:* $17,300 includes full-time tuition ($13,400) and room and board ($3900). Part-time tuition: $215 per semester hour.

Financial Aid Of all full-time matriculated undergraduates who enrolled in 2001, 180 Federal Work-Study jobs (averaging $1200). *Average indebtedness upon graduation:* $20,500.

Applying *Options:* early admission, deferred entrance. *Application fee:* $25. *Required:* high school transcript. *Required for some:* 2 letters of recommendation, interview. *Recommended:* essay or personal statement, minimum 2.0 GPA. *Application deadline:* rolling (freshmen), rolling (transfers). *Notification:* continuous (freshmen).

Admissions Contact Mr. Greg A. Fritz, Associate Vice President of Admissions and Marketing, University of Sioux Falls, Sioux Falls, SD 57105. *Phone:* 605-331-6600. *Toll-free phone:* 800-888-1047 Ext. 6. *Fax:* 605-331-6615. *E-mail:* admissions@usiouxfalls.edu.

UNIVERSITY OF SOUTH DAKOTA

Vermillion, South Dakota

- **State-supported** university, founded 1862
- **Calendar** semesters
- **Degrees** associate, bachelor's, master's, doctoral, first professional, and post-master's certificates
- **Small-town** 216-acre campus
- **Endowment** $64.9 million
- **Coed,** 5,363 undergraduate students, 75% full-time, 59% women, 41% men
- **Moderately difficult** entrance level, 56% of applicants were admitted

Undergraduates 4,005 full-time, 1,358 part-time. Students come from 34 states and territories, 33 other countries, 27% are from out of state, 0.9% African American, 0.6% Asian American or Pacific Islander, 0.6% Hispanic American, 3% Native American, 2% international, 10% transferred in, 34% live on campus. *Retention:* 74% of 2001 full-time freshmen returned.

Freshmen *Admission:* 2,762 applied, 1,559 admitted, 1,044 enrolled. *Average high school GPA:* 3.18. *Test scores:* ACT scores over 18: 87%; ACT scores over 24: 33%; ACT scores over 30: 4%.

Faculty *Total:* 249, 95% full-time, 84% with terminal degrees. *Student/faculty ratio:* 15:1.

Majors Accounting; advertising; alcohol/drug abuse counseling; anthropology; applied art; art; art education; arts management; biology; broadcast journalism; business administration; business economics; business marketing and marketing management; ceramic arts; chemistry; classics; computer science; creative writing; criminal justice/law enforcement administration; dental hygiene; drawing; earth sciences; economics; education; elementary education; English; film/video production; finance; fine/studio arts; fish/game management; French; German; graphic design/commercial art/illustration; health services administration; history; human resources management; information sciences/systems; journalism; Latin (ancient and medieval); liberal arts and sciences/liberal studies; mass communications; mathematical statistics; mathematics; medical technology; middle school education; music; music (piano and organ performance); music teacher education; music (voice and choral/opera performance); nursing; philosophy; photography; physical education; physician assistant; physics; political science; pre-dentistry; pre-engineering; pre-law; pre-medicine; pre-veterinary studies; printmaking; psychology; public relations; radio/television broadcasting; recreation/leisure studies; science education; sculpture; secondary education; social work; sociology; Spanish; special education; speech-language pathology/audiology; speech/rhetorical studies; stringed instruments; theater arts/drama; wind/percussion instruments; zoology.

Academic Programs *Special study options:* advanced placement credit, distance learning, double majors, English as a second language, honors programs, independent study, internships, off-campus study, part-time degree program, services for LD students, study abroad, summer session for credit. *ROTC:* Army (b). *Unusual degree programs:* 3-2 accounting.

Library I. D. Weeks Library plus 2 others with 1.5 million titles, 2,862 serial subscriptions, 3,766 audiovisual materials, an OPAC.

Computers on Campus 1800 computers available on campus for general student use. A campuswide network can be accessed from student residence rooms and from off campus. Internet access, at least one staffed computer lab available.

Student Life *Housing:* on-campus residence required through sophomore year. *Options:* coed, men-only, women-only. *Activities and Organizations:* drama/theater group, student-run newspaper, radio station, choral group, marching band, Program Council, Residence Hall Association, Interfraternity/Panhellenic Council, Student Ambassadors, Delta Sigma Pi, national fraternities, national sororities. *Campus security:* 24-hour emergency response devices and patrols, student patrols, late-night transport/escort service, controlled dormitory access. *Student Services:* health clinic, personal/psychological counseling, legal services.

Athletics Member NCAA. All Division II. *Intercollegiate sports:* baseball M(s), basketball M(s)/W(s), cross-country running M(s)/W(s), football M(s), softball W(s), swimming M(s)/W, tennis M(s)/W(s), track and field M(s)/W(s), volleyball W(s). *Intramural sports:* badminton M/W, basketball M(c)/W(c), bowling M/W, cross-country running M/W, fencing M(c)/W(c), football M(c)/W(c), golf M/W, ice hockey M(c), racquetball M(c)/W(c), riflery M/W, rugby M(c), soccer M(c)/W(c), softball M(c)/W(c), swimming M/W, table tennis M/W, tennis M/W, track and field M/W, volleyball M/W, water polo M/W.

Standardized Tests *Required:* SAT I or ACT (for admission).

Costs (2001–02) *Tuition:* state resident $1997 full-time, $62 per credit hour part-time; nonresident $6352 full-time, $199 per credit hour part-time. *Required fees:* $1888 full-time, $59 per credit hour. *Room and board:* $3151; room only: $1521. *Payment plan:* deferred payment. *Waivers:* senior citizens.

Financial Aid Of all full-time matriculated undergraduates who enrolled in 2001, 3564 applied for aid, 3350 were judged to have need, 2680 had their need fully met. 595 Federal Work-Study jobs (averaging $1200). In 2001, 262 non-need-based awards were made. *Average percent of need met:* 80%. *Average financial aid package:* $6595. *Average need-based loan:* $4205. *Average need-based gift aid:* $1580. *Average non-need based aid:* $3909. *Average indebtedness upon graduation:* $17,646.

University of South Dakota (continued)

Applying *Options:* electronic application, early admission, deferred entrance. *Application fee:* $15. *Required:* high school transcript. *Required for some:* letters of recommendation. *Recommended:* minimum 2.6 GPA. *Application deadline:* rolling (freshmen), rolling (transfers). *Notification:* continuous (freshmen).

Admissions Contact Ms. Paula Tacke, Director of Admissions, University of South Dakota, 414 East Clark Street, Vermillion, SD 57069. *Phone:* 605-677-5434. *Toll-free phone:* 877-269-6837. *Fax:* 605-677-6753. *E-mail:* admiss@usd.edu.

TENNESSEE

AMERICAN BAPTIST COLLEGE OF AMERICAN BAPTIST THEOLOGICAL SEMINARY

Nashville, Tennessee

- **Independent Baptist** 4-year, founded 1924
- **Calendar** semesters
- **Degrees** associate and bachelor's
- **Urban** 52-acre campus
- **Endowment** $528,472
- **Coed,** 106 undergraduate students, 82% full-time, 23% women, 77% men
- **Noncompetitive** entrance level, 100% of applicants were admitted

Undergraduates 87 full-time, 19 part-time. Students come from 10 states and territories, 5 other countries, 15% are from out of state, 92% African American, 8% international, 5% transferred in, 20% live on campus. *Retention:* 85% of 2001 full-time freshmen returned.

Freshmen *Admission:* 45 applied, 45 admitted, 41 enrolled. *Average high school GPA:* 2.25.

Faculty *Total:* 13, 38% full-time, 77% with terminal degrees. *Student/faculty ratio:* 8:1.

Majors Biblical studies; theology.

Academic Programs *Special study options:* academic remediation for entering students, accelerated degree program, adult/continuing education programs, cooperative education, English as a second language, part-time degree program, student-designed majors, summer session for credit.

Library 40,000 titles, 200 serial subscriptions.

Computers on Campus 8 computers available on campus for general student use. At least one staffed computer lab available.

Student Life *Housing Options:* coed, men-only, women-only. *Activities and Organizations:* choral group, Student Government Association, Vespers Service, national fraternities. *Campus security:* student patrols, security patrols from 10 p.m. to 7 a.m. *Student Services:* personal/psychological counseling.

Athletics *Intramural sports:* basketball M, football M, golf M.

Standardized Tests *Recommended:* SAT I or ACT (for admission).

Costs (2002–03) *One-time required fee:* $5. *Tuition:* $3000 full-time, $125 per credit hour part-time. Full-time tuition and fees vary according to course load. Part-time tuition and fees vary according to course load. *Required fees:* $45 full-time, $45 per year part-time. *Room only:* $1600. Room and board charges vary according to housing facility. *Payment plan:* deferred payment.

Financial Aid Of all full-time matriculated undergraduates who enrolled in 2001, 40 applied for aid, 35 were judged to have need. *Average financial aid package:* $1650. *Financial aid deadline:* 7/23.

Applying *Options:* electronic application, deferred entrance. *Application fee:* $20. *Required:* high school transcript, 3 letters of recommendation, interview. *Recommended:* essay or personal statement. *Application deadlines:* 7/1 (freshmen), 7/1 (transfers). *Notification:* continuous until 8/15 (freshmen).

Admissions Contact Ms. Marcella Lockhart, Director of Enrollment Management, American Baptist College of American Baptist Theological Seminary, 1800 Baptist World Center Drive, Nashville, TN 37207. *Phone:* 615-228-7877 Ext. 35. *Fax:* 615-226-7855.

AQUINAS COLLEGE

Nashville, Tennessee

- **Independent Roman Catholic** 4-year, founded 1961
- **Calendar** semesters
- **Degrees** diplomas, associate, and bachelor's
- **Urban** 92-acre campus
- **Endowment** $2.3 million
- **Coed,** 635 undergraduate students
- **Moderately difficult** entrance level, 13% of applicants were admitted

Undergraduates Students come from 5 states and territories, 2 other countries, 10% are from out of state. *Retention:* 70% of 2001 full-time freshmen returned.

Freshmen *Admission:* 1,800 applied, 226 admitted. *Average high school GPA:* 2.00. *Test scores:* ACT scores over 18: 56%; ACT scores over 24: 1%.

Faculty *Total:* 60, 18% with terminal degrees. *Student/faculty ratio:* 15:1.

Majors Elementary education; liberal arts and sciences/liberal studies; nursing.

Academic Programs *Special study options:* academic remediation for entering students, advanced placement credit, independent study, internships, part-time degree program, summer session for credit. *ROTC:* Army (c), Air Force (c).

Library Aquinas College Library plus 1 other with 45,762 titles, 301 serial subscriptions, an OPAC, a Web page.

Computers on Campus 52 computers available on campus for general student use. Internet access, at least one staffed computer lab available.

Student Life *Housing:* college housing not available. *Activities and Organizations:* student-run newspaper, Student Council. *Campus security:* 24-hour emergency response devices, patrols by security after class hours. *Student Services:* personal/psychological counseling.

Athletics Member NJCAA. *Intercollegiate sports:* baseball M(s), basketball M(s).

Standardized Tests *Required:* SAT I or ACT (for admission).

Costs (2002–03) *Tuition:* $8500 full-time, $360 per credit hour part-time. Full-time tuition and fees vary according to program. Part-time tuition and fees vary according to program. *Required fees:* $330 full-time, $165 per term. *Payment plan:* installment.

Financial Aid Of all full-time matriculated undergraduates who enrolled in 2001, 324 applied for aid, 208 were judged to have need, 57 had their need fully met. 9 Federal Work-Study jobs (averaging $2905). *Average percent of need met:* 76%. *Average financial aid package:* $8560. *Average need-based gift aid:* $2550. *Average indebtedness upon graduation:* $8500.

Applying *Options:* deferred entrance. *Application fee:* $10. *Required:* essay or personal statement, high school transcript, minimum 2.0 GPA, interview. *Application deadline:* rolling (freshmen), rolling (transfers). *Notification:* continuous (freshmen).

Admissions Contact Neil J. Devine, Director of Career Planning and Admission, Aquinas College, 4210 Harding Road, Nashville, TN 37205-2005. *Phone:* 615-297-7545 Ext. 426. *Fax:* 615-297-7970 Ext. 460.

AUSTIN PEAY STATE UNIVERSITY

Clarksville, Tennessee

- **State-supported** comprehensive, founded 1927, part of Tennessee Board of Regents
- **Calendar** semesters
- **Degrees** associate, bachelor's, master's, and post-master's certificates
- **Suburban** 200-acre campus with easy access to Nashville
- **Endowment** $3.1 million
- **Coed,** 6,617 undergraduate students, 73% full-time, 60% women, 40% men
- **Moderately difficult** entrance level, 48% of applicants were admitted

Undergraduates 4,842 full-time, 1,775 part-time. Students come from 37 states and territories, 17 other countries, 3% are from out of state, 20% African American, 3% Asian American or Pacific Islander, 5% Hispanic American, 0.8% Native American, 0.2% international, 12% transferred in, 15% live on campus. *Retention:* 64% of 2001 full-time freshmen returned.

Freshmen *Admission:* 2,666 applied, 1,279 admitted, 1,047 enrolled. *Average high school GPA:* 3.03. *Test scores:* SAT verbal scores over 500: 52%; SAT math scores over 500: 43%; ACT scores over 18: 83%; SAT verbal scores over 600: 13%; SAT math scores over 600: 12%; ACT scores over 24: 24%; SAT verbal scores over 700: 1%; SAT math scores over 700: 3%; ACT scores over 30: 2%.

Faculty *Total:* 463, 59% full-time, 60% with terminal degrees. *Student/faculty ratio:* 18:1.

Majors Agricultural sciences; art; biology; business; business administration; chemistry; computer/information sciences; data processing; engineering technology; English; foreign languages/literatures; general studies; geography; geology; health education; health/physical education; history; industrial arts; interdisciplinary studies; mass communications; mathematics; medical technology; music; nonprofit/public management; nursing; philosophy; physics; political science; psychology; radiological science; social work; sociology; Spanish; special education.

Academic Programs *Special study options:* academic remediation for entering students, adult/continuing education programs, advanced placement credit, dis-

tance learning, double majors, English as a second language, honors programs, independent study, internships, part-time degree program, services for LD students, study abroad, summer session for credit. *ROTC:* Army (b).

Library Felix G. Woodward Library with 174,474 titles, 1,787 serial subscriptions, 7,374 audiovisual materials, an OPAC, a Web page.

Computers on Campus 411 computers available on campus for general student use. A campuswide network can be accessed from student residence rooms and from off campus. At least one staffed computer lab available.

Student Life *Housing:* on-campus residence required for freshman year. *Options:* coed, men-only, women-only. *Activities and Organizations:* drama/theater group, student-run newspaper, radio and television station, choral group, marching band, national fraternities, national sororities. *Campus security:* 24-hour patrols, late-night transport/escort service, controlled dormitory access. *Student Services:* health clinic, personal/psychological counseling.

Athletics Member NCAA. All Division I except football (Division I-AA). *Intercollegiate sports:* baseball M(s), basketball M(s)/W(s), cross-country running M(s)/W(s), golf M(s), riflery W(s), softball W(s), tennis M(s)/W(s), track and field W(s), volleyball W(s). *Intramural sports:* basketball M/W, football M/W, golf M, gymnastics M/W, racquetball M/W, riflery W, soccer M, swimming M/W, tennis M/W, track and field M, volleyball M/W.

Standardized Tests *Required:* SAT I or ACT (for admission).

Costs (2001–02) *Tuition:* state resident $2556 full-time, $112 per credit hour part-time; nonresident $9028 full-time, $392 per credit hour part-time. Part-time tuition and fees vary according to course load. *Required fees:* $652 full-time, $28 per credit hour, $30 per term part-time. *Room and board:* $3670; room only: $2180. Room and board charges vary according to board plan and housing facility. *Payment plans:* installment, deferred payment. *Waivers:* senior citizens and employees or children of employees.

Financial Aid Of all full-time matriculated undergraduates who enrolled in 2001, 3460 applied for aid, 3302 were judged to have need. 353 Federal Work-Study jobs, 586 State and other part-time jobs. In 2001, 238 non-need-based awards were made. *Average percent of need met:* 65%. *Average financial aid package:* $6975. *Average need-based loan:* $3925. *Average need-based gift aid:* $3200. *Average non-need based aid:* $750. *Average indebtedness upon graduation:* $16,225.

Applying *Options:* early admission, deferred entrance. *Application fee:* $15. *Required:* high school transcript, 2.75 high school GPA, minimum ACT composite score of 19. *Application deadline:* 8/15 (freshmen), rolling (transfers). *Notification:* continuous (freshmen).

Admissions Contact Mr. Charles McCorkle, Director of Admissions, Austin Peay State University, PO Box 4548, Clarksville, TN 37044-4548. *Phone:* 931-221-7661. *Toll-free phone:* 800-844-2778. *Fax:* 931-221-6168. *E-mail:* admissions@apsu01.apsu.edu.

BAPTIST MEMORIAL COLLEGE OF HEALTH SCIENCES

Memphis, Tennessee

Admissions Contact 1003 Monroe Avenue, Memphis, TN 38104. *Toll-free phone:* 800-796-7171.

BELMONT UNIVERSITY

Nashville, Tennessee

- **Independent Baptist** comprehensive, founded 1951
- **Calendar** semesters
- **Degrees** bachelor's, master's, doctoral, and postbachelor's certificates
- **Urban** 34-acre campus
- **Endowment** $39.4 million
- **Coed,** 2,617 undergraduate students, 89% full-time, 60% women, 40% men
- **Moderately difficult** entrance level, 74% of applicants were admitted

Undergraduates 2,321 full-time, 296 part-time. Students come from 51 states and territories, 11 other countries, 59% are from out of state, 3% African American, 1% Asian American or Pacific Islander, 1% Hispanic American, 0.2% Native American, 0.4% international, 11% transferred in, 50% live on campus. *Retention:* 73% of 2001 full-time freshmen returned.

Freshmen *Admission:* 1,265 applied, 938 admitted, 510 enrolled. *Average high school GPA:* 3.24. *Test scores:* SAT verbal scores over 500: 85%; SAT math scores over 500: 77%; ACT scores over 18: 99%; SAT verbal scores over 600: 39%; SAT math scores over 600: 33%; ACT scores over 24: 56%; SAT verbal scores over 700: 7%; SAT math scores over 700: 5%; ACT scores over 30: 7%.

Faculty *Total:* 387, 53% full-time. *Student/faculty ratio:* 11:1.

Majors Accounting; advertising; applied mathematics; art; art education; behavioral sciences; biblical languages/literatures; biblical studies; bilingual/bicultural education; biochemistry; biological/physical sciences; biology; broadcast journalism; business administration; business economics; business education; business marketing and marketing management; chemistry; computer management; computer programming; computer science; counselor education/guidance; developmental/child psychology; divinity/ministry; early childhood education; economics; education; education (K-12); elementary education; engineering science; English; finance; fine/studio arts; Greek (modern); health education; health services administration; history; hospitality management; hotel and restaurant management; information sciences/systems; international business; journalism; mass communications; mathematics; medical technology; music; music business management/merchandising; music history; music (piano and organ performance); music teacher education; music (voice and choral/opera performance); nursing; pastoral counseling; pharmacology; philosophy; physical education; physics; political science; psychology; radio/television broadcasting; reading education; recreation/leisure studies; religious music; retail management; secretarial science; social work; sociology; Spanish; special education; speech/rhetorical studies; theater arts/drama; western civilization.

Academic Programs *Special study options:* accelerated degree program, adult/continuing education programs, advanced placement credit, cooperative education, distance learning, double majors, honors programs, independent study, internships, part-time degree program, services for LD students, student-designed majors, study abroad, summer session for credit. *ROTC:* Army (c). *Unusual degree programs:* 3-2 engineering with Auburn University, Georgia Institute of Technology, University of Tennessee.

Library Lila D. Bunch Library with 178,660 titles, 1,476 serial subscriptions, 23,922 audiovisual materials, an OPAC, a Web page.

Computers on Campus 250 computers available on campus for general student use. A campuswide network can be accessed from student residence rooms and from off campus. Internet access, online (class) registration, at least one staffed computer lab available.

Student Life *Housing:* on-campus residence required through sophomore year. *Options:* men-only, women-only. *Activities and Organizations:* drama/theater group, student-run newspaper, radio and television station, choral group, marching band, national fraternities, national sororities. *Campus security:* 24-hour emergency response devices and patrols, late-night transport/escort service, controlled dormitory access, bicycle patrol. *Student Services:* health clinic, personal/psychological counseling.

Athletics Member NCAA. All Division I. *Intercollegiate sports:* baseball M(s), basketball M(s)/W(s), cross-country running M(s)/W(s), golf M(s)/W(s), soccer M(s)/W(s), softball W(s), tennis M(s)/W(s), track and field M(s)/W(s), volleyball W(s). *Intramural sports:* basketball M/W, bowling M/W, football M, golf M, racquetball M/W, table tennis M/W, tennis M/W, volleyball M/W.

Standardized Tests *Required:* SAT I or ACT (for admission).

Costs (2001–02) *Comprehensive fee:* $19,066 includes full-time tuition ($13,040), mandatory fees ($360), and room and board ($5666). Full-time tuition and fees vary according to class time and course load. Part-time tuition: $495 per semester hour. Part-time tuition and fees vary according to course load. *Required fees:* $120 per term part-time. *Room and board:* College room only: $2656. Room and board charges vary according to board plan, housing facility, and location. *Payment plans:* installment, deferred payment. *Waivers:* senior citizens and employees or children of employees.

Financial Aid Of all full-time matriculated undergraduates who enrolled in 2001, 1767 applied for aid, 1052 were judged to have need, 264 had their need fully met. 593 Federal Work-Study jobs. *Average percent of need met:* 46%. *Average financial aid package:* $7123. *Average need-based loan:* $5266. *Average need-based gift aid:* $4025. *Average indebtedness upon graduation:* $11,274.

Applying *Options:* common application, early admission, deferred entrance. *Application fee:* $35. *Required:* essay or personal statement, high school transcript, minimum 3.0 GPA, letters of recommendation, resume of activities. *Required for some:* interview. *Application deadlines:* 5/1 (freshmen), 5/1 (transfers). *Notification:* continuous (freshmen).

Admissions Contact Dr. Kathryn Baugher, Dean of Enrollment Services, Belmont University, 1900 Belmont Boulevard, Nashville, TN 37212-3757. *Phone:* 615-460-6785. *Toll-free phone:* 800-56E-NROL. *Fax:* 615-460-5434. *E-mail:* buadmission@mail.belmont.edu.

BETHEL COLLEGE

McKenzie, Tennessee

- **Independent Cumberland Presbyterian** comprehensive, founded 1842
- **Calendar** semesters
- **Degrees** bachelor's and master's

Bethel College (continued)
- **Small-town** 100-acre campus
- **Endowment** $6.6 million
- **Coed,** 840 undergraduate students, 88% full-time, 53% women, 47% men
- **Minimally difficult** entrance level, 63% of applicants were admitted

Undergraduates Students come from 28 states and territories, 2 other countries, 19% are from out of state, 19% African American, 0.3% Asian American or Pacific Islander, 1% Hispanic American, 0.5% Native American, 1% international, 50% live on campus. *Retention:* 54% of 2001 full-time freshmen returned.

Freshmen *Admission:* 473 applied, 299 admitted. *Average high school GPA:* 2.85. *Test scores:* SAT verbal scores over 500: 40%; SAT math scores over 500: 40%; ACT scores over 18: 72%; SAT math scores over 600: 10%; ACT scores over 24: 17%.

Faculty *Total:* 67, 55% full-time, 48% with terminal degrees. *Student/faculty ratio:* 14:1.

Majors Accounting; biology; biology education; business administration; chemistry; education; education (K-12); elementary education; English; English education; health/physical education; history; history education; human services; interdisciplinary studies; liberal arts and sciences/liberal studies; mathematics; physical education; physician assistant; pre-dentistry; pre-medicine; psychology; special education; theater arts/drama.

Academic Programs *Special study options:* academic remediation for entering students, accelerated degree program, adult/continuing education programs, advanced placement credit, double majors, internships, off-campus study, part-time degree program, services for LD students, student-designed majors, summer session for credit. *Unusual degree programs:* 3-2 engineering with Tennessee Technological University, The University of Memphis; religion with Memphis Theological Seminary.

Library Burroughs Learning Center with 73,288 titles, 254 serial subscriptions.

Computers on Campus 35 computers available on campus for general student use. Internet access, at least one staffed computer lab available.

Student Life *Housing:* on-campus residence required through sophomore year. *Options:* coed, men-only, women-only, disabled students. *Activities and Organizations:* drama/theater group, choral group, FCA, SETA (Education), Black Student Union, Honor Club. *Campus security:* night patrols by trained security personnel. *Student Services:* personal/psychological counseling.

Athletics Member NAIA. *Intercollegiate sports:* baseball M(s), basketball M(s)/W(s), cross-country running M(s)/W(s), football M(s), golf M(s), soccer M(s)/W(s), softball W(s), tennis M(s)/W(s), track and field M(s)/W(s), volleyball W(s). *Intramural sports:* basketball M/W, football M, golf M/W, soccer M/W, softball M/W, table tennis M/W, tennis M/W, volleyball M/W, weight lifting M/W.

Standardized Tests *Required:* SAT I or ACT (for admission).

Costs (2002–03) *Comprehensive fee:* $13,580 includes full-time tuition ($8180), mandatory fees ($850), and room and board ($4550). Part-time tuition: $245 per semester hour. Part-time tuition and fees vary according to course load. *Required fees:* $10 per semester hour. *Payment plan:* installment. *Waivers:* employees or children of employees.

Financial Aid Of all full-time matriculated undergraduates who enrolled in 2001, 398 applied for aid, 262 were judged to have need, 226 had their need fully met. In 2001, 44 non-need-based awards were made. *Average financial aid package:* $9891. *Average need-based loan:* $1774. *Average need-based gift aid:* $9488. *Average non-need based aid:* $3540. *Financial aid deadline:* 8/21.

Applying *Options:* early admission, deferred entrance. *Application fee:* $30. *Required:* high school transcript, minimum 2.5 GPA. *Required for some:* essay or personal statement, 1 letter of recommendation, interview. *Application deadline:* rolling (freshmen), rolling (transfers). *Notification:* continuous (freshmen).

Admissions Contact Mrs. Tina Hodges, Director of Admissions and Marketing, Bethel College, 325 Cherry Avenue, McKenzie, TN 38201. *Phone:* 731-352-4030. *Fax:* 731-352-4069. *E-mail:* admissions@bethel-college.edu.

BRYAN COLLEGE
Dayton, Tennessee

- **Independent interdenominational** 4-year, founded 1930
- **Calendar** semesters
- **Degrees** associate and bachelor's
- **Small-town** 100-acre campus
- **Endowment** $2.0 million
- **Coed,** 558 undergraduate students
- **Moderately difficult** entrance level, 34% of applicants were admitted

Bryan College is a 4-year, interdenominational, Christian liberal arts college. High-quality academics, spiritual atmosphere, and close interpersonal relationships highlight the reasons students choose Bryan College. Bryan's unique Biblical Worldview approach to education equips students to see the world through the lens of scripture. As a result, students are better able to understand and interpret the world around them through a biblical worldview. Visits to the Bryan campus are encouraged.

Undergraduates Students come from 33 states and territories, 15 other countries, 2% African American, 0.5% Asian American or Pacific Islander, 0.9% Hispanic American, 0.4% Native American, 2% international, 74% live on campus. *Retention:* 77% of 2001 full-time freshmen returned.

Freshmen *Admission:* 484 applied, 164 admitted. *Average high school GPA:* 3.64. *Test scores:* SAT verbal scores over 500: 76%; SAT math scores over 500: 68%; ACT scores over 18: 87%; SAT verbal scores over 600: 31%; SAT math scores over 600: 23%; ACT scores over 24: 49%; SAT verbal scores over 700: 11%; SAT math scores over 700: 6%; ACT scores over 30: 7%.

Faculty *Total:* 58, 64% full-time, 53% with terminal degrees. *Student/faculty ratio:* 14:1.

Majors Biblical studies; biology; business administration; computer science; early childhood education; education; elementary education; English; history; liberal arts and sciences/liberal studies; literature; mass communications; mathematics; middle school education; music; music business management/merchandising; music (piano and organ performance); music teacher education; music (voice and choral/opera performance); physical education; pre-medicine; psychology; religious education; religious music; science education; secondary education; wind/percussion instruments.

Academic Programs *Special study options:* academic remediation for entering students, adult/continuing education programs, advanced placement credit, double majors, honors programs, independent study, internships, part-time degree program, study abroad, summer session for credit. *Unusual degree programs:* 3-2 nursing with Vanderbilt University.

Library Ironside Memorial Library with 119,348 titles, 949 serial subscriptions, 3,786 audiovisual materials, an OPAC, a Web page.

Computers on Campus 74 computers available on campus for general student use. A campuswide network can be accessed from student residence rooms. Internet access, at least one staffed computer lab available.

Student Life *Housing:* on-campus residence required through senior year. *Options:* men-only, women-only. *Activities and Organizations:* drama/theater group, student-run newspaper, choral group, Practical Christian Involvement, Student Government Association, Fellowship of Christian Athletes, Hilltop Players, chorale. *Campus security:* student patrols, late-night transport/escort service, controlled dormitory access, police patrols. *Student Services:* personal/psychological counseling.

Athletics Member NAIA, NCCAA. *Intercollegiate sports:* basketball M(s)/W(s), soccer M(s)/W(s), tennis M/W, volleyball W(s). *Intramural sports:* basketball M/W, football M, golf M, soccer M/W, softball M/W, tennis M/W, volleyball M/W.

Standardized Tests *Required:* ACT (for admission). *Recommended:* SAT I (for admission).

Costs (2002–03) *Comprehensive fee:* $17,100 includes full-time tuition ($12,700) and room and board ($4400). Part-time tuition: $500 per credit hour.

Financial Aid Of all full-time matriculated undergraduates who enrolled in 2001, 539 applied for aid, 410 were judged to have need, 205 had their need fully met. 215 Federal Work-Study jobs (averaging $810). In 2001, 27 non-need-based awards were made. *Average percent of need met:* 72%. *Average financial aid package:* $11,700. *Average need-based loan:* $5439. *Average need-based gift aid:* $5000. *Average non-need based aid:* $1500. *Average indebtedness upon graduation:* $14,504.

Applying *Options:* electronic application, early admission, deferred entrance. *Application fee:* $20. *Required:* essay or personal statement, high school transcript, minimum 2.0 GPA, 3 letters of recommendation. *Required for some:* interview. *Application deadline:* rolling (freshmen), rolling (transfers).

Admissions Contact Mr. Ronald D. Petitte, Registrar, Bryan College, PO Box 7000, Dayton, TN 37321-7000. *Phone:* 423-775-7237. *Toll-free phone:* 800-277-9522. *Fax:* 423-775-7330. *E-mail:* admiss@bryannet.bryan.edu.

CARSON-NEWMAN COLLEGE
Jefferson City, Tennessee

- **Independent Southern Baptist** comprehensive, founded 1851
- **Calendar** semesters
- **Degrees** associate, bachelor's, and master's
- **Small-town** 90-acre campus with easy access to Knoxville
- **Endowment** $26.6 million
- **Coed,** 1,991 undergraduate students, 91% full-time, 58% women, 42% men
- **Moderately difficult** entrance level, 89% of applicants were admitted

Undergraduates 1,807 full-time, 184 part-time. Students come from 42 states and territories, 15 other countries, 35% are from out of state, 8% African American, 0.3% Asian American or Pacific Islander, 0.4% Hispanic American, 0.2% Native American, 3% international, 9% transferred in, 51% live on campus. *Retention:* 77% of 2001 full-time freshmen returned.

Freshmen *Admission:* 1,131 applied, 1,006 admitted, 410 enrolled. *Average high school GPA:* 3.23. *Test scores:* ACT scores over 18: 89%; ACT scores over 24: 39%; ACT scores over 30: 6%.

Faculty *Total:* 177, 69% full-time, 37% with terminal degrees. *Student/faculty ratio:* 13:1.

Majors Accounting; art; art education; athletic training/sports medicine; biblical languages/literatures; biblical studies; biology; broadcast journalism; business administration; business economics; business education; business marketing and marketing management; chemistry; child care/development; computer science; consumer services; creative writing; developmental/child psychology; dietetics; divinity/ministry; drawing; early childhood education; economics; education; elementary education; English; exercise sciences; family/consumer studies; fashion merchandising; film studies; French; graphic design/commercial art/illustration; health facilities administration; history; home economics; home economics education; human services; information sciences/systems; interdisciplinary studies; interior design; international economics; journalism; liberal arts and sciences/liberal studies; literature; management information systems/business data processing; mass communications; mathematics; medical technology; music; music (piano and organ performance); music teacher education; music theory and composition; music (voice and choral/opera performance); nursing; nutrition science; philosophy; photography; physical education; political science; psychology; recreation/leisure studies; religious studies; secondary education; sociology; Spanish; special education; speech/rhetorical studies; theater arts/drama.

Academic Programs *Special study options:* academic remediation for entering students, accelerated degree program, adult/continuing education programs, advanced placement credit, English as a second language, honors programs, internships, off-campus study, part-time degree program, services for LD students, student-designed majors, study abroad, summer session for credit. *ROTC:* Army (b), Air Force (c). *Unusual degree programs:* 3-2 engineering with Georgia Institute of Technology, University of Tennessee, Tennessee Technological University; pharmacy with Campbell University, Mercer University, University of Georgia.

Library Stephens-Burnett Library plus 1 other with 2,245 serial subscriptions, 14,008 audiovisual materials, an OPAC, a Web page.

Computers on Campus 200 computers available on campus for general student use. A campuswide network can be accessed from student residence rooms and from off campus. Internet access, at least one staffed computer lab available.

Student Life *Housing:* on-campus residence required through junior year. *Options:* men-only, women-only. *Activities and Organizations:* drama/theater group, student-run newspaper, choral group, marching band, Baptist Student Union, Fellowship of Christian Athletes, Student Government Association, Student Ambassadors Association, Columbians, national fraternities, national sororities. *Campus security:* 24-hour emergency response devices and patrols, late-night transport/escort service, controlled dormitory access. *Student Services:* health clinic, personal/psychological counseling.

Athletics Member NCAA. All Division II. *Intercollegiate sports:* baseball M(s), basketball M(s)/W(s), cross-country running M(s)/W(s), football M(s), golf M(s), soccer M(s)/W(s), softball W(s), tennis M(s)/W(s), track and field M(s)/W(s), volleyball W(s), wrestling M(s). *Intramural sports:* badminton M/W, baseball M/W, basketball M/W, football M/W, golf M/W, racquetball M/W, skiing (downhill) M/W, soccer M/W, softball M/W, table tennis M/W, tennis M/W, volleyball M/W.

Standardized Tests *Required:* SAT I or ACT (for admission).

Costs (2002–03) *Comprehensive fee:* $17,240 includes full-time tuition ($12,200), mandatory fees ($690), and room and board ($4350). Full-time tuition and fees vary according to class time. Part-time tuition: $500 per semester hour. Part-time tuition and fees vary according to class time. *Required fees:* $200 per term part-time. *Room and board:* College room only: $1750. Room and board charges vary according to board plan. *Payment plan:* installment. *Waivers:* senior citizens and employees or children of employees.

Financial Aid Of all full-time matriculated undergraduates who enrolled in 2001, 1731 applied for aid, 1262 were judged to have need, 340 had their need fully met. 350 Federal Work-Study jobs (averaging $1498). 300 State and other part-time jobs (averaging $1532). In 2001, 450 non-need-based awards were made. *Average percent of need met:* 82%. *Average financial aid package:* $12,332. *Average need-based loan:* $4632. *Average need-based gift aid:* $8192. *Average non-need based aid:* $4022. *Average indebtedness upon graduation:* $14,315.

Applying *Options:* electronic application, deferred entrance. *Application fee:* $25. *Required:* high school transcript, minimum 2.25 GPA, medical history. *Required for some:* essay or personal statement, letters of recommendation, interview. *Recommended:* interview. *Application deadlines:* 8/1 (freshmen), 8/1 (transfers). *Notification:* continuous (freshmen).

Admissions Contact Mrs. Sheryl M. Gray, Director of Undergraduate Admissions, Carson-Newman College, PO Box 72025, Jefferson City, TN 37760. *Phone:* 865-471-3223. *Toll-free phone:* 800-678-9061. *Fax:* 865-471-3502. *E-mail:* cnadmiss@cn.edu.

CHRISTIAN BROTHERS UNIVERSITY
Memphis, Tennessee

- **Independent Roman Catholic** comprehensive, founded 1871
- **Calendar** semesters
- **Degrees** bachelor's and master's
- **Urban** 70-acre campus
- **Endowment** $21.3 million
- **Coed,** 1,659 undergraduate students, 79% full-time, 55% women, 45% men
- **Moderately difficult** entrance level, 82% of applicants were admitted

Undergraduates 1,315 full-time, 344 part-time. Students come from 30 states and territories, 28 other countries, 17% are from out of state, 28% African American, 4% Asian American or Pacific Islander, 2% Hispanic American, 0.3% Native American, 5% international, 7% transferred in, 31% live on campus. *Retention:* 73% of 2001 full-time freshmen returned.

Freshmen *Admission:* 888 applied, 730 admitted, 289 enrolled. *Average high school GPA:* 3.38. *Test scores:* SAT verbal scores over 500: 73%; SAT math scores over 500: 72%; ACT scores over 18: 97%; SAT verbal scores over 600: 27%; SAT math scores over 600: 42%; ACT scores over 24: 46%; SAT verbal scores over 700: 8%; SAT math scores over 700: 13%; ACT scores over 30: 10%.

Faculty *Total:* 196, 57% full-time, 64% with terminal degrees. *Student/faculty ratio:* 14:1.

Majors Accounting; biology; biology education; business; business administration; business marketing and marketing management; chemical engineering; chemistry; chemistry education; civil engineering; computer engineering; computer science; economics; education; educational psychology; electrical engineering; elementary education; engineering physics; English; English education; environmental engineering; finance; history; history education; management information systems/business data processing; mathematics; mathematics education; mechanical engineering; natural sciences; physics; physics education; predentistry; pre-law; pre-medicine; pre-pharmacy studies; pre-theology; psychology; religious studies; technical/business writing.

Academic Programs *Special study options:* accelerated degree program, advanced placement credit, double majors, honors programs, internships, off-campus study, part-time degree program, study abroad, summer session for credit. *ROTC:* Army (c), Navy (c), Air Force (c).

Library Plough Memorial Library and Media Center with 100,000 titles, 537 serial subscriptions, an OPAC, a Web page.

Computers on Campus 300 computers available on campus for general student use. A campuswide network can be accessed from student residence rooms and from off campus that provide access to on-line class listings, e-mail, course assignments. Internet access, online (class) registration, at least one staffed computer lab available.

Student Life *Housing:* on-campus residence required for freshman year. *Options:* coed. *Activities and Organizations:* drama/theater group, student-run newspaper, choral group, Black Student Association, BACCHUS Alcohol Awareness Group, Intercultural Club, College Republicans, Beta Beta Beta, national fraternities, national sororities. *Campus security:* 24-hour emergency response devices and patrols, student patrols, late-night transport/escort service, controlled dormitory access. *Student Services:* health clinic, personal/psychological counseling.

Athletics Member NCAA. All Division II. *Intercollegiate sports:* baseball M(s), basketball M(s)/W(s), cross-country running M/W, golf M, soccer M(s)/W(s), softball W(s), tennis M/W, volleyball W(s). *Intramural sports:* basketball M/W, bowling M/W, cross-country running M/W, football M/W, golf M, racquetball M/W, soccer M/W, softball M/W, swimming M/W, table tennis M/W, volleyball M/W.

Standardized Tests *Required:* SAT I or ACT (for admission).

Costs (2001–02) *Comprehensive fee:* $19,820 includes full-time tuition ($14,900), mandatory fees ($400), and room and board ($4520). Part-time tuition: $465 per credit hour. Part-time tuition and fees vary according to class time. *Room and board:* Room and board charges vary according to board plan and housing facility. *Payment plans:* installment, deferred payment. *Waivers:* children of alumni and employees or children of employees.

Financial Aid Of all full-time matriculated undergraduates who enrolled in 2001, 912 applied for aid, 748 were judged to have need, 152 had their need fully

Christian Brothers University (continued)
met. In 2001, 471 non-need-based awards were made. *Average percent of need met:* 74%. *Average financial aid package:* $11,887. *Average need-based loan:* $4056. *Average need-based gift aid:* $5611. *Average non-need based aid:* $7778. *Average indebtedness upon graduation:* $16,579.

Applying *Options:* common application, electronic application, early admission, deferred entrance. *Application fee:* $25. *Required:* essay or personal statement, high school transcript, minimum 2.5 GPA. *Required for some:* letters of recommendation. *Recommended:* interview. *Application deadlines:* 8/23 (freshmen), 8/23 (transfers).

Admissions Contact Ms. Courtney Fee, Dean of Admission, Christian Brothers University, 650 East Parkway South, Memphis, TN 38104. *Phone:* 901-321-3205. *Toll-free phone:* 800-288-7576. *Fax:* 901-321-3202. *E-mail:* admissions@cbu.edu.

CRICHTON COLLEGE
Memphis, Tennessee

- **Independent** 4-year, founded 1941
- **Calendar** semesters
- **Degree** certificates and bachelor's
- **Urban** 55-acre campus
- **Endowment** $483,133
- **Coed,** 1,043 undergraduate students, 82% full-time, 54% women, 46% men
- **Moderately difficult** entrance level, 76% of applicants were admitted

Undergraduates 857 full-time, 186 part-time. Students come from 10 states and territories, 4 other countries, 14% are from out of state, 47% African American, 0.4% Asian American or Pacific Islander, 0.4% Hispanic American, 0.8% Native American, 0.6% international, 85% transferred in, 5% live on campus. *Retention:* 45% of 2001 full-time freshmen returned.

Freshmen *Admission:* 170 applied, 130 admitted, 48 enrolled. *Average high school GPA:* 3.21.

Faculty *Total:* 92, 30% full-time, 32% with terminal degrees. *Student/faculty ratio:* 17:1.

Majors Biblical studies; biology; biology education; business administration; chemistry; clinical psychology; communications; counseling psychology; elementary education; English; English education; history; liberal arts and sciences/liberal studies; pre-law; psychology; school psychology; secondary education.

Academic Programs *Special study options:* academic remediation for entering students, accelerated degree program, adult/continuing education programs, advanced placement credit, cooperative education, distance learning, double majors, independent study, internships, part-time degree program, student-designed majors, study abroad, summer session for credit.

Library Crichton College Library with 45,484 titles, 289 serial subscriptions, 797 audiovisual materials, an OPAC.

Computers on Campus 30 computers available on campus for general student use. Internet access, at least one staffed computer lab available.

Student Life *Housing Options:* men-only, women-only. *Activities and Organizations:* drama/theater group, choral group, Student Government Association, Orientation Staff, Presidential Ambassadors, Psychology Club, Crichton Student Teacher Education Association. *Campus security:* 24-hour patrols, controlled dormitory access, security alarms in campus apartments. *Student Services:* personal/psychological counseling.

Athletics Member NCCAA. *Intercollegiate sports:* baseball M(s). *Intramural sports:* basketball M/W, football M/W, softball M/W, volleyball M/W.

Standardized Tests *Required:* SAT I or ACT (for admission).

Costs (2001–02) *One-time required fee:* $5. *Tuition:* $9480 full-time, $395 per hour part-time. Full-time tuition and fees vary according to program. Part-time tuition and fees vary according to program. *Room only:* $3200. *Waivers:* children of alumni and employees or children of employees.

Financial Aid Of all full-time matriculated undergraduates who enrolled in 2001, 847 applied for aid, 730 were judged to have need, 29 had their need fully met. 35 Federal Work-Study jobs (averaging $2655). In 2001, 15 non-need-based awards were made. *Average percent of need met:* 35%. *Average financial aid package:* $4080. *Average need-based loan:* $3302. *Average need-based gift aid:* $2698. *Average non-need based aid:* $2500. *Average indebtedness upon graduation:* $11,492.

Applying *Options:* electronic application, early admission, deferred entrance. *Application fee:* $25. *Required:* high school transcript, 3 letters of recommendation. *Required for some:* essay or personal statement. *Recommended:* minimum 2.0 GPA, interview. *Application deadlines:* 8/31 (freshmen), 8/31 (transfers). *Notification:* continuous (freshmen).

Admissions Contact Mr. David Wilson, Associate Director of Admissions, Crichton College, 6655 Winchester Road, PO Box 757830, Memphis, TN 38175-7830. *Phone:* 901-367-3888. *Toll-free phone:* 800-960-9777. *Fax:* 901-366-2650. *E-mail:* info@crichton.edu.

CUMBERLAND UNIVERSITY
Lebanon, Tennessee

- **Independent** comprehensive, founded 1842
- **Calendar** semesters
- **Degrees** associate, bachelor's, and master's
- **Small-town** 44-acre campus with easy access to Nashville
- **Endowment** $5.5 million
- **Coed,** 908 undergraduate students, 84% full-time, 52% women, 48% men
- **Moderately difficult** entrance level, 78% of applicants were admitted

Undergraduates 767 full-time, 141 part-time. Students come from 25 states and territories, 18 other countries, 21% are from out of state, 11% African American, 1% Asian American or Pacific Islander, 3% Hispanic American, 0.1% Native American, 0.4% international, 6% transferred in, 39% live on campus. *Retention:* 60% of 2001 full-time freshmen returned.

Freshmen *Admission:* 522 applied, 407 admitted, 226 enrolled. *Average high school GPA:* 3.10. *Test scores:* SAT verbal scores over 500: 35%; SAT math scores over 500: 33%; ACT scores over 18: 80%; SAT verbal scores over 600: 7%; SAT math scores over 600: 10%; ACT scores over 24: 17%; SAT verbal scores over 700: 3%; SAT math scores over 700: 2%; ACT scores over 30: 2%.

Faculty *Total:* 122, 60% full-time, 49% with terminal degrees. *Student/faculty ratio:* 13:1.

Majors Accounting; American studies; athletic training/sports medicine; biology; biology education; business; criminal justice/law enforcement administration; education; elementary education; English; fine/studio arts; history; history education; liberal arts and sciences/liberal studies; mathematics; mathematics education; music; music teacher education; nursing; physical education; physics; political science; pre-dentistry; pre-medicine; pre-veterinary studies; psychology; secondary education; social sciences; sociology; special education; theater arts/drama.

Academic Programs *Special study options:* academic remediation for entering students, adult/continuing education programs, advanced placement credit, cooperative education, double majors, freshman honors college, honors programs, internships, part-time degree program, services for LD students, summer session for credit.

Library Doris and Harry Vise Library with 50,000 titles, 130 serial subscriptions, 250 audiovisual materials, a Web page.

Computers on Campus 50 computers available on campus for general student use. A campuswide network can be accessed from student residence rooms and from off campus. Internet access, at least one staffed computer lab available.

Student Life *Housing Options:* coed, men-only, women-only. *Activities and Organizations:* drama/theater group, student-run newspaper, radio station, choral group, marching band, Alpha Chi Honor Society, Alpha Lambda Delta Honor Society, Baptist Student Union, campus radio station, Student Government Association, national fraternities, national sororities. *Campus security:* 24-hour patrols. *Student Services:* health clinic, personal/psychological counseling.

Athletics Member NAIA. *Intercollegiate sports:* baseball M(s), basketball M(s)/W(s), cross-country running M(s)/W(s), football M(s), golf M, soccer M(s)/W(s), softball W(s), tennis M(s)/W(s), volleyball W(s), wrestling M(s). *Intramural sports:* basketball M/W, bowling M/W, football M/W, golf M, softball W, table tennis M/W, volleyball M/W, weight lifting M.

Standardized Tests *Required:* SAT I or ACT (for admission).

Costs (2001–02) *Comprehensive fee:* $15,330 includes full-time tuition ($10,950) and room and board ($4380). Full-time tuition and fees vary according to course load. Part-time tuition: $457 per semester hour. *Room and board:* College room only: $1700. Room and board charges vary according to board plan and housing facility. *Waivers:* employees or children of employees.

Applying *Options:* deferred entrance. *Application fee:* $25. *Required:* high school transcript. *Required for some:* 3 letters of recommendation. *Recommended:* minimum 2.0 GPA. *Application deadline:* rolling (freshmen), rolling (transfers). *Notification:* continuous (freshmen).

Admissions Contact Mr. Edward Freytag, Director of Admissions, Cumberland University, One Cumberland Square, Lebanon, TN 37087. *Phone:* 615-444-2562 Ext. 1232. *Toll-free phone:* 800-467-0562. *Fax:* 615-444-2569. *E-mail:* admissions@cumberland.edu.

EAST TENNESSEE STATE UNIVERSITY
Johnson City, Tennessee

- **State-supported** university, founded 1911, part of State University and Community College System of Tennessee, Tennessee Board of Regents
- **Calendar** semesters
- **Degrees** associate, bachelor's, master's, doctoral, first professional, post-master's, and postbachelor's certificates
- **Small-town** 366-acre campus
- **Coed,** 9,328 undergraduate students, 81% full-time, 58% women, 42% men
- **Moderately difficult** entrance level, 80% of applicants were admitted

East Tennessee State University serves 12,000 students in the beautiful mountain and lake region of northeast Tennessee. Programs are offered in arts and sciences, business, medicine, education, applied science and technology, public and allied health, and nursing. Extensive graduate study includes a master's in physical therapy. An astronomy observatory and a $28-million library recently opened. Unique programs include bluegrass music, Appalachian studies, storytelling, and computer animation.

Undergraduates 7,564 full-time, 1,764 part-time. Students come from 38 states and territories, 44 other countries, 9% are from out of state, 5% African American, 1% Asian American or Pacific Islander, 0.9% Hispanic American, 0.4% Native American, 0.8% international, 8% transferred in, 20% live on campus. *Retention:* 69% of 2001 full-time freshmen returned.

Freshmen *Admission:* 3,316 applied, 2,646 admitted, 1,520 enrolled. *Average high school GPA:* 3.16. *Test scores:* SAT verbal scores over 500: 52%; SAT math scores over 500: 47%; ACT scores over 18: 85%; SAT verbal scores over 600: 19%; SAT math scores over 600: 14%; ACT scores over 24: 29%; SAT verbal scores over 700: 4%; SAT math scores over 700: 2%; ACT scores over 30: 3%.

Faculty *Total:* 703, 59% full-time, 55% with terminal degrees. *Student/faculty ratio:* 18:1.

Majors Accounting; art; biology; business administration; business economics; business marketing and marketing management; chemistry; child care/development; computer/information sciences; criminal justice/law enforcement administration; dental hygiene; economics; engineering-related technology; English; environmental health; finance; foreign languages/literatures; general studies; geography; health/physical education; health professions and related sciences; history; home economics; mass communications; mathematics; multi/interdisciplinary studies related; music; nursing; philosophy; physics; political science; psychology; public health; social work; sociology; special education; speech/rhetorical studies; surveying.

Academic Programs *Special study options:* academic remediation for entering students, accelerated degree program, adult/continuing education programs, advanced placement credit, cooperative education, distance learning, double majors, external degree program, freshman honors college, honors programs, independent study, internships, off-campus study, part-time degree program, services for LD students, study abroad, summer session for credit. *ROTC:* Army (b).

Library Sherrod Library plus 2 others with 594,080 titles, 3,403 serial subscriptions, an OPAC, a Web page.

Computers on Campus 550 computers available on campus for general student use. Internet access, online (class) registration, at least one staffed computer lab available.

Student Life *Housing Options:* men-only, women-only. *Activities and Organizations:* drama/theater group, student-run newspaper, radio and television station, choral group, marching band, honor societies, Volunteer ETSU, Greek organizations, religious groups, Residence Hall Councils, national fraternities, national sororities. *Campus security:* 24-hour emergency response devices and patrols, student patrols, late-night transport/escort service, controlled dormitory access. *Student Services:* health clinic, personal/psychological counseling, women's center.

Athletics Member NCAA. All Division I except football (Division I-AA). *Intercollegiate sports:* baseball M(s), basketball M(s)/W(s), cross-country running M(s)/W(s), golf M(s)/W(s), soccer W(s), softball W(s), tennis M(s)/W(s), track and field M(s)/W(s), volleyball W(s). *Intramural sports:* archery M/W, badminton M/W, baseball M, basketball M/W, bowling M/W, cross-country running M/W, football M/W, golf M/W, racquetball M/W, riflery M/W, skiing (downhill) M/W, softball M/W, swimming M/W, table tennis M/W, tennis M/W, track and field M/W, volleyball W.

Standardized Tests *Required:* SAT I or ACT (for admission).

Costs (2001–02) *Tuition:* state resident $2556 full-time, $112 per credit part-time; nonresident $9028 full-time, $382 per credit part-time. *Required fees:* $563 full-time, $35 per credit, $4 per term part-time. *Room and board:* $4008; room only: $1840. Room and board charges vary according to board plan and housing facility. *Payment plan:* deferred payment. *Waivers:* senior citizens and employees or children of employees.

Financial Aid Of all full-time matriculated undergraduates who enrolled in 2001, 5508 applied for aid, 3895 were judged to have need, 1447 had their need fully met. 765 Federal Work-Study jobs (averaging $1231). 468 State and other part-time jobs (averaging $824). In 2001, 1151 non-need-based awards were made. *Average percent of need met:* 83%. *Average financial aid package:* $4425. *Average need-based loan:* $1616. *Average need-based gift aid:* $2515. *Average non-need based aid:* $2546. *Average indebtedness upon graduation:* $18,425.

Applying *Options:* electronic application, early admission. *Application fee:* $15. *Required:* high school transcript, minimum 2.3 GPA, minimum High School GPA of 2.3 or minimum ACT score of 19. *Application deadline:* rolling (freshmen), rolling (transfers). *Notification:* continuous (freshmen).

Admissions Contact Mr. Mike Pitts, Director of Admissions, East Tennessee State University, PO Box 70731, Johnson City, TN 37614-0734. *Phone:* 423-439-4213. *Toll-free phone:* 800-462-3878. *Fax:* 423-439-4630. *E-mail:* go2etsu@etsu.edu.

EDUCATION AMERICA, SOUTHEAST COLLEGE OF TECHNOLOGY, MEMPHIS CAMPUS
Memphis, Tennessee

- **Proprietary** primarily 2-year
- **Calendar** quarters
- **Degrees** associate and bachelor's
- 600 undergraduate students, 100% full-time
- 71% of applicants were admitted

Admissions Contact David Cunningham, Director of Academics, Education America, Southeast College of Technology, Memphis Campus, 2731 Nonconnah Boulevard, Suite 160, Memphis, TN 38132-2131. *Phone:* 901-291-4234.

FISK UNIVERSITY
Nashville, Tennessee

- **Independent** comprehensive, founded 1866, affiliated with United Church of Christ
- **Calendar** semesters
- **Degrees** bachelor's and master's
- **Urban** 40-acre campus
- **Endowment** $12.0 million
- **Coed,** 786 undergraduate students, 98% full-time, 69% women, 31% men
- **Moderately difficult** entrance level, 71% of applicants were admitted

Undergraduates 768 full-time, 18 part-time. Students come from 32 states and territories, 7 other countries, 75% are from out of state, 94% African American, 0.4% Asian American or Pacific Islander, 4% international, 3% transferred in, 66% live on campus. *Retention:* 88% of 2001 full-time freshmen returned.

Freshmen *Admission:* 1,270 applied, 903 admitted, 152 enrolled. *Average high school GPA:* 3.05. *Test scores:* SAT verbal scores over 500: 45%; SAT math scores over 500: 28%; ACT scores over 18: 60%; SAT verbal scores over 600: 7%; SAT math scores over 600: 7%; ACT scores over 24: 6%.

Faculty *Total:* 83, 65% full-time, 59% with terminal degrees. *Student/faculty ratio:* 12:1.

Majors Accounting; art; biology; business administration; chemistry; computer science; economics; English; finance; French; health services administration; history; mathematics; music; music teacher education; philosophy; physics; political science; psychology; public administration; religious studies; sociology; Spanish; speech/rhetorical studies; theater arts/drama.

Academic Programs *Special study options:* advanced placement credit, cooperative education, honors programs, internships, off-campus study, student-designed majors. *ROTC:* Army (c), Air Force (c). *Unusual degree programs:* 3-2 business administration with Vanderbilt University; engineering with Vanderbilt University, Florida Agricultural and Mechanical University, University of Alabama in Huntsville; management, public administration with Vanderbilt University, pharmacy with Howard University.

Library Fisk University Main Library with 210,000 titles, 425 serial subscriptions, an OPAC, a Web page.

Computers on Campus 40 computers available on campus for general student use. A campuswide network can be accessed from student residence rooms and from off campus. At least one staffed computer lab available.

Student Life *Housing:* on-campus residence required through senior year. *Activities and Organizations:* drama/theater group, student-run newspaper, radio

Fisk University (continued)
station, choral group, Student Government Association, State clubs, Panhellenic Council, national fraternities, national sororities. *Campus security:* 24-hour patrols, late-night transport/escort service. *Student Services:* personal/psychological counseling.

Athletics Member NCAA. All Division III. *Intercollegiate sports:* baseball M, basketball M/W, cross-country running M/W, tennis M/W, track and field M/W, volleyball W. *Intramural sports:* badminton M/W, baseball M, basketball M/W, tennis M/W, track and field M/W, volleyball M/W.

Standardized Tests *Required:* SAT I or ACT (for admission).

Costs (2001–02) *Comprehensive fee:* $15,271 includes full-time tuition ($9789), mandatory fees ($300), and room and board ($5182). Full-time tuition and fees vary according to course load and degree level. Part-time tuition and fees vary according to course load and degree level. *Room and board:* Room and board charges vary according to board plan. *Payment plan:* installment. *Waivers:* employees or children of employees.

Financial Aid Of all full-time matriculated undergraduates who enrolled in 2001, 745 applied for aid, 733 were judged to have need, 350 had their need fully met. 180 Federal Work-Study jobs. In 2001, 35 non-need-based awards were made. *Average percent of need met:* 60%. *Average financial aid package:* $12,500. *Average need-based loan:* $4250. *Average need-based gift aid:* $2250. *Average non-need based aid:* $2200.

Applying *Options:* common application, electronic application, early admission. *Application fee:* $25. *Required:* essay or personal statement, high school transcript, minimum 2.5 GPA, 2 letters of recommendation. *Application deadlines:* 6/15 (freshmen), 6/15 (transfers). *Notification:* continuous (freshmen).

Admissions Contact Director of Admissions, Fisk University, Admissions Office, Fisk University, 1000 17th Avenue North, Nashville, TN 37208. *Phone:* 615-329-8666. *Toll-free phone:* 800-443-FISK. *E-mail:* admit@fisk.edu.

FREED-HARDEMAN UNIVERSITY
Henderson, Tennessee

- **Independent** comprehensive, founded 1869, affiliated with Church of Christ
- **Calendar** semesters
- **Degrees** bachelor's and master's
- **Small-town** 96-acre campus
- **Endowment** $24.0 million
- **Coed,** 1,414 undergraduate students, 93% full-time, 52% women, 48% men
- **Moderately difficult** entrance level, 56% of applicants were admitted

Undergraduates 1,319 full-time, 95 part-time. Students come from 36 states and territories, 21 other countries, 51% are from out of state, 5% African American, 0.6% Asian American or Pacific Islander, 0.7% Hispanic American, 0.4% Native American, 3% international, 7% transferred in, 77% live on campus. *Retention:* 69% of 2001 full-time freshmen returned.

Freshmen *Admission:* 822 applied, 459 admitted, 346 enrolled. *Average high school GPA:* 3.45. *Test scores:* ACT scores over 18: 93%; ACT scores over 24: 50%; ACT scores over 30: 9%.

Faculty *Total:* 143, 65% full-time, 61% with terminal degrees. *Student/faculty ratio:* 13:1.

Majors Accounting; agricultural business; American studies; art; art education; behavioral sciences; biblical studies; biological/physical sciences; biology; biology education; business administration; business economics; business marketing and marketing management; chemistry; child care/development; clothing/apparel/textile studies; communications; computer/information sciences; computer science; education; elementary education; English; English education; fashion merchandising; finance; graphic design/commercial art/illustration; health education; health/physical education; history; home economics; humanities; human resources management; information sciences/systems; interdisciplinary studies; liberal arts and sciences/liberal studies; mass communications; mathematics; mathematics education; missionary studies; music; music teacher education; philosophy; physical education; physical sciences; pre-dentistry; pre-law; premedicine; pre-pharmacy studies; pre-veterinary studies; psychology; public relations; radio/television broadcasting; science education; secondary education; social sciences; social work; special education; theater arts/drama.

Academic Programs *Special study options:* academic remediation for entering students, accelerated degree program, advanced placement credit, cooperative education, double majors, honors programs, independent study, internships, off-campus study, part-time degree program, services for LD students, student-designed majors, study abroad, summer session for credit. *Unusual degree programs:* 3-2 engineering with Tennessee Technological University, Auburn University, Vanderbilt University, University of Tennessee, Oklahoma Christian University, The University of Memphis.

Library Loden-Daniel Library with 155,394 titles, 1,634 serial subscriptions, 41,478 audiovisual materials, an OPAC, a Web page.

Computers on Campus 238 computers available on campus for general student use. A campuswide network can be accessed from student residence rooms and from off campus. Internet access, at least one staffed computer lab available.

Student Life *Housing:* on-campus residence required through senior year. *Options:* men-only, women-only. *Activities and Organizations:* drama/theater group, student-run newspaper, radio and television station, choral group, Student Alumni Association, University Program Council, University Student Ambassadors, Evangelism Forum. *Campus security:* 24-hour emergency response devices and patrols, late-night transport/escort service. *Student Services:* health clinic, personal/psychological counseling.

Athletics Member NAIA. *Intercollegiate sports:* baseball M(s), basketball M(s)/W(s), cross-country running M(s)/W(s), golf M(s)/W(s), soccer M(s)/W(s), softball W(s), tennis M(s)/W(s), volleyball W(s). *Intramural sports:* basketball M/W, football M/W, racquetball M/W, softball M/W, table tennis M/W, tennis M/W, volleyball M/W.

Standardized Tests *Required:* ACT (for admission).

Costs (2001–02) *Comprehensive fee:* $14,290 includes full-time tuition ($8080), mandatory fees ($1500), and room and board ($4710). Full-time tuition and fees vary according to course load. Part-time tuition: $312 per credit. Part-time tuition and fees vary according to course load. *Required fees:* $41 per semester hour, $180 per term part-time. *Room and board:* College room only: $2560. Room and board charges vary according to board plan. *Payment plans:* tuition prepayment, installment. *Waivers:* senior citizens and employees or children of employees.

Applying *Options:* early admission, deferred entrance. *Required:* high school transcript, minimum 2.25 GPA. *Required for some:* interview. *Recommended:* essay or personal statement, letters of recommendation. *Application deadline:* rolling (freshmen), rolling (transfers). *Notification:* continuous until 9/1 (freshmen).

Admissions Contact Mr. Jim Brown, Director of Admissions, Freed-Hardeman University, 158 East Main Street, Henderson, TN 38340-2399. *Phone:* 731-989-6651. *Toll-free phone:* 800-630-3480. *Fax:* 731-989-6047. *E-mail:* admissions@fhu.edu.

FREE WILL BAPTIST BIBLE COLLEGE
Nashville, Tennessee

- **Independent Free Will Baptist** 4-year, founded 1942
- **Calendar** semesters
- **Degrees** associate and bachelor's
- **Suburban** 10-acre campus
- **Coed**
- **Noncompetitive** entrance level

Student Life *Campus security:* 24-hour emergency response devices, student patrols, late-night transport/escort service, controlled dormitory access.

Athletics Member NCCAA.

Standardized Tests *Required:* ACT (for admission).

Financial Aid Of all full-time matriculated undergraduates who enrolled in 2001, 18 Federal Work-Study jobs (averaging $1291). *Average indebtedness upon graduation:* $14,509.

Applying *Options:* early admission, deferred entrance. *Application fee:* $25. *Required:* essay or personal statement, high school transcript, 3 letters of recommendation, medical history.

Admissions Contact Dr. Milton Fields, Academic Dean, Free Will Baptist Bible College, 3606 West End Avenue, Nashville, TN 37205-2498. *Phone:* 615-383-1340. *Toll-free phone:* 800-763-9222. *Fax:* 615-269-6028.

ITT TECHNICAL INSTITUTE
Nashville, Tennessee

- **Proprietary** primarily 2-year, founded 1984, part of ITT Educational Services, Inc
- **Calendar** quarters
- **Degrees** associate and bachelor's
- **Urban** 21-acre campus
- **Coed,** 560 undergraduate students
- **Minimally difficult** entrance level

Majors Computer/information sciences related; computer programming; drafting; electrical/electronic engineering technologies related; information technology.

Student Life *Housing:* college housing not available.
Costs (2001–02) *Tuition:* Full-time tuition and fees vary according to program. Part-time tuition and fees vary according to program. $260—$330 per credit hour.
Applying *Options:* deferred entrance. *Application fee:* $100. *Required:* high school transcript, interview. *Recommended:* letters of recommendation. *Application deadline:* rolling (freshmen), rolling (transfers). *Notification:* continuous (freshmen).
Admissions Contact Mr. Ronald Binkley, Director of Recruitment, ITT Technical Institute, 441 Donnelson Pike, Nashville, TN 37214. *Phone:* 615-889-8700. *Toll-free phone:* 800-331-8386. *Fax:* 615-872-7209.

ITT TECHNICAL INSTITUTE
Knoxville, Tennessee

- **Proprietary** primarily 2-year, founded 1988, part of ITT Educational Services, Inc
- **Calendar** quarters
- **Degrees** associate and bachelor's
- **Suburban** 5-acre campus
- **Coed,** 475 undergraduate students
- **Minimally difficult** entrance level

Majors Computer/information sciences related; computer programming; drafting; electrical/electronic engineering technologies related; information technology.
Student Life *Housing:* college housing not available.
Costs (2001–02) *Tuition:* Full-time tuition and fees vary according to program. Part-time tuition and fees vary according to program. $260—$330 per credit hour.
Applying *Options:* deferred entrance. *Application fee:* $100. *Required:* high school transcript, interview. *Recommended:* letters of recommendation. *Application deadline:* rolling (freshmen), rolling (transfers). *Notification:* continuous (freshmen).
Admissions Contact Mr. Mike Burke, Director of Recruitment, ITT Technical Institute, 10208 Technology Drive, Knoxville, TX 37932. *Phone:* 865-671-2800. *Toll-free phone:* 800-671-2801.

JOHNSON BIBLE COLLEGE
Knoxville, Tennessee

- **Independent** comprehensive, founded 1893, affiliated with Christian Churches and Churches of Christ
- **Calendar** semesters
- **Degrees** certificates, diplomas, associate, bachelor's, and master's
- **Rural** 75-acre campus
- **Coed,** 588 undergraduate students, 98% full-time, 48% women, 52% men
- **Minimally difficult** entrance level, 87% of applicants were admitted

Undergraduates 574 full-time, 14 part-time. Students come from 34 states and territories, 8 other countries, 73% are from out of state, 2% African American, 0.3% Asian American or Pacific Islander, 0.5% Hispanic American, 0.2% Native American, 3% international, 11% transferred in, 80% live on campus. *Retention:* 75% of 2001 full-time freshmen returned.
Freshmen *Admission:* 188 applied, 163 admitted, 123 enrolled. *Average high school GPA:* 3.10. *Test scores:* SAT verbal scores over 500: 62%; SAT math scores over 500: 59%; ACT scores over 18: 88%; SAT verbal scores over 600: 26%; SAT math scores over 600: 25%; ACT scores over 24: 27%; SAT verbal scores over 700: 6%; SAT math scores over 700: 4%; ACT scores over 30: 5%.
Faculty *Total:* 45, 51% full-time, 51% with terminal degrees. *Student/faculty ratio:* 16:1.
Majors Biblical studies; early childhood education; elementary education; middle school education; religious music; teacher assistant/aide.
Academic Programs *Special study options:* academic remediation for entering students, accelerated degree program, adult/continuing education programs, advanced placement credit, cooperative education, distance learning, double majors, English as a second language, independent study, internships, part-time degree program, services for LD students, summer session for credit.
Library Glass Memorial Library plus 1 other with 94,178 titles, 421 serial subscriptions, 11,542 audiovisual materials, an OPAC, a Web page.
Computers on Campus 18 computers available on campus for general student use. A campuswide network can be accessed from student residence rooms and from off campus. At least one staffed computer lab available.
Student Life *Housing:* on-campus residence required through senior year. *Options:* men-only, women-only. *Activities and Organizations:* student-run radio station, choral group, Quest, Timothy club, International Harvesters. *Campus security:* 24-hour emergency response devices, student patrols. *Student Services:* health clinic, personal/psychological counseling.
Athletics Member NCCAA. *Intercollegiate sports:* baseball M, basketball M/W, soccer M/W, volleyball W. *Intramural sports:* basketball M, tennis M/W, volleyball M/W.
Standardized Tests *Required:* SAT I or ACT (for admission). *Required for some:* ACT (for admission).
Costs (2001–02) *One-time required fee:* $50. *Comprehensive fee:* $9000 includes full-time tuition ($4930), mandatory fees ($570), and room and board ($3500). Part-time tuition: $205 per semester hour. Part-time tuition and fees vary according to course load. *Required fees:* $18 per semester hour. *Room and board:* Room and board charges vary according to board plan and housing facility. *Payment plan:* installment. *Waivers:* employees or children of employees.
Financial Aid Of all full-time matriculated undergraduates who enrolled in 2001, 524 applied for aid, 499 were judged to have need, 23 had their need fully met. 110 Federal Work-Study jobs (averaging $940). *Average percent of need met:* 57%. *Average financial aid package:* $3137. *Average need-based loan:* $2324. *Average need-based gift aid:* $3034. *Average indebtedness upon graduation:* $12,007.
Applying *Options:* deferred entrance. *Application fee:* $35. *Required:* essay or personal statement, high school transcript, 3 letters of recommendation. *Required for some:* interview. *Application deadlines:* 8/1 (freshmen), 8/1 (transfers). *Notification:* continuous (freshmen).
Admissions Contact Mr. Tim Wingfield, Director of Admissions, Johnson Bible College, 7900 Johnson Drive, Knoxville, TN 37998. *Phone:* 865-251-2346. *Toll-free phone:* 800-827-2122. *Fax:* 423-251-2336. *E-mail:* twingfield@jbc.edu.

KING COLLEGE
Bristol, Tennessee

- **Independent** comprehensive, founded 1867, affiliated with Presbyterian Church (U.S.A.)
- **Calendar** semesters
- **Degrees** bachelor's and master's
- **Suburban** 135-acre campus
- **Endowment** $25.0 million
- **Coed,** 655 undergraduate students, 88% full-time, 58% women, 42% men
- **Moderately difficult** entrance level, 64% of applicants were admitted

Undergraduates 574 full-time, 81 part-time. Students come from 29 states and territories, 31 other countries, 50% are from out of state, 2% African American, 0.4% Asian American or Pacific Islander, 0.9% Hispanic American, 6% international, 5% transferred in, 80% live on campus. *Retention:* 77% of 2001 full-time freshmen returned.
Freshmen *Admission:* 583 applied, 373 admitted, 146 enrolled. *Average high school GPA:* 3.53. *Test scores:* SAT verbal scores over 500: 72%; SAT math scores over 500: 64%; ACT scores over 18: 95%; SAT verbal scores over 600: 29%; SAT math scores over 600: 27%; ACT scores over 24: 48%; SAT verbal scores over 700: 7%; SAT math scores over 700: 3%; ACT scores over 30: 6%.
Faculty *Total:* 71, 59% full-time, 49% with terminal degrees. *Student/faculty ratio:* 11:1.
Majors Accounting; American studies; behavioral sciences; biblical studies; biochemistry; biological/physical sciences; biological specializations related; biology; biology education; biophysics; business administration; chemistry; chemistry education; communications; creative writing; early childhood education; economics; education; elementary education; English; English education; fine/studio arts; French; French language education; health professions and related sciences; history; history education; information sciences/systems; international business; mathematics; mathematics/computer science; mathematics education; medical technology; middle school education; modern languages; music; nursing; physics; physics education; political science; pre-law; pre-medicine; pre-pharmacy studies; pre-veterinary studies; psychology; religious studies; secondary education; Spanish; Spanish language education; speech/theater education.
Academic Programs *Special study options:* accelerated degree program, advanced placement credit, double majors, English as a second language, honors programs, independent study, internships, off-campus study, part-time degree program, study abroad, summer session for credit. *ROTC:* Army (c). *Unusual degree programs:* 3-2 engineering with University of Tennessee, Vanderbilt University.
Library E. W. King Library with 95,136 titles, 605 serial subscriptions, 5,290 audiovisual materials, an OPAC, a Web page.

King College (continued)

Computers on Campus 80 computers available on campus for general student use. A campuswide network can be accessed from student residence rooms and from off campus. Internet access, at least one staffed computer lab available.

Student Life *Housing:* on-campus residence required for freshman year. *Options:* men-only, women-only, disabled students. *Activities and Organizations:* drama/theater group, student-run newspaper, choral group, Student Government Association, Campus Life Committee, World Christian Fellowship, Fellowship of Christian Athletes, Drama Club. *Campus security:* late-night transport/escort service. *Student Services:* health clinic, personal/psychological counseling.

Athletics Member NAIA. *Intercollegiate sports:* baseball M(s), basketball M(s)/W(s), golf M(s), soccer M(s)/W(s), tennis M(s)/W(s), volleyball W(s). *Intramural sports:* badminton M/W, basketball M/W, cross-country running M(c)/W(c), soccer M/W, softball M/W, table tennis M/W, tennis M/W, volleyball M/W, weight lifting M.

Standardized Tests *Required:* SAT I or ACT (for admission).

Costs (2001–02) *Comprehensive fee:* $17,800 includes full-time tuition ($12,390), mandatory fees ($950), and room and board ($4460). Part-time tuition: $300 per credit hour. Part-time tuition and fees vary according to course load and program. No tuition increase for student's term of enrollment. *Required fees:* $100 per term part-time. *Room and board:* College room only: $2100. *Payment plans:* tuition prepayment, installment. *Waivers:* employees or children of employees.

Financial Aid Of all full-time matriculated undergraduates who enrolled in 2001, 428 applied for aid, 385 were judged to have need, 66 had their need fully met. 119 Federal Work-Study jobs (averaging $1243). 201 State and other part-time jobs (averaging $1365). In 2001, 140 non-need-based awards were made. *Average percent of need met:* 81%. *Average financial aid package:* $12,765. *Average need-based loan:* $3677. *Average need-based gift aid:* $9163. *Average non-need based aid:* $6510. *Average indebtedness upon graduation:* $3875.

Applying *Options:* common application, electronic application, early admission, deferred entrance. *Application fee:* $20. *Required:* essay or personal statement, high school transcript, minimum 2.4 GPA. *Required for some:* letters of recommendation, interview. *Recommended:* letters of recommendation, interview. *Application deadline:* rolling (freshmen), rolling (transfers). *Notification:* continuous (freshmen).

Admissions Contact Mr. Micah Crews, Director of Admissions, King College, 1350 King College Road, Bristol, TN 37620-2699. *Phone:* 423-652-4773. *Toll-free phone:* 800-362-0014. *Fax:* 423-652-4727. *E-mail:* admissions@king.edu.

LAMBUTH UNIVERSITY

Jackson, Tennessee

- **Independent United Methodist** 4-year, founded 1843
- **Calendar** semesters
- **Degree** bachelor's
- **Urban** 50-acre campus with easy access to Memphis
- **Endowment** $8.5 million
- **Coed,** 904 undergraduate students, 91% full-time, 58% women, 42% men
- **Moderately difficult** entrance level, 68% of applicants were admitted

Undergraduates 826 full-time, 78 part-time. Students come from 26 states and territories, 13 other countries, 20% are from out of state, 16% African American, 0.2% Asian American or Pacific Islander, 0.8% Hispanic American, 0.2% Native American, 2% international, 9% transferred in, 59% live on campus. *Retention:* 63% of 2001 full-time freshmen returned.

Freshmen *Admission:* 917 applied, 621 admitted, 210 enrolled. *Average high school GPA:* 3.20. *Test scores:* SAT verbal scores over 500: 70%; SAT math scores over 500: 61%; ACT scores over 18: 99%; SAT verbal scores over 600: 9%; SAT math scores over 600: 26%; ACT scores over 24: 31%; SAT verbal scores over 700: 4%; ACT scores over 30: 3%.

Faculty *Total:* 96, 53% full-time, 48% with terminal degrees. *Student/faculty ratio:* 14:1.

Majors Accounting; art; art education; art history; athletic training/sports medicine; biology; business administration; business marketing and marketing management; chemistry; criminal justice/law enforcement administration; education; education (K-12); education of the hearing impaired; elementary education; English; family/consumer studies; fashion merchandising; fine/studio arts; general studies; graphic design/commercial art/illustration; history; human ecology; humanities; information sciences/systems; interdisciplinary studies; interior design; interior environments; international relations; marketing operations; mass communications; mathematics; middle school education; modern languages; music; music (piano and organ performance); music teacher education; music (voice and choral/opera performance); nutrition studies; physical education; political science; pre-dentistry; pre-law; pre-medicine; psychology; public relations; religious music; religious studies; secondary education; sociology; special education; speech-language pathology/audiology; speech therapy; theater arts/drama; wind/percussion instruments.

Academic Programs *Special study options:* academic remediation for entering students, adult/continuing education programs, advanced placement credit, double majors, English as a second language, independent study, internships, off-campus study, part-time degree program, services for LD students, student-designed majors, study abroad, summer session for credit.

Library Luther L. Gobbel Library with 198,000 titles, 7,000 serial subscriptions, 109 audiovisual materials, an OPAC.

Computers on Campus 60 computers available on campus for general student use. A campuswide network can be accessed from student residence rooms and from off campus. Internet access, at least one staffed computer lab available.

Student Life *Housing:* on-campus residence required through senior year. *Options:* coed, men-only, women-only. *Activities and Organizations:* drama/theater group, student-run newspaper, choral group, student government, Student Activities Committee, Black Student Union, Religious Life Council, International Students Organization, national fraternities, national sororities. *Campus security:* 24-hour emergency response devices and patrols, late-night transport/escort service, controlled dormitory access. *Student Services:* health clinic, personal/psychological counseling.

Athletics Member NAIA. *Intercollegiate sports:* baseball M(s), basketball M(s)/W(s), cross-country running M(s)/W(s), football M(s), golf M(s), soccer M(s)/W(s), softball W(s), tennis M(s)/W(s), volleyball W(s).

Standardized Tests *Required:* SAT I or ACT (for admission).

Costs (2001–02) *Comprehensive fee:* $14,254 includes full-time tuition ($9398), mandatory fees ($150), and room and board ($4706). Part-time tuition: $372 per credit hour. Part-time tuition and fees vary according to class time and course load. *Required fees:* $75 per term part-time. *Room and board:* College room only: $2148. Room and board charges vary according to board plan and housing facility. *Payment plans:* installment, deferred payment. *Waivers:* adult students, senior citizens, and employees or children of employees.

Financial Aid Of all full-time matriculated undergraduates who enrolled in 2001, 828 applied for aid, 537 were judged to have need, 199 had their need fully met. 116 Federal Work-Study jobs (averaging $1040). 46 State and other part-time jobs (averaging $1172). *Average percent of need met:* 72%. *Average financial aid package:* $8107. *Average need-based loan:* $3545. *Average need-based gift aid:* $5450. *Average indebtedness upon graduation:* $11,000.

Applying *Options:* common application, electronic application, early admission, deferred entrance. *Application fee:* $25. *Required:* essay or personal statement, high school transcript, minimum 2.0 GPA. *Required for some:* 3 letters of recommendation. *Recommended:* interview. *Application deadline:* rolling (freshmen), rolling (transfers). *Notification:* continuous (freshmen).

Admissions Contact Ms. Denes Bardos, Director of Admissions, Lambuth University, 705 Lambuth Boulevard, Jackson, TN 38301. *Phone:* 731-425-3323. *Toll-free phone:* 800-526-2884. *Fax:* 731-425-3496. *E-mail:* admit@lambuth.edu.

LANE COLLEGE

Jackson, Tennessee

- **Independent** 4-year, founded 1882, affiliated with Christian Methodist Episcopal Church
- **Calendar** semesters
- **Degree** bachelor's
- **Suburban** 25-acre campus with easy access to Memphis
- **Endowment** $2.8 million
- **Coed**
- **Minimally difficult** entrance level

Faculty *Student/faculty ratio:* 15:1.

Student Life *Campus security:* 24-hour emergency response devices and patrols, surveillance cameras, lighted parking areas.

Athletics Member NCAA. All Division II.

Standardized Tests *Required:* SAT I or ACT (for admission).

Costs (2001–02) *Comprehensive fee:* $10,150 includes full-time tuition ($5800), mandatory fees ($550), and room and board ($3800). Full-time tuition and fees vary according to course load. Part-time tuition: $250 per semester hour. Part-time tuition and fees vary according to course load. *Required fees:* $275 per term. *Payment plans:* installment, deferred payment.

Financial Aid Of all full-time matriculated undergraduates who enrolled in 2001, 660 applied for aid, 620 were judged to have need, 41 had their need fully met. 338 Federal Work-Study jobs (averaging $908). *Average percent of need met:* 88. *Average financial aid package:* $8468. *Average need-based loan:* $2986. *Average need-based gift aid:* $5563. *Average indebtedness upon graduation:* $17,525.

Applying *Options:* common application, electronic application, early admission. *Required:* high school transcript, minimum 2.0 GPA, 2 letters of recommendation.

Admissions Contact Ms. E. Brown, Director of Admissions, Lane College, 545 Lane Avenue, Bray Administration Building 2nd Floor, Jackson, TN 38301-4598. *Phone:* 901-426-7532. *Toll-free phone:* 800-960-7533. *Fax:* 901-426-7559. *E-mail:* admissions@lanecollege.edu.

LEE UNIVERSITY
Cleveland, Tennessee

- **Independent** comprehensive, founded 1918, affiliated with Church of God
- **Calendar** semesters
- **Degrees** bachelor's and master's
- **Small-town** 45-acre campus
- **Endowment** $6.8 million
- **Coed,** 3,325 undergraduate students, 93% full-time, 57% women, 43% men
- **Minimally difficult** entrance level, 62% of applicants were admitted

Undergraduates 3,084 full-time, 241 part-time. Students come from 48 states and territories, 39 other countries, 62% are from out of state, 3% African American, 0.9% Asian American or Pacific Islander, 3% Hispanic American, 0.5% Native American, 3% international, 9% transferred in, 49% live on campus. *Retention:* 72% of 2001 full-time freshmen returned.

Freshmen *Admission:* 1,142 applied, 705 admitted, 846 enrolled. *Average high school GPA:* 3.10. *Test scores:* SAT verbal scores over 500: 63%; SAT math scores over 500: 58%; ACT scores over 18: 85%; SAT verbal scores over 600: 28%; SAT math scores over 600: 20%; ACT scores over 24: 47%; SAT verbal scores over 700: 5%; SAT math scores over 700: 3%; ACT scores over 30: 7%.

Faculty *Total:* 248, 47% full-time, 35% with terminal degrees. *Student/faculty ratio:* 20:1.

Majors Accounting; biblical studies; biological/physical sciences; biology; business administration; business education; chemistry; education; elementary education; English; health education; history; individual/family development; information sciences/systems; international relations; mass communications; mathematics; medical technology; modern languages; music; music (piano and organ performance); music teacher education; music (voice and choral/opera performance); natural sciences; pastoral counseling; physical education; psychology; religious education; respiratory therapy; secondary education; secretarial science; social sciences; sociology; special education; theology.

Academic Programs *Special study options:* academic remediation for entering students, adult/continuing education programs, advanced placement credit, cooperative education, distance learning, double majors, English as a second language, external degree program, honors programs, independent study, internships, part-time degree program, services for LD students, study abroad, summer session for credit.

Library William G. Squires Library with 158,896 titles, 20,000 serial subscriptions, 13,156 audiovisual materials, an OPAC, a Web page.

Computers on Campus A campuswide network can be accessed from off campus. Internet access, at least one staffed computer lab available.

Student Life *Housing:* on-campus residence required for freshman year. *Options:* men-only, women-only, disabled students. *Activities and Organizations:* drama/theater group, student-run newspaper, choral group, Student Leadership Council, Pioneers for Christ, International Student Fellowship, Umoja, Back Yard Ministry. *Campus security:* 24-hour emergency response devices and patrols, late-night transport/escort service. *Student Services:* health clinic, personal/psychological counseling.

Athletics Member NAIA, NCCAA. *Intercollegiate sports:* basketball M(s)/W(s), cross-country running M(s)/W(s), golf M(s), soccer M(s)/W(s), softball W(s), tennis M(s)/W(s), volleyball W(s). *Intramural sports:* badminton M/W, basketball M/W, bowling M/W, football M/W, racquetball M/W, soccer M/W, softball M/W, table tennis M/W, tennis M/W, volleyball M/W.

Standardized Tests *Required:* SAT I or ACT (for admission). *Recommended:* ACT (for admission).

Costs (2002–03) *Tuition:* $335 per credit hour part-time. *Required fees:* $25 per term part-time. *Room only:* Room and board charges vary according to board plan and housing facility. *Payment plan:* deferred payment. *Waivers:* employees or children of employees.

Financial Aid Of all full-time matriculated undergraduates who enrolled in 2001, 2203 applied for aid, 1890 were judged to have need, 244 had their need fully met. In 2001, 617 non-need-based awards were made. *Average percent of need met:* 45%. *Average financial aid package:* $6705. *Average need-based loan:* $3874. *Average need-based gift aid:* $4483. *Average indebtedness upon graduation:* $10,750.

Applying *Options:* common application, electronic application, early admission, deferred entrance. *Application fee:* $25. *Required:* high school transcript, minimum 2.0 GPA, MMR immunization record. *Required for some:* 1 letter of recommendation. *Recommended:* 3 letters of recommendation. *Application deadline:* 9/1 (freshmen), rolling (transfers). *Notification:* continuous (freshmen).

Admissions Contact Admissions Coordinator, Lee University, PO Box 3450, Cleveland, TN 37311. *Phone:* 423-614-8500. *Toll-free phone:* 800-LEE-9930. *Fax:* 423-614-8533. *E-mail:* admissions@leeuniversity.edu.

LEMOYNE-OWEN COLLEGE
Memphis, Tennessee

- **Independent** 4-year, founded 1862, affiliated with United Church of Christ
- **Calendar** semesters
- **Degrees** bachelor's and postbachelor's certificates
- **Urban** 15-acre campus
- **Endowment** $10.0 million
- **Coed,** 734 undergraduate students, 85% full-time, 70% women, 30% men
- **Minimally difficult** entrance level, 100% of applicants were admitted

Undergraduates 623 full-time, 111 part-time. Students come from 20 states and territories, 6 other countries, 7% are from out of state, 95% African American, 0.3% Asian American or Pacific Islander, 2% international, 14% transferred in, 20% live on campus. *Retention:* 65% of 2001 full-time freshmen returned.

Freshmen *Admission:* 203 applied, 203 admitted, 162 enrolled. *Average high school GPA:* 2.64. *Test scores:* ACT scores over 18: 24%; ACT scores over 24: 1%.

Faculty *Total:* 59, 97% full-time, 59% with terminal degrees. *Student/faculty ratio:* 14:1.

Majors Accounting; art; biology; business administration; chemistry; computer science; education; education (K-12); elementary education; English; history; humanities; mathematics; natural sciences; physical education; political science; secondary education; social sciences; social work; sociology.

Academic Programs *Special study options:* academic remediation for entering students, accelerated degree program, adult/continuing education programs, advanced placement credit, cooperative education, double majors, honors programs, independent study, internships, off-campus study, part-time degree program, services for LD students, study abroad, summer session for credit. *ROTC:* Army (c), Air Force (c). *Unusual degree programs:* 3-2 engineering with Christian Brothers University, Tuskegee University, Tennessee State University; nursing with University of Tennessee at Memphis; mass communications with Rust College, pharmacy with Xavier University of Louisiana.

Library Hollis F. Price Library with 90,000 titles, 350 serial subscriptions.

Computers on Campus 223 computers available on campus for general student use. A campuswide network can be accessed from off campus. Internet access, at least one staffed computer lab available.

Student Life *Housing Options:* men-only, women-only. *Activities and Organizations:* drama/theater group, student-run newspaper, choral group, Students in Free Enterprise, National Black Student Accountant Club, Gospel Choir, Pre-Alumni, National Panhellenic Council, national fraternities, national sororities. *Campus security:* 24-hour patrols, late-night transport/escort service, controlled dormitory access. *Student Services:* health clinic, personal/psychological counseling.

Athletics Member NCAA, NAIA. All NCAA Division I except baseball (Division II), men's and women's basketball (Division II), cross-country running (Division II). *Intercollegiate sports:* baseball M(s), basketball M(s)/W(s), cross-country running M(s), golf M(s)/W(s), softball W(s), tennis M(s)/W(s), volleyball W(s). *Intramural sports:* soccer M/W.

Standardized Tests *Required:* SAT I or ACT (for admission).

Costs (2001–02) *Comprehensive fee:* $13,070 includes full-time tuition ($8250), mandatory fees ($200), and room and board ($4620). Full-time tuition and fees vary according to course load. Part-time tuition: $345 per credit hour. Part-time tuition and fees vary according to course load. *Room and board:* College room only: $2420. Room and board charges vary according to housing facility. *Payment plans:* installment, deferred payment. *Waivers:* employees or children of employees.

Financial Aid Of all full-time matriculated undergraduates who enrolled in 2001, 504 applied for aid, 487 were judged to have need, 35 had their need fully met. 290 Federal Work-Study jobs. In 2001, 23 non-need-based awards were made. *Average percent of need met:* 66%. *Average financial aid package:* $9710. *Average need-based loan:* $3053. *Average need-based gift aid:* $7000. *Average non-need based aid:* $7856. *Average indebtedness upon graduation:* $10,500.

LeMoyne-Owen College (continued)

Applying *Options:* common application. *Application fee:* $25. *Required:* essay or personal statement, high school transcript, minimum 2.0 GPA, 2 letters of recommendation, interview. *Application deadline:* 4/1 (freshmen), rolling (transfers).

Admissions Contact LeMoyne-Owen College, 807 Walker Avenue, Memphis, TN 38126. *Phone:* 901-942-7302. *Toll-free phone:* 800-737-7778. *E-mail:* admissions@nile.lemoyne-owen.edu.

LINCOLN MEMORIAL UNIVERSITY

Harrogate, Tennessee

- **Independent** comprehensive, founded 1897
- **Calendar** semesters
- **Degrees** associate, bachelor's, and master's
- **Small-town** 1000-acre campus
- **Endowment** $31.1 million
- **Coed,** 943 undergraduate students, 76% full-time, 67% women, 33% men
- **Moderately difficult** entrance level, 72% of applicants were admitted

Undergraduates 721 full-time, 222 part-time. Students come from 30 states and territories, 15 other countries, 54% are from out of state, 3% African American, 0.3% Asian American or Pacific Islander, 0.1% Hispanic American, 0.3% Native American, 5% international, 19% transferred in, 32% live on campus. *Retention:* 54% of 2001 full-time freshmen returned.

Freshmen *Admission:* 539 applied, 388 admitted, 168 enrolled. *Average high school GPA:* 3.43. *Test scores:* ACT scores over 18: 91%; ACT scores over 24: 42%; ACT scores over 30: 3%.

Faculty *Total:* 135, 64% full-time, 56% with terminal degrees. *Student/faculty ratio:* 9:1.

Majors Accounting; art; athletic training/sports medicine; biology; business administration; business economics; business education; business marketing and marketing management; chemistry; early childhood education; education; elementary education; English; environmental science; finance; fish/game management; health education; history; humanities; liberal arts and sciences/liberal studies; mass communications; mathematics; medical technology; nursing; physical education; pre-law; pre-medicine; pre-veterinary studies; psychology; science education; secondary education; social work; veterinary sciences; veterinary technology; wildlife management.

Academic Programs *Special study options:* accelerated degree program, adult/continuing education programs, advanced placement credit, double majors, English as a second language, honors programs, independent study, part-time degree program, student-designed majors, summer session for credit.

Library Carnegie Library with 145,537 titles, 251 serial subscriptions, 3,369 audiovisual materials, an OPAC, a Web page.

Computers on Campus 150 computers available on campus for general student use. A campuswide network can be accessed from student residence rooms. Internet access, at least one staffed computer lab available.

Student Life *Housing Options:* coed, men-only, women-only. *Activities and Organizations:* drama/theater group, student-run newspaper, radio and television station, choral group, Baptist Student Association, Wesleyan Association, Student Nurses Association, Student National Education Association, Student Alumni Association. *Campus security:* 24-hour emergency response devices and patrols. *Student Services:* personal/psychological counseling.

Athletics Member NCAA. All Division II. *Intercollegiate sports:* baseball M(s), basketball M(s)/W(s), cross-country running M(s)/W(s), golf M(s)/W, soccer M(s)/W(s), softball W(s), tennis M(s)/W(s), volleyball W(s). *Intramural sports:* basketball M/W, football M, golf M/W, soccer M/W, softball M/W, tennis M/W, volleyball M/W.

Standardized Tests *Required:* SAT I or ACT (for admission).

Costs (2002–03) *Comprehensive fee:* $16,140 includes full-time tuition ($11,760) and room and board ($4380). Part-time tuition: $490 per semester hour. *Room and board:* Room and board charges vary according to board plan and housing facility. *Payment plans:* installment, deferred payment. *Waivers:* senior citizens and employees or children of employees.

Financial Aid Of all full-time matriculated undergraduates who enrolled in 2001, 683 applied for aid, 458 were judged to have need, 402 had their need fully met. 164 Federal Work-Study jobs (averaging $1134). In 2001, 129 non-need-based awards were made. *Average percent of need met:* 90%. *Average financial aid package:* $9800. *Average need-based loan:* $3000. *Average need-based gift aid:* $5620. *Average non-need based aid:* $5725. *Average indebtedness upon graduation:* $11,500.

Applying *Options:* common application. *Application fee:* $25. *Required:* high school transcript, minimum 2.3 GPA. *Required for some:* essay or personal statement. *Recommended:* interview. *Application deadline:* rolling (freshmen), rolling (transfers).

Admissions Contact Mr. Conrad Daniels, Dean of Admissions and Recruitment, Lincoln Memorial University, Cumberland Gap Parkway, Harrogate, TN 37752-1901. *Phone:* 423-869-6280. *Toll-free phone:* 800-325-0900. *Fax:* 423-869-6250. *E-mail:* admissions@inetlmu.lmunet.edu.

LIPSCOMB UNIVERSITY

Nashville, Tennessee

- **Independent** comprehensive, founded 1891, affiliated with Church of Christ
- **Calendar** semesters
- **Degrees** bachelor's, master's, and first professional
- **Urban** 65-acre campus
- **Endowment** $46.3 million
- **Coed,** 2,408 undergraduate students, 88% full-time, 57% women, 43% men
- **Moderately difficult** entrance level, 85% of applicants were admitted

Founded in 1891, Lipscomb University is a distinctly Christian university with a sterling academic reputation. More than 100 major programs of study are offered. Lipscomb's twenty-first century, campuswide, fiber-optic network provides PC connections in every dorm room and many other locations for Internet access to resources worldwide.

Undergraduates 2,111 full-time, 297 part-time. Students come from 42 states and territories, 41 other countries, 38% are from out of state, 6% transferred in, 49% live on campus. *Retention:* 74% of 2001 full-time freshmen returned.

Freshmen *Admission:* 1,601 applied, 1,358 admitted, 596 enrolled. *Average high school GPA:* 3.46. *Test scores:* SAT verbal scores over 500: 76%; SAT math scores over 500: 70%; ACT scores over 18: 93%; SAT verbal scores over 600: 30%; SAT math scores over 600: 28%; ACT scores over 24: 48%; SAT verbal scores over 700: 7%; SAT math scores over 700: 7%; ACT scores over 30: 10%.

Faculty *Total:* 231, 50% full-time, 59% with terminal degrees. *Student/faculty ratio:* 16:1.

Majors Accounting; American government; American studies; art; athletic training/sports medicine; biblical languages/literatures; biblical studies; biochemistry; biology; biology education; business administration; business economics; business marketing and marketing management; chemistry; computer science; dietetics; divinity/ministry; education; elementary education; engineering science; English; environmental science; exercise sciences; family/consumer studies; fashion merchandising; finance; fine/studio arts; food products retailing; French; French language education; German; graphic design/commercial art/illustration; health education; history; home economics; information sciences/systems; liberal arts and sciences/liberal studies; mass communications; mathematics; middle school education; music; music (piano and organ performance); music teacher education; music (voice and choral/opera performance); nursing; philosophy; physical education; physics; political science; pre-dentistry; pre-law; pre-medicine; pre-veterinary studies; psychology; public administration; public relations; secondary education; social work; Spanish; speech/rhetorical studies; stringed instruments; theology; urban studies; wind/percussion instruments.

Academic Programs *Special study options:* academic remediation for entering students, accelerated degree program, adult/continuing education programs, advanced placement credit, distance learning, double majors, honors programs, independent study, internships, part-time degree program, services for LD students, study abroad, summer session for credit. *ROTC:* Army (c), Air Force (c). *Unusual degree programs:* 3-2 engineering with Auburn University, Vanderbilt University, Tennessee Technical University, University of Tennessee; nursing with Vanderbilt University, Belmont University.

Library Beaman Library plus 1 other with 199,400 titles, 886 serial subscriptions, 724 audiovisual materials, an OPAC.

Computers on Campus 232 computers available on campus for general student use. A campuswide network can be accessed from student residence rooms and from off campus. Internet access, online (class) registration, at least one staffed computer lab available.

Student Life *Housing:* on-campus residence required through senior year. *Options:* men-only, women-only. *Activities and Organizations:* drama/theater group, student-run newspaper, radio station, choral group, social clubs, Sigma Pi Beta, Circle K, business fraternities, intramural program. *Campus security:* 24-hour emergency response devices and patrols, late-night transport/escort service, controlled dormitory access. *Student Services:* health clinic, personal/psychological counseling.

Athletics Member NCAA. All Division I. *Intercollegiate sports:* baseball M(s), basketball M(s)/W(s), cross-country running M(s)/W(s), golf M(s)/W(s), soccer

M(s)/W(s), softball W(s), tennis M(s)/W(s), volleyball W(s). *Intramural sports:* basketball M/W, football M/W, racquetball M/W, soccer M/W, softball M/W, table tennis M/W, tennis M/W, volleyball M/W.

Standardized Tests *Required:* SAT I or ACT (for admission).

Costs (2001–02) *Comprehensive fee:* $16,248 includes full-time tuition ($10,440), mandatory fees ($388), and room and board ($5420). Full-time tuition and fees vary according to degree level and location. Part-time tuition: $348 per hour. Part-time tuition and fees vary according to class time, degree level, and location. *Required fees:* $12 per hour. *Room and board:* Room and board charges vary according to board plan, housing facility, and location. *Payment plan:* installment. *Waivers:* minority students and employees or children of employees.

Financial Aid Of all full-time matriculated undergraduates who enrolled in 2001, 1700 applied for aid, 1400 were judged to have need. 48 Federal Work-Study jobs (averaging $1545). *Average financial aid package:* $12,000. *Average need-based gift aid:* $7000.

Applying *Options:* electronic application, early admission, early action. *Application fee:* $50. *Required:* high school transcript, minimum 2.25 GPA, 2 letters of recommendation. *Recommended:* essay or personal statement, interview. *Application deadline:* rolling (freshmen), rolling (transfers). *Notification:* continuous (freshmen), 12/15 (early action).

Admissions Contact Mr. Scott Gilmer, Director of Admissions, Lipscomb University, 3901 Granny White Pike, Nashville, TN 37204-3951. *Phone:* 615-269-1776. *Toll-free phone:* 800-333-4358. *Fax:* 615-269-1804. *E-mail:* admissions@lipscom.edu.

MARTIN METHODIST COLLEGE

Pulaski, Tennessee

- **Independent United Methodist** 4-year, founded 1870
- **Calendar** semesters
- **Degree** diplomas and bachelor's
- **Small-town** 6-acre campus with easy access to Nashville
- **Endowment** $6.6 million
- **Coed,** 631 undergraduate students, 65% full-time, 61% women, 39% men
- **Minimally difficult** entrance level, 97% of applicants were admitted

Undergraduates 408 full-time, 223 part-time. Students come from 25 states and territories, 13 other countries, 24% are from out of state, 9% African American, 0.3% Asian American or Pacific Islander, 1.0% Hispanic American, 0.8% Native American, 16% international, 10% transferred in, 35% live on campus. *Retention:* 29% of 2001 full-time freshmen returned.

Freshmen *Admission:* 377 applied, 364 admitted, 157 enrolled. *Average high school GPA:* 2.85.

Faculty *Total:* 62, 53% full-time, 47% with terminal degrees. *Student/faculty ratio:* 17:1.

Majors Advertising; agricultural business; American studies; art; art education; behavioral sciences; biological/physical sciences; biology; broadcast journalism; business administration; business education; business marketing and marketing management; chemistry; community services; computer programming; computer science; counselor education/guidance; criminal justice/law enforcement administration; divinity/ministry; early childhood education; economics; education; elementary education; English; health education; health science; health services administration; history; history of philosophy; humanities; human services; interior design; law enforcement/police science; legal administrative assistant; liberal arts and sciences/liberal studies; maritime science; marriage/family counseling; mass communications; mathematics; medical administrative assistant; medical laboratory technician; music; music teacher education; pharmacy; philosophy; physical education; physical sciences; physical therapy; physiology; psychology; public health; recreation/leisure facilities management; religious studies; science education; secretarial science; social work; sociology; teacher assistant/aide; theater arts/drama; theology; veterinary sciences; wildlife biology; wildlife management; zoology.

Academic Programs *Special study options:* academic remediation for entering students, adult/continuing education programs, advanced placement credit, English as a second language, part-time degree program, services for LD students, student-designed majors, summer session for credit.

Library Warden Memorial Library with 80,000 titles, 252 serial subscriptions, 668 audiovisual materials, an OPAC, a Web page.

Computers on Campus 40 computers available on campus for general student use. Internet access, at least one staffed computer lab available.

Student Life *Housing:* on-campus residence required through sophomore year. *Options:* men-only, women-only. *Activities and Organizations:* drama/theater group, choral group, Student Christian Association, Fellowship of Christian Athletes, Drama Club, International Club, Students for Environment Awareness. *Campus security:* controlled dormitory access.

Athletics Member NAIA. *Intercollegiate sports:* baseball M(s), basketball M(s)/W(s), cross-country running M/W, golf M(s), soccer M(s)/W(s), softball W(s), tennis M(s)/W(s), volleyball W(s). *Intramural sports:* badminton M/W, basketball M/W, football M, racquetball M/W, soccer M/W, softball M/W, swimming M/W, table tennis M/W, volleyball M/W.

Standardized Tests *Required:* SAT I or ACT (for admission).

Costs (2001–02) *Comprehensive fee:* $14,540 includes full-time tuition ($10,800), mandatory fees ($40), and room and board ($3700). Part-time tuition: $450 per credit hour. Part-time tuition and fees vary according to class time. *Room and board:* Room and board charges vary according to housing facility. *Waivers:* employees or children of employees.

Financial Aid Of all full-time matriculated undergraduates who enrolled in 2001, 488 applied for aid, 347 were judged to have need, 242 had their need fully met. 53 Federal Work-Study jobs (averaging $770). 27 State and other part-time jobs (averaging $813). In 2001, 81 non-need-based awards were made. *Average percent of need met:* 84%. *Average financial aid package:* $5640. *Average need-based loan:* $3010. *Average need-based gift aid:* $3711. *Average non-need based aid:* $2270. *Average indebtedness upon graduation:* $9048.

Applying *Options:* common application, early admission, deferred entrance. *Application fee:* $25. *Required:* high school transcript, minimum 2.0 GPA. *Recommended:* essay or personal statement, interview. *Application deadlines:* 8/30 (freshmen), 8/30 (transfers). *Notification:* continuous (freshmen).

Admissions Contact Tony Booker, Director of Admissions, Martin Methodist College, 433 West Madison Street, Pulaski, TN 38478-2716. *Phone:* 931-363-9804. *Toll-free phone:* 800-467-1273. *Fax:* 931-363-9818. *E-mail:* admissions@martinmethodist.edu.

MARYVILLE COLLEGE

Maryville, Tennessee

- **Independent Presbyterian** 4-year, founded 1819
- **Calendar** 4-1-4
- **Degree** bachelor's
- **Suburban** 350-acre campus with easy access to Knoxville
- **Endowment** $24.4 million
- **Coed,** 1,026 undergraduate students, 97% full-time, 58% women, 42% men
- **Moderately difficult** entrance level, 79% of applicants were admitted

Undergraduates 998 full-time, 28 part-time. Students come from 29 states and territories, 19 other countries, 30% are from out of state, 6% African American, 1% Asian American or Pacific Islander, 0.8% Hispanic American, 0.6% Native American, 3% international, 6% transferred in, 70% live on campus. *Retention:* 70% of 2001 full-time freshmen returned.

Freshmen *Admission:* 1,494 applied, 1,173 admitted, 288 enrolled. *Average high school GPA:* 3.49. *Test scores:* SAT verbal scores over 500: 74%; SAT math scores over 500: 75%; ACT scores over 18: 92%; SAT verbal scores over 600: 39%; SAT math scores over 600: 25%; ACT scores over 24: 50%; SAT verbal scores over 700: 10%; SAT math scores over 700: 2%; ACT scores over 30: 10%.

Faculty *Total:* 97, 65% full-time, 72% with terminal degrees. *Student/faculty ratio:* 14:1.

Majors Area studies related; art; art education; biochemistry; biology; biology education; business administration; chemical and atomic/molecular physics; chemistry; chemistry education; computer science; developmental/child psychology; economics; education; engineering; English; English education; environmental science; fine/studio arts; history; history education; international business; international relations; mathematics; mathematics/computer science; mathematics education; music; music (piano and organ performance); music teacher education; music (voice and choral/opera performance); nursing; physical education; physics education; political science; psychology; recreation/leisure studies; religious studies; sign language interpretation; social science education; sociology; Spanish; Spanish language education; teaching English as a second language; technical/business writing; theater arts/drama; wind/percussion instruments.

Academic Programs *Special study options:* adult/continuing education programs, advanced placement credit, double majors, English as a second language, honors programs, independent study, internships, off-campus study, part-time degree program, services for LD students, student-designed majors, study abroad, summer session for credit. *Unusual degree programs:* 3-2 business administration with University of Tennessee, Knoxville; engineering with Vanderbilt University, Washington University in St. Louis, Auburn University, Tennessee Technological University; nursing with Vanderbilt University.

Library Lamar Memorial Library plus 1 other with 83,573 titles, 672 serial subscriptions, 672 audiovisual materials, an OPAC, a Web page.

Computers on Campus 62 computers available on campus for general student use. A campuswide network can be accessed from student residence rooms and from off campus. Internet access, at least one staffed computer lab available.

Maryville College (continued)

Student Life *Housing:* on-campus residence required through senior year. *Options:* coed, men-only, women-only, disabled students. *Activities and Organizations:* drama/theater group, student-run newspaper, choral group, Voices of Praise, student government, Student Programming Board, Equestrian Club, Peer Mentors. *Campus security:* 24-hour emergency response devices and patrols, late-night transport/escort service, controlled dormitory access. *Student Services:* health clinic, personal/psychological counseling.

Athletics Member NCAA. All Division III. *Intercollegiate sports:* baseball M, basketball M/W, cross-country running M/W, equestrian sports M/W, football M, soccer M/W, softball W, tennis M/W, volleyball W. *Intramural sports:* baseball M, basketball M/W, football M/W, golf M/W, racquetball M/W, soccer M/W, softball M/W, swimming M/W, table tennis M/W, tennis M/W, volleyball M/W, weight lifting M/W.

Standardized Tests *Required:* SAT I or ACT (for admission).

Costs (2001–02) *Comprehensive fee:* $23,210 includes full-time tuition ($16,985), mandatory fees ($575), and room and board ($5650). Part-time tuition: $708 per hour. *Room and board:* College room only: $2750. Room and board charges vary according to board plan and housing facility. *Payment plans:* installment, deferred payment. *Waivers:* employees or children of employees.

Financial Aid Of all full-time matriculated undergraduates who enrolled in 2001, 998 applied for aid, 782 were judged to have need, 340 had their need fully met. 353 Federal Work-Study jobs (averaging $1192). 375 State and other part-time jobs (averaging $1320). In 2001, 210 non-need-based awards were made. *Average percent of need met:* 92%. *Average financial aid package:* $18,573. *Average need-based loan:* $1133. *Average need-based gift aid:* $14,123. *Average non-need based aid:* $11,524.

Applying *Options:* common application, electronic application, early admission, early decision, early action, deferred entrance. *Application fee:* $25. *Required:* high school transcript, minimum 2.5 GPA. *Required for some:* essay or personal statement, letters of recommendation, interview. *Recommended:* minimum 3.0 GPA. *Application deadline:* 3/1 (freshmen), rolling (transfers). *Early decision:* 11/15. *Notification:* 4/1 (freshmen), 12/1 (early decision), 10/1 (early action).

Admissions Contact Ms. Linda L. Moore, Administrative Assistant of Admissions, Maryville College, 502 East Lamar Alexander Parkway, Maryville, TN 37804-5907. *Phone:* 865-981-8092. *Toll-free phone:* 800-597-2687. *Fax:* 865-981-8005. *E-mail:* admissions@maryvillecollege.edu.

MEMPHIS COLLEGE OF ART
Memphis, Tennessee

- **Independent** comprehensive, founded 1936
- **Calendar** semesters
- **Degrees** bachelor's and master's
- **Urban** 200-acre campus
- **Coed,** 265 undergraduate students, 91% full-time, 49% women, 51% men
- **Moderately difficult** entrance level, 73% of applicants were admitted

For more than half a century, Memphis College of Art has been a small, distinctive community of artists. Students of diverse backgrounds work together in the shared pursuit of a challenging professional education in the visual arts. The College is situated in 340-acre Overton Park in midtown Memphis. Students have access to excellent equipment—from looms and presses to the latest in computer technology. Degrees are offered in both fine arts and commercial arts.

Undergraduates 241 full-time, 24 part-time. Students come from 29 states and territories, 10 other countries, 50% are from out of state, 12% African American, 0.8% Asian American or Pacific Islander, 2% Hispanic American, 0.4% Native American, 5% international, 14% transferred in, 11% live on campus. *Retention:* 46% of 2001 full-time freshmen returned.

Freshmen *Admission:* 207 applied, 152 admitted, 74 enrolled. *Average high school GPA:* 2.68. *Test scores:* ACT scores over 18: 85%; ACT scores over 24: 23%; ACT scores over 30: 2%.

Faculty *Total:* 41, 41% full-time, 41% with terminal degrees. *Student/faculty ratio:* 11:1.

Majors Advertising; applied art; art; ceramic arts; commercial photography; computer graphics; drawing; fine/studio arts; graphic design/commercial art/illustration; metal/jewelry arts; painting; photography; printmaking; sculpture; textile arts; wood science/paper technology.

Academic Programs *Special study options:* adult/continuing education programs, advanced placement credit, double majors, independent study, internships, off-campus study, part-time degree program, summer session for credit.

Library G. Pillow Lewis Library with 14,500 titles, 102 serial subscriptions.

Computers on Campus 40 computers available on campus for general student use. Internet access, at least one staffed computer lab available.

Student Life *Housing Options:* coed. *Activities and Organizations:* student-run newspaper, student government. *Campus security:* late-night transport/escort service, late night security patrols by trained personnel. *Student Services:* personal/psychological counseling.

Standardized Tests *Required:* SAT I or ACT (for admission).

Costs (2002–03) *Comprehensive fee:* $19,000 includes full-time tuition ($13,540), mandatory fees ($260), and room and board ($5200). Part-time tuition: $580 per credit hour. Part-time tuition and fees vary according to course load. *Room and board:* College room only: $3200. Room and board charges vary according to housing facility. *Payment plans:* installment, deferred payment. *Waivers:* employees or children of employees.

Financial Aid Of all full-time matriculated undergraduates who enrolled in 2001, 163 applied for aid, 139 were judged to have need, 90 had their need fully met. In 2001, 80 non-need-based awards were made. *Average percent of need met:* 80%. *Average financial aid package:* $6500. *Average need-based loan:* $5500. *Average need-based gift aid:* $3000. *Average non-need based aid:* $5500. *Average indebtedness upon graduation:* $16,500.

Applying *Options:* common application, electronic application, early admission, deferred entrance. *Application fee:* $25. *Required:* essay or personal statement, high school transcript, portfolio. *Recommended:* interview. *Application deadline:* rolling (freshmen), rolling (transfers). *Notification:* continuous (freshmen).

Admissions Contact Ms. Annette Moore, Director of Admission, Memphis College of Art, 1930 Poplar Avenue, Memphis, TN 38104. *Phone:* 901-272-5153. *Toll-free phone:* 800-727-1088. *Fax:* 901-272-5158. *E-mail:* info@mca.edu.

MIDDLE TENNESSEE STATE UNIVERSITY
Murfreesboro, Tennessee

- **State-supported** university, founded 1911, part of Tennessee Board of Regents
- **Calendar** semesters
- **Degrees** certificates, associate, bachelor's, master's, doctoral, and post-master's certificates
- **Urban** 500-acre campus with easy access to Nashville
- **Endowment** $880,840
- **Coed,** 18,130 undergraduate students, 83% full-time, 54% women, 46% men
- **Moderately difficult** entrance level, 78% of applicants were admitted

Undergraduates 15,100 full-time, 3,030 part-time. Students come from 47 states and territories, 8% are from out of state, 11% African American, 2% Asian American or Pacific Islander, 1% Hispanic American, 0.5% Native American, 11% transferred in, 20% live on campus. *Retention:* 68% of 2001 full-time freshmen returned.

Freshmen *Admission:* 6,322 applied, 4,939 admitted, 2,904 enrolled. *Average high school GPA:* 3.1. *Test scores:* ACT scores over 18: 90%; ACT scores over 24: 29%; ACT scores over 30: 3%.

Faculty *Total:* 963, 71% full-time. *Student/faculty ratio:* 23:1.

Majors Accounting; agribusiness; animal sciences; anthropology; art; art education; athletic training/sports medicine; aviation/airway science; biological/physical sciences; biology; business administration; business economics; business education; business marketing and marketing management; chemistry; clothing/apparel/textile studies; computer science; criminal justice/law enforcement administration; early childhood education; economics; engineering-related technology; English; entrepreneurship; environmental technology; family resource management studies; finance; foreign languages/literatures; geology; health education; health/physical education; history; industrial arts education; industrial technology; interdisciplinary studies; interior design; international relations; law enforcement/police science; management information systems/business data processing; marketing/distribution education; mass communications; mathematics; music; music business management/merchandising; nursing; nutrition science; office management; organizational psychology; philosophy; physics; plant sciences; political science; psychology; public relations; recreation/leisure facilities management; social work; sociology; special education; theater arts/drama.

Academic Programs *Special study options:* academic remediation for entering students, accelerated degree program, adult/continuing education programs, advanced placement credit, cooperative education, distance learning, double majors, English as a second language, freshman honors college, honors programs, independent study, internships, off-campus study, part-time degree program, services for LD students, student-designed majors, study abroad, summer session for credit. *ROTC:* Army (b), Air Force (c). *Unusual degree programs:* 3-2 engineering with University of Tennessee, Knoxville; Georgia Institute of Technology; Tennessee Technological University; The University of Memphis; Tennessee State University; Vanderbilt University.

Library University Library with 651,744 titles, 3,608 serial subscriptions, an OPAC, a Web page.

Computers on Campus 2200 computers available on campus for general student use. A campuswide network can be accessed from off campus. Internet access, online (class) registration, at least one staffed computer lab available.

Student Life *Housing Options:* men-only, women-only. *Activities and Organizations:* drama/theater group, student-run newspaper, radio station, choral group, marching band, African-American Student Association, Student Tennessee Education Association, Gamma Beta Phi, Golden Key National Honor Society, Inter-Fraternity Council, national fraternities, national sororities. *Campus security:* 24-hour emergency response devices and patrols, student patrols, late-night transport/escort service, controlled dormitory access. *Student Services:* health clinic, personal/psychological counseling, women's center, legal services.

Athletics Member NCAA. All Division I except football (Division I-A). *Intercollegiate sports:* baseball M(s), basketball M(s)/W(s), cross-country running M(s)/W(s), equestrian sports M/W, golf M(s), soccer W(s), softball W(s), tennis M(s)/W(s), track and field M(s)/W(s), volleyball W(s). *Intramural sports:* basketball M/W, bowling M(c)/W(c), fencing M(c)/W(c), field hockey M(c)/W(c), football M, lacrosse M(c)/W(c), racquetball M(c)/W(c), riflery M, rugby M(c)/W(c), soccer M(c)/W, softball M/W, swimming M/W, tennis M/W, volleyball M(c)/W(c), wrestling M(c)/W(c).

Standardized Tests *Required:* SAT I or ACT (for admission).

Costs (2001–02) *Tuition:* state resident $2556 full-time, $112 per semester hour part-time; nonresident $9028 full-time, $392 per semester hour part-time. Part-time tuition and fees vary according to course load. *Required fees:* $638 full-time, $21 per semester hour, $23 per term part-time. *Room and board:* $3800; room only: $2140. Room and board charges vary according to board plan and housing facility. *Payment plan:* deferred payment. *Waivers:* senior citizens and employees or children of employees.

Financial Aid Of all full-time matriculated undergraduates who enrolled in 2001, 9926 applied for aid, 6275 were judged to have need, 3068 had their need fully met. 393 Federal Work-Study jobs (averaging $1897). In 2001, 1334 non-need-based awards were made. *Average percent of need met:* 82%. *Average financial aid package:* $4785. *Average need-based gift aid:* $2465. *Average non-need based aid:* $2143. *Average indebtedness upon graduation:* $17,536.

Applying *Options:* electronic application, early admission, deferred entrance. *Application fee:* $15. *Required:* high school transcript, minimum 2.8 GPA. *Required for some:* essay or personal statement. *Application deadline:* rolling (freshmen), rolling (transfers). *Notification:* continuous (freshmen).

Admissions Contact Ms. Lynn Palmer, Director of Admissions, Middle Tennessee State University, 1301 East Main Street, MTSU-CAB 208, Murfreesboro, TN 37132. *Phone:* 615-898-2111. *Toll-free phone:* 800-331-MTSU (in-state); 800-433-MTSU (out-of-state). *Fax:* 615-898-5478. *E-mail:* admissions@mtsu.edu.

MILLIGAN COLLEGE

Milligan College, Tennessee

- **Independent Christian** comprehensive, founded 1866
- **Calendar** semesters
- **Degrees** bachelor's and master's
- **Suburban** 145-acre campus
- **Endowment** $6.1 million
- **Coed,** 789 undergraduate students, 97% full-time, 60% women, 40% men
- **Moderately difficult** entrance level, 76% of applicants were admitted

Undergraduates 769 full-time, 20 part-time. Students come from 38 states and territories, 8 other countries, 59% are from out of state, 2% African American, 0.5% Asian American or Pacific Islander, 0.8% Hispanic American, 0.4% Native American, 2% international, 6% transferred in, 69% live on campus. *Retention:* 73% of 2001 full-time freshmen returned.

Freshmen *Admission:* 712 applied, 543 admitted, 192 enrolled. *Average high school GPA:* 3.50. *Test scores:* SAT verbal scores over 500: 71%; SAT math scores over 500: 65%; ACT scores over 18: 94%; SAT verbal scores over 600: 24%; SAT math scores over 600: 21%; ACT scores over 24: 40%; SAT verbal scores over 700: 3%; SAT math scores over 700: 2%; ACT scores over 30: 4%.

Faculty *Total:* 101, 64% full-time, 55% with terminal degrees. *Student/faculty ratio:* 11:1.

Majors Accounting; advertising; art; biblical studies; biological/physical sciences; biology; broadcast journalism; business administration; business economics; chemistry; computer science; early childhood education; education; English; exercise sciences; health science; health services administration; history; humanities; journalism; mathematics; music; music (piano and organ performance); music teacher education; music (voice and choral/opera performance); nursing; pastoral counseling; physical education; pre-dentistry; pre-medicine; pre-veterinary studies; psychology; public relations; radio/television broadcasting; religious education; religious music; science education; secondary education; sociology; theater arts/drama.

Academic Programs *Special study options:* academic remediation for entering students, accelerated degree program, adult/continuing education programs, advanced placement credit, cooperative education, double majors, independent study, internships, off-campus study, part-time degree program, study abroad, summer session for credit. *ROTC:* Army (c). *Unusual degree programs:* 3-2 engineering with Tennessee Technological University.

Library P. H. Welshimer Memorial Library with 107,464 titles, 2,478 serial subscriptions, 2,951 audiovisual materials, an OPAC, a Web page.

Computers on Campus 79 computers available on campus for general student use. A campuswide network can be accessed from student residence rooms and from off campus. Internet access, at least one staffed computer lab available.

Student Life *Housing:* on-campus residence required through senior year. *Options:* men-only, women-only. *Activities and Organizations:* drama/theater group, student-run newspaper, radio station, choral group, Social Affairs Committee, Buffalo Ramblers, Concert Council, Volunteer Milligan, Students for Life. *Campus security:* 24-hour patrols, late-night transport/escort service. *Student Services:* health clinic, personal/psychological counseling.

Athletics Member NAIA. *Intercollegiate sports:* baseball M(s), basketball M(s)/W(s), cross-country running M(s)/W(s), golf M(s), soccer M(s)/W(s), softball W(s), tennis M(s)/W(s), volleyball W(s). *Intramural sports:* basketball M/W, football M/W, softball M/W, volleyball M/W, water polo M/W.

Standardized Tests *Required:* SAT I or ACT (for admission).

Costs (2001–02) *One-time required fee:* $20. *Comprehensive fee:* $17,550 includes full-time tuition ($12,750), mandatory fees ($500), and room and board ($4300). Full-time tuition and fees vary according to class time. Part-time tuition: $530 per credit. Part-time tuition and fees vary according to class time and course load. *Required fees:* $140 per term part-time. *Room and board:* College room only: $2100. Room and board charges vary according to board plan and housing facility. *Payment plan:* installment. *Waivers:* employees or children of employees.

Financial Aid Of all full-time matriculated undergraduates who enrolled in 2001, 760 applied for aid, 616 were judged to have need, 269 had their need fully met. 162 Federal Work-Study jobs (averaging $1080). 239 State and other part-time jobs (averaging $960). In 2001, 73 non-need-based awards were made. *Average percent of need met:* 84%. *Average financial aid package:* $11,182. *Average need-based loan:* $3377. *Average need-based gift aid:* $2752. *Average non-need based aid:* $4283. *Average indebtedness upon graduation:* $16,373.

Applying *Options:* deferred entrance. *Application fee:* $30. *Required:* essay or personal statement, high school transcript, minimum 2.0 GPA, 2 letters of recommendation. *Required for some:* interview. *Recommended:* minimum 3.0 GPA. *Application deadline:* rolling (freshmen), rolling (transfers). *Notification:* continuous (freshmen).

Admissions Contact Mr. David Mee, Vice President for Enrollment Management, Milligan College, PO Box 210, Milligan College, TN 37682. *Phone:* 423-461-8730. *Toll-free phone:* 800-262-8337. *Fax:* 423-461-8982. *E-mail:* admissions@milligan.edu.

O'MORE COLLEGE OF DESIGN

Franklin, Tennessee

- **Independent** 4-year, founded 1970
- **Calendar** semesters
- **Degree** bachelor's
- **Small-town** 6-acre campus with easy access to Nashville
- **Coed,** 132 undergraduate students, 70% full-time, 90% women, 10% men
- **Moderately difficult** entrance level, 72% of applicants were admitted

Undergraduates Students come from 7 states and territories, 2 other countries, 11% are from out of state, 3% African American, 2% Asian American or Pacific Islander, 2% Hispanic American, 2% international, 30% live on campus. *Retention:* 85% of 2001 full-time freshmen returned.

Freshmen *Admission:* 90 applied, 65 admitted. *Average high school GPA:* 3.00.

Faculty *Total:* 42, 17% full-time. *Student/faculty ratio:* 3:1.

Majors Fashion design/illustration; fashion merchandising; graphic design/commercial art/illustration; interior design.

Academic Programs *Special study options:* academic remediation for entering students, adult/continuing education programs, advanced placement credit, cooperative education, independent study, internships, part-time degree program, services for LD students, summer session for credit.

Library Fleming-Farrar Hall with 4,000 titles, 60 serial subscriptions.

Computers on Campus 20 computers available on campus for general student use. Internet access, at least one staffed computer lab available.

O'More College of Design (continued)

Student Life *Housing Options:* cooperative. *Campus security:* 24-hour emergency response devices.

Standardized Tests *Required:* ACT (for admission).

Costs (2001–02) *Tuition:* $9920 full-time. *Required fees:* $350 full-time.

Applying *Options:* common application, deferred entrance. *Application fee:* $25. *Required:* essay or personal statement, high school transcript, minimum 2.5 GPA, interview. *Required for some:* 3 letters of recommendation, portfolio. *Application deadlines:* 8/1 (freshmen), 8/1 (transfers). *Notification:* continuous until 8/1 (freshmen).

Admissions Contact Chris Lee, Director of Enrollment Management, O'More College of Design, 423 South Margin Street, Franklin, TN 37064-2816. *Phone:* 615-794-4254 Ext. 32. *Fax:* 615-790-1662.

RHODES COLLEGE
Memphis, Tennessee

- **Independent Presbyterian** comprehensive, founded 1848
- **Calendar** semesters
- **Degrees** bachelor's and master's (master's degree in accounting only)
- **Suburban** 100-acre campus
- **Endowment** $202.0 million
- **Coed,** 1,535 undergraduate students, 98% full-time, 57% women, 43% men
- **Very difficult** entrance level, 64% of applicants were admitted

Undergraduates 1,508 full-time, 27 part-time. Students come from 43 states and territories, 73% are from out of state, 4% African American, 3% Asian American or Pacific Islander, 2% Hispanic American, 0.1% Native American, 0.5% international, 1% transferred in, 74% live on campus. *Retention:* 89% of 2001 full-time freshmen returned.

Freshmen *Admission:* 2,426 applied, 1,558 admitted, 417 enrolled. *Average high school GPA:* 3.60. *Test scores:* SAT verbal scores over 500: 99%; SAT math scores over 500: 100%; ACT scores over 18: 100%; SAT verbal scores over 600: 76%; SAT math scores over 600: 79%; ACT scores over 24: 96%; SAT verbal scores over 700: 26%; SAT math scores over 700: 17%; ACT scores over 30: 33%.

Faculty *Total:* 155, 77% full-time, 82% with terminal degrees. *Student/faculty ratio:* 12:1.

Majors Anthropology; art; art history; biochemistry; biology; business administration; chemistry; classics; computer science; economics; English; fine/studio arts; French; German; Greek (modern); history; interdisciplinary studies; international business; international economics; international relations; Latin (ancient and medieval); mathematics; music; philosophy; physics; political science; psychology; religious studies; Russian/Slavic studies; sociology; Spanish; theater arts/drama; urban studies.

Academic Programs *Special study options:* accelerated degree program, advanced placement credit, double majors, honors programs, independent study, internships, off-campus study, part-time degree program, services for LD students, student-designed majors, study abroad, summer session for credit. *ROTC:* Army (c), Air Force (c). *Unusual degree programs:* 3-2 engineering with Washington University in St. Louis.

Library Burrow Library plus 3 others with 263,000 titles, 1,200 serial subscriptions, 96,000 audiovisual materials, an OPAC, a Web page.

Computers on Campus 125 computers available on campus for general student use. A campuswide network can be accessed from student residence rooms and from off campus. At least one staffed computer lab available.

Student Life *Housing:* on-campus residence required through sophomore year. *Options:* coed, men-only, women-only. *Activities and Organizations:* drama/theater group, student-run newspaper, choral group, Kinney Volunteer Program, Habitat for Humanity, Adopt A Friend, Foster, national fraternities, national sororities. *Campus security:* 24-hour emergency response devices and patrols, student patrols, late-night transport/escort service, 24-hour monitored security cameras in parking areas, fenced campus with monitored access at night. *Student Services:* health clinic, personal/psychological counseling.

Athletics Member NCAA. All Division III. *Intercollegiate sports:* baseball M, basketball M/W, cross-country running M/W, equestrian sports M(c)/W(c), field hockey W, football M, golf M/W, lacrosse M(c), rugby M(c), soccer M/W, softball W, swimming M/W, tennis M/W, track and field M/W, volleyball W. *Intramural sports:* basketball M/W, football M/W, racquetball M/W, soccer M/W, softball M/W, squash M/W, tennis M/W, volleyball M/W, water polo M/W.

Standardized Tests *Required:* SAT I or ACT (for admission).

Costs (2001–02) *Comprehensive fee:* $26,436 includes full-time tuition ($20,336), mandatory fees ($200), and room and board ($5900). Part-time tuition: $850 per credit hour. *Room and board:* Room and board charges vary according to board plan. *Payment plan:* installment. *Waivers:* employees or children of employees.

Financial Aid Of all full-time matriculated undergraduates who enrolled in 2001, 714 applied for aid, 536 were judged to have need, 224 had their need fully met. 191 Federal Work-Study jobs (averaging $1537). 271 State and other part-time jobs (averaging $1395). In 2001, 461 non-need-based awards were made. *Average percent of need met:* 94%. *Average financial aid package:* $18,123. *Average need-based loan:* $4317. *Average need-based gift aid:* $11,702. *Average non-need based aid:* $8917. *Average indebtedness upon graduation:* $14,900.

Applying *Options:* common application, electronic application, early admission, early decision, deferred entrance. *Application fee:* $40. *Required:* essay or personal statement, high school transcript, 2 letters of recommendation. *Recommended:* interview. *Application deadlines:* 2/1 (freshmen), 2/1 (transfers). *Early decision:* 11/1 (for plan 1), 1/1 (for plan 2). *Notification:* 4/1 (freshmen), 12/1 (early decision plan 1), 2/1 (early decision plan 2).

Admissions Contact Mr. David J. Wottle, Dean of Admissions and Financial Aid, Rhodes College, 2000 North Parkway, Memphis, TN 38112. *Phone:* 901-843-3700. *Toll-free phone:* 800-844-5969. *Fax:* 901-843-3631. *E-mail:* adminfo@rhodes.edu.

SOUTHERN ADVENTIST UNIVERSITY
Collegedale, Tennessee

- **Independent Seventh-day Adventist** comprehensive, founded 1892
- **Calendar** semesters
- **Degrees** certificates, associate, bachelor's, and master's
- **Small-town** 1000-acre campus with easy access to Chattanooga
- **Endowment** $19.8 million
- **Coed,** 2,098 undergraduate students, 86% full-time, 55% women, 45% men
- **Moderately difficult** entrance level, 77% of applicants were admitted

Undergraduates 1,810 full-time, 288 part-time. Students come from 46 states and territories, 55 other countries, 78% are from out of state, 7% African American, 4% Asian American or Pacific Islander, 10% Hispanic American, 0.4% Native American, 5% international, 10% transferred in, 65% live on campus. *Retention:* 67% of 2001 full-time freshmen returned.

Freshmen *Admission:* 1,195 applied, 919 admitted, 511 enrolled. *Average high school GPA:* 3.20. *Test scores:* ACT scores over 18: 89%; ACT scores over 24: 40%; ACT scores over 30: 6%.

Faculty *Total:* 161, 67% full-time, 50% with terminal degrees. *Student/faculty ratio:* 16:1.

Majors Accounting; actuarial science; art; auto body repair; auto mechanic/technician; biochemistry; biology; broadcast journalism; business administration; business marketing and marketing management; chemistry; computer graphics; computer science; dental hygiene; early childhood education; elementary education; engineering; English; English education; exercise sciences; family studies; film/video production; foreign languages/literatures; general studies; health services administration; history; international business; journalism; management information systems/business data processing; management science; mass communications; mathematics; medical radiologic technology; medical technology; music; music (general performance); music teacher education; music theory and composition; nonprofit/public management; nursing; nursing science; nutrition studies; occupational therapy; physical education; physical therapy; physician assistant; physics; psychology; public relations; radio/television broadcasting technology; religious education; religious studies; respiratory therapy; secretarial science; social work; speech-language pathology; sport/fitness administration; theology.

Academic Programs *Special study options:* advanced placement credit, double majors, English as a second language, honors programs, independent study, internships, part-time degree program, services for LD students, study abroad, summer session for credit.

Library McKee Library with 151,045 titles, 6,746 serial subscriptions, 3,606 audiovisual materials, an OPAC, a Web page.

Computers on Campus 200 computers available on campus for general student use. A campuswide network can be accessed from student residence rooms and from off campus. Internet access, at least one staffed computer lab available.

Student Life *Housing:* on-campus residence required through senior year. *Options:* men-only, women-only. *Activities and Organizations:* drama/theater group, student-run newspaper, radio and television station, choral group, Student Association, Black Christian Union, Campus Ministries. *Campus security:* 24-hour patrols, late-night transport/escort service, controlled dormitory access. *Student Services:* health clinic, personal/psychological counseling.

Athletics *Intramural sports:* badminton M/W, basketball M/W, gymnastics M/W, racquetball M/W, soccer M/W, softball M/W, table tennis M/W, tennis M/W, volleyball M/W.

Standardized Tests *Required:* SAT I or ACT (for admission).

Costs (2002–03) *Comprehensive fee:* $16,330 includes full-time tuition ($11,840), mandatory fees ($380), and room and board ($4110). Part-time tuition: $500 per semester hour. Part-time tuition and fees vary according to course load. *Required fees:* $190 per term part-time. *Room and board:* College room only: $2160. Room and board charges vary according to housing facility. *Payment plans:* tuition prepayment, installment, deferred payment. *Waivers:* adult students, senior citizens, and employees or children of employees.

Financial Aid Of all full-time matriculated undergraduates who enrolled in 2001, 1484 applied for aid, 897 were judged to have need, 129 had their need fully met. In 2001, 544 non-need-based awards were made. *Average percent of need met:* 64%. *Average financial aid package:* $8718. *Average need-based loan:* $2886. *Average need-based gift aid:* $3830. *Average indebtedness upon graduation:* $14,900.

Applying *Options:* early admission, deferred entrance. *Application fee:* $25. *Required:* high school transcript, minimum 2.0 GPA, 2 letters of recommendation. *Required for some:* essay or personal statement. *Recommended:* interview. *Application deadline:* rolling (freshmen), rolling (transfers). *Notification:* continuous (freshmen).

Admissions Contact Mr. Victor Czerkasij, Director of Admissions and Recruitment, Southern Adventist University, PO Box 370, Collegedale, TN 37315-0370. *Phone:* 423-238-2843. *Toll-free phone:* 800-768-8437. *Fax:* 423-238-3005. *E-mail:* admissions@southern.edu.

TENNESSEE INSTITUTE OF ELECTRONICS

Knoxville, Tennessee

- **Proprietary** primarily 2-year, founded 1947
- **Calendar** quarters
- **Degrees** associate and bachelor's
- **Suburban** 1-acre campus
- **Coed**
- **Noncompetitive** entrance level

Student Life *Campus security:* 24-hour emergency response devices.

Applying *Application fee:* $100. *Recommended:* high school transcript.

Admissions Contact Mr. Richard Rackley, Assistant Director, Tennessee Institute of Electronics, 3203 Tazewell Pike, Knoxville, TN 37918-2530. *Phone:* 865-688-9422.

TENNESSEE STATE UNIVERSITY

Nashville, Tennessee

- **State-supported** comprehensive, founded 1912, part of Tennessee Board of Regents
- **Calendar** semesters
- **Degrees** associate, bachelor's, master's, and doctoral
- **Urban** 450-acre campus
- **Coed,** 7,061 undergraduate students, 85% full-time, 62% women, 38% men
- **Minimally difficult** entrance level, 48% of applicants were admitted

Undergraduates 6,027 full-time, 1,034 part-time. Students come from 45 states and territories, 42% are from out of state, 82% African American, 1.0% Asian American or Pacific Islander, 0.5% Hispanic American, 0.0% Native American, 1% international, 7% transferred in, 39% live on campus. *Retention:* 76% of 2001 full-time freshmen returned.

Freshmen *Admission:* 6,610 applied, 3,165 admitted, 1,271 enrolled. *Average high school GPA:* 2.98. *Test scores:* ACT scores over 18: 70%; ACT scores over 24: 11%.

Faculty *Total:* 517, 68% full-time. *Student/faculty ratio:* 26:1.

Majors Accounting; adult/continuing education; African studies; agricultural sciences; animal sciences; architectural engineering; art; biology; business administration; business economics; business education; chemistry; civil engineering; clinical psychology; computer science; consumer services; criminal justice/law enforcement administration; dental hygiene; early childhood education; education; education administration; electrical engineering; elementary education; engineering; English; family/consumer studies; food services technology; French; health education; health services administration; history; humanities; industrial arts; industrial/manufacturing engineering; industrial technology; liberal arts and sciences/liberal studies; mass communications; mathematics; mechanical engineering; medical records administration; medical technology; music; nursing; physical education; physical therapy; physics; political science; psychology; public administration; reading education; recreation/leisure studies; respiratory therapy; secretarial science; social work; sociology; Spanish; special education; speech-language pathology/audiology; transportation technology.

Academic Programs *Special study options:* academic remediation for entering students, accelerated degree program, adult/continuing education programs, cooperative education, external degree program, freshman honors college, honors programs, independent study, internships, off-campus study, part-time degree program, services for LD students, summer session for credit. *ROTC:* Army (c), Navy (c), Air Force (b).

Library Martha M. Brown/Lois H. Daniel Library plus 1 other with 580,650 titles, 23,668 audiovisual materials, an OPAC, a Web page.

Computers on Campus 320 computers available on campus for general student use. A campuswide network can be accessed from student residence rooms and from off campus. At least one staffed computer lab available.

Student Life *Housing Options:* coed, men-only, women-only. *Activities and Organizations:* drama/theater group, student-run newspaper, radio station, choral group, marching band, SADD, Pre Alumni Council, Baptist Student Union, T. E. Poag Players, national fraternities, national sororities. *Campus security:* 24-hour patrols, controlled dormitory access. *Student Services:* health clinic, personal/psychological counseling, women's center.

Athletics Member NCAA. All Division I except football (Division I-AA). *Intercollegiate sports:* basketball M(s)/W(s), cross-country running M(s)/W(s), golf M(s), softball W, tennis M(s)/W(s), track and field M(s)/W(s), volleyball W. *Intramural sports:* baseball M, basketball M/W, football M, softball W, track and field M/W, volleyball M/W.

Standardized Tests *Required:* SAT I or ACT (for admission).

Costs (2001–02) *Tuition:* state resident $3008 full-time, $163 per credit hour part-time; nonresident $9480 full-time, $433 per credit hour part-time. Full-time tuition and fees vary according to course load. Part-time tuition and fees vary according to course load. *Required fees:* $25 full-time. *Room and board:* $3600; room only: $2090. Room and board charges vary according to board plan and housing facility. *Payment plan:* deferred payment. *Waivers:* minority students and employees or children of employees.

Financial Aid Of all full-time matriculated undergraduates who enrolled in 2001, 5076 applied for aid, 4387 were judged to have need, 844 had their need fully met. In 2001, 420 non-need-based awards were made. *Average percent of need met:* 77%. *Average financial aid package:* $3572. *Average need-based gift aid:* $1606. *Average non-need based aid:* $1850.

Applying *Options:* electronic application. *Application fee:* $15. *Required:* high school transcript. *Required for some:* 3 letters of recommendation. *Application deadlines:* 8/1 (freshmen), 8/1 (transfers). *Notification:* continuous until 8/15 (freshmen).

Admissions Contact Ms. Vernella Smith, Admissions Coordinator, Tennessee State University, 3500 John A Merritt Boulevard, Nashville, TN 37209-1561. *Phone:* 615-963-5104. *Fax:* 615-963-5108. *E-mail:* jcade@tnstate.edu.

TENNESSEE TECHNOLOGICAL UNIVERSITY

Cookeville, Tennessee

- **State-supported** university, founded 1915, part of Tennessee Board of Regents
- **Calendar** semesters
- **Degrees** certificates, bachelor's, master's, and doctoral
- **Small-town** 235-acre campus
- **Endowment** $26.8 million
- **Coed,** 7,099 undergraduate students, 88% full-time, 46% women, 54% men
- **Moderately difficult** entrance level, 98% of applicants were admitted

Undergraduates 6,226 full-time, 873 part-time. Students come from 41 states and territories, 21 other countries, 5% are from out of state, 4% African American, 1% Asian American or Pacific Islander, 0.9% Hispanic American, 0.3% Native American, 0.8% international, 8% transferred in, 25% live on campus. *Retention:* 71% of 2001 full-time freshmen returned.

Freshmen *Admission:* 2,357 applied, 2,306 admitted, 1,323 enrolled. *Average high school GPA:* 3.11. *Test scores:* SAT verbal scores over 500: 73%; SAT math scores over 500: 78%; ACT scores over 18: 90%; SAT verbal scores over 600: 31%; SAT math scores over 600: 36%; ACT scores over 24: 37%; SAT verbal scores over 700: 6%; SAT math scores over 700: 9%; ACT scores over 30: 7%.

Faculty *Total:* 500, 72% full-time, 68% with terminal degrees. *Student/faculty ratio:* 18:1.

Majors Accounting; agricultural business; agricultural education; agricultural engineering; agronomy/crop science; animal sciences; art; art education; biochemistry; biology; business administration; business marketing and marketing management; chemical engineering; chemistry; child care/development; civil engineering; clothing/textiles; computer engineering; computer science; dietetics; early childhood education; economics; education; electrical engineering; elementary education; English; fashion merchandising; finance; French; geology; Ger-

Tennessee Technological University (continued)

man; health education; history; home economics; home economics education; horticulture science; industrial/manufacturing engineering; industrial technology; information sciences/systems; international business; journalism; labor/personnel relations; landscaping management; mathematics; mechanical engineering; music; music teacher education; music therapy; nursing; nutrition science; operations management; physical education; physics; political science; pre-dentistry; pre-law; pre-medicine; pre-veterinary studies; psychology; secondary education; social work; sociology; Spanish; special education; technical/business writing; wildlife management.

Academic Programs *Special study options:* academic remediation for entering students, accelerated degree program, adult/continuing education programs, advanced placement credit, cooperative education, double majors, English as a second language, honors programs, internships, part-time degree program, services for LD students, study abroad, summer session for credit. *ROTC:* Army (b), Air Force (c).

Library University Library with 593,431 titles, 3,752 serial subscriptions, 17,695 audiovisual materials, an OPAC, a Web page.

Computers on Campus 407 computers available on campus for general student use. A campuswide network can be accessed from student residence rooms and from off campus. Internet access, online (class) registration, at least one staffed computer lab available.

Student Life *Housing:* on-campus residence required through sophomore year. *Options:* coed, men-only, women-only. *Activities and Organizations:* drama/theater group, student-run newspaper, radio station, choral group, marching band, Baptist Student Union, Fellowship of Christian Athletes, University Christian Student Center, Interfraternity Council, Residence Hall Association, national fraternities, national sororities. *Campus security:* 24-hour emergency response devices and patrols, late-night transport/escort service, student safety organization, lighted pathways. *Student Services:* health clinic, personal/psychological counseling, women's center.

Athletics Member NCAA. All Division I except football (Division I-AA). *Intercollegiate sports:* baseball M(s), basketball M(s)/W(s), cross-country running M(s)/W(s), golf M(s)/W(s), riflery M(s)/W(s), soccer W(s), softball W(s), tennis M(s)/W(s), track and field W(s), volleyball W(s). *Intramural sports:* basketball M/W, equestrian sports M(c)/W(c), fencing M(c)/W(c), football M/W, golf M/W, racquetball M/W, rugby M(c)/W(c), soccer M/W, softball M/W, tennis M/W, volleyball M/W, wrestling M.

Standardized Tests *Required:* SAT I or ACT (for admission). *Recommended:* ACT (for admission).

Costs (2001–02) *Tuition:* state resident $2556 full-time, $112 per hour part-time; nonresident $9028 full-time, $392 per hour part-time. Part-time tuition and fees vary according to course load. *Required fees:* $266 full-time, $34 per hour. *Room and board:* $3880; room only: $1980. Room and board charges vary according to board plan and housing facility. *Waivers:* employees or children of employees.

Financial Aid Of all full-time matriculated undergraduates who enrolled in 2001, 4632 applied for aid, 2496 were judged to have need, 760 had their need fully met. 408 Federal Work-Study jobs (averaging $1598). In 2001, 1290 non-need-based awards were made. *Average percent of need met:* 75%. *Average financial aid package:* $3379. *Average need-based loan:* $1439. *Average need-based gift aid:* $2560. *Average non-need based aid:* $2356. *Average indebtedness upon graduation:* $13,100.

Applying *Options:* early admission, deferred entrance. *Application fee:* $15. *Required:* high school transcript, 2.35 high school GPA or ACT composite score of 19. *Recommended:* interview. *Application deadline:* rolling (freshmen), rolling (transfers). *Notification:* continuous (freshmen).

Admissions Contact Mrs. Rebecca Tolbert, Associate Vice President for Enrollment and Records, Tennessee Technological University, TTU Box 5006, Cookeville, TN 38505. *Phone:* 931-372-3888. *Toll-free phone:* 800-255-8881. *Fax:* 931-372-6250. *E-mail:* u_admissions@tntech.edu.

TENNESSEE TEMPLE UNIVERSITY
Chattanooga, Tennessee

- **Independent Baptist** comprehensive, founded 1946
- **Calendar** semesters
- **Degrees** certificates, diplomas, associate, bachelor's, and master's
- **Urban** 55-acre campus
- **Endowment** $600,000
- **Coed,** 682 undergraduate students, 97% full-time, 47% women, 53% men
- **Minimally difficult** entrance level, 99% of applicants were admitted

Undergraduates 664 full-time, 18 part-time. Students come from 40 states and territories, 1 other country, 69% are from out of state, 5% African American, 1% Asian American or Pacific Islander, 2% Hispanic American, 0.7% Native American, 4% international, 10% transferred in, 70% live on campus. *Retention:* 64% of 2001 full-time freshmen returned.

Freshmen *Admission:* 274 applied, 270 admitted, 112 enrolled.

Faculty *Total:* 60, 62% full-time, 17% with terminal degrees. *Student/faculty ratio:* 15:1.

Majors Accounting; biblical studies; biological/physical sciences; biology; business administration; earth sciences; education; elementary education; English; history; information sciences/systems; interdisciplinary studies; liberal arts and sciences/liberal studies; music; music (piano and organ performance); music teacher education; music (voice and choral/opera performance); pastoral counseling; psychology; religious education; religious music; science education; secondary education; secretarial science; sign language interpretation; speech/theater education.

Academic Programs *Special study options:* academic remediation for entering students, adult/continuing education programs, advanced placement credit, cooperative education, distance learning, double majors, external degree program, honors programs, independent study, internships, part-time degree program, summer session for credit.

Library Cierpke Memorial Library with 150,711 titles, 76 serial subscriptions.

Computers on Campus 150 computers available on campus for general student use. A campuswide network can be accessed from student residence rooms and from off campus. Internet access, at least one staffed computer lab available.

Student Life *Housing:* on-campus residence required through senior year. *Options:* men-only, women-only. *Activities and Organizations:* drama/theater group, choral group. *Campus security:* 24-hour emergency response devices and patrols, late-night transport/escort service. *Student Services:* health clinic, personal/psychological counseling.

Athletics Member NCCAA. *Intercollegiate sports:* baseball M(s), basketball M(s)/W(s), soccer M(s)/W, volleyball W(s), wrestling M. *Intramural sports:* basketball M/W, football M/W, soccer M/W, softball M/W, tennis M/W, volleyball M/W.

Standardized Tests *Required:* SAT I or ACT (for placement).

Costs (2001–02) *Comprehensive fee:* $11,570 includes full-time tuition ($5500), mandatory fees ($950), and room and board ($5120). Part-time tuition: $250 per credit. *Room and board:* Room and board charges vary according to board plan. *Payment plan:* installment. *Waivers:* employees or children of employees.

Financial Aid Of all full-time matriculated undergraduates who enrolled in 2001, 707 applied for aid, 396 were judged to have need, 175 had their need fully met. 82 Federal Work-Study jobs (averaging $1500). 88 State and other part-time jobs (averaging $1440). In 2001, 275 non-need-based awards were made. *Average percent of need met:* 72%. *Average financial aid package:* $8425. *Average need-based loan:* $4500. *Average need-based gift aid:* $2100. *Average non-need based aid:* $4000. *Average indebtedness upon graduation:* $9000. *Financial aid deadline:* 5/15.

Applying *Options:* electronic application, deferred entrance. *Application fee:* $30. *Required:* high school transcript, minimum 2.0 GPA, 3 letters of recommendation, interview. *Required for some:* essay or personal statement. *Application deadlines:* 8/20 (freshmen), 8/15 (transfers).

Admissions Contact Tennessee Temple University, 1815 Union Avenue, Chattanooga, TN 37404-3587. *Phone:* 423-493-4371. *Toll-free phone:* 800-553-4050. *Fax:* 423-493-4497. *E-mail:* ttuinfo@tntemple.edu.

TENNESSEE WESLEYAN COLLEGE
Athens, Tennessee

- **Independent United Methodist** 4-year, founded 1857
- **Calendar** semesters
- **Degrees** bachelor's (all information given is for both main and branch campuses)
- **Small-town** 40-acre campus
- **Endowment** $8.6 million
- **Coed,** 786 undergraduate students, 77% full-time, 63% women, 37% men
- **Moderately difficult** entrance level, 71% of applicants were admitted

Undergraduates 606 full-time, 180 part-time. Students come from 15 states and territories, 11 other countries, 8% are from out of state, 3% African American, 0.1% Asian American or Pacific Islander, 0.3% Hispanic American, 4% international, 19% transferred in, 33% live on campus. *Retention:* 65% of 2001 full-time freshmen returned.

Freshmen *Admission:* 466 applied, 333 admitted, 118 enrolled. *Average high school GPA:* 3.20.

Faculty *Total:* 81, 51% full-time, 48% with terminal degrees. *Student/faculty ratio:* 17:1.

Majors Accounting; athletic training/sports medicine; behavioral sciences; biology; biology education; business administration; chemistry; chemistry education; education; education (K-12); elementary education; English; English education; exercise sciences; finance; health/physical education; health science; history; history education; human resources management; human services; interdisciplinary studies; mathematics; mathematics education; music; music teacher education; nursing; ophthalmic/optometric services related; physical education; pre-dentistry; pre-law; pre-medicine; pre-pharmacy studies; pre-theology; pre-veterinary studies; psychology; recreation/leisure studies; religious studies; secondary education; sport/fitness administration.

Academic Programs *Special study options:* academic remediation for entering students, accelerated degree program, adult/continuing education programs, advanced placement credit, double majors, English as a second language, freshman honors college, honors programs, independent study, internships, off-campus study, part-time degree program, student-designed majors, study abroad, summer session for credit.

Library Merner-Pfeifer Library with 79,328 titles, 408 serial subscriptions, 3,610 audiovisual materials, an OPAC, a Web page.

Computers on Campus 35 computers available on campus for general student use. Internet access, at least one staffed computer lab available.

Student Life *Housing:* on-campus residence required through senior year. *Options:* men-only, women-only. *Activities and Organizations:* drama/theater group, student-run newspaper, choral group, Wesleyan Christian Fellowship, Circle K, Baptist Student Union, Student Government Association, choir, national sororities. *Campus security:* controlled dormitory access, night patrols by trained security personnel. *Student Services:* health clinic, personal/psychological counseling.

Athletics Member NAIA. *Intercollegiate sports:* baseball M(s), basketball M(s)/W(s), golf M(s), soccer M(s)/W(s), softball W(s), tennis M(s)/W(s), volleyball W(s). *Intramural sports:* basketball M/W, table tennis M/W, tennis M/W, volleyball M/W.

Standardized Tests *Required:* SAT I or ACT (for admission).

Costs (2002–03) *Comprehensive fee:* $14,620 includes full-time tuition ($10,000), mandatory fees ($240), and room and board ($4380). Part-time tuition: $280 per semester hour. Part-time tuition and fees vary according to class time and location. *Required fees:* $25 per credit hour. *Room and board:* College room only: $1640. Room and board charges vary according to housing facility. *Payment plans:* installment, deferred payment. *Waivers:* employees or children of employees.

Financial Aid Of all full-time matriculated undergraduates who enrolled in 2001, 372 applied for aid, 319 were judged to have need, 64 had their need fully met. 111 Federal Work-Study jobs (averaging $542). 33 State and other part-time jobs (averaging $886). In 2001, 80 non-need-based awards were made. *Average percent of need met:* 72%. *Average financial aid package:* $7171. *Average need-based loan:* $2859. *Average need-based gift aid:* $5282. *Average non-need based aid:* $5097. *Average indebtedness upon graduation:* $5602. *Financial aid deadline:* 5/1.

Applying *Options:* early admission, deferred entrance. *Application fee:* $25. *Required:* high school transcript, minimum 2.25 GPA, 1 letter of recommendation. *Required for some:* interview. *Recommended:* essay or personal statement. *Application deadline:* rolling (freshmen), rolling (transfers). *Notification:* continuous (freshmen).

Admissions Contact Mrs. Ruthie Cawood, Director of Admission, Tennessee Wesleyan College, PO Box 40, Athens, TN 37371-0040. *Phone:* 423-746-5287. *Toll-free phone:* 800-PICK-TWC. *Fax:* 423-745-9335.

TREVECCA NAZARENE UNIVERSITY
Nashville, Tennessee

- **Independent Nazarene** comprehensive, founded 1901
- **Calendar** semesters
- **Degrees** associate, bachelor's, master's, doctoral, and post-master's certificates
- **Urban** 65-acre campus
- **Endowment** $10.2 million
- **Coed,** 1,159 undergraduate students, 77% full-time, 55% women, 45% men
- **Noncompetitive** entrance level, 79% of applicants were admitted

Undergraduates 896 full-time, 263 part-time. Students come from 36 states and territories, 41% are from out of state, 6% African American, 0.5% Asian American or Pacific Islander, 2% Hispanic American, 0.5% Native American, 1% international, 6% transferred in, 75% live on campus. *Retention:* 58% of 2001 full-time freshmen returned.

Freshmen *Admission:* 571 applied, 449 admitted, 237 enrolled. *Average high school GPA:* 3.00. *Test scores:* ACT scores over 18: 88%; ACT scores over 24: 36%; ACT scores over 30: 6%.

Faculty *Total:* 166, 43% full-time, 48% with terminal degrees. *Student/faculty ratio:* 16:1.

Majors Accounting; behavioral sciences; biological/physical sciences; biology; biology education; broadcast journalism; business administration; business marketing and marketing management; chemistry; chemistry education; child care/development; communications; early childhood education; education (K-12); English; English education; exercise sciences; general studies; history; history education; information sciences/systems; mass communications; mathematics; mathematics education; medical technology; music; music business management/merchandising; music teacher education; physical education; physics; psychology; radio/television broadcasting technology; religious music; religious studies; secondary education; social sciences; speech/rhetorical studies; theater arts/drama.

Academic Programs *Special study options:* academic remediation for entering students, accelerated degree program, adult/continuing education programs, advanced placement credit, double majors, internships, part-time degree program, services for LD students, summer session for credit. *ROTC:* Army (c).

Library Mackey Library with 102,419 titles, 2,353 serial subscriptions, 3,731 audiovisual materials, an OPAC, a Web page.

Computers on Campus 200 computers available on campus for general student use. A campuswide network can be accessed from student residence rooms and from off campus. Internet access, at least one staffed computer lab available.

Student Life *Housing:* on-campus residence required through junior year. *Options:* men-only, women-only. *Activities and Organizations:* drama/theater group, student-run newspaper, radio station, choral group. *Campus security:* 24-hour patrols, student patrols, late-night transport/escort service. *Student Services:* health clinic, personal/psychological counseling.

Athletics Member NAIA. *Intercollegiate sports:* baseball M(s), basketball M(s)/W(s), golf M(s)/W(s), soccer M(s)/W(s), softball W(s), volleyball W(s). *Intramural sports:* badminton M/W, basketball M/W, football M/W, golf M/W, racquetball M/W, softball M/W, table tennis M/W, track and field M/W, volleyball M/W.

Standardized Tests *Required:* SAT I or ACT (for admission).

Costs (2001–02) *Comprehensive fee:* $16,540 includes full-time tuition ($11,390) and room and board ($5150). Full-time tuition and fees vary according to course load. Part-time tuition: $438 per credit hour. Part-time tuition and fees vary according to course load. *Room and board:* College room only: $2230. Room and board charges vary according to board plan. *Payment plan:* installment. *Waivers:* senior citizens and employees or children of employees.

Financial Aid Of all full-time matriculated undergraduates who enrolled in 2001, 438 applied for aid, 386 were judged to have need, 279 had their need fully met. In 2001, 57 non-need-based awards were made. *Average percent of need met:* 49%. *Average financial aid package:* $9647. *Average need-based gift aid:* $3869. *Average non-need based aid:* $3015. *Average indebtedness upon graduation:* $20,508.

Applying *Options:* early admission, deferred entrance. *Application fee:* $25. *Required:* high school transcript, minimum 2.5 GPA, medical history and immunization records. *Recommended:* letters of recommendation. *Application deadline:* rolling (freshmen), rolling (transfers).

Admissions Contact Ms. Patricia D. Cook, Director of Admissions, Trevecca Nazarene University, 333 Murfreesboro Road, Nashville, TN 37210-2834. *Phone:* 615-248-1320. *Toll-free phone:* 888-210-4TNU. *Fax:* 615-248-7406. *E-mail:* admissions_und@trevecca.edu.

TUSCULUM COLLEGE
Greeneville, Tennessee

- **Independent Presbyterian** comprehensive, founded 1794
- **Calendar** semesters
- **Degrees** bachelor's and master's
- **Small-town** 140-acre campus
- **Endowment** $12.4 million
- **Coed,** 1,556 undergraduate students, 100% full-time, 53% women, 47% men
- **Moderately difficult** entrance level, 85% of applicants were admitted

Imagine an education that goes far beyond the 4 walls of a classroom. Tusculum believes that to actually learn something, students need to experience it. With the focused calendar (1 course at a time for 3 weeks), students have hands-on experiences that allow them to travel to such places as Costa Rica, England, Mexico, Scotland, and Spain.

Undergraduates 1,551 full-time, 5 part-time. Students come from 29 states and territories, 15 other countries, 17% are from out of state, 9% African American,

Tusculum College (continued)
0.3% Asian American or Pacific Islander, 0.8% Hispanic American, 0.1% Native American, 2% international, 13% transferred in, 23% live on campus. *Retention:* 68% of 2001 full-time freshmen returned.

Freshmen *Admission:* 917 applied, 779 admitted, 268 enrolled. *Average high school GPA:* 2.89. *Test scores:* SAT verbal scores over 500: 38%; SAT math scores over 500: 43%; ACT scores over 18: 80%; SAT verbal scores over 600: 8%; SAT math scores over 600: 11%; ACT scores over 24: 26%; ACT scores over 30: 2%.

Faculty *Total:* 120, 68% full-time, 59% with terminal degrees. *Student/faculty ratio:* 15:1.

Majors Accounting; art; art education; athletic training/sports medicine; biology; business administration; computer science; early childhood education; education; elementary education; English; environmental science; history; information sciences/systems; mathematics; medical technology; middle school education; museum studies; physical education; pre-law; pre-medicine; pre-veterinary studies; psychology; secondary education; special education; sport/fitness administration; telecommunications.

Academic Programs *Special study options:* academic remediation for entering students, adult/continuing education programs, advanced placement credit, double majors, English as a second language, independent study, internships, part-time degree program, student-designed majors, study abroad, summer session for credit.

Library Albert Columbus Tate Library plus 2 others with 68,573 titles, 1,000 serial subscriptions, 832 audiovisual materials, an OPAC, a Web page.

Computers on Campus 60 computers available on campus for general student use. A campuswide network can be accessed from student residence rooms and from off campus. Internet access, at least one staffed computer lab available.

Student Life *Housing:* on-campus residence required through senior year. *Options:* coed, men-only, women-only. *Activities and Organizations:* drama/theater group, student-run newspaper, radio station, choral group, Pioneer Newspaper, Bonwondi, Campus Activities Board, Fellowship of Christian Athletes, "Tusculana" (yearbook). *Campus security:* 24-hour patrols, student patrols, trained security personnel on duty. *Student Services:* health clinic, personal/psychological counseling, women's center.

Athletics Member NCAA. All Division II. *Intercollegiate sports:* baseball M(s), basketball M(s)/W(s), cross-country running M(s)/W(s), football M(s), golf M/W, soccer M(s)/W(s), softball W(s), tennis M(s)/W(s), volleyball W(s). *Intramural sports:* baseball M, basketball M/W, football M, softball M, tennis M/W, volleyball M/W.

Standardized Tests *Required:* SAT I or ACT (for admission).

Costs (2001–02) *Comprehensive fee:* $17,900 includes full-time tuition ($13,400) and room and board ($4500). Full-time tuition and fees vary according to degree level and reciprocity agreements. Part-time tuition: $580 per credit hour. Part-time tuition and fees vary according to degree level and reciprocity agreements. *Payment plan:* installment. *Waivers:* employees or children of employees.

Financial Aid Of all full-time matriculated undergraduates who enrolled in 2001, 1155 applied for aid, 755 were judged to have need, 173 had their need fully met. 121 Federal Work-Study jobs (averaging $1107). 160 State and other part-time jobs (averaging $1667). In 2001, 281 non-need-based awards were made. *Average percent of need met:* 80%. *Average financial aid package:* $7522. *Average need-based loan:* $3307. *Average need-based gift aid:* $1720. *Average non-need based aid:* $4834. *Average indebtedness upon graduation:* $14,633.

Applying *Options:* early admission, deferred entrance. *Required:* essay or personal statement, high school transcript, minimum 2.0 GPA, letters of recommendation. *Recommended:* interview. *Application deadline:* rolling (freshmen), rolling (transfers).

Admissions Contact Mr. George Wolf, Director of Admissions, Tusculum College, PO Box 5047, Greeneville, TN 37743-9997. *Phone:* 423-636-7300 Ext. 611. *Toll-free phone:* 800-729-0256. *Fax:* 423-638-7166 Ext. 312. *E-mail:* admissions@tusculum.edu.

UNION UNIVERSITY
Jackson, Tennessee

- **Independent Southern Baptist** comprehensive, founded 1823
- **Calendar** 4-1-4
- **Degrees** diplomas, associate, bachelor's, master's, and post-master's certificates
- **Small-town** 290-acre campus with easy access to Memphis
- **Endowment** $16.3 million
- **Coed,** 1,965 undergraduate students, 84% full-time, 59% women, 41% men
- **Moderately difficult** entrance level, 86% of applicants were admitted

Undergraduates 1,657 full-time, 308 part-time. Students come from 40 states and territories, 28 other countries, 27% are from out of state, 6% African American, 0.8% Asian American or Pacific Islander, 0.6% Hispanic American, 0.2% Native American, 2% international, 9% transferred in, 72% live on campus. *Retention:* 93% of 2001 full-time freshmen returned.

Freshmen *Admission:* 1,042 applied, 901 admitted, 430 enrolled. *Average high school GPA:* 3.52. *Test scores:* SAT verbal scores over 500: 80%; SAT math scores over 500: 74%; ACT scores over 18: 96%; SAT verbal scores over 600: 42%; SAT math scores over 600: 35%; ACT scores over 24: 53%; SAT verbal scores over 700: 10%; SAT math scores over 700: 13%; ACT scores over 30: 14%.

Faculty *Total:* 222, 66% full-time, 49% with terminal degrees. *Student/faculty ratio:* 12:1.

Majors Accounting; advertising; art; art education; athletic training/sports medicine; biblical languages/literatures; biblical studies; biological/physical sciences; biology; broadcast journalism; business administration; business economics; business education; business marketing and marketing management; chemistry; computer science; early childhood education; economics; education; elementary education; English; exercise sciences; family/community studies; finance; foreign languages/literatures; French; history; information sciences/systems; journalism; mass communications; mathematics; medical technology; music; music business management/merchandising; music (general performance); music (piano and organ performance); music teacher education; music (voice and choral/opera performance); nursing; philosophy; philosophy and religion related; physical education; physics; political science; pre-dentistry; pre-law; pre-medicine; pre-pharmacy studies; psychology; public relations; radio/television broadcasting; recreation/leisure facilities management; religious music; religious studies; science education; secondary education; social work; sociology; Spanish; special education; speech/rhetorical studies; sport/fitness administration; teaching English as a second language; theater arts/drama; theological studies/religious vocations related; theology.

Academic Programs *Special study options:* accelerated degree program, adult/continuing education programs, advanced placement credit, distance learning, double majors, English as a second language, honors programs, independent study, internships, off-campus study, part-time degree program, services for LD students, study abroad, summer session for credit. *Unusual degree programs:* 3-2 engineering with Tennessee Technological University, The University of Memphis, University of Tennessee.

Library Emma Waters Summar Library with 135,877 titles, 4,655 serial subscriptions, 11,526 audiovisual materials, an OPAC, a Web page.

Computers on Campus 236 computers available on campus for general student use. A campuswide network can be accessed from student residence rooms and from off campus. Internet access, at least one staffed computer lab available.

Student Life *Housing:* on-campus residence required through senior year. *Options:* men-only, women-only, disabled students. *Activities and Organizations:* drama/theater group, student-run newspaper, choral group, Campus Ministries, Student Government Association, Student Activities Council, SIFE, national fraternities, national sororities. *Campus security:* 24-hour emergency response devices and patrols, student patrols, late-night transport/escort service. *Student Services:* health clinic, personal/psychological counseling.

Athletics Member NAIA, NCCAA. *Intercollegiate sports:* baseball M(s), basketball M(s)/W(s), cross-country running M/W(s), golf M(s), soccer M(s), softball W(s), tennis M(s)/W(s), volleyball W(s). *Intramural sports:* basketball M/W, bowling M/W, cross-country running M/W, football M/W, golf M/W, racquetball M/W, soccer W, softball M/W, table tennis M/W, tennis M/W, volleyball M/W, weight lifting M/W.

Standardized Tests *Required:* SAT I or ACT (for admission).

Costs (2002–03) *Comprehensive fee:* $18,930 includes full-time tuition ($14,080), mandatory fees ($500), and room and board ($4350). Full-time tuition and fees vary according to class time, course load, location, and program. Part-time tuition: $440 per credit hour. *Room and board:* Room and board charges vary according to board plan and location. *Payment plans:* tuition prepayment, installment, deferred payment. *Waivers:* employees or children of employees.

Financial Aid Of all full-time matriculated undergraduates who enrolled in 2001, 1418 applied for aid, 840 were judged to have need. 205 Federal Work-Study jobs (averaging $610). 150 State and other part-time jobs (averaging $660). In 2001, 150 non-need-based awards were made. *Average need-based loan:* $3859. *Average need-based gift aid:* $1471. *Average non-need based aid:* $2400. *Average indebtedness upon graduation:* $7800.

Applying *Options:* common application, electronic application, early admission, early action. *Application fee:* $25. *Required:* high school transcript, minimum 2.5 GPA. *Required for some:* letters of recommendation. *Recommended:* essay or personal statement, interview. *Application deadline:* rolling (freshmen), rolling (transfers). *Notification:* continuous until 8/15 (freshmen).

Admissions Contact Mr. Robbie Graves, Director of Enrollment Services, Union University, 1050 Union University Drive, Jackson, TN 38305-3697. *Phone:* 731-661-5008. *Toll-free phone:* 800-33-UNION. *Fax:* 731-661-5017. *E-mail:* info@uu.edu.

THE UNIVERSITY OF MEMPHIS
Memphis, Tennessee

- **State-supported** university, founded 1912, part of Tennessee Board of Regents
- **Calendar** semesters
- **Degrees** certificates, diplomas, bachelor's, master's, doctoral, first professional, post-master's, postbachelor's, and first professional certificates
- **Urban** 1100-acre campus
- **Endowment** $171.8 million
- **Coed,** 15,612 undergraduate students, 72% full-time, 59% women, 41% men
- **Moderately difficult** entrance level, 74% of applicants were admitted

Undergraduates Students come from 44 states and territories, 94 other countries, 9% are from out of state, 34% African American, 2% Asian American or Pacific Islander, 1% Hispanic American, 0.3% Native American, 2% international, 13% live on campus. *Retention:* 72% of 2001 full-time freshmen returned.

Freshmen *Admission:* 4,513 applied, 3,338 admitted. *Average high school GPA:* 3.03. *Test scores:* SAT verbal scores over 500: 69%; SAT math scores over 500: 68%; ACT scores over 18: 89%; SAT verbal scores over 600: 26%; SAT math scores over 600: 29%; ACT scores over 24: 33%; SAT verbal scores over 700: 8%; SAT math scores over 700: 5%; ACT scores over 30: 3%.

Faculty *Total:* 1,268, 67% full-time, 54% with terminal degrees. *Student/faculty ratio:* 18:1.

Majors Accounting; anthropology; architecture; art; art history; biology; business administration; business economics; business marketing and marketing management; chemistry; civil engineering; communications; computer engineering; computer engineering technology; computer science; consumer services; criminal justice/law enforcement administration; criminology; economics; electrical/electronic engineering technology; electrical engineering; English; exercise sciences; finance; foreign languages/literatures; geography; geology; history; hospitality management; individual/family development; industrial/manufacturing engineering; insurance/risk management; interdisciplinary studies; international business; international relations; journalism; management information systems/business data processing; management science; mathematics; mechanical engineering; microbiology/bacteriology; molecular biology; music; music business management/merchandising; nursing; philosophy; physics; political science; professional studies; psychology; real estate; recreation/leisure studies; retail management; social work; sociology; special education; systems engineering; theater arts/drama.

Academic Programs *Special study options:* academic remediation for entering students, accelerated degree program, adult/continuing education programs, advanced placement credit, cooperative education, distance learning, double majors, English as a second language, honors programs, independent study, internships, part-time degree program, services for LD students, student-designed majors, study abroad, summer session for credit. *ROTC:* Army (b), Navy (b), Air Force (b).

Library McWherter Library plus 6 others with 10,578 serial subscriptions, an OPAC, a Web page.

Computers on Campus 2000 computers available on campus for general student use. A campuswide network can be accessed from off campus. Internet access, online (class) registration, at least one staffed computer lab available.

Student Life *Housing Options:* coed, men-only, women-only, disabled students. *Activities and Organizations:* drama/theater group, student-run newspaper, radio station, choral group, marching band, national fraternities, national sororities. *Campus security:* 24-hour emergency response devices and patrols, student patrols, late-night transport/escort service. *Student Services:* health clinic, personal/psychological counseling, women's center, legal services.

Athletics Member NCAA. All Division I except football (Division I-A). *Intercollegiate sports:* baseball M(s), basketball M(s)/W(s), cross-country running M(s)/W(s), golf M(s)/W(s), racquetball M(c)/W(c), riflery M(s)/W(s), soccer M(s)/W(s), swimming M(c)/W(c), tennis M(s)/W(s), track and field M/W, volleyball W(s). *Intramural sports:* archery M/W, badminton M/W, basketball M/W, bowling M/W, fencing M, golf M/W, rugby M/W, soccer M, softball M/W, swimming M/W, table tennis M/W, tennis M/W, track and field M/W, volleyball M/W.

Standardized Tests *Required:* SAT I or ACT (for admission).

Costs (2001–02) *Tuition:* state resident $2856 full-time, $165 per credit hour part-time; nonresident $9510 full-time, $443 per credit hour part-time. Part-time tuition and fees vary according to course load. *Required fees:* $614 full-time. *Room and board:* $3801; room only: $1801. Room and board charges vary according to housing facility. *Payment plan:* installment. *Waivers:* senior citizens and employees or children of employees.

Financial Aid Of all full-time matriculated undergraduates who enrolled in 2001, 7201 applied for aid, 6297 were judged to have need, 1010 had their need fully met. 381 Federal Work-Study jobs (averaging $1360). In 2001, 1216 non-need-based awards were made. *Average percent of need met:* 76%. *Average financial aid package:* $3316. *Average need-based loan:* $1738. *Average need-based gift aid:* $2701. *Average indebtedness upon graduation:* $18,344.

Applying *Options:* early admission. *Application fee:* $15. *Required:* high school transcript. *Required for some:* minimum 2.0 GPA, 2 letters of recommendation, interview. *Application deadlines:* 8/1 (freshmen), 8/1 (transfers). *Notification:* continuous (freshmen).

Admissions Contact Mr. David Wallace, Director of Admissions, The University of Memphis, Memphis, TN 38152. *Phone:* 901-678-2101. *Fax:* 901-678-3053. *E-mail:* dwallace@memphis.edu.

THE UNIVERSITY OF TENNESSEE
Knoxville, Tennessee

- **State-supported** university, founded 1794, part of University of Tennessee System
- **Calendar** semesters
- **Degrees** bachelor's, master's, doctoral, and first professional
- **Urban** 533-acre campus
- **Endowment** $420.5 million
- **Coed,** 20,124 undergraduate students, 90% full-time, 52% women, 48% men
- **Moderately difficult** entrance level, 69% of applicants were admitted

Undergraduates 18,135 full-time, 1,989 part-time. Students come from 50 states and territories, 101 other countries, 14% are from out of state, 6% African American, 2% Asian American or Pacific Islander, 1% Hispanic American, 0.3% Native American, 1% international, 6% transferred in, 37% live on campus. *Retention:* 78% of 2001 full-time freshmen returned.

Freshmen *Admission:* 8,263 applied, 5,675 admitted, 3,958 enrolled. *Average high school GPA:* 3.31. *Test scores:* SAT verbal scores over 500: 70%; SAT math scores over 500: 70%; ACT scores over 18: 96%; SAT verbal scores over 600: 28%; SAT math scores over 600: 31%; ACT scores over 24: 45%; SAT verbal scores over 700: 6%; SAT math scores over 700: 5%; ACT scores over 30: 9%.

Faculty *Total:* 1,244, 98% full-time, 85% with terminal degrees. *Student/faculty ratio:* 14:1.

Majors Accounting; advertising; aerospace engineering; agricultural business related; agricultural economics; agricultural education; agricultural engineering; animal sciences; anthropology; architecture; area, ethnic, and cultural studies related; art education; art history; biochemistry; biology; botany; business; business administration; business economics; business education; business marketing and marketing management; chemical engineering; chemistry; civil engineering; classics; computer engineering; computer science; consumer economics; cultural studies; ecology; economics; electrical engineering; engineering physics; engineering science; English; exercise sciences; family studies; finance; fine/studio arts; food sciences; forestry; French; geography; geology; German; graphic design/commercial art/illustration; health education; hearing sciences; history; home economics education; hotel and restaurant management; individual/family development; industrial/manufacturing engineering; interior design; Italian; journalism; logistics/materials management; materials engineering; mathematical statistics; mathematics; mechanical engineering; medical technology; microbiology/bacteriology; multi/interdisciplinary studies related; music; music teacher education; nuclear engineering; nursing; nutrition science; ornamental horticulture; philosophy; physics; plant protection; plant sciences; political science; psychology; public administration; radio/television broadcasting; recreation/leisure facilities management; religious studies; Russian; social work; sociology; Spanish; special education; speech-language pathology; speech/rhetorical studies; sport/fitness administration; technical education; theater arts/drama; wildlife management; zoology.

Academic Programs *Special study options:* accelerated degree program, adult/continuing education programs, advanced placement credit, cooperative education, distance learning, double majors, English as a second language, honors programs, independent study, internships, off-campus study, part-time degree program, services for LD students, student-designed majors, study abroad, summer session for credit. *ROTC:* Army (b), Air Force (b).

Library John C. Hodges Library plus 6 others with 24.4 million titles, 17,628 serial subscriptions, 175,541 audiovisual materials, an OPAC, a Web page.

Computers on Campus 1000 computers available on campus for general student use. A campuswide network can be accessed from student residence rooms and from off campus. Internet access, online (class) registration, at least one staffed computer lab available.

Student Life *Housing:* on-campus residence required for freshman year. *Options:* coed. *Activities and Organizations:* drama/theater group, student-run newspaper, radio station, choral group, marching band, Central Program Council, religious organizations, Volunteer Outreach for Leadership and Service, Student

The University of Tennessee (continued)
Government Association, Dance Marathon, national fraternities, national sororities. *Campus security:* 24-hour emergency response devices and patrols, late-night transport/escort service. *Student Services:* health clinic, personal/psychological counseling, women's center, legal services.

Athletics Member NCAA. All Division I except football (Division I-A). *Intercollegiate sports:* baseball M(s), basketball M(s)/W(s), crew W(s), cross-country running M(s)/W(s), golf M(s)/W(s), soccer W(s), softball W(s), swimming M(s)/W(s), tennis M(s)/W(s), track and field M(s)/W(s), volleyball W(s). *Intramural sports:* badminton M/W, basketball M/W, bowling M/W, crew M(c)/W(c), cross-country running M/W, equestrian sports M(c)/W(c), fencing M(c)/W(c), field hockey M/W, football M/W, golf M/W, gymnastics M(c)/W(c), ice hockey M(c)/W(c), lacrosse M(c)/W(c), racquetball M/W, riflery M(c)/W(c), rugby M(c)/W(c), sailing M(c)/W(c), skiing (downhill) M(c)/W(c), soccer M/W, softball M/W, swimming M/W, table tennis M/W, tennis M/W, track and field M/W, volleyball M(c)/W, water polo M/W, weight lifting M(c)/W(c).

Standardized Tests *Required:* SAT I or ACT (for admission).

Costs (2001–02) *Tuition:* state resident $3234 full-time, $160 per semester hour part-time; nonresident $10,770 full-time, $488 per semester hour part-time. *Required fees:* $800 full-time, $25 per semester hour. *Room and board:* $4402; room only: $2250. Room and board charges vary according to board plan and housing facility. *Payment plans:* installment, deferred payment. *Waivers:* senior citizens and employees or children of employees.

Financial Aid Of all full-time matriculated undergraduates who enrolled in 2001, 8442 applied for aid, 6090 were judged to have need, 1003 had their need fully met. *Average percent of need met:* 69%. *Average financial aid package:* $6220. *Average need-based loan:* $3499. *Average need-based gift aid:* $3990. *Average indebtedness upon graduation:* $21,221.

Applying *Options:* early admission, deferred entrance. *Application fee:* $25. *Required:* essay or personal statement, high school transcript, minimum 2.0 GPA, specific high school units. *Application deadlines:* 1/21 (freshmen), 6/1 (transfers). *Notification:* continuous (freshmen).

Admissions Contact Mr. Marshall Rose, Acting Director of Admissions, The University of Tennessee, 320 Student Services Building, Knoxville, TN 37996-0230. *Phone:* 865-974-2184. *Toll-free phone:* 800-221-8657. *Fax:* 865-974-6341. *E-mail:* admissions@tennessee.edu.

THE UNIVERSITY OF TENNESSEE AT CHATTANOOGA

Chattanooga, Tennessee

- **State-supported** comprehensive, founded 1886, part of University of Tennessee System
- **Calendar** semesters
- **Degrees** bachelor's, master's, and post-master's certificates
- **Urban** 102-acre campus with easy access to Atlanta
- **Endowment** $101.2 million
- **Coed,** 7,105 undergraduate students, 81% full-time, 58% women, 42% men
- **Moderately difficult** entrance level, 51% of applicants were admitted

Undergraduates 5,744 full-time, 1,361 part-time. Students come from 41 states and territories, 49 other countries, 7% are from out of state, 18% African American, 3% Asian American or Pacific Islander, 0.9% Hispanic American, 0.3% Native American, 1% international, 9% transferred in, 26% live on campus. *Retention:* 74% of 2001 full-time freshmen returned.

Freshmen *Admission:* 2,501 applied, 1,272 admitted, 1,081 enrolled. *Average high school GPA:* 3.19. *Test scores:* SAT verbal scores over 500: 61%; SAT math scores over 500: 79%; ACT scores over 18: 83%; SAT verbal scores over 600: 28%; SAT math scores over 600: 44%; ACT scores over 24: 29%; SAT verbal scores over 700: 6%; SAT math scores over 700: 8%; ACT scores over 30: 3%.

Faculty *Total:* 608, 56% full-time, 54% with terminal degrees. *Student/faculty ratio:* 16:1.

Majors Accounting; applied mathematics; art; art education; biology; broadcast journalism; business administration; business marketing and marketing management; chemical engineering; chemistry; civil engineering; computer science; corrections; creative writing; criminal justice/law enforcement administration; early childhood education; economics; education; electrical engineering; elementary education; engineering; engineering/industrial management; English; environmental science; family/consumer studies; finance; French; geology; Greek (modern); history; home economics; humanities; human services; industrial/manufacturing engineering; information sciences/systems; interdisciplinary studies; Latin (ancient and medieval); law enforcement/police science; legal studies; mass communications; mathematics; mechanical engineering; medical technology; music; music (piano and organ performance); music teacher education; music (voice and choral/opera performance); nursing; occupational therapy; paralegal/legal assistant; philosophy; physical education; physical therapy; physics; political science; pre-medicine; pre-veterinary studies; psychology; recreation/leisure studies; science education; sculpture; secondary education; social work; sociology; Spanish; special education; theater arts/drama; urban studies.

Academic Programs *Special study options:* academic remediation for entering students, adult/continuing education programs, advanced placement credit, cooperative education, distance learning, double majors, English as a second language, honors programs, independent study, internships, off-campus study, part-time degree program, services for LD students, study abroad, summer session for credit. *Unusual degree programs:* 3-2 engineering with Georgia Institute of Technology, University of Tennessee, Knoxville.

Library Lupton Library with 479,007 titles, 2,768 serial subscriptions, 15,448 audiovisual materials, an OPAC, a Web page.

Computers on Campus 300 computers available on campus for general student use. A campuswide network can be accessed from student residence rooms and from off campus. Internet access, online (class) registration, at least one staffed computer lab available.

Student Life *Housing Options:* coed. *Activities and Organizations:* drama/theater group, student-run newspaper, radio station, choral group, marching band, Student Government Association, Black Student Association, Association for Campus Entertainment, International Student Association, Baptist Student Union, national fraternities, national sororities. *Campus security:* 24-hour emergency response devices and patrols, late-night transport/escort service. *Student Services:* health clinic, personal/psychological counseling.

Athletics Member NCAA. All Division I except football (Division I-AA). *Intercollegiate sports:* basketball M(s)/W(s), crew M/W, cross-country running M(s)/W(s), golf M(s)/W, soccer M(s)/W(s), softball W(s), tennis M(s)/W(s), track and field M/W, volleyball W(s), wrestling M(s). *Intramural sports:* badminton M/W, basketball M/W, bowling M/W, cross-country running M/W, fencing M, football M, golf M, racquetball M/W, swimming M/W, tennis M/W, volleyball W, weight lifting M, wrestling M.

Standardized Tests *Required:* SAT I or ACT (for admission).

Costs (2001–02) *Tuition:* state resident $3236 full-time, $162 per hour part-time; nonresident $9766 full-time, $464 per hour part-time. *Room and board:* room only: $2400. Room and board charges vary according to housing facility. *Payment plan:* deferred payment. *Waivers:* senior citizens and employees or children of employees.

Financial Aid Of all full-time matriculated undergraduates who enrolled in 2001, 3752 applied for aid, 3208 were judged to have need, 409 had their need fully met. 210 Federal Work-Study jobs (averaging $1667). 400 State and other part-time jobs (averaging $1875). In 2001, 789 non-need-based awards were made. *Average percent of need met:* 82%. *Average financial aid package:* $8215. *Average need-based loan:* $4300. *Average need-based gift aid:* $3430. *Average non-need based aid:* $3900. *Average indebtedness upon graduation:* $14,250.

Applying *Options:* early admission, deferred entrance. *Application fee:* $25. *Required:* high school transcript, 1 letter of recommendation. *Recommended:* essay or personal statement. *Application deadlines:* 8/1 (freshmen), 8/1 (transfers). *Notification:* continuous (freshmen).

Admissions Contact Mr. Yancy Freeman, Director of Student Recruitment, The University of Tennessee at Chattanooga, 131 Hooper Hall, Chattanooga, TN 37403. *Phone:* 423-755-4597. *Toll-free phone:* 800-UTC-6627. *Fax:* 423-755-4157. *E-mail:* yancy-freeman@utc.edu.

THE UNIVERSITY OF TENNESSEE AT MARTIN

Martin, Tennessee

- **State-supported** comprehensive, founded 1900, part of University of Tennessee System
- **Calendar** semesters
- **Degrees** bachelor's and master's
- **Small-town** 250-acre campus
- **Endowment** $12.2 million
- **Coed,** 5,478 undergraduate students, 85% full-time, 56% women, 44% men
- **Moderately difficult** entrance level, 55% of applicants were admitted

Undergraduates 4,662 full-time, 816 part-time. Students come from 35 states and territories, 30 other countries, 8% are from out of state, 15% African American, 0.5% Asian American or Pacific Islander, 0.5% Hispanic American, 0.3% Native American, 4% international, 7% transferred in, 40% live on campus. *Retention:* 66% of 2001 full-time freshmen returned.

Freshmen *Admission:* 2,294 applied, 1,272 admitted, 1,080 enrolled. *Average high school GPA:* 3.16. *Test scores:* ACT scores over 18: 82%; ACT scores over 24: 27%; ACT scores over 30: 3%.

Faculty *Total:* 414, 61% full-time, 48% with terminal degrees. *Student/faculty ratio:* 18:1.

Majors Accounting; agricultural animal husbandry/production management; agricultural business; agricultural education; agricultural sciences; agronomy/crop science; animal sciences; art education; athletic training/sports medicine; biology; biology education; broadcast journalism; business administration; business economics; business education; business marketing and marketing management; chemistry; chemistry education; child care/development; computer science; criminal justice/law enforcement administration; dietetics; early childhood education; economics; education (K-12); elementary education; engineering; English; English education; environmental science; fashion merchandising; finance; French; French language education; geography; geology; German language education; graphic design/commercial art/illustration; health/physical education; history; history education; home economics; home economics education; interdisciplinary studies; interior design; international business; international relations; journalism; landscaping management; management information systems/business data processing; mathematics; mathematics education; music; music (piano and organ performance); music teacher education; music (voice and choral/opera performance); nursing; philosophy; political science; pre-dentistry; pre-medicine; pre-pharmacy studies; pre-veterinary studies; professional studies; psychology; public administration; public relations; recreation/leisure facilities management; science education; social work; sociology; soil conservation; Spanish; Spanish language education; special education; sport/fitness administration; stringed instruments; visual/performing arts; wildlife management; wind/percussion instruments.

Academic Programs *Special study options:* academic remediation for entering students, accelerated degree program, adult/continuing education programs, advanced placement credit, cooperative education, distance learning, double majors, English as a second language, honors programs, independent study, internships, off-campus study, part-time degree program, services for LD students, student-designed majors, study abroad, summer session for credit. *ROTC:* Army (b).

Library Paul Meek Library plus 1 other with 436,366 titles, 2,654 serial subscriptions, 10,858 audiovisual materials, an OPAC, a Web page.

Computers on Campus 185 computers available on campus for general student use. A campuswide network can be accessed from student residence rooms and from off campus. At least one staffed computer lab available.

Student Life *Housing:* on-campus residence required through sophomore year. *Options:* coed, men-only, women-only, disabled students. *Activities and Organizations:* drama/theater group, student-run newspaper, radio and television station, choral group, marching band, Student Government Association, Greek organizations, religious affiliated groups, Student Activities Council, Black Student Association (BSA), national fraternities, national sororities. *Campus security:* 24-hour emergency response devices and patrols, student patrols, late-night transport/escort service, controlled dormitory access. *Student Services:* health clinic, personal/psychological counseling.

Athletics Member NCAA. All Division I except football (Division I-AA). *Intercollegiate sports:* baseball M(s), basketball M(s)/W(s), cross-country running W(s), golf M(s), riflery M(s)/W(s), soccer W(s), softball W(s), tennis M(s)/W(s), track and field M(s)/W(s), volleyball W(s). *Intramural sports:* basketball M/W, cross-country running M/W, equestrian sports W, football M/W, golf M/W, racquetball M/W, soccer M/W, softball M/W, swimming M/W, tennis M/W, track and field M/W, volleyball M/W.

Standardized Tests *Required:* SAT I or ACT (for admission).

Costs (2001–02) *Tuition:* state resident $3860 full-time, $161 per semester hour part-time; nonresident $9810 full-time, $409 per semester hour part-time. *Required fees:* $582 full-time. *Room and board:* $3820; room only: $1840. Room and board charges vary according to board plan and housing facility. *Payment plan:* deferred payment. *Waivers:* senior citizens and employees or children of employees.

Financial Aid Of all full-time matriculated undergraduates who enrolled in 2001, 3933 applied for aid, 2304 were judged to have need, 558 had their need fully met. 236 Federal Work-Study jobs (averaging $1900). In 2001, 882 non-need-based awards were made. *Average percent of need met:* 76%. *Average financial aid package:* $6571. *Average need-based loan:* $3968. *Average need-based gift aid:* $3354. *Average non-need based aid:* $3211. *Average indebtedness upon graduation:* $10,500.

Applying *Options:* common application, electronic application, deferred entrance. *Application fee:* $25. *Required:* high school transcript, minimum 2.25 GPA. *Application deadline:* rolling (freshmen), rolling (transfers). *Notification:* continuous until 8/1 (freshmen).

Admissions Contact Ms. Judy Rayburn, Director of Admission, The University of Tennessee at Martin, 200 Hall-Moody Administration Building, Martin, TN 38238. *Phone:* 901-587-7032. *Toll-free phone:* 800-829-8861. *Fax:* 731-587-7029. *E-mail:* jrayburn@utm.edu.

THE UNIVERSITY OF TENNESSEE HEALTH SCIENCE CENTER
Memphis, Tennessee

Admissions Contact Ms. June Peoples, Director of Admissions, The University of Tennessee Health Science Center, 800 Madison Avenue, Memphis, TN 38163-0002. *Phone:* 901-448-5560. *Fax:* 901-448-7585. *E-mail:* jpeoples@utmen1.utmem.edu.

UNIVERSITY OF THE SOUTH
Sewanee, Tennessee

- **Independent Episcopal** comprehensive, founded 1857
- **Calendar** semesters
- **Degrees** certificates, bachelor's, master's, doctoral, and first professional
- **Small-town** 10,000-acre campus
- **Endowment** $232.9 million
- **Coed,** 1,329 undergraduate students, 98% full-time, 53% women, 47% men
- **Very difficult** entrance level, 74% of applicants were admitted

Undergraduates 1,309 full-time, 20 part-time. Students come from 44 states and territories, 75% are from out of state, 4% African American, 1% Asian American or Pacific Islander, 0.7% Hispanic American, 0.2% Native American, 1% international, 1% transferred in, 92% live on campus. *Retention:* 85% of 2001 full-time freshmen returned.

Freshmen *Admission:* 1,620 applied, 1,194 admitted, 355 enrolled. *Average high school GPA:* 3.46. *Test scores:* SAT verbal scores over 500: 96%; SAT math scores over 500: 98%; ACT scores over 18: 100%; SAT verbal scores over 600: 61%; SAT math scores over 600: 59%; ACT scores over 24: 78%; SAT verbal scores over 700: 13%; SAT math scores over 700: 8%; ACT scores over 30: 17%.

Faculty *Total:* 163, 78% full-time, 85% with terminal degrees. *Student/faculty ratio:* 10:1.

Majors American studies; anthropology; applied art; art; art history; Asian studies; biology; chemistry; classics; comparative literature; computer science; drawing; economics; English; environmental science; European studies; fine/studio arts; forestry; French; geology; German; Greek (modern); history; international relations; Latin (ancient and medieval); literature; mathematics; medieval/renaissance studies; music; music history; natural resources management; philosophy; physics; political science; psychology; religious studies; Russian; Russian/Slavic studies; social sciences; Spanish; theater arts/drama.

Academic Programs *Special study options:* advanced placement credit, double majors, independent study, internships, services for LD students, student-designed majors, study abroad, summer session for credit. *Unusual degree programs:* 3-2 engineering with Georgia Institute of Technology, Washington University in St. Louis, Vanderbilt University, Rensselaer Polytechnic Institute, Columbia University; forestry with Duke University, Yale University.

Library Jessie Ball duPont Library with 457,526 titles, 6,495 serial subscriptions, 72,964 audiovisual materials, an OPAC, a Web page.

Computers on Campus 92 computers available on campus for general student use. A campuswide network can be accessed from student residence rooms and from off campus. At least one staffed computer lab available.

Student Life *Housing:* on-campus residence required through senior year. *Options:* coed. *Activities and Organizations:* drama/theater group, student-run newspaper, radio station, choral group, Sewanee Outing Program, Community Service Council, Student Activities Programming Board, student radio station, BACCHUS (Alcohol and Drug Education), national fraternities. *Campus security:* 24-hour emergency response devices and patrols, late-night transport/escort service, security lighting. *Student Services:* health clinic, personal/psychological counseling, women's center, legal services.

Athletics Member NCAA. All Division III. *Intercollegiate sports:* baseball M, basketball M/W, crew M(c)/W(c), cross-country running M/W, equestrian sports M(c)/W(c), fencing M(c)/W(c), field hockey W, football M, golf M/W, lacrosse M(c)/W(c), rugby M(c), soccer M/W, softball W(c), swimming M/W, tennis M/W, track and field M/W, volleyball W. *Intramural sports:* basketball M/W, cross-country running M/W, football M, golf M/W, racquetball M/W, soccer M/W, softball M/W, swimming M/W, table tennis M/W, tennis M/W, track and field M/W, volleyball M/W.

Standardized Tests *Required:* SAT I or ACT (for admission). *Recommended:* SAT II: Subject Tests (for admission).

Costs (2001–02) *Comprehensive fee:* $27,290 includes full-time tuition ($21,140), mandatory fees ($200), and room and board ($5950). Part-time tuition: $770 per semester hour. *Room and board:* College room only: $3050. *Payment plans:* installment, deferred payment. *Waivers:* employees or children of employees.

University of the South (continued)

Financial Aid Of all full-time matriculated undergraduates who enrolled in 2001, 627 applied for aid, 518 were judged to have need, 518 had their need fully met. 385 Federal Work-Study jobs (averaging $1135). 157 State and other part-time jobs (averaging $1088). In 2001, 114 non-need-based awards were made. *Average percent of need met:* 100%. *Average financial aid package:* $21,067. *Average need-based loan:* $3414. *Average need-based gift aid:* $15,289. *Average non-need based aid:* $6165. *Average indebtedness upon graduation:* $13,213.

Applying *Options:* common application, electronic application, early admission, early decision, deferred entrance. *Application fee:* $45. *Required:* essay or personal statement, high school transcript, 2 letters of recommendation. *Recommended:* interview. *Application deadlines:* 2/1 (freshmen), 4/1 (transfers). *Early decision:* 11/15. *Notification:* 4/1 (freshmen), 12/15 (early decision).

Admissions Contact Mr. David Lesesne, Dean of Admission, University of the South, 735 University Avenue, Sewanee, TN 37383. *Phone:* 931-598-1238. *Toll-free phone:* 800-522-2234. *Fax:* 931-598-3248. *E-mail:* admiss@sewanee.edu.

VANDERBILT UNIVERSITY
Nashville, Tennessee

- **Independent** university, founded 1873
- **Calendar** semesters
- **Degrees** bachelor's, master's, doctoral, and first professional
- **Urban** 330-acre campus
- **Endowment** $1.4 billion
- **Coed,** 6,077 undergraduate students, 99% full-time, 52% women, 48% men
- **Very difficult** entrance level, 46% of applicants were admitted

Undergraduates 6,017 full-time, 60 part-time. Students come from 54 states and territories, 36 other countries, 80% are from out of state, 6% African American, 6% Asian American or Pacific Islander, 4% Hispanic American, 0.2% Native American, 3% international, 1% transferred in, 84% live on campus. *Retention:* 94% of 2001 full-time freshmen returned.

Freshmen *Admission:* 9,746 applied, 4,528 admitted, 1,557 enrolled. *Test scores:* SAT verbal scores over 500: 98%; SAT math scores over 500: 99%; ACT scores over 18: 100%; SAT verbal scores over 600: 79%; SAT math scores over 600: 87%; ACT scores over 24: 96%; SAT verbal scores over 700: 24%; SAT math scores over 700: 36%; ACT scores over 30: 46%.

Faculty *Total:* 938, 74% full-time. *Student/faculty ratio:* 9:1.

Majors African-American studies; African studies; American studies; anthropology; art; astronomy; bioengineering; biology; chemical engineering; chemistry; civil engineering; classics; cognitive psychology/psycholinguistics; computer engineering; computer science; early childhood education; East Asian studies; ecology; economics; education; electrical engineering; elementary education; engineering; engineering science; English; European studies; French; geology; German; history; human resources management; individual/family development; interdisciplinary studies; Latin American studies; mass communications; mathematics; mechanical engineering; molecular biology; music; music (piano and organ performance); music (voice and choral/opera performance); philosophy; physics; political science; Portuguese; psychology; religious studies; Russian; secondary education; sociology; Spanish; special education; stringed instruments; theater arts/drama; urban studies; wind/percussion instruments.

Academic Programs *Special study options:* accelerated degree program, advanced placement credit, cooperative education, double majors, English as a second language, honors programs, independent study, off-campus study, services for LD students, student-designed majors, study abroad, summer session for credit. *ROTC:* Army (b), Navy (b), Air Force (c).

Library Jean and Alexander Heard Library plus 7 others with 1.7 million titles, 21,608 serial subscriptions, 43,182 audiovisual materials.

Computers on Campus 400 computers available on campus for general student use. A campuswide network can be accessed from student residence rooms and from off campus that provide access to productivity and educational software. At least one staffed computer lab available.

Student Life *Housing:* on-campus residence required through senior year. *Options:* coed, men-only, women-only, disabled students. *Activities and Organizations:* drama/theater group, student-run newspaper, radio station, choral group, marching band, national fraternities, national sororities. *Campus security:* 24-hour emergency response devices and patrols, student patrols, late-night transport/escort service, controlled dormitory access. *Student Services:* health clinic, personal/psychological counseling, women's center.

Athletics Member NCAA. All Division I except football (Division I-A). *Intercollegiate sports:* baseball M(s), basketball M(s)/W(s), crew M(c)/W(c), cross-country running M(s)/W(s), equestrian sports M(c)/W(c), fencing M(c)/W(c), field hockey M(c)/W(c), golf M(s)/W(s), ice hockey M(c)/W(c), lacrosse M(c)/W(s), rugby M(c)/W(c), sailing M(c)/W(c), soccer M(s)/W(s), squash M(c)/W(c), tennis M(s)/W(s), track and field M(c)/W(s), volleyball M(c)/W(c), water polo M(c)/W(c), wrestling M(c)/W(c). *Intramural sports:* badminton M/W, baseball M, basketball M/W, bowling M/W, football M/W, golf M/W, racquetball M/W, soccer M/W, softball M/W, squash M/W, swimming M/W, table tennis M/W, tennis M/W, volleyball M/W, water polo M/W, weight lifting M/W.

Standardized Tests *Required:* SAT I or ACT (for admission). *Recommended:* SAT II: Subject Tests (for admission), SAT II: Writing Test (for admission).

Costs (2001–02) *Comprehensive fee:* $34,482 includes full-time tuition ($25,190), mandatory fees ($657), and room and board ($8635). Part-time tuition: $1050 per credit hour. Part-time tuition and fees vary according to course load. *Room and board:* College room only: $5585. Room and board charges vary according to board plan and housing facility. *Payment plans:* tuition prepayment, installment, deferred payment. *Waivers:* employees or children of employees.

Financial Aid Of all full-time matriculated undergraduates who enrolled in 2001, 2537 applied for aid, 2267 were judged to have need, 2187 had their need fully met. In 2001, 871 non-need-based awards were made. *Average percent of need met:* 99%. *Average financial aid package:* $24,812. *Average need-based loan:* $5423. *Average need-based gift aid:* $16,622. *Average indebtedness upon graduation:* $21,015.

Applying *Options:* common application, electronic application, early admission, early decision, deferred entrance. *Application fee:* $50. *Required:* essay or personal statement, high school transcript, 2 letters of recommendation. *Application deadline:* 1/4 (freshmen). *Early decision:* 11/1 (for plan 1), 1/4 (for plan 2). *Notification:* 4/1 (freshmen), 12/15 (early decision plan 1), 2/15 (early decision plan 2).

Admissions Contact Mr. Bill Shain, Dean of Undergraduate Admissions, Vanderbilt University, Nashville, TN 37240-1001. *Phone:* 615-322-2561. *Toll-free phone:* 800-288-0432. *Fax:* 615-343-7765. *E-mail:* admissions@vanderbilt.edu.

WATKINS COLLEGE OF ART AND DESIGN
Nashville, Tennessee

- **Independent** primarily 2-year, founded 1885
- **Calendar** semesters
- **Degrees** associate, bachelor's, and postbachelor's certificates
- **Urban** campus
- **Endowment** $7.0 million
- **Coed,** 357 undergraduate students, 35% full-time, 51% women, 49% men
- **Moderately difficult** entrance level, 73% of applicants were admitted

Undergraduates 124 full-time, 233 part-time. Students come from 9 states and territories, 3 other countries, 35% are from out of state, 8% African American, 0.5% Asian American or Pacific Islander, 2% Hispanic American, 0.7% international, 22% transferred in. *Retention:* 75% of 2001 full-time freshmen returned.

Freshmen *Admission:* 80 applied, 58 admitted, 24 enrolled. *Average high school GPA:* 2.95.

Faculty *Total:* 35, 29% full-time, 69% with terminal degrees.

Majors Art; film studies; graphic design/commercial art/illustration; interior design; photography.

Academic Programs *Special study options:* cooperative education, double majors, internships, summer session for credit.

Library The George B. Allen Library with 4,000 titles, 35 serial subscriptions.

Computers on Campus 10 computers available on campus for general student use. At least one staffed computer lab available.

Student Life *Housing:* college housing not available. *Activities and Organizations:* student-run newspaper. *Student Services:* personal/psychological counseling.

Standardized Tests *Required for some:* SAT I or ACT (for admission).

Costs (2002–03) *Tuition:* $8500 full-time, $340 per hour part-time. Full-time tuition and fees vary according to course load and program. Part-time tuition and fees vary according to course load and program. *Payment plan:* deferred payment. *Waivers:* employees or children of employees.

Financial Aid Of all full-time matriculated undergraduates who enrolled in 2001, 15 Federal Work-Study jobs (averaging $1500). 15 State and other part-time jobs (averaging $1500). *Financial aid deadline:* 6/1.

Applying *Options:* early decision, early action, deferred entrance. *Application fee:* $35. *Required:* essay or personal statement, high school transcript, minimum 2.5 GPA, letters of recommendation. *Required for some:* interview, statement of good standing from prior institution(s), portfolio. *Application deadlines:* 4/1 (freshmen), 4/1 (transfers). *Notification:* 4/30 (freshmen).

Admissions Contact Mr. Ted Gray, Director of Admissions, Watkins College of Art and Design, 100 Powell Place, Nashville, TN 37204. *Phone:* 615-383-4848. *Fax:* 615-383-4849. *E-mail:* tgray@watkins.edu.

TEXAS

ABILENE CHRISTIAN UNIVERSITY
Abilene, Texas

- **Independent** comprehensive, founded 1906, affiliated with Church of Christ
- **Calendar** semesters
- **Degrees** certificates, associate, bachelor's, master's, doctoral, first professional, and postbachelor's certificates
- **Urban** 208-acre campus
- **Endowment** $137.1 million
- **Coed,** 4,234 undergraduate students, 92% full-time, 55% women, 45% men
- **Moderately difficult** entrance level, 66% of applicants were admitted

Undergraduates 3,908 full-time, 326 part-time. Students come from 49 states and territories, 49 other countries, 20% are from out of state, 6% African American, 0.8% Asian American or Pacific Islander, 6% Hispanic American, 0.4% Native American, 4% international, 5% transferred in, 43% live on campus. *Retention:* 76% of 2001 full-time freshmen returned.

Freshmen *Admission:* 3,056 applied, 2,004 admitted, 1,031 enrolled. *Average high school GPA:* 3.50. *Test scores:* SAT verbal scores over 500: 73%; SAT math scores over 500: 74%; ACT scores over 18: 93%; SAT verbal scores over 600: 33%; SAT math scores over 600: 34%; ACT scores over 24: 45%; SAT verbal scores over 700: 8%; SAT math scores over 700: 7%; ACT scores over 30: 8%.

Faculty *Total:* 323, 71% full-time, 59% with terminal degrees. *Student/faculty ratio:* 17:1.

Majors Accounting; advertising; agribusiness; animal sciences; architectural engineering technology; area studies; art; art education; biblical studies; biochemistry; biology; biology education; business administration; business education; business marketing and marketing management; chemistry; chemistry education; child care/development; computer education; computer/information sciences; computer science; construction technology; criminal justice/law enforcement administration; dietetics; drafting; drama/dance education; electrical engineering; elementary education; engineering physics; engineering science; English; English education; environmental science; exercise sciences; fashion merchandising; finance; fine/studio arts; French; French language education; geology; graphic design/commercial art/illustration; health education; health/physical education; history; history education; home economics; home economics education; human resources management; individual/family development; industrial arts education; industrial technology; interdisciplinary studies; interior design; international relations; journalism; liberal arts and sciences/liberal studies; management science; mathematics; mathematics education; missionary studies; music; music (piano and organ performance); music teacher education; music (voice and choral/opera performance); nursing; organizational psychology; pastoral counseling; physical education; physics; physics education; political science; pre-dentistry; pre-law; pre-medicine; pre-pharmacy studies; pre-veterinary studies; psychology; public administration; range management; reading education; science education; secondary education; social science education; social studies education; social work; sociology; Spanish; Spanish language education; special education; speech education; speech-language pathology/audiology; speech/rhetorical studies; theater arts/drama.

Academic Programs *Special study options:* academic remediation for entering students, adult/continuing education programs, advanced placement credit, distance learning, double majors, English as a second language, external degree program, honors programs, independent study, internships, off-campus study, part-time degree program, services for LD students, student-designed majors, study abroad, summer session for credit. *Unusual degree programs:* 3-2 engineering with The University of Texas at Dallas, The University of Texas at Arlington.

Library Brown Library with 478,831 titles, 2,387 serial subscriptions, 57,395 audiovisual materials, an OPAC, a Web page.

Computers on Campus 650 computers available on campus for general student use. A campuswide network can be accessed from student residence rooms and from off campus. Internet access, online (class) registration, at least one staffed computer lab available.

Student Life *Housing:* on-campus residence required through sophomore year. *Options:* men-only, women-only. *Activities and Organizations:* drama/theater group, student-run newspaper, radio and television station, choral group, marching band, Student Association, Alpha Phi Omega, "W" Club, Spring Break Campaign, Student Alumni Association. *Campus security:* 24-hour emergency response devices and patrols, late-night transport/escort service. *Student Services:* health clinic, personal/psychological counseling.

Athletics Member NCAA. All Division II. *Intercollegiate sports:* baseball M(s), basketball M(s)/W(s), cross-country running M(s)/W(s), football M(s), golf M(s), soccer M(c)/W(c), softball W(s), tennis M(s)/W(s), track and field M(s)/W(s), volleyball W(s). *Intramural sports:* badminton M/W, basketball M/W, bowling M/W, cross-country running M/W, football M/W, racquetball M/W, soccer M/W, softball M/W, table tennis M/W, tennis M/W, track and field M/W, volleyball M/W, water polo M.

Standardized Tests *Required:* SAT I or ACT (for admission).

Costs (2001–02) *Comprehensive fee:* $16,300 includes full-time tuition ($11,130), mandatory fees ($520), and room and board ($4650). Full-time tuition and fees vary according to course load. Part-time tuition: $371 per semester hour. Part-time tuition and fees vary according to course load. *Required fees:* $17 per semester hour, $5 per term part-time. *Room and board:* College room only: $1950. Room and board charges vary according to board plan and housing facility. *Payment plans:* tuition prepayment, installment. *Waivers:* employees or children of employees.

Financial Aid Of all full-time matriculated undergraduates who enrolled in 2001, 3453 applied for aid, 2094 were judged to have need, 1184 had their need fully met. 741 Federal Work-Study jobs (averaging $1302). In 2001, 560 non-need-based awards were made. *Average percent of need met:* 80%. *Average financial aid package:* $9914. *Average need-based loan:* $3602. *Average need-based gift aid:* $6485. *Average non-need based aid:* $8521. *Average indebtedness upon graduation:* $24,572.

Applying *Options:* common application, electronic application. *Application fee:* $25. *Required:* high school transcript, 2 letters of recommendation. *Recommended:* minimum 2.0 GPA, interview. *Application deadline:* 8/1 (freshmen), rolling (transfers). *Notification:* continuous until 9/1 (freshmen).

Admissions Contact Abilene Christian University, ACU Box 29100, Abilene, TX 79699-9100. *Phone:* 915-674-2650. *Toll-free phone:* 800-460-6228 Ext. 2650. *E-mail:* info@admissions.acu.edu.

AMBERTON UNIVERSITY
Garland, Texas

- **Independent nondenominational** upper-level, founded 1971
- **Calendar** 4 10-week terms
- **Degrees** bachelor's and master's
- **Suburban** 5-acre campus with easy access to Dallas-Fort Worth
- **Endowment** $5.0 million
- **Coed**
- **Minimally difficult** entrance level

Faculty *Student/faculty ratio:* 25:1.

Student Life *Campus security:* 24-hour emergency response devices and patrols.

Applying *Options:* common application, deferred entrance. *Application fee:* $25.

Admissions Contact Dr. Algia Allen, Vice President for Academic Services, Amberton University, 1700 Eastgate Drive, Garland, TX 75041-5595. *Phone:* 972-279-6511 Ext. 135. *E-mail:* webteam@amberu.edu.

ANGELO STATE UNIVERSITY
San Angelo, Texas

- **State-supported** comprehensive, founded 1928, part of Texas State University System
- **Calendar** semesters
- **Degrees** associate, bachelor's, and master's
- **Urban** 268-acre campus
- **Endowment** $68.7 million
- **Coed,** 5,829 undergraduate students, 81% full-time, 56% women, 44% men
- **Moderately difficult** entrance level, 76% of applicants were admitted

Undergraduates 4,730 full-time, 1,099 part-time. Students come from 33 states and territories, 20 other countries, 2% are from out of state, 5% African American, 1.0% Asian American or Pacific Islander, 20% Hispanic American, 0.3% Native American, 1% international, 7% transferred in, 25% live on campus. *Retention:* 58% of 2001 full-time freshmen returned.

Freshmen *Admission:* 3,534 applied, 2,690 admitted, 1,246 enrolled. *Test scores:* SAT verbal scores over 500: 45%; SAT math scores over 500: 51%; ACT scores over 18: 77%; SAT verbal scores over 600: 13%; SAT math scores over

Angelo State University (continued)
600: 12%; ACT scores over 24: 21%; SAT verbal scores over 700: 1%; SAT math scores over 700: 2%; ACT scores over 30: 1%.

Faculty *Total:* 261, 83% full-time, 66% with terminal degrees. *Student/faculty ratio:* 22:1.

Majors Accounting; agricultural animal husbandry/production management; animal sciences; aquaculture operations/production management; art; athletic training/sports medicine; biochemistry; biology; business administration; business marketing and marketing management; chemistry; communications; computer science; criminal justice studies; English; finance; fine arts and art studies related; fine/studio arts; French; general studies; German; health/physical education; history; humanities; interdisciplinary studies; journalism; liberal arts and sciences/liberal studies; management information systems/business data processing; mathematics; mathematics/computer science; medical technology; music; nursing; physics; physics related; political science; psychology; range management; real estate; social sciences; sociology; Spanish; theater arts/drama.

Academic Programs *Special study options:* academic remediation for entering students, accelerated degree program, adult/continuing education programs, advanced placement credit, distance learning, double majors, independent study, internships, off-campus study, part-time degree program, services for LD students, study abroad, summer session for credit. *ROTC:* Air Force (b). *Unusual degree programs:* 3-2 engineering with University of Texas at El Paso, Texas A&M University, Lamar University.

Library Portor Henderson Library plus 1 other with 452,232 titles, 1,850 serial subscriptions, 28,781 audiovisual materials, an OPAC, a Web page.

Computers on Campus 325 computers available on campus for general student use. A campuswide network can be accessed from student residence rooms and from off campus. Internet access, online (class) registration, at least one staffed computer lab available.

Student Life *Housing:* on-campus residence required through sophomore year. *Options:* coed, men-only, women-only, disabled students. *Activities and Organizations:* drama/theater group, student-run newspaper, choral group, marching band, Block and Bridle Club, Baptist Student Union, Delta Sigma Pi, Air Force ROTC, Association of Mexican-American Students, national fraternities, national sororities. *Campus security:* 24-hour emergency response devices and patrols, student patrols, late-night transport/escort service, controlled dormitory access. *Student Services:* health clinic, personal/psychological counseling.

Athletics Member NCAA. All Division II. *Intercollegiate sports:* basketball M(s)/W(s), cross-country running M(s)/W(s), football M(s), rugby M(c), soccer W(s), softball W(s), track and field M(s)/W(s), volleyball W(s). *Intramural sports:* archery M/W, badminton M/W, basketball M/W, bowling M/W, football M/W, golf M/W, racquetball M/W, rugby M, soccer M/W, softball M/W, swimming M/W, table tennis M/W, tennis M/W, volleyball M/W, weight lifting M/W.

Standardized Tests *Required:* SAT I or ACT (for admission).

Costs (2001–02) *Tuition:* state resident $1260 full-time, $67 per semester hour part-time; nonresident $7590 full-time, $280 per semester hour part-time. Full-time tuition and fees vary according to course load. Part-time tuition and fees vary according to course load. *Required fees:* $1462 full-time, $24 per semester hour, $71 per term part-time. *Room and board:* $4810; room only: $3268. Room and board charges vary according to board plan and housing facility. *Payment plan:* installment. *Waivers:* senior citizens.

Financial Aid Of all full-time matriculated undergraduates who enrolled in 2001, 4194 applied for aid, 2851 were judged to have need, 1906 had their need fully met. 124 Federal Work-Study jobs (averaging $1982). 20 State and other part-time jobs (averaging $1186). In 2001, 184 non-need-based awards were made. *Average percent of need met:* 66%. *Average financial aid package:* $4238. *Average need-based gift aid:* $1380. *Average non-need based aid:* $1603. *Average indebtedness upon graduation:* $15,000.

Applying *Options:* common application, electronic application, early admission, deferred entrance. *Required:* high school transcript. *Application deadlines:* 8/1 (freshmen), 8/1 (transfers). *Notification:* continuous (freshmen).

Admissions Contact Mrs. Monique Cossich, Director of Admissions, Angelo State University, Box 11014, ASU Station, Hardeman Administration and Journalism Building, San Angelo, TX 76909. *Phone:* 915-942-2185 Ext. 231. *Toll-free phone:* 800-946-8627. *Fax:* 915-942-2078. *E-mail:* admissions@angelo.edu.

ARLINGTON BAPTIST COLLEGE
Arlington, Texas

- **Independent Baptist** 4-year, founded 1939
- **Calendar** semesters
- **Degree** certificates, diplomas, and bachelor's
- **Urban** 32-acre campus with easy access to Dallas-Fort Worth
- **Endowment** $19,332
- **Coed,** 242 undergraduate students, 81% full-time, 38% women, 62% men
- **Minimally difficult** entrance level, 100% of applicants were admitted

Undergraduates 195 full-time, 47 part-time. Students come from 18 states and territories, 4 other countries, 24% are from out of state, 1% African American, 0.8% Asian American or Pacific Islander, 6% Hispanic American, 5% international, 35% transferred in, 55% live on campus. *Retention:* 71% of 2001 full-time freshmen returned.

Freshmen *Admission:* 73 applied, 73 admitted, 52 enrolled. *Average high school GPA:* 3.00.

Faculty *Total:* 20, 35% full-time, 10% with terminal degrees. *Student/faculty ratio:* 18:1.

Majors Biblical studies; divinity/ministry; education; music; music teacher education; religious studies.

Academic Programs *Special study options:* academic remediation for entering students, accelerated degree program, advanced placement credit, distance learning, double majors, external degree program, independent study, internships, part-time degree program, summer session for credit.

Library Dr. Earl K. Oldham Library with 26,405 titles, 116 serial subscriptions, 939 audiovisual materials.

Computers on Campus 6 computers available on campus for general student use. At least one staffed computer lab available.

Student Life *Housing:* on-campus residence required through senior year. *Options:* men-only, women-only. *Activities and Organizations:* drama/theater group, student-run newspaper, choral group, Preachers Fellowship, Student Missionary Association, L.I.F.T., International Students Association, 4-12 Group. *Campus security:* student patrols, controlled dormitory access. *Student Services:* personal/psychological counseling.

Athletics Member NCCAA. *Intercollegiate sports:* baseball M, basketball M, volleyball W. *Intramural sports:* baseball M, basketball M/W, volleyball W.

Standardized Tests *Recommended:* SAT I and SAT II or ACT (for placement).

Costs (2001–02) *Tuition:* $4160 full-time, $130 per semester hour part-time. *Required fees:* $540 full-time, $270 per term part-time. *Room only:* $1800. *Payment plans:* installment, deferred payment. *Waivers:* employees or children of employees.

Financial Aid Of all full-time matriculated undergraduates who enrolled in 2001, 152 applied for aid, 152 were judged to have need. *Average percent of need met:* 75%. *Average need-based gift aid:* $5248.

Applying *Options:* common application, electronic application, early admission, deferred entrance. *Application fee:* $15. *Required:* essay or personal statement, high school transcript, 1 letter of recommendation, pastoral recommendation, medical examination. *Required for some:* interview. *Application deadline:* rolling (freshmen), rolling (transfers). *Notification:* continuous (freshmen).

Admissions Contact Ms. Janie Hall, Registrar/Admissions, Arlington Baptist College, 3001 West Division, Arlington, TX 76012-3425. *Phone:* 817-461-8741 Ext. 105. *Fax:* 817-274-1138. *E-mail:* jhall@abconline.edu.

AUSTIN COLLEGE
Sherman, Texas

- **Independent Presbyterian** comprehensive, founded 1849
- **Calendar** 4-1-4
- **Degrees** bachelor's and master's
- **Suburban** 60-acre campus with easy access to Dallas-Fort Worth
- **Endowment** $104.9 million
- **Coed,** 1,227 undergraduate students, 99% full-time, 56% women, 44% men
- **Very difficult** entrance level, 80% of applicants were admitted

Undergraduates 1,219 full-time, 8 part-time. Students come from 30 states and territories, 28 other countries, 11% are from out of state, 5% African American, 8% Asian American or Pacific Islander, 7% Hispanic American, 0.8% Native American, 2% international, 4% transferred in, 74% live on campus. *Retention:* 83% of 2001 full-time freshmen returned.

Freshmen *Admission:* 1,004 applied, 806 admitted, 313 enrolled. *Test scores:* SAT verbal scores over 500: 92%; SAT math scores over 500: 93%; ACT scores over 18: 99%; SAT verbal scores over 600: 53%; SAT math scores over 600: 53%; ACT scores over 24: 73%; SAT verbal scores over 700: 9%; SAT math scores over 700: 11%; ACT scores over 30: 17%.

Faculty *Total:* 116, 73% full-time, 93% with terminal degrees. *Student/faculty ratio:* 13:1.

Majors American studies; art; biology; business administration; chemistry; classical and ancient Near Eastern languages related; classics; communications; computer science; economics; English; French; German; history; international economics; international relations; Latin American studies; Latin (ancient and medieval); mathematics; multi/interdisciplinary studies related; music; philosophy; physical education; physics; political science; psychology; religious studies; sociology; Spanish.

Academic Programs *Special study options:* accelerated degree program, adult/continuing education programs, advanced placement credit, double majors, honors programs, independent study, internships, off-campus study, part-time degree program, student-designed majors, study abroad, summer session for credit. *Unusual degree programs:* 3-2 engineering with University of Texas at Dallas; Texas A&M University; Washington University in St. Louis; Columbia University, The Fu Foundation School of Engineering and Applied Science.

Library Abell Library with 201,354 titles, 1,364 serial subscriptions, 6,913 audiovisual materials, an OPAC, a Web page.

Computers on Campus 165 computers available on campus for general student use. A campuswide network can be accessed from student residence rooms and from off campus. Internet access, at least one staffed computer lab available.

Student Life *Housing:* on-campus residence required through junior year. *Options:* coed, men-only, women-only, disabled students. *Activities and Organizations:* drama/theater group, student-run newspaper, choral group, Fellowship of Christian Athletes, Campus Activity Board, Indian Cultural Association, Student Development Board, International Relations Club. *Campus security:* 24-hour emergency response devices and patrols, late-night transport/escort service, controlled dormitory access. *Student Services:* health clinic, personal/psychological counseling.

Athletics Member NCAA. All Division III. *Intercollegiate sports:* baseball M, basketball M/W, cross-country running M/W, football M, golf M, soccer M/W, swimming M/W, tennis M/W, track and field M/W, volleyball W. *Intramural sports:* basketball M/W, bowling M/W, football M/W, lacrosse M(c), racquetball M/W, soccer M/W, softball M/W, table tennis M/W, tennis M/W, volleyball M/W.

Standardized Tests *Required:* SAT I or ACT (for admission).

Costs (2002–03) *One-time required fee:* $25. *Comprehensive fee:* $22,771 includes full-time tuition ($16,392), mandatory fees ($145), and room and board ($6234). Part-time tuition: $2375 per course. *Room and board:* College room only: $2952. Room and board charges vary according to board plan. *Payment plan:* installment. *Waivers:* employees or children of employees.

Financial Aid Of all full-time matriculated undergraduates who enrolled in 2001, 1152 applied for aid, 731 were judged to have need, 594 had their need fully met. In 2001, 396 non-need-based awards were made. *Average percent of need met:* 97%. *Average financial aid package:* $16,447. *Average need-based loan:* $3764. *Average need-based gift aid:* $11,379. *Average non-need based aid:* $7883. *Average indebtedness upon graduation:* $23,892.

Applying *Options:* common application, electronic application, early admission, early decision, early action, deferred entrance. *Application fee:* $35. *Required:* essay or personal statement, high school transcript, 2 letters of recommendation. *Required for some:* interview. *Recommended:* minimum 3.0 GPA, interview. *Application deadlines:* 8/15 (freshmen), 8/15 (transfers). *Early decision:* 12/1. *Notification:* 1/10 (early decision), 3/1 (early action).

Admissions Contact Ms. Nan Massingill, Vice President for Institutional Enrollment, Austin College, 900 North Grand Avenue, Suite 6N, Sherman, TX 75090-4400. *Phone:* 903-813-3000. *Toll-free phone:* 800-442-5363. *Fax:* 903-813-3198. *E-mail:* admission@austinc.edu.

AUSTIN GRADUATE SCHOOL OF THEOLOGY
Austin, Texas

- **Independent** upper-level, founded 1917, affiliated with Church of Christ
- **Calendar** semesters
- **Degrees** bachelor's and master's
- **Urban** campus
- **Endowment** $4.0 million
- **Coed,** 48 undergraduate students, 33% full-time, 31% women, 69% men
- **Minimally difficult** entrance level

Undergraduates 16 full-time, 32 part-time. Students come from 2 states and territories, 1 other country, 32% are from out of state, 23% African American, 10% Hispanic American, 42% transferred in, 0% live on campus.

Faculty *Total:* 11, 45% full-time, 55% with terminal degrees. *Student/faculty ratio:* 9:1.

Majors Biblical studies.

Academic Programs *Special study options:* adult/continuing education programs, advanced placement credit, part-time degree program, summer session for credit.

Library ICS Library plus 1 other with 25,000 titles, 95 serial subscriptions, an OPAC, a Web page.

Computers on Campus 5 computers available on campus for general student use. A campuswide network can be accessed from off campus. Internet access, at least one staffed computer lab available.

Student Life *Housing:* college housing not available. *Activities and Organizations:* student-run newspaper, student government. *Campus security:* 24-hour emergency response devices.

Standardized Tests *Required for some:* SAT I or ACT (for admission).

Costs (2001–02) *Tuition:* $2400 full-time, $300 per course part-time. *Payment plan:* installment. *Waivers:* employees or children of employees.

Financial Aid Of all full-time matriculated undergraduates who enrolled in 2001, 14 applied for aid, 12 were judged to have need. 4 Federal Work-Study jobs (averaging $1062). *Average need-based loan:* $4103. *Average need-based gift aid:* $2727.

Applying *Application deadline:* rolling (transfers).

Admissions Contact Ms. Laura Najera, Director of Admissions, Austin Graduate School of Theology, 1909 University Avenue, Austin, TX 78705. *Phone:* 512-476-2772 Ext. 203. *Toll-free phone:* 866-AUS-GRAD. *Fax:* 512-476-3919. *E-mail:* registrar@austingrad.edu.

BAPTIST MISSIONARY ASSOCIATION THEOLOGICAL SEMINARY
Jacksonville, Texas

- **Independent Baptist** comprehensive, founded 1955
- **Calendar** semesters
- **Degrees** associate, bachelor's, master's, and first professional
- **Small-town** 17-acre campus
- **Endowment** $448,505
- **Coed, primarily men**
- **Noncompetitive** entrance level

Faculty *Student/faculty ratio:* 14:1.

Costs (2001–02) *Tuition:* $2100 full-time, $70 per credit hour part-time. *Required fees:* $120 full-time, $30 per term part-time. *Room only:* $3580.

Financial Aid Of all full-time matriculated undergraduates who enrolled in 2001, 2 applied for aid, 2 were judged to have need. *Average percent of need met:* 50. *Average financial aid package:* $1098.

Applying *Application fee:* $20. *Required:* 3 letters of recommendation, interview.

Admissions Contact Dr. Philip Attebery, Dean and Registrar, Baptist Missionary Association Theological Seminary, 1530 East Pine Street, Jacksonville, TX 75766-5407. *Phone:* 903-586-2501. *Fax:* 903-586-0378. *E-mail:* bmatsem@flash.net.

BAYLOR UNIVERSITY
Waco, Texas

- **Independent Baptist** university, founded 1845
- **Calendar** semesters
- **Degrees** bachelor's, master's, doctoral, first professional, and post-master's certificates
- **Urban** 432-acre campus with easy access to Dallas-Fort Worth
- **Endowment** $614.0 million
- **Coed,** 12,190 undergraduate students, 96% full-time, 58% women, 42% men
- **Moderately difficult** entrance level, 79% of applicants were admitted

The oldest university in Texas, Baylor is proud of its strong Christian heritage. Teaching, scholarly attention to discovery, and service to others are emphasized. Baylor University is the largest Baptist institution of higher education in the world. Students can choose from 162 baccalaureate, 73 master's, 18 doctoral, and 4 professional programs with the assurance of individual attention due to the low student-faculty ratio and small classes.

Undergraduates 11,689 full-time, 501 part-time. Students come from 50 states and territories, 70 other countries, 17% are from out of state, 6% African American, 5% Asian American or Pacific Islander, 7% Hispanic American, 0.5% Native American, 2% international, 4% transferred in, 32% live on campus. *Retention:* 85% of 2001 full-time freshmen returned.

Freshmen *Admission:* 7,986 applied, 6,336 admitted, 2,801 enrolled. *Test scores:* SAT verbal scores over 500: 87%; SAT math scores over 500: 92%; ACT scores over 18: 99%; SAT verbal scores over 600: 39%; SAT math scores over 600: 48%; ACT scores over 24: 61%; SAT verbal scores over 700: 8%; SAT math scores over 700: 10%; ACT scores over 30: 8%.

Baylor University (continued)

Faculty *Total:* 813, 86% full-time. *Student/faculty ratio:* 18:1.

Majors Accounting; acting/directing; aircraft pilot (professional); American studies; anthropology; applied mathematics; archaeology; architecture; art; art education; art history; Asian studies; biblical languages/literatures; biochemistry; biology; biology education; business; business administration; business economics; business education; business marketing and marketing management; business statistics; chemistry; chemistry education; classics; clothing/apparel/textile studies; communication disorders; communications; computer education; computer science; dietetics; drama/dance education; early childhood education; earth sciences; economics; education; education of the speech impaired; electrical engineering; elementary education; engineering; English; English composition; English education; enterprise management; environmental science; fashion design/illustration; finance; financial planning; fine/studio arts; foreign languages education; forensic technology; forestry; French; French language education; geography; geology; geophysics/seismology; German; German language education; Greek (ancient and medieval); health education; health/physical education; history; history education; home economics; human resources management; individual/family development; insurance/risk management; interdisciplinary studies; interior design; international business; international relations; journalism; Latin American studies; Latin (ancient and medieval); linguistics; management information systems/business data processing; mathematics; mathematics education; mechanical engineering; museum studies; music; music (general performance); music history; music teacher education; music theory and composition; nursing; operations management; philosophy; physical education; physics; physics education; physiological psychology/psychobiology; political science; pre-dentistry; pre-law; pre-medicine; psychology; public administration; reading education; real estate; religious music; religious studies; Russian; Russian/Slavic studies; science education; secondary education; social science education; social studies education; social work; sociology; Spanish; Spanish language education; special education; speech education; speech/rhetorical studies; sport/fitness administration; telecommunications; theater arts/drama; theater design; urban studies.

Academic Programs *Special study options:* accelerated degree program, advanced placement credit, double majors, English as a second language, honors programs, internships, part-time degree program, services for LD students, student-designed majors, study abroad, summer session for credit. *ROTC:* Air Force (b). *Unusual degree programs:* 3-2 forestry with Duke University; architecture with Washington University in St. Louis, medical technology and biology, medicine, dentistry, optometry.

Library Moody Memorial Library plus 8 others with 1.1 million titles, 9,106 serial subscriptions, 71,076 audiovisual materials, an OPAC, a Web page.

Computers on Campus 1300 computers available on campus for general student use. A campuswide network can be accessed from student residence rooms and from off campus. Internet access, online (class) registration, at least one staffed computer lab available.

Student Life *Housing Options:* men-only, women-only, disabled students. *Activities and Organizations:* drama/theater group, student-run newspaper, radio and television station, choral group, marching band, Alpha Phi Omega, College Republicans, Gamma Beta Phi, student government, national fraternities, national sororities. *Campus security:* 24-hour emergency response devices and patrols, late-night transport/escort service, controlled dormitory access, bicycle patrols. *Student Services:* health clinic, personal/psychological counseling, legal services.

Athletics Member NCAA. All Division I except football (Division I-A). *Intercollegiate sports:* badminton M(c)/W(c), baseball M(s), basketball M(s)/W(s), crew M(c)/W(c), cross-country running M(s)/W(s), fencing M(c)/W(c), golf M(s)/W(s), lacrosse M(c)/W(c), rugby M(c)/W(c), sailing M(c)/W(c), soccer M(c)/W(s), softball W(s), tennis M(s)/W(s), track and field M(s)/W(s), volleyball M(c)/W(s). *Intramural sports:* basketball M/W, bowling M/W, football M/W, golf M/W, racquetball M/W, soccer M/W, softball M/W, swimming M/W, table tennis M/W, tennis M/W, track and field M/W, volleyball M/W, weight lifting M/W.

Standardized Tests *Required:* SAT I or ACT (for admission).

Costs (2002–03) *Comprehensive fee:* $22,928 includes full-time tuition ($15,700), mandatory fees ($1514), and room and board ($5714). Part-time tuition: $654 per semester hour. No tuition increase for student's term of enrollment. *Required fees:* $47 per semester hour. *Room and board:* College room only: $2728. Room and board charges vary according to board plan and housing facility. *Payment plan:* installment. *Waivers:* employees or children of employees.

Financial Aid Of all full-time matriculated undergraduates who enrolled in 2001, 9389 applied for aid, 5079 were judged to have need, 865 had their need fully met. 2877 Federal Work-Study jobs (averaging $2483). 562 State and other part-time jobs (averaging $2663). In 2001, 3900 non-need-based awards were made. *Average percent of need met:* 66%. *Average financial aid package:* $9975. *Average need-based loan:* $3546. *Average need-based gift aid:* $5446.

Applying *Options:* electronic application, early admission, deferred entrance. *Application fee:* $35. *Required:* essay or personal statement, high school transcript. *Recommended:* interview. *Application deadline:* rolling (freshmen), rolling (transfers). *Notification:* continuous (freshmen).

Admissions Contact Mr. James Steen, Director of Admission Services, Baylor University, PO Box 97056, Waco, TX 76798-7056. *Phone:* 254-710-3435. *Toll-free phone:* 800-BAYLOR U. *Fax:* 254-710-3436. *E-mail:* admissions_office@baylor.edu.

COLLEGE OF BIBLICAL STUDIES-HOUSTON
Houston, Texas

Admissions Contact 6000 Dale Carnegie Drive, Houston, TX 77036.

THE COLLEGE OF SAINT THOMAS MORE
Fort Worth, Texas

- **Independent** primarily 2-year, founded 1981, affiliated with Roman Catholic Church
- **Calendar** semesters
- **Degrees** associate and bachelor's
- **Urban** campus with easy access to Dallas
- **Coed**
- **Moderately difficult** entrance level

Faculty *Student/faculty ratio:* 4:1.

Student Life *Campus security:* 24-hour patrols, student patrols, late-night transport/escort service.

Standardized Tests *Required:* SAT I or ACT (for admission).

Financial Aid Available in 2001, 6 State and other part-time jobs (averaging $500).

Applying *Options:* common application, early admission, early decision, deferred entrance. *Application fee:* $35. *Required:* essay or personal statement, high school transcript, minimum 2.0 GPA, 1 letter of recommendation. *Recommended:* interview.

Admissions Contact Mr. Kenneth B. McIntyre, Dean of Students and Registrar, The College of Saint Thomas More, 3013 Lubbock Avenue, Fort Worth, TX 76109-2323. *Phone:* 817-921-2728. *Toll-free phone:* 800-583-6489. *Fax:* 817-924-3206. *E-mail:* more-info@cstm.edu.

CONCORDIA UNIVERSITY AT AUSTIN
Austin, Texas

- **Independent** comprehensive, founded 1926, affiliated with Lutheran Church-Missouri Synod, part of Concordia University System
- **Calendar** semesters
- **Degrees** certificates, diplomas, associate, bachelor's, master's, and postbachelor's certificates
- **Urban** 20-acre campus with easy access to San Antonio
- **Endowment** $6.1 million
- **Coed**
- **Moderately difficult** entrance level

Faculty *Student/faculty ratio:* 12:1.

Student Life *Campus security:* 24-hour emergency response devices, student patrols, late-night transport/escort service.

Athletics Member NCAA. All Division III.

Standardized Tests *Required:* SAT I or ACT (for admission).

Financial Aid Of all full-time matriculated undergraduates who enrolled in 2001, 404 applied for aid, 351 were judged to have need, 219 had their need fully met. 83 Federal Work-Study jobs (averaging $1120). In 2001, 150. *Average percent of need met:* 87. *Average financial aid package:* $10,318. *Average need-based gift aid:* $2756. *Average non-need based aid:* $3795. *Average indebtedness upon graduation:* $11,917.

Applying *Options:* early admission. *Application fee:* $25. *Required:* high school transcript, minimum 2.5 GPA. *Required for some:* letters of recommendation, interview.

Admissions Contact Mr. Jay Krause, Vice President for Enrollment Services, Concordia University at Austin, 3400 Interstate 35 North, Austin, TX 78705-2799. *Phone:* 512-486-2000 Ext. 1107. *Toll-free phone:* 800-285-4252. *Fax:* 512-459-8517. *E-mail:* ctxadmis@crf.cuis.edu.

THE CRISWELL COLLEGE
Dallas, Texas

- **Independent** comprehensive, founded 1970, affiliated with Southern Baptist Convention

■ **Calendar** semesters
■ **Degrees** associate, bachelor's, master's, and first professional
■ **Urban** 1-acre campus
■ **Endowment** $6.0 million
■ **Coed**
■ **Minimally difficult** entrance level

Student Life *Campus security:* 24-hour emergency response devices and patrols, late-night transport/escort service.

Standardized Tests *Required:* SAT I or ACT (for admission).

Costs (2001–02) *Tuition:* $3720 full-time, $155 per credit part-time. *Required fees:* $180 full-time, $90 per term part-time.

Applying *Options:* early admission, deferred entrance. *Application fee:* $30. *Required:* essay or personal statement, high school transcript, 2 letters of recommendation, church recommendation. *Recommended:* minimum 2.0 GPA, interview.

Admissions Contact Mr. Tommy Weir, Vice President for Institutional Advancement, The Criswell College, 4010 Gaston Avenue, Dallas, TX 75246-1537. *Phone:* 214-818-1302. *Toll-free phone:* 800-899-0012. *Fax:* 214-818-1310.

DALLAS BAPTIST UNIVERSITY
Dallas, Texas

■ **Independent** comprehensive, founded 1965, affiliated with Baptist Church
■ **Calendar** 4-1-4
■ **Degrees** associate, bachelor's, master's, and postbachelor's certificates
■ **Urban** 288-acre campus
■ **Endowment** $18.6 million
■ **Coed,** 3,340 undergraduate students, 46% full-time, 61% women, 39% men
■ **Moderately difficult** entrance level, 93% of applicants were admitted

Undergraduates 1,540 full-time, 1,800 part-time. Students come from 32 states and territories, 44 other countries, 7% are from out of state, 20% African American, 1% Asian American or Pacific Islander, 8% Hispanic American, 3% Native American, 6% international, 9% transferred in, 24% live on campus.

Freshmen *Admission:* 630 applied, 586 admitted, 246 enrolled. *Average high school GPA:* 3.50. *Test scores:* SAT verbal scores over 500: 64%; SAT math scores over 500: 65%; ACT scores over 18: 92%; SAT verbal scores over 600: 19%; SAT math scores over 600: 13%; ACT scores over 24: 23%; SAT verbal scores over 700: 1%; SAT math scores over 700: 3%; ACT scores over 30: 1%.

Faculty *Total:* 319, 26% full-time, 44% with terminal degrees. *Student/faculty ratio:* 19:1.

Majors Accounting; art; biblical studies; biology; business administration; business economics; business marketing and marketing management; computer/information sciences; computer science; criminal justice/law enforcement administration; early childhood education; education; elementary education; English; finance; health services administration; history; interdisciplinary studies; liberal arts and sciences/liberal studies; management information systems/business data processing; mathematics; music; music (piano and organ performance); music teacher education; music theory and composition; music (voice and choral/opera performance); pastoral counseling; philosophy; physical education; political science; psychology; religious education; religious music; science education; secondary education; sociology.

Academic Programs *Special study options:* adult/continuing education programs, advanced placement credit, distance learning, double majors, English as a second language, independent study, internships, off-campus study, part-time degree program, services for LD students, study abroad, summer session for credit. *ROTC:* Army (c), Air Force (c).

Library Vance Memorial Library with 213,072 titles, 664 serial subscriptions, 5,992 audiovisual materials, an OPAC, a Web page.

Computers on Campus 109 computers available on campus for general student use. A campuswide network can be accessed from student residence rooms and from off campus. Internet access, at least one staffed computer lab available.

Student Life *Housing:* on-campus residence required through senior year. *Options:* men-only, women-only. *Activities and Organizations:* drama/theater group, choral group, Student Activities Board, Baptist Student Ministry, Student Government Association, Student Education Association, International Student Organization. *Campus security:* 24-hour emergency response devices and patrols, late-night transport/escort service, controlled dormitory access. *Student Services:* health clinic, personal/psychological counseling.

Athletics Member NCAA, NAIA, NCCAA. All NCAA Division II. *Intercollegiate sports:* baseball M(s), cross-country running M/W(s), soccer M/W(s), tennis M/W(s), track and field M/W(s), volleyball M/W(s). *Intramural sports:* basketball M/W, football M/W, softball M/W, table tennis M/W, tennis M/W, volleyball M/W.

Standardized Tests *Required:* SAT I or ACT (for admission).

Costs (2001–02) *Comprehensive fee:* $13,682 includes full-time tuition ($9750) and room and board ($3932). Part-time tuition: $325 per credit hour. *Room and board:* College room only: $1600. Room and board charges vary according to board plan. *Payment plan:* installment. *Waivers:* employees or children of employees.

Financial Aid Of all full-time matriculated undergraduates who enrolled in 2001, 1171 applied for aid, 755 were judged to have need, 153 had their need fully met. 95 Federal Work-Study jobs (averaging $1752). 10 State and other part-time jobs (averaging $1581). In 2001, 323 non-need-based awards were made. *Average percent of need met:* 71%. *Average financial aid package:* $6946. *Average need-based loan:* $3166. *Average need-based gift aid:* $2604. *Average non-need based aid:* $6946. *Average indebtedness upon graduation:* $13,669.

Applying *Options:* common application. *Application fee:* $25. *Required:* essay or personal statement, high school transcript, rank in upper 50% of high school class or 3.0 high school GPA, minimum ACT score of 20, combined SAT score of 950. *Recommended:* letters of recommendation, interview. *Application deadline:* rolling (freshmen), rolling (transfers). *Notification:* continuous (freshmen).

Admissions Contact Dr. Duke Jones, Director of Admissions, Dallas Baptist University, 3000 Mountain Creek Parkway, Dallas, TX 75211-9299. *Phone:* 214-333-5360. *Toll-free phone:* 800-460-1328. *Fax:* 214-333-5447. *E-mail:* admiss@dbu.edu.

DALLAS CHRISTIAN COLLEGE
Dallas, Texas

■ **Independent** 4-year, founded 1950, affiliated with Christian Churches and Churches of Christ
■ **Calendar** semesters
■ **Degree** diplomas and bachelor's
■ **Urban** 22-acre campus with easy access to Fort Worth
■ **Endowment** $91,418
■ **Coed,** 281 undergraduate students, 63% full-time, 46% women, 54% men
■ **Minimally difficult** entrance level, 49% of applicants were admitted

Undergraduates 178 full-time, 103 part-time. Students come from 15 states and territories, 3 other countries, 15% are from out of state, 16% African American, 0.4% Asian American or Pacific Islander, 7% Hispanic American, 1% Native American, 2% international, 8% transferred in, 36% live on campus. *Retention:* 45% of 2001 full-time freshmen returned.

Freshmen *Admission:* 85 applied, 42 admitted, 43 enrolled. *Average high school GPA:* 3.14. *Test scores:* SAT verbal scores over 500: 41%; SAT math scores over 500: 50%; ACT scores over 18: 69%; SAT verbal scores over 600: 8%; ACT scores over 24: 31%.

Faculty *Total:* 46, 20% full-time, 20% with terminal degrees. *Student/faculty ratio:* 13:1.

Majors Biblical studies; business administration; education.

Academic Programs *Special study options:* academic remediation for entering students, accelerated degree program, adult/continuing education programs, advanced placement credit, distance learning, double majors, independent study, internships, part-time degree program, summer session for credit.

Library C. C. Crawford Memorial Library with 24,853 titles, 291 serial subscriptions, 1,643 audiovisual materials, an OPAC.

Computers on Campus 16 computers available on campus for general student use. Internet access, at least one staffed computer lab available.

Student Life *Housing:* on-campus residence required through senior year. *Options:* men-only, women-only. *Activities and Organizations:* choral group. *Campus security:* controlled dormitory access. *Student Services:* personal/psychological counseling.

Athletics Member NCCAA. *Intercollegiate sports:* basketball M/W, soccer M, volleyball W. *Intramural sports:* volleyball M/W.

Standardized Tests *Required:* SAT I or ACT (for admission).

Costs (2002–03) *Comprehensive fee:* $10,480 includes full-time tuition ($6080), mandatory fees ($500), and room and board ($3900). Part-time tuition: $190 per semester hour. *Required fees:* $125 per term part-time.

Financial Aid Of all full-time matriculated undergraduates who enrolled in 2001, 135 applied for aid, 103 were judged to have need. 32 Federal Work-Study jobs (averaging $1505). In 2001, 21 non-need-based awards were made. *Average financial aid package:* $5526. *Average non-need based aid:* $1421.

Applying *Options:* deferred entrance. *Application fee:* $20. *Required:* high school transcript, 2 letters of recommendation. *Required for some:* essay or personal statement, interview. *Application deadline:* rolling (freshmen), rolling (transfers).

Dallas Christian College (continued)
Admissions Contact Mr. Marty McKee, Director of Admissions, Dallas Christian College, 2700 Christian Parkway, Dallas, TX 75234-7299. *Phone:* 972-241-3371 Ext. 153. *Fax:* 972-241-8021. *E-mail:* dcc@dallas.edu.

DeVry University
Irving, Texas

- **Proprietary** 4-year, founded 1969, part of DeVry, Inc
- **Calendar** semesters
- **Degrees** associate and bachelor's
- **Suburban** 13-acre campus with easy access to Dallas
- **Coed,** 3,569 undergraduate students, 63% full-time, 28% women, 72% men
- **Minimally difficult** entrance level, 86% of applicants were admitted

Undergraduates 2,232 full-time, 1,337 part-time. Students come from 36 states and territories, 14 other countries, 10% are from out of state, 32% African American, 7% Asian American or Pacific Islander, 16% Hispanic American, 0.5% Native American, 2% international, 8% transferred in. *Retention:* 39% of 2001 full-time freshmen returned.
Freshmen *Admission:* 1,643 applied, 1,410 admitted, 1,037 enrolled.
Faculty *Total:* 179, 43% full-time. *Student/faculty ratio:* 20:1.
Majors Business administration/management related; business systems analysis/design; business systems networking/ telecommunications; computer engineering technology; electrical/electronic engineering technology; information sciences/systems; operations management.
Academic Programs *Special study options:* academic remediation for entering students, accelerated degree program, adult/continuing education programs, advanced placement credit, cooperative education, part-time degree program, services for LD students, summer session for credit.
Library Learning Resource Center with 14,700 titles, 73 serial subscriptions, 885 audiovisual materials.
Computers on Campus 325 computers available on campus for general student use. A campuswide network can be accessed from off campus. Internet access, online (class) registration, at least one staffed computer lab available.
Student Life *Housing:* college housing not available. *Activities and Organizations:* student-run newspaper, Association of Information Technology Professionals, Gamers, Business Information Systems, Toastmasters, Telecommunications Management and Associations. *Campus security:* 24-hour emergency response devices, student patrols, late-night transport/escort service, lighted pathways/sidewalks.
Athletics *Intramural sports:* basketball M, football M, golf M, softball M, volleyball M.
Standardized Tests *Recommended:* SAT I or ACT (for admission).
Costs (2001–02) *Tuition:* $8740 full-time, $310 per credit hour part-time. Full-time tuition and fees vary according to course load. Part-time tuition and fees vary according to course load. *Payment plans:* installment, deferred payment. *Waivers:* employees or children of employees.
Financial Aid Of all full-time matriculated undergraduates who enrolled in 2001, 2849 applied for aid, 2691 were judged to have need, 72 had their need fully met. In 2001, 155 non-need-based awards were made. *Average percent of need met:* 41%. *Average financial aid package:* $7394. *Average need-based loan:* $5462. *Average need-based gift aid:* $3595.
Applying *Options:* electronic application, deferred entrance. *Application fee:* $50. *Required:* high school transcript, interview. *Application deadline:* rolling (freshmen), rolling (transfers). *Notification:* continuous (freshmen).
Admissions Contact Ms. Vicki Carroll, New Student Coordinator, DeVry University, 4000 Millenia Drive, Orlando, FL 32839. *Phone:* 972-929-5777. *Toll-free phone:* 800-443-3879 (in-state); 800-633-3879 (out-of-state).

East Texas Baptist University
Marshall, Texas

- **Independent Baptist** 4-year, founded 1912
- **Calendar** 4-1-4
- **Degrees** associate and bachelor's
- **Small-town** 200-acre campus
- **Endowment** $46.8 million
- **Coed,** 1,509 undergraduate students, 89% full-time, 53% women, 47% men
- **Moderately difficult** entrance level, 75% of applicants were admitted

Undergraduates 1,339 full-time, 170 part-time. Students come from 27 states and territories, 23 other countries, 8% are from out of state, 13% African American, 4% Hispanic American, 0.6% Native American, 2% international, 9% transferred in, 69% live on campus. *Retention:* 65% of 2001 full-time freshmen returned.
Freshmen *Admission:* 766 applied, 575 admitted, 368 enrolled. *Test scores:* ACT scores over 18: 80%; ACT scores over 24: 24%; ACT scores over 30: 2%.
Faculty *Total:* 118, 62% full-time, 53% with terminal degrees. *Student/faculty ratio:* 16:1.
Majors Accounting; athletic training/sports medicine; behavioral sciences; biology; biology education; business; business administration; business marketing and marketing management; chemistry; chemistry education; computer/information sciences; drama/dance education; early childhood education; education (multiple levels); elementary education; English; English education; finance; health/physical education; history; history education; liberal arts and sciences/liberal studies; mathematics; mathematics education; medical technology; music; music (piano and organ performance); music teacher education; music (voice and choral/opera performance); nursing; pastoral counseling; physical education; psychology; religious education; religious music; religious studies; science education; secondary education; social studies education; sociology; Spanish; Spanish language education; speech education; speech/rhetorical studies; theater arts/drama; theology.
Academic Programs *Special study options:* academic remediation for entering students, accelerated degree program, adult/continuing education programs, advanced placement credit, double majors, English as a second language, external degree program, honors programs, independent study, internships, off-campus study, part-time degree program, study abroad, summer session for credit.
Library Mamye Jarrett Library with 116,895 titles, 668 serial subscriptions, an OPAC.
Computers on Campus 203 computers available on campus for general student use. A campuswide network can be accessed from student residence rooms and from off campus. Internet access, online (class) registration, at least one staffed computer lab available.
Student Life *Housing:* on-campus residence required through senior year. *Options:* men-only, women-only, disabled students. *Activities and Organizations:* drama/theater group, student-run newspaper, choral group, Baptist Student Ministries, Phi Beta Lambda, Student Government Association, national fraternities. *Campus security:* 24-hour emergency response devices, controlled dormitory access. *Student Services:* health clinic, personal/psychological counseling.
Athletics Member NCAA. All Division III. *Intercollegiate sports:* baseball M, basketball M/W, cross-country running M/W, football M, soccer M/W, softball W, volleyball W. *Intramural sports:* basketball M/W, football M, racquetball M/W, soccer M/W, softball M/W, table tennis M/W, volleyball M/W.
Standardized Tests *Required:* ACT (for admission).
Costs (2001–02) *Comprehensive fee:* $12,349 includes full-time tuition ($8250), mandatory fees ($800), and room and board ($3299). Part-time tuition: $275 per semester hour. *Required fees:* $35 per semester hour. *Room and board:* Room and board charges vary according to board plan and housing facility. *Payment plan:* installment. *Waivers:* employees or children of employees.
Financial Aid Of all full-time matriculated undergraduates who enrolled in 2001, 1316 applied for aid, 837 were judged to have need, 405 had their need fully met. 171 Federal Work-Study jobs (averaging $1218). 471 State and other part-time jobs (averaging $1226). In 2001, 297 non-need-based awards were made. *Average percent of need met:* 70%. *Average financial aid package:* $10,305. *Average need-based loan:* $3106. *Average need-based gift aid:* $5040. *Average non-need based aid:* $4212. *Average indebtedness upon graduation:* $13,480.
Applying *Options:* common application, deferred entrance. *Application fee:* $25. *Required:* essay or personal statement, high school transcript, minimum 2.0 GPA. *Required for some:* interview. *Application deadline:* rolling (freshmen), rolling (transfers). *Notification:* continuous (freshmen).
Admissions Contact Mr. Vince Blankenship, Director of Admissions, East Texas Baptist University, 1209 North Grove, Marshall, TX 75670-1498. *Phone:* 903-923-2000. *Toll-free phone:* 800-804-ETBU. *Fax:* 903-938-1705. *E-mail:* admissions@etbu.edu.

Hardin-Simmons University
Abilene, Texas

- **Independent Baptist** comprehensive, founded 1891
- **Calendar** semesters
- **Degrees** bachelor's, master's, and first professional
- **Urban** 40-acre campus
- **Endowment** $73.9 million
- **Coed,** 1,902 undergraduate students, 88% full-time, 53% women, 47% men
- **Moderately difficult** entrance level, 69% of applicants were admitted

Undergraduates 1,670 full-time, 232 part-time. Students come from 26 states and territories, 7% are from out of state, 4% African American, 0.6% Asian American or Pacific Islander, 7% Hispanic American, 0.4% Native American, 0.2% international, 7% transferred in, 49% live on campus. *Retention:* 66% of 2001 full-time freshmen returned.

Freshmen *Admission:* 1,234 applied, 856 admitted, 378 enrolled. *Test scores:* SAT verbal scores over 500: 57%; SAT math scores over 500: 57%; ACT scores over 18: 91%; SAT verbal scores over 600: 15%; SAT math scores over 600: 16%; ACT scores over 24: 31%; SAT math scores over 700: 2%; ACT scores over 30: 2%.

Faculty *Total:* 193, 66% full-time, 55% with terminal degrees. *Student/faculty ratio:* 13:1.

Majors Accounting; agricultural sciences; art; art education; biblical studies; biology; biology education; business administration; business education; business marketing and marketing management; chemistry; chemistry education; computer education; computer science; corrections; divinity/ministry; elementary education; English; English education; exercise sciences; finance; French; French language education; geology; German; German language education; history; history education; interdisciplinary studies; law enforcement/police science; mass communications; mathematics; mathematics education; medical technology; music; music business management/merchandising; music (piano and organ performance); music teacher education; music (voice and choral/opera performance); nursing; pastoral counseling; philosophy; physical education; physical sciences; physics; physics education; political science; pre-dentistry; pre-law; pre-medicine; psychology; reading education; religious music; science education; secondary education; social studies education; social work; sociology; Spanish; Spanish language education; speech-language pathology/audiology; speech/rhetorical studies; stringed instruments; theater arts/drama; theology; wind/percussion instruments.

Academic Programs *Special study options:* academic remediation for entering students, accelerated degree program, adult/continuing education programs, advanced placement credit, double majors, independent study, internships, off-campus study, part-time degree program, services for LD students, study abroad, summer session for credit. *Unusual degree programs:* 3-2 biology, physical therapy.

Library Richardson Library plus 1 other with 194,433 titles, 4,015 serial subscriptions, 16,007 audiovisual materials, an OPAC, a Web page.

Computers on Campus 224 computers available on campus for general student use. A campuswide network can be accessed from student residence rooms and from off campus. Internet access, at least one staffed computer lab available.

Student Life *Housing:* on-campus residence required through sophomore year. *Options:* men-only, women-only. *Activities and Organizations:* drama/theater group, student-run newspaper, choral group, marching band, Baptist Student Union, Student Foundation, Student Congress, Fellowship Christian Athletes, national fraternities. *Campus security:* 24-hour patrols, controlled dormitory access. *Student Services:* health clinic, personal/psychological counseling.

Athletics Member NCAA. All Division III. *Intercollegiate sports:* baseball M, basketball M/W, football M, golf M/W, soccer M/W, tennis M/W, volleyball W. *Intramural sports:* badminton M/W, basketball M/W, bowling M/W, cross-country running M(c)/W(c), football M/W, golf M/W, racquetball M/W, soccer M/W, softball M/W, table tennis M(c)/W(c), tennis M/W, volleyball M/W.

Standardized Tests *Required:* SAT I or ACT (for admission).

Costs (2001–02) *Comprehensive fee:* $14,765 includes full-time tuition ($10,500), mandatory fees ($750), and room and board ($3515). Full-time tuition and fees vary according to program. Part-time tuition: $330 per semester hour. Part-time tuition and fees vary according to course load and program. No tuition increase for student's term of enrollment. *Required fees:* $55 per term part-time. *Room and board:* College room only: $1730. Room and board charges vary according to board plan and housing facility. *Payment plans:* tuition prepayment, installment, deferred payment. *Waivers:* employees or children of employees.

Financial Aid Of all full-time matriculated undergraduates who enrolled in 2001, 1532 applied for aid, 1050 were judged to have need, 255 had their need fully met. 61 Federal Work-Study jobs (averaging $1884). 348 State and other part-time jobs (averaging $2094). *Average percent of need met:* 24%. *Average financial aid package:* $9413. *Average need-based loan:* $3900. *Average need-based gift aid:* $4157.

Applying *Options:* early admission, deferred entrance. *Application fee:* $25. *Required:* high school transcript, minimum 2.0 GPA. *Application deadline:* rolling (freshmen), rolling (transfers). *Notification:* continuous (freshmen).

Admissions Contact Mrs. Stacey Martin, Enrollment Services Counselor, Hardin-Simmons University, Box 16050, Abilene, TX 79698-6050. *Phone:* 915-670-5813. *Toll-free phone:* 800-568-2692. *Fax:* 915-670-1527. *E-mail:* enroll.services@hsutx.edu.

HOUSTON BAPTIST UNIVERSITY
Houston, Texas

- **Independent Baptist** comprehensive, founded 1960
- **Calendar** quarters
- **Degrees** associate, bachelor's, and master's
- **Urban** 158-acre campus
- **Endowment** $47.1 million
- **Coed,** 1,953 undergraduate students, 86% full-time, 69% women, 31% men
- **Moderately difficult** entrance level, 76% of applicants were admitted

Undergraduates 1,679 full-time, 274 part-time. Students come from 17 states and territories, 36 other countries, 5% are from out of state, 13% transferred in, 37% live on campus. *Retention:* 80% of 2001 full-time freshmen returned.

Freshmen *Admission:* 747 applied, 568 admitted, 328 enrolled. *Test scores:* SAT verbal scores over 500: 65%; SAT math scores over 500: 66%; ACT scores over 18: 89%; SAT verbal scores over 600: 21%; SAT math scores over 600: 24%; ACT scores over 24: 30%; SAT verbal scores over 700: 2%; SAT math scores over 700: 4%; ACT scores over 30: 2%.

Faculty *Total:* 189, 60% full-time, 56% with terminal degrees. *Student/faculty ratio:* 16:1.

Majors Accounting; art; art education; biblical studies; bilingual/bicultural education; biology; broadcast journalism; business administration; business economics; business marketing and marketing management; chemistry; computer science; counselor education/guidance; developmental/child psychology; early childhood education; economics; education; elementary education; engineering; engineering physics; engineering science; English; exercise sciences; finance; French; history; information sciences/systems; interdisciplinary studies; journalism; liberal arts and sciences/liberal studies; mass communications; mathematics; medical technology; music; music teacher education; nuclear medical technology; nursing; physics; political science; pre-dentistry; pre-law; pre-medicine; pre-veterinary studies; psychology; recreation/leisure studies; religious music; religious studies; secondary education; sociology; Spanish; special education; speech/rhetorical studies.

Academic Programs *Special study options:* academic remediation for entering students, adult/continuing education programs, advanced placement credit, double majors, English as a second language, honors programs, independent study, internships, part-time degree program, study abroad, summer session for credit. *ROTC:* Army (c), Navy (c). *Unusual degree programs:* 3-2 engineering with University of Houston, Baylor University.

Library Moody Library with 140,292 titles, 1,415 serial subscriptions, 9,700 audiovisual materials.

Computers on Campus 115 computers available on campus for general student use. A campuswide network can be accessed from off campus. At least one staffed computer lab available.

Student Life *Housing:* on-campus residence required for freshman year. *Options:* men-only, women-only. *Activities and Organizations:* drama/theater group, student-run newspaper, choral group, Christian Life on Campus, International Friends, Amnesty International, Students in Free Enterprise, Alpha Phi Omega, national fraternities, national sororities. *Campus security:* 24-hour emergency response devices and patrols, late-night transport/escort service. *Student Services:* personal/psychological counseling.

Athletics Member NAIA. *Intercollegiate sports:* baseball M(s), basketball M(s)/W(s), softball W(s), volleyball W(s). *Intramural sports:* badminton M/W, basketball M/W, bowling M/W, football M/W, golf M/W, soccer M/W, softball M/W, table tennis M/W, tennis M/W, track and field M/W, volleyball M/W.

Standardized Tests *Required:* SAT I or ACT (for admission).

Costs (2002–03) *Comprehensive fee:* $15,798 includes full-time tuition ($10,500), mandatory fees ($855), and room and board ($4443). Full-time tuition and fees vary according to course load and student level. Part-time tuition: $350 per credit hour. Part-time tuition and fees vary according to course load and student level. *Room and board:* College room only: $2070. Room and board charges vary according to board plan. *Waivers:* senior citizens and employees or children of employees.

Financial Aid Of all full-time matriculated undergraduates who enrolled in 2001, 971 applied for aid, 857 were judged to have need, 133 had their need fully met. In 2001, 111 non-need-based awards were made. *Average percent of need met:* 56%. *Average financial aid package:* $9908. *Average need-based loan:* $3218. *Average need-based gift aid:* $6884. *Average indebtedness upon graduation:* $15,782.

Applying *Options:* early admission, deferred entrance. *Application fee:* $25. *Required:* essay or personal statement, high school transcript, 1 letter of recommendation. *Recommended:* interview. *Application deadline:* rolling (freshmen), rolling (transfers). *Notification:* continuous (freshmen).

Houston Baptist University (continued)

Admissions Contact Mr. David Melton, Director of Admissions, Houston Baptist University, 7502 Fondren Road, Houston, TX 77074-3298. *Phone:* 281-649-3211 Ext. 3208. *Toll-free phone:* 800-969-3210. *Fax:* 281-649-3217. *E-mail:* unadm@hbu.edu.

HOWARD PAYNE UNIVERSITY

Brownwood, Texas

- **Independent Southern Baptist** 4-year, founded 1889
- **Calendar** semesters
- **Degrees** certificates, associate, and bachelor's
- **Small-town** 30-acre campus
- **Endowment** $33.5 million
- **Coed,** 1,526 undergraduate students
- **Minimally difficult** entrance level, 88% of applicants were admitted

Undergraduates Students come from 12 states and territories, 2% are from out of state, 9% African American, 2% Asian American or Pacific Islander, 12% Hispanic American, 0.2% Native American, 0.1% international, 48% live on campus. *Retention:* 58% of 2001 full-time freshmen returned.

Freshmen *Admission:* 553 applied, 488 admitted. *Average high school GPA:* 3.10. *Test scores:* SAT verbal scores over 500: 49%; SAT math scores over 500: 49%; ACT scores over 18: 71%; SAT verbal scores over 600: 17%; SAT math scores over 600: 13%; ACT scores over 24: 27%; SAT verbal scores over 700: 2%; SAT math scores over 700: 1%; ACT scores over 30: 5%.

Faculty *Total:* 134, 55% full-time, 46% with terminal degrees. *Student/faculty ratio:* 14:1.

Majors Accounting; American studies; applied art; art; art education; athletic training/sports medicine; behavioral sciences; biblical languages/literatures; biblical studies; biology; biology education; business; business administration; business education; business marketing and marketing management; chemistry; communications; drama/dance education; early childhood education; education; education (multiple levels); elementary education; English; English education; European studies; exercise sciences; finance; fine/studio arts; general studies; health/physical education; health science; health services administration; history; history education; information sciences/systems; liberal arts and sciences/liberal studies; mathematics; modern languages; music; music (general performance); music (piano and organ performance); music teacher education; music (voice and choral/opera performance); paralegal/legal assistant; philosophy; physical education; political science; pre-law; pre-medicine; psychology; public relations; recreation/leisure studies; religious education; religious music; religious studies; science education; secondary education; social science education; social sciences; social work; sociology; Spanish; speech education; speech/rhetorical studies; sport/fitness administration; stringed instruments; teaching English as a second language; telecommunications; theater arts/drama; theology; wind/percussion instruments.

Academic Programs *Special study options:* academic remediation for entering students, adult/continuing education programs, advanced placement credit, double majors, English as a second language, honors programs, independent study, internships, part-time degree program, services for LD students, study abroad, summer session for credit.

Library Walker Memorial Library with 72,788 titles, 2,369 serial subscriptions, 6,821 audiovisual materials, an OPAC.

Computers on Campus 220 computers available on campus for general student use. A campuswide network can be accessed from student residence rooms and from off campus. Internet access, at least one staffed computer lab available.

Student Life *Housing:* on-campus residence required through junior year. *Options:* men-only, women-only. *Activities and Organizations:* drama/theater group, student-run newspaper, radio and television station, choral group, marching band, Baptist Student Ministry, Zeta Zeta Zeta, Delta Chi Ro, Student Foundation, Iota Chi Alpha. *Campus security:* 24-hour emergency response devices, controlled dormitory access, 12-hour patrols by trained security personnel. *Student Services:* health clinic, personal/psychological counseling.

Athletics Member NCAA. All Division III. *Intercollegiate sports:* baseball M, basketball M/W, cross-country running M/W, football M, golf M/W, soccer M(c), softball W, tennis M/W, track and field M/W, volleyball M(c)/W. *Intramural sports:* basketball M/W, football M/W, softball M/W, tennis M/W, volleyball M/W.

Standardized Tests *Required:* SAT I or ACT (for admission).

Costs (2001–02) *Comprehensive fee:* $13,834 includes full-time tuition ($9200), mandatory fees ($800), and room and board ($3834). Part-time tuition: $195 per semester hour. Part-time tuition and fees vary according to course load. *Room and board:* College room only: $1660. Room and board charges vary according to board plan, gender, and housing facility. *Payment plan:* deferred payment. *Waivers:* senior citizens and employees or children of employees.

Financial Aid Of all full-time matriculated undergraduates who enrolled in 2001, 1046 applied for aid, 810 were judged to have need, 337 had their need fully met. 166 Federal Work-Study jobs (averaging $800). 105 State and other part-time jobs (averaging $1511). In 2001, 48 non-need-based awards were made. *Average percent of need met:* 69%. *Average financial aid package:* $7359. *Average need-based loan:* $2300. *Average need-based gift aid:* $4735. *Average non-need based aid:* $4400. *Average indebtedness upon graduation:* $15,000.

Applying *Options:* common application, early admission. *Application fee:* $25. *Required:* high school transcript, minimum 3.0 GPA. *Required for some:* letters of recommendation, interview. *Application deadline:* rolling (freshmen), rolling (transfers).

Admissions Contact Ms. Cheryl Mangrum, Coordinator of Admission Services, Howard Payne University, HPU Station Box 828, 1000 Fisk Avenue, Brownwood, TX 76801. *Phone:* 915-649-8027. *Toll-free phone:* 800-880-4478. *Fax:* 915-649-8901. *E-mail:* enroll@hputx.edu.

HUSTON-TILLOTSON COLLEGE

Austin, Texas

- **Independent interdenominational** 4-year, founded 1875
- **Calendar** semesters
- **Degree** bachelor's
- **Urban** 23-acre campus
- **Endowment** $6.1 million
- **Coed,** 618 undergraduate students, 76% full-time, 55% women, 45% men
- **Moderately difficult** entrance level, 89% of applicants were admitted

Undergraduates Students come from 17 states and territories, 15 other countries, 9% are from out of state, 75% African American, 4% Asian American or Pacific Islander, 7% Hispanic American, 7% international, 40% live on campus. *Retention:* 49% of 2001 full-time freshmen returned.

Freshmen *Admission:* 201 applied, 179 admitted. *Average high school GPA:* 2.53. *Test scores:* ACT scores over 18: 20%.

Faculty *Total:* 37. *Student/faculty ratio:* 16:1.

Majors Accounting; American government; biology; business administration; chemistry; computer science; education; elementary education; English; mathematics; music; physical education; political science; pre-medicine; psychology; secondary education; social studies education; sociology.

Academic Programs *Special study options:* academic remediation for entering students, accelerated degree program, advanced placement credit, cooperative education, double majors, English as a second language, internships, part-time degree program, services for LD students, summer session for credit. *Unusual degree programs:* 3-2 engineering with Prairie View A&M University.

Library Downs-Jones Library with 84,200 titles, 349 serial subscriptions.

Computers on Campus 250 computers available on campus for general student use. Internet access, at least one staffed computer lab available.

Student Life *Housing Options:* men-only, women-only. *Activities and Organizations:* choral group, Student Government Association, Campus Pals, national fraternities, national sororities. *Campus security:* 24-hour patrols. *Student Services:* health clinic, personal/psychological counseling, women's center.

Athletics Member NAIA. *Intercollegiate sports:* baseball M, basketball M/W, cross-country running W, soccer M, track and field M/W, volleyball W. *Intramural sports:* basketball M/W, football M, volleyball M/W.

Costs (2001–02) *Comprehensive fee:* $12,977 includes full-time tuition ($6690), mandatory fees ($1260), and room and board ($5027). Part-time tuition: $223 per hour. *Required fees:* $70 per term part-time.

Financial Aid Of all full-time matriculated undergraduates who enrolled in 2001, 568 applied for aid, 542 were judged to have need, 105 had their need fully met. 75 Federal Work-Study jobs (averaging $1498). *Average financial aid package:* $9142. *Average need-based loan:* $3256. *Average need-based gift aid:* $8786.

Applying *Options:* common application. *Application fee:* $25. *Required:* essay or personal statement, high school transcript, minimum 2.0 GPA. *Required for some:* interview. *Application deadlines:* 3/1 (freshmen), 3/1 (transfers).

Admissions Contact Huston-Tillotson College, 900 Chicon Street, Austin, TX 78702. *Phone:* 512-505-3027. *Fax:* 512-505-3192. *E-mail:* taglenn@htc.edu.

JARVIS CHRISTIAN COLLEGE

Hawkins, Texas

- **Independent** 4-year, founded 1912, affiliated with Christian Church (Disciples of Christ)

- **Calendar** semesters
- **Degree** bachelor's
- **Rural** 465-acre campus
- **Endowment** $14.0 million
- **Coed,** 571 undergraduate students, 99% full-time, 58% women, 42% men
- **Minimally difficult** entrance level, 100% of applicants were admitted

Undergraduates 564 full-time, 7 part-time. Students come from 15 states and territories, 9 other countries, 92% are from out of state, 95% African American, 2% Hispanic American, 3% international, 6% transferred in, 85% live on campus. *Retention:* 50% of 2001 full-time freshmen returned.

Freshmen *Admission:* 272 applied, 272 admitted, 137 enrolled. *Average high school GPA:* 2.87. *Test scores:* SAT math scores over 500: 1%; ACT scores over 18: 1%; SAT math scores over 600: 1%.

Faculty *Total:* 58, 69% full-time, 50% with terminal degrees. *Student/faculty ratio:* 14:1.

Majors Accounting; biology; business administration; business education; business marketing and marketing management; chemistry; computer science; early childhood education; economics; elementary education; English; history; mathematics; music; music teacher education; physical education; physics; political science; reading education; religious studies; secondary education; sociology; special education.

Academic Programs *Special study options:* academic remediation for entering students, advanced placement credit, cooperative education, distance learning, honors programs, internships, off-campus study, part-time degree program. *Unusual degree programs:* 3-2 engineering with University of Texas at Arlington; nursing with University of Texas at Tyler.

Library Olin Library with 74,002 titles, 495 serial subscriptions.

Computers on Campus 75 computers available on campus for general student use. At least one staffed computer lab available.

Student Life *Housing:* on-campus residence required through senior year. *Options:* men-only, women-only. *Activities and Organizations:* drama/theater group, student-run newspaper, choral group, Student Government Association, SIFE, national fraternities, national sororities. *Campus security:* 24-hour patrols. *Student Services:* health clinic, personal/psychological counseling.

Athletics Member NAIA. *Intercollegiate sports:* baseball M/W, basketball M/W, cross-country running M/W, softball W, track and field M/W, volleyball M/W. *Intramural sports:* basketball M/W, football M, golf M, swimming M/W, tennis M/W.

Standardized Tests *Required:* SAT I or ACT (for admission). *Recommended:* ACT (for admission).

Costs (2002–03) *Comprehensive fee:* $9535 includes full-time tuition ($5200), mandatory fees ($350), and room and board ($3985). Full-time tuition and fees vary according to program. Part-time tuition: $173 per credit hour. Part-time tuition and fees vary according to program. No tuition increase for student's term of enrollment. *Room and board:* College room only: $1610. *Payment plans:* installment, deferred payment.

Financial Aid Of all full-time matriculated undergraduates who enrolled in 2001, 505 applied for aid, 495 were judged to have need, 316 had their need fully met. 197 Federal Work-Study jobs (averaging $1440). 6 State and other part-time jobs (averaging $1440). In 2001, 10 non-need-based awards were made. *Average percent of need met:* 85%. *Average financial aid package:* $8670. *Average need-based loan:* $3850. *Average need-based gift aid:* $5751. *Average non-need based aid:* $8500.

Applying *Options:* common application, early admission, deferred entrance. *Application fee:* $25. *Required:* high school transcript. *Recommended:* minimum 2.0 GPA. *Application deadline:* rolling (freshmen), rolling (transfers).

Admissions Contact Ms. Serena Sentell, Admissions Counselor, Jarvis Christian College, P.O. Box 1970, Hawkins, TX 75765-9989. *Phone:* 903-769-0417. *Toll-free phone:* 800-292-9517. *Fax:* 903-769-4842.

LAMAR UNIVERSITY
Beaumont, Texas

- **State-supported** university, founded 1923, part of Texas State University System
- **Calendar** semesters
- **Degrees** associate, bachelor's, master's, and doctoral
- **Suburban** 200-acre campus with easy access to Houston
- **Coed,** 8,026 undergraduate students, 66% full-time, 60% women, 40% men
- **Minimally difficult** entrance level, 69% of applicants were admitted

Undergraduates 5,314 full-time, 2,712 part-time. Students come from 39 states and territories, 19% African American, 3% Asian American or Pacific Islander, 5% Hispanic American, 0.4% Native American, 0.7% international, 5% transferred in. *Retention:* 67% of 2001 full-time freshmen returned.

Freshmen *Admission:* 3,269 applied, 2,262 admitted, 1,330 enrolled. *Average high school GPA:* 3.0. *Test scores:* SAT verbal scores over 500: 37%; SAT math scores over 500: 38%; ACT scores over 18: 74%; SAT verbal scores over 600: 10%; SAT math scores over 600: 12%; ACT scores over 24: 19%; SAT verbal scores over 700: 1%; SAT math scores over 700: 2%; ACT scores over 30: 3%.

Faculty *Total:* 421, 51% with terminal degrees. *Student/faculty ratio:* 25:1.

Majors Accounting; applied art; applied mathematics; art; art education; auto mechanic/technician; biology; broadcast journalism; business administration; business machine repair; business marketing and marketing management; chemical engineering; chemistry; child care/development; civil engineering; clinical psychology; computer programming; computer science; corrections; cosmetology; counselor education/guidance; criminal justice/law enforcement administration; dance; data processing technology; dental hygiene; dietetics; drafting; early childhood education; economics; education; education administration; electrical/electronic engineering technology; electrical engineering; elementary education; energy management technology; engineering science; English; environmental science; fashion design/illustration; fashion merchandising; finance; fine/studio arts; fire science; food products retailing; food sciences; French; geology; graphic design/commercial art/illustration; health education; health science; heating/air conditioning/refrigeration; history; home economics; home economics education; industrial/manufacturing engineering; industrial radiologic technology; industrial technology; information sciences/systems; interdisciplinary studies; interior design; jazz; journalism; law enforcement/police science; legal administrative assistant; liberal arts and sciences/liberal studies; machine technology; marine technology; mass communications; mathematics; mechanical engineering; medical administrative assistant; medical technology; music; music (piano and organ performance); music teacher education; music (voice and choral/opera performance); nursing; occupational safety/health technology; oceanography; physical education; physics; political science; practical nurse; pre-dentistry; psychology; radio/television broadcasting; real estate; respiratory therapy; robotics; safety/security technology; secondary education; secretarial science; social work; sociology; Spanish; special education; speech-language pathology/audiology; speech therapy; stringed instruments; teacher assistant/aide; theater arts/drama; welding technology.

Academic Programs *Special study options:* academic remediation for entering students, accelerated degree program, adult/continuing education programs, advanced placement credit, cooperative education, English as a second language, honors programs, internships, off-campus study, part-time degree program, services for LD students, student-designed majors, study abroad, summer session for credit.

Library Mary and John Gray Library with 600,000 titles, 2,900 serial subscriptions, an OPAC, a Web page.

Computers on Campus 120 computers available on campus for general student use. A campuswide network can be accessed from student residence rooms and from off campus. At least one staffed computer lab available.

Student Life *Housing Options:* coed. *Activities and Organizations:* drama/theater group, student-run newspaper, choral group, national fraternities, national sororities. *Campus security:* 24-hour emergency response devices and patrols, student patrols, late-night transport/escort service. *Student Services:* health clinic, personal/psychological counseling.

Athletics Member NCAA. All Division I except football (Division I-AA). *Intercollegiate sports:* baseball M(s), basketball M(s)/W(s), cross-country running M(s)/W(s), golf M(s)/W(s), tennis M(s)/W(s), track and field M(s)/W(s), volleyball W(s). *Intramural sports:* basketball M/W, cross-country running M/W, football M, golf M/W, gymnastics W, racquetball M/W, rugby M, sailing M/W, soccer M, swimming M/W, tennis M/W, track and field M/W, volleyball M/W, weight lifting M/W.

Standardized Tests *Required:* SAT I or ACT (for admission). *Required for some:* SAT II: Subject Tests (for admission).

Costs (2001–02) *Tuition:* state resident $2160 full-time, $432 per term part-time; nonresident $8490 full-time, $1698 per term part-time. Part-time tuition and fees vary according to course load. *Required fees:* $596 full-time, $214 per term part-time. *Room and board:* $4854; room only: $3200. Room and board charges vary according to board plan and housing facility. *Payment plan:* installment. *Waivers:* senior citizens.

Financial Aid Of all full-time matriculated undergraduates who enrolled in 2001, 3696 applied for aid, 2500 were judged to have need, 159 had their need fully met. 123 Federal Work-Study jobs, 9 State and other part-time jobs (averaging $3000). In 2001, 1055 non-need-based awards were made. *Average percent of need met:* 13%. *Average financial aid package:* $1175. *Average non-need based aid:* $880. *Average indebtedness upon graduation:* $8800.

Lamar University (continued)

Applying *Options:* electronic application, early admission. *Required:* high school transcript. *Required for some:* essay or personal statement. *Application deadlines:* 8/1 (freshmen), 8/1 (transfers). *Notification:* continuous (freshmen).

Admissions Contact Ms. Melissa Chesser, Director of Recruitment, Lamar University, PO Box 10009, Beaumont, TX 77710. *Phone:* 409-880-8888. *Fax:* 409-880-8463. *E-mail:* admissions@hal.lamar.edu.

LETOURNEAU UNIVERSITY
Longview, Texas

- **Independent nondenominational** comprehensive, founded 1946
- **Calendar** semesters
- **Degrees** associate, bachelor's, and master's
- **Suburban** 162-acre campus
- **Endowment** $4.5 million
- **Coed,** 2,807 undergraduate students, 44% full-time, 50% women, 50% men
- **Moderately difficult** entrance level, 85% of applicants were admitted

Undergraduates 1,239 full-time, 1,568 part-time. Students come from 49 states and territories, 19 other countries, 50% are from out of state, 17% African American, 1% Asian American or Pacific Islander, 5% Hispanic American, 0.6% Native American, 2% international, 4% transferred in, 72% live on campus. *Retention:* 75% of 2001 full-time freshmen returned.

Freshmen *Admission:* 765 applied, 651 admitted, 244 enrolled. *Average high school GPA:* 3.51. *Test scores:* SAT verbal scores over 500: 89%; SAT math scores over 500: 87%; ACT scores over 18: 99%; SAT verbal scores over 600: 45%; SAT math scores over 600: 46%; ACT scores over 24: 68%; SAT verbal scores over 700: 13%; SAT math scores over 700: 11%; ACT scores over 30: 19%.

Faculty *Total:* 310, 22% full-time. *Student/faculty ratio:* 15:1.

Majors Accounting; aircraft mechanic/airframe; aircraft pilot (professional); aviation technology; biblical studies; bioengineering; biology; business administration; business marketing and marketing management; chemistry; computer engineering; computer engineering technology; computer science; drafting/design technology; electrical/electronic engineering technology; electrical engineering; elementary education; engineering; engineering technology; English; finance; history; information sciences/systems; interdisciplinary studies; international business; management information systems/business data processing; mathematics; mechanical engineering; mechanical engineering technology; missionary studies; natural sciences; physical education; pre-dentistry; pre-law; pre-medicine; pre-veterinary studies; psychology; religious studies; secondary education; sport/fitness administration; welding technology.

Academic Programs *Special study options:* academic remediation for entering students, adult/continuing education programs, advanced placement credit, cooperative education, distance learning, double majors, honors programs, independent study, internships, off-campus study, part-time degree program, services for LD students, study abroad, summer session for credit.

Library Margaret Estes Resource Center with 72,957 titles, 459 serial subscriptions, 3,136 audiovisual materials, an OPAC, a Web page.

Computers on Campus 120 computers available on campus for general student use. A campuswide network can be accessed from student residence rooms and from off campus. At least one staffed computer lab available.

Student Life *Housing:* on-campus residence required through junior year. *Options:* men-only, women-only. *Activities and Organizations:* drama/theater group, student-run newspaper, choral group, student ministries, Themelios, Student Foundation, Student Senate, Roller Hockey Club. *Campus security:* 24-hour emergency response devices and patrols, late-night transport/escort service, controlled dormitory access. *Student Services:* health clinic, personal/psychological counseling.

Athletics Member NCAA, NCCAA. All NCAA Division III. *Intercollegiate sports:* baseball M, basketball M/W, cross-country running M/W, golf M/W, soccer M/W, softball W, tennis M/W, volleyball W. *Intramural sports:* badminton M/W, basketball M/W, bowling M/W, cross-country running M/W, football M/W, golf M/W, racquetball M/W, soccer M/W, softball M/W, swimming M/W, table tennis M/W, tennis M/W, volleyball M/W.

Standardized Tests *Required:* SAT I or ACT (for admission).

Costs (2002–03) *Comprehensive fee:* $19,020 includes full-time tuition ($13,240), mandatory fees ($170), and room and board ($5610). Part-time tuition: $250 per hour. Part-time tuition and fees vary according to course load. *Room and board:* Room and board charges vary according to board plan. *Payment plan:* installment. *Waivers:* employees or children of employees.

Financial Aid Of all full-time matriculated undergraduates who enrolled in 2001, 1151 applied for aid, 891 were judged to have need, 286 had their need fully met. In 2001, 59 non-need-based awards were made. *Average percent of need met:* 76%. *Average financial aid package:* $10,073. *Average need-based loan:* $3969. *Average need-based gift aid:* $3477. *Average non-need based aid:* $3529. *Average indebtedness upon graduation:* $17,950.

Applying *Options:* deferred entrance. *Application fee:* $25. *Required:* essay or personal statement, high school transcript, minimum 2.5 GPA, 2 letters of recommendation. *Required for some:* interview. *Application deadlines:* 8/1 (freshmen), 8/1 (transfers). *Notification:* continuous (freshmen).

Admissions Contact Mr. James Townsend, Director of Admissions, LeTourneau University, PO Box 7001, Longview, TX 75607. *Phone:* 903-233-3400. *Toll-free phone:* 800-759-8811. *Fax:* 903-233-3411. *E-mail:* admissions@letu.edu.

LUBBOCK CHRISTIAN UNIVERSITY
Lubbock, Texas

- **Independent** comprehensive, founded 1957, affiliated with Church of Christ
- **Calendar** semesters
- **Degrees** bachelor's and master's
- **Suburban** 120-acre campus
- **Endowment** $3.2 million
- **Coed,** 1,701 undergraduate students, 84% full-time, 57% women, 43% men
- **Moderately difficult** entrance level, 77% of applicants were admitted

Undergraduates 1,432 full-time, 269 part-time. Students come from 30 states and territories, 17 other countries, 16% are from out of state, 5% African American, 0.4% Asian American or Pacific Islander, 10% Hispanic American, 0.4% Native American, 4% international, 14% transferred in. *Retention:* 69% of 2001 full-time freshmen returned.

Freshmen *Admission:* 962 applied, 745 admitted, 567 enrolled. *Average high school GPA:* 3.34. *Test scores:* SAT verbal scores over 500: 52%; SAT math scores over 500: 45%; ACT scores over 18: 80%; SAT verbal scores over 600: 17%; SAT math scores over 600: 9%; ACT scores over 24: 27%; SAT verbal scores over 700: 2%; SAT math scores over 700: 1%; ACT scores over 30: 4%.

Faculty *Total:* 139, 53% full-time. *Student/faculty ratio:* 16:1.

Majors Accounting; agricultural business; agricultural sciences; applied art; athletic training/sports medicine; biblical languages/literatures; biblical studies; biology; business administration; chemistry; computer science; education; elementary education; English; finance; graphic design/commercial art/illustration; history; humanities; journalism; liberal arts and sciences/liberal studies; mass communications; mathematics; music; music teacher education; physical education; pre-dentistry; pre-law; pre-veterinary studies; psychology; secondary education; social work; Spanish.

Academic Programs *Special study options:* academic remediation for entering students, accelerated degree program, adult/continuing education programs, advanced placement credit, distance learning, freshman honors college, honors programs, internships, part-time degree program, services for LD students, student-designed majors, study abroad, summer session for credit. *ROTC:* Army (c), Air Force (c). *Unusual degree programs:* 3-2 engineering with Texas Tech University.

Library University Library with 108,000 titles, 556 serial subscriptions.

Computers on Campus 130 computers available on campus for general student use. A campuswide network can be accessed from student residence rooms and from off campus that provide access to e-mail. Internet access, online (class) registration, at least one staffed computer lab available.

Student Life *Housing:* on-campus residence required through sophomore year. *Options:* men-only, women-only. *Activities and Organizations:* drama/theater group, student-run newspaper, choral group, Primary Ministry Groups. *Campus security:* 24-hour patrols. *Student Services:* health clinic, personal/psychological counseling.

Athletics Member NAIA. *Intercollegiate sports:* baseball M(s), basketball M(s)/W(s), soccer M, track and field M/W, volleyball W(s). *Intramural sports:* badminton M/W, basketball M/W, bowling M/W, cross-country running M/W, football M/W, golf M/W, racquetball M/W, soccer M/W, softball M/W, table tennis M/W, tennis M/W, track and field M/W, volleyball M/W.

Standardized Tests *Required:* SAT I or ACT (for admission).

Costs (2001–02) *Comprehensive fee:* $14,894 includes full-time tuition ($10,326), mandatory fees ($668), and room and board ($3900). Full-time tuition and fees vary according to program. Part-time tuition: $142 per credit hour. Part-time tuition and fees vary according to course load and program. *Required fees:* $193 per term part-time. *Room and board:* College room only: $1560. Room and board charges vary according to board plan and housing facility. *Payment plan:* installment. *Waivers:* employees or children of employees.

Financial Aid Of all full-time matriculated undergraduates who enrolled in 2001, 992 applied for aid, 885 were judged to have need, 91 had their need fully met. In 2001, 185 non-need-based awards were made. *Average percent of need*

met: 74%. *Average financial aid package:* $10,268. *Average need-based loan:* $3466. *Average need-based gift aid:* $7044. *Average indebtedness upon graduation:* $20,312.

Applying *Options:* common application, electronic application, early admission, deferred entrance. *Application fee:* $20. *Required:* high school transcript. *Application deadline:* rolling (freshmen), rolling (transfers).

Admissions Contact Mrs. Rhonda Crawford, Director of Admissions, Lubbock Christian University, 5601 19th Street, Lubbock, TX 79407. *Phone:* 806-796-8800 Ext. 260. *Toll-free phone:* 800-933-7601 Ext. 260. *Fax:* 806-796-8917 Ext. 260. *E-mail:* admissions@lcu.edu.

McMurry University
Abilene, Texas

- **Independent United Methodist** 4-year, founded 1923
- **Calendar** 4-4-1
- **Degree** bachelor's
- **Urban** 41-acre campus
- **Endowment** $42.3 million
- **Coed,** 1,378 undergraduate students, 85% full-time, 51% women, 49% men
- **Moderately difficult** entrance level, 74% of applicants were admitted

Undergraduates 1,172 full-time, 206 part-time. Students come from 11 states and territories, 4 other countries, 4% are from out of state, 8% African American, 1% Asian American or Pacific Islander, 13% Hispanic American, 2% Native American, 0.9% international, 10% transferred in, 43% live on campus. *Retention:* 66% of 2001 full-time freshmen returned.

Freshmen *Admission:* 828 applied, 616 admitted, 358 enrolled. *Average high school GPA:* 3.42. *Test scores:* SAT verbal scores over 500: 52%; SAT math scores over 500: 54%; ACT scores over 18: 87%; SAT verbal scores over 600: 14%; SAT math scores over 600: 16%; ACT scores over 24: 31%; SAT verbal scores over 700: 1%; SAT math scores over 700: 1%; ACT scores over 30: 2%.

Faculty *Total:* 110, 69% full-time, 63% with terminal degrees. *Student/faculty ratio:* 15:1.

Majors Accounting; art; art education; biochemistry; biology; biology education; business; business economics; business education; business marketing and marketing management; chemistry; communications; computer education; computer science; creative writing; criminal justice/law enforcement administration; drama/dance education; elementary education; English; English education; environmental science; finance; foreign languages education; history; history education; mathematics; mathematics/computer science; mathematics education; music; music teacher education; paralegal/legal assistant; philosophy; physical education; physics; political science; psychology; religious education; religious studies; science education; social science education; social studies education; sociology; Spanish; speech education; theater arts/drama.

Academic Programs *Special study options:* academic remediation for entering students, accelerated degree program, advanced placement credit, double majors, honors programs, independent study, internships, part-time degree program, services for LD students, study abroad, summer session for credit. *Unusual degree programs:* 3-2 engineering with Texas Tech University.

Library Jay-Rollins Library with 115,704 titles, 603 serial subscriptions, 7,519 audiovisual materials, an OPAC, a Web page.

Computers on Campus 165 computers available on campus for general student use. Internet access, at least one staffed computer lab available.

Student Life *Housing:* on-campus residence required through junior year. *Options:* men-only, women-only. *Activities and Organizations:* drama/theater group, student-run newspaper, television station, choral group, marching band, Alpha Phi Omega, McMurry Christian Ministries, Indian Insight Service Club, Campus Activity Board, Vision Quest Tribe Guides. *Campus security:* 24-hour emergency response devices and patrols, late-night transport/escort service, controlled dormitory access. *Student Services:* health clinic, personal/psychological counseling.

Athletics Member NCAA. All Division III. *Intercollegiate sports:* baseball M, basketball M/W, cross-country running M/W, football M, golf M/W, soccer M/W, swimming M/W, tennis M/W, track and field M/W, volleyball W. *Intramural sports:* basketball M/W, football M/W, soccer M/W, softball M/W, tennis M/W, volleyball M/W.

Standardized Tests *Required:* SAT I or ACT (for admission).

Costs (2001–02) *Comprehensive fee:* $15,417 includes full-time tuition ($9600), mandatory fees ($1305), and room and board ($4512). Full-time tuition and fees vary according to course load. Part-time tuition: $320 per semester hour. Part-time tuition and fees vary according to course load. *Required fees:* $38 per term. *Room and board:* College room only: $2150. Room and board charges vary according to board plan. *Payment plan:* installment. *Waivers:* employees or children of employees.

Financial Aid Of all full-time matriculated undergraduates who enrolled in 2001, 1151 applied for aid, 934 were judged to have need, 192 had their need fully met. 218 Federal Work-Study jobs (averaging $709). 207 State and other part-time jobs (averaging $683). In 2001, 187 non-need-based awards were made. *Average percent of need met:* 73%. *Average financial aid package:* $10,545. *Average need-based loan:* $4570. *Average need-based gift aid:* $6219. *Average non-need based aid:* $4393. *Average indebtedness upon graduation:* $16,771.

Applying *Options:* common application, electronic application, deferred entrance. *Application fee:* $20. *Required:* high school transcript, minimum 2.0 GPA. *Required for some:* essay or personal statement, 3 letters of recommendation. *Recommended:* interview. *Application deadline:* rolling (freshmen), rolling (transfers). *Notification:* continuous (freshmen).

Admissions Contact Ms. Amy Weyant, Director of Admissions, McMurry University, Box 947, Abilene, TX 79697. *Phone:* 915-793-4705. *Toll-free phone:* 800-477-0077. *Fax:* 915-793-4718. *E-mail:* admissions@mcm.edu.

Midwestern State University
Wichita Falls, Texas

- **State-supported** comprehensive, founded 1922
- **Calendar** semesters
- **Degrees** associate, bachelor's, and master's
- **Urban** 172-acre campus
- **Endowment** $6.1 million
- **Coed,** 5,288 undergraduate students, 72% full-time, 57% women, 43% men
- **Minimally difficult** entrance level, 55% of applicants were admitted

Undergraduates 3,806 full-time, 1,482 part-time. Students come from 44 states and territories, 46 other countries, 6% are from out of state, 8% African American, 3% Asian American or Pacific Islander, 9% Hispanic American, 1% Native American, 6% international, 11% transferred in, 15% live on campus. *Retention:* 64% of 2001 full-time freshmen returned.

Freshmen *Admission:* 2,420 applied, 1,328 admitted, 803 enrolled. *Test scores:* SAT verbal scores over 500: 42%; SAT math scores over 500: 48%; ACT scores over 18: 82%; SAT verbal scores over 600: 10%; SAT math scores over 600: 12%; ACT scores over 24: 17%; SAT verbal scores over 700: 2%; SAT math scores over 700: 1%; ACT scores over 30: 1%.

Faculty *Total:* 330, 63% full-time, 51% with terminal degrees. *Student/faculty ratio:* 19:1.

Majors Accounting; applied art; art; art education; biology; business administration; business education; business marketing and marketing management; chemical engineering technology; chemistry; computer science; criminal justice/law enforcement administration; dental hygiene; economics; electrical/electronic engineering technology; elementary education; engineering technology; English; environmental science; exercise sciences; finance; geology; history; humanities; industrial/manufacturing engineering; information sciences/systems; interdisciplinary studies; international relations; mass communications; mathematics; medical technology; music; music teacher education; nursing; physical sciences; physics; political science; pre-dentistry; pre-law; pre-medicine; pre-veterinary studies; psychology; radiological science; respiratory therapy; secondary education; social work; sociology; Spanish; theater arts/drama; wildlife biology.

Academic Programs *Special study options:* academic remediation for entering students, accelerated degree program, adult/continuing education programs, advanced placement credit, distance learning, English as a second language, honors programs, internships, part-time degree program, services for LD students, study abroad, summer session for credit.

Library Moffett Library with 366,350 titles, 1,100 serial subscriptions, an OPAC, a Web page.

Computers on Campus 220 computers available on campus for general student use. A campuswide network can be accessed from student residence rooms and from off campus. At least one staffed computer lab available.

Student Life *Housing:* on-campus residence required through sophomore year. *Options:* coed. *Activities and Organizations:* drama/theater group, student-run newspaper, television station, choral group, marching band, honor societies, Greek Organizations, political groups, national fraternities, national sororities. *Campus security:* 24-hour emergency response devices and patrols, controlled dormitory access. *Student Services:* health clinic, personal/psychological counseling, legal services.

Athletics Member NCAA. All Division II. *Intercollegiate sports:* basketball M(s)/W(s), football M(s), soccer M(s)/W(s), tennis M(s)/W(s), volleyball W(s). *Intramural sports:* archery M/W, badminton M/W, basketball M/W, bowling M/W, football M/W, golf M/W, soccer M, table tennis M/W, tennis M/W, track and field M/W, volleyball M/W.

Standardized Tests *Required:* SAT I or ACT (for admission).

Midwestern State University (continued)

Costs (2001–02) *Tuition:* state resident $1980 full-time, $66 per credit hour part-time; nonresident $8310 full-time, $277 per credit hour part-time. Part-time tuition and fees vary according to course load. *Required fees:* $596 full-time, $37 per credit hour, $77 per term part-time. *Room and board:* $4392; room only: $2200. Room and board charges vary according to board plan and housing facility. *Payment plan:* installment.

Applying *Options:* common application, early admission, early action, deferred entrance. *Required:* high school transcript. *Application deadlines:* 8/7 (freshmen), 8/7 (transfers). *Notification:* continuous until 8/31 (freshmen).

Admissions Contact Barbara Merkle, Director of Admissions, Midwestern State University, 3410 Taft Boulevard, Wichita Falls, TX 76308. *Phone:* 940-397-4334. *Toll-free phone:* 800-842-1922. *E-mail:* school.relations@mwsu.edu.

NORTHWOOD UNIVERSITY, TEXAS CAMPUS

Cedar Hill, Texas

- **Independent** 4-year, founded 1966
- **Calendar** quarters
- **Degrees** associate and bachelor's
- **Small-town** 360-acre campus with easy access to Dallas
- **Endowment** $52.4 million
- **Coed,** 1,114 undergraduate students, 75% full-time, 57% women, 43% men
- **Moderately difficult** entrance level, 67% of applicants were admitted

Undergraduates 840 full-time, 274 part-time. Students come from 13 states and territories, 19 other countries, 9% are from out of state, 22% African American, 2% Asian American or Pacific Islander, 18% Hispanic American, 0.1% Native American, 5% international, 7% transferred in, 17% live on campus. *Retention:* 68% of 2001 full-time freshmen returned.

Freshmen *Admission:* 717 applied, 480 admitted, 258 enrolled. *Average high school GPA:* 3.1. *Test scores:* SAT verbal scores over 500: 40%; SAT math scores over 500: 41%; ACT scores over 18: 61%; SAT verbal scores over 600: 11%; SAT math scores over 600: 11%; ACT scores over 24: 7%; SAT verbal scores over 700: 2%.

Faculty *Total:* 25, 60% full-time, 76% with terminal degrees. *Student/faculty ratio:* 25:1.

Majors Accounting; advertising; business administration; business marketing and marketing management; court reporting; enterprise management; fashion merchandising; finance; hotel and restaurant management; international business; management information systems/business data processing; vehicle marketing operations; vehicle parts/accessories marketing operations.

Academic Programs *Special study options:* academic remediation for entering students, adult/continuing education programs, advanced placement credit, distance learning, double majors, external degree program, honors programs, independent study, internships, off-campus study, part-time degree program, study abroad, summer session for credit.

Library Hach Library with 13,000 titles, 160 serial subscriptions, an OPAC.

Computers on Campus 20 computers available on campus for general student use. A campuswide network can be accessed from student residence rooms and from off campus. Internet access, at least one staffed computer lab available.

Student Life *Housing:* on-campus residence required for freshman year. *Options:* men-only, women-only. *Activities and Organizations:* Student Senate, Students in Free Enterprise, Student Programming Board, Black Student Alliance, Hispanic Students Association. *Campus security:* 24-hour emergency response devices and patrols, student patrols. *Student Services:* health clinic, personal/psychological counseling.

Athletics Member NAIA. *Intercollegiate sports:* baseball M(s), cross-country running M(s)/W(s), golf M(s)/W(s), soccer M(s)/W(s), softball W(s), track and field M(s)/W(s). *Intramural sports:* basketball M/W, bowling M/W, football M, tennis M/W, volleyball M/W, weight lifting M/W.

Standardized Tests *Required:* SAT I or ACT (for admission).

Costs (2001–02) *Comprehensive fee:* $18,135 includes full-time tuition ($12,231), mandatory fees ($300), and room and board ($5604). Part-time tuition: $255 per credit. Part-time tuition and fees vary according to course load. *Room and board:* Room and board charges vary according to board plan. *Payment plan:* installment. *Waivers:* children of alumni and employees or children of employees.

Financial Aid Of all full-time matriculated undergraduates who enrolled in 2001, 480 applied for aid, 435 were judged to have need, 369 had their need fully met. In 2001, 106 non-need-based awards were made. *Average percent of need met:* 85%. *Average financial aid package:* $18,136. *Average need-based loan:* $3530. *Average need-based gift aid:* $5235. *Average non-need based aid:* $4660. *Average indebtedness upon graduation:* $17,901.

Applying *Options:* common application, electronic application, deferred entrance. *Application fee:* $25. *Required:* high school transcript. *Recommended:* essay or personal statement, minimum 2.0 GPA, 1 letter of recommendation, interview. *Application deadlines:* 9/1 (freshmen), 9/1 (transfers). *Notification:* continuous (freshmen).

Admissions Contact Mr. James R. Hickerson, Director of Admissions, Northwood University, Texas Campus, P.O. Box 58, Cedar Hill, TX 75104. *Phone:* 972-293-5400. *Toll-free phone:* 800-927-9663. *Fax:* 972-291-3824. *E-mail:* txadmit@northwood.edu.

OUR LADY OF THE LAKE UNIVERSITY OF SAN ANTONIO

San Antonio, Texas

- **Independent Roman Catholic** comprehensive, founded 1895
- **Calendar** semesters
- **Degrees** bachelor's, master's, and doctoral
- **Urban** 75-acre campus
- **Endowment** $25.9 million
- **Coed,** 2,196 undergraduate students, 61% full-time, 78% women, 22% men
- **Moderately difficult** entrance level, 61% of applicants were admitted

Undergraduates 1,330 full-time, 866 part-time. Students come from 28 states and territories, 17 other countries, 1% are from out of state, 7% African American, 0.7% Asian American or Pacific Islander, 67% Hispanic American, 0.4% Native American, 1% international, 6% transferred in, 29% live on campus. *Retention:* 68% of 2001 full-time freshmen returned.

Freshmen *Admission:* 2,285 applied, 1,405 admitted, 408 enrolled. *Average high school GPA:* 3.24. *Test scores:* SAT verbal scores over 500: 32%; SAT math scores over 500: 24%; ACT scores over 18: 68%; SAT verbal scores over 600: 5%; SAT math scores over 600: 3%; ACT scores over 24: 6%.

Faculty *Total:* 264, 48% full-time. *Student/faculty ratio:* 15:1.

Majors Accounting; American studies; art; biology; business administration; business marketing and marketing management; business systems networking/telecommunications; chemistry; communications; early childhood education; English; family/community studies; fashion merchandising; fine arts and art studies related; history; human resources management; liberal arts and sciences/liberal studies; mathematics; Mexican-American studies; natural sciences; philosophy; political science; psychology; religious studies; social sciences; social work; sociology; Spanish; special education; speech-language pathology/audiology; theater arts/drama.

Academic Programs *Special study options:* academic remediation for entering students, adult/continuing education programs, advanced placement credit, double majors, English as a second language, internships, off-campus study, part-time degree program, services for LD students, summer session for credit. *ROTC:* Army (c), Air Force (c). *Unusual degree programs:* 3-2 engineering with Texas Tech University, Washington University in St. Louis.

Library Saint Florence Library plus 2 others with 122,784 titles, 30,143 serial subscriptions, 6,774 audiovisual materials, an OPAC, a Web page.

Computers on Campus 200 computers available on campus for general student use. A campuswide network can be accessed from off campus. At least one staffed computer lab available.

Student Life *Housing Options:* coed, men-only, women-only, disabled students. *Activities and Organizations:* drama/theater group, student-run newspaper, television station, choral group. *Campus security:* 24-hour emergency response devices and patrols, late-night transport/escort service, controlled dormitory access. *Student Services:* health clinic, personal/psychological counseling, women's center.

Athletics *Intramural sports:* basketball M/W, football M/W, golf M/W, racquetball M/W, soccer M/W, softball M/W, swimming M/W, tennis M/W, track and field M/W, volleyball M/W.

Standardized Tests *Required:* SAT I or ACT (for admission).

Costs (2001–02) *Comprehensive fee:* $17,336 includes full-time tuition ($12,528), mandatory fees ($258), and room and board ($4550). Part-time tuition: $407 per credit hour. *Required fees:* $4 per credit hour, $76 per year part-time. *Room and board:* College room only: $2558. Room and board charges vary according to board plan and housing facility. *Payment plan:* installment. *Waivers:* employees or children of employees.

Financial Aid Of all full-time matriculated undergraduates who enrolled in 2001, 1236 applied for aid, 1183 were judged to have need. In 2001, 65 non-need-based awards were made. *Average financial aid package:* $12,944. *Average need-based loan:* $3857. *Average need-based gift aid:* $3032. *Average non-need based aid:* $7256. *Average indebtedness upon graduation:* $17,650.

Applying *Options:* common application, deferred entrance. *Application fee:* $25. *Required:* high school transcript. *Required for some:* interview. *Application deadline:* rolling (freshmen), rolling (transfers). *Notification:* continuous (freshmen).

Admissions Contact Mr. Michael Boatner, Acting Director of Admissions, Our Lady of the Lake University of San Antonio, 411 Southwest 24th Street, San Antonio, TX 78207-4689. *Phone:* 210-434-6711 Ext. 314. *Toll-free phone:* 800-436-6558. *Fax:* 210-431-4036. *E-mail:* admission@lake.ollusa.edu.

PAUL QUINN COLLEGE
Dallas, Texas

Admissions Contact Don Robinson, Director of Admissions, Paul Quinn College, 3837 Simpson-Stuart Road, Dallas, TX 75241-4331. *Phone:* 214-302-3520. *Toll-free phone:* 800-237-2648. *Fax:* 214-302-3559.

PRAIRIE VIEW A&M UNIVERSITY
Prairie View, Texas

- **State-supported** comprehensive, founded 1878, part of Texas A&M University System
- **Calendar** semesters
- **Degrees** bachelor's, master's, and doctoral
- **Small-town** 1440-acre campus with easy access to Houston
- **Coed,** 5,387 undergraduate students, 91% full-time, 56% women, 44% men
- **Moderately difficult** entrance level, 97% of applicants were admitted

Prairie View A&M University is the second-oldest public institution of higher education in Texas, originating in the Texas Constitution of 1876. The University opened in 1878 as the Agricultural and Mechanical College of Texas for Colored Youth, with 8 students and 2 faculty members. Today, the University enrolls more than 6,700 students and offers undergraduate and graduate degrees. Its most prominent programs are in accounting, computer science, criminal justice, education, engineering, nursing, and premedicine. Major academic units include the School of Architecture, the College of Agriculture and Human Sciences, the College of Arts and Sciences, the College of Business, the College of Education, the College of Engineering, The School of Juvenile Justice, the College of Nursing, and the Graduate School. The University is fully accredited by the Southern Association of Colleges and Schools and has specialized accreditation in several areas, including computer science, education, engineering, nursing, nutrition, and social work.

Undergraduates 4,890 full-time, 497 part-time. Students come from 44 states and territories, 39 other countries, 7% are from out of state, 94% African American, 0.6% Asian American or Pacific Islander, 2% Hispanic American, 0.0% Native American, 2% international. *Retention:* 70% of 2001 full-time freshmen returned.

Freshmen *Admission:* 2,143 applied, 2,073 admitted, 1,274 enrolled. *Average high school GPA:* 2.83. *Test scores:* SAT verbal scores over 500: 16%; SAT math scores over 500: 16%; ACT scores over 18: 39%; SAT verbal scores over 600: 2%; SAT math scores over 600: 2%; ACT scores over 24: 5%.

Faculty *Total:* 299, 88% full-time, 64% with terminal degrees. *Student/faculty ratio:* 18:1.

Majors Accounting; agricultural education; agricultural sciences; architecture; biology; business administration; business marketing and marketing management; chemical engineering; chemistry; civil engineering; community health liaison; computer engineering technology; computer science; criminal justice studies; drafting; electrical/electronic engineering technology; electrical engineering; engineering technology; English; family/community studies; finance; history; industrial technology; interdisciplinary studies; mathematics; mechanical engineering; medical technology; music; music (piano and organ performance); music (voice and choral/opera performance); nursing; nutrition science; physics; political science; psychology; social work; sociology; Spanish; theater arts/drama; trade/industrial education; wind/percussion instruments.

Academic Programs *Special study options:* academic remediation for entering students, accelerated degree program, advanced placement credit, cooperative education, distance learning, double majors, English as a second language, honors programs, independent study, internships, part-time degree program, summer session for credit. *ROTC:* Army (b).

Library John B. Coleman Library with an OPAC, a Web page.

Computers on Campus 102 computers available on campus for general student use. At least one staffed computer lab available.

Student Life *Housing:* on-campus residence required for freshman year. *Options:* coed, men-only, women-only. *Activities and Organizations:* drama/theater group, student-run newspaper, radio station, choral group, marching band, National Society of Black Engineers, National Association of Black Accountants, National Organization of Black Chemists and Chemical Engineers, Toastmasters International, Baptist Student Movement, national fraternities, national sororities. *Campus security:* 24-hour emergency response devices and patrols. *Student Services:* health clinic, personal/psychological counseling.

Athletics Member NCAA. All Division I except football (Division I-AA). *Intercollegiate sports:* baseball M(s), basketball M(s)/W(s), bowling W(s), cross-country running M/W, equestrian sports M/W, golf M(s)/W(s), softball W(s), tennis M(s)/W(s), track and field M(s)/W(s), volleyball W(s). *Intramural sports:* basketball M/W, golf M/W, lacrosse M/W, softball M/W, swimming M/W, table tennis M, tennis M/W, track and field M/W, volleyball M/W, weight lifting M(c).

Standardized Tests *Required:* SAT I or ACT (for admission).

Costs (2002–03) *Tuition:* state resident $1320 full-time, $44 per credit hour part-time; nonresident $7860 full-time, $262 per credit hour part-time. Full-time tuition and fees vary according to course load and degree level. Part-time tuition and fees vary according to course load and degree level. *Required fees:* $1912 full-time, $59 per credit hour, $131 per term part-time. *Room and board:* $6461; room only: $4170. Room and board charges vary according to board plan and housing facility. *Payment plans:* installment, deferred payment. *Waivers:* senior citizens.

Financial Aid Of all full-time matriculated undergraduates who enrolled in 2001, 4622 applied for aid, 4311 were judged to have need. 732 Federal Work-Study jobs (averaging $1934). 328 State and other part-time jobs (averaging $1146). In 2001, 271 non-need-based awards were made. *Average percent of need met:* 75%. *Average financial aid package:* $6920. *Average need-based loan:* $4000. *Average need-based gift aid:* $3300. *Average non-need based aid:* $1400. *Average indebtedness upon graduation:* $11,000.

Applying *Options:* early admission, deferred entrance. *Application fee:* $25. *Required:* high school transcript, minimum 2.5 GPA, letters of recommendation. *Application deadline:* 7/1 (transfers). *Notification:* continuous (freshmen).

Admissions Contact Ms. Mary Gooch, Director of Admissions, Prairie View A&M University, PO Box 3089, Prairie View, TX 77446-0188. *Phone:* 936-857-2626. *Fax:* 936-857-2699. *E-mail:* mary_gooch@pvamu.edu.

RICE UNIVERSITY
Houston, Texas

- **Independent** university, founded 1912
- **Calendar** semesters
- **Degrees** bachelor's, master's, and doctoral
- **Urban** 300-acre campus
- **Endowment** $3.2 billion
- **Coed,** 2,890 undergraduate students, 94% full-time, 48% women, 52% men
- **Most difficult** entrance level, 23% of applicants were admitted

Undergraduates 2,713 full-time, 177 part-time. Students come from 52 states and territories, 32 other countries, 46% are from out of state, 7% African American, 14% Asian American or Pacific Islander, 10% Hispanic American, 0.5% Native American, 3% international, 2% transferred in, 64% live on campus. *Retention:* 96% of 2001 full-time freshmen returned.

Freshmen *Admission:* 6,740 applied, 1,578 admitted, 657 enrolled. *Test scores:* SAT verbal scores over 500: 98%; SAT math scores over 500: 99%; ACT scores over 18: 100%; SAT verbal scores over 600: 88%; SAT math scores over 600: 92%; ACT scores over 24: 97%; SAT verbal scores over 700: 57%; SAT math scores over 700: 63%; ACT scores over 30: 70%.

Faculty *Total:* 741, 64% full-time, 90% with terminal degrees. *Student/faculty ratio:* 5:1.

Majors Anthropology; applied mathematics; architecture; art; art history; Asian studies; astronomy; astrophysics; biochemistry; bioengineering; biology; business administration; chemical engineering; chemistry; civil engineering; classics; computer engineering; computer/information sciences; ecology; economics; electrical engineering; English; environmental engineering; evolutionary biology; fine/studio arts; French; geology; geophysics/seismology; German; Greek (ancient and medieval); history; Latin American studies; Latin (ancient and medieval); linguistics; materials engineering; materials science; mathematical statistics; mathematics; mechanical engineering; multi/interdisciplinary studies related; music; music (general performance); music history; music theory and composition; neuroscience; philosophy; physical education; physical/theoretical chemistry; physics; political science; psychology; public policy analysis; religious studies; Russian; Russian/Slavic studies; sociology; Spanish; visual and performing arts related; women's studies.

Academic Programs *Special study options:* accelerated degree program, advanced placement credit, double majors, honors programs, independent study, internships, off-campus study, services for LD students, student-designed majors, study abroad, summer session for credit. *ROTC:* Army (c), Navy (b). *Unusual degree programs:* 3-2 law with Columbia University School of Law.

Library Fondren Library with 2.0 million titles, 14,000 serial subscriptions, an OPAC, a Web page.

Rice University (continued)

Computers on Campus 600 computers available on campus for general student use. A campuswide network can be accessed from student residence rooms and from off campus. Internet access, at least one staffed computer lab available.

Student Life *Housing Options:* coed. *Activities and Organizations:* drama/theater group, student-run newspaper, radio and television station, choral group, marching band, Drama Club, volunteer program, intramural sports, college government, Marching Owl Band. *Campus security:* 24-hour emergency response devices and patrols, late-night transport/escort service, controlled dormitory access. *Student Services:* health clinic, personal/psychological counseling, women's center.

Athletics Member NCAA. All Division I except football (Division I-A). *Intercollegiate sports:* badminton M(c)/W(c), baseball M(s), basketball M(s)/W(s), crew M(c)/W(c), cross-country running M(s)/W(s), fencing M(c)/W(c), field hockey W(c), golf M(s), lacrosse M(c)/W(c), rugby M(c)/W(c), sailing M(c)/W(c), soccer M(c)/W(s), swimming W(s), tennis M(s)/W(s), track and field M(s)/W(s), volleyball M(c)/W(s), water polo M(c)/W(c), wrestling M(c). *Intramural sports:* badminton M/W, basketball M/W, football M/W, racquetball M/W, soccer M/W, softball M/W, squash M, swimming M/W, table tennis M/W, tennis M/W, track and field M/W, volleyball M/W.

Standardized Tests *Required:* SAT I or ACT (for admission), SAT II: Subject Tests (for admission), SAT II: Writing Test (for admission).

Costs (2001–02) *Comprehensive fee:* $24,335 includes full-time tuition ($16,600), mandatory fees ($535), and room and board ($7200). Full-time tuition and fees vary according to student level. Part-time tuition: $692 per semester hour. Part-time tuition and fees vary according to student level. No tuition increase for student's term of enrollment. *Required fees:* $140 per term part-time. *Room and board:* College room only: $4200. Room and board charges vary according to board plan. *Payment plan:* installment. *Waivers:* employees or children of employees.

Financial Aid Of all full-time matriculated undergraduates who enrolled in 2001, 2186 applied for aid, 1068 were judged to have need, 1068 had their need fully met. In 2001, 1118 non-need-based awards were made. *Average percent of need met:* 100%. *Average financial aid package:* $16,448. *Average need-based loan:* $2441. *Average need-based gift aid:* $12,440. *Average non-need based aid:* $2965. *Average indebtedness upon graduation:* $12,525.

Applying *Options:* common application, electronic application, early admission, early decision, early action, deferred entrance. *Application fee:* $35. *Required:* essay or personal statement, high school transcript, 2 letters of recommendation. *Recommended:* interview. *Application deadlines:* 1/2 (freshmen), 4/1 (transfers). *Early decision:* 11/1. *Notification:* 4/1 (freshmen), 12/15 (early decision), 2/10 (early action).

Admissions Contact Ms. Julie M. Browning, Dean for Undergraduate Admission, Rice University, PO Box 1892, MS 17, Houston, TX 77251-1892. *Phone:* 713-348-RICE. *Toll-free phone:* 800-527-OWLS. *E-mail:* admission@rice.edu.

ST. EDWARD'S UNIVERSITY
Austin, Texas

- **Independent Roman Catholic** comprehensive, founded 1885
- **Calendar** semesters
- **Degrees** bachelor's, master's, and postbachelor's certificates
- **Urban** 180-acre campus
- **Endowment** $37.3 million
- **Coed,** 3,369 undergraduate students, 69% full-time, 57% women, 43% men
- **Moderately difficult** entrance level, 74% of applicants were admitted

Undergraduates 2,324 full-time, 1,045 part-time. Students come from 35 states and territories, 40 other countries, 5% are from out of state, 5% African American, 2% Asian American or Pacific Islander, 28% Hispanic American, 0.5% Native American, 4% international, 10% transferred in, 36% live on campus. *Retention:* 78% of 2001 full-time freshmen returned.

Freshmen *Admission:* 1,413 applied, 1,042 admitted, 431 enrolled. *Test scores:* SAT verbal scores over 500: 69%; SAT math scores over 500: 71%; ACT scores over 18: 91%; SAT verbal scores over 600: 24%; SAT math scores over 600: 21%; ACT scores over 24: 34%; SAT verbal scores over 700: 2%; SAT math scores over 700: 3%; ACT scores over 30: 2%.

Faculty *Total:* 336, 39% full-time, 46% with terminal degrees. *Student/faculty ratio:* 15:1.

Majors Accounting; accounting related; art; bilingual/bicultural education; biochemistry; biology; business administration; chemistry; communications; computer/information sciences; computer science; creative writing; criminal justice/law enforcement administration; economics; elementary education; English; English education; finance; history; international business; international relations; liberal arts and sciences/liberal studies; literature; marketing management and research related; mathematics; philosophy; photography; physical education; political science; psychology; religious studies; social sciences; social work; sociology; Spanish; theater arts/drama.

Academic Programs *Special study options:* academic remediation for entering students, accelerated degree program, adult/continuing education programs, advanced placement credit, cooperative education, distance learning, double majors, honors programs, independent study, internships, part-time degree program, services for LD students, study abroad, summer session for credit. *ROTC:* Army (c), Air Force (c).

Library Scarborough-Phillips Library with 107,231 titles, 4,122 serial subscriptions, 2,152 audiovisual materials, an OPAC, a Web page.

Computers on Campus 288 computers available on campus for general student use. A campuswide network can be accessed from student residence rooms and from off campus. Internet access, online (class) registration, at least one staffed computer lab available.

Student Life *Housing:* on-campus residence required for freshman year. *Options:* coed, men-only, women-only. *Activities and Organizations:* drama/theater group, student-run newspaper, choral group, Student Government Association, University Programming Board, Student Leadership Training Program, Alpha Phi Omega, Delta Sigma Pi. *Campus security:* 24-hour emergency response devices and patrols, late-night transport/escort service, controlled dormitory access. *Student Services:* health clinic, personal/psychological counseling.

Athletics Member NCAA. All Division II. *Intercollegiate sports:* baseball M(s), basketball M(s)/W(s), golf M(s), soccer M(s)/W(s), softball W(s), tennis M(s)/W(s), volleyball W(s). *Intramural sports:* basketball M/W, football M/W, golf M/W, racquetball M/W, soccer M/W, softball M/W, tennis M/W, volleyball M/W.

Standardized Tests *Required:* SAT I or ACT (for admission).

Costs (2001–02) *Comprehensive fee:* $17,846 includes full-time tuition ($12,728) and room and board ($5118). Part-time tuition: $424 per credit hour. *Room and board:* Room and board charges vary according to housing facility. *Payment plan:* installment. *Waivers:* employees or children of employees.

Financial Aid Of all full-time matriculated undergraduates who enrolled in 2001, 1610 applied for aid, 1279 were judged to have need, 192 had their need fully met. 205 Federal Work-Study jobs (averaging $1859). 60 State and other part-time jobs (averaging $1912). In 2001, 73 non-need-based awards were made. *Average percent of need met:* 69%. *Average financial aid package:* $10,072. *Average need-based loan:* $4165. *Average need-based gift aid:* $6767. *Average non-need based aid:* $3515. *Average indebtedness upon graduation:* $21,033.

Applying *Options:* common application, deferred entrance. *Application fee:* $30. *Required:* essay or personal statement, high school transcript. *Recommended:* letters of recommendation, interview. *Application deadlines:* 7/1 (freshmen), 7/1 (transfers). *Notification:* continuous until 10/1 (freshmen).

Admissions Contact Ms. Tracy Manier, Director of Admission, St. Edward's University, 3001 South Congress Avenue, Austin, TX 78704-6489. *Phone:* 512-448-8602. *Toll-free phone:* 800-555-0164. *Fax:* 512-464-8877. *E-mail:* seu.admit@admin.stedwards.edu.

ST. MARY'S UNIVERSITY OF SAN ANTONIO
San Antonio, Texas

- **Independent Roman Catholic** comprehensive, founded 1852
- **Calendar** semesters
- **Degrees** bachelor's, master's, doctoral, and first professional
- **Urban** 135-acre campus
- **Endowment** $83.0 million
- **Coed,** 2,613 undergraduate students, 90% full-time, 59% women, 41% men
- **Moderately difficult** entrance level, 81% of applicants were admitted

Undergraduates 2,342 full-time, 271 part-time. Students come from 35 states and territories, 50 other countries, 4% are from out of state, 3% African American, 2% Asian American or Pacific Islander, 69% Hispanic American, 0.4% Native American, 3% international, 6% transferred in, 42% live on campus. *Retention:* 79% of 2001 full-time freshmen returned.

Freshmen *Admission:* 1,674 applied, 1,364 admitted, 536 enrolled. *Average high school GPA:* 3.15. *Test scores:* SAT verbal scores over 500: 67%; SAT math scores over 500: 70%; ACT scores over 18: 94%; SAT verbal scores over 600: 16%; SAT math scores over 600: 16%; ACT scores over 24: 30%; SAT verbal scores over 700: 1%; SAT math scores over 700: 1%; ACT scores over 30: 1%.

Faculty *Total:* 337, 54% full-time, 76% with terminal degrees. *Student/faculty ratio:* 15:1.

Majors Accounting; art education; biochemistry; biology; business administration; business education; business marketing and marketing management; chemistry; communications; computer engineering; computer management; computer science; criminal justice/law enforcement administration; criminology; earth sciences; economics; education; electrical engineering; engineering; engineering science; English; entrepreneurship; exercise sciences; finance; French; geology; health/physical education; history; human resources management; industrial/manufacturing engineering; information sciences/systems; international business; mass communications; mathematical statistics; mathematics; music; philosophy; physics; political science; pre-dentistry; psychology; reading education; social studies education; sociology; Spanish; speech/rhetorical studies; theology.

Academic Programs *Special study options:* academic remediation for entering students, adult/continuing education programs, advanced placement credit, cooperative education, distance learning, double majors, English as a second language, honors programs, independent study, internships, off-campus study, part-time degree program, study abroad, summer session for credit. *ROTC:* Army (b).

Library Academic Library plus 1 other with 837,287 titles, 1,126 serial subscriptions, 3,104 audiovisual materials, an OPAC, a Web page.

Computers on Campus 100 computers available on campus for general student use. A campuswide network can be accessed from student residence rooms and from off campus. At least one staffed computer lab available.

Student Life *Housing:* on-campus residence required for freshman year. *Options:* coed, men-only, women-only, disabled students. *Activities and Organizations:* drama/theater group, student-run newspaper, choral group, Alpha Phi Omega, Rotoract, Student Government Association, International Student Association, Delta Sigma Pi, national fraternities, national sororities. *Campus security:* 24-hour emergency response devices and patrols, late-night transport/escort service, controlled dormitory access. *Student Services:* health clinic, personal/psychological counseling.

Athletics Member NCAA, NAIA. All NCAA Division II. *Intercollegiate sports:* baseball M(s), basketball M(s)/W(s), golf M(s), rugby M(c), soccer M(s)/W(s), softball W, tennis M(s)/W(s), volleyball W(s). *Intramural sports:* badminton M/W, basketball M/W, bowling M/W, cross-country running M/W, football M/W, softball M/W, table tennis M/W, tennis M/W, volleyball M/W, water polo M/W.

Standardized Tests *Required:* SAT I or ACT (for admission).

Costs (2002–03) *Comprehensive fee:* $20,235 includes full-time tuition ($14,200), mandatory fees ($500), and room and board ($5535). Part-time tuition: $426 per credit hour. *Required fees:* $250 per term part-time. *Room and board:* College room only: $3380. *Waivers:* employees or children of employees.

Financial Aid Of all full-time matriculated undergraduates who enrolled in 2001, 1751 applied for aid, 1592 were judged to have need, 374 had their need fully met. 731 Federal Work-Study jobs (averaging $1821). 134 State and other part-time jobs (averaging $1486). In 2001, 171 non-need-based awards were made. *Average percent of need met:* 60%. *Average financial aid package:* $10,930. *Average need-based loan:* $4348. *Average need-based gift aid:* $6562. *Average non-need based aid:* $6204. *Average indebtedness upon graduation:* $22,023.

Applying *Options:* common application, deferred entrance. *Application fee:* $30. *Required:* essay or personal statement, high school transcript. *Required for some:* letters of recommendation. *Recommended:* interview. *Application deadline:* rolling (freshmen), rolling (transfers). *Notification:* continuous (freshmen).

Admissions Contact Mr. Richard Castillo, Director of Admissions, St. Mary's University of San Antonio, 1 Camino Santa Maria, San Antonio, TX 78228-8503. *Phone:* 210-436-3126. *Toll-free phone:* 800-FOR-STMU. *Fax:* 210-431-6742. *E-mail:* uadm@stmarytx.edu.

Sam Houston State University

Huntsville, Texas

- **State-supported** comprehensive, founded 1879, part of Texas State University System
- **Calendar** semesters
- **Degrees** bachelor's, master's, and doctoral
- **Small-town** 2143-acre campus with easy access to Houston
- **Endowment** $22.8 million
- **Coed,** 11,273 undergraduate students, 82% full-time, 57% women, 43% men
- **Moderately difficult** entrance level, 86% of applicants were admitted

Undergraduates 9,214 full-time, 2,059 part-time. Students come from 43 states and territories, 46 other countries, 1% are from out of state, 15% African American, 0.9% Asian American or Pacific Islander, 9% Hispanic American, 0.5% Native American, 0.5% international, 13% transferred in, 25% live on campus. *Retention:* 67% of 2001 full-time freshmen returned.

Freshmen *Admission:* 4,708 applied, 4,072 admitted, 1,770 enrolled. *Test scores:* SAT verbal scores over 500: 46%; SAT math scores over 500: 44%; ACT scores over 18: 79%; SAT verbal scores over 600: 10%; SAT math scores over 600: 9%; ACT scores over 24: 17%; SAT verbal scores over 700: 1%; SAT math scores over 700: 1%; ACT scores over 30: 1%.

Faculty *Total:* 528, 72% full-time, 70% with terminal degrees. *Student/faculty ratio:* 21:1.

Majors Accounting; advertising; agricultural business; agricultural education; agricultural mechanization; agricultural sciences; animal sciences; art; biology; business; business administration; business economics; business education; business marketing and marketing management; chemistry; community health liaison; computer/information sciences; construction management; corrections; criminal justice studies; dance; drafting; electrical/electronic engineering technology; English; environmental science; exercise sciences; fashion merchandising; finance; French; geography; geology; German; graphic design/commercial art/illustration; history; home economics; home economics education; horticulture science; humanities; human resources management; industrial technology; interior design; international business; journalism; law enforcement/police science; mathematics; medical technology; music; music teacher education; music therapy; nutrition science; operations management; painting; philosophy; photography; physics; political science; psychology; public relations; radio/television broadcasting; sociology; Spanish; speech/rhetorical studies; theater arts/drama.

Academic Programs *Special study options:* academic remediation for entering students, accelerated degree program, adult/continuing education programs, advanced placement credit, cooperative education, distance learning, double majors, English as a second language, honors programs, independent study, internships, part-time degree program, services for LD students, summer session for credit. *ROTC:* Army (b). *Unusual degree programs:* 3-2 engineering with Texas A&M University.

Library Newton Gresham Library with 1.8 million titles, 3,297 serial subscriptions, 18,427 audiovisual materials, an OPAC.

Computers on Campus 200 computers available on campus for general student use. A campuswide network can be accessed from off campus. Internet access, at least one staffed computer lab available.

Student Life *Housing:* on-campus residence required for freshman year. *Options:* coed. *Activities and Organizations:* drama/theater group, student-run newspaper, radio and television station, choral group, marching band, Residence Hall Association, Inter-Fraternal Council, Pan-Hellenic Council, NAACP, Baptist student ministry, national fraternities, national sororities. *Campus security:* 24-hour emergency response devices and patrols, student patrols, late-night transport/escort service. *Student Services:* health clinic, personal/psychological counseling, legal services.

Athletics Member NCAA. All Division I except football (Division I-AA). *Intercollegiate sports:* baseball M(s), basketball M(s)/W(s), cross-country running M/W, equestrian sports M/W, golf M(s), lacrosse M(c), riflery M(c)/W(c), rugby M(c), soccer M(c), tennis M(s)/W(s), track and field M/W, volleyball W(s). *Intramural sports:* basketball M/W, bowling M/W, football M, gymnastics W(c), racquetball M/W, soccer M/W, softball M/W, swimming M/W, tennis M/W, volleyball M/W, water polo M/W.

Standardized Tests *Required:* SAT I or ACT (for admission).

Costs (2001–02) *Tuition:* state resident $2070 full-time, $69 per semester hour part-time; nonresident $8400 full-time, $280 per semester hour part-time. Full-time tuition and fees vary according to course load. Part-time tuition and fees vary according to course load. *Required fees:* $748 full-time, $371 per term part-time. *Room and board:* $3672; room only: $1904. Room and board charges vary according to board plan and housing facility. *Payment plan:* installment.

Financial Aid Of all full-time matriculated undergraduates who enrolled in 2001, 4749 applied for aid, 3099 were judged to have need. 27 State and other part-time jobs (averaging $1494). In 2001, 706 non-need-based awards were made. *Average financial aid package:* $4796. *Average need-based loan:* $3399. *Average need-based gift aid:* $2474. *Average non-need based aid:* $1483. *Average indebtedness upon graduation:* $10,266. *Financial aid deadline:* 6/30.

Applying *Options:* common application, early admission. *Application fee:* $20. *Required:* high school transcript, minimum 2.0 GPA. *Application deadline:* rolling (freshmen), rolling (transfers). *Notification:* continuous (freshmen).

Admissions Contact Ms. Joey Chandler, Director of Admissions and Recruitment, Sam Houston State University, PO Box 2418, Huntsville, TX 77341. *Phone:* 936-294-1828. *Fax:* 936-294-3758.

Schreiner University

Kerrville, Texas

- **Independent Presbyterian** comprehensive, founded 1923
- **Calendar** semesters
- **Degrees** certificates, associate, bachelor's, master's, and postbachelor's certificates
- **Small-town** 175-acre campus with easy access to San Antonio and Austin
- **Endowment** $29.2 million
- **Coed,** 791 undergraduate students, 86% full-time, 62% women, 38% men

Schreiner University (continued)

- **Moderately difficult** entrance level, 71% of applicants were admitted

Undergraduates 680 full-time, 111 part-time. Students come from 21 states and territories, 0% are from out of state, 2% African American, 0.9% Asian American or Pacific Islander, 15% Hispanic American, 1% Native American, 0.8% international, 10% transferred in, 47% live on campus. *Retention:* 66% of 2001 full-time freshmen returned.

Freshmen *Admission:* 654 applied, 464 admitted, 207 enrolled. *Average high school GPA:* 3.40. *Test scores:* SAT verbal scores over 500: 53%; SAT math scores over 500: 49%; ACT scores over 18: 79%; SAT verbal scores over 600: 17%; SAT math scores over 600: 19%; ACT scores over 24: 31%; SAT verbal scores over 700: 5%; ACT scores over 30: 2%.

Faculty *Total:* 87, 64% full-time, 43% with terminal degrees. *Student/faculty ratio:* 11:1.

Majors Accounting; art; biochemistry; biology; business; business administration; business marketing and marketing management; chemistry; engineering; English; exercise sciences; finance; graphic design/commercial art/illustration; health/physical education; history; humanities; legal studies; liberal arts and sciences/liberal studies; literature; mathematics; philosophy; pre-dentistry; pre-engineering; pre-law; pre-medicine; psychology; real estate; religious studies.

Academic Programs *Special study options:* academic remediation for entering students, advanced placement credit, cooperative education, distance learning, double majors, English as a second language, freshman honors college, honors programs, independent study, internships, part-time degree program, services for LD students, student-designed majors, study abroad, summer session for credit. *Unusual degree programs:* 3-2 engineering with University of Texas at Austin, Texas A&M University.

Library W. M. Logan Library with 73,335 titles, 702 serial subscriptions, 613 audiovisual materials, an OPAC, a Web page.

Computers on Campus 62 computers available on campus for general student use. A campuswide network can be accessed from student residence rooms and from off campus. Internet access, at least one staffed computer lab available.

Student Life *Housing:* on-campus residence required through junior year. *Options:* coed, disabled students. *Activities and Organizations:* drama/theater group, student-run newspaper, choral group, Student Senate, Back on Campus Again (nontraditional student organization), Campus Ministry, International Club, Best Buddies, national fraternities. *Campus security:* 24-hour emergency response devices and patrols, late-night transport/escort service, 18-hour patrols by trained security personnel. *Student Services:* health clinic, personal/psychological counseling.

Athletics Member NCAA, NAIA. All NCAA Division III. *Intercollegiate sports:* baseball M, basketball M/W, golf M/W, soccer M/W, softball W, tennis M/W, volleyball W. *Intramural sports:* basketball M/W, cross-country running M/W, football M/W, racquetball M/W, soccer M/W, softball M/W, table tennis M/W, tennis M/W, volleyball M/W.

Standardized Tests *Required:* SAT I or ACT (for admission).

Costs (2001–02) *Comprehensive fee:* $19,254 includes full-time tuition ($12,118), mandatory fees ($200), and room and board ($6936). Part-time tuition: $517 per credit hour. *Room and board:* College room only: $3244. Room and board charges vary according to board plan and housing facility. *Payment plan:* installment. *Waivers:* employees or children of employees.

Financial Aid Of all full-time matriculated undergraduates who enrolled in 2001, 513 applied for aid, 481 were judged to have need, 82 had their need fully met. 149 Federal Work-Study jobs (averaging $1034). 165 State and other part-time jobs (averaging $984). In 2001, 112 non-need-based awards were made. *Average percent of need met:* 67%. *Average financial aid package:* $10,582. *Average need-based loan:* $2708. *Average need-based gift aid:* $7897. *Average non-need based aid:* $6769. *Average indebtedness upon graduation:* $18,562.

Applying *Options:* common application, early admission. *Application fee:* $25. *Required:* high school transcript. *Required for some:* essay or personal statement, 1 letter of recommendation. *Recommended:* essay or personal statement, minimum 2.0 GPA, interview. *Application deadlines:* 8/1 (freshmen), 8/15 (transfers). *Notification:* continuous (freshmen).

Admissions Contact Ms. Peg Lexton, Dean of Admission and Financial Aid, Schreiner University, 2100 Memorial Boulevard, Kerrville, TX 78028. *Phone:* 830-792-7277. *Toll-free phone:* 800-343-4919. *Fax:* 830-792-7226. *E-mail:* admissions@schreiner.edu.

SOUTHERN METHODIST UNIVERSITY
Dallas, Texas

- **Independent** university, founded 1911, affiliated with United Methodist Church
- **Calendar** semesters
- **Degrees** bachelor's, master's, doctoral, first professional, and postbachelor's certificates
- **Suburban** 163-acre campus
- **Endowment** $790.1 million
- **Coed,** 5,836 undergraduate students, 94% full-time, 54% women, 46% men
- **Moderately difficult** entrance level, 75% of applicants were admitted

Undergraduates 5,497 full-time, 339 part-time. Students come from 48 states and territories, 54 other countries, 35% are from out of state, 6% African American, 6% Asian American or Pacific Islander, 8% Hispanic American, 0.7% Native American, 4% international, 5% transferred in, 48% live on campus. *Retention:* 86% of 2001 full-time freshmen returned.

Freshmen *Admission:* 5,322 applied, 3,984 admitted, 1,353 enrolled. *Average high school GPA:* 3.33. *Test scores:* SAT verbal scores over 500: 85%; SAT math scores over 500: 91%; ACT scores over 18: 99%; SAT verbal scores over 600: 39%; SAT math scores over 600: 47%; ACT scores over 24: 69%; SAT verbal scores over 700: 7%; SAT math scores over 700: 9%; ACT scores over 30: 10%.

Faculty *Total:* 732, 71% full-time. *Student/faculty ratio:* 12:1.

Majors Accounting; advertising; African-American studies; anthropology; applied economics; art history; biochemistry; biology; broadcast journalism; business administration; business marketing and marketing management; chemistry; computer engineering; computer science; creative writing; dance; economics; electrical engineering; English; environmental engineering; environmental science; European studies; film studies; finance; fine/studio arts; foreign languages/literatures; French; geology; geophysics/seismology; German; history; humanities; international relations; journalism; Latin American studies; management information systems/business data processing; management science; mathematical statistics; mathematics; mechanical engineering; medieval/renaissance studies; Mexican-American studies; music; music (general performance); music (piano and organ performance); music teacher education; music theory and composition; music therapy; organizational behavior; philosophy; physics; political science; psychology; public policy analysis; public relations; quantitative economics; radio/television broadcasting; real estate; religious studies; Russian; Russian/Slavic studies; social sciences; sociology; Spanish; theater arts/drama.

Academic Programs *Special study options:* academic remediation for entering students, accelerated degree program, adult/continuing education programs, advanced placement credit, cooperative education, distance learning, double majors, English as a second language, honors programs, independent study, internships, part-time degree program, services for LD students, student-designed majors, study abroad, summer session for credit. *ROTC:* Army (b), Air Force (c).

Library Central University Library plus 7 others with 3.1 million titles, 11,216 serial subscriptions, an OPAC, a Web page.

Computers on Campus 409 computers available on campus for general student use. A campuswide network can be accessed from student residence rooms and from off campus. At least one staffed computer lab available.

Student Life *Housing:* on-campus residence required for freshman year. *Options:* coed, disabled students. *Activities and Organizations:* drama/theater group, student-run newspaper, radio station, choral group, marching band, Program Council, student senate, student foundation, Residence Hall Association, United Methodist Campus Ministries, national fraternities, national sororities. *Campus security:* 24-hour emergency response devices and patrols, late-night transport/escort service, controlled dormitory access. *Student Services:* health clinic, personal/psychological counseling, women's center.

Athletics Member NCAA. All Division I except football (Division I-A). *Intercollegiate sports:* baseball M(c), basketball M(s)/W(s), crew M(c)/W(s), cross-country running M(s)/W(s), fencing M(c)/W(c), golf M(s)/W(s), ice hockey M(c), lacrosse M(c)/W(c), rugby M(c), sailing M(c)/W(c), soccer M(s)/W(s), swimming M(s)/W(s), tennis M(s)/W(s), track and field M(s)/W(s), volleyball M(c)/W(s), wrestling M(c). *Intramural sports:* badminton M/W, basketball M/W, bowling M/W, football M/W, golf M/W, racquetball M/W, soccer M/W, softball M/W, swimming M/W, tennis M/W, track and field M/W, volleyball M/W, weight lifting M/W.

Standardized Tests *Required:* SAT I or ACT (for admission). *Required for some:* SAT II: Subject Tests (for admission).

Costs (2001–02) *Comprehensive fee:* $28,349 includes full-time tuition ($18,450), mandatory fees ($2346), and room and board ($7553). Part-time tuition: $771 per credit hour. Part-time tuition and fees vary according to class time and course load. *Required fees:* $99 per credit hour. *Room and board:* Room and board charges vary according to board plan and housing facility. *Payment plans:* tuition prepayment, installment. *Waivers:* employees or children of employees.

Financial Aid Of all full-time matriculated undergraduates who enrolled in 2001, 2262 applied for aid, 1892 were judged to have need, 1263 had their need fully met. In 2001, 1652 non-need-based awards were made. *Average percent of need met:* 94%. *Average financial aid package:* $20,604. *Average need-based* loan: $3918. *Average need-based gift aid:* $12,294. *Average non-need based aid:* $5241. *Average indebtedness upon graduation:* $19,792.

Applying *Options:* common application, early admission, early action, deferred entrance. *Application fee:* $50. *Required:* essay or personal statement, high school transcript, 1 letter of recommendation. *Application deadlines:* 1/15 (freshmen), 7/1 (transfers). *Notification:* continuous (freshmen), 12/31 (early action).

Admissions Contact Mr. Ron W. Moss, Director of Admission and Enrollment Management, Southern Methodist University, PO Box 750181, Dallas, TX 75275-0181. *Phone:* 214-768-2058. *Toll-free phone:* 800-323-0672. *Fax:* 214-768-0103. *E-mail:* enrol_serv@mail.smu.edu.

SOUTHWESTERN ADVENTIST UNIVERSITY

Keene, Texas

- **Independent Seventh-day Adventist** comprehensive, founded 1894
- **Calendar** semesters
- **Degrees** associate, bachelor's, and master's
- **Rural** 150-acre campus with easy access to Dallas-Fort Worth
- **Endowment** $7.6 million
- **Coed,** 1,163 undergraduate students, 71% full-time, 60% women, 40% men
- **Minimally difficult** entrance level, 64% of applicants were admitted

Undergraduates 821 full-time, 342 part-time. Students come from 50 states and territories, 53 other countries, 39% are from out of state, 14% African American, 6% Asian American or Pacific Islander, 15% Hispanic American, 1% Native American, 13% international, 21% transferred in, 31% live on campus. *Retention:* 61% of 2001 full-time freshmen returned.

Freshmen *Admission:* 657 applied, 422 admitted, 168 enrolled. *Average high school GPA:* 3.22. *Test scores:* SAT verbal scores over 500: 48%; SAT math scores over 500: 32%; ACT scores over 18: 84%; SAT verbal scores over 600: 19%; SAT math scores over 600: 6%; ACT scores over 24: 21%; SAT verbal scores over 700: 1%; SAT math scores over 700: 1%; ACT scores over 30: 1%.

Faculty *Total:* 92, 54% full-time, 40% with terminal degrees. *Student/faculty ratio:* 15:1.

Majors Accounting; biology; broadcast journalism; business administration; chemistry; computer science; criminal justice/law enforcement administration; elementary education; English; exercise sciences; health/physical education; health services administration; history; information sciences/systems; international business; international relations; journalism; mass communications; mathematics; medical technology; music; nursing; physics; psychology; religious studies; secretarial science; social sciences; social work; theology.

Academic Programs *Special study options:* academic remediation for entering students, accelerated degree program, cooperative education, English as a second language, external degree program, honors programs, independent study, internships, off-campus study, part-time degree program, student-designed majors, study abroad, summer session for credit.

Library Chan Shun Centennial Library with 108,481 titles, 457 serial subscriptions, an OPAC, a Web page.

Computers on Campus 50 computers available on campus for general student use. A campuswide network can be accessed from student residence rooms and from off campus. Internet access, at least one staffed computer lab available.

Student Life *Housing:* on-campus residence required for freshman year. *Options:* men-only, women-only, cooperative. *Activities and Organizations:* drama/theater group, student-run newspaper, radio and television station, choral group, Student Association, SIFE, Education/Psychology Club, Theology Club, Nursing Club. *Campus security:* 24-hour emergency response devices, student patrols. *Student Services:* health clinic, personal/psychological counseling.

Athletics Member NAIA. *Intercollegiate sports:* baseball M(s), basketball M(s)/W(s), soccer M(s), softball W(c), volleyball M(c)/W(s). *Intramural sports:* basketball M/W, football M/W, skiing (downhill) M(c)/W(c), soccer M/W, softball M/W, volleyball M/W.

Standardized Tests *Required:* SAT I or ACT (for admission).

Costs (2001–02) *Comprehensive fee:* $14,798 includes full-time tuition ($9880), mandatory fees ($140), and room and board ($4778). Part-time tuition: $412 per semester hour. Part-time tuition and fees vary according to course load. *Required fees:* $140 per year part-time. *Room and board:* Room and board charges vary according to board plan. *Payment plan:* installment. *Waivers:* employees or children of employees.

Financial Aid Of all full-time matriculated undergraduates who enrolled in 2001, 664 applied for aid, 445 were judged to have need, 109 had their need fully met. 84 Federal Work-Study jobs (averaging $1331). 5 State and other part-time jobs (averaging $1058). In 2001, 157 non-need-based awards were made. *Average percent of need met:* 81%. *Average financial aid package:* $9622. *Average need-based loan:* $4862. *Average need-based gift aid:* $3529. *Average non-need based aid:* $3762. *Average indebtedness upon graduation:* $18,223.

Applying *Options:* deferred entrance. *Required:* high school transcript, minimum 2.0 GPA. *Required for some:* essay or personal statement, 1 letter of recommendation, interview. *Application deadlines:* 8/31 (freshmen), 8/31 (transfers). *Notification:* 9/1 (freshmen).

Admissions Contact Mrs. Sylvia Peterson, Admissions Counselor, Southwestern Adventist University, PO Box 567, Keene, TX 76059. *Phone:* 817-645-3921 Ext. 294. *Toll-free phone:* 800-433-2240. *Fax:* 817-556-4744. *E-mail:* sylviap@swau.edu.

SOUTHWESTERN ASSEMBLIES OF GOD UNIVERSITY

Waxahachie, Texas

- **Independent** comprehensive, founded 1927, affiliated with Assemblies of God
- **Calendar** semesters
- **Degrees** associate, bachelor's, and master's
- **Small-town** 70-acre campus with easy access to Dallas
- **Endowment** $853,777
- **Coed,** 1,607 undergraduate students, 87% full-time, 52% women, 48% men
- **Noncompetitive** entrance level, 60% of applicants were admitted

Undergraduates 1,398 full-time, 209 part-time. Students come from 42 states and territories, 11 other countries, 35% are from out of state, 6% African American, 1% Asian American or Pacific Islander, 15% Hispanic American, 2% Native American, 0.8% international, 14% transferred in, 55% live on campus. *Retention:* 61% of 2001 full-time freshmen returned.

Freshmen *Admission:* 971 applied, 579 admitted, 360 enrolled. *Average high school GPA:* 2.8. *Test scores:* SAT verbal scores over 500: 56%; SAT math scores over 500: 48%; ACT scores over 18: 70%; SAT verbal scores over 600: 20%; SAT math scores over 600: 20%; ACT scores over 24: 17%; SAT verbal scores over 700: 8%; SAT math scores over 700: 4%; ACT scores over 30: 1%.

Faculty *Total:* 90, 69% full-time, 41% with terminal degrees. *Student/faculty ratio:* 20:1.

Majors Accounting; biblical languages/literatures; biblical studies; business; business administration; communications; divinity/ministry; education; elementary education; general studies; missionary studies; music; pastoral counseling; psychology; religious education; religious music; religious studies; secondary education; social sciences.

Academic Programs *Special study options:* academic remediation for entering students, adult/continuing education programs, advanced placement credit, distance learning, double majors, external degree program, independent study, internships, part-time degree program, services for LD students, summer session for credit.

Library P. C. Nelson Memorial Library plus 1 other with 110,000 titles, 600 serial subscriptions, a Web page.

Computers on Campus 45 computers available on campus for general student use. A campuswide network can be accessed from off campus. Internet access, at least one staffed computer lab available.

Student Life *Housing:* on-campus residence required through senior year. *Options:* coed. *Activities and Organizations:* drama/theater group, student-run newspaper, choral group, Gold Jackets/Blazers, Intramurals, Mission Association, Student Congress, SOCS. *Campus security:* student patrols, late-night transport/escort service. *Student Services:* health clinic, personal/psychological counseling.

Athletics Member NAIA, NCCAA. *Intercollegiate sports:* basketball M/W, football M, volleyball W. *Intramural sports:* basketball M/W, soccer M(c), softball M/W, table tennis M/W, tennis M/W, volleyball M/W.

Standardized Tests *Required:* SAT I or ACT (for admission).

Costs (2002–03) *Comprehensive fee:* $13,070 includes full-time tuition ($7800), mandatory fees ($800), and room and board ($4470). Part-time tuition: $260 per credit hour. *Required fees:* $30 per hour.

Financial Aid Of all full-time matriculated undergraduates who enrolled in 2001, 1116 applied for aid, 1002 were judged to have need, 110 had their need fully met. 178 Federal Work-Study jobs, 7 State and other part-time jobs (averaging $890). In 2001, 316 non-need-based awards were made. *Average percent of need met:* 64%. *Average financial aid package:* $6728. *Average need-based loan:* $3177. *Average need-based gift aid:* $3511. *Average indebtedness upon graduation:* $13,938. *Financial aid deadline:* 7/1.

Applying *Options:* early admission, deferred entrance. *Application fee:* $35. *Required:* essay or personal statement, high school transcript, 2 letters of recommendation, medical history, evidence of approved Christian character. *Application deadline:* rolling (freshmen), rolling (transfers).

Southwestern Assemblies of God University (continued)
Admissions Contact Eddie Davis, Enrollment Services, Southwestern Assemblies of God University, 1200 Sycamore Street, Waxahachie, TX 75165-2397. *Phone:* 972-937-4010 Ext. 1121. *Toll-free phone:* 800-262-SAGU.

SOUTHWESTERN CHRISTIAN COLLEGE
Terrell, Texas

Admissions Contact Admissions Department, Southwestern Christian College, Box 10, 200 Bowser Street, Terrell, TX 75160. *Phone:* 214-524-3341.

SOUTHWESTERN UNIVERSITY
Georgetown, Texas

- **Independent Methodist** 4-year, founded 1840
- **Calendar** semesters
- **Degree** bachelor's
- **Suburban** 500-acre campus with easy access to Austin
- **Endowment** $317.0 million
- **Coed,** 1,320 undergraduate students, 98% full-time, 57% women, 43% men
- **Very difficult** entrance level, 59% of applicants were admitted

Undergraduates 1,294 full-time, 26 part-time. Students come from 31 states and territories, 7 other countries, 8% are from out of state, 3% African American, 2% Asian American or Pacific Islander, 12% Hispanic American, 0.5% Native American, 0.1% international, 3% transferred in, 81% live on campus. *Retention:* 88% of 2001 full-time freshmen returned.

Freshmen *Admission:* 1,561 applied, 928 admitted, 325 enrolled. *Average high school GPA:* 3.5. *Test scores:* SAT verbal scores over 500: 94%; SAT math scores over 500: 94%; ACT scores over 18: 99%; SAT verbal scores over 600: 63%; SAT math scores over 600: 62%; ACT scores over 24: 75%; SAT verbal scores over 700: 14%; SAT math scores over 700: 12%; ACT scores over 30: 19%.

Faculty *Total:* 156, 71% full-time, 90% with terminal degrees. *Student/faculty ratio:* 11:1.

Majors Accounting; American studies; animal sciences; art; art education; art history; biology; business administration; chemistry; computer science; economics; English; experimental psychology; fine/studio arts; French; German; history; international relations; literature; mass communications; mathematics; modern languages; music; music history; music (piano and organ performance); music teacher education; philosophy; physical education; physics; political science; psychology; religious music; religious studies; social sciences; sociology; Spanish; theater arts/drama; women's studies.

Academic Programs *Special study options:* accelerated degree program, advanced placement credit, double majors, freshman honors college, honors programs, independent study, internships, off-campus study, part-time degree program, student-designed majors, study abroad, summer session for credit. *Unusual degree programs:* 3-2 engineering with Washington University in St. Louis, Arizona State University, Texas A&M University.

Library A. Frank Smith Jr. Library Center with 303,017 titles, 1,425 serial subscriptions, 9,820 audiovisual materials, an OPAC, a Web page.

Computers on Campus 223 computers available on campus for general student use. A campuswide network can be accessed from student residence rooms and from off campus. Internet access, at least one staffed computer lab available.

Student Life *Housing:* on-campus residence required for freshman year. *Options:* coed, men-only, women-only. *Activities and Organizations:* drama/theater group, student-run newspaper, television station, choral group, Alpha Phi Omega, International Club, Latinos Unidos, national fraternities, national sororities. *Campus security:* 24-hour emergency response devices and patrols, student patrols, late-night transport/escort service, controlled dormitory access. *Student Services:* health clinic, personal/psychological counseling, women's center.

Athletics Member NCAA. All Division III. *Intercollegiate sports:* baseball M, basketball M/W, cross-country running M/W, golf M/W, soccer M/W, swimming M/W, tennis M/W, volleyball W. *Intramural sports:* basketball M/W, bowling M/W, football M, golf M/W, racquetball M/W, soccer M/W, softball M, swimming M/W, table tennis M, tennis M/W, volleyball W.

Standardized Tests *Required:* SAT I or ACT (for admission).

Costs (2001–02) *Comprehensive fee:* $22,550 includes full-time tuition ($16,650) and room and board ($5900). Part-time tuition: $690 per semester hour. *Room and board:* College room only: $2930. Room and board charges vary according to board plan, housing facility, and student level. *Payment plans:* installment, deferred payment. *Waivers:* employees or children of employees.

Financial Aid Of all full-time matriculated undergraduates who enrolled in 2001, 779 applied for aid, 657 were judged to have need, 656 had their need fully met. 274 Federal Work-Study jobs (averaging $1659). 307 State and other part-time jobs (averaging $1899). In 2001, 341 non-need-based awards were made. *Average percent of need met:* 98%. *Average financial aid package:* $14,613. *Average need-based loan:* $2872. *Average need-based gift aid:* $10,544. *Average non-need based aid:* $6350. *Average indebtedness upon graduation:* $19,627. *Financial aid deadline:* 3/1.

Applying *Options:* common application, electronic application, early admission, early decision, deferred entrance. *Application fee:* $40. *Required:* essay or personal statement, high school transcript, 1 letter of recommendation. *Required for some:* interview. *Recommended:* interview. *Application deadlines:* 2/15 (freshmen), 4/1 (transfers). *Early decision:* 11/1. *Notification:* 3/31 (freshmen), 12/1 (early decision).

Admissions Contact Mr. John W. Lind, Vice President for Enrollment Management, Southwestern University, 1001 East University Avenue, Georgetown, TX 78626. *Phone:* 512-863-1200. *Toll-free phone:* 800-252-3166. *Fax:* 512-863-9601. *E-mail:* admission@southwestern.edu.

SOUTHWEST TEXAS STATE UNIVERSITY
San Marcos, Texas

- **State-supported** comprehensive, founded 1899, part of Texas State University System
- **Calendar** semesters
- **Degrees** bachelor's, master's, doctoral, and postbachelor's certificates
- **Small-town** 423-acre campus with easy access to San Antonio and Austin
- **Endowment** $18.4 million
- **Coed,** 20,179 undergraduate students, 80% full-time, 55% women, 45% men
- **Moderately difficult** entrance level, 58% of applicants were admitted

Undergraduates 16,090 full-time, 4,089 part-time. Students come from 47 states and territories, 76 other countries, 2% are from out of state, 5% African American, 2% Asian American or Pacific Islander, 19% Hispanic American, 0.5% Native American, 0.9% international, 13% transferred in, 21% live on campus. *Retention:* 74% of 2001 full-time freshmen returned.

Freshmen *Admission:* 9,354 applied, 5,400 admitted, 2,527 enrolled. *Test scores:* SAT verbal scores over 500: 61%; SAT math scores over 500: 64%; ACT scores over 18: 91%; SAT verbal scores over 600: 14%; SAT math scores over 600: 15%; ACT scores over 24: 26%; SAT verbal scores over 700: 1%; SAT math scores over 700: 1%; ACT scores over 30: 1%.

Faculty *Total:* 989, 68% full-time, 62% with terminal degrees. *Student/faculty ratio:* 25:1.

Majors Accounting; advertising; agribusiness; agricultural sciences; American studies; animal sciences; animal sciences related; anthropology; art; Asian studies; athletic training/sports medicine; biology; botany; broadcast journalism; business administration; business computer facilities operation; business economics; business marketing and marketing management; cartography; chemistry; city/community/regional planning; community health liaison; computer/information sciences; construction technology; corrections; criminal justice studies; dance; economics; engineering-related technology; engineering technology; English; environmental science; European studies; fashion merchandising; finance; fine/studio arts; French; geography; German; graphic design/commercial art/illustration; graphic/printing equipment; health facilities administration; health/physical education; health services administration; history; home economics; individual/family development; industrial/manufacturing engineering; industrial technology; interior architecture; international relations; jazz; journalism; law enforcement/police science; management information systems/business data processing; marine biology; mass communications; mathematics; medical radiologic technology; medical records administration; medical technology; microbiology/bacteriology; Middle Eastern studies; multi/interdisciplinary studies related; music; music (general performance); music related; nutrition studies; philosophy; physics; physiology; political science; psychology; public administration; public relations; recreation/leisure facilities management; respiratory therapy; Russian/Slavic studies; social work; sociology; Spanish; speech-language pathology/audiology; speech/rhetorical studies; theater arts/drama; zoology.

Academic Programs *Special study options:* academic remediation for entering students, accelerated degree program, adult/continuing education programs, advanced placement credit, distance learning, double majors, English as a second language, honors programs, independent study, internships, off-campus study, part-time degree program, services for LD students, study abroad, summer session for credit. *ROTC:* Army (b), Air Force (b). *Unusual degree programs:* 3-2 engineering with University of Texas at Austin, Texas A&M University, Texas Tech University, University of Texas at San Antonio; dentistry with University of Texas Health Science Center at San Antonio.

Library Alkek Library with 710,223 titles, 6,252 serial subscriptions, 276,299 audiovisual materials, an OPAC, a Web page.

Computers on Campus 731 computers available on campus for general student use. A campuswide network can be accessed from student residence rooms and from off campus. Internet access, at least one staffed computer lab available.
Student Life *Housing:* on-campus residence required through sophomore year. *Options:* coed, men-only, women-only. *Activities and Organizations:* drama/theater group, student-run newspaper, radio station, choral group, marching band, Non-traditional Students Association (NTSO), Panhellenic Council (PC), Student Association for Campus Activities (SACA), Association Student Government (ASG), Interfraternity Council (IFC), national fraternities, national sororities. *Campus security:* 24-hour emergency response devices and patrols, late-night transport/escort service, controlled dormitory access. *Student Services:* health clinic, personal/psychological counseling, legal services.
Athletics Member NCAA. All Division I except football (Division I-AA). *Intercollegiate sports:* baseball M(s), basketball M(s)/W(s), bowling M(c)/W(c), cross-country running M(s)/W(s), fencing M(c)/W(c), golf M(s), gymnastics M(c)/W(c), ice hockey M(c), lacrosse M(c)/W(c), rugby M(c), soccer M(c)/W(s)(c), softball W(s), tennis M(c)/W(s), track and field M(s)/W(s), volleyball M(c)/W(s). *Intramural sports:* basketball M/W, bowling M/W, cross-country running M/W, football M/W, golf M/W, racquetball M/W, soccer M/W, softball M/W, tennis M/W, volleyball M/W.
Standardized Tests *Required:* SAT I or ACT (for admission).
Costs (2001–02) *Tuition:* state resident $2520 full-time, $84 per semester hour part-time; nonresident $8850 full-time, $295 per semester hour part-time. Full-time tuition and fees vary according to course load. Part-time tuition and fees vary according to course load. *Required fees:* $1058 full-time, $14 per credit hour. *Room and board:* $5152; room only: $3126. Room and board charges vary according to board plan and housing facility. *Payment plan:* installment. *Waivers:* employees or children of employees.
Financial Aid Of all full-time matriculated undergraduates who enrolled in 2001, 9477 applied for aid, 6945 were judged to have need, 667 had their need fully met. 824 Federal Work-Study jobs (averaging $1485). 70 State and other part-time jobs (averaging $1046). In 2001, 2118 non-need-based awards were made. *Average percent of need met:* 69%. *Average financial aid package:* $6715. *Average need-based loan:* $3724. *Average need-based gift aid:* $2770. *Average indebtedness upon graduation:* $14,549.
Applying *Options:* electronic application, early admission, deferred entrance. *Application fee:* $40. *Required:* essay or personal statement, high school transcript. *Required for some:* interview. *Application deadlines:* 7/1 (freshmen), 7/1 (transfers). *Notification:* continuous (freshmen).
Admissions Contact Mrs. Christie Kangas, Director of Admissions, Southwest Texas State University, Admissions and Visitors Center, San Marcos, TX 78666. *Phone:* 512-245-2364 Ext. 2803. *Fax:* 512-245-8044. *E-mail:* admissions@swt.edu.

STEPHEN F. AUSTIN STATE UNIVERSITY
Nacogdoches, Texas

- **State-supported** comprehensive, founded 1923
- **Calendar** semesters
- **Degrees** bachelor's, master's, and doctoral
- **Small-town** 400-acre campus
- **Coed,** 10,283 undergraduate students, 88% full-time, 58% women, 42% men
- **Moderately difficult** entrance level, 67% of applicants were admitted

Undergraduates 9,001 full-time, 1,282 part-time. Students come from 31 states and territories, 54 other countries, 2% are from out of state, 15% African American, 0.9% Asian American or Pacific Islander, 6% Hispanic American, 0.5% Native American, 0.4% international, 9% transferred in, 35% live on campus. *Retention:* 60% of 2001 full-time freshmen returned.
Freshmen *Admission:* 9,621 applied, 6,486 admitted, 2,161 enrolled. *Test scores:* SAT verbal scores over 500: 46%; SAT math scores over 500: 47%; ACT scores over 18: 76%; SAT verbal scores over 600: 9%; SAT math scores over 600: 8%; ACT scores over 24: 18%; SAT verbal scores over 700: 1%; SAT math scores over 700: 1%.
Faculty *Total:* 582, 72% full-time, 65% with terminal degrees. *Student/faculty ratio:* 15:1.
Majors Accounting; agribusiness; agricultural mechanization; agricultural production; agricultural sciences; agronomy/crop science; animal sciences; art; art history; biology; business; business administration; business economics; business marketing and marketing management; chemistry; communications; community health liaison; computer/information sciences; conservation and renewable natural resources related; corrections; criminal justice studies; dance; data processing technology; economics; English; environmental science; fashion merchandising; finance; forest management; forestry; French; geography; geology; gerontology; health/physical education; hearing sciences; history; home economics; horticulture science; horticulture services; hospitality management; humanities; individual/family development; interdisciplinary studies; interior architecture; international business; journalism; law enforcement/police science; mathematics; medical technology; multi/interdisciplinary studies related; music; music (general performance); music teacher education; nursing; nutrition studies; office management; paralegal/legal assistant; physics; political science; poultry science; psychology; public administration; radio/television broadcasting; rehabilitation therapy; social sciences; social work; sociology; Spanish; speech-language pathology/audiology; speech/rhetorical studies; theater arts/drama; wildlife management.
Academic Programs *Special study options:* academic remediation for entering students, accelerated degree program, adult/continuing education programs, advanced placement credit, cooperative education, distance learning, double majors, English as a second language, freshman honors college, honors programs, independent study, internships, off-campus study, part-time degree program, services for LD students, student-designed majors, summer session for credit. *ROTC:* Army (b).
Library Ralph W. Steen Library with 694,812 titles, 4,083 serial subscriptions, 48,902 audiovisual materials, an OPAC, a Web page.
Computers on Campus 800 computers available on campus for general student use. A campuswide network can be accessed from student residence rooms and from off campus. Internet access, online (class) registration, at least one staffed computer lab available.
Student Life *Housing:* on-campus residence required through sophomore year. *Options:* coed, men-only, women-only, disabled students. *Activities and Organizations:* drama/theater group, student-run newspaper, radio and television station, choral group, marching band, Texas Student Education Association, American Marketing Association, Baptist Student Union, national fraternities, national sororities. *Campus security:* 24-hour emergency response devices and patrols, student patrols, late-night transport/escort service, controlled dormitory access. *Student Services:* health clinic, personal/psychological counseling, legal services.
Athletics Member NCAA. All Division I except football (Division I-AA). *Intercollegiate sports:* basketball M(s)/W(s), cross-country running M(s)/W(s), golf M(s), soccer W(s), softball W(s), tennis W(s), track and field M(s)/W(s), volleyball W(s). *Intramural sports:* badminton M/W, baseball M(c), cross-country running M/W, football M/W, lacrosse M(c), racquetball M(c)/W(c), rugby M(c)/W(c), soccer M(c), softball M/W, table tennis M/W, tennis M/W, volleyball M(c), water polo M/W, wrestling M(c)/W(c).
Standardized Tests *Required:* SAT I or ACT (for admission).
Costs (2001–02) *One-time required fee:* $10. *Tuition:* state resident $1728 full-time, $72 per semester hour part-time; nonresident $6792 full-time, $283 per semester hour part-time. Part-time tuition and fees vary according to course load. *Required fees:* $602 full-time, $22 per semester hour, $13 per term part-time. *Room and board:* $4575; room only: $2342. Room and board charges vary according to board plan and housing facility. *Payment plan:* installment.
Financial Aid Of all full-time matriculated undergraduates who enrolled in 2001, 5428 applied for aid, 3726 were judged to have need, 3160 had their need fully met. 515 Federal Work-Study jobs (averaging $1295). 47 State and other part-time jobs (averaging $1156). In 2001, 359 non-need-based awards were made. *Average percent of need met:* 72%. *Average financial aid package:* $6856. *Average need-based loan:* $3278. *Average need-based gift aid:* $3326. *Average non-need based aid:* $1365. *Average indebtedness upon graduation:* $6894.
Applying *Options:* common application. *Application fee:* $25. *Required:* high school transcript. *Application deadline:* rolling (freshmen), rolling (transfers).
Admissions Contact Ms. Beth Smith, Assistant Director of Admissions, Stephen F. Austin State University, SFA Box 13051, Nacogdoches, TX 75962. *Phone:* 936-468-2504. *Toll-free phone:* 800-259-9SFA. *Fax:* 936-468-3849. *E-mail:* admissions@sfasu.edu.

SUL ROSS STATE UNIVERSITY
Alpine, Texas

- **State-supported** comprehensive, founded 1920, part of Texas State University System
- **Calendar** semesters
- **Degrees** certificates, associate, bachelor's, and master's
- **Small-town** 640-acre campus
- **Endowment** $5.9 million
- **Coed,** 1,488 undergraduate students, 85% full-time, 48% women, 52% men
- **Noncompetitive** entrance level

Undergraduates 1,259 full-time, 229 part-time. Students come from 12 states and territories, 2 other countries, 2% are from out of state, 5% African American, 0.6% Asian American or Pacific Islander, 47% Hispanic American, 0.4% Native American, 0.4% international, 8% transferred in. *Retention:* 50% of 2001 full-time freshmen returned.

Sul Ross State University (continued)

Freshmen *Admission:* 339 admitted, 339 enrolled. *Test scores:* SAT verbal scores over 500: 19%; SAT math scores over 500: 19%; ACT scores over 18: 54%; SAT verbal scores over 600: 3%; SAT math scores over 600: 3%; ACT scores over 24: 6%; SAT verbal scores over 700: 1%.

Faculty *Total:* 113, 75% full-time, 69% with terminal degrees. *Student/faculty ratio:* 17:1.

Majors Accounting; agricultural animal health; agricultural business; animal sciences; art; biology; business administration; chemistry; criminal justice/law enforcement administration; elementary education; English; environmental science; equestrian studies; geology; history; industrial arts; mass communications; mathematics; Mexican-American studies; music; nursing; physical education; political science; pre-dentistry; pre-law; pre-medicine; pre-veterinary studies; psychology; range management; secretarial science; social sciences; Spanish; theater arts/drama; veterinary technology; wildlife management.

Academic Programs *Special study options:* academic remediation for entering students, advanced placement credit, distance learning, honors programs, internships, part-time degree program, summer session for credit.

Library Bryan Wildenthal Memorial Library with 262,466 titles, an OPAC, a Web page.

Computers on Campus 200 computers available on campus for general student use. A campuswide network can be accessed from student residence rooms and from off campus. Internet access, at least one staffed computer lab available.

Student Life *Housing:* on-campus residence required through sophomore year. *Options:* coed. *Activities and Organizations:* drama/theater group, student-run newspaper, radio station, choral group, Baptist Student Union, Wesley Center, rodeo club, Wildlife Society, MECHA. *Campus security:* 24-hour patrols, late-night transport/escort service. *Student Services:* health clinic, personal/psychological counseling.

Athletics Member NCAA. All Division III. *Intercollegiate sports:* baseball M, basketball M/W, football M, softball W, tennis M/W, track and field M/W, volleyball W. *Intramural sports:* basketball M/W, football M/W, softball M, volleyball M/W.

Standardized Tests *Required:* SAT I or ACT (for admission).

Costs (2001–02) *Tuition:* state resident $1920 full-time, $64 per credit part-time; nonresident $8250 full-time, $275 per credit part-time. *Required fees:* $872 full-time, $32 per credit, $71 per term part-time. *Room and board:* $3790.

Applying *Options:* early admission, deferred entrance. *Required:* high school transcript. *Recommended:* interview. *Application deadline:* rolling (freshmen), rolling (transfers). *Notification:* continuous (freshmen).

Admissions Contact Mr. Robert Cullins, Dean of Admissions and Records, Sul Ross State University, Box C-2, Alpine, TX 79832. *Phone:* 915-837-8050. *Fax:* 915-837-8431. *E-mail:* rcullins@sulross.edu.

TARLETON STATE UNIVERSITY
Stephenville, Texas

- **State-supported** comprehensive, founded 1899, part of Texas A&M University System
- **Calendar** semesters
- **Degrees** bachelor's and master's
- **Small-town** 165-acre campus with easy access to Dallas-Fort Worth
- **Endowment** $5.4 million
- **Coed,** 6,715 undergraduate students, 77% full-time, 54% women, 46% men
- **Moderately difficult** entrance level, 67% of applicants were admitted

Undergraduates 5,171 full-time, 1,544 part-time. Students come from 45 states and territories, 31 other countries, 4% are from out of state, 7% African American, 0.7% Asian American or Pacific Islander, 7% Hispanic American, 0.9% Native American, 0.6% international, 13% transferred in, 22% live on campus. *Retention:* 61% of 2001 full-time freshmen returned.

Freshmen *Admission:* 2,282 applied, 1,540 admitted, 1,128 enrolled. *Test scores:* SAT verbal scores over 500: 42%; SAT math scores over 500: 44%; ACT scores over 18: 83%; SAT verbal scores over 600: 9%; SAT math scores over 600: 10%; ACT scores over 24: 18%; SAT verbal scores over 700: 1%; SAT math scores over 700: 1%; ACT scores over 30: 2%.

Faculty *Total:* 428, 71% full-time, 54% with terminal degrees. *Student/faculty ratio:* 18:1.

Majors Accounting; agricultural business; agricultural economics; agricultural education; agricultural sciences; agricultural supplies; aircraft pilot (professional); animal sciences; art; art education; aviation management; biology; business administration; business education; business marketing and marketing management; chemistry; counselor education/guidance; criminal justice/law enforcement administration; dietetics; economics; education; education administration; elementary education; English; exercise sciences; farm/ranch management; fashion merchandising; finance; geology; history; home economics; horticulture science; human resources management; industrial arts; industrial technology; information sciences/systems; interdisciplinary studies; international agriculture; international business; liberal arts and sciences/liberal studies; management information systems/business data processing; mathematics; medical technology; music; music teacher education; nursing; office management; physical education; physics; political science; psychology; range management; science education; social work; sociology; Spanish; speech/rhetorical studies; theater arts/drama; water resources; zoology.

Academic Programs *Special study options:* academic remediation for entering students, accelerated degree program, adult/continuing education programs, advanced placement credit, cooperative education, distance learning, double majors, honors programs, internships, off-campus study, part-time degree program, services for LD students, study abroad, summer session for credit. *ROTC:* Army (b).

Library Dick Smith Library plus 1 other with 288,000 titles, 2,198 serial subscriptions, 6,945 audiovisual materials, a Web page.

Computers on Campus 500 computers available on campus for general student use. A campuswide network can be accessed from off campus. Internet access, online (class) registration, at least one staffed computer lab available.

Student Life *Housing:* on-campus residence required through sophomore year. *Options:* coed, men-only, women-only. *Activities and Organizations:* drama/theater group, student-run newspaper, choral group, marching band, Student Government Association, Student Programming Association, Plowboys Association, Student Organizational Forum, Tarleton Association of Student Leaders, national fraternities, national sororities. *Campus security:* 24-hour emergency response devices and patrols, late-night transport/escort service. *Student Services:* health clinic, personal/psychological counseling, legal services.

Athletics Member NCAA. All Division II. *Intercollegiate sports:* baseball M(s), basketball M(s)/W(s), cross-country running M/W, football M(s), golf W, softball W(s), tennis W, track and field M(s)/W(s), volleyball W(s). *Intramural sports:* archery M/W, basketball M/W, football M/W, golf M/W, racquetball M/W, softball M/W, tennis M/W, volleyball M/W.

Standardized Tests *Required:* SAT I or ACT (for admission).

Costs (2001–02) *Tuition:* state resident $2160 full-time, $72 per semester hour part-time; nonresident $8490 full-time, $283 per semester hour part-time. Full-time tuition and fees vary according to course load. Part-time tuition and fees vary according to course load. *Required fees:* $760 full-time, $40 per semester hour, $25 per term part-time. *Room and board:* $4486; room only: $2470. Room and board charges vary according to board plan and housing facility. *Payment plan:* installment. *Waivers:* senior citizens and employees or children of employees.

Financial Aid Of all full-time matriculated undergraduates who enrolled in 2001, 3426 applied for aid, 2702 were judged to have need, 2269 had their need fully met. 73 Federal Work-Study jobs, 10 State and other part-time jobs (averaging $3300). *Average percent of need met:* 61%. *Average financial aid package:* $6323. *Average need-based loan:* $3258. *Average need-based gift aid:* $2461. *Average indebtedness upon graduation:* $15,522.

Applying *Options:* electronic application, early admission, deferred entrance. *Application fee:* $25. *Required:* high school transcript. *Required for some:* interview. *Application deadlines:* 8/1 (freshmen), 8/1 (transfers).

Admissions Contact Ms. Denise Siler, Director of Admissions, Tarleton State University, Box T-0030, Tarleton Station, Stephenville, TX 76402. *Phone:* 254-968-9125. *Toll-free phone:* 800-687-4878. *Fax:* 254-968-9951.

TEXAS A&M INTERNATIONAL UNIVERSITY
Laredo, Texas

- **State-supported** comprehensive, founded 1969, part of Texas A&M University System
- **Calendar** semesters
- **Degrees** bachelor's and master's
- **Urban** 300-acre campus
- **Endowment** $4.4 million
- **Coed,** 2,609 undergraduate students, 64% full-time, 64% women, 36% men
- **Moderately difficult** entrance level, 92% of applicants were admitted

Undergraduates 1,682 full-time, 927 part-time. Students come from 30 states and territories, 9 other countries, 1% are from out of state, 0.4% African American, 0.2% Asian American or Pacific Islander, 94% Hispanic American, 0.1% Native American, 3% international, 9% transferred in. *Retention:* 66% of 2001 full-time freshmen returned.

Freshmen *Admission:* 378 applied, 349 admitted, 417 enrolled. *Average high school GPA:* 3.00. *Test scores:* SAT verbal scores over 500: 28%; SAT math scores

over 500: 34%; SAT verbal scores over 600: 8%; SAT math scores over 600: 8%; SAT verbal scores over 700: 1%; SAT math scores over 700: 1%.

Faculty *Total:* 196, 62% with terminal degrees. *Student/faculty ratio:* 12:1.

Majors Accounting; bilingual/bicultural education; biology; biology education; business administration; business economics; business marketing and marketing management; chemistry; communications; criminal justice studies; early childhood education; English; English education; finance; health/physical education; history; history education; information sciences/systems; mathematics; mathematics education; nursing; nursing (surgical); physical education; physical sciences; political science; psychology; reading education; science education; social sciences; social studies education; sociology; Spanish; Spanish language education; special education.

Academic Programs *Special study options:* academic remediation for entering students, advanced placement credit, English as a second language, honors programs, internships, part-time degree program, services for LD students, study abroad, summer session for credit.

Library Sue and Radcliff Killam Library with 166,951 titles, 8,492 serial subscriptions, 1,040 audiovisual materials, an OPAC, a Web page.

Computers on Campus 200 computers available on campus for general student use. A campuswide network can be accessed from off campus. At least one staffed computer lab available.

Student Life *Activities and Organizations:* student-run newspaper, choral group, TAMIU Ambassadors, Electronic Commerce Association, Rainbow Education Association of Laredo, Student Finance Society, Psychology Club. *Campus security:* 24-hour emergency response devices and patrols. *Student Services:* health clinic, personal/psychological counseling.

Standardized Tests *Required:* SAT I or ACT (for admission).

Costs (2002–03) *Tuition:* state resident $2220 full-time, $74 per credit part-time; nonresident $8490 full-time, $283 per credit part-time. Full-time tuition and fees vary according to course load. Part-time tuition and fees vary according to course load. *Required fees:* $649 full-time, $22 per credit. *Room and board:* room only: $3210. *Payment plan:* installment. *Waivers:* senior citizens and employees or children of employees.

Financial Aid Of all full-time matriculated undergraduates who enrolled in 2001, 2280 applied for aid, 1709 were judged to have need, 940 had their need fully met. 4 State and other part-time jobs (averaging $3000). *Average percent of need met:* 55%. *Average financial aid package:* $9438. *Average need-based gift aid:* $1000. *Average indebtedness upon graduation:* $10,000.

Applying *Options:* common application, electronic application, early admission, deferred entrance. *Required:* high school transcript. *Application deadlines:* 7/1 (freshmen), 7/1 (transfers). *Notification:* 7/15 (freshmen).

Admissions Contact Ms. Veronica Gonzalez, Director of Enrollment Management and School Relations, Texas A&M International University, 5201 University Boulevard, Laredo, TX 78041-1900. *Phone:* 956-326-2270. *Fax:* 956-326-2199. *E-mail:* enroll@tamiu.edu.

TEXAS A&M UNIVERSITY
College Station, Texas

- **State-supported** university, founded 1876, part of Texas A&M University System
- **Calendar** semesters
- **Degrees** bachelor's, master's, doctoral, first professional, and postbachelor's certificates
- **Suburban** 5200-acre campus with easy access to Houston
- **Endowment** $4.0 billion
- **Coed,** 36,603 undergraduate students, 92% full-time, 49% women, 51% men
- **Moderately difficult** entrance level, 69% of applicants were admitted

Undergraduates 33,776 full-time, 2,827 part-time. Students come from 52 states and territories, 111 other countries, 4% are from out of state, 2% African American, 3% Asian American or Pacific Islander, 9% Hispanic American, 0.5% Native American, 1% international, 5% transferred in, 14% live on campus. *Retention:* 88% of 2001 full-time freshmen returned.

Freshmen *Admission:* 16,685 applied, 11,531 admitted, 6,760 enrolled. *Test scores:* SAT verbal scores over 500: 80%; SAT math scores over 500: 90%; ACT scores over 18: 98%; SAT verbal scores over 600: 40%; SAT math scores over 600: 50%; ACT scores over 24: 65%; SAT verbal scores over 700: 7%; SAT math scores over 700: 13%; ACT scores over 30: 15%.

Faculty *Total:* 2,178, 86% full-time, 87% with terminal degrees. *Student/faculty ratio:* 22:1.

Majors Accounting; aerospace engineering; agribusiness; agricultural animal breeding; agricultural animal husbandry/production management; agricultural business; agricultural economics; agricultural engineering; agricultural mechanization; agricultural sciences; agronomy/crop science; American studies; animal sciences; anthropology; applied mathematics; aquaculture operations/production management; architectural environmental design; atmospheric sciences; biochemistry; bioengineering; biological/physical sciences; biology; botany; business administration; business marketing and marketing management; cell biology; chemical engineering; chemistry; civil engineering; community health liaison; computer engineering; computer/information sciences; construction technology; curriculum and instruction; dairy science; earth sciences; economics; electrical engineering; engineering-related technology; English; entomology; environmental science; finance; food sciences; foreign languages/literatures; forestry; French; genetics; geography; geology; geophysics/seismology; German; health education; health/physical education; history; horticulture services; industrial/manufacturing engineering; interdisciplinary studies; journalism; landscape architecture; logistics/materials management; mathematics; mechanical engineering; microbiology/bacteriology; molecular biology; music; natural resources conservation; nuclear engineering; nutrition studies; ocean engineering; operations research; ornamental horticulture; petroleum engineering; philosophy; physics; plant sciences; political science; poultry science; psychology; range management; recreation/leisure facilities management; Russian; sales operations; sociology; Spanish; speech/rhetorical studies; theater arts/drama; zoology.

Academic Programs *Special study options:* academic remediation for entering students, advanced placement credit, cooperative education, distance learning, double majors, English as a second language, honors programs, independent study, internships, off-campus study, part-time degree program, services for LD students, study abroad, summer session for credit. *ROTC:* Army (b), Navy (b), Air Force (b).

Library Sterling C. Evans Library plus 4 others with 1.5 million titles, 26,625 serial subscriptions, 253,951 audiovisual materials, an OPAC, a Web page.

Computers on Campus 1500 computers available on campus for general student use. A campuswide network can be accessed from student residence rooms and from off campus. At least one staffed computer lab available.

Student Life *Housing Options:* coed, men-only, women-only, disabled students. *Activities and Organizations:* drama/theater group, student-run newspaper, radio and television station, choral group, marching band, Memorial Student Center, Corps of Cadets, Greek organizations, Fish Camp, student government, national fraternities, national sororities. *Campus security:* 24-hour emergency response devices and patrols, late-night transport/escort service, controlled dormitory access, student escorts. *Student Services:* health clinic, personal/psychological counseling, women's center, legal services.

Athletics Member NCAA. All Division I except football (Division I-A). *Intercollegiate sports:* archery W(s), baseball M(s), basketball M(s)/W(s), cross-country running M(s)/W(s), equestrian sports W, golf M(s)/W(s), soccer W(s), softball W(s), swimming M(s)/W(s), tennis M(s)/W(s), track and field M(s)/W(s), volleyball W(s). *Intramural sports:* archery M/W, badminton M/W, basketball M/W, bowling M/W, cross-country running M/W, fencing M(c)/W(c), field hockey M(c)/W(c), football M/W, golf M/W, gymnastics M(c)/W(c), lacrosse M(c)/W(c), racquetball M(c)/W(c), riflery M/W, rugby M(c)/W(c), sailing M(c)/W(c), soccer M/W, softball M/W, squash M/W, swimming M/W, table tennis M/W, tennis M/W, track and field M/W, volleyball M/W, water polo M/W, weight lifting M(c)/W(c), wrestling M(c).

Standardized Tests *Required:* SAT I or ACT (for admission).

Costs (2001–02) *Tuition:* state resident $2520 full-time, $84 per credit hour part-time; nonresident $8850 full-time, $295 per credit hour part-time. Full-time tuition and fees vary according to course load, location, and program. *Required fees:* $1202 full-time. *Room and board:* $5266; room only: $2754. Room and board charges vary according to board plan and housing facility. *Payment plan:* installment. *Waivers:* employees or children of employees.

Financial Aid Of all full-time matriculated undergraduates who enrolled in 2001, 14337 applied for aid, 9525 were judged to have need, 8647 had their need fully met. In 2001, 4173 non-need-based awards were made. *Average percent of need met:* 81%. *Average financial aid package:* $8016. *Average need-based loan:* $3411. *Average need-based gift aid:* $4694. *Average non-need based aid:* $6442. *Average indebtedness upon graduation:* $13,143.

Applying *Options:* electronic application. *Application fee:* $50. *Required:* essay or personal statement, high school transcript. *Application deadlines:* 2/15 (freshmen), 4/1 (transfers). *Notification:* continuous (freshmen).

Admissions Contact Texas A&M University, 217 John J. Koldus Building, College Station, TX 77843-1265. *Phone:* 979-845-3741. *Fax:* 979-845-8737. *E-mail:* admissions@tamu.edu.

TEXAS A&M UNIVERSITY AT GALVESTON
Galveston, Texas

- **State-supported** 4-year, founded 1962, part of Texas A&M University System

Texas A&M University at Galveston (continued)

- **Calendar** semesters
- **Degree** bachelor's
- **Suburban** 100-acre campus with easy access to Houston
- **Endowment** $1.4 million
- **Coed,** 1,366 undergraduate students, 90% full-time, 51% women, 49% men
- **Moderately difficult** entrance level, 87% of applicants were admitted

Undergraduates 1,235 full-time, 131 part-time. Students come from 50 states and territories, 22% are from out of state, 1% African American, 2% Asian American or Pacific Islander, 9% Hispanic American, 0.8% Native American, 0.5% international, 11% transferred in, 54% live on campus. *Retention:* 70% of 2001 full-time freshmen returned.

Freshmen *Admission:* 895 applied, 783 admitted, 405 enrolled. *Test scores:* SAT verbal scores over 500: 64%; SAT math scores over 500: 67%; ACT scores over 18: 90%; SAT verbal scores over 600: 21%; SAT math scores over 600: 19%; ACT scores over 24: 31%; SAT verbal scores over 700: 2%; SAT math scores over 700: 1%; ACT scores over 30: 2%.

Faculty *Total:* 129, 83% with terminal degrees. *Student/faculty ratio:* 16:1.

Majors Business administration; fish/game management; marine biology; marine science; maritime science; naval architecture/marine engineering; ocean engineering; oceanography; transportation technology.

Academic Programs *Special study options:* academic remediation for entering students, accelerated degree program, advanced placement credit, cooperative education, double majors, English as a second language, independent study, internships, part-time degree program, study abroad, summer session for credit. *ROTC:* Navy (b).

Library Jack K. Williams Library with 61,436 titles, an OPAC, a Web page.

Computers on Campus 122 computers available on campus for general student use. A campuswide network can be accessed from student residence rooms and from off campus. At least one staffed computer lab available.

Student Life *Housing:* on-campus residence required through sophomore year. *Options:* coed, men-only, women-only, disabled students. *Activities and Organizations:* drama/theater group, student-run newspaper, choral group, Sail Club, Caving Club, Dive Club, Rowing Club, Drill Team. *Campus security:* 24-hour emergency response devices and patrols. *Student Services:* health clinic, personal/psychological counseling.

Athletics *Intercollegiate sports:* crew M/W, lacrosse M, sailing M/W. *Intramural sports:* basketball M, football M/W, golf M/W, rugby M, soccer M, softball M/W, table tennis M/W, tennis M/W, volleyball M/W, water polo M.

Standardized Tests *Required:* SAT I or ACT (for admission). *Recommended:* SAT II: Subject Tests (for admission), SAT II: Writing Test (for admission).

Costs (2001–02) *Tuition:* state resident $1260 full-time, $42 per credit hour part-time; nonresident $7590 full-time, $253 per credit hour part-time. Part-time tuition and fees vary according to program. *Required fees:* $1983 full-time, $1983 per year part-time. *Room and board:* $3977; room only: $1780. Room and board charges vary according to board plan. *Payment plan:* installment.

Financial Aid Of all full-time matriculated undergraduates who enrolled in 2001, 623 applied for aid, 539 were judged to have need, 284 had their need fully met. In 2001, 33 non-need-based awards were made. *Average percent of need met:* 74%. *Average financial aid package:* $6161. *Average need-based loan:* $2040. *Average need-based gift aid:* $2885. *Average non-need based aid:* $3651. *Average indebtedness upon graduation:* $7885.

Applying *Options:* electronic application, early admission, deferred entrance. *Application fee:* $35. *Required:* high school transcript. *Required for some:* interview. *Recommended:* essay or personal statement, letters of recommendation. *Application deadline:* rolling (freshmen), rolling (transfers). *Notification:* continuous (freshmen).

Admissions Contact Sarah Wilson, Academic Advisor II, Texas A&M University at Galveston, PO Box 1675, Galveston, TX 77553-1675. *Phone:* 409-740-4448. *Toll-free phone:* 87—SEAAGIE. *Fax:* 409-740-4731. *E-mail:* seaaggie@tamug.tamu.edu.

TEXAS A&M UNIVERSITY-COMMERCE

Commerce, Texas

- **State-supported** university, founded 1889, part of Texas A&M University System
- **Calendar** semesters
- **Degrees** bachelor's, master's, and doctoral
- **Small-town** 140-acre campus with easy access to Dallas-Fort Worth
- **Endowment** $8.0 million
- **Coed,** 4,448 undergraduate students, 78% full-time, 59% women, 41% men
- **Moderately difficult** entrance level, 63% of applicants were admitted

Undergraduates Students come from 29 states and territories, 25 other countries, 4% are from out of state, 16% African American, 0.9% Asian American or Pacific Islander, 5% Hispanic American, 1% Native American, 0.9% international, 24% live on campus. *Retention:* 65% of 2001 full-time freshmen returned.

Freshmen *Admission:* 1,485 applied, 942 admitted. *Test scores:* SAT verbal scores over 500: 49%; SAT math scores over 500: 42%; ACT scores over 18: 81%; SAT verbal scores over 600: 10%; SAT math scores over 600: 12%; ACT scores over 24: 20%; SAT verbal scores over 700: 1%; SAT math scores over 700: 1%; ACT scores over 30: 1%.

Faculty *Total:* 518, 47% full-time, 38% with terminal degrees. *Student/faculty ratio:* 17:1.

Majors Accounting; advertising; agricultural economics; agricultural education; agricultural sciences; agronomy/crop science; animal sciences; anthropology; art; art education; art history; biology; business administration; business education; business marketing and marketing management; chemistry; computer science; construction engineering; counselor education/guidance; criminal justice/law enforcement administration; drawing; early childhood education; earth sciences; economics; education; elementary education; English; finance; French; geography; geology; graphic design/commercial art/illustration; graphic/printing equipment; health education; history; human resources management; industrial arts; industrial/manufacturing engineering; information sciences/systems; interdisciplinary studies; journalism; labor/personnel relations; law enforcement/police science; legal administrative assistant; liberal arts and sciences/liberal studies; management information systems/business data processing; mathematics; music; music (piano and organ performance); music teacher education; music (voice and choral/opera performance); photography; physical education; physics; political science; psychology; radio/television broadcasting; reading education; sculpture; secondary education; secretarial science; social sciences; social work; sociology; Spanish; special education; theater arts/drama; trade/industrial education.

Academic Programs *Special study options:* academic remediation for entering students, adult/continuing education programs, advanced placement credit, cooperative education, distance learning, double majors, honors programs, independent study, internships, off-campus study, part-time degree program, services for LD students, study abroad, summer session for credit. *Unusual degree programs:* 3-2 engineering with Texas A&M University.

Library Gee Library with 2.7 million titles, 1,779 serial subscriptions, 44,492 audiovisual materials, an OPAC, a Web page.

Computers on Campus 405 computers available on campus for general student use. A campuswide network can be accessed from student residence rooms and from off campus. Internet access, online (class) registration, at least one staffed computer lab available.

Student Life *Housing:* on-campus residence required for freshman year. *Options:* coed, men-only, women-only, disabled students. *Activities and Organizations:* drama/theater group, student-run newspaper, radio and television station, choral group, marching band, national fraternities, national sororities. *Campus security:* 24-hour emergency response devices and patrols, controlled dormitory access. *Student Services:* health clinic, personal/psychological counseling, legal services.

Athletics Member NCAA. All Division II. *Intercollegiate sports:* basketball M(s)/W(s), cross-country running M(s)/W(s), football M(s), golf M(s)/W(s), soccer W(s), track and field M(s)/W(s), volleyball W(s). *Intramural sports:* badminton M/W, basketball M/W, cross-country running M/W, football M/W, racquetball M/W, soccer M, softball M/W, table tennis M/W, tennis M/W, track and field M/W, volleyball M/W.

Standardized Tests *Required:* SAT I or ACT (for admission).

Costs (2001–02) *Tuition:* state resident $2776 full-time, $145 per semester hour part-time; nonresident $9106 full-time, $356 per semester hour part-time. Full-time tuition and fees vary according to course load. Part-time tuition and fees vary according to course load. *Room and board:* $4800. Room and board charges vary according to board plan and housing facility. *Payment plan:* installment. *Waivers:* senior citizens.

Applying *Options:* common application, early admission. *Required:* high school transcript. *Application deadline:* 8/1 (freshmen), rolling (transfers). *Notification:* continuous (freshmen).

Admissions Contact Mr. Randy McDonald, Director of School Relations, Texas A&M University-Commerce, PO Box 3011, Commerce, TX 75429. *Phone:* 903-886-5072. *Toll-free phone:* 800-331-3878. *Fax:* 903-886-5888. *E-mail:* admissions@tamu-commerce.edu.

TEXAS A&M UNIVERSITY-CORPUS CHRISTI

Corpus Christi, Texas

- **State-supported** comprehensive, founded 1947, part of Texas A&M University System

- **Calendar** semesters
- **Degrees** bachelor's, master's, and doctoral
- **Suburban** 240-acre campus
- **Endowment** $2.6 million
- **Coed,** 5,966 undergraduate students, 77% full-time, 59% women, 41% men
- **Moderately difficult** entrance level, 89% of applicants were admitted

Undergraduates 4,567 full-time, 1,399 part-time. Students come from 35 states and territories, 22 other countries, 2% are from out of state, 2% African American, 2% Asian American or Pacific Islander, 37% Hispanic American, 0.4% Native American, 0.8% international, 16% transferred in, 14% live on campus. *Retention:* 71% of 2001 full-time freshmen returned.

Freshmen *Admission:* 2,880 applied, 2,552 admitted, 1,055 enrolled. *Test scores:* SAT verbal scores over 500: 52%; SAT math scores over 500: 54%; ACT scores over 18: 80%; SAT verbal scores over 600: 11%; SAT math scores over 600: 11%; ACT scores over 24: 19%; SAT verbal scores over 700: 1%; SAT math scores over 700: 1%; ACT scores over 30: 1%.

Faculty *Total:* 304, 79% full-time, 69% with terminal degrees. *Student/faculty ratio:* 22:1.

Majors Accounting; art; biology; business administration; business marketing and marketing management; cartography; chemistry; communications; computer science; criminal justice/law enforcement administration; engineering technology; English; environmental science; finance; fine/studio arts; geology; health science; history; information sciences/systems; interdisciplinary studies; mathematics; medical technology; music; nursing; physical education; political science; psychology; sociology; Spanish; surveying; trade/industrial education.

Academic Programs *Special study options:* academic remediation for entering students, advanced placement credit, cooperative education, distance learning, double majors, independent study, internships, off-campus study, part-time degree program, services for LD students, summer session for credit. *ROTC:* Army (b).

Library Mary and Jeff Bell Library with 319,757 titles, 1,901 serial subscriptions, 6,012 audiovisual materials, an OPAC, a Web page.

Computers on Campus 300 computers available on campus for general student use. A campuswide network can be accessed from off campus. At least one staffed computer lab available.

Student Life *Housing Options:* coed, men-only, women-only. *Activities and Organizations:* drama/theater group, student-run newspaper, choral group, marching band, Student Accounting Society, Student Art Association, science clubs, national fraternities, national sororities. *Campus security:* 24-hour emergency response devices and patrols, late-night transport/escort service, security gate access with card after 10 p.m. *Student Services:* health clinic, personal/psychological counseling, women's center.

Athletics Member NCAA. *Intercollegiate sports:* baseball M(s), basketball M(s)/W(s), golf W, softball W, tennis M/W, track and field M/W, volleyball W. *Intramural sports:* baseball M/W, basketball M/W, cross-country running M/W, football M/W, golf M/W, racquetball M/W, sailing M/W, soccer M/W, softball M/W, swimming M/W, tennis M/W, track and field M/W, volleyball M/W.

Standardized Tests *Required:* SAT I or ACT (for admission).

Costs (2002–03) *Tuition:* state resident $2340 full-time, $78 per credit part-time; nonresident $8670 full-time, $289 per credit part-time. Full-time tuition and fees vary according to course load. Part-time tuition and fees vary according to course load. No tuition increase for student's term of enrollment. *Required fees:* $698 full-time. *Room and board:* $7020; room only: $4860. Room and board charges vary according to housing facility. *Payment plans:* installment, deferred payment. *Waivers:* employees or children of employees.

Financial Aid Of all full-time matriculated undergraduates who enrolled in 2001, 2887 applied for aid, 2310 were judged to have need, 245 had their need fully met. 6 State and other part-time jobs (averaging $2400). In 2001, 585 non-need-based awards were made. *Average percent of need met:* 75%. *Average financial aid package:* $5751. *Average need-based loan:* $3558. *Average need-based gift aid:* $3455. *Financial aid deadline:* 4/1.

Applying *Application fee:* $20. *Required:* high school transcript, minimum 2.0 GPA. *Application deadline:* rolling (freshmen), rolling (transfers).

Admissions Contact Ms. Margaret Dechant, Director of Admissions, Texas A&M University-Corpus Christi, 6300 Ocean Drive, Corpus Christi, TX 78412-5503. *Phone:* 361-825-2414. *Toll-free phone:* 800-482-6822. *Fax:* 361-825-5887. *E-mail:* judith.perales@mail.tamucc.edu.

TEXAS A&M UNIVERSITY-KINGSVILLE

Kingsville, Texas

- **State-supported** university, founded 1925, part of Texas A&M University System
- **Calendar** semesters
- **Degrees** bachelor's, master's, doctoral, and post-master's certificates
- **Small-town** 255-acre campus
- **Coed,** 5,008 undergraduate students, 78% full-time, 49% women, 51% men
- **Moderately difficult** entrance level, 99% of applicants were admitted

Undergraduates 3,883 full-time, 1,125 part-time. Students come from 37 states and territories, 58 other countries, 2% are from out of state, 5% African American, 0.5% Asian American or Pacific Islander, 66% Hispanic American, 0.2% Native American, 2% international, 9% transferred in, 30% live on campus. *Retention:* 61% of 2001 full-time freshmen returned.

Freshmen *Admission:* 1,420 applied, 1,400 admitted, 880 enrolled. *Average high school GPA:* 3.34. *Test scores:* SAT verbal scores over 500: 22%; SAT math scores over 500: 31%; ACT scores over 18: 54%; SAT verbal scores over 600: 4%; SAT math scores over 600: 5%; ACT scores over 24: 9%; SAT math scores over 700: 1%.

Faculty *Total:* 365, 75% full-time, 64% with terminal degrees. *Student/faculty ratio:* 16:1.

Majors Accounting; agricultural business; agricultural education; agricultural sciences; agronomy/crop science; animal sciences; anthropology; art; bilingual/bicultural education; biology; business administration; business economics; business marketing and marketing management; chemical engineering; chemistry; child care/development; civil engineering; computer science; criminology; dietetics; early childhood education; economics; education; electrical engineering; elementary education; English; environmental engineering; fashion merchandising; finance; fish/game management; food sciences; geography; geology; health education; history; home economics; home economics education; horticulture science; hotel and restaurant management; human services; industrial/manufacturing engineering; industrial technology; information sciences/systems; interior design; international business; journalism; mass communications; mathematics; mechanical engineering; music; music teacher education; nutrition science; petroleum engineering; physical education; physics; political science; pre-dentistry; pre-law; pre-medicine; pre-veterinary studies; psychology; public administration; range management; real estate; secondary education; social work; sociology; Spanish; speech/rhetorical studies; speech therapy; theater arts/drama; wildlife management.

Academic Programs *Special study options:* academic remediation for entering students, adult/continuing education programs, advanced placement credit, cooperative education, distance learning, double majors, English as a second language, internships, part-time degree program, services for LD students, study abroad, summer session for credit. *ROTC:* Army (b).

Library James C. Jernigan Library with 358,466 titles, 2,304 serial subscriptions, 3,224 audiovisual materials, an OPAC.

Computers on Campus 600 computers available on campus for general student use. A campuswide network can be accessed from student residence rooms and from off campus. At least one staffed computer lab available.

Student Life *Housing:* on-campus residence required through sophomore year. *Options:* coed, men-only, women-only. *Activities and Organizations:* drama/theater group, student-run newspaper, radio and television station, choral group, marching band, Aggie Club, rodeo club, educational association, child development club, resident's hall club, national fraternities, national sororities. *Campus security:* 24-hour emergency response devices and patrols, late-night transport/escort service. *Student Services:* health clinic, personal/psychological counseling, women's center.

Athletics Member NCAA, NAIA. All NCAA Division II. *Intercollegiate sports:* baseball M(s), basketball M(s)/W(s), cross-country running M(s)/W(s), equestrian sports M/W, football M(s), riflery M/W, softball W(s), tennis M(s)/W(s), track and field M(s)/W(s), volleyball W(s). *Intramural sports:* badminton M/W, basketball M/W, bowling M/W, fencing M/W, football M/W, golf M/W, racquetball M/W, soccer M/W, swimming M/W, tennis M/W, volleyball W, weight lifting M/W.

Standardized Tests *Required for some:* SAT I or ACT (for admission).

Costs (2001–02) *Tuition:* state resident $2862 full-time, $227 per credit hour part-time; nonresident $9192 full-time, $360 per credit hour part-time. *Room and board:* $3584.

Financial Aid Of all full-time matriculated undergraduates who enrolled in 2001, 4200 applied for aid, 3800 were judged to have need, 3658 had their need fully met. *Average percent of need met:* 86%. *Average financial aid package:* $6575. *Average need-based loan:* $3500. *Average indebtedness upon graduation:* $23,000.

Applying *Options:* common application, early admission, deferred entrance. *Application fee:* $15. *Required:* high school transcript. *Required for some:* interview. *Recommended:* minimum 2.0 GPA. *Application deadline:* rolling (freshmen), rolling (transfers). *Notification:* continuous (freshmen).

Texas A&M University-Kingsville (continued)

Admissions Contact Texas A&M University-Kingsville, Campus Box 105, Kingsville, TX 78363. *Phone:* 361-593-2811. *Toll-free phone:* 800-687-6000. *Fax:* 361-593-2195.

TEXAS A&M UNIVERSITY SYSTEM HEALTH SCIENCE CENTER

College Station, Texas

- **State-supported** upper-level, founded 1999
- **Calendar** semesters
- **Degrees** bachelor's, master's, doctoral, first professional, post-master's, and first professional certificates (Profile only includes information for the Baylor College of Dentistry)
- **Coed,** 60 undergraduate students, 100% full-time, 97% women, 3% men

Undergraduates 60 full-time. 1% are from out of state, 3% African American, 3% Asian American or Pacific Islander, 12% Hispanic American.

Majors Dental hygiene.

Academic Programs *Special study options:* services for LD students.

Library Baylor Hospital.

Student Life *Housing:* college housing not available. *Campus security:* 24-hour emergency response devices and patrols, late-night transport/escort service, electronically operated building access. *Student Services:* health clinic, personal/psychological counseling.

Costs (2001–02) *Tuition:* state resident $1500 full-time; nonresident $8600 full-time. *Required fees:* $3530 full-time.

Applying *Application fee:* $35. *Application deadline:* rolling (transfers).

Admissions Contact Dr. Jack L. Long, Director of Admissions and Records, Texas A&M University System Health Science Center, PO Box 660677, Dallas, TX 75266-0677. *Phone:* 214-828-8230. *Fax:* 214-874-4567.

TEXAS A&M UNIVERSITY-TEXARKANA

Texarkana, Texas

- **State-supported** upper-level, founded 1971, part of Texas A&M University System
- **Calendar** semesters
- **Degrees** bachelor's and master's
- **Small-town** 1-acre campus
- **Coed,** 828 undergraduate students
- **Noncompetitive** entrance level

Undergraduates Students come from 4 states and territories.

Faculty *Total:* 73, 55% full-time, 63% with terminal degrees. *Student/faculty ratio:* 14:1.

Majors Accounting; biology; business; business administration; business marketing and marketing management; criminal justice studies; English; finance; general studies; history; human resources management; interdisciplinary studies; international business; management information systems/business data processing; mathematics; psychology.

Academic Programs *Special study options:* advanced placement credit, distance learning, independent study, internships, part-time degree program, services for LD students, student-designed majors, summer session for credit.

Library John F. Moss Library plus 1 other with 325,388 titles, 164,250 serial subscriptions, 3,620 audiovisual materials, an OPAC, a Web page.

Computers on Campus 170 computers available on campus for general student use. A campuswide network can be accessed from off campus. Internet access, online (class) registration, at least one staffed computer lab available.

Student Life *Housing:* college housing not available. *Activities and Organizations:* student-run newspaper, Education Club, Psychology Club, Science Club, Multicultural Association, Reading Club. *Campus security:* 24-hour patrols, late-night transport/escort service.

Costs (2001–02) *One-time required fee:* $10. *Tuition:* state resident $1536 full-time, $64 per credit hour part-time; nonresident $6600 full-time, $84 per credit hour part-time. Part-time tuition and fees vary according to course load. *Required fees:* $360 full-time, $15 per credit hour, $6 per term part-time. *Payment plan:* installment. *Waivers:* senior citizens.

Financial Aid Of all full-time matriculated undergraduates who enrolled in 2001, 143 applied for aid, 126 were judged to have need. 19 Federal Work-Study jobs (averaging $1106).

Applying *Options:* common application, electronic application. *Application deadline:* rolling (transfers). *Notification:* continuous (transfers).

Admissions Contact Mrs. Patricia E. Black, Director of Admissions and Registrar, Texas A&M University-Texarkana, PO Box 5518, Texarkana, TX 75505-5518. *Phone:* 903-223-3068. *Fax:* 903-223-3140. *E-mail:* admissions@tamut.edu.

TEXAS CHIROPRACTIC COLLEGE

Pasadena, Texas

Admissions Contact Mr. Robert Cooper, Director of Admissions, Texas Chiropractic College, 5912 Spencer Highway, Pasadena, TX 77505-1699. *Phone:* 281-998-6017. *Toll-free phone:* 800-468-6839.

TEXAS CHRISTIAN UNIVERSITY

Fort Worth, Texas

- **Independent** university, founded 1873, affiliated with Christian Church (Disciples of Christ)
- **Calendar** semesters
- **Degrees** certificates, diplomas, bachelor's, master's, doctoral, and first professional
- **Suburban** 237-acre campus
- **Endowment** $1.0 billion
- **Coed,** 6,885 undergraduate students, 92% full-time, 57% women, 43% men
- **Moderately difficult** entrance level, 72% of applicants were admitted

TCU's mission—to educate individuals to think and act as ethical leaders and responsible citizens in the global community—influences every area of this person-centered private university. From leadership development to one of the top study-abroad programs in the nation, TCU graduates earn more than degrees that will improve their lives. They learn to change their world.

Undergraduates 6,344 full-time, 541 part-time. Students come from 50 states and territories, 75 other countries, 22% are from out of state, 4% African American, 2% Asian American or Pacific Islander, 6% Hispanic American, 0.5% Native American, 4% international, 6% transferred in, 48% live on campus. *Retention:* 82% of 2001 full-time freshmen returned.

Freshmen *Admission:* 5,822 applied, 4,187 admitted, 1,514 enrolled. *Average high school GPA:* 3.0.

Faculty *Total:* 593, 66% full-time. *Student/faculty ratio:* 15:1.

Majors Accounting; advertising; aerospace engineering; art; art education; art history; Asian studies; astronomy; astrophysics; bilingual/bicultural education; biochemistry; biology; broadcast journalism; business administration; business marketing and marketing management; chemistry; classics; computer science; criminal justice studies; dance; dietetics; economics; education of the hearing impaired; elementary education; engineering; English; English education; enterprise management; entrepreneurship; environmental science; fashion design/illustration; fashion merchandising; finance; fine/studio arts; French; general studies; geology; graphic design/commercial art/illustration; health science; history; interior design; international business; international relations; journalism; Latin American studies; liberal arts and sciences/liberal studies; marketing research; mass communications; mathematics; mathematics education; middle school education; military studies; music; music (general performance); music history; musicology; music (piano and organ performance); music teacher education; music theory and composition; music (voice and choral/opera performance); neuroscience; nursing; nutrition studies; philosophy; photography; physical education; physics; political science; printmaking; psychology; radio/television broadcasting; real estate; religious studies; science education; sculpture; secondary education; social studies education; social work; sociology; Spanish; special education; speech-language pathology/audiology; speech/rhetorical studies; teaching English as a second language; technical education; theater arts/drama; women's studies.

Academic Programs *Special study options:* accelerated degree program, adult/continuing education programs, advanced placement credit, distance learning, double majors, English as a second language, honors programs, independent study, internships, part-time degree program, services for LD students, student-designed majors, study abroad, summer session for credit. *ROTC:* Army (b), Air Force (b). *Unusual degree programs:* 3-2 education, economics.

Library Mary Couts Burnett Library with 1.3 million titles, 4,734 serial subscriptions, 55,702 audiovisual materials, an OPAC, a Web page.

Computers on Campus 4225 computers available on campus for general student use. A campuswide network can be accessed from student residence rooms and from off campus. Internet access, online (class) registration, at least one staffed computer lab available.

Student Life *Housing:* on-campus residence required for freshman year. *Options:* coed, men-only, women-only, disabled students. *Activities and Organizations:* drama/theater group, student-run newspaper, radio and television station, choral group, marching band, national fraternities, national sororities. *Campus security:* 24-hour emergency response devices and patrols, student patrols, late-night transport/escort service, controlled dormitory access, emergency call boxes, video camera surveillance in parking lots. *Student Services:* health clinic, personal/psychological counseling, women's center, legal services.

Athletics Member NCAA. All Division I except football (Division I-A). *Intercollegiate sports:* baseball M(s), basketball M(s)/W(s), cross-country running M(s)/W(s), golf M(s)/W(s), riflery W, soccer M/W(s), swimming M(s)/W(s), tennis M(s)/W(s), track and field M(s)/W(s), volleyball W(s). *Intramural sports:* badminton M/W, basketball M/W, bowling M/W, lacrosse M(c)/W(c), rugby M(c)/W(c), soccer M/W, softball M/W, table tennis M/W, tennis M/W, volleyball M(c).

Standardized Tests *Required:* SAT I or ACT (for admission). *Recommended:* SAT II: Subject Tests (for admission), SAT II: Writing Test (for admission).

Costs (2001–02) *One-time required fee:* $200. *Comprehensive fee:* $19,910 includes full-time tuition ($13,500), mandatory fees ($1540), and room and board ($4870). Part-time tuition: $420 per semester hour. *Required fees:* $65 per semester hour. *Room and board:* College room only: $3270. Room and board charges vary according to board plan and housing facility. *Payment plan:* installment. *Waivers:* employees or children of employees.

Financial Aid Of all full-time matriculated undergraduates who enrolled in 2001, 3233 applied for aid, 2452 were judged to have need, 1342 had their need fully met. 1022 Federal Work-Study jobs (averaging $1992). 16 State and other part-time jobs (averaging $1924). In 2001, 1358 non-need-based awards were made. *Average percent of need met:* 94%. *Average financial aid package:* $10,828. *Average need-based loan:* $4527. *Average need-based gift aid:* $7194. *Average non-need based aid:* $6208.

Applying *Options:* common application, electronic application, early action, deferred entrance. *Application fee:* $35. *Required:* essay or personal statement, high school transcript, minimum 2.0 GPA, 2 letters of recommendation. *Recommended:* minimum 3.0 GPA, interview. *Application deadlines:* 2/15 (freshmen), 6/15 (transfers). *Notification:* 4/1 (freshmen), 1/1 (early action).

Admissions Contact Mr. Ray Brown, Dean of Admissions, Texas Christian University, TCU Box 297013, Fort Worth, TX 76129-0002. *Phone:* 817-257-7490. *Toll-free phone:* 800-828-3764. *Fax:* 817-257-7268. *E-mail:* frogmail@tcu.edu.

TEXAS COLLEGE
Tyler, Texas

- **Independent** 4-year, founded 1894, affiliated with Christian Methodist Episcopal Church
- **Calendar** semesters
- **Degree** certificates and bachelor's
- **Coed,** 511 undergraduate students, 97% full-time, 62% women, 38% men
- 41% of applicants were admitted

Undergraduates 496 full-time, 15 part-time. 97% African American, 0.6% Asian American or Pacific Islander, 2% Hispanic American, 0.2% Native American.

Freshmen *Admission:* 1,239 applied, 511 admitted, 174 enrolled.

Faculty *Total:* 39, 74% full-time, 44% with terminal degrees. *Student/faculty ratio:* 10:1.

Majors Art; biology; business; business administration; computer science; elementary education; English; health/physical education; history; mathematics; music; political science; social work; sociology.

Costs (2001–02) *Comprehensive fee:* $13,820 includes full-time tuition ($8375) and room and board ($5445). Part-time tuition: $208 per credit hour. *Room and board:* College room only: $700.

Admissions Contact Anetha Francis, Enrollment Services Director, Texas College, 2404 North Grand Avenue, PO Box 4500, Tyler, TX 75712-4500. *Phone:* 903-593-8311 Ext. 2297.

TEXAS LUTHERAN UNIVERSITY
Seguin, Texas

- **Independent** 4-year, founded 1891, affiliated with Evangelical Lutheran Church
- **Calendar** semesters
- **Degree** bachelor's
- **Suburban** 196-acre campus with easy access to San Antonio
- **Endowment** $30.7 million
- **Coed,** 1,473 undergraduate students, 86% full-time, 54% women, 46% men
- **Moderately difficult** entrance level, 81% of applicants were admitted

The high-quality education that TLU provides has been recognized repeatedly in *U.S. News & World Report*'s survey of America's best colleges and universities. The magazine also recognized TLU as one of the best values for the money among its peers in the Western United States. This recognition affirms the high-quality education offered at Texas Lutheran.

Undergraduates 1,266 full-time, 207 part-time. Students come from 27 states and territories, 16 other countries, 5% are from out of state, 6% African American, 2% Asian American or Pacific Islander, 17% Hispanic American, 0.8% Native American, 3% international, 4% transferred in, 70% live on campus. *Retention:* 78% of 2001 full-time freshmen returned.

Freshmen *Admission:* 1,015 applied, 826 admitted, 375 enrolled. *Average high school GPA:* 3.37. *Test scores:* SAT verbal scores over 500: 59%; SAT math scores over 500: 68%; ACT scores over 18: 92%; SAT verbal scores over 600: 20%; SAT math scores over 600: 18%; ACT scores over 24: 39%; SAT verbal scores over 700: 3%; SAT math scores over 700: 1%; ACT scores over 30: 3%.

Faculty *Total:* 128, 50% full-time, 59% with terminal degrees. *Student/faculty ratio:* 15:1.

Majors Accounting; art; art education; athletic training/sports medicine; biology; business administration; chemistry; communications; computer science; economics; education; education (multiple levels); elementary education; English; exercise sciences; finance; health/physical education/fitness related; history; history education; information sciences/systems; international relations; mathematics; mathematics education; middle school education; molecular biology; music; music teacher education; philosophy; physical education; physics; political science; pre-dentistry; pre-law; pre-medicine; pre-veterinary studies; psychology; social studies education; sociology; Spanish; sport/fitness administration; theater arts/drama; theology.

Academic Programs *Special study options:* accelerated degree program, adult/continuing education programs, advanced placement credit, double majors, English as a second language, honors programs, independent study, internships, part-time degree program, study abroad, summer session for credit. *ROTC:* Army (c), Air Force (c). *Unusual degree programs:* 3-2 engineering with Texas A&M University, Texas Tech University.

Library Blumberg Memorial Library with 156,321 titles, 633 serial subscriptions, 10,298 audiovisual materials, an OPAC, a Web page.

Computers on Campus 90 computers available on campus for general student use. A campuswide network can be accessed from student residence rooms and from off campus. Internet access, at least one staffed computer lab available.

Student Life *Housing:* on-campus residence required through senior year. *Options:* coed, men-only, women-only. *Activities and Organizations:* drama/theater group, student-run newspaper, choral group, Campus Ministry, Mexican American Student Association, Student Government Association. *Campus security:* 24-hour emergency response devices and patrols, late-night transport/escort service, controlled dormitory access. *Student Services:* health clinic, personal/psychological counseling, women's center.

Athletics Member NCAA. except baseball (Division III), men's and women's basketball (Division III), cross-country running (Division III), football (Division III), men's and women's golf (Division III), men's and women's soccer (Division III), softball (Division III), men's and women's tennis (Division III), track and field (Division III), volleyball (Division III) *Intercollegiate sports:* baseball M, basketball M/W, cross-country running W, football M, golf M/W, soccer M/W, softball W, tennis M/W, track and field W, volleyball W. *Intramural sports:* basketball M/W, football M, golf M/W, racquetball M/W, softball M/W, swimming M/W, tennis M/W, volleyball M/W.

Standardized Tests *Required:* SAT I or ACT (for admission).

Costs (2001–02) *Comprehensive fee:* $17,690 includes full-time tuition ($13,440), mandatory fees ($100), and room and board ($4150). Full-time tuition and fees vary according to course load. Part-time tuition: $450 per credit hour. Part-time tuition and fees vary according to course load. *Required fees:* $50 per term part-time. *Room and board:* College room only: $1840. Room and board charges vary according to board plan and housing facility. *Payment plan:* installment. *Waivers:* children of alumni and employees or children of employees.

Financial Aid Of all full-time matriculated undergraduates who enrolled in 2001, 1163 applied for aid, 776 were judged to have need, 200 had their need fully met. 142 Federal Work-Study jobs (averaging $1181). In 2001, 367 non-need-based awards were made. *Average percent of need met:* 80%. *Average financial aid package:* $10,743. *Average need-based loan:* $3160. *Average need-based gift aid:* $7428. *Average non-need based aid:* $4871. *Average indebtedness upon graduation:* $19,750.

Texas Lutheran University (continued)

Applying *Options:* common application, electronic application, deferred entrance. *Application fee:* $25. *Required:* essay or personal statement, high school transcript, letters of recommendation. *Required for some:* minimum 2.0 GPA, 2 letters of recommendation, interview. *Application deadline:* rolling (freshmen), rolling (transfers). *Notification:* continuous until 8/1 (freshmen).

Admissions Contact Mr. E. Norman Jones, Vice President for Enrollment Services, Texas Lutheran University, 1000 West Court Street, Seguin, TX 78155-5999. *Phone:* 830-372-8050. *Toll-free phone:* 800-771-8521. *Fax:* 830-372-8096. *E-mail:* admissions@tlu.edu.

TEXAS SOUTHERN UNIVERSITY
Houston, Texas

- **State-supported** university, founded 1947, part of Texas Higher Education Coordinating Board
- **Calendar** semesters
- **Degrees** bachelor's, master's, doctoral, and first professional
- **Urban** 147-acre campus
- **Endowment** $12.0 million
- **Coed,** 6,485 undergraduate students, 84% full-time, 55% women, 45% men
- **Noncompetitive** entrance level, 21% of applicants were admitted

Undergraduates 5,448 full-time, 1,037 part-time. Students come from 48 states and territories, 56 other countries, 13% are from out of state, 90% African American, 2% Asian American or Pacific Islander, 2% Hispanic American, 0.1% Native American, 5% international, 11% transferred in, 97% live on campus. *Retention:* 62% of 2001 full-time freshmen returned.

Freshmen *Admission:* 7,358 applied, 1,562 admitted, 1,562 enrolled.

Faculty *Total:* 291, 86% full-time, 57% with terminal degrees. *Student/faculty ratio:* 22:1.

Majors Accounting; architectural engineering technology; art; art education; aviation management; bilingual/bicultural education; biology; business administration; business education; business marketing and marketing management; chemistry; child care/development; city/community/regional planning; civil engineering technology; clothing/textiles; computer engineering technology; computer programming; computer science; construction technology; counselor education/guidance; criminal justice/law enforcement administration; curriculum and instruction; dietetics; drafting; drafting/design technology; early childhood education; economics; education; education administration; educational media design; electrical/electronic engineering technology; elementary education; engineering-related technology; English; environmental health; environmental technology; fashion merchandising; finance; French; German; health education; health/physical education; health science; health services administration; history; home economics; industrial arts education; industrial technology; insurance/risk management; interdisciplinary studies; jazz; journalism; law enforcement/police science; mass communications; mathematics; medical records administration; medical technology; music; music (piano and organ performance); music teacher education; music (voice and choral/opera performance); nursing; nutrition studies; occupational safety/health technology; office management; operations management; pharmacy; photography; physical education; physical therapy; physics; political science; pre-dentistry; pre-medicine; psychology; public administration; public policy analysis; radio/television broadcasting; reading education; respiratory therapy; science/technology and society; secondary education; social/philosophical foundations of education; social work; sociology; Spanish; special education; speech/rhetorical studies; speech therapy; telecommunications; theater arts/drama; toxicology; transportation technology; wind/percussion instruments.

Academic Programs *Special study options:* academic remediation for entering students, accelerated degree program, adult/continuing education programs, cooperative education, distance learning, English as a second language, honors programs, internships, part-time degree program, services for LD students, summer session for credit. *ROTC:* Army (c), Navy (c).

Library Robert J. Terry Library plus 2 others with 473,499 titles, 1,715 serial subscriptions, an OPAC.

Computers on Campus 410 computers available on campus for general student use. Internet access, at least one staffed computer lab available.

Student Life *Housing:* on-campus residence required for freshman year. *Options:* men-only, women-only. *Activities and Organizations:* drama/theater group, student-run newspaper, radio station, choral group, marching band, Debate Team, University Program Council, Student Government Association, national fraternities, national sororities. *Campus security:* 24-hour emergency response devices and patrols, student patrols. *Student Services:* health clinic, personal/psychological counseling, legal services.

Athletics Member NCAA. All Division I except football (Division I-AA). *Intercollegiate sports:* baseball M, basketball M(s)/W(s), cross-country running M(s)/W(s), golf M(s), soccer M, softball W, tennis M(s), track and field M(s)/W(s), volleyball M. *Intramural sports:* bowling W, softball M/W, swimming M/W, volleyball M/W.

Standardized Tests *Required:* SAT I or ACT (for placement).

Costs (2001–02) *Tuition:* state resident $1008 full-time, $42 per semester hour part-time; nonresident $6072 full-time, $253 per semester hour part-time. Full-time tuition and fees vary according to course load and program. Part-time tuition and fees vary according to course load and program. *Required fees:* $1070 full-time, $21 per hour. *Room and board:* $4498; room only: $2278. *Payment plan:* installment. *Waivers:* minority students and senior citizens.

Applying *Options:* common application, electronic application. *Application fee:* $25. *Required:* high school transcript. *Application deadlines:* 8/10 (freshmen), 8/10 (transfers). *Notification:* continuous until 8/28 (freshmen).

Admissions Contact Texas Southern University, 3100 Cleburne, Houston, TX 77004-4598. *Phone:* 713-313-7472.

TEXAS TECH UNIVERSITY
Lubbock, Texas

- **State-supported** university, founded 1923, part of Texas Tech University System
- **Calendar** semesters
- **Degrees** bachelor's, master's, doctoral, and first professional
- **Urban** 1839-acre campus
- **Endowment** $318.4 million
- **Coed,** 21,269 undergraduate students, 89% full-time, 46% women, 54% men
- **Moderately difficult** entrance level, 74% of applicants were admitted

Undergraduates 18,904 full-time, 2,365 part-time. Students come from 53 states and territories, 79 other countries, 5% are from out of state, 3% African American, 2% Asian American or Pacific Islander, 10% Hispanic American, 0.5% Native American, 0.7% international, 12% transferred in, 26% live on campus. *Retention:* 81% of 2001 full-time freshmen returned.

Freshmen *Admission:* 12,008 applied, 8,837 admitted, 4,257 enrolled. *Test scores:* SAT verbal scores over 500: 72%; SAT math scores over 500: 79%; ACT scores over 18: 96%; SAT verbal scores over 600: 22%; SAT math scores over 600: 29%; ACT scores over 24: 47%; SAT verbal scores over 700: 3%; SAT math scores over 700: 4%; ACT scores over 30: 6%.

Faculty *Total:* 1,005, 90% full-time, 88% with terminal degrees. *Student/faculty ratio:* 20:1.

Majors Accounting; acting/directing; advertising; agricultural animal husbandry/production management; agricultural business; agricultural economics; agricultural production; agricultural sciences; agronomy/crop science; animal sciences; anthropology; architectural engineering technology; architecture; art; art history; biochemistry; biological/physical sciences; biology; business administration; business administration/management related; business marketing and marketing management; cell biology; chemical engineering; chemistry; child care/development; civil engineering; classics; clothing/apparel/textile studies; community health liaison; computer engineering; computer/information sciences; dance; dietetics; earth sciences; economics; electrical/electronic engineering technology; electrical engineering; engineering; engineering physics; engineering-related technology; engineering technology; English; environmental engineering; exercise sciences; family studies; fashion design/illustration; fashion merchandising; finance; fine/studio arts; fishing sciences; food sciences; French; general studies; geography; geology; geophysics/seismology; German; graphic design/commercial art/illustration; health/physical education; hearing sciences; history; home economics; horticulture science; horticulture services; hotel and restaurant management; individual/family development; industrial/manufacturing engineering; interdisciplinary studies; interior architecture; international business; journalism; landscape architecture; Latin American studies; liberal arts and sciences/liberal studies; management information systems/business data processing; mathematics; mechanical engineering; mechanical engineering technology; microbiology/bacteriology; molecular biology; music; music (general performance); music theory and composition; natural resources conservation; nutrition studies; petroleum engineering; philosophy; physics; plant protection; political science; psychology; public relations; radio/television broadcasting; radio/television broadcasting technology; range management; recreation/leisure studies; Russian/Slavic studies; social work; sociology; Spanish; speech/rhetorical studies; textile sciences/engineering; theater arts/drama; theater design; wildlife management; zoology.

Academic Programs *Special study options:* academic remediation for entering students, accelerated degree program, adult/continuing education programs, advanced placement credit, cooperative education, distance learning, double majors, English as a second language, external degree program, freshman honors college, honors programs, independent study, internships, off-campus study, services for LD students, student-designed majors, study abroad, summer session for credit. *ROTC:* Army (b), Air Force (b).

Library Texas Tech Library plus 3 others with 4.2 million titles, 27,054 serial subscriptions, 80,953 audiovisual materials, an OPAC, a Web page.

Computers on Campus 2000 computers available on campus for general student use. A campuswide network can be accessed from student residence rooms and from off campus. Internet access, online (class) registration, at least one staffed computer lab available.

Student Life *Housing:* on-campus residence required for freshman year. *Options:* coed, men-only, women-only. *Activities and Organizations:* drama/theater group, student-run newspaper, radio station, choral group, marching band, national fraternities, national sororities. *Campus security:* 24-hour emergency response devices and patrols, late-night transport/escort service, controlled dormitory access. *Student Services:* health clinic, personal/psychological counseling, legal services.

Athletics Member NCAA. All Division I except football (Division I-A). *Intercollegiate sports:* baseball M(s), basketball M(s)/W(s), cross-country running M(s)/W(s), golf M(s)/W(s), soccer W(s), softball W(s), tennis M(s)/W(s), track and field M(s)/W(s), volleyball W(s). *Intramural sports:* archery M, baseball M/W, basketball M/W, bowling M/W, cross-country running M/W, equestrian sports M, fencing M/W, football M/W, golf M/W, gymnastics M/W, racquetball M, riflery M, rugby M, sailing M, soccer M, softball M/W, squash M/W, swimming M/W, table tennis M/W, tennis M/W, track and field M/W, volleyball M/W, water polo M/W, weight lifting M, wrestling M.

Standardized Tests *Required:* SAT I or ACT (for admission).

Costs (2001–02) *Tuition:* state resident $2520 full-time, $84 per credit hour part-time; nonresident $8850 full-time, $295 per credit hour part-time. Full-time tuition and fees vary according to course load. Part-time tuition and fees vary according to course load. *Required fees:* $969 full-time, $484 per year part-time. *Room and board:* $5337; room only: $2887. Room and board charges vary according to board plan and housing facility. *Payment plan:* installment. *Waivers:* senior citizens.

Financial Aid Of all full-time matriculated undergraduates who enrolled in 2001, 10903 applied for aid, 7108 were judged to have need, 1413 had their need fully met. 395 Federal Work-Study jobs (averaging $1576). In 2001, 1358 non-need-based awards were made. *Average percent of need met:* 62%. *Average financial aid package:* $5441. *Average need-based loan:* $3438. *Average need-based gift aid:* $2821. *Average non-need based aid:* $2097. *Average indebtedness upon graduation:* $13,805.

Applying *Options:* electronic application, early admission, deferred entrance. *Application fee:* $40. *Required:* high school transcript, minimum 2.0 GPA. *Required for some:* essay or personal statement. *Application deadline:* rolling (freshmen), rolling (transfers). *Notification:* continuous (freshmen).

Admissions Contact Director Admissions and School Relations, Texas Tech University, Box 45005, Lubbock, TX 79409-5005. *Phone:* 806-742-1480. *Fax:* 806-742-0980. *E-mail:* admissions@ttu.edu.

TEXAS WESLEYAN UNIVERSITY

Fort Worth, Texas

- **Independent United Methodist** comprehensive, founded 1890
- **Calendar** semesters
- **Degrees** bachelor's, master's, and first professional
- **Urban** 74-acre campus
- **Endowment** $41.2 million
- **Coed,** 1,714 undergraduate students, 64% full-time, 65% women, 35% men
- **Moderately difficult** entrance level, 83% of applicants were admitted

Undergraduates 1,092 full-time, 622 part-time. Students come from 16 states and territories, 31 other countries, 4% are from out of state, 19% African American, 2% Asian American or Pacific Islander, 18% Hispanic American, 1% Native American, 2% international, 12% transferred in, 10% live on campus. *Retention:* 50% of 2001 full-time freshmen returned.

Freshmen *Admission:* 602 applied, 501 admitted, 229 enrolled. *Average high school GPA:* 3.28. *Test scores:* SAT verbal scores over 500: 40%; SAT math scores over 500: 38%; ACT scores over 18: 68%; SAT verbal scores over 600: 8%; SAT math scores over 600: 10%; ACT scores over 24: 11%; SAT verbal scores over 700: 1%; SAT math scores over 700: 1%.

Faculty *Total:* 226, 49% full-time, 50% with terminal degrees. *Student/faculty ratio:* 15:1.

Majors Accounting; advertising; art; art education; athletic training/sports medicine; behavioral sciences; bilingual/bicultural education; biochemistry; biological sciences/life sciences related; biology; biology education; business administration; business economics; business education; business management/administrative services related; business marketing and marketing management; chemistry; chemistry related; computer/information sciences; counseling psychology; criminal justice studies; drama/dance education; economics; education; elementary education; engineering related; English; English education; foreign languages education; health/physical education; history; history education; humanities; industrial arts education; international business; international relations; journalism; law and legal studies related; management information systems/business data processing; mathematics; mathematics education; multi/interdisciplinary studies related; music; music teacher education; music (voice and choral/opera performance); organizational psychology; physical education; political science; pre-dentistry; pre-law; pre-medicine; psychology; radio/television broadcasting; reading education; religious education; religious studies; school psychology; science education; social sciences; social studies education; sociology; Spanish; speech education; speech/rhetorical studies; sport/fitness administration; teaching English as a second language; theater arts/drama; visual/performing arts; wind/percussion instruments.

Academic Programs *Special study options:* academic remediation for entering students, adult/continuing education programs, advanced placement credit, distance learning, English as a second language, internships, part-time degree program, services for LD students, study abroad, summer session for credit. *ROTC:* Army (c), Air Force (c). *Unusual degree programs:* 3-2 engineering with Case Western Reserve University, Southern Methodist University, University of Texas at Arlington, Vanderbilt University, Washington University in St. Louis.

Library Eunice and James L. West Library plus 1 other with 192,044 titles, 632 serial subscriptions, 5,302 audiovisual materials, an OPAC.

Computers on Campus 65 computers available on campus for general student use. Internet access, at least one staffed computer lab available.

Student Life *Housing Options:* coed, men-only, women-only. *Activities and Organizations:* drama/theater group, student-run newspaper, choral group, national fraternities, national sororities. *Campus security:* 24-hour emergency response devices and patrols, student patrols, late-night transport/escort service, controlled dormitory access. *Student Services:* health clinic, personal/psychological counseling.

Athletics Member NCAA. All Division III. *Intercollegiate sports:* baseball M, basketball M/W, golf M(s), soccer M/W, softball W, table tennis M, tennis M/W, volleyball W. *Intramural sports:* badminton M/W, basketball M/W, bowling M/W, field hockey M/W, football M, golf M, racquetball M/W, soccer M/W, swimming M/W, table tennis M/W, tennis M/W, track and field M, volleyball W.

Standardized Tests *Required:* SAT I or ACT (for admission).

Costs (2001–02) *Comprehensive fee:* $14,680 includes full-time tuition ($9720), mandatory fees ($970), and room and board ($3990). Full-time tuition and fees vary according to program. Part-time tuition: $320 per credit hour. Part-time tuition and fees vary according to program. *Room and board:* College room only: $1560. Room and board charges vary according to board plan and student level. *Payment plans:* installment, deferred payment. *Waivers:* employees or children of employees.

Financial Aid Of all full-time matriculated undergraduates who enrolled in 2001, 146 Federal Work-Study jobs (averaging $1689). 11 State and other part-time jobs (averaging $2362).

Applying *Options:* common application, deferred entrance. *Application fee:* $25. *Required:* essay or personal statement, high school transcript, minimum 2.5 GPA. *Required for some:* interview. *Application deadline:* rolling (freshmen), rolling (transfers). *Notification:* continuous (freshmen).

Admissions Contact Ms. Stephanie Lewis-Boatner, Director of Freshman Admissions, Texas Wesleyan University, 1201 Wesleyan Street, Fort Worth, TX 76105-1536. *Phone:* 817-531-4422. *Toll-free phone:* 800-580-8980. *Fax:* 817-531-7515. *E-mail:* freshman@txwesleyan.edu.

TEXAS WOMAN'S UNIVERSITY

Denton, Texas

- **State-supported** university, founded 1901
- **Calendar** semesters
- **Degrees** bachelor's, master's, doctoral, and post-master's certificates
- **Suburban** 270-acre campus with easy access to Dallas-Fort Worth
- **Endowment** $7.1 million
- **Coed, primarily women,** 4,405 undergraduate students, 72% full-time, 94% women, 6% men
- **Minimally difficult** entrance level, 70% of applicants were admitted

TWU offers bachelor's, master's, and doctoral degree programs to approximately 8,000 students. A teaching and research institution, TWU emphasizes the health sciences, education, and the liberal arts. TWU offers a university experience focusing on the priorities and potential of all students. TWU welcomes women and men and traditional and nontraditional students to its three campuses in Denton, Dallas, and Houston. TWU offers more than 100 degree programs.

Texas Woman's University (continued)

Undergraduates 3,189 full-time, 1,216 part-time. Students come from 26 states and territories, 29 other countries, 1% are from out of state, 21% African American, 5% Asian American or Pacific Islander, 11% Hispanic American, 0.7% Native American, 2% international, 14% transferred in, 22% live on campus. *Retention:* 67% of 2001 full-time freshmen returned.

Freshmen *Admission:* 1,237 applied, 862 admitted, 504 enrolled. *Average high school GPA:* 3.20.

Faculty *Total:* 443, 85% full-time. *Student/faculty ratio:* 13:1.

Majors Accounting; art; art history; biology; business administration; business marketing and marketing management; ceramic arts; chemistry; child care/development; clothing/apparel/textile studies; community health liaison; computer/information sciences; consumer economics; criminal justice studies; dance; dental hygiene; design/visual communications; dietetics; economics; English; fashion design/illustration; fashion merchandising; fine/studio arts; health/physical education; history; home economics; individual/family development; interdisciplinary studies; library science; mass communications; mathematics; medical illustrating; medical technology; metal/jewelry arts; music; music (general performance); music therapy; nursing; nutritional sciences; nutrition studies; occupational therapy; office management; painting; paralegal/legal assistant; photography; political science; psychology; public administration; sculpture; secretarial science; sociology; Spanish; speech-language pathology/audiology; textile arts; theater arts/drama.

Academic Programs *Special study options:* academic remediation for entering students, accelerated degree program, adult/continuing education programs, advanced placement credit, cooperative education, distance learning, double majors, honors programs, independent study, internships, off-campus study, part-time degree program, services for LD students, summer session for credit. *Unusual degree programs:* 3-2 engineering with The University of Texas at Dallas; physical therapy, human biology, kinesiology.

Library Blagg-Huey Library with 559,116 titles, 8,287 serial subscriptions, 84,120 audiovisual materials, an OPAC, a Web page.

Computers on Campus 332 computers available on campus for general student use. A campuswide network can be accessed from student residence rooms and from off campus. Internet access, at least one staffed computer lab available.

Student Life *Housing:* on-campus residence required through sophomore year. *Options:* coed. *Activities and Organizations:* drama/theater group, student-run newspaper, choral group, national sororities. *Campus security:* 24-hour emergency response devices and patrols, late-night transport/escort service, controlled dormitory access. *Student Services:* health clinic, personal/psychological counseling.

Athletics Member NCAA. All Division II. *Intercollegiate sports:* basketball W(s), gymnastics W(s), softball W(s), tennis W(s), volleyball W(s). *Intramural sports:* badminton M(c)/W(c), basketball M(c)/W(c), bowling M(c)/W(c), football M(c)/W(c), golf M(c)/W(c), soccer M(c)/W(c), softball M(c)/W(c), tennis M(c)/W(c), volleyball M(c)/W(c).

Standardized Tests *Required:* SAT I or ACT (for admission).

Costs (2001–02) *Tuition:* state resident $1872 full-time, $78 per semester hour part-time; nonresident $6936 full-time, $289 per semester hour part-time. Full-time tuition and fees vary according to course load, degree level, location, program, and reciprocity agreements. Part-time tuition and fees vary according to course load, degree level, location, program, and reciprocity agreements. *Required fees:* $632 full-time, $132 per semester hour. *Room and board:* $4427; room only: $2240. Room and board charges vary according to board plan and housing facility. *Payment plan:* installment.

Financial Aid Of all full-time matriculated undergraduates who enrolled in 2001, 3135 applied for aid, 2483 were judged to have need, 2239 had their need fully met. 159 Federal Work-Study jobs (averaging $1259). 362 State and other part-time jobs (averaging $2911). In 2001, 183 non-need-based awards were made. *Average percent of need met:* 98%. *Average financial aid package:* $8214. *Average need-based loan:* $3726. *Average need-based gift aid:* $3338. *Average non-need based aid:* $4569. *Average indebtedness upon graduation:* $20,023.

Applying *Options:* electronic application, early admission, deferred entrance. *Application fee:* $30. *Required:* high school transcript, minimum 2.0 GPA. *Application deadlines:* 7/15 (freshmen), 7/15 (transfers). *Notification:* continuous until 8/15 (freshmen).

Admissions Contact Ms. Teresa Mauk, Director of Admissions, Texas Woman's University, PO Box 425589, Denton, TX 76204-5589. *Phone:* 940-898-3040. *Toll-free phone:* 888-948-9984. *Fax:* 940-898-3081. *E-mail:* admissions@twu.edu.

TRINITY UNIVERSITY
San Antonio, Texas

- **Independent** comprehensive, founded 1869, affiliated with Presbyterian Church
- **Calendar** semesters
- **Degrees** bachelor's and master's
- **Urban** 113-acre campus
- **Endowment** $649.9 million
- **Coed,** 2,386 undergraduate students, 98% full-time, 51% women, 49% men
- **Very difficult** entrance level, 75% of applicants were admitted

Undergraduates 2,328 full-time, 58 part-time. Students come from 51 states and territories, 18 other countries, 29% are from out of state, 2% African American, 7% Asian American or Pacific Islander, 10% Hispanic American, 0.6% Native American, 2% international, 1% transferred in, 77% live on campus. *Retention:* 86% of 2001 full-time freshmen returned.

Freshmen *Admission:* 2,683 applied, 2,013 admitted, 630 enrolled. *Average high school GPA:* 3.80. *Test scores:* SAT verbal scores over 500: 99%; SAT math scores over 500: 100%; ACT scores over 18: 101%; SAT verbal scores over 600: 66%; SAT math scores over 600: 74%; ACT scores over 24: 95%; SAT verbal scores over 700: 18%; SAT math scores over 700: 17%; ACT scores over 30: 40%.

Faculty *Total:* 271, 78% full-time. *Student/faculty ratio:* 11:1.

Majors Accounting; acting/directing; anthropology; art; art history; Asian studies; biochemistry; biology; business administration; business marketing and marketing management; chemistry; Chinese; classics; communications; computer/information sciences; economics; engineering science; English; European studies; finance; French; geology; German; history; humanities; international business; Latin American studies; management science; mathematics; music; music (general performance); music theory and composition; music (voice and choral/opera performance); philosophy; physics; political science; pre-dentistry; pre-law; pre-medicine; pre-veterinary studies; psychology; religious studies; Russian; sociology; Spanish; speech/rhetorical studies; theater arts/drama; theater design; urban studies.

Academic Programs *Special study options:* accelerated degree program, advanced placement credit, double majors, honors programs, independent study, internships, part-time degree program, services for LD students, study abroad, summer session for credit. *ROTC:* Air Force (c).

Library Elizabeth Huth Coates Library with 871,081 titles, 3,450 serial subscriptions, 61,179 audiovisual materials, an OPAC, a Web page.

Computers on Campus 100 computers available on campus for general student use. A campuswide network can be accessed from student residence rooms and from off campus. Internet access, at least one staffed computer lab available.

Student Life *Housing:* on-campus residence required through junior year. *Options:* coed. *Activities and Organizations:* drama/theater group, student-run newspaper, radio and television station, choral group, Voluntary Action Center, Alpha Phi Omega, Association of Student Representatives, Activities Council, Multicultural Network. *Campus security:* 24-hour emergency response devices and patrols, late-night transport/escort service, controlled dormitory access. *Student Services:* health clinic, personal/psychological counseling.

Athletics Member NCAA. All Division III. *Intercollegiate sports:* baseball M, basketball M/W, cross-country running M/W, football M, golf M/W, lacrosse M(c)/W(c), riflery M(c)/W(c), soccer M/W, softball W, swimming M/W, tennis M/W, track and field M/W, volleyball M(c)/W. *Intramural sports:* basketball M/W, cross-country running M/W, football M/W, golf M, racquetball M/W, soccer M/W, softball M/W, swimming M/W, table tennis M/W, tennis M/W, track and field M/W, volleyball M/W, water polo M/W, wrestling M.

Standardized Tests *Required:* SAT I or ACT (for admission).

Costs (2001–02) *Comprehensive fee:* $23,114 includes full-time tuition ($16,410), mandatory fees ($144), and room and board ($6560). Part-time tuition: $684 per semester hour. *Required fees:* $6 per semester hour. *Room and board:* College room only: $4220. Room and board charges vary according to board plan. *Payment plans:* tuition prepayment, installment. *Waivers:* employees or children of employees.

Financial Aid Of all full-time matriculated undergraduates who enrolled in 2001, 1958 applied for aid, 984 were judged to have need, 709 had their need fully met. 10 State and other part-time jobs (averaging $1435). In 2001, 974 non-need-based awards were made. *Average percent of need met:* 90%. *Average financial aid package:* $14,550. *Average need-based loan:* $3402. *Average need-based gift aid:* $11,135. *Average non-need based aid:* $4881. *Average indebtedness upon graduation:* $16,724.

Applying *Options:* common application, electronic application, early decision, early action, deferred entrance. *Application fee:* $30. *Required:* essay or personal statement, high school transcript, 2 letters of recommendation. *Recommended:* interview. *Application deadlines:* 2/1 (freshmen), 2/1 (transfers). *Early decision:* 11/1. *Notification:* 4/1 (freshmen), 12/15 (early decision), 2/1 (early action).

Admissions Contact Christopher Ellertson, Dean of Admissions and Financial Aid, Trinity University, 715 Stadium Drive, San Antonio, TX 78212-7200. *Phone:* 210-999-7207. *Toll-free phone:* 800-TRINITY. *Fax:* 210-999-8164. *E-mail:* admissions@trinity.edu.

UNIVERSITY OF DALLAS

Irving, Texas

- **Independent Roman Catholic** university, founded 1955
- **Calendar** semesters
- **Degrees** certificates, bachelor's, master's, and doctoral
- **Suburban** 750-acre campus with easy access to Dallas-Fort Worth
- **Endowment** $52.3 million
- **Coed,** 1,255 undergraduate students, 94% full-time, 58% women, 42% men
- **Very difficult** entrance level, 85% of applicants were admitted

Undergraduates 1,185 full-time, 70 part-time. Students come from 48 states and territories, 21 other countries, 40% are from out of state, 2% African American, 6% Asian American or Pacific Islander, 14% Hispanic American, 0.7% Native American, 2% international, 5% transferred in, 57% live on campus. *Retention:* 78% of 2001 full-time freshmen returned.

Freshmen *Admission:* 1,410 applied, 1,204 admitted, 311 enrolled. *Average high school GPA:* 3.80. *Test scores:* SAT verbal scores over 500: 91%; SAT math scores over 500: 88%; ACT scores over 18: 97%; SAT verbal scores over 600: 58%; SAT math scores over 600: 51%; ACT scores over 24: 70%; SAT verbal scores over 700: 19%; SAT math scores over 700: 11%; ACT scores over 30: 20%.

Faculty *Total:* 237, 54% full-time. *Student/faculty ratio:* 11:1.

Majors Art; art education; art history; biochemistry; biology; ceramic arts; chemistry; classics; computer science; economics; economics related; education; elementary education; English; fine/studio arts; French; German; history; mathematics; painting; philosophy; physics; political science; pre-dentistry; pre-law; pre-medicine; pre-theology; printmaking; psychology; sculpture; secondary education; Spanish; theater arts/drama; theology.

Academic Programs *Special study options:* academic remediation for entering students, accelerated degree program, adult/continuing education programs, advanced placement credit, double majors, English as a second language, independent study, internships, off-campus study, part-time degree program, services for LD students, student-designed majors, study abroad, summer session for credit. *ROTC:* Army (c), Air Force (c). *Unusual degree programs:* 3-2 engineering with Washington University in St. Louis, The University of Texas at Dallas; architecture with Washington University in St. Louis, The University of Texas at Arlington.

Library William A. Blakley Library with 192,468 titles, 1,819 serial subscriptions, 1,223 audiovisual materials, an OPAC.

Computers on Campus 70 computers available on campus for general student use. A campuswide network can be accessed from student residence rooms and from off campus. At least one staffed computer lab available.

Student Life *Housing:* on-campus residence required through junior year. *Options:* coed, men-only, women-only. *Activities and Organizations:* drama/theater group, student-run newspaper, choral group, student government, Student Foundation, Program Board, Crusaders for Life, Residence Hall Association. *Campus security:* 24-hour emergency response devices and patrols, late-night transport/escort service, controlled dormitory access. *Student Services:* health clinic, personal/psychological counseling.

Athletics Member NCAA. All Division III. *Intercollegiate sports:* baseball M, basketball M/W, cross-country running M/W, golf M/W, soccer M/W, softball W, tennis M/W, track and field M/W, volleyball W. *Intramural sports:* badminton M/W, basketball M/W, football M/W, rugby M(c), sailing M(c)/W(c), soccer M/W, softball M/W, tennis M/W, volleyball M/W.

Standardized Tests *Required:* SAT I or ACT (for admission).

Costs (2001–02) *Comprehensive fee:* $22,034 includes full-time tuition ($15,824), mandatory fees ($260), and room and board ($5950). Part-time tuition: $650 per credit. *Required fees:* $130 per term part-time. *Room and board:* Room and board charges vary according to board plan and housing facility. *Payment plans:* installment, deferred payment. *Waivers:* employees or children of employees.

Financial Aid Of all full-time matriculated undergraduates who enrolled in 2001, 1115 applied for aid, 661 were judged to have need, 182 had their need fully met. In 2001, 56 non-need-based awards were made. *Average percent of need met:* 84%. *Average financial aid package:* $12,367. *Average need-based loan:* $3615. *Average need-based gift aid:* $8563. *Average non-need based aid:* $5520. *Average indebtedness upon graduation:* $15,300.

Applying *Options:* early admission, early action, deferred entrance. *Application fee:* $40. *Required:* essay or personal statement, high school transcript, 1 letter of recommendation. *Required for some:* interview. *Recommended:* interview. *Application deadlines:* 2/15 (freshmen), 7/1 (transfers). *Notification:* continuous (freshmen), 1/15 (early action).

Admissions Contact Mr. Larry Webb, Director of Enrollment, University of Dallas, 1845 East Northgate Drive, Irving, TX 75062-4799. *Phone:* 972-721-5266. *Toll-free phone:* 800-628-6999. *Fax:* 972-721-5017. *E-mail:* ugadmis@mailadmin.udallas.edu.

UNIVERSITY OF HOUSTON

Houston, Texas

- **State-supported** university, founded 1927, part of University of Houston System
- **Calendar** semesters
- **Degrees** bachelor's, master's, doctoral, and first professional
- **Urban** 550-acre campus
- **Endowment** $299.7 million
- **Coed,** 25,230 undergraduate students, 70% full-time, 53% women, 47% men
- **Moderately difficult** entrance level, 79% of applicants were admitted

Undergraduates 17,642 full-time, 7,588 part-time. Students come from 52 states and territories, 130 other countries, 2% are from out of state, 15% African American, 20% Asian American or Pacific Islander, 20% Hispanic American, 0.4% Native American, 4% international, 10% transferred in, 9% live on campus. *Retention:* 78% of 2001 full-time freshmen returned.

Freshmen *Admission:* 7,734 applied, 6,121 admitted, 3,475 enrolled. *Average high school GPA:* 3.10. *Test scores:* SAT verbal scores over 500: 53%; SAT math scores over 500: 63%; ACT scores over 18: 83%; SAT verbal scores over 600: 16%; SAT math scores over 600: 23%; ACT scores over 24: 23%; SAT verbal scores over 700: 2%; SAT math scores over 700: 4%; ACT scores over 30: 3%.

Faculty *Total:* 2,039, 54% full-time, 48% with terminal degrees. *Student/faculty ratio:* 18:1.

Majors Accounting; anthropology; applied mathematics; architectural environmental design; architecture; art; art history; biochemistry; biology; business administration; business communications; business home economics; business statistics; chemical engineering; chemistry; civil engineering; civil engineering technology; classics; communications; community health liaison; computer engineering technology; computer/information sciences; computer systems analysis; construction technology; creative writing; drafting; economics; electrical engineering; electromechanical technology; English; entrepreneurship; exercise sciences; finance; fine/studio arts; French; geology; geophysics/seismology; German; health/physical education; history; home economics; hotel and restaurant management; individual/family development; industrial/manufacturing engineering; industrial technology; information sciences/systems; interdisciplinary studies; interior architecture; interior design; Italian; journalism; Latin (ancient and medieval); management information systems/business data processing; mathematical statistics; mathematics; mechanical engineering; medical technology; music; music (general performance); music theory and composition; nutrition studies; operations management; organizational behavior; painting; pharmacy; philosophy; photography; physics; political science; pre-dentistry; pre-law; pre-medicine; pre-veterinary studies; printmaking; psychology; public relations; radio/television broadcasting; Russian/Slavic studies; sculpture; sociology; Spanish; speech-language pathology/audiology; speech/rhetorical studies; theater arts/drama; Western European studies.

Academic Programs *Special study options:* academic remediation for entering students, accelerated degree program, adult/continuing education programs, advanced placement credit, cooperative education, distance learning, double majors, English as a second language, freshman honors college, honors programs, independent study, internships, off-campus study, part-time degree program, services for LD students, study abroad, summer session for credit. *ROTC:* Army (b), Navy (c).

Library M.D. Anderson Library plus 5 others with 2.1 million titles, 15,203 serial subscriptions, 13,385 audiovisual materials, an OPAC, a Web page.

Computers on Campus 825 computers available on campus for general student use. A campuswide network can be accessed from student residence rooms and from off campus. Internet access, online (class) registration, at least one staffed computer lab available.

Student Life *Housing Options:* coed. *Activities and Organizations:* drama/theater group, student-run newspaper, radio and television station, choral group, marching band, Council of Ethnic Organizations, Greek Life, Frontier Fiesta

University of Houston (continued)
Association, intramural sports, Golden Key National Honor Society, national fraternities, national sororities. *Campus security:* 24-hour emergency response devices and patrols, student patrols, late-night transport/escort service, controlled dormitory access, vehicle assistance. *Student Services:* health clinic, personal/psychological counseling, women's center, legal services.

Athletics Member NCAA. All Division I except football (Division I-A). *Intercollegiate sports:* baseball M(s), basketball M(s)/W(s), cross-country running M(s)/W(s), golf M(s), soccer W(s), softball W(s), swimming W(s), tennis W(s), track and field M(s)/W(s), volleyball W(s). *Intramural sports:* badminton M/W, basketball M/W, bowling M(c)/W(c), cross-country running M/W, football M/W, golf M/W, lacrosse M, racquetball M/W, soccer M(c), swimming M/W, tennis M/W, track and field M/W, volleyball M/W, water polo M/W, weight lifting M.

Standardized Tests *Required:* SAT I or ACT (for admission). *Recommended:* SAT I (for admission), SAT II: Subject Tests (for admission).

Costs (2001–02) *Tuition:* state resident $1260 full-time, $42 per credit hour part-time; nonresident $7590 full-time, $253 per credit hour part-time. Full-time tuition and fees vary according to class time, course load, degree level, location, program, reciprocity agreements, and student level. Part-time tuition and fees vary according to class time, course load, degree level, location, program, reciprocity agreements, and student level. *Required fees:* $1908 full-time. *Room and board:* $5242; room only: $3072. Room and board charges vary according to board plan and housing facility. *Payment plan:* installment. *Waivers:* senior citizens.

Applying *Options:* common application, electronic application. *Application fee:* $40. *Required:* high school transcript, minimum 2.0 GPA. *Recommended:* letters of recommendation. *Application deadlines:* 5/1 (freshmen), 5/1 (transfers). *Notification:* continuous (freshmen).

Admissions Contact Mr. Jose Cantu, Co-Assistant Director of Student Outreach Services, University of Houston, 4800 Calhoun, Houston, TX 77204-2161. *Phone:* 713-743-9617. *Fax:* 713-743-9633. *E-mail:* admissions@uh.edu.

UNIVERSITY OF HOUSTON-CLEAR LAKE
Houston, Texas

- **State-supported** upper-level, founded 1974, part of University of Houston System
- **Calendar** semesters
- **Degrees** bachelor's and master's
- **Suburban** 487-acre campus
- **Endowment** $7.4 million
- **Coed,** 4,128 undergraduate students, 49% full-time, 64% women, 36% men
- **Minimally difficult** entrance level, 67% of applicants were admitted

Undergraduates Students come from 66 other countries, 1% are from out of state, 8% African American, 6% Asian American or Pacific Islander, 15% Hispanic American, 0.4% Native American, 3% international.

Freshmen *Admission:* 1,836 applied, 1,221 admitted.

Faculty *Total:* 583, 37% full-time. *Student/faculty ratio:* 14:1.

Majors Accounting; anthropology; applied art; behavioral sciences; biological/physical sciences; biology; business; business administration; business marketing and marketing management; chemistry; communications; computer engineering; computer engineering technology; computer science; education; environmental science; exercise sciences; finance; geography; health services administration; history; humanities; information sciences/systems; interdisciplinary studies; legal studies; literature; marketing research; mathematics/computer science; natural resources management; physical sciences; psychology; social work; sociology.

Academic Programs *Special study options:* accelerated degree program, cooperative education, distance learning, double majors, English as a second language, independent study, internships, part-time degree program, services for LD students, student-designed majors, summer session for credit.

Library Neumann Library with 405,797 titles, an OPAC.

Computers on Campus 383 computers available on campus for general student use. A campuswide network can be accessed from off campus. Internet access, online (class) registration, at least one staffed computer lab available.

Student Life *Housing:* college housing not available. *Activities and Organizations:* student-run newspaper, Beta Alpha Psi, International Student Organization, Family Therapy Student Association, Texas Student Education Association, Accounting Association. *Campus security:* 24-hour emergency response devices and patrols, late-night transport/escort service. *Student Services:* health clinic, personal/psychological counseling, women's center, legal services.

Athletics *Intramural sports:* football M/W, golf M/W, rugby M(c), soccer M(c)/W(c), softball M/W, tennis M/W, volleyball M/W.

Costs (2001–02) *Tuition:* state resident $2284 full-time, $40 per credit hour part-time; nonresident $7444 full-time, $253 per credit hour part-time. Part-time tuition and fees vary according to course load. *Required fees:* $1172 full-time, $479 per term part-time. *Payment plan:* installment. *Waivers:* senior citizens.

Financial Aid Of all full-time matriculated undergraduates who enrolled in 2001, 58 Federal Work-Study jobs, 5 State and other part-time jobs.

Applying *Options:* common application, electronic application, deferred entrance. *Application fee:* $30. *Application deadline:* rolling (transfers). *Notification:* continuous (transfers).

Admissions Contact Mr. John Smith, Executive Director of Enrollment Services, University of Houston-Clear Lake, 2700 Bay Area Boulevard, Box 13, Houston, TX 77058-1098. *Phone:* 281-283-2517. *Fax:* 281-283-2530. *E-mail:* admissions@cl.uh.edu.

UNIVERSITY OF HOUSTON-DOWNTOWN
Houston, Texas

- **State-supported** 4-year, founded 1974, part of University of Houston System
- **Calendar** semesters
- **Degree** bachelor's
- **Urban** 20-acre campus
- **Endowment** $8.3 million
- **Coed**
- **Noncompetitive** entrance level

Faculty *Student/faculty ratio:* 25:1.

Student Life *Campus security:* 24-hour emergency response devices and patrols, late-night transport/escort service.

Financial Aid Of all full-time matriculated undergraduates who enrolled in 2001, 2543 applied for aid, 2006 were judged to have need, 342 had their need fully met. 120 Federal Work-Study jobs (averaging $2500). 8 State and other part-time jobs (averaging $2196). *Average percent of need met:* 71. *Average financial aid package:* $5490. *Average need-based gift aid:* $3662. *Average non-need based aid:* $2316.

Applying *Options:* common application, deferred entrance. *Application fee:* $10. *Required:* high school transcript.

Admissions Contact Mr. Mike Kerrendal, Director, Admissions and Records, University of Houston-Downtown, One Main Street, Houston, TX 77002. *Phone:* 713-221-8931. *Fax:* 713-221-8157. *E-mail:* uhdadmit@dt.uh.edu.

UNIVERSITY OF HOUSTON-VICTORIA
Victoria, Texas

- **State-supported** upper-level, founded 1973, part of University of Houston System
- **Calendar** semesters
- **Degrees** bachelor's and master's
- **Small-town** campus
- **Endowment** $5.7 million
- **Coed,** 893 undergraduate students, 37% full-time, 72% women, 28% men
- **Minimally difficult** entrance level, 85% of applicants were admitted

Undergraduates 329 full-time, 564 part-time. Students come from 1 other state, 6 other countries, 0% are from out of state, 8% African American, 5% Asian American or Pacific Islander, 18% Hispanic American, 0.2% Native American, 0.8% international, 21% transferred in.

Freshmen *Admission:* 290 applied, 247 admitted.

Faculty *Total:* 88, 65% full-time, 73% with terminal degrees. *Student/faculty ratio:* 16:1.

Majors Business administration; computer science; education; humanities; mathematics; social sciences.

Academic Programs *Special study options:* adult/continuing education programs, distance learning, double majors, independent study, internships, off-campus study, part-time degree program, services for LD students, study abroad, summer session for credit.

Library VC/UHV Library plus 1 other with 202,484 titles, 1,051 serial subscriptions, 7,477 audiovisual materials, an OPAC, a Web page.

Computers on Campus 150 computers available on campus for general student use. A campuswide network can be accessed from off campus. Internet access, online (class) registration, at least one staffed computer lab available.

Student Life *Housing:* college housing not available. *Activities and Organizations:* Texas Student Education Association. *Campus security:* 24-hour emergency response devices and patrols.

Costs (2001–02) *Tuition:* state resident $1008 full-time, $42 per credit hour part-time; nonresident $6072 full-time, $253 per credit hour part-time. Full-time tuition and fees vary according to course load. Part-time tuition and fees vary according to course load. *Required fees:* $1296 full-time, $54 per credit hour. *Payment plans:* tuition prepayment, installment. *Waivers:* senior citizens.

Financial Aid Of all full-time matriculated undergraduates who enrolled in 2001, 131 applied for aid, 125 were judged to have need, 4 had their need fully met. 20 Federal Work-Study jobs (averaging $1951). 1 State and other part-time jobs (averaging $3207). In 2001, 18 non-need-based awards were made. *Average percent of need met:* 56%. *Average financial aid package:* $5746. *Average need-based loan:* $3996. *Average need-based gift aid:* $2916. *Average non-need based aid:* $2616. *Average indebtedness upon graduation:* $15,950.

Applying *Application deadline:* rolling (transfers). *Notification:* continuous (transfers).

Admissions Contact Mr. Richard Phillips, Director of Enrollment Management, University of Houston-Victoria, 3007 North Ben Wilson, Victoria, TX 77901-4450. *Phone:* 361-570-4110. *Toll-free phone:* 800-687-8648. *Fax:* 361-570-4114. *E-mail:* urbanom@jade.vic.uh.edu.

UNIVERSITY OF MARY HARDIN-BAYLOR

Belton, Texas

- **Independent Southern Baptist** comprehensive, founded 1845
- **Calendar** semesters
- **Degrees** bachelor's and master's
- **Small-town** 100-acre campus with easy access to Austin
- **Endowment** $40.6 million
- **Coed,** 2,437 undergraduate students, 85% full-time, 64% women, 36% men
- **Moderately difficult** entrance level, 90% of applicants were admitted

Undergraduates 2,070 full-time, 367 part-time. Students come from 23 states and territories, 13 other countries, 3% are from out of state, 10% African American, 2% Asian American or Pacific Islander, 10% Hispanic American, 0.7% Native American, 0.8% international, 13% transferred in, 45% live on campus. *Retention:* 62% of 2001 full-time freshmen returned.

Freshmen *Admission:* 941 applied, 851 admitted, 459 enrolled. *Test scores:* SAT verbal scores over 500: 59%; SAT math scores over 500: 55%; ACT scores over 18: 89%; SAT verbal scores over 600: 14%; SAT math scores over 600: 14%; ACT scores over 24: 30%; SAT verbal scores over 700: 4%; SAT math scores over 700: 1%; ACT scores over 30: 3%.

Faculty *Total:* 225, 53% full-time, 43% with terminal degrees. *Student/faculty ratio:* 17:1.

Majors Accounting; art; art education; biology; business administration; business education; business marketing and marketing management; chemistry; communications; computer graphics; computer/information sciences; computer science; criminal justice/law enforcement administration; early childhood education; economics; education; elementary education; English; finance; history; information sciences/systems; mass communications; mathematics; medical technology; music (general performance); music teacher education; nursing; physical education; political science; pre-dentistry; pre-law; pre-medicine; pre-pharmacy studies; pre-veterinary studies; psychology; reading education; recreation/leisure studies; religious music; religious studies; secondary education; social work; sociology; Spanish; special education.

Academic Programs *Special study options:* academic remediation for entering students, accelerated degree program, adult/continuing education programs, advanced placement credit, distance learning, double majors, English as a second language, honors programs, independent study, internships, part-time degree program, services for LD students, summer session for credit. *ROTC:* Air Force (c).

Library Townsend Memorial Library with 116,678 titles, 1,724 serial subscriptions, 6,382 audiovisual materials, an OPAC, a Web page.

Computers on Campus 221 computers available on campus for general student use. A campuswide network can be accessed from student residence rooms. Internet access, at least one staffed computer lab available.

Student Life *Housing:* on-campus residence required through junior year. *Options:* men-only, women-only, disabled students. *Activities and Organizations:* drama/theater group, student-run newspaper, choral group, marching band, Baptist Student Ministry, Student Government Association, Residence Hall Association, Campus Activities Board, Crusaders for Christ. *Campus security:* 24-hour emergency response devices and patrols, controlled dormitory access. *Student Services:* health clinic, personal/psychological counseling.

Athletics Member NCAA. All Division III. *Intercollegiate sports:* baseball M, basketball M/W, cross-country running M/W, football M, golf M/W, soccer M/W, softball W, tennis M/W, volleyball W. *Intramural sports:* badminton M/W, basketball M/W, cross-country running M/W, football M/W, soccer M/W, softball M/W, swimming M/W, table tennis M/W, tennis M/W, track and field M/W, volleyball M/W, water polo M/W.

Standardized Tests *Required:* SAT I or ACT (for admission).

Costs (2001–02) *Comprehensive fee:* $13,929 includes full-time tuition ($9000), mandatory fees ($890), and room and board ($4039). Part-time tuition: $300 per semester hour. *Required fees:* $20 per semester hour. *Room and board:* College room only: $1993. Room and board charges vary according to housing facility. *Payment plan:* installment. *Waivers:* employees or children of employees.

Financial Aid Of all full-time matriculated undergraduates who enrolled in 2001, 1881 applied for aid, 1580 were judged to have need, 717 had their need fully met. 219 Federal Work-Study jobs (averaging $2300). 193 State and other part-time jobs (averaging $2300). In 2001, 50 non-need-based awards were made. *Average percent of need met:* 51%. *Average financial aid package:* $7675. *Average need-based loan:* $4000. *Average need-based gift aid:* $3550. *Average non-need based aid:* $3700. *Average indebtedness upon graduation:* $13,509.

Applying *Options:* common application, early admission, deferred entrance. *Application fee:* $35. *Required:* high school transcript. *Required for some:* interview. *Application deadline:* rolling (freshmen), rolling (transfers). *Notification:* continuous (freshmen).

Admissions Contact Ms. Valerie Hampton, Admissions Clerk, University of Mary Hardin-Baylor, UMHB Station Box 8004, 900 College Street, Belton, TX 76513-2599. *Phone:* 254-295-4520. *Toll-free phone:* 800-727-8642. *Fax:* 254-295-5049. *E-mail:* admission@umhb.edu.

UNIVERSITY OF NORTH TEXAS

Denton, Texas

- **State-supported** university, founded 1890
- **Calendar** semesters
- **Degrees** bachelor's, master's, and doctoral
- **Urban** 500-acre campus with easy access to Dallas-Fort Worth
- **Endowment** $10.2 million
- **Coed,** 21,675 undergraduate students, 78% full-time, 55% women, 45% men
- **Moderately difficult** entrance level, 72% of applicants were admitted

Undergraduates 16,935 full-time, 4,740 part-time. Students come from 49 states and territories, 115 other countries, 10% are from out of state, 10% African American, 4% Asian American or Pacific Islander, 9% Hispanic American, 0.8% Native American, 3% international, 13% transferred in, 22% live on campus. *Retention:* 69% of 2001 full-time freshmen returned.

Freshmen *Admission:* 8,172 applied, 5,874 admitted, 2,902 enrolled. *Test scores:* SAT verbal scores over 500: 66%; SAT math scores over 500: 67%; ACT scores over 18: 72%; SAT verbal scores over 600: 23%; SAT math scores over 600: 26%; ACT scores over 24: 23%; SAT verbal scores over 700: 3%; SAT math scores over 700: 5%; ACT scores over 30: 1%.

Faculty *Total:* 1,072, 76% full-time, 66% with terminal degrees. *Student/faculty ratio:* 17:1.

Majors Accounting; advertising; anthropology; applied art; art; art education; art history; behavioral sciences; biochemistry; biology; biology education; broadcast journalism; business; business computer programming; business education; business marketing and marketing management; ceramic arts; chemistry; chemistry education; child guidance; civil engineering technology; communications; computer education; computer/information sciences; counselor education/guidance; criminal justice/law enforcement administration; cytotechnology; dance; drawing; early childhood education; economics; electrical/electronic engineering technology; engineering technology; English; English composition; English education; entrepreneurship; exercise sciences; family living/parenthood; fashion design/illustration; fashion merchandising; finance; French; French language education; general studies; geography; German; German language education; gerontology; health education; history; history education; home economics education; hotel and restaurant management; industrial technology; information sciences/systems; insurance/risk management; interdisciplinary studies; interior design; jazz; journalism; literature; logistics/materials management; mass communications; mathematics; mathematics education; mechanical engineering technology; medical technology; metal/jewelry arts; music; music (general performance); music history; music (piano and organ performance); music teacher education; music theory and composition; music (voice and choral/opera performance); operations management; organizational behavior; painting; philosophy; photography; physical education; physics; physics education; political science; pre-dentistry; pre-medicine; pre-theology; printmaking; psychology; public health education/promotion; public relations; radio/television broadcasting; reading education; real estate; recreation/leisure studies; rehabilitation therapy; science education; sculpture; secondary education; social sciences; social work; sociology; Spanish; Spanish language education; special education; speech education; speech-language pathology/audiology; stringed instruments; textile arts; theater arts/drama; visual/performing arts; wind/percussion instruments.

Academic Programs *Special study options:* academic remediation for entering students, accelerated degree program, advanced placement credit, cooperative

University of North Texas (continued)

education, English as a second language, freshman honors college, honors programs, internships, part-time degree program, services for LD students, student-designed majors, study abroad, summer session for credit. *ROTC:* Army (c), Air Force (b).

Library Willis Library plus 4 others with 1.8 million titles, 12,243 serial subscriptions, 63,338 audiovisual materials, an OPAC, a Web page.

Computers on Campus 2006 computers available on campus for general student use. A campuswide network can be accessed from student residence rooms and from off campus. At least one staffed computer lab available.

Student Life *Housing:* on-campus residence required for freshman year. *Options:* coed, women-only, disabled students. *Activities and Organizations:* drama/theater group, student-run newspaper, radio and television station, choral group, marching band, national fraternities, national sororities. *Campus security:* 24-hour emergency response devices, late-night transport/escort service, controlled dormitory access. *Student Services:* health clinic, personal/psychological counseling, legal services.

Athletics Member NCAA. All Division I. *Intercollegiate sports:* badminton M(c)/W(c), baseball M(c), basketball M(s)/W(s), cross-country running M(s)/W(s), fencing M(c)/W(c), football M(s), golf M(s)/W(s), lacrosse M(c)/W(c), racquetball M(c)/W(c), rugby M(c)/W(c), sailing M(c)/W(c), soccer W, swimming M(c)/W(c), table tennis M(c)/W(c), tennis W(s), track and field M(s)/W(s), volleyball M(c)/W(s), weight lifting M(c)/W(c). *Intramural sports:* badminton M/W, basketball M/W, bowling M/W, fencing M(c)/W(c), football M/W, golf M/W, racquetball M/W, soccer M/W, softball M/W, tennis M/W, track and field M/W, volleyball M/W, water polo M/W, weight lifting M(c)/W(c).

Standardized Tests *Required:* SAT I or ACT (for admission).

Costs (2001–02) *One-time required fee:* $10. *Tuition:* state resident $2080 full-time, $80 per credit part-time; nonresident $8280 full-time, $293 per credit part-time. Full-time tuition and fees vary according to course load and location. Part-time tuition and fees vary according to course load and location. *Required fees:* $970 full-time, $114 per term part-time. *Room and board:* $4400; room only: $2375. Room and board charges vary according to board plan. *Payment plan:* installment. *Waivers:* senior citizens and employees or children of employees.

Financial Aid Of all full-time matriculated undergraduates who enrolled in 2001, 9134 applied for aid, 6357 were judged to have need, 1280 had their need fully met. In 2001, 1985 non-need-based awards were made. *Average percent of need met:* 70%. *Average financial aid package:* $5788. *Average need-based loan:* $3231. *Average need-based gift aid:* $3132. *Average non-need based aid:* $2079. *Average indebtedness upon graduation:* $16,000.

Applying *Options:* common application, electronic application, early admission, deferred entrance. *Application fee:* $40. *Required:* high school transcript. *Required for some:* essay or personal statement, 3 letters of recommendation, interview. *Application deadlines:* 6/15 (freshmen), 6/15 (transfers). *Notification:* continuous (freshmen).

Admissions Contact Ms. Janet Trepka, Coordinator or New Student Mentoring Programs and Vice President of Student Development, University of North Texas, Box 311277, Denton, TX 76203-9988. *Phone:* 940-565-3190. *Toll-free phone:* 800-868-8211. *Fax:* 940-565-2408. *E-mail:* undergrad@abn.unt.edu.

UNIVERSITY OF PHOENIX-DALLAS/FT. WORTH CAMPUS
Dallas, Texas

- **Proprietary** comprehensive, founded 2001
- **Calendar** continuous
- **Degrees** certificates, associate, bachelor's, master's, doctoral, post-master's, and postbachelor's certificates (courses conducted at 54 campuses and learning centers in 13 states)
- **Coed,** 295 undergraduate students, 100% full-time, 38% women, 62% men

Undergraduates Students come from 5 states and territories, 1% are from out of state.

Freshmen *Admission:* 9 admitted.

Faculty *Total:* 86, 2% full-time, 16% with terminal degrees. *Student/faculty ratio:* 17:1.

Majors Business administration; management information systems/business data processing; management science.

Student Life *Housing:* college housing not available.

Costs (2001–02) *Tuition:* $8310 full-time. Full-time tuition and fees vary according to location and program. *Payment plan:* deferred payment. *Waivers:* employees or children of employees.

Applying *Application fee:* $85. *Required:* 2 years of work experience. *Required for some:* high school transcript. *Application deadline:* rolling (freshmen), rolling (transfers).

Admissions Contact Ms. Beth Barilla, Director of Admissions, University of Phoenix-Dallas/Ft. Worth Campus, 4615 East Elwood Street, Phoenix, AZ 85040-1958. *Phone:* 480-927-0099 Ext. 1218. *Toll-free phone:* 800-228-7240. *Fax:* 480-594-1758. *E-mail:* beth.barilla@apollogrp.edu.

UNIVERSITY OF PHOENIX-HOUSTON CAMPUS
Houston, Texas

- **Proprietary** comprehensive, founded 2001
- **Calendar** continuous
- **Degrees** certificates, associate, bachelor's, master's, doctoral, post-master's, and postbachelor's certificates (courses conducted at 54 campuses and learning centers in 13 states)
- **Coed,** 386 undergraduate students, 100% full-time, 66% women, 34% men

Undergraduates Students come from 2 states and territories.

Freshmen *Admission:* 23 admitted.

Faculty *Total:* 69, 6% full-time, 10% with terminal degrees. *Student/faculty ratio:* 18:1.

Majors Business administration; management information systems/business data processing; management science.

Student Life *Housing:* college housing not available.

Costs (2001–02) *Tuition:* $8310 full-time. Full-time tuition and fees vary according to location and program. *Payment plan:* deferred payment. *Waivers:* employees or children of employees.

Applying *Application fee:* $85. *Required:* 2 years of work experience. *Required for some:* high school transcript. *Application deadline:* rolling (freshmen), rolling (transfers).

Admissions Contact Ms. Beth Barilla, Director of Admissions, University of Phoenix-Houston Campus, 4615 East Elwood Street, Phoenix, AZ 85040-1958. *Phone:* 480-927-0099 Ext. 1218. *Toll-free phone:* 800-228-7240. *Fax:* 480-594-1758. *E-mail:* beth.barilla@apollogrp.edu.

UNIVERSITY OF ST. THOMAS
Houston, Texas

- **Independent Roman Catholic** comprehensive, founded 1947
- **Calendar** semesters
- **Degrees** diplomas, bachelor's, master's, doctoral, and first professional
- **Urban** 20-acre campus
- **Endowment** $42.1 million
- **Coed,** 1,851 undergraduate students, 70% full-time, 65% women, 35% men
- 78% of applicants were admitted

Undergraduates 1,293 full-time, 558 part-time. Students come from 23 states and territories, 46 other countries, 3% are from out of state, 6% African American, 13% Asian American or Pacific Islander, 30% Hispanic American, 0.7% Native American, 5% international, 11% transferred in, 10% live on campus. *Retention:* 76% of 2001 full-time freshmen returned.

Freshmen *Admission:* 768 applied, 598 admitted, 284 enrolled. *Average high school GPA:* 3.63. *Test scores:* SAT verbal scores over 500: 87%; SAT math scores over 500: 87%; ACT scores over 18: 98%; SAT verbal scores over 600: 31%; SAT math scores over 600: 37%; ACT scores over 24: 65%; SAT verbal scores over 700: 2%; SAT math scores over 700: 7%; ACT scores over 30: 11%.

Faculty *Total:* 242, 46% full-time, 40% with terminal degrees. *Student/faculty ratio:* 14:1.

Majors Accounting; biology; business administration; business marketing and marketing management; chemistry; communications; economics; education; elementary education; English; environmental science; finance; fine/studio arts; French; general studies; history; international relations; liberal arts and sciences/liberal studies; management information systems/business data processing; mathematics; music; music teacher education; pastoral counseling; philosophy; political science; pre-dentistry; pre-law; pre-medicine; psychology; secondary education; Spanish; theater arts/drama; theology.

Academic Programs *Special study options:* academic remediation for entering students, accelerated degree program, adult/continuing education programs, advanced placement credit, cooperative education, double majors, English as a second language, honors programs, independent study, internships, off-campus study, part-time degree program, services for LD students, student-designed majors, study abroad, summer session for credit. *ROTC:* Army (c). *Unusual degree programs:* 3-2 engineering with University of Notre Dame, University of Houston, Texas A&M University.

Library Doherty Library plus 1 other with 226,593 titles, 3,400 serial subscriptions, 1,148 audiovisual materials, an OPAC, a Web page.

Computers on Campus 143 computers available on campus for general student use. A campuswide network can be accessed from student residence rooms and from off campus. Internet access, at least one staffed computer lab available.

Student Life *Housing Options:* coed. *Activities and Organizations:* drama/theater group, student-run newspaper, choral group. *Campus security:* 24-hour emergency response devices and patrols, late-night transport/escort service. *Student Services:* health clinic, personal/psychological counseling.

Athletics *Intramural sports:* baseball M(c), basketball M/W(c), fencing M(c)/W(c), racquetball M/W, soccer M(c)/W(c), softball M/W, table tennis M/W, tennis M/W, volleyball M(c)/W(c).

Standardized Tests *Required:* SAT I or ACT (for admission).

Costs (2001–02) *Comprehensive fee:* $19,082 includes full-time tuition ($13,050), mandatory fees ($112), and room and board ($5920). Full-time tuition and fees vary according to course load and degree level. Part-time tuition: $435 per credit hour. Part-time tuition and fees vary according to course load and degree level. *Required fees:* $30 per term part-time. *Room and board:* College room only: $3020. Room and board charges vary according to board plan and housing facility. *Payment plans:* installment, deferred payment. *Waivers:* senior citizens and employees or children of employees.

Financial Aid Of all full-time matriculated undergraduates who enrolled in 2001, 800 applied for aid, 701 were judged to have need, 81 had their need fully met. 48 Federal Work-Study jobs (averaging $2959). 1 State and other part-time jobs (averaging $1949). In 2001, 288 non-need-based awards were made. *Average percent of need met:* 62%. *Average financial aid package:* $10,275. *Average need-based loan:* $3947. *Average need-based gift aid:* $7263. *Average non-need based aid:* $6550. *Average indebtedness upon graduation:* $19,837.

Applying *Options:* common application, electronic application, deferred entrance. *Application fee:* $35. *Required:* high school transcript, minimum 2.25 GPA. *Required for some:* essay or personal statement, 2 letters of recommendation, interview. *Application deadline:* rolling (freshmen), rolling (transfers). *Notification:* continuous (freshmen).

Admissions Contact Mr. Gerald E. Warren, Assistant Director of Admissions, University of St. Thomas, 3800 Montrose Boulevard, Houston, TX 77006-4696. *Phone:* 713-525-3500. *Toll-free phone:* 800-856-8565. *Fax:* 713-525-3558. *E-mail:* admissions@stthom.edu.

THE UNIVERSITY OF TEXAS AT ARLINGTON

Arlington, Texas

- **State-supported** university, founded 1895, part of University of Texas System
- **Calendar** semesters
- **Degrees** bachelor's, master's, doctoral, post-master's, and postbachelor's certificates
- **Urban** 395-acre campus with easy access to Dallas-Fort Worth
- **Endowment** $31.4 million
- **Coed,** 16,330 undergraduate students, 68% full-time, 53% women, 47% men
- **Moderately difficult** entrance level, 85% of applicants were admitted

Undergraduates 11,185 full-time, 5,145 part-time. Students come from 45 states and territories, 88 other countries, 3% are from out of state, 13% African American, 11% Asian American or Pacific Islander, 12% Hispanic American, 0.8% Native American, 5% international, 18% transferred in, 14% live on campus. *Retention:* 69% of 2001 full-time freshmen returned.

Freshmen *Admission:* 4,404 applied, 3,724 admitted, 1,959 enrolled. *Test scores:* SAT verbal scores over 500: 61%; SAT math scores over 500: 67%; ACT scores over 18: 88%; SAT verbal scores over 600: 16%; SAT math scores over 600: 23%; ACT scores over 24: 26%; SAT verbal scores over 700: 2%; SAT math scores over 700: 3%; ACT scores over 30: 1%.

Faculty *Total:* 951, 64% full-time. *Student/faculty ratio:* 21:1.

Majors Accounting; advertising; aerospace engineering; anthropology; architecture; art; art history; athletic training/sports medicine; banking; biochemistry; biology; business administration; business economics; business marketing and marketing management; chemistry; child care/development; civil engineering; classics; communications; computer engineering; criminal justice studies; economics; electrical engineering; English; film/video production; fine/studio arts; French; geology; German; health/physical education; history; industrial/manufacturing engineering; interdisciplinary studies; interior architecture; international business; journalism; management information systems/business data processing; mathematics; mechanical engineering; medical technology; microbiology/bacteriology; music; nursing; philosophy; photography; physics; political science; psychology; public relations; radio/television broadcasting; real estate; Russian; social work; sociology; Spanish; speech/rhetorical studies; theater arts/drama.

Academic Programs *Special study options:* academic remediation for entering students, adult/continuing education programs, advanced placement credit, cooperative education, distance learning, double majors, English as a second language, freshman honors college, honors programs, independent study, internships, part-time degree program, services for LD students, student-designed majors, study abroad, summer session for credit. *ROTC:* Army (b), Air Force (c).

Library Central Library plus 2 others with 694,357 titles, 4,738 serial subscriptions, 3,097 audiovisual materials, an OPAC, a Web page.

Computers on Campus 700 computers available on campus for general student use. A campuswide network can be accessed from student residence rooms and from off campus. Online (class) registration, at least one staffed computer lab available.

Student Life *Housing Options:* coed, men-only, women-only. *Activities and Organizations:* drama/theater group, student-run newspaper, radio station, choral group, marching band, Medical/Dental Preparatory Association, IMAX (Indian Music and Culture Society), Baptist Student Ministry, Friendship Association of Chinese Students, Association of Information Technology Professionals, national fraternities, national sororities. *Campus security:* 24-hour emergency response devices and patrols, late-night transport/escort service, controlled dormitory access, remote emergency telephones, bicycle patrols, crime prevention program, student shuttle service from 7:30 a.m. to 4:30 p.m. *Student Services:* health clinic, personal/psychological counseling, legal services.

Athletics Member NCAA. All Division I. *Intercollegiate sports:* baseball M(s), basketball M(s)/W(s), cross-country running M(s)/W(s), golf M(s), softball W(s), tennis M(s)/W(s), track and field M(s)/W(s), volleyball W(s). *Intramural sports:* badminton M/W, basketball M/W, bowling M/W, football M/W, golf M/W, racquetball M/W, soccer M/W, softball M/W, table tennis M/W, volleyball M/W.

Standardized Tests *Required:* SAT I or ACT (for admission).

Costs (2001–02) *Tuition:* state resident $2016 full-time; nonresident $7080 full-time. Full-time tuition and fees vary according to course load. Part-time tuition and fees vary according to course load. *Required fees:* $1052 full-time. *Room and board:* $4124; room only: $2163. Room and board charges vary according to board plan and housing facility. *Payment plan:* installment. *Waivers:* employees or children of employees.

Financial Aid Of all full-time matriculated undergraduates who enrolled in 2001, 5939 applied for aid, 4563 were judged to have need, 950 had their need fully met. 1245 Federal Work-Study jobs (averaging $2444). In 2001, 1478 non-need-based awards were made. *Average percent of need met:* 82%. *Average financial aid package:* $7663. *Average need-based loan:* $4827. *Average need-based gift aid:* $3883. *Average non-need based aid:* $1926. *Average indebtedness upon graduation:* $12,671.

Applying *Options:* early admission, deferred entrance. *Application fee:* $25. *Required:* high school transcript, class rank. *Application deadline:* rolling (freshmen), rolling (transfers). *Notification:* continuous (freshmen).

Admissions Contact Mr. George E. Norton, Interim Director of Admissions, The University of Texas at Arlington, PO Box 19111, 701 South Nedderman Drive, Room 110, Davis Hall, Arlington, TX 76019-0088. *Phone:* 817-272-3254. *Fax:* 817-272-3435. *E-mail:* admissions@uta.edu.

THE UNIVERSITY OF TEXAS AT AUSTIN

Austin, Texas

- **State-supported** university, founded 1883, part of University of Texas System
- **Calendar** semesters
- **Degrees** bachelor's, master's, doctoral, and first professional
- **Urban** 350-acre campus with easy access to San Antonio
- **Endowment** $1.5 billion
- **Coed,** 38,609 undergraduate students, 88% full-time, 51% women, 49% men
- **Very difficult** entrance level, 64% of applicants were admitted

Undergraduates 34,027 full-time, 4,582 part-time. Students come from 54 states and territories, 118 other countries, 5% are from out of state, 4% African American, 16% Asian American or Pacific Islander, 14% Hispanic American, 0.4% Native American, 3% international, 5% transferred in, 17% live on campus. *Retention:* 92% of 2001 full-time freshmen returned.

Freshmen *Admission:* 20,954 applied, 13,326 admitted, 7,337 enrolled. *Test scores:* SAT verbal scores over 500: 89%; SAT math scores over 500: 93%; ACT scores over 18: 98%; SAT verbal scores over 600: 50%; SAT math scores over 600: 63%; ACT scores over 24: 69%; SAT verbal scores over 700: 12%; SAT math scores over 700: 20%; ACT scores over 30: 14%.

The University of Texas at Austin (continued)

Faculty *Total:* 2,653, 90% full-time, 89% with terminal degrees. *Student/faculty ratio:* 19:1.

Majors Accounting; advertising; aerospace engineering; American studies; anthropology; Arabic; archaeology; architectural engineering; architecture; art; art history; Asian studies; astronomy; biochemistry; bioengineering; biology; botany; business; business administration; business administration/management related; business marketing and marketing management; chemical engineering; chemistry; civil engineering; classics; clothing/apparel/textile studies; communication disorders; communications; community health liaison; computer/information sciences; dance; design/visual communications; ecology; economics; electrical engineering; English; ethnic/cultural studies related; finance; fine/studio arts; foreign languages/literatures; French; geography; geological sciences related; geology; geophysics/seismology; German; Greek (ancient and medieval); health/physical education; Hebrew; history; home economics; humanities; individual/family development; interior design; Islamic studies; Italian; journalism; Latin American studies; Latin (ancient and medieval); liberal arts and sciences/liberal studies; linguistics; management information systems/business data processing; mathematics; mechanical engineering; medical technology; microbiology/bacteriology; Middle Eastern studies; molecular biology; music; music (general performance); music history; music theory and composition; nursing; nutrition studies; petroleum engineering; pharmacy; philosophy; physical sciences related; physics; political science; Portuguese; psychology; public relations; radio/television broadcasting; religious studies; Russian; Russian/Slavic studies; Scandinavian languages; Slavic languages; social work; sociology; Spanish; theater arts/drama; visual/performing arts; zoology.

Academic Programs *Special study options:* academic remediation for entering students, accelerated degree program, adult/continuing education programs, advanced placement credit, cooperative education, distance learning, double majors, English as a second language, honors programs, independent study, internships, part-time degree program, services for LD students, student-designed majors, study abroad, summer session for credit. *ROTC:* Army (b), Navy (b), Air Force (b). *Unusual degree programs:* 3-2 architecture.

Library Perry-Castañeda Library plus 18 others with 4.3 million titles, 50,165 serial subscriptions, 573,254 audiovisual materials, an OPAC, a Web page.

Computers on Campus 4000 computers available on campus for general student use. A campuswide network can be accessed from student residence rooms and from off campus that provide access to e-mail. Internet access, at least one staffed computer lab available.

Student Life *Housing Options:* coed, men-only, women-only, cooperative. *Activities and Organizations:* drama/theater group, student-run newspaper, radio and television station, choral group, marching band, Alpha Phi Omega, Orange Jackets, Baptist Student Ministry, Longhorn Band Student Organization, Student Volunteer Board, national fraternities, national sororities. *Campus security:* 24-hour emergency response devices and patrols, student patrols, late-night transport/escort service, controlled dormitory access. *Student Services:* health clinic, personal/psychological counseling, legal services.

Athletics Member NCAA. All Division I except football (Division I-A). *Intercollegiate sports:* baseball M(s), basketball M(s)/W(s), crew W(s), cross-country running M(s)/W(s), golf M(s)/W(s), soccer W(s), softball W(s), swimming M(s)/W(s), tennis M(s)/W(s), track and field M(s)/W(s), volleyball W(s). *Intramural sports:* archery M(c)/W(c), badminton M/W, baseball M(c), basketball M/W, bowling M/W, crew M(c), cross-country running M/W, equestrian sports M(c)/W(c), fencing M/W, football M/W, golf M/W, gymnastics M(c)/W(c), lacrosse M(c)/W(c), racquetball M/W, riflery M(c)/W(c), rugby M(c), sailing M(c)/W(c), soccer M/W, softball M/W, squash M/W, swimming M/W, table tennis M/W, tennis M/W, track and field M/W, volleyball M/W, water polo M(c)/W(c), weight lifting M/W, wrestling M(c)/W(c).

Standardized Tests *Required:* SAT I or ACT (for admission).

Costs (2001–02) *Tuition:* state resident $2520 full-time, $84 per semester hour part-time; nonresident $8850 full-time, $295 per semester hour part-time. Full-time tuition and fees vary according to course load and program. Part-time tuition and fees vary according to course load and program. *Required fees:* $1246 full-time, $33 per semester hour, $158 per term part-time. *Room and board:* $5671; room only: $3114. Room and board charges vary according to board plan and housing facility. *Payment plans:* tuition prepayment, installment. *Waivers:* senior citizens and employees or children of employees.

Financial Aid Of all full-time matriculated undergraduates who enrolled in 2001, 21870 applied for aid, 17400 were judged to have need, 14100 had their need fully met. In 2001, 7930 non-need-based awards were made. *Average percent of need met:* 95%. *Average financial aid package:* $7320. *Average need-based loan:* $4430. *Average need-based gift aid:* $4400. *Average non-need based aid:* $4460. *Average indebtedness upon graduation:* $17,100.

Applying *Options:* common application, electronic application, deferred entrance. *Application fee:* $50. *Required:* high school transcript. *Required for some:* essay or personal statement. *Application deadlines:* 2/1 (freshmen), 3/1 (transfers). *Notification:* continuous (freshmen).

Admissions Contact Freshman Admissions Center, The University of Texas at Austin, John Hargis Hall, Campus Mail Code D0700, Austin, TX 78712-1111. *Phone:* 512-475-7440. *Fax:* 512-475-7475. *E-mail:* frmn@uts.cc.utexas.edu.

THE UNIVERSITY OF TEXAS AT BROWNSVILLE

Brownsville, Texas

- **State-supported** upper-level, founded 1973, part of University of Texas System
- **Calendar** semesters
- **Degrees** certificates, associate, bachelor's, and master's
- **Urban** 65-acre campus
- **Endowment** $926,806
- **Coed,** 8,607 undergraduate students, 46% full-time, 62% women, 38% men
- **Noncompetitive** entrance level, 100% of applicants were admitted

Undergraduates 3,938 full-time, 4,669 part-time. 0.3% African American, 0.2% Asian American or Pacific Islander, 94% Hispanic American, 0.1% Native American, 0.6% international.

Freshmen *Admission:* 1,511 applied, 1,511 admitted.

Faculty *Total:* 489, 57% full-time. *Student/faculty ratio:* 15:1.

Majors Accounting; applied art; bilingual/bicultural education; biology; business administration; business marketing and marketing management; corrections; criminal justice/law enforcement administration; early childhood education; English; exercise sciences; finance; history; law enforcement/police science; liberal arts and sciences/liberal studies; mathematics; nursing; political science; sociology; Spanish; special education.

Academic Programs *Special study options:* academic remediation for entering students, advanced placement credit, cooperative education, part-time degree program, summer session for credit.

Library Arnulfo L. Oliveira Library with 147,216 titles, 4,447 serial subscriptions, 1,000 audiovisual materials, an OPAC, a Web page.

Computers on Campus 580 computers available on campus for general student use. A campuswide network can be accessed from off campus. Internet access available.

Student Life *Housing:* college housing not available. *Activities and Organizations:* student-run newspaper, choral group, Student Activities Programming Board, Criminal Justice Club, Gorgas Science Club, Club Cultural Latinoamericano. *Campus security:* 24-hour emergency response devices and patrols. *Student Services:* health clinic, personal/psychological counseling.

Athletics Member NJCAA. *Intercollegiate sports:* baseball M(s), golf M(s)/W(s), volleyball W(s). *Intramural sports:* badminton W.

Costs (2001–02) *Tuition:* area resident $576 full-time, $24 per hour part-time; state resident $1008 full-time, $42 per hour part-time; nonresident $6072 full-time, $253 per hour part-time. Full-time tuition and fees vary according to class time. Part-time tuition and fees vary according to class time. *Required fees:* $1106 full-time, $40 per hour. *Payment plan:* installment.

Financial Aid Of all full-time matriculated undergraduates who enrolled in 2001, 3349 applied for aid, 3151 were judged to have need, 1031 had their need fully met. *Average percent of need met:* 71%. *Average financial aid package:* $2467. *Average need-based loan:* $1369. *Average need-based gift aid:* $1725. *Average indebtedness upon graduation:* $8295.

Applying *Options:* common application. *Application deadline:* 8/1 (transfers). *Notification:* continuous (transfers).

Admissions Contact Carlo Tamayo, New Student Relations Coordinator, The University of Texas at Brownsville, 80 Fort Brown, Brownsville, TX 78520-4991. *Phone:* 956-544-8860. *Toll-free phone:* 800-850-0160. *Fax:* 956-544-8832. *E-mail:* cata01@utb.edu.

THE UNIVERSITY OF TEXAS AT DALLAS

Richardson, Texas

- **State-supported** university, founded 1969, part of University of Texas System
- **Calendar** semesters
- **Degrees** bachelor's, master's, and doctoral
- **Suburban** 455-acre campus with easy access to Dallas
- **Endowment** $190.3 million
- **Coed,** 7,491 undergraduate students, 65% full-time, 48% women, 52% men

■ **Very difficult** entrance level, 56% of applicants were admitted

Undergraduates 4,871 full-time, 2,620 part-time. Students come from 35 states and territories, 129 other countries, 10% are from out of state, 7% African American, 21% Asian American or Pacific Islander, 9% Hispanic American, 0.5% Native American, 4% international, 18% transferred in, 18% live on campus. *Retention:* 78% of 2001 full-time freshmen returned.

Freshmen *Admission:* 4,105 applied, 2,294 admitted, 1,010 enrolled. *Average high school GPA:* 3.40. *Test scores:* SAT verbal scores over 500: 81%; SAT math scores over 500: 88%; ACT scores over 18: 100%; SAT verbal scores over 600: 38%; SAT math scores over 600: 52%; ACT scores over 24: 56%; SAT verbal scores over 700: 8%; SAT math scores over 700: 14%; ACT scores over 30: 12%.

Faculty *Total:* 537, 63% full-time, 97% with terminal degrees. *Student/faculty ratio:* 19:1.

Majors Accounting; American studies; applied mathematics; art; biology; business; business marketing and marketing management; chemistry; cognitive psychology/psycholinguistics; computer engineering; computer/information sciences; computer science; criminology; economics; electrical engineering; ethnic/cultural studies related; geography; geology; history; humanities; industrial/manufacturing engineering; interdisciplinary studies; international business; literature; management information systems/business data processing; mathematical statistics; mathematics; neuroscience; organizational behavior; physics; political science; psychology; public administration; sociology; speech-language pathology/audiology; visual/performing arts.

Academic Programs *Special study options:* academic remediation for entering students, accelerated degree program, adult/continuing education programs, advanced placement credit, cooperative education, distance learning, double majors, honors programs, independent study, internships, part-time degree program, services for LD students, student-designed majors, study abroad, summer session for credit. *ROTC:* Army (c), Air Force (c). *Unusual degree programs:* engineering with Abilene Christian University, Austin College, Paul Quinn College, Texas Woman's University.

Library Eugene McDermott Library plus 2 others with 447,496 titles, 3,831 serial subscriptions, 2,011 audiovisual materials, an OPAC, a Web page.

Computers on Campus 428 computers available on campus for general student use. A campuswide network can be accessed from student residence rooms and from off campus. Internet access, online (class) registration, at least one staffed computer lab available.

Student Life *Housing Options:* coed. *Activities and Organizations:* drama/theater group, student-run newspaper, Friendship Association of Chinese Students and Scholars, Golden Key National Honor Society, Muslim Students Association, Indian Student Association, Black Student Alliance, national fraternities, national sororities. *Campus security:* 24-hour emergency response devices and patrols, late-night transport/escort service. *Student Services:* health clinic, personal/psychological counseling, women's center, legal services.

Athletics Member NCAA. All Division III. *Intercollegiate sports:* baseball M, basketball M/W, cross-country running M/W, golf M/W, soccer M/W, softball W, tennis M/W. *Intramural sports:* basketball M/W, football M/W, golf M/W, racquetball M/W, softball M/W, squash M/W, swimming M/W, table tennis M/W, tennis M/W, volleyball M/W, weight lifting M/W.

Standardized Tests *Required:* SAT I or ACT (for admission). *Recommended:* SAT II: Writing Test (for admission).

Costs (2001–02) *One-time required fee:* $10. *Tuition:* state resident $1260 full-time, $42 per credit part-time; nonresident $7590 full-time, $253 per credit part-time. Full-time tuition and fees vary according to course load, degree level, and program. Part-time tuition and fees vary according to course load, degree level, and program. *Required fees:* $2398 full-time, $93 per credit, $138 per term part-time. *Room and board:* $5914. Room and board charges vary according to board plan and housing facility. *Payment plan:* installment. *Waivers:* senior citizens.

Financial Aid Of all full-time matriculated undergraduates who enrolled in 2001, 2349 applied for aid, 2188 were judged to have need, 477 had their need fully met. 16 Federal Work-Study jobs (averaging $5317). In 2001, 423 non-need-based awards were made. *Average percent of need met:* 80%. *Average financial aid package:* $7940. *Average need-based loan:* $3999. *Average need-based gift aid:* $2546.

Applying *Options:* electronic application, deferred entrance. *Application fee:* $25. *Required:* essay or personal statement, high school transcript. *Required for some:* interview. *Recommended:* 3 letters of recommendation. *Application deadline:* 8/1 (freshmen). *Notification:* continuous (freshmen).

Admissions Contact Admissions Office, The University of Texas at Dallas, PO Box 830688 Mail Station MC11, Richardson, TX 75083-0688. *Phone:* 972-883-2342. *Toll-free phone:* 800-889-2443. *Fax:* 972-883-2599. *E-mail:* ugrad-admissions@utdallas.edu.

THE UNIVERSITY OF TEXAS AT EL PASO
El Paso, Texas

■ **State-supported** university, founded 1913
■ **Calendar** semesters
■ **Degrees** bachelor's, master's, and doctoral
■ **Urban** 360-acre campus
■ **Coed,** 13,642 undergraduate students, 73% full-time, 54% women, 46% men
■ **Minimally difficult** entrance level, 94% of applicants were admitted

Undergraduates 10,013 full-time, 3,629 part-time. Students come from 47 states and territories, 67 other countries, 3% are from out of state, 2% African American, 1% Asian American or Pacific Islander, 72% Hispanic American, 0.3% Native American, 12% international, 7% transferred in, 2% live on campus. *Retention:* 68% of 2001 full-time freshmen returned.

Freshmen *Admission:* 3,414 applied, 3,215 admitted, 2,286 enrolled. *Average high school GPA:* 3.33. *Test scores:* SAT verbal scores over 500: 32%; SAT math scores over 500: 35%; ACT scores over 18: 69%; SAT verbal scores over 600: 5%; SAT math scores over 600: 5%; ACT scores over 24: 12%.

Faculty *Total:* 877, 63% full-time. *Student/faculty ratio:* 19:1.

Majors Accounting; anthropology; applied mathematics; art; art education; biology; botany; broadcast journalism; business administration; business marketing and marketing management; ceramic arts; chemistry; civil engineering; community services; computer science; creative writing; criminal justice/law enforcement administration; drawing; economics; electrical engineering; English; finance; fine/studio arts; French; geography; geology; geophysics/seismology; German; graphic design/commercial art/illustration; health science; health services administration; history; industrial/manufacturing engineering; information sciences/systems; interdisciplinary studies; journalism; Latin American studies; linguistics; mass communications; mathematical statistics; mathematics; mechanical engineering; medical technology; metallurgical engineering; Mexican-American studies; microbiology/bacteriology; music; nursing; philosophy; physics; political science; printmaking; psychology; real estate; sculpture; social work; sociology; Spanish; speech-language pathology/audiology; speech/rhetorical studies; theater arts/drama; zoology.

Academic Programs *Special study options:* academic remediation for entering students, accelerated degree program, adult/continuing education programs, advanced placement credit, cooperative education, English as a second language, honors programs, internships, off-campus study, part-time degree program, services for LD students, summer session for credit. *ROTC:* Army (b), Air Force (b).

Library University Library with 961,247 titles, 3,005 serial subscriptions.

Computers on Campus A campuswide network can be accessed from student residence rooms and from off campus. At least one staffed computer lab available.

Student Life *Housing Options:* coed. *Activities and Organizations:* drama/theater group, student-run newspaper, radio station, choral group, marching band, national fraternities, national sororities. *Campus security:* 24-hour emergency response devices and patrols, late-night transport/escort service. *Student Services:* health clinic, personal/psychological counseling, women's center, legal services.

Athletics Member NCAA. All Division I except football (Division I-A). *Intercollegiate sports:* basketball M(s)/W(s), cross-country running M(s)/W(s), golf M(s), riflery M/W, tennis W(s), track and field M(s)/W(s), volleyball W(s). *Intramural sports:* archery M/W, badminton M/W, basketball M/W, bowling M/W, fencing M/W, field hockey M, golf M/W, gymnastics M/W, racquetball M/W, skiing (downhill) M, soccer M/W, squash M/W, swimming M/W, tennis M/W, track and field M/W, volleyball M/W, water polo M/W, weight lifting M, wrestling M/W.

Standardized Tests *Required for some:* SAT I or ACT (for admission).

Costs (2002–03) *Tuition:* state resident $1920 full-time, $80 per credit hour part-time; nonresident $6984 full-time, $291 per credit hour part-time. Full-time tuition and fees vary according to reciprocity agreements. Part-time tuition and fees vary according to course load and reciprocity agreements. *Required fees:* $636 full-time. *Room and board:* $4120; room only: $2520. Room and board charges vary according to housing facility. *Payment plan:* installment.

Financial Aid Of all full-time matriculated undergraduates who enrolled in 2001, 5706 applied for aid, 4576 were judged to have need, 839 had their need fully met. In 2001, 309 non-need-based awards were made. *Average percent of need met:* 67%. *Average financial aid package:* $7593. *Average need-based loan:* $4666. *Average need-based gift aid:* $3446. *Average non-need based aid:* $1661. *Average indebtedness upon graduation:* $12,825.

Applying *Required:* high school transcript. *Application deadlines:* 7/1 (freshmen), 7/31 (transfers). *Notification:* continuous until 4/1 (freshmen).

Admissions Contact Ms. Diana Guerrero, Director of Admissions, The University of Texas at El Paso, 500 West University Avenue, El Paso, TX 79968-0001. *Phone:* 915-747-5588. *Fax:* 915-747-5122. *E-mail:* admission@utep.edu.

THE UNIVERSITY OF TEXAS AT SAN ANTONIO
San Antonio, Texas

- **State-supported** university, founded 1969, part of University of Texas System
- **Calendar** semesters
- **Degrees** bachelor's, master's, and doctoral
- **Suburban** 600-acre campus
- **Endowment** $23.7 million
- **Coed,** 17,425 undergraduate students, 69% full-time, 55% women, 45% men
- **Moderately difficult** entrance level, 99% of applicants were admitted

Undergraduates 12,034 full-time, 5,391 part-time. Students come from 52 states and territories, 83 other countries, 2% are from out of state, 6% African American, 4% Asian American or Pacific Islander, 47% Hispanic American, 0.5% Native American, 2% international, 15% transferred in, 13% live on campus. *Retention:* 64% of 2001 full-time freshmen returned.

Freshmen *Admission:* 5,519 applied, 5,486 admitted, 2,294 enrolled. *Test scores:* SAT verbal scores over 500: 48%; SAT math scores over 500: 50%; ACT scores over 18: 81%; SAT verbal scores over 600: 11%; SAT math scores over 600: 12%; ACT scores over 24: 18%; SAT verbal scores over 700: 1%; SAT math scores over 700: 1%; ACT scores over 30: 1%.

Faculty *Total:* 963, 48% full-time, 70% with terminal degrees. *Student/faculty ratio:* 24:1.

Majors Accounting; American studies; anthropology; art; art history; bilingual/bicultural education; biological/physical sciences; biology; business; business administration; business economics; business marketing and marketing management; chemistry; civil engineering; classics; communications; community health liaison; computer/information sciences; corrections; criminal justice/law enforcement administration; electrical engineering; English; finance; French; geography; geology; German; health/physical education; health science; Hispanic-American studies; history; humanities; human resources management; information sciences/systems; interdisciplinary studies; interior architecture; interior design; international business; journalism; management information systems/business data processing; management science; mass communications; mathematical statistics; mathematics; mechanical engineering; medical technology; music; musical instrument technology; occupational therapy; operations management; philosophy; physical therapy; physics; political science; psychology; sociology; Spanish; travel/tourism management.

Academic Programs *Special study options:* academic remediation for entering students, accelerated degree program, adult/continuing education programs, advanced placement credit, cooperative education, distance learning, English as a second language, freshman honors college, honors programs, independent study, internships, part-time degree program, services for LD students, study abroad, summer session for credit. *ROTC:* Army (b), Air Force (b).

Library John Peace Library plus 1 other with 521,009 titles, 2,665 serial subscriptions, 24,752 audiovisual materials, an OPAC, a Web page.

Computers on Campus 800 computers available on campus for general student use. A campuswide network can be accessed from student residence rooms and from off campus. Internet access, online (class) registration, at least one staffed computer lab available.

Student Life *Housing Options:* coed. *Activities and Organizations:* drama/theater group, student-run newspaper, choral group, Pre-Med Society, MPA Student Association, Intervarsity Christian Fellowship, Catholic Student Association, national fraternities, national sororities. *Campus security:* 24-hour emergency response devices and patrols, student patrols, late-night transport/escort service, controlled dormitory access. *Student Services:* health clinic, personal/psychological counseling, legal services.

Athletics Member NCAA. All Division I. *Intercollegiate sports:* baseball M(s), basketball M(s)/W(s), cross-country running M(s)/W(s), golf M(s), softball W(s), tennis M(s)/W(s), track and field M(s)/W(s), volleyball W(s). *Intramural sports:* badminton M/W, baseball M, basketball M/W, cross-country running M/W, football M/W, golf M, soccer M/W, softball M/W, table tennis M/W, tennis M/W, track and field M/W, volleyball M/W, weight lifting M/W.

Standardized Tests *Required:* SAT I or ACT (for admission).

Costs (2001–02) *Tuition:* state resident $2520 full-time, $84 per semester hour part-time; nonresident $8850 full-time, $295 per semester hour part-time. Full-time tuition and fees vary according to course load. Part-time tuition and fees vary according to course load. *Required fees:* $983 full-time. *Room and board:* $6113. Room and board charges vary according to housing facility. *Payment plan:* installment.

Financial Aid Of all full-time matriculated undergraduates who enrolled in 2001, 6456 applied for aid. 525 Federal Work-Study jobs (averaging $2042). 41 State and other part-time jobs (averaging $2094). *Average percent of need met:* 65%.

Applying *Options:* common application, electronic application. *Application fee:* $25. *Required:* high school transcript. *Application deadlines:* 7/1 (freshmen), 7/1 (transfers).

Admissions Contact Mr. John Wallace, Interim Director, The University of Texas at San Antonio, 6900 North Loop 1604 West, San Antonio, TX 78249. *Phone:* 210-458-4530. *Toll-free phone:* 800-669-0916 (in-state); 800-669-0919 (out-of-state). *E-mail:* prospects@utsa.edu.

THE UNIVERSITY OF TEXAS AT TYLER
Tyler, Texas

- **State-supported** comprehensive, founded 1971, part of University of Texas System
- **Calendar** semesters
- **Degrees** bachelor's and master's
- **Urban** 200-acre campus
- **Endowment** $43.4 million
- **Coed,** 2,702 undergraduate students, 66% full-time, 65% women, 35% men
- 85% of applicants were admitted

The University of Texas at Tyler, a broad-spectrum liberal arts university, also offers academic programs that support professional and specialized careers. Seventy-four bachelor's and master's degree programs are offered through the University's 5 colleges, which include the Schools of Business Administration, Education and Psychology, Engineering, Health Sciences, and Arts and Sciences. For more information, students should call 800-UTTYLER.

Undergraduates 1,773 full-time, 929 part-time. Students come from 24 states and territories, 27 other countries, 2% are from out of state, 9% African American, 1% Asian American or Pacific Islander, 4% Hispanic American, 1% Native American, 1% international, 88% transferred in. *Retention:* 58% of 2001 full-time freshmen returned.

Freshmen *Admission:* 998 applied, 847 admitted, 259 enrolled. *Test scores:* SAT verbal scores over 500: 77%; SAT math scores over 500: 75%; ACT scores over 18: 96%; SAT verbal scores over 600: 24%; SAT math scores over 600: 21%; ACT scores over 24: 46%; SAT verbal scores over 700: 3%; SAT math scores over 700: 2%; ACT scores over 30: 2%.

Faculty *Total:* 271, 65% full-time, 57% with terminal degrees. *Student/faculty ratio:* 10:1.

Majors Accounting; art; biology; business administration; business marketing and marketing management; chemistry; computer science; criminal justice/law enforcement administration; economics; electrical engineering; English; exercise sciences; finance; health science; history; interdisciplinary studies; journalism; liberal arts and sciences/liberal studies; mathematics; mechanical engineering; medical technology; music; nursing; political science; psychology; sociology; Spanish; speech/rhetorical studies; theater arts/drama.

Academic Programs *Special study options:* adult/continuing education programs, advanced placement credit, cooperative education, distance learning, double majors, English as a second language, honors programs, independent study, internships, off-campus study, part-time degree program, services for LD students, student-designed majors, study abroad, summer session for credit.

Library Robert Muntz Library with 216,365 titles, 1,534 serial subscriptions, 10,772 audiovisual materials, an OPAC, a Web page.

Computers on Campus 300 computers available on campus for general student use. A campuswide network can be accessed from student residence rooms and from off campus. Internet access, at least one staffed computer lab available.

Student Life *Housing Options:* coed. *Activities and Organizations:* drama/theater group, student-run newspaper, choral group, Beta Beta Beta, Pre-Med/Pre-Dental, American Chemistry Society, Press Club, Association for Computing Machinery. *Campus security:* 24-hour emergency response devices and patrols, late-night transport/escort service, controlled dormitory access. *Student Services:* personal/psychological counseling.

Athletics *Intercollegiate sports:* tennis M/W. *Intramural sports:* basketball M/W, bowling M, football M, golf M/W, racquetball M/W, softball M, volleyball W.

Standardized Tests *Required:* SAT I or ACT (for admission).

Costs (2002–03) *Tuition:* state resident $3062 full-time; nonresident $9392 full-time. Full-time tuition and fees vary according to course load. *Room and board:* room only: $3267. Room and board charges vary according to board plan and housing facility. *Payment plan:* installment. *Waivers:* employees or children of employees.

Financial Aid Of all full-time matriculated undergraduates who enrolled in 2001, 963 applied for aid, 906 were judged to have need, 300 had their need fully met. 66 Federal Work-Study jobs (averaging $1596). 12 State and other part-time jobs (averaging $1039). In 2001, 336 non-need-based awards were made. *Average*

percent of need met: 70%. *Average financial aid package:* $6900. *Average need-based loan:* $4500. *Average need-based gift aid:* $2100. *Average non-need based aid:* $1000. *Average indebtedness upon graduation:* $6500.

Applying *Options:* common application, electronic application, deferred entrance. *Notification:* continuous (freshmen).

Admissions Contact The University of Texas at Tyler, 3900 University Boulevard, Tyler, TX 75799-0001. *Phone:* 903-566-7195. *Toll-free phone:* 800-UTTYLER. *Fax:* 903-566-7068.

THE UNIVERSITY OF TEXAS HEALTH SCIENCE CENTER AT HOUSTON

Houston, Texas

- **State-supported** upper-level, founded 1972, part of University of Texas System
- **Calendar** semesters
- **Degrees** certificates, bachelor's, master's, doctoral, first professional, and post-master's certificates
- **Urban** campus
- **Endowment** $88.7 million
- **Coed,** 330 undergraduate students, 98% full-time, 90% women, 10% men
- **Moderately difficult** entrance level, 30% of applicants were admitted

Undergraduates 323 full-time, 7 part-time. Students come from 3 states and territories, 1% are from out of state, 14% African American, 12% Asian American or Pacific Islander, 13% Hispanic American, 0.9% international, 100% transferred in.

Freshmen *Admission:* 702 applied, 212 admitted.

Faculty *Total:* 1,115, 78% full-time.

Majors Dental hygiene; nursing.

Academic Programs *Special study options:* accelerated degree program, distance learning, independent study, part-time degree program. *ROTC:* Army (c).

Library Houston Academy of Medicine-Texas Medical Center Library plus 3 others with 270,649 titles, 2,778 serial subscriptions, an OPAC, a Web page.

Computers on Campus A campuswide network can be accessed from off campus. Internet access, online (class) registration, at least one staffed computer lab available.

Student Life *Housing Options:* coed. *Activities and Organizations:* student-run newspaper. *Campus security:* 24-hour emergency response devices and patrols, late-night transport/escort service, controlled access to all buildings. *Student Services:* health clinic, personal/psychological counseling.

Costs (2001–02) *Tuition:* state resident $3150 full-time, $70 per hour part-time; nonresident $12,645 full-time, $281 per hour part-time. Part-time tuition and fees vary according to course load. *Required fees:* $624 full-time, $14 per semester hour, $20 per term part-time. *Payment plan:* installment.

Financial Aid Of all full-time matriculated undergraduates who enrolled in 2001, 225 applied for aid, 179 were judged to have need. *Average percent of need met:* 95%. *Average financial aid package:* $11,924. *Average need-based loan:* $4657. *Average need-based gift aid:* $3908. *Average indebtedness upon graduation:* $14,820.

Applying *Options:* electronic application. *Application fee:* $10. *Application deadline:* 12/31 (transfers).

Admissions Contact Mr. Robert L. Jenkins, Associate Registrar, The University of Texas Health Science Center at Houston, 7000 Fannin, PO Box 20036, Houston, TX 77225-0036. *Phone:* 713-500-3361. *Fax:* 713-500-3356. *E-mail:* uthschro@admin4.hsc.uth.tmc.edu.

THE UNIVERSITY OF TEXAS HEALTH SCIENCE CENTER AT SAN ANTONIO

San Antonio, Texas

Admissions Contact Mr. James Peak, Registrar, The University of Texas Health Science Center at San Antonio, 7703 Floyd Curl Drive, San Antonio, TX 78229-3900. *Phone:* 210-567-2629.

THE UNIVERSITY OF TEXAS MEDICAL BRANCH

Galveston, Texas

- **State-supported** upper-level, founded 1891, part of University of Texas System
- **Calendar** semesters
- **Degrees** bachelor's, master's, doctoral, and first professional
- **Small-town** 100-acre campus with easy access to Houston
- **Endowment** $330.9 million
- **Coed,** 562 undergraduate students, 64% full-time, 85% women, 15% men
- **Most difficult** entrance level, 69% of applicants were admitted

Undergraduates 357 full-time, 205 part-time. Students come from 3 states and territories, 1 other country, 1% are from out of state, 12% African American, 7% Asian American or Pacific Islander, 15% Hispanic American, 0.5% Native American, 0.7% international, 34% transferred in, 20% live on campus.

Freshmen *Admission:* 394 applied, 272 admitted.

Faculty *Total:* 134, 90% full-time. *Student/faculty ratio:* 7:1.

Majors Medical technology; nursing; occupational therapy; respiratory therapy.

Academic Programs *Special study options:* advanced placement credit, distance learning, internships, part-time degree program, services for LD students, summer session for credit.

Library Moody Medical Library with 247,096 titles, 1,986 serial subscriptions, an OPAC, a Web page.

Computers on Campus 160 computers available on campus for general student use. A campuswide network can be accessed from student residence rooms and from off campus. Internet access, at least one staffed computer lab available.

Student Life *Housing Options:* coed. *Activities and Organizations:* student-run newspaper, Texas Medical Association, American Medical Student Association, American Medical Women's Association, Texas Association Latin American Medical Students, National Medical Student Association, national fraternities. *Campus security:* 24-hour emergency response devices and patrols, late-night transport/escort service. *Student Services:* health clinic, personal/psychological counseling, legal services.

Athletics *Intramural sports:* basketball M/W, football M/W, soccer M/W, softball M/W, volleyball M/W.

Costs (2001–02) *One-time required fee:* $31. *Tuition:* state resident $1512 full-time, $40 per credit hour part-time; nonresident $9108 full-time, $253 per credit hour part-time. Full-time tuition and fees vary according to course load and program. Part-time tuition and fees vary according to course load and program. *Required fees:* $707 full-time, $333 per credit hour, $63 per credit hour part-time. *Room and board:* room only: $2400. Room and board charges vary according to housing facility. *Payment plan:* installment.

Financial Aid Of all full-time matriculated undergraduates who enrolled in 2001, 25 Federal Work-Study jobs (averaging $1234).

Applying *Options:* electronic application. *Application fee:* $25.

Admissions Contact Ms. Vicki L. Brewer, Interim Registrar, The University of Texas Medical Branch, 301 University Boulevard, Galveston, TX 77555-1305. *Phone:* 409-772-1215. *Fax:* 409-772-5056. *E-mail:* student.admissions@utmb.edu.

THE UNIVERSITY OF TEXAS OF THE PERMIAN BASIN

Odessa, Texas

- **State-supported** comprehensive, founded 1969, part of University of Texas System
- **Calendar** semesters
- **Degrees** bachelor's and master's
- **Urban** 600-acre campus
- **Coed,** 1,783 undergraduate students, 67% full-time, 66% women, 34% men
- **Moderately difficult** entrance level, 89% of applicants were admitted

Undergraduates 1,197 full-time, 586 part-time. Students come from 3 other countries, 3% African American, 0.9% Asian American or Pacific Islander, 36% Hispanic American, 0.6% Native American, 0.2% international. *Retention:* 59% of 2001 full-time freshmen returned.

Freshmen *Admission:* 298 applied, 266 admitted, 168 enrolled.

Faculty *Total:* 146, 56% full-time, 62% with terminal degrees. *Student/faculty ratio:* 17:1.

Majors Accounting; art; biology; business administration; business marketing and marketing management; chemistry; computer science; criminology; earth sciences; economics; English; environmental science; exercise sciences; finance; geology; history; humanities; interdisciplinary studies; mass communications; mathematics; political science; psychology; sociology; Spanish; speech/rhetorical studies.

Academic Programs *Special study options:* academic remediation for entering students, advanced placement credit, internships, part-time degree program, summer session for credit.

Library 267,531 titles, 723 serial subscriptions.

The University of Texas of the Permian Basin (continued)

Computers on Campus 130 computers available on campus for general student use. A campuswide network can be accessed from student residence rooms and from off campus. Internet access, at least one staffed computer lab available.

Student Life *Activities and Organizations:* student-run newspaper. *Campus security:* 24-hour patrols, late-night transport/escort service. *Student Services:* personal/psychological counseling.

Athletics Member NAIA. *Intercollegiate sports:* soccer M, softball W, volleyball W. *Intramural sports:* basketball M, football M, golf M/W, racquetball M/W, riflery M/W, rugby M, soccer M, swimming M/W, tennis M/W, volleyball M/W.

Standardized Tests *Required:* SAT I or ACT (for admission).

Costs (2001–02) *Tuition:* $75 per credit hour part-time; state resident $1800 full-time, $336 per credit hour part-time; nonresident $6864 full-time. Full-time tuition and fees vary according to course load and student level. Part-time tuition and fees vary according to course load and student level. *Required fees:* $634 full-time, $50 per credit hour. *Room and board:* room only: $1900. *Payment plan:* installment.

Financial Aid Of all full-time matriculated undergraduates who enrolled in 2001, 1145 applied for aid, 941 were judged to have need, 383 had their need fully met. 77 Federal Work-Study jobs (averaging $1418). 8 State and other part-time jobs (averaging $1154). In 2001, 183 non-need-based awards were made. *Average percent of need met:* 81%. *Average financial aid package:* $7960. *Average need-based loan:* $3964. *Average need-based gift aid:* $7012. *Average indebtedness upon graduation:* $13,697.

Applying *Options:* deferred entrance. *Required:* high school transcript. *Application deadline:* 8/1 (freshmen), rolling (transfers).

Admissions Contact Ms. Vicki Gomez, Assistant Vice President for Admissions, The University of Texas of the Permian Basin, 4901 East University, Odessa, TX 79762-0001. *Phone:* 915-552-2605. *Fax:* 915-552-2374. *E-mail:* gomez-v@gusher.pb.utexas.edu.

The University of Texas-Pan American

Edinburg, Texas

- **State-supported** comprehensive, founded 1927, part of University of Texas System
- **Calendar** semesters
- **Degrees** bachelor's, master's, and doctoral
- **Rural** 200-acre campus
- **Endowment** $21.8 million
- **Coed,** 11,971 undergraduate students, 66% full-time, 59% women, 41% men
- **Noncompetitive** entrance level, 77% of applicants were admitted

Undergraduates 7,896 full-time, 4,075 part-time. Students come from 30 states and territories, 10 other countries, 1% are from out of state, 0.4% African American, 1% Asian American or Pacific Islander, 85% Hispanic American, 0.2% Native American, 2% international, 5% transferred in. *Retention:* 61% of 2001 full-time freshmen returned.

Freshmen *Admission:* 4,050 applied, 3,104 admitted, 1,886 enrolled. *Test scores:* SAT verbal scores over 500: 28%; SAT math scores over 500: 30%; ACT scores over 18: 49%; SAT verbal scores over 600: 5%; SAT math scores over 600: 6%; ACT scores over 24: 8%; SAT math scores over 700: 1%.

Faculty *Total:* 601, 70% full-time. *Student/faculty ratio:* 29:1.

Majors Accounting; American studies; anthropology; Army R.O.T.C./military science; art; art education; art history; biology; business; business administration; business marketing and marketing management; chemistry; communications; community health liaison; computer/information sciences; computer science; corrections; criminal justice/law enforcement administration; cultural studies; dietetics; early childhood education; economics; electrical engineering; elementary education; English; finance; fine/studio arts; French; health education; health/physical education; history; human services; industrial/manufacturing engineering; information sciences/systems; interdisciplinary studies; international business; journalism; law enforcement/police science; management information systems/business data processing; mass communications; mathematics; mechanical engineering; medical technology; Mexican-American studies; music; nursing; philosophy; physical education; physical therapy; physics; political science; pre-dentistry; pre-medicine; psychology; public administration; reading education; recreation/leisure studies; rehabilitation therapy; secondary education; secretarial science; social work; sociology; Spanish; special education; speech-language pathology/audiology; speech/rhetorical studies; speech therapy; theater arts/drama.

Academic Programs *Special study options:* academic remediation for entering students, adult/continuing education programs, cooperative education, distance learning, double majors, external degree program, honors programs, independent study, internships, part-time degree program, services for LD students, study abroad, summer session for credit. *ROTC:* Army (b).

Library Learning Resource Library with 418,750 titles, 2,669 serial subscriptions, 24,412 audiovisual materials.

Computers on Campus 500 computers available on campus for general student use. A campuswide network can be accessed from off campus. Internet access, online (class) registration, at least one staffed computer lab available.

Student Life *Housing Options:* men-only, women-only. *Activities and Organizations:* drama/theater group, student-run newspaper, television station, choral group, Accounting Society, American Marketing Association, Pre-Medical/Bio Medical Society, Association of Texas Professional Educators, Financial Management Association, national fraternities, national sororities. *Campus security:* 24-hour emergency response devices and patrols, late-night transport/escort service. *Student Services:* health clinic, personal/psychological counseling.

Athletics Member NCAA. All Division I. *Intercollegiate sports:* baseball M(s), basketball M(s)/W(s), cross-country running M(s)/W(s), golf M(s)/W(s), riflery M/W, soccer M, tennis M(s)/W(s), track and field M(s)/W(s), volleyball W. *Intramural sports:* badminton M/W, basketball M/W, football M/W, gymnastics M/W, racquetball M/W, soccer M, softball M/W, swimming M/W, table tennis M/W, tennis M/W, volleyball M/W, weight lifting M/W.

Standardized Tests *Required:* SAT I or ACT (for admission). *Recommended:* ACT (for admission).

Costs (2001–02) *Tuition:* state resident $2040 full-time, $68 per semester hour part-time; nonresident $8370 full-time, $279 per semester hour part-time. Part-time tuition and fees vary according to course load. *Required fees:* $664 full-time, $299 per term part-time. *Room and board:* $5531; room only: $3367. Room and board charges vary according to housing facility.

Financial Aid Of all full-time matriculated undergraduates who enrolled in 2001, 6226 applied for aid, 5554 were judged to have need. 895 Federal Work-Study jobs (averaging $1882). 61 State and other part-time jobs (averaging $1073). *Average financial aid package:* $3254. *Average need-based loan:* $3960. *Average need-based gift aid:* $3122.

Applying *Options:* common application, electronic application, early admission. *Required:* high school transcript. *Required for some:* interview. *Application deadlines:* 7/10 (freshmen), 7/10 (transfers). *Notification:* continuous (freshmen).

Admissions Contact Mr. David Zuniga, Director of Admissions, The University of Texas-Pan American, Office of Admissions and Records, 1201 West University Drive, Edinburg, TX 78539. *Phone:* 956-381-2201. *Fax:* 956-381-2212. *E-mail:* admissions@panam.edu.

The University of Texas Southwestern Medical Center at Dallas

Dallas, Texas

- **State-supported** upper-level, founded 1943, part of University of Texas System
- **Calendar** trimesters
- **Degrees** bachelor's, master's, doctoral, first professional, and postbachelor's certificates
- **Urban** 98-acre campus
- **Endowment** $586.0 million
- **Coed,** 215 undergraduate students, 67% full-time, 73% women, 27% men
- **Moderately difficult** entrance level, 74% of applicants were admitted

Undergraduates 145 full-time, 70 part-time. Students come from 7 states and territories, 4 other countries, 7% are from out of state, 12% African American, 6% Asian American or Pacific Islander, 11% Hispanic American, 1.0% Native American, 2% international, 19% transferred in.

Freshmen *Admission:* 61 applied, 45 admitted.

Faculty *Total:* 103, 57% full-time, 55% with terminal degrees. *Student/faculty ratio:* 3:1.

Majors Dietetics; health facilities administration; health services administration; medical technology; orthotics/prosthetics; rehabilitation/therapeutic services related.

Academic Programs *Special study options:* advanced placement credit, independent study, internships, part-time degree program.

Library University of Texas Southwestern Library with 257,782 titles, 2,865 serial subscriptions, an OPAC, a Web page.

Computers on Campus 150 computers available on campus for general student use. A campuswide network can be accessed from off campus. Internet access, at least one staffed computer lab available.

Student Life *Housing:* college housing not available. *Campus security:* 24-hour patrols, late-night transport/escort service. *Student Services:* health clinic.

Athletics *Intramural sports:* basketball M/W, football M, golf M/W, soccer M/W, tennis M/W, volleyball M/W, weight lifting M/W.

Costs (2002–03) *Tuition:* state resident $1620 full-time, $54 per semester hour part-time; nonresident $8160 full-time, $272 per semester hour part-time. Full-time tuition and fees vary according to course load. Part-time tuition and fees vary according to course load. *Required fees:* $725 full-time. *Payment plan:* installment.

Financial Aid Of all full-time matriculated undergraduates who enrolled in 2001, 147 applied for aid, 147 were judged to have need. 1 Federal Work-Study jobs (averaging $379). *Average indebtedness upon graduation:* $20,144.

Applying *Options:* electronic application. *Application fee:* $10. *Application deadline:* rolling (transfers). *Notification:* continuous (transfers).

Admissions Contact Dr. Scott Wright, Director of Admissions, The University of Texas Southwestern Medical Center at Dallas, 5323 Harry Hines Boulevard, Dallas, TX 75390-9096. *Phone:* 214-648-5617. *Fax:* 214-648-3289. *E-mail:* admissions@utsouthwestern.edu.

UNIVERSITY OF THE INCARNATE WORD

San Antonio, Texas

- **Independent Roman Catholic** comprehensive, founded 1881
- **Calendar** semesters
- **Degrees** bachelor's, master's, and doctoral
- **Urban** 200-acre campus
- **Endowment** $23.9 million
- **Coed,** 3,519 undergraduate students, 60% full-time, 66% women, 34% men
- **Moderately difficult** entrance level, 37% of applicants were admitted

Undergraduates 2,116 full-time, 1,403 part-time. Students come from 27 states and territories, 37 other countries, 1% are from out of state, 6% African American, 2% Asian American or Pacific Islander, 53% Hispanic American, 0.5% Native American, 7% international, 10% transferred in, 21% live on campus. *Retention:* 70% of 2001 full-time freshmen returned.

Freshmen *Admission:* 1,276 applied, 472 admitted, 433 enrolled. *Average high school GPA:* 3.26. *Test scores:* SAT verbal scores over 500: 37%; SAT math scores over 500: 34%; ACT scores over 18: 66%; SAT verbal scores over 600: 9%; SAT math scores over 600: 7%; ACT scores over 24: 11%; SAT verbal scores over 700: 2%; ACT scores over 30: 3%.

Faculty *Total:* 418, 29% full-time. *Student/faculty ratio:* 14:1.

Majors Accounting; adult/continuing education; art; art education; biology; business; business administration; business marketing and marketing management; chemistry; communications; computer management; developmental/child psychology; early childhood education; education; elementary education; English; environmental science; fashion design/illustration; fashion merchandising; finance; graphic design/commercial art/illustration; history; hotel and restaurant management; interdisciplinary studies; interior design; interior environments; international business; liberal arts and sciences/liberal studies; management information systems/business data processing; management science; mass communications; mathematics; medical technology; music; music business management/merchandising; music history; music teacher education; music therapy; Native American studies; nuclear medical technology; nursing; nutrition science; organizational behavior; philosophy; physical education; political science; predentistry; pre-law; pre-medicine; psychology; reading education; religious studies; secondary education; sociology; Spanish; special education; speech/rhetorical studies; sport/fitness administration; theater arts/drama.

Academic Programs *Special study options:* academic remediation for entering students, accelerated degree program, adult/continuing education programs, advanced placement credit, double majors, English as a second language, external degree program, independent study, internships, off-campus study, part-time degree program, services for LD students, study abroad, summer session for credit. *ROTC:* Army (c), Air Force (c).

Library J.E. and L.E. Mabee Library plus 1 other with 235,000 titles, 3,436 serial subscriptions, 36,441 audiovisual materials, an OPAC, a Web page.

Computers on Campus 200 computers available on campus for general student use. A campuswide network can be accessed from student residence rooms and from off campus. Internet access, online (class) registration, at least one staffed computer lab available.

Student Life *Housing Options:* coed, men-only, women-only. *Activities and Organizations:* drama/theater group, student-run newspaper, choral group, Alpha Phi Omega, Dietetics Club, Red Alert, Student Nurses Association, Crusaders Seeking Christ, national fraternities, national sororities. *Campus security:* 24-hour emergency response devices and patrols, late-night transport/escort service, controlled dormitory access. *Student Services:* health clinic, personal/psychological counseling.

Athletics Member NCAA, NAIA. All NCAA Division II. *Intercollegiate sports:* baseball M(s), basketball M(s)/W(s), cross-country running M(s)/W(s), golf M(s)/W(s), soccer M(s)/W(s), softball W(s), tennis M(s)/W(s), volleyball W(s). *Intramural sports:* archery M/W, badminton M/W, basketball M/W, bowling M/W, cross-country running M/W, football M/W, golf M/W, racquetball M/W, soccer M/W, swimming M/W, table tennis M/W, tennis M/W, track and field M/W, volleyball M/W.

Standardized Tests *Required:* SAT I or ACT (for admission).

Costs (2002–03) *One-time required fee:* $30. *Comprehensive fee:* $18,748 includes full-time tuition ($13,220), mandatory fees ($278), and room and board ($5250). Part-time tuition: $414 per semester hour. Part-time tuition and fees vary according to course load. *Required fees:* $97 per term part-time. *Room and board:* College room only: $3110. Room and board charges vary according to board plan. *Payment plan:* installment. *Waivers:* employees or children of employees.

Financial Aid Of all full-time matriculated undergraduates who enrolled in 2001, 2261 applied for aid, 1831 were judged to have need, 306 had their need fully met. 506 Federal Work-Study jobs (averaging $1752). 26 State and other part-time jobs (averaging $1000). In 2001, 407 non-need-based awards were made. *Average percent of need met:* 85%. *Average financial aid package:* $13,546. *Average need-based loan:* $4000. *Average need-based gift aid:* $8215. *Average non-need based aid:* $6800.

Applying *Options:* electronic application, early admission, deferred entrance. *Application fee:* $20. *Required:* high school transcript. *Required for some:* essay or personal statement, interview. *Recommended:* minimum 2.0 GPA, 1 letter of recommendation, interview. *Application deadline:* rolling (freshmen), rolling (transfers).

Admissions Contact Ms. Andrea Cyterski, Director of Admissions, University of the Incarnate Word, Box 285, San Antonio, TX 78209-6397. *Phone:* 210-829-6005. *Toll-free phone:* 800-749-WORD. *Fax:* 210-829-3921. *E-mail:* admis@universe.uiwtx.edu.

WAYLAND BAPTIST UNIVERSITY

Plainview, Texas

- **Independent Baptist** comprehensive, founded 1908
- **Calendar** 4-1-4
- **Degrees** associate, bachelor's, and master's (branch locations: Anchorage, AK; Amarillo, TX; Luke Airforce Base, AZ; Glorieta, NM; Aiea, HI; Lubbock, TX; San Antonio, TX; Wichita Falls, TX)
- **Small-town** 80-acre campus
- **Endowment** $32.1 million
- **Coed,** 932 undergraduate students, 79% full-time, 60% women, 40% men
- **Minimally difficult** entrance level, 97% of applicants were admitted

Undergraduates 739 full-time, 193 part-time. Students come from 22 states and territories, 6 other countries, 12% are from out of state, 3% African American, 0.4% Asian American or Pacific Islander, 17% Hispanic American, 0.4% Native American, 1% international, 6% transferred in, 54% live on campus. *Retention:* 58% of 2001 full-time freshmen returned.

Freshmen *Admission:* 278 applied, 271 admitted, 212 enrolled. *Average high school GPA:* 3.32. *Test scores:* SAT verbal scores over 500: 40%; SAT math scores over 500: 42%; ACT scores over 18: 68%; SAT verbal scores over 600: 18%; SAT math scores over 600: 15%; ACT scores over 24: 25%; SAT verbal scores over 700: 1%; SAT math scores over 700: 2%; ACT scores over 30: 2%.

Faculty *Total:* 95, 67% full-time. *Student/faculty ratio:* 12:1.

Majors Art; biological/physical sciences; biology; business administration; chemistry; criminal justice studies; education; elementary education; English; history; mass communications; mathematics; music; music teacher education; physical education; physical sciences; political science; psychology; religious education; religious music; religious studies; social sciences; Spanish; theater arts/drama; trade/industrial education.

Academic Programs *Special study options:* academic remediation for entering students, accelerated degree program, adult/continuing education programs, advanced placement credit, distance learning, double majors, external degree program, honors programs, internships, part-time degree program, summer session for credit. *Unusual degree programs:* 3-2 engineering with Texas Tech University.

Library J.E. and L.E. Mabee Learning Resource Center with 111,824 titles, 360 serial subscriptions, 13,239 audiovisual materials, an OPAC, a Web page.

Computers on Campus 297 computers available on campus for general student use. A campuswide network can be accessed from student residence rooms and from off campus. Internet access, at least one staffed computer lab available.

Student Life *Housing:* on-campus residence required through junior year. *Options:* men-only, women-only. *Activities and Organizations:* drama/theater

Wayland Baptist University (continued)
group, student-run newspaper, radio and television station, choral group, marching band, student government, national fraternities, national sororities. *Campus security:* 24-hour emergency response devices and patrols, security lighting. *Student Services:* health clinic, personal/psychological counseling.

Athletics Member NAIA. *Intercollegiate sports:* baseball M(s), basketball M(s)/W(s), cross-country running M(s)/W(s), golf M, soccer W, track and field M(s)/W(s), volleyball W(s). *Intramural sports:* basketball M/W, football M/W, golf M/W, softball M/W, volleyball M/W.

Standardized Tests *Required for some:* SAT I or ACT (for admission).

Costs (2001–02) *Comprehensive fee:* $11,271 includes full-time tuition ($7800), mandatory fees ($350), and room and board ($3121). Part-time tuition: $260 per credit hour. Part-time tuition and fees vary according to course load. *Required fees:* $40 per term part-time. *Room and board:* College room only: $1216. Room and board charges vary according to board plan and housing facility. *Payment plan:* installment. *Waivers:* employees or children of employees.

Financial Aid Of all full-time matriculated undergraduates who enrolled in 2001, 732 applied for aid, 624 were judged to have need, 154 had their need fully met. In 2001, 77 non-need-based awards were made. *Average percent of need met:* 82%. *Average financial aid package:* $9484. *Average need-based loan:* $4321. *Average need-based gift aid:* $4979.

Applying *Application fee:* $35. *Required:* high school transcript. *Recommended:* interview. *Application deadline:* rolling (freshmen), rolling (transfers). *Notification:* continuous (freshmen).

Admissions Contact Mr. Shawn Thomas, Director of Student Admissions, Wayland Baptist University, 1900 West 7th Street #712, Plainview, TX 79072. *Phone:* 806-291-3508. *Toll-free phone:* 800-588-1-WBU. *E-mail:* admityou@mail.wbu.edu.

West Texas A&M University

Canyon, Texas

- **State-supported** comprehensive, founded 1909, part of Texas A&M University System
- **Calendar** semesters
- **Degrees** bachelor's and master's
- **Small-town** 128-acre campus
- **Endowment** $13.7 million
- **Coed,** 5,395 undergraduate students, 79% full-time, 56% women, 44% men
- **Moderately difficult** entrance level, 88% of applicants were admitted

Undergraduates 4,278 full-time, 1,117 part-time. Students come from 38 states and territories, 26 other countries, 8% are from out of state, 3% African American, 1% Asian American or Pacific Islander, 13% Hispanic American, 0.7% Native American, 2% international, 13% transferred in, 29% live on campus. *Retention:* 66% of 2001 full-time freshmen returned.

Freshmen *Admission:* 2,147 applied, 1,888 admitted, 798 enrolled. *Average high school GPA:* 3.80. *Test scores:* SAT verbal scores over 500: 52%; SAT math scores over 500: 47%; ACT scores over 18: 81%; SAT verbal scores over 600: 13%; SAT math scores over 600: 13%; ACT scores over 24: 23%; SAT verbal scores over 700: 1%; ACT scores over 30: 1%.

Faculty *Total:* 315, 69% full-time, 52% with terminal degrees. *Student/faculty ratio:* 23:1.

Majors Accounting; advertising; agribusiness; agricultural business; animal sciences; art; biology; broadcast journalism; business; business administration; business economics; business marketing and marketing management; chemistry; communication disorders; computer/information sciences; criminal justice/law enforcement administration; dance; economics; English; environmental science; equestrian studies; finance; fine/studio arts; general studies; geography; geology; graphic design/commercial art/illustration; health/physical education; history; industrial technology; interdisciplinary studies; journalism; liberal arts and sciences/liberal studies; management information systems/business data processing; mass communications; mathematics; medical technology; multi/interdisciplinary studies related; music; music (general performance); music theory and composition; music therapy; nursing; physics; plant protection; plant sciences related; political science; psychology; public administration; recreation/leisure studies; social sciences; social work; sociology; Spanish; speech/rhetorical studies; theater arts/drama; wildlife biology.

Academic Programs *Special study options:* academic remediation for entering students, adult/continuing education programs, advanced placement credit, cooperative education, distance learning, double majors, English as a second language, honors programs, independent study, internships, part-time degree program, services for LD students, student-designed majors, summer session for credit. *Unusual degree programs:* 3-2 engineering with Texas Tech University, Texas A&M University; accounting.

Library Cornette Library with 301,412 titles, 5,905 serial subscriptions, 1,464 audiovisual materials, an OPAC, a Web page.

Computers on Campus 800 computers available on campus for general student use. A campuswide network can be accessed from student residence rooms and from off campus. Internet access, online (class) registration, at least one staffed computer lab available.

Student Life *Housing:* on-campus residence required through sophomore year. *Options:* coed, men-only, women-only, disabled students. *Activities and Organizations:* drama/theater group, student-run newspaper, radio station, choral group, marching band, Residence Hall Association, Greek System, Student Organizations' Roundtable, student government, Students in Free Enterprise, national fraternities, national sororities. *Campus security:* 24-hour emergency response devices and patrols, student patrols, late-night transport/escort service, controlled dormitory access. *Student Services:* health clinic, personal/psychological counseling.

Athletics Member NCAA. All Division II. *Intercollegiate sports:* baseball M(s), basketball M(s)/W(s), bowling M(s)(c)/W(s)(c), cross-country running M(s)/W(s), equestrian sports M(c)/W(s), football M(s), golf M(s)/W(s), soccer M(s)/W(s), tennis M(s)/W(s), volleyball W(s). *Intramural sports:* badminton M/W, basketball M/W, bowling M/W, football M/W, golf M/W, racquetball M/W, soccer M/W, softball M/W, swimming M/W, table tennis M/W, tennis M/W, volleyball M/W, wrestling M.

Standardized Tests *Required:* SAT I or ACT (for admission).

Costs (2001–02) *One-time required fee:* $10. *Tuition:* state resident $1668 full-time, $70 per hour part-time; nonresident $6732 full-time, $281 per hour part-time. Full-time tuition and fees vary according to course load. Part-time tuition and fees vary according to course load. *Required fees:* $633 full-time, $21 per hour, $80 per term part-time. *Room and board:* $3831; room only: $1836. Room and board charges vary according to board plan and housing facility. *Payment plan:* installment. *Waivers:* senior citizens.

Financial Aid Of all full-time matriculated undergraduates who enrolled in 2001, 2921 applied for aid, 2452 were judged to have need, 2359 had their need fully met. 208 Federal Work-Study jobs (averaging $1403). 41 State and other part-time jobs (averaging $507). In 2001, 371 non-need-based awards were made. *Average percent of need met:* 62%. *Average financial aid package:* $5043. *Average need-based loan:* $3665. *Average need-based gift aid:* $2405. *Average non-need based aid:* $3874.

Applying *Options:* common application, electronic application. *Application fee:* $25. *Required:* high school transcript, class rank. *Application deadline:* rolling (freshmen), rolling (transfers). *Notification:* continuous (freshmen).

Admissions Contact Ms. Lila Vars, Director of Admissions, West Texas A&M University, WT Box 60907, Canyon, TX 79016-0001. *Phone:* 806-651-2020. *Toll-free phone:* 800-99-WTAMU (in-state); 800-99-WTMAU (out-of-state). *Fax:* 806-651-5268. *E-mail:* lvars@mail.wtamu.edu.

Wiley College

Marshall, Texas

- **Independent** 4-year, founded 1873, affiliated with United Methodist Church
- **Calendar** semesters
- **Degrees** associate and bachelor's
- **Small-town** 58-acre campus
- **Endowment** $5.1 million
- **Coed,** 584 undergraduate students, 95% full-time, 52% women, 48% men
- **Noncompetitive** entrance level

Undergraduates 557 full-time, 27 part-time. Students come from 16 states and territories, 7 other countries, 35% are from out of state, 88% African American, 0.7% Hispanic American, 0.3% Native American, 9% international, 93% transferred in. *Retention:* 50% of 2001 full-time freshmen returned.

Freshmen *Admission:* 141 enrolled. *Average high school GPA:* 2.7.

Faculty *Total:* 57, 79% full-time, 58% with terminal degrees. *Student/faculty ratio:* 8:1.

Majors Biology; business administration; business education; chemistry; computer/information sciences; computer science; elementary education; English; history; hotel and restaurant management; mass communications; mathematics; music; music teacher education; philosophy; physical education; physical sciences; physics; pre-dentistry; pre-law; pre-medicine; religious studies; secretarial science; social sciences; social work; sociology; special education.

Academic Programs *Special study options:* academic remediation for entering students, adult/continuing education programs, off-campus study, part-time degree program, student-designed majors, study abroad, summer session for credit.

Library T. Winston Cole, Sr. Library with 24,000 titles, 23,000 serial subscriptions, 8,000 audiovisual materials.

Computers on Campus 30 computers available on campus for general student use.
Student Life *Activities and Organizations:* drama/theater group, student-run newspaper, national fraternities, national sororities. *Student Services:* health clinic, personal/psychological counseling.
Athletics *Intercollegiate sports:* basketball M(s)/W(s), track and field M(s)/W(s), volleyball W. *Intramural sports:* basketball M/W, track and field M/W, volleyball W.
Standardized Tests *Recommended:* SAT I or ACT (for admission).
Costs (2001–02) *Comprehensive fee:* $9572 includes full-time tuition ($4816), mandatory fees ($1024), and room and board ($3732). Part-time tuition: $163 per semester hour. *Required fees:* $498 per term part-time. *Room and board:* College room only: $1794. *Payment plan:* installment. *Waivers:* employees or children of employees.
Applying *Options:* early admission, deferred entrance. *Application fee:* $10. *Required:* high school transcript, 1 letter of recommendation. *Application deadlines:* 8/1 (freshmen), 8/1 (transfers). *Notification:* continuous until 8/10 (freshmen).
Admissions Contact Dr. Rory Bedford, Director of Admissions, Wiley College, 711 Wiley Avenue, Marshall, TX 75670. *Phone:* 903-927-3356. *Toll-free phone:* 800-658-6889. *E-mail:* vvalentine@wileyc.edu.

UTAH

BRIGHAM YOUNG UNIVERSITY
Provo, Utah

- **Independent** university, founded 1875, affiliated with Church of Jesus Christ of Latter-day Saints
- **Calendar** 4-4-2-2
- **Degrees** bachelor's, master's, doctoral, and first professional
- **Suburban** 638-acre campus with easy access to Salt Lake City
- **Coed,** 29,815 undergraduate students, 89% full-time, 51% women, 49% men
- **Moderately difficult** entrance level, 65% of applicants were admitted

Undergraduates 26,537 full-time, 3,278 part-time. Students come from 53 states and territories, 107 other countries, 70% are from out of state, 0.3% African American, 3% Asian American or Pacific Islander, 3% Hispanic American, 0.6% Native American, 3% international, 4% transferred in, 20% live on campus. *Retention:* 91% of 2001 full-time freshmen returned.
Freshmen *Admission:* 10,293 applied, 6,739 admitted, 5,186 enrolled. *Average high school GPA:* 3.76. *Test scores:* ACT scores over 18: 99%; ACT scores over 24: 88%; ACT scores over 30: 25%.
Faculty *Total:* 2,066, 76% full-time, 51% with terminal degrees. *Student/faculty ratio:* 20:1.
Majors Accounting; agronomy/crop science; American studies; animal sciences; anthropology; art; art education; art history; Asian studies; astrophysics; biochemistry; biology; botany; business administration; business marketing and marketing management; chemical engineering; chemistry; chemistry education; Chinese; civil engineering; classics; communications; comparative literature; computer engineering; computer science; construction management; dance; design/visual communications; dietetics; drama/dance education; early childhood education; earth sciences; economics; electrical/electronic engineering technology; electrical engineering; elementary education; engineering; engineering technology; English; English education; European studies; family/community studies; family studies; food sciences; foreign languages education; French; French language education; geography; geology; German; German language education; graphic design/commercial art/illustration; health/physical education; health science; hearing sciences; history; history education; horticulture science; humanities; industrial arts education; industrial design; interior design; international relations; Italian; Japanese; Latin American studies; Latin (ancient and medieval); linguistics; mathematical statistics; mathematics; mathematics education; mechanical engineering; microbiology/bacteriology; Middle Eastern studies; molecular biology; music; music (general performance); music teacher education; music theory and composition; nursing; nutritional sciences; philosophy; photography; physical education; physics; physics education; plant breeding; political science; Portuguese; psychology; range management; recreation/leisure facilities management; Russian; social studies education; social work; sociology; Spanish; Spanish language education; speech-language pathology; theater arts/drama; visual/performing arts; wildlife biology; wildlife management; zoology.
Academic Programs *Special study options:* academic remediation for entering students, accelerated degree program, adult/continuing education programs, advanced placement credit, cooperative education, distance learning, double majors, English as a second language, external degree program, freshman honors college, honors programs, independent study, internships, off-campus study, part-time degree program, services for LD students, study abroad, summer session for credit. *ROTC:* Army (b), Air Force (b).
Library Harold B. Lee Library plus 2 others with 2.6 million titles, 16,201 serial subscriptions, 56,353 audiovisual materials, an OPAC, a Web page.
Computers on Campus 1800 computers available on campus for general student use. A campuswide network can be accessed from student residence rooms and from off campus. Internet access, online (class) registration, at least one staffed computer lab available.
Student Life *Housing Options:* men-only, women-only. *Activities and Organizations:* drama/theater group, student-run newspaper, radio and television station, choral group, marching band, Swing Kids, Adaptive Aquatics, ACCESS, Young Republicans. *Campus security:* 24-hour emergency response devices and patrols, late-night transport/escort service, controlled dormitory access. *Student Services:* health clinic, personal/psychological counseling, women's center, legal services.
Athletics Member NCAA. All Division I except football (Division I-A). *Intercollegiate sports:* baseball M(s), basketball M(s)/W(s), cross-country running M(s)/W(s), golf M(s)/W(s), gymnastics W(s), lacrosse M(c), racquetball M(c)/W(c), rugby M(c), soccer M(c)/W(s), softball W(c), swimming M(s)/W(s), tennis M(s)/W(s), track and field M(s)/W(s), volleyball M(s)/W(s). *Intramural sports:* badminton M/W, basketball M/W, field hockey M, football M/W, golf M/W, racquetball M/W, soccer M/W, softball M/W, tennis M/W, volleyball M/W, water polo M/W.
Standardized Tests *Required:* ACT (for admission).
Costs (2002–03) *Comprehensive fee:* $7840 includes full-time tuition ($3060) and room and board ($4780). Full-time tuition and fees vary according to reciprocity agreements. Part-time tuition: $156 per credit hour. Part-time tuition and fees vary according to course load and reciprocity agreements. *Room and board:* Room and board charges vary according to board plan and housing facility. *Waivers:* employees or children of employees.
Financial Aid Of all full-time matriculated undergraduates who enrolled in 2001, 21847 applied for aid, 11281 were judged to have need, 8 had their need fully met. 56 State and other part-time jobs (averaging $1318). In 2001, 7262 non-need-based awards were made. *Average percent of need met:* 37%. *Average financial aid package:* $3602. *Average need-based loan:* $1806. *Average need-based gift aid:* $1797. *Average non-need based aid:* $2838. *Average indebtedness upon graduation:* $11,591.
Applying *Options:* electronic application, early admission, deferred entrance. *Application fee:* $25. *Required:* essay or personal statement, high school transcript, 1 letter of recommendation, interview. *Application deadlines:* 2/15 (freshmen), 3/15 (transfers). *Notification:* continuous (freshmen).
Admissions Contact Mr. Erlend D. Peterson, Dean of Admissions and Records, Brigham Young University, 84602-1110. *Phone:* 801-378-2539. *Fax:* 801-378-4264. *E-mail:* admissions@byu.edu.

DIXIE STATE COLLEGE OF UTAH
St. George, Utah

- **State-supported** primarily 2-year, founded 1911
- **Calendar** semesters
- **Degrees** certificates, diplomas, associate, and bachelor's
- **Small-town** 60-acre campus
- **Endowment** $6.2 million
- **Coed,** 7,001 undergraduate students, 45% full-time, 51% women, 49% men
- **Noncompetitive** entrance level, 93% of applicants were admitted

Undergraduates 3,170 full-time, 3,831 part-time. Students come from 47 states and territories, 12 other countries, 14% are from out of state, 0.6% African American, 1% Asian American or Pacific Islander, 2% Hispanic American, 1% Native American, 0.6% international, 4% transferred in, 2% live on campus. *Retention:* 41% of 2001 full-time freshmen returned.
Freshmen *Admission:* 2,473 applied, 2,292 admitted, 1,501 enrolled. *Average high school GPA:* 3.21. *Test scores:* SAT verbal scores over 500: 31%; SAT math scores over 500: 31%; ACT scores over 18: 72%; SAT verbal scores over 600: 5%; ACT scores over 24: 17%; ACT scores over 30: 1%.
Faculty *Total:* 302, 34% full-time, 44% with terminal degrees. *Student/faculty ratio:* 22:1.
Majors Accounting; agricultural sciences; aircraft pilot (professional); architectural drafting; art; art history; auto body repair; auto mechanic/technician; aviation management; biology; biotechnology research; botany; broadcast journalism; business administration; cartography; ceramic arts; chemistry; child care/guidance; communications; computer science; criminal justice studies; dance; data processing technology; dental hygiene; diesel engine mechanic; drawing;

Dixie State College of Utah (continued)
early childhood education; ecology; economics; elementary education; emergency medical technology; engineering; English; environmental science; foreign languages/literatures; forestry; general retailing/wholesaling; geology; graphic design/commercial art/illustration; health professions and related sciences; history; humanities; interior design; journalism; liberal arts and sciences/liberal studies; marine biology; mathematics; mechanical drafting; music; natural resources conservation; natural resources management; nursing; painting; philosophy; photographic technology; photography; physical education; physics; plant pathology; plant protection; political science; pre-law; printmaking; psychology; radio/television broadcasting; range management; sculpture; secondary education; secretarial science; social work; sociology; soil sciences; theater arts/drama; tourism/travel marketing related; water resources engineering; Web page, digital/multimedia and information resources design; wildlife management; zoology.

Academic Programs *Special study options:* academic remediation for entering students, adult/continuing education programs, advanced placement credit, cooperative education, distance learning, English as a second language, honors programs, part-time degree program, services for LD students, summer session for credit.

Library Val A. Browning Library with 83,160 titles, 343 serial subscriptions, 12,321 audiovisual materials, an OPAC, a Web page.

Computers on Campus A campuswide network can be accessed from student residence rooms. Internet access, online (class) registration, at least one staffed computer lab available.

Student Life *Housing Options:* coed, men-only. *Activities and Organizations:* drama/theater group, student-run newspaper, radio and television station, choral group, Dixie Spirit, Outdoor Club, Association of Women Students. *Campus security:* 24-hour emergency response devices and patrols. *Student Services:* health clinic, personal/psychological counseling.

Athletics Member NJCAA. *Intercollegiate sports:* baseball M(s), basketball M(s)/W(s), football M(s), golf M(s), soccer W(s), softball W(s), volleyball W(s). *Intramural sports:* basketball M/W, football M, golf M, soccer M/W, softball M/W, tennis M/W, volleyball M/W.

Standardized Tests *Required:* CPT or ACT COMPASS (if not submitting SAT I or ACT). *Recommended:* SAT I or ACT (for placement).

Costs (2001–02) *Tuition:* state resident $1252 full-time, $54 per credit part-time; nonresident $5476 full-time, $230 per credit part-time. Full-time tuition and fees vary according to class time. Part-time tuition and fees vary according to class time and course load. *Required fees:* $292 full-time. *Room and board:* $2850. Room and board charges vary according to board plan. *Payment plan:* installment. *Waivers:* senior citizens and employees or children of employees.

Financial Aid Of all full-time matriculated undergraduates who enrolled in 2001, 100 Federal Work-Study jobs (averaging $2200). 20 State and other part-time jobs (averaging $2200).

Applying *Options:* electronic application, early admission, deferred entrance. *Application fee:* $25. *Required:* high school transcript. *Application deadline:* rolling (freshmen), rolling (transfers).

Admissions Contact Ms. Darla Rollins, Admissions Coordinator, Dixie State College of Utah, 225 South 700 East, St. George, UT 84770-3876. *Phone:* 435-652-7702. *Toll-free phone:* 888-GO2DIXIE. *Fax:* 435-656-4005. *E-mail:* rollins@dixie.edu.

ITT Technical Institute
Murray, Utah

- **Proprietary** primarily 2-year, founded 1984, part of ITT Educational Services, Inc
- **Calendar** quarters
- **Degrees** associate and bachelor's
- **Suburban** 3-acre campus with easy access to Salt Lake City
- **Coed,** 472 undergraduate students
- **Minimally difficult** entrance level

Majors Computer/information sciences related; computer programming; drafting; electrical/electronic engineering technologies related; industrial design; information technology.

Student Life *Housing:* college housing not available.

Costs (2001–02) *Tuition:* Full-time tuition and fees vary according to program. Part-time tuition and fees vary according to program. $260—$330 per credit hour.

Applying *Options:* deferred entrance. *Application fee:* $100. *Required:* high school transcript, interview. *Recommended:* letters of recommendation. *Application deadline:* rolling (freshmen), rolling (transfers). *Notification:* continuous (freshmen).

Admissions Contact Mr. Gary Lafe, Director of Recruitment, ITT Technical Institute, 920 West LeVoy Drive, Murray, UT 84123-2500. *Phone:* 801-263-3313. *Toll-free phone:* 800-365-2136.

Southern Utah University
Cedar City, Utah

- **State-supported** comprehensive, founded 1897, part of Utah System of Higher Education
- **Calendar** semesters
- **Degrees** certificates, diplomas, associate, bachelor's, and master's
- **Small-town** 113-acre campus
- **Endowment** $5.1 million
- **Coed,** 5,884 undergraduate students, 78% full-time, 56% women, 44% men
- **Moderately difficult** entrance level, 84% of applicants were admitted

Undergraduates 4,601 full-time, 1,283 part-time. Students come from 40 states and territories, 14 other countries, 17% are from out of state, 0.5% African American, 1% Asian American or Pacific Islander, 2% Hispanic American, 1% Native American, 2% international, 9% transferred in, 6% live on campus. *Retention:* 63% of 2001 full-time freshmen returned.

Freshmen *Admission:* 1,507 applied, 1,269 admitted, 813 enrolled. *Average high school GPA:* 3.42. *Test scores:* SAT verbal scores over 500: 54%; SAT math scores over 500: 52%; ACT scores over 18: 79%; SAT verbal scores over 600: 15%; SAT math scores over 600: 17%; ACT scores over 24: 27%; SAT verbal scores over 700: 2%; SAT math scores over 700: 3%; ACT scores over 30: 2%.

Faculty *Total:* 300, 68% full-time, 44% with terminal degrees. *Student/faculty ratio:* 21:1.

Majors Accounting; agricultural sciences; art; art education; auto mechanic/technician; biology; botany; business administration; business education; carpentry; chemistry; child care/development; computer science; construction technology; criminal justice/law enforcement administration; dance; drafting; economics; education; electrical/electronic engineering technology; elementary education; English; family/community studies; French; geology; German; history; home economics; home economics education; industrial arts; information sciences/systems; interior design; mass communications; mathematics; music; music teacher education; physical education; physical sciences; political science; pre-engineering; psychology; secondary education; social sciences; sociology; Spanish; special education; speech/rhetorical studies; theater arts/drama; zoology.

Academic Programs *Special study options:* academic remediation for entering students, adult/continuing education programs, advanced placement credit, cooperative education, distance learning, double majors, English as a second language, honors programs, independent study, internships, part-time degree program, services for LD students, summer session for credit. *ROTC:* Army (b).

Library Southern Utah University Library with 180,424 titles, 6,165 serial subscriptions, 13,352 audiovisual materials, an OPAC, a Web page.

Computers on Campus 300 computers available on campus for general student use. A campuswide network can be accessed from student residence rooms and from off campus. At least one staffed computer lab available.

Student Life *Housing Options:* coed, men-only, women-only, disabled students. *Activities and Organizations:* drama/theater group, student-run newspaper, radio and television station, choral group, marching band, Outdoor Club, Intertribal Club, Latter Day Saints Student Association, Ski Club, Residence Halls Association, national fraternities, national sororities. *Campus security:* 24-hour emergency response devices, student patrols, late-night transport/escort service, controlled dormitory access. *Student Services:* health clinic, personal/psychological counseling, women's center.

Athletics Member NCAA. All Division I except football (Division I-AA). *Intercollegiate sports:* baseball M(s), basketball M(s)/W(s), cross-country running M/W, golf M(s), gymnastics W(s), softball W(s), tennis W(s), track and field M(s)/W(s). *Intramural sports:* basketball M/W, football M, golf M/W, soccer M/W, tennis M/W, track and field M/W, volleyball M/W.

Standardized Tests *Required:* SAT I or ACT (for admission). *Recommended:* ACT (for admission).

Costs (2001–02) *Tuition:* state resident $1732 full-time, $86 per credit hour part-time; nonresident $6314 full-time, $315 per credit hour part-time. Part-time tuition and fees vary according to course load. *Required fees:* $462 full-time. *Room and board:* $2866; room only: $1260. Room and board charges vary according to board plan and housing facility. *Waivers:* senior citizens and employees or children of employees.

Financial Aid Of all full-time matriculated undergraduates who enrolled in 2001, 2335 applied for aid, 2161 were judged to have need. *Average percent of need met:* 84%. *Average financial aid package:* $4371. *Average indebtedness upon graduation:* $10,285.

Applying *Options:* electronic application, early admission, deferred entrance. *Application fee:* $25. *Required:* high school transcript, minimum 2.0 GPA. *Application deadline:* 7/1 (freshmen), rolling (transfers).

Admissions Contact Mr. Dale S. Orton, Director of Admissions, Southern Utah University, 351 West Center Street, Cedar City, UT 84720. *Phone:* 801-586-7740. *Fax:* 435-865-8223. *E-mail:* adminfo@suu.edu.

UNIVERSITY OF PHOENIX-UTAH CAMPUS

Salt Lake City, Utah

- **Proprietary** comprehensive
- **Calendar** continuous
- **Degrees** certificates, associate, bachelor's, master's, doctoral, post-master's, and postbachelor's certificates (courses conducted at 54 campuses and learning centers in 13 states)
- **Coed,** 1,734 undergraduate students, 100% full-time, 39% women, 61% men
- **Noncompetitive** entrance level

Undergraduates Students come from 28 states and territories, 3% are from out of state.

Freshmen *Admission:* 48 admitted.

Faculty *Total:* 304, 3% full-time, 25% with terminal degrees. *Student/faculty ratio:* 14:1.

Majors Accounting; business administration; business marketing and marketing management; computer/information sciences; management information systems/business data processing; management science; nursing; nursing science; public administration and services related.

Academic Programs *Special study options:* accelerated degree program, adult/continuing education programs, advanced placement credit, distance learning, external degree program, independent study.

Library University Library with 17.5 million titles, 9,000 serial subscriptions, an OPAC, a Web page.

Computers on Campus A campuswide network can be accessed from off campus. Internet access, at least one staffed computer lab available.

Student Life *Housing:* college housing not available.

Costs (2001–02) *Tuition:* $8220 full-time. Full-time tuition and fees vary according to location and program. *Payment plan:* deferred payment. *Waivers:* employees or children of employees.

Applying *Options:* deferred entrance. *Application fee:* $85. *Required:* 2 years of work experience. *Required for some:* high school transcript. *Application deadline:* rolling (freshmen), rolling (transfers).

Admissions Contact Ms. Beth Barilla, Director of Admissions, University of Phoenix-Utah Campus, 4615 East Elwood Street, Phoenix, AZ 85040-1958. *Phone:* 480-927-0099 Ext. 1218. *Toll-free phone:* 800-224-2844. *Fax:* 480-594-1758. *E-mail:* beth.barilla@apollogrp.edu.

UNIVERSITY OF UTAH

Salt Lake City, Utah

- **State-supported** university, founded 1850, part of Utah System of Higher Education
- **Calendar** semesters
- **Degrees** certificates, bachelor's, master's, doctoral, and first professional
- **Urban** 1500-acre campus
- **Endowment** $297.8 million
- **Coed,** 22,234 undergraduate students, 63% full-time, 46% women, 54% men
- **Moderately difficult** entrance level, 91% of applicants were admitted

Undergraduates 14,109 full-time, 8,125 part-time. Students come from 54 states and territories, 120 other countries, 7% are from out of state, 0.7% African American, 4% Asian American or Pacific Islander, 3% Hispanic American, 0.6% Native American, 3% international, 10% transferred in, 11% live on campus. *Retention:* 75% of 2001 full-time freshmen returned.

Freshmen *Admission:* 5,926 applied, 5,392 admitted, 2,737 enrolled. *Average high school GPA:* 3.42. *Test scores:* ACT scores over 18: 92%; ACT scores over 24: 47%; ACT scores over 30: 8%.

Faculty *Total:* 1,246, 84% full-time. *Student/faculty ratio:* 14:1.

Majors Accounting; anthropology; Arabic; architecture; art; art history; Asian studies; atmospheric sciences; behavioral sciences; biology; biology education; biomedical science; broadcast journalism; business administration; business management/administrative services related; business marketing and marketing management; chemical engineering; chemistry; child care/development; Chinese; civil engineering; classics; communications; computer engineering; computer science; dance; developmental/child psychology; drama/dance education; early childhood education; economics; electrical engineering; elementary education; English; environmental engineering; environmental health; environmental science; exercise sciences; family/community studies; family/consumer studies; film studies; finance; food sciences; French; French language education; geography; geological engineering; geological sciences related; geology; geophysics/seismology; German; German language education; Greek (modern); health education; health/physical education; health professions and related sciences; history; history education; home economics; home economics education; individual/family development; Japanese; journalism; liberal arts and sciences/liberal studies; liberal arts and studies related; linguistics; marketing management and research related; mass communications; materials engineering; materials science; mathematics; mathematics education; mechanical engineering; medical cell biology; medical laboratory technician; medical technology; metallurgical engineering; Middle Eastern studies; mining/mineral engineering; music; music teacher education; nursing; pharmacy; philosophy; physical education; physical therapy; physics; physics education; political science; psychology; public relations; radio/television broadcasting; recreation/leisure facilities management; recreation/leisure studies; Russian; science education; secondary education; social science education; social sciences; social studies education; social work; sociology; Spanish; Spanish language education; speech-language pathology/audiology; speech/rhetorical studies; theater arts/drama; urban studies; women's studies.

Academic Programs *Special study options:* academic remediation for entering students, accelerated degree program, adult/continuing education programs, advanced placement credit, cooperative education, distance learning, double majors, English as a second language, honors programs, independent study, internships, off-campus study, part-time degree program, services for LD students, student-designed majors, study abroad, summer session for credit. *ROTC:* Army (b), Navy (b), Air Force (b). *Unusual degree programs:* 3-2 physical therapy, occupational therapy.

Library Marriott Library plus 2 others with 3.3 million titles, 21,853 serial subscriptions, 56,427 audiovisual materials, an OPAC, a Web page.

Computers on Campus 5000 computers available on campus for general student use. A campuswide network can be accessed from student residence rooms and from off campus that provide access to on-line classes. Internet access, online (class) registration, at least one staffed computer lab available.

Student Life *Housing Options:* coed. *Activities and Organizations:* drama/theater group, student-run newspaper, radio and television station, choral group, marching band, Bennion Center, Latter-Day Saints Student Association, Newman Center, Greek System, Center for Ethnic Student Affairs, national fraternities, national sororities. *Campus security:* 24-hour emergency response devices and patrols, student patrols, late-night transport/escort service, controlled dormitory access. *Student Services:* health clinic, personal/psychological counseling, women's center, legal services.

Athletics Member NCAA. All Division I except football (Division I-A). *Intercollegiate sports:* baseball M(s), basketball M(s)/W(s), bowling M(c)/W(c), cross-country running M(s)/W(s), golf M(s), gymnastics W(s), ice hockey M(c), racquetball M(c)/W(c), rugby M(c), skiing (cross-country) M(s)/W(s), skiing (downhill) M(s)/W(s), soccer M(c)/W(s), softball W, swimming M(s)/W(s), table tennis M(c)/W(c), tennis M(s)/W(s), track and field M(s)/W(s), volleyball W(s). *Intramural sports:* badminton M/W, basketball M/W, bowling M/W, cross-country running M/W, football M/W, golf M/W, racquetball M/W, riflery M/W, rugby M/W, skiing (cross-country) M/W, skiing (downhill) M/W, soccer M/W, softball M/W, squash M/W, swimming M/W, table tennis M/W, tennis M/W, track and field M/W, volleyball M/W, water polo M/W, weight lifting M/W, wrestling M.

Standardized Tests *Required:* SAT I or ACT (for admission).

Costs (2001–02) *Tuition:* state resident $2517 full-time, $136 per credit part-time; nonresident $8813 full-time, $493 per credit part-time. Full-time tuition and fees vary according to course load and student level. Part-time tuition and fees vary according to course load and student level. *Required fees:* $540 full-time, $52 per credit part-time. *Room and board:* $4646; room only: $2193. Room and board charges vary according to board plan and housing facility. *Payment plans:* installment, deferred payment. *Waivers:* senior citizens and employees or children of employees.

Financial Aid Of all full-time matriculated undergraduates who enrolled in 2001, 6689 applied for aid, 4955 were judged to have need, 907 had their need fully met. 416 Federal Work-Study jobs (averaging $2307). 25 State and other part-time jobs (averaging $4480). In 2001, 289 non-need-based awards were made. *Average percent of need met:* 63%. *Average financial aid package:* $6446. *Average need-based loan:* $3482. *Average need-based gift aid:* $3849. *Average indebtedness upon graduation:* $12,300.

Applying *Options:* common application, electronic application, early admission, deferred entrance. *Application fee:* $30. *Required:* high school transcript, minimum 2.0 GPA. *Recommended:* minimum 3.0 GPA. *Application deadlines:* 5/1 (freshmen), 5/1 (transfers).

University of Utah (continued)

Admissions Contact Ms. Suzanne Espinoza, Director of High School Services, University of Utah, 250 South Student Services Building, 201 South, 460 E Room 205, Salt Lake City, UT 84112. *Phone:* 801-581-8761. *Toll-free phone:* 800-444-8638. *Fax:* 801-585-7864.

UTAH STATE UNIVERSITY

Logan, Utah

- **State-supported** university, founded 1888, part of Utah System of Higher Education
- **Calendar** semesters
- **Degrees** certificates, associate, bachelor's, master's, and doctoral
- **Urban** 456-acre campus
- **Endowment** $79.2 million
- **Coed,** 19,295 undergraduate students, 66% full-time, 52% women, 48% men
- **Moderately difficult** entrance level, 97% of applicants were admitted

Undergraduates 12,760 full-time, 6,535 part-time. Students come from 53 states and territories, 62 other countries, 31% are from out of state, 0.5% African American, 1% Asian American or Pacific Islander, 2% Hispanic American, 0.6% Native American, 3% international, 8% transferred in.

Freshmen *Admission:* 5,573 applied, 5,431 admitted, 2,919 enrolled. *Average high school GPA:* 3.37. *Test scores:* SAT verbal scores over 500: 58%; SAT math scores over 500: 61%; ACT scores over 18: 88%; SAT verbal scores over 600: 20%; SAT math scores over 600: 23%; ACT scores over 24: 36%; SAT verbal scores over 700: 4%; SAT math scores over 700: 4%; ACT scores over 30: 6%.

Faculty *Total:* 673, 96% full-time, 79% with terminal degrees. *Student/faculty ratio:* 26:1.

Majors Accounting; aerospace engineering; aerospace engineering technology; agricultural business; agricultural business related; agricultural economics; agricultural education; agricultural engineering; agricultural sciences; agronomy/crop science; aircraft mechanic/airframe; American studies; animal sciences; anthropology; area studies related; art; Asian studies; biological specializations related; biology; biology education; botany; business; business administration; business education; business marketing and marketing management; chemistry; chemistry education; civil engineering; computer engineering; computer engineering technology; computer/information sciences; computer/information sciences related; conservation and renewable natural resources related; curriculum and instruction; dairy science; dance; drafting; early childhood education; ecology; economics; education (multiple levels); electrical engineering; elementary education; English; entomology; environmental engineering; family/consumer resource management related; fashion merchandising; finance; foods/nutrition studies related; forestry; forestry sciences related; French; general studies; geography; geology; German; health education; history; home economics education; horticulture science; housing studies; human resources management; individual/family development; individual/family development related; industrial arts education; industrial production technologies related; information sciences/systems; interior design; international agriculture; journalism; landscape architecture; liberal arts and sciences/liberal studies; marketing/distribution education; mathematical statistics; mathematics; mathematics education; mechanical engineering; medical technology; microbiology/bacteriology; multi/interdisciplinary studies related; music; music teacher education; music therapy; occupational safety/health technology; operations management; ornamental horticulture; parks, recreation, leisure and fitness studies related; philosophy; physical education; physics; physics education; physiology; plant sciences; plant sciences related; political science; pre-dentistry; pre-law; pre-medicine; pre-veterinary studies; psychology; public health related; range management; recreation/leisure studies; science education; secondary education; secretarial science; social studies education; social work; sociology; soil sciences; Spanish; special education; speech-language pathology/audiology; speech/rhetorical studies; teacher education, specific programs related; technical education; theater arts/drama; tool/die making; wildlife management; zoology.

Academic Programs *Special study options:* academic remediation for entering students, accelerated degree program, adult/continuing education programs, advanced placement credit, cooperative education, distance learning, double majors, English as a second language, external degree program, freshman honors college, honors programs, internships, off-campus study, part-time degree program, services for LD students, student-designed majors, study abroad, summer session for credit. *ROTC:* Air Force (b).

Library Merrill Library plus 4 others with 1.0 million titles, 14,449 serial subscriptions, 27,594 audiovisual materials, an OPAC, a Web page.

Computers on Campus 850 computers available on campus for general student use. A campuswide network can be accessed from student residence rooms and from off campus. Internet access, online (class) registration, at least one staffed computer lab available.

Student Life *Housing Options:* coed, men-only, women-only, disabled students. *Activities and Organizations:* drama/theater group, student-run newspaper, choral group, marching band, Latter-Day Saints Student Association, Greek organizations, multicultural clubs, volunteer groups, college councils, national fraternities, national sororities. *Campus security:* 24-hour emergency response devices and patrols, student patrols, late-night transport/escort service, video monitor in pedestrian tunnels. *Student Services:* health clinic, personal/psychological counseling, women's center, legal services.

Athletics Member NCAA. All Division I except football (Division I-A). *Intercollegiate sports:* baseball M(c), basketball M(s)/W(c), cross-country running M(s)/W(s), golf M(s), gymnastics W(s), ice hockey M(c), rugby M(c)/W(c), soccer M(c)/W(s), softball W(s), tennis M(s)/W(s), track and field M(s)/W(s), volleyball M(c)/W(s). *Intramural sports:* badminton M/W, basketball M/W, cross-country running M/W, equestrian sports M(c)/W(c), fencing M(c)/W(c), football M/W, golf M/W, ice hockey W(c), lacrosse M(c), racquetball M(c)/W(c), skiing (cross-country) M(c)/W(c), skiing (downhill) M(c)/W(c), soccer M/W, softball M/W, squash M/W, swimming M/W, table tennis M/W, tennis M/W, volleyball M/W, water polo M(c)/W(c).

Standardized Tests *Required:* SAT I or ACT (for admission). *Recommended:* ACT (for admission).

Costs (2001–02) *Tuition:* state resident $2123 full-time; nonresident $7429 full-time. *Required fees:* $468 full-time. *Room and board:* $4180; room only: $1600. Room and board charges vary according to board plan and housing facility. *Payment plan:* deferred payment. *Waivers:* minority students, children of alumni, adult students, senior citizens, and employees or children of employees.

Financial Aid Of all full-time matriculated undergraduates who enrolled in 2001, 6618 applied for aid, 5922 were judged to have need, 732 had their need fully met. 483 Federal Work-Study jobs (averaging $2778). 65 State and other part-time jobs (averaging $2784). In 2001, 1349 non-need-based awards were made. *Average percent of need met:* 59%. *Average financial aid package:* $4500. *Average need-based loan:* $3600. *Average need-based gift aid:* $2500. *Average non-need based aid:* $2100. *Average indebtedness upon graduation:* $11,500.

Applying *Options:* electronic application, early admission, deferred entrance. *Application fee:* $35. *Required:* high school transcript. *Recommended:* minimum 2.75 GPA. *Application deadline:* rolling (transfers). *Notification:* continuous (freshmen).

Admissions Contact Mr. Lynn Poulsen, Associate Vice President, Student Services, Utah State University, 1600 Old Main Hill, Logan, UT 84322-1600. *Phone:* 435-797-1107. *Fax:* 435-797-4077. *E-mail:* admit@cc.usu.edu.

UTAH VALLEY STATE COLLEGE

Orem, Utah

- **State-supported** primarily 2-year, founded 1941, part of Utah System of Higher Education
- **Calendar** semesters
- **Degrees** diplomas, associate, and bachelor's
- **Suburban** 200-acre campus with easy access to Salt Lake City
- **Endowment** $1.7 million
- **Coed**
- **Noncompetitive** entrance level

Faculty *Student/faculty ratio:* 20:1.

Student Life *Campus security:* 24-hour patrols.

Athletics Member NJCAA.

Standardized Tests *Required:* SAT I, ACT, or in-house tests.

Applying *Options:* electronic application, early admission, deferred entrance. *Application fee:* $30. *Recommended:* high school transcript.

Admissions Contact Mr. David Chappell, Registrar and Director of Admissions, Utah Valley State College, 800 West 1200 South Street, Orem, UT 84058-5999. *Phone:* 801-222-8460. *Fax:* 801-225-4677. *E-mail:* info@uvsc.edu.

WEBER STATE UNIVERSITY

Ogden, Utah

- **State-supported** comprehensive, founded 1889, part of Utah System of Higher Education
- **Calendar** semesters
- **Degrees** certificates, associate, bachelor's, master's, and postbachelor's certificates
- **Urban** 526-acre campus with easy access to Salt Lake City
- **Endowment** $24.0 million
- **Coed,** 16,619 undergraduate students, 59% full-time, 51% women, 49% men

■ **Noncompetitive** entrance level, 100% of applicants were admitted

Undergraduates 9,813 full-time, 6,806 part-time. Students come from 52 states and territories, 45 other countries, 6% are from out of state, 0.9% African American, 2% Asian American or Pacific Islander, 3% Hispanic American, 0.8% Native American, 2% international, 10% transferred in, 3% live on campus. *Retention:* 69% of 2001 full-time freshmen returned.

Freshmen *Admission:* 4,705 applied, 4,705 admitted, 2,665 enrolled. *Average high school GPA:* 3.24. *Test scores:* SAT verbal scores over 500: 58%; SAT math scores over 500: 60%; ACT scores over 18: 81%; SAT verbal scores over 600: 19%; SAT math scores over 600: 24%; ACT scores over 24: 30%; SAT verbal scores over 700: 3%; SAT math scores over 700: 4%; ACT scores over 30: 2%.

Faculty *Total:* 705, 64% full-time. *Student/faculty ratio:* 22:1.

Majors Accounting; aerospace engineering; Air Force R.O.T.C./air science; applied mathematics; archaeology; art; art education; athletic training/sports medicine; auto body repair; auto mechanic/technician; automotive engineering technology; bilingual/bicultural education; biological technology; biology education; botany; business administration; business economics; business education; business marketing and marketing management; business systems networking/ telecommunications; chemical technology; chemistry; chemistry education; child care/development; child care/guidance; computer engineering technology; computer/ information sciences; computer science; corrections; criminal justice studies; dance; dental hygiene; design/visual communications; diagnostic medical sonography; diesel engine mechanic; drafting; drama/dance education; early childhood education; economics; electrical/electronic engineering technology; elementary education; emergency medical technology; English; English education; exercise sciences; family studies; fashion merchandising; finance; French; French language education; geography; geology; German; German language education; gerontology; graphic design/commercial art/illustration; health/ physical education; health services administration; history; history education; human resources management; industrial arts; industrial technology; information sciences/systems; interior design; journalism; law enforcement/police science; liberal arts and sciences/liberal studies; logistics/materials management; machine technology; management information systems/business data processing; mathematics; mechanical engineering technology; medical laboratory technician; medical radiologic technology; medical records technology; medical technology; microbiology/bacteriology; music; music (general performance); music (piano and organ performance); music teacher education; nuclear medical technology; nursing; office management; photography; physical education; physics; physics education; political science; psychology; public relations; radio/television broadcasting; respiratory therapy; science education; secondary education; secretarial science; social science education; social studies education; social work; sociology; Spanish; Spanish language education; technical/business writing; theater arts/drama; zoology.

Academic Programs *Special study options:* academic remediation for entering students, accelerated degree program, adult/continuing education programs, advanced placement credit, cooperative education, distance learning, double majors, English as a second language, external degree program, freshman honors college, honors programs, independent study, internships, off-campus study, part-time degree program, services for LD students, student-designed majors, study abroad, summer session for credit. *ROTC:* Army (b), Navy (b), Air Force (b).

Library Stewart Library plus 1 other with 648,743 titles, 2,278 serial subscriptions, 15,383 audiovisual materials, an OPAC, a Web page.

Computers on Campus 558 computers available on campus for general student use. A campuswide network can be accessed from student residence rooms and from off campus that provide access to Online Grades. Internet access, online (class) registration, at least one staffed computer lab available.

Student Life *Housing Options:* men-only, women-only, disabled students. *Activities and Organizations:* drama/theater group, student-run newspaper, radio and television station, choral group, marching band, LDSSA, mountaineering club, rodeo club, Beta Alpha Psi, Student Nurses, national fraternities, national sororities. *Campus security:* 24-hour emergency response devices and patrols, student patrols, late-night transport/escort service, controlled dormitory access. *Student Services:* health clinic, personal/psychological counseling, women's center, legal services.

Athletics Member NCAA. All Division I except football (Division I-AA). *Intercollegiate sports:* baseball M(c), basketball M(s)/W(s), bowling M(c)/W(c), cross-country running M(s)/W(s), fencing M(c)/W(c), golf M(s)/W(s), ice hockey M(c), lacrosse M(c)/W(c), racquetball M(c)/W(c), rugby M(c)/W(c), skiing (downhill) M(c)/W(c), soccer M(c)/W(s), softball W(c), swimming M(c)/W(c), tennis M(s)/W(s), track and field M(s)/W(s), volleyball W(s), water polo M(c)/ W(c). *Intramural sports:* baseball M/W, basketball M/W, bowling M/W, cross-country running M/W, football M/W, golf M/W, racquetball M/W, soccer M/W, softball M/W, tennis M/W, volleyball M/W.

Standardized Tests *Required:* SAT I or ACT (for placement).

Costs (2001–02) *Tuition:* state resident $1786 full-time; nonresident $6252 full-time. Part-time tuition and fees vary according to course load. *Required fees:* $466 full-time. *Room and board:* $4645; room only: $1645. Room and board charges vary according to board plan and housing facility. *Payment plans:* installment, deferred payment. *Waivers:* senior citizens and employees or children of employees.

Financial Aid Of all full-time matriculated undergraduates who enrolled in 2001, 7850 applied for aid, 6908 were judged to have need, 5089 had their need fully met. *Average percent of need met:* 86%. *Average financial aid package:* $5100. *Average need-based loan:* $2620. *Average need-based gift aid:* $3600. *Average indebtedness upon graduation:* $8500.

Applying *Options:* electronic application, early admission, deferred entrance. *Application fee:* $30. *Required:* high school transcript. *Application deadline:* 8/24 (freshmen), rolling (transfers). *Notification:* continuous (freshmen).

Admissions Contact John Allred, Admissions Advisor, Weber State University, 1137 University Circle, 3750 Harrison Boulevard, Ogden, UT 84408-1137. *Phone:* 801-626-6050. *Toll-free phone:* 800-634-6568. *Fax:* 801-626-6744. *E-mail:* admissions@weber.edu.

WESTERN GOVERNORS UNIVERSITY

Salt Lake City, Utah

■ **Independent** comprehensive, founded 1998
■ **Calendar** continuous
■ **Degrees** certificates, diplomas, associate, bachelor's, master's, and post-master's certificates
■ **Coed,** 1,683 undergraduate students, 100% full-time, 52% women, 48% men
■ 30% of applicants were admitted

Undergraduates 1,683 full-time. Students come from 42 states and territories, 5% African American, 2% Asian American or Pacific Islander, 6% Hispanic American, 2% Native American.

Freshmen *Admission:* 387 applied, 118 admitted.

Faculty *Total:* 9. *Student/faculty ratio:* 49:1.

Majors Business; computer engineering related; information sciences/systems; information technology; system administration.

Academic Programs *Special study options:* accelerated degree program, adult/continuing education programs, distance learning, double majors, external degree program, independent study, part-time degree program, services for LD students.

Library WGU Central Library (online) with a Web page.

Computers on Campus Internet access, online (class) registration available.

Costs (2001–02) *Tuition:* $3200 full-time. Full-time tuition and fees vary according to degree level. Part-time tuition and fees vary according to degree level. No tuition increase for student's term of enrollment. *Required fees:* $50 full-time. *Payment plans:* tuition prepayment, installment.

Applying *Options:* electronic application. *Application fee:* $100.

Admissions Contact Ms. Wendy Gregory, Enrollment Director, Western Governors University, 2040 East Murray Holladay Road, Suite 106, Salt Lake City, UT 84117. *Phone:* 801-274-3280 Ext. 315. *Toll-free phone:* 877-435-7948. *Fax:* 801-274-3305. *E-mail:* info@wgu.edu.

WESTMINSTER COLLEGE

Salt Lake City, Utah

■ **Independent** comprehensive, founded 1875
■ **Calendar** 4-4-1
■ **Degrees** bachelor's, master's, and postbachelor's certificates
■ **Suburban** 27-acre campus
■ **Endowment** $46.6 million
■ **Coed,** 1,979 undergraduate students, 85% full-time, 59% women, 41% men
■ **Moderately difficult** entrance level, 90% of applicants were admitted

Undergraduates 1,677 full-time, 302 part-time. Students come from 29 states and territories, 20 other countries, 8% are from out of state, 0.3% African American, 3% Asian American or Pacific Islander, 5% Hispanic American, 0.8% Native American, 1% international, 13% transferred in, 18% live on campus. *Retention:* 77% of 2001 full-time freshmen returned.

Freshmen *Admission:* 774 applied, 700 admitted, 333 enrolled. *Average high school GPA:* 3.65. *Test scores:* ACT scores over 18: 97%; ACT scores over 24: 51%; ACT scores over 30: 7%.

Faculty *Total:* 257, 44% full-time, 48% with terminal degrees. *Student/faculty ratio:* 11:1.

Westminster College (continued)

Majors Accounting; aircraft pilot (professional); art; aviation management; biology; biology education; business; business administration; business economics; business information/data processing related; business marketing and marketing management; chemistry; communications; computer science; early childhood education; elementary education; English; finance; history; human resources management; international business; mathematics; nursing; philosophy; physics; political science; psychology; social science education; social sciences; sociology; special education.

Academic Programs *Special study options:* academic remediation for entering students, accelerated degree program, advanced placement credit, double majors, English as a second language, honors programs, independent study, internships, part-time degree program, services for LD students, student-designed majors, summer session for credit. *ROTC:* Army (c), Navy (c), Air Force (c). *Unusual degree programs:* 3-2 engineering with University of Southern California, Washington University in St. Louis.

Library Giovale Library plus 1 other with 102,632 titles, 1,807 serial subscriptions, 3,930 audiovisual materials, an OPAC, a Web page.

Computers on Campus 238 computers available on campus for general student use. A campuswide network can be accessed from student residence rooms. Internet access, online (class) registration, at least one staffed computer lab available.

Student Life *Housing:* on-campus residence required for freshman year. *Options:* coed. *Activities and Organizations:* drama/theater group, student-run newspaper, choral group, Outdoor Club, Pre-Med Society, English club, Theatre Society, Students Educators Association. *Campus security:* 24-hour emergency response devices and patrols, student patrols, late-night transport/escort service, controlled dormitory access. *Student Services:* personal/psychological counseling.

Athletics Member NAIA. *Intercollegiate sports:* basketball M/W, golf M/W, soccer M, volleyball W. *Intramural sports:* basketball M/W, cross-country running M/W, football M/W, skiing (cross-country) M/W, soccer M/W, table tennis M/W, tennis M/W, volleyball M/W, weight lifting M/W.

Standardized Tests *Required:* SAT I or ACT (for admission).

Costs (2001–02) *Comprehensive fee:* $19,430 includes full-time tuition ($14,500), mandatory fees ($280), and room and board ($4650). Full-time tuition and fees vary according to course load. Part-time tuition: $592 per credit hour. Part-time tuition and fees vary according to course load. *Required fees:* $70 per term part-time. *Room and board:* Room and board charges vary according to board plan and housing facility. *Payment plans:* installment, deferred payment. *Waivers:* employees or children of employees.

Financial Aid Of all full-time matriculated undergraduates who enrolled in 2001, 1637 applied for aid, 1129 were judged to have need, 515 had their need fully met. In 2001, 490 non-need-based awards were made. *Average percent of need met:* 91%. *Average financial aid package:* $13,891. *Average need-based loan:* $4680. *Average need-based gift aid:* $7580. *Average non-need based aid:* $5200. *Average indebtedness upon graduation:* $14,550.

Applying *Options:* common application, electronic application, early admission, deferred entrance. *Application fee:* $30. *Required:* high school transcript, minimum 2.5 GPA. *Recommended:* essay or personal statement, minimum 3.0 GPA, 1 letter of recommendation, interview. *Application deadline:* rolling (freshmen), rolling (transfers). *Notification:* continuous (freshmen).

Admissions Contact Mr. Philip J. Alletto, Vice President of Student Development and Enrollment Management, Westminster College, 1840 South 1300 East, Salt Lake City, UT 84105-3697. *Phone:* 801-832-2200. *Toll-free phone:* 800-748-4753. *Fax:* 801-484-3252. *E-mail:* admispub@wsclc.edu.

VERMONT

BENNINGTON COLLEGE
Bennington, Vermont

- **Independent** comprehensive, founded 1932
- **Calendar** semesters
- **Degrees** bachelor's, master's, and postbachelor's certificates
- **Small-town** 550-acre campus with easy access to Albany
- **Endowment** $9.4 million
- **Coed,** 537 undergraduate students, 100% full-time, 68% women, 32% men
- **Very difficult** entrance level, 65% of applicants were admitted

Bennington regards education as a sensual and ethical, no less than intellectual, process. It seeks to liberate and nurture the individuality, the creative intelligence, and the ethical and aesthetic sensibility of its students, to the end that their richly varied natural endowments will be directed toward self-fulfillment and toward constructive social purposes.

Undergraduates 536 full-time, 1 part-time. Students come from 48 states and territories, 23 other countries, 96% are from out of state, 1% African American, 2% Asian American or Pacific Islander, 2% Hispanic American, 0.2% Native American, 11% international, 4% transferred in, 98% live on campus. *Retention:* 79% of 2001 full-time freshmen returned.

Freshmen *Admission:* 719 applied, 468 admitted, 182 enrolled. *Average high school GPA:* 3.54. *Test scores:* SAT verbal scores over 500: 95%; SAT math scores over 500: 81%; SAT verbal scores over 600: 64%; SAT math scores over 600: 41%; SAT verbal scores over 700: 19%; SAT math scores over 700: 8%.

Faculty *Total:* 93, 66% full-time, 56% with terminal degrees. *Student/faculty ratio:* 9:1.

Majors Anthropology; architecture; art; biochemistry; biological/physical sciences; biology; ceramic arts; chemistry; Chinese; comparative literature; computer science; creative writing; dance; design/applied arts related; developmental/child psychology; drawing; early childhood education; ecology; English; environmental biology; environmental science; European studies; film studies; fine/studio arts; French; German; history; history of philosophy; humanities; interdisciplinary studies; international relations; Italian studies; Japanese; jazz; liberal arts and sciences/liberal studies; literature; mathematics; modern languages; music; music history; music (voice and choral/opera performance); natural sciences; philosophy; photography; physics; pre-medicine; pre-veterinary studies; printmaking; psychology; sculpture; social sciences; sociology; Spanish; stringed instruments; theater arts/drama; visual/performing arts.

Academic Programs *Special study options:* English as a second language, independent study, internships, off-campus study, student-designed majors, study abroad.

Library Crossett Library plus 2 others with 121,000 titles, 500 serial subscriptions, 27,500 audiovisual materials, an OPAC, a Web page.

Computers on Campus 60 computers available on campus for general student use. A campuswide network can be accessed from student residence rooms and from off campus. Internet access, at least one staffed computer lab available.

Student Life *Housing:* on-campus residence required through senior year. *Options:* coed, cooperative. *Activities and Organizations:* drama/theater group, student-run newspaper, radio station, choral group, literary magazine, Amnesty International, Campus Activities Board, film society, student newspaper. *Campus security:* 24-hour emergency response devices and patrols, late-night transport/escort service. *Student Services:* health clinic, personal/psychological counseling.

Athletics *Intercollegiate sports:* soccer M(c)/W(c). *Intramural sports:* archery M/W, badminton M/W, basketball M/W, football M/W, skiing (cross-country) M/W, skiing (downhill) M/W, soccer M/W, tennis M/W, volleyball M/W, weight lifting M/W.

Standardized Tests *Required:* SAT I or ACT (for admission).

Costs (2001–02) *Comprehensive fee:* $31,350 includes full-time tuition ($24,450), mandatory fees ($550), and room and board ($6350). Part-time tuition: $3100 per course. *Room and board:* College room only: $3300. *Payment plan:* installment. *Waivers:* employees or children of employees.

Financial Aid Of all full-time matriculated undergraduates who enrolled in 2001, 390 applied for aid, 361 were judged to have need, 25 had their need fully met. 58 State and other part-time jobs (averaging $1487). *Average percent of need met:* 75%. *Average financial aid package:* $19,417. *Average need-based loan:* $3781. *Average need-based gift aid:* $15,009. *Average indebtedness upon graduation:* $18,475.

Applying *Options:* common application, early admission, early decision, deferred entrance. *Application fee:* $50. *Required:* essay or personal statement, high school transcript, 2 letters of recommendation, interview. *Application deadlines:* 1/1 (freshmen), 6/1 (transfers). *Early decision:* 11/15. *Notification:* 4/1 (freshmen), 12/1 (early decision).

Admissions Contact Mr. Deane Bogardus, Director of Admissions, Bennington College, One College Drive, Bennington, VT 05201. *Phone:* 802-440-4312. *Toll-free phone:* 800-833-6845. *Fax:* 802-440-4320. *E-mail:* admissions@bennington.edu.

BURLINGTON COLLEGE
Burlington, Vermont

- **Independent** 4-year, founded 1972
- **Calendar** semesters
- **Degrees** certificates, associate, and bachelor's
- **Urban** 1-acre campus
- **Endowment** $134,180
- **Coed,** 267 undergraduate students, 63% full-time, 63% women, 37% men

■ **Noncompetitive** entrance level, 95% of applicants were admitted

A small, progressive liberal arts college offering flexible learning options within a friendly, supportive environment. A third of students self-design their liberal arts majors. A distance learning degree program is also offered. New paralegal, cinema studies, and film production programs enhance a curriculum already strong in social sciences and the humanities.

Undergraduates 167 full-time, 100 part-time. Students come from 20 states and territories, 8 other countries, 46% are from out of state, 22% transferred in, 10% live on campus. *Retention:* 60% of 2001 full-time freshmen returned.

Freshmen *Admission:* 63 applied, 60 admitted, 42 enrolled.

Faculty *Total:* 54. *Student/faculty ratio:* 8:1.

Majors Art; film studies; film/video production; humanities; human services; interdisciplinary studies; liberal arts and sciences/liberal studies; literature; psychology; women's studies.

Academic Programs *Special study options:* academic remediation for entering students, accelerated degree program, adult/continuing education programs, cooperative education, distance learning, double majors, external degree program, independent study, internships, off-campus study, part-time degree program, services for LD students, student-designed majors, summer session for credit.

Library Burlington College Library with 43,500 titles, 1,650 serial subscriptions, 1,754 audiovisual materials, a Web page.

Computers on Campus 17 computers available on campus for general student use. Internet access, at least one staffed computer lab available.

Student Life *Housing Options:* coed, cooperative. *Activities and Organizations:* student-run newspaper, Student Association. *Campus security:* 24-hour emergency response devices. *Student Services:* personal/psychological counseling.

Costs (2001–02) *Tuition:* $10,350 full-time, $345 per credit hour part-time. *Required fees:* $290 full-time, $290 per year part-time. *Room only:* $5500.

Financial Aid Of all full-time matriculated undergraduates who enrolled in 2001, 99 applied for aid, 96 were judged to have need, 5 had their need fully met. 67 Federal Work-Study jobs (averaging $1765). *Average percent of need met:* 60%. *Average financial aid package:* $8003. *Average need-based loan:* $3420. *Average need-based gift aid:* $4977. *Average indebtedness upon graduation:* $14,748.

Applying *Options:* common application, electronic application, deferred entrance. *Application fee:* $30. *Required:* essay or personal statement, high school transcript, 2 letters of recommendation, interview. *Application deadlines:* 8/1 (freshmen), 8/1 (transfers). *Notification:* continuous (freshmen).

Admissions Contact Ms. Cathleen Sullivan, Assistant Director of Admissions, Burlington College, 95 North Avenue, Burlington, VT 05401-2998. *Phone:* 802-862-9616 Ext. 24. *Toll-free phone:* 800-862-9616. *Fax:* 802-660-4331. *E-mail:* admissions@burlcol.edu.

CASTLETON STATE COLLEGE

Castleton, Vermont

- **State-supported** comprehensive, founded 1787, part of Vermont State Colleges System
- **Calendar** semesters
- **Degrees** associate, bachelor's, master's, and post-master's certificates
- **Rural** 130-acre campus
- **Endowment** $3.5 million
- **Coed,** 1,542 undergraduate students, 88% full-time, 61% women, 39% men
- **Moderately difficult** entrance level, 93% of applicants were admitted

Located in a historic Vermont village close to skiing, Castleton is small enough to be a community where individuals matter yet large enough to offer 30 academic programs, 12 intercollegiate sports, and more than 40 clubs and student organizations. Castleton stresses community service and internships and provides exceptional programs for first-year students.

Undergraduates 1,358 full-time, 184 part-time. Students come from 29 states and territories, 35% are from out of state, 0.4% African American, 0.3% Asian American or Pacific Islander, 1% Hispanic American, 0.1% Native American, 0.1% international, 10% transferred in, 41% live on campus. *Retention:* 70% of 2001 full-time freshmen returned.

Freshmen *Admission:* 1,082 applied, 1,007 admitted, 393 enrolled. *Test scores:* SAT verbal scores over 500: 43%; SAT math scores over 500: 5%; SAT verbal scores over 600: 7%; SAT math scores over 600: 2%; SAT verbal scores over 700: 1%; SAT math scores over 700: 1%.

Faculty *Total:* 167, 51% full-time, 58% with terminal degrees. *Student/faculty ratio:* 13:1.

Majors Accounting; American literature; art; athletic training/sports medicine; biological/physical sciences; biology; business; business administration; business marketing and marketing management; chemistry; communications; computer/information sciences; computer programming; criminal justice/law enforcement administration; criminology; developmental/child psychology; environmental science; exercise sciences; finance; general studies; geology; health/physical education; health science; history; journalism; literature; mathematics; mathematics education; music; music teacher education; natural sciences; nursing; physical education; psychology; radio/television broadcasting; science education; social sciences; social studies education; social work; sociology; Spanish; theater arts/drama.

Academic Programs *Special study options:* academic remediation for entering students, advanced placement credit, cooperative education, double majors, honors programs, independent study, internships, off-campus study, part-time degree program, services for LD students, student-designed majors, study abroad, summer session for credit. *ROTC:* Army (b). *Unusual degree programs:* 3-2 business administration with Clarkson University; engineering with Clarkson University.

Library Calvin Coolidge Library with 161,480 titles, 1,858 serial subscriptions, 2,626 audiovisual materials, an OPAC, a Web page.

Computers on Campus 215 computers available on campus for general student use. A campuswide network can be accessed from student residence rooms. Internet access, at least one staffed computer lab available.

Student Life *Housing:* on-campus residence required for freshman year. *Options:* coed. *Activities and Organizations:* drama/theater group, student-run newspaper, radio station, choral group, student radio station, community service, women's issues, Rugby, Snowboarding. *Campus security:* 24-hour emergency response devices and patrols, student patrols, late-night transport/escort service, controlled dormitory access. *Student Services:* health clinic, personal/psychological counseling.

Athletics Member NCAA. All Division III. *Intercollegiate sports:* baseball M, basketball M/W, cross-country running M/W, field hockey W, gymnastics M(c)/W(c), ice hockey M/W(c), lacrosse M/W, rugby M(c)/W(c), soccer M/W, softball W, tennis M/W, volleyball M(c)/W(c). *Intramural sports:* basketball M/W, equestrian sports M/W, football M/W, golf M/W, racquetball M/W, skiing (cross-country) M/W, skiing (downhill) M/W, soccer M/W, softball M/W, swimming M/W, table tennis M/W, tennis M/W, volleyball M/W, water polo M/W, weight lifting M/W.

Standardized Tests *Required:* SAT I or ACT (for admission).

Costs (2001–02) *Tuition:* state resident $4404 full-time, $184 per credit part-time; nonresident $10,320 full-time, $430 per credit part-time. Full-time tuition and fees vary according to reciprocity agreements. Part-time tuition and fees vary according to course load and reciprocity agreements. *Required fees:* $988 full-time, $31 per credit. *Room and board:* $5530. Room and board charges vary according to board plan. *Payment plan:* installment. *Waivers:* senior citizens and employees or children of employees.

Financial Aid Of all full-time matriculated undergraduates who enrolled in 2001, 1129 applied for aid, 945 were judged to have need, 140 had their need fully met. 360 Federal Work-Study jobs (averaging $1121). In 2001, 21 non-need-based awards were made. *Average percent of need met:* 68%. *Average financial aid package:* $6500. *Average need-based loan:* $3700. *Average need-based gift aid:* $3200. *Average non-need based aid:* $2500. *Average indebtedness upon graduation:* $17,200.

Applying *Options:* common application, electronic application, deferred entrance. *Application fee:* $30. *Required:* essay or personal statement, high school transcript, minimum 2.5 GPA, letters of recommendation. *Recommended:* interview. *Application deadline:* rolling (freshmen), rolling (transfers). *Notification:* continuous (freshmen).

Admissions Contact Ms. Heather Atwell, Director of Undergraduate Admissions, Castleton State College, Seminary Street, Castleton, VT 05735. *Phone:* 802-468-1351. *Toll-free phone:* 800-639-8521. *Fax:* 802-468-1476. *E-mail:* info@castleton.edu.

CHAMPLAIN COLLEGE

Burlington, Vermont

- **Independent** comprehensive, founded 1878
- **Calendar** semesters
- **Degrees** certificates, associate, and bachelor's (the baccalaureate programs are part of the 2+2 curriculum)
- **Suburban** 19-acre campus
- **Endowment** $6.1 million
- **Coed,** 2,523 undergraduate students, 59% full-time, 54% women, 46% men
- **Moderately difficult** entrance level, 64% of applicants were admitted

Champlain College (continued)

Since 1878, Champlain College has championed independent thinking, teaching academic skills and practical knowledge required for professional success. Students earn their bachelor's degree, plus an embedded associate degree, in one of 23 career-focused majors with built-in internship opportunities. Located in a classic college town, world-class skiing and outdoor recreation are available nearby.

Undergraduates 1,494 full-time, 1,029 part-time. Students come from 29 states and territories, 42% are from out of state, 1% African American, 2% Asian American or Pacific Islander, 1.0% Hispanic American, 1% Native American, 0.8% international, 6% transferred in, 42% live on campus. *Retention:* 71% of 2001 full-time freshmen returned.

Freshmen *Admission:* 1,445 applied, 919 admitted, 428 enrolled. *Average high school GPA:* 2.80. *Test scores:* SAT verbal scores over 500: 43%; SAT math scores over 500: 39%; ACT scores over 18: 79%; SAT verbal scores over 600: 8%; SAT math scores over 600: 8%; ACT scores over 24: 22%; SAT verbal scores over 700: 1%; SAT math scores over 700: 1%; ACT scores over 30: 2%.

Faculty *Total:* 193, 39% full-time, 24% with terminal degrees. *Student/faculty ratio:* 13:1.

Majors Accounting; business; business administration; business marketing and marketing management; business systems networking/ telecommunications; communications; computer management; computer software and media applications related; computer software engineering; criminal justice/law enforcement administration; criminal justice studies; early childhood education; elementary education; graphic design/commercial art/illustration; hospitality management; hospitality/ recreation marketing operations; hotel and restaurant management; hotel/motel services marketing operations; human services; information sciences/systems; international business; liberal arts and sciences/liberal studies; marketing operations; mass communications; multimedia; paralegal/legal assistant; professional studies; public relations; radiological science; respiratory therapy; social work; sport/fitness administration; system/networking/LAN/WAN management; telecommunications; tourism promotion operations; travel services marketing operations; travel/tourism management; Web/multimedia management/webmaster.

Academic Programs *Special study options:* adult/continuing education programs, advanced placement credit, cooperative education, distance learning, double majors, freshman honors college, honors programs, internships, off-campus study, part-time degree program, services for LD students, study abroad, summer session for credit. *ROTC:* Army (c).

Library Miller Information Commons with 63,000 titles, 8,831 serial subscriptions, an OPAC, a Web page.

Computers on Campus 200 computers available on campus for general student use. A campuswide network can be accessed from student residence rooms and from off campus. Internet access, online (class) registration, at least one staffed computer lab available.

Student Life *Housing Options:* coed, men-only, women-only. *Activities and Organizations:* drama/theater group, choral group, Diversity Champlain, International Club, Community Service Organization, Theater Group/Champlain Players, Outing Club/Skiing Snowboarding Club. *Campus security:* 24-hour emergency response devices and patrols, late-night transport/escort service, controlled dormitory access. *Student Services:* health clinic, personal/psychological counseling.

Athletics Member NJCAA. *Intramural sports:* basketball M/W, golf M/W, ice hockey M/W, sailing M/W, skiing (cross-country) M/W, skiing (downhill) M/W, soccer M/W, table tennis M/W, volleyball M/W.

Standardized Tests *Required:* SAT I or ACT (for admission).

Costs (2001–02) *Comprehensive fee:* $19,680 includes full-time tuition ($11,505), mandatory fees ($100), and room and board ($8075). Full-time tuition and fees vary according to course load and program. Part-time tuition: $350 per credit hour. Part-time tuition and fees vary according to course load and program. *Required fees:* $100 per year part-time. *Room and board:* College room only: $4825. Room and board charges vary according to board plan. *Payment plan:* installment. *Waivers:* senior citizens and employees or children of employees.

Financial Aid Of all full-time matriculated undergraduates who enrolled in 2001, 1138 applied for aid, 976 were judged to have need, 126 had their need fully met. 414 Federal Work-Study jobs. In 2001, 192 non-need-based awards were made. *Average percent of need met:* 66%. *Average financial aid package:* $7936. *Average need-based loan:* $3641. *Average need-based gift aid:* $4738.

Applying *Options:* common application, early admission, deferred entrance. *Application fee:* $35. *Required:* essay or personal statement, high school transcript. *Recommended:* minimum 2.0 GPA, 1 letter of recommendation, interview. *Application deadline:* rolling (freshmen), rolling (transfers). *Notification:* continuous (freshmen).

Admissions Contact Ms. Josephine H. Churchill, Director of Admissions, Champlain College, 163 South Willard Street, Burlington, VT 05401. *Phone:* 802-860-2727. *Toll-free phone:* 800-570-5858. *Fax:* 802-860-2767. *E-mail:* admission@champlain.edu.

COLLEGE OF ST. JOSEPH

Rutland, Vermont

- **Independent Roman Catholic** comprehensive, founded 1950
- **Calendar** semesters
- **Degrees** certificates, associate, bachelor's, master's, and postbachelor's certificates
- **Small-town** 90-acre campus
- **Endowment** $1.2 million
- **Coed,** 314 undergraduate students, 57% full-time, 66% women, 34% men
- **Minimally difficult** entrance level, 89% of applicants were admitted

Undergraduates 180 full-time, 134 part-time. Students come from 15 states and territories, 30% are from out of state, 12% transferred in, 29% live on campus. *Retention:* 71% of 2001 full-time freshmen returned.

Freshmen *Admission:* 128 applied, 114 admitted, 40 enrolled. *Average high school GPA:* 2.6. *Test scores:* SAT verbal scores over 500: 35%; SAT math scores over 500: 27%; SAT verbal scores over 600: 4%; SAT math scores over 600: 6%.

Faculty *Total:* 59, 19% full-time, 24% with terminal degrees. *Student/faculty ratio:* 12:1.

Majors Accounting; American studies; business administration; communications; early childhood education; education; elementary education; English; finance; history; human services; information sciences/systems; journalism; liberal arts and sciences/liberal studies; political science; pre-law; psychology; recreation/leisure facilities management; secondary education; special education.

Academic Programs *Special study options:* academic remediation for entering students, accelerated degree program, adult/continuing education programs, advanced placement credit, double majors, English as a second language, internships, part-time degree program, services for LD students, study abroad, summer session for credit.

Library St. Joseph Library plus 1 other with 45,000 titles, 256 serial subscriptions, 5,504 audiovisual materials, an OPAC.

Computers on Campus 30 computers available on campus for general student use. A campuswide network can be accessed from student residence rooms. Internet access, at least one staffed computer lab available.

Student Life *Housing:* on-campus residence required through sophomore year. *Options:* men-only, women-only. *Activities and Organizations:* drama/theater group, student-run newspaper, choral group, Human Services Club, Campus Ministry Club, Psi Chi, Ambassadors, chorus. *Campus security:* 24-hour emergency response devices. *Student Services:* personal/psychological counseling.

Athletics Member NAIA. *Intercollegiate sports:* basketball M(s)/W(s), cross-country running M(s)/W(s), soccer M(s)/W(s). *Intramural sports:* baseball M, basketball M/W, bowling M/W, racquetball M/W, skiing (cross-country) M/W, skiing (downhill) M/W, soccer M/W, softball M/W, tennis M/W, volleyball M/W, weight lifting M/W.

Standardized Tests *Required:* SAT I or ACT (for admission).

Costs (2002–03) *Comprehensive fee:* $18,600 includes full-time tuition ($12,000), mandatory fees ($200), and room and board ($6400). Full-time tuition and fees vary according to program. Part-time tuition: $215 per credit. Part-time tuition and fees vary according to program. *Required fees:* $45 per credit. *Room and board:* College room only: $3100. Room and board charges vary according to housing facility. *Payment plan:* installment. *Waivers:* senior citizens and employees or children of employees.

Financial Aid Of all full-time matriculated undergraduates who enrolled in 2001, 166 applied for aid, 152 were judged to have need, 13 had their need fully met. 47 Federal Work-Study jobs (averaging $725). 70 State and other part-time jobs (averaging $885). In 2001, 8 non-need-based awards were made. *Average percent of need met:* 82%. *Average financial aid package:* $12,221. *Average need-based loan:* $3817. *Average need-based gift aid:* $6302. *Average non-need based aid:* $1500. *Average indebtedness upon graduation:* $17,606.

Applying *Options:* early admission, deferred entrance. *Application fee:* $25. *Required:* essay or personal statement, high school transcript, minimum 2.0 GPA, 2 letters of recommendation. *Recommended:* interview. *Application deadline:* rolling (freshmen), rolling (transfers). *Notification:* continuous (freshmen).

Admissions Contact Mr. Maurice Ouimet, Assistant Dean of Admissions, College of St. Joseph, 71 Clement Road, Rutland, VT 05701-3899. *Phone:* 802-773-5900 Ext. 217. *Fax:* 802-773-5900 Ext. 258. *E-mail:* admissions@csj.edu.

GODDARD COLLEGE
Plainfield, Vermont

- **Independent** comprehensive, founded 1938
- **Calendar** semesters
- **Degrees** bachelor's and master's
- **Rural** 250-acre campus
- **Endowment** $500,000
- **Coed,** 319 undergraduate students, 100% full-time, 59% women, 41% men
- **Moderately difficult** entrance level, 99% of applicants were admitted

Undergraduates 319 full-time. Students come from 34 states and territories, 5 other countries, 87% are from out of state, 2% African American, 1% Asian American or Pacific Islander, 2% Hispanic American, 0.6% Native American, 2% international, 22% transferred in, 80% live on campus. *Retention:* 57% of 2001 full-time freshmen returned.

Freshmen *Admission:* 104 applied, 103 admitted, 48 enrolled. *Average high school GPA:* 3.13. *Test scores:* SAT verbal scores over 500: 78%; SAT math scores over 500: 62%; ACT scores over 18: 100%; SAT verbal scores over 600: 46%; SAT math scores over 600: 16%; SAT verbal scores over 700: 5%; SAT math scores over 700: 3%.

Faculty *Total:* 75, 19% full-time, 33% with terminal degrees. *Student/faculty ratio:* 11:1.

Majors African-American studies; American studies; anthropology; applied art; art; art education; art history; behavioral sciences; biological/physical sciences; biology; ceramic arts; child care/development; community services; comparative literature; creative writing; cultural studies; developmental/child psychology; drawing; early childhood education; ecology; education; elementary education; English; environmental education; environmental science; fine/studio arts; history; human ecology; humanities; individual/family development; interdisciplinary studies; jazz; journalism; liberal arts and sciences/liberal studies; literature; medieval/renaissance studies; middle school education; music; music history; natural sciences; peace/conflict studies; philosophy; photography; physical sciences; political science; psychology; sculpture; secondary education; social sciences; sociology; theater arts/drama; women's studies.

Academic Programs *Special study options:* adult/continuing education programs, advanced placement credit, cooperative education, distance learning, double majors, external degree program, independent study, internships, off-campus study, services for LD students, student-designed majors.

Library Eliot Pratt Center with 70,000 titles, 280 serial subscriptions, 175 audiovisual materials, a Web page.

Computers on Campus 27 computers available on campus for general student use. A campuswide network can be accessed from student residence rooms and from off campus. Internet access, at least one staffed computer lab available.

Student Life *Housing:* on-campus residence required through sophomore year. *Options:* coed, women-only, cooperative. *Activities and Organizations:* drama/theater group, student-run newspaper, radio station, women's center, student newspaper, Student Art Group, multicultural center, student theatre. *Campus security:* 24-hour patrols, patrols by trained security personnel 9 p.m. to 6 a.m. *Student Services:* personal/psychological counseling, women's center.

Standardized Tests *Recommended:* SAT I and SAT II or ACT (for admission).

Costs (2001–02) *Comprehensive fee:* $19,448 includes full-time tuition ($17,840), mandatory fees ($126), and room and board ($1482). *Room and board:* College room only: $539. *Payment plan:* installment. *Waivers:* employees or children of employees.

Financial Aid Of all full-time matriculated undergraduates who enrolled in 2001, 220 applied for aid, 155 were judged to have need. 130 Federal Work-Study jobs (averaging $1496). In 2001, 65 non-need-based awards were made. *Average percent of need met:* 77%. *Average financial aid package:* $17,100. *Average need-based loan:* $5500. *Average need-based gift aid:* $8700. *Average non-need based aid:* $3000. *Average indebtedness upon graduation:* $17,125.

Applying *Options:* electronic application, deferred entrance. *Application fee:* $40. *Required:* essay or personal statement, high school transcript, 2 letters of recommendation, interview. *Application deadline:* rolling (freshmen), rolling (transfers). *Notification:* continuous (freshmen).

Admissions Contact Mr. Josh Castle, Admissions Counselor, Goddard College, 123 Pitkin Road, Plainfield, VT 05667-9432. *Phone:* 802-454-8311 Ext. 322. *Toll-free phone:* 800-468-4888 Ext. 307. *Fax:* 802-454-1029. *E-mail:* admissions@earth.goddard.edu.

GREEN MOUNTAIN COLLEGE
Poultney, Vermont

- **Independent** 4-year, founded 1834, affiliated with United Methodist Church
- **Calendar** semesters
- **Degree** bachelor's
- **Small-town** 155-acre campus
- **Endowment** $1.7 million
- **Coed,** 659 undergraduate students, 96% full-time, 47% women, 53% men
- **Moderately difficult** entrance level, 72% of applicants were admitted

Undergraduates 633 full-time, 26 part-time. Students come from 28 states and territories, 19 other countries, 90% are from out of state, 2% African American, 0.2% Asian American or Pacific Islander, 2% Hispanic American, 0.8% Native American, 8% international, 8% transferred in, 85% live on campus. *Retention:* 57% of 2001 full-time freshmen returned.

Freshmen *Admission:* 738 applied, 532 admitted, 193 enrolled. *Average high school GPA:* 2.60. *Test scores:* SAT verbal scores over 500: 50%; SAT math scores over 500: 46%; ACT scores over 18: 75%; SAT verbal scores over 600: 15%; SAT math scores over 600: 11%; ACT scores over 24: 29%; SAT verbal scores over 700: 2%; SAT math scores over 700: 1%.

Faculty *Total:* 64, 59% full-time, 53% with terminal degrees. *Student/faculty ratio:* 14:1.

Majors Art; arts management; behavioral sciences; biology; business; business administration; business economics; communications; creative writing; elementary education; English; environmental science; fine/studio arts; history; international business; liberal arts and sciences/liberal studies; natural resources management; philosophy; psychology; recreational therapy; recreation/leisure facilities management; recreation/leisure studies; secondary education; special education; theater arts/drama; visual/performing arts.

Academic Programs *Special study options:* accelerated degree program, adult/continuing education programs, advanced placement credit, cooperative education, double majors, English as a second language, external degree program, honors programs, independent study, internships, off-campus study, part-time degree program, services for LD students, student-designed majors, study abroad, summer session for credit. *ROTC:* Army (c), Navy (c), Air Force (c).

Library Griswold Library with 62,000 titles, 230 serial subscriptions, 4,350 audiovisual materials, an OPAC, a Web page.

Computers on Campus 80 computers available on campus for general student use. A campuswide network can be accessed from student residence rooms and from off campus. Internet access, online (class) registration, at least one staffed computer lab available.

Student Life *Housing:* on-campus residence required through junior year. *Options:* coed. *Activities and Organizations:* drama/theater group, student-run newspaper, choral group, Student National Education Association, Student Government Association, Outing Club, Intercultural Club, Peer Majors Club. *Campus security:* 24-hour emergency response devices and patrols, student patrols, late-night transport/escort service, controlled dormitory access. *Student Services:* health clinic, personal/psychological counseling.

Athletics Member NCAA. All Division II. *Intercollegiate sports:* basketball M(s)/W(s), cross-country running M(s)/W(s), golf M(s)/W(s), lacrosse M, skiing (downhill) M(s)/W(s), soccer M(s)/W(s), softball W(s), tennis M(s)/W(s), volleyball W(s). *Intramural sports:* badminton M/W, basketball M/W, bowling M/W, football M/W, lacrosse M, rugby M/W, skiing (cross-country) M/W, skiing (downhill) M/W, soccer M/W, softball W, swimming M/W, table tennis M/W, tennis M/W, volleyball M/W, weight lifting M/W.

Standardized Tests *Required:* SAT I or ACT (for admission).

Costs (2001–02) *Comprehensive fee:* $24,130 includes full-time tuition ($17,880), mandatory fees ($400), and room and board ($5850). Full-time tuition and fees vary according to program. Part-time tuition: $596 per credit. Part-time tuition and fees vary according to course load. *Required fees:* $200 per term part-time. *Room and board:* Room and board charges vary according to board plan. *Payment plans:* tuition prepayment, installment. *Waivers:* employees or children of employees.

Financial Aid Of all full-time matriculated undergraduates who enrolled in 2001, 500 applied for aid, 410 were judged to have need, 220 had their need fully met. In 2001, 130 non-need-based awards were made. *Average percent of need met:* 75%. *Average financial aid package:* $11,000. *Average need-based loan:* $3583. *Average need-based gift aid:* $4700. *Average non-need based aid:* $4320. *Average indebtedness upon graduation:* $14,000.

Applying *Options:* common application, electronic application, deferred entrance. *Application fee:* $30. *Required:* high school transcript. *Recommended:* essay or personal statement, minimum 2.4 GPA, 2 letters of recommendation, interview. *Application deadline:* rolling (freshmen), rolling (transfers). *Notification:* continuous until 8/1 (freshmen).

Green Mountain College (continued)

Admissions Contact Ms. Merrilyn Tatarczuch-Koff, Dean of Enrollment Services, Green Mountain College, Poultney, VT 05764. *Phone:* 802-287-8000 Ext. 8305. *Toll-free phone:* 800-776-6675. *Fax:* 802-287-8099. *E-mail:* admiss@greenmtn.edu.

JOHNSON STATE COLLEGE
Johnson, Vermont

- **State-supported** comprehensive, founded 1828, part of Vermont State Colleges System
- **Calendar** semesters
- **Degrees** certificates, associate, bachelor's, and master's
- **Rural** 350-acre campus with easy access to Montreal
- **Coed,** 1,387 undergraduate students, 72% full-time, 58% women, 42% men
- **Moderately difficult** entrance level, 83% of applicants were admitted

Undergraduates 998 full-time, 389 part-time. Students come from 25 states and territories, 16 other countries, 40% are from out of state, 0.5% African American, 0.2% Asian American or Pacific Islander, 0.8% Hispanic American, 2% Native American, 2% international, 11% transferred in, 57% live on campus. *Retention:* 61% of 2001 full-time freshmen returned.

Freshmen *Admission:* 948 applied, 788 admitted, 223 enrolled. *Test scores:* SAT verbal scores over 500: 55%; SAT math scores over 500: 48%; SAT verbal scores over 600: 11%; SAT math scores over 600: 5%; SAT verbal scores over 700: 2%; SAT math scores over 700: 1%.

Faculty *Total:* 181, 34% full-time. *Student/faculty ratio:* 16:1.

Majors Accounting; acting/directing; anthropology; art; art education; athletic training/sports medicine; biology; biology education; business; business administration; business marketing and marketing management; creative writing; dance; drama/dance education; education; elementary education; English; English education; environmental education; environmental science; exercise sciences; fine/studio arts; general studies; health/physical education; health science; history; history education; hospitality management; humanities; information sciences/systems; jazz; journalism; liberal arts and sciences/liberal studies; literature; management information systems/business data processing; mathematics; mathematics education; middle school education; music; music business management/merchandising; music (general performance); music teacher education; natural resources management; physical education; political science; pre-medicine; psychology; recreation/leisure studies; secondary education; social science education; social studies education; sociology; sport/fitness administration; theater arts/drama; theater design; travel/tourism management; visual/performing arts.

Academic Programs *Special study options:* accelerated degree program, advanced placement credit, cooperative education, distance learning, double majors, English as a second language, external degree program, honors programs, independent study, internships, off-campus study, part-time degree program, services for LD students, summer session for credit. *ROTC:* Army (c).

Library Library and Learning Center with 100,053 titles, 522 serial subscriptions, 7,200 audiovisual materials, an OPAC.

Computers on Campus 131 computers available on campus for general student use. A campuswide network can be accessed from student residence rooms and from off campus. Internet access, at least one staffed computer lab available.

Student Life *Housing:* on-campus residence required through sophomore year. *Options:* coed. *Activities and Organizations:* drama/theater group, student-run newspaper, radio station, choral group, SERVE (Break Away, Habitat for Humanity), Outing Club, Snowboarding, Earth Action Club, Gay Straight Alliance. *Campus security:* 24-hour emergency response devices and patrols, student patrols, late-night transport/escort service, controlled dormitory access. *Student Services:* health clinic, personal/psychological counseling.

Athletics Member NCAA. All Division III. *Intercollegiate sports:* basketball M/W, cross-country running M/W, lacrosse M, soccer M/W, softball W, tennis M/W. *Intramural sports:* basketball M/W, cross-country running M/W, golf M(c), lacrosse M, racquetball M/W, rugby M(c)/W(c), soccer M/W, softball M/W, swimming M(c)/W(c), table tennis M/W, tennis M/W, volleyball M/W, water polo M/W, weight lifting M/W.

Standardized Tests *Required:* SAT I or ACT (for admission).

Costs (2001–02) *Tuition:* state resident $4404 full-time, $184 per credit part-time; nonresident $10,320 full-time, $430 per credit part-time. Full-time tuition and fees vary according to reciprocity agreements. Part-time tuition and fees vary according to course load and reciprocity agreements. *Required fees:* $848 full-time, $424 per term part-time. *Room and board:* $5520; room only: $3252. Room and board charges vary according to board plan and housing facility. *Payment plans:* installment, deferred payment. *Waivers:* senior citizens and employees or children of employees.

Financial Aid Of all full-time matriculated undergraduates who enrolled in 2001, 832 applied for aid, 685 were judged to have need, 167 had their need fully met. 395 Federal Work-Study jobs (averaging $1583). *Average percent of need met:* 81%. *Average financial aid package:* $7835. *Average need-based loan:* $3294. *Average need-based gift aid:* $4426. *Average indebtedness upon graduation:* $16,910.

Applying *Options:* electronic application, deferred entrance. *Application fee:* $30. *Required:* essay or personal statement, high school transcript, minimum 2.0 GPA, 1 letter of recommendation. *Recommended:* minimum 2.5 GPA, interview. *Application deadline:* rolling (freshmen), rolling (transfers). *Notification:* continuous (freshmen).

Admissions Contact Ms. Kellie Rose, Assistant Director of Admissions, Johnson State College, 337 College Hill, Johnson, VT 05656-9405. *Phone:* 802-635-1219. *Toll-free phone:* 800-635-2356. *Fax:* 802-635-1230. *E-mail:* jscapply@badger.jsc.vsc.edu.

LYNDON STATE COLLEGE
Lyndonville, Vermont

- **State-supported** comprehensive, founded 1911, part of Vermont State Colleges System
- **Calendar** semesters
- **Degrees** associate, bachelor's, and master's
- **Rural** 175-acre campus
- **Coed,** 1,130 undergraduate students
- **Moderately difficult** entrance level, 96% of applicants were admitted

Undergraduates Students come from 20 states and territories, 48% are from out of state, 50% live on campus. *Retention:* 57% of 2001 full-time freshmen returned.

Freshmen *Admission:* 943 applied, 903 admitted. *Average high school GPA:* 2.5. *Test scores:* SAT verbal scores over 500: 42%; SAT math scores over 500: 39%; SAT verbal scores over 600: 8%; SAT math scores over 600: 7%.

Faculty *Total:* 122, 52% full-time, 32% with terminal degrees. *Student/faculty ratio:* 17:1.

Majors Accounting; athletic training/sports medicine; atmospheric sciences; biological/physical sciences; business administration; communications; computer/information sciences; computer science; elementary education; English; English education; enterprise management; graphic design/commercial art/illustration; health/physical education; journalism; liberal arts and sciences/liberal studies; mathematics; mathematics education; physical education; physical sciences; psychology; radio/television broadcasting; radio/television broadcasting technology; reading education; recreation/leisure facilities management; recreation/leisure studies; science education; social science education; social sciences; special education; sport/fitness administration.

Academic Programs *Special study options:* academic remediation for entering students, adult/continuing education programs, advanced placement credit, cooperative education, double majors, independent study, internships, part-time degree program, services for LD students, student-designed majors, study abroad, summer session for credit. *ROTC:* Air Force (b).

Library Samuel Read Hall Library with 101,872 titles, 16,468 serial subscriptions, 4,883 audiovisual materials, an OPAC, a Web page.

Computers on Campus 125 computers available on campus for general student use. A campuswide network can be accessed from student residence rooms and from off campus. Internet access, at least one staffed computer lab available.

Student Life *Housing:* on-campus residence required through sophomore year. *Options:* coed, women-only, disabled students. *Activities and Organizations:* drama/theater group, student-run newspaper, radio station, choral group, American Meteorological Society, ASSIST (A Society of Students in Service Together), Student Senate, Campus Activities Board, Outing Club. *Campus security:* 24-hour emergency response devices, student patrols, late-night transport/escort service, controlled dormitory access. *Student Services:* health clinic, personal/psychological counseling.

Athletics Member NAIA. *Intercollegiate sports:* baseball M, basketball M/W, cross-country running M/W, soccer M/W, softball W, tennis M/W. *Intramural sports:* basketball M/W, cross-country running M/W, field hockey M/W, football M/W, golf M/W, ice hockey M/W, racquetball M/W, rugby M/W, skiing (cross-country) M/W, skiing (downhill) M/W, softball M/W, squash M/W, swimming M/W, table tennis M/W, tennis M/W, volleyball M/W, water polo M/W.

Standardized Tests *Required:* SAT I or ACT (for admission).

Costs (2001–02) *One-time required fee:* $150. *Tuition:* state resident $4404 full-time, $184 per credit hour part-time; nonresident $10,320 full-time. Full-time tuition and fees vary according to reciprocity agreements. Part-time tuition and fees vary according to reciprocity agreements. *Required fees:* $848 full-time, $37 per credit hour. *Room and board:* $5520; room only: $3348. Room and board charges vary according to board plan and housing facility. *Waivers:* senior citizens and employees or children of employees.

Financial Aid Of all full-time matriculated undergraduates who enrolled in 2001, 839 applied for aid, 729 were judged to have need, 83 had their need fully met. 223 Federal Work-Study jobs (averaging $1129). In 2001, 139 non-need-based awards were made. *Average percent of need met:* 87%. *Average financial aid package:* $12,563. *Average need-based loan:* $4186. *Average need-based gift aid:* $1583. *Average non-need based aid:* $1232.

Applying *Options:* common application, electronic application, early admission, deferred entrance. *Application fee:* $30. *Required:* high school transcript, minimum 2.0 GPA, 1 letter of recommendation. *Required for some:* minimum 3.0 GPA. *Recommended:* essay or personal statement, minimum 3.0 GPA, interview. *Application deadline:* rolling (freshmen), rolling (transfers). *Notification:* continuous (freshmen).

Admissions Contact Ms. Michelle McCaffrey, Director of Admissions, Lyndon State College, 1001 College Road, PO Box 919, Lyndonville, VT 05851. *Phone:* 802-626-6413. *Toll-free phone:* 800-225-1998. *Fax:* 802-626-6335. *E-mail:* admissions@mail.lsc.vsc.edu.

MARLBORO COLLEGE

Marlboro, Vermont

- **Independent** comprehensive, founded 1946
- **Calendar** semesters
- **Degrees** bachelor's and master's
- **Rural** 350-acre campus
- **Endowment** $15.4 million
- **Coed,** 331 undergraduate students, 97% full-time, 57% women, 43% men
- **Moderately difficult** entrance level, 87% of applicants were admitted

Undergraduates 321 full-time, 10 part-time. Students come from 36 states and territories, 89% are from out of state, 0.9% African American, 2% Hispanic American, 0.9% Native American, 0.9% international, 6% transferred in, 74% live on campus. *Retention:* 71% of 2001 full-time freshmen returned.

Freshmen *Admission:* 205 applied, 179 admitted, 80 enrolled. *Average high school GPA:* 3.33. *Test scores:* SAT verbal scores over 500: 94%; SAT math scores over 500: 86%; SAT verbal scores over 600: 69%; SAT math scores over 600: 31%; ACT scores over 24: 100%; SAT verbal scores over 700: 24%; SAT math scores over 700: 5%; ACT scores over 30: 25%.

Faculty *Total:* 52, 67% full-time, 62% with terminal degrees. *Student/faculty ratio:* 8:1.

Majors African studies; American studies; anthropology; applied mathematics; art; art history; Asian studies; astronomy; astrophysics; behavioral sciences; biblical studies; biochemistry; biology; botany; cell biology; ceramic arts; chemistry; classics; comparative literature; computer science; creative writing; cultural studies; dance; developmental/child psychology; drawing; East Asian studies; Eastern European area studies; ecology; economics; English; environmental biology; environmental science; European studies; experimental psychology; film studies; fine/studio arts; folklore; French; German; Greek (modern); history; history of philosophy; humanities; interdisciplinary studies; international economics; international relations; Italian; Latin American studies; Latin (ancient and medieval); linguistics; literature; mathematics; medieval/renaissance studies; modern languages; molecular biology; music; music history; natural resources conservation; natural sciences; philosophy; photography; physics; political science; Portuguese; pre-law; pre-medicine; pre-veterinary studies; psychology; religious studies; romance languages; Russian/Slavic studies; sculpture; social sciences; sociology; Spanish; theater arts/drama; women's studies.

Academic Programs *Special study options:* accelerated degree program, advanced placement credit, double majors, independent study, internships, off-campus study, part-time degree program, services for LD students, student-designed majors, study abroad.

Library Rice Memorial Library with 54,289 titles, 250 serial subscriptions, 746 audiovisual materials, an OPAC, a Web page.

Computers on Campus 42 computers available on campus for general student use. A campuswide network can be accessed from student residence rooms and from off campus. Internet access, at least one staffed computer lab available.

Student Life *Housing:* on-campus residence required for freshman year. *Options:* coed, women-only, cooperative. *Activities and Organizations:* drama/theater group, student-run newspaper, choral group, Theater Club, outdoor program, Fencing Club, Gay/Lesbian/Bisexual Alliance, Women's Chorus. *Campus security:* 24-hour emergency response devices. *Student Services:* health clinic, personal/psychological counseling.

Athletics *Intercollegiate sports:* skiing (downhill) M/W, soccer M/W. *Intramural sports:* basketball M/W, fencing M/W, ice hockey M/W, skiing (cross-country) M/W, skiing (downhill) M/W, soccer M/W, softball M/W, table tennis M/W, volleyball M/W, weight lifting M/W.

Standardized Tests *Required:* SAT I or ACT (for admission). *Recommended:* SAT II: Subject Tests (for admission).

Costs (2002–03) *Comprehensive fee:* $26,410 includes full-time tuition ($18,800), mandatory fees ($860), and room and board ($6750). Full-time tuition and fees vary according to course load and program. Part-time tuition: $630 per credit. Part-time tuition and fees vary according to course load and program. *Required fees:* $165 per term part-time. *Room and board:* College room only: $3300. *Payment plan:* installment. *Waivers:* senior citizens and employees or children of employees.

Financial Aid Of all full-time matriculated undergraduates who enrolled in 2001, 240 applied for aid, 213 were judged to have need, 114 had their need fully met. 189 Federal Work-Study jobs (averaging $1647). 3 State and other part-time jobs (averaging $1930). In 2001, 3 non-need-based awards were made. *Average percent of need met:* 94%. *Average financial aid package:* $15,091. *Average need-based loan:* $3754. *Average need-based gift aid:* $9346. *Average non-need based aid:* $1416. *Average indebtedness upon graduation:* $18,212.

Applying *Options:* common application, electronic application, early admission, early decision, early action, deferred entrance. *Application fee:* $50. *Required:* essay or personal statement, high school transcript, 2 letters of recommendation, interview, graded expository essay. *Recommended:* minimum 3.0 GPA. *Application deadlines:* 3/1 (freshmen), 4/1 (transfers). *Early decision:* 11/15. *Notification:* 4/1 (freshmen), 12/15 (early decision), 2/1 (early action).

Admissions Contact Ms. Julie E. Richardson, Vice President, Enrollment and Financial Aid, Marlboro College, PO Box A, South Road, Marlboro, VT 05344-0300. *Phone:* 802-258-9261. *Toll-free phone:* 800-343-0049. *Fax:* 802-451-7555. *E-mail:* admissions@marlboro.edu.

MIDDLEBURY COLLEGE

Middlebury, Vermont

- **Independent** comprehensive, founded 1800
- **Calendar** 4-1-4
- **Degrees** bachelor's, master's, and doctoral
- **Small-town** 350-acre campus
- **Endowment** $666.8 million
- **Coed,** 2,307 undergraduate students, 98% full-time, 52% women, 48% men
- **Very difficult** entrance level, 23% of applicants were admitted

Undergraduates 2,270 full-time, 37 part-time. Students come from 50 states and territories, 83 other countries, 93% are from out of state, 2% African American, 6% Asian American or Pacific Islander, 6% Hispanic American, 0.6% Native American, 8% international, 0.1% transferred in, 94% live on campus. *Retention:* 97% of 2001 full-time freshmen returned.

Freshmen *Admission:* 5,411 applied, 1,222 admitted, 513 enrolled. *Test scores:* SAT verbal scores over 500: 98%; SAT math scores over 500: 99%; SAT verbal scores over 600: 94%; SAT math scores over 600: 95%; SAT verbal scores over 700: 57%; SAT math scores over 700: 56%.

Faculty *Total:* 237, 92% full-time, 91% with terminal degrees. *Student/faculty ratio:* 11:1.

Majors American studies; anthropology; art; art history; biochemistry; biological/physical sciences; biology; chemistry; Chinese; classics; computer science; dance; drawing; East Asian studies; Eastern European area studies; economics; education; English; environmental science; film studies; fine/studio arts; French; geography; geology; German; history; humanities; international economics; international relations; Italian; Japanese; liberal arts and sciences/liberal studies; literature; mathematics; modern languages; molecular biology; music; natural sciences; philosophy; physical sciences; physics; political science; pre-dentistry; pre-law; pre-medicine; pre-veterinary studies; psychology; religious studies; romance languages; Russian; Russian/Slavic studies; secondary education; social sciences; sociology; Southeast Asian studies; Spanish; theater arts/drama; women's studies.

Academic Programs *Special study options:* accelerated degree program, advanced placement credit, double majors, honors programs, independent study, internships, off-campus study, services for LD students, student-designed majors, study abroad, summer session for credit. *ROTC:* Army (c). *Unusual degree programs:* 3-2 business administration with University of Chicago; New York University; Rutgers, The State University of New Jersey, Graduate School of Management; University of Rochester; Columbia University; Boston University; Dartmouth College; engineering with Columbia University, Rensselaer Polytechnic Institute, University of Rochester; forestry with Duke University; nursing with Columbia University.

Middlebury College (continued)

Library Egbert Starr Library plus 3 others with 1.5 million titles, 2,496 serial subscriptions, 27,697 audiovisual materials, an OPAC, a Web page.

Computers on Campus 225 computers available on campus for general student use. A campuswide network can be accessed from student residence rooms and from off campus that provide access to computer helpline. Internet access, online (class) registration, at least one staffed computer lab available.

Student Life *Housing:* on-campus residence required through junior year. *Options:* coed, disabled students. *Activities and Organizations:* drama/theater group, student-run newspaper, radio station, choral group, Volunteer Service Organization, International Students Organization, Mountain Club, Activities Board, WRMC Radio. *Campus security:* 24-hour patrols, student patrols, late-night transport/escort service. *Student Services:* health clinic, personal/psychological counseling, women's center.

Athletics Member NCAA. All Division III except men's and women's skiing (cross-country) (Division I), men's and women's skiing (downhill) (Division I). *Intercollegiate sports:* baseball M, basketball M/W, cross-country running M/W, field hockey W, football M, golf M/W, ice hockey M/W, lacrosse M/W, skiing (cross-country) M/W, skiing (downhill) M/W, soccer M/W, softball W, squash W, swimming M/W, tennis M/W, track and field M/W, volleyball W. *Intramural sports:* archery M/W, badminton M/W, basketball M(c)/W(c), crew M/W, cross-country running M/W, equestrian sports M(c)/W(c), football M/W, golf M/W, ice hockey M/W, rugby M(c)/W(c), sailing M(c)/W(c), skiing (downhill) M/W, soccer M/W, softball M/W, squash M/W, swimming M/W, table tennis M/W, tennis M/W, volleyball M/W, water polo M(c)/W(c).

Costs (2001–02) *Payment plans:* tuition prepayment, installment. *Waivers:* employees or children of employees.

Financial Aid Of all full-time matriculated undergraduates who enrolled in 2001, 928 applied for aid, 792 were judged to have need, 792 had their need fully met. 477 Federal Work-Study jobs (averaging $1579). 123 State and other part-time jobs (averaging $1558). *Average percent of need met:* 100%. *Average financial aid package:* $26,039. *Average need-based loan:* $5774. *Average need-based gift aid:* $19,931. *Average indebtedness upon graduation:* $20,824.

Applying *Options:* common application, early admission, early decision, deferred entrance. *Application fee:* $55. *Required:* essay or personal statement, high school transcript, 3 letters of recommendation. *Recommended:* interview. *Application deadlines:* 12/15 (freshmen), 3/1 (transfers). *Early decision:* 11/15 (for plan 1), 12/15 (for plan 2). *Notification:* 4/1 (freshmen), 12/15 (early decision plan 1), 1/31 (early decision plan 2).

Admissions Contact Mr. John Hanson, Director of Admissions, Middlebury College, Emma Willard House, Middlebury, VT 05753-6002. *Phone:* 802-443-3000. *Fax:* 802-443-2056. *E-mail:* admissions@middlebury.edu.

NEW ENGLAND CULINARY INSTITUTE

Montpelier, Vermont

- **Proprietary** primarily 2-year, founded 1980
- **Calendar** quarters
- **Degrees** certificates, diplomas, associate, and bachelor's
- **Small-town** campus
- **Endowment** $50,000
- **Coed,** 639 undergraduate students, 100% full-time, 28% women, 72% men
- **Moderately difficult** entrance level

Undergraduates 639 full-time. Students come from 50 states and territories, 8 other countries, 77% are from out of state, 2% African American, 0.8% Asian American or Pacific Islander, 3% Hispanic American, 0.2% Native American, 2% transferred in, 80% live on campus.

Freshmen *Admission:* 210 enrolled. *Average high school GPA:* 2.5.

Faculty *Total:* 77, 88% full-time, 4% with terminal degrees. *Student/faculty ratio:* 6:1.

Majors Culinary arts; food products retailing; hotel and restaurant management.

Academic Programs *Special study options:* internships.

Library New England Culinary Institute Library with 800 titles, 100 serial subscriptions, 100 audiovisual materials, an OPAC.

Computers on Campus 14 computers available on campus for general student use. A campuswide network can be accessed from student residence rooms. Internet access, at least one staffed computer lab available.

Student Life *Housing Options:* coed, men-only, women-only. *Activities and Organizations:* student-run newspaper, American Culinary Federation, Toastmasters, Ice Carving Club. *Campus security:* 24-hour emergency response devices. *Student Services:* personal/psychological counseling.

Standardized Tests *Recommended:* SAT I (for placement).

Costs (2001–02) *Comprehensive fee:* $23,875 includes full-time tuition ($19,660), mandatory fees ($200), and room and board ($4015). Full-time tuition and fees vary according to degree level and program. *Room and board:* College room only: $2370. *Payment plan:* installment. *Waivers:* children of alumni and employees or children of employees.

Applying *Options:* common application, electronic application, deferred entrance. *Required:* essay or personal statement, high school transcript, interview. *Application deadline:* rolling (freshmen).

Admissions Contact Ms. Linda Cooper, Director of Admissions, New England Culinary Institute, 250 Main Street, Montpelier, VT 05602. *Phone:* 802-223-9295. *Toll-free phone:* 877-223-6324. *Fax:* 802-223-0634. *E-mail:* IntInq@neci.edu.

NORWICH UNIVERSITY

Northfield, Vermont

- **Independent** comprehensive, founded 1819
- **Calendar** semesters
- **Degrees** bachelor's, master's, and post-master's certificates
- **Small-town** 1125-acre campus
- **Endowment** $110.9 million
- **Coed,** 2,129 undergraduate students
- **Moderately difficult** entrance level, 91% of applicants were admitted

Undergraduates Students come from 41 states and territories, 10 other countries, 74% are from out of state, 84% live on campus. *Retention:* 71% of 2001 full-time freshmen returned.

Freshmen *Admission:* 1,472 applied, 1,340 admitted. *Average high school GPA:* 3.01. *Test scores:* SAT verbal scores over 500: 50%; SAT math scores over 500: 52%; SAT verbal scores over 600: 15%; SAT math scores over 600: 15%; SAT verbal scores over 700: 3%; SAT math scores over 700: 1%.

Faculty *Total:* 272, 51% full-time. *Student/faculty ratio:* 12:1.

Majors Architecture; athletic training/sports medicine; biochemical technology; biology; business administration; chemistry; civil engineering; communications; computer science; criminal justice/law enforcement administration; economics; educational media design; electrical engineering; English; environmental science; geology; history; information sciences/systems; international relations; mathematics; mechanical engineering; nursing; peace/conflict studies; physical education; physics; political science; psychology.

Academic Programs *Special study options:* academic remediation for entering students, adult/continuing education programs, advanced placement credit, cooperative education, distance learning, double majors, English as a second language, external degree program, independent study, internships, part-time degree program, services for LD students, study abroad, summer session for credit. *ROTC:* Army (b), Navy (b), Air Force (b).

Library Kreitzberg Library with 256,530 titles, 904 serial subscriptions, 1,501 audiovisual materials, an OPAC, a Web page.

Computers on Campus 142 computers available on campus for general student use. A campuswide network can be accessed from student residence rooms and from off campus. Internet access, at least one staffed computer lab available.

Student Life *Housing:* on-campus residence required through senior year. *Options:* coed. *Activities and Organizations:* drama/theater group, student-run newspaper, radio station, choral group, marching band, Rugby Club, National Eagle Scout Association, Mountain and Cold Weather Company, Outing Club, band. *Campus security:* 24-hour emergency response devices and patrols, late-night transport/escort service. *Student Services:* health clinic, personal/psychological counseling.

Athletics Member NCAA. All Division III. *Intercollegiate sports:* baseball M, basketball M/W, cross-country running M/W, fencing M(c)/W(c), football M, ice hockey M/W(c), lacrosse M, riflery M/W, rugby M(c)/W(c), sailing M(c)/W(c), skiing (cross-country) M(c)/W(c), skiing (downhill) M(c)/W(c), soccer M/W, softball W, swimming M/W, tennis M/W(c), track and field M/W, volleyball M(c)/W(c), weight lifting M(c)/W(c), wrestling M. *Intramural sports:* basketball M/W, cross-country running M/W, football M, golf M/W, ice hockey M/W, lacrosse M/W, racquetball M/W, rugby M/W, soccer M/W, softball W, swimming M/W, tennis M/W, track and field M/W, volleyball M/W, water polo M/W, weight lifting M/W, wrestling M.

Standardized Tests *Required:* SAT I or ACT (for admission). *Recommended:* SAT II: Subject Tests (for admission).

Costs (2001–02) *Comprehensive fee:* $22,262 includes full-time tuition ($15,914), mandatory fees ($280), and room and board ($6068). Full-time tuition and fees vary according to location and program. Part-time tuition: $425 per credit hour. Part-time tuition and fees vary according to course load, location, and program. *Room and board:* Room and board charges vary according to board plan and location. *Payment plan:* installment. *Waivers:* employees or children of employees.

Applying *Options:* electronic application, early admission, early decision, deferred entrance. *Application fee:* $35. *Required:* high school transcript. *Required for some:* essay or personal statement, portfolio. *Recommended:* essay or personal statement, minimum 2.0 GPA, 2 letters of recommendation, interview. *Application deadline:* rolling (freshmen), rolling (transfers). *Early decision:* 11/15. *Notification:* continuous (freshmen), 12/15 (early decision).

Admissions Contact Ms. Karen McGrath, Dean of Enrollment Management, Norwich University, 158 Harmon Drive, Northfield, VT 05663. *Phone:* 802-485-2013. *Toll-free phone:* 800-468-6679. *Fax:* 802-485-2580. *E-mail:* nuadm@norwich.edu.

SAINT MICHAEL'S COLLEGE
Colchester, Vermont

- **Independent Roman Catholic** comprehensive, founded 1904
- **Calendar** semesters
- **Degrees** bachelor's, master's, and post-master's certificates
- **Small-town** 440-acre campus with easy access to Montreal
- **Endowment** $60.6 million
- **Coed,** 2,021 undergraduate students, 96% full-time, 55% women, 45% men
- **Moderately difficult** entrance level, 64% of applicants were admitted

Undergraduates 1,944 full-time, 77 part-time. Students come from 32 states and territories, 17 other countries, 77% are from out of state, 1.0% African American, 1% Asian American or Pacific Islander, 1% Hispanic American, 2% international, 1% transferred in, 89% live on campus. *Retention:* 89% of 2001 full-time freshmen returned.

Freshmen *Admission:* 2,550 applied, 1,636 admitted, 518 enrolled. *Test scores:* SAT verbal scores over 500: 84%; SAT math scores over 500: 83%; SAT verbal scores over 600: 31%; SAT math scores over 600: 29%; SAT verbal scores over 700: 4%; SAT math scores over 700: 3%.

Faculty *Total:* 190, 73% full-time, 71% with terminal degrees. *Student/faculty ratio:* 13:1.

Majors Accounting; American studies; art; art education; biochemistry; biology; business administration; chemistry; classics; computer science; economics; education; elementary education; English; environmental science; French; history; journalism; mathematics; modern languages; music; music teacher education; philosophy; physical sciences; physics; political science; pre-dentistry; pre-law; pre-medicine; pre-veterinary studies; psychology; religious studies; secondary education; sociology; Spanish; theater arts/drama.

Academic Programs *Special study options:* advanced placement credit, double majors, English as a second language, honors programs, independent study, internships, off-campus study, part-time degree program, student-designed majors, study abroad, summer session for credit. *ROTC:* Army (c), Air Force (c). *Unusual degree programs:* 3-2 engineering with University of Vermont, Clarkson University.

Library Durick Library with 206,124 titles, 3,312 serial subscriptions, 6,195 audiovisual materials, an OPAC, a Web page.

Computers on Campus 180 computers available on campus for general student use. A campuswide network can be accessed from student residence rooms and from off campus. Internet access, at least one staffed computer lab available.

Student Life *Housing:* on-campus residence required through senior year. *Options:* coed, men-only, women-only, cooperative, disabled students. *Activities and Organizations:* drama/theater group, student-run newspaper, radio station, choral group, Student Association, Mobilization of Volunteer Efforts (MOVE), student radio station, wilderness program, student newspaper. *Campus security:* 24-hour emergency response devices and patrols, student patrols, late-night transport/escort service, bicycle patrols. *Student Services:* health clinic, personal/psychological counseling, women's center.

Athletics Member NCAA. All Division II. *Intercollegiate sports:* baseball M, basketball M(s)/W(s), cross-country running M/W, field hockey W, golf M, ice hockey M/W, lacrosse M/W, rugby M(c)/W(c), skiing (cross-country) M/W, skiing (downhill) M/W, soccer M/W, softball W, swimming M/W, tennis M/W, volleyball W. *Intramural sports:* badminton M/W, basketball M/W, racquetball M/W, skiing (cross-country) M/W, skiing (downhill) M/W, soccer M/W, softball M/W, squash M/W, swimming M/W, table tennis M/W, tennis M/W, volleyball M/W, water polo M/W.

Standardized Tests *Required:* SAT I or ACT (for admission).

Costs (2002–03) *Comprehensive fee:* $28,455 includes full-time tuition ($21,010), mandatory fees ($190), and room and board ($7255). Part-time tuition: $700 per semester hour. *Room and board:* College room only: $4510. Room and board charges vary according to board plan and housing facility. *Payment plan:* installment. *Waivers:* employees or children of employees.

Financial Aid Of all full-time matriculated undergraduates who enrolled in 2001, 1427 applied for aid, 1179 were judged to have need, 403 had their need fully met. 540 State and other part-time jobs (averaging $1300). In 2001, 332 non-need-based awards were made. *Average percent of need met:* 91%. *Average financial aid package:* $15,686. *Average need-based loan:* $4280. *Average need-based gift aid:* $6417. *Average non-need based aid:* $6039. *Average indebtedness upon graduation:* $17,180.

Applying *Options:* common application, electronic application, early admission, early action, deferred entrance. *Application fee:* $45. *Required:* essay or personal statement, high school transcript. *Recommended:* minimum 3.0 GPA, letters of recommendation, interview. *Application deadlines:* 2/1 (freshmen), 2/1 (transfers). *Notification:* 4/1 (freshmen), 2/1 (early action).

Admissions Contact Ms. Jacqueline Murphy, Director of Admission, Saint Michael's College, One Winooski Park, Colchester, VT 05439. *Phone:* 802-654-3000. *Toll-free phone:* 800-762-8000. *Fax:* 802-654-2906. *E-mail:* admission@smcvt.edu.

SOUTHERN VERMONT COLLEGE
Bennington, Vermont

- **Independent** 4-year, founded 1926
- **Calendar** semesters
- **Degrees** associate and bachelor's
- **Small-town** 371-acre campus with easy access to Albany
- **Endowment** $1.2 million
- **Coed,** 457 undergraduate students, 67% full-time, 63% women, 37% men
- **Minimally difficult** entrance level, 68% of applicants were admitted

Undergraduates Students come from 18 states and territories, 2 other countries, 61% are from out of state, 5% African American, 0.2% Asian American or Pacific Islander, 2% Hispanic American, 0.9% international, 32% live on campus. *Retention:* 64% of 2001 full-time freshmen returned.

Freshmen *Admission:* 345 applied, 236 admitted. *Average high school GPA:* 2.70. *Test scores:* SAT verbal scores over 500: 25%; SAT math scores over 500: 24%; ACT scores over 18: 56%; SAT verbal scores over 600: 4%; SAT math scores over 600: 4%; ACT scores over 24: 11%.

Faculty *Total:* 61, 34% full-time, 10% with terminal degrees. *Student/faculty ratio:* 11:1.

Majors Accounting; business administration; child care/development; communications; creative writing; criminal justice/law enforcement administration; developmental/child psychology; English; environmental science; hospitality management; hotel and restaurant management; human services; liberal arts and sciences/liberal studies; literature; mass communications; nursing; psychology; social work.

Academic Programs *Special study options:* academic remediation for entering students, accelerated degree program, adult/continuing education programs, advanced placement credit, cooperative education, distance learning, double majors, external degree program, honors programs, independent study, internships, part-time degree program, services for LD students, student-designed majors, study abroad, summer session for credit.

Library Southern Vermont College Library with 26,000 titles, 250 serial subscriptions, 500 audiovisual materials, a Web page.

Computers on Campus 35 computers available on campus for general student use. A campuswide network can be accessed from student residence rooms and from off campus. Internet access, at least one staffed computer lab available.

Student Life *Housing:* on-campus residence required for freshman year. *Options:* coed. *Activities and Organizations:* drama/theater group, student-run newspaper, Student Association, Environmental Association, business club, Criminal Justice Association, Madhatters (drama club). *Campus security:* 24-hour patrols, late-night transport/escort service, controlled dormitory access. *Student Services:* health clinic, personal/psychological counseling.

Athletics Member NCAA. All Division III. *Intercollegiate sports:* baseball M, basketball M/W, cross-country running M/W, soccer M/W, softball W. *Intramural sports:* badminton M/W, baseball M/W, basketball M/W, football M/W, golf M/W, ice hockey M/W, lacrosse M/W, skiing (cross-country) M/W, skiing (downhill) M/W, soccer M/W, softball M/W, table tennis M/W, tennis M/W, volleyball M/W, weight lifting M/W.

Standardized Tests *Required:* SAT I or ACT (for admission).

Costs (2002–03) *Comprehensive fee:* $17,685 includes full-time tuition ($11,695) and room and board ($5990). Part-time tuition: $285 per credit. *Room and board:* College room only: $2995.

Financial Aid Of all full-time matriculated undergraduates who enrolled in 2001, 282 applied for aid, 253 were judged to have need, 75 had their need fully met. In 2001, 16 non-need-based awards were made. *Average percent of need met:* 90%. *Average financial aid package:* $12,512. *Average need-based gift aid:* $8717. *Average non-need based aid:* $3954. *Average indebtedness upon graduation:* $13,500.

Southern Vermont College (continued)

Applying *Options:* common application, electronic application, early admission, deferred entrance. *Application fee:* $30. *Required:* essay or personal statement, high school transcript, 2 letters of recommendation. *Required for some:* interview. *Recommended:* minimum 2.0 GPA, interview. *Application deadline:* rolling (freshmen), rolling (transfers). *Notification:* continuous (freshmen).

Admissions Contact Elizabeth Gatti, Director of Admissions, Southern Vermont College, 982 Mansion Drive, Bennington, VT 05201. *Phone:* 802-447-6304. *Toll-free phone:* 800-378-2782. *Fax:* 802-447-4695. *E-mail:* admis@svc.edu.

STERLING COLLEGE
Craftsbury Common, Vermont

- **Independent** 4-year, founded 1958
- **Calendar** semesters
- **Degrees** associate and bachelor's
- **Rural** 150-acre campus
- **Endowment** $581,589
- **Coed,** 80 undergraduate students, 100% full-time, 39% women, 61% men
- **Moderately difficult** entrance level, 61% of applicants were admitted

Undergraduates 80 full-time. Students come from 18 states and territories, 82% are from out of state, 8% transferred in, 74% live on campus. *Retention:* 83% of 2001 full-time freshmen returned.

Freshmen *Admission:* 59 applied, 36 admitted, 19 enrolled. *Average high school GPA:* 2.62. *Test scores:* SAT verbal scores over 500: 67%; SAT math scores over 500: 61%; SAT verbal scores over 600: 33%; SAT math scores over 600: 14%; SAT verbal scores over 700: 6%.

Faculty *Total:* 28, 36% full-time, 7% with terminal degrees. *Student/faculty ratio:* 10:1.

Majors Agricultural sciences; ecology; environmental science; forestry; human ecology; natural resources conservation; natural resources management; recreation/leisure facilities management; recreation/leisure studies; wildlife management.

Academic Programs *Special study options:* honors programs, independent study, internships, off-campus study, part-time degree program, services for LD students, student-designed majors, study abroad, summer session for credit.

Library Brown Library plus 1 other with 8,062 titles, 101 serial subscriptions, 244 audiovisual materials, an OPAC.

Computers on Campus 15 computers available on campus for general student use. A campuswide network can be accessed from student residence rooms. Internet access, at least one staffed computer lab available.

Student Life *Housing:* on-campus residence required for freshman year. *Options:* coed, men-only, women-only. *Activities and Organizations:* Outing Club, Timbersports Team, Student Life, Art Club. *Campus security:* student patrols. *Student Services:* health clinic, personal/psychological counseling.

Athletics *Intramural sports:* basketball M/W, skiing (cross-country) M/W, table tennis M/W, volleyball M/W.

Costs (2002–03) *Comprehensive fee:* $25,490 includes full-time tuition ($19,695), mandatory fees ($125), and room and board ($5670). Full-time tuition and fees vary according to course load, program, and student level. Part-time tuition: $425 per credit. *Room and board:* College room only: $2381. *Payment plan:* installment. *Waivers:* employees or children of employees.

Financial Aid Of all full-time matriculated undergraduates who enrolled in 2001, 80 applied for aid, 46 were judged to have need, 2 had their need fully met. 30 Federal Work-Study jobs (averaging $450). In 2001, 6 non-need-based awards were made. *Average percent of need met:* 75%. *Average financial aid package:* $10,920. *Average need-based loan:* $2726. *Average need-based gift aid:* $6422. *Average non-need based aid:* $1333. *Average indebtedness upon graduation:* $18,464.

Applying *Options:* common application, electronic application, early admission, deferred entrance. *Application fee:* $35. *Required:* essay or personal statement, high school transcript, 3 letters of recommendation, interview. *Recommended:* minimum 2.0 GPA. *Application deadline:* rolling (freshmen), rolling (transfers). *Notification:* continuous until 8/30 (freshmen).

Admissions Contact John Zaber, Director of Admissions, Sterling College, PO Box 72, Craftsbury Common, VT 05827. *Phone:* 802-586-7711 Ext. 35. *Toll-free phone:* 800-648-3591. *Fax:* 802-586-2596. *E-mail:* admissions@sterlingcollege.edu.

UNIVERSITY OF VERMONT
Burlington, Vermont

- **State-supported** university, founded 1791
- **Calendar** semesters
- **Degrees** certificates, associate, bachelor's, master's, doctoral, first professional, post-master's, and postbachelor's certificates
- **Suburban** 425-acre campus
- **Endowment** $219.6 million
- **Coed,** 8,592 undergraduate students, 84% full-time, 56% women, 44% men
- **Moderately difficult** entrance level, 80% of applicants were admitted

Undergraduates 7,214 full-time, 1,378 part-time. Students come from 51 states and territories, 36 other countries, 61% are from out of state, 0.6% African American, 2% Asian American or Pacific Islander, 2% Hispanic American, 0.2% Native American, 1% international, 4% transferred in, 52% live on campus. *Retention:* 82% of 2001 full-time freshmen returned.

Freshmen *Admission:* 8,268 applied, 6,578 admitted, 1,849 enrolled. *Test scores:* SAT verbal scores over 500: 82%; SAT math scores over 500: 84%; ACT scores over 18: 97%; SAT verbal scores over 600: 32%; SAT math scores over 600: 36%; ACT scores over 24: 55%; SAT verbal scores over 700: 3%; SAT math scores over 700: 3%; ACT scores over 30: 8%.

Faculty *Total:* 680, 77% full-time, 74% with terminal degrees. *Student/faculty ratio:* 13:1.

Majors Agricultural business; agricultural economics; agricultural sciences; animal sciences; anthropology; applied mathematics; art education; art history; Asian studies; athletic training/sports medicine; biochemistry; biology; botany; business administration; Canadian studies; cell biology; chemistry; child care/development; civil engineering; classics; communication disorders; computer science; dairy science; dietetics; early childhood education; Eastern European area studies; ecology; economics; education; electrical engineering; elementary education; engineering/industrial management; English; English education; environmental biology; environmental science; European studies; family/community studies; family/consumer studies; fine/studio arts; fish/game management; foreign languages education; forestry; French; geography; geology; German; Greek (ancient and medieval); history; horticulture science; horticulture services; individual/family development; information sciences/systems; interdisciplinary studies; international relations; landscaping management; Latin American studies; Latin (ancient and medieval); mathematical statistics; mathematics; mathematics education; mechanical engineering; medical laboratory assistant; medical radiologic technology; medical technology; microbiology/bacteriology; middle school education; molecular biology; music; music (general performance); music history; music teacher education; natural resources conservation; natural resources management; nursing; nutritional sciences; nutrition science; nutrition studies; philosophy; physical education; physics; plant sciences; political science; pre-veterinary studies; psychology; recreation/leisure facilities management; recreation/leisure studies; religious studies; romance languages; Russian; Russian/Slavic studies; science education; secondary education; social science education; social work; sociology; soil sciences; Spanish; speech-language pathology/audiology; theater arts/drama; water resources; wildlife biology; wildlife management; women's studies; zoology.

Academic Programs *Special study options:* academic remediation for entering students, advanced placement credit, cooperative education, distance learning, double majors, English as a second language, honors programs, independent study, internships, off-campus study, part-time degree program, services for LD students, student-designed majors, study abroad, summer session for credit. *ROTC:* Army (b).

Library Bailey-Howe Library plus 3 others with 2.4 million titles, 20,216 serial subscriptions, 36,531 audiovisual materials, an OPAC, a Web page.

Computers on Campus 685 computers available on campus for general student use. A campuswide network can be accessed from student residence rooms and from off campus that provide access to e-mail, Web pages, on-line course support. Internet access, at least one staffed computer lab available.

Student Life *Housing:* on-campus residence required through sophomore year. *Options:* coed. *Activities and Organizations:* drama/theater group, student-run newspaper, radio and television station, choral group, Volunteers in Action, Outing Club, club sports, national fraternities, national sororities. *Campus security:* 24-hour emergency response devices and patrols, late-night transport/escort service, controlled dormitory access. *Student Services:* health clinic, personal/psychological counseling, women's center, legal services.

Athletics Member NCAA. All Division I. *Intercollegiate sports:* baseball M, basketball M(s)/W(s), crew M(c)/W(c), cross-country running M/W, equestrian sports M(c)/W(c), field hockey W(s), golf M, gymnastics M(c)/W(c), ice hockey M(s)/W, lacrosse M/W, rugby M(c)/W(c), sailing M(c)/W(c), skiing (cross-country) M(s)/W(s), skiing (downhill) M(s)/W(s), soccer M(s)/W(s), softball W(s), swimming M/W, tennis M/W, track and field M(c)/W(s), volleyball M(c)/W(c), wrestling M(c). *Intramural sports:* basketball M/W, ice hockey M/W, racquetball M/W, soccer M/W, softball M/W, tennis M/W, volleyball M/W.

Standardized Tests *Required:* SAT I or ACT (for admission).

Costs (2001–02) *Tuition:* state resident $8040 full-time, $335 per credit part-time; nonresident $20,100 full-time, $838 per credit part-time. Part-time tuition and fees vary according to course load. *Required fees:* $625 full-time, $142 per term part-time. *Room and board:* $6096; room only: $4040. Room and board charges vary according to board plan. *Payment plans:* installment, deferred payment. *Waivers:* senior citizens and employees or children of employees.

Financial Aid Of all full-time matriculated undergraduates who enrolled in 2001, 4166 applied for aid, 3164 were judged to have need, 1692 had their need fully met. 1862 Federal Work-Study jobs. In 2001, 748 non-need-based awards were made. *Average percent of need met:* 94%. *Average financial aid package:* $13,442. *Average need-based loan:* $4780. *Average need-based gift aid:* $8226. *Average non-need based aid:* $3228. *Average indebtedness upon graduation:* $22,425.

Applying *Options:* electronic application, early decision, early action, deferred entrance. *Application fee:* $45. *Required:* essay or personal statement, high school transcript, letters of recommendation. *Recommended:* 2 letters of recommendation, interview. *Application deadlines:* 1/15 (freshmen), 4/1 (transfers). *Early decision:* 11/1. *Notification:* continuous until 3/31 (freshmen), 12/15 (early decision), 12/15 (early action).

Admissions Contact Mr. Donald M. Honeman, Director of Admissions, University of Vermont, Office of Admissions, Burlington, VT 05401-3596. *Phone:* 802-656-3370. *Fax:* 802-656-8611.

VERMONT TECHNICAL COLLEGE
Randolph Center, Vermont

- **State-supported** 4-year, founded 1866, part of Vermont State Colleges System
- **Calendar** semesters
- **Degrees** certificates, associate, and bachelor's
- **Rural** 544-acre campus
- **Endowment** $3.9 million
- **Coed,** 1,272 undergraduate students, 70% full-time, 31% women, 69% men
- **Minimally difficult** entrance level, 71% of applicants were admitted

Vermont Tech offers education for careers in today's technology-driven workplace. Articulation agreements with other regional institutions simplify the transfer process for graduates who want to pursue higher degrees. VTC has averaged at least 98% placement for every graduating class since 1982. Vermont Tech is a residential, coeducational college offering associate and bachelor's degree programs on its 544-acre campus in central Vermont.

Undergraduates 889 full-time, 383 part-time. Students come from 10 states and territories, 19% are from out of state, 0.2% African American, 1% Asian American or Pacific Islander, 0.6% Hispanic American, 0.2% Native American, 0.1% international, 10% transferred in, 66% live on campus. *Retention:* 65% of 2001 full-time freshmen returned.

Freshmen *Admission:* 734 applied, 524 admitted, 290 enrolled. *Average high school GPA:* 3.00. *Test scores:* SAT verbal scores over 500: 41%; SAT math scores over 500: 50%; ACT scores over 18: 100%; SAT verbal scores over 600: 11%; SAT math scores over 600: 14%; SAT verbal scores over 700: 1%; SAT math scores over 700: 1%.

Faculty *Total:* 113, 62% full-time, 23% with terminal degrees. *Student/faculty ratio:* 11:1.

Majors Accounting; agribusiness; architectural engineering technology; automotive engineering technology; bioengineering; biotechnology research; business administration; business systems networking/ telecommunications; civil engineering technology; computer engineering technology; construction technology; dairy science; electrical/electronic engineering technology; electromechanical technology; engineering technology; environmental technology; horticulture science; landscaping management; mechanical engineering technology; nursing; ornamental horticulture; practical nurse; secretarial science; telecommunications; veterinary technology.

Academic Programs *Special study options:* academic remediation for entering students, accelerated degree program, advanced placement credit, cooperative education, distance learning, double majors, English as a second language, honors programs, independent study, internships, part-time degree program, services for LD students, summer session for credit. *ROTC:* Army (c).

Library Hartness Library with 57,568 titles, 1,724 serial subscriptions, 2,030 audiovisual materials, an OPAC, a Web page.

Computers on Campus 225 computers available on campus for general student use. A campuswide network can be accessed from student residence rooms and from off campus. Internet access, at least one staffed computer lab available.

Student Life *Housing:* on-campus residence required through senior year. *Options:* coed, men-only, women-only. *Activities and Organizations:* drama/ theater group, student-run radio station, ASVTC (student government), Hockey Club, student radio station, American Institute of Architecture Students, Golf Club. *Campus security:* 24-hour emergency response devices and patrols, late-night transport/escort service, controlled dormitory access. *Student Services:* health clinic, personal/psychological counseling, women's center.

Athletics Member NSCAA. *Intercollegiate sports:* baseball M, basketball M/W, ice hockey M(c)/W(c), soccer M/W, softball W, volleyball M/W. *Intramural sports:* basketball M/W, bowling M(c)/W(c), cross-country running M/W, football M/W, golf M(c)/W(c), racquetball M/W, riflery M(c)/W(c), skiing (cross-country) M(c)/W(c), soccer M/W, softball M/W, squash M/W, swimming M/W, table tennis M/W, tennis M/W, volleyball M/W, water polo M/W, weight lifting M(c)/W(c).

Standardized Tests *Required for some:* SAT I (for admission), SAT I or ACT (for admission). *Recommended:* SAT I or ACT (for admission).

Costs (2001–02) *Tuition:* state resident $5340 full-time, $223 per credit hour part-time; nonresident $10,788 full-time, $450 per credit hour part-time. Full-time tuition and fees vary according to course load, program, and reciprocity agreements. Part-time tuition and fees vary according to program and reciprocity agreements. *Required fees:* $32 per credit hour. *Room and board:* $5520; room only: $3252. Room and board charges vary according to board plan. *Payment plans:* installment, deferred payment. *Waivers:* employees or children of employees.

Financial Aid Of all full-time matriculated undergraduates who enrolled in 2001, 716 applied for aid, 604 were judged to have need. 200 Federal Work-Study jobs (averaging $1003). *Average percent of need met:* 78%. *Average financial aid package:* $9200. *Average need-based loan:* $2788. *Average need-based gift aid:* $3700. *Average non-need based aid:* $1000.

Applying *Options:* common application, electronic application. *Application fee:* $30. *Required:* high school transcript. *Required for some:* essay or personal statement, letters of recommendation, interview. *Recommended:* minimum 3.0 GPA, letters of recommendation, interview. *Application deadline:* rolling (freshmen), rolling (transfers). *Notification:* continuous until 9/1 (freshmen).

Admissions Contact Ms. Rosemary W. Distel, Director of Admissions, Vermont Technical College, PO Box 500, Randolph Center, VT 05061. *Phone:* 802-728-1245. *Toll-free phone:* 800-442-VTC1. *Fax:* 802-728-1390. *E-mail:* admissions@vtc.edu.

VIRGINIA

AMERICAN MILITARY UNIVERSITY
Manassas, Virginia

- **Proprietary** comprehensive, founded 1991
- **Calendar** trimesters
- **Degrees** certificates, associate, bachelor's, and master's
- **Coed, primarily men**
- **Noncompetitive** entrance level, 100% of applicants were admitted

Undergraduates Students come from 52 states and territories, 90% are from out of state, 16% African American, 2% Asian American or Pacific Islander, 6% Hispanic American, 1.0% Native American. *Retention:* 68% of 2001 full-time freshmen returned.

Freshmen *Admission:* 72 applied, 72 admitted. *Average high school GPA:* 2.50.

Faculty *Total:* 403, 21% with terminal degrees. *Student/faculty ratio:* 11:1.

Majors Army R.O.T.C./military science; business services marketing; computer science; criminal justice studies; general studies; history; management science.

Academic Programs *Special study options:* adult/continuing education programs, distance learning, external degree program, independent study, part-time degree program.

Student Life *Housing:* college housing not available.

Costs (2001–02) *One-time required fee:* $75. *Tuition:* $9000 full-time, $750 per course part-time. Full-time tuition and fees vary according to course load. *Payment plan:* installment.

Applying *Options:* common application, deferred entrance. *Required:* high school transcript. *Application deadline:* rolling (freshmen), rolling (transfers).

Admissions Contact Ms. Nancy Tilton, Director of Admissions, American Military University, 10648 Wakeman Court, Manassas, VA 20110. *Phone:* 703-330-5398 Ext. 882. *Toll-free phone:* 877-468-6268. *Fax:* 703-330-5109. *E-mail:* admissions@amunet.edu.

THE ART INSTITUTE OF WASHINGTON
Arlington, Virginia

- **Proprietary** 4-year, founded 2000, part of The Art Institutes International
- **Calendar** quarters

The Art Institute of Washington (continued)
- **Degrees** associate and bachelor's
- **Coed**

Faculty *Student/faculty ratio:* 20:1.
Majors Computer graphics; graphic design/commercial art/illustration; multimedia.
Student Life *Housing:* college housing not available.
Costs (2001–02) *Tuition:* $12,000 full-time.
Applying *Options:* electronic application. *Application fee:* $50. *Required:* essay or personal statement, high school transcript, interview.
Admissions Contact Ms. Ann Marie Drucker, Director of Admissions, The Art Institute of Washington, 1820 North Fort Myer Drive, Arlington, VA 22209. *Phone:* 703-358-9550. *Toll-free phone:* 877-303-3771.

AVERETT UNIVERSITY
Danville, Virginia

- **Independent Baptist** comprehensive, founded 1859
- **Calendar** semesters
- **Degrees** associate, bachelor's, and master's
- **Suburban** 25-acre campus
- **Endowment** $18.8 million
- **Coed,** 1,763 undergraduate students, 65% full-time, 61% women, 39% men
- **Moderately difficult** entrance level, 89% of applicants were admitted

Undergraduates 1,138 full-time, 625 part-time. Students come from 25 states and territories, 11 other countries, 16% are from out of state, 28% African American, 1% Asian American or Pacific Islander, 1% Hispanic American, 0.7% Native American, 2% international, 12% transferred in, 49% live on campus. *Retention:* 57% of 2001 full-time freshmen returned.
Freshmen *Admission:* 603 applied, 536 admitted, 227 enrolled. *Average high school GPA:* 2.99. *Test scores:* SAT verbal scores over 500: 44%; SAT math scores over 500: 35%; ACT scores over 18: 65%; SAT verbal scores over 600: 10%; SAT math scores over 600: 8%; ACT scores over 24: 13%; SAT verbal scores over 700: 2%.
Faculty *Total:* 244, 25% full-time, 59% with terminal degrees. *Student/faculty ratio:* 14:1.
Majors Accounting; aircraft pilot (professional); air traffic control; air transportation related; applied mathematics related; art; art education; athletic training/sports medicine; aviation management; aviation technology; behavioral sciences; biological/physical sciences; biology; biology education; business; business administration; business administration/management related; business computer programming; business marketing and marketing management; chemistry; chemistry education; clinical psychology; cognitive psychology/psycholinguistics; criminal justice/corrections related; criminal justice/law enforcement administration; drama/theater literature; ecology; education (multiple levels); English; English education; environmental science; equestrian studies; finance; health education; health/physical education; health/physical education/fitness related; history; information sciences/systems; journalism; journalism and mass communication related; liberal arts and sciences/liberal studies; mathematics; mathematics/computer science; mathematics education; medical radiologic technology; medical technology; music; music (general performance); organizational psychology; physical education; physiological psychology/psychobiology; political science; pre-medicine; psychology related; religious music; religious studies; social sciences; social studies education; sociology; sport/fitness administration; teacher education, specific programs related; theater arts/drama; transportation and materials moving related.
Academic Programs *Special study options:* academic remediation for entering students, accelerated degree program, adult/continuing education programs, advanced placement credit, double majors, honors programs, internships, off-campus study, part-time degree program, services for LD students, student-designed majors, study abroad, summer session for credit.
Library Mary B. Blount Library with 202,044 titles, 502 serial subscriptions, 19 audiovisual materials, an OPAC, a Web page.
Computers on Campus 100 computers available on campus for general student use. Internet access, at least one staffed computer lab available.
Student Life *Housing:* on-campus residence required through junior year. *Options:* coed, men-only, women-only. *Activities and Organizations:* drama/theater group, student-run newspaper, choral group, Baptist Student Union, Student Government Association, Alpha Psi Omega, Phi Sigma Sigma, national fraternities, national sororities. *Campus security:* 24-hour emergency response devices and patrols, controlled dormitory access. *Student Services:* personal/psychological counseling.
Athletics Member NCAA. All Division III. *Intercollegiate sports:* baseball M, basketball M/W, cross-country running M/W, equestrian sports M/W, football M, golf M, lacrosse W, soccer M/W, softball W, tennis M/W, volleyball W. *Intramural sports:* basketball M/W, soccer M, softball M/W, table tennis M/W, tennis M/W, volleyball M/W.
Standardized Tests *Required:* SAT I or ACT (for admission).
Costs (2001–02) *Comprehensive fee:* $19,990 includes full-time tuition ($14,490), mandatory fees ($500), and room and board ($5000). Full-time tuition and fees vary according to program. Part-time tuition: $255 per credit. Part-time tuition and fees vary according to course load. *Room and board:* College room only: $3560. Room and board charges vary according to board plan and housing facility. *Payment plan:* installment. *Waivers:* senior citizens and employees or children of employees.
Financial Aid Of all full-time matriculated undergraduates who enrolled in 2001, 847 applied for aid, 765 were judged to have need, 133 had their need fully met. 135 Federal Work-Study jobs (averaging $1317). In 2001, 207 non-need-based awards were made. *Average percent of need met:* 68%. *Average financial aid package:* $9982. *Average need-based loan:* $3705. *Average need-based gift aid:* $7440. *Average indebtedness upon graduation:* $16,848.
Applying *Options:* common application, electronic application, early admission, deferred entrance. *Required:* essay or personal statement, high school transcript, minimum 2.0 GPA, 1 letter of recommendation. *Recommended:* interview. *Application deadline:* rolling (freshmen), rolling (transfers). *Notification:* continuous until 9/1 (freshmen).
Admissions Contact Mr. Gary Sherman, Vice President of Enrollment Management, Averett University, English Hall, Danville, VA 24541. *Phone:* 804-791-5660. *Toll-free phone:* 800-AVERETT. *Fax:* 804-797-2784. *E-mail:* admit@averett.edu.

BLUEFIELD COLLEGE
Bluefield, Virginia

- **Independent Southern Baptist** 4-year, founded 1922
- **Calendar** semesters
- **Degrees** associate and bachelor's
- **Small-town** 85-acre campus
- **Endowment** $3.0 million
- **Coed,** 841 undergraduate students, 96% full-time, 52% women, 48% men
- **Moderately difficult** entrance level, 76% of applicants were admitted

Undergraduates 805 full-time, 36 part-time. Students come from 17 states and territories, 20% are from out of state, 13% African American, 1.0% Asian American or Pacific Islander, 0.6% Hispanic American, 2% Native American, 0.2% international, 51% transferred in, 17% live on campus. *Retention:* 71% of 2001 full-time freshmen returned.
Freshmen *Admission:* 516 applied, 393 admitted, 165 enrolled. *Average high school GPA:* 3.1. *Test scores:* SAT verbal scores over 500: 37%; SAT math scores over 500: 34%; ACT scores over 18: 61%; SAT verbal scores over 600: 5%; SAT math scores over 600: 5%; ACT scores over 24: 16%; SAT verbal scores over 700: 2%.
Faculty *Total:* 102, 31% full-time. *Student/faculty ratio:* 24:1.
Majors Art; athletic training/sports medicine; biblical studies; biology; business administration; business education; chemistry; computer science; criminal justice/law enforcement administration; early childhood education; education; elementary education; English; exercise sciences; history; human resources management; interdisciplinary studies; liberal arts and sciences/liberal studies; mass communications; mathematics; medical laboratory technician; middle school education; music; music teacher education; philosophy; physical education; psychology; religious music; religious studies; science education; secondary education; social sciences; sociology; theater arts/drama.
Academic Programs *Special study options:* academic remediation for entering students, accelerated degree program, adult/continuing education programs, advanced placement credit, double majors, external degree program, freshman honors college, honors programs, internships, part-time degree program, services for LD students, student-designed majors, study abroad, summer session for credit.
Library Easley Library with 49,000 titles, 215 serial subscriptions, 900 audiovisual materials, a Web page.
Computers on Campus 100 computers available on campus for general student use. Internet access, at least one staffed computer lab available.
Student Life *Housing:* on-campus residence required through junior year. *Options:* coed, men-only, women-only. *Activities and Organizations:* drama/theater group, student-run newspaper, radio station, choral group, Baptist Student Union, Fellowship of Christian Athletes, Student Union Board, Student Govern-

ment Association, Bluefield Singers. *Campus security:* controlled dormitory access, night security patrols. *Student Services:* health clinic, personal/psychological counseling.

Athletics Member NAIA. *Intercollegiate sports:* baseball M(s), basketball M(s)/W(s), golf M(s), soccer M(s), softball W(s), tennis M(s)/W(s), volleyball W(s). *Intramural sports:* badminton M/W, baseball M, basketball M/W, football M, soccer W, softball M/W, table tennis M/W, tennis M/W, volleyball M/W.

Standardized Tests *Required:* SAT I or ACT (for admission).

Costs (2002–03) *Comprehensive fee:* $15,000 includes full-time tuition ($9345), mandatory fees ($450), and room and board ($5205). Part-time tuition: $310 per hour. *Room and board:* College room only: $2010.

Applying *Options:* deferred entrance. *Application fee:* $20. *Required:* high school transcript, minimum 2.0 GPA. *Required for some:* letters of recommendation, interview. *Recommended:* interview. *Application deadline:* rolling (freshmen), rolling (transfers). *Notification:* continuous (freshmen).

Admissions Contact Office of Admissions, Bluefield College, 3000 College Drive, Bluefield, VA 24605-1799. *Phone:* 276-326-4214. *Toll-free phone:* 800-872-0175. *Fax:* 276-326-4288. *E-mail:* admissions@mail.bluefield.edu.

BRIDGEWATER COLLEGE
Bridgewater, Virginia

- **Independent** 4-year, founded 1880, affiliated with Church of the Brethren
- **Calendar** 4-1-4
- **Degree** bachelor's
- **Small-town** 190-acre campus
- **Endowment** $44.7 million
- **Coed,** 1,260 undergraduate students, 98% full-time, 57% women, 43% men
- **Moderately difficult** entrance level, 87% of applicants were admitted

Bridgewater College offers a balanced liberal arts and sciences program in a challenging and supportive environment. The general education curriculum for first-year students and sophomores focuses on effective writing, oral communication, quantitative reasoning, critical thinking, and wellness. In the College's award-winning Personal Development Portfolio program, each student is paired with a faculty mentor who aids the student's development in intellect, character, citizenship, and wellness. The program culminates in an enhanced resume, documenting achievement in these areas and supplementing the academic transcript. Excellent facilities include the new 34,00-square-foot Funkhouser Center for Health and Wellness and residence halls that are fully wired for Internet, phone, and cable television access.

Undergraduates 1,240 full-time, 20 part-time. Students come from 22 states and territories, 5 other countries, 23% are from out of state, 6% African American, 1% Asian American or Pacific Islander, 1% Hispanic American, 0.5% Native American, 0.6% international, 3% transferred in, 83% live on campus. *Retention:* 75% of 2001 full-time freshmen returned.

Freshmen *Admission:* 1,156 applied, 1,004 admitted, 340 enrolled. *Average high school GPA:* 3.40. *Test scores:* SAT verbal scores over 500: 58%; SAT math scores over 500: 59%; ACT scores over 18: 84%; SAT verbal scores over 600: 19%; SAT math scores over 600: 23%; ACT scores over 24: 41%; SAT verbal scores over 700: 3%; SAT math scores over 700: 3%; ACT scores over 30: 6%.

Faculty *Total:* 97, 80% full-time, 67% with terminal degrees. *Student/faculty ratio:* 15:1.

Majors Accounting; American history; art; art education; athletic training/sports medicine; biology; biology education; business administration; business economics; business marketing and marketing management; chemistry; chemistry education; computer education; computer science; cultural studies; driver/safety education; economics; elementary education; English; English education; exercise sciences; fashion merchandising; finance; French; French language education; general studies; German language education; health/physical education; health/physical education/fitness related; history; history education; home economics; home economics education; interior design; international business; international relations; management information systems/business data processing; mathematics; mathematics education; medical technology; music; music teacher education; organizational behavior; philosophy and religion related; physical sciences; physics; physics education; political science; psychology; secondary education; social science education; social studies education; sociology; Spanish; Spanish language education; special education; teaching English as a second language.

Academic Programs *Special study options:* adult/continuing education programs, advanced placement credit, double majors, honors programs, independent study, internships, part-time degree program, study abroad, summer session for credit. *Unusual degree programs:* 3-2 forestry with Duke University.

Library Alexander Mack Memorial Library with 127,472 titles, 637 serial subscriptions, 8,326 audiovisual materials, an OPAC, a Web page.

Computers on Campus 144 computers available on campus for general student use. A campuswide network can be accessed from student residence rooms and from off campus that provide access to on-line course and grade information. Internet access, at least one staffed computer lab available.

Student Life *Housing:* on-campus residence required through senior year. *Options:* men-only, women-only, disabled students. *Activities and Organizations:* drama/theater group, student-run newspaper, radio station, choral group, Eagle Productions, Pep Band, Oratorio Choir, Baptist Student Union, Brethren Student Fellowship. *Campus security:* 24-hour emergency response devices and patrols, controlled dormitory access. *Student Services:* health clinic, personal/psychological counseling.

Athletics Member NCAA. All Division III. *Intercollegiate sports:* baseball M, basketball M/W, cross-country running M/W, field hockey W, football M, golf M, lacrosse W, soccer M/W, softball W, tennis M/W, track and field M/W, volleyball W. *Intramural sports:* basketball M/W, bowling M/W, football M/W, golf M/W, racquetball M/W, soccer M/W, softball M/W, swimming M/W, table tennis M/W, tennis M/W, track and field M/W, volleyball M/W.

Standardized Tests *Required:* SAT I or ACT (for admission). *Recommended:* SAT I (for admission).

Costs (2002–03) *Comprehensive fee:* $23,950 includes full-time tuition ($16,090) and room and board ($7860). Part-time tuition: $550 per credit. *Required fees:* $30 per term part-time. *Room and board:* College room only: $3860. Room and board charges vary according to housing facility. *Payment plan:* installment. *Waivers:* minority students and employees or children of employees.

Financial Aid Of all full-time matriculated undergraduates who enrolled in 2001, 978 applied for aid, 861 were judged to have need, 251 had their need fully met. 342 Federal Work-Study jobs (averaging $998). 56 State and other part-time jobs (averaging $862). In 2001, 344 non-need-based awards were made. *Average percent of need met:* 93%. *Average financial aid package:* $15,488. *Average need-based loan:* $4439. *Average need-based gift aid:* $11,856. *Average non-need based aid:* $9851. *Average indebtedness upon graduation:* $18,668.

Applying *Options:* common application, electronic application, deferred entrance. *Application fee:* $30. *Required:* essay or personal statement, high school transcript, minimum 2.0 GPA, 2 letters of recommendation. *Required for some:* interview. *Recommended:* minimum 3.0 GPA, interview. *Application deadline:* rolling (freshmen), rolling (transfers).

Admissions Contact Ms. Linda F. Stout, Director of Enrollment Operations, Bridgewater College, 402 East College Street, Bridgewater, VA 22812-1599. *Phone:* 540-828-5375. *Toll-free phone:* 800-759-8328. *Fax:* 540-828-5481. *E-mail:* admissions@bridgewater.edu.

BRYANT AND STRATTON COLLEGE, VIRGINIA BEACH
Virginia Beach, Virginia

- **Proprietary** primarily 2-year, founded 1952, part of Bryant and Stratton Business Institute, Inc
- **Calendar** semesters
- **Degrees** diplomas, associate, and bachelor's
- **Suburban** campus
- **Coed,** 159 undergraduate students, 82% full-time, 81% women, 19% men
- **Minimally difficult** entrance level, 77% of applicants were admitted

Undergraduates 130 full-time, 29 part-time. Students come from 1 other state, 50% African American, 2% Asian American or Pacific Islander, 8% Hispanic American, 0.6% Native American.

Freshmen *Admission:* 74 applied, 57 admitted, 57 enrolled.

Faculty *Total:* 36, 14% full-time, 8% with terminal degrees. *Student/faculty ratio:* 8:1.

Majors Accounting; business administration; hotel and restaurant management; information sciences/systems; legal administrative assistant; medical administrative assistant; medical assistant; paralegal/legal assistant; retail management; secretarial science; travel/tourism management.

Academic Programs *Special study options:* academic remediation for entering students, adult/continuing education programs, advanced placement credit, internships, part-time degree program, summer session for credit.

Library campus library with 9,646 titles, 131 serial subscriptions, 359 audiovisual materials.

Computers on Campus 55 computers available on campus for general student use. Internet access, at least one staffed computer lab available.

Student Life *Housing:* college housing not available. *Activities and Organizations:* student-run newspaper, Phi Beta Lambda, Alpha Beta Gamma, Student Government Association, Medical Club, Law Society. *Campus security:* late-night transport/escort service.

Bryant and Stratton College, Virginia Beach (continued)

Applying *Options:* common application, electronic application, deferred entrance. *Application fee:* $25. *Required:* high school transcript, interview. *Application deadline:* rolling (freshmen), rolling (transfers).

Admissions Contact Mr. Greg Smith, Director of Admissions, Bryant and Stratton College, Virginia Beach, 301 Centre Pointe Drive, Virginia Beach, VA 23462-4417. *Phone:* 757-499-7900.

CHRISTENDOM COLLEGE
Front Royal, Virginia

- **Independent Roman Catholic** comprehensive, founded 1977
- **Calendar** semesters
- **Degrees** associate, bachelor's, and master's
- **Rural** 100-acre campus with easy access to Washington, DC
- **Endowment** $2.3 million
- **Coed,** 331 undergraduate students, 99% full-time, 57% women, 43% men
- **Moderately difficult** entrance level, 81% of applicants were admitted

Undergraduates 329 full-time, 2 part-time. Students come from 48 states and territories, 4 other countries, 79% are from out of state, 0.6% African American, 2% Asian American or Pacific Islander, 3% Hispanic American, 0.3% Native American, 3% international, 3% transferred in, 93% live on campus. *Retention:* 83% of 2001 full-time freshmen returned.

Freshmen *Admission:* 197 applied, 159 admitted, 102 enrolled. *Average high school GPA:* 3.50. *Test scores:* SAT verbal scores over 500: 80%; SAT math scores over 500: 85%; ACT scores over 18: 100%; SAT verbal scores over 600: 54%; SAT math scores over 600: 46%; ACT scores over 24: 66%; SAT verbal scores over 700: 26%; SAT math scores over 700: 8%; ACT scores over 30: 14%.

Faculty *Total:* 34, 59% full-time, 68% with terminal degrees. *Student/faculty ratio:* 12:1.

Majors Classics; French; history; liberal arts and sciences/liberal studies; literature; philosophy; political science; theology.

Academic Programs *Special study options:* academic remediation for entering students, accelerated degree program, advanced placement credit, cooperative education, double majors, internships, services for LD students, study abroad, summer session for credit.

Library O'Reilly Memorial Library with 70,850 titles, 395 serial subscriptions, 1,238 audiovisual materials, an OPAC.

Computers on Campus 17 computers available on campus for general student use. Internet access, at least one staffed computer lab available.

Student Life *Housing:* on-campus residence required through senior year. *Options:* men-only, women-only. *Activities and Organizations:* drama/theater group, student-run newspaper, choral group, drama, choir, Shield of Roses, Legion of Mary, debate. *Campus security:* 24-hour emergency response devices, late-night transport/escort service, night patrols by trained security personnel. *Student Services:* health clinic, personal/psychological counseling.

Athletics *Intercollegiate sports:* baseball M(c), basketball M(c)/W(c), soccer M(c)/W(c). *Intramural sports:* basketball M/W, fencing M/W, football M/W, golf M/W, racquetball M/W, soccer M/W, softball M/W, table tennis M/W, tennis M/W, volleyball M/W.

Standardized Tests *Required:* SAT I or ACT (for admission).

Costs (2001–02) *Comprehensive fee:* $16,680 includes full-time tuition ($11,750), mandatory fees ($230), and room and board ($4700). Part-time tuition: $525 per credit. *Required fees:* $115 per term part-time. *Payment plans:* tuition prepayment, installment. *Waivers:* employees or children of employees.

Financial Aid Of all full-time matriculated undergraduates who enrolled in 2001, 213 applied for aid, 164 were judged to have need, 153 had their need fully met. 114 State and other part-time jobs (averaging $1750). In 2001, 57 non-need-based awards were made. *Average percent of need met:* 90%. *Average financial aid package:* $9125. *Average need-based loan:* $3335. *Average need-based gift aid:* $4070. *Average non-need based aid:* $4475. *Average indebtedness upon graduation:* $8000.

Applying *Options:* common application, electronic application, early admission, early action. *Application fee:* $25. *Required:* essay or personal statement, high school transcript, 2 letters of recommendation. *Recommended:* minimum 3.0 GPA, interview. *Application deadline:* rolling (freshmen), rolling (transfers). *Notification:* continuous (freshmen), 12/15 (early action).

Admissions Contact Mr. Paul Heisler, Director of Admissions, Christendom College, 134 Christendom Drive, Front Royal, VA 22630-5103. *Phone:* 540-636-2900 Ext. 290. *Toll-free phone:* 800-877-5456 Ext. 290. *Fax:* 540-636-1655. *E-mail:* admissions@christendom.edu.

CHRISTOPHER NEWPORT UNIVERSITY
Newport News, Virginia

- **State-supported** comprehensive, founded 1960
- **Calendar** semesters
- **Degrees** bachelor's and master's
- **Suburban** 113-acre campus with easy access to Norfolk
- **Endowment** $2.5 million
- **Coed,** 5,158 undergraduate students, 78% full-time, 61% women, 39% men
- **Moderately difficult** entrance level, 48% of applicants were admitted

Undergraduates 4,041 full-time, 1,117 part-time. Students come from 28 states and territories, 10 other countries, 3% are from out of state, 14% African American, 3% Asian American or Pacific Islander, 3% Hispanic American, 0.4% Native American, 0.3% international, 6% transferred in, 30% live on campus. *Retention:* 81% of 2001 full-time freshmen returned.

Freshmen *Admission:* 4,270 applied, 2,069 admitted, 1,048 enrolled. *Average high school GPA:* 3.30. *Test scores:* SAT verbal scores over 500: 87%; SAT math scores over 500: 83%; ACT scores over 18: 85%; SAT verbal scores over 600: 31%; SAT math scores over 600: 25%; ACT scores over 24: 8%; SAT verbal scores over 700: 3%; SAT math scores over 700: 1%.

Faculty *Total:* 315, 58% full-time, 55% with terminal degrees. *Student/faculty ratio:* 20:1.

Majors Accounting; art; biology; business administration; business economics; business marketing and marketing management; communications; computer engineering; computer/information sciences; computer science; criminal justice/law enforcement administration; developmental/child psychology; economics; education; elementary education; English; environmental science; finance; French; German; health education; health/physical education; history; horticulture science; information sciences/systems; interdisciplinary studies; international business; international relations; legal studies; literature; mathematics; middle school education; music; music history; music teacher education; music theory and composition; nursing; philosophy; physical education; physics; political science; pre-law; psychology; public administration; real estate; recreation/leisure studies; religious studies; science education; secondary education; social work; sociology; Spanish; sport/fitness administration; theater arts/drama; visual/performing arts.

Academic Programs *Special study options:* academic remediation for entering students, accelerated degree program, adult/continuing education programs, advanced placement credit, cooperative education, distance learning, double majors, honors programs, independent study, internships, off-campus study, part-time degree program, services for LD students, student-designed majors, study abroad, summer session for credit. *ROTC:* Army (b). *Unusual degree programs:* 3-2 engineering with Old Dominion University; forestry with Duke University; environmental management with Duke University.

Library Captain John Smith Library with 430,502 titles, 10,353 serial subscriptions, 9,292 audiovisual materials, an OPAC, a Web page.

Computers on Campus 1000 computers available on campus for general student use. A campuswide network can be accessed from student residence rooms and from off campus. Internet access, at least one staffed computer lab available.

Student Life *Housing:* on-campus residence required for freshman year. *Options:* coed. *Activities and Organizations:* drama/theater group, student-run newspaper, radio station, choral group, Student Virginia Education Association, Student Government Association, national fraternities, national sororities. *Campus security:* 24-hour emergency response devices and patrols, late-night transport/escort service, controlled dormitory access, campus police. *Student Services:* health clinic, personal/psychological counseling.

Athletics Member NCAA. All Division III. *Intercollegiate sports:* baseball M, basketball M/W, cross-country running M/W, equestrian sports M(c)/W(c), field hockey W, football M, golf M, lacrosse M(c)/W(c), rugby M(c), sailing M/W, soccer M/W, softball W, tennis M/W, track and field M/W, volleyball W. *Intramural sports:* badminton M/W, basketball M/W, bowling M/W, cross-country running M/W, football M/W, golf M/W, softball M/W, table tennis M/W, tennis M/W, volleyball M/W, weight lifting M/W.

Standardized Tests *Required:* SAT I or ACT (for admission).

Costs (2001–02) *Tuition:* state resident $1888 full-time, $130 per semester hour part-time; nonresident $7910 full-time, $381 per semester hour part-time. Full-time tuition and fees vary according to course load. Part-time tuition and fees vary according to course load. *Required fees:* $1224 full-time, $20 per term part-time. *Room and board:* $5750; room only: $3500. Room and board charges vary according to housing facility. *Payment plan:* installment. *Waivers:* senior citizens and employees or children of employees.

Financial Aid Of all full-time matriculated undergraduates who enrolled in 2001, 2851 applied for aid, 1762 were judged to have need, 276 had their need fully met. 118 Federal Work-Study jobs (averaging $1217). 740 State and other part-time jobs (averaging $1519). In 2001, 432 non-need-based awards were made. *Average percent of need met:* 65%. *Average financial aid package:* $4701. *Average need-based loan:* $1672. *Average need-based gift aid:* $2798. *Average non-need based aid:* $1462.

Applying *Options:* common application, electronic application, early admission, early action, deferred entrance. *Application fee:* $25. *Required:* high school transcript, minimum 3.0 GPA. *Required for some:* essay or personal statement, 3 letters of recommendation, interview. *Application deadlines:* 3/1 (freshmen), 6/1 (transfers). *Notification:* continuous (freshmen).

Admissions Contact Ms. Rebecca Ducknuall, Assistant Director of Admissions, Christopher Newport University, 1 University Place, Newport News, VA 23606-2998. *Phone:* 757-594-7205. *Toll-free phone:* 800-333-4CNU. *Fax:* 757-594-7333. *E-mail:* admit@cnu.edu.

THE COLLEGE OF WILLIAM AND MARY

Williamsburg, Virginia

- **State-supported** university, founded 1693
- **Calendar** semesters
- **Degrees** bachelor's, master's, doctoral, and first professional
- **Small-town** 1200-acre campus with easy access to Richmond
- **Endowment** $367.5 million
- **Coed,** 5,604 undergraduate students, 99% full-time, 57% women, 43% men
- **Very difficult** entrance level, 37% of applicants were admitted

Undergraduates 5,527 full-time, 77 part-time. Students come from 50 states and territories, 52 other countries, 35% are from out of state, 5% African American, 7% Asian American or Pacific Islander, 3% Hispanic American, 0.3% Native American, 1% international, 3% transferred in, 77% live on campus. *Retention:* 95% of 2001 full-time freshmen returned.

Freshmen *Admission:* 8,610 applied, 3,222 admitted, 1,348 enrolled. *Average high school GPA:* 4.0. *Test scores:* SAT verbal scores over 500: 95%; SAT math scores over 500: 96%; ACT scores over 18: 100%; SAT verbal scores over 600: 81%; SAT math scores over 600: 80%; ACT scores over 24: 98%; SAT verbal scores over 700: 36%; SAT math scores over 700: 30%; ACT scores over 30: 57%.

Faculty *Total:* 743, 78% full-time, 80% with terminal degrees. *Student/faculty ratio:* 12:1.

Majors African-American studies; American studies; anthropology; art; art history; biology; biopsychology; business administration; chemistry; classics; computer science; cultural studies; East Asian studies; economics; English; environmental science; European studies; French; geology; German; Greek (modern); history; interdisciplinary studies; international relations; Latin American studies; Latin (ancient and medieval); linguistics; mathematics; medieval/renaissance studies; modern languages; music; philosophy; physical education; physics; political science; psychology; public policy analysis; religious studies; Russian/Slavic studies; sociology; Spanish; theater arts/drama; women's studies.

Academic Programs *Special study options:* accelerated degree program, advanced placement credit, double majors, honors programs, independent study, part-time degree program, services for LD students, student-designed majors, study abroad, summer session for credit. *ROTC:* Army (b). *Unusual degree programs:* 3-2 engineering with Columbia University, Washington University in St. Louis, Rensselaer Polytechnic Institute, Case Western Reserve University, University of Virginia; forestry with Duke University.

Library Swem Library plus 9 others with 2.0 million titles, 11,541 serial subscriptions, 28,002 audiovisual materials, an OPAC, a Web page.

Computers on Campus 300 computers available on campus for general student use. A campuswide network can be accessed from student residence rooms and from off campus. Internet access, at least one staffed computer lab available.

Student Life *Housing:* on-campus residence required for freshman year. *Options:* coed, women-only. *Activities and Organizations:* drama/theater group, student-run newspaper, radio and television station, choral group, Alpha Phi Omega, College Partnership for Kids, student assembly, Flat Hat (student newspaper), Resident Housing Association, national fraternities, national sororities. *Campus security:* 24-hour emergency response devices and patrols, student patrols, late-night transport/escort service, controlled dormitory access. *Student Services:* health clinic, personal/psychological counseling, legal services.

Athletics Member NCAA. All Division I except football (Division I-AA). *Intercollegiate sports:* baseball M(s), basketball M(s)/W(s), cross-country running M(s)/W(s), field hockey W(s), golf M/W, gymnastics M(s)/W(s), lacrosse W(s), soccer M(s)/W(s), swimming M(s)/W, tennis M(s)/W(s), track and field M(s)/W(s), volleyball W(s). *Intramural sports:* badminton M(c)/W(c), baseball M(c), basketball M/W, bowling M/W, crew M(c)/W(c), cross-country running M(c)/W(c), equestrian sports M(c)/W(c), fencing M(c)/W(c), field hockey W(c), football M/W, golf M/W, gymnastics M(c)/W(c), ice hockey M(c), lacrosse M(c)/W(c), racquetball M(c)/W(c), rugby M(c)/W(c), sailing M(c)/W(c), soccer M(c)/W(c), softball M(c)/W, swimming M(c)/W(c), table tennis M/W, tennis M(c)/W(c), volleyball M(c)/W(c), weight lifting M(c)/W(c), wrestling M.

Standardized Tests *Required:* SAT I or ACT (for admission). *Recommended:* SAT II: Subject Tests (for admission), SAT II: Writing Test (for admission).

Costs (2001–02) *Tuition:* state resident $4780 full-time, $122 per credit hour part-time; nonresident $17,808 full-time, $550 per credit hour part-time. *Room and board:* $5222; room only: $3052. Room and board charges vary according to board plan and housing facility. *Payment plan:* installment. *Waivers:* senior citizens and employees or children of employees.

Financial Aid Of all full-time matriculated undergraduates who enrolled in 2001, 2576 applied for aid, 1491 were judged to have need, 796 had their need fully met. 256 Federal Work-Study jobs (averaging $924). In 2001, 916 non-need-based awards were made. *Average percent of need met:* 88%. *Average financial aid package:* $8701. *Average need-based loan:* $3191. *Average need-based gift aid:* $6496. *Financial aid deadline:* 3/15.

Applying *Options:* common application, electronic application, early admission, early decision, deferred entrance. *Application fee:* $40. *Required:* essay or personal statement, high school transcript. *Recommended:* 1 letter of recommendation. *Application deadlines:* 1/5 (freshmen), 2/15 (transfers). *Early decision:* 11/1. *Notification:* 4/1 (freshmen), 12/1 (early decision).

Admissions Contact Dr. Karen R. Cottrell, Associate Provost for Enrollment, The College of William and Mary, PO Box 8795, Williamsburg, VA 23187-8795. *Phone:* 757-221-4223. *Fax:* 757-221-1242. *E-mail:* admiss@facstaff.wm.edu.

COMMUNITY HOSPITAL OF ROANOKE VALLEY-COLLEGE OF HEALTH SCIENCES

Roanoke, Virginia

- **Independent** 4-year, founded 1982
- **Calendar** semesters
- **Degrees** certificates, associate, and bachelor's
- **Urban** 1-acre campus
- **Endowment** $3.8 million
- **Coed,** 642 undergraduate students, 67% full-time, 77% women, 23% men
- **Moderately difficult** entrance level, 95% of applicants were admitted

Undergraduates 427 full-time, 215 part-time. Students come from 7 states and territories, 7% are from out of state, 10% African American, 2% Asian American or Pacific Islander, 0.6% Hispanic American, 0.2% Native American, 23% transferred in, 15% live on campus. *Retention:* 51% of 2001 full-time freshmen returned.

Freshmen *Admission:* 130 applied, 124 admitted, 124 enrolled.

Faculty *Total:* 90, 50% full-time, 20% with terminal degrees. *Student/faculty ratio:* 11:1.

Majors Athletic training/sports medicine; biomedical science; emergency medical technology; fire protection/safety technology; health science; health services administration; nursing; occupational therapy assistant; physical therapy assistant; physician assistant; practical nurse; radiological science; respiratory therapy.

Academic Programs *Special study options:* academic remediation for entering students, accelerated degree program, adult/continuing education programs, advanced placement credit, distance learning, internships, part-time degree program, services for LD students, summer session for credit.

Library Learning Resource Center with 11,256 titles, 380 serial subscriptions, 819 audiovisual materials, an OPAC, a Web page.

Computers on Campus 56 computers available on campus for general student use. A campuswide network can be accessed from off campus. Internet access, at least one staffed computer lab available.

Student Life *Housing Options:* coed. *Activities and Organizations:* Student Government Association, Student Nurse Association, Student Occupational Therapy Association, Student Physical Therapist Assistant Assembly, Crossroads. *Campus security:* 24-hour emergency response devices and patrols, late-night transport/escort service, controlled dormitory access. *Student Services:* health clinic, personal/psychological counseling.

Standardized Tests *Required for some:* SAT I or ACT (for admission). *Recommended:* SAT I (for admission).

Costs (2002–03) *Tuition:* $5280 full-time, $220 per credit hour part-time. Full-time tuition and fees vary according to class time, course load, degree level, and program. Part-time tuition and fees vary according to class time, course load, degree level, and program. *Required fees:* $150 full-time. *Room only:* $2000. *Payment plan:* installment. *Waivers:* employees or children of employees.

Financial Aid Of all full-time matriculated undergraduates who enrolled in 2001, 235 applied for aid, 227 were judged to have need, 12 had their need fully met. In 2001, 29 non-need-based awards were made. *Average percent of need met:* 45%. *Average financial aid package:* $8684. *Average need-based loan:* $4444. *Average need-based gift aid:* $5869. *Average non-need based aid:* $4515. *Average indebtedness upon graduation:* $5520.

Community Hospital of Roanoke Valley-College of Health Sciences (continued)

Applying *Options:* early decision. *Application fee:* $25. *Required:* essay or personal statement, high school transcript, minimum 2.0 GPA. *Required for some:* letters of recommendation, interview, volunteer experience. *Application deadline:* 7/31 (freshmen). *Early decision:* 10/15. *Notification:* continuous until 7/31 (freshmen), 12/1 (early decision).

Admissions Contact Ms. Connie Cook, Admissions Representative, Community Hospital of Roanoke Valley-College of Health Sciences, PO Box 13186, Roanoke, VA 24031-3186. *Phone:* 540-985-8563. *Toll-free phone:* 888-985-8483. *Fax:* 540-985-9773.

DEVRY UNIVERSITY
Arlington, Virginia

- **Proprietary** 4-year, founded 2001, part of DeVry, Inc
- **Calendar** semesters
- **Degrees** associate and bachelor's
- **Coed,** 243 undergraduate students, 39% full-time, 18% women, 82% men
- 71% of applicants were admitted

Undergraduates 94 full-time, 149 part-time. Students come from 9 states and territories, 5 other countries, 65% are from out of state, 54% African American, 5% Asian American or Pacific Islander, 4% Hispanic American, 0.4% Native American, 2% international, 7% transferred in.

Freshmen *Admission:* 756 applied, 538 admitted, 204 enrolled.

Faculty *Total:* 16, 75% full-time. *Student/faculty ratio:* 6:1.

Majors Business administration/management related; business systems analysis/design; business systems networking/ telecommunications; computer engineering technology; electrical/electronic engineering technology; information sciences/systems.

Student Life *Housing:* college housing not available.

Standardized Tests *Recommended:* SAT I or ACT (for admission).

Costs (2001–02) *Tuition:* $10,000 full-time, $355 per credit hour part-time. Full-time tuition and fees vary according to course load. Part-time tuition and fees vary according to course load. *Payment plans:* installment, deferred payment. *Waivers:* employees or children of employees.

Financial Aid Of all full-time matriculated undergraduates who enrolled in 2001, 289 applied for aid, 261 were judged to have need. In 2001, 29 non-need-based awards were made. *Average percent of need met:* 30%. *Average financial aid package:* $4351. *Average need-based loan:* $2796. *Average need-based gift aid:* $3024.

Applying *Application fee:* $50. *Required:* high school transcript, interview. *Application deadline:* rolling (freshmen), rolling (transfers). *Notification:* continuous (freshmen).

Admissions Contact Mr. Todd Marshburn, Director of Enrollment Services, DeVry University, Century Building I, Suite 200, 2341 Jefferson Davis Highway, Arlington, VA 22202. *Phone:* 866-338-7932.

EASTERN MENNONITE UNIVERSITY
Harrisonburg, Virginia

- **Independent Mennonite** comprehensive, founded 1917
- **Calendar** semesters
- **Degrees** certificates, associate, bachelor's, master's, first professional, and postbachelor's certificates
- **Small-town** 92-acre campus
- **Endowment** $15.9 million
- **Coed,** 1,020 undergraduate students, 95% full-time, 60% women, 40% men
- **Moderately difficult** entrance level, 70% of applicants were admitted

International education is a special mission of Eastern Mennonite University. The University's distinctive Global Village curriculum builds an outstanding liberal arts education on a foundation of Christian values and cross-cultural understanding. Every student engages in cross-cultural study in locations such as Latin America, Europe, the Middle East, Russia, China, Africa, and an American Indian reservation.

Undergraduates 970 full-time, 50 part-time. Students come from 37 states and territories, 17 other countries, 59% are from out of state, 6% African American, 1% Asian American or Pacific Islander, 2% Hispanic American, 0.4% Native American, 5% international, 8% transferred in, 61% live on campus. *Retention:* 76% of 2001 full-time freshmen returned.

Freshmen *Admission:* 587 applied, 410 admitted, 208 enrolled. *Average high school GPA:* 3.46. *Test scores:* SAT verbal scores over 500: 62%; SAT math scores over 500: 59%; ACT scores over 18: 88%; SAT verbal scores over 600: 32%; SAT math scores over 600: 28%; ACT scores over 24: 48%; SAT verbal scores over 700: 11%; SAT math scores over 700: 8%; ACT scores over 30: 8%.

Faculty *Total:* 141, 68% full-time, 58% with terminal degrees. *Student/faculty ratio:* 13:1.

Majors Accounting; art; art education; biblical studies; biochemistry; biology; biology education; business administration; chemistry; chemistry education; communications; computer science; computer systems analysis; development economics; early childhood education; economics; education of the emotionally handicapped; education of the mentally handicapped; education of the specific learning disabled; elementary education; English; English education; environmental science; French; French language education; general studies; German; German language education; health education; history; international agriculture; international business; liberal arts and sciences/liberal studies; mathematics; mathematics education; medical technology; middle school education; multi/interdisciplinary studies related; music; music teacher education; nursing; peace/conflict studies; philosophy and religion related; physical education; pre-dentistry; pre-medicine; pre-veterinary studies; psychology; secondary education; social science education; social sciences; social work; sociology; Spanish; Spanish language education; sport/fitness administration; theater arts/drama; theology.

Academic Programs *Special study options:* academic remediation for entering students, adult/continuing education programs, advanced placement credit, distance learning, double majors, English as a second language, honors programs, independent study, internships, off-campus study, part-time degree program, services for LD students, study abroad, summer session for credit. *Unusual degree programs:* 3-2 engineering with Pennsylvania State University University Park Campus; appropriate technology with Drexel University.

Library Sadie Hartzler Library with 175,362 titles, 1,157 serial subscriptions, 10,723 audiovisual materials, an OPAC, a Web page.

Computers on Campus 138 computers available on campus for general student use. A campuswide network can be accessed from student residence rooms. Internet access, at least one staffed computer lab available.

Student Life *Housing:* on-campus residence required through junior year. *Options:* coed, men-only, women-only. *Activities and Organizations:* drama/theater group, student-run newspaper, radio station, choral group, YPCA, Campus Activities Council, Student Government Association, University Chorale, International Student Organization. *Campus security:* 24-hour emergency response devices, controlled dormitory access, night watchman. *Student Services:* health clinic, personal/psychological counseling.

Athletics Member NCAA. All Division III. *Intercollegiate sports:* baseball M, basketball M/W, cross-country running M/W, field hockey W, soccer M/W, softball W, tennis M/W, track and field M/W, volleyball M/W. *Intramural sports:* basketball M/W, soccer M/W, softball M/W, tennis M/W, volleyball M/W.

Standardized Tests *Required:* SAT I or ACT (for admission).

Costs (2001–02) *Comprehensive fee:* $20,700 includes full-time tuition ($15,300) and room and board ($5400). Full-time tuition and fees vary according to program. Part-time tuition: $640 per credit hour. Part-time tuition and fees vary according to program. *Required fees:* $2 per semester hour. *Room and board:* College room only: $2770. Room and board charges vary according to board plan, housing facility, and student level. *Payment plan:* installment. *Waivers:* employees or children of employees.

Financial Aid Of all full-time matriculated undergraduates who enrolled in 2001, 918 applied for aid, 629 were judged to have need, 85 had their need fully met. 326 Federal Work-Study jobs (averaging $1787). In 2001, 277 non-need-based awards were made. *Average percent of need met:* 87%. *Average financial aid package:* $13,241. *Average need-based loan:* $5057. *Average need-based gift aid:* $7722. *Average non-need based aid:* $6285. *Average indebtedness upon graduation:* $19,169.

Applying *Options:* common application, electronic application, early admission, deferred entrance. *Application fee:* $25. *Required:* high school transcript, minimum 2.2 GPA, 1 letter of recommendation, statement of commitment. *Recommended:* interview. *Application deadlines:* 8/1 (freshmen), 8/1 (transfers). *Notification:* continuous (freshmen).

Admissions Contact Ms. Ellen B. Miller, Director of Admissions, Eastern Mennonite University, 1200 Park Road, Harrisonburg, VA 22802-2462. *Phone:* 540-432-4118. *Toll-free phone:* 800-368-2665. *Fax:* 540-432-4444. *E-mail:* admiss@emu.edu.

EMORY & HENRY COLLEGE
Emory, Virginia

- **Independent United Methodist** comprehensive, founded 1836
- **Calendar** semesters
- **Degrees** bachelor's and master's

- **Rural** 163-acre campus
- **Endowment** $65.3 million
- **Coed,** 989 undergraduate students, 97% full-time, 52% women, 48% men
- **Moderately difficult** entrance level, 78% of applicants were admitted

Emory & Henry continues to build on a long-standing tradition of excellence. The College recently completed the construction of a 70,000-square-foot academic center, which provides high-tech science laboratories and modern classroom space. Emory & Henry also has joined with Barter Theater, the state theater of Virginia, to create the Barter Conservatory at Emory & Henry, integrating college-level studies in theater with professional stage experience. Founded in 1836, Emory & Henry offers small classes, a wide range of academic programs, and a variety of student life activities in one of the nation's most beautiful settings.

Undergraduates 961 full-time, 28 part-time. Students come from 24 states and territories, 26% are from out of state, 6% African American, 1% Asian American or Pacific Islander, 0.6% Hispanic American, 0.1% Native American, 1% international, 6% transferred in, 69% live on campus. *Retention:* 73% of 2001 full-time freshmen returned.

Freshmen *Admission:* 1,127 applied, 875 admitted, 267 enrolled. *Average high school GPA:* 3.37. *Test scores:* SAT verbal scores over 500: 64%; SAT math scores over 500: 53%; ACT scores over 18: 96%; SAT verbal scores over 600: 18%; SAT math scores over 600: 15%; ACT scores over 24: 47%; SAT verbal scores over 700: 4%; SAT math scores over 700: 2%; ACT scores over 30: 4%.

Faculty *Total:* 87, 67% full-time, 69% with terminal degrees. *Student/faculty ratio:* 14:1.

Majors Accounting; applied mathematics; art; biology; business administration; chemistry; community services; computer science; creative writing; East Asian studies; economics; English; environmental science; French; geography; health/physical education; history; interdisciplinary studies; international relations; mass communications; mathematics; medical technology; Middle Eastern studies; music; philosophy; physics; political science; pre-dentistry; pre-law; pre-medicine; pre-veterinary studies; psychology; religious studies; sociology; Spanish; theater arts/drama.

Academic Programs *Special study options:* advanced placement credit, double majors, English as a second language, honors programs, independent study, internships, off-campus study, services for LD students, student-designed majors, study abroad, summer session for credit. *Unusual degree programs:* 3-2 engineering with University of Virginia, University of Tennessee, Tennessee Technical Institute; forestry with Duke University.

Library Kelly Library with 176,450 titles, 5,129 serial subscriptions, 6,169 audiovisual materials, an OPAC, a Web page.

Computers on Campus 121 computers available on campus for general student use. A campuswide network can be accessed from student residence rooms and from off campus. Internet access, at least one staffed computer lab available.

Student Life *Housing:* on-campus residence required through senior year. *Options:* men-only, women-only. *Activities and Organizations:* drama/theater group, student-run newspaper, radio station, choral group, Alpha Phi Omega, Student Virginia Education Association, student radio station, Campus Christian Fellowship, Greek organizations. *Campus security:* 24-hour emergency response devices and patrols, student patrols, late-night transport/escort service. *Student Services:* health clinic, personal/psychological counseling, women's center.

Athletics Member NCAA. All Division III. *Intercollegiate sports:* baseball M, basketball M/W, cross-country running M/W, football M, golf M, soccer M/W, softball W, tennis M/W, volleyball W. *Intramural sports:* basketball M/W, football M/W, golf M/W, racquetball M/W, skiing (cross-country) M(c)/W(c), skiing (downhill) M(c), soccer M/W, softball M/W, table tennis M/W, tennis M/W, volleyball M/W, water polo M/W, weight lifting M/W.

Standardized Tests *Required:* SAT I or ACT (for admission).

Costs (2002–03) *Comprehensive fee:* $20,350 includes full-time tuition ($14,600), mandatory fees ($200), and room and board ($5550). Full-time tuition and fees vary according to course load. Part-time tuition: $610 per semester hour. Part-time tuition and fees vary according to course load. *Required fees:* $10 per semester hour. *Room and board:* College room only: $2688. Room and board charges vary according to board plan. *Payment plan:* installment. *Waivers:* employees or children of employees.

Financial Aid Of all full-time matriculated undergraduates who enrolled in 2001, 818 applied for aid, 704 were judged to have need, 67 had their need fully met. 164 Federal Work-Study jobs (averaging $1387). 28 State and other part-time jobs (averaging $1806). In 2001, 234 non-need-based awards were made. *Average percent of need met:* 78%. *Average financial aid package:* $11,404. *Average need-based loan:* $2804. *Average need-based gift aid:* $2670. *Average non-need based aid:* $6313. *Average indebtedness upon graduation:* $10,625. *Financial aid deadline:* 8/1.

Applying *Options:* common application, electronic application, early admission, early decision, deferred entrance. *Application fee:* $30. *Required:* essay or personal statement, high school transcript. *Required for some:* 2 letters of recommendation. *Recommended:* interview. *Application deadline:* rolling (freshmen), rolling (transfers). *Early decision:* 12/1. *Notification:* continuous (freshmen), 12/20 (early decision).

Admissions Contact Ms. Debbie Jones Thompson, Dean of Admissions and Financial Aid, Emory & Henry College, 30479 Armbrister Drive, PO Box 10, Emory, VA 24327. *Phone:* 276-944-6133. *Toll-free phone:* 800-848-5493. *Fax:* 276-944-6935. *E-mail:* ehadmiss@ehc.edu.

FERRUM COLLEGE

Ferrum, Virginia

- **Independent United Methodist** 4-year, founded 1913
- **Calendar** semesters
- **Degree** bachelor's
- **Rural** 720-acre campus
- **Endowment** $40.8 million
- **Coed,** 920 undergraduate students, 96% full-time, 42% women, 58% men
- **Minimally difficult** entrance level, 70% of applicants were admitted

Undergraduates 882 full-time, 38 part-time. Students come from 29 states and territories, 5 other countries, 16% are from out of state, 19% African American, 1% Asian American or Pacific Islander, 1% Hispanic American, 0.3% Native American, 1.0% international, 8% transferred in, 81% live on campus. *Retention:* 56% of 2001 full-time freshmen returned.

Freshmen *Admission:* 1,053 applied, 734 admitted, 276 enrolled. *Average high school GPA:* 2.63. *Test scores:* SAT verbal scores over 500: 28%; SAT math scores over 500: 27%; SAT verbal scores over 600: 5%; SAT math scores over 600: 3%; SAT verbal scores over 700: 1%.

Faculty *Total:* 95, 68% full-time, 47% with terminal degrees. *Student/faculty ratio:* 13:1.

Majors Accounting; agricultural sciences; art; athletic training/sports medicine; biology; business administration; chemistry; computer science; criminal justice studies; education; English; environmental science; finance; fine/studio arts; French; general studies; history; information sciences/systems; international business; international relations; liberal arts and sciences/liberal studies; mathematics; medical technology; philosophy; physical education; political science; psychology; recreation/leisure studies; religious studies; Russian; social sciences; social work; Spanish; theater arts/drama.

Academic Programs *Special study options:* adult/continuing education programs, advanced placement credit, cooperative education, distance learning, double majors, independent study, internships, part-time degree program, services for LD students, student-designed majors, study abroad, summer session for credit.

Library Stanley Library with 7,739 serial subscriptions, 1,610 audiovisual materials, an OPAC, a Web page.

Computers on Campus 470 computers available on campus for general student use. A campuswide network can be accessed from student residence rooms and from off campus. Internet access, at least one staffed computer lab available.

Student Life *Housing:* on-campus residence required through senior year. *Options:* coed, women-only. *Activities and Organizations:* drama/theater group, student-run newspaper, radio station, choral group, Student Government Association, Agriculture Club, BACCHUS, Panther Productions, African American Student Association, Students in Free Enterprise. *Campus security:* 24-hour emergency response devices and patrols, student patrols, late-night transport/escort service, controlled dormitory access. *Student Services:* health clinic.

Athletics Member NCAA. All Division III. *Intercollegiate sports:* baseball M, basketball M/W, cross-country running M/W, equestrian sports M/W, football M, golf M, lacrosse W, soccer M/W, softball W, tennis M/W, volleyball W. *Intramural sports:* basketball M/W, bowling M/W, football M/W, golf M, racquetball M/W, soccer M/W, softball M/W, swimming M/W, table tennis M/W, tennis M/W, volleyball M/W.

Standardized Tests *Required:* SAT I or ACT (for admission).

Costs (2001–02) *Comprehensive fee:* $18,550 includes full-time tuition ($12,950) and room and board ($5600). Part-time tuition: $390 per credit hour. Part-time tuition and fees vary according to course load. *Payment plan:* installment. *Waivers:* senior citizens and employees or children of employees.

Financial Aid Of all full-time matriculated undergraduates who enrolled in 2001, 762 applied for aid, 693 were judged to have need, 385 had their need fully met. 272 Federal Work-Study jobs (averaging $1425). 84 State and other part-time jobs (averaging $1310). In 2001, 184 non-need-based awards were made. *Average*

Ferrum College (continued)
percent of need met: 84%. *Average financial aid package:* $10,022. *Average need-based loan:* $4026. *Average need-based gift aid:* $6473. *Average indebtedness upon graduation:* $17,093.

Applying *Options:* common application, electronic application, early admission, deferred entrance. *Application fee:* $25. *Required:* high school transcript. *Required for some:* interview. *Recommended:* essay or personal statement, minimum 2.0 GPA, 2 letters of recommendation, interview. *Application deadline:* rolling (freshmen), rolling (transfers). *Notification:* continuous (freshmen).

Admissions Contact Ms. Gilda Q. Woods, Director of Admissions, Ferrum College, Spilman-Daniel House, PO Box 1000, Ferrum, VA 24088-9001. *Phone:* 540-365-4290. *Toll-free phone:* 800-868-9797. *Fax:* 540-365-4266. *E-mail:* admissions@ferrum.edu.

GEORGE MASON UNIVERSITY
Fairfax, Virginia

- **State-supported** university, founded 1957
- **Calendar** semesters
- **Degrees** certificates, bachelor's, master's, doctoral, first professional, and postbachelor's certificates
- **Suburban** 677-acre campus with easy access to Washington, DC
- **Endowment** $33.5 million
- **Coed,** 15,802 undergraduate students, 72% full-time, 56% women, 44% men
- **Moderately difficult** entrance level, 68% of applicants were admitted

Undergraduates 11,329 full-time, 4,473 part-time. Students come from 54 states and territories, 127 other countries, 10% are from out of state, 9% African American, 16% Asian American or Pacific Islander, 7% Hispanic American, 0.4% Native American, 5% international, 13% transferred in, 19% live on campus. *Retention:* 79% of 2001 full-time freshmen returned.

Freshmen *Admission:* 8,106 applied, 5,519 admitted, 2,146 enrolled. *Average high school GPA:* 3.20. *Test scores:* SAT verbal scores over 500: 68%; SAT math scores over 500: 72%; ACT scores over 18: 87%; SAT verbal scores over 600: 21%; SAT math scores over 600: 23%; ACT scores over 24: 21%; SAT verbal scores over 700: 3%; SAT math scores over 700: 3%; ACT scores over 30: 2%.

Faculty *Total:* 1,512, 56% full-time, 53% with terminal degrees. *Student/faculty ratio:* 16:1.

Majors Accounting; anthropology; art; art history; biology; business administration; business management/administrative services related; business marketing and marketing management; chemistry; civil engineering related; computer engineering; computer/information sciences; dance; economics; electrical engineering; English; finance; fine/studio arts; foreign languages/literatures; geography; geology; health education; health professions and related sciences; history; interdisciplinary studies; international relations; law enforcement/police science; liberal arts and sciences/liberal studies; mathematics; medical technology; music (general performance); nursing; philosophy; physical education; physics; political science; psychology; public administration; religious studies; Russian/Slavic studies; social work; sociology; solid state and low-temperature physics; speech/rhetorical studies; systems engineering; theater arts/drama; visual/performing arts.

Academic Programs *Special study options:* accelerated degree program, adult/continuing education programs, advanced placement credit, cooperative education, distance learning, double majors, English as a second language, external degree program, honors programs, independent study, internships, off-campus study, part-time degree program, services for LD students, student-designed majors, study abroad, summer session for credit. *ROTC:* Army (b), Air Force (c).

Library Fenwick Library plus 1 other with 947,288 titles, 18,820 serial subscriptions, 233,891 audiovisual materials, an OPAC, a Web page.

Computers on Campus 1500 computers available on campus for general student use. A campuswide network can be accessed from student residence rooms and from off campus that provide access to telephone registration. Internet access, at least one staffed computer lab available.

Student Life *Housing Options:* coed, men-only, women-only, disabled students. *Activities and Organizations:* drama/theater group, student-run newspaper, radio and television station, choral group, Intramurals, Greek Life, Student Government, club sports, volunteer and community service, national fraternities, national sororities. *Campus security:* 24-hour emergency response devices and patrols, student patrols, late-night transport/escort service, controlled dormitory access. *Student Services:* health clinic, personal/psychological counseling, women's center.

Athletics Member NCAA. All Division I. *Intercollegiate sports:* baseball M(s), basketball M(s)/W(s), cross-country running M(s)/W(s), golf M(s), lacrosse W(s), soccer M(s)/W(s), softball W(s), swimming M(s)/W(s), tennis M(s)/W(s), track and field M(s)/W(s), volleyball M(s)/W(s), wrestling M(s). *Intramural sports:* basketball M/W, crew M/W, cross-country running M/W, field hockey W, football M, ice hockey M, racquetball M/W, rugby M/W, soccer M/W, tennis M/W, track and field M/W, volleyball M/W.

Standardized Tests *Required:* SAT I or ACT (for admission). *Recommended:* SAT II: Subject Tests (for admission).

Costs (2001–02) *Tuition:* state resident $2376 full-time, $158 per credit hour part-time; nonresident $11,280 full-time, $529 per credit hour part-time. Full-time tuition and fees vary according to course load. Part-time tuition and fees vary according to course load. *Required fees:* $1416 full-time. *Room and board:* $5400; room only: $3280. Room and board charges vary according to board plan and housing facility. *Payment plans:* installment, deferred payment. *Waivers:* senior citizens and employees or children of employees.

Financial Aid Of all full-time matriculated undergraduates who enrolled in 2001, 8355 applied for aid, 5560 were judged to have need, 2888 had their need fully met. 407 Federal Work-Study jobs (averaging $2180). In 2001, 1671 non-need-based awards were made. *Average percent of need met:* 59%. *Average financial aid package:* $6344. *Average need-based loan:* $3594. *Average need-based gift aid:* $3976. *Average indebtedness upon graduation:* $14,110.

Applying *Options:* common application, electronic application, early admission, deferred entrance. *Application fee:* $35. *Required:* essay or personal statement, high school transcript, minimum 2.0 GPA, interview. *Recommended:* minimum 3.0 GPA, letters of recommendation. *Application deadlines:* 2/1 (freshmen), 3/15 (transfers). *Notification:* 4/1 (freshmen).

Admissions Contact Mr. Eddie Tallent, Director of Admissions, George Mason University, 4400 University Drive, MSN 3A4, Fairfax, VA 22030-4444. *Phone:* 703-993-2398. *Fax:* 703-993-2392. *E-mail:* admissions@gmu.edu.

HAMPDEN-SYDNEY COLLEGE
Hampden-Sydney, Virginia

- **Independent Presbyterian** 4-year, founded 1776
- **Calendar** semesters
- **Degree** bachelor's
- **Rural** 660-acre campus with easy access to Richmond
- **Endowment** $101.7 million
- **Men only,** 1,026 undergraduate students, 100% full-time
- **Moderately difficult** entrance level, 77% of applicants were admitted

Undergraduates 1,026 full-time. Students come from 33 states and territories, 37% are from out of state, 4% African American, 0.6% Asian American or Pacific Islander, 1% Hispanic American, 0.4% Native American, 0.1% international, 1% transferred in, 94% live on campus. *Retention:* 79% of 2001 full-time freshmen returned.

Freshmen *Admission:* 329 enrolled. *Average high school GPA:* 3.1. *Test scores:* SAT verbal scores over 500: 75%; SAT math scores over 500: 82%; SAT verbal scores over 600: 34%; SAT math scores over 600: 35%; SAT verbal scores over 700: 6%; SAT math scores over 700: 4%.

Faculty *Total:* 107, 74% full-time, 75% with terminal degrees. *Student/faculty ratio:* 10:1.

Majors Biochemistry; biology; biophysics; business economics; chemistry; classics; computer science; economics; English; fine/studio arts; French; German; Greek (modern); history; humanities; Latin (ancient and medieval); mathematics; philosophy; physics; political science; psychology; public policy analysis; religious studies; Spanish.

Academic Programs *Special study options:* academic remediation for entering students, accelerated degree program, advanced placement credit, double majors, honors programs, independent study, internships, off-campus study, study abroad, summer session for credit. *ROTC:* Army (c). *Unusual degree programs:* 3-2 engineering with University of Virginia.

Library Eggleston Library with 219,221 titles, 948 serial subscriptions, an OPAC, a Web page.

Computers on Campus 140 computers available on campus for general student use. A campuswide network can be accessed from student residence rooms and from off campus. At least one staffed computer lab available.

Student Life *Housing:* on-campus residence required through senior year. *Options:* men-only. *Activities and Organizations:* drama/theater group, student-run newspaper, radio station, choral group, Good Men-Good Citizens, Fellowship of Christian Athletes, Rugby Club, College Republicans, Society for the Preservation of Southern Heritage, national fraternities. *Campus security:* 24-hour emergency response devices and patrols. *Student Services:* health clinic, personal/psychological counseling.

Athletics Member NCAA. All Division III. *Intercollegiate sports:* baseball M, basketball M, cross-country running M, football M, golf M, lacrosse M, rugby

M(c), soccer M, tennis M, volleyball M(c), water polo M(c). *Intramural sports:* basketball M, football M, soccer M, softball M, water polo M.

Standardized Tests *Required:* SAT I or ACT (for admission). *Recommended:* SAT II: Subject Tests (for admission), SAT II: Writing Test (for admission).

Costs (2001–02) *Comprehensive fee:* $24,871 includes full-time tuition ($17,858), mandatory fees ($627), and room and board ($6386). Part-time tuition: $586 per semester hour. *Room and board:* College room only: $2640. Room and board charges vary according to board plan and housing facility. *Payment plan:* installment. *Waivers:* employees or children of employees.

Financial Aid Of all full-time matriculated undergraduates who enrolled in 2001, 633 applied for aid, 477 were judged to have need, 155 had their need fully met. 200 Federal Work-Study jobs (averaging $1160). *Average percent of need met:* 88%. *Average financial aid package:* $14,518. *Average need-based loan:* $3781. *Average need-based gift aid:* $11,248.

Applying *Options:* common application, electronic application, early admission, early decision, early action. *Application fee:* $30. *Required:* essay or personal statement, high school transcript, minimum 2.0 GPA, 2 letters of recommendation. *Recommended:* minimum 3.0 GPA, interview. *Application deadlines:* 3/1 (freshmen), 7/1 (transfers). *Early decision:* 11/15. *Notification:* continuous until 4/15 (freshmen), 12/15 (early decision), 2/15 (early action).

Admissions Contact Ms. Anita H. Garland, Dean of Admissions, Hampden-Sydney College, PO Box 667, Hampden-Sydney, VA 23943-0667. *Phone:* 434-223-6120. *Toll-free phone:* 800-755-0733. *Fax:* 434-223-6346. *E-mail:* hsapp@hsc.edu.

HAMPTON UNIVERSITY
Hampton, Virginia

- **Independent** university, founded 1868
- **Calendar** semesters
- **Degrees** certificates, associate, bachelor's, master's, doctoral, first professional, and post-master's certificates
- **Urban** 210-acre campus with easy access to Norfolk
- **Endowment** $174.6 million
- **Coed,** 4,953 undergraduate students, 93% full-time, 62% women, 38% men
- **Moderately difficult** entrance level, 57% of applicants were admitted

Undergraduates 4,586 full-time, 367 part-time. Students come from 65 states and territories, 33 other countries, 70% are from out of state, 96% African American, 0.4% Asian American or Pacific Islander, 0.5% Hispanic American, 0.2% Native American, 0.8% international, 3% transferred in, 59% live on campus. *Retention:* 85% of 2001 full-time freshmen returned.

Freshmen *Admission:* 5,754 applied, 3,280 admitted, 1,243 enrolled. *Average high school GPA:* 3.00. *Test scores:* SAT verbal scores over 500: 66%; SAT math scores over 500: 51%; ACT scores over 18: 64%; SAT verbal scores over 600: 19%; SAT math scores over 600: 6%; ACT scores over 24: 4%; SAT verbal scores over 700: 1%; SAT math scores over 700: 1%; ACT scores over 30: 1%.

Faculty *Total:* 388, 84% full-time. *Student/faculty ratio:* 16:1.

Majors Accounting; advertising; air traffic control; architecture; Army R.O.T.C./military science; art; art education; aviation management; aviation technology; biology; broadcast journalism; business administration; business education; business marketing and marketing management; ceramic arts; chemical engineering; chemistry; child care/development; computer science; construction management; construction technology; criminal justice/law enforcement administration; developmental/child psychology; drawing; early childhood education; economics; education; electrical/electronic engineering technology; electrical engineering; elementary education; English; entrepreneurship; environmental science; fashion design/illustration; fashion merchandising; finance; fire science; general studies; graphic design/commercial art/illustration; health education; history; home economics education; hotel and restaurant management; information sciences/systems; interior design; jazz; journalism; marine biology; marine science; mass communications; mathematics; middle school education; modern languages; molecular biology; music; music related; music teacher education; Navy/Marine Corps R.O.T.C./naval science; nursing; paralegal/legal assistant; photography; physical education; physical sciences; physical therapy; physics; political science; pre-dentistry; pre-law; pre-medicine; pre-veterinary studies; psychology; public relations; recreational therapy; religious studies; secondary education; social sciences; social work; sociology; special education; speech-language pathology/audiology; speech therapy; sport/fitness administration; theater arts/drama.

Academic Programs *Special study options:* academic remediation for entering students, accelerated degree program, adult/continuing education programs, advanced placement credit, cooperative education, distance learning, honors programs, independent study, internships, off-campus study, part-time degree program, services for LD students, study abroad, summer session for credit. *ROTC:* Army (b), Navy (b).

Library William R. and Norma B. Harvey Library with 196,913 titles, 1,564 serial subscriptions, 55 audiovisual materials, an OPAC.

Computers on Campus 1300 computers available on campus for general student use. A campuswide network can be accessed from student residence rooms and from off campus. Internet access, at least one staffed computer lab available.

Student Life *Housing Options:* coed, men-only, women-only. *Activities and Organizations:* drama/theater group, student-run newspaper, radio station, choral group, marching band, student government, Student Leaders, Student Union Board, student recruitment team, Resident Assistants, national fraternities, national sororities. *Campus security:* 24-hour emergency response devices and patrols, controlled dormitory access, emergency call boxes. *Student Services:* health clinic, personal/psychological counseling, women's center.

Athletics Member NCAA. All Division I. *Intercollegiate sports:* basketball M(s)/W(s), bowling M, cross-country running M(s)/W(s), football M(s), golf M, sailing M, softball W(s), tennis M(s)/W(s), track and field M(s)/W(s), volleyball W(s). *Intramural sports:* basketball M/W, bowling M/W, cross-country running M/W, football M, golf M/W, sailing M/W, softball W, swimming M/W, tennis M/W, track and field M/W, volleyball M/W.

Standardized Tests *Required:* SAT I or ACT (for admission).

Costs (2001–02) *Comprehensive fee:* $17,112 includes full-time tuition ($10,464), mandatory fees ($1202), and room and board ($5446). Part-time tuition: $260 per credit hour. *Room and board:* College room only: $2846. Room and board charges vary according to housing facility. *Payment plan:* deferred payment. *Waivers:* employees or children of employees.

Financial Aid Of all full-time matriculated undergraduates who enrolled in 2001, 3748 applied for aid, 2692 were judged to have need, 2043 had their need fully met. 354 Federal Work-Study jobs (averaging $1545). In 2001, 914 non-need-based awards were made. *Average percent of need met:* 18%. *Average financial aid package:* $15,326. *Average need-based loan:* $1809. *Average need-based gift aid:* $2170. *Average non-need based aid:* $4405. *Average indebtedness upon graduation:* $23,000. *Financial aid deadline:* 3/1.

Applying *Options:* common application, early admission, deferred entrance. *Application fee:* $25. *Required:* essay or personal statement, high school transcript, minimum 2.0 GPA, 2 letters of recommendation. *Application deadlines:* 3/15 (freshmen), 3/15 (transfers). *Notification:* continuous until 7/31 (freshmen).

Admissions Contact Mr. Leonard M. Jones Jr., Director of Admissions, Hampton University, Office of Admissions, Hampton, VA 23668. *Phone:* 757-727-5328. *Toll-free phone:* 800-624-3328. *Fax:* 757-727-5095. *E-mail:* admit@hamptonu.edu.

HOLLINS UNIVERSITY
Roanoke, Virginia

- **Independent** comprehensive, founded 1842
- **Calendar** 4-1-4
- **Degrees** bachelor's, master's, and post-master's certificates
- **Suburban** 475-acre campus
- **Endowment** $91.3 million
- **Women only,** 818 undergraduate students, 95% full-time
- **Moderately difficult** entrance level, 81% of applicants were admitted

Undergraduates 777 full-time, 41 part-time. Students come from 45 states and territories, 9 other countries, 58% are from out of state, 5% African American, 2% Asian American or Pacific Islander, 2% Hispanic American, 0.1% Native American, 3% international, 4% transferred in, 89% live on campus. *Retention:* 81% of 2001 full-time freshmen returned.

Freshmen *Admission:* 191 enrolled. *Average high school GPA:* 3.30. *Test scores:* SAT verbal scores over 500: 85%; SAT math scores over 500: 72%; ACT scores over 18: 94%; SAT verbal scores over 600: 48%; SAT math scores over 600: 25%; ACT scores over 24: 61%; SAT verbal scores over 700: 13%; SAT math scores over 700: 2%; ACT scores over 30: 11%.

Faculty *Total:* 100, 75% full-time, 84% with terminal degrees. *Student/faculty ratio:* 9:1.

Majors Art history; biology; business; chemistry; classics; communications; computer science; creative writing; dance; economics; English; fine/studio arts; French; German; history; information sciences/systems; interdisciplinary studies; international relations; liberal arts and sciences/liberal studies; mathematics; music; philosophy; physics; political science; psychology; religious studies; sociology; Spanish; theater arts/drama; women's studies.

Academic Programs *Special study options:* accelerated degree program, adult/continuing education programs, advanced placement credit, double majors, honors programs, independent study, internships, off-campus study, part-time degree program, student-designed majors, study abroad. *Unusual degree programs:* 3-2 engineering with Virginia Polytechnic Institute and State University, Washington University in St. Louis.

Hollins University (continued)

Library Wyndham Robertson Library plus 1 other with 186,835 titles, 6,382 serial subscriptions, 3,402 audiovisual materials, an OPAC, a Web page.

Computers on Campus 100 computers available on campus for general student use. A campuswide network can be accessed from student residence rooms and from off campus that provide access to applications software. Internet access, at least one staffed computer lab available.

Student Life *Housing:* on-campus residence required through senior year. *Options:* women-only. *Activities and Organizations:* drama/theater group, student-run newspaper, choral group, Student Government Association, SHARE (volunteer group), Religious Life Association, Student Athletic Association, campus political organizations. *Campus security:* 24-hour emergency response devices and patrols, late-night transport/escort service, controlled dormitory access, emergency call boxes. *Student Services:* health clinic, personal/psychological counseling, women's center.

Athletics Member NCAA. All Division III. *Intercollegiate sports:* basketball W, cross-country running W, equestrian sports W, fencing W, field hockey W, golf W, lacrosse W, soccer W, softball W(c), swimming W, tennis W, volleyball W.

Standardized Tests *Required:* SAT I or ACT (for admission). *Recommended:* SAT II: Subject Tests (for admission).

Costs (2001–02) *Comprehensive fee:* $24,328 includes full-time tuition ($17,470), mandatory fees ($250), and room and board ($6608). Part-time tuition: $546 per credit. *Required fees:* $125 per year part-time. *Room and board:* College room only: $3966. *Payment plan:* installment.

Financial Aid Of all full-time matriculated undergraduates who enrolled in 2001, 693 applied for aid, 439 were judged to have need, 44 had their need fully met. 258 Federal Work-Study jobs (averaging $1892). 56 State and other part-time jobs (averaging $2073). In 2001, 250 non-need-based awards were made. *Average percent of need met:* 83%. *Average financial aid package:* $15,190. *Average need-based loan:* $4380. *Average need-based gift aid:* $11,123. *Average non-need based aid:* $8485. *Average indebtedness upon graduation:* $13,907. *Financial aid deadline:* 2/15.

Applying *Options:* common application, electronic application, early admission, early decision, deferred entrance. *Application fee:* $35. *Required:* essay or personal statement, high school transcript, 1 letter of recommendation. *Recommended:* interview. *Application deadlines:* 2/15 (freshmen), 6/1 (transfers). *Early decision:* 12/1. *Notification:* continuous (freshmen), 12/15 (early decision).

Admissions Contact Ms. Celia McCormick, Dean of Admissions, Hollins University, PO Box 9707, Roanoke, VA 24020-1707. *Phone:* 540-362-6401. *Toll-free phone:* 800-456-9595. *Fax:* 540-362-6218. *E-mail:* huadm@hollins.edu.

ITT Technical Institute
Norfolk, Virginia

- **Proprietary** primarily 2-year, founded 1988, part of ITT Educational Services, Inc
- **Calendar** quarters
- **Degrees** associate and bachelor's
- **Suburban** 2-acre campus
- **Coed,** 381 undergraduate students
- **Minimally difficult** entrance level

Majors Computer/information sciences related; computer programming; drafting; electrical/electronic engineering technologies related; robotics technology.

Student Life *Housing:* college housing not available. *Activities and Organizations:* student-run newspaper.

Costs (2001–02) *Tuition:* Full-time tuition and fees vary according to program. Part-time tuition and fees vary according to program. $260—$330 per credit hour.

Financial Aid Of all full-time matriculated undergraduates who enrolled in 2001, 3 Federal Work-Study jobs (averaging $5000).

Applying *Options:* deferred entrance. *Application fee:* $100. *Required:* high school transcript, interview. *Recommended:* letters of recommendation. *Application deadline:* rolling (freshmen), rolling (transfers). *Notification:* continuous (freshmen).

Admissions Contact Mr. Jack Keesee, Director of Recruitment, ITT Technical Institute, 863 Glenrock Road, Suite 100, Norfolk, VA 23502-3701. *Phone:* 757-466-1260.

James Madison University
Harrisonburg, Virginia

- **State-supported** comprehensive, founded 1908
- **Calendar** semesters
- **Degrees** bachelor's, master's, and doctoral (also offers specialist in education degree)
- **Small-town** 472-acre campus
- **Endowment** $24.1 million
- **Coed,** 14,590 undergraduate students, 94% full-time, 58% women, 42% men
- **Very difficult** entrance level, 64% of applicants were admitted

Undergraduates 13,720 full-time, 870 part-time. Students come from 49 states and territories, 54 other countries, 29% are from out of state, 4% African American, 5% Asian American or Pacific Islander, 2% Hispanic American, 0.2% Native American, 1% international, 4% transferred in, 41% live on campus. *Retention:* 90% of 2001 full-time freshmen returned.

Freshmen *Admission:* 14,114 applied, 9,080 admitted, 3,249 enrolled. *Average high school GPA:* 3.58. *Test scores:* SAT verbal scores over 500: 87%; SAT math scores over 500: 89%; SAT verbal scores over 600: 33%; SAT math scores over 600: 39%; SAT verbal scores over 700: 3%; SAT math scores over 700: 3%.

Faculty *Total:* 938, 73% full-time, 64% with terminal degrees. *Student/faculty ratio:* 17:1.

Majors Accounting; adult/continuing education; anthropology; art; art history; biology; business administration; business economics; business education; business marketing and marketing management; chemistry; communications; community health liaison; computer/information sciences; early childhood education; economics; education; educational media design; elementary education; English; finance; foreign languages/literatures; French; geography; geology; German; health/physical education; history; hotel and restaurant management; information sciences/systems; international business; international relations; liberal arts and sciences/liberal studies; mathematics; music (general performance); nursing; nutrition studies; philosophy; physics; political science; psychology; public administration; religious studies; Russian; science/technology and society; social sciences; social work; sociology; Spanish; special education; speech-language pathology; technical/business writing; theater arts/drama.

Academic Programs *Special study options:* accelerated degree program, adult/continuing education programs, advanced placement credit, distance learning, double majors, English as a second language, freshman honors college, honors programs, independent study, internships, part-time degree program, services for LD students, study abroad, summer session for credit. *ROTC:* Army (b).

Library Carrier Library plus 2 others with 1.3 million titles, 3,367 serial subscriptions, 28,465 audiovisual materials, an OPAC, a Web page.

Computers on Campus 500 computers available on campus for general student use. A campuswide network can be accessed from student residence rooms and from off campus. Internet access, online (class) registration, at least one staffed computer lab available.

Student Life *Housing:* on-campus residence required for freshman year. *Options:* coed. *Activities and Organizations:* drama/theater group, student-run newspaper, radio station, choral group, marching band, Student Ambassadors, sports clubs, Greek organizations, service organizations, special interest groups, national fraternities, national sororities. *Campus security:* 24-hour emergency response devices and patrols, student patrols, late-night transport/escort service, controlled dormitory access, lighted pathways. *Student Services:* health clinic, personal/psychological counseling.

Athletics Member NCAA. All Division I except football (Division I-AA). *Intercollegiate sports:* archery M/W, baseball M(s), basketball M(s)/W(s), cross-country running M(s)/W(s), fencing W, field hockey W(s), golf M(s)/W(s), gymnastics M(s)/W(s), lacrosse W(s), soccer M(s)/W(s), softball W(s), swimming M(s)/W(s), tennis M(s)/W(s), track and field M(s)/W(s), volleyball W(s), wrestling M(s). *Intramural sports:* badminton M/W, baseball M(c), basketball M(c)/W(c), bowling M(c)/W(c), equestrian sports M(c)/W(c), fencing M(c)/W(c), field hockey M(c)/W(c), football M/W, golf M/W, gymnastics M(c)/W(c), lacrosse M(c)/W(c), racquetball M/W, rugby M(c)/W(c), skiing (downhill) M(c)/W(c), soccer M(c)/W(c), softball M/W(c), swimming M(c)/W(c), table tennis M(c)/W(c), tennis M(c)/W(c), volleyball M(c)/W(c), water polo M(c)/W(c).

Standardized Tests *Required:* SAT I or ACT (for admission). *Required for some:* SAT II: Subject Tests (for admission). *Recommended:* SAT I (for admission).

Costs (2001–02) *Tuition:* state resident $4094 full-time; nonresident $10,606 full-time. *Room and board:* $5458; room only: $2932. Room and board charges vary according to board plan and housing facility. *Payment plan:* installment. *Waivers:* senior citizens and employees or children of employees.

Financial Aid Of all full-time matriculated undergraduates who enrolled in 2001, 10104 applied for aid, 6039 were judged to have need, 1478 had their need fully met. In 2001, 432 non-need-based awards were made. *Average percent of need met:* 57%. *Average financial aid package:* $5814. *Average need-based loan:* $3359. *Average need-based gift aid:* $4085. *Average non-need based aid:* $1461. *Average indebtedness upon graduation:* $12,474.

Applying *Options:* electronic application, early action. *Application fee:* $30. *Required:* essay or personal statement, high school transcript. *Recommended:* minimum 3.0 GPA. *Application deadlines:* 1/15 (freshmen), 3/1 (transfers). *Notification:* 4/1 (freshmen), 1/15 (early action).

Admissions Contact Ms. Laika Tamny, Associate Director of Admissions, James Madison University, Office of Admission, Sonner Hall MSC 0101, Harrisonburg, VA 22807. *Phone:* 540-568-6147. *Fax:* 540-568-3332. *E-mail:* gotojmu@jmu.edu.

JOHNSON & WALES UNIVERSITY
Norfolk, Virginia

- **Independent** 4-year, founded 1986
- **Calendar** quarters
- **Degrees** certificates, diplomas, associate, and bachelor's
- **Urban** campus
- **Endowment** $80.3 million
- **Coed,** 635 undergraduate students, 95% full-time, 45% women, 55% men
- **Minimally difficult** entrance level, 68% of applicants were admitted

Undergraduates 604 full-time, 31 part-time. Students come from 23 states and territories, 36% African American, 2% Asian American or Pacific Islander, 5% Hispanic American, 0.2% Native American, 9% transferred in.

Freshmen *Admission:* 170 applied, 115 admitted, 173 enrolled. *Average high school GPA:* 2.53. *Test scores:* SAT verbal scores over 500: 27%; SAT math scores over 500: 24%; SAT verbal scores over 600: 11%; SAT math scores over 600: 4%.

Faculty *Total:* 33, 55% full-time. *Student/faculty ratio:* 18:1.

Majors Culinary arts; food systems administration.

Academic Programs *Special study options:* academic remediation for entering students, accelerated degree program, cooperative education, internships, part-time degree program, services for LD students, summer session for credit.

Library Johnson & Wales at Norfolk Library with 3,281 titles, 47 serial subscriptions, 134 audiovisual materials, an OPAC.

Computers on Campus 15 computers available on campus for general student use. A campuswide network can be accessed from off campus. Internet access, at least one staffed computer lab available.

Student Life *Housing:* on-campus residence required for freshman year. *Options:* coed. *Activities and Organizations:* ACF, Garde Manger and Food Styling Club, Team J-W, Griffin Society, Baking and Pastry Club. *Campus security:* late-night transport/escort service, controlled dormitory access, trained evening security personnel. *Student Services:* health clinic, personal/psychological counseling.

Standardized Tests *Required for some:* SAT I or ACT (for admission).

Costs (2002–03) *Comprehensive fee:* $23,016 includes full-time tuition ($16,050), mandatory fees ($630), and room and board ($6336). *Room and board:* College room only: $4542.

Financial Aid Of all full-time matriculated undergraduates who enrolled in 2001, 574 applied for aid, 523 were judged to have need, 17 had their need fully met. In 2001, 10 non-need-based awards were made. *Average percent of need met:* 65%. *Average financial aid package:* $9624. *Average need-based loan:* $4888. *Average need-based gift aid:* $3419. *Average non-need based aid:* $2180. *Average indebtedness upon graduation:* $13,695.

Applying *Options:* common application, electronic application, early admission, deferred entrance. *Required:* high school transcript. *Required for some:* letters of recommendation. *Recommended:* essay or personal statement, minimum 2.0 GPA, interview. *Application deadline:* rolling (freshmen), rolling (transfers). *Notification:* continuous (freshmen).

Admissions Contact Ms. Torri Butler, Director of Student Affairs, Johnson & Wales University, 2428 Almeda Avenue, Suite 316, Norfolk, VA 23513. *Phone:* 757-853-3508 Ext. 222. *Toll-free phone:* 800-277-2433. *Fax:* 757-857-4869. *E-mail:* admissions@jwu.edu.

LIBERTY UNIVERSITY
Lynchburg, Virginia

- **Independent nondenominational** comprehensive, founded 1971
- **Calendar** semesters
- **Degrees** associate, bachelor's, master's, doctoral, and first professional (also offers external degree program with significant enrollment not reflected in profile)
- **Suburban** 160-acre campus
- **Endowment** $2.7 million
- **Coed,** 5,391 undergraduate students, 84% full-time, 51% women, 49% men
- **Minimally difficult** entrance level, 58% of applicants were admitted

Undergraduates 4,548 full-time, 843 part-time. Students come from 52 states and territories, 52 other countries, 62% are from out of state, 8% African American, 2% Asian American or Pacific Islander, 2% Hispanic American, 0.5% Native American, 3% international, 10% transferred in, 68% live on campus.

Freshmen *Admission:* 2,642 applied, 1,530 admitted, 1,179 enrolled. *Average high school GPA:* 3.13.

Faculty *Total:* 265, 65% full-time, 50% with terminal degrees. *Student/faculty ratio:* 21:1.

Majors Accounting; athletic training/sports medicine; biology; biology education; business administration; communications; computer/information sciences; elementary education; English; English education; exercise sciences; family/community studies; general studies; health education; health/physical education; history; history education; interdisciplinary studies; mathematics; mathematics education; music; music teacher education; nursing; physical education; political science; psychology; religious studies; science education; secondary education; social science education; social sciences; Spanish; special education; sport/fitness administration; teaching English as a second language.

Academic Programs *Special study options:* academic remediation for entering students, accelerated degree program, advanced placement credit, distance learning, double majors, English as a second language, external degree program, honors programs, independent study, internships, part-time degree program, services for LD students, student-designed majors, summer session for credit.

Library A. Pierre Guillermin Library plus 1 other with 296,601 titles, 7,739 serial subscriptions, 5,555 audiovisual materials, an OPAC, a Web page.

Computers on Campus 245 computers available on campus for general student use. A campuswide network can be accessed from student residence rooms and from off campus. Internet access, online (class) registration, at least one staffed computer lab available.

Student Life *Housing:* on-campus residence required through junior year. *Options:* men-only, women-only. *Activities and Organizations:* drama/theater group, student-run newspaper, radio station, choral group, marching band, College Republicans, Youthquest, Circle K. *Campus security:* 24-hour patrols, late-night transport/escort service, 24-hour emergency dispatch. *Student Services:* health clinic, personal/psychological counseling.

Athletics Member NCAA. All Division I except football (Division I-AA). *Intercollegiate sports:* baseball M(s), basketball M(s)/W(s), cross-country running M(s)/W(s), field hockey W(c), golf M(s), ice hockey M(c), soccer M(s)/W(s), softball W(s), tennis M(s)/W(s), track and field M(s)/W(s), volleyball W(s). *Intramural sports:* basketball M/W, football M, soccer M/W, softball M/W, tennis M/W, volleyball M/W.

Standardized Tests *Required:* SAT I or ACT (for admission). *Required for some:* ACT (for admission).

Costs (2002–03) *Comprehensive fee:* $15,440 includes full-time tuition ($9840), mandatory fees ($500), and room and board ($5100). Full-time tuition and fees vary according to course load. Part-time tuition: $328 per semester hour. Part-time tuition and fees vary according to course load. *Required fees:* $328 per semester hour, $250 per term part-time. *Payment plan:* installment. *Waivers:* employees or children of employees.

Financial Aid Of all full-time matriculated undergraduates who enrolled in 2001, 4234 applied for aid, 3295 were judged to have need, 231 had their need fully met. 418 Federal Work-Study jobs (averaging $1250). In 2001, 1157 non-need-based awards were made. *Average percent of need met:* 64%. *Average financial aid package:* $7765. *Average need-based loan:* $4139. *Average need-based gift aid:* $2780. *Average non-need based aid:* $3623. *Average indebtedness upon graduation:* $14,484.

Applying *Options:* electronic application, early admission, deferred entrance. *Application fee:* $35. *Required:* essay or personal statement, high school transcript. *Required for some:* 1 letter of recommendation, interview. *Recommended:* minimum 2.0 GPA, 1 letter of recommendation. *Application deadlines:* 6/30 (freshmen), 6/30 (transfers). *Notification:* continuous until 8/15 (freshmen).

Admissions Contact Mr. David Hart, Associate Director of Admissions, Liberty University, 1971 University Boulevard, Lynchburg, VA 24502. *Phone:* 434-582-7307. *Toll-free phone:* 800-543-5317. *Fax:* 434-582-2421. *E-mail:* admissions@liberty.edu.

LONGWOOD COLLEGE
Farmville, Virginia

- **State-supported** comprehensive, founded 1839, part of The State Council of Higher Education for Virginia (SCHEV)
- **Calendar** semesters
- **Degrees** bachelor's and master's

Longwood College (continued)

- **Small-town** 160-acre campus with easy access to Richmond
- **Endowment** $24.7 million
- **Coed,** 3,560 undergraduate students, 97% full-time, 66% women, 34% men
- **Moderately difficult** entrance level, 78% of applicants were admitted

Undergraduates 3,440 full-time, 120 part-time. Students come from 25 states and territories, 15 other countries, 10% are from out of state, 8% African American, 2% Asian American or Pacific Islander, 2% Hispanic American, 0.2% Native American, 0.4% international, 5% transferred in, 77% live on campus. *Retention:* 83% of 2001 full-time freshmen returned.

Freshmen *Admission:* 2,792 applied, 2,175 admitted, 894 enrolled. *Average high school GPA:* 3.20. *Test scores:* SAT verbal scores over 500: 74%; SAT math scores over 500: 70%; SAT verbal scores over 600: 19%; SAT math scores over 600: 15%; SAT verbal scores over 700: 2%; SAT math scores over 700: 1%.

Faculty *Total:* 232, 74% full-time, 63% with terminal degrees. *Student/faculty ratio:* 19:1.

Majors Accounting; anthropology; applied mathematics; Army R.O.T.C./military science; art; art education; art history; athletic training/sports medicine; biology; biophysics; business administration; business economics; business marketing and marketing management; chemistry; communication disorders; communications; community health liaison; computer science; criminal justice/law enforcement administration; dance; developmental/child psychology; drawing; early childhood education; earth sciences; economics; education; elementary education; English; environmental science; exercise sciences; experimental psychology; finance; fine/studio arts; French; geography; German; graphic design/commercial art/illustration; health education; health science; history; interior design; international economics; international relations; journalism; liberal arts and sciences/liberal studies; library science; management information systems/business data processing; mathematics; medical laboratory technician; medical technology; modern languages; music; music teacher education; natural sciences; pharmacy; physical education; physics; political science; pre-dentistry; pre-law; pre-medicine; pre-veterinary studies; printmaking; psychology; reading education; recreational therapy; science education; sculpture; secondary education; social work; sociology; Spanish; special education; sport/fitness administration; theater arts/drama; women's studies.

Academic Programs *Special study options:* academic remediation for entering students, accelerated degree program, adult/continuing education programs, advanced placement credit, distance learning, double majors, English as a second language, honors programs, independent study, internships, off-campus study, part-time degree program, services for LD students, study abroad, summer session for credit. *ROTC:* Army (b). *Unusual degree programs:* 3-2 engineering with University of Virginia, Old Dominion University, Georgia Institute of Technology, University of Tennessee, Virginia Polytechnic Institute and University, Christopher Newport University.

Library Longwood Library with 241,641 titles, 2,505 serial subscriptions, 36,398 audiovisual materials, an OPAC, a Web page.

Computers on Campus 270 computers available on campus for general student use. A campuswide network can be accessed from student residence rooms and from off campus. Internet access, at least one staffed computer lab available.

Student Life *Housing:* on-campus residence required through junior year. *Options:* coed, women-only, disabled students. *Activities and Organizations:* drama/theater group, student-run newspaper, radio station, choral group, Student Government Association, Alpha Phi Omega, Intervarsity Christian, Longwood Ambassadors, Wellness Advocates, national fraternities, national sororities. *Campus security:* 24-hour emergency response devices and patrols, late-night transport/escort service, controlled dormitory access, security lighting. *Student Services:* health clinic, personal/psychological counseling.

Athletics Member NCAA. All Division II. *Intercollegiate sports:* baseball M(s), basketball M(s)/W(s), equestrian sports M(c)/W(c), field hockey W(s), golf M(s)/W(s), lacrosse W, rugby M(c)/W(c), soccer M(s)/W, softball W, swimming M(c)/W(c), tennis M/W(s), track and field M(c)/W(c), volleyball M(c)/W(c), wrestling M(c). *Intramural sports:* badminton M/W, basketball W, bowling M/W, football M/W, golf M/W, racquetball M/W, soccer M/W, softball M/W, table tennis M/W, tennis M/W, volleyball M/W.

Standardized Tests *Required:* SAT I or ACT (for admission). *Required for some:* SAT II: Subject Tests (for admission).

Costs (2001–02) *Tuition:* state resident $1970 full-time, $83 per credit hour part-time; nonresident $7690 full-time, $320 per credit hour part-time. *Required fees:* $2256 full-time, $88 per credit hour. *Room and board:* $4724; room only: $2852. Room and board charges vary according to board plan. *Payment plan:* installment. *Waivers:* senior citizens and employees or children of employees.

Financial Aid Of all full-time matriculated undergraduates who enrolled in 2001, 2024 applied for aid, 1355 were judged to have need, 457 had their need fully met. 392 Federal Work-Study jobs (averaging $792). 327 State and other part-time jobs (averaging $823). In 2001, 669 non-need-based awards were made. *Average percent of need met:* 80%. *Average financial aid package:* $6132. *Average need-based loan:* $2863. *Average need-based gift aid:* $3048. *Average indebtedness upon graduation:* $14,987.

Applying *Options:* common application, electronic application, early admission, early action, deferred entrance. *Application fee:* $30. *Required:* essay or personal statement, high school transcript. *Required for some:* letters of recommendation, interview. *Recommended:* minimum 2.6 GPA. *Application deadlines:* 3/1 (freshmen), 6/1 (transfers). *Notification:* continuous until 6/1 (freshmen), 1/1 (early action).

Admissions Contact Mr. Robert J. Chonko, Director of Admissions, Longwood College, 201 High Street, Farmville, VA 23909. *Phone:* 434-395-2060. *Toll-free phone:* 800-281-4677 Ext. 2. *Fax:* 434-395-2332. *E-mail:* lcadmit@longwood.edu.

LYNCHBURG COLLEGE

Lynchburg, Virginia

- **Independent** comprehensive, founded 1903, affiliated with Christian Church (Disciples of Christ)
- **Calendar** semesters
- **Degrees** bachelor's and master's
- **Suburban** 214-acre campus
- **Endowment** $67.8 million
- **Coed,** 1,733 undergraduate students, 92% full-time, 61% women, 39% men
- **Moderately difficult** entrance level, 75% of applicants were admitted

Undergraduates 1,588 full-time, 145 part-time. Students come from 31 states and territories, 10 other countries, 43% are from out of state, 8% African American, 0.9% Asian American or Pacific Islander, 2% Hispanic American, 0.5% Native American, 0.8% international, 72% live on campus. *Retention:* 69% of 2001 full-time freshmen returned.

Freshmen *Admission:* 2,310 applied, 1,724 admitted, 475 enrolled. *Average high school GPA:* 2.99. *Test scores:* SAT verbal scores over 500: 54%; SAT math scores over 500: 53%; ACT scores over 18: 81%; SAT verbal scores over 600: 11%; SAT math scores over 600: 12%; ACT scores over 24: 25%; SAT verbal scores over 700: 1%; SAT math scores over 700: 1%.

Faculty *Total:* 194, 56% full-time. *Student/faculty ratio:* 12:1.

Majors Accounting; athletic training/sports medicine; biology; business administration; business marketing and marketing management; chemistry; computer science; creative writing; developmental/child psychology; early childhood education; economics; education; elementary education; English; environmental science; exercise sciences; fine/studio arts; French; health education; history; international relations; journalism; mass communications; mathematics; music; nursing; philosophy; physical education; physics; physiological psychology/psychobiology; political science; pre-dentistry; pre-law; pre-medicine; pre-veterinary studies; psychology; recreation/leisure studies; religious studies; secondary education; social sciences; sociology; Spanish; special education; speech/rhetorical studies; sport/fitness administration; theater arts/drama.

Academic Programs *Special study options:* accelerated degree program, adult/continuing education programs, advanced placement credit, double majors, honors programs, internships, off-campus study, part-time degree program, services for LD students, summer session for credit. *Unusual degree programs:* 3-2 engineering with Old Dominion University, University of Virginia.

Library Knight-Capron Library with 287,601 titles, 636 serial subscriptions, 9,360 audiovisual materials, an OPAC, a Web page.

Computers on Campus 217 computers available on campus for general student use. A campuswide network can be accessed from student residence rooms. Internet access, at least one staffed computer lab available.

Student Life *Housing:* on-campus residence required through junior year. *Options:* coed. *Activities and Organizations:* drama/theater group, student-run newspaper, choral group, Student Activities Board, SGA, Black Student Association, Habitat for Humanity, gospel ensemble, national fraternities, national sororities. *Campus security:* 24-hour emergency response devices and patrols, late-night transport/escort service, controlled dormitory access. *Student Services:* health clinic, personal/psychological counseling.

Athletics Member NCAA. All Division III. *Intercollegiate sports:* baseball M, basketball M/W, cross-country running M/W, equestrian sports M/W, field hockey W, golf M, lacrosse M/W, soccer M/W, softball W, tennis M/W, track and field M/W, volleyball W. *Intramural sports:* badminton M/W, baseball M, basketball M/W, bowling M/W, equestrian sports M/W, football M, golf M, racquetball M/W, rugby M/W, soccer M/W, softball W, tennis M/W, track and field M/W, volleyball M/W.

Standardized Tests *Required:* SAT I or ACT (for admission). *Recommended:* SAT II: Subject Tests (for admission), SAT II: Writing Test (for admission).

Costs (2002–03) *Comprehensive fee:* $24,765 includes full-time tuition ($20,040), mandatory fees ($125), and room and board ($4600). Part-time tuition: $300 per credit hour. Part-time tuition and fees vary according to course load. *Room and board:* College room only: $2700. Room and board charges vary according to board plan. *Payment plan:* installment. *Waivers:* adult students, senior citizens, and employees or children of employees.

Applying *Options:* common application, electronic application, early admission, early decision, deferred entrance. *Application fee:* $30. *Required:* essay or personal statement, high school transcript. *Recommended:* 2 letters of recommendation, interview. *Application deadline:* rolling (freshmen), rolling (transfers). *Early decision:* 11/15. *Notification:* continuous (freshmen), 12/15 (early decision).

Admissions Contact Ms. Sharon Walters-Bower, Director of Recruitment, Lynchburg College, 1501 Lakeside Drive, Lynchburg, VA 24501-3199. *Phone:* 434-544-8300. *Toll-free phone:* 800-426-8101. *Fax:* 804-544-8653. *E-mail:* admissions@lynchburg.edu.

MARY BALDWIN COLLEGE

Staunton, Virginia

- **Independent** comprehensive, founded 1842, affiliated with Presbyterian Church (U.S.A.)
- **Calendar** 4-4-1
- **Degrees** certificates, bachelor's, and master's
- **Small-town** 54-acre campus
- **Endowment** $33.9 million
- **Coed, primarily women,** 1,489 undergraduate students, 74% full-time, 96% women, 4% men
- **Moderately difficult** entrance level, 82% of applicants were admitted

Undergraduates 1,096 full-time, 393 part-time. Students come from 39 states and territories, 7 other countries, 23% are from out of state, 18% African American, 2% Asian American or Pacific Islander, 4% Hispanic American, 0.2% Native American, 2% international, 10% transferred in, 87% live on campus. *Retention:* 74% of 2001 full-time freshmen returned.

Freshmen *Admission:* 1,228 applied, 1,005 admitted, 260 enrolled. *Average high school GPA:* 3.17. *Test scores:* SAT verbal scores over 500: 73%; SAT math scores over 500: 49%; ACT scores over 18: 72%; SAT verbal scores over 600: 25%; SAT math scores over 600: 11%; ACT scores over 24: 26%; SAT verbal scores over 700: 4%; ACT scores over 30: 5%.

Faculty *Total:* 130, 55% full-time, 49% with terminal degrees. *Student/faculty ratio:* 11:1.

Majors Accounting; advertising; applied mathematics; art; art history; arts management; Asian studies; biochemistry; biology; business administration; business economics; chemistry; communications; computer management; economics; English; fine/studio arts; French; German; graphic design/commercial art/illustration; health services administration; history; interdisciplinary studies; international relations; journalism; mass communications; mathematics; medical technology; music; philosophy; physics; political science; psychology; public relations; religious studies; social work; sociology; Spanish; theater arts/drama.

Academic Programs *Special study options:* academic remediation for entering students, accelerated degree program, adult/continuing education programs, advanced placement credit, distance learning, double majors, English as a second language, external degree program, freshman honors college, honors programs, independent study, internships, off-campus study, part-time degree program, services for LD students, student-designed majors, study abroad. *ROTC:* Army (b), Navy (c), Air Force (c). *Unusual degree programs:* 3-2 engineering with University of Virginia; nursing with Vanderbilt University.

Library Grafton Library with 166,797 titles, 7,000 serial subscriptions, 9,000 audiovisual materials, an OPAC, a Web page.

Computers on Campus 175 computers available on campus for general student use. A campuswide network can be accessed from student residence rooms and from off campus. Internet access, online (class) registration, at least one staffed computer lab available.

Student Life *Housing:* on-campus residence required through senior year. *Options:* women-only. *Activities and Organizations:* drama/theater group, student-run newspaper, radio station, choral group, marching band, Student Senate, Baldwin Program Board, President's Society, Black Student Alliance, Stars. *Campus security:* 24-hour emergency response devices and patrols, late-night transport/escort service, controlled dormitory access. *Student Services:* health clinic, personal/psychological counseling.

Athletics Member NCAA. All Division III. *Intercollegiate sports:* basketball W, cross-country running W(c), fencing W(c), field hockey W(c), lacrosse W(c), soccer W, softball W, swimming W, tennis W, volleyball W. *Intramural sports:* equestrian sports W(c).

Standardized Tests *Required:* SAT I or ACT (for admission).

Costs (2001–02) *Comprehensive fee:* $23,440 includes full-time tuition ($15,815), mandatory fees ($175), and room and board ($7450). Full-time tuition and fees vary according to degree level and program. Part-time tuition: $307 per semester hour. Part-time tuition and fees vary according to degree level. *Room and board:* College room only: $3450. Room and board charges vary according to housing facility. *Payment plan:* installment. *Waivers:* employees or children of employees.

Financial Aid Of all full-time matriculated undergraduates who enrolled in 2001, 795 applied for aid, 695 were judged to have need, 312 had their need fully met. 288 Federal Work-Study jobs (averaging $1421). 117 State and other part-time jobs (averaging $1255). *Average percent of need met:* 89%. *Average financial aid package:* $17,638. *Average need-based loan:* $3945. *Average need-based gift aid:* $9927. *Average indebtedness upon graduation:* $19,148. *Financial aid deadline:* 5/15.

Applying *Options:* common application, electronic application, early admission, early decision, deferred entrance. *Application fee:* $25. *Required:* high school transcript, minimum 2.0 GPA, 1 letter of recommendation. *Recommended:* interview. *Application deadline:* rolling (freshmen), rolling (transfers). *Early decision:* 11/15. *Notification:* continuous (freshmen), 12/1 (early decision).

Admissions Contact Ms. Lisa Branson, Assistant Director for Freshmen Services, Mary Baldwin College, Frederick and New Streets, Staunton, VA 24401. *Phone:* 540-887-7221 Ext. 7287. *Toll-free phone:* 800-468-2262. *Fax:* 540-886-6634. *E-mail:* admit@mbc.edu.

MARYMOUNT UNIVERSITY

Arlington, Virginia

- **Independent** comprehensive, founded 1950, affiliated with Roman Catholic Church
- **Calendar** semesters
- **Degrees** certificates, associate, bachelor's, master's, post-master's, and postbachelor's certificates
- **Suburban** 21-acre campus with easy access to Washington, DC
- **Endowment** $22.1 million
- **Coed,** 2,041 undergraduate students, 75% full-time, 71% women, 29% men
- **Moderately difficult** entrance level, 87% of applicants were admitted

Marymount is a comprehensive, coeducational Catholic university that emphasizes excellence in teaching, attention to the individual, and values and ethics across the curriculum. The University offers thirty-seven undergraduate majors and twenty-six graduate degree programs. Marymount serves approximately 2,100 undergraduate and 1,500 graduate students. With two campuses in Arlington, Virginia, and the Loudoun Academic Center in Sterling, Virginia, Marymount University is just minutes from the resources of Washington, D.C.

Undergraduates 1,523 full-time, 518 part-time. Students come from 36 states and territories, 75 other countries, 51% are from out of state, 15% African American, 8% Asian American or Pacific Islander, 8% Hispanic American, 0.2% Native American, 12% international, 15% transferred in, 32% live on campus. *Retention:* 73% of 2001 full-time freshmen returned.

Freshmen *Admission:* 1,407 applied, 1,220 admitted, 363 enrolled. *Average high school GPA:* 2.95. *Test scores:* SAT verbal scores over 500: 53%; SAT math scores over 500: 49%; ACT scores over 18: 69%; SAT verbal scores over 600: 13%; SAT math scores over 600: 10%; ACT scores over 24: 12%; SAT verbal scores over 700: 2%; SAT math scores over 700: 1%.

Faculty *Total:* 372, 33% full-time, 59% with terminal degrees. *Student/faculty ratio:* 13:1.

Majors Accounting; art; biological specializations related; biology; business administration; business administration/management related; business marketing and marketing management; cell and molecular biology related; communications; computer/information sciences; computer science; criminology; economics; economics related; educational psychology; English; environmental science; fashion design/illustration; fashion merchandising; finance; graphic design/commercial art/illustration; health science; history; human resources management; interior design; international business; liberal arts and sciences/liberal studies; management science; mathematics; mental health services related; nursing; organizational psychology; paralegal/legal assistant; philosophy; political science; psychology; public policy analysis; recreation/leisure studies; religious studies; retail management; social psychology; sociology; sport/fitness administration.

Academic Programs *Special study options:* academic remediation for entering students, advanced placement credit, double majors, English as a second language, independent study, internships, off-campus study, part-time degree program, services for LD students, student-designed majors, study abroad, summer session for credit. *ROTC:* Army (c).

Marymount University (continued)

Library Emerson C. Reinsch Library plus 1 other with 176,986 titles, 1,067 serial subscriptions, 920 audiovisual materials, an OPAC.

Computers on Campus 260 computers available on campus for general student use. A campuswide network can be accessed from off campus that provide access to on-line registration for graduate students. At least one staffed computer lab available.

Student Life *Housing:* on-campus residence required through sophomore year. *Options:* coed, men-only, women-only. *Activities and Organizations:* drama/theater group, student-run newspaper, choral group, American Society of Interior Design, Student Nurses Association, Fashion Club, International Club, One 2 One (Drama Club). *Campus security:* 24-hour emergency response devices and patrols, late-night transport/escort service, controlled dormitory access. *Student Services:* health clinic, personal/psychological counseling.

Athletics Member NCAA. All Division III. *Intercollegiate sports:* basketball M/W, golf M, lacrosse M/W, soccer M/W, swimming M/W, volleyball W. *Intramural sports:* basketball M/W, football M/W, golf M, soccer M/W, softball M/W, swimming M/W, table tennis M/W, volleyball M/W, water polo M/W.

Standardized Tests *Required:* SAT I or ACT (for admission).

Costs (2001–02) *Comprehensive fee:* $21,560 includes full-time tuition ($14,850), mandatory fees ($120), and room and board ($6590). Part-time tuition: $481 per credit hour. *Required fees:* $5 per credit hour. *Payment plans:* installment, deferred payment. *Waivers:* senior citizens and employees or children of employees.

Financial Aid Of all full-time matriculated undergraduates who enrolled in 2001, 1239 applied for aid, 833 were judged to have need, 172 had their need fully met. 264 Federal Work-Study jobs (averaging $1800). In 2001, 340 non-need-based awards were made. *Average percent of need met:* 80%. *Average financial aid package:* $12,999. *Average need-based loan:* $3714. *Average need-based gift aid:* $7191. *Average non-need based aid:* $5639.

Applying *Options:* common application, electronic application, early admission, deferred entrance. *Application fee:* $35. *Required:* high school transcript, minimum 2.0 GPA, 1 letter of recommendation. *Recommended:* essay or personal statement, interview. *Application deadline:* rolling (freshmen), rolling (transfers). *Notification:* 10/15 (freshmen).

Admissions Contact Mr. Mike Canfield, Associate Director of Undergraduate Admissions, Marymount University, 2807 North Glebe Road, Arlington, VA 22207-4299. *Phone:* 703-284-1500. *Toll-free phone:* 800-548-7638. *Fax:* 703-522-0349. *E-mail:* admissions@marymount.edu.

MARY WASHINGTON COLLEGE

Fredericksburg, Virginia

- **State-supported** comprehensive, founded 1908
- **Calendar** semesters
- **Degrees** bachelor's and master's
- **Small-town** 176-acre campus with easy access to Richmond and Washington, DC
- **Endowment** $27.7 million
- **Coed,** 4,173 undergraduate students, 81% full-time, 67% women, 33% men
- **Very difficult** entrance level, 55% of applicants were admitted

Undergraduates 3,400 full-time, 773 part-time. Students come from 46 states and territories, 14 other countries, 35% are from out of state, 4% African American, 4% Asian American or Pacific Islander, 3% Hispanic American, 0.3% Native American, 0.3% international, 4% transferred in, 70% live on campus. *Retention:* 87% of 2001 full-time freshmen returned.

Freshmen *Admission:* 4,320 applied, 2,397 admitted, 843 enrolled. *Average high school GPA:* 3.72. *Test scores:* SAT verbal scores over 500: 96%; SAT math scores over 500: 94%; SAT verbal scores over 600: 59%; SAT math scores over 600: 47%; SAT verbal scores over 700: 11%; SAT math scores over 700: 4%.

Faculty *Total:* 321, 63% full-time, 51% with terminal degrees. *Student/faculty ratio:* 17:1.

Majors American studies; architectural history; art; art history; biology; business administration; chemistry; classics; computer science; economics; elementary education; English; environmental science; fine/studio arts; French; geography; geology; German; history; interdisciplinary studies; international relations; Latin (ancient and medieval); liberal arts and sciences/liberal studies; mathematics; modern languages; music; music teacher education; philosophy; physics; political science; pre-dentistry; pre-law; pre-medicine; pre-veterinary studies; psychology; religious studies; secondary education; sociology; Spanish; theater arts/drama.

Academic Programs *Special study options:* accelerated degree program, adult/continuing education programs, advanced placement credit, cooperative education, double majors, independent study, internships, part-time degree program, services for LD students, student-designed majors, study abroad, summer session for credit.

Library Simpson Library with 354,326 titles, 1,713 serial subscriptions, 342 audiovisual materials, an OPAC, a Web page.

Computers on Campus 238 computers available on campus for general student use. A campuswide network can be accessed from student residence rooms and from off campus. At least one staffed computer lab available.

Student Life *Housing Options:* coed, men-only, women-only. *Activities and Organizations:* drama/theater group, student-run newspaper, radio station, choral group, Community Outreach, debate team, Washington Guides, Trek Club, entertainment committee. *Campus security:* 24-hour emergency response devices and patrols, student patrols, late-night transport/escort service, controlled dormitory access, self-defense and safety classes. *Student Services:* health clinic, personal/psychological counseling, women's center.

Athletics Member NCAA. All Division III. *Intercollegiate sports:* baseball M, basketball M/W, crew M/W, cross-country running M/W, equestrian sports M/W, field hockey W, lacrosse M/W, rugby M(c)/W(c), soccer M/W, softball W, swimming M/W, tennis M/W, track and field M/W, volleyball M(c)/W. *Intramural sports:* baseball M/W, basketball M/W, fencing M/W, football M/W, golf M/W, soccer M/W, softball M/W, tennis M/W, volleyball M/W, water polo M/W.

Standardized Tests *Required:* SAT I or ACT (for admission). *Recommended:* SAT II: Subject Tests (for admission).

Costs (2001–02) *Tuition:* state resident $1550 full-time, $117 per credit hour part-time; nonresident $8220 full-time, $395 per credit hour part-time. Part-time tuition and fees vary according to course load. *Required fees:* $1790 full-time. *Room and board:* $5692; room only: $3218. Room and board charges vary according to board plan. *Payment plan:* installment. *Waivers:* employees or children of employees.

Financial Aid Of all full-time matriculated undergraduates who enrolled in 2001, 2386 applied for aid, 1545 were judged to have need, 88 had their need fully met. 88 Federal Work-Study jobs (averaging $623). 1459 State and other part-time jobs (averaging $696). In 2001, 387 non-need-based awards were made. *Average percent of need met:* 57%. *Average financial aid package:* $5375. *Average need-based loan:* $4456. *Average need-based gift aid:* $2610. *Average indebtedness upon graduation:* $12,200. *Financial aid deadline:* 3/1.

Applying *Options:* electronic application, early decision, deferred entrance. *Application fee:* $35. *Required:* essay or personal statement, high school transcript. *Application deadlines:* 2/1 (freshmen), 3/1 (transfers). *Early decision:* 11/1. *Notification:* 4/1 (freshmen), 12/15 (early decision).

Admissions Contact Dr. Jenifer Blair, Dean of Undergraduate Admissions, Mary Washington College, 1301 College Avenue, Fredericksburg, VA 22401-5358. *Phone:* 540-654-2000. *Toll-free phone:* 800-468-5614. *E-mail:* admit@mwc.edu.

NATIONAL COLLEGE OF BUSINESS & TECHNOLOGY

Salem, Virginia

- **Proprietary** primarily 2-year, founded 1886, part of National College of Business and Technology
- **Calendar** quarters
- **Degrees** certificates, diplomas, associate, and bachelor's
- **Urban** 3-acre campus
- **Coed**
- **Noncompetitive** entrance level, 100% of applicants were admitted

Undergraduates Students come from 15 other countries, 24% are from out of state. *Retention:* 70% of 2001 full-time freshmen returned.

Freshmen *Admission:* 346 applied, 346 admitted.

Faculty *Student/faculty ratio:* 12:1.

Majors Accounting; accounting technician; business; business marketing and marketing management; computer/information sciences; executive assistant; hospitality management; hotel and restaurant management; medical assistant; office management; secretarial science; tourism/travel marketing.

Academic Programs *Special study options:* academic remediation for entering students, advanced placement credit, double majors, internships, part-time degree program, summer session for credit.

Library Main Library plus 1 other with 25,867 titles, 40 serial subscriptions.

Computers on Campus 35 computers available on campus for general student use. Internet access, at least one staffed computer lab available.

Student Life *Housing Options:* coed.

Costs (2001–02) *Comprehensive fee:* $7308 includes full-time tuition ($5013), mandatory fees ($45), and room and board ($2250). Full-time tuition and fees vary according to course load. Part-time tuition: $148 per credit hour. Part-time tuition and fees vary according to course load. *Required fees:* $15 per term part-time. *Payment plans:* installment, deferred payment. *Waivers:* employees or children of employees.

Financial Aid Of all full-time matriculated undergraduates who enrolled in 2001, 6 Federal Work-Study jobs.

Applying *Application fee:* $30. *Required:* high school transcript. *Recommended:* interview. *Application deadline:* rolling (freshmen), rolling (transfers).

Admissions Contact Ms. Bunnie Hancock, Admissions Representative, National College of Business & Technology, PO Box 6400, Roanoke, VA 24017. *Phone:* 540-986-1800. *Toll-free phone:* 800-664-1886. *Fax:* 540-986-1344. *E-mail:* market@educorp.edu.

NORFOLK STATE UNIVERSITY

Norfolk, Virginia

- **State-supported** comprehensive, founded 1935, part of State Council of Higher Education for Virginia
- **Calendar** semesters
- **Degrees** certificates, associate, bachelor's, master's, doctoral, and postbachelor's certificates
- **Urban** 130-acre campus
- **Endowment** $4.9 million
- **Coed,** 5,963 undergraduate students, 80% full-time, 63% women, 37% men
- **Moderately difficult** entrance level, 80% of applicants were admitted

Undergraduates 4,764 full-time, 1,199 part-time. Students come from 45 states and territories, 37 other countries, 32% are from out of state, 92% African American, 0.7% Asian American or Pacific Islander, 1% Hispanic American, 0.2% Native American, 0.9% international, 5% transferred in, 35% live on campus. *Retention:* 66% of 2001 full-time freshmen returned.

Freshmen *Admission:* 3,989 applied, 3,204 admitted, 1,133 enrolled. *Average high school GPA:* 2.58. *Test scores:* SAT verbal scores over 500: 17%; SAT math scores over 500: 13%; ACT scores over 18: 38%; SAT verbal scores over 600: 1%; SAT math scores over 600: 1%; ACT scores over 24: 2%.

Faculty *Total:* 466, 64% full-time. *Student/faculty ratio:* 15:1.

Majors Accounting; architectural engineering technology; art; biology; business; business education; chemistry; computer engineering technology; computer/information sciences; computer science; construction technology; drafting/design technology; early childhood education; economics; electrical/electronic engineering technology; electrical engineering; English; exercise sciences; health services administration; history; home economics; home economics related; interdisciplinary studies; journalism; labor/personnel relations; mass communications; mathematics; medical records administration; medical technology; multi/interdisciplinary studies related; music; nursing; office management; physics; political science; psychology; social work; sociology; special education; trade/industrial education.

Academic Programs *Special study options:* accelerated degree program, adult/continuing education programs, advanced placement credit, cooperative education, freshman honors college, honors programs, independent study, internships, off-campus study, part-time degree program, services for LD students, student-designed majors, summer session for credit. *ROTC:* Army (b), Navy (b).

Library Lymon Beecher Brooks Library with 597,878 titles, an OPAC.

Computers on Campus 512 computers available on campus for general student use. A campuswide network can be accessed from student residence rooms and from off campus. Internet access, online (class) registration, at least one staffed computer lab available.

Student Life *Housing Options:* men-only, women-only. *Activities and Organizations:* drama/theater group, student-run newspaper, radio and television station, choral group, marching band, Student Virginia Education Association, National Society of Minority Hospitality Management, national fraternities, national sororities. *Campus security:* 24-hour patrols, late-night transport/escort service, campus call boxes. *Student Services:* health clinic, personal/psychological counseling, women's center.

Athletics Member NCAA. All Division I except football (Division I-AA). *Intercollegiate sports:* baseball M, basketball M(s)/W(s), cross-country running M(s)/W(s), softball W(s), tennis M(s)/W(s), track and field M(s)/W(s), volleyball W(s), wrestling M(s). *Intramural sports:* badminton M, basketball M/W, bowling M/W, cross-country running M/W, football M, riflery M/W, soccer M, softball M/W, swimming M/W, table tennis M/W, tennis M/W, track and field M/W, volleyball M/W, weight lifting M/W, wrestling M.

Standardized Tests *Required:* SAT I or ACT (for admission).

Costs (2001–02) *One-time required fee:* $35. *Tuition:* state resident $1326 full-time, $51 per credit part-time; nonresident $7228 full-time, $278 per credit part-time. Full-time tuition and fees vary according to course load. Part-time tuition and fees vary according to course load. *Required fees:* $1590 full-time, $57 per credit part-time. *Room and board:* $5466; room only: $3416. Room and board charges vary according to board plan and housing facility. *Payment plans:* installment, deferred payment. *Waivers:* senior citizens and employees or children of employees.

Financial Aid Of all full-time matriculated undergraduates who enrolled in 2001, 4258 applied for aid, 3591 were judged to have need. 324 Federal Work-Study jobs (averaging $1308). 181 State and other part-time jobs (averaging $1189). *Average financial aid package:* $6950. *Average need-based loan:* $3238. *Average need-based gift aid:* $4270. *Average indebtedness upon graduation:* $15,000.

Applying *Options:* common application, deferred entrance. *Application fee:* $25. *Required:* high school transcript, minimum 2.0 GPA. *Required for some:* letters of recommendation. *Application deadline:* rolling (freshmen), rolling (transfers).

Admissions Contact Ms. Michelle Marable, Director of Admissions, Norfolk State University, 700 Park Avenue, Norfolk, VA 23504. *Phone:* 757-823-8396. *Fax:* 757-823-2078. *E-mail:* admissions@nsu.edu.

OLD DOMINION UNIVERSITY

Norfolk, Virginia

- **State-supported** university, founded 1930
- **Calendar** semesters
- **Degrees** bachelor's, master's, doctoral, and post-master's certificates
- **Urban** 186-acre campus with easy access to Virginia Beach
- **Endowment** $73.2 million
- **Coed,** 13,098 undergraduate students, 67% full-time, 57% women, 43% men
- **Moderately difficult** entrance level, 70% of applicants were admitted

Undergraduates 8,741 full-time, 4,357 part-time. Students come from 48 states and territories, 95 other countries, 8% are from out of state, 23% African American, 7% Asian American or Pacific Islander, 3% Hispanic American, 0.7% Native American, 3% international, 11% transferred in, 23% live on campus. *Retention:* 77% of 2001 full-time freshmen returned.

Freshmen *Admission:* 5,780 applied, 4,073 admitted, 1,559 enrolled. *Average high school GPA:* 3.14. *Test scores:* SAT verbal scores over 500: 59%; SAT math scores over 500: 55%; SAT verbal scores over 600: 15%; SAT math scores over 600: 14%; SAT verbal scores over 700: 1%; SAT math scores over 700: 1%.

Faculty *Total:* 934, 65% full-time. *Student/faculty ratio:* 16:1.

Majors Accounting; art; art history; biochemistry; biology; business administration; business economics; business marketing and marketing management; chemistry; civil engineering; computer engineering; computer/information sciences; criminology; dental hygiene; economics; electrical engineering; engineering technologies related; English; environmental engineering; finance; foreign languages/literatures; geography; geology; health professions and related sciences; history; international relations; management information systems/business data processing; mathematics; mechanical engineering; medical technology; mental health services related; multi/interdisciplinary studies related; music (general performance); nuclear medical technology; nursing; philosophy; physical education; physics; political science; psychology; recreation/leisure facilities management; sociology; speech-language pathology/audiology; speech/rhetorical studies; teacher education, specific programs related; theater arts/drama; women's studies.

Academic Programs *Special study options:* accelerated degree program, adult/continuing education programs, advanced placement credit, cooperative education, distance learning, double majors, English as a second language, external degree program, freshman honors college, honors programs, independent study, internships, off-campus study, part-time degree program, services for LD students, student-designed majors, study abroad, summer session for credit. *ROTC:* Army (b), Navy (b).

Library Douglas and Patricia Perry Library plus 2 others with 585,396 titles, 7,985 serial subscriptions, 39,050 audiovisual materials, an OPAC, a Web page.

Computers on Campus 790 computers available on campus for general student use. A campuswide network can be accessed from student residence rooms and from off campus that provide access to on-line courses. Internet access, online (class) registration, at least one staffed computer lab available.

Student Life *Housing Options:* coed. *Activities and Organizations:* drama/theater group, student-run newspaper, radio station, choral group, Black Student Alliance, Council of International Student Organizations, WODU (radio station), Golden Key National Honor Society, Filipino American Student Association, national fraternities, national sororities. *Campus security:* 24-hour emergency response devices and patrols, late-night transport/escort service, controlled dormitory access. *Student Services:* health clinic, personal/psychological counseling, women's center.

Old Dominion University (continued)

Athletics Member NCAA. All Division I. *Intercollegiate sports:* baseball M(s), basketball M(s)/W(s)(c), crew M(c)/W(c), cross-country running W(s), fencing M(c)/W(c), field hockey M(c)/W(s)(c), golf M(s), lacrosse M(c)/W(s), rugby M(c)/W(c), sailing M/W, soccer M(s)/W(s), swimming M(s)/W(s), tennis M(s)/W(s), wrestling M(s). *Intramural sports:* badminton M/W, basketball M/W, bowling M/W, golf M/W, soccer M/W, softball M/W, swimming M/W, table tennis M/W, tennis M/W, volleyball M/W, water polo M/W, wrestling M/W.

Standardized Tests *Required:* SAT I or ACT (for admission).

Costs (2001–02) *Tuition:* state resident $3870 full-time, $129 per credit hour part-time; nonresident $12,240 full-time, $408 per credit hour part-time. Full-time tuition and fees vary according to class time, course load, and location. Part-time tuition and fees vary according to class time, course load, and location. *Required fees:* $152 full-time, $55 per credit hour, $30 per term part-time. *Room and board:* $5364; room only: $3102. Room and board charges vary according to board plan and housing facility. *Payment plans:* installment, deferred payment. *Waivers:* senior citizens and employees or children of employees.

Financial Aid Of all full-time matriculated undergraduates who enrolled in 2001, 6973 applied for aid, 4866 were judged to have need, 1804 had their need fully met. In 2001, 755 non-need-based awards were made. *Average percent of need met:* 72%. *Average financial aid package:* $6821. *Average need-based loan:* $3668. *Average need-based gift aid:* $3916. *Average non-need based aid:* $2894. *Average indebtedness upon graduation:* $16,500. *Financial aid deadline:* 3/15.

Applying *Options:* common application, electronic application, early admission, early action, deferred entrance. *Application fee:* $30. *Required:* high school transcript, minimum 2.5 GPA. *Required for some:* essay or personal statement, interview. *Recommended:* essay or personal statement, 2 letters of recommendation, interview. *Application deadlines:* 2/15 (freshmen), 6/1 (transfers). *Notification:* 3/15 (freshmen), 1/15 (early action).

Admissions Contact Ms. Alice McAdory, (Acting) Director of Admissions, Old Dominion University, 108 Rollins Hall, Norfolk, VA 23529-0050. *Phone:* 757-683-3637. *Toll-free phone:* 800-348-7926. *Fax:* 757-683-3255. *E-mail:* admit@odu.edu.

RADFORD UNIVERSITY
Radford, Virginia

- **State-supported** comprehensive, founded 1910
- **Calendar** semesters
- **Degrees** bachelor's, master's, and post-master's certificates
- **Small-town** 177-acre campus
- **Endowment** $25.8 million
- **Coed,** 8,061 undergraduate students, 93% full-time, 60% women, 40% men
- **Moderately difficult** entrance level, 75% of applicants were admitted

Undergraduates 7,526 full-time, 535 part-time. Students come from 45 states and territories, 65 other countries, 12% are from out of state, 6% African American, 2% Asian American or Pacific Islander, 2% Hispanic American, 0.3% Native American, 1% international, 9% transferred in, 40% live on campus. *Retention:* 79% of 2001 full-time freshmen returned.

Freshmen *Admission:* 6,278 applied, 4,710 admitted, 1,877 enrolled. *Average high school GPA:* 3.03. *Test scores:* SAT verbal scores over 500: 50%; SAT math scores over 500: 47%; ACT scores over 18: 83%; SAT verbal scores over 600: 9%; SAT math scores over 600: 9%; SAT verbal scores over 700: 1%.

Faculty *Total:* 551, 65% full-time, 59% with terminal degrees. *Student/faculty ratio:* 20:1.

Majors Accounting; anthropology; art; biology; business administration; business marketing and marketing management; chemistry; communication disorders; communications; computer science; criminal justice/law enforcement administration; dance; dietetics; economics; English; fashion design/illustration; finance; foreign languages/literatures; geography; geology; health education; history; individual/family development; interdisciplinary studies; interior design; journalism; liberal arts and sciences/liberal studies; management information systems/business data processing; mathematics; medical technology; music; music therapy; nursing; office management; philosophy; physical education; physical sciences; political science; psychology; recreation/leisure studies; religious studies; social sciences; social work; sociology; theater arts/drama.

Academic Programs *Special study options:* accelerated degree program, adult/continuing education programs, advanced placement credit, distance learning, double majors, English as a second language, honors programs, independent study, internships, off-campus study, part-time degree program, services for LD students, student-designed majors, study abroad, summer session for credit. *ROTC:* Army (b), Navy (c).

Library McConnell Library with 527,789 titles, 14,914 audiovisual materials, an OPAC, a Web page.

Computers on Campus 460 computers available on campus for general student use. A campuswide network can be accessed from student residence rooms and from off campus. Internet access, at least one staffed computer lab available.

Student Life *Housing:* on-campus residence required for freshman year. *Options:* coed, women-only. *Activities and Organizations:* drama/theater group, student-run newspaper, radio and television station, choral group, Student Government Association, Student Education Association, international club, ski club, Student Life Committee, national fraternities, national sororities. *Campus security:* 24-hour emergency response devices and patrols, student patrols, late-night transport/escort service, controlled dormitory access. *Student Services:* health clinic, personal/psychological counseling.

Athletics Member NCAA. All Division I. *Intercollegiate sports:* baseball M(s), basketball M(s)/W(s), cross-country running M(s)/W(s), field hockey W(s), golf M(s)/W(s), lacrosse M(s), soccer M(s)/W(s), softball W(s), tennis M(s)/W(s), track and field M(s)/W(s), volleyball W(s). *Intramural sports:* basketball M/W, bowling M/W, cross-country running M/W, equestrian sports M(c)/W(c), football M, ice hockey M(c), racquetball M/W, rugby M(c)/W(c), skiing (downhill) M(c)/W(c), soccer M/W, softball M/W, swimming M/W, tennis M/W, volleyball M/W, water polo M/W.

Standardized Tests *Required:* SAT I or ACT (for admission).

Costs (2001–02) *Tuition:* state resident $1629 full-time, $128 per credit hour part-time; nonresident $7768 full-time, $384 per credit hour part-time. *Required fees:* $1440 full-time. *Room and board:* $5233; room only: $2835. Room and board charges vary according to board plan and housing facility. *Payment plan:* installment. *Waivers:* employees or children of employees.

Financial Aid Of all full-time matriculated undergraduates who enrolled in 2001, 4673 applied for aid, 3149 were judged to have need, 2118 had their need fully met. 482 Federal Work-Study jobs (averaging $1445). 795 State and other part-time jobs (averaging $1310). *Average percent of need met:* 85%. *Average financial aid package:* $7360. *Average need-based loan:* $3243. *Average need-based gift aid:* $3410. *Average indebtedness upon graduation:* $13,442.

Applying *Options:* common application, electronic application, early admission. *Application fee:* $20. *Required:* high school transcript, minimum 2.0 GPA. *Required for some:* essay or personal statement. *Recommended:* 1 letter of recommendation, interview. *Application deadline:* 5/1 (freshmen), rolling (transfers). *Notification:* continuous until 6/1 (freshmen).

Admissions Contact Dr. David Kraus, Director of Admissions and Records, Radford University, PO Box 6903, RU Station, Radford, VA 24142. *Phone:* 540-831-5371. *Toll-free phone:* 800-890-4265. *Fax:* 540-831-5038. *E-mail:* ruadmiss@runet.edu.

RANDOLPH-MACON COLLEGE
Ashland, Virginia

- **Independent United Methodist** 4-year, founded 1830
- **Calendar** 4-1-4
- **Degree** bachelor's
- **Suburban** 110-acre campus with easy access to Richmond
- **Endowment** $83.8 million
- **Coed,** 1,150 undergraduate students, 97% full-time, 49% women, 51% men
- **Moderately difficult** entrance level, 80% of applicants were admitted

Undergraduates 1,113 full-time, 37 part-time. Students come from 33 states and territories, 16 other countries, 40% are from out of state, 5% African American, 1.0% Asian American or Pacific Islander, 1% Hispanic American, 0.1% Native American, 1% international, 2% transferred in, 90% live on campus. *Retention:* 78% of 2001 full-time freshmen returned.

Freshmen *Admission:* 1,744 applied, 1,392 admitted, 311 enrolled. *Average high school GPA:* 3.11. *Test scores:* SAT verbal scores over 500: 80%; SAT math scores over 500: 78%; SAT verbal scores over 600: 24%; SAT math scores over 600: 21%; SAT verbal scores over 700: 5%.

Faculty *Total:* 137, 61% full-time, 74% with terminal degrees. *Student/faculty ratio:* 11:1.

Majors Accounting; art; art history; arts management; biology; business economics; chemistry; classics; computer science; economics; English; environmental science; fine/studio arts; French; German; Greek (ancient and medieval); history; international relations; Latin (ancient and medieval); mathematics; music; philosophy; physics; political science; psychology; religious studies; sociology; Spanish; theater arts/drama; women's studies.

Academic Programs *Special study options:* academic remediation for entering students, accelerated degree program, advanced placement credit, double majors, honors programs, independent study, internships, off-campus study, part-time degree program, services for LD students, study abroad, summer session for credit. *ROTC:* Army (c). *Unusual degree programs:* 3-2 engineering with Columbia University, University of Virginia; forestry with Duke University.

Library McGraw-Page Library with 171,531 titles, 1,455 serial subscriptions, 7,819 audiovisual materials, an OPAC, a Web page.

Computers on Campus 185 computers available on campus for general student use. A campuswide network can be accessed from student residence rooms and from off campus. Internet access, at least one staffed computer lab available.

Student Life *Housing:* on-campus residence required through junior year. *Options:* coed, men-only, women-only. *Activities and Organizations:* drama/theater group, student-run newspaper, radio and television station, choral group, Christian Fellowship, Campus Activities Board/Student Government Association, Drama Guild, intramural sports, Student Honors Association, national fraternities, national sororities. *Campus security:* 24-hour emergency response devices and patrols, late-night transport/escort service, controlled dormitory access. *Student Services:* health clinic, personal/psychological counseling, women's center.

Athletics Member NCAA. All Division III. *Intercollegiate sports:* baseball M, basketball M/W, field hockey W, football M, golf M, lacrosse M/W, soccer M/W, softball W, swimming W, tennis M/W, volleyball W. *Intramural sports:* basketball M/W, football M/W, lacrosse M/W, racquetball M/W, soccer M/W, softball M/W, table tennis M/W, volleyball M/W.

Standardized Tests *Required:* SAT I or ACT (for admission). *Recommended:* SAT II: Subject Tests (for admission), SAT II: Writing Test (for admission).

Costs (2001–02) *One-time required fee:* $75. *Comprehensive fee:* $24,395 includes full-time tuition ($18,570), mandatory fees ($525), and room and board ($5300). Part-time tuition: $186 per credit hour. Part-time tuition and fees vary according to course load. *Room and board:* College room only: $2760. Room and board charges vary according to board plan and housing facility. *Payment plan:* installment. *Waivers:* employees or children of employees.

Financial Aid Of all full-time matriculated undergraduates who enrolled in 2001, 729 applied for aid, 607 were judged to have need, 180 had their need fully met. 265 Federal Work-Study jobs (averaging $1110). In 2001, 383 non-need-based awards were made. *Average percent of need met:* 87%. *Average financial aid package:* $14,242. *Average need-based loan:* $4404. *Average need-based gift aid:* $10,089. *Average indebtedness upon graduation:* $17,416.

Applying *Options:* common application, electronic application, early admission, early decision, deferred entrance. *Application fee:* $30. *Required:* essay or personal statement, high school transcript, 1 letter of recommendation. *Recommended:* interview. *Application deadlines:* 3/1 (freshmen), 3/1 (transfers). *Early decision:* 12/1. *Notification:* continuous until 4/1 (freshmen), 12/20 (early decision).

Admissions Contact Mr. John C. Conkright, Dean of Admissions and Financial Aid, Randolph-Macon College, PO Box 5005, Ashland, VA 23005-5505. *Phone:* 804-752-7305. *Toll-free phone:* 800-888-1762. *Fax:* 804-752-4707. *E-mail:* admissions@rmc.edu.

RANDOLPH-MACON WOMAN'S COLLEGE
Lynchburg, Virginia

- **Independent Methodist** 4-year, founded 1891
- **Calendar** semesters
- **Degree** bachelor's
- **Suburban** 100-acre campus
- **Endowment** $133.9 million
- **Women only,** 721 undergraduate students, 95% full-time
- **Moderately difficult** entrance level, 87% of applicants were admitted

Undergraduates 688 full-time, 33 part-time. Students come from 47 states and territories, 44 other countries, 50% are from out of state, 7% African American, 3% Asian American or Pacific Islander, 3% Hispanic American, 0.6% Native American, 11% international, 5% transferred in, 90% live on campus. *Retention:* 76% of 2001 full-time freshmen returned.

Freshmen *Admission:* 189 enrolled. *Average high school GPA:* 3.44. *Test scores:* SAT verbal scores over 500: 89%; SAT math scores over 500: 80%; ACT scores over 18: 96%; SAT verbal scores over 600: 56%; SAT math scores over 600: 34%; ACT scores over 24: 70%; SAT verbal scores over 700: 19%; SAT math scores over 700: 3%; ACT scores over 30: 21%.

Faculty *Total:* 94, 77% full-time, 76% with terminal degrees. *Student/faculty ratio:* 9:1.

Majors American studies; art; art history; biology; chemistry; classics; creative writing; dance; economics; English; environmental science; fine/studio arts; French; German; Greek (ancient and medieval); health professions and related sciences; history; international relations; Latin (ancient and medieval); liberal arts and sciences/liberal studies; mass communications; mathematics; museum studies; music; music history; music (voice and choral/opera performance); philosophy; physics; political science; psychology; religious studies; Russian/Slavic studies; sociology; Spanish; theater arts/drama.

Academic Programs *Special study options:* accelerated degree program, adult/continuing education programs, advanced placement credit, double majors, honors programs, independent study, internships, off-campus study, part-time degree program, services for LD students, student-designed majors, study abroad. *Unusual degree programs:* 3-2 nursing with Johns Hopkins University.

Library Lipscomb Library with 123,500 titles, 1,200 serial subscriptions, 3,000 audiovisual materials, an OPAC, a Web page.

Computers on Campus 154 computers available on campus for general student use. A campuswide network can be accessed from student residence rooms and from off campus. Internet access, online (class) registration, at least one staffed computer lab available.

Student Life *Housing:* on-campus residence required through senior year. *Options:* women-only. *Activities and Organizations:* drama/theater group, student-run newspaper, radio station, choral group, Pan World Club, Macon Activities Council, Model United Nations, BIONIC (Believe It or Not, I Care volunteer organization), Black Woman's Alliance. *Campus security:* 24-hour emergency response devices and patrols, late-night transport/escort service. *Student Services:* health clinic, personal/psychological counseling.

Athletics Member NCAA. All Division III. *Intercollegiate sports:* basketball W, equestrian sports W, field hockey W, lacrosse W, soccer W, softball W, swimming W, tennis W, volleyball W.

Standardized Tests *Required:* SAT I or ACT (for admission).

Costs (2001–02) *Comprehensive fee:* $25,820 includes full-time tuition ($18,090), mandatory fees ($380), and room and board ($7350). Part-time tuition: $750 per semester hour. Part-time tuition and fees vary according to course load. *Required fees:* $45 per term part-time. *Payment plan:* installment. *Waivers:* adult students and employees or children of employees.

Financial Aid Of all full-time matriculated undergraduates who enrolled in 2001, 462 applied for aid, 402 were judged to have need, 170 had their need fully met. 78 Federal Work-Study jobs (averaging $1860). 320 State and other part-time jobs (averaging $1174). In 2001, 262 non-need-based awards were made. *Average percent of need met:* 91%. *Average financial aid package:* $18,268. *Average need-based loan:* $3862. *Average need-based gift aid:* $13,103. *Average indebtedness upon graduation:* $19,100.

Applying *Options:* common application, electronic application, early admission, early decision, deferred entrance. *Application fee:* $35. *Required:* essay or personal statement, high school transcript, 2 letters of recommendation. *Recommended:* interview. *Application deadlines:* 3/1 (freshmen), 6/1 (transfers). *Early decision:* 11/15. *Notification:* continuous (freshmen), 12/15 (early decision).

Admissions Contact Pat LeDonne, Director of Admissions, Randolph-Macon Woman's College, 2500 Rivermont Avenue, Lynchburg, VA 24503-1526. *Phone:* 434-947-8100. *Toll-free phone:* 800-745-7692. *Fax:* 434-947-8996. *E-mail:* admissions@rmwc.edu.

ROANOKE COLLEGE
Salem, Virginia

- **Independent** 4-year, founded 1842, affiliated with Evangelical Lutheran Church in America
- **Calendar** semesters
- **Degree** bachelor's
- **Suburban** 68-acre campus
- **Endowment** $90.0 million
- **Coed,** 1,790 undergraduate students, 93% full-time, 62% women, 38% men
- **Moderately difficult** entrance level, 74% of applicants were admitted

Undergraduates 1,666 full-time, 124 part-time. Students come from 40 states and territories, 16 other countries, 42% are from out of state, 4% African American, 1% Asian American or Pacific Islander, 2% Hispanic American, 0.3% Native American, 1% international, 5% transferred in, 57% live on campus. *Retention:* 79% of 2001 full-time freshmen returned.

Freshmen *Admission:* 2,687 applied, 1,990 admitted, 498 enrolled. *Average high school GPA:* 3.25. *Test scores:* SAT verbal scores over 500: 80%; SAT math scores over 500: 80%; SAT verbal scores over 600: 33%; SAT math scores over 600: 24%; SAT verbal scores over 700: 4%; SAT math scores over 700: 2%.

Faculty *Total:* 176, 69% full-time, 65% with terminal degrees. *Student/faculty ratio:* 14:1.

Majors Art; athletic training/sports medicine; biochemistry; biology; business administration; chemistry; computer science; criminal justice studies; economics; English; environmental science; French; health/physical education; history; information sciences/systems; international relations; mathematics; medical technology; music; philosophy; physics; political science; psychology; religious studies; sociology; Spanish; theater arts/drama; theology.

Academic Programs *Special study options:* accelerated degree program, adult/continuing education programs, advanced placement credit, double majors,

Roanoke College (continued)
English as a second language, honors programs, independent study, internships, off-campus study, part-time degree program, services for LD students, study abroad, summer session for credit. *Unusual degree programs:* 3-2 engineering with Washington University in St. Louis, Virginia Polytechnic Institute and State University.

Library Fintel Library plus 1 other with 425,000 titles, 15,200 serial subscriptions, 6,000 audiovisual materials, an OPAC, a Web page.

Computers on Campus 150 computers available on campus for general student use. A campuswide network can be accessed from student residence rooms and from off campus. Internet access, at least one staffed computer lab available.

Student Life *Housing:* on-campus residence required through senior year. *Options:* coed, men-only, women-only. *Activities and Organizations:* drama/theater group, student-run newspaper, radio station, choral group, Alpha Phi Omega, Habitat for Humanity, Earthbound Environment Group, Campus Activities Board, Hiking Club, national fraternities, national sororities. *Campus security:* 24-hour emergency response devices and patrols, late-night transport/escort service, controlled dormitory access. *Student Services:* health clinic, personal/psychological counseling.

Athletics Member NCAA. All Division III. *Intercollegiate sports:* baseball M, basketball M/W, cross-country running M/W, field hockey W, golf M/W(c), ice hockey M(c), lacrosse M/W, soccer M/W, softball W, tennis M/W, track and field M/W, volleyball M(c)/W. *Intramural sports:* badminton M/W, basketball M/W, field hockey W, football M/W, ice hockey M, lacrosse M, racquetball M/W, soccer M/W, softball M/W, table tennis M/W, tennis M/W, volleyball M/W, water polo M/W.

Standardized Tests *Required:* SAT I or ACT (for admission).

Costs (2001–02) *Comprehensive fee:* $24,689 includes full-time tuition ($18,186), mandatory fees ($495), and room and board ($6008). Part-time tuition: $865 per course. *Required fees:* $25 per term part-time. *Room and board:* College room only: $3092. *Payment plan:* installment. *Waivers:* senior citizens and employees or children of employees.

Financial Aid Of all full-time matriculated undergraduates who enrolled in 2001, 1163 applied for aid, 1154 were judged to have need, 341 had their need fully met. In 2001, 417 non-need-based awards were made. *Average percent of need met:* 95%. *Average financial aid package:* $16,390. *Average need-based loan:* $4185. *Average need-based gift aid:* $12,813. *Average non-need based aid:* $9540. *Average indebtedness upon graduation:* $15,284.

Applying *Options:* common application, electronic application, early admission, early decision, early action, deferred entrance. *Application fee:* $30. *Required:* high school transcript. *Recommended:* essay or personal statement, 3 letters of recommendation, interview. *Application deadlines:* 3/1 (freshmen), 8/1 (transfers). *Early decision:* 11/15. *Notification:* 4/1 (freshmen), 11/30 (early decision), 10/15 (early action).

Admissions Contact Mr. Michael C. Maxey, Vice President of Admissions, Roanoke College, 221 College Lane, Salem, VA 24153. *Phone:* 540-375-2270. *Toll-free phone:* 800-388-2276. *Fax:* 540-375-2267. *E-mail:* admissions@roanoke.edu.

SAINT PAUL'S COLLEGE
Lawrenceville, Virginia

- **Independent Episcopal** 4-year, founded 1888
- **Calendar** semesters
- **Degree** bachelor's
- **Small-town** 75-acre campus with easy access to Richmond
- **Coed**
- **Minimally difficult** entrance level

Faculty *Student/faculty ratio:* 17:1.

Student Life *Campus security:* 24-hour emergency response devices and patrols, late-night transport/escort service, alarms on doors.

Athletics Member NCAA. All Division II.

Standardized Tests *Required:* SAT I or ACT (for placement).

Financial Aid Of all full-time matriculated undergraduates who enrolled in 2001, 409 applied for aid, 386 were judged to have need, 3 had their need fully met. 245 Federal Work-Study jobs (averaging $1514). *Average percent of need met:* 90. *Average financial aid package:* $11,564. *Average need-based loan:* $2887. *Average need-based gift aid:* $7702. *Average indebtedness upon graduation:* $13,258.

Applying *Options:* common application, deferred entrance. *Application fee:* $20. *Required:* high school transcript, 1 letter of recommendation. *Recommended:* essay or personal statement, interview.

Admissions Contact Mr. Michael C. Taylor, Director of Admissions, Saint Paul's College, 115 College Drive, Lawrenceville, VA 23868. *Phone:* 804-848-4268. *Toll-free phone:* 800-678-7071.

SHENANDOAH UNIVERSITY
Winchester, Virginia

- **Independent United Methodist** comprehensive, founded 1875
- **Calendar** semesters
- **Degrees** certificates, associate, bachelor's, master's, doctoral, first professional, and postbachelor's certificates
- **Small-town** 100-acre campus with easy access to Baltimore and Washington, DC
- **Endowment** $41.5 million
- **Coed,** 1,361 undergraduate students, 91% full-time, 57% women, 43% men
- **Moderately difficult** entrance level, 100% of applicants were admitted

Undergraduates 1,241 full-time, 120 part-time. Students come from 38 states and territories, 21 other countries, 37% are from out of state, 9% African American, 1% Asian American or Pacific Islander, 2% Hispanic American, 0.3% Native American, 4% international, 10% transferred in, 42% live on campus. *Retention:* 68% of 2001 full-time freshmen returned.

Freshmen *Admission:* 1,055 applied, 1,055 admitted, 314 enrolled. *Average high school GPA:* 3.09. *Test scores:* SAT verbal scores over 500: 56%; SAT math scores over 500: 47%; ACT scores over 18: 68%; SAT verbal scores over 600: 17%; SAT math scores over 600: 12%; ACT scores over 24: 18%; SAT verbal scores over 700: 4%; SAT math scores over 700: 1%; ACT scores over 30: 9%.

Faculty *Total:* 288, 55% full-time, 53% with terminal degrees. *Student/faculty ratio:* 10:1.

Majors American studies; arts management; biology; business administration; chemistry; communications; criminal justice/law enforcement administration; dance; educational psychology; English; environmental science; history; liberal arts and sciences/liberal studies; mathematics; music; music (general performance); music (piano and organ performance); music related; music teacher education; music theory and composition; music therapy; nursing; physical education; psychology; public administration; religious studies; respiratory therapy; sociology; theater arts/drama; theater arts/drama and stagecraft related; visual/performing arts.

Academic Programs *Special study options:* accelerated degree program, adult/continuing education programs, advanced placement credit, distance learning, double majors, English as a second language, independent study, internships, off-campus study, part-time degree program, services for LD students, study abroad, summer session for credit.

Library Alson H. Smith Jr. Library plus 1 other with 117,800 titles, 9,160 serial subscriptions, 17,100 audiovisual materials, an OPAC, a Web page.

Computers on Campus 170 computers available on campus for general student use. A campuswide network can be accessed from student residence rooms and from off campus. Internet access, online (class) registration, at least one staffed computer lab available.

Student Life *Housing:* on-campus residence required through senior year. *Options:* coed, women-only, disabled students. *Activities and Organizations:* drama/theater group, student-run newspaper, radio and television station, choral group, Harambee Singers, Alpha Psi Omega, Phi Mu Alpha, Student Government Association, Intervarsity Student Council. *Campus security:* 24-hour emergency response devices and patrols, late-night transport/escort service, controlled dormitory access, side door alarms, guard gate house, bike patrols. *Student Services:* health clinic, personal/psychological counseling.

Athletics Member NCAA. All Division III. *Intercollegiate sports:* baseball M, basketball M/W, cross-country running M/W, football M, golf M, lacrosse M/W, soccer M/W, softball W, tennis M/W, volleyball W. *Intramural sports:* basketball M/W, bowling M/W, soccer M/W, softball M/W, table tennis M/W, tennis M/W, volleyball M/W.

Standardized Tests *Required:* SAT I or ACT (for admission).

Costs (2001–02) *Comprehensive fee:* $23,400 includes full-time tuition ($17,000) and room and board ($6400). Full-time tuition and fees vary according to course load. Part-time tuition: $520 per credit hour. Part-time tuition and fees vary according to course load. *Room and board:* Room and board charges vary according to board plan. *Payment plan:* deferred payment. *Waivers:* employees or children of employees.

Financial Aid Of all full-time matriculated undergraduates who enrolled in 2001, 1154 applied for aid, 1078 were judged to have need, 171 had their need fully met. 389 Federal Work-Study jobs (averaging $1093). 223 State and other part-time jobs (averaging $1565). *Average percent of need met:* 84%. *Average financial aid package:* $11,720. *Average need-based loan:* $5604. *Average* *need-based gift aid:* $2580. *Average non-need based aid:* $6212. *Average indebtedness upon graduation:* $16,160.

Applying *Options:* common application, electronic application, deferred entrance. *Application fee:* $30. *Required:* high school transcript. *Required for some:* interview, audition. *Recommended:* minimum 2.0 GPA. *Application deadline:* rolling (freshmen), rolling (transfers).

Admissions Contact Mr. Michael Carpenter, Director of Admissions, Shenandoah University, 1460 University Drive, Winchester, VA 22601-5195. *Phone:* 540-665-4581. *Toll-free phone:* 800-432-2266. *Fax:* 540-665-4627. *E-mail:* admit@su.edu.

SOUTHERN VIRGINIA UNIVERSITY

Buena Vista, Virginia

- **Independent** 4-year, founded 1867
- **Calendar** semesters
- **Degree** bachelor's
- **Endowment** $600,000
- **Coed,** 481 undergraduate students, 100% full-time, 67% women, 33% men
- 52% of applicants were admitted

Undergraduates 481 full-time. Students come from 43 states and territories, 10 other countries, 75% are from out of state, 0.6% African American, 1% Asian American or Pacific Islander, 2% Hispanic American, 1% Native American, 3% international, 10% transferred in.

Freshmen *Admission:* 398 applied, 206 admitted, 204 enrolled. *Average high school GPA:* 3.10.

Faculty *Total:* 44, 50% with terminal degrees. *Student/faculty ratio:* 14:1.

Majors Art; business administration; English; health/physical education; history; liberal arts and sciences/liberal studies; music; philosophy; Spanish; sport/fitness administration; visual/performing arts; Web page, digital/multimedia and information resources design.

Academic Programs *Special study options:* cooperative education, summer session for credit.

Library an OPAC.

Computers on Campus A campuswide network can be accessed from student residence rooms and from off campus. Internet access, online (class) registration, at least one staffed computer lab available.

Student Life *Activities and Organizations:* drama/theater group, student-run newspaper, choral group. *Campus security:* 24-hour patrols. *Student Services:* health clinic, personal/psychological counseling.

Athletics Member NAIA, NSCAA. *Intercollegiate sports:* baseball M, basketball M/W, cross-country running M/W, lacrosse M, soccer M/W, softball W, track and field M/W, volleyball W, wrestling M.

Standardized Tests *Required:* SAT I or ACT (for admission).

Costs (2002–03) *Comprehensive fee:* $23,500 includes full-time tuition ($18,500) and room and board ($5000). *Payment plan:* installment. *Waivers:* employees or children of employees.

Applying *Options:* common application. *Application fee:* $35. *Recommended:* high school transcript, minimum 2.5 GPA. *Application deadline:* 8/15 (freshmen).

Admissions Contact Tony Caputo, Dean of Admissions, Southern Virginia University, One University Hill Drive, Buena Vista, VA 24416. *Phone:* 540-261-2756. *Toll-free phone:* 800-229-8420. *E-mail:* admissions@southernvirginia.edu.

SWEET BRIAR COLLEGE

Sweet Briar, Virginia

- **Independent** 4-year, founded 1901
- **Calendar** semesters
- **Degree** bachelor's
- **Rural** 3300-acre campus
- **Endowment** $112.4 million
- **Women only,** 738 undergraduate students, 92% full-time
- **Moderately difficult** entrance level, 81% of applicants were admitted

Undergraduates 682 full-time, 56 part-time. Students come from 44 states and territories, 11 other countries, 60% are from out of state, 4% African American, 2% Asian American or Pacific Islander, 3% Hispanic American, 0.7% Native American, 2% international, 2% transferred in, 92% live on campus. *Retention:* 82% of 2001 full-time freshmen returned.

Freshmen *Admission:* 159 enrolled. *Average high school GPA:* 3.43. *Test scores:* SAT verbal scores over 500: 79%; SAT math scores over 500: 72%; ACT scores over 18: 92%; SAT verbal scores over 600: 40%; SAT math scores over 600: 28%; ACT scores over 24: 54%; SAT verbal scores over 700: 5%; SAT math scores over 700: 2%; ACT scores over 30: 9%.

Faculty *Total:* 116, 61% full-time, 74% with terminal degrees. *Student/faculty ratio:* 7:1.

Majors Anthropology; art history; biochemistry; biology; business administration/management related; chemistry; classics; computer science; creative writing; dance; economics; English; environmental science; European studies; fine/studio arts; French; general studies; German; Greek (ancient and medieval); history; interdisciplinary studies; international relations; Italian; Italian studies; Latin (ancient and medieval); mathematics; mathematics related; modern languages; music; philosophy; physics; political science; psychology; religious studies; sociology; Spanish; theater arts/drama.

Academic Programs *Special study options:* accelerated degree program, adult/continuing education programs, advanced placement credit, double majors, honors programs, independent study, internships, off-campus study, part-time degree program, services for LD students, student-designed majors, study abroad, summer session for credit. *Unusual degree programs:* 3-2 engineering with Virginia Polytechnic Institute and State University, University of Virginia, Columbia University, Washington University in St. Louis.

Library Mary Helen Cochran Library plus 3 others with 474,818 titles, 9,792 serial subscriptions, 6,634 audiovisual materials, an OPAC, a Web page.

Computers on Campus 117 computers available on campus for general student use. A campuswide network can be accessed from student residence rooms and from off campus. Internet access, at least one staffed computer lab available.

Student Life *Housing:* on-campus residence required through senior year. *Options:* women-only. *Activities and Organizations:* drama/theater group, student-run newspaper, radio and television station, choral group, WNRS radio station, American Chemical Society, cheerleaders, Sweet Tones, Student Government Association/Campus Events Organization. *Campus security:* 24-hour emergency response devices and patrols, late-night transport/escort service, controlled dormitory access, front gate security. *Student Services:* health clinic, personal/psychological counseling.

Athletics Member NCAA. All Division III. *Intercollegiate sports:* equestrian sports W(c), fencing W(c), field hockey W, lacrosse W, soccer W, softball W(c), swimming W, tennis W, volleyball W.

Standardized Tests *Required:* SAT I or ACT (for admission). *Recommended:* SAT II: Subject Tests (for admission).

Costs (2001–02) *Comprehensive fee:* $25,310 includes full-time tuition ($17,860), mandatory fees ($150), and room and board ($7300). Full-time tuition and fees vary according to program. Part-time tuition: $595 per credit hour. Part-time tuition and fees vary according to program. *Room and board:* College room only: $2940. *Payment plan:* installment. *Waivers:* adult students, senior citizens, and employees or children of employees.

Financial Aid Of all full-time matriculated undergraduates who enrolled in 2001, 372 applied for aid, 299 were judged to have need, 160 had their need fully met. 67 Federal Work-Study jobs (averaging $929). In 2001, 267 non-need-based awards were made. *Average percent of need met:* 92%. *Average financial aid package:* $16,690. *Average need-based loan:* $3088. *Average need-based gift aid:* $13,088. *Average indebtedness upon graduation:* $18,718.

Applying *Options:* common application, electronic application, early admission, early decision, deferred entrance. *Application fee:* $25. *Required:* essay or personal statement, high school transcript, 2 letters of recommendation. *Required for some:* interview. *Application deadlines:* 2/1 (freshmen), 7/1 (transfers). *Early decision:* 12/1. *Notification:* continuous until 4/1 (freshmen), 12/15 (early decision).

Admissions Contact Ms. Margaret Williams Blount, Director of Admissions, Sweet Briar College, PO Box B, Sweet Briar, VA 24595. *Phone:* 434-381-6142. *Toll-free phone:* 800-381-6142. *Fax:* 434-381-6152. *E-mail:* admissions@sbc.edu.

UNIVERSITY OF RICHMOND

Richmond, Virginia

- **Independent** comprehensive, founded 1830
- **Calendar** semesters
- **Degrees** certificates, diplomas, associate, bachelor's, master's, first professional, and postbachelor's certificates
- **Suburban** 350-acre campus
- **Endowment** $1.1 billion
- **Coed,** 3,021 undergraduate students, 99% full-time, 52% women, 48% men
- **Very difficult** entrance level, 44% of applicants were admitted

Undergraduates 2,989 full-time, 32 part-time. Students come from 49 states and territories, 72 other countries, 85% are from out of state, 5% African

University of Richmond (continued)
American, 3% Asian American or Pacific Islander, 2% Hispanic American, 0.1% Native American, 4% international, 1% transferred in, 92% live on campus. *Retention:* 89% of 2001 full-time freshmen returned.

Freshmen *Admission:* 5,622 applied, 2,498 admitted, 792 enrolled. *Test scores:* SAT verbal scores over 500: 96%; SAT math scores over 500: 98%; ACT scores over 18: 100%; SAT verbal scores over 600: 74%; SAT math scores over 600: 84%; ACT scores over 24: 95%; SAT verbal scores over 700: 18%; SAT math scores over 700: 20%; ACT scores over 30: 35%.

Faculty *Total:* 337, 80% full-time, 79% with terminal degrees. *Student/faculty ratio:* 10:1.

Majors Accounting; American studies; art; art education; art history; biology; business administration; business economics; business marketing and marketing management; chemistry; classics; computer science; criminal justice/law enforcement administration; Eastern European area studies; economics; education; elementary education; English; environmental science; European studies; finance; fine/studio arts; French; German; Greek (modern); health education; history; human resources management; interdisciplinary studies; international business; international economics; international relations; journalism; Latin American studies; Latin (ancient and medieval); legal administrative assistant; management information systems/business data processing; mathematics; middle school education; molecular biology; music; music history; philosophy; physical education; physics; political science; psychology; religious studies; secondary education; sociology; Spanish; speech/rhetorical studies; theater arts/drama; urban studies; women's studies.

Academic Programs *Special study options:* accelerated degree program, adult/continuing education programs, advanced placement credit, cooperative education, distance learning, double majors, English as a second language, honors programs, independent study, internships, off-campus study, part-time degree program, services for LD students, student-designed majors, study abroad, summer session for credit. *ROTC:* Army (b).

Library Boatwright Memorial Library plus 4 others with 716,677 titles, 3,579 serial subscriptions, 24,916 audiovisual materials, an OPAC, a Web page.

Computers on Campus 500 computers available on campus for general student use. A campuswide network can be accessed from student residence rooms and from off campus. At least one staffed computer lab available.

Student Life *Housing Options:* coed, men-only, women-only. *Activities and Organizations:* drama/theater group, student-run newspaper, radio and television station, choral group, Volunteer Action Council, Student Government Association, Campus Activities Board, Multicultural Student Union, Intramurals, national fraternities, national sororities. *Campus security:* 24-hour emergency response devices and patrols, late-night transport/escort service, controlled dormitory access, campus police. *Student Services:* health clinic, personal/psychological counseling, women's center.

Athletics Member NCAA. All Division I except football (Division I-AA). *Intercollegiate sports:* baseball M(s), basketball M(s)/W(s), crew M(c)/W(c), cross-country running M/W(s), equestrian sports W(c), fencing M(c)/W(c), field hockey W(s), golf M, lacrosse M(c)/W(s), rugby M(c), soccer M(s)/W(s), swimming M(c)/W(s), tennis M/W(s), track and field M/W, volleyball M(c)/W(c), water polo M(c)/W(c). *Intramural sports:* archery M/W, badminton M/W, basketball M/W, fencing M/W, field hockey W(c), football M/W, golf M/W, lacrosse W(c), racquetball M/W, skiing (downhill) M(c)/W(c), soccer M(c)/W(c), softball M/W, squash M/W, swimming M/W, table tennis M/W, tennis M/W, volleyball M/W, water polo M, wrestling M.

Standardized Tests *Required:* SAT II: Writing Test (for admission).

Costs (2001–02) *Comprehensive fee:* $27,300 includes full-time tuition ($22,570) and room and board ($4730). Part-time tuition: $1030 per semester hour. Part-time tuition and fees vary according to class time. *Room and board:* College room only: $2250. Room and board charges vary according to board plan and housing facility. *Payment plan:* installment. *Waivers:* employees or children of employees.

Financial Aid Of all full-time matriculated undergraduates who enrolled in 2001, 1228 applied for aid, 821 were judged to have need, 410 had their need fully met. 250 Federal Work-Study jobs (averaging $1225). In 2001, 881 non-need-based awards were made. *Average percent of need met:* 96%. *Average financial aid package:* $16,134. *Average need-based loan:* $4271. *Average need-based gift aid:* $12,097. *Average indebtedness upon graduation:* $14,370. *Financial aid deadline:* 2/25.

Applying *Options:* common application, electronic application, early admission, early decision, deferred entrance. *Application fee:* $40. *Required:* essay or personal statement, high school transcript, minimum 2.0 GPA, 1 letter of recommendation, signed character statement. *Application deadlines:* 1/15 (freshmen), 2/1 (transfers). *Early decision:* 11/15 (for plan 1), 1/15 (for plan 2). *Notification:* 4/1 (freshmen), 12/15 (early decision plan 1), 2/15 (early decision plan 2).

Admissions Contact Ms. Pamela Spence, Dean of Admission, University of Richmond, 28 Westhampton Way, University of Richmond, VA 23173. *Phone:* 804-289-8640. *Toll-free phone:* 800-700-1662. *Fax:* 804-287-6003.

UNIVERSITY OF VIRGINIA
Charlottesville, Virginia

- **State-supported** university, founded 1819
- **Calendar** semesters
- **Degrees** bachelor's, master's, doctoral, first professional, and post-master's certificates
- **Suburban** 1133-acre campus with easy access to Richmond
- **Endowment** $1.7 billion
- **Coed,** 13,764 undergraduate students, 93% full-time, 54% women, 46% men
- **Most difficult** entrance level, 38% of applicants were admitted

Undergraduates 12,796 full-time, 968 part-time. Students come from 51 states and territories, 101 other countries, 29% are from out of state, 9% African American, 11% Asian American or Pacific Islander, 3% Hispanic American, 0.4% Native American, 4% international, 4% transferred in, 47% live on campus. *Retention:* 96% of 2001 full-time freshmen returned.

Freshmen *Admission:* 14,739 applied, 5,534 admitted, 2,980 enrolled. *Average high school GPA:* 3.97. *Test scores:* SAT verbal scores over 500: 96%; SAT math scores over 500: 98%; ACT scores over 18: 100%; SAT verbal scores over 600: 77%; SAT math scores over 600: 82%; ACT scores over 24: 83%; SAT verbal scores over 700: 30%; SAT math scores over 700: 37%; ACT scores over 30: 44%.

Faculty *Total:* 1,265, 86% full-time, 86% with terminal degrees. *Student/faculty ratio:* 16:1.

Majors Aerospace engineering; African-American studies; anthropology; applied mathematics; architecture; art; astronomy; biology; business; chemical engineering; chemistry; city/community/regional planning; civil engineering; classics; comparative literature; computer engineering; computer/information sciences; cultural studies; economics; electrical engineering; engineering; English; environmental science; French; German; history; international relations; Italian; liberal arts and sciences/liberal studies; mathematics; mechanical engineering; music; nursing; philosophy; physical education; physics; political science; psychology; religious studies; Slavic languages; sociology; Spanish; speech-language pathology/audiology; systems engineering; theater arts/drama.

Academic Programs *Special study options:* accelerated degree program, adult/continuing education programs, advanced placement credit, cooperative education, double majors, honors programs, independent study, internships, part-time degree program, services for LD students, student-designed majors, study abroad, summer session for credit. *ROTC:* Army (b), Navy (b), Air Force (b).

Library Alderman Library plus 14 others with 3.3 million titles, 51,237 serial subscriptions, 282,798 audiovisual materials, an OPAC, a Web page.

Computers on Campus 1859 computers available on campus for general student use. A campuswide network can be accessed from student residence rooms and from off campus. Internet access, online (class) registration, at least one staffed computer lab available.

Student Life *Housing:* on-campus residence required for freshman year. *Options:* coed. *Activities and Organizations:* drama/theater group, student-run newspaper, radio and television station, choral group, Madison House, student government, university guides, University Union, The Cavalier Daily, national fraternities, national sororities. *Campus security:* 24-hour emergency response devices and patrols, late-night transport/escort service, controlled dormitory access. *Student Services:* health clinic, personal/psychological counseling, women's center, legal services.

Athletics Member NCAA. All Division I except football (Division I-A). *Intercollegiate sports:* baseball M(s), basketball M(s)/W(s), crew W(s), cross-country running M(s)/W(s), field hockey W(s), golf M(s), ice hockey M(c), lacrosse M(s)/W(s), soccer M(s)/W(s), softball W(s), swimming M(s)/W(s), tennis M(s)/W(s), track and field M(s)/W(s), volleyball W(s), wrestling M(s). *Intramural sports:* archery M/W, badminton M/W, basketball M/W, bowling M/W, crew M(c)/W, cross-country running M/W, equestrian sports M/W, fencing M(c)/W(c), field hockey W, football M/W, golf M/W, gymnastics M(c)/W(c), lacrosse M/W, racquetball M(c)/W(c), riflery M(c)/W(c), rugby M(c)/W(c), sailing M(c)/W(c), skiing (cross-country) M/W, skiing (downhill) M(c)/W(c), soccer M(c)/W(c), softball M/W, squash M(c)/W(c), swimming M/W, tennis M/W(c), track and field M/W, volleyball M(c)/W(c), water polo M(c), weight lifting M(c)/W(c), wrestling M.

Standardized Tests *Required:* SAT I or ACT (for admission), SAT II: Subject Tests (for admission), SAT II: Writing Test (for admission).

Costs (2001–02) *Tuition:* state resident $3046 full-time; nonresident $17,078 full-time. Full-time tuition and fees vary according to program. *Required fees:*

$1375 full-time. *Room and board:* $4970; room only: $2260. Room and board charges vary according to board plan and housing facility. *Payment plan:* installment. *Waivers:* senior citizens and employees or children of employees.

Financial Aid Of all full-time matriculated undergraduates who enrolled in 2001, 4763 applied for aid, 2845 were judged to have need, 1447 had their need fully met. 423 Federal Work-Study jobs (averaging $1431). *Average percent of need met:* 92%. *Average financial aid package:* $10,774. *Average need-based loan:* $3728. *Average need-based gift aid:* $8608. *Average indebtedness upon graduation:* $13,890.

Applying *Options:* electronic application, early decision, deferred entrance. *Application fee:* $40. *Required:* essay or personal statement, high school transcript, 1 letter of recommendation. *Application deadlines:* 1/2 (freshmen), 3/1 (transfers). *Early decision:* 11/1. *Notification:* 4/1 (freshmen), 12/1 (early decision).

Admissions Contact Mr. John A. Blackburn, Dean of Admission, University of Virginia, PO Box 400160, Charlottesville, VA 22904-4160. *Phone:* 434-982-3200. *Fax:* 434-924-3587. *E-mail:* undergrad-admission@virginia.edu.

THE UNIVERSITY OF VIRGINIA'S COLLEGE AT WISE

Wise, Virginia

- **State-supported** 4-year, founded 1954, part of University of Virginia
- **Calendar** semesters
- **Degrees** bachelor's and postbachelor's certificates
- **Small-town** 350-acre campus
- **Endowment** $19.4 million
- **Coed,** 1,480 undergraduate students, 82% full-time, 54% women, 46% men
- **Moderately difficult** entrance level, 77% of applicants were admitted

Undergraduates 1,209 full-time, 271 part-time. Students come from 10 states and territories, 8 other countries, 6% are from out of state, 5% African American, 1% Asian American or Pacific Islander, 0.5% Hispanic American, 0.3% Native American, 0.9% international, 11% transferred in, 30% live on campus. *Retention:* 74% of 2001 full-time freshmen returned.

Freshmen *Admission:* 841 applied, 647 admitted, 325 enrolled. *Average high school GPA:* 3.10. *Test scores:* SAT verbal scores over 500: 41%; SAT math scores over 500: 36%; ACT scores over 18: 81%; SAT verbal scores over 600: 10%; SAT math scores over 600: 6%; ACT scores over 24: 32%; SAT verbal scores over 700: 2%; SAT math scores over 700: 1%.

Faculty *Total:* 95, 69% full-time, 64% with terminal degrees. *Student/faculty ratio:* 17:1.

Majors Accounting; art; biology; business administration; chemistry; communications; computer/information sciences; criminal justice studies; economics; English; environmental science; foreign languages/literatures; French; history; interdisciplinary studies; liberal arts and sciences/liberal studies; mathematics; medical technology; nursing (family practice); political science; psychology; sociology; Spanish; theater arts/drama.

Academic Programs *Special study options:* academic remediation for entering students, accelerated degree program, adult/continuing education programs, advanced placement credit, cooperative education, distance learning, double majors, honors programs, independent study, internships, part-time degree program, services for LD students, student-designed majors, study abroad, summer session for credit.

Library Wyllie Library with 95,861 titles, 1,029 serial subscriptions, 11,582 audiovisual materials, an OPAC, a Web page.

Computers on Campus 130 computers available on campus for general student use. A campuswide network can be accessed from student residence rooms and from off campus. Internet access, at least one staffed computer lab available.

Student Life *Housing Options:* coed, men-only, women-only. *Activities and Organizations:* drama/theater group, student-run newspaper, radio and television station, choral group, student government, SAB (Student Activities Board), Inter Greek Council, MCA (Multi-Cultural Association), RHA (Residence Hall Association), national fraternities, national sororities. *Campus security:* 24-hour emergency response devices and patrols, student patrols, late-night transport/escort service. *Student Services:* health clinic, personal/psychological counseling.

Athletics Member NAIA. *Intercollegiate sports:* baseball M(s), basketball M(s)/W(s), cross-country running M(s)/W(s), football M(s), golf M/W, softball W(s), tennis M(s)/W(s), track and field M/W, volleyball W(s). *Intramural sports:* basketball M/W, football M/W, softball M/W, table tennis M/W, tennis M/W, volleyball M/W.

Standardized Tests *Required:* SAT I or ACT (for admission).

Costs (2001–02) *Tuition:* state resident $1885 full-time, $77 per semester hour part-time; nonresident $8379 full-time, $368 per semester hour part-time. Part-time tuition and fees vary according to course load. *Required fees:* $1585 full-time, $190 per semester hour. *Room and board:* $5226; room only: $2932. Room and board charges vary according to housing facility. *Payment plans:* installment, deferred payment. *Waivers:* employees or children of employees.

Financial Aid Of all full-time matriculated undergraduates who enrolled in 2001, 1082 applied for aid, 883 were judged to have need, 791 had their need fully met. 186 Federal Work-Study jobs (averaging $1365). In 2001, 214 non-need-based awards were made. *Average percent of need met:* 95%. *Average financial aid package:* $5149. *Average need-based loan:* $2439. *Average need-based gift aid:* $3536. *Average non-need based aid:* $1344. *Average indebtedness upon graduation:* $6179.

Applying *Options:* early admission. *Application fee:* $15. *Required:* high school transcript, minimum 2.3 GPA. *Required for some:* interview. *Recommended:* 2 letters of recommendation. *Application deadlines:* 8/1 (freshmen), 8/15 (transfers). *Notification:* continuous until 8/20 (freshmen), 2/15 (early action).

Admissions Contact Mr. Russell Necessary, Director of Admissions and Financial Aid, The University of Virginia's College at Wise, 1 College Avenue, Wise, VA 24293. *Phone:* 276-328-0322. *Toll-free phone:* 888-282-9324. *Fax:* 540-328-0251. *E-mail:* admissions@uvawise.edu.

VIRGINIA COMMONWEALTH UNIVERSITY

Richmond, Virginia

- **State-supported** university, founded 1838
- **Calendar** semesters
- **Degrees** bachelor's, master's, doctoral, first professional, post-master's, and postbachelor's certificates
- **Urban** 126-acre campus
- **Endowment** $148.0 million
- **Coed,** 17,148 undergraduate students, 70% full-time, 59% women, 41% men
- **Moderately difficult** entrance level, 74% of applicants were admitted

Virginia Commonwealth University (VCU) is noted for excellent programs in the arts, business, education, engineering, humanities, life sciences, mass communications, pre-health sciences, and social work and for its diverse student body and faculty. Honors and guaranteed admission programs, cooperative education and internship programs, and undergraduate research and study-abroad opportunities are also offered.

Undergraduates 12,048 full-time, 5,100 part-time. Students come from 45 states and territories, 75 other countries, 5% are from out of state, 22% African American, 8% Asian American or Pacific Islander, 3% Hispanic American, 0.6% Native American, 1% international, 9% transferred in, 10% live on campus. *Retention:* 77% of 2001 full-time freshmen returned.

Freshmen *Admission:* 7,926 applied, 5,856 admitted, 2,740 enrolled. *Average high school GPA:* 3.07. *Test scores:* SAT verbal scores over 500: 62%; SAT math scores over 500: 56%; ACT scores over 18: 85%; SAT verbal scores over 600: 21%; SAT math scores over 600: 16%; ACT scores over 24: 19%; SAT verbal scores over 700: 2%; SAT math scores over 700: 2%; ACT scores over 30: 1%.

Faculty *Total:* 2,029, 53% full-time. *Student/faculty ratio:* 13:1.

Majors Accounting; art education; art history; bioengineering; biological/physical sciences; biology; business administration; business economics; business marketing and marketing management; chemical engineering; chemistry; computer/information sciences; craft/folk art; criminal justice/law enforcement administration; dance; dental hygiene; design/visual communications; education; electrical engineering; English; fashion design/illustration; foreign languages/literatures; general studies; health education; health/medical diagnostic and treatment services related; history; information sciences/systems; interior design; mass communications; mathematics; mechanical engineering; medical technology; music (general performance); nursing; painting; pharmacy; philosophy; photography; physics; political science; psychology; recreation/leisure facilities management; religious studies; sculpture; social work; sociology; theater arts/drama; urban studies.

Academic Programs *Special study options:* academic remediation for entering students, accelerated degree program, adult/continuing education programs, advanced placement credit, cooperative education, distance learning, double majors, English as a second language, honors programs, independent study, internships, off-campus study, part-time degree program, services for LD students, student-designed majors, study abroad, summer session for credit. *ROTC:* Army (b).

Library James Branch Cabell and Tompkins-McCaw Library with 1.2 million titles, 18,315 serial subscriptions, 39,090 audiovisual materials, an OPAC, a Web page.

Computers on Campus 900 computers available on campus for general student use. A campuswide network can be accessed from student residence rooms and from off campus. At least one staffed computer lab available.

Virginia Commonwealth University (continued)

Student Life *Housing Options:* coed, men-only, women-only, disabled students. *Activities and Organizations:* drama/theater group, student-run newspaper, radio station, choral group, Student Government Organization, Activities Programming Board, Latino Student Alliance, Black Caucus, Greek Council, national fraternities, national sororities. *Campus security:* 24-hour emergency response devices and patrols, student patrols, late-night transport/escort service, controlled dormitory access, security personnel in residence halls. *Student Services:* health clinic, personal/psychological counseling.

Athletics Member NCAA. All Division I. *Intercollegiate sports:* baseball M(s), basketball M(s)/W(s), cross-country running M(s)/W(s), field hockey W(s), golf M(s), rugby M(c), soccer M(s)/W(s), tennis M(s)/W(s), track and field M(s)/W(s), volleyball W(s), weight lifting M(c)/W(c). *Intramural sports:* badminton M/W, basketball M/W, cross-country running M(c), fencing M(c)/W(c), football M, racquetball M/W, soccer M/W, softball M/W, table tennis M/W, tennis M/W, volleyball M/W, water polo M/W.

Standardized Tests *Required:* SAT I or ACT (for admission).

Costs (2001–02) *Tuition:* state resident $2492 full-time, $104 per credit part-time; nonresident $12,672 full-time, $528 per credit part-time. Full-time tuition and fees vary according to program. Part-time tuition and fees vary according to course load and location. *Required fees:* $1183 full-time, $43 per credit. *Room and board:* $5355; room only: $3217. Room and board charges vary according to board plan and housing facility. *Payment plan:* installment. *Waivers:* senior citizens.

Financial Aid Of all full-time matriculated undergraduates who enrolled in 2001, 8618 applied for aid, 6236 were judged to have need, 604 had their need fully met. 740 Federal Work-Study jobs (averaging $1588). In 2001, 1223 non-need-based awards were made. *Average percent of need met:* 57%. *Average financial aid package:* $6458. *Average need-based loan:* $3536. *Average need-based gift aid:* $3187. *Average non-need based aid:* $2359. *Average indebtedness upon graduation:* $21,994.

Applying *Options:* common application, electronic application, early admission, early decision, deferred entrance. *Application fee:* $25. *Required:* high school transcript. *Required for some:* minimum 3.0 GPA, 2 letters of recommendation, interview. *Recommended:* essay or personal statement, minimum 2.5 GPA. *Application deadlines:* 2/1 (freshmen), 8/1 (transfers). *Early decision:* 11/1. *Notification:* continuous until 4/1 (freshmen), 12/1 (early decision).

Admissions Contact Counseling Staff, Virginia Commonwealth University, 821 West Franklin Street, Box 842526. *Phone:* 804-828-1222. *Toll-free phone:* 800-841-3638. *Fax:* 804-828-1899. *E-mail:* vcuinfo@vcu.edu.

VIRGINIA INTERMONT COLLEGE
Bristol, Virginia

- **Independent** 4-year, founded 1884, affiliated with Baptist Church
- **Calendar** semesters
- **Degrees** associate and bachelor's
- **Small-town** 27-acre campus
- **Endowment** $2.3 million
- **Coed,** 918 undergraduate students, 87% full-time, 75% women, 25% men
- **Minimally difficult** entrance level, 67% of applicants were admitted

Students from all over the world who are looking for a solid liberal arts background with a variety of academic majors come to Virginia Intermont. They appreciate the individualized instruction and challenging academic atmosphere. Specialized areas, such as photography and digital imaging, equine studies, paralegal studies, and sport management are invaluable assets to the educational background and practical experience that Virginia Intermont College has to offer.

Undergraduates 795 full-time, 123 part-time. Students come from 32 states and territories, 17 other countries, 36% are from out of state, 5% African American, 0.3% Asian American or Pacific Islander, 0.3% Hispanic American, 0.3% Native American, 4% international, 8% transferred in, 52% live on campus. *Retention:* 50% of 2001 full-time freshmen returned.

Freshmen *Admission:* 661 applied, 443 admitted, 158 enrolled. *Average high school GPA:* 2.91. *Test scores:* SAT verbal scores over 500: 47%; SAT math scores over 500: 25%; ACT scores over 18: 72%; SAT verbal scores over 600: 12%; SAT math scores over 600: 2%; ACT scores over 24: 3%; SAT verbal scores over 700: 3%.

Faculty *Total:* 163, 26% full-time, 16% with terminal degrees. *Student/faculty ratio:* 11:1.

Majors Art; art education; biology; biology education; business administration; business education; business marketing and marketing management; dance; elementary education; English; English education; environmental science; equestrian studies; graphic design/commercial art/illustration; history; interdisciplinary studies; liberal arts and sciences/liberal studies; mathematics; paralegal/legal assistant; photography; physical education; political science; pre-law; pre-medicine; pre-veterinary studies; psychology; religious studies; secondary education; social studies education; social work; sport/fitness administration; theater arts/drama.

Academic Programs *Special study options:* academic remediation for entering students, adult/continuing education programs, advanced placement credit, double majors, independent study, internships, off-campus study, part-time degree program, services for LD students, study abroad, summer session for credit.

Library J. F. Hicks Library with 59,714 titles, 276 serial subscriptions, 5,582 audiovisual materials, an OPAC, a Web page.

Computers on Campus 80 computers available on campus for general student use. A campuswide network can be accessed from student residence rooms and from off campus. Internet access, online (class) registration, at least one staffed computer lab available.

Student Life *Housing:* on-campus residence required through junior year. *Options:* coed, men-only, women-only. *Activities and Organizations:* drama/theater group, student-run newspaper, choral group, Student Government Association, Student Activities Committee, Baptist Student Union, equestrian club, Business Organization for Student Success. *Campus security:* late-night transport/escort service, 17-hour patrols by trained security personnel. *Student Services:* personal/psychological counseling, women's center.

Athletics Member NAIA. *Intercollegiate sports:* baseball M(s), basketball M(s)/W(s), equestrian sports M(s)/W(s), golf M(s), soccer M(s)/W(s), softball W(s), tennis M(s)/W(s). *Intramural sports:* basketball M/W, bowling M/W, football M/W, golf M/W, skiing (downhill) M/W, softball M/W, swimming M/W, table tennis M/W, tennis M/W, volleyball M/W, weight lifting M/W.

Standardized Tests *Required:* SAT I or ACT (for admission).

Costs (2001–02) *Comprehensive fee:* $17,510 includes full-time tuition ($11,890), mandatory fees ($320), and room and board ($5300). Part-time tuition: $150 per credit. Part-time tuition and fees vary according to course load. *Required fees:* $60 per term part-time. *Room and board:* College room only: $2600. *Payment plan:* installment. *Waivers:* employees or children of employees.

Financial Aid Of all full-time matriculated undergraduates who enrolled in 2001, 693 applied for aid, 560 were judged to have need, 117 had their need fully met. 272 Federal Work-Study jobs (averaging $681). In 2001, 133 non-need-based awards were made. *Average percent of need met:* 66%. *Average financial aid package:* $11,744. *Average need-based loan:* $4139. *Average need-based gift aid:* $7476. *Average non-need based aid:* $6135. *Average indebtedness upon graduation:* $17,125.

Applying *Options:* common application, electronic application, early admission, deferred entrance. *Application fee:* $15. *Required:* high school transcript, minimum 2.0 GPA. *Required for some:* essay or personal statement. *Recommended:* interview. *Application deadline:* rolling (freshmen), rolling (transfers). *Notification:* continuous (freshmen).

Admissions Contact Ms. Robin B. Cozart, Director of Admissions, Virginia Intermont College, 1013 Moore Street, Campus Box D-460, Bristol, VA 24201. *Phone:* 540-466-7854. *Toll-free phone:* 800-451-1842. *Fax:* 540-466-7855. *E-mail:* viadmit@vic.edu.

VIRGINIA MILITARY INSTITUTE
Lexington, Virginia

- **State-supported** 4-year, founded 1839
- **Calendar** semesters
- **Degree** bachelor's
- **Small-town** 140-acre campus
- **Endowment** $281.4 million
- **Coed, primarily men,** 1,311 undergraduate students
- **Moderately difficult** entrance level, 63% of applicants were admitted

Undergraduates Students come from 44 states and territories, 19 other countries, 47% are from out of state, 5% African American, 4% Asian American or Pacific Islander, 3% Hispanic American, 0.5% Native American, 3% international, 100% live on campus. *Retention:* 86% of 2001 full-time freshmen returned.

Freshmen *Admission:* 1,349 applied, 847 admitted. *Average high school GPA:* 3.28. *Test scores:* SAT verbal scores over 500: 85%; SAT math scores over 500: 89%; ACT scores over 18: 97%; SAT verbal scores over 600: 29%; SAT math scores over 600: 37%; ACT scores over 24: 42%; SAT verbal scores over 700: 5%; SAT math scores over 700: 3%; ACT scores over 30: 7%.

Faculty *Total:* 145, 69% full-time, 74% with terminal degrees. *Student/faculty ratio:* 11:1.

Majors Biology; chemistry; civil engineering; computer science; economics; electrical engineering; English; history; international relations; mathematics; mechanical engineering; modern languages; physics; psychology.

Academic Programs *Special study options:* accelerated degree program, advanced placement credit, double majors, honors programs, independent study, internships, services for LD students, study abroad, summer session for credit. *ROTC:* Army (b), Navy (b), Air Force (b).

Library Preston Library plus 1 other with 507,133 titles, 162,053 serial subscriptions, 4,896 audiovisual materials, an OPAC, a Web page.

Computers on Campus 200 computers available on campus for general student use. A campuswide network can be accessed from student residence rooms and from off campus. Internet access, at least one staffed computer lab available.

Student Life *Housing:* on-campus residence required through senior year. *Options:* coed. *Activities and Organizations:* drama/theater group, student-run newspaper, choral group, marching band, Newman Club, Officers Christian Fellowship, Strength & Fitness, Promaji, Pre-law Society. *Campus security:* 24-hour emergency response devices and patrols, student patrols. *Student Services:* health clinic, personal/psychological counseling.

Athletics Member NCAA. All Division I except football (Division I-AA). *Intercollegiate sports:* baseball M(s), basketball M(s), cross-country running M(s)/W(s), fencing M(c)/W(c), golf M(s), ice hockey M(c), lacrosse M(s), racquetball M(c)/W(c), riflery M(s)/W(s), rugby M(c)/W(c), soccer M(s), swimming M(s)/W, tennis M(s), track and field M(s)/W(s), volleyball M(c)/W(c), water polo M(c)/W(c), weight lifting M(c)/W(c), wrestling M(s). *Intramural sports:* basketball M/W, football M/W, soccer M/W, softball M/W.

Standardized Tests *Required:* SAT I or ACT (for admission).

Costs (2001–02) *Tuition:* state resident $2924 full-time, $90 per credit hour part-time; nonresident $13,992 full-time, $270 per credit hour part-time. *Required fees:* $2206 full-time. *Room and board:* $4838; room only: $1476. *Payment plan:* installment.

Financial Aid Of all full-time matriculated undergraduates who enrolled in 2001, 681 applied for aid, 503 were judged to have need, 319 had their need fully met. 65 Federal Work-Study jobs (averaging $1070). In 2001, 297 non-need-based awards were made. *Average percent of need met:* 93%. *Average financial aid package:* $12,838. *Average need-based loan:* $4087. *Average need-based gift aid:* $10,682. *Average non-need based aid:* $11,388. *Average indebtedness upon graduation:* $12,867.

Applying *Options:* electronic application, early decision. *Application fee:* $25. *Required:* high school transcript. *Recommended:* essay or personal statement, 2 letters of recommendation, interview. *Application deadlines:* 3/1 (freshmen), 3/1 (transfers). *Early decision:* 11/15. *Notification:* continuous (freshmen), 12/15 (early decision).

Admissions Contact Lt. Col. Tom Mortenson, Associate Director of Admissions, Virginia Military Institute, 309 Letcher Avenue, Lexington, VA 24450. *Phone:* 540-464-7211. *Toll-free phone:* 800-767-4207. *Fax:* 540-464-7746. *E-mail:* admissions@vmi.edu.

VIRGINIA POLYTECHNIC INSTITUTE AND STATE UNIVERSITY

Blacksburg, Virginia

- **State-supported** university, founded 1872
- **Calendar** semesters
- **Degrees** associate, bachelor's, master's, doctoral, and first professional
- **Small-town** 2600-acre campus
- **Endowment** $368.2 million
- **Coed,** 21,869 undergraduate students, 97% full-time, 40% women, 60% men
- **Moderately difficult** entrance level, 66% of applicants were admitted

Undergraduates 21,203 full-time, 666 part-time. Students come from 52 states and territories, 104 other countries, 27% are from out of state, 5% African American, 7% Asian American or Pacific Islander, 2% Hispanic American, 0.2% Native American, 3% international, 4% transferred in, 44% live on campus. *Retention:* 90% of 2001 full-time freshmen returned.

Freshmen *Admission:* 18,800 applied, 12,500 admitted, 5,007 enrolled. *Average high school GPA:* 3.56. *Test scores:* SAT verbal scores over 500: 88%; SAT math scores over 500: 91%; SAT verbal scores over 600: 39%; SAT math scores over 600: 52%; SAT verbal scores over 700: 5%; SAT math scores over 700: 11%.

Faculty *Total:* 1,491, 83% full-time. *Student/faculty ratio:* 23:1.

Majors Accounting; aerospace engineering; agricultural economics; agricultural education; agricultural mechanization; agronomy/crop science; animal sciences; architecture; art; biochemistry; biology; business; business administration; business education; business marketing and marketing management; chemical engineering; chemistry; civil engineering; clothing/textiles; communications; computer engineering; computer science; construction technology; consumer/homemaking education; dairy science; dietetics; early childhood education; economics; electrical engineering; engineering; engineering science; English; environmental science; finance; food sciences; forestry; French; geography; geology; German; health education; history; horticulture science; human resources management; human services; industrial arts education; industrial design; industrial/manufacturing engineering; information sciences/systems; interdisciplinary studies; international relations; landscape architecture; management information systems/business data processing; marketing/distribution education; materials engineering; mathematical statistics; mathematics; mechanical engineering; mining/mineral engineering; music; nutrition science; ocean engineering; philosophy; physics; political science; poultry science; psychology; sociology; Spanish; theater arts/drama; trade/industrial education; travel/tourism management; urban studies.

Academic Programs *Special study options:* accelerated degree program, adult/continuing education programs, advanced placement credit, cooperative education, distance learning, double majors, English as a second language, honors programs, independent study, internships, off-campus study, part-time degree program, services for LD students, study abroad, summer session for credit. *ROTC:* Army (b), Air Force (b).

Library Newman Library plus 4 others with 2.0 million titles, 18,281 serial subscriptions, 17,510 audiovisual materials, an OPAC, a Web page.

Computers on Campus A campuswide network can be accessed from student residence rooms and from off campus. Internet access, online (class) registration, at least one staffed computer lab available.

Student Life *Housing:* on-campus residence required for freshman year. *Options:* coed, men-only, women-only. *Activities and Organizations:* drama/theater group, student-run newspaper, radio and television station, choral group, marching band, Virginia Tech Union, Student Government Association, international student organizations, national fraternities, national sororities. *Campus security:* 24-hour emergency response devices and patrols, student patrols, late-night transport/escort service, controlled dormitory access. *Student Services:* health clinic, personal/psychological counseling, women's center, legal services.

Athletics Member NCAA. All Division I except football (Division I-A). *Intercollegiate sports:* baseball M(s), basketball M(s)/W(s), bowling M(c)/W(c), crew M(c)/W(c), cross-country running M(s)/W(s), equestrian sports M(c)/W(c), fencing M(c)/W(c), field hockey M(c)/W(c), golf M(s), gymnastics M(c)/W(c), ice hockey M(c)/W(c), lacrosse M(c)/W(s), rugby M(c)/W(c), skiing (downhill) M(c)/W(c), soccer M(s)/W(s), softball W, swimming M(s)/W(s), tennis M(s)/W(s), track and field M(s)/W(s), volleyball M(c)/W(s), water polo M(c)/W(c), weight lifting M(c)/W(c), wrestling M(s). *Intramural sports:* badminton M/W, basketball M/W, cross-country running M/W, football M/W, golf M/W, ice hockey M/W, racquetball M/W, riflery M/W, skiing (downhill) M/W, soccer M/W, softball W, squash M/W, swimming M/W, table tennis M/W, tennis M/W, track and field M/W, volleyball M/W, wrestling M.

Standardized Tests *Required:* SAT I or ACT (for admission).

Costs (2001–02) *Tuition:* state resident $2792 full-time, $117 per credit hour part-time; nonresident $11,616 full-time, $484 per credit hour part-time. Full-time tuition and fees vary according to location. Part-time tuition and fees vary according to course load. *Required fees:* $872 full-time, $109 per term part-time. *Room and board:* $4032; room only: $2008. Room and board charges vary according to board plan and housing facility. *Payment plan:* installment. *Waivers:* employees or children of employees.

Financial Aid Of all full-time matriculated undergraduates who enrolled in 2001, 17467 applied for aid, 16054 were judged to have need, 3614 had their need fully met. 2094 Federal Work-Study jobs (averaging $2000). In 2001, 8611 non-need-based awards were made. *Average percent of need met:* 68%. *Average financial aid package:* $7488. *Average need-based loan:* $4176. *Average need-based gift aid:* $4005. *Average indebtedness upon graduation:* $17,580.

Applying *Options:* electronic application, early admission, early decision, deferred entrance. *Application fee:* $25. *Required:* high school transcript, minimum 2.0 GPA. *Recommended:* minimum 3.3 GPA. *Application deadlines:* 1/15 (freshmen), 3/1 (transfers). *Early decision:* 11/1. *Notification:* 4/1 (freshmen), 12/15 (early decision).

Admissions Contact Ms. Mildred Johnson, Associate Director for Freshmen Admissions, Virginia Polytechnic Institute and State University, 201 Burruss Hall, Blacksburg, VA 24061. *Phone:* 540-231-6267. *Fax:* 540-231-3242. *E-mail:* vtadmiss@vt.edu.

VIRGINIA STATE UNIVERSITY

Petersburg, Virginia

- **State-supported** comprehensive, founded 1882, part of State Council of Higher Education for Virginia

Virginia State University (continued)
- **Calendar** semesters
- **Degrees** bachelor's, master's, and post-master's certificates
- **Suburban** 236-acre campus with easy access to Richmond
- **Endowment** $7.8 million
- **Coed,** 3,853 undergraduate students, 91% full-time, 56% women, 44% men
- **Minimally difficult** entrance level, 87% of applicants were admitted

Undergraduates 3,521 full-time, 332 part-time. Students come from 27 states and territories, 35% are from out of state, 96% African American, 0.2% Asian American or Pacific Islander, 1% Hispanic American, 0.1% Native American, 0.1% international, 4% transferred in, 52% live on campus. *Retention:* 72% of 2001 full-time freshmen returned.

Freshmen *Admission:* 3,347 applied, 2,917 admitted, 1,087 enrolled. *Average high school GPA:* 2.55. *Test scores:* SAT verbal scores over 500: 10%; SAT math scores over 500: 7%; ACT scores over 18: 21%; SAT verbal scores over 600: 1%; SAT math scores over 600: 1%.

Faculty *Total:* 180. *Student/faculty ratio:* 17:1.

Majors Accounting; agricultural sciences; biology; business administration; business economics; business education; business marketing and marketing management; chemistry; computer engineering; computer science; criminal justice studies; engineering technology; English; family/consumer resource management related; history; hotel and restaurant management; industrial/manufacturing engineering; interdisciplinary studies; management information systems/business data processing; mass communications; mathematics; music (general performance); physical education; physics; political science; psychology; public administration; social work; sociology; trade/industrial education; visual/performing arts.

Academic Programs *Special study options:* adult/continuing education programs, advanced placement credit, cooperative education, double majors, honors programs, independent study, internships, part-time degree program, services for LD students, student-designed majors, summer session for credit. *ROTC:* Army (b). *Unusual degree programs:* 3-2 engineering with Old Dominion University.

Library Johnston Memorial Library with 282,353 titles, 1,150 serial subscriptions, an OPAC, a Web page.

Computers on Campus 491 computers available on campus for general student use. Internet access, at least one staffed computer lab available.

Student Life *Housing:* on-campus residence required for freshman year. *Options:* men-only, women-only. *Activities and Organizations:* drama/theater group, student-run newspaper, choral group, marching band, NAACP, Betterment of Brothers/Sisters, Student Government Association, dormitory cabinets, pre-alumni associations, national fraternities, national sororities. *Campus security:* 24-hour emergency response devices and patrols. *Student Services:* health clinic, personal/psychological counseling.

Athletics Member NCAA. All Division II. *Intercollegiate sports:* baseball M, basketball M(s)/W(s), cross-country running M(s)/W(s), football M(s), golf M/W, softball W(s), tennis M(s)/W(s), track and field M(s)/W(s), volleyball W(s). *Intramural sports:* basketball M/W, football M, tennis M/W, track and field M/W, volleyball W.

Standardized Tests *Required:* SAT I or ACT (for admission).

Costs (2001–02) *Tuition:* state resident $1588 full-time, $69 per credit part-time; nonresident $8014 full-time, $350 per credit part-time. Full-time tuition and fees vary according to class time, course load, and program. Part-time tuition and fees vary according to class time, course load, and program. *Required fees:* $1724 full-time, $31 per term part-time. *Room and board:* $5594; room only: $3180. Room and board charges vary according to board plan and housing facility. *Payment plan:* deferred payment. *Waivers:* senior citizens.

Financial Aid Of all full-time matriculated undergraduates who enrolled in 2001, 2989 applied for aid, 2690 were judged to have need. 290 Federal Work-Study jobs (averaging $1200). 75 State and other part-time jobs (averaging $4398). In 2001, 158 non-need-based awards were made. *Average percent of need met:* 78%. *Average financial aid package:* $6413. *Average need-based loan:* $2815. *Average need-based gift aid:* $2122. *Average non-need based aid:* $3478. *Average indebtedness upon graduation:* $18,500. *Financial aid deadline:* 5/1.

Applying *Options:* common application, electronic application. *Application fee:* $25. *Required:* high school transcript, minimum 2.0 GPA, 2 letters of recommendation. *Application deadlines:* 5/1 (freshmen), 5/1 (transfers). *Notification:* continuous (freshmen).

Admissions Contact Mrs. Irene Logan, Director of Admissions (Interim), Virginia State University, PO Box 9018, Petersburg, VA 23806-2096. *Phone:* 804-524-5902. *Toll-free phone:* 800-871-7611. *E-mail:* lwinn@vsu.edu.

VIRGINIA UNION UNIVERSITY
Richmond, Virginia

- **Independent Baptist** comprehensive, founded 1865
- **Calendar** semesters
- **Degrees** bachelor's, master's, doctoral, and first professional
- **Urban** 72-acre campus
- **Coed,** 1,377 undergraduate students, 96% full-time, 59% women, 41% men
- **Moderately difficult** entrance level, 48% of applicants were admitted

Undergraduates 1,318 full-time, 59 part-time. Students come from 21 states and territories, 2 other countries, 99% African American, 0.1% Hispanic American. *Retention:* 70% of 2001 full-time freshmen returned.

Freshmen *Admission:* 2,572 applied, 1,232 admitted, 668 enrolled. *Average high school GPA:* 2.45.

Faculty *Total:* 85, 95% full-time. *Student/faculty ratio:* 11:1.

Majors Accounting; biology; business administration; business education; business marketing and marketing management; chemistry; criminology; drama therapy; early childhood education; elementary education; English; history; jazz; journalism; management information systems/business data processing; mathematics; music; political science; psychology; social work; sociology; special education.

Academic Programs *Special study options:* academic remediation for entering students, adult/continuing education programs, advanced placement credit, cooperative education, English as a second language, honors programs, internships, off-campus study, summer session for credit. *ROTC:* Army (c). *Unusual degree programs:* 3-2 engineering with Howard University, University of Michigan (Ann Arbor), University of Iowa, Virginia Commonwealth University.

Library L. Douglas Wilder Learning Resource Center and Library with 147,611 titles, 311 serial subscriptions, an OPAC.

Computers on Campus 128 computers available on campus for general student use. Internet access, at least one staffed computer lab available.

Student Life *Housing Options:* coed. *Activities and Organizations:* drama/theater group, student-run newspaper, choral group, marching band, national fraternities, national sororities. *Campus security:* 24-hour emergency response devices and patrols, controlled dormitory access. *Student Services:* health clinic, personal/psychological counseling.

Athletics Member NCAA. All Division II. *Intercollegiate sports:* basketball M(s)/W(s), cross-country running M(s)/W(s), football M(s), golf M(s), softball W(s), tennis M(s), track and field M(s)/W(s), volleyball W(s). *Intramural sports:* basketball M, softball W.

Standardized Tests *Required:* SAT I or ACT (for placement).

Costs (2001–02) *Comprehensive fee:* $15,354 includes full-time tuition ($9640), mandatory fees ($1050), and room and board ($4664). Part-time tuition: $402 per credit. *Required fees:* $525 per term part-time. *Room and board:* College room only: $2460. *Payment plans:* installment, deferred payment. *Waivers:* employees or children of employees.

Financial Aid Of all full-time matriculated undergraduates who enrolled in 2001, 933 applied for aid, 870 were judged to have need, 178 had their need fully met. 347 Federal Work-Study jobs (averaging $1835). In 2001, 35 non-need-based awards were made. *Average percent of need met:* 82%. *Average financial aid package:* $9386. *Average non-need based aid:* $8199.

Applying *Options:* common application, early admission, deferred entrance. *Application fee:* $15. *Required:* high school transcript. *Recommended:* essay or personal statement, 3 letters of recommendation. *Application deadline:* rolling (freshmen), rolling (transfers). *Notification:* continuous (freshmen).

Admissions Contact Mr. Gil Powell, Director of Admissions, Virginia Union University, 1500 North Lombardy Street, Richmond, VA 23220-1170. *Phone:* 804-257-5881. *Toll-free phone:* 800-368-3227.

VIRGINIA WESLEYAN COLLEGE
Norfolk, Virginia

- **Independent United Methodist** 4-year, founded 1961
- **Calendar** 4-1-4
- **Degree** bachelor's
- **Urban** 300-acre campus
- **Endowment** $20.3 million
- **Coed,** 1,408 undergraduate students, 75% full-time, 68% women, 32% men
- **Moderately difficult** entrance level, 80% of applicants were admitted

Undergraduates 1,056 full-time, 352 part-time. Students come from 53 states and territories, 29% are from out of state, 13% African American, 3% Asian American or Pacific Islander, 3% Hispanic American, 0.6% Native American, 0.7% international, 10% transferred in, 40% live on campus.

Freshmen *Admission:* 982 applied, 786 admitted, 295 enrolled. *Average high school GPA:* 2.85. *Test scores:* SAT verbal scores over 500: 56%; SAT math scores over 500: 37%; SAT verbal scores over 600: 13%; SAT math scores over 600: 9%; SAT verbal scores over 700: 1%; SAT math scores over 700: 1%.

Faculty *Total:* 109, 69% full-time, 59% with terminal degrees. *Student/faculty ratio:* 13:1.

Majors American studies; art; art education; biological/physical sciences; biology; business administration; chemistry; communications; computer science; criminal justice studies; drama/theater literature; earth sciences; education; education (K-12); elementary education; English; environmental science; foreign languages/literatures; French; German; history; humanities; human services; interdisciplinary studies; international relations; liberal arts and sciences/liberal studies; mathematics; middle school education; music; music teacher education; natural sciences; philosophy; political science; pre-dentistry; pre-law; pre-medicine; pre-veterinary studies; psychology; recreation/leisure studies; religious studies; science education; science/technology and society; secondary education; social sciences; sociology; Spanish; theater arts/drama.

Academic Programs *Special study options:* academic remediation for entering students, adult/continuing education programs, advanced placement credit, double majors, freshman honors college, honors programs, independent study, internships, off-campus study, part-time degree program, services for LD students, student-designed majors, study abroad, summer session for credit. *ROTC:* Army (c).

Library H. C. Hofheimer II Library with 111,067 titles, 651 serial subscriptions, 2,851 audiovisual materials, an OPAC, a Web page.

Computers on Campus 114 computers available on campus for general student use. A campuswide network can be accessed from student residence rooms that provide access to network programs, Web pages, on-line grades. Internet access, at least one staffed computer lab available.

Student Life *Housing:* on-campus residence required through senior year. *Options:* coed. *Activities and Organizations:* drama/theater group, student-run newspaper, radio station, choral group, student government, student radio station, student newspaper, Habitat for Humanity, national fraternities, national sororities. *Campus security:* 24-hour emergency response devices and patrols, late-night transport/escort service, controlled dormitory access, well-lit pathways. *Student Services:* health clinic, personal/psychological counseling, women's center.

Athletics Member NCAA. All Division III. *Intercollegiate sports:* baseball M, basketball M/W, cross-country running M/W, field hockey W, golf M, lacrosse M/W, soccer M/W, softball W, tennis M/W. *Intramural sports:* badminton M/W, basketball M/W, football M/W, golf M/W, racquetball M/W, skiing (downhill) M/W, soccer M/W, softball M/W, table tennis M/W, volleyball M/W, water polo M/W, weight lifting M/W.

Standardized Tests *Required:* SAT I or ACT (for admission).

Costs (2001–02) *Comprehensive fee:* $22,350 includes full-time tuition ($16,500) and room and board ($5850). Full-time tuition and fees vary according to class time. Part-time tuition: $688 per semester hour. Part-time tuition and fees vary according to class time and course load. *Room and board:* Room and board charges vary according to board plan and housing facility. *Payment plans:* installment, deferred payment. *Waivers:* senior citizens and employees or children of employees.

Financial Aid Of all full-time matriculated undergraduates who enrolled in 2001, 1023 applied for aid, 821 were judged to have need, 268 had their need fully met. 157 Federal Work-Study jobs. In 2001, 101 non-need-based awards were made. *Average percent of need met:* 92%. *Average financial aid package:* $14,860. *Average need-based loan:* $3309. *Average need-based gift aid:* $2752. *Average non-need based aid:* $9945. *Average indebtedness upon graduation:* $19,387.

Applying *Options:* common application, electronic application, early admission, deferred entrance. *Application fee:* $40. *Required:* essay or personal statement, high school transcript, minimum 2.0 GPA. *Recommended:* minimum 2.5 GPA, interview. *Application deadline:* rolling (freshmen), rolling (transfers). *Notification:* continuous (freshmen).

Admissions Contact Mr. Richard T. Hinshaw, Vice President for Enrollment Management, Dean of Admissions, Virginia Wesleyan College, Office of Admissions, Virginia Wesleyan College, 1584 Wesleyan Drive, Norfolk, VA 23502-5599. *Phone:* 757-455-3208. *Toll-free phone:* 800-737-8684. *Fax:* 757-461-5238. *E-mail:* admissions@vwc.edu.

WASHINGTON AND LEE UNIVERSITY

Lexington, Virginia

- **Independent** comprehensive, founded 1749
- **Calendar** 4-4-2
- **Degrees** bachelor's and first professional
- **Small-town** 322-acre campus
- **Endowment** $639.0 million
- **Coed,** 1,764 undergraduate students, 100% full-time, 46% women, 54% men
- **Most difficult** entrance level, 35% of applicants were admitted

Undergraduates 1,761 full-time, 3 part-time. Students come from 46 states and territories, 36 other countries, 87% are from out of state, 3% African American, 2% Asian American or Pacific Islander, 1.0% Hispanic American, 0.1% Native American, 4% international, 0.3% transferred in, 61% live on campus. *Retention:* 94% of 2001 full-time freshmen returned.

Freshmen *Admission:* 2,939 applied, 1,016 admitted, 488 enrolled. *Average high school GPA:* 3.90. *Test scores:* SAT verbal scores over 500: 99%; SAT math scores over 500: 99%; ACT scores over 18: 100%; SAT verbal scores over 600: 89%; SAT math scores over 600: 90%; ACT scores over 24: 100%; SAT verbal scores over 700: 36%; SAT math scores over 700: 36%; ACT scores over 30: 49%.

Faculty *Total:* 254, 93% full-time, 73% with terminal degrees. *Student/faculty ratio:* 9:1.

Majors Accounting; anthropology; archaeology; art history; biology; business administration; chemical engineering; chemistry; classics; computer science; East Asian studies; economics; engineering physics; English; fine/studio arts; foreign languages/literatures; forestry; French; geology; German; history; interdisciplinary studies; journalism; mathematics; medieval/renaissance studies; music; neuroscience; philosophy; physics; political science; psychology; public policy analysis; religious studies; Russian/Slavic studies; sociology; Spanish; theater arts/drama.

Academic Programs *Special study options:* accelerated degree program, advanced placement credit, double majors, honors programs, independent study, internships, off-campus study, services for LD students, student-designed majors, study abroad. *ROTC:* Army (c). *Unusual degree programs:* 3-2 forestry with Duke University.

Library James G. Leyburn Library plus 4 others with 603,758 titles, 2,856 serial subscriptions, 8,190 audiovisual materials, an OPAC, a Web page.

Computers on Campus 224 computers available on campus for general student use. A campuswide network can be accessed from student residence rooms and from off campus that provide access to e-mail. Internet access, online (class) registration, at least one staffed computer lab available.

Student Life *Housing:* on-campus residence required through sophomore year. *Options:* coed, men-only, women-only. *Activities and Organizations:* drama/theater group, student-run newspaper, radio and television station, choral group, Outing Club, Student Activities Board, Nabors Service League, Freshman Orientation Committee, student recruitment, national fraternities, national sororities. *Campus security:* 24-hour emergency response devices and patrols, late-night transport/escort service, controlled dormitory access. *Student Services:* health clinic, personal/psychological counseling, women's center.

Athletics Member NCAA. All Division III. *Intercollegiate sports:* baseball M, basketball M/W, cross-country running M/W, equestrian sports M/W, field hockey W, football M, golf M, ice hockey M(c)/W(c), lacrosse M/W, rugby M(c), soccer M/W, softball W(c), swimming M/W, tennis M/W, track and field M/W, volleyball M(c)/W, water polo M(c), wrestling M. *Intramural sports:* badminton M/W, baseball M/W, basketball M/W, bowling M/W, cross-country running M/W, fencing M(c)/W(c), football M/W, golf M/W, lacrosse M(c)/W(c), racquetball M(c)/W(c), skiing (cross-country) M(c)/W(c), skiing (downhill) M(c)/W(c), soccer M(c)/W(c), softball M/W, squash M(c)/W(c), swimming M/W, table tennis M/W, tennis M/W, track and field M/W, volleyball M/W, weight lifting M(c), wrestling M.

Standardized Tests *Required:* SAT I or ACT (for admission).

Costs (2001–02) *Comprehensive fee:* $25,095 includes full-time tuition ($19,170), mandatory fees ($175), and room and board ($5750). Part-time tuition: $639 per credit hour. *Room and board:* College room only: $2625. Room and board charges vary according to board plan and housing facility. *Waivers:* employees or children of employees.

Financial Aid Of all full-time matriculated undergraduates who enrolled in 2001, 658 applied for aid, 470 were judged to have need, 388 had their need fully met. 175 Federal Work-Study jobs (averaging $1380). 226 State and other part-time jobs (averaging $1342). In 2001, 344 non-need-based awards were made. *Average percent of need met:* 99%. *Average financial aid package:*

Washington and Lee University (continued)
$15,930. *Average need-based loan:* $3695. *Average need-based gift aid:* $15,149. *Average non-need based aid:* $7366. *Average indebtedness upon graduation:* $15,673.
Applying *Options:* common application, electronic application, early decision, deferred entrance. *Application fee:* $40. *Required:* essay or personal statement, high school transcript, 3 letters of recommendation. *Recommended:* interview. *Application deadlines:* 1/15 (freshmen), 4/1 (transfers). *Early decision:* 12/1. *Notification:* 4/1 (freshmen), 12/22 (early decision).
Admissions Contact Mr. William M. Hartog, Dean of Admissions and Financial Aid, Washington and Lee University, Lexington, VA 24450-0303. *Phone:* 540-463-8710. *Fax:* 540-463-8062. *E-mail:* admissions@wlu.edu.

World College
Virginia Beach, Virginia

- **Proprietary** 4-year, founded 1992
- **Calendar** semesters
- **Degrees** bachelor's (offers only external degree programs)
- **Suburban** campus
- **Coed,** 376 undergraduate students
- **Noncompetitive** entrance level

Undergraduates Students come from 50 states and territories, 25 other countries.
Faculty *Total:* 8, 100% full-time.
Majors Electrical/electronic engineering technology.
Academic Programs *Special study options:* academic remediation for entering students, accelerated degree program, adult/continuing education programs, distance learning, external degree program, part-time degree program.
Student Life *Housing:* college housing not available.
Applying *Options:* common application, early admission. *Required:* high school transcript. *Application deadline:* rolling (freshmen). *Notification:* continuous (freshmen).
Admissions Contact Michael Smith, Director of Operations and Registrar, World College, 5193 Shore Drive, Suite 105, Virginia Beach, VA 23455. *Phone:* 757-464-4600. *Toll-free phone:* 800-696-7532. *Fax:* 757-464-3687. *E-mail:* instruct@cie-wc.edu.

WASHINGTON

Antioch University Seattle
Seattle, Washington

- **Independent** upper-level, founded 1975, part of Antioch University
- **Calendar** quarters
- **Degrees** bachelor's and master's
- **Urban** campus
- **Coed,** 190 undergraduate students, 14% full-time, 75% women, 25% men
- **Noncompetitive** entrance level

Undergraduates Students come from 6 states and territories, 21% African American, 9% Asian American or Pacific Islander, 2% Hispanic American, 4% Native American.
Faculty *Total:* 15, 53% full-time, 47% with terminal degrees. *Student/faculty ratio:* 8:1.
Majors Liberal arts and sciences/liberal studies.
Academic Programs *Special study options:* academic remediation for entering students, accelerated degree program, adult/continuing education programs, advanced placement credit, external degree program, part-time degree program, student-designed majors, study abroad, summer session for credit.
Library Antioch Seattle Library with 4,750 titles, 85 serial subscriptions, an OPAC, a Web page.
Computers on Campus 8 computers available on campus for general student use. At least one staffed computer lab available.
Student Life *Housing:* college housing not available. *Activities and Organizations:* student-run newspaper.
Costs (2001–02) *Tuition:* $12,420 full-time, $355 per credit part-time. Full-time tuition and fees vary according to course load. Part-time tuition and fees vary according to course load and program. *Required fees:* $90 full-time, $15 per term part-time. *Payment plan:* installment. *Waivers:* employees or children of employees.
Financial Aid Of all full-time matriculated undergraduates who enrolled in 2001, 291 applied for aid, 280 were judged to have need, 200 had their need fully met. 22 Federal Work-Study jobs. *Average financial aid package:* $10,250. *Average need-based loan:* $5500. *Average indebtedness upon graduation:* $13,999.
Applying *Options:* electronic application, deferred entrance. *Application fee:* $50. *Application deadline:* 9/15 (transfers). *Notification:* continuous until 10/1 (transfers).
Admissions Contact Ms. Dianne Larsen, Admissions Director, Antioch University Seattle, 2326 Sixth Avenue, Seattle, WA 98121. *Phone:* 206-441-5352 Ext. 5200.

Bastyr University
Kenmore, Washington

- **Independent** upper-level, founded 1978
- **Calendar** quarters
- **Degrees** bachelor's, master's, first professional, and first professional certificates
- **Suburban** 50-acre campus with easy access to Seattle
- **Endowment** $361,142
- **Coed,** 193 undergraduate students, 82% full-time, 82% women, 18% men
- 66% of applicants were admitted

Undergraduates 159 full-time, 34 part-time. Students come from 7 other countries, 4% Asian American or Pacific Islander, 2% Hispanic American, 2% international, 42% transferred in, 6% live on campus.
Freshmen *Admission:* 179 applied, 119 admitted.
Faculty *Total:* 45, 40% full-time, 91% with terminal degrees. *Student/faculty ratio:* 15:1.
Majors Dietetics; exercise sciences; health science; nutrition science; psychology.
Academic Programs *Special study options:* cooperative education, double majors, independent study, internships, part-time degree program, summer session for credit.
Library Bastyr University Library with 11,000 titles, 250 serial subscriptions, 2,000 audiovisual materials, an OPAC, a Web page.
Computers on Campus 16 computers available on campus for general student use. Internet access, at least one staffed computer lab available.
Student Life *Housing Options:* coed. *Activities and Organizations:* student-run newspaper, Parent Resource Center, nature club, Spirituality in Focus, Environmental Action Team, Toastmasters. *Campus security:* student patrols, late-night transport/escort service. *Student Services:* health clinic, personal/psychological counseling.
Athletics *Intramural sports:* basketball M, soccer M/W, volleyball M/W.
Costs (2002–03) *Tuition:* $11,100 full-time, $243 per credit part-time. Full-time tuition and fees vary according to course load and program. Part-time tuition and fees vary according to course load and program. *Required fees:* $918 full-time. *Room only:* $4050. Room and board charges vary according to board plan and housing facility. *Waivers:* employees or children of employees.
Financial Aid Of all full-time matriculated undergraduates who enrolled in 2001, 146 applied for aid, 146 were judged to have need. 49 Federal Work-Study jobs (averaging $3066). 44 State and other part-time jobs (averaging $2648). *Average percent of need met:* 50%. *Average financial aid package:* $10,260. *Average need-based gift aid:* $750. *Average indebtedness upon graduation:* $21,000.
Applying *Options:* deferred entrance. *Application fee:* $60. *Application deadline:* 3/15 (transfers). *Notification:* continuous until 9/1 (transfers).
Admissions Contact Mr. Richard Dent, Director of Student Enrollment, Bastyr University, 14500 Juanita Drive, NE, Kenmore, WA 98028-4966. *Phone:* 425-602-3080. *Fax:* 425-823-6222.

Central Washington University
Ellensburg, Washington

- **State-supported** comprehensive, founded 1891
- **Calendar** quarters
- **Degrees** bachelor's, master's, and postbachelor's certificates
- **Small-town** 380-acre campus
- **Endowment** $8.5 million
- **Coed,** 8,306 undergraduate students, 88% full-time, 53% women, 47% men

■ **Moderately difficult** entrance level, 89% of applicants were admitted

Undergraduates 7,292 full-time, 1,014 part-time. Students come from 36 states and territories, 24 other countries, 4% are from out of state, 2% African American, 4% Asian American or Pacific Islander, 5% Hispanic American, 2% Native American, 2% international, 14% transferred in, 29% live on campus. *Retention:* 73% of 2001 full-time freshmen returned.

Freshmen *Admission:* 2,985 applied, 2,658 admitted, 1,260 enrolled. *Average high school GPA:* 3.17. *Test scores:* SAT verbal scores over 500: 51%; SAT math scores over 500: 47%; ACT scores over 18: 77%; SAT verbal scores over 600: 13%; SAT math scores over 600: 12%; ACT scores over 24: 22%; SAT verbal scores over 700: 2%; SAT math scores over 700: 1%; ACT scores over 30: 2%.

Faculty *Total:* 507, 66% full-time, 59% with terminal degrees. *Student/faculty ratio:* 20:1.

Majors Accounting; anthropology; art; art education; aviation/airway science; biology; biology education; business administration; business education; chemistry; chemistry education; community health liaison; computer/information sciences; criminal justice/law enforcement administration; drama/dance education; early childhood education; earth sciences; economics; electrical/electronic engineering technology; elementary education; emergency medical technology; English; English education; exercise sciences; fashion merchandising; foreign languages/literatures; geography; geology; gerontology; health education; history; history education; home economics; industrial arts education; industrial technology; journalism; mass communications; mathematics; mathematics education; mechanical engineering technology; music; music business management/merchandising; music (piano and organ performance); music teacher education; music theory and composition; music (voice and choral/opera performance); nutrition studies; occupational safety/health technology; office management; operations management; philosophy; physical education; physics; political science; psychology; public policy analysis; public relations; radio/television broadcasting; recreation/leisure studies; science education; social science education; sociology; special education; sport/fitness administration; theater arts/drama; trade/industrial education.

Academic Programs *Special study options:* academic remediation for entering students, adult/continuing education programs, advanced placement credit, cooperative education, distance learning, double majors, English as a second language, honors programs, independent study, internships, off-campus study, part-time degree program, services for LD students, student-designed majors, study abroad, summer session for credit. *ROTC:* Army (b), Air Force (b). *Unusual degree programs:* 3-2 engineering with University of Washington, Washington State University.

Library Central Washington University Library with 537,718 titles, 1,469 serial subscriptions, 9,230 audiovisual materials, an OPAC, a Web page.

Computers on Campus 659 computers available on campus for general student use. A campuswide network can be accessed from student residence rooms and from off campus. Internet access, at least one staffed computer lab available.

Student Life *Housing:* on-campus residence required for freshman year. *Options:* coed, disabled students. *Activities and Organizations:* drama/theater group, student-run newspaper, radio station, choral group, marching band, International Business Club, Marketing Club, Associated Students of CWU. *Campus security:* 24-hour emergency response devices and patrols, late-night transport/escort service, controlled dormitory access. *Student Services:* health clinic, personal/psychological counseling.

Athletics Member NCAA. All Division II. *Intercollegiate sports:* baseball M(s), basketball M(s)/W(s), cross-country running M(s)/W(s), fencing M(c), football M(s), rugby M(c)/W(c), soccer W(s), softball W(s), swimming M(s)/W(s), track and field M(s)/W(s), volleyball W(s), water polo M(c), wrestling M(s). *Intramural sports:* badminton M/W, basketball M/W, football M/W, golf M/W, racquetball M/W, rugby M/W, skiing (cross-country) M/W, skiing (downhill) M/W, soccer M/W, softball M/W, tennis M/W, volleyball M/W, wrestling M.

Standardized Tests *Required:* SAT I or ACT (for admission).

Costs (2001–02) *Tuition:* state resident $3024 full-time, $101 per credit part-time; nonresident $10,761 full-time, $359 per credit part-time. Full-time tuition and fees vary according to location. Part-time tuition and fees vary according to course load and location. *Required fees:* $324 full-time. *Room and board:* $5220. Room and board charges vary according to board plan and housing facility. *Waivers:* senior citizens and employees or children of employees.

Financial Aid Of all full-time matriculated undergraduates who enrolled in 2001, 4432 applied for aid, 3233 were judged to have need, 333 had their need fully met. 240 Federal Work-Study jobs (averaging $1658). *Average percent of need met:* 27%. *Average financial aid package:* $3712. *Average need-based loan:* $3663. *Average need-based gift aid:* $4190. *Average indebtedness upon graduation:* $18,461.

Applying *Options:* electronic application. *Application fee:* $35. *Required:* high school transcript, minimum 2.0 GPA. *Required for some:* essay or personal statement, letters of recommendation, interview. *Application deadline:* rolling (freshmen), rolling (transfers). *Notification:* continuous (freshmen).

Admissions Contact Mr. Mike Reilly, Director of Admissions, Central Washington University, 400 East 8th Avenue, Ellensburg, WA 98926-7463. *Phone:* 509-963-1211. *Toll-free phone:* 866-298-4968. *Fax:* 509-963-3022. *E-mail:* cwuadmis@cwu.edu.

CITY UNIVERSITY
Bellevue, Washington

■ **Independent** comprehensive, founded 1973
■ **Calendar** quarters
■ **Degrees** certificates, diplomas, associate, bachelor's, master's, and postbachelor's certificates
■ **Suburban** campus with easy access to Seattle
■ **Endowment** $195,000
■ **Coed,** 2,877 undergraduate students, 10% full-time, 45% women, 55% men
■ **Noncompetitive** entrance level, 100% of applicants were admitted

Undergraduates 297 full-time, 2,580 part-time. Students come from 47 states and territories, 33 other countries, 35% are from out of state, 6% African American, 9% Asian American or Pacific Islander, 3% Hispanic American, 1% Native American, 5% international, 73% transferred in.

Freshmen *Admission:* 1,460 applied, 1,460 admitted.

Faculty *Total:* 1,095, 5% full-time, 98% with terminal degrees.

Majors Accounting; business administration; computer/information sciences related; computer programming; elementary education; general studies; international business; journalism and mass communication related; mass communications; medical laboratory technician; psychology; special education.

Academic Programs *Special study options:* accelerated degree program, adult/continuing education programs, advanced placement credit, distance learning, double majors, English as a second language, external degree program, honors programs, independent study, internships, part-time degree program, services for LD students, summer session for credit.

Library City University Library with 32,329 titles, 1,518 serial subscriptions, 5,184 audiovisual materials, an OPAC, a Web page.

Computers on Campus 145 computers available on campus for general student use. A campuswide network can be accessed from off campus. Internet access, at least one staffed computer lab available.

Student Life *Housing:* college housing not available. *Campus security:* 24-hour emergency response devices.

Costs (2001–02) *Tuition:* $7280 full-time, $182 per credit hour part-time.

Financial Aid Of all full-time matriculated undergraduates who enrolled in 2001, 344 applied for aid, 287 were judged to have need. In 2001, 5 non-need-based awards were made. *Average financial aid package:* $4629. *Average need-based loan:* $4208. *Average need-based gift aid:* $2058. *Average non-need based aid:* $3708. *Average indebtedness upon graduation:* $17,308.

Applying *Options:* common application, electronic application, deferred entrance. *Application fee:* $75. *Recommended:* high school transcript. *Application deadline:* rolling (freshmen), rolling (transfers).

Admissions Contact Mr. Kent Gibson, Interim Vice President, Admissions and Student Services, City University, 11900 NE First Street, Bellevue, WA 98005. *Phone:* 800-426-5596 Ext. 4661. *Toll-free phone:* 800-426-5596. *Fax:* 425-709-5361. *E-mail:* info@cityu.edu.

CORNISH COLLEGE OF THE ARTS
Seattle, Washington

■ **Independent** 4-year, founded 1914
■ **Calendar** semesters
■ **Degree** certificates and bachelor's
■ **Urban** 4-acre campus
■ **Endowment** $636,870
■ **Coed,** 650 undergraduate students, 94% full-time, 62% women, 38% men
■ **Moderately difficult** entrance level, 76% of applicants were admitted

Undergraduates 614 full-time, 36 part-time. Students come from 27 states and territories, 14 other countries, 40% are from out of state, 4% transferred in. *Retention:* 72% of 2001 full-time freshmen returned.

Freshmen *Admission:* 566 applied, 431 admitted, 128 enrolled. *Average high school GPA:* 3.10.

Faculty *Total:* 158, 68% full-time. *Student/faculty ratio:* 9:1.

Majors Art; dance; fine/studio arts; graphic design/commercial art/illustration; interior design; music; music (piano and organ performance); music (voice and choral/opera performance); stringed instruments; theater arts/drama.

Cornish College of the Arts (continued)

Academic Programs *Special study options:* academic remediation for entering students, advanced placement credit, independent study, internships, services for LD students, study abroad, summer session for credit.

Library Cornish College of the Arts Library plus 2 others with 12,000 titles, 3,000 serial subscriptions, an OPAC.

Computers on Campus 20 computers available on campus for general student use. Internet access, at least one staffed computer lab available.

Student Life *Housing:* college housing not available. *Activities and Organizations:* drama/theater group, choral group, Student Union, Film Society, Black Student Alliance. *Campus security:* 24-hour emergency response devices and patrols, late-night transport/escort service. *Student Services:* personal/psychological counseling.

Standardized Tests *Recommended:* SAT I or ACT (for admission).

Costs (2001–02) *Tuition:* $16,000 full-time, $675 per credit part-time. Part-time tuition and fees vary according to program. *Required fees:* $200 full-time, $100 per term part-time. *Payment plan:* installment. *Waivers:* employees or children of employees.

Financial Aid Of all full-time matriculated undergraduates who enrolled in 2001, 573 applied for aid, 485 were judged to have need, 24 had their need fully met. *Average percent of need met:* 51%. *Average financial aid package:* $10,240. *Average need-based loan:* $4005. *Average need-based gift aid:* $5265. *Average indebtedness upon graduation:* $23,000.

Applying *Options:* electronic application, deferred entrance. *Application fee:* $35. *Required:* essay or personal statement, high school transcript, minimum 2.0 GPA, portfolio or audition. *Required for some:* 2 letters of recommendation. *Recommended:* 2 letters of recommendation, interview. *Application deadlines:* 8/15 (freshmen), 8/15 (transfers). *Notification:* continuous (freshmen).

Admissions Contact Ms. Sharron Starling, Associate Director of Admissions, Cornish College of the Arts, 710 East Roy Street, Seattle, WA 98102-4696. *Phone:* 206-726-5017. *Toll-free phone:* 800-726-ARTS. *Fax:* 206-720-1011. *E-mail:* admissions@cornish.edu.

CROWN COLLEGE

Tacoma, Washington

- **Proprietary** primarily 2-year, founded 1969
- **Calendar** continuous
- **Degrees** associate and bachelor's (bachelor's degree in public administration only)
- **Urban** campus with easy access to Seattle
- **Coed**
- 95% of applicants were admitted

Faculty *Student/faculty ratio:* 20:1.

Student Life *Campus security:* 24-hour emergency response devices.

Standardized Tests *Required:* ABLE.

Costs (2001–02) *Tuition:* $7072 full-time. No tuition increase for student's term of enrollment. *Required fees:* $200 full-time.

Applying *Options:* common application, electronic application. *Required:* essay or personal statement, high school transcript, interview.

Admissions Contact Ms. Sheila Millineaux, Admissions Director, Crown College, 8739 South Hosmer, Tacoma, WA 98444. *Phone:* 253-531-3123. *Toll-free phone:* 800-755-9525. *Fax:* 253-531-3521. *E-mail:* admissions@crowncollege.edu.

DEVRY UNIVERSITY

Federal Way, Washington

- **Proprietary** 4-year, founded 2001, part of DeVry, Inc
- **Calendar** semesters
- **Degrees** associate and bachelor's
- **Coed,** 561 undergraduate students, 72% full-time, 19% women, 81% men
- 89% of applicants were admitted

Undergraduates 403 full-time, 158 part-time. Students come from 15 states and territories, 1 other country, 9% are from out of state, 12% African American, 14% Asian American or Pacific Islander, 9% Hispanic American, 3% Native American, 0.7% international, 7% transferred in.

Freshmen *Admission:* 689 applied, 612 admitted, 487 enrolled.

Faculty *Total:* 19, 58% full-time. *Student/faculty ratio:* 32:1.

Majors Business administration/management related; business systems analysis/design; business systems networking/ telecommunications; computer engineering technology; electrical/electronic engineering technology; information sciences/systems.

Student Life *Housing:* college housing not available. *Activities and Organizations:* student-run newspaper, Associated Student Body (ASB), Ski Club, Computer Information Club, Basketball Club. *Campus security:* 24-hour emergency response devices and patrols, lighted pathways, emergency response team.

Athletics *Intramural sports:* basketball M/W.

Standardized Tests *Recommended:* SAT I or ACT (for admission).

Costs (2001–02) *Tuition:* $10,000 full-time, $355 per credit hour part-time. Full-time tuition and fees vary according to course load. Part-time tuition and fees vary according to course load. *Payment plans:* installment, deferred payment. *Waivers:* employees or children of employees.

Financial Aid Of all full-time matriculated undergraduates who enrolled in 2001, 699 applied for aid, 648 were judged to have need, 11 had their need fully met. In 2001, 51 non-need-based awards were made. *Average percent of need met:* 35%. *Average financial aid package:* $6026. *Average need-based loan:* $4510. *Average need-based gift aid:* $3360.

Applying *Application fee:* $50. *Application deadline:* rolling (freshmen), rolling (transfers). *Notification:* continuous (freshmen).

Admissions Contact Ms. Latanya Kibby, Assistant New Student Coordinator, DeVry University, 3600 South 344th Way, Federal Way, WA 98001-2995. *Phone:* 253-943-2800.

EASTERN WASHINGTON UNIVERSITY

Cheney, Washington

- **State-supported** comprehensive, founded 1882
- **Calendar** quarters
- **Degrees** bachelor's and master's
- **Small-town** 335-acre campus
- **Endowment** $4.0 million
- **Coed,** 7,958 undergraduate students, 89% full-time, 57% women, 43% men
- **Moderately difficult** entrance level, 84% of applicants were admitted

Undergraduates 7,072 full-time, 886 part-time. Students come from 40 states and territories, 26 other countries, 9% are from out of state, 2% African American, 3% Asian American or Pacific Islander, 4% Hispanic American, 2% Native American, 2% international, 14% transferred in, 21% live on campus. *Retention:* 81% of 2001 full-time freshmen returned.

Freshmen *Admission:* 3,116 applied, 2,608 admitted, 1,199 enrolled. *Average high school GPA:* 3.26. *Test scores:* SAT verbal scores over 500: 51%; SAT math scores over 500: 50%; ACT scores over 18: 84%; SAT verbal scores over 600: 14%; SAT math scores over 600: 12%; ACT scores over 24: 23%; SAT verbal scores over 700: 1%; SAT math scores over 700: 1%; ACT scores over 30: 2%.

Faculty *Total:* 636, 56% full-time, 43% with terminal degrees. *Student/faculty ratio:* 21:1.

Majors Accounting; anthropology; Army R.O.T.C./military science; art; art education; art history; athletic training/sports medicine; biochemistry; biological/physical sciences; biology; botany; broadcast journalism; business administration; business economics; business education; business marketing and marketing management; chemistry; city/community/regional planning; computer engineering technology; computer/information sciences; computer science; construction technology; corrections; creative writing; criminal justice/law enforcement administration; dance; dental hygiene; developmental/child psychology; earth sciences; economics; education; electrical/electronic engineering technology; elementary education; English; environmental biology; exercise sciences; finance; fine/studio arts; French; geography; geology; health education; health services administration; history; humanities; human resources management; industrial technology; information sciences/systems; interdisciplinary studies; international relations; journalism; liberal arts and sciences/liberal studies; literature; management information systems/business data processing; mass communications; mathematics; mechanical engineering technology; medical technology; microbiology/bacteriology; modern languages; music; music (piano and organ performance); music teacher education; music (voice and choral/opera performance); natural sciences; nursing; occupational therapy; philosophy; physical education; physical sciences; physical therapy; physics; political science; pre-dentistry; pre-law; pre-medicine; pre-veterinary studies; psychology; public administration; public health; public policy analysis; public relations; radio/television broadcasting; reading education; recreational therapy; recreation/leisure facilities management; recreation/leisure studies; science education; secondary education; social sciences; social work; sociology; Spanish; special education; speech-language pathology/audiology; speech/rhetorical studies; speech therapy; stringed instruments; theater arts/drama; urban studies; wind/percussion instruments; zoology.

Academic Programs *Special study options:* advanced placement credit, cooperative education, distance learning, double majors, English as a second language, external degree program, honors programs, independent study, internships, off-campus study, part-time degree program, services for LD students, student-designed majors, study abroad, summer session for credit. *ROTC:* Army (b).

Library John F. Kennedy Library plus 2 others with 1.4 million titles, 6,429 serial subscriptions, 31,832 audiovisual materials, an OPAC, a Web page.

Computers on Campus 125 computers available on campus for general student use. A campuswide network can be accessed from student residence rooms and from off campus that provide access to e-mail. Internet access, at least one staffed computer lab available.

Student Life *Housing Options:* coed, men-only, women-only, disabled students. *Activities and Organizations:* drama/theater group, student-run newspaper, radio and television station, choral group, marching band, International Student Association, cultural heritage groups, Eagle Ambassadors, business/honor fraternities, religious organizations, national fraternities, national sororities. *Campus security:* 24-hour emergency response devices and patrols, student patrols, late-night transport/escort service, controlled dormitory access, emergency call boxes. *Student Services:* health clinic, personal/psychological counseling, women's center.

Athletics Member NCAA. All Division I except football (Division I-AA). *Intercollegiate sports:* badminton M(c), baseball M(c), basketball M(s)/W(s), cross-country running M(s)/W(s), golf M(s)/W(s), ice hockey M(c), soccer W(s), tennis M(s)/W(s), track and field M(s)/W(s), volleyball W(s). *Intramural sports:* baseball M/W, basketball M/W, bowling M/W, cross-country running M/W, football M/W, golf M/W, racquetball M/W, soccer M/W, softball M/W, tennis M/W, track and field M/W, volleyball M/W.

Standardized Tests *Required:* SAT I or ACT (for admission).

Costs (2001–02) *Tuition:* state resident $2964 full-time, $99 per credit hour part-time; nonresident $10,230 full-time, $341 per credit hour part-time. Full-time tuition and fees vary according to reciprocity agreements. Part-time tuition and fees vary according to course load and reciprocity agreements. *Required fees:* $222 full-time. *Room and board:* $4786. Room and board charges vary according to board plan and housing facility. *Payment plan:* installment. *Waivers:* employees or children of employees.

Financial Aid Of all full-time matriculated undergraduates who enrolled in 2001, 4429 applied for aid, 3680 were judged to have need, 560 had their need fully met. 331 Federal Work-Study jobs (averaging $1762). In 2001, 435 non-need-based awards were made. *Average percent of need met:* 40%. *Average financial aid package:* $13,512. *Average need-based loan:* $3659. *Average need-based gift aid:* $3980. *Average non-need based aid:* $2457. *Average indebtedness upon graduation:* $15,340.

Applying *Options:* common application, electronic application, early admission, deferred entrance. *Application fee:* $35. *Required:* high school transcript, minimum 2.0 GPA. *Required for some:* essay or personal statement, letters of recommendation, interview. *Recommended:* minimum 3.0 GPA. *Application deadline:* rolling (freshmen), rolling (transfers). *Notification:* continuous (freshmen).

Admissions Contact Ms. Michelle Whittingham, Director of Admissions, Eastern Washington University, 526 Fifth Street, SUT 101, Cheney, WA 99004-2447. *Phone:* 509-359-6582. *Toll-free phone:* 888-740-1914. *Fax:* 509-359-6692. *E-mail:* admissions@mail.ewu.edu.

THE EVERGREEN STATE COLLEGE

Olympia, Washington

- **State-supported** comprehensive, founded 1967
- **Calendar** quarters
- **Degrees** bachelor's and master's
- **Small-town** 1000-acre campus with easy access to Seattle
- **Endowment** $2.3 million
- **Coed,** 4,001 undergraduate students, 87% full-time, 58% women, 42% men
- **Moderately difficult** entrance level, 82% of applicants were admitted

Undergraduates 3,486 full-time, 515 part-time. Students come from 46 states and territories, 14 other countries, 24% are from out of state, 4% African American, 4% Asian American or Pacific Islander, 4% Hispanic American, 4% Native American, 0.9% international, 24% transferred in, 22% live on campus. *Retention:* 69% of 2001 full-time freshmen returned.

Freshmen *Admission:* 1,237 applied, 1,013 admitted, 469 enrolled. *Average high school GPA:* 3.13. *Test scores:* SAT verbal scores over 500: 85%; SAT math scores over 500: 69%; ACT scores over 18: 79%; SAT verbal scores over 600: 52%; SAT math scores over 600: 26%; ACT scores over 24: 31%; SAT verbal scores over 700: 9%; SAT math scores over 700: 2%; ACT scores over 30: 3%.

Faculty *Total:* 276, 79% full-time, 69% with terminal degrees. *Student/faculty ratio:* 22:1.

Majors Agricultural sciences; American studies; anthropology; art; art history; arts management; Asian studies; audio engineering; biochemistry; biological/physical sciences; biology; business administration; ceramic arts; chemistry; classics; community services; comparative literature; computer science; counselor education/guidance; creative writing; cultural studies; dance; earth sciences; ecology; economics; education; energy management technology; English; environmental biology; environmental education; environmental science; European studies; film studies; film/video production; fine/studio arts; fish/game management; French; genetics; geology; Hispanic-American studies; history; history of philosophy; human ecology; humanities; human services; interdisciplinary studies; Japanese; land use management; Latin American studies; liberal arts and sciences/liberal studies; literature; marine biology; marine science; mass communications; mathematics; Mexican-American studies; microbiology/bacteriology; molecular biology; music; Native American studies; natural resources conservation; natural resources management; natural sciences; philosophy; photography; physical sciences; physics; political science; pre-dentistry; pre-law; pre-medicine; pre-veterinary studies; psychology; public administration; public policy analysis; Russian; Russian/Slavic studies; social sciences; sociology; Spanish; theater arts/drama; urban studies; water resources; western civilization; wildlife biology; women's studies; zoology.

Academic Programs *Special study options:* advanced placement credit, cooperative education, double majors, independent study, internships, off-campus study, part-time degree program, services for LD students, student-designed majors, study abroad, summer session for credit.

Library Daniel J. Evans Library with 320,100 titles, 5,100 serial subscriptions, 85,344 audiovisual materials, an OPAC, a Web page.

Computers on Campus 150 computers available on campus for general student use. A campuswide network can be accessed from student residence rooms and from off campus. Internet access, at least one staffed computer lab available.

Student Life *Housing Options:* coed. *Activities and Organizations:* drama/theater group, student-run newspaper, radio station, choral group, Environmental Resource Center, Women's Resource Center, Evergreen Queer Alliance, Evergreen Political Information Center. *Campus security:* 24-hour emergency response devices and patrols, student patrols, late-night transport/escort service, controlled dormitory access. *Student Services:* health clinic, personal/psychological counseling, women's center.

Athletics Member NAIA. *Intercollegiate sports:* basketball M/W, cross-country running M/W, soccer M/W, swimming M/W, tennis M/W, volleyball M/W. *Intramural sports:* basketball M/W, crew M/W, fencing M/W, racquetball M/W, sailing M/W, skiing (downhill) M/W, soccer M/W, swimming M/W, tennis M/W, volleyball M/W, weight lifting M/W.

Standardized Tests *Required:* SAT I or ACT (for admission).

Costs (2001–02) *Tuition:* state resident $3024 full-time, $101 per quarter hour part-time; nonresident $10,764 full-time, $359 per quarter hour part-time. *Required fees:* $167 full-time. *Room and board:* $5610. Room and board charges vary according to board plan and housing facility. *Payment plan:* installment.

Financial Aid Of all full-time matriculated undergraduates who enrolled in 2001, 2701 applied for aid, 2266 were judged to have need, 1057 had their need fully met. 320 Federal Work-Study jobs (averaging $1116). 172 State and other part-time jobs (averaging $1673). In 2001, 45 non-need-based awards were made. *Average percent of need met:* 78%. *Average financial aid package:* $8059. *Average need-based loan:* $3868. *Average need-based gift aid:* $4219. *Average non-need based aid:* $1879. *Average indebtedness upon graduation:* $12,000.

Applying *Options:* electronic application, early admission. *Application fee:* $35. *Required:* high school transcript, minimum 2.0 GPA. *Required for some:* interview. *Recommended:* essay or personal statement. *Application deadlines:* 3/1 (freshmen), 3/1 (transfers). *Notification:* 4/1 (freshmen).

Admissions Contact Mr. Doug P. Scrima, Director of Admissions, The Evergreen State College, 2700 Evergreen Parkway NW, Olympia, WA 98505. *Phone:* 360-867-6170. *Fax:* 360-867-6576. *E-mail:* admissions@evergreen.edu.

GONZAGA UNIVERSITY

Spokane, Washington

- **Independent Roman Catholic** comprehensive, founded 1887
- **Calendar** semesters
- **Degrees** bachelor's, master's, doctoral, first professional, and post-master's certificates
- **Urban** 94-acre campus
- **Endowment** $110.7 million
- **Coed,** 3,483 undergraduate students, 95% full-time, 54% women, 46% men
- **Moderately difficult** entrance level, 82% of applicants were admitted

Gonzaga's nationally dominant debate team, exceptional medical school acceptance rate, and CPA examination pass rates exemplify Gonzaga's commitment to academic excellence. Outstanding facilities supporting these programs include Foley Center Library, featuring 782,000 volumes and microform

Gonzaga University (continued)
titles, Jundt Art Center and Museum, and Gonzaga's new School of Law building, completed in spring of 2000.

Undergraduates 3,295 full-time, 188 part-time. Students come from 34 states and territories, 35 other countries, 54% are from out of state, 1% African American, 5% Asian American or Pacific Islander, 3% Hispanic American, 1% Native American, 2% international, 7% transferred in, 53% live on campus. *Retention:* 90% of 2001 full-time freshmen returned.
Freshmen *Admission:* 3,042 applied, 2,495 admitted, 971 enrolled. *Average high school GPA:* 3.62. *Test scores:* SAT verbal scores over 500: 87%; SAT math scores over 500: 89%; ACT scores over 18: 99%; SAT verbal scores over 600: 40%; SAT math scores over 600: 49%; ACT scores over 24: 73%; SAT verbal scores over 700: 9%; SAT math scores over 700: 8%; ACT scores over 30: 15%.
Faculty *Total:* 501, 56% full-time, 46% with terminal degrees. *Student/faculty ratio:* 11:1.
Majors Accounting; art; Asian studies; biochemistry; biology; broadcast journalism; business administration; business economics; business marketing and marketing management; chemistry; civil engineering; computer engineering; computer science; criminal justice/law enforcement administration; economics; electrical engineering; elementary education; engineering; English; exercise sciences; finance; French; German; history; information sciences/systems; international business; international relations; Italian; journalism; liberal arts and sciences/liberal studies; literature; mass communications; mathematics; mechanical engineering; music; music teacher education; nursing; philosophy; physical education; physics; political science; psychology; public relations; religious studies; secondary education; sociology; Spanish; special education; speech/rhetorical studies; sport/fitness administration; theater arts/drama.
Academic Programs *Special study options:* adult/continuing education programs, advanced placement credit, distance learning, double majors, English as a second language, honors programs, independent study, internships, off-campus study, part-time degree program, services for LD students, student-designed majors, study abroad, summer session for credit. *ROTC:* Army (b).
Library Ralph E. and Helen Higgins Foley Center plus 1 other with 351,616 titles, 1,470 serial subscriptions, 2,597 audiovisual materials, an OPAC, a Web page.
Computers on Campus 340 computers available on campus for general student use. A campuswide network can be accessed from student residence rooms and from off campus. Internet access, online (class) registration, at least one staffed computer lab available.
Student Life *Housing:* on-campus residence required through sophomore year. *Options:* coed, men-only, women-only. *Activities and Organizations:* drama/theater group, student-run newspaper, radio and television station, choral group, Student Body Association, Search, Circle K, Encore, Knights and Setons. *Campus security:* 24-hour emergency response devices and patrols, late-night transport/escort service, controlled dormitory access. *Student Services:* health clinic, personal/psychological counseling.
Athletics Member NCAA. All Division I. *Intercollegiate sports:* baseball M(s), basketball M(s)/W(s), crew M(c)/W(c), cross-country running M/W, golf M/W, skiing (cross-country) M(c)/W(c), skiing (downhill) M(c)/W(c), soccer M(s)/W(s), tennis M(s)/W(s), track and field M/W, volleyball W(s). *Intramural sports:* basketball M(c)/W(c), football M(c)/W(c), racquetball M(c)/W(c), softball M(c)/W(c), volleyball M(c)/W(c).
Standardized Tests *Required:* SAT I or ACT (for admission).
Costs (2001–02) *Comprehensive fee:* $24,221 includes full-time tuition ($18,300), mandatory fees ($241), and room and board ($5680). Full-time tuition and fees vary according to course load. Part-time tuition: $525 per credit. Part-time tuition and fees vary according to course load. *Required fees:* $35 per term part-time. *Room and board:* College room only: $2850. Room and board charges vary according to board plan and housing facility. *Payment plans:* installment, deferred payment. *Waivers:* senior citizens and employees or children of employees.
Financial Aid Of all full-time matriculated undergraduates who enrolled in 2001, 1959 applied for aid, 1606 were judged to have need, 419 had their need fully met. 391 Federal Work-Study jobs (averaging $2586). 393 State and other part-time jobs (averaging $4232). In 2001, 838 non-need-based awards were made. *Average percent of need met:* 82%. *Average financial aid package:* $15,735. *Average need-based loan:* $5130. *Average need-based gift aid:* $9470. *Average non-need based aid:* $5887. *Average indebtedness upon graduation:* $21,511.
Applying *Options:* common application, electronic application, early admission, early action, deferred entrance. *Application fee:* $40. *Required:* essay or personal statement, high school transcript, minimum 3.0 GPA, 1 letter of recommendation. *Recommended:* interview. *Application deadlines:* 2/1 (freshmen), 6/1 (transfers). *Notification:* continuous (freshmen), 1/1 (early action).
Admissions Contact Ms. Julie McCulloh, Associate Dean of Admission, Gonzaga University, Ad Box 102, Spokane, WA 99258-0102. *Phone:* 509-323-6591. *Toll-free phone:* 800-322-2584 Ext. 6572. *Fax:* 509-323-5780. *E-mail:* ballinger@gu.gonzaga.edu.

HENRY COGSWELL COLLEGE
Everett, Washington

- **Independent** 4-year, founded 1979
- **Calendar** trimesters
- **Degree** bachelor's
- **Urban** 1-acre campus with easy access to Seattle
- **Endowment** $138,743
- **Coed, primarily men,** 258 undergraduate students, 64% full-time, 21% women, 79% men
- **Noncompetitive** entrance level, 79% of applicants were admitted

Undergraduates 165 full-time, 93 part-time. Students come from 3 states and territories, 2 other countries, 2% are from out of state, 2% African American, 8% Asian American or Pacific Islander, 3% Hispanic American, 0.8% Native American, 0.8% international, 93% transferred in. *Retention:* 86% of 2001 full-time freshmen returned.
Freshmen *Admission:* 28 applied, 22 admitted, 17 enrolled. *Average high school GPA:* 3.10.
Faculty *Total:* 36, 28% full-time, 36% with terminal degrees. *Student/faculty ratio:* 7:1.
Majors Business administration; computer graphics; computer science; electrical engineering; mechanical engineering.
Academic Programs *Special study options:* academic remediation for entering students, accelerated degree program, adult/continuing education programs, advanced placement credit, double majors, internships, part-time degree program, summer session for credit.
Library Henry Cogswell College Library with 6,774 titles, 60 serial subscriptions, 85 audiovisual materials, an OPAC.
Computers on Campus 40 computers available on campus for general student use. A campuswide network can be accessed from off campus. Internet access, at least one staffed computer lab available.
Student Life *Housing:* college housing not available. *Activities and Organizations:* Student Senate, climbing logs (indoor wall climbing). *Campus security:* controlled dormitory access.
Standardized Tests *Required:* SAT I or ACT (for admission).
Costs (2002–03) *One-time required fee:* $75. *Tuition:* $13,080 full-time, $545 per credit part-time. No tuition increase for student's term of enrollment. *Payment plans:* installment, deferred payment. *Waivers:* employees or children of employees.
Financial Aid Of all full-time matriculated undergraduates who enrolled in 2001, 67 applied for aid, 59 were judged to have need. 6 Federal Work-Study jobs (averaging $590). *Average percent of need met:* 36%. *Average financial aid package:* $6902. *Average need-based loan:* $4130. *Average need-based gift aid:* $3476. *Average indebtedness upon graduation:* $22,650.
Applying *Options:* common application, electronic application, deferred entrance. *Application fee:* $50. *Required:* essay or personal statement, high school transcript. *Required for some:* 3 letters of recommendation, portfolio. *Recommended:* interview. *Application deadline:* rolling (freshmen), rolling (transfers). *Notification:* continuous (freshmen).
Admissions Contact Henry Cogswell College, 3002 Colby Avenue, Everett, WA 98201. *Phone:* 425-258-3351 Ext. 116. *Toll-free phone:* 866-411-HCC1. *Fax:* 425-257-0405. *E-mail:* information@henrycogswell.edu.

HERITAGE COLLEGE
Toppenish, Washington

- **Independent** comprehensive, founded 1982
- **Calendar** semesters
- **Degrees** associate, bachelor's, and master's
- **Rural** 10-acre campus
- **Endowment** $3.1 million
- **Coed**
- **Noncompetitive** entrance level

Faculty *Student/faculty ratio:* 9:1.
Student Life *Campus security:* 24-hour emergency response devices.
Standardized Tests *Recommended:* SAT I or ACT (for placement).

Financial Aid Of all full-time matriculated undergraduates who enrolled in 2001, 268 applied for aid, 264 were judged to have need, 23 had their need fully met. 126 Federal Work-Study jobs (averaging $1331). 66 State and other part-time jobs (averaging $2623). In 2001, 4. *Average percent of need met:* 65. *Average financial aid package:* $7393. *Average need-based loan:* $3112. *Average need-based gift aid:* $5429. *Average non-need based aid:* $6954.

Applying *Options:* common application, early admission, deferred entrance. *Required:* high school transcript.

Admissions Contact Mr. Norberto T. Espindola, Director of Admissions and Recruitment, Heritage College, 3240 Fort Road, Toppenish, WA 98948-9599. *Phone:* 509-865-8500 Ext. 2002. *Toll-free phone:* 509-865-8508. *Fax:* 509-865-4469. *E-mail:* espindola_b@heritage.edu.

ITT TECHNICAL INSTITUTE
Seattle, Washington

- **Proprietary** primarily 2-year, founded 1932, part of ITT Educational Services, Inc
- **Calendar** quarters
- **Degrees** associate and bachelor's
- **Urban** campus
- **Coed,** 436 undergraduate students
- **Minimally difficult** entrance level

Majors Computer/information sciences related; computer programming; computer systems analysis; electrical/electronic engineering technologies related; information technology.

Student Life *Housing:* college housing not available.

Costs (2001–02) *Tuition:* Full-time tuition and fees vary according to program. Part-time tuition and fees vary according to program. $260—$330 per credit hour.

Applying *Options:* deferred entrance. *Application fee:* $100. *Required:* high school transcript, interview. *Recommended:* letters of recommendation. *Application deadline:* rolling (freshmen), rolling (transfers). *Notification:* continuous (freshmen).

Admissions Contact Mr. Gary Rentel, Director of Recruitment, ITT Technical Institute, 12720 Gateway Drive, Seattle, WA 98168. *Phone:* 206-244-3300. *Toll-free phone:* 800-422-2029.

THE LEADERSHIP INSTITUTE OF SEATTLE
Kenmore, Washington

Admissions Contact Mr. Don Werner, Coordinator of Undergraduate Admissions, The Leadership Institute of Seattle, 1450 114th Avenue SE, Suite 230, Bellevue, WA 98004-6934. *Phone:* 425-635-1187 Ext. 254. *Toll-free phone:* 800-789-5467. *E-mail:* lios@lios.org.

NORTHWEST COLLEGE
Kirkland, Washington

- **Independent** comprehensive, founded 1934, affiliated with Assemblies of God
- **Calendar** semesters
- **Degrees** certificates, diplomas, associate, bachelor's, and master's
- **Suburban** 65-acre campus with easy access to Seattle
- **Endowment** $7.7 million
- **Coed,** 1,096 undergraduate students, 95% full-time, 56% women, 44% men
- **Moderately difficult** entrance level, 26% of applicants were admitted

Undergraduates 1,039 full-time, 57 part-time. Students come from 30 states and territories, 22% are from out of state, 3% African American, 6% Asian American or Pacific Islander, 3% Hispanic American, 1% Native American, 0.2% international, 20% transferred in, 61% live on campus. *Retention:* 65% of 2001 full-time freshmen returned.

Freshmen *Admission:* 774 applied, 199 admitted, 207 enrolled. *Average high school GPA:* 3.1. *Test scores:* SAT verbal scores over 500: 74%; SAT math scores over 500: 26%; ACT scores over 18: 78%; SAT verbal scores over 600: 20%; SAT math scores over 600: 5%; ACT scores over 24: 23%; SAT verbal scores over 700: 1%; ACT scores over 30: 1%.

Faculty *Total:* 82, 56% full-time, 37% with terminal degrees. *Student/faculty ratio:* 18:1.

Majors Behavioral sciences; biblical studies; business administration; divinity/ministry; education; elementary education; English; English education; environmental biology; health science; history; history education; interdisciplinary studies; liberal arts and sciences/liberal studies; management science; middle school education; music; music (piano and organ performance); music teacher education; music (voice and choral/opera performance); pastoral counseling; philosophy; physical education; pre-law; psychology; religious education; religious music; religious studies; secondary education; social sciences; special education; teaching English as a second language; theater arts/drama; theology.

Academic Programs *Special study options:* academic remediation for entering students, accelerated degree program, adult/continuing education programs, advanced placement credit, cooperative education, double majors, English as a second language, independent study, internships, part-time degree program, student-designed majors, study abroad, summer session for credit.

Library D. V. Hurst Library with 159,115 titles, 814 serial subscriptions, 16,887 audiovisual materials, an OPAC.

Computers on Campus 40 computers available on campus for general student use. A campuswide network can be accessed from student residence rooms and from off campus. At least one staffed computer lab available.

Student Life *Housing:* on-campus residence required through sophomore year. *Options:* men-only, women-only. *Activities and Organizations:* drama/theater group, student-run newspaper, radio station, choral group, Environmental Club, Psychology Club, Association of Business Students, Drama Club, student ministries. *Campus security:* 24-hour emergency response devices and patrols, late-night transport/escort service, controlled dormitory access. *Student Services:* health clinic, personal/psychological counseling.

Athletics Member NAIA, NCCAA. *Intercollegiate sports:* basketball M(s)/W(s), cross-country running M(s)/W(s), soccer M(s), track and field M(s)/W(s), volleyball W(s). *Intramural sports:* baseball M, basketball M/W, football M, golf M, table tennis M/W, tennis M/W, track and field M/W, volleyball M/W.

Standardized Tests *Required:* SAT I or ACT (for admission).

Costs (2002–03) *Comprehensive fee:* $18,849 includes full-time tuition ($12,550), mandatory fees ($303), and room and board ($5996). Part-time tuition: $525 per credit hour. Part-time tuition and fees vary according to course load. *Required fees:* $163 per term part-time. *Room and board:* Room and board charges vary according to board plan. *Payment plans:* installment, deferred payment. *Waivers:* senior citizens and employees or children of employees.

Financial Aid Of all full-time matriculated undergraduates who enrolled in 2001, 654 applied for aid, 570 were judged to have need, 117 had their need fully met. 101 Federal Work-Study jobs (averaging $1250). 36 State and other part-time jobs (averaging $3303). In 2001, 146 non-need-based awards were made. *Average percent of need met:* 70%. *Average financial aid package:* $9399. *Average need-based loan:* $3502. *Average need-based gift aid:* $6054.

Applying *Options:* common application, early admission, early decision, deferred entrance. *Application fee:* $30. *Required:* essay or personal statement, high school transcript, minimum 2.3 GPA, 2 letters of recommendation. *Required for some:* interview. *Application deadlines:* 8/1 (freshmen), 8/1 (transfers). *Early decision:* 11/15. *Notification:* continuous (freshmen), 12/31 (early decision).

Admissions Contact Mr. Myles Corrigan, Associate Vice President of Enrollment, Northwest College, PO Box 579, Kirkland, WA 98083-0579. *Phone:* 425-889-5209. *Toll-free phone:* 800-669-3781. *Fax:* 425-889-5224. *E-mail:* admissions@ncag.edu.

NORTHWEST COLLEGE OF ART
Poulsbo, Washington

- **Proprietary** 4-year, founded 1982
- **Calendar** semesters
- **Degree** bachelor's
- **Small-town** 26-acre campus with easy access to Seattle
- **Coed,** 83 undergraduate students
- **Moderately difficult** entrance level

Undergraduates Students come from 1 other country.

Freshmen *Average high school GPA:* 3.0.

Faculty *Total:* 7, 29% full-time.

Majors Art; graphic design/commercial art/illustration.

Academic Programs *Special study options:* double majors, internships, summer session for credit.

Library Northwest College of Art Library.

Computers on Campus 28 computers available on campus for general student use. Internet access, at least one staffed computer lab available.

Student Life *Housing:* college housing not available.

Costs (2002–03) *Tuition:* $11,800 full-time, $510 per credit part-time. Part-time tuition and fees vary according to course load. *Required fees:* $100 full-time, $100 per term part-time. *Payment plan:* installment. *Waivers:* employees or children of employees.

Northwest College of Art (continued)

Applying *Options:* deferred entrance. *Application fee:* $50. *Required:* essay or personal statement, high school transcript, minimum 2.0 GPA, 3 letters of recommendation, interview, portfolio. *Application deadlines:* 6/1 (freshmen), 6/1 (transfers). *Notification:* continuous (freshmen).

Admissions Contact Mr. Craig Freeman, President, Northwest College of Art, 16464 State Highway 305, Poulsbo, WA 98370. *Phone:* 360-779-9993. *Toll-free phone:* 800-769-ARTS. *Fax:* 360-779-9933. *E-mail:* kimatnca@silverlink.net.

PACIFIC LUTHERAN UNIVERSITY
Tacoma, Washington

- **Independent** comprehensive, founded 1890, affiliated with Evangelical Lutheran Church in America
- **Calendar** 4-1-4
- **Degrees** bachelor's, master's, and postbachelor's certificates
- **Suburban** 126-acre campus with easy access to Seattle
- **Endowment** $42.6 million
- **Coed,** 3,144 undergraduate students, 92% full-time, 61% women, 39% men
- **Moderately difficult** entrance level, 80% of applicants were admitted

Pacific Lutheran University (PLU) believes that a keener understanding of the global community is vital. A recent report in *The Chronicle of Higher Education* reported that PLU ranked tenth in the master's category of U.S. Institutions with the Largest Numbers of Students Studying Abroad. Forty-three percent of PLU students who graduated in 2000 studied abroad.

Undergraduates 2,905 full-time, 239 part-time. Students come from 40 states and territories, 26 other countries, 26% are from out of state, 2% African American, 5% Asian American or Pacific Islander, 2% Hispanic American, 0.6% Native American, 8% international, 10% transferred in, 50% live on campus. *Retention:* 82% of 2001 full-time freshmen returned.

Freshmen *Admission:* 1,808 applied, 1,455 admitted, 581 enrolled. *Average high school GPA:* 3.60. *Test scores:* SAT verbal scores over 500: 76%; SAT math scores over 500: 73%; ACT scores over 18: 93%; SAT verbal scores over 600: 31%; SAT math scores over 600: 29%; ACT scores over 24: 58%; SAT verbal scores over 700: 4%; SAT math scores over 700: 5%; ACT scores over 30: 8%.

Faculty *Total:* 280, 81% full-time, 76% with terminal degrees. *Student/faculty ratio:* 13:1.

Majors Accounting; anthropology; art; art education; art history; biochemistry; biology; broadcast journalism; business administration; business marketing and marketing management; chemistry; Chinese; classics; computer engineering; computer science; early childhood education; earth sciences; economics; education; electrical engineering; elementary education; engineering physics; engineering science; English; environmental science; finance; fine/studio arts; French; geology; German; history; international business; international relations; journalism; literature; management information systems/business data processing; mass communications; mathematics; modern languages; music; music (piano and organ performance); music teacher education; music (voice and choral/opera performance); nursing; philosophy; physical education; physics; political science; psychology; radio/television broadcasting; reading education; recreational therapy; religious music; religious studies; Scandinavian languages; science education; secondary education; social work; sociology; Spanish; special education; theater arts/drama; women's studies.

Academic Programs *Special study options:* accelerated degree program, adult/continuing education programs, advanced placement credit, cooperative education, double majors, English as a second language, freshman honors college, honors programs, independent study, internships, part-time degree program, services for LD students, student-designed majors, study abroad, summer session for credit. *ROTC:* Army (b). *Unusual degree programs:* 3-2 engineering with Columbia University, Washington University in St. Louis.

Library Mortvedt Library with 365,021 titles, 2,186 serial subscriptions, 12,648 audiovisual materials, an OPAC, a Web page.

Computers on Campus 200 computers available on campus for general student use. A campuswide network can be accessed from student residence rooms and from off campus. Internet access, online (class) registration, at least one staffed computer lab available.

Student Life *Housing:* on-campus residence required through sophomore year. *Options:* coed, women-only. *Activities and Organizations:* drama/theater group, student-run newspaper, radio and television station, choral group, Rejoice, Circle K, adult students club, Residence Hall Government, Inter-varsity Fellowship. *Campus security:* 24-hour emergency response devices and patrols, student patrols, late-night transport/escort service. *Student Services:* health clinic, personal/psychological counseling, women's center.

Athletics Member NCAA. All Division III. *Intercollegiate sports:* baseball M, basketball M/W, crew M/W, cross-country running M/W, football M, golf M/W, lacrosse M(c)/W(c), rugby M(c), skiing (cross-country) M(c)/W(c), skiing (downhill) M(c)/W(c), soccer M/W, softball W, swimming M/W, tennis M/W, track and field M/W, volleyball M(c)/W, wrestling M. *Intramural sports:* badminton M/W, basketball M/W, bowling M/W, cross-country running M/W, football M/W, golf M/W, racquetball M/W, soccer M/W, softball M/W, squash M/W, swimming M/W, table tennis M/W, tennis M/W, track and field M/W, volleyball M/W.

Standardized Tests *Required:* SAT I or ACT (for admission).

Costs (2001–02) *Comprehensive fee:* $23,318 includes full-time tuition ($17,728) and room and board ($5590). Part-time tuition: $554 per semester hour. *Room and board:* College room only: $2740. Room and board charges vary according to board plan. *Payment plan:* installment. *Waivers:* senior citizens and employees or children of employees.

Financial Aid Of all full-time matriculated undergraduates who enrolled in 2001, 2353 applied for aid, 2009 were judged to have need, 786 had their need fully met. 627 Federal Work-Study jobs (averaging $1235). 1037 State and other part-time jobs (averaging $2435). In 2001, 559 non-need-based awards were made. *Average percent of need met:* 92%. *Average financial aid package:* $15,168. *Average need-based loan:* $6144. *Average need-based gift aid:* $7339. *Average non-need based aid:* $5103. *Average indebtedness upon graduation:* $19,279.

Applying *Options:* common application, early admission, early action, deferred entrance. *Application fee:* $35. *Required:* essay or personal statement, high school transcript, minimum 2.5 GPA, 1 letter of recommendation. *Required for some:* interview. *Application deadline:* rolling (freshmen), rolling (transfers). *Notification:* continuous (freshmen), 12/1 (early action).

Admissions Contact Office of Admissions, Pacific Lutheran University, Tacoma, WA 98447. *Phone:* 253-535-7151. *Toll-free phone:* 800-274-6758. *Fax:* 253-536-5136. *E-mail:* admissions@plu.edu.

PUGET SOUND CHRISTIAN COLLEGE
Mountlake Terrace, Washington

- **Independent Christian** 4-year, founded 1950
- **Calendar** semesters
- **Degrees** certificates, associate, and bachelor's
- **Suburban** 4-acre campus with easy access to Seattle
- **Endowment** $321,391
- **Coed,** 227 undergraduate students, 84% full-time, 52% women, 48% men
- **Minimally difficult** entrance level, 71% of applicants were admitted

Undergraduates 191 full-time, 36 part-time. Students come from 8 states and territories, 1 other country, 35% are from out of state, 8% transferred in, 34% live on campus. *Retention:* 59% of 2001 full-time freshmen returned.

Freshmen *Admission:* 59 applied, 42 admitted, 38 enrolled. *Average high school GPA:* 3.03. *Test scores:* SAT verbal scores over 500: 68%; SAT math scores over 500: 50%; SAT verbal scores over 600: 18%; SAT math scores over 600: 3%.

Faculty *Total:* 28, 36% full-time.

Majors Biblical studies; divinity/ministry; education; music; pastoral counseling; religious education; religious music; social sciences; theology.

Academic Programs *Special study options:* academic remediation for entering students, adult/continuing education programs, advanced placement credit, double majors, external degree program, independent study, internships, part-time degree program, summer session for credit.

Library C. H. Phillips Library with 37,500 titles, 130 serial subscriptions.

Computers on Campus 8 computers available on campus for general student use. Internet access, at least one staffed computer lab available.

Student Life *Housing:* on-campus residence required for freshman year. *Options:* men-only, women-only. *Activities and Organizations:* student-run newspaper, choral group, Team Macedonia, ASB Outreach Committee. *Campus security:* 24-hour emergency response devices, student patrols. *Student Services:* personal/psychological counseling.

Athletics Member NCCAA. *Intercollegiate sports:* basketball M/W, volleyball W. *Intramural sports:* basketball M/W, tennis M/W, volleyball M/W.

Standardized Tests *Required for some:* SAT I and SAT II or ACT (for placement). *Recommended:* SAT I and SAT II or ACT (for placement), SAT II: Writing Test (for placement).

Costs (2001–02) *Comprehensive fee:* $6200 includes full-time tuition ($3850) and room and board ($2350).

Applying *Options:* deferred entrance. *Application fee:* $25. *Required:* essay or personal statement, high school transcript, minimum 2.0 GPA, letters of recommendation. *Required for some:* interview. *Application deadlines:* 7/15 (freshmen), 7/15 (transfers). *Notification:* continuous until 8/15 (freshmen).

Admissions Contact Mr. Ben Maxson, Admissions Counselor, Puget Sound Christian College, 7011 226th Place, SW, Mountlake Terrace, WA 98043. *Phone:* 425-775-8686 Ext. 506. *Toll-free phone:* 888-775-8699. *Fax:* 425-775-8688 Ext. 506. *E-mail:* admissions@pscc.edu.

SAINT MARTIN'S COLLEGE
Lacey, Washington

- **Independent Roman Catholic** comprehensive, founded 1895
- **Calendar** semesters
- **Degrees** associate, bachelor's, and master's
- **Suburban** 380-acre campus with easy access to Tacoma
- **Endowment** $7.6 million
- **Coed,** 1,201 undergraduate students, 66% full-time, 53% women, 47% men
- **Moderately difficult** entrance level, 98% of applicants were admitted

Undergraduates 794 full-time, 407 part-time. Students come from 17 states and territories, 13 other countries, 8% are from out of state, 7% African American, 6% Asian American or Pacific Islander, 5% Hispanic American, 1% Native American, 5% International, 9% transferred in, 25% live on campus. *Retention:* 72% of 2001 full-time freshmen returned.

Freshmen *Admission:* 364 applied, 357 admitted, 147 enrolled. *Average high school GPA:* 3.31. *Test scores:* SAT verbal scores over 500: 52%; SAT math scores over 500: 46%; ACT scores over 18: 71%; SAT verbal scores over 600: 11%; SAT math scores over 600: 12%; ACT scores over 24: 21%; SAT verbal scores over 700: 3%.

Faculty *Total:* 75, 80% full-time, 76% with terminal degrees. *Student/faculty ratio:* 13:1.

Majors Accounting; biology; business administration; business marketing and marketing management; chemistry; civil engineering; community services; computer science; criminal justice/law enforcement administration; economics; education; elementary education; English; finance; history; humanities; information sciences/systems; liberal arts and sciences/liberal studies; management information systems/business data processing; mathematics; mechanical engineering; political science; pre-dentistry; pre-law; pre-medicine; pre-pharmacy studies; pre-veterinary studies; psychology; religious studies; secondary education; special education; theater arts/drama.

Academic Programs *Special study options:* academic remediation for entering students, accelerated degree program, adult/continuing education programs, advanced placement credit, cooperative education, double majors, English as a second language, independent study, internships, off-campus study, part-time degree program, services for LD students, study abroad, summer session for credit. *ROTC:* Army (c).

Library Saint Martin's College Library with 84,220 titles, 852 serial subscriptions, 1,239 audiovisual materials, an OPAC, a Web page.

Computers on Campus 110 computers available on campus for general student use. A campuswide network can be accessed from student residence rooms and from off campus. Internet access, at least one staffed computer lab available.

Student Life *Housing:* on-campus residence required through sophomore year. *Options:* coed. *Activities and Organizations:* drama/theater group, student-run newspaper, choral group, Hawaiian Club, Education Club, ASME, SWE. *Campus security:* 24-hour emergency response devices and patrols, late-night transport/escort service, night patrols by security personnel. *Student Services:* personal/psychological counseling.

Athletics Member NCAA. All Division II. *Intercollegiate sports:* baseball M(s), basketball M(s)/W(s), cross-country running M(s)/W(s), golf M(s)/W(s), softball W(s), track and field M(s)/W(s), volleyball W(s). *Intramural sports:* basketball M/W, soccer M/W, softball M/W, table tennis M/W, tennis M/W, volleyball M/W, weight lifting M/W.

Standardized Tests *Required:* SAT I or ACT (for admission).

Costs (2002–03) *Comprehensive fee:* $21,958 includes full-time tuition ($16,600), mandatory fees ($260), and room and board ($5098). Part-time tuition: $553 per credit. Part-time tuition and fees vary according to course load. *Required fees:* $25 per term part-time. *Room and board:* College room only: $1844.

Financial Aid Of all full-time matriculated undergraduates who enrolled in 2001, 483 applied for aid, 447 were judged to have need, 221 had their need fully met. In 2001, 61 non-need-based awards were made. *Average percent of need met:* 89%. *Average financial aid package:* $14,336. *Average need-based loan:* $5463. *Average need-based gift aid:* $7566. *Average non-need based aid:* $4996. *Average indebtedness upon graduation:* $12,813.

Applying *Options:* common application, electronic application. *Application fee:* $35. *Required:* essay or personal statement, high school transcript, minimum 2.5 GPA, 1 letter of recommendation. *Required for some:* interview. *Application deadlines:* 8/1 (freshmen), 8/1 (transfers). *Notification:* continuous until 8/15 (freshmen).

Admissions Contact Mr. Todd Abbott, Director of Admission, Saint Martin's College, 5300 Pacific Avenue, SE, Lacey, WA 98503. *Phone:* 360-438-4590. *Toll-free phone:* 800-368-8803. *Fax:* 37—412-6189. *E-mail:* admissions@stmartin.edu.

SEATTLE PACIFIC UNIVERSITY
Seattle, Washington

- **Independent Free Methodist** comprehensive, founded 1891
- **Calendar** quarters
- **Degrees** certificates, bachelor's, master's, doctoral, and post-master's certificates
- **Urban** 35-acre campus
- **Endowment** $24.0 million
- **Coed,** 2,828 undergraduate students, 89% full-time, 66% women, 34% men
- **Moderately difficult** entrance level, 83% of applicants were admitted

At the heart of an SPU education is the Common Curriculum, an innovative 4-year core program. Consisting of 7 required courses over 4 years, the program explicitly connects the liberal arts, the Chirstian faith, and human issues. Another feature of the Common Curriculum is a group of literary and artistic works reflecting the University's core values that all students study.

Undergraduates 2,531 full-time, 297 part-time. Students come from 39 states and territories, 34 other countries, 35% are from out of state, 2% African American, 5% Asian American or Pacific Islander, 2% Hispanic American, 0.8% Native American, 2% international, 8% transferred in, 61% live on campus. *Retention:* 80% of 2001 full-time freshmen returned.

Freshmen *Admission:* 1,769 applied, 1,469 admitted, 647 enrolled. *Average high school GPA:* 3.58. *Test scores:* SAT verbal scores over 500: 82%; SAT math scores over 500: 78%; ACT scores over 18: 97%; SAT verbal scores over 600: 38%; SAT math scores over 600: 36%; ACT scores over 24: 55%; SAT verbal scores over 700: 8%; SAT math scores over 700: 5%; ACT scores over 30: 13%.

Faculty *Total:* 267, 65% full-time. *Student/faculty ratio:* 16:1.

Majors Accounting; art; art education; biochemistry; biology; biology education; business administration; business computer facilities operation; business economics; business systems analysis/design; chemistry; classics; clothing/apparel/textile studies; communications; computer science; economics; electrical engineering; engineering science; English; English education; European studies; exercise sciences; family/consumer studies; French; general studies; German; history; home economics education; Latin American studies; Latin (ancient and medieval); mathematics; mathematics education; mathematics related; music; music teacher education; nursing; nutrition science; organizational behavior; philosophy; physical education; physics; political science; pre-dentistry; pre-law; pre-medicine; psychology; religious education; religious studies; Russian; science education; social science education; sociology; Spanish; special education; theater arts/drama; theology.

Academic Programs *Special study options:* academic remediation for entering students, adult/continuing education programs, advanced placement credit, cooperative education, distance learning, double majors, English as a second language, external degree program, honors programs, independent study, internships, off-campus study, part-time degree program, services for LD students, student-designed majors, study abroad, summer session for credit. *ROTC:* Army (c), Navy (c), Air Force (c).

Library Seattle Pacific University Library with 141,712 titles, 1,192 serial subscriptions, 2,670 audiovisual materials, an OPAC, a Web page.

Computers on Campus 150 computers available on campus for general student use. A campuswide network can be accessed from student residence rooms and from off campus. Internet access, online (class) registration, at least one staffed computer lab available.

Student Life *Housing:* on-campus residence required through senior year. *Options:* coed, women-only. *Activities and Organizations:* drama/theater group, student-run newspaper, radio station, choral group, Centurions, Falconettes, Forensics, Amnesty International, University Players. *Campus security:* 24-hour emergency response devices and patrols, student patrols, late-night transport/escort service, closed circuit TV monitors. *Student Services:* health clinic, personal/psychological counseling.

Athletics Member NCAA. All Division II. *Intercollegiate sports:* basketball M(s)/W(s), crew M/W, cross-country running M(s)/W(s), gymnastics W(s), soccer M(s)/W, track and field M(s)/W(s), volleyball W(s). *Intramural sports:* badminton M/W, basketball M/W, bowling M/W, cross-country running M/W, football M/W, golf M/W, skiing (cross-country) M(c)/W(c), skiing (downhill) M(c)/W(c), soccer M/W(c), softball M/W, swimming M/W, table tennis M/W, tennis M/W, track and field M/W, volleyball M(c)/W(c), weight lifting M/W, wrestling M.

Seattle Pacific University (continued)

Standardized Tests *Required:* SAT I or ACT (for admission). *Recommended:* SAT I (for admission).

Costs (2001–02) *Comprehensive fee:* $22,674 includes full-time tuition ($16,335), mandatory fees ($90), and room and board ($6249). Part-time tuition: $354 per credit. Part-time tuition and fees vary according to course load. *Required fees:* $30 per term. *Room and board:* College room only: $3255. Room and board charges vary according to board plan and housing facility. *Payment plan:* installment. *Waivers:* senior citizens and employees or children of employees.

Financial Aid Of all full-time matriculated undergraduates who enrolled in 2001, 1806 applied for aid, 1499 were judged to have need, 332 had their need fully met. 390 Federal Work-Study jobs (averaging $1295). 280 State and other part-time jobs (averaging $2784). In 2001, 713 non-need-based awards were made. *Average percent of need met:* 78%. *Average financial aid package:* $12,845. *Average need-based loan:* $5395. *Average need-based gift aid:* $9649. *Average indebtedness upon graduation:* $18,498.

Applying *Options:* common application, electronic application, early admission, early action, deferred entrance. *Application fee:* $35. *Required:* essay or personal statement, high school transcript, minimum 2.5 GPA, 2 letters of recommendation. *Application deadlines:* 6/1 (freshmen), 8/1 (transfers). *Notification:* continuous (freshmen), 2/15 (early action).

Admissions Contact Mrs. Jennifer Feddern Kenney, Director of Admissions, Seattle Pacific University, 3307 Third Avenue West, Seattle, WA 98119-1997. *Phone:* 206-281-2517. *Toll-free phone:* 800-366-3344. *Fax:* 206-281-2669. *E-mail:* admissions@spu.edu.

SEATTLE UNIVERSITY

Seattle, Washington

- **Independent Roman Catholic** comprehensive, founded 1891
- **Calendar** quarters
- **Degrees** certificates, bachelor's, master's, doctoral, first professional, post-master's, and postbachelor's certificates
- **Urban** 46-acre campus
- **Endowment** $137.4 million
- **Coed,** 3,352 undergraduate students, 91% full-time, 61% women, 39% men
- **Moderately difficult** entrance level, 80% of applicants were admitted

Undergraduates 3,047 full-time, 305 part-time. Students come from 58 states and territories, 69 other countries, 17% are from out of state, 4% African American, 21% Asian American or Pacific Islander, 6% Hispanic American, 1% Native American, 9% international, 8% transferred in, 36% live on campus. *Retention:* 83% of 2001 full-time freshmen returned.

Freshmen *Admission:* 2,634 applied, 2,110 admitted, 643 enrolled. *Average high school GPA:* 3.50. *Test scores:* SAT verbal scores over 500: 80%; SAT math scores over 500: 83%; ACT scores over 18: 98%; SAT verbal scores over 600: 40%; SAT math scores over 600: 36%; ACT scores over 24: 65%; SAT verbal scores over 700: 6%; SAT math scores over 700: 4%; ACT scores over 30: 11%.

Faculty *Total:* 480, 69% full-time, 82% with terminal degrees. *Student/faculty ratio:* 12:1.

Majors Accounting; applied mathematics; art; art history; biochemistry; biological/physical sciences; biology; business administration; business economics; business marketing and marketing management; chemistry; civil engineering; computer science; creative writing; criminal justice/law enforcement administration; diagnostic medical sonography; East Asian studies; economics; electrical engineering; English; environmental engineering; environmental science; finance; fine/studio arts; French; German; history; humanities; industrial/manufacturing engineering; insurance/risk management; international business; international economics; international relations; journalism; liberal arts and sciences/liberal studies; management information systems/business data processing; mass communications; mathematics; mechanical engineering; medical technology; nursing; operations management; philosophy; photography; physics; political science; psychology; public administration; public relations; religious studies; social work; sociology; Spanish; theater arts/drama; Western European studies.

Academic Programs *Special study options:* accelerated degree program, adult/continuing education programs, advanced placement credit, double majors, English as a second language, freshman honors college, honors programs, independent study, internships, off-campus study, part-time degree program, services for LD students, student-designed majors, study abroad, summer session for credit. *ROTC:* Army (b), Navy (c), Air Force (c).

Library Lemieux Library plus 1 other with 502,438 titles, 6,504 serial subscriptions, 5,857 audiovisual materials, an OPAC, a Web page.

Computers on Campus 401 computers available on campus for general student use. A campuswide network can be accessed from student residence rooms and from off campus. At least one staffed computer lab available.

Student Life *Housing:* on-campus residence required through sophomore year. *Options:* coed, disabled students. *Activities and Organizations:* drama/theater group, student-run newspaper, radio station, choral group, student government, volunteer center, Hawaiian Club, International Student Club. *Campus security:* 24-hour emergency response devices and patrols, late-night transport/escort service, controlled dormitory access, bicycle patrols. *Student Services:* health clinic, personal/psychological counseling, women's center.

Athletics Member NCAA, NAIA. All NCAA Division II. *Intercollegiate sports:* baseball M(c)/W(c), basketball M/W, crew M(c)/W(c), cross-country running M/W, golf M(c)/W(c), riflery M(c)/W(c), skiing (downhill) M(c)/W(c), soccer M/W, softball W, swimming M/W, tennis M/W, volleyball M(c)/W, water polo M(c)/W(c). *Intramural sports:* basketball M/W, field hockey M/W, football M/W, racquetball M/W, soccer M/W, softball M/W, volleyball M/W.

Standardized Tests *Required:* SAT I or ACT (for admission).

Costs (2001–02) *One-time required fee:* $75. *Comprehensive fee:* $24,183 includes full-time tuition ($17,865) and room and board ($6318). Full-time tuition and fees vary according to course load. Part-time tuition: $397 per credit hour. Part-time tuition and fees vary according to course load. *Room and board:* College room only: $4098. Room and board charges vary according to board plan and housing facility. *Payment plan:* installment. *Waivers:* employees or children of employees.

Financial Aid Of all full-time matriculated undergraduates who enrolled in 2001, 2808 applied for aid, 2355 were judged to have need, 312 had their need fully met. In 2001, 40 non-need-based awards were made. *Average percent of need met:* 81%. *Average financial aid package:* $15,506. *Average need-based loan:* $4372. *Average need-based gift aid:* $8692. *Average non-need based aid:* $7182.

Applying *Options:* common application, electronic application, early admission, deferred entrance. *Application fee:* $45. *Required:* essay or personal statement, high school transcript, minimum 2.5 GPA, 2 letters of recommendation. *Application deadlines:* 7/1 (freshmen), 8/1 (transfers). *Notification:* continuous (freshmen).

Admissions Contact Mr. Michael K. McKeon, Dean of Admissions, Seattle University, 900 Broadway, Seattle, WA 98122-4340. *Phone:* 206-296-2000. *Toll-free phone:* 800-542-0833 (in-state); 800-426-7123 (out-of-state). *Fax:* 206-296-5656. *E-mail:* admissions@seattleu.edu.

TRINITY LUTHERAN COLLEGE

Issaquah, Washington

- **Independent Lutheran** 4-year, founded 1944
- **Calendar** quarters
- **Degrees** associate, bachelor's, and postbachelor's certificates
- **Suburban** 46-acre campus with easy access to Seattle
- **Endowment** $1.2 million
- **Coed**
- **Minimally difficult** entrance level

Faculty *Student/faculty ratio:* 9:1.

Student Life *Campus security:* 24-hour emergency response devices, student patrols, controlled dormitory access.

Standardized Tests *Required:* SAT I or ACT (for admission).

Applying *Options:* early admission, deferred entrance. *Application fee:* $30. *Required:* essay or personal statement, high school transcript, minimum 2.0 GPA, 2 letters of recommendation. *Required for some:* interview. *Recommended:* interview.

Admissions Contact Ms. Sigrid Olsen Cutler, Trinity Lutheran College, 4221 228th Avenue, SE, Issaquah, WA 98029-9299. *Phone:* 425-961-5516. *Toll-free phone:* 800-843-5659. *Fax:* 425-392-0404. *E-mail:* admission@tlc.edu.

UNIVERSITY OF PHOENIX-WASHINGTON CAMPUS

Seattle, Washington

- **Proprietary** comprehensive
- **Calendar** continuous
- **Degrees** certificates, associate, bachelor's, master's, doctoral, post-master's, and postbachelor's certificates (courses conducted at 54 campuses and learning centers in 13 states)
- **Coed,** 1,207 undergraduate students, 100% full-time, 57% women, 43% men
- **Noncompetitive** entrance level

Undergraduates Students come from 12 states and territories, 1% are from out of state.

Freshmen *Admission:* 11 admitted.
Faculty *Total:* 286, 2% full-time, 23% with terminal degrees. *Student/faculty ratio:* 13:1.
Majors Computer/information sciences; enterprise management; management information systems/business data processing; management science.
Academic Programs *Special study options:* accelerated degree program, adult/continuing education programs, advanced placement credit, distance learning, external degree program, independent study.
Library University Library with 17.5 million titles, 9,000 serial subscriptions, an OPAC, a Web page.
Computers on Campus A campuswide network can be accessed from off campus. Internet access, at least one staffed computer lab available.
Student Life *Housing:* college housing not available.
Costs (2001–02) *Tuition:* $8940 full-time. Full-time tuition and fees vary according to location and program. *Payment plan:* deferred payment. *Waivers:* employees or children of employees.
Applying *Options:* deferred entrance. *Application fee:* $85. *Required:* 2 years of work experience. *Required for some:* high school transcript. *Application deadline:* rolling (freshmen), rolling (transfers).
Admissions Contact Ms. Beth Barilla, Director of Admissions, University of Phoenix-Washington Campus, 4615 East Elwood Street, Phoenix, AZ 85040-1958. *Phone:* 480-927-0099 Ext. 1218. *Toll-free phone:* 800-228-7240. *Fax:* 480-894-1758. *E-mail:* beth.barilla@apollogrp.edu.

UNIVERSITY OF PUGET SOUND
Tacoma, Washington

- **Independent** comprehensive, founded 1888
- **Calendar** semesters
- **Degrees** bachelor's, master's, and doctoral
- **Suburban** 97-acre campus with easy access to Seattle
- **Endowment** $188.4 million
- **Coed,** 2,604 undergraduate students, 97% full-time, 61% women, 39% men
- **Very difficult** entrance level, 67% of applicants were admitted

Undergraduates 2,518 full-time, 86 part-time. Students come from 48 states and territories, 20 other countries, 69% are from out of state, 2% African American, 11% Asian American or Pacific Islander, 3% Hispanic American, 1% Native American, 1% international, 3% transferred in, 54% live on campus. *Retention:* 84% of 2001 full-time freshmen returned.
Freshmen *Admission:* 4,377 applied, 2,915 admitted, 703 enrolled. *Average high school GPA:* 3.59. *Test scores:* SAT verbal scores over 500: 98%; SAT math scores over 500: 96%; ACT scores over 18: 100%; SAT verbal scores over 600: 70%; SAT math scores over 600: 64%; ACT scores over 24: 83%; SAT verbal scores over 700: 16%; SAT math scores over 700: 11%; ACT scores over 30: 21%.
Faculty *Total:* 259, 83% full-time, 77% with terminal degrees. *Student/faculty ratio:* 11:1.
Majors Art; Asian studies; biology; business; business computer programming; chemistry; classics; communications; computer science; creative writing; economics; English; exercise sciences; French; geology; German; history; interdisciplinary studies; international business; international economics; international relations; mathematics; music; music business management/merchandising; music (general performance); music teacher education; natural sciences; occupational therapy; philosophy; physics; political science; pre-dentistry; pre-law; premedicine; pre-veterinary studies; psychology; religious studies; sociology; Spanish; theater arts/drama.
Academic Programs *Special study options:* advanced placement credit, cooperative education, double majors, honors programs, independent study, internships, part-time degree program, student-designed majors, study abroad, summer session for credit. *ROTC:* Army (c). *Unusual degree programs:* 3-2 engineering with Washington University in St. Louis, Columbia University, Duke University, Boston University, University of Southern California.
Library Collins Memorial Library with 326,438 titles, 4,510 serial subscriptions, 15,846 audiovisual materials, an OPAC, a Web page.
Computers on Campus 180 computers available on campus for general student use. A campuswide network can be accessed from student residence rooms and from off campus. Internet access, at least one staffed computer lab available.
Student Life *Housing Options:* coed, women-only, disabled students. *Activities and Organizations:* drama/theater group, student-run newspaper, radio station, choral group, Hui-O-Hawaii, Repertory Dance Group, Circle K, outdoor programs, Lighthouse, national fraternities, national sororities. *Campus security:* 24-hour emergency response devices and patrols, student patrols, late-night transport/escort service, controlled dormitory access, 24-hour locked residence hall entrances. *Student Services:* health clinic, personal/psychological counseling.
Athletics Member NCAA. All Division III. *Intercollegiate sports:* baseball M, basketball M/W, crew M/W, cross-country running M/W, football M, golf M/W, lacrosse M(c)/W, skiing (downhill) M/W, soccer M/W, softball W, swimming M/W, tennis M/W, track and field M/W, volleyball W. *Intramural sports:* basketball M/W, bowling M/W, football M/W, golf M/W, racquetball M/W, soccer M/W, softball M/W, tennis M/W, track and field M/W, volleyball M/W.
Standardized Tests *Required:* SAT I or ACT (for admission).
Costs (2001–02) *Comprehensive fee:* $28,285 includes full-time tuition ($22,350), mandatory fees ($155), and room and board ($5780). Part-time tuition: $2820 per unit. *Room and board:* College room only: $3160. Room and board charges vary according to board plan. *Payment plans:* installment, deferred payment. *Waivers:* employees or children of employees.
Financial Aid Of all full-time matriculated undergraduates who enrolled in 2001, 1656 applied for aid, 1401 were judged to have need, 679 had their need fully met. 621 Federal Work-Study jobs, 253 State and other part-time jobs. In 2001, 676 non-need-based awards were made. *Average percent of need met:* 90%. *Average financial aid package:* $18,401. *Average need-based loan:* $5661. *Average need-based gift aid:* $12,121. *Average non-need based aid:* $6218. *Average indebtedness upon graduation:* $22,535.
Applying *Options:* common application, electronic application, early admission, early decision, deferred entrance. *Application fee:* $40. *Required:* essay or personal statement, high school transcript, 2 letters of recommendation. *Recommended:* minimum 3.0 GPA, interview. *Application deadlines:* 2/1 (freshmen), 6/1 (transfers). *Early decision:* 11/15 (for plan 1), 12/15 (for plan 2). *Notification:* continuous until 5/1 (freshmen), 12/15 (early decision plan 1), 1/15 (early decision plan 2).
Admissions Contact University of Puget Sound, 1500 North Warner Street, Tacoma, WA 98416-0005. *Phone:* 253-879-3211. *Toll-free phone:* 800-396-7191. *Fax:* 253-879-3993. *E-mail:* admission@ups.edu.

UNIVERSITY OF WASHINGTON
Seattle, Washington

- **State-supported** university, founded 1861
- **Calendar** quarters
- **Degrees** bachelor's, master's, doctoral, and first professional
- **Urban** 703-acre campus
- **Endowment** $963.0 million
- **Coed,** 26,860 undergraduate students, 87% full-time, 51% women, 49% men
- **Moderately difficult** entrance level, 79% of applicants were admitted

Undergraduates 23,281 full-time, 3,579 part-time. Students come from 52 states and territories, 59 other countries, 11% are from out of state, 3% African American, 23% Asian American or Pacific Islander, 4% Hispanic American, 1% Native American, 3% international, 7% transferred in, 17% live on campus. *Retention:* 90% of 2001 full-time freshmen returned.
Freshmen *Admission:* 14,666 applied, 11,523 admitted, 5,210 enrolled. *Average high school GPA:* 3.67. *Test scores:* SAT verbal scores over 500: 76%; SAT math scores over 500: 82%; ACT scores over 18: 21%; SAT verbal scores over 600: 37%; SAT math scores over 600: 48%; ACT scores over 24: 14%; SAT verbal scores over 700: 7%; SAT math scores over 700: 11%; ACT scores over 30: 3%.
Faculty *Total:* 3,282, 81% full-time, 87% with terminal degrees. *Student/faculty ratio:* 11:1.
Majors Accounting; aerospace engineering; African-American studies; Air Force R.O.T.C./air science; anthropology; applied mathematics; architectural urban design; architecture; Army R.O.T.C./military science; art; art history; Asian studies; astronomy; atmospheric sciences; bilingual/bicultural education; biochemistry; biology; biology education; biostatistics; botany; business; business administration; Canadian studies; cell biology; ceramic arts; ceramic sciences/engineering; chemical engineering; chemistry; Chinese; city/community/regional planning; civil engineering; classics; communications; comparative literature; computer engineering; computer/information sciences; computer science; construction management; creative writing; criminal justice/law enforcement administration; cultural studies; dance; data processing technology; dental hygiene; East Asian studies; economics; education; education (multiple levels); electrical engineering; elementary education; engineering; English; environmental health; environmental science; European studies; fishing sciences; forest engineering; forest management; forestry; forestry sciences; French; general studies; geography; geology; geophysics/seismology; German; graphic design/commercial art/illustration; Greek (ancient and medieval); history; history of science and technology; humanities; industrial design; industrial/manufacturing engineering; information sciences/systems; interdisciplinary studies; interior architecture; international business; international relations; Italian; Japanese; Judaic studies; landscape architecture; Latin American studies; Latin (ancient and medieval); liberal arts and sciences/liberal studies; linguistics; management information systems/

University of Washington (continued)
business data processing; management science; materials engineering; mathematical statistics; mathematics; mechanical engineering; medical technology; metal/jewelry arts; metallurgical engineering; Mexican-American studies; microbiology/bacteriology; Middle Eastern studies; molecular biology; music; musical instrument technology; music (general performance); music history; musicology; music (piano and organ performance); music teacher education; music theory and composition; music (voice and choral/opera performance); Native American studies; natural resources management; Navy/Marine Corps R.O.T.C./naval science; nursing; nursing (maternal/child health); nursing (public health); occupational therapy; oceanography; orthotics/prosthetics; painting; pharmacy; philosophy; photography; physical therapy; physician assistant; physics; political science; printmaking; psychology; public administration; public health; religious studies; romance languages; Russian; Russian/Slavic studies; Scandinavian languages; Scandinavian studies; science education; sculpture; secondary education; Slavic languages; social sciences; social work; sociology; South Asian studies; Southeast Asian studies; Spanish; speech-language pathology/audiology; speech/rhetorical studies; stringed instruments; teaching English as a second language; technical/business writing; textile arts; theater arts/drama; wildlife management; women's studies; wood science/paper technology; zoology.

Academic Programs *Special study options:* academic remediation for entering students, accelerated degree program, adult/continuing education programs, advanced placement credit, cooperative education, distance learning, double majors, English as a second language, external degree program, honors programs, independent study, internships, part-time degree program, services for LD students, student-designed majors, study abroad, summer session for credit. *ROTC:* Army (b), Navy (b), Air Force (b).

Library Suzzallo/Allen Library plus 21 others with 5.8 million titles, 50,245 serial subscriptions, 1.4 million audiovisual materials, a Web page.

Computers on Campus 285 computers available on campus for general student use. A campuswide network can be accessed from student residence rooms and from off campus. At least one staffed computer lab available.

Student Life *Housing Options:* coed, disabled students. *Activities and Organizations:* drama/theater group, student-run newspaper, radio and television station, choral group, marching band, national fraternities, national sororities. *Campus security:* 24-hour emergency response devices and patrols, late-night transport/escort service, controlled dormitory access. *Student Services:* health clinic, personal/psychological counseling, women's center, legal services.

Athletics Member NCAA. All Division I except football (Division I-A). *Intercollegiate sports:* baseball M(s), basketball M(s)/W(s), crew M(s)/W(s), cross-country running M(s)/W(s), golf M(s)/W(s), gymnastics W(s), soccer M(s)/W, softball W(s), swimming M(s)/W(s), tennis M(s)/W(s), track and field M(s)/W(s), volleyball W(s), wrestling M(c). *Intramural sports:* archery M(c)/W(c), badminton M/W, basketball M/W, bowling M/W, crew M(c)/W(c), fencing M(c)/W(c), field hockey M(c)/W(c), football M/W, golf M/W, gymnastics M(c)/W(c), ice hockey M(c), lacrosse M(c)/W(c), racquetball M(c)/W(c), rugby M(c), sailing M(c)/W(c), skiing (cross-country) M(c)/W(c), skiing (downhill) M(c)/W(c), soccer M(c)/W(c), squash M(c)/W(c), swimming M/W, table tennis M/W, tennis M/W, track and field M/W, volleyball M/W, water polo M(c)/W(c), wrestling M.

Standardized Tests *Required:* SAT I or ACT (for admission).

Costs (2001–02) *Tuition:* state resident $3983 full-time, $134 per credit part-time; nonresident $13,258 full-time, $448 per credit part-time. Part-time tuition and fees vary according to course load. *Room and board:* $6378. Room and board charges vary according to board plan. *Payment plan:* installment. *Waivers:* employees or children of employees.

Financial Aid Of all full-time matriculated undergraduates who enrolled in 2001, 15075 applied for aid, 10698 were judged to have need, 4805 had their need fully met. In 2001, 1214 non-need-based awards were made. *Average percent of need met:* 88%. *Average financial aid package:* $9815. *Average need-based loan:* $3857. *Average need-based gift aid:* $6454. *Average non-need based aid:* $2418. *Average indebtedness upon graduation:* $14,500.

Applying *Options:* electronic application, early admission. *Application fee:* $35. *Required:* essay or personal statement, high school transcript, minimum 2.0 GPA. *Application deadlines:* 1/15 (freshmen), 4/15 (transfers). *Notification:* continuous until 4/15 (freshmen).

Admissions Contact Ms. Stephanie Preston, Assistant Director of Admissions, University of Washington, Box 355840, Seattle, WA 98195-5840. *Phone:* 206-543-9686. *E-mail:* askuwadm@u.washington.edu.

WALLA WALLA COLLEGE
College Place, Washington

- **Independent Seventh-day Adventist** comprehensive, founded 1892
- **Calendar** quarters
- **Degrees** associate, bachelor's, and master's
- **Small-town** 77-acre campus
- **Endowment** $9.7 million
- **Coed,** 1,577 undergraduate students, 87% full-time, 50% women, 50% men
- **Moderately difficult** entrance level, 52% of applicants were admitted

Undergraduates 1,365 full-time, 212 part-time. Students come from 49 states and territories, 26 other countries, 58% are from out of state, 2% African American, 5% Asian American or Pacific Islander, 5% Hispanic American, 0.2% Native American, 2% international, 10% transferred in, 58% live on campus. *Retention:* 100% of 2001 full-time freshmen returned.

Freshmen *Admission:* 634 applied, 328 admitted, 287 enrolled. *Average high school GPA:* 3.10. *Test scores:* ACT scores over 18: 81%; ACT scores over 24: 43%; ACT scores over 30: 7%.

Faculty *Total:* 203, 60% full-time, 44% with terminal degrees. *Student/faculty ratio:* 12:1.

Majors Accounting; art; art education; auto mechanic/technician; aviation technology; biblical languages/literatures; bioengineering; biology; biomedical technology; biophysics; business administration; business education; business marketing and marketing management; chemistry; civil engineering; computer programming; computer science; economics; education (K-12); electrical engineering; electromechanical technology; elementary education; engineering; engineering-related technology; English; environmental science; exercise sciences; French; German; graphic design/commercial art/illustration; health/physical education; health science; history; humanities; industrial arts; journalism; management information systems/business data processing; mass communications; mathematics; mechanical engineering; medical technology; modern languages; music; music (piano and organ performance); music teacher education; music (voice and choral/opera performance); nursing; philosophy; physical education; physics; pre-dentistry; pre-law; pre-medicine; pre-veterinary studies; psychology; public health education/promotion; public relations; radio/television broadcasting; religious studies; social work; sociology; Spanish; speech/rhetorical studies; theology.

Academic Programs *Special study options:* academic remediation for entering students, advanced placement credit, cooperative education, double majors, English as a second language, freshman honors college, honors programs, independent study, internships, part-time degree program, services for LD students, study abroad, summer session for credit.

Library Peterson Memorial Library plus 3 others with 128,747 titles, 1,317 serial subscriptions, 3,483 audiovisual materials, an OPAC, a Web page.

Computers on Campus 108 computers available on campus for general student use. A campuswide network can be accessed from student residence rooms and from off campus. Internet access, online (class) registration, at least one staffed computer lab available.

Student Life *Housing:* on-campus residence required through junior year. *Options:* men-only, women-only. *Activities and Organizations:* drama/theater group, student-run newspaper, radio station, choral group, Associated Students of Walla Walla College (ASWWC), Village Singles' Club, Aleph Gimel Ain (women's club), Amnesty International, Omicron Pi Sigma (men's club). *Campus security:* 24-hour emergency response devices and patrols, student patrols, late-night transport/escort service, controlled dormitory access. *Student Services:* health clinic, personal/psychological counseling.

Athletics Member NCCAA. *Intercollegiate sports:* basketball M/W, golf M, ice hockey M, soccer M, softball W, volleyball M/W. *Intramural sports:* basketball M/W, football M/W, gymnastics M/W, ice hockey M, racquetball M/W, softball M/W, table tennis M/W, tennis M/W, volleyball M/W.

Standardized Tests *Required:* SAT I or ACT (for admission). *Recommended:* ACT (for admission).

Costs (2002–03) *Comprehensive fee:* $20,925 includes full-time tuition ($16,440), mandatory fees ($159), and room and board ($4326). Full-time tuition and fees vary according to course load, degree level, and location. Part-time tuition: $423 per credit hour. *Room and board:* College room only: $2226. Room and board charges vary according to gender, housing facility, and location. *Payment plan:* installment. *Waivers:* senior citizens and employees or children of employees.

Financial Aid Of all full-time matriculated undergraduates who enrolled in 2001, 1241 applied for aid, 933 were judged to have need, 141 had their need fully met. 713 Federal Work-Study jobs (averaging $2172). 42 State and other part-time jobs (averaging $2510). In 2001, 240 non-need-based awards were made. *Average percent of need met:* 83%. *Average financial aid package:* $13,381. *Average need-based loan:* $4429. *Average need-based gift aid:* $5209. *Average non-need based aid:* $5016. *Average indebtedness upon graduation:* $20,738.

Applying *Options:* common application, electronic application, deferred entrance. *Application fee:* $30. *Required:* high school transcript, minimum 2.0 GPA, 3 letters of recommendation. *Application deadline:* rolling (freshmen), rolling (transfers). *Notification:* continuous (freshmen).

Admissions Contact Mr. Dallas Weis, Director of Admissions, Walla Walla College, 204 South College Avenue, College Place, WA 99324. *Phone:* 509-527-2327. *Toll-free phone:* 800-541-8900. *Fax:* 509-527-2397. *E-mail:* info@wwc.edu.

WASHINGTON STATE UNIVERSITY
Pullman, Washington

- **State-supported** university, founded 1890
- **Calendar** semesters
- **Degrees** bachelor's, master's, doctoral, first professional, and postbachelor's certificates
- **Rural** 620-acre campus
- **Endowment** $480.8 million
- **Coed,** 17,476 undergraduate students, 83% full-time, 52% women, 48% men
- **Moderately difficult** entrance level, 81% of applicants were admitted

Undergraduates 14,560 full-time, 2,916 part-time. Students come from 57 states and territories, 64 other countries, 10% are from out of state, 3% African American, 5% Asian American or Pacific Islander, 3% Hispanic American, 1% Native American, 3% international, 14% transferred in, 49% live on campus. *Retention:* 83% of 2001 full-time freshmen returned.

Freshmen *Admission:* 7,968 applied, 6,484 admitted, 2,630 enrolled. *Average high school GPA:* 3.40. *Test scores:* SAT verbal scores over 500: 58%; SAT math scores over 500: 59%; SAT verbal scores over 600: 17%; SAT math scores over 600: 19%; SAT verbal scores over 700: 2%; SAT math scores over 700: 2%.

Faculty *Total:* 1,255, 85% full-time, 82% with terminal degrees. *Student/faculty ratio:* 17:1.

Majors Accounting; advertising; agricultural business; agricultural economics; agricultural education; agricultural engineering; agricultural mechanization; agricultural production; agronomy/crop science; American studies; animal sciences; anthropology; architecture; art; Asian studies; athletic training/sports medicine; biochemistry; biological/physical sciences; biology; biophysics; business administration; business marketing and marketing management; chemical engineering; chemistry; civil engineering; classics; clothing/apparel/textile studies; computer engineering; computer science; construction technology; criminal justice/law enforcement administration; economics; education; electrical engineering; elementary education; English; entomology; environmental science; exercise sciences; finance; forestry; French; genetics; geology; German; health education; history; home economics; home economics education; horticulture science; hotel and restaurant management; humanities; individual/family development; industrial/manufacturing engineering; insurance/risk management; interior architecture; international business; journalism; liberal arts and sciences/liberal studies; linguistics; management information systems/business data processing; mass communications; materials engineering; mathematics; mathematics/computer science; mechanical engineering; microbiology/bacteriology; music; music (general performance); music theory and composition; natural resources conservation; natural resources management; neuroscience; nursing; nutrition studies; philosophy; physical education; physics; plant sciences; political science; pre-dentistry; pre-law; pre-medicine; psychology; public administration; public relations; radio/television broadcasting; range management; real estate; recreation/leisure facilities management; recreation/leisure studies; religious studies; Russian; secondary education; social sciences; social work; sociology; soil sciences; Spanish; special education; speech-language pathology/audiology; sport/fitness administration; theater arts/drama; veterinary sciences; wildlife biology; wildlife management; women's studies; zoology.

Academic Programs *Special study options:* academic remediation for entering students, adult/continuing education programs, advanced placement credit, cooperative education, distance learning, double majors, English as a second language, external degree program, honors programs, internships, off-campus study, part-time degree program, services for LD students, study abroad, summer session for credit. *ROTC:* Army (b), Navy (b), Air Force (b).

Library Holland Library plus 5 others with 2.0 million titles, 28,026 serial subscriptions, 316,707 audiovisual materials, an OPAC, a Web page.

Computers on Campus 10000 computers available on campus for general student use. A campuswide network can be accessed from student residence rooms and from off campus. Internet access, online (class) registration, at least one staffed computer lab available.

Student Life *Housing:* on-campus residence required for freshman year. *Options:* coed, men-only, women-only. *Activities and Organizations:* drama/theater group, student-run newspaper, radio and television station, choral group, marching band, national fraternities, national sororities. *Campus security:* 24-hour emergency response devices and patrols, student patrols, late-night transport/escort service, controlled dormitory access. *Student Services:* health clinic, personal/psychological counseling, women's center, legal services.

Athletics Member NCAA. All Division I except football (Division I-A). *Intercollegiate sports:* baseball M(s), basketball M(s)/W(s), bowling M(c)/W(c), crew M(c)/W(s), cross-country running M(s)/W(s), equestrian sports M(c)/W(c), golf M(s)/W(s), ice hockey M(c)/W(c), lacrosse M(c)/W(c), rugby M(c)/W(c), skiing (cross-country) M(c)/W(c), skiing (downhill) M(c)/W(c), soccer M(c)/W(s), softball W(c), swimming W(s), tennis W(s), track and field M(s)/W(s), volleyball M(c)/W(s), water polo M(c). *Intramural sports:* badminton M/W, basketball M/W, bowling M/W, cross-country running M/W, fencing M(c)/W(c), football M/W, golf M/W, racquetball M/W, soccer M/W, softball M/W, table tennis M/W, tennis M/W, track and field M/W, volleyball M/W, wrestling M.

Standardized Tests *Required:* SAT I or ACT (for admission).

Costs (2001–02) *Tuition:* state resident $3574 full-time, $195 per credit part-time; nonresident $10,955 full-time, $563 per credit part-time. Part-time tuition and fees vary according to course load. *Required fees:* $662 full-time. *Room and board:* $5152. Room and board charges vary according to board plan and housing facility. *Payment plans:* tuition prepayment, installment. *Waivers:* children of alumni, senior citizens, and employees or children of employees.

Financial Aid Of all full-time matriculated undergraduates who enrolled in 2001, 10342 applied for aid, 6711 were judged to have need, 3398 had their need fully met. 865 Federal Work-Study jobs. In 2001, 2003 non-need-based awards were made. *Average percent of need met:* 98%. *Average financial aid package:* $9053. *Average need-based loan:* $4093. *Average need-based gift aid:* $4364. *Average non-need based aid:* $2253. *Average indebtedness upon graduation:* $15,000.

Applying *Options:* common application, electronic application, early admission. *Application fee:* $35. *Required:* high school transcript, minimum 2.0 GPA. *Required for some:* 3 letters of recommendation.

Admissions Contact Ms. Wendy Peterson, Director of Admissions, Washington State University, Pullman, WA 99164. *Phone:* 509-335-5586. *Toll-free phone:* 888-468-6978. *Fax:* 509-335-7468. *E-mail:* ir@wsu.edu.

WESTERN WASHINGTON UNIVERSITY
Bellingham, Washington

- **State-supported** comprehensive, founded 1893
- **Calendar** quarters
- **Degrees** bachelor's, master's, and postbachelor's certificates
- **Small-town** 223-acre campus with easy access to Seattle and Vancouver
- **Endowment** $3.7 million
- **Coed,** 11,050 undergraduate students, 95% full-time, 56% women, 44% men
- **Moderately difficult** entrance level, 78% of applicants were admitted

Western Washington University is an innovative public university considered to be among the best in the Pacific Northwest. Western is recognized for excellence in undergraduate education, an increasingly diverse and multicultural learning environment, and a strong sense of community. Primary reasons for attending Western are academic quality, location, size, job placement, and cost.

Undergraduates 10,513 full-time, 537 part-time. Students come from 47 states and territories, 41 other countries, 8% are from out of state, 2% African American, 7% Asian American or Pacific Islander, 3% Hispanic American, 2% Native American, 1.0% international, 9% transferred in, 33% live on campus. *Retention:* 79% of 2001 full-time freshmen returned.

Freshmen *Admission:* 6,862 applied, 5,355 admitted, 2,086 enrolled. *Average high school GPA:* 3.50. *Test scores:* SAT verbal scores over 500: 74%; SAT math scores over 500: 73%; ACT scores over 18: 93%; SAT verbal scores over 600: 28%; SAT math scores over 600: 25%; ACT scores over 24: 44%; SAT verbal scores over 700: 4%; SAT math scores over 700: 2%; ACT scores over 30: 4%.

Faculty *Total:* 630, 71% full-time, 72% with terminal degrees. *Student/faculty ratio:* 21:1.

Majors Accounting; American studies; anthropology; archaeology; art; art education; art history; Asian studies; athletic training/sports medicine; automotive engineering technology; biochemistry; biological/physical sciences; biology; broadcast journalism; business administration; business economics; business marketing and marketing management; Canadian studies; cell biology; ceramic arts; chemistry; city/community/regional planning; classics; communications; comparative literature; computer management; computer programming; computer science; counselor education/guidance; creative writing; cultural studies; developmental/child psychology; early childhood education; earth sciences; East Asian studies; ecology; economics; education; education administration; education (multiple levels); electrical/electronic engineering technology; elementary education; engineering design; engineering technology; English; environmental biology; environmental education; environmental science; exercise sciences; finance; fine/studio arts; French; general studies; geography; geology; geophysics/

Western Washington University (continued)

seismology; German; graphic design/commercial art/illustration; health education; history; humanities; human resources management; human services; industrial design; industrial technology; interdisciplinary studies; international business; jazz; journalism; Latin American studies; liberal arts and sciences/liberal studies; linguistics; literature; management information systems/business data processing; marine biology; mass communications; mathematics; molecular biology; music; music history; music teacher education; natural resources management; operations management; philosophy; physical education; physics; plastics technology; political science; pre-law; psychology; public health education/promotion; recreation/leisure studies; science education; secondary education; sociology; Spanish; special education; speech-language pathology/audiology; theater arts/drama; western civilization; women's studies.

Academic Programs *Special study options:* accelerated degree program, adult/continuing education programs, advanced placement credit, cooperative education, distance learning, double majors, English as a second language, honors programs, independent study, internships, off-campus study, services for LD students, student-designed majors, study abroad, summer session for credit.

Library Wilson Library plus 3 others with 1.3 million titles, 4,805 serial subscriptions, 24,825 audiovisual materials, an OPAC, a Web page.

Computers on Campus 1500 computers available on campus for general student use. A campuswide network can be accessed from student residence rooms and from off campus. Internet access, online (class) registration, at least one staffed computer lab available.

Student Life *Housing Options:* coed. *Activities and Organizations:* drama/theater group, student-run newspaper, radio and television station, choral group, Intramurals, Residence Hall Association, Associated Students, Outdoor Center, Ethnic Student Center. *Campus security:* 24-hour emergency response devices and patrols, student patrols, late-night transport/escort service, controlled dormitory access. *Student Services:* health clinic, personal/psychological counseling, women's center, legal services.

Athletics Member NCAA. All Division II. *Intercollegiate sports:* basketball M(s)/W(s), crew M/W, cross-country running M(s)/W(s), football M(s), golf M(s)/W, soccer M(s)/W(s), softball W(s), track and field M(s)/W(s), volleyball W(s). *Intramural sports:* badminton M/W, baseball M, basketball M/W, ice hockey M, lacrosse M/W, racquetball M/W, rugby M/W, sailing M/W, skiing (downhill) M/W, soccer M/W, softball M/W, swimming M/W, table tennis M/W, tennis M/W, volleyball M/W, water polo M/W, wrestling M.

Standardized Tests *Required:* SAT I or ACT (for admission).

Costs (2001–02) *Tuition:* state resident $3015 full-time, $101 per credit part-time; nonresident $10,755 full-time, $359 per credit part-time. Part-time tuition and fees vary according to course load. *Required fees:* $273 full-time, $91 per term part-time. *Room and board:* $5700; room only: $3420. Room and board charges vary according to board plan and housing facility. *Payment plan:* installment. *Waivers:* senior citizens and employees or children of employees.

Financial Aid Of all full-time matriculated undergraduates who enrolled in 2001, 8742 applied for aid, 4010 were judged to have need, 1519 had their need fully met. In 2001, 930 non-need-based awards were made. *Average percent of need met:* 89%. *Average financial aid package:* $7637. *Average need-based loan:* $3445. *Average need-based gift aid:* $4626. *Average indebtedness upon graduation:* $14,063.

Applying *Options:* electronic application. *Application fee:* $35. *Required:* high school transcript, minimum 2.5 GPA. *Recommended:* essay or personal statement. *Application deadlines:* 3/1 (freshmen), 4/1 (transfers). *Notification:* continuous until 4/15 (freshmen).

Admissions Contact Ms. Karen Copetas, Director of Admissions, Western Washington University, 516 High Street, Bellingham, WA 98225-9009. *Phone:* 360-650-3440 Ext. 3440. *Fax:* 360-650-7369. *E-mail:* admit@cc.wwu.edu.

WHITMAN COLLEGE
Walla Walla, Washington

- **Independent** 4-year, founded 1859
- **Calendar** semesters
- **Degree** bachelor's
- **Small-town** 55-acre campus
- **Endowment** $268.9 million
- **Coed,** 1,439 undergraduate students, 97% full-time, 56% women, 44% men
- **Very difficult** entrance level, 54% of applicants were admitted

Whitman College, one of the nation's leading liberal arts colleges, develops its students' capacities to analyze, interpret, criticize, communicate, and engage. Strong residential life and active cocurricular programs encourage personal and social development. A Whitman education is intended to foster intellectual vitality, confidence, leadership, and the flexibility to succeed in a changing technological, multicultural world. Whitman's location in Walla Walla, Washington, offers an ideal setting for a rigorous education, an active campus life, and a strong sense of community in the beautiful Pacific Northwest.

Undergraduates 1,399 full-time, 40 part-time. Students come from 45 states and territories, 22 other countries, 55% are from out of state, 2% African American, 7% Asian American or Pacific Islander, 3% Hispanic American, 0.9% Native American, 2% international, 2% transferred in, 65% live on campus. *Retention:* 94% of 2001 full-time freshmen returned.

Freshmen *Admission:* 2,144 applied, 1,161 admitted, 362 enrolled. *Average high school GPA:* 3.72. *Test scores:* SAT verbal scores over 500: 100%; SAT math scores over 500: 98%; ACT scores over 18: 100%; SAT verbal scores over 600: 81%; SAT math scores over 600: 82%; ACT scores over 24: 95%; SAT verbal scores over 700: 30%; SAT math scores over 700: 24%; ACT scores over 30: 45%.

Faculty *Total:* 165, 70% full-time, 85% with terminal degrees. *Student/faculty ratio:* 10:1.

Majors Anthropology; art; art history; Asian studies; astronomy; biochemistry; biology; biophysics; chemistry; classics; economics; English; environmental science; French; geology; German; history; mathematics; molecular biology; music; philosophy; physics; political science; psychology; sociology; Spanish; theater arts/drama.

Academic Programs *Special study options:* advanced placement credit, double majors, honors programs, independent study, internships, off-campus study, services for LD students, student-designed majors, study abroad. *Unusual degree programs:* 3-2 engineering with California Institute of Technology, Columbia University, Duke University, University of Washington; forestry with Duke University, Washington University in St. Louis; international studies with Monterey Institute of International Studies, oceanography with University of Washington, teacher education with Bank Street College of Education.

Library Penrose Library plus 1 other with 325,245 titles, 2,333 serial subscriptions, 2,250 audiovisual materials, an OPAC, a Web page.

Computers on Campus 300 computers available on campus for general student use. A campuswide network can be accessed from student residence rooms and from off campus that provide access to course registration information. Internet access, at least one staffed computer lab available.

Student Life *Housing:* on-campus residence required through sophomore year. *Options:* coed, women-only. *Activities and Organizations:* drama/theater group, student-run newspaper, radio station, choral group, Associated Students, outdoor program, Center for Community Service, national fraternities, national sororities. *Campus security:* 24-hour emergency response devices and patrols, student patrols, late-night transport/escort service, controlled dormitory access. *Student Services:* health clinic, personal/psychological counseling, women's center.

Athletics Member NCAA. All Division III. *Intercollegiate sports:* baseball M, basketball M/W, bowling M(c)/W(c), cross-country running M/W, fencing M(c)/W(c), golf M/W, ice hockey M(c), lacrosse M(c)/W(c), rugby M(c)/W(c), skiing (cross-country) M/W, skiing (downhill) M/W, soccer M/W, swimming M/W, tennis M/W, track and field M/W, volleyball M(c)/W, water polo M(c)/W(c). *Intramural sports:* basketball M/W, bowling M/W, football M/W, racquetball M/W, soccer M/W, softball M/W, tennis M/W, volleyball M/W.

Standardized Tests *Required:* SAT I or ACT (for admission). *Recommended:* SAT II: Writing Test (for admission).

Costs (2002–03) *Comprehensive fee:* $30,824 includes full-time tuition ($24,070), mandatory fees ($204), and room and board ($6550). Part-time tuition: $1000 per credit. *Room and board:* College room only: $3000. Room and board charges vary according to board plan and housing facility. *Payment plan:* deferred payment. *Waivers:* employees or children of employees.

Financial Aid Of all full-time matriculated undergraduates who enrolled in 2001, 770 applied for aid, 595 were judged to have need, 333 had their need fully met. 458 Federal Work-Study jobs (averaging $1750). 243 State and other part-time jobs (averaging $1450). In 2001, 607 non-need-based awards were made. *Average percent of need met:* 96%. *Average financial aid package:* $16,700. *Average need-based loan:* $3850. *Average need-based gift aid:* $12,100. *Average non-need based aid:* $7250. *Average indebtedness upon graduation:* $12,578.

Applying *Options:* common application, electronic application, early admission, early decision, deferred entrance. *Application fee:* $45. *Required:* essay or personal statement, high school transcript, 1 letter of recommendation. *Recommended:* interview. *Application deadlines:* 2/1 (freshmen), 2/1 (transfers). *Early decision:* 11/15 (for plan 1), 1/1 (for plan 2). *Notification:* 4/1 (freshmen), 12/15 (early decision plan 1), 1/24 (early decision plan 2).

Admissions Contact Mr. John Bogley, Dean of Admission and Financial Aid, Whitman College, 345 Boyer Avenue, Walla Walla, WA 99362-2083. *Phone:* 509-527-5176. *Toll-free phone:* 877-462-9448. *Fax:* 509-527-4967. *E-mail:* admission@whitman.edu.

Whitworth College
Spokane, Washington

- **Independent Presbyterian** comprehensive, founded 1890
- **Calendar** 4-1-4
- **Degrees** bachelor's and master's
- **Suburban** 200-acre campus
- **Endowment** $54.0 million
- **Coed,** 1,650 undergraduate students
- **Very difficult** entrance level, 90% of applicants were admitted

Undergraduates Students come from 31 states and territories, 24 other countries, 45% are from out of state, 60% live on campus. *Retention:* 85% of 2001 full-time freshmen returned.

Freshmen *Admission:* 1,115 applied, 1,001 admitted. *Average high school GPA:* 3.60. *Test scores:* SAT verbal scores over 500: 76%; SAT math scores over 500: 79%; SAT verbal scores over 600: 39%; SAT math scores over 600: 40%; SAT verbal scores over 700: 7%; SAT math scores over 700: 5%.

Faculty *Total:* 110, 84% full-time, 77% with terminal degrees. *Student/faculty ratio:* 15:1.

Majors Accounting; American studies; art; art education; art history; arts management; athletic training/sports medicine; biology; business administration; chemistry; computer science; economics; elementary education; English; fine/studio arts; French; history; international business; international relations; journalism; mass communications; mathematics; music; music (piano and organ performance); music teacher education; music (voice and choral/opera performance); nursing; peace/conflict studies; philosophy; physical education; physics; political science; pre-dentistry; pre-law; pre-medicine; pre-veterinary studies; psychology; religious studies; secondary education; sociology; Spanish; special education; speech/rhetorical studies; theater arts/drama.

Academic Programs *Special study options:* academic remediation for entering students, adult/continuing education programs, advanced placement credit, cooperative education, English as a second language, internships, off-campus study, part-time degree program, student-designed majors, study abroad, summer session for credit. *ROTC:* Army (c). *Unusual degree programs:* 3-2 engineering with Seattle Pacific University, University of Southern California, Washington University in St. Louis, Columbia University.

Library Harriet Cheney Cowles Library with 135,373 titles, 725 serial subscriptions, an OPAC, a Web page.

Computers on Campus 150 computers available on campus for general student use. A campuswide network can be accessed from student residence rooms and from off campus. At least one staffed computer lab available.

Student Life *Housing:* on-campus residence required through sophomore year. *Options:* coed. *Activities and Organizations:* drama/theater group, student-run newspaper, radio station, choral group, International Club, Habitat for Humanity, En Christo, Hawaiian club, Ski Club. *Campus security:* 24-hour emergency response devices and patrols, late-night transport/escort service. *Student Services:* health clinic, personal/psychological counseling.

Athletics Member NCAA. All Division III. *Intercollegiate sports:* baseball M, basketball M/W, cross-country running M/W, football M, soccer M/W, swimming M/W, tennis M/W, track and field M/W, volleyball W. *Intramural sports:* basketball M/W, football M/W, golf M/W, rugby M, skiing (cross-country) M/W, skiing (downhill) M/W, softball M/W, table tennis M/W, volleyball M/W, water polo M/W.

Standardized Tests *Required:* SAT I or ACT (for admission).

Costs (2001–02) *Comprehensive fee:* $23,938 includes full-time tuition ($17,800), mandatory fees ($238), and room and board ($5900). Part-time tuition and fees vary according to class time. *Room and board:* Room and board charges vary according to board plan and housing facility. *Payment plans:* tuition prepayment, installment. *Waivers:* children of alumni and employees or children of employees.

Financial Aid Of all full-time matriculated undergraduates who enrolled in 2001, 1648 applied for aid, 1196 were judged to have need, 295 had their need fully met. 392 Federal Work-Study jobs (averaging $2148). 303 State and other part-time jobs (averaging $2564). In 2001, 389 non-need-based awards were made. *Average percent of need met:* 86%. *Average financial aid package:* $15,543. *Average need-based loan:* $4418. *Average need-based gift aid:* $10,064. *Average non-need based aid:* $6517.

Applying *Options:* common application, electronic application, early admission, early action, deferred entrance. *Required:* essay or personal statement, high school transcript, letters of recommendation. *Required for some:* interview. *Application deadlines:* 3/1 (freshmen), 7/1 (transfers). *Notification:* 12/15 (early action).

Admissions Contact Admissions Office, Whitworth College, 300 West Hawthorne Road, Spokane, WA 99251-0001. *Phone:* 800-533-4668. *Toll-free phone:* 800-533-4668. *Fax:* 509-777-3758. *E-mail:* admission@whitworth.edu.

WEST VIRGINIA

Alderson-Broaddus College
Philippi, West Virginia

- **Independent** comprehensive, founded 1871, affiliated with American Baptist Churches in the U.S.A.
- **Calendar** semesters
- **Degrees** associate, bachelor's, and master's
- **Rural** 170-acre campus
- **Endowment** $12.0 million
- **Coed,** 741 undergraduate students, 91% full-time, 64% women, 36% men
- **Moderately difficult** entrance level, 64% of applicants were admitted

Undergraduates 678 full-time, 63 part-time. Students come from 26 states and territories, 5 other countries, 25% are from out of state, 3% African American, 2% Asian American or Pacific Islander, 0.9% Hispanic American, 1% Native American, 1% international, 7% transferred in. *Retention:* 69% of 2001 full-time freshmen returned.

Freshmen *Admission:* 1,047 applied, 674 admitted, 245 enrolled. *Average high school GPA:* 3.26. *Test scores:* SAT verbal scores over 500: 57%; SAT math scores over 500: 41%; SAT verbal scores over 600: 14%; SAT math scores over 600: 12%.

Faculty *Total:* 96, 61% full-time, 44% with terminal degrees. *Student/faculty ratio:* 13:1.

Majors Accounting; applied mathematics; athletic training/sports medicine; biology; broadcast journalism; business administration; business marketing and marketing management; chemistry; computer/information sciences; computer science; creative writing; cytotechnology; education; elementary education; environmental science; finance; history; industrial radiologic technology; liberal arts and sciences/liberal studies; literature; management information systems/business data processing; mass communications; mathematics; medical technology; music; music teacher education; natural sciences; nursing; physical education; physician assistant; political science; pre-dentistry; pre-law; pre-medicine; pre-veterinary studies; psychology; recreational therapy; recreation/leisure studies; religious music; religious studies; science education; secondary education; sociology; special education; speech/rhetorical studies; technical/business writing; theater arts/drama.

Academic Programs *Special study options:* academic remediation for entering students, advanced placement credit, double majors, honors programs, independent study, internships, off-campus study, part-time degree program, student-designed majors, study abroad, summer session for credit. *ROTC:* Army (c).

Library Pickett Library with 82,685 titles, 270 serial subscriptions, an OPAC, a Web page.

Computers on Campus 92 computers available on campus for general student use. A campuswide network can be accessed from student residence rooms and from off campus. Internet access, at least one staffed computer lab available.

Student Life *Housing:* on-campus residence required through senior year. *Options:* coed, women-only. *Activities and Organizations:* drama/theater group, student-run newspaper, radio and television station, choral group, Baptist Campus Ministry, Collegiate 4-H, American Academy of Physician Assistants, S.L.I.C.E. (Students Learning in Community Education), Association of Women Students. *Campus security:* 24-hour patrols, late-night transport/escort service, controlled dormitory access. *Student Services:* health clinic, personal/psychological counseling.

Athletics Member NCAA. All Division II. *Intercollegiate sports:* baseball M(s), basketball M(s)/W(s), cross-country running M(s)/W(s), soccer M(s), softball W(s), volleyball W(s). *Intramural sports:* archery M/W, badminton M/W, baseball M, basketball M/W, bowling M/W, football M, golf M, racquetball M/W, soccer M/W, softball W, swimming M/W, table tennis M/W, tennis M/W, volleyball M/W, water polo M/W, weight lifting M/W.

Standardized Tests *Required:* SAT I or ACT (for admission).

Costs (2001–02) *Comprehensive fee:* $19,640 includes full-time tuition ($14,290), mandatory fees ($150), and room and board ($5200). Part-time tuition: $472 per credit hour. *Payment plan:* installment. *Waivers:* employees or children of employees.

Applying *Options:* electronic application, deferred entrance. *Application fee:* $10. *Required:* high school transcript, minimum 2.0 GPA. *Required for some:* 3

Alderson-Broaddus College (continued)
letters of recommendation, interview. *Application deadline:* rolling (freshmen), rolling (transfers). *Notification:* continuous until 8/31 (freshmen).

Admissions Contact Ms. Kimberly Klaus, Associate Director of Admissions, Alderson-Broaddus College, PO Box 2003, Philippi, WV 26416. *Phone:* 304-457-1700 Ext. 6255. *Toll-free phone:* 800-263-1549. *Fax:* 304-457-6239. *E-mail:* admissions@ab.edu.

APPALACHIAN BIBLE COLLEGE

Bradley, West Virginia

- **Independent nondenominational** 4-year, founded 1950
- **Calendar** semesters
- **Degrees** certificates, associate, and bachelor's
- **Small-town** 110-acre campus
- **Endowment** $242,376
- **Coed,** 243 undergraduate students, 81% full-time, 51% women, 49% men
- **Minimally difficult** entrance level, 46% of applicants were admitted

Freshmen *Admission:* 108 applied, 50 admitted.

Faculty *Total:* 31, 42% full-time, 23% with terminal degrees. *Student/faculty ratio:* 17:1.

Majors Biblical studies; theology.

Academic Programs *Special study options:* academic remediation for entering students, adult/continuing education programs, advanced placement credit, independent study, internships, part-time degree program, summer session for credit.

Library John Van Pufflen Library with 44,944 titles, 347 serial subscriptions, 4,268 audiovisual materials, an OPAC, a Web page.

Computers on Campus 7 computers available on campus for general student use. Internet access, at least one staffed computer lab available.

Student Life *Housing:* on-campus residence required through senior year. *Options:* men-only, women-only. *Activities and Organizations:* drama/theater group, choral group, Campus Missionary Fellowship. *Campus security:* 24-hour emergency response devices, patrols by trained security personnel. *Student Services:* health clinic, personal/psychological counseling.

Athletics Member NCCAA. *Intercollegiate sports:* basketball M/W, soccer M, volleyball W.

Standardized Tests *Required:* SAT I or ACT (for admission).

Costs (2001–02) *Comprehensive fee:* $10,160 includes full-time tuition ($6710) and room and board ($3450). Part-time tuition: $235 per credit hour. *Required fees:* $27 per credit hour. *Payment plan:* installment. *Waivers:* employees or children of employees.

Financial Aid Of all full-time matriculated undergraduates who enrolled in 2001, 261 applied for aid, 261 were judged to have need. 32 Federal Work-Study jobs (averaging $543). *Average percent of need met:* 85%. *Average financial aid package:* $3000. *Average need-based loan:* $3500. *Average need-based gift aid:* $3000. *Average indebtedness upon graduation:* $15,857.

Applying *Application fee:* $10. *Required:* essay or personal statement, high school transcript, 3 letters of recommendation. *Recommended:* minimum 2.5 GPA, interview. *Application deadline:* rolling (freshmen), rolling (transfers).

Admissions Contact Ms. Sara Stout, Admissions Counselor, Appalachian Bible College, PO Box ABC, Bradley, WV 25818. *Phone:* 800-678-9ABC Ext. 3213. *Toll-free phone:* 800-678-9ABC. *Fax:* 304-877-5082. *E-mail:* admissions@abc.edu.

BETHANY COLLEGE

Bethany, West Virginia

- **Independent** 4-year, founded 1840, affiliated with Christian Church (Disciples of Christ)
- **Calendar** 4-1-4
- **Degree** bachelor's
- **Rural** 1600-acre campus with easy access to Pittsburgh
- **Endowment** $56.0 million
- **Coed,** 774 undergraduate students, 98% full-time, 45% women, 55% men
- **Moderately difficult** entrance level, 71% of applicants were admitted

Undergraduates 761 full-time, 13 part-time. Students come from 28 states and territories, 16 other countries, 70% are from out of state, 4% African American, 0.6% Asian American or Pacific Islander, 1% Hispanic American, 0.3% Native American, 5% international, 2% transferred in, 88% live on campus. *Retention:* 84% of 2001 full-time freshmen returned.

Freshmen *Admission:* 929 applied, 658 admitted, 197 enrolled. *Average high school GPA:* 3.31. *Test scores:* SAT verbal scores over 500: 51%; SAT math scores over 500: 57%; ACT scores over 18: 90%; SAT verbal scores over 600: 20%; SAT math scores over 600: 21%; ACT scores over 24: 45%; SAT verbal scores over 700: 3%; SAT math scores over 700: 4%; ACT scores over 30: 7%.

Faculty *Total:* 67, 87% full-time, 67% with terminal degrees. *Student/faculty ratio:* 12:1.

Majors Accounting; art; biology; business administration; business economics; chemistry; communications; computer science; economics; education; education (K-12); elementary education; English; environmental science; fine/studio arts; French; German; history; interdisciplinary studies; international relations; liberal arts and sciences/liberal studies; mathematics; music; philosophy; physical education; physics; political science; pre-dentistry; pre-law; pre-medicine; pre-veterinary studies; psychology; religious studies; social work; Spanish; sport/fitness administration; theater arts/drama.

Academic Programs *Special study options:* academic remediation for entering students, advanced placement credit, double majors, English as a second language, independent study, internships, off-campus study, services for LD students, student-designed majors, study abroad. *Unusual degree programs:* 3-2 engineering with Columbia University, Washington University in St. Louis, Case Western Reserve University.

Library T. W. Phillips Memorial Library with 190,983 titles, 529 serial subscriptions, 1,388 audiovisual materials, an OPAC, a Web page.

Computers on Campus 136 computers available on campus for general student use. A campuswide network can be accessed from off campus. At least one staffed computer lab available.

Student Life *Housing:* on-campus residence required through senior year. *Options:* coed, men-only, women-only, disabled students. *Activities and Organizations:* drama/theater group, student-run newspaper, radio and television station, choral group, Student Board of Governors, Outdoor Club, Model United Nations, Public Relations Society, International Student Association, national fraternities, national sororities. *Campus security:* 24-hour emergency response devices and patrols, late-night transport/escort service. *Student Services:* health clinic, personal/psychological counseling.

Athletics Member NCAA. All Division III. *Intercollegiate sports:* baseball M, basketball M/W, cross-country running M/W, football M, golf M/W, ice hockey M(c), lacrosse M(c)/W(c), rugby M(c), soccer M/W, softball W, swimming M/W, tennis M/W, track and field M/W, volleyball W, weight lifting M(c). *Intramural sports:* basketball M/W, football M/W, racquetball M/W, soccer M/W, softball M/W, swimming M/W, table tennis M/W, tennis M/W, volleyball M/W, weight lifting M/W.

Standardized Tests *Required:* SAT I or ACT (for admission).

Costs (2001–02) *Comprehensive fee:* $27,004 includes full-time tuition ($20,650), mandatory fees ($354), and room and board ($6000). Part-time tuition: $742 per credit hour. *Required fees:* $354 per year part-time. *Room and board:* College room only: $3000. *Payment plan:* installment. *Waivers:* employees or children of employees.

Financial Aid Of all full-time matriculated undergraduates who enrolled in 2001, 703 applied for aid, 653 were judged to have need, 301 had their need fully met. 221 State and other part-time jobs (averaging $345). In 2001, 32 non-need-based awards were made. *Average percent of need met:* 90%. *Average financial aid package:* $17,875. *Average need-based loan:* $4700. *Average indebtedness upon graduation:* $18,200.

Applying *Options:* common application, electronic application. *Application fee:* $25. *Required:* essay or personal statement, high school transcript, minimum 2.0 GPA, 1 letter of recommendation. *Required for some:* interview. *Recommended:* interview. *Application deadline:* 8/15 (freshmen), rolling (transfers). *Notification:* continuous until 8/15 (freshmen).

Admissions Contact Brian Ralph, Vice President for Enrollment Management, Bethany College, Office of Admission, Bethany, WV 26032. *Phone:* 304-829-7611. *Toll-free phone:* 800-922-7611. *Fax:* 304-829-7142. *E-mail:* admission@mail.bethanywv.edu.

BLUEFIELD STATE COLLEGE

Bluefield, West Virginia

- **State-supported** 4-year, founded 1895, part of Higher Education Policy Commission System
- **Calendar** semesters
- **Degrees** certificates, associate, and bachelor's
- **Small-town** 45-acre campus
- **Endowment** $5.1 million
- **Coed,** 2,768 undergraduate students, 65% full-time, 62% women, 38% men
- **Noncompetitive** entrance level, 99% of applicants were admitted

Undergraduates 1,799 full-time, 969 part-time. Students come from 10 states and territories, 6% are from out of state, 7% transferred in. *Retention:* 53% of 2001 full-time freshmen returned.
Freshmen *Admission:* 1,021 applied, 1,012 admitted, 492 enrolled. *Average high school GPA:* 3.15. *Test scores:* ACT scores over 18: 67%; ACT scores over 24: 6%.
Faculty *Total:* 198, 39% full-time, 21% with terminal degrees. *Student/faculty ratio:* 17:1.
Majors Accounting; architectural engineering technology; biological/physical sciences; business; business administration; business marketing and marketing management; civil engineering technology; communication equipment technology; computer/information sciences; corrections; criminal justice studies; electrical/electronic engineering technology; elementary education; general studies; hotel and restaurant management; humanities; interdisciplinary studies; law enforcement/police science; liberal arts and sciences/liberal studies; mechanical engineering technology; medical assistant; medical radiologic technology; mining technology; nursing; paralegal/legal assistant; psychology; secretarial science; social sciences.
Academic Programs *Special study options:* academic remediation for entering students, adult/continuing education programs, advanced placement credit, distance learning, double majors, external degree program, internships, part-time degree program, student-designed majors, summer session for credit.
Library Hardway Library with 90,436 titles, 462 serial subscriptions, 341 audiovisual materials, an OPAC, a Web page.
Computers on Campus 355 computers available on campus for general student use. A campuswide network can be accessed from off campus. Internet access, at least one staffed computer lab available.
Student Life *Housing:* college housing not available. *Activities and Organizations:* student-run newspaper, choral group, Phi Eta Sigma, Student Nurses Association, Student Government Association, Minorities on the Move, national fraternities, national sororities. *Campus security:* 24-hour emergency response devices and patrols, student patrols. *Student Services:* health clinic, personal/psychological counseling.
Athletics Member NCAA. All Division II. *Intercollegiate sports:* baseball M(s), basketball M(s)/W(s), cross-country running M(s)/W(s), golf M(s), softball W(s), tennis M(s)/W(s). *Intramural sports:* badminton M/W, basketball M/W, football M/W, soccer M/W, softball M/W, swimming M/W, table tennis M/W, tennis M/W, volleyball M/W, water polo M/W, weight lifting M/W.
Standardized Tests *Recommended:* SAT I or ACT (for admission).
Costs (2001–02) *Tuition:* state resident $2288 full-time, $96 per credit hour part-time; nonresident $5766 full-time, $242 per credit hour part-time. Full-time tuition and fees vary according to program and reciprocity agreements. Part-time tuition and fees vary according to course load, program, and reciprocity agreements. *Payment plan:* deferred payment. *Waivers:* senior citizens.
Financial Aid Of all full-time matriculated undergraduates who enrolled in 2001, 1200 applied for aid, 725 were judged to have need, 130 had their need fully met. 103 Federal Work-Study jobs (averaging $1400). In 2001, 215 non-need-based awards were made. *Average percent of need met:* 70%. *Average financial aid package:* $4600. *Average need-based loan:* $2250. *Average need-based gift aid:* $700. *Average non-need based aid:* $1450. *Average indebtedness upon graduation:* $6500.
Applying *Options:* common application, electronic application, deferred entrance. *Required:* high school transcript, minimum 2.0 GPA. *Application deadline:* rolling (freshmen), rolling (transfers).
Admissions Contact Mr. John C. Cardwell, Director of Enrollment Management, Bluefield State College, 219 Rock Street, Bluefield, WV 24701-2198. *Phone:* 304-327-4567. *Toll-free phone:* 800-344-8892 Ext. 4065 (in-state); 800-654-7798 Ext. 4065 (out-of-state). *Fax:* 304-325-7747. *E-mail:* bscadmit@bluefield.wvnet.edu.

CONCORD COLLEGE
Athens, West Virginia

- **State-supported** 4-year, founded 1872, part of State College System of West Virginia
- **Calendar** semesters
- **Degrees** associate and bachelor's
- **Rural** 100-acre campus
- **Endowment** $15.0 million
- **Coed,** 3,055 undergraduate students, 81% full-time, 57% women, 43% men
- **Minimally difficult** entrance level, 65% of applicants were admitted

Undergraduates 2,475 full-time, 580 part-time. Students come from 26 states and territories, 11% are from out of state, 5% African American, 1% Asian American or Pacific Islander, 0.5% Hispanic American, 0.2% Native American, 5% transferred in, 39% live on campus. *Retention:* 64% of 2001 full-time freshmen returned.
Freshmen *Admission:* 2,330 applied, 1,521 admitted, 562 enrolled. *Average high school GPA:* 3.69. *Test scores:* SAT verbal scores over 500: 44%; SAT math scores over 500: 45%; ACT scores over 18: 79%; SAT verbal scores over 600: 19%; SAT math scores over 600: 15%; ACT scores over 24: 24%; SAT verbal scores over 700: 3%; SAT math scores over 700: 3%; ACT scores over 30: 2%.
Faculty *Total:* 167, 50% full-time, 41% with terminal degrees. *Student/faculty ratio:* 24:1.
Majors Accounting; art education; biology; business administration; business education; ceramic arts; chemistry; computer science; early childhood education; education; elementary education; English; food products retailing; geography; graphic design/commercial art/illustration; health education; history; hospitality management; hotel and restaurant management; information sciences/systems; library science; mass communications; mathematics; medical technology; music teacher education; physical education; political science; pre-medicine; pre-veterinary studies; psychology; recreation/leisure facilities management; secondary education; social work; sociology; special education; travel/tourism management.
Academic Programs *Special study options:* academic remediation for entering students, advanced placement credit, double majors, English as a second language, honors programs, part-time degree program, services for LD students, student-designed majors, summer session for credit.
Library J. Frank Marsh Library with 96,787 titles, 552 serial subscriptions, 1,077 audiovisual materials, an OPAC.
Computers on Campus 250 computers available on campus for general student use. A campuswide network can be accessed from off campus. At least one staffed computer lab available.
Student Life *Housing:* on-campus residence required through senior year. *Options:* coed, men-only, women-only. *Activities and Organizations:* drama/theater group, student-run newspaper, radio and television station, choral group, Student Union Board, student government, student-run publications, Greek organizations, music groups, national fraternities, national sororities. *Campus security:* 24-hour patrols, late-night transport/escort service. *Student Services:* health clinic.
Athletics Member NCAA, NAIA. All NCAA Division II. *Intercollegiate sports:* baseball M(s), basketball M(s)/W(s), cross-country running M/W, football M(s), golf M/W, softball W, tennis M/W, track and field M/W, volleyball W(s). *Intramural sports:* archery M/W, badminton M/W, basketball M/W, bowling M/W, football M, golf M/W, racquetball M/W, soccer M/W, swimming M/W, tennis M/W, track and field M/W, volleyball M/W, water polo M/W, wrestling M.
Standardized Tests *Required:* SAT I or ACT (for admission). *Recommended:* ACT (for admission).
Costs (2001–02) *One-time required fee:* $40. *Tuition:* state resident $2724 full-time, $114 per credit hour part-time; nonresident $6116 full-time, $255 per credit hour part-time. Full-time tuition and fees vary according to program. Part-time tuition and fees vary according to program. *Room and board:* $4358; room only: $1996. Room and board charges vary according to board plan and housing facility. *Payment plans:* installment, deferred payment. *Waivers:* employees or children of employees.
Financial Aid *Average indebtedness upon graduation:* $10,000.
Applying *Options:* common application, early admission. *Required:* high school transcript, minimum 2.0 GPA. *Recommended:* interview. *Application deadline:* rolling (freshmen), rolling (transfers). *Notification:* continuous (freshmen).
Admissions Contact Mr. Michael Curry, Vice President of Admissions and Financial Aid, Concord College, 1000 Vermillion Street, Athens, WV 24712. *Phone:* 304-384-5248. *Toll-free phone:* 888-384-5249. *Fax:* 304-384-9044. *E-mail:* admissions@concord.edu.

DAVIS & ELKINS COLLEGE
Elkins, West Virginia

- **Independent Presbyterian** 4-year, founded 1904
- **Calendar** semesters
- **Degrees** associate and bachelor's
- **Small-town** 170-acre campus
- **Endowment** $17.6 million
- **Coed,** 668 undergraduate students, 89% full-time, 61% women, 39% men
- **Minimally difficult** entrance level, 83% of applicants were admitted

Undergraduates Students come from 22 states and territories, 12 other countries, 45% are from out of state, 4% African American, 0.7% Asian American or Pacific Islander, 3% Hispanic American, 44% live on campus. *Retention:* 64% of 2001 full-time freshmen returned.

Davis & Elkins College (continued)

Freshmen *Admission:* 421 applied, 348 admitted. *Average high school GPA:* 3.07. *Test scores:* SAT verbal scores over 500: 43%; SAT math scores over 500: 37%; ACT scores over 18: 68%; SAT verbal scores over 600: 13%; SAT math scores over 600: 12%; ACT scores over 24: 16%; SAT verbal scores over 700: 3%; ACT scores over 30: 1%.

Faculty *Total:* 56, 82% full-time. *Student/faculty ratio:* 12:1.

Majors Accounting; art; biology; business administration; business education; business marketing and marketing management; chemistry; computer science; computer typography/composition; creative writing; economics; education; elementary education; English; environmental science; exercise sciences; French; health education; health services administration; history; hospitality management; international business; journalism; literature; mass communications; mathematics; music; music business management/merchandising; music teacher education; natural sciences; nursing; occupational therapy; physical education; political science; pre-dentistry; pre-law; pre-medicine; pre-veterinary studies; psychology; recreation/leisure studies; religious education; secondary education; secretarial science; social sciences; sociology; Spanish; sport/fitness administration; theater arts/drama; travel/tourism management.

Academic Programs *Special study options:* accelerated degree program, adult/continuing education programs, advanced placement credit, cooperative education, double majors, English as a second language, external degree program, honors programs, independent study, internships, part-time degree program, services for LD students, student-designed majors, study abroad, summer session for credit. *Unusual degree programs:* 3-2 engineering with West Virginia University, Washington University in St. Louis; forestry with Duke University, State University of New York College of Environmental Science and Forestry.

Library Booth Library with 12,540 audiovisual materials, an OPAC, a Web page.

Computers on Campus 101 computers available on campus for general student use. A campuswide network can be accessed from student residence rooms and from off campus. At least one staffed computer lab available.

Student Life *Housing:* on-campus residence required through senior year. *Options:* coed, men-only, women-only, disabled students. *Activities and Organizations:* drama/theater group, student-run newspaper, radio station, choral group, Beta Alpha Beta, campus radio station, Student Nurses Association, Student Education Association, International Student Organization, national fraternities, national sororities. *Campus security:* late-night transport/escort service, controlled dormitory access, late night security personnel. *Student Services:* health clinic, personal/psychological counseling.

Athletics Member NCAA. All Division II except field hockey (Division I). *Intercollegiate sports:* baseball M(s), basketball M(s)/W(s), cross-country running M(s)/W(s), field hockey W(s), golf M(s), soccer M(s)/W(s), softball W(s), tennis M(s)/W(s), volleyball W(s). *Intramural sports:* basketball M/W, football M/W, lacrosse M(c)/W, skiing (cross-country) M/W, skiing (downhill) M/W, soccer M/W, softball M/W, swimming M/W, tennis M/W, track and field M/W, volleyball M/W(c), water polo M/W.

Standardized Tests *Required:* SAT I or ACT (for admission).

Costs (2001–02) *Comprehensive fee:* $19,490 includes full-time tuition ($13,644), mandatory fees ($220), and room and board ($5626). Part-time tuition: $507 per credit. Part-time tuition and fees vary according to course load. *Required fees:* $50 per term part-time. *Payment plan:* installment. *Waivers:* employees or children of employees.

Financial Aid Of all full-time matriculated undergraduates who enrolled in 2001, 423 applied for aid, 360 were judged to have need, 67 had their need fully met. 176 Federal Work-Study jobs (averaging $1196). 84 State and other part-time jobs (averaging $1201). In 2001, 117 non-need-based awards were made. *Average percent of need met:* 79%. *Average financial aid package:* $11,043. *Average need-based loan:* $3289. *Average need-based gift aid:* $7704. *Average non-need based aid:* $6077.

Applying *Options:* common application, electronic application, early admission, deferred entrance. *Application fee:* $35. *Required:* high school transcript, minimum 2.0 GPA. *Recommended:* interview. *Application deadline:* rolling (freshmen), rolling (transfers). *Notification:* continuous (freshmen).

Admissions Contact Mr. Matt Shiflett, Director of Admissions, Davis & Elkins College, Elkins, WV 26241. *Phone:* 304-637-1332. *Toll-free phone:* 800-624-3157. *Fax:* 304-637-1800. *E-mail:* admis@dne.edu.

FAIRMONT STATE COLLEGE
Fairmont, West Virginia

- **State-supported** 4-year, founded 1865, part of State College System of West Virginia
- **Calendar** semesters
- **Degrees** certificates, associate, bachelor's, and master's
- **Small-town** 80-acre campus
- **Endowment** $6.4 million
- **Coed,** 6,724 undergraduate students, 68% full-time, 55% women, 45% men
- **Minimally difficult** entrance level, 97% of applicants were admitted

Undergraduates 4,600 full-time, 2,124 part-time. Students come from 22 states and territories, 23 other countries, 6% are from out of state, 4% African American, 0.4% Asian American or Pacific Islander, 0.6% Hispanic American, 0.3% Native American, 1% international, 5% transferred in, 6% live on campus. *Retention:* 64% of 2001 full-time freshmen returned.

Freshmen *Admission:* 2,057 applied, 1,986 admitted, 1,200 enrolled. *Average high school GPA:* 2.60. *Test scores:* ACT scores over 18: 60%; ACT scores over 24: 11%; ACT scores over 30: 1%.

Faculty *Total:* 517, 54% full-time, 24% with terminal degrees. *Student/faculty ratio:* 18:1.

Majors Accounting; art education; aviation management; aviation technology; biology; business administration; business education; chemistry; child care/development; civil engineering technology; community services; computer science; construction technology; drafting; economics; education; electrical/electronic engineering technology; elementary education; engineering technology; English; family/consumer studies; fashion merchandising; finance; French; graphic design/commercial art/illustration; graphic/printing equipment; health science; history; home economics; home economics education; human services; industrial arts; industrial technology; information sciences/systems; institutional food workers; interior design; law enforcement/police science; liberal arts and sciences/liberal studies; mathematics; mechanical engineering technology; medical laboratory technician; medical records administration; music teacher education; nursing; occupational safety/health technology; physical education; physical therapy; political science; psychology; real estate; retail management; science education; secondary education; secretarial science; sign language interpretation; sociology; special education; speech/rhetorical studies; theater arts/drama; veterinary technology.

Academic Programs *Special study options:* academic remediation for entering students, accelerated degree program, adult/continuing education programs, advanced placement credit, double majors, English as a second language, honors programs, internships, part-time degree program, services for LD students, summer session for credit. *ROTC:* Army (b).

Library Musick Library with 276,722 titles, 883 serial subscriptions, 2,066 audiovisual materials, an OPAC, a Web page.

Computers on Campus 1300 computers available on campus for general student use. A campuswide network can be accessed from off campus. Internet access, at least one staffed computer lab available.

Student Life *Housing Options:* coed, men-only, women-only. *Activities and Organizations:* drama/theater group, student-run newspaper, choral group, marching band, Alpha Phi Omega, Circle K, Society for Non-traditional Students, Criminal Justice Club, Honors Association, national fraternities, national sororities. *Campus security:* 24-hour emergency response devices and patrols, student patrols, controlled dormitory access. *Student Services:* health clinic, personal/psychological counseling, legal services.

Athletics Member NCAA. All Division II. *Intercollegiate sports:* baseball M, basketball M(s)/W(s), cross-country running M/W, football M(s), golf M(s)/W, softball W, swimming M(s)/W(s), tennis M(s)/W(s), volleyball W. *Intramural sports:* archery M/W, basketball M/W, bowling M/W, cross-country running M/W, football M, golf M/W, swimming M/W, table tennis M/W, tennis M/W, volleyball M/W, wrestling M.

Standardized Tests *Required:* SAT I or ACT (for admission).

Costs (2001–02) *Tuition:* state resident $2408 full-time, $101 per credit hour part-time; nonresident $5672 full-time, $237 per credit hour part-time. Full-time tuition and fees vary according to program. Part-time tuition and fees vary according to program. *Room and board:* Room and board charges vary according to board plan. *Payment plan:* installment. *Waivers:* senior citizens and employees or children of employees.

Financial Aid Of all full-time matriculated undergraduates who enrolled in 2001, 2638 applied for aid, 2310 were judged to have need, 327 had their need fully met. 403 Federal Work-Study jobs (averaging $1017). 410 State and other part-time jobs (averaging $1428). In 2001, 304 non-need-based awards were made. *Average percent of need met:* 65%. *Average financial aid package:* $4439. *Average need-based loan:* $2494. *Average need-based gift aid:* $2865. *Average indebtedness upon graduation:* $5313.

Applying *Options:* common application, electronic application, early admission. *Required:* high school transcript. *Recommended:* minimum 2.0 GPA. *Application deadlines:* 6/15 (freshmen), 6/15 (transfers).

Admissions Contact Mr. Douglas Dobbins, Executive Director of Enrollment Services, Fairmont State College, 1201 Locust Avenue, Fairmont, WV 26554. *Phone:* 304-367-4000. *Toll-free phone:* 800-641-5678. *Fax:* 304-367-4789. *E-mail:* admit@mail.fscwv.edu.

GLENVILLE STATE COLLEGE
Glenville, West Virginia

- **State-supported** 4-year, founded 1872, part of West Virginia Higher Education Policy Commission
- **Calendar** semesters
- **Degrees** associate and bachelor's
- **Rural** 331-acre campus
- **Endowment** $4.7 million
- **Coed,** 2,144 undergraduate students, 77% full-time, 59% women, 41% men
- **Noncompetitive** entrance level, 100% of applicants were admitted

Glenville State is a small, state-assisted college in central West Virginia. Major academic emphasis is on traditional 4-year baccalaureate degree programs such as education, behavioral science, and business administration. In addition, Glenville State offers highly successful associate-level programs in a variety of fields, including the nationally accredited forestry program. The campus is student-centered, and located in a safe, rural environment.

Undergraduates 1,650 full-time, 494 part-time. 3% African American, 1% Asian American or Pacific Islander, 0.3% Hispanic American, 0.3% Native American, 30% live on campus.

Freshmen *Admission:* 1,225 applied, 1,225 admitted, 538 enrolled.

Faculty *Total:* 175, 38% full-time, 21% with terminal degrees.

Majors Accounting; behavioral sciences; biology; business administration; business education; business marketing and marketing management; chemistry; computer engineering technology; computer science; criminal justice/law enforcement administration; early childhood education; education; elementary education; English; environmental technology; finance; forest harvesting production technology; history; information sciences/systems; liberal arts and sciences/liberal studies; music business management/merchandising; music teacher education; nursing; paralegal/legal assistant; physical education; science education; secondary education; secretarial science; special education; surveying.

Academic Programs *Special study options:* academic remediation for entering students, accelerated degree program, adult/continuing education programs, advanced placement credit, cooperative education, distance learning, double majors, English as a second language, honors programs, internships, part-time degree program, services for LD students, student-designed majors, summer session for credit. *ROTC:* Army (b).

Library Robert F. Kidd Library with 115,892 titles, 1,853 serial subscriptions, 20,145 audiovisual materials, an OPAC, a Web page.

Computers on Campus 120 computers available on campus for general student use. A campuswide network can be accessed from off campus. Internet access, at least one staffed computer lab available.

Student Life *Housing:* on-campus residence required for freshman year. *Options:* coed, men-only, women-only, disabled students. *Activities and Organizations:* drama/theater group, student-run newspaper, choral group, marching band, percussion ensemble, student government, band, choir, Fellowship of Christian Athletes, national fraternities. *Campus security:* 24-hour emergency response devices and patrols, student patrols, late-night transport/escort service. *Student Services:* health clinic.

Athletics Member NCAA. All Division II. *Intercollegiate sports:* basketball M(s)/W(s), cross-country running M(s)/W(s), football M(s), golf M(s)/W(s), track and field M(s)/W(s), volleyball W(s).

Standardized Tests *Required:* SAT I or ACT (for admission).

Costs (2001–02) *Tuition:* state resident $2488 full-time, $104 per credit hour part-time; nonresident $6120 full-time, $255 per credit hour part-time. *Room and board:* $4100. Room and board charges vary according to housing facility. *Payment plan:* installment. *Waivers:* senior citizens.

Financial Aid Of all full-time matriculated undergraduates who enrolled in 2001, 1362 applied for aid, 1207 were judged to have need, 327 had their need fully met. 207 Federal Work-Study jobs (averaging $731). 350 State and other part-time jobs. In 2001, 128 non-need-based awards were made. *Average percent of need met:* 80%. *Average financial aid package:* $6370. *Average need-based loan:* $3218. *Average need-based gift aid:* $3724. *Average non-need based aid:* $1948. *Average indebtedness upon graduation:* $12,117.

Applying *Options:* common application, electronic application, deferred entrance. *Application fee:* $10. *Required:* high school transcript, minimum 2.0 GPA, completion of college-preparatory program. *Application deadlines:* 8/1 (freshmen), 6/1 (transfers). *Notification:* continuous (freshmen).

Admissions Contact Ms. Brenda McCartney, Associate Registrar, Glenville State College, 200 High Street, Glenville, WV 26351-1200. *Phone:* 304-462-4117 Ext. 347. *Toll-free phone:* 800-924-2010. *Fax:* 304-462-8619. *E-mail:* visitor@glenville.edu.

MARSHALL UNIVERSITY
Huntington, West Virginia

- **State-supported** university, founded 1837, part of University System of West Virginia
- **Calendar** semesters
- **Degrees** certificates, associate, bachelor's, master's, doctoral, first professional, and post-master's certificates
- **Urban** 70-acre campus
- **Endowment** $43.3 million
- **Coed,** 9,653 undergraduate students, 84% full-time, 55% women, 45% men
- **Minimally difficult** entrance level, 91% of applicants were admitted

Undergraduates 8,126 full-time, 1,527 part-time. Students come from 40 states and territories, 36 other countries, 16% are from out of state, 4% African American, 0.9% Asian American or Pacific Islander, 0.5% Hispanic American, 0.7% Native American, 0.8% international, 6% transferred in, 20% live on campus. *Retention:* 75% of 2001 full-time freshmen returned.

Freshmen *Admission:* 2,416 applied, 2,198 admitted, 1,796 enrolled. *Average high school GPA:* 3.30. *Test scores:* ACT scores over 18: 86%; ACT scores over 24: 26%; ACT scores over 30: 4%.

Faculty *Total:* 708, 64% full-time, 50% with terminal degrees. *Student/faculty ratio:* 20:1.

Majors Accounting; adult/continuing education administration; biology; business administration; business economics; business marketing and marketing management; business systems analysis/design; chemistry; communication disorders; counselor education/guidance; criminal justice studies; cytotechnology; dietetics; economics; education; elementary education; English; environmental science; finance; foreign languages/literatures; general studies; geography; geology; history; home economics; humanities; international relations; journalism; mathematics; medical laboratory technician; medical technology; multi/interdisciplinary studies related; nursing; occupational safety/health technology; physical education; physics; political science; psychology; recreation/leisure facilities management; secondary education; social work; sociology; speech/rhetorical studies; systems science/theory.

Academic Programs *Special study options:* academic remediation for entering students, accelerated degree program, adult/continuing education programs, advanced placement credit, cooperative education, distance learning, double majors, English as a second language, honors programs, independent study, internships, off-campus study, part-time degree program, services for LD students, study abroad, summer session for credit. *ROTC:* Army (b). *Unusual degree programs:* 3-2 forestry with Duke University.

Library John Deaver Drinko Library plus 2 others with 1.4 million titles, 13,405 serial subscriptions, 18,524 audiovisual materials, an OPAC, a Web page.

Computers on Campus 1330 computers available on campus for general student use. A campuswide network can be accessed from student residence rooms and from off campus. Internet access, online (class) registration, at least one staffed computer lab available.

Student Life *Housing:* on-campus residence required through sophomore year. *Options:* coed, men-only, women-only, disabled students. *Activities and Organizations:* drama/theater group, student-run newspaper, radio and television station, choral group, marching band, Gamma Beta Phi, Habitat for Humanity, Men's and Women's Rugby, Phi Eta Sigma, Campus Crusade for Christ, national fraternities, national sororities. *Campus security:* 24-hour emergency response devices and patrols, student patrols, late-night transport/escort service. *Student Services:* health clinic, personal/psychological counseling, women's center, legal services.

Athletics Member NCAA. All Division I except football (Division I-A). *Intercollegiate sports:* baseball M(s), basketball M(s)/W(s), cross-country running M(s)/W(s), golf M(s), soccer M(s)/W(s), softball W(s), tennis W(s), track and field M(s)/W(s), volleyball W(s). *Intramural sports:* badminton M/W, baseball M, basketball M/W, bowling M/W, cross-country running M/W, football M, golf M/W, ice hockey M(c), racquetball M/W, rugby M(c)/W(c), skiing (cross-country) M(c)/W(c), skiing (downhill) M(c)/W(c), soccer M/W, softball W, swimming M/W, table tennis M/W, tennis M/W, track and field M/W, volleyball M/W, water polo M/W, wrestling M.

Standardized Tests *Required:* SAT I or ACT (for admission).

Costs (2001–02) *Tuition:* state resident $2724 full-time, $93 per semester hour part-time; nonresident $7294 full-time, $284 per semester hour part-time. Full-time tuition and fees vary according to program and reciprocity agreements. Part-time tuition and fees vary according to program and reciprocity agreements.

Marshall University (continued)
Required fees: $488 full-time, $21 per semester hour. *Room and board:* $5028; room only: $2688. Room and board charges vary according to board plan and housing facility. *Payment plans:* installment, deferred payment.

Financial Aid Of all full-time matriculated undergraduates who enrolled in 2001, 5492 applied for aid, 4211 were judged to have need, 1627 had their need fully met. 394 Federal Work-Study jobs (averaging $1719). 53 State and other part-time jobs (averaging $4884). In 2001, 1270 non-need-based awards were made. *Average percent of need met:* 70%. *Average financial aid package:* $5999. *Average need-based loan:* $4117. *Average need-based gift aid:* $3574. *Average non-need based aid:* $2784. *Average indebtedness upon graduation:* $15,169.

Applying *Options:* common application, electronic application, early admission, deferred entrance. *Application fee:* $35 (non-residents). *Required:* high school transcript, minimum 2.0 GPA. *Application deadline:* rolling (freshmen), rolling (transfers). *Notification:* continuous (freshmen).

Admissions Contact Dr. Barbara J. Tarter, Interim Admissions Director, Marshall University, 1 John Marshall Drive, Huntington, WV 25755. *Phone:* 304-696-3160. *Toll-free phone:* 800-642-3499. *Fax:* 304-696-3135. *E-mail:* admissions@marshall.edu.

MOUNTAIN STATE UNIVERSITY
Beckley, West Virginia

- **Independent** comprehensive, founded 1933
- **Calendar** semesters
- **Degrees** certificates, associate, bachelor's, and master's
- **Small-town** 7-acre campus
- **Endowment** $3.6 million
- **Coed,** 2,422 undergraduate students, 71% full-time, 65% women, 35% men
- **Noncompetitive** entrance level, 100% of applicants were admitted

Undergraduates 1,722 full-time, 700 part-time. 12% are from out of state, 8% African American, 1% Asian American or Pacific Islander, 0.8% Hispanic American, 1% Native American, 6% international, 7% transferred in, 5% live on campus. *Retention:* 67% of 2001 full-time freshmen returned.

Freshmen *Admission:* 401 applied, 401 admitted, 401 enrolled. *Average high school GPA:* 2.50. *Test scores:* SAT verbal scores over 500: 41%; SAT math scores over 500: 48%; ACT scores over 18: 55%; SAT verbal scores over 600: 6%; SAT math scores over 600: 13%; ACT scores over 24: 8%; SAT verbal scores over 700: 2%.

Faculty *Total:* 126, 43% full-time, 18% with terminal degrees. *Student/faculty ratio:* 19:1.

Majors Aviation technology; banking; behavioral sciences; business administration; computer science; criminal justice studies; diagnostic medical sonography; education; engineering; environmental science; health services administration; information sciences/systems; interdisciplinary studies; legal administrative assistant; legal studies; medical assistant; nursing; occupational therapy assistant; paralegal/legal assistant; physical therapy assistant; physician assistant; radio/television broadcasting technology; respiratory therapy; secretarial science; social work; travel/tourism management.

Academic Programs *Special study options:* academic remediation for entering students, accelerated degree program, adult/continuing education programs, advanced placement credit, cooperative education, distance learning, double majors, English as a second language, external degree program, independent study, internships, part-time degree program, student-designed majors, summer session for credit.

Library Robert C. Byrd Learning Resource Center plus 1 other with 90,929 titles, 2,300 serial subscriptions, 2,405 audiovisual materials, an OPAC.

Computers on Campus 90 computers available on campus for general student use. A campuswide network can be accessed from off campus. Internet access, online (class) registration, at least one staffed computer lab available.

Student Life *Housing:* on-campus residence required through sophomore year. *Options:* coed. *Activities and Organizations:* drama/theater group, Student Christian Organization, astronomy club, Creative Writing Group, Gay, Lesbian, and Bisexual Student Support Group, Student Government Association. *Campus security:* 24-hour emergency response devices, late-night transport/escort service, controlled dormitory access, night patrols by security.

Athletics Member NAIA. *Intercollegiate sports:* basketball M(s), softball W(s), volleyball W. *Intramural sports:* basketball M/W, racquetball M/W, soccer M, swimming M/W, table tennis M, tennis M/W, volleyball M/W.

Standardized Tests *Required for some:* SAT I or ACT (for admission).

Costs (2001–02) *Comprehensive fee:* $8542 includes full-time tuition ($3600), mandatory fees ($960), and room and board ($3982). Full-time tuition and fees vary according to program. Part-time tuition: $145 per credit hour. Part-time tuition and fees vary according to program. *Required fees:* $35 per credit hour. *Room and board:* College room only: $2382. Room and board charges vary according to board plan. *Payment plan:* installment. *Waivers:* adult students and employees or children of employees.

Financial Aid Of all full-time matriculated undergraduates who enrolled in 2001, 2012 applied for aid, 1865 were judged to have need, 59 had their need fully met. 120 Federal Work-Study jobs. In 2001, 147 non-need-based awards were made. *Average percent of need met:* 49%. *Average financial aid package:* $5877. *Average need-based loan:* $3661. *Average need-based gift aid:* $3438. *Average indebtedness upon graduation:* $8933.

Applying *Options:* common application, electronic application, early admission, deferred entrance. *Required:* high school transcript. *Application deadline:* rolling (freshmen), rolling (transfers).

Admissions Contact Marketing Department, Mountain State University, P.O. Box 9003, Beckley, WV 25802-9003. *Phone:* 304-253-7351 Ext. 1433. *Toll-free phone:* 800-766-6067. *Fax:* 304-253-5072. *E-mail:* gocwv@cwv.edu.

OHIO VALLEY COLLEGE
Vienna, West Virginia

- **Independent** 4-year, founded 1960, affiliated with Church of Christ
- **Calendar** semesters
- **Degrees** associate and bachelor's
- **Small-town** 299-acre campus
- **Endowment** $561,086
- **Coed,** 453 undergraduate students, 98% full-time, 53% women, 47% men
- **Minimally difficult** entrance level, 48% of applicants were admitted

Undergraduates 442 full-time, 11 part-time. Students come from 23 states and territories, 13 other countries, 61% are from out of state, 5% African American, 0.2% Asian American or Pacific Islander, 0.9% Hispanic American, 0.4% Native American, 5% international, 13% transferred in, 60% live on campus. *Retention:* 65% of 2001 full-time freshmen returned.

Freshmen *Admission:* 399 applied, 190 admitted, 94 enrolled. *Average high school GPA:* 3.00. *Test scores:* SAT verbal scores over 500: 41%; SAT math scores over 500: 35%; ACT scores over 18: 82%; SAT verbal scores over 600: 13%; SAT math scores over 600: 13%; ACT scores over 24: 17%; SAT verbal scores over 700: 3%; ACT scores over 30: 2%.

Faculty *Total:* 50, 36% full-time, 90% with terminal degrees. *Student/faculty ratio:* 16:1.

Majors Accounting; biblical studies; business administration; business communications; education; education (multiple levels); elementary education; English education; human resources management; liberal arts and sciences/liberal studies; mathematics education; physical education; professional studies; psychology; religious studies; science education; science technologies related; secondary education; social studies education; special education.

Academic Programs *Special study options:* academic remediation for entering students, adult/continuing education programs, advanced placement credit, English as a second language, external degree program, honors programs, internships, part-time degree program, study abroad, summer session for credit. *ROTC:* Air Force (c).

Library Icy Belle Library with 34,000 titles, 313 serial subscriptions, 6,303 audiovisual materials, an OPAC.

Computers on Campus 34 computers available on campus for general student use. A campuswide network can be accessed from student residence rooms that provide access to e-mail. Internet access, at least one staffed computer lab available.

Student Life *Housing:* on-campus residence required through junior year. *Options:* men-only, women-only. *Activities and Organizations:* drama/theater group, student-run newspaper, choral group, Mission Club, Women for Christ, Timothy Club, Ambassador. *Campus security:* 24-hour emergency response devices, late-night transport/escort service. *Student Services:* health clinic, personal/psychological counseling.

Athletics Member NCAA, NAIA, NCCAA. All NCAA Division II. *Intercollegiate sports:* baseball M(s), basketball M(s)/W(s), cross-country running M(s)/W(s), golf M(s), soccer M(s), softball W(s), volleyball W(s). *Intramural sports:* baseball M, basketball M/W, bowling M/W, cross-country running M/W, football M/W, golf M/W, soccer M/W, softball M/W, table tennis M/W, track and field M/W, volleyball M/W.

Standardized Tests *Required:* SAT I or ACT (for admission).

Costs (2001–02) *One-time required fee:* $20. *Comprehensive fee:* $13,650 includes full-time tuition ($8380), mandatory fees ($1060), and room and board ($4210). Full-time tuition and fees vary according to course load. Part-time tuition: $306 per hour. Part-time tuition and fees vary according to course load.

Required fees: $42 per hour. *Room and board:* College room only: $2030. Room and board charges vary according to board plan. *Payment plan:* installment. *Waivers:* senior citizens and employees or children of employees.

Financial Aid Of all full-time matriculated undergraduates who enrolled in 2001, 341 applied for aid, 300 were judged to have need, 102 had their need fully met. 168 Federal Work-Study jobs (averaging $800). 54 State and other part-time jobs (averaging $800). In 2001, 62 non-need-based awards were made. *Average percent of need met:* 74%. *Average financial aid package:* $8423. *Average need-based loan:* $3774. *Average need-based gift aid:* $3570. *Average non-need based aid:* $3515. *Average indebtedness upon graduation:* $14,900.

Applying *Options:* common application, electronic application, early admission, early action, deferred entrance. *Application fee:* $20. *Required:* high school transcript. *Required for some:* essay or personal statement, interview. *Recommended:* letters of recommendation. *Application deadline:* rolling (freshmen), rolling (transfers). *Notification:* continuous (freshmen), 10/1 (early action).

Admissions Contact Mr. Denver Lucky, Director of Admissions, Vice President for Enrollment, Ohio Valley College, #1 Campus View Drive, Vienna, WV 26105. *Phone:* 304-865-6202. *Toll-free phone:* 877-446-8668 Ext. 6200. *Fax:* 304-865-6001. *E-mail:* admissions@ovc.edu.

SALEM INTERNATIONAL UNIVERSITY

Salem, West Virginia

- **Independent** comprehensive, founded 1888
- **Calendar** modular
- **Degrees** associate, bachelor's, and master's
- **Rural** 300-acre campus
- **Coed,** 455 undergraduate students, 98% full-time, 43% women, 57% men
- **Minimally difficult** entrance level, 22% of applicants were admitted

Undergraduates 445 full-time, 10 part-time. Students come from 39 states and territories, 15 other countries, 70% are from out of state, 9% African American, 0.7% Asian American or Pacific Islander, 3% Hispanic American, 0.4% Native American, 26% international, 8% transferred in, 64% live on campus. *Retention:* 68% of 2001 full-time freshmen returned.

Freshmen *Admission:* 454 applied, 99 admitted, 99 enrolled. *Average high school GPA:* 2.90. *Test scores:* SAT verbal scores over 500: 44%; SAT math scores over 500: 38%; ACT scores over 18: 68%; SAT verbal scores over 600: 12%; SAT math scores over 600: 12%; ACT scores over 24: 18%; SAT verbal scores over 700: 2%; SAT math scores over 700: 2%.

Faculty *Total:* 60, 55% full-time, 57% with terminal degrees. *Student/faculty ratio:* 13:1.

Majors Aircraft pilot (professional); Asian studies; athletic training/sports medicine; biological technology; biology; business administration; computer science; criminal justice/law enforcement administration; education; education (K-12); elementary education; environmental science; equestrian studies; human services; international business; Japanese; liberal arts and sciences/liberal studies; mass communications; mathematics; molecular biology; physical education; psychology; public health; radio/television broadcasting; secondary education; sport/fitness administration; telecommunications.

Academic Programs *Special study options:* academic remediation for entering students, accelerated degree program, advanced placement credit, double majors, English as a second language, independent study, internships, off-campus study, part-time degree program, services for LD students, study abroad. *Unusual degree programs:* 3-2 molecular biology/biotechnology.

Library Benedum Library with 179,096 titles, 625 serial subscriptions, 798 audiovisual materials, an OPAC.

Computers on Campus 79 computers available on campus for general student use. A campuswide network can be accessed from off campus. At least one staffed computer lab available.

Student Life *Housing:* on-campus residence required through junior year. *Options:* coed, men-only, women-only. *Activities and Organizations:* student-run newspaper, radio and television station, choral group, National Honor Society, Humanics Student Association, equestrian club, Alpha Phi Omega service fraternity, LIGHT, national fraternities, national sororities. *Campus security:* 24-hour emergency response devices and patrols, late-night transport/escort service, controlled dormitory access. *Student Services:* health clinic, personal/psychological counseling.

Athletics Member NCAA. All Division II. *Intercollegiate sports:* baseball M(s), basketball M(s)/W(s), cross-country running M(s)/W(s), equestrian sports M/W, golf M, soccer M(s), softball W(s), swimming M(s)/W(s), tennis M(s)/W(s), volleyball W(s), water polo M(s)/W(s). *Intramural sports:* basketball M/W, football M/W, racquetball M/W, rugby M, soccer M/W, softball M/W, swimming M/W, table tennis M/W, tennis M/W.

Standardized Tests *Required:* SAT I or ACT (for admission).

Costs (2001–02) *Comprehensive fee:* $18,072 includes full-time tuition ($13,500), mandatory fees ($140), and room and board ($4432). Full-time tuition and fees vary according to course load and program. Part-time tuition: $250 per credit. Part-time tuition and fees vary according to course load and program. *Required fees:* $20 per term part-time. *Payment plan:* installment. *Waivers:* senior citizens and employees or children of employees.

Financial Aid Of all full-time matriculated undergraduates who enrolled in 2001, 358 applied for aid, 274 were judged to have need, 165 had their need fully met. 191 Federal Work-Study jobs (averaging $1995). In 2001, 25 non-need-based awards were made. *Average percent of need met:* 89%. *Average financial aid package:* $13,299. *Average need-based loan:* $7034. *Average need-based gift aid:* $4611. *Average non-need based aid:* $3750. *Average indebtedness upon graduation:* $21,182.

Applying *Options:* electronic application, deferred entrance. *Application fee:* $25. *Required:* high school transcript, minimum 2.00 GPA. *Required for some:* interview. *Recommended:* essay or personal statement, interview. *Application deadline:* rolling (freshmen), rolling (transfers).

Admissions Contact Director of Admissions, Salem International University, PO Box 500, Salem, WV 26426-0500. *Phone:* 304-782-5336 Ext. 336. *Toll-free phone:* 800-283-4562. *E-mail:* admiss_new@salemiu.edu.

SHEPHERD COLLEGE

Shepherdstown, West Virginia

- **State-supported** 4-year, founded 1871, part of West Virginia Higher Education Policy Commission
- **Calendar** semesters
- **Degrees** associate and bachelor's
- **Small-town** 320-acre campus with easy access to Washington, DC
- **Endowment** $15.6 million
- **Coed,** 4,391 undergraduate students, 67% full-time, 60% women, 40% men
- **Moderately difficult** entrance level, 94% of applicants were admitted

Shepherd College, a public liberal arts college, has a long-standing reputation for providing high-quality education at a reasonable cost. Recently, the College was number 12 on *Money* magazine's list of the 25 public schools providing the best buys in education, marking the 5th time Shepherd has been named to one of *Money*'s best buys in education lists.

Undergraduates 2,930 full-time, 1,461 part-time. Students come from 48 states and territories, 20 other countries, 33% are from out of state, 5% African American, 0.9% Asian American or Pacific Islander, 2% Hispanic American, 0.5% Native American, 1.0% international, 7% transferred in, 25% live on campus. *Retention:* 69% of 2001 full-time freshmen returned.

Freshmen *Admission:* 1,527 applied, 1,434 admitted, 714 enrolled. *Average high school GPA:* 3.01. *Test scores:* SAT verbal scores over 500: 50%; SAT math scores over 500: 51%; ACT scores over 18: 76%; SAT verbal scores over 600: 14%; SAT math scores over 600: 11%; ACT scores over 24: 20%; SAT verbal scores over 700: 2%; ACT scores over 30: 2%.

Faculty *Total:* 330, 42% full-time, 39% with terminal degrees. *Student/faculty ratio:* 17:1.

Majors Accounting; art; biology; business administration; chemistry; communications; computer/information sciences; criminal justice studies; culinary arts and services related; design/visual communications; economics; electrical/electronic engineering technology; electromechanical technology; elementary education; emergency medical technology; engineering technologies related; English; environmental science; fashion merchandising; general studies; history; home economics; information sciences/systems; mathematics; multi/interdisciplinary studies related; music; nursing; occupational safety/health technology; paralegal/legal assistant; political science; psychology; recreation/leisure studies; secondary education; social work; sociology.

Academic Programs *Special study options:* academic remediation for entering students, accelerated degree program, adult/continuing education programs, advanced placement credit, cooperative education, double majors, English as a second language, honors programs, internships, part-time degree program, services for LD students, summer session for credit. *ROTC:* Army (c), Air Force (c).

Library Ruth Scarborough Library with 185,273 titles, 2,629 serial subscriptions, 11,393 audiovisual materials, an OPAC, a Web page.

Computers on Campus 300 computers available on campus for general student use. A campuswide network can be accessed from student residence rooms and from off campus that provide access to personal web pages. Internet access, online (class) registration, at least one staffed computer lab available.

Student Life *Housing:* on-campus residence required through senior year. *Options:* coed. *Activities and Organizations:* drama/theater group, student-run newspaper, radio station, choral group, marching band, Student Government

Shepherd College (continued)
Association, Outdoors Club, Christian Student Union, NAACP, Living Learning Center, national fraternities, national sororities. *Campus security:* 24-hour emergency response devices and patrols, late-night transport/escort service, controlled dormitory access. *Student Services:* health clinic, personal/psychological counseling.

Athletics Member NCAA. All Division II. *Intercollegiate sports:* baseball M, basketball M(s)/W(s), cross-country running M/W, football M(s), golf M, soccer M/W, softball W, tennis M/W, volleyball W(s). *Intramural sports:* basketball M/W, bowling M/W, football M/W, racquetball M/W, soccer M/W, softball M/W, tennis M/W, volleyball M/W, weight lifting M/W.

Standardized Tests *Required:* SAT I or ACT (for admission).

Costs (2001–02) *Tuition:* state resident $2608 full-time, $109 per semester hour part-time; nonresident $6294 full-time, $262 per semester hour part-time. Full-time tuition and fees vary according to degree level, location, and reciprocity agreements. Part-time tuition and fees vary according to degree level and location. *Room and board:* $4454; room only: $2335. Room and board charges vary according to board plan and housing facility. *Payment plan:* installment. *Waivers:* minority students and senior citizens.

Financial Aid Of all full-time matriculated undergraduates who enrolled in 2001, 2116 applied for aid, 1392 were judged to have need, 290 had their need fully met. 179 Federal Work-Study jobs (averaging $1269). 316 State and other part-time jobs (averaging $1377). In 2001, 358 non-need-based awards were made. *Average percent of need met:* 80%. *Average financial aid package:* $7028. *Average need-based loan:* $3522. *Average need-based gift aid:* $3065. *Average indebtedness upon graduation:* $14,556.

Applying *Options:* early admission, early action, deferred entrance. *Application fee:* $30. *Required:* high school transcript, minimum 2.5 GPA. *Recommended:* essay or personal statement, minimum 3.0 GPA, 3 letters of recommendation, interview. *Application deadlines:* 2/1 (freshmen), 3/15 (transfers). *Notification:* continuous until 6/15 (freshmen), 12/15 (early action).

Admissions Contact Mr. Karl L. Wolf, Director of Admissions, Shepherd College, PO Box 3210, Shepherdstown, WV 25443-3210. *Phone:* 304-876-5212. *Toll-free phone:* 800-344-5231. *Fax:* 304-876-5165. *E-mail:* admoff@shepherd.edu.

UNIVERSITY OF CHARLESTON
Charleston, West Virginia

- **Independent** comprehensive, founded 1888
- **Calendar** semesters
- **Degrees** associate, bachelor's, and master's
- **Urban** 40-acre campus
- **Endowment** $32.4 million
- **Coed,** 1,089 undergraduate students, 79% full-time, 69% women, 31% men
- **Moderately difficult** entrance level, 71% of applicants were admitted

Undergraduates 857 full-time, 232 part-time. Students come from 27 states and territories, 26 other countries, 19% are from out of state, 5% African American, 0.7% Asian American or Pacific Islander, 1% Hispanic American, 0.5% Native American, 5% international, 12% transferred in, 29% live on campus. *Retention:* 66% of 2001 full-time freshmen returned.

Freshmen *Admission:* 1,534 applied, 1,088 admitted, 187 enrolled. *Average high school GPA:* 3.21. *Test scores:* SAT verbal scores over 500: 50%; SAT math scores over 500: 41%; ACT scores over 18: 84%; SAT verbal scores over 600: 7%; SAT math scores over 600: 13%; ACT scores over 24: 20%; SAT verbal scores over 700: 1%; ACT scores over 30: 1%.

Faculty *Total:* 108, 65% full-time, 45% with terminal degrees. *Student/faculty ratio:* 15:1.

Majors Accounting; art; athletic training/sports medicine; biological/physical sciences; biology; business administration; business marketing and marketing management; chemistry; computer/information sciences; creative writing; education; elementary education; English; environmental biology; environmental science; history; humanities; information sciences/systems; interior design; liberal arts and sciences/liberal studies; mass communications; music; music business management/merchandising; music teacher education; music (voice and choral/opera performance); nursing; philosophy; political science; psychology; radiological science; religious studies; respiratory therapy; science education; social studies education.

Academic Programs *Special study options:* academic remediation for entering students, accelerated degree program, adult/continuing education programs, advanced placement credit, distance learning, double majors, English as a second language, independent study, internships, part-time degree program, student-designed majors, study abroad, summer session for credit. *ROTC:* Army (b).

Library Schoenbaum Library with 111,264 titles, 2,011 serial subscriptions, 2,505 audiovisual materials, an OPAC, a Web page.

Computers on Campus 200 computers available on campus for general student use. A campuswide network can be accessed from student residence rooms and from off campus. At least one staffed computer lab available.

Student Life *Housing:* on-campus residence required through sophomore year. *Options:* coed. *Activities and Organizations:* drama/theater group, student-run newspaper, choral group, Student Activities Board, American Society of Interior Designers, Student Government Association, Capito Association of Nursing Students, International Student Organization, national fraternities, national sororities. *Campus security:* 24-hour emergency response devices and patrols, student patrols, late-night transport/escort service, controlled dormitory access, radio connection to city police and ambulance. *Student Services:* personal/psychological counseling.

Athletics Member NCAA. All Division II. *Intercollegiate sports:* baseball M(s), basketball M(s)/W(s), crew M(s)/W(s), cross-country running M(s)/W(s), golf M(s), soccer M(s)/W(s), softball W(s), swimming M(s)/W(s), tennis M(s)/W(s), track and field M(s)/W(s), volleyball W(s). *Intramural sports:* basketball M/W, bowling M/W, football M/W, racquetball M/W, soccer M, swimming M/W, tennis M/W, volleyball M/W.

Standardized Tests *Required:* SAT I or ACT (for admission).

Costs (2001–02) *Comprehensive fee:* $20,640 includes full-time tuition ($14,900) and room and board ($5740). Part-time tuition: $620 per credit hour. Part-time tuition and fees vary according to course load and program. No tuition increase for student's term of enrollment. *Required fees:* $75 per term part-time. *Room and board:* College room only: $2990. Room and board charges vary according to board plan and housing facility. *Payment plan:* installment. *Waivers:* senior citizens and employees or children of employees.

Financial Aid Of all full-time matriculated undergraduates who enrolled in 2001, 835 applied for aid, 615 were judged to have need, 399 had their need fully met. In 2001, 110 non-need-based awards were made. *Average percent of need met:* 85%. *Average financial aid package:* $13,800. *Average need-based loan:* $4318. *Average need-based gift aid:* $4935. *Average non-need based aid:* $4910. *Average indebtedness upon graduation:* $18,500.

Applying *Options:* electronic application, early admission, deferred entrance. *Application fee:* $25. *Required:* high school transcript, minimum 2.25 GPA. *Recommended:* essay or personal statement, letters of recommendation. *Application deadline:* rolling (freshmen), rolling (transfers). *Notification:* continuous (freshmen).

Admissions Contact Ms. Kim Scranage, Associate Director of Admissions, University of Charleston, 2300 MacCorkle Avenue, SE, Charleston, WV 25304. *Phone:* 304-357-4750. *Toll-free phone:* 800-995-GOUC. *Fax:* 304-357-4781. *E-mail:* admissions@uchaswv.edu.

WEST LIBERTY STATE COLLEGE
West Liberty, West Virginia

- **State-supported** 4-year, founded 1837, part of West Virginia Higher Education Policy Commission
- **Calendar** semesters
- **Degrees** associate and bachelor's
- **Rural** 290-acre campus with easy access to Pittsburgh
- **Endowment** $6.9 million
- **Coed,** 2,633 undergraduate students, 90% full-time, 55% women, 45% men
- **Minimally difficult** entrance level, 97% of applicants were admitted

Undergraduates 2,375 full-time, 258 part-time. Students come from 22 states and territories, 9 other countries, 28% are from out of state, 3% African American, 0.3% Asian American or Pacific Islander, 0.6% Hispanic American, 0.1% Native American, 0.6% international, 11% transferred in, 45% live on campus. *Retention:* 68% of 2001 full-time freshmen returned.

Freshmen *Admission:* 1,301 applied, 1,259 admitted, 531 enrolled. *Average high school GPA:* 3.03. *Test scores:* SAT verbal scores over 500: 35%; SAT math scores over 500: 34%; ACT scores over 18: 66%; SAT verbal scores over 600: 7%; SAT math scores over 600: 8%; ACT scores over 24: 11%; SAT verbal scores over 700: 1%.

Faculty *Total:* 166, 67% full-time, 31% with terminal degrees. *Student/faculty ratio:* 19:1.

Majors Accounting; art education; banking; biology; business administration; business economics; business marketing and marketing management; chemistry; criminal justice/law enforcement administration; dental hygiene; early childhood education; education; elementary education; English; exercise sciences; graphic design/commercial art/illustration; health education; health science; history; information sciences/systems; interdisciplinary studies; mass communications;

mathematics; medical technology; music teacher education; nursing; physical education; political science; pre-dentistry; pre-law; pre-medicine; psychology; secondary education; social sciences; sociology.

Academic Programs *Special study options:* academic remediation for entering students, accelerated degree program, adult/continuing education programs, advanced placement credit, double majors, external degree program, honors programs, independent study, internships, off-campus study, part-time degree program, student-designed majors, summer session for credit.

Library Paul N. Elbin Library plus 1 other with 194,447 titles, 512 serial subscriptions, 13,037 audiovisual materials, an OPAC, a Web page.

Computers on Campus 300 computers available on campus for general student use. A campuswide network can be accessed from student residence rooms and from off campus. Internet access, at least one staffed computer lab available.

Student Life *Housing Options:* coed, men-only, women-only, disabled students. *Activities and Organizations:* drama/theater group, student-run newspaper, radio and television station, choral group, marching band, Delta Sigma Pi, Student Senate, Drama Club, Students in Free Enterprise, Chi Omega Sorority, national fraternities, national sororities. *Campus security:* 24-hour emergency response devices and patrols, late-night transport/escort service. *Student Services:* health clinic, personal/psychological counseling.

Athletics Member NCAA. All Division II. *Intercollegiate sports:* baseball M(s), basketball M(s)/W(s), cross-country running M(s)/W(s), football M(s), golf M(s)/W(s), softball W(s), tennis M(s)/W(s), track and field M(s)/W(s), volleyball W(s), wrestling M(s). *Intramural sports:* basketball M/W, golf M/W, racquetball M/W, softball M/W, table tennis M/W, tennis M/W, volleyball M/W.

Standardized Tests *Required:* SAT I or ACT (for admission).

Costs (2001–02) *Tuition:* state resident $2516 full-time, $105 per semester hour part-time; nonresident $6248 full-time, $260 per semester hour part-time. *Room and board:* $3540; room only: $1500. Room and board charges vary according to board plan and housing facility. *Payment plans:* installment, deferred payment. *Waivers:* senior citizens and employees or children of employees.

Financial Aid Of all full-time matriculated undergraduates who enrolled in 2001, 1726 applied for aid, 1337 were judged to have need, 428 had their need fully met. 140 Federal Work-Study jobs (averaging $955). 51 State and other part-time jobs (averaging $3585). In 2001, 238 non-need-based awards were made. *Average percent of need met:* 79%. *Average financial aid package:* $5389. *Average need-based loan:* $3093. *Average need-based gift aid:* $3244. *Average indebtedness upon graduation:* $12,568.

Applying *Options:* electronic application. *Required:* high school transcript, minimum 2.0 GPA. *Recommended:* interview. *Notification:* continuous (freshmen).

Admissions Contact Ms. Stephanie North, Admissions Counselor, West Liberty State College, PO Box 295, West Liberty, WV 26074. *Phone:* 304-336-8078. *Toll-free phone:* 800-732-6204 Ext. 8076. *Fax:* 304-336-8403. *E-mail:* wladmsn1@wlsc.wvnet.edu.

WEST VIRGINIA STATE COLLEGE
Institute, West Virginia

- **State-supported** 4-year, founded 1891, part of State College System of West Virginia
- **Calendar** semesters
- **Degrees** certificates, diplomas, associate, and bachelor's
- **Suburban** 90-acre campus
- **Coed,** 4,836 undergraduate students, 64% full-time, 59% women, 41% men
- **Minimally difficult** entrance level, 100% of applicants were admitted

Undergraduates Students come from 34 states and territories, 3% are from out of state, 15% African American, 1% Asian American or Pacific Islander, 0.5% Hispanic American, 0.5% Native American, 7% live on campus.

Freshmen *Admission:* 719 applied, 719 admitted. *Average high school GPA:* 2.84.

Faculty *Total:* 282, 53% full-time, 33% with terminal degrees. *Student/faculty ratio:* 23:1.

Majors Accounting; advertising; applied mathematics; architectural engineering technology; art; art education; biology; business administration; business education; business marketing and marketing management; chemical engineering technology; chemistry; computer programming; computer science; criminal justice/law enforcement administration; drafting; early childhood education; economics; education; electrical/electronic engineering technology; elementary education; English; fashion merchandising; finance; gerontology; health education; history; hotel and restaurant management; liberal arts and sciences/liberal studies; mass communications; mathematics; medical assistant; music teacher education; nuclear medical technology; physical education; political science; pre-dentistry; pre-engineering; pre-medicine; pre-veterinary studies; psychology; recreational therapy; recreation/leisure studies; science education; secondary education; secretarial science; social work; sociology.

Academic Programs *Special study options:* academic remediation for entering students, accelerated degree program, adult/continuing education programs, advanced placement credit, cooperative education, external degree program, internships, part-time degree program, services for LD students, summer session for credit. *ROTC:* Army (b).

Library Drain-Jordan Library with 194,706 titles, 1,678 serial subscriptions, 3,290 audiovisual materials, an OPAC.

Computers on Campus A campuswide network can be accessed from student residence rooms and from off campus. At least one staffed computer lab available.

Student Life *Housing:* on-campus residence required for freshman year. *Options:* men-only, women-only. *Activities and Organizations:* student-run newspaper, choral group, marching band, national fraternities, national sororities. *Campus security:* 24-hour emergency response devices and patrols, late-night transport/escort service. *Student Services:* health clinic, personal/psychological counseling.

Athletics Member NCAA. All Division II. *Intercollegiate sports:* baseball M, basketball M(s)/W(s), cross-country running M/W, football M(s), golf M(s), softball W(s), tennis M/W, track and field M/W, volleyball W. *Intramural sports:* basketball M/W, bowling M/W, football M, golf M.

Standardized Tests *Required:* SAT I or ACT (for placement).

Costs (2001–02) *Tuition:* state resident $2562 full-time, $106 per credit hour part-time; nonresident $5892 full-time, $246 per credit hour part-time. Full-time tuition and fees vary according to program. Part-time tuition and fees vary according to course load and program. *Room and board:* $4300; room only: $2000. *Payment plans:* tuition prepayment, installment.

Financial Aid *Financial aid deadline:* 6/15.

Applying *Options:* common application, early admission. *Required:* high school transcript. *Application deadlines:* 8/11 (freshmen), 8/11 (transfers). *Notification:* continuous (freshmen).

Admissions Contact Ms. Alice Ruhnke, Director of Admissions, West Virginia State College, Campus Box 197, PO Box 1000, Ferrell Hall, Room 106, Institute, WV 25112-1000. *Phone:* 304-766-3221. *Toll-free phone:* 800-987-2112. *Fax:* 304-766-4158. *E-mail:* ruhnkeam@mail.wvsc.edu.

WEST VIRGINIA UNIVERSITY
Morgantown, West Virginia

- **State-supported** university, founded 1867, part of West Virginia Higher Education System
- **Calendar** semesters
- **Degrees** bachelor's, master's, doctoral, and first professional
- **Small-town** 541-acre campus with easy access to Pittsburgh
- **Endowment** $313.0 million
- **Coed,** 16,121 undergraduate students, 94% full-time, 46% women, 54% men
- **Moderately difficult** entrance level, 94% of applicants were admitted

Undergraduates 15,181 full-time, 940 part-time. Students come from 50 states and territories, 68 other countries, 38% are from out of state, 4% African American, 2% Asian American or Pacific Islander, 1% Hispanic American, 0.4% Native American, 2% international, 5% transferred in, 21% live on campus. *Retention:* 76% of 2001 full-time freshmen returned.

Freshmen *Admission:* 8,786 applied, 8,238 admitted, 3,661 enrolled. *Average high school GPA:* 3.18. *Test scores:* SAT verbal scores over 500: 57%; SAT math scores over 500: 62%; ACT scores over 18: 92%; SAT verbal scores over 600: 13%; SAT math scores over 600: 16%; ACT scores over 24: 38%; SAT verbal scores over 700: 2%; SAT math scores over 700: 2%; ACT scores over 30: 4%.

Faculty *Total:* 1,766, 74% full-time, 65% with terminal degrees. *Student/faculty ratio:* 19:1.

Majors Accounting; advertising; aerospace engineering; agricultural education; agronomy/crop science; animal sciences; anthropology; art; biology; business administration; business marketing and marketing management; chemical engineering; chemistry; civil engineering; computer engineering; computer science; dental hygiene; economics; electrical engineering; elementary education; English; environmental science; exercise sciences; finance; fish/game management; foreign languages/literatures; forensic technology; forestry; geography; geology; history; home economics; horticulture science; industrial/manufacturing engineering; interdisciplinary studies; international relations; journalism; landscape architecture; liberal arts and sciences/liberal studies; mass communications; mathematical statistics; mathematics; mechanical engineering; medical technology; mining/mineral engineering; music; natural resources management; nursing; occupational therapy; petroleum engineering; pharmacy; philosophy; physical

West Virginia University (continued)

education; physical therapy; physics; plant sciences; political science; psychology; recreation/leisure facilities management; recreation/leisure studies; secondary education; social work; sociology; speech-language pathology/audiology; sport/fitness administration; theater arts/drama; visual/performing arts; wildlife management; wood science/paper technology.

Academic Programs *Special study options:* academic remediation for entering students, accelerated degree program, adult/continuing education programs, advanced placement credit, distance learning, double majors, English as a second language, external degree program, honors programs, independent study, internships, off-campus study, part-time degree program, services for LD students, student-designed majors, study abroad, summer session for credit. *ROTC:* Army (b), Air Force (b). *Unusual degree programs:* 3-2 education, business foreign language, occupational therapy, physical therapy, social work.

Library Wise Library plus 9 others with 1.4 million titles, 7,905 serial subscriptions, 42,040 audiovisual materials, an OPAC, a Web page.

Computers on Campus 1600 computers available on campus for general student use. A campuswide network can be accessed from student residence rooms and from off campus. Internet access, at least one staffed computer lab available.

Student Life *Housing:* on-campus residence required for freshman year. *Options:* coed, men-only, women-only, disabled students. *Activities and Organizations:* drama/theater group, student-run newspaper, radio station, choral group, marching band, Residential Hall Association, Gamma Beta Phi, Alpha Beta Phi, national fraternities, national sororities. *Campus security:* 24-hour emergency response devices and patrols, student patrols, late-night transport/escort service. *Student Services:* health clinic, personal/psychological counseling, women's center, legal services.

Athletics Member NCAA. All Division I except football (Division I-A). *Intercollegiate sports:* baseball M(s), basketball M(s)/W(s), cross-country running M(s)/W(s), gymnastics W(s), riflery M(s)/W(s), soccer M(s)/W(s), swimming M(s)/W(s), tennis M(s)/W(s), track and field M(s)/W(s), volleyball W(s), wrestling M(s). *Intramural sports:* badminton M/W, basketball M/W, bowling M/W, crew M(c)/W(c), equestrian sports M(c)/W(c), fencing M(c)/W(c), football M, golf M/W, ice hockey M(c), lacrosse M(c), racquetball M/W, riflery M/W, rugby M(c)/W(c), skiing (cross-country) M(c)/W(c), skiing (downhill) M(c)/W(c), soccer M/W, softball M/W, swimming M/W, table tennis M/W, tennis M/W, track and field M/W, volleyball M/W, wrestling M.

Standardized Tests *Required:* SAT I or ACT (for admission).

Costs (2001–02) *Tuition:* state resident $2076 full-time, $125 per credit hour part-time; nonresident $7960 full-time, $370 per credit hour part-time. Full-time tuition and fees vary according to location, program, and reciprocity agreements. Part-time tuition and fees vary according to course load, location, program, and reciprocity agreements. *Required fees:* $872 full-time. *Room and board:* $5326. Room and board charges vary according to board plan, housing facility, and location. *Payment plans:* installment, deferred payment. *Waivers:* senior citizens.

Financial Aid Of all full-time matriculated undergraduates who enrolled in 2001, 10003 applied for aid, 7256 were judged to have need, 2012 had their need fully met. 1545 Federal Work-Study jobs (averaging $1006). 1132 State and other part-time jobs (averaging $912). In 2001, 5692 non-need-based awards were made. *Average percent of need met:* 88%. *Average financial aid package:* $7076. *Average need-based loan:* $3997. *Average need-based gift aid:* $3284. *Average indebtedness upon graduation:* $18,273. *Financial aid deadline:* 3/1.

Applying *Options:* common application, electronic application, early admission, deferred entrance. *Application fee:* $40 (non-residents). *Required:* high school transcript, minimum 2.0 GPA, 2.0 for West Virginia residents; 2.25 required for non-residents. *Required for some:* essay or personal statement, minimum 2.25 GPA. *Application deadlines:* 8/1 (freshmen), 8/1 (transfers).

Admissions Contact Mr. Cheng H. Khoo, Director of Admissions and Records, West Virginia University, Box 6009, Morgantown, WV 26506-6009. *Phone:* 304-293-2121 Ext. 1511. *Toll-free phone:* 800-344-9881. *Fax:* 304-293-3080. *E-mail:* wvuadmissions@arc.wvu.edu.

WEST VIRGINIA UNIVERSITY AT PARKERSBURG

Parkersburg, West Virginia

- **State-supported** primarily 2-year, founded 1961, part of University System of West Virginia
- **Calendar** semesters
- **Degrees** certificates, diplomas, associate, and bachelor's
- **Small-town** 140-acre campus
- **Coed**
- **Noncompetitive** entrance level

Faculty *Student/faculty ratio:* 22:1.

Standardized Tests *Required:* ACT (for placement).

Applying *Options:* common application, electronic application, early admission, deferred entrance. *Required for some:* high school transcript.

Admissions Contact Criss McCauley, Senior Admissions Counselor, West Virginia University at Parkersburg, 300 Campus Drive, Parkersburg, WV 26101. *Phone:* 304-424-8223. *Toll-free phone:* 800-WVA-WVUP. *Fax:* 304-424-8332.

WEST VIRGINIA UNIVERSITY INSTITUTE OF TECHNOLOGY

Montgomery, West Virginia

- **State-supported** comprehensive, founded 1895, part of University System of West Virginia
- **Calendar** semesters
- **Degrees** certificates, associate, bachelor's, and master's
- **Small-town** 200-acre campus
- **Endowment** $5.2 million
- **Coed,** 2,353 undergraduate students, 70% full-time, 38% women, 62% men
- **Noncompetitive** entrance level, 100% of applicants were admitted

Tech's home is in scenic, wild-and-wonderful West Virginia, with opportunities for snow skiing and white-water rafting nearby. Tech offers more than 35 majors, including engineering, engineering technologies, business, computer science, social sciences, nursing, dental hygiene, health service administration, and printing. In addition, Tech offers an optional 5-year program in cooperative education and a practicum experience in social science. The low student-faculty ratio ensures a personalized education for Tech students.

Undergraduates 1,645 full-time, 708 part-time. Students come from 25 states and territories, 24 other countries, 9% are from out of state, 7% African American, 0.9% Asian American or Pacific Islander, 0.6% Hispanic American, 0.4% Native American, 4% international, 8% transferred in, 26% live on campus. *Retention:* 60% of 2001 full-time freshmen returned.

Freshmen *Admission:* 957 applied, 954 admitted, 457 enrolled. *Average high school GPA:* 3.20. *Test scores:* SAT verbal scores over 500: 50%; SAT math scores over 500: 40%; ACT scores over 18: 71%; SAT verbal scores over 600: 15%; SAT math scores over 600: 15%; ACT scores over 24: 15%; SAT math scores over 700: 2%; ACT scores over 30: 1%.

Faculty *Total:* 177, 68% full-time, 37% with terminal degrees. *Student/faculty ratio:* 16:1.

Majors Accounting; aerospace engineering; auto mechanic/technician; automotive engineering technology; biology; business administration; chemical engineering; chemistry; city/community/regional planning; civil engineering; civil engineering technology; community services; computer management; computer programming; computer science; corrections; culinary arts; data processing technology; dental hygiene; drafting; electrical/electronic engineering technology; electrical engineering; engineering; engineering physics; engineering technology; graphic/printing equipment; health education; health services administration; history; industrial technology; labor/personnel relations; legal administrative assistant; liberal arts and sciences/liberal studies; mathematics; mechanical engineering; mechanical engineering technology; medical administrative assistant; multi/interdisciplinary studies related; nursing; operating room technician; physical education; public administration; respiratory therapy; secretarial science.

Academic Programs *Special study options:* academic remediation for entering students, accelerated degree program, adult/continuing education programs, advanced placement credit, cooperative education, English as a second language, external degree program, internships, part-time degree program, services for LD students, student-designed majors, summer session for credit. *ROTC:* Army (b). *Unusual degree programs:* 3-2 education with West Virginia University.

Library Vining Library plus 1 other with 166,292 titles, 605 serial subscriptions, an OPAC, a Web page.

Computers on Campus 625 computers available on campus for general student use. A campuswide network can be accessed from student residence rooms and from off campus. Internet access, at least one staffed computer lab available.

Student Life *Housing:* on-campus residence required through sophomore year. *Options:* coed. *Activities and Organizations:* drama/theater group, student-run newspaper, choral group, marching band, Student Government Association, Christian Student Union, Alpha Phi Omega, national fraternities, national sororities. *Campus security:* 24-hour emergency response devices and patrols, late-night transport/escort service. *Student Services:* health clinic, personal/psychological counseling, women's center.

Athletics Member NCAA. All Division II. *Intercollegiate sports:* baseball M(s), basketball M(s)/W(s), football M(s), golf M(s), softball W(s), tennis M(s)/W(s), volleyball W(s). *Intramural sports:* badminton M/W, basketball M/W, crew M/W, football M/W, soccer M/W, swimming M/W, table tennis M/W, tennis M/W, volleyball M/W, water polo M/W, wrestling M.

Standardized Tests *Required:* SAT I or ACT (for admission).

Costs (2001–02) *Tuition:* state resident $2836 full-time, $118 per hour part-time; nonresident $7020 full-time, $293 per hour part-time. Full-time tuition and fees vary according to location and program. Part-time tuition and fees vary according to location. *Room and board:* $4682; room only: $2194. Room and board charges vary according to board plan. *Payment plan:* installment. *Waivers:* senior citizens and employees or children of employees.

Financial Aid Of all full-time matriculated undergraduates who enrolled in 2001, 1311 applied for aid, 897 were judged to have need, 95 had their need fully met. 250 Federal Work-Study jobs. In 2001, 132 non-need-based awards were made. *Average percent of need met:* 92%. *Average financial aid package:* $6045. *Average need-based loan:* $3085. *Average need-based gift aid:* $3690. *Average non-need based aid:* $2819. *Average indebtedness upon graduation:* $13,421.

Applying *Options:* common application, electronic application, early admission. *Required:* high school transcript. *Required for some:* minimum 2.0 GPA. *Application deadline:* rolling (freshmen), rolling (transfers). *Notification:* continuous until 8/15 (freshmen).

Admissions Contact Ms. Donna Varney, Director of Admissions I, West Virginia University Institute of Technology, Box 10, Old Main, Montgomery, WV 25136. *Phone:* 304-442-3167. *Toll-free phone:* 888-554-8324. *Fax:* 304-442-3097. *E-mail:* admissions@wvutech.edu.

WEST VIRGINIA WESLEYAN COLLEGE

Buckhannon, West Virginia

- **Independent** comprehensive, founded 1890, affiliated with United Methodist Church
- **Calendar** 4-1-4
- **Degrees** bachelor's and master's
- **Small-town** 80-acre campus
- **Endowment** $35.0 million
- **Coed,** 1,537 undergraduate students, 95% full-time, 54% women, 46% men
- **Moderately difficult** entrance level, 86% of applicants were admitted

West Virginia Wesleyan's new programs of study include arts administration, musical theater, and the five-year undergraduate/Master of Business Administration program in accounting, business, economics, finance, international business, management, and marketing. All Wesleyan students receive an IBM ThinkPad laptop computer.

Undergraduates 1,457 full-time, 80 part-time. Students come from 26 other countries, 47% are from out of state, 5% African American, 1% Asian American or Pacific Islander, 0.8% Hispanic American, 0.2% Native American, 3% international, 3% transferred in, 85% live on campus. *Retention:* 74% of 2001 full-time freshmen returned.

Freshmen *Admission:* 1,123 applied, 961 admitted, 402 enrolled. *Average high school GPA:* 3.28. *Test scores:* SAT verbal scores over 500: 57%; SAT math scores over 500: 55%; ACT scores over 18: 99%; SAT verbal scores over 600: 16%; SAT math scores over 600: 15%; ACT scores over 24: 42%; SAT verbal scores over 700: 1%; SAT math scores over 700: 2%; ACT scores over 30: 12%.

Faculty *Total:* 144, 58% full-time. *Student/faculty ratio:* 14:1.

Majors Accounting; art; art education; art history; athletic training/sports medicine; biology; business administration; business economics; business marketing and marketing management; ceramic arts; chemistry; computer science; creative writing; drawing; early childhood education; economics; education; education (K-12); elementary education; engineering mechanics; engineering physics; English; fine/studio arts; graphic design/commercial art/illustration; health education; history; information sciences/systems; international relations; literature; mathematics; middle school education; music; music teacher education; nursing; philosophy; physical education; physics; political science; pre-dentistry; pre-law; pre-medicine; pre-veterinary studies; psychology; public relations; religious education; religious studies; secondary education; sociology; speech/rhetorical studies; theater arts/drama.

Academic Programs *Special study options:* academic remediation for entering students, accelerated degree program, adult/continuing education programs, advanced placement credit, double majors, English as a second language, honors programs, independent study, internships, off-campus study, part-time degree program, services for LD students, student-designed majors, study abroad, summer session for credit.

Library A. M. Pfeiffer Library with 7,605 audiovisual materials, an OPAC, a Web page.

Computers on Campus A campuswide network can be accessed from student residence rooms and from off campus that provide access to laptop computer provided to all full time students. Internet access, at least one staffed computer lab available.

Student Life *Housing:* on-campus residence required through senior year. *Options:* coed, men-only, women-only, disabled students. *Activities and Organizations:* drama/theater group, student-run newspaper, radio station, choral group, Campus Activities Board, environmental club, American Marketing Club, Wesleyan Ambassadors, national fraternities, national sororities. *Campus security:* 24-hour emergency response devices and patrols, student patrols, late-night transport/escort service, controlled dormitory access. *Student Services:* health clinic, personal/psychological counseling.

Athletics Member NCAA. All Division II. *Intercollegiate sports:* baseball M, basketball M(s)/W(s), cross-country running M(s)/W(s), football M(s), golf M(s), lacrosse M(c)/W(c), soccer M(s)/W(s), softball W(s), swimming M(s)/W(s), tennis M(s)/W(s), track and field M(s)/W(s), volleyball W(s). *Intramural sports:* basketball M/W, bowling M/W, football M/W, golf M/W, racquetball M/W, soccer M/W, softball M/W, table tennis M/W, volleyball M/W, water polo M/W.

Standardized Tests *Required:* SAT I or ACT (for admission).

Costs (2002–03) *Comprehensive fee:* $24,120 includes full-time tuition ($17,900), mandatory fees ($1400), and room and board ($4820). Part-time tuition: $320 per credit hour.

Financial Aid Of all full-time matriculated undergraduates who enrolled in 2001, 1430 applied for aid, 1125 were judged to have need, 713 had their need fully met. 675 State and other part-time jobs. In 2001, 217 non-need-based awards were made. *Average percent of need met:* 94%. *Average financial aid package:* $17,300. *Average need-based loan:* $3288. *Average need-based gift aid:* $12,320. *Average non-need based aid:* $9398. *Average indebtedness upon graduation:* $15,160.

Applying *Options:* electronic application, early admission, early decision, deferred entrance. *Application fee:* $25. *Required:* high school transcript. *Recommended:* essay or personal statement, letters of recommendation, interview. *Application deadline:* 8/1 (freshmen), rolling (transfers). *Early decision:* 12/1. *Notification:* continuous until 9/1 (freshmen), 1/31 (early decision).

Admissions Contact Mr. Robert N. Skinner II, Director of Admission, West Virginia Wesleyan College, 59 College Avenue, Buckhannon, WV 26201. *Phone:* 304-473-8510. *Toll-free phone:* 800-722-9933. *Fax:* 304-472-2571. *E-mail:* admissions@academ.wvwc.edu.

WHEELING JESUIT UNIVERSITY

Wheeling, West Virginia

- **Independent Roman Catholic (Jesuit)** comprehensive, founded 1954
- **Calendar** semesters
- **Degrees** bachelor's and master's
- **Suburban** 70-acre campus with easy access to Pittsburgh
- **Endowment** $19.5 million
- **Coed,** 1,249 undergraduate students, 83% full-time, 60% women, 40% men
- **Moderately difficult** entrance level, 88% of applicants were admitted

WJU, the youngest school of the 60 best regional universities recognized by *U.S. News & World Report* 5 years in a row, broke ground in spring 2000 for a new $8.5 million science center. The 50,000-square-foot building will house several faculty offices, classrooms, research rooms, and a computer science center and is targeted for completion in fall 2001.

Undergraduates 1,040 full-time, 209 part-time. Students come from 32 states and territories, 28 other countries, 67% are from out of state, 2% African American, 1.0% Asian American or Pacific Islander, 0.7% Hispanic American, 0.1% Native American, 3% international, 10% transferred in, 78% live on campus. *Retention:* 70% of 2001 full-time freshmen returned.

Freshmen *Admission:* 933 applied, 818 admitted, 258 enrolled. *Average high school GPA:* 3.20. *Test scores:* SAT verbal scores over 500: 61%; SAT math scores over 500: 58%; ACT scores over 18: 91%; SAT verbal scores over 600: 14%; SAT math scores over 600: 17%; ACT scores over 24: 36%; SAT verbal scores over 700: 1%; SAT math scores over 700: 3%; ACT scores over 30: 4%.

Faculty *Total:* 95, 91% full-time, 77% with terminal degrees. *Student/faculty ratio:* 11:1.

Majors Accounting; aviation management; biology; biology education; business administration; business marketing and marketing management; chemistry; chemistry education; computer programming; computer science; criminal justice/law enforcement administration; education; education of the specific learning disabled; elementary education; English; English education; environmental science; foreign languages education; French; French language education; health services administration; history; history education; international business; inter-

Wheeling Jesuit University (continued)
national relations; liberal arts and sciences/liberal studies; management science; mathematics; mathematics education; middle school education; music (general performance); nuclear medical technology; nursing; nursing administration; nursing (surgical); philosophy; physical therapy; physics; physics education; political science; psychology; religious studies; respiratory therapy; romance languages; science education; secondary education; social studies education; Spanish; Spanish language education; sport/fitness administration.

Academic Programs *Special study options:* academic remediation for entering students, adult/continuing education programs, advanced placement credit, cooperative education, English as a second language, external degree program, honors programs, internships, off-campus study, part-time degree program, student-designed majors, summer session for credit. *Unusual degree programs:* 3-2 engineering with Case Western Reserve University.

Library Bishop Hodges Learning Center plus 1 other with 153,094 titles, 487 serial subscriptions, 5,308 audiovisual materials, an OPAC.

Computers on Campus 75 computers available on campus for general student use. A campuswide network can be accessed from student residence rooms and from off campus. Internet access, at least one staffed computer lab available.

Student Life *Housing:* on-campus residence required through sophomore year. *Options:* men-only, women-only, disabled students. *Activities and Organizations:* drama/theater group, student-run newspaper, choral group. *Campus security:* 24-hour patrols, student patrols, late-night transport/escort service, controlled dormitory access. *Student Services:* health clinic, personal/psychological counseling.

Athletics Member NCAA, NAIA. All NCAA Division II. *Intercollegiate sports:* basketball M(s)/W(s), cross-country running M(s)/W(s), golf M(s)/W(s), lacrosse M(s)(c), rugby M(c), soccer M(s)/W(s), softball W(s), swimming M(s)/W(s), track and field M(s)/W(s), volleyball W(s). *Intramural sports:* basketball M/W, football M/W, golf M/W, ice hockey M(c), lacrosse M(c), rugby M(c), soccer M/W, softball M/W, tennis M/W, volleyball M/W.

Standardized Tests *Required:* SAT I or ACT (for admission).

Costs (2001–02) *Comprehensive fee:* $22,660 includes full-time tuition ($17,000), mandatory fees ($240), and room and board ($5420). Full-time tuition and fees vary according to course load and program. Part-time tuition: $440 per credit hour. Part-time tuition and fees vary according to class time, course load, and program. No tuition increase for student's term of enrollment. *Required fees:* $120 per term part-time. *Room and board:* College room only: $2420. Room and board charges vary according to board plan, gender, and housing facility. *Payment plan:* installment. *Waivers:* senior citizens and employees or children of employees.

Financial Aid Of all full-time matriculated undergraduates who enrolled in 2001, 945 applied for aid, 816 were judged to have need, 223 had their need fully met. 287 Federal Work-Study jobs (averaging $1473). 618 State and other part-time jobs (averaging $1804). In 2001, 161 non-need-based awards were made. *Average percent of need met:* 99%. *Average financial aid package:* $14,918. *Average need-based loan:* $3680. *Average need-based gift aid:* $5523. *Average non-need based aid:* $7950. *Average indebtedness upon graduation:* $9934.

Applying *Options:* common application, electronic application, early admission, deferred entrance. *Application fee:* $25. *Required:* high school transcript, minimum 2.2 GPA. *Required for some:* minimum 3.0 GPA, letters of recommendation, interview. *Recommended:* letters of recommendation, interview. *Application deadline:* rolling (freshmen), rolling (transfers).

Admissions Contact Mr. Thomas M. Pie, Director of Admissions, Wheeling Jesuit University, 316 Washington Avenue, Wheeling, WV 26003-6295. *Phone:* 304-243-2359. *Toll-free phone:* 800-624-6992. *Fax:* 304-243-2397. *E-mail:* admiss@wju.edu.

WISCONSIN

ALVERNO COLLEGE
Milwaukee, Wisconsin

- **Independent Roman Catholic** comprehensive, founded 1887
- **Calendar** semesters
- **Degrees** associate, bachelor's, and master's (also offers weekend program with significant enrollment not reflected in profile)
- **Suburban** 46-acre campus
- **Endowment** $21.8 million
- **Women only,** 1,779 undergraduate students, 56% full-time
- **Moderately difficult** entrance level, 90% of applicants were admitted

Undergraduates 997 full-time, 782 part-time. Students come from 13 states and territories, 12 other countries, 3% are from out of state, 4% transferred in, 9% live on campus. *Retention:* 71% of 2001 full-time freshmen returned.

Freshmen *Admission:* 201 enrolled.

Faculty *Total:* 191, 50% full-time, 72% with terminal degrees. *Student/faculty ratio:* 14:1.

Majors Art; art education; art therapy; biology; business administration; chemistry; child care/development; communications; communications technologies related; community services; computer science; education; elementary education; English; English education; environmental science; general studies; history; international business; international relations; liberal arts and sciences/liberal studies; mathematics; middle school education; music; music teacher education; music therapy; nuclear medical technology; nursing; nursing related; philosophy; psychology; religious studies; science education; secondary education; social science education; social sciences; social studies education; teacher assistant/aide.

Academic Programs *Special study options:* academic remediation for entering students, adult/continuing education programs, advanced placement credit, double majors, internships, part-time degree program, services for LD students, study abroad, summer session for credit. *ROTC:* Army (c), Air Force (c).

Library Library Media Center with 89,683 titles, 1,197 serial subscriptions, 20,409 audiovisual materials, an OPAC, a Web page.

Computers on Campus 250 computers available on campus for general student use. A campuswide network can be accessed from student residence rooms and from off campus that provide access to email. Internet access, at least one staffed computer lab available.

Student Life *Housing:* on-campus residence required for freshman year. *Options:* women-only. *Activities and Organizations:* drama/theater group, student-run newspaper, choral group, Student Nurses Association, Women in Communication, Pi Sigma Epsilon, Students in Free Enterprise, Alverno Student Educators Organization. *Campus security:* 24-hour emergency response devices and patrols, late-night transport/escort service, controlled dormitory access, video camera surveillance at entrances of residence halls, emergency telephones, well-lit parking lots and pathways, security personnel. *Student Services:* health clinic.

Athletics Member NCAA. All Division III. *Intercollegiate sports:* basketball W, cross-country running W, soccer W, softball W, volleyball W. *Intramural sports:* basketball W, volleyball W.

Standardized Tests *Recommended:* ACT (for admission).

Costs (2001–02) *One-time required fee:* $15. *Comprehensive fee:* $16,930 includes full-time tuition ($12,000), mandatory fees ($150), and room and board ($4780). Full-time tuition and fees vary according to class time and program. Part-time tuition: $500 per credit hour. Part-time tuition and fees vary according to class time and program. *Required fees:* $75 per term part-time. *Room and board:* College room only: $1780. Room and board charges vary according to board plan. *Payment plans:* installment, deferred payment. *Waivers:* employees or children of employees.

Financial Aid Of all full-time matriculated undergraduates who enrolled in 2001, 202 Federal Work-Study jobs (averaging $718). 150 State and other part-time jobs (averaging $1011).

Applying *Options:* common application, electronic application, deferred entrance. *Application fee:* $20. *Required:* essay or personal statement, high school transcript. *Required for some:* letters of recommendation, Alverno Communication Placement Assessment. *Recommended:* interview. *Application deadlines:* 8/1 (freshmen), 8/1 (transfers). *Notification:* continuous (freshmen).

Admissions Contact Ms. Mary Kay Farrell, Director of Admissions, Alverno College, 3400 South 43 Street, PO Box 343922, Milwaukee, WI 53234-3922. *Phone:* 414-382-6113. *Toll-free phone:* 800-933-3401. *Fax:* 414-382-6354. *E-mail:* admissions@alverno.edu.

BELLIN COLLEGE OF NURSING
Green Bay, Wisconsin

- **Independent** 4-year, founded 1909
- **Calendar** semesters
- **Degree** bachelor's
- **Urban** campus
- **Endowment** $7.7 million
- **Coed, primarily women,** 160 undergraduate students, 85% full-time, 93% women, 8% men
- **Moderately difficult** entrance level, 60% of applicants were admitted

Undergraduates 136 full-time, 24 part-time. Students come from 3 states and territories, 1 other country, 3% are from out of state, 0.6% African American, 3% Asian American or Pacific Islander, 0.6% Hispanic American, 1% Native American, 0.6% international, 13% transferred in. *Retention:* 92% of 2001 full-time freshmen returned.

Freshmen *Admission:* 42 applied, 25 admitted, 18 enrolled. *Average high school GPA:* 3.43. *Test scores:* ACT scores over 18: 100%; ACT scores over 24: 41%.
Faculty *Total:* 18, 78% full-time, 6% with terminal degrees. *Student/faculty ratio:* 10:1.
Majors Nursing.
Academic Programs *Special study options:* accelerated degree program, advanced placement credit, independent study, off-campus study, summer session for credit. *ROTC:* Army (c).
Library Meredith B. and John M. Rose Library with 5,000 titles, 233 serial subscriptions.
Computers on Campus 15 computers available on campus for general student use. Internet access, at least one staffed computer lab available.
Student Life *Housing:* college housing not available. *Activities and Organizations:* Student Senate, Student Nurses Association. *Campus security:* 24-hour patrols, late-night transport/escort service, electronically operated building access after hours. *Student Services:* health clinic, personal/psychological counseling.
Standardized Tests *Required:* ACT (for admission).
Costs (2001–02) *Tuition:* $10,240 full-time, $497 per credit part-time. Full-time tuition and fees vary according to student level. *Required fees:* $214 full-time. *Payment plan:* installment.
Financial Aid Of all full-time matriculated undergraduates who enrolled in 2001, 85 applied for aid, 74 were judged to have need, 35 had their need fully met. 5 Federal Work-Study jobs (averaging $1988). In 2001, 5 non-need-based awards were made. *Average percent of need met:* 87%. *Average financial aid package:* $12,016. *Average need-based loan:* $6189. *Average need-based gift aid:* $6666. *Average non-need based aid:* $1877. *Average indebtedness upon graduation:* $18,752.
Applying *Options:* electronic application. *Application fee:* $20. *Required:* high school transcript, 3 letters of recommendation, interview. *Recommended:* minimum 3.0 GPA. *Application deadline:* rolling (freshmen), rolling (transfers). *Notification:* continuous (freshmen).
Admissions Contact Dr. Penny Croghan, Admissions Director, Bellin College of Nursing, 725 South Webster Avenue, Green Bay, WI 54301. *Phone:* 920-433-5803. *Toll-free phone:* 800-236-8707. *Fax:* 920-433-7416. *E-mail:* admissio@bcon.edu.

BELOIT COLLEGE
Beloit, Wisconsin

- **Independent** 4-year, founded 1846
- **Calendar** semesters
- **Degree** bachelor's
- **Small-town** 65-acre campus with easy access to Chicago and Milwaukee
- **Endowment** $99.7 million
- **Coed,** 1,273 undergraduate students, 96% full-time, 59% women, 41% men
- **Very difficult** entrance level, 66% of applicants were admitted

Beloit College is an uncommonly diverse academic, residential, and international community where, through investigation and scholarship, students invent themselves. Featuring an extraordinary teaching faculty, Beloit's curriculum integrates rigorous academic programs with interdisciplinary studies and hands-on learning opportunities. Beloit students complement classroom activities by studying abroad, conducting independent research, participating in internships, and engaging in student government and a host of other campus clubs and activities. With the support of enthusiastic faculty advisers and the College's extensive resources, students tailor their Beloit experience to reach their fullest intellectual, professional, and personal development.

Undergraduates 1,221 full-time, 52 part-time. Students come from 49 states and territories, 58 other countries, 80% are from out of state, 4% African American, 4% Asian American or Pacific Islander, 4% Hispanic American, 0.5% Native American, 10% international, 3% transferred in, 93% live on campus. *Retention:* 89% of 2001 full-time freshmen returned.
Freshmen *Admission:* 1,529 applied, 1,004 admitted, 309 enrolled. *Average high school GPA:* 3.54. *Test scores:* SAT verbal scores over 500: 92%; SAT math scores over 500: 87%; ACT scores over 18: 100%; SAT verbal scores over 600: 67%; SAT math scores over 600: 50%; ACT scores over 24: 75%; SAT verbal scores over 700: 20%; SAT math scores over 700: 8%; ACT scores over 30: 25%.
Faculty *Total:* 122, 76% full-time, 98% with terminal degrees. *Student/faculty ratio:* 11:1.
Majors Anthropology; art education; art history; Asian studies; biochemistry; biology; business administration; business economics; cell biology; chemistry; classics; comparative literature; computer science; creative writing; economics; education; elementary education; engineering; English; environmental biology; environmental science; European studies; fine/studio arts; French; geology; German; history; interdisciplinary studies; international relations; Latin American studies; literature; mass communications; mathematics; modern languages; molecular biology; museum studies; music; music teacher education; philosophy; physics; political science; pre-dentistry; pre-law; pre-medicine; psychology; religious studies; romance languages; Russian; Russian/Slavic studies; science education; secondary education; sociobiology; sociology; Spanish; theater arts/drama; women's studies.
Academic Programs *Special study options:* adult/continuing education programs, advanced placement credit, double majors, English as a second language, independent study, internships, off-campus study, services for LD students, student-designed majors, study abroad, summer session for credit. *Unusual degree programs:* 3-2 engineering with University of Illinois at Urbana-Champaign, University of Michigan, Rensselaer Polytechnic Institute, Georgia Institute of Technology; forestry with Duke University; medical technology with Rush University.
Library Morse Library and Black Information Center with 243,779 titles, 980 serial subscriptions, an OPAC, a Web page.
Computers on Campus 152 computers available on campus for general student use. A campuswide network can be accessed from student residence rooms and from off campus. Internet access, at least one staffed computer lab available.
Student Life *Housing:* on-campus residence required through junior year. *Options:* coed, men-only, women-only, cooperative. *Activities and Organizations:* drama/theater group, student-run newspaper, radio and television station, choral group, Science Fiction and Fantasy Association, Anthropology Club, International Club, WBEL (student radio station), Outdoor Environmental Club, national fraternities. *Campus security:* 24-hour emergency response devices and patrols, late-night transport/escort service, controlled dormitory access. *Student Services:* health clinic, personal/psychological counseling, women's center.
Athletics Member NCAA. All Division III. *Intercollegiate sports:* baseball M, basketball M/W, crew M(c)/W(c), cross-country running M/W, fencing M(c)/W(c), football M, golf M/W, ice hockey M(c)/W(c), lacrosse M(c)/W(c), soccer M/W, softball W, swimming M/W, tennis M/W, track and field M/W, volleyball W. *Intramural sports:* badminton M/W, basketball M/W, bowling M/W, football M, racquetball M/W, sailing M/W, soccer M/W, tennis M/W, volleyball M/W, water polo M/W.
Standardized Tests *Required:* SAT I or ACT (for admission).
Costs (2002–03) *Comprehensive fee:* $28,504 includes full-time tuition ($23,016), mandatory fees ($220), and room and board ($5268). *Room and board:* College room only: $2570.
Financial Aid Of all full-time matriculated undergraduates who enrolled in 2001, 1118 applied for aid, 886 were judged to have need, 886 had their need fully met. 453 Federal Work-Study jobs (averaging $1414). 520 State and other part-time jobs (averaging $1099). In 2001, 79 non-need-based awards were made. *Average percent of need met:* 100%. *Average financial aid package:* $17,560. *Average need-based loan:* $4675. *Average need-based gift aid:* $11,998. *Average non-need based aid:* $7898. *Average indebtedness upon graduation:* $14,895.
Applying *Options:* common application, electronic application, early admission, early decision, early action, deferred entrance. *Application fee:* $30. *Required:* essay or personal statement, high school transcript, 1 letter of recommendation. *Required for some:* interview. *Recommended:* interview. *Application deadline:* 2/1 (freshmen), rolling (transfers). *Early decision:* 11/15. *Notification:* continuous (freshmen), 12/15 (early decision), 1/15 (early action).
Admissions Contact Mr. James S. Zielinski, Director of Admissions, Beloit College, 700 College Street, Beloit, WI 53511-5596. *Phone:* 608-363-2500. *Toll-free phone:* 800-356-0751. *Fax:* 608-363-2075. *E-mail:* admiss@beloit.edu.

CARDINAL STRITCH UNIVERSITY
Milwaukee, Wisconsin

- **Independent Roman Catholic** comprehensive, founded 1937
- **Calendar** semesters
- **Degrees** certificates, associate, bachelor's, master's, doctoral, and postbachelor's certificates
- **Suburban** 40-acre campus
- **Endowment** $17.7 million
- **Coed,** 3,123 undergraduate students, 93% full-time, 69% women, 31% men
- **Moderately difficult** entrance level, 71% of applicants were admitted

Cardinal Stritch University is a Catholic, coeducational institution rooted in the liberal arts. The University provides all of the resources associated with a large university yet offers the benefits of personal attention and 1-on-1 instruction associated with a smaller institution. Graduate and undergraduate programs,

Cardinal Stritch University (continued)
offered in traditional and nontraditional formats, range from business and education to religious studies and art.

Undergraduates 2,900 full-time, 223 part-time. Students come from 16 states and territories, 27 other countries, 11% are from out of state, 16% African American, 2% Asian American or Pacific Islander, 3% Hispanic American, 0.5% Native American, 1% international, 5% transferred in, 5% live on campus. *Retention:* 73% of 2001 full-time freshmen returned.

Freshmen *Admission:* 387 applied, 276 admitted, 138 enrolled. *Average high school GPA:* 2.98. *Test scores:* ACT scores over 18: 84%; ACT scores over 24: 28%; ACT scores over 30: 3%.

Faculty *Total:* 397, 25% full-time, 28% with terminal degrees. *Student/faculty ratio:* 18:1.

Majors Accounting; art; art education; biology; business administration; business economics; chemistry; communications; computer science; creative writing; divinity/ministry; early childhood education; education; elementary education; English; fine/studio arts; French; graphic design/commercial art/illustration; history; interdisciplinary studies; international business; liberal arts and sciences/liberal studies; mathematics; mathematics/computer science; music; nursing; political science; pre-dentistry; pre-law; pre-medicine; pre-veterinary studies; psychology; public relations; religious education; religious studies; science education; secondary education; social sciences; sociology; Spanish; special education; theater arts/drama.

Academic Programs *Special study options:* academic remediation for entering students, accelerated degree program, adult/continuing education programs, advanced placement credit, cooperative education, distance learning, double majors, English as a second language, external degree program, honors programs, independent study, internships, off-campus study, part-time degree program, services for LD students, student-designed majors, study abroad, summer session for credit.

Library Cardinal Stritch University Library with 96,864 titles, 688 serial subscriptions, 6,138 audiovisual materials, an OPAC, a Web page.

Computers on Campus 236 computers available on campus for general student use. A campuswide network can be accessed from student residence rooms and from off campus. Internet access, at least one staffed computer lab available.

Student Life *Housing Options:* coed. *Activities and Organizations:* drama/theater group, student-run newspaper, radio station, choral group, Residence Hall Association, Student Government Association, Student Activities Board. *Campus security:* 24-hour emergency response devices and patrols, late-night transport/escort service. *Student Services:* health clinic, personal/psychological counseling.

Athletics Member NAIA. *Intercollegiate sports:* baseball M, basketball M/W, cross-country running M/W, soccer M/W, softball W, volleyball M/W. *Intramural sports:* basketball M/W, volleyball M/W.

Standardized Tests *Required:* SAT I or ACT (for admission).

Costs (2001–02) *Comprehensive fee:* $17,620 includes full-time tuition ($12,480), mandatory fees ($300), and room and board ($4840). Full-time tuition and fees vary according to program. Part-time tuition: $390 per credit. Part-time tuition and fees vary according to course load and program. *Required fees:* $100 per term part-time. *Room and board:* Room and board charges vary according to board plan. *Payment plan:* installment. *Waivers:* employees or children of employees.

Financial Aid Of all full-time matriculated undergraduates who enrolled in 2001, 2043 applied for aid, 1767 were judged to have need, 339 had their need fully met. In 2001, 341 non-need-based awards were made. *Average percent of need met:* 61%. *Average financial aid package:* $7115. *Average need-based loan:* $3224. *Average need-based gift aid:* $4649.

Applying *Options:* common application, electronic application, early admission, deferred entrance. *Application fee:* $25. *Required:* essay or personal statement, high school transcript, minimum 2.0 GPA. *Required for some:* letters of recommendation. *Recommended:* interview. *Application deadline:* rolling (freshmen), rolling (transfers).

Admissions Contact Mr. David Wegener, Director of Admissions, Cardinal Stritch University, 6801 North Yates Road, Milwaukee, WI 53217-3985. *Phone:* 414-410-4040. *Toll-free phone:* 800-347-8822. *Fax:* 414-410-4058. *E-mail:* admityou@stritch.edu.

CARROLL COLLEGE
Waukesha, Wisconsin

- **Independent Presbyterian** comprehensive, founded 1846
- **Calendar** semesters
- **Degrees** bachelor's and master's (master's degrees in education and physical therapy)
- **Suburban** 52-acre campus with easy access to Milwaukee
- **Endowment** $31.5 million
- **Coed,** 2,680 undergraduate students, 71% full-time, 67% women, 33% men
- **Moderately difficult** entrance level, 85% of applicants were admitted

Carroll College gives its students the support they need to learn and grow—small classes and individual attention provide a quality educational experience at Wisconsin's oldest college. Students are encouraged to explore the world around them by studying in other countries or participating in internships. An Honors Program is available to academically talented students.

Undergraduates 1,915 full-time, 765 part-time. Students come from 28 states and territories, 24 other countries, 19% are from out of state, 2% African American, 0.9% Asian American or Pacific Islander, 2% Hispanic American, 0.4% Native American, 3% international, 6% transferred in, 58% live on campus. *Retention:* 78% of 2001 full-time freshmen returned.

Freshmen *Admission:* 1,711 applied, 1,457 admitted, 485 enrolled. *Test scores:* ACT scores over 18: 91%; ACT scores over 24: 45%; ACT scores over 30: 5%.

Faculty *Total:* 243, 42% full-time, 51% with terminal degrees. *Student/faculty ratio:* 20:1.

Majors Accounting; actuarial science; art; art education; athletic training/sports medicine; biochemistry; biology; business administration; business information/data processing related; business marketing and marketing management; chemistry; communications; computer/information sciences; computer science; computer software and media applications related; creative writing; criminal justice/law enforcement administration; design/visual communications; early childhood education; education; elementary education; English; environmental science; exercise sciences; finance; fine/studio arts; forensic technology; geography; graphic design/commercial art/illustration; health education; history; information sciences/systems; international relations; journalism; mathematics; medical technology; music; music teacher education; music (voice and choral/opera performance); nursing; organizational behavior; physical education; political science; pre-medicine; psychology; public relations; religious studies; science education; social work; sociology; Spanish; theater arts/drama.

Academic Programs *Special study options:* academic remediation for entering students, adult/continuing education programs, advanced placement credit, distance learning, double majors, honors programs, independent study, internships, part-time degree program, services for LD students, student-designed majors, study abroad, summer session for credit. *ROTC:* Air Force (c).

Library Todd Wehr Memorial Library with 200,000 titles, 520 serial subscriptions, 362 audiovisual materials, an OPAC, a Web page.

Computers on Campus 250 computers available on campus for general student use. A campuswide network can be accessed from student residence rooms and from off campus. Internet access, at least one staffed computer lab available.

Student Life *Housing:* on-campus residence required through sophomore year. *Options:* coed, women-only. *Activities and Organizations:* drama/theater group, student-run newspaper, radio station, choral group, College Activities Board, Student Senate, Black Student Union, Carroll College Christian Fellowship, Residence Hall Association, national sororities. *Campus security:* 24-hour emergency response devices and patrols, student patrols, late-night transport/escort service, controlled dormitory access. *Student Services:* health clinic, personal/psychological counseling.

Athletics Member NCAA. All Division III. *Intercollegiate sports:* baseball M, basketball M/W, cross-country running M/W, football M, golf M/W, soccer M/W, softball W, swimming M/W, tennis M/W, track and field M/W, volleyball W. *Intramural sports:* badminton M/W, basketball M/W, football M/W, soccer M/W, softball M/W, table tennis M/W, volleyball M/W, water polo M/W.

Costs (2001–02) *One-time required fee:* $60. *Comprehensive fee:* $21,170 includes full-time tuition ($15,860), mandatory fees ($340), and room and board ($4970). Full-time tuition and fees vary according to program. Part-time tuition: $198 per credit. Part-time tuition and fees vary according to course load and program. *Room and board:* College room only: $2700. Room and board charges vary according to board plan and housing facility. *Payment plan:* installment. *Waivers:* employees or children of employees.

Financial Aid Of all full-time matriculated undergraduates who enrolled in 2001, 1877 applied for aid, 1408 were judged to have need, 1408 had their need fully met. 454 Federal Work-Study jobs (averaging $1599). 677 State and other part-time jobs (averaging $1516). In 2001, 507 non-need-based awards were made. *Average percent of need met:* 100%. *Average financial aid package:* $12,174. *Average need-based loan:* $3493. *Average need-based gift aid:* $9988. *Average non-need based aid:* $6303. *Average indebtedness upon graduation:* $16,000.

Applying *Options:* common application, electronic application, early admission, deferred entrance. *Required:* high school transcript, minimum 2.0 GPA, 1 letter of recommendation. *Required for some:* essay or personal statement.

Recommended: interview. *Application deadline:* rolling (freshmen), rolling (transfers). *Notification:* continuous until 8/20 (freshmen).

Admissions Contact Mr. James V. Wiseman III, Vice President of Enrollment, Carroll College, 100 North East Avenue, Waukesha, WI 53186-5593. *Phone:* 262-524-7221. *Toll-free phone:* 800-CARROLL. *Fax:* 262-524-7139. *E-mail:* cc.info@ccadmin.cc.edu.

CARTHAGE COLLEGE
Kenosha, Wisconsin

- **Independent** comprehensive, founded 1847, affiliated with Evangelical Lutheran Church in America
- **Calendar** 4-1-4
- **Degrees** bachelor's and master's
- **Suburban** 72-acre campus with easy access to Chicago and Milwaukee
- **Endowment** $36.0 million
- **Coed,** 2,260 undergraduate students, 76% full-time, 55% women, 45% men
- **Moderately difficult** entrance level, 88% of applicants were admitted

Undergraduates 1,721 full-time, 539 part-time. Students come from 24 states and territories, 52% are from out of state, 6% African American, 1% Asian American or Pacific Islander, 4% Hispanic American, 0.4% Native American, 3% transferred in, 74% live on campus. *Retention:* 72% of 2001 full-time freshmen returned.

Freshmen *Admission:* 2,356 applied, 2,085 admitted, 577 enrolled. *Average high school GPA:* 3.05. *Test scores:* SAT verbal scores over 500: 61%; SAT math scores over 500: 56%; ACT scores over 18: 88%; SAT verbal scores over 600: 20%; SAT math scores over 600: 25%; ACT scores over 24: 35%; SAT verbal scores over 700: 3%; SAT math scores over 700: 5%; ACT scores over 30: 6%.

Faculty *Total:* 147, 69% full-time, 61% with terminal degrees. *Student/faculty ratio:* 16:1.

Majors Accounting; applied art; athletic training/sports medicine; biology; business administration; chemistry; classics; computer science; criminal justice/law enforcement administration; economics; education; elementary education; engineering; English; environmental science; fine/studio arts; French; geography; German; graphic design/commercial art/illustration; history; international economics; marketing research; mathematics; middle school education; modern languages; music; music teacher education; natural sciences; neuroscience; occupational therapy; philosophy; physical education; physics; political science; pre-dentistry; pre-law; pre-medicine; pre-veterinary studies; psychology; recreation/leisure studies; religious studies; science education; secondary education; social sciences; social work; sociology; Spanish; special education; speech/rhetorical studies; theater arts/drama.

Academic Programs *Special study options:* accelerated degree program, adult/continuing education programs, advanced placement credit, cooperative education, double majors, honors programs, independent study, internships, off-campus study, part-time degree program, services for LD students, student-designed majors, study abroad, summer session for credit. *ROTC:* Army (c), Air Force (c). *Unusual degree programs:* 3-2 engineering with Case Western Reserve University, Washington University in St. Louis, University of Wisconsin-Madison, University of Minnesota; occupational therapy with Washington University in St. Louis.

Library Hedberg Library with 141,187 titles, 615 serial subscriptions, 3,194 audiovisual materials, an OPAC, a Web page.

Computers on Campus 200 computers available on campus for general student use. A campuswide network can be accessed from student residence rooms and from off campus. Internet access, at least one staffed computer lab available.

Student Life *Housing:* on-campus residence required through senior year. *Options:* coed, women-only. *Activities and Organizations:* drama/theater group, student-run newspaper, radio station, choral group, Residence Life Council, Alpha Lambda Delta, Circle K, Intervarsity Christian Fellowship, Pals-n-Partners, national fraternities, national sororities. *Campus security:* 24-hour emergency response devices and patrols, student patrols, late-night transport/escort service, controlled dormitory access. *Student Services:* health clinic, personal/psychological counseling.

Athletics Member NCAA. All Division III. *Intercollegiate sports:* baseball M, basketball M/W, cross-country running M/W, football M, golf M/W, ice hockey M(c), soccer M/W, softball W, swimming M/W, tennis M/W, track and field M/W, volleyball W. *Intramural sports:* badminton M/W, basketball M/W, bowling M/W, football M/W, golf M/W, skiing (downhill) M/W, soccer M/W, softball M/W, table tennis M/W, tennis M/W, volleyball M/W, weight lifting M/W.

Standardized Tests *Required:* SAT I or ACT (for admission).

Costs (2001–02) *Comprehensive fee:* $23,670 includes full-time tuition ($18,205) and room and board ($5465). Part-time tuition: $270 per credit hour. Part-time tuition and fees vary according to class time. *Room and board:* Room and board charges vary according to board plan. *Payment plan:* installment. *Waivers:* children of alumni and employees or children of employees.

Financial Aid Of all full-time matriculated undergraduates who enrolled in 2001, 1461 applied for aid, 1155 were judged to have need, 637 had their need fully met. In 2001, 303 non-need-based awards were made. *Average percent of need met:* 93%. *Average financial aid package:* $15,253. *Average need-based loan:* $4350. *Average need-based gift aid:* $10,784. *Average non-need based aid:* $7166.

Applying *Options:* electronic application, early action, deferred entrance. *Application fee:* $25. *Required:* high school transcript, minimum 2.0 GPA. *Required for some:* essay or personal statement, 2 letters of recommendation. *Recommended:* essay or personal statement, minimum 3.0 GPA, interview. *Application deadline:* rolling (freshmen), rolling (transfers). *Notification:* continuous (freshmen), 7/15 (early action).

Admissions Contact Mr. Tom Augustine, Director of Admission, Carthage College, 2001 Alford Park Drive, Kenosha, WI 53140-1994. *Phone:* 262-551-6000. *Toll-free phone:* 800-351-4058. *Fax:* 262-551-5762. *E-mail:* admissions@carthage.edu.

COLUMBIA COLLEGE OF NURSING
Milwaukee, Wisconsin

- **Independent** 4-year, founded 1901
- **Calendar** semesters
- **Degree** bachelor's
- **Urban** campus
- **Endowment** $1.7 million
- **Coed, primarily women,** 190 undergraduate students, 82% full-time, 96% women, 4% men
- **Moderately difficult** entrance level

Undergraduates 155 full-time, 35 part-time. Students come from 4 states and territories, 13% are from out of state, 2% African American, 1% Hispanic American, 0.5% international, 6% transferred in, 18% live on campus. *Retention:* 63% of 2001 full-time freshmen returned.

Freshmen *Average high school GPA:* 3.34. *Test scores:* ACT scores over 18: 96%; ACT scores over 24: 34%.

Faculty *Total:* 13, 54% full-time, 31% with terminal degrees. *Student/faculty ratio:* 18:1.

Majors Nursing.

Academic Programs *Special study options:* advanced placement credit, double majors, honors programs, independent study, off-campus study, part-time degree program, summer session for credit.

Library Ellen Bacon Library plus 1 other with 9,060 titles, 253 serial subscriptions, 508 audiovisual materials, an OPAC.

Computers on Campus 18 computers available on campus for general student use. Internet access, at least one staffed computer lab available.

Student Life *Housing:* on-campus residence required through sophomore year. *Options:* coed. *Activities and Organizations:* Student Senate, Student Nurses Association. *Campus security:* 24-hour emergency response devices and patrols, student patrols, late-night transport/escort service, controlled dormitory access. *Student Services:* health clinic, personal/psychological counseling.

Standardized Tests *Required:* SAT I or ACT (for admission).

Costs (2002–03) *Comprehensive fee:* $20,150 includes full-time tuition ($16,400) and room and board ($3750). Part-time tuition: $275 per credit. Part-time tuition and fees vary according to program. *Required fees:* $360 per year part-time. *Room and board:* College room only: $2750. Room and board charges vary according to board plan, housing facility, location, and student level. *Payment plan:* installment. *Waivers:* employees or children of employees.

Financial Aid Of all full-time matriculated undergraduates who enrolled in 2001, 1782 applied for aid, 1336 were judged to have need, 1336 had their need fully met. In 2001, 426 non-need-based awards were made. *Average percent of need met:* 100%. *Average financial aid package:* $13,219. *Average need-based loan:* $3186. *Average need-based gift aid:* $9050. *Average non-need based aid:* $7051. *Average indebtedness upon graduation:* $16,000.

Applying *Options:* common application. *Required:* high school transcript. *Required for some:* essay or personal statement. *Recommended:* essay or personal statement, 1 letter of recommendation, interview. *Application deadline:* rolling (freshmen), rolling (transfers).

Admissions Contact Mr. James Wiseman, Dean of Admissions, Columbia College of Nursing, Carroll College, 100 North East Avenue, Milwaukee, WI 53186. *Phone:* 262-524-7220. *Fax:* 262-524-7646. *E-mail:* jwiseman@ccadmin.cc.edu.

CONCORDIA UNIVERSITY WISCONSIN
Mequon, Wisconsin

- **Independent** comprehensive, founded 1881, affiliated with Lutheran Church-Missouri Synod
- **Calendar** 4-1-4
- **Degrees** bachelor's and master's
- **Suburban** 155-acre campus with easy access to Milwaukee
- **Endowment** $37.0 million
- **Coed,** 3,921 undergraduate students, 77% full-time, 65% women, 35% men
- **Moderately difficult** entrance level, 64% of applicants were admitted

Undergraduates 3,009 full-time, 912 part-time. Students come from 41 states and territories, 21 other countries, 34% are from out of state, 16% African American, 0.9% Asian American or Pacific Islander, 1% Hispanic American, 0.6% Native American, 0.1% international, 71% live on campus. *Retention:* 75% of 2001 full-time freshmen returned.

Freshmen *Admission:* 1,216 applied, 773 admitted, 353 enrolled. *Average high school GPA:* 3.10. *Test scores:* ACT scores over 18: 93%; ACT scores over 24: 39%; ACT scores over 30: 6%.

Faculty *Total:* 164, 57% full-time, 41% with terminal degrees. *Student/faculty ratio:* 11:1.

Majors Accounting; agricultural business; aircraft pilot (professional); art; art education; athletic training/sports medicine; biblical languages/literatures; biology; business administration; business education; business marketing and marketing management; computer science; criminal justice/law enforcement administration; early childhood education; economics; education; elementary education; English; German; graphic design/commercial art/illustration; Greek (modern); health services administration; Hebrew; history; humanities; industrial radiologic technology; interior design; liberal arts and sciences/liberal studies; mass communications; mathematics; middle school education; music; music teacher education; nursing; occupational therapy; paralegal/legal assistant; pastoral counseling; physical education; physical therapy; pre-dentistry; pre-law; pre-medicine; psychology; religious studies; science education; secondary education; social work; Spanish; teaching English as a second language; theater arts/drama; theology.

Academic Programs *Special study options:* academic remediation for entering students, accelerated degree program, adult/continuing education programs, advanced placement credit, distance learning, double majors, English as a second language, honors programs, independent study, internships, off-campus study, part-time degree program, services for LD students, student-designed majors, study abroad, summer session for credit.

Library Rinker Memorial Library with 110,929 titles, 1,411 serial subscriptions, 4,645 audiovisual materials, an OPAC.

Computers on Campus 100 computers available on campus for general student use. A campuswide network can be accessed from student residence rooms and from off campus. Internet access, at least one staffed computer lab available.

Student Life *Housing Options:* men-only, women-only. *Activities and Organizations:* drama/theater group, student-run newspaper, radio station, choral group, Fellowship of Christian Athletes, Kammerchor, Youth Ministry, band. *Campus security:* student patrols, controlled dormitory access. *Student Services:* health clinic, personal/psychological counseling.

Athletics Member NCAA. All Division III. *Intercollegiate sports:* baseball M, basketball M/W, cross-country running M/W, football M, golf M/W, soccer M/W, softball W, tennis M/W, track and field M/W, volleyball W, wrestling M. *Intramural sports:* basketball M/W, softball M/W, volleyball M/W.

Standardized Tests *Required:* SAT I or ACT (for admission).

Costs (2001–02) *Comprehensive fee:* $18,680 includes full-time tuition ($13,550), mandatory fees ($60), and room and board ($5070). Part-time tuition: $565 per credit hour. Part-time tuition and fees vary according to class time and program. No tuition increase for student's term of enrollment. *Payment plans:* installment, deferred payment. *Waivers:* employees or children of employees.

Financial Aid Of all full-time matriculated undergraduates who enrolled in 2001, 1242 applied for aid, 1204 were judged to have need, 842 had their need fully met. 75 Federal Work-Study jobs (averaging $1574). 114 State and other part-time jobs (averaging $2500). In 2001, 39 non-need-based awards were made. *Average percent of need met:* 90%. *Average financial aid package:* $12,121. *Average need-based loan:* $3380. *Average need-based gift aid:* $8210. *Average non-need based aid:* $3500. *Average indebtedness upon graduation:* $14,075.

Applying *Options:* deferred entrance. *Application fee:* $35. *Required:* high school transcript, minimum 2.0 GPA. *Required for some:* essay or personal statement, minimum 3.0 GPA, 3 letters of recommendation. *Recommended:* interview. *Application deadlines:* 8/15 (freshmen), 8/15 (transfers). *Notification:* continuous until 8/15 (freshmen).

Admissions Contact Mr. Ken Gaschk, Director of Admissions, Concordia University Wisconsin, 12800 North Lake Shore Drive, Mequon, WI 53097-2402. *Phone:* 262-243-4305 Ext. 4305. *E-mail:* kgaschk@bach.cuw.edu.

EDGEWOOD COLLEGE
Madison, Wisconsin

- **Independent Roman Catholic** comprehensive, founded 1927
- **Calendar** 4-1-4
- **Degrees** associate, bachelor's, and master's
- **Urban** 55-acre campus
- **Endowment** $4.2 million
- **Coed,** 1,632 undergraduate students, 75% full-time, 72% women, 28% men
- **Moderately difficult** entrance level, 78% of applicants were admitted

Undergraduates Students come from 16 states and territories, 10 other countries, 7% are from out of state, 1% African American, 1% Asian American or Pacific Islander, 1% Hispanic American, 0.2% Native American, 3% international, 15% live on campus. *Retention:* 75% of 2001 full-time freshmen returned.

Freshmen *Admission:* 904 applied, 708 admitted. *Average high school GPA:* 3.21. *Test scores:* SAT verbal scores over 500: 50%; ACT scores over 18: 92%; SAT verbal scores over 600: 21%; ACT scores over 24: 36%; ACT scores over 30: 2%.

Faculty *Total:* 190, 42% full-time, 28% with terminal degrees. *Student/faculty ratio:* 13:1.

Majors Accounting; art; art education; art therapy; biology; business administration; chemistry; criminal justice/law enforcement administration; cytotechnology; developmental/child psychology; early childhood education; economics; education; elementary education; English; French; graphic design/commercial art/illustration; history; information sciences/systems; international relations; liberal arts and sciences/liberal studies; mass communications; mathematics; medical technology; music; natural sciences; nursing; political science; pre-dentistry; pre-engineering; pre-law; pre-medicine; pre-veterinary studies; psychology; public administration; public policy analysis; religious studies; social sciences; sociology; Spanish; theater arts/drama.

Academic Programs *Special study options:* academic remediation for entering students, adult/continuing education programs, advanced placement credit, independent study, off-campus study, part-time degree program, services for LD students, summer session for credit. *Unusual degree programs:* 3-2 engineering with University of Wisconsin-Madison.

Library Oscar Rennebohm Library with 90,253 titles, 447 serial subscriptions, 4,359 audiovisual materials, an OPAC, a Web page.

Computers on Campus 85 computers available on campus for general student use. A campuswide network can be accessed from student residence rooms and from off campus. Internet access, at least one staffed computer lab available.

Student Life *Housing Options:* coed, women-only, disabled students. *Activities and Organizations:* drama/theater group, student-run newspaper, choral group, Student Government Association, Student Programming Board, Resident Life Association, Chalk Talk, Student Nurses Association. *Campus security:* 24-hour emergency response devices and patrols, student patrols, late-night transport/escort service, controlled dormitory access. *Student Services:* health clinic, personal/psychological counseling.

Athletics Member NCAA. All Division III. *Intercollegiate sports:* baseball M, basketball M/W, cross-country running M/W, golf M/W, soccer M/W, softball W, tennis M/W, volleyball W. *Intramural sports:* basketball M/W, bowling M/W, golf M/W, soccer M/W, softball M/W, table tennis M/W, volleyball M/W, weight lifting M/W.

Standardized Tests *Required:* SAT I or ACT (for admission).

Costs (2001–02) *Comprehensive fee:* $18,304 includes full-time tuition ($13,300) and room and board ($5004). Full-time tuition and fees vary according to program. Part-time tuition: $400 per credit. Part-time tuition and fees vary according to course load and program. *Required fees:* $55 per term part-time. *Room and board:* College room only: $2352. Room and board charges vary according to board plan and housing facility. *Payment plans:* installment, deferred payment. *Waivers:* employees or children of employees.

Financial Aid Of all full-time matriculated undergraduates who enrolled in 2001, 876 applied for aid, 750 were judged to have need, 155 had their need fully met. 177 Federal Work-Study jobs (averaging $1619). 399 State and other part-time jobs (averaging $1713). *Average percent of need met:* 71%. *Average financial aid package:* $9420. *Average need-based loan:* $3642. *Average need-based gift aid:* $5355. *Average indebtedness upon graduation:* $18,318.

Applying *Options:* deferred entrance. *Application fee:* $25. *Required:* high school transcript, minimum 2.5 GPA. *Required for some:* essay or personal statement, 2 letters of recommendation, interview. *Application deadline:* rolling (freshmen), rolling (transfers). *Notification:* continuous (freshmen).

Admissions Contact Mr. Scott Flanagan, Dean of Admissions and Financial Aid, Edgewood College, 1000 Edgewood College Drive, Madison, WI 53711-1997. *Phone:* 608-663-2254. *Toll-free phone:* 800-444-4861. *Fax:* 608-663-3291. *E-mail:* admissions@edgewood.edu.

HERZING COLLEGE
Madison, Wisconsin

- **Proprietary** primarily 2-year, founded 1948, part of Herzing Institutes, Inc
- **Calendar** semesters
- **Degrees** diplomas, associate, and bachelor's
- **Suburban** campus with easy access to Milwaukee
- **Coed, primarily men**
- **Moderately difficult** entrance level

Faculty *Student/faculty ratio:* 25:1.
Student Life *Campus security:* 24-hour emergency response devices.
Costs (2001–02) *One-time required fee:* $50. *Tuition:* $240 per credit part-time. Full-time tuition and fees vary according to class time and program. Part-time tuition and fees vary according to class time and program. $3,600-$4,010 per semester, including books.
Financial Aid *Financial aid deadline:* 6/30.
Applying *Options:* common application, electronic application, early admission. *Required:* high school transcript, interview.
Admissions Contact Ms. Renee Herzing, Admissions Director, Herzing College, 5218 E. Terrace Drive, Madison, WI 53718. *Phone:* 608-249-6611 Ext. 0842. *Toll-free phone:* 800-582-1227. *E-mail:* mailbag@msn.herzing.edu.

ITT TECHNICAL INSTITUTE
Greenfield, Wisconsin

- **Proprietary** primarily 2-year, founded 1968, part of ITT Educational Services, Inc
- **Calendar** quarters
- **Degrees** associate and bachelor's
- **Suburban** campus with easy access to Milwaukee
- **Coed,** 421 undergraduate students
- **Minimally difficult** entrance level

Majors Computer/information sciences related; computer programming; drafting; electrical/electronic engineering technologies related; information technology.
Student Life *Housing:* college housing not available.
Costs (2001–02) *Tuition:* Full-time tuition and fees vary according to program. Part-time tuition and fees vary according to program. $260—$330 per credit hour.
Applying *Options:* deferred entrance. *Application fee:* $100. *Required:* high school transcript, interview. *Recommended:* letters of recommendation. *Application deadline:* rolling (freshmen), rolling (transfers).
Admissions Contact Mr. Russel Gill, Director of Recruitment, ITT Technical Institute, 6300 West Layton Avenue, Greenfield, WI 53220. *Phone:* 414-282-9494.

LAKELAND COLLEGE
Sheboygan, Wisconsin

- **Independent** comprehensive, founded 1862, affiliated with United Church of Christ
- **Calendar** 4-4-1
- **Degrees** bachelor's and master's
- **Rural** 240-acre campus with easy access to Milwaukee
- **Endowment** $7.8 million
- **Coed,** 3,344 undergraduate students, 37% full-time, 60% women, 40% men
- **Moderately difficult** entrance level, 70% of applicants were admitted

Undergraduates 1,250 full-time, 2,094 part-time. Students come from 16 states and territories, 38 other countries, 17% are from out of state, 5% African American, 2% Asian American or Pacific Islander, 1% Hispanic American, 0.6% Native American, 4% international, 3% transferred in, 65% live on campus. *Retention:* 59% of 2001 full-time freshmen returned.
Freshmen *Admission:* 587 applied, 408 admitted, 186 enrolled. *Average high school GPA:* 2.87. *Test scores:* ACT scores over 18: 71%; ACT scores over 24: 18%; ACT scores over 30: 1%.
Faculty *Total:* 48, 92% full-time, 65% with terminal degrees. *Student/faculty ratio:* 19:1.
Majors Accounting; art; arts management; behavioral sciences; biology; business administration; business economics; business education; business marketing and marketing management; chemistry; computer science; creative writing; early childhood education; economics; education; elementary education; English; exercise sciences; finance; German; history; hospitality management; international business; mathematics; middle school education; music; music teacher education; philosophy; pre-law; psychology; public administration; religious studies; science education; secondary education; social sciences; sociology; Spanish; theater arts/drama.
Academic Programs *Special study options:* academic remediation for entering students, adult/continuing education programs, advanced placement credit, distance learning, English as a second language, honors programs, internships, part-time degree program, study abroad, summer session for credit. *Unusual degree programs:* 3-2 engineering with University of Wisconsin-Madison; nursing with Bellin College of Nursing.
Library Esch Memorial Library with 64,970 titles, 317 serial subscriptions, 647 audiovisual materials, a Web page.
Computers on Campus 100 computers available on campus for general student use. A campuswide network can be accessed from student residence rooms. Internet access, at least one staffed computer lab available.
Student Life *Housing:* on-campus residence required through senior year. *Options:* coed, men-only, women-only. *Activities and Organizations:* drama/theater group, student-run newspaper, television station, choral group, Lakeland College Campus Activities Board, Student Association, Habitat for Humanity, Mortar Board, Global Students Association. *Campus security:* student patrols, late-night transport/escort service, controlled dormitory access. *Student Services:* health clinic, personal/psychological counseling.
Athletics Member NCAA. All Division III. *Intercollegiate sports:* baseball M, basketball M/W, cross-country running M/W, football M, golf M/W, soccer M/W, softball W, tennis M/W, volleyball M(c)/W, wrestling M. *Intramural sports:* bowling M/W, football M/W.
Standardized Tests *Required:* SAT I or ACT (for admission).
Costs (2002–03) *Comprehensive fee:* $19,193 includes full-time tuition ($13,250), mandatory fees ($585), and room and board ($5358). Full-time tuition and fees vary according to location. Part-time tuition: $1325 per course. Part-time tuition and fees vary according to class time and location. *Room and board:* College room only: $2513. Room and board charges vary according to board plan and housing facility. *Payment plan:* installment. *Waivers:* senior citizens and employees or children of employees.
Financial Aid Of all full-time matriculated undergraduates who enrolled in 2001, 899 applied for aid, 782 were judged to have need, 244 had their need fully met. *Average percent of need met:* 84%. *Average financial aid package:* $9673. *Average need-based loan:* $3343. *Average need-based gift aid:* $6925. *Financial aid deadline:* 7/1.
Applying *Options:* common application, electronic application, deferred entrance. *Application fee:* $20. *Required:* essay or personal statement, high school transcript, minimum 2.0 GPA. *Required for some:* interview. *Recommended:* letters of recommendation. *Application deadlines:* 7/15 (freshmen), 7/15 (transfers). *Notification:* 8/1 (freshmen).
Admissions Contact Mr. Leo Gavrilos, Director of Admissions, Lakeland College, PO Box 359, Nash Visitors Center, Sheboygan, WI 53082-0359. *Phone:* 920-565-1217. *Toll-free phone:* 800-242-3347. *E-mail:* admissions@lakeland.edu.

LAWRENCE UNIVERSITY
Appleton, Wisconsin

- **Independent** 4-year, founded 1847
- **Calendar** trimesters
- **Degree** bachelor's
- **Small-town** 84-acre campus
- **Endowment** $176.2 million
- **Coed,** 1,323 undergraduate students, 94% full-time, 54% women, 46% men
- **Very difficult** entrance level, 68% of applicants were admitted

Lawrence is committed to development of intellect and talent, acquisition of knowledge and understanding, and cultivation of judgment and values. Research opportunities and independent study with faculty members, an academic honor code, a conservatory of music, a freshman seminar that focuses on developing communication and analysis skills, and weekend retreats to the college's 425-acre estate on Lake Michigan are among the programs that contribute to "the Lawrence Difference."

Lawrence University (continued)

Undergraduates 1,247 full-time, 76 part-time. Students come from 49 states and territories, 39 other countries, 58% are from out of state, 1% African American, 2% Asian American or Pacific Islander, 2% Hispanic American, 0.5% Native American, 9% international, 3% transferred in, 98% live on campus. *Retention:* 87% of 2001 full-time freshmen returned.

Freshmen *Admission:* 1,629 applied, 1,102 admitted, 320 enrolled. *Average high school GPA:* 3.67. *Test scores:* SAT verbal scores over 500: 91%; SAT math scores over 500: 98%; ACT scores over 18: 99%; SAT verbal scores over 600: 63%; SAT math scores over 600: 66%; ACT scores over 24: 85%; SAT verbal scores over 700: 30%; SAT math scores over 700: 27%; ACT scores over 30: 30%.

Faculty *Total:* 166, 78% full-time, 86% with terminal degrees. *Student/faculty ratio:* 11:1.

Majors Anthropology; art history; biology; chemistry; classics; cognitive psychology/psycholinguistics; computer science; East Asian studies; ecology; economics; English; environmental science; fine/studio arts; French; geology; German; history; international economics; international relations; linguistics; mathematics; music; music (piano and organ performance); music teacher education; music (voice and choral/opera performance); neuroscience; philosophy; physics; political science; pre-dentistry; pre-law; pre-medicine; pre-veterinary studies; psychology; religious studies; Russian; Russian/Slavic studies; secondary education; Spanish; stringed instruments; theater arts/drama; wind/percussion instruments.

Academic Programs *Special study options:* advanced placement credit, double majors, independent study, internships, off-campus study, part-time degree program, services for LD students, student-designed majors, study abroad. *Unusual degree programs:* 3-2 engineering with Rensselaer Polytechnic Institute, University of Michigan, Washington University in St. Louis, Columbia University; forestry with Duke University; nursing with Rush University; medical technology with Rush University, occupational therapy with Washington University.

Library Seeley G. Mudd Library with 365,612 titles, 1,406 serial subscriptions, 17,550 audiovisual materials, an OPAC, a Web page.

Computers on Campus 140 computers available on campus for general student use. A campuswide network can be accessed from student residence rooms. At least one staffed computer lab available.

Student Life *Housing:* on-campus residence required through senior year. *Options:* coed. *Activities and Organizations:* drama/theater group, student-run newspaper, radio station, choral group, Psychology Student Association, Outdoor Recreation Club, Lawrence International, Christian Fellowship, Political Science Club, national fraternities, national sororities. *Campus security:* 24-hour emergency response devices, student patrols, late-night transport/escort service, controlled dormitory access, evening patrols by trained security personnel. *Student Services:* health clinic, personal/psychological counseling.

Athletics Member NCAA. All Division III. *Intercollegiate sports:* baseball M, basketball M/W, crew M(c)/W(c), cross-country running M/W, fencing M/W, football M, golf M, ice hockey M, lacrosse M(c)/W(c), rugby W(c), soccer M/W, softball W, swimming M/W, tennis M/W, track and field M/W, volleyball W, wrestling M. *Intramural sports:* badminton M/W, basketball M/W, bowling M/W, cross-country running M/W, fencing M/W, football M/W, golf M/W, racquetball M/W, sailing M/W, skiing (cross-country) M/W, skiing (downhill) M/W, squash M/W, swimming M/W, table tennis M/W, tennis M/W, track and field M/W, volleyball M/W, weight lifting M/W, wrestling M.

Standardized Tests *Required:* SAT I or ACT (for admission).

Costs (2001–02) *Comprehensive fee:* $27,711 includes full-time tuition ($22,584), mandatory fees ($144), and room and board ($4983). *Room and board:* College room only: $2316. Room and board charges vary according to board plan. *Payment plan:* installment. *Waivers:* employees or children of employees.

Financial Aid Of all full-time matriculated undergraduates who enrolled in 2001, 999 applied for aid, 877 were judged to have need, 877 had their need fully met. 654 Federal Work-Study jobs (averaging $2174). 214 State and other part-time jobs (averaging $2454). In 2001, 280 non-need-based awards were made. *Average percent of need met:* 100%. *Average financial aid package:* $20,530. *Average need-based loan:* $4908. *Average need-based gift aid:* $14,202. *Average non-need based aid:* $8363. *Average indebtedness upon graduation:* $18,688.

Applying *Options:* common application, electronic application, early admission, early decision, early action, deferred entrance. *Application fee:* $30. *Required:* essay or personal statement, high school transcript, 2 letters of recommendation, audition for music program. *Recommended:* minimum 3.0 GPA, interview. *Application deadline:* 1/15 (freshmen), rolling (transfers). *Early decision:* 11/15. *Notification:* 4/1 (freshmen), 12/1 (early decision), 1/15 (early action).

Admissions Contact Mr. Steven T. Syverson, Dean of Admissions and Financial Aid, Lawrence University, PO Box 599, Appleton, WI 54912-0599. *Phone:* 920-832-6500. *Toll-free phone:* 800-227-0982. *Fax:* 920-832-6782. *E-mail:* excel@lawrence.edu.

MARANATHA BAPTIST BIBLE COLLEGE
Watertown, Wisconsin

- **Independent Baptist** comprehensive, founded 1968
- **Calendar** semesters
- **Degrees** certificates, associate, bachelor's, and master's
- **Small-town** 60-acre campus with easy access to Milwaukee
- **Endowment** $151,276
- **Coed,** 752 undergraduate students, 100% full-time, 52% women, 48% men
- **Noncompetitive** entrance level, 79% of applicants were admitted

Undergraduates 752 full-time. Students come from 29 states and territories, 5 other countries, 66% are from out of state, 1% African American, 0.9% Asian American or Pacific Islander, 2% Hispanic American, 0.1% Native American, 1% international, 3% transferred in, 80% live on campus. *Retention:* 64% of 2001 full-time freshmen returned.

Freshmen *Admission:* 358 applied, 284 admitted, 284 enrolled. *Test scores:* ACT scores over 18: 78%; ACT scores over 24: 24%; ACT scores over 30: 2%.

Faculty *Total:* 64. *Student/faculty ratio:* 16:1.

Majors Biblical studies; business administration; business education; early childhood education; education; elementary education; humanities; liberal arts and sciences/liberal studies; music; music teacher education; nursing; physical education; religious education; religious music; religious studies; science education; secondary education; secretarial science; speech/rhetorical studies.

Academic Programs *Special study options:* academic remediation for entering students, accelerated degree program, distance learning, double majors, independent study, internships, off-campus study, part-time degree program, summer session for credit. *ROTC:* Air Force (c).

Library Cedarholm Library and Resource Center plus 1 other with 99,390 titles, 515 serial subscriptions, 3,441 audiovisual materials, an OPAC.

Computers on Campus 61 computers available on campus for general student use. A campuswide network can be accessed from student residence rooms and from off campus. Internet access, at least one staffed computer lab available.

Student Life *Housing:* on-campus residence required through senior year. *Options:* men-only, women-only. *Activities and Organizations:* drama/theater group, choral group. *Campus security:* student patrols, late-night transport/escort service, controlled dormitory access. *Student Services:* health clinic, personal/psychological counseling.

Athletics Member NCAA, NCCAA. All NCAA Division III. *Intercollegiate sports:* baseball M, basketball M/W, cross-country running M/W, football M, soccer M/W, softball W, volleyball W, wrestling M. *Intramural sports:* basketball M, softball M, volleyball M(c).

Standardized Tests *Recommended:* ACT (for admission).

Costs (2001–02) *Required fees:* $350 full-time. *Room and board:* $4050.

Financial Aid Of all full-time matriculated undergraduates who enrolled in 2001, 562 applied for aid, 518 were judged to have need, 24 had their need fully met. 327 State and other part-time jobs (averaging $2543). In 2001, 16 non-need-based awards were made. *Average percent of need met:* 47%. *Average financial aid package:* $4320. *Average need-based loan:* $3213. *Average need-based gift aid:* $2822. *Average non-need based aid:* $1885. *Average indebtedness upon graduation:* $11,791.

Applying *Options:* common application, early admission, deferred entrance. *Application fee:* $25. *Required:* essay or personal statement, high school transcript, 3 letters of recommendation. *Application deadline:* rolling (freshmen), rolling (transfers).

Admissions Contact Mr. James H. Harrison, Director of Admissions, Maranatha Baptist Bible College, 745 West Main Street, Watertown, WI 53094. *Phone:* 920-206-2327. *Toll-free phone:* 800-622-2947. *Fax:* 920-261-9109. *E-mail:* admissions@mbbc.edu.

MARIAN COLLEGE OF FOND DU LAC
Fond du Lac, Wisconsin

- **Independent Roman Catholic** comprehensive, founded 1936
- **Calendar** semesters
- **Degrees** bachelor's and master's
- **Small-town** 50-acre campus with easy access to Milwaukee
- **Coed,** 1,628 undergraduate students, 66% full-time, 69% women, 31% men
- **Moderately difficult** entrance level, 76% of applicants were admitted

Marian College distinguishes itself from other institutions with extensive clinical, internship, and cooperative education experiences. As a result of these experiences, students develop the knowledge and skills necessary to be competent and marketable in their chosen fields. In fact, 97 percent of Marian

graduates find employment or enter graduate schools of their choice. Marian students enjoy the benefits of a truly personal education and make their home away from home in unique housing options, including residence halls, townhouses, and courtyard suites.

Undergraduates 1,075 full-time, 553 part-time. 3% African American, 0.7% Asian American or Pacific Islander, 2% Hispanic American, 0.6% Native American, 2% international, 55% live on campus.

Freshmen *Admission:* 761 applied, 580 admitted, 224 enrolled. *Average high school GPA:* 2.93.

Faculty *Total:* 81, 88% full-time, 56% with terminal degrees. *Student/faculty ratio:* 13:1.

Majors Accounting; art; art education; biological/physical sciences; biology; business administration; business economics; business marketing and marketing management; chemistry; criminal justice/law enforcement administration; cytotechnology; early childhood education; education; elementary education; English; environmental science; finance; history; human services; industrial radiologic technology; international relations; liberal arts and sciences/liberal studies; mass communications; mathematics; medical technology; middle school education; modern languages; music; music business management/merchandising; music teacher education; nursing; political science; pre-dentistry; pre-law; pre-medicine; pre-veterinary studies; psychology; science education; secondary education; social work; Spanish; sport/fitness administration.

Academic Programs *Special study options:* academic remediation for entering students, accelerated degree program, adult/continuing education programs, advanced placement credit, cooperative education, distance learning, double majors, external degree program, honors programs, independent study, internships, part-time degree program, services for LD students, student-designed majors, study abroad, summer session for credit. *ROTC:* Army (b).

Library Cardinal Meyer Library with 91,708 titles, 698 serial subscriptions, 397 audiovisual materials, an OPAC, a Web page.

Computers on Campus 125 computers available on campus for general student use. A campuswide network can be accessed from student residence rooms. Internet access, online (class) registration, at least one staffed computer lab available.

Student Life *Housing:* on-campus residence required through sophomore year. *Options:* coed. *Activities and Organizations:* drama/theater group, student-run newspaper, choral group, Student Senate, Student Nurses Association, Student Education Association, Arts and Humanities Club, Music Performance Organization, national fraternities, national sororities. *Campus security:* 24-hour emergency response devices and patrols, student patrols, late-night transport/escort service, controlled dormitory access. *Student Services:* health clinic, personal/psychological counseling.

Athletics Member NCAA. All Division III. *Intercollegiate sports:* baseball M, basketball M/W, golf M/W, ice hockey M, soccer M/W, softball W, tennis M/W, volleyball W. *Intramural sports:* basketball M/W, bowling M/W, skiing (downhill) M/W, tennis M/W, volleyball M/W.

Standardized Tests *Required:* SAT I or ACT (for admission).

Costs (2001–02) *Comprehensive fee:* $17,935 includes full-time tuition ($13,230), mandatory fees ($315), and room and board ($4390). Part-time tuition: $270 per credit. Part-time tuition and fees vary according to class time, course load, and program. *Room and board:* Room and board charges vary according to board plan, housing facility, and location. *Payment plan:* installment. *Waivers:* senior citizens and employees or children of employees.

Financial Aid Of all full-time matriculated undergraduates who enrolled in 2001, 1025 applied for aid, 836 were judged to have need, 341 had their need fully met. 85 Federal Work-Study jobs (averaging $1100). 195 State and other part-time jobs (averaging $900). In 2001, 165 non-need-based awards were made. *Average percent of need met:* 95%. *Average financial aid package:* $13,951. *Average need-based loan:* $3627. *Average need-based gift aid:* $4984. *Average non-need based aid:* $4110. *Average indebtedness upon graduation:* $19,500.

Applying *Options:* common application, electronic application, deferred entrance. *Application fee:* $15. *Required:* high school transcript. *Required for some:* interview. *Recommended:* minimum 2.0 GPA, letters of recommendation. *Application deadline:* rolling (freshmen), rolling (transfers). *Notification:* continuous until 8/15 (freshmen).

Admissions Contact Stacey L. Akey, Dean of Admissions, Marian College of Fond du Lac, Fond du Lac, WI 54935. *Phone:* 920-923-7652. *Toll-free phone:* 800-2-MARIAN Ext. 7652. *Fax:* 920-923-8755. *E-mail:* admit@mariancollege.edu.

MARQUETTE UNIVERSITY
Milwaukee, Wisconsin

- **Independent Roman Catholic (Jesuit)** university, founded 1881
- **Calendar** semesters
- **Degrees** certificates, associate, bachelor's, master's, doctoral, first professional, post-master's, and postbachelor's certificates
- **Urban** 80-acre campus
- **Endowment** $227.0 million
- **Coed,** 7,499 undergraduate students, 93% full-time, 55% women, 45% men
- **Moderately difficult** entrance level, 84% of applicants were admitted

Undergraduates 6,955 full-time, 544 part-time. Students come from 54 states and territories, 54 other countries, 52% are from out of state, 5% African American, 4% Asian American or Pacific Islander, 4% Hispanic American, 0.3% Native American, 2% international, 2% transferred in, 50% live on campus. *Retention:* 89% of 2001 full-time freshmen returned.

Freshmen *Admission:* 6,743 applied, 5,657 admitted, 1,665 enrolled. *Test scores:* SAT verbal scores over 500: 85%; SAT math scores over 500: 83%; ACT scores over 18: 99%; SAT verbal scores over 600: 42%; SAT math scores over 600: 42%; ACT scores over 24: 68%; SAT verbal scores over 700: 7%; SAT math scores over 700: 7%; ACT scores over 30: 11%.

Faculty *Total:* 1,115, 53% full-time. *Student/faculty ratio:* 15:1.

Majors Accounting; advertising; African-American studies; anthropology; athletic training/sports medicine; bilingual/bicultural education; biochemistry; bioengineering; biology; biomedical science; broadcast journalism; business administration; business economics; business marketing and marketing management; chemistry; civil engineering; classics; communications; computer engineering; computer science; creative writing; criminology; dental hygiene; economics; education; electrical engineering; elementary education; engineering; English; environmental engineering; exercise sciences; finance; French; German; history; history of philosophy; human resources management; industrial/manufacturing engineering; information sciences/systems; interdisciplinary studies; international business; international relations; journalism; management information systems/business data processing; mass communications; mathematical statistics; mathematics; mechanical engineering; medical laboratory technician; middle school education; molecular biology; nursing; nursing (midwifery); philosophy; physical therapy; physician assistant; physics; political science; pre-dentistry; pre-law; pre-medicine; psychology; public relations; secondary education; social work; sociology; Spanish; speech-language pathology/audiology; speech/rhetorical studies; theater arts/drama; theology; women's studies.

Academic Programs *Special study options:* accelerated degree program, adult/continuing education programs, advanced placement credit, cooperative education, distance learning, double majors, English as a second language, honors programs, independent study, internships, off-campus study, part-time degree program, services for LD students, study abroad, summer session for credit. *ROTC:* Army (b), Navy (b), Air Force (b).

Library Memorial Library plus 2 others with 719,906 titles, 9,225 serial subscriptions, 7,276 audiovisual materials, an OPAC, a Web page.

Computers on Campus 600 computers available on campus for general student use. A campuswide network can be accessed from student residence rooms and from off campus. Internet access, at least one staffed computer lab available.

Student Life *Housing:* on-campus residence required through sophomore year. *Options:* coed, men-only, women-only, disabled students. *Activities and Organizations:* drama/theater group, student-run newspaper, radio and television station, choral group, student government, club sports, community service organizations, band/jazz/orchestra, national fraternities, national sororities. *Campus security:* 24-hour emergency response devices and patrols, student patrols, late-night transport/escort service, 24-hour desk attendants in residence halls. *Student Services:* health clinic, personal/psychological counseling.

Athletics Member NCAA. All Division I. *Intercollegiate sports:* baseball M(c), basketball M(s)/W(s), crew M(c)/W(c), cross-country running M(s)/W(s), fencing M(c)/W(c), football M(c), golf M(s), lacrosse M(c), rugby M(c)/W(c), sailing M(c)/W(c), skiing (downhill) M(c)/W(c), soccer M(s)/W(s), softball W(c), swimming M(c)/W(c), tennis M(s)/W(s), track and field M(s)/W(s), volleyball M(c)/W(s). *Intramural sports:* badminton M/W, basketball M/W, bowling M/W, football W, golf M/W, racquetball M/W, soccer M/W, softball M/W, squash M/W, tennis M/W, track and field M/W, volleyball M/W, water polo M/W, weight lifting M/W.

Standardized Tests *Required:* SAT I or ACT (for admission).

Costs (2002–03) *Comprehensive fee:* $26,056 includes full-time tuition ($19,400), mandatory fees ($306), and room and board ($6350). Full-time tuition and fees vary according to course load and program. Part-time tuition: $570 per credit. Part-time tuition and fees vary according to program. *Room and board:* College room only: $3810. Room and board charges vary according to board plan, housing facility, and location. *Payment plans:* tuition prepayment, installment. *Waivers:* adult students, senior citizens, and employees or children of employees.

Financial Aid Of all full-time matriculated undergraduates who enrolled in 2001, 4799 applied for aid, 4284 were judged to have need, 2703 had their need fully met. In 2001, 739 non-need-based awards were made. *Average percent of*

Marquette University (continued)
need met: 90%. *Average financial aid package:* $15,483. *Average need-based loan:* $5276. *Average need-based gift aid:* $10,013. *Average non-need based aid:* $7654.

Applying *Options:* common application, electronic application, early admission, deferred entrance. *Application fee:* $30. *Required:* essay or personal statement, high school transcript, minimum 2.5 GPA. *Recommended:* minimum 3.4 GPA, 1 letter of recommendation, interview. *Application deadline:* rolling (freshmen), rolling (transfers). *Notification:* 11/15 (freshmen).

Admissions Contact Mr. Robert Blust, Dean of Undergraduate Admissions, Marquette University, PO Box 1881, Milwaukee, WI 53201-1881. *Phone:* 414-288-7004. *Toll-free phone:* 800-222-6544. *Fax:* 414-288-3764. *E-mail:* admissions@marquette.edu.

MILWAUKEE INSTITUTE OF ART AND DESIGN
Milwaukee, Wisconsin

- **Independent** 4-year, founded 1974
- **Calendar** semesters
- **Degree** bachelor's
- **Urban** campus
- **Endowment** $1.8 million
- **Coed,** 650 undergraduate students, 90% full-time, 50% women, 50% men
- **Moderately difficult** entrance level, 66% of applicants were admitted

Undergraduates 585 full-time, 65 part-time. Students come from 20 states and territories, 28% are from out of state, 2% African American, 2% Asian American or Pacific Islander, 6% Hispanic American, 0.8% Native American, 9% transferred in, 22% live on campus. *Retention:* 73% of 2001 full-time freshmen returned.

Freshmen *Admission:* 409 applied, 271 admitted, 137 enrolled. *Average high school GPA:* 2.92. *Test scores:* ACT scores over 18: 86%; ACT scores over 24: 35%; ACT scores over 30: 4%.

Faculty *Total:* 100, 36% full-time, 69% with terminal degrees. *Student/faculty ratio:* 16:1.

Majors Art; drawing; graphic design/commercial art/illustration; industrial design; interior design; painting; photography; printmaking; sculpture.

Academic Programs *Special study options:* academic remediation for entering students, adult/continuing education programs, advanced placement credit, cooperative education, double majors, independent study, internships, off-campus study, part-time degree program, services for LD students, study abroad, summer session for credit.

Library 23,000 titles, 84 serial subscriptions, 360 audiovisual materials, an OPAC, a Web page.

Computers on Campus 99 computers available on campus for general student use. Internet access, at least one staffed computer lab available.

Student Life *Housing:* on-campus residence required for freshman year. *Options:* coed. *Activities and Organizations:* student government, Student Gallery Committee, Student Activities Committee, Minority Student Organization, community service. *Campus security:* 24-hour emergency response devices, late-night transport/escort service. *Student Services:* health clinic, personal/psychological counseling.

Standardized Tests *Recommended:* SAT I or ACT (for placement).

Costs (2002–03) *Comprehensive fee:* $26,568 includes full-time tuition ($19,900), mandatory fees ($130), and room and board ($6538). Part-time tuition: $665 per credit. Part-time tuition and fees vary according to course load. *Required fees:* $65 per term part-time. *Room and board:* Room and board charges vary according to board plan. *Payment plan:* deferred payment. *Waivers:* employees or children of employees.

Financial Aid Of all full-time matriculated undergraduates who enrolled in 2001, 676 applied for aid, 620 were judged to have need, 95 had their need fully met. In 2001, 118 non-need-based awards were made. *Average percent of need met:* 58%. *Average financial aid package:* $12,142. *Average need-based loan:* $5399. *Average need-based gift aid:* $6770. *Financial aid deadline:* 3/1.

Applying *Options:* common application, electronic application, deferred entrance. *Application fee:* $25. *Required:* essay or personal statement, high school transcript, interview, portfolio. *Required for some:* letters of recommendation. *Recommended:* minimum 2.0 GPA. *Application deadline:* rolling (freshmen), rolling (transfers).

Admissions Contact Ms. Mary Schopp, Vice President of Enrollment Management, Milwaukee Institute of Art and Design, 273 East Erie Street, Milwaukee, WI 53202. *Phone:* 414-291-8070. *Toll-free phone:* 888-749-MIAD. *Fax:* 414-291-8077. *E-mail:* miadadm@miad.edu.

MILWAUKEE SCHOOL OF ENGINEERING
Milwaukee, Wisconsin

- **Independent** comprehensive, founded 1903
- **Calendar** quarters
- **Degrees** bachelor's and master's
- **Urban** 12-acre campus
- **Endowment** $24.4 million
- **Coed, primarily men,** 2,246 undergraduate students, 79% full-time, 15% women, 85% men
- **Moderately difficult** entrance level, 69% of applicants were admitted

Undergraduates 1,765 full-time, 481 part-time. Students come from 37 states and territories, 26 other countries, 22% are from out of state, 3% African American, 3% Asian American or Pacific Islander, 2% Hispanic American, 0.3% Native American, 4% international, 8% transferred in, 40% live on campus. *Retention:* 77% of 2001 full-time freshmen returned.

Freshmen *Admission:* 2,093 applied, 1,436 admitted, 488 enrolled. *Average high school GPA:* 3.50. *Test scores:* SAT verbal scores over 500: 78%; SAT math scores over 500: 96%; ACT scores over 18: 99%; SAT verbal scores over 600: 35%; SAT math scores over 600: 74%; ACT scores over 24: 84%; SAT verbal scores over 700: 7%; SAT math scores over 700: 14%; ACT scores over 30: 31%.

Faculty *Total:* 227, 52% full-time, 35% with terminal degrees. *Student/faculty ratio:* 11:1.

Majors Architectural engineering; bioengineering; business; communications related; computer engineering; computer software engineering; electrical/electronic engineering technology; electrical engineering; industrial/manufacturing engineering; international business; management information systems/business data processing; mechanical engineering; mechanical engineering technology; nursing.

Academic Programs *Special study options:* academic remediation for entering students, accelerated degree program, adult/continuing education programs, advanced placement credit, distance learning, double majors, independent study, internships, part-time degree program, services for LD students, study abroad, summer session for credit. *ROTC:* Army (c), Air Force (c).

Library Walter Schroeder Library with 45,638 titles, 430 serial subscriptions, 467 audiovisual materials, an OPAC, a Web page.

Computers on Campus 105 computers available on campus for general student use. A campuswide network can be accessed from student residence rooms and from off campus that provide access to e-mail. Internet access, at least one staffed computer lab available.

Student Life *Housing:* on-campus residence required through sophomore year. *Options:* coed, disabled students. *Activities and Organizations:* drama/theater group, student-run newspaper, radio station, Architectural Engineering Society, Society of Automotive Engineers, Student Government Association, Circle K, Student Union Board, national fraternities, national sororities. *Campus security:* 24-hour emergency response devices and patrols, late-night transport/escort service, controlled dormitory access. *Student Services:* health clinic, personal/psychological counseling.

Athletics Member NCAA. All Division III. *Intercollegiate sports:* baseball M, basketball M/W, cross-country running M/W, golf M/W, ice hockey M, soccer M/W, softball W, tennis M/W, track and field M/W, volleyball M/W, wrestling M. *Intramural sports:* basketball M/W, bowling M(c)/W(c), football M/W, soccer M/W, softball M/W, volleyball M/W.

Standardized Tests *Required:* SAT I or ACT (for admission).

Costs (2002–03) *Comprehensive fee:* $26,970 includes full-time tuition ($21,855) and room and board ($5115). Full-time tuition and fees vary according to student level. Part-time tuition: $382 per quarter hour. Part-time tuition and fees vary according to course load. *Room and board:* College room only: $3255. Room and board charges vary according to board plan and housing facility. *Payment plan:* installment. *Waivers:* employees or children of employees.

Financial Aid Of all full-time matriculated undergraduates who enrolled in 2001, 1532 applied for aid, 1302 were judged to have need, 141 had their need fully met. In 2001, 254 non-need-based awards were made. *Average percent of need met:* 62%. *Average financial aid package:* $13,713. *Average need-based loan:* $3519. *Average need-based gift aid:* $4496. *Average non-need based aid:* $4505. *Average indebtedness upon graduation:* $25,000.

Applying *Options:* common application, electronic application, deferred entrance. *Application fee:* $25. *Required:* high school transcript, minimum 2.5 GPA. *Required for some:* essay or personal statement, interview. *Application deadline:* rolling (freshmen), rolling (transfers). *Notification:* continuous (freshmen).

Admissions Contact Mr. Tim A. Valley, Dean of Enrollment Management, Milwaukee School of Engineering, 1025 North Broadway, Milwaukee, WI 53202-3109. *Phone:* 414-277-6763. *Toll-free phone:* 800-332-6763. *Fax:* 414-277-7475. *E-mail:* explore@msoe.edu.

MOUNT MARY COLLEGE
Milwaukee, Wisconsin

- **Independent Roman Catholic** comprehensive, founded 1913
- **Calendar** semesters
- **Degrees** bachelor's and master's
- **Suburban** 80-acre campus
- **Endowment** $14.8 million
- **Women only,** 1,080 undergraduate students, 49% full-time
- **Moderately difficult** entrance level, 89% of applicants were admitted

Undergraduates 527 full-time, 553 part-time. Students come from 7 states and territories, 6 other countries, 5% are from out of state, 16% African American, 4% Asian American or Pacific Islander, 4% Hispanic American, 0.7% Native American, 1% international, 6% transferred in, 27% live on campus. *Retention:* 66% of 2001 full-time freshmen returned.

Freshmen *Admission:* 95 enrolled. *Average high school GPA:* 3.14. *Test scores:* ACT scores over 18: 79%; ACT scores over 24: 21%.

Faculty *Total:* 164, 42% full-time, 41% with terminal degrees. *Student/faculty ratio:* 8:1.

Majors Accounting; art; art education; art therapy; behavioral sciences; bilingual/bicultural education; biology; business administration; business education; chemistry; communications; computer science; criminal justice/corrections related; dietetics; early childhood education; education; elementary education; English; fashion design/illustration; fashion merchandising; French; graphic design/commercial art/illustration; history; interior design; international relations; mathematics; music; music teacher education; occupational therapy; philosophy; pre-dentistry; pre-law; pre-medicine; pre-veterinary studies; public relations; religious education; religious studies; secondary education; social work; Spanish; technical/business writing.

Academic Programs *Special study options:* academic remediation for entering students, accelerated degree program, adult/continuing education programs, advanced placement credit, double majors, English as a second language, honors programs, independent study, internships, part-time degree program, services for LD students, student-designed majors, summer session for credit. *ROTC:* Army (c). *Unusual degree programs:* 3-2 dentistry with Marquette University.

Library Haggerty Library with 104,000 titles, 675 serial subscriptions, 8,910 audiovisual materials, an OPAC, a Web page.

Computers on Campus 74 computers available on campus for general student use. A campuswide network can be accessed from student residence rooms and from off campus. Internet access, at least one staffed computer lab available.

Student Life *Housing Options:* women-only. *Activities and Organizations:* drama/theater group, student-run newspaper, choral group, Student Association, campus ministry, Student Occupational Therapy Association, ARTS Organization. *Campus security:* 24-hour patrols, late-night transport/escort service, controlled dormitory access. *Student Services:* health clinic, personal/psychological counseling, women's center.

Athletics *Intercollegiate sports:* basketball W, soccer W, softball W, tennis W, volleyball W. *Intramural sports:* basketball W, soccer W, volleyball W.

Standardized Tests *Required:* SAT I or ACT (for admission).

Costs (2001–02) *Comprehensive fee:* $18,024 includes full-time tuition ($13,234), mandatory fees ($160), and room and board ($4630). Part-time tuition: $398 per credit. Part-time tuition and fees vary according to course load. *Required fees:* $40 per term part-time. *Room and board:* College room only: $2010. Room and board charges vary according to board plan. *Payment plan:* installment. *Waivers:* senior citizens and employees or children of employees.

Financial Aid Of all full-time matriculated undergraduates who enrolled in 2001, 422 applied for aid, 373 were judged to have need, 83 had their need fully met. 111 Federal Work-Study jobs, 74 State and other part-time jobs (averaging $1037). *Average percent of need met:* 71%. *Average financial aid package:* $10,035. *Average need-based loan:* $4390. *Average need-based gift aid:* $6131. *Average indebtedness upon graduation:* $22,366.

Applying *Options:* common application, electronic application, early admission. *Application fee:* $25. *Required:* high school transcript, minimum 2.5 GPA. *Required for some:* essay or personal statement, 2 letters of recommendation. *Recommended:* interview. *Application deadline:* rolling (freshmen), rolling (transfers). *Notification:* continuous (freshmen).

Admissions Contact Ms. Amy Dobson, Director of Enrollment, Mount Mary College, 2900 North Menomonee River Parkway, Milwaukee, WI 53222-4597. *Phone:* 414-258-4810 Ext. 360. *Fax:* 414-256-1205. *E-mail:* admiss@mtmary.edu.

NORTHLAND COLLEGE
Ashland, Wisconsin

- **Independent** 4-year, founded 1892, affiliated with United Church of Christ
- **Calendar** 4-4-1
- **Degree** bachelor's
- **Small-town** 130-acre campus
- **Endowment** $18.7 million
- **Coed,** 797 undergraduate students, 100% full-time, 56% women, 44% men
- **Moderately difficult** entrance level, 89% of applicants were admitted

Undergraduates 797 full-time. Students come from 46 states and territories, 9 other countries, 65% are from out of state, 0.9% African American, 0.8% Asian American or Pacific Islander, 2% Hispanic American, 2% Native American, 3% international, 8% transferred in, 61% live on campus. *Retention:* 72% of 2001 full-time freshmen returned.

Freshmen *Admission:* 821 applied, 730 admitted, 194 enrolled. *Test scores:* SAT verbal scores over 500: 78%; SAT math scores over 500: 80%; ACT scores over 18: 94%; SAT verbal scores over 600: 45%; SAT math scores over 600: 35%; ACT scores over 24: 49%; SAT verbal scores over 700: 9%; SAT math scores over 700: 4%; ACT scores over 30: 9%.

Faculty *Total:* 84, 55% full-time, 55% with terminal degrees. *Student/faculty ratio:* 14:1.

Majors Applied mathematics; art; art education; atmospheric sciences; biological/physical sciences; biology; business administration; business economics; chemistry; creative writing; early childhood education; earth sciences; ecology; economics; education; elementary education; English; environmental biology; environmental education; environmental science; fine/studio arts; fish/game management; forestry; geology; history; information sciences/systems; interdisciplinary studies; land use management; mathematics; middle school education; music; music teacher education; Native American studies; natural resources conservation; natural resources management; natural sciences; peace/conflict studies; philosophy; pre-dentistry; pre-law; pre-medicine; pre-veterinary studies; psychology; recreational therapy; recreation/leisure facilities management; recreation/leisure studies; religious studies; science education; secondary education; social sciences; sociology; water resources; wildlife biology; wildlife management; zoology.

Academic Programs *Special study options:* accelerated degree program, adult/continuing education programs, advanced placement credit, cooperative education, distance learning, double majors, independent study, internships, off-campus study, part-time degree program, student-designed majors, study abroad, summer session for credit. *Unusual degree programs:* 3-2 engineering with Michigan Technological University, Washington University in St. Louis; forestry with Michigan Technological University.

Library Dexter Library with 81,000 titles, 340 serial subscriptions, an OPAC.

Computers on Campus 120 computers available on campus for general student use. A campuswide network can be accessed from student residence rooms and from off campus. At least one staffed computer lab available.

Student Life *Housing:* on-campus residence required through sophomore year. *Options:* coed, men-only, women-only. *Activities and Organizations:* drama/theater group, student-run newspaper, radio station, choral group, Psi Chi, the National Honor Society in Psychology, Northland College student association, Native American student association, Northland Greens, "N" Club. *Campus security:* 24-hour emergency response devices, controlled dormitory access. *Student Services:* health clinic, personal/psychological counseling, women's center.

Athletics Member NAIA. *Intercollegiate sports:* baseball M, basketball M/W, cross-country running M/W, ice hockey M, soccer M/W, softball W, volleyball W. *Intramural sports:* archery M/W, badminton M/W, basketball M/W, football M/W, golf M/W, ice hockey M/W, lacrosse M, racquetball M/W, rugby M(c)/W(c), skiing (cross-country) M(c)/W(c), skiing (downhill) M(c)/W(c), soccer M/W, softball M/W, swimming M/W, table tennis M/W, tennis M/W, volleyball M/W, water polo M/W, weight lifting M/W.

Standardized Tests *Required:* SAT I or ACT (for admission).

Costs (2002–03) *Comprehensive fee:* $21,435 includes full-time tuition ($16,260), mandatory fees ($340), and room and board ($4835). Part-time tuition: $330 per credit. *Room and board:* Room and board charges vary according to board plan and housing facility. *Payment plan:* installment. *Waivers:* employees or children of employees.

Financial Aid Of all full-time matriculated undergraduates who enrolled in 2001, 707 applied for aid, 644 were judged to have need, 65 had their need fully met. 323 Federal Work-Study jobs (averaging $987). 280 State and other part-time

Northland College (continued)
jobs (averaging $1082). In 2001, 26 non-need-based awards were made. *Average percent of need met:* 76%. *Average financial aid package:* $12,445. *Average need-based loan:* $3659. *Average need-based gift aid:* $7446. *Average non-need based aid:* $3690. *Average indebtedness upon graduation:* $18,943.

Applying *Options:* common application, electronic application, early admission, deferred entrance. *Required:* essay or personal statement, high school transcript, 1 letter of recommendation. *Recommended:* minimum 2.0 GPA, interview. *Application deadlines:* 8/1 (freshmen), 8/1 (transfers). *Notification:* continuous (freshmen).

Admissions Contact Mr. Eric Peterson, Director of Admission, Northland College, 1411 Ellis Avenue, Ashland, WI 54806. *Phone:* 715-682-1224. *Toll-free phone:* 800-753-1840 (in-state); 800-753-1040 (out-of-state). *Fax:* 715-682-1258. *E-mail:* admit@northland.edu.

RIPON COLLEGE
Ripon, Wisconsin

- **Independent** 4-year, founded 1851
- **Calendar** semesters
- **Degree** bachelor's
- **Small-town** 250-acre campus with easy access to Milwaukee
- **Endowment** $31.9 million
- **Coed,** 903 undergraduate students, 98% full-time, 53% women, 47% men
- **Moderately difficult** entrance level, 84% of applicants were admitted

Undergraduates 884 full-time, 19 part-time. Students come from 33 states and territories, 17 other countries, 30% are from out of state, 2% African American, 1% Asian American or Pacific Islander, 4% Hispanic American, 0.5% Native American, 1% international, 2% transferred in, 94% live on campus. *Retention:* 88% of 2001 full-time freshmen returned.

Freshmen *Admission:* 847 applied, 710 admitted, 201 enrolled. *Average high school GPA:* 3.42. *Test scores:* SAT verbal scores over 500: 80%; SAT math scores over 500: 88%; ACT scores over 18: 99%; SAT verbal scores over 600: 48%; SAT math scores over 600: 56%; ACT scores over 24: 50%; SAT verbal scores over 700: 4%; SAT math scores over 700: 12%; ACT scores over 30: 7%.

Faculty *Total:* 85, 67% full-time, 74% with terminal degrees. *Student/faculty ratio:* 15:1.

Majors Anthropology; art; biochemistry; biology; business administration; chemistry; computer science; early childhood education; economics; education; elementary education; English; environmental science; French; German; history; interdisciplinary studies; Latin American studies; mathematics; music; music teacher education; philosophy; physical education; physics; physiological psychology/psychobiology; political science; pre-dentistry; pre-law; pre-medicine; pre-veterinary studies; psychology; religious studies; romance languages; secondary education; sociology; Spanish; speech/rhetorical studies; theater arts/drama.

Academic Programs *Special study options:* accelerated degree program, advanced placement credit, double majors, internships, off-campus study, part-time degree program, services for LD students, student-designed majors, study abroad. *ROTC:* Army (b). *Unusual degree programs:* 3-2 engineering with Rensselaer Polytechnic Institute, Washington University in St. Louis, University of Wisconsin-Madison; forestry with Duke University; nursing with Rush University; environmental studies with Duke University.

Library Lane Library with 164,232 titles, 794 serial subscriptions, 8,200 audiovisual materials, an OPAC, a Web page.

Computers on Campus 150 computers available on campus for general student use. A campuswide network can be accessed from student residence rooms and from off campus. Internet access, at least one staffed computer lab available.

Student Life *Housing:* on-campus residence required through senior year. *Options:* coed, men-only, women-only. *Activities and Organizations:* drama/theater group, student-run newspaper, radio station, choral group, Environmental Group, Student Senate, Community Service Coalition, SMAC (Student Media and Activities Committee), national fraternities, national sororities. *Campus security:* 24-hour emergency response devices and patrols, student patrols, late-night transport/escort service, controlled dormitory access. *Student Services:* health clinic, personal/psychological counseling, legal services.

Athletics Member NCAA. All Division III. *Intercollegiate sports:* baseball M, basketball M/W, cross-country running M/W, football M, golf M/W, ice hockey M(c)/W(c), rugby M(c), soccer M/W, softball W, swimming M/W, tennis M/W, track and field M/W, volleyball W, wrestling M(c)/W(c). *Intramural sports:* basketball M/W, bowling M/W, fencing M/W, football M/W, golf M/W, racquetball M/W, soccer M/W, softball M/W, table tennis M/W, tennis M/W, volleyball M/W, water polo M(c)/W(c).

Standardized Tests *Required:* SAT I or ACT (for admission).

Costs (2001–02) *Comprehensive fee:* $24,180 includes full-time tuition ($19,260), mandatory fees ($240), and room and board ($4680). Part-time tuition: $825 per credit. No tuition increase for student's term of enrollment. *Room and board:* College room only: $2130. *Payment plan:* installment. *Waivers:* children of alumni and employees or children of employees.

Financial Aid Of all full-time matriculated undergraduates who enrolled in 2001, 743 applied for aid, 670 were judged to have need, 546 had their need fully met. 186 Federal Work-Study jobs (averaging $1250). 406 State and other part-time jobs (averaging $1135). In 2001, 180 non-need-based awards were made. *Average percent of need met:* 98%. *Average financial aid package:* $16,158. *Average need-based loan:* $3377. *Average need-based gift aid:* $13,382. *Average non-need based aid:* $12,811. *Average indebtedness upon graduation:* $14,957.

Applying *Options:* common application, electronic application, deferred entrance. *Application fee:* $30. *Required:* high school transcript, minimum 2.0 GPA, 1 letter of recommendation. *Recommended:* essay or personal statement, interview. *Application deadline:* rolling (freshmen), rolling (transfers). *Notification:* continuous (freshmen).

Admissions Contact Mr. Scott J. Goplin, Vice President and Dean of Admission and Financial Aid, Ripon College, 300 Seward Street, PO Box 248, Ripon, WI 54971. *Phone:* 920-748-8185. *Toll-free phone:* 800-947-4766. *Fax:* 920-748-8335. *E-mail:* adminfo@ripon.edu.

ST. NORBERT COLLEGE
De Pere, Wisconsin

- **Independent Roman Catholic** comprehensive, founded 1898
- **Calendar** semesters
- **Degrees** bachelor's and master's
- **Suburban** 84-acre campus
- **Endowment** $46.8 million
- **Coed,** 2,059 undergraduate students, 96% full-time, 57% women, 43% men
- **Moderately difficult** entrance level, 84% of applicants were admitted

To firmly address the concerns associated with financing a private school education, St. Norbert College offers a 4-year graduation guarantee. This guarantee reflects the strengths of the College's advisement program, the flexibility and integrity of the curriculum, and St. Norbert's commitment to making private education affordable. The College also guarantees campus employment to all first-year students, regardless of need.

Undergraduates 1,971 full-time, 88 part-time. Students come from 27 states and territories, 27 other countries, 28% are from out of state, 1% African American, 2% Asian American or Pacific Islander, 1% Hispanic American, 0.9% Native American, 3% international, 3% transferred in, 75% live on campus. *Retention:* 82% of 2001 full-time freshmen returned.

Freshmen *Admission:* 1,603 applied, 1,347 admitted, 558 enrolled. *Average high school GPA:* 3.29. *Test scores:* ACT scores over 18: 99%; ACT scores over 24: 56%; ACT scores over 30: 6%.

Faculty *Total:* 175, 66% full-time, 66% with terminal degrees. *Student/faculty ratio:* 14:1.

Majors Accounting; art; biological/physical sciences; biology; business; business computer programming; chemistry; communications; economics; education (K-12); elementary education; English; French; geology; German; graphic design/commercial art/illustration; history; humanities; interdisciplinary studies; international business; international relations; management information systems/business data processing; mathematics; mathematics/computer science; medical technology; music; music teacher education; philosophy; physics; political science; pre-dentistry; pre-engineering; pre-law; pre-medicine; pre-veterinary studies; psychology; religious studies; sociology; Spanish.

Academic Programs *Special study options:* academic remediation for entering students, accelerated degree program, advanced placement credit, cooperative education, distance learning, double majors, English as a second language, honors programs, independent study, internships, off-campus study, part-time degree program, services for LD students, student-designed majors, study abroad, summer session for credit. *ROTC:* Army (b).

Library Todd Wehr Library with 140,514 titles, 10,000 serial subscriptions, 7,625 audiovisual materials, an OPAC, a Web page.

Computers on Campus 179 computers available on campus for general student use. A campuswide network can be accessed from student residence rooms and from off campus. Internet access, online (class) registration, at least one staffed computer lab available.

Student Life *Housing:* on-campus residence required through senior year. *Options:* coed, women-only, disabled students. *Activities and Organizations:* drama/theater group, student-run newspaper, radio and television station, choral group, Yes! Your Entertainment Service, Student Government Association, Residence Hall Association, national fraternities, national sororities. *Campus security:* 24-hour emergency response devices and patrols, student patrols, late-night transport/escort service, controlled dormitory access, crime prevention programs. *Student Services:* health clinic, personal/psychological counseling, women's center.

Athletics Member NCAA. All Division III. *Intercollegiate sports:* baseball M, basketball M/W, cross-country running M/W, football M, golf M/W, ice hockey M, soccer M/W, softball W, swimming W, tennis M/W, track and field M/W, volleyball W. *Intramural sports:* basketball M/W, crew M(c)/W(c), football M/W, racquetball M/W, soccer M/W, softball M/W, volleyball M/W.

Standardized Tests *Required:* SAT I or ACT (for admission).

Costs (2001–02) *One-time required fee:* $100. *Comprehensive fee:* $23,169 includes full-time tuition ($17,757), mandatory fees ($250), and room and board ($5162). Full-time tuition and fees vary according to course load. Part-time tuition: $2220 per course. Part-time tuition and fees vary according to course load. No tuition increase for student's term of enrollment. *Required fees:* $13 per course, $50 per term part-time. *Room and board:* College room only: $2742. Room and board charges vary according to board plan, housing facility, and student level. *Payment plans:* installment, deferred payment. *Waivers:* employees or children of employees.

Financial Aid Of all full-time matriculated undergraduates who enrolled in 2001, 1477 applied for aid, 1253 were judged to have need, 498 had their need fully met. 380 Federal Work-Study jobs, 715 State and other part-time jobs. In 2001, 616 non-need-based awards were made. *Average percent of need met:* 88%. *Average financial aid package:* $13,971. *Average need-based loan:* $4209. *Average need-based gift aid:* $9839. *Average indebtedness upon graduation:* $16,715.

Applying *Options:* common application, electronic application, early decision, deferred entrance. *Application fee:* $25. *Required:* essay or personal statement, high school transcript, 1 letter of recommendation. *Recommended:* interview. *Application deadline:* rolling (freshmen), rolling (transfers). *Early decision:* 12/1. *Notification:* continuous (freshmen), 12/15 (early decision).

Admissions Contact Mr. Daniel L. Meyer, Dean of Admission and Enrollment Management, St. Norbert College, 100 Grant Street, De Pere, WI 54115-2099. *Phone:* 920-403-3005. *Toll-free phone:* 800-236-4878. *Fax:* 920-403-4072. *E-mail:* admit@mail.snc.edu.

SILVER LAKE COLLEGE
Manitowoc, Wisconsin

- **Independent Roman Catholic** comprehensive, founded 1869
- **Calendar** semesters
- **Degrees** certificates, associate, bachelor's, master's, and postbachelor's certificates
- **Rural** 30-acre campus with easy access to Milwaukee
- **Endowment** $4.9 million
- **Coed,** 663 undergraduate students, 40% full-time, 72% women, 28% men
- **Minimally difficult** entrance level, 89% of applicants were admitted

In a recent survey of Silver Lake College (SLC) graduates, 99 percent of those responding said that they are very satisfied or satisfied with their education. For information about the College's outstanding programs of study, students should contact the admissions office at 800-236-4SLC Ext. 175 (toll-free) or visit the College's Web site at http://www.sl.edu.

Undergraduates 263 full-time, 400 part-time. Students come from 3 states and territories, 1 other country, 2% are from out of state, 0.4% African American, 1% Asian American or Pacific Islander, 1.0% Hispanic American, 2% Native American, 0.4% international, 13% transferred in, 3% live on campus. *Retention:* 66% of 2001 full-time freshmen returned.

Freshmen *Admission:* 72 applied, 64 admitted, 35 enrolled. *Average high school GPA:* 2.91. *Test scores:* ACT scores over 18: 63%.

Faculty *Total:* 112, 37% full-time, 30% with terminal degrees. *Student/faculty ratio:* 8:1.

Majors Accounting; art; art education; biology; business administration; computer/information sciences; early childhood education; education of the mentally handicapped; education of the specific learning disabled; elementary education; English; general studies; graphic design/commercial art/illustration; history; human resources management; interdisciplinary studies; mathematics; music; music teacher education; psychology; social sciences; theology.

Academic Programs *Special study options:* academic remediation for entering students, accelerated degree program, adult/continuing education programs, advanced placement credit, cooperative education, distance learning, double majors, English as a second language, independent study, internships, part-time degree program, student-designed majors, summer session for credit.

Library The Erma M. and Theodore M. Zigmunt Library with 64,668 titles, 306 serial subscriptions, 17,983 audiovisual materials, an OPAC.

Computers on Campus 50 computers available on campus for general student use. A campuswide network can be accessed from off campus. Internet access, at least one staffed computer lab available.

Student Life *Housing:* on-campus residence required through sophomore year. *Options:* men-only, women-only. *Activities and Organizations:* student-run newspaper, choral group. *Campus security:* 24-hour emergency response devices. *Student Services:* personal/psychological counseling.

Athletics *Intercollegiate sports:* basketball W. *Intramural sports:* table tennis M/W, volleyball M/W.

Standardized Tests *Required:* SAT I or ACT (for admission).

Costs (2002–03) *Tuition:* $13,650 full-time, $340 per credit part-time. Full-time tuition and fees vary according to location and program. Part-time tuition and fees vary according to course load, location, and program. *Room only:* $3800. Room and board charges vary according to board plan. *Waivers:* children of alumni, senior citizens, and employees or children of employees.

Financial Aid Of all full-time matriculated undergraduates who enrolled in 2001, 215 applied for aid, 199 were judged to have need, 6 had their need fully met. 73 Federal Work-Study jobs (averaging $1079). In 2001, 7 non-need-based awards were made. *Average percent of need met:* 68%. *Average financial aid package:* $10,607. *Average need-based loan:* $4060. *Average need-based gift aid:* $7040. *Average non-need based aid:* $3529. *Average indebtedness upon graduation:* $16,517.

Applying *Options:* electronic application, early admission, deferred entrance. *Application fee:* $35. *Required:* high school transcript, minimum 2.0 GPA. *Required for some:* interview, audition. *Application deadlines:* 8/31 (freshmen), 8/31 (transfers). *Notification:* continuous (freshmen).

Admissions Contact Ms. Janis Algozine, Vice President, Dean of Students, Silver Lake College, 2406 South Alverno Road, Manitowoc, WI 54220-9319. *Phone:* 920-684-5955 Ext. 175. *Toll-free phone:* 800-236-4752 Ext. 175. *Fax:* 920-684-7082. *E-mail:* admslc@silver.sl.edu.

UNIVERSITY OF PHOENIX-WISCONSIN CAMPUS
Brookfield, Wisconsin

- **Proprietary** comprehensive
- **Calendar** continuous
- **Degrees** certificates, associate, bachelor's, master's, doctoral, post-master's, and postbachelor's certificates (courses conducted at 54 campuses and learning centers in 13 states)
- **Coed**

Undergraduates Students come from 2 states and territories, 1% are from out of state.

Freshmen *Admission:* 6 admitted.

Faculty *Total:* 31, 3% full-time, 13% with terminal degrees. *Student/faculty ratio:* 13:1.

Majors Accounting; business administration; computer/information sciences.

Student Life *Housing:* college housing not available.

Costs (2001–02) *Tuition:* $8850 full-time. Full-time tuition and fees vary according to location and program. *Payment plan:* deferred payment. *Waivers:* employees or children of employees.

Admissions Contact 4615 East Elwood Street, Phoenix, AZ 85040-1948. *Toll-free phone:* 800-228-7240. *E-mail:* beth.barilla@apollogrp.edu.

UNIVERSITY OF WISCONSIN-EAU CLAIRE
Eau Claire, Wisconsin

- **State-supported** comprehensive, founded 1916, part of University of Wisconsin System
- **Calendar** semesters
- **Degrees** associate, bachelor's, master's, post-master's, and postbachelor's certificates
- **Urban** 333-acre campus
- **Endowment** $21.4 million
- **Coed,** 10,218 undergraduate students, 92% full-time, 60% women, 40% men
- **Moderately difficult** entrance level, 75% of applicants were admitted

Undergraduates 9,376 full-time, 842 part-time. Students come from 25 states and territories, 48 other countries, 22% are from out of state, 0.7% African American, 3% Asian American or Pacific Islander, 1.0% Hispanic American,

University of Wisconsin-Eau Claire (continued)
0.6% Native American, 1% international, 5% transferred in, 39% live on campus. *Retention:* 78% of 2001 full-time freshmen returned.

Freshmen *Admission:* 6,206 applied, 4,677 admitted, 2,136 enrolled. *Test scores:* SAT verbal scores over 500: 75%; SAT math scores over 500: 89%; ACT scores over 18: 99%; SAT verbal scores over 600: 54%; SAT math scores over 600: 57%; ACT scores over 24: 49%; SAT verbal scores over 700: 9%; SAT math scores over 700: 8%; ACT scores over 30: 4%.

Faculty *Total:* 487, 85% full-time, 79% with terminal degrees. *Student/faculty ratio:* 20:1.

Majors Accounting; art; biochemistry; biology; business administration; business marketing and marketing management; chemistry; communication disorders; communications; computer/information sciences; criminal justice studies; economics; elementary education; English; environmental health; exercise sciences; finance; French; geography; geology; German; health services administration; history; journalism; Latin American studies; liberal arts and sciences/liberal studies; management information systems/business data processing; mass communications; mathematics; music; music therapy; Native American studies; nursing; philosophy; physics; political science; psychology; public health; religious studies; science education; social studies education; social work; sociology; Spanish; special education; theater arts/drama.

Academic Programs *Special study options:* academic remediation for entering students, adult/continuing education programs, advanced placement credit, cooperative education, distance learning, double majors, English as a second language, honors programs, independent study, internships, off-campus study, part-time degree program, services for LD students, study abroad, summer session for credit.

Library William D. McIntyre Library plus 1 other with 703,340 titles, 3,376 serial subscriptions, 12,052 audiovisual materials, an OPAC, a Web page.

Computers on Campus 925 computers available on campus for general student use. A campuswide network can be accessed from student residence rooms and from off campus. Internet access, online (class) registration, at least one staffed computer lab available.

Student Life *Housing:* on-campus residence required for freshman year. *Options:* coed, men-only, women-only. *Activities and Organizations:* drama/theater group, student-run newspaper, radio and television station, choral group, marching band, American Marketing Association, Beta Upsilon Sigma, International Greek Association, Student Information Management Society, Hobnailers, national fraternities, national sororities. *Campus security:* 24-hour emergency response devices and patrols, late-night transport/escort service, controlled dormitory access. *Student Services:* health clinic, personal/psychological counseling, legal services.

Athletics Member NCAA. All Division III. *Intercollegiate sports:* basketball M/W, cross-country running M/W, football M, golf M/W, gymnastics W, ice hockey M/W, soccer W, softball W, swimming M/W, tennis M/W, track and field M/W, volleyball W, wrestling M. *Intramural sports:* badminton M/W, baseball M, basketball M/W, bowling M/W, football M/W, golf M/W, ice hockey M/W, racquetball M/W, rugby M/W, skiing (cross-country) M/W, skiing (downhill) M/W, soccer M/W, softball M/W, swimming M/W, table tennis M/W, tennis M/W, volleyball M/W, water polo M, weight lifting M/W.

Standardized Tests *Required:* SAT I or ACT (for admission).

Costs (2001–02) *Tuition:* state resident $3472 full-time, $145 per credit part-time; nonresident $12,112 full-time, $507 per credit part-time. Full-time tuition and fees vary according to reciprocity agreements. Part-time tuition and fees vary according to reciprocity agreements. *Room and board:* $3560; room only: $2150. Room and board charges vary according to board plan. *Payment plan:* installment. *Waivers:* minority students and senior citizens.

Financial Aid Of all full-time matriculated undergraduates who enrolled in 2001, 5639 applied for aid, 3626 were judged to have need, 2834 had their need fully met. 1701 Federal Work-Study jobs (averaging $1515). 2236 State and other part-time jobs (averaging $1060). In 2001, 811 non-need-based awards were made. *Average percent of need met:* 79%. *Average financial aid package:* $5596. *Average need-based loan:* $3259. *Average need-based gift aid:* $3568. *Average non-need based aid:* $1689. *Average indebtedness upon graduation:* $14,536.

Applying *Options:* electronic application, early admission. *Application fee:* $35. *Required:* high school transcript, rank in upper 50% of high school class. *Application deadlines:* rolling (freshmen), 7/1 (transfers). *Notification:* continuous (freshmen).

Admissions Contact Mr. Robert Lopez, Director of Admissions, University of Wisconsin-Eau Claire, PO Box 4004, Eau Claire, WI 54702-4004. *Phone:* 715-836-5415. *E-mail:* ask-uwec@uwec.edu.

UNIVERSITY OF WISCONSIN-GREEN BAY
Green Bay, Wisconsin

- **State-supported** comprehensive, founded 1968, part of University of Wisconsin System
- **Calendar** semesters
- **Degrees** associate, bachelor's, master's, and postbachelor's certificates
- **Suburban** 700-acre campus
- **Endowment** $7.7 million
- **Coed,** 5,383 undergraduate students, 80% full-time, 66% women, 34% men
- **Moderately difficult** entrance level, 80% of applicants were admitted

Undergraduates 4,327 full-time, 1,056 part-time. Students come from 29 states and territories, 32 other countries, 5% are from out of state, 0.7% African American, 2% Asian American or Pacific Islander, 0.6% Hispanic American, 2% Native American, 1% international, 9% transferred in, 30% live on campus. *Retention:* 74% of 2001 full-time freshmen returned.

Freshmen *Admission:* 2,405 applied, 1,930 admitted, 909 enrolled. *Average high school GPA:* 3.33. *Test scores:* ACT scores over 18: 93%; ACT scores over 24: 40%; ACT scores over 30: 2%.

Faculty *Total:* 279, 61% full-time, 58% with terminal degrees. *Student/faculty ratio:* 23:1.

Majors Accounting; art; biology; business administration; chemistry; communications; computer science; developmental/child psychology; earth sciences; economics; elementary education; English; environmental science; French; general studies; German; history; humanities; information sciences/systems; interdisciplinary studies; mathematics; music; nursing science; nutritional sciences; philosophy; political science; pre-dentistry; psychology; public administration; social work; Spanish; theater arts/drama; urban studies.

Academic Programs *Special study options:* academic remediation for entering students, accelerated degree program, adult/continuing education programs, advanced placement credit, cooperative education, distance learning, double majors, English as a second language, external degree program, independent study, internships, off-campus study, part-time degree program, services for LD students, student-designed majors, study abroad, summer session for credit. *ROTC:* Army (b).

Library Cofrin Library with 259,941 titles, 8,012 serial subscriptions, 45,396 audiovisual materials, an OPAC, a Web page.

Computers on Campus 550 computers available on campus for general student use. A campuswide network can be accessed from student residence rooms and from off campus that provide access to on-line degree progress. Internet access, online (class) registration, at least one staffed computer lab available.

Student Life *Housing Options:* coed. *Activities and Organizations:* drama/theater group, student-run newspaper, choral group, marching band, Good Times, Concerned, Ambassadors, SUFAC, 4th Estate, national fraternities, national sororities. *Campus security:* 24-hour emergency response devices and patrols, late-night transport/escort service, controlled dormitory access. *Student Services:* health clinic, personal/psychological counseling, legal services.

Athletics Member NCAA. All Division I. *Intercollegiate sports:* basketball M(s)/W(s), cross-country running M(s)/W(s), skiing (cross-country) M(s)/W(s), soccer M(s)/W(s), softball W(s), swimming M(s)/W(s), tennis M(s)/W(s), volleyball W(s). *Intramural sports:* basketball M/W, football M/W, racquetball M/W, sailing M/W, skiing (cross-country) M/W, soccer M/W, softball M/W, swimming M/W, tennis M/W, volleyball M/W, weight lifting M/W.

Standardized Tests *Required:* SAT I or ACT (for admission).

Costs (2001–02) *Tuition:* state resident $2776 full-time, $116 per credit part-time; nonresident $11,034 full-time, $460 per credit part-time. *Required fees:* $872 full-time, $21 per credit. *Room and board:* room only: $2200. Room and board charges vary according to board plan and housing facility. *Payment plan:* installment.

Financial Aid Of all full-time matriculated undergraduates who enrolled in 2001, 2762 applied for aid, 1938 were judged to have need, 1129 had their need fully met. In 2001, 817 non-need-based awards were made. *Average percent of need met:* 93%. *Average financial aid package:* $5913. *Average need-based loan:* $3754. *Average need-based gift aid:* $4222. *Average indebtedness upon graduation:* $12,591.

Applying *Options:* electronic application, deferred entrance. *Application fee:* $35. *Required:* essay or personal statement, high school transcript, rank in upper 45% of high school class. *Required for some:* letters of recommendation, interview. *Application deadlines:* 2/1 (freshmen), 4/15 (transfers). *Notification:* continuous until 8/15 (freshmen).

Admissions Contact Ms. Pam Harvey-Jacobs, Interim Director of Admissions, University of Wisconsin-Green Bay, 2420 Nicolet Drive, Green Bay, WI 54311-7001. *Phone:* 920-465-2111. *Toll-free phone:* 888-367-8942. *Fax:* 920-465-5754. *E-mail:* admissns@uwgb.edu.

UNIVERSITY OF WISCONSIN-LA CROSSE

La Crosse, Wisconsin

- **State-supported** comprehensive, founded 1909, part of University of Wisconsin System
- **Calendar** semesters
- **Degrees** associate, bachelor's, and master's
- **Suburban** 121-acre campus
- **Endowment** $13.0 million
- **Coed,** 8,486 undergraduate students, 93% full-time, 58% women, 42% men
- **Moderately difficult** entrance level, 69% of applicants were admitted

Undergraduates 7,866 full-time, 620 part-time. Students come from 33 states and territories, 43 other countries, 17% are from out of state, 0.9% African American, 2% Asian American or Pacific Islander, 1% Hispanic American, 0.6% Native American, 0.6% international, 4% transferred in, 32% live on campus. *Retention:* 85% of 2001 full-time freshmen returned.

Freshmen *Admission:* 5,028 applied, 3,457 admitted, 1,604 enrolled. *Test scores:* ACT scores over 18: 99%; ACT scores over 24: 57%; ACT scores over 30: 4%.

Faculty *Total:* 491, 80% full-time, 68% with terminal degrees. *Student/faculty ratio:* 21:1.

Majors Accounting; archaeology; art; art education; athletic training/sports medicine; biology; business administration; business marketing and marketing management; chemistry; communications; computer science; early childhood education; economics; education; elementary education; English; exercise sciences; finance; French; geography; German; health education; history; international business; liberal arts and sciences/liberal studies; management information systems/business data processing; mathematics; medical microbiology; medical technology; microbiology/bacteriology; music; music teacher education; nuclear medical technology; occupational therapy; philosophy; physical education; physician assistant; physics; political science; psychology; public administration; public health education/promotion; recreational therapy; recreation/leisure facilities management; science education; secondary education; social studies education; sociology; Spanish; speech/rhetorical studies; sport/fitness administration; theater arts/drama.

Academic Programs *Special study options:* academic remediation for entering students, adult/continuing education programs, advanced placement credit, distance learning, double majors, English as a second language, freshman honors college, honors programs, internships, off-campus study, part-time degree program, services for LD students, study abroad, summer session for credit. *ROTC:* Army (b). *Unusual degree programs:* 3-2 engineering with University of Wisconsin-Madison, University of Wisconsin-Milwaukee.

Library Murphy Library with 650,332 titles, 5,705 serial subscriptions, 1,235 audiovisual materials, an OPAC, a Web page.

Computers on Campus 560 computers available on campus for general student use. A campuswide network can be accessed from student residence rooms and from off campus. At least one staffed computer lab available.

Student Life *Housing:* on-campus residence required for freshman year. *Options:* coed, women-only. *Activities and Organizations:* drama/theater group, student-run newspaper, radio station, choral group, marching band, Greek Organization Council, Sports and Activities Club, Residential Hall Council, national fraternities, national sororities. *Campus security:* 24-hour emergency response devices and patrols, late-night transport/escort service, controlled dormitory access. *Student Services:* health clinic, personal/psychological counseling, women's center, legal services.

Athletics Member NCAA. All Division III. *Intercollegiate sports:* baseball M, basketball M/W, cross-country running M/W, football M, gymnastics W, soccer W, softball W, swimming M/W, tennis M/W, track and field M/W, volleyball W, wrestling M. *Intramural sports:* basketball M/W, bowling M/W, football M/W, golf M/W, lacrosse M, racquetball M/W, rugby M/W, sailing M/W, skiing (downhill) M/W, soccer M, softball M/W, tennis M/W, volleyball M/W, weight lifting M/W.

Standardized Tests *Required:* SAT I or ACT (for admission).

Costs (2002–03) *Tuition:* state resident $3777 full-time, $124 per credit part-time; nonresident $12,885 full-time, $503 per credit part-time. Full-time tuition and fees vary according to program and reciprocity agreements. Part-time tuition and fees vary according to course load, program, and reciprocity agreements. *Required fees:* $36 per credit hour. *Room and board:* $3766; room only: $2033. *Payment plan:* installment. *Waivers:* minority students.

Financial Aid Of all full-time matriculated undergraduates who enrolled in 2001, 5855 applied for aid, 4420 were judged to have need, 4112 had their need fully met. 456 Federal Work-Study jobs (averaging $1234). 1002 State and other part-time jobs (averaging $1542). In 2001, 412 non-need-based awards were made. *Average percent of need met:* 93%. *Average financial aid package:* $5493. *Average need-based loan:* $3295. *Average need-based gift aid:* $1845. *Average non-need based aid:* $745. *Average indebtedness upon graduation:* $14,450.

Applying *Options:* electronic application, early admission, deferred entrance. *Application fee:* $35. *Required:* high school transcript. *Required for some:* interview. *Recommended:* essay or personal statement. *Application deadline:* rolling (freshmen), rolling (transfers). *Notification:* continuous (freshmen).

Admissions Contact Mr. Tim Lewis, Director of Admissions, University of Wisconsin-La Crosse, 1725 State Street, LaCrosse, WI 54601. *Phone:* 608-785-8939. *Fax:* 608-785-8940. *E-mail:* admissions@uwlax.edu.

UNIVERSITY OF WISCONSIN-MADISON

Madison, Wisconsin

- **State-supported** university, founded 1848, part of University of Wisconsin System
- **Calendar** semesters
- **Degrees** bachelor's, master's, doctoral, and first professional
- **Urban** 1050-acre campus
- **Endowment** $650.8 million
- **Coed,** 28,788 undergraduate students
- **Very difficult** entrance level, 57% of applicants were admitted

Undergraduates Students come from 52 states and territories, 116 other countries, 39% are from out of state, 2% African American, 4% Asian American or Pacific Islander, 2% Hispanic American, 0.5% Native American, 4% international. *Retention:* 96% of 2001 full-time freshmen returned.

Freshmen *Admission:* 20,330 applied, 11,500 admitted. *Average high school GPA:* 3.80. *Test scores:* SAT verbal scores over 500: 96%; SAT math scores over 500: 97%; ACT scores over 18: 100%; SAT verbal scores over 600: 69%; SAT math scores over 600: 76%; ACT scores over 24: 86%; SAT verbal scores over 700: 25%; SAT math scores over 700: 23%; ACT scores over 30: 35%.

Faculty *Total:* 2,219. *Student/faculty ratio:* 14:1.

Majors Accounting; actuarial science; advertising; African-American studies; African languages; African studies; agricultural business; agricultural economics; agricultural education; agricultural engineering; agricultural sciences; agronomy/crop science; American studies; animal sciences; anthropology; applied art; applied mathematics; art; art education; art history; Asian studies; astronomy; biochemistry; bioengineering; biology; botany; broadcast journalism; business administration; cartography; cell biology; chemical engineering; chemistry; child care/development; Chinese; civil engineering; classics; clothing/textiles; comparative literature; computer engineering; computer science; construction management; consumer services; dairy science; developmental/child psychology; dietetics; early childhood education; earth sciences; economics; electrical engineering; elementary education; engineering; engineering mechanics; engineering physics; English; entomology; environmental engineering; experimental psychology; family/consumer studies; farm/ranch management; fashion merchandising; finance; food sciences; forestry; French; genetics; geography; geology; geophysics/seismology; German; Greek (modern); Hebrew; Hispanic-American studies; history; history of science and technology; home economics; home economics education; horticulture science; industrial/manufacturing engineering; insurance/risk management; interior design; international relations; Italian; Japanese; journalism; labor/personnel relations; landscape architecture; Latin American studies; Latin (ancient and medieval); linguistics; mass communications; mathematical statistics; mathematics; mechanical engineering; medical technology; metallurgical engineering; microbiology/bacteriology; mining/mineral engineering; molecular biology; music; music teacher education; natural resources management; nuclear engineering; nursing; nutrition science; occupational therapy; pharmacology; pharmacy; philosophy; physical education; physician assistant; physics; political science; Portuguese; poultry science; psychology; public relations; radio/television broadcasting; real estate; recreation/leisure studies; Russian; Scandinavian languages; science education; secondary education; Slavic languages; social sciences; social work; sociology; Southeast Asian studies; Spanish; special education; speech therapy; surveying; theater arts/drama; toxicology; urban studies; water resources; wildlife management; women's studies; zoology.

Academic Programs *Special study options:* accelerated degree program, adult/continuing education programs, advanced placement credit, cooperative education, distance learning, double majors, English as a second language, external degree program, freshman honors college, honors programs, independent study, internships, part-time degree program, services for LD students, student-designed majors, study abroad, summer session for credit. *ROTC:* Army (b), Navy (b), Air Force (b).

University of Wisconsin-Madison (continued)

Library Memorial Library plus 40 others with 6.1 million titles, 66,000 serial subscriptions, an OPAC, a Web page.

Computers on Campus 2800 computers available on campus for general student use. A campuswide network can be accessed from student residence rooms and from off campus. Internet access, at least one staffed computer lab available.

Student Life *Housing Options:* coed, men-only, women-only, cooperative, disabled students. *Activities and Organizations:* drama/theater group, student-run newspaper, radio station, choral group, marching band, national fraternities, national sororities. *Campus security:* 24-hour emergency response devices and patrols, late-night transport/escort service, controlled dormitory access, free cab rides throughout city. *Student Services:* health clinic, personal/psychological counseling, women's center, legal services.

Athletics Member NCAA. All Division I except football (Division I-A). *Intercollegiate sports:* basketball M(s)/W(s), crew M(s)/W(s), cross-country running M(s)/W(s), golf M(s)/W(s), ice hockey M(s)/W(s), lacrosse W(s), rugby M(c), sailing M(c)/W(c), soccer M(s)/W(s), softball W(s), swimming M(s)/W(s), tennis M(s)/W(s), track and field M(s)/W(s), volleyball W(s), wrestling M(s). *Intramural sports:* archery M/W, badminton M/W, basketball M/W, bowling M/W, crew M/W, equestrian sports M/W, fencing M/W, football M, golf M/W, gymnastics M/W, ice hockey M/W, lacrosse M/W, racquetball M/W, riflery M/W, rugby M/W, sailing M/W, skiing (cross-country) M/W, skiing (downhill) M/W, soccer M/W, softball M/W, squash M/W, swimming M/W, table tennis M/W, tennis M/W, track and field M/W, volleyball M/W, water polo M/W, wrestling M.

Standardized Tests *Required:* SAT I or ACT (for admission). *Required for some:* SAT II: Subject Tests (for admission). *Recommended:* SAT II: Subject Tests (for admission).

Costs (2001–02) *Tuition:* state resident $4086 full-time, $1075 per term part-time; nonresident $15,972 full-time, $4295 per term part-time. Full-time tuition and fees vary according to reciprocity agreements. Part-time tuition and fees vary according to course load and reciprocity agreements. *Room and board:* $5700. Room and board charges vary according to board plan.

Financial Aid Of all full-time matriculated undergraduates who enrolled in 2001, 13120 applied for aid, 7812 were judged to have need, 1650 had their need fully met. 2432 Federal Work-Study jobs (averaging $1922). In 2001, 3706 non-need-based awards were made. *Average financial aid package:* $7926. *Average need-based loan:* $3926. *Average need-based gift aid:* $4924. *Average non-need based aid:* $2360. *Average indebtedness upon graduation:* $15,140.

Applying *Options:* electronic application, early admission, deferred entrance. *Application fee:* $35. *Required:* essay or personal statement, high school transcript. *Application deadlines:* 2/1 (freshmen), 2/1 (transfers). *Notification:* continuous (freshmen).

Admissions Contact Mr. Keith White, Office of Admissions, University of Wisconsin-Madison, 716 Langdon Street, Madison, WI 53706-1400. *Phone:* 608-262-3961. *Fax:* 608-262-7706. *E-mail:* on.wisconsin@mail.admin.wisc.edu.

UNIVERSITY OF WISCONSIN-MILWAUKEE

Milwaukee, Wisconsin

- **State-supported** university, founded 1956, part of University of Wisconsin System
- **Calendar** semesters
- **Degrees** certificates, bachelor's, master's, and doctoral
- **Urban** 90-acre campus
- **Coed,** 19,959 undergraduate students, 75% full-time, 55% women, 45% men
- **Moderately difficult** entrance level, 79% of applicants were admitted

Undergraduates 15,034 full-time, 4,925 part-time. Students come from 53 states and territories, 3% are from out of state, 9% African American, 4% Asian American or Pacific Islander, 4% Hispanic American, 0.9% Native American, 1% international, 9% transferred in, 13% live on campus. *Retention:* 76% of 2001 full-time freshmen returned.

Freshmen *Admission:* 7,340 applied, 5,771 admitted, 3,016 enrolled. *Average high school GPA:* 2.84. *Test scores:* SAT verbal scores over 500: 62%; SAT math scores over 500: 71%; ACT scores over 18: 88%; SAT verbal scores over 600: 20%; SAT math scores over 600: 29%; ACT scores over 24: 33%; SAT verbal scores over 700: 1%; SAT math scores over 700: 4%; ACT scores over 30: 3%.

Faculty *Total:* 1,333, 59% full-time. *Student/faculty ratio:* 19:1.

Majors Accounting; African-American studies; anthropology; applied mathematics; architecture; art; art education; art history; atmospheric sciences; bilingual/bicultural education; biochemistry; biology; broadcast journalism; business administration; business marketing and marketing management; ceramic arts; chemistry; civil engineering; classics; comparative literature; computer science; criminal justice/law enforcement administration; cultural studies; dance; early childhood education; earth sciences; ecology; economics; education; electrical engineering; elementary education; engineering; English; film studies; finance; fine/studio arts; forestry; French; geography; geology; German; Greek (modern); health science; health services administration; Hebrew; history; human resources management; industrial/manufacturing engineering; interdisciplinary studies; international relations; Italian; journalism; labor/personnel relations; Latin American studies; Latin (ancient and medieval); law enforcement/police science; linguistics; literature; management information systems/business data processing; mass communications; materials engineering; mathematical statistics; mathematics; mechanical engineering; medical records administration; medical technology; metal/jewelry arts; music; music history; music teacher education; music therapy; music (voice and choral/opera performance); Native American studies; natural resources conservation; nursing; occupational therapy; peace/conflict studies; philosophy; physical therapy; physics; political science; pre-dentistry; pre-law; pre-medicine; psychology; real estate; recreational therapy; recreation/leisure studies; religious studies; Russian; Russian/Slavic studies; sculpture; secondary education; Slavic languages; social work; sociology; Spanish; special education; speech-language pathology/audiology; stringed instruments; textile arts; theater arts/drama; urban studies; wind/percussion instruments; women's studies; zoology.

Academic Programs *Special study options:* academic remediation for entering students, adult/continuing education programs, advanced placement credit, cooperative education, distance learning, double majors, English as a second language, honors programs, independent study, internships, off-campus study, part-time degree program, services for LD students, student-designed majors, study abroad, summer session for credit.

Library Golda Meir Library with 1.3 million titles, 9,986 serial subscriptions, 31,501 audiovisual materials, an OPAC, a Web page.

Computers on Campus 310 computers available on campus for general student use. A campuswide network can be accessed from off campus. At least one staffed computer lab available.

Student Life *Housing Options:* coed. *Activities and Organizations:* drama/theater group, student-run newspaper, radio station, choral group, national fraternities, national sororities. *Campus security:* 24-hour emergency response devices, late-night transport/escort service. *Student Services:* health clinic, personal/psychological counseling, women's center, legal services.

Athletics Member NCAA. All Division I. *Intercollegiate sports:* baseball M, basketball M(s)/W(s), cross-country running M(s)/W(s), soccer M(s)/W(s), swimming M(s)/W(s), tennis M(s)/W(s), track and field M(s)/W(s), volleyball M/W(s). *Intramural sports:* badminton M/W, basketball M/W, bowling M(c)/W(c), fencing M(c)/W(c), field hockey M/W, football M, golf M/W, racquetball M/W, riflery M(c)/W(c), rugby M(c)/W(c), sailing M(c)/W(c), skiing (downhill) M(c)/W(c), soccer M/W, swimming M/W, tennis M/W, volleyball M/W, water polo M/W, weight lifting M/W, wrestling M.

Standardized Tests *Required:* SAT I or ACT (for admission).

Costs (2001–02) *Tuition:* state resident $4057 full-time, $144 per credit part-time; nonresident $15,028 full-time, $595 per credit part-time. Full-time tuition and fees vary according to location, program, and reciprocity agreements. Part-time tuition and fees vary according to course load, location, program, and reciprocity agreements. *Room and board:* room only: $2700. Room and board charges vary according to board plan. *Payment plan:* installment.

Financial Aid Of all full-time matriculated undergraduates who enrolled in 2001, 8377 applied for aid, 6217 were judged to have need, 2854 had their need fully met. In 2001, 1702 non-need-based awards were made. *Average percent of need met:* 74%. *Average financial aid package:* $6669. *Average need-based loan:* $3506. *Average need-based gift aid:* $3819. *Average indebtedness upon graduation:* $15,452.

Applying *Options:* deferred entrance. *Application fee:* $35. *Required:* high school transcript. *Application deadline:* rolling (freshmen), rolling (transfers). *Notification:* continuous (freshmen).

Admissions Contact Ms. Jan Ford, Director, Recruitment and Outreach, University of Wisconsin-Milwaukee, PO Box 749, Milwaukee, WI 53201. *Phone:* 414-229-4397. *Fax:* 414-229-6940. *E-mail:* uwmlook@des.uwm.edu.

UNIVERSITY OF WISCONSIN-OSHKOSH

Oshkosh, Wisconsin

- **State-supported** comprehensive, founded 1871, part of University of Wisconsin System
- **Calendar** semesters
- **Degrees** associate, bachelor's, and master's
- **Suburban** 192-acre campus with easy access to Milwaukee
- **Endowment** $350,000
- **Coed,** 9,414 undergraduate students, 86% full-time, 59% women, 41% men

■ **Moderately difficult** entrance level, 82% of applicants were admitted

Undergraduates 8,120 full-time, 1,294 part-time. Students come from 30 states and territories, 32 other countries, 4% are from out of state, 1.0% African American, 2% Asian American or Pacific Islander, 1% Hispanic American, 0.6% Native American, 0.9% international, 8% transferred in, 34% live on campus. *Retention:* 71% of 2001 full-time freshmen returned.

Freshmen *Admission:* 4,300 applied, 3,534 admitted, 1,863 enrolled. *Test scores:* ACT scores over 18: 92%; ACT scores over 24: 28%; ACT scores over 30: 2%.

Faculty *Total:* 593, 61% full-time, 71% with terminal degrees. *Student/faculty ratio:* 15:1.

Majors Accounting; anthropology; art; art education; biology; broadcast journalism; business administration; business marketing and marketing management; chemistry; computer science; criminal justice/law enforcement administration; early childhood education; economics; education; elementary education; English; finance; fine/studio arts; French; geography; geology; German; history; human services; international relations; journalism; liberal arts and sciences/liberal studies; management information systems/business data processing; mass communications; mathematics; medical technology; microbiology/bacteriology; music; music teacher education; music therapy; nursing; philosophy; physical education; physics; political science; pre-dentistry; pre-law; pre-medicine; pre-veterinary studies; psychology; radio/television broadcasting; religious studies; secondary education; social work; sociology; Spanish; special education; speech-language pathology/audiology; teaching English as a second language; theater arts/drama; urban studies.

Academic Programs *Special study options:* academic remediation for entering students, accelerated degree program, adult/continuing education programs, advanced placement credit, cooperative education, distance learning, double majors, English as a second language, honors programs, independent study, internships, part-time degree program, services for LD students, student-designed majors, study abroad, summer session for credit. *ROTC:* Army (b).

Library Forrest R. Polk Library with 446,774 titles, 5,219 serial subscriptions, 9,102 audiovisual materials, an OPAC, a Web page.

Computers on Campus 475 computers available on campus for general student use. A campuswide network can be accessed from student residence rooms and from off campus. Internet access, online (class) registration, at least one staffed computer lab available.

Student Life *Housing:* on-campus residence required through sophomore year. *Options:* coed, women-only. *Activities and Organizations:* drama/theater group, student-run newspaper, radio station, choral group, USRH, Model UN, Pi Sigma Epsilon, Panhellenic, Human Services Organization, national fraternities, national sororities. *Campus security:* 24-hour emergency response devices and patrols, student patrols, late-night transport/escort service, controlled dormitory access. *Student Services:* health clinic, personal/psychological counseling, women's center, legal services.

Athletics Member NCAA. All Division III. *Intercollegiate sports:* baseball M, basketball M/W, cross-country running M/W, football M, golf W, gymnastics W, riflery M/W, soccer M/W, softball W, swimming M/W, tennis M/W, track and field M/W, volleyball W, wrestling M. *Intramural sports:* basketball M/W, bowling M(c)/W(c), cross-country running M/W, football M/W, golf M/W, gymnastics M(c), ice hockey M(c), lacrosse M(c)/W(c), racquetball M/W, skiing (downhill) M/W, soccer M/W, softball M/W, tennis M/W, volleyball M(c)/W, wrestling M.

Costs (2001–02) *Tuition:* state resident $3228 full-time, $136 per credit part-time; nonresident $11,740 full-time, $501 per credit part-time. Full-time tuition and fees vary according to reciprocity agreements. Part-time tuition and fees vary according to reciprocity agreements. *Room and board:* $3816. Room and board charges vary according to housing facility. *Payment plan:* installment.

Applying *Options:* electronic application, deferred entrance. *Application fee:* $35. *Required:* high school transcript, rank in upper 50% of high school class or ACT composite score of 23 or above. *Recommended:* essay or personal statement. *Application deadlines:* 8/1 (freshmen), 8/1 (transfers). *Notification:* continuous (freshmen).

Admissions Contact Mr. Richard Hillman, Associate Director of Admissions, University of Wisconsin-Oshkosh, Oshkosh, WI 54901-8602. *Phone:* 920-424-0202. *Fax:* 920-424-1098. *E-mail:* oshadmuw@uwosh.edu.

UNIVERSITY OF WISCONSIN-PARKSIDE
Kenosha, Wisconsin

■ **State-supported** comprehensive, founded 1968, part of University of Wisconsin System
■ **Calendar** semesters
■ **Degrees** certificates, bachelor's, and master's
■ **Suburban** 700-acre campus with easy access to Chicago and Milwaukee
■ **Coed**, 4,934 undergraduate students, 69% full-time, 59% women, 41% men
■ **Moderately difficult** entrance level, 76% of applicants were admitted

Undergraduates 3,398 full-time, 1,536 part-time. Students come from 21 states and territories, 21 other countries, 12% are from out of state, 9% African American, 2% Asian American or Pacific Islander, 7% Hispanic American, 0.7% Native American, 2% international, 7% transferred in, 18% live on campus. *Retention:* 61% of 2001 full-time freshmen returned.

Freshmen *Admission:* 1,966 applied, 1,492 admitted, 929 enrolled. *Test scores:* ACT scores over 18: 75%; ACT scores over 24: 17%; ACT scores over 30: 1%.

Faculty *Total:* 187, 98% full-time, 76% with terminal degrees. *Student/faculty ratio:* 20:1.

Majors Accounting; art; biological sciences/life sciences related; business administration; chemistry; communications; computer science; creative writing; criminal justice/law enforcement administration; economics; English; finance; French; geography; geology; German; history; humanities; interdisciplinary studies; international relations; mathematics; molecular biology; music; nursing; philosophy; physics; political science; pre-dentistry; pre-law; pre-medicine; pre-pharmacy studies; pre-veterinary studies; psychology; sociology; Spanish; sport/fitness administration; theater arts/drama.

Academic Programs *Special study options:* academic remediation for entering students, accelerated degree program, adult/continuing education programs, advanced placement credit, distance learning, double majors, English as a second language, external degree program, honors programs, independent study, internships, off-campus study, part-time degree program, services for LD students, summer session for credit. *ROTC:* Army (c). *Unusual degree programs:* 3-2 molecular biology.

Library Library-Learning Center with 265,110 titles, 4,096 serial subscriptions, 18,007 audiovisual materials, an OPAC, a Web page.

Computers on Campus 180 computers available on campus for general student use. A campuswide network can be accessed from student residence rooms and from off campus. At least one staffed computer lab available.

Student Life *Housing Options:* coed, disabled students. *Activities and Organizations:* drama/theater group, student-run newspaper, radio station, choral group, Black Student Union, Latinos Unidos, Parkside Student Government Association, Asian American Club, Parkside Adult Student Alliance, national fraternities, national sororities. *Campus security:* 24-hour emergency response devices and patrols, late-night transport/escort service, controlled dormitory access. *Student Services:* health clinic, personal/psychological counseling, women's center.

Athletics Member NCAA, NAIA. All NCAA Division II. *Intercollegiate sports:* baseball M(s), basketball M(s)/W(s), cross-country running M(s)/W(s), golf M(s), soccer M(s)/W(s), softball W(s), track and field M(s)/W(s), volleyball W(s), wrestling M(s). *Intramural sports:* badminton M/W, basketball M/W, bowling M(c)/W(c), football M/W, racquetball M/W, rugby M(c), soccer M/W, softball M/W, swimming M/W, table tennis M/W, tennis M/W, volleyball M/W.

Standardized Tests *Required for some:* SAT I or ACT (for admission).

Costs (2001–02) *Tuition:* state resident $3298 full-time, $154 per credit part-time; nonresident $12,066 full-time, $519 per credit part-time. Full-time tuition and fees vary according to course load and reciprocity agreements. Part-time tuition and fees vary according to course load. *Room and board:* $4960; room only: $3060. Room and board charges vary according to board plan and housing facility. *Payment plan:* installment. *Waivers:* senior citizens.

Financial Aid Of all full-time matriculated undergraduates who enrolled in 2001, 2486 applied for aid, 1822 were judged to have need, 733 had their need fully met. In 2001, 121 non-need-based awards were made. *Average percent of need met:* 79%. *Average financial aid package:* $6063. *Average need-based loan:* $3367. *Average need-based gift aid:* $4113. *Average non-need based aid:* $2048. *Average indebtedness upon graduation:* $12,500.

Applying *Options:* electronic application, deferred entrance. *Application fee:* $35. *Required:* high school transcript, mnimum of 17 high school units distributed as specified in the UW-Parkside catalog. *Application deadlines:* 8/1 (freshmen), 8/1 (transfers). *Notification:* continuous (freshmen).

Admissions Contact Mr. Matthew Jensen, Director of Admissions, University of Wisconsin-Parkside, 900 Wood Road, PO Box 2000, Kenosha, WI 53141-2000. *Phone:* 262-595-2757. *Toll-free phone:* 877-633-3897. *Fax:* 262-595-2008. *E-mail:* matthew.jensen@uwp.edu.

UNIVERSITY OF WISCONSIN-PLATTEVILLE
Platteville, Wisconsin

■ **State-supported** comprehensive, founded 1866, part of University of Wisconsin System
■ **Calendar** semesters
■ **Degrees** certificates, associate, bachelor's, and master's

University of Wisconsin-Platteville (continued)

- **Small-town** 380-acre campus
- **Endowment** $3.0 million
- **Coed,** 5,154 undergraduate students, 91% full-time, 39% women, 61% men
- **Moderately difficult** entrance level, 45% of applicants were admitted

Undergraduates 4,669 full-time, 485 part-time. Students come from 34 states and territories, 47 other countries, 1% are from out of state, 0.9% African American, 0.8% Asian American or Pacific Islander, 0.7% Hispanic American, 0.2% Native American, 0.9% international, 5% transferred in, 55% live on campus. *Retention:* 60% of 2001 full-time freshmen returned.

Freshmen *Admission:* 2,459 applied, 1,118 admitted, 1,511 enrolled. *Test scores:* ACT scores over 18: 95%; ACT scores over 24: 39%; ACT scores over 30: 3%.

Faculty *Total:* 347, 75% full-time, 60% with terminal degrees. *Student/faculty ratio:* 22:1.

Majors Accounting; agricultural business; agronomy/crop science; animal sciences; art; biological/physical sciences; biology; broadcast journalism; business administration; business economics; cartography; civil engineering; computer science; construction management; criminal justice/law enforcement administration; early childhood education; economics; education; electrical engineering; elementary education; English; French; geography; geology; German; graphic design/commercial art/illustration; history; industrial arts; industrial design; industrial/manufacturing engineering; industrial technology; international relations; land use management; liberal arts and sciences/liberal studies; mass communications; mathematics; mechanical engineering; middle school education; music; philosophy; political science; psychology; science education; secondary education; social sciences; Spanish; speech/rhetorical studies; telecommunications.

Academic Programs *Special study options:* academic remediation for entering students, accelerated degree program, adult/continuing education programs, advanced placement credit, cooperative education, English as a second language, external degree program, honors programs, internships, off-campus study, part-time degree program, services for LD students, student-designed majors, study abroad, summer session for credit.

Library Karrmann Library with 257,566 titles, 1,499 serial subscriptions, an OPAC, a Web page.

Computers on Campus 250 computers available on campus for general student use. A campuswide network can be accessed from student residence rooms and from off campus. Internet access, at least one staffed computer lab available.

Student Life *Housing:* on-campus residence required through sophomore year. *Options:* coed, men-only, women-only. *Activities and Organizations:* drama/theater group, student-run newspaper, radio station, choral group, marching band, national fraternities, national sororities. *Campus security:* 24-hour emergency response devices and patrols, student patrols, late-night transport/escort service. *Student Services:* health clinic, personal/psychological counseling, women's center.

Athletics Member NCAA. All Division III. *Intercollegiate sports:* baseball M, basketball M/W, cross-country running M/W, football M, golf M, ice hockey M(c), rugby M(c), soccer M/W, softball W, track and field M/W, volleyball M(c)/W, wrestling M. *Intramural sports:* badminton M/W, basketball M/W, bowling M/W, football M, golf M, racquetball M/W, soccer M/W, softball M/W, table tennis M/W, tennis M/W, volleyball M/W, water polo M/W.

Standardized Tests *Required:* SAT I or ACT (for admission). *Recommended:* ACT (for admission).

Costs (2001–02) *Tuition:* state resident $2766 full-time, $151 per credit part-time; nonresident $11,288 full-time, $506 per credit part-time. No tuition increase for student's term of enrollment. *Required fees:* $707 full-time. *Room and board:* $3799; room only: $1915. *Payment plan:* installment.

Financial Aid Of all full-time matriculated undergraduates who enrolled in 2001, 3332 applied for aid, 2469 were judged to have need. 485 Federal Work-Study jobs (averaging $1230). 1132 State and other part-time jobs (averaging $989). *Average percent of need met:* 85%. *Average financial aid package:* $4836. *Average need-based loan:* $2612. *Average need-based gift aid:* $1523. *Average indebtedness upon graduation:* $14,647.

Applying *Options:* electronic application. *Application fee:* $35. *Required:* high school transcript. *Required for some:* letters of recommendation. *Application deadline:* rolling (freshmen), rolling (transfers).

Admissions Contact Dr. Richard Schumacher, Dean of Admissions and Enrollment Management, University of Wisconsin-Platteville, 1 University Plaza, Platteville, WI 53818-3099. *Phone:* 608-342-1125. *Toll-free phone:* 800-362-5515. *E-mail:* admit@uwplatt.edu.

UNIVERSITY OF WISCONSIN-RIVER FALLS
River Falls, Wisconsin

- **State-supported** comprehensive, founded 1874, part of University of Wisconsin System
- **Calendar** semesters
- **Degrees** certificates, bachelor's, and master's
- **Suburban** 225-acre campus with easy access to Minneapolis-St. Paul
- **Coed,** 5,447 undergraduate students, 93% full-time, 61% women, 39% men
- **Moderately difficult** entrance level, 43% of applicants were admitted

Undergraduates Students come from 26 states and territories, 12 other countries, 48% are from out of state, 38% live on campus. *Retention:* 70% of 2001 full-time freshmen returned.

Freshmen *Admission:* 2,733 applied, 1,175 admitted. *Test scores:* ACT scores over 18: 96%; ACT scores over 24: 36%; ACT scores over 30: 3%.

Faculty *Total:* 248. *Student/faculty ratio:* 19:1.

Majors Accounting; agricultural business; agricultural education; agricultural engineering; agricultural sciences; agronomy/crop science; animal sciences; art; art education; biochemistry; biology; biology education; biotechnology research; broadcast journalism; business administration; business marketing and marketing management; chemistry; chemistry education; communication disorders; computer education; computer/information sciences; computer science; dairy science; economics; education; elementary education; engineering technology; English; English education; environmental science; equestrian studies; finance; food sciences; French; French language education; geography; geology; German; German language education; history; history education; horticulture science; information sciences/systems; journalism; land use management; liberal arts and sciences/liberal studies; management information systems/business data processing; mathematics; mathematics education; music; music teacher education; natural resources conservation; natural sciences; physical education; physical sciences; physics; physics education; political science; pre-dentistry; pre-law; pre-medicine; pre-pharmacy studies; pre-veterinary studies; psychology; public relations; radio/television broadcasting; science education; secondary education; social science education; social sciences; social studies education; social work; sociology; soil sciences; Spanish; Spanish language education; speech/rhetorical studies; speech therapy; teaching English as a second language; theater arts/drama.

Academic Programs *Special study options:* academic remediation for entering students, accelerated degree program, adult/continuing education programs, advanced placement credit, cooperative education, distance learning, double majors, external degree program, honors programs, independent study, internships, off-campus study, part-time degree program, services for LD students, student-designed majors, study abroad, summer session for credit. *Unusual degree programs:* 3-2 engineering with University of Wisconsin, Madison and University of Minnesota, Twin Cities.

Library Chalmer Davee Library with 448,088 titles, 1,660 serial subscriptions, 7,500 audiovisual materials, an OPAC, a Web page.

Computers on Campus 387 computers available on campus for general student use. A campuswide network can be accessed from student residence rooms and from off campus. Internet access, online (class) registration, at least one staffed computer lab available.

Student Life *Housing:* on-campus residence required through sophomore year. *Options:* coed, women-only. *Activities and Organizations:* drama/theater group, student-run newspaper, radio and television station, choral group, Bushwackers (High Adventure Club), Habitat for Humanity, Agricultural Education Society, Dairy Club, Rodeo Club, national fraternities, national sororities. *Campus security:* 24-hour emergency response devices and patrols, student patrols, late-night transport/escort service, controlled dormitory access. *Student Services:* health clinic, personal/psychological counseling, women's center.

Athletics Member NCAA. All Division III. *Intercollegiate sports:* baseball M, basketball M/W, cross-country running M/W, equestrian sports M(c)/W(c), football M, gymnastics W, ice hockey M/W, rugby M(c)/W(c), soccer M(c)/W, softball W, swimming M/W, tennis W, track and field M(c)/W, volleyball M(c)/W, weight lifting M(c)/W(c), wrestling M. *Intramural sports:* badminton M/W, basketball M/W, football M/W, golf M/W, softball M/W, tennis M/W, volleyball M/W.

Standardized Tests *Required:* ACT (for admission).

Costs (2001–02) *Tuition:* state resident $3384 full-time, $178 per credit part-time; nonresident $11,896 full-time, $532 per credit part-time. Full-time tuition and fees vary according to course load and reciprocity agreements. Part-time tuition and fees vary according to course load and reciprocity agreements. *Required fees:* $606 full-time. *Room and board:* $3582; room only: $2046. Room and board charges vary according to board plan. *Payment plan:* installment.

Financial Aid Of all full-time matriculated undergraduates who enrolled in 2001, 3631 applied for aid, 2727 were judged to have need, 1240 had their need

fully met. *Average percent of need met:* 77%. *Average financial aid package:* $4429. *Average need-based loan:* $2353. *Average need-based gift aid:* $1652. *Average non-need based aid:* $3738. *Average indebtedness upon graduation:* $12,500.

Applying *Options:* common application, electronic application, deferred entrance. *Application fee:* $35. *Required:* high school transcript. *Recommended:* rank in upper 40% of high school class. *Application deadline:* rolling (freshmen), rolling (transfers). *Notification:* continuous (freshmen).

Admissions Contact Mr. Alan Tuchtenhagen, Director of Admissions, University of Wisconsin-River Falls, 410 South Third Street, 112 South Hall, River Falls, WI 54022-5001. *Phone:* 715-425-3500. *Fax:* 715-425-0676. *E-mail:* admit@uwrf.edu.

UNIVERSITY OF WISCONSIN-STEVENS POINT
Stevens Point, Wisconsin

- **State-supported** comprehensive, founded 1894, part of University of Wisconsin System
- **Calendar** semesters
- **Degrees** associate, bachelor's, and master's
- **Small-town** 335-acre campus
- **Endowment** $9.2 million
- **Coed,** 8,512 undergraduate students, 90% full-time, 57% women, 43% men
- **Moderately difficult** entrance level, 77% of applicants were admitted

Undergraduates 7,697 full-time, 815 part-time. Students come from 35 states and territories, 30 other countries, 6% are from out of state, 0.5% African American, 1% Asian American or Pacific Islander, 0.6% Hispanic American, 0.7% Native American, 2% international, 8% transferred in, 36% live on campus. *Retention:* 78% of 2001 full-time freshmen returned.

Freshmen *Admission:* 4,151 applied, 3,184 admitted, 1,499 enrolled. *Average high school GPA:* 3.40. *Test scores:* SAT verbal scores over 500: 68%; SAT math scores over 500: 74%; ACT scores over 18: 96%; SAT verbal scores over 600: 24%; SAT math scores over 600: 18%; ACT scores over 24: 38%; SAT verbal scores over 700: 5%; ACT scores over 30: 3%.

Faculty *Total:* 430, 83% full-time, 76% with terminal degrees. *Student/faculty ratio:* 20:1.

Majors Accounting; actuarial science; art; arts management; athletic training/sports medicine; biology; business administration; chemistry; communications; computer/information sciences; dance; dietetics; early childhood education; economics; education; elementary education; English; family/consumer studies; fine/studio arts; forestry; French; general studies; geography; German; graphic design/commercial art/illustration; health/physical education; history; home economics education; interior design; international relations; liberal arts and sciences/liberal studies; mathematics; medical technology; music; music teacher education; natural resources conservation; natural resources management; natural sciences; philosophy; physical education; physics; political science; polymer chemistry; psychology; public administration; secondary education; social sciences; sociology; soil conservation; Spanish; speech-language pathology/audiology; theater arts/drama; water resources; wildlife management; wood science/paper technology.

Academic Programs *Special study options:* academic remediation for entering students, accelerated degree program, adult/continuing education programs, advanced placement credit, cooperative education, distance learning, double majors, English as a second language, independent study, internships, off-campus study, part-time degree program, services for LD students, student-designed majors, study abroad, summer session for credit. *ROTC:* Army (b).

Library Learning Resources Center with 362,788 titles, 1,816 serial subscriptions, an OPAC, a Web page.

Computers on Campus 700 computers available on campus for general student use. A campuswide network can be accessed from student residence rooms and from off campus. Internet access, at least one staffed computer lab available.

Student Life *Housing:* on-campus residence required through sophomore year. *Options:* coed, men-only, women-only. *Activities and Organizations:* drama/theater group, student-run newspaper, radio and television station, choral group, marching band, national fraternities, national sororities. *Campus security:* 24-hour emergency response devices and patrols, student patrols, late-night transport/escort service, controlled dormitory access. *Student Services:* health clinic, personal/psychological counseling, women's center, legal services.

Athletics Member NCAA. All Division III. *Intercollegiate sports:* baseball M, basketball M/W, cross-country running M/W, football M, golf W, ice hockey M/W, soccer W, softball W, swimming M/W, tennis W, track and field M/W, volleyball W, wrestling M. *Intramural sports:* badminton M/W, basketball M/W, football M/W, golf M/W, ice hockey M/W, racquetball M/W, soccer M/W, softball M/W, table tennis M/W, tennis M/W, volleyball M/W, wrestling M/W.

Standardized Tests *Required:* SAT I or ACT (for admission).

Costs (2001–02) *Tuition:* state resident $2776 full-time, $116 per credit part-time; nonresident $11,288 full-time, $470 per credit part-time. Full-time tuition and fees vary according to reciprocity agreements. Part-time tuition and fees vary according to course load and reciprocity agreements. *Required fees:* $599 full-time, $54 per credit. *Room and board:* $3738; room only: $2200. Room and board charges vary according to board plan. *Payment plan:* deferred payment.

Financial Aid Of all full-time matriculated undergraduates who enrolled in 2001, 6633 applied for aid, 3546 were judged to have need, 2623 had their need fully met. In 2001, 529 non-need-based awards were made. *Average percent of need met:* 89%. *Average financial aid package:* $5598. *Average need-based loan:* $3398. *Average need-based gift aid:* $3807. *Average non-need based aid:* $1364. *Average indebtedness upon graduation:* $13,062.

Applying *Options:* deferred entrance. *Application fee:* $35. *Required:* high school transcript. *Recommended:* campus visit. *Application deadline:* rolling (freshmen), rolling (transfers). *Notification:* continuous (freshmen).

Admissions Contact Dr. David Eckholm, Director of Admissions, University of Wisconsin-Stevens Point, 2100 Main Street, Stevens Point, WI 54481-3897. *Phone:* 715-346-2441. *Fax:* 715-346-3296. *E-mail:* admiss@uwsp.edu.

UNIVERSITY OF WISCONSIN-STOUT
Menomonie, Wisconsin

- **State-supported** comprehensive, founded 1891, part of University of Wisconsin System
- **Calendar** semesters
- **Degrees** bachelor's, master's, and post-master's certificates
- **Small-town** 120-acre campus with easy access to Minneapolis-St. Paul
- **Endowment** $465,954
- **Coed,** 7,258 undergraduate students, 89% full-time, 48% women, 52% men
- **Moderately difficult** entrance level, 71% of applicants were admitted

Undergraduates 6,451 full-time, 807 part-time. Students come from 22 states and territories, 33 other countries, 28% are from out of state, 0.9% African American, 1% Asian American or Pacific Islander, 0.8% Hispanic American, 0.4% Native American, 0.7% international, 8% transferred in, 35% live on campus. *Retention:* 75% of 2001 full-time freshmen returned.

Freshmen *Admission:* 3,162 applied, 2,243 admitted, 1,299 enrolled. *Average high school GPA:* 3.15. *Test scores:* ACT scores over 18: 92%; ACT scores over 24: 28%; ACT scores over 30: 2%.

Faculty *Total:* 395, 79% full-time, 63% with terminal degrees. *Student/faculty ratio:* 20:1.

Majors Applied mathematics; art education; business administration; business administration/management related; business marketing and marketing management; business systems networking/ telecommunications; clothing/apparel/textile studies; construction technology; design/applied arts related; dietetics; early childhood education; engineering/industrial management; foods/nutrition studies related; home economics education; hotel and restaurant management; individual/family development; industrial arts education; industrial/manufacturing engineering; industrial production technologies related; industrial technology; marketing/distribution education; nutrition studies; psychology; science technologies related; technical/business writing; technical education; vocational rehabilitation counseling.

Academic Programs *Special study options:* academic remediation for entering students, accelerated degree program, adult/continuing education programs, advanced placement credit, cooperative education, distance learning, double majors, English as a second language, honors programs, independent study, internships, off-campus study, part-time degree program, services for LD students, study abroad, summer session for credit.

Library Library Learning Center with 219,270 titles, 6,205 serial subscriptions, 16,047 audiovisual materials, an OPAC, a Web page.

Computers on Campus 590 computers available on campus for general student use. A campuswide network can be accessed from student residence rooms and from off campus. Internet access, online (class) registration, at least one staffed computer lab available.

Student Life *Housing:* on-campus residence required through sophomore year. *Options:* coed. *Activities and Organizations:* drama/theater group, student-run newspaper, radio station, choral group, marching band, Hotel/Motel Management Association, Intergreek Council, DECA-District Educational Clubs of America, Recreation Commission, OASIS, national fraternities, national sororities. *Campus security:* 24-hour emergency response devices and patrols, student patrols, late-night transport/escort service. *Student Services:* health clinic, personal/psychological counseling, legal services.

Athletics Member NCAA. All Division III. *Intercollegiate sports:* baseball M, basketball M/W, cross-country running M/W, football M, gymnastics W, ice

University of Wisconsin-Stout (continued)
hockey M/W(c), soccer M(c)/W, softball W, tennis W, track and field M/W, volleyball M(c)/W. *Intramural sports:* baseball M, basketball M/W, bowling M(c)/W(c), football M/W, golf M/W, ice hockey M/W, racquetball M/W, rugby M(c)/W(c), skiing (cross-country) M(c)/W(c), skiing (downhill) M(c)/W(c), softball M/W, volleyball M/W.

Standardized Tests *Required:* SAT I or ACT (for admission).

Costs (2001–02) *Tuition:* state resident $2916 full-time, $122 per credit part-time; nonresident $11,440 full-time, $477 per credit part-time. Full-time tuition and fees vary according to reciprocity agreements. Part-time tuition and fees vary according to reciprocity agreements. *Required fees:* $586 full-time. *Room and board:* $3690; room only: $2036. Room and board charges vary according to board plan. *Payment plan:* installment.

Financial Aid Of all full-time matriculated undergraduates who enrolled in 2001, 4390 applied for aid, 3008 were judged to have need, 1761 had their need fully met. In 2001, 421 non-need-based awards were made. *Average percent of need met:* 84%. *Average financial aid package:* $5972. *Average need-based loan:* $3215. *Average need-based gift aid:* $3755. *Average non-need based aid:* $1757. *Average indebtedness upon graduation:* $15,961.

Applying *Options:* electronic application, early admission, deferred entrance. *Application fee:* $35. *Required:* high school transcript. *Required for some:* minimum 2.75 GPA. *Application deadline:* rolling (freshmen), rolling (transfers).

Admissions Contact Ms. Cynthia Jenkins, Director of Admissions, University of Wisconsin-Stout, Menomonie, WI 54751. *Phone:* 715-232-2639. *Toll-free phone:* 800-HI-STOUT. *Fax:* 715-232-1667. *E-mail:* admissions@uwstout.edu.

UNIVERSITY OF WISCONSIN-SUPERIOR
Superior, Wisconsin

- **State-supported** comprehensive, founded 1893, part of University of Wisconsin System
- **Calendar** semesters
- **Degrees** certificates, associate, bachelor's, master's, and post-master's certificates
- **Small-town** 230-acre campus
- **Endowment** $9.3 million
- **Coed,** 2,434 undergraduate students, 82% full-time, 61% women, 39% men
- **Moderately difficult** entrance level, 81% of applicants were admitted

Undergraduates 2,003 full-time, 431 part-time. Students come from 29 states and territories, 18 other countries, 50% are from out of state, 0.9% African American, 0.7% Asian American or Pacific Islander, 0.7% Hispanic American, 2% Native American, 5% international, 12% transferred in, 25% live on campus. *Retention:* 65% of 2001 full-time freshmen returned.

Freshmen *Admission:* 771 applied, 622 admitted, 342 enrolled. *Test scores:* SAT verbal scores over 500: 75%; SAT math scores over 500: 100%; ACT scores over 18: 93%; SAT verbal scores over 600: 50%; SAT math scores over 600: 25%; ACT scores over 24: 30%; ACT scores over 30: 1%.

Faculty *Total:* 175, 61% full-time, 56% with terminal degrees. *Student/faculty ratio:* 16:1.

Majors Accounting; art education; art history; art therapy; biological/physical sciences; biology; biology education; broadcast journalism; business administration; business economics; business education; business marketing and marketing management; cell biology; chemistry; chemistry education; communications; computer/information sciences; computer science; counselor education/guidance; criminal justice studies; distribution operations; economics; education; education administration; educational media technology; education (K-12); elementary education; English; English education; fine/studio arts; history; history education; information sciences/systems; journalism; law enforcement/police science; legal studies; liberal arts and sciences/liberal studies; marine biology; marketing operations; mass communications; mathematics; mathematics education; molecular biology; music; music teacher education; paralegal/legal assistant; physical education; physical sciences; political science; pre-law; psychology; radio/television broadcasting; reading education; science education; secretarial science; social psychology; social science education; social sciences; social studies education; social work; sociology; special education; speech/rhetorical studies; theater arts/drama.

Academic Programs *Special study options:* academic remediation for entering students, adult/continuing education programs, advanced placement credit, cooperative education, distance learning, double majors, English as a second language, external degree program, freshman honors college, honors programs, independent study, internships, off-campus study, part-time degree program, services for LD students, student-designed majors, study abroad, summer session for credit. *ROTC:* Air Force (c). *Unusual degree programs:* 3-2 engineering with Michigan Technological University, University of Wisconsin-Madison; forestry with Michigan Technological University.

Library Jim Dan Hill Library with an OPAC, a Web page.

Computers on Campus 125 computers available on campus for general student use. A campuswide network can be accessed from student residence rooms and from off campus. Internet access, online (class) registration, at least one staffed computer lab available.

Student Life *Housing:* on-campus residence required for freshman year. *Options:* coed, men-only, women-only, disabled students. *Activities and Organizations:* drama/theater group, student-run newspaper, radio and television station, choral group, Student Senate, Student Activities Board, Residence Hall Association, Intervarsity Christian Fellowship. *Campus security:* 24-hour emergency response devices and patrols, student patrols, late-night transport/escort service, controlled dormitory access. *Student Services:* health clinic, personal/psychological counseling, women's center.

Athletics Member NCAA. All Division III. *Intercollegiate sports:* baseball M, basketball M/W, cross-country running M/W, ice hockey M/W, soccer M/W, softball W, track and field M/W, volleyball W. *Intramural sports:* badminton M/W, baseball M/W, basketball M/W, bowling M/W, cross-country running M/W, golf M/W, ice hockey M, racquetball M/W, riflery M/W, skiing (cross-country) M/W, skiing (downhill) M/W, softball M/W, table tennis M/W, tennis M/W, volleyball M/W.

Standardized Tests *Recommended:* ACT (for admission).

Costs (2001–02) *Tuition:* state resident $2776 full-time, $116 per credit part-time; nonresident $8512 full-time, $354 per credit part-time. Full-time tuition and fees vary according to course load and reciprocity agreements. Part-time tuition and fees vary according to course load and reciprocity agreements. *Required fees:* $457 full-time, $144 per term part-time. *Room and board:* $3818; room only: $2090. Room and board charges vary according to housing facility. *Payment plan:* installment. *Waivers:* minority students and senior citizens.

Financial Aid Of all full-time matriculated undergraduates who enrolled in 2001, 1310 applied for aid, 1013 were judged to have need, 664 had their need fully met. 260 Federal Work-Study jobs (averaging $1320). In 2001, 71 non-need-based awards were made. *Average financial aid package:* $7390. *Average need-based loan:* $3189. *Average need-based gift aid:* $3807. *Average non-need based aid:* $2559. *Average indebtedness upon graduation:* $13,749. *Financial aid deadline:* 5/15.

Applying *Options:* electronic application, deferred entrance. *Application fee:* $35. *Required:* high school transcript. *Required for some:* minimum 2.6 GPA, letters of recommendation. *Recommended:* interview. *Application deadlines:* 5/1 (freshmen), 5/1 (transfers). *Notification:* continuous (freshmen).

Admissions Contact Ms. Lorraine Washa, Student Application Contact, University of Wisconsin-Superior, Belknap and Catlin, PO Box 2000, Superior, WI 54880-4500. *Phone:* 715-394-8230. *Fax:* 715-394-8407. *E-mail:* admissions@uwsuper.edu.

UNIVERSITY OF WISCONSIN-WHITEWATER
Whitewater, Wisconsin

- **State-supported** comprehensive, founded 1868, part of University of Wisconsin System
- **Calendar** semesters
- **Degrees** associate, bachelor's, and master's
- **Small-town** 385-acre campus with easy access to Milwaukee
- **Endowment** $8.6 million
- **Coed,** 9,351 undergraduate students, 90% full-time, 53% women, 47% men
- **Moderately difficult** entrance level, 77% of applicants were admitted

Undergraduates 8,388 full-time, 963 part-time. Students come from 29 states and territories, 37 other countries, 5% are from out of state, 4% African American, 2% Asian American or Pacific Islander, 2% Hispanic American, 0.4% Native American, 0.9% international, 5% transferred in, 40% live on campus. *Retention:* 75% of 2001 full-time freshmen returned.

Freshmen *Admission:* 4,885 applied, 3,748 admitted, 1,841 enrolled. *Average high school GPA:* 2.66.

Faculty *Total:* 494, 78% full-time, 72% with terminal degrees. *Student/faculty ratio:* 20:1.

Majors Accounting; art; art education; art history; biological/physical sciences; biology; business; business administration; business economics; business education; business marketing and marketing management; chemistry; computer science; early childhood education; economics; education; elementary education; English; finance; French; geography; German; history; human resources management; international relations; journalism; liberal arts and sciences/liberal studies; management information systems/business data processing; mass communications; mathematics; music; music teacher education; physical education; physics; political science; pre-law; psychology; public administration; public policy analysis; safety/security technology; secondary education; social work; sociology; Spanish; special education; speech/rhetorical studies; theater arts/drama; women's studies.

Academic Programs *Special study options:* academic remediation for entering students, accelerated degree program, adult/continuing education programs, advanced placement credit, distance learning, double majors, external degree program, honors programs, independent study, internships, part-time degree program, services for LD students, student-designed majors, study abroad, summer session for credit. *ROTC:* Army (b), Air Force (b).

Library Andersen Library with 436,521 titles, 2,206 serial subscriptions, 18,617 audiovisual materials, an OPAC, a Web page.

Computers on Campus 700 computers available on campus for general student use. A campuswide network can be accessed from student residence rooms and from off campus. At least one staffed computer lab available.

Student Life *Housing:* on-campus residence required through sophomore year. *Options:* coed. *Activities and Organizations:* drama/theater group, student-run newspaper, radio station, choral group, marching band, Finance Association, American Marketing Association, Black Student Union, P.S.E., Wisconsin Education Association, national fraternities, national sororities. *Campus security:* 24-hour emergency response devices, late-night transport/escort service. *Student Services:* health clinic, personal/psychological counseling, women's center, legal services.

Athletics Member NCAA. All Division III. *Intercollegiate sports:* baseball M, basketball M/W, bowling M(c)/W(c), cross-country running M/W, football M, golf W, gymnastics W, ice hockey M(c), lacrosse M(c), rugby M(c), soccer M/W, softball W, swimming M/W, tennis M/W, track and field M/W, volleyball M(c)/W, wrestling M. *Intramural sports:* basketball M/W, bowling M/W, football M/W, riflery M(c)/W(c), skiing (cross-country) M(c)/W(c), skiing (downhill) M(c)/W(c), softball M/W, tennis M/W, volleyball M/W, water polo M/W, wrestling M.

Standardized Tests *Required:* ACT (for admission). *Required for some:* SAT I (for admission).

Costs (2001–02) *Tuition:* state resident $3367 full-time, $140 per credit part-time; nonresident $11,878 full-time, $506 per credit part-time. Full-time tuition and fees vary according to reciprocity agreements. Part-time tuition and fees vary according to reciprocity agreements. *Room and board:* $3570; room only: $2070. Room and board charges vary according to board plan. *Payment plan:* installment.

Financial Aid Of all full-time matriculated undergraduates who enrolled in 2001, 5500 applied for aid, 3792 were judged to have need, 1975 had their need fully met. 500 Federal Work-Study jobs (averaging $1000). 2000 State and other part-time jobs (averaging $1300). *Average percent of need met:* 83%. *Average financial aid package:* $6021. *Average need-based loan:* $4147. *Average need-based gift aid:* $3577. *Average indebtedness upon graduation:* $10,451.

Applying *Options:* early admission. *Application fee:* $35. *Required:* high school transcript. *Required for some:* letters of recommendation. *Application deadline:* rolling (freshmen), rolling (transfers).

Admissions Contact Dr. Tori A. McGuire, Executive Director of Admissions, University of Wisconsin-Whitewater, 800 West Main Street, Whitewater, WI 53190-1790. *Phone:* 262-472-1440 Ext. 1512. *Fax:* 262-472-1515. *E-mail:* uwwadmit@uwwvax.uww.edu.

VITERBO UNIVERSITY
La Crosse, Wisconsin

- **Independent Roman Catholic** comprehensive, founded 1890
- **Calendar** semesters
- **Degrees** bachelor's and master's
- **Urban** 5-acre campus
- **Endowment** $10.6 million
- **Coed,** 1,714 undergraduate students, 83% full-time, 74% women, 26% men
- **Moderately difficult** entrance level, 85% of applicants were admitted

Undergraduates 1,418 full-time, 296 part-time. Students come from 24 states and territories, 13 other countries, 24% are from out of state, 1% African American, 1% Asian American or Pacific Islander, 2% Hispanic American, 0.5% Native American, 1.0% international, 8% transferred in, 35% live on campus. *Retention:* 71% of 2001 full-time freshmen returned.

Freshmen *Admission:* 1,245 applied, 1,055 admitted, 337 enrolled. *Average high school GPA:* 3.19. *Test scores:* ACT scores over 18: 91%; ACT scores over 24: 23%; ACT scores over 30: 2%.

Faculty *Total:* 160, 65% full-time, 48% with terminal degrees. *Student/faculty ratio:* 13:1.

Majors Accounting; applied art; art; art education; arts management; biochemistry; biology; biology education; business administration; business education; business marketing and marketing management; chemistry; chemistry education; computer education; criminal justice/law enforcement administration; dietetics; drama/dance education; elementary education; English; English education; graphic design/commercial art/illustration; health services administration; humanities; human resources management; industrial arts education; information sciences/systems; liberal arts and sciences/liberal studies; mathematics; mathematics education; middle school education; music; music (general performance); music (piano and organ performance); music teacher education; music theory and composition; music (voice and choral/opera performance); nursing; optometric/ophthalmic laboratory technician; pre-dentistry; pre-law; pre-medicine; pre-pharmacy studies; pre-veterinary studies; psychology; religious education; religious studies; science education; social studies education; social work; sociology; Spanish; Spanish language education; speech/theater education; theater arts/drama; theology.

Academic Programs *Special study options:* academic remediation for entering students, accelerated degree program, adult/continuing education programs, advanced placement credit, cooperative education, double majors, independent study, internships, off-campus study, part-time degree program, student-designed majors, study abroad, summer session for credit. *ROTC:* Army (c).

Library Todd Wehr Memorial Library with 100,000 titles, 3,000 serial subscriptions, 6,000 audiovisual materials, an OPAC, a Web page.

Computers on Campus 180 computers available on campus for general student use. A campuswide network can be accessed from student residence rooms and from off campus that provide access to e-mail. Internet access, at least one staffed computer lab available.

Student Life *Housing:* on-campus residence required through sophomore year. *Options:* coed. *Activities and Organizations:* drama/theater group, student-run newspaper, choral group, Viterbo Student Nurses Association, Viterbo Education Students Club, Connect—AODA Peer Counselors, Campus Ministry—Volunteer Services and Service Trips, Sigma Pi Delta. *Campus security:* 24-hour emergency response devices, late-night transport/escort service, controlled dormitory access, Security officers on campus 5:00 p.m. to 7:00 a.m. *Student Services:* health clinic, personal/psychological counseling.

Athletics Member NAIA. *Intercollegiate sports:* baseball M, basketball M/W, soccer M/W, softball W, volleyball W. *Intramural sports:* basketball M/W, bowling M/W, football M, golf M/W, racquetball M/W, skiing (cross-country) M/W, skiing (downhill) M/W, soccer M/W, softball M/W, swimming M/W, table tennis M/W, tennis M/W, volleyball M/W.

Standardized Tests *Required:* ACT (for admission).

Costs (2001–02) *Comprehensive fee:* $18,340 includes full-time tuition ($13,350), mandatory fees ($280), and room and board ($4710). Part-time tuition: $390 per credit. Part-time tuition and fees vary according to course load. *Required fees:* $15 per credit. *Room and board:* College room only: $2070. Room and board charges vary according to board plan and housing facility. *Payment plan:* installment. *Waivers:* senior citizens and employees or children of employees.

Financial Aid Of all full-time matriculated undergraduates who enrolled in 2001, 1230 applied for aid, 1141 were judged to have need, 351 had their need fully met. 301 Federal Work-Study jobs (averaging $1522). 55 State and other part-time jobs (averaging $1418). In 2001, 251 non-need-based awards were made. *Average percent of need met:* 76%. *Average financial aid package:* $12,325. *Average need-based loan:* $3758. *Average need-based gift aid:* $8109. *Average indebtedness upon graduation:* $15,602.

Applying *Options:* early admission, deferred entrance. *Application fee:* $15. *Required:* high school transcript, minimum 2.0 GPA, audition for theater and music; portfolio for art. *Required for some:* 1 letter of recommendation, interview. *Application deadline:* rolling (freshmen), rolling (transfers). *Notification:* 8/15 (freshmen).

Admissions Contact Mr. Joe Fischer, Admission Counselor, Viterbo University, 815 South 9th Street, LaCrosse, WI 54601. *Phone:* 608-796-3016 Ext. 3016. *Toll-free phone:* 800-VIT-ERBO Ext. 3010. *Fax:* 608-796-3020. *E-mail:* admission@viterbo.edu.

WISCONSIN LUTHERAN COLLEGE
Milwaukee, Wisconsin

- **Independent** 4-year, founded 1973, affiliated with Wisconsin Evangelical Lutheran Synod
- **Calendar** semesters
- **Degree** bachelor's
- **Suburban** 16-acre campus
- **Endowment** $6.8 million
- **Coed,** 716 undergraduate students, 91% full-time, 63% women, 37% men
- **Moderately difficult** entrance level, 86% of applicants were admitted

Undergraduates 650 full-time, 66 part-time. Students come from 25 states and territories, 7 other countries, 21% are from out of state, 1% African American,

Wisconsin Lutheran College (continued)
0.8% Asian American or Pacific Islander, 0.9% Hispanic American, 2% international, 3% transferred in, 80% live on campus. *Retention:* 79% of 2001 full-time freshmen returned.

Freshmen *Admission:* 447 applied, 383 admitted, 200 enrolled. *Average high school GPA:* 3.45. *Test scores:* ACT scores over 18: 99%; ACT scores over 24: 66%; ACT scores over 30: 15%.

Faculty *Total:* 77, 57% full-time, 47% with terminal degrees. *Student/faculty ratio:* 12:1.

Majors Art; biology; business economics; chemistry; communications; communications related; elementary education; English; history; interdisciplinary studies; mathematics; music; political science; psychology; social sciences; Spanish; theology.

Academic Programs *Special study options:* advanced placement credit, double majors, independent study, internships, off-campus study, part-time degree program, student-designed majors, study abroad, summer session for credit.

Library Marvin M. Schwan Library with 58,026 titles, 585 serial subscriptions, 3,929 audiovisual materials, an OPAC, a Web page.

Computers on Campus 125 computers available on campus for general student use. A campuswide network can be accessed from student residence rooms and from off campus. Internet access, at least one staffed computer lab available.

Student Life *Housing:* on-campus residence required through senior year. *Options:* men-only, women-only. *Activities and Organizations:* drama/theater group, student-run newspaper, choral group. *Campus security:* 24-hour emergency response devices and patrols, late-night transport/escort service, controlled dormitory access, closed circuit TV monitors. *Student Services:* health clinic, personal/psychological counseling.

Athletics Member NCAA. All Division III. *Intercollegiate sports:* baseball M, basketball M/W, cross-country running M/W, football M, golf M/W, soccer M/W, softball W, tennis W, track and field M/W, volleyball M(c)/W. *Intramural sports:* badminton M/W, basketball M/W, bowling M/W, tennis M/W, volleyball M/W.

Standardized Tests *Required:* SAT I or ACT (for admission).

Costs (2002–03) *Comprehensive fee:* $20,416 includes full-time tuition ($14,970), mandatory fees ($126), and room and board ($5320). Part-time tuition: $450 per credit. *Required fees:* $50 per year part-time. *Room and board:* College room only: $2820. Room and board charges vary according to board plan and housing facility. *Payment plan:* installment. *Waivers:* employees or children of employees.

Financial Aid Of all full-time matriculated undergraduates who enrolled in 2001, 531 applied for aid, 485 were judged to have need, 209 had their need fully met. 252 Federal Work-Study jobs (averaging $1618). 22 State and other part-time jobs (averaging $4845). In 2001, 146 non-need-based awards were made. *Average percent of need met:* 88%. *Average financial aid package:* $12,149. *Average need-based loan:* $3309. *Average need-based gift aid:* $8507. *Average non-need based aid:* $8194. *Average indebtedness upon graduation:* $13,602.

Applying *Options:* electronic application, early admission. *Application fee:* $20. *Required:* high school transcript, minimum 2.70 GPA, 1 letter of recommendation, minimum ACT score of 21. *Required for some:* interview. *Notification:* continuous (freshmen).

Admissions Contact Mr. Craig Swiontek, Director of Admissions, Wisconsin Lutheran College, 8800 West Bluemound Road, Milwaukee, WI 53226-9942. *Phone:* 414-443-8713. *Toll-free phone:* 888-WIS LUTH. *Fax:* 414-443-8514. *E-mail:* admissions@wlc.edu.

WYOMING

UNIVERSITY OF WYOMING
Laramie, Wyoming

- **State-supported** university, founded 1886
- **Calendar** semesters
- **Degrees** certificates, bachelor's, master's, doctoral, first professional, and post-master's certificates
- **Small-town** campus
- **Endowment** $69.3 million
- **Coed,** 8,857 undergraduate students
- **Moderately difficult** entrance level, 97% of applicants were admitted

Undergraduates Students come from 55 states and territories, 53 other countries, 26% are from out of state, 1.0% African American, 1.0% Asian American or Pacific Islander, 3% Hispanic American, 1% Native American, 1% international, 26% live on campus. *Retention:* 78% of 2001 full-time freshmen returned.

Freshmen *Admission:* 2,560 applied, 2,481 admitted. *Average high school GPA:* 3.42. *Test scores:* SAT verbal scores over 500: 69%; SAT math scores over 500: 72%; ACT scores over 18: 92%; SAT verbal scores over 600: 26%; SAT math scores over 600: 31%; ACT scores over 24: 45%; SAT verbal scores over 700: 3%; SAT math scores over 700: 7%; ACT scores over 30: 6%.

Faculty *Total:* 643, 93% full-time, 86% with terminal degrees. *Student/faculty ratio:* 14:1.

Majors Accounting; agricultural business; agricultural education; agricultural extension; agricultural sciences related; American studies; animal sciences related; anthropology; architectural engineering; art; astronomy; astrophysics; biology; botany; business administration; business economics; business marketing and marketing management; chemical engineering; chemistry; civil engineering; communications; computer engineering; computer/information sciences; criminal justice/law enforcement administration; dental hygiene; electrical engineering; elementary education; English; enterprise management; environmental science; exercise sciences; family/community studies; finance; fine arts and art studies related; French; geography; geological sciences related; geology; German; health education; health professions and related sciences; history; humanities; industrial arts education; information sciences/systems; international relations; journalism; management science; mathematical statistics; mathematics; mathematics related; mechanical engineering; microbiology/bacteriology; molecular biology; multi/interdisciplinary studies related; music; music (general performance); music teacher education; music theory and composition; nursing; philosophy; physical education; physics; political science; psychology; range management; recreation/leisure facilities management; Russian; secondary education; social sciences; social work; sociology; Spanish; special education; special education related; speech-language pathology/audiology; theater arts/drama; trade/industrial education; wildlife management; women's studies; zoology.

Academic Programs *Special study options:* academic remediation for entering students, accelerated degree program, adult/continuing education programs, advanced placement credit, distance learning, double majors, external degree program, honors programs, independent study, internships, off-campus study, part-time degree program, services for LD students, student-designed majors, study abroad, summer session for credit. *ROTC:* Army (b), Air Force (b).

Library Coe Library plus 7 others with 19,720 titles, 14,737 serial subscriptions, 3,701 audiovisual materials, an OPAC, a Web page.

Computers on Campus 1270 computers available on campus for general student use. A campuswide network can be accessed from student residence rooms and from off campus. Internet access, online (class) registration, at least one staffed computer lab available.

Student Life *Housing:* on-campus residence required for freshman year. *Options:* coed, women-only, disabled students. *Activities and Organizations:* drama/theater group, student-run newspaper, radio and television station, choral group, marching band, Golden Key, SPURS, Fellowship of Christian Athletes, MECHA, national fraternities, national sororities. *Campus security:* 24-hour emergency response devices and patrols, student patrols, late-night transport/escort service, controlled dormitory access. *Student Services:* health clinic, personal/psychological counseling, women's center, legal services.

Athletics Member NCAA. All Division I except football (Division I-A). *Intercollegiate sports:* badminton M(c)/W(c), baseball M(c), basketball M(s)/W(s), cross-country running M(s)/W(s), fencing M(c)/W(c), golf M(s)/W(s), ice hockey M(c)/W(c), riflery M(c)/W(c), rugby M(c)/W(c), skiing (downhill) M(c)/W(c), soccer M(c)/W(s), swimming M(s)/W(s), tennis W(s), track and field M(s)/W(s), volleyball M(c)/W(s), wrestling M(s). *Intramural sports:* badminton M/W, basketball M/W, bowling M/W, cross-country running M/W, fencing M/W, football M/W, golf M/W, racquetball M/W, skiing (downhill) M/W, soccer M/W, softball M/W, swimming M/W, table tennis M/W, tennis M/W, volleyball M/W, water polo M/W, weight lifting M/W, wrestling M/W.

Standardized Tests *Required for some:* SAT I or ACT (for admission).

Costs (2001–02) *Tuition:* state resident $2316 full-time, $106 per semester hour part-time; nonresident $7788 full-time, $334 per semester hour part-time. Full-time tuition and fees vary according to course load and reciprocity agreements. Part-time tuition and fees vary according to course load and reciprocity agreements. *Required fees:* $491 full-time. *Room and board:* $4748; room only: $2012. Room and board charges vary according to board plan and housing facility. *Payment plans:* installment, deferred payment. *Waivers:* children of alumni, senior citizens, and employees or children of employees.

Financial Aid Of all full-time matriculated undergraduates who enrolled in 2001, 4633 applied for aid, 3185 were judged to have need, 2186 had their need fully met. 471 Federal Work-Study jobs (averaging $1101). In 2001, 2481 non-need-based awards were made. *Average percent of need met:* 74%. *Average financial aid package:* $6900. *Average need-based loan:* $4426. *Average need-based gift aid:* $2513. *Average non-need based aid:* $3322. *Average indebtedness upon graduation:* $18,321.

Applying *Options:* deferred entrance. *Application fee:* $30. *Required:* high school transcript, minimum 2.75 GPA, 3.0 high school GPA for nonresidents. *Required for some:* minimum 3.0 GPA. *Recommended:* interview. *Application deadlines:* 8/10 (freshmen), 8/10 (transfers). *Notification:* continuous (freshmen).

Admissions Contact Ms. Sara Axelson, Associate Vice President Enrollment and Director of Admissions, University of Wyoming, Box 3435, Laramie, WY 82071. *Phone:* 307-766-5160. *Toll-free phone:* 800-342-5996. *Fax:* 307-766-4042. *E-mail:* why-wyo@uwyo.edu.

GUAM

UNIVERSITY OF GUAM
Mangilao, Guam

Admissions Contact Ms. Katherine King-Nwosisi, Director of Admissions and Records, University of Guam, UOG Station, Mangilao, GU 96923. *Phone:* 671-735-2213. *E-mail:* admrecs@uog.edu.

PUERTO RICO

AMERICAN UNIVERSITY OF PUERTO RICO
Bayamón, Puerto Rico

- **Independent** 4-year, founded 1963
- **Calendar** semesters
- **Degrees** certificates, diplomas, associate, and bachelor's
- 21-acre campus with easy access to San Juan
- **Coed,** 4,537 undergraduate students, 80% full-time, 55% women, 45% men
- **Noncompetitive** entrance level, 100% of applicants were admitted

Undergraduates Students come from 1 other state, 1 other country, 100% Hispanic American.

Freshmen *Admission:* 937 applied, 937 admitted.

Faculty *Total:* 222, 47% full-time.

Majors Accounting; business administration; education; elementary education; liberal arts and sciences/liberal studies; physical education; purchasing/contracts management; secretarial science; special education.

Academic Programs *Special study options:* adult/continuing education programs, advanced placement credit, cooperative education, freshman honors college, honors programs, internships, part-time degree program, services for LD students, summer session for credit. *ROTC:* Army (c).

Library Loida Figueroa Meacado with 91,835 titles, 231 serial subscriptions, 2,091 audiovisual materials.

Computers on Campus 85 computers available on campus for general student use. At least one staffed computer lab available.

Student Life *Housing:* college housing not available. *Activities and Organizations:* drama/theater group. *Campus security:* 24-hour patrols. *Student Services:* health clinic.

Athletics *Intercollegiate sports:* basketball M, cross-country running M/W, swimming M/W, tennis M/W, track and field M/W, volleyball M/W. *Intramural sports:* basketball M, softball M/W, table tennis M/W, volleyball M/W.

Standardized Tests *Required:* SAT I (for placement), CEEB.

Costs (2001–02) *Tuition:* $3364 full-time, $1181 per term part-time. Full-time tuition and fees vary according to program. Part-time tuition and fees vary according to program. No tuition increase for student's term of enrollment. *Required fees:* $214 full-time, $114 per term part-time.

Financial Aid *Financial aid deadline:* 5/30.

Applying *Options:* deferred entrance. *Application fee:* $15. *Required:* high school transcript. *Application deadlines:* 7/1 (freshmen), 7/1 (transfers). *Notification:* continuous (freshmen).

Admissions Contact Ms. Margarita Cruz, Director of Admissions, American University of Puerto Rico, PO Box 2037, Bayamón, PR 00960-2037. *Phone:* 787-740-6410. *Fax:* 787-785-7377.

ATLANTIC COLLEGE
Guaynabo, Puerto Rico

- **Independent** 4-year
- **Calendar** semesters
- **Degree** bachelor's
- 370 undergraduate students, 84% full-time
- 96% of applicants were admitted

Faculty *Student/faculty ratio:* 19:1.

Costs (2001–02) *One-time required fee:* $80. *Tuition:* $3593 full-time, $88 per credit part-time. Full-time tuition and fees vary according to course load. Part-time tuition and fees vary according to course load. *Required fees:* $253 full-time, $40 per term part-time.

Financial Aid Of all full-time matriculated undergraduates who enrolled in 2001, 459 applied for aid, 454 were judged to have need, 9 had their need fully met. 3 Federal Work-Study jobs (averaging $5000).

Applying *Options:* common application. *Required:* high school transcript. *Required for some:* interview.

Admissions Contact Zaida Perez, Admission's Officer, Atlantic College, PO Box 3918, Colton Street No. 9, Guaynabo, PR 00970. *Phone:* 787-720-1022 Ext. 13. *Fax:* 787-720-1022 Ext. 13. *E-mail:* atlancole@coqui.net.

BAYAMÓN CENTRAL UNIVERSITY
Bayamón, Puerto Rico

- **Independent Roman Catholic** comprehensive, founded 1970
- **Calendar** semesters
- **Degrees** certificates, associate, bachelor's, and master's
- **Suburban** 55-acre campus with easy access to San Juan
- **Endowment** $6.6 million
- **Coed,** 2,935 undergraduate students, 80% full-time, 67% women, 33% men
- **Moderately difficult** entrance level, 62% of applicants were admitted

Undergraduates 2,335 full-time, 600 part-time. Students come from 1 other state, 0% are from out of commonwealth, 100% Hispanic American, 7% transferred in. *Retention:* 70% of 2001 full-time freshmen returned.

Freshmen *Admission:* 901 applied, 559 admitted, 452 enrolled. *Average high school GPA:* 2.58.

Faculty *Total:* 203, 31% full-time, 23% with terminal degrees. *Student/faculty ratio:* 24:1.

Majors Accounting; biological/physical sciences; biology; business; business administration; business marketing and marketing management; chemistry; computer science; early childhood education; educational media design; elementary education; English education; environmental science; human resources management; journalism; management information systems/business data processing; mathematics education; nursing; occupational safety/health technology; philosophy; physical education; psychology; public administration; religious studies; science education; secretarial science; social work; Spanish language education; special education.

Academic Programs *Special study options:* academic remediation for entering students, accelerated degree program, adult/continuing education programs, advanced placement credit, English as a second language, honors programs, independent study, internships, part-time degree program, services for LD students, student-designed majors, summer session for credit. *ROTC:* Army (c), Air Force (c).

Library BCU Library plus 1 other with 51,011 titles, 3,027 serial subscriptions, 900 audiovisual materials, an OPAC.

Computers on Campus 130 computers available on campus for general student use. Internet access, at least one staffed computer lab available.

Student Life *Housing:* college housing not available. *Activities and Organizations:* student-run newspaper, choral group, Business Students Association, Nursing Students Association, Journalism Students Association, Psychology Students Association, Biology Students Association. *Campus security:* 24-hour patrols. *Student Services:* health clinic, personal/psychological counseling, legal services.

Athletics *Intercollegiate sports:* basketball M(s)/W(s), cross-country running M(s)/W(s), softball M(s)/W(s), swimming M(s)/W(s), track and field M(s)/W(s), volleyball M(s)/W(s), water polo M(s)/W(s). *Intramural sports:* basketball M/W, cross-country running M/W, softball M/W, swimming M/W, table tennis M/W, track and field M/W, volleyball M/W, weight lifting M/W.

Costs (2002–03) *Tuition:* $3420 full-time, $115 per credit part-time. *Required fees:* $320 full-time, $160 per term part-time. *Payment plan:* deferred payment. *Waivers:* employees or children of employees.

Financial Aid Of all full-time matriculated undergraduates who enrolled in 2001, 2172 applied for aid, 2105 were judged to have need, 105 had their need fully met. 378 Federal Work-Study jobs (averaging $1020). *Average percent of need met:* 75%. *Average need-based loan:* $3600. *Average need-based gift aid:* $6452. *Average indebtedness upon graduation:* $8200.

Bayamón Central University (continued)
Applying *Options:* common application. *Application fee:* $15. *Required:* high school transcript, medical history. *Required for some:* letters of recommendation, interview. *Application deadlines:* 8/15 (freshmen), 8/15 (transfers).
Admissions Contact Sra. Christine M. Hernandez, Director of Admissions, Bayamón Central University, PO Box 1725, Bayamón, PR 00960-1725. *Phone:* 787-786-3030 Ext. 2102. *Fax:* 787-740-2200. *E-mail:* chernandez@ucb.edu.pr.

CARIBBEAN UNIVERSITY
Bayamón, Puerto Rico

- **Independent** 4-year, founded 1969
- **Calendar** trimesters
- **Degrees** associate, bachelor's, and master's
- 16-acre campus with easy access to San Juan
- **Coed,** 2,762 undergraduate students
- **Minimally difficult** entrance level, 82% of applicants were admitted

Freshmen *Admission:* 1,932 applied, 1,577 admitted.
Faculty *Total:* 158, 28% full-time.
Majors Accounting; biology education; business administration; civil engineering; civil engineering technology; computer programming; computer programming related; computer science; criminal justice/law enforcement administration; criminology; drafting/design technology; early childhood education; education; education administration; education (K-12); electrical/electronic engineering technologies related; elementary education; elementary/middle/secondary education administration; engineering/industrial management; English education; executive assistant; finance; human resources management; human services; industrial/manufacturing engineering; information sciences/systems; insurance marketing; law enforcement/police science; legal administrative assistant; liberal arts and sciences/liberal studies; marketing operations; marketing operations/marketing and distribution related; mathematics education; medical administrative assistant; nursing; nursing related; pre-law; pre-medicine; real estate; secondary education; secretarial science; social work; special education; surveying.
Academic Programs *Special study options:* academic remediation for entering students, accelerated degree program, adult/continuing education programs, English as a second language, part-time degree program, services for LD students, summer session for credit. *ROTC:* Army (c).
Library 17,632 titles, 153 serial subscriptions.
Computers on Campus 90 computers available on campus for general student use.
Student Life *Housing:* college housing not available. *Student Services:* health clinic, personal/psychological counseling.
Athletics *Intercollegiate sports:* basketball M, cross-country running M/W, tennis M/W, track and field M/W, volleyball M/W, weight lifting M. *Intramural sports:* basketball M, cross-country running M/W, gymnastics M/W, table tennis M/W, tennis M/W, track and field M/W, volleyball M/W, weight lifting M.
Standardized Tests *Required:* SAT I (for placement), SAT II: Subject Tests (for placement).
Costs (2001–02) *Tuition:* $3000 full-time.
Applying *Options:* deferred entrance. *Required:* high school transcript. *Application deadlines:* rolling (freshmen), 8/1 (transfers).
Admissions Contact Mr. Hector Gracia, Director of Admissions, Caribbean University, Box 493, Bayamón, PR 00960-0493. *Phone:* 787-780-0070 Ext. 226.

CARLOS ALBIZU UNIVERSITY
San Juan, Puerto Rico

Admissions Contact PO Box 9023711, San Juan, PR 00902-3711.

COLEGIO BIBLICO PENTECOSTAL
St. Just, Puerto Rico

Admissions Contact Ms. Gladys Santiago, Registrar, Colegio Biblico Pentecostal, PO Box 901, St. Just, PR 00978-0901. *Phone:* 787-761-0640.

COLEGIO PENTECOSTAL MIZPA
Río Piedras, Puerto Rico

Admissions Contact Km. 0 Hm. 2, Bo. Caimito, Apartado 20966, Río Piedras, PR 00928-0966.

COLEGIO UNIVERSITARIO DEL ESTE
Carolina, Puerto Rico

Admissions Contact Carmen Rodríguez, Associate Director, Colegio Universitario del Este, PO Box 2010, Carolina, PR 00984-2010. *Phone:* 787-257-7373 Ext. 3300. *Fax:* 787-257-7373 Ext. 4000.

COLUMBIA COLLEGE
Caguas, Puerto Rico

- **Proprietary** 4-year, founded 1966
- **Calendar** semesters
- **Degrees** certificates, associate, and bachelor's
- **Rural** 6-acre campus with easy access to San Juan
- **Coed,** 899 undergraduate students, 56% full-time, 66% women, 34% men
- **Noncompetitive** entrance level, 50% of applicants were admitted

Undergraduates 503 full-time, 396 part-time. 100% Hispanic American.
Freshmen *Admission:* 432 applied, 214 admitted, 86 enrolled. *Average high school GPA:* 2.00.
Faculty *Total:* 30, 47% full-time, 17% with terminal degrees. *Student/faculty ratio:* 18:1.
Majors Business; business administration; electrical/electronic engineering technology; management information systems/business data processing; nursing; nursing science; secretarial science.
Academic Programs *Special study options:* accelerated degree program, adult/continuing education programs, external degree program, independent study, part-time degree program.
Library Efrain Sola Bezares Library with 10,200 titles, 164 serial subscriptions, an OPAC.
Computers on Campus 55 computers available on campus for general student use. Internet access, at least one staffed computer lab available.
Student Life *Housing:* college housing not available. *Campus security:* 24-hour patrols. *Student Services:* personal/psychological counseling.
Costs (2002–03) *Tuition:* $2880 full-time, $720 part-time. *Required fees:* $400 full-time, $200 per term part-time.
Applying *Options:* common application. *Application fee:* $50. *Required:* high school transcript. *Recommended:* essay or personal statement. *Application deadline:* rolling (freshmen).
Admissions Contact Ms. Ana Rosa Burgos, Admission Director, Columbia College, PO Box 8517, Caguas, PR 00726. *Phone:* 787-743-4041 Ext. 234. *Toll-free phone:* 800-981-4877 Ext. 239. *Fax:* 787-744-7031. *E-mail:* arburgos@columbiaco.edu.

CONSERVATORY OF MUSIC OF PUERTO RICO
San Juan, Puerto Rico

- **Commonwealth-supported** 4-year, founded 1959
- **Calendar** semesters
- **Degree** bachelor's
- **Urban** 6-acre campus
- **Endowment** $12,520
- **Coed**
- **Very difficult** entrance level

Faculty *Student/faculty ratio:* 4:1.
Student Life *Campus security:* 24-hour patrols.
Standardized Tests *Required:* SAT I (for admission), SAT II: Subject Tests (for admission).
Costs (2001–02) *Tuition:* $45 per credit part-time. Full-time tuition and fees vary according to program.
Financial Aid Of all full-time matriculated undergraduates who enrolled in 2001, 130 applied for aid, 130 were judged to have need. *Average percent of need met:* 62. *Average financial aid package:* $3060. *Average need-based gift aid:* $4951. *Average indebtedness upon graduation:* $5500.
Applying *Options:* common application, early admission. *Application fee:* $25. *Required:* high school transcript, minimum 2.0 GPA, interview, audition, music and theory examinations. *Required for some:* minimum 2.50 GPA.
Admissions Contact Ana Marta Graiza, Marketing and Recruitment Officer, Conservatory of Music of Puerto Rico, 350 Rafael Lamar St at FDR Ave, San Juan, PR 00918. *Phone:* 787-751-6180 Ext. 274. *Fax:* 787-758-8268. *E-mail:* aarraiza@cmpr.prstar.net.

Electronic Data Processing College of Puerto Rico

San Juan, Puerto Rico

Admissions Contact Mrs. Elsie Zayas, Admissions Director, Electronic Data Processing College of Puerto Rico, 555 Munoz Rivera Avenue, San Juan, PR 00919-2303. *Phone:* 787-765-3560 Ext. 138.

Escuela de Artes Plasticas de Puerto Rico

San Juan, Puerto Rico

- **Commonwealth-supported** 4-year, founded 1966
- **Calendar** semesters
- **Degree** bachelor's
- **Urban** campus
- **Coed,** 313 undergraduate students, 76% full-time, 35% women, 65% men
- **Moderately difficult** entrance level, 52% of applicants were admitted

Undergraduates 237 full-time, 76 part-time. Students come from 1 other state, 100% Hispanic American, 8% transferred in. *Retention:* 81% of 2001 full-time freshmen returned.

Freshmen *Admission:* 159 applied, 83 admitted, 55 enrolled. *Average high school GPA:* 2.77. *Test scores:* SAT verbal scores over 500: 39%; SAT math scores over 500: 48%; SAT verbal scores over 600: 6%; SAT math scores over 600: 7%.

Faculty *Total:* 50, 42% full-time, 10% with terminal degrees. *Student/faculty ratio:* 9:1.

Majors Art education; graphic design/commercial art/illustration; painting; printmaking; sculpture.

Academic Programs *Special study options:* cooperative education, services for LD students, summer session for credit.

Library Francisco Oller Library with 24,582 titles, 111 serial subscriptions, 34,082 audiovisual materials, an OPAC.

Computers on Campus 36 computers available on campus for general student use. Internet access, at least one staffed computer lab available.

Student Life *Housing:* college housing not available. *Activities and Organizations:* student government. *Campus security:* 24-hour patrols.

Standardized Tests *Required:* SAT I (for placement).

Costs (2001–02) *Tuition:* $112 per credit part-time. Full-time tuition and fees vary according to course load and program. Part-time tuition and fees vary according to course load and program. *Required fees:* $1200 full-time, $50 per credit. *Room only:* Room and board charges vary according to housing facility. *Payment plan:* deferred payment. *Waivers:* employees or children of employees.

Financial Aid Of all full-time matriculated undergraduates who enrolled in 2001, 256 applied for aid, 256 were judged to have need. 10 Federal Work-Study jobs (averaging $1800). *Average percent of need met:* 82%.

Applying *Options:* common application. *Application fee:* $20. *Required:* essay or personal statement, high school transcript, minimum 2.0 GPA, interview, portfolio. *Application deadlines:* 4/1 (freshmen), 5/1 (transfers). *Notification:* 5/1 (freshmen).

Admissions Contact Milagros Lugo, Admission Assistant, Escuela de Artes Plasticas de Puerto Rico, PO Box 9021112, San Juan, PR 00902-1112. *Phone:* 787-725-8120 Ext. 250. *Fax:* 787-725-8111. *E-mail:* eap@coqui.net.

Inter American University of Puerto Rico, Aguadilla Campus

Aguadilla, Puerto Rico

- **Independent** 4-year, founded 1957, part of Inter American University of Puerto Rico
- **Calendar** semesters
- **Degrees** certificates, associate, and bachelor's
- **Small-town** 50-acre campus
- **Endowment** $669,694
- **Coed,** 3,800 undergraduate students
- **Moderately difficult** entrance level, 78% of applicants were admitted

Undergraduates 100% Hispanic American.

Freshmen *Admission:* 1,003 applied, 786 admitted. *Average high school GPA:* 2.75.

Faculty *Total:* 209, 36% full-time. *Student/faculty ratio:* 21:1.

Majors Accounting; biology; biology education; business administration; business marketing and marketing management; computer science; criminal justice studies; early childhood education; electrical/electronic engineering technology; elementary education; hotel and restaurant management; human services; nursing science; secretarial science; Spanish language education; teaching English as a second language.

Academic Programs *Special study options:* academic remediation for entering students, adult/continuing education programs, advanced placement credit, cooperative education, distance learning, double majors, external degree program, honors programs, independent study, internships, off-campus study, part-time degree program, services for LD students, summer session for credit. *ROTC:* Army (b).

Library Access Information Center with 46,880 titles, 515 serial subscriptions, 24,434 audiovisual materials, an OPAC.

Computers on Campus 292 computers available on campus for general student use. A campuswide network can be accessed from off campus. Internet access, online (class) registration, at least one staffed computer lab available.

Student Life *Housing:* college housing not available. *Activities and Organizations:* drama/theater group, student-run newspaper, radio station, choral group, Criminal Justice Association, Secretarial Sciences Association, Future Teachers Association, Psychosocial Human Services Association, IPDAS (Drugs, Alcohol and Aids Prevention Institute). *Campus security:* 24-hour emergency response devices and patrols. *Student Services:* health clinic, personal/psychological counseling.

Athletics *Intercollegiate sports:* baseball M(s), basketball M(s)/W(s), cross-country running M(s)/W(s), soccer M(s), softball M(s)/W(s), table tennis M(s)/W(s), tennis M(s)/W(s), track and field M(s)/W(s), volleyball M(s)/W(s), weight lifting M(s)/W(s). *Intramural sports:* basketball M/W, cross-country running M/W, softball M/W, table tennis M/W, tennis M/W, track and field M/W, volleyball M/W, weight lifting M/W.

Standardized Tests *Required for some:* SAT I (for admission).

Costs (2001–02) *Tuition:* $2880 full-time, $120 per credit hour part-time. Full-time tuition and fees vary according to course load. Part-time tuition and fees vary according to course load. *Required fees:* $398 full-time, $131 per term part-time. *Payment plan:* deferred payment. *Waivers:* employees or children of employees.

Applying *Options:* common application, electronic application, early admission. *Required:* high school transcript, minimum 2.00 GPA. *Application deadline:* rolling (freshmen), rolling (transfers).

Admissions Contact Ms. Doris Pérez, Director of Admissions, Inter American University of Puerto Rico, Aguadilla Campus, PO Box 20,000, Road 459 Interstate 463, Aguadilla, PR 00605. *Phone:* 787-891-0925 Ext. 2101. *Fax:* 787-882-3020.

Inter American University of Puerto Rico, Arecibo Campus

Arecibo, Puerto Rico

- **Independent** comprehensive, founded 1957, part of Inter American University of Puerto Rico
- **Calendar** semesters
- **Degrees** associate, bachelor's, master's, and postbachelor's certificates
- **Urban** 20-acre campus with easy access to San Juan
- **Endowment** $40.5 million
- **Coed**
- **Moderately difficult** entrance level

Faculty *Student/faculty ratio:* 24:1.

Student Life *Campus security:* 24-hour emergency response devices and patrols.

Financial Aid Of all full-time matriculated undergraduates who enrolled in 2001, 3019 applied for aid, 2835 were judged to have need, 6 had their need fully met. *Average percent of need met:* 11. *Average financial aid package:* $2207. *Average need-based loan:* $1325. *Average need-based gift aid:* $1653.

Applying *Options:* electronic application, early admission, deferred entrance. *Required:* high school transcript, minimum 2.0 GPA. *Required for some:* interview. *Recommended:* minimum 3.0 GPA.

Admissions Contact Ms. Provi Montalvo, Admission Director, Inter American University of Puerto Rico, Arecibo Campus, PO Box 4050, Arecibo, PR 00614-4050. *Phone:* 787-878-5475 Ext. 2268.

INTER AMERICAN UNIVERSITY OF PUERTO RICO, BARRANQUITAS CAMPUS
Barranquitas, Puerto Rico

- **Independent** 4-year, founded 1957, part of Inter American University of Puerto Rico, Inc.
- **Calendar** semesters
- **Degrees** associate and bachelor's
- **Small-town** campus with easy access to San Juan
- **Coed,** 1,710 undergraduate students, 91% full-time, 71% women, 29% men
- **Moderately difficult** entrance level

Undergraduates Students come from 1 other state, 100% Hispanic American. *Retention:* 76% of 2001 full-time freshmen returned.

Faculty *Total:* 90, 41% full-time.

Majors Accounting; business administration; computer science; criminal justice/law enforcement administration; elementary education; nursing; secondary education; secretarial science.

Academic Programs *Special study options:* academic remediation for entering students, adult/continuing education programs, advanced placement credit, English as a second language, part-time degree program, study abroad, summer session for credit. *ROTC:* Army (c).

Library Luis Muñoz Marín with 32,863 titles, 224 serial subscriptions.

Computers on Campus 65 computers available on campus for general student use. Internet access, at least one staffed computer lab available.

Student Life *Housing:* college housing not available. *Campus security:* 24-hour patrols.

Athletics *Intercollegiate sports:* basketball M/W, cross-country running M/W, softball M/W, table tennis M/W, tennis M/W, track and field M/W, volleyball M/W, weight lifting M. *Intramural sports:* basketball M/W, cross-country running M/W, softball M, table tennis M/W, track and field M/W, volleyball M/W.

Standardized Tests *Required:* SAT I or ACT (for admission).

Costs (2001–02) *Tuition:* Part-time tuition and fees vary according to course load. No tuition increase for student's term of enrollment. *Payment plan:* deferred payment. *Waivers:* minority students.

Financial Aid Of all full-time matriculated undergraduates who enrolled in 2001, 1350 applied for aid, 1350 were judged to have need. 466 Federal Work-Study jobs.

Applying *Options:* common application, deferred entrance. *Application fee:* $19. *Required:* high school transcript, interview. *Application deadlines:* 5/15 (freshmen), 5/15 (transfers).

Admissions Contact Ms. Carmen L. Ortiz, Admission Director, Inter American University of Puerto Rico, Barranquitas Campus, PO Box 517, Barranquitas, PR 00794. *Phone:* 787-857-3600 Ext. 2011. *Fax:* 787-857-2244. *E-mail:* clortiz@inter.edu.

INTER AMERICAN UNIVERSITY OF PUERTO RICO, BAYAMÓN CAMPUS
Bayamón, Puerto Rico

- **Independent** 4-year, founded 1912, part of Inter American University of Puerto Rico
- **Calendar** semesters
- **Degrees** certificates, associate, and bachelor's
- **Urban** 51-acre campus with easy access to San Juan
- **Endowment** $2.0 million
- **Coed**
- 65% of applicants were admitted

Student Life *Campus security:* 24-hour patrols.

Standardized Tests *Required for some:* SAT I (for admission).

Applying *Options:* common application. *Application fee:* $25. *Required:* high school transcript, minimum 2.0 GPA, 2.50 GPA for engineering programs. *Recommended:* interview.

Admissions Contact Mr. Celestino De Hoyos, Dean of Admissions, Inter American University of Puerto Rico, Bayamón Campus, 500 Road 830, Bayamón, PR 00957. *Phone:* 787-279-1912 Ext. 2018. *Fax:* 787-279-2205 Ext. 2017. *E-mail:* cdehoyos@bc.inter.edu.

INTER AMERICAN UNIVERSITY OF PUERTO RICO, FAJARDO CAMPUS
Fajardo, Puerto Rico

- **Independent** 4-year, founded 1965, part of Inter American University of Puerto Rico
- **Calendar** semesters
- **Degrees** associate and bachelor's
- **Small-town** campus with easy access to San Juan
- **Coed**
- **Moderately difficult** entrance level

Student Life *Campus security:* 24-hour patrols.

Standardized Tests *Required:* SAT I (for admission).

Applying *Options:* early admission, deferred entrance. *Required:* high school transcript, minimum 2.0 GPA. *Required for some:* letters of recommendation.

Admissions Contact Ms. Jackeline Melèndez, Technician, Inter American University of Puerto Rico, Fajardo Campus, Call Box 70003, Fajaido, PR 00738-7003. *Phone:* 787-863-2390 Ext. 2210. *E-mail:* adcaraba@inter.edu.

INTER AMERICAN UNIVERSITY OF PUERTO RICO, GUAYAMA CAMPUS
Guayama, Puerto Rico

Admissions Contact Mrs. Laura E. Ferrer, Director of Admissions, Inter American University of Puerto Rico, Guayama Campus, Call Box 10004, Guayama, PR 00785. *Phone:* 787-864-2222 Ext. 220. *Fax:* 787-864-8232.

INTER AMERICAN UNIVERSITY OF PUERTO RICO, METROPOLITAN CAMPUS
San Juan, Puerto Rico

- **Independent** comprehensive, founded 1960, part of Inter American University of Puerto Rico
- **Calendar** semesters
- **Degrees** certificates, associate, bachelor's, master's, doctoral, postbachelor's, and first professional certificates
- **Coed**
- **Moderately difficult** entrance level

Faculty *Student/faculty ratio:* 40:1.

Student Life *Campus security:* 24-hour emergency response devices and patrols, video security system.

Standardized Tests *Required for some:* SAT I (for admission), SAT I (for placement).

Costs (2001–02) *Tuition:* $3300 full-time, $990 per term part-time. *Required fees:* $566 full-time, $145 per term part-time.

Financial Aid Of all full-time matriculated undergraduates who enrolled in 2001, 4328 applied for aid, 3935 were judged to have need, 29 had their need fully met. *Average percent of need met:* 11. *Average financial aid package:* $2144. *Average need-based loan:* $1149. *Average need-based gift aid:* $1617. *Financial aid deadline:* 4/30.

Applying *Required:* high school transcript, minimum 2.0 GPA.

Admissions Contact Ms. Ida G. Betancourt, Official Admission, Inter American University of Puerto Rico, Metropolitan Campus, Metropolitan Campus—Admission Ofc, PO Box 191293, San Juan, PR 00919-1293. *Phone:* 787-250-1912 Ext. 2100. *Fax:* 787-764-6963.

INTER AMERICAN UNIVERSITY OF PUERTO RICO, PONCE CAMPUS
Mercedita, Puerto Rico

- **Independent** 4-year, founded 1962, part of Inter American University of Puerto Rico
- **Calendar** semesters
- **Degrees** associate and bachelor's
- **Urban** 50-acre campus with easy access to San Juan

■ **Coed**
■ **Moderately difficult** entrance level

Faculty *Student/faculty ratio:* 34:1.
Standardized Tests *Required for some:* SAT I (for admission).
Costs (2001–02) *Tuition:* $3600 full-time, $120 per credit part-time. *Required fees:* $600 full-time.
Applying *Options:* common application, deferred entrance. *Required:* high school transcript, minimum 2.00 GPA.
Admissions Contact Mr. Fanco Diaz, Admissions Officer, Inter American University of Puerto Rico, Ponce Campus, Ponce Campus, 104 Turpo Industrial Park Road #1, Mercedita, PR 00715-1602. *Phone:* 787-284-1912 Ext. 2025. *Fax:* 787-841-0103. *E-mail:* jmuniz@ponce.inter.edu.

INTER AMERICAN UNIVERSITY OF PUERTO RICO, SAN GERMÁN CAMPUS
San Germán, Puerto Rico

■ **Independent** university, founded 1912, part of Inter American University of Puerto Rico
■ **Calendar** semesters
■ **Degrees** certificates, associate, bachelor's, master's, doctoral, and postbachelor's certificates
■ **Small-town** 260-acre campus
■ **Coed,** 4,810 undergraduate students, 83% full-time, 53% women, 47% men
■ **Moderately difficult** entrance level, 33% of applicants were admitted

Undergraduates 4,005 full-time, 805 part-time. Students come from 15 states and territories, 1% are from out of commonwealth, 100% Hispanic American, 2% transferred in, 10% live on campus.
Freshmen *Admission:* 4,705 applied, 1,570 admitted, 485 enrolled. *Average high school GPA:* 2.73. *Test scores:* SAT verbal scores over 500: 29%; SAT math scores over 500: 33%; SAT verbal scores over 600: 6%; SAT math scores over 600: 9%; SAT math scores over 700: 1%.
Faculty *Total:* 309, 41% full-time, 25% with terminal degrees. *Student/faculty ratio:* 25:1.
Majors Accounting; applied art; applied mathematics; art; art education; art history; behavioral sciences; biology; biomedical science; business administration; business economics; business marketing and marketing management; ceramic arts; chemistry; computer programming; computer science; drawing; early childhood education; economics; education; electrical/electronic engineering technology; elementary education; English; environmental science; exercise sciences; finance; health science; Hispanic-American studies; human resources management; industrial radiologic technology; information sciences/systems; linguistics; literature; marketing management and research related; mathematics; medical records administration; medical technology; microbiology/bacteriology; music; music (piano and organ performance); music teacher education; music (voice and choral/opera performance); natural sciences; nursing; photography; physical education; political science; psychology; public administration; science education; sculpture; secondary education; secretarial science; social sciences; sociology; stringed instruments; teaching English as a second language; wind/percussion instruments.
Academic Programs *Special study options:* academic remediation for entering students, accelerated degree program, adult/continuing education programs, advanced placement credit, cooperative education, distance learning, double majors, English as a second language, external degree program, honors programs, independent study, internships, off-campus study, part-time degree program, services for LD students, summer session for credit. *ROTC:* Army (c), Navy (c), Air Force (c).
Library Juan Cancio Ortiz Library with 162,544 titles, 1,748 serial subscriptions, 2,836 audiovisual materials, an OPAC, a Web page.
Computers on Campus 520 computers available on campus for general student use. Internet access, online (class) registration, at least one staffed computer lab available.
Student Life *Housing Options:* men-only, women-only. *Activities and Organizations:* drama/theater group, student-run newspaper, choral group, Future Teachers Association, PolyNature, Association for Computer Machinery, International Association of Administrative Professionals, Biology Honor Society, national fraternities, national sororities. *Campus security:* 24-hour emergency response devices and patrols. *Student Services:* personal/psychological counseling.
Athletics *Intercollegiate sports:* baseball M(s), basketball M(s)/W(s), cross-country running M(s)/W(s), soccer M(s), swimming M/W, table tennis M(s)/W(s), tennis M(s)/W(s), track and field M(s)/W(s), volleyball M(s)/W(s), weight lifting M(s), wrestling M(s). *Intramural sports:* badminton M/W, basketball M/W, cross-country running M/W, table tennis M/W, tennis M/W, track and field M/W, volleyball M/W.
Costs (2001–02) *Comprehensive fee:* $6390 includes full-time tuition ($3600), mandatory fees ($390), and room and board ($2400). Part-time tuition: $120 per credit. *Required fees:* $195 per term part-time. *Room and board:* College room only: $900. Room and board charges vary according to housing facility. *Payment plan:* deferred payment. *Waivers:* employees or children of employees.
Financial Aid Of all full-time matriculated undergraduates who enrolled in 2001, 3992 applied for aid, 3535 were judged to have need, 46 had their need fully met. *Average percent of need met:* 36%. *Average financial aid package:* $1592.
Applying *Options:* early admission. *Required:* high school transcript, medical history. *Required for some:* 1 letter of recommendation, interview. *Recommended:* essay or personal statement, minimum 2.0 GPA. *Application deadlines:* 5/13 (freshmen), 5/15 (transfers). *Notification:* continuous (freshmen).
Admissions Contact Mrs. Mildred Camacho, Director of Admissions, Inter American University of Puerto Rico, San Germán Campus, PO Box 5100, San Germán, PR 00683-5008. *Phone:* 787-264-1912 Ext. 7283. *Fax:* 787-892-6350. *E-mail:* milcama@sg.inter.edu.

POLYTECHNIC UNIVERSITY OF PUERTO RICO
Hato Rey, Puerto Rico

■ **Independent** comprehensive, founded 1966
■ **Calendar** trimesters
■ **Degrees** bachelor's and master's
■ **Urban** 10-acre campus with easy access to San Juan
■ **Endowment** $12.9 million
■ **Coed,** 4,895 undergraduate students, 53% full-time, 22% women, 78% men
■ **Minimally difficult** entrance level, 90% of applicants were admitted

Undergraduates 2,587 full-time, 2,308 part-time. Students come from 1 other state, 0% are from out of commonwealth, 100% Hispanic American, 9% transferred in. *Retention:* 70% of 2001 full-time freshmen returned.
Freshmen *Admission:* 1,000 applied, 897 admitted, 897 enrolled. *Average high school GPA:* 3.00.
Faculty *Total:* 279, 43% full-time, 15% with terminal degrees. *Student/faculty ratio:* 19:1.
Majors Architecture; business administration; chemical engineering; civil engineering; electrical engineering; environmental engineering; industrial/manufacturing engineering; mechanical engineering; surveying.
Academic Programs *Special study options:* academic remediation for entering students, English as a second language, part-time degree program, student-designed majors, summer session for credit. *ROTC:* Army (c).
Library Main Library plus 1 other with 81,899 titles, 2,025 serial subscriptions, 1,728 audiovisual materials, an OPAC, a Web page.
Computers on Campus 375 computers available on campus for general student use. A campuswide network can be accessed from student residence rooms and from off campus. At least one staffed computer lab available.
Student Life *Housing:* college housing not available. *Activities and Organizations:* drama/theater group, choral group, Society of Women Engineers, American Civil Engineering—Student Chapter, Society of Hispanic Professional Engineers, Society of Automotive Engineers, Capitulo Estudiantil Ingenieros Electricos. *Campus security:* 24-hour patrols. *Student Services:* health clinic, personal/psychological counseling.
Athletics *Intercollegiate sports:* basketball M/W, cross-country running M/W, soccer M, softball M/W, table tennis M/W, tennis M/W, track and field M/W, volleyball M/W. *Intramural sports:* basketball M, cross-country running M/W, soccer M/W, table tennis M/W, tennis M/W, volleyball M/W.
Standardized Tests *Required for some:* SAT I (for admission).
Costs (2002–03) *One-time required fee:* $10. *Tuition:* $4695 full-time, $120 per credit part-time. Full-time tuition and fees vary according to program. Part-time tuition and fees vary according to program. *Required fees:* $330 full-time, $110 per term part-time. *Payment plan:* deferred payment. *Waivers:* employees or children of employees.
Financial Aid Of all full-time matriculated undergraduates who enrolled in 2001, 1928 applied for aid, 1928 were judged to have need. *Financial aid deadline:* 5/15.
Applying *Options:* early admission, deferred entrance. *Application fee:* $30. *Required:* high school transcript. *Application deadline:* 8/15 (freshmen).
Admissions Contact Ms. Teresa Cardona, Director of Admissions, Polytechnic University of Puerto Rico, PO Box 192017, San Juan, PR 00919-2017. *Phone:* 787-754-8000 Ext. 240. *E-mail:* rbelvis@pupr.edu.

PONTIFICAL CATHOLIC UNIVERSITY OF PUERTO RICO

Ponce, Puerto Rico

- **Independent Roman Catholic** university, founded 1948
- **Calendar** semesters
- **Degrees** associate, bachelor's, master's, doctoral, and first professional (branch locations: Arecibo, Guayana, Mayagüez)
- **Urban** 120-acre campus with easy access to San Juan
- **Endowment** $13.7 million
- **Coed,** 5,530 undergraduate students, 83% full-time, 65% women, 35% men
- **Moderately difficult** entrance level, 87% of applicants were admitted

Undergraduates 4,577 full-time, 953 part-time. Students come from 1 other state, 0% are from out of commonwealth, 100% Hispanic American, 3% transferred in, 4% live on campus.

Freshmen *Admission:* 1,317 applied, 1,143 admitted, 980 enrolled. *Average high school GPA:* 2.75. *Test scores:* SAT verbal scores over 500: 30%; SAT math scores over 500: 31%; SAT verbal scores over 600: 7%; SAT math scores over 600: 9%; SAT math scores over 700: 1%.

Faculty *Total:* 248, 100% full-time. *Student/faculty ratio:* 33:1.

Majors Accounting; art; art education; biological/physical sciences; biology; biology education; business administration; business education; business marketing and marketing management; chemistry; computer education; computer management; computer programming; computer science; criminal justice/law enforcement administration; criminology; early childhood education; economics; education; elementary education; English; English education; environmental science; fashion design/illustration; finance; French; gerontology; health education; Hispanic-American studies; history; history education; home economics; home economics education; human resources management; international business; liberal arts and sciences/liberal studies; mass communications; mathematics; mathematics education; medical technology; music; music teacher education; nursing; philosophy; physical education; physics; political science; pre-law; pre-medicine; psychology; public administration; public relations; publishing; radio/television broadcasting; science education; secondary education; secretarial science; social studies education; social work; sociology; Spanish; special education; theology; tourism/travel marketing; travel/tourism management; veterinary sciences.

Academic Programs *Special study options:* academic remediation for entering students, adult/continuing education programs, advanced placement credit, cooperative education, double majors, English as a second language, honors programs, independent study, off-campus study, part-time degree program, services for LD students, summer session for credit. *ROTC:* Army (c). *Unusual degree programs:* 3-2 engineering with Case Western Reserve University; pharmacy with Massachusetts College of Pharmacy and Allied Health Sciences.

Library Encarnacion Valdes Library plus 1 other with 48,580 serial subscriptions, an OPAC, a Web page.

Computers on Campus 419 computers available on campus for general student use. A campuswide network can be accessed from off campus. Internet access, at least one staffed computer lab available.

Student Life *Housing Options:* men-only, women-only. *Activities and Organizations:* drama/theater group, student-run newspaper, radio and television station, choral group, Accounting Students Club, Foreign Students Club, Christ Heralds, national fraternities, national sororities. *Campus security:* 24-hour emergency response devices and patrols. *Student Services:* health clinic, personal/psychological counseling.

Athletics *Intercollegiate sports:* basketball M/W, cross-country running M/W, soccer M/W, swimming M/W, table tennis M/W, tennis M/W, track and field M(s)/W(s), volleyball M/W, water polo M, weight lifting M, wrestling M. *Intramural sports:* archery M/W, baseball M, basketball M/W, bowling M/W, cross-country running M/W, softball M/W, swimming M/W, table tennis M/W, tennis M/W, track and field M/W, volleyball M/W, weight lifting M, wrestling M.

Standardized Tests *Required:* SAT I (for admission).

Costs (2001–02) *Comprehensive fee:* $7000 includes full-time tuition ($3840), mandatory fees ($320), and room and board ($2840). Full-time tuition and fees vary according to course load. Part-time tuition: $120 per credit. Part-time tuition and fees vary according to course load. *Required fees:* $198 per term part-time. *Room and board:* College room only: $800. *Payment plan:* deferred payment. *Waivers:* employees or children of employees.

Financial Aid Of all full-time matriculated undergraduates who enrolled in 2001, 6169 applied for aid, 6096 were judged to have need, 73 had their need fully met. 975 Federal Work-Study jobs (averaging $613). *Average percent of need met:* 71%. *Average need-based loan:* $3108. *Average need-based gift aid:* $3961.

Applying *Options:* early admission, deferred entrance. *Application fee:* $15. *Required:* high school transcript, minimum 2.0 GPA. *Required for some:* essay or personal statement, minimum 3.0 GPA, 1 letter of recommendation, interview. *Application deadlines:* 3/15 (freshmen), 3/15 (transfers). *Notification:* continuous (freshmen).

Admissions Contact Sra. Ana O. Bonilla, Director of Admissions, Pontifical Catholic University of Puerto Rico, 2250 Avenida Las Americas, Ponce, PR 00717-0777. *Phone:* 787-841-2000 Ext. 1004. *Toll-free phone:* 800-981-5040. *Fax:* 787-840-4295. *E-mail:* admissions@pucpr.edu.

UNIVERSIDAD ADVENTISTA DE LAS ANTILLAS

Mayagüez, Puerto Rico

- **Independent Seventh-day Adventist** comprehensive, founded 1957
- **Calendar** semesters
- **Degrees** associate, bachelor's, and master's
- **Rural** 284-acre campus
- **Coed,** 719 undergraduate students, 89% full-time, 60% women, 40% men
- **Minimally difficult** entrance level, 78% of applicants were admitted

Undergraduates 642 full-time, 77 part-time. Students come from 10 states and territories, 22 other countries, 24% are from out of commonwealth, 0.8% African American, 96% Hispanic American, 3% international, 11% transferred in, 27% live on campus. *Retention:* 72% of 2001 full-time freshmen returned.

Freshmen *Admission:* 380 applied, 298 admitted, 128 enrolled. *Average high school GPA:* 2.83.

Faculty *Total:* 63, 62% full-time, 11% with terminal degrees. *Student/faculty ratio:* 14:1.

Majors Biblical studies; biology; business administration; chemistry; computer science; elementary education; history; medical administrative assistant; medical records administration; music; music teacher education; nursing; pastoral counseling; religious education; respiratory therapy; secondary education; secretarial science; Spanish; theology.

Academic Programs *Special study options:* academic remediation for entering students, adult/continuing education programs, advanced placement credit, cooperative education, double majors, English as a second language, internships, part-time degree program, services for LD students, summer session for credit. *Unusual degree programs:* 3-2 engineering with Walla Walla College; nursing with Loma Linda University.

Library Biblioteca Dennis Soto plus 1 other with 86,465 titles, 452 serial subscriptions, 325 audiovisual materials, an OPAC, a Web page.

Computers on Campus 62 computers available on campus for general student use. Internet access, at least one staffed computer lab available.

Student Life *Housing:* on-campus residence required for freshman year. *Options:* coed, men-only, women-only. *Activities and Organizations:* student-run newspaper, choral group, Score Group, Gymnastic Club, Student Council, Group Life. *Campus security:* 24-hour emergency response devices and patrols, student patrols, controlled dormitory access. *Student Services:* health clinic, personal/psychological counseling.

Athletics *Intercollegiate sports:* softball M. *Intramural sports:* basketball M/W, gymnastics M/W, soccer M, softball M, swimming M/W, tennis M/W, volleyball M/W.

Standardized Tests *Recommended:* SAT I or ACT (for admission).

Costs (2002–03) *Comprehensive fee:* $6580 includes full-time tuition ($3475), mandatory fees ($605), and room and board ($2500). Full-time tuition and fees vary according to course load. Part-time tuition: $120 per credit. Part-time tuition and fees vary according to course load. *Room and board:* College room only: $700. Room and board charges vary according to board plan. *Payment plans:* tuition prepayment, installment, deferred payment. *Waivers:* employees or children of employees.

Financial Aid Of all full-time matriculated undergraduates who enrolled in 2001, 612 applied for aid, 609 were judged to have need, 2 had their need fully met. 93 State and other part-time jobs (averaging $386). *Average percent of need met:* 60%. *Average financial aid package:* $6700. *Average need-based loan:* $1792. *Average need-based gift aid:* $4795.

Applying *Options:* common application, early admission. *Application fee:* $20. *Required:* high school transcript, minimum 2.0 GPA, letters of recommendation. *Required for some:* interview.

Admissions Contact Universidad Adventista de las Antillas, Universidad Adventista de las Antillas oficina de Admisiones, PO Box 118, Mayaguez, PR 00681-0118. *Phone:* 787-834-9595 Ext. 2208. *Fax:* 787-834-9597. *E-mail:* admissions@uaa.edu.

UNIVERSIDAD DEL TURABO
Turabo, Puerto Rico

Admissions Contact Sr. Jesús Torres, Director of Admissions, Universidad del Turabo, PO Box 3030, Turabo, PR 00778-3030. *Phone:* 787-743-7979 Ext. 201.

UNIVERSIDAD METROPOLITANA
Río Piedras, Puerto Rico

Admissions Contact Ms. Carmen Rosado, Director of Admissions, Universidad Metropolitana, Call Box 21150, Río Piedras, PR 00928-1150. *Phone:* 787-766-1717 Ext. 540. *Toll-free phone:* 800-747-8362. *E-mail:* um_frivera@suagm1.suagm.edu.

UNIVERSITY OF PHOENIX-PUERTO RICO CAMPUS
Guaynabo, Puerto Rico

- **Proprietary** comprehensive
- **Calendar** continuous
- **Degrees** certificates, associate, bachelor's, master's, doctoral, post-master's, and postbachelor's certificates (courses conducted at 54 campuses and learning centers in 13 states)
- **Coed,** 299 undergraduate students, 100% full-time, 54% women, 46% men
- **Noncompetitive** entrance level

Undergraduates Students come from 2 states and territories, 1% are from out of commonwealth.
Freshmen *Admission:* 32 admitted.
Faculty *Total:* 166, 3% full-time, 45% with terminal degrees. *Student/faculty ratio:* 12:1.
Majors Accounting; business administration; information technology; management science.
Academic Programs *Special study options:* accelerated degree program, adult/continuing education programs, advanced placement credit, distance learning, external degree program, independent study.
Library University Library with 17.5 million titles, 9,000 serial subscriptions, an OPAC, a Web page.
Computers on Campus A campuswide network can be accessed from off campus. Internet access, at least one staffed computer lab available.
Student Life *Housing:* college housing not available.
Costs (2001–02) *Tuition:* $4740 full-time. Full-time tuition and fees vary according to location and program. *Payment plan:* deferred payment. *Waivers:* employees or children of employees.
Applying *Options:* deferred entrance. *Application fee:* $85. *Required:* 2 years of work experience. *Required for some:* high school transcript. *Application deadline:* rolling (freshmen), rolling (transfers).
Admissions Contact Ms. Beth Barilla, Director of Admissions, University of Phoenix-Puerto Rico Campus, 4615 East Elwood Street, Phoenix, AZ 85040-1958. *Phone:* 480-927-0099 Ext. 1218. *Toll-free phone:* 800-228-7240. *Fax:* 480-594-1758. *E-mail:* beth.barilla@apollogrp.edu.

UNIVERSITY OF PUERTO RICO, AGUADILLA UNIVERSITY COLLEGE
Aguadilla, Puerto Rico

- **Commonwealth-supported** 4-year, founded 1972, part of University of Puerto Rico System
- **Calendar** semesters
- **Degrees** associate and bachelor's
- **Suburban** 32-acre campus
- **Coed**
- **Moderately difficult** entrance level

Student Life *Campus security:* 24-hour patrols.
Standardized Tests *Required:* SAT I (for admission), SAT II: Subject Tests (for admission).
Applying *Options:* common application, early admission, deferred entrance. *Required:* high school transcript.
Admissions Contact Ms. Melba Serrano Lugo, Admissions Officer, University of Puerto Rico, Aguadilla University College, Admission Office, PO Box 250160, Aguadilla, PR 00604-0160. *Phone:* 787-890-2681 Ext. 280. *E-mail:* m_serrano@upr.clue.edu.

UNIVERSITY OF PUERTO RICO AT ARECIBO
Arecibo, Puerto Rico

Admissions Contact Mrs. Margarita Sáenz, Director of Admissions, University of Puerto Rico at Arecibo, PO Box 4010, Arecibo, PR 00614-4010. *Phone:* 787-878-2830 Ext. 3023. *E-mail:* m_saenz@cuta.upr.clu.edu.

UNIVERSITY OF PUERTO RICO AT BAYAMÓN
Bayamón, Puerto Rico

Admissions Contact Ms. Vivian Rivera, Officer of Admission, University of Puerto Rico at Bayamón, 170 Carr 174 Parque Indust Minillas, Bayamón, PR 00959-1919. *Phone:* 787-786-2885 Ext. 2425. *E-mail:* e_velez@cutb.upr.clu.edu.

UNIVERSITY OF PUERTO RICO AT CAROLINA
Carolina, Puerto Rico

Admissions Contact Mrs. Ivonne Calderon, Admissions Officer, University of Puerto Rico at Carolina, PO Box 4800, Carolina, PR 00984-4800. *Phone:* 787-257-0000 Ext. 3347.

UNIVERSITY OF PUERTO RICO AT HUMACAO
Humacao, Puerto Rico

- **Commonwealth-supported** 4-year, founded 1962, part of University of Puerto Rico System
- **Calendar** semesters
- **Degrees** associate and bachelor's
- **Suburban** 62-acre campus with easy access to San Juan
- **Coed,** 4,476 undergraduate students, 78% full-time, 72% women, 28% men
- **Moderately difficult** entrance level, 65% of applicants were admitted

Undergraduates 3,513 full-time, 963 part-time. Students come from 5 states and territories, 0% are from out of commonwealth, 100% Hispanic American, 0.6% transferred in. *Retention:* 87% of 2001 full-time freshmen returned.
Freshmen *Admission:* 1,491 applied, 966 admitted, 822 enrolled. *Average high school GPA:* 3.44.
Faculty *Total:* 284, 91% full-time, 37% with terminal degrees. *Student/faculty ratio:* 15:1.
Majors Accounting; biology; business; business administration; chemical technology; chemistry; electrical/electronic engineering technology; elementary education; human resources management; marine biology; mathematics/computer science; microbiology/bacteriology; nursing; occupational therapy assistant; physical therapy assistant; physics; secretarial science; social work; teaching English as a second language; wildlife management.
Academic Programs *Special study options:* academic remediation for entering students, English as a second language, freshman honors college, honors programs, internships, off-campus study, part-time degree program, services for LD students, summer session for credit. *ROTC:* Army (b).
Library 64,557 titles, 2,526 serial subscriptions, 752 audiovisual materials, an OPAC, a Web page.
Computers on Campus 271 computers available on campus for general student use. A campuswide network can be accessed from off campus. Internet access, online (class) registration, at least one staffed computer lab available.
Student Life *Housing:* college housing not available. *Activities and Organizations:* drama/theater group, student-run radio station, choral group, marching band, Recreational Organization, Accounting Students Association, Management Students Association, Microbiology Students Association, Human Resources Students Association, national fraternities. *Campus security:* 24-hour patrols, 24-hour gate security. *Student Services:* personal/psychological counseling.
Athletics *Intercollegiate sports:* baseball M(s), basketball M(s)/W(s), cross-country running M(s)/W(s), softball W, swimming M/W, tennis W, track and field M(s)/W(s), volleyball M/W, wrestling M. *Intramural sports:* basketball M/W, volleyball M/W.
Standardized Tests *Required for some:* SAT I (for admission), SAT II: Subject Tests (for admission).

University of Puerto Rico at Humacao (continued)

Costs (2001–02) *Tuition:* commonwealth resident $1020 full-time, $30 per credit part-time. Full-time tuition and fees vary according to course load. Part-time tuition and fees vary according to course load. Nonresidents who are U.S. citizens pay an amount equal to the rate for nonresidents at a state university in their home state. *Required fees:* $225 full-time, $40 per term part-time. *Payment plan:* deferred payment. *Waivers:* employees or children of employees.

Financial Aid Of all full-time matriculated undergraduates who enrolled in 2001, 2898 applied for aid, 2839 were judged to have need. 278 Federal Work-Study jobs (averaging $1318). In 2001, 29 non-need-based awards were made. *Average percent of need met:* 55%. *Average non-need based aid:* $1066. *Financial aid deadline:* 6/30.

Applying *Options:* deferred entrance. *Application fee:* $15. *Required:* high school transcript, minimum 2.0 GPA. *Application deadlines:* 11/30 (freshmen), 2/15 (transfers). *Notification:* continuous until 4/30 (freshmen).

Admissions Contact Mrs. Inara Ferrer, Director of Admissions, University of Puerto Rico at Humacao, HUC Station, Humacao, PR 00791. *Phone:* 787-850-9301. *E-mail:* i_ferrer@cuhac.upr.clu.edu.

UNIVERSITY OF PUERTO RICO AT PONCE

Ponce, Puerto Rico

- **Commonwealth-supported** 4-year, founded 1970, part of University of Puerto Rico System
- **Calendar** semesters
- **Degrees** associate and bachelor's
- **Urban** 86-acre campus with easy access to San Juan
- **Coed,** 4,070 undergraduate students, 84% full-time, 66% women, 34% men
- **Moderately difficult** entrance level, 61% of applicants were admitted

Undergraduates 3,403 full-time, 667 part-time. Students come from 1 other state, 100% Hispanic American, 2% transferred in. *Retention:* 74% of 2001 full-time freshmen returned.

Freshmen *Admission:* 1,668 applied, 1,021 admitted, 1,643 enrolled. *Average high school GPA:* 3.2.

Faculty *Total:* 178, 76% full-time, 12% with terminal degrees. *Student/faculty ratio:* 19:1.

Majors Accounting; athletic training/sports medicine; business administration; civil engineering technology; computer science; drafting; elementary education; industrial technology; liberal arts and sciences/liberal studies; natural sciences; occupational therapy; physical therapy; secretarial science.

Academic Programs *Special study options:* academic remediation for entering students, accelerated degree program, adult/continuing education programs, advanced placement credit, English as a second language, freshman honors college, honors programs, internships, part-time degree program, summer session for credit. *ROTC:* Army (b).

Library 53,000 titles, 1,643 serial subscriptions, an OPAC.

Computers on Campus 231 computers available on campus for general student use. Internet access, at least one staffed computer lab available.

Student Life *Housing:* college housing not available. *Activities and Organizations:* drama/theater group, choral group, American Marketing Association, Secretarial Sciences Association, drama club, Alfa Computer Club. *Campus security:* 24-hour patrols. *Student Services:* health clinic.

Athletics *Intercollegiate sports:* basketball M(s)/W(s), cross-country running M(s)/W(s), tennis M(s)/W(s), track and field M(s)/W(s), volleyball M(s)/W(s), weight lifting M(s)/W(s). *Intramural sports:* basketball M/W, cross-country running M/W, racquetball M/W, softball M/W, table tennis M/W, tennis M/W, track and field M/W, volleyball M/W, weight lifting M/W.

Standardized Tests *Required:* SAT I (for admission).

Costs (2001–02) *Tuition:* commonwealth resident $1245 full-time, $30 per credit part-time. *Required fees:* $1000 full-time, $1000 per year part-time. *Payment plan:* installment. *Waivers:* employees or children of employees.

Financial Aid Of all full-time matriculated undergraduates who enrolled in 2001, 3461 applied for aid, 3133 were judged to have need. *Average percent of need met:* 40%. *Financial aid deadline:* 6/30.

Applying *Options:* common application, early admission, early decision. *Application fee:* $15. *Required:* high school transcript. *Application deadlines:* 11/15 (freshmen), 2/23 (transfers). *Early decision:* 1/15. *Notification:* 3/4 (freshmen), 1/20 (early decision).

Admissions Contact Mr. William Rodriguez Mercado, Admissions Officer, University of Puerto Rico at Ponce, PO Box 7186, Ponce, PR 00732-7186. *Phone:* 787-844-8181 Ext. 2530. *Fax:* 787-842-3875.

UNIVERSITY OF PUERTO RICO AT UTUADO

Utuado, Puerto Rico

- **Commonwealth-supported** 4-year, founded 1979, part of University of Puerto Rico System
- **Calendar** semesters
- **Degrees** associate and bachelor's
- **Small-town** 180-acre campus with easy access to San Juan
- **Coed**
- **Moderately difficult** entrance level

Faculty *Student/faculty ratio:* 21:1.

Student Life *Campus security:* 24-hour emergency response devices and patrols.

Costs (2001–02) *Tuition:* commonwealth resident $1245 full-time, $30 per credit part-time; nonresident $2400 full-time. Full-time tuition and fees vary according to program. Part-time tuition and fees vary according to program. *Required fees:* $70 full-time.

Financial Aid Of all full-time matriculated undergraduates who enrolled in 2001, 143 Federal Work-Study jobs. *Financial aid deadline:* 6/15.

Applying *Options:* common application. *Application fee:* $15.

Admissions Contact Ms. Maria V. Robles Serrano, Admissions Officer, University of Puerto Rico at Utuado, PO Box 2500, Utuado, PR 00641-2500. *Phone:* 787-894-2828 Ext. 2240.

UNIVERSITY OF PUERTO RICO, CAYEY UNIVERSITY COLLEGE

Cayey, Puerto Rico

- **Commonwealth-supported** 4-year, founded 1967, part of University of Puerto Rico System
- **Calendar** semesters
- **Degrees** associate and bachelor's
- **Urban** 177-acre campus with easy access to San Juan
- **Coed,** 4,019 undergraduate students, 91% full-time, 71% women, 29% men
- **Very difficult** entrance level, 36% of applicants were admitted

Undergraduates 3,665 full-time, 354 part-time. Students come from 1 other state, 100% Hispanic American, 0.5% transferred in. *Retention:* 89% of 2001 full-time freshmen returned.

Freshmen *Admission:* 3,365 applied, 1,217 admitted, 907 enrolled. *Average high school GPA:* 3.3.

Faculty *Total:* 230, 79% full-time. *Student/faculty ratio:* 18:1.

Majors Accounting; Army R.O.T.C./military science; biology; biology education; business administration; chemistry; chemistry education; economics; elementary education; English; English education; history; history education; humanities; mathematics; mathematics education; mental health/rehabilitation; natural sciences; physical education; physics education; psychology; science education; secondary education; secretarial science; social science education; social sciences; social studies education; sociology; Spanish; Spanish language education.

Academic Programs *Special study options:* academic remediation for entering students, accelerated degree program, advanced placement credit, honors programs, off-campus study, part-time degree program, study abroad, summer session for credit. *ROTC:* Army (b).

Library Victor M. Pons Library with 109,776 titles, 2,013 serial subscriptions, 2,286 audiovisual materials, an OPAC, a Web page.

Computers on Campus 450 computers available on campus for general student use. A campuswide network can be accessed from off campus. Internet access, online (class) registration, at least one staffed computer lab available.

Student Life *Housing:* college housing not available. *Activities and Organizations:* drama/theater group, choral group, Business Administration Circle, Christian University Association, national fraternities, national sororities. *Campus security:* 24-hour emergency response devices and patrols, late-night transport/escort service. *Student Services:* health clinic, personal/psychological counseling, women's center.

Athletics *Intercollegiate sports:* basketball M(s)/W(s), cross-country running M(s)/W(s), fencing M(s)/W(s), football M(s), golf M(s), soccer M(s), swimming M(s), table tennis M(s), tennis M(s)/W(s), track and field M(s)/W(s), volleyball M(s)/W(s). *Intramural sports:* basketball M/W, cross-country running M/W, fencing M/W, football M, golf M, soccer M/W, swimming M/W, tennis M/W, track and field M/W, volleyball M/W.

Standardized Tests *Required for some:* SAT I (for admission).

Costs (2002–03) *Tuition:* area resident $1020 full-time, $30 per credit part-time. Full-time tuition and fees vary according to degree level and program. *Required fees:* $225 full-time, $225 per year part-time. *Waivers:* employees or children of employees.

Financial Aid Of all full-time matriculated undergraduates who enrolled in 2001, 2866 applied for aid, 2819 were judged to have need. 281 Federal Work-Study jobs. *Average financial aid package:* $4200. *Average need-based loan:* $3000. *Average need-based gift aid:* $3300.

Applying *Options:* common application, early admission. *Application fee:* $15. *Required:* high school transcript, minimum 2.0 GPA. *Application deadlines:* 12/1 (freshmen), 2/15 (transfers). *Notification:* continuous until 5/5 (freshmen).

Admissions Contact Admissions Officer, University of Puerto Rico, Cayey University College, Avenue Antonio R. Barcelo, Cayey, PR 00736. *Phone:* 787-738-2161 Ext. 2208.

UNIVERSITY OF PUERTO RICO, MAYAGÜEZ CAMPUS

Mayagüez, Puerto Rico

- **Commonwealth-supported** university, founded 1911, part of University of Puerto Rico System
- **Calendar** semesters
- **Degrees** bachelor's, master's, and doctoral
- **Urban** 315-acre campus
- **Coed**
- **Very difficult** entrance level

Faculty *Student/faculty ratio:* 16:1.

Student Life *Campus security:* 24-hour emergency response devices and patrols.

Standardized Tests *Required:* SAT I (for admission), SAT II: Subject Tests (for admission).

Costs (2001–02) *Tuition:* $30 per credit part-time; commonwealth resident $1050 full-time. *Required fees:* $110 full-time.

Financial Aid Of all full-time matriculated undergraduates who enrolled in 2001, 8004 applied for aid, 7112 were judged to have need. 398 Federal Work-Study jobs (averaging $1172). 428 State and other part-time jobs (averaging $3827). *Average percent of need met:* 52. *Average financial aid package:* $4200. *Average need-based gift aid:* $900. *Average indebtedness upon graduation:* $6400.

Applying *Options:* common application, early action. *Application fee:* $15. *Required:* high school transcript.

Admissions Contact Ms. Norma Torres, Director, Admissions Office, University of Puerto Rico, Mayagüez Campus, PO Box 9021, Mayaguez, PR 00681-9021. *Phone:* 787-265-3811. *Fax:* 787-834-5265. *E-mail:* norma_t@dediego.uprm.edu.

UNIVERSITY OF PUERTO RICO, MEDICAL SCIENCES CAMPUS

San Juan, Puerto Rico

- **Commonwealth-supported** upper-level, founded 1950, part of University of Puerto Rico System
- **Calendar** semesters
- **Degrees** certificates, associate, bachelor's, master's, doctoral, first professional, postbachelor's, and first professional certificates (bachelor's degree is upper-level)
- **Urban** 11-acre campus
- **Coed, primarily women,** 904 undergraduate students, 87% full-time, 88% women, 12% men
- **Moderately difficult** entrance level, 70% of applicants were admitted

Undergraduates 782 full-time, 122 part-time. Students come from 1 other state, 100% Hispanic American, 40% transferred in.

Freshmen *Admission:* 430 applied, 300 admitted.

Faculty *Total:* 605, 70% full-time.

Majors Dental assistant; dental hygiene; health education; health science; medical laboratory technology; medical radiologic technology; nuclear medical technology; nursing; occupational therapy; optometric/ophthalmic laboratory technician; pharmacy; physical therapy; speech-language pathology/audiology; veterinary technology.

Academic Programs *Special study options:* academic remediation for entering students, adult/continuing education programs, internships, off-campus study, summer session for credit.

Library Medical Sciences Library plus 1 other with 42,092 titles, 1,132 serial subscriptions, 1,702 audiovisual materials, an OPAC, a Web page.

Computers on Campus A campuswide network can be accessed from off campus. Internet access, at least one staffed computer lab available.

Student Life *Housing:* college housing not available. *Activities and Organizations:* drama/theater group, choral group, General Council of Students, Academy of Pharmacy Students, Council of medicine students, Council of Public Health Students, American Medical Association-Puerto Rico Chapter-Student Section, national fraternities, national sororities. *Campus security:* 24-hour emergency response devices. *Student Services:* health clinic, personal/psychological counseling, women's center, legal services.

Athletics *Intramural sports:* basketball M, volleyball M.

Standardized Tests *Required:* SAT I (for placement). *Required for some:* PCAT, MCAT, DAT, ASPHAT, GRE, PAEG.

Costs (2001–02) *Tuition:* commonwealth resident $1080 full-time, $30 per credit part-time. Full-time tuition and fees vary according to course load, degree level, and program. Part-time tuition and fees vary according to course load, degree level, and program. *Required fees:* $1018 full-time. *Room and board:* Room and board charges vary according to housing facility. *Payment plan:* deferred payment. *Waivers:* employees or children of employees.

Financial Aid Of all full-time matriculated undergraduates who enrolled in 2001, 915 applied for aid, 806 were judged to have need, 484 had their need fully met. 94 Federal Work-Study jobs (averaging $618). *Average percent of need met:* 68%. *Average financial aid package:* $4644. *Average need-based loan:* $5500. *Average need-based gift aid:* $3450. *Average indebtedness upon graduation:* $4500. *Financial aid deadline:* 6/9.

Applying *Application fee:* $15. *Application deadline:* 2/28 (transfers). *Notification:* continuous until 5/30 (transfers).

Admissions Contact Mrs. Rosa Vèlez, Acting Director of Admission Office, University of Puerto Rico, Medical Sciences Campus, P.O. Box 365067, San Juan, PR 00936-5067. *Phone:* 787-758-2525 Ext. 5211. *E-mail:* rvelez@rcm.upr.edu.

UNIVERSITY OF PUERTO RICO, RÍO PIEDRAS

San Juan, Puerto Rico

- **Commonwealth-supported** university, founded 1903, part of University of Puerto Rico System
- **Calendar** semesters
- **Degrees** bachelor's, master's, doctoral, first professional, and post-master's certificates
- **Urban** 281-acre campus
- **Coed**
- **Very difficult** entrance level

Faculty *Student/faculty ratio:* 17:1.

Student Life *Campus security:* 24-hour emergency response devices, late-night transport/escort service.

Athletics Member NCAA, NAIA. All NCAA Division II.

Standardized Tests *Required:* SAT I (for admission), SAT II: Subject Tests (for admission).

Applying *Options:* common application. *Application fee:* $15. *Required:* high school transcript, minimum 2.0 GPA. *Required for some:* interview.

Admissions Contact Mrs. Cruz B. Valentìn, Director of Admissions, University of Puerto Rico, Río Piedras, PO Box 21907, San Juan, PR 00931-1907. *Phone:* 787-764-0000 Ext. 5666. *Fax:* 787-764-3680 Ext. 5352.

UNIVERSITY OF THE SACRED HEART

San Juan, Puerto Rico

- **Independent Roman Catholic** comprehensive, founded 1935
- **Calendar** semesters
- **Degrees** certificates, associate, bachelor's, and master's
- **Urban** 33-acre campus
- **Endowment** $16.5 million
- **Coed**
- **Moderately difficult** entrance level

Faculty *Student/faculty ratio:* 22:1.

Student Life *Campus security:* 24-hour patrols.

Costs (2001–02) *One-time required fee:* $10. *Tuition:* $4610 full-time, $140 per credit part-time. Full-time tuition and fees vary according to student level. Part-time tuition and fees vary according to student level. *Required fees:* $400 full-time, $160 per term part-time. *Room only:* $1800. Room and board charges vary according to student level.

University of the Sacred Heart (continued)

Applying *Options:* common application, early admission. *Application fee:* $15. *Required:* high school transcript, minimum 2.5 GPA, 1 letter of recommendation.

Admissions Contact Mr. Daniel Rodriguez, Director of Admissions, University of the Sacred Heart, Admissions Office, PO Box 12383, San Juan, PR 00914-0383. *Phone:* 787-728-1515 Ext. 3237.

VIRGIN ISLANDS

UNIVERSITY OF THE VIRGIN ISLANDS

Charlotte Amalie, Virgin Islands

- **Territory-supported** comprehensive, founded 1962
- **Calendar** semesters
- **Degrees** associate, bachelor's, and master's
- **Small-town** 175-acre campus
- **Endowment** $6.3 million
- **Coed,** 2,104 undergraduate students, 52% full-time, 77% women, 23% men
- **Minimally difficult** entrance level, 97% of applicants were admitted

Undergraduates 1,101 full-time, 1,003 part-time. Students come from 29 states and territories, 10 other countries, 3% are from out of territory, 3% transferred in.

Freshmen *Admission:* 473 applied, 457 admitted, 282 enrolled. *Test scores:* SAT verbal scores over 500: 18%; SAT math scores over 500: 11%; SAT verbal scores over 600: 2%.

Faculty *Total:* 246, 45% full-time, 39% with terminal degrees. *Student/faculty ratio:* 9:1.

Majors Accounting; biology; business administration; chemistry; computer science; data processing technology; elementary education; English; hotel and restaurant management; humanities; law enforcement/police science; marine biology; mathematics; music teacher education; nursing; physics; psychology; secretarial science; social sciences; social work; speech/rhetorical studies; theater arts/drama; trade/industrial education.

Academic Programs *Special study options:* academic remediation for entering students, adult/continuing education programs, advanced placement credit, internships, off-campus study, part-time degree program, summer session for credit.

Library Ralph M. Paiewonsky Library with 106,361 titles, 940 serial subscriptions, an OPAC, a Web page.

Computers on Campus 100 computers available on campus for general student use. A campuswide network can be accessed from off campus. At least one staffed computer lab available.

Student Life *Housing Options:* men-only, women-only. *Activities and Organizations:* drama/theater group, student-run newspaper, choral group, The Squad, Predators, Golden Key Honor Society, National Student Exchange Club, St. Kitts and Nevis, national fraternities, national sororities. *Campus security:* 24-hour patrols. *Student Services:* health clinic, personal/psychological counseling.

Athletics *Intercollegiate sports:* basketball M/W, cross-country running M/W, tennis M/W, volleyball M/W. *Intramural sports:* basketball M/W, tennis M/W, volleyball M/W.

Costs (2001–02) *Tuition:* territory resident $2730 full-time, $91 per credit part-time; nonresident $8190 full-time, $273 per credit part-time. *Required fees:* $2216 full-time, $65 per term part-time. *Room and board:* $5830; room only: $2000. *Waivers:* senior citizens and employees or children of employees.

Financial Aid Of all full-time matriculated undergraduates who enrolled in 2001, 994 applied for aid, 688 were judged to have need, 83 had their need fully met. 44 Federal Work-Study jobs (averaging $2500). 42 State and other part-time jobs (averaging $2500). *Average percent of need met:* 50%. *Average financial aid package:* $2400. *Average need-based loan:* $1383. *Average need-based gift aid:* $1770. *Average indebtedness upon graduation:* $2000.

Applying *Options:* early admission, deferred entrance. *Application fee:* $20. *Required:* essay or personal statement, high school transcript, 2 letters of recommendation. *Application deadlines:* 4/15 (freshmen), 4/15 (transfers).

Admissions Contact Ms. Carolyn Cook, Director of Admissions & New Student Services, University of the Virgin Islands, No. 2 John Brewers Bay, St. Thomas, VI 00802. *Phone:* 340-693-1224. *E-mail:* admissions@uvi.edu.

CANADA

ACADIA UNIVERSITY

Wolfville, Nova Scotia, Canada

- **Province-supported** comprehensive, founded 1838
- **Calendar** Canadian standard year
- **Degrees** bachelor's and master's
- **Small-town** 250-acre campus
- **Endowment** $22.0 million
- **Coed,** 3,821 undergraduate students, 96% full-time, 56% women, 44% men
- **Moderately difficult** entrance level, 48% of applicants were admitted

Undergraduates 3,658 full-time, 163 part-time. Students come from 12 provinces and territories, 64 other countries, 39% are from out of province, 6% transferred in, 40% live on campus. *Retention:* 89% of 2001 full-time freshmen returned.

Freshmen *Admission:* 1,936 applied, 936 admitted, 1,097 enrolled.

Faculty *Total:* 278, 67% full-time. *Student/faculty ratio:* 17:1.

Majors Biology; business administration; Canadian studies; chemistry; classics; computer science; dietetics; economics; education; elementary education; English; environmental science; exercise sciences; food sciences; French; geology; history; Latin (ancient and medieval); mathematics; music; music (piano and organ performance); music teacher education; music (voice and choral/opera performance); nutrition science; philosophy; physics; political science; predentistry; pre-law; pre-medicine; pre-veterinary studies; psychology; secondary education; sociology; stringed instruments; theater arts/drama; wind/percussion instruments.

Academic Programs *Special study options:* academic remediation for entering students, advanced placement credit, cooperative education, distance learning, double majors, English as a second language, honors programs, internships, off-campus study, part-time degree program, study abroad, summer session for credit.

Library Vaughan Memorial Library with 822,030 titles, 4,106 serial subscriptions, 4,406 audiovisual materials, an OPAC, a Web page.

Computers on Campus 3700 computers available on campus for general student use. A campuswide network can be accessed from student residence rooms and from off campus that provide access to online course and grade information. Internet access, online (class) registration, at least one staffed computer lab available.

Student Life *Housing Options:* coed, men-only, women-only. *Activities and Organizations:* drama/theater group, student-run newspaper, radio station, choral group, marching band, Acadia Recreation Club, Acadia Ski Club, Education Society, Computer Science Club, Caricom. *Campus security:* 24-hour emergency response devices and patrols, student patrols, late-night transport/escort service, controlled dormitory access. *Student Services:* health clinic, personal/psychological counseling, women's center, legal services.

Athletics Member CIAU. *Intercollegiate sports:* baseball M(c), basketball M/W, football M, ice hockey M/W, rugby M(c)/W(c), soccer M/W, track and field M/W, volleyball W. *Intramural sports:* badminton M/W, baseball M/W, basketball M/W, cross-country running M/W, ice hockey M/W, racquetball M/W, rugby M/W, skiing (cross-country) M/W, skiing (downhill) M/W, soccer M/W, squash M/W, swimming M/W, table tennis M/W, tennis M/W, track and field M/W, volleyball M/W, water polo M/W, wrestling M.

Standardized Tests *Required:* SAT I (for admission). *Required for some:* SAT II: Subject Tests (for admission).

Costs (2001–02) *Tuition:* nonresident $6182 Canadian dollars full-time, $684 Canadian dollars per course part-time; International tuition $11,003 Canadian dollars full-time. *Required fees:* $147 Canadian dollars full-time, $5 Canadian dollars per course. *Room and board:* $5270 Canadian dollars; room only: $2860 Canadian dollars. Room and board charges vary according to board plan and housing facility. *Payment plan:* installment. *Waivers:* employees or children of employees.

Applying *Options:* electronic application, deferred entrance. *Application fee:* $25. *Required:* high school transcript, minimum 2.5 GPA. *Required for some:* essay or personal statement, letters of recommendation, interview. *Application deadlines:* 7/1 (freshmen), 5/31 (out-of-state freshmen), 7/1 (transfers). *Notification:* continuous (freshmen).

Admissions Contact Ms. Anne Scott, Manager of Admissions, Acadia University, Wolfville, NS B0P 1X0, Canada. *Phone:* 902-585-1222. *Fax:* 902-585-1081. *E-mail:* admissions@acadiau.ca.

ALBERTA COLLEGE OF ART & DESIGN
Calgary, Alberta, Canada

- **Province-supported** 4-year, founded 1926
- **Calendar** semesters
- **Degree** diplomas and bachelor's
- **Urban** 1-acre campus
- **Coed,** 955 undergraduate students
- **Moderately difficult** entrance level, 50% of applicants were admitted

Undergraduates Students come from 4 provinces and territories, 6 other countries. *Retention:* 92% of 2001 full-time freshmen returned.

Freshmen *Admission:* 520 applied, 260 admitted.

Faculty *Total:* 117, 43% full-time.

Majors Art; ceramic arts; computer graphics; drawing; fine/studio arts; graphic design/commercial art/illustration; metal/jewelry arts; photography; printmaking; sculpture; textile arts.

Academic Programs *Special study options:* academic remediation for entering students, adult/continuing education programs, advanced placement credit, external degree program, independent study, internships, part-time degree program, services for LD students, study abroad, summer session for credit.

Library Luke Lindo Library with 20,000 titles, 65 serial subscriptions.

Computers on Campus 65 computers available on campus for general student use. Internet access, at least one staffed computer lab available.

Student Life *Housing:* college housing not available. *Campus security:* 24-hour emergency response devices and patrols, late-night transport/escort service. *Student Services:* health clinic, personal/psychological counseling.

Costs (2001–02) *Tuition:* province resident $446 Canadian dollars per credit part-time; nonresident $3495 Canadian dollars full-time; International tuition $9141 Canadian dollars full-time. Full-time tuition and fees vary according to course load and program. Part-time tuition and fees vary according to course load and program. *Required fees:* $441 Canadian dollars full-time. *Room and board:* Room and board charges vary according to housing facility. *Payment plan:* installment. *Waivers:* senior citizens and employees or children of employees.

Applying *Options:* early admission, early decision, early action. *Application fee:* $25. *Required:* essay or personal statement, high school transcript, portfolio of artwork. *Recommended:* minimum 2.0 GPA. *Application deadlines:* 4/1 (freshmen), 4/1 (transfers). *Early decision:* 3/1. *Notification:* 6/15 (freshmen), 4/1 (early decision), 4/30 (early action).

Admissions Contact Ms. Joy Borman, Associate Director of Admissions, Alberta College of Art & Design, 1407-14 Avenue NW, Calgary, AB T2N 4R3, Canada. *Phone:* 403-284-7689. *Toll-free phone:* 800-251-8290. *Fax:* 403-284-7644. *E-mail:* admissions@acad.ab.ca.

ATHABASCA UNIVERSITY
Athabasca, Alberta, Canada

- **Province-supported** comprehensive, founded 1970
- **Calendar** continuous
- **Degrees** certificates, diplomas, bachelor's, and master's (offers only external degree programs)
- **Small-town** 480-acre campus
- **Endowment** $1.1 million
- **Coed,** 23,472 undergraduate students, 69% women, 31% men
- **Noncompetitive** entrance level

Undergraduates 23,472 part-time. Students come from 26 provinces and territories, 34 other countries, 52% are from out of province.

Freshmen *Admission:* 1,640 enrolled.

Faculty *Total:* 445, 21% full-time.

Majors Accounting; anthropology; applied art; biological/physical sciences; business administration; Canadian studies; computer/information sciences; English; French; history; information sciences/systems; labor/personnel relations; liberal arts and sciences/liberal studies; nursing; psychology; public administration; sociology; women's studies.

Academic Programs *Special study options:* academic remediation for entering students, accelerated degree program, adult/continuing education programs, advanced placement credit, cooperative education, distance learning, English as a second language, external degree program, off-campus study, part-time degree program, services for LD students, student-designed majors, study abroad, summer session for credit.

Library Athabasca University Library plus 1 other with 130,000 titles, 4,000 serial subscriptions, 3,345 audiovisual materials.

Computers on Campus 28 computers available on campus for general student use. A campuswide network can be accessed from off campus that provide access to computing services help desk. Internet access, online (class) registration, at least one staffed computer lab available.

Student Life *Housing:* college housing not available. *Activities and Organizations:* student-run newspaper. *Campus security:* 24-hour emergency response devices.

Costs (2001–02) *Tuition:* province resident $4760 full-time, $476 per course part-time; nonresident $726 per course part-time; International tuition $7260 full-time. *Waivers:* senior citizens and employees or children of employees.

Applying *Options:* common application, electronic application. *Application fee:* $50. *Required:* high school transcript. *Application deadline:* rolling (freshmen), rolling (transfers). *Notification:* continuous (freshmen).

Admissions Contact Ms. Margaret Carmichael, Assistant Registrar, Admissions, Athabasca University, 1 University Drive, Athabasca, AB T9S 3A3. *Phone:* 780-675-6377. *Toll-free phone:* 800-788-9041. *Fax:* 780-675-6437. *E-mail:* auinfo@athabascau.ca.

ATLANTIC BAPTIST UNIVERSITY
Moncton, New Brunswick, Canada

- **Independent Baptist** 4-year, founded 1949
- **Calendar** semesters
- **Degree** certificates and bachelor's
- **Urban** campus
- **Endowment** $1.0 million
- **Coed,** 469 undergraduate students, 88% full-time, 68% women, 32% men
- **Minimally difficult** entrance level, 90% of applicants were admitted

Undergraduates 412 full-time, 57 part-time. Students come from 11 provinces and territories, 1 other country, 76% are from out of province, 9% transferred in, 29% live on campus. *Retention:* 91% of 2001 full-time freshmen returned.

Freshmen *Admission:* 201 applied, 180 admitted, 158 enrolled.

Faculty *Total:* 44, 50% full-time, 43% with terminal degrees. *Student/faculty ratio:* 10:1.

Majors Biblical studies; biology; business administration; education; education (K-12); English; history; interdisciplinary studies; mass communications; psychology; religious studies; sociology.

Academic Programs *Special study options:* double majors, honors programs, part-time degree program, summer session for credit.

Library George A. Rawlyk Library with 40,000 titles, 150 serial subscriptions, an OPAC.

Computers on Campus 35 computers available on campus for general student use. A campuswide network can be accessed from student residence rooms. At least one staffed computer lab available.

Student Life *Housing Options:* men-only, women-only, disabled students. *Activities and Organizations:* drama/theater group, student-run newspaper, choral group, Student Association, Debate Team, Intra Murals, Drama, Choir. *Campus security:* 24-hour emergency response devices, student patrols, controlled dormitory access. *Student Services:* personal/psychological counseling.

Athletics *Intercollegiate sports:* basketball M/W, soccer M/W, softball M/W, volleyball M/W. *Intramural sports:* badminton M/W, basketball M/W, bowling M/W, football M, ice hockey M, skiing (downhill) M/W, softball M/W, table tennis M/W, volleyball M/W, weight lifting M/W.

Costs (2001–02) *Comprehensive fee:* $9290 Canadian dollars includes full-time tuition ($4610 Canadian dollars), mandatory fees ($530 Canadian dollars), and room and board ($4150 Canadian dollars). Part-time tuition: $495 Canadian dollars per course. Part-time tuition and fees vary according to course load. *Room and board:* College room only: $1860 Canadian dollars. Room and board charges vary according to board plan and student level. *Payment plan:* installment. *Waivers:* senior citizens and employees or children of employees.

Applying *Options:* common application, deferred entrance. *Application fee:* $35. *Required:* essay or personal statement, high school transcript, 3 letters of recommendation. *Required for some:* interview. *Application deadline:* rolling (freshmen), rolling (transfers). *Notification:* continuous until 9/15 (freshmen).

Admissions Contact Ms. Giselle Tranquilla, Assistant for Student Recruitment, Atlantic Baptist University, Box 6004, Moncton, NB E1C 9L7, Canada. *Phone:* 506-858-8970 Ext. 6434. *Toll-free phone:* 888-YOU-N-ABU. *Fax:* 506-858-9694. *E-mail:* admissions@abu.nb.ca.

AUGUSTANA UNIVERSITY COLLEGE
Camrose, Alberta, Canada

- **Province-supported** 4-year
- **Degree** bachelor's
- **Endowment** $2.0 million
- **Coed**
- **Minimally difficult** entrance level

Faculty *Student/faculty ratio:* 15:1.
Standardized Tests *Required for some:* SAT I and SAT II or ACT (for admission), SAT II: Subject Tests (for admission), SAT II: Writing Test (for admission).
Costs (2001–02) *Tuition:* nonresident $5120 Canadian dollars full-time, $244 Canadian dollars per credit part-time; International tuition $6830 Canadian dollars full-time. *Required fees:* $5253 Canadian dollars full-time. *Room and board:* $4240 Canadian dollars.
Applying *Options:* electronic application, early admission, early decision, early action, deferred entrance. *Application fee:* $30. *Required:* high school transcript, minimum 2.0 GPA.
Admissions Contact Mr. Tim Hanson, Director of Admissions, Augustana University College, 4901-46 Ave, Camrose, AB T4V 2R3. *Phone:* 780-649-1135 Ext. 1135. *Toll-free phone:* 800-661-8714. *E-mail:* admissions@augustana.ab.ca.

BETHANY BIBLE COLLEGE
Sussex, New Brunswick, Canada

Admissions Contact Rev. Jon Steppe, Director of Admissions and Marketing, Bethany Bible College, 26 Western Street, Sussex, NB E4E 1E6, Canada. *Phone:* 506-432-4402. *Toll-free phone:* 888-432-4422. *Fax:* 506-432-4425. *E-mail:* steppej@bethany-ca.edu.

BETHANY BIBLE INSTITUTE
Hepburn, Saskatchewan, Canada

- **Independent** 4-year, founded 1927, affiliated with Mennonite Brethren Church
- **Calendar** semesters
- **Degrees** certificates, diplomas, associate, and bachelor's
- **Coed,** 135 undergraduate students, 100% full-time, 48% women, 52% men
- 86% of applicants were admitted

Undergraduates 135 full-time.
Freshmen *Admission:* 72 applied, 62 admitted, 62 enrolled.
Faculty *Total:* 11, 73% full-time, 9% with terminal degrees.
Majors Pastoral counseling; theological studies/religious vocations related.
Student Life *Housing Options:* men-only, women-only. *Activities and Organizations:* drama/theater group, student-run newspaper, choral group.
Athletics *Intercollegiate sports:* basketball M/W, ice hockey M, soccer M/W, volleyball M/W. *Intramural sports:* badminton M/W.
Costs (2002–03) *Comprehensive fee:* $8530 Canadian dollars includes full-time tuition ($4160 Canadian dollars), mandatory fees ($600 Canadian dollars), and room and board ($3770 Canadian dollars). Full-time tuition and fees vary according to course load. Part-time tuition: $130 Canadian dollars per credit. Part-time tuition and fees vary according to course load. *Waivers:* employees or children of employees.
Applying *Application fee:* $55. *Required:* essay or personal statement, high school transcript, letters of recommendation.
Admissions Contact Mr. Dave Carey, Admissions Director, Bethany Bible Institute, Box 166, Hepburn, SK 50K I20, Canada. *Phone:* 306-947-2129. *E-mail:* info@bethany.sk.ca.

BISHOP'S UNIVERSITY
Lennoxville, Quebec, Canada

- **Province-supported** comprehensive, founded 1843
- **Calendar** Canadian standard year
- **Degrees** certificates, bachelor's, and master's
- **Small-town** 500-acre campus
- **Endowment** $13.0 million
- **Coed,** 2,396 undergraduate students, 79% full-time, 57% women, 43% men
- **Moderately difficult** entrance level, 82% of applicants were admitted

Undergraduates 1,885 full-time, 511 part-time. Students come from 12 provinces and territories, 32 other countries, 47% are from out of province, 4% transferred in, 27% live on campus. *Retention:* 85% of 2001 full-time freshmen returned.
Freshmen *Admission:* 1,344 applied, 1,107 admitted, 502 enrolled.
Faculty *Total:* 162, 74% full-time, 52% with terminal degrees. *Student/faculty ratio:* 12:1.
Majors Accounting; aerospace science; art; arts management; biochemistry; biological/physical sciences; biology; business administration; business economics; business marketing and marketing management; Canadian studies; chemistry; classics; computer/information sciences; computer science; economics; education; English; finance; French; geography; German; gerontology; history; humanities; human resources management; international business; Italian; liberal arts and sciences/liberal studies; literature; management information systems/business data processing; mathematics; modern languages; music; natural sciences; neuroscience; philosophy; physics; political science; psychology; religious studies; social sciences; sociology; Spanish; theater arts/drama; women's studies.
Academic Programs *Special study options:* academic remediation for entering students, accelerated degree program, adult/continuing education programs, advanced placement credit, double majors, English as a second language, honors programs, independent study, off-campus study, part-time degree program, services for LD students, student-designed majors, study abroad, summer session for credit.
Library John Bassett Memorial Library plus 1 other with 443,345 titles, 1,742 serial subscriptions, 15,356 audiovisual materials, an OPAC.
Computers on Campus 160 computers available on campus for general student use. A campuswide network can be accessed from student residence rooms. Internet access, at least one staffed computer lab available.
Student Life *Housing Options:* coed, women-only. *Activities and Organizations:* drama/theater group, student-run newspaper, radio station, choral group, Big Buddies, The Campus, Psychology Club, Student Patrol, Intervarsity Christian Fellowship, national fraternities, national sororities. *Campus security:* 24-hour emergency response devices and patrols, student patrols, late-night transport/escort service, controlled dormitory access. *Student Services:* health clinic, personal/psychological counseling, women's center.
Athletics Member CIAU. *Intercollegiate sports:* basketball M/W, field hockey W(c), football M, golf M, ice hockey W(c), lacrosse M(c)/W(c), rugby M/W, skiing (downhill) M/W, soccer W, volleyball W(c). *Intramural sports:* badminton M/W, basketball M/W, cross-country running M/W, equestrian sports M(c)/W(c), football M, golf M/W, ice hockey M/W, riflery M(c)/W(c), soccer M/W, softball M/W, squash M/W, swimming M/W, table tennis M/W, tennis M/W, volleyball M/W, water polo M/W, weight lifting M/W.
Standardized Tests *Required for some:* SAT I or ACT (for admission). *Recommended:* SAT II: Subject Tests (for admission).
Costs (2001–02) *Tuition:* $56 Canadian dollars per credit part-time; province resident $1668 Canadian dollars full-time, $129 Canadian dollars per credit part-time; nonresident $3858 Canadian dollars full-time; International tuition $9168 Canadian dollars full-time. Full-time tuition and fees vary according to program. Part-time tuition and fees vary according to program. *Required fees:* $758 Canadian dollars full-time, $26 Canadian dollars per term part-time. *Room and board:* $6240 Canadian dollars. Room and board charges vary according to board plan, housing facility, and location. *Payment plan:* installment. *Waivers:* senior citizens and employees or children of employees.
Applying *Application fee:* $55. *Required:* high school transcript, minimum 3.0 GPA, birth certificate, copy of student visa. *Required for some:* 1 letter of recommendation. *Application deadlines:* 3/1 (freshmen), 3/1 (transfers). *Notification:* continuous until 8/31 (freshmen).
Admissions Contact Mr. Hans Rouleau, Coordinator of Liaison, Bishop's University, Lennoxville, QC J1M 1Z7, Canada. *Phone:* 819-822-9600 Ext. 2217. *Toll-free phone:* 800-567-2792 Ext. 2681. *Fax:* 819-822-9661. *E-mail:* liaison@ubishops.ca.

BRANDON UNIVERSITY
Brandon, Manitoba, Canada

- **Province-supported** comprehensive, founded 1899
- **Calendar** Canadian standard year
- **Degrees** certificates, bachelor's, and master's
- **Small-town** 30-acre campus
- **Endowment** $14.0 million
- **Coed,** 2,867 undergraduate students, 66% full-time, 67% women, 33% men
- **Noncompetitive** entrance level, 79% of applicants were admitted

Undergraduates 1,883 full-time, 984 part-time. Students come from 32 other countries, 8% are from out of province, 9% live on campus. *Retention:* 47% of 2001 full-time freshmen returned.
Freshmen *Admission:* 1,890 applied, 1,499 admitted, 1,177 enrolled. *Average high school GPA:* 3.50.
Faculty *Total:* 231, 85% full-time. *Student/faculty ratio:* 11:1.
Majors Biology; botany; business administration; Canadian studies; chemistry; community services; computer science; counselor education/guidance; early childhood education; economics; education; elementary education; English; family/community studies; French; general studies; geography; geology; history; liberal arts and sciences/liberal studies; mathematics; mathematics/computer science; mental health/rehabilitation; middle school education; music; music (general performance); music history; music (piano and organ performance); music teacher education; music theory and composition; music (voice and choral/opera performance); Native American studies; nursing (psychiatric/mental health); nursing science; philosophy; physics; political science; pre-dentistry; pre-law; pre-medicine; pre-veterinary studies; psychology; religious studies; secondary education; sociology; zoology.
Academic Programs *Special study options:* academic remediation for entering students, accelerated degree program, distance learning, double majors, English as a second language, honors programs, part-time degree program, services for LD students, summer session for credit. *Unusual degree programs:* 3-2 education.
Library John E. Robbins Library with 238,816 titles, 1,699 serial subscriptions, 12,233 audiovisual materials, an OPAC, a Web page.
Computers on Campus 160 computers available on campus for general student use. A campuswide network can be accessed from student residence rooms and from off campus. Internet access, at least one staffed computer lab available.
Student Life *Housing Options:* coed, men-only, women-only. *Activities and Organizations:* drama/theater group, student-run newspaper, radio station, choral group, Psychology Club, Zoology Club, Intervarsity Christian Fellowship, International Students Club, Business Administration Club. *Campus security:* 24-hour emergency response devices, controlled dormitory access, night residence hall security personnel. *Student Services:* personal/psychological counseling.
Athletics Member CIAU. *Intercollegiate sports:* bowling M(s)/W(s), ice hockey M. *Intramural sports:* badminton M/W, baseball M/W, bowling M/W, ice hockey M/W, soccer M/W, volleyball M/W, weight lifting M/W.
Costs (2001–02) *One-time required fee:* $30 Canadian dollars. *Tuition:* province resident $110 Canadian dollars per credit part-time; nonresident $3354 Canadian dollars full-time, $319 Canadian dollars per credit part-time; International tuition $5870 Canadian dollars full-time. Full-time tuition and fees vary according to course load, location, program, and reciprocity agreements. Part-time tuition and fees vary according to course load, location, program, and reciprocity agreements. *Required fees:* $185 Canadian dollars full-time, $30 Canadian dollars per credit. *Room and board:* $5561 Canadian dollars; room only: $3275 Canadian dollars. Room and board charges vary according to housing facility. *Payment plan:* installment. *Waivers:* senior citizens.
Applying *Options:* common application, deferred entrance. *Application fee:* $35. *Required:* high school transcript. *Required for some:* letters of recommendation, criminal and child abuse registry checks. *Application deadline:* rolling (freshmen), rolling (transfers). *Notification:* continuous until 9/30 (freshmen).
Admissions Contact Faye Douglas, Director of Admissions, Brandon University, 270 18th Street, Brandon, MB R7A 6A9, Canada. *Phone:* 204-727-7352. *Toll-free phone:* 800-644-7644. *Fax:* 204-728-3221. *E-mail:* douglas@brandonu.ca.

BRIERCREST BIBLE COLLEGE
Caronport, Saskatchewan, Canada

- **Independent interdenominational** 4-year, founded 1935, part of Briercrest Family of Schools
- **Calendar** semesters
- **Degrees** certificates, diplomas, associate, and bachelor's
- **Rural** 300-acre campus
- **Endowment** $764,628
- **Coed,** 750 undergraduate students, 90% full-time, 48% women, 52% men
- **Noncompetitive** entrance level

Undergraduates Students come from 11 provinces and territories, 7 other countries, 74% are from out of province, 75% live on campus. *Retention:* 77% of 2001 full-time freshmen returned.
Freshmen *Admission:* 598 applied. *Average high school GPA:* 2.88.
Faculty *Total:* 47, 36% full-time, 30% with terminal degrees. *Student/faculty ratio:* 26:1.
Majors Accounting; biblical studies; business administration; child care/development; cultural studies; divinity/ministry; missionary studies; music; pastoral counseling; religious music; religious studies; theology.
Academic Programs *Special study options:* academic remediation for entering students, accelerated degree program, adult/continuing education programs, distance learning, double majors, external degree program, independent study, internships, off-campus study, part-time degree program, summer session for credit.
Library Archibald Library with 61,450 titles, 384 serial subscriptions, 3,327 audiovisual materials, an OPAC, a Web page.
Computers on Campus 30 computers available on campus for general student use. A campuswide network can be accessed from off campus. Internet access, online (class) registration, at least one staffed computer lab available.
Student Life *Housing:* on-campus residence required through senior year. *Options:* men-only, women-only. *Activities and Organizations:* drama/theater group, student-run radio station, choral group, Student Missions Fellowship, Titus II, Student Families Association, Yearbook Committee, Weekend Activities Committee. *Campus security:* 24-hour patrols. *Student Services:* health clinic, personal/psychological counseling, legal services.
Athletics *Intercollegiate sports:* basketball M/W, ice hockey M, soccer M/W, volleyball M/W. *Intramural sports:* badminton M/W, basketball M/W, football M/W, golf M/W, ice hockey M/W, soccer M/W, softball M/W, table tennis M/W, tennis M/W, volleyball M/W, weight lifting M/W.
Costs (2002–03) *Comprehensive fee:* $9824 Canadian dollars includes full-time tuition ($5824 Canadian dollars) and room and board ($4000 Canadian dollars). Part-time tuition: $182 Canadian dollars per credit. *Room and board:* College room only: $2400 Canadian dollars. Room and board charges vary according to housing facility. *Payment plan:* installment. *Waivers:* senior citizens and employees or children of employees.
Applying *Options:* common application, electronic application, early admission, deferred entrance. *Application fee:* $25. *Required:* essay or personal statement, high school transcript, 2 letters of recommendation. *Required for some:* interview. *Application deadlines:* 8/15 (freshmen), 8/15 (transfers). *Notification:* continuous until 9/1 (freshmen).
Admissions Contact Mr. Jay Sills, Director of Enrollment Management, Briercrest Bible College, 510 College Drive, Caronport, SK S0H 0S0, Canada. *Phone:* 306-756-3200 Ext. 257. *Toll-free phone:* 800-667-5199. *E-mail:* enrollment@briercrest.ca.

BRITISH COLUMBIA INSTITUTE OF TECHNOLOGY
Burnaby, British Columbia, Canada

- **Province-supported** 4-year, founded 1964
- **Calendar** quarters
- **Degree** certificates, diplomas, and bachelor's
- **Endowment** $6.0 million
- **Coed,** 24,576 undergraduate students

Undergraduates 0% are from out of province, 5% live on campus.
Faculty *Total:* 1,162, 52% full-time.
Majors Accounting; accounting technician; aerospace engineering technology; aircraft mechanic/airframe; aircraft mechanic/powerplant; architectural drafting; architectural engineering technology; auto body repair; auto mechanic/technician; aviation technology; biological technology; biotechnology research; business administration; business marketing and marketing management; cabinet making; cardiovascular technology; carpentry; chemical technology; civil engineering technology; civil/structural drafting; computer science; computer systems analysis; construction management; construction technology; construction trades related; data processing technology; diesel engine mechanic; drafting; electrical/electronic engineering technology; electrical/power transmission installation; engineering related; enterprise management; environmental engineering; environmental health; environmental technology; finance; financial management and services related; financial planning; fire protection/safety technology; forensic technology; forest management; forest products technology; graphic design/commercial art/illustration; health/medical administrative services related; health/medical diagnostic and treatment services related; health professions and related sciences; health services administration; heating/air conditioning/refrigeration; heavy equipment maintenance; human resources management; industrial machinery maintenance/repair; industrial technology; information sciences/systems; interior design; international business; machine technology; management science; mechanical drafting; mechanical engineering technology; mechanics and repair related; medical administrative assistant; medical laboratory technician; medical laboratory technology; medical radiologic technology; mining technology; naval

British Columbia Institute of Technology (continued)
architecture/marine engineering; nuclear medical technology; nursing; nursing administration; nursing (pediatric); nursing related; nursing (surgical); occupational health/industrial hygiene; operations management; petroleum technology; plastics technology; plumbing; radio/television broadcasting technology; real estate; robotics technology; science technologies related; secretarial science; sheet metal working; small engine mechanic; surveying; taxation; trade/industrial education; transportation engineering; travel/tourism management; vehicle/mobile equipment mechanics and repair related; welding technology; wildlife management.

Student Life *Housing Options:* coed, men-only, women-only, disabled students. *Activities and Organizations:* student-run newspaper, radio station. *Campus security:* 24-hour emergency response devices and patrols, student patrols, late-night transport/escort service. *Student Services:* health clinic, personal/psychological counseling.

Athletics *Intramural sports:* archery M(c)/W(c), basketball M/W, crew M(c)/W(c), football M/W, ice hockey M/W, rugby M(c)/W(c), soccer M/W, softball M/W, volleyball M/W.

Costs (2001–02) *Tuition:* $81 Canadian dollars per credit part-time; province resident $2126 Canadian dollars full-time; International tuition $8600 Canadian dollars full-time. Full-time tuition and fees vary according to class time, course load, degree level, location, and program. Part-time tuition and fees vary according to class time, course load, degree level, location, and program. No tuition increase for student's term of enrollment. *Required fees:* $103 Canadian dollars full-time, $5 Canadian dollars per credit. *Room and board:* room only: $3375 Canadian dollars. *Payment plan:* deferred payment. *Waivers:* minority students.

Admissions Contact Ms. Anna Dosen, Supervisor of Admissions, British Columbia Institute of Technology, 3700 Willingdon Avenue, Burnaby, BC V5G 3H2, Canada. *Phone:* 604-432-8576. *Fax:* 604-431-6917.

BROCK UNIVERSITY
St. Catharines, Ontario, Canada

- **Province-supported** comprehensive, founded 1964
- **Calendar** Canadian standard year
- **Degrees** certificates, bachelor's, master's, and doctoral
- **Urban** 540-acre campus with easy access to Toronto
- **Coed,** 10,777 undergraduate students
- **Moderately difficult** entrance level, 23% of applicants were admitted

Undergraduates Students come from 12 provinces and territories, 18 other countries, 16% live on campus.

Freshmen *Admission:* 9,800 applied, 2,250 admitted. *Average high school GPA:* 3.00.

Faculty *Total:* 366, 100% full-time, 93% with terminal degrees. *Student/faculty ratio:* 23:1.

Majors Accounting; adult/continuing education; applied mathematics; archaeology; art; biochemistry; biological/physical sciences; biology; biotechnology research; business; business administration; business communications; business economics; business marketing and marketing management; Canadian studies; chemistry; classics; communication disorders; communications; computer engineering technology; computer programming; computer science; drawing; earth sciences; economics; education; elementary education; English; entrepreneurship; environmental science; European studies; exercise sciences; film studies; finance; fine/studio arts; French; geography; geology; German; Greek (ancient and medieval); health science; health services administration; history; humanities; human resources management; information sciences/systems; interdisciplinary studies; international business; international economics; Italian; labor/personnel relations; liberal arts and sciences/liberal studies; linguistics; literature; mass communications; mathematical statistics; mathematics; mathematics education; movement therapy; music; music teacher education; neuroscience; nursing science; philosophy; physical education; physical sciences; physics; political science; psychology; public administration; public health; recreation/leisure studies; Russian/Slavic studies; science education; secondary education; social sciences; sociology; Spanish; sport/fitness administration; theater arts/drama; travel/tourism management; women's studies.

Academic Programs *Special study options:* academic remediation for entering students, accelerated degree program, adult/continuing education programs, advanced placement credit, cooperative education, double majors, English as a second language, honors programs, internships, part-time degree program, services for LD students, student-designed majors, study abroad, summer session for credit.

Library James A-Gibson Library plus 1 other with 1.4 million titles, 2,900 serial subscriptions, 19,500 audiovisual materials, an OPAC, a Web page.

Computers on Campus 275 computers available on campus for general student use. A campuswide network can be accessed from student residence rooms and from off campus. Internet access, online (class) registration, at least one staffed computer lab available.

Student Life *Housing Options:* coed. *Activities and Organizations:* drama/theater group, student-run newspaper, radio station, choral group, International Students Association, Brock University Student Association, Business Administration Association, Brock Christian Fellowship. *Campus security:* 24-hour emergency response devices and patrols, student patrols, late-night transport/escort service, controlled dormitory access. *Student Services:* health clinic, personal/psychological counseling, women's center.

Athletics Member CIAU. *Intercollegiate sports:* badminton M/W, baseball M(c), basketball M/W, crew M/W, cross-country running M/W, fencing M/W, field hockey W(c), golf M, ice hockey M/W, lacrosse M, rugby M/W, soccer M/W, squash M, swimming M/W, tennis M, volleyball M/W, wrestling M/W. *Intramural sports:* badminton M/W, basketball M/W, cross-country running M/W, fencing M/W, field hockey M/W, football M/W, golf M/W, gymnastics M/W, ice hockey M/W, lacrosse M, racquetball M/W, sailing M/W, skiing (cross-country) M/W, skiing (downhill) M/W, soccer M/W, softball M/W, squash M/W, swimming M/W, tennis M/W, volleyball M/W, water polo M/W, weight lifting M/W.

Standardized Tests *Recommended:* SAT I and SAT II or ACT (for admission).

Costs (2001–02) *Tuition:* nonresident $4444 Canadian dollars full-time, $889 Canadian dollars per credit part-time; International tuition $10,114 Canadian dollars full-time. Full-time tuition and fees vary according to course load and degree level. Part-time tuition and fees vary according to course load and degree level. *Room and board:* $5390 Canadian dollars; room only: $2640 Canadian dollars. Room and board charges vary according to board plan and housing facility. *Payment plan:* installment. *Waivers:* senior citizens and employees or children of employees.

Financial Aid Available in 2001, 80 State and other part-time jobs.

Applying *Options:* common application, electronic application. *Application fee:* $90. *Required:* high school transcript, minimum 3.0 GPA. *Required for some:* essay or personal statement, minimum 3.0 GPA, letters of recommendation, interview, audition, portfolio. *Application deadlines:* 6/1 (freshmen), 6/1 (transfers). *Notification:* continuous (freshmen).

Admissions Contact Ms. Jeanette Davis, Undergraduate Admissions Officer, Brock University, 500 Glenridge Avenue, St. Catharines, St. Catharines, ON L2S 3A1, Canada. *Phone:* 905-688-5550 Ext. 3434. *E-mail:* barb@spartan.ac.brocku.ca.

CANADIAN BIBLE COLLEGE
Regina, Saskatchewan, Canada

- **Independent** 4-year, founded 1941, affiliated with The Christian and Missionary Alliance
- **Calendar** semesters
- **Degrees** certificates, diplomas, and bachelor's (Graduate and professional degrees are offered by Canadian Theological Seminary)
- **Urban** 16-acre campus
- **Endowment** $1.2 million
- **Coed,** 329 undergraduate students, 74% full-time, 47% women, 53% men
- **Noncompetitive** entrance level, 100% of applicants were admitted

Undergraduates 245 full-time, 84 part-time. Students come from 11 provinces and territories, 36% are from out of province, 0.6% African American, 4% Asian American or Pacific Islander, 0.9% Hispanic American, 2% Native American, 2% international, 66% live on campus. *Retention:* 64% of 2001 full-time freshmen returned.

Freshmen *Admission:* 129 applied, 129 admitted, 129 enrolled.

Faculty *Total:* 49, 76% with terminal degrees.

Majors Biblical studies; missionary studies; religious education; religious music; theology.

Academic Programs *Special study options:* academic remediation for entering students, accelerated degree program, adult/continuing education programs, advanced placement credit, cooperative education, distance learning, double majors, English as a second language, external degree program, honors programs, independent study, internships, off-campus study, part-time degree program, services for LD students, study abroad, summer session for credit.

Library Archibald Foundation Library with 65,000 titles, 546 serial subscriptions, an OPAC.

Computers on Campus 14 computers available on campus for general student use. Internet access available.

Student Life *Housing:* on-campus residence required through sophomore year. *Options:* men-only, women-only. *Activities and Organizations:* drama/theater group, student-run newspaper, choral group, International Students Fellowship,

Missions Group. *Campus security:* 24-hour emergency response devices, controlled dormitory access. *Student Services:* health clinic, personal/psychological counseling, women's center.

Athletics *Intercollegiate sports:* basketball M/W, ice hockey M, soccer M/W, volleyball M/W. *Intramural sports:* badminton M/W, basketball M/W, football M/W, golf M/W, ice hockey M, soccer M/W, table tennis M/W, volleyball M/W, weight lifting M/W.

Costs (2001–02) *Comprehensive fee:* $7140 Canadian dollars includes full-time tuition ($5100 Canadian dollars), mandatory fees ($60 Canadian dollars), and room and board ($1980 Canadian dollars). Part-time tuition: $170 Canadian dollars per credit. *Required fees:* $30 Canadian dollars per term part-time. *Room and board:* Room and board charges vary according to board plan and housing facility. *Waivers:* employees or children of employees.

Applying *Options:* common application, electronic application, early admission, deferred entrance. *Application fee:* $30. *Required:* essay or personal statement, high school transcript, 2 letters of recommendation. *Required for some:* interview. *Recommended:* medical history. *Application deadline:* rolling (freshmen), rolling (transfers). *Notification:* continuous until 9/1 (freshmen).

Admissions Contact Canadian Bible College, 440 Fourth Avenue, Regina, SK S4T 0H8, Canada. *Phone:* 306-545-1515 Ext. 305. *Toll-free phone:* 800-461-1222. *Fax:* 306-545-0210. *E-mail:* enrollment@cbccts.sk.ca.

CANADIAN MENNONITE UNIVERSITY
Winnipeg, Manitoba, Canada

- **Independent Mennonite Brethren** comprehensive, founded 1943
- **Calendar** semesters
- **Degree** certificates, diplomas, and bachelor's
- **Urban** 2-acre campus
- **Coed**
- **Moderately difficult** entrance level

Student Life *Campus security:* student patrols, late-night transport/escort service, controlled dormitory access, combination door locks to sections of the campus.

Financial Aid *Financial aid deadline:* 9/30.

Applying *Options:* common application, deferred entrance. *Application fee:* $20. *Required:* high school transcript, minimum 2.0 GPA. *Required for some:* essay or personal statement.

Admissions Contact Mr. Joe Moder, Recruitment Coordinator, Canadian Mennonite University, 500 Shaftesbury Boulevard, Winnipeg, MB R3P 2N2, Canada. *Phone:* 204-669-6583 Ext. 246. *E-mail:* recruitment@concordcollege.mb.ca.

CARLETON UNIVERSITY
Ottawa, Ontario, Canada

- **Province-supported** university, founded 1942
- **Calendar** Canadian standard year
- **Degrees** diplomas, bachelor's, master's, and doctoral
- **Urban** 152-acre campus
- **Endowment** $62.9 million
- **Coed,** 16,140 undergraduate students, 76% full-time, 50% women, 50% men
- **Moderately difficult** entrance level, 72% of applicants were admitted

Undergraduates 12,329 full-time, 3,811 part-time. Students come from 13 provinces and territories, 116 other countries, 11% are from out of province, 4% transferred in, 10% live on campus. *Retention:* 85% of 2001 full-time freshmen returned.

Freshmen *Admission:* 14,095 applied, 10,106 admitted, 3,477 enrolled.

Faculty *Total:* 695, 98% full-time, 80% with terminal degrees. *Student/faculty ratio:* 24:1.

Majors Accounting; aerospace engineering; African studies; anthropology; applied mathematics; architecture; art history; Asian studies; biochemistry; biological/physical sciences; biological technology; biology; botany; business administration; business marketing and marketing management; Canadian studies; chemistry; child care/development; city/community/regional planning; civil engineering; classics; cognitive psychology/psycholinguistics; comparative literature; computer engineering; computer programming; computer science; criminal justice/law enforcement administration; criminology; earth sciences; East Asian studies; Eastern European area studies; ecology; economics; electrical engineering; engineering; English; environmental engineering; environmental science; European studies; film studies; finance; French; geography; geology; German; Greek (modern); history; humanities; human resources management; industrial design; information sciences/systems; interdisciplinary studies; international business; international relations; Italian; journalism; labor/personnel relations; Latin American studies; Latin (ancient and medieval); law enforcement/police science; linguistics; management information systems/business data processing; mass communications; mathematical statistics; mathematics; mechanical engineering; medieval/renaissance studies; Middle Eastern studies; modern languages; music; operations research; philosophy; physics; political science; pre-law; psychology; public administration; religious studies; Russian; Russian/Slavic studies; social work; sociology; Spanish; systems engineering; teaching English as a second language; theater arts/drama; urban studies; women's studies.

Academic Programs *Special study options:* academic remediation for entering students, accelerated degree program, adult/continuing education programs, cooperative education, distance learning, double majors, English as a second language, honors programs, internships, off-campus study, part-time degree program, services for LD students, student-designed majors, study abroad, summer session for credit.

Library MacOdrum Library with 10,174 serial subscriptions, 19,994 audiovisual materials, an OPAC, a Web page.

Computers on Campus 504 computers available on campus for general student use. A campuswide network can be accessed from student residence rooms and from off campus. Internet access, at least one staffed computer lab available.

Student Life *Housing Options:* coed. *Activities and Organizations:* drama/theater group, student-run newspaper, radio station. *Campus security:* 24-hour emergency response devices and patrols, student patrols, late-night transport/escort service, controlled dormitory access. *Student Services:* health clinic, personal/psychological counseling, women's center.

Athletics Member CIAU. *Intercollegiate sports:* basketball M(s)/W(s), crew M/W, fencing M(s)/W(s), field hockey W(s), football M, golf M, ice hockey M(c)/W(c), lacrosse M(c), rugby M(s)/W(c), skiing (cross-country) M(s)/W(s), soccer M(s)/W(s), swimming M/W, volleyball W(c), water polo M(s)/W(s). *Intramural sports:* badminton M/W, baseball W, basketball M/W, football M/W, golf M/W, ice hockey M, skiing (downhill) M/W, soccer M/W, softball M/W, squash M/W, swimming M/W, tennis M/W, volleyball M/W, water polo M/W.

Standardized Tests *Required for some:* SAT I and SAT II or ACT (for admission).

Costs (2001–02) *Tuition:* area resident $3990 Canadian dollars full-time, $785 Canadian dollars per credit part-time; International tuition $9180 Canadian dollars full-time. Full-time tuition and fees vary according to program. Part-time tuition and fees vary according to program. *Required fees:* $526 Canadian dollars full-time. *Room and board:* $5537 Canadian dollars; room only: $2810 Canadian dollars. Room and board charges vary according to board plan. *Waivers:* senior citizens and employees or children of employees.

Applying *Options:* common application, deferred entrance. *Application fee:* $85. *Required:* high school transcript, minimum 2.0 GPA. *Required for some:* minimum 3.0 GPA, letters of recommendation, interview. *Application deadlines:* 6/1 (freshmen), 4/1 (out-of-state freshmen), 6/1 (transfers). *Notification:* continuous (freshmen), continuous (out-of-state freshmen).

Admissions Contact Douglas Huckvale, Manager, Undergraduate Recruitment Office, Carleton University, 1125 Colonel By Drive, Ottawa, ON K1S 5B6, Canada. *Phone:* 613-520-3663. *Toll-free phone:* 888-354-4414. *Fax:* 613-520-3847. *E-mail:* liaison@admissions.carleton.ca.

CENTRAL PENTECOSTAL COLLEGE
Saskatoon, Saskatchewan, Canada

- **Independent** 4-year, founded 1930, affiliated with Pentecostal Assemblies of Canada
- **Calendar** semesters
- **Degree** certificates, diplomas, and bachelor's
- **Urban** 5-acre campus
- **Coed,** 84 undergraduate students, 75% full-time, 52% women, 48% men
- **Minimally difficult** entrance level, 100% of applicants were admitted

Undergraduates 63 full-time, 21 part-time. Students come from 4 provinces and territories, 3 other countries, 41% are from out of province, 1% transferred in, 56% live on campus. *Retention:* 76% of 2001 full-time freshmen returned.

Freshmen *Admission:* 8 applied, 8 admitted, 7 enrolled.

Faculty *Total:* 11, 64% full-time, 73% with terminal degrees. *Student/faculty ratio:* 12:1.

Majors Religious studies.

Academic Programs *Special study options:* academic remediation for entering students, independent study, internships, part-time degree program, student-designed majors, study abroad.

Library A. C. Schindel Library with 16,600 titles, 140 serial subscriptions, 323 audiovisual materials, an OPAC.

Central Pentecostal College (continued)
Computers on Campus 23 computers available on campus for general student use. Internet access, at least one staffed computer lab available.
Student Life *Housing:* on-campus residence required through sophomore year. *Activities and Organizations:* drama/theater group, student-run newspaper, choral group. *Campus security:* 24-hour emergency response devices, late-night transport/escort service. *Student Services:* personal/psychological counseling.
Athletics *Intramural sports:* basketball M/W, ice hockey M, soccer M/W, volleyball M/W.
Costs (2002–03) *Comprehensive fee:* $7936 Canadian dollars includes full-time tuition ($4160 Canadian dollars), mandatory fees ($376 Canadian dollars), and room and board ($3400 Canadian dollars). Part-time tuition: $130 Canadian dollars per credit hour. *Required fees:* $12 Canadian dollars per credit hour. *Room and board:* College room only: $2000 Canadian dollars. *Payment plans:* installment, deferred payment. *Waivers:* senior citizens and employees or children of employees.
Applying *Options:* common application, electronic application, deferred entrance. *Application fee:* $40 (non-residents). *Required:* essay or personal statement, high school transcript, 3 letters of recommendation. *Required for some:* interview. *Application deadline:* 8/15 (freshmen).
Admissions Contact Ms. Angie Hume, Assistant Registrar, Central Pentecostal College, 1303 Jackson Avenue, Saskatoon, SK S7H 2M9, Canada. *Phone:* 306-374-6655. *Fax:* 306-373-6968. *E-mail:* admissions@cpc-paoc.edu.

Collège Dominicain de Philosophie et de Théologie
Ottawa, Ontario, Canada

- **Independent Roman Catholic** comprehensive, founded 1909
- **Calendar** semesters
- **Degrees** certificates, bachelor's, master's, and doctoral
- **Urban** campus
- **Coed,** 203 undergraduate students, 37% full-time, 49% women, 51% men
- **Noncompetitive** entrance level, 100% of applicants were admitted

Undergraduates 75 full-time, 128 part-time. Students come from 6 provinces and territories, 8 other countries. *Retention:* 72% of 2001 full-time freshmen returned.
Freshmen *Admission:* 22 applied, 22 admitted, 21 enrolled.
Faculty *Total:* 64, 39% full-time, 38% with terminal degrees.
Majors Pastoral counseling; philosophy; theology.
Academic Programs *Special study options:* accelerated degree program, part-time degree program, summer session for credit.
Library Bibliothéque du College Dominicain with 85,000 titles, 500 serial subscriptions, an OPAC.
Computers on Campus 1 computer available on campus for general student use. . At least one staffed computer lab available.
Student Life *Activities and Organizations:* Association Etudiant College Dominicain. *Campus security:* late-night transport/escort service.
Costs (2001–02) *Comprehensive fee:* $7400 includes full-time tuition ($2600) and room and board ($4800). Part-time tuition: $100 per credit hour. Part-time tuition and fees vary according to course load. International tuition: $6600 full-time. *Required fees:* $100 per credit. *Payment plan:* installment. *Waivers:* senior citizens.
Applying *Options:* common application. *Application fee:* $20. *Required:* high school transcript. *Recommended:* interview. *Application deadline:* 7/15 (freshmen), rolling (transfers).
Admissions Contact Fr. Jacques Lison OP, Registrar, Collège Dominicain de Philosophie et de Théologie, 96, Avenue Empress, Ottawa, ON K1R 7G3, Canada. *Phone:* 613-233-5696.

College of Emmanuel and St. Chad
Saskatoon, Saskatchewan, Canada

Admissions Contact Ms. Susan M. Avant, Registrar, College of Emmanuel and St. Chad, 1337 College Drive, Saskatoon, SK S7N 0W6, Canada. *Phone:* 306-975-1553.

Collège universitaire de Saint-Boniface
Saint-Boniface, Manitoba, Canada

Admissions Contact 200 avenue de la Cathèdrale, Saint-Boniface, MB R2H 0H7, Canada.

Columbia Bible College
Abbotsford, British Columbia, Canada

- **Independent Mennonite Brethren** 4-year, founded 1936
- **Calendar** semesters
- **Degree** certificates, diplomas, and bachelor's
- **Urban** 9-acre campus with easy access to Vancouver
- **Coed,** 502 undergraduate students, 80% full-time, 45% women, 55% men
- **Noncompetitive** entrance level, 83% of applicants were admitted

Undergraduates 400 full-time, 102 part-time. Students come from 5 provinces and territories, 11 other countries, 40% are from out of province, 16% international, 4% transferred in, 65% live on campus. *Retention:* 100% of 2001 full-time freshmen returned.
Freshmen *Admission:* 339 applied, 280 admitted, 354 enrolled.
Faculty *Total:* 59, 32% full-time, 83% with terminal degrees. *Student/faculty ratio:* 22:1.
Majors Biblical studies; early childhood education; missionary studies; pastoral counseling; pre-theology; recreation/leisure studies; religious studies.
Academic Programs *Special study options:* academic remediation for entering students, advanced placement credit, cooperative education, distance learning, double majors, English as a second language, independent study, internships, part-time degree program, services for LD students.
Library Columbia Resource Center plus 1 other with 44,000 titles, 100 serial subscriptions, a Web page.
Computers on Campus 20 computers available on campus for general student use. Internet access, at least one staffed computer lab available.
Student Life *Housing:* on-campus residence required through sophomore year. *Options:* men-only, women-only. *Activities and Organizations:* drama/theater group, student-run newspaper, choral group. *Campus security:* late-night transport/escort service, night watchman 11 p.m. to 6 a.m. *Student Services:* personal/psychological counseling.
Athletics *Intercollegiate sports:* basketball M/W, ice hockey M, soccer M, volleyball M/W.
Costs (2002–03) *Comprehensive fee:* $9000 includes full-time tuition ($4200), mandatory fees ($400), and room and board ($4400). Part-time tuition: $175 per credit hour. *Required fees:* $15 per credit hour.
Applying *Application fee:* $50. *Required:* essay or personal statement, high school transcript, letters of recommendation. *Required for some:* interview. *Application deadlines:* 8/15 (freshmen), 8/15 (transfers). *Notification:* continuous (freshmen).
Admissions Contact Ms. Esther Martens, Academic Assistant, Columbia Bible College, 2940 Clearbrook Road, Abbotsford, BC V2T 2Z8. *Phone:* 604-853-3358 Ext. 306. *Toll-free phone:* 800-283-0881. *Fax:* 604-853-3063. *E-mail:* admissions@columbiabc.edu.

Concordia University
Montréal, Quebec, Canada

- **Province-supported** university, founded 1974
- **Calendar** trimesters
- **Degrees** certificates, diplomas, bachelor's, master's, doctoral, post-master's, and postbachelor's certificates
- **Urban** 110-acre campus
- **Endowment** $32.2 million
- **Coed,** 24,262 undergraduate students, 52% full-time, 53% women, 47% men
- **Moderately difficult** entrance level, 65% of applicants were admitted

Undergraduates Students come from 10 provinces and territories, 122 other countries, 1% live on campus. *Retention:* 76% of 2001 full-time freshmen returned.
Freshmen *Admission:* 13,064 applied, 8,452 admitted. *Average high school GPA:* 2.76. *Test scores:* SAT verbal scores over 500: 52%; SAT math scores over 500: 79%; SAT verbal scores over 600: 20%; SAT math scores over 600: 36%; SAT verbal scores over 700: 2%; SAT math scores over 700: 4%.
Faculty *Total:* 1,399, 50% full-time, 93% with terminal degrees. *Student/faculty ratio:* 20:1.
Majors Accounting; acting/directing; actuarial science; anthropology; applied mathematics; archaeology; art; art education; art history; art therapy; athletic training/sports medicine; behavioral sciences; biochemistry; biology; botany; business administration; business economics; business marketing and marketing management; cell biology; ceramic arts; chemistry; civil engineering; classics; communications; computer engineering; computer science; construction engineering; creative writing; cultural studies; dance; developmental/child psychology; drama/dance education; drawing; early childhood education; ecology; economics;

electrical engineering; elementary education; English; enterprise management; environmental biology; environmental engineering; environmental science; exercise sciences; film studies; film/video production; finance; fine/studio arts; foreign language translation; French; geography; German; graphic design/ commercial art/illustration; Hebrew; history; human ecology; human resources management; industrial/manufacturing engineering; interdisciplinary studies; international business; Italian; jazz; journalism; Latin (ancient and medieval); linguistics; literature; management information systems/business data processing; marketing research; mass communications; mathematical statistics; mathematics; mechanical engineering; modern languages; molecular biology; music; music (general performance); neuroscience; operations research; painting; philosophy; photography; physics; play/screenwriting; political science; printmaking; psychology; public administration; public policy analysis; recreational therapy; recreation/ leisure studies; religious studies; sculpture; social sciences; sociology; South Asian studies; Spanish; teaching English as a second language; textile arts; theater arts/drama; theater design; theology; urban studies; western civilization; women's studies; zoology.

Academic Programs *Special study options:* academic remediation for entering students, accelerated degree program, adult/continuing education programs, advanced placement credit, cooperative education, distance learning, double majors, English as a second language, external degree program, honors programs, independent study, internships, off-campus study, part-time degree program, services for LD students, student-designed majors, study abroad, summer session for credit.

Library Webster Library plus 2 others with 1.3 million titles, 5,894 serial subscriptions, an OPAC, a Web page.

Computers on Campus 350 computers available on campus for general student use. A campuswide network can be accessed from student residence rooms and from off campus that provide access to specialized software applications. Internet access, online (class) registration, at least one staffed computer lab available.

Student Life *Housing Options:* coed. *Activities and Organizations:* drama/ theater group, student-run newspaper, radio and television station, choral group, ethnic clubs, student media, departmental clubs, national fraternities, national sororities. *Campus security:* 24-hour emergency response devices and patrols, student patrols, late-night transport/escort service, controlled dormitory access. *Student Services:* health clinic, personal/psychological counseling, women's center, legal services.

Athletics Member CIAU. *Intercollegiate sports:* baseball M, basketball M/W, cross-country running M/W, football M, golf M, ice hockey M/W, rugby M/W, skiing (downhill) M/W, soccer M/W, track and field M/W, wrestling M/W. *Intramural sports:* badminton M/W, baseball M, basketball M/W, crew M/W, cross-country running M/W, football M/W, golf M/W, ice hockey M/W, soccer M/W, softball M/W, swimming M/W, volleyball M/W, weight lifting M/W.

Standardized Tests *Recommended:* SAT I and SAT II or ACT (for placement), SAT II: Writing Test (for placement).

Costs (2002–03) *Tuition:* province resident $1670 Canadian dollars full-time, $56 Canadian dollars per credit part-time; nonresident $3860 Canadian dollars full-time, $129 Canadian dollars per credit part-time; International tuition $10,435 Canadian dollars full-time. Full-time tuition and fees vary according to program. Part-time tuition and fees vary according to program. *Required fees:* $925 Canadian dollars full-time, $30 Canadian dollars per credit. *Room and board:* $6500 Canadian dollars. Room and board charges vary according to housing facility. *Payment plan:* installment. *Waivers:* senior citizens and employees or children of employees.

Applying *Options:* common application, electronic application, early action. *Application fee:* $50. *Required:* high school transcript. *Required for some:* essay or personal statement, 3 letters of recommendation, interview, CEGEP transcript. *Application deadlines:* 3/1 (freshmen), 3/1 (transfers). *Notification:* continuous until 9/1 (freshmen), 4/15 (early action).

Admissions Contact Ms. Assunta Fargnoli, Assistant Registrar, Concordia University, Admissions Application Center, PO Box 2900, Montréal, QC H3G 2S2, Canada. *Phone:* 514-848-2628. *Fax:* 514-848-8621. *E-mail:* admreg@ alcor.concordia.ca.

CONCORDIA UNIVERSITY COLLEGE OF ALBERTA

Edmonton, Alberta, Canada

- **Independent religious** 4-year, founded 1921
- **Degrees** certificates, diplomas, bachelor's, and postbachelor's certificates
- **Coed**
- 65% of applicants were admitted

Faculty *Student/faculty ratio:* 18:1.

Student Life *Campus security:* 24-hour patrols, late-night transport/escort service.

Costs (2001–02) *Comprehensive fee:* $9617 Canadian dollars includes full-time tuition ($4925 Canadian dollars), mandatory fees ($262 Canadian dollars), and room and board ($4430 Canadian dollars). Full-time tuition and fees vary according to class time, course load, and program. Part-time tuition: $616 Canadian dollars per credit. Part-time tuition and fees vary according to class time, course load, and program. International tuition: $6925 Canadian dollars full-time. *Required fees:* $44 Canadian dollars per credit. *Room and board:* Room and board charges vary according to board plan.

Applying *Options:* common application, electronic application, early admission. *Required:* high school transcript, minimum 2.0 GPA. *Required for some:* essay or personal statement, 2 letters of recommendation, interview.

Admissions Contact Mr. Tony Norrad, Dean of Admissions and Financial Aid, Concordia University College of Alberta, 7128 Ada Boulevard, Edmonton, AB T5B 4E4. *Phone:* 780-479-9224. *Fax:* 780-474-1933. *E-mail:* admits@ concordia.ab.ca.

DALHOUSIE UNIVERSITY

Halifax, Nova Scotia, Canada

- **Province-supported** university, founded 1818
- **Calendar** semesters
- **Degrees** diplomas, bachelor's, master's, doctoral, and first professional
- **Urban** 80-acre campus
- **Endowment** $230.3 million
- **Coed,** 9,313 undergraduate students, 87% full-time, 56% women, 44% men
- **Moderately difficult** entrance level, 73% of applicants were admitted

Serving Canada and the international community, Dalhousie University has a worldwide reputation and offers undergraduate, graduate, and professional programs. With an enrollment of 13,500, the University offers a unique combination of personal attention with a variety of programs at the undergraduate and graduate levels. For further information about programs in the arts, social sciences, science, engineering, architecture, computer science, health professions, law, medicine, graduate studies, and dentistry, students should contact the Registrar's Office, Dalhousie University, Halifax, NS B3H 4H6 Canada (e-mail: admissions@dal.ca; Web site: http://www.dal.ca).

Undergraduates Students come from 13 provinces and territories, 84 other countries, 14% live on campus. *Retention:* 80% of 2001 full-time freshmen returned.

Freshmen *Admission:* 4,570 applied, 3,337 admitted. *Test scores:* SAT verbal scores over 500: 67%; SAT math scores over 500: 72%; SAT verbal scores over 600: 32%; SAT math scores over 600: 26%; SAT verbal scores over 700: 6%; SAT math scores over 700: 4%.

Faculty *Total:* 1,516. *Student/faculty ratio:* 12:1.

Majors Accounting; agricultural engineering; anthropology; architecture; biochemistry; biology; business administration; Canadian studies; chemical engineering; chemistry; civil engineering; classics; computer engineering; computer/ information technology services administration and management related; computer science; dental hygiene; earth sciences; economics; engineering; English; exercise sciences; food sciences; French; German; health education; health science; history; history of science and technology; industrial/manufacturing engineering; international relations; linguistics; literature; management science; marine biology; mathematical statistics; mathematics; mechanical engineering; metallurgical engineering; microbiology/bacteriology; mining/mineral engineering; music; neuroscience; nursing; occupational therapy; pharmacy; philosophy; physical therapy; physics; political science; pre-dentistry; pre-law; pre-medicine; pre-veterinary studies; psychology; recreation/leisure studies; religious studies; Russian; social work; sociology; Spanish; theater arts/drama; women's studies.

Academic Programs *Special study options:* academic remediation for entering students, adult/continuing education programs, advanced placement credit, cooperative education, distance learning, double majors, English as a second language, honors programs, off-campus study, part-time degree program, services for LD students, study abroad, summer session for credit.

Library The Killam Memorial Library plus 4 others with 1.7 million titles, 8,306 serial subscriptions, 6,001 audiovisual materials, an OPAC, a Web page.

Computers on Campus 710 computers available on campus for general student use. A campuswide network can be accessed from student residence rooms and from off campus. Internet access, at least one staffed computer lab available.

Student Life *Housing Options:* coed, men-only, women-only, disabled students. *Activities and Organizations:* drama/theater group, student-run newspaper, radio station, choral group, International Students Association, Arts Society, Science Society, Commerce Society, Dalhousie Outdoors Club, national fraterni-

Dalhousie University (continued)
ties, national sororities. *Campus security:* 24-hour emergency response devices and patrols, student patrols, late-night transport/escort service. *Student Services:* health clinic, personal/psychological counseling, women's center, legal services.

Athletics Member CIAU. *Intercollegiate sports:* basketball M/W, cross-country running M/W, field hockey W(c), ice hockey M, soccer M/W, swimming M/W, track and field M/W, volleyball M/W. *Intramural sports:* badminton M/W, baseball M(c), basketball M/W, crew M(c)/W(c), cross-country running M/W, fencing M/W, field hockey W, football M/W, golf M/W, gymnastics M/W, ice hockey M/W(c), lacrosse M, racquetball M/W, rugby M(c)/W(c), sailing M(c)/W(c), skiing (cross-country) M/W, skiing (downhill) M/W, soccer M/W, softball M/W, squash M(c)/W(c), swimming M/W, tennis M/W, track and field M/W, volleyball M/W, water polo M/W, weight lifting M/W, wrestling M/W.

Standardized Tests *Required:* SAT I (for admission).

Costs (2001–02) *Comprehensive fee:* $10,526 Canadian dollars includes full-time tuition ($4901 Canadian dollars) and room and board ($5625 Canadian dollars). Full-time tuition and fees vary according to course load. Part-time tuition: $900 Canadian dollars per year. Part-time tuition and fees vary according to course load. International tuition: $9351 Canadian dollars full-time. *Room and board:* Room and board charges vary according to board plan and housing facility. *Waivers:* minority students, senior citizens, and employees or children of employees.

Applying *Options:* electronic application, deferred entrance. *Application fee:* $40. *Required:* high school transcript, minimum 3.0 GPA. *Required for some:* essay or personal statement, 1 letter of recommendation, interview, minimum 1100 comprehensive score on SAT I for U.S. applicants. *Application deadlines:* 6/1 (freshmen), 6/1 (transfers). *Notification:* continuous (freshmen).

Admissions Contact Ms. Susan Tanner, Associate Registrar of Admissions, Dalhousie University, Halifax, NS B3H 4H6. *Phone:* 902-494-6572. *Fax:* 902-494-1630. *E-mail:* admissions@dal.ca.

École des Hautes Études Commerciales de Montréal
Montréal, Quebec, Canada

- **Province-supported** comprehensive, founded 1910, part of Université de Montréal
- **Calendar** trimesters
- **Degrees** certificates, diplomas, bachelor's, master's, and doctoral
- **Urban** 9-acre campus
- **Coed,** 7,900 undergraduate students, 53% full-time, 50% women, 50% men
- **Moderately difficult** entrance level, 46% of applicants were admitted

Undergraduates 4,187 full-time, 3,713 part-time. Students come from 8 provinces and territories, 80 other countries, 1% are from out of province. *Retention:* 84% of 2001 full-time freshmen returned.

Freshmen *Admission:* 2,304 applied, 1,068 admitted, 997 enrolled.

Faculty *Total:* 535, 36% full-time, 29% with terminal degrees.

Majors Accounting; applied economics; business; business administration; business economics; business marketing and marketing management; business statistics; business systems analysis/design; computer management; enterprise management; entrepreneurship; finance; human resources management; information sciences/systems; international business; international economics; international finance; management information systems/business data processing; management science; retail management.

Academic Programs *Special study options:* academic remediation for entering students, adult/continuing education programs, English as a second language, honors programs, independent study, off-campus study, part-time degree program, student-designed majors, study abroad, summer session for credit.

Library Myriam et J.-Robert Ouimet Library plus 1 other with 343,456 titles, 6,018 serial subscriptions, 2,211 audiovisual materials, an OPAC, a Web page.

Computers on Campus 250 computers available on campus for general student use. A campuswide network can be accessed from off campus. Internet access, online (class) registration, at least one staffed computer lab available.

Student Life *Housing:* college housing not available. *Activities and Organizations:* student-run newspaper. *Campus security:* 24-hour emergency response devices and patrols. *Student Services:* health clinic, personal/psychological counseling, legal services.

Costs (2001–02) *Tuition:* province resident $1680 Canadian dollars full-time, $56 Canadian dollars per credit part-time; nonresident $3870 Canadian dollars full-time, $129 Canadian dollars per credit part-time; International tuition $9870 Canadian dollars full-time. Full-time tuition and fees vary according to program. Part-time tuition and fees vary according to program. college room and board is available through the Université de Montréal. *Required fees:* $310 Canadian dollars full-time, $3 Canadian dollars per credit, $60 Canadian dollars per term part-time. *Room and board:* room only: $3000 Canadian dollars. *Payment plan:* installment. *Waivers:* employees or children of employees.

Applying *Options:* common application, deferred entrance. *Application fee:* $40. *Required:* high school transcript. *Required for some:* cote de rendement collégial. *Application deadlines:* 3/1 (freshmen), 5/1 (out-of-state freshmen), 3/1 (transfers). *Notification:* 3/15 (freshmen), 6/1 (out-of-state freshmen).

Admissions Contact Ms. Lyne Héroux, Administrative Director of Bachelor Program, École des Hautes Études Commerciales de Montréal, 3000 chemin de la Côte-Sainte-Catherine, Montréal, QC H3T 2A7. *Phone:* 514-340-6139. *Fax:* 514-340-5640. *E-mail:* registraire.info@hec.ca.

Emmanuel Bible College
Kitchener, Ontario, Canada

Admissions Contact Mrs. Ruth Scott, Recruitment Officer, Emmanuel Bible College, 100 Fergus Avenue, Kitchener, ON N2A 2H2, Canada. *Phone:* 519-894-8900 Ext. 30.

Heritage Baptist College and Heritage Theological Seminary
Cambridge, Ontario, Canada

Admissions Contact Mr. Alan Wiseman, Registrar/Director of Admissions, Heritage Baptist College and Heritage Theological Seminary, 175 Holiday Inn Drive, Cambridge, ON N3C 3T2, Canada. *Phone:* 519-651-2869 Ext. 227. *Fax:* 519-651-2870. *E-mail:* admissions@heritage-theo.edu.

The King's University College
Edmonton, Alberta, Canada

- **Independent interdenominational** 4-year, founded 1979
- **Calendar** Canadian standard year
- **Degree** bachelor's
- **Suburban** 20-acre campus
- **Endowment** $413,411
- **Coed,** 570 undergraduate students, 92% full-time, 60% women, 40% men
- **Moderately difficult** entrance level, 91% of applicants were admitted

Undergraduates 526 full-time, 44 part-time. Students come from 7 provinces and territories, 11 other countries, 21% are from out of province, 18% transferred in, 20% live on campus. *Retention:* 73% of 2001 full-time freshmen returned.

Freshmen *Admission:* 461 applied, 418 admitted, 146 enrolled. *Average high school GPA:* 3.00.

Faculty *Total:* 88, 38% full-time, 45% with terminal degrees. *Student/faculty ratio:* 17:1.

Majors Biology; business administration; chemistry; computer science; elementary education; English; environmental science; history; music; philosophy; psychology; social sciences; sociology.

Academic Programs *Special study options:* adult/continuing education programs, advanced placement credit, double majors, independent study, internships, off-campus study, part-time degree program, services for LD students, study abroad. *Unusual degree programs:* 3-2 elementary education.

Library Simona Maaskant with 64,448 titles, 1,507 serial subscriptions, 4,426 audiovisual materials, an OPAC, a Web page.

Computers on Campus 37 computers available on campus for general student use. Internet access, at least one staffed computer lab available.

Student Life *Housing Options:* coed, women-only. *Activities and Organizations:* drama/theater group, student-run newspaper, choral group, Swing Dance Club, The King's Players (drama club), chamber and concert choirs, King's Science Society, The Political Studies Club. *Campus security:* 24-hour emergency response devices, student patrols, controlled dormitory access. *Student Services:* personal/psychological counseling.

Athletics *Intercollegiate sports:* basketball M(s)/W(s), soccer M/W, volleyball M(s)/W(s). *Intramural sports:* ice hockey M.

Standardized Tests *Recommended:* SAT I and SAT II or ACT (for admission).

Costs (2001–02) *Comprehensive fee:* $11,068 Canadian dollars includes full-time tuition ($5704 Canadian dollars), mandatory fees ($240 Canadian dollars), and room and board ($5124 Canadian dollars). Full-time tuition and fees vary according to course load and degree level. Part-time tuition: $184 Canadian dollars per credit. Part-time tuition and fees vary according to course load and degree level. *Required fees:* $60 Canadian dollars per term part-time. *Room and board:* Room and board charges vary according to board plan. *Waivers:* employees or children of employees.

Financial Aid Available in 2001, 58 State and other part-time jobs. *Financial aid deadline:* 3/31.

Applying *Options:* electronic application. *Application fee:* $35. *Required:* high school transcript, minimum 2.0 GPA, 1 letter of recommendation. *Required for some:* essay or personal statement, interview. *Application deadline:* rolling (freshmen), rolling (transfers). *Notification:* continuous until 8/15 (freshmen).

Admissions Contact Mr. Glenn J. Keeler, Registrar/Director of Admissions, The King's University College, 9125-50 Street, Edmonton, AB T6B 2H3. *Phone:* 780-465-8335. *Toll-free phone:* 800-661-8582. *Fax:* 780-465-3534. *E-mail:* admissions@kingsu.ab.ca.

KWANTLEN UNIVERSITY COLLEGE
Surrey, British Columbia, Canada

Admissions Contact 1266 72nd Avenue, Surrey, BC V3W 2M8, Canada.

LAKEHEAD UNIVERSITY
Thunder Bay, Ontario, Canada

- **Province-supported** comprehensive, founded 1965
- **Calendar** Canadian standard year
- **Degrees** bachelor's, master's, and doctoral
- **Suburban** 345-acre campus
- **Endowment** $10.3 million
- **Coed,** 5,854 undergraduate students, 80% full-time, 57% women, 43% men
- **Moderately difficult** entrance level, 35% of applicants were admitted

Undergraduates Students come from 10 provinces and territories, 52 other countries, 6% are from out of province, 22% live on campus.

Freshmen *Admission:* 5,759 applied, 2,028 admitted. *Average high school GPA:* 3.1.

Faculty *Total:* 537, 45% full-time. *Student/faculty ratio:* 19:1.

Majors Accounting; anthropology; archaeology; art; athletic training/sports medicine; biological/physical sciences; biology; business administration; business marketing and marketing management; chemical engineering; chemical engineering technology; chemistry; civil engineering; civil engineering technology; clinical psychology; computer engineering; computer science; economics; education; electrical/electronic engineering technology; electrical engineering; elementary education; engineering; English; environmental biology; environmental science; finance; forest harvesting production technology; forestry; French; geography; geology; history; human resources management; information sciences/systems; labor/personnel relations; liberal arts and sciences/liberal studies; library science; management information systems/business data processing; mathematics; mechanical engineering; mechanical engineering technology; music; natural sciences; nursing; philosophy; physical education; physics; political science; psychology; recreation/leisure studies; science education; secondary education; social work; sociology; women's studies.

Academic Programs *Special study options:* academic remediation for entering students, accelerated degree program, adult/continuing education programs, advanced placement credit, cooperative education, distance learning, double majors, English as a second language, honors programs, part-time degree program, services for LD students, student-designed majors, study abroad, summer session for credit.

Library Chancellor Norman M. Paterson Library plus 1 other with 719,253 titles, 2,100 serial subscriptions, 260 audiovisual materials, an OPAC, a Web page.

Computers on Campus 700 computers available on campus for general student use. A campuswide network can be accessed from student residence rooms and from off campus. Internet access, online (class) registration, at least one staffed computer lab available.

Student Life *Housing Options:* coed, women-only. *Activities and Organizations:* drama/theater group, student-run newspaper, Outdoor Recreation Students Association, Engineering Students Society, Business Association, ECHO/LUFROG, Educational Students Association. *Campus security:* 24-hour emergency response devices and patrols, student patrols, late-night transport/escort service, controlled dormitory access. *Student Services:* health clinic, personal/psychological counseling, women's center.

Athletics Member CIAU. *Intercollegiate sports:* basketball M/W, crew M/W, cross-country running M/W, rugby M/W, skiing (cross-country) M/W, soccer M(c), track and field M/W, volleyball M/W, wrestling M/W. *Intramural sports:* badminton M/W, baseball M/W, basketball M/W, bowling M/W, ice hockey M/W, soccer M/W, volleyball M/W.

Costs (2001–02) *Tuition:* nonresident $3988 Canadian dollars full-time, $798 Canadian dollars per course part-time; International tuition $8670 Canadian dollars full-time. Full-time tuition and fees vary according to program. Part-time tuition and fees vary according to program. *Required fees:* $428 Canadian dollars full-time, $65 Canadian dollars per course. *Room and board:* $5497 Canadian dollars. Room and board charges vary according to housing facility. *Payment plans:* installment, deferred payment. *Waivers:* senior citizens and employees or children of employees.

Applying *Options:* common application, early admission, deferred entrance. *Application fee:* $85. *Required for some:* essay or personal statement, high school transcript, letters of recommendation. *Application deadline:* rolling (freshmen), rolling (transfers). *Notification:* continuous until 9/23 (freshmen).

Admissions Contact Ms. Sarena Knapik, Chief Admissions Officer, Lakehead University, 955 Oliver Road, Thunder Bay, ON P7B 5E1, Canada. *Phone:* 807-343-8500. *Toll-free phone:* 800-465-3959. *Fax:* 807-343-8156. *E-mail:* admissions@lakeheadu.ca.

LAURENTIAN UNIVERSITY
Sudbury, Ontario, Canada

- **Independent nondenominational** comprehensive, founded 1960
- **Calendar** Canadian standard year
- **Degrees** bachelor's and master's
- **Suburban** 700-acre campus
- **Endowment** $8.1 million
- **Coed,** 5,454 undergraduate students
- **Minimally difficult** entrance level, 78% of applicants were admitted

Undergraduates Students come from 12 provinces and territories, 15 other countries.

Freshmen *Admission:* 4,374 applied, 3,400 admitted.

Faculty *Total:* 390, 69% full-time. *Student/faculty ratio:* 20:1.

Majors Adult/continuing education; anthropology; astronomy; behavioral sciences; biochemistry; biology; business administration; chemistry; classics; computer science; earth sciences; economics; education; English; exercise sciences; film studies; folklore; foreign language translation; French; geography; geological engineering; geology; history; Italian; legal studies; liberal arts and sciences/liberal studies; mathematics; medical physics/biophysics; metallurgical engineering; mining/mineral engineering; modern languages; music; Native American studies; nursing; philosophy; physical education; physics; political science; psychology; public health education/promotion; religious studies; social work; sociology; Spanish; sport/fitness administration; theater arts/drama; women's studies.

Academic Programs *Special study options:* academic remediation for entering students, accelerated degree program, adult/continuing education programs, cooperative education, external degree program, honors programs, off-campus study, part-time degree program, services for LD students, summer session for credit.

Library J. N. Desmarais Library plus 3 others with 696,838 titles, a Web page.

Computers on Campus 125 computers available on campus for general student use. Internet access, at least one staffed computer lab available.

Student Life *Housing Options:* coed. *Activities and Organizations:* drama/theater group, student-run newspaper, radio station, Students General Association, Association des Etudiants Francophone, Association of Laurentian Part-time Students. *Campus security:* 24-hour emergency response devices and patrols, late-night transport/escort service. *Student Services:* health clinic, personal/psychological counseling.

Athletics Member CIAU. *Intercollegiate sports:* basketball M/W, cross-country running M/W, field hockey W, ice hockey M/W, skiing (cross-country) M/W, skiing (downhill) M/W, soccer M, swimming M/W, track and field M/W, volleyball M. *Intramural sports:* basketball M/W, cross-country running M/W, football M/W, golf M/W, gymnastics M/W, ice hockey M/W, skiing (cross-country) M/W, skiing (downhill) M/W, swimming M/W, tennis M/W, volleyball M/W.

Costs (2001–02) *Comprehensive fee:* $9068 Canadian dollars includes full-time tuition ($4029 Canadian dollars), mandatory fees ($319 Canadian dollars), and room and board ($4720 Canadian dollars). Full-time tuition and fees vary according to program. Part-time tuition: $403 Canadian dollars per course. Part-time tuition and fees vary according to program. *Required fees:* $4 Canadian dollars per term part-time.

Financial Aid Available in 2001, 180 State and other part-time jobs (averaging $1700).

Applying *Options:* common application, early admission. *Application fee:* $50. *Required:* high school transcript. *Required for some:* essay or personal statement, 2 letters of recommendation, interview. *Application deadlines:* rolling (freshmen), 6/30 (out-of-state freshmen), rolling (transfers).

Laurentian University (continued)

Admissions Contact Mr. Ron Smith, Registrar, Laurentian University, Ramsey Lake Road, Sudbury, ON P3E 2C6. *Phone:* 705-675-1151 Ext. 3919. *Fax:* 705-675-4891. *E-mail:* admissions@nickel.laurentian.ca.

MALASPINA UNIVERSITY-COLLEGE
Nanaimo, British Columbia, Canada

- **Province-supported** 4-year, founded 1969
- **Calendar** semesters
- **Degrees** certificates, diplomas, associate, bachelor's, and postbachelor's certificates
- **Coed,** 6,422 undergraduate students, 100% full-time, 60% women, 40% men

Undergraduates 6,422 full-time.

Faculty *Total:* 1,022, 40% full-time. *Student/faculty ratio:* 17:1.

Majors Anthropology; biology; business; child care/guidance; computer/information sciences; creative writing; education; fishing sciences; history; liberal arts and sciences/liberal studies; nursing related; psychology; sociology; travel/tourism management.

Costs (2002–03) *Tuition:* area resident $2370 Canadian dollars full-time, $79 Canadian dollars per credit hour part-time.

Admissions Contact Mr. Fred Jarklin, Admissions Manager, Malaspina University-College, 900 Fifth Street, Nanaimo, BC V9R 5S5, Canada. *Phone:* 250-740-6356 Ext. 6356.

MASTER'S COLLEGE AND SEMINARY
Peterborough, Ontario, Canada

- **Independent Pentecostal** 4-year, founded 1939
- **Calendar** semesters
- **Degree** certificates, diplomas, and bachelor's
- **Small-town** 7-acre campus with easy access to Toronto
- **Endowment** $320,000
- **Coed,** 416 undergraduate students
- **Noncompetitive** entrance level, 87% of applicants were admitted

Undergraduates Students come from 8 provinces and territories, 5 other countries. *Retention:* 66% of 2001 full-time freshmen returned.

Freshmen *Admission:* 78 applied, 68 admitted.

Faculty *Total:* 33, 24% full-time, 15% with terminal degrees. *Student/faculty ratio:* 22:1.

Majors Divinity/ministry; missionary studies; religious education; theology.

Academic Programs *Special study options:* academic remediation for entering students, accelerated degree program, distance learning, independent study, internships, off-campus study, part-time degree program, services for LD students, study abroad, summer session for credit. *Unusual degree programs:* theology.

Library 43,197 titles, 243 serial subscriptions, 2,537 audiovisual materials, an OPAC.

Computers on Campus 14 computers available on campus for general student use. A campuswide network can be accessed from off campus that provide access to e-mail. Internet access, at least one staffed computer lab available.

Student Life *Housing:* on-campus residence required through sophomore year. *Options:* men-only, women-only. *Activities and Organizations:* choral group. *Campus security:* student patrols.

Athletics *Intercollegiate sports:* basketball M/W, ice hockey M, soccer M, volleyball M/W. *Intramural sports:* badminton M/W, baseball M/W, basketball M/W, golf M/W, ice hockey M, table tennis M/W, volleyball M/W.

Costs (2001–02) *Comprehensive fee:* $9310 Canadian dollars includes full-time tuition ($4650 Canadian dollars), mandatory fees ($450 Canadian dollars), and room and board ($4210 Canadian dollars). Full-time tuition and fees vary according to course load. Part-time tuition: $155 Canadian dollars per credit hour. Part-time tuition and fees vary according to course load. *Required fees:* $45 Canadian dollars per course. *Payment plan:* installment. *Waivers:* employees or children of employees.

Applying *Options:* deferred entrance. *Application fee:* $50. *Required:* essay or personal statement, high school transcript, 3 letters of recommendation, medical history, Christian commitment. *Required for some:* interview. *Recommended:* minimum 2.0 GPA. *Application deadlines:* 8/31 (freshmen), 8/31 (transfers).

Admissions Contact Mrs. Joan Mann, Director of Enrollment Management, Master's College and Seminary, 780 Argyle Street, Peterborough, ON K9H 5T2, Canada. *Phone:* 705-748-9111 Ext. 145. *Toll-free phone:* 800-295-6368. *E-mail:* jmann@epbc.edu.

MCGILL UNIVERSITY
Montréal, Quebec, Canada

- **Independent** university, founded 1821
- **Calendar** semesters
- **Degrees** certificates, diplomas, bachelor's, master's, doctoral, first professional, and postbachelor's certificates
- **Urban** 80-acre campus
- **Endowment** $496.3 million
- **Coed,** 21,544 undergraduate students, 75% full-time, 60% women, 40% men
- **Very difficult** entrance level, 57% of applicants were admitted

Undergraduates 16,138 full-time, 5,406 part-time. Students come from 12 provinces and territories, 150 other countries, 26% are from out of province, 6% transferred in, 7% live on campus.

Freshmen *Admission:* 15,885 applied, 9,077 admitted, 4,313 enrolled. *Average high school GPA:* 3.50.

Faculty *Total:* 2,124, 67% full-time, 95% with terminal degrees. *Student/faculty ratio:* 15:1.

Majors Accounting; African studies; agribusiness; agricultural business; agricultural economics; agricultural engineering; animal sciences; animal sciences related; anthropology; applied mathematics; architecture; area studies related; art history; atmospheric sciences; biochemistry; biology; biology education; botany; botany related; business administration; business economics; business education; Canadian studies; chemical engineering; chemistry; chemistry education; chemistry related; classics; computer engineering; computer/information sciences; computer science; computer science related; dietetics; earth sciences; East Asian studies; Eastern European area studies; ecology; economics; education; electrical engineering; elementary education; engineering related; English; English education; English related; enterprise management; entrepreneurship; environmental biology; environmental science; exercise sciences; finance; food sciences; foreign languages/literatures; French; French language education; genetics; geography; geophysics/seismology; German; history; history education; humanities; human resources management; information sciences/systems; international agriculture; international business; Italian; jazz; Judaic studies; labor/personnel relations; Latin American studies; linguistics; management science; marine biology; marketing research; mathematical statistics; mathematics; mathematics/computer science; mathematics education; mechanical engineering; metallurgical engineering; microbiology/bacteriology; Middle Eastern studies; mining/mineral engineering; molecular biology; music; music (general performance); music history; music (piano and organ performance); music related; music teacher education; music theory and composition; music (voice and choral/opera performance); natural resources conservation; natural resources management; natural resources management/protective services related; nursing; nutritional sciences; nutrition science; occupational therapy; organizational behavior; philosophy; philosophy and religion related; physical education; physical therapy; physics; physics education; physiological psychology/psychobiology; physiology; plant sciences; political science; psychology; religious education; religious studies; Russian; Russian/Slavic studies; science education; secondary education; social science education; social studies education; social work; sociology; soil sciences; Spanish; special education; teaching English as a second language; theater arts/drama; urban studies; wildlife biology; wildlife management; women's studies; zoology; zoology related.

Academic Programs *Special study options:* adult/continuing education programs, advanced placement credit, double majors, English as a second language, honors programs, internships, off-campus study, part-time degree program, services for LD students, student-designed majors, study abroad, summer session for credit.

Library Humanities and Social Sciences Library plus 16 others with 3.0 million titles, 15,919 serial subscriptions, 553,469 audiovisual materials, an OPAC, a Web page.

Computers on Campus 1500 computers available on campus for general student use. A campuswide network can be accessed from student residence rooms and from off campus. Internet access, online (class) registration, at least one staffed computer lab available.

Student Life *Housing Options:* coed, women-only, cooperative. *Activities and Organizations:* drama/theater group, student-run newspaper, radio station, choral group, Debating Union, UNSAM (Model United Nations), Sexual Assault Centre, Walksafe, Queer McGill, national fraternities, national sororities. *Campus security:* 24-hour emergency response devices and patrols, student patrols, late-night transport/escort service, controlled dormitory access. *Student Services:* health clinic, personal/psychological counseling, women's center, legal services.

Athletics Member CIAU. *Intercollegiate sports:* badminton M/W, baseball M, basketball M/W, crew M/W, cross-country running M/W, fencing M/W, field hockey W, football M, ice hockey M/W, lacrosse M/W, rugby M/W, sailing M/W, skiing (cross-country) M/W, skiing (downhill) M/W, soccer M/W, squash M/W, swimming M/W, tennis M/W, track and field M/W, volleyball M/W, wrestling M/W. *Intramural sports:* badminton M/W, basketball M/W, football M/W, ice hockey M/W, soccer M/W, squash M/W, table tennis M/W, tennis M/W, volleyball M/W.

Costs (2002–03) *Tuition:* province resident $1668 Canadian dollars full-time, $56 Canadian dollars per credit part-time; nonresident $4012 Canadian dollars full-time, $134 Canadian dollars per credit part-time; International tuition $8763 Canadian dollars full-time. Full-time tuition and fees vary according to course load and program. Part-time tuition and fees vary according to course load and program. *Required fees:* $1050 Canadian dollars full-time. *Room and board:* $7000 Canadian dollars. Room and board charges vary according to board plan, gender, housing facility, and location. *Payment plan:* installment. *Waivers:* senior citizens and employees or children of employees.

Applying *Options:* electronic application, deferred entrance. *Application fee:* $60. *Required:* high school transcript, minimum 3.3 GPA. *Required for some:* letters of recommendation, audition for music program, portfolio for architecture program. *Application deadlines:* 1/15 (freshmen), 1/15 (transfers). *Notification:* continuous (freshmen).

Admissions Contact Ms. Robin Geller, Registrar and Director of Admissions, Recruitment and Registrar's Office, McGill University, 845 Sherbrooke Street West, Montreal, QC H3A 2T5, Canada. *Phone:* 514-398-6424. *Fax:* 514-398-8939. *E-mail:* admissions@mcgill.ca.

McMaster University
Hamilton, Ontario, Canada

- **Province-supported** university, founded 1887
- **Calendar** Canadian standard year
- **Degrees** bachelor's, master's, doctoral, and first professional
- **Suburban** 300-acre campus with easy access to Toronto
- **Coed,** 15,500 undergraduate students, 82% full-time, 57% women, 43% men
- **Very difficult** entrance level, 76% of applicants were admitted

Undergraduates 12,700 full-time, 2,800 part-time. Students come from 12 provinces and territories, 79 other countries, 23% live on campus.

Freshmen *Admission:* 20,254 applied, 15,490 admitted, 4,510 enrolled.

Faculty *Total:* 1,258, 98% full-time.

Majors Anthropology; applied mathematics; art; art history; astrophysics; biochemistry; biological/physical sciences; biological technology; biology; business administration; chemical engineering; chemistry; civil engineering; classics; communications related; comparative literature; computer engineering; computer science; earth sciences; economics; electrical engineering; engineering/industrial management; engineering physics; English; environmental science; exercise sciences; French; geography; geology; German; gerontology; Hispanic-American studies; history; industrial/manufacturing engineering; Japanese; labor/personnel relations; Latin American studies; linguistics; materials engineering; materials science; mathematical statistics; mathematics; mechanical engineering; modern languages; molecular biology; multimedia; music; music history; music teacher education; nursing; nursing (midwifery); pharmacology; philosophy; physical sciences; physics; political science; psychology; religious education; religious studies; Russian; Russian/Slavic studies; social work; sociology; theater arts/drama; women's studies.

Academic Programs *Special study options:* academic remediation for entering students, accelerated degree program, adult/continuing education programs, cooperative education, honors programs, independent study, internships, off-campus study, part-time degree program, services for LD students, student-designed majors, study abroad, summer session for credit.

Library Mills Memorial Library plus 4 others with 1.7 million titles, 11,976 serial subscriptions, an OPAC, a Web page.

Computers on Campus 400 computers available on campus for general student use. A campuswide network can be accessed from student residence rooms and from off campus. Internet access, at least one staffed computer lab available.

Student Life *Housing Options:* coed, men-only, women-only. *Activities and Organizations:* drama/theater group, student-run newspaper, radio station, choral group, Inter-Varsity Christian Fellowship Club, African-Caribbean Student Association, Chinese Students' Association, AIESEC (international leadership organization), South East Asian Society. *Campus security:* 24-hour emergency response devices and patrols, student patrols, late-night transport/escort service, controlled dormitory access. *Student Services:* health clinic, personal/psychological counseling, women's center, legal services.

Athletics Member CIAU. *Intercollegiate sports:* badminton M/W, baseball M, basketball M/W, cross-country running M/W, fencing M/W, football M, golf M/W, lacrosse M/W, rugby M/W, soccer M/W, squash M/W, swimming M/W, tennis M/W, track and field M/W, volleyball M/W, water polo M/W, wrestling M/W. *Intramural sports:* badminton M/W, baseball M/W, basketball M/W, cross-country running M/W, football M/W, golf M, gymnastics M/W, ice hockey M/W, lacrosse M/W, soccer M/W, softball M/W, squash M/W, table tennis M/W, tennis M/W, volleyball M/W, water polo M/W.

Costs (2001–02) *Tuition:* area resident $4700 Canadian dollars full-time; International tuition $13,000 Canadian dollars full-time. *Room and board:* $6000 Canadian dollars.

Applying *Options:* early action. *Application fee:* $95. *Required:* high school transcript. *Required for some:* essay or personal statement, interview. *Application deadlines:* 7/15 (freshmen), 5/1 (out-of-state freshmen), 7/15 (transfers). *Notification:* continuous until 9/1 (freshmen), 6/12 (early action).

Admissions Contact Mrs. Lynn Giordano, Associate Registrar, Admissions, McMaster University, 1280 Main Street West, Hamilton, ON L8S 4M2, Canada. *Phone:* 905-525-9140 Ext. 24034. *Fax:* 905-527-1105. *E-mail:* macadmit@mcmaster.ca.

Memorial University of Newfoundland
St. John's, Newfoundland, Canada

- **Province-supported** university, founded 1925
- **Calendar** trimesters
- **Degrees** bachelor's, master's, doctoral, and postbachelor's certificates
- **Urban** 220-acre campus
- **Coed,** 14,037 undergraduate students, 85% full-time, 60% women, 40% men
- **Moderately difficult** entrance level, 76% of applicants were admitted

Undergraduates Students come from 12 provinces and territories, 5% are from out of province, 10% live on campus. *Retention:* 80% of 2001 full-time freshmen returned.

Freshmen *Admission:* 2,981 applied, 2,269 admitted.

Faculty *Total:* 907, 92% full-time, 68% with terminal degrees. *Student/faculty ratio:* 12:1.

Majors Accounting; acting/directing; adult/continuing education; anthropology; applied mathematics; archaeology; area studies; art; art history; athletic training/sports medicine; biochemistry; biological/physical sciences; biology; business administration; business marketing and marketing management; Canadian studies; cartography; cell biology; chemical engineering; chemistry; civil engineering; classics; computer programming; computer science; counselor education/guidance; criminology; dietetics; drama/theater literature; drawing; earth sciences; ecology; economics; education; electrical engineering; elementary education; engineering; English; entomology; environmental biology; environmental science; exercise sciences; finance; folklore; food sciences; forestry sciences; French; geography; geological engineering; geology; geophysics/seismology; German; Greek (modern); history; humanities; industrial/manufacturing engineering; information sciences/systems; labor/personnel relations; Latin (ancient and medieval); law enforcement/police science; linguistics; literature; marine biology; marine science; mathematical statistics; mathematics; mechanical engineering; medieval/renaissance studies; microbiology/bacteriology; middle school education; music; music history; music (piano and organ performance); music teacher education; music theory and composition; music (voice and choral/opera performance); naval architecture/marine engineering; neuroscience; nursing; nutrition science; ocean engineering; oceanography; organizational behavior; painting; pharmacy; philosophy; photography; physical education; physics; political science; pre-medicine; printmaking; psychology; recreation/leisure studies; religious studies; Russian; science education; sculpture; secondary education; social sciences; social work; sociology; Spanish; special education; stringed instruments; theater arts/drama; theater design; trade/industrial education; wind/percussion instruments; women's studies; zoology.

Academic Programs *Special study options:* academic remediation for entering students, accelerated degree program, adult/continuing education programs, advanced placement credit, cooperative education, distance learning, double majors, English as a second language, honors programs, internships, off-campus study, part-time degree program, services for LD students, study abroad, summer session for credit. *Unusual degree programs:* 3-2 forestry with University of New Brunswick; pharmacy, music.

Library Queen Elizabeth II Library plus 2 others with 1.2 million titles, 17,000 serial subscriptions, an OPAC, a Web page.

Computers on Campus 800 computers available on campus for general student use. A campuswide network can be accessed from student residence rooms and from off campus. Internet access, at least one staffed computer lab available.

Student Life *Housing Options:* coed, men-only, women-only, disabled students. *Activities and Organizations:* drama/theater group, student-run newspaper, radio station, choral group, International Student Center, Students Older Than Average, Memorial's Organization for the Disabled, Biology Society, Student Parents at MUN. *Campus security:* 24-hour emergency response devices and patrols, student patrols, late-night transport/escort service. *Student Services:* health clinic, personal/psychological counseling, women's center, legal services.

Memorial University of Newfoundland (continued)

Athletics Member CIAU. *Intercollegiate sports:* basketball M/W, cross-country running M/W, soccer M/W, swimming M/W, volleyball M/W, wrestling M/W. *Intramural sports:* badminton M/W, basketball M/W, cross-country running M/W, soccer M/W, softball M/W, squash M/W, swimming M/W, table tennis M/W, tennis M/W, volleyball M/W, water polo M/W, weight lifting M(c).

Costs (2002–03) *Tuition:* nonresident $2673 Canadian dollars full-time, $220 Canadian dollars per credit hour part-time; International tuition $6600 Canadian dollars full-time. *Required fees:* $254 Canadian dollars full-time, $5 Canadian dollars per term part-time. *Room and board:* $4400 Canadian dollars; room only: $1600 Canadian dollars. Room and board charges vary according to board plan, housing facility, and location. *Waivers:* employees or children of employees.

Applying *Options:* electronic application. *Application fee:* $80. *Required:* high school transcript. *Required for some:* essay or personal statement, 2 letters of recommendation, interview, audition, portfolio. *Application deadlines:* rolling (freshmen), 3/1 (out-of-state freshmen), 3/1 (transfers). *Notification:* continuous (freshmen), continuous (out-of-state freshmen).

Admissions Contact Ms. Phyllis McCann, Admissions Manager, Memorial University of Newfoundland, Elizabeth Avenue, St. John's, NF A1C 5S7, Canada. *Phone:* 709-737-3705. *E-mail:* sturecru@morgan.ucs.mun.ca.

MOUNT ALLISON UNIVERSITY

Sackville, New Brunswick, Canada

- **Province-supported** comprehensive, founded 1839
- **Calendar** Canadian standard year
- **Degrees** bachelor's and master's
- **Small-town** 50-acre campus
- **Endowment** $65.0 million
- **Coed,** 2,554 undergraduate students, 89% full-time, 62% women, 38% men
- **Moderately difficult** entrance level, 77% of applicants were admitted

Undergraduates 2,278 full-time, 276 part-time. Students come from 13 provinces and territories, 40 other countries, 66% are from out of province, 4% transferred in, 65% live on campus. *Retention:* 90% of 2001 full-time freshmen returned.

Freshmen *Admission:* 2,084 applied, 1,603 admitted, 781 enrolled. *Average high school GPA:* 3.80.

Faculty *Total:* 165, 75% full-time. *Student/faculty ratio:* 18:1.

Majors Accounting; American studies; anthropology; applied mathematics; art history; biochemistry; biological/physical sciences; biology; biopsychology; business; business administration; business economics; Canadian studies; chemistry; classics; computer science; drawing; economics; English; environmental science; fine/studio arts; French; geography; geology; German; Greek (ancient and medieval); history; humanities; interdisciplinary studies; international business; international relations; Latin (ancient and medieval); liberal arts and sciences/liberal studies; literature; mathematics; mathematics/computer science; medieval/renaissance studies; modern languages; music; music (general performance); music history; music (piano and organ performance); music (voice and choral/opera performance); natural sciences; philosophy; photography; physics; physiological psychology/psychobiology; political science; pre-dentistry; pre-law; pre-medicine; pre-pharmacy studies; pre-theology; pre-veterinary studies; printmaking; psychology; religious studies; romance languages; sculpture; sociology; Spanish; stringed instruments; theater arts/drama; wind/percussion instruments.

Academic Programs *Special study options:* academic remediation for entering students, adult/continuing education programs, advanced placement credit, distance learning, double majors, English as a second language, honors programs, independent study, internships, off-campus study, part-time degree program, services for LD students, student-designed majors, study abroad, summer session for credit.

Library Ralph Pickard Bell Library plus 3 others with 400,000 titles, 1,700 serial subscriptions, an OPAC, a Web page.

Computers on Campus 100 computers available on campus for general student use. A campuswide network can be accessed from student residence rooms and from off campus. Internet access, at least one staffed computer lab available.

Student Life *Housing:* on-campus residence required through senior year. *Options:* coed, women-only. *Activities and Organizations:* drama/theater group, student-run newspaper, radio station, choral group, Commerce Society, Windsor Theatre, President's Leadership Development Certificate, Newfoundland Society, Garnet and Gold Society. *Campus security:* 24-hour emergency response devices, late-night transport/escort service. *Student Services:* health clinic, personal/psychological counseling.

Athletics Member CIAU. *Intercollegiate sports:* badminton M/W, baseball M/W, basketball M/W, field hockey W, football M, rugby M/W, soccer M/W, swimming M/W, volleyball M/W. *Intramural sports:* badminton M/W, baseball M/W, basketball M/W, football M/W, golf M/W, ice hockey M/W, racquetball M/W, rugby M/W, skiing (cross-country) M/W, skiing (downhill) M/W, soccer M/W, softball M/W, tennis M/W, volleyball M/W, weight lifting M/W.

Standardized Tests *Required for some:* SAT I and SAT II or ACT (for admission), SAT II: Writing Test (for admission).

Costs (2001–02) *Tuition:* province resident $4610 Canadian dollars full-time, $461 Canadian dollars per course part-time; nonresident $922 Canadian dollars per course part-time; International tuition $9220 Canadian dollars full-time. Full-time tuition and fees vary according to course load. Part-time tuition and fees vary according to course load. *Required fees:* $184 Canadian dollars full-time. *Room and board:* $6050 Canadian dollars. Room and board charges vary according to board plan and housing facility. *Payment plan:* installment. *Waivers:* senior citizens and employees or children of employees.

Applying *Options:* deferred entrance. *Application fee:* $40. *Required:* high school transcript, minimum 3.0 GPA. *Required for some:* essay or personal statement, interview. *Recommended:* 2 letters of recommendation. *Application deadline:* rolling (freshmen), rolling (transfers). *Notification:* continuous (freshmen).

Admissions Contact Mr. Mark Bishop, Admissions Counselor, Mount Allison University, 65 York Street, Sackville, NB E4L 1E4, Canada. *Phone:* 506-364-2269. *E-mail:* admissions@mta.ca.

MOUNT SAINT VINCENT UNIVERSITY

Halifax, Nova Scotia, Canada

- **Province-supported** comprehensive, founded 1873
- **Calendar** Canadian standard year
- **Degrees** certificates, diplomas, bachelor's, master's, first professional, and postbachelor's certificates
- **Suburban** 40-acre campus
- **Endowment** $15.4 million
- **Coed, primarily women,** 2,953 undergraduate students, 62% full-time, 84% women, 16% men
- **Moderately difficult** entrance level, 77% of applicants were admitted

Undergraduates 1,832 full-time, 1,121 part-time. Students come from 13 provinces and territories, 30 other countries, 10% are from out of province, 23% transferred in, 6% live on campus. *Retention:* 70% of 2001 full-time freshmen returned.

Freshmen *Admission:* 1,949 applied, 1,495 admitted, 425 enrolled. *Average high school GPA:* 3.50.

Faculty *Total:* 264, 53% full-time. *Student/faculty ratio:* 15:1.

Majors Accounting; anthropology; applied mathematics; art education; biological/physical sciences; biology; business administration; business marketing and marketing management; business systems analysis/design; chemistry; child care/development; computer/information sciences; developmental/child psychology; dietetics; early childhood education; economics; education; elementary education; English; family/consumer studies; fine/studio arts; food products retailing; French; German; gerontological services; gerontology; history; hospitality management; hotel and restaurant management; human ecology; humanities; information sciences/systems; interdisciplinary studies; liberal arts and sciences/liberal studies; linguistics; literature; management information systems/business data processing; marketing research; mathematical statistics; mathematics; mathematics/computer science; modern languages; nutritional sciences; nutrition science; peace/conflict studies; philosophy; political science; psychology; public relations; reading education; religious studies; secondary education; social sciences; sociology; Spanish; tourism/travel marketing; travel/tourism management; women's studies.

Academic Programs *Special study options:* academic remediation for entering students, accelerated degree program, adult/continuing education programs, advanced placement credit, cooperative education, distance learning, double majors, English as a second language, external degree program, honors programs, independent study, internships, off-campus study, part-time degree program, services for LD students, student-designed majors, study abroad, summer session for credit. *Unusual degree programs:* 3-2 computer science with Dalhousie University.

Library E. Margaret Fulton Communications Centre Library plus 3 others with 194,531 titles, 2,682 serial subscriptions, 967 audiovisual materials, an OPAC, a Web page.

Computers on Campus 125 computers available on campus for general student use. A campuswide network can be accessed from student residence rooms. Internet access, online (class) registration, at least one staffed computer lab available.

Student Life *Housing Options:* men-only, women-only. *Activities and Organizations:* student-run newspaper, choral group, Business Society, Residence Society, Science Society, History Society, Queer/Straight Alliance. *Campus security:* 24-hour emergency response devices and patrols, late-night transport/escort service, controlled dormitory access. *Student Services:* health clinic, personal/psychological counseling, women's center.

Athletics *Intercollegiate sports:* badminton M/W, basketball M/W, soccer W, volleyball W. *Intramural sports:* badminton M/W, basketball M/W, soccer M, volleyball M/W.

Standardized Tests *Required for some:* SAT I and SAT II or ACT (for admission).

Costs (2001–02) *Tuition:* nonresident $4315 Canadian dollars full-time, $863 Canadian dollars per unit part-time; International tuition $7615 Canadian dollars full-time. Full-time tuition and fees vary according to course load, degree level, and location. Part-time tuition and fees vary according to course load, degree level, and location. *Required fees:* $131 Canadian dollars full-time, $26 Canadian dollars per unit. *Room and board:* $4775 Canadian dollars; room only: $3355 Canadian dollars. Room and board charges vary according to housing facility. *Payment plan:* installment. *Waivers:* senior citizens and employees or children of employees.

Applying *Options:* common application, electronic application, deferred entrance. *Application fee:* $30. *Required:* high school transcript, minimum 2.0 GPA. *Required for some:* essay or personal statement, minimum 3.0 GPA, 2 letters of recommendation, interview. *Application deadlines:* 8/14 (freshmen), 5/30 (out-of-state freshmen), 8/14 (transfers). *Notification:* continuous until 9/1 (freshmen), 6/1 (out-of-state freshmen).

Admissions Contact Ms. Tara Wigglesworth-Hines, Assistant Registrar/Admissions, Mount Saint Vincent University, 166 Bedford Highway, Halifax, NS B3M 2J6, Canada. *Phone:* 902-457-6128. *Fax:* 902-457-6498. *E-mail:* admissions@msvu.ca.

NER ISRAEL YESHIVA COLLEGE OF TORONTO
Thornhill, Ontario, Canada

Admissions Contact Rabbi Y. Kravetz, Director of Admissions, Ner Israel Yeshiva College of Toronto, 8950 Bathurst Street, Thornhill, ON L4J 8A7, Canada. *Phone:* 905-731-1224.

NIPISSING UNIVERSITY
North Bay, Ontario, Canada

- **Province-supported** comprehensive, founded 1992
- **Calendar** semesters
- **Degrees** bachelor's and master's
- **Suburban** 290-hectare campus
- **Endowment** $3.9 million
- **Coed,** 1,957 undergraduate students
- 28% of applicants were admitted

Undergraduates Students come from 9 provinces and territories, 16 other countries, 34% live on campus. *Retention:* 82% of 2001 full-time freshmen returned.

Freshmen *Admission:* 1,964 applied, 544 admitted. *Average high school GPA:* 3.5.

Faculty *Total:* 168, 40% full-time, 38% with terminal degrees. *Student/faculty ratio:* 17:1.

Majors Biology; business administration; classics; computer science; economics; education; English; environmental biology; environmental science; financial services marketing; geography; history; liberal arts and sciences/liberal studies; mathematics; nursing; philosophy; psychology; sociology; women's studies.

Academic Programs *Special study options:* academic remediation for entering students, distance learning, double majors, external degree program, honors programs, independent study, off-campus study, part-time degree program, services for LD students, study abroad, summer session for credit.

Library Education Centre Library with 166,675 titles, 4,083 serial subscriptions, 229 audiovisual materials, an OPAC, a Web page.

Computers on Campus 163 computers available on campus for general student use. A campuswide network can be accessed from student residence rooms and from off campus. Internet access, online (class) registration, at least one staffed computer lab available.

Student Life *Housing Options:* coed, disabled students. *Activities and Organizations:* drama/theater group, student-run newspaper, BACCHUS, NUSAC (Nipissing University Student Athletic Counsel), Business Society, drama club, ski club. *Campus security:* 24-hour emergency response devices and patrols, student patrols, late-night transport/escort service, controlled dormitory access. *Student Services:* health clinic, personal/psychological counseling, women's center.

Athletics Member CIAU. *Intercollegiate sports:* cross-country running M/W, golf M, skiing (cross-country) M/W, soccer M/W, track and field M, volleyball M/W. *Intramural sports:* badminton M/W, baseball M/W, basketball M/W, ice hockey M/W, softball M/W.

Costs (2001–02) *Tuition:* nonresident $3720 full-time, $744 per course part-time; International tuition $6500 full-time. Full-time tuition and fees vary according to course load. Part-time tuition and fees vary according to course load and location. *Required fees:* $1300 full-time, $71 per course. *Room and board:* room only: $3500. Room and board charges vary according to housing facility and location. *Payment plan:* installment. *Waivers:* employees or children of employees.

Applying *Application fee:* $40. *Required:* high school transcript. *Application deadlines:* 8/31 (freshmen), 8/31 (transfers). *Notification:* continuous until 9/11 (freshmen).

Admissions Contact Ms. Diane Huber, Manager of Liaison Services, Nipissing University, 100 College Drive, Box 5002, North Bay, ON P1B 8L7, Canada. *Phone:* 705-474-3461 Ext. 4518. *Fax:* 705-495-1772. *E-mail:* liaison@nipissingu.ca.

NORTH AMERICAN BAPTIST COLLEGE AND EDMONTON BAPTIST SEMINARY
Edmonton, Alberta, Canada

- **Independent North American Baptist** comprehensive, founded 1940
- **Calendar** semesters
- **Degrees** associate, bachelor's, and master's
- **Urban** 27-acre campus
- **Endowment** $1.6 million
- **Coed,** 269 undergraduate students, 75% full-time, 48% women, 52% men
- **Minimally difficult** entrance level, 78% of applicants were admitted

Undergraduates 202 full-time, 67 part-time. Students come from 4 provinces and territories, 4 other countries, 28% are from out of province, 5% transferred in, 55% live on campus. *Retention:* 88% of 2001 full-time freshmen returned.

Freshmen *Admission:* 152 applied, 119 admitted, 117 enrolled.

Faculty *Total:* 30, 23% full-time, 60% with terminal degrees. *Student/faculty ratio:* 16:1.

Majors Biblical studies; divinity/ministry; education; English; liberal arts and sciences/liberal studies; music; religious studies.

Academic Programs *Special study options:* academic remediation for entering students, adult/continuing education programs, advanced placement credit, cooperative education, English as a second language, internships, off-campus study, part-time degree program, student-designed majors.

Library Schalm Library with 50,083 titles, 303 serial subscriptions, an OPAC.

Computers on Campus 16 computers available on campus for general student use. Internet access, at least one staffed computer lab available.

Student Life *Housing:* on-campus residence required for freshman year. *Options:* coed. *Activities and Organizations:* drama/theater group, student-run newspaper, choral group, Choristers (choral group), Student Union, prayer groups, Sacrifice of Praise (band). *Campus security:* evening and late night patrols by security. *Student Services:* personal/psychological counseling.

Athletics *Intercollegiate sports:* basketball M/W, ice hockey M, volleyball M/W. *Intramural sports:* badminton M/W, basketball M/W, football M, golf M, soccer M/W, table tennis M/W, volleyball M/W, weight lifting M/W.

Standardized Tests *Recommended:* SAT I or ACT (for admission).

Costs (2002–03) *Comprehensive fee:* $9210 Canadian dollars includes full-time tuition ($5400 Canadian dollars), mandatory fees ($260 Canadian dollars), and room and board ($3550 Canadian dollars). Part-time tuition: $225 Canadian dollars per credit hour. Part-time tuition and fees vary according to course load. *Required fees:* $9 Canadian dollars per credit hour, $10 Canadian dollars per term part-time. *Room and board:* Room and board charges vary according to board plan and housing facility.

Financial Aid *Financial aid deadline:* 7/1.

Applying *Options:* common application, deferred entrance. *Application fee:* $35. *Required:* essay or personal statement, high school transcript, 3 letters of recommendation. *Required for some:* minimum 3.0 GPA, interview. *Application deadlines:* 8/1 (freshmen), 8/1 (transfers). *Notification:* continuous until 8/31 (freshmen).

Admissions Contact Mrs. Dawn Cunningham Hall, Admissions Counselor, North American Baptist College and Edmonton Baptist Seminary, 11525 Twenty-

North American Baptist College and Edmonton Baptist Seminary (continued)
third Avenue, AB T6J 4T3, Canada. *Phone:* 780-431-5200 Ext. 231. *Toll-free phone:* 800-567-4988. *Fax:* 780-436-9416. *E-mail:* nabc@nabcebs.ab.ca.

NORTHWEST BIBLE COLLEGE
Edmonton, Alberta, Canada

- **Independent** 4-year, founded 1946, affiliated with Pentecostal Assemblies of Canada
- **Calendar** semesters
- **Degree** certificates, diplomas, and bachelor's
- **Coed,** 261 undergraduate students, 83% full-time, 42% women, 58% men
- 99% of applicants were admitted

Undergraduates Students come from 9 provinces and territories, 3 other countries, 21% are from out of province. *Retention:* 55% of 2001 full-time freshmen returned.
Freshmen *Admission:* 127 applied, 126 admitted.
Faculty *Total:* 30, 33% full-time, 87% with terminal degrees. *Student/faculty ratio:* 15:1.
Majors Biblical studies; religious music; theology.
Student Life *Housing:* college housing not available. *Activities and Organizations:* student-run newspaper, choral group.
Athletics *Intercollegiate sports:* ice hockey M. *Intramural sports:* ice hockey M, volleyball M.
Costs (2001–02) *Tuition:* $4125 Canadian dollars full-time, $130 Canadian dollars per credit hour part-time. Full-time tuition and fees vary according to course load and program. Part-time tuition and fees vary according to course load. *Required fees:* $350 Canadian dollars full-time.
Applying *Application fee:* $50. *Required:* essay or personal statement, high school transcript. *Application deadline:* 8/20 (freshmen).
Admissions Contact Ingrid Thompson, Registrar, Northwest Bible College, 11617-106 Avenue, Edmonton, AB T5H 0S1, Canada. *Phone:* 780-452-0808. *Toll-free phone:* 866-222-0808. *E-mail:* info@nwbc.ab.ca.

NOVA SCOTIA AGRICULTURAL COLLEGE
Truro, Nova Scotia, Canada

- **Province-supported** comprehensive, founded 1905
- **Calendar** semesters
- **Degrees** diplomas, bachelor's, and master's
- **Small-town** 408-acre campus with easy access to Halifax
- **Coed,** 667 undergraduate students
- **Minimally difficult** entrance level, 63% of applicants were admitted

Undergraduates Students come from 14 provinces and territories, 25% are from out of province. *Retention:* 85% of 2001 full-time freshmen returned.
Freshmen *Admission:* 563 applied, 352 admitted.
Faculty *Total:* 74, 81% full-time, 73% with terminal degrees. *Student/faculty ratio:* 7:1.
Majors Agricultural business; agricultural economics; agricultural mechanization; agricultural sciences; animal sciences; engineering; environmental science; horticulture services; plant sciences; pre-veterinary studies.
Academic Programs *Special study options:* academic remediation for entering students, adult/continuing education programs, advanced placement credit, cooperative education, internships, off-campus study, part-time degree program.
Library MacRae Library with 23,000 titles, 800 serial subscriptions.
Computers on Campus 110 computers available on campus for general student use. Internet access, at least one staffed computer lab available.
Student Life *Housing Options:* coed. *Activities and Organizations:* student-run newspaper. *Campus security:* 24-hour patrols, student patrols. *Student Services:* health clinic, personal/psychological counseling.
Athletics *Intercollegiate sports:* badminton M/W, basketball M/W, soccer M/W, volleyball M/W. *Intramural sports:* badminton M/W, basketball M/W, ice hockey M, racquetball M/W, rugby M/W, skiing (cross-country) M/W, skiing (downhill) M/W, soccer M/W, softball M/W, squash M/W, volleyball M/W.
Costs (2001–02) *Tuition:* nonresident $4100 Canadian dollars full-time, $410 Canadian dollars per course part-time; International tuition $8000 Canadian dollars full-time. *Required fees:* $362 Canadian dollars full-time, $10 Canadian dollars per course. *Room and board:* $4566 Canadian dollars. Room and board charges vary according to board plan. *Payment plan:* installment.
Applying *Options:* common application. *Application fee:* $25. *Required:* high school transcript. *Required for some:* interview. *Application deadline:* 8/1 (freshmen).
Admissions Contact Ms. Elizabeth Johnson, Admissions Officer, Nova Scotia Agricultural College, PO Box 550, Truro, NS B2N 5E3, Canada. *Phone:* 902-893-8212. *E-mail:* reg_info@nsac.ns.ca.

NOVA SCOTIA COLLEGE OF ART AND DESIGN
Halifax, Nova Scotia, Canada

- **Province-supported** comprehensive, founded 1887
- **Calendar** semesters
- **Degrees** bachelor's and master's
- **Urban** 1-acre campus
- **Endowment** $965,928
- **Coed,** 842 undergraduate students, 83% full-time, 68% women, 32% men
- **Very difficult** entrance level, 43% of applicants were admitted

Undergraduates 698 full-time, 144 part-time. Students come from 12 provinces and territories, 19 other countries.
Freshmen *Admission:* 247 applied, 105 admitted, 141 enrolled.
Faculty *Total:* 92, 48% full-time, 41% with terminal degrees. *Student/faculty ratio:* 11:1.
Majors Architectural environmental design; art; art education; art history; ceramic arts; city/community/regional planning; drawing; education; fine/studio arts; graphic design/commercial art/illustration; metal/jewelry arts; painting; photography; printmaking; sculpture; textile arts.
Academic Programs *Special study options:* cooperative education, distance learning, double majors, external degree program, honors programs, independent study, internships, off-campus study, part-time degree program, services for LD students, student-designed majors, study abroad, summer session for credit. *Unusual degree programs:* 3-2 environmental planning.
Library Nova Scotia College of Art and Design Library with 32,000 titles, 235 serial subscriptions, 120,000 audiovisual materials, an OPAC.
Computers on Campus 60 computers available on campus for general student use. Internet access, at least one staffed computer lab available.
Student Life *Housing:* college housing not available. *Campus security:* evening patrols by trained security personnel. *Student Services:* personal/psychological counseling.
Costs (2001–02) *Tuition:* nonresident $4624 Canadian dollars full-time, $174 Canadian dollars per credit part-time; International tuition $7884 Canadian dollars full-time. Full-time tuition and fees vary according to course load. Part-time tuition and fees vary according to course load. *Required fees:* $21 Canadian dollars per term part-time. *Room and board:* $4000 Canadian dollars. Room and board charges vary according to housing facility. *Payment plan:* deferred payment. *Waivers:* employees or children of employees.
Applying *Options:* deferred entrance. *Application fee:* $35. *Required:* essay or personal statement, high school transcript, portfolio. *Required for some:* 2 letters of recommendation, interview. *Recommended:* minimum 3.0 GPA. *Application deadlines:* 5/15 (freshmen), 4/1 (transfers). *Notification:* 6/30 (freshmen).
Admissions Contact Mr. Terry Bailey, Coordinator of Admissions, Off Campus and Recruitment, Nova Scotia College of Art and Design, 5163 Duke Street, Halifax, NS B3J 3J6, Canada. *Phone:* 902-494-8129. *Fax:* 902-425-2987. *E-mail:* admiss@nscad.ns.ca.

OKANAGAN UNIVERSITY COLLEGE
Kelowna, British Columbia, Canada

- **Province-supported** 4-year, part of British Columbia Provincial Government Institution
- **Degree** certificates, diplomas, and bachelor's
- **Endowment** $4.5 million
- **Coed,** 5,553 undergraduate students, 67% full-time, 62% women, 38% men

Undergraduates 3,742 full-time, 1,811 part-time. Students come from 14 provinces and territories, 2 other countries, 1% are from out of province. *Retention:* 57% of 2001 full-time freshmen returned.
Freshmen *Admission:* 932 enrolled.
Faculty *Total:* 302, 82% full-time, 74% with terminal degrees. *Student/faculty ratio:* 14:1.
Majors Anthropology; biological specializations related; biology; business administration; cell biology; chemistry; chemistry related; ecology; economics; education; English; fine arts and art studies related; general studies; history; international relations; liberal arts and sciences/liberal studies; mathematics; nursing (adult health); philosophy; physics; physiology; political science; psychology; social work.

Academic Programs *Special study options:* adult/continuing education programs, advanced placement credit, cooperative education, distance learning, double majors, English as a second language, honors programs, independent study, off-campus study, part-time degree program, services for LD students, study abroad, summer session for credit.
Library 241,536 titles, 1,689 serial subscriptions, 10,000 audiovisual materials, an OPAC, a Web page.
Computers on Campus 422 computers available on campus for general student use. Internet access, online (class) registration, at least one staffed computer lab available.
Student Life *Housing Options:* coed, disabled students. *Activities and Organizations:* student-run newspaper, choral group. *Campus security:* 24-hour emergency response devices and patrols, controlled dormitory access. *Student Services:* health clinic, personal/psychological counseling.
Athletics *Intercollegiate sports:* basketball M/W, soccer M/W, volleyball M/W. *Intramural sports:* badminton M/W, basketball M/W, bowling M/W, crew M/W, football M/W, ice hockey M/W, rugby M/W, sailing M/W, skiing (downhill) M/W, soccer M/W, softball M/W, swimming M/W, table tennis M/W, tennis M/W, volleyball M/W, weight lifting M/W.
Costs (2001–02) *Tuition:* area resident $670 Canadian dollars full-time, $150 Canadian dollars per course part-time; International tuition $3183 Canadian dollars full-time. Full-time tuition and fees vary according to course load and location. Part-time tuition and fees vary according to course load and location. *Required fees:* $190 Canadian dollars full-time, $120 Canadian dollars per term part-time. *Room and board:* room only: $2920 Canadian dollars. Room and board charges vary according to board plan, housing facility, and location. *Payment plan:* deferred payment. *Waivers:* senior citizens and employees or children of employees.
Applying *Options:* common application, electronic application. *Application fee:* $20. *Required for some:* essay or personal statement, high school transcript, minimum 2.0 GPA, interview. *Application deadline:* rolling (freshmen), rolling (transfers). *Notification:* continuous (freshmen).
Admissions Contact Ms. Deborah Matheson, Manager of Admissions, Okanagan University College, 1000 K. L. O. Road, Kelowna, BC V1Y 4X8, Canada. *Phone:* 250-862-5417 Ext. 4213. *Toll-free phone:* 888-733-6533. *Fax:* 250-862-5466.

OPEN LEARNING AGENCY
Burnaby, British Columbia, Canada

- **Province-supported** 4-year, founded 1978, part of province of British Columbia, Canada public post-secondary system
- **Calendar** continuous
- **Degrees** certificates, diplomas, and bachelor's (offers only distance learning degree programs)
- **Suburban** campus with easy access to Vancouver
- **Coed,** 13,950 undergraduate students, 64% women, 36% men
- **Noncompetitive** entrance level

Faculty *Student/faculty ratio:* 1:1.
Majors Art; biological sciences/life sciences related; business administration; business administration/management related; design/applied arts related; electrical/electronic engineering technologies related; fine/studio arts; general studies; health science; jazz; music (general performance); music therapy; nursing (psychiatric/mental health); respiratory therapy; tourism promotion operations.
Academic Programs *Special study options:* academic remediation for entering students, adult/continuing education programs, distance learning, double majors, English as a second language, external degree program, honors programs, independent study, off-campus study, part-time degree program, services for LD students, student-designed majors.
Library Open Learning Agency Library plus 1 other with an OPAC, a Web page.
Computers on Campus A campuswide network can be accessed from off campus. Internet access, online (class) registration available.
Student Life *Housing:* college housing not available.
Costs (2001–02) *Tuition:* province resident $60 Canadian dollars per credit part-time; nonresident $120 Canadian dollars per credit part-time. Part-time tuition and fees vary according to class time, course load, degree level, program, and reciprocity agreements. *Required fees:* $45 Canadian dollars per credit. *Payment plan:* deferred payment. *Waivers:* senior citizens and employees or children of employees.
Applying *Options:* common application, electronic application, deferred entrance. *Required for some:* program specific. *Application deadline:* rolling (freshmen), rolling (transfers).
Admissions Contact Mr. Robert Ruff, Registrar, Open Learning Agency, 4355 Mathissi Place, Burnaby, BC V5G 4S8, Canada. *Phone:* 604-431-3000 Ext. 3055. *Toll-free phone:* 800-663-9711. *Fax:* 604-431-3344. *E-mail:* student@ola.bc.ca.

PRAIRIE BIBLE COLLEGE
Three Hills, Alberta, Canada

- **Independent interdenominational** 4-year, founded 1922
- **Calendar** semesters
- **Degree** certificates, diplomas, and bachelor's
- **Small-town** 130-acre campus with easy access to Calgary
- **Coed,** 490 undergraduate students
- **Minimally difficult** entrance level, 96% of applicants were admitted

Undergraduates Students come from 7 other countries, 78% live on campus. *Retention:* 43% of 2001 full-time freshmen returned.
Freshmen *Admission:* 248 applied, 239 admitted.
Faculty *Total:* 42, 74% full-time, 26% with terminal degrees. *Student/faculty ratio:* 12:1.
Majors Biblical languages/literatures; international relations; music; religious education; theology.
Academic Programs *Special study options:* accelerated degree program, adult/continuing education programs, advanced placement credit, English as a second language, internships, part-time degree program, study abroad.
Library T. S. Rendall Library with 60,745 titles, 458 serial subscriptions.
Computers on Campus 30 computers available on campus for general student use. Internet access, at least one staffed computer lab available.
Student Life *Housing:* on-campus residence required for freshman year. *Options:* men-only, women-only. *Activities and Organizations:* drama/theater group, student-run newspaper, radio station, choral group, WIN, SMF, student government, Off-Campus. *Campus security:* 24-hour emergency response devices and patrols, late-night transport/escort service, controlled dormitory access. *Student Services:* health clinic, personal/psychological counseling.
Athletics *Intercollegiate sports:* basketball M/W, cross-country running M/W, volleyball M/W. *Intramural sports:* badminton M/W, basketball M/W, football M, ice hockey M, soccer M, volleyball M/W.
Costs (2002–03) *Comprehensive fee:* $9276 Canadian dollars includes full-time tuition ($5088 Canadian dollars), mandatory fees ($758 Canadian dollars), and room and board ($3430 Canadian dollars). Part-time tuition: $159 Canadian dollars per credit. *Required fees:* $19 Canadian dollars per credit, $75 Canadian dollars per term part-time.
Applying *Options:* common application, electronic application, early decision. *Required:* essay or personal statement, high school transcript, 2 letters of recommendation. *Required for some:* minimum 3.0 GPA. *Recommended:* minimum 2.0 GPA. *Application deadlines:* 8/15 (freshmen), 8/15 (transfers). *Early decision:* 3/1.
Admissions Contact Mr. Vance Neudorf, Director of Enrollment, Prairie Bible College, 319 Fifth Avenue North, PO Box 4000, Three Hills, AB T0M 2N0. *Phone:* 403-443-5511 Ext. 3033. *Toll-free phone:* 800-661-2425. *Fax:* 403-443-5540. *E-mail:* vance.neudorf@pbi.ab.ca.

PROVIDENCE COLLEGE AND THEOLOGICAL SEMINARY
Otterburne, Manitoba, Canada

- **Independent interdenominational** comprehensive, founded 1925
- **Calendar** semesters
- **Degrees** bachelor's, master's, and doctoral
- **Rural** 100-acre campus with easy access to Winnipeg
- **Endowment** $687,655
- **Coed,** 415 undergraduate students, 85% full-time, 50% women, 50% men
- **Noncompetitive** entrance level

Undergraduates Students come from 4 provinces and territories, 18 other countries, 30% are from out of province, 60% live on campus. *Retention:* 70% of 2001 full-time freshmen returned.
Faculty *Total:* 54, 37% full-time. *Student/faculty ratio:* 22:1.
Majors Aircraft pilot (professional); aviation technology; biblical studies; business administration; divinity/ministry; education; history; humanities; liberal arts and sciences/liberal studies; music; pastoral counseling; religious education; religious studies; social sciences; teaching English as a second language; theater arts/drama; theology.

Providence College and Theological Seminary (continued)

Academic Programs *Special study options:* academic remediation for entering students, accelerated degree program, distance learning, double majors, English as a second language, freshman honors college, independent study, internships, part-time degree program.

Library 47,756 titles, 635 serial subscriptions.

Computers on Campus 14 computers available on campus for general student use. A campuswide network can be accessed from off campus. Internet access, at least one staffed computer lab available.

Student Life *Housing:* on-campus residence required for freshman year. *Options:* men-only, women-only. *Activities and Organizations:* drama/theater group, student-run newspaper, choral group. *Campus security:* student patrols, controlled dormitory access. *Student Services:* health clinic, personal/psychological counseling.

Athletics Member NCCAA. *Intercollegiate sports:* badminton M/W, basketball M/W, ice hockey M, soccer M, table tennis M/W, volleyball M/W. *Intramural sports:* badminton M/W, basketball M/W, cross-country running M/W, football M, golf M, ice hockey W, skiing (cross-country) M/W, soccer M/W, table tennis M/W, tennis M/W, volleyball M/W, weight lifting M/W.

Standardized Tests *Recommended:* SAT I or ACT (for placement).

Costs (2002–03) *Comprehensive fee:* $8876 Canadian dollars includes full-time tuition ($4800 Canadian dollars), mandatory fees ($376 Canadian dollars), and room and board ($3700 Canadian dollars). Part-time tuition: $172 Canadian dollars per credit hour. *Required fees:* $16 Canadian dollars per credit hour. *Payment plan:* installment. *Waivers:* children of alumni and employees or children of employees.

Applying *Options:* deferred entrance. *Application fee:* $25. *Required:* high school transcript, 4 letters of recommendation. *Application deadline:* rolling (freshmen), rolling (transfers).

Admissions Contact Mr. Mark Little, Dean of Admissions and Records, Providence College and Theological Seminary, General Delivery, Otterburne, MB R0A 1G0, Canada. *Phone:* 204-433-7488 Ext. 249. *Toll-free phone:* 800-668-7768. *E-mail:* mlittle@providence.mb.ca.

QUEEN'S UNIVERSITY AT KINGSTON

Kingston, Ontario, Canada

- **Province-supported** university, founded 1841
- **Calendar** Canadian standard year
- **Degrees** bachelor's, master's, and doctoral
- **Urban** 160-acre campus
- **Coed,** 14,546 undergraduate students
- **Most difficult** entrance level, 57% of applicants were admitted

Undergraduates Students come from 13 provinces and territories, 80 other countries, 11% are from out of province, 25% live on campus.

Freshmen *Admission:* 21,779 applied, 12,420 admitted. *Average high school GPA:* 3.48. *Test scores:* SAT verbal scores over 500: 83%; SAT math scores over 500: 85%; SAT verbal scores over 600: 43%; SAT math scores over 600: 50%; SAT verbal scores over 700: 14%; SAT math scores over 700: 17%.

Faculty *Total:* 973. *Student/faculty ratio:* 12:1.

Majors Art education; art history; astrophysics; biochemistry; biology; business administration; Canadian studies; chemical and atomic/molecular physics; chemical engineering; chemistry; civil engineering; classics; cognitive psychology/psycholinguistics; computer engineering; computer engineering related; computer hardware engineering; computer/information sciences; computer science; computer science related; computer software engineering; economics; education; electrical engineering; elementary education; engineering; engineering physics; engineering science; English; environmental science; film studies; fine/studio arts; French; geography; geological engineering; geology; German; Greek (modern); health education; health/physical education; health science; Hispanic-American studies; history; interdisciplinary studies; Italian; Judaic studies; Latin American studies; Latin (ancient and medieval); linguistics; mathematical statistics; mathematics; mechanical engineering; medieval/renaissance studies; mining/mineral engineering; music; music teacher education; nursing; occupational therapy; philosophy; physical education; physical therapy; physics; physiology; political science; psychology; rehabilitation therapy; religious studies; robotics; science education; secondary education; sociology; Spanish; stringed instruments; theater arts/drama; women's studies.

Academic Programs *Special study options:* accelerated degree program, adult/continuing education programs, cooperative education, distance learning, double majors, English as a second language, honors programs, internships, part-time degree program, services for LD students, student-designed majors, study abroad, summer session for credit.

Library Joseph S. Stauffer Library plus 7 others with 3.2 million titles, 10,825 serial subscriptions, an OPAC, a Web page.

Computers on Campus 400 computers available on campus for general student use. A campuswide network can be accessed from student residence rooms and from off campus. At least one staffed computer lab available.

Student Life *Housing Options:* coed, men-only, women-only, cooperative. *Activities and Organizations:* drama/theater group, student-run newspaper, radio station, choral group, marching band, Arts and Sciences Undergraduate Society, Alma Mater Society, Engineering Society, Commerce Society. *Campus security:* 24-hour emergency response devices and patrols, student patrols, late-night transport/escort service, controlled dormitory access. *Student Services:* health clinic, personal/psychological counseling, women's center, legal services.

Athletics Member CIAU. *Intercollegiate sports:* badminton M/W, baseball M(c), basketball M/W, crew M/W, cross-country running M/W, fencing M/W, field hockey W, football M, golf M, gymnastics M(c)/W(c), ice hockey M/W, lacrosse M(c)/W(c), rugby M/W, sailing M(c)/W(c), skiing (cross-country) M/W, skiing (downhill) M(c)/W(c), soccer M/W, squash M/W, swimming M/W, table tennis M(c)/W(c), tennis M/W, track and field M/W, volleyball M/W, water polo M/W, wrestling M/W. *Intramural sports:* archery M(c)/W(c), badminton M/W, basketball M/W, crew M(c)/W(c), equestrian sports M(c)/W(c), fencing M(c)/W(c), football M, golf M, ice hockey M/W, rugby M/W, skiing (cross-country) M(c)/W(c), soccer M/W, squash M/W, swimming M/W, tennis M/W, volleyball M/W, water polo M/W.

Standardized Tests *Required:* SAT I (for admission). *Required for some:* SAT II: Subject Tests (for admission).

Costs (2002–03) *Tuition:* nonresident $4030 Canadian dollars full-time, $806 Canadian dollars per course part-time; International tuition $11,220 Canadian dollars full-time. *Required fees:* $698 Canadian dollars full-time. *Room and board;* $4711 Canadian dollars; room only: $3980 Canadian dollars.

Applying *Options:* common application, deferred entrance. *Application fee:* $85. *Required:* high school transcript, minimum 2.0 GPA. *Required for some:* essay or personal statement, 1 letter of recommendation, interview. *Application deadlines:* 3/31 (freshmen), 6/1 (transfers). *Notification:* 5/15 (freshmen).

Admissions Contact Mr. Nicholas Snider, Manager of Student Recruitment, Queen's University at Kingston, Richardson Hall, Kingston, ON K7L 3N6, Canada. *Phone:* 613-533-2217. *Fax:* 613-533-6810. *E-mail:* admissn@post.queensu.ca.

REDEEMER UNIVERSITY COLLEGE

Ancaster, Ontario, Canada

- **Independent interdenominational** 4-year, founded 1980
- **Calendar** semesters
- **Degrees** certificates, bachelor's, and postbachelor's certificates
- **Small-town** 78-acre campus with easy access to Toronto
- **Endowment** $507,705
- **Coed,** 704 undergraduate students, 93% full-time, 62% women, 38% men
- **Moderately difficult** entrance level, 80% of applicants were admitted

Undergraduates Students come from 14 provinces and territories, 7 other countries, 60% live on campus. *Retention:* 82% of 2001 full-time freshmen returned.

Freshmen *Admission:* 424 applied, 341 admitted. *Average high school GPA:* 3.3. *Test scores:* ACT scores over 18: 100%; ACT scores over 24: 64%.

Faculty *Total:* 60, 58% full-time, 57% with terminal degrees. *Student/faculty ratio:* 17:1.

Majors Accounting; art; biblical studies; biological/physical sciences; biology; business administration; computer science; education; education (K-12); elementary education; English; exercise sciences; French; health/physical education; history; humanities; human resources management; liberal arts and sciences/liberal studies; mathematics; music; natural sciences; philosophy; political science; pre-dentistry; pre-law; pre-medicine; pre-theology; pre-veterinary studies; psychology; recreation/leisure studies; religious studies; social work; sociology; theater arts/drama; theology.

Academic Programs *Special study options:* academic remediation for entering students, cooperative education, double majors, English as a second language, honors programs, independent study, internships, off-campus study, part-time degree program, services for LD students, study abroad, summer session for credit. *Unusual degree programs:* 3-2 chemistry with University of Guelph.

Library Redeemer College Library with 93,500 titles, 419 serial subscriptions, an OPAC, a Web page.

Computers on Campus 35 computers available on campus for general student use. A campuswide network can be accessed from off campus. Internet access, at least one staffed computer lab available.

Student Life *Housing:* on-campus residence required through sophomore year. *Options:* men-only, women-only. *Activities and Organizations:* drama/theater group, student-run newspaper, choral group, Church in the Box, mission trips, Bible study groups, Choir, iIntramurals. *Campus security:* 24-hour emergency response devices, student patrols, late-night transport/escort service, controlled dormitory access, path lighting. *Student Services:* health clinic, personal/psychological counseling.
Athletics *Intercollegiate sports:* basketball M/W, golf M/W, soccer M/W, volleyball M/W. *Intramural sports:* badminton M/W, basketball M/W, bowling M/W, football M/W, ice hockey M, racquetball M/W, skiing (cross-country) M/W, skiing (downhill) M/W, soccer M/W, softball M/W, squash M/W, table tennis M/W, tennis M/W, volleyball M/W, weight lifting M/W.
Standardized Tests *Required for some:* SAT I or ACT (for admission).
Costs (2002–03) *Comprehensive fee:* $15,013 Canadian dollars includes full-time tuition ($9854 Canadian dollars), mandatory fees ($373 Canadian dollars), and room and board ($4786 Canadian dollars). Part-time tuition: $985 Canadian dollars per course. *Required fees:* $27 Canadian dollars per course, $273 Canadian dollars per term part-time. *Room and board:* Room and board charges vary according to housing facility. *Payment plans:* installment, deferred payment. *Waivers:* minority students, senior citizens, and employees or children of employees.
Applying *Options:* deferred entrance. *Application fee:* $35. *Required:* essay or personal statement, high school transcript, minimum 2.0 GPA, 2 letters of recommendation, pastoral reference. *Required for some:* essay or personal statement, interview. *Application deadlines:* 5/31 (freshmen), 5/31 (transfers). *Notification:* continuous (freshmen).
Admissions Contact Office of Admissions, Redeemer University College, 777 Garner Road East, Ancaster, ON L9K 1J4, Canada. *Phone:* 905-648-2131 Ext. 4280. *Toll-free phone:* 800-263-6467 Ext. 4280. *Fax:* 905-648-2134. *E-mail:* adm@redeemer.on.ca.

ROCKY MOUNTAIN COLLEGE
Calgary, Alberta, Canada

- **Independent** 4-year, founded 1992, affiliated with Missionary Church
- **Calendar** semesters
- **Degree** certificates, diplomas, and bachelor's
- **Suburban** 1-acre campus
- **Endowment** $238,300
- **Coed,** 342 undergraduate students
- **Noncompetitive** entrance level, 96% of applicants were admitted

Undergraduates Students come from 6 provinces and territories, 2 other countries, 20% live on campus. *Retention:* 62% of 2001 full-time freshmen returned.
Freshmen *Admission:* 169 applied, 163 admitted.
Faculty *Total:* 27, 52% full-time, 22% with terminal degrees.
Majors Biblical studies; education; music; pastoral counseling; social sciences.
Academic Programs *Special study options:* academic remediation for entering students, adult/continuing education programs, advanced placement credit, internships, part-time degree program, summer session for credit.
Library Main Library plus 1 other with 25,280 titles, 135 serial subscriptions.
Computers on Campus 5 computers available on campus for general student use. At least one staffed computer lab available.
Student Life *Housing Options:* coed. *Activities and Organizations:* drama/theater group, choral group. *Campus security:* 24-hour emergency response devices. *Student Services:* personal/psychological counseling.
Athletics *Intramural sports:* basketball M/W, volleyball M/W.
Costs (2001–02) *Tuition:* $5146 full-time, $166 per credit hour part-time.
Applying *Options:* deferred entrance. *Application fee:* $25. *Required:* essay or personal statement, high school transcript, 2 letters of recommendation. *Required for some:* interview. *Application deadline:* rolling (freshmen), rolling (transfers).
Admissions Contact Mr. Randy Young, Rocky Mountain College, 4039 Brentwood Drive NW, Calgary, AB T2L 1L1. *Phone:* 403-284-5100 Ext. 222. *E-mail:* rockymc@telusplanet.net.

ROYAL MILITARY COLLEGE OF CANADA
Kingston, Ontario, Canada

- **Federally supported** comprehensive, founded 1876
- **Calendar** Canadian standard year
- **Degrees** bachelor's, master's, and doctoral
- **Suburban** 90-acre campus
- **Coed**
- **Most difficult** entrance level

Student Life *Campus security:* 24-hour emergency response devices and patrols.
Athletics Member CIAU.
Applying *Required:* high school transcript, letters of recommendation, interview, medical, aptitude and physical fitness testing for full-time students; Canadian residency.
Admissions Contact Mr. J. Ross McKenzie, Assistant Registrar (Liaison), Royal Military College of Canada, PO Box 17000, Station Forces, Kingston, ON K7K 7B4, Canada. *Phone:* 613-541-6000 Ext. 6652. *Fax:* 613-542-3565. *E-mail:* registrar@rmc.ca.

ROYAL ROADS UNIVERSITY
Victoria, British Columbia, Canada

- **Province-supported** upper-level, founded 1996
- **Calendar** continuous
- **Degrees** certificates, diplomas, bachelor's, and master's
- **Suburban** 125-acre campus
- **Endowment** $2.0 million
- **Coed,** 412 undergraduate students, 54% full-time, 39% women, 61% men
- **Moderately difficult** entrance level

Undergraduates 224 full-time, 188 part-time. Students come from 7 provinces and territories, 6 other countries, 9% are from out of province, 3% international, 57% transferred in, 0% live on campus.
Faculty *Total:* 130, 12% full-time. *Student/faculty ratio:* 23:1.
Majors Business administration; environmental science.
Academic Programs *Special study options:* accelerated degree program, adult/continuing education programs, advanced placement credit, distance learning, part-time degree program, summer session for credit.
Library Learning Resource Centre plus 1 other with 40,000 titles, 609 audiovisual materials, an OPAC, a Web page.
Computers on Campus 100 computers available on campus for general student use. A campuswide network can be accessed from student residence rooms and from off campus. Internet access, online (class) registration, at least one staffed computer lab available.
Student Life *Housing:* college housing not available. *Activities and Organizations:* student-run newspaper, rowing, mountain biking, recycling club. *Campus security:* 24-hour emergency response devices and patrols, late-night transport/escort service, controlled dormitory access. *Student Services:* personal/psychological counseling.
Athletics *Intramural sports:* badminton M/W, basketball M/W, crew M/W, cross-country running M/W, racquetball M/W, sailing M/W, soccer M/W, softball M/W, squash M/W, swimming M/W, tennis M/W, volleyball M/W, weight lifting M/W.
Costs (2001–02) *Tuition:* nonresident $5800 Canadian dollars full-time, $485 Canadian dollars per course part-time; International tuition $11,600 Canadian dollars full-time. Full-time tuition and fees vary according to course load and program. Part-time tuition and fees vary according to course load and program. No tuition increase for student's term of enrollment. *Required fees:* $360 Canadian dollars full-time, $30 Canadian dollars per course. *Payment plans:* tuition prepayment, installment.
Applying *Options:* common application, electronic application. *Application fee:* $50. *Application deadline:* rolling (transfers). *Notification:* 5/30 (transfers).
Admissions Contact Ms. Ann Nightingale, Registrar and Director, Learner Services, Royal Roads University, Office of Learner Services and Registrar, 2005 Sooke Road, Victoria, BC V9B 5Y2, Canada. *Phone:* 250-391-2552. *Toll-free phone:* 800-788-8028. *E-mail:* rruregistrar@royalroads.ca.

RYERSON UNIVERSITY
Toronto, Ontario, Canada

- **Province-supported** 4-year, founded 1948
- **Calendar** Canadian standard year or semesters depending on program
- **Degrees** certificates, diplomas, bachelor's, and master's
- **Urban** 20-acre campus
- **Coed**
- **Moderately difficult** entrance level

Student Life *Campus security:* 24-hour emergency response devices and patrols, late-night transport/escort service, controlled dormitory access.

Ryerson University (continued)

Athletics Member CIAU.

Financial Aid *Financial aid deadline:* 1/15.

Applying *Options:* electronic application. *Application fee:* $95. *Required:* high school transcript. *Required for some:* essay or personal statement, letters of recommendation, interview, portfolio, audition, entrance examination.

Admissions Contact Office of Admissions, Ryerson University, 350 Victoria Street, Toronto, ON M5B 2K3, Canada. *Phone:* 416-979-5036. *Fax:* 416-979-5221. *E-mail:* inquire@acs.ryerson.ca.

St. Francis Xavier University

Antigonish, Nova Scotia, Canada

- **Independent Roman Catholic** comprehensive, founded 1853
- **Calendar** Canadian standard year
- **Degrees** bachelor's and master's
- **Small-town** 100-acre campus
- **Endowment** $34.1 million
- **Coed,** 3,787 undergraduate students, 89% full-time, 61% women, 39% men
- **Moderately difficult** entrance level, 64% of applicants were admitted

Undergraduates Students come from 12 provinces and territories, 25 other countries, 41% are from out of province, 43% live on campus. *Retention:* 88% of 2001 full-time freshmen returned.

Freshmen *Admission:* 2,737 applied, 1,753 admitted.

Faculty *Total:* 265, 84% full-time, 66% with terminal degrees. *Student/faculty ratio:* 16:1.

Majors Accounting; anthropology; biological/physical sciences; biology; business administration; Canadian studies; chemistry; classics; computer/information sciences; cultural studies; economics; education; elementary education; English; environmental science; exercise sciences; French; geology; history; information sciences/systems; jazz; liberal arts and sciences/liberal studies; management information systems/business data processing; mathematics; modern languages; music; nursing; nursing science; nutrition science; philosophy; physical education; physical sciences; physics; political science; pre-dentistry; pre-law; pre-medicine; pre-veterinary studies; psychology; religious studies; secondary education; sociology; water resources; women's studies.

Academic Programs *Special study options:* academic remediation for entering students, accelerated degree program, adult/continuing education programs, distance learning, double majors, English as a second language, honors programs, independent study, internships, off-campus study, part-time degree program, services for LD students, student-designed majors, study abroad, summer session for credit.

Library Angus L. MacDonald Library plus 1 other with 632,575 titles, 3,282 serial subscriptions, 6,598 audiovisual materials, an OPAC, a Web page.

Computers on Campus 300 computers available on campus for general student use. A campuswide network can be accessed from student residence rooms and from off campus. Internet access, online (class) registration, at least one staffed computer lab available.

Student Life *Housing Options:* coed, men-only, women-only, disabled students. *Activities and Organizations:* drama/theater group, student-run newspaper, radio station, choral group, X-Project, Walkhome Program, orientation committee, Exekoi Tutoring, Off-Campus Society. *Campus security:* 24-hour emergency response devices and patrols, student patrols, late-night transport/escort service, controlled dormitory access. *Student Services:* health clinic, personal/psychological counseling.

Athletics Member CIAU. *Intercollegiate sports:* basketball M/W, cross-country running M/W, football M, ice hockey M/W, rugby M/W, soccer M, tennis M/W, volleyball W. *Intramural sports:* badminton M/W, basketball M/W, cross-country running M/W, football M/W, golf M/W, ice hockey M/W, racquetball M/W, rugby M/W, soccer M/W, softball M/W, squash M/W, swimming M/W, table tennis M/W, tennis M/W, track and field M/W, volleyball M/W, water polo M/W, weight lifting M/W.

Standardized Tests *Required for some:* SAT I or ACT (for admission), SAT II: Writing Test (for admission). *Recommended:* SAT I or ACT (for admission), SAT II: Subject Tests (for admission), SAT II: Writing Test (for admission).

Costs (2001–02) *Comprehensive fee:* $10,436 Canadian dollars includes full-time tuition ($4600 Canadian dollars), mandatory fees ($341 Canadian dollars), and room and board ($5495 Canadian dollars). Full-time tuition and fees vary according to course load. Part-time tuition: $980 Canadian dollars per course. Part-time tuition and fees vary according to course load. International tuition: $7900 Canadian dollars full-time. *Room and board:* Room and board charges vary according to board plan and housing facility. *Payment plan:* installment. *Waivers:* senior citizens and employees or children of employees.

Applying *Options:* common application. *Application fee:* $30. *Required:* high school transcript. *Application deadline:* rolling (freshmen), rolling (transfers). *Notification:* continuous until 8/15 (freshmen).

Admissions Contact Ms. Rose Ann Septon, Admissions Officer, St. Francis Xavier University, PO Box 5000, Antigonish, NS B2G 2L1. *Phone:* 902-867-2219. *Toll-free phone:* 877-867 Ext. 7839. *Fax:* 902-867-2329. *E-mail:* admit@stfx.ca.

Saint Mary's University

Halifax, Nova Scotia, Canada

- **Province-supported** comprehensive, founded 1802
- **Calendar** semesters
- **Degrees** certificates, diplomas, bachelor's, master's, and doctoral
- **Urban** 30-acre campus
- **Endowment** $36.2 million
- **Coed,** 6,946 undergraduate students, 74% full-time, 53% women, 47% men
- **Moderately difficult** entrance level, 87% of applicants were admitted

Undergraduates Students come from 11 provinces and territories, 57 other countries, 12% are from out of province, 15% live on campus.

Freshmen *Admission:* 3,519 applied, 3,066 admitted.

Faculty *Total:* 442, 49% full-time, 61% with terminal degrees. *Student/faculty ratio:* 24:1.

Majors Accounting; anthropology; Asian studies; astronomy; astrophysics; biology; business administration; business economics; business marketing and marketing management; Canadian studies; chemistry; classics; computer science; criminology; data processing technology; economics; engineering; English; finance; French; geography; geology; German; history; human resources management; interdisciplinary studies; international relations; mathematics; modern languages; philosophy; physics; political science; psychology; religious studies; sociology; women's studies.

Academic Programs *Special study options:* academic remediation for entering students, accelerated degree program, adult/continuing education programs, cooperative education, distance learning, double majors, English as a second language, honors programs, independent study, internships, off-campus study, part-time degree program, services for LD students, student-designed majors, study abroad, summer session for credit.

Library Patrick Power Library plus 1 other with 385,310 titles, 1,973 serial subscriptions, an OPAC, a Web page.

Computers on Campus 300 computers available on campus for general student use. A campuswide network can be accessed from student residence rooms and from off campus. Internet access, at least one staffed computer lab available.

Student Life *Housing Options:* coed, women-only. *Activities and Organizations:* drama/theater group, student-run newspaper, International Students Organization, commerce society, AIESEC, journal society, political science society. *Campus security:* 24-hour emergency response devices and patrols, student patrols, late-night transport/escort service, controlled dormitory access, electronic surveillance of labs and key areas. *Student Services:* health clinic, personal/psychological counseling.

Athletics Member CIAU. *Intercollegiate sports:* basketball M/W, cross-country running M/W, field hockey W, football M, ice hockey M/W, rugby W, soccer M/W, track and field M/W, volleyball W. *Intramural sports:* badminton M/W, baseball M, basketball M/W, fencing M/W, football M/W, golf M/W, ice hockey M/W, racquetball M/W, rugby M/W, soccer M/W, softball M/W, squash M/W, table tennis M/W, tennis M/W, volleyball M/W.

Costs (2001–02) *Tuition:* nonresident $4440 Canadian dollars full-time; International tuition $8880 Canadian dollars full-time. Full-time tuition and fees vary according to class time and course load. Part-time tuition and fees vary according to class time and course load. *Required fees:* $120 Canadian dollars full-time, $40 Canadian dollars per term. *Room and board:* $5030 Canadian dollars; room only: $2650 Canadian dollars. Room and board charges vary according to board plan and housing facility. *Payment plan:* installment. *Waivers:* senior citizens and employees or children of employees.

Applying *Options:* early action. *Application fee:* $35. *Required:* high school transcript, minimum 2.0 GPA. *Required for some:* interview. *Application deadlines:* 7/1 (freshmen), 6/1 (transfers). *Notification:* continuous (freshmen), 4/1 (early action).

Admissions Contact Mr. Greg Ferguson, Director of Admissions, Saint Mary's University, Halifax, NS B3H 3C3. *Phone:* 902-420-5415. *Fax:* 902-496-8100. *E-mail:* jim.dunn@stmarys.edu.

Saint Paul University
Ottawa, Ontario, Canada

- **Province-supported** university, founded 1848
- **Calendar** Canadian standard year
- **Degrees** bachelor's, master's, and doctoral
- **Urban** 4-acre campus
- **Coed**
- **Moderately difficult** entrance level

Standardized Tests *Recommended:* SAT I (for admission).
Applying *Options:* common application, deferred entrance. *Application fee:* $20. *Required:* high school transcript.
Admissions Contact Ms. Evelyn G. Dutrisac, Registrar, Saint Paul University, 223 Main Street, Ottawa, ON K1S 1C4, Canada. *Phone:* 613-236-1393 Ext. 2238. *Fax:* 613-782-3014. *E-mail:* edutrisac@ustpaul.ca.

St. Thomas University
Fredericton, New Brunswick, Canada

- **Independent Roman Catholic** 4-year, founded 1910
- **Calendar** Canadian standard year
- **Degrees** bachelor's and postbachelor's certificates
- **Small-town** 202-acre campus
- **Endowment** $18.9 million
- **Coed,** 2,837 undergraduate students
- **Moderately difficult** entrance level, 55% of applicants were admitted

Undergraduates Students come from 10 provinces and territories, 8 other countries, 28% live on campus.
Freshmen *Admission:* 2,100 applied, 1,155 admitted. *Average high school GPA:* 3.0. *Test scores:* SAT verbal scores over 500: 63%; SAT math scores over 500: 63%; SAT math scores over 600: 13%.
Faculty *Total:* 190, 47% full-time. *Student/faculty ratio:* 15:1.
Majors Anthropology; criminology; economics; education; English; French; gerontological services; gerontology; history; journalism; mathematics; Native American studies; philosophy; political science; psychology; religious studies; Russian; social work; sociology; Spanish.
Academic Programs *Special study options:* academic remediation for entering students, accelerated degree program, cooperative education, distance learning, double majors, English as a second language, honors programs, independent study, internships, off-campus study, part-time degree program, services for LD students, student-designed majors, summer session for credit. *Unusual degree programs:* 3-2 education.
Library Harriet Irving Library plus 1 other with 1.1 million titles, 4,912 serial subscriptions, an OPAC, a Web page.
Computers on Campus 78 computers available on campus for general student use. A campuswide network can be accessed from off campus. Internet access, at least one staffed computer lab available.
Student Life *Activities and Organizations:* drama/theater group, student-run newspaper, radio station, choral group, Theatre St. Thomas, St. Thomas Student Union, Political Science Society, Economics Society, Student Help Centre. *Campus security:* 24-hour emergency response devices and patrols, late-night transport/escort service, controlled dormitory access. *Student Services:* health clinic, personal/psychological counseling.
Athletics Member CIAU. *Intercollegiate sports:* basketball M/W, cross-country running M/W, ice hockey M(s), rugby M/W, soccer M/W, volleyball W. *Intramural sports:* badminton M/W, basketball M/W, cross-country running M/W, football M/W, ice hockey M/W, racquetball M/W, skiing (cross-country) M/W, soccer M/W, softball M/W, squash M/W, swimming M/W, tennis M/W, track and field M/W, volleyball M/W, water polo M/W.
Standardized Tests *Required for some:* SAT I (for admission), SAT II: Subject Tests (for admission), SAT II: Writing Test (for admission).
Costs (2001–02) *Comprehensive fee:* $7816 includes full-time tuition ($3290), mandatory fees ($96), and room and board ($4430). Part-time tuition: $378 per course. International tuition: $6580 full-time. *Required fees:* $35 per credit.
Applying *Options:* electronic application, early action, deferred entrance. *Application fee:* $25. *Required:* high school transcript, minimum 2.5 GPA. *Required for some:* essay or personal statement, letters of recommendation, interview. *Recommended:* minimum 3.0 GPA. *Application deadlines:* 7/31 (freshmen), 7/31 (transfers). *Notification:* continuous until 8/31 (freshmen), 5/15 (early action).
Admissions Contact Mr. Jason Elliott, High School Relations Officer, St. Thomas University, Fredericton, NB E3B 5G3. *Phone:* 506-452-0532 Ext. 514. *Fax:* 506-452-0617. *E-mail:* admissions@stthomasu.ca.

Simon Fraser University
Burnaby, British Columbia, Canada

- **Province-supported** university, founded 1965
- **Calendar** trimesters
- **Degrees** certificates, diplomas, bachelor's, master's, doctoral, post-master's, and postbachelor's certificates
- **Suburban** 1200-acre campus with easy access to Vancouver
- **Endowment** $93.9 million
- **Coed,** 17,185 undergraduate students, 51% full-time, 57% women, 43% men
- **Moderately difficult** entrance level

Undergraduates 8,805 full-time, 8,380 part-time. Students come from 11 provinces and territories, 76 other countries, 7% are from out of province, 6% transferred in, 8% live on campus. *Retention:* 83% of 2001 full-time freshmen returned.
Freshmen *Admission:* 5,452 admitted, 2,171 enrolled. *Average high school GPA:* 3.20.
Faculty *Total:* 681, 89% with terminal degrees. *Student/faculty ratio:* 22:1.
Majors Actuarial science; anthropology; applied mathematics; archaeology; art; biochemistry; biological/physical sciences; biology; business administration; Canadian studies; chemical and atomic/molecular physics; chemistry; cognitive psychology/psycholinguistics; communications; computer science; criminology; dance; earth sciences; economics; education; engineering science; English; environmental science; exercise sciences; film studies; French; general studies; geography; history; humanities; Latin American studies; liberal arts and sciences/liberal studies; linguistics; management science; mathematics; music; philosophy; physics; political science; psychology; sociology; Spanish; theater arts/drama; visual and performing arts related; women's studies.
Academic Programs *Special study options:* adult/continuing education programs, advanced placement credit, cooperative education, distance learning, double majors, honors programs, internships, off-campus study, part-time degree program, student-designed majors, study abroad, summer session for credit.
Library W. A. C. Bennett Library with 1.6 million titles, 12,534 serial subscriptions, 58,674 audiovisual materials, an OPAC, a Web page.
Computers on Campus 900 computers available on campus for general student use. A campuswide network can be accessed from off campus. Internet access, online (class) registration, at least one staffed computer lab available.
Student Life *Housing Options:* coed, women-only, disabled students. *Activities and Organizations:* student-run newspaper, radio station, choral group, The Peak Newspaper, orientation leaders, crisis line, Women's Centre, Simon Fraser Public Interest Research Group. *Campus security:* 24-hour emergency response devices and patrols, student patrols, late-night transport/escort service, controlled dormitory access, safe-walk stations, 24-hour safe study area. *Student Services:* health clinic, personal/psychological counseling, women's center, legal services.
Athletics Member NAIA. *Intercollegiate sports:* basketball M(s)/W(s), cross-country running M(s)/W(s), field hockey W(s), football M(s), golf M(s), soccer M(s)/W(s), softball W(s), swimming M(s)/W(s), track and field M(s)/W(s), volleyball W(s), wrestling M(s). *Intramural sports:* badminton M(c)/W(c), basketball M/W, crew M(c)/W(c), fencing M(c)/W(c), football M, golf W(c), ice hockey W, lacrosse M(c), rugby M(c)/W(c), soccer M(c)/W(c), softball M/W, squash M(c)/W(c), table tennis M(c)/W(c), tennis M(c)/W(c), volleyball M(c)/W(c), water polo W(c).
Standardized Tests *Required:* SAT I or ACT (for admission).
Costs (2001–02) *Tuition:* province resident $73 Canadian dollars per credit hour part-time; nonresident $2195 Canadian dollars full-time, $231 Canadian dollars per credit hour part-time; International tuition $6930 Canadian dollars full-time. *Required fees:* $209 Canadian dollars full-time. *Room and board:* room only: $2712 Canadian dollars. Room and board charges vary according to housing facility. *Waivers:* senior citizens and employees or children of employees.
Financial Aid Available in 2001, 346 State and other part-time jobs (averaging $895).
Applying *Options:* electronic application, early admission, early decision, deferred entrance. *Application fee:* $25. *Required:* high school transcript, minimum 3.2 GPA. *Required for some:* essay or personal statement, letters of recommendation, interview. *Application deadline:* 4/30 (freshmen), rolling (transfers). *Early decision:* 5/1. *Notification:* 5/1 (early decision).

Simon Fraser University (continued)

Admissions Contact Mr. Nick Heath, Director of Admissions, Simon Fraser University, 8888 University Drive, Burnaby, BC V5A 1S6, Canada. *Phone:* 604-291-3224. *Fax:* 604-291-4969. *E-mail:* undergraduate-admissions@sfu.ca.

STEINBACH BIBLE COLLEGE
Steinbach, Manitoba, Canada

- **Independent Mennonite** 4-year, founded 1936
- **Calendar** semesters
- **Degree** certificates, diplomas, and bachelor's
- **Small-town** campus with easy access to Winnipeg
- **Coed,** 98 undergraduate students, 91% full-time, 45% women, 55% men
- **Minimally difficult** entrance level

Faculty *Total:* 15, 40% full-time, 27% with terminal degrees. *Student/faculty ratio:* 11:1.

Majors Biblical studies; music; religious studies.

Computers on Campus 24 computers available on campus for general student use.

Costs (2001–02) *Comprehensive fee:* $7392 includes full-time tuition ($3746) and room and board ($3646). Part-time tuition: $117 per credit hour. *Required fees:* $60 per year.

Admissions Contact Dr. Terry Hiebert, Registrar, Steinbach Bible College, PO Box 1420, Steinbach, MB R0A 2A0, Canada. *Phone:* 204-326-6451 Ext. 230. *E-mail:* inof@sbcollege.mb.ca.

TÉLÉ-UNIVERSITÉ
Québec, Quebec, Canada

Admissions Contact Ms. Louise Bertrand, Registraire, Télé-université, 455, rue de l'Église, C.P. 4800, succ. Terminus, Québec, QC G1K 9H5, Canada. *Phone:* 418-657-2262 Ext. 5307. *Toll-free phone:* 888-843-4333. *E-mail:* info@teluq.uquebec.ca.

TRENT UNIVERSITY
Peterborough, Ontario, Canada

- **Province-supported** comprehensive, founded 1963
- **Calendar** Canadian standard year
- **Degrees** diplomas, bachelor's, master's, and doctoral
- **Suburban** 1400-acre campus with easy access to Toronto
- **Endowment** $5.1 million
- **Coed,** 5,358 undergraduate students, 76% full-time, 67% women, 33% men
- **Moderately difficult** entrance level, 80% of applicants were admitted

Undergraduates 4,063 full-time, 1,295 part-time. Students come from 13 provinces and territories, 62 other countries. *Retention:* 86% of 2001 full-time freshmen returned.

Freshmen *Admission:* 4,212 applied, 3,362 admitted, 1,523 enrolled. *Average high school GPA:* 3.04.

Faculty *Total:* 260, 84% full-time, 87% with terminal degrees. *Student/faculty ratio:* 22:1.

Majors Anthropology; applied mathematics; biochemistry; biological/physical sciences; biology; business administration; Canadian studies; chemistry; classics; computer science; economics; education; elementary education; English; environmental science; French; geography; German; Greek (modern); Hispanic-American studies; history; humanities; interdisciplinary studies; international relations; Latin (ancient and medieval); liberal arts and sciences/liberal studies; literature; mathematics; modern languages; Native American studies; natural sciences; nursing; philosophy; physical sciences; physics; political science; psychology; secondary education; social sciences; sociology; Spanish; women's studies.

Academic Programs *Special study options:* academic remediation for entering students, accelerated degree program, adult/continuing education programs, advanced placement credit, double majors, honors programs, off-campus study, part-time degree program, services for LD students, student-designed majors, study abroad, summer session for credit.

Library Thomas J. Bata Library plus 2 others with 579,557 titles, 2,312 serial subscriptions, an OPAC, a Web page.

Computers on Campus 250 computers available on campus for general student use. A campuswide network can be accessed from student residence rooms and from off campus. Internet access, at least one staffed computer lab available.

Student Life *Housing Options:* coed, women-only. *Activities and Organizations:* drama/theater group, student-run newspaper, radio station, choral group, Trent Radio, Trent International Program, Trent Central Student Association, Arthur (student newspaper), Excalibur (yearbook). *Campus security:* 24-hour emergency response devices and patrols, student patrols, late-night transport/escort service. *Student Services:* health clinic, personal/psychological counseling, women's center.

Athletics Member CIAU. *Intercollegiate sports:* basketball M(c)/W(c), crew M/W, cross-country running M/W, fencing M/W, field hockey W, golf M/W, rugby M/W, skiing (cross-country) M/W, soccer M/W, squash M/W, swimming M/W, volleyball M(c)/W(c). *Intramural sports:* badminton M/W, basketball M/W, cross-country running M/W, football M/W, ice hockey M/W, soccer M/W, softball M/W, squash M/W, swimming M/W, tennis M/W, track and field M/W, volleyball M/W, water polo M/W.

Standardized Tests *Required for some:* SAT I or ACT (for admission).

Costs (2002–03) *Tuition:* area resident $4110 Canadian dollars full-time, $890 Canadian dollars per course part-time; International tuition $10,940 Canadian dollars full-time. Part-time tuition and fees vary according to course load. *Required fees:* $475 Canadian dollars full-time. *Room and board:* $6208 Canadian dollars; room only: $3482 Canadian dollars. Room and board charges vary according to board plan and housing facility. *Payment plan:* installment. *Waivers:* senior citizens and employees or children of employees.

Applying *Options:* deferred entrance. *Application fee:* $95. *Required:* high school transcript, minimum 2.8 GPA. *Required for some:* essay or personal statement, letters of recommendation, interview. *Application deadlines:* 6/1 (freshmen), 6/1 (transfers).

Admissions Contact Mrs. Carol Murray, Admissions Officer, Trent University, Office of the Registrar, Peterborough, ON K9J 7B8, Canada. *Phone:* 705-748-1215. *Fax:* 705-748-1629. *E-mail:* leaders@trentu.ca.

TRINITY WESTERN UNIVERSITY
Langley, British Columbia, Canada

- **Independent** comprehensive, founded 1962, affiliated with Evangelical Free Church of America
- **Calendar** semesters
- **Degrees** bachelor's and master's
- **Suburban** 110-acre campus with easy access to Vancouver
- **Endowment** $3.0 million
- **Coed,** 2,600 undergraduate students
- **Moderately difficult** entrance level, 77% of applicants were admitted

Undergraduates Students come from 10 provinces and territories, 29 other countries, 33% are from out of province, 40% live on campus. *Retention:* 80% of 2001 full-time freshmen returned.

Freshmen *Admission:* 1,633 applied, 1,256 admitted. *Average high school GPA:* 3.30.

Faculty *Total:* 138, 56% full-time, 61% with terminal degrees. *Student/faculty ratio:* 18:1.

Majors Aircraft pilot (professional); applied mathematics; biblical studies; biological/physical sciences; biology; business administration; chemistry; communications; computer science; divinity/ministry; education; elementary education; English; environmental biology; environmental science; general studies; geography; health/physical education; history; humanities; human services; international relations; liberal arts and sciences/liberal studies; linguistics; mathematics; mathematics/computer science; missionary studies; music; natural sciences; nursing; philosophy; physical education; political science; pre-dentistry; pre-law; pre-medicine; pre-veterinary studies; psychology; religious studies; secondary education; social sciences; theater arts/drama.

Academic Programs *Special study options:* academic remediation for entering students, adult/continuing education programs, advanced placement credit, cooperative education, double majors, English as a second language, honors programs, independent study, internships, off-campus study, part-time degree program, study abroad, summer session for credit.

Library Norma Marion Alloway Library with 115,626 titles, 2,316 serial subscriptions, 3,002 audiovisual materials, an OPAC, a Web page.

Computers on Campus 50 computers available on campus for general student use. A campuswide network can be accessed from student residence rooms and from off campus. Internet access, at least one staffed computer lab available.

Student Life *Housing:* on-campus residence required through sophomore year. *Options:* coed, men-only, women-only, disabled students. *Activities and Organizations:* drama/theater group, student-run newspaper, choral group, Campus Ministries, choir, student newspaper, discipleship program. *Campus security:*

24-hour emergency response devices and patrols, late-night transport/escort service, controlled dormitory access. *Student Services:* health clinic, personal/psychological counseling.

Athletics Member CIAU. *Intercollegiate sports:* basketball M/W, golf M, ice hockey M/W, rugby M/W, soccer M/W, track and field M/W, volleyball M/W. *Intramural sports:* badminton M/W, basketball M/W, football M, soccer M/W, softball M/W, table tennis M/W, tennis M/W, volleyball M/W, weight lifting M/W, wrestling M/W.

Standardized Tests *Required for some:* SAT I or ACT (for admission).

Costs (2002–03) *Comprehensive fee:* $18,780 Canadian dollars includes full-time tuition ($11,850 Canadian dollars), mandatory fees ($110 Canadian dollars), and room and board ($6820 Canadian dollars). Full-time tuition and fees vary according to class time and program. Part-time tuition: $395 Canadian dollars per semester hour. Part-time tuition and fees vary according to class time and program. *Required fees:* $50 Canadian dollars per term part-time. *Room and board:* Room and board charges vary according to board plan, housing facility, and student level. *Payment plan:* installment. *Waivers:* employees or children of employees.

Financial Aid Of all full-time matriculated undergraduates who enrolled in 2001, 45 Federal Work-Study jobs.

Applying *Options:* common application, electronic application, deferred entrance. *Application fee:* $35. *Required:* essay or personal statement, high school transcript, minimum 2.5 GPA, 2 letters of recommendation, community standards document. *Required for some:* interview. *Application deadlines:* 6/15 (freshmen), 6/15 (transfers). *Notification:* continuous (freshmen).

Admissions Contact Mr. Jeff Suderman, Director of Undergraduate Admissions, Trinity Western University, 7600 Glover Road, Langley, BC V24 141, Canada. *Phone:* 604-513-2019. *Toll-free phone:* 888-468-6898. *Fax:* 604-513-2064. *E-mail:* admissions@twu.ca.

TYNDALE COLLEGE & SEMINARY

Toronto, Ontario, Canada

- **Independent interdenominational** comprehensive, founded 1894
- **Calendar** semesters
- **Degrees** bachelor's, master's, and first professional
- **Urban** 10-acre campus with easy access to Toronto
- **Coed,** 485 undergraduate students, 49% full-time, 52% women, 48% men
- **Moderately difficult** entrance level

Undergraduates 238 full-time, 247 part-time. Students come from 7 provinces and territories, 12 other countries, 13% African American, 23% Asian American or Pacific Islander, 2% Hispanic American, 30% live on campus. *Retention:* 49% of 2001 full-time freshmen returned.

Freshmen *Admission:* 104 enrolled.

Faculty *Total:* 44, 27% full-time, 100% with terminal degrees. *Student/faculty ratio:* 10:1.

Majors Biblical studies; business; divinity/ministry; English; history; human services; liberal arts and sciences/liberal studies; pastoral counseling; philosophy; psychology; recreation/leisure studies; recreation products/services marketing operations; religious education.

Academic Programs *Special study options:* academic remediation for entering students, accelerated degree program, adult/continuing education programs, internships, off-campus study, part-time degree program, student-designed majors, study abroad, summer session for credit.

Library J. William Horsey Library with 65,013 titles, 410 serial subscriptions, an OPAC.

Computers on Campus 4 computers available on campus for general student use. Internet access, at least one staffed computer lab available.

Student Life *Housing Options:* coed. *Activities and Organizations:* drama/theater group, student-run newspaper, choral group, Choir, Student Government, Urban Ministry Team, ""Steadfast" Drama Team. *Campus security:* student patrols, late-night transport/escort service, controlled dormitory access. *Student Services:* personal/psychological counseling.

Athletics *Intercollegiate sports:* basketball M/W, ice hockey M, volleyball M/W. *Intramural sports:* badminton M(c)/W(c), basketball M(c), football M, golf M, skiing (cross-country) M(c)/W(c), skiing (downhill) M(c)/W(c), soccer M(c)/W(c), softball M/W, swimming M(c)/W(c), volleyball W, weight lifting M(c)/W(c).

Costs (2002–03) *Comprehensive fee:* $10,445 Canadian dollars includes full-time tuition ($6450 Canadian dollars) and room and board ($3995 Canadian dollars). Part-time tuition: $196 Canadian dollars per credit hour. *Required fees:* $19 Canadian dollars per credit hour. *Payment plan:* installment. *Waivers:* employees or children of employees.

Applying *Options:* deferred entrance. *Application fee:* $50. *Required:* essay or personal statement, high school transcript, 3 letters of recommendation. *Required for some:* interview. *Application deadlines:* 8/15 (freshmen), 8/15 (transfers).

Admissions Contact Ms. Kathleen Steadman, Assistant Registrar, Tyndale College & Seminary, 25 Ballyconnor Court, Toronto, ON M2M 4B3, Canada. *Phone:* 416-226-6620 Ext. 6738. *Toll-free phone:* 800-663-6052. *E-mail:* enroll@tyndale.ca.

UNIVERSITÉ DE MONCTON

Moncton, New Brunswick, Canada

Admissions Contact Miss Nicole Savois, Chief Admission Officer, Université de Moncton, Moncton, NB E1A 3E9, Canada. *Phone:* 506-858-4115. *Toll-free phone:* 800-363-8336. *Fax:* 506-858-4544. *E-mail:* registrariat@umoncton.ca.

UNIVERSITÉ DE MONTRÉAL

Montréal, Quebec, Canada

- **Independent** university, founded 1920
- **Calendar** trimesters
- **Degrees** certificates, bachelor's, master's, and doctoral
- **Urban** 150-acre campus
- **Coed,** 24,930 undergraduate students, 67% full-time, 70% women, 30% men
- **Moderately difficult** entrance level

Undergraduates *Retention:* 83% of 2001 full-time freshmen returned.

Majors Actuarial science; anthropology; applied mathematics; archaeology; architecture; art; art history; biblical studies; biochemistry; biology; biomedical science; chemical engineering; chemistry; classics; computer science; criminology; developmental/child psychology; early childhood education; East Asian studies; ecology; economics; education; elementary education; English; film studies; French; geography; geology; German; Hispanic-American studies; history; human resources management; industrial design; interdisciplinary studies; jazz; labor/personnel relations; landscape architecture; legal studies; linguistics; literature; mass communications; mathematical statistics; mathematics; microbiology/bacteriology; modern languages; music; nursing; nutrition science; occupational therapy; operations research; ophthalmic/optometric services; pharmacy; philosophy; physical education; physical therapy; physics; political science; predentistry; pre-medicine; psychology; rehabilitation therapy; religious studies; secondary education; social sciences; social work; sociology; Spanish; special education; speech-language pathology/audiology; theology; urban studies; veterinary sciences.

Academic Programs *Special study options:* accelerated degree program, adult/continuing education programs, distance learning, English as a second language, internships, off-campus study, part-time degree program, summer session for credit.

Library Main Library plus 18 others with 15,300 serial subscriptions, 164,079 audiovisual materials, an OPAC, a Web page.

Computers on Campus 600 computers available on campus for general student use. A campuswide network can be accessed from student residence rooms and from off campus. Internet access, at least one staffed computer lab available.

Student Life *Housing Options:* coed. *Activities and Organizations:* drama/theater group, student-run newspaper, radio station, choral group, Federation des Associations Etudiantes du Campus. *Campus security:* 24-hour emergency response devices and patrols, student patrols, late-night transport/escort service, controlled dormitory access, cameras, alarm systems, crime prevention programs. *Student Services:* health clinic, personal/psychological counseling, legal services.

Athletics Member CIAU. *Intercollegiate sports:* badminton M/W, skiing (downhill) M/W, soccer M/W, swimming M/W, volleyball M/W. *Intramural sports:* archery M/W, badminton M/W, basketball M/W, fencing M/W, golf M/W, gymnastics M/W, ice hockey M/W, racquetball M/W, soccer M/W, squash M/W, swimming M/W, table tennis M/W, tennis M/W, volleyball M/W, water polo M/W.

Financial Aid Available in 2001, 400 State and other part-time jobs.

Applying *Options:* common application. *Application fee:* $30. *Required:* Diploma of Collegiate Studies (and transcript) or equivalent. *Required for some:* interview. *Application deadlines:* 3/1 (freshmen), 3/1 (transfers). *Notification:* 5/15 (freshmen).

Admissions Contact Mr. Fernand Boucher, Registrar, Université de Montréal, Case postale 6205, Succursale Centre-ville, Montréal, QC H3C 3T5, Canada. *Phone:* 514-343-7076. *Fax:* 514-343-5788. *E-mail:* fernand.boucher@umontreal.ca.

Université de Sherbrooke
Sherbrooke, Quebec, Canada

- **Independent** university, founded 1954
- **Calendar** Canadian standard year
- **Degrees** certificates, diplomas, bachelor's, master's, doctoral, and first professional
- **Urban** 800-acre campus with easy access to Montreal
- **Coed**
- **Moderately difficult** entrance level

Undergraduates Students come from 3 provinces and territories, 62 other countries.

Majors Accounting; adult/continuing education; applied mathematics; athletic training/sports medicine; biochemistry; biological technology; biology; business administration; business marketing and marketing management; chemical engineering; chemistry; civil engineering; computer engineering; computer management; computer science; counselor education/guidance; early childhood education; ecology; economics; education; electrical engineering; elementary education; engineering; English; exercise sciences; finance; French; geography; geophysics/seismology; history; information sciences/systems; interdisciplinary studies; legal studies; liberal arts and sciences/liberal studies; management information systems/business data processing; mass communications; mathematical statistics; mathematics; mechanical engineering; microbiology/bacteriology; music; nursing; operations research; philosophy; physical education; physics; pre-medicine; psychology; secondary education; social work; special education; textile sciences/engineering; theology.

Academic Programs *Special study options:* accelerated degree program, adult/continuing education programs, cooperative education, internships, off-campus study, part-time degree program, services for LD students, student-designed majors, summer session for credit.

Library Bibliothéque Generale plus 3 others with 1.2 million titles, 5,937 serial subscriptions.

Computers on Campus 300 computers available on campus for general student use.

Student Life *Housing Options:* coed. *Activities and Organizations:* drama/theater group, student-run newspaper, radio station. *Campus security:* 24-hour emergency response devices and patrols. *Student Services:* health clinic, personal/psychological counseling, legal services.

Athletics Member CIAU. *Intercollegiate sports:* badminton M/W, cross-country running M(s)/W(s), skiing (cross-country) M/W, soccer M(s)/W(s), swimming M(s)/W(s), track and field M(s)/W(s), volleyball M(s)/W(s). *Intramural sports:* badminton M/W, basketball M/W, cross-country running M/W, ice hockey M, racquetball M/W, skiing (cross-country) M/W, skiing (downhill) M/W, soccer M/W, softball M/W, squash M/W, swimming M/W, tennis M/W, track and field M/W, volleyball M/W.

Financial Aid Available in 2001, 332 State and other part-time jobs. *Financial aid deadline:* 3/31.

Applying *Options:* early admission. *Application fee:* $30. *Required:* high school transcript. *Required for some:* letters of recommendation, interview. *Application deadline:* 3/1 (freshmen). *Notification:* continuous until 5/15 (freshmen).

Admissions Contact Ms. Lisa Bedard, Admissions Officer, Université de Sherbrooke, 2500, Boulevard de l'Université, Sherbrooke, QC J1K 2R1, Canada. *Phone:* 819-821-7681. *Toll-free phone:* 800-267-UDES. *E-mail:* information@courrier.usherb.ca.

Université du Québec à Chicoutimi
Chicoutimi, Quebec, Canada

Admissions Contact Mr. Claudio Zoccastello, Admissions Officer, Université du Québec à Chicoutimi, 555, boulevard de L'Université, Chicoutimi, PQ G7H 2B1, Canada. *Phone:* 418-545-5005. *E-mail:* czoccast@uqac.uquebec.ca.

Université du Québec à Hull
Hull, Quebec, Canada

Admissions Contact Ms. Lene Blais, Admissions Officer, Université du Québec à Hull, C.P. 1250, Station "B" Hull, Quebec J8X 3X7, Canada. *Phone:* 819-595-3900 Ext. 1841. *Fax:* 819-773-1835. *E-mail:* lene_blais@uqah.uquebec.ca.

Université du Québec à Montréal
Montréal, Quebec, Canada

Admissions Contact Ms. Lucille Boisselle-Roy, Admissions Officer, Université du Québec à Montréal, CP 8888, Succursale Centre-ville, Montréal, QC H2L 4S8, Canada. *Phone:* 514-987-3132. *Fax:* 514-987-7728. *E-mail:* admission@uqam.ca.

Université du Québec à Rimouski
Rimouski, Quebec, Canada

Admissions Contact Mr. Conrad Lavoie, Admissions Officer, Université du Québec à Rimouski, 300, Allee des Ursulines, CP 3300, Rimouski, PQ G5L 3A1, Canada. *Phone:* 418-724-1433. *E-mail:* raymond_cote@uqar.uquebec.ca.

Université du Québec à Trois-Rivières
Trois-Rivières, Quebec, Canada

- **Province-supported** university, founded 1969, part of Université du Québec
- **Calendar** trimesters
- **Degrees** certificates, bachelor's, master's, and doctoral
- **Urban** campus with easy access to Montreal
- **Endowment** $3.3 million
- **Coed**
- **Noncompetitive** entrance level

Student Life *Campus security:* 24-hour emergency response devices and patrols, late-night transport/escort service, controlled dormitory access.

Athletics Member CIAU.

Applying *Application fee:* $30. *Required:* Diploma of Collegiate Studies (and transcript) or equivalent. *Required for some:* interview.

Admissions Contact Mrs. Suzanne Camirand, Admissions Officer, Université du Québec à Trois-Rivières, Bureau du registraire, Service des admissions, 3350 Boulevard Des Forges, Trois Rivieres, QC G9A 5H7, Canada. *Phone:* 819-376-5045. *Toll-free phone:* 800-365-0922. *Fax:* 819-376-5210. *E-mail:* registraire@uqtr.uquebec.ca.

Université du Québec, École de Technologie Supérieure
Montréal, Quebec, Canada

- **Province-supported** comprehensive, founded 1974, part of Université du Québec
- **Calendar** trimesters
- **Degrees** bachelor's, master's, and doctoral
- **Urban** campus
- **Coed, primarily men,** 3,421 undergraduate students, 70% full-time, 9% women, 91% men
- **Noncompetitive** entrance level, 86% of applicants were admitted

Undergraduates 2,394 full-time, 1,027 part-time.

Freshmen *Admission:* 1,606 applied, 1,374 admitted, 828 enrolled.

Faculty *Total:* 190, 55% full-time.

Majors Construction engineering; electrical engineering; engineering; mechanical engineering; robotics.

Academic Programs *Special study options:* accelerated degree program, adult/continuing education programs, cooperative education, off-campus study, part-time degree program, services for LD students, summer session for credit.

Library 44,195 titles, 630 serial subscriptions, an OPAC, a Web page.

Student Life *Activities and Organizations:* student-run newspaper, radio station. *Student Services:* health clinic, personal/psychological counseling.

Athletics *Intercollegiate sports:* rugby M. *Intramural sports:* badminton M/W, basketball M/W, ice hockey M, soccer M/W, table tennis M/W, tennis M/W, volleyball M/W.

Costs (2001–02) *Tuition:* nonresident $7716 Canadian dollars full-time, $128 Canadian dollars per credit part-time; International tuition $18,726 Canadian dollars full-time. *Room and board:* $6390 Canadian dollars; room only: $4050 Canadian dollars.

Applying *Application fee:* $30. *Required:* Diploma of Collegiate Studies (and transcript) or equivalent. *Application deadline:* 3/1 (freshmen). *Notification:* 5/15 (freshmen).

Admissions Contact Mme. Francine Gamache, Registraire, Université du Québec, École de technologie supérieure, 1100, rue Notre Dame Ouest, Montréal, PQ H3C 1K3, Canada. *Phone:* 514-396-8885. *E-mail:* admission@ets.mtl.ca.

UNIVERSITÉ DU QUÉBEC EN ABITIBI-TÉMISCAMINGUE
Rouyn-Noranda, Quebec, Canada

Admissions Contact Mrs. Monique Fay, Admissions Officer, Université du Québec en Abitibi-Témiscamingue, 445 boulevard de l'Université, Rouyn-Noranda, PQ J9X 5E4, Canada. *Phone:* 819-762-0971. *Fax:* 819-797-4727. *E-mail:* micheline.chevalier@uqat.uquebec.ca.

UNIVERSITÉ LAVAL
Québec, Quebec, Canada

- **Independent** university, founded 1852
- **Calendar** trimesters
- **Degrees** certificates, diplomas, associate, bachelor's, master's, doctoral, first professional, postbachelor's, and first professional certificates
- **Urban** 465-acre campus with easy access to Québec City
- **Endowment** $45.2 million
- **Coed,** 28,458 undergraduate students, 65% full-time, 59% women, 41% men
- **Minimally difficult** entrance level, 80% of applicants were admitted

Undergraduates Students come from 11 provinces and territories, 79 other countries, 2% are from out of province, 7% live on campus. *Retention:* 83% of 2001 full-time freshmen returned.

Freshmen *Admission:* 16,770 applied, 13,400 admitted.

Faculty *Total:* 1,446. *Student/faculty ratio:* 19:1.

Majors Actuarial science; agricultural economics; agronomy/crop science; anthropology; archaeology; architecture; art education; art history; biochemistry; biology; business administration; chemical engineering; chemistry; civil engineering; classical and ancient Near Eastern languages related; computer engineering; computer science; consumer services; counselor education/guidance; early childhood education; economics; electrical engineering; elementary education; engineering physics; engineering related; English; environmental engineering; environmental science; exercise sciences; fine/studio arts; folklore; food sciences; foreign language translation; forest management; forest production and processing related; French; French language education; geography; geological engineering; geology; graphic design/commercial art/illustration; history; insurance/risk management; interdisciplinary studies; international economics; international relations; jazz; labor/personnel relations; legal studies; linguistics; literature; mass communications; mathematical statistics; mathematics; mechanical engineering; metallurgical engineering; microbiology/bacteriology; mining/mineral engineering; modern languages; music; music teacher education; nursing; nutritional sciences; nutrition science; occupational therapy; pharmacy; philosophy; physical education; physical therapy; physics; political science; pre-dentistry; pre-medicine; psychology; quantitative economics; rabbinical/Talmudic studies; secondary education; social work; sociology; Spanish; surveying; teaching English as a second language; technical education; theater arts/drama; theology; wood science/paper technology.

Academic Programs *Special study options:* academic remediation for entering students, accelerated degree program, adult/continuing education programs, cooperative education, honors programs, internships, off-campus study, part-time degree program, student-designed majors, summer session for credit.

Library Bibliothéque Générale plus 2 others with 2.2 million titles, 13,655 serial subscriptions, 19,700 audiovisual materials, an OPAC, a Web page.

Computers on Campus 7000 computers available on campus for general student use. A campuswide network can be accessed from student residence rooms and from off campus. Internet access, at least one staffed computer lab available.

Student Life *Housing Options:* coed, men-only, women-only, disabled students. *Activities and Organizations:* drama/theater group, student-run newspaper, radio station, choral group, Drama Club, Improvisation Ligue, Création Littéraire, Chorale de L'université Laval, Amnistie Internationale, national fraternities. *Campus security:* 24-hour emergency response devices and patrols, student patrols, late-night transport/escort service, controlled dormitory access, video cameras in most buildings, underground walkways. *Student Services:* health clinic, personal/psychological counseling.

Athletics Member CIAU. *Intercollegiate sports:* badminton M(s)/W(s), baseball M(s), basketball M(s)/W(s), cross-country running M(s)/W(s), football M(s), golf M(s), gymnastics M(s)/W(s), skiing (downhill) M(s)/W(s), soccer M(s)/W(s), swimming M(s)/W(s), track and field M(s)/W(s), volleyball M(s)/W(s). *Intramural sports:* badminton M/W, baseball M, basketball M/W, cross-country running M/W, golf M/W, ice hockey M/W, soccer M/W, softball M/W, squash M/W, swimming M/W, tennis M/W, volleyball M/W, water polo M/W, weight lifting M/W.

Costs (2001–02) *Tuition:* province resident $1830 Canadian dollars full-time, $62 Canadian dollars per credit part-time; nonresident $4020 Canadian dollars full-time, $135 Canadian dollars per credit part-time; International tuition $10,020 Canadian dollars full-time. Full-time tuition and fees vary according to course load and program. Part-time tuition and fees vary according to course load and program. *Required fees:* $750 Canadian dollars full-time, $7 Canadian dollars per credit. *Room and board:* $8000 Canadian dollars; room only: $2696 Canadian dollars. Room and board charges vary according to housing facility. *Payment plan:* deferred payment. *Waivers:* employees or children of employees.

Applying *Options:* common application. *Application fee:* $30. *Required:* high school transcript, general knowledge of French language. *Required for some:* interview. *Application deadlines:* 3/1 (freshmen), 5/1 (transfers).

Admissions Contact Mrs. Claire Sormany, Responsable des Communications, Université Laval, C. P. 2208, Succ. Terminus, Sainte-Foy, QC G1K 7P4, Canada. *Phone:* 418-656-3080 Ext. 2119. *Toll-free phone:* 877-785-2825. *Fax:* 418-656-5216. *E-mail:* reg@reg.ulaval.ca.

UNIVERSITÉ SAINTE-ANNE
Church Point, Nova Scotia, Canada

Admissions Contact Mrs. Blanche Thériault, Admissions Officer, Université Sainte-Anne, Church Point, NS B0W 1M0. *Phone:* 902-769-2114 Ext. 116. *Fax:* 902-769-2930. *E-mail:* admission@ustanne.ednet.ns.ca.

UNIVERSITY COLLEGE OF CAPE BRETON
Sydney, Nova Scotia, Canada

- **Province-supported** comprehensive, founded 1974
- **Calendar** Canadian standard year
- **Degrees** certificates, diplomas, bachelor's, master's, and postbachelor's certificates
- **Small-town** 57-hectare campus
- **Endowment** $6.8 million
- **Coed,** 3,070 undergraduate students, 79% full-time, 56% women, 44% men
- **Moderately difficult** entrance level, 96% of applicants were admitted

Undergraduates 2,410 full-time, 660 part-time. Students come from 11 provinces and territories, 25 other countries, 9% are from out of province, 5% transferred in, 5% live on campus. *Retention:* 63% of 2001 full-time freshmen returned.

Freshmen *Admission:* 2,320 applied, 2,222 admitted, 907 enrolled.

Faculty *Total:* 225, 76% full-time, 45% with terminal degrees. *Student/faculty ratio:* 12:1.

Majors Accounting; anthropology; biological/physical sciences; biology; business; business administration; business economics; business marketing and marketing management; chemical technology; chemistry; communications; community services; computer/information sciences; computer science; economics; electrical equipment installation/repair; engineering; English; environmental health; environmental science; environmental technology; finance; French; history; hospitality management; hospitality/recreation marketing operations; information sciences/systems; labor/personnel relations; liberal arts and sciences/liberal studies; machine shop assistant; management information systems/business data processing; marketing operations; mathematics; Native American studies; nursing; organizational behavior; petroleum products retailing operations; petroleum technology; philosophy; political science; pre-dentistry; pre-law; pre-medicine; pre-veterinary studies; psychology; recreation/leisure studies; religious studies; sociology; speech/rhetorical studies; sport/fitness administration; tourism promotion operations; travel/tourism management.

Academic Programs *Special study options:* academic remediation for entering students, accelerated degree program, advanced placement credit, cooperative education, distance learning, double majors, honors programs, internships, part-time degree program, services for LD students, student-designed majors, study abroad, summer session for credit.

Library University College Library with 451,271 titles, 800 serial subscriptions, 1,850 audiovisual materials, an OPAC, a Web page.

Computers on Campus 206 computers available on campus for general student use. A campuswide network can be accessed from off campus. Internet access, at least one staffed computer lab available.

Student Life *Housing Options:* coed. *Activities and Organizations:* drama/theater group, student-run newspaper, radio and television station, Marketing

University College of Cape Breton (continued)
Society, International Students Society, Music Society, MacKenzie Residence Society, Nursing Society. *Campus security:* 24-hour patrols, controlled dormitory access, security for social events, escort service. *Student Services:* health clinic, personal/psychological counseling, women's center, legal services.

Athletics Member CIAU. *Intercollegiate sports:* badminton M/W, basketball M/W, soccer M/W, volleyball M/W. *Intramural sports:* baseball M, rugby M/W.

Costs (2001–02) *Tuition:* nonresident $4310 Canadian dollars full-time, $862 Canadian dollars per course part-time; International tuition $7010 Canadian dollars full-time. Full-time tuition and fees vary according to course load and program. Part-time tuition and fees vary according to course load. *Required fees:* $415 Canadian dollars full-time, $143 Canadian dollars per course. *Room and board:* $6180 Canadian dollars; room only: $3120 Canadian dollars. Room and board charges vary according to board plan and housing facility. *Payment plan:* installment. *Waivers:* senior citizens and employees or children of employees.

Applying *Options:* electronic application. *Application fee:* $20. *Required:* high school transcript. *Required for some:* essay or personal statement, 3 letters of recommendation, interview. *Application deadlines:* 8/1 (freshmen), 3/31 (out-of-state freshmen). *Notification:* continuous (freshmen).

Admissions Contact Ms. Cheryl Livingstone, Admissions Officer, University College of Cape Breton, PO Box 5300, Sydney, NS B1P 6L2, Canada. *Phone:* 902-563-1166. *Toll-free phone:* 888-959-9995. *Fax:* 902-563-1371. *E-mail:* admissions@uccb.ns.ca.

University College of the Cariboo
Kamloops, British Columbia, Canada

- **Province-supported** 4-year, founded 1970
- **Degrees** certificates, diplomas, associate, bachelor's, and postbachelor's certificates
- **Endowment** $4.0 million
- **Coed,** 4,820 undergraduate students, 70% full-time, 61% women, 39% men
- 57% of applicants were admitted

Undergraduates Students come from 10 provinces and territories, 43 other countries, 7% are from out of province, 9% live on campus.

Freshmen *Admission:* 2,190 applied, 1,250 admitted.

Faculty *Total:* 571, 65% full-time. *Student/faculty ratio:* 13:1.

Majors Accounting; agricultural animal husbandry/production management; animal sciences; biochemistry; biology; business administration; business marketing and marketing management; Canadian studies; cell biology; chemistry; child care services management; communication systems installation/repair; computer installation/repair; computer science; drafting/design technology; ecology; economics; electrical equipment installation/repair; elementary education; English; environmental biology; finance; fine/studio arts; geography; history; hospitality/recreation marketing operations; hotel/motel services marketing operations; human resources management; industrial electronics installation/repair; journalism; marketing operations; mathematics; molecular biology; natural resources conservation; nursing science; physics; psychology; recreation products/services marketing operations; respiratory therapy; social work; sociology; tourism promotion operations; tourism/travel marketing; visual/performing arts.

Academic Programs *Special study options:* adult/continuing education programs, advanced placement credit, cooperative education, distance learning, double majors, English as a second language, honors programs, independent study, internships, off-campus study, part-time degree program, services for LD students, study abroad, summer session for credit.

Library University College of the Cariboo Library with 207,200 titles, 920 serial subscriptions, 8,200 audiovisual materials, an OPAC, a Web page.

Computers on Campus 300 computers available on campus for general student use. A campuswide network can be accessed from student residence rooms and from off campus that provide access to Web CT. Internet access, online (class) registration available.

Student Life *Housing:* college housing not available. *Options:* coed. *Activities and Organizations:* student-run newspaper, radio station, choral group. *Campus security:* 24-hour emergency response devices and patrols, student patrols, late-night transport/escort service. *Student Services:* health clinic, personal/psychological counseling.

Athletics *Intercollegiate sports:* badminton M(s)/W(s), baseball M, basketball M(s)/W(s), soccer M(s)/W(s), volleyball M(s)/W(s). *Intramural sports:* cross-country running M/W, football M, ice hockey M, racquetball M/W, rugby M, skiing (cross-country) M/W, skiing (downhill) M/W, softball M/W, squash M/W, swimming M/W, table tennis M/W, track and field M.

Costs (2001–02) *Tuition:* province resident $41 Canadian dollars per credit part-time; nonresident $1200 Canadian dollars full-time, $41 Canadian dollars per credit part-time; International tuition $7600 Canadian dollars full-time. Full-time tuition and fees vary according to class time and program. Part-time tuition and fees vary according to class time and program. *Required fees:* $500 Canadian dollars full-time. *Room and board:* room only: $2600 Canadian dollars. *Waivers:* senior citizens.

Applying *Options:* electronic application. *Application fee:* $100 (non-residents). *Required:* high school transcript. *Required for some:* letters of recommendation, interview. *Application deadlines:* 3/1 (freshmen), 3/1 (transfers). *Notification:* continuous until 3/1 (freshmen).

Admissions Contact Mr. Josh Keller, Director, Public Relations and Student Recruitment, University College of the Cariboo, PO Box 3010, 900 McGill Road, Kamloops, BC V2C 5N3, Canada. *Phone:* 250-828-5008. *Toll-free phone:* 250-828-5071. *Fax:* 250-828-5159. *E-mail:* admissions@cariboo.bc.ca.

University College of the Fraser Valley
Abbotsford, British Columbia, Canada

- **Province-supported** 4-year, founded 1974, part of B.C. provincial education
- **Calendar** semesters
- **Degrees** certificates, diplomas, associate, and bachelor's
- **Urban** campus with easy access to Vancouver
- **Endowment** $1.1 million
- **Coed,** 5,987 undergraduate students, 39% full-time, 60% women, 40% men

Faculty *Total:* 322, 83% full-time, 15% with terminal degrees. *Student/faculty ratio:* 13:1.

Majors Adult/continuing education; adult/continuing education administration; anthropology; aviation management; biology; business administration; chemistry; child care/guidance; computer/information sciences; computer systems analysis; criminal justice studies; English; geography; history; interdisciplinary studies; Latin American studies; mass communications; mathematical statistics; mathematics; nursing; physical education; physics; psychology; social work; sociology; theater arts/drama.

Academic Programs *Special study options:* academic remediation for entering students, adult/continuing education programs, advanced placement credit, cooperative education, distance learning, double majors, English as a second language, independent study, internships, part-time degree program, services for LD students, summer session for credit.

Library Peter Jones Library plus 3 others with an OPAC, a Web page.

Computers on Campus 850 computers available on campus for general student use. Internet access, at least one staffed computer lab available.

Student Life *Housing:* college housing not available. *Activities and Organizations:* drama/theater group, student-run newspaper. *Campus security:* late-night transport/escort service. *Student Services:* personal/psychological counseling.

Athletics *Intercollegiate sports:* basketball M(s)/W(s), soccer M(s)/W(s). *Intramural sports:* badminton M/W, basketball M/W, cross-country running M(c)/W(c), soccer M/W, volleyball M/W, wrestling M(c)/W(c).

Costs (2001–02) *Tuition:* $120 Canadian dollars per course part-time; nonresident $1144 Canadian dollars full-time; International tuition $3500 Canadian dollars full-time. Full-time tuition and fees vary according to class time and course load. Part-time tuition and fees vary according to class time and course load. *Required fees:* $125 Canadian dollars full-time, $2 Canadian dollars per credit. *Payment plan:* deferred payment. *Waivers:* senior citizens and employees or children of employees.

Applying *Options:* common application, electronic application, deferred entrance. *Application fee:* $15. *Required for some:* essay or personal statement, high school transcript, minimum 2.5 GPA, 2 letters of recommendation, interview. *Application deadlines:* 2/28 (freshmen), 2/28 (transfers). *Notification:* continuous until 9/1 (freshmen).

Admissions Contact Ms. Robin Smith, Admissions Coordinator, University College of the Fraser Valley, 33844 King Road, Abbotsford, BC V2S 7M8, Canada. *Phone:* -853-7441 Ext. 4242. *E-mail:* reginfo@ucfv.bc.ca.

University of Alberta
Edmonton, Alberta, Canada

- **Province-supported** university, founded 1906
- **Calendar** Canadian standard year
- **Degrees** certificates, diplomas, bachelor's, master's, doctoral, and first professional
- **Urban** 154-acre campus
- **Endowment** $524.2 million
- **Coed,** 27,404 undergraduate students

■ **Moderately difficult** entrance level, 47% of applicants were admitted

Undergraduates Students come from 13 provinces and territories, 110 other countries, 5% are from out of province, 15% live on campus.

Freshmen *Admission:* 11,005 applied, 5,147 admitted. *Average high school GPA:* 3.16.

Faculty *Total:* 1,456. *Student/faculty ratio:* 14:1.

Majors Accounting; adult/continuing education; agricultural business; agricultural economics; agricultural sciences; agronomy/crop science; animal sciences; anthropology; applied mathematics; Arabic; art; art education; art history; athletic training/sports medicine; atmospheric sciences; bilingual/bicultural education; biochemistry; biological/physical sciences; biological technology; biology; botany; business administration; business education; business marketing and marketing management; Canadian studies; cartography; cell biology; chemical engineering; chemistry; child care/development; Chinese; civil engineering; classics; clinical psychology; clothing/textiles; comparative literature; computer engineering; computer science; construction engineering; criminal justice/law enforcement administration; criminology; dairy science; dance; dental hygiene; developmental/child psychology; drawing; early childhood education; earth sciences; East Asian studies; Eastern European area studies; economics; education; electrical engineering; elementary education; engineering; engineering physics; English; entomology; environmental biology; environmental engineering; environmental science; exercise sciences; experimental psychology; family/consumer studies; farm/ranch management; finance; fine/studio arts; folklore; food products retailing; food sciences; forestry; French; genetics; geography; geology; geophysics/seismology; German; Greek (modern); Hebrew; history; home economics; home economics education; human ecology; humanities; human resources management; industrial arts; industrial design; information sciences/systems; international business; international relations; Italian; Japanese; labor/personnel relations; land use management; Latin American studies; Latin (ancient and medieval); legal studies; liberal arts and sciences/liberal studies; linguistics; literature; management information systems/business data processing; mathematical statistics; mathematics; mechanical engineering; medical laboratory technician; metallurgical engineering; microbiology/bacteriology; mining/mineral engineering; modern languages; molecular biology; music; music history; music (piano and organ performance); music teacher education; music (voice and choral/opera performance); Native American studies; natural resources conservation; natural resources management; nursing; nutrition science; occupational therapy; paleontology; petroleum engineering; pharmacology; pharmacy; philosophy; physical education; physical sciences; physical therapy; physics; physiology; political science; pre-dentistry; pre-law; pre-medicine; pre-veterinary studies; printmaking; psychology; range management; reading education; recreation/leisure facilities management; recreation/leisure studies; religious studies; romance languages; Russian; Russian/Slavic studies; Scandinavian languages; science education; sculpture; secondary education; Slavic languages; sociology; Spanish; special education; sport/fitness administration; stringed instruments; teaching English as a second language; theater arts/drama; trade/industrial education; urban studies; wildlife management; wind/percussion instruments; women's studies; zoology.

Academic Programs *Special study options:* academic remediation for entering students, adult/continuing education programs, advanced placement credit, cooperative education, distance learning, double majors, English as a second language, honors programs, internships, off-campus study, part-time degree program, services for LD students, study abroad, summer session for credit. *Unusual degree programs:* 3-2 education.

Library Cameron Library plus 10 others with 5.3 million titles, 26,000 serial subscriptions, an OPAC, a Web page.

Computers on Campus 721 computers available on campus for general student use. A campuswide network can be accessed from student residence rooms and from off campus that provide access to e-mail. Internet access, at least one staffed computer lab available.

Student Life *Housing:* on-campus residence required through senior year. *Options:* coed, disabled students. *Activities and Organizations:* drama/theater group, student-run newspaper, radio station, choral group, national fraternities, national sororities. *Campus security:* 24-hour emergency response devices, student patrols, late-night transport/escort service. *Student Services:* health clinic, personal/psychological counseling, women's center, legal services.

Athletics Member CIAU. *Intercollegiate sports:* basketball M(s)/W(s), field hockey M(s)/W(s), football M(s), gymnastics M(s)/W(s), ice hockey M(s), soccer M(s)/W(s), swimming M(s)/W(s), volleyball M(s)/W(s), wrestling M(s). *Intramural sports:* archery M(c)/W(c), badminton M(c)/W(c), basketball M/W, bowling M/W, crew M(c)/W(c), cross-country running M(c)/W(c), fencing M(c)/W(c), field hockey W, football M, golf M/W, gymnastics M/W, ice hockey M/W(c), racquetball M/W, rugby M(c)/W(c), skiing (cross-country) M(c)/W(c), skiing (downhill) M(c)/W(c), soccer M/W, squash M/W, swimming M/W, table tennis M/W, tennis M/W, track and field M(c)/W(c), volleyball M/W, water polo M/W, weight lifting M(c)/W(c), wrestling M.

Costs (2001–02) *Tuition:* province resident $389 Canadian dollars per course part-time; nonresident $3890 Canadian dollars full-time; International tuition $10,000 Canadian dollars full-time. Full-time tuition and fees vary according to course load and program. Part-time tuition and fees vary according to course load and program. *Required fees:* $440 Canadian dollars full-time, $119 Canadian dollars per year part-time. *Room and board:* $4500 Canadian dollars. Room and board charges vary according to board plan and housing facility. *Payment plan:* installment.

Applying *Options:* electronic application, deferred entrance. *Application fee:* $60. *Required:* high school transcript. *Required for some:* essay or personal statement, letters of recommendation, interview. *Recommended:* minimum 2.0 GPA. *Application deadlines:* 5/1 (freshmen), 5/1 (transfers). *Notification:* continuous until 9/1 (freshmen).

Admissions Contact Ms. Carole Byrne, Associate Registrar/Director of Admissions, University of Alberta, 201 Administration Building, Edmonton, AB T6G 2M7, Canada. *Phone:* 780-492-3113. *Fax:* 780-492-7172. *E-mail:* registrar@ualberta.ca.

THE UNIVERSITY OF BRITISH COLUMBIA
Vancouver, British Columbia, Canada

■ **Province-supported** university, founded 1915
■ **Calendar** Canadian standard year
■ **Degrees** certificates, diplomas, bachelor's, master's, doctoral, first professional, and postbachelor's certificates
■ **Urban** 1000-acre campus
■ **Endowment** $631,460
■ **Coed,** 25,694 undergraduate students, 70% full-time, 57% women, 43% men
■ **Very difficult** entrance level, 41% of applicants were admitted

Undergraduates 18,074 full-time, 7,620 part-time. Students come from 12 provinces and territories, 114 other countries, 6% are from out of province, 23% live on campus.

Freshmen *Admission:* 24,298 applied, 9,880 admitted, 4,735 enrolled.

Faculty *Total:* 2,595, 67% full-time. *Student/faculty ratio:* 15:1.

Majors Accounting; agricultural economics; agricultural sciences; animal sciences; anthropology; applied mathematics; aquaculture operations/production management; art education; art history; Asian studies; astronomy; atmospheric sciences; biochemistry; bioengineering; biology; business administration; business education; business marketing and marketing management; Canadian studies; cell biology; chemical engineering; chemistry; Chinese; civil engineering; classics; clinical psychology; computer engineering; computer science; counselor education/guidance; creative writing; cultural studies; dental hygiene; developmental/child psychology; dietetics; early childhood education; earth sciences; economics; education; education administration; electrical engineering; elementary education; engineering physics; engineering technologies related; English; environmental biology; environmental science; exercise sciences; experimental psychology; film studies; finance; fine/studio arts; fish/game management; food sciences; forest products technology; forestry; French; genetics; geography; geological engineering; geology; geophysics/seismology; German; history; home economics; home economics education; horticulture science; industrial arts; interdisciplinary studies; international business; international relations; Italian; Japanese; labor/personnel relations; landscape architecture; Latin American studies; Latin (ancient and medieval); liberal arts and sciences/liberal studies; linguistics; management information systems/business data processing; marine biology; materials engineering; mathematical statistics; mathematics; mechanical engineering; medical laboratory technician; metallurgical engineering; microbiology/bacteriology; mining/mineral engineering; music; music history; music (piano and organ performance); music teacher education; music theory and composition; music (voice and choral/opera performance); natural resources conservation; natural resources management; natural resources management/protective services related; nursing; nutrition science; occupational therapy; oceanography; pharmacology; pharmacy; philosophy; physical therapy; physics; political science; pre-dentistry; pre-law; pre-medicine; pre-veterinary studies; psychology; reading education; recreation/leisure facilities management; rehabilitation therapy; religious studies; romance languages; Russian; Russian/Slavic studies; science education; secondary education; Slavic languages; social sciences; social work; sociology; soil sciences; Spanish; special education; speech therapy; stringed instruments; teaching English as a second language; theater arts/drama; transportation technology; urban studies; wildlife management; women's studies; wood science/paper technology.

Academic Programs *Special study options:* academic remediation for entering students, adult/continuing education programs, advanced placement credit, cooperative education, distance learning, double majors, English as a second language, external degree program, freshman honors college, honors programs, internships,

The University of British Columbia (continued)
off-campus study, part-time degree program, services for LD students, study abroad, summer session for credit. *ROTC:* Army (c), Navy (c), Air Force (c).

Library Walter C. Koerner Library plus 16 others with 3.9 million titles, 25,966 serial subscriptions, an OPAC, a Web page.

Computers on Campus 1100 computers available on campus for general student use. A campuswide network can be accessed from student residence rooms and from off campus. At least one staffed computer lab available.

Student Life *Housing Options:* coed, men-only, women-only, disabled students. *Activities and Organizations:* drama/theater group, student-run newspaper, radio station, choral group, Ski and Board Club, Dance Club, AIESEC Club, UBC Film Society, Varsity Outdoors Club, national fraternities, national sororities. *Campus security:* 24-hour emergency response devices and patrols, student patrols, late-night transport/escort service, 24-hour desk attendants in residence halls. *Student Services:* health clinic, personal/psychological counseling, women's center, legal services.

Athletics Member NAIA, CIAU. *Intercollegiate sports:* baseball M(s), basketball M(s)/W(s), crew M(s)/W(s), cross-country running M(s)/W(s), fencing W(c), field hockey M/W(s), football M(s), golf M(s)/W(s), ice hockey M(s)/W(s), rugby M(s)/W(s), skiing (cross-country) M/W, skiing (downhill) M/W, soccer M(s)/W(s), swimming M(s)/W(s), track and field M(s)/W(s), volleyball M(s)/W(s), water polo M(c)/W(c). *Intramural sports:* badminton M/W, basketball M/W, cross-country running M/W, football M/W, ice hockey M/W, racquetball M/W, soccer M/W, softball M/W, squash M/W, swimming M/W, table tennis M/W, tennis M/W, volleyball M/W.

Standardized Tests *Recommended:* SAT I (for admission).

Costs (2002–03) *Tuition:* $73 Canadian dollars per credit part-time; province resident $73 Canadian dollars per credit part-time; nonresident $73 Canadian dollars per credit part-time.

Financial Aid Available in 2001, 875 State and other part-time jobs (averaging $2500). *Financial aid deadline:* 10/1.

Applying *Options:* electronic application, early admission. *Application fee:* $100. *Required:* high school transcript, minimum 2.6 GPA. *Required for some:* essay or personal statement, letters of recommendation. *Application deadlines:* 3/31 (freshmen), 3/31 (transfers). *Notification:* continuous until 8/31 (freshmen).

Admissions Contact The University of British Columbia, 1874 East Mall, Vancouver, BC V6T 1Z1, Canada. *Phone:* 604-822-3014. *Toll-free phone:* 877-292-1422. *Fax:* 604-822-3599. *E-mail:* student.information@ubc.ca.

UNIVERSITY OF CALGARY
Calgary, Alberta, Canada

- **Province-supported** university, founded 1945
- **Calendar** semesters
- **Degrees** bachelor's, master's, and doctoral
- **Urban** 304-acre campus
- **Coed,** 22,457 undergraduate students, 85% full-time, 56% women, 44% men
- **Moderately difficult** entrance level, 65% of applicants were admitted

Undergraduates Students come from 12 provinces and territories, 70 other countries.

Freshmen *Admission:* 5,925 applied, 3,871 admitted.

Faculty *Total:* 1,965, 72% full-time. *Student/faculty ratio:* 14:1.

Majors Accounting; actuarial science; anthropology; applied mathematics; archaeology; art; art education; art history; astrophysics; biochemistry; biology; botany; business administration; business marketing and marketing management; Canadian studies; cell biology; chemical engineering; chemistry; civil engineering; classics; communications; computer engineering; computer science; dance; development economics; drama/dance education; early childhood education; earth sciences; East Asian studies; ecology; economics; education; electrical engineering; elementary education; English; environmental science; exercise sciences; finance; French; general studies; geography; geological engineering; geology; geophysics/seismology; German; history; hotel and restaurant management; humanities; industrial/manufacturing engineering; insurance/risk management; international relations; Latin American studies; legal studies; liberal arts and sciences/liberal studies; linguistics; management information systems/business data processing; mathematical statistics; mathematics; mechanical engineering; medieval/renaissance studies; molecular biology; music; nursing; philosophy; physics; political science; psychology; recreation/leisure studies; rehabilitation therapy; religious studies; Russian; secondary education; social work; sociology; Spanish; theater arts/drama; travel/tourism management; urban studies; women's studies; zoology.

Academic Programs *Special study options:* adult/continuing education programs, cooperative education, distance learning, double majors, English as a second language, honors programs, internships, part-time degree program, services for LD students, summer session for credit.

Library MacKimmie Library plus 4 others with 2.3 million titles, 14,776 serial subscriptions, 111,445 audiovisual materials, an OPAC, a Web page.

Computers on Campus 1000 computers available on campus for general student use. A campuswide network can be accessed from student residence rooms and from off campus. Internet access, online (class) registration, at least one staffed computer lab available.

Student Life *Housing Options:* coed, disabled students. *Activities and Organizations:* student-run newspaper, radio and television station, choral group. *Campus security:* 24-hour emergency response devices and patrols, late-night transport/escort service, controlled dormitory access. *Student Services:* health clinic, personal/psychological counseling, legal services.

Athletics Member CIAU. *Intercollegiate sports:* basketball M(s)/W(s), cross-country running W(s), field hockey W(s), football M(s), golf M(s), ice hockey M(s), soccer M(s)/W(s), swimming M(s)/W(s), track and field M(s)/W(s), volleyball M(s)/W(s), wrestling M(s). *Intramural sports:* badminton M(c)/W(c), basketball M/W, fencing M(c)/W(c), field hockey M(c)/W(c), football M, golf M, ice hockey M/W, lacrosse W(c), racquetball M(c)/W(c), soccer M/W, softball M/W, squash M(c)/W(c), swimming M(c)/W(c), table tennis M(c)/W(c), volleyball M/W.

Standardized Tests *Required for some:* SAT I (for admission), SAT II: Subject Tests (for admission), SAT II: Writing Test (for admission).

Costs (2001–02) *Tuition:* $412 Canadian dollars per course part-time; International tuition $8240 Canadian dollars full-time. Full-time tuition and fees vary according to course load. Part-time tuition and fees vary according to course load. *Required fees:* $420 Canadian dollars full-time, $140 Canadian dollars per year part-time. *Room only:* Room and board charges vary according to board plan and housing facility. *Waivers:* senior citizens and employees or children of employees.

Applying *Options:* electronic application, early admission. *Application fee:* $65. *Required:* high school transcript. *Application deadline:* 6/1 (freshmen). *Notification:* continuous (freshmen).

Admissions Contact Director of Recruitment and Admissions, University of Calgary, Office of Admissions, Calgary, AB T2N 1N4, Canada. *Phone:* 403-220-6645. *Fax:* 403-220-0762. *E-mail:* applinfo@ucalgary.ca.

UNIVERSITY OF GUELPH
Guelph, Ontario, Canada

- **Province-supported** university, founded 1964
- **Calendar** trimesters
- **Degrees** certificates, diplomas, bachelor's, master's, doctoral, and first professional
- **Urban** 817-acre campus with easy access to Toronto
- **Coed,** 13,302 undergraduate students, 87% full-time, 62% women, 38% men
- **Moderately difficult** entrance level, 63% of applicants were admitted

Undergraduates 11,513 full-time, 1,789 part-time. Students come from 12 provinces and territories, 85 other countries, 6% transferred in, 38% live on campus. *Retention:* 94% of 2001 full-time freshmen returned.

Freshmen *Admission:* 14,813 applied, 9,343 admitted, 3,088 enrolled.

Faculty *Total:* 791, 79% full-time. *Student/faculty ratio:* 20:1.

Majors Agricultural business; agricultural economics; agricultural sciences; agronomy/crop science; animal sciences; anthropology; applied mathematics; art history; biochemistry; bioengineering; biological/physical sciences; biology; biomedical science; biophysics; botany; business economics; business marketing and marketing management; chemical and atomic/molecular physics; chemistry; child care/development; classics; computer engineering technology; computer science; criminal justice/law enforcement administration; development economics; dietetics; earth sciences; ecology; economics; English; environmental biology; environmental engineering; environmental science; environmental technology; European studies; exercise sciences; family studies; fine/studio arts; French; geography; gerontology; history; horticulture science; hotel and restaurant management; human resources management; information sciences/systems; landscape architecture; marine biology; mathematical statistics; mathematics; microbiology/bacteriology; molecular biology; music; natural resources management; nonprofit/public management; nutritional sciences; nutrition science; philosophy; physical sciences; physics; political science; psychology; quantitative economics; real estate; sociology; Spanish; theater arts/drama; theoretical/mathematical physics; tourism/travel marketing; toxicology; veterinary sciences; water resources engineering; wildlife biology; women's studies; zoology.

Academic Programs *Special study options:* academic remediation for entering students, accelerated degree program, adult/continuing education programs, advanced placement credit, cooperative education, distance learning, double majors, freshman honors college, honors programs, independent study, part-time degree program, services for LD students, student-designed majors, study abroad, summer session for credit.

Library McLaughlin Library plus 1 other with 2.1 million titles, 7,294 serial subscriptions, 16,437 audiovisual materials, an OPAC, a Web page.

Computers on Campus 1200 computers available on campus for general student use. A campuswide network can be accessed from student residence rooms and from off campus. Internet access, at least one staffed computer lab available.

Student Life *Housing Options:* coed, men-only, women-only, cooperative. *Activities and Organizations:* drama/theater group, student-run newspaper, radio station, choral group. *Campus security:* 24-hour emergency response devices and patrols, late-night transport/escort service, video camera surveillance in parking lots, alarms in women's locker room. *Student Services:* health clinic, personal/psychological counseling, women's center, legal services.

Athletics Member CIAU. *Intercollegiate sports:* baseball M, basketball M/W, crew M/W, cross-country running M/W, field hockey W, football M, golf M, ice hockey M/W, lacrosse M/W, rugby M/W, skiing (cross-country) M/W, soccer M/W, swimming M/W, track and field M/W, volleyball M/W, wrestling M/W. *Intramural sports:* archery M(c)/W(c), badminton M(c)/W(c), baseball M(c), basketball M/W, fencing M(c)/W(c), football M, ice hockey M/W, lacrosse M(c)/W(c), skiing (cross-country) M(c)/W(c), soccer M/W, softball M/W, squash M(c)/W(c), tennis M(c)/W(c), volleyball M/W, water polo M/W.

Standardized Tests *Required for some:* SAT I or ACT (for admission).

Costs (2001–02) *Tuition:* nonresident $4029 Canadian dollars full-time, $403 Canadian dollars per course part-time. Full-time tuition and fees vary according to program. Part-time tuition and fees vary according to course load. *Required fees:* $678 Canadian dollars full-time, $14 Canadian dollars per course, $99 Canadian dollars per term part-time. *Room and board:* $6014 Canadian dollars; room only: $3000 Canadian dollars. Room and board charges vary according to board plan and housing facility. *Waivers:* senior citizens and employees or children of employees.

Financial Aid Available in 2001, 600 State and other part-time jobs (averaging $800).

Applying *Options:* early admission. *Application fee:* $85. *Required:* high school transcript. *Required for some:* essay or personal statement. *Recommended:* minimum 3.0 GPA, letters of recommendation. *Application deadlines:* 4/1 (freshmen), 6/1 (transfers). *Notification:* 6/5 (freshmen).

Admissions Contact Mr. Hugh Clark, Admissions Coordinator, University of Guelph, L-3 University Centre, Guelph, ON N1G 2W1, Canada. *Phone:* 519-824-4120 Ext. 6066. *E-mail:* internat@registrar.uoguelph.ca.

UNIVERSITY OF KING'S COLLEGE
Halifax, Nova Scotia, Canada

- **Province-supported** 4-year, founded 1789
- **Calendar** Canadian standard year
- **Degree** bachelor's
- **Urban** 4-acre campus
- **Endowment** $19.0 million
- **Coed,** 914 undergraduate students, 97% full-time, 59% women, 41% men
- **Moderately difficult** entrance level, 47% of applicants were admitted

Undergraduates 886 full-time, 28 part-time. Students come from 10 provinces and territories, 8 other countries, 54% are from out of province, 2% transferred in, 28% live on campus. *Retention:* 56% of 2001 full-time freshmen returned.

Freshmen *Admission:* 1,055 applied, 498 admitted, 306 enrolled.

Faculty *Total:* 40, 100% full-time, 70% with terminal degrees.

Majors Anthropology; biochemistry; biology; chemistry; classics; computer science; development economics; earth sciences; economics; English; French; German; history; journalism; linguistics; marine biology; mathematical statistics; mathematics; microbiology/bacteriology; neuroscience; philosophy; physics; political science; psychology; religious studies; Russian; sociology; Spanish; theater arts/drama; western civilization; women's studies.

Academic Programs *Special study options:* accelerated degree program, advanced placement credit, cooperative education, double majors, honors programs, independent study, internships, off-campus study, part-time degree program, services for LD students, student-designed majors, study abroad, summer session for credit.

Library University of King's College Library with 80,000 titles, 192 serial subscriptions, 74 audiovisual materials, an OPAC.

Computers on Campus 51 computers available on campus for general student use. A campuswide network can be accessed from student residence rooms and from off campus. Internet access, at least one staffed computer lab available.

Student Life *Housing Options:* coed, men-only, women-only. *Activities and Organizations:* drama/theater group, student-run newspaper, radio station, choral group, King's Theatrical Society, student newspaper, King's College Dance Collective, St. Andrew's Missionary Society, King's Independent Film-Makers Society. *Campus security:* student patrols, late-night transport/escort service. *Student Services:* health clinic, personal/psychological counseling, women's center, legal services.

Athletics *Intercollegiate sports:* basketball M/W, rugby M/W, soccer M/W, volleyball M/W. *Intramural sports:* badminton M/W, basketball M/W, soccer M/W, softball M/W, squash M/W, tennis M/W, volleyball M/W, water polo M/W.

Standardized Tests *Required for some:* SAT I (for admission).

Costs (2001–02) *Tuition:* province resident $4500 Canadian dollars full-time, $150 Canadian dollars per credit hour part-time; nonresident $4500 Canadian dollars full-time, $150 Canadian dollars per credit hour part-time. Full-time tuition and fees vary according to program. Part-time tuition and fees vary according to program. *Required fees:* $600 Canadian dollars full-time, $304 Canadian dollars per term part-time. *Room and board:* $5565 Canadian dollars. Room and board charges vary according to housing facility. *Waivers:* employees or children of employees.

Applying *Application fee:* $40. *Required:* high school transcript, minimum 3.0 GPA. *Required for some:* essay or personal statement, letters of recommendation, writing sample. *Application deadlines:* 6/1 (freshmen), 6/1 (transfers). *Notification:* continuous until 3/15 (freshmen).

Admissions Contact Karl Turner, Admissions Officer, University of King's College, Registrar's Office, Halifax, NS B3H 2A1, Canada. *Phone:* 902-422-1271 Ext. 193. *Fax:* 902-423-3357. *E-mail:* admissions@ukings.ns.ca.

THE UNIVERSITY OF LETHBRIDGE
Lethbridge, Alberta, Canada

- **Province-supported** comprehensive, founded 1967
- **Calendar** semesters
- **Degrees** certificates, diplomas, bachelor's, master's, and doctoral
- **Urban** 576-acre campus
- **Endowment** $10.7 million
- **Coed,** 6,718 undergraduate students, 90% full-time, 57% women, 43% men
- **Moderately difficult** entrance level, 57% of applicants were admitted

Undergraduates Students come from 12 provinces and territories, 39 other countries, 17% are from out of province, 10% live on campus. *Retention:* 72% of 2001 full-time freshmen returned.

Freshmen *Admission:* 1,564 applied, 887 admitted. *Average high school GPA:* 3.30.

Faculty *Total:* 299, 99% full-time, 76% with terminal degrees. *Student/faculty ratio:* 19:1.

Majors Accounting; agricultural business; agricultural sciences; anthropology; art; art education; biochemistry; biological/physical sciences; biology; business administration; business education; business marketing and marketing management; Canadian studies; chemistry; computer science; earth sciences; economics; education; education administration; education (K-12); English; environmental science; finance; French; geography; German; health education; history; humanities; human resources management; international business; management information systems/business data processing; mathematics; modern languages; music; music teacher education; Native American languages; Native American studies; neuroscience; nursing; philosophy; physical education; physics; political science; psychology; public administration; religious studies; science education; social sciences; sociology; special education; theater arts/drama; urban studies.

Academic Programs *Special study options:* academic remediation for entering students, accelerated degree program, cooperative education, distance learning, double majors, English as a second language, independent study, internships, off-campus study, part-time degree program, student-designed majors, study abroad, summer session for credit. *Unusual degree programs:* 3-2 education.

Library The University of Lethbridge Library with 484,657 titles, 3,331 audiovisual materials, an OPAC, a Web page.

Computers on Campus 550 computers available on campus for general student use. A campuswide network can be accessed from student residence rooms and from off campus. Internet access, online (class) registration, at least one staffed computer lab available.

Student Life *Housing:* on-campus residence required through senior year. *Options:* coed. *Activities and Organizations:* drama/theater group, student-run newspaper, radio station, choral group, Management Students Society, Inter-Varsity Christian Fellowship, Organization of Residence Students, The University of Lethbridge Geography Club, Education Undergraduate Society. *Campus security:* 24-hour emergency response devices and patrols, student patrols, late-night transport/escort service, video camera monitored entrances, hallways. *Student Services:* health clinic, personal/psychological counseling, women's center.

The University of Lethbridge (continued)

Athletics Member CIAU. *Intercollegiate sports:* basketball M(s)/W(s), cross-country running M(s)/W(s), ice hockey M(s), soccer M(s)/W(s), swimming M(s)/W(s), track and field M(s)/W(s), volleyball W. *Intramural sports:* badminton M/W, basketball M/W, fencing M(c)/W(c), football M/W, golf M/W, gymnastics M/W, ice hockey M, racquetball M/W, rugby M(c)/W(c), skiing (cross-country) M/W, skiing (downhill) M/W, soccer M/W, softball M/W, squash M/W, tennis M(c)/W(c), volleyball M/W, water polo M/W, weight lifting M/W.

Standardized Tests *Required for some:* SAT I and SAT II or ACT (for admission), SAT II: Writing Test (for admission).

Costs (2002–03) *Tuition:* nonresident $3470 Canadian dollars full-time, $347 Canadian dollars per course part-time; International tuition $6940 Canadian dollars full-time. *Required fees:* $645 Canadian dollars full-time, $85 Canadian dollars per course. *Room and board:* $5000 Canadian dollars; room only: $2432 Canadian dollars.

Applying *Options:* common application, electronic application, early admission, early decision, deferred entrance. *Application fee:* $75. *Required:* high school transcript, minimum 2.0 GPA. *Required for some:* minimum 3.0 GPA, letters of recommendation, interview. *Application deadlines:* 8/26 (freshmen), 8/26 (transfers). *Early decision:* 4/1. *Notification:* continuous (freshmen), 4/22 (early decision).

Admissions Contact Mr. Peter Haney, Assistant Registrar, The University of Lethbridge, Lethbridge, AB T1K 3M4, Canada. *Phone:* 403-382-7134. *Toll-free phone:* 403-320-5700. *Fax:* 403-329-5159. *E-mail:* inquiries@uleth.ca.

UNIVERSITY OF MANITOBA

Winnipeg, Manitoba, Canada

- **Province-supported** university, founded 1877
- **Calendar** 8-month academic year plus 6-week summer session
- **Degrees** bachelor's, master's, and doctoral
- **Suburban** 685-acre campus
- **Coed,** 20,534 undergraduate students, 75% full-time, 57% women, 43% men
- **Moderately difficult** entrance level, 66% of applicants were admitted

Undergraduates 15,376 full-time, 5,158 part-time.

Freshmen *Admission:* 5,173 applied, 3,416 admitted, 7,156 enrolled.

Faculty *Total:* 1,060.

Majors Accounting; actuarial science; agricultural economics; agricultural engineering; agricultural sciences; agronomy/crop science; animal sciences; anthropology; applied mathematics; architectural environmental design; architecture; art; art history; astronomy; biology; botany; business administration; business economics; Canadian studies; chemistry; child care/development; civil engineering; classics; clothing/textiles; computer engineering; computer science; dental hygiene; early childhood education; earth sciences; ecology; economics; education; electrical engineering; elementary education; engineering science; English; entomology; environmental science; film studies; finance; food sciences; French; genetics; geography; geological engineering; geology; German; Greek (modern); history; home economics; human ecology; industrial/manufacturing engineering; interior design; Judaic studies; labor/personnel relations; Latin (ancient and medieval); mathematical statistics; mathematics; mechanical engineering; medieval/renaissance studies; microbiology/bacteriology; music; nursing; nutrition science; occupational therapy; pharmacy; philosophy; physical education; physical therapy; physics; political science; pre-dentistry; pre-law; pre-medicine; pre-veterinary studies; psychology; public administration; rehabilitation therapy; religious studies; Russian; Russian/Slavic studies; science education; secondary education; Slavic languages; social work; sociology; South Asian studies; Spanish; theater arts/drama; women's studies; zoology.

Academic Programs *Special study options:* academic remediation for entering students, adult/continuing education programs, external degree program, honors programs, internships, off-campus study, part-time degree program, summer session for credit. *ROTC:* Army (b), Navy (b), Air Force (b).

Library Elizabeth Dafoe Library plus 12 others with 1.6 million titles, 12,800 serial subscriptions.

Computers on Campus A campuswide network can be accessed from student residence rooms and from off campus.

Student Life *Housing Options:* coed. *Activities and Organizations:* drama/theater group, student-run newspaper, national fraternities. *Campus security:* 24-hour emergency response devices, student patrols, late-night transport/escort service. *Student Services:* health clinic, personal/psychological counseling, women's center.

Athletics Member CIAU. *Intercollegiate sports:* basketball M/W, cross-country running M/W, field hockey M/W, football M/W, gymnastics M/W, ice hockey M/W, swimming M/W, track and field M/W, volleyball M/W. *Intramural sports:* basketball M/W, cross-country running M/W, fencing M/W, field hockey M/W, football M/W, golf M/W, gymnastics M/W, ice hockey M/W, lacrosse M/W, skiing (cross-country) M/W, skiing (downhill) M/W, soccer M/W, squash M/W, swimming M/W, tennis M/W, track and field M/W, volleyball M/W, wrestling M/W.

Costs (2001–02) *Tuition:* nonresident $3000 Canadian dollars full-time, $100 Canadian dollars per credit hour part-time. Full-time tuition and fees vary according to degree level and program. Part-time tuition and fees vary according to degree level and program. *Room and board:* $5137 Canadian dollars. Room and board charges vary according to board plan, housing facility, and location. *Waivers:* senior citizens and employees or children of employees.

Financial Aid Available in 2001, 50 State and other part-time jobs (averaging $980).

Applying *Application fee:* $35. *Required:* high school transcript. *Application deadlines:* 7/1 (freshmen), 7/1 (transfers). *Notification:* continuous (freshmen).

Admissions Contact Mr. Peter Dueck, Director of Enrollment Services, University of Manitoba, Winnipeg, MB R3T 2N2, Canada. *Phone:* 204-474-6382.

UNIVERSITY OF NEW BRUNSWICK

Fredericton, New Brunswick, Canada

- **Province-supported** university, founded 1785
- **Calendar** Canadian standard year
- **Degrees** bachelor's, master's, and doctoral
- **Urban** 7100-acre campus
- **Coed**
- **Moderately difficult** entrance level

Faculty *Student/faculty ratio:* 15:1.

Student Life *Campus security:* late-night transport/escort service.

Athletics Member CIAU.

Standardized Tests *Required for some:* SAT I (for admission).

Applying *Options:* early admission, deferred entrance. *Application fee:* $35. *Required:* high school transcript. *Required for some:* essay or personal statement, 1 letter of recommendation, interview.

Admissions Contact Ms. Kathryn E. Monti, Assistant Registrar/Admissions, University of New Brunswick, PO Box 4400, Sir Howard Douglas Hall, Fredericton, NB E3B 5Z8, Canada. *Phone:* 506-453-4865. *Fax:* 506-453-5016. *E-mail:* unbfacts@unb.ca.

UNIVERSITY OF NEW BRUNSWICK

Saint John, New Brunswick, Canada

- **Province-supported** comprehensive, founded 1964
- **Calendar** Canadian standard year
- **Degrees** certificates, diplomas, bachelor's, master's, doctoral, and postbachelor's certificates
- **Urban** 250-acre campus
- **Coed**
- **Moderately difficult** entrance level

Faculty *Student/faculty ratio:* 10:1.

Student Life *Campus security:* 24-hour emergency response devices and patrols, student patrols, late-night transport/escort service, controlled dormitory access.

Standardized Tests *Required:* SAT I (for admission).

Financial Aid Of all full-time matriculated undergraduates who enrolled in 2001, 100 State and other part-time jobs (averaging $500).

Applying *Options:* electronic application, early admission, deferred entrance. *Application fee:* $35. *Required:* high school transcript. *Required for some:* letters of recommendation.

Admissions Contact Ms. Sue Ellis Loparco, Admissions Officer, University of New Brunswick, PO Box 5050, Tucker Park Road, Saint John, NB E2L 4L5. *Phone:* 506-648-5674. *Toll-free phone:* 800-743-4333 (in-state); 800-743-5691 (out-of-state). *Fax:* 506-648-5691. *E-mail:* apply@unbsj.ca.

UNIVERSITY OF NORTHERN BRITISH COLUMBIA

Prince George, British Columbia, Canada

Admissions Contact 3333 University Way, Prince George, BC V2N 4Z9, Canada.

UNIVERSITY OF OTTAWA
Ottawa, Ontario, Canada

- **Province-supported** university, founded 1848
- **Calendar** Canadian standard year
- **Degrees** bachelor's, master's, and doctoral
- **Urban** 70-acre campus
- **Coed,** 22,442 undergraduate students
- **Moderately difficult** entrance level

Undergraduates Students come from 12 provinces and territories.
Faculty *Total:* 1,431, 60% full-time.
Majors Accounting; advertising; applied art; applied mathematics; art; arts management; behavioral sciences; bilingual/bicultural education; biochemistry; biological/physical sciences; biological technology; biology; biomedical science; business administration; business economics; business marketing and marketing management; Canadian studies; chemical engineering; chemistry; civil engineering; classics; computer engineering; computer/information sciences; computer science; criminal justice/law enforcement administration; criminology; developmental/child psychology; dietetics; early childhood education; earth sciences; economics; education; electrical engineering; elementary education; engineering; engineering/industrial management; engineering science; English; environmental science; finance; fine/studio arts; French; geography; geology; geophysics/seismology; German; Hispanic-American studies; history; humanities; human resources management; information sciences/systems; interdisciplinary studies; international business; international relations; Italian; Latin (ancient and medieval); liberal arts and sciences/liberal studies; linguistics; literature; management information systems/business data processing; mass communications; mathematical statistics; mathematics; mechanical engineering; medieval/renaissance studies; microbiology/bacteriology; modern languages; music; music history; music teacher education; music (voice and choral/opera performance); natural sciences; nursing; nutrition science; occupational therapy; pastoral counseling; philosophy; photography; physical education; physical sciences; physical therapy; physics; physiology; political science; pre-law; pre-medicine; psychology; public administration; public policy analysis; public relations; recreation/leisure studies; rehabilitation therapy; religious studies; Russian; Russian/Slavic studies; secondary education; Slavic languages; social sciences; sociology; Spanish; special education; systems science/theory; teaching English as a second language; theater arts/drama; theology; women's studies.
Academic Programs *Special study options:* academic remediation for entering students, accelerated degree program, adult/continuing education programs, cooperative education, English as a second language, external degree program, honors programs, internships, off-campus study, part-time degree program, services for LD students, student-designed majors, study abroad, summer session for credit.
Library Morisset Library plus 5 others with 2.6 million titles, 9,183 serial subscriptions, an OPAC, a Web page.
Computers on Campus 1500 computers available on campus for general student use. A campuswide network can be accessed from student residence rooms and from off campus. At least one staffed computer lab available.
Student Life *Housing Options:* coed. *Activities and Organizations:* drama/theater group, student-run newspaper, radio station, choral group, Student Federation. *Campus security:* 24-hour emergency response devices and patrols, student patrols, late-night transport/escort service, controlled dormitory access. *Student Services:* health clinic, personal/psychological counseling, women's center, legal services.
Athletics Member CIAU. *Intercollegiate sports:* badminton M/W, basketball M/W, cross-country running M/W, fencing M/W, football M, ice hockey M, soccer W, swimming M/W, volleyball W. *Intramural sports:* badminton M/W, basketball M/W, fencing M/W, golf M/W, gymnastics M/W, ice hockey M/W, racquetball M/W, skiing (cross-country) M/W, skiing (downhill) M/W, soccer M/W, squash M/W, swimming M/W, table tennis M/W, volleyball M/W, water polo M/W, weight lifting M/W.
Standardized Tests *Required:* SAT I (for admission).
Costs (2002–03) *Tuition:* $158 Canadian dollars per credit part-time; International tuition $11,250 Canadian dollars full-time. Full-time tuition and fees vary according to program. Part-time tuition and fees vary according to program. *Required fees:* $344 Canadian dollars full-time.
Applying *Options:* early admission. *Application fee:* $95. *Required:* high school transcript, minimum 3.0 GPA. *Required for some:* interview. *Application deadline:* 4/30 (freshmen). *Notification:* continuous until 8/30 (freshmen).
Admissions Contact Mr. André Pierre Lepage, Director of Admissions, University of Ottawa, PO Box 450, Station A, Ottawa, ON K1N 6N5, Canada. *Phone:* 613-562-5800 Ext. 1593. *E-mail:* liaison@uottawa.ca.

UNIVERSITY OF PHOENIX-VANCOUVER CAMPUS
Burnaby, British Columbia, Canada

- **Proprietary** comprehensive
- **Calendar** continuous
- **Degrees** certificates, associate, bachelor's, master's, doctoral, post-master's, and postbachelor's certificates (courses conducted at 54 campuses and learning centers in 13 states)
- **Coed,** 114 undergraduate students, 100% full-time, 41% women, 59% men
- **Noncompetitive** entrance level

Undergraduates Students come from 1 other province, 1 other country, 5% are from out of province.
Freshmen *Admission:* 5 admitted.
Faculty *Total:* 85, 1% full-time, 12% with terminal degrees. *Student/faculty ratio:* 13:1.
Majors Computer/information sciences; management information systems/business data processing.
Academic Programs *Special study options:* accelerated degree program, adult/continuing education programs, advanced placement credit, distance learning, external degree program, independent study.
Library University Library with 17.5 million titles, 9,000 serial subscriptions, an OPAC, a Web page.
Computers on Campus A campuswide network can be accessed from off campus. Internet access, at least one staffed computer lab available.
Student Life *Housing:* college housing not available.
Costs (2001–02) *Tuition:* $7500 full-time. Full-time tuition and fees vary according to location and program. *Payment plan:* deferred payment. *Waivers:* employees or children of employees.
Applying *Options:* deferred entrance. *Application fee:* $85. *Required:* 2 years of work experience. *Required for some:* high school transcript. *Application deadline:* rolling (freshmen), rolling (transfers).
Admissions Contact Ms. Beth Barilla, Director of Admissions, University of Phoenix-Vancouver Campus, 4615 East Elwood Street, Phoenix, AZ 85040-1958. *Phone:* 480-927-0099 Ext. 1218. *Fax:* 480-594-1758. *E-mail:* beth.barilla@apollogrp.edu.

UNIVERSITY OF PRINCE EDWARD ISLAND
Charlottetown, Prince Edward Island, Canada

- **Province-supported** comprehensive, founded 1834
- **Calendar** Canadian standard year
- **Degrees** certificates, diplomas, bachelor's, master's, doctoral, and first professional
- **Small-town** 130-acre campus
- **Coed,** 3,019 undergraduate students, 83% full-time, 65% women, 35% men
- **Moderately difficult** entrance level, 63% of applicants were admitted

Undergraduates Students come from 8 provinces and territories, 6 other countries, 14% live on campus. *Retention:* 69% of 2001 full-time freshmen returned.
Freshmen *Admission:* 1,575 applied, 997 admitted.
Faculty *Total:* 177.
Majors Anthropology; biology; business administration; Canadian studies; chemistry; computer science; economics; education; elementary education; English; family/consumer studies; French; German; history; hospitality management; mathematics; medical radiologic technology; music; music teacher education; nursing; nutrition science; philosophy; physics; political science; pre-dentistry; pre-medicine; pre-veterinary studies; psychology; religious studies; secondary education; sociology; Spanish.
Academic Programs *Special study options:* distance learning, double majors, English as a second language, honors programs, part-time degree program, summer session for credit.
Library Robertson Library with 394,000 titles, 1,700 serial subscriptions, an OPAC, a Web page.
Computers on Campus 120 computers available on campus for general student use. A campuswide network can be accessed from student residence rooms and from off campus. Internet access, at least one staffed computer lab available.
Student Life *Housing Options:* coed. *Activities and Organizations:* drama/theater group, student-run newspaper, choral group, Business Society, Biology Club, Music Society, Intramurals, Theatre Society. *Campus security:* 24-hour emergency response devices and patrols, late-night transport/escort service, controlled dormitory access, late night residence hall security personnel. *Student Services:* health clinic, personal/psychological counseling, women's center.

University of Prince Edward Island (continued)

Athletics Member CIAU. *Intercollegiate sports:* basketball M/W, field hockey W, ice hockey M, soccer M/W, volleyball W. *Intramural sports:* badminton M/W, basketball M/W, fencing M(c)/W(c), ice hockey M, racquetball M(c)/W(c), rugby M(c)/W(c), skiing (cross-country) M(c)/W(c), skiing (downhill) M(c)/W(c), soccer M, squash M(c)/W(c), tennis M(c)/W(c), volleyball M/W, weight lifting M(c)/W(c).

Costs (2001–02) *Tuition:* province resident $8044 Canadian dollars full-time; International tuition $14,014 Canadian dollars full-time.

Applying *Options:* common application, early admission. *Application fee:* $35. *Required:* high school transcript, minimum 2.0 GPA. *Required for some:* 3 letters of recommendation. *Application deadlines:* 8/15 (freshmen), 4/1 (out-of-state freshmen), 8/15 (transfers). *Notification:* continuous until 8/31 (freshmen), continuous until 6/30 (out-of-state freshmen).

Admissions Contact Mr. Paul Cantilo, Liaison Officer, University of Prince Edward Island, Registrar's Office, Charlottetown, PE C1A 4D3, Canada. *Phone:* 902-628-4353. *Fax:* 902-566-0795. *E-mail:* registrar@upei.ca.

UNIVERSITY OF REGINA
Regina, Saskatchewan, Canada

- **Province-supported** university, founded 1974
- **Calendar** semesters
- **Degrees** certificates, bachelor's, master's, and doctoral
- **Urban** 330-acre campus
- **Endowment** $62.8 million
- **Coed,** 10,818 undergraduate students
- **Minimally difficult** entrance level

Undergraduates Students come from 12 provinces and territories, 57 other countries.

Freshmen *Admission:* 4,446 admitted.

Faculty *Total:* 654, 59% full-time, 45% with terminal degrees. *Student/faculty ratio:* 26:1.

Majors Accounting; adult/continuing education; anthropology; art; art education; art history; bilingual/bicultural education; biochemistry; biological/physical sciences; biology; business administration; business education; business marketing and marketing management; Canadian studies; chemistry; classics; computer science; criminal justice/law enforcement administration; criminal justice studies; early childhood education; economics; education; electrical/electronic engineering technology; electrical engineering; elementary education; engineering; English; environmental biology; environmental engineering; exercise sciences; film studies; film/video production; finance; geography; geology; German; health education; history; history of philosophy; humanities; industrial/manufacturing engineering; journalism; law enforcement/police science; liberal arts and sciences/liberal studies; linguistics; mathematical statistics; mathematics; middle school education; music; music teacher education; Native American studies; petroleum engineering; philosophy; physical education; physics; political science; pre-dentistry; pre-law; pre-medicine; pre-veterinary studies; psychology; public administration; religious studies; science education; secondary education; social sciences; social work; sociology; sport/fitness administration; systems engineering; theater arts/drama; trade/industrial education; women's studies.

Academic Programs *Special study options:* academic remediation for entering students, adult/continuing education programs, advanced placement credit, cooperative education, English as a second language, honors programs, internships, off-campus study, part-time degree program, services for LD students, student-designed majors, summer session for credit.

Library Dr. John Archer Library plus 6 others with 2.3 million titles.

Computers on Campus 150 computers available on campus for general student use. A campuswide network can be accessed from student residence rooms and from off campus. Internet access, at least one staffed computer lab available.

Student Life *Housing Options:* coed. *Activities and Organizations:* drama/theater group, student-run newspaper, choral group, Administration Students' Society, Education Students' Society, Engineering Students Society, Amnesty International, Plumb Flower Society. *Campus security:* 24-hour emergency response devices, student patrols, late-night transport/escort service, controlled dormitory access. *Student Services:* health clinic, personal/psychological counseling, women's center.

Athletics *Intercollegiate sports:* basketball M(s)/W(s), football M(s), ice hockey M(s)/W(s), soccer W, swimming M/W, track and field M/W, volleyball M/W, wrestling M(s)/W(s). *Intramural sports:* badminton M/W, basketball M/W, ice hockey M/W, soccer M/W, softball M/W, volleyball M/W, water polo M/W.

Costs (2001–02) *Tuition:* nonresident $3300 Canadian dollars full-time, $110 Canadian dollars per credit hour part-time; International tuition $6600 Canadian dollars full-time. Full-time tuition and fees vary according to course load. Part-time tuition and fees vary according to course load. *Required fees:* $275 Canadian dollars full-time, $2 Canadian dollars per credit hour, $54 Canadian dollars per term part-time. *Room and board:* $5000 Canadian dollars; room only: $2800 Canadian dollars. Room and board charges vary according to board plan and housing facility. *Waivers:* senior citizens and employees or children of employees.

Applying *Options:* early admission, deferred entrance. *Application fee:* $60. *Required:* high school transcript, minimum 2.5 GPA. *Required for some:* essay or personal statement, letters of recommendation, interview. *Application deadlines:* 7/1 (freshmen), 4/1 (out-of-state freshmen), 7/1 (transfers).

Admissions Contact Mr. Clarence Gray, Assistant Registrar/Admissions and Awards, University of Regina, Regina, SK S4S 0A2, Canada. *Phone:* 306-585-4591. *E-mail:* admissions.office@uregina.ca.

UNIVERSITY OF SASKATCHEWAN
Saskatoon, Saskatchewan, Canada

- **Province-supported** university, founded 1907
- **Calendar** Canadian standard year
- **Degrees** diplomas, bachelor's, master's, doctoral, and first professional
- **Urban** 363-acre campus
- **Endowment** $36.7 million
- **Coed,** 17,715 undergraduate students
- **Moderately difficult** entrance level, 66% of applicants were admitted

Undergraduates Students come from 67 other countries, 4% are from out of province.

Freshmen *Admission:* 8,816 applied, 5,815 admitted. *Average high school GPA:* 3.26.

Faculty *Total:* 934, 100% full-time.

Majors Accounting; agricultural economics; agricultural engineering; agricultural sciences; agronomy/crop science; American studies; anatomy; animal sciences; anthropology; archaeology; art history; biochemistry; biology; business; business economics; business marketing and marketing management; chemical engineering; chemistry; civil engineering; classics; computer science; economics; education; electrical engineering; elementary education; engineering physics; English; environmental science; finance; fine/studio arts; food sciences; French; geography; geological engineering; geology; geophysical engineering; geophysics/seismology; German; Greek (modern); health services administration; history; home economics education; horticulture science; human resources management; information sciences/systems; international relations; land use management; Latin (ancient and medieval); linguistics; mathematical statistics; mathematics; mechanical engineering; microbiology/bacteriology; music; music teacher education; Native American studies; nursing; nursing administration; nutritional sciences; operations management; pharmacy; philosophy; physical education; physical therapy; physics; physiology; plant sciences; political science; pre-dentistry; pre-law; pre-medicine; pre-pharmacy studies; pre-veterinary studies; psychology; public administration; range management; recreation/leisure studies; religious studies; Russian; secondary education; Slavic languages; sociology; soil sciences; Spanish; technical education; theater arts/drama; theoretical/mathematical physics; trade/industrial education; urban studies; women's studies.

Academic Programs *Special study options:* academic remediation for entering students, accelerated degree program, adult/continuing education programs, advanced placement credit, cooperative education, distance learning, double majors, English as a second language, honors programs, independent study, internships, off-campus study, part-time degree program, services for LD students, study abroad, summer session for credit.

Library University of Saskatchewan Main Library plus 7 others with 1.7 million titles, 14,170 serial subscriptions, an OPAC, a Web page.

Computers on Campus 900 computers available on campus for general student use. A campuswide network can be accessed from off campus. Internet access, at least one staffed computer lab available.

Student Life *Housing Options:* coed, men-only, women-only. *Activities and Organizations:* drama/theater group, student-run newspaper, choral group, Ballroom Dancing Club, Ski Club, AIESEC. *Campus security:* 24-hour patrols, late-night transport/escort service. *Student Services:* health clinic, personal/psychological counseling, women's center.

Athletics Member CIAU. *Intercollegiate sports:* basketball M/W, cross-country running M/W, football M, gymnastics M(c), ice hockey M/W, soccer M/W, track and field M/W, volleyball M/W, wrestling M/W(c). *Intramural sports:* badminton M/W, baseball M/W, basketball M/W, bowling M/W, crew M(c)/W(c), cross-country running M/W, football M/W, golf M/W, gymnastics M/W, ice hockey M/W, racquetball M/W, skiing (downhill) M/W, soccer M/W, softball M/W, squash M/W, swimming M/W, tennis M/W, volleyball M/W, water polo M/W, weight lifting M/W.

Costs (2001–02) *Tuition:* area resident $4610 Canadian dollars full-time; International tuition $9911 Canadian dollars full-time. *Required fees:* $307 Canadian dollars full-time. *Room and board:* $4600 Canadian dollars.
Financial Aid *Financial aid deadline:* 4/1.
Applying *Options:* electronic application, early admission. *Application fee:* $50. *Required:* high school transcript. *Required for some:* essay or personal statement, interview. *Application deadlines:* 5/15 (freshmen), 5/15 (transfers). *Notification:* continuous (freshmen).
Admissions Contact Ms. Emily B. Farnham, Director of Admissions, Office of the Registrar, University of Saskatchewan, Office of the Registrar, Saskatoon, SK S7N 5A2. *Phone:* 306-966-6749. *Fax:* 306-966-6730. *E-mail:* admissions@usask.ca.

UNIVERSITY OF TORONTO
Toronto, Ontario, Canada

- **Province-supported** university, founded 1827
- **Calendar** Canadian standard year
- **Degrees** certificates, diplomas, bachelor's, master's, doctoral, and first professional
- **Urban** 900-acre campus
- **Endowment** $1.0 billion
- **Coed,** 32,984 undergraduate students, 73% full-time, 59% women, 41% men
- **Very difficult** entrance level

Undergraduates 24,114 full-time, 8,870 part-time. Students come from 12 provinces and territories, 126 other countries, 3% are from out of province. *Retention:* 94% of 2001 full-time freshmen returned.
Freshmen *Admission:* 10,029 enrolled.
Faculty *Total:* 2,937, 90% full-time. *Student/faculty ratio:* 15:1.
Majors Actuarial science; aerospace engineering; African studies; American studies; anatomy; anthropology; applied mathematics; Arabic; archaeology; architecture; art; art education; art history; arts management; Asian studies; astronomy; biblical languages/literatures; biochemistry; bioengineering; biological/physical sciences; biology; biophysics; botany; business administration; Canadian studies; chemical engineering; chemistry; Chinese; civil engineering; classics; computer engineering; computer science; counselor education/guidance; cultural studies; earth sciences; East Asian studies; Eastern European area studies; ecology; economics; education; electrical engineering; engineering; engineering physics; engineering science; English; environmental science; European studies; film studies; finance; fine/studio arts; forestry; French; genetics; geography; geological engineering; geology; geophysical engineering; geophysics/seismology; German; Greek (modern); health education; Hebrew; Hispanic-American studies; history; history of philosophy; history of science and technology; humanities; industrial/manufacturing engineering; international relations; Islamic studies; Italian; Japanese; Judaic studies; labor/personnel relations; landscape architecture; Latin American studies; Latin (ancient and medieval); law enforcement/police science; linguistics; literature; mass communications; materials engineering; materials science; mathematical statistics; mathematics; mechanical engineering; medical illustrating; medieval/renaissance studies; metallurgical engineering; metallurgy; microbiology/bacteriology; Middle Eastern studies; modern languages; molecular biology; music; music history; music teacher education; Native American studies; neuroscience; nuclear engineering; nursing; nutrition science; occupational therapy; paleontology; petroleum engineering; pharmacology; pharmacy; philosophy; physical education; physical therapy; physics; physiology; plastics engineering; political science; Portuguese; pre-dentistry; pre-law; pre-medicine; psychology; public administration; rehabilitation therapy; religious studies; romance languages; Russian; Russian/Slavic studies; Slavic languages; sociology; South Asian studies; Spanish; surveying; theater arts/drama; theology; toxicology; urban studies; women's studies; wood science/paper technology; zoology.
Academic Programs *Special study options:* adult/continuing education programs, cooperative education, double majors, English as a second language, off-campus study, part-time degree program, services for LD students, study abroad, summer session for credit.
Library Robart's Library plus 31 others with 8.9 million titles, 51,248 serial subscriptions, 901,452 audiovisual materials, an OPAC, a Web page.
Computers on Campus 2000 computers available on campus for general student use. A campuswide network can be accessed from student residence rooms and from off campus. Internet access, at least one staffed computer lab available.
Student Life *Housing Options:* coed. *Activities and Organizations:* drama/theater group, student-run newspaper, radio station, choral group, national fraternities, national sororities. *Campus security:* 24-hour emergency response devices and patrols, student patrols, late-night transport/escort service. *Student Services:* health clinic, personal/psychological counseling, women's center, legal services.
Athletics Member CIAU. *Intercollegiate sports:* archery M/W, badminton M/W, basketball M/W, crew M, cross-country running M/W, fencing M/W, field hockey W, football M, golf M, gymnastics M/W, ice hockey M/W, rugby M, skiing (cross-country) M/W, skiing (downhill) M/W, soccer M/W, squash M/W, swimming M/W, tennis M/W, track and field M/W, volleyball M/W, wrestling M. *Intramural sports:* archery M/W, badminton M/W, basketball M/W, crew M, fencing M/W, field hockey W, football M/W, gymnastics M/W, ice hockey M/W, lacrosse M/W, racquetball M, rugby M, skiing (downhill) M/W, soccer M/W, squash M/W, swimming M/W, tennis M/W, track and field M/W, volleyball M/W, water polo M/W.
Standardized Tests *Required for some:* SAT I (for admission), SAT II: Subject Tests (for admission).
Costs (2001–02) *Tuition:* nonresident $2512 full-time, $500 per course part-time; International tuition $5507 full-time. Full-time tuition and fees vary according to program. Part-time tuition and fees vary according to program. *Required fees:* $437 full-time, $145 per term part-time. *Room and board:* $4364; room only: $2500. *Payment plan:* installment. *Waivers:* senior citizens and employees or children of employees.
Applying *Options:* deferred entrance. *Required:* high school transcript. *Required for some:* interview. *Application deadlines:* 7/1 (freshmen), 7/1 (transfers). *Notification:* continuous (freshmen).
Admissions Contact Admissions and Awards, University of Toronto, Toronto, ON M5S 1A1, Canada. *Phone:* 416-978-2190. *E-mail:* ask@adm.utoronto.ca.

UNIVERSITY OF VICTORIA
Victoria, British Columbia, Canada

- **Province-supported** university, founded 1963
- **Calendar** Canadian standard year
- **Degrees** certificates, diplomas, bachelor's, master's, doctoral, and first professional
- **Suburban** 380-acre campus with easy access to Vancouver
- **Coed,** 16,073 undergraduate students, 62% full-time, 59% women, 41% men
- **Moderately difficult** entrance level, 62% of applicants were admitted

Undergraduates 9,894 full-time, 6,179 part-time. Students come from 11 provinces and territories, 93 other countries, 13% are from out of province, 6% transferred in, 12% live on campus.
Freshmen *Admission:* 7,044 applied, 4,402 admitted, 3,572 enrolled. *Average high school GPA:* 3.69.
Faculty *Total:* 623, 94% full-time. *Student/faculty ratio:* 27:1.
Majors Anthropology; art education; art history; Asian studies; astronomy; atmospheric sciences; biochemistry; biology; botany; business; chemistry; child care/development; Chinese; classics; computer engineering; computer science; creative writing; early childhood education; earth sciences; Eastern European area studies; ecology; economics; education; electrical engineering; elementary education; English; environmental science; exercise sciences; fine/studio arts; French; geography; geology; geophysics/seismology; German; Greek (ancient and medieval); health services administration; history; hotel and restaurant management; international business; Italian; Japanese; Latin (ancient and medieval); liberal arts and sciences/liberal studies; linguistics; literature; marine biology; mathematical statistics; mathematics; mechanical engineering; medieval/renaissance studies; microbiology/bacteriology; modern languages; music; music history; music (piano and organ performance); music teacher education; music theory and composition; music (voice and choral/opera performance); nursing science; oceanography; philosophy; physical education; physics; political science; pre-dentistry; pre-law; pre-medicine; pre-veterinary studies; psychology; public administration; romance languages; Russian; Russian/Slavic studies; secondary education; Slavic languages; social work; sociology; Spanish; special education; sport/fitness administration; teaching English as a second language; technical/business writing; theater arts/drama; women's studies; zoology.
Academic Programs *Special study options:* academic remediation for entering students, adult/continuing education programs, advanced placement credit, cooperative education, distance learning, double majors, English as a second language, honors programs, independent study, internships, off-campus study, part-time degree program, services for LD students, study abroad, summer session for credit.
Library McPherson Library plus 2 others with 1.6 million titles, 12,000 serial subscriptions, an OPAC, a Web page.
Computers on Campus 400 computers available on campus for general student use. A campuswide network can be accessed from student residence rooms and from off campus. Internet access, at least one staffed computer lab available.
Student Life *Housing Options:* coed. *Activities and Organizations:* drama/theater group, student-run newspaper, radio station, choral group. *Campus secu-*

University of Victoria (continued)
rity: 24-hour emergency response devices and patrols, student patrols, late-night transport/escort service. *Student Services:* health clinic, personal/psychological counseling, women's center, legal services.

Athletics Member CIAU. *Intercollegiate sports:* basketball M/W, crew M/W, cross-country running M/W, field hockey W, rugby M/W, soccer M/W, swimming M/W, track and field M/W, volleyball M/W. *Intramural sports:* basketball M/W, cross-country running M/W, fencing M/W, field hockey M/W, football M/W, golf M/W, ice hockey M/W, racquetball M/W, rugby M/W, sailing M/W, skiing (downhill) M/W, soccer M/W, softball M/W, squash M/W, swimming M/W, table tennis M/W, tennis M/W, volleyball M/W, water polo M/W, weight lifting M/W.

Costs (2001–02) *Tuition:* province resident $1435 full-time, $38 per credit part-time; nonresident $1435 full-time, $38 per credit part-time; International tuition $4472 full-time. *Required fees:* $738 full-time. *Room and board:* $3811.

Applying *Options:* electronic application, early admission, early action, deferred entrance. *Application fee:* $65 (non-residents). *Required:* high school transcript, minimum 2.5 GPA. *Required for some:* essay or personal statement, minimum 3.0 GPA, interview, audition, portfolio. *Application deadlines:* 4/30 (freshmen), 4/30 (transfers). *Notification:* continuous (freshmen), 5/1 (early action).

Admissions Contact Mr. Bruno Rocca, Admission Services Office, University of Victoria, PO Box 3025, Victoria, BC V8W 3P2. *Phone:* 250-721-8121 Ext. 8109. *Fax:* 250-721-6225. *E-mail:* srsad13@uvvm.uvic.ca.

UNIVERSITY OF WATERLOO
Waterloo, Ontario, Canada

- **Province-supported** university, founded 1957
- **Calendar** trimesters
- **Degrees** certificates, diplomas, bachelor's, master's, doctoral, and first professional
- **Suburban** 900-acre campus with easy access to Toronto
- **Coed,** 20,064 undergraduate students, 87% full-time, 48% women, 52% men
- **Moderately difficult** entrance level, 61% of applicants were admitted

Undergraduates Students come from 12 provinces and territories, 73 other countries, 1% are from out of province, 39% live on campus. *Retention:* 85% of 2001 full-time freshmen returned.

Freshmen *Admission:* 23,557 applied, 14,437 admitted. *Average high school GPA:* 3.50.

Faculty *Total:* 1,417, 54% full-time. *Student/faculty ratio:* 15:1.

Majors Accounting; actuarial science; anthropology; applied mathematics; architecture; art history; arts management; biochemistry; biological/physical sciences; biology; biology education; biotechnology research; business administration; business administration/management related; Canadian studies; chemical and atomic/molecular physics; chemical engineering; chemistry; chemistry education; city/community/regional planning; civil engineering; classics; computer engineering; computer science; computer software engineering; earth sciences; economics; electrical engineering; engineering; English; environmental engineering; environmental science; exercise sciences; film studies; fine/studio arts; French; French language education; geochemistry; geography; geological engineering; geology; German; health science; history; human resources management; interdisciplinary studies; international relations; liberal arts and sciences/liberal studies; mathematical statistics; mathematics; mathematics/computer science; mathematics education; mechanical engineering; medieval/renaissance studies; music; operations research; ophthalmic/optometric services; philosophy; physics; physics education; political science; psychology; recreation/leisure studies; religious studies; Russian; Russian/Slavic studies; social work; sociology; Spanish; speech/rhetorical studies; systems engineering; theater arts/drama; women's studies.

Academic Programs *Special study options:* academic remediation for entering students, accelerated degree program, adult/continuing education programs, cooperative education, distance learning, double majors, external degree program, honors programs, independent study, internships, off-campus study, part-time degree program, services for LD students, student-designed majors, study abroad, summer session for credit.

Library Dana Porter Library plus 7 others with 2.9 million titles, 13,228 serial subscriptions, an OPAC, a Web page.

Computers on Campus 6000 computers available on campus for general student use. A campuswide network can be accessed from student residence rooms and from off campus that provide access to e-mail. Internet access, at least one staffed computer lab available.

Student Life *Housing Options:* coed. *Activities and Organizations:* drama/theater group, student-run newspaper, radio station, choral group, Chinese Students Association, South Asian Students Association, Entrepreneurs Association of UW, national fraternities, national sororities. *Campus security:* 24-hour emergency response devices and patrols, student patrols, late-night transport/escort service. *Student Services:* health clinic, personal/psychological counseling, women's center, legal services.

Athletics Member CIAU. *Intercollegiate sports:* badminton M/W, baseball M, basketball M/W, cross-country running M/W, field hockey W, football M, golf M, ice hockey M/W, rugby M/W, skiing (downhill) M/W, soccer M/W, squash M, swimming M/W, tennis M/W, track and field M/W, volleyball M/W. *Intramural sports:* archery M(c)/W(c), badminton M(c)/W(c), basketball M/W, crew M(c)/W(c), fencing M(c)/W(c), golf M(c)/W(c), ice hockey M/W, racquetball M(c)/W(c), skiing (cross-country) M(c)/W(c), skiing (downhill) M(c)/W(c), soccer M/W, squash M(c)/W(c), table tennis M(c)/W, volleyball M/W, water polo M/W, weight lifting M/W.

Standardized Tests *Required for some:* SAT I or ACT (for admission), SAT II: Subject Tests (for admission).

Costs (2001–02) *Tuition:* nonresident $4030 Canadian dollars full-time, $453 Canadian dollars per course part-time; International tuition $12,666 Canadian dollars full-time. Full-time tuition and fees vary according to program. Part-time tuition and fees vary according to program. *Required fees:* $515 Canadian dollars full-time. *Room and board:* $5950 Canadian dollars. Room and board charges vary according to board plan and housing facility. *Waivers:* senior citizens and employees or children of employees.

Financial Aid Available in 2001, 450 State and other part-time jobs (averaging $1000).

Applying *Options:* electronic application, early admission. *Application fee:* $95. *Required:* high school transcript. *Required for some:* essay or personal statement, minimum 3.0 GPA, letters of recommendation, interview. *Notification:* continuous until 7/30 (freshmen).

Admissions Contact Mr. P. Burroughs, Director of Admissions, University of Waterloo, 200 University Avenue West, Waterloo, ON N2L 3G1, Canada. *Phone:* 519-888-4567 Ext. 2265. *Fax:* 519-746-8088 Ext. 3614. *E-mail:* watquest@uwaterloo.ca.

THE UNIVERSITY OF WESTERN ONTARIO
London, Ontario, Canada

- **Province-supported** university, founded 1878
- **Calendar** Canadian standard year
- **Degrees** certificates, diplomas, bachelor's, master's, doctoral, and first professional
- **Suburban** 420-acre campus
- **Coed,** 20,548 undergraduate students, 84% full-time, 54% women, 46% men
- **Very difficult** entrance level, 17% of applicants were admitted

Undergraduates Students come from 12 provinces and territories, 13% live on campus. *Retention:* 93% of 2001 full-time freshmen returned.

Freshmen *Admission:* 25,776 applied, 4,397 admitted.

Faculty *Total:* 1,204, 100% full-time. *Student/faculty ratio:* 18:1.

Majors Actuarial science; anthropology; applied mathematics; art; art education; art history; astronomy; biochemistry; biological/physical sciences; biology; biophysics; business administration; business education; cell biology; chemical engineering; chemistry; city/community/regional planning; civil engineering; classics; clothing/textiles; computer/information sciences; computer science; computer software engineering; dietetics; early childhood education; earth sciences; ecology; economics; education; electrical engineering; elementary education; English; environmental science; film studies; fine/studio arts; French; genetics; geography; geology; geophysics/seismology; German; Greek (ancient and medieval); health science; history; home economics; journalism and mass communication related; Latin (ancient and medieval); linguistics; materials engineering; mathematical statistics; mathematics; mechanical engineering; microbiology/bacteriology; music; music history; music (piano and organ performance); music teacher education; music (voice and choral/opera performance); natural resources management; nursing; nursing administration; nutrition science; occupational therapy; pharmacology; philosophy; physical education; physical therapy; physics; physiology; plant sciences; political science; psychology; public administration; religious studies; Russian; secondary education; social work; sociology; Spanish; special education; stringed instruments; toxicology; urban studies; western civilization; wind/percussion instruments; women's studies; zoology.

Academic Programs *Special study options:* academic remediation for entering students, adult/continuing education programs, cooperative education, distance learning, double majors, honors programs, internships, off-campus study, part-time degree program, services for LD students, student-designed majors, study abroad, summer session for credit.

Library The University of Western Ontario Library System plus 7 others with 2.5 million titles, 12,558 serial subscriptions, 1.3 million audiovisual materials, an OPAC.

Computers on Campus 100 computers available on campus for general student use. A campuswide network can be accessed from student residence rooms and from off campus. Internet access, online (class) registration, at least one staffed computer lab available.

Student Life *Housing Options:* coed. *Activities and Organizations:* drama/theater group, student-run newspaper, radio station, choral group, marching band, national fraternities, national sororities. *Campus security:* 24-hour emergency response devices and patrols, student patrols, late-night transport/escort service. *Student Services:* health clinic, personal/psychological counseling, women's center, legal services.

Athletics Member CIAU. *Intercollegiate sports:* badminton M/W, basketball M/W, crew M/W, cross-country running M/W, fencing M/W, field hockey W, football M, golf M, ice hockey M, rugby M/W, skiing (cross-country) M/W, soccer M/W, squash M/W, swimming M/W, tennis M/W, track and field M/W, volleyball M/W, water polo M, wrestling M. *Intramural sports:* badminton M/W, basketball M/W, equestrian sports M(c)/W(c), fencing M(c)/W(c), football M, ice hockey M/W, racquetball M/W, riflery M(c)/W(c), rugby W, skiing (cross-country) M(c)/W(c), skiing (downhill) M(c)/W(c), soccer M/W, softball M/W, squash M(c)/W(c), swimming M(c)/W(c), table tennis M(c)/W(c), tennis M/W, volleyball M/W, water polo M/W.

Standardized Tests *Required for some:* SAT I (for admission).

Costs (2001–02) *Tuition:* nonresident $4000 Canadian dollars full-time, $800 Canadian dollars per course part-time; International tuition $9300 Canadian dollars full-time. Full-time tuition and fees vary according to program. Part-time tuition and fees vary according to program. *Required fees:* $845 Canadian dollars full-time, $120 Canadian dollars per course. *Room and board:* $5600 Canadian dollars. Room and board charges vary according to board plan and housing facility. *Payment plans:* installment, deferred payment. *Waivers:* children of alumni, senior citizens, and employees or children of employees.

Applying *Options:* deferred entrance. *Application fee:* $85. *Required:* high school transcript, minimum 3.0 GPA. *Application deadlines:* 6/1 (freshmen), 5/15 (out-of-state freshmen), 6/1 (transfers).

Admissions Contact Ms. Lori Gribbon, Manager, Admissions, The University of Western Ontario, London, ON N6A 5B8, Canada. *Phone:* 519-661-2116. *Fax:* 519-661-3710. *E-mail:* reg-admissions@uwo.ca.

UNIVERSITY OF WINDSOR
Windsor, Ontario, Canada

- **Province-supported** university, founded 1857
- **Calendar** semesters
- **Degrees** certificates, bachelor's, master's, doctoral, and first professional
- **Urban** 125-acre campus with easy access to Detroit
- **Endowment** $14.6 million
- **Coed,** 11,404 undergraduate students, 74% full-time, 53% women, 47% men
- **Moderately difficult** entrance level, 87% of applicants were admitted

Undergraduates 8,448 full-time, 2,956 part-time. Students come from 24 provinces and territories, 75 other countries, 7% transferred in, 16% live on campus. *Retention:* 76% of 2001 full-time freshmen returned.

Freshmen *Admission:* 12,874 applied, 11,206 admitted, 3,080 enrolled. *Average high school GPA:* 3.40.

Faculty *Total:* 596, 71% full-time. *Student/faculty ratio:* 24:1.

Majors Accounting; acting/directing; anthropology; applied mathematics; art; art education; art history; arts management; athletic training/sports medicine; automotive engineering technology; biochemical technology; biochemistry; biological/physical sciences; biological technology; biology; biology education; biophysics; biopsychology; biotechnology research; broadcast journalism; business administration; business computer programming; business economics; business marketing and marketing management; chemistry; chemistry education; city/community/regional planning; civil engineering; classics; clinical psychology; communications; communications technologies related; comparative literature; computer engineering; computer science; computer software and media applications related; counselor education/guidance; creative writing; criminal justice studies; criminology; development economics; drama/dance education; drawing; early childhood education; earth sciences; economics; education; education administration; education (K-12); electrical engineering; elementary education; engineering; engineering mechanics; English; English education; environmental biology; environmental engineering; environmental science; exercise sciences; family/consumer studies; film studies; finance; fine/studio arts; French; French language education; general studies; geology; German; German language education; gerontology; Greek (modern); health/physical education; Hispanic-American studies; history; history education; humanities; human resources management; industrial/manufacturing engineering; information sciences/systems; international relations; Italian; Italian studies; Japanese; journalism; labor/personnel relations; Latin (ancient and medieval); legal studies; linguistics; literature; management science; marketing research; mass communications; materials engineering; mathematical statistics; mathematics; mathematics/computer science; mathematics education; mechanical engineering; medical laboratory technology; microbiology/bacteriology; modern languages; multimedia; music; music (general performance); music history; music teacher education; music theory and composition; music therapy; natural resources management; neuroscience; nursing; nursing administration; painting; philosophy; physical education; physics; physics education; political science; pre-dentistry; pre-law; pre-medicine; pre-pharmacy studies; psychology; radio/television broadcasting; recreation/leisure studies; romance languages; Russian; science education; science/technology and society; sculpture; secondary education; Slavic languages; social sciences; social work; sociology; Spanish; special education; speech/theater education; sport/fitness administration; theater arts/drama; visual/performing arts; women's studies.

Academic Programs *Special study options:* academic remediation for entering students, accelerated degree program, adult/continuing education programs, advanced placement credit, cooperative education, distance learning, double majors, external degree program, honors programs, internships, off-campus study, part-time degree program, services for LD students, student-designed majors, study abroad, summer session for credit.

Library Leddy Library plus 2 others with 2.4 million titles, 9,104 serial subscriptions, 1,920 audiovisual materials, an OPAC, a Web page.

Computers on Campus 700 computers available on campus for general student use. A campuswide network can be accessed from student residence rooms and from off campus that provide access to online transcripts, degree audits, grades. Internet access, online (class) registration, at least one staffed computer lab available.

Student Life *Housing Options:* coed. *Activities and Organizations:* drama/theater group, student-run newspaper, radio station, choral group, University of Windsor Student Alliance, Environmental Awareness Association, Social Science Society, Commerce Society, Science Society. *Campus security:* 24-hour emergency response devices and patrols, student patrols, late-night transport/escort service, controlled dormitory access. *Student Services:* health clinic, personal/psychological counseling, women's center, legal services.

Athletics Member CIAU. *Intercollegiate sports:* basketball M/W, cross-country running M/W, football M, golf M, ice hockey M/W, rugby M/W, soccer M/W, track and field M/W, volleyball M/W. *Intramural sports:* badminton M/W, baseball M/W, basketball M/W, bowling M/W, football M/W, golf M/W, ice hockey M/W, rugby M/W, soccer M/W, softball M/W, swimming M/W, table tennis M/W, tennis M/W, track and field M/W, volleyball M/W, water polo M/W, weight lifting M/W.

Standardized Tests *Required for some:* SAT I (for admission), SAT I and SAT II or ACT (for admission).

Costs (2001–02) *Tuition:* nonresident $4896 Canadian dollars full-time, $393 Canadian dollars per course part-time; International tuition $11,250 Canadian dollars full-time. Full-time tuition and fees vary according to program. Part-time tuition and fees vary according to program. *Required fees:* $613 Canadian dollars full-time, $10 Canadian dollars per course, $51 Canadian dollars per term part-time. *Room and board:* $6673 Canadian dollars. Room and board charges vary according to board plan and housing facility. *Payment plan:* installment. *Waivers:* senior citizens and employees or children of employees.

Applying *Options:* common application, electronic application, early admission. *Application fee:* $30. *Required:* high school transcript, minimum 2.3 GPA. *Required for some:* essay or personal statement, minimum 3.3 GPA, 1 letter of recommendation, interview. *Recommended:* minimum 2.7 GPA. *Application deadlines:* rolling (freshmen), 7/1 (out-of-state freshmen), rolling (transfers).

Admissions Contact Ms. Charlene Yates, Assistant Registrar, University of Windsor, 401 Sunset Avenue, Windsor, ON N9B 3P4, Canada. *Phone:* 519-253-3000 Ext. 3332. *Toll-free phone:* 800-864-2860. *Fax:* 519-971-3653. *E-mail:* registr@uwindsor.ca.

THE UNIVERSITY OF WINNIPEG
Winnipeg, Manitoba, Canada

- **Province-supported** comprehensive, founded 1967
- **Calendar** Canadian standard year
- **Degrees** bachelor's and master's
- **Urban** 2-acre campus
- **Coed**
- **Moderately difficult** entrance level

The University of Winnipeg (continued)

Student Life *Campus security:* 24-hour emergency response devices and patrols, student patrols, video controlled external access.

Athletics Member CIAU.

Financial Aid *Financial aid deadline:* 3/1.

Applying *Options:* early admission, deferred entrance. *Application fee:* $55 (non-residents). *Required:* high school transcript. *Required for some:* interview.

Admissions Contact Ms. Nancy Latocki, Director of Admissions, The University of Winnipeg, 515 Portage Avenue, Winnipeg, MB R3B 2E9, Canada. *Phone:* 204-786-9740. *E-mail:* admissions@uwinnipeg.ca.

WESTERN PENTECOSTAL BIBLE COLLEGE
Abbotsford, British Columbia, Canada

Admissions Contact Ms. Melody Deeley, Registrar, Western Pentecostal Bible College, Box 1700, Abbotsford, BC V2S 7E7, Canada. *Phone:* 604-853-7491. *Toll-free phone:* 800-976-8388.

WILFRID LAURIER UNIVERSITY
Waterloo, Ontario, Canada

- **Province-supported** comprehensive, founded 1911
- **Calendar** Canadian standard year
- **Degrees** diplomas, bachelor's, master's, and doctoral
- **Urban** 40-acre campus with easy access to Toronto
- **Coed,** 9,362 undergraduate students, 84% full-time, 58% women, 42% men
- **Moderately difficult** entrance level, 68% of applicants were admitted

Undergraduates 7,824 full-time, 1,538 part-time. Students come from 13 provinces and territories, 49 other countries.

Freshmen *Admission:* 12,892 applied, 8,767 admitted, 2,657 enrolled.

Faculty *Total:* 309. *Student/faculty ratio:* 23:1.

Majors Anthropology; archaeology; art; biology; business administration; Canadian studies; chemistry; classics; computer science; economics; English; film studies; French; geography; German; Greek (modern); history; international relations; Latin (ancient and medieval); mass communications; mathematical statistics; mathematics; music; music therapy; philosophy; physical education; physics; political science; psychology; religious studies; sociology; Spanish; theater arts/drama; women's studies.

Academic Programs *Special study options:* accelerated degree program, adult/continuing education programs, cooperative education, honors programs, internships, off-campus study, part-time degree program, services for LD students, study abroad, summer session for credit.

Library Wilfrid Laurier University Library with 580,000 titles, 4,500 serial subscriptions.

Computers on Campus 450 computers available on campus for general student use. A campuswide network can be accessed from off campus. Internet access available.

Student Life *Housing Options:* coed. *Activities and Organizations:* drama/theater group, student-run newspaper, radio station, choral group, Water Buffaloes, TAMIAE, ski club, Musicians' Network, Laurier Christian Fellowship. *Campus security:* 24-hour emergency response devices and patrols, student patrols, late-night transport/escort service, controlled dormitory access. *Student Services:* health clinic, personal/psychological counseling, women's center, legal services.

Athletics Member CIAU. *Intercollegiate sports:* basketball M/W, cross-country running M, football M, golf M, ice hockey M/W, rugby M, soccer M/W, swimming M/W, tennis W, volleyball M/W. *Intramural sports:* badminton M/W, basketball M/W, football M/W, golf M, ice hockey M/W, lacrosse M(c), skiing (cross-country) M(c)/W(c), skiing (downhill) M(c)/W(c), soccer M/W, softball M/W, squash M/W, swimming M/W, tennis M/W, volleyball M/W, weight lifting W.

Standardized Tests *Required for some:* SAT I (for admission).

Costs (2001–02) *Tuition:* province resident $903 Canadian dollars per course part-time; nonresident $9015 Canadian dollars full-time, $1803 Canadian dollars per course part-time; International tuition $13,482 Canadian dollars full-time. *Required fees:* $258 Canadian dollars full-time. *Room and board:* $5760 Canadian dollars; room only: $3160 Canadian dollars. Room and board charges vary according to board plan and housing facility. *Payment plan:* installment. *Waivers:* senior citizens and employees or children of employees.

Applying *Options:* common application. *Application fee:* $80. *Required:* high school transcript. *Required for some:* letters of recommendation, interview. *Application deadlines:* 4/1 (freshmen), 4/1 (transfers). *Notification:* continuous (freshmen).

Admissions Contact Ms. Gail Forsyth, Manager of Admissions, Wilfrid Laurier University, 75 University Avenue West, Waterloo, ON N2L 3C5, Canada. *Phone:* 519-884-0710 Ext. 6099. *Fax:* 519-884-8826. *E-mail:* admissions@mach1.wlu.ca.

WILLIAM AND CATHERINE BOOTH COLLEGE
Winnipeg, Manitoba, Canada

Admissions Contact Ms. Mary Ann Austin, Registrar, William and Catherine Booth College, 447 Webb Place, Winnipeg, MB R3B 2P2, Canada. *Phone:* 204-947-6701. *Toll-free phone:* 800-781-6044.

YORK UNIVERSITY
Toronto, Ontario, Canada

- **Province-supported** university, founded 1959
- **Calendar** Canadian standard year
- **Degrees** certificates, bachelor's, master's, doctoral, first professional, post-master's, and postbachelor's certificates
- **Urban** 650-acre campus
- **Endowment** $145.2 million
- **Coed,** 34,248 undergraduate students, 79% full-time, 62% women, 38% men
- **Moderately difficult** entrance level, 24% of applicants were admitted

Undergraduates Students come from 150 other countries, 2% are from out of province, 6% live on campus.

Freshmen *Admission:* 35,817 applied, 8,743 admitted.

Faculty *Total:* 2,973, 39% full-time, 98% with terminal degrees.

Majors Accounting; acting/directing; actuarial science; aerospace engineering; aerospace science; African studies; anthropology; applied art; applied mathematics; art; art education; art history; Asian studies; astronomy; atmospheric sciences; behavioral sciences; biblical languages/literatures; bilingual/bicultural education; biological/physical sciences; biology; biology education; biotechnology research; business; business administration; business economics; business marketing and marketing management; business statistics; Canadian studies; chemistry; chemistry education; classics; communications; computer engineering; computer hardware engineering; computer/information sciences; computer programming; computer science; computer software engineering; creative writing; cultural studies; curriculum and instruction; dance; design/visual communications; development economics; drama/dance education; drawing; early childhood education; earth sciences; East Asian studies; ecology; economics; education; education (K-12); elementary education; engineering physics; English; English education; entrepreneurship; environmental biology; environmental education; environmental science; film studies; film/video production; finance; fine/studio arts; foreign language translation; French; geography; geotechnical engineering; German; gerontology; graphic design/commercial art/illustration; Greek (modern); health facilities administration; health/physical education; health science; Hebrew; Hispanic-American studies; history; history education; humanities; human resources management; information technology; interdisciplinary studies; international business; international business marketing; international finance; international relations; Italian; Italian studies; Japanese; jazz; Judaic studies; labor/personnel relations; Latin American studies; Latin (ancient and medieval); legal studies; liberal arts and sciences/liberal studies; linguistics; literature; management information systems/business data processing; management science; marketing operations; marketing research; mass communications; mathematical statistics; mathematics; mathematics/computer science; mathematics education; middle school education; modern languages; molecular biology; music; music (general performance); music history; musicology; music (piano and organ performance); music teacher education; music theory and composition; music (voice and choral/opera performance); natural sciences; nursing science; operations research; organizational behavior; painting; philosophy; photography; physical education; physical sciences; physics; physics education; play/screenwriting; political science; pre-dentistry; pre-law; pre-medicine; pre-pharmacy studies; pre-veterinary studies; printmaking; psychology; public administration; public health; public policy analysis; rehabilitation therapy; religious studies; romance languages; Russian; Russian/Slavic studies; science education; science/technology and society; sculpture; secondary education; sign language interpretation; social science education; social sciences; social studies education; social work; sociology; Spanish; special education; speech/theater education; sport/fitness administration; teaching English as a second language; technical/business writing; theater arts/drama; theater design; urban studies; visual/performing arts; women's studies.

Academic Programs *Special study options:* academic remediation for entering students, accelerated degree program, adult/continuing education programs,

advanced placement credit, distance learning, double majors, English as a second language, honors programs, independent study, internships, off-campus study, part-time degree program, services for LD students, student-designed majors, study abroad, summer session for credit. *Unusual degree programs:* 3-2 education.

Library Scott Library plus 4 others with 2.2 million titles, 13,651 serial subscriptions, an OPAC, a Web page.

Computers on Campus 1200 computers available on campus for general student use. A campuswide network can be accessed from student residence rooms and from off campus. Internet access, online (class) registration, at least one staffed computer lab available.

Student Life *Housing Options:* coed, disabled students. *Activities and Organizations:* drama/theater group, student-run newspaper, radio station, choral group, college student councils, York Federation of Students, Jewish Student Association, First Nations and Aboriginal Student Association, International and Exchange Students Club. *Campus security:* 24-hour emergency response devices and patrols, student patrols, late-night transport/escort service, controlled dormitory access. *Student Services:* health clinic, personal/psychological counseling, women's center, legal services.

Athletics Member CIAU. *Intercollegiate sports:* badminton M/W, basketball M/W, cross-country running M/W, fencing M/W, field hockey W, football M, golf M, ice hockey M/W, lacrosse W, rugby M/W, soccer M/W, swimming M/W, tennis M/W, track and field M/W, volleyball M/W, water polo M/W. *Intramural sports:* badminton M/W, baseball M/W, basketball M/W, bowling M/W, cross-country running M/W, football M/W, golf M/W, ice hockey M/W, soccer M/W, softball M/W, squash M/W, swimming M/W, table tennis M/W, tennis M/W, volleyball M/W, water polo M/W.

Standardized Tests *Required:* SAT I or ACT (for admission).

Costs (2001–02) *Tuition:* nonresident $4636 Canadian dollars full-time, $927 Canadian dollars per course part-time; International tuition $11,195 Canadian dollars full-time. Full-time tuition and fees vary according to course load, degree level, and program. Part-time tuition and fees vary according to course load, degree level, and program. *Required fees:* $703 Canadian dollars full-time. *Room and board:* $4693 Canadian dollars; room only: $2893 Canadian dollars. Room and board charges vary according to board plan and housing facility. *Payment plans:* installment, deferred payment. *Waivers:* senior citizens and employees or children of employees.

Applying *Options:* electronic application, early admission, early action, deferred entrance. *Application fee:* $80. *Required:* high school transcript, minimum 3.0 GPA, audition/evaluation for fine arts program, supplemental applications for business and environmental studies. *Required for some:* essay or personal statement, 1 letter of recommendation, interview. *Application deadlines:* 4/1 (freshmen), 4/1 (transfers). *Notification:* 6/1 (early action).

Admissions Contact Vanessa Grafi, International Recruitment Officer, York University, 140 Atkinson Building, Toronto, ON M3J 1P3, Canada. *Phone:* 416-736-5825. *Fax:* 416-650-8195. *E-mail:* intlenq@yorku.ca.

CAYMAN ISLANDS

INTERNATIONAL COLLEGE OF THE CAYMAN ISLANDS

Newlands, Cayman Islands

- **Independent** comprehensive, founded 1970
- **Calendar** quarters
- **Degrees** associate, bachelor's, and master's
- **Rural** 3-acre campus
- **Coed**
- **Moderately difficult** entrance level

Faculty *Student/faculty ratio:* 15:1.

Student Life *Campus security:* 24-hour emergency response devices.

Standardized Tests *Required:* SAT I or ACT (for admission).

Financial Aid *Financial aid deadline:* 8/15.

Applying *Options:* common application, deferred entrance. *Application fee:* $38. *Required:* essay or personal statement, high school transcript, minimum 2.0 GPA, 2 letters of recommendation, rank in upper 50% of high school class. *Required for some:* interview.

Admissions Contact Ms. Dianne Levy, Admissions Representative, International College of the Cayman Islands, PO Box 136, Savannah Post Office, Newlands, Grand Cayman, Cayman Islands. *Phone:* 345-947-1100 Ext. 301. *Fax:* 345-947-1210. *E-mail:* icci@candw.ky.

EGYPT

AMERICAN UNIVERSITY IN CAIRO

Cairo, Egypt

- **Independent** comprehensive, founded 1919
- **Calendar** semesters
- **Degrees** certificates, diplomas, bachelor's, and master's (majority of students are Egyptians; enrollment open to all nationalities)
- **Urban** 26-acre campus
- **Endowment** $392.3 million
- **Coed,** 4,164 undergraduate students, 88% full-time, 54% women, 46% men
- **Very difficult** entrance level, 44% of applicants were admitted

Undergraduates 3,659 full-time, 505 part-time. Students come from 65 other countries, 0.3% transferred in, 6% live on campus. *Retention:* 95% of 2001 full-time freshmen returned.

Freshmen *Admission:* 2,075 applied, 905 admitted, 603 enrolled. *Average high school GPA:* 3.20. *Test scores:* SAT verbal scores over 500: 75%; SAT math scores over 500: 40%; SAT verbal scores over 600: 26%; SAT math scores over 600: 10%; SAT verbal scores over 700: 3%; SAT math scores over 700: 1%.

Faculty *Total:* 498, 61% full-time. *Student/faculty ratio:* 13:1.

Majors Accounting; anthropology; archaeology; area studies; art; biology; business administration; chemistry; comparative literature; computer science; construction engineering; economics; electrical engineering; English; history; journalism; mass communications; mathematics; mechanical engineering; Middle Eastern studies; philosophy; physics; political science; psychology; sociology; theater arts/drama.

Academic Programs *Special study options:* academic remediation for entering students, adult/continuing education programs, advanced placement credit, double majors, independent study, off-campus study, part-time degree program, study abroad, summer session for credit.

Library American University in Cairo Library plus 2 others with 297,100 titles, 2,000 serial subscriptions, an OPAC, a Web page.

Computers on Campus 500 computers available on campus for general student use. A campuswide network can be accessed from student residence rooms and from off campus. Internet access, online (class) registration, at least one staffed computer lab available.

Student Life *Housing Options:* men-only, women-only. *Activities and Organizations:* drama/theater group, student-run newspaper, radio station, choral group, student government, choral groups/folklore dancing groups, community service groups, Model UN and Model Arab League Clubs, intramural sports. *Campus security:* 24-hour emergency response devices and patrols, controlled dormitory access. *Student Services:* health clinic, personal/psychological counseling.

Athletics *Intercollegiate sports:* basketball M/W, crew M/W, fencing M/W, gymnastics M/W, soccer M/W, squash M/W, swimming M/W, table tennis M/W, tennis M/W, track and field M/W, volleyball M/W, water polo M, wrestling M. *Intramural sports:* basketball M/W, soccer M/W, squash M/W, table tennis M/W, tennis M/W, volleyball M/W, weight lifting M.

Standardized Tests *Required for some:* SAT I or ACT (for admission).

Costs (2001–02) *Tuition:* $11,500 full-time, $479 per credit part-time. Part-time tuition and fees vary according to course load. *Required fees:* $110 full-time, $55 per term part-time. *Room only:* $2900. Room and board charges vary according to housing facility. *Payment plan:* deferred payment. *Waivers:* employees or children of employees.

Applying *Options:* electronic application, early decision. *Application fee:* $50. *Required:* essay or personal statement, high school transcript, minimum 2.00 GPA. *Application deadlines:* 6/15 (freshmen), 6/15 (transfers). *Early decision:* 3/1.

Admissions Contact Randa Kamel, Associate Director of Admissions, American University in Cairo, The Office of Student Affairs, 420 Fifth Avenue, 3rd Floor, New York, NY 10018-2728. *Phone:* 202-357-5199. *Fax:* 212-730-1600. *E-mail:* davidson@aucnyu.edu.

FRANCE

THE AMERICAN UNIVERSITY OF PARIS

Paris, France

- **Independent** 4-year, founded 1962
- **Calendar** semesters

The American University of Paris (continued)
- **Degree** bachelor's
- **Urban** campus
- **Coed,** 835 undergraduate students, 92% full-time, 66% women, 34% men
- **Moderately difficult** entrance level, 75% of applicants were admitted

Undergraduates 769 full-time, 66 part-time. Students come from 41 states and territories, 87 other countries, 9% transferred in.
Freshmen *Admission:* 831 applied, 623 admitted, 162 enrolled. *Test scores:* SAT verbal scores over 500: 87%; SAT math scores over 500: 81%; SAT verbal scores over 600: 51%; SAT math scores over 600: 33%; SAT verbal scores over 700: 6%; SAT math scores over 700: 6%.
Faculty *Total:* 123, 41% full-time. *Student/faculty ratio:* 15:1.
Majors Art history; comparative literature; computer science; economics; European studies; French; history; international business; international economics; international relations; mass communications.
Academic Programs *Special study options:* advanced placement credit, double majors, English as a second language, honors programs, internships, part-time degree program, study abroad, summer session for credit.
Library The American University of Paris Library with 70,000 titles, 1,000 serial subscriptions, an OPAC, a Web page.
Computers on Campus 107 computers available on campus for general student use. A campuswide network can be accessed from off campus. Internet access, at least one staffed computer lab available.
Student Life *Housing:* college housing not available. *Activities and Organizations:* drama/theater group, student-run newspaper, Safe Haven Aids Information, Publications Board, Student Senate, International Business Student Association, Sports Association. *Campus security:* 24-hour emergency response devices. *Student Services:* personal/psychological counseling.
Athletics *Intramural sports:* basketball M/W, fencing M, football M, golf M, racquetball M/W, soccer M, squash M/W, tennis M/W, volleyball M/W.
Standardized Tests *Required for some:* SAT I or ACT (for admission).
Costs (2001–02) *Tuition:* $19,000 full-time, $604 per credit part-time. Full-time tuition and fees vary according to course load. Part-time tuition and fees vary according to course load. *Payment plan:* installment. *Waivers:* children of alumni and employees or children of employees.
Applying *Options:* electronic application, deferred entrance. *Application fee:* $50. *Required:* essay or personal statement, high school transcript, 2 letters of recommendation. *Recommended:* minimum 3.0 GPA, interview. *Application deadlines:* 5/1 (freshmen), 7/1 (out-of-state freshmen), 5/1 (transfers). *Notification:* continuous (freshmen), continuous (out-of-state freshmen).
Admissions Contact Ms. Candace McLaughlin, The American University of Paris, 60 East 42nd Street, Suite 1463, New York, NY 10165. *Phone:* 212-983-1414. *Fax:* 212-983-0444. *E-mail:* nyoffice@aup.fr.

SCHILLER INTERNATIONAL UNIVERSITY
Paris, France

- **Independent** comprehensive, founded 1967, part of Schiller International University
- **Calendar** semesters
- **Degrees** associate, bachelor's, and master's
- **Urban** campus
- **Coed,** 74 undergraduate students
- **Noncompetitive** entrance level

Schiller International University (SIU) is an independent American university with campuses in England, France, Germany, Spain, Switzerland, and the United States. In addition, students can transfer without loss of credit. English is the language of instruction at all campuses. SIU offers undergraduate and graduate students an American education in an international setting.

Majors Business administration; interdisciplinary studies; international business; international relations; liberal arts and sciences/liberal studies.
Academic Programs *Special study options:* accelerated degree program, adult/continuing education programs, advanced placement credit, English as a second language, internships, part-time degree program, student-designed majors, study abroad, summer session for credit.
Library 3,797 titles, 41 serial subscriptions.
Computers on Campus 11 computers available on campus for general student use. At least one staffed computer lab available.
Student Life *Housing:* college housing not available. *Activities and Organizations:* student-run newspaper, student government, student newspaper, yearbook staff. *Student Services:* personal/psychological counseling.
Athletics *Intramural sports:* soccer M/W.
Costs (2002–03) *Comprehensive fee:* $21,760 includes full-time tuition ($14,560) and room and board ($7200).
Financial Aid *Financial aid deadline:* 6/1.
Applying *Options:* common application, deferred entrance. *Application fee:* $35. *Required:* essay or personal statement, high school transcript. *Recommended:* minimum 2.0 GPA. *Application deadline:* rolling (freshmen), rolling (transfers).
Admissions Contact Ms. Francoise Barody, Acting Campus Director, Schiller International University, 32 Boulevard de Vaugirard, 75015 Paris, France. *Phone:* 14-538-5601.

GERMANY

SCHILLER INTERNATIONAL UNIVERSITY
Heidelberg, Germany

- **Independent** comprehensive, founded 1969, part of Schiller International University
- **Calendar** semesters
- **Degrees** associate, bachelor's, and master's
- **Urban** campus with easy access to Frankfurt
- **Coed,** 121 undergraduate students
- **Noncompetitive** entrance level

Schiller International University (SIU) is an independent American university with campuses in England, France, Germany, Spain, Switzerland, and the United States. In addition, students can transfer without loss of credit. English is the language of instruction at all campuses. SIU offers undergraduate and graduate students an American education in an international setting.

Undergraduates Students come from 130 other countries.
Faculty *Total:* 28, 29% full-time.
Majors Economics; interdisciplinary studies; international business; international relations; liberal arts and sciences/liberal studies.
Academic Programs *Special study options:* accelerated degree program, adult/continuing education programs, advanced placement credit, English as a second language, part-time degree program, student-designed majors, study abroad, summer session for credit.
Library 8,000 titles, 94 serial subscriptions.
Computers on Campus 16 computers available on campus for general student use. At least one staffed computer lab available.
Student Life *Housing Options:* coed. *Activities and Organizations:* student-run newspaper, student government, yearbook staff. *Campus security:* 24-hour emergency response devices. *Student Services:* personal/psychological counseling.
Athletics *Intramural sports:* basketball M/W, soccer M/W, swimming M/W, table tennis M/W, volleyball M/W.
Costs (2002–03) *Comprehensive fee:* $21,760 includes full-time tuition ($14,560) and room and board ($7200). *Payment plan:* deferred payment. *Waivers:* employees or children of employees.
Financial Aid *Financial aid deadline:* 6/1.
Applying *Options:* common application, deferred entrance. *Application fee:* $35. *Required:* essay or personal statement, high school transcript. *Recommended:* minimum 2.0 GPA. *Application deadline:* rolling (freshmen), rolling (transfers).
Admissions Contact Dr. Nicolle Macho, Campus Director, Schiller International University, Bergstrasse 106, 69121 Heidelberg, Germany. *Phone:* 49-6221-45810 Ext. 35. *E-mail:* siu_hd@compuserve.com.

GREECE

AMERICAN COLLEGE OF THESSALONIKI
Thessaloniki, Greece

- **Independent** 4-year
- **Calendar** semesters
- **Degree** certificates and bachelor's
- **Suburban** 40-acre campus
- **Coed,** 705 undergraduate students, 69% full-time, 59% women, 41% men
- **Minimally difficult** entrance level, 67% of applicants were admitted

Undergraduates 489 full-time, 216 part-time. Students come from 22 other countries, 1.0% transferred in, 1% live on campus. *Retention:* 90% of 2001 full-time freshmen returned.

Freshmen *Admission:* 181 applied, 122 admitted, 138 enrolled. *Average high school GPA:* 2.50.

Faculty *Total:* 74, 35% full-time, 34% with terminal degrees. *Student/faculty ratio:* 10:1.

Majors Business administration; English; history; international relations; liberal arts and sciences/liberal studies; management information systems/business data processing; psychology.

Academic Programs *Special study options:* academic remediation for entering students, advanced placement credit, double majors, English as a second language, independent study, internships, part-time degree program, study abroad, summer session for credit.

Library Eleftheriadis Library with 35,000 titles, 3,000 serial subscriptions, an OPAC, a Web page.

Computers on Campus 80 computers available on campus for general student use. Internet access, at least one staffed computer lab available.

Student Life *Activities and Organizations:* drama/theater group, student-run newspaper, choral group, Drama Club, Marketing Club, Sailing Club, Investments Club, student newspaper. *Campus security:* 24-hour patrols. *Student Services:* personal/psychological counseling.

Athletics *Intramural sports:* basketball M/W, sailing M/W, soccer M, volleyball M/W.

Costs (2001–02) *Tuition:* 4960 euros full-time, 160 euros per credit hour part-time. *Required fees:* 300 euros full-time, 80 euros per term part-time. *Room only:* 2650 euros. *Payment plan:* installment. *Waivers:* employees or children of employees.

Applying *Options:* common application, early admission, deferred entrance. *Application fee:* $40. *Required:* high school transcript, proficiency in English. *Required for some:* essay or personal statement, interview. *Recommended:* minimum 2.0 GPA. *Application deadlines:* 9/1 (freshmen), 9/1 (transfers). *Notification:* 9/10 (freshmen).

Admissions Contact Ms. Roula Lebetli, Admissions Officer, American College of Thessaloniki, PO Box 21021, Pylea, Thessaloniki 55510, Greece. *Phone:* 30-31398239. *Fax:* 30-31301076. *E-mail:* rleb@ac.anatolia.edu.gr.

The College of Southeastern Europe, The American University of Athens

Athens, Greece

- **Independent** 4-year, founded 1982
- **Calendar** semesters
- **Degree** bachelor's
- **Urban** campus
- **Endowment** $5.6 million
- **Coed,** 341 undergraduate students, 88% full-time, 40% women, 60% men
- **Moderately difficult** entrance level, 86% of applicants were admitted

Undergraduates 299 full-time, 42 part-time. Students come from 12 other countries, 3% Asian American or Pacific Islander, 21% transferred in. *Retention:* 90% of 2001 full-time freshmen returned.

Freshmen *Admission:* 65 applied, 56 admitted, 56 enrolled. *Average high school GPA:* 2.80.

Faculty *Total:* 54, 76% full-time, 44% with terminal degrees. *Student/faculty ratio:* 12:1.

Majors Accounting; advertising; American literature; archaeology; architectural engineering; architectural environmental design; architectural urban design; art history; biochemistry; biology; British literature; broadcast journalism; business; business administration; business economics; business marketing and marketing management; business quantitative methods/management science related; chemistry; civil engineering; clinical psychology; computer graphics; computer/information sciences; computer science; computer systems networking/telecommunications; electrical engineering; finance; foreign languages/literatures; graphic design/commercial art/illustration; history; hospitality management; hotel and restaurant management; human resources management; industrial/manufacturing engineering; insurance/risk management; interior architecture; international business; journalism; management science; mathematics; mechanical engineering; molecular biology; philosophy; physics; political science; psychology; public relations; sociology; structural engineering; travel/tourism management; western civilization.

Academic Programs *Special study options:* accelerated degree program, cooperative education, double majors, English as a second language, independent study, internships, part-time degree program, study abroad, summer session for credit.

Library The College of Southeastern Europe Library with 36,100 titles, 219 serial subscriptions, 51 audiovisual materials, an OPAC.

Computers on Campus A campuswide network can be accessed from off campus. Internet access, at least one staffed computer lab available.

Student Life *Activities and Organizations:* drama/theater group, student-run newspaper, Poetry & Literature Society, journalism association, drama club, political science association, Parliamentary Debating Society. *Campus security:* 24-hour emergency response devices and patrols, closed-circuit TV. *Student Services:* personal/psychological counseling.

Athletics *Intramural sports:* basketball M, sailing M, skiing (downhill) M/W, soccer M, swimming M/W, volleyball M/W, water polo M/W.

Costs (2001–02) *Tuition:* $4650 full-time, $192 per credit part-time. *Payment plan:* deferred payment.

Financial Aid Available in 2001, 15 State and other part-time jobs (averaging $1125).

Applying *Options:* common application. *Application fee:* $90. *Required:* essay or personal statement, high school transcript, 2 letters of recommendation, interview. *Application deadline:* rolling (freshmen).

Admissions Contact Ms. Thalia Poulos, Director of Admissions, The College of Southeastern Europe, The American University of Athens, 17 Patriarchou Ieremiou Street, Athens 11475, Greece. *Phone:* 301-725-9301. *Toll-free phone:* 30-1-725-9301-2. *Fax:* 30-1-725-9304. *E-mail:* admissions@southeastern.edu.gr.

Deree College

Athens, Greece

Admissions Contact Mr. Nick Jiavaras, Director of Enrollment Management, Deree College, 6 Gravias Street, GR-153 42 Aghia Paraskevi, Athens, Greece. *Phone:* 301-600-9800 Ext. 1322. *Fax:* 301-600-9811. *E-mail:* dereeadm@hol.gr.

IRELAND

Institute of Public Administration

Dublin, Ireland

Admissions Contact Ms. Mary T. Coolahan, Registrar, Institute of Public Administration, 52-61 Lansdowne Road, Dublin 4, Ireland. *Phone:* 01-668-6233. *Fax:* 01-269-8644.

ITALY

American University of Rome

Rome, Italy

- **Independent** 4-year, founded 1969
- **Calendar** semesters
- **Degrees** associate and bachelor's
- **Urban** 1-acre campus
- **Coed,** 310 undergraduate students
- **Moderately difficult** entrance level, 23% of applicants were admitted

Undergraduates 57% live on campus. *Retention:* 52% of 2001 full-time freshmen returned.

Freshmen *Admission:* 247 applied, 58 admitted.

Faculty *Total:* 47, 13% full-time, 26% with terminal degrees. *Student/faculty ratio:* 7:1.

Majors Business administration; communications; interdisciplinary studies; international business; international relations; Italian; liberal arts and sciences/liberal studies.

Academic Programs *Special study options:* accelerated degree program, advanced placement credit, double majors, English as a second language, internships, part-time degree program, student-designed majors, study abroad, summer session for credit.

American University of Rome (continued)

Library American University of Rome Library with 5,000 titles, 15 serial subscriptions.

Computers on Campus 22 computers available on campus for general student use. Internet access, at least one staffed computer lab available.

Student Life *Housing Options:* men-only, women-only. *Activities and Organizations:* drama/theater group, student-run newspaper, International Business Clubs, International Liberal Arts Club, Drama Club. *Student Services:* personal/psychological counseling.

Athletics *Intercollegiate sports:* soccer M. *Intramural sports:* soccer W.

Standardized Tests *Required for some:* SAT I (for admission).

Costs (2002–03) *Tuition:* $9822 full-time, $1228 per course part-time. Full-time tuition and fees vary according to course load. Part-time tuition and fees vary according to course load. *Required fees:* $230 full-time, $120 per term part-time. *Room only:* $5660. Room and board charges vary according to housing facility and location.

Applying *Options:* common application, deferred entrance. *Application fee:* $55. *Required:* essay or personal statement, high school transcript, minimum 2.0 GPA, letters of recommendation. *Recommended:* minimum 2.5 GPA, interview.

Admissions Contact James Lynch, Director, Admissions, Student Services and Placement, American University of Rome, Via Pietro Roselli 4, Rome 00153, Italy. *Phone:* 39-06-58330919 Ext. 219. *Fax:* 202-296-9577. *E-mail:* aurinfo@aur.edu.

JOHN CABOT UNIVERSITY

Rome, Italy

- **Independent** 4-year, founded 1972
- **Degree** bachelor's
- **Coed,** 406 undergraduate students, 100% full-time, 61% women, 39% men
- **Moderately difficult** entrance level, 88% of applicants were admitted

Undergraduates 406 full-time. Students come from 40 other countries. *Retention:* 62% of 2001 full-time freshmen returned.

Freshmen *Admission:* 110 applied, 97 admitted, 90 enrolled. *Average high school GPA:* 3.0.

Faculty *Total:* 60, 18% full-time, 43% with terminal degrees. *Student/faculty ratio:* 12:1.

Majors Art history; business administration; international relations; literature; political science.

Academic Programs *Special study options:* advanced placement credit, cooperative education, double majors, English as a second language, freshman honors college, honors programs, independent study, internships, part-time degree program, study abroad, summer session for credit.

Library Frohring Library with 16,000 titles, 35,000 serial subscriptions, 50 audiovisual materials, an OPAC, a Web page.

Computers on Campus 40 computers available on campus for general student use. Internet access, at least one staffed computer lab available.

Standardized Tests *Required for some:* SAT I (for admission), ACT (for admission).

Costs (2001–02) *Comprehensive fee:* $19,400 includes full-time tuition ($11,000), mandatory fees ($400), and room and board ($8000). Full-time tuition and fees vary according to course load. Part-time tuition: $500 per credit. Part-time tuition and fees vary according to course load. *Room and board:* College room only: $5400. *Waivers:* employees or children of employees.

Applying *Options:* common application, electronic application, deferred entrance. *Application fee:* $50. *Required:* essay or personal statement, high school transcript, 2 letters of recommendation. *Recommended:* minimum 3.0 GPA, interview. *Application deadlines:* 7/15 (freshmen), 7/15 (transfers). *Notification:* continuous until 8/1 (freshmen).

Admissions Contact Karin Tyack, Admissions Counselor, John Cabot University, via della Lungara 233, Roma 00165, Italy. *Phone:* 39-06 68191221. *Fax:* 39-06 6832088. *E-mail:* jcu@johncabot.edu.

KENYA

UNITED STATES INTERNATIONAL UNIVERSITY

Nairobi, Kenya

Admissions Contact Ms. Susan Topham, Associate Director of Admissions, United States International University, 10455 Pomerado Road, San Diego, CA 92131-1799. *Phone:* 619-635-4772. *Fax:* 619-635-4739. *E-mail:* admission@usiu.edu.

LEBANON

LEBANESE AMERICAN UNIVERSITY

Beirut, Lebanon

Admissions Contact PO Box 13-5053, Beirut, Lebanon.

MEXICO

ALLIANT INTERNATIONAL UNIVERSITY-MÉXICO CITY

Mexico City, Mexico

Admissions Contact Ms. Susan Topham, Director of Admissions, Alliant International University-México City, 10455 Pomerado Road, San Diego, CA 92131-1799. *Phone:* -619-635-4772. *Fax:* 619-635-4739. *E-mail:* admissions@usiu.edu.

INSTITUTO TECNOLÓGICO Y DE ESTUDIOS SUPERIORES DE MONTERREY, CAMPUS CENTRAL DE VERACRUZ

Córdoba, Mexico

Admissions Contact Ing. Luis Pablo Villareal, Registrar, Instituto Tecnológico y de Estudios Superiores de Monterrey, Campus Central de Veracruz, Avenida Eugenio Garza Sada 1, Apartado Postal 314, 94500 Córdoba, Veracruz, Mexico. *Phone:* -27-13-23-40 Ext. 123. *Fax:* 83-58-19-54.

INSTITUTO TECNOLÓGICO Y DE ESTUDIOS SUPERIORES DE MONTERREY, CAMPUS CHIAPAS

Tuxtla Gutiérrez, Mexico

Admissions Contact Lic. Luis Enrique Cancino, Registrar, Instituto Tecnológico y de Estudios Superiores de Monterrey, Campus Chiapas, Carretera a Tapanatepec Km 149&746, Apartado Postal 312, 29000 Tuxtla Gutiérrez, Chiapas, Mexico. *Phone:* -96-15-1723. *Fax:* 83-58-19-54.

INSTITUTO TECNOLÓGICO Y DE ESTUDIOS SUPERIORES DE MONTERREY, CAMPUS CHIHUAHUA

Chihuahua, Mexico

Admissions Contact Ing. Juan Manuel Fernandez, Registrar, Instituto Tecnológico y de Estudios Superiores de Monterrey, Campus Chihuahua, Colegio Militar 4700, Colonia Nombre de Dios, Apartado Postal 728, 31300 Chihuahua, Chihuahua, Mexico. *Phone:* -14-17-48-58 Ext. 117. *Fax:* 83-58-19-54.

INSTITUTO TECNOLÓGICO Y DE ESTUDIOS SUPERIORES DE MONTERREY, CAMPUS CIUDAD DE MÉXICO

Ciudad de Mexico, Mexico

Admissions Contact Admissions Office, Instituto Tecnológico y de Estudios Superiores de Monterrey, Campus Ciudad de México, Calle del Puente #222 esquina con Periférico, 14380 Colonia Huipulco, Tlalpan, MDF, Mexico. *Phone:* 5-673-6488. *Fax:* 83-58-19-54.

Instituto Tecnológico y de Estudios Superiores de Monterrey, Campus Ciudad Juárez

Ciudad Juárez, Mexico

Admissions Contact Lic. Alberto Trejo, Registrar, Instituto Tecnológico y de Estudios Superiores de Monterrey, Campus Ciudad Juárez, Boulevard Tomas Fernandez y Avenida A J Bermudez, Apartado Postal 3105-J, 32320 Ciudad Juárez, Chihuahua, Mexico. *Phone:* -16-17-88-07 Ext. 113. *Fax:* 83-58-19-54.

Instituto Tecnológico y de Estudios Superiores de Monterrey, Campus Ciudad Obregón

Ciudad Obregón, Mexico

Admissions Contact Lic. Judith Almeida, Registrar, Instituto Tecnológico y de Estudios Superiores de Monterrey, Campus Ciudad Obregón, Dr Norman E Borlaug Km 14, Apartado Postal 662, 85000 Ciudad Obregón, Sonora, Mexico. *Phone:* -64-15-03-12. *Fax:* 83-58-19-54.

Instituto Tecnológico y de Estudios Superiores de Monterrey, Campus Colima

Colima, Mexico

Admissions Contact Lic. Manuel Perez Rivera, Registrar, Instituto Tecnológico y de Estudios Superiores de Monterrey, Campus Colima, Prolongacion Ignacio Sandoval s/n, Fraccionamiento Jardines de Vista Hermosa, Apartado Postal 190, 28010 Colima, Colima, Mexico. *Phone:* -33-12-53-39. *Fax:* 83-58-19-54.

Instituto Tecnológico y de Estudios Superiores de Monterrey, Campus Estado de México

Atizapán de Zaragoza, Mexico

Admissions Contact Prof. Jose de Jesus Molina, Registrar, Instituto Tecnológico y de Estudios Superiores de Monterrey, Campus Estado de México, Camino al Lago de Guadalupe Km 4, Apartado Postal 214, 52926 Atizapán de Zaragoza, Mexico. *Phone:* -5-873-3600. *Fax:* 83-58-19-54.

Instituto Tecnológico y de Estudios Superiores de Monterrey, Campus Guadalajara

Zapopan, Mexico

Admissions Contact Ms. Janet Martell Sotomayor, Registration Director, Instituto Tecnológico y de Estudios Superiores de Monterrey, Campus Guadalajara, Avenida General Ramón Corona 2514, 44100 Zapopan, Jalisco, Mexico. *Phone:* -3-669-3006.

Instituto Tecnológico y de Estudios Superiores de Monterrey, Campus Hidalgo

Pachuca, Mexico

Admissions Contact Lic. Lizbet Melo, Registrar, Instituto Tecnológico y de Estudios Superiores de Monterrey, Campus Hidalgo, Apartado Postal 237. *Phone:* -714-25-00 Ext. 128. *Fax:* 83-58-19-54. *E-mail:* lizmelo@campus.hgo.itesm.mx.

Instituto Tecnológico y de Estudios Superiores de Monterrey, Campus Irapuato

Irapuato, Mexico

Admissions Contact Ing. Marcela Beltrán, Registrar, Instituto Tecnológico y de Estudios Superiores de Monterrey, Campus Irapuato, Paseo Mirador del Valle No. 445, Col. Villas de Irapuato, Apartado Postal 568, 36660 Irapuato, Guanajuato, Mexico. *Phone:* -46-230342. *Fax:* 83-58-19-54.

Instituto Tecnológico y de Estudios Superiores de Monterrey, Campus Laguna

Torreón, Mexico

Admissions Contact Ing. Aroldo Camargo Soto, Registrar, Instituto Tecnológico y de Estudios Superiores de Monterrey, Campus Laguna, Paseo del Tecnologico s/n Ampliacion La Rosita, Apartado Postal 506, 27250 Torreón, Coahuila, Mexico. *Phone:* -17-20-66-61 Ext. 23. *Fax:* 83-58-19-54.

Instituto Tecnológico y de Estudios Superiores de Monterrey, Campus León

León, Mexico

Admissions Contact Lic. Eddie Villegas, Registrar, Instituto Tecnológico y de Estudios Superiores de Monterrey, Campus León, Apdo. Postal No. 872, Leon 37120, Mexico. *Phone:* -47-17-10-00 Ext. 131. *Fax:* 83-58-19-54.

Instituto Tecnológico y de Estudios Superiores de Monterrey, Campus Mazatlán

Mazatlán, Mexico

Admissions Contact Ing. Martin Ley Urias, Registrar, Instituto Tecnológico y de Estudios Superiores de Monterrey, Campus Mazatlán, Carretera Mazatlan-Higueras, Km 3, Camino al Conchi, Apartado Postal 799, 82000 Mazatlán, Sinaloa, Mexico. *Phone:* -69-80-1143. *Fax:* 83-58-19-54.

Instituto Tecnológico y de Estudios Superiores de Monterrey, Campus Monterrey

Monterrey, Mexico

Admissions Contact Lic. Julieta Miery Teran, Director of Admissions, Instituto Tecnológico y de Estudios Superiores de Monterrey, Campus Monterrey, Avenida Eugenio Garza Sada 2501 Sur Colonia Tecnnologico, Sucursal de Correos J, 64849 Monterrey, Nuevo León, Mexico. *Phone:* -83-58-46-50. *Fax:* 83-58-19-54.

Instituto Tecnológico y de Estudios Superiores de Monterrey, Campus Morelos

Temixco, Mexico

Admissions Contact Lic. Miguel Angel Machua S., Registrar, Instituto Tecnológico y de Estudios Superiores de Monterrey, Campus Morelos, Paseo de la Reforma 182-A, Colonia Lomas de Cuernavaca, 62000 Temixco, Morelos, Mexico. *Phone:* -73 18-49-57. *Fax:* 83-58-19-54.

Instituto Tecnológico y de Estudios Superiores de Monterrey, Campus Querétaro

Santiago de Querétaro, Mexico

Admissions Contact Lic. Marco Vinicio Lopez, Registrar, Instituto Tecnológico y de Estudios Superiores de Monterrey, Campus Querétaro, Avenida Epigmenio Gonzalez #500, Fracc. San Pablo, Queretaro 76130, Mexico. *Phone:* -42-17-38-25 Ext. 156. *Fax:* 83-58-19-54.

INSTITUTO TECNOLÓGICO Y DE ESTUDIOS SUPERIORES DE MONTERREY, CAMPUS SALTILLO

Saltillo, Mexico

Admissions Contact Lic. Esteban Ramos, Registrar, Instituto Tecnológico y de Estudios Superiores de Monterrey, Campus Saltillo, Prolongacion Juan de la Barrera 1241 Ote, Apartado Postal 539, 25270 Saltillo, Coahuila, Mexico. *Phone:* -84-15-06-90 Ext. 12. *Fax:* 83-58-19-54.

INSTITUTO TECNOLÓGICO Y DE ESTUDIOS SUPERIORES DE MONTERREY, CAMPUS SAN LUIS POTOSÍ

San Luis Potosí, Mexico

Admissions Contact Ing. Consuelo Gonzalez, Registrar, Instituto Tecnológico y de Estudios Superiores de Monterrey, Campus San Luis Potosí, Avenida Robles 600, Colonia Jacarandas, Apartado Postal 1473 Suc E, 78140 San Luis Potosí, SLP, Mexico. *Phone:* 48-13-3441 Ext. 14. *Fax:* 83-58-19-54.

INSTITUTO TECNOLÓGICO Y DE ESTUDIOS SUPERIORES DE MONTERREY, CAMPUS SINALOA

Culiacán, Mexico

Admissions Contact Lic. Hugo Guerrero, Registrar, Instituto Tecnológico y de Estudios Superiores de Monterrey, Campus Sinaloa, Boulevard Culiacán 3773, Apartado Postal 69-F, 80800 Culiacán, Sinaloa, Mexico. *Phone:* -67-14-03-69. *Fax:* 83-58-19-54.

INSTITUTO TECNOLÓGICO Y DE ESTUDIOS SUPERIORES DE MONTERREY, CAMPUS SONORA NORTE

Hermosillo, Mexico

Admissions Contact Ing. Victor Eduardo Perez Orozco, Library and Admissions/ Registration Director, Instituto Tecnológico y de Estudios Superiores de Monterrey, Campus Sonora Norte, Carretera Hermosillo-Nogales Km 9, Apartado Postal 216, 83000 Hermosillo, Sonora, Mexico. *Phone:* -62-15-52-05 Ext. 131. *Fax:* 83-58-19-54.

INSTITUTO TECNOLÓGICO Y DE ESTUDIOS SUPERIORES DE MONTERREY, CAMPUS TAMPICO

Altimira, Mexico

Admissions Contact Ing. Javier Ponce, Registrar, Instituto Tecnológico y de Estudios Superiores de Monterrey, Campus Tampico, Apdo. Postal 7, Conedor Industrial, Canekra Tampico-Mark, Altamira 89600, Mexico. *Phone:* 126-4-19-79.

INSTITUTO TECNOLÓGICO Y DE ESTUDIOS SUPERIORES DE MONTERREY, CAMPUS TOLUCA

Toluca, Mexico

Admissions Contact Ing. Victor M. Martinez Orta, Registrar, Instituto Tecnológico y de Estudios Superiores de Monterrey, Campus Toluca, Ex-hacienda La Pila, 100 metros al norte de San Antonio Buenavista, 50252 Toluca, Estado de Mexico, Mexico. *Phone:* -72-74-11-92. *Fax:* 83-58-19-54.

INSTITUTO TECNOLÓGICO Y DE ESTUDIOS SUPERIORES DE MONTERREY, CAMPUS ZACATECAS

Zacatecas, Mexico

Admissions Contact Lic. Ma. de Lourdes Zorrilla, Business Affairs Director and Registrar, Instituto Tecnológico y de Estudios Superiores de Monterrey, Campus Zacatecas, Calzada Pedro Coronel #16, Frente al Club Bernades, Municipio de Guadalupe, 98000 Zacatecas, Zacatecas, Mexico. *Phone:* 49-23-00-40.

UNIVERSIDAD DE LAS AMERICAS, A.C.

Mexico City, Mexico

Admissions Contact Calle de Puebla 223, Col. Roma, Mexico City 06700, Mexico.

UNIVERSIDAD DE LAS AMÉRICAS-PUEBLA

Puebla, Mexico

Admissions Contact Lic. Jorge A. Varela Olivares, Chief of Admissions, Universidad de las Américas-Puebla, Cholula Apartado 359, 72820 Cholula, Mexico. *Phone:* 22-29-20-17 Ext. 4015. *Fax:* 22-29-20-18. *E-mail:* jvarela@udlapvms.pue.udlap.mx.

NICARAGUA

AVE MARIA COLLEGE OF THE AMERICAS

San Marcos, Nicaragua

Admissions Contact Mr. Patrick Clark, Director of Admissions, Ave Maria College of the Americas, San Marcos, Carazo, Nicaragua. *Phone:* 43-22314-138.

NIGERIA

THE NIGERIAN BAPTIST THEOLOGICAL SEMINARY

Ogbomoso, Nigeria

Admissions Contact Mr. Daniel F. Oroniran, Registrar, The Nigerian Baptist Theological Seminary, PO Box 30, Ogbomoso, Oyo, Nigeria. *Phone:* -038-710011.

SPAIN

SCHILLER INTERNATIONAL UNIVERSITY

Madrid, Spain

- **Independent** comprehensive, founded 1967, part of Schiller International University
- **Calendar** semesters
- **Degrees** associate, bachelor's, and master's
- **Urban** campus
- **Coed,** 204 undergraduate students
- **Noncompetitive** entrance level

Schiller International University (SIU) is an independent American university with campuses in England, France, Germany, Spain, Switzerland, and the United States. In addition, students can transfer without loss of credit. English is the language of instruction at all campuses. SIU offers undergraduate and graduate students an American education in an international setting.

Majors Business administration; business marketing and marketing management; hotel and restaurant management; interdisciplinary studies; international business; international relations; liberal arts and sciences/liberal studies; premedicine; pre-veterinary studies.

Academic Programs *Special study options:* accelerated degree program, adult/continuing education programs, advanced placement credit, English as a second language, internships, part-time degree program, student-designed majors, study abroad, summer session for credit.

Library 4,216 titles, 58 serial subscriptions.

Computers on Campus 8 computers available on campus for general student use. At least one staffed computer lab available.

Student Life *Housing:* college housing not available. *Activities and Organizations:* student-run newspaper, student government, campus newspaper, yearbook staff. *Student Services:* personal/psychological counseling.

Athletics *Intramural sports:* soccer M/W, volleyball M/W.

Costs (2002–03) *Comprehensive fee:* $21,760 includes full-time tuition ($14,560) and room and board ($7200).

Financial Aid Of all full-time matriculated undergraduates who enrolled in 2001, 3 Federal Work-Study jobs (averaging $4880). *Financial aid deadline:* 4/15.

Applying *Options:* common application, deferred entrance. *Application fee:* $35. *Required:* essay or personal statement, high school transcript. *Recommended:* minimum 2.0 GPA. *Application deadline:* rolling (freshmen), rolling (transfers).

Admissions Contact Mr. Carlos Lizardi, Associate Director of Public Affairs and Admissions, Schiller International University, San Bernardo 97-99, Edif. Colomina, 28015 Madrid, Spain. *Phone:* 1-448-2488.

SWITZERLAND

ECOLE HÔTELIÈRE DE LAUSANNE
Lausanne, Switzerland

Admissions Contact Le Chalet-a-Gobet, 1000 Lausanne 25, Switzerland.

FRANKLIN COLLEGE SWITZERLAND
Sorengo, Switzerland

- **Independent** 4-year, founded 1969
- **Calendar** semesters
- **Degrees** associate and bachelor's
- **Suburban** 5-acre campus
- **Coed,** 273 undergraduate students, 99% full-time, 60% women, 40% men
- **Moderately difficult** entrance level, 85% of applicants were admitted

Franklin College is a 4-year, coeducational, residential American liberal arts college located in southern Switzerland and specializing in international studies. Students from more than 50 countries attend. Semester and Year Abroad students are welcome. Summer sessions are offered May-July. Every semester, students take faculty-led Academic Travel trips to destinations worldwide.

Undergraduates 270 full-time, 3 part-time. Students come from 25 states and territories, 63 other countries, 100% are from out of state, 4% transferred in, 70% live on campus. *Retention:* 48% of 2001 full-time freshmen returned.

Freshmen *Admission:* 288 applied, 246 admitted, 97 enrolled. *Average high school GPA:* 3.11. *Test scores:* SAT verbal scores over 500: 94%; SAT math scores over 500: 82%; ACT scores over 18: 88%; SAT verbal scores over 600: 44%; SAT math scores over 600: 38%; ACT scores over 24: 63%; SAT verbal scores over 700: 7%; SAT math scores over 700: 8%; ACT scores over 30: 13%.

Faculty *Total:* 46, 37% full-time, 41% with terminal degrees. *Student/faculty ratio:* 9:1.

Majors Art history; communications; European studies; history; international business; international economics; international finance; international relations; liberal arts and sciences/liberal studies; literature; modern languages; romance languages.

Academic Programs *Special study options:* accelerated degree program, advanced placement credit, double majors, English as a second language, honors programs, independent study, internships, part-time degree program, study abroad, summer session for credit.

Library David R. Grace Library with 31,910 titles, 158 serial subscriptions, 1,506 audiovisual materials, an OPAC, a Web page.

Computers on Campus 38 computers available on campus for general student use. A campuswide network can be accessed from off campus. Internet access, at least one staffed computer lab available.

Student Life *Housing:* on-campus residence required through sophomore year. *Options:* coed, men-only, women-only. *Activities and Organizations:* drama/theater group, student-run newspaper, radio station, Student Union, Newspaper, Literary Society, Drama Society, Photography Club. *Student Services:* personal/psychological counseling.

Athletics *Intramural sports:* badminton M(c)/W(c), basketball M(c)/W(c), crew M(c)/W(c), equestrian sports W(c), ice hockey M(c)/W(c), sailing M(c)/W(c), skiing (cross-country) M(c)/W(c), skiing (downhill) M(c)/W(c), soccer M(c)/W(c), swimming M(c)/W(c), tennis M(c)/W(c), volleyball M(c)/W(c), weight lifting M(c)/W(c).

Standardized Tests *Required:* SAT I or ACT (for admission). *Recommended:* SAT II: Subject Tests (for admission), SAT II: Writing Test (for admission).

Costs (2001–02) *Comprehensive fee:* $28,710 includes full-time tuition ($19,700), mandatory fees ($1160), and room and board ($7850). Full-time tuition and fees vary according to course load. Part-time tuition: $1970 per course. Part-time tuition and fees vary according to course load. *Required fees:* $115 per course. *Room and board:* College room only: $5600. Room and board charges vary according to board plan and housing facility. *Payment plans:* installment, deferred payment. *Waivers:* employees or children of employees.

Applying *Options:* common application, early admission, early decision, early action, deferred entrance. *Application fee:* $50. *Required:* essay or personal statement, high school transcript, minimum 2.0 GPA, 3 letters of recommendation. *Recommended:* interview. *Application deadlines:* 3/15 (freshmen), 6/15 (transfers). *Early decision:* 12/1. *Notification:* continuous (freshmen), 1/1 (early decision), 1/15 (early action).

Admissions Contact Ms. Karen Ballard, Director of Admissions, Franklin College Switzerland, 135 East 65th Street, New York, NY 10021. *Phone:* 212-772-2090. *Fax:* 212-772-2718. *E-mail:* info@fc.edu.

SCHILLER INTERNATIONAL UNIVERSITY, AMERICAN COLLEGE OF SWITZERLAND
Leysin, Switzerland

- **Independent** comprehensive, founded 1963, part of Schiller International University
- **Calendar** semesters
- **Degrees** associate, bachelor's, and master's
- **Small-town** 15-acre campus with easy access to Geneva
- **Coed,** 82 undergraduate students, 95% full-time, 45% women, 55% men
- **Minimally difficult** entrance level

Schiller International University (SIU) is an independent American university with campuses in England, France, Germany, Spain, Switzerland, and the United States. In addition, students can transfer without loss of credit. English is the language of instruction at all campuses. SIU offers undergraduate and graduate students an American education in an international setting.

Undergraduates 78 full-time, 4 part-time. Students come from 7 states and territories, 25 other countries, 17% transferred in, 90% live on campus. *Retention:* 75% of 2001 full-time freshmen returned.

Freshmen *Admission:* 31 enrolled.

Faculty *Total:* 15, 33% full-time.

Majors Business administration; economics; hotel and restaurant management; interdisciplinary studies; international business; international economics; international relations; liberal arts and sciences/liberal studies; travel/tourism management.

Academic Programs *Special study options:* academic remediation for entering students, accelerated degree program, advanced placement credit, English as a second language, internships, part-time degree program, student-designed majors, study abroad, summer session for credit.

Library 48,355 titles, 200 serial subscriptions.

Computers on Campus 17 computers available on campus for general student use. Internet access, at least one staffed computer lab available.

Student Life *Housing:* on-campus residence required through sophomore year. *Options:* coed. *Campus security:* 24-hour patrols. *Student Services:* health clinic, personal/psychological counseling.

Athletics *Intramural sports:* badminton M/W, basketball M/W, equestrian sports M/W, skiing (cross-country) M/W, skiing (downhill) M/W, soccer M/W, squash M/W, swimming M/W, table tennis M/W, tennis M/W, volleyball M/W.

Costs (2002–03) *Comprehensive fee:* 38,400 Swiss francs includes full-time tuition (22,000 Swiss francs) and room and board (16,400 Swiss francs).

Schiller International University, American College of Switzerland (continued)

Applying *Options:* common application, deferred entrance. *Application fee:* $50. *Required:* essay or personal statement, high school transcript, minimum 2.0 GPA, 1 letter of recommendation. *Application deadline:* rolling (freshmen), rolling (transfers).

Admissions Contact United States Admissions Representative (ACS), Schiller International University, American College of Switzerland, 453 Edgewater Drive, Dunedin, FL 34698. *Phone:* -813-736-5082. *Toll-free phone:* 800-336-4133. *Fax:* 813-734-0359.

Swiss Hotel Association, Hotel Management School, "Les Roches"

Crans-Montana, Switzerland

Admissions Contact CH 3975 Bluche, Switzerland.

UNITED ARAB EMIRATES

The American University in Dubai

Dubai, United Arab Emirates

Admissions Contact The American University in Dubai, PO Box 28282, Dubai, United Arab Emirates. *Fax:* 971-4-3948887. *E-mail:* info@aud.edu.

UNITED KINGDOM

American InterContinental University-London

London, United Kingdom

- **Proprietary** comprehensive, founded 1970, part of American Intercontinental University
- **Calendar** 3 8-week terms, 2 8-week summer terms
- **Degrees** associate, bachelor's, and master's
- **Urban** campus
- **Coed**
- **Noncompetitive** entrance level

Faculty *Student/faculty ratio:* 12:1.

Student Life *Campus security:* 24-hour emergency response devices.

Applying *Options:* early admission, deferred entrance. *Application fee:* $35. *Required:* essay or personal statement, high school transcript, 2 letters of recommendation, interview.

Admissions Contact Mr. Geoff Hazell, Director of Admissions and Marketing, American InterContinental University-London, 110 Marylebone High Street, London W1M 3DB, United Kingdom. *Phone:* 207-467-5642. *Fax:* 207-467-5641. *E-mail:* admissions@aiulondon.ac.uk.

Huron University USA in London

London, United Kingdom

- **Independent** comprehensive
- **Degrees** certificates, diplomas, bachelor's, and master's
- **Coed**
- **Moderately difficult** entrance level, 63% of applicants were admitted

Undergraduates 70% live on campus.

Freshmen *Admission:* 80 applied, 50 admitted. *Average high school GPA:* 2.5.

Faculty *Total:* 25. *Student/faculty ratio:* 10:1.

Majors Art; art history; business administration; communications; humanities; international relations.

Student Life *Housing Options:* coed. *Activities and Organizations:* student-run newspaper. *Student Services:* personal/psychological counseling.

Standardized Tests *Required for some:* SAT I or ACT (for admission).

Costs (2001–02) *Tuition:* 8250 British pounds full-time. *Room only:* 4000 British pounds.

Applying *Required:* essay or personal statement, high school transcript, minimum 2.0 GPA. *Required for some:* interview. *Application deadline:* 7/1 (freshmen). *Notification:* 7/15 (freshmen).

Admissions Contact Mr. Rob Atkinson, Director of Admissions, Huron University USA in London, 58 Princes Gate-Exhibition Road, London SW7 2PG, United Kingdom. *Phone:* 207-584-9696.

Richmond, The American International University in London

Richmond, United Kingdom

- **Independent** comprehensive, founded 1972
- **Calendar** semesters
- **Degrees** associate, bachelor's, master's, and postbachelor's certificates
- **Urban** 5-acre campus with easy access to London
- **Coed,** 904 undergraduate students, 100% full-time, 56% women, 44% men
- **Moderately difficult** entrance level, 46% of applicants were admitted

Undergraduates 904 full-time. Students come from 40 states and territories, 110 other countries. *Retention:* 73% of 2001 full-time freshmen returned.

Freshmen *Admission:* 1,348 applied, 623 admitted, 162 enrolled. *Average high school GPA:* 3.20. *Test scores:* SAT verbal scores over 500: 75%; SAT math scores over 500: 80%; ACT scores over 18: 100%; SAT verbal scores over 600: 25%; SAT math scores over 600: 5%; ACT scores over 24: 60%; ACT scores over 30: 10%.

Faculty *Total:* 128, 70% with terminal degrees. *Student/faculty ratio:* 17:1.

Majors Anthropology; art; art history; business administration; computer engineering; computer programming; computer science; economics; English; environmental science; European studies; fine/studio arts; history; information sciences/systems; international business; international relations; liberal arts and sciences/liberal studies; literature; mass communications; mathematics; political science; pre-engineering; psychology; social sciences; sociology; systems engineering; theater arts/drama.

Academic Programs *Special study options:* academic remediation for entering students, advanced placement credit, double majors, English as a second language, honors programs, independent study, internships, study abroad, summer session for credit. *Unusual degree programs:* 3-2 engineering with George Washington University.

Library Taylor Library plus 2 others with 80,000 titles, 277 serial subscriptions, an OPAC.

Computers on Campus 400 computers available on campus for general student use. A campuswide network can be accessed from off campus. Internet access, online (class) registration, at least one staffed computer lab available.

Student Life *Housing Options:* coed. *Activities and Organizations:* drama/theater group, student-run newspaper, radio station, International Club, Computer Club, ethnic clubs, Debate Society, sports clubs. *Campus security:* 24-hour patrols. *Student Services:* health clinic, personal/psychological counseling.

Athletics *Intercollegiate sports:* rugby M, soccer M/W, table tennis M, tennis M. *Intramural sports:* badminton M/W, basketball M/W, crew M/W, cross-country running M/W, equestrian sports M, rugby M, soccer M/W, squash M/W, swimming M/W, table tennis M/W, tennis M/W, volleyball M/W, weight lifting M/W.

Standardized Tests *Required:* SAT I or ACT (for admission).

Costs (2002–03) *Comprehensive fee:* $24,117 includes full-time tuition ($14,140), mandatory fees ($1410), and room and board ($8567). Part-time tuition: $1800 per course. *Required fees:* $705 per term part-time.

Applying *Options:* common application, electronic application, deferred entrance. *Application fee:* $60. *Required:* essay or personal statement, high school transcript, 1 letter of recommendation. *Application deadline:* 8/1 (freshmen). *Notification:* 8/15 (freshmen).

Admissions Contact Mr. Brian E. Davis, Director of United States Admissions, Richmond, The American International University in London, 19 Bay State Road, Boston, MA 02215. *Phone:* 617-954-9942. *Fax:* 617-236-4703. *E-mail:* us_admissions@richmond.ac.uk.

Schiller International University

London, United Kingdom

- **Independent** comprehensive, founded 1970, part of Schiller International University
- **Calendar** semesters
- **Degrees** associate, bachelor's, and master's
- **Urban** campus

- **Coed,** 283 undergraduate students
- **Noncompetitive** entrance level

Schiller International University (SIU) is an independent American university with campuses in England, France, Germany, Spain, Switzerland, and the United States. In addition, students can transfer without loss of credit. English is the language of instruction at all campuses. SIU offers undergraduate and graduate students an American education in an international setting.

Undergraduates Students come from 60 other countries.

Majors Economics; hotel and restaurant management; interdisciplinary studies; international business; international relations; liberal arts and sciences/liberal studies; pre-medicine; pre-veterinary studies; psychology.

Academic Programs *Special study options:* accelerated degree program, adult/continuing education programs, advanced placement credit, double majors, English as a second language, independent study, internships, part-time degree program, student-designed majors, study abroad, summer session for credit.

Library 21,603 titles, 143 serial subscriptions.

Computers on Campus 39 computers available on campus for general student use. At least one staffed computer lab available.

Student Life *Housing Options:* coed. *Activities and Organizations:* student-run newspaper, Student Government, campus newspaper, yearbook staff. *Campus security:* 24-hour patrols. *Student Services:* personal/psychological counseling.

Athletics *Intramural sports:* archery M/W, baseball M/W, rugby M, soccer M/W, volleyball M/W.

Costs (2002–03) *Comprehensive fee:* $21,760 includes full-time tuition ($14,560) and room and board ($7200).

Financial Aid Of all full-time matriculated undergraduates who enrolled in 2001, 2 Federal Work-Study jobs (averaging $4330).

Applying *Options:* common application, deferred entrance. *Application fee:* $35. *Required:* essay or personal statement, high school transcript. *Recommended:* minimum 2.0 GPA. *Application deadline:* rolling (freshmen), rolling (transfers).

Admissions Contact Mr. Christoph Leibrecht, Director of Admissions, Schiller International University, 51-55 Waterloo Road, London SE1 8TX, United Kingdom. *Phone:* 813-736-5082.

Quick-Reference College Search Indexes

Majors Index

ACCOUNTING
Abilene Christian U (TX)
Adams State Coll (CO)
Adelphi U (NY)
Adrian Coll (MI)
Alabama State U (AL)
Alaska Pacific U (AK)
Albany State U (GA)
Albertson Coll of Idaho (ID)
Albertus Magnus Coll (CT)
Albright Coll (PA)
Alcorn State U (MS)
Alderson-Broaddus Coll (WV)
Alfred U (NY)
Alma Coll (MI)
Alvernia Coll (PA)
American International Coll (MA)
American U in Cairo(Egypt)
American U of Puerto Rico (PR)
Anderson Coll (SC)
Anderson U (IN)
Andrews U (MI)
Angelo State U (TX)
Appalachian State U (NC)
Aquinas Coll (MI)
Arcadia U (PA)
Arizona State U (AZ)
Arizona State U West (AZ)
Arkansas State U (AR)
Arkansas Tech U (AR)
Asbury Coll (KY)
Ashland U (OH)
Assumption Coll (MA)
Athabasca U (AB, Canada)
Athens State U (AL)
Atlantic Union Coll (MA)
Auburn U (AL)
Auburn U Montgomery (AL)
Augsburg Coll (MN)
Augustana Coll (IL)
Augustana Coll (SD)
Augusta State U (GA)
Aurora U (IL)
Averett U (VA)
Avila Coll (MO)
Azusa Pacific U (CA)
Babson Coll (MA)
Baker Coll of Auburn Hills (MI)
Baker Coll of Cadillac (MI)
Baker Coll of Flint (MI)
Baker Coll of Jackson (MI)
Baker Coll of Muskegon (MI)
Baker Coll of Owosso (MI)
Baker Coll of Port Huron (MI)
Baker U (KS)
Baldwin-Wallace Coll (OH)
Ball State U (IN)
Barber-Scotia Coll (NC)
Barry U (FL)
Barton Coll (NC)
Bayamón Central U (PR)
Baylor U (TX)
Becker Coll (MA)
Belhaven Coll (MS)
Bellarmine U (KY)
Bellevue U (NE)
Belmont Abbey Coll (NC)
Belmont U (TN)
Bemidji State U (MN)
Benedict Coll (SC)
Benedictine Coll (KS)
Benedictine U (IL)
Bennett Coll (NC)
Bentley Coll (MA)
Berkeley Coll, New York (NY)
Berkeley Coll, White Plains (NY)
Baruch Coll of the City U of NY (NY)
Berry Coll (GA)
Bethany Coll (KS)
Bethany Coll (WV)
Bethel Coll (IN)
Bethel Coll (KS)
Bethel Coll (MN)
Bethel Coll (TN)
Bethune-Cookman Coll (FL)
Birmingham-Southern Coll (AL)
Bishop's U (PQ, Canada)
Black Hills State U (SD)
Bloomfield Coll (NJ)
Bloomsburg U of Pennsylvania (PA)
Bluefield State Coll (WV)
Bluffton Coll (OH)
Boise State U (ID)
Boston Coll (MA)
Boston U (MA)
Bowie State U (MD)
Bowling Green State U (OH)
Bradley U (IL)
Brenau U (GA)
Brescia U (KY)
Brewton-Parker Coll (GA)
Briar Cliff U (IA)
Bridgewater Coll (VA)
Bridgewater State Coll (MA)
Briercrest Bible Coll (SK, Canada)
Brigham Young U (UT)
Brigham Young U–Hawaii (HI)
Brock U (ON, Canada)
Brooklyn Coll of the City U of NY (NY)
Bryant Coll (RI)
Bucknell U (PA)
Buena Vista U (IA)
Butler U (IN)
Cabrini Coll (PA)
Caldwell Coll (NJ)
California Coll for Health Sciences (CA)
California Lutheran U (CA)
California State Polytechnic U, Pomona (CA)
California State U, Dominguez Hills (CA)
California State U, Fresno (CA)
California State U, Fullerton (CA)
California State U, Hayward (CA)
California State U, Long Beach (CA)
California State U, Northridge (CA)
California State U, Sacramento (CA)
California State U, San Bernardino (CA)
California State U, San Marcos (CA)
California State U, Stanislaus (CA)
California U of Pennsylvania (PA)
Calvin Coll (MI)
Cameron U (OK)
Campbellsville U (KY)
Campbell U (NC)
Canisius Coll (NY)
Capital U (OH)
Cardinal Stritch U (WI)
Caribbean U (PR)
Carleton U (ON, Canada)
Carlow Coll (PA)
Carroll Coll (MT)
Carroll Coll (WI)
Carson-Newman Coll (TN)
Carthage Coll (WI)
Case Western Reserve U (OH)
Castleton State Coll (VT)
The Catholic U of America (DC)
Cazenovia Coll (NY)
Cedar Crest Coll (PA)
Cedarville U (OH)
Centenary Coll (NJ)
Centenary Coll of Louisiana (LA)
Central Christian Coll of Kansas (KS)
Central Coll (IA)
Central Connecticut State U (CT)
Central Methodist Coll (MO)
Central Michigan U (MI)
Central Missouri State U (MO)
Central State U (OH)
Central Washington U (WA)
Chaminade U of Honolulu (HI)
Champlain Coll (VT)
Chapman U (CA)
Charleston Southern U (SC)
Chatham Coll (PA)
Chestnut Hill Coll (PA)
Chicago State U (IL)
Chowan Coll (NC)
Christian Brothers U (TN)
Christopher Newport U (VA)
City U (WA)
Claremont McKenna Coll (CA)
Clarion U of Pennsylvania (PA)
Clark Atlanta U (GA)
Clarke Coll (IA)
Clarkson U (NY)
Clayton Coll & State U (GA)
Clearwater Christian Coll (FL)
Cleary Coll (MI)
Clemson U (SC)
Cleveland State U (OH)
Coastal Carolina U (SC)
Coe Coll (IA)
Coker Coll (SC)
Coll Misericordia (PA)
Coll of Charleston (SC)
Coll of Mount St. Joseph (OH)
The Coll of New Jersey (NJ)
Coll of Saint Benedict (MN)
Coll of St. Catherine (MN)
Coll of Saint Elizabeth (NJ)
Coll of St. Joseph (VT)
The Coll of Saint Rose (NY)
The Coll of St. Scholastica (MN)
Coll of Santa Fe (NM)
The Coll of Southeastern Europe, The American U of Athens(Greece)
Coll of Staten Island of the City U of NY (NY)
Coll of the Holy Cross (MA)
Coll of the Ozarks (MO)
Coll of the Southwest (NM)
Colorado Christian U (CO)
Colorado State U (CO)
Colorado Tech U Sioux Falls Campus (SD)
Columbia Coll (MO)
Columbia Coll (SC)
Columbia Union Coll (MD)
Columbus State U (GA)
Concord Coll (WV)
Concordia Coll (MN)
Concordia U (IL)
Concordia U (MN)
Concordia U (NE)
Concordia U (QC, Canada)
Concordia U Wisconsin (WI)
Converse Coll (SC)
Cornerstone U (MI)
Creighton U (NE)
Culver-Stockton Coll (MO)
Cumberland Coll (KY)
Cumberland U (TN)
Daemen Coll (NY)
Dakota State U (SD)
Dakota Wesleyan U (SD)
Dalhousie U (NS, Canada)
Dallas Baptist U (TX)
Davenport U, Dearborn (MI)
Davenport U, Grand Rapids (MI)
Davenport U, Kalamazoo (MI)
Davenport U, Lansing (MI)
Davenport U, Warren (MI)
David N. Myers U (OH)
Davis & Elkins Coll (WV)
Defiance Coll (OH)
Delaware State U (DE)
Delaware Valley Coll (PA)
Delta State U (MS)
DePaul U (IL)
DeSales U (PA)
Dickinson State U (ND)
Dillard U (LA)
Doane Coll (NE)
Dominican Coll (NY)
Dominican U (IL)
Dordt Coll (IA)
Dowling Coll (NY)
Drake U (IA)
Drexel U (PA)
Drury U (MO)
Duquesne U (PA)
D'Youville Coll (NY)
East Carolina U (NC)
East Central U (OK)
Eastern Connecticut State U (CT)
Eastern Illinois U (IL)
Eastern Kentucky U (KY)
Eastern Mennonite U (VA)
Eastern Michigan U (MI)
Eastern New Mexico U (NM)
Eastern Oregon U (OR)
Eastern U (PA)
Eastern Washington U (WA)
East Tennessee State U (TN)
East Texas Baptist U (TX)
East-West U (IL)
École des Hautes Études Commerciales de Montréal (PQ, Canada)
Edgewood Coll (WI)
Elizabeth City State U (NC)
Elizabethtown Coll (PA)
Elmhurst Coll (IL)
Elmira Coll (NY)
Elms Coll (MA)
Elon U (NC)
Emmanuel Coll (MA)
Emory & Henry Coll (VA)
Emory U (GA)
Emporia State U (KS)
Eureka Coll (IL)
Evangel U (MO)
Excelsior Coll (NY)
Fairfield U (CT)
Fairleigh Dickinson U, Florham-Madison Campus (NJ)
Fairleigh Dickinson U, Teaneck-Hackensack Campus (NJ)
Fairmont State Coll (WV)
Faulkner U (AL)
Fayetteville State U (NC)
Felician Coll (NJ)
Ferris State U (MI)
Ferrum Coll (VA)
Fisk U (TN)
Fitchburg State Coll (MA)
Flagler Coll (FL)
Florida A&M U (FL)
Florida Atlantic U (FL)
Florida Gulf Coast U (FL)
Florida International U (FL)
Florida Metropolitan U-Fort Lauderdale Coll (FL)
Florida Metropolitan U-Orlando Coll, North (FL)
Florida Metropolitan U-Orlando Coll, South (FL)
Florida Metropolitan U-Tampa Coll (FL)
Florida Southern Coll (FL)
Florida State U (FL)
Fontbonne U (MO)
Fordham U (NY)
Fort Hays State U (KS)
Fort Lewis Coll (CO)
Fort Valley State U (GA)
Framingham State Coll (MA)
Franciscan U of Steubenville (OH)
Francis Marion U (SC)
Franklin Coll of Indiana (IN)
Franklin Pierce Coll (NH)
Franklin U (OH)
Freed-Hardeman U (TN)
Fresno Pacific U (CA)
Friends U (KS)
Frostburg State U (MD)
Furman U (SC)
Gallaudet U (DC)
Gannon U (PA)
Gardner-Webb U (NC)
Geneva Coll (PA)
George Mason U (VA)
Georgetown Coll (KY)
Georgetown U (DC)
The George Washington U (DC)
Georgia Coll and State U (GA)
Georgian Court Coll (NJ)
Georgia Southern U (GA)
Georgia Southwestern State U (GA)
Georgia State U (GA)
Gettysburg Coll (PA)
Glenville State Coll (WV)
Golden Gate U (CA)
Goldey-Beacom Coll (DE)
Gonzaga U (WA)
Gordon Coll (MA)
Goshen Coll (IN)
Governors State U (IL)
Grace Coll (IN)
Graceland U (IA)
Grace U (NE)
Grambling State U (LA)
Grand Canyon U (AZ)
Grand Valley State U (MI)
Grand View Coll (IA)
Greensboro Coll (NC)
Greenville Coll (IL)
Grove City Coll (PA)
Guilford Coll (NC)
Gustavus Adolphus Coll (MN)
Gwynedd-Mercy Coll (PA)
Hampton U (VA)
Hannibal-LaGrange Coll (MO)
Harding U (AR)
Hardin-Simmons U (TX)
Harris-Stowe State Coll (MO)
Hartwick Coll (NY)
Hastings Coll (NE)
Hawai'i Pacific U (HI)
Heidelberg Coll (OH)
Henderson State U (AR)
Hendrix Coll (AR)
Hesser Coll (NH)
High Point U (NC)
Hilbert Coll (NY)
Hillsdale Coll (MI)
Hofstra U (NY)
Holy Family Coll (PA)
Hope Coll (MI)
Houghton Coll (NY)
Houston Baptist U (TX)
Howard Payne U (TX)
Howard U (DC)
Humboldt State U (CA)
Hunter Coll of the City U of NY (NY)
Huntingdon Coll (AL)
Huntington Coll (IN)
Huron U (SD)
Husson Coll (ME)
Huston-Tillotson Coll (TX)
Idaho State U (ID)
Illinois Coll (IL)
Illinois State U (IL)
Illinois Wesleyan U (IL)
Immaculata Coll (PA)
Indiana Inst of Technology (IN)
Indiana State U (IN)
Indiana U Bloomington (IN)
Indiana U Northwest (IN)
Indiana U of Pennsylvania (PA)
Indiana U–Purdue U Fort Wayne (IN)
Indiana Wesleyan U (IN)
Inter American U of PR, Aguadilla Campus (PR)
Inter Amer U of PR, Barranquitas Campus (PR)
Inter American U of PR, San Germán Campus (PR)
International Business Coll, Fort Wayne (IN)
International Coll (FL)
Iona Coll (NY)
Iowa State U of Science and Technology (IA)
Iowa Wesleyan Coll (IA)
Ithaca Coll (NY)
Jackson State U (MS)
Jacksonville State U (AL)
Jacksonville U (FL)
James Madison U (VA)
Jamestown Coll (ND)
Jarvis Christian Coll (TX)
John Brown U (AR)

ACCOUNTING RELATED

ACCOUNTING TECHNICIAN

ACTING/DIRECTING

ACTUARIAL SCIENCE

ADAPTED PHYSICAL EDUCATION

ADMINISTRATIVE/SECRETARIAL SERVICES

ADULT/CONTINUING EDUCATION

U of Virginia (VA)
U of Washington (WA)
U of Wisconsin–Madison (WI)
U of Wisconsin–Milwaukee (WI)
Vanderbilt U (TN)
Washington U in St. Louis (MO)
Wayne State U (MI)
Wellesley Coll (MA)
Wells Coll (NY)
Wesleyan U (CT)
Western Michigan U (MI)
William Paterson U of New Jersey (NJ)
Yale U (CT)
York Coll of the City U of New York (NY)
Youngstown State U (OH)

AFRICAN LANGUAGES
Harvard U (MA)
Lincoln U (PA)
Long Island U, Southampton Coll, Friends World Program (NY)
Ohio U (OH)
U of Calif, Los Angeles (CA)
U of Wisconsin–Madison (WI)

AFRICAN STUDIES
American U (DC)
Bard Coll (NY)
Barnard Coll (NY)
Bates Coll (ME)
Bowdoin Coll (ME)
Bowling Green State U (OH)
Brandeis U (MA)
Brooklyn Coll of the City U of NY (NY)
California State U, Northridge (CA)
Carleton Coll (MN)
Carleton U (ON, Canada)
Chicago State U (IL)
Colgate U (NY)
Coll of the Holy Cross (MA)
The Coll of Wooster (OH)
Connecticut Coll (CT)
Cornell U (NY)
Dartmouth Coll (NH)
DePaul U (IL)
Emory U (GA)
Fordham U (NY)
Franklin and Marshall Coll (PA)
Hamilton Coll (NY)
Hampshire Coll (MA)
Harvard U (MA)
Haverford Coll (PA)
Hobart and William Smith Colls (NY)
Indiana U Bloomington (IN)
Lake Forest Coll (IL)
Lehigh U (PA)
Long Island U, Southampton Coll, Friends World Program (NY)
Luther Coll (IA)
Marlboro Coll (VT)
McGill U (PQ, Canada)
Morgan State U (MD)
Oakland U (MI)
The Ohio State U (OH)
Ohio U (OH)
Portland State U (OR)
Queens Coll of the City U of NY (NY)
Rutgers, The State U of New Jersey, New Brunswick (NJ)
St. Lawrence U (NY)
Shaw U (NC)
Stanford U (CA)
State U of NY at Binghamton (NY)
State U of NY Coll at Brockport (NY)
State U of NY at Stony Brook (NY)
Tennessee State U (TN)
Tulane U (LA)
U of Calif, Davis (CA)
U of Chicago (IL)
The U of Iowa (IA)
U of Kansas (KS)
U of Michigan (MI)
U of Minnesota, Twin Cities Campus (MN)
U of Pennsylvania (PA)
U of Toronto (ON, Canada)
U of Wisconsin–Madison (WI)
Vanderbilt U (TN)
Vassar Coll (NY)
Washington U in St. Louis (MO)
Wellesley Coll (MA)
William Paterson U of New Jersey (NJ)
Yale U (CT)
York U (ON, Canada)
Youngstown State U (OH)

AGRIBUSINESS
Abilene Christian U (TX)
Arkansas State U (AR)
Central Missouri State U (MO)
Coll of the Ozarks (MO)
Colorado State U (CO)
Cornell U (NY)
Illinois State U (IL)
McGill U (PQ, Canada)
Michigan State U (MI)
Middle Tennessee State U (TN)
Mississippi State U (MS)
North Carolina State U (NC)
North Dakota State U (ND)
Northwestern Coll (IA)
Penn State U Univ Park Campus (PA)
South Dakota State U (SD)
Southwest Missouri State U (MO)
Southwest Texas State U (TX)
Stephen F. Austin State U (TX)
Texas A&M U (TX)
U of Arkansas (AR)
U of Delaware (DE)
West Texas A&M U (TX)

AGRICULTURAL ANIMAL BREEDING
Texas A&M U (TX)

AGRICULTURAL ANIMAL HEALTH
Sul Ross State U (TX)

AGRICULTURAL ANIMAL HUSBANDRY/PRODUCTION MANAGEMENT
Angelo State U (TX)
Dordt Coll (IA)
North Dakota State U (ND)
Saint Mary-of-the-Woods Coll (IN)
Texas A&M U (TX)
Texas Tech U (TX)
U of New Hampshire (NH)
The U of Tennessee at Martin (TN)

AGRICULTURAL BUSINESS
Alcorn State U (MS)
Andrews U (MI)
Arizona State U East (AZ)
Arkansas Tech U (AR)
Berea Coll (KY)
California Polytechnic State U, San Luis Obispo (CA)
California State Polytechnic U, Pomona (CA)
California State U, Chico (CA)
California State U, Fresno (CA)
Cameron U (OK)
Central Missouri State U (MO)
Clemson U (SC)
Concordia U Wisconsin (WI)
Cornell U (NY)
Delaware State U (DE)
Delaware Valley Coll (PA)
Dickinson State U (ND)
Dordt Coll (IA)
Eastern Kentucky U (KY)
Eastern New Mexico U (NM)
Eastern Oregon U (OR)
Florida A&M U (FL)
Florida Southern Coll (FL)
Fort Hays State U (KS)
Fort Lewis Coll (CO)
Freed-Hardeman U (TN)
Hannibal-LaGrange Coll (MO)
Iowa State U of Science and Technology (IA)
Kansas State U (KS)
Lincoln U (MO)
Louisiana State U and A&M Coll (LA)
Louisiana Tech U (LA)
Lubbock Christian U (TX)
McGill U (PQ, Canada)
McPherson Coll (KS)
Michigan State U (MI)
MidAmerica Nazarene U (KS)
Missouri Valley Coll (MO)
Montana State U–Bozeman (MT)
Murray State U (KY)
New Mexico State U (NM)
Nicholls State U (LA)
North Carolina Ag and Tech State U (NC)
Northwestern Oklahoma State U (OK)
Northwest Missouri State U (MO)
Nova Scotia Ag Coll (NS, Canada)
The Ohio State U (OH)
Oklahoma Panhandle State U (OK)
Oklahoma State U (OK)
Oregon State U (OR)
Penn State U Univ Park Campus (PA)
Rocky Mountain Coll (MT)
Sam Houston State U (TX)
San Diego State U (CA)
Simon's Rock Coll of Bard (MA)
South Carolina State U (SC)
Southeast Missouri State U (MO)
Southern Arkansas U–Magnolia (AR)
Southwest State U (MN)
State U of NY Coll of A&T at Cobleskill (NY)
Sul Ross State U (TX)
Tabor Coll (KS)
Tarleton State U (TX)
Tennessee Technological U (TN)
Texas A&M U (TX)
Texas A&M U–Kingsville (TX)
Texas Tech U (TX)
Tuskegee U (AL)
U of Alberta (AB, Canada)
U of Calif, Davis (CA)
U of Delaware (DE)
U of Georgia (GA)
U of Guelph (ON, Canada)
U of Hawaii at Hilo (HI)
U of Idaho (ID)
The U of Lethbridge (AB, Canada)
U of Louisiana at Monroe (LA)
U of Maryland Eastern Shore (MD)
U of Minnesota, Crookston (MN)
U of Minnesota, Twin Cities Campus (MN)
U of Missouri–Columbia (MO)
U of Nebraska at Kearney (NE)
U of Nebraska–Lincoln (NE)
U of New Hampshire (NH)
The U of Tennessee at Martin (TN)
U of Vermont (VT)
U of Wisconsin–Madison (WI)
U of Wisconsin–Platteville (WI)
U of Wisconsin–River Falls (WI)
U of Wyoming (WY)
Utah State U (UT)
Washington State U (WA)
Wayne State Coll (NE)
West Texas A&M U (TX)
Wilmington Coll (OH)

AGRICULTURAL BUSINESS AND PRODUCTION RELATED
Michigan State U (MI)
U of Nebraska–Lincoln (NE)

AGRICULTURAL BUSINESS RELATED
U of Nebraska–Lincoln (NE)
The U of Tennessee (TN)
Utah State U (UT)

AGRICULTURAL ECONOMICS
Alcorn State U (MS)
Auburn U (AL)
Central Missouri State U (MO)
Clemson U (SC)
Colorado State U (CO)
Cornell U (NY)
Eastern Oregon U (OR)
Fort Valley State U (GA)
Kansas State U (KS)
McGill U (PQ, Canada)
McPherson Coll (KS)
Michigan State U (MI)
Mississippi State U (MS)
Murray State U (KY)
New Mexico State U (NM)
North Carolina Ag and Tech State U (NC)
North Dakota State U (ND)
Northwest Missouri State U (MO)
Nova Scotia Ag Coll (NS, Canada)
The Ohio State U (OH)
Oklahoma State U (OK)
Oregon State U (OR)
Purdue U (IN)
South Dakota State U (SD)
Southern Illinois U Carbondale (IL)
Southern U and A&M Coll (LA)
Tarleton State U (TX)
Texas A&M U (TX)
Texas A&M U–Commerce (TX)
Texas Tech U (TX)
Truman State U (MO)
Université Laval (QC, Canada)
U of Alberta (AB, Canada)
The U of Arizona (AZ)
U of Arkansas at Pine Bluff (AR)
U of Calif, Davis (CA)
U of Connecticut (CT)
U of Delaware (DE)
U of Florida (FL)
U of Georgia (GA)
U of Guelph (ON, Canada)
U of Hawaii at Manoa (HI)
U of Idaho (ID)
U of Illinois at Urbana–Champaign (IL)
U of Kentucky (KY)
U of Maine (ME)
U of Manitoba (MB, Canada)
U of Maryland, Coll Park (MD)
U of Missouri–Columbia (MO)
U of Nebraska–Lincoln (NE)
U of Nevada, Reno (NV)
U of Saskatchewan (SK, Canada)
The U of Tennessee (TN)
U of Vermont (VT)
U of Wisconsin–Madison (WI)
Utah State U (UT)
Virginia Polytechnic Inst and State U (VA)
Washington State U (WA)

AGRICULTURAL EDUCATION
Andrews U (MI)
Arkansas State U (AR)
Auburn U (AL)
California State Polytechnic U, Pomona (CA)
California State U, Chico (CA)
California State U, Fresno (CA)
Central Missouri State U (MO)
Clemson U (SC)
Coll of the Ozarks (MO)
Colorado State U (CO)
Cornell U (NY)
Delaware State U (DE)
Eastern New Mexico U (NM)
Iowa State U of Science and Technology (IA)
Mississippi State U (MS)
Montana State U–Bozeman (MT)
Morehead State U (KY)
Murray State U (KY)
New Mexico State U (NM)
North Carolina Ag and Tech State U (NC)
North Carolina State U (NC)
North Dakota State U (ND)
Northwest Missouri State U (MO)
The Ohio State U (OH)
Oklahoma Panhandle State U (OK)
Oklahoma State U (OK)
Prairie View A&M U (TX)
Purdue U (IN)
Sam Houston State U (TX)
South Dakota State U (SD)
Southern Arkansas U–Magnolia (AR)
Southwest Missouri State U (MO)
Tarleton State U (TX)
Tennessee Technological U (TN)
Texas A&M U–Commerce (TX)
Texas A&M U–Kingsville (TX)
The U of Arizona (AZ)
U of Arkansas (AR)
U of Arkansas at Pine Bluff (AR)
U of Calif, Davis (CA)
U of Connecticut (CT)
U of Delaware (DE)
U of Florida (FL)
U of Georgia (GA)
U of Hawaii at Manoa (HI)
U of Idaho (ID)
U of Illinois at Urbana–Champaign (IL)
U of Maryland Eastern Shore (MD)
U of Minnesota, Twin Cities Campus (MN)
U of Missouri–Columbia (MO)
U of Nebraska–Lincoln (NE)
U of Nevada, Reno (NV)
The U of Tennessee (TN)
The U of Tennessee at Martin (TN)
U of Wisconsin–Madison (WI)
U of Wisconsin–River Falls (WI)
U of Wyoming (WY)
Utah State U (UT)
Virginia Polytechnic Inst and State U (VA)
Washington State U (WA)
West Virginia U (WV)
Wilmington Coll (OH)

AGRICULTURAL ENGINEERING
Auburn U (AL)
California Polytechnic State U, San Luis Obispo (CA)
California State Polytechnic U, Pomona (CA)
Clemson U (SC)
Colorado State U (CO)
Cornell U (NY)
Dalhousie U (NS, Canada)
Fort Valley State U (GA)
Iowa State U of Science and Technology (IA)
Kansas State U (KS)
McGill U (PQ, Canada)
Michigan State U (MI)
Mississippi State U (MS)
Murray State U (KY)
North Carolina State U (NC)
North Dakota State U (ND)
The Ohio State U (OH)
Penn State U Univ Park Campus (PA)
Purdue U (IN)
South Dakota State U (SD)
Tennessee Technological U (TN)
Texas A&M U (TX)
The U of Arizona (AZ)
U of Arkansas (AR)
U of Calif, Davis (CA)
U of Delaware (DE)
U of Florida (FL)
U of Georgia (GA)
U of Hawaii at Manoa (HI)
U of Idaho (ID)
U of Illinois at Urbana–Champaign (IL)
U of Kentucky (KY)
U of Maine (ME)
U of Manitoba (MB, Canada)
U of Minnesota, Twin Cities Campus (MN)
U of Nebraska–Lincoln (NE)
U of Saskatchewan (SK, Canada)
The U of Tennessee (TN)
U of Wisconsin–Madison (WI)
U of Wisconsin–River Falls (WI)
Utah State U (UT)
Washington State U (WA)

AGRICULTURAL EXTENSION
Colorado State U (CO)
U of Wyoming (WY)

AGRICULTURAL/FOOD PRODUCTS PROCESSING
Kansas State U (KS)
Michigan State U (MI)
The Ohio State U (OH)
U of Illinois at Urbana–Champaign (IL)

AGRICULTURAL MECHANIZATION
Andrews U (MI)
Cameron U (OK)
Central Missouri State U (MO)
Coll of the Ozarks (MO)
Cornell U (NY)
Eastern Kentucky U (KY)
Iowa State U of Science and Technology (IA)
Kansas State U (KS)
Lewis-Clark State Coll (ID)
Montana State U–Bozeman (MT)
North Carolina Ag and Tech State U (NC)
North Dakota State U (ND)
Northwest Missouri State U (MO)
Nova Scotia Ag Coll (NS, Canada)
Penn State U Univ Park Campus (PA)
Purdue U (IN)
Sam Houston State U (TX)
South Dakota State U (SD)
State U of NY Coll of A&T at Cobleskill (NY)
Stephen F. Austin State U (TX)
Texas A&M U (TX)
U of Idaho (ID)

ANATOMY

ANIMAL SCIENCES

ANIMAL SCIENCES RELATED

ANTHROPOLOGY

Miami U (OH)
Michigan State U (MI)
Middlebury Coll (VT)
Middle Tennessee State U (TN)
Millersville U of Pennsylvania (PA)
Millsaps Coll (MS)
Mills Coll (CA)
Minnesota State U, Mankato (MN)
Minnesota State U Moorhead (MN)
Mississippi State U (MS)
Monmouth U (NJ)
Montana State U–Bozeman (MT)
Montclair State U (NJ)
Mount Allison U (NB, Canada)
Mount Holyoke Coll (MA)
Mount Saint Vincent U (NS, Canada)
Muhlenberg Coll (PA)
National-Louis U (IL)
New Coll of Florida (FL)
New Mexico Highlands U (NM)
New Mexico State U (NM)
New York U (NY)
North Carolina Wesleyan Coll (NC)
North Central Coll (IL)
North Dakota State U (ND)
Northeastern Illinois U (IL)
Northeastern U (MA)
Northern Arizona U (AZ)
Northern Illinois U (IL)
Northern Kentucky U (KY)
North Park U (IL)
Northwestern State U of Louisiana (LA)
Northwestern U (IL)
Oakland U (MI)
Oberlin Coll (OH)
Occidental Coll (CA)
The Ohio State U (OH)
Ohio U (OH)
Ohio Wesleyan U (OH)
Okanagan U Coll (BC, Canada)
Oregon State U (OR)
Pacific Lutheran U (WA)
Penn State U Univ Park Campus (PA)
Pitzer Coll (CA)
Plattsburgh State U of NY (NY)
Pomona Coll (CA)
Portland State U (OR)
Prescott Coll (AZ)
Princeton U (NJ)
Principia Coll (IL)
Purchase Coll, State U of NY (NY)
Queens Coll of the City U of NY (NY)
Radford U (VA)
Reed Coll (OR)
Rhode Island Coll (RI)
Rhodes Coll (TN)
Rice U (TX)
Richmond, The American International U in London(United Kingdom)
Ripon Coll (WI)
Rockford Coll (IL)
Rollins Coll (FL)
Rutgers, The State U of New Jersey, New Brunswick (NJ)
St. Cloud State U (MN)
Saint Francis U (PA)
St. Francis Xavier U (NS, Canada)
St. John Fisher Coll (NY)
St. John's U (NY)
St. Lawrence U (NY)
Saint Mary's Coll (IN)
Saint Mary's Coll of California (CA)
St. Mary's Coll of Maryland (MD)
Saint Mary's U (NS, Canada)
St. Thomas U (NB, Canada)
Saint Vincent Coll (PA)
Salve Regina U (RI)
San Diego State U (CA)
San Francisco State U (CA)
San Jose State U (CA)
Santa Clara U (CA)
Sarah Lawrence Coll (NY)
Scripps Coll (CA)
Seton Hall U (NJ)
Simon Fraser U (BC, Canada)
Simon's Rock Coll of Bard (MA)
Skidmore Coll (NY)
Slippery Rock U of Pennsylvania (PA)
Smith Coll (MA)
Sonoma State U (CA)
Southeast Missouri State U (MO)
Southern Illinois U Carbondale (IL)
Southern Illinois U Edwardsville (IL)
Southern Methodist U (TX)
Southern Oregon U (OR)
Southwest Missouri State U (MO)
Southwest Texas State U (TX)
Stanford U (CA)
State U of NY at Albany (NY)
State U of NY at Binghamton (NY)
State U of NY at New Paltz (NY)
State U of NY at Oswego (NY)
State U of NY Coll at Brockport (NY)
State U of NY Coll at Buffalo (NY)
State U of NY Coll at Cortland (NY)
State U of NY Coll at Geneseo (NY)
State U of NY Coll at Oneonta (NY)
State U of NY Coll at Potsdam (NY)
State U of West Georgia (GA)
State U of NY at Stony Brook (NY)
Swarthmore Coll (PA)
Sweet Briar Coll (VA)
Syracuse U (NY)
Temple U (PA)
Texas A&M U (TX)
Texas A&M U–Commerce (TX)
Texas A&M U–Kingsville (TX)
Texas Tech U (TX)
Thomas Edison State Coll (NJ)
Thomas U (GA)
Towson U (MD)
Transylvania U (KY)
Trent U (ON, Canada)
Trinity Coll (CT)
Trinity U (TX)
Tufts U (MA)
Tulane U (LA)
Union Coll (NY)
Université de Montréal (QC, Canada)
Université Laval (QC, Canada)
State U of NY at Buffalo (NY)
U Coll of Cape Breton (NS, Canada)
U Coll of the Fraser Valley (BC, Canada)
The U of Alabama (AL)
The U of Alabama at Birmingham (AL)
U of Alaska Anchorage (AK)
U of Alaska Fairbanks (AK)
U of Alberta (AB, Canada)
The U of Arizona (AZ)
U of Arkansas (AR)
U of Arkansas at Little Rock (AR)
The U of British Columbia (BC, Canada)
U of Calgary (AB, Canada)
U of Calif, Berkeley (CA)
U of Calif, Davis (CA)
U of Calif, Irvine (CA)
U of Calif, Los Angeles (CA)
U of Calif, Riverside (CA)
U of Calif, San Diego (CA)
U of Calif, Santa Barbara (CA)
U of Calif, Santa Cruz (CA)
U of Central Florida (FL)
U of Chicago (IL)
U of Cincinnati (OH)
U of Colorado at Boulder (CO)
U of Colorado at Colorado Springs (CO)
U of Colorado at Denver (CO)
U of Connecticut (CT)
U of Delaware (DE)
U of Denver (CO)
U of Evansville (IN)
U of Florida (FL)
U of Georgia (GA)
U of Guelph (ON, Canada)
U of Hawaii at Hilo (HI)
U of Hawaii at Manoa (HI)
U of Hawaii–West Oahu (HI)
U of Houston (TX)
U of Houston–Clear Lake (TX)
U of Idaho (ID)
U of Illinois at Chicago (IL)
U of Illinois at Springfield (IL)
U of Illinois at Urbana–Champaign (IL)
U of Indianapolis (IN)
The U of Iowa (IA)
U of Kansas (KS)
U of Kentucky (KY)
U of King's Coll (NS, Canada)
U of La Verne (CA)
The U of Lethbridge (AB, Canada)
U of Louisiana at Lafayette (LA)
U of Louisville (KY)
U of Maine (ME)
U of Maine at Farmington (ME)
U of Manitoba (MB, Canada)
U of Maryland, Baltimore County (MD)
U of Maryland, Coll Park (MD)
U of Massachusetts Amherst (MA)
U of Massachusetts Boston (MA)
The U of Memphis (TN)
U of Miami (FL)
U of Michigan (MI)
U of Michigan–Dearborn (MI)
U of Michigan–Flint (MI)
U of Minnesota, Duluth (MN)
U of Minnesota, Twin Cities Campus (MN)
U of Mississippi (MS)
U of Missouri–Columbia (MO)
U of Missouri–St. Louis (MO)
The U of Montana–Missoula (MT)
U of Nebraska–Lincoln (NE)
U of Nevada, Las Vegas (NV)
U of Nevada, Reno (NV)
U of New Hampshire (NH)
U of New Mexico (NM)
U of New Orleans (LA)
The U of North Carolina at Chapel Hill (NC)
The U of North Carolina at Charlotte (NC)
The U of North Carolina at Greensboro (NC)
The U of North Carolina at Wilmington (NC)
U of North Dakota (ND)
U of Northern Iowa (IA)
U of North Florida (FL)
U of North Texas (TX)
U of Notre Dame (IN)
U of Oklahoma (OK)
U of Oregon (OR)
U of Pennsylvania (PA)
U of Pittsburgh (PA)
U of Pittsburgh at Greensburg (PA)
U of Prince Edward Island (PE, Canada)
U of Redlands (CA)
U of Regina (SK, Canada)
U of Rhode Island (RI)
U of Rochester (NY)
U of San Diego (CA)
U of Saskatchewan (SK, Canada)
U of South Alabama (AL)
U of South Carolina (SC)
U of South Dakota (SD)
U of Southern California (CA)
U of Southern Maine (ME)
U of Southern Mississippi (MS)
U of South Florida (FL)
The U of Tennessee (TN)
The U of Texas at Arlington (TX)
The U of Texas at Austin (TX)
The U of Texas at El Paso (TX)
The U of Texas at San Antonio (TX)
The U of Texas–Pan American (TX)
U of the District of Columbia (DC)
U of the South (TN)
U of Toledo (OH)
U of Toronto (ON, Canada)
U of Tulsa (OK)
U of Utah (UT)
U of Vermont (VT)
U of Victoria (BC, Canada)
U of Virginia (VA)
U of Washington (WA)
U of Waterloo (ON, Canada)
The U of Western Ontario (ON, Canada)
U of West Florida (FL)
U of Windsor (ON, Canada)
U of Wisconsin–Madison (WI)
U of Wisconsin–Milwaukee (WI)
U of Wisconsin–Oshkosh (WI)
U of Wyoming (WY)
Ursinus Coll (PA)
Utah State U (UT)
Valdosta State U (GA)
Vanderbilt U (TN)
Vanguard U of Southern California (CA)
Vassar Coll (NY)
Wagner Coll (NY)
Wake Forest U (NC)
Warren Wilson Coll (NC)
Washburn U of Topeka (KS)
Washington and Lee U (VA)
Washington Coll (MD)
Washington State U (WA)
Washington U in St. Louis (MO)
Wayne State U (MI)
Webster U (MO)
Wellesley Coll (MA)
Wells Coll (NY)
Wesleyan U (CT)
West Chester U of Pennsylvania (PA)
Western Carolina U (NC)
Western Connecticut State U (CT)
Western Kentucky U (KY)
Western Michigan U (MI)
Western Oregon U (OR)
Western State Coll of Colorado (CO)
Western Washington U (WA)
Westminster Coll (MO)
Westmont Coll (CA)
West Virginia U (WV)
Wheaton Coll (IL)
Wheaton Coll (MA)
Whitman Coll (WA)
Wichita State U (KS)
Widener U (PA)
Wilfrid Laurier U (ON, Canada)
William Paterson U of New Jersey (NJ)
Williams Coll (MA)
Wright State U (OH)
Yale U (CT)
York Coll of the City U of New York (NY)
York U (ON, Canada)
Youngstown State U (OH)

APPAREL MARKETING

Concordia Coll (MN)
Philadelphia U (PA)
U of Rhode Island (RI)
Youngstown State U (OH)

APPLIED ART

Academy of Art Coll (CA)
Alfred U (NY)
American Academy of Art (IL)
Athabasca U (AB, Canada)
Azusa Pacific U (CA)
Bemidji State U (MN)
Berry Coll (GA)
California Coll of Arts and Crafts (CA)
California Polytechnic State U, San Luis Obispo (CA)
California State U, Dominguez Hills (CA)
California State U, Northridge (CA)
Carthage Coll (WI)
Chicago State U (IL)
Cleveland State U (OH)
Ctr for Creative Studies—Coll of Art and Design (MI)
The Coll of New Rochelle (NY)
Coll of Staten Island of the City U of NY (NY)
Columbia Coll (MO)
Columbia Coll (SC)
Columbia U, School of General Studies (NY)
Columbus Coll of Art and Design (OH)
Converse Coll (SC)
Corcoran Coll of Art and Design (DC)
Cornell U (NY)
Daemen Coll (NY)
DePaul U (IL)
Dowling Coll (NY)
Elizabeth City State U (NC)
Elms Coll (MA)
Franklin Pierce Coll (NH)
Friends U (KS)
Georgia Southwestern State U (GA)
Goddard Coll (VT)
Howard Payne U (TX)
Howard U (DC)
Huntingdon Coll (AL)
Illinois Wesleyan U (IL)
Indiana U Bloomington (IN)
Inter American U of PR, San Germán Campus (PR)
Iowa Wesleyan Coll (IA)
Lamar U (TX)
Lindenwood U (MO)
Long Island U, C.W. Post Campus (NY)
Long Island U, Southampton Coll, Friends World Program (NY)
Lubbock Christian U (TX)
Mansfield U of Pennsylvania (PA)
Marygrove Coll (MI)
Marywood U (PA)
McNeese State U (LA)
Memphis Coll of Art (TN)
Mesa State Coll (CO)
Midwestern State U (TX)
Minnesota State U, Mankato (MN)
Minnesota State U Moorhead (MN)
Mississippi Coll (MS)
Mount Vernon Nazarene U (OH)
Muskingum Coll (OH)
National American U (NM)
New World School of the Arts (FL)
Northern Michigan U (MI)
Oakland City U (IN)
Oklahoma Baptist U (OK)
Olivet Coll (MI)
Oregon State U (OR)
Otis Coll of Art and Design (CA)
Peru State Coll (NE)
Point Park Coll (PA)
Portland State U (OR)
Pratt Inst (NY)
Rochester Inst of Technology (NY)
St. Cloud State U (MN)
St. Thomas Aquinas Coll (NY)
Savannah Coll of Art and Design (GA)
School of the Museum of Fine Arts (MA)
School of Visual Arts (NY)
Seton Hill Coll (PA)
Springfield Coll (MA)
State U of NY Coll at Buffalo (NY)
State U of NY Coll at Fredonia (NY)
Syracuse U (NY)
Truman State U (MO)
The U of Akron (OH)
U of Calif, Los Angeles (CA)
U of Dayton (OH)
U of Delaware (DE)
U of Houston–Clear Lake (TX)
U of Michigan (MI)
Western Montana Coll of The U of Montana (MT)
U of North Texas (TX)
U of Oregon (OR)
U of Ottawa (ON, Canada)
U of Sioux Falls (SD)
U of South Dakota (SD)
U of Southern Colorado (CO)
The U of Texas at Brownsville (TX)
U of the South (TN)
U of Toledo (OH)
U of Wisconsin–Madison (WI)
Viterbo U (WI)
Washington U in St. Louis (MO)
William Carey Coll (MS)
William Paterson U of New Jersey (NJ)
Winona State U (MN)
York U (ON, Canada)

APPLIED ECONOMICS

Cornell U (NY)
École des Hautes Études Commerciales de Montréal (PQ, Canada)
Florida State U (FL)
Ithaca Coll (NY)
Penn State U Univ Park Campus (PA)
Plymouth State Coll (NH)
Saint Joseph's Coll (IN)
Southern Methodist U (TX)
U of Massachusetts Amherst (MA)
U of Northern Iowa (IA)
U of Rhode Island (RI)
U of San Francisco (CA)

APPLIED HISTORY

East Carolina U (NC)
Meredith Coll (NC)
U of Calif, Santa Barbara (CA)
U of Hawaii at Manoa (HI)
Western Michigan U (MI)

APPLIED MATHEMATICS

Alderson-Broaddus Coll (WV)
American U (DC)
Asbury Coll (KY)
Auburn U (AL)
Barnard Coll (NY)
Baylor U (TX)
Belmont U (TN)
Bowie State U (MD)

Brescia U (KY)
Brock U (ON, Canada)
Brown U (RI)
California Inst of Technology (CA)
California State Polytechnic U, Pomona (CA)
California State U, Chico (CA)
California State U, Fullerton (CA)
California State U, Hayward (CA)
California State U, Long Beach (CA)
California State U, Northridge (CA)
Carleton U (ON, Canada)
Carnegie Mellon U (PA)
Case Western Reserve U (OH)
Chapman U (CA)
Charleston Southern U (SC)
Clarkson U (NY)
Coastal Carolina U (SC)
Colorado State U (CO)
Columbia U, School of General Studies (NY)
Columbia U, School of Engineering & Applied Sci (NY)
Concordia U (QC, Canada)
DePaul U (IL)
Dowling Coll (NY)
Eastern Kentucky U (KY)
Elizabeth City State U (NC)
Elms Coll (MA)
Emory & Henry Coll (VA)
Ferris State U (MI)
Florida Inst of Technology (FL)
Florida International U (FL)
Florida State U (FL)
Franklin Coll of Indiana (IN)
Fresno Pacific U (CA)
Geneva Coll (PA)
The George Washington U (DC)
Grand Valley State U (MI)
Grand View Coll (IA)
Hampshire Coll (MA)
Harvard U (MA)
Hawai'i Pacific U (HI)
Hofstra U (NY)
Humboldt State U (CA)
Illinois Inst of Technology (IL)
Indiana U of Pennsylvania (PA)
Indiana U South Bend (IN)
Inter American U of PR, San Germán Campus (PR)
Ithaca Coll (NY)
Johns Hopkins U (MD)
Johnson C. Smith U (NC)
Kent State U (OH)
Kentucky State U (KY)
Kettering U (MI)
Lamar U (TX)
La Roche Coll (PA)
La Salle U (PA)
Le Moyne Coll (NY)
Limestone Coll (SC)
Long Island U, C.W. Post Campus (NY)
Longwood Coll (VA)
Loyola Coll in Maryland (MD)
Marlboro Coll (VT)
Mary Baldwin Coll (VA)
Maryville U of Saint Louis (MO)
Massachusetts Inst of Technology (MA)
The Master's Coll and Seminary (CA)
McGill U (PQ, Canada)
McMaster U (ON, Canada)
Medgar Evers Coll of the City U of NY (NY)
Memorial U of Newfoundland (NF, Canada)
Mesa State Coll (CO)
Metropolitan State U (MN)
Michigan State U (MI)
Michigan Technological U (MI)
Montana Tech of The U of Montana (MT)
Montclair State U (NJ)
Mount Allison U (NB, Canada)
Mount Saint Vincent U (NS, Canada)
Murray State U (KY)
New Jersey Inst of Technology (NJ)
New Mexico Inst of Mining and Technology (NM)
North Carolina Ag and Tech State U (NC)
North Carolina State U (NC)
North Central Coll (IL)
Northland Coll (WI)
Northwestern U (IL)
Oakland City U (IN)
Oakwood Coll (AL)
Ohio U (OH)
Oregon State U (OR)
Pacific Union Coll (CA)
Penn State U Harrisburg Campus of the Capital Coll (PA)
Penn State U Univ Park Campus (PA)
Queens Coll (NC)
Queens Coll of the City U of NY (NY)
Quinnipiac U (CT)
Rensselaer Polytechnic Inst (NY)
Rice U (TX)
Robert Morris U (PA)
Rochester Inst of Technology (NY)
Saint Joseph's Coll (IN)
Saint Louis U (MO)
Saint Mary's Coll (IN)
St. Thomas Aquinas Coll (NY)
Salem State Coll (MA)
San Diego State U (CA)
San Francisco State U (CA)
San Jose State U (CA)
Seattle U (WA)
Shawnee State U (OH)
Simon Fraser U (BC, Canada)
Simon's Rock Coll of Bard (MA)
Sonoma State U (CA)
Southeast Missouri State U (MO)
State U of NY at Albany (NY)
State U of NY at New Paltz (NY)
State U of NY at Oswego (NY)
State U of NY Inst of Tech at Utica/Rome (NY)
State U of NY at Stony Brook (NY)
Texas A&M U (TX)
Trent U (ON, Canada)
Trinity Western U (BC, Canada)
United States Military Academy (NY)
Université de Montréal (QC, Canada)
Université de Sherbrooke (PQ, Canada)
The U of Akron (OH)
U of Alberta (AB, Canada)
The U of British Columbia (BC, Canada)
U of Calgary (AB, Canada)
U of Calif, Berkeley (CA)
U of Calif, Los Angeles (CA)
U of Calif, San Diego (CA)
U of Calif, Santa Cruz (CA)
U of Central Oklahoma (OK)
U of Chicago (IL)
U of Colorado at Boulder (CO)
U of Colorado at Colorado Springs (CO)
U of Colorado at Denver (CO)
U of Connecticut (CT)
U of Guelph (ON, Canada)
U of Houston (TX)
U of Idaho (ID)
U of Manitoba (MB, Canada)
U of Maryland, Baltimore County (MD)
U of Massachusetts Boston (MA)
U of Massachusetts Lowell (MA)
U of Michigan (MI)
U of Missouri–Rolla (MO)
U of Missouri–St. Louis (MO)
The U of Montana–Missoula (MT)
Western Montana Coll of The U of Montana (MT)
U of Nevada, Las Vegas (NV)
The U of North Carolina at Chapel Hill (NC)
The U of North Carolina at Greensboro (NC)
U of Ottawa (ON, Canada)
U of Pittsburgh (PA)
U of Pittsburgh at Bradford (PA)
U of Pittsburgh at Greensburg (PA)
U of Rochester (NY)
U of Sioux Falls (SD)
U of South Carolina Aiken (SC)
The U of Tennessee at Chattanooga (TN)
The U of Texas at Dallas (TX)
The U of Texas at El Paso (TX)
U of Toronto (ON, Canada)
U of Tulsa (OK)
U of Vermont (VT)
U of Virginia (VA)
U of Washington (WA)
U of Waterloo (ON, Canada)
The U of Western Ontario (ON, Canada)
U of Windsor (ON, Canada)
U of Wisconsin–Madison (WI)
U of Wisconsin–Milwaukee (WI)
U of Wisconsin–Stout (WI)
Ursinus Coll (PA)
Valdosta State U (GA)
Wake Forest U (NC)
Washington U in St. Louis (MO)
Wayne State Coll (NE)
Weber State U (UT)
Western Michigan U (MI)
West Virginia State Coll (WV)
William Paterson U of New Jersey (NJ)
Winona State U (MN)
Worcester Polytechnic Inst (MA)
Yale U (CT)
York U (ON, Canada)

APPLIED MATHEMATICS RELATED

Averett U (VA)
Georgia Inst of Technology (GA)
U of Dayton (OH)

AQUACULTURE OPERATIONS/ PRODUCTION MANAGEMENT

Angelo State U (TX)
Clemson U (SC)
Lake Erie Coll (OH)
Purdue U (IN)
Texas A&M U (TX)

ARABIC

Dartmouth Coll (NH)
Georgetown U (DC)
Harvard U (MA)
Long Island U, Southampton Coll, Friends World Program (NY)
The Ohio State U (OH)
State U of NY at Binghamton (NY)
United States Military Academy (NY)
U of Alberta (AB, Canada)
U of Calif, Los Angeles (CA)
U of Chicago (IL)
U of Miami (FL)
U of Michigan (MI)
U of Notre Dame (IN)
The U of Texas at Austin (TX)
U of Toronto (ON, Canada)
U of Utah (UT)
Washington U in St. Louis (MO)

ARCHAEOLOGY

American U in Cairo(Egypt)
Appalachian State U (NC)
Baltimore Hebrew U (MD)
Bard Coll (NY)
Baylor U (TX)
Boston U (MA)
Bowdoin Coll (ME)
Bridgewater State Coll (MA)
Brock U (ON, Canada)
Brown U (RI)
Bryn Mawr Coll (PA)
The Coll of Southeastern Europe, The American U of Athens(Greece)
The Coll of Wooster (OH)
Columbia Coll (NY)
Concordia U (QC, Canada)
Cornell U (NY)
Dartmouth Coll (NH)
Fort Lewis Coll (CO)
Franklin Pierce Coll (NH)
The George Washington U (DC)
Hampshire Coll (MA)
Harvard U (MA)
Haverford Coll (PA)
Hunter Coll of the City U of NY (NY)
Kent State U (OH)
Lakehead U (ON, Canada)
Long Island U, Southampton Coll, Friends World Program (NY)
Lycoming Coll (PA)
Massachusetts Inst of Technology (MA)
Memorial U of Newfoundland (NF, Canada)
Mercyhurst Coll (PA)
Minnesota State U Moorhead (MN)
New York U (NY)
Oberlin Coll (OH)
Oregon State U (OR)
Simon Fraser U (BC, Canada)
Stanford U (CA)
State U of NY Coll at Potsdam (NY)
Tufts U (MA)
Université de Montréal (QC, Canada)
U of Calgary (AB, Canada)
U of Calif, San Diego (CA)
U of Evansville (IN)
U of Hawaii at Manoa (HI)
U of Indianapolis (IN)
U of Kansas (KS)
U of Michigan (MI)
U of Missouri–Columbia (MO)
The U of North Carolina at Greensboro (NC)
U of Saskatchewan (SK, Canada)
The U of Texas at Austin (TX)
U of Toronto (ON, Canada)
U of Wisconsin–La Crosse (WI)
Washington and Lee U (VA)
Washington U in St. Louis (MO)
Wellesley Coll (MA)
Western Washington U (WA)
Wheaton Coll (IL)
Wilfrid Laurier U (ON, Canada)
Yale U (CT)

ARCHITECTURAL ENGINEERING

Andrews U (MI)
Auburn U (AL)
California Polytechnic State U, San Luis Obispo (CA)
The Coll of Southeastern Europe, The American U of Athens(Greece)
Drexel U (PA)
Harvard U (MA)
Illinois Inst of Technology (IL)
Kansas State U (KS)
Milwaukee School of Engineering (WI)
North Carolina Ag and Tech State U (NC)
Oklahoma State U (OK)
Penn State U Univ Park Campus (PA)
Tennessee State U (TN)
Tufts U (MA)
U of Cincinnati (OH)
U of Colorado at Boulder (CO)
U of Kansas (KS)
U of Miami (FL)
U of Missouri–Rolla (MO)
U of Nebraska–Lincoln (NE)
U of Southern California (CA)
The U of Texas at Austin (TX)
U of Wyoming (WY)

ARCHITECTURAL ENGINEERING TECHNOLOGY

Abilene Christian U (TX)
Andrews U (MI)
Bluefield State Coll (WV)
British Columbia Inst of Technology (BC, Canada)
California State U, Chico (CA)
Central Missouri State U (MO)
Cornell U (NY)
Delaware State U (DE)
Fitchburg State Coll (MA)
Florida A&M U (FL)
Grambling State U (LA)
Indiana State U (IN)
Indiana U–Purdue U Indianapolis (IN)
Louisiana State U and A&M Coll (LA)
Purdue U (IN)
Southern Polytechnic State U (GA)
State U of NY Coll of Technology at Alfred (NY)
Texas Southern U (TX)
Texas Tech U (TX)
Thomas Edison State Coll (NJ)
U of Cincinnati (OH)
U of Hartford (CT)
U of Southern Mississippi (MS)
Vermont Tech Coll (VT)
Washington U in St. Louis (MO)
Wentworth Inst of Technology (MA)

ARCHITECTURAL ENVIRONMENTAL DESIGN

Art Center Coll of Design (CA)
Auburn U (AL)
Ball State U (IN)
Bowling Green State U (OH)
Ctr for Creative Studies—Coll of Art and Design (MI)
The Coll of Southeastern Europe, The American U of Athens(Greece)
Coll of the Atlantic (ME)
Cornell U (NY)
Florida International U (FL)
Hampshire Coll (MA)
Harvard U (MA)
Miami U (OH)
Montana State U–Bozeman (MT)
North Dakota State U (ND)
Nova Scotia Coll of Art and Design (NS, Canada)
Otis Coll of Art and Design (CA)
Parsons School of Design, New School U (NY)
Prescott Coll (AZ)
State U of NY Coll of Environ Sci and Forestry (NY)
Texas A&M U (TX)
State U of NY at Buffalo (NY)
U of Colorado at Boulder (CO)
U of Hawaii at Manoa (HI)
U of Houston (TX)
U of Manitoba (MB, Canada)
U of Massachusetts Amherst (MA)
U of New Mexico (NM)
U of Oklahoma (OK)
U of Pennsylvania (PA)

ARCHITECTURAL HISTORY

Coll of Charleston (SC)
Goucher Coll (MD)
Mary Washington Coll (VA)
Roger Williams U (RI)
Salve Regina U (RI)
Savannah Coll of Art and Design (GA)
U of Delaware (DE)
U of Hawaii at Manoa (HI)
Ursuline Coll (OH)

ARCHITECTURAL URBAN DESIGN

The Coll of Southeastern Europe, The American U of Athens(Greece)
U of Hawaii at Manoa (HI)
U of Nevada, Las Vegas (NV)
U of Washington (WA)

ARCHITECTURE

Alliant International U (CA)
Andrews U (MI)
Arizona State U (AZ)
Auburn U (AL)
Ball State U (IN)
Barnard Coll (NY)
Baylor U (TX)
Bennington Coll (VT)
Boston Architectural Center (MA)
Brown U (RI)
California Coll of Arts and Crafts (CA)
California Polytechnic State U, San Luis Obispo (CA)
California State Polytechnic U, Pomona (CA)
Carleton U (ON, Canada)
Carnegie Mellon U (PA)
The Catholic U of America (DC)
City Coll of the City U of NY (NY)
Clemson U (SC)
Coe Coll (IA)
Columbia Coll (NY)
Columbia U, School of General Studies (NY)
Concordia Coll (MN)
Connecticut Coll (CT)
Cooper Union for the Advancement of Science & Art (NY)
Cornell Coll (IA)
Cornell U (NY)
Dalhousie U (NS, Canada)
Drexel U (PA)
Drury U (MO)
Eastern Michigan U (MI)
Florida A&M U (FL)
Florida Atlantic U (FL)
Georgia Inst of Technology (GA)
Hampshire Coll (MA)
Hampton U (VA)
Hobart and William Smith Colls (NY)
Howard U (DC)

Illinois Inst of Technology (IL)
Iowa State U of Science and Technology (IA)
Judson Coll (IL)
Kansas State U (KS)
Kent State U (OH)
Lawrence Technological U (MI)
Lehigh U (PA)
Louisiana State U and A&M Coll (LA)
Louisiana Tech U (LA)
Massachusetts Coll of Art (MA)
Massachusetts Inst of Technology (MA)
McGill U (PQ, Canada)
Miami U (OH)
Mississippi State U (MS)
New Jersey Inst of Technology (NJ)
Newschool of Architecture & Design (CA)
New York Inst of Technology (NY)
North Carolina State U (NC)
North Dakota State U (ND)
Northeastern U (MA)
Norwich U (VT)
The Ohio State U (OH)
Oklahoma State U (OK)
Parsons School of Design, New School U (NY)
Penn State U Univ Park Campus (PA)
Philadelphia U (PA)
Polytechnic U of Puerto Rico (PR)
Portland State U (OR)
Prairie View A&M U (TX)
Pratt Inst (NY)
Princeton U (NJ)
Rensselaer Polytechnic Inst (NY)
Rhode Island School of Design (RI)
Rice U (TX)
Roger Williams U (RI)
Savannah Coll of Art and Design (GA)
Smith Coll (MA)
Southern California Inst of Architecture (CA)
Southern Illinois U Carbondale (IL)
Southern Polytechnic State U (GA)
Southern U and A&M Coll (LA)
Syracuse U (NY)
Temple U (PA)
Texas Tech U (TX)
Tulane U (LA)
Tuskegee U (AL)
Université de Montréal (QC, Canada)
Université Laval (QC, Canada)
State U of NY at Buffalo (NY)
The U of Arizona (AZ)
U of Arkansas (AR)
U of Calif, Berkeley (CA)
U of Cincinnati (OH)
U of Florida (FL)
U of Hawaii at Manoa (HI)
U of Houston (TX)
U of Idaho (ID)
U of Illinois at Chicago (IL)
U of Kansas (KS)
U of Kentucky (KY)
U of Manitoba (MB, Canada)
U of Maryland, Coll Park (MD)
The U of Memphis (TN)
U of Miami (FL)
U of Michigan (MI)
U of Minnesota, Twin Cities Campus (MN)
U of Nebraska–Lincoln (NE)
U of Nevada, Las Vegas (NV)
U of New Mexico (NM)
The U of North Carolina at Charlotte (NC)
U of Notre Dame (IN)
U of Oklahoma (OK)
U of Oregon (OR)
U of Pennsylvania (PA)
U of San Francisco (CA)
U of Southern California (CA)
The U of Tennessee (TN)
The U of Texas at Arlington (TX)
The U of Texas at Austin (TX)
U of the District of Columbia (DC)
U of Toronto (ON, Canada)
U of Utah (UT)
U of Virginia (VA)
U of Washington (WA)
U of Waterloo (ON, Canada)
U of Wisconsin–Milwaukee (WI)
Virginia Polytechnic Inst and State U (VA)
Washington State U (WA)
Washington U in St. Louis (MO)
Wellesley Coll (MA)
Wentworth Inst of Technology (MA)
Woodbury U (CA)
Yale U (CT)

ARCHITECTURE RELATED

Clemson U (SC)
Columbia Coll (NY)
New York Inst of Technology (NY)
U of Illinois at Urbana–Champaign (IL)
U of Kansas (KS)
U of Louisiana at Lafayette (LA)
Washington U in St. Louis (MO)

AREA, ETHNIC, AND CULTURAL STUDIES RELATED

Brandeis U (MA)
Linfield Coll (OR)
Pratt Inst (NY)
Queens Coll of the City U of NY (NY)
Skidmore Coll (NY)
Touro Coll (NY)
U of Hawaii at Manoa (HI)
The U of North Carolina at Chapel Hill (NC)
The U of North Carolina at Charlotte (NC)
The U of Tennessee (TN)
Washington U in St. Louis (MO)

AREA STUDIES

Abilene Christian U (TX)
American U in Cairo(Egypt)
Bard Coll (NY)
Bucknell U (PA)
Denison U (OH)
Eastern Michigan U (MI)
Excelsior Coll (NY)
Gettysburg Coll (PA)
Hawai'i Pacific U (HI)
Marymount Coll of Fordham U (NY)
Memorial U of Newfoundland (NF, Canada)
Millersville U of Pennsylvania (PA)
United States Air Force Academy (CO)
The U of Montana–Missoula (MT)
U of Oklahoma (OK)

AREA STUDIES RELATED

Boston U (MA)
Drexel U (PA)
Holy Names Coll (CA)
Lewis U (IL)
Maryville Coll (TN)
McGill U (PQ, Canada)
Swarthmore Coll (PA)
U of Alaska Fairbanks (AK)
U of Illinois at Urbana–Champaign (IL)
Utah State U (UT)

ARMY R.O.T.C./MILITARY SCIENCE

American Military U (VA)
Campbell U (NC)
Drake U (IA)
Eastern Washington U (WA)
Hampton U (VA)
Jacksonville State U (AL)
La Salle U (PA)
Longwood Coll (VA)
Minnesota State U, Mankato (MN)
Monmouth Coll (IL)
Northwest Missouri State U (MO)
Ohio U (OH)
Purdue U Calumet (IN)
Rensselaer Polytechnic Inst (NY)
Rhode Island Coll (RI)
United States Military Academy (NY)
The U of Iowa (IA)
U of Puerto Rico, Cayey U Coll (PR)
The U of Texas–Pan American (TX)
U of Washington (WA)

ART

Abilene Christian U (TX)
Academy of Art Coll (CA)
Adams State Coll (CO)
Adrian Coll (MI)
Agnes Scott Coll (GA)
Alabama State U (AL)
Albany State U (GA)
Alberta Coll of Art & Design (AB, Canada)
Albertson Coll of Idaho (ID)
Albertus Magnus Coll (CT)
Albion Coll (MI)
Albright Coll (PA)
Alfred U (NY)
Alma Coll (MI)
Alverno Coll (WI)
American Academy of Art (IL)
American U (DC)
American U in Cairo(Egypt)
Amherst Coll (MA)
Anderson Coll (SC)
Andrews U (MI)
Angelo State U (TX)
Anna Maria Coll (MA)
Appalachian State U (NC)
Aquinas Coll (MI)
Arcadia U (PA)
Arizona State U (AZ)
Arkansas State U (AR)
Arkansas Tech U (AR)
Armstrong Atlantic State U (GA)
Art Academy of Cincinnati (OH)
Art Center Coll of Design (CA)
The Art Inst of Boston at Lesley U (MA)
The Art Inst of Colorado (CO)
Art Inst of Southern California (CA)
Ashland U (OH)
Athens State U (AL)
Atlantic Union Coll (MA)
Auburn U (AL)
Auburn U Montgomery (AL)
Augsburg Coll (MN)
Augustana Coll (IL)
Augustana Coll (SD)
Austin Coll (TX)
Austin Peay State U (TN)
Averett U (VA)
Avila Coll (MO)
Azusa Pacific U (CA)
Baldwin-Wallace Coll (OH)
Ball State U (IN)
Bard Coll (NY)
Bates Coll (ME)
Baylor U (TX)
Belhaven Coll (MS)
Bellarmine U (KY)
Bellevue U (NE)
Belmont U (TN)
Bemidji State U (MN)
Benedict Coll (SC)
Bennett Coll (NC)
Bennington Coll (VT)
Berea Coll (KY)
Berry Coll (GA)
Bethany Coll (KS)
Bethany Coll (WV)
Bethany Lutheran Coll (MN)
Bethel Coll (IN)
Bethel Coll (KS)
Bethel Coll (MN)
Biola U (CA)
Birmingham-Southern Coll (AL)
Bishop's U (PQ, Canada)
Blackburn Coll (IL)
Black Hills State U (SD)
Bloomfield Coll (NJ)
Bluefield Coll (VA)
Bluffton Coll (OH)
Boise State U (ID)
Bowdoin Coll (ME)
Bowie State U (MD)
Bowling Green State U (OH)
Bradley U (IL)
Brandeis U (MA)
Brescia U (KY)
Brevard Coll (NC)
Briar Cliff U (IA)
Bridgewater Coll (VA)
Bridgewater State Coll (MA)
Brigham Young U (UT)
Brigham Young U–Hawaii (HI)
Brock U (ON, Canada)
Brooklyn Coll of the City U of NY (NY)
Brown U (RI)
Bryn Mawr Coll (PA)
Bucknell U (PA)
Buena Vista U (IA)
Burlington Coll (VT)
Caldwell Coll (NJ)
California Baptist U (CA)
California Coll of Arts and Crafts (CA)
California Inst of the Arts (CA)
California Lutheran U (CA)
California Polytechnic State U, San Luis Obispo (CA)
California State Polytechnic U, Pomona (CA)
California State U, Bakersfield (CA)
California State U, Chico (CA)
California State U, Dominguez Hills (CA)
California State U, Fresno (CA)
California State U, Fullerton (CA)
California State U, Long Beach (CA)
California State U, Los Angeles (CA)
California State U, Monterey Bay (CA)
California State U, Northridge (CA)
California State U, Sacramento (CA)
California State U, San Bernardino (CA)
California State U, Stanislaus (CA)
California U of Pennsylvania (PA)
Calvin Coll (MI)
Cameron U (OK)
Campbellsville U (KY)
Campbell U (NC)
Capital U (OH)
Cardinal Stritch U (WI)
Carlow Coll (PA)
Carnegie Mellon U (PA)
Carroll Coll (WI)
Carson-Newman Coll (TN)
Castleton State Coll (VT)
The Catholic U of America (DC)
Cedar Crest Coll (PA)
Centenary Coll of Louisiana (LA)
Central Coll (IA)
Central Connecticut State U (CT)
Central Michigan U (MI)
Central State U (OH)
Central Washington U (WA)
Centre Coll (KY)
Chadron State Coll (NE)
Chapman U (CA)
Cheyney U of Pennsylvania (PA)
Chowan Coll (NC)
Christopher Newport U (VA)
City Coll of the City U of NY (NY)
Claflin U (SC)
Claremont McKenna Coll (CA)
Clarion U of Pennsylvania (PA)
Clark Atlanta U (GA)
Clarke Coll (IA)
Clark U (MA)
Clemson U (SC)
Cleveland State U (OH)
Coastal Carolina U (SC)
Coe Coll (IA)
Coker Coll (SC)
Colby Coll (ME)
Colby-Sawyer Coll (NH)
Colgate U (NY)
Ctr for Creative Studies—Coll of Art and Design (MI)
Coll of Mount St. Joseph (OH)
The Coll of New Jersey (NJ)
Coll of Notre Dame of Maryland (MD)
Coll of Saint Benedict (MN)
Coll of St. Catherine (MN)
Coll of Saint Elizabeth (NJ)
Coll of the Atlantic (ME)
Coll of Visual Arts (MN)
The Coll of William and Mary (VA)
The Coll of Wooster (OH)
Colorado Christian U (CO)
Colorado State U (CO)
Columbia Coll (MO)
Columbia Coll (SC)
Columbia Coll Chicago (IL)
Columbus Coll of Art and Design (OH)
Columbus State U (GA)
Concordia Coll (MN)
Concordia U (CA)
Concordia U (IL)
Concordia U (MI)
Concordia U (NE)
Concordia U (QC, Canada)
Concordia U Wisconsin (WI)
Connecticut Coll (CT)
Converse Coll (SC)
Cooper Union for the Advancement of Science & Art (NY)
Corcoran Coll of Art and Design (DC)
Cornell Coll (IA)
Cornell U (NY)
Cornish Coll of the Arts (WA)
Creighton U (NE)
Culver-Stockton Coll (MO)
Curry Coll (MA)
Daemen Coll (NY)
Dakota Wesleyan U (SD)
Dallas Baptist U (TX)
Dana Coll (NE)
Davidson Coll (NC)
Davis & Elkins Coll (WV)
Defiance Coll (OH)
Delaware State U (DE)
Denison U (OH)
DePaul U (IL)
Dickinson State U (ND)
Dillard U (LA)
Doane Coll (NE)
Dominican U (IL)
Dominican U of California (CA)
Dordt Coll (IA)
Dowling Coll (NY)
Drake U (IA)
Drew U (NJ)
Drury U (MO)
Duke U (NC)
Earlham Coll (IN)
East Carolina U (NC)
East Central U (OK)
Eastern Connecticut State U (CT)
Eastern Illinois U (IL)
Eastern Kentucky U (KY)
Eastern Mennonite U (VA)
Eastern Michigan U (MI)
Eastern New Mexico U (NM)
Eastern Oregon U (OR)
Eastern Washington U (WA)
East Tennessee State U (TN)
Eckerd Coll (FL)
Edgewood Coll (WI)
Elizabeth City State U (NC)
Elizabethtown Coll (PA)
Elmhurst Coll (IL)
Elmira Coll (NY)
Elms Coll (MA)
Elon U (NC)
Emmanuel Coll (MA)
Emory & Henry Coll (VA)
Emporia State U (KS)
Eureka Coll (IL)
Evangel U (MO)
The Evergreen State Coll (WA)
Fairfield U (CT)
Fayetteville State U (NC)
Felician Coll (NJ)
Ferrum Coll (VA)
Finlandia U (MI)
Fisk U (TN)
Florida A&M U (FL)
Florida Atlantic U (FL)
Florida Southern Coll (FL)
Florida State U (FL)
Fontbonne U (MO)
Fordham U (NY)
Fort Hays State U (KS)
Fort Lewis Coll (CO)
Francis Marion U (SC)
Franklin and Marshall Coll (PA)
Franklin Pierce Coll (NH)
Freed-Hardeman U (TN)
Friends U (KS)
Furman U (SC)
Gallaudet U (DC)
Gardner-Webb U (NC)
George Fox U (OR)
George Mason U (VA)
Georgetown Coll (KY)
Georgetown U (DC)
The George Washington U (DC)
Georgia Coll and State U (GA)
Georgian Court Coll (NJ)
Georgia Southern U (GA)
Georgia Southwestern State U (GA)
Gettysburg Coll (PA)
Goddard Coll (VT)
Gonzaga U (WA)
Gordon Coll (MA)
Goshen Coll (IN)
Goucher Coll (MD)
Governors State U (IL)
Grace Coll (IN)
Graceland U (IA)
Grambling State U (LA)
Grand Canyon U (AZ)
Grand Valley State U (MI)
Grand View Coll (IA)
Green Mountain Coll (VT)
Greensboro Coll (NC)

Greenville Coll (IL)
Grinnell Coll (IA)
Guilford Coll (NC)
Gustavus Adolphus Coll (MN)
Hamilton Coll (NY)
Hamline U (MN)
Hampshire Coll (MA)
Hampton U (VA)
Hannibal-LaGrange Coll (MO)
Hanover Coll (IN)
Harding U (AR)
Hardin-Simmons U (TX)
Hartwick Coll (NY)
Harvard U (MA)
Hastings Coll (NE)
Haverford Coll (PA)
Henderson State U (AR)
Hendrix Coll (AR)
Hillsdale Coll (MI)
Hiram Coll (OH)
Hobart and William Smith Colls (NY)
Holy Family Coll (PA)
Hood Coll (MD)
Houghton Coll (NY)
Houston Baptist U (TX)
Howard Payne U (TX)
Howard U (DC)
Humboldt State U (CA)
Hunter Coll of the City U of NY (NY)
Huntingdon Coll (AL)
Huntington Coll (IN)
Huron U USA in London(United Kingdom)
Idaho State U (ID)
Illinois Coll (IL)
Illinois State U (IL)
Illinois Wesleyan U (IL)
Indiana State U (IN)
Indiana U Bloomington (IN)
Indiana U Northwest (IN)
Indiana U of Pennsylvania (PA)
Indiana U South Bend (IN)
Indiana U Southeast (IN)
Indiana Wesleyan U (IN)
Inter American U of PR, San Germán Campus (PR)
Iona Coll (NY)
Iowa State U of Science and Technology (IA)
Iowa Wesleyan Coll (IA)
Ithaca Coll (NY)
Jackson State U (MS)
Jacksonville State U (AL)
Jacksonville U (FL)
James Madison U (VA)
Jamestown Coll (ND)
Johnson State Coll (VT)
Judson Coll (AL)
Judson Coll (IL)
Kalamazoo Coll (MI)
Kansas State U (KS)
Kansas Wesleyan U (KS)
Kean U (NJ)
Keene State Coll (NH)
Kennesaw State U (GA)
Kenyon Coll (OH)
Knox Coll (IL)
Lafayette Coll (PA)
LaGrange Coll (GA)
Lake Erie Coll (OH)
Lakehead U (ON, Canada)
Lakeland Coll (WI)
Lamar U (TX)
Lambuth U (TN)
Lander U (SC)
La Salle U (PA)
Lehigh U (PA)
Lehman Coll of the City U of NY (NY)
LeMoyne-Owen Coll (TN)
Lewis & Clark Coll (OR)
Lewis U (IL)
Lincoln Memorial U (TN)
Lincoln U (MO)
Lindenwood U (MO)
Lindsey Wilson Coll (KY)
Linfield Coll (OR)
Lipscomb U (TN)
Lock Haven U of Pennsylvania (PA)
Long Island U, Brooklyn Campus (NY)
Long Island U, C.W. Post Campus (NY)
Long Island U, Southampton Coll (NY)
Long Island U, Southampton Coll, Friends World Program (NY)
Longwood Coll (VA)
Louisiana Coll (LA)
Louisiana State U in Shreveport (LA)
Louisiana Tech U (LA)
Lourdes Coll (OH)
Loyola Coll in Maryland (MD)
Loyola U Chicago (IL)
Loyola U New Orleans (LA)
Luther Coll (IA)
Lycoming Coll (PA)
Lyon Coll (AR)
MacMurray Coll (IL)
Maharishi U of Management (IA)
Malone Coll (OH)
Manchester Coll (IN)
Manhattanville Coll (NY)
Mansfield U of Pennsylvania (PA)
Marian Coll (IN)
Marian Coll of Fond du Lac (WI)
Marietta Coll (OH)
Marist Coll (NY)
Marlboro Coll (VT)
Mars Hill Coll (NC)
Mary Baldwin Coll (VA)
Marygrove Coll (MI)
Maryland Inst, Coll of Art (MD)
Marylhurst U (OR)
Marymount Coll of Fordham U (NY)
Marymount Manhattan Coll (NY)
Marymount U (VA)
Maryville Coll (TN)
Mary Washington Coll (VA)
Massachusetts Coll of Liberal Arts (MA)
McKendree Coll (IL)
McMaster U (ON, Canada)
McMurry U (TX)
McPherson Coll (KS)
Memorial U of Newfoundland (NF, Canada)
Memphis Coll of Art (TN)
Mercer U (GA)
Mercy Coll (NY)
Mercyhurst Coll (PA)
Mesa State Coll (CO)
Methodist Coll (NC)
Metropolitan State Coll of Denver (CO)
Miami U (OH)
Michigan State U (MI)
Middlebury Coll (VT)
Middle Tennessee State U (TN)
Midland Lutheran Coll (NE)
Midwestern State U (TX)
Millersville U of Pennsylvania (PA)
Milligan Coll (TN)
Millsaps Coll (MS)
Mills Coll (CA)
Milwaukee Inst of Art and Design (WI)
Minnesota State U, Mankato (MN)
Minnesota State U Moorhead (MN)
Minot State U (ND)
Mississippi Coll (MS)
Mississippi U for Women (MS)
Mississippi Valley State U (MS)
Missouri Valley Coll (MO)
Missouri Western State Coll (MO)
Molloy Coll (NY)
Monmouth Coll (IL)
Monmouth U (NJ)
Montana State U–Billings (MT)
Montana State U–Bozeman (MT)
Montclair State U (NJ)
Montserrat Coll of Art (MA)
Moore Coll of Art and Design (PA)
Moravian Coll (PA)
Morehouse Coll (GA)
Morgan State U (MD)
Morningside Coll (IA)
Morris Brown Coll (GA)
Mount Mary Coll (WI)
Mount Mercy Coll (IA)
Mount Olive Coll (NC)
Mount St. Mary's Coll (CA)
Mount Union Coll (OH)
Mount Vernon Nazarene U (OH)
Muhlenberg Coll (PA)
Murray State U (KY)
Muskingum Coll (OH)
Naropa U (CO)
National-Louis U (IL)
Nazareth Coll of Rochester (NY)
Nebraska Wesleyan U (NE)
Newberry Coll (SC)
New Coll of Florida (FL)
New England Coll (NH)
New Jersey City U (NJ)
New Mexico Highlands U (NM)
New Mexico State U (NM)
New World School of the Arts (FL)
New York U (NY)
Nicholls State U (LA)
Norfolk State U (VA)
North Carolina Central U (NC)
North Central Coll (IL)
North Dakota State U (ND)
Northeastern Illinois U (IL)
Northeastern State U (OK)
Northeastern U (MA)
Northern Arizona U (AZ)
Northern Illinois U (IL)
Northern Kentucky U (KY)
Northern Michigan U (MI)
Northern State U (SD)
North Georgia Coll & State U (GA)
Northland Coll (WI)
North Park U (IL)
Northwest Coll of Art (WA)
Northwestern Coll (IA)
Northwestern State U of Louisiana (LA)
Northwestern U (IL)
Northwest Missouri State U (MO)
Northwest Nazarene U (ID)
Notre Dame Coll (OH)
Notre Dame de Namur U (CA)
Nova Scotia Coll of Art and Design (NS, Canada)
Oakland City U (IN)
Oberlin Coll (OH)
Oglethorpe U (GA)
Ohio Northern U (OH)
The Ohio State U (OH)
Ohio U (OH)
Oklahoma Baptist U (OK)
Oklahoma Christian U of Science and Arts (OK)
Oklahoma City U (OK)
Oklahoma State U (OK)
Old Dominion U (VA)
Olivet Coll (MI)
Olivet Nazarene U (IL)
Oregon State U (OR)
Otis Coll of Art and Design (CA)
Ottawa U (KS)
Otterbein Coll (OH)
Ouachita Baptist U (AR)
Our Lady of the Lake U of San Antonio (TX)
Pace U (NY)
Pacific Lutheran U (WA)
Pacific Northwest Coll of Art (OR)
Pacific Union Coll (CA)
Pacific U (OR)
Paier Coll of Art, Inc. (CT)
Palm Beach Atlantic Coll (FL)
Parsons School of Design, New School U (NY)
Penn State U Univ Park Campus (PA)
Pepperdine U, Malibu (CA)
Peru State Coll (NE)
Pikeville Coll (KY)
Pittsburg State U (KS)
Pitzer Coll (CA)
Plymouth State Coll (NH)
Point Loma Nazarene U (CA)
Pomona Coll (CA)
Pontifical Catholic U of Puerto Rico (PR)
Portland State U (OR)
Pratt Inst (NY)
Presbyterian Coll (SC)
Prescott Coll (AZ)
Purchase Coll, State U of NY (NY)
Purdue U (IN)
Queens Coll (NC)
Queens Coll of the City U of NY (NY)
Quincy U (IL)
Radford U (VA)
Ramapo Coll of New Jersey (NJ)
Randolph-Macon Coll (VA)
Randolph-Macon Woman's Coll (VA)
Redeemer U Coll (ON, Canada)
Reed Coll (OR)
Regis Coll (MA)
Rhode Island Coll (RI)
Rhode Island School of Design (RI)
Rhodes Coll (TN)
Rice U (TX)
Richmond, The American International U in London(United Kingdom)
Ripon Coll (WI)
Rivier Coll (NH)
Roanoke Coll (VA)
Roberts Wesleyan Coll (NY)
Rochester Inst of Technology (NY)
Rockford Coll (IL)
Rocky Mountain Coll (MT)
Rollins Coll (FL)
Rowan U (NJ)
Rutgers, The State U of New Jersey, New Brunswick (NJ)
Sacred Heart U (CT)
Saginaw Valley State U (MI)
St. Ambrose U (IA)
St. Andrews Presbyterian Coll (NC)
Saint Anselm Coll (NH)
St. Cloud State U (MN)
St. Edward's U (TX)
Saint John's U (MN)
Saint Joseph's U (PA)
St. Lawrence U (NY)
Saint Mary Coll (KS)
Saint Mary-of-the-Woods Coll (IN)
Saint Mary's Coll (IN)
Saint Mary's Coll of California (CA)
St. Mary's Coll of Maryland (MD)
Saint Michael's Coll (VT)
St. Norbert Coll (WI)
St. Olaf Coll (MN)
Saint Peter's Coll (NJ)
St. Thomas Aquinas Coll (NY)
Saint Xavier U (IL)
Salem State Coll (MA)
Salisbury U (MD)
Samford U (AL)
Sam Houston State U (TX)
San Diego State U (CA)
San Francisco Art Inst (CA)
San Francisco State U (CA)
San Jose State U (CA)
Santa Clara U (CA)
Sarah Lawrence Coll (NY)
Savannah Coll of Art and Design (GA)
School of the Art Inst of Chicago (IL)
School of the Museum of Fine Arts (MA)
School of Visual Arts (NY)
Schreiner U (TX)
Scripps Coll (CA)
Seattle Pacific U (WA)
Seattle U (WA)
Seton Hill Coll (PA)
Shawnee State U (OH)
Shepherd Coll (WV)
Shippensburg U of Pennsylvania (PA)
Shorter Coll (GA)
Siena Heights U (MI)
Sierra Nevada Coll (NV)
Silver Lake Coll (WI)
Simmons Coll (MA)
Simon Fraser U (BC, Canada)
Simpson Coll (IA)
Slippery Rock U of Pennsylvania (PA)
Smith Coll (MA)
Sonoma State U (CA)
South Dakota State U (SD)
Southeastern Louisiana U (LA)
Southeastern Oklahoma State U (OK)
Southeast Missouri State U (MO)
Southern Adventist U (TN)
Southern Arkansas U–Magnolia (AR)
Southern Illinois U Carbondale (IL)
Southern Illinois U Edwardsville (IL)
Southern Oregon U (OR)
Southern U and A&M Coll (LA)
Southern Utah U (UT)
Southern Virginia U (VA)
Southwest Baptist U (MO)
Southwestern U (TX)
Southwest Missouri State U (MO)
Southwest State U (MN)
Southwest Texas State U (TX)
Spelman Coll (GA)
Spring Arbor U (MI)
Stanford U (CA)
State U of NY at Albany (NY)
State U of NY at Binghamton (NY)
State U of NY at New Paltz (NY)
State U of NY at Oswego (NY)
State U of NY Coll at Brockport (NY)
State U of NY Coll at Buffalo (NY)
State U of NY Coll at Fredonia (NY)
State U of NY Coll at Geneseo (NY)
State U of NY Coll at Old Westbury (NY)
State U of NY Coll at Oneonta (NY)
State U of NY Coll at Potsdam (NY)
State U of NY Empire State Coll (NY)
State U of West Georgia (GA)
Stephen F. Austin State U (TX)
Sterling Coll (KS)
Stetson U (FL)
Suffolk U (MA)
Sul Ross State U (TX)
Susquehanna U (PA)
Syracuse U (NY)
Tarleton State U (TX)
Taylor U (IN)
Temple U (PA)
Tennessee State U (TN)
Tennessee Technological U (TN)
Texas A&M U–Commerce (TX)
Texas A&M U–Corpus Christi (TX)
Texas A&M U–Kingsville (TX)
Texas Christian U (TX)
Texas Coll (TX)
Texas Lutheran U (TX)
Texas Southern U (TX)
Texas Tech U (TX)
Texas Wesleyan U (TX)
Texas Woman's U (TX)
Thiel Coll (PA)
Thomas Edison State Coll (NJ)
Thomas U (GA)
Tougaloo Coll (MS)
Towson U (MD)
Transylvania U (KY)
Trinity Christian Coll (IL)
Trinity Coll (CT)
Trinity U (TX)
Troy State U (AL)
Truman State U (MO)
Tulane U (LA)
Tusculum Coll (TN)
Union U (TN)
Université de Montréal (QC, Canada)
State U of NY at Buffalo (NY)
The U of Akron (OH)
The U of Alabama in Huntsville (AL)
U of Alaska Anchorage (AK)
U of Alaska Fairbanks (AK)
U of Alberta (AB, Canada)
U of Arkansas (AR)
U of Arkansas at Little Rock (AR)
U of Arkansas at Pine Bluff (AR)
U of Bridgeport (CT)
U of Calgary (AB, Canada)
U of Calif, Berkeley (CA)
U of Calif, Davis (CA)
U of Calif, Irvine (CA)
U of Calif, Los Angeles (CA)
U of Calif, San Diego (CA)
U of Calif, Santa Cruz (CA)
U of Central Arkansas (AR)
U of Central Florida (FL)
U of Central Oklahoma (OK)
U of Charleston (WV)
U of Chicago (IL)
U of Cincinnati (OH)
U of Colorado at Boulder (CO)
U of Colorado at Colorado Springs (CO)
U of Dallas (TX)
U of Dayton (OH)
U of Delaware (DE)
U of Denver (CO)
U of Evansville (IN)
The U of Findlay (OH)
U of Georgia (GA)
U of Great Falls (MT)
U of Hawaii at Hilo (HI)
U of Hawaii at Manoa (HI)
U of Houston (TX)
U of Idaho (ID)
U of Illinois at Springfield (IL)
U of Indianapolis (IN)
The U of Iowa (IA)
U of Kansas (KS)
U of La Verne (CA)
The U of Lethbridge (AB, Canada)

U of Louisiana at Lafayette (LA)
U of Louisiana at Monroe (LA)
U of Maine (ME)
U of Maine at Farmington (ME)
U of Maine at Presque Isle (ME)
U of Manitoba (MB, Canada)
U of Mary Hardin-Baylor (TX)
U of Maryland, Baltimore County (MD)
U of Massachusetts Boston (MA)
U of Massachusetts Dartmouth (MA)
The U of Memphis (TN)
U of Miami (FL)
U of Michigan–Flint (MI)
U of Minnesota, Duluth (MN)
U of Minnesota, Twin Cities Campus (MN)
U of Mississippi (MS)
U of Missouri–Columbia (MO)
U of Missouri–Kansas City (MO)
U of Missouri–St. Louis (MO)
U of Mobile (AL)
The U of Montana–Missoula (MT)
Western Montana Coll of The U of Montana (MT)
U of Montevallo (AL)
U of Nebraska at Kearney (NE)
U of Nebraska at Omaha (NE)
U of Nevada, Las Vegas (NV)
U of Nevada, Reno (NV)
U of New Hampshire (NH)
U of New Haven (CT)
U of New Mexico (NM)
The U of North Carolina at Asheville (NC)
The U of North Carolina at Charlotte (NC)
The U of North Carolina at Greensboro (NC)
The U of North Carolina at Pembroke (NC)
U of North Dakota (ND)
U of Northern Colorado (CO)
U of Northern Iowa (IA)
U of North Florida (FL)
U of North Texas (TX)
U of Oklahoma (OK)
U of Oregon (OR)
U of Ottawa (ON, Canada)
U of Pennsylvania (PA)
U of Puget Sound (WA)
U of Regina (SK, Canada)
U of Rhode Island (RI)
U of Richmond (VA)
U of Rio Grande (OH)
U of Saint Francis (IN)
U of San Diego (CA)
U of Science and Arts of Oklahoma (OK)
U of South Alabama (AL)
U of South Dakota (SD)
U of Southern California (CA)
U of Southern Colorado (CO)
U of Southern Indiana (IN)
U of Southern Maine (ME)
U of South Florida (FL)
The U of Tampa (FL)
The U of Tennessee at Chattanooga (TN)
The U of Texas at Arlington (TX)
The U of Texas at Austin (TX)
The U of Texas at Dallas (TX)
The U of Texas at El Paso (TX)
The U of Texas at San Antonio (TX)
The U of Texas at Tyler (TX)
The U of Texas of the Permian Basin (TX)
The U of Texas–Pan American (TX)
U of the District of Columbia (DC)
U of the Incarnate Word (TX)
U of the Ozarks (AR)
U of the Pacific (CA)
U of the South (TN)
U of Toledo (OH)
U of Toronto (ON, Canada)
U of Tulsa (OK)
U of Utah (UT)
U of Virginia (VA)
The U of Virginia's Coll at Wise (VA)
U of Washington (WA)
The U of Western Ontario (ON, Canada)
U of West Florida (FL)
U of Windsor (ON, Canada)
U of Wisconsin–Eau Claire (WI)
U of Wisconsin–Green Bay (WI)
U of Wisconsin–La Crosse (WI)
U of Wisconsin–Madison (WI)
U of Wisconsin–Milwaukee (WI)
U of Wisconsin–Oshkosh (WI)
U of Wisconsin–Parkside (WI)
U of Wisconsin–Platteville (WI)
U of Wisconsin–River Falls (WI)
U of Wisconsin–Stevens Point (WI)
U of Wisconsin–Whitewater (WI)
U of Wyoming (WY)
Upper Iowa U (IA)
Ursinus Coll (PA)
Ursuline Coll (OH)
Utah State U (UT)
Valdosta State U (GA)
Valley City State U (ND)
Valparaiso U (IN)
Vanderbilt U (TN)
Virginia Intermont Coll (VA)
Virginia Polytechnic Inst and State U (VA)
Virginia Wesleyan Coll (VA)
Viterbo U (WI)
Wabash Coll (IN)
Wagner Coll (NY)
Wake Forest U (NC)
Walla Walla Coll (WA)
Warren Wilson Coll (NC)
Wartburg Coll (IA)
Washburn U of Topeka (KS)
Washington & Jefferson Coll (PA)
Washington Coll (MD)
Washington State U (WA)
Washington U in St. Louis (MO)
Watkins Coll of Art and Design (TN)
Wayland Baptist U (TX)
Waynesburg Coll (PA)
Wayne State Coll (NE)
Wayne State U (MI)
Weber State U (UT)
Webster U (MO)
Wells Coll (NY)
West Chester U of Pennsylvania (PA)
Western Carolina U (NC)
Western Connecticut State U (CT)
Western Illinois U (IL)
Western Maryland Coll (MD)
Western Michigan U (MI)
Western Oregon U (OR)
Western State Coll of Colorado (CO)
Western Washington U (WA)
Westfield State Coll (MA)
Westminster Coll (PA)
Westminster Coll (UT)
Westmont Coll (CA)
West Texas A&M U (TX)
West Virginia State Coll (WV)
West Virginia U (WV)
West Virginia Wesleyan Coll (WV)
Wheaton Coll (IL)
Wheaton Coll (MA)
White Pines Coll (NH)
Whitman Coll (WA)
Whittier Coll (CA)
Whitworth Coll (WA)
Wichita State U (KS)
Wilfrid Laurier U (ON, Canada)
Willamette U (OR)
William Carey Coll (MS)
William Jewell Coll (MO)
William Paterson U of New Jersey (NJ)
Williams Baptist Coll (AR)
William Woods U (MO)
Wilson Coll (PA)
Wingate U (NC)
Winona State U (MN)
Winston-Salem State U (NC)
Winthrop U (SC)
Wisconsin Lutheran Coll (WI)
Wittenberg U (OH)
Wright State U (OH)
Xavier U (OH)
Xavier U of Louisiana (LA)
Yale U (CT)
York Coll of Pennsylvania (PA)
York Coll of the City U of New York (NY)
York U (ON, Canada)
Youngstown State U (OH)

ART EDUCATION

Abilene Christian U (TX)
Adams State Coll (CO)
Adelphi U (NY)
Adrian Coll (MI)
Alabama State U (AL)
Albright Coll (PA)
Alfred U (NY)
Alma Coll (MI)
Alverno Coll (WI)
Anderson Coll (SC)
Anderson U (IN)
Andrews U (MI)
Anna Maria Coll (MA)
Appalachian State U (NC)
Aquinas Coll (MI)
Arcadia U (PA)
Arkansas State U (AR)
Arkansas Tech U (AR)
Armstrong Atlantic State U (GA)
Asbury Coll (KY)
Ashland U (OH)
Atlantic Union Coll (MA)
Augsburg Coll (MN)
Augustana Coll (IL)
Augustana Coll (SD)
Averett U (VA)
Avila Coll (MO)
Baker U (KS)
Baldwin-Wallace Coll (OH)
Ball State U (IN)
Barton Coll (NC)
Baylor U (TX)
Belmont U (TN)
Beloit Coll (WI)
Bemidji State U (MN)
Benedict Coll (SC)
Berea Coll (KY)
Berry Coll (GA)
Bethany Coll (KS)
Bethel Coll (MN)
Birmingham-Southern Coll (AL)
Bloomfield Coll (NJ)
Bluffton Coll (OH)
Boise State U (ID)
Boston U (MA)
Bowling Green State U (OH)
Brenau U (GA)
Brescia U (KY)
Briar Cliff U (IA)
Bridgewater Coll (VA)
Brigham Young U (UT)
Brigham Young U–Hawaii (HI)
Brooklyn Coll of the City U of NY (NY)
California State U, Chico (CA)
California State U, Fullerton (CA)
California State U, Long Beach (CA)
California State U, Northridge (CA)
Calvin Coll (MI)
Cameron U (OK)
Campbellsville U (KY)
Capital U (OH)
Cardinal Stritch U (WI)
Carlow Coll (PA)
Carroll Coll (WI)
Carson-Newman Coll (TN)
Case Western Reserve U (OH)
The Catholic U of America (DC)
Centenary Coll of Louisiana (LA)
Central Connecticut State U (CT)
Central Michigan U (MI)
Central Missouri State U (MO)
Central State U (OH)
Central Washington U (WA)
Chadron State Coll (NE)
Chicago State U (IL)
City Coll of the City U of NY (NY)
Claflin U (SC)
Clark Atlanta U (GA)
Clarke Coll (IA)
Cleveland State U (OH)
Coastal Carolina U (SC)
Coe Coll (IA)
Coker Coll (SC)
Colby-Sawyer Coll (NH)
Coll of Mount St. Joseph (OH)
The Coll of New Jersey (NJ)
The Coll of New Rochelle (NY)
Coll of Saint Benedict (MN)
Coll of St. Catherine (MN)
The Coll of Saint Rose (NY)
Coll of the Ozarks (MO)
Colorado State U (CO)
Columbia Coll (MO)
Columbia Coll (SC)
Columbus State U (GA)
Concord Coll (WV)
Concordia Coll (MN)
Concordia U (IL)
Concordia U (NE)
Concordia U (QC, Canada)
Concordia U Wisconsin (WI)
Converse Coll (SC)
Cornell Coll (IA)
Creighton U (NE)
Culver-Stockton Coll (MO)
Cumberland Coll (KY)
Daemen Coll (NY)
Dakota State U (SD)
Dakota Wesleyan U (SD)
Dana Coll (NE)
Defiance Coll (OH)
Delaware State U (DE)
Delta State U (MS)
Dickinson State U (ND)
Dillard U (LA)
Drury U (MO)
East Carolina U (NC)
East Central U (OK)
Eastern Kentucky U (KY)
Eastern Mennonite U (VA)
Eastern Michigan U (MI)
Eastern Washington U (WA)
Edgewood Coll (WI)
Edinboro U of Pennsylvania (PA)
Elmhurst Coll (IL)
Elmira Coll (NY)
Elms Coll (MA)
Emmanuel Coll (MA)
Emporia State U (KS)
Escuela de Artes Plasticas de Puerto Rico (PR)
Evangel U (MO)
Fairmont State Coll (WV)
Flagler Coll (FL)
Florida A&M U (FL)
Florida International U (FL)
Florida Southern Coll (FL)
Florida State U (FL)
Fontbonne U (MO)
Fort Hays State U (KS)
Fort Lewis Coll (CO)
Framingham State Coll (MA)
Francis Marion U (SC)
Franklin Pierce Coll (NH)
Freed-Hardeman U (TN)
Friends U (KS)
Frostburg State U (MD)
Gallaudet U (DC)
Georgian Court Coll (NJ)
Georgia Southern U (GA)
Georgia Southwestern State U (GA)
Georgia State U (GA)
Goddard Coll (VT)
Goshen Coll (IN)
Grace Coll (IN)
Graceland U (IA)
Grambling State U (LA)
Grand Canyon U (AZ)
Grand Valley State U (MI)
Grand View Coll (IA)
Greensboro Coll (NC)
Greenville Coll (IL)
Gustavus Adolphus Coll (MN)
Hampton U (VA)
Hannibal-LaGrange Coll (MO)
Harding U (AR)
Hardin-Simmons U (TX)
Hastings Coll (NE)
Henderson State U (AR)
High Point U (NC)
Hofstra U (NY)
Houghton Coll (NY)
Houston Baptist U (TX)
Howard Payne U (TX)
Humboldt State U (CA)
Huntingdon Coll (AL)
Huntington Coll (IN)
Indiana State U (IN)
Indiana U Bloomington (IN)
Indiana U of Pennsylvania (PA)
Indiana U–Purdue U Indianapolis (IN)
Indiana Wesleyan U (IN)
Inter American U of PR, San Germán Campus (PR)
Iowa Wesleyan Coll (IA)
Jackson State U (MS)
Jacksonville U (FL)
Johnson State Coll (VT)
Kansas Wesleyan U (KS)
Kennesaw State U (GA)
Kent State U (OH)
Kentucky State U (KY)
Kentucky Wesleyan Coll (KY)
Kutztown U of Pennsylvania (PA)
LaGrange Coll (GA)
Lamar U (TX)
Lambuth U (TN)
Lenoir-Rhyne Coll (NC)
Lewis U (IL)
Limestone Coll (SC)
Lincoln U (MO)
Lincoln U (PA)
Lindenwood U (MO)
Long Island U, Brooklyn Campus (NY)
Long Island U, C.W. Post Campus (NY)
Long Island U, Southampton Coll (NY)
Long Island U, Southampton Coll, Friends World Program (NY)
Longwood Coll (VA)
Loras Coll (IA)
Louisiana Coll (LA)
Louisiana State U in Shreveport (LA)
Louisiana Tech U (LA)
Luther Coll (IA)
Lycoming Coll (PA)
Malone Coll (OH)
Manchester Coll (IN)
Manhattanville Coll (NY)
Mansfield U of Pennsylvania (PA)
Marian Coll (IN)
Marian Coll of Fond du Lac (WI)
Mars Hill Coll (NC)
Maryland Inst, Coll of Art (MD)
Marymount Coll of Fordham U (NY)
Maryville Coll (TN)
Maryville U of Saint Louis (MO)
Marywood U (PA)
Massachusetts Coll of Art (MA)
McKendree Coll (IL)
McMurry U (TX)
McPherson Coll (KS)
Mercer U (GA)
Mercyhurst Coll (PA)
Meredith Coll (NC)
Messiah Coll (PA)
Methodist Coll (NC)
Miami U (OH)
Michigan State U (MI)
Middle Tennessee State U (TN)
Midland Lutheran Coll (NE)
Midwestern State U (TX)
Millersville U of Pennsylvania (PA)
Millikin U (IL)
Minnesota State U, Mankato (MN)
Minnesota State U Moorhead (MN)
Minot State U (ND)
Mississippi Coll (MS)
Mississippi U for Women (MS)
Missouri Western State Coll (MO)
Montana State U–Billings (MT)
Montclair State U (NJ)
Montserrat Coll of Art (MA)
Moore Coll of Art and Design (PA)
Moravian Coll (PA)
Morningside Coll (IA)
Mount Mary Coll (WI)
Mount Mercy Coll (IA)
Mount St. Mary's Coll (CA)
Mount Saint Vincent U (NS, Canada)
Mount Vernon Nazarene U (OH)
Murray State U (KY)
Muskingum Coll (OH)
Nazareth Coll of Rochester (NY)
New Jersey City U (NJ)
New Mexico Highlands U (NM)
New York Inst of Technology (NY)
Nicholls State U (LA)
North Carolina Ag and Tech State U (NC)
North Carolina Central U (NC)
North Central Coll (IL)
Northeastern State U (OK)
Northern Arizona U (AZ)
Northern Illinois U (IL)
Northern Michigan U (MI)
Northern State U (SD)
North Georgia Coll & State U (GA)
Northland Coll (WI)
North Park U (IL)
Northwestern Coll (IA)
Northwestern Coll (MN)
Northwest Missouri State U (MO)
Northwest Nazarene U (ID)
Nova Scotia Coll of Art and Design (NS, Canada)
Oakland City U (IN)
Ohio Dominican Coll (OH)
Ohio Northern U (OH)
The Ohio State U (OH)
Ohio U (OH)
Ohio Wesleyan U (OH)
Oklahoma Baptist U (OK)

Oklahoma Christian U of Science and Arts (OK)
Oklahoma City U (OK)
Olivet Coll (MI)
Olivet Nazarene U (IL)
Oral Roberts U (OK)
Ottawa U (KS)
Otterbein Coll (OH)
Ouachita Baptist U (AR)
Pace U (NY)
Pacific Lutheran U (WA)
Pacific U (OR)
Palm Beach Atlantic Coll (FL)
Parsons School of Design, New School U (NY)
Penn State U Univ Park Campus (PA)
Peru State Coll (NE)
Pittsburg State U (KS)
Plymouth State Coll (NH)
Pontifical Catholic U of Puerto Rico (PR)
Pratt Inst (NY)
Queens Coll of the City U of NY (NY)
Queen's U at Kingston (ON, Canada)
Quincy U (IL)
Rhode Island Coll (RI)
Roberts Wesleyan Coll (NY)
Rockford Coll (IL)
Rocky Mountain Coll (MT)
Rocky Mountain Coll of Art & Design (CO)
Rowan U (NJ)
St. Ambrose U (IA)
St. Bonaventure U (NY)
St. Cloud State U (MN)
Saint John's U (MN)
St. John's U (NY)
Saint Joseph Coll (CT)
Saint Mary-of-the-Woods Coll (IN)
Saint Mary's Coll (IN)
Saint Mary's Coll of California (CA)
St. Mary's U of San Antonio (TX)
Saint Michael's Coll (VT)
St. Thomas Aquinas Coll (NY)
Saint Vincent Coll (PA)
Saint Xavier U (IL)
Salem State Coll (MA)
San Diego State U (CA)
School of the Art Inst of Chicago (IL)
School of the Museum of Fine Arts (MA)
School of Visual Arts (NY)
Seattle Pacific U (WA)
Seton Hall U (NJ)
Seton Hill Coll (PA)
Shorter Coll (GA)
Siena Heights U (MI)
Silver Lake Coll (WI)
Simpson Coll (IA)
South Carolina State U (SC)
South Dakota State U (SD)
Southeastern Louisiana U (LA)
Southeastern Oklahoma State U (OK)
Southeast Missouri State U (MO)
Southern Arkansas U–Magnolia (AR)
Southern Connecticut State U (CT)
Southern Nazarene U (OK)
Southern Utah U (UT)
Southwest Baptist U (MO)
Southwestern Oklahoma State U (OK)
Southwestern U (TX)
Southwest Missouri State U (MO)
Southwest State U (MN)
State U of NY at New Paltz (NY)
State U of NY Coll at Buffalo (NY)
State U of West Georgia (GA)
Syracuse U (NY)
Tabor Coll (KS)
Tarleton State U (TX)
Taylor U (IN)
Temple U (PA)
Tennessee Technological U (TN)
Texas A&M U–Commerce (TX)
Texas Christian U (TX)
Texas Lutheran U (TX)
Texas Southern U (TX)
Texas Wesleyan U (TX)
Thomas More Coll (KY)
Towson U (MD)
Transylvania U (KY)
Trinity Christian Coll (IL)
Troy State U (AL)
Tusculum Coll (TN)
Union Coll (NE)
Union U (TN)
Université Laval (QC, Canada)
The U of Akron (OH)
U of Alberta (AB, Canada)
The U of Arizona (AZ)
U of Arkansas at Pine Bluff (AR)
The U of British Columbia (BC, Canada)
U of Calgary (AB, Canada)
U of Central Florida (FL)
U of Central Oklahoma (OK)
U of Cincinnati (OH)
U of Dallas (TX)
U of Dayton (OH)
U of Denver (CO)
U of Evansville (IN)
The U of Findlay (OH)
U of Florida (FL)
U of Georgia (GA)
U of Great Falls (MT)
U of Hawaii at Manoa (HI)
U of Idaho (ID)
U of Illinois at Chicago (IL)
U of Illinois at Urbana–Champaign (IL)
U of Indianapolis (IN)
The U of Iowa (IA)
U of Kansas (KS)
U of Kentucky (KY)
The U of Lethbridge (AB, Canada)
U of Louisiana at Monroe (LA)
U of Maine (ME)
U of Maine at Presque Isle (ME)
U of Mary Hardin-Baylor (TX)
U of Maryland, Coll Park (MD)
U of Maryland Eastern Shore (MD)
U of Massachusetts Dartmouth (MA)
U of Michigan (MI)
U of Michigan–Dearborn (MI)
U of Michigan–Flint (MI)
U of Minnesota, Duluth (MN)
U of Minnesota, Twin Cities Campus (MN)
U of Missouri–Columbia (MO)
The U of Montana–Missoula (MT)
Western Montana Coll of The U of Montana (MT)
U of Montevallo (AL)
U of Nebraska–Lincoln (NE)
U of Nevada, Reno (NV)
U of New England (ME)
U of New Hampshire (NH)
U of New Mexico (NM)
The U of North Carolina at Charlotte (NC)
The U of North Carolina at Greensboro (NC)
The U of North Carolina at Pembroke (NC)
U of Northern Iowa (IA)
U of North Florida (FL)
U of North Texas (TX)
U of Regina (SK, Canada)
U of Richmond (VA)
U of Rio Grande (OH)
U of Saint Francis (IN)
U of Sioux Falls (SD)
U of South Carolina (SC)
U of South Dakota (SD)
U of Southern Colorado (CO)
U of Southern Maine (ME)
U of South Florida (FL)
The U of Tennessee (TN)
The U of Tennessee at Chattanooga (TN)
The U of Tennessee at Martin (TN)
The U of Texas at El Paso (TX)
The U of Texas–Pan American (TX)
U of the District of Columbia (DC)
U of the Incarnate Word (TX)
U of the Ozarks (AR)
U of Toledo (OH)
U of Toronto (ON, Canada)
U of Vermont (VT)
U of Victoria (BC, Canada)
The U of Western Ontario (ON, Canada)
U of West Florida (FL)
U of Windsor (ON, Canada)
U of Wisconsin–La Crosse (WI)
U of Wisconsin–Madison (WI)
U of Wisconsin–Milwaukee (WI)
U of Wisconsin–Oshkosh (WI)
U of Wisconsin–River Falls (WI)
U of Wisconsin–Stout (WI)
U of Wisconsin–Superior (WI)
U of Wisconsin–Whitewater (WI)
Upper Iowa U (IA)
Ursuline Coll (OH)
Valdosta State U (GA)
Valley City State U (ND)
Valparaiso U (IN)
Virginia Commonwealth U (VA)
Virginia Intermont Coll (VA)
Virginia Wesleyan Coll (VA)
Viterbo U (WI)
Walla Walla Coll (WA)
Wartburg Coll (IA)
Washburn U of Topeka (KS)
Washington & Jefferson Coll (PA)
Washington U in St. Louis (MO)
Wayne State U (MI)
Weber State U (UT)
Western Carolina U (NC)
Western Kentucky U (KY)
Western Michigan U (MI)
Western State Coll of Colorado (CO)
Western Washington U (WA)
Westfield State Coll (MA)
West Liberty State Coll (WV)
Westmont Coll (CA)
West Virginia State Coll (WV)
West Virginia Wesleyan Coll (WV)
Whitworth Coll (WA)
Wichita State U (KS)
William Carey Coll (MS)
William Paterson U of New Jersey (NJ)
Williams Baptist Coll (AR)
William Woods U (MO)
Wilmington Coll (OH)
Wingate U (NC)
Winona State U (MN)
Winston-Salem State U (NC)
Wittenberg U (OH)
Wright State U (OH)
Xavier U of Louisiana (LA)
York U (ON, Canada)
Youngstown State U (OH)

ART HISTORY

Adams State Coll (CO)
Albertus Magnus Coll (CT)
Alfred U (NY)
Allegheny Coll (PA)
American U (DC)
The American U of Paris(France)
Andrews U (MI)
Appalachian State U (NC)
Aquinas Coll (MI)
Arcadia U (PA)
Arizona State U (AZ)
Art Academy of Cincinnati (OH)
Augsburg Coll (MN)
Augustana Coll (IL)
Baker U (KS)
Baldwin-Wallace Coll (OH)
Bard Coll (NY)
Barnard Coll (NY)
Baylor U (TX)
Beloit Coll (WI)
Berea Coll (KY)
Berry Coll (GA)
Bethel Coll (MN)
Birmingham-Southern Coll (AL)
Blackburn Coll (IL)
Bloomsburg U of Pennsylvania (PA)
Boise State U (ID)
Boston Coll (MA)
Boston U (MA)
Bowdoin Coll (ME)
Bowling Green State U (OH)
Bradley U (IL)
Brigham Young U (UT)
Brooklyn Coll of the City U of NY (NY)
Brown U (RI)
Bryn Mawr Coll (PA)
Bucknell U (PA)
California State U, Chico (CA)
California State U, Dominguez Hills (CA)
California State U, Fullerton (CA)
California State U, Hayward (CA)
California State U, Long Beach (CA)
California State U, Northridge (CA)
California State U, San Bernardino (CA)
Calvin Coll (MI)
Canisius Coll (NY)
Carleton Coll (MN)
Carleton U (ON, Canada)
Carlow Coll (PA)
Case Western Reserve U (OH)
The Catholic U of America (DC)
Centre Coll (KY)
Chapman U (CA)
Chatham Coll (PA)
Chestnut Hill Coll (PA)
Chicago State U (IL)
City Coll of the City U of NY (NY)
Clarke Coll (IA)
Clark U (MA)
Cleveland State U (OH)
Colby Coll (ME)
Colgate U (NY)
Coll of Charleston (SC)
The Coll of New Rochelle (NY)
Coll of Saint Benedict (MN)
Coll of St. Catherine (MN)
Coll of Santa Fe (NM)
The Coll of Southeastern Europe, The American U of Athens(Greece)
Coll of the Holy Cross (MA)
The Coll of William and Mary (VA)
The Coll of Wooster (OH)
The Colorado Coll (CO)
Colorado State U (CO)
Columbia Coll (NY)
Columbia Coll (SC)
Columbia U, School of General Studies (NY)
Concordia Coll (MN)
Concordia U (MN)
Concordia U (QC, Canada)
Connecticut Coll (CT)
Converse Coll (SC)
Cornell Coll (IA)
Cornell U (NY)
Creighton U (NE)
Dartmouth Coll (NH)
Denison U (OH)
DePaul U (IL)
DePauw U (IN)
Dominican U (IL)
Dominican U of California (CA)
Drake U (IA)
Drury U (MO)
Duke U (NC)
Duquesne U (PA)
East Carolina U (NC)
Eastern Michigan U (MI)
Eastern U (PA)
Eastern Washington U (WA)
Edinboro U of Pennsylvania (PA)
Emmanuel Coll (MA)
Emory U (GA)
The Evergreen State Coll (WA)
Florida International U (FL)
Florida State U (FL)
Fordham U (NY)
Framingham State Coll (MA)
Franklin Coll Switzerland(Switzerland)
Furman U (SC)
Gallaudet U (DC)
George Mason U (VA)
The George Washington U (DC)
Georgian Court Coll (NJ)
Gettysburg Coll (PA)
Goddard Coll (VT)
Governors State U (IL)
Grand Valley State U (MI)
Gustavus Adolphus Coll (MN)
Hamilton Coll (NY)
Hamline U (MN)
Hampshire Coll (MA)
Hanover Coll (IN)
Hartwick Coll (NY)
Harvard U (MA)
Hastings Coll (NE)
Haverford Coll (PA)
Hiram Coll (OH)
Hobart and William Smith Colls (NY)
Hofstra U (NY)
Hollins U (VA)
Hope Coll (MI)
Humboldt State U (CA)
Hunter Coll of the City U of NY (NY)
Huron U USA in London(United Kingdom)
Illinois Wesleyan U (IL)
Indiana State U (IN)
Indiana U Bloomington (IN)
Indiana U–Purdue U Indianapolis (IN)
Inter American U of PR, San Germán Campus (PR)
Ithaca Coll (NY)
Jacksonville U (FL)
James Madison U (VA)
John Cabot U(Italy)
John Carroll U (OH)
Johns Hopkins U (MD)
Juniata Coll (PA)
Kalamazoo Coll (MI)
Kansas City Art Inst (MO)
Kean U (NJ)
Kendall Coll of Art and Design of Ferris State U (MI)
Kent State U (OH)
Kenyon Coll (OH)
Knox Coll (IL)
Lafayette Coll (PA)
Lake Forest Coll (IL)
Lambuth U (TN)
La Salle U (PA)
Lawrence U (WI)
Lehman Coll of the City U of NY (NY)
Lindenwood U (MO)
Long Island U, C.W. Post Campus (NY)
Long Island U, Southampton Coll, Friends World Program (NY)
Longwood Coll (VA)
Lourdes Coll (OH)
Loyola Marymount U (CA)
Loyola U Chicago (IL)
Lycoming Coll (PA)
Macalester Coll (MN)
MacMurray Coll (IL)
Manhattanville Coll (NY)
Mansfield U of Pennsylvania (PA)
Marian Coll (IN)
Marlboro Coll (VT)
Mars Hill Coll (NC)
Mary Baldwin Coll (VA)
Marymount Coll of Fordham U (NY)
Marymount Manhattan Coll (NY)
Mary Washington Coll (VA)
Massachusetts Coll of Art (MA)
McGill U (PQ, Canada)
McMaster U (ON, Canada)
Memorial U of Newfoundland (NF, Canada)
Meredith Coll (NC)
Messiah Coll (PA)
Miami U (OH)
Michigan State U (MI)
Middlebury Coll (VT)
Mills Coll (CA)
Minnesota State U, Mankato (MN)
Minnesota State U Moorhead (MN)
Mississippi Coll (MS)
Monmouth U (NJ)
Montclair State U (NJ)
Moore Coll of Art and Design (PA)
Moravian Coll (PA)
Morgan State U (MD)
Mount Allison U (NB, Canada)
Mount Holyoke Coll (MA)
Muhlenberg Coll (PA)
Nazareth Coll of Rochester (NY)
New England Coll (NH)
New York U (NY)
Northern Arizona U (AZ)
Northern Illinois U (IL)
Northwestern U (IL)
Notre Dame Coll (OH)
Nova Scotia Coll of Art and Design (NS, Canada)
Oakland U (MI)
Oberlin Coll (OH)
Occidental Coll (CA)
The Ohio State U (OH)
Ohio U (OH)
Ohio Wesleyan U (OH)
Oklahoma City U (OK)
Old Dominion U (VA)
Oregon State U (OR)
Pace U (NY)
Pacific Lutheran U (WA)
Pacific Union Coll (CA)
Penn State U Univ Park Campus (PA)
Pine Manor Coll (MA)
Pitzer Coll (CA)
Plattsburgh State U of NY (NY)
Pomona Coll (CA)
Portland State U (OR)
Pratt Inst (NY)
Princeton U (NJ)
Principia Coll (IL)
Providence Coll (RI)
Purchase Coll, State U of NY (NY)
Queens Coll (NC)

Queens Coll of the City U of NY (NY)
Queen's U at Kingston (ON, Canada)
Randolph-Macon Coll (VA)
Randolph-Macon Woman's Coll (VA)
Rhode Island Coll (RI)
Rhodes Coll (TN)
Rice U (TX)
Richmond, The American International U in London(United Kingdom)
Rockford Coll (IL)
Roger Williams U (RI)
Rollins Coll (FL)
Roosevelt U (IL)
Rosemont Coll (PA)
Rutgers, The State U of New Jersey, New Brunswick (NJ)
St. Cloud State U (MN)
Saint John's U (MN)
Saint Joseph Coll (CT)
St. Lawrence U (NY)
Saint Louis U (MO)
Saint Mary's Coll of California (CA)
St. Olaf Coll (MN)
Saint Vincent Coll (PA)
Salem Coll (NC)
Salve Regina U (RI)
San Diego State U (CA)
San Jose State U (CA)
Santa Clara U (CA)
Sarah Lawrence Coll (NY)
Savannah Coll of Art and Design (GA)
School of the Art Inst of Chicago (IL)
Scripps Coll (CA)
Seattle U (WA)
Seton Hall U (NJ)
Seton Hill Coll (PA)
Simon's Rock Coll of Bard (MA)
Skidmore Coll (NY)
Smith Coll (MA)
Sonoma State U (CA)
Southern Connecticut State U (CT)
Southern Methodist U (TX)
Southwestern U (TX)
State U of NY at Albany (NY)
State U of NY at Binghamton (NY)
State U of NY at New Paltz (NY)
State U of NY Coll at Buffalo (NY)
State U of NY Coll at Cortland (NY)
State U of NY Coll at Fredonia (NY)
State U of NY Coll at Geneseo (NY)
State U of NY Coll at Oneonta (NY)
State U of NY Coll at Potsdam (NY)
Stephen F. Austin State U (TX)
State U of NY at Stony Brook (NY)
Susquehanna U (PA)
Swarthmore Coll (PA)
Sweet Briar Coll (VA)
Syracuse U (NY)
Temple U (PA)
Texas A&M U–Commerce (TX)
Texas Christian U (TX)
Texas Tech U (TX)
Texas Woman's U (TX)
Trinity Coll (CT)
Trinity Coll (DC)
Trinity U (TX)
Troy State U (AL)
Truman State U (MO)
Tufts U (MA)
Tulane U (LA)
Université de Montréal (QC, Canada)
Université Laval (QC, Canada)
State U of NY at Buffalo (NY)
The U of Akron (OH)
The U of Alabama (AL)
U of Alberta (AB, Canada)
The U of Arizona (AZ)
U of Arkansas at Little Rock (AR)
The U of British Columbia (BC, Canada)
U of Calgary (AB, Canada)
U of Calif, Berkeley (CA)
U of Calif, Davis (CA)
U of Calif, Irvine (CA)
U of Calif, Los Angeles (CA)
U of Calif, Riverside (CA)
U of Calif, San Diego (CA)
U of Calif, Santa Barbara (CA)
U of Calif, Santa Cruz (CA)
U of Chicago (IL)
U of Cincinnati (OH)
U of Connecticut (CT)
U of Dallas (TX)
U of Dayton (OH)
U of Delaware (DE)
U of Denver (CO)
U of Evansville (IN)
U of Florida (FL)
U of Georgia (GA)
U of Guelph (ON, Canada)
U of Hartford (CT)
U of Hawaii at Manoa (HI)
U of Houston (TX)
U of Illinois at Chicago (IL)
U of Illinois at Urbana–Champaign (IL)
U of Indianapolis (IN)
The U of Iowa (IA)
U of Kansas (KS)
U of Kentucky (KY)
U of Louisville (KY)
U of Maine (ME)
U of Manitoba (MB, Canada)
U of Maryland, Baltimore County (MD)
U of Maryland, Coll Park (MD)
U of Massachusetts Amherst (MA)
U of Massachusetts Dartmouth (MA)
The U of Memphis (TN)
U of Miami (FL)
U of Michigan (MI)
U of Michigan–Dearborn (MI)
U of Minnesota, Duluth (MN)
U of Minnesota, Morris (MN)
U of Minnesota, Twin Cities Campus (MN)
U of Mississippi (MS)
U of Missouri–Kansas City (MO)
U of Missouri–St. Louis (MO)
The U of Montana–Missoula (MT)
U of Nebraska at Omaha (NE)
U of Nebraska–Lincoln (NE)
U of Nevada, Las Vegas (NV)
U of Nevada, Reno (NV)
U of New Hampshire (NH)
U of New Mexico (NM)
U of New Orleans (LA)
The U of North Carolina at Chapel Hill (NC)
The U of North Carolina at Greensboro (NC)
The U of North Carolina at Wilmington (NC)
U of Northern Iowa (IA)
U of North Texas (TX)
U of Notre Dame (IN)
U of Oklahoma (OK)
U of Oregon (OR)
U of Pennsylvania (PA)
U of Pittsburgh (PA)
U of Redlands (CA)
U of Regina (SK, Canada)
U of Rhode Island (RI)
U of Richmond (VA)
U of Rochester (NY)
U of St. Thomas (MN)
U of Saskatchewan (SK, Canada)
U of South Alabama (AL)
U of South Carolina (SC)
U of Southern California (CA)
The U of Tennessee (TN)
The U of Texas at Arlington (TX)
The U of Texas at Austin (TX)
The U of Texas at San Antonio (TX)
The U of Texas–Pan American (TX)
U of the Pacific (CA)
U of the South (TN)
U of Toledo (OH)
U of Toronto (ON, Canada)
U of Tulsa (OK)
U of Utah (UT)
U of Vermont (VT)
U of Victoria (BC, Canada)
U of Washington (WA)
U of Waterloo (ON, Canada)
The U of Western Ontario (ON, Canada)
U of West Florida (FL)
U of Windsor (ON, Canada)
U of Wisconsin–Madison (WI)
U of Wisconsin–Milwaukee (WI)
U of Wisconsin–Superior (WI)
U of Wisconsin–Whitewater (WI)
Ursuline Coll (OH)
Valparaiso U (IN)
Vassar Coll (NY)
Villanova U (PA)
Virginia Commonwealth U (VA)
Wake Forest U (NC)
Washburn U of Topeka (KS)
Washington and Lee U (VA)
Washington U in St. Louis (MO)
Wayne State U (MI)
Webster U (MO)
Wellesley Coll (MA)
Wells Coll (NY)
Wesleyan Coll (GA)
Wesleyan U (CT)
Western Maryland Coll (MD)
Western Michigan U (MI)
Western Washington U (WA)
West Virginia Wesleyan Coll (WV)
Wheaton Coll (MA)
Whitman Coll (WA)
Whitworth Coll (WA)
Wichita State U (KS)
Willamette U (OR)
William Paterson U of New Jersey (NJ)
Williams Coll (MA)
Winthrop U (SC)
Wittenberg U (OH)
Wofford Coll (SC)
Wright State U (OH)
Yale U (CT)
York U (ON, Canada)
Youngstown State U (OH)

ARTS MANAGEMENT

Adrian Coll (MI)
Appalachian State U (NC)
Baldwin-Wallace Coll (OH)
Bellarmine U (KY)
Benedictine Coll (KS)
Benedictine U (IL)
Bennett Coll (NC)
Baruch Coll of the City U of NY (NY)
Bishop's U (PQ, Canada)
Brenau U (GA)
Buena Vista U (IA)
Butler U (IN)
California State U, Hayward (CA)
Centenary Coll of Louisiana (LA)
Chatham Coll (PA)
Coll of Charleston (SC)
Coll of Santa Fe (NM)
Columbia Coll (SC)
Columbia Coll Chicago (IL)
Concordia Coll (NY)
Culver-Stockton Coll (MO)
Dakota State U (SD)
DePaul U (IL)
Eastern Michigan U (MI)
The Evergreen State Coll (WA)
Fontbonne U (MO)
Georgia Coll and State U (GA)
Green Mountain Coll (VT)
Illinois Wesleyan U (IL)
Ithaca Coll (NY)
Kansas Wesleyan U (KS)
Lakeland Coll (WI)
Long Island U, C.W. Post Campus (NY)
Long Island U, Southampton Coll, Friends World Program (NY)
Luther Coll (IA)
Mary Baldwin Coll (VA)
Marywood U (PA)
Mercyhurst Coll (PA)
Millikin U (IL)
Newberry Coll (SC)
North Carolina State U (NC)
Northern Arizona U (AZ)
Ohio U (OH)
Oklahoma City U (OK)
Pfeiffer U (NC)
Point Park Coll (PA)
Quincy U (IL)
Randolph-Macon Coll (VA)
Salem Coll (NC)
Seton Hill Coll (PA)
Shenandoah U (VA)
Simmons Coll (MA)
Southeastern Louisiana U (LA)
Spring Hill Coll (AL)
State U of NY Coll at Brockport (NY)
State U of NY Coll at Fredonia (NY)
U of Evansville (IN)
The U of Iowa (IA)
U of Kentucky (KY)
U of Michigan–Dearborn (MI)
U of Ottawa (ON, Canada)
U of Portland (OR)
U of South Dakota (SD)
U of Toronto (ON, Canada)
U of Tulsa (OK)
U of Waterloo (ON, Canada)
U of Windsor (ON, Canada)
U of Wisconsin–Stevens Point (WI)
Upper Iowa U (IA)
Viterbo U (WI)
Wagner Coll (NY)
Wartburg Coll (IA)
Waynesburg Coll (PA)
Whitworth Coll (WA)

ART THERAPY

Albertus Magnus Coll (CT)
Alverno Coll (WI)
Anna Maria Coll (MA)
Arcadia U (PA)
Avila Coll (MO)
Bowling Green State U (OH)
Brescia U (KY)
Capital U (OH)
The Coll of New Rochelle (NY)
Coll of Santa Fe (NM)
Concordia U (QC, Canada)
Converse Coll (SC)
Edgewood Coll (WI)
Elms Coll (MA)
Emmanuel Coll (MA)
Goshen Coll (IN)
Harding U (AR)
Howard U (DC)
Long Island U, C.W. Post Campus (NY)
Long Island U, Southampton Coll, Friends World Program (NY)
Marygrove Coll (MI)
Marymount Coll of Fordham U (NY)
Marywood U (PA)
Mercyhurst Coll (PA)
Millikin U (IL)
Mount Mary Coll (WI)
Nazareth Coll of Rochester (NY)
Ohio U (OH)
Ohio Wesleyan U (OH)
Pittsburg State U (KS)
Prescott Coll (AZ)
Russell Sage Coll (NY)
St. Thomas Aquinas Coll (NY)
School of the Art Inst of Chicago (IL)
School of Visual Arts (NY)
Seton Hill Coll (PA)
Springfield Coll (MA)
Spring Hill Coll (AL)
U of Indianapolis (IN)
U of Wisconsin–Superior (WI)
Webster U (MO)

ASIAN-AMERICAN STUDIES

California State U, Fullerton (CA)
California State U, Hayward (CA)
Columbia Coll (NY)
The Ohio State U (OH)
Pitzer Coll (CA)
Scripps Coll (CA)
U of Calif, Berkeley (CA)
U of Calif, Los Angeles (CA)
U of Calif, Riverside (CA)
U of Calif, Santa Barbara (CA)
U of Denver (CO)
U of Southern California (CA)

ASIAN STUDIES

American U (DC)
Amherst Coll (MA)
Augustana Coll (IL)
Bard Coll (NY)
Barnard Coll (NY)
Baylor U (TX)
Beloit Coll (WI)
Birmingham-Southern Coll (AL)
Bowdoin Coll (ME)
Bowling Green State U (OH)
Brigham Young U (UT)
California State U, Chico (CA)
California State U, Long Beach (CA)
California State U, Sacramento (CA)
Carleton Coll (MN)
Carleton U (ON, Canada)
Case Western Reserve U (OH)
City Coll of the City U of NY (NY)
Claremont McKenna Coll (CA)
Clark U (MA)
Coe Coll (IA)
Colgate U (NY)
Coll of the Holy Cross (MA)
The Coll of Wooster (OH)
The Colorado Coll (CO)
Colorado State U (CO)
Cornell U (NY)
Dartmouth Coll (NH)
Duke U (NC)
Earlham Coll (IN)
Emory U (GA)
The Evergreen State Coll (WA)
Florida State U (FL)
Fort Lewis Coll (CO)
Furman U (SC)
The George Washington U (DC)
Gonzaga U (WA)
Hamilton Coll (NY)
Hamline U (MN)
Hampshire Coll (MA)
Harvard U (MA)
Hobart and William Smith Colls (NY)
Hofstra U (NY)
Indiana U Bloomington (IN)
John Carroll U (OH)
Kenyon Coll (OH)
Lake Forest Coll (IL)
Lehigh U (PA)
Long Island U, Southampton Coll, Friends World Program (NY)
Macalester Coll (MN)
Manhattanville Coll (NY)
Marlboro Coll (VT)
Mary Baldwin Coll (VA)
Mount Holyoke Coll (MA)
Mount Union Coll (OH)
Northwestern U (IL)
Occidental Coll (CA)
Ohio U (OH)
Pitzer Coll (CA)
Pomona Coll (CA)
Queens Coll of the City U of NY (NY)
Rice U (TX)
St. Andrews Presbyterian Coll (NC)
St. John's U (NY)
St. Lawrence U (NY)
Saint Mary's U (NS, Canada)
St. Olaf Coll (MN)
Salem International U (WV)
Samford U (AL)
San Diego State U (CA)
Sarah Lawrence Coll (NY)
Scripps Coll (CA)
Seton Hall U (NJ)
Simon's Rock Coll of Bard (MA)
Skidmore Coll (NY)
Southwest Texas State U (TX)
Stanford U (CA)
State U of NY at Albany (NY)
State U of NY Coll at Brockport (NY)
Swarthmore Coll (PA)
Temple U (PA)
Texas Christian U (TX)
Trinity U (TX)
Tufts U (MA)
Tulane U (LA)
The U of Alabama (AL)
The U of British Columbia (BC, Canada)
U of Calif, Berkeley (CA)
U of Calif, Riverside (CA)
U of Calif, Santa Barbara (CA)
U of Calif, Santa Cruz (CA)
U of Chicago (IL)
U of Cincinnati (OH)
U of Colorado at Boulder (CO)
U of Florida (FL)
U of Hawaii at Manoa (HI)
U of Hawaii–West Oahu (HI)
U of Illinois at Urbana–Champaign (IL)
The U of Iowa (IA)
U of Michigan (MI)
The U of Montana–Missoula (MT)
U of New Mexico (NM)
The U of North Carolina at Chapel Hill (NC)
U of Northern Iowa (IA)
U of Oregon (OR)
U of Puget Sound (WA)
U of Redlands (CA)
The U of Texas at Austin (TX)
U of the South (TN)
U of Toledo (OH)
U of Toronto (ON, Canada)
U of Utah (UT)
U of Vermont (VT)

U of Victoria (BC, Canada)
U of Washington (WA)
U of Wisconsin–Madison (WI)
Utah State U (UT)
Vassar Coll (NY)
Washington State U (WA)
Washington U in St. Louis (MO)
Wayne State U (MI)
Western Michigan U (MI)
Western Washington U (WA)
Wheaton Coll (MA)
Whitman Coll (WA)
Willamette U (OR)
Williams Coll (MA)
Wittenberg U (OH)
York U (ON, Canada)

ASTRONOMY
Amherst Coll (MA)
Barnard Coll (NY)
Benedictine Coll (KS)
Boston U (MA)
Bryn Mawr Coll (PA)
California Inst of Technology (CA)
Case Western Reserve U (OH)
Central Michigan U (MI)
Colgate U (NY)
Columbia Coll (NY)
Columbia U, School of General Studies (NY)
Cornell U (NY)
Dartmouth Coll (NH)
Drake U (IA)
Eastern U (PA)
Hampshire Coll (MA)
Harvard U (MA)
Haverford Coll (PA)
Indiana U Bloomington (IN)
Laurentian U (ON, Canada)
Lycoming Coll (PA)
Marlboro Coll (VT)
Minnesota State U, Mankato (MN)
Mount Holyoke Coll (MA)
Mount Union Coll (OH)
Northern Arizona U (AZ)
Northwestern U (IL)
The Ohio State U (OH)
Ohio Wesleyan U (OH)
Penn State U Univ Park Campus (PA)
Pomona Coll (CA)
Rice U (TX)
Saint Mary's U (NS, Canada)
San Diego State U (CA)
San Francisco State U (CA)
Smith Coll (MA)
State U of NY Coll at Brockport (NY)
State U of NY at Stony Brook (NY)
Swarthmore Coll (PA)
Texas Christian U (TX)
Tufts U (MA)
The U of Arizona (AZ)
The U of British Columbia (BC, Canada)
U of Colorado at Boulder (CO)
U of Delaware (DE)
U of Florida (FL)
U of Georgia (GA)
U of Hawaii at Manoa (HI)
U of Illinois at Urbana–Champaign (IL)
The U of Iowa (IA)
U of Kansas (KS)
U of Manitoba (MB, Canada)
U of Maryland, Coll Park (MD)
U of Massachusetts Amherst (MA)
U of Michigan (MI)
U of Minnesota, Twin Cities Campus (MN)
The U of Montana–Missoula (MT)
U of Oklahoma (OK)
U of Rochester (NY)
U of Southern California (CA)
The U of Texas at Austin (TX)
U of Toronto (ON, Canada)
U of Victoria (BC, Canada)
U of Virginia (VA)
U of Washington (WA)
The U of Western Ontario (ON, Canada)
U of Wisconsin–Madison (WI)
U of Wyoming (WY)
Valdosta State U (GA)
Valparaiso U (IN)
Vanderbilt U (TN)
Vassar Coll (NY)
Villanova U (PA)
Wellesley Coll (MA)
Wesleyan U (CT)
Wheaton Coll (MA)
Whitman Coll (WA)
Williams Coll (MA)
Yale U (CT)
York U (ON, Canada)
Youngstown State U (OH)

ASTROPHYSICS
Agnes Scott Coll (GA)
Augsburg Coll (MN)
Boston U (MA)
Brigham Young U (UT)
California Inst of Technology (CA)
California State U, Northridge (CA)
Colgate U (NY)
Columbia Coll (NY)
Connecticut Coll (CT)
Florida Inst of Technology (FL)
Hampshire Coll (MA)
Harvard U (MA)
Indiana U Bloomington (IN)
Marlboro Coll (VT)
McMaster U (ON, Canada)
Michigan State U (MI)
New Mexico Inst of Mining and Technology (NM)
Ohio U (OH)
Pacific Union Coll (CA)
Penn State U Univ Park Campus (PA)
Princeton U (NJ)
Queen's U at Kingston (ON, Canada)
Rice U (TX)
Saint Mary's U (NS, Canada)
San Francisco State U (CA)
Swarthmore Coll (PA)
Texas Christian U (TX)
U of Calgary (AB, Canada)
U of Calif, Berkeley (CA)
U of Calif, Los Angeles (CA)
U of Calif, Santa Cruz (CA)
U of Delaware (DE)
U of Minnesota, Twin Cities Campus (MN)
U of Missouri–St. Louis (MO)
U of New Mexico (NM)
U of Oklahoma (OK)
U of Wyoming (WY)
Villanova U (PA)
Wellesley Coll (MA)
Williams Coll (MA)
Yale U (CT)

ATHLETIC TRAINING/SPORTS MEDICINE
Adams State Coll (CO)
Alderson-Broaddus Coll (WV)
Alfred U (NY)
Alma Coll (MI)
Anderson U (IN)
Angelo State U (TX)
Appalachian State U (NC)
Aquinas Coll (MI)
Arkansas State U (AR)
Ashland U (OH)
Augsburg Coll (MN)
Augustana Coll (SD)
Averett U (VA)
Azusa Pacific U (CA)
Baldwin-Wallace Coll (OH)
Ball State U (IN)
Barton Coll (NC)
Belhaven Coll (MS)
Bethany Coll (KS)
Bethel Coll (MN)
Bluefield Coll (VA)
Boise State U (ID)
Boston U (MA)
Bowling Green State U (OH)
Bridgewater Coll (VA)
Bridgewater State Coll (MA)
Buena Vista U (IA)
Butler U (IN)
California Lutheran U (CA)
California State U, Hayward (CA)
California State U, Long Beach (CA)
California State U, Northridge (CA)
Calvin Coll (MI)
Campbellsville U (KY)
Campbell U (NC)
Canisius Coll (NY)
Capital U (OH)
Carroll Coll (WI)
Carson-Newman Coll (TN)
Carthage Coll (WI)
Castleton State Coll (VT)
Catawba Coll (NC)
Cedarville U (OH)
Central Connecticut State U (CT)
Central Methodist Coll (MO)
Central Michigan U (MI)
Chapman U (CA)
Chowan Coll (NC)
Christian Heritage Coll (CA)
Clarke Coll (IA)
Coe Coll (IA)
Coker Coll (SC)
Colby-Sawyer Coll (NH)
Coll of the Southwest (NM)
Colorado State U (CO)
Columbus State U (GA)
Comm Hospital Roanoke Valley–Coll of Health Scis (VA)
Concordia U (NE)
Concordia U (QC, Canada)
Concordia U Wisconsin (WI)
Culver-Stockton Coll (MO)
Cumberland U (TN)
Dakota Wesleyan U (SD)
Defiance Coll (OH)
DePauw U (IN)
Dominican Coll (NY)
Duquesne U (PA)
East Carolina U (NC)
Eastern Kentucky U (KY)
Eastern Michigan U (MI)
Eastern Washington U (WA)
East Stroudsburg U of Pennsylvania (PA)
East Texas Baptist U (TX)
Elon U (NC)
Endicott Coll (MA)
Erskine Coll (SC)
Eureka Coll (IL)
Faulkner U (AL)
Ferrum Coll (VA)
Florida Southern Coll (FL)
Franklin Coll of Indiana (IN)
Fresno Pacific U (CA)
Gardner-Webb U (NC)
George Fox U (OR)
Georgia Southern U (GA)
Graceland U (IA)
Grand Canyon U (AZ)
Grand Valley State U (MI)
Greensboro Coll (NC)
Guilford Coll (NC)
Gustavus Adolphus Coll (MN)
Hamline U (MN)
Heidelberg Coll (OH)
Henderson State U (AR)
High Point U (NC)
Hope Coll (MI)
Hope International U (CA)
Houghton Coll (NY)
Howard Payne U (TX)
Huntingdon Coll (AL)
Indiana State U (IN)
Indiana U Bloomington (IN)
Indiana Wesleyan U (IN)
Ithaca Coll (NY)
John Brown U (AR)
Johnson State Coll (VT)
Keene State Coll (NH)
Kent State U (OH)
King's Coll (PA)
Lakehead U (ON, Canada)
Lake Superior State U (MI)
Lambuth U (TN)
Lees-McRae Coll (NC)
Lenoir-Rhyne Coll (NC)
Liberty U (VA)
Limestone Coll (SC)
Lincoln Memorial U (TN)
Lindenwood U (MO)
Linfield Coll (OR)
Lipscomb U (TN)
Lock Haven U of Pennsylvania (PA)
Long Island U, Brooklyn Campus (NY)
Longwood Coll (VA)
Loras Coll (IA)
Louisiana Coll (LA)
Lubbock Christian U (TX)
Lynchburg Coll (VA)
Lyndon State Coll (VT)
Manchester Coll (IN)
Marietta Coll (OH)
Marist Coll (NY)
Marquette U (WI)
Mars Hill Coll (NC)
Marywood U (PA)
Massachusetts Coll of Liberal Arts (MA)
McKendree Coll (IL)
Memorial U of Newfoundland (NF, Canada)
Mercyhurst Coll (PA)
Merrimack Coll (MA)
Messiah Coll (PA)
Methodist Coll (NC)
Miami U (OH)
MidAmerica Nazarene U (KS)
Middle Tennessee State U (TN)
Midland Lutheran Coll (NE)
Millikin U (IL)
Minnesota State U, Mankato (MN)
Missouri Baptist Coll (MO)
Mount Marty Coll (SD)
Mount Olive Coll (NC)
Mount St. Clare Coll (IA)
Mount Union Coll (OH)
Mount Vernon Nazarene U (OH)
National American U (SD)
Nebraska Wesleyan U (NE)
Newberry Coll (SC)
New England Coll (NH)
Newman U (KS)
New Mexico State U (NM)
North Carolina Central U (NC)
North Central Coll (IL)
North Dakota State U (ND)
Northeastern U (MA)
Northern Michigan U (MI)
North Park U (IL)
Northwestern Coll (MN)
Northwest Nazarene U (ID)
Norwich U (VT)
Ohio Northern U (OH)
The Ohio State U (OH)
Ohio U (OH)
Oklahoma Baptist U (OK)
Oklahoma Wesleyan U (OK)
Olivet Coll (MI)
Olivet Nazarene U (IL)
Oregon State U (OR)
Otterbein Coll (OH)
Pacific U (OR)
Park U (MO)
Pepperdine U, Malibu (CA)
Pfeiffer U (NC)
Plymouth State Coll (NH)
Point Loma Nazarene U (CA)
Quincy U (IL)
Quinnipiac U (CT)
Roanoke Coll (VA)
Rocky Mountain Coll (MT)
Russell Sage Coll (NY)
Sacred Heart U (CT)
St. Ambrose U (IA)
Salem International U (WV)
Salisbury U (MD)
Samford U (AL)
San Jose State U (CA)
Shawnee State U (OH)
Simpson Coll (IA)
Slippery Rock U of Pennsylvania (PA)
South Dakota State U (SD)
Southeast Missouri State U (MO)
Southern Connecticut State U (CT)
Southern Nazarene U (OK)
Southwest Baptist U (MO)
Southwestern Coll (KS)
Southwest Missouri State U (MO)
Southwest Texas State U (TX)
Springfield Coll (MA)
State U of NY Coll at Brockport (NY)
State U of NY Coll at Cortland (NY)
Sterling Coll (KS)
Stetson U (FL)
Tabor Coll (KS)
Taylor U (IN)
Temple U (PA)
Tennessee Wesleyan Coll (TN)
Texas Lutheran U (TX)
Texas Wesleyan U (TX)
Towson U (MD)
Trinity International U (IL)
Troy State U (AL)
Tusculum Coll (TN)
Union U (TN)
Université de Sherbrooke (PQ, Canada)
The U of Akron (OH)
The U of Alabama (AL)
U of Alberta (AB, Canada)
U of Central Arkansas (AR)
U of Charleston (WV)
U of Delaware (DE)
U of Evansville (IN)
The U of Findlay (OH)
U of Hawaii at Manoa (HI)
U of Idaho (ID)
U of Indianapolis (IN)
The U of Iowa (IA)
U of Maine at Presque Isle (ME)
U of Mary (ND)
U of Miami (FL)
U of Michigan (MI)
U of Mobile (AL)
U of Nebraska–Lincoln (NE)
U of Nevada, Las Vegas (NV)
U of New Hampshire (NH)
The U of North Carolina at Wilmington (NC)
U of North Dakota (ND)
U of Pittsburgh at Bradford (PA)
U of Puerto Rico at Ponce (PR)
U of San Francisco (CA)
U of Southern Colorado (CO)
U of Southern Maine (ME)
The U of Tennessee at Martin (TN)
The U of Texas at Arlington (TX)
U of Tulsa (OK)
U of Vermont (VT)
The U of West Alabama (AL)
U of Windsor (ON, Canada)
U of Wisconsin–La Crosse (WI)
U of Wisconsin–Stevens Point (WI)
Upper Iowa U (IA)
Urbana U (OH)
Ursinus Coll (PA)
Valdosta State U (GA)
Valparaiso U (IN)
Vanguard U of Southern California (CA)
Walsh U (OH)
Washington State U (WA)
Waynesburg Coll (PA)
Weber State U (UT)
West Chester U of Pennsylvania (PA)
Western State Coll of Colorado (CO)
Western Washington U (WA)
Westminster Coll (MO)
West Virginia Wesleyan Coll (WV)
Whitworth Coll (WA)
William Woods U (MO)
Wilmington Coll (OH)
Wingate U (NC)
Winona State U (MN)
Xavier U (OH)
Youngstown State U (OH)

ATMOSPHERIC SCIENCES
California State U, Chico (CA)
Cornell U (NY)
Creighton U (NE)
Florida Inst of Technology (FL)
Florida State U (FL)
Harvard U (MA)
Iowa State U of Science and Technology (IA)
Jackson State U (MS)
Lyndon State Coll (VT)
McGill U (PQ, Canada)
Metropolitan State Coll of Denver (CO)
Millersville U of Pennsylvania (PA)
New Mexico Inst of Mining and Technology (NM)
North Carolina State U (NC)
Northern Illinois U (IL)
Northland Coll (WI)
Ohio U (OH)
Penn State U Univ Park Campus (PA)
Plymouth State Coll (NH)
Rutgers, The State U of New Jersey, New Brunswick (NJ)
St. Cloud State U (MN)
Saint Louis U (MO)
San Francisco State U (CA)
San Jose State U (CA)
State U of NY at Albany (NY)
State U of NY at Oswego (NY)
State U of NY Coll at Brockport (NY)
State U of NY Coll at Oneonta (NY)
State U of NY Maritime Coll (NY)
State U of NY at Stony Brook (NY)
Texas A&M U (TX)
United States Air Force Academy (CO)
U of Alberta (AB, Canada)
The U of Arizona (AZ)

The U of British Columbia (BC, Canada)
U of Calif, Davis (CA)
U of Calif, Los Angeles (CA)
U of Hawaii at Manoa (HI)
U of Kansas (KS)
U of Louisiana at Monroe (LA)
U of Miami (FL)
U of Michigan (MI)
U of Missouri–Columbia (MO)
U of Nebraska–Lincoln (NE)
The U of North Carolina at Asheville (NC)
U of North Dakota (ND)
U of Oklahoma (OK)
U of South Alabama (AL)
U of Utah (UT)
U of Victoria (BC, Canada)
U of Washington (WA)
U of Wisconsin–Milwaukee (WI)
Valparaiso U (IN)
Western Connecticut State U (CT)
York U (ON, Canada)

AUDIO ENGINEERING
American U (DC)
Berklee Coll of Music (MA)
Cleveland Inst of Music (OH)
Cogswell Polytechnical Coll (CA)
The Evergreen State Coll (WA)
Five Towns Coll (NY)
Mount Vernon Nazarene U (OH)
New England School of Communications (ME)
Peabody Conserv of Music of Johns Hopkins U (MD)
State U of NY Coll at Fredonia (NY)
U of Hartford (CT)
U of Southern California (CA)
Webster U (MO)

AUTO MECHANIC/TECHNICIAN
Andrews U (MI)
Ferris State U (MI)
Lewis-Clark State Coll (ID)
Montana State U–Northern (MT)
Pittsburg State U (KS)
U of Arkansas at Pine Bluff (AR)
U of Southern Colorado (CO)
Walla Walla Coll (WA)
Weber State U (UT)

AUTOMOTIVE ENGINEERING TECHNOLOGY
Central Michigan U (MI)
Central Missouri State U (MO)
Grambling State U (LA)
Indiana State U (IN)
Minnesota State U, Mankato (MN)
Pennsylvania Coll of Technology (PA)
Rochester Inst of Technology (NY)
Southern Illinois U Carbondale (IL)
U of Windsor (ON, Canada)
Weber State U (UT)
Western Michigan U (MI)
Western Washington U (WA)

AVIATION/AIRWAY SCIENCE
Central Washington U (WA)
Delta State U (MS)
Embry-Riddle Aeronautical U (AZ)
Embry-Riddle Aeronautical U (FL)
Embry-Riddle Aeronautical U, Extended Campus (FL)
Florida Inst of Technology (FL)
Kansas State U (KS)
Kent State U (OH)
Louisiana Tech U (LA)
Middle Tennessee State U (TN)
Ohio U (OH)
Purdue U (IN)
Quincy U (IL)
San Jose State U (CA)
U of North Dakota (ND)
Western Michigan U (MI)

AVIATION MANAGEMENT
Averett U (VA)
Baker Coll of Muskegon (MI)
Bowling Green State U (OH)
Bridgewater State Coll (MA)
Coll of Aeronautics (NY)
Daniel Webster Coll (NH)
Delaware State U (DE)
Dowling Coll (NY)
Eastern Kentucky U (KY)
Embry-Riddle Aeronautical U (AZ)
Embry-Riddle Aeronautical U (FL)
Embry-Riddle Aeronautical U, Extended Campus (FL)
Everglades Coll (FL)
Fairmont State Coll (WV)
Florida Inst of Technology (FL)
Geneva Coll (PA)
Hampton U (VA)
Indiana State U (IN)
Jacksonville U (FL)
Lewis U (IL)
Louisiana Tech U (LA)
Lynn U (FL)
Marywood U (PA)
Metropolitan State Coll of Denver (CO)
Minnesota State U, Mankato (MN)
The Ohio State U (OH)
Ohio U (OH)
Oklahoma State U (OK)
Park U (MO)
Quincy U (IL)
Robert Morris U (PA)
Rocky Mountain Coll (MT)
St. Cloud State U (MN)
St. Francis Coll (NY)
Saint Louis U (MO)
Salem State Coll (MA)
San Jose State U (CA)
Southeastern Oklahoma State U (OK)
Southern Illinois U Carbondale (IL)
Southern Nazarene U (OK)
State U of NY at Farmingdale (NY)
Tarleton State U (TX)
Texas Southern U (TX)
U Coll of the Fraser Valley (BC, Canada)
U of Dubuque (IA)
U of Nebraska at Kearney (NE)
U of Nebraska at Omaha (NE)
U of New Haven (CT)
U of North Dakota (ND)
Western Michigan U (MI)
Westminster Coll (UT)
Wheeling Jesuit U (WV)
Wilmington Coll (DE)
Winona State U (MN)

AVIATION TECHNOLOGY
Andrews U (MI)
Averett U (VA)
Christian Heritage Coll (CA)
Coll of Aeronautics (NY)
Coll of the Ozarks (MO)
Elizabeth City State U (NC)
Fairmont State Coll (WV)
Grace U (NE)
Hampton U (VA)
LeTourneau U (TX)
Lewis U (IL)
Moody Bible Inst (IL)
The Ohio State U (OH)
Oklahoma State U (OK)
Providence Coll and Theological Seminary (MB, Canada)
San Jose State U (CA)
Southern Illinois U Carbondale (IL)
Walla Walla Coll (WA)
Western Michigan U (MI)
Wilmington Coll (DE)

BAKER/PASTRY CHEF
Johnson & Wales U (RI)

BANKING
Central Michigan U (MI)
Clearwater Christian Coll (FL)
Delaware State U (DE)
Husson Coll (ME)
National U (CA)
Southeastern U (DC)
Southeast Missouri State U (MO)
Thomas Edison State Coll (NJ)
U of Indianapolis (IN)
U of Nebraska at Omaha (NE)
U of North Florida (FL)
The U of Texas at Arlington (TX)
West Liberty State Coll (WV)
Youngstown State U (OH)

BEHAVIORAL SCIENCES
Andrews U (MI)
Anna Maria Coll (MA)
Athens State U (AL)
Augsburg Coll (MN)
Averett U (VA)
Avila Coll (MO)
Belmont U (TN)
Bemidji State U (MN)
Brown U (RI)
California Baptist U (CA)
California State Polytechnic U, Pomona (CA)
California State U, Dominguez Hills (CA)
California State U, Monterey Bay (CA)
Cedar Crest Coll (PA)
Chaminade U of Honolulu (HI)
Circleville Bible Coll (OH)
Coker Coll (SC)
Columbia Coll (MO)
Concordia U (CA)
Concordia U (NE)
Concordia U (QC, Canada)
Cornell U (NY)
Dakota Wesleyan U (SD)
Drew U (NJ)
Drury U (MO)
East Texas Baptist U (TX)
East-West U (IL)
Erskine Coll (SC)
Evangel U (MO)
Felician Coll (NJ)
Freed-Hardeman U (TN)
Georgia Southwestern State U (GA)
Glenville State Coll (WV)
Goddard Coll (VT)
Grand Valley State U (MI)
Green Mountain Coll (VT)
Gwynedd-Mercy Coll (PA)
Hampshire Coll (MA)
Harvard U (MA)
Hawai'i Pacific U (HI)
Howard Payne U (TX)
Indiana U Kokomo (IN)
Inter American U of PR, San Germán Campus (PR)
Iona Coll (NY)
John Jay Coll of Criminal Justice, the City U of NY (NY)
Johns Hopkins U (MD)
King Coll (TN)
Lakeland Coll (WI)
Laurentian U (ON, Canada)
Lincoln U (PA)
Long Island U, Southampton Coll (NY)
Long Island U, Southampton Coll, Friends World Program (NY)
Loyola U New Orleans (LA)
Marist Coll (NY)
Marlboro Coll (VT)
Mars Hill Coll (NC)
McPherson Coll (KS)
Mercy Coll (NY)
Mesa State Coll (CO)
Methodist Coll (NC)
Metropolitan State Coll of Denver (CO)
Mid-Continent Coll (KY)
Midland Lutheran Coll (NE)
Minnesota State U, Mankato (MN)
Morgan State U (MD)
Mountain State U (WV)
Mount Aloysius Coll (PA)
Mount Marty Coll (SD)
Mount Mary Coll (WI)
National-Louis U (IL)
National U (CA)
New Mexico Inst of Mining and Technology (NM)
Northeastern U (MA)
Northwest Coll (WA)
Northwest Missouri State U (MO)
Notre Dame de Namur U (CA)
Oklahoma Wesleyan U (OK)
Our Lady of Holy Cross Coll (LA)
Pacific Union Coll (CA)
Point Park Coll (PA)
Purdue U Calumet (IN)
Rhode Island Coll (RI)
Rochester Coll (MI)
St. Cloud State U (MN)
St. Joseph's Coll, Suffolk Campus (NY)
San Jose State U (CA)
Sojourner-Douglass Coll (MD)
Sterling Coll (KS)
Syracuse U (NY)
Tennessee Wesleyan Coll (TN)
Texas Wesleyan U (TX)
Trevecca Nazarene U (TN)
Tufts U (MA)
United States Air Force Academy (CO)
United States Military Academy (NY)
The U of Akron (OH)
U of Chicago (IL)
U of Houston–Clear Lake (TX)
U of La Verne (CA)
U of Maine at Fort Kent (ME)
U of Maine at Machias (ME)
U of Maine at Presque Isle (ME)
U of Mary (ND)
U of Michigan–Dearborn (MI)
U of Missouri–St. Louis (MO)
U of Mobile (AL)
U of North Texas (TX)
U of Ottawa (ON, Canada)
U of St. Thomas (MN)
U of Sioux Falls (SD)
U of Utah (UT)
U System Coll for Lifelong Learning (NH)
Walsh U (OH)
Western International U (AZ)
Westminster Coll (PA)
Widener U (PA)
William Paterson U of New Jersey (NJ)
Wilmington Coll (DE)
Wilson Coll (PA)
Wittenberg U (OH)
York Coll of Pennsylvania (PA)
York U (ON, Canada)

BIBLICAL LANGUAGES/ LITERATURES
American Christian Coll and Seminary (OK)
Baltimore Hebrew U (MD)
Baylor U (TX)
Belmont U (TN)
Bethany Coll of the Assemblies of God (CA)
Bethel Coll (IN)
Carson-Newman Coll (TN)
Central Bible Coll (MO)
Columbia International U (SC)
Concordia U (IL)
Concordia U (MI)
Concordia U Wisconsin (WI)
Cornerstone U (MI)
Harding U (AR)
Harvard U (MA)
Howard Payne U (TX)
Indiana Wesleyan U (IN)
Laura and Alvin Siegal Coll of Judaic Studies (OH)
Lipscomb U (TN)
Long Island U, Southampton Coll, Friends World Program (NY)
Lubbock Christian U (TX)
Luther Coll (IA)
The Master's Coll and Seminary (CA)
Mid-Continent Coll (KY)
Multnomah Bible Coll and Biblical Seminary (OR)
North Greenville Coll (SC)
Northwest Nazarene U (ID)
Oklahoma Baptist U (OK)
Ozark Christian Coll (MO)
Prairie Bible Coll (AB, Canada)
Southeastern Bible Coll (AL)
Southern Christian U (AL)
Southwestern Assemblies of God U (TX)
Taylor U (IN)
Toccoa Falls Coll (GA)
Union U (TN)
U of Chicago (IL)
U of Toronto (ON, Canada)
Walla Walla Coll (WA)
York Coll (NE)
York U (ON, Canada)

BIBLICAL STUDIES
Abilene Christian U (TX)
Alaska Bible Coll (AK)
American Baptist Coll of American Baptist Theol Sem (TN)
Anderson U (IN)
Andrews U (MI)
Appalachian Bible Coll (WV)
Arlington Baptist Coll (TX)
Asbury Coll (KY)
Atlanta Christian Coll (GA)
Atlantic Baptist U (NB, Canada)
Austin Graduate School of Theology (TX)
Azusa Pacific U (CA)
Baltimore Hebrew U (MD)
Baptist Bible Coll of Pennsylvania (PA)
The Baptist Coll of Florida (FL)
Barclay Coll (KS)
Beacon Coll and Graduate School (GA)
Belhaven Coll (MS)
Belmont U (TN)
Bethany Coll of the Assemblies of God (CA)
Bethel Coll (IN)
Bethel Coll (MN)
Beulah Heights Bible Coll (GA)
Biola U (CA)
Bluefield Coll (VA)
Blue Mountain Coll (MS)
Boise Bible Coll (ID)
Briercrest Bible Coll (SK, Canada)
Bryan Coll (TN)
California Christian Coll (CA)
Calvary Bible Coll and Theological Seminary (MO)
Calvin Coll (MI)
Campbellsville U (KY)
Canadian Bible Coll (SK, Canada)
Carson-Newman Coll (TN)
Cascade Coll (OR)
Cedarville U (OH)
Central Baptist Coll (AR)
Central Bible Coll (MO)
Central Christian Coll of Kansas (KS)
Central Christian Coll of the Bible (MO)
Christian Heritage Coll (CA)
Cincinnati Bible Coll and Seminary (OH)
Circleville Bible Coll (OH)
Clear Creek Baptist Bible Coll (KY)
Clearwater Christian Coll (FL)
Colorado Christian U (CO)
Columbia Bible Coll (BC, Canada)
Columbia International U (SC)
Cornerstone U (MI)
Covenant Coll (GA)
Crichton Coll (TN)
Crown Coll (MN)
Dallas Baptist U (TX)
Dallas Christian Coll (TX)
Eastern Mennonite U (VA)
Eastern U (PA)
Emmanuel Coll (GA)
Emmaus Bible Coll (IA)
Erskine Coll (SC)
Eugene Bible Coll (OR)
Evangel U (MO)
Faith Baptist Bible Coll and Theological Seminary (IA)
Faulkner U (AL)
Florida Christian Coll (FL)
Florida Coll (FL)
Freed-Hardeman U (TN)
Fresno Pacific U (CA)
Friends U (KS)
Geneva Coll (PA)
George Fox U (OR)
Global U of the Assemblies of God (MO)
God's Bible School and Coll (OH)
Gordon Coll (MA)
Goshen Coll (IN)
Grace Bible Coll (MI)
Grace Coll (IN)
Grace U (NE)
Grand Canyon U (AZ)
Great Lakes Christian Coll (MI)
Hannibal-LaGrange Coll (MO)
Harding U (AR)
Hardin-Simmons U (TX)
Harvard U (MA)
Heritage Christian U (AL)
Hobe Sound Bible Coll (FL)
Holy Apostles Coll and Seminary (CT)
Hope International U (CA)
Houghton Coll (NY)
Houston Baptist U (TX)
Howard Payne U (TX)
Huntington Coll (IN)
Indiana Wesleyan U (IN)
Jewish Theological Seminary of America (NY)
John Brown U (AR)
Johnson Bible Coll (TN)
John Wesley Coll (NC)

Judson Coll (IL)
King Coll (TN)
Lancaster Bible Coll (PA)
Laura and Alvin Siegal Coll of Judaic Studies (OH)
Lee U (TN)
LeTourneau U (TX)
LIFE Bible Coll (CA)
Lincoln Christian Coll (IL)
Lipscomb U (TN)
Long Island U, Southampton Coll, Friends World Program (NY)
Lubbock Christian U (TX)
Magnolia Bible Coll (MS)
Malone Coll (OH)
Manhattan Christian Coll (KS)
Maranatha Baptist Bible Coll (WI)
Marlboro Coll (VT)
The Master's Coll and Seminary (CA)
Messiah Coll (PA)
Methodist Coll (NC)
Mid-Continent Coll (KY)
Milligan Coll (TN)
Minnesota Bible Coll (MN)
Montreat Coll (NC)
Moody Bible Inst (IL)
Mount Vernon Nazarene U (OH)
Multnomah Bible Coll and Biblical Seminary (OR)
Nazarene Bible Coll (CO)
North American Baptist Coll & Edmonton Baptist Sem (AB, Canada)
North Greenville Coll (SC)
North Park U (IL)
Northwest Bible Coll (AB, Canada)
Northwest Christian Coll (OR)
Northwest Coll (WA)
Northwestern Coll (MN)
Nyack Coll (NY)
Oak Hills Christian Coll (MN)
Oakland City U (IN)
Ohio Valley Coll (WV)
Oklahoma Baptist U (OK)
Oklahoma Christian U of Science and Arts (OK)
Olivet Nazarene U (IL)
Oral Roberts U (OK)
Ouachita Baptist U (AR)
Ozark Christian Coll (MO)
Patten Coll (CA)
Philadelphia Biblical U (PA)
Pillsbury Baptist Bible Coll (MN)
Practical Bible Coll (NY)
Providence Coll and Theological Seminary (MB, Canada)
Puget Sound Christian Coll (WA)
Redeemer U Coll (ON, Canada)
Reformed Bible Coll (MI)
Roanoke Bible Coll (NC)
Rochester Coll (MI)
Rocky Mountain Coll (AB, Canada)
St. Louis Christian Coll (MO)
Samford U (AL)
San Jose Christian Coll (CA)
Shasta Bible Coll (CA)
Simpson Coll and Graduate School (CA)
Southeastern Bible Coll (AL)
Southeastern Coll of the Assemblies of God (FL)
Southern Christian U (AL)
Southern Methodist Coll (SC)
Southern Nazarene U (OK)
Southwest Baptist U (MO)
Southwestern Assemblies of God U (TX)
Southwestern Coll (AZ)
Steinbach Bible Coll (MB, Canada)
Tabor Coll (KS)
Taylor U (IN)
Taylor U, Fort Wayne Campus (IN)
Tennessee Temple U (TN)
Toccoa Falls Coll (GA)
Touro Coll (NY)
Trinity Baptist Coll (FL)
Trinity Bible Coll (ND)
Trinity Coll of Florida (FL)
Trinity International U (IL)
Trinity Western U (BC, Canada)
Tyndale Coll & Seminary (ON, Canada)
Union U (TN)
Universidad Adventista de las Antillas (PR)
Université de Montréal (QC, Canada)
U of Evansville (IN)
U of Michigan (MI)
Valley Forge Christian Coll (PA)
Vanguard U of Southern California (CA)
Warner Pacific Coll (OR)
Warner Southern Coll (FL)
Washington Bible Coll (MD)
Wesley Coll (MS)
Western Baptist Coll (OR)
Wheaton Coll (IL)
William Carey Coll (MS)
William Tyndale Coll (MI)
York Coll (NE)

BILINGUAL/BICULTURAL EDUCATION

Adrian Coll (MI)
Alfred U (NY)
Belmont U (TN)
Biola U (CA)
Boise State U (ID)
Boston U (MA)
Brooklyn Coll of the City U of NY (NY)
California State Polytechnic U, Pomona (CA)
California State U, Dominguez Hills (CA)
California State U, Sacramento (CA)
Calvin Coll (MI)
Chicago State U (IL)
Coll of the Southwest (NM)
Eastern Michigan U (MI)
Elms Coll (MA)
Florida State U (FL)
Fordham U (NY)
Fresno Pacific U (CA)
Goshen Coll (IN)
Houston Baptist U (TX)
Indiana U Bloomington (IN)
Long Island U, Southampton Coll, Friends World Program (NY)
Marquette U (WI)
Mercy Coll (NY)
Mount Mary Coll (WI)
New Mexico Highlands U (NM)
Northeastern Illinois U (IL)
Prescott Coll (AZ)
Rider U (NJ)
St. Edward's U (TX)
State U of NY Coll at Old Westbury (NY)
Texas A&M International U (TX)
Texas A&M U–Kingsville (TX)
Texas Christian U (TX)
Texas Southern U (TX)
Texas Wesleyan U (TX)
U of Alberta (AB, Canada)
U of Delaware (DE)
The U of Findlay (OH)
U of Michigan–Dearborn (MI)
U of Ottawa (ON, Canada)
U of Regina (SK, Canada)
U of San Francisco (CA)
The U of Texas at Brownsville (TX)
The U of Texas at San Antonio (TX)
U of Washington (WA)
U of Wisconsin–Milwaukee (WI)
Weber State U (UT)
Western Illinois U (IL)
York U (ON, Canada)

BIOCHEMICAL TECHNOLOGY

Norwich U (VT)
State U of NY at Buffalo (NY)
U of Windsor (ON, Canada)

BIOCHEMISTRY

Abilene Christian U (TX)
Adelphi U (NY)
Agnes Scott Coll (GA)
Albright Coll (PA)
Alma Coll (MI)
Alvernia Coll (PA)
American International Coll (MA)
American U (DC)
Andrews U (MI)
Angelo State U (TX)
Arizona State U (AZ)
Asbury Coll (KY)
Atlantic Union Coll (MA)
Auburn U (AL)
Azusa Pacific U (CA)
Bard Coll (NY)
Barnard Coll (NY)
Bates Coll (ME)
Baylor U (TX)
Belmont U (TN)
Beloit Coll (WI)
Benedictine Coll (KS)
Benedictine U (IL)
Bennington Coll (VT)
Berry Coll (GA)
Bethel Coll (MN)
Biola U (CA)
Bishop's U (PQ, Canada)
Bloomfield Coll (NJ)
Boston Coll (MA)
Boston U (MA)
Bowdoin Coll (ME)
Bowling Green State U (OH)
Bradley U (IL)
Brandeis U (MA)
Bridgewater State Coll (MA)
Brigham Young U (UT)
Brock U (ON, Canada)
Brown U (RI)
California Inst of Technology (CA)
California Lutheran U (CA)
California Polytechnic State U, San Luis Obispo (CA)
California State U, Chico (CA)
California State U, Dominguez Hills (CA)
California State U, Fullerton (CA)
California State U, Hayward (CA)
California State U, Long Beach (CA)
California State U, Los Angeles (CA)
California State U, Northridge (CA)
California State U, San Bernardino (CA)
California State U, San Marcos (CA)
Calvin Coll (MI)
Campbell U (NC)
Canisius Coll (NY)
Carleton U (ON, Canada)
Carnegie Mellon U (PA)
Carroll Coll (WI)
Case Western Reserve U (OH)
The Catholic U of America (DC)
Cedar Crest Coll (PA)
Centenary Coll of Louisiana (LA)
Centre Coll (KY)
Chapman U (CA)
Charleston Southern U (SC)
Chatham Coll (PA)
Chestnut Hill Coll (PA)
City Coll of the City U of NY (NY)
Claremont McKenna Coll (CA)
Clarkson U (NY)
Clark U (MA)
Clemson U (SC)
Coe Coll (IA)
Colby Coll (ME)
Colgate U (NY)
Coll Misericordia (PA)
Coll of Charleston (SC)
Coll of Mount St. Joseph (OH)
Coll of Mount Saint Vincent (NY)
Coll of Saint Benedict (MN)
Coll of St. Catherine (MN)
Coll of Saint Elizabeth (NJ)
The Coll of Saint Rose (NY)
The Coll of St. Scholastica (MN)
The Coll of Southeastern Europe, The American U of Athens(Greece)
Coll of Staten Island of the City U of NY (NY)
Coll of the Holy Cross (MA)
The Coll of Wooster (OH)
The Colorado Coll (CO)
Colorado State U (CO)
Columbia Coll (NY)
Columbia Union Coll (MD)
Concordia U (QC, Canada)
Connecticut Coll (CT)
Converse Coll (SC)
Cornell Coll (IA)
Cornell U (NY)
Daemen Coll (NY)
Dalhousie U (NS, Canada)
Dartmouth Coll (NH)
Denison U (OH)
DePaul U (IL)
Dickinson Coll (PA)
Dominican U (IL)
Drew U (NJ)
Duquesne U (PA)
East Carolina U (NC)
Eastern Kentucky U (KY)
Eastern Mennonite U (VA)
Eastern Michigan U (MI)
Eastern U (PA)
Eastern Washington U (WA)
East Stroudsburg U of Pennsylvania (PA)
Edinboro U of Pennsylvania (PA)
Elizabethtown Coll (PA)
Elmira Coll (NY)
Emmanuel Coll (MA)
The Evergreen State Coll (WA)
Fairleigh Dickinson U, Teaneck-Hackensack Campus (NJ)
Felician Coll (NJ)
Florida Inst of Technology (FL)
Florida State U (FL)
Fort Lewis Coll (CO)
Franklin and Marshall Coll (PA)
Furman U (SC)
Georgetown U (DC)
Georgian Court Coll (NJ)
Gettysburg Coll (PA)
Gonzaga U (WA)
Grinnell Coll (IA)
Grove City Coll (PA)
Gustavus Adolphus Coll (MN)
Hamilton Coll (NY)
Hampden-Sydney Coll (VA)
Hampshire Coll (MA)
Harding U (AR)
Hartwick Coll (NY)
Harvard U (MA)
Haverford Coll (PA)
Hobart and William Smith Colls (NY)
Hofstra U (NY)
Holy Family Coll (PA)
Hood Coll (MD)
Hope Coll (MI)
Humboldt State U (CA)
Idaho State U (ID)
Immaculata Coll (PA)
Indiana U Bloomington (IN)
Indiana U of Pennsylvania (PA)
Iona Coll (NY)
Iowa State U of Science and Technology (IA)
Ithaca Coll (NY)
Jamestown Coll (ND)
John Brown U (AR)
Juniata Coll (PA)
Kansas State U (KS)
Kenyon Coll (OH)
Keuka Coll (NY)
King Coll (TN)
Knox Coll (IL)
Lafayette Coll (PA)
LaGrange Coll (GA)
La Salle U (PA)
Laurentian U (ON, Canada)
Lebanon Valley Coll (PA)
Lehigh U (PA)
Lehman Coll of the City U of NY (NY)
Le Moyne Coll (NY)
Lewis & Clark Coll (OR)
Lewis U (IL)
Lipscomb U (TN)
Loras Coll (IA)
Louisiana State U and A&M Coll (LA)
Loyola Marymount U (CA)
Loyola U Chicago (IL)
Maharishi U of Management (IA)
Manhattan Coll (NY)
Manhattanville Coll (NY)
Mansfield U of Pennsylvania (PA)
Marietta Coll (OH)
Marist Coll (NY)
Marlboro Coll (VT)
Marquette U (WI)
Mary Baldwin Coll (VA)
Maryville Coll (TN)
McGill U (PQ, Canada)
McMaster U (ON, Canada)
McMurry U (TX)
Memorial U of Newfoundland (NF, Canada)
Merrimack Coll (MA)
Messiah Coll (PA)
Miami U (OH)
Michigan State U (MI)
Michigan Technological U (MI)
Middlebury Coll (VT)
Mills Coll (CA)
Minnesota State U, Mankato (MN)
Mississippi State U (MS)
Montclair State U (NJ)
Mount Allison U (NB, Canada)
Mount Holyoke Coll (MA)
Mount St. Mary's Coll (CA)
Mount Saint Mary's Coll and Seminary (MD)
Muhlenberg Coll (PA)
Nazareth Coll of Rochester (NY)
Nebraska Wesleyan U (NE)
New Mexico State U (NM)
New York U (NY)
Niagara U (NY)
North Carolina State U (NC)
North Central Coll (IL)
North Dakota State U (ND)
Northeastern U (MA)
Northern Michigan U (MI)
Northwestern U (IL)
Notre Dame Coll (OH)
Notre Dame de Namur U (CA)
Oakland U (MI)
Oakwood Coll (AL)
Oberlin Coll (OH)
Occidental Coll (CA)
Ohio Northern U (OH)
The Ohio State U (OH)
Ohio U (OH)
Oklahoma Christian U of Science and Arts (OK)
Oklahoma City U (OK)
Oklahoma State U (OK)
Old Dominion U (VA)
Olivet Coll (MI)
Olivet Nazarene U (IL)
Oral Roberts U (OK)
Oregon State U (OR)
Otterbein Coll (OH)
Pace U (NY)
Pacific Lutheran U (WA)
Pacific Union Coll (CA)
Penn State U Univ Park Campus (PA)
Philadelphia U (PA)
Plattsburgh State U of NY (NY)
Point Loma Nazarene U (CA)
Pomona Coll (CA)
Portland State U (OR)
Purdue U (IN)
Queens Coll (NC)
Queens Coll of the City U of NY (NY)
Queen's U at Kingston (ON, Canada)
Quinnipiac U (CT)
Ramapo Coll of New Jersey (NJ)
Reed Coll (OR)
Regis Coll (MA)
Regis U (CO)
Rensselaer Polytechnic Inst (NY)
Rhodes Coll (TN)
Rice U (TX)
The Richard Stockton Coll of New Jersey (NJ)
Rider U (NJ)
Ripon Coll (WI)
Roanoke Coll (VA)
Roberts Wesleyan Coll (NY)
Rochester Inst of Technology (NY)
Rockford Coll (IL)
Rosemont Coll (PA)
Russell Sage Coll (NY)
Sacred Heart U (CT)
Saginaw Valley State U (MI)
Saint Anselm Coll (NH)
St. Bonaventure U (NY)
St. Edward's U (TX)
St. John Fisher Coll (NY)
Saint John's U (MN)
Saint Joseph Coll (CT)
Saint Joseph's Coll (IN)
St. Lawrence U (NY)
St. Mary's U of San Antonio (TX)
Saint Michael's Coll (VT)
Saint Peter's Coll (NJ)
Saint Vincent Coll (PA)
Samford U (AL)
San Francisco State U (CA)
San Jose State U (CA)
Schreiner U (TX)
Scripps Coll (CA)
Seattle Pacific U (WA)
Seattle U (WA)
Seton Hall U (NJ)
Seton Hill Coll (PA)
Simmons Coll (MA)
Simon Fraser U (BC, Canada)
Simpson Coll (IA)
Skidmore Coll (NY)
Smith Coll (MA)
South Dakota State U (SD)
Southern Adventist U (TN)
Southern Connecticut State U (CT)

Southern Methodist U (TX)
Southern Oregon U (OR)
Southwestern Coll (KS)
Spelman Coll (GA)
Spring Arbor U (MI)
State U of NY at Albany (NY)
State U of NY at Binghamton (NY)
State U of NY at New Paltz (NY)
State U of NY Coll at Brockport (NY)
State U of NY Coll at Fredonia (NY)
State U of NY Coll at Geneseo (NY)
State U of NY Coll of Environ Sci and Forestry (NY)
Stetson U (FL)
Stevens Inst of Technology (NJ)
Stonehill Coll (MA)
State U of NY at Stony Brook (NY)
Suffolk U (MA)
Susquehanna U (PA)
Swarthmore Coll (PA)
Sweet Briar Coll (VA)
Syracuse U (NY)
Temple U (PA)
Tennessee Technological U (TN)
Texas A&M U (TX)
Texas Christian U (TX)
Texas Tech U (TX)
Texas Wesleyan U (TX)
Towson U (MD)
Trent U (ON, Canada)
Trinity Coll (CT)
Trinity Coll (DC)
Trinity U (TX)
Tulane U (LA)
Union Coll (NE)
Union Coll (NY)
United States Air Force Academy (CO)
Université de Montréal (QC, Canada)
Université de Sherbrooke (PQ, Canada)
Université Laval (QC, Canada)
State U of NY at Buffalo (NY)
U Coll of the Cariboo (BC, Canada)
U of Alberta (AB, Canada)
The U of Arizona (AZ)
The U of British Columbia (BC, Canada)
U of Calgary (AB, Canada)
U of Calif, Davis (CA)
U of Calif, Los Angeles (CA)
U of Calif, Riverside (CA)
U of Calif, San Diego (CA)
U of Calif, Santa Barbara (CA)
U of Calif, Santa Cruz (CA)
U of Chicago (IL)
U of Cincinnati (OH)
U of Colorado at Boulder (CO)
U of Dallas (TX)
U of Dayton (OH)
U of Delaware (DE)
U of Denver (CO)
U of Evansville (IN)
U of Georgia (GA)
U of Guelph (ON, Canada)
U of Hawaii at Manoa (HI)
U of Houston (TX)
U of Illinois at Chicago (IL)
U of Illinois at Urbana–Champaign (IL)
The U of Iowa (IA)
U of Kansas (KS)
U of King's Coll (NS, Canada)
The U of Lethbridge (AB, Canada)
U of Maine (ME)
U of Maryland, Baltimore County (MD)
U of Maryland, Coll Park (MD)
U of Massachusetts Amherst (MA)
U of Massachusetts Boston (MA)
U of Miami (FL)
U of Michigan (MI)
U of Michigan–Dearborn (MI)
U of Minnesota, Duluth (MN)
U of Minnesota, Twin Cities Campus (MN)
U of Missouri–Columbia (MO)
U of Missouri–St. Louis (MO)
The U of Montana–Missoula (MT)
U of Nebraska–Lincoln (NE)
U of Nevada, Las Vegas (NV)
U of Nevada, Reno (NV)
U of New England (ME)
U of New Hampshire (NH)
U of New Mexico (NM)
U of Northern Iowa (IA)
U of North Texas (TX)
U of Notre Dame (IN)
U of Oklahoma (OK)
U of Oregon (OR)
U of Ottawa (ON, Canada)
U of Pennsylvania (PA)
U of Regina (SK, Canada)
U of Rochester (NY)
U of St. Thomas (MN)
U of San Francisco (CA)
U of Saskatchewan (SK, Canada)
U of Southern California (CA)
The U of Tampa (FL)
The U of Tennessee (TN)
The U of Texas at Arlington (TX)
The U of Texas at Austin (TX)
U of the Pacific (CA)
U of the Sciences in Philadelphia (PA)
U of Toronto (ON, Canada)
U of Tulsa (OK)
U of Vermont (VT)
U of Victoria (BC, Canada)
U of Washington (WA)
U of Waterloo (ON, Canada)
The U of Western Ontario (ON, Canada)
U of Windsor (ON, Canada)
U of Wisconsin–Eau Claire (WI)
U of Wisconsin–Madison (WI)
U of Wisconsin–Milwaukee (WI)
U of Wisconsin–River Falls (WI)
Ursinus Coll (PA)
Vassar Coll (NY)
Virginia Polytechnic Inst and State U (VA)
Viterbo U (WI)
Warren Wilson Coll (NC)
Wartburg Coll (IA)
Washington State U (WA)
Washington U in St. Louis (MO)
Wellesley Coll (MA)
Wells Coll (NY)
Wesleyan U (CT)
West Chester U of Pennsylvania (PA)
Western Kentucky U (KY)
Western Maryland Coll (MD)
Western Michigan U (MI)
Western Washington U (WA)
Wheaton Coll (MA)
Whitman Coll (WA)
Whittier Coll (CA)
Wilkes U (PA)
William Jewell Coll (MO)
Wittenberg U (OH)
Worcester Polytechnic Inst (MA)
Xavier U of Louisiana (LA)

BIOENGINEERING

Arizona State U (AZ)
Auburn U (AL)
Boston U (MA)
Brown U (RI)
California State U, Long Beach (CA)
Carnegie Mellon U (PA)
Case Western Reserve U (OH)
The Catholic U of America (DC)
Cedar Crest Coll (PA)
Columbia U, School of Engineering & Applied Sci (NY)
Cornell U (NY)
Drexel U (PA)
Duke U (NC)
Eastern Nazarene Coll (MA)
Florida State U (FL)
Harvard U (MA)
Illinois Inst of Technology (IL)
Indiana U–Purdue U Indianapolis (IN)
Johns Hopkins U (MD)
LeTourneau U (TX)
Louisiana State U and A&M Coll (LA)
Louisiana Tech U (LA)
Marquette U (WI)
Massachusetts Inst of Technology (MA)
Mercer U (GA)
Michigan State U (MI)
Milwaukee School of Engineering (WI)
Mississippi State U (MS)
New Jersey Inst of Technology (NJ)
North Dakota State U (ND)
Northwestern U (IL)
Oklahoma State U (OK)
Oral Roberts U (OK)
Penn State U Univ Park Campus (PA)
Rensselaer Polytechnic Inst (NY)
Rice U (TX)
Saint Louis U (MO)
Stevens Inst of Technology (NJ)
State U of NY at Stony Brook (NY)
Syracuse U (NY)
Texas A&M U (TX)
Trinity Coll (CT)
Trinity Coll (DC)
Tulane U (LA)
The U of Akron (OH)
The U of Alabama at Birmingham (AL)
The U of British Columbia (BC, Canada)
U of Calif, Berkeley (CA)
U of Calif, Davis (CA)
U of Calif, San Diego (CA)
U of Central Oklahoma (OK)
U of Connecticut (CT)
U of Guelph (ON, Canada)
U of Hartford (CT)
U of Idaho (ID)
U of Illinois at Chicago (IL)
U of Illinois at Urbana–Champaign (IL)
The U of Iowa (IA)
U of Miami (FL)
U of Missouri–Columbia (MO)
U of Nebraska–Lincoln (NE)
U of Pennsylvania (PA)
U of Pittsburgh (PA)
U of Rhode Island (RI)
U of Rochester (NY)
U of Southern California (CA)
The U of Texas at Austin (TX)
U of the Pacific (CA)
U of Toledo (OH)
U of Toronto (ON, Canada)
U of Wisconsin–Madison (WI)
Vanderbilt U (TN)
Virginia Commonwealth U (VA)
Walla Walla Coll (WA)
Washington U in St. Louis (MO)
Western New England Coll (MA)
Worcester Polytechnic Inst (MA)
Wright State U (OH)
Yale U (CT)

BIOLOGICAL/PHYSICAL SCIENCES

Adams State Coll (CO)
Adelphi U (NY)
Alfred U (NY)
Alice Lloyd Coll (KY)
Alma Coll (MI)
Alvernia Coll (PA)
Athabasca U (AB, Canada)
Atlantic Union Coll (MA)
Augsburg Coll (MN)
Averett U (VA)
Bard Coll (NY)
Bayamón Central U (PR)
Belmont U (TN)
Bemidji State U (MN)
Benedictine Coll (KS)
Bennington Coll (VT)
Bishop's U (PQ, Canada)
Bluefield State Coll (WV)
Brescia U (KY)
Brock U (ON, Canada)
Buena Vista U (IA)
California State U, Fresno (CA)
California U of Pennsylvania (PA)
Calvin Coll (MI)
Cameron U (OK)
Carleton U (ON, Canada)
Case Western Reserve U (OH)
Castleton State Coll (VT)
Cedar Crest Coll (PA)
Cedarville U (OH)
Cheyney U of Pennsylvania (PA)
Chowan Coll (NC)
Clarion U of Pennsylvania (PA)
Coe Coll (IA)
Coll of Santa Fe (NM)
Coll of the Atlantic (ME)
Concordia U (IL)
Concordia U (MI)
Concordia U (OR)
Delta State U (MS)
Dowling Coll (NY)
Drexel U (PA)
Eastern Michigan U (MI)
Eastern Nazarene Coll (MA)
Eastern Oregon U (OR)
Eastern Washington U (WA)
Edinboro U of Pennsylvania (PA)
Erskine Coll (SC)
Eureka Coll (IL)
The Evergreen State Coll (WA)
Fairleigh Dickinson U, Teaneck-Hackensack Campus (NJ)
Fordham U (NY)
Fort Hays State U (KS)
Framingham State Coll (MA)
Freed-Hardeman U (TN)
Gannon U (PA)
Georgia Southwestern State U (GA)
Gettysburg Coll (PA)
Goddard Coll (VT)
Grand Valley State U (MI)
Grand View Coll (IA)
Grinnell Coll (IA)
Hampshire Coll (MA)
Harding U (AR)
Harvard U (MA)
Hofstra U (NY)
Houghton Coll (NY)
Huntington Coll (IN)
Indiana U Kokomo (IN)
Indiana U of Pennsylvania (PA)
Iowa Wesleyan Coll (IA)
John Carroll U (OH)
Johns Hopkins U (MD)
Johnson C. Smith U (NC)
Judson Coll (IL)
Juniata Coll (PA)
King Coll (TN)
King's Coll (PA)
Kutztown U of Pennsylvania (PA)
Lakehead U (ON, Canada)
Lees-McRae Coll (NC)
Lee U (TN)
Le Moyne Coll (NY)
Lewis-Clark State Coll (ID)
Lock Haven U of Pennsylvania (PA)
Long Island U, Brooklyn Campus (NY)
Louisiana State U in Shreveport (LA)
Lyndon State Coll (VT)
Mansfield U of Pennsylvania (PA)
Marian Coll of Fond du Lac (WI)
Mars Hill Coll (NC)
Marygrove Coll (MI)
Marylhurst U (OR)
Marymount Coll of Fordham U (NY)
Maryville U of Saint Louis (MO)
Massachusetts Coll of Liberal Arts (MA)
The Master's Coll and Seminary (CA)
McMaster U (ON, Canada)
Memorial U of Newfoundland (NF, Canada)
Methodist Coll (NC)
Michigan State U (MI)
Middlebury Coll (VT)
Middle Tennessee State U (TN)
Midland Lutheran Coll (NE)
Milligan Coll (TN)
Minnesota State U, Mankato (MN)
Mississippi State U (MS)
Mississippi U for Women (MS)
Montana State U–Northern (MT)
Montana Tech of The U of Montana (MT)
Mount Allison U (NB, Canada)
Mount Saint Vincent U (NS, Canada)
Mount Vernon Nazarene U (OH)
National-Louis U (IL)
Nebraska Wesleyan U (NE)
New Mexico Inst of Mining and Technology (NM)
Northern State U (SD)
Northland Coll (WI)
North Park U (IL)
Northwestern U (IL)
Northwest Missouri State U (MO)
Oakland City U (IN)
Oklahoma Baptist U (OK)
Oklahoma Christian U of Science and Arts (OK)
Oklahoma City U (OK)
Oklahoma Panhandle State U (OK)
Oklahoma Wesleyan U (OK)
Olivet Nazarene U (IL)
Oregon State U (OR)
Palmer Coll of Chiropractic (IA)
Penn State U Abington Coll (PA)
Penn State U Berks Cmps of Berks-Lehigh Valley Coll (PA)
Penn State U Univ Park Campus (PA)
Peru State Coll (NE)
Philander Smith Coll (AR)
Pillsbury Baptist Bible Coll (MN)
Point Park Coll (PA)
Pontifical Catholic U of Puerto Rico (PR)
Portland State U (OR)
Purdue U (IN)
Purdue U Calumet (IN)
Quinnipiac U (CT)
Redeemer U Coll (ON, Canada)
Rensselaer Polytechnic Inst (NY)
Rhode Island Coll (RI)
Roberts Wesleyan Coll (NY)
Rochester Coll (MI)
Rochester Inst of Technology (NY)
Rockford Coll (IL)
Rocky Mountain Coll (MT)
Saginaw Valley State U (MI)
Saint Anselm Coll (NH)
St. Francis Xavier U (NS, Canada)
Saint Mary-of-the-Woods Coll (IN)
St. Norbert Coll (WI)
Saint Peter's Coll (NJ)
Saint Xavier U (IL)
San Francisco State U (CA)
Santa Clara U (CA)
Sarah Lawrence Coll (NY)
Seattle U (WA)
Shawnee State U (OH)
Sierra Nevada Coll (NV)
Simon Fraser U (BC, Canada)
Simpson Coll (IA)
Southeast Missouri State U (MO)
Southern Arkansas U–Magnolia (AR)
Southern Nazarene U (OK)
State U of NY Coll at Fredonia (NY)
State U of NY Coll of Environ Sci and Forestry (NY)
State U of NY Empire State Coll (NY)
Tabor Coll (KS)
Tennessee Temple U (TN)
Texas A&M U (TX)
Texas Tech U (TX)
Towson U (MD)
Trent U (ON, Canada)
Trevecca Nazarene U (TN)
Trinity Western U (BC, Canada)
Union Coll (NY)
Union U (TN)
United States Air Force Academy (CO)
United States Military Academy (NY)
U Coll of Cape Breton (NS, Canada)
The U of Akron (OH)
The U of Alabama (AL)
The U of Alabama at Birmingham (AL)
U of Alaska Anchorage (AK)
U of Alaska Fairbanks (AK)
U of Alberta (AB, Canada)
U of Central Arkansas (AR)
U of Charleston (WV)
U of Denver (CO)
U of Dubuque (IA)
The U of Findlay (OH)
U of Georgia (GA)
U of Guelph (ON, Canada)
U of Houston–Clear Lake (TX)
U of Kansas (KS)
U of La Verne (CA)
The U of Lethbridge (AB, Canada)
The U of Maine at Augusta (ME)
U of Mary (ND)
U of Massachusetts Amherst (MA)
U of Michigan–Dearborn (MI)
U of Mobile (AL)
U of Nebraska at Omaha (NE)
U of New Hampshire (NH)
U of New Orleans (LA)
U of Northern Iowa (IA)
U of North Florida (FL)
U of Oregon (OR)
U of Ottawa (ON, Canada)
U of Pittsburgh (PA)
U of Regina (SK, Canada)
U of Rochester (NY)
U of Saint Francis (IN)
U of Southern Indiana (IN)
U of South Florida (FL)

The U of Texas at San Antonio (TX)
U of Toledo (OH)
U of Toronto (ON, Canada)
U of Waterloo (ON, Canada)
The U of Western Ontario (ON, Canada)
U of West Florida (FL)
U of Windsor (ON, Canada)
U of Wisconsin–Platteville (WI)
U of Wisconsin–Superior (WI)
U of Wisconsin–Whitewater (WI)
Upper Iowa U (IA)
Vanguard U of Southern California (CA)
Villa Julie Coll (MD)
Virginia Commonwealth U (VA)
Virginia Wesleyan Coll (VA)
Walsh U (OH)
Warner Pacific Coll (OR)
Washington State U (WA)
Washington U in St. Louis (MO)
Wayland Baptist U (TX)
West Chester U of Pennsylvania (PA)
Western Washington U (WA)
William Carey Coll (MS)
Wilmington Coll (OH)
Winona State U (MN)
Wittenberg U (OH)
Worcester State Coll (MA)
Xavier U (OH)
York Coll (NE)
York U (ON, Canada)
Youngstown State U (OH)

BIOLOGICAL SCIENCES/LIFE SCIENCES RELATED
Arizona State U (AZ)
Boston U (MA)
Brandeis U (MA)
Canisius Coll (NY)
Guilford Coll (NC)
Holy Names Coll (CA)
Kent State U (OH)
Loras Coll (IA)
Louisiana State U and A&M Coll (LA)
National U (CA)
Open Learning Agency (BC, Canada)
Park U (MO)
Rochester Inst of Technology (NY)
Skidmore Coll (NY)
Swarthmore Coll (PA)
Texas Wesleyan U (TX)
U of Nebraska–Lincoln (NE)
U of North Alabama (AL)
U of Wisconsin–Parkside (WI)
Ursuline Coll (OH)
Washington U in St. Louis (MO)

BIOLOGICAL SPECIALIZATIONS RELATED
Arizona State U (AZ)
King Coll (TN)
Marymount U (VA)
Marywood U (PA)
Okanagan U Coll (BC, Canada)
Saint Mary's U of Minnesota (MN)
U of Hawaii at Manoa (HI)
U of Louisiana at Lafayette (LA)
Utah State U (UT)
Wilson Coll (PA)

BIOLOGICAL TECHNOLOGY
British Columbia Inst of Technology (BC, Canada)
California State Polytechnic U, Pomona (CA)
Carleton U (ON, Canada)
Harvard U (MA)
McMaster U (ON, Canada)
Michigan Technological U (MI)
Minnesota State U, Mankato (MN)
Niagara U (NY)
Northeastern U (MA)
Penn State U Univ Park Campus (PA)
Purdue U Calumet (IN)
St. Cloud State U (MN)
Salem International U (WV)
State U of NY Coll at Brockport (NY)
State U of NY Coll at Fredonia (NY)
State U of NY Coll at Oneonta (NY)
Suffolk U (MA)
Université de Sherbrooke (PQ, Canada)
U of Alberta (AB, Canada)
U of Delaware (DE)
U of Missouri–St. Louis (MO)
U of Nebraska at Omaha (NE)
U of New Haven (CT)
U of Ottawa (ON, Canada)
U of Windsor (ON, Canada)
Villa Julie Coll (MD)
Westminster Coll (PA)
Worcester Polytechnic Inst (MA)
Worcester State Coll (MA)
York Coll of the City U of New York (NY)

BIOLOGY
Abilene Christian U (TX)
Acadia U (NS, Canada)
Adams State Coll (CO)
Adelphi U (NY)
Adrian Coll (MI)
Agnes Scott Coll (GA)
Alabama State U (AL)
Albany State U (GA)
Albertson Coll of Idaho (ID)
Albertus Magnus Coll (CT)
Albion Coll (MI)
Albright Coll (PA)
Alcorn State U (MS)
Alderson-Broaddus Coll (WV)
Alfred U (NY)
Alice Lloyd Coll (KY)
Allegheny Coll (PA)
Alma Coll (MI)
Alvernia Coll (PA)
Alverno Coll (WI)
American International Coll (MA)
American U (DC)
American U in Cairo(Egypt)
Amherst Coll (MA)
Anderson Coll (SC)
Anderson U (IN)
Andrews U (MI)
Angelo State U (TX)
Anna Maria Coll (MA)
Appalachian State U (NC)
Aquinas Coll (MI)
Arcadia U (PA)
Arizona State U (AZ)
Arizona State U West (AZ)
Arkansas State U (AR)
Arkansas Tech U (AR)
Armstrong Atlantic State U (GA)
Asbury Coll (KY)
Ashland U (OH)
Assumption Coll (MA)
Athens State U (AL)
Atlantic Baptist U (NB, Canada)
Atlantic Union Coll (MA)
Auburn U (AL)
Auburn U Montgomery (AL)
Augsburg Coll (MN)
Augustana Coll (IL)
Augustana Coll (SD)
Augusta State U (GA)
Aurora U (IL)
Austin Coll (TX)
Austin Peay State U (TN)
Averett U (VA)
Avila Coll (MO)
Azusa Pacific U (CA)
Baker U (KS)
Baldwin-Wallace Coll (OH)
Ball State U (IN)
Barber-Scotia Coll (NC)
Bard Coll (NY)
Barnard Coll (NY)
Barry U (FL)
Barton Coll (NC)
Bates Coll (ME)
Bayamón Central U (PR)
Baylor U (TX)
Belhaven Coll (MS)
Bellarmine U (KY)
Belmont Abbey Coll (NC)
Belmont U (TN)
Beloit Coll (WI)
Bemidji State U (MN)
Benedict Coll (SC)
Benedictine Coll (KS)
Benedictine U (IL)
Bennett Coll (NC)
Bennington Coll (VT)
Berea Coll (KY)
Berry Coll (GA)
Bethany Coll (KS)
Bethany Coll (WV)
Bethany Lutheran Coll (MN)
Bethel Coll (IN)
Bethel Coll (KS)
Bethel Coll (MN)
Bethel Coll (TN)
Bethune-Cookman Coll (FL)
Biola U (CA)
Birmingham-Southern Coll (AL)
Bishop's U (PQ, Canada)
Blackburn Coll (IL)
Black Hills State U (SD)
Bloomfield Coll (NJ)
Bloomsburg U of Pennsylvania (PA)
Bluefield Coll (VA)
Blue Mountain Coll (MS)
Bluffton Coll (OH)
Boise State U (ID)
Boston Coll (MA)
Boston U (MA)
Bowdoin Coll (ME)
Bowie State U (MD)
Bowling Green State U (OH)
Bradley U (IL)
Brandeis U (MA)
Brandon U (MB, Canada)
Brenau U (GA)
Brescia U (KY)
Brewton-Parker Coll (GA)
Briar Cliff U (IA)
Bridgewater Coll (VA)
Bridgewater State Coll (MA)
Brigham Young U (UT)
Brigham Young U–Hawaii (HI)
Brock U (ON, Canada)
Brooklyn Coll of the City U of NY (NY)
Brown U (RI)
Bryan Coll (TN)
Bryn Athyn Coll of the New Church (PA)
Bryn Mawr Coll (PA)
Bucknell U (PA)
Buena Vista U (IA)
Butler U (IN)
Cabrini Coll (PA)
Caldwell Coll (NJ)
California Baptist U (CA)
California Inst of Technology (CA)
California Lutheran U (CA)
California Polytechnic State U, San Luis Obispo (CA)
California State Polytechnic U, Pomona (CA)
California State U, Bakersfield (CA)
California State U, Chico (CA)
California State U, Dominguez Hills (CA)
California State U, Fresno (CA)
California State U, Fullerton (CA)
California State U, Hayward (CA)
California State U, Long Beach (CA)
California State U, Los Angeles (CA)
California State U, Northridge (CA)
California State U, Sacramento (CA)
California State U, San Bernardino (CA)
California State U, San Marcos (CA)
California State U, Stanislaus (CA)
California U of Pennsylvania (PA)
Calvin Coll (MI)
Cameron U (OK)
Campbellsville U (KY)
Campbell U (NC)
Canisius Coll (NY)
Capital U (OH)
Cardinal Stritch U (WI)
Carleton Coll (MN)
Carleton U (ON, Canada)
Carlow Coll (PA)
Carnegie Mellon U (PA)
Carroll Coll (MT)
Carroll Coll (WI)
Carson-Newman Coll (TN)
Carthage Coll (WI)
Case Western Reserve U (OH)
Castleton State Coll (VT)
Catawba Coll (NC)
The Catholic U of America (DC)
Cedar Crest Coll (PA)
Cedarville U (OH)
Centenary Coll (NJ)
Centenary Coll of Louisiana (LA)
Central Coll (IA)
Central Connecticut State U (CT)
Central Methodist Coll (MO)
Central Michigan U (MI)
Central Missouri State U (MO)
Central State U (OH)
Central Washington U (WA)
Centre Coll (KY)
Chadron State Coll (NE)
Chaminade U of Honolulu (HI)
Chapman U (CA)
Charleston Southern U (SC)
Chatham Coll (PA)
Chestnut Hill Coll (PA)
Cheyney U of Pennsylvania (PA)
Chicago State U (IL)
Chowan Coll (NC)
Christian Brothers U (TN)
Christian Heritage Coll (CA)
Christopher Newport U (VA)
Citadel, The Military Coll of South Carolina (SC)
City Coll of the City U of NY (NY)
Claflin U (SC)
Claremont McKenna Coll (CA)
Clarion U of Pennsylvania (PA)
Clark Atlanta U (GA)
Clarke Coll (IA)
Clarkson U (NY)
Clark U (MA)
Clearwater Christian Coll (FL)
Clemson U (SC)
Cleveland State U (OH)
Coastal Carolina U (SC)
Coe Coll (IA)
Coker Coll (SC)
Colby Coll (ME)
Colby-Sawyer Coll (NH)
Colgate U (NY)
Coll Misericordia (PA)
Coll of Charleston (SC)
Coll of Mount St. Joseph (OH)
Coll of Mount Saint Vincent (NY)
The Coll of New Jersey (NJ)
The Coll of New Rochelle (NY)
Coll of Notre Dame of Maryland (MD)
Coll of Saint Benedict (MN)
Coll of St. Catherine (MN)
Coll of Saint Elizabeth (NJ)
Coll of Saint Mary (NE)
The Coll of Saint Rose (NY)
The Coll of St. Scholastica (MN)
Coll of Santa Fe (NM)
The Coll of Southeastern Europe, The American U of Athens(Greece)
Coll of Staten Island of the City U of NY (NY)
Coll of the Atlantic (ME)
Coll of the Holy Cross (MA)
Coll of the Ozarks (MO)
Coll of the Southwest (NM)
The Coll of William and Mary (VA)
The Coll of Wooster (OH)
Colorado Christian U (CO)
The Colorado Coll (CO)
Colorado State U (CO)
Columbia Coll (MO)
Columbia Coll (NY)
Columbia Coll (SC)
Columbia Union Coll (MD)
Columbia U, School of General Studies (NY)
Columbus State U (GA)
Concord Coll (WV)
Concordia Coll (MN)
Concordia Coll (NY)
Concordia U (CA)
Concordia U (IL)
Concordia U (MI)
Concordia U (MN)
Concordia U (NE)
Concordia U (OR)
Concordia U (QC, Canada)
Concordia U Wisconsin (WI)
Connecticut Coll (CT)
Converse Coll (SC)
Coppin State Coll (MD)
Cornell Coll (IA)
Cornell U (NY)
Cornerstone U (MI)
Covenant Coll (GA)
Creighton U (NE)
Crichton Coll (TN)
Culver-Stockton Coll (MO)
Cumberland Coll (KY)
Cumberland U (TN)
Curry Coll (MA)
Daemen Coll (NY)
Dakota State U (SD)
Dakota Wesleyan U (SD)
Dalhousie U (NS, Canada)
Dallas Baptist U (TX)
Dana Coll (NE)
Dartmouth Coll (NH)
Davidson Coll (NC)
Davis & Elkins Coll (WV)
Defiance Coll (OH)
Delaware State U (DE)
Delaware Valley Coll (PA)
Delta State U (MS)
Denison U (OH)
DePaul U (IL)
DePauw U (IN)
DeSales U (PA)
Dickinson Coll (PA)
Dickinson State U (ND)
Dillard U (LA)
Doane Coll (NE)
Dominican Coll (NY)
Dominican U (IL)
Dominican U of California (CA)
Dordt Coll (IA)
Dowling Coll (NY)
Drake U (IA)
Drew U (NJ)
Drexel U (PA)
Drury U (MO)
Duke U (NC)
Duquesne U (PA)
D'Youville Coll (NY)
Earlham Coll (IN)
East Carolina U (NC)
East Central U (OK)
Eastern Connecticut State U (CT)
Eastern Illinois U (IL)
Eastern Kentucky U (KY)
Eastern Mennonite U (VA)
Eastern Michigan U (MI)
Eastern Nazarene Coll (MA)
Eastern New Mexico U (NM)
Eastern Oregon U (OR)
Eastern U (PA)
Eastern Washington U (WA)
East Stroudsburg U of Pennsylvania (PA)
East Tennessee State U (TN)
East Texas Baptist U (TX)
East-West U (IL)
Eckerd Coll (FL)
Edgewood Coll (WI)
Edinboro U of Pennsylvania (PA)
Edward Waters Coll (FL)
Elizabeth City State U (NC)
Elizabethtown Coll (PA)
Elmhurst Coll (IL)
Elmira Coll (NY)
Elms Coll (MA)
Elon U (NC)
Emmanuel Coll (MA)
Emory & Henry Coll (VA)
Emory U (GA)
Emporia State U (KS)
Erskine Coll (SC)
Eureka Coll (IL)
Evangel U (MO)
The Evergreen State Coll (WA)
Excelsior Coll (NY)
Fairfield U (CT)
Fairleigh Dickinson U, Florham-Madison Campus (NJ)
Fairleigh Dickinson U, Teaneck-Hackensack Campus (NJ)
Fairmont State Coll (WV)
Faulkner U (AL)
Fayetteville State U (NC)
Felician Coll (NJ)
Ferris State U (MI)
Ferrum Coll (VA)
Fisk U (TN)
Fitchburg State Coll (MA)
Florida A&M U (FL)
Florida Atlantic U (FL)
Florida Inst of Technology (FL)
Florida International U (FL)
Florida Southern Coll (FL)
Florida State U (FL)
Fontbonne U (MO)
Fordham U (NY)
Fort Hays State U (KS)
Fort Lewis Coll (CO)
Fort Valley State U (GA)
Framingham State Coll (MA)
Franciscan U of Steubenville (OH)
Francis Marion U (SC)
Franklin and Marshall Coll (PA)
Franklin Coll of Indiana (IN)
Franklin Pierce Coll (NH)
Freed-Hardeman U (TN)

Fresno Pacific U (CA)
Friends U (KS)
Frostburg State U (MD)
Furman U (SC)
Gallaudet U (DC)
Gannon U (PA)
Gardner-Webb U (NC)
Geneva Coll (PA)
George Fox U (OR)
George Mason U (VA)
Georgetown Coll (KY)
Georgetown U (DC)
The George Washington U (DC)
Georgia Coll and State U (GA)
Georgia Inst of Technology (GA)
Georgian Court Coll (NJ)
Georgia Southern U (GA)
Georgia Southwestern State U (GA)
Georgia State U (GA)
Gettysburg Coll (PA)
Glenville State Coll (WV)
Goddard Coll (VT)
Gonzaga U (WA)
Gordon Coll (MA)
Goshen Coll (IN)
Goucher Coll (MD)
Governors State U (IL)
Grace Coll (IN)
Graceland U (IA)
Grambling State U (LA)
Grand Canyon U (AZ)
Grand Valley State U (MI)
Grand View Coll (IA)
Green Mountain Coll (VT)
Greensboro Coll (NC)
Greenville Coll (IL)
Grinnell Coll (IA)
Grove City Coll (PA)
Guilford Coll (NC)
Gustavus Adolphus Coll (MN)
Gwynedd-Mercy Coll (PA)
Hamilton Coll (NY)
Hamline U (MN)
Hampden-Sydney Coll (VA)
Hampshire Coll (MA)
Hampton U (VA)
Hannibal-LaGrange Coll (MO)
Hanover Coll (IN)
Harding U (AR)
Hardin-Simmons U (TX)
Hartwick Coll (NY)
Harvard U (MA)
Harvey Mudd Coll (CA)
Hastings Coll (NE)
Haverford Coll (PA)
Hawai'i Pacific U (HI)
Heidelberg Coll (OH)
Henderson State U (AR)
Hendrix Coll (AR)
High Point U (NC)
Hillsdale Coll (MI)
Hiram Coll (OH)
Hobart and William Smith Colls (NY)
Hofstra U (NY)
Hollins U (VA)
Holy Family Coll (PA)
Hood Coll (MD)
Hope Coll (MI)
Houghton Coll (NY)
Houston Baptist U (TX)
Howard Payne U (TX)
Howard U (DC)
Humboldt State U (CA)
Hunter Coll of the City U of NY (NY)
Huntingdon Coll (AL)
Huntington Coll (IN)
Husson Coll (ME)
Huston-Tillotson Coll (TX)
Idaho State U (ID)
Illinois Coll (IL)
Illinois Inst of Technology (IL)
Illinois State U (IL)
Illinois Wesleyan U (IL)
Immaculata Coll (PA)
Indiana State U (IN)
Indiana U Bloomington (IN)
Indiana U East (IN)
Indiana U Kokomo (IN)
Indiana U Northwest (IN)
Indiana U of Pennsylvania (PA)
Indiana U–Purdue U Fort Wayne (IN)
Indiana U–Purdue U Indianapolis (IN)
Indiana U South Bend (IN)
Indiana U Southeast (IN)
Indiana Wesleyan U (IN)
Inter American U of PR, Aguadilla Campus (PR)
Inter American U of PR, San Germán Campus (PR)
Iona Coll (NY)
Iowa State U of Science and Technology (IA)
Iowa Wesleyan Coll (IA)
Ithaca Coll (NY)
Jackson State U (MS)
Jacksonville State U (AL)
Jacksonville U (FL)
James Madison U (VA)
Jamestown Coll (ND)
Jarvis Christian Coll (TX)
John Brown U (AR)
John Carroll U (OH)
Johns Hopkins U (MD)
Johnson C. Smith U (NC)
Johnson State Coll (VT)
Judson Coll (AL)
Judson Coll (IL)
Juniata Coll (PA)
Kalamazoo Coll (MI)
Kansas State U (KS)
Kansas Wesleyan U (KS)
Kean U (NJ)
Keene State Coll (NH)
Kennesaw State U (GA)
Kent State U (OH)
Kentucky State U (KY)
Kentucky Wesleyan Coll (KY)
Kenyon Coll (OH)
Keuka Coll (NY)
King Coll (TN)
King's Coll (PA)
The King's U Coll (AB, Canada)
Knox Coll (IL)
Kutztown U of Pennsylvania (PA)
Lafayette Coll (PA)
LaGrange Coll (GA)
Lake Erie Coll (OH)
Lake Forest Coll (IL)
Lakehead U (ON, Canada)
Lakeland Coll (WI)
Lake Superior State U (MI)
Lamar U (TX)
Lambuth U (TN)
Lander U (SC)
La Roche Coll (PA)
La Salle U (PA)
Laurentian U (ON, Canada)
Lawrence U (WI)
Lebanon Valley Coll (PA)
Lees-McRae Coll (NC)
Lee U (TN)
Lehigh U (PA)
Lehman Coll of the City U of NY (NY)
Le Moyne Coll (NY)
LeMoyne-Owen Coll (TN)
Lenoir-Rhyne Coll (NC)
LeTourneau U (TX)
Lewis & Clark Coll (OR)
Lewis-Clark State Coll (ID)
Lewis U (IL)
Liberty U (VA)
Limestone Coll (SC)
Lincoln Memorial U (TN)
Lincoln U (MO)
Lincoln U (PA)
Lindenwood U (MO)
Lindsey Wilson Coll (KY)
Linfield Coll (OR)
Lipscomb U (TN)
Lock Haven U of Pennsylvania (PA)
Long Island U, Brooklyn Campus (NY)
Long Island U, C.W. Post Campus (NY)
Long Island U, Southampton Coll (NY)
Longwood Coll (VA)
Loras Coll (IA)
Louisiana Coll (LA)
Louisiana State U in Shreveport (LA)
Louisiana Tech U (LA)
Lourdes Coll (OH)
Loyola Coll in Maryland (MD)
Loyola Marymount U (CA)
Loyola U Chicago (IL)
Loyola U New Orleans (LA)
Lubbock Christian U (TX)
Luther Coll (IA)
Lycoming Coll (PA)
Lynchburg Coll (VA)
Lyon Coll (AR)
Macalester Coll (MN)
MacMurray Coll (IL)
Maharishi U of Management (IA)
Malaspina U-Coll (BC, Canada)
Malone Coll (OH)
Manchester Coll (IN)
Manhattan Coll (NY)
Manhattanville Coll (NY)
Mansfield U of Pennsylvania (PA)
Marian Coll (IN)
Marian Coll of Fond du Lac (WI)
Marietta Coll (OH)
Marist Coll (NY)
Marlboro Coll (VT)
Marquette U (WI)
Marshall U (WV)
Mars Hill Coll (NC)
Mary Baldwin Coll (VA)
Marygrove Coll (MI)
Marymount Coll of Fordham U (NY)
Marymount Manhattan Coll (NY)
Marymount U (VA)
Maryville Coll (TN)
Maryville U of Saint Louis (MO)
Mary Washington Coll (VA)
Marywood U (PA)
Massachusetts Coll of Liberal Arts (MA)
Massachusetts Inst of Technology (MA)
The Master's Coll and Seminary (CA)
Mayville State U (ND)
McGill U (PQ, Canada)
McKendree Coll (IL)
McMaster U (ON, Canada)
McMurry U (TX)
McNeese State U (LA)
McPherson Coll (KS)
Medaille Coll (NY)
Medgar Evers Coll of the City U of NY (NY)
Memorial U of Newfoundland (NF, Canada)
Mercer U (GA)
Mercy Coll (NY)
Mercyhurst Coll (PA)
Meredith Coll (NC)
Merrimack Coll (MA)
Mesa State Coll (CO)
Messiah Coll (PA)
Methodist Coll (NC)
Metropolitan State Coll of Denver (CO)
Metropolitan State U (MN)
Miami U (OH)
Michigan State U (MI)
Michigan Technological U (MI)
MidAmerica Nazarene U (KS)
Middlebury Coll (VT)
Middle Tennessee State U (TN)
Midland Lutheran Coll (NE)
Midway Coll (KY)
Midwestern State U (TX)
Millersville U of Pennsylvania (PA)
Milligan Coll (TN)
Millikin U (IL)
Millsaps Coll (MS)
Mills Coll (CA)
Minnesota State U, Mankato (MN)
Minnesota State U Moorhead (MN)
Minot State U (ND)
Mississippi Coll (MS)
Mississippi State U (MS)
Mississippi U for Women (MS)
Mississippi Valley State U (MS)
Missouri Baptist Coll (MO)
Missouri Southern State Coll (MO)
Missouri Valley Coll (MO)
Missouri Western State Coll (MO)
Molloy Coll (NY)
Monmouth Coll (IL)
Monmouth U (NJ)
Montana State U–Billings (MT)
Montana State U–Bozeman (MT)
Montana State U–Northern (MT)
Montana Tech of The U of Montana (MT)
Montclair State U (NJ)
Moravian Coll (PA)
Morehead State U (KY)
Morehouse Coll (GA)
Morgan State U (MD)
Morningside Coll (IA)
Morris Brown Coll (GA)
Morris Coll (SC)
Mount Allison U (NB, Canada)
Mount Holyoke Coll (MA)
Mount Marty Coll (SD)
Mount Mary Coll (WI)
Mount Mercy Coll (IA)
Mount Olive Coll (NC)
Mount St. Clare Coll (IA)
Mount Saint Mary Coll (NY)
Mount St. Mary's Coll (CA)
Mount Saint Mary's Coll and Seminary (MD)
Mount Saint Vincent U (NS, Canada)
Mount Union Coll (OH)
Mount Vernon Nazarene U (OH)
Muhlenberg Coll (PA)
Murray State U (KY)
Muskingum Coll (OH)
National-Louis U (IL)
Nazareth Coll of Rochester (NY)
Nebraska Wesleyan U (NE)
Neumann Coll (PA)
Newberry Coll (SC)
New Coll of Florida (FL)
New England Coll (NH)
New Jersey City U (NJ)
New Jersey Inst of Technology (NJ)
Newman U (KS)
New Mexico Highlands U (NM)
New Mexico Inst of Mining and Technology (NM)
New Mexico State U (NM)
New York Inst of Technology (NY)
New York U (NY)
Niagara U (NY)
Nicholls State U (LA)
Nipissing U (ON, Canada)
Norfolk State U (VA)
North Carolina Ag and Tech State U (NC)
North Carolina Central U (NC)
North Carolina State U (NC)
North Carolina Wesleyan Coll (NC)
North Central Coll (IL)
North Dakota State U (ND)
Northeastern Illinois U (IL)
Northeastern State U (OK)
Northeastern U (MA)
Northern Arizona U (AZ)
Northern Illinois U (IL)
Northern Kentucky U (KY)
Northern Michigan U (MI)
Northern State U (SD)
North Georgia Coll & State U (GA)
Northland Coll (WI)
North Park U (IL)
Northwestern Coll (IA)
Northwestern Coll (MN)
Northwestern Oklahoma State U (OK)
Northwestern State U of Louisiana (LA)
Northwestern U (IL)
Northwest Missouri State U (MO)
Northwest Nazarene U (ID)
Norwich U (VT)
Notre Dame Coll (OH)
Notre Dame de Namur U (CA)
Nova Southeastern U (FL)
Oakland City U (IN)
Oakland U (MI)
Oakwood Coll (AL)
Oberlin Coll (OH)
Occidental Coll (CA)
Oglethorpe U (GA)
Ohio Dominican Coll (OH)
Ohio Northern U (OH)
The Ohio State U (OH)
Ohio Wesleyan U (OH)
Okanagan U Coll (BC, Canada)
Oklahoma Baptist U (OK)
Oklahoma Christian U of Science and Arts (OK)
Oklahoma City U (OK)
Oklahoma Panhandle State U (OK)
Oklahoma State U (OK)
Oklahoma Wesleyan U (OK)
Old Dominion U (VA)
Olivet Coll (MI)
Olivet Nazarene U (IL)
Oral Roberts U (OK)
Oregon State U (OR)
Ottawa U (KS)
Otterbein Coll (OH)
Ouachita Baptist U (AR)
Our Lady of Holy Cross Coll (LA)
Our Lady of the Lake U of San Antonio (TX)
Pace U (NY)
Pacific Lutheran U (WA)
Pacific Union Coll (CA)
Pacific U (OR)
Paine Coll (GA)
Palm Beach Atlantic Coll (FL)
Park U (MO)
Peace Coll (NC)
Penn State U at Erie, The Behrend Coll (PA)
Penn State U Univ Park Campus (PA)
Pepperdine U, Malibu (CA)
Peru State Coll (NE)
Pfeiffer U (NC)
Philadelphia U (PA)
Philander Smith Coll (AR)
Piedmont Coll (GA)
Pikeville Coll (KY)
Pine Manor Coll (MA)
Pittsburg State U (KS)
Pitzer Coll (CA)
Plattsburgh State U of NY (NY)
Plymouth State Coll (NH)
Point Loma Nazarene U (CA)
Point Park Coll (PA)
Pomona Coll (CA)
Pontifical Catholic U of Puerto Rico (PR)
Portland State U (OR)
Prairie View A&M U (TX)
Presbyterian Coll (SC)
Prescott Coll (AZ)
Principia Coll (IL)
Providence Coll (RI)
Purchase Coll, State U of NY (NY)
Purdue U (IN)
Purdue U Calumet (IN)
Purdue U North Central (IN)
Queens Coll (NC)
Queens Coll of the City U of NY (NY)
Queen's U at Kingston (ON, Canada)
Quincy U (IL)
Quinnipiac U (CT)
Radford U (VA)
Ramapo Coll of New Jersey (NJ)
Randolph-Macon Coll (VA)
Randolph-Macon Woman's Coll (VA)
Redeemer U Coll (ON, Canada)
Reed Coll (OR)
Regis Coll (MA)
Regis U (CO)
Reinhardt Coll (GA)
Rensselaer Polytechnic Inst (NY)
Rhode Island Coll (RI)
Rhodes Coll (TN)
Rice U (TX)
The Richard Stockton Coll of New Jersey (NJ)
Rider U (NJ)
Ripon Coll (WI)
Rivier Coll (NH)
Roanoke Coll (VA)
Roberts Wesleyan Coll (NY)
Rochester Inst of Technology (NY)
Rockford Coll (IL)
Rockhurst U (MO)
Rocky Mountain Coll (MT)
Rogers State U (OK)
Roger Williams U (RI)
Rollins Coll (FL)
Roosevelt U (IL)
Rose-Hulman Inst of Technology (IN)
Rosemont Coll (PA)
Rowan U (NJ)
Russell Sage Coll (NY)
Rust Coll (MS)
Rutgers, The State U of New Jersey, New Brunswick (NJ)
Sacred Heart U (CT)
Saginaw Valley State U (MI)
St. Ambrose U (IA)
St. Andrews Presbyterian Coll (NC)
Saint Anselm Coll (NH)
Saint Augustine's Coll (NC)
St. Bonaventure U (NY)
St. Cloud State U (MN)
St. Edward's U (TX)
St. Francis Coll (NY)
Saint Francis U (PA)
St. Francis Xavier U (NS, Canada)
St. John Fisher Coll (NY)
Saint John's U (MN)
St. John's U (NY)
Saint Joseph Coll (CT)
Saint Joseph's Coll (IN)
Saint Joseph's Coll (ME)
St. Joseph's Coll, New York (NY)

St. Joseph's Coll, Suffolk Campus (NY)
Saint Joseph's U (PA)
St. Lawrence U (NY)
Saint Leo U (FL)
Saint Louis U (MO)
Saint Martin's Coll (WA)
Saint Mary Coll (KS)
Saint Mary-of-the-Woods Coll (IN)
Saint Mary's Coll (IN)
Saint Mary's Coll of Ave Maria U (MI)
Saint Mary's Coll of California (CA)
St. Mary's Coll of Maryland (MD)
Saint Mary's U (NS, Canada)
Saint Mary's U of Minnesota (MN)
St. Mary's U of San Antonio (TX)
Saint Michael's Coll (VT)
St. Norbert Coll (WI)
St. Olaf Coll (MN)
Saint Peter's Coll (NJ)
St. Thomas Aquinas Coll (NY)
St. Thomas U (FL)
Saint Vincent Coll (PA)
Saint Xavier U (IL)
Salem Coll (NC)
Salem International U (WV)
Salem State Coll (MA)
Salisbury U (MD)
Salve Regina U (RI)
Samford U (AL)
Sam Houston State U (TX)
San Diego State U (CA)
San Francisco State U (CA)
San Jose State U (CA)
Santa Clara U (CA)
Sarah Lawrence Coll (NY)
Savannah State U (GA)
Dr. William M. Scholl Coll of Podiatric Medicine (IL)
Schreiner U (TX)
Scripps Coll (CA)
Seattle Pacific U (WA)
Seattle U (WA)
Seton Hall U (NJ)
Seton Hill Coll (PA)
Shawnee State U (OH)
Shaw U (NC)
Shenandoah U (VA)
Shepherd Coll (WV)
Shippensburg U of Pennsylvania (PA)
Shorter Coll (GA)
Siena Coll (NY)
Siena Heights U (MI)
Silver Lake Coll (WI)
Simmons Coll (MA)
Simon Fraser U (BC, Canada)
Simon's Rock Coll of Bard (MA)
Simpson Coll (IA)
Skidmore Coll (NY)
Slippery Rock U of Pennsylvania (PA)
Smith Coll (MA)
Sonoma State U (CA)
South Carolina State U (SC)
South Dakota State U (SD)
Southeastern Coll of the Assemblies of God (FL)
Southeastern Louisiana U (LA)
Southeastern Oklahoma State U (OK)
Southeast Missouri State U (MO)
Southern Adventist U (TN)
Southern Arkansas U–Magnolia (AR)
Southern Connecticut State U (CT)
Southern Illinois U Carbondale (IL)
Southern Illinois U Edwardsville (IL)
Southern Methodist U (TX)
Southern Nazarene U (OK)
Southern Oregon U (OR)
Southern U and A&M Coll (LA)
Southern Utah U (UT)
Southern Wesleyan U (SC)
Southwest Baptist U (MO)
Southwestern Adventist U (TX)
Southwestern Coll (KS)
Southwestern Oklahoma State U (OK)
Southwestern U (TX)
Southwest Missouri State U (MO)
Southwest State U (MN)
Southwest Texas State U (TX)
Spelman Coll (GA)
Spring Arbor U (MI)
Springfield Coll (MA)
Spring Hill Coll (AL)
Stanford U (CA)
State U of NY at Albany (NY)
State U of NY at Binghamton (NY)
State U of NY at New Paltz (NY)
State U of NY at Oswego (NY)
State U of NY Coll at Brockport (NY)
State U of NY Coll at Buffalo (NY)
State U of NY Coll at Cortland (NY)
State U of NY Coll at Fredonia (NY)
State U of NY Coll at Geneseo (NY)
State U of NY Coll at Old Westbury (NY)
State U of NY Coll at Oneonta (NY)
State U of NY Coll at Potsdam (NY)
State U of NY Coll of Environ Sci and Forestry (NY)
State U of West Georgia (GA)
Stephen F. Austin State U (TX)
Stephens Coll (MO)
Sterling Coll (KS)
Stetson U (FL)
Stonehill Coll (MA)
State U of NY at Stony Brook (NY)
Suffolk U (MA)
Sul Ross State U (TX)
Susquehanna U (PA)
Swarthmore Coll (PA)
Sweet Briar Coll (VA)
Syracuse U (NY)
Tabor Coll (KS)
Talladega Coll (AL)
Tarleton State U (TX)
Taylor U (IN)
Teikyo Post U (CT)
Temple U (PA)
Tennessee State U (TN)
Tennessee Technological U (TN)
Tennessee Temple U (TN)
Tennessee Wesleyan Coll (TN)
Texas A&M International U (TX)
Texas A&M U (TX)
Texas A&M U–Commerce (TX)
Texas A&M U–Corpus Christi (TX)
Texas A&M U–Kingsville (TX)
Texas A&M U–Texarkana (TX)
Texas Christian U (TX)
Texas Coll (TX)
Texas Lutheran U (TX)
Texas Southern U (TX)
Texas Tech U (TX)
Texas Wesleyan U (TX)
Texas Woman's U (TX)
Thiel Coll (PA)
Thomas Edison State Coll (NJ)
Thomas More Coll (KY)
Thomas More Coll of Liberal Arts (NH)
Thomas U (GA)
Tougaloo Coll (MS)
Touro Coll (NY)
Towson U (MD)
Transylvania U (KY)
Trent U (ON, Canada)
Trevecca Nazarene U (TN)
Trinity Christian Coll (IL)
Trinity Coll (CT)
Trinity Coll (DC)
Trinity International U (IL)
Trinity U (TX)
Trinity Western U (BC, Canada)
Tri-State U (IN)
Troy State U (AL)
Troy State U Dothan (AL)
Truman State U (MO)
Tufts U (MA)
Tulane U (LA)
Tusculum Coll (TN)
Tuskegee U (AL)
Union Coll (KY)
Union Coll (NE)
Union Coll (NY)
Union U (TN)
United States Air Force Academy (CO)
United States Military Academy (NY)
Universidad Adventista de las Antillas (PR)
Université de Montréal (QC, Canada)
Université de Sherbrooke (PQ, Canada)
Université Laval (QC, Canada)
State U of NY at Buffalo (NY)
U Coll of Cape Breton (NS, Canada)
U Coll of the Cariboo (BC, Canada)
U Coll of the Fraser Valley (BC, Canada)
The U of Akron (OH)
The U of Alabama (AL)
The U of Alabama at Birmingham (AL)
The U of Alabama in Huntsville (AL)
U of Alaska Fairbanks (AK)
U of Alaska Southeast (AK)
U of Alberta (AB, Canada)
The U of Arizona (AZ)
U of Arkansas (AR)
U of Arkansas at Little Rock (AR)
U of Arkansas at Pine Bluff (AR)
U of Bridgeport (CT)
The U of British Columbia (BC, Canada)
U of Calgary (AB, Canada)
U of Calif, Davis (CA)
U of Calif, Irvine (CA)
U of Calif, Los Angeles (CA)
U of Calif, Riverside (CA)
U of Calif, San Diego (CA)
U of Calif, Santa Barbara (CA)
U of Calif, Santa Cruz (CA)
U of Central Arkansas (AR)
U of Central Florida (FL)
U of Central Oklahoma (OK)
U of Charleston (WV)
U of Chicago (IL)
U of Cincinnati (OH)
U of Colorado at Boulder (CO)
U of Colorado at Colorado Springs (CO)
U of Colorado at Denver (CO)
U of Connecticut (CT)
U of Dallas (TX)
U of Dayton (OH)
U of Delaware (DE)
U of Denver (CO)
U of Dubuque (IA)
U of Evansville (IN)
The U of Findlay (OH)
U of Georgia (GA)
U of Great Falls (MT)
U of Guelph (ON, Canada)
U of Hartford (CT)
U of Hawaii at Hilo (HI)
U of Hawaii at Manoa (HI)
U of Houston (TX)
U of Houston–Clear Lake (TX)
U of Idaho (ID)
U of Illinois at Chicago (IL)
U of Illinois at Springfield (IL)
U of Illinois at Urbana–Champaign (IL)
U of Indianapolis (IN)
The U of Iowa (IA)
U of Kansas (KS)
U of Kentucky (KY)
U of King's Coll (NS, Canada)
U of La Verne (CA)
The U of Lethbridge (AB, Canada)
U of Louisiana at Lafayette (LA)
U of Louisiana at Monroe (LA)
U of Louisville (KY)
U of Maine (ME)
U of Maine at Farmington (ME)
U of Maine at Fort Kent (ME)
U of Maine at Machias (ME)
U of Maine at Presque Isle (ME)
U of Manitoba (MB, Canada)
U of Mary (ND)
U of Mary Hardin-Baylor (TX)
U of Maryland, Baltimore County (MD)
U of Maryland, Coll Park (MD)
U of Maryland Eastern Shore (MD)
U of Massachusetts Amherst (MA)
U of Massachusetts Boston (MA)
U of Massachusetts Dartmouth (MA)
U of Massachusetts Lowell (MA)
The U of Memphis (TN)
U of Miami (FL)
U of Michigan (MI)
U of Michigan–Dearborn (MI)
U of Michigan–Flint (MI)
U of Minnesota, Duluth (MN)
U of Minnesota, Morris (MN)
U of Minnesota, Twin Cities Campus (MN)
U of Mississippi (MS)
U of Missouri–Columbia (MO)
U of Missouri–Kansas City (MO)
U of Missouri–Rolla (MO)
U of Missouri–St. Louis (MO)
U of Mobile (AL)
The U of Montana–Missoula (MT)
Western Montana Coll of The U of Montana (MT)
U of Montevallo (AL)
U of Nebraska at Kearney (NE)
U of Nebraska at Omaha (NE)
U of Nevada, Las Vegas (NV)
U of Nevada, Reno (NV)
U of New England (ME)
U of New Hampshire (NH)
U of New Mexico (NM)
U of New Orleans (LA)
U of North Alabama (AL)
The U of North Carolina at Asheville (NC)
The U of North Carolina at Chapel Hill (NC)
The U of North Carolina at Charlotte (NC)
The U of North Carolina at Greensboro (NC)
The U of North Carolina at Pembroke (NC)
The U of North Carolina at Wilmington (NC)
U of North Dakota (ND)
U of Northern Colorado (CO)
U of Northern Iowa (IA)
U of North Florida (FL)
U of North Texas (TX)
U of Notre Dame (IN)
U of Oregon (OR)
U of Ottawa (ON, Canada)
U of Pennsylvania (PA)
U of Pittsburgh (PA)
U of Pittsburgh at Bradford (PA)
U of Pittsburgh at Greensburg (PA)
U of Pittsburgh at Johnstown (PA)
U of Portland (OR)
U of Prince Edward Island (PE, Canada)
U of Puerto Rico, Humacao U Coll (PR)
U of Puerto Rico, Cayey U Coll (PR)
U of Puget Sound (WA)
U of Redlands (CA)
U of Regina (SK, Canada)
U of Rhode Island (RI)
U of Richmond (VA)
U of Rio Grande (OH)
U of Rochester (NY)
U of St. Francis (IL)
U of Saint Francis (IN)
U of St. Thomas (MN)
U of St. Thomas (TX)
U of San Diego (CA)
U of San Francisco (CA)
U of Saskatchewan (SK, Canada)
U of Science and Arts of Oklahoma (OK)
The U of Scranton (PA)
U of Sioux Falls (SD)
U of South Alabama (AL)
U of South Carolina (SC)
U of South Carolina Aiken (SC)
U of South Carolina Spartanburg (SC)
U of South Dakota (SD)
U of Southern California (CA)
U of Southern Colorado (CO)
U of Southern Indiana (IN)
U of Southern Maine (ME)
U of Southern Mississippi (MS)
U of South Florida (FL)
The U of Tampa (FL)
The U of Tennessee (TN)
The U of Tennessee at Chattanooga (TN)
The U of Tennessee at Martin (TN)
The U of Texas at Arlington (TX)
The U of Texas at Austin (TX)
The U of Texas at Brownsville (TX)
The U of Texas at Dallas (TX)
The U of Texas at El Paso (TX)
The U of Texas at San Antonio (TX)
The U of Texas at Tyler (TX)
The U of Texas of the Permian Basin (TX)
The U of Texas–Pan American (TX)
U of the District of Columbia (DC)
U of the Incarnate Word (TX)
U of the Ozarks (AR)
U of the Pacific (CA)
U of the Sciences in Philadelphia (PA)
U of the South (TN)
U of the Virgin Islands (VI)
U of Toledo (OH)
U of Toronto (ON, Canada)
U of Tulsa (OK)
U of Utah (UT)
U of Vermont (VT)
U of Victoria (BC, Canada)
U of Virginia (VA)
The U of Virginia's Coll at Wise (VA)
U of Washington (WA)
U of Waterloo (ON, Canada)
The U of West Alabama (AL)
The U of Western Ontario (ON, Canada)
U of West Florida (FL)
U of Windsor (ON, Canada)
U of Wisconsin–Eau Claire (WI)
U of Wisconsin–Green Bay (WI)
U of Wisconsin–La Crosse (WI)
U of Wisconsin–Madison (WI)
U of Wisconsin–Milwaukee (WI)
U of Wisconsin–Oshkosh (WI)
U of Wisconsin–Platteville (WI)
U of Wisconsin–River Falls (WI)
U of Wisconsin–Stevens Point (WI)
U of Wisconsin–Superior (WI)
U of Wisconsin–Whitewater (WI)
U of Wyoming (WY)
Upper Iowa U (IA)
Urbana U (OH)
Ursinus Coll (PA)
Ursuline Coll (OH)
Utah State U (UT)
Utica Coll of Syracuse U (NY)
Valdosta State U (GA)
Valley City State U (ND)
Valparaiso U (IN)
Vanderbilt U (TN)
Vanguard U of Southern California (CA)
Vassar Coll (NY)
Villa Julie Coll (MD)
Villanova U (PA)
Virginia Commonwealth U (VA)
Virginia Intermont Coll (VA)
Virginia Military Inst (VA)
Virginia Polytechnic Inst and State U (VA)
Virginia State U (VA)
Virginia Union U (VA)
Virginia Wesleyan Coll (VA)
Viterbo U (WI)
Voorhees Coll (SC)
Wabash Coll (IN)
Wagner Coll (NY)
Wake Forest U (NC)
Walla Walla Coll (WA)
Walsh U (OH)
Warner Pacific Coll (OR)
Warner Southern Coll (FL)
Warren Wilson Coll (NC)
Wartburg Coll (IA)
Washburn U of Topeka (KS)
Washington & Jefferson Coll (PA)
Washington and Lee U (VA)
Washington Coll (MD)
Washington State U (WA)
Washington U in St. Louis (MO)
Wayland Baptist U (TX)
Waynesburg Coll (PA)
Wayne State Coll (NE)
Wayne State U (MI)
Webster U (MO)
Wellesley Coll (MA)
Wells Coll (NY)
Wesleyan Coll (GA)
Wesleyan U (CT)
Wesley Coll (DE)
West Chester U of Pennsylvania (PA)
Western Carolina U (NC)
Western Connecticut State U (CT)
Western Illinois U (IL)
Western Kentucky U (KY)
Western Maryland Coll (MD)
Western Michigan U (MI)
Western New England Coll (MA)
Western Oregon U (OR)
Western State Coll of Colorado (CO)
Western States Chiropractic Coll (OR)
Western Washington U (WA)
Westfield State Coll (MA)
West Liberty State Coll (WV)

Westminster Coll (MO)
Westminster Coll (PA)
Westminster Coll (UT)
Westmont Coll (CA)
West Texas A&M U (TX)
West Virginia State Coll (WV)
West Virginia U (WV)
West Virginia U Inst of Technology (WV)
West Virginia Wesleyan Coll (WV)
Wheaton Coll (IL)
Wheaton Coll (MA)
Wheeling Jesuit U (WV)
Whitman Coll (WA)
Whittier Coll (CA)
Whitworth Coll (WA)
Wichita State U (KS)
Widener U (PA)
Wilberforce U (OH)
Wiley Coll (TX)
Wilfrid Laurier U (ON, Canada)
Wilkes U (PA)
Willamette U (OR)
William Carey Coll (MS)
William Jewell Coll (MO)
William Paterson U of New Jersey (NJ)
William Penn U (IA)
Williams Baptist Coll (AR)
Williams Coll (MA)
William Woods U (MO)
Wilmington Coll (OH)
Wilson Coll (PA)
Wingate U (NC)
Winona State U (MN)
Winston-Salem State U (NC)
Winthrop U (SC)
Wisconsin Lutheran Coll (WI)
Wittenberg U (OH)
Wofford Coll (SC)
Worcester Polytechnic Inst (MA)
Worcester State Coll (MA)
Wright State U (OH)
Xavier U (OH)
Xavier U of Louisiana (LA)
Yale U (CT)
Yeshiva U (NY)
York Coll (NE)
York Coll of Pennsylvania (PA)
York Coll of the City U of New York (NY)
York U (ON, Canada)
Youngstown State U (OH)

BIOLOGY EDUCATION

Abilene Christian U (TX)
Adams State Coll (CO)
Alvernia Coll (PA)
Anderson Coll (SC)
Arkansas State U (AR)
Arkansas Tech U (AR)
Averett U (VA)
Baylor U (TX)
Berea Coll (KY)
Berry Coll (GA)
Bethany Coll (KS)
Bethel Coll (TN)
Bethune-Cookman Coll (FL)
Bloomfield Coll (NJ)
Blue Mountain Coll (MS)
Bowling Green State U (OH)
Bridgewater Coll (VA)
Brigham Young U–Hawaii (HI)
Cabrini Coll (PA)
Campbell U (NC)
Canisius Coll (NY)
Caribbean U (PR)
Carroll Coll (MT)
The Catholic U of America (DC)
Cedarville U (OH)
Central Methodist Coll (MO)
Central Michigan U (MI)
Central Missouri State U (MO)
Central Washington U (WA)
Chadron State Coll (NE)
Christian Brothers U (TN)
Citadel, The Military Coll of South Carolina (SC)
Clearwater Christian Coll (FL)
Colby-Sawyer Coll (NH)
The Coll of New Jersey (NJ)
Coll of St. Catherine (MN)
Coll of the Ozarks (MO)
Colorado State U (CO)
Concordia Coll (MN)
Concordia U (IL)
Concordia U (NE)
Crichton Coll (TN)
Cumberland U (TN)
Daemen Coll (NY)
Dakota Wesleyan U (SD)
Delta State U (MS)
Dillard U (LA)
Dominican Coll (NY)
Duquesne U (PA)
Eastern Mennonite U (VA)
Eastern Michigan U (MI)
East Texas Baptist U (TX)
Elmhurst Coll (IL)
Elmira Coll (NY)
Florida Inst of Technology (FL)
Framingham State Coll (MA)
Franklin Coll of Indiana (IN)
Freed-Hardeman U (TN)
George Fox U (OR)
Georgia Southern U (GA)
Greensboro Coll (NC)
Greenville Coll (IL)
Gustavus Adolphus Coll (MN)
Hardin-Simmons U (TX)
Hastings Coll (NE)
Henderson State U (AR)
Hofstra U (NY)
Howard Payne U (TX)
Husson Coll (ME)
Indiana U Bloomington (IN)
Indiana U Northwest (IN)
Indiana U–Purdue U Fort Wayne (IN)
Indiana U South Bend (IN)
Indiana U Southeast (IN)
Inter American U of PR, Aguadilla Campus (PR)
Ithaca Coll (NY)
Johnson State Coll (VT)
Juniata Coll (PA)
Kennesaw State U (GA)
Keuka Coll (NY)
King Coll (TN)
La Roche Coll (PA)
Liberty U (VA)
Limestone Coll (SC)
Lipscomb U (TN)
Long Island U, C.W. Post Campus (NY)
Louisiana State U in Shreveport (LA)
Luther Coll (IA)
Malone Coll (OH)
Manhattanville Coll (NY)
Mansfield U of Pennsylvania (PA)
Marymount Coll of Fordham U (NY)
Maryville Coll (TN)
Mayville State U (ND)
McGill U (PQ, Canada)
McKendree Coll (IL)
McMurry U (TX)
Messiah Coll (PA)
Miami U (OH)
Minot State U (ND)
Molloy Coll (NY)
Montana State U–Billings (MT)
Nazareth Coll of Rochester (NY)
New York Inst of Technology (NY)
New York U (NY)
Niagara U (NY)
North Carolina Central U (NC)
North Carolina State U (NC)
North Dakota State U (ND)
Northern Arizona U (AZ)
Northwest Nazarene U (ID)
Ohio U (OH)
Oklahoma Baptist U (OK)
Pace U (NY)
Pikeville Coll (KY)
Point Park Coll (PA)
Pontifical Catholic U of Puerto Rico (PR)
Rivier Coll (NH)
Rust Coll (MS)
St. Ambrose U (IA)
Saint Augustine's Coll (NC)
St. John's U (NY)
Saint Joseph's Coll (ME)
Saint Xavier U (IL)
Salve Regina U (RI)
San Diego State U (CA)
Seattle Pacific U (WA)
Seton Hill Coll (PA)
Shaw U (NC)
Southern Arkansas U–Magnolia (AR)
Southern Nazarene U (OK)
Southwest Missouri State U (MO)
Southwest State U (MN)
State U of NY at Albany (NY)
State U of NY Coll at Potsdam (NY)
State U of NY Coll of Environ Sci and Forestry (NY)
State U of West Georgia (GA)
Talladega Coll (AL)
Tennessee Wesleyan Coll (TN)
Texas A&M International U (TX)
Texas Wesleyan U (TX)
Trevecca Nazarene U (TN)
Trinity Christian Coll (IL)
Union Coll (NE)
The U of Arizona (AZ)
U of Delaware (DE)
U of Illinois at Chicago (IL)
U of Maine at Farmington (ME)
U of Mary (ND)
U of Nebraska–Lincoln (NE)
The U of North Carolina at Wilmington (NC)
U of North Texas (TX)
U of Puerto Rico, Cayey U Coll (PR)
U of Rio Grande (OH)
The U of Tennessee at Martin (TN)
U of Utah (UT)
U of Washington (WA)
U of Waterloo (ON, Canada)
U of Windsor (ON, Canada)
U of Wisconsin–River Falls (WI)
U of Wisconsin–Superior (WI)
Utah State U (UT)
Utica Coll of Syracuse U (NY)
Valley City State U (ND)
Virginia Intermont Coll (VA)
Viterbo U (WI)
Washington U in St. Louis (MO)
Weber State U (UT)
Westminster Coll (UT)
Wheeling Jesuit U (WV)
Xavier U (OH)
York U (ON, Canada)
Youngstown State U (OH)

BIOMEDICAL ENGINEERING-RELATED TECHNOLOGY

Indiana State U (IN)
New York Inst of Technology (NY)
Oral Roberts U (OK)
Thomas Edison State Coll (NJ)

BIOMEDICAL SCIENCE

Brown U (RI)
Cedar Crest Coll (PA)
City Coll of the City U of NY (NY)
Comm Hospital Roanoke Valley–Coll of Health Scis (VA)
Emory U (GA)
Framingham State Coll (MA)
Grand Valley State U (MI)
Harvard U (MA)
Howard U (DC)
Immaculata Coll (PA)
Inter American U of PR, San Germán Campus (PR)
Marquette U (WI)
MCP Hahnemann U (PA)
Rutgers, The State U of New Jersey, New Brunswick (NJ)
St. Cloud State U (MN)
St. Francis Coll (NY)
State U of NY Coll at Fredonia (NY)
Stephens Coll (MO)
Suffolk U (MA)
Université de Montréal (QC, Canada)
U of Calif, Riverside (CA)
U of Guelph (ON, Canada)
U of Michigan (MI)
U of Mississippi (MS)
The U of North Carolina at Pembroke (NC)
U of Ottawa (ON, Canada)
U of South Alabama (AL)
U of Utah (UT)
Western Michigan U (MI)
Worcester Polytechnic Inst (MA)

BIOMEDICAL TECHNOLOGY

Alfred U (NY)
Alvernia Coll (PA)
Andrews U (MI)
California State U, Hayward (CA)
Cedar Crest Coll (PA)
Cleveland State U (OH)
Northwest Missouri State U (MO)
Suffolk U (MA)
U of New Hampshire (NH)
U of Southern Colorado (CO)
Walla Walla Coll (WA)

BIOMETRICS

Cornell U (NY)
Harvard U (MA)
Rutgers, The State U of New Jersey, New Brunswick (NJ)
U of Michigan (MI)

BIOPHYSICS

Andrews U (MI)
Brandeis U (MA)
Brown U (RI)
Carnegie Mellon U (PA)
Centenary Coll of Louisiana (LA)
Claremont McKenna Coll (CA)
Clarkson U (NY)
Columbia Coll (NY)
Hampden-Sydney Coll (VA)
Hampshire Coll (MA)
Harvard U (MA)
Haverford Coll (PA)
Howard U (DC)
Illinois Inst of Technology (IL)
Iowa State U of Science and Technology (IA)
Johns Hopkins U (MD)
King Coll (TN)
Longwood Coll (VA)
Oregon State U (OR)
Pacific Union Coll (CA)
Rensselaer Polytechnic Inst (NY)
St. Bonaventure U (NY)
St. Lawrence U (NY)
Saint Mary's U of Minnesota (MN)
Southwestern Oklahoma State U (OK)
State U of NY Coll at Geneseo (NY)
Suffolk U (MA)
State U of NY at Buffalo (NY)
U of Calif, San Diego (CA)
U of Connecticut (CT)
U of Guelph (ON, Canada)
U of Hawaii at Manoa (HI)
U of Illinois at Urbana–Champaign (IL)
U of Michigan (MI)
U of Pennsylvania (PA)
U of San Francisco (CA)
The U of Scranton (PA)
U of Southern California (CA)
U of Southern Indiana (IN)
U of Toronto (ON, Canada)
The U of Western Ontario (ON, Canada)
U of Windsor (ON, Canada)
Walla Walla Coll (WA)
Washington State U (WA)
Washington U in St. Louis (MO)
Whitman Coll (WA)

BIOPSYCHOLOGY

Barnard Coll (NY)
Bucknell U (PA)
Coll of the Holy Cross (MA)
The Coll of William and Mary (VA)
Columbia Coll (NY)
Morningside Coll (IA)
Mount Allison U (NB, Canada)
Nebraska Wesleyan U (NE)
Philadelphia U (PA)
Rider U (NJ)
Russell Sage Coll (NY)
U of Calif, Santa Barbara (CA)
U of Denver (CO)
U of Pittsburgh at Johnstown (PA)
U of Windsor (ON, Canada)
Washington U in St. Louis (MO)

BIOSTATISTICS

Cornell U (NY)
U of Hawaii at Manoa (HI)
U of Washington (WA)

BIOTECHNOLOGY RESEARCH

Assumption Coll (MA)
Brock U (ON, Canada)
Cabrini Coll (PA)
Calvin Coll (MI)
Clarkson U (NY)
Cleveland State U (OH)
East Stroudsburg U of Pennsylvania (PA)
Elizabethtown Coll (PA)
Manhattan Coll (NY)
Missouri Southern State Coll (MO)
Montana State U–Bozeman (MT)
North Dakota State U (ND)
The Ohio State U (OH)
Plymouth State Coll (NH)
Rochester Inst of Technology (NY)
Rutgers, The State U of New Jersey, New Brunswick (NJ)
State U of NY Coll of Environ Sci and Forestry (NY)
Thomas Jefferson U (PA)
State U of NY at Buffalo (NY)
U of Calif, San Diego (CA)
U of Delaware (DE)
U of Nebraska at Omaha (NE)
U of Southern Maine (ME)
U of Waterloo (ON, Canada)
U of Windsor (ON, Canada)
U of Wisconsin–River Falls (WI)
York U (ON, Canada)

BOTANY

Andrews U (MI)
Arizona State U (AZ)
Ball State U (IN)
Brandon U (MB, Canada)
Brigham Young U (UT)
California State Polytechnic U, Pomona (CA)
Carleton U (ON, Canada)
Coll of the Atlantic (ME)
Colorado State U (CO)
Concordia U (QC, Canada)
Connecticut Coll (CT)
Cornell U (NY)
Eastern Washington U (WA)
Fort Valley State U (GA)
Hampshire Coll (MA)
Howard U (DC)
Humboldt State U (CA)
Idaho State U (ID)
Iowa State U of Science and Technology (IA)
Juniata Coll (PA)
Kent State U (OH)
Marlboro Coll (VT)
Mars Hill Coll (NC)
McGill U (PQ, Canada)
Miami U (OH)
Michigan State U (MI)
Minnesota State U, Mankato (MN)
North Carolina State U (NC)
North Dakota State U (ND)
Northern Arizona U (AZ)
Northern Michigan U (MI)
Northwest Missouri State U (MO)
The Ohio State U (OH)
Ohio U (OH)
Ohio Wesleyan U (OH)
Oklahoma State U (OK)
Oregon State U (OR)
Purdue U (IN)
Purdue U Calumet (IN)
St. Cloud State U (MN)
Saint Xavier U (IL)
San Francisco State U (CA)
Sonoma State U (CA)
Southeastern Oklahoma State U (OK)
Southern Connecticut State U (CT)
Southern Illinois U Carbondale (IL)
Southern Utah U (UT)
Southwest Texas State U (TX)
State U of NY Coll of Environ Sci and Forestry (NY)
Texas A&M U (TX)
The U of Akron (OH)
U of Alberta (AB, Canada)
U of Arkansas (AR)
U of Calgary (AB, Canada)
U of Calif, Davis (CA)
U of Calif, Riverside (CA)
U of Calif, Santa Cruz (CA)
U of Delaware (DE)
U of Florida (FL)
U of Georgia (GA)
U of Great Falls (MT)
U of Guelph (ON, Canada)
U of Hawaii at Manoa (HI)
U of Idaho (ID)
U of Illinois at Urbana–Champaign (IL)
U of Maine (ME)
U of Manitoba (MB, Canada)
U of Michigan (MI)
U of Minnesota, Twin Cities Campus (MN)
The U of Montana–Missoula (MT)
U of Nevada, Reno (NV)
U of New Hampshire (NH)
U of Oklahoma (OK)
The U of Tennessee (TN)

The U of Texas at Austin (TX)
The U of Texas at El Paso (TX)
U of Toronto (ON, Canada)
U of Vermont (VT)
U of Victoria (BC, Canada)
U of Washington (WA)
U of Wisconsin–Madison (WI)
U of Wyoming (WY)
Utah State U (UT)
Weber State U (UT)
Wittenberg U (OH)

BOTANY RELATED
McGill U (PQ, Canada)

BRITISH LITERATURE
The Coll of Southeastern Europe, The American U of Athens(Greece)
Gannon U (PA)
Maharishi U of Management (IA)
Marylhurst U (OR)
Oral Roberts U (OK)
Point Loma Nazarene U (CA)
U of Pittsburgh (PA)
U of Southern California (CA)
Washington U in St. Louis (MO)

BROADCAST JOURNALISM
Adrian Coll (MI)
Alderson-Broaddus Coll (WV)
American U (DC)
Auburn U (AL)
Baldwin-Wallace Coll (OH)
Barry U (FL)
Barton Coll (NC)
Belmont U (TN)
Bemidji State U (MN)
Benedict Coll (SC)
Berry Coll (GA)
Bowie State U (MD)
Bowling Green State U (OH)
Bradley U (IL)
Brooklyn Coll of the City U of NY (NY)
California State U, Hayward (CA)
California State U, Long Beach (CA)
California State U, Northridge (CA)
Calvary Bible Coll and Theological Seminary (MO)
Carson-Newman Coll (TN)
Cedarville U (OH)
Chapman U (CA)
Chicago State U (IL)
The Coll of New Rochelle (NY)
The Coll of Southeastern Europe, The American U of Athens(Greece)
Coll of the Ozarks (MO)
Colorado Christian U (CO)
Columbia Coll Chicago (IL)
Columbia Coll–Hollywood (CA)
Columbia Union Coll (MD)
Concordia Coll (MN)
Drake U (IA)
East Carolina U (NC)
Eastern Kentucky U (KY)
Eastern Michigan U (MI)
Eastern Washington U (WA)
Edinboro U of Pennsylvania (PA)
Elizabeth City State U (NC)
Elon U (NC)
Emerson Coll (MA)
Evangel U (MO)
Florida International U (FL)
Florida Southern Coll (FL)
Fontbonne U (MO)
Fordham U (NY)
Franklin Coll of Indiana (IN)
Gonzaga U (WA)
Goshen Coll (IN)
Grace U (NE)
Grand Valley State U (MI)
Hampton U (VA)
Hofstra U (NY)
Houston Baptist U (TX)
Howard U (DC)
Humboldt State U (CA)
Huntington Coll (IN)
Indiana U Bloomington (IN)
Iona Coll (NY)
Ithaca Coll (NY)
John Brown U (AR)
Lamar U (TX)
La Salle U (PA)
Lewis U (IL)
Lindenwood U (MO)
Lock Haven U of Pennsylvania (PA)
Long Island U, C.W. Post Campus (NY)
Louisiana Coll (LA)
Malone Coll (OH)
Mansfield U of Pennsylvania (PA)
Marist Coll (NY)
Marquette U (WI)
Massachusetts Coll of Liberal Arts (MA)
Mercyhurst Coll (PA)
Mesa State Coll (CO)
Midland Lutheran Coll (NE)
Milligan Coll (TN)
Minnesota State U Moorhead (MN)
Montclair State U (NJ)
Morris Coll (SC)
Mount Vernon Nazarene U (OH)
New England School of Communications (ME)
North Central Coll (IL)
Northern Michigan U (MI)
Northwest Missouri State U (MO)
Ohio Northern U (OH)
Ohio U (OH)
Ohio Wesleyan U (OH)
Oklahoma Baptist U (OK)
Oklahoma Christian U of Science and Arts (OK)
Oklahoma City U (OK)
Oklahoma State U (OK)
Olivet Nazarene U (IL)
Pacific Lutheran U (WA)
Pacific U (OR)
Pittsburg State U (KS)
Plattsburgh State U of NY (NY)
Point Park Coll (PA)
Quinnipiac U (CT)
Reformed Bible Coll (MI)
Rust Coll (MS)
St. Cloud State U (MN)
St. Francis Coll (NY)
San Jose State U (CA)
Shorter Coll (GA)
Southern Adventist U (TN)
Southern Arkansas U–Magnolia (AR)
Southern Methodist U (TX)
Southern Nazarene U (OK)
Southwestern Adventist U (TX)
Southwest Texas State U (TX)
State U of NY at New Paltz (NY)
State U of NY Coll at Brockport (NY)
State U of NY Coll at Buffalo (NY)
State U of NY Coll at Fredonia (NY)
Stephens Coll (MO)
Suffolk U (MA)
Syracuse U (NY)
Temple U (PA)
Texas Christian U (TX)
Troy State U (AL)
Union U (TN)
The U of Akron (OH)
U of Central Oklahoma (OK)
U of Cincinnati (OH)
U of Colorado at Boulder (CO)
U of Dayton (OH)
The U of Findlay (OH)
U of Georgia (GA)
U of Illinois at Urbana–Champaign (IL)
The U of Iowa (IA)
U of Kansas (KS)
U of La Verne (CA)
U of Maryland, Coll Park (MD)
U of Miami (FL)
U of Missouri–Columbia (MO)
U of Montevallo (AL)
U of Nebraska at Omaha (NE)
U of Nebraska–Lincoln (NE)
U of Nevada, Reno (NV)
The U of North Carolina at Pembroke (NC)
U of Northern Iowa (IA)
U of North Texas (TX)
U of Oklahoma (OK)
U of Oregon (OR)
U of St. Francis (IL)
U of St. Thomas (MN)
U of San Francisco (CA)
U of South Carolina (SC)
U of South Dakota (SD)
U of Southern California (CA)
U of Southern Colorado (CO)
The U of Tennessee at Chattanooga (TN)
The U of Tennessee at Martin (TN)
The U of Texas at El Paso (TX)
U of Tulsa (OK)
U of Utah (UT)
U of Windsor (ON, Canada)
U of Wisconsin–Madison (WI)
U of Wisconsin–Milwaukee (WI)
U of Wisconsin–Oshkosh (WI)
U of Wisconsin–Platteville (WI)
U of Wisconsin–River Falls (WI)
U of Wisconsin–Superior (WI)
Valdosta State U (GA)
Waldorf Coll (IA)
Wartburg Coll (IA)
Webster U (MO)
Western Washington U (WA)
Westminster Coll (PA)
West Texas A&M U (TX)
William Woods U (MO)
Winona State U (MN)

BUILDING MAINTENANCE/ MANAGEMENT
Peirce Coll (PA)

BUSINESS
Andrew Jackson U (AL)
Arizona State U East (AZ)
Asbury Coll (KY)
Auburn U Montgomery (AL)
Aurora U (IL)
Austin Peay State U (TN)
Averett U (VA)
Baker Coll of Jackson (MI)
Bayamón Central U (PR)
Baylor U (TX)
Bay Path Coll (MA)
Benedictine U (IL)
Bentley Coll (MA)
Berkeley Coll, New York (NY)
Berkeley Coll, White Plains (NY)
Blue Mountain Coll (MS)
Bowling Green State U (OH)
Brescia U (KY)
Brevard Coll (NC)
Briarcliffe Coll (NY)
Brock U (ON, Canada)
California Coll for Health Sciences (CA)
California State U, Chico (CA)
California State U, Stanislaus (CA)
Cameron U (OK)
Campbell U (NC)
Capella U (MN)
Carlow Coll (PA)
The Catholic U of America (DC)
Central Michigan U (MI)
Champlain Coll (VT)
Christian Brothers U (TN)
Circleville Bible Coll (OH)
The Coll of Southeastern Europe, The American U of Athens(Greece)
Coll of Staten Island of the City U of NY (NY)
Colorado Christian U (CO)
Columbia Coll (PR)
Concordia Coll (MN)
Concordia U (NE)
Cumberland Coll (KY)
Cumberland U (TN)
Delta State U (MS)
DePaul U (IL)
Dominican Coll (NY)
Drake U (IA)
Drexel U (PA)
Duquesne U (PA)
Eastern Connecticut State U (CT)
Eastern Illinois U (IL)
Eastern Michigan U (MI)
East Texas Baptist U (TX)
École des Hautes Études Commerciales de Montréal (PQ, Canada)
Florida Southern Coll (FL)
Florida State U (FL)
Franklin Coll of Indiana (IN)
Georgia Coll and State U (GA)
Grace Coll (IN)
Green Mountain Coll (VT)
Henderson State U (AR)
Hillsdale Free Will Baptist Coll (OK)
Hollins U (VA)
Howard Payne U (TX)
Indiana U Bloomington (IN)
Indiana U East (IN)
Indiana U Kokomo (IN)
Indiana U–Purdue U Indianapolis (IN)
Indiana U South Bend (IN)
Indiana U Southeast (IN)
Ithaca Coll (NY)
Jacksonville U (FL)
Johns Hopkins U (MD)
Johnson State Coll (VT)
Judson Coll (AL)
Limestone Coll (SC)
Linfield Coll (OR)
Loras Coll (IA)
Loyola Coll in Maryland (MD)
Luther Coll (IA)
Maharishi U of Management (IA)
Malaspina U-Coll (BC, Canada)
Manchester Coll (IN)
Marygrove Coll (MI)
Maryville U of Saint Louis (MO)
McMurry U (TX)
Mercer U (GA)
Miami U (OH)
Milwaukee School of Engineering (WI)
Monroe Coll, Bronx (NY)
Monroe Coll, New Rochelle (NY)
Montana State U–Billings (MT)
Montana State U–Bozeman (MT)
Montana Tech of The U of Montana (MT)
Mount Allison U (NB, Canada)
Murray State U (KY)
National Coll of Business & Technology, Salem (VA)
New Mexico State U (NM)
Norfolk State U (VA)
Northeastern Illinois U (IL)
Northeastern U (MA)
Northern Arizona U (AZ)
Northern Illinois U (IL)
Ohio U (OH)
Oklahoma Christian U of Science and Arts (OK)
Oklahoma City U (OK)
Oklahoma State U (OK)
Peirce Coll (PA)
Penn State U Abington Coll (PA)
Penn State U Altoona Coll (PA)
Penn State U Beaver Campus of the Commonwealth Coll (PA)
Penn State U Berks Cmps of Berks-Lehigh Valley Coll (PA)
Penn State U Delaware County Campus of the Commonwealth Coll (PA)
Penn State U DuBois Campus of the Commonwealth Coll (PA)
Penn State U Fayette Campus of the Commonwealth Coll (PA)
Penn State U Hazleton Campus of the Commonwealth Coll (PA)
Penn State U Lehigh Valley Cmps of Berks-Lehigh Valley Coll (PA)
Penn State U McKeesport Campus of the Commonwealth Coll (PA)
Penn State U Mont Alto Campus of the Commonwealth Coll (PA)
Penn State U New Kensington Campus of the Commonwealth Coll (PA)
Penn State U Schuylkill Campus of the Capital Coll (PA)
Penn State U Shenango Campus of the Commonwealth Coll (PA)
Penn State U Worthington Scranton Cmps Commonwealth Coll (PA)
Penn State U York Campus of the Commonwealth Coll (PA)
Regis Coll (MA)
Rockhurst U (MO)
Roger Williams U (RI)
Saginaw Valley State U (MI)
St. Ambrose U (IA)
Saint Anselm Coll (NH)
Saint Mary's U of Minnesota (MN)
St. Norbert Coll (WI)
Saint Xavier U (IL)
Sam Houston State U (TX)
Schreiner U (TX)
Skidmore Coll (NY)
Southern Arkansas U–Magnolia (AR)
Southern Illinois U Carbondale (IL)
Southern Illinois U Edwardsville (IL)
Southwest Missouri State U (MO)
Stephen F. Austin State U (TX)
Texas A&M U–Texarkana (TX)
Texas Coll (TX)
Thomas More Coll (KY)
Touro U International (CA)
Trinity Christian Coll (IL)
Troy State U Montgomery (AL)
Tyndale Coll & Seminary (ON, Canada)
Union Inst & U (OH)
U Coll of Cape Breton (NS, Canada)
The U of Akron (OH)
The U of Arizona (AZ)
U of Arkansas (AR)
U of Arkansas at Little Rock (AR)
U of Central Arkansas (AR)
U of Central Florida (FL)
U of Central Oklahoma (OK)
U of Connecticut (CT)
U of Denver (CO)
U of Georgia (GA)
U of Hawaii at Manoa (HI)
U of Houston–Clear Lake (TX)
U of Illinois at Urbana–Champaign (IL)
U of Kansas (KS)
U of Kentucky (KY)
U of Maryland, Coll Park (MD)
U of Mississippi (MS)
U of Missouri–Rolla (MO)
The U of Montana–Missoula (MT)
Western Montana Coll of The U of Montana (MT)
U of Nevada, Reno (NV)
U of North Dakota (ND)
U of North Texas (TX)
U of Notre Dame (IN)
U of Pittsburgh (PA)
U of Puerto Rico, Humacao U Coll (PR)
U of Puget Sound (WA)
U of Redlands (CA)
U of San Francisco (CA)
U of Saskatchewan (SK, Canada)
U of Science and Arts of Oklahoma (OK)
U of South Alabama (AL)
U of Southern Indiana (IN)
U of South Florida (FL)
The U of Tennessee (TN)
The U of Texas at Austin (TX)
The U of Texas at Dallas (TX)
The U of Texas at San Antonio (TX)
The U of Texas–Pan American (TX)
U of the Incarnate Word (TX)
U of Victoria (BC, Canada)
U of Virginia (VA)
U of Washington (WA)
U of Wisconsin–Whitewater (WI)
Utah State U (UT)
Virginia Polytechnic Inst and State U (VA)
Wake Forest U (NC)
Washington U in St. Louis (MO)
Webber International U (FL)
Webster U (MO)
Western Governors U (UT)
Western Illinois U (IL)
Western Michigan U (MI)
Western Oregon U (OR)
Westminster Coll (UT)
Westmont Coll (CA)
West Texas A&M U (TX)
Xavier U (OH)
York U (ON, Canada)
Youngstown State U (OH)

BUSINESS ADMINISTRATION
Abilene Christian U (TX)
Acadia U (NS, Canada)
Adams State Coll (CO)
Adelphi U (NY)
Adrian Coll (MI)
AIBT International Inst of the Americas (AZ)
Alabama State U (AL)
Alaska Pacific U (AK)
Albany State U (GA)
Albertson Coll of Idaho (ID)
Albion Coll (MI)
Albright Coll (PA)
Alcorn State U (MS)
Alderson-Broaddus Coll (WV)
Alfred U (NY)
Alice Lloyd Coll (KY)
Alliant International U (CA)
Alma Coll (MI)
Alvernia Coll (PA)
Alverno Coll (WI)

Indiana U–Purdue U Fort Wayne (IN)
Indiana Wesleyan U (IN)
Inst of Computer Technology (CA)
Inter American U of PR, Aguadilla Campus (PR)
Inter Amer U of PR, Barranquitas Campus (PR)
Inter American U of PR, San Germán Campus (PR)
International Business Coll, Fort Wayne (IN)
International Coll (FL)
Iona Coll (NY)
Iowa State U of Science and Technology (IA)
Iowa Wesleyan Coll (IA)
Ithaca Coll (NY)
Jackson State U (MS)
Jacksonville State U (AL)
Jacksonville U (FL)
James Madison U (VA)
Jamestown Coll (ND)
Jarvis Christian Coll (TX)
John Brown U (AR)
John Cabot U(Italy)
John Carroll U (OH)
John F. Kennedy U (CA)
Johnson & Wales U (RI)
Johnson C. Smith U (NC)
Johnson State Coll (VT)
John Wesley Coll (NC)
Jones Coll (FL)
Judson Coll (IL)
Juniata Coll (PA)
Kansas State U (KS)
Kansas Wesleyan U (KS)
Kean U (NJ)
Keene State Coll (NH)
Kendall Coll (IL)
Kennesaw State U (GA)
Kent State U (OH)
Kent State U, Geauga Campus (OH)
Kent State U, Tuscarawas Campus (OH)
Kentucky Christian Coll (KY)
Kentucky State U (KY)
Kentucky Wesleyan Coll (KY)
Kettering U (MI)
Keuka Coll (NY)
King Coll (TN)
King's Coll (PA)
The King's U Coll (AB, Canada)
LaGrange Coll (GA)
Lake Erie Coll (OH)
Lakehead U (ON, Canada)
Lakeland Coll (WI)
Lake Superior State U (MI)
Lamar U (TX)
Lambuth U (TN)
Lander U (SC)
La Roche Coll (PA)
La Salle U (PA)
Lasell Coll (MA)
Laurentian U (ON, Canada)
Lawrence Technological U (MI)
Lebanon Valley Coll (PA)
Lees-McRae Coll (NC)
Lee U (TN)
Lehigh U (PA)
Lehman Coll of the City U of NY (NY)
Le Moyne Coll (NY)
LeMoyne-Owen Coll (TN)
Lenoir-Rhyne Coll (NC)
Lesley U (MA)
LeTourneau U (TX)
Lewis-Clark State Coll (ID)
Lewis U (IL)
Liberty U (VA)
Limestone Coll (SC)
Lincoln Christian Coll (IL)
Lincoln Memorial U (TN)
Lincoln U (CA)
Lincoln U (MO)
Lincoln U (PA)
Lindenwood U (MO)
Lindsey Wilson Coll (KY)
Lipscomb U (TN)
Lock Haven U of Pennsylvania (PA)
Long Island U, Brentwood Campus (NY)
Long Island U, Brooklyn Campus (NY)
Long Island U, C.W. Post Campus (NY)
Long Island U, Southampton Coll (NY)
Longwood Coll (VA)
Loras Coll (IA)
Louisiana Coll (LA)
Louisiana State U and A&M Coll (LA)
Louisiana State U in Shreveport (LA)
Louisiana Tech U (LA)
Lourdes Coll (OH)
Loyola Marymount U (CA)
Loyola U Chicago (IL)
Loyola U New Orleans (LA)
Lubbock Christian U (TX)
Luther Coll (IA)
Lycoming Coll (PA)
Lynchburg Coll (VA)
Lyndon State Coll (VT)
Lynn U (FL)
Lyon Coll (AR)
MacMurray Coll (IL)
Maharishi U of Management (IA)
Maine Maritime Academy (ME)
Malone Coll (OH)
Manchester Coll (IN)
Manhattan Christian Coll (KS)
Manhattanville Coll (NY)
Mansfield U of Pennsylvania (PA)
Maranatha Baptist Bible Coll (WI)
Marian Coll (IN)
Marian Coll of Fond du Lac (WI)
Marietta Coll (OH)
Marist Coll (NY)
Marquette U (WI)
Marshall U (WV)
Mars Hill Coll (NC)
Martin Methodist Coll (TN)
Mary Baldwin Coll (VA)
Marygrove Coll (MI)
Marylhurst U (OR)
Marymount Coll of Fordham U (NY)
Marymount Manhattan Coll (NY)
Marymount U (VA)
Maryville Coll (TN)
Maryville U of Saint Louis (MO)
Mary Washington Coll (VA)
Marywood U (PA)
Massachusetts Coll of Liberal Arts (MA)
Massachusetts Inst of Technology (MA)
The Master's Coll and Seminary (CA)
Mayville State U (ND)
McGill U (PQ, Canada)
McKendree Coll (IL)
McMaster U (ON, Canada)
McNeese State U (LA)
McPherson Coll (KS)
Medaille Coll (NY)
Medgar Evers Coll of the City U of NY (NY)
Memorial U of Newfoundland (NF, Canada)
Menlo Coll (CA)
Mercer U (GA)
Mercy Coll (NY)
Mercyhurst Coll (PA)
Meredith Coll (NC)
Merrimack Coll (MA)
Mesa State Coll (CO)
Messiah Coll (PA)
Methodist Coll (NC)
Metropolitan State U (MN)
Miami U (OH)
Michigan State U (MI)
Michigan Technological U (MI)
MidAmerica Nazarene U (KS)
Middle Tennessee State U (TN)
Midland Lutheran Coll (NE)
Midway Coll (KY)
Midwestern State U (TX)
Millersville U of Pennsylvania (PA)
Milligan Coll (TN)
Millikin U (IL)
Millsaps Coll (MS)
Minnesota State U, Mankato (MN)
Minnesota State U Moorhead (MN)
Minot State U (ND)
Mississippi Coll (MS)
Mississippi State U (MS)
Mississippi U for Women (MS)
Mississippi Valley State U (MS)
Missouri Baptist Coll (MO)
Missouri Southern State Coll (MO)
Missouri Valley Coll (MO)
Missouri Western State Coll (MO)
Mitchell Coll (CT)
Molloy Coll (NY)
Monmouth Coll (IL)
Monmouth U (NJ)
Monroe Coll, Bronx (NY)
Monroe Coll, New Rochelle (NY)
Montana State U–Billings (MT)
Montana State U–Northern (MT)
Montana Tech of The U of Montana (MT)
Montclair State U (NJ)
Montreat Coll (NC)
Moravian Coll (PA)
Morehead State U (KY)
Morehouse Coll (GA)
Morgan State U (MD)
Morningside Coll (IA)
Morris Brown Coll (GA)
Morris Coll (SC)
Mount Allison U (NB, Canada)
Mount Aloysius Coll (PA)
Mount Ida Coll (MA)
Mount Marty Coll (SD)
Mount Mary Coll (WI)
Mount Mercy Coll (IA)
Mount Olive Coll (NC)
Mount St. Clare Coll (IA)
Mount Saint Mary Coll (NY)
Mount St. Mary's Coll (CA)
Mount Saint Mary's Coll and Seminary (MD)
Mount Saint Vincent U (NS, Canada)
Mount Union Coll (OH)
Mount Vernon Nazarene U (OH)
Muhlenberg Coll (PA)
Murray State U (KY)
Muskingum Coll (OH)
National American U, Colorado Springs (CO)
National American U (NM)
National American U (SD)
National American U–St. Paul Campus (MN)
National American U–Sioux Falls Branch (SD)
The National Hispanic U (CA)
National-Louis U (IL)
National U (CA)
Nazareth Coll of Rochester (NY)
Nebraska Wesleyan U (NE)
Neumann Coll (PA)
Newberry Coll (SC)
Newbury Coll (MA)
New England Coll (NH)
New Jersey City U (NJ)
New Jersey Inst of Technology (NJ)
Newman U (KS)
New Mexico Highlands U (NM)
New Mexico Inst of Mining and Technology (NM)
New Mexico State U (NM)
New York Inst of Technology (NY)
New York U (NY)
Niagara U (NY)
Nicholls State U (LA)
Nipissing U (ON, Canada)
North Carolina Ag and Tech State U (NC)
North Carolina Central U (NC)
North Carolina State U (NC)
North Carolina Wesleyan Coll (NC)
North Central Coll (IL)
North Dakota State U (ND)
Northeastern State U (OK)
Northern Arizona U (AZ)
Northern Illinois U (IL)
Northern Kentucky U (KY)
Northern Michigan U (MI)
Northern State U (SD)
North Georgia Coll & State U (GA)
North Greenville Coll (SC)
Northland Coll (WI)
North Park U (IL)
Northwest Christian Coll (OR)
Northwest Coll (WA)
Northwestern Coll (IA)
Northwestern Coll (MN)
Northwestern Oklahoma State U (OK)
Northwestern Polytechnic U (CA)
Northwestern State U of Louisiana (LA)
Northwest Missouri State U (MO)
Northwest Nazarene U (ID)
Northwood U (MI)
Northwood U, Florida Campus (FL)
Northwood U, Texas Campus (TX)
Norwich U (VT)
Notre Dame Coll (OH)
Notre Dame de Namur U (CA)
Nova Southeastern U (FL)
Nyack Coll (NY)
Oak Hills Christian Coll (MN)
Oakland City U (IN)
Oakland U (MI)
Oakwood Coll (AL)
Oglethorpe U (GA)
Ohio Dominican Coll (OH)
Ohio Northern U (OH)
The Ohio State U (OH)
Ohio U (OH)
Ohio U–Chillicothe (OH)
Ohio U–Lancaster (OH)
Ohio U–Southern Campus (OH)
Ohio Valley Coll (WV)
Ohio Wesleyan U (OH)
Okanagan U Coll (BC, Canada)
Oklahoma Baptist U (OK)
Oklahoma Christian U of Science and Arts (OK)
Oklahoma City U (OK)
Oklahoma Panhandle State U (OK)
Oklahoma Wesleyan U (OK)
Old Dominion U (VA)
Olivet Coll (MI)
Olivet Nazarene U (IL)
Open Learning Agency (BC, Canada)
Oral Roberts U (OK)
Oregon Inst of Technology (OR)
Oregon State U (OR)
Ottawa U (KS)
Otterbein Coll (OH)
Ouachita Baptist U (AR)
Our Lady of Holy Cross Coll (LA)
Our Lady of the Lake U of San Antonio (TX)
Pace U (NY)
Pacific Lutheran U (WA)
Pacific States U (CA)
Pacific Union Coll (CA)
Pacific U (OR)
Paine Coll (GA)
Palm Beach Atlantic Coll (FL)
Park U (MO)
Patten Coll (CA)
Peace Coll (NC)
Peirce Coll (PA)
Pennsylvania Coll of Technology (PA)
Penn State U at Erie, The Behrend Coll (PA)
Penn State U Harrisburg Campus of the Capital Coll (PA)
Penn State U Univ Park Campus (PA)
Pepperdine U, Malibu (CA)
Peru State Coll (NE)
Pfeiffer U (NC)
Philadelphia Biblical U (PA)
Philadelphia U (PA)
Philander Smith Coll (AR)
Piedmont Coll (GA)
Pikeville Coll (KY)
Pillsbury Baptist Bible Coll (MN)
Pine Manor Coll (MA)
Pittsburg State U (KS)
Plattsburgh State U of NY (NY)
Plymouth State Coll (NH)
Point Loma Nazarene U (CA)
Point Park Coll (PA)
Polytechnic U of Puerto Rico (PR)
Pontifical Catholic U of Puerto Rico (PR)
Portland State U (OR)
Potomac Coll (DC)
Prairie View A&M U (TX)
Presbyterian Coll (SC)
Presentation Coll (SD)
Principia Coll (IL)
Providence Coll (RI)
Providence Coll and Theological Seminary (MB, Canada)
Purdue U (IN)
Purdue U Calumet (IN)
Purdue U North Central (IN)
Queens Coll (NC)
Queen's U at Kingston (ON, Canada)
Quincy U (IL)
Quinnipiac U (CT)
Radford U (VA)
Ramapo Coll of New Jersey (NJ)
Redeemer U Coll (ON, Canada)
Reformed Bible Coll (MI)
Regis U (CO)
Reinhardt Coll (GA)
Rensselaer Polytechnic Inst (NY)
Rhode Island Coll (RI)
Rhodes Coll (TN)
Rice U (TX)
The Richard Stockton Coll of New Jersey (NJ)
Richmond, The American International U in London(United Kingdom)
Rider U (NJ)
Ripon Coll (WI)
Rivier Coll (NH)
Roanoke Coll (VA)
Robert Morris Coll (IL)
Robert Morris U (PA)
Roberts Wesleyan Coll (NY)
Rochester Coll (MI)
Rochester Inst of Technology (NY)
Rockford Coll (IL)
Rockhurst U (MO)
Rocky Mountain Coll (MT)
Roger Williams U (RI)
Roosevelt U (IL)
Rosemont Coll (PA)
Rowan U (NJ)
Royal Roads U (BC, Canada)
Russell Sage Coll (NY)
Rust Coll (MS)
Rutgers, The State U of New Jersey, New Brunswick (NJ)
Sacred Heart U (CT)
Sage Coll of Albany (NY)
Saginaw Valley State U (MI)
St. Ambrose U (IA)
St. Andrews Presbyterian Coll (NC)
Saint Augustine's Coll (NC)
St. Bonaventure U (NY)
St. Cloud State U (MN)
St. Edward's U (TX)
St. Francis Coll (NY)
Saint Francis U (PA)
St. Francis Xavier U (NS, Canada)
St. Gregory's U (OK)
St. John Fisher Coll (NY)
Saint John's U (MN)
St. John's U (NY)
Saint Joseph Coll (CT)
Saint Joseph's Coll (IN)
Saint Joseph's Coll (ME)
St. Joseph's Coll, New York (NY)
St. Joseph's Coll, Suffolk Campus (NY)
Saint Joseph's U (PA)
Saint Leo U (FL)
Saint Louis U (MO)
Saint Martin's Coll (WA)
Saint Mary Coll (KS)
Saint Mary-of-the-Woods Coll (IN)
Saint Mary's Coll (IN)
Saint Mary's Coll of Ave Maria U (MI)
Saint Mary's Coll of California (CA)
Saint Mary's U (NS, Canada)
Saint Mary's U of Minnesota (MN)
St. Mary's U of San Antonio (TX)
Saint Michael's Coll (VT)
Saint Peter's Coll (NJ)
St. Thomas Aquinas Coll (NY)
St. Thomas U (FL)
Saint Vincent Coll (PA)
Salem Coll (NC)
Salem International U (WV)
Salem State Coll (MA)
Salisbury U (MD)
Salve Regina U (RI)
Samford U (AL)
Sam Houston State U (TX)
San Diego State U (CA)
San Francisco State U (CA)
San Jose State U (CA)
Santa Clara U (CA)
Savannah State U (GA)
Schiller International U(France)
Schiller International U(Spain)
Schiller International U, American Coll of Switzerland(Switzerland)
Schreiner U (TX)
Seattle Pacific U (WA)
Seattle U (WA)
Seton Hall U (NJ)
Seton Hill Coll (PA)
Shawnee State U (OH)
Shaw U (NC)
Sheldon Jackson Coll (AK)
Shenandoah U (VA)
Shepherd Coll (WV)
Shippensburg U of Pennsylvania (PA)
Shorter Coll (GA)
Siena Heights U (MI)

Sierra Nevada Coll (NV)
Silver Lake Coll (WI)
Simmons Coll (MA)
Simon Fraser U (BC, Canada)
Simpson Coll (IA)
Simpson Coll and Graduate School (CA)
Sinte Gleska U (SD)
Slippery Rock U of Pennsylvania (PA)
Sojourner-Douglass Coll (MD)
Sonoma State U (CA)
South Carolina State U (SC)
Southeastern Louisiana U (LA)
Southeastern Oklahoma State U (OK)
Southeastern U (DC)
Southeast Missouri State U (MO)
Southern Adventist U (TN)
Southern Connecticut State U (CT)
Southern Illinois U Carbondale (IL)
Southern Methodist U (TX)
Southern Nazarene U (OK)
Southern New Hampshire U (NH)
Southern Oregon U (OR)
Southern U and A&M Coll (LA)
Southern Utah U (UT)
Southern Vermont Coll (VT)
Southern Virginia U (VA)
Southern Wesleyan U (SC)
Southwest Baptist U (MO)
Southwestern Adventist U (TX)
Southwestern Assemblies of God U (TX)
Southwestern Coll (AZ)
Southwestern Coll (KS)
Southwestern Oklahoma State U (OK)
Southwestern U (TX)
Southwest Missouri State U (MO)
Southwest State U (MN)
Southwest Texas State U (TX)
Spring Arbor U (MI)
Springfield Coll (MA)
Spring Hill Coll (AL)
State U of NY at Albany (NY)
State U of NY at New Paltz (NY)
State U of NY at Oswego (NY)
State U of NY Coll at Brockport (NY)
State U of NY Coll at Buffalo (NY)
State U of NY Coll at Fredonia (NY)
State U of NY Coll at Geneseo (NY)
State U of NY Coll at Old Westbury (NY)
State U of NY Coll at Potsdam (NY)
State U of NY Empire State Coll (NY)
State U of NY Inst of Tech at Utica/Rome (NY)
State U of NY Maritime Coll (NY)
State U of West Georgia (GA)
Stephen F. Austin State U (TX)
Stephens Coll (MO)
Sterling Coll (KS)
Stetson U (FL)
Stonehill Coll (MA)
State U of NY at Stony Brook (NY)
Strayer U (DC)
Suffolk U (MA)
Sullivan U (KY)
Sul Ross State U (TX)
Susquehanna U (PA)
Syracuse U (NY)
Tabor Coll (KS)
Talladega Coll (AL)
Tarleton State U (TX)
Taylor U (IN)
Taylor U, Fort Wayne Campus (IN)
Teikyo Post U (CT)
Temple U (PA)
Tennessee State U (TN)
Tennessee Technological U (TN)
Tennessee Temple U (TN)
Tennessee Wesleyan Coll (TN)
Texas A&M International U (TX)
Texas A&M U (TX)
Texas A&M U at Galveston (TX)
Texas A&M U–Commerce (TX)
Texas A&M U–Corpus Christi (TX)
Texas A&M U–Kingsville (TX)
Texas A&M U–Texarkana (TX)
Texas Christian U (TX)
Texas Coll (TX)
Texas Lutheran U (TX)
Texas Southern U (TX)
Texas Tech U (TX)
Texas Wesleyan U (TX)
Texas Woman's U (TX)
Thiel Coll (PA)
Thomas Coll (ME)
Thomas Edison State Coll (NJ)
Thomas U (GA)
Tiffin U (OH)
Toccoa Falls Coll (GA)
Tougaloo Coll (MS)
Touro Coll (NY)
Towson U (MD)
Transylvania U (KY)
Trent U (ON, Canada)
Trevecca Nazarene U (TN)
Trinity Bible Coll (ND)
Trinity Christian Coll (IL)
Trinity Coll (DC)
Trinity International U (IL)
Trinity U (TX)
Trinity Western U (BC, Canada)
Tri-State U (IN)
Troy State U (AL)
Troy State U Dothan (AL)
Troy State U Montgomery (AL)
Truman State U (MO)
Tulane U (LA)
Tusculum Coll (TN)
Tuskegee U (AL)
Union Coll (KY)
Union Coll (NE)
Union U (TN)
United States Air Force Academy (CO)
United States Military Academy (NY)
Universidad Adventista de las Antillas (PR)
Université de Sherbrooke (PQ, Canada)
Université Laval (QC, Canada)
State U of NY at Buffalo (NY)
U Coll of Cape Breton (NS, Canada)
U Coll of the Cariboo (BC, Canada)
U Coll of the Fraser Valley (BC, Canada)
The U of Akron (OH)
The U of Alabama (AL)
The U of Alabama at Birmingham (AL)
The U of Alabama in Huntsville (AL)
U of Alaska Anchorage (AK)
U of Alaska Fairbanks (AK)
U of Alaska Southeast (AK)
U of Alberta (AB, Canada)
U of Arkansas (AR)
U of Arkansas at Little Rock (AR)
U of Arkansas at Pine Bluff (AR)
U of Baltimore (MD)
U of Bridgeport (CT)
The U of British Columbia (BC, Canada)
U of Calgary (AB, Canada)
U of Calif, Berkeley (CA)
U of Calif, Riverside (CA)
U of Central Arkansas (AR)
U of Central Florida (FL)
U of Central Oklahoma (OK)
U of Charleston (WV)
U of Cincinnati (OH)
U of Colorado at Boulder (CO)
U of Colorado at Colorado Springs (CO)
U of Colorado at Denver (CO)
U of Dayton (OH)
U of Delaware (DE)
U of Denver (CO)
U of Dubuque (IA)
U of Evansville (IN)
The U of Findlay (OH)
U of Florida (FL)
U of Georgia (GA)
U of Great Falls (MT)
U of Hartford (CT)
U of Hawaii at Hilo (HI)
U of Hawaii at Manoa (HI)
U of Hawaii–West Oahu (HI)
U of Houston (TX)
U of Houston–Clear Lake (TX)
U of Houston–Victoria (TX)
U of Illinois at Chicago (IL)
U of Illinois at Springfield (IL)
U of Indianapolis (IN)
The U of Iowa (IA)
U of La Verne (CA)
The U of Lethbridge (AB, Canada)
U of Louisiana at Lafayette (LA)
U of Louisiana at Monroe (LA)
U of Louisville (KY)
U of Maine (ME)
The U of Maine at Augusta (ME)
U of Maine at Fort Kent (ME)
U of Maine at Machias (ME)
U of Maine at Presque Isle (ME)
U of Manitoba (MB, Canada)
U of Mary (ND)
U of Mary Hardin-Baylor (TX)
U of Maryland Eastern Shore (MD)
U of Maryland University Coll (MD)
U of Massachusetts Amherst (MA)
U of Massachusetts Boston (MA)
U of Massachusetts Dartmouth (MA)
U of Massachusetts Lowell (MA)
The U of Memphis (TN)
U of Miami (FL)
U of Michigan (MI)
U of Michigan–Dearborn (MI)
U of Michigan–Flint (MI)
U of Minnesota, Crookston (MN)
U of Minnesota, Duluth (MN)
U of Minnesota, Morris (MN)
U of Mississippi (MS)
U of Missouri–Columbia (MO)
U of Missouri–Kansas City (MO)
U of Missouri–Rolla (MO)
U of Missouri–St. Louis (MO)
U of Mobile (AL)
U of Montevallo (AL)
U of Nebraska at Kearney (NE)
U of Nebraska–Lincoln (NE)
U of Nevada, Las Vegas (NV)
U of New England (ME)
U of New Hampshire (NH)
U of New Haven (CT)
U of New Mexico (NM)
U of New Orleans (LA)
U of North Alabama (AL)
The U of North Carolina at Asheville (NC)
The U of North Carolina at Chapel Hill (NC)
The U of North Carolina at Charlotte (NC)
The U of North Carolina at Greensboro (NC)
The U of North Carolina at Pembroke (NC)
The U of North Carolina at Wilmington (NC)
U of Northern Colorado (CO)
U of Northern Iowa (IA)
U of North Florida (FL)
U of Northwestern Ohio (OH)
U of Oklahoma (OK)
U of Oregon (OR)
U of Ottawa (ON, Canada)
U of Pennsylvania (PA)
U of Phoenix-Atlanta Campus (GA)
U of Phoenix–Boston Campus (MA)
U of Phoenix–Colorado Campus (CO)
U of Phoenix–Dallas/Ft. Worth Campus (TX)
U of Phoenix–Fort Lauderdale Campus (FL)
U of Phoenix–Houston Campus (TX)
U of Phoenix–Jacksonville Campus (FL)
U of Phoenix–Louisiana Campus (LA)
U of Phoenix–Maryland Campus (MD)
U of Phoenix–Metro Detroit Campus (MI)
U of Phoenix–Nevada Campus (NV)
U of Phoenix–New Mexico Campus (NM)
U of Phoenix–Northern California Campus (CA)
U of Phoenix–Ohio Campus (OH)
U of Phoenix–Oklahoma City Campus (OK)
U of Phoenix–Oregon Campus (OR)
U of Phoenix–Orlando Campus (FL)
U of Phoenix–Philadelphia Campus (PA)
U of Phoenix–Phoenix Campus (AZ)
U of Phoenix–Pittsburgh Campus (PA)
U of Phoenix–Puerto Rico Campus (PR)
U of Phoenix–Sacramento Campus (CA)
U of Phoenix–Saint Louis Campus (MO)
U of Phoenix–San Diego Campus (CA)
U of Phoenix–Southern Arizona Campus (AZ)
U of Phoenix–Southern California Campus (CA)
U of Phoenix–Southern Colorado Campus (CO)
U of Phoenix–Tampa Campus (FL)
U of Phoenix–Tulsa Campus (OK)
U of Phoenix–Utah Campus (UT)
U of Phoenix–West Michigan Campus (MI)
U of Phoenix-Wisconsin Campus (WI)
U of Pittsburgh at Bradford (PA)
U of Pittsburgh at Greensburg (PA)
U of Pittsburgh at Johnstown (PA)
U of Portland (OR)
U of Prince Edward Island (PE, Canada)
U of Puerto Rico, Humacao U Coll (PR)
U of Puerto Rico at Ponce (PR)
U of Puerto Rico, Cayey U Coll (PR)
U of Redlands (CA)
U of Regina (SK, Canada)
U of Rhode Island (RI)
U of Richmond (VA)
U of Rio Grande (OH)
U of St. Francis (IL)
U of Saint Francis (IN)
U of St. Thomas (MN)
U of St. Thomas (TX)
U of San Diego (CA)
U of San Francisco (CA)
U of Science and Arts of Oklahoma (OK)
The U of Scranton (PA)
U of Sioux Falls (SD)
U of South Alabama (AL)
U of South Carolina (SC)
U of South Carolina Aiken (SC)
U of South Carolina Spartanburg (SC)
U of South Dakota (SD)
U of Southern California (CA)
U of Southern Colorado (CO)
U of Southern Indiana (IN)
U of Southern Maine (ME)
U of Southern Mississippi (MS)
U of South Florida (FL)
The U of Tampa (FL)
The U of Tennessee (TN)
The U of Tennessee at Chattanooga (TN)
The U of Tennessee at Martin (TN)
The U of Texas at Arlington (TX)
The U of Texas at Austin (TX)
The U of Texas at Brownsville (TX)
The U of Texas at El Paso (TX)
The U of Texas at San Antonio (TX)
The U of Texas at Tyler (TX)
The U of Texas of the Permian Basin (TX)
The U of Texas–Pan American (TX)
U of the District of Columbia (DC)
U of the Incarnate Word (TX)
U of the Ozarks (AR)
U of the Pacific (CA)
U of the Virgin Islands (VI)
U of Toledo (OH)
U of Toronto (ON, Canada)
U of Tulsa (OK)
U of Utah (UT)
U of Vermont (VT)
The U of Virginia's Coll at Wise (VA)
U of Washington (WA)
U of Waterloo (ON, Canada)
The U of West Alabama (AL)
The U of Western Ontario (ON, Canada)
U of West Florida (FL)
U of Windsor (ON, Canada)
U of Wisconsin–Eau Claire (WI)
U of Wisconsin–Green Bay (WI)
U of Wisconsin–La Crosse (WI)
U of Wisconsin–Madison (WI)
U of Wisconsin–Milwaukee (WI)
U of Wisconsin–Oshkosh (WI)
U of Wisconsin–Parkside (WI)
U of Wisconsin–Platteville (WI)
U of Wisconsin–River Falls (WI)
U of Wisconsin–Stevens Point (WI)
U of Wisconsin–Stout (WI)
U of Wisconsin–Superior (WI)
U of Wisconsin–Whitewater (WI)
U of Wyoming (WY)
U System Coll for Lifelong Learning (NH)
Upper Iowa U (IA)
Urbana U (OH)
Ursinus Coll (PA)
Ursuline Coll (OH)
Utah State U (UT)
Utica Coll of Syracuse U (NY)
Valdosta State U (GA)
Valley City State U (ND)
Valparaiso U (IN)
Vanguard U of Southern California (CA)
Villa Julie Coll (MD)
Villanova U (PA)
Virginia Coll at Birmingham (AL)
Virginia Commonwealth U (VA)
Virginia Intermont Coll (VA)
Virginia Polytechnic Inst and State U (VA)
Virginia State U (VA)
Virginia Union U (VA)
Virginia Wesleyan Coll (VA)
Viterbo U (WI)
Voorhees Coll (SC)
Wagner Coll (NY)
Waldorf Coll (IA)
Walla Walla Coll (WA)
Walsh Coll of Accountancy and Business Admin (MI)
Walsh U (OH)
Warner Pacific Coll (OR)
Warner Southern Coll (FL)
Warren Wilson Coll (NC)
Wartburg Coll (IA)
Washburn U of Topeka (KS)
Washington & Jefferson Coll (PA)
Washington and Lee U (VA)
Washington Coll (MD)
Washington State U (WA)
Washington U in St. Louis (MO)
Wayland Baptist U (TX)
Waynesburg Coll (PA)
Wayne State Coll (NE)
Wayne State U (MI)
Webber International U (FL)
Weber State U (UT)
Webster U (MO)
Wells Coll (NY)
Wentworth Inst of Technology (MA)
Wesleyan Coll (GA)
Wesley Coll (DE)
West Chester U of Pennsylvania (PA)
Western Baptist Coll (OR)
Western Carolina U (NC)
Western Connecticut State U (CT)
Western International U (AZ)
Western Kentucky U (KY)
Western Maryland Coll (MD)
Western Michigan U (MI)
Western New England Coll (MA)
Western State Coll of Colorado (CO)
Western Washington U (WA)
Westfield State Coll (MA)
West Liberty State Coll (WV)
Westminster Coll (MO)
Westminster Coll (PA)
Westminster Coll (UT)
West Texas A&M U (TX)
West Virginia State Coll (WV)
West Virginia U (WV)
West Virginia U Inst of Technology (WV)
West Virginia Wesleyan Coll (WV)
Wheeling Jesuit U (WV)
Whittier Coll (CA)
Whitworth Coll (WA)
Wichita State U (KS)
Widener U (PA)
Wilberforce U (OH)
Wiley Coll (TX)
Wilfrid Laurier U (ON, Canada)
Wilkes U (PA)
William Carey Coll (MS)
William Jewell Coll (MO)
William Paterson U of New Jersey (NJ)
William Penn U (IA)
Williams Baptist Coll (AR)

BUSINESS QUANTITATIVE METHODS/MANAGEMENT SCIENCE RELATED

BUSINESS SERVICES MARKETING

BUSINESS STATISTICS

BUSINESS SYSTEMS ANALYSIS/DESIGN

BUSINESS SYSTEMS NETWORKING/ TELECOMMUNICATIONS

BUYING OPERATIONS

CANADIAN STUDIES

CARDIOVASCULAR TECHNOLOGY

CARPENTRY

CARTOGRAPHY

CELL AND MOLECULAR BIOLOGY RELATED

CELL BIOLOGY

CERAMIC ARTS

CERAMIC SCIENCES/ ENGINEERING

CHEMICAL AND ATOMIC/ MOLECULAR PHYSICS

CHEMICAL ENGINEERING

CHEMICAL ENGINEERING TECHNOLOGY

CHEMICAL TECHNOLOGY

CHEMISTRY

Newman U (KS)
New Mexico Highlands U (NM)
New Mexico Inst of Mining and Technology (NM)
New Mexico State U (NM)
New York Inst of Technology (NY)
New York U (NY)
Niagara U (NY)
Nicholls State U (LA)
Norfolk State U (VA)
North Carolina Ag and Tech State U (NC)
North Carolina Central U (NC)
North Carolina State U (NC)
North Carolina Wesleyan Coll (NC)
North Central Coll (IL)
North Dakota State U (ND)
Northeastern Illinois U (IL)
Northeastern State U (OK)
Northeastern U (MA)
Northern Arizona U (AZ)
Northern Illinois U (IL)
Northern Kentucky U (KY)
Northern Michigan U (MI)
Northern State U (SD)
North Georgia Coll & State U (GA)
Northland Coll (WI)
North Park U (IL)
Northwestern Coll (IA)
Northwestern Oklahoma State U (OK)
Northwestern State U of Louisiana (LA)
Northwestern U (IL)
Northwest Missouri State U (MO)
Northwest Nazarene U (ID)
Norwich U (VT)
Notre Dame Coll (OH)
Oakland City U (IN)
Oakland U (MI)
Oakwood Coll (AL)
Oberlin Coll (OH)
Occidental Coll (CA)
Oglethorpe U (GA)
Ohio Dominican Coll (OH)
Ohio Northern U (OH)
The Ohio State U (OH)
Ohio U (OH)
Ohio Wesleyan U (OH)
Okanagan U Coll (BC, Canada)
Oklahoma Baptist U (OK)
Oklahoma Christian U of Science and Arts (OK)
Oklahoma City U (OK)
Oklahoma Panhandle State U (OK)
Oklahoma State U (OK)
Oklahoma Wesleyan U (OK)
Old Dominion U (VA)
Olivet Coll (MI)
Olivet Nazarene U (IL)
Oral Roberts U (OK)
Oregon State U (OR)
Otterbein Coll (OH)
Ouachita Baptist U (AR)
Our Lady of the Lake U of San Antonio (TX)
Pace U (NY)
Pacific Lutheran U (WA)
Pacific Union Coll (CA)
Pacific U (OR)
Paine Coll (GA)
Park U (MO)
Penn State U at Erie, The Behrend Coll (PA)
Penn State U Univ Park Campus (PA)
Pepperdine U, Malibu (CA)
Peru State Coll (NE)
Pfeiffer U (NC)
Philadelphia U (PA)
Philander Smith Coll (AR)
Piedmont Coll (GA)
Pikeville Coll (KY)
Pittsburg State U (KS)
Pitzer Coll (CA)
Plattsburgh State U of NY (NY)
Plymouth State Coll (NH)
Point Loma Nazarene U (CA)
Polytechnic U, Brooklyn Campus (NY)
Pomona Coll (CA)
Pontifical Catholic U of Puerto Rico (PR)
Portland State U (OR)
Prairie View A&M U (TX)
Presbyterian Coll (SC)
Princeton U (NJ)
Principia Coll (IL)
Providence Coll (RI)
Purchase Coll, State U of NY (NY)
Purdue U (IN)
Purdue U Calumet (IN)
Queens Coll of the City U of NY (NY)
Queen's U at Kingston (ON, Canada)
Quincy U (IL)
Quinnipiac U (CT)
Radford U (VA)
Ramapo Coll of New Jersey (NJ)
Randolph-Macon Coll (VA)
Randolph-Macon Woman's Coll (VA)
Reed Coll (OR)
Regis Coll (MA)
Regis U (CO)
Rensselaer Polytechnic Inst (NY)
Rhode Island Coll (RI)
Rhodes Coll (TN)
Rice U (TX)
The Richard Stockton Coll of New Jersey (NJ)
Rider U (NJ)
Ripon Coll (WI)
Rivier Coll (NH)
Roanoke Coll (VA)
Roberts Wesleyan Coll (NY)
Rochester Inst of Technology (NY)
Rockford Coll (IL)
Rockhurst U (MO)
Rocky Mountain Coll (MT)
Roger Williams U (RI)
Rollins Coll (FL)
Roosevelt U (IL)
Rose-Hulman Inst of Technology (IN)
Rosemont Coll (PA)
Rowan U (NJ)
Russell Sage Coll (NY)
Rust Coll (MS)
Rutgers, The State U of New Jersey, New Brunswick (NJ)
Sacred Heart U (CT)
Saginaw Valley State U (MI)
St. Ambrose U (IA)
St. Andrews Presbyterian Coll (NC)
Saint Augustine's Coll (NC)
St. Bonaventure U (NY)
St. Cloud State U (MN)
St. Edward's U (TX)
Saint Francis U (PA)
St. Francis Xavier U (NS, Canada)
St. John Fisher Coll (NY)
Saint John's U (MN)
St. John's U (NY)
Saint Joseph Coll (CT)
Saint Joseph's Coll (IN)
Saint Joseph's Coll (ME)
St. Joseph's Coll, New York (NY)
Saint Joseph's U (PA)
St. Lawrence U (NY)
Saint Louis U (MO)
Saint Martin's Coll (WA)
Saint Mary Coll (KS)
Saint Mary's Coll (IN)
Saint Mary's Coll of Ave Maria U (MI)
Saint Mary's Coll of California (CA)
St. Mary's Coll of Maryland (MD)
Saint Mary's U (NS, Canada)
Saint Mary's U of Minnesota (MN)
St. Mary's U of San Antonio (TX)
Saint Michael's Coll (VT)
St. Norbert Coll (WI)
St. Olaf Coll (MN)
Saint Peter's Coll (NJ)
St. Thomas U (FL)
Saint Vincent Coll (PA)
Saint Xavier U (IL)
Salem Coll (NC)
Salem State Coll (MA)
Salisbury U (MD)
Salve Regina U (RI)
Samford U (AL)
Sam Houston State U (TX)
San Diego State U (CA)
San Francisco State U (CA)
San Jose State U (CA)
Santa Clara U (CA)
Sarah Lawrence Coll (NY)
Savannah State U (GA)
Schreiner U (TX)
Scripps Coll (CA)
Seattle Pacific U (WA)
Seattle U (WA)
Seton Hall U (NJ)
Seton Hill Coll (PA)
Shawnee State U (OH)
Shaw U (NC)
Shenandoah U (VA)
Shepherd Coll (WV)
Shippensburg U of Pennsylvania (PA)
Shorter Coll (GA)
Siena Coll (NY)
Siena Heights U (MI)
Simmons Coll (MA)
Simon Fraser U (BC, Canada)
Simon's Rock Coll of Bard (MA)
Simpson Coll (IA)
Skidmore Coll (NY)
Slippery Rock U of Pennsylvania (PA)
Smith Coll (MA)
Sonoma State U (CA)
South Carolina State U (SC)
South Dakota School of Mines and Technology (SD)
South Dakota State U (SD)
Southeastern Louisiana U (LA)
Southeastern Oklahoma State U (OK)
Southeast Missouri State U (MO)
Southern Adventist U (TN)
Southern Arkansas U–Magnolia (AR)
Southern Connecticut State U (CT)
Southern Illinois U Carbondale (IL)
Southern Illinois U Edwardsville (IL)
Southern Methodist U (TX)
Southern Nazarene U (OK)
Southern Oregon U (OR)
Southern U and A&M Coll (LA)
Southern Utah U (UT)
Southern Wesleyan U (SC)
Southwest Baptist U (MO)
Southwestern Adventist U (TX)
Southwestern Coll (KS)
Southwestern Oklahoma State U (OK)
Southwestern U (TX)
Southwest Missouri State U (MO)
Southwest State U (MN)
Southwest Texas State U (TX)
Spelman Coll (GA)
Spring Arbor U (MI)
Springfield Coll (MA)
Spring Hill Coll (AL)
Stanford U (CA)
State U of NY at Albany (NY)
State U of NY at Binghamton (NY)
State U of NY at New Paltz (NY)
State U of NY at Oswego (NY)
State U of NY Coll at Brockport (NY)
State U of NY Coll at Buffalo (NY)
State U of NY Coll at Cortland (NY)
State U of NY Coll at Fredonia (NY)
State U of NY Coll at Geneseo (NY)
State U of NY Coll at Old Westbury (NY)
State U of NY Coll at Oneonta (NY)
State U of NY Coll at Potsdam (NY)
State U of NY Coll of Environ Sci and Forestry (NY)
State U of West Georgia (GA)
Stephen F. Austin State U (TX)
Stetson U (FL)
Stevens Inst of Technology (NJ)
Stonehill Coll (MA)
State U of NY at Stony Brook (NY)
Suffolk U (MA)
Sul Ross State U (TX)
Susquehanna U (PA)
Swarthmore Coll (PA)
Sweet Briar Coll (VA)
Syracuse U (NY)
Tabor Coll (KS)
Talladega Coll (AL)
Tarleton State U (TX)
Taylor U (IN)
Temple U (PA)
Tennessee State U (TN)
Tennessee Technological U (TN)
Tennessee Wesleyan Coll (TN)
Texas A&M International U (TX)
Texas A&M U (TX)
Texas A&M U–Commerce (TX)
Texas A&M U–Corpus Christi (TX)
Texas A&M U–Kingsville (TX)
Texas Christian U (TX)
Texas Lutheran U (TX)
Texas Southern U (TX)
Texas Tech U (TX)
Texas Wesleyan U (TX)
Texas Woman's U (TX)
Thiel Coll (PA)
Thomas Edison State Coll (NJ)
Thomas More Coll (KY)
Tougaloo Coll (MS)
Touro Coll (NY)
Towson U (MD)
Transylvania U (KY)
Trent U (ON, Canada)
Trevecca Nazarene U (TN)
Trinity Christian Coll (IL)
Trinity Coll (CT)
Trinity Coll (DC)
Trinity International U (IL)
Trinity U (TX)
Trinity Western U (BC, Canada)
Tri-State U (IN)
Troy State U (AL)
Truman State U (MO)
Tufts U (MA)
Tulane U (LA)
Tuskegee U (AL)
Union Coll (KY)
Union Coll (NE)
Union Coll (NY)
Union U (TN)
United States Air Force Academy (CO)
United States Military Academy (NY)
United States Naval Academy (MD)
Universidad Adventista de las Antillas (PR)
Université de Montréal (QC, Canada)
Université de Sherbrooke (PQ, Canada)
Université Laval (QC, Canada)
State U of NY at Buffalo (NY)
U Coll of Cape Breton (NS, Canada)
U Coll of the Cariboo (BC, Canada)
U Coll of the Fraser Valley (BC, Canada)
The U of Akron (OH)
The U of Alabama (AL)
The U of Alabama at Birmingham (AL)
The U of Alabama in Huntsville (AL)
U of Alaska Anchorage (AK)
U of Alaska Fairbanks (AK)
U of Alberta (AB, Canada)
The U of Arizona (AZ)
U of Arkansas (AR)
U of Arkansas at Little Rock (AR)
U of Arkansas at Pine Bluff (AR)
The U of British Columbia (BC, Canada)
U of Calgary (AB, Canada)
U of Calif, Berkeley (CA)
U of Calif, Davis (CA)
U of Calif, Irvine (CA)
U of Calif, Los Angeles (CA)
U of Calif, Riverside (CA)
U of Calif, San Diego (CA)
U of Calif, Santa Barbara (CA)
U of Calif, Santa Cruz (CA)
U of Central Arkansas (AR)
U of Central Florida (FL)
U of Central Oklahoma (OK)
U of Charleston (WV)
U of Chicago (IL)
U of Cincinnati (OH)
U of Colorado at Boulder (CO)
U of Colorado at Colorado Springs (CO)
U of Colorado at Denver (CO)
U of Connecticut (CT)
U of Dallas (TX)
U of Dayton (OH)
U of Delaware (DE)
U of Denver (CO)
U of Evansville (IN)
U of Florida (FL)
U of Georgia (GA)
U of Guelph (ON, Canada)
U of Hartford (CT)
U of Hawaii at Hilo (HI)
U of Hawaii at Manoa (HI)
U of Houston (TX)
U of Houston–Clear Lake (TX)
U of Idaho (ID)
U of Illinois at Chicago (IL)
U of Illinois at Springfield (IL)
U of Illinois at Urbana–Champaign (IL)
U of Indianapolis (IN)
The U of Iowa (IA)
U of Kansas (KS)
U of Kentucky (KY)
U of King's Coll (NS, Canada)
U of La Verne (CA)
The U of Lethbridge (AB, Canada)
U of Louisiana at Lafayette (LA)
U of Louisiana at Monroe (LA)
U of Louisville (KY)
U of Maine (ME)
U of Maine at Farmington (ME)
U of Manitoba (MB, Canada)
U of Mary Hardin-Baylor (TX)
U of Maryland, Baltimore County (MD)
U of Maryland, Coll Park (MD)
U of Maryland Eastern Shore (MD)
U of Massachusetts Amherst (MA)
U of Massachusetts Boston (MA)
U of Massachusetts Dartmouth (MA)
U of Massachusetts Lowell (MA)
The U of Memphis (TN)
U of Miami (FL)
U of Michigan (MI)
U of Michigan–Dearborn (MI)
U of Michigan–Flint (MI)
U of Minnesota, Duluth (MN)
U of Minnesota, Morris (MN)
U of Minnesota, Twin Cities Campus (MN)
U of Mississippi (MS)
U of Missouri–Columbia (MO)
U of Missouri–Kansas City (MO)
U of Missouri–Rolla (MO)
U of Missouri–St. Louis (MO)
U of Mobile (AL)
The U of Montana–Missoula (MT)
Western Montana Coll of The U of Montana (MT)
U of Montevallo (AL)
U of Nebraska at Kearney (NE)
U of Nebraska at Omaha (NE)
U of Nebraska–Lincoln (NE)
U of Nevada, Las Vegas (NV)
U of Nevada, Reno (NV)
U of New Hampshire (NH)
U of New Haven (CT)
U of New Mexico (NM)
U of New Orleans (LA)
U of North Alabama (AL)
The U of North Carolina at Asheville (NC)
The U of North Carolina at Chapel Hill (NC)
The U of North Carolina at Charlotte (NC)
The U of North Carolina at Greensboro (NC)
The U of North Carolina at Pembroke (NC)
The U of North Carolina at Wilmington (NC)
U of North Dakota (ND)
U of Northern Colorado (CO)
U of Northern Iowa (IA)
U of North Florida (FL)
U of North Texas (TX)
U of Notre Dame (IN)
U of Oklahoma (OK)
U of Oregon (OR)
U of Ottawa (ON, Canada)
U of Pennsylvania (PA)
U of Pittsburgh (PA)
U of Pittsburgh at Bradford (PA)
U of Pittsburgh at Johnstown (PA)
U of Portland (OR)
U of Prince Edward Island (PE, Canada)
U of Puerto Rico, Humacao U Coll (PR)
U of Puerto Rico, Cayey U Coll (PR)
U of Puget Sound (WA)
U of Redlands (CA)
U of Regina (SK, Canada)
U of Rhode Island (RI)
U of Richmond (VA)
U of Rio Grande (OH)
U of Rochester (NY)
U of Saint Francis (IN)
U of St. Thomas (MN)
U of St. Thomas (TX)
U of San Diego (CA)
U of San Francisco (CA)
U of Saskatchewan (SK, Canada)
U of Science and Arts of Oklahoma (OK)

CHEMISTRY EDUCATION

CHEMISTRY RELATED

CHILD CARE/DEVELOPMENT

CHILD CARE/GUIDANCE

CHILD CARE SERVICES MANAGEMENT

CHILD GUIDANCE

CHINESE

CITY/COMMUNITY/REGIONAL PLANNING

CIVIL ENGINEERING

CIVIL ENGINEERING RELATED

CIVIL ENGINEERING TECHNOLOGY

CLASSICAL AND ANCIENT NEAR EASTERN LANGUAGES RELATED

CLASSICS

CLINICAL PSYCHOLOGY

CLOTHING/APPAREL/TEXTILE

CLOTHING/APPAREL/TEXTILE STUDIES

CLOTHING/TEXTILES

COGNITIVE PSYCHOLOGY/ PSYCHOLINGUISTICS

COLLEGE/POSTSECONDARY STUDENT COUNSELING

COMMERCIAL PHOTOGRAPHY

COMMUNICATION DISORDERS

COMMUNICATION DISORDERS SCIENCES/SERVICES RELATED

COMMUNICATION EQUIPMENT TECHNOLOGY

COMMUNICATIONS

COMMUNICATIONS RELATED

COMMUNICATIONS TECHNOLOGIES RELATED

COMMUNITY HEALTH LIAISON

COMMUNITY PSYCHOLOGY

COMMUNITY SERVICES

COMPARATIVE LITERATURE

COMPUTER EDUCATION

COMPUTER ENGINEERING

COMPUTER ENGINEERING RELATED

COMPUTER ENGINEERING TECHNOLOGY

COMPUTER GRAPHICS

COMPUTER HARDWARE ENGINEERING

COMPUTER/INFORMATION SCIENCES

COMPUTER/INFORMATION SCIENCES RELATED

COMPUTER/INFORMATION SYSTEMS SECURITY

COMPUTER/INFORMATION TECHNOLOGY SERVICES ADMINISTRATION AND MANAGEMENT RELATED

COMPUTER MAINTENANCE TECHNOLOGY

COMPUTER MANAGEMENT

COMPUTER PROGRAMMING

COMPUTER PROGRAMMING RELATED

COMPUTER SCIENCE

Northeastern U (MA)
Northern Illinois U (IL)
Northern Kentucky U (KY)
Northern Michigan U (MI)
North Georgia Coll & State U (GA)
Northwestern Coll (IA)
Northwestern Oklahoma State U (OK)
Northwestern Polytechnic U (CA)
Northwestern U (IL)
Northwest Missouri State U (MO)
Northwest Nazarene U (ID)
Norwich U (VT)
Notre Dame de Namur U (CA)
Nova Southeastern U (FL)
Nyack Coll (NY)
Oakwood Coll (AL)
Oberlin Coll (OH)
Oglethorpe U (GA)
Ohio Dominican Coll (OH)
Ohio Northern U (OH)
The Ohio State U (OH)
Ohio U (OH)
Ohio Wesleyan U (OH)
Oklahoma Baptist U (OK)
Oklahoma Christian U of Science and Arts (OK)
Oklahoma City U (OK)
Oklahoma State U (OK)
Olivet Coll (MI)
Olivet Nazarene U (IL)
Oral Roberts U (OK)
Oregon State U (OR)
Otterbein Coll (OH)
Ouachita Baptist U (AR)
Pacific Lutheran U (WA)
Pacific States U (CA)
Pacific Union Coll (CA)
Pacific U (OR)
Park U (MO)
Pepperdine U, Malibu (CA)
Peru State Coll (NE)
Philadelphia U (PA)
Philander Smith Coll (AR)
Piedmont Coll (GA)
Pikeville Coll (KY)
Pittsburg State U (KS)
Plattsburgh State U of NY (NY)
Plymouth State Coll (NH)
Point Loma Nazarene U (CA)
Point Park Coll (PA)
Polytechnic U, Brooklyn Campus (NY)
Pomona Coll (CA)
Pontifical Catholic U of Puerto Rico (PR)
Portland State U (OR)
Prairie View A&M U (TX)
Presbyterian Coll (SC)
Providence Coll (RI)
Purdue U Calumet (IN)
Queens Coll of the City U of NY (NY)
Queen's U at Kingston (ON, Canada)
Quincy U (IL)
Quinnipiac U (CT)
Radford U (VA)
Randolph-Macon Coll (VA)
Redeemer U Coll (ON, Canada)
Regis U (CO)
Rensselaer Polytechnic Inst (NY)
Rhode Island Coll (RI)
Rhodes Coll (TN)
The Richard Stockton Coll of New Jersey (NJ)
Richmond, The American International U in London(United Kingdom)
Rider U (NJ)
Ripon Coll (WI)
Rivier Coll (NH)
Roanoke Coll (VA)
Roberts Wesleyan Coll (NY)
Rochester Inst of Technology (NY)
Rockford Coll (IL)
Rockhurst U (MO)
Rocky Mountain Coll (MT)
Roger Williams U (RI)
Rollins Coll (FL)
Roosevelt U (IL)
Rose-Hulman Inst of Technology (IN)
Rowan U (NJ)
Russell Sage Coll (NY)
Rust Coll (MS)
Rutgers, The State U of New Jersey, New Brunswick (NJ)
Sacred Heart U (CT)
St. Ambrose U (IA)
Saint Anselm Coll (NH)
Saint Augustine's Coll (NC)
St. Bonaventure U (NY)
St. Cloud State U (MN)
St. Edward's U (TX)
Saint Francis U (PA)
St. John Fisher Coll (NY)
Saint John's U (MN)
Saint Joseph Coll (CT)
Saint Joseph's Coll (IN)
St. Joseph's Coll, Suffolk Campus (NY)
Saint Joseph's U (PA)
St. Lawrence U (NY)
Saint Martin's Coll (WA)
St. Mary's Coll of Maryland (MD)
Saint Mary's U (NS, Canada)
Saint Mary's U of Minnesota (MN)
St. Mary's U of San Antonio (TX)
Saint Michael's Coll (VT)
St. Thomas U (FL)
Saint Xavier U (IL)
Salem International U (WV)
Salem State Coll (MA)
Samford U (AL)
San Francisco State U (CA)
San Jose State U (CA)
Santa Clara U (CA)
Sarah Lawrence Coll (NY)
Scripps Coll (CA)
Seattle Pacific U (WA)
Seattle U (WA)
Seton Hill Coll (PA)
Shaw U (NC)
Siena Coll (NY)
Simmons Coll (MA)
Simon Fraser U (BC, Canada)
Simon's Rock Coll of Bard (MA)
Simpson Coll (IA)
Slippery Rock U of Pennsylvania (PA)
Smith Coll (MA)
Sonoma State U (CA)
South Carolina State U (SC)
South Dakota School of Mines and Technology (SD)
Southeastern Louisiana U (LA)
Southeastern U (DC)
Southern Adventist U (TN)
Southern Connecticut State U (CT)
Southern Methodist U (TX)
Southern Nazarene U (OK)
Southern Oregon U (OR)
Southern U and A&M Coll (LA)
Southern Utah U (UT)
Southwest Baptist U (MO)
Southwestern Adventist U (TX)
Southwestern Oklahoma State U (OK)
Southwestern U (TX)
Southwest Missouri State U (MO)
Southwest State U (MN)
Spelman Coll (GA)
Spring Arbor U (MI)
Springfield Coll (MA)
Stanford U (CA)
State U of NY at Albany (NY)
State U of NY at Binghamton (NY)
State U of NY at New Paltz (NY)
State U of NY at Oswego (NY)
State U of NY Coll at Brockport (NY)
State U of NY Coll at Fredonia (NY)
State U of NY Coll at Geneseo (NY)
State U of NY Coll at Oneonta (NY)
State U of NY Inst of Tech at Utica/Rome (NY)
State U of West Georgia (GA)
Stetson U (FL)
Stevens Inst of Technology (NJ)
Stonehill Coll (MA)
State U of NY at Stony Brook (NY)
Suffolk U (MA)
Sullivan U (KY)
Susquehanna U (PA)
Sweet Briar Coll (VA)
Syracuse U (NY)
Tabor Coll (KS)
Talladega Coll (AL)
Taylor U (IN)
Taylor U, Fort Wayne Campus (IN)
Temple U (PA)
Tennessee State U (TN)
Tennessee Technological U (TN)
Texas A&M U–Commerce (TX)
Texas A&M U–Corpus Christi (TX)
Texas A&M U–Kingsville (TX)
Texas Christian U (TX)
Texas Coll (TX)
Texas Lutheran U (TX)
Texas Southern U (TX)
Thiel Coll (PA)
Thomas Coll (ME)
Thomas Edison State Coll (NJ)
Tougaloo Coll (MS)
Touro Coll (NY)
Transylvania U (KY)
Trent U (ON, Canada)
Trinity Christian Coll (IL)
Trinity Coll (CT)
Trinity International U (IL)
Trinity Western U (BC, Canada)
Tri-State U (IN)
Truman State U (MO)
Tufts U (MA)
Tulane U (LA)
Tusculum Coll (TN)
Tuskegee U (AL)
Union Coll (NE)
Union U (TN)
United States Air Force Academy (CO)
United States Military Academy (NY)
United States Naval Academy (MD)
Universidad Adventista de las Antillas (PR)
Université de Montréal (QC, Canada)
Université de Sherbrooke (PQ, Canada)
Université Laval (QC, Canada)
State U of NY at Buffalo (NY)
U Coll of Cape Breton (NS, Canada)
U Coll of the Cariboo (BC, Canada)
The U of Akron (OH)
U of Alaska Anchorage (AK)
U of Alaska Fairbanks (AK)
U of Alberta (AB, Canada)
U of Arkansas at Little Rock (AR)
U of Arkansas at Pine Bluff (AR)
U of Bridgeport (CT)
The U of British Columbia (BC, Canada)
U of Calgary (AB, Canada)
U of Calif, Irvine (CA)
U of Calif, Los Angeles (CA)
U of Calif, Riverside (CA)
U of Calif, San Diego (CA)
U of Calif, Santa Barbara (CA)
U of Calif, Santa Cruz (CA)
U of Central Oklahoma (OK)
U of Chicago (IL)
U of Cincinnati (OH)
U of Colorado at Boulder (CO)
U of Colorado at Colorado Springs (CO)
U of Colorado at Denver (CO)
U of Connecticut (CT)
U of Dallas (TX)
U of Dayton (OH)
U of Delaware (DE)
U of Dubuque (IA)
U of Evansville (IN)
The U of Findlay (OH)
U of Guelph (ON, Canada)
U of Hawaii at Hilo (HI)
U of Houston–Clear Lake (TX)
U of Houston–Victoria (TX)
U of Idaho (ID)
U of Illinois at Springfield (IL)
U of Indianapolis (IN)
The U of Iowa (IA)
U of King's Coll (NS, Canada)
U of La Verne (CA)
The U of Lethbridge (AB, Canada)
U of Louisiana at Lafayette (LA)
U of Louisiana at Monroe (LA)
U of Maine (ME)
U of Maine at Farmington (ME)
U of Maine at Fort Kent (ME)
U of Manitoba (MB, Canada)
U of Mary Hardin-Baylor (TX)
U of Maryland, Baltimore County (MD)
U of Maryland, Coll Park (MD)
U of Maryland Eastern Shore (MD)
U of Maryland University Coll (MD)
U of Massachusetts Amherst (MA)
U of Massachusetts Boston (MA)
U of Massachusetts Lowell (MA)
The U of Memphis (TN)
U of Miami (FL)
U of Michigan (MI)
U of Michigan–Dearborn (MI)
U of Michigan–Flint (MI)
U of Minnesota, Duluth (MN)
U of Minnesota, Morris (MN)
U of Minnesota, Twin Cities Campus (MN)
U of Missouri–Columbia (MO)
U of Missouri–Kansas City (MO)
U of Missouri–Rolla (MO)
U of Missouri–St. Louis (MO)
U of Mobile (AL)
The U of Montana–Missoula (MT)
U of Nebraska at Omaha (NE)
U of Nebraska–Lincoln (NE)
U of Nevada, Las Vegas (NV)
U of Nevada, Reno (NV)
U of New Hampshire (NH)
U of New Mexico (NM)
U of New Orleans (LA)
The U of North Carolina at Asheville (NC)
The U of North Carolina at Charlotte (NC)
The U of North Carolina at Pembroke (NC)
U of Northern Iowa (IA)
U of Oklahoma (OK)
U of Oregon (OR)
U of Ottawa (ON, Canada)
U of Pittsburgh (PA)
U of Pittsburgh at Bradford (PA)
U of Pittsburgh at Johnstown (PA)
U of Portland (OR)
U of Prince Edward Island (PE, Canada)
U of Puerto Rico at Ponce (PR)
U of Puget Sound (WA)
U of Redlands (CA)
U of Regina (SK, Canada)
U of Richmond (VA)
U of Rio Grande (OH)
U of Rochester (NY)
U of St. Francis (IL)
U of San Diego (CA)
U of San Francisco (CA)
U of Saskatchewan (SK, Canada)
U of Science and Arts of Oklahoma (OK)
The U of Scranton (PA)
U of Sioux Falls (SD)
U of South Dakota (SD)
U of Southern California (CA)
U of Southern Colorado (CO)
U of Southern Maine (ME)
The U of Tennessee (TN)
The U of Tennessee at Chattanooga (TN)
The U of Tennessee at Martin (TN)
The U of Texas at Dallas (TX)
The U of Texas at El Paso (TX)
The U of Texas at Tyler (TX)
The U of Texas of the Permian Basin (TX)
The U of Texas–Pan American (TX)
U of the District of Columbia (DC)
U of the Pacific (CA)
U of the Sciences in Philadelphia (PA)
U of the South (TN)
U of Toledo (OH)
U of Toronto (ON, Canada)
U of Tulsa (OK)
U of Utah (UT)
U of Vermont (VT)
U of Victoria (BC, Canada)
U of Washington (WA)
U of Waterloo (ON, Canada)
The U of Western Ontario (ON, Canada)
U of Windsor (ON, Canada)
U of Wisconsin–Green Bay (WI)
U of Wisconsin–La Crosse (WI)
U of Wisconsin–Madison (WI)
U of Wisconsin–Milwaukee (WI)
U of Wisconsin–Oshkosh (WI)
U of Wisconsin–Parkside (WI)
U of Wisconsin–Platteville (WI)
U of Wisconsin–River Falls (WI)
U of Wisconsin–Superior (WI)
U of Wisconsin–Whitewater (WI)
Ursinus Coll (PA)
Valdosta State U (GA)
Valparaiso U (IN)
Vanderbilt U (TN)
Vassar Coll (NY)
Villanova U (PA)
Virginia Military Inst (VA)
Virginia Polytechnic Inst and State U (VA)
Virginia State U (VA)
Virginia Wesleyan Coll (VA)
Voorhees Coll (SC)
Wagner Coll (NY)
Walla Walla Coll (WA)
Walsh U (OH)
Wartburg Coll (IA)
Washington and Lee U (VA)
Washington State U (WA)
Washington U in St. Louis (MO)
Waynesburg Coll (PA)
Wayne State Coll (NE)
Weber State U (UT)
Webster U (MO)
Wellesley Coll (MA)
Wells Coll (NY)
Wentworth Inst of Technology (MA)
Wesleyan U (CT)
West Chester U of Pennsylvania (PA)
Western Baptist Coll (OR)
Western Carolina U (NC)
Western Connecticut State U (CT)
Western Michigan U (MI)
Western New England Coll (MA)
Western Oregon U (OR)
Western State Coll of Colorado (CO)
Western Washington U (WA)
Westfield State Coll (MA)
Westminster Coll (MO)
Westminster Coll (PA)
Westminster Coll (UT)
Westmont Coll (CA)
West Virginia U (WV)
West Virginia U Inst of Technology (WV)
West Virginia Wesleyan Coll (WV)
Wheaton Coll (IL)
Wheaton Coll (MA)
Wheeling Jesuit U (WV)
Whitworth Coll (WA)
Widener U (PA)
Wilberforce U (OH)
Wiley Coll (TX)
Wilfrid Laurier U (ON, Canada)
Willamette U (OR)
William Jewell Coll (MO)
William Paterson U of New Jersey (NJ)
William Penn U (IA)
Williams Coll (MA)
Wilmington Coll (OH)
Winona State U (MN)
Winston-Salem State U (NC)
Winthrop U (SC)
Wittenberg U (OH)
Wofford Coll (SC)
Worcester Polytechnic Inst (MA)
Worcester State Coll (MA)
Wright State U (OH)
Xavier U (OH)
Xavier U of Louisiana (LA)
Yeshiva U (NY)
York U (ON, Canada)
Youngstown State U (OH)

COMPUTER SCIENCE RELATED

Allegheny Coll (PA)
Holy Names Coll (CA)
Indiana State U (IN)
Kenyon Coll (OH)
McGill U (PQ, Canada)
Queen's U at Kingston (ON, Canada)

COMPUTER SOFTWARE AND MEDIA APPLICATIONS RELATED

Carroll Coll (WI)
Champlain Coll (VT)
Dakota Wesleyan U (SD)
Grand View Coll (IA)
New England School of Communications (ME)
U of Windsor (ON, Canada)

COMPUTER SOFTWARE ENGINEERING

Champlain Coll (VT)
Clarkson U (NY)
Fairfield U (CT)
Florida State U (FL)
Milwaukee School of Engineering (WI)
Mississippi State U (MS)
Notre Dame de Namur U (CA)

Queen's U at Kingston (ON, Canada)
Saint Louis U (MO)
U of Waterloo (ON, Canada)
The U of Western Ontario (ON, Canada)
York U (ON, Canada)

COMPUTER SYSTEMS ANALYSIS
Baker Coll of Flint (MI)
British Columbia Inst of Technology (BC, Canada)
Eastern Mennonite U (VA)
Kent State U (OH)
Miami U (OH)
Montana Tech of The U of Montana (MT)
Oklahoma Baptist U (OK)
Rockhurst U (MO)
Saginaw Valley State U (MI)
St. Ambrose U (IA)
U Coll of the Fraser Valley (BC, Canada)
U of Advancing Computer Technology (AZ)
U of Houston (TX)
U of Louisville (KY)
U of Miami (FL)

COMPUTER SYSTEMS NETWORKING/ TELECOMMUNICATIONS
Boise State U (ID)
Capella U (MN)
Chaparral Coll (AZ)
The Coll of Southeastern Europe, The American U of Athens(Greece)
Sage Coll of Albany (NY)
Strayer U (DC)
Westwood Coll of Technology–Denver North (CO)

COMPUTER TYPOGRAPHY/ COMPOSITION
Baltimore Hebrew U (MD)
David N. Myers U (OH)

CONSERVATION AND RENEWABLE NATURAL RESOURCES RELATED
Stephen F. Austin State U (TX)
U of Alaska Fairbanks (AK)
U of Louisiana at Lafayette (LA)
Utah State U (UT)

CONSTRUCTION/BUILDING INSPECTION
Tuskegee U (AL)

CONSTRUCTION ENGINEERING
American U in Cairo(Egypt)
Andrews U (MI)
Bradley U (IL)
The Catholic U of America (DC)
Concordia U (QC, Canada)
John Brown U (AR)
Lawrence Technological U (MI)
Michigan Technological U (MI)
North Carolina State U (NC)
North Dakota State U (ND)
Oregon State U (OR)
State U of NY Coll of Environ Sci and Forestry (NY)
State U of NY Coll of Technology at Alfred (NY)
Temple U (PA)
Texas A&M U–Commerce (TX)
U du Québec, École de technologie supérieure (PQ, Canada)
U of Alberta (AB, Canada)
U of Cincinnati (OH)
U of Nevada, Las Vegas (NV)
Western Michigan U (MI)

CONSTRUCTION MANAGEMENT
Andrews U (MI)
Boise State U (ID)
Brigham Young U (UT)
California State U, Long Beach (CA)
Ferris State U (MI)
Hampton U (VA)
John Brown U (AR)
Minnesota State U, Mankato (MN)
Mississippi State U (MS)
North Carolina Ag and Tech State U (NC)
North Dakota State U (ND)
Oklahoma State U (OK)
Oregon State U (OR)
Pittsburg State U (KS)
Pratt Inst (NY)
Roger Williams U (RI)
Sam Houston State U (TX)
State U of NY at Farmingdale (NY)
U of Cincinnati (OH)
U of Denver (CO)
U of Maryland Eastern Shore (MD)
U of Minnesota, Twin Cities Campus (MN)
U of the District of Columbia (DC)
U of Washington (WA)
U of Wisconsin–Madison (WI)
U of Wisconsin–Platteville (WI)
Utica Coll of Syracuse U (NY)
Wentworth Inst of Technology (MA)
Western Michigan U (MI)

CONSTRUCTION TECHNOLOGY
Andrews U (MI)
Arizona State U (AZ)
Bemidji State U (MN)
Bowling Green State U (OH)
California State Polytechnic U, Pomona (CA)
California State U, Fresno (CA)
California State U, Long Beach (CA)
California State U, Sacramento (CA)
Central Connecticut State U (CT)
Central Michigan U (MI)
Central Missouri State U (MO)
Colorado State U (CO)
Eastern Kentucky U (KY)
Eastern Washington U (WA)
Fairleigh Dickinson U, Teaneck-Hackensack Campus (NJ)
Fitchburg State Coll (MA)
Florida A&M U (FL)
Florida International U (FL)
Georgia Inst of Technology (GA)
Georgia Southern U (GA)
Grambling State U (LA)
Hampton U (VA)
Indiana U–Purdue U Fort Wayne (IN)
Minnesota State U Moorhead (MN)
Montana State U–Bozeman (MT)
Murray State U (KY)
Norfolk State U (VA)
Northern Arizona U (AZ)
Northern Michigan U (MI)
Oklahoma State U (OK)
Pittsburg State U (KS)
Purdue U Calumet (IN)
South Dakota State U (SD)
Southern Illinois U Carbondale (IL)
Southern Illinois U Edwardsville (IL)
Southern Polytechnic State U (GA)
Southern Utah U (UT)
Southwest Missouri State U (MO)
Southwest Texas State U (TX)
Texas A&M U (TX)
Texas Southern U (TX)
Thomas Edison State Coll (NJ)
Tuskegee U (AL)
U of Arkansas at Little Rock (AR)
U of Cincinnati (OH)
U of Florida (FL)
U of Houston (TX)
U of Louisiana at Monroe (LA)
U of Maine (ME)
U of Maryland Eastern Shore (MD)
U of Nebraska–Lincoln (NE)
U of New Mexico (NM)
U of North Florida (FL)
U of Oklahoma (OK)
U of Southern Colorado (CO)
U of Toledo (OH)
U of Wisconsin–Stout (WI)
Virginia Polytechnic Inst and State U (VA)
Washington State U (WA)
Wentworth Inst of Technology (MA)

CONSUMER ECONOMICS
Indiana U of Pennsylvania (PA)
Louisiana Tech U (LA)
Southeastern Louisiana U (LA)
Texas Woman's U (TX)
The U of Alabama (AL)
The U of Arizona (AZ)
U of Delaware (DE)
U of Georgia (GA)
U of Illinois at Urbana–Champaign (IL)
U of Rhode Island (RI)
The U of Tennessee (TN)

CONSUMER/HOMEMAKING EDUCATION
Virginia Polytechnic Inst and State U (VA)

CONSUMER SERVICES
Carson-Newman Coll (TN)
Coll of the Ozarks (MO)
Cornell U (NY)
Iowa State U of Science and Technology (IA)
Pacific Union Coll (CA)
South Dakota State U (SD)
State U of NY Coll at Oneonta (NY)
Syracuse U (NY)
Tennessee State U (TN)
Université Laval (QC, Canada)
The U of Memphis (TN)
U of Wisconsin–Madison (WI)

CORRECTIONS
Bluefield State Coll (WV)
California State U, Hayward (CA)
Chicago State U (IL)
Coll of the Ozarks (MO)
Eastern Kentucky U (KY)
Eastern Washington U (WA)
Hardin-Simmons U (TX)
Jacksonville State U (AL)
John Jay Coll of Criminal Justice, the City U of NY (NY)
Lake Superior State U (MI)
Lamar U (TX)
Mercyhurst Coll (PA)
Minnesota State U, Mankato (MN)
Murray State U (KY)
Northeastern U (MA)
Oklahoma City U (OK)
St. Cloud State U (MN)
Saint Louis U (MO)
Sam Houston State U (TX)
Southeast Missouri State U (MO)
Southwest Texas State U (TX)
State U of NY Coll at Brockport (NY)
Stephen F. Austin State U (TX)
Tiffin U (OH)
Troy State U (AL)
The U of Akron (OH)
U of Arkansas at Pine Bluff (AR)
U of Indianapolis (IN)
U of New Mexico (NM)
U of Pittsburgh (PA)
U of Southern Colorado (CO)
The U of Tennessee at Chattanooga (TN)
The U of Texas at Brownsville (TX)
The U of Texas at San Antonio (TX)
The U of Texas–Pan American (TX)
Washburn U of Topeka (KS)
Weber State U (UT)
Western Oregon U (OR)
Westfield State Coll (MA)
Winona State U (MN)
York Coll of Pennsylvania (PA)
Youngstown State U (OH)

COUNSELING PSYCHOLOGY
Atlanta Christian Coll (GA)
Central Baptist Coll (AR)
Crichton Coll (TN)
Grace Coll (IN)
Limestone Coll (SC)
Mid-Continent Coll (KY)
Minnesota Bible Coll (MN)
Morningside Coll (IA)
Northwestern U (IL)
Oregon Inst of Technology (OR)
Rochester Coll (MI)
Saint Xavier U (IL)
Samford U (AL)
Southwestern Coll (AZ)
Texas Wesleyan U (TX)
Toccoa Falls Coll (GA)
U of Great Falls (MT)
U of North Alabama (AL)
U of Phoenix–Phoenix Campus (AZ)

COUNSELOR EDUCATION/ GUIDANCE
Belmont U (TN)
Bowling Green State U (OH)
Brandon U (MB, Canada)
California State Polytechnic U, Pomona (CA)
Circleville Bible Coll (OH)
DePaul U (IL)
East Central U (OK)
The Evergreen State Coll (WA)
Franklin Pierce Coll (NH)
Houston Baptist U (TX)
Howard U (DC)
Lamar U (TX)
Marshall U (WV)
Memorial U of Newfoundland (NF, Canada)
Mesa State Coll (CO)
Northern Arizona U (AZ)
Northwest Missouri State U (MO)
Ohio U (OH)
Pittsburg State U (KS)
Purdue U Calumet (IN)
St. Cloud State U (MN)
Southern Christian U (AL)
Tarleton State U (TX)
Texas A&M U–Commerce (TX)
Texas Southern U (TX)
Université de Sherbrooke (PQ, Canada)
Université Laval (QC, Canada)
The U of British Columbia (BC, Canada)
U of Central Oklahoma (OK)
U of Hawaii at Manoa (HI)
U of North Texas (TX)
U of Toronto (ON, Canada)
U of Windsor (ON, Canada)
U of Wisconsin–Superior (WI)
Valdosta State U (GA)
Wayne State Coll (NE)
Western Washington U (WA)
Westfield State Coll (MA)

COURT REPORTING
Central Michigan U (MI)
Johnson & Wales U (RI)
Kansas City Coll of Legal Studies (MO)
Metropolitan Coll, Tulsa (OK)
Northwood U, Texas Campus (TX)
U of Mississippi (MS)

CRAFT/FOLK ART
Bowling Green State U (OH)
Bridgewater State Coll (MA)
The Cleveland Inst of Art (OH)
Kent State U (OH)
Kutztown U of Pennsylvania (PA)
Oregon Coll of Art & Craft (OR)
Rochester Inst of Technology (NY)
U of Illinois at Urbana–Champaign (IL)
The U of the Arts (PA)
Virginia Commonwealth U (VA)

CREATIVE WRITING
Agnes Scott Coll (GA)
Albertson Coll of Idaho (ID)
Alderson-Broaddus Coll (WV)
Anderson Coll (SC)
Arkansas Tech U (AR)
Ashland U (OH)
Augustana Coll (IL)
Bard Coll (NY)
Beloit Coll (WI)
Bennington Coll (VT)
Baruch Coll of the City U of NY (NY)
Bethel Coll (MN)
Bloomfield Coll (NJ)
Bowie State U (MD)
Bowling Green State U (OH)
Briar Cliff U (IA)
Bridgewater State Coll (MA)
Brooklyn Coll of the City U of NY (NY)
Brown U (RI)
California State U, Hayward (CA)
California State U, Long Beach (CA)
California State U, Northridge (CA)
California State U, San Bernardino (CA)
Cardinal Stritch U (WI)
Carlow Coll (PA)
Carnegie Mellon U (PA)
Carroll Coll (WI)
Carson-Newman Coll (TN)
Central Michigan U (MI)
Chapman U (CA)
Chicago State U (IL)
City Coll of the City U of NY (NY)
Coll of St. Catherine (MN)
Coll of Santa Fe (NM)
The Colorado Coll (CO)
Colorado State U (CO)
Columbia Coll (SC)
Columbia Coll Chicago (IL)
Concordia Coll (MN)
Concordia U (QC, Canada)
Cornell U (NY)
Dartmouth Coll (NH)
Davis & Elkins Coll (WV)
Denison U (OH)
DePaul U (IL)
Dominican U of California (CA)
Eastern U (PA)
Eastern Washington U (WA)
Eckerd Coll (FL)
Emerson Coll (MA)
Emory & Henry Coll (VA)
Emory U (GA)
Eugene Lang Coll, New School U (NY)
The Evergreen State Coll (WA)
Florida State U (FL)
Fordham U (NY)
Franklin Pierce Coll (NH)
Geneva Coll (PA)
Goddard Coll (VT)
Grand Valley State U (MI)
Green Mountain Coll (VT)
Hamilton Coll (NY)
Hampshire Coll (MA)
Harvard U (MA)
Hastings Coll (NE)
High Point U (NC)
Hollins U (VA)
Houghton Coll (NY)
Huntingdon Coll (AL)
Indiana Wesleyan U (IN)
Ithaca Coll (NY)
Johns Hopkins U (MD)
Johnson State Coll (VT)
Kenyon Coll (OH)
King Coll (TN)
Knox Coll (IL)
Lakeland Coll (WI)
La Salle U (PA)
Lehman Coll of the City U of NY (NY)
Le Moyne Coll (NY)
Linfield Coll (OR)
Long Island U, Southampton Coll (NY)
Long Island U, Southampton Coll, Friends World Program (NY)
Loras Coll (IA)
Loyola Coll in Maryland (MD)
Loyola U New Orleans (LA)
Lycoming Coll (PA)
Lynchburg Coll (VA)
Malaspina U-Coll (BC, Canada)
Marlboro Coll (VT)
Marquette U (WI)
Marylhurst U (OR)
Marymount Coll of Fordham U (NY)
Massachusetts Coll of Liberal Arts (MA)
McMurry U (TX)
Mercyhurst Coll (PA)
Methodist Coll (NC)
Miami U (OH)
Millikin U (IL)
Mills Coll (CA)
Minnesota State U, Mankato (MN)
Montclair State U (NJ)
Mount Saint Mary's Coll and Seminary (MD)
Naropa U (CO)
Nazareth Coll of Rochester (NY)
North Carolina State U (NC)
Northern Michigan U (MI)
Northland Coll (WI)
Northwestern Coll (MN)
Oberlin Coll (OH)
Ohio Northern U (OH)
The Ohio State U (OH)
Ohio U (OH)
Ohio Wesleyan U (OH)
Oklahoma Christian U of Science and Arts (OK)
Pacific U (OR)
Pine Manor Coll (MA)
Pratt Inst (NY)

Purchase Coll, State U of NY (NY)
Randolph-Macon Woman's Coll (VA)
Rockhurst U (MO)
Roger Williams U (RI)
St. Andrews Presbyterian Coll (NC)
St. Cloud State U (MN)
St. Edward's U (TX)
Saint Joseph's Coll (IN)
St. Lawrence U (NY)
Saint Leo U (FL)
Saint Mary's Coll (IN)
San Diego State U (CA)
San Francisco State U (CA)
Sarah Lawrence Coll (NY)
Seattle U (WA)
Seton Hill Coll (PA)
Simon's Rock Coll of Bard (MA)
Southern Connecticut State U (CT)
Southern Methodist U (TX)
Southern Vermont Coll (VT)
Southwest State U (MN)
State U of NY at New Paltz (NY)
State U of NY at Oswego (NY)
State U of NY Coll at Brockport (NY)
Stephens Coll (MO)
Susquehanna U (PA)
Sweet Briar Coll (VA)
Taylor U (IN)
Trinity Coll (CT)
The U of Arizona (AZ)
The U of British Columbia (BC, Canada)
U of Calif, Riverside (CA)
U of Calif, San Diego (CA)
U of Calif, Santa Cruz (CA)
U of Charleston (WV)
U of Chicago (IL)
U of Denver (CO)
U of Evansville (IN)
The U of Findlay (OH)
U of Houston (TX)
The U of Iowa (IA)
U of Maine at Farmington (ME)
U of Miami (FL)
U of Michigan (MI)
The U of Montana–Missoula (MT)
U of Nebraska at Omaha (NE)
U of New Mexico (NM)
The U of North Carolina at Wilmington (NC)
U of Pittsburgh (PA)
U of Pittsburgh at Bradford (PA)
U of Pittsburgh at Greensburg (PA)
U of Pittsburgh at Johnstown (PA)
U of Puget Sound (WA)
U of Redlands (CA)
U of St. Thomas (MN)
U of South Dakota (SD)
U of Southern California (CA)
The U of Tampa (FL)
The U of Tennessee at Chattanooga (TN)
The U of Texas at El Paso (TX)
U of Victoria (BC, Canada)
U of Washington (WA)
U of Windsor (ON, Canada)
U of Wisconsin–Parkside (WI)
Ursinus Coll (PA)
Warren Wilson Coll (NC)
Washington U in St. Louis (MO)
Wayne State Coll (NE)
Webster U (MO)
Wells Coll (NY)
Western Michigan U (MI)
Western Washington U (WA)
Westminster Coll (MO)
Westminster Coll (PA)
West Virginia Wesleyan Coll (WV)
White Pines Coll (NH)
Wittenberg U (OH)
York U (ON, Canada)

CRIMINAL JUSTICE/ CORRECTIONS RELATED

Averett U (VA)
Chadron State Coll (NE)
Mount Mary Coll (WI)
The U of Alabama at Birmingham (AL)
U of Alaska Fairbanks (AK)
U of Phoenix–Southern Colorado Campus (CO)

CRIMINAL JUSTICE/LAW ENFORCEMENT ADMINISTRATION

Abilene Christian U (TX)
Adrian Coll (MI)
Alabama State U (AL)
Albertus Magnus Coll (CT)
Alvernia Coll (PA)
American International Coll (MA)
Anderson U (IN)
Anna Maria Coll (MA)
Appalachian State U (NC)
Arizona State U West (AZ)
Armstrong Atlantic State U (GA)
Ashland U (OH)
Athens State U (AL)
Aurora U (IL)
Averett U (VA)
Baldwin-Wallace Coll (OH)
Ball State U (IN)
Barber-Scotia Coll (NC)
Bay Path Coll (MA)
Becker Coll (MA)
Bellevue U (NE)
Bemidji State U (MN)
Benedict Coll (SC)
Benedictine Coll (KS)
Bethune-Cookman Coll (FL)
Blackburn Coll (IL)
Bloomfield Coll (NJ)
Bluefield Coll (VA)
Bluffton Coll (OH)
Boise State U (ID)
Bowie State U (MD)
Bradley U (IL)
Briar Cliff U (IA)
Buena Vista U (IA)
California Lutheran U (CA)
California State U, Bakersfield (CA)
California State U, Chico (CA)
California State U, Dominguez Hills (CA)
California State U, Fullerton (CA)
California State U, Hayward (CA)
California State U, Long Beach (CA)
California State U, Los Angeles (CA)
California State U, Sacramento (CA)
California State U, San Bernardino (CA)
California State U, Stanislaus (CA)
Calvin Coll (MI)
Cameron U (OK)
Campbellsville U (KY)
Campbell U (NC)
Canisius Coll (NY)
Caribbean U (PR)
Carleton U (ON, Canada)
Carroll Coll (WI)
Carthage Coll (WI)
Castleton State Coll (VT)
Cedarville U (OH)
Central Missouri State U (MO)
Central Washington U (WA)
Chaminade U of Honolulu (HI)
Champlain Coll (VT)
Chapman U (CA)
Charleston Southern U (SC)
Chestnut Hill Coll (PA)
Chicago State U (IL)
Christopher Newport U (VA)
Citadel, The Military Coll of South Carolina (SC)
Clark Atlanta U (GA)
Coker Coll (SC)
The Coll of New Jersey (NJ)
Coll of the Ozarks (MO)
Columbia Coll (MO)
Columbus State U (GA)
Concordia U (MI)
Concordia U Wisconsin (WI)
Coppin State Coll (MD)
Culver-Stockton Coll (MO)
Cumberland U (TN)
Curry Coll (MA)
Dakota Wesleyan U (SD)
Dallas Baptist U (TX)
Defiance Coll (OH)
Delaware State U (DE)
Delaware Valley Coll (PA)
DeSales U (PA)
Dordt Coll (IA)
East Central U (OK)
Eastern Kentucky U (KY)
Eastern Michigan U (MI)
Eastern Washington U (WA)
East Tennessee State U (TN)
Edgewood Coll (WI)
Edward Waters Coll (FL)
Elizabeth City State U (NC)
Elmira Coll (NY)
Evangel U (MO)
Faulkner U (AL)
Fayetteville State U (NC)
Ferris State U (MI)
Fitchburg State Coll (MA)
Florida A&M U (FL)
Florida Metropolitan U-Tampa Coll (FL)
Fordham U (NY)
Fort Valley State U (GA)
Franklin Pierce Coll (NH)
Gardner-Webb U (NC)
The George Washington U (DC)
Georgia Coll and State U (GA)
Gonzaga U (WA)
Governors State U (IL)
Grace Coll (IN)
Graceland U (IA)
Grambling State U (LA)
Grand Canyon U (AZ)
Grand Valley State U (MI)
Grand View Coll (IA)
Gustavus Adolphus Coll (MN)
Hamline U (MN)
Hampton U (VA)
Hannibal-LaGrange Coll (MO)
Harris-Stowe State Coll (MO)
Hawai'i Pacific U (HI)
Hesser Coll (NH)
Hilbert Coll (NY)
Holy Family Coll (PA)
Huron U (SD)
Indiana U Northwest (IN)
Indiana U South Bend (IN)
Inter Amer U of PR, Barranquitas Campus (PR)
International Coll (FL)
Iona Coll (NY)
Iowa Wesleyan Coll (IA)
Jackson State U (MS)
Jacksonville State U (AL)
John Jay Coll of Criminal Justice, the City U of NY (NY)
Johnson & Wales U (RI)
Johnson C. Smith U (NC)
Kansas Wesleyan U (KS)
Kean U (NJ)
Keuka Coll (NY)
Keystone Coll (PA)
Lake Superior State U (MI)
Lamar U (TX)
Lambuth U (TN)
Lees-McRae Coll (NC)
Lewis-Clark State Coll (ID)
Lewis U (IL)
Lincoln U (MO)
Lincoln U (PA)
Lindenwood U (MO)
Lindsey Wilson Coll (KY)
Lock Haven U of Pennsylvania (PA)
Long Island U, C.W. Post Campus (NY)
Longwood Coll (VA)
Louisiana Coll (LA)
Lourdes Coll (OH)
Lycoming Coll (PA)
MacMurray Coll (IL)
Mansfield U of Pennsylvania (PA)
Marian Coll of Fond du Lac (WI)
Marist Coll (NY)
Mars Hill Coll (NC)
McKendree Coll (IL)
McMurry U (TX)
Mercer U (GA)
Mercy Coll (NY)
Mercyhurst Coll (PA)
Methodist Coll (NC)
Metropolitan State Coll of Denver (CO)
MidAmerica Nazarene U (KS)
Middle Tennessee State U (TN)
Midland Lutheran Coll (NE)
Midwestern State U (TX)
Mississippi Coll (MS)
Mississippi Valley State U (MS)
Missouri Southern State Coll (MO)
Missouri Valley Coll (MO)
Mitchell Coll (CT)
Moravian Coll (PA)
Morris Brown Coll (GA)
Morris Coll (SC)
Mount Ida Coll (MA)
Mount Mercy Coll (IA)
Mount Olive Coll (NC)
Mount Vernon Nazarene U (OH)
National U (CA)
Newbury Coll (MA)
New England Coll (NH)
New Mexico State U (NM)
New York Inst of Technology (NY)
Niagara U (NY)
North Carolina Central U (NC)
North Carolina State U (NC)
North Carolina Wesleyan Coll (NC)
North Dakota State U (ND)
Northeastern State U (OK)
Northern Arizona U (AZ)
Northern Kentucky U (KY)
Northern Michigan U (MI)
North Georgia Coll & State U (GA)
Norwich U (VT)
Oakland City U (IN)
Oakland U (MI)
Ohio Dominican Coll (OH)
Ohio Northern U (OH)
Ohio U (OH)
Ohio U–Chillicothe (OH)
Ohio U–Lancaster (OH)
Ohio U–Zanesville (OH)
Oklahoma City U (OK)
Olivet Nazarene U (IL)
Pace U (NY)
Park U (MO)
Penn State U Univ Park Campus (PA)
Peru State Coll (NE)
Pfeiffer U (NC)
Pittsburg State U (KS)
Pontifical Catholic U of Puerto Rico (PR)
Portland State U (OR)
Purdue U Calumet (IN)
Quincy U (IL)
Radford U (VA)
Regis U (CO)
Roberts Wesleyan Coll (NY)
Rochester Inst of Technology (NY)
Rockford Coll (IL)
Roger Williams U (RI)
Russell Sage Coll (NY)
Rutgers, The State U of New Jersey, New Brunswick (NJ)
Sacred Heart U (CT)
Sage Coll of Albany (NY)
St. Cloud State U (MN)
St. Edward's U (TX)
Saint Francis U (PA)
St. John's U (NY)
Saint Joseph's U (PA)
Saint Martin's Coll (WA)
Saint Mary's U of Minnesota (MN)
St. Mary's U of San Antonio (TX)
St. Thomas Aquinas Coll (NY)
St. Thomas U (FL)
Salem International U (WV)
Salem State Coll (MA)
Salve Regina U (RI)
Samford U (AL)
San Diego State U (CA)
San Francisco State U (CA)
San Jose State U (CA)
Savannah State U (GA)
Seattle U (WA)
Shenandoah U (VA)
Siena Heights U (MI)
Simpson Coll (IA)
Sinte Gleska U (SD)
Sojourner-Douglass Coll (MD)
Sonoma State U (CA)
South Carolina State U (SC)
Southeast Missouri State U (MO)
Southern Illinois U Carbondale (IL)
Southern Vermont Coll (VT)
Southwest Baptist U (MO)
Southwestern Adventist U (TX)
Southwestern Oklahoma State U (OK)
State U of NY at Albany (NY)
State U of NY at Oswego (NY)
State U of NY Coll at Brockport (NY)
State U of NY Coll at Buffalo (NY)
State U of NY Coll at Fredonia (NY)
State U of West Georgia (GA)
Suffolk U (MA)
Sul Ross State U (TX)
Tarleton State U (TX)
Taylor U, Fort Wayne Campus (IN)
Teikyo Post U (CT)
Temple U (PA)
Tennessee State U (TN)
Texas A&M U–Commerce (TX)
Texas A&M U–Corpus Christi (TX)
Texas Southern U (TX)
Thomas Coll (ME)
Thomas Edison State Coll (NJ)
Thomas More Coll (KY)
Thomas U (GA)
Tiffin U (OH)
Tri-State U (IN)
Truman State U (MO)
Union Coll (KY)
Union Inst & U (OH)
The U of Akron (OH)
U of Alaska Anchorage (AK)
U of Alberta (AB, Canada)
The U of Arizona (AZ)
U of Arkansas at Little Rock (AR)
U of Arkansas at Pine Bluff (AR)
U of Baltimore (MD)
U of Central Oklahoma (OK)
U of Cincinnati (OH)
U of Dayton (OH)
U of Delaware (DE)
U of Dubuque (IA)
U of Evansville (IN)
The U of Findlay (OH)
U of Guelph (ON, Canada)
U of Hartford (CT)
U of Hawaii–West Oahu (HI)
U of Illinois at Springfield (IL)
U of Indianapolis (IN)
U of Louisville (KY)
The U of Maine at Augusta (ME)
U of Maine at Presque Isle (ME)
U of Mary Hardin-Baylor (TX)
U of Maryland Eastern Shore (MD)
U of Maryland University Coll (MD)
U of Massachusetts Lowell (MA)
The U of Memphis (TN)
U of Michigan–Flint (MI)
U of Missouri–Kansas City (MO)
U of Missouri–St. Louis (MO)
U of Nebraska at Omaha (NE)
U of Nevada, Las Vegas (NV)
U of New Haven (CT)
U of North Alabama (AL)
The U of North Carolina at Pembroke (NC)
U of North Texas (TX)
U of Ottawa (ON, Canada)
U of Phoenix–Colorado Campus (CO)
U of Phoenix–New Mexico Campus (NM)
U of Phoenix–Phoenix Campus (AZ)
U of Phoenix–Tulsa Campus (OK)
U of Pittsburgh at Bradford (PA)
U of Pittsburgh at Greensburg (PA)
U of Regina (SK, Canada)
U of Richmond (VA)
U of South Alabama (AL)
U of South Carolina (SC)
U of South Carolina Spartanburg (SC)
U of South Dakota (SD)
The U of Tennessee at Chattanooga (TN)
The U of Tennessee at Martin (TN)
The U of Texas at Brownsville (TX)
The U of Texas at El Paso (TX)
The U of Texas at San Antonio (TX)
The U of Texas at Tyler (TX)
The U of Texas–Pan American (TX)
U of the District of Columbia (DC)
U of Washington (WA)
U of Wisconsin–Milwaukee (WI)
U of Wisconsin–Oshkosh (WI)
U of Wisconsin–Parkside (WI)
U of Wisconsin–Platteville (WI)
U of Wyoming (WY)
U System Coll for Lifelong Learning (NH)
Urbana U (OH)
Utica Coll of Syracuse U (NY)
Valdosta State U (GA)
Villanova U (PA)
Virginia Commonwealth U (VA)
Viterbo U (WI)
Voorhees Coll (SC)
Washburn U of Topeka (KS)
Washington State U (WA)
Waynesburg Coll (PA)
Wayne State Coll (NE)
West Chester U of Pennsylvania (PA)
Western Illinois U (IL)
Western International U (AZ)

Western New England Coll (MA)
Western Oregon U (OR)
Westfield State Coll (MA)
West Liberty State Coll (WV)
Westminster Coll (PA)
West Texas A&M U (TX)
West Virginia State Coll (WV)
Wheeling Jesuit U (WV)
Widener U (PA)
Wilmington Coll (DE)
Wilmington Coll (OH)
Winona State U (MN)
York Coll of Pennsylvania (PA)
Youngstown State U (OH)

CRIMINAL JUSTICE STUDIES

Albany State U (GA)
Alcorn State U (MS)
Alfred U (NY)
American Military U (VA)
American U (DC)
Andrew Jackson U (AL)
Angelo State U (TX)
Appalachian State U (NC)
Arizona State U (AZ)
Auburn U Montgomery (AL)
Augsburg Coll (MN)
Augusta State U (GA)
Aurora U (IL)
Avila Coll (MO)
Barton Coll (NC)
Bellarmine U (KY)
Bethany Coll (KS)
Bethel Coll (IN)
Bethel Coll (KS)
Bloomsburg U of Pennsylvania (PA)
Bluefield State Coll (WV)
Bridgewater State Coll (MA)
Butler U (IN)
Caldwell Coll (NJ)
California Baptist U (CA)
Cazenovia Coll (NY)
Central Methodist Coll (MO)
Champlain Coll (VT)
Chaparral Coll (AZ)
Chowan Coll (NC)
Coll of Saint Elizabeth (NJ)
Coll of the Southwest (NM)
Colorado State U (CO)
Colorado Tech U Sioux Falls Campus (SD)
Columbia Southern U (AL)
Concordia Coll (MN)
Delta State U (MS)
DeSales U (PA)
East Carolina U (NC)
Eastern New Mexico U (NM)
Edinboro U of Pennsylvania (PA)
Elizabethtown Coll (PA)
Endicott Coll (MA)
Fairleigh Dickinson U, Teaneck-Hackensack Campus (NJ)
Ferrum Coll (VA)
Florida Atlantic U (FL)
Florida Gulf Coast U (FL)
Florida International U (FL)
Florida Metropolitan U-Tampa Coll, Lakeland (FL)
Florida Metropolitan U-Orlando Coll, South (FL)
Florida Southern Coll (FL)
Fort Hays State U (KS)
Frostburg State U (MD)
Gannon U (PA)
Georgia Southern U (GA)
Georgia State U (GA)
Guilford Coll (NC)
Harding U (AR)
Hesser Coll (NH)
High Point U (NC)
Illinois State U (IL)
Indiana U Bloomington (IN)
Indiana U Kokomo (IN)
Indiana U–Purdue U Fort Wayne (IN)
Indiana U–Purdue U Indianapolis (IN)
Indiana Wesleyan U (IN)
Inter American U of PR, Aguadilla Campus (PR)
International Coll (FL)
Jackson State U (MS)
Jamestown Coll (ND)
Judson Coll (AL)
Judson Coll (IL)
Juniata Coll (PA)
Kendall Coll (IL)
Kent State U (OH)
Kentucky State U (KY)
Kentucky Wesleyan Coll (KY)
King's Coll (PA)
Kutztown U of Pennsylvania (PA)
La Roche Coll (PA)
La Salle U (PA)
Lasell Coll (MA)
Limestone Coll (SC)
Long Island U, Brentwood Campus (NY)
Loras Coll (IA)
Louisiana State U in Shreveport (LA)
Loyola U Chicago (IL)
Loyola U New Orleans (LA)
Marshall U (WV)
McNeese State U (LA)
Medaille Coll (NY)
Metropolitan State U (MN)
Michigan State U (MI)
Minnesota State U Moorhead (MN)
Minot State U (ND)
Missouri Baptist Coll (MO)
Missouri Western State Coll (MO)
Molloy Coll (NY)
Monmouth U (NJ)
Mountain State U (WV)
Mount Aloysius Coll (PA)
Mount Marty Coll (SD)
Mount St. Clare Coll (IA)
Mount Saint Mary Coll (NY)
Murray State U (KY)
National U (CA)
New Jersey City U (NJ)
New Mexico Highlands U (NM)
Northeastern Illinois U (IL)
Northeastern U (MA)
Northern Kentucky U (KY)
Northwestern Coll (MN)
Northwestern State U of Louisiana (LA)
The Ohio State U (OH)
Ohio U (OH)
Olivet Coll (MI)
Penn State U Abington Coll (PA)
Penn State U Altoona Coll (PA)
Penn State U Fayette Campus of the Commonwealth Coll (PA)
Penn State U Harrisburg Campus of the Capital Coll (PA)
Penn State U Schuylkill Campus of the Capital Coll (PA)
Penn State U Univ Park Campus (PA)
Pikeville Coll (KY)
Pittsburg State U (KS)
Point Park Coll (PA)
Prairie View A&M U (TX)
Prescott Coll (AZ)
Quinnipiac U (CT)
Rhode Island Coll (RI)
Roanoke Coll (VA)
Rochester Inst of Technology (NY)
Roosevelt U (IL)
Saginaw Valley State U (MI)
St. Ambrose U (IA)
Saint Anselm Coll (NH)
Saint Joseph's Coll (IN)
Saint Joseph's Coll (ME)
Saint Louis U (MO)
Saint Peter's Coll (NJ)
Saint Xavier U (IL)
Sam Houston State U (TX)
Seton Hall U (NJ)
Seton Hill Coll (PA)
Shaw U (NC)
Shippensburg U of Pennsylvania (PA)
Southeastern Louisiana U (LA)
Southeastern Oklahoma State U (OK)
Southeast Missouri State U (MO)
Southern Arkansas U–Magnolia (AR)
Southern Illinois U Edwardsville (IL)
Southern Nazarene U (OK)
Southern U and A&M Coll (LA)
Southwestern Coll (KS)
Southwest Missouri State U (MO)
Southwest State U (MN)
Southwest Texas State U (TX)
State U of NY Coll at Potsdam (NY)
Stephen F. Austin State U (TX)
Stonehill Coll (MA)
Taylor U, Fort Wayne Campus (IN)
Texas A&M International U (TX)
Texas A&M U–Texarkana (TX)
Texas Christian U (TX)
Texas Wesleyan U (TX)
Texas Woman's U (TX)
Thiel Coll (PA)
Troy State U Dothan (AL)
U Coll of the Fraser Valley (BC, Canada)
The U of Akron (OH)
The U of Alabama (AL)
U of Arkansas (AR)
U of Central Florida (FL)
U of Central Oklahoma (OK)
U of Florida (FL)
U of Georgia (GA)
U of Idaho (ID)
U of Illinois at Chicago (IL)
U of Louisiana at Lafayette (LA)
U of Louisiana at Monroe (LA)
U of Massachusetts Boston (MA)
U of Nebraska at Kearney (NE)
U of Nebraska at Omaha (NE)
The U of North Carolina at Charlotte (NC)
The U of North Carolina at Wilmington (NC)
U of North Dakota (ND)
U of North Florida (FL)
U of Portland (OR)
U of Regina (SK, Canada)
The U of Scranton (PA)
U of Southern Mississippi (MS)
U of South Florida (FL)
The U of Texas at Arlington (TX)
U of Toledo (OH)
The U of Virginia's Coll at Wise (VA)
U of West Florida (FL)
U of Windsor (ON, Canada)
U of Wisconsin–Eau Claire (WI)
U of Wisconsin–Superior (WI)
Virginia State U (VA)
Virginia Wesleyan Coll (VA)
Wayland Baptist U (TX)
Wayne State U (MI)
Weber State U (UT)
Western Carolina U (NC)
Western Michigan U (MI)
Wichita State U (KS)
Xavier U (OH)
Youngstown State U (OH)

CRIMINOLOGY

Adams State Coll (CO)
Albright Coll (PA)
Arkansas State U (AR)
Auburn U (AL)
Ball State U (IN)
Barry U (FL)
Bridgewater State Coll (MA)
California State U, Fresno (CA)
Capital U (OH)
Caribbean U (PR)
Carleton U (ON, Canada)
Castleton State Coll (VT)
Centenary Coll (NJ)
Central Connecticut State U (CT)
Central Michigan U (MI)
Coll of the Ozarks (MO)
Dominican U (IL)
Drury U (MO)
Eastern Michigan U (MI)
Florida State U (FL)
Gallaudet U (DC)
Husson Coll (ME)
Indiana State U (IN)
Indiana U of Pennsylvania (PA)
Kent State U (OH)
Le Moyne Coll (NY)
Lindenwood U (MO)
Marquette U (WI)
Marymount U (VA)
Maryville U of Saint Louis (MO)
Memorial U of Newfoundland (NF, Canada)
Mesa State Coll (CO)
Midland Lutheran Coll (NE)
New Mexico Highlands U (NM)
Niagara U (NY)
The Ohio State U (OH)
Ohio U (OH)
Old Dominion U (VA)
Plattsburgh State U of NY (NY)
Pontifical Catholic U of Puerto Rico (PR)
The Richard Stockton Coll of New Jersey (NJ)
Saint Augustine's Coll (NC)
St. Cloud State U (MN)
Saint Leo U (FL)
Saint Mary's U (NS, Canada)
St. Mary's U of San Antonio (TX)
St. Thomas U (NB, Canada)
San Jose State U (CA)
Simon Fraser U (BC, Canada)
Southern Oregon U (OR)
State U of NY Coll at Brockport (NY)
State U of NY Coll at Old Westbury (NY)
Texas A&M U–Kingsville (TX)
Université de Montréal (QC, Canada)
U of Alberta (AB, Canada)
U of Calif, Irvine (CA)
U of La Verne (CA)
U of Maryland, Coll Park (MD)
The U of Memphis (TN)
U of Miami (FL)
U of Minnesota, Duluth (MN)
U of Missouri–St. Louis (MO)
U of Nevada, Reno (NV)
U of Northern Iowa (IA)
U of Oklahoma (OK)
U of Ottawa (ON, Canada)
U of St. Thomas (MN)
U of Southern Colorado (CO)
U of Southern Maine (ME)
The U of Tampa (FL)
The U of Texas at Dallas (TX)
The U of Texas of the Permian Basin (TX)
U of Windsor (ON, Canada)
Upper Iowa U (IA)
Valparaiso U (IN)
Virginia Union U (VA)
Western Michigan U (MI)
William Penn U (IA)

CROP PRODUCTION MANAGEMENT

Cornell U (NY)

CULINARY ARTS

The Art Inst of Colorado (CO)
Baltimore International Coll (MD)
The Culinary Inst of America (NY)
Drexel U (PA)
Johnson & Wales U (RI)
Kendall Coll (IL)
Mercyhurst Coll (PA)
Metropolitan State U (MN)
Mississippi U for Women (MS)
Northern Michigan U (MI)
Paul Smith's Coll of Arts and Sciences (NY)
Pennsylvania Coll of Technology (PA)
State U of NY Coll of Technology at Delhi (NY)
Sullivan U (KY)
U of Nevada, Las Vegas (NV)

CULINARY ARTS AND SERVICES RELATED

Newbury Coll (MA)

CULTURAL STUDIES

Azusa Pacific U (CA)
Baltimore Hebrew U (MD)
Bard Coll (NY)
Bethel Coll (MN)
Boise State U (ID)
Bridgewater Coll (VA)
Briercrest Bible Coll (SK, Canada)
Brigham Young U–Hawaii (HI)
California State Polytechnic U, Pomona (CA)
California State U, Chico (CA)
California State U, Fullerton (CA)
California State U, Hayward (CA)
California State U, Northridge (CA)
California State U, Sacramento (CA)
Clark U (MA)
The Coll of William and Mary (VA)
Columbia International U (SC)
Concordia U (QC, Canada)
Cornell Coll (IA)
The Evergreen State Coll (WA)
Fort Lewis Coll (CO)
Goddard Coll (VT)
Hampshire Coll (MA)
Harvard U (MA)
Houghton Coll (NY)
Indiana Wesleyan U (IN)
Kent State U (OH)
Long Island U, Southampton Coll, Friends World Program (NY)
Marlboro Coll (VT)
Mills Coll (CA)
Minnesota State U, Mankato (MN)
The Ohio State U (OH)
Ohio Wesleyan U (OH)
Oregon State U (OR)
Penn State U Univ Park Campus (PA)
Reformed Bible Coll (MI)
St. Francis Xavier U (NS, Canada)
Saint Mary-of-the-Woods Coll (IN)
St. Olaf Coll (MN)
Simon's Rock Coll of Bard (MA)
Sonoma State U (CA)
The U of British Columbia (BC, Canada)
U of Calif, Berkeley (CA)
U of Calif, Irvine (CA)
U of Calif, Riverside (CA)
U of Calif, San Diego (CA)
U of Colorado at Boulder (CO)
U of Nevada, Las Vegas (NV)
U of Oregon (OR)
U of Southern California (CA)
The U of Tennessee (TN)
The U of Texas–Pan American (TX)
U of Toronto (ON, Canada)
U of Virginia (VA)
U of Washington (WA)
U of Wisconsin–Milwaukee (WI)
Washington U in St. Louis (MO)
Western Washington U (WA)
Yale U (CT)
York U (ON, Canada)

CURRICULUM AND INSTRUCTION

Long Island U, C.W. Post Campus (NY)
Ohio U (OH)
Texas A&M U (TX)
Texas Southern U (TX)
U of Hawaii at Manoa (HI)
The U of Montana–Missoula (MT)
Utah State U (UT)
York U (ON, Canada)

CYTOTECHNOLOGY

Alderson-Broaddus Coll (WV)
Anderson Coll (SC)
Barry U (FL)
Bloomfield Coll (NJ)
California State U, Dominguez Hills (CA)
Coll of Saint Elizabeth (NJ)
The Coll of Saint Rose (NY)
Eastern Kentucky U (KY)
Eastern Michigan U (MI)
Edgewood Coll (WI)
Elmhurst Coll (IL)
Felician Coll (NJ)
Illinois Coll (IL)
Indiana U–Purdue U Indianapolis (IN)
Indiana U Southeast (IN)
Jewish Hospital Coll of Nursing and Allied Health (MO)
Loma Linda U (CA)
Long Island U, Brooklyn Campus (NY)
Long Island U, C.W. Post Campus (NY)
Luther Coll (IA)
Marian Coll of Fond du Lac (WI)
Marshall U (WV)
Mayo School of Health Sciences (MN)
Minnesota State U Moorhead (MN)
Monmouth U (NJ)
Mount St. Clare Coll (IA)
Northern Michigan U (MI)
Oakland U (MI)
Roosevelt U (IL)
St. John's U (NY)
Saint Mary's Coll (IN)
Saint Mary's U of Minnesota (MN)
Salve Regina U (RI)
Slippery Rock U of Pennsylvania (PA)
State U of New York Upstate Medical University (NY)
State U of NY at Stony Brook (NY)
Suffolk U (MA)
Thiel Coll (PA)
Thomas Edison State Coll (NJ)
Thomas Jefferson U (PA)
The U of Akron (OH)

The U of Alabama at Birmingham (AL)
U of Arkansas for Medical Sciences (AR)
U of Connecticut (CT)
U of Kansas (KS)
U of Louisville (KY)
U of Mississippi Medical Center (MS)
U of Missouri–St. Louis (MO)
U of North Dakota (ND)
U of North Texas (TX)
Winona State U (MN)

DAIRY SCIENCE
California Polytechnic State U, San Luis Obispo (CA)
Cornell U (NY)
Delaware Valley Coll (PA)
Eastern Kentucky U (KY)
Iowa State U of Science and Technology (IA)
Oregon State U (OR)
South Dakota State U (SD)
State U of NY Coll of A&T at Cobleskill (NY)
Texas A&M U (TX)
U of Alberta (AB, Canada)
U of Florida (FL)
U of Georgia (GA)
U of New Hampshire (NH)
U of Vermont (VT)
U of Wisconsin–Madison (WI)
U of Wisconsin–River Falls (WI)
Utah State U (UT)
Virginia Polytechnic Inst and State U (VA)

DANCE
Adelphi U (NY)
Alma Coll (MI)
Amherst Coll (MA)
Arizona State U (AZ)
Baldwin-Wallace Coll (OH)
Ball State U (IN)
Bard Coll (NY)
Barnard Coll (NY)
Belhaven Coll (MS)
Bennington Coll (VT)
Birmingham-Southern Coll (AL)
The Boston Conservatory (MA)
Bowling Green State U (OH)
Brenau U (GA)
Brigham Young U (UT)
Butler U (IN)
California Inst of the Arts (CA)
California State U, Fresno (CA)
California State U, Fullerton (CA)
California State U, Hayward (CA)
California State U, Long Beach (CA)
California State U, Los Angeles (CA)
California State U, Northridge (CA)
Cedar Crest Coll (PA)
Centenary Coll of Louisiana (LA)
Chapman U (CA)
Coker Coll (SC)
The Colorado Coll (CO)
Colorado State U (CO)
Columbia Coll (NY)
Columbia Coll (SC)
Columbia Coll Chicago (IL)
Columbia U, School of General Studies (NY)
Concordia U (QC, Canada)
Connecticut Coll (CT)
Cornell U (NY)
Cornish Coll of the Arts (WA)
Denison U (OH)
DeSales U (PA)
Dickinson Coll (PA)
East Carolina U (NC)
Eastern Kentucky U (KY)
Eastern Michigan U (MI)
Eastern Washington U (WA)
Emerson Coll (MA)
Emory U (GA)
The Evergreen State Coll (WA)
Florida International U (FL)
Florida State U (FL)
Fordham U (NY)
Friends U (KS)
Frostburg State U (MD)
George Mason U (VA)
The George Washington U (DC)
Goucher Coll (MD)
Gustavus Adolphus Coll (MN)
Hamilton Coll (NY)
Hampshire Coll (MA)
Hobart and William Smith Colls (NY)
Hofstra U (NY)
Hollins U (VA)
Hope Coll (MI)
Hunter Coll of the City U of NY (NY)
Huntingdon Coll (AL)
Indiana U Bloomington (IN)
Ithaca Coll (NY)
Jacksonville U (FL)
Johnson State Coll (VT)
The Juilliard School (NY)
Kent State U (OH)
Kenyon Coll (OH)
Lake Erie Coll (OH)
Lamar U (TX)
La Roche Coll (PA)
Lehman Coll of the City U of NY (NY)
Lindenwood U (MO)
Long Island U, Brooklyn Campus (NY)
Long Island U, C.W. Post Campus (NY)
Long Island U, Southampton Coll, Friends World Program (NY)
Longwood Coll (VA)
Loyola Marymount U (CA)
Luther Coll (IA)
Manhattanville Coll (NY)
Marlboro Coll (VT)
Marygrove Coll (MI)
Marymount Manhattan Coll (NY)
Mercyhurst Coll (PA)
Meredith Coll (NC)
Middlebury Coll (VT)
Mills Coll (CA)
Montclair State U (NJ)
Mount Holyoke Coll (MA)
Muhlenberg Coll (PA)
Naropa U (CO)
New Mexico State U (NM)
New World School of the Arts (FL)
New York U (NY)
North Carolina School of the Arts (NC)
Northwestern U (IL)
Oakland U (MI)
Oberlin Coll (OH)
The Ohio State U (OH)
Ohio U (OH)
Oklahoma City U (OK)
Otterbein Coll (OH)
Pitzer Coll (CA)
Point Park Coll (PA)
Pomona Coll (CA)
Prescott Coll (AZ)
Purchase Coll, State U of NY (NY)
Queens Coll of the City U of NY (NY)
Radford U (VA)
Randolph-Macon Woman's Coll (VA)
Reed Coll (OR)
Rhode Island Coll (RI)
Roger Williams U (RI)
Rutgers, The State U of New Jersey, New Brunswick (NJ)
Saint Mary's Coll of California (CA)
St. Olaf Coll (MN)
Sam Houston State U (TX)
San Diego State U (CA)
San Francisco State U (CA)
San Jose State U (CA)
Sarah Lawrence Coll (NY)
Scripps Coll (CA)
Shenandoah U (VA)
Simon Fraser U (BC, Canada)
Simon's Rock Coll of Bard (MA)
Skidmore Coll (NY)
Slippery Rock U of Pennsylvania (PA)
Smith Coll (MA)
Southern Illinois U Edwardsville (IL)
Southern Methodist U (TX)
Southern Utah U (UT)
Southwest Missouri State U (MO)
Southwest Texas State U (TX)
State U of NY Coll at Brockport (NY)
State U of NY Coll at Fredonia (NY)
State U of NY Coll at Potsdam (NY)
Stephen F. Austin State U (TX)
Stephens Coll (MO)
Swarthmore Coll (PA)
Sweet Briar Coll (VA)
Temple U (PA)
Texas Christian U (TX)
Texas Tech U (TX)
Texas Woman's U (TX)
Thomas Edison State Coll (NJ)
Towson U (MD)
Trinity Coll (CT)
State U of NY at Buffalo (NY)
The U of Akron (OH)
The U of Alabama (AL)
U of Alberta (AB, Canada)
The U of Arizona (AZ)
U of Calgary (AB, Canada)
U of Calif, Irvine (CA)
U of Calif, Riverside (CA)
U of Calif, San Diego (CA)
U of Calif, Santa Barbara (CA)
U of Calif, Santa Cruz (CA)
U of Central Oklahoma (OK)
U of Cincinnati (OH)
U of Colorado at Boulder (CO)
U of Florida (FL)
U of Hartford (CT)
U of Hawaii at Manoa (HI)
U of Idaho (ID)
U of Illinois at Urbana–Champaign (IL)
The U of Iowa (IA)
U of Kansas (KS)
U of Maryland, Baltimore County (MD)
U of Maryland, Coll Park (MD)
U of Massachusetts Amherst (MA)
U of Miami (FL)
U of Michigan (MI)
U of Minnesota, Twin Cities Campus (MN)
U of Missouri–Kansas City (MO)
The U of Montana–Missoula (MT)
U of Nebraska–Lincoln (NE)
U of Nevada, Las Vegas (NV)
U of New Mexico (NM)
The U of North Carolina at Charlotte (NC)
The U of North Carolina at Greensboro (NC)
U of North Texas (TX)
U of Oklahoma (OK)
U of Oregon (OR)
U of Southern Mississippi (MS)
U of South Florida (FL)
The U of Texas at Austin (TX)
The U of the Arts (PA)
U of Utah (UT)
U of Washington (WA)
U of Wisconsin–Milwaukee (WI)
U of Wisconsin–Stevens Point (WI)
Utah State U (UT)
Virginia Commonwealth U (VA)
Virginia Intermont Coll (VA)
Washington U in St. Louis (MO)
Wayne State U (MI)
Weber State U (UT)
Webster U (MO)
Wells Coll (NY)
Wesleyan U (CT)
Western Michigan U (MI)
Western Oregon U (OR)
Westmont Coll (CA)
West Texas A&M U (TX)
Winthrop U (SC)
Wright State U (OH)
York U (ON, Canada)

DANCE THERAPY
Long Island U, Southampton Coll, Friends World Program (NY)
Mercyhurst Coll (PA)
Naropa U (CO)

DATA PROCESSING
East Carolina U (NC)
Eastern Michigan U (MI)
Peirce Coll (PA)

DATA PROCESSING TECHNOLOGY
Arkansas State U (AR)
Bemidji State U (MN)
Central Baptist Coll (AR)
Chicago State U (IL)
Cleary Coll (MI)
Florida Metropolitan U-Orlando Coll, North (FL)
Florida Metropolitan U-Tampa Coll (FL)
Gardner-Webb U (NC)
Hannibal-LaGrange Coll (MO)
Harding U (AR)
Indiana U Kokomo (IN)
Indiana U Northwest (IN)
Minnesota State U, Mankato (MN)
Mount Vernon Nazarene U (OH)
Murray State U (KY)
Northern Michigan U (MI)
Northwest Missouri State U (MO)
Pacific Union Coll (CA)
Peirce Coll (PA)
Saint Mary's U (NS, Canada)
Stephen F. Austin State U (TX)
U of Advancing Computer Technology (AZ)
U of Arkansas (AR)
U of Southern Indiana (IN)
U of Southern Mississippi (MS)
U of Washington (WA)
West Virginia U Inst of Technology (WV)

DENTAL HYGIENE
Armstrong Atlantic State U (GA)
Dalhousie U (NS, Canada)
Eastern Washington U (WA)
East Tennessee State U (TN)
Howard U (DC)
Idaho State U (ID)
Indiana U–Purdue U Indianapolis (IN)
Loma Linda U (CA)
Louisiana State U Health Sciences Center (LA)
Marquette U (WI)
Mars Hill Coll (NC)
Medical Coll of Georgia (GA)
Midwestern State U (TX)
Minnesota State U, Mankato (MN)
New York U (NY)
Northeastern U (MA)
Northern Arizona U (AZ)
The Ohio State U (OH)
Old Dominion U (VA)
Oregon Health & Science U (OR)
Oregon Inst of Technology (OR)
Pennsylvania Coll of Technology (PA)
Southern Illinois U Carbondale (IL)
Tennessee State U (TN)
Texas A&M U System Health Science Center (TX)
Texas Woman's U (TX)
Thomas Edison State Coll (NJ)
U of Alberta (AB, Canada)
U of Arkansas for Medical Sciences (AR)
U of Bridgeport (CT)
The U of British Columbia (BC, Canada)
U of Colorado Health Sciences Center (CO)
U of Hawaii at Manoa (HI)
U of Louisiana at Lafayette (LA)
U of Louisiana at Monroe (LA)
U of Louisville (KY)
U of Manitoba (MB, Canada)
U of Michigan (MI)
U of Minnesota, Twin Cities Campus (MN)
U of Mississippi Medical Center (MS)
U of Missouri–Kansas City (MO)
U of Nebraska Medical Center (NE)
U of New England (ME)
U of New Haven (CT)
U of New Mexico (NM)
The U of North Carolina at Chapel Hill (NC)
U of Oklahoma Health Sciences Center (OK)
U of Pittsburgh (PA)
U of Rhode Island (RI)
U of South Dakota (SD)
U of Southern California (CA)
U of Texas-Houston Health Science Center (TX)
U of Washington (WA)
U of Wyoming (WY)
Virginia Commonwealth U (VA)
Weber State U (UT)
Western Kentucky U (KY)
West Liberty State Coll (WV)
West Virginia U (WV)
Wichita State U (KS)

DENTAL LABORATORY TECHNICIAN
Boston U (MA)
Louisiana State U Health Sciences Center (LA)

DESIGN/APPLIED ARTS RELATED
The Art Inst of California (CA)
Bennington Coll (VT)
Drexel U (PA)
ITT Tech Inst, Sylmar (CA)
ITT Tech Inst, Indianapolis (IN)
ITT Tech Inst (OR)
Maine Coll of Art (ME)
New York Inst of Technology (NY)
Ohio U (OH)
Open Learning Agency (BC, Canada)
Ringling School of Art and Design (FL)
Robert Morris Coll (IL)
The U of Akron (OH)
U of Saint Francis (IN)
U of Wisconsin–Stout (WI)

DESIGN/VISUAL COMMUNICATIONS
Adams State Coll (CO)
American Academy of Art (IL)
American InterContinental U, Atlanta (GA)
The Art Inst of Phoenix (AZ)
Art Inst of Southern California (CA)
Atlanta Coll of Art (GA)
Bethel Coll (IN)
Bowling Green State U (OH)
Brigham Young U (UT)
California State U, Chico (CA)
Calvin Coll (MI)
Canisius Coll (NY)
Carlow Coll (PA)
Carroll Coll (WI)
Cazenovia Coll (NY)
Central Connecticut State U (CT)
Collins Coll: A School of Design and Technology (AZ)
The Illinois Inst of Art-Schaumburg (IL)
International Academy of Design & Technology (FL)
International Acad of Merchandising & Design, Ltd (IL)
Iowa State U of Science and Technology (IA)
ITT Tech Inst, Rancho Cordova (CA)
Jacksonville U (FL)
Kean U (NJ)
Kendall Coll of Art and Design of Ferris State U (MI)
Maharishi U of Management (IA)
Marywood U (PA)
Mount Union Coll (OH)
Mount Vernon Nazarene U (OH)
North Carolina State U (NC)
Northwestern State U of Louisiana (LA)
Ohio Dominican Coll (OH)
The Ohio State U (OH)
Ohio U (OH)
Paier Coll of Art, Inc. (CT)
Peace Coll (NC)
Purdue U (IN)
Rochester Inst of Technology (NY)
Saginaw Valley State U (MI)
St. Ambrose U (IA)
Saint Mary-of-the-Woods Coll (IN)
San Diego State U (CA)
Southern Illinois U Carbondale (IL)
Southwest Missouri State U (MO)
Syracuse U (NY)
Texas Woman's U (TX)
U of Advancing Computer Technology (AZ)
U of Calif, Davis (CA)
U of Calif, Los Angeles (CA)
U of Kansas (KS)
U of Massachusetts Dartmouth (MA)
U of Michigan (MI)
U of Notre Dame (IN)
The U of Texas at Austin (TX)
Ursuline Coll (OH)
Virginia Commonwealth U (VA)
Washington U in St. Louis (MO)
Weber State U (UT)

Westwood Coll of Technology–Denver North (CO)
William Woods U (MO)
York U (ON, Canada)

DEVELOPMENTAL/CHILD PSYCHOLOGY
Appalachian State U (NC)
Auburn U (AL)
Becker Coll (MA)
Belmont U (TN)
Bennington Coll (VT)
Berea Coll (KY)
Bluffton Coll (OH)
California Polytechnic State U, San Luis Obispo (CA)
California State U, Bakersfield (CA)
California State U, Hayward (CA)
California State U, Northridge (CA)
California State U, San Bernardino (CA)
Carson-Newman Coll (TN)
Castleton State Coll (VT)
Christopher Newport U (VA)
Clark Atlanta U (GA)
Colby-Sawyer Coll (NH)
Concordia U (QC, Canada)
Cornell U (NY)
Eastern Washington U (WA)
Edgewood Coll (WI)
Fitchburg State Coll (MA)
Fort Valley State U (GA)
Framingham State Coll (MA)
Fresno Pacific U (CA)
Goddard Coll (VT)
Hampshire Coll (MA)
Hampton U (VA)
Houston Baptist U (TX)
Humboldt State U (CA)
Iowa State U of Science and Technology (IA)
Long Island U, Southampton Coll, Friends World Program (NY)
Longwood Coll (VA)
Lynchburg Coll (VA)
Marlboro Coll (VT)
Maryville Coll (TN)
Metropolitan State U (MN)
Mills Coll (CA)
Minnesota State U, Mankato (MN)
Mount St. Mary's Coll (CA)
Mount Saint Vincent U (NS, Canada)
Northwest Missouri State U (MO)
Oklahoma Baptist U (OK)
Olivet Nazarene U (IL)
Quinnipiac U (CT)
Rockford Coll (IL)
St. Joseph's Coll, New York (NY)
St. Joseph's Coll, Suffolk Campus (NY)
San Jose State U (CA)
Sarah Lawrence Coll (NY)
Simon's Rock Coll of Bard (MA)
Sonoma State U (CA)
Spelman Coll (GA)
Suffolk U (MA)
Tufts U (MA)
Université de Montréal (QC, Canada)
The U of Akron (OH)
U of Alberta (AB, Canada)
The U of British Columbia (BC, Canada)
U of Calif, Santa Cruz (CA)
U of Delaware (DE)
U of Kansas (KS)
U of La Verne (CA)
U of Michigan–Dearborn (MI)
U of Minnesota, Twin Cities Campus (MN)
U of Missouri–Columbia (MO)
U of New England (ME)
U of Ottawa (ON, Canada)
U of Southern Colorado (CO)
U of the District of Columbia (DC)
U of the Incarnate Word (TX)
U of Toledo (OH)
U of Utah (UT)
U of Wisconsin–Green Bay (WI)
U of Wisconsin–Madison (WI)
Utica Coll of Syracuse U (NY)
Villa Julie Coll (MD)
Western Washington U (WA)
Whittier Coll (CA)
Wittenberg U (OH)

DEVELOPMENT ECONOMICS
American U (DC)
Arkansas State U (AR)
Brown U (RI)
Clark U (MA)
Eastern Mennonite U (VA)
Fitchburg State Coll (MA)
Georgia Southern U (GA)
The Ohio State U (OH)
U of Calgary (AB, Canada)
U of Guelph (ON, Canada)
U of King's Coll (NS, Canada)
U of Windsor (ON, Canada)
York U (ON, Canada)

DIAGNOSTIC MEDICAL SONOGRAPHY
Medical Coll of Georgia (GA)
Mountain State U (WV)
Nebraska Methodist Coll of Nursing & Allied Health (NE)
Rochester Inst of Technology (NY)
Seattle U (WA)
U of Nebraska Medical Center (NE)
Weber State U (UT)

DIETETICS
Abilene Christian U (TX)
Acadia U (NS, Canada)
Andrews U (MI)
Arizona State U East (AZ)
Ashland U (OH)
Ball State U (IN)
Bastyr U (WA)
Baylor U (TX)
Bennett Coll (NC)
Berea Coll (KY)
Bluffton Coll (OH)
Bowling Green State U (OH)
Brigham Young U (UT)
California State Polytechnic U, Pomona (CA)
California State U, Fresno (CA)
California State U, Long Beach (CA)
California State U, Northridge (CA)
California State U, San Bernardino (CA)
Carson-Newman Coll (TN)
Case Western Reserve U (OH)
Central Michigan U (MI)
Central Missouri State U (MO)
Coll of Saint Benedict (MN)
Coll of St. Catherine (MN)
Coll of Saint Elizabeth (NJ)
Coll of the Ozarks (MO)
Colorado State U (CO)
Concordia Coll (MN)
Cornell U (NY)
Dominican U (IL)
D'Youville Coll (NY)
East Carolina U (NC)
Eastern Kentucky U (KY)
Eastern Michigan U (MI)
Florida International U (FL)
Florida State U (FL)
Fontbonne U (MO)
Framingham State Coll (MA)
Gannon U (PA)
Georgia State U (GA)
Harding U (AR)
Immaculata Coll (PA)
Indiana U Bloomington (IN)
Indiana U of Pennsylvania (PA)
Iowa State U of Science and Technology (IA)
Jacksonville State U (AL)
Kansas State U (KS)
Keene State Coll (NH)
Lamar U (TX)
Lehman Coll of the City U of NY (NY)
Lipscomb U (TN)
Loma Linda U (CA)
Louisiana State U and A&M Coll (LA)
Louisiana Tech U (LA)
Mansfield U of Pennsylvania (PA)
Marshall U (WV)
Marymount Coll of Fordham U (NY)
Marywood U (PA)
McGill U (PQ, Canada)
Memorial U of Newfoundland (NF, Canada)
Mercyhurst Coll (PA)
Meredith Coll (NC)
Messiah Coll (PA)
Miami U (OH)
Michigan State U (MI)
Minnesota State U, Mankato (MN)
Montclair State U (NJ)
Morgan State U (MD)
Mount Mary Coll (WI)
Mount Saint Vincent U (NS, Canada)
Nicholls State U (LA)
North Carolina Ag and Tech State U (NC)
North Dakota State U (ND)
Northern Michigan U (MI)
Northwest Missouri State U (MO)
Notre Dame Coll (OH)
Oakwood Coll (AL)
The Ohio State U (OH)
Ohio U (OH)
Olivet Nazarene U (IL)
Oregon State U (OR)
Ouachita Baptist U (AR)
Pacific Union Coll (CA)
Point Loma Nazarene U (CA)
Queens Coll of the City U of NY (NY)
Radford U (VA)
Rochester Inst of Technology (NY)
Saint John's U (MN)
Saint Joseph Coll (CT)
Saint Louis U (MO)
Samford U (AL)
San Francisco State U (CA)
San Jose State U (CA)
Seton Hill Coll (PA)
Simmons Coll (MA)
South Dakota State U (SD)
Southwest Missouri State U (MO)
State U of NY Coll at Buffalo (NY)
State U of NY Coll at Oneonta (NY)
Syracuse U (NY)
Tarleton State U (TX)
Tennessee Technological U (TN)
Texas A&M U–Kingsville (TX)
Texas Christian U (TX)
Texas Southern U (TX)
Texas Tech U (TX)
Texas Woman's U (TX)
Tuskegee U (AL)
The U of Akron (OH)
U of Arkansas at Pine Bluff (AR)
The U of British Columbia (BC, Canada)
U of Central Oklahoma (OK)
U of Connecticut (CT)
U of Dayton (OH)
U of Delaware (DE)
U of Georgia (GA)
U of Guelph (ON, Canada)
U of Louisiana at Lafayette (LA)
U of Maryland, Coll Park (MD)
U of Maryland Eastern Shore (MD)
U of Missouri–Columbia (MO)
U of Montevallo (AL)
U of Nebraska at Kearney (NE)
U of New Hampshire (NH)
U of New Haven (CT)
The U of North Carolina at Greensboro (NC)
U of North Dakota (ND)
U of Northern Colorado (CO)
U of Northern Iowa (IA)
U of Oklahoma Health Sciences Center (OK)
U of Ottawa (ON, Canada)
U of Pittsburgh (PA)
U of Rhode Island (RI)
U of Southern Mississippi (MS)
The U of Tennessee at Martin (TN)
The U of Texas–Pan American (TX)
U of Texas Southwestern Medical Center at Dallas (TX)
U of Vermont (VT)
The U of Western Ontario (ON, Canada)
U of Wisconsin–Madison (WI)
U of Wisconsin–Stevens Point (WI)
U of Wisconsin–Stout (WI)
Virginia Polytechnic Inst and State U (VA)
Viterbo U (WI)
Wayne State U (MI)
Western Carolina U (NC)
Western Michigan U (MI)
Youngstown State U (OH)

DISTRIBUTION OPERATIONS
McKendree Coll (IL)
U of Wisconsin–Superior (WI)
Youngstown State U (OH)

DIVINITY/MINISTRY
Arlington Baptist Coll (TX)
Atlantic Union Coll (MA)
Azusa Pacific U (CA)
Baptist Bible Coll (MO)
Baptist Bible Coll of Pennsylvania (PA)
Barclay Coll (KS)
Belmont U (TN)
Bethany Coll of the Assemblies of God (CA)
Bethel Coll (IN)
Biola U (CA)
Bluffton Coll (OH)
Boise Bible Coll (ID)
Brewton-Parker Coll (GA)
Briercrest Bible Coll (SK, Canada)
Calvary Bible Coll and Theological Seminary (MO)
Campbellsville U (KY)
Cardinal Stritch U (WI)
Central Christian Coll of Kansas (KS)
Central Christian Coll of the Bible (MO)
Christian Heritage Coll (CA)
Cincinnati Bible Coll and Seminary (OH)
Clear Creek Baptist Bible Coll (KY)
Colorado Christian U (CO)
Concordia U (CA)
Cornerstone U (MI)
Emmanuel Coll (GA)
Eugene Bible Coll (OR)
Faith Baptist Bible Coll and Theological Seminary (IA)
Faulkner U (AL)
Florida Christian Coll (FL)
Fresno Pacific U (CA)
Friends U (KS)
Global U of the Assemblies of God (MO)
Grace Coll (IN)
Grace U (NE)
Grand Canyon U (AZ)
Great Lakes Christian Coll (MI)
Greenville Coll (IL)
Grove City Coll (PA)
Hannibal-LaGrange Coll (MO)
Hardin-Simmons U (TX)
Huntington Coll (IN)
John Brown U (AR)
John Wesley Coll (NC)
Lincoln Christian Coll (IL)
Lipscomb U (TN)
Manhattan Christian Coll (KS)
Martin Methodist Coll (TN)
Marylhurst U (OR)
The Master's Coll and Seminary (CA)
Master's Coll and Seminary (ON, Canada)
Mount Olive Coll (NC)
Multnomah Bible Coll and Biblical Seminary (OR)
Nebraska Christian Coll (NE)
North American Baptist Coll & Edmonton Baptist Sem (AB, Canada)
North Park U (IL)
Northwest Coll (WA)
Northwest Nazarene U (ID)
Oakland City U (IN)
Oklahoma Baptist U (OK)
Oklahoma Christian U of Science and Arts (OK)
Oklahoma Wesleyan U (OK)
Patten Coll (CA)
Pillsbury Baptist Bible Coll (MN)
Providence Coll and Theological Seminary (MB, Canada)
Puget Sound Christian Coll (WA)
Reformed Bible Coll (MI)
Roberts Wesleyan Coll (NY)
St. Louis Christian Coll (MO)
San Jose Christian Coll (CA)
Shorter Coll (GA)
Southeastern Bible Coll (AL)
Southern Wesleyan U (SC)
Southwestern Assemblies of God U (TX)
Southwestern Coll (AZ)
Tabor Coll (KS)
Taylor U, Fort Wayne Campus (IN)
Trinity International U (IL)
Trinity Western U (BC, Canada)
Tyndale Coll & Seminary (ON, Canada)
U of Mary (ND)
U of Saint Francis (IN)
Warner Pacific Coll (OR)
Western Baptist Coll (OR)
Williams Baptist Coll (AR)

DRAFTING
Baker Coll of Flint (MI)
Baker Coll of Owosso (MI)
Central Missouri State U (MO)
Columbus Coll of Art and Design (OH)
East Central U (OK)
Grambling State U (LA)
Keene State Coll (NH)
Lewis-Clark State Coll (ID)
Lynn U (FL)
Montana State U–Northern (MT)
Murray State U (KY)
Northern Michigan U (MI)
Northern State U (SD)
Pacific Union Coll (CA)
Prairie View A&M U (TX)
Robert Morris Coll (IL)
Sam Houston State U (TX)
Southwest Missouri State U (MO)
Texas Southern U (TX)
Thomas Edison State Coll (NJ)
Tri-State U (IN)
U of Houston (TX)
U of Nebraska at Omaha (NE)
U of Rio Grande (OH)
Western Michigan U (MI)

DRAFTING/DESIGN TECHNOLOGY
Caribbean U (PR)
Hillsdale Coll (MI)
Lewis-Clark State Coll (ID)
Norfolk State U (VA)
Texas Southern U (TX)
Tri-State U (IN)

DRAMA/DANCE EDUCATION
Abilene Christian U (TX)
Appalachian State U (NC)
Baylor U (TX)
Boston U (MA)
Bowling Green State U (OH)
Brenau U (GA)
Bridgewater State Coll (MA)
Brigham Young U (UT)
The Catholic U of America (DC)
Central Washington U (WA)
Chadron State Coll (NE)
Coll of St. Catherine (MN)
Concordia U (QC, Canada)
Dana Coll (NE)
East Carolina U (NC)
Eastern Michigan U (MI)
East Texas Baptist U (TX)
Emerson Coll (MA)
Greensboro Coll (NC)
Greenville Coll (IL)
Hastings Coll (NE)
Howard Payne U (TX)
Huntingdon Coll (AL)
Indiana U–Purdue U Fort Wayne (IN)
Jacksonville U (FL)
Johnson State Coll (VT)
Luther Coll (IA)
Marywood U (PA)
McMurry U (TX)
Meredith Coll (NC)
Minnesota State U Moorhead (MN)
New York U (NY)
Northern Arizona U (AZ)
The Ohio State U (OH)
Oklahoma Baptist U (OK)
Point Park Coll (PA)
Salve Regina U (RI)
San Diego State U (CA)
Southwestern Coll (KS)
Southwest State U (MN)
Texas Wesleyan U (TX)
The U of Akron (OH)
The U of Arizona (AZ)
U of Calgary (AB, Canada)
U of Georgia (GA)
The U of Iowa (IA)
U of Maryland, Coll Park (MD)
The U of North Carolina at Charlotte (NC)
U of St. Thomas (MN)
U of South Florida (FL)
U of Utah (UT)
U of Windsor (ON, Canada)

Viterbo U (WI)
Washington U in St. Louis (MO)
Weber State U (UT)
William Jewell Coll (MO)
York U (ON, Canada)
Youngstown State U (OH)

DRAMA/THEATER LITERATURE
Averett U (VA)
Bard Coll (NY)
Barnard Coll (NY)
Boston U (MA)
DePaul U (IL)
Marymount Manhattan Coll (NY)
Memorial U of Newfoundland (NF, Canada)
Northwestern U (IL)
Ohio U (OH)
U of Connecticut (CT)
U of Northern Iowa (IA)
Virginia Wesleyan Coll (VA)
Washington U in St. Louis (MO)

DRAMA THERAPY
Howard U (DC)
Long Island U, Southampton Coll, Friends World Program (NY)
Virginia Union U (VA)

DRAWING
Academy of Art Coll (CA)
Adams State Coll (CO)
Alberta Coll of Art & Design (AB, Canada)
Alfred U (NY)
Alma Coll (MI)
American Academy of Art (IL)
Anderson Coll (SC)
Aquinas Coll (MI)
Arcadia U (PA)
Arizona State U (AZ)
Art Academy of Cincinnati (OH)
Art Inst of Southern California (CA)
Atlanta Coll of Art (GA)
Ball State U (IN)
Bard Coll (NY)
Bennington Coll (VT)
Bethany Coll (KS)
Biola U (CA)
Birmingham-Southern Coll (AL)
Boise State U (ID)
Boston U (MA)
Bowling Green State U (OH)
Brock U (ON, Canada)
California Coll of Arts and Crafts (CA)
California State U, Fullerton (CA)
California State U, Hayward (CA)
California State U, Long Beach (CA)
California State U, Northridge (CA)
Carson-Newman Coll (TN)
Centenary Coll of Louisiana (LA)
Chicago State U (IL)
The Cleveland Inst of Art (OH)
Ctr for Creative Studies—Coll of Art and Design (MI)
Coll of the Atlantic (ME)
Coll of Visual Arts (MN)
Colorado State U (CO)
Columbia Coll (MO)
Columbus Coll of Art and Design (OH)
Concordia U (QC, Canada)
Corcoran Coll of Art and Design (DC)
Cornell U (NY)
DePaul U (IL)
Drake U (IA)
Eastern Kentucky U (KY)
Framingham State Coll (MA)
Georgia Southwestern State U (GA)
Georgia State U (GA)
Goddard Coll (VT)
Governors State U (IL)
Grace Coll (IN)
Grand Valley State U (MI)
Hampshire Coll (MA)
Hampton U (VA)
Illinois Wesleyan U (IL)
Indiana U Bloomington (IN)
Inter American U of PR, San Germán Campus (PR)
Judson Coll (IL)
Lewis U (IL)
Lindenwood U (MO)
Long Island U, Southampton Coll, Friends World Program (NY)
Longwood Coll (VA)
Lyme Academy Coll of Fine Arts (CT)
Maharishi U of Management (IA)
Marlboro Coll (VT)
Maryland Inst, Coll of Art (MD)
McNeese State U (LA)
Memorial U of Newfoundland (NF, Canada)
Memphis Coll of Art (TN)
Middlebury Coll (VT)
Milwaukee Inst of Art and Design (WI)
Minneapolis Coll of Art and Design (MN)
Minnesota State U, Mankato (MN)
Mississippi U for Women (MS)
Montserrat Coll of Art (MA)
Mount Allison U (NB, Canada)
Nazareth Coll of Rochester (NY)
New England Coll (NH)
New York U (NY)
Northern Michigan U (MI)
Northwest Missouri State U (MO)
Nova Scotia Coll of Art and Design (NS, Canada)
The Ohio State U (OH)
Ohio U (OH)
Otis Coll of Art and Design (CA)
Pacific Northwest Coll of Art (OR)
Parsons School of Design, New School U (NY)
Portland State U (OR)
Pratt Inst (NY)
Rhode Island School of Design (RI)
Rivier Coll (NH)
Rowan U (NJ)
Rutgers, The State U of New Jersey, New Brunswick (NJ)
Sacred Heart U (CT)
St. Cloud State U (MN)
Salem State Coll (MA)
San Francisco Art Inst (CA)
Sarah Lawrence Coll (NY)
School of the Art Inst of Chicago (IL)
School of the Museum of Fine Arts (MA)
School of Visual Arts (NY)
Seton Hill Coll (PA)
Shawnee State U (OH)
Simon's Rock Coll of Bard (MA)
Sonoma State U (CA)
State U of NY at Binghamton (NY)
State U of NY at New Paltz (NY)
State U of NY Coll at Brockport (NY)
State U of NY Coll at Buffalo (NY)
State U of NY Coll at Fredonia (NY)
Temple U (PA)
Texas A&M U–Commerce (TX)
Trinity Christian Coll (IL)
The U of Akron (OH)
U of Alberta (AB, Canada)
U of Calif, Santa Cruz (CA)
U of Evansville (IN)
U of Hartford (CT)
The U of Iowa (IA)
U of Michigan (MI)
The U of Montana–Missoula (MT)
U of Montevallo (AL)
U of North Texas (TX)
U of Oregon (OR)
U of San Francisco (CA)
U of South Dakota (SD)
The U of Texas at El Paso (TX)
U of the South (TN)
U of Toledo (OH)
U of Windsor (ON, Canada)
Washington U in St. Louis (MO)
Webster U (MO)
West Virginia Wesleyan Coll (WV)
William Carey Coll (MS)
Wingate U (NC)
Winona State U (MN)
Wittenberg U (OH)
Wright State U (OH)
York U (ON, Canada)

DRIVER/SAFETY EDUCATION
Bridgewater Coll (VA)
William Penn U (IA)

EARLY CHILDHOOD EDUCATION
Alabama State U (AL)
Albany State U (GA)
Albright Coll (PA)
Alma Coll (MI)
Alvernia Coll (PA)
American International Coll (MA)
Anderson Coll (SC)
Anna Maria Coll (MA)
Appalachian State U (NC)
Arcadia U (PA)
Arizona State U (AZ)
Arkansas State U (AR)
Arkansas Tech U (AR)
Armstrong Atlantic State U (GA)
Ashland U (OH)
Athens State U (AL)
Atlanta Christian Coll (GA)
Atlantic Union Coll (MA)
Auburn U (AL)
Augsburg Coll (MN)
Augusta State U (GA)
Ball State U (IN)
Barry U (FL)
Bayamón Central U (PR)
Baylor U (TX)
Bay Path Coll (MA)
Becker Coll (MA)
Belmont U (TN)
Benedict Coll (SC)
Bennett Coll (NC)
Bennington Coll (VT)
Berea Coll (KY)
Berry Coll (GA)
Bethany Coll of the Assemblies of God (CA)
Bethel Coll (MN)
Birmingham-Southern Coll (AL)
Black Hills State U (SD)
Bloomsburg U of Pennsylvania (PA)
Bluefield Coll (VA)
Bluffton Coll (OH)
Boise State U (ID)
Boston Coll (MA)
Boston U (MA)
Bowie State U (MD)
Bowling Green State U (OH)
Bradley U (IL)
Brandon U (MB, Canada)
Brenau U (GA)
Brewton-Parker Coll (GA)
Bridgewater State Coll (MA)
Brigham Young U (UT)
Brooklyn Coll of the City U of NY (NY)
Bryan Coll (TN)
Bucknell U (PA)
Cabrini Coll (PA)
California Polytechnic State U, San Luis Obispo (CA)
California State U, Chico (CA)
California State U, Sacramento (CA)
California U of Pennsylvania (PA)
Cardinal Stritch U (WI)
Caribbean U (PR)
Carlow Coll (PA)
Carroll Coll (WI)
Carson-Newman Coll (TN)
The Catholic U of America (DC)
Cazenovia Coll (NY)
Cedarville U (OH)
Centenary Coll of Louisiana (LA)
Central Connecticut State U (CT)
Central Methodist Coll (MO)
Central State U (OH)
Central Washington U (WA)
Chaminade U of Honolulu (HI)
Champlain Coll (VT)
Charleston Southern U (SC)
Chestnut Hill Coll (PA)
Cheyney U of Pennsylvania (PA)
Chicago State U (IL)
Cincinnati Bible Coll and Seminary (OH)
City Coll of the City U of NY (NY)
Clarion U of Pennsylvania (PA)
Clark Atlanta U (GA)
Clarke Coll (IA)
Clemson U (SC)
Cleveland State U (OH)
Coastal Carolina U (SC)
Coker Coll (SC)
Coll Misericordia (PA)
Coll of Mount St. Joseph (OH)
The Coll of New Jersey (NJ)
Coll of Notre Dame of Maryland (MD)
Coll of St. Catherine (MN)
Coll of St. Joseph (VT)
Coll of Saint Mary (NE)
Coll of Santa Fe (NM)
Columbia Bible Coll (BC, Canada)
Columbia Coll (SC)
Columbia Coll Chicago (IL)
Columbia International U (SC)
Columbia Union Coll (MD)
Columbus State U (GA)
Concord Coll (WV)
Concordia Coll (MN)
Concordia U (CA)
Concordia U (IL)
Concordia U (MN)
Concordia U (NE)
Concordia U (OR)
Concordia U (QC, Canada)
Concordia U Wisconsin (WI)
Converse Coll (SC)
Coppin State Coll (MD)
Cornerstone U (MI)
Crown Coll (MN)
Curry Coll (MA)
Daemen Coll (NY)
Dallas Baptist U (TX)
Delaware State U (DE)
Delta State U (MS)
DePaul U (IL)
Dillard U (LA)
Duquesne U (PA)
East Carolina U (NC)
East Central U (OK)
Eastern Connecticut State U (CT)
Eastern Illinois U (IL)
Eastern Kentucky U (KY)
Eastern Mennonite U (VA)
Eastern Nazarene Coll (MA)
Eastern New Mexico U (NM)
East Stroudsburg U of Pennsylvania (PA)
East Texas Baptist U (TX)
Edgewood Coll (WI)
Edinboro U of Pennsylvania (PA)
Edward Waters Coll (FL)
Elizabeth City State U (NC)
Elizabethtown Coll (PA)
Elmhurst Coll (IL)
Elms Coll (MA)
Endicott Coll (MA)
Erskine Coll (SC)
Evangel U (MO)
Faulkner U (AL)
Fayetteville State U (NC)
Fitchburg State Coll (MA)
Florida A&M U (FL)
Florida Gulf Coast U (FL)
Florida Southern Coll (FL)
Florida State U (FL)
Fontbonne U (MO)
Fort Hays State U (KS)
Fort Lewis Coll (CO)
Fort Valley State U (GA)
Framingham State Coll (MA)
Francis Marion U (SC)
Franklin Pierce Coll (NH)
Friends U (KS)
Frostburg State U (MD)
Furman U (SC)
Gallaudet U (DC)
Gannon U (PA)
Gardner-Webb U (NC)
Georgetown Coll (KY)
Georgia Coll and State U (GA)
Georgia Southern U (GA)
Georgia Southwestern State U (GA)
Georgia State U (GA)
Glenville State Coll (WV)
Goddard Coll (VT)
Gordon Coll (MA)
Goshen Coll (IN)
Governors State U (IL)
Grace Bible Coll (MI)
Grambling State U (LA)
Greensboro Coll (NC)
Greenville Coll (IL)
Grove City Coll (PA)
Gwynedd-Mercy Coll (PA)
Hampshire Coll (MA)
Hampton U (VA)
Hannibal-LaGrange Coll (MO)
Harding U (AR)
Harris-Stowe State Coll (MO)
Henderson State U (AR)
High Point U (NC)
Hillsdale Coll (MI)
Hofstra U (NY)
Holy Family Coll (PA)
Hood Coll (MD)
Houston Baptist U (TX)
Howard Payne U (TX)
Howard U (DC)
Humboldt State U (CA)
Hunter Coll of the City U of NY (NY)
Idaho State U (ID)
Illinois State U (IL)
Immaculata Coll (PA)
Indiana State U (IN)
Indiana U Bloomington (IN)
Indiana U of Pennsylvania (PA)
Inter American U of PR, Aguadilla Campus (PR)
Inter American U of PR, San Germán Campus (PR)
Iowa State U of Science and Technology (IA)
Iowa Wesleyan Coll (IA)
Jacksonville State U (AL)
James Madison U (VA)
Jarvis Christian Coll (TX)
John Brown U (AR)
John Carroll U (OH)
Johnson Bible Coll (TN)
Johnson C. Smith U (NC)
Judson Coll (IL)
Juniata Coll (PA)
Kean U (NJ)
Keene State Coll (NH)
Kendall Coll (IL)
Kennesaw State U (GA)
Kent State U (OH)
Keystone Coll (PA)
King Coll (TN)
King's Coll (PA)
LaGrange Coll (GA)
Lakeland Coll (WI)
Lamar U (TX)
Lander U (SC)
La Roche Coll (PA)
Lasell Coll (MA)
Lenoir-Rhyne Coll (NC)
Lesley U (MA)
Lincoln Christian Coll (IL)
Lincoln Memorial U (TN)
Lincoln U (PA)
Lindenwood U (MO)
Lock Haven U of Pennsylvania (PA)
Long Island U, Brooklyn Campus (NY)
Long Island U, C.W. Post Campus (NY)
Long Island U, Southampton Coll, Friends World Program (NY)
Longwood Coll (VA)
Loras Coll (IA)
Louisiana Coll (LA)
Louisiana Tech U (LA)
Lourdes Coll (OH)
Loyola U Chicago (IL)
Luther Coll (IA)
Lynchburg Coll (VA)
Lynn U (FL)
Malone Coll (OH)
Mansfield U of Pennsylvania (PA)
Maranatha Baptist Bible Coll (WI)
Marian Coll (IN)
Marian Coll of Fond du Lac (WI)
Mars Hill Coll (NC)
Martin Luther Coll (MN)
Marygrove Coll (MI)
Maryville U of Saint Louis (MO)
Massachusetts Coll of Liberal Arts (MA)
McNeese State U (LA)
McPherson Coll (KS)
Medaille Coll (NY)
Mercer U (GA)
Mercy Coll (NY)
Mercyhurst Coll (PA)
Messiah Coll (PA)
Methodist Coll (NC)
Miami U (OH)
Middle Tennessee State U (TN)
Midland Lutheran Coll (NE)
Midway Coll (KY)
Millersville U of Pennsylvania (PA)
Milligan Coll (TN)
Mills Coll (CA)
Minnesota State U, Mankato (MN)
Minnesota State U Moorhead (MN)
Mississippi Valley State U (MS)
Missouri Baptist Coll (MO)
Missouri Southern State Coll (MO)
Mitchell Coll (CT)
Montclair State U (NJ)
Morehead State U (KY)
Morris Brown Coll (GA)
Morris Coll (SC)
Mount Aloysius Coll (PA)
Mount Ida Coll (MA)

Mount Mary Coll (WI)
Mount St. Clare Coll (IA)
Mount Saint Vincent U (NS, Canada)
Mount Union Coll (OH)
Mount Vernon Nazarene U (OH)
Muskingum Coll (OH)
Naropa U (CO)
National-Louis U (IL)
Neumann Coll (PA)
Newberry Coll (SC)
New Jersey City U (NJ)
New Mexico Highlands U (NM)
New Mexico State U (NM)
New York U (NY)
Nicholls State U (LA)
Norfolk State U (VA)
North Carolina Ag and Tech State U (NC)
North Carolina Central U (NC)
North Central Coll (IL)
Northeastern Illinois U (IL)
Northeastern State U (OK)
Northeastern U (MA)
Northern Illinois U (IL)
Northern Kentucky U (KY)
North Georgia Coll & State U (GA)
North Greenville Coll (SC)
Northland Coll (WI)
North Park U (IL)
Northwestern Coll (MN)
Northwestern Oklahoma State U (OK)
Northwestern State U of Louisiana (LA)
Northwest Missouri State U (MO)
Notre Dame Coll (OH)
Nova Southeastern U (FL)
Oglethorpe U (GA)
Ohio Northern U (OH)
Ohio U (OH)
Oklahoma Baptist U (OK)
Oklahoma Christian U of Science and Arts (OK)
Oklahoma City U (OK)
Olivet Nazarene U (IL)
Oral Roberts U (OK)
Oregon State U (OR)
Ouachita Baptist U (AR)
Our Lady of the Lake U of San Antonio (TX)
Pacific Lutheran U (WA)
Pacific Oaks Coll (CA)
Pacific Union Coll (CA)
Pacific U (OR)
Paine Coll (GA)
Palm Beach Atlantic Coll (FL)
Park U (MO)
Patten Coll (CA)
Peru State Coll (NE)
Philadelphia Biblical U (PA)
Philander Smith Coll (AR)
Piedmont Coll (GA)
Pine Manor Coll (MA)
Pittsburg State U (KS)
Plymouth State Coll (NH)
Point Park Coll (PA)
Pontifical Catholic U of Puerto Rico (PR)
Presbyterian Coll (SC)
Prescott Coll (AZ)
Purdue U (IN)
Queens Coll (NC)
Queens Coll of the City U of NY (NY)
Reinhardt Coll (GA)
Rhode Island Coll (RI)
Rider U (NJ)
Ripon Coll (WI)
Rivier Coll (NH)
Roosevelt U (IL)
Rowan U (NJ)
Sacred Heart U (CT)
St. Ambrose U (IA)
St. Cloud State U (MN)
Saint Joseph Coll (CT)
St. Joseph's Coll, Suffolk Campus (NY)
Saint Mary-of-the-Woods Coll (IN)
Saint Mary's U of Minnesota (MN)
St. Thomas Aquinas Coll (NY)
Saint Xavier U (IL)
Salem State Coll (MA)
Salve Regina U (RI)
Samford U (AL)
Sarah Lawrence Coll (NY)
Seton Hall U (NJ)
Seton Hill Coll (PA)
Siena Heights U (MI)
Silver Lake Coll (WI)
Simmons Coll (MA)
Simpson Coll (IA)
Sinte Gleska U (SD)
Slippery Rock U of Pennsylvania (PA)
Sojourner-Douglass Coll (MD)
South Carolina State U (SC)
South Dakota State U (SD)
Southeastern Oklahoma State U (OK)
Southeast Missouri State U (MO)
Southern Adventist U (TN)
Southern Arkansas U–Magnolia (AR)
Southern Connecticut State U (CT)
Southern Illinois U Carbondale (IL)
Southern Illinois U Edwardsville (IL)
Southern Nazarene U (OK)
Southern New Hampshire U (NH)
Southern Wesleyan U (SC)
Southwestern Coll (KS)
Southwest Missouri State U (MO)
Southwest State U (MN)
Spring Arbor U (MI)
Springfield Coll (MA)
Spring Hill Coll (AL)
State U of NY at New Paltz (NY)
State U of NY Coll at Buffalo (NY)
State U of NY Coll at Cortland (NY)
State U of NY Coll at Fredonia (NY)
State U of NY Coll at Geneseo (NY)
Stephens Coll (MO)
Stonehill Coll (MA)
Susquehanna U (PA)
Syracuse U (NY)
Tabor Coll (KS)
Temple U (PA)
Tennessee State U (TN)
Tennessee Technological U (TN)
Texas A&M International U (TX)
Texas A&M U–Commerce (TX)
Texas A&M U–Kingsville (TX)
Texas Southern U (TX)
Thomas U (GA)
Toccoa Falls Coll (GA)
Tougaloo Coll (MS)
Touro Coll (NY)
Towson U (MD)
Trevecca Nazarene U (TN)
Trinity Coll (DC)
Troy State U (AL)
Troy State U Dothan (AL)
Tufts U (MA)
Tusculum Coll (TN)
Union U (TN)
Université de Montréal (QC, Canada)
Université de Sherbrooke (PQ, Canada)
Université Laval (QC, Canada)
The U of Akron (OH)
The U of Alabama (AL)
The U of Alabama at Birmingham (AL)
U of Alaska Anchorage (AK)
U of Alaska Southeast (AK)
U of Alberta (AB, Canada)
The U of Arizona (AZ)
U of Arkansas at Little Rock (AR)
U of Arkansas at Pine Bluff (AR)
The U of British Columbia (BC, Canada)
U of Calgary (AB, Canada)
U of Central Arkansas (AR)
U of Central Florida (FL)
U of Central Oklahoma (OK)
U of Cincinnati (OH)
U of Dayton (OH)
U of Delaware (DE)
U of Georgia (GA)
U of Great Falls (MT)
U of Hartford (CT)
U of Hawaii at Manoa (HI)
U of Illinois at Urbana–Champaign (IL)
U of Kentucky (KY)
U of La Verne (CA)
U of Louisiana at Monroe (LA)
U of Maine (ME)
U of Maine at Farmington (ME)
U of Manitoba (MB, Canada)
U of Mary (ND)
U of Mary Hardin-Baylor (TX)
U of Maryland, Coll Park (MD)
U of Maryland Eastern Shore (MD)
U of Michigan–Dearborn (MI)
U of Michigan–Flint (MI)
U of Minnesota, Crookston (MN)
U of Minnesota, Duluth (MN)
U of Minnesota, Twin Cities Campus (MN)
U of Missouri–Columbia (MO)
U of Missouri–Kansas City (MO)
U of Missouri–St. Louis (MO)
U of Mobile (AL)
U of Montevallo (AL)
U of Nevada, Las Vegas (NV)
U of New Hampshire (NH)
U of New Mexico (NM)
U of North Alabama (AL)
The U of North Carolina at Chapel Hill (NC)
The U of North Carolina at Charlotte (NC)
The U of North Carolina at Pembroke (NC)
The U of North Carolina at Wilmington (NC)
U of North Dakota (ND)
U of Northern Iowa (IA)
U of North Texas (TX)
U of Oklahoma (OK)
U of Ottawa (ON, Canada)
U of Regina (SK, Canada)
U of Science and Arts of Oklahoma (OK)
The U of Scranton (PA)
U of South Alabama (AL)
U of South Carolina Aiken (SC)
U of South Carolina Spartanburg (SC)
U of South Florida (FL)
The U of Tennessee at Chattanooga (TN)
The U of Tennessee at Martin (TN)
The U of Texas at Brownsville (TX)
The U of Texas–Pan American (TX)
U of the District of Columbia (DC)
U of the Incarnate Word (TX)
U of the Ozarks (AR)
U of Toledo (OH)
U of Utah (UT)
U of Vermont (VT)
U of Victoria (BC, Canada)
The U of West Alabama (AL)
The U of Western Ontario (ON, Canada)
U of West Florida (FL)
U of Windsor (ON, Canada)
U of Wisconsin–La Crosse (WI)
U of Wisconsin–Madison (WI)
U of Wisconsin–Milwaukee (WI)
U of Wisconsin–Oshkosh (WI)
U of Wisconsin–Platteville (WI)
U of Wisconsin–Stevens Point (WI)
U of Wisconsin–Stout (WI)
U of Wisconsin–Whitewater (WI)
U System Coll for Lifelong Learning (NH)
Utah State U (UT)
Valdosta State U (GA)
Vanderbilt U (TN)
Villa Julie Coll (MD)
Virginia Polytechnic Inst and State U (VA)
Virginia Union U (VA)
Voorhees Coll (SC)
Wagner Coll (NY)
Waldorf Coll (IA)
Walsh U (OH)
Warner Pacific Coll (OR)
Wartburg Coll (IA)
Washburn U of Topeka (KS)
Washington Bible Coll (MD)
Wayne State Coll (NE)
Weber State U (UT)
Webster U (MO)
Wesleyan Coll (GA)
West Chester U of Pennsylvania (PA)
Western Carolina U (NC)
Western Kentucky U (KY)
Western Washington U (WA)
Westfield State Coll (MA)
West Liberty State Coll (WV)
Westminster Coll (MO)
Westminster Coll (UT)
West Virginia State Coll (WV)
West Virginia Wesleyan Coll (WV)
Wheelock Coll (MA)
Whittier Coll (CA)
Widener U (PA)
Williams Baptist Coll (AR)
Wingate U (NC)
Winona State U (MN)
Winston-Salem State U (NC)
Winthrop U (SC)
Worcester State Coll (MA)
Wright State U (OH)
Xavier U of Louisiana (LA)
Yeshiva U (NY)
York U (ON, Canada)
Youngstown State U (OH)

EARTH SCIENCES

Adams State Coll (CO)
Adelphi U (NY)
Adrian Coll (MI)
Alfred U (NY)
Augustana Coll (IL)
Baylor U (TX)
Bemidji State U (MN)
Bloomsburg U of Pennsylvania (PA)
Boise State U (ID)
Boston U (MA)
Bridgewater State Coll (MA)
Brigham Young U (UT)
Brock U (ON, Canada)
Brooklyn Coll of the City U of NY (NY)
California Inst of Technology (CA)
California State Polytechnic U, Pomona (CA)
California State U, Chico (CA)
California State U, Dominguez Hills (CA)
California State U, Long Beach (CA)
California State U, Los Angeles (CA)
California State U, Monterey Bay (CA)
California State U, Northridge (CA)
California U of Pennsylvania (PA)
Carleton U (ON, Canada)
Central Connecticut State U (CT)
Central Michigan U (MI)
Central Missouri State U (MO)
Central Washington U (WA)
City Coll of the City U of NY (NY)
Clarion U of Pennsylvania (PA)
Clark U (MA)
Colby Coll (ME)
Dalhousie U (NS, Canada)
Dartmouth Coll (NH)
DePauw U (IN)
Dickinson State U (ND)
Eastern Kentucky U (KY)
Eastern Michigan U (MI)
Eastern Washington U (WA)
East Stroudsburg U of Pennsylvania (PA)
Edinboro U of Pennsylvania (PA)
Emporia State U (KS)
The Evergreen State Coll (WA)
Fitchburg State Coll (MA)
Framingham State Coll (MA)
Frostburg State U (MD)
Gannon U (PA)
Georgia Inst of Technology (GA)
Georgia Southwestern State U (GA)
Grand Valley State U (MI)
Guilford Coll (NC)
Hampshire Coll (MA)
Harvard U (MA)
Indiana U of Pennsylvania (PA)
Iowa State U of Science and Technology (IA)
Johns Hopkins U (MD)
Kean U (NJ)
Kent State U (OH)
Kutztown U of Pennsylvania (PA)
Laurentian U (ON, Canada)
Lewis-Clark State Coll (ID)
Lock Haven U of Pennsylvania (PA)
Long Island U, C.W. Post Campus (NY)
Longwood Coll (VA)
Mansfield U of Pennsylvania (PA)
Massachusetts Inst of Technology (MA)
McGill U (PQ, Canada)
McMaster U (ON, Canada)
Memorial U of Newfoundland (NF, Canada)
Mercer U (GA)
Mercyhurst Coll (PA)
Miami U (OH)
Michigan State U (MI)
Michigan Technological U (MI)
Millersville U of Pennsylvania (PA)
Minnesota State U, Mankato (MN)
Montana State U–Bozeman (MT)
Montclair State U (NJ)
Murray State U (KY)
Muskingum Coll (OH)
National U (CA)
North Dakota State U (ND)
Northeastern Illinois U (IL)
Northern Michigan U (MI)
Northland Coll (WI)
Northwest Missouri State U (MO)
Ohio Wesleyan U (OH)
Olivet Nazarene U (IL)
Pacific Lutheran U (WA)
Penn State U Univ Park Campus (PA)
Queens Coll of the City U of NY (NY)
St. Cloud State U (MN)
St. Mary's U of San Antonio (TX)
Salem State Coll (MA)
Shippensburg U of Pennsylvania (PA)
Simon Fraser U (BC, Canada)
Slippery Rock U of Pennsylvania (PA)
Sonoma State U (CA)
Southeast Missouri State U (MO)
Southern Connecticut State U (CT)
Stanford U (CA)
State U of NY at Albany (NY)
State U of NY at New Paltz (NY)
State U of NY Coll at Brockport (NY)
State U of NY Coll at Buffalo (NY)
State U of NY Coll at Cortland (NY)
State U of NY Coll at Fredonia (NY)
State U of NY Coll at Oneonta (NY)
State U of West Georgia (GA)
State U of NY at Stony Brook (NY)
Tennessee Temple U (TN)
Texas A&M U (TX)
Texas A&M U–Commerce (TX)
Texas Tech U (TX)
Tulane U (LA)
U of Alaska Fairbanks (AK)
U of Alberta (AB, Canada)
The U of Arizona (AZ)
U of Arkansas (AR)
The U of British Columbia (BC, Canada)
U of Calgary (AB, Canada)
U of Calif, Berkeley (CA)
U of Calif, Los Angeles (CA)
U of Calif, San Diego (CA)
U of Calif, Santa Cruz (CA)
U of Guelph (ON, Canada)
U of Indianapolis (IN)
The U of Iowa (IA)
U of King's Coll (NS, Canada)
The U of Lethbridge (AB, Canada)
U of Manitoba (MB, Canada)
U of Massachusetts Amherst (MA)
U of Michigan–Flint (MI)
U of Missouri–Kansas City (MO)
U of Nebraska at Omaha (NE)
U of Nevada, Las Vegas (NV)
U of New Hampshire (NH)
U of New Mexico (NM)
The U of North Carolina at Charlotte (NC)
U of Northern Colorado (CO)
U of Ottawa (ON, Canada)
U of Rochester (NY)
U of South Dakota (SD)
The U of Texas of the Permian Basin (TX)
U of Toronto (ON, Canada)
U of Victoria (BC, Canada)
U of Waterloo (ON, Canada)
The U of Western Ontario (ON, Canada)
U of Windsor (ON, Canada)
U of Wisconsin–Green Bay (WI)
U of Wisconsin–Madison (WI)
U of Wisconsin–Milwaukee (WI)
Virginia Wesleyan Coll (VA)
Washington U in St. Louis (MO)
Wesleyan U (CT)
West Chester U of Pennsylvania (PA)
Western Connecticut State U (CT)
Western Michigan U (MI)
Western Washington U (WA)
Wilkes U (PA)
Winona State U (MN)
Wittenberg U (OH)

York U (ON, Canada)
Youngstown State U (OH)

EAST AND SOUTHEAST ASIAN LANGUAGES RELATED

Dartmouth Coll (NH)
Michigan State U (MI)
U of Hawaii at Manoa (HI)
U of Kansas (KS)
Washington U in St. Louis (MO)

EAST ASIAN STUDIES

Augsburg Coll (MN)
Barnard Coll (NY)
Bates Coll (ME)
Boston U (MA)
Brown U (RI)
Bryn Mawr Coll (PA)
Bucknell U (PA)
Carleton U (ON, Canada)
Colby Coll (ME)
Colgate U (NY)
The Coll of William and Mary (VA)
Columbia Coll (NY)
Columbia U, School of General Studies (NY)
Connecticut Coll (CT)
Cornell U (NY)
Denison U (OH)
DePaul U (IL)
DePauw U (IN)
Dickinson Coll (PA)
Emory & Henry Coll (VA)
The George Washington U (DC)
Hamilton Coll (NY)
Hamline U (MN)
Hampshire Coll (MA)
Harvard U (MA)
Haverford Coll (PA)
Indiana U Bloomington (IN)
John Carroll U (OH)
Johns Hopkins U (MD)
Lawrence U (WI)
Lewis & Clark Coll (OR)
Long Island U, Southampton Coll, Friends World Program (NY)
Marlboro Coll (VT)
Massachusetts Inst of Technology (MA)
McGill U (PQ, Canada)
Middlebury Coll (VT)
New York U (NY)
Oakland U (MI)
Oberlin Coll (OH)
The Ohio State U (OH)
Ohio Wesleyan U (OH)
Penn State U Univ Park Campus (PA)
Pomona Coll (CA)
Portland State U (OR)
Princeton U (NJ)
Queens Coll of the City U of NY (NY)
Rutgers, The State U of New Jersey, New Brunswick (NJ)
San Jose State U (CA)
Scripps Coll (CA)
Seattle U (WA)
Simmons Coll (MA)
Smith Coll (MA)
Stanford U (CA)
State U of NY at Albany (NY)
United States Military Academy (NY)
Université de Montréal (QC, Canada)
U of Alberta (AB, Canada)
The U of Arizona (AZ)
U of Calgary (AB, Canada)
U of Calif, Davis (CA)
U of Calif, Irvine (CA)
U of Calif, Los Angeles (CA)
U of Calif, Santa Cruz (CA)
U of Chicago (IL)
U of Delaware (DE)
U of Hawaii at Manoa (HI)
U of Minnesota, Twin Cities Campus (MN)
The U of Montana–Missoula (MT)
U of Oregon (OR)
U of Pennsylvania (PA)
U of St. Thomas (MN)
U of Southern California (CA)
U of Toronto (ON, Canada)
U of Washington (WA)
Ursinus Coll (PA)
Valparaiso U (IN)
Vanderbilt U (TN)
Washington and Lee U (VA)
Washington U in St. Louis (MO)
Wayne State U (MI)
Wellesley Coll (MA)
Wesleyan U (CT)
Western Washington U (WA)
Wittenberg U (OH)
Yale U (CT)
York U (ON, Canada)

EASTERN EUROPEAN AREA STUDIES

Baltimore Hebrew U (MD)
Bard Coll (NY)
Barnard Coll (NY)
Carleton U (ON, Canada)
Connecticut Coll (CT)
Cornell U (NY)
Emory U (GA)
Florida State U (FL)
Fordham U (NY)
Hamline U (MN)
Hampshire Coll (MA)
Harvard U (MA)
Indiana U Bloomington (IN)
Kent State U (OH)
Long Island U, Southampton Coll, Friends World Program (NY)
Marlboro Coll (VT)
McGill U (PQ, Canada)
Middlebury Coll (VT)
Portland State U (OR)
Rutgers, The State U of New Jersey, New Brunswick (NJ)
Salem State Coll (MA)
Sarah Lawrence Coll (NY)
State U of NY at Albany (NY)
United States Military Academy (NY)
U of Alberta (AB, Canada)
U of Chicago (IL)
U of Connecticut (CT)
The U of Iowa (IA)
U of Oregon (OR)
U of Richmond (VA)
U of Toronto (ON, Canada)
U of Vermont (VT)
U of Victoria (BC, Canada)
Wesleyan U (CT)

EAST EUROPEAN LANGUAGES RELATED

Princeton U (NJ)
The U of North Carolina at Chapel Hill (NC)

ECOLOGY

Adelphi U (NY)
Alma Coll (MI)
Appalachian State U (NC)
Averett U (VA)
Ball State U (IN)
Bard Coll (NY)
Barry U (FL)
Bemidji State U (MN)
Bennington Coll (VT)
Boston U (MA)
Bradley U (IL)
Brevard Coll (NC)
California State U, Fresno (CA)
California State U, Hayward (CA)
California State U, Sacramento (CA)
California State U, San Marcos (CA)
Carleton U (ON, Canada)
Carlow Coll (PA)
The Catholic U of America (DC)
Clark U (MA)
Coll of the Atlantic (ME)
Concordia Coll (NY)
Concordia U (QC, Canada)
Connecticut Coll (CT)
Cornell U (NY)
Dartmouth Coll (NH)
Defiance Coll (OH)
East Central U (OK)
Eastern Kentucky U (KY)
East Stroudsburg U of Pennsylvania (PA)
The Evergreen State Coll (WA)
Florida Inst of Technology (FL)
Florida State U (FL)
Franklin Pierce Coll (NH)
Friends U (KS)
Frostburg State U (MD)
Georgetown Coll (KY)
Goddard Coll (VT)
Hampshire Coll (MA)
Harvard U (MA)
Huntingdon Coll (AL)
Idaho State U (ID)
Iona Coll (NY)
Iowa State U of Science and Technology (IA)
Jacksonville State U (AL)
Juniata Coll (PA)
Keene State Coll (NH)
Lawrence U (WI)
Lenoir-Rhyne Coll (NC)
Lock Haven U of Pennsylvania (PA)
Long Island U, Southampton Coll, Friends World Program (NY)
Maharishi U of Management (IA)
Manchester Coll (IN)
Marlboro Coll (VT)
McGill U (PQ, Canada)
Memorial U of Newfoundland (NF, Canada)
Michigan Technological U (MI)
Minnesota State U, Mankato (MN)
Missouri Southern State Coll (MO)
Montreat Coll (NC)
Morehead State U (KY)
Naropa U (CO)
New England Coll (NH)
Northern Arizona U (AZ)
Northern Michigan U (MI)
Northland Coll (WI)
Northwestern U (IL)
Northwest Missouri State U (MO)
Oberlin Coll (OH)
Okanagan U Coll (BC, Canada)
Pace U (NY)
Plymouth State Coll (NH)
Pomona Coll (CA)
Prescott Coll (AZ)
Princeton U (NJ)
Rice U (TX)
Rutgers, The State U of New Jersey, New Brunswick (NJ)
St. Bonaventure U (NY)
St. Cloud State U (MN)
St. John's U (NY)
St. Lawrence U (NY)
San Diego State U (CA)
San Francisco State U (CA)
San Jose State U (CA)
Sarah Lawrence Coll (NY)
Sierra Nevada Coll (NV)
Simon's Rock Coll of Bard (MA)
Slippery Rock U of Pennsylvania (PA)
Sonoma State U (CA)
Springfield Coll (MA)
State U of NY Coll of Environ Sci and Forestry (NY)
State U of West Georgia (GA)
Sterling Coll (VT)
Towson U (MD)
Tufts U (MA)
Tulane U (LA)
Unity Coll (ME)
Université de Montréal (QC, Canada)
Université de Sherbrooke (PQ, Canada)
U Coll of the Cariboo (BC, Canada)
The U of Arizona (AZ)
U of Calgary (AB, Canada)
U of Calif, Irvine (CA)
U of Calif, Los Angeles (CA)
U of Calif, San Diego (CA)
U of Calif, Santa Barbara (CA)
U of Calif, Santa Cruz (CA)
U of Colorado at Colorado Springs (CO)
U of Connecticut (CT)
U of Delaware (DE)
U of Georgia (GA)
U of Guelph (ON, Canada)
U of Illinois at Urbana–Champaign (IL)
U of Maine at Machias (ME)
U of Manitoba (MB, Canada)
U of Maryland, Coll Park (MD)
U of Maryland Eastern Shore (MD)
U of Miami (FL)
U of Michigan (MI)
U of Minnesota, Twin Cities Campus (MN)
U of Missouri–St. Louis (MO)
U of New Hampshire (NH)
U of Pittsburgh (PA)
U of Pittsburgh at Johnstown (PA)
U of Rio Grande (OH)
The U of Tennessee (TN)
The U of Texas at Austin (TX)
U of Toronto (ON, Canada)
U of Vermont (VT)
U of Victoria (BC, Canada)
The U of Western Ontario (ON, Canada)
U of Wisconsin–Milwaukee (WI)
Ursinus Coll (PA)
Utah State U (UT)
Vanderbilt U (TN)
West Chester U of Pennsylvania (PA)
Western Washington U (WA)
William Paterson U of New Jersey (NJ)
Winona State U (MN)
Yale U (CT)
York U (ON, Canada)

ECONOMICS

Acadia U (NS, Canada)
Adams State Coll (CO)
Adelphi U (NY)
Adrian Coll (MI)
Agnes Scott Coll (GA)
Alabama State U (AL)
Albertson Coll of Idaho (ID)
Albertus Magnus Coll (CT)
Albion Coll (MI)
Albright Coll (PA)
Alcorn State U (MS)
Alfred U (NY)
Allegheny Coll (PA)
Alma Coll (MI)
American International Coll (MA)
American U (DC)
American U in Cairo(Egypt)
The American U of Paris(France)
Amherst Coll (MA)
Andrews U (MI)
Appalachian State U (NC)
Aquinas Coll (MI)
Arizona State U (AZ)
Arkansas State U (AR)
Arkansas Tech U (AR)
Armstrong Atlantic State U (GA)
Ashland U (OH)
Assumption Coll (MA)
Auburn U (AL)
Augsburg Coll (MN)
Augustana Coll (IL)
Augustana Coll (SD)
Aurora U (IL)
Austin Coll (TX)
Ave Maria Coll (MI)
Babson Coll (MA)
Baker U (KS)
Baldwin-Wallace Coll (OH)
Ball State U (IN)
Bard Coll (NY)
Barnard Coll (NY)
Barry U (FL)
Bates Coll (ME)
Baylor U (TX)
Bellarmine U (KY)
Belmont Abbey Coll (NC)
Belmont U (TN)
Beloit Coll (WI)
Bemidji State U (MN)
Benedictine Coll (KS)
Benedictine U (IL)
Bentley Coll (MA)
Berea Coll (KY)
Baruch Coll of the City U of NY (NY)
Berry Coll (GA)
Bethany Coll (WV)
Bethel Coll (MN)
Birmingham-Southern Coll (AL)
Bishop's U (PQ, Canada)
Bloomfield Coll (NJ)
Bloomsburg U of Pennsylvania (PA)
Bluffton Coll (OH)
Boise State U (ID)
Boston Coll (MA)
Boston U (MA)
Bowdoin Coll (ME)
Bowie State U (MD)
Bowling Green State U (OH)
Bradley U (IL)
Brandeis U (MA)
Brandon U (MB, Canada)
Bridgewater Coll (VA)
Bridgewater State Coll (MA)
Brigham Young U (UT)
Brock U (ON, Canada)
Brooklyn Coll of the City U of NY (NY)
Brown U (RI)
Bryant Coll (RI)
Bryn Mawr Coll (PA)
Bucknell U (PA)
Buena Vista U (IA)
Butler U (IN)
California Inst of Technology (CA)
California Lutheran U (CA)
California Polytechnic State U, San Luis Obispo (CA)
California State Polytechnic U, Pomona (CA)
California State U, Bakersfield (CA)
California State U, Chico (CA)
California State U, Dominguez Hills (CA)
California State U, Fresno (CA)
California State U, Fullerton (CA)
California State U, Hayward (CA)
California State U, Long Beach (CA)
California State U, Los Angeles (CA)
California State U, Northridge (CA)
California State U, Sacramento (CA)
California State U, San Bernardino (CA)
California State U, San Marcos (CA)
California State U, Stanislaus (CA)
California U of Pennsylvania (PA)
Calvin Coll (MI)
Campbellsville U (KY)
Campbell U (NC)
Canisius Coll (NY)
Capital U (OH)
Carleton Coll (MN)
Carleton U (ON, Canada)
Carnegie Mellon U (PA)
Carson-Newman Coll (TN)
Carthage Coll (WI)
Case Western Reserve U (OH)
The Catholic U of America (DC)
Centenary Coll of Louisiana (LA)
Central Coll (IA)
Central Connecticut State U (CT)
Central Methodist Coll (MO)
Central Michigan U (MI)
Central Missouri State U (MO)
Central State U (OH)
Central Washington U (WA)
Centre Coll (KY)
Chapman U (CA)
Chatham Coll (PA)
Chestnut Hill Coll (PA)
Cheyney U of Pennsylvania (PA)
Chicago State U (IL)
Christian Brothers U (TN)
Christopher Newport U (VA)
City Coll of the City U of NY (NY)
Claremont McKenna Coll (CA)
Clarion U of Pennsylvania (PA)
Clark Atlanta U (GA)
Clarke Coll (IA)
Clarkson U (NY)
Clark U (MA)
Clemson U (SC)
Cleveland State U (OH)
Coe Coll (IA)
Colby Coll (ME)
Colgate U (NY)
Coll of Charleston (SC)
Coll of Mount Saint Vincent (NY)
The Coll of New Jersey (NJ)
The Coll of New Rochelle (NY)
Coll of Notre Dame of Maryland (MD)
Coll of Saint Benedict (MN)
Coll of St. Catherine (MN)
Coll of Saint Elizabeth (NJ)
The Coll of St. Scholastica (MN)
The Coll of Staten Island of the City U of NY (NY)
Coll of the Atlantic (ME)
Coll of the Holy Cross (MA)
The Coll of William and Mary (VA)
The Coll of Wooster (OH)
The Colorado Coll (CO)
Colorado School of Mines (CO)
Colorado State U (CO)
Columbia Coll (NY)
Columbia U, School of General Studies (NY)
Concordia Coll (MN)
Concordia U (MN)
Concordia U (QC, Canada)

Concordia U Wisconsin (WI)
Connecticut Coll (CT)
Converse Coll (SC)
Cornell Coll (IA)
Cornell U (NY)
Covenant Coll (GA)
Creighton U (NE)
Dalhousie U (NS, Canada)
Dartmouth Coll (NH)
David N. Myers U (OH)
Davidson Coll (NC)
Davis & Elkins Coll (WV)
Delaware State U (DE)
Denison U (OH)
DePaul U (IL)
DePauw U (IN)
Dickinson Coll (PA)
Dillard U (LA)
Doane Coll (NE)
Dominican Coll (NY)
Dominican U (IL)
Dowling Coll (NY)
Drake U (IA)
Drew U (NJ)
Drury U (MO)
Duke U (NC)
Earlham Coll (IN)
East Carolina U (NC)
Eastern Connecticut State U (CT)
Eastern Illinois U (IL)
Eastern Kentucky U (KY)
Eastern Mennonite U (VA)
Eastern Michigan U (MI)
Eastern Oregon U (OR)
Eastern Washington U (WA)
East Stroudsburg U of Pennsylvania (PA)
East Tennessee State U (TN)
Eckerd Coll (FL)
Edgewood Coll (WI)
Edinboro U of Pennsylvania (PA)
Elizabethtown Coll (PA)
Elmhurst Coll (IL)
Elmira Coll (NY)
Elon U (NC)
Emmanuel Coll (MA)
Emory & Henry Coll (VA)
Emory U (GA)
Emporia State U (KS)
Eugene Lang Coll, New School U (NY)
Eureka Coll (IL)
The Evergreen State Coll (WA)
Excelsior Coll (NY)
Fairfield U (CT)
Fairleigh Dickinson U, Florham-Madison Campus (NJ)
Fairmont State Coll (WV)
Fayetteville State U (NC)
Fisk U (TN)
Fitchburg State Coll (MA)
Florida A&M U (FL)
Florida Atlantic U (FL)
Florida International U (FL)
Florida Southern Coll (FL)
Florida State U (FL)
Fordham U (NY)
Fort Hays State U (KS)
Fort Lewis Coll (CO)
Fort Valley State U (GA)
Framingham State Coll (MA)
Franciscan U of Steubenville (OH)
Francis Marion U (SC)
Franklin and Marshall Coll (PA)
Franklin Coll of Indiana (IN)
Franklin Pierce Coll (NH)
Frostburg State U (MD)
Furman U (SC)
Gallaudet U (DC)
George Mason U (VA)
Georgetown U (DC)
The George Washington U (DC)
Georgia Southern U (GA)
Georgia State U (GA)
Gettysburg Coll (PA)
Gonzaga U (WA)
Gordon Coll (MA)
Goshen Coll (IN)
Goucher Coll (MD)
Graceland U (IA)
Grand Canyon U (AZ)
Grand Valley State U (MI)
Grinnell Coll (IA)
Grove City Coll (PA)
Guilford Coll (NC)
Gustavus Adolphus Coll (MN)
Hamilton Coll (NY)
Hamline U (MN)
Hampden-Sydney Coll (VA)
Hampshire Coll (MA)
Hampton U (VA)
Hanover Coll (IN)
Harding U (AR)
Hartwick Coll (NY)
Harvard U (MA)
Hastings Coll (NE)
Haverford Coll (PA)
Hawai'i Pacific U (HI)
Heidelberg Coll (OH)
Hendrix Coll (AR)
Hillsdale Coll (MI)
Hiram Coll (OH)
Hobart and William Smith Colls (NY)
Hofstra U (NY)
Hollins U (VA)
Holy Family Coll (PA)
Hood Coll (MD)
Hope Coll (MI)
Houston Baptist U (TX)
Howard U (DC)
Humboldt State U (CA)
Hunter Coll of the City U of NY (NY)
Huntington Coll (IN)
Idaho State U (ID)
Illinois Coll (IL)
Illinois State U (IL)
Illinois Wesleyan U (IL)
Immaculata Coll (PA)
Indiana State U (IN)
Indiana U Bloomington (IN)
Indiana U Northwest (IN)
Indiana U of Pennsylvania (PA)
Indiana U–Purdue U Fort Wayne (IN)
Indiana U–Purdue U Indianapolis (IN)
Indiana U South Bend (IN)
Indiana U Southeast (IN)
Indiana Wesleyan U (IN)
Inter American U of PR, San Germán Campus (PR)
Iona Coll (NY)
Iowa State U of Science and Technology (IA)
Ithaca Coll (NY)
Jackson State U (MS)
Jacksonville State U (AL)
Jacksonville U (FL)
James Madison U (VA)
Jarvis Christian Coll (TX)
John Carroll U (OH)
Johns Hopkins U (MD)
Johnson C. Smith U (NC)
Juniata Coll (PA)
Kansas State U (KS)
Kean U (NJ)
Keene State Coll (NH)
Kennesaw State U (GA)
Kent State U (OH)
Kenyon Coll (OH)
King Coll (TN)
King's Coll (PA)
Knox Coll (IL)
Lafayette Coll (PA)
LaGrange Coll (GA)
Lake Forest Coll (IL)
Lakehead U (ON, Canada)
Lakeland Coll (WI)
Lake Superior State U (MI)
Lamar U (TX)
La Salle U (PA)
Laurentian U (ON, Canada)
Lawrence U (WI)
Lebanon Valley Coll (PA)
Lehigh U (PA)
Lehman Coll of the City U of NY (NY)
Le Moyne Coll (NY)
Lenoir-Rhyne Coll (NC)
Lewis & Clark Coll (OR)
Lewis U (IL)
Lincoln U (CA)
Lincoln U (MO)
Lincoln U (PA)
Lindenwood U (MO)
Linfield Coll (OR)
Lock Haven U of Pennsylvania (PA)
Long Island U, Brooklyn Campus (NY)
Long Island U, C.W. Post Campus (NY)
Longwood Coll (VA)
Loras Coll (IA)
Louisiana Coll (LA)
Louisiana State U and A&M Coll (LA)
Loyola Coll in Maryland (MD)
Loyola Marymount U (CA)
Loyola U Chicago (IL)
Loyola U New Orleans (LA)
Luther Coll (IA)
Lycoming Coll (PA)
Lynchburg Coll (VA)
Lyon Coll (AR)
Macalester Coll (MN)
Manchester Coll (IN)
Manhattan Coll (NY)
Manhattanville Coll (NY)
Mansfield U of Pennsylvania (PA)
Marietta Coll (OH)
Marist Coll (NY)
Marlboro Coll (VT)
Marquette U (WI)
Marshall U (WV)
Mary Baldwin Coll (VA)
Marymount Coll of Fordham U (NY)
Marymount U (VA)
Maryville Coll (TN)
Mary Washington Coll (VA)
Massachusetts Coll of Liberal Arts (MA)
Massachusetts Inst of Technology (MA)
McGill U (PQ, Canada)
McKendree Coll (IL)
McMaster U (ON, Canada)
Memorial U of Newfoundland (NF, Canada)
Mercer U (GA)
Meredith Coll (NC)
Merrimack Coll (MA)
Messiah Coll (PA)
Methodist Coll (NC)
Metropolitan State Coll of Denver (CO)
Metropolitan State U (MN)
Miami U (OH)
Michigan State U (MI)
Middlebury Coll (VT)
Middle Tennessee State U (TN)
Midland Lutheran Coll (NE)
Midwestern State U (TX)
Millersville U of Pennsylvania (PA)
Millsaps Coll (MS)
Mills Coll (CA)
Minnesota State U, Mankato (MN)
Minnesota State U Moorhead (MN)
Minot State U (ND)
Mississippi State U (MS)
Missouri Valley Coll (MO)
Missouri Western State Coll (MO)
Monmouth Coll (IL)
Monmouth U (NJ)
Montana State U–Bozeman (MT)
Montclair State U (NJ)
Montreat Coll (NC)
Moravian Coll (PA)
Morehouse Coll (GA)
Morgan State U (MD)
Mount Allison U (NB, Canada)
Mount Holyoke Coll (MA)
Mount Saint Mary's Coll and Seminary (MD)
Mount Saint Vincent U (NS, Canada)
Mount Union Coll (OH)
Muhlenberg Coll (PA)
Murray State U (KY)
Muskingum Coll (OH)
Nazareth Coll of Rochester (NY)
Nebraska Wesleyan U (NE)
Newberry Coll (SC)
New Coll of Florida (FL)
New Jersey City U (NJ)
New Mexico State U (NM)
New York Inst of Technology (NY)
New York U (NY)
Niagara U (NY)
Nipissing U (ON, Canada)
Norfolk State U (VA)
North Carolina Ag and Tech State U (NC)
North Carolina State U (NC)
North Central Coll (IL)
North Dakota State U (ND)
Northeastern Illinois U (IL)
Northeastern U (MA)
Northern Arizona U (AZ)
Northern Illinois U (IL)
Northern Kentucky U (KY)
Northern Michigan U (MI)
Northern State U (SD)
Northland Coll (WI)
North Park U (IL)
Northwestern Coll (IA)
Northwestern U (IL)
Northwest Missouri State U (MO)
Northwood U (MI)
Norwich U (VT)
Oakland U (MI)
Oakwood Coll (AL)
Oberlin Coll (OH)
Occidental Coll (CA)
Oglethorpe U (GA)
Ohio Dominican Coll (OH)
The Ohio State U (OH)
Ohio U (OH)
Ohio Wesleyan U (OH)
Okanagan U Coll (BC, Canada)
Oklahoma State U (OK)
Old Dominion U (VA)
Olivet Coll (MI)
Olivet Nazarene U (IL)
Oregon State U (OR)
Otterbein Coll (OH)
Pace U (NY)
Pacific Lutheran U (WA)
Pacific U (OR)
Park U (MO)
Penn State U at Erie, The Behrend Coll (PA)
Penn State U Univ Park Campus (PA)
Pepperdine U, Malibu (CA)
Pittsburg State U (KS)
Pitzer Coll (CA)
Plattsburgh State U of NY (NY)
Point Loma Nazarene U (CA)
Pomona Coll (CA)
Pontifical Catholic U of Puerto Rico (PR)
Portland State U (OR)
Presbyterian Coll (SC)
Princeton U (NJ)
Principia Coll (IL)
Providence Coll (RI)
Purchase Coll, State U of NY (NY)
Purdue U (IN)
Purdue U Calumet (IN)
Queens Coll of the City U of NY (NY)
Queen's U at Kingston (ON, Canada)
Quinnipiac U (CT)
Radford U (VA)
Ramapo Coll of New Jersey (NJ)
Randolph-Macon Coll (VA)
Randolph-Macon Woman's Coll (VA)
Reed Coll (OR)
Regis Coll (MA)
Regis U (CO)
Rensselaer Polytechnic Inst (NY)
Rhode Island Coll (RI)
Rhodes Coll (TN)
Rice U (TX)
The Richard Stockton Coll of New Jersey (NJ)
Richmond, The American International U in London(United Kingdom)
Rider U (NJ)
Ripon Coll (WI)
Roanoke Coll (VA)
Robert Morris U (PA)
Rochester Inst of Technology (NY)
Rockford Coll (IL)
Rockhurst U (MO)
Rocky Mountain Coll (MT)
Rollins Coll (FL)
Roosevelt U (IL)
Rose-Hulman Inst of Technology (IN)
Rosemont Coll (PA)
Rowan U (NJ)
Russell Sage Coll (NY)
Rutgers, The State U of New Jersey, New Brunswick (NJ)
Sacred Heart U (CT)
Saginaw Valley State U (MI)
St. Ambrose U (IA)
Saint Anselm Coll (NH)
St. Cloud State U (MN)
St. Edward's U (TX)
St. Francis Coll (NY)
Saint Francis U (PA)
St. Francis Xavier U (NS, Canada)
St. John Fisher Coll (NY)
Saint John's U (MN)
St. John's U (NY)
Saint Joseph Coll (CT)
Saint Joseph's Coll (IN)
Saint Joseph's U (PA)
St. Lawrence U (NY)
Saint Louis U (MO)
Saint Martin's Coll (WA)
Saint Mary's Coll (IN)
Saint Mary's Coll of California (CA)
St. Mary's Coll of Maryland (MD)
Saint Mary's U (NS, Canada)
St. Mary's U of San Antonio (TX)
Saint Michael's Coll (VT)
St. Norbert Coll (WI)
St. Olaf Coll (MN)
Saint Peter's Coll (NJ)
St. Thomas U (NB, Canada)
Saint Vincent Coll (PA)
Salem Coll (NC)
Salem State Coll (MA)
Salisbury U (MD)
Salve Regina U (RI)
San Diego State U (CA)
San Francisco State U (CA)
San Jose State U (CA)
Santa Clara U (CA)
Sarah Lawrence Coll (NY)
Schiller International U(Germany)
Schiller International U(United Kingdom)
Schiller International U, American Coll of Switzerland(Switzerland)
Scripps Coll (CA)
Seattle Pacific U (WA)
Seattle U (WA)
Seton Hall U (NJ)
Seton Hill Coll (PA)
Shepherd Coll (WV)
Shippensburg U of Pennsylvania (PA)
Shorter Coll (GA)
Siena Coll (NY)
Simmons Coll (MA)
Simon Fraser U (BC, Canada)
Simpson Coll (IA)
Skidmore Coll (NY)
Slippery Rock U of Pennsylvania (PA)
Smith Coll (MA)
Sojourner-Douglass Coll (MD)
Sonoma State U (CA)
South Carolina State U (SC)
South Dakota State U (SD)
Southeast Missouri State U (MO)
Southern Connecticut State U (CT)
Southern Illinois U Carbondale (IL)
Southern Illinois U Edwardsville (IL)
Southern Methodist U (TX)
Southern New Hampshire U (NH)
Southern Oregon U (OR)
Southern Utah U (UT)
Southwestern U (TX)
Southwest Missouri State U (MO)
Southwest Texas State U (TX)
Spelman Coll (GA)
Stanford U (CA)
State U of NY at Albany (NY)
State U of NY at Binghamton (NY)
State U of NY at New Paltz (NY)
State U of NY at Oswego (NY)
State U of NY Coll at Buffalo (NY)
State U of NY Coll at Cortland (NY)
State U of NY Coll at Fredonia (NY)
State U of NY Coll at Geneseo (NY)
State U of NY Coll at Oneonta (NY)
State U of NY Coll at Potsdam (NY)
State U of NY Empire State Coll (NY)
State U of West Georgia (GA)
Stephen F. Austin State U (TX)
Stetson U (FL)
Stonehill Coll (MA)
State U of NY at Stony Brook (NY)
Strayer U (DC)
Suffolk U (MA)
Susquehanna U (PA)
Swarthmore Coll (PA)
Sweet Briar Coll (VA)
Syracuse U (NY)
Talladega Coll (AL)
Tarleton State U (TX)
Taylor U (IN)
Temple U (PA)
Tennessee Technological U (TN)
Texas A&M U (TX)
Texas A&M U–Commerce (TX)
Texas A&M U–Kingsville (TX)
Texas Christian U (TX)

Texas Lutheran U (TX)
Texas Southern U (TX)
Texas Tech U (TX)
Texas Wesleyan U (TX)
Texas Woman's U (TX)
Thomas Edison State Coll (NJ)
Thomas More Coll (KY)
Tiffin U (OH)
Tougaloo Coll (MS)
Touro Coll (NY)
Towson U (MD)
Transylvania U (KY)
Trent U (ON, Canada)
Trinity Coll (CT)
Trinity Coll (DC)
Trinity International U (IL)
Trinity U (TX)
Truman State U (MO)
Tufts U (MA)
Tulane U (LA)
Tuskegee U (AL)
Union Coll (NY)
Union U (TN)
United States Air Force Academy (CO)
United States Military Academy (NY)
United States Naval Academy (MD)
Université de Montréal (QC, Canada)
Université de Sherbrooke (PQ, Canada)
Université Laval (QC, Canada)
State U of NY at Buffalo (NY)
U Coll of Cape Breton (NS, Canada)
U Coll of the Cariboo (BC, Canada)
The U of Akron (OH)
U of Alaska Anchorage (AK)
U of Alaska Fairbanks (AK)
U of Alberta (AB, Canada)
The U of Arizona (AZ)
U of Arkansas (AR)
U of Arkansas at Little Rock (AR)
U of Arkansas at Pine Bluff (AR)
U of Baltimore (MD)
U of Bridgeport (CT)
The U of British Columbia (BC, Canada)
U of Calgary (AB, Canada)
U of Calif, Berkeley (CA)
U of Calif, Davis (CA)
U of Calif, Irvine (CA)
U of Calif, Los Angeles (CA)
U of Calif, Riverside (CA)
U of Calif, San Diego (CA)
U of Calif, Santa Barbara (CA)
U of Calif, Santa Cruz (CA)
U of Central Arkansas (AR)
U of Central Florida (FL)
U of Central Oklahoma (OK)
U of Chicago (IL)
U of Cincinnati (OH)
U of Colorado at Boulder (CO)
U of Colorado at Colorado Springs (CO)
U of Colorado at Denver (CO)
U of Connecticut (CT)
U of Dallas (TX)
U of Dayton (OH)
U of Delaware (DE)
U of Denver (CO)
U of Evansville (IN)
The U of Findlay (OH)
U of Florida (FL)
U of Georgia (GA)
U of Guelph (ON, Canada)
U of Hartford (CT)
U of Hawaii at Hilo (HI)
U of Hawaii at Manoa (HI)
U of Hawaii–West Oahu (HI)
U of Houston (TX)
U of Idaho (ID)
U of Illinois at Chicago (IL)
U of Illinois at Springfield (IL)
U of Illinois at Urbana–Champaign (IL)
The U of Iowa (IA)
U of Kansas (KS)
U of Kentucky (KY)
U of King's Coll (NS, Canada)
The U of Lethbridge (AB, Canada)
U of Louisville (KY)
U of Maine (ME)
U of Maine at Farmington (ME)
U of Manitoba (MB, Canada)
U of Mary Hardin-Baylor (TX)
U of Maryland, Baltimore County (MD)
U of Maryland, Coll Park (MD)
U of Massachusetts Amherst (MA)
U of Massachusetts Boston (MA)
U of Massachusetts Dartmouth (MA)
U of Massachusetts Lowell (MA)
The U of Memphis (TN)
U of Michigan (MI)
U of Michigan–Dearborn (MI)
U of Michigan–Flint (MI)
U of Minnesota, Duluth (MN)
U of Minnesota, Morris (MN)
U of Minnesota, Twin Cities Campus (MN)
U of Mississippi (MS)
U of Missouri–Columbia (MO)
U of Missouri–Kansas City (MO)
U of Missouri–Rolla (MO)
U of Missouri–St. Louis (MO)
U of Mobile (AL)
The U of Montana–Missoula (MT)
U of Nebraska at Kearney (NE)
U of Nebraska at Omaha (NE)
U of Nebraska–Lincoln (NE)
U of Nevada, Las Vegas (NV)
U of New Hampshire (NH)
U of New Haven (CT)
U of New Mexico (NM)
U of New Orleans (LA)
The U of North Carolina at Asheville (NC)
The U of North Carolina at Chapel Hill (NC)
The U of North Carolina at Charlotte (NC)
The U of North Carolina at Greensboro (NC)
The U of North Carolina at Pembroke (NC)
The U of North Carolina at Wilmington (NC)
U of North Dakota (ND)
U of Northern Colorado (CO)
U of Northern Iowa (IA)
U of North Florida (FL)
U of North Texas (TX)
U of Notre Dame (IN)
U of Oklahoma (OK)
U of Oregon (OR)
U of Ottawa (ON, Canada)
U of Pennsylvania (PA)
U of Pittsburgh (PA)
U of Pittsburgh at Bradford (PA)
U of Pittsburgh at Johnstown (PA)
U of Prince Edward Island (PE, Canada)
U of Puerto Rico, Cayey U Coll (PR)
U of Puget Sound (WA)
U of Redlands (CA)
U of Regina (SK, Canada)
U of Rhode Island (RI)
U of Richmond (VA)
U of Rio Grande (OH)
U of Rochester (NY)
U of Saint Francis (IN)
U of St. Thomas (MN)
U of St. Thomas (TX)
U of San Diego (CA)
U of San Francisco (CA)
U of Saskatchewan (SK, Canada)
U of Science and Arts of Oklahoma (OK)
The U of Scranton (PA)
U of Sioux Falls (SD)
U of South Carolina (SC)
U of South Dakota (SD)
U of Southern California (CA)
U of Southern Indiana (IN)
U of Southern Maine (ME)
U of South Florida (FL)
The U of Tampa (FL)
The U of Tennessee (TN)
The U of Tennessee at Chattanooga (TN)
The U of Tennessee at Martin (TN)
The U of Texas at Arlington (TX)
The U of Texas at Austin (TX)
The U of Texas at Dallas (TX)
The U of Texas at El Paso (TX)
The U of Texas at Tyler (TX)
The U of Texas of the Permian Basin (TX)
The U of Texas–Pan American (TX)
U of the District of Columbia (DC)
U of the Pacific (CA)
U of the South (TN)
U of Toledo (OH)
U of Toronto (ON, Canada)
U of Tulsa (OK)
U of Utah (UT)
U of Vermont (VT)
U of Victoria (BC, Canada)
U of Virginia (VA)
The U of Virginia's Coll at Wise (VA)
U of Washington (WA)
U of Waterloo (ON, Canada)
The U of Western Ontario (ON, Canada)
U of Windsor (ON, Canada)
U of Wisconsin–Eau Claire (WI)
U of Wisconsin–Green Bay (WI)
U of Wisconsin–La Crosse (WI)
U of Wisconsin–Madison (WI)
U of Wisconsin–Milwaukee (WI)
U of Wisconsin–Oshkosh (WI)
U of Wisconsin–Parkside (WI)
U of Wisconsin–Platteville (WI)
U of Wisconsin–River Falls (WI)
U of Wisconsin–Stevens Point (WI)
U of Wisconsin–Superior (WI)
U of Wisconsin–Whitewater (WI)
Ursinus Coll (PA)
Utah State U (UT)
Utica Coll of Syracuse U (NY)
Valdosta State U (GA)
Valparaiso U (IN)
Vanderbilt U (TN)
Vassar Coll (NY)
Villanova U (PA)
Virginia Military Inst (VA)
Virginia Polytechnic Inst and State U (VA)
Wabash Coll (IN)
Wake Forest U (NC)
Walla Walla Coll (WA)
Warren Wilson Coll (NC)
Wartburg Coll (IA)
Washburn U of Topeka (KS)
Washington & Jefferson Coll (PA)
Washington and Lee U (VA)
Washington Coll (MD)
Washington State U (WA)
Washington U in St. Louis (MO)
Wayne State U (MI)
Weber State U (UT)
Webster U (MO)
Wellesley Coll (MA)
Wells Coll (NY)
Wesleyan Coll (GA)
Wesleyan U (CT)
West Chester U of Pennsylvania (PA)
Western Connecticut State U (CT)
Western Illinois U (IL)
Western Kentucky U (KY)
Western Maryland Coll (MD)
Western Michigan U (MI)
Western New England Coll (MA)
Western Oregon U (OR)
Western State Coll of Colorado (CO)
Western Washington U (WA)
Westfield State Coll (MA)
Westminster Coll (MO)
Westminster Coll (PA)
Westmont Coll (CA)
West Texas A&M U (TX)
West Virginia State Coll (WV)
West Virginia U (WV)
West Virginia Wesleyan Coll (WV)
Wheaton Coll (IL)
Wheaton Coll (MA)
Whitman Coll (WA)
Whittier Coll (CA)
Whitworth Coll (WA)
Wichita State U (KS)
Widener U (PA)
Wilberforce U (OH)
Wilfrid Laurier U (ON, Canada)
Willamette U (OR)
William Carey Coll (MS)
William Jewell Coll (MO)
Williams Coll (MA)
Wilmington Coll (OH)
Wingate U (NC)
Winona State U (MN)
Winston-Salem State U (NC)
Wittenberg U (OH)
Wofford Coll (SC)
Worcester Polytechnic Inst (MA)
Worcester State Coll (MA)
Wright State U (OH)
Xavier U (OH)
Xavier U of Louisiana (LA)
Yale U (CT)
Yeshiva U (NY)
York Coll of Pennsylvania (PA)
York Coll of the City U of New York (NY)
York U (ON, Canada)
Youngstown State U (OH)

ECONOMICS RELATED

Bloomsburg U of Pennsylvania (PA)
The Colorado Coll (CO)
Marymount U (VA)
State U of West Georgia (GA)
The U of Akron (OH)
U of Dallas (TX)

EDUCATION

Acadia U (NS, Canada)
Adrian Coll (MI)
Alabama State U (AL)
Albion Coll (MI)
Alderson-Broaddus Coll (WV)
Alfred U (NY)
Alma Coll (MI)
Alvernia Coll (PA)
Alverno Coll (WI)
American International Coll (MA)
American U of Puerto Rico (PR)
Anderson Coll (SC)
Anderson U (IN)
Andrews U (MI)
Arcadia U (PA)
Arlington Baptist Coll (TX)
Armstrong Atlantic State U (GA)
Ashland U (OH)
Assumption Coll (MA)
Atlantic Baptist U (NB, Canada)
Atlantic Union Coll (MA)
Augsburg Coll (MN)
Augustana Coll (IL)
Baldwin-Wallace Coll (OH)
Ball State U (IN)
Baltimore Hebrew U (MD)
Baptist Bible Coll of Pennsylvania (PA)
The Baptist Coll of Florida (FL)
Barry U (FL)
Barton Coll (NC)
Baylor U (TX)
Bellarmine U (KY)
Belmont Abbey Coll (NC)
Belmont U (TN)
Beloit Coll (WI)
Bemidji State U (MN)
Benedictine U (IL)
Berea Coll (KY)
Baruch Coll of the City U of NY (NY)
Berry Coll (GA)
Bethany Coll (KS)
Bethany Coll (WV)
Bethany Coll of the Assemblies of God (CA)
Bethel Coll (IN)
Bethel Coll (MN)
Bethel Coll (TN)
Biola U (CA)
Birmingham-Southern Coll (AL)
Bishop's U (PQ, Canada)
Bluefield Coll (VA)
Bluffton Coll (OH)
Boise State U (ID)
Boston U (MA)
Bowie State U (MD)
Bowling Green State U (OH)
Brandon U (MB, Canada)
Brenau U (GA)
Brescia U (KY)
Brewton-Parker Coll (GA)
Briar Cliff U (IA)
Bridgewater State Coll (MA)
Brigham Young U–Hawaii (HI)
Brock U (ON, Canada)
Brooklyn Coll of the City U of NY (NY)
Brown U (RI)
Bryan Coll (TN)
Bucknell U (PA)
Buena Vista U (IA)
Cabrini Coll (PA)
California State U, Sacramento (CA)
California U of Pennsylvania (PA)
Calvary Bible Coll and Theological Seminary (MO)
Cameron U (OK)
Campbell U (NC)
Canisius Coll (NY)
Capital U (OH)
Cardinal Stritch U (WI)
Caribbean U (PR)
Carroll Coll (MT)
Carroll Coll (WI)
Carson-Newman Coll (TN)
Carthage Coll (WI)
Catawba Coll (NC)
The Catholic U of America (DC)
Cedar Crest Coll (PA)
Cedarville U (OH)
Centenary Coll (NJ)
Centenary Coll of Louisiana (LA)
Central Methodist Coll (MO)
Central Missouri State U (MO)
Charleston Southern U (SC)
Cheyney U of Pennsylvania (PA)
Chicago State U (IL)
Christian Brothers U (TN)
Christian Heritage Coll (CA)
Christopher Newport U (VA)
Cincinnati Bible Coll and Seminary (OH)
Circleville Bible Coll (OH)
City Coll of the City U of NY (NY)
Clarion U of Pennsylvania (PA)
Clark Atlanta U (GA)
Clarke Coll (IA)
Clark U (MA)
Clearwater Christian Coll (FL)
Cleveland State U (OH)
Coe Coll (IA)
Coker Coll (SC)
Colgate U (NY)
Coll of Mount Saint Vincent (NY)
The Coll of New Jersey (NJ)
The Coll of New Rochelle (NY)
Coll of Notre Dame of Maryland (MD)
Coll of Saint Benedict (MN)
Coll of St. Catherine (MN)
Coll of St. Joseph (VT)
Coll of Saint Mary (NE)
The Coll of Saint Rose (NY)
The Coll of St. Scholastica (MN)
Coll of Staten Island of the City U of NY (NY)
Coll of the Atlantic (ME)
Coll of the Ozarks (MO)
Coll of the Southwest (NM)
Columbia Coll (MO)
Columbia Coll (SC)
Columbus State U (GA)
Concord Coll (WV)
Concordia Coll (MN)
Concordia Coll (NY)
Concordia U (IL)
Concordia U (MN)
Concordia U (NE)
Concordia U (OR)
Concordia U Wisconsin (WI)
Converse Coll (SC)
Coppin State Coll (MD)
Cornell Coll (IA)
Cornell U (NY)
Cornerstone U (MI)
Creighton U (NE)
Cumberland U (TN)
Curry Coll (MA)
Dakota State U (SD)
Dallas Baptist U (TX)
Dallas Christian Coll (TX)
Dana Coll (NE)
Davis & Elkins Coll (WV)
Defiance Coll (OH)
Delaware State U (DE)
Delta State U (MS)
DePaul U (IL)
Dickinson State U (ND)
Dillard U (LA)
Dominican Coll (NY)
Dordt Coll (IA)
Dowling Coll (NY)
Drury U (MO)
Duquesne U (PA)
D'Youville Coll (NY)
Earlham Coll (IN)
East Central U (OK)
Eastern Kentucky U (KY)
Eastern Nazarene Coll (MA)
Eastern Oregon U (OR)
Eastern Washington U (WA)
Edgewood Coll (WI)
Edward Waters Coll (FL)
Elizabeth City State U (NC)
Elizabethtown Coll (PA)
Elmhurst Coll (IL)
Elmira Coll (NY)
Elms Coll (MA)
Elon U (NC)
Emmanuel Coll (MA)

Emory U (GA)
Endicott Coll (MA)
Eugene Lang Coll, New School U (NY)
Eureka Coll (IL)
Evangel U (MO)
The Evergreen State Coll (WA)
Fairmont State Coll (WV)
Faulkner U (AL)
Fayetteville State U (NC)
Felician Coll (NJ)
Ferris State U (MI)
Ferrum Coll (VA)
Finlandia U (MI)
Fitchburg State Coll (MA)
Florida A&M U (FL)
Florida Southern Coll (FL)
Fontbonne U (MO)
Fordham U (NY)
Fort Lewis Coll (CO)
Framingham State Coll (MA)
Franklin Pierce Coll (NH)
Freed-Hardeman U (TN)
Fresno Pacific U (CA)
Friends U (KS)
Frostburg State U (MD)
Furman U (SC)
Gallaudet U (DC)
Gardner-Webb U (NC)
Georgetown Coll (KY)
Georgia Southwestern State U (GA)
Gettysburg Coll (PA)
Glenville State Coll (WV)
Goddard Coll (VT)
Gordon Coll (MA)
Goshen Coll (IN)
Goucher Coll (MD)
Graceland U (IA)
Grand Valley State U (MI)
Grand View Coll (IA)
Great Lakes Christian Coll (MI)
Greensboro Coll (NC)
Greenville Coll (IL)
Gustavus Adolphus Coll (MN)
Gwynedd-Mercy Coll (PA)
Hamline U (MN)
Hampshire Coll (MA)
Hampton U (VA)
Hannibal-LaGrange Coll (MO)
Hastings Coll (NE)
Haverford Coll (PA)
Heidelberg Coll (OH)
High Point U (NC)
Hillsdale Coll (MI)
Holy Family Coll (PA)
Houston Baptist U (TX)
Howard Payne U (TX)
Howard U (DC)
Humboldt State U (CA)
Huntingdon Coll (AL)
Huntington Coll (IN)
Huston-Tillotson Coll (TX)
Idaho State U (ID)
Illinois Coll (IL)
Illinois Wesleyan U (IL)
Immaculata Coll (PA)
Indiana U Bloomington (IN)
Indiana U East (IN)
Indiana U Northwest (IN)
Indiana U–Purdue U Fort Wayne (IN)
Indiana U–Purdue U Indianapolis (IN)
Indiana U South Bend (IN)
Indiana U Southeast (IN)
Indiana Wesleyan U (IN)
Inter American U of PR, San Germán Campus (PR)
Iona Coll (NY)
Iowa State U of Science and Technology (IA)
Iowa Wesleyan Coll (IA)
Jacksonville State U (AL)
Jacksonville U (FL)
James Madison U (VA)
John Brown U (AR)
John Carroll U (OH)
Johnson C. Smith U (NC)
Johnson State Coll (VT)
Judson Coll (AL)
Judson Coll (IL)
Juniata Coll (PA)
Kansas Wesleyan U (KS)
Keene State Coll (NH)
Kennesaw State U (GA)
Kent State U (OH)
King Coll (TN)
Knox Coll (IL)
Kutztown U of Pennsylvania (PA)
LaGrange Coll (GA)
Lake Forest Coll (IL)
Lakehead U (ON, Canada)
Lakeland Coll (WI)
Lake Superior State U (MI)
Lamar U (TX)
Lambuth U (TN)
Lancaster Bible Coll (PA)
Lander U (SC)
La Salle U (PA)
Lasell Coll (MA)
Laura and Alvin Siegal Coll of Judaic Studies (OH)
Laurentian U (ON, Canada)
Lees-McRae Coll (NC)
Lee U (TN)
LeMoyne-Owen Coll (TN)
Lenoir-Rhyne Coll (NC)
Lesley U (MA)
Lewis-Clark State Coll (ID)
Lewis U (IL)
Limestone Coll (SC)
Lincoln Memorial U (TN)
Lincoln U (PA)
Lindenwood U (MO)
Lindsey Wilson Coll (KY)
Lipscomb U (TN)
Lock Haven U of Pennsylvania (PA)
Long Island U, Brooklyn Campus (NY)
Long Island U, C.W. Post Campus (NY)
Long Island U, Southampton Coll, Friends World Program (NY)
Longwood Coll (VA)
Loras Coll (IA)
Loyola Coll in Maryland (MD)
Loyola U New Orleans (LA)
Lubbock Christian U (TX)
Luther Coll (IA)
Lycoming Coll (PA)
Lynchburg Coll (VA)
Lynn U (FL)
Maharishi U of Management (IA)
Malaspina U-Coll (BC, Canada)
Manchester Coll (IN)
Manhattan Coll (NY)
Manhattanville Coll (NY)
Mansfield U of Pennsylvania (PA)
Maranatha Baptist Bible Coll (WI)
Marian Coll (IN)
Marian Coll of Fond du Lac (WI)
Marietta Coll (OH)
Marquette U (WI)
Marshall U (WV)
Mars Hill Coll (NC)
Marymount Coll of Fordham U (NY)
Maryville Coll (TN)
Marywood U (PA)
Massachusetts Coll of Liberal Arts (MA)
The Master's Coll and Seminary (CA)
Mayville State U (ND)
McGill U (PQ, Canada)
McNeese State U (LA)
McPherson Coll (KS)
Medaille Coll (NY)
Medgar Evers Coll of the City U of NY (NY)
Memorial U of Newfoundland (NF, Canada)
Mercy Coll (NY)
Mercyhurst Coll (PA)
Mesa State Coll (CO)
Methodist Coll (NC)
Middlebury Coll (VT)
Midland Lutheran Coll (NE)
Midway Coll (KY)
Milligan Coll (TN)
Millsaps Coll (MS)
Mills Coll (CA)
Minnesota State U, Mankato (MN)
Mississippi Coll (MS)
Mississippi U for Women (MS)
Mississippi Valley State U (MS)
Missouri Southern State Coll (MO)
Missouri Valley Coll (MO)
Molloy Coll (NY)
Monmouth Coll (IL)
Monmouth U (NJ)
Montana State U–Billings (MT)
Montana State U–Northern (MT)
Montreat Coll (NC)
Moravian Coll (PA)
Morgan State U (MD)
Morningside Coll (IA)
Mount Holyoke Coll (MA)
Mount Marty Coll (SD)
Mount Mary Coll (WI)
Mount Mercy Coll (IA)
Mount St. Clare Coll (IA)
Mount Saint Mary Coll (NY)
Mount St. Mary's Coll (CA)
Mount Saint Vincent U (NS, Canada)
Mount Vernon Nazarene U (OH)
Muskingum Coll (OH)
The National Hispanic U (CA)
Nazareth Coll of Rochester (NY)
Newberry Coll (SC)
New England Coll (NH)
Newman U (KS)
New Mexico Highlands U (NM)
New York Inst of Technology (NY)
New York U (NY)
Niagara U (NY)
Nicholls State U (LA)
Nipissing U (ON, Canada)
North Carolina Ag and Tech State U (NC)
North Carolina State U (NC)
North Carolina Wesleyan Coll (NC)
North Central Coll (IL)
North Dakota State U (ND)
Northeastern State U (OK)
Northeastern U (MA)
Northern Arizona U (AZ)
Northern Illinois U (IL)
Northern Kentucky U (KY)
Northern Michigan U (MI)
Northern State U (SD)
North Georgia Coll & State U (GA)
Northland Coll (WI)
North Park U (IL)
Northwest Coll (WA)
Northwestern Coll (IA)
Northwestern U (IL)
Northwest Missouri State U (MO)
Notre Dame de Namur U (CA)
Nova Scotia Coll of Art and Design (NS, Canada)
Oakland City U (IN)
Oglethorpe U (GA)
Ohio Dominican Coll (OH)
Ohio U (OH)
Ohio U–Lancaster (OH)
Ohio U–Southern Campus (OH)
Ohio Valley Coll (WV)
Ohio Wesleyan U (OH)
Okanagan U Coll (BC, Canada)
Oklahoma Baptist U (OK)
Oklahoma City U (OK)
Oklahoma State U (OK)
Oklahoma Wesleyan U (OK)
Olivet Coll (MI)
Olivet Nazarene U (IL)
Oral Roberts U (OK)
Otterbein Coll (OH)
Ouachita Baptist U (AR)
Our Lady of Holy Cross Coll (LA)
Pacific Lutheran U (WA)
Pacific Union Coll (CA)
Pacific U (OR)
Palm Beach Atlantic Coll (FL)
Pepperdine U, Malibu (CA)
Peru State Coll (NE)
Pfeiffer U (NC)
Pillsbury Baptist Bible Coll (MN)
Pittsburg State U (KS)
Plattsburgh State U of NY (NY)
Point Park Coll (PA)
Pontifical Catholic U of Puerto Rico (PR)
Presbyterian Coll (SC)
Prescott Coll (AZ)
Providence Coll and Theological Seminary (MB, Canada)
Purdue U (IN)
Purdue U Calumet (IN)
Queens Coll (NC)
Queens Coll of the City U of NY (NY)
Queen's U at Kingston (ON, Canada)
Quinnipiac U (CT)
Redeemer U Coll (ON, Canada)
Regis U (CO)
Rhode Island Coll (RI)
Rider U (NJ)
Ripon Coll (WI)
Rivier Coll (NH)
Roberts Wesleyan Coll (NY)
Rockford Coll (IL)
Rockhurst U (MO)
Rocky Mountain Coll (MT)
Rocky Mountain Coll (AB, Canada)
Rollins Coll (FL)
Roosevelt U (IL)
Sacred Heart U (CT)
St. Ambrose U (IA)
St. Cloud State U (MN)
Saint Francis U (PA)
St. Francis Xavier U (NS, Canada)
Saint John's U (MN)
Saint Joseph Coll (CT)
Saint Joseph's Coll (ME)
St. Joseph's Coll, New York (NY)
St. Joseph's Coll, Suffolk Campus (NY)
Saint Joseph's U (PA)
Saint Leo U (FL)
Saint Martin's Coll (WA)
Saint Mary-of-the-Woods Coll (IN)
Saint Mary's Coll (IN)
Saint Mary's Coll of California (CA)
St. Mary's U of San Antonio (TX)
Saint Michael's Coll (VT)
St. Petersburg Coll (FL)
St. Thomas Aquinas Coll (NY)
St. Thomas U (NB, Canada)
Salem Coll (NC)
Salem International U (WV)
Salem State Coll (MA)
Salisbury U (MD)
San Jose Christian Coll (CA)
Sarah Lawrence Coll (NY)
Seton Hill Coll (PA)
Shasta Bible Coll (CA)
Shawnee State U (OH)
Sheldon Jackson Coll (AK)
Simmons Coll (MA)
Simon Fraser U (BC, Canada)
Simpson Coll (IA)
Simpson Coll and Graduate School (CA)
Slippery Rock U of Pennsylvania (PA)
Smith Coll (MA)
South Carolina State U (SC)
South Dakota State U (SD)
Southeastern Bible Coll (AL)
Southeastern Oklahoma State U (OK)
Southern Connecticut State U (CT)
Southern Nazarene U (OK)
Southern Utah U (UT)
Southern Wesleyan U (SC)
Southwestern Oklahoma State U (OK)
Southwest State U (MN)
Springfield Coll (MA)
State U of NY at New Paltz (NY)
State U of NY at Oswego (NY)
State U of NY Coll at Brockport (NY)
State U of NY Coll at Fredonia (NY)
State U of NY Coll at Geneseo (NY)
State U of NY Coll at Oneonta (NY)
State U of NY Empire State Coll (NY)
Stetson U (FL)
Stonehill Coll (MA)
Suffolk U (MA)
Syracuse U (NY)
Tabor Coll (KS)
Talladega Coll (AL)
Tarleton State U (TX)
Taylor U (IN)
Temple U (PA)
Tennessee State U (TN)
Tennessee Technological U (TN)
Tennessee Temple U (TN)
Tennessee Wesleyan Coll (TN)
Texas A&M U–Commerce (TX)
Texas A&M U–Kingsville (TX)
Texas Lutheran U (TX)
Texas Southern U (TX)
Texas Wesleyan U (TX)
Tougaloo Coll (MS)
Touro Coll (NY)
Trent U (ON, Canada)
Trinity Christian Coll (IL)
Trinity Coll (CT)
Trinity Coll (DC)
Trinity International U (IL)
Trinity Western U (BC, Canada)
Tri-State U (IN)
Troy State U (AL)
Tusculum Coll (TN)
Union Coll (KY)
Union Coll (NE)
Union Inst & U (OH)
Union U (TN)
Université de Montréal (QC, Canada)
Université de Sherbrooke (PQ, Canada)
The U of Akron (OH)
U of Alaska Anchorage (AK)
U of Alaska Fairbanks (AK)
U of Alaska Southeast (AK)
U of Alberta (AB, Canada)
U of Arkansas at Little Rock (AR)
The U of British Columbia (BC, Canada)
U of Calgary (AB, Canada)
U of Charleston (WV)
U of Cincinnati (OH)
U of Dallas (TX)
U of Dayton (OH)
U of Delaware (DE)
The U of Findlay (OH)
U of Hawaii at Manoa (HI)
U of Houston–Clear Lake (TX)
U of Houston–Victoria (TX)
U of Indianapolis (IN)
The U of Iowa (IA)
U of La Verne (CA)
The U of Lethbridge (AB, Canada)
U of Maine (ME)
U of Maine at Fort Kent (ME)
U of Maine at Machias (ME)
U of Maine at Presque Isle (ME)
U of Manitoba (MB, Canada)
U of Mary (ND)
U of Mary Hardin-Baylor (TX)
U of Maryland, Coll Park (MD)
U of Maryland Eastern Shore (MD)
U of Massachusetts Amherst (MA)
U of Miami (FL)
U of Michigan (MI)
U of Michigan–Dearborn (MI)
U of Michigan–Flint (MI)
U of Minnesota, Duluth (MN)
U of Minnesota, Morris (MN)
U of Minnesota, Twin Cities Campus (MN)
U of Missouri–Columbia (MO)
U of Missouri–Kansas City (MO)
U of Missouri–St. Louis (MO)
The U of Montana–Missoula (MT)
Western Montana Coll of The U of Montana (MT)
U of Nebraska at Omaha (NE)
U of Nevada, Las Vegas (NV)
U of New England (ME)
U of New Mexico (NM)
The U of North Carolina at Pembroke (NC)
U of Oregon (OR)
U of Ottawa (ON, Canada)
U of Pittsburgh at Greensburg (PA)
U of Pittsburgh at Johnstown (PA)
U of Portland (OR)
U of Prince Edward Island (PE, Canada)
U of Redlands (CA)
U of Regina (SK, Canada)
U of Richmond (VA)
U of Rio Grande (OH)
U of Saint Francis (IN)
U of St. Thomas (TX)
U of San Diego (CA)
U of San Francisco (CA)
U of Saskatchewan (SK, Canada)
U of Sioux Falls (SD)
U of South Dakota (SD)
U of Southern California (CA)
U of Southern Colorado (CO)
U of South Florida (FL)
The U of Tennessee at Chattanooga (TN)
U of the Incarnate Word (TX)
U of the Pacific (CA)
U of Toledo (OH)
U of Toronto (ON, Canada)
U of Tulsa (OK)
U of Vermont (VT)
U of Victoria (BC, Canada)
U of Washington (WA)
The U of Western Ontario (ON, Canada)
U of Windsor (ON, Canada)
U of Wisconsin–La Crosse (WI)
U of Wisconsin–Milwaukee (WI)
U of Wisconsin–Oshkosh (WI)
U of Wisconsin–Platteville (WI)
U of Wisconsin–River Falls (WI)
U of Wisconsin–Stevens Point (WI)
U of Wisconsin–Superior (WI)

U of Wisconsin–Whitewater (WI)
Upper Iowa U (IA)
Urbana U (OH)
Ursinus Coll (PA)
Ursuline Coll (OH)
Valdosta State U (GA)
Valley City State U (ND)
Valparaiso U (IN)
Vanderbilt U (TN)
Vanguard U of Southern California (CA)
Villanova U (PA)
Virginia Commonwealth U (VA)
Virginia Wesleyan Coll (VA)
Voorhees Coll (SC)
Wagner Coll (NY)
Wake Forest U (NC)
Walsh U (OH)
Warner Pacific Coll (OR)
Warren Wilson Coll (NC)
Washburn U of Topeka (KS)
Washington State U (WA)
Washington U in St. Louis (MO)
Wayland Baptist U (TX)
Wayne State Coll (NE)
Webster U (MO)
Wells Coll (NY)
Wesleyan Coll (GA)
Wesley Coll (DE)
West Chester U of Pennsylvania (PA)
Western Baptist Coll (OR)
Western Connecticut State U (CT)
Western State Coll of Colorado (CO)
Western Washington U (WA)
Westfield State Coll (MA)
West Liberty State Coll (WV)
Westminster Coll (MO)
Westminster Coll (PA)
Westmont Coll (CA)
West Virginia State Coll (WV)
West Virginia Wesleyan Coll (WV)
Wheeling Jesuit U (WV)
Wheelock Coll (MA)
Wilkes U (PA)
William Carey Coll (MS)
William Jewell Coll (MO)
William Paterson U of New Jersey (NJ)
William Penn U (IA)
Williams Baptist Coll (AR)
William Woods U (MO)
Wilmington Coll (OH)
Wingate U (NC)
Winona State U (MN)
Winston-Salem State U (NC)
Wittenberg U (OH)
Wright State U (OH)
Xavier U (OH)
Xavier U of Louisiana (LA)
Yeshiva U (NY)
York Coll (NE)
York Coll of Pennsylvania (PA)
York U (ON, Canada)
Youngstown State U (OH)

EDUCATION ADMINISTRATION

Campbell U (NC)
Caribbean U (PR)
Eureka Coll (IL)
Lamar U (TX)
Laura and Alvin Siegal Coll of Judaic Studies (OH)
Lindenwood U (MO)
Long Island U, Brooklyn Campus (NY)
McNeese State U (LA)
Northern Arizona U (AZ)
Northwest Missouri State U (MO)
Ohio U (OH)
Oral Roberts U (OK)
Purdue U Calumet (IN)
St. Cloud State U (MN)
Tarleton State U (TX)
Tennessee State U (TN)
Texas Southern U (TX)
The U of British Columbia (BC, Canada)
U of Central Oklahoma (OK)
U of Hawaii at Manoa (HI)
The U of Lethbridge (AB, Canada)
U of Nebraska at Omaha (NE)
U of Oregon (OR)
U of San Francisco (CA)
U of Windsor (ON, Canada)
U of Wisconsin–Superior (WI)
Valdosta State U (GA)
Western Washington U (WA)
William Carey Coll (MS)

EDUCATION ADMINISTRATION/ SUPERVISION RELATED

Philander Smith Coll (AR)
U of Miami (FL)

EDUCATIONAL MEDIA DESIGN

Ball State U (IN)
Bayamón Central U (PR)
California State U, Chico (CA)
The Coll of St. Scholastica (MN)
Indiana State U (IN)
Ithaca Coll (NY)
Jacksonville State U (AL)
James Madison U (VA)
Norwich U (VT)
Ohio U (OH)
St. Cloud State U (MN)
Texas Southern U (TX)
U of Central Oklahoma (OK)
U of Hawaii at Manoa (HI)
U of Nebraska at Omaha (NE)
U of Toledo (OH)
Western Illinois U (IL)
Western Oregon U (OR)
Widener U (PA)

EDUCATIONAL MEDIA TECHNOLOGY

Duquesne U (PA)
Salve Regina U (RI)
Seton Hill Coll (PA)
U of Maine (ME)
U of Wisconsin–Superior (WI)

EDUCATIONAL PSYCHOLOGY

Alcorn State U (MS)
Christian Brothers U (TN)
Jacksonville State U (AL)
Marymount U (VA)
Mississippi State U (MS)
St. Mary's Coll of Maryland (MD)
Shenandoah U (VA)
U of Hawaii at Manoa (HI)

EDUCATIONAL STATISTICS/ RESEARCH METHODS

Bucknell U (PA)
Ohio U (OH)

EDUCATION (K-12)

Adrian Coll (MI)
Atlantic Baptist U (NB, Canada)
Augustana Coll (SD)
Belmont U (TN)
Bethany Coll (WV)
Bethel Coll (TN)
Biola U (CA)
Briar Cliff U (IA)
Campbell U (NC)
Caribbean U (PR)
Centenary Coll of Louisiana (LA)
Charleston Southern U (SC)
Christian Heritage Coll (CA)
Clearwater Christian Coll (FL)
Coll of Saint Mary (NE)
The Coll of St. Scholastica (MN)
Columbia Coll (MO)
Columbia Coll (NY)
Columbus State U (GA)
Creighton U (NE)
Dickinson State U (ND)
Dominican U (IL)
Dordt Coll (IA)
D'Youville Coll (NY)
Felician Coll (NJ)
Finlandia U (MI)
Franklin Coll of Indiana (IN)
Graceland U (IA)
Grace U (NE)
Gwynedd-Mercy Coll (PA)
Hamline U (MN)
Hastings Coll (NE)
Hillsdale Coll (MI)
Illinois Coll (IL)
Indiana Wesleyan U (IN)
Ithaca Coll (NY)
Jamestown Coll (ND)
John Carroll U (OH)
Keystone Coll (PA)
Lake Erie Coll (OH)
Lambuth U (TN)
LeMoyne-Owen Coll (TN)
Lewis-Clark State Coll (ID)
Lewis U (IL)
Lindenwood U (MO)
McKendree Coll (IL)
McPherson Coll (KS)
Methodist Coll (NC)
Metropolitan State Coll of Denver (CO)
Midland Lutheran Coll (NE)
Mount Saint Mary Coll (NY)
New England Coll (NH)
Northwestern Oklahoma State U (OK)
Ohio Dominican Coll (OH)
Ohio Wesleyan U (OH)
Our Lady of Holy Cross Coll (LA)
Pacific Union Coll (CA)
Pikeville Coll (KY)
Queens Coll of the City U of NY (NY)
Quincy U (IL)
Redeemer U Coll (ON, Canada)
Rocky Mountain Coll (MT)
St. Ambrose U (IA)
Saint Augustine's Coll (NC)
Saint Mary-of-the-Woods Coll (IN)
St. Norbert Coll (WI)
Salem International U (WV)
Southern New Hampshire U (NH)
Southwest Baptist U (MO)
Syracuse U (NY)
Tabor Coll (KS)
Tennessee Wesleyan Coll (TN)
Thomas Coll (ME)
Transylvania U (KY)
Trevecca Nazarene U (TN)
Trinity International U (IL)
The U of Lethbridge (AB, Canada)
U of Maine at Fort Kent (ME)
U of Minnesota, Morris (MN)
Western Montana Coll of The U of Montana (MT)
U of St. Thomas (MN)
U of Southern California (CA)
The U of Tampa (FL)
The U of Tennessee at Martin (TN)
U of Windsor (ON, Canada)
U of Wisconsin–Superior (WI)
Walla Walla Coll (WA)
Washington U in St. Louis (MO)
West Virginia Wesleyan Coll (WV)
York U (ON, Canada)

EDUCATION (MULTIPLE LEVELS)

Averett U (VA)
California State U, Sacramento (CA)
Chestnut Hill Coll (PA)
Coll of Saint Elizabeth (NJ)
East Texas Baptist U (TX)
George Fox U (OR)
Howard Payne U (TX)
Ithaca Coll (NY)
Lake Superior State U (MI)
Manhattan Coll (NY)
Martin Luther Coll (MN)
Ohio Valley Coll (WV)
Oral Roberts U (OK)
The Richard Stockton Coll of New Jersey (NJ)
Saint Louis U (MO)
Texas Lutheran U (TX)
U of Nebraska–Lincoln (NE)
U of North Alabama (AL)
U of Rio Grande (OH)
U of Washington (WA)
Utah State U (UT)
Western Washington U (WA)
York Coll (NE)
Youngstown State U (OH)

EDUCATION OF THE EMOTIONALLY HANDICAPPED

Bradley U (IL)
Central Michigan U (MI)
East Carolina U (NC)
Eastern Mennonite U (VA)
Eastern Michigan U (MI)
Florida International U (FL)
Florida State U (FL)
Greensboro Coll (NC)
Hope Coll (MI)
Loras Coll (IA)
Marygrove Coll (MI)
Minnesota State U Moorhead (MN)
Oklahoma Baptist U (OK)
Trinity Christian Coll (IL)
U of Maine at Farmington (ME)
U of Nebraska at Omaha (NE)
The U of North Carolina at Wilmington (NC)
U of South Florida (FL)
Western Michigan U (MI)

EDUCATION OF THE GIFTED/ TALENTED

U of Great Falls (MT)

EDUCATION OF THE HEARING IMPAIRED

Augustana Coll (SD)
Barton Coll (NC)
Boston U (MA)
Bowling Green State U (OH)
The Coll of New Jersey (NJ)
Eastern Michigan U (MI)
Flagler Coll (FL)
Indiana U of Pennsylvania (PA)
Lambuth U (TN)
Minot State U (ND)
Texas Christian U (TX)
U of Arkansas at Little Rock (AR)
U of Nebraska at Omaha (NE)
U of Nebraska–Lincoln (NE)
The U of North Carolina at Greensboro (NC)
U of Science and Arts of Oklahoma (OK)
U of Southern Mississippi (MS)

EDUCATION OF THE MENTALLY HANDICAPPED

Augusta State U (GA)
Bowling Green State U (OH)
Bradley U (IL)
Central Michigan U (MI)
East Carolina U (NC)
Eastern Mennonite U (VA)
Eastern Michigan U (MI)
Flagler Coll (FL)
Florida International U (FL)
Florida State U (FL)
Greensboro Coll (NC)
Loras Coll (IA)
Minnesota State U Moorhead (MN)
Minot State U (ND)
Oklahoma Baptist U (OK)
Shaw U (NC)
Silver Lake Coll (WI)
State U of West Georgia (GA)
Trinity Christian Coll (IL)
U of Maine at Farmington (ME)
The U of North Carolina at Charlotte (NC)
The U of North Carolina at Wilmington (NC)
U of Northern Iowa (IA)
U of Rio Grande (OH)
U of South Florida (FL)
Western Michigan U (MI)
York Coll (NE)

EDUCATION OF THE MULTIPLE HANDICAPPED

Bowling Green State U (OH)
The U of Akron (OH)
U of Northern Iowa (IA)

EDUCATION OF THE PHYSICALLY HANDICAPPED

Eastern Michigan U (MI)
Indiana U of Pennsylvania (PA)

EDUCATION OF THE SPECIFIC LEARNING DISABLED

Appalachian State U (NC)
Aquinas Coll (MI)
Bethune-Cookman Coll (FL)
Bowling Green State U (OH)
Bradley U (IL)
East Carolina U (NC)
Eastern Mennonite U (VA)
Flagler Coll (FL)
Florida International U (FL)
Florida Southern Coll (FL)
Florida State U (FL)
Greensboro Coll (NC)
Harding U (AR)
Hope Coll (MI)
Malone Coll (OH)
Mercer U (GA)
Minnesota State U Moorhead (MN)
Northwestern U (IL)
Oklahoma Baptist U (OK)
Pace U (NY)
Silver Lake Coll (WI)
Trinity Christian Coll (IL)
The U of Akron (OH)
U of Maine at Farmington (ME)
The U of North Carolina at Wilmington (NC)
U of Rio Grande (OH)
U of South Florida (FL)
Wheeling Jesuit U (WV)
Winston-Salem State U (NC)
Youngstown State U (OH)

EDUCATION OF THE SPEECH IMPAIRED

Baylor U (TX)
Bloomsburg U of Pennsylvania (PA)
Eastern Michigan U (MI)
Emerson Coll (MA)
Indiana U of Pennsylvania (PA)
Ithaca Coll (NY)
Kutztown U of Pennsylvania (PA)
Louisiana Tech U (LA)
Minot State U (ND)
New York U (NY)
Northern Arizona U (AZ)
St. John's U (NY)
Southeastern Louisiana U (LA)
State U of NY Coll at Cortland (NY)
The U of Akron (OH)
U of Toledo (OH)
Wayne State U (MI)
Western Kentucky U (KY)

EDUCATION OF THE VISUALLY HANDICAPPED

Auburn U (AL)
Dominican Coll (NY)
Eastern Michigan U (MI)
Florida State U (FL)
Western Michigan U (MI)

EDUCATION RELATED

Albany State U (GA)
Arkansas State U (AR)
Eastern Illinois U (IL)
Marylhurst U (OR)
Marywood U (PA)
Park U (MO)
State U of NY Coll at Potsdam (NY)
Swarthmore Coll (PA)
U of Missouri–St. Louis (MO)
The U of the Arts (PA)

ELECTRICAL/ELECTRONIC ENGINEERING TECHNOLOGIES RELATED

Caribbean U (PR)
Embry-Riddle Aeronautical U (FL)
ITT Tech Inst (AL)
ITT Tech Inst, Phoenix (AZ)
ITT Tech Inst, Anaheim (CA)
ITT Tech Inst, Rancho Cordova (CA)
ITT Tech Inst, San Diego (CA)
ITT Tech Inst (CO)
ITT Tech Inst, Fort Lauderdale (FL)
ITT Tech Inst, Jacksonville (FL)
ITT Tech Inst, Tampa (FL)
ITT Tech Inst (ID)
ITT Tech Inst, Mount Prospect (IL)
ITT Tech Inst, Indianapolis (IN)
ITT Tech Inst, Earth City (MO)
ITT Tech Inst (NM)
ITT Tech Inst, Knoxville (TN)
ITT Tech Inst, Nashville (TN)
ITT Tech Inst (UT)
ITT Tech Inst, Greenfield (WI)
New York Inst of Technology (NY)
Open Learning Agency (BC, Canada)
Pennsylvania Coll of Technology (PA)
Southern Illinois U Carbondale (IL)

ELECTRICAL/ELECTRONIC ENGINEERING TECHNOLOGY

Andrews U (MI)
Appalachian State U (NC)
Arizona State U East (AZ)
Baker Coll of Muskegon (MI)
Baker Coll of Owosso (MI)
Bluefield State Coll (WV)
Bowling Green State U (OH)
Bradley U (IL)
Brigham Young U (UT)
British Columbia Inst of Technology (BC, Canada)
California State Polytechnic U, Pomona (CA)

California State U, Long Beach (CA)
California U of Pennsylvania (PA)
Cameron U (OK)
Capitol Coll (MD)
Central Michigan U (MI)
Central Missouri State U (MO)
Central Washington U (WA)
Cleveland State U (OH)
Cogswell Polytechnical Coll (CA)
Colorado Tech U (CO)
Delaware State U (DE)
Denver Tech Coll (CO)
DeVry Coll of Technology (NJ)
DeVry Inst of Technology (NY)
DeVry U (AZ)
DeVry U, Fremont (CA)
DeVry U, Long Beach (CA)
DeVry U, Pomona (CA)
DeVry U, West Hills (CA)
DeVry U, Colorado Springs (CO)
DeVry U (FL)
DeVry U, Alpharetta (GA)
DeVry U, Decatur (GA)
DeVry U, Addison (IL)
DeVry U, Chicago (IL)
DeVry U, Tinley Park (IL)
DeVry U (MO)
DeVry U (OH)
DeVry U (TX)
DeVry U (VA)
DeVry U (WA)
East Central U (OK)
Eastern Washington U (WA)
East-West U (IL)
Edinboro U of Pennsylvania (PA)
Elizabeth City State U (NC)
Embry-Riddle Aeronautical U (FL)
Excelsior Coll (NY)
Fairleigh Dickinson U, Teaneck-Hackensack Campus (NJ)
Fairmont State Coll (WV)
Ferris State U (MI)
Fitchburg State Coll (MA)
Florida A&M U (FL)
Fort Valley State U (GA)
Francis Marion U (SC)
Georgia Southern U (GA)
Grambling State U (LA)
Hamilton Tech Coll (IA)
Hampton U (VA)
Herzing Coll (AL)
Indiana State U (IN)
Indiana U–Purdue U Fort Wayne (IN)
Indiana U–Purdue U Indianapolis (IN)
Inter American U of PR, Aguadilla Campus (PR)
Inter American U of PR, San Germán Campus (PR)
ITT Tech Inst, Hayward (CA)
ITT Tech Inst, Oxnard (CA)
ITT Tech Inst, Mount Prospect (IL)
Jackson State U (MS)
Jacksonville State U (AL)
Johnson & Wales U (RI)
Kansas State U (KS)
Keene State Coll (NH)
Lakehead U (ON, Canada)
Lake Superior State U (MI)
LeTourneau U (TX)
Lewis-Clark State Coll (ID)
Louisiana Tech U (LA)
Maharishi U of Management (IA)
McNeese State U (LA)
Metropolitan State Coll of Denver (CO)
Michigan Technological U (MI)
Midwestern State U (TX)
Milwaukee School of Engineering (WI)
Minnesota State U, Mankato (MN)
Missouri Western State Coll (MO)
Montana State U–Bozeman (MT)
Montana State U–Northern (MT)
Murray State U (KY)
New York Inst of Technology (NY)
Norfolk State U (VA)
Northeastern State U (OK)
Northeastern U (MA)
Northern Kentucky U (KY)
Northern Michigan U (MI)
Northern State U (SD)
Northwestern State U of Louisiana (LA)
Oklahoma State U (OK)
Oregon Inst of Technology (OR)
Pacific Union Coll (CA)
Penn State U Berks Cmps of Berks-Lehigh Valley Coll (PA)
Penn State U Harrisburg Campus of the Capital Coll (PA)
Pittsburg State U (KS)
Point Park Coll (PA)
Prairie View A&M U (TX)
Purdue U (IN)
Purdue U Calumet (IN)
Rochester Inst of Technology (NY)
Roosevelt U (IL)
St. Cloud State U (MN)
Sam Houston State U (TX)
Savannah State U (GA)
South Carolina State U (SC)
South Dakota State U (SD)
Southeastern Oklahoma State U (OK)
Southeast Missouri State U (MO)
Southern Polytechnic State U (GA)
Southern U and A&M Coll (LA)
Southern Utah U (UT)
Southwest Missouri State U (MO)
State U of NY at Farmingdale (NY)
State U of NY Coll at Buffalo (NY)
State U of NY Coll of Technology at Alfred (NY)
State U of NY Inst of Tech at Utica/Rome (NY)
Temple U (PA)
Texas Southern U (TX)
Texas Tech U (TX)
Thomas Edison State Coll (NJ)
U of Arkansas at Little Rock (AR)
U of Calif, Santa Barbara (CA)
U of Central Florida (FL)
U of Cincinnati (OH)
U of Dayton (OH)
U of Hartford (CT)
U of Maine (ME)
U of Maryland Eastern Shore (MD)
U of Massachusetts Dartmouth (MA)
U of Massachusetts Lowell (MA)
The U of Memphis (TN)
U of New Hampshire (NH)
The U of North Carolina at Charlotte (NC)
U of North Texas (TX)
U of Pittsburgh at Johnstown (PA)
U of Regina (SK, Canada)
U of Southern Colorado (CO)
U of Southern Mississippi (MS)
U of Toledo (OH)
Wayne State U (MI)
Weber State U (UT)
Wentworth Inst of Technology (MA)
Western Carolina U (NC)
Western Washington U (WA)
Westwood Coll of Technology–Denver North (CO)
World Coll (VA)
Youngstown State U (OH)

ELECTRICAL/ELECTRONICS DRAFTING

Idaho State U (ID)

ELECTRICAL ENGINEERING

Abilene Christian U (TX)
Alfred U (NY)
American U in Cairo(Egypt)
Arizona State U (AZ)
Arkansas Tech U (AR)
Auburn U (AL)
Baylor U (TX)
Bloomsburg U of Pennsylvania (PA)
Boise State U (ID)
Boston U (MA)
Bradley U (IL)
Brigham Young U (UT)
Brown U (RI)
Bucknell U (PA)
California Inst of Technology (CA)
California Polytechnic State U, San Luis Obispo (CA)
California State Polytechnic U, Pomona (CA)
California State U, Chico (CA)
California State U, Fresno (CA)
California State U, Fullerton (CA)
California State U, Long Beach (CA)
California State U, Los Angeles (CA)
California State U, Northridge (CA)
California State U, Sacramento (CA)
Calvin Coll (MI)
Capitol Coll (MD)
Carleton U (ON, Canada)
Carnegie Mellon U (PA)
Case Western Reserve U (OH)
The Catholic U of America (DC)
Cedarville U (OH)
Christian Brothers U (TN)
Citadel, The Military Coll of South Carolina (SC)
City Coll of the City U of NY (NY)
Clarkson U (NY)
Clemson U (SC)
Cleveland State U (OH)
Cogswell Polytechnical Coll (CA)
The Coll of Southeastern Europe, The American U of Athens(Greece)
Colorado School of Mines (CO)
Colorado State U (CO)
Colorado Tech U (CO)
Columbia U, School of Engineering & Applied Sci (NY)
Concordia U (QC, Canada)
Cooper Union for the Advancement of Science & Art (NY)
Cornell U (NY)
Dominican U (IL)
Dordt Coll (IA)
Drexel U (PA)
Duke U (NC)
Eastern Nazarene Coll (MA)
East-West U (IL)
Embry-Riddle Aeronautical U (AZ)
Fairfield U (CT)
Fairleigh Dickinson U, Teaneck-Hackensack Campus (NJ)
Florida A&M U (FL)
Florida Atlantic U (FL)
Florida Inst of Technology (FL)
Florida International U (FL)
Florida State U (FL)
Frostburg State U (MD)
Gallaudet U (DC)
Gannon U (PA)
George Mason U (VA)
The George Washington U (DC)
Georgia Inst of Technology (GA)
Gonzaga U (WA)
Grand Valley State U (MI)
Grove City Coll (PA)
Hampton U (VA)
Harvard U (MA)
Henry Cogswell Coll (WA)
Hofstra U (NY)
Howard U (DC)
Illinois Inst of Technology (IL)
Indiana Inst of Technology (IN)
Indiana U–Purdue U Fort Wayne (IN)
Indiana U–Purdue U Indianapolis (IN)
Iowa State U of Science and Technology (IA)
Jacksonville U (FL)
John Brown U (AR)
Johns Hopkins U (MD)
Johnson & Wales U (RI)
Kansas State U (KS)
Kettering U (MI)
Lafayette Coll (PA)
Lakehead U (ON, Canada)
Lake Superior State U (MI)
Lamar U (TX)
Lawrence Technological U (MI)
Lehigh U (PA)
LeTourneau U (TX)
Louisiana State U and A&M Coll (LA)
Louisiana Tech U (LA)
Loyola Coll in Maryland (MD)
Loyola Marymount U (CA)
Maharishi U of Management (IA)
Manhattan Coll (NY)
Marquette U (WI)
Massachusetts Inst of Technology (MA)
McGill U (PQ, Canada)
McMaster U (ON, Canada)
McNeese State U (LA)
Memorial U of Newfoundland (NF, Canada)
Mercer U (GA)
Merrimack Coll (MA)
Michigan State U (MI)
Michigan Technological U (MI)
Milwaukee School of Engineering (WI)
Minnesota State U, Mankato (MN)
Mississippi State U (MS)
Missouri Tech (MO)
Montana State U–Bozeman (MT)
Morgan State U (MD)
New Jersey Inst of Technology (NJ)
New Mexico Inst of Mining and Technology (NM)
New Mexico State U (NM)
New York Inst of Technology (NY)
New York U (NY)
Norfolk State U (VA)
North Carolina Ag and Tech State U (NC)
North Carolina State U (NC)
North Dakota State U (ND)
Northeastern U (MA)
Northern Arizona U (AZ)
Northern Illinois U (IL)
Northwestern Polytechnic U (CA)
Northwestern U (IL)
Norwich U (VT)
Oakland U (MI)
Ohio Northern U (OH)
The Ohio State U (OH)
Ohio U (OH)
Oklahoma Christian U of Science and Arts (OK)
Oklahoma State U (OK)
Old Dominion U (VA)
Oral Roberts U (OK)
Oregon State U (OR)
Pacific Lutheran U (WA)
Pacific States U (CA)
Penn State U Altoona Coll (PA)
Penn State U at Erie, The Behrend Coll (PA)
Penn State U Harrisburg Campus of the Capital Coll (PA)
Penn State U Univ Park Campus (PA)
Polytechnic U, Brooklyn Campus (NY)
Polytechnic U of Puerto Rico (PR)
Portland State U (OR)
Prairie View A&M U (TX)
Princeton U (NJ)
Purdue U (IN)
Purdue U Calumet (IN)
Queen's U at Kingston (ON, Canada)
Rensselaer Polytechnic Inst (NY)
Rice U (TX)
Rochester Inst of Technology (NY)
Rose-Hulman Inst of Technology (IN)
Rowan U (NJ)
Saginaw Valley State U (MI)
St. Cloud State U (MN)
Saint Louis U (MO)
St. Mary's U of San Antonio (TX)
San Diego State U (CA)
San Francisco State U (CA)
San Jose State U (CA)
Santa Clara U (CA)
Seattle Pacific U (WA)
Seattle U (WA)
South Dakota School of Mines and Technology (SD)
South Dakota State U (SD)
Southern Illinois U Carbondale (IL)
Southern Illinois U Edwardsville (IL)
Southern Methodist U (TX)
Southern U and A&M Coll (LA)
Stanford U (CA)
State U of NY at Binghamton (NY)
State U of NY at New Paltz (NY)
State U of NY Maritime Coll (NY)
Stevens Inst of Technology (NJ)
Suffolk U (MA)
Syracuse U (NY)
Temple U (PA)
Tennessee State U (TN)
Tennessee Technological U (TN)
Texas A&M U (TX)
Texas A&M U–Kingsville (TX)
Texas Tech U (TX)
Tri-State U (IN)
Tufts U (MA)
Tulane U (LA)
Tuskegee U (AL)
Union Coll (NY)
United States Air Force Academy (CO)
United States Coast Guard Academy (CT)
United States Military Academy (NY)
United States Naval Academy (MD)
Université de Sherbrooke (PQ, Canada)
U du Québec, École de technologie supérieure (PQ, Canada)
Université Laval (QC, Canada)
State U of NY at Buffalo (NY)
The U of Akron (OH)
The U of Alabama (AL)
The U of Alabama at Birmingham (AL)
The U of Alabama in Huntsville (AL)
U of Alaska Fairbanks (AK)
U of Alberta (AB, Canada)
The U of Arizona (AZ)
U of Arkansas (AR)
The U of British Columbia (BC, Canada)
U of Calgary (AB, Canada)
U of Calif, Berkeley (CA)
U of Calif, Davis (CA)
U of Calif, Irvine (CA)
U of Calif, Los Angeles (CA)
U of Calif, Riverside (CA)
U of Calif, San Diego (CA)
U of Calif, Santa Barbara (CA)
U of Calif, Santa Cruz (CA)
U of Central Florida (FL)
U of Cincinnati (OH)
U of Colorado at Boulder (CO)
U of Colorado at Colorado Springs (CO)
U of Colorado at Denver (CO)
U of Connecticut (CT)
U of Dayton (OH)
U of Delaware (DE)
U of Denver (CO)
U of Evansville (IN)
U of Florida (FL)
U of Hartford (CT)
U of Hawaii at Manoa (HI)
U of Houston (TX)
U of Idaho (ID)
U of Illinois at Chicago (IL)
U of Illinois at Urbana–Champaign (IL)
U of Indianapolis (IN)
The U of Iowa (IA)
U of Kansas (KS)
U of Kentucky (KY)
U of Louisiana at Lafayette (LA)
U of Louisville (KY)
U of Maine (ME)
U of Manitoba (MB, Canada)
U of Maryland, Coll Park (MD)
U of Massachusetts Amherst (MA)
U of Massachusetts Dartmouth (MA)
U of Massachusetts Lowell (MA)
The U of Memphis (TN)
U of Miami (FL)
U of Michigan (MI)
U of Michigan–Dearborn (MI)
U of Minnesota, Duluth (MN)
U of Minnesota, Twin Cities Campus (MN)
U of Mississippi (MS)
U of Missouri–Columbia (MO)
U of Missouri–Kansas City (MO)
U of Missouri–Rolla (MO)
U of Missouri–St. Louis (MO)
U of Nebraska–Lincoln (NE)
U of Nevada, Las Vegas (NV)
U of Nevada, Reno (NV)
U of New Hampshire (NH)
U of New Haven (CT)
U of New Mexico (NM)
U of New Orleans (LA)
The U of North Carolina at Charlotte (NC)
U of North Dakota (ND)
U of North Florida (FL)
U of Notre Dame (IN)
U of Oklahoma (OK)
U of Ottawa (ON, Canada)
U of Pennsylvania (PA)
U of Pittsburgh (PA)
U of Portland (OR)
U of Regina (SK, Canada)
U of Rhode Island (RI)
U of Rochester (NY)
U of St. Thomas (MN)
U of San Diego (CA)
U of Saskatchewan (SK, Canada)
The U of Scranton (PA)

U of South Alabama (AL)
U of South Carolina (SC)
U of Southern California (CA)
U of Southern Maine (ME)
U of South Florida (FL)
The U of Tennessee (TN)
The U of Tennessee at Chattanooga (TN)
The U of Texas at Arlington (TX)
The U of Texas at Austin (TX)
The U of Texas at Dallas (TX)
The U of Texas at El Paso (TX)
The U of Texas at San Antonio (TX)
The U of Texas at Tyler (TX)
The U of Texas–Pan American (TX)
U of the District of Columbia (DC)
U of the Pacific (CA)
U of Toledo (OH)
U of Toronto (ON, Canada)
U of Tulsa (OK)
U of Utah (UT)
U of Vermont (VT)
U of Victoria (BC, Canada)
U of Virginia (VA)
U of Washington (WA)
U of Waterloo (ON, Canada)
The U of Western Ontario (ON, Canada)
U of Windsor (ON, Canada)
U of Wisconsin–Madison (WI)
U of Wisconsin–Milwaukee (WI)
U of Wisconsin–Platteville (WI)
U of Wyoming (WY)
Utah State U (UT)
Valparaiso U (IN)
Vanderbilt U (TN)
Villanova U (PA)
Virginia Commonwealth U (VA)
Virginia Military Inst (VA)
Virginia Polytechnic Inst and State U (VA)
Walla Walla Coll (WA)
Washington State U (WA)
Washington U in St. Louis (MO)
Wayne State U (MI)
Wentworth Inst of Technology (MA)
Western Kentucky U (KY)
Western Michigan U (MI)
Western New England Coll (MA)
West Virginia U (WV)
West Virginia U Inst of Technology (WV)
Wichita State U (KS)
Widener U (PA)
Wilberforce U (OH)
Wilkes U (PA)
Worcester Polytechnic Inst (MA)
Wright State U (OH)
Yale U (CT)
Youngstown State U (OH)

ELECTRICAL EQUIPMENT INSTALLATION/REPAIR
U Coll of Cape Breton (NS, Canada)

ELECTROENCEPHALOGRAPH TECHNOLOGY
Johns Hopkins U (MD)

ELECTROMECHANICAL INSTRUMENTATION AND MAINTENANCE TECHNOLOGIES RELATED
ITT Tech Inst, Rancho Cordova (CA)

ELECTROMECHANICAL TECHNOLOGY
Excelsior Coll (NY)
Penn State U Berks Cmps of Berks-Lehigh Valley Coll (PA)
Penn State U New Kensington Campus of the Commonwealth Coll (PA)
State U of NY Coll of Technology at Alfred (NY)
U of Houston (TX)
U of the District of Columbia (DC)
U of Toledo (OH)
Vermont Tech Coll (VT)
Wayne State U (MI)

ELEMENTARY EDUCATION
Abilene Christian U (TX)
Acadia U (NS, Canada)
Adams State Coll (CO)
Adelphi U (NY)
Adrian Coll (MI)
Alabama State U (AL)
Alaska Pacific U (AK)
Albion Coll (MI)
Albright Coll (PA)
Alcorn State U (MS)
Alderson-Broaddus Coll (WV)
Alfred U (NY)
Alice Lloyd Coll (KY)
Alliant International U (CA)
Alma Coll (MI)
Alvernia Coll (PA)
Alverno Coll (WI)
American Indian Coll of the Assemblies of God, Inc (AZ)
American International Coll (MA)
American U (DC)
American U of Puerto Rico (PR)
Anderson Coll (SC)
Anderson U (IN)
Andrews U (MI)
Anna Maria Coll (MA)
Aquinas Coll (MI)
Aquinas Coll (TN)
Arcadia U (PA)
Arizona State U (AZ)
Arizona State U East (AZ)
Arizona State U West (AZ)
Arkansas Baptist Coll (AR)
Arkansas Tech U (AR)
Armstrong Atlantic State U (GA)
Asbury Coll (KY)
Ashland U (OH)
Assumption Coll (MA)
Athens State U (AL)
Atlantic Union Coll (MA)
Auburn U (AL)
Auburn U Montgomery (AL)
Augsburg Coll (MN)
Augustana Coll (IL)
Augustana Coll (SD)
Augusta State U (GA)
Aurora U (IL)
Avila Coll (MO)
Baker U (KS)
Baldwin-Wallace Coll (OH)
Ball State U (IN)
Baptist Bible Coll (MO)
Baptist Bible Coll of Pennsylvania (PA)
The Baptist Coll of Florida (FL)
Barber-Scotia Coll (NC)
Barclay Coll (KS)
Barry U (FL)
Barton Coll (NC)
Bayamón Central U (PR)
Baylor U (TX)
Bay Path Coll (MA)
Becker Coll (MA)
Belhaven Coll (MS)
Bellarmine U (KY)
Belmont Abbey Coll (NC)
Belmont U (TN)
Beloit Coll (WI)
Bemidji State U (MN)
Benedict Coll (SC)
Benedictine Coll (KS)
Benedictine U (IL)
Bennett Coll (NC)
Berea Coll (KY)
Berry Coll (GA)
Bethany Coll (KS)
Bethany Coll (WV)
Bethany Coll of the Assemblies of God (CA)
Bethel Coll (IN)
Bethel Coll (KS)
Bethel Coll (MN)
Bethel Coll (TN)
Bethune-Cookman Coll (FL)
Biola U (CA)
Birmingham-Southern Coll (AL)
Blackburn Coll (IL)
Black Hills State U (SD)
Bloomsburg U of Pennsylvania (PA)
Bluefield Coll (VA)
Bluefield State Coll (WV)
Blue Mountain Coll (MS)
Bluffton Coll (OH)
Boise State U (ID)
Boston Coll (MA)
Boston U (MA)
Bowie State U (MD)
Bowling Green State U (OH)
Bradley U (IL)
Brandon U (MB, Canada)
Brescia U (KY)
Brewton-Parker Coll (GA)
Briar Cliff U (IA)
Bridgewater Coll (VA)
Bridgewater State Coll (MA)
Brigham Young U (UT)
Brigham Young U–Hawaii (HI)
Brock U (ON, Canada)
Brooklyn Coll of the City U of NY (NY)
Bryan Coll (TN)
Bryn Athyn Coll of the New Church (PA)
Bucknell U (PA)
Buena Vista U (IA)
Butler U (IN)
Cabrini Coll (PA)
Caldwell Coll (NJ)
California State U, Fresno (CA)
California U of Pennsylvania (PA)
Calvary Bible Coll and Theological Seminary (MO)
Calvin Coll (MI)
Cameron U (OK)
Campbellsville U (KY)
Campbell U (NC)
Canisius Coll (NY)
Capital U (OH)
Cardinal Stritch U (WI)
Caribbean U (PR)
Caribbean Ctr for Advanced Studies/ Miami Inst of Psych (FL)
Carlow Coll (PA)
Carroll Coll (MT)
Carroll Coll (WI)
Carson-Newman Coll (TN)
Carthage Coll (WI)
Catawba Coll (NC)
The Catholic U of America (DC)
Cedar Crest Coll (PA)
Cedarville U (OH)
Centenary Coll (NJ)
Centenary Coll of Louisiana (LA)
Central Coll (IA)
Central Connecticut State U (CT)
Central Methodist Coll (MO)
Central Michigan U (MI)
Central Missouri State U (MO)
Central Washington U (WA)
Centre Coll (KY)
Chadron State Coll (NE)
Chaminade U of Honolulu (HI)
Champlain Coll (VT)
Charleston Southern U (SC)
Chestnut Hill Coll (PA)
Cheyney U of Pennsylvania (PA)
Chicago State U (IL)
Chowan Coll (NC)
Christian Brothers U (TN)
Christian Heritage Coll (CA)
Christopher Newport U (VA)
Circleville Bible Coll (OH)
City Coll of the City U of NY (NY)
City U (WA)
Claflin U (SC)
Clarion U of Pennsylvania (PA)
Clark Atlanta U (GA)
Clarke Coll (IA)
Clark U (MA)
Clearwater Christian Coll (FL)
Clemson U (SC)
Cleveland State U (OH)
Coastal Carolina U (SC)
Coe Coll (IA)
Coker Coll (SC)
Colby-Sawyer Coll (NH)
Coll Misericordia (PA)
Coll of Charleston (SC)
Coll of Mount Saint Vincent (NY)
The Coll of New Jersey (NJ)
The Coll of New Rochelle (NY)
Coll of Notre Dame of Maryland (MD)
Coll of Saint Benedict (MN)
Coll of St. Catherine (MN)
Coll of St. Joseph (VT)
Coll of Saint Mary (NE)
The Coll of Saint Rose (NY)
Coll of Santa Fe (NM)
Coll of the Atlantic (ME)
Coll of the Ozarks (MO)
Coll of the Southwest (NM)
Columbia Coll (MO)
Columbia Coll (SC)
Columbia International U (SC)
Columbia Union Coll (MD)
Columbus State U (GA)
Concord Coll (WV)
Concordia Coll (MN)
Concordia Coll (NY)
Concordia U (CA)
Concordia U (IL)
Concordia U (MI)
Concordia U (MN)
Concordia U (NE)
Concordia U (OR)
Concordia U (QC, Canada)
Concordia U Wisconsin (WI)
Converse Coll (SC)
Coppin State Coll (MD)
Cornell Coll (IA)
Cornerstone U (MI)
Covenant Coll (GA)
Creighton U (NE)
Crichton Coll (TN)
Crown Coll (MN)
Culver-Stockton Coll (MO)
Cumberland Coll (KY)
Cumberland U (TN)
Curry Coll (MA)
Daemen Coll (NY)
Dakota State U (SD)
Dakota Wesleyan U (SD)
Dallas Baptist U (TX)
Dana Coll (NE)
Davis & Elkins Coll (WV)
Defiance Coll (OH)
Delaware State U (DE)
Delta State U (MS)
DePaul U (IL)
DePauw U (IN)
DeSales U (PA)
Dickinson State U (ND)
Dillard U (LA)
Doane Coll (NE)
Dominican Coll (NY)
Dominican U (IL)
Dordt Coll (IA)
Dowling Coll (NY)
Drake U (IA)
Drury U (MO)
Duquesne U (PA)
D'Youville Coll (NY)
East Carolina U (NC)
East Central U (OK)
Eastern Connecticut State U (CT)
Eastern Illinois U (IL)
Eastern Kentucky U (KY)
Eastern Mennonite U (VA)
Eastern Michigan U (MI)
Eastern Nazarene Coll (MA)
Eastern New Mexico U (NM)
Eastern U (PA)
Eastern Washington U (WA)
East Stroudsburg U of Pennsylvania (PA)
East Texas Baptist U (TX)
Edgewood Coll (WI)
Edinboro U of Pennsylvania (PA)
Edward Waters Coll (FL)
Elizabeth City State U (NC)
Elizabethtown Coll (PA)
Elmhurst Coll (IL)
Elmira Coll (NY)
Elms Coll (MA)
Elon U (NC)
Emmanuel Coll (GA)
Emmanuel Coll (MA)
Emmaus Bible Coll (IA)
Emory U (GA)
Emporia State U (KS)
Endicott Coll (MA)
Erskine Coll (SC)
Eureka Coll (IL)
Evangel U (MO)
Fairmont State Coll (WV)
Faith Baptist Bible Coll and Theological Seminary (IA)
Faulkner U (AL)
Fayetteville State U (NC)
Felician Coll (NJ)
Fitchburg State Coll (MA)
Five Towns Coll (NY)
Flagler Coll (FL)
Florida A&M U (FL)
Florida Atlantic U (FL)
Florida Coll (FL)
Florida Gulf Coast U (FL)
Florida International U (FL)
Florida Southern Coll (FL)
Florida State U (FL)
Fontbonne U (MO)
Fordham U (NY)
Fort Hays State U (KS)
Fort Lewis Coll (CO)
Framingham State Coll (MA)
Franciscan U of Steubenville (OH)
Francis Marion U (SC)
Franklin Coll of Indiana (IN)
Franklin Pierce Coll (NH)
Freed-Hardeman U (TN)
Fresno Pacific U (CA)
Friends U (KS)
Frostburg State U (MD)
Furman U (SC)
Gallaudet U (DC)
Gannon U (PA)
Gardner-Webb U (NC)
Geneva Coll (PA)
George Fox U (OR)
Georgetown Coll (KY)
Georgian Court Coll (NJ)
Georgia Southwestern State U (GA)
Gettysburg Coll (PA)
Glenville State Coll (WV)
Goddard Coll (VT)
Gonzaga U (WA)
Gordon Coll (MA)
Goshen Coll (IN)
Goucher Coll (MD)
Governors State U (IL)
Grace Bible Coll (MI)
Grace Coll (IN)
Graceland U (IA)
Grace U (NE)
Grambling State U (LA)
Grand Canyon U (AZ)
Grand Valley State U (MI)
Grand View Coll (IA)
Green Mountain Coll (VT)
Greensboro Coll (NC)
Greenville Coll (IL)
Grove City Coll (PA)
Guilford Coll (NC)
Gustavus Adolphus Coll (MN)
Gwynedd-Mercy Coll (PA)
Hamline U (MN)
Hampshire Coll (MA)
Hampton U (VA)
Hannibal-LaGrange Coll (MO)
Hanover Coll (IN)
Harding U (AR)
Hardin-Simmons U (TX)
Harris-Stowe State Coll (MO)
Haskell Indian Nations U (KS)
Hastings Coll (NE)
Heidelberg Coll (OH)
Hellenic Coll (MA)
Henderson State U (AR)
Hendrix Coll (AR)
High Point U (NC)
Hillsdale Coll (MI)
Hiram Coll (OH)
Hobe Sound Bible Coll (FL)
Hofstra U (NY)
Holy Family Coll (PA)
Hope Coll (MI)
Hope International U (CA)
Houghton Coll (NY)
Houston Baptist U (TX)
Howard Payne U (TX)
Humboldt State U (CA)
Hunter Coll of the City U of NY (NY)
Huntington Coll (IN)
Huron U (SD)
Husson Coll (ME)
Huston-Tillotson Coll (TX)
Idaho State U (ID)
Illinois Coll (IL)
Illinois State U (IL)
Illinois Wesleyan U (IL)
Immaculata Coll (PA)
Indiana State U (IN)
Indiana U Bloomington (IN)
Indiana U East (IN)
Indiana U Kokomo (IN)
Indiana U Northwest (IN)
Indiana U of Pennsylvania (PA)
Indiana U–Purdue U Fort Wayne (IN)
Indiana U–Purdue U Indianapolis (IN)
Indiana U South Bend (IN)
Indiana U Southeast (IN)
Indiana Wesleyan U (IN)
Inter American U of PR, Aguadilla Campus (PR)
Inter Amer U of PR, Barranquitas Campus (PR)
Inter American U of PR, San Germán Campus (PR)
Iona Coll (NY)
Iowa State U of Science and Technology (IA)
Iowa Wesleyan Coll (IA)
Jackson State U (MS)

ELEMENTARY/MIDDLE/ SECONDARY EDUCATION ADMINISTRATION

EMERGENCY MEDICAL TECHNOLOGY

ENERGY MANAGEMENT TECHNOLOGY

ENGINEERING

ENGINEERING DESIGN

ENGINEERING/INDUSTRIAL MANAGEMENT

Brevard Coll (NC)
Brewton-Parker Coll (GA)
Briar Cliff U (IA)
Bridgewater Coll (VA)
Bridgewater State Coll (MA)
Brigham Young U (UT)
Brigham Young U–Hawaii (HI)
Brock U (ON, Canada)
Brooklyn Coll of the City U of NY (NY)
Brown U (RI)
Bryan Coll (TN)
Bryant Coll (RI)
Bryn Athyn Coll of the New Church (PA)
Bryn Mawr Coll (PA)
Bucknell U (PA)
Buena Vista U (IA)
Butler U (IN)
Cabrini Coll (PA)
Caldwell Coll (NJ)
California Baptist U (CA)
California Lutheran U (CA)
California Polytechnic State U, San Luis Obispo (CA)
California State Polytechnic U, Pomona (CA)
California State U, Bakersfield (CA)
California State U, Chico (CA)
California State U, Dominguez Hills (CA)
California State U, Fresno (CA)
California State U, Fullerton (CA)
California State U, Hayward (CA)
California State U, Long Beach (CA)
California State U, Los Angeles (CA)
California State U, Northridge (CA)
California State U, Sacramento (CA)
California State U, San Bernardino (CA)
California State U, San Marcos (CA)
California State U, Stanislaus (CA)
California U of Pennsylvania (PA)
Calvin Coll (MI)
Cameron U (OK)
Campbellsville U (KY)
Campbell U (NC)
Canisius Coll (NY)
Capital U (OH)
Cardinal Stritch U (WI)
Carleton Coll (MN)
Carleton U (ON, Canada)
Carlow Coll (PA)
Carnegie Mellon U (PA)
Carroll Coll (MT)
Carroll Coll (WI)
Carson-Newman Coll (TN)
Carthage Coll (WI)
Case Western Reserve U (OH)
Catawba Coll (NC)
The Catholic U of America (DC)
Cazenovia Coll (NY)
Cedar Crest Coll (PA)
Cedarville U (OH)
Centenary Coll (NJ)
Centenary Coll of Louisiana (LA)
Central Coll (IA)
Central Connecticut State U (CT)
Central Methodist Coll (MO)
Central Michigan U (MI)
Central Missouri State U (MO)
Central State U (OH)
Central Washington U (WA)
Centre Coll (KY)
Chadron State Coll (NE)
Chaminade U of Honolulu (HI)
Chapman U (CA)
Charleston Southern U (SC)
Chatham Coll (PA)
Chestnut Hill Coll (PA)
Cheyney U of Pennsylvania (PA)
Chicago State U (IL)
Chowan Coll (NC)
Christian Brothers U (TN)
Christian Heritage Coll (CA)
Christopher Newport U (VA)
Citadel, The Military Coll of South Carolina (SC)
City Coll of the City U of NY (NY)
Claflin U (SC)
Claremont McKenna Coll (CA)
Clarion U of Pennsylvania (PA)
Clark Atlanta U (GA)
Clarke Coll (IA)
Clark U (MA)
Clearwater Christian Coll (FL)
Clemson U (SC)
Cleveland State U (OH)
Coastal Carolina U (SC)
Coe Coll (IA)
Coker Coll (SC)
Colby Coll (ME)
Colby-Sawyer Coll (NH)
Colgate U (NY)
Coll Misericordia (PA)
Coll of Charleston (SC)
Coll of Mount St. Joseph (OH)
Coll of Mount Saint Vincent (NY)
The Coll of New Jersey (NJ)
The Coll of New Rochelle (NY)
Coll of Notre Dame of Maryland (MD)
Coll of Saint Benedict (MN)
Coll of St. Catherine (MN)
Coll of Saint Elizabeth (NJ)
Coll of St. Joseph (VT)
Coll of Saint Mary (NE)
The Coll of Saint Rose (NY)
The Coll of St. Scholastica (MN)
Coll of Santa Fe (NM)
Coll of Staten Island of the City U of NY (NY)
Coll of the Atlantic (ME)
Coll of the Holy Cross (MA)
Coll of the Ozarks (MO)
Coll of the Southwest (NM)
The Coll of William and Mary (VA)
The Coll of Wooster (OH)
Colorado Christian U (CO)
The Colorado Coll (CO)
Colorado State U (CO)
Columbia Coll (MO)
Columbia Coll (NY)
Columbia Coll (SC)
Columbia Union Coll (MD)
Columbia U, School of General Studies (NY)
Columbus State U (GA)
Concord Coll (WV)
Concordia Coll (MN)
Concordia Coll (NY)
Concordia U (CA)
Concordia U (IL)
Concordia U (MI)
Concordia U (MN)
Concordia U (NE)
Concordia U (OR)
Concordia U (QC, Canada)
Concordia U Wisconsin (WI)
Connecticut Coll (CT)
Converse Coll (SC)
Coppin State Coll (MD)
Cornell Coll (IA)
Cornell U (NY)
Cornerstone U (MI)
Covenant Coll (GA)
Creighton U (NE)
Crichton Coll (TN)
Crown Coll (MN)
Culver-Stockton Coll (MO)
Cumberland Coll (KY)
Cumberland U (TN)
Curry Coll (MA)
Daemen Coll (NY)
Dakota State U (SD)
Dakota Wesleyan U (SD)
Dalhousie U (NS, Canada)
Dallas Baptist U (TX)
Dana Coll (NE)
Dartmouth Coll (NH)
Davidson Coll (NC)
Davis & Elkins Coll (WV)
Defiance Coll (OH)
Delaware State U (DE)
Delaware Valley Coll (PA)
Delta State U (MS)
Denison U (OH)
DePaul U (IL)
DePauw U (IN)
DeSales U (PA)
Dickinson Coll (PA)
Dickinson State U (ND)
Dillard U (LA)
Doane Coll (NE)
Dominican Coll (NY)
Dominican U (IL)
Dominican U of California (CA)
Dordt Coll (IA)
Dowling Coll (NY)
Drake U (IA)
Drew U (NJ)
Drury U (MO)
Duke U (NC)
Duquesne U (PA)
D'Youville Coll (NY)
Earlham Coll (IN)
East Carolina U (NC)
East Central U (OK)
Eastern Connecticut State U (CT)
Eastern Illinois U (IL)
Eastern Kentucky U (KY)
Eastern Mennonite U (VA)
Eastern Michigan U (MI)
Eastern Nazarene Coll (MA)
Eastern New Mexico U (NM)
Eastern Oregon U (OR)
Eastern U (PA)
Eastern Washington U (WA)
East Stroudsburg U of Pennsylvania (PA)
East Tennessee State U (TN)
East Texas Baptist U (TX)
East-West U (IL)
Eckerd Coll (FL)
Edgewood Coll (WI)
Edinboro U of Pennsylvania (PA)
Edward Waters Coll (FL)
Elizabeth City State U (NC)
Elizabethtown Coll (PA)
Elmhurst Coll (IL)
Elmira Coll (NY)
Elms Coll (MA)
Elon U (NC)
Emmanuel Coll (GA)
Emmanuel Coll (MA)
Emory & Henry Coll (VA)
Emory U (GA)
Emporia State U (KS)
Erskine Coll (SC)
Eugene Lang Coll, New School U (NY)
Eureka Coll (IL)
Evangel U (MO)
The Evergreen State Coll (WA)
Fairfield U (CT)
Fairleigh Dickinson U, Florham-Madison Campus (NJ)
Fairleigh Dickinson U, Teaneck-Hackensack Campus (NJ)
Fairmont State Coll (WV)
Faulkner U (AL)
Fayetteville State U (NC)
Felician Coll (NJ)
Ferrum Coll (VA)
Fisk U (TN)
Fitchburg State Coll (MA)
Flagler Coll (FL)
Florida A&M U (FL)
Florida Atlantic U (FL)
Florida International U (FL)
Florida Southern Coll (FL)
Florida State U (FL)
Fontbonne U (MO)
Fordham U (NY)
Fort Hays State U (KS)
Fort Lewis Coll (CO)
Framingham State Coll (MA)
Franciscan U of Steubenville (OH)
Francis Marion U (SC)
Franklin and Marshall Coll (PA)
Franklin Coll of Indiana (IN)
Franklin Pierce Coll (NH)
Freed-Hardeman U (TN)
Fresno Pacific U (CA)
Friends U (KS)
Frostburg State U (MD)
Furman U (SC)
Gallaudet U (DC)
Gardner-Webb U (NC)
Geneva Coll (PA)
George Fox U (OR)
George Mason U (VA)
Georgetown Coll (KY)
Georgetown U (DC)
The George Washington U (DC)
Georgia Coll and State U (GA)
Georgian Court Coll (NJ)
Georgia Southern U (GA)
Georgia Southwestern State U (GA)
Georgia State U (GA)
Gettysburg Coll (PA)
Glenville State Coll (WV)
Goddard Coll (VT)
Gonzaga U (WA)
Gordon Coll (MA)
Goshen Coll (IN)
Goucher Coll (MD)
Governors State U (IL)
Grace Coll (IN)
Graceland U (IA)
Grambling State U (LA)
Grand Canyon U (AZ)
Grand Valley State U (MI)
Grand View Coll (IA)
Green Mountain Coll (VT)
Greensboro Coll (NC)
Greenville Coll (IL)
Grinnell Coll (IA)
Grove City Coll (PA)
Guilford Coll (NC)
Gustavus Adolphus Coll (MN)
Gwynedd-Mercy Coll (PA)
Hamilton Coll (NY)
Hamline U (MN)
Hampden-Sydney Coll (VA)
Hampshire Coll (MA)
Hampton U (VA)
Hannibal-LaGrange Coll (MO)
Hanover Coll (IN)
Harding U (AR)
Hardin-Simmons U (TX)
Hartwick Coll (NY)
Harvard U (MA)
Hastings Coll (NE)
Haverford Coll (PA)
Heidelberg Coll (OH)
Henderson State U (AR)
Hendrix Coll (AR)
High Point U (NC)
Hilbert Coll (NY)
Hillsdale Coll (MI)
Hiram Coll (OH)
Hobart and William Smith Colls (NY)
Hofstra U (NY)
Hollins U (VA)
Holy Family Coll (PA)
Holy Names Coll (CA)
Hood Coll (MD)
Hope Coll (MI)
Houghton Coll (NY)
Houston Baptist U (TX)
Howard Payne U (TX)
Howard U (DC)
Humboldt State U (CA)
Hunter Coll of the City U of NY (NY)
Huntingdon Coll (AL)
Huntington Coll (IN)
Huston-Tillotson Coll (TX)
Idaho State U (ID)
Illinois Coll (IL)
Illinois State U (IL)
Illinois Wesleyan U (IL)
Immaculata Coll (PA)
Indiana State U (IN)
Indiana U Bloomington (IN)
Indiana U East (IN)
Indiana U Kokomo (IN)
Indiana U Northwest (IN)
Indiana U of Pennsylvania (PA)
Indiana U–Purdue U Fort Wayne (IN)
Indiana U–Purdue U Indianapolis (IN)
Indiana U South Bend (IN)
Indiana U Southeast (IN)
Indiana Wesleyan U (IN)
Inter American U of PR, San Germán Campus (PR)
Iona Coll (NY)
Iowa State U of Science and Technology (IA)
Iowa Wesleyan Coll (IA)
Ithaca Coll (NY)
Jackson State U (MS)
Jacksonville State U (AL)
Jacksonville U (FL)
James Madison U (VA)
Jamestown Coll (ND)
Jarvis Christian Coll (TX)
John Brown U (AR)
John Carroll U (OH)
Johns Hopkins U (MD)
Johnson C. Smith U (NC)
Johnson State Coll (VT)
Judson Coll (AL)
Judson Coll (IL)
Juniata Coll (PA)
Kalamazoo Coll (MI)
Kansas State U (KS)
Kansas Wesleyan U (KS)
Kean U (NJ)
Keene State Coll (NH)
Kennesaw State U (GA)
Kent State U (OH)
Kentucky State U (KY)
Kentucky Wesleyan Coll (KY)
Kenyon Coll (OH)
Keuka Coll (NY)
King Coll (TN)
King's Coll (PA)
The King's U Coll (AB, Canada)
Knox Coll (IL)
Kutztown U of Pennsylvania (PA)
Lafayette Coll (PA)
LaGrange Coll (GA)
Lake Erie Coll (OH)
Lake Forest Coll (IL)
Lakehead U (ON, Canada)
Lakeland Coll (WI)
Lake Superior State U (MI)
Lamar U (TX)
Lambuth U (TN)
Lander U (SC)
La Roche Coll (PA)
La Salle U (PA)
Laurentian U (ON, Canada)
Lawrence U (WI)
Lebanon Valley Coll (PA)
Lees-McRae Coll (NC)
Lee U (TN)
Lehigh U (PA)
Lehman Coll of the City U of NY (NY)
Le Moyne Coll (NY)
LeMoyne-Owen Coll (TN)
Lenoir-Rhyne Coll (NC)
LeTourneau U (TX)
Lewis & Clark Coll (OR)
Lewis-Clark State Coll (ID)
Lewis U (IL)
Liberty U (VA)
Limestone Coll (SC)
Lincoln Memorial U (TN)
Lincoln U (MO)
Lincoln U (PA)
Lindenwood U (MO)
Lindsey Wilson Coll (KY)
Linfield Coll (OR)
Lipscomb U (TN)
Lock Haven U of Pennsylvania (PA)
Long Island U, Brooklyn Campus (NY)
Long Island U, C.W. Post Campus (NY)
Long Island U, Southampton Coll (NY)
Long Island U, Southampton Coll, Friends World Program (NY)
Longwood Coll (VA)
Loras Coll (IA)
Louisiana Coll (LA)
Louisiana State U and A&M Coll (LA)
Louisiana State U in Shreveport (LA)
Louisiana Tech U (LA)
Lourdes Coll (OH)
Loyola Coll in Maryland (MD)
Loyola Marymount U (CA)
Loyola U Chicago (IL)
Loyola U New Orleans (LA)
Lubbock Christian U (TX)
Luther Coll (IA)
Lycoming Coll (PA)
Lynchburg Coll (VA)
Lyndon State Coll (VT)
Lynn U (FL)
Lyon Coll (AR)
Macalester Coll (MN)
MacMurray Coll (IL)
Maharishi U of Management (IA)
Malone Coll (OH)
Manchester Coll (IN)
Manhattan Coll (NY)
Manhattanville Coll (NY)
Mansfield U of Pennsylvania (PA)
Marian Coll (IN)
Marian Coll of Fond du Lac (WI)
Marietta Coll (OH)
Marist Coll (NY)
Marlboro Coll (VT)
Marquette U (WI)
Marshall U (WV)
Mars Hill Coll (NC)
Martin Methodist Coll (TN)
Mary Baldwin Coll (VA)
Marygrove Coll (MI)
Marymount Coll of Fordham U (NY)
Marymount Manhattan Coll (NY)
Marymount U (VA)
Maryville Coll (TN)
Maryville U of Saint Louis (MO)
Mary Washington Coll (VA)
Marywood U (PA)
Massachusetts Coll of Liberal Arts (MA)

The Master's Coll and Seminary (CA)
Mayville State U (ND)
McGill U (PQ, Canada)
McKendree Coll (IL)
McMaster U (ON, Canada)
McMurry U (TX)
McNeese State U (LA)
McPherson Coll (KS)
Memorial U of Newfoundland (NF, Canada)
Mercer U (GA)
Mercy Coll (NY)
Mercyhurst Coll (PA)
Meredith Coll (NC)
Merrimack Coll (MA)
Mesa State Coll (CO)
Messiah Coll (PA)
Methodist Coll (NC)
Metropolitan State Coll of Denver (CO)
Metropolitan State U (MN)
Miami U (OH)
Michigan State U (MI)
Michigan Technological U (MI)
MidAmerica Nazarene U (KS)
Mid-Continent Coll (KY)
Middlebury Coll (VT)
Middle Tennessee State U (TN)
Midland Lutheran Coll (NE)
Midway Coll (KY)
Midwestern State U (TX)
Millersville U of Pennsylvania (PA)
Milligan Coll (TN)
Millikin U (IL)
Millsaps Coll (MS)
Mills Coll (CA)
Minnesota State U, Mankato (MN)
Minnesota State U Moorhead (MN)
Minot State U (ND)
Mississippi Coll (MS)
Mississippi State U (MS)
Mississippi U for Women (MS)
Mississippi Valley State U (MS)
Missouri Baptist Coll (MO)
Missouri Southern State Coll (MO)
Missouri Valley Coll (MO)
Missouri Western State Coll (MO)
Molloy Coll (NY)
Monmouth Coll (IL)
Monmouth U (NJ)
Montana State U–Billings (MT)
Montana State U–Bozeman (MT)
Montclair State U (NJ)
Montreat Coll (NC)
Moravian Coll (PA)
Morehead State U (KY)
Morehouse Coll (GA)
Morgan State U (MD)
Morningside Coll (IA)
Morris Brown Coll (GA)
Morris Coll (SC)
Mount Allison U (NB, Canada)
Mount Aloysius Coll (PA)
Mount Holyoke Coll (MA)
Mount Marty Coll (SD)
Mount Mary Coll (WI)
Mount Mercy Coll (IA)
Mount Olive Coll (NC)
Mount St. Clare Coll (IA)
Mount Saint Mary Coll (NY)
Mount St. Mary's Coll (CA)
Mount Saint Mary's Coll and Seminary (MD)
Mount Saint Vincent U (NS, Canada)
Mount Union Coll (OH)
Mount Vernon Nazarene U (OH)
Muhlenberg Coll (PA)
Murray State U (KY)
Muskingum Coll (OH)
National-Louis U (IL)
Nazareth Coll of Rochester (NY)
Nebraska Wesleyan U (NE)
Neumann Coll (PA)
Newberry Coll (SC)
New England Coll (NH)
New Jersey City U (NJ)
Newman U (KS)
New Mexico Highlands U (NM)
New Mexico State U (NM)
New York Inst of Technology (NY)
New York U (NY)
Niagara U (NY)
Nicholls State U (LA)
Nipissing U (ON, Canada)
Norfolk State U (VA)
North American Baptist Coll & Edmonton Baptist Sem (AB, Canada)
North Carolina Ag and Tech State U (NC)
North Carolina Central U (NC)
North Carolina State U (NC)
North Carolina Wesleyan Coll (NC)
North Central Coll (IL)
North Dakota State U (ND)
Northeastern Illinois U (IL)
Northeastern State U (OK)
Northeastern U (MA)
Northern Arizona U (AZ)
Northern Illinois U (IL)
Northern Kentucky U (KY)
Northern Michigan U (MI)
Northern State U (SD)
North Georgia Coll & State U (GA)
Northland Coll (WI)
North Park U (IL)
Northwest Coll (WA)
Northwestern Coll (IA)
Northwestern Coll (MN)
Northwestern Oklahoma State U (OK)
Northwestern State U of Louisiana (LA)
Northwestern U (IL)
Northwest Missouri State U (MO)
Northwest Nazarene U (ID)
Norwich U (VT)
Notre Dame Coll (OH)
Notre Dame de Namur U (CA)
Nyack Coll (NY)
Oakland City U (IN)
Oakland U (MI)
Oakwood Coll (AL)
Oberlin Coll (OH)
Oglethorpe U (GA)
Ohio Dominican Coll (OH)
Ohio Northern U (OH)
The Ohio State U (OH)
The Ohio State U at Lima (OH)
Ohio U (OH)
Ohio Wesleyan U (OH)
Okanagan U Coll (BC, Canada)
Oklahoma Baptist U (OK)
Oklahoma Christian U of Science and Arts (OK)
Oklahoma City U (OK)
Oklahoma Panhandle State U (OK)
Oklahoma State U (OK)
Oklahoma Wesleyan U (OK)
Old Dominion U (VA)
Olivet Coll (MI)
Olivet Nazarene U (IL)
Oregon State U (OR)
Ottawa U (KS)
Otterbein Coll (OH)
Ouachita Baptist U (AR)
Our Lady of Holy Cross Coll (LA)
Our Lady of the Lake U of San Antonio (TX)
Pace U (NY)
Pacific Lutheran U (WA)
Pacific Union Coll (CA)
Pacific U (OR)
Paine Coll (GA)
Palm Beach Atlantic Coll (FL)
Park U (MO)
Peace Coll (NC)
Penn State U Abington Coll (PA)
Penn State U Altoona Coll (PA)
Penn State U at Erie, The Behrend Coll (PA)
Penn State U Delaware County Campus of the Commonwealth Coll (PA)
Penn State U Univ Park Campus (PA)
Pepperdine U, Malibu (CA)
Peru State Coll (NE)
Pfeiffer U (NC)
Philander Smith Coll (AR)
Piedmont Coll (GA)
Pikeville Coll (KY)
Pillsbury Baptist Bible Coll (MN)
Pine Manor Coll (MA)
Pittsburg State U (KS)
Pitzer Coll (CA)
Plattsburgh State U of NY (NY)
Plymouth State Coll (NH)
Point Park Coll (PA)
Pomona Coll (CA)
Pontifical Catholic U of Puerto Rico (PR)
Pontifical Coll Josephinum (OH)
Portland State U (OR)
Prairie View A&M U (TX)
Presbyterian Coll (SC)
Princeton U (NJ)
Principia Coll (IL)
Providence Coll (RI)
Purdue U (IN)
Purdue U Calumet (IN)
Purdue U North Central (IN)
Queens Coll (NC)
Queens Coll of the City U of NY (NY)
Queen's U at Kingston (ON, Canada)
Quincy U (IL)
Quinnipiac U (CT)
Radford U (VA)
Randolph-Macon Coll (VA)
Randolph-Macon Woman's Coll (VA)
Redeemer U Coll (ON, Canada)
Reed Coll (OR)
Regis Coll (MA)
Regis U (CO)
Rhode Island Coll (RI)
Rhodes Coll (TN)
Rice U (TX)
The Richard Stockton Coll of New Jersey (NJ)
Richmond, The American International U in London(United Kingdom)
Rider U (NJ)
Ripon Coll (WI)
Rivier Coll (NH)
Roanoke Coll (VA)
Robert Morris U (PA)
Roberts Wesleyan Coll (NY)
Rochester Coll (MI)
Rockford Coll (IL)
Rockhurst U (MO)
Rocky Mountain Coll (MT)
Roger Williams U (RI)
Rollins Coll (FL)
Roosevelt U (IL)
Rosemont Coll (PA)
Rowan U (NJ)
Russell Sage Coll (NY)
Rutgers, The State U of New Jersey, New Brunswick (NJ)
Sacred Heart U (CT)
Saginaw Valley State U (MI)
St. Ambrose U (IA)
St. Andrews Presbyterian Coll (NC)
Saint Anselm Coll (NH)
Saint Augustine's Coll (NC)
St. Bonaventure U (NY)
St. Cloud State U (MN)
St. Edward's U (TX)
St. Francis Coll (NY)
Saint Francis U (PA)
St. Francis Xavier U (NS, Canada)
St. John Fisher Coll (NY)
St. John's Seminary Coll (CA)
Saint John's U (MN)
St. John's U (NY)
Saint Joseph Coll (CT)
Saint Joseph's Coll (IN)
Saint Joseph's Coll (ME)
St. Joseph's Coll, New York (NY)
St. Joseph's Coll, Suffolk Campus (NY)
Saint Joseph's U (PA)
St. Lawrence U (NY)
Saint Leo U (FL)
Saint Louis U (MO)
Saint Martin's Coll (WA)
Saint Mary Coll (KS)
Saint Mary-of-the-Woods Coll (IN)
Saint Mary's Coll (IN)
Saint Mary's Coll of Ave Maria U (MI)
Saint Mary's Coll of California (CA)
St. Mary's Coll of Maryland (MD)
Saint Mary's U (NS, Canada)
Saint Mary's U of Minnesota (MN)
St. Mary's U of San Antonio (TX)
Saint Michael's Coll (VT)
St. Norbert Coll (WI)
St. Olaf Coll (MN)
Saint Peter's Coll (NJ)
St. Thomas Aquinas Coll (NY)
St. Thomas U (FL)
St. Thomas U (NB, Canada)
Saint Vincent Coll (PA)
Saint Xavier U (IL)
Salem Coll (NC)
Salem State Coll (MA)
Salisbury U (MD)
Salve Regina U (RI)
Samford U (AL)
Sam Houston State U (TX)
San Diego State U (CA)
San Francisco State U (CA)
San Jose State U (CA)
Santa Clara U (CA)
Sarah Lawrence Coll (NY)
Savannah State U (GA)
Schreiner U (TX)
Scripps Coll (CA)
Seattle Pacific U (WA)
Seattle U (WA)
Seton Hall U (NJ)
Seton Hill Coll (PA)
Shawnee State U (OH)
Shaw U (NC)
Shenandoah U (VA)
Shepherd Coll (WV)
Shippensburg U of Pennsylvania (PA)
Shorter Coll (GA)
Siena Coll (NY)
Siena Heights U (MI)
Silver Lake Coll (WI)
Simmons Coll (MA)
Simon Fraser U (BC, Canada)
Simpson Coll (IA)
Simpson Coll and Graduate School (CA)
Slippery Rock U of Pennsylvania (PA)
Smith Coll (MA)
Sonoma State U (CA)
South Carolina State U (SC)
South Dakota State U (SD)
Southeastern Coll of the Assemblies of God (FL)
Southeastern Louisiana U (LA)
Southeastern Oklahoma State U (OK)
Southeast Missouri State U (MO)
Southern Adventist U (TN)
Southern Arkansas U–Magnolia (AR)
Southern Connecticut State U (CT)
Southern Illinois U Carbondale (IL)
Southern Illinois U Edwardsville (IL)
Southern Methodist U (TX)
Southern Nazarene U (OK)
Southern New Hampshire U (NH)
Southern Oregon U (OR)
Southern U and A&M Coll (LA)
Southern Utah U (UT)
Southern Vermont Coll (VT)
Southern Virginia U (VA)
Southern Wesleyan U (SC)
Southwest Baptist U (MO)
Southwestern Adventist U (TX)
Southwestern Coll (KS)
Southwestern Oklahoma State U (OK)
Southwestern U (TX)
Southwest Missouri State U (MO)
Southwest State U (MN)
Southwest Texas State U (TX)
Spelman Coll (GA)
Spring Arbor U (MI)
Springfield Coll (MA)
Spring Hill Coll (AL)
Stanford U (CA)
State U of NY at Albany (NY)
State U of NY at Binghamton (NY)
State U of NY at New Paltz (NY)
State U of NY at Oswego (NY)
State U of NY Coll at Brockport (NY)
State U of NY Coll at Buffalo (NY)
State U of NY Coll at Cortland (NY)
State U of NY Coll at Fredonia (NY)
State U of NY Coll at Geneseo (NY)
State U of NY Coll at Oneonta (NY)
State U of NY Coll at Potsdam (NY)
State U of West Georgia (GA)
Stephen F. Austin State U (TX)
Stephens Coll (MO)
Sterling Coll (KS)
Stetson U (FL)
Stevens Inst of Technology (NJ)
Stonehill Coll (MA)
State U of NY at Stony Brook (NY)
Suffolk U (MA)
Sul Ross State U (TX)
Susquehanna U (PA)
Swarthmore Coll (PA)
Sweet Briar Coll (VA)
Syracuse U (NY)
Tabor Coll (KS)
Talladega Coll (AL)
Tarleton State U (TX)
Taylor U (IN)
Taylor U, Fort Wayne Campus (IN)
Teikyo Post U (CT)
Temple U (PA)
Tennessee State U (TN)
Tennessee Technological U (TN)
Tennessee Temple U (TN)
Tennessee Wesleyan Coll (TN)
Texas A&M International U (TX)
Texas A&M U (TX)
Texas A&M U–Commerce (TX)
Texas A&M U–Corpus Christi (TX)
Texas A&M U–Kingsville (TX)
Texas A&M U–Texarkana (TX)
Texas Christian U (TX)
Texas Coll (TX)
Texas Lutheran U (TX)
Texas Southern U (TX)
Texas Tech U (TX)
Texas Wesleyan U (TX)
Texas Woman's U (TX)
Thiel Coll (PA)
Thomas Edison State Coll (NJ)
Thomas More Coll (KY)
Thomas U (GA)
Toccoa Falls Coll (GA)
Tougaloo Coll (MS)
Touro Coll (NY)
Towson U (MD)
Transylvania U (KY)
Trent U (ON, Canada)
Trevecca Nazarene U (TN)
Trinity Christian Coll (IL)
Trinity Coll (CT)
Trinity Coll (DC)
Trinity International U (IL)
Trinity U (TX)
Trinity Western U (BC, Canada)
Troy State U (AL)
Troy State U Dothan (AL)
Troy State U Montgomery (AL)
Truman State U (MO)
Tufts U (MA)
Tulane U (LA)
Tusculum Coll (TN)
Tuskegee U (AL)
Tyndale Coll & Seminary (ON, Canada)
Union Coll (KY)
Union Coll (NE)
Union Coll (NY)
Union U (TN)
United States Air Force Academy (CO)
United States Naval Academy (MD)
Université de Montréal (QC, Canada)
Université de Sherbrooke (PQ, Canada)
Université Laval (QC, Canada)
State U of NY at Buffalo (NY)
U Coll of Cape Breton (NS, Canada)
U Coll of the Cariboo (BC, Canada)
U Coll of the Fraser Valley (BC, Canada)
The U of Akron (OH)
The U of Alabama (AL)
The U of Alabama at Birmingham (AL)
The U of Alabama in Huntsville (AL)
U of Alaska Anchorage (AK)
U of Alaska Fairbanks (AK)
U of Alberta (AB, Canada)
The U of Arizona (AZ)
U of Arkansas (AR)
U of Arkansas at Little Rock (AR)
U of Arkansas at Pine Bluff (AR)
U of Baltimore (MD)
U of Bridgeport (CT)
The U of British Columbia (BC, Canada)
U of Calgary (AB, Canada)
U of Calif, Berkeley (CA)
U of Calif, Davis (CA)
U of Calif, Irvine (CA)
U of Calif, Los Angeles (CA)
U of Calif, Riverside (CA)
U of Calif, San Diego (CA)
U of Calif, Santa Barbara (CA)
U of Central Arkansas (AR)
U of Central Florida (FL)
U of Central Oklahoma (OK)
U of Charleston (WV)

ENGLISH COMPOSITION

ENGLISH EDUCATION

ENGLISH RELATED

ENTERPRISE MANAGEMENT

ENTOMOLOGY

ENTREPRENEURSHIP

ENVIRONMENTAL BIOLOGY

ENVIRONMENTAL CONTROL TECHNOLOGIES RELATED

ENVIRONMENTAL EDUCATION

ENVIRONMENTAL ENGINEERING

U of Miami (FL)
U of Michigan (MI)
U of Nevada, Reno (NV)
U of New Hampshire (NH)
U of North Dakota (ND)
U of Notre Dame (IN)
U of Oklahoma (OK)
U of Regina (SK, Canada)
U of Southern California (CA)
U of Utah (UT)
U of Waterloo (ON, Canada)
U of Windsor (ON, Canada)
U of Wisconsin–Madison (WI)
Utah State U (UT)
Wentworth Inst of Technology (MA)
Western Michigan U (MI)
Wilkes U (PA)
Worcester Polytechnic Inst (MA)
Yale U (CT)
Youngstown State U (OH)

ENVIRONMENTAL HEALTH
Benedict Coll (SC)
Boise State U (ID)
Bowling Green State U (OH)
British Columbia Inst of Technology (BC, Canada)
California State U, Northridge (CA)
California State U, Sacramento (CA)
Clarkson U (NY)
Colorado State U (CO)
Delaware State U (DE)
East Carolina U (NC)
East Central U (OK)
Eastern Kentucky U (KY)
East Tennessee State U (TN)
Ferris State U (MI)
Hampshire Coll (MA)
Illinois State U (IL)
Indiana State U (IN)
Indiana U of Pennsylvania (PA)
Iowa Wesleyan Coll (IA)
Missouri Southern State Coll (MO)
New Mexico State U (NM)
Oakland U (MI)
Ohio U (OH)
Oregon State U (OR)
Salisbury U (MD)
San Jose State U (CA)
Springfield Coll (MA)
Texas Southern U (TX)
U Coll of Cape Breton (NS, Canada)
U of Arkansas at Little Rock (AR)
U of Georgia (GA)
U of Miami (FL)
U of Michigan–Flint (MI)
The U of North Carolina at Chapel Hill (NC)
U of Southern Colorado (CO)
U of Southern Maine (ME)
U of Utah (UT)
U of Washington (WA)
U of Wisconsin–Eau Claire (WI)
West Chester U of Pennsylvania (PA)
Western Carolina U (NC)
Wright State U (OH)
York Coll of the City U of New York (NY)

ENVIRONMENTAL SCIENCE
Abilene Christian U (TX)
Acadia U (NS, Canada)
Adams State Coll (CO)
Adrian Coll (MI)
Alaska Pacific U (AK)
Albion Coll (MI)
Albright Coll (PA)
Alderson-Broaddus Coll (WV)
Alfred U (NY)
Allegheny Coll (PA)
Alliant International U (CA)
Alverno Coll (WI)
American U (DC)
Aquinas Coll (MI)
Ashland U (OH)
Assumption Coll (MA)
Auburn U (AL)
Augustana Coll (IL)
Aurora U (IL)
Averett U (VA)
Baldwin-Wallace Coll (OH)
Ball State U (IN)
Bard Coll (NY)
Barnard Coll (NY)
Barton Coll (NC)
Bates Coll (ME)
Bayamón Central U (PR)
Baylor U (TX)
Bellevue U (NE)
Beloit Coll (WI)
Bemidji State U (MN)
Benedictine U (IL)
Bennington Coll (VT)
Berry Coll (GA)
Bethany Coll (WV)
Bethel Coll (MN)
Black Hills State U (SD)
Boise State U (ID)
Boston Coll (MA)
Boston U (MA)
Bowdoin Coll (ME)
Brenau U (GA)
Brevard Coll (NC)
Briar Cliff U (IA)
Brock U (ON, Canada)
Brown U (RI)
Bucknell U (PA)
Cabrini Coll (PA)
California State U, Chico (CA)
California State U, Hayward (CA)
California State U, Monterey Bay (CA)
California State U, San Bernardino (CA)
California U of Pennsylvania (PA)
Calvin Coll (MI)
Cameron U (OK)
Canisius Coll (NY)
Capital U (OH)
Carleton U (ON, Canada)
Carroll Coll (MT)
Carroll Coll (WI)
Carthage Coll (WI)
Case Western Reserve U (OH)
Castleton State Coll (VT)
Catawba Coll (NC)
Cedar Crest Coll (PA)
Centenary Coll of Louisiana (LA)
Central Coll (IA)
Central Methodist Coll (MO)
Central Michigan U (MI)
Chapman U (CA)
Charleston Southern U (SC)
Chatham Coll (PA)
Chestnut Hill Coll (PA)
Christopher Newport U (VA)
Claremont McKenna Coll (CA)
Clarion U of Pennsylvania (PA)
Clarkson U (NY)
Clark U (MA)
Cleveland State U (OH)
Coe Coll (IA)
Colby Coll (ME)
Colby-Sawyer Coll (NH)
Colgate U (NY)
The Coll of Saint Rose (NY)
Coll of Santa Fe (NM)
Coll of the Atlantic (ME)
Coll of the Holy Cross (MA)
Coll of the Southwest (NM)
The Coll of William and Mary (VA)
The Colorado Coll (CO)
Columbia Coll (NY)
Columbia Southern U (AL)
Concordia Coll (MN)
Concordia U (IL)
Concordia U (MN)
Concordia U (OR)
Concordia U (QC, Canada)
Cornell Coll (IA)
Cornell U (NY)
Creighton U (NE)
Curry Coll (MA)
Dana Coll (NE)
Dartmouth Coll (NH)
Davis & Elkins Coll (WV)
Defiance Coll (OH)
Delaware Valley Coll (PA)
Denison U (OH)
DePaul U (IL)
DeSales U (PA)
Dickinson Coll (PA)
Dickinson State U (ND)
Doane Coll (NE)
Dominican Coll (NY)
Dominican U (IL)
Dominican U of California (CA)
Dordt Coll (IA)
Drake U (IA)
Drexel U (PA)
Drury U (MO)
Duke U (NC)
Duquesne U (PA)
Earlham Coll (IN)
East Central U (OK)
Eastern Kentucky U (KY)
Eastern Mennonite U (VA)
Eastern U (PA)
Eckerd Coll (FL)
Edinboro U of Pennsylvania (PA)
Elizabethtown Coll (PA)
Elmhurst Coll (IL)
Elmira Coll (NY)
Elon U (NC)
Emory & Henry Coll (VA)
The Evergreen State Coll (WA)
Fairleigh Dickinson U, Teaneck-Hackensack Campus (NJ)
Felician Coll (NJ)
Ferrum Coll (VA)
Fitchburg State Coll (MA)
Florida Inst of Technology (FL)
Florida International U (FL)
Florida Southern Coll (FL)
Florida State U (FL)
Framingham State Coll (MA)
Franklin Pierce Coll (NH)
Frostburg State U (MD)
Furman U (SC)
Georgetown Coll (KY)
The George Washington U (DC)
Gettysburg Coll (PA)
Goddard Coll (VT)
Goshen Coll (IN)
Green Mountain Coll (VT)
Grinnell Coll (IA)
Guilford Coll (NC)
Gustavus Adolphus Coll (MN)
Hamline U (MN)
Hampshire Coll (MA)
Hampton U (VA)
Harvard U (MA)
Hawai'i Pacific U (HI)
Hiram Coll (OH)
Hobart and William Smith Colls (NY)
Hofstra U (NY)
Hood Coll (MD)
Hope Coll (MI)
Humboldt State U (CA)
Huntingdon Coll (AL)
Illinois Coll (IL)
Indiana U Bloomington (IN)
Indiana U of Pennsylvania (PA)
Inter American U of PR, San Germán Campus (PR)
Iowa State U of Science and Technology (IA)
Ithaca Coll (NY)
Jacksonville U (FL)
John Brown U (AR)
John Carroll U (OH)
Johns Hopkins U (MD)
Johnson State Coll (VT)
Juniata Coll (PA)
Keene State Coll (NH)
Kentucky Wesleyan Coll (KY)
Kenyon Coll (OH)
Kettering U (MI)
Keystone Coll (PA)
King's Coll (PA)
The King's U Coll (AB, Canada)
Knox Coll (IL)
Kutztown U of Pennsylvania (PA)
Lake Erie Coll (OH)
Lake Forest Coll (IL)
Lakehead U (ON, Canada)
Lake Superior State U (MI)
Lamar U (TX)
Lander U (SC)
La Salle U (PA)
Lawrence U (WI)
Lees-McRae Coll (NC)
Lehigh U (PA)
Lenoir-Rhyne Coll (NC)
Lewis & Clark Coll (OR)
Lewis U (IL)
Lincoln Memorial U (TN)
Lipscomb U (TN)
Long Island U, C.W. Post Campus (NY)
Long Island U, Southampton Coll (NY)
Long Island U, Southampton Coll, Friends World Program (NY)
Longwood Coll (VA)
Louisiana State U and A&M Coll (LA)
Louisiana State U in Shreveport (LA)
Louisiana Tech U (LA)
Loyola U Chicago (IL)
Lynchburg Coll (VA)
Lynn U (FL)
Lyon Coll (AR)
Macalester Coll (MN)
Maharishi U of Management (IA)
Manchester Coll (IN)
Mansfield U of Pennsylvania (PA)
Marian Coll of Fond du Lac (WI)
Marietta Coll (OH)
Marist Coll (NY)
Marlboro Coll (VT)
Marshall U (WV)
Marygrove Coll (MI)
Marylhurst U (OR)
Marymount U (VA)
Maryville Coll (TN)
Maryville U of Saint Louis (MO)
Mary Washington Coll (VA)
Marywood U (PA)
Massachusetts Coll of Liberal Arts (MA)
Massachusetts Inst of Technology (MA)
Massachusetts Maritime Academy (MA)
McGill U (PQ, Canada)
McMaster U (ON, Canada)
McMurry U (TX)
McNeese State U (LA)
McPherson Coll (KS)
Medgar Evers Coll of the City U of NY (NY)
Memorial U of Newfoundland (NF, Canada)
Mercer U (GA)
Meredith Coll (NC)
Merrimack Coll (MA)
Messiah Coll (PA)
Metropolitan State Coll of Denver (CO)
Middlebury Coll (VT)
Midland Lutheran Coll (NE)
Midwestern State U (TX)
Mills Coll (CA)
Minnesota State U, Mankato (MN)
Molloy Coll (NY)
Monmouth Coll (IL)
Montana State U–Billings (MT)
Montana State U–Bozeman (MT)
Montclair State U (NJ)
Montreat Coll (NC)
Mount Allison U (NB, Canada)
Mount Holyoke Coll (MA)
Mount Marty Coll (SD)
Mount Olive Coll (NC)
Muhlenberg Coll (PA)
Muskingum Coll (OH)
Naropa U (CO)
Nazareth Coll of Rochester (NY)
New Coll of Florida (FL)
New England Coll (NH)
New Jersey Inst of Technology (NJ)
New Mexico Highlands U (NM)
New Mexico Inst of Mining and Technology (NM)
New Mexico State U (NM)
Nipissing U (ON, Canada)
North Carolina Central U (NC)
North Carolina State U (NC)
North Carolina Wesleyan Coll (NC)
Northeastern Illinois U (IL)
Northeastern U (MA)
Northern Arizona U (AZ)
Northern Kentucky U (KY)
Northern Michigan U (MI)
Northern State U (SD)
Northland Coll (WI)
Northwestern Coll (IA)
Northwestern U (IL)
Norwich U (VT)
Notre Dame Coll (OH)
Nova Scotia Ag Coll (NS, Canada)
Oberlin Coll (OH)
Occidental Coll (CA)
Ohio Northern U (OH)
The Ohio State U (OH)
Ohio Wesleyan U (OH)
Oklahoma State U (OK)
Olivet Coll (MI)
Olivet Nazarene U (IL)
Oregon Inst of Technology (OR)
Oregon State U (OR)
Pacific Lutheran U (WA)
Pacific U (OR)
Paul Smith's Coll of Arts and Sciences (NY)
Penn State U Altoona Coll (PA)
Pfeiffer U (NC)
Piedmont Coll (GA)
Pittsburg State U (KS)
Pitzer Coll (CA)
Plattsburgh State U of NY (NY)
Point Park Coll (PA)
Pomona Coll (CA)
Pontifical Catholic U of Puerto Rico (PR)
Portland State U (OR)
Prescott Coll (AZ)
Principia Coll (IL)
Providence Coll (RI)
Purchase Coll, State U of NY (NY)
Queens Coll of the City U of NY (NY)
Queen's U at Kingston (ON, Canada)
Quincy U (IL)
Ramapo Coll of New Jersey (NJ)
Randolph-Macon Coll (VA)
Randolph-Macon Woman's Coll (VA)
Regis U (CO)
Rensselaer Polytechnic Inst (NY)
The Richard Stockton Coll of New Jersey (NJ)
Richmond, The American International U in London(United Kingdom)
Rider U (NJ)
Ripon Coll (WI)
Roanoke Coll (VA)
Rochester Inst of Technology (NY)
Rocky Mountain Coll (MT)
Roger Williams U (RI)
Rollins Coll (FL)
Roosevelt U (IL)
Royal Roads U (BC, Canada)
Rutgers, The State U of New Jersey, New Brunswick (NJ)
Sacred Heart U (CT)
Saint Anselm Coll (NH)
St. Bonaventure U (NY)
Saint Francis U (PA)
St. Francis Xavier U (NS, Canada)
Saint Joseph Coll (CT)
Saint Joseph's Coll (IN)
Saint Joseph's Coll (ME)
Saint Joseph's U (PA)
St. Lawrence U (NY)
Saint Leo U (FL)
Saint Louis U (MO)
Saint Mary's Coll of Ave Maria U (MI)
Saint Michael's Coll (VT)
Saint Vincent Coll (PA)
Salem International U (WV)
Samford U (AL)
Sam Houston State U (TX)
San Diego State U (CA)
San Jose State U (CA)
Sarah Lawrence Coll (NY)
Savannah State U (GA)
Scripps Coll (CA)
Seattle U (WA)
Shaw U (NC)
Shenandoah U (VA)
Shepherd Coll (WV)
Shippensburg U of Pennsylvania (PA)
Shorter Coll (GA)
Siena Coll (NY)
Sierra Nevada Coll (NV)
Simmons Coll (MA)
Simon Fraser U (BC, Canada)
Simon's Rock Coll of Bard (MA)
Slippery Rock U of Pennsylvania (PA)
Sonoma State U (CA)
Southeastern Oklahoma State U (OK)
Southeast Missouri State U (MO)
Southern Methodist U (TX)
Southern Nazarene U (OK)
Southern Oregon U (OR)
Southern Vermont Coll (VT)
Southwest State U (MN)
Southwest Texas State U (TX)
Spelman Coll (GA)
Springfield Coll (MA)
Spring Hill Coll (AL)
Stanford U (CA)
State U of NY at Binghamton (NY)
State U of NY at New Paltz (NY)
State U of NY Coll at Brockport (NY)
State U of NY Coll at Fredonia (NY)
State U of NY Coll at Oneonta (NY)
State U of NY Coll of A&T at Cobleskill (NY)

State U of NY Coll of Environ Sci and Forestry (NY)
State U of NY Maritime Coll (NY)
State U of West Georgia (GA)
Stephen F. Austin State U (TX)
Stephens Coll (MO)
Sterling Coll (VT)
Stetson U (FL)
State U of NY at Stony Brook (NY)
Suffolk U (MA)
Sul Ross State U (TX)
Sweet Briar Coll (VA)
Syracuse U (NY)
Taylor U (IN)
Teikyo Post U (CT)
Texas A&M U (TX)
Texas A&M U–Corpus Christi (TX)
Texas Christian U (TX)
Thiel Coll (PA)
Thomas Edison State Coll (NJ)
Trent U (ON, Canada)
Trinity Coll (DC)
Trinity Western U (BC, Canada)
Tri-State U (IN)
Tufts U (MA)
Tulane U (LA)
Tusculum Coll (TN)
Tuskegee U (AL)
United States Military Academy (NY)
Unity Coll (ME)
Université Laval (QC, Canada)
U Coll of Cape Breton (NS, Canada)
U of Alaska Southeast (AK)
U of Alberta (AB, Canada)
The U of Arizona (AZ)
The U of British Columbia (BC, Canada)
U of Calgary (AB, Canada)
U of Calif, Berkeley (CA)
U of Calif, Riverside (CA)
U of Calif, San Diego (CA)
U of Calif, Santa Barbara (CA)
U of Calif, Santa Cruz (CA)
U of Central Arkansas (AR)
U of Charleston (WV)
U of Chicago (IL)
U of Colorado at Boulder (CO)
U of Connecticut (CT)
U of Dayton (OH)
U of Delaware (DE)
U of Denver (CO)
U of Dubuque (IA)
U of Evansville (IN)
The U of Findlay (OH)
U of Florida (FL)
U of Guelph (ON, Canada)
U of Houston–Clear Lake (TX)
U of Idaho (ID)
U of Illinois at Urbana–Champaign (IL)
U of Indianapolis (IN)
The U of Iowa (IA)
The U of Lethbridge (AB, Canada)
U of Maine at Farmington (ME)
U of Maine at Fort Kent (ME)
U of Maine at Machias (ME)
U of Maine at Presque Isle (ME)
U of Manitoba (MB, Canada)
U of Maryland, Baltimore County (MD)
U of Maryland, Coll Park (MD)
U of Maryland Eastern Shore (MD)
U of Maryland University Coll (MD)
U of Massachusetts Amherst (MA)
U of Miami (FL)
U of Michigan (MI)
U of Michigan–Dearborn (MI)
U of Michigan–Flint (MI)
U of Minnesota, Crookston (MN)
U of Minnesota, Duluth (MN)
U of Minnesota, Twin Cities Campus (MN)
U of Mobile (AL)
The U of Montana–Missoula (MT)
Western Montana Coll of The U of Montana (MT)
U of Nebraska–Lincoln (NE)
U of Nevada, Las Vegas (NV)
U of New England (ME)
U of New Hampshire (NH)
U of New Haven (CT)
The U of North Carolina at Asheville (NC)
The U of North Carolina at Chapel Hill (NC)
The U of North Carolina at Wilmington (NC)
U of Northern Iowa (IA)
U of Notre Dame (IN)
U of Oklahoma (OK)
U of Oregon (OR)
U of Ottawa (ON, Canada)
U of Pittsburgh at Bradford (PA)
U of Pittsburgh at Johnstown (PA)
U of Portland (OR)
U of Redlands (CA)
U of Rhode Island (RI)
U of Richmond (VA)
U of Rochester (NY)
U of St. Francis (IL)
U of Saint Francis (IN)
U of St. Thomas (MN)
U of St. Thomas (TX)
U of San Francisco (CA)
U of Saskatchewan (SK, Canada)
The U of Scranton (PA)
U of Southern California (CA)
U of Southern Maine (ME)
U of South Florida (FL)
The U of Tampa (FL)
The U of Tennessee at Chattanooga (TN)
The U of Tennessee at Martin (TN)
The U of Texas of the Permian Basin (TX)
U of the District of Columbia (DC)
U of the Incarnate Word (TX)
U of the Ozarks (AR)
U of the Pacific (CA)
U of the Sciences in Philadelphia (PA)
U of the South (TN)
U of Toledo (OH)
U of Toronto (ON, Canada)
U of Tulsa (OK)
U of Utah (UT)
U of Vermont (VT)
U of Victoria (BC, Canada)
U of Virginia (VA)
The U of Virginia's Coll at Wise (VA)
U of Washington (WA)
U of Waterloo (ON, Canada)
The U of Western Ontario (ON, Canada)
U of West Florida (FL)
U of Windsor (ON, Canada)
U of Wisconsin–Green Bay (WI)
U of Wisconsin–River Falls (WI)
U of Wyoming (WY)
Ursinus Coll (PA)
Valdosta State U (GA)
Valparaiso U (IN)
Vassar Coll (NY)
Villa Julie Coll (MD)
Virginia Intermont Coll (VA)
Virginia Polytechnic Inst and State U (VA)
Virginia Wesleyan Coll (VA)
Walla Walla Coll (WA)
Warren Wilson Coll (NC)
Washington Coll (MD)
Washington State U (WA)
Washington U in St. Louis (MO)
Waynesburg Coll (PA)
Webster U (MO)
Wellesley Coll (MA)
Wells Coll (NY)
Wesleyan U (CT)
Wesley Coll (DE)
West Chester U of Pennsylvania (PA)
Western Connecticut State U (CT)
Western Michigan U (MI)
Western New England Coll (MA)
Western State Coll of Colorado (CO)
Western Washington U (WA)
Westminster Coll (MO)
Westminster Coll (PA)
West Texas A&M U (TX)
West Virginia U (WV)
Wheaton Coll (IL)
Wheaton Coll (MA)
Wheeling Jesuit U (WV)
Whitman Coll (WA)
Widener U (PA)
Willamette U (OR)
William Paterson U of New Jersey (NJ)
Wilson Coll (PA)
Wittenberg U (OH)
Worcester Polytechnic Inst (MA)
Xavier U (OH)
Xavier U of Louisiana (LA)
Yale U (CT)
York U (ON, Canada)
Youngstown State U (OH)

ENVIRONMENTAL TECHNOLOGY

Arizona State U East (AZ)
British Columbia Inst of Technology (BC, Canada)
California State U, Long Beach (CA)
East Carolina U (NC)
Lake Superior State U (MI)
Middle Tennessee State U (TN)
New York Inst of Technology (NY)
San Jose State U (CA)
Shawnee State U (OH)
Texas Southern U (TX)
Unity Coll (ME)
U Coll of Cape Breton (NS, Canada)
U of Delaware (DE)
U of Guelph (ON, Canada)
U of North Dakota (ND)
Western Kentucky U (KY)

EQUESTRIAN STUDIES

Averett U (VA)
Cazenovia Coll (NY)
Centenary Coll (NJ)
Colorado State U (CO)
Delaware Valley Coll (PA)
Johnson & Wales U (RI)
Lake Erie Coll (OH)
Midway Coll (KY)
Mount Ida Coll (MA)
National American U (SD)
North Dakota State U (ND)
Oregon State U (OR)
Otterbein Coll (OH)
Rocky Mountain Coll (MT)
St. Andrews Presbyterian Coll (NC)
Saint Mary-of-the-Woods Coll (IN)
Salem International U (WV)
Stephens Coll (MO)
Sul Ross State U (TX)
Teikyo Post U (CT)
Truman State U (MO)
The U of Findlay (OH)
U of Louisville (KY)
U of Minnesota, Crookston (MN)
U of New Hampshire (NH)
U of Wisconsin–River Falls (WI)
Virginia Intermont Coll (VA)
West Texas A&M U (TX)
William Woods U (MO)

ETHNIC/CULTURAL STUDIES RELATED

Boston U (MA)
The Colorado Coll (CO)
Connecticut Coll (CT)
Marylhurst U (OR)
Metropolitan State U (MN)
St. Olaf Coll (MN)
U of Hawaii at Manoa (HI)
U of Pittsburgh (PA)
The U of Texas at Austin (TX)
The U of Texas at Dallas (TX)
Washington U in St. Louis (MO)
Wellesley Coll (MA)
Yale U (CT)

EUROPEAN HISTORY

Bard Coll (NY)
Calvin Coll (MI)
Pitzer Coll (CA)
U of Calif, Santa Cruz (CA)

EUROPEAN STUDIES

American U (DC)
The American U of Paris(France)
Amherst Coll (MA)
Bard Coll (NY)
Barnard Coll (NY)
Beloit Coll (WI)
Bennington Coll (VT)
Brandeis U (MA)
Brigham Young U (UT)
Brock U (ON, Canada)
Canisius Coll (NY)
Carleton U (ON, Canada)
Carnegie Mellon U (PA)
Case Western Reserve U (OH)
Central Michigan U (MI)
Chapman U (CA)
Claremont McKenna Coll (CA)
The Coll of William and Mary (VA)
The Coll of Wooster (OH)
Cornell U (NY)
Elmira Coll (NY)
The Evergreen State Coll (WA)
Fort Lewis Coll (CO)
Franklin Coll Switzerland(Switzerland)
Georgetown Coll (KY)
The George Washington U (DC)
Grace U (NE)
Hamline U (MN)
Hampshire Coll (MA)
Harvard U (MA)
Hillsdale Coll (MI)
Hobart and William Smith Colls (NY)
Howard Payne U (TX)
Huntingdon Coll (AL)
Illinois Wesleyan U (IL)
Lake Forest Coll (IL)
Long Island U, Southampton Coll, Friends World Program (NY)
Loyola Marymount U (CA)
Marlboro Coll (VT)
Millsaps Coll (MS)
Mount Holyoke Coll (MA)
New York U (NY)
Ohio U (OH)
Pitzer Coll (CA)
Richmond, The American International U in London(United Kingdom)
Salem State Coll (MA)
San Diego State U (CA)
San Jose State U (CA)
Sarah Lawrence Coll (NY)
Scripps Coll (CA)
Seattle Pacific U (WA)
Simon's Rock Coll of Bard (MA)
Southern Methodist U (TX)
Southwest Texas State U (TX)
State U of NY Coll at Brockport (NY)
Sweet Briar Coll (VA)
Trinity U (TX)
United States Military Academy (NY)
U of Calif, Los Angeles (CA)
U of Guelph (ON, Canada)
U of Hawaii–West Oahu (HI)
U of Kansas (KS)
U of Michigan (MI)
U of Minnesota, Morris (MN)
U of Minnesota, Twin Cities Campus (MN)
U of New Mexico (NM)
The U of North Carolina at Greensboro (NC)
U of Northern Iowa (IA)
U of Richmond (VA)
U of South Carolina (SC)
U of the South (TN)
U of Toledo (OH)
U of Toronto (ON, Canada)
U of Vermont (VT)
U of Washington (WA)
Valparaiso U (IN)
Vanderbilt U (TN)
Washington U in St. Louis (MO)
Western Michigan U (MI)

EVOLUTIONARY BIOLOGY

Case Western Reserve U (OH)
Coll of the Atlantic (ME)
Dartmouth Coll (NH)
Florida State U (FL)
Hampshire Coll (MA)
Harvard U (MA)
Oregon State U (OR)
Rice U (TX)
Rutgers, The State U of New Jersey, New Brunswick (NJ)
San Diego State U (CA)
Tulane U (LA)
The U of Arizona (AZ)
U of New Hampshire (NH)
U of Rochester (NY)
Yale U (CT)

EXECUTIVE ASSISTANT

Caribbean U (PR)
Cumberland Coll (KY)
Eastern Michigan U (MI)
Youngstown State U (OH)

EXERCISE SCIENCES

Abilene Christian U (TX)
Acadia U (NS, Canada)
Adams State Coll (CO)
Adrian Coll (MI)
Albertson Coll of Idaho (ID)
Alma Coll (MI)
Andrews U (MI)
Arizona State U (AZ)
Arkansas State U (AR)
Augustana Coll (SD)
Avila Coll (MO)
Ball State U (IN)
Barry U (FL)
Bastyr U (WA)
Becker Coll (MA)
Bethel Coll (IN)
Biola U (CA)
Bloomsburg U of Pennsylvania (PA)
Bluefield Coll (VA)
Bluffton Coll (OH)
Boise State U (ID)
Boston U (MA)
Bowling Green State U (OH)
Brevard Coll (NC)
Bridgewater Coll (VA)
Bridgewater State Coll (MA)
Brock U (ON, Canada)
Cabrini Coll (PA)
California Baptist U (CA)
California State U, Chico (CA)
California State U, Hayward (CA)
California State U, Long Beach (CA)
Calvin Coll (MI)
Carroll Coll (WI)
Carson-Newman Coll (TN)
Castleton State Coll (VT)
Central Coll (IA)
Central Washington U (WA)
Chapman U (CA)
Chowan Coll (NC)
Coker Coll (SC)
Colby-Sawyer Coll (NH)
Coll of Mount Saint Vincent (NY)
The Coll of St. Scholastica (MN)
Colorado State U (CO)
Columbia Union Coll (MD)
Columbus State U (GA)
Concordia Coll (MN)
Concordia U (CA)
Concordia U (IL)
Concordia U (NE)
Concordia U (QC, Canada)
Cornell Coll (IA)
Creighton U (NE)
Dakota State U (SD)
Dalhousie U (NS, Canada)
Davis & Elkins Coll (WV)
Defiance Coll (OH)
Dordt Coll (IA)
Drury U (MO)
East Carolina U (NC)
Eastern Kentucky U (KY)
Eastern Washington U (WA)
East Stroudsburg U of Pennsylvania (PA)
Elmhurst Coll (IL)
Emmanuel Coll (GA)
Eureka Coll (IL)
Fitchburg State Coll (MA)
Florida Atlantic U (FL)
Florida International U (FL)
Frostburg State U (MD)
Furman U (SC)
The George Washington U (DC)
Georgia Southern U (GA)
Gonzaga U (WA)
Gordon Coll (MA)
Grand Canyon U (AZ)
Guilford Coll (NC)
Hamline U (MN)
Hampshire Coll (MA)
Harding U (AR)
Hardin-Simmons U (TX)
High Point U (NC)
Hofstra U (NY)
Hope Coll (MI)
Houston Baptist U (TX)
Howard Payne U (TX)
Humboldt State U (CA)
Huntingdon Coll (AL)
Huntington Coll (IN)
Indiana Wesleyan U (IN)
Inter American U of PR, San Germán Campus (PR)
Iowa Wesleyan Coll (IA)
Ithaca Coll (NY)
Jacksonville State U (AL)
John Brown U (AR)
Johnson State Coll (VT)
Judson Coll (AL)
Kansas State U (KS)
Kennesaw State U (GA)

Kent State U (OH)
Lakeland Coll (WI)
Lake Superior State U (MI)
Lander U (SC)
Lasell Coll (MA)
Laurentian U (ON, Canada)
Lenoir-Rhyne Coll (NC)
Lewis-Clark State Coll (ID)
Liberty U (VA)
Linfield Coll (OR)
Lipscomb U (TN)
Longwood Coll (VA)
Loras Coll (IA)
Louisiana Coll (LA)
Lynchburg Coll (VA)
Malone Coll (OH)
Marquette U (WI)
McGill U (PQ, Canada)
McMaster U (ON, Canada)
Memorial U of Newfoundland (NF, Canada)
Meredith Coll (NC)
Mesa State Coll (CO)
Messiah Coll (PA)
Metropolitan State Coll of Denver (CO)
Miami U (OH)
MidAmerica Nazarene U (KS)
Midwestern State U (TX)
Milligan Coll (TN)
Mississippi U for Women (MS)
Missouri Southern State Coll (MO)
Missouri Western State Coll (MO)
Montclair State U (NJ)
Mount Union Coll (OH)
Mount Vernon Nazarene U (OH)
Murray State U (KY)
Nebraska Wesleyan U (NE)
Norfolk State U (VA)
North Central Coll (IL)
Northern Arizona U (AZ)
Northern Kentucky U (KY)
Northern Michigan U (MI)
North Park U (IL)
Northwestern Coll (IA)
Oakland U (MI)
Occidental Coll (CA)
The Ohio State U (OH)
Ohio U (OH)
Oklahoma Baptist U (OK)
Oklahoma Wesleyan U (OK)
Olivet Nazarene U (IL)
Oral Roberts U (OK)
Oregon State U (OR)
Pacific Union Coll (CA)
Pacific U (OR)
Redeemer U Coll (ON, Canada)
Rocky Mountain Coll (MT)
Rutgers, The State U of New Jersey, New Brunswick (NJ)
St. Cloud State U (MN)
St. Francis Xavier U (NS, Canada)
Saint Joseph's Coll (ME)
Saint Louis U (MO)
St. Mary's U of San Antonio (TX)
Salem State Coll (MA)
Samford U (AL)
Sam Houston State U (TX)
San Jose State U (CA)
Schreiner U (TX)
Seattle Pacific U (WA)
Simon Fraser U (BC, Canada)
Skidmore Coll (NY)
Slippery Rock U of Pennsylvania (PA)
Southern Adventist U (TN)
Southern Arkansas U–Magnolia (AR)
Southern Nazarene U (OK)
Southwestern Adventist U (TX)
Springfield Coll (MA)
State U of NY Coll at Brockport (NY)
State U of NY Coll at Buffalo (NY)
Stetson U (FL)
Syracuse U (NY)
Tarleton State U (TX)
Tennessee Wesleyan Coll (TN)
Texas Lutheran U (TX)
Texas Tech U (TX)
Towson U (MD)
Transylvania U (KY)
Trevecca Nazarene U (TN)
Truman State U (MO)
Tulane U (LA)
Union U (TN)
Université de Sherbrooke (PQ, Canada)
Université Laval (QC, Canada)
State U of NY at Buffalo (NY)
U of Alberta (AB, Canada)
The U of British Columbia (BC, Canada)
U of Calgary (AB, Canada)
U of Calif, Los Angeles (CA)
U of Central Arkansas (AR)
U of Colorado at Boulder (CO)
U of Dayton (OH)
U of Delaware (DE)
U of Evansville (IN)
U of Florida (FL)
U of Guelph (ON, Canada)
U of Hawaii at Manoa (HI)
U of Houston (TX)
U of Houston–Clear Lake (TX)
The U of Iowa (IA)
U of Mary (ND)
U of Massachusetts Amherst (MA)
U of Massachusetts Lowell (MA)
The U of Memphis (TN)
U of Miami (FL)
U of Michigan (MI)
U of Minnesota, Duluth (MN)
U of Mississippi (MS)
U of Nebraska–Lincoln (NE)
U of Nevada, Las Vegas (NV)
U of New Hampshire (NH)
U of Northern Colorado (CO)
U of North Texas (TX)
U of Oregon (OR)
U of Puget Sound (WA)
U of Regina (SK, Canada)
U of San Francisco (CA)
The U of Scranton (PA)
U of Sioux Falls (SD)
U of South Carolina (SC)
U of South Carolina Aiken (SC)
U of Southern California (CA)
U of Southern Colorado (CO)
U of Southern Indiana (IN)
The U of Tampa (FL)
The U of Tennessee (TN)
The U of Texas at Brownsville (TX)
The U of Texas at Tyler (TX)
The U of Texas of the Permian Basin (TX)
U of the Pacific (CA)
U of Toledo (OH)
U of Tulsa (OK)
U of Utah (UT)
U of Victoria (BC, Canada)
U of Waterloo (ON, Canada)
U of Windsor (ON, Canada)
U of Wisconsin–Eau Claire (WI)
U of Wisconsin–La Crosse (WI)
U of Wyoming (WY)
Upper Iowa U (IA)
Valparaiso U (IN)
Vanguard U of Southern California (CA)
Voorhees Coll (SC)
Wake Forest U (NC)
Walla Walla Coll (WA)
Warner Pacific Coll (OR)
Warner Southern Coll (FL)
Washington State U (WA)
Waynesburg Coll (PA)
Wayne State Coll (NE)
Weber State U (UT)
Wesley Coll (DE)
West Chester U of Pennsylvania (PA)
Western Maryland Coll (MD)
Western Michigan U (MI)
Western State Coll of Colorado (CO)
Western Washington U (WA)
West Liberty State Coll (WV)
Westmont Coll (CA)
West Virginia U (WV)
Wheaton Coll (IL)
Willamette U (OR)
William Paterson U of New Jersey (NJ)
Wilson Coll (PA)
Winona State U (MN)
Youngstown State U (OH)

EXPERIMENTAL PSYCHOLOGY

Alfred U (NY)
Cedar Crest Coll (PA)
Embry-Riddle Aeronautical U (FL)
Longwood Coll (VA)
Marlboro Coll (VT)
Millikin U (IL)
Moravian Coll (PA)
New Mexico Inst of Mining and Technology (NM)
Southwestern U (TX)
Tufts U (MA)
U of Alberta (AB, Canada)
The U of British Columbia (BC, Canada)
U of South Carolina (SC)
U of Southern Colorado (CO)
U of Toledo (OH)
U of Wisconsin–Madison (WI)

FAMILY/COMMUNITY STUDIES

Andrews U (MI)
Bowling Green State U (OH)
Brandon U (MB, Canada)
Brigham Young U (UT)
Cornell U (NY)
Eastern Illinois U (IL)
Eastern Kentucky U (KY)
Goshen Coll (IN)
Iowa State U of Science and Technology (IA)
Liberty U (VA)
Long Island U, Southampton Coll, Friends World Program (NY)
Messiah Coll (PA)
Oklahoma Christian U of Science and Arts (OK)
Oklahoma State U (OK)
Olivet Nazarene U (IL)
Oregon State U (OR)
Our Lady of the Lake U of San Antonio (TX)
Pacific Union Coll (CA)
Prairie View A&M U (TX)
Seton Hill Coll (PA)
Southern Utah U (UT)
Syracuse U (NY)
Toccoa Falls Coll (GA)
Union U (TN)
U of Calif, Santa Cruz (CA)
U of Delaware (DE)
U of Florida (FL)
U of Maryland, Coll Park (MD)
U of Minnesota, Twin Cities Campus (MN)
The U of North Carolina at Greensboro (NC)
U of Northern Iowa (IA)
U of Utah (UT)
U of Vermont (VT)
U of Wyoming (WY)
Ursuline Coll (OH)
Youngstown State U (OH)

FAMILY/CONSUMER RESOURCE MANAGEMENT RELATED

U of Hawaii at Manoa (HI)
U of Nebraska–Lincoln (NE)
Utah State U (UT)
Virginia State U (VA)

FAMILY/CONSUMER STUDIES

Andrews U (MI)
Ashland U (OH)
Baldwin-Wallace Coll (OH)
Ball State U (IN)
Berea Coll (KY)
California State U, Fresno (CA)
California State U, Northridge (CA)
California State U, Sacramento (CA)
Carson-Newman Coll (TN)
Chadron State Coll (NE)
Concordia Coll (MN)
Cornell U (NY)
Fairmont State Coll (WV)
Florida State U (FL)
Framingham State Coll (MA)
Hampshire Coll (MA)
Harding U (AR)
Howard U (DC)
Illinois State U (IL)
Indiana U Bloomington (IN)
Iowa State U of Science and Technology (IA)
Lambuth U (TN)
Lipscomb U (TN)
Louisiana Coll (LA)
Miami U (OH)
Minnesota State U, Mankato (MN)
Mississippi Coll (MS)
Montclair State U (NJ)
Mount Saint Vincent U (NS, Canada)
Murray State U (KY)
New Mexico State U (NM)
North Carolina Central U (NC)
North Dakota State U (ND)
Northern Michigan U (MI)
Northwest Missouri State U (MO)
Oklahoma State U (OK)
Oregon State U (OR)
Pacific Union Coll (CA)
Saint Joseph Coll (CT)
Seattle Pacific U (WA)
Seton Hill Coll (PA)
Southeast Missouri State U (MO)
Southern Illinois U Carbondale (IL)
Tennessee State U (TN)
Towson U (MD)
The U of Akron (OH)
U of Alberta (AB, Canada)
U of Delaware (DE)
U of Hawaii at Manoa (HI)
U of Maryland Eastern Shore (MD)
U of Missouri–Columbia (MO)
U of Montevallo (AL)
U of Nebraska at Kearney (NE)
U of New Hampshire (NH)
U of Northern Iowa (IA)
U of Prince Edward Island (PE, Canada)
The U of Tennessee at Chattanooga (TN)
U of Utah (UT)
U of Vermont (VT)
U of Windsor (ON, Canada)
U of Wisconsin–Madison (WI)
U of Wisconsin–Stevens Point (WI)
Wayne State Coll (NE)

FAMILY LIVING/PARENTHOOD

U of North Texas (TX)

FAMILY RESOURCE MANAGEMENT STUDIES

Arizona State U (AZ)
Bradley U (IL)
Central Michigan U (MI)
Cornell U (NY)
Eastern Michigan U (MI)
George Fox U (OR)
Iowa State U of Science and Technology (IA)
Michigan State U (MI)
Middle Tennessee State U (TN)
New Mexico State U (NM)
The Ohio State U (OH)
Ohio U (OH)

FAMILY STUDIES

Anderson U (IN)
Brigham Young U (UT)
Central Michigan U (MI)
Gallaudet U (DC)
Michigan State U (MI)
Point Loma Nazarene U (CA)
Southern Adventist U (TN)
Spring Arbor U (MI)
Syracuse U (NY)
Texas Tech U (TX)
The U of Akron (OH)
U of Guelph (ON, Canada)
U of Southern Mississippi (MS)
The U of Tennessee (TN)
Weber State U (UT)
Western Michigan U (MI)

FARM/RANCH MANAGEMENT

California Polytechnic State U, San Luis Obispo (CA)
California State Polytechnic U, Pomona (CA)
Colorado State U (CO)
Cornell U (NY)
Eastern Kentucky U (KY)
Iowa State U of Science and Technology (IA)
Johnson & Wales U (RI)
North Dakota State U (ND)
Northwest Missouri State U (MO)
Tarleton State U (TX)
U of Alberta (AB, Canada)
The U of Findlay (OH)
U of Wisconsin–Madison (WI)

FASHION DESIGN/ ILLUSTRATION

Academy of Art Coll (CA)
American InterContinental U (CA)
American InterContinental U, Atlanta (GA)
The Art Inst of California-San Francisco (CA)
The Art Inst of Portland (OR)
Baylor U (TX)
Bluffton Coll (OH)
Bowling Green State U (OH)
California Coll of Arts and Crafts (CA)
Centenary Coll (NJ)
Clark Atlanta U (GA)
Columbia Coll Chicago (IL)
Columbus Coll of Art and Design (OH)
Dominican U (IL)
Drexel U (PA)
Fashion Inst of Technology (NY)
Florida State U (FL)
Framingham State Coll (MA)
Hampton U (VA)
Howard U (DC)
The Illinois Inst of Art (IL)
Indiana U Bloomington (IN)
International Academy of Design & Technology (FL)
International Acad of Merchandising & Design, Ltd (IL)
Iowa State U of Science and Technology (IA)
Kent State U (OH)
Lamar U (TX)
Lasell Coll (MA)
Lindenwood U (MO)
Long Island U, Southampton Coll, Friends World Program (NY)
Lynn U (FL)
Marist Coll (NY)
Marymount Coll of Fordham U (NY)
Marymount U (VA)
Massachusetts Coll of Art (MA)
Meredith Coll (NC)
Minnesota State U, Mankato (MN)
Moore Coll of Art and Design (PA)
Mount Ida Coll (MA)
Mount Mary Coll (WI)
North Dakota State U (ND)
Northwest Missouri State U (MO)
O'More Coll of Design (TN)
Oregon State U (OR)
Otis Coll of Art and Design (CA)
Parsons School of Design, New School U (NY)
Philadelphia U (PA)
Pontifical Catholic U of Puerto Rico (PR)
Pratt Inst (NY)
Radford U (VA)
Rhode Island School of Design (RI)
Savannah Coll of Art and Design (GA)
School of the Art Inst of Chicago (IL)
State U of NY Coll at Buffalo (NY)
Stephens Coll (MO)
Syracuse U (NY)
Texas Christian U (TX)
Texas Tech U (TX)
Texas Woman's U (TX)
U of Cincinnati (OH)
U of Delaware (DE)
U of Maryland Eastern Shore (MD)
U of North Texas (TX)
U of San Francisco (CA)
U of the Incarnate Word (TX)
Ursuline Coll (OH)
Virginia Commonwealth U (VA)
Washington U in St. Louis (MO)
Woodbury U (CA)

FASHION MERCHANDISING

Abilene Christian U (TX)
Academy of Art Coll (CA)
American InterContinental U (CA)
American InterContinental U, Atlanta (GA)
Ashland U (OH)
Ball State U (IN)
Bennett Coll (NC)
Bluffton Coll (OH)
Bowling Green State U (OH)
Brenau U (GA)
Bridgewater Coll (VA)
California State U, Long Beach (CA)
California State U, Northridge (CA)
Carson-Newman Coll (TN)
Central Michigan U (MI)
Central Washington U (WA)
Coll of St. Catherine (MN)
Delta State U (MS)
Dominican U (IL)
East Central U (OK)
Eastern Kentucky U (KY)
Eastern Michigan U (MI)

Fashion Inst of Technology (NY)
Florida State U (FL)
Fontbonne U (MO)
Framingham State Coll (MA)
Freed-Hardeman U (TN)
George Fox U (OR)
Hampton U (VA)
Harding U (AR)
The Illinois Inst of Art (IL)
Immaculata Coll (PA)
Indiana U Bloomington (IN)
Indiana U of Pennsylvania (PA)
International Acad of Merchandising & Design, Ltd (IL)
Judson Coll (AL)
Kent State U (OH)
Laboratory Inst of Merchandising (NY)
Lamar U (TX)
Lambuth U (TN)
Lasell Coll (MA)
Lincoln U (MO)
Lindenwood U (MO)
Lipscomb U (TN)
Louisiana State U and A&M Coll (LA)
Lynn U (FL)
Marist Coll (NY)
Mars Hill Coll (NC)
Marygrove Coll (MI)
Marymount Coll of Fordham U (NY)
Marymount U (VA)
Mercyhurst Coll (PA)
Meredith Coll (NC)
Mississippi Coll (MS)
Montclair State U (NJ)
Mount Ida Coll (MA)
Mount Mary Coll (WI)
New Mexico State U (NM)
North Dakota State U (ND)
Northeastern State U (OK)
Northwest Missouri State U (MO)
Northwood U (MI)
Northwood U, Texas Campus (TX)
Oklahoma State U (OK)
Olivet Nazarene U (IL)
O'More Coll of Design (TN)
Oregon State U (OR)
Our Lady of the Lake U of San Antonio (TX)
Pacific Union Coll (CA)
Parsons School of Design, New School U (NY)
Philadelphia U (PA)
Pittsburg State U (KS)
Sam Houston State U (TX)
South Carolina State U (SC)
South Dakota State U (SD)
Southeast Missouri State U (MO)
Southwest Texas State U (TX)
State U of NY Coll at Buffalo (NY)
State U of NY Coll at Oneonta (NY)
Stephen F. Austin State U (TX)
Stephens Coll (MO)
Tarleton State U (TX)
Tennessee Technological U (TN)
Texas A&M U–Kingsville (TX)
Texas Christian U (TX)
Texas Southern U (TX)
Texas Tech U (TX)
Texas Woman's U (TX)
The U of Akron (OH)
U of Arkansas at Pine Bluff (AR)
U of Bridgeport (CT)
U of Central Oklahoma (OK)
U of Delaware (DE)
U of Georgia (GA)
U of Louisiana at Lafayette (LA)
U of Maryland Eastern Shore (MD)
The U of Montana–Missoula (MT)
U of Montevallo (AL)
U of Nebraska at Omaha (NE)
U of North Texas (TX)
The U of Tennessee at Martin (TN)
U of the Incarnate Word (TX)
U of Wisconsin–Madison (WI)
Ursuline Coll (OH)
Utah State U (UT)
Warren Wilson Coll (NC)
Wayne State Coll (NE)
Woodbury U (CA)
Youngstown State U (OH)

FILM STUDIES

Academy of Art Coll (CA)
Art Center Coll of Design (CA)
Bard Coll (NY)
Bennington Coll (VT)
Bowling Green State U (OH)
Brock U (ON, Canada)
Brooklyn Coll of the City U of NY (NY)
Brown U (RI)
Burlington Coll (VT)
California Coll of Arts and Crafts (CA)
California Inst of the Arts (CA)
California State U, Long Beach (CA)
California State U, Northridge (CA)
Calvin Coll (MI)
Carleton U (ON, Canada)
Carson-Newman Coll (TN)
Centenary Coll of Louisiana (LA)
Chapman U (CA)
Claremont McKenna Coll (CA)
Clark U (MA)
Coll of Santa Fe (NM)
The Colorado Coll (CO)
Columbia Coll (NY)
Columbia Coll Chicago (IL)
Columbia Coll–Hollywood (CA)
Columbia U, School of General Studies (NY)
Concordia U (QC, Canada)
Connecticut Coll (CT)
Curry Coll (MA)
Dartmouth Coll (NH)
Denison U (OH)
Emerson Coll (MA)
Emory U (GA)
The Evergreen State Coll (WA)
Florida State U (FL)
Fordham U (NY)
Georgia State U (GA)
Grand Valley State U (MI)
Hampshire Coll (MA)
Harvard U (MA)
Hofstra U (NY)
Howard U (DC)
Hunter Coll of the City U of NY (NY)
Iona Coll (NY)
Ithaca Coll (NY)
Johns Hopkins U (MD)
Keene State Coll (NH)
La Salle U (PA)
Laurentian U (ON, Canada)
Long Island U, C.W. Post Campus (NY)
Long Island U, Southampton Coll, Friends World Program (NY)
Marlboro Coll (VT)
Middlebury Coll (VT)
Mount Holyoke Coll (MA)
New York U (NY)
North Carolina School of the Arts (NC)
Northern Michigan U (MI)
Northwestern U (IL)
Olivet Nazarene U (IL)
Penn State U Univ Park Campus (PA)
Pitzer Coll (CA)
Pomona Coll (CA)
Prescott Coll (AZ)
Purchase Coll, State U of NY (NY)
Queens Coll of the City U of NY (NY)
Queen's U at Kingston (ON, Canada)
Quinnipiac U (CT)
Rhode Island Coll (RI)
Rhode Island School of Design (RI)
Rutgers, The State U of New Jersey, New Brunswick (NJ)
Sacred Heart U (CT)
St. Cloud State U (MN)
San Francisco Art Inst (CA)
San Francisco State U (CA)
San Jose State U (CA)
Sarah Lawrence Coll (NY)
School of the Art Inst of Chicago (IL)
School of the Museum of Fine Arts (MA)
School of Visual Arts (NY)
Simon Fraser U (BC, Canada)
Southern Methodist U (TX)
State U of NY at Binghamton (NY)
State U of NY Coll at Brockport (NY)
State U of NY Coll at Cortland (NY)
State U of NY Coll at Fredonia (NY)
State U of NY at Stony Brook (NY)
Syracuse U (NY)
Temple U (PA)
Université de Montréal (QC, Canada)
State U of NY at Buffalo (NY)
The U of British Columbia (BC, Canada)
U of Calif, Irvine (CA)
U of Calif, Los Angeles (CA)
U of Calif, San Diego (CA)
U of Calif, Santa Barbara (CA)
U of Calif, Santa Cruz (CA)
U of Chicago (IL)
U of Colorado at Boulder (CO)
U of Delaware (DE)
U of Hartford (CT)
The U of Iowa (IA)
U of Manitoba (MB, Canada)
U of Maryland, Baltimore County (MD)
U of Miami (FL)
U of Michigan (MI)
U of Minnesota, Twin Cities Campus (MN)
U of Nebraska–Lincoln (NE)
U of Nevada, Las Vegas (NV)
U of New Mexico (NM)
U of Pittsburgh (PA)
U of Regina (SK, Canada)
U of Rochester (NY)
U of Southern California (CA)
U of Toledo (OH)
U of Toronto (ON, Canada)
U of Utah (UT)
U of Waterloo (ON, Canada)
The U of Western Ontario (ON, Canada)
U of Windsor (ON, Canada)
U of Wisconsin–Milwaukee (WI)
Vassar Coll (NY)
Washington U in St. Louis (MO)
Watkins Coll of Art and Design (TN)
Wayne State U (MI)
Webster U (MO)
Wellesley Coll (MA)
Wesleyan U (CT)
Wilfrid Laurier U (ON, Canada)
Wright State U (OH)
Yale U (CT)
York U (ON, Canada)

FILM/VIDEO AND PHOTOGRAPHIC ARTS RELATED

The Art Inst of Philadelphia (PA)
Bloomfield Coll (NJ)
Ctr for Creative Studies—Coll of Art and Design (MI)
New England School of Communications (ME)
Rocky Mountain Coll of Art & Design (CO)
Scripps Coll (CA)
Southern Illinois U Carbondale (IL)
The U of the Arts (PA)

FILM/VIDEO PRODUCTION

Academy of Art Coll (CA)
American InterContinental U (CA)
American InterContinental U, Atlanta (GA)
American U (DC)
The Art Inst of Phoenix (AZ)
Atlanta Coll of Art (GA)
Bard Coll (NY)
Boston U (MA)
Burlington Coll (VT)
California State U, Long Beach (CA)
California State U, Northridge (CA)
Chapman U (CA)
City Coll of the City U of NY (NY)
Coll of Santa Fe (NM)
Coll of Staten Island of the City U of NY (NY)
Columbia Coll Chicago (IL)
Columbia Coll–Hollywood (CA)
Concordia U (QC, Canada)
DeSales U (PA)
Drexel U (PA)
Emerson Coll (MA)
The Evergreen State Coll (WA)
Fairleigh Dickinson U, Florham-Madison Campus (NJ)
Fitchburg State Coll (MA)
Five Towns Coll (NY)
Florida State U (FL)
Grand Valley State U (MI)
Hampshire Coll (MA)
Hofstra U (NY)
The Illinois Inst of Art-Schaumburg (IL)
Iowa Wesleyan Coll (IA)
Ithaca Coll (NY)
Long Island U, C.W. Post Campus (NY)
Long Island U, Southampton Coll, Friends World Program (NY)
Loyola Marymount U (CA)
Maharishi U of Management (IA)
Massachusetts Coll of Art (MA)
Minneapolis Coll of Art and Design (MN)
Montana State U–Bozeman (MT)
New England School of Communications (ME)
New York U (NY)
North Carolina School of the Arts (NC)
Northern Michigan U (MI)
Ohio U (OH)
Oklahoma City U (OK)
Point Park Coll (PA)
Pratt Inst (NY)
Purchase Coll, State U of NY (NY)
Quinnipiac U (CT)
Rochester Inst of Technology (NY)
Sacred Heart U (CT)
Sarah Lawrence Coll (NY)
Savannah Coll of Art and Design (GA)
School of the Art Inst of Chicago (IL)
School of the Museum of Fine Arts (MA)
School of Visual Arts (NY)
Southern Adventist U (TN)
Syracuse U (NY)
Temple U (PA)
U of Advancing Computer Technology (AZ)
U of Calif, Berkeley (CA)
U of Calif, Santa Cruz (CA)
U of Central Florida (FL)
U of Hartford (CT)
U of Illinois at Chicago (IL)
The U of Iowa (IA)
U of Miami (FL)
The U of North Carolina at Greensboro (NC)
The U of North Carolina at Wilmington (NC)
U of Oklahoma (OK)
U of Regina (SK, Canada)
U of South Dakota (SD)
U of Southern California (CA)
U of Southern Colorado (CO)
The U of Texas at Arlington (TX)
The U of the Arts (PA)
Vanguard U of Southern California (CA)
Villa Julie Coll (MD)
Waldorf Coll (IA)
Webster U (MO)
York U (ON, Canada)

FINANCE

Abilene Christian U (TX)
Adams State Coll (CO)
Adelphi U (NY)
Alabama State U (AL)
Albertus Magnus Coll (CT)
Albright Coll (PA)
Alderson-Broaddus Coll (WV)
Alfred U (NY)
American International Coll (MA)
American U (DC)
Anderson Coll (SC)
Anderson U (IN)
Angelo State U (TX)
Appalachian State U (NC)
Arcadia U (PA)
Arizona State U (AZ)
Arkansas State U (AR)
Ashland U (OH)
Auburn U (AL)
Auburn U Montgomery (AL)
Augustana Coll (IL)
Augusta State U (GA)
Aurora U (IL)
Averett U (VA)
Avila Coll (MO)
Babson Coll (MA)
Baldwin-Wallace Coll (OH)
Ball State U (IN)
Barber-Scotia Coll (NC)
Barry U (FL)
Barton Coll (NC)
Baylor U (TX)
Belmont U (TN)
Benedict Coll (SC)
Benedictine Coll (KS)
Benedictine U (IL)
Bentley Coll (MA)
Baruch Coll of the City U of NY (NY)
Berry Coll (GA)
Bethel Coll (MN)
Bishop's U (PQ, Canada)
Bloomfield Coll (NJ)
Boise State U (ID)
Boston Coll (MA)
Boston U (MA)
Bowling Green State U (OH)
Bradley U (IL)
Brescia U (KY)
Bridgewater Coll (VA)
Bridgewater State Coll (MA)
Brock U (ON, Canada)
Bryant Coll (RI)
Buena Vista U (IA)
Butler U (IN)
Cabrini Coll (PA)
California Coll for Health Sciences (CA)
California State Polytechnic U, Pomona (CA)
California State U, Bakersfield (CA)
California State U, Chico (CA)
California State U, Dominguez Hills (CA)
California State U, Fresno (CA)
California State U, Fullerton (CA)
California State U, Hayward (CA)
California State U, Long Beach (CA)
California State U, Northridge (CA)
California State U, San Bernardino (CA)
California State U, Stanislaus (CA)
Cameron U (OK)
Campbell U (NC)
Canisius Coll (NY)
Capital U (OH)
Carleton U (ON, Canada)
Carroll Coll (MT)
Carroll Coll (WI)
Castleton State Coll (VT)
The Catholic U of America (DC)
Cedarville U (OH)
Central Connecticut State U (CT)
Central Michigan U (MI)
Central Missouri State U (MO)
Central Pennsylvania Coll (PA)
Central State U (OH)
Chapman U (CA)
Chicago State U (IL)
Christian Brothers U (TN)
Christopher Newport U (VA)
Clarion U of Pennsylvania (PA)
Clarkson U (NY)
Cleary Coll (MI)
Clemson U (SC)
Cleveland State U (OH)
Coastal Carolina U (SC)
Coker Coll (SC)
The Coll of New Jersey (NJ)
Coll of St. Joseph (VT)
The Coll of Southeastern Europe, The American U of Athens(Greece)
Colorado State U (CO)
Colorado Tech U Sioux Falls Campus (SD)
Columbia Coll (MO)
Columbus State U (GA)
Concordia U (MN)
Concordia U (QC, Canada)
Creighton U (NE)
Culver-Stockton Coll (MO)
Dakota State U (SD)
Dakota Wesleyan U (SD)
Dallas Baptist U (TX)
Davenport U, Dearborn (MI)
Davenport U, Grand Rapids (MI)
Davenport U, Lansing (MI)
David N. Myers U (OH)
Defiance Coll (OH)
Delta State U (MS)
DePaul U (IL)
DeSales U (PA)
Dickinson State U (ND)
Dominican Coll (NY)
Dowling Coll (NY)
Drake U (IA)
Drexel U (PA)

Duquesne U (PA)
East Carolina U (NC)
East Central U (OK)
Eastern Illinois U (IL)
Eastern Kentucky U (KY)
Eastern Michigan U (MI)
Eastern New Mexico U (NM)
Eastern U (PA)
Eastern Washington U (WA)
East Tennessee State U (TN)
East Texas Baptist U (TX)
East-West U (IL)
École des Hautes Études Commerciales de Montréal (PQ, Canada)
Elmhurst Coll (IL)
Emory U (GA)
Eureka Coll (IL)
Excelsior Coll (NY)
Fairfield U (CT)
Fairmont State Coll (WV)
Fayetteville State U (NC)
Ferris State U (MI)
Ferrum Coll (VA)
Fisk U (TN)
Florida A&M U (FL)
Florida Atlantic U (FL)
Florida Gulf Coast U (FL)
Florida International U (FL)
Florida Southern Coll (FL)
Florida State U (FL)
Fontbonne U (MO)
Fordham U (NY)
Fort Hays State U (KS)
Fort Lewis Coll (CO)
Framingham State Coll (MA)
Francis Marion U (SC)
Franklin and Marshall Coll (PA)
Franklin Coll of Indiana (IN)
Franklin Pierce Coll (NH)
Franklin U (OH)
Freed-Hardeman U (TN)
Fresno Pacific U (CA)
Gannon U (PA)
George Mason U (VA)
Georgetown Coll (KY)
Georgetown U (DC)
The George Washington U (DC)
Georgia Southern U (GA)
Georgia State U (GA)
Glenville State Coll (WV)
Golden Gate U (CA)
Goldey-Beacom Coll (DE)
Gonzaga U (WA)
Governors State U (IL)
Grand Canyon U (AZ)
Grand Valley State U (MI)
Grove City Coll (PA)
Gwynedd-Mercy Coll (PA)
Hampton U (VA)
Harding U (AR)
Hardin-Simmons U (TX)
Hawai'i Pacific U (HI)
Hillsdale Coll (MI)
Hofstra U (NY)
Houston Baptist U (TX)
Howard Payne U (TX)
Howard U (DC)
Huron U (SD)
Husson Coll (ME)
Idaho State U (ID)
Illinois Coll (IL)
Illinois State U (IL)
Indiana Inst of Technology (IN)
Indiana State U (IN)
Indiana U Bloomington (IN)
Indiana U of Pennsylvania (PA)
Indiana U–Purdue U Fort Wayne (IN)
Indiana Wesleyan U (IN)
Inter American U of PR, San Germán Campus (PR)
International Business Coll, Fort Wayne (IN)
Iona Coll (NY)
Iowa State U of Science and Technology (IA)
Ithaca Coll (NY)
Jackson State U (MS)
Jacksonville State U (AL)
Jacksonville U (FL)
James Madison U (VA)
John Carroll U (OH)
Johnson C. Smith U (NC)
Juniata Coll (PA)
Kansas State U (KS)
Kean U (NJ)
Kennesaw State U (GA)
Kent State U (OH)
Kettering U (MI)
King's Coll (PA)
Kutztown U of Pennsylvania (PA)
Lake Forest Coll (IL)
Lakehead U (ON, Canada)
Lakeland Coll (WI)
Lake Superior State U (MI)
Lamar U (TX)
La Roche Coll (PA)
La Salle U (PA)
Lasell Coll (MA)
Lehigh U (PA)
LeTourneau U (TX)
Lewis U (IL)
Lincoln Memorial U (TN)
Lincoln U (PA)
Lindenwood U (MO)
Linfield Coll (OR)
Lipscomb U (TN)
Long Island U, Brentwood Campus (NY)
Long Island U, Brooklyn Campus (NY)
Long Island U, C.W. Post Campus (NY)
Longwood Coll (VA)
Loras Coll (IA)
Louisiana Coll (LA)
Louisiana State U and A&M Coll (LA)
Louisiana State U in Shreveport (LA)
Louisiana Tech U (LA)
Loyola Coll in Maryland (MD)
Loyola U Chicago (IL)
Loyola U New Orleans (LA)
Lubbock Christian U (TX)
Lycoming Coll (PA)
Manchester Coll (IN)
Manhattan Coll (NY)
Manhattanville Coll (NY)
Marian Coll (IN)
Marian Coll of Fond du Lac (WI)
Marquette U (WI)
Marshall U (WV)
Mars Hill Coll (NC)
Marymount Coll of Fordham U (NY)
Marymount U (VA)
Massachusetts Coll of Liberal Arts (MA)
The Master's Coll and Seminary (CA)
McGill U (PQ, Canada)
McKendree Coll (IL)
McMurry U (TX)
McNeese State U (LA)
McPherson Coll (KS)
Memorial U of Newfoundland (NF, Canada)
Mercer U (GA)
Mercy Coll (NY)
Mercyhurst Coll (PA)
Meredith Coll (NC)
Merrimack Coll (MA)
Mesa State Coll (CO)
Methodist Coll (NC)
Metropolitan State Coll of Denver (CO)
Metropolitan State U (MN)
Miami U (OH)
Michigan State U (MI)
Michigan Technological U (MI)
Middle Tennessee State U (TN)
Midwestern State U (TX)
Millikin U (IL)
Minnesota State U, Mankato (MN)
Minnesota State U Moorhead (MN)
Minot State U (ND)
Mississippi State U (MS)
Missouri Southern State Coll (MO)
Missouri Western State Coll (MO)
Monmouth U (NJ)
Montana State U–Billings (MT)
Montana Tech of The U of Montana (MT)
Montclair State U (NJ)
Morehead State U (KY)
Morehouse Coll (GA)
Morgan State U (MD)
Murray State U (KY)
National U (CA)
Newbury Coll (MA)
New Mexico State U (NM)
New York Inst of Technology (NY)
New York U (NY)
Nicholls State U (LA)
North Central Coll (IL)
Northeastern Illinois U (IL)
Northeastern State U (OK)
Northeastern U (MA)
Northern Arizona U (AZ)
Northern Illinois U (IL)
Northern Kentucky U (KY)
Northern Michigan U (MI)
Northern State U (SD)
North Georgia Coll & State U (GA)
North Park U (IL)
Northwestern Coll (MN)
Northwest Missouri State U (MO)
Northwest Nazarene U (ID)
Northwood U (MI)
Northwood U, Florida Campus (FL)
Northwood U, Texas Campus (TX)
Notre Dame Coll (OH)
Notre Dame de Namur U (CA)
Oakland U (MI)
The Ohio State U (OH)
Ohio U (OH)
Oklahoma Baptist U (OK)
Oklahoma City U (OK)
Oklahoma State U (OK)
Old Dominion U (VA)
Olivet Coll (MI)
Olivet Nazarene U (IL)
Oral Roberts U (OK)
Oregon State U (OR)
Otterbein Coll (OH)
Ouachita Baptist U (AR)
Pace U (NY)
Pacific Lutheran U (WA)
Pacific Union Coll (CA)
Pacific U (OR)
Palm Beach Atlantic Coll (FL)
Penn State U at Erie, The Behrend Coll (PA)
Penn State U Harrisburg Campus of the Capital Coll (PA)
Penn State U Univ Park Campus (PA)
Philadelphia U (PA)
Pittsburg State U (KS)
Pontifical Catholic U of Puerto Rico (PR)
Portland State U (OR)
Prairie View A&M U (TX)
Providence Coll (RI)
Quincy U (IL)
Quinnipiac U (CT)
Radford U (VA)
Rhode Island Coll (RI)
Rider U (NJ)
Robert Morris U (PA)
Rochester Inst of Technology (NY)
Rockford Coll (IL)
Rockhurst U (MO)
Roosevelt U (IL)
Rowan U (NJ)
Rutgers, The State U of New Jersey, New Brunswick (NJ)
Sacred Heart U (CT)
Saginaw Valley State U (MI)
St. Ambrose U (IA)
Saint Anselm Coll (NH)
St. Bonaventure U (NY)
St. Cloud State U (MN)
St. Edward's U (TX)
Saint Francis U (PA)
St. John Fisher Coll (NY)
St. John's U (NY)
Saint Joseph's Coll (IN)
Saint Joseph's Coll (ME)
Saint Joseph's U (PA)
Saint Louis U (MO)
Saint Martin's Coll (WA)
Saint Mary's Coll (IN)
Saint Mary's U (NS, Canada)
St. Mary's U of San Antonio (TX)
St. Thomas Aquinas Coll (NY)
St. Thomas U (FL)
Saint Vincent Coll (PA)
Salem State Coll (MA)
Sam Houston State U (TX)
San Diego State U (CA)
San Francisco State U (CA)
San Jose State U (CA)
Santa Clara U (CA)
Schreiner U (TX)
Seattle U (WA)
Seton Hall U (NJ)
Seton Hill Coll (PA)
Shippensburg U of Pennsylvania (PA)
Siena Coll (NY)
Simmons Coll (MA)
Slippery Rock U of Pennsylvania (PA)
Southeastern Louisiana U (LA)
Southeastern Oklahoma State U (OK)
Southeastern U (DC)
Southeast Missouri State U (MO)
Southern Connecticut State U (CT)
Southern Illinois U Carbondale (IL)
Southern Methodist U (TX)
Southern Nazarene U (OK)
Southern New Hampshire U (NH)
Southwestern Oklahoma State U (OK)
Southwest Missouri State U (MO)
Southwest Texas State U (TX)
Spring Hill Coll (AL)
State U of NY at New Paltz (NY)
State U of NY at Oswego (NY)
State U of NY Coll at Brockport (NY)
State U of NY Coll at Fredonia (NY)
State U of NY Coll at Old Westbury (NY)
State U of NY Inst of Tech at Utica/Rome (NY)
State U of West Georgia (GA)
Stephen F. Austin State U (TX)
Stetson U (FL)
Stonehill Coll (MA)
Suffolk U (MA)
Susquehanna U (PA)
Syracuse U (NY)
Talladega Coll (AL)
Tarleton State U (TX)
Taylor U (IN)
Teikyo Post U (CT)
Temple U (PA)
Tennessee Technological U (TN)
Tennessee Wesleyan Coll (TN)
Texas A&M International U (TX)
Texas A&M U (TX)
Texas A&M U–Commerce (TX)
Texas A&M U–Corpus Christi (TX)
Texas A&M U–Kingsville (TX)
Texas A&M U–Texarkana (TX)
Texas Christian U (TX)
Texas Lutheran U (TX)
Texas Southern U (TX)
Texas Tech U (TX)
Thomas Coll (ME)
Thomas Edison State Coll (NJ)
Tiffin U (OH)
Touro Coll (NY)
Trinity U (TX)
Troy State U (AL)
Troy State U Montgomery (AL)
Truman State U (MO)
Tulane U (LA)
Tuskegee U (AL)
Union U (TN)
Université de Sherbrooke (PQ, Canada)
U Coll of Cape Breton (NS, Canada)
U Coll of the Cariboo (BC, Canada)
The U of Akron (OH)
The U of Alabama (AL)
The U of Alabama at Birmingham (AL)
The U of Alabama in Huntsville (AL)
U of Alaska Anchorage (AK)
U of Alberta (AB, Canada)
The U of Arizona (AZ)
U of Arkansas (AR)
U of Arkansas at Little Rock (AR)
U of Baltimore (MD)
U of Bridgeport (CT)
The U of British Columbia (BC, Canada)
U of Calgary (AB, Canada)
U of Central Arkansas (AR)
U of Central Florida (FL)
U of Central Oklahoma (OK)
U of Cincinnati (OH)
U of Colorado at Boulder (CO)
U of Colorado at Colorado Springs (CO)
U of Connecticut (CT)
U of Dayton (OH)
U of Delaware (DE)
U of Denver (CO)
U of Evansville (IN)
U of Florida (FL)
U of Georgia (GA)
U of Hartford (CT)
U of Hawaii at Manoa (HI)
U of Houston (TX)
U of Houston–Clear Lake (TX)
U of Idaho (ID)
U of Illinois at Chicago (IL)
U of Illinois at Urbana–Champaign (IL)
The U of Iowa (IA)
U of Kentucky (KY)
The U of Lethbridge (AB, Canada)
U of Louisiana at Lafayette (LA)
U of Louisiana at Monroe (LA)
U of Louisville (KY)
U of Manitoba (MB, Canada)
U of Mary Hardin-Baylor (TX)
U of Maryland, Coll Park (MD)
U of Massachusetts Amherst (MA)
U of Massachusetts Dartmouth (MA)
The U of Memphis (TN)
U of Miami (FL)
U of Michigan–Dearborn (MI)
U of Michigan–Flint (MI)
U of Minnesota, Duluth (MN)
U of Minnesota, Twin Cities Campus (MN)
U of Mississippi (MS)
U of Missouri–Columbia (MO)
U of Missouri–St. Louis (MO)
U of Nebraska at Omaha (NE)
U of Nebraska–Lincoln (NE)
U of Nevada, Las Vegas (NV)
U of Nevada, Reno (NV)
U of New Hampshire (NH)
U of New Haven (CT)
U of New Orleans (LA)
U of North Alabama (AL)
The U of North Carolina at Charlotte (NC)
The U of North Carolina at Greensboro (NC)
The U of North Carolina at Wilmington (NC)
U of North Dakota (ND)
U of Northern Iowa (IA)
U of North Florida (FL)
U of North Texas (TX)
U of Notre Dame (IN)
U of Oklahoma (OK)
U of Oregon (OR)
U of Ottawa (ON, Canada)
U of Pennsylvania (PA)
U of Pittsburgh (PA)
U of Pittsburgh at Johnstown (PA)
U of Portland (OR)
U of Regina (SK, Canada)
U of Rhode Island (RI)
U of Richmond (VA)
U of St. Francis (IL)
U of Saint Francis (IN)
U of St. Thomas (MN)
U of St. Thomas (TX)
U of San Francisco (CA)
U of Saskatchewan (SK, Canada)
The U of Scranton (PA)
U of South Alabama (AL)
U of South Carolina (SC)
U of South Dakota (SD)
U of Southern Colorado (CO)
U of Southern Indiana (IN)
U of Southern Mississippi (MS)
U of South Florida (FL)
The U of Tampa (FL)
The U of Tennessee (TN)
The U of Tennessee at Chattanooga (TN)
The U of Tennessee at Martin (TN)
The U of Texas at Austin (TX)
The U of Texas at Brownsville (TX)
The U of Texas at El Paso (TX)
The U of Texas at San Antonio (TX)
The U of Texas at Tyler (TX)
The U of Texas of the Permian Basin (TX)
The U of Texas–Pan American (TX)
U of the District of Columbia (DC)
U of the Incarnate Word (TX)
U of Toledo (OH)
U of Toronto (ON, Canada)
U of Tulsa (OK)
U of Utah (UT)
U of West Florida (FL)
U of Windsor (ON, Canada)
U of Wisconsin–Eau Claire (WI)
U of Wisconsin–La Crosse (WI)
U of Wisconsin–Madison (WI)
U of Wisconsin–Milwaukee (WI)
U of Wisconsin–Oshkosh (WI)
U of Wisconsin–Parkside (WI)
U of Wisconsin–River Falls (WI)
U of Wisconsin–Whitewater (WI)
U of Wyoming (WY)

Utah State U (UT)
Valdosta State U (GA)
Valparaiso U (IN)
Vanguard U of Southern California (CA)
Villanova U (PA)
Virginia Polytechnic Inst and State U (VA)
Wagner Coll (NY)
Wake Forest U (NC)
Waldorf Coll (IA)
Walsh Coll of Accountancy and Business Admin (MI)
Walsh U (OH)
Warner Southern Coll (FL)
Wartburg Coll (IA)
Washburn U of Topeka (KS)
Washington State U (WA)
Washington U in St. Louis (MO)
Waynesburg Coll (PA)
Wayne State Coll (NE)
Wayne State U (MI)
Webber International U (FL)
Weber State U (UT)
Western Baptist Coll (OR)
Western Carolina U (NC)
Western Connecticut State U (CT)
Western Illinois U (IL)
Western International U (AZ)
Western Kentucky U (KY)
Western Michigan U (MI)
Western New England Coll (MA)
Western Washington U (WA)
Westfield State Coll (MA)
Westminster Coll (MO)
Westminster Coll (UT)
West Texas A&M U (TX)
West Virginia U (WV)
Wichita State U (KS)
Wilberforce U (OH)
William Carey Coll (MS)
Wilmington Coll (DE)
Wingate U (NC)
Winona State U (MN)
Wittenberg U (OH)
Wofford Coll (SC)
Wright State U (OH)
Xavier U (OH)
Yeshiva U (NY)
York Coll (NE)
York Coll of Pennsylvania (PA)
York U (ON, Canada)
Youngstown State U (OH)

FINANCIAL MANAGEMENT AND SERVICES RELATED
Bryant Coll (RI)
Park U (MO)
San Diego State U (CA)
The U of Akron (OH)

FINANCIAL PLANNING
Baylor U (TX)
Bethany Coll (KS)
British Columbia Inst of Technology (BC, Canada)
Central Michigan U (MI)
Marywood U (PA)
Medaille Coll (NY)
The Ohio State U at Lima (OH)
Roger Williams U (RI)
Trinity Christian Coll (IL)

FINANCIAL SERVICES MARKETING
Nipissing U (ON, Canada)

FINE ARTS AND ART STUDIES RELATED
Allegheny Coll (PA)
Angelo State U (TX)
The Catholic U of America (DC)
Chestnut Hill Coll (PA)
Coll of Staten Island of the City U of NY (NY)
Indiana State U (IN)
Kentucky Wesleyan Coll (KY)
Loyola U Chicago (IL)
Okanagan U Coll (BC, Canada)
Oregon Coll of Art & Craft (OR)
Our Lady of the Lake U of San Antonio (TX)
San Diego State U (CA)
Skidmore Coll (NY)
The U of Akron (OH)
U of North Alabama (AL)
U of Saint Francis (IN)
U of Wyoming (WY)

FINE/STUDIO ARTS
Abilene Christian U (TX)
Academy of Art Coll (CA)
Adams State Coll (CO)
Alberta Coll of Art & Design (AB, Canada)
Albertus Magnus Coll (CT)
Alfred U (NY)
Allegheny Coll (PA)
American Academy of Art (IL)
American U (DC)
Amherst Coll (MA)
Anderson Coll (SC)
Anderson U (IN)
Angelo State U (TX)
Anna Maria Coll (MA)
Appalachian State U (NC)
Aquinas Coll (MI)
Arcadia U (PA)
Arizona State U (AZ)
Art Academy of Cincinnati (OH)
Asbury Coll (KY)
Ashland U (OH)
Atlanta Coll of Art (GA)
Auburn U (AL)
Augsburg Coll (MN)
Augustana Coll (IL)
Baker U (KS)
Baldwin-Wallace Coll (OH)
Ball State U (IN)
Bard Coll (NY)
Barton Coll (NC)
Baylor U (TX)
Bay Path Coll (MA)
Belmont U (TN)
Beloit Coll (WI)
Bemidji State U (MN)
Benedictine U (IL)
Bennington Coll (VT)
Berea Coll (KY)
Berry Coll (GA)
Bethany Coll (WV)
Bethel Coll (MN)
Biola U (CA)
Birmingham-Southern Coll (AL)
Bloomsburg U of Pennsylvania (PA)
Boston Coll (MA)
Bowdoin Coll (ME)
Bradley U (IL)
Brandeis U (MA)
Brenau U (GA)
Briarcliffe Coll (NY)
Bridgewater State Coll (MA)
Brock U (ON, Canada)
Brown U (RI)
Bucknell U (PA)
Cabrini Coll (PA)
California Baptist U (CA)
California Coll of Arts and Crafts (CA)
California Inst of the Arts (CA)
California State U, Chico (CA)
California State U, Dominguez Hills (CA)
California State U, Fullerton (CA)
California State U, Hayward (CA)
California State U, Long Beach (CA)
California State U, Northridge (CA)
Calvin Coll (MI)
Campbell U (NC)
Capital U (OH)
Cardinal Stritch U (WI)
Carleton Coll (MN)
Carnegie Mellon U (PA)
Carroll Coll (WI)
Carthage Coll (WI)
Cedar Crest Coll (PA)
Centenary Coll of Louisiana (LA)
Central Missouri State U (MO)
Chapman U (CA)
Chatham Coll (PA)
Chestnut Hill Coll (PA)
Chicago State U (IL)
Chowan Coll (NC)
Clarke Coll (IA)
Clark U (MA)
Coe Coll (IA)
Coker Coll (SC)
Ctr for Creative Studies—Coll of Art and Design (MI)
Coll of Charleston (SC)
Coll of Mount St. Joseph (OH)
The Coll of New Jersey (NJ)
The Coll of New Rochelle (NY)
Coll of Saint Benedict (MN)
Coll of St. Catherine (MN)
The Coll of Saint Rose (NY)
Coll of Santa Fe (NM)
Coll of the Holy Cross (MA)
Coll of the Ozarks (MO)
The Coll of Wooster (OH)
The Colorado Coll (CO)
Colorado State U (CO)
Columbia Coll (MO)
Columbia Coll (SC)
Columbia Coll Chicago (IL)
Columbus Coll of Art and Design (OH)
Concordia Coll (MN)
Concordia U (NE)
Concordia U (QC, Canada)
Converse Coll (SC)
Corcoran Coll of Art and Design (DC)
Cornell U (NY)
Cornish Coll of the Arts (WA)
Cumberland Coll (KY)
Cumberland U (TN)
Daemen Coll (NY)
Dartmouth Coll (NH)
Denison U (OH)
DePaul U (IL)
DePauw U (IN)
Dickinson Coll (PA)
Dominican U (IL)
Drake U (IA)
Drury U (MO)
Duquesne U (PA)
East Carolina U (NC)
Eastern Washington U (WA)
Edinboro U of Pennsylvania (PA)
Elmira Coll (NY)
Emmanuel Coll (MA)
Endicott Coll (MA)
The Evergreen State Coll (WA)
Felician Coll (NJ)
Ferris State U (MI)
Ferrum Coll (VA)
Finlandia U (MI)
Flagler Coll (FL)
Florida International U (FL)
Florida Southern Coll (FL)
Florida State U (FL)
Fontbonne U (MO)
Fordham U (NY)
Fort Lewis Coll (CO)
Framingham State Coll (MA)
Franklin Pierce Coll (NH)
Furman U (SC)
Gallaudet U (DC)
George Mason U (VA)
The George Washington U (DC)
Georgia Southwestern State U (GA)
Gettysburg Coll (PA)
Goddard Coll (VT)
Governors State U (IL)
Graceland U (IA)
Grand Canyon U (AZ)
Grand Valley State U (MI)
Grand View Coll (IA)
Green Mountain Coll (VT)
Hamilton Coll (NY)
Hamline U (MN)
Hampden-Sydney Coll (VA)
Hampshire Coll (MA)
Harvard U (MA)
High Point U (NC)
Hiram Coll (OH)
Hobart and William Smith Colls (NY)
Hofstra U (NY)
Hollins U (VA)
Hope Coll (MI)
Howard Payne U (TX)
Humboldt State U (CA)
Hunter Coll of the City U of NY (NY)
Illinois Wesleyan U (IL)
Indiana State U (IN)
Indiana U Bloomington (IN)
Indiana U–Purdue U Fort Wayne (IN)
Indiana U–Purdue U Indianapolis (IN)
Indiana U South Bend (IN)
Indiana U Southeast (IN)
Iowa Wesleyan Coll (IA)
Ithaca Coll (NY)
Jacksonville U (FL)
Johnson State Coll (VT)
Judson Coll (IL)
Juniata Coll (PA)
Kean U (NJ)
Kendall Coll of Art and Design of Ferris State U (MI)
Kennesaw State U (GA)
Kent State U (OH)
Kentucky State U (KY)
Kenyon Coll (OH)
King Coll (TN)
Kutztown U of Pennsylvania (PA)
Lafayette Coll (PA)
Lake Erie Coll (OH)
Lake Forest Coll (IL)
Lamar U (TX)
Lambuth U (TN)
Lawrence U (WI)
Lewis U (IL)
Limestone Coll (SC)
Lindenwood U (MO)
Lipscomb U (TN)
Long Island U, C.W. Post Campus (NY)
Long Island U, Southampton Coll (NY)
Long Island U, Southampton Coll, Friends World Program (NY)
Longwood Coll (VA)
Loras Coll (IA)
Louisiana Coll (LA)
Louisiana State U and A&M Coll (LA)
Loyola Marymount U (CA)
Lycoming Coll (PA)
Lynchburg Coll (VA)
Macalester Coll (MN)
MacMurray Coll (IL)
Manchester Coll (IN)
Manhattanville Coll (NY)
Mansfield U of Pennsylvania (PA)
Marian Coll (IN)
Marietta Coll (OH)
Marist Coll (NY)
Marlboro Coll (VT)
Mary Baldwin Coll (VA)
Marygrove Coll (MI)
Maryland Inst, Coll of Art (MD)
Marymount Coll of Fordham U (NY)
Marymount Manhattan Coll (NY)
Maryville Coll (TN)
Maryville U of Saint Louis (MO)
Mary Washington Coll (VA)
Marywood U (PA)
Massachusetts Coll of Art (MA)
Memphis Coll of Art (TN)
Mercyhurst Coll (PA)
Meredith Coll (NC)
Merrimack Coll (MA)
Messiah Coll (PA)
Miami U (OH)
Middlebury Coll (VT)
Millikin U (IL)
Mills Coll (CA)
Minneapolis Coll of Art and Design (MN)
Minnesota State U, Mankato (MN)
Minnesota State U Moorhead (MN)
Monmouth U (NJ)
Montana State U–Bozeman (MT)
Montclair State U (NJ)
Montserrat Coll of Art (MA)
Moore Coll of Art and Design (PA)
Moravian Coll (PA)
Morehead State U (KY)
Morningside Coll (IA)
Mount Allison U (NB, Canada)
Mount Holyoke Coll (MA)
Mount Saint Vincent U (NS, Canada)
Muhlenberg Coll (PA)
Murray State U (KY)
Nazareth Coll of Rochester (NY)
New Coll of Florida (FL)
New England Coll (NH)
New Mexico State U (NM)
New World School of the Arts (FL)
New York Inst of Technology (NY)
New York U (NY)
North Carolina Central U (NC)
Northeastern State U (OK)
Northern Illinois U (IL)
Northern Kentucky U (KY)
Northern Michigan U (MI)
Northland Coll (WI)
North Park U (IL)
Northwestern Coll (MN)
Northwest Missouri State U (MO)
Notre Dame Coll (OH)
Notre Dame de Namur U (CA)
Nova Scotia Coll of Art and Design (NS, Canada)
Oberlin Coll (OH)
Occidental Coll (CA)
Ohio Dominican Coll (OH)
The Ohio State U (OH)
Ohio U (OH)
Ohio Wesleyan U (OH)
Oklahoma Baptist U (OK)
Oklahoma City U (OK)
Oklahoma State U (OK)
Olivet Coll (MI)
Open Learning Agency (BC, Canada)
Oral Roberts U (OK)
Oregon State U (OR)
Otis Coll of Art and Design (CA)
Pacific Lutheran U (WA)
Pacific Northwest Coll of Art (OR)
Pacific Union Coll (CA)
Paier Coll of Art, Inc. (CT)
Park U (MO)
Pennsylvania School of Art & Design (PA)
Piedmont Coll (GA)
Pine Manor Coll (MA)
Pittsburg State U (KS)
Pitzer Coll (CA)
Plattsburgh State U of NY (NY)
Plymouth State Coll (NH)
Pomona Coll (CA)
Pratt Inst (NY)
Principia Coll (IL)
Providence Coll (RI)
Queens Coll (NC)
Queens Coll of the City U of NY (NY)
Queen's U at Kingston (ON, Canada)
Quincy U (IL)
Ramapo Coll of New Jersey (NJ)
Randolph-Macon Coll (VA)
Randolph-Macon Woman's Coll (VA)
Reed Coll (OR)
Rhode Island Coll (RI)
Rhodes Coll (TN)
Rice U (TX)
Richmond, The American International U in London(United Kingdom)
Ringling School of Art and Design (FL)
Rivier Coll (NH)
Roberts Wesleyan Coll (NY)
Rochester Inst of Technology (NY)
Rockford Coll (IL)
Rollins Coll (FL)
Rosemont Coll (PA)
Rowan U (NJ)
Saginaw Valley State U (MI)
St. Ambrose U (IA)
St. Andrews Presbyterian Coll (NC)
St. Cloud State U (MN)
Saint John's U (MN)
St. John's U (NY)
Saint Louis U (MO)
Saint Mary-of-the-Woods Coll (IN)
Saint Mary's U of Minnesota (MN)
Saint Peter's Coll (NJ)
St. Thomas Aquinas Coll (NY)
Saint Vincent Coll (PA)
Salem Coll (NC)
Salve Regina U (RI)
San Francisco Art Inst (CA)
San Jose State U (CA)
Sarah Lawrence Coll (NY)
School of the Art Inst of Chicago (IL)
School of the Museum of Fine Arts (MA)
School of Visual Arts (NY)
Scripps Coll (CA)
Seattle U (WA)
Seton Hill Coll (PA)
Shawnee State U (OH)
Shorter Coll (GA)
Sierra Nevada Coll (NV)
Simon's Rock Coll of Bard (MA)
Smith Coll (MA)
Sonoma State U (CA)
Southern Connecticut State U (CT)
Southern Illinois U Carbondale (IL)
Southern Illinois U Edwardsville (IL)
Southern Methodist U (TX)
Southwestern U (TX)
Southwest State U (MN)
Southwest Texas State U (TX)
Spring Hill Coll (AL)
State U of NY at Binghamton (NY)
State U of NY at New Paltz (NY)

State U of NY Coll at Brockport (NY)
State U of NY Coll at Buffalo (NY)
State U of NY Coll at Cortland (NY)
State U of NY Coll at Fredonia (NY)
State U of NY Coll at Geneseo (NY)
State U of NY Coll at Oneonta (NY)
Stonehill Coll (MA)
State U of NY at Stony Brook (NY)
Swarthmore Coll (PA)
Sweet Briar Coll (VA)
Syracuse U (NY)
Texas A&M U–Corpus Christi (TX)
Texas Christian U (TX)
Texas Tech U (TX)
Texas Woman's U (TX)
Thomas More Coll (KY)
Transylvania U (KY)
Trinity Coll (CT)
Troy State U (AL)
Truman State U (MO)
Tulane U (LA)
Union Coll (NE)
Union Coll (NY)
Université Laval (QC, Canada)
State U of NY at Buffalo (NY)
U Coll of the Cariboo (BC, Canada)
The U of Akron (OH)
The U of Alabama (AL)
The U of Alabama at Birmingham (AL)
U of Alberta (AB, Canada)
The U of Arizona (AZ)
The U of British Columbia (BC, Canada)
U of Calif, Irvine (CA)
U of Calif, Riverside (CA)
U of Calif, San Diego (CA)
U of Calif, Santa Barbara (CA)
U of Central Florida (FL)
U of Chicago (IL)
U of Colorado at Boulder (CO)
U of Colorado at Colorado Springs (CO)
U of Colorado at Denver (CO)
U of Connecticut (CT)
U of Dallas (TX)
U of Dayton (OH)
U of Denver (CO)
U of Florida (FL)
U of Georgia (GA)
U of Great Falls (MT)
U of Guelph (ON, Canada)
U of Houston (TX)
U of Idaho (ID)
U of Illinois at Chicago (IL)
U of Indianapolis (IN)
The U of Iowa (IA)
U of Kansas (KS)
U of Kentucky (KY)
U of Louisville (KY)
U of Maine (ME)
U of Maine at Presque Isle (ME)
U of Maryland, Coll Park (MD)
U of Massachusetts Amherst (MA)
U of Miami (FL)
U of Minnesota, Duluth (MN)
U of Minnesota, Morris (MN)
U of Missouri–Kansas City (MO)
U of Missouri–St. Louis (MO)
U of Montevallo (AL)
U of Nebraska at Omaha (NE)
U of Nebraska–Lincoln (NE)
U of New Hampshire (NH)
U of North Alabama (AL)
The U of North Carolina at Asheville (NC)
The U of North Carolina at Chapel Hill (NC)
The U of North Carolina at Charlotte (NC)
The U of North Carolina at Greensboro (NC)
The U of North Carolina at Wilmington (NC)
U of Northern Iowa (IA)
U of North Florida (FL)
U of Notre Dame (IN)
U of Oklahoma (OK)
U of Ottawa (ON, Canada)
U of Pittsburgh (PA)
U of Redlands (CA)
U of Richmond (VA)
U of Rochester (NY)
U of St. Thomas (TX)
U of San Francisco (CA)
U of Saskatchewan (SK, Canada)
U of South Carolina (SC)
U of South Carolina Aiken (SC)
U of South Dakota (SD)
U of Southern California (CA)
The U of Tennessee (TN)
The U of Texas at Arlington (TX)
The U of Texas at Austin (TX)
The U of Texas at El Paso (TX)
The U of Texas–Pan American (TX)
U of the District of Columbia (DC)
U of the Pacific (CA)
U of the South (TN)
U of Toledo (OH)
U of Toronto (ON, Canada)
U of Vermont (VT)
U of Victoria (BC, Canada)
U of Waterloo (ON, Canada)
The U of Western Ontario (ON, Canada)
U of West Florida (FL)
U of Windsor (ON, Canada)
U of Wisconsin–Milwaukee (WI)
U of Wisconsin–Oshkosh (WI)
U of Wisconsin–Stevens Point (WI)
U of Wisconsin–Superior (WI)
Utica Coll of Syracuse U (NY)
Valdosta State U (GA)
Valparaiso U (IN)
Vassar Coll (NY)
Washburn U of Topeka (KS)
Washington and Lee U (VA)
Washington U in St. Louis (MO)
Webster U (MO)
Wellesley Coll (MA)
Wells Coll (NY)
Wesleyan Coll (GA)
Wesleyan U (CT)
West Chester U of Pennsylvania (PA)
Western Carolina U (NC)
Western Illinois U (IL)
Western Kentucky U (KY)
Western State Coll of Colorado (CO)
Western Washington U (WA)
West Texas A&M U (TX)
West Virginia Wesleyan Coll (WV)
Wheaton Coll (MA)
Whitworth Coll (WA)
Wilberforce U (OH)
Willamette U (OR)
William Carey Coll (MS)
William Paterson U of New Jersey (NJ)
Williams Baptist Coll (AR)
Williams Coll (MA)
William Woods U (MO)
Wingate U (NC)
Winona State U (MN)
Wittenberg U (OH)
Xavier U (OH)
York U (ON, Canada)
Youngstown State U (OH)

FIRE PROTECTION RELATED

The U of Akron (OH)

FIRE PROTECTION/SAFETY TECHNOLOGY

California State U, Los Angeles (CA)
Columbia Southern U (AL)
Eastern Kentucky U (KY)
Oklahoma State U (OK)
Thomas Edison State Coll (NJ)
U of Cincinnati (OH)
U of New Haven (CT)

FIRE SCIENCE

Anna Maria Coll (MA)
Cogswell Polytechnical Coll (CA)
Eastern Kentucky U (KY)
Eastern Oregon U (OR)
Hampton U (VA)
Holy Family Coll (PA)
Jackson State U (MS)
John Jay Coll of Criminal Justice, the City U of NY (NY)
Lake Superior State U (MI)
Mercy Coll (NY)
U of Maryland University Coll (MD)
U of the District of Columbia (DC)

FIRE SERVICES ADMINISTRATION

Columbia Southern U (AL)
Southern Illinois U Carbondale (IL)
Western Oregon U (OR)

FISH/GAME MANAGEMENT

Delaware State U (DE)
The Evergreen State Coll (WA)
Humboldt State U (CA)
Iowa State U of Science and Technology (IA)
Lake Superior State U (MI)
Lincoln Memorial U (TN)
North Dakota State U (ND)
Northland Coll (WI)
Oregon State U (OR)
Pittsburg State U (KS)
South Dakota State U (SD)
Southeastern Oklahoma State U (OK)
State U of NY Coll of Environ Sci and Forestry (NY)
Texas A&M U at Galveston (TX)
Texas A&M U–Kingsville (TX)
U of Arkansas at Pine Bluff (AR)
The U of British Columbia (BC, Canada)
U of Idaho (ID)
U of Minnesota, Duluth (MN)
U of Minnesota, Twin Cities Campus (MN)
U of Missouri–Columbia (MO)
U of South Dakota (SD)
U of Vermont (VT)
West Virginia U (WV)

FISHING SCIENCES

Colorado State U (CO)
Malaspina U-Coll (BC, Canada)
Mansfield U of Pennsylvania (PA)
Murray State U (KY)
The Ohio State U (OH)
Penn State U Univ Park Campus (PA)
State U of NY Coll of A&T at Cobleskill (NY)
State U of NY Coll of Environ Sci and Forestry (NY)
Texas Tech U (TX)
Unity Coll (ME)
U of Alaska Fairbanks (AK)
U of Georgia (GA)
U of Nebraska–Lincoln (NE)
U of Rhode Island (RI)
U of Washington (WA)

FLUID/THERMAL SCIENCES

Harvard U (MA)
Worcester Polytechnic Inst (MA)

FOLKLORE

Harvard U (MA)
Indiana U Bloomington (IN)
Laurentian U (ON, Canada)
Long Island U, Southampton Coll, Friends World Program (NY)
Marlboro Coll (VT)
Memorial U of Newfoundland (NF, Canada)
The Ohio State U (OH)
U of Alberta (AB, Canada)
U of Oregon (OR)
U of Pennsylvania (PA)

FOOD PRODUCTS RETAILING

Ball State U (IN)
California State U, Northridge (CA)
Concord Coll (WV)
Delaware Valley Coll (PA)
Dominican U (IL)
Immaculata Coll (PA)
Iowa State U of Science and Technology (IA)
Johnson & Wales U (RI)
Lindenwood U (MO)
Lipscomb U (TN)
Lynn U (FL)
Montclair State U (NJ)
Mount Saint Vincent U (NS, Canada)
New England Culinary Inst (VT)
North Carolina Wesleyan Coll (NC)
Northern Michigan U (MI)
Oregon State U (OR)
Rochester Inst of Technology (NY)
San Francisco State U (CA)
State U of NY Coll at Buffalo (NY)
Syracuse U (NY)
U of Alberta (AB, Canada)
U of Maryland Eastern Shore (MD)
Wayne State Coll (NE)

FOOD SALES OPERATIONS

Immaculata Coll (PA)
Johnson & Wales U (RI)
Northwest Missouri State U (MO)
Rochester Inst of Technology (NY)
Saint Joseph's U (PA)
U of Delaware (DE)

FOOD SCIENCES

Acadia U (NS, Canada)
Arizona State U East (AZ)
Auburn U (AL)
Brigham Young U (UT)
California Polytechnic State U, San Luis Obispo (CA)
California State U, Northridge (CA)
Chapman U (CA)
Clemson U (SC)
Cornell U (NY)
Dalhousie U (NS, Canada)
Delaware Valley Coll (PA)
Dominican U (IL)
Framingham State Coll (MA)
Kansas State U (KS)
Lamar U (TX)
Louisiana State U and A&M Coll (LA)
Marymount Coll of Fordham U (NY)
McGill U (PQ, Canada)
Memorial U of Newfoundland (NF, Canada)
Michigan State U (MI)
Mississippi State U (MS)
North Carolina Ag and Tech State U (NC)
North Carolina State U (NC)
North Dakota State U (ND)
Northwest Missouri State U (MO)
The Ohio State U (OH)
Olivet Nazarene U (IL)
Oregon State U (OR)
Penn State U Univ Park Campus (PA)
Purdue U (IN)
Rutgers, The State U of New Jersey, New Brunswick (NJ)
San Jose State U (CA)
South Dakota State U (SD)
Texas A&M U (TX)
Texas A&M U–Kingsville (TX)
Texas Tech U (TX)
Tuskegee U (AL)
Université Laval (QC, Canada)
The U of Akron (OH)
U of Alberta (AB, Canada)
U of Arkansas (AR)
The U of British Columbia (BC, Canada)
U of Calif, Davis (CA)
U of Delaware (DE)
U of Florida (FL)
U of Georgia (GA)
U of Hawaii at Manoa (HI)
U of Idaho (ID)
U of Illinois at Urbana–Champaign (IL)
U of Kentucky (KY)
U of Maine (ME)
U of Manitoba (MB, Canada)
U of Maryland, Coll Park (MD)
U of Massachusetts Amherst (MA)
U of Missouri–Columbia (MO)
U of Nebraska–Lincoln (NE)
U of Saskatchewan (SK, Canada)
The U of Tennessee (TN)
U of the District of Columbia (DC)
U of Utah (UT)
U of Wisconsin–Madison (WI)
U of Wisconsin–River Falls (WI)
Virginia Polytechnic Inst and State U (VA)

FOOD SERVICES TECHNOLOGY

California State U, Northridge (CA)
Delaware Valley Coll (PA)
Iowa State U of Science and Technology (IA)
Johnson & Wales U (RI)
Mansfield U of Pennsylvania (PA)
San Jose State U (CA)
Tennessee State U (TN)

FOODS/NUTRITION STUDIES RELATED

U of Wisconsin–Stout (WI)
Utah State U (UT)

FOOD SYSTEMS ADMINISTRATION

Johnson & Wales U (VA)
Western Michigan U (MI)

FOREIGN LANGUAGES EDUCATION

Arkansas Tech U (AR)
Baylor U (TX)
Berea Coll (KY)
Bethune-Cookman Coll (FL)
Boston U (MA)
Bowling Green State U (OH)
Brigham Young U (UT)
Central Methodist Coll (MO)
Dana Coll (NE)
Delta State U (MS)
Duquesne U (PA)
Eastern Michigan U (MI)
Elmira Coll (NY)
Florida International U (FL)
Florida State U (FL)
Gannon U (PA)
Greenville Coll (IL)
Hastings Coll (NE)
Juniata Coll (PA)
Le Moyne Coll (NY)
Lincoln U (PA)
Long Island U, C.W. Post Campus (NY)
Luther Coll (IA)
McMurry U (TX)
Mercer U (GA)
Millersville U of Pennsylvania (PA)
Nazareth Coll of Rochester (NY)
New York U (NY)
Rivier Coll (NH)
St. John's U (NY)
San Diego State U (CA)
Seton Hill Coll (PA)
Southwestern Coll (KS)
Southwest Missouri State U (MO)
State U of NY at Albany (NY)
State U of NY Coll at Potsdam (NY)
State U of West Georgia (GA)
Texas Wesleyan U (TX)
The U of Akron (OH)
The U of Arizona (AZ)
U of Central Florida (FL)
U of Delaware (DE)
U of Georgia (GA)
U of Hawaii at Manoa (HI)
U of Illinois at Chicago (IL)
U of Illinois at Urbana–Champaign (IL)
U of Louisiana at Monroe (LA)
U of Maryland, Coll Park (MD)
U of Minnesota, Twin Cities Campus (MN)
U of Nebraska–Lincoln (NE)
U of Nevada, Reno (NV)
U of New Orleans (LA)
U of Northern Iowa (IA)
U of Oklahoma (OK)
U of South Florida (FL)
U of Vermont (VT)
U of West Florida (FL)
Wheeling Jesuit U (WV)
Youngstown State U (OH)

FOREIGN LANGUAGES/ LITERATURES

Adelphi U (NY)
Arkansas Tech U (AR)
Assumption Coll (MA)
Auburn U Montgomery (AL)
Augustana Coll (SD)
Austin Peay State U (TN)
Bethune-Cookman Coll (FL)
Boston U (MA)
California State U, Monterey Bay (CA)
Central Methodist Coll (MO)
Central Washington U (WA)
Clemson U (SC)
The Coll of Southeastern Europe, The American U of Athens(Greece)
Delta State U (MS)
Duquesne U (PA)
Eastern Illinois U (IL)
East Tennessee State U (TN)
Elmira Coll (NY)
Elon U (NC)
Emporia State U (KS)
Excelsior Coll (NY)
Frostburg State U (MD)

Gannon U (PA)
George Mason U (VA)
Gordon Coll (MA)
Graceland U (IA)
Hastings Coll (NE)
Indiana State U (IN)
James Madison U (VA)
Juniata Coll (PA)
Kansas State U (KS)
Kentucky Wesleyan Coll (KY)
Knox Coll (IL)
Marshall U (WV)
Massachusetts Inst of Technology (MA)
McGill U (PQ, Canada)
Metropolitan State Coll of Denver (CO)
Middle Tennessee State U (TN)
Millikin U (IL)
Minnesota State U Moorhead (MN)
Mississippi Coll (MS)
Mississippi State U (MS)
Monmouth U (NJ)
Montana State U–Bozeman (MT)
New Mexico State U (NM)
Oakland U (MI)
Old Dominion U (VA)
Pace U (NY)
Principia Coll (IL)
Purdue U (IN)
Radford U (VA)
The Richard Stockton Coll of New Jersey (NJ)
Roger Williams U (RI)
Rutgers, The State U of New Jersey, New Brunswick (NJ)
St. Lawrence U (NY)
Saint Peter's Coll (NJ)
Samford U (AL)
Scripps Coll (CA)
Seton Hall U (NJ)
Simon's Rock Coll of Bard (MA)
Southern Adventist U (TN)
Southern Illinois U Edwardsville (IL)
Southern Methodist U (TX)
Southwestern Coll (KS)
Stonehill Coll (MA)
Syracuse U (NY)
Texas A&M U (TX)
Thomas Edison State Coll (NJ)
Union Coll (NY)
Union U (TN)
The U of Alabama in Huntsville (AL)
U of Alaska Anchorage (AK)
U of Alaska Fairbanks (AK)
U of Calif, San Diego (CA)
U of Calif, Santa Cruz (CA)
U of Central Florida (FL)
U of Delaware (DE)
U of Georgia (GA)
U of Hartford (CT)
U of Idaho (ID)
U of Massachusetts Lowell (MA)
The U of Memphis (TN)
The U of Montana–Missoula (MT)
U of New Mexico (NM)
U of North Alabama (AL)
U of North Dakota (ND)
U of Northern Iowa (IA)
The U of Scranton (PA)
U of South Alabama (AL)
U of Southern Mississippi (MS)
The U of Texas at Austin (TX)
The U of Virginia's Coll at Wise (VA)
Virginia Commonwealth U (VA)
Virginia Wesleyan Coll (VA)
Washington and Lee U (VA)
Wayne State U (MI)
West Virginia U (WV)
Widener U (PA)
Wilson Coll (PA)
Youngstown State U (OH)

FOREIGN LANGUAGES/ LITERATURES RELATED
Clemson U (SC)
Southern Illinois U Carbondale (IL)
U of Hawaii at Manoa (HI)
Yale U (CT)

FOREIGN LANGUAGE TRANSLATION
Concordia U (QC, Canada)
Laurentian U (ON, Canada)
Université Laval (QC, Canada)
York U (ON, Canada)

FORENSIC TECHNOLOGY
Alvernia Coll (PA)
Baylor U (TX)
Carroll Coll (WI)
Chaminade U of Honolulu (HI)
Coll of the Ozarks (MO)
Columbia Coll (MO)
Eastern Kentucky U (KY)
Indiana U Bloomington (IN)
Jacksonville State U (AL)
John Jay Coll of Criminal Justice, the City U of NY (NY)
Loyola U New Orleans (LA)
State U of NY Coll at Buffalo (NY)
U of Baltimore (MD)
U of Central Florida (FL)
U of Central Oklahoma (OK)
U of Mississippi (MS)
U of New Haven (CT)
Waynesburg Coll (PA)
West Chester U of Pennsylvania (PA)
West Virginia U (WV)

FOREST ENGINEERING
Oregon State U (OR)
State U of NY Coll of Environ Sci and Forestry (NY)
U of Maine (ME)
U of Washington (WA)

FOREST HARVESTING PRODUCTION TECHNOLOGY
Lakehead U (ON, Canada)

FOREST MANAGEMENT
Clemson U (SC)
Louisiana State U and A&M Coll (LA)
North Carolina State U (NC)
State U of NY Coll of Environ Sci and Forestry (NY)
Stephen F. Austin State U (TX)
Université Laval (QC, Canada)
U of Minnesota, Twin Cities Campus (MN)
The U of Montana–Missoula (MT)
U of Washington (WA)
Warren Wilson Coll (NC)

FOREST PRODUCTION AND PROCESSING RELATED
Université Laval (QC, Canada)

FOREST PRODUCTS TECHNOLOGY
Penn State U Univ Park Campus (PA)
Southern U and A&M Coll (LA)

FORESTRY
Albright Coll (PA)
Baylor U (TX)
California Polytechnic State U, San Luis Obispo (CA)
Coll of Saint Benedict (MN)
Humboldt State U (CA)
Iowa State U of Science and Technology (IA)
Lakehead U (ON, Canada)
Lees-McRae Coll (NC)
Louisiana Tech U (LA)
Michigan State U (MI)
Michigan Technological U (MI)
Mississippi State U (MS)
North Dakota State U (ND)
Northland Coll (WI)
Northwest Missouri State U (MO)
The Ohio State U (OH)
Oklahoma State U (OK)
Oregon State U (OR)
Purdue U (IN)
Saint John's U (MN)
Southern Illinois U Carbondale (IL)
State U of NY Coll of Environ Sci and Forestry (NY)
Stephen F. Austin State U (TX)
Sterling Coll (VT)
Texas A&M U (TX)
Thomas Edison State Coll (NJ)
Unity Coll (ME)
U of Alberta (AB, Canada)
The U of British Columbia (BC, Canada)
U of Florida (FL)
U of Georgia (GA)
U of Idaho (ID)
U of Illinois at Urbana–Champaign (IL)
U of Maine (ME)
U of Massachusetts Amherst (MA)
U of Minnesota, Twin Cities Campus (MN)
U of Missouri–Columbia (MO)
The U of Montana–Missoula (MT)
U of Nevada, Reno (NV)
U of New Hampshire (NH)
The U of Tennessee (TN)
U of the District of Columbia (DC)
U of the South (TN)
U of Toronto (ON, Canada)
U of Vermont (VT)
U of Washington (WA)
U of Wisconsin–Madison (WI)
U of Wisconsin–Milwaukee (WI)
U of Wisconsin–Stevens Point (WI)
Utah State U (UT)
Virginia Polytechnic Inst and State U (VA)
Washington and Lee U (VA)
Washington State U (WA)
West Virginia U (WV)

FORESTRY SCIENCES
Auburn U (AL)
Colorado State U (CO)
Memorial U of Newfoundland (NF, Canada)
Northern Arizona U (AZ)
Penn State U Univ Park Campus (PA)
U of Calif, Berkeley (CA)
U of Georgia (GA)
U of Kentucky (KY)
U of Washington (WA)

FORESTRY SCIENCES RELATED
Utah State U (UT)

FRENCH
Abilene Christian U (TX)
Acadia U (NS, Canada)
Adelphi U (NY)
Adrian Coll (MI)
Agnes Scott Coll (GA)
Alabama State U (AL)
Albany State U (GA)
Albertus Magnus Coll (CT)
Albion Coll (MI)
Albright Coll (PA)
Alfred U (NY)
Allegheny Coll (PA)
Alma Coll (MI)
American U (DC)
The American U of Paris(France)
Amherst Coll (MA)
Anderson U (IN)
Andrews U (MI)
Angelo State U (TX)
Appalachian State U (NC)
Aquinas Coll (MI)
Arizona State U (AZ)
Arkansas State U (AR)
Arkansas Tech U (AR)
Asbury Coll (KY)
Ashland U (OH)
Assumption Coll (MA)
Athabasca U (AB, Canada)
Atlantic Union Coll (MA)
Auburn U (AL)
Augsburg Coll (MN)
Augustana Coll (IL)
Augustana Coll (SD)
Augusta State U (GA)
Austin Coll (TX)
Baker U (KS)
Baldwin-Wallace Coll (OH)
Ball State U (IN)
Bard Coll (NY)
Barnard Coll (NY)
Barry U (FL)
Bates Coll (ME)
Baylor U (TX)
Bellarmine U (KY)
Beloit Coll (WI)
Benedictine Coll (KS)
Bennington Coll (VT)
Berea Coll (KY)
Berry Coll (GA)
Bethany Coll (WV)
Birmingham-Southern Coll (AL)
Bishop's U (PQ, Canada)
Bloomsburg U of Pennsylvania (PA)
Blue Mountain Coll (MS)
Boise State U (ID)
Boston Coll (MA)
Boston U (MA)
Bowdoin Coll (ME)
Bowling Green State U (OH)
Bradley U (IL)
Brandeis U (MA)
Brandon U (MB, Canada)
Bridgewater Coll (VA)
Brigham Young U (UT)
Brock U (ON, Canada)
Brooklyn Coll of the City U of NY (NY)
Brown U (RI)
Bryn Mawr Coll (PA)
Bucknell U (PA)
Butler U (IN)
Cabrini Coll (PA)
Caldwell Coll (NJ)
California Lutheran U (CA)
California State U, Chico (CA)
California State U, Dominguez Hills (CA)
California State U, Fresno (CA)
California State U, Fullerton (CA)
California State U, Hayward (CA)
California State U, Long Beach (CA)
California State U, Los Angeles (CA)
California State U, Northridge (CA)
California State U, Sacramento (CA)
California State U, San Bernardino (CA)
California State U, Stanislaus (CA)
California U of Pennsylvania (PA)
Calvin Coll (MI)
Campbell U (NC)
Canisius Coll (NY)
Capital U (OH)
Cardinal Stritch U (WI)
Carleton Coll (MN)
Carleton U (ON, Canada)
Carnegie Mellon U (PA)
Carroll Coll (MT)
Carson-Newman Coll (TN)
Carthage Coll (WI)
Case Western Reserve U (OH)
Catawba Coll (NC)
The Catholic U of America (DC)
Cedar Crest Coll (PA)
Centenary Coll of Louisiana (LA)
Central Coll (IA)
Central Connecticut State U (CT)
Central Methodist Coll (MO)
Central Michigan U (MI)
Central Missouri State U (MO)
Centre Coll (KY)
Chapman U (CA)
Chatham Coll (PA)
Chestnut Hill Coll (PA)
Cheyney U of Pennsylvania (PA)
Christendom Coll (VA)
Christopher Newport U (VA)
Citadel, The Military Coll of South Carolina (SC)
City Coll of the City U of NY (NY)
Claremont McKenna Coll (CA)
Clarion U of Pennsylvania (PA)
Clark Atlanta U (GA)
Clarke Coll (IA)
Clark U (MA)
Cleveland State U (OH)
Coe Coll (IA)
Coker Coll (SC)
Colby Coll (ME)
Colgate U (NY)
Coll of Charleston (SC)
Coll of Mount Saint Vincent (NY)
The Coll of New Rochelle (NY)
Coll of Saint Benedict (MN)
Coll of St. Catherine (MN)
Coll of the Holy Cross (MA)
Coll of the Ozarks (MO)
The Coll of William and Mary (VA)
The Coll of Wooster (OH)
The Colorado Coll (CO)
Colorado State U (CO)
Columbia Coll (NY)
Columbia Coll (SC)
Columbia U, School of General Studies (NY)
Concordia Coll (MN)
Concordia U (QC, Canada)
Connecticut Coll (CT)
Converse Coll (SC)
Cornell Coll (IA)
Cornell U (NY)
Creighton U (NE)
Daemen Coll (NY)
Dalhousie U (NS, Canada)
Dartmouth Coll (NH)
Davidson Coll (NC)
Davis & Elkins Coll (WV)
Delaware State U (DE)
Denison U (OH)
DePaul U (IL)
DePauw U (IN)
Dickinson Coll (PA)
Dillard U (LA)
Doane Coll (NE)
Dominican U (IL)
Drew U (NJ)
Drury U (MO)
Duke U (NC)
Earlham Coll (IN)
East Carolina U (NC)
Eastern Kentucky U (KY)
Eastern Mennonite U (VA)
Eastern Michigan U (MI)
Eastern U (PA)
Eastern Washington U (WA)
East Stroudsburg U of Pennsylvania (PA)
Eckerd Coll (FL)
Edgewood Coll (WI)
Elizabethtown Coll (PA)
Elmhurst Coll (IL)
Elmira Coll (NY)
Elms Coll (MA)
Elon U (NC)
Emory & Henry Coll (VA)
Emory U (GA)
Erskine Coll (SC)
The Evergreen State Coll (WA)
Fairfield U (CT)
Fairleigh Dickinson U, Florham-Madison Campus (NJ)
Fairleigh Dickinson U, Teaneck-Hackensack Campus (NJ)
Fairmont State Coll (WV)
Ferrum Coll (VA)
Fisk U (TN)
Florida A&M U (FL)
Florida Atlantic U (FL)
Florida International U (FL)
Florida State U (FL)
Fordham U (NY)
Fort Hays State U (KS)
Fort Valley State U (GA)
Framingham State Coll (MA)
Franciscan U of Steubenville (OH)
Francis Marion U (SC)
Franklin and Marshall Coll (PA)
Franklin Coll of Indiana (IN)
Furman U (SC)
Gallaudet U (DC)
Gardner-Webb U (NC)
Georgetown Coll (KY)
Georgetown U (DC)
The George Washington U (DC)
Georgia Coll and State U (GA)
Georgian Court Coll (NJ)
Georgia Southern U (GA)
Georgia Southwestern State U (GA)
Georgia State U (GA)
Gettysburg Coll (PA)
Gonzaga U (WA)
Gordon Coll (MA)
Goucher Coll (MD)
Grace Coll (IN)
Grambling State U (LA)
Grand Valley State U (MI)
Greensboro Coll (NC)
Grinnell Coll (IA)
Grove City Coll (PA)
Guilford Coll (NC)
Gustavus Adolphus Coll (MN)
Hamilton Coll (NY)
Hamline U (MN)
Hampden-Sydney Coll (VA)
Hanover Coll (IN)
Harding U (AR)
Hardin-Simmons U (TX)
Hartwick Coll (NY)
Harvard U (MA)
Haverford Coll (PA)
Hendrix Coll (AR)
High Point U (NC)
Hillsdale Coll (MI)
Hiram Coll (OH)
Hobart and William Smith Colls (NY)
Hofstra U (NY)
Hollins U (VA)
Holy Family Coll (PA)
Hood Coll (MD)

Hope Coll (MI)
Houghton Coll (NY)
Houston Baptist U (TX)
Howard U (DC)
Humboldt State U (CA)
Hunter Coll of the City U of NY (NY)
Idaho State U (ID)
Illinois Coll (IL)
Illinois State U (IL)
Illinois Wesleyan U (IL)
Immaculata Coll (PA)
Indiana State U (IN)
Indiana U Bloomington (IN)
Indiana U Northwest (IN)
Indiana U of Pennsylvania (PA)
Indiana U–Purdue U Fort Wayne (IN)
Indiana U–Purdue U Indianapolis (IN)
Indiana U South Bend (IN)
Indiana U Southeast (IN)
Iona Coll (NY)
Iowa State U of Science and Technology (IA)
Ithaca Coll (NY)
Jacksonville State U (AL)
Jacksonville U (FL)
James Madison U (VA)
John Carroll U (OH)
Johns Hopkins U (MD)
Juniata Coll (PA)
Kalamazoo Coll (MI)
Keene State Coll (NH)
Kennesaw State U (GA)
Kent State U (OH)
Kenyon Coll (OH)
King Coll (TN)
King's Coll (PA)
Knox Coll (IL)
Kutztown U of Pennsylvania (PA)
Lafayette Coll (PA)
Lake Erie Coll (OH)
Lake Forest Coll (IL)
Lakehead U (ON, Canada)
Lamar U (TX)
La Salle U (PA)
Laurentian U (ON, Canada)
Lawrence U (WI)
Lebanon Valley Coll (PA)
Lehigh U (PA)
Lehman Coll of the City U of NY (NY)
Le Moyne Coll (NY)
Lenoir-Rhyne Coll (NC)
Lewis & Clark Coll (OR)
Lincoln U (MO)
Lincoln U (PA)
Lindenwood U (MO)
Linfield Coll (OR)
Lipscomb U (TN)
Lock Haven U of Pennsylvania (PA)
Long Island U, C.W. Post Campus (NY)
Long Island U, Southampton Coll, Friends World Program (NY)
Longwood Coll (VA)
Loras Coll (IA)
Louisiana Coll (LA)
Louisiana State U and A&M Coll (LA)
Louisiana State U in Shreveport (LA)
Louisiana Tech U (LA)
Loyola Coll in Maryland (MD)
Loyola Marymount U (CA)
Loyola U Chicago (IL)
Loyola U New Orleans (LA)
Luther Coll (IA)
Lycoming Coll (PA)
Lynchburg Coll (VA)
Macalester Coll (MN)
Manchester Coll (IN)
Manhattan Coll (NY)
Manhattanville Coll (NY)
Mansfield U of Pennsylvania (PA)
Marian Coll (IN)
Marist Coll (NY)
Marlboro Coll (VT)
Marquette U (WI)
Mary Baldwin Coll (VA)
Marymount Coll of Fordham U (NY)
Mary Washington Coll (VA)
Marywood U (PA)
McGill U (PQ, Canada)
McMaster U (ON, Canada)
McNeese State U (LA)
Memorial U of Newfoundland (NF, Canada)
Mercer U (GA)
Mercy Coll (NY)
Mercyhurst Coll (PA)
Meredith Coll (NC)
Merrimack Coll (MA)
Messiah Coll (PA)
Methodist Coll (NC)
Miami U (OH)
Michigan State U (MI)
Middlebury Coll (VT)
Millersville U of Pennsylvania (PA)
Millikin U (IL)
Millsaps Coll (MS)
Mills Coll (CA)
Minnesota State U, Mankato (MN)
Minot State U (ND)
Mississippi Coll (MS)
Missouri Southern State Coll (MO)
Missouri Western State Coll (MO)
Molloy Coll (NY)
Monmouth Coll (IL)
Montclair State U (NJ)
Moravian Coll (PA)
Morehead State U (KY)
Morehouse Coll (GA)
Morris Brown Coll (GA)
Mount Allison U (NB, Canada)
Mount Holyoke Coll (MA)
Mount Mary Coll (WI)
Mount St. Mary's Coll (CA)
Mount Saint Mary's Coll and Seminary (MD)
Mount Saint Vincent U (NS, Canada)
Mount Union Coll (OH)
Muhlenberg Coll (PA)
Murray State U (KY)
Muskingum Coll (OH)
Nazareth Coll of Rochester (NY)
Nebraska Wesleyan U (NE)
Newberry Coll (SC)
New Coll of Florida (FL)
New York U (NY)
Niagara U (NY)
Nicholls State U (LA)
North Carolina Ag and Tech State U (NC)
North Carolina Central U (NC)
North Carolina State U (NC)
North Central Coll (IL)
North Dakota State U (ND)
Northeastern Illinois U (IL)
Northeastern State U (OK)
Northeastern U (MA)
Northern Arizona U (AZ)
Northern Illinois U (IL)
Northern Kentucky U (KY)
Northern Michigan U (MI)
Northern State U (SD)
North Georgia Coll & State U (GA)
North Park U (IL)
Northwestern U (IL)
Northwest Missouri State U (MO)
Notre Dame de Namur U (CA)
Oakland U (MI)
Oakwood Coll (AL)
Oberlin Coll (OH)
Occidental Coll (CA)
Ohio Northern U (OH)
The Ohio State U (OH)
Ohio U (OH)
Ohio Wesleyan U (OH)
Oklahoma Baptist U (OK)
Oklahoma City U (OK)
Oklahoma State U (OK)
Oral Roberts U (OK)
Oregon State U (OR)
Otterbein Coll (OH)
Ouachita Baptist U (AR)
Pacific Lutheran U (WA)
Pacific Union Coll (CA)
Pacific U (OR)
Penn State U Univ Park Campus (PA)
Pepperdine U, Malibu (CA)
Pittsburg State U (KS)
Pitzer Coll (CA)
Plattsburgh State U of NY (NY)
Plymouth State Coll (NH)
Pomona Coll (CA)
Pontifical Catholic U of Puerto Rico (PR)
Portland State U (OR)
Presbyterian Coll (SC)
Principia Coll (IL)
Providence Coll (RI)
Purchase Coll, State U of NY (NY)
Purdue U Calumet (IN)
Queens Coll (NC)
Queens Coll of the City U of NY (NY)
Queen's U at Kingston (ON, Canada)
Randolph-Macon Coll (VA)
Randolph-Macon Woman's Coll (VA)
Redeemer U Coll (ON, Canada)
Reed Coll (OR)
Regis Coll (MA)
Regis U (CO)
Rhode Island Coll (RI)
Rhodes Coll (TN)
Rice U (TX)
Rider U (NJ)
Ripon Coll (WI)
Rivier Coll (NH)
Roanoke Coll (VA)
Rockford Coll (IL)
Rockhurst U (MO)
Rollins Coll (FL)
Rosemont Coll (PA)
Rutgers, The State U of New Jersey, New Brunswick (NJ)
Saginaw Valley State U (MI)
St. Ambrose U (IA)
Saint Anselm Coll (NH)
Saint Augustine's Coll (NC)
St. Bonaventure U (NY)
St. Cloud State U (MN)
Saint Francis U (PA)
St. Francis Xavier U (NS, Canada)
St. John Fisher Coll (NY)
Saint John's U (MN)
St. John's U (NY)
Saint Joseph Coll (CT)
Saint Joseph's U (PA)
St. Lawrence U (NY)
Saint Louis U (MO)
Saint Mary-of-the-Woods Coll (IN)
Saint Mary's Coll (IN)
Saint Mary's Coll of California (CA)
Saint Mary's U (NS, Canada)
Saint Mary's U of Minnesota (MN)
St. Mary's U of San Antonio (TX)
Saint Michael's Coll (VT)
St. Norbert Coll (WI)
St. Olaf Coll (MN)
St. Thomas U (NB, Canada)
Salem Coll (NC)
Salisbury U (MD)
Salve Regina U (RI)
Samford U (AL)
Sam Houston State U (TX)
San Diego State U (CA)
San Francisco State U (CA)
San Jose State U (CA)
Santa Clara U (CA)
Sarah Lawrence Coll (NY)
Scripps Coll (CA)
Seattle Pacific U (WA)
Seattle U (WA)
Seton Hall U (NJ)
Shippensburg U of Pennsylvania (PA)
Shorter Coll (GA)
Siena Coll (NY)
Simmons Coll (MA)
Simon Fraser U (BC, Canada)
Simon's Rock Coll of Bard (MA)
Simpson Coll (IA)
Skidmore Coll (NY)
Slippery Rock U of Pennsylvania (PA)
Smith Coll (MA)
Sonoma State U (CA)
South Carolina State U (SC)
South Dakota State U (SD)
Southeastern Louisiana U (LA)
Southeast Missouri State U (MO)
Southern Connecticut State U (CT)
Southern Illinois U Carbondale (IL)
Southern Methodist U (TX)
Southern U and A&M Coll (LA)
Southern Utah U (UT)
Southwestern U (TX)
Southwest Missouri State U (MO)
Southwest Texas State U (TX)
Spelman Coll (GA)
Stanford U (CA)
State U of NY at Albany (NY)
State U of NY at Binghamton (NY)
State U of NY at New Paltz (NY)
State U of NY at Oswego (NY)
State U of NY Coll at Brockport (NY)
State U of NY Coll at Buffalo (NY)
State U of NY Coll at Cortland (NY)
State U of NY Coll at Fredonia (NY)
State U of NY Coll at Geneseo (NY)
State U of NY Coll at Oneonta (NY)
State U of NY Coll at Potsdam (NY)
State U of West Georgia (GA)
Stephen F. Austin State U (TX)
Stetson U (FL)
State U of NY at Stony Brook (NY)
Suffolk U (MA)
Susquehanna U (PA)
Swarthmore Coll (PA)
Sweet Briar Coll (VA)
Syracuse U (NY)
Talladega Coll (AL)
Taylor U (IN)
Temple U (PA)
Tennessee State U (TN)
Tennessee Technological U (TN)
Texas A&M U (TX)
Texas A&M U–Commerce (TX)
Texas Christian U (TX)
Texas Southern U (TX)
Texas Tech U (TX)
Thiel Coll (PA)
Towson U (MD)
Transylvania U (KY)
Trent U (ON, Canada)
Trinity Coll (CT)
Trinity Coll (DC)
Trinity U (TX)
Truman State U (MO)
Tufts U (MA)
Tulane U (LA)
Union Coll (NE)
Union U (TN)
United States Military Academy (NY)
Université de Montréal (QC, Canada)
Université de Sherbrooke (PQ, Canada)
Université Laval (QC, Canada)
State U of NY at Buffalo (NY)
U Coll of Cape Breton (NS, Canada)
The U of Akron (OH)
The U of Alabama (AL)
The U of Alabama at Birmingham (AL)
U of Alberta (AB, Canada)
The U of Arizona (AZ)
U of Arkansas (AR)
U of Arkansas at Little Rock (AR)
The U of British Columbia (BC, Canada)
U of Calgary (AB, Canada)
U of Calif, Berkeley (CA)
U of Calif, Davis (CA)
U of Calif, Irvine (CA)
U of Calif, Los Angeles (CA)
U of Calif, Riverside (CA)
U of Calif, San Diego (CA)
U of Calif, Santa Barbara (CA)
U of Calif, Santa Cruz (CA)
U of Central Arkansas (AR)
U of Central Florida (FL)
U of Central Oklahoma (OK)
U of Chicago (IL)
U of Cincinnati (OH)
U of Colorado at Boulder (CO)
U of Colorado at Denver (CO)
U of Connecticut (CT)
U of Dallas (TX)
U of Dayton (OH)
U of Delaware (DE)
U of Denver (CO)
U of Evansville (IN)
U of Florida (FL)
U of Georgia (GA)
U of Guelph (ON, Canada)
U of Hawaii at Manoa (HI)
U of Houston (TX)
U of Idaho (ID)
U of Illinois at Chicago (IL)
U of Illinois at Urbana–Champaign (IL)
U of Indianapolis (IN)
The U of Iowa (IA)
U of Kansas (KS)
U of Kentucky (KY)
U of King's Coll (NS, Canada)
U of La Verne (CA)
The U of Lethbridge (AB, Canada)
U of Louisiana at Monroe (LA)
U of Louisville (KY)
U of Maine (ME)
U of Maine at Fort Kent (ME)
U of Maine at Presque Isle (ME)
U of Manitoba (MB, Canada)
U of Maryland, Baltimore County (MD)
U of Maryland, Coll Park (MD)
U of Massachusetts Amherst (MA)
U of Massachusetts Boston (MA)
U of Massachusetts Dartmouth (MA)
U of Miami (FL)
U of Michigan (MI)
U of Michigan–Dearborn (MI)
U of Michigan–Flint (MI)
U of Minnesota, Morris (MN)
U of Minnesota, Twin Cities Campus (MN)
U of Mississippi (MS)
U of Missouri–Columbia (MO)
U of Missouri–Kansas City (MO)
U of Missouri–St. Louis (MO)
The U of Montana–Missoula (MT)
U of Montevallo (AL)
U of Nebraska at Kearney (NE)
U of Nebraska at Omaha (NE)
U of Nebraska–Lincoln (NE)
U of Nevada, Las Vegas (NV)
U of Nevada, Reno (NV)
U of New Hampshire (NH)
U of New Mexico (NM)
U of New Orleans (LA)
The U of North Carolina at Asheville (NC)
The U of North Carolina at Charlotte (NC)
The U of North Carolina at Greensboro (NC)
The U of North Carolina at Wilmington (NC)
U of North Dakota (ND)
U of Northern Colorado (CO)
U of Northern Iowa (IA)
U of North Texas (TX)
U of Notre Dame (IN)
U of Oklahoma (OK)
U of Oregon (OR)
U of Ottawa (ON, Canada)
U of Pennsylvania (PA)
U of Pittsburgh (PA)
U of Prince Edward Island (PE, Canada)
U of Puget Sound (WA)
U of Redlands (CA)
U of Rhode Island (RI)
U of Richmond (VA)
U of Rochester (NY)
U of St. Thomas (MN)
U of St. Thomas (TX)
U of San Diego (CA)
U of San Francisco (CA)
U of Saskatchewan (SK, Canada)
The U of Scranton (PA)
U of South Carolina (SC)
U of South Carolina Spartanburg (SC)
U of South Dakota (SD)
U of Southern California (CA)
U of Southern Indiana (IN)
U of Southern Maine (ME)
U of South Florida (FL)
The U of Tennessee (TN)
The U of Tennessee at Chattanooga (TN)
The U of Tennessee at Martin (TN)
The U of Texas at Arlington (TX)
The U of Texas at Austin (TX)
The U of Texas at El Paso (TX)
The U of Texas at San Antonio (TX)
The U of Texas–Pan American (TX)
U of the District of Columbia (DC)
U of the Pacific (CA)
U of the South (TN)
U of Toledo (OH)
U of Toronto (ON, Canada)
U of Tulsa (OK)
U of Utah (UT)
U of Vermont (VT)
U of Victoria (BC, Canada)
U of Virginia (VA)
The U of Virginia's Coll at Wise (VA)
U of Washington (WA)
U of Waterloo (ON, Canada)
The U of Western Ontario (ON, Canada)
U of Windsor (ON, Canada)

U of Wisconsin–Eau Claire (WI)
U of Wisconsin–Green Bay (WI)
U of Wisconsin–La Crosse (WI)
U of Wisconsin–Madison (WI)
U of Wisconsin–Milwaukee (WI)
U of Wisconsin–Oshkosh (WI)
U of Wisconsin–Parkside (WI)
U of Wisconsin–Platteville (WI)
U of Wisconsin–River Falls (WI)
U of Wisconsin–Stevens Point (WI)
U of Wisconsin–Whitewater (WI)
U of Wyoming (WY)
Ursinus Coll (PA)
Utah State U (UT)
Valdosta State U (GA)
Valparaiso U (IN)
Vanderbilt U (TN)
Vassar Coll (NY)
Villanova U (PA)
Virginia Polytechnic Inst and State U (VA)
Virginia Wesleyan Coll (VA)
Wabash Coll (IN)
Wake Forest U (NC)
Walla Walla Coll (WA)
Walsh U (OH)
Wartburg Coll (IA)
Washburn U of Topeka (KS)
Washington & Jefferson Coll (PA)
Washington and Lee U (VA)
Washington Coll (MD)
Washington State U (WA)
Washington U in St. Louis (MO)
Wayne State Coll (NE)
Wayne State U (MI)
Weber State U (UT)
Webster U (MO)
Wellesley Coll (MA)
Wells Coll (NY)
Wesleyan U (CT)
West Chester U of Pennsylvania (PA)
Western Illinois U (IL)
Western Kentucky U (KY)
Western Maryland Coll (MD)
Western Michigan U (MI)
Western State Coll of Colorado (CO)
Western Washington U (WA)
Westminster Coll (MO)
Westminster Coll (PA)
Westmont Coll (CA)
Wheaton Coll (IL)
Wheaton Coll (MA)
Wheeling Jesuit U (WV)
Whitman Coll (WA)
Whittier Coll (CA)
Whitworth Coll (WA)
Wichita State U (KS)
Widener U (PA)
Wilfrid Laurier U (ON, Canada)
Wilkes U (PA)
Willamette U (OR)
William Jewell Coll (MO)
Williams Coll (MA)
Winona State U (MN)
Wittenberg U (OH)
Wofford Coll (SC)
Wright State U (OH)
Xavier U (OH)
Xavier U of Louisiana (LA)
Yale U (CT)
Yeshiva U (NY)
York Coll of the City U of New York (NY)
York U (ON, Canada)
Youngstown State U (OH)

FRENCH LANGUAGE EDUCATION
Abilene Christian U (TX)
Anderson U (IN)
Arkansas State U (AR)
Baylor U (TX)
Berea Coll (KY)
Berry Coll (GA)
Blue Mountain Coll (MS)
Bowling Green State U (OH)
Bridgewater Coll (VA)
Brigham Young U (UT)
Canisius Coll (NY)
The Catholic U of America (DC)
Central Michigan U (MI)
Central Missouri State U (MO)
Coll of St. Catherine (MN)
Colorado State U (CO)
Concordia Coll (MN)
Daemen Coll (NY)
Duquesne U (PA)
East Carolina U (NC)
Eastern Mennonite U (VA)
Eastern Michigan U (MI)
Elmhurst Coll (IL)
Elmira Coll (NY)
Framingham State Coll (MA)
Franklin Coll of Indiana (IN)
Georgia Southern U (GA)
Grace Coll (IN)
Grambling State U (LA)
Hardin-Simmons U (TX)
Hofstra U (NY)
Indiana U Bloomington (IN)
Indiana U Northwest (IN)
Indiana U–Purdue U Fort Wayne (IN)
Indiana U–Purdue U Indianapolis (IN)
Indiana U South Bend (IN)
Ithaca Coll (NY)
Juniata Coll (PA)
Kennesaw State U (GA)
King Coll (TN)
Lipscomb U (TN)
Long Island U, C.W. Post Campus (NY)
Louisiana State U in Shreveport (LA)
Louisiana Tech U (LA)
Luther Coll (IA)
Manhattanville Coll (NY)
Mansfield U of Pennsylvania (PA)
Marymount Coll of Fordham U (NY)
McGill U (PQ, Canada)
Messiah Coll (PA)
Minot State U (ND)
Missouri Western State Coll (MO)
Molloy Coll (NY)
New York U (NY)
Niagara U (NY)
North Carolina Central U (NC)
North Carolina State U (NC)
North Dakota State U (ND)
Ohio U (OH)
Oklahoma Baptist U (OK)
Oral Roberts U (OK)
Pace U (NY)
St. Ambrose U (IA)
St. John's U (NY)
Saint Mary's U of Minnesota (MN)
Salve Regina U (RI)
San Diego State U (CA)
Southeastern Louisiana U (LA)
Southwest Missouri State U (MO)
State U of NY at Albany (NY)
State U of NY Coll at Potsdam (NY)
Talladega Coll (AL)
Université Laval (QC, Canada)
The U of Arizona (AZ)
U of Illinois at Chicago (IL)
U of Illinois at Urbana–Champaign (IL)
U of Indianapolis (IN)
The U of Iowa (IA)
U of Minnesota, Duluth (MN)
U of Nebraska–Lincoln (NE)
The U of North Carolina at Charlotte (NC)
The U of North Carolina at Wilmington (NC)
U of North Texas (TX)
The U of Tennessee at Martin (TN)
U of Toledo (OH)
U of Utah (UT)
U of Waterloo (ON, Canada)
U of Windsor (ON, Canada)
U of Wisconsin–River Falls (WI)
Washington U in St. Louis (MO)
Weber State U (UT)
Western Carolina U (NC)
Wheeling Jesuit U (WV)
William Woods U (MO)
Youngstown State U (OH)

FURNITURE DESIGN
Ferris State U (MI)
Rochester Inst of Technology (NY)

GENERAL RETAILING/ WHOLESALING
U of New Haven (CT)
U of South Carolina (SC)

GENERAL RETAILING/ WHOLESALING RELATED
The U of Akron (OH)

GENERAL STUDIES
Alfred U (NY)
Alverno Coll (WI)
Angelo State U (TX)
Antioch U Santa Barbara (CA)
Arkansas State U (AR)
Arkansas Tech U (AR)
Avila Coll (MO)
Bluefield State Coll (WV)
Brandon U (MB, Canada)
Brenau U (GA)
Bridgewater Coll (VA)
Carroll Coll (MT)
The Catholic U of America (DC)
Central Christian Coll of Kansas (KS)
Central Coll (IA)
City U (WA)
Clearwater Christian Coll (FL)
Coll of Mount St. Joseph (OH)
Columbia International U (SC)
Crown Coll (MN)
Cumberland Coll (KY)
DePaul U (IL)
Drexel U (PA)
East Tennessee State U (TN)
Emporia State U (KS)
Fairleigh Dickinson U, Teaneck-Hackensack Campus (NJ)
Ferrum Coll (VA)
Fitchburg State Coll (MA)
Georgia Southern U (GA)
Hampton U (VA)
Harding U (AR)
Howard Payne U (TX)
Idaho State U (ID)
Indiana State U (IN)
Indiana U Bloomington (IN)
Indiana U East (IN)
Indiana U Kokomo (IN)
Indiana U Northwest (IN)
Indiana U of Pennsylvania (PA)
Indiana U–Purdue U Fort Wayne (IN)
Indiana U–Purdue U Indianapolis (IN)
Indiana U South Bend (IN)
Indiana U Southeast (IN)
Indiana Wesleyan U (IN)
Kent State U (OH)
Lambuth U (TN)
La Roche Coll (PA)
Liberty U (VA)
Louisiana State U and A&M Coll (LA)
Louisiana State U in Shreveport (LA)
Louisiana Tech U (LA)
Loyola U New Orleans (LA)
Marshall U (WV)
Metropolitan State U (MN)
Michigan Technological U (MI)
Mid-Continent Coll (KY)
Minot State U (ND)
Missouri Western State Coll (MO)
Morehead State U (KY)
Mount Marty Coll (SD)
Mount St. Clare Coll (IA)
Mount Saint Mary's Coll and Seminary (MD)
Nicholls State U (LA)
Northern Arizona U (AZ)
Northwestern State U of Louisiana (LA)
Nova Southeastern U (FL)
Ohio U (OH)
Ohio Wesleyan U (OH)
Open Learning Agency (BC, Canada)
Our Lady of Holy Cross Coll (LA)
Point Park Coll (PA)
Rochester Inst of Technology (NY)
Saginaw Valley State U (MI)
St. Joseph's Coll, New York (NY)
Samford U (AL)
Seattle Pacific U (WA)
Seton Hill Coll (PA)
Shepherd Coll (WV)
Siena Heights U (MI)
Simon Fraser U (BC, Canada)
Southeastern Louisiana U (LA)
Southeastern U (DC)
Southern Nazarene U (OK)
Southwestern Assemblies of God U (TX)
Southwestern Coll (KS)
Springfield Coll (MA)
Spring Hill Coll (AL)
State U of NY Inst of Tech at Utica/Rome (NY)
Sweet Briar Coll (VA)
Texas A&M U–Texarkana (TX)
Texas Christian U (TX)
Texas Tech U (TX)
Trinity Western U (BC, Canada)
U of Calgary (AB, Canada)
U of Connecticut (CT)
U of Dayton (OH)
U of Idaho (ID)
U of Louisiana at Lafayette (LA)
U of Louisiana at Monroe (LA)
U of Maine at Farmington (ME)
U of Maine at Machias (ME)
U of Massachusetts Amherst (MA)
U of Miami (FL)
U of Michigan (MI)
U of Missouri–St. Louis (MO)
U of Mobile (AL)
U of Nebraska at Kearney (NE)
U of Nebraska at Omaha (NE)
U of Nevada, Reno (NV)
U of New Mexico (NM)
U of New Orleans (LA)
U of North Alabama (AL)
U of North Texas (TX)
U of St. Thomas (TX)
U of South Florida (FL)
U of Washington (WA)
U of Windsor (ON, Canada)
U of Wisconsin–Green Bay (WI)
U of Wisconsin–Stevens Point (WI)
U System Coll for Lifelong Learning (NH)
Virginia Commonwealth U (VA)
Western Kentucky U (KY)
Western Washington U (WA)
West Texas A&M U (TX)
Winston-Salem State U (NC)
York Coll (NE)

GENETICS
Ball State U (IN)
Cedar Crest Coll (PA)
Cornell U (NY)
Dartmouth Coll (NH)
The Evergreen State Coll (WA)
Florida State U (FL)
Hampshire Coll (MA)
Harvard U (MA)
Iowa State U of Science and Technology (IA)
Jacksonville State U (AL)
McGill U (PQ, Canada)
Missouri Southern State Coll (MO)
North Dakota State U (ND)
The Ohio State U (OH)
Ohio Wesleyan U (OH)
Rochester Inst of Technology (NY)
Rutgers, The State U of New Jersey, New Brunswick (NJ)
St. Cloud State U (MN)
Sarah Lawrence Coll (NY)
Texas A&M U (TX)
U of Alberta (AB, Canada)
The U of British Columbia (BC, Canada)
U of Calif, Berkeley (CA)
U of Calif, Davis (CA)
U of Georgia (GA)
U of Hawaii at Manoa (HI)
U of Manitoba (MB, Canada)
U of Minnesota, Twin Cities Campus (MN)
U of Rochester (NY)
U of Toronto (ON, Canada)
The U of Western Ontario (ON, Canada)
U of Wisconsin–Madison (WI)
Washington State U (WA)
Worcester Polytechnic Inst (MA)

GEOCHEMISTRY
Bridgewater State Coll (MA)
Brown U (RI)
California Inst of Technology (CA)
Columbia Coll (NY)
Hampshire Coll (MA)
Harvard U (MA)
New Mexico Inst of Mining and Technology (NM)
Northern Arizona U (AZ)
Pomona Coll (CA)
San Diego State U (CA)
State U of NY at Oswego (NY)
State U of NY Coll at Cortland (NY)
State U of NY Coll at Fredonia (NY)
State U of NY Coll at Geneseo (NY)
U of Calif, Los Angeles (CA)
U of Waterloo (ON, Canada)
West Chester U of Pennsylvania (PA)

GEOGRAPHY
Appalachian State U (NC)
Aquinas Coll (MI)
Arizona State U (AZ)
Arkansas State U (AR)
Auburn U (AL)
Augustana Coll (IL)
Austin Peay State U (TN)
Ball State U (IN)
Baylor U (TX)
Bellevue U (NE)
Bemidji State U (MN)
Bishop's U (PQ, Canada)
Bloomsburg U of Pennsylvania (PA)
Boston U (MA)
Bowling Green State U (OH)
Brandon U (MB, Canada)
Bridgewater State Coll (MA)
Brigham Young U (UT)
Brock U (ON, Canada)
Bucknell U (PA)
California State Polytechnic U, Pomona (CA)
California State U, Chico (CA)
California State U, Dominguez Hills (CA)
California State U, Fresno (CA)
California State U, Fullerton (CA)
California State U, Hayward (CA)
California State U, Long Beach (CA)
California State U, Los Angeles (CA)
California State U, Northridge (CA)
California State U, Sacramento (CA)
California State U, San Bernardino (CA)
California State U, Stanislaus (CA)
California U of Pennsylvania (PA)
Calvin Coll (MI)
Carleton U (ON, Canada)
Carroll Coll (WI)
Carthage Coll (WI)
Central Connecticut State U (CT)
Central Michigan U (MI)
Central Missouri State U (MO)
Central Washington U (WA)
Cheyney U of Pennsylvania (PA)
Chicago State U (IL)
City Coll of the City U of NY (NY)
Clarion U of Pennsylvania (PA)
Clark U (MA)
Colgate U (NY)
Concord Coll (WV)
Concordia U (IL)
Concordia U (NE)
Concordia U (QC, Canada)
Dartmouth Coll (NH)
DePaul U (IL)
DePauw U (IN)
Dickinson State U (ND)
East Carolina U (NC)
Eastern Illinois U (IL)
Eastern Kentucky U (KY)
Eastern Michigan U (MI)
Eastern Washington U (WA)
East Stroudsburg U of Pennsylvania (PA)
East Tennessee State U (TN)
Edinboro U of Pennsylvania (PA)
Elmhurst Coll (IL)
Emory & Henry Coll (VA)
Excelsior Coll (NY)
Fayetteville State U (NC)
Fitchburg State Coll (MA)
Florida Atlantic U (FL)
Florida International U (FL)
Florida State U (FL)
Framingham State Coll (MA)
Francis Marion U (SC)
Frostburg State U (MD)
George Mason U (VA)
The George Washington U (DC)
Georgia Southern U (GA)
Georgia State U (GA)
Grambling State U (LA)
Gustavus Adolphus Coll (MN)
Hampshire Coll (MA)
Hofstra U (NY)
Humboldt State U (CA)

Hunter Coll of the City U of NY (NY)
Illinois State U (IL)
Indiana State U (IN)
Indiana U Bloomington (IN)
Indiana U of Pennsylvania (PA)
Indiana U–Purdue U Indianapolis (IN)
Indiana U Southeast (IN)
Jacksonville State U (AL)
Jacksonville U (FL)
James Madison U (VA)
Johns Hopkins U (MD)
Kansas State U (KS)
Keene State Coll (NH)
Kent State U (OH)
Kutztown U of Pennsylvania (PA)
Lakehead U (ON, Canada)
Laurentian U (ON, Canada)
Lehman Coll of the City U of NY (NY)
Lock Haven U of Pennsylvania (PA)
Long Island U, C.W. Post Campus (NY)
Long Island U, Southampton Coll, Friends World Program (NY)
Longwood Coll (VA)
Louisiana State U and A&M Coll (LA)
Louisiana State U in Shreveport (LA)
Louisiana Tech U (LA)
Macalester Coll (MN)
Mansfield U of Pennsylvania (PA)
Marshall U (WV)
Mary Washington Coll (VA)
McGill U (PQ, Canada)
McMaster U (ON, Canada)
Memorial U of Newfoundland (NF, Canada)
Miami U (OH)
Michigan State U (MI)
Middlebury Coll (VT)
Millersville U of Pennsylvania (PA)
Minnesota State U, Mankato (MN)
Montclair State U (NJ)
Morehead State U (KY)
Mount Allison U (NB, Canada)
Mount Holyoke Coll (MA)
Murray State U (KY)
New Mexico State U (NM)
Nipissing U (ON, Canada)
North Carolina Central U (NC)
Northeastern Illinois U (IL)
Northeastern State U (OK)
Northern Arizona U (AZ)
Northern Illinois U (IL)
Northern Kentucky U (KY)
Northern Michigan U (MI)
Northwestern U (IL)
Northwest Missouri State U (MO)
The Ohio State U (OH)
Ohio U (OH)
Ohio Wesleyan U (OH)
Oklahoma State U (OK)
Old Dominion U (VA)
Oregon State U (OR)
Penn State U Univ Park Campus (PA)
Pittsburg State U (KS)
Plattsburgh State U of NY (NY)
Plymouth State Coll (NH)
Portland State U (OR)
Queen's U at Kingston (ON, Canada)
Radford U (VA)
Rhode Island Coll (RI)
Rowan U (NJ)
Rutgers, The State U of New Jersey, New Brunswick (NJ)
St. Cloud State U (MN)
Saint Mary's U (NS, Canada)
Salem State Coll (MA)
Salisbury U (MD)
Samford U (AL)
Sam Houston State U (TX)
San Diego State U (CA)
San Francisco State U (CA)
San Jose State U (CA)
Shippensburg U of Pennsylvania (PA)
Simon Fraser U (BC, Canada)
Simon's Rock Coll of Bard (MA)
Slippery Rock U of Pennsylvania (PA)
Sonoma State U (CA)
South Dakota State U (SD)
Southeast Missouri State U (MO)
Southern Connecticut State U (CT)
Southern Illinois U Carbondale (IL)
Southern Illinois U Edwardsville (IL)
Southern Oregon U (OR)
Southwest Missouri State U (MO)
Southwest Texas State U (TX)
State U of NY at Albany (NY)
State U of NY at Binghamton (NY)
State U of NY at New Paltz (NY)
State U of NY Coll at Buffalo (NY)
State U of NY Coll at Cortland (NY)
State U of NY Coll at Geneseo (NY)
State U of NY Coll at Oneonta (NY)
State U of NY Coll at Potsdam (NY)
State U of West Georgia (GA)
Stephen F. Austin State U (TX)
Stetson U (FL)
Syracuse U (NY)
Temple U (PA)
Texas A&M U (TX)
Texas A&M U–Commerce (TX)
Texas A&M U–Kingsville (TX)
Texas Tech U (TX)
Towson U (MD)
Trent U (ON, Canada)
Trinity Western U (BC, Canada)
United States Air Force Academy (CO)
United States Military Academy (NY)
Université de Montréal (QC, Canada)
Université de Sherbrooke (PQ, Canada)
Université Laval (QC, Canada)
State U of NY at Buffalo (NY)
U Coll of the Cariboo (BC, Canada)
U Coll of the Fraser Valley (BC, Canada)
The U of Akron (OH)
The U of Alabama (AL)
U of Alaska Fairbanks (AK)
U of Alberta (AB, Canada)
The U of Arizona (AZ)
U of Arkansas (AR)
The U of British Columbia (BC, Canada)
U of Calgary (AB, Canada)
U of Calif, Berkeley (CA)
U of Calif, Irvine (CA)
U of Calif, Los Angeles (CA)
U of Calif, Santa Barbara (CA)
U of Central Arkansas (AR)
U of Central Oklahoma (OK)
U of Chicago (IL)
U of Cincinnati (OH)
U of Colorado at Boulder (CO)
U of Colorado at Colorado Springs (CO)
U of Colorado at Denver (CO)
U of Connecticut (CT)
U of Delaware (DE)
U of Denver (CO)
U of Florida (FL)
U of Georgia (GA)
U of Guelph (ON, Canada)
U of Hawaii at Hilo (HI)
U of Hawaii at Manoa (HI)
U of Houston–Clear Lake (TX)
U of Idaho (ID)
U of Illinois at Chicago (IL)
U of Illinois at Urbana–Champaign (IL)
The U of Iowa (IA)
U of Kansas (KS)
U of Kentucky (KY)
The U of Lethbridge (AB, Canada)
U of Louisiana at Monroe (LA)
U of Louisville (KY)
U of Maine at Farmington (ME)
U of Manitoba (MB, Canada)
U of Maryland, Baltimore County (MD)
U of Maryland, Coll Park (MD)
U of Massachusetts Amherst (MA)
U of Massachusetts Boston (MA)
The U of Memphis (TN)
U of Miami (FL)
U of Michigan (MI)
U of Michigan–Flint (MI)
U of Minnesota, Duluth (MN)
U of Minnesota, Twin Cities Campus (MN)
U of Missouri–Columbia (MO)
U of Missouri–Kansas City (MO)
The U of Montana–Missoula (MT)
U of Nebraska at Kearney (NE)
U of Nebraska at Omaha (NE)
U of Nebraska–Lincoln (NE)
U of Nevada, Reno (NV)
U of New Hampshire (NH)
U of New Mexico (NM)
U of New Orleans (LA)
U of North Alabama (AL)
The U of North Carolina at Chapel Hill (NC)
The U of North Carolina at Charlotte (NC)
The U of North Carolina at Greensboro (NC)
The U of North Carolina at Wilmington (NC)
U of North Dakota (ND)
U of Northern Colorado (CO)
U of Northern Iowa (IA)
U of North Texas (TX)
U of Oklahoma (OK)
U of Oregon (OR)
U of Ottawa (ON, Canada)
U of Pittsburgh at Johnstown (PA)
U of Regina (SK, Canada)
U of St. Thomas (MN)
U of Saskatchewan (SK, Canada)
U of South Alabama (AL)
U of South Carolina (SC)
U of Southern California (CA)
U of Southern Maine (ME)
U of Southern Mississippi (MS)
U of South Florida (FL)
The U of Tennessee (TN)
The U of Tennessee at Martin (TN)
The U of Texas at Austin (TX)
The U of Texas at Dallas (TX)
The U of Texas at El Paso (TX)
The U of Texas at San Antonio (TX)
U of the District of Columbia (DC)
U of Toledo (OH)
U of Toronto (ON, Canada)
U of Utah (UT)
U of Vermont (VT)
U of Victoria (BC, Canada)
U of Washington (WA)
U of Waterloo (ON, Canada)
The U of Western Ontario (ON, Canada)
U of Wisconsin–Eau Claire (WI)
U of Wisconsin–La Crosse (WI)
U of Wisconsin–Madison (WI)
U of Wisconsin–Milwaukee (WI)
U of Wisconsin–Oshkosh (WI)
U of Wisconsin–Parkside (WI)
U of Wisconsin–Platteville (WI)
U of Wisconsin–River Falls (WI)
U of Wisconsin–Stevens Point (WI)
U of Wisconsin–Whitewater (WI)
U of Wyoming (WY)
Utah State U (UT)
Valparaiso U (IN)
Vassar Coll (NY)
Villanova U (PA)
Virginia Polytechnic Inst and State U (VA)
Wayne State Coll (NE)
Wayne State U (MI)
Weber State U (UT)
West Chester U of Pennsylvania (PA)
Western Illinois U (IL)
Western Kentucky U (KY)
Western Michigan U (MI)
Western Oregon U (OR)
Western Washington U (WA)
Westfield State Coll (MA)
West Texas A&M U (TX)
West Virginia U (WV)
Wilfrid Laurier U (ON, Canada)
William Paterson U of New Jersey (NJ)
Wittenberg U (OH)
Worcester State Coll (MA)
Wright State U (OH)
York U (ON, Canada)
Youngstown State U (OH)

GEOLOGICAL ENGINEERING

Auburn U (AL)
Colorado School of Mines (CO)
Cornell U (NY)
Harvard U (MA)
Laurentian U (ON, Canada)
Memorial U of Newfoundland (NF, Canada)
Michigan Technological U (MI)
Montana Tech of The U of Montana (MT)
New Mexico State U (NM)
Oregon State U (OR)
Queen's U at Kingston (ON, Canada)
South Dakota School of Mines and Technology (SD)
Université Laval (QC, Canada)
The U of Akron (OH)
U of Alaska Fairbanks (AK)
The U of Arizona (AZ)
The U of British Columbia (BC, Canada)
U of Calgary (AB, Canada)
U of Calif, Los Angeles (CA)
U of Idaho (ID)
U of Manitoba (MB, Canada)
U of Minnesota, Twin Cities Campus (MN)
U of Mississippi (MS)
U of Missouri–Rolla (MO)
U of Nevada, Reno (NV)
U of North Dakota (ND)
U of Oklahoma (OK)
U of Saskatchewan (SK, Canada)
U of Toronto (ON, Canada)
U of Utah (UT)
U of Waterloo (ON, Canada)

GEOLOGICAL SCIENCES RELATED

Ohio U (OH)
San Diego State U (CA)
The U of Akron (OH)
U of Hawaii at Manoa (HI)
U of Miami (FL)
U of Nevada, Las Vegas (NV)
U of Pittsburgh (PA)
The U of Texas at Austin (TX)
U of Utah (UT)
U of Wyoming (WY)
Western Michigan U (MI)
Yale U (CT)

GEOLOGY

Abilene Christian U (TX)
Acadia U (NS, Canada)
Adams State Coll (CO)
Albion Coll (MI)
Alfred U (NY)
Allegheny Coll (PA)
Amherst Coll (MA)
Appalachian State U (NC)
Arizona State U (AZ)
Arkansas Tech U (AR)
Ashland U (OH)
Auburn U (AL)
Augustana Coll (IL)
Austin Peay State U (TN)
Baldwin-Wallace Coll (OH)
Ball State U (IN)
Bates Coll (ME)
Baylor U (TX)
Beloit Coll (WI)
Bemidji State U (MN)
Bloomsburg U of Pennsylvania (PA)
Boise State U (ID)
Boston Coll (MA)
Boston U (MA)
Bowdoin Coll (ME)
Bowling Green State U (OH)
Bradley U (IL)
Brandon U (MB, Canada)
Bridgewater State Coll (MA)
Brigham Young U (UT)
Brock U (ON, Canada)
Brooklyn Coll of the City U of NY (NY)
Brown U (RI)
Bryn Mawr Coll (PA)
Bucknell U (PA)
California Inst of Technology (CA)
California Lutheran U (CA)
California State Polytechnic U, Pomona (CA)
California State U, Bakersfield (CA)
California State U, Chico (CA)
California State U, Dominguez Hills (CA)
California State U, Fresno (CA)
California State U, Fullerton (CA)
California State U, Hayward (CA)
California State U, Long Beach (CA)
California State U, Los Angeles (CA)
California State U, Northridge (CA)
California State U, Sacramento (CA)
California State U, San Bernardino (CA)
California State U, Stanislaus (CA)
California U of Pennsylvania (PA)
Calvin Coll (MI)
Carleton Coll (MN)
Carleton U (ON, Canada)
Case Western Reserve U (OH)
Castleton State Coll (VT)
Centenary Coll of Louisiana (LA)
Central Michigan U (MI)
Central Missouri State U (MO)
Central Washington U (WA)
City Coll of the City U of NY (NY)
Clarion U of Pennsylvania (PA)
Clemson U (SC)
Cleveland State U (OH)
Colby Coll (ME)
Colgate U (NY)
Coll of Charleston (SC)
The Coll of William and Mary (VA)
The Coll of Wooster (OH)
The Colorado Coll (CO)
Colorado State U (CO)
Columbia Coll (MO)
Columbia Coll (NY)
Columbia U, School of General Studies (NY)
Columbus State U (GA)
Cornell Coll (IA)
Cornell U (NY)
Denison U (OH)
DePauw U (IN)
Dickinson Coll (PA)
Duke U (NC)
Earlham Coll (IN)
East Carolina U (NC)
Eastern Illinois U (IL)
Eastern Kentucky U (KY)
Eastern Michigan U (MI)
Eastern New Mexico U (NM)
Eastern Washington U (WA)
Edinboro U of Pennsylvania (PA)
Elizabeth City State U (NC)
The Evergreen State Coll (WA)
Excelsior Coll (NY)
Florida Atlantic U (FL)
Florida International U (FL)
Florida State U (FL)
Fort Hays State U (KS)
Fort Lewis Coll (CO)
Franklin and Marshall Coll (PA)
Furman U (SC)
George Mason U (VA)
The George Washington U (DC)
Georgia Southern U (GA)
Georgia Southwestern State U (GA)
Georgia State U (GA)
Grand Valley State U (MI)
Guilford Coll (NC)
Gustavus Adolphus Coll (MN)
Hamilton Coll (NY)
Hampshire Coll (MA)
Hanover Coll (IN)
Hardin-Simmons U (TX)
Hartwick Coll (NY)
Harvard U (MA)
Haverford Coll (PA)
Hobart and William Smith Colls (NY)
Hofstra U (NY)
Hope Coll (MI)
Howard U (DC)
Humboldt State U (CA)
Idaho State U (ID)
Illinois State U (IL)
Indiana State U (IN)
Indiana U Bloomington (IN)
Indiana U Northwest (IN)
Indiana U of Pennsylvania (PA)
Indiana U–Purdue U Fort Wayne (IN)
Indiana U–Purdue U Indianapolis (IN)
Iowa State U of Science and Technology (IA)
Jacksonville State U (AL)
James Madison U (VA)
Juniata Coll (PA)
Kansas State U (KS)
Keene State Coll (NH)
Kent State U (OH)
Kutztown U of Pennsylvania (PA)
Lafayette Coll (PA)
Lakehead U (ON, Canada)

Lake Superior State U (MI)
Lamar U (TX)
La Salle U (PA)
Laurentian U (ON, Canada)
Lawrence U (WI)
Lehman Coll of the City U of NY (NY)
Lewis-Clark State Coll (ID)
Lock Haven U of Pennsylvania (PA)
Long Island U, C.W. Post Campus (NY)
Long Island U, Southampton Coll, Friends World Program (NY)
Louisiana State U and A&M Coll (LA)
Louisiana Tech U (LA)
Macalester Coll (MN)
Marietta Coll (OH)
Marshall U (WV)
Mary Washington Coll (VA)
McMaster U (ON, Canada)
Memorial U of Newfoundland (NF, Canada)
Mercyhurst Coll (PA)
Mesa State Coll (CO)
Miami U (OH)
Michigan State U (MI)
Michigan Technological U (MI)
Middlebury Coll (VT)
Middle Tennessee State U (TN)
Midwestern State U (TX)
Millersville U of Pennsylvania (PA)
Millsaps Coll (MS)
Minot State U (ND)
Mississippi State U (MS)
Moravian Coll (PA)
Morehead State U (KY)
Mount Allison U (NB, Canada)
Mount Holyoke Coll (MA)
Mount Union Coll (OH)
Murray State U (KY)
Muskingum Coll (OH)
New Jersey City U (NJ)
New Mexico Inst of Mining and Technology (NM)
New Mexico State U (NM)
North Carolina State U (NC)
North Dakota State U (ND)
Northeastern U (MA)
Northern Arizona U (AZ)
Northern Illinois U (IL)
Northern Kentucky U (KY)
Northland Coll (WI)
Northwestern U (IL)
Northwest Missouri State U (MO)
Norwich U (VT)
Oberlin Coll (OH)
Occidental Coll (CA)
The Ohio State U (OH)
Ohio U (OH)
Ohio Wesleyan U (OH)
Oklahoma State U (OK)
Old Dominion U (VA)
Olivet Nazarene U (IL)
Oregon State U (OR)
Pacific Lutheran U (WA)
Penn State U Univ Park Campus (PA)
Plattsburgh State U of NY (NY)
Pomona Coll (CA)
Portland State U (OR)
Princeton U (NJ)
Purdue U (IN)
Queens Coll of the City U of NY (NY)
Queen's U at Kingston (ON, Canada)
Radford U (VA)
Rensselaer Polytechnic Inst (NY)
Rice U (TX)
The Richard Stockton Coll of New Jersey (NJ)
Rider U (NJ)
Rocky Mountain Coll (MT)
Rutgers, The State U of New Jersey, New Brunswick (NJ)
St. Francis Xavier U (NS, Canada)
St. Lawrence U (NY)
Saint Louis U (MO)
Saint Mary's U (NS, Canada)
St. Mary's U of San Antonio (TX)
St. Norbert Coll (WI)
Salem State Coll (MA)
Sam Houston State U (TX)
San Diego State U (CA)
San Francisco State U (CA)
San Jose State U (CA)
Sarah Lawrence Coll (NY)
Scripps Coll (CA)
Simon's Rock Coll of Bard (MA)
Skidmore Coll (NY)
Slippery Rock U of Pennsylvania (PA)
Smith Coll (MA)
Sonoma State U (CA)
South Dakota School of Mines and Technology (SD)
Southeast Missouri State U (MO)
Southern Illinois U Carbondale (IL)
Southern Methodist U (TX)
Southern Oregon U (OR)
Southern Utah U (UT)
Southwest Missouri State U (MO)
Stanford U (CA)
State U of NY at Albany (NY)
State U of NY at Binghamton (NY)
State U of NY at New Paltz (NY)
State U of NY at Oswego (NY)
State U of NY Coll at Brockport (NY)
State U of NY Coll at Buffalo (NY)
State U of NY Coll at Cortland (NY)
State U of NY Coll at Fredonia (NY)
State U of NY Coll at Geneseo (NY)
State U of NY Coll at Oneonta (NY)
State U of NY Coll at Potsdam (NY)
State U of West Georgia (GA)
Stephen F. Austin State U (TX)
State U of NY at Stony Brook (NY)
Sul Ross State U (TX)
Susquehanna U (PA)
Syracuse U (NY)
Tarleton State U (TX)
Temple U (PA)
Tennessee Technological U (TN)
Texas A&M U (TX)
Texas A&M U–Commerce (TX)
Texas A&M U–Corpus Christi (TX)
Texas A&M U–Kingsville (TX)
Texas Christian U (TX)
Texas Tech U (TX)
Towson U (MD)
Trinity U (TX)
Tufts U (MA)
Tulane U (LA)
Union Coll (NY)
Université de Montréal (QC, Canada)
Université Laval (QC, Canada)
State U of NY at Buffalo (NY)
The U of Akron (OH)
The U of Alabama (AL)
U of Alaska Fairbanks (AK)
U of Alberta (AB, Canada)
The U of Arizona (AZ)
U of Arkansas (AR)
U of Arkansas at Little Rock (AR)
The U of British Columbia (BC, Canada)
U of Calgary (AB, Canada)
U of Calif, Berkeley (CA)
U of Calif, Davis (CA)
U of Calif, Los Angeles (CA)
U of Calif, Riverside (CA)
U of Calif, Santa Barbara (CA)
U of Calif, Santa Cruz (CA)
U of Cincinnati (OH)
U of Colorado at Boulder (CO)
U of Colorado at Denver (CO)
U of Connecticut (CT)
U of Dayton (OH)
U of Delaware (DE)
U of Florida (FL)
U of Georgia (GA)
U of Hawaii at Hilo (HI)
U of Hawaii at Manoa (HI)
U of Houston (TX)
U of Idaho (ID)
U of Illinois at Chicago (IL)
U of Illinois at Urbana–Champaign (IL)
The U of Iowa (IA)
U of Kansas (KS)
U of Kentucky (KY)
U of Louisiana at Lafayette (LA)
U of Louisiana at Monroe (LA)
U of Maine (ME)
U of Maine at Farmington (ME)
U of Maine at Presque Isle (ME)
U of Manitoba (MB, Canada)
U of Maryland, Coll Park (MD)
U of Massachusetts Amherst (MA)
The U of Memphis (TN)
U of Miami (FL)
U of Michigan (MI)
U of Minnesota, Duluth (MN)
U of Minnesota, Morris (MN)
U of Minnesota, Twin Cities Campus (MN)
U of Mississippi (MS)
U of Missouri–Columbia (MO)
U of Missouri–Kansas City (MO)
U of Missouri–Rolla (MO)
The U of Montana–Missoula (MT)
Western Montana Coll of The U of Montana (MT)
U of Nebraska at Omaha (NE)
U of Nebraska–Lincoln (NE)
U of Nevada, Las Vegas (NV)
U of Nevada, Reno (NV)
U of New Hampshire (NH)
U of New Mexico (NM)
U of New Orleans (LA)
U of North Alabama (AL)
The U of North Carolina at Chapel Hill (NC)
The U of North Carolina at Charlotte (NC)
The U of North Carolina at Wilmington (NC)
U of North Dakota (ND)
U of Northern Iowa (IA)
U of Notre Dame (IN)
U of Oklahoma (OK)
U of Oregon (OR)
U of Ottawa (ON, Canada)
U of Pennsylvania (PA)
U of Pittsburgh (PA)
U of Pittsburgh at Bradford (PA)
U of Pittsburgh at Johnstown (PA)
U of Puget Sound (WA)
U of Regina (SK, Canada)
U of Rhode Island (RI)
U of Rochester (NY)
U of St. Thomas (MN)
U of Saskatchewan (SK, Canada)
U of South Alabama (AL)
U of South Carolina (SC)
U of Southern California (CA)
U of Southern Indiana (IN)
U of Southern Maine (ME)
U of Southern Mississippi (MS)
U of South Florida (FL)
The U of Tennessee (TN)
The U of Tennessee at Chattanooga (TN)
The U of Tennessee at Martin (TN)
The U of Texas at Arlington (TX)
The U of Texas at Austin (TX)
The U of Texas at Dallas (TX)
The U of Texas at El Paso (TX)
The U of Texas at San Antonio (TX)
The U of Texas of the Permian Basin (TX)
U of the Pacific (CA)
U of the South (TN)
U of Toledo (OH)
U of Toronto (ON, Canada)
U of Tulsa (OK)
U of Utah (UT)
U of Vermont (VT)
U of Victoria (BC, Canada)
U of Washington (WA)
U of Waterloo (ON, Canada)
The U of Western Ontario (ON, Canada)
U of Windsor (ON, Canada)
U of Wisconsin–Eau Claire (WI)
U of Wisconsin–Madison (WI)
U of Wisconsin–Milwaukee (WI)
U of Wisconsin–Oshkosh (WI)
U of Wisconsin–Parkside (WI)
U of Wisconsin–Platteville (WI)
U of Wisconsin–River Falls (WI)
U of Wyoming (WY)
Utah State U (UT)
Valparaiso U (IN)
Vanderbilt U (TN)
Vassar Coll (NY)
Virginia Polytechnic Inst and State U (VA)
Washington and Lee U (VA)
Washington State U (WA)
Wayne State U (MI)
Weber State U (UT)
Wellesley Coll (MA)
West Chester U of Pennsylvania (PA)
Western Illinois U (IL)
Western Kentucky U (KY)
Western Michigan U (MI)
Western State Coll of Colorado (CO)
Western Washington U (WA)
West Texas A&M U (TX)
West Virginia U (WV)
Wheaton Coll (IL)
Whitman Coll (WA)
Wichita State U (KS)
Williams Coll (MA)
Winona State U (MN)
Wittenberg U (OH)
Wright State U (OH)
York Coll of the City U of New York (NY)
Youngstown State U (OH)

GEOPHYSICAL ENGINEERING
Colorado School of Mines (CO)
Harvard U (MA)
Montana Tech of The U of Montana (MT)
New Jersey Inst of Technology (NJ)
Tufts U (MA)
U of Calif, Los Angeles (CA)
U of Saskatchewan (SK, Canada)
U of Toronto (ON, Canada)

GEOPHYSICS/SEISMOLOGY
Baylor U (TX)
Boise State U (ID)
Boston Coll (MA)
Bowling Green State U (OH)
Brown U (RI)
California Inst of Technology (CA)
California State U, Northridge (CA)
Eastern Michigan U (MI)
Hampshire Coll (MA)
Harvard U (MA)
Hope Coll (MI)
Kansas State U (KS)
McGill U (PQ, Canada)
Memorial U of Newfoundland (NF, Canada)
Michigan Technological U (MI)
New Mexico Inst of Mining and Technology (NM)
Oregon State U (OR)
Rice U (TX)
St. Lawrence U (NY)
Saint Louis U (MO)
San Jose State U (CA)
Southern Methodist U (TX)
Stanford U (CA)
State U of NY Coll at Fredonia (NY)
State U of NY Coll at Geneseo (NY)
Texas A&M U (TX)
Texas Tech U (TX)
Université de Sherbrooke (PQ, Canada)
The U of Akron (OH)
U of Alberta (AB, Canada)
The U of British Columbia (BC, Canada)
U of Calgary (AB, Canada)
U of Calif, Berkeley (CA)
U of Calif, Los Angeles (CA)
U of Calif, Riverside (CA)
U of Calif, Santa Barbara (CA)
U of Calif, Santa Cruz (CA)
U of Chicago (IL)
U of Delaware (DE)
U of Houston (TX)
U of Minnesota, Twin Cities Campus (MN)
U of Missouri–Rolla (MO)
U of Nevada, Reno (NV)
U of New Orleans (LA)
U of Oklahoma (OK)
U of Ottawa (ON, Canada)
U of Saskatchewan (SK, Canada)
U of South Carolina (SC)
The U of Texas at Austin (TX)
The U of Texas at El Paso (TX)
U of Toronto (ON, Canada)
U of Tulsa (OK)
U of Utah (UT)
U of Victoria (BC, Canada)
U of Washington (WA)
The U of Western Ontario (ON, Canada)
U of Wisconsin–Madison (WI)
Western Michigan U (MI)
Western Washington U (WA)

GEOTECHNICAL ENGINEERING
Montana Tech of The U of Montana (MT)
York U (ON, Canada)

GERMAN
Adrian Coll (MI)
Agnes Scott Coll (GA)
Albion Coll (MI)
Alfred U (NY)
Allegheny Coll (PA)
Alma Coll (MI)
American U (DC)
Amherst Coll (MA)
Anderson U (IN)
Angelo State U (TX)
Aquinas Coll (MI)
Arizona State U (AZ)
Arkansas Tech U (AR)
Auburn U (AL)
Augsburg Coll (MN)
Augustana Coll (IL)
Augustana Coll (SD)
Austin Coll (TX)
Baker U (KS)
Baldwin-Wallace Coll (OH)
Ball State U (IN)
Bard Coll (NY)
Barnard Coll (NY)
Bates Coll (ME)
Baylor U (TX)
Bellarmine U (KY)
Beloit Coll (WI)
Bemidji State U (MN)
Bennington Coll (VT)
Berea Coll (KY)
Berry Coll (GA)
Bethany Coll (WV)
Bethel Coll (KS)
Birmingham-Southern Coll (AL)
Bishop's U (PQ, Canada)
Bloomsburg U of Pennsylvania (PA)
Boise State U (ID)
Boston Coll (MA)
Boston U (MA)
Bowdoin Coll (ME)
Bowling Green State U (OH)
Bradley U (IL)
Brandeis U (MA)
Brigham Young U (UT)
Brock U (ON, Canada)
Brooklyn Coll of the City U of NY (NY)
Brown U (RI)
Bryn Mawr Coll (PA)
Bucknell U (PA)
Butler U (IN)
California Lutheran U (CA)
California State U, Chico (CA)
California State U, Fullerton (CA)
California State U, Long Beach (CA)
California State U, Northridge (CA)
California State U, Sacramento (CA)
California U of Pennsylvania (PA)
Calvin Coll (MI)
Canisius Coll (NY)
Carleton Coll (MN)
Carleton U (ON, Canada)
Carnegie Mellon U (PA)
Carthage Coll (WI)
Case Western Reserve U (OH)
The Catholic U of America (DC)
Centenary Coll of Louisiana (LA)
Central Coll (IA)
Central Connecticut State U (CT)
Central Michigan U (MI)
Central Missouri State U (MO)
Centre Coll (KY)
Christopher Newport U (VA)
Citadel, The Military Coll of South Carolina (SC)
Claremont McKenna Coll (CA)
Clark Atlanta U (GA)
Cleveland State U (OH)
Coe Coll (IA)
Colby Coll (ME)
Colgate U (NY)
Coll of Charleston (SC)
Coll of Saint Benedict (MN)
Coll of the Holy Cross (MA)
Coll of the Ozarks (MO)
The Coll of William and Mary (VA)
The Coll of Wooster (OH)
The Colorado Coll (CO)
Colorado State U (CO)
Columbia Coll (NY)
Columbia U, School of General Studies (NY)
Concordia Coll (MN)

Concordia U (NE)
Concordia U (QC, Canada)
Concordia U Wisconsin (WI)
Connecticut Coll (CT)
Cornell Coll (IA)
Cornell U (NY)
Creighton U (NE)
Dalhousie U (NS, Canada)
Dana Coll (NE)
Dartmouth Coll (NH)
Davidson Coll (NC)
Denison U (OH)
DePaul U (IL)
DePauw U (IN)
Dickinson Coll (PA)
Dillard U (LA)
Doane Coll (NE)
Dordt Coll (IA)
Drew U (NJ)
Drury U (MO)
Duke U (NC)
Earlham Coll (IN)
East Carolina U (NC)
Eastern Kentucky U (KY)
Eastern Mennonite U (VA)
Eastern Michigan U (MI)
Eckerd Coll (FL)
Edinboro U of Pennsylvania (PA)
Elizabethtown Coll (PA)
Elmhurst Coll (IL)
Emory U (GA)
Fairfield U (CT)
Florida Atlantic U (FL)
Florida International U (FL)
Florida State U (FL)
Fordham U (NY)
Fort Hays State U (KS)
Francis Marion U (SC)
Franklin and Marshall Coll (PA)
Furman U (SC)
Georgetown Coll (KY)
Georgetown U (DC)
The George Washington U (DC)
Georgia Southern U (GA)
Georgia State U (GA)
Gettysburg Coll (PA)
Gonzaga U (WA)
Gordon Coll (MA)
Goshen Coll (IN)
Grace Coll (IN)
Graceland U (IA)
Grand Valley State U (MI)
Grinnell Coll (IA)
Guilford Coll (NC)
Gustavus Adolphus Coll (MN)
Hamilton Coll (NY)
Hamline U (MN)
Hampden-Sydney Coll (VA)
Hanover Coll (IN)
Hardin-Simmons U (TX)
Hartwick Coll (NY)
Harvard U (MA)
Hastings Coll (NE)
Haverford Coll (PA)
Heidelberg Coll (OH)
Hendrix Coll (AR)
Hillsdale Coll (MI)
Hiram Coll (OH)
Hofstra U (NY)
Hollins U (VA)
Hope Coll (MI)
Howard U (DC)
Humboldt State U (CA)
Hunter Coll of the City U of NY (NY)
Idaho State U (ID)
Illinois Coll (IL)
Illinois State U (IL)
Illinois Wesleyan U (IL)
Immaculata Coll (PA)
Indiana State U (IN)
Indiana U Bloomington (IN)
Indiana U of Pennsylvania (PA)
Indiana U–Purdue U Fort Wayne (IN)
Indiana U–Purdue U Indianapolis (IN)
Indiana U South Bend (IN)
Indiana U Southeast (IN)
Iowa State U of Science and Technology (IA)
Ithaca Coll (NY)
Jacksonville State U (AL)
James Madison U (VA)
John Carroll U (OH)
Johns Hopkins U (MD)
Juniata Coll (PA)
Kalamazoo Coll (MI)
Kansas Wesleyan U (KS)
Kent State U (OH)
Kenyon Coll (OH)
Knox Coll (IL)
Lafayette Coll (PA)
Lake Erie Coll (OH)
Lake Forest Coll (IL)
Lakeland Coll (WI)
La Salle U (PA)
Lawrence U (WI)
Lebanon Valley Coll (PA)
Lehigh U (PA)
Lenoir-Rhyne Coll (NC)
Lewis & Clark Coll (OR)
Linfield Coll (OR)
Lipscomb U (TN)
Lock Haven U of Pennsylvania (PA)
Long Island U, C.W. Post Campus (NY)
Long Island U, Southampton Coll, Friends World Program (NY)
Longwood Coll (VA)
Louisiana State U and A&M Coll (LA)
Loyola Coll in Maryland (MD)
Loyola U Chicago (IL)
Loyola U New Orleans (LA)
Luther Coll (IA)
Lycoming Coll (PA)
Manchester Coll (IN)
Mansfield U of Pennsylvania (PA)
Marlboro Coll (VT)
Marquette U (WI)
Mary Baldwin Coll (VA)
Mary Washington Coll (VA)
Massachusetts Inst of Technology (MA)
McGill U (PQ, Canada)
McMaster U (ON, Canada)
Memorial U of Newfoundland (NF, Canada)
Mercer U (GA)
Mercyhurst Coll (PA)
Messiah Coll (PA)
Miami U (OH)
Michigan State U (MI)
Middlebury Coll (VT)
Millersville U of Pennsylvania (PA)
Millikin U (IL)
Millsaps Coll (MS)
Mills Coll (CA)
Minnesota State U, Mankato (MN)
Minot State U (ND)
Missouri Southern State Coll (MO)
Montclair State U (NJ)
Moravian Coll (PA)
Morehouse Coll (GA)
Mount Allison U (NB, Canada)
Mount Holyoke Coll (MA)
Mount Saint Mary's Coll and Seminary (MD)
Mount Saint Vincent U (NS, Canada)
Mount Union Coll (OH)
Muhlenberg Coll (PA)
Murray State U (KY)
Muskingum Coll (OH)
Nazareth Coll of Rochester (NY)
Nebraska Wesleyan U (NE)
Newberry Coll (SC)
New Coll of Florida (FL)
New York U (NY)
North Carolina State U (NC)
North Central Coll (IL)
Northeastern State U (OK)
Northeastern U (MA)
Northern Arizona U (AZ)
Northern Illinois U (IL)
Northern State U (SD)
Northwestern U (IL)
Oakland U (MI)
Oberlin Coll (OH)
The Ohio State U (OH)
Ohio U (OH)
Ohio Wesleyan U (OH)
Oklahoma Baptist U (OK)
Oklahoma City U (OK)
Oklahoma State U (OK)
Oral Roberts U (OK)
Oregon State U (OR)
Pacific Lutheran U (WA)
Pacific U (OR)
Penn State U Univ Park Campus (PA)
Pepperdine U, Malibu (CA)
Pitzer Coll (CA)
Pomona Coll (CA)
Portland State U (OR)
Presbyterian Coll (SC)
Princeton U (NJ)
Principia Coll (IL)
Purdue U Calumet (IN)
Queens Coll of the City U of NY (NY)
Queen's U at Kingston (ON, Canada)
Randolph-Macon Coll (VA)
Randolph-Macon Woman's Coll (VA)
Reed Coll (OR)
Rensselaer Polytechnic Inst (NY)
Rhodes Coll (TN)
Rice U (TX)
Rider U (NJ)
Ripon Coll (WI)
Rockford Coll (IL)
Rollins Coll (FL)
Rosemont Coll (PA)
Rutgers, The State U of New Jersey, New Brunswick (NJ)
St. Ambrose U (IA)
St. Cloud State U (MN)
St. John Fisher Coll (NY)
Saint John's U (MN)
Saint Joseph's U (PA)
St. Lawrence U (NY)
Saint Louis U (MO)
Saint Mary's Coll of California (CA)
Saint Mary's U (NS, Canada)
St. Norbert Coll (WI)
St. Olaf Coll (MN)
Salem Coll (NC)
Samford U (AL)
Sam Houston State U (TX)
San Diego State U (CA)
San Francisco State U (CA)
San Jose State U (CA)
Sarah Lawrence Coll (NY)
Scripps Coll (CA)
Seattle Pacific U (WA)
Seattle U (WA)
Simon's Rock Coll of Bard (MA)
Simpson Coll (IA)
Skidmore Coll (NY)
Smith Coll (MA)
Sonoma State U (CA)
South Dakota State U (SD)
Southeast Missouri State U (MO)
Southern Connecticut State U (CT)
Southern Illinois U Carbondale (IL)
Southern Methodist U (TX)
Southern Utah U (UT)
Southwestern U (TX)
Southwest Missouri State U (MO)
Southwest Texas State U (TX)
Stanford U (CA)
State U of NY at Binghamton (NY)
State U of NY at New Paltz (NY)
State U of NY at Oswego (NY)
State U of NY Coll at Cortland (NY)
Stetson U (FL)
State U of NY at Stony Brook (NY)
Susquehanna U (PA)
Swarthmore Coll (PA)
Sweet Briar Coll (VA)
Syracuse U (NY)
Temple U (PA)
Tennessee Technological U (TN)
Texas A&M U (TX)
Texas Southern U (TX)
Texas Tech U (TX)
Towson U (MD)
Trent U (ON, Canada)
Trinity Coll (CT)
Trinity U (TX)
Truman State U (MO)
Tufts U (MA)
Tulane U (LA)
Union Coll (NE)
United States Military Academy (NY)
Université de Montréal (QC, Canada)
State U of NY at Buffalo (NY)
The U of Akron (OH)
The U of Alabama (AL)
U of Alberta (AB, Canada)
The U of Arizona (AZ)
U of Arkansas (AR)
The U of British Columbia (BC, Canada)
U of Calgary (AB, Canada)
U of Calif, Berkeley (CA)
U of Calif, Davis (CA)
U of Calif, Irvine (CA)
U of Calif, Los Angeles (CA)
U of Calif, Riverside (CA)
U of Calif, San Diego (CA)
U of Calif, Santa Barbara (CA)
U of Calif, Santa Cruz (CA)
U of Central Oklahoma (OK)
U of Chicago (IL)
U of Cincinnati (OH)
U of Colorado at Boulder (CO)
U of Colorado at Denver (CO)
U of Connecticut (CT)
U of Dallas (TX)
U of Dayton (OH)
U of Delaware (DE)
U of Denver (CO)
U of Evansville (IN)
U of Florida (FL)
U of Georgia (GA)
U of Hawaii at Manoa (HI)
U of Houston (TX)
U of Idaho (ID)
U of Illinois at Chicago (IL)
U of Illinois at Urbana–Champaign (IL)
U of Indianapolis (IN)
The U of Iowa (IA)
U of Kansas (KS)
U of Kentucky (KY)
U of King's Coll (NS, Canada)
U of La Verne (CA)
The U of Lethbridge (AB, Canada)
U of Louisville (KY)
U of Maine (ME)
U of Manitoba (MB, Canada)
U of Maryland, Baltimore County (MD)
U of Maryland, Coll Park (MD)
U of Massachusetts Amherst (MA)
U of Massachusetts Boston (MA)
U of Miami (FL)
U of Michigan (MI)
U of Michigan–Dearborn (MI)
U of Michigan–Flint (MI)
U of Minnesota, Morris (MN)
U of Minnesota, Twin Cities Campus (MN)
U of Mississippi (MS)
U of Missouri–Columbia (MO)
U of Missouri–Kansas City (MO)
U of Missouri–St. Louis (MO)
The U of Montana–Missoula (MT)
U of Nebraska at Kearney (NE)
U of Nebraska at Omaha (NE)
U of Nebraska–Lincoln (NE)
U of Nevada, Las Vegas (NV)
U of Nevada, Reno (NV)
U of New Hampshire (NH)
U of New Mexico (NM)
The U of North Carolina at Asheville (NC)
The U of North Carolina at Chapel Hill (NC)
The U of North Carolina at Charlotte (NC)
The U of North Carolina at Greensboro (NC)
U of North Dakota (ND)
U of Northern Colorado (CO)
U of Northern Iowa (IA)
U of North Texas (TX)
U of Notre Dame (IN)
U of Oklahoma (OK)
U of Oregon (OR)
U of Ottawa (ON, Canada)
U of Pennsylvania (PA)
U of Pittsburgh (PA)
U of Prince Edward Island (PE, Canada)
U of Puget Sound (WA)
U of Redlands (CA)
U of Regina (SK, Canada)
U of Rhode Island (RI)
U of Richmond (VA)
U of Rochester (NY)
U of St. Thomas (MN)
U of Saskatchewan (SK, Canada)
The U of Scranton (PA)
U of South Carolina (SC)
U of South Dakota (SD)
U of Southern California (CA)
U of Southern Indiana (IN)
U of South Florida (FL)
The U of Tennessee (TN)
The U of Texas at Arlington (TX)
The U of Texas at Austin (TX)
The U of Texas at El Paso (TX)
The U of Texas at San Antonio (TX)
U of the Pacific (CA)
U of the South (TN)
U of Toledo (OH)
U of Toronto (ON, Canada)
U of Tulsa (OK)
U of Utah (UT)
U of Vermont (VT)
U of Victoria (BC, Canada)
U of Virginia (VA)
U of Washington (WA)
U of Waterloo (ON, Canada)
The U of Western Ontario (ON, Canada)
U of Windsor (ON, Canada)
U of Wisconsin–Eau Claire (WI)
U of Wisconsin–Green Bay (WI)
U of Wisconsin–La Crosse (WI)
U of Wisconsin–Madison (WI)
U of Wisconsin–Milwaukee (WI)
U of Wisconsin–Oshkosh (WI)
U of Wisconsin–Parkside (WI)
U of Wisconsin–Platteville (WI)
U of Wisconsin–River Falls (WI)
U of Wisconsin–Stevens Point (WI)
U of Wisconsin–Whitewater (WI)
U of Wyoming (WY)
Ursinus Coll (PA)
Utah State U (UT)
Valparaiso U (IN)
Vanderbilt U (TN)
Vassar Coll (NY)
Villanova U (PA)
Virginia Polytechnic Inst and State U (VA)
Virginia Wesleyan Coll (VA)
Wabash Coll (IN)
Wake Forest U (NC)
Walla Walla Coll (WA)
Wartburg Coll (IA)
Washburn U of Topeka (KS)
Washington & Jefferson Coll (PA)
Washington and Lee U (VA)
Washington Coll (MD)
Washington State U (WA)
Washington U in St. Louis (MO)
Wayne State Coll (NE)
Wayne State U (MI)
Weber State U (UT)
Webster U (MO)
Wellesley Coll (MA)
Wells Coll (NY)
Wesleyan U (CT)
West Chester U of Pennsylvania (PA)
Western Carolina U (NC)
Western Kentucky U (KY)
Western Maryland Coll (MD)
Western Michigan U (MI)
Western Washington U (WA)
Westminster Coll (PA)
Wheaton Coll (IL)
Wheaton Coll (MA)
Whitman Coll (WA)
Wilfrid Laurier U (ON, Canada)
Willamette U (OR)
Williams Coll (MA)
Winona State U (MN)
Wittenberg U (OH)
Wofford Coll (SC)
Wright State U (OH)
Xavier U (OH)
Yale U (CT)
York U (ON, Canada)

GERMAN LANGUAGE EDUCATION

Anderson U (IN)
Baylor U (TX)
Berea Coll (KY)
Berry Coll (GA)
Bridgewater Coll (VA)
Brigham Young U (UT)
Canisius Coll (NY)
The Catholic U of America (DC)
Central Michigan U (MI)
Central Missouri State U (MO)
Colorado State U (CO)
Concordia Coll (MN)
Duquesne U (PA)
East Carolina U (NC)
Eastern Mennonite U (VA)
Eastern Michigan U (MI)
Elmhurst Coll (IL)
Georgia Southern U (GA)
Grace Coll (IN)
Hardin-Simmons U (TX)
Hofstra U (NY)
Indiana U Bloomington (IN)
Indiana U–Purdue U Fort Wayne (IN)
Indiana U–Purdue U Indianapolis (IN)

Indiana U South Bend (IN)
Ithaca Coll (NY)
Juniata Coll (PA)
Luther Coll (IA)
Mansfield U of Pennsylvania (PA)
Messiah Coll (PA)
Minot State U (ND)
Ohio U (OH)
Oklahoma Baptist U (OK)
Oral Roberts U (OK)
St. Ambrose U (IA)
San Diego State U (CA)
Southwest Missouri State U (MO)
The U of Akron (OH)
The U of Arizona (AZ)
U of Illinois at Chicago (IL)
U of Illinois at Urbana–Champaign (IL)
The U of Iowa (IA)
U of Minnesota, Duluth (MN)
U of Nebraska–Lincoln (NE)
The U of North Carolina at Charlotte (NC)
U of North Texas (TX)
The U of Tennessee at Martin (TN)
U of Utah (UT)
U of Windsor (ON, Canada)
U of Wisconsin–River Falls (WI)
Washington U in St. Louis (MO)
Weber State U (UT)
Western Carolina U (NC)
Youngstown State U (OH)

GERONTOLOGICAL SERVICES

Bowling Green State U (OH)
Mount Saint Vincent U (NS, Canada)
Ohio U (OH)
Saint Mary-of-the-Woods Coll (IN)
St. Thomas U (NB, Canada)
U of Northern Colorado (CO)

GERONTOLOGY

Alfred U (NY)
Alma Coll (MI)
Avila Coll (MO)
Bethune-Cookman Coll (FL)
Bishop's U (PQ, Canada)
Bowling Green State U (OH)
California State U, Dominguez Hills (CA)
California State U, Hayward (CA)
California State U, Northridge (CA)
California State U, Sacramento (CA)
California U of Pennsylvania (PA)
Case Western Reserve U (OH)
Cedar Crest Coll (PA)
Central Washington U (WA)
Chestnut Hill Coll (PA)
Coll of Mount St. Joseph (OH)
Coll of the Holy Cross (MA)
Coll of the Ozarks (MO)
Dominican U (IL)
Felician Coll (NJ)
Framingham State Coll (MA)
Gwynedd-Mercy Coll (PA)
Iona Coll (NY)
Ithaca Coll (NY)
John Carroll U (OH)
King's Coll (PA)
Lindenwood U (MO)
Long Island U, Southampton Coll, Friends World Program (NY)
Lourdes Coll (OH)
Lynn U (FL)
Mars Hill Coll (NC)
McMaster U (ON, Canada)
Mercy Coll (NY)
Mount St. Mary's Coll (CA)
Mount Saint Vincent U (NS, Canada)
National-Louis U (IL)
Nazareth Coll of Rochester (NY)
Pontifical Catholic U of Puerto Rico (PR)
Quinnipiac U (CT)
Roosevelt U (IL)
St. Cloud State U (MN)
Saint Mary-of-the-Woods Coll (IN)
St. Thomas U (NB, Canada)
San Diego State U (CA)
Shaw U (NC)
Sojourner-Douglass Coll (MD)
Southeastern Oklahoma State U (OK)
Southwest Missouri State U (MO)
Springfield Coll (MA)
State U of NY Coll at Brockport (NY)
State U of NY Coll at Fredonia (NY)
State U of NY Coll at Oneonta (NY)
Stephen F. Austin State U (TX)
Thomas Edison State Coll (NJ)
Towson U (MD)
The U of Akron (OH)
U of Arkansas at Pine Bluff (AR)
U of Evansville (IN)
U of Guelph (ON, Canada)
U of Hawaii at Manoa (HI)
U of Massachusetts Boston (MA)
U of Missouri–St. Louis (MO)
U of Nebraska at Omaha (NE)
U of Nevada, Las Vegas (NV)
The U of North Carolina at Greensboro (NC)
U of North Texas (TX)
The U of Scranton (PA)
U of Southern California (CA)
U of South Florida (FL)
U of Windsor (ON, Canada)
Wagner Coll (NY)
Weber State U (UT)
Western Michigan U (MI)
Wichita State U (KS)
Winston-Salem State U (NC)
York Coll of the City U of New York (NY)
York U (ON, Canada)

GRAPHIC DESIGN/COMMERCIAL ART/ILLUSTRATION

Abilene Christian U (TX)
Academy of Art Coll (CA)
Alberta Coll of Art & Design (AB, Canada)
Albertus Magnus Coll (CT)
Alfred U (NY)
American Academy of Art (IL)
American InterContinental U (CA)
American InterContinental U, Atlanta (GA)
American U (DC)
Anderson Coll (SC)
Anderson U (IN)
Andrews U (MI)
Appalachian State U (NC)
Arcadia U (PA)
Arizona State U (AZ)
Arkansas State U (AR)
Art Academy of Cincinnati (OH)
Art Center Coll of Design (CA)
The Art Inst of Atlanta (GA)
The Art Inst of Boston at Lesley U (MA)
The Art Inst of California (CA)
The Art Inst of California-San Francisco (CA)
The Art Inst of Colorado (CO)
The Art Inst of Philadelphia (PA)
The Art Inst of Phoenix (AZ)
The Art Inst of Portland (OR)
Art Inst of Southern California (CA)
The Art Inst of Washington (VA)
The Art Insts International Minnesota (MN)
Ashland U (OH)
Atlanta Coll of Art (GA)
Auburn U (AL)
Avila Coll (MO)
Baker Coll of Flint (MI)
Baker Coll of Owosso (MI)
Ball State U (IN)
Barton Coll (NC)
Becker Coll (MA)
Bellevue U (NE)
Bemidji State U (MN)
Benedict Coll (SC)
Biola U (CA)
Black Hills State U (SD)
Bluffton Coll (OH)
Boise State U (ID)
Boston U (MA)
Brenau U (GA)
Brescia U (KY)
Briar Cliff U (IA)
Bridgewater State Coll (MA)
Brigham Young U (UT)
Buena Vista U (IA)
Cabrini Coll (PA)
California Coll of Arts and Crafts (CA)
California Inst of the Arts (CA)
California Polytechnic State U, San Luis Obispo (CA)
California State Polytechnic U, Pomona (CA)
California State U, Dominguez Hills (CA)
California State U, Fresno (CA)
California State U, Fullerton (CA)
California State U, Hayward (CA)
California State U, Long Beach (CA)
California State U, Northridge (CA)
California State U, San Bernardino (CA)
Campbell U (NC)
Cardinal Stritch U (WI)
Carnegie Mellon U (PA)
Carroll Coll (WI)
Carson-Newman Coll (TN)
Carthage Coll (WI)
Centenary Coll (NJ)
Central Michigan U (MI)
Central Missouri State U (MO)
Champlain Coll (VT)
Chapman U (CA)
Chatham Coll (PA)
Chicago State U (IL)
Chowan Coll (NC)
Clark U (MA)
The Cleveland Inst of Art (OH)
Cogswell Polytechnical Coll (CA)
Coker Coll (SC)
Colby-Sawyer Coll (NH)
Ctr for Creative Studies—Coll of Art and Design (MI)
Coll of Mount St. Joseph (OH)
The Coll of New Jersey (NJ)
The Coll of Saint Rose (NY)
The Coll of Southeastern Europe, The American U of Athens(Greece)
Coll of Visual Arts (MN)
Colorado State U (CO)
Columbia Coll (MO)
Columbia Coll (SC)
Columbia Coll Chicago (IL)
Columbus Coll of Art and Design (OH)
Concord Coll (WV)
Concordia U (IL)
Concordia U (NE)
Concordia U (QC, Canada)
Concordia U Wisconsin (WI)
Cooper Union for the Advancement of Science & Art (NY)
Corcoran Coll of Art and Design (DC)
Cornish Coll of the Arts (WA)
Creighton U (NE)
Curry Coll (MA)
Daemen Coll (NY)
DePaul U (IL)
Dominican U (IL)
Dordt Coll (IA)
Drake U (IA)
Drexel U (PA)
Eastern Kentucky U (KY)
Edgewood Coll (WI)
Elms Coll (MA)
Emmanuel Coll (MA)
Endicott Coll (MA)
Escuela de Artes Plasticas de Puerto Rico (PR)
Fairmont State Coll (WV)
Fashion Inst of Technology (NY)
Felician Coll (NJ)
Fitchburg State Coll (MA)
Flagler Coll (FL)
Florida A&M U (FL)
Florida Southern Coll (FL)
Florida State U (FL)
Fontbonne U (MO)
Fordham U (NY)
Fort Hays State U (KS)
Franklin Pierce Coll (NH)
Freed-Hardeman U (TN)
Gallaudet U (DC)
Georgian Court Coll (NJ)
Georgia Southwestern State U (GA)
Grace Coll (IN)
Graceland U (IA)
Grand Canyon U (AZ)
Grand Valley State U (MI)
Grand View Coll (IA)
Hampshire Coll (MA)
Hampton U (VA)
Harding U (AR)
Howard U (DC)
Huntington Coll (IN)
The Illinois Inst of Art (IL)
Illinois Wesleyan U (IL)
Indiana U Bloomington (IN)
Indiana U–Purdue U Fort Wayne (IN)
International Academy of Design & Technology (FL)
International Business Coll, Fort Wayne (IN)
Iowa State U of Science and Technology (IA)
Iowa Wesleyan Coll (IA)
John Brown U (AR)
Judson Coll (IL)
Kansas City Art Inst (MO)
Keene State Coll (NH)
Kendall Coll of Art and Design of Ferris State U (MI)
Kent State U (OH)
Kutztown U of Pennsylvania (PA)
Lamar U (TX)
Lambuth U (TN)
La Roche Coll (PA)
La Salle U (PA)
Lasell Coll (MA)
Lewis U (IL)
Limestone Coll (SC)
Lipscomb U (TN)
Long Island U, C.W. Post Campus (NY)
Long Island U, Southampton Coll (NY)
Longwood Coll (VA)
Louisiana Coll (LA)
Louisiana Tech U (LA)
Loyola U New Orleans (LA)
Lubbock Christian U (TX)
Lycoming Coll (PA)
Lyndon State Coll (VT)
Lynn U (FL)
Maharishi U of Management (IA)
Maine Coll of Art (ME)
Marietta Coll (OH)
Mary Baldwin Coll (VA)
Maryland Inst, Coll of Art (MD)
Marymount U (VA)
Maryville U of Saint Louis (MO)
Massachusetts Coll of Art (MA)
Memphis Coll of Art (TN)
Mercy Coll (NY)
Meredith Coll (NC)
MidAmerica Nazarene U (KS)
Millikin U (IL)
Milwaukee Inst of Art and Design (WI)
Minneapolis Coll of Art and Design (MN)
Minnesota State U, Mankato (MN)
Minnesota State U Moorhead (MN)
Mississippi Coll (MS)
Missouri Southern State Coll (MO)
Missouri Western State Coll (MO)
Monmouth U (NJ)
Montana State U–Northern (MT)
Montserrat Coll of Art (MA)
Moore Coll of Art and Design (PA)
Moravian Coll (PA)
Morningside Coll (IA)
Mount Ida Coll (MA)
Mount Mary Coll (WI)
Mount Olive Coll (NC)
Nazareth Coll of Rochester (NY)
New Mexico Highlands U (NM)
New World School of the Arts (FL)
New York Inst of Technology (NY)
New York U (NY)
North Carolina State U (NC)
Northeastern State U (OK)
Northeastern U (MA)
Northern Kentucky U (KY)
Northern Michigan U (MI)
Northwest Coll of Art (WA)
Northwestern Coll (MN)
Northwest Missouri State U (MO)
Northwest Nazarene U (ID)
Notre Dame de Namur U (CA)
Nova Scotia Coll of Art and Design (NS, Canada)
Ohio Northern U (OH)
The Ohio State U (OH)
Ohio U (OH)
Oklahoma Christian U of Science and Arts (OK)
Oklahoma City U (OK)
Oklahoma State U (OK)
Olivet Coll (MI)
Olivet Nazarene U (IL)
O'More Coll of Design (TN)
Oral Roberts U (OK)
Otis Coll of Art and Design (CA)
Pacific Northwest Coll of Art (OR)
Paier Coll of Art, Inc. (CT)
Park U (MO)
Parsons School of Design, New School U (NY)
Pennsylvania Coll of Technology (PA)
Pennsylvania School of Art & Design (PA)
Penn State U Univ Park Campus (PA)
Peru State Coll (NE)
Philadelphia U (PA)
Pittsburg State U (KS)
Platt Coll (CO)
Plymouth State Coll (NH)
Point Loma Nazarene U (CA)
Portland State U (OR)
Pratt Inst (NY)
Rhode Island School of Design (RI)
Ringling School of Art and Design (FL)
Rivier Coll (NH)
Roberts Wesleyan Coll (NY)
Rochester Inst of Technology (NY)
Rocky Mountain Coll of Art & Design (CO)
Rowan U (NJ)
Rutgers, The State U of New Jersey, New Brunswick (NJ)
Sacred Heart U (CT)
St. Cloud State U (MN)
St. John's U (NY)
Saint Mary's U of Minnesota (MN)
St. Norbert Coll (WI)
St. Thomas Aquinas Coll (NY)
Salem State Coll (MA)
Samford U (AL)
Sam Houston State U (TX)
San Jose State U (CA)
Savannah Coll of Art and Design (GA)
School of the Art Inst of Chicago (IL)
School of the Museum of Fine Arts (MA)
School of Visual Arts (NY)
Schreiner U (TX)
Seton Hall U (NJ)
Seton Hill Coll (PA)
Simmons Coll (MA)
Simpson Coll (IA)
Southern Connecticut State U (CT)
Southwest Baptist U (MO)
Southwestern Oklahoma State U (OK)
Southwest Texas State U (TX)
Spring Hill Coll (AL)
State U of NY at Farmingdale (NY)
State U of NY at New Paltz (NY)
State U of NY at Oswego (NY)
State U of NY Coll at Buffalo (NY)
State U of NY Coll at Fredonia (NY)
Suffolk U (MA)
Syracuse U (NY)
Taylor U (IN)
Temple U (PA)
Texas A&M U–Commerce (TX)
Texas Christian U (TX)
Texas Tech U (TX)
Trinity Christian Coll (IL)
Truman State U (MO)
Union Coll (NE)
Université Laval (QC, Canada)
U of Advancing Computer Technology (AZ)
The U of Akron (OH)
U of Bridgeport (CT)
U of Central Oklahoma (OK)
U of Cincinnati (OH)
U of Dayton (OH)
U of Delaware (DE)
U of Denver (CO)
U of Evansville (IN)
U of Florida (FL)
U of Hartford (CT)
U of Illinois at Chicago (IL)
U of Illinois at Urbana–Champaign (IL)
U of Indianapolis (IN)
U of Massachusetts Dartmouth (MA)
U of Miami (FL)
U of Michigan (MI)
U of Minnesota, Duluth (MN)

U of Minnesota, Twin Cities Campus (MN)
U of Missouri–St. Louis (MO)
U of Montevallo (AL)
U of Oregon (OR)
U of Saint Francis (IN)
U of San Francisco (CA)
U of Sioux Falls (SD)
U of South Dakota (SD)
The U of Tennessee (TN)
The U of Tennessee at Martin (TN)
The U of Texas at El Paso (TX)
The U of the Arts (PA)
U of the Incarnate Word (TX)
U of the Pacific (CA)
U of Washington (WA)
U of Wisconsin–Platteville (WI)
U of Wisconsin–Stevens Point (WI)
Upper Iowa U (IA)
Villa Julie Coll (MD)
Viterbo U (WI)
Walla Walla Coll (WA)
Wartburg Coll (IA)
Washington U in St. Louis (MO)
Watkins Coll of Art and Design (TN)
Waynesburg Coll (PA)
Wayne State Coll (NE)
Weber State U (UT)
Webster U (MO)
Western Connecticut State U (CT)
Western Kentucky U (KY)
Western Michigan U (MI)
Western State Coll of Colorado (CO)
Western Washington U (WA)
Westfield State Coll (MA)
West Liberty State Coll (WV)
West Texas A&M U (TX)
West Virginia Wesleyan Coll (WV)
White Pines Coll (NH)
Wichita State U (KS)
William Paterson U of New Jersey (NJ)
William Woods U (MO)
Winona State U (MN)
Wittenberg U (OH)
Woodbury U (CA)
York Coll of Pennsylvania (PA)
York U (ON, Canada)
Youngstown State U (OH)

GRAPHIC/PRINTING EQUIPMENT
Andrews U (MI)
Appalachian State U (NC)
Arkansas State U (AR)
California Polytechnic State U, San Luis Obispo (CA)
Central Missouri State U (MO)
Chowan Coll (NC)
Fairmont State Coll (WV)
Ferris State U (MI)
Florida A&M U (FL)
Georgia Southern U (GA)
Indiana State U (IN)
Kean U (NJ)
Murray State U (KY)
Pennsylvania Coll of Technology (PA)
Pittsburg State U (KS)
Rochester Inst of Technology (NY)
Southwest Texas State U (TX)
Texas A&M U–Commerce (TX)
U of the District of Columbia (DC)
West Virginia U Inst of Technology (WV)

GREEK (ANCIENT AND MEDIEVAL)
Amherst Coll (MA)
Asbury Coll (KY)
Bard Coll (NY)
Barnard Coll (NY)
Baylor U (TX)
Boston U (MA)
Brandeis U (MA)
Brock U (ON, Canada)
Bryn Mawr Coll (PA)
Calvary Bible Coll and Theological Seminary (MO)
Carleton Coll (MN)
Columbia Coll (NY)
Dartmouth Coll (NH)
Dickinson Coll (PA)
Duke U (NC)
Duquesne U (PA)
Elmira Coll (NY)
Franklin and Marshall Coll (PA)
Hobart and William Smith Colls (NY)
Hunter Coll of the City U of NY (NY)
Indiana U Bloomington (IN)
Loyola U Chicago (IL)
Miami U (OH)
Mount Allison U (NB, Canada)
Multnomah Bible Coll and Biblical Seminary (OR)
New Coll of Florida (FL)
Ohio U (OH)
Randolph-Macon Coll (VA)
Randolph-Macon Woman's Coll (VA)
Rice U (TX)
Rutgers, The State U of New Jersey, New Brunswick (NJ)
Saint Louis U (MO)
St. Olaf Coll (MN)
Samford U (AL)
Santa Clara U (CA)
Smith Coll (MA)
Swarthmore Coll (PA)
Sweet Briar Coll (VA)
U of Calif, Berkeley (CA)
U of Calif, Santa Cruz (CA)
U of Chicago (IL)
U of Georgia (GA)
U of Hawaii at Manoa (HI)
U of Nebraska–Lincoln (NE)
U of Notre Dame (IN)
U of St. Thomas (MN)
The U of Scranton (PA)
U of Southern California (CA)
The U of Texas at Austin (TX)
U of Vermont (VT)
U of Victoria (BC, Canada)
U of Washington (WA)
The U of Western Ontario (ON, Canada)
Wake Forest U (NC)
Washington U in St. Louis (MO)
Wellesley Coll (MA)
Yale U (CT)

GREEK (MODERN)
Ball State U (IN)
Bard Coll (NY)
Belmont U (TN)
Boise Bible Coll (ID)
Boston U (MA)
Brooklyn Coll of the City U of NY (NY)
Butler U (IN)
Calvin Coll (MI)
Carleton U (ON, Canada)
Claremont McKenna Coll (CA)
Colgate U (NY)
The Coll of William and Mary (VA)
The Coll of Wooster (OH)
Columbia Coll (NY)
Concordia U Wisconsin (WI)
Cornell Coll (IA)
Cornell U (NY)
Creighton U (NE)
DePauw U (IN)
Emory U (GA)
Florida State U (FL)
Fordham U (NY)
Furman U (SC)
Gettysburg Coll (PA)
Hamilton Coll (NY)
Hampden-Sydney Coll (VA)
Harvard U (MA)
Haverford Coll (PA)
John Carroll U (OH)
Kenyon Coll (OH)
La Salle U (PA)
Lehman Coll of the City U of NY (NY)
Long Island U, Southampton Coll, Friends World Program (NY)
Loyola Marymount U (CA)
Luther Coll (IA)
Macalester Coll (MN)
Marlboro Coll (VT)
Memorial U of Newfoundland (NF, Canada)
Monmouth Coll (IL)
Mount Holyoke Coll (MA)
New York U (NY)
Oberlin Coll (OH)
The Ohio State U (OH)
Queens Coll of the City U of NY (NY)
Queen's U at Kingston (ON, Canada)
Rhodes Coll (TN)
Rockford Coll (IL)
Saint Mary's Coll of California (CA)
Southern Wesleyan U (SC)
Syracuse U (NY)
Trent U (ON, Canada)
Tufts U (MA)
Tulane U (LA)
U of Alberta (AB, Canada)
U of Calif, Los Angeles (CA)
The U of Iowa (IA)
U of Manitoba (MB, Canada)
U of Michigan (MI)
U of Minnesota, Twin Cities Campus (MN)
U of New Hampshire (NH)
U of Oregon (OR)
U of Richmond (VA)
U of Saskatchewan (SK, Canada)
The U of Tennessee at Chattanooga (TN)
U of the South (TN)
U of Toronto (ON, Canada)
U of Utah (UT)
U of Windsor (ON, Canada)
U of Wisconsin–Madison (WI)
U of Wisconsin–Milwaukee (WI)
Ursinus Coll (PA)
Wabash Coll (IN)
Wilfrid Laurier U (ON, Canada)
Wright State U (OH)
York U (ON, Canada)

HEALTH AIDE
Campbell U (NC)

HEALTH EDUCATION
Abilene Christian U (TX)
Anderson U (IN)
Appalachian State U (NC)
Aquinas Coll (MI)
Arkansas State U (AR)
Armstrong Atlantic State U (GA)
Ashland U (OH)
Auburn U (AL)
Augsburg Coll (MN)
Austin Peay State U (TN)
Averett U (VA)
Baldwin-Wallace Coll (OH)
Ball State U (IN)
Baylor U (TX)
Belmont U (TN)
Bemidji State U (MN)
Berry Coll (GA)
Bethel Coll (MN)
Bluffton Coll (OH)
Bowling Green State U (OH)
Briar Cliff U (IA)
Bridgewater State Coll (MA)
California State U, Chico (CA)
California State U, Northridge (CA)
California State U, San Bernardino (CA)
Campbellsville U (KY)
Capital U (OH)
Carroll Coll (WI)
Cedarville U (OH)
Centenary Coll of Louisiana (LA)
Central Michigan U (MI)
Central State U (OH)
Central Washington U (WA)
Chicago State U (IL)
Christopher Newport U (VA)
Clark Atlanta U (GA)
Coll of Mount Saint Vincent (NY)
Concord Coll (WV)
Concordia Coll (MN)
Concordia U (MN)
Concordia U (NE)
Cumberland Coll (KY)
Curry Coll (MA)
Dalhousie U (NS, Canada)
Davis & Elkins Coll (WV)
Defiance Coll (OH)
Delaware State U (DE)
Dillard U (LA)
East Carolina U (NC)
Eastern Illinois U (IL)
Eastern Kentucky U (KY)
Eastern Mennonite U (VA)
Eastern Washington U (WA)
East Stroudsburg U of Pennsylvania (PA)
Elon U (NC)
Emporia State U (KS)
Fayetteville State U (NC)
Florida A&M U (FL)
Florida International U (FL)
Florida State U (FL)
Fort Valley State U (GA)
Freed-Hardeman U (TN)
Friends U (KS)
Gardner-Webb U (NC)
George Fox U (OR)
George Mason U (VA)
Georgia Coll and State U (GA)
Graceland U (IA)
Gustavus Adolphus Coll (MN)
Gwynedd-Mercy Coll (PA)
Hamline U (MN)
Hampton U (VA)
Heidelberg Coll (OH)
Hofstra U (NY)
Hunter Coll of the City U of NY (NY)
Idaho State U (ID)
Illinois State U (IL)
Indiana State U (IN)
Indiana U–Purdue U Indianapolis (IN)
Iowa State U of Science and Technology (IA)
Ithaca Coll (NY)
Jackson State U (MS)
Jacksonville State U (AL)
John Brown U (AR)
Johnson C. Smith U (NC)
Kansas Wesleyan U (KS)
Keene State Coll (NH)
Kennesaw State U (GA)
Kent State U (OH)
Lamar U (TX)
Lee U (TN)
Lehman Coll of the City U of NY (NY)
Liberty U (VA)
Lincoln Memorial U (TN)
Lincoln U (PA)
Lipscomb U (TN)
Lock Haven U of Pennsylvania (PA)
Long Island U, C.W. Post Campus (NY)
Longwood Coll (VA)
Louisiana Coll (LA)
Luther Coll (IA)
Lynchburg Coll (VA)
Malone Coll (OH)
Manchester Coll (IN)
Marywood U (PA)
Mayville State U (ND)
Miami U (OH)
MidAmerica Nazarene U (KS)
Middle Tennessee State U (TN)
Minnesota State U, Mankato (MN)
Minnesota State U Moorhead (MN)
Missouri Baptist Coll (MO)
Missouri Valley Coll (MO)
Montana State U–Billings (MT)
Montclair State U (NJ)
Morehead State U (KY)
Morgan State U (MD)
Morris Brown Coll (GA)
Mount Vernon Nazarene U (OH)
Murray State U (KY)
Muskingum Coll (OH)
New Mexico Highlands U (NM)
Nicholls State U (LA)
North Carolina Ag and Tech State U (NC)
North Carolina Central U (NC)
North Central Coll (IL)
Northeastern State U (OK)
Northern Arizona U (AZ)
Northern Illinois U (IL)
Northern Michigan U (MI)
Northern State U (SD)
Northwestern Oklahoma State U (OK)
Northwest Missouri State U (MO)
Ohio Northern U (OH)
Ohio Wesleyan U (OH)
Otterbein Coll (OH)
Peru State Coll (NE)
Pittsburg State U (KS)
Pontifical Catholic U of Puerto Rico (PR)
Portland State U (OR)
Queen's U at Kingston (ON, Canada)
Radford U (VA)
Rhode Island Coll (RI)
Rocky Mountain Coll (MT)
St. Ambrose U (IA)
St. Cloud State U (MN)
Saint Mary's Coll of California (CA)
Salem State Coll (MA)
Salisbury U (MD)
San Francisco State U (CA)
Slippery Rock U of Pennsylvania (PA)
South Carolina State U (SC)
Southeastern Oklahoma State U (OK)
Southern Illinois U Carbondale (IL)
Southern Illinois U Edwardsville (IL)
Southern Nazarene U (OK)
Southern Oregon U (OR)
Southwest State U (MN)
Springfield Coll (MA)
State U of NY Coll at Brockport (NY)
State U of NY Coll at Cortland (NY)
Syracuse U (NY)
Tabor Coll (KS)
Temple U (PA)
Tennessee State U (TN)
Tennessee Technological U (TN)
Texas A&M U (TX)
Texas A&M U–Commerce (TX)
Texas A&M U–Kingsville (TX)
Texas Southern U (TX)
Touro U International (CA)
Troy State U (AL)
Union Coll (KY)
The U of Akron (OH)
The U of Alabama at Birmingham (AL)
The U of Arizona (AZ)
U of Arkansas at Little Rock (AR)
U of Central Arkansas (AR)
U of Cincinnati (OH)
U of Dayton (OH)
U of Delaware (DE)
U of Florida (FL)
U of Georgia (GA)
U of Hawaii at Manoa (HI)
The U of Iowa (IA)
U of Kansas (KS)
U of Kentucky (KY)
The U of Lethbridge (AB, Canada)
U of Maine (ME)
U of Maine at Farmington (ME)
U of Maine at Presque Isle (ME)
U of Maryland, Coll Park (MD)
U of Massachusetts Lowell (MA)
U of Minnesota, Duluth (MN)
The U of Montana–Missoula (MT)
Western Montana Coll of The U of Montana (MT)
U of Nebraska at Omaha (NE)
U of Nebraska–Lincoln (NE)
U of Nevada, Las Vegas (NV)
U of Nevada, Reno (NV)
U of New Mexico (NM)
The U of North Carolina at Greensboro (NC)
The U of North Carolina at Pembroke (NC)
U of Northern Iowa (IA)
U of North Texas (TX)
U of Puerto Rico Medical Sciences Campus (PR)
U of Regina (SK, Canada)
U of Richmond (VA)
U of Rio Grande (OH)
U of Saint Francis (IN)
U of St. Thomas (MN)
U of Sioux Falls (SD)
The U of Tennessee (TN)
The U of Texas–Pan American (TX)
U of the District of Columbia (DC)
U of Toledo (OH)
U of Toronto (ON, Canada)
U of Utah (UT)
U of Wisconsin–La Crosse (WI)
U of Wyoming (WY)
Upper Iowa U (IA)
Urbana U (OH)
Ursinus Coll (PA)
Utah State U (UT)
Valley City State U (ND)
Virginia Commonwealth U (VA)
Virginia Polytechnic Inst and State U (VA)
Washburn U of Topeka (KS)
Washington State U (WA)
West Chester U of Pennsylvania (PA)
Western Connecticut State U (CT)
Western Illinois U (IL)
Western Michigan U (MI)
Western Washington U (WA)
West Liberty State Coll (WV)
West Virginia State Coll (WV)
West Virginia U Inst of Technology (WV)
West Virginia Wesleyan Coll (WV)

William Carey Coll (MS)
William Paterson U of New Jersey (NJ)
William Penn U (IA)
Wilmington Coll (OH)
Winona State U (MN)
Wright State U (OH)
Xavier U of Louisiana (LA)
York Coll of the City U of New York (NY)
Youngstown State U (OH)

HEALTH FACILITIES ADMINISTRATION
Carson-Newman Coll (TN)
Central Michigan U (MI)
Coll of Mount Saint Vincent (NY)
Eastern U (PA)
Ithaca Coll (NY)
Long Island U, C.W. Post Campus (NY)
Ohio U (OH)
St. John's U (NY)
Southern Illinois U Carbondale (IL)
Southwest Texas State U (TX)
The U of Alabama (AL)
U of Pennsylvania (PA)
U of Texas Southwestern Medical Center at Dallas (TX)
U of Toledo (OH)
Worcester State Coll (MA)
York U (ON, Canada)

HEALTH/MEDICAL ADMINISTRATIVE SERVICES RELATED
Pennsylvania Coll of Technology (PA)
Robert Morris U (PA)
U of Baltimore (MD)
Ursuline Coll (OH)

HEALTH/MEDICAL ASSISTANTS RELATED
Wayne State U (MI)

HEALTH/MEDICAL BIOSTATISTICS
The U of North Carolina at Chapel Hill (NC)

HEALTH/MEDICAL DIAGNOSTIC AND TREATMENT SERVICES RELATED
Fairleigh Dickinson U, Florham-Madison Campus (NJ)
Fairleigh Dickinson U, Teaneck-Hackensack Campus (NJ)
Florida Gulf Coast U (FL)
Georgian Court Coll (NJ)
U of Connecticut (CT)
U of Toledo (OH)
Virginia Commonwealth U (VA)

HEALTH/MEDICAL LABORATORY TECHNOLOGIES RELATED
Saint Louis U (MO)

HEALTH/MEDICAL PREPARATORY PROGRAMS RELATED
Aurora U (IL)
Chadron State Coll (NE)
Duquesne U (PA)
Guilford Coll (NC)
Ithaca Coll (NY)
Juniata Coll (PA)
Lander U (SC)
Rhode Island Coll (RI)
The U of Akron (OH)
U of Louisville (KY)
U of Miami (FL)
U of South Alabama (AL)
Utica Coll of Syracuse U (NY)

HEALTH OCCUPATIONS EDUCATION
New York Inst of Technology (NY)
North Carolina State U (NC)
U of Central Oklahoma (OK)
U of Louisville (KY)
U of Maine at Farmington (ME)

HEALTH/PHYSICAL EDUCATION
Abilene Christian U (TX)
Anderson U (IN)
Angelo State U (TX)
Arkansas State U (AR)
Asbury Coll (KY)
Austin Peay State U (TN)
Averett U (VA)
Baylor U (TX)
Bethel Coll (KS)
Bethel Coll (TN)
Black Hills State U (SD)
Bridgewater Coll (VA)
Bridgewater State Coll (MA)
Brigham Young U (UT)
Brigham Young U–Hawaii (HI)
California State U, Fullerton (CA)
California State U, Sacramento (CA)
Cameron U (OK)
Campbell U (NC)
Castleton State Coll (VT)
Cedarville U (OH)
Central Michigan U (MI)
Christopher Newport U (VA)
Coll of St. Catherine (MN)
Coll of the Ozarks (MO)
Concordia Coll (MN)
Concordia U (NE)
Dana Coll (NE)
Doane Coll (NE)
Eastern Michigan U (MI)
Eastern U (PA)
East Tennessee State U (TN)
East Texas Baptist U (TX)
Edinboro U of Pennsylvania (PA)
Elmhurst Coll (IL)
Emory & Henry Coll (VA)
Freed-Hardeman U (TN)
Georgia Southern U (GA)
Hastings Coll (NE)
Houghton Coll (NY)
Howard Payne U (TX)
Indiana U of Pennsylvania (PA)
Iowa State U of Science and Technology (IA)
Ithaca Coll (NY)
Jacksonville State U (AL)
James Madison U (VA)
Johnson State Coll (VT)
Kentucky State U (KY)
Liberty U (VA)
Linfield Coll (OR)
Louisiana Tech U (LA)
Luther Coll (IA)
Lyndon State Coll (VT)
Malone Coll (OH)
Marywood U (PA)
Mayville State U (ND)
Miami U (OH)
Middle Tennessee State U (TN)
Minnesota State U Moorhead (MN)
Montana State U–Bozeman (MT)
New England Coll (NH)
North Carolina Central U (NC)
North Dakota State U (ND)
Northwest Nazarene U (ID)
Ohio U (OH)
Oklahoma Baptist U (OK)
Oklahoma State U (OK)
Olivet Coll (MI)
Philander Smith Coll (AR)
Pillsbury Baptist Bible Coll (MN)
Point Loma Nazarene U (CA)
Queen's U at Kingston (ON, Canada)
Redeemer U Coll (ON, Canada)
Roanoke Coll (VA)
St. Mary's U of San Antonio (TX)
Salisbury U (MD)
Samford U (AL)
San Jose State U (CA)
Schreiner U (TX)
South Dakota State U (SD)
Southeast Missouri State U (MO)
Southern Illinois U Edwardsville (IL)
Southern Virginia U (VA)
Southwestern Adventist U (TX)
Southwestern Coll (KS)
Southwest State U (MN)
Southwest Texas State U (TX)
Spring Arbor U (MI)
Stephen F. Austin State U (TX)
Tennessee Wesleyan Coll (TN)
Texas A&M International U (TX)
Texas A&M U (TX)
Texas Coll (TX)
Texas Southern U (TX)
Texas Tech U (TX)
Texas Wesleyan U (TX)
Texas Woman's U (TX)
Trinity Western U (BC, Canada)
U of Arkansas (AR)
U of Delaware (DE)
U of Great Falls (MT)
U of Hawaii at Manoa (HI)
U of Houston (TX)
U of Illinois at Chicago (IL)
U of Illinois at Urbana–Champaign (IL)
U of Kansas (KS)
U of Louisiana at Monroe (LA)
U of Louisville (KY)
U of Missouri–Kansas City (MO)
U of Montevallo (AL)
The U of North Carolina at Chapel Hill (NC)
The U of North Carolina at Charlotte (NC)
The U of North Carolina at Wilmington (NC)
U of Oklahoma (OK)
U of Rio Grande (OH)
U of St. Thomas (MN)
U of San Francisco (CA)
U of Science and Arts of Oklahoma (OK)
U of Southern Mississippi (MS)
The U of Tennessee at Martin (TN)
The U of Texas at Arlington (TX)
The U of Texas at Austin (TX)
The U of Texas at San Antonio (TX)
The U of Texas–Pan American (TX)
U of Utah (UT)
U of West Florida (FL)
U of Windsor (ON, Canada)
U of Wisconsin–Stevens Point (WI)
Valparaiso U (IN)
Vanguard U of Southern California (CA)
Walla Walla Coll (WA)
Weber State U (UT)
West Texas A&M U (TX)
William Penn U (IA)
York U (ON, Canada)
Youngstown State U (OH)

HEALTH/PHYSICAL EDUCATION/ FITNESS RELATED
Arizona State U East (AZ)
Averett U (VA)
Briar Cliff U (IA)
Colorado Christian U (CO)
East Carolina U (NC)
Mayville State U (ND)
Reinhardt Coll (GA)
Texas Lutheran U (TX)
The U of Akron (OH)
U of Central Oklahoma (OK)

HEALTH PHYSICS/RADIOLOGIC HEALTH
Bloomsburg U of Pennsylvania (PA)
U of Nevada, Las Vegas (NV)

HEALTH PRODUCTS/SERVICES MARKETING
Carlow Coll (PA)
Quinnipiac U (CT)

HEALTH PROFESSIONS AND RELATED SCIENCES
Albany State U (GA)
Alcorn State U (MS)
Bradley U (IL)
California State U, Fullerton (CA)
Clemson U (SC)
East Tennessee State U (TN)
George Mason U (VA)
Hofstra U (NY)
King Coll (TN)
King's Coll (PA)
Lebanon Valley Coll (PA)
Maharishi U of Management (IA)
Mass Coll of Pharmacy and Allied Health Sciences (MA)
The Ohio State U (OH)
Ohio U (OH)
Old Dominion U (VA)
Pennsylvania Coll of Technology (PA)
Randolph-Macon Woman's Coll (VA)
San Diego State U (CA)
Touro Coll (NY)
The U of Alabama (AL)
U of Arkansas (AR)
U of Miami (FL)
U of Pennsylvania (PA)
U of Pittsburgh (PA)
U of Utah (UT)
U of Wyoming (WY)
Washington U in St. Louis (MO)

HEALTH SCIENCE
Alma Coll (MI)
American U (DC)
Armstrong Atlantic State U (GA)
Athens State U (AL)
Azusa Pacific U (CA)
Ball State U (IN)
Bastyr U (WA)
Benedictine U (IL)
Boise State U (ID)
Boston U (MA)
Bradley U (IL)
Brigham Young U (UT)
Brock U (ON, Canada)
Brooklyn Coll of the City U of NY (NY)
California State U, Chico (CA)
California State U, Dominguez Hills (CA)
California State U, Fresno (CA)
California State U, Hayward (CA)
California State U, Long Beach (CA)
California State U, Los Angeles (CA)
California State U, Northridge (CA)
California State U, San Bernardino (CA)
Campbell U (NC)
Carlow Coll (PA)
Castleton State Coll (VT)
Cedar Crest Coll (PA)
Centenary Coll of Louisiana (LA)
Chapman U (CA)
Coll Misericordia (PA)
Coll of Mount Saint Vincent (NY)
The Coll of St. Scholastica (MN)
Coll of the Ozarks (MO)
Columbus State U (GA)
Dalhousie U (NS, Canada)
Delaware State U (DE)
Eastern Nazarene Coll (MA)
Erskine Coll (SC)
Fairmont State Coll (WV)
Florida Atlantic U (FL)
Florida International U (FL)
Gannon U (PA)
Gettysburg Coll (PA)
Graceland U (IA)
Grand Valley State U (MI)
Gwynedd-Mercy Coll (PA)
Hampshire Coll (MA)
Hiram Coll (OH)
Inter American U of PR, San Germán Campus (PR)
Johnson State Coll (VT)
Kalamazoo Coll (MI)
Kansas State U (KS)
Lamar U (TX)
Lock Haven U of Pennsylvania (PA)
Long Island U, Brooklyn Campus (NY)
Longwood Coll (VA)
Manchester Coll (IN)
Marymount U (VA)
Maryville U of Saint Louis (MO)
MCP Hahnemann U (PA)
Medical U of South Carolina (SC)
Merrimack Coll (MA)
Milligan Coll (TN)
Minnesota State U, Mankato (MN)
Montana Tech of The U of Montana (MT)
Montclair State U (NJ)
Morris Coll (SC)
Mount Olive Coll (NC)
New Jersey City U (NJ)
Newman U (KS)
Northeastern U (MA)
Northern Illinois U (IL)
Northwest Missouri State U (MO)
Oakland U (MI)
Ohio U (OH)
Oklahoma State U (OK)
Oregon State U (OR)
Our Lady of Holy Cross Coll (LA)
Pacific U (OR)
Queen's U at Kingston (ON, Canada)
Roosevelt U (IL)
Samuel Merritt Coll (CA)
San Francisco State U (CA)
San Jose State U (CA)
Sonoma State U (CA)
State U of NY Coll at Brockport (NY)
State U of NY Coll at Cortland (NY)
State U of NY at Stony Brook (NY)
Syracuse U (NY)
Tennessee Wesleyan Coll (TN)
Texas A&M U–Corpus Christi (TX)
Texas Christian U (TX)
Texas Southern U (TX)
Touro Coll (NY)
Towson U (MD)
Truman State U (MO)
Union Inst & U (OH)
U of Alaska Anchorage (AK)
U of Arkansas at Little Rock (AR)
U of Central Florida (FL)
U of Colorado at Colorado Springs (CO)
U of Florida (FL)
U of Hartford (CT)
U of Maryland, Baltimore County (MD)
U of Missouri–St. Louis (MO)
U of Nevada, Las Vegas (NV)
U of New England (ME)
U of North Florida (FL)
U of Puerto Rico Medical Sciences Campus (PR)
U of Rochester (NY)
U of St. Francis (IL)
U of Saint Francis (IN)
U of St. Thomas (MN)
U of Southern California (CA)
U of Southern Maine (ME)
The U of Texas at El Paso (TX)
The U of Texas at San Antonio (TX)
The U of Texas at Tyler (TX)
U of the Sciences in Philadelphia (PA)
U of Waterloo (ON, Canada)
The U of Western Ontario (ON, Canada)
U of Wisconsin–Milwaukee (WI)
Ursinus Coll (PA)
Ursuline Coll (OH)
Valdosta State U (GA)
Waldorf Coll (IA)
Walla Walla Coll (WA)
Warner Pacific Coll (OR)
Wayne State U (MI)
West Chester U of Pennsylvania (PA)
Western Baptist Coll (OR)
West Liberty State Coll (WV)
William Paterson U of New Jersey (NJ)
Winona State U (MN)
York U (ON, Canada)
Youngstown State U (OH)

HEALTH SERVICES ADMINISTRATION
Albertus Magnus Coll (CT)
Alfred U (NY)
Alvernia Coll (PA)
Appalachian State U (NC)
Arcadia U (PA)
Auburn U (AL)
Augustana Coll (SD)
Baker Coll of Auburn Hills (MI)
Baker Coll of Flint (MI)
Baker Coll of Muskegon (MI)
Baker Coll of Owosso (MI)
Baker Coll of Port Huron (MI)
Bellevue U (NE)
Belmont U (TN)
Benedictine U (IL)
Black Hills State U (SD)
Bowling Green State U (OH)
British Columbia Inst of Technology (BC, Canada)
Brock U (ON, Canada)
California Coll for Health Sciences (CA)
California State U, Chico (CA)
California State U, Dominguez Hills (CA)
California State U, Long Beach (CA)
California State U, Northridge (CA)
California State U, San Bernardino (CA)
Cedar Crest Coll (PA)
Chestnut Hill Coll (PA)
Clayton Coll & State U (GA)

Cleary Coll (MI)
Coll of Mount St. Joseph (OH)
The Coll of St. Scholastica (MN)
Columbia Southern U (AL)
Columbia Union Coll (MD)
Comm Hospital Roanoke Valley–Coll of Health Scis (VA)
Concordia Coll (MN)
Concordia U (MI)
Concordia U (NE)
Concordia U (OR)
Concordia U Wisconsin (WI)
Creighton U (NE)
Dallas Baptist U (TX)
Davenport U, Dearborn (MI)
Davenport U, Grand Rapids (MI)
Davenport U, Kalamazoo (MI)
David N. Myers U (OH)
Davis & Elkins Coll (WV)
Dillard U (LA)
Dominican Coll (NY)
Drexel U (PA)
Duquesne U (PA)
D'Youville Coll (NY)
Eastern Kentucky U (KY)
Eastern Michigan U (MI)
Eastern Washington U (WA)
Ferris State U (MI)
Fisk U (TN)
Florida A&M U (FL)
Florida Atlantic U (FL)
Florida International U (FL)
Florida Metropolitan U-Orlando Coll, South (FL)
Franklin U (OH)
Friends U (KS)
Frostburg State U (MD)
Governors State U (IL)
Gwynedd-Mercy Coll (PA)
Harding U (AR)
Harris-Stowe State Coll (MO)
Hastings Coll (NE)
Heidelberg Coll (OH)
Howard Payne U (TX)
Idaho State U (ID)
Indiana U Northwest (IN)
Indiana U–Purdue U Fort Wayne (IN)
Indiana U–Purdue U Indianapolis (IN)
Indiana U South Bend (IN)
Iona Coll (NY)
Ithaca Coll (NY)
John Brown U (AR)
Johnson & Wales U (RI)
King's Coll (PA)
Lander U (SC)
Lehman Coll of the City U of NY (NY)
Lewis U (IL)
Lindenwood U (MO)
Long Island U, C.W. Post Campus (NY)
Lynn U (FL)
Macon State Coll (GA)
Martin Methodist Coll (TN)
Mary Baldwin Coll (VA)
Maryville U of Saint Louis (MO)
Marywood U (PA)
Mercy Coll (NY)
Mercy Coll of Health Sciences (IA)
Methodist Coll (NC)
Metropolitan State Coll of Denver (CO)
Milligan Coll (TN)
Minnesota State U Moorhead (MN)
Montana State U–Billings (MT)
Montana State U–Bozeman (MT)
Mountain State U (WV)
Mount St. Clare Coll (IA)
Mount St. Mary's Coll (CA)
National-Louis U (IL)
National U (CA)
Newbury Coll (MA)
New Mexico Highlands U (NM)
Norfolk State U (VA)
Northeastern State U (OK)
Northeastern U (MA)
Ohio U (OH)
Oregon State U (OR)
Peirce Coll (PA)
Penn State U Univ Park Campus (PA)
Point Park Coll (PA)
Presentation Coll (SD)
Providence Coll (RI)
Quinnipiac U (CT)
Robert Morris U (PA)
Roosevelt U (IL)
St. Francis Coll (NY)
St. Joseph's Coll, New York (NY)
St. Joseph's Coll, Suffolk Campus (NY)
Saint Joseph's U (PA)
Saint Leo U (FL)
Saint Louis U (MO)
Saint Mary's U of Minnesota (MN)
Saint Peter's Coll (NJ)
San Jose State U (CA)
Slippery Rock U of Pennsylvania (PA)
Sojourner-Douglass Coll (MD)
Southeastern U (DC)
Southern Adventist U (TN)
Southwestern Adventist U (TX)
Southwestern Oklahoma State U (OK)
Southwest Texas State U (TX)
Spring Arbor U (MI)
Springfield Coll (MA)
State U of NY Coll at Fredonia (NY)
State U of NY Inst of Tech at Utica/Rome (NY)
Stonehill Coll (MA)
Tennessee State U (TN)
Texas Southern U (TX)
Thomas Edison State Coll (NJ)
Touro U International (CA)
Towson U (MD)
The U of Arizona (AZ)
U of Central Florida (FL)
U of Cincinnati (OH)
U of Connecticut (CT)
U of Evansville (IN)
U of Great Falls (MT)
U of Hawaii–West Oahu (HI)
U of Houston–Clear Lake (TX)
U of Illinois at Springfield (IL)
U of Kentucky (KY)
U of La Verne (CA)
U of Maryland, Baltimore County (MD)
U of Michigan–Dearborn (MI)
U of Michigan–Flint (MI)
U of Nevada, Las Vegas (NV)
U of New England (ME)
U of New Hampshire (NH)
The U of North Carolina at Chapel Hill (NC)
U of Northwestern Ohio (OH)
U of Rhode Island (RI)
U of Saskatchewan (SK, Canada)
The U of Scranton (PA)
U of South Dakota (SD)
U of Southern Indiana (IN)
The U of Texas at El Paso (TX)
U of Texas Southwestern Medical Center at Dallas (TX)
U of Victoria (BC, Canada)
U of Wisconsin–Eau Claire (WI)
U of Wisconsin–Milwaukee (WI)
U System Coll for Lifelong Learning (NH)
Ursuline Coll (OH)
Viterbo U (WI)
Waynesburg Coll (PA)
Weber State U (UT)
Webster U (MO)
Western International U (AZ)
Western Kentucky U (KY)
West Virginia U Inst of Technology (WV)
Wheeling Jesuit U (WV)
Wichita State U (KS)
Wilberforce U (OH)
Winona State U (MN)
Worcester State Coll (MA)
York Coll of Pennsylvania (PA)

HEALTH UNIT MANAGEMENT
Ursuline Coll (OH)

HEARING SCIENCES
Arizona State U (AZ)
Brigham Young U (UT)
Indiana U Bloomington (IN)
Northwestern U (IL)
Stephen F. Austin State U (TX)
Texas Tech U (TX)
U of Northern Colorado (CO)
The U of Tennessee (TN)

HEATING/AIR CONDITIONING/ REFRIGERATION
Ferris State U (MI)

HEATING/AIR CONDITIONING/ REFRIGERATION TECHNOLOGY
Pennsylvania Coll of Technology (PA)

HEAVY EQUIPMENT MAINTENANCE
Ferris State U (MI)
Pittsburg State U (KS)

HEBREW
Baltimore Hebrew U (MD)
Bard Coll (NY)
Calvary Bible Coll and Theological Seminary (MO)
Concordia U (QC, Canada)
Concordia U Wisconsin (WI)
Cornell U (NY)
Dartmouth Coll (NH)
Harvard U (MA)
Hofstra U (NY)
Hunter Coll of the City U of NY (NY)
Laura and Alvin Siegal Coll of Judaic Studies (OH)
Lehman Coll of the City U of NY (NY)
Long Island U, Southampton Coll, Friends World Program (NY)
Luther Coll (IA)
New York U (NY)
The Ohio State U (OH)
Queens Coll of the City U of NY (NY)
State U of NY at Binghamton (NY)
Temple U (PA)
Touro Coll (NY)
U of Alberta (AB, Canada)
U of Calif, Los Angeles (CA)
U of Michigan (MI)
U of Minnesota, Twin Cities Campus (MN)
U of Oregon (OR)
The U of Texas at Austin (TX)
U of Toronto (ON, Canada)
U of Wisconsin–Madison (WI)
U of Wisconsin–Milwaukee (WI)
Washington U in St. Louis (MO)
Yeshiva U (NY)
York U (ON, Canada)

HIGHER EDUCATION ADMINISTRATION
Bowling Green State U (OH)

HISPANIC-AMERICAN STUDIES
Arizona State U (AZ)
Barton Coll (NC)
Boston Coll (MA)
Brown U (RI)
California State U, Fullerton (CA)
California State U, Northridge (CA)
Columbia Coll (NY)
Columbia U, School of General Studies (NY)
Cornell U (NY)
Dartmouth Coll (NH)
The Evergreen State Coll (WA)
Fordham U (NY)
Goshen Coll (IN)
Hampshire Coll (MA)
Harvard U (MA)
Hofstra U (NY)
Hunter Coll of the City U of NY (NY)
Inter American U of PR, San Germán Campus (PR)
Lewis & Clark Coll (OR)
Long Island U, Southampton Coll, Friends World Program (NY)
McMaster U (ON, Canada)
Mills Coll (CA)
Mount Saint Mary Coll (NY)
Pomona Coll (CA)
Pontifical Catholic U of Puerto Rico (PR)
Queen's U at Kingston (ON, Canada)
Rutgers, The State U of New Jersey, New Brunswick (NJ)
St. Francis Coll (NY)
St. Olaf Coll (MN)
San Diego State U (CA)
Scripps Coll (CA)
Sonoma State U (CA)
State U of NY at Albany (NY)
State U of NY Coll at Oneonta (NY)
Trent U (ON, Canada)
Tulane U (LA)
Université de Montréal (QC, Canada)
The U of Arizona (AZ)
U of Calif, Berkeley (CA)
U of Calif, Santa Cruz (CA)
U of Michigan (MI)
U of Michigan–Dearborn (MI)
U of Northern Colorado (CO)
U of Ottawa (ON, Canada)
U of San Diego (CA)
U of Southern California (CA)
U of Southern Maine (ME)
The U of Texas at San Antonio (TX)
U of Toronto (ON, Canada)
U of Windsor (ON, Canada)
U of Wisconsin–Madison (WI)
Vassar Coll (NY)
Wayne State U (MI)
Wheaton Coll (MA)
Willamette U (OR)
York U (ON, Canada)

HISTORY
Abilene Christian U (TX)
Acadia U (NS, Canada)
Adams State Coll (CO)
Adelphi U (NY)
Adrian Coll (MI)
Agnes Scott Coll (GA)
Alabama State U (AL)
Albany State U (GA)
Albertson Coll of Idaho (ID)
Albertus Magnus Coll (CT)
Albion Coll (MI)
Albright Coll (PA)
Alcorn State U (MS)
Alderson-Broaddus Coll (WV)
Alfred U (NY)
Alice Lloyd Coll (KY)
Allegheny Coll (PA)
Alma Coll (MI)
Alvernia Coll (PA)
Alverno Coll (WI)
American Coll of Thessaloniki(Greece)
American International Coll (MA)
American Military U (VA)
American U (DC)
American U in Cairo(Egypt)
The American U of Paris(France)
Amherst Coll (MA)
Anderson Coll (SC)
Anderson U (IN)
Andrews U (MI)
Angelo State U (TX)
Anna Maria Coll (MA)
Appalachian State U (NC)
Aquinas Coll (MI)
Arcadia U (PA)
Arizona State U (AZ)
Arizona State U West (AZ)
Arkansas State U (AR)
Arkansas Tech U (AR)
Armstrong Atlantic State U (GA)
Asbury Coll (KY)
Ashland U (OH)
Assumption Coll (MA)
Athabasca U (AB, Canada)
Athens State U (AL)
Atlantic Baptist U (NB, Canada)
Atlantic Union Coll (MA)
Auburn U (AL)
Auburn U Montgomery (AL)
Augsburg Coll (MN)
Augustana Coll (IL)
Augustana Coll (SD)
Augusta State U (GA)
Aurora U (IL)
Austin Coll (TX)
Austin Peay State U (TN)
Ave Maria Coll (MI)
Averett U (VA)
Avila Coll (MO)
Azusa Pacific U (CA)
Baker U (KS)
Baldwin-Wallace Coll (OH)
Ball State U (IN)
Bard Coll (NY)
Barnard Coll (NY)
Barry U (FL)
Barton Coll (NC)
Bates Coll (ME)
Baylor U (TX)
Bay Path Coll (MA)
Belhaven Coll (MS)
Bellarmine U (KY)
Bellevue U (NE)
Belmont Abbey Coll (NC)
Belmont U (TN)
Beloit Coll (WI)
Bemidji State U (MN)
Benedict Coll (SC)
Benedictine Coll (KS)
Benedictine U (IL)
Bennington Coll (VT)
Bentley Coll (MA)
Berea Coll (KY)
Baruch Coll of the City U of NY (NY)
Berry Coll (GA)
Bethany Coll (KS)
Bethany Coll (WV)
Bethel Coll (IN)
Bethel Coll (KS)
Bethel Coll (MN)
Bethel Coll (TN)
Bethune-Cookman Coll (FL)
Biola U (CA)
Birmingham-Southern Coll (AL)
Bishop's U (PQ, Canada)
Blackburn Coll (IL)
Black Hills State U (SD)
Bloomfield Coll (NJ)
Bloomsburg U of Pennsylvania (PA)
Bluefield Coll (VA)
Blue Mountain Coll (MS)
Bluffton Coll (OH)
Boise State U (ID)
Boston Coll (MA)
Boston U (MA)
Bowdoin Coll (ME)
Bowie State U (MD)
Bowling Green State U (OH)
Bradley U (IL)
Brandeis U (MA)
Brandon U (MB, Canada)
Brenau U (GA)
Brescia U (KY)
Brevard Coll (NC)
Brewton-Parker Coll (GA)
Briar Cliff U (IA)
Bridgewater Coll (VA)
Bridgewater State Coll (MA)
Brigham Young U (UT)
Brigham Young U–Hawaii (HI)
Brock U (ON, Canada)
Brooklyn Coll of the City U of NY (NY)
Brown U (RI)
Bryan Coll (TN)
Bryant Coll (RI)
Bryn Athyn Coll of the New Church (PA)
Bryn Mawr Coll (PA)
Bucknell U (PA)
Buena Vista U (IA)
Butler U (IN)
Cabrini Coll (PA)
Caldwell Coll (NJ)
California Baptist U (CA)
California Inst of Technology (CA)
California Lutheran U (CA)
California Polytechnic State U, San Luis Obispo (CA)
California State Polytechnic U, Pomona (CA)
California State U, Bakersfield (CA)
California State U, Chico (CA)
California State U, Dominguez Hills (CA)
California State U, Fresno (CA)
California State U, Fullerton (CA)
California State U, Hayward (CA)
California State U, Long Beach (CA)
California State U, Los Angeles (CA)
California State U, Northridge (CA)
California State U, Sacramento (CA)
California State U, San Bernardino (CA)
California State U, San Marcos (CA)
California State U, Stanislaus (CA)
California U of Pennsylvania (PA)
Calvin Coll (MI)
Cameron U (OK)
Campbellsville U (KY)
Campbell U (NC)
Canisius Coll (NY)
Capital U (OH)
Cardinal Stritch U (WI)
Carleton Coll (MN)

Carleton U (ON, Canada)
Carlow Coll (PA)
Carnegie Mellon U (PA)
Carroll Coll (MT)
Carroll Coll (WI)
Carson-Newman Coll (TN)
Carthage Coll (WI)
Case Western Reserve U (OH)
Castleton State Coll (VT)
Catawba Coll (NC)
The Catholic U of America (DC)
Cedar Crest Coll (PA)
Cedarville U (OH)
Centenary Coll (NJ)
Centenary Coll of Louisiana (LA)
Central Coll (IA)
Central Connecticut State U (CT)
Central Methodist Coll (MO)
Central Michigan U (MI)
Central Missouri State U (MO)
Central State U (OH)
Central Washington U (WA)
Centre Coll (KY)
Chadron State Coll (NE)
Chaminade U of Honolulu (HI)
Chapman U (CA)
Charleston Southern U (SC)
Chatham Coll (PA)
Chestnut Hill Coll (PA)
Chicago State U (IL)
Chowan Coll (NC)
Christendom Coll (VA)
Christian Brothers U (TN)
Christian Heritage Coll (CA)
Christopher Newport U (VA)
Citadel, The Military Coll of South Carolina (SC)
City Coll of the City U of NY (NY)
Claflin U (SC)
Claremont McKenna Coll (CA)
Clarion U of Pennsylvania (PA)
Clark Atlanta U (GA)
Clarke Coll (IA)
Clarkson U (NY)
Clark U (MA)
Clearwater Christian Coll (FL)
Clemson U (SC)
Cleveland State U (OH)
Coastal Carolina U (SC)
Coe Coll (IA)
Coker Coll (SC)
Colby Coll (ME)
Colgate U (NY)
Coll Misericordia (PA)
Coll of Charleston (SC)
Coll of Mount St. Joseph (OH)
Coll of Mount Saint Vincent (NY)
The Coll of New Jersey (NJ)
The Coll of New Rochelle (NY)
Coll of Notre Dame of Maryland (MD)
Coll of Saint Benedict (MN)
Coll of St. Catherine (MN)
Coll of Saint Elizabeth (NJ)
Coll of St. Joseph (VT)
The Coll of Saint Rose (NY)
The Coll of St. Scholastica (MN)
The Coll of Southeastern Europe, The American U of Athens(Greece)
Coll of Staten Island of the City U of NY (NY)
Coll of the Holy Cross (MA)
Coll of the Ozarks (MO)
Coll of the Southwest (NM)
The Coll of William and Mary (VA)
The Coll of Wooster (OH)
Colorado Christian U (CO)
The Colorado Coll (CO)
Colorado State U (CO)
Columbia Coll (MO)
Columbia Coll (NY)
Columbia Coll (SC)
Columbia Union Coll (MD)
Columbia U, School of General Studies (NY)
Columbus State U (GA)
Concord Coll (WV)
Concordia Coll (MN)
Concordia Coll (NY)
Concordia U (CA)
Concordia U (IL)
Concordia U (MN)
Concordia U (NE)
Concordia U (QC, Canada)
Concordia U Wisconsin (WI)
Connecticut Coll (CT)
Converse Coll (SC)
Coppin State Coll (MD)
Cornell Coll (IA)
Cornell U (NY)
Cornerstone U (MI)
Covenant Coll (GA)
Creighton U (NE)
Crichton Coll (TN)
Crown Coll (MN)
Culver-Stockton Coll (MO)
Cumberland Coll (KY)
Cumberland U (TN)
Curry Coll (MA)
Daemen Coll (NY)
Dakota Wesleyan U (SD)
Dalhousie U (NS, Canada)
Dallas Baptist U (TX)
Dana Coll (NE)
Dartmouth Coll (NH)
Davidson Coll (NC)
Davis & Elkins Coll (WV)
Defiance Coll (OH)
Delaware State U (DE)
Delta State U (MS)
Denison U (OH)
DePaul U (IL)
DePauw U (IN)
DeSales U (PA)
Dickinson Coll (PA)
Dickinson State U (ND)
Dillard U (LA)
Doane Coll (NE)
Dominican Coll (NY)
Dominican U (IL)
Dominican U of California (CA)
Dordt Coll (IA)
Dowling Coll (NY)
Drake U (IA)
Drew U (NJ)
Drexel U (PA)
Drury U (MO)
Duke U (NC)
Duquesne U (PA)
D'Youville Coll (NY)
Earlham Coll (IN)
East Carolina U (NC)
East Central U (OK)
Eastern Connecticut State U (CT)
Eastern Illinois U (IL)
Eastern Kentucky U (KY)
Eastern Mennonite U (VA)
Eastern Michigan U (MI)
Eastern Nazarene Coll (MA)
Eastern New Mexico U (NM)
Eastern Oregon U (OR)
Eastern U (PA)
Eastern Washington U (WA)
East Stroudsburg U of Pennsylvania (PA)
East Tennessee State U (TN)
East Texas Baptist U (TX)
Eckerd Coll (FL)
Edgewood Coll (WI)
Edinboro U of Pennsylvania (PA)
Edward Waters Coll (FL)
Elizabeth City State U (NC)
Elizabethtown Coll (PA)
Elmhurst Coll (IL)
Elmira Coll (NY)
Elms Coll (MA)
Elon U (NC)
Emmanuel Coll (GA)
Emmanuel Coll (MA)
Emory & Henry Coll (VA)
Emory U (GA)
Emporia State U (KS)
Erskine Coll (SC)
Eugene Lang Coll, New School U (NY)
Eureka Coll (IL)
Evangel U (MO)
The Evergreen State Coll (WA)
Excelsior Coll (NY)
Fairfield U (CT)
Fairleigh Dickinson U, Florham-Madison Campus (NJ)
Fairleigh Dickinson U, Teaneck-Hackensack Campus (NJ)
Fairmont State Coll (WV)
Faulkner U (AL)
Fayetteville State U (NC)
Felician Coll (NJ)
Ferrum Coll (VA)
Fisk U (TN)
Fitchburg State Coll (MA)
Flagler Coll (FL)
Florida A&M U (FL)
Florida Atlantic U (FL)
Florida International U (FL)
Florida Southern Coll (FL)
Florida State U (FL)
Fontbonne U (MO)
Fordham U (NY)
Fort Hays State U (KS)
Fort Lewis Coll (CO)
Framingham State Coll (MA)
Franciscan U of Steubenville (OH)
Francis Marion U (SC)
Franklin and Marshall Coll (PA)
Franklin Coll of Indiana (IN)
Franklin Coll Switzerland(Switzerland)
Franklin Pierce Coll (NH)
Freed-Hardeman U (TN)
Fresno Pacific U (CA)
Friends U (KS)
Frostburg State U (MD)
Furman U (SC)
Gallaudet U (DC)
Gannon U (PA)
Gardner-Webb U (NC)
Geneva Coll (PA)
George Fox U (OR)
George Mason U (VA)
Georgetown Coll (KY)
Georgetown U (DC)
The George Washington U (DC)
Georgia Coll and State U (GA)
Georgian Court Coll (NJ)
Georgia Southern U (GA)
Georgia Southwestern State U (GA)
Georgia State U (GA)
Gettysburg Coll (PA)
Glenville State Coll (WV)
Goddard Coll (VT)
Gonzaga U (WA)
Gordon Coll (MA)
Goshen Coll (IN)
Goucher Coll (MD)
Graceland U (IA)
Grambling State U (LA)
Grand Canyon U (AZ)
Grand Valley State U (MI)
Grand View Coll (IA)
Green Mountain Coll (VT)
Greensboro Coll (NC)
Greenville Coll (IL)
Grinnell Coll (IA)
Grove City Coll (PA)
Guilford Coll (NC)
Gustavus Adolphus Coll (MN)
Gwynedd-Mercy Coll (PA)
Hamilton Coll (NY)
Hamline U (MN)
Hampden-Sydney Coll (VA)
Hampshire Coll (MA)
Hampton U (VA)
Hannibal-LaGrange Coll (MO)
Hanover Coll (IN)
Harding U (AR)
Hardin-Simmons U (TX)
Hartwick Coll (NY)
Harvard U (MA)
Hastings Coll (NE)
Haverford Coll (PA)
Hawai'i Pacific U (HI)
Heidelberg Coll (OH)
Henderson State U (AR)
Hendrix Coll (AR)
High Point U (NC)
Hillsdale Coll (MI)
Hiram Coll (OH)
Hobart and William Smith Colls (NY)
Hofstra U (NY)
Hollins U (VA)
Holy Family Coll (PA)
Holy Names Coll (CA)
Hood Coll (MD)
Hope Coll (MI)
Houghton Coll (NY)
Houston Baptist U (TX)
Howard Payne U (TX)
Howard U (DC)
Humboldt State U (CA)
Hunter Coll of the City U of NY (NY)
Huntingdon Coll (AL)
Huntington Coll (IN)
Idaho State U (ID)
Illinois Coll (IL)
Illinois State U (IL)
Illinois Wesleyan U (IL)
Immaculata Coll (PA)
Indiana State U (IN)
Indiana U Bloomington (IN)
Indiana U Northwest (IN)
Indiana U of Pennsylvania (PA)
Indiana U–Purdue U Fort Wayne (IN)
Indiana U–Purdue U Indianapolis (IN)
Indiana U South Bend (IN)
Indiana U Southeast (IN)
Indiana Wesleyan U (IN)
Iona Coll (NY)
Iowa State U of Science and Technology (IA)
Iowa Wesleyan Coll (IA)
Ithaca Coll (NY)
Jackson State U (MS)
Jacksonville State U (AL)
Jacksonville U (FL)
James Madison U (VA)
Jamestown Coll (ND)
Jarvis Christian Coll (TX)
Jewish Theological Seminary of America (NY)
John Brown U (AR)
John Carroll U (OH)
Johns Hopkins U (MD)
Johnson C. Smith U (NC)
Johnson State Coll (VT)
Judson Coll (AL)
Judson Coll (IL)
Juniata Coll (PA)
Kalamazoo Coll (MI)
Kansas State U (KS)
Kansas Wesleyan U (KS)
Kean U (NJ)
Keene State Coll (NH)
Kennesaw State U (GA)
Kent State U (OH)
Kentucky Christian Coll (KY)
Kentucky State U (KY)
Kentucky Wesleyan Coll (KY)
Kenyon Coll (OH)
Keuka Coll (NY)
King Coll (TN)
King's Coll (PA)
The King's U Coll (AB, Canada)
Knox Coll (IL)
Kutztown U of Pennsylvania (PA)
Lafayette Coll (PA)
LaGrange Coll (GA)
Lake Forest Coll (IL)
Lakehead U (ON, Canada)
Lakeland Coll (WI)
Lake Superior State U (MI)
Lamar U (TX)
Lambuth U (TN)
Lander U (SC)
La Roche Coll (PA)
La Salle U (PA)
Laura and Alvin Siegal Coll of Judaic Studies (OH)
Laurentian U (ON, Canada)
Lawrence U (WI)
Lebanon Valley Coll (PA)
Lees-McRae Coll (NC)
Lee U (TN)
Lehigh U (PA)
Lehman Coll of the City U of NY (NY)
Le Moyne Coll (NY)
LeMoyne-Owen Coll (TN)
Lenoir-Rhyne Coll (NC)
LeTourneau U (TX)
Lewis & Clark Coll (OR)
Lewis-Clark State Coll (ID)
Lewis U (IL)
Liberty U (VA)
Limestone Coll (SC)
Lincoln Memorial U (TN)
Lincoln U (MO)
Lincoln U (PA)
Lindenwood U (MO)
Lindsey Wilson Coll (KY)
Linfield Coll (OR)
Lipscomb U (TN)
Lock Haven U of Pennsylvania (PA)
Long Island U, Brooklyn Campus (NY)
Long Island U, C.W. Post Campus (NY)
Long Island U, Southampton Coll (NY)
Long Island U, Southampton Coll, Friends World Program (NY)
Longwood Coll (VA)
Loras Coll (IA)
Louisiana Coll (LA)
Louisiana State U and A&M Coll (LA)
Louisiana State U in Shreveport (LA)
Louisiana Tech U (LA)
Lourdes Coll (OH)
Loyola Coll in Maryland (MD)
Loyola Marymount U (CA)
Loyola U Chicago (IL)
Loyola U New Orleans (LA)
Lubbock Christian U (TX)
Luther Coll (IA)
Lycoming Coll (PA)
Lynchburg Coll (VA)
Lynn U (FL)
Lyon Coll (AR)
Macalester Coll (MN)
MacMurray Coll (IL)
Malaspina U-Coll (BC, Canada)
Malone Coll (OH)
Manchester Coll (IN)
Manhattan Coll (NY)
Manhattanville Coll (NY)
Mansfield U of Pennsylvania (PA)
Marian Coll (IN)
Marian Coll of Fond du Lac (WI)
Marietta Coll (OH)
Marist Coll (NY)
Marlboro Coll (VT)
Marquette U (WI)
Marshall U (WV)
Mars Hill Coll (NC)
Mary Baldwin Coll (VA)
Marygrove Coll (MI)
Marymount Coll of Fordham U (NY)
Marymount Manhattan Coll (NY)
Marymount U (VA)
Maryville Coll (TN)
Maryville U of Saint Louis (MO)
Mary Washington Coll (VA)
Massachusetts Coll of Liberal Arts (MA)
Massachusetts Inst of Technology (MA)
The Master's Coll and Seminary (CA)
McGill U (PQ, Canada)
McKendree Coll (IL)
McMaster U (ON, Canada)
McMurry U (TX)
McNeese State U (LA)
McPherson Coll (KS)
Memorial U of Newfoundland (NF, Canada)
Mercer U (GA)
Mercy Coll (NY)
Mercyhurst Coll (PA)
Meredith Coll (NC)
Merrimack Coll (MA)
Mesa State Coll (CO)
Messiah Coll (PA)
Methodist Coll (NC)
Metropolitan State Coll of Denver (CO)
Metropolitan State U (MN)
Miami U (OH)
Michigan State U (MI)
Michigan Technological U (MI)
MidAmerica Nazarene U (KS)
Middlebury Coll (VT)
Middle Tennessee State U (TN)
Midland Lutheran Coll (NE)
Midwestern State U (TX)
Millersville U of Pennsylvania (PA)
Milligan Coll (TN)
Millikin U (IL)
Millsaps Coll (MS)
Mills Coll (CA)
Minnesota State U, Mankato (MN)
Minnesota State U Moorhead (MN)
Minot State U (ND)
Mississippi Coll (MS)
Mississippi State U (MS)
Mississippi U for Women (MS)
Mississippi Valley State U (MS)
Missouri Baptist Coll (MO)
Missouri Southern State Coll (MO)
Missouri Valley Coll (MO)
Missouri Western State Coll (MO)
Molloy Coll (NY)
Monmouth Coll (IL)
Monmouth U (NJ)
Montana State U–Billings (MT)
Montana State U–Bozeman (MT)
Montclair State U (NJ)
Montreat Coll (NC)
Moravian Coll (PA)
Morehead State U (KY)
Morehouse Coll (GA)
Morgan State U (MD)
Morningside Coll (IA)
Morris Brown Coll (GA)
Morris Coll (SC)

Mount Allison U (NB, Canada)
Mount Holyoke Coll (MA)
Mount Marty Coll (SD)
Mount Mary Coll (WI)
Mount Mercy Coll (IA)
Mount Olive Coll (NC)
Mount Saint Mary Coll (NY)
Mount St. Mary's Coll (CA)
Mount Saint Mary's Coll and Seminary (MD)
Mount Saint Vincent U (NS, Canada)
Mount Union Coll (OH)
Mount Vernon Nazarene U (OH)
Muhlenberg Coll (PA)
Multnomah Bible Coll and Biblical Seminary (OR)
Murray State U (KY)
Muskingum Coll (OH)
Nazareth Coll of Rochester (NY)
Nebraska Wesleyan U (NE)
Newberry Coll (SC)
New Coll of Florida (FL)
New England Coll (NH)
New Jersey City U (NJ)
New Jersey Inst of Technology (NJ)
Newman U (KS)
New Mexico Highlands U (NM)
New Mexico State U (NM)
New York U (NY)
Niagara U (NY)
Nicholls State U (LA)
Nipissing U (ON, Canada)
Norfolk State U (VA)
North Carolina Ag and Tech State U (NC)
North Carolina Central U (NC)
North Carolina State U (NC)
North Carolina Wesleyan Coll (NC)
North Central Coll (IL)
North Dakota State U (ND)
Northeastern Illinois U (IL)
Northeastern State U (OK)
Northeastern U (MA)
Northern Arizona U (AZ)
Northern Illinois U (IL)
Northern Kentucky U (KY)
Northern Michigan U (MI)
Northern State U (SD)
North Georgia Coll & State U (GA)
Northland Coll (WI)
North Park U (IL)
Northwest Coll (WA)
Northwestern Coll (IA)
Northwestern Coll (MN)
Northwestern Oklahoma State U (OK)
Northwestern State U of Louisiana (LA)
Northwestern U (IL)
Northwest Missouri State U (MO)
Northwest Nazarene U (ID)
Norwich U (VT)
Notre Dame Coll (OH)
Notre Dame de Namur U (CA)
Nyack Coll (NY)
Oakland U (MI)
Oakwood Coll (AL)
Oberlin Coll (OH)
Occidental Coll (CA)
Oglethorpe U (GA)
Ohio Dominican Coll (OH)
Ohio Northern U (OH)
The Ohio State U (OH)
Ohio U (OH)
Ohio Wesleyan U (OH)
Okanagan U Coll (BC, Canada)
Oklahoma Baptist U (OK)
Oklahoma Christian U of Science and Arts (OK)
Oklahoma City U (OK)
Oklahoma Panhandle State U (OK)
Oklahoma State U (OK)
Oklahoma Wesleyan U (OK)
Old Dominion U (VA)
Olivet Coll (MI)
Olivet Nazarene U (IL)
Oral Roberts U (OK)
Oregon State U (OR)
Ottawa U (KS)
Otterbein Coll (OH)
Ouachita Baptist U (AR)
Our Lady of Holy Cross Coll (LA)
Our Lady of the Lake U of San Antonio (TX)
Pace U (NY)
Pacific Lutheran U (WA)
Pacific Union Coll (CA)
Pacific U (OR)
Paine Coll (GA)
Palm Beach Atlantic Coll (FL)
Park U (MO)
Penn State U Abington Coll (PA)
Penn State U at Erie, The Behrend Coll (PA)
Penn State U Univ Park Campus (PA)
Pepperdine U, Malibu (CA)
Peru State Coll (NE)
Pfeiffer U (NC)
Piedmont Coll (GA)
Pikeville Coll (KY)
Pillsbury Baptist Bible Coll (MN)
Pine Manor Coll (MA)
Pittsburg State U (KS)
Pitzer Coll (CA)
Plattsburgh State U of NY (NY)
Plymouth State Coll (NH)
Point Loma Nazarene U (CA)
Point Park Coll (PA)
Pomona Coll (CA)
Pontifical Catholic U of Puerto Rico (PR)
Portland State U (OR)
Prairie View A&M U (TX)
Presbyterian Coll (SC)
Prescott Coll (AZ)
Princeton U (NJ)
Principia Coll (IL)
Providence Coll (RI)
Providence Coll and Theological Seminary (MB, Canada)
Purchase Coll, State U of NY (NY)
Purdue U (IN)
Purdue U Calumet (IN)
Queens Coll (NC)
Queens Coll of the City U of NY (NY)
Queen's U at Kingston (ON, Canada)
Quincy U (IL)
Quinnipiac U (CT)
Radford U (VA)
Ramapo Coll of New Jersey (NJ)
Randolph-Macon Coll (VA)
Randolph-Macon Woman's Coll (VA)
Redeemer U Coll (ON, Canada)
Reed Coll (OR)
Regis Coll (MA)
Regis U (CO)
Rhode Island Coll (RI)
Rhodes Coll (TN)
Rice U (TX)
The Richard Stockton Coll of New Jersey (NJ)
Richmond, The American International U in London(United Kingdom)
Rider U (NJ)
Ripon Coll (WI)
Rivier Coll (NH)
Roanoke Coll (VA)
Roberts Wesleyan Coll (NY)
Rochester Coll (MI)
Rockford Coll (IL)
Rockhurst U (MO)
Rocky Mountain Coll (MT)
Roger Williams U (RI)
Rollins Coll (FL)
Roosevelt U (IL)
Rosemont Coll (PA)
Rowan U (NJ)
Russell Sage Coll (NY)
Rutgers, The State U of New Jersey, New Brunswick (NJ)
Sacred Heart U (CT)
Saginaw Valley State U (MI)
St. Ambrose U (IA)
St. Andrews Presbyterian Coll (NC)
Saint Anselm Coll (NH)
Saint Augustine's Coll (NC)
St. Bonaventure U (NY)
St. Cloud State U (MN)
St. Edward's U (TX)
St. Francis Coll (NY)
Saint Francis U (PA)
St. Francis Xavier U (NS, Canada)
St. John Fisher Coll (NY)
Saint John's U (MN)
St. John's U (NY)
Saint Joseph Coll (CT)
Saint Joseph's Coll (IN)
St. Joseph's Coll, New York (NY)
St. Joseph's Coll, Suffolk Campus (NY)
Saint Joseph's U (PA)
St. Lawrence U (NY)
Saint Leo U (FL)
Saint Louis U (MO)
Saint Martin's Coll (WA)
Saint Mary Coll (KS)
Saint Mary-of-the-Woods Coll (IN)
Saint Mary's Coll (IN)
Saint Mary's Coll of California (CA)
St. Mary's Coll of Maryland (MD)
Saint Mary's U (NS, Canada)
Saint Mary's U of Minnesota (MN)
St. Mary's U of San Antonio (TX)
Saint Michael's Coll (VT)
St. Norbert Coll (WI)
St. Olaf Coll (MN)
Saint Peter's Coll (NJ)
St. Thomas Aquinas Coll (NY)
St. Thomas U (FL)
St. Thomas U (NB, Canada)
Saint Vincent Coll (PA)
Saint Xavier U (IL)
Salem Coll (NC)
Salem State Coll (MA)
Salisbury U (MD)
Salve Regina U (RI)
Samford U (AL)
Sam Houston State U (TX)
San Diego State U (CA)
San Francisco State U (CA)
San Jose State U (CA)
Santa Clara U (CA)
Sarah Lawrence Coll (NY)
Savannah State U (GA)
Schreiner U (TX)
Scripps Coll (CA)
Seattle Pacific U (WA)
Seattle U (WA)
Seton Hall U (NJ)
Seton Hill Coll (PA)
Shawnee State U (OH)
Shenandoah U (VA)
Shepherd Coll (WV)
Shippensburg U of Pennsylvania (PA)
Shorter Coll (GA)
Siena Coll (NY)
Siena Heights U (MI)
Silver Lake Coll (WI)
Simmons Coll (MA)
Simon Fraser U (BC, Canada)
Simpson Coll (IA)
Simpson Coll and Graduate School (CA)
Skidmore Coll (NY)
Slippery Rock U of Pennsylvania (PA)
Smith Coll (MA)
Sonoma State U (CA)
South Carolina State U (SC)
South Dakota State U (SD)
Southeastern Louisiana U (LA)
Southeastern Oklahoma State U (OK)
Southeast Missouri State U (MO)
Southern Adventist U (TN)
Southern Arkansas U–Magnolia (AR)
Southern Connecticut State U (CT)
Southern Illinois U Carbondale (IL)
Southern Illinois U Edwardsville (IL)
Southern Methodist U (TX)
Southern Nazarene U (OK)
Southern Oregon U (OR)
Southern U and A&M Coll (LA)
Southern Utah U (UT)
Southern Virginia U (VA)
Southern Wesleyan U (SC)
Southwest Baptist U (MO)
Southwestern Adventist U (TX)
Southwestern Coll (KS)
Southwestern Oklahoma State U (OK)
Southwestern U (TX)
Southwest Missouri State U (MO)
Southwest State U (MN)
Southwest Texas State U (TX)
Spelman Coll (GA)
Spring Arbor U (MI)
Springfield Coll (MA)
Spring Hill Coll (AL)
Stanford U (CA)
State U of NY at Albany (NY)
State U of NY at Binghamton (NY)
State U of NY at New Paltz (NY)
State U of NY at Oswego (NY)
State U of NY Coll at Brockport (NY)
State U of NY Coll at Buffalo (NY)
State U of NY Coll at Cortland (NY)
State U of NY Coll at Fredonia (NY)
State U of NY Coll at Geneseo (NY)
State U of NY Coll at Oneonta (NY)
State U of NY Coll at Potsdam (NY)
State U of NY Empire State Coll (NY)
State U of West Georgia (GA)
Stephen F. Austin State U (TX)
Stephens Coll (MO)
Sterling Coll (KS)
Stetson U (FL)
Stevens Inst of Technology (NJ)
Stonehill Coll (MA)
State U of NY at Stony Brook (NY)
Suffolk U (MA)
Sul Ross State U (TX)
Susquehanna U (PA)
Swarthmore Coll (PA)
Sweet Briar Coll (VA)
Syracuse U (NY)
Tabor Coll (KS)
Talladega Coll (AL)
Tarleton State U (TX)
Taylor U (IN)
Teikyo Post U (CT)
Temple U (PA)
Tennessee State U (TN)
Tennessee Technological U (TN)
Tennessee Temple U (TN)
Tennessee Wesleyan Coll (TN)
Texas A&M International U (TX)
Texas A&M U (TX)
Texas A&M U–Commerce (TX)
Texas A&M U–Corpus Christi (TX)
Texas A&M U–Kingsville (TX)
Texas A&M U–Texarkana (TX)
Texas Christian U (TX)
Texas Coll (TX)
Texas Lutheran U (TX)
Texas Southern U (TX)
Texas Tech U (TX)
Texas Wesleyan U (TX)
Texas Woman's U (TX)
Thiel Coll (PA)
Thomas Edison State Coll (NJ)
Thomas More Coll (KY)
Thomas U (GA)
Tougaloo Coll (MS)
Touro Coll (NY)
Towson U (MD)
Transylvania U (KY)
Trent U (ON, Canada)
Trevecca Nazarene U (TN)
Trinity Christian Coll (IL)
Trinity Coll (CT)
Trinity Coll (DC)
Trinity International U (IL)
Trinity U (TX)
Trinity Western U (BC, Canada)
Troy State U (AL)
Troy State U Dothan (AL)
Troy State U Montgomery (AL)
Truman State U (MO)
Tufts U (MA)
Tulane U (LA)
Tusculum Coll (TN)
Tuskegee U (AL)
Tyndale Coll & Seminary (ON, Canada)
Union Coll (KY)
Union Coll (NE)
Union Coll (NY)
Union Inst & U (OH)
Union U (TN)
United States Air Force Academy (CO)
United States Military Academy (NY)
United States Naval Academy (MD)
Universidad Adventista de las Antillas (PR)
Université de Montréal (QC, Canada)
Université de Sherbrooke (PQ, Canada)
Université Laval (QC, Canada)
State U of NY at Buffalo (NY)
U Coll of Cape Breton (NS, Canada)
U Coll of the Cariboo (BC, Canada)
U Coll of the Fraser Valley (BC, Canada)
The U of Akron (OH)
The U of Alabama (AL)
The U of Alabama at Birmingham (AL)
The U of Alabama in Huntsville (AL)
U of Alaska Anchorage (AK)
U of Alaska Fairbanks (AK)
U of Alberta (AB, Canada)
The U of Arizona (AZ)
U of Arkansas (AR)
U of Arkansas at Little Rock (AR)
U of Arkansas at Pine Bluff (AR)
U of Baltimore (MD)
The U of British Columbia (BC, Canada)
U of Calgary (AB, Canada)
U of Calif, Berkeley (CA)
U of Calif, Davis (CA)
U of Calif, Irvine (CA)
U of Calif, Los Angeles (CA)
U of Calif, Riverside (CA)
U of Calif, San Diego (CA)
U of Calif, Santa Barbara (CA)
U of Calif, Santa Cruz (CA)
U of Central Arkansas (AR)
U of Central Florida (FL)
U of Central Oklahoma (OK)
U of Charleston (WV)
U of Chicago (IL)
U of Cincinnati (OH)
U of Colorado at Boulder (CO)
U of Colorado at Colorado Springs (CO)
U of Colorado at Denver (CO)
U of Connecticut (CT)
U of Dallas (TX)
U of Dayton (OH)
U of Delaware (DE)
U of Denver (CO)
U of Evansville (IN)
The U of Findlay (OH)
U of Florida (FL)
U of Georgia (GA)
U of Great Falls (MT)
U of Guelph (ON, Canada)
U of Hartford (CT)
U of Hawaii at Hilo (HI)
U of Hawaii at Manoa (HI)
U of Hawaii–West Oahu (HI)
U of Houston (TX)
U of Houston–Clear Lake (TX)
U of Idaho (ID)
U of Illinois at Chicago (IL)
U of Illinois at Springfield (IL)
U of Illinois at Urbana–Champaign (IL)
U of Indianapolis (IN)
The U of Iowa (IA)
U of Kansas (KS)
U of Kentucky (KY)
U of King's Coll (NS, Canada)
U of La Verne (CA)
The U of Lethbridge (AB, Canada)
U of Louisiana at Lafayette (LA)
U of Louisiana at Monroe (LA)
U of Louisville (KY)
U of Maine (ME)
U of Maine at Farmington (ME)
U of Maine at Machias (ME)
U of Maine at Presque Isle (ME)
U of Manitoba (MB, Canada)
U of Mary Hardin-Baylor (TX)
U of Maryland, Baltimore County (MD)
U of Maryland, Coll Park (MD)
U of Maryland Eastern Shore (MD)
U of Maryland University Coll (MD)
U of Massachusetts Amherst (MA)
U of Massachusetts Boston (MA)
U of Massachusetts Dartmouth (MA)
U of Massachusetts Lowell (MA)
The U of Memphis (TN)
U of Miami (FL)
U of Michigan (MI)
U of Michigan–Dearborn (MI)
U of Michigan–Flint (MI)
U of Minnesota, Duluth (MN)
U of Minnesota, Morris (MN)
U of Minnesota, Twin Cities Campus (MN)
U of Mississippi (MS)
U of Missouri–Columbia (MO)
U of Missouri–Kansas City (MO)
U of Missouri–Rolla (MO)
U of Missouri–St. Louis (MO)
U of Mobile (AL)
The U of Montana–Missoula (MT)
U of Montevallo (AL)
U of Nebraska at Kearney (NE)

U of Nebraska at Omaha (NE)
U of Nebraska–Lincoln (NE)
U of Nevada, Las Vegas (NV)
U of Nevada, Reno (NV)
U of New England (ME)
U of New Hampshire (NH)
U of New Haven (CT)
U of New Mexico (NM)
U of New Orleans (LA)
U of North Alabama (AL)
The U of North Carolina at Asheville (NC)
The U of North Carolina at Chapel Hill (NC)
The U of North Carolina at Charlotte (NC)
The U of North Carolina at Greensboro (NC)
The U of North Carolina at Pembroke (NC)
The U of North Carolina at Wilmington (NC)
U of North Dakota (ND)
U of Northern Colorado (CO)
U of Northern Iowa (IA)
U of North Florida (FL)
U of North Texas (TX)
U of Notre Dame (IN)
U of Oklahoma (OK)
U of Oregon (OR)
U of Ottawa (ON, Canada)
U of Pennsylvania (PA)
U of Pittsburgh (PA)
U of Pittsburgh at Bradford (PA)
U of Pittsburgh at Johnstown (PA)
U of Portland (OR)
U of Prince Edward Island (PE, Canada)
U of Puerto Rico, Cayey U Coll (PR)
U of Puget Sound (WA)
U of Redlands (CA)
U of Regina (SK, Canada)
U of Rhode Island (RI)
U of Richmond (VA)
U of Rio Grande (OH)
U of Rochester (NY)
U of St. Francis (IL)
U of Saint Francis (IN)
U of St. Thomas (MN)
U of St. Thomas (TX)
U of San Diego (CA)
U of San Francisco (CA)
U of Saskatchewan (SK, Canada)
U of Science and Arts of Oklahoma (OK)
The U of Scranton (PA)
U of Sioux Falls (SD)
U of South Alabama (AL)
U of South Carolina (SC)
U of South Carolina Aiken (SC)
U of South Carolina Spartanburg (SC)
U of South Dakota (SD)
U of Southern California (CA)
U of Southern Colorado (CO)
U of Southern Indiana (IN)
U of Southern Maine (ME)
U of Southern Mississippi (MS)
U of South Florida (FL)
The U of Tampa (FL)
The U of Tennessee (TN)
The U of Tennessee at Chattanooga (TN)
The U of Tennessee at Martin (TN)
The U of Texas at Arlington (TX)
The U of Texas at Austin (TX)
The U of Texas at Brownsville (TX)
The U of Texas at Dallas (TX)
The U of Texas at El Paso (TX)
The U of Texas at San Antonio (TX)
The U of Texas at Tyler (TX)
The U of Texas of the Permian Basin (TX)
The U of Texas–Pan American (TX)
U of the District of Columbia (DC)
U of the Incarnate Word (TX)
U of the Ozarks (AR)
U of the Pacific (CA)
U of the South (TN)
U of Toledo (OH)
U of Toronto (ON, Canada)
U of Tulsa (OK)
U of Utah (UT)
U of Vermont (VT)
U of Victoria (BC, Canada)
U of Virginia (VA)
The U of Virginia's Coll at Wise (VA)
U of Washington (WA)
U of Waterloo (ON, Canada)
The U of West Alabama (AL)
The U of Western Ontario (ON, Canada)
U of West Florida (FL)
U of Windsor (ON, Canada)
U of Wisconsin–Eau Claire (WI)
U of Wisconsin–Green Bay (WI)
U of Wisconsin–La Crosse (WI)
U of Wisconsin–Madison (WI)
U of Wisconsin–Milwaukee (WI)
U of Wisconsin–Oshkosh (WI)
U of Wisconsin–Parkside (WI)
U of Wisconsin–Platteville (WI)
U of Wisconsin–River Falls (WI)
U of Wisconsin–Stevens Point (WI)
U of Wisconsin–Superior (WI)
U of Wisconsin–Whitewater (WI)
U of Wyoming (WY)
Urbana U (OH)
Ursinus Coll (PA)
Ursuline Coll (OH)
Utah State U (UT)
Utica Coll of Syracuse U (NY)
Valdosta State U (GA)
Valley City State U (ND)
Valparaiso U (IN)
Vanderbilt U (TN)
Vanguard U of Southern California (CA)
Vassar Coll (NY)
Villanova U (PA)
Virginia Commonwealth U (VA)
Virginia Intermont Coll (VA)
Virginia Military Inst (VA)
Virginia Polytechnic Inst and State U (VA)
Virginia State U (VA)
Virginia Union U (VA)
Virginia Wesleyan Coll (VA)
Wabash Coll (IN)
Wagner Coll (NY)
Wake Forest U (NC)
Waldorf Coll (IA)
Walla Walla Coll (WA)
Walsh U (OH)
Warner Pacific Coll (OR)
Warner Southern Coll (FL)
Warren Wilson Coll (NC)
Wartburg Coll (IA)
Washburn U of Topeka (KS)
Washington & Jefferson Coll (PA)
Washington and Lee U (VA)
Washington Coll (MD)
Washington State U (WA)
Washington U in St. Louis (MO)
Wayland Baptist U (TX)
Waynesburg Coll (PA)
Wayne State Coll (NE)
Wayne State U (MI)
Weber State U (UT)
Webster U (MO)
Wellesley Coll (MA)
Wells Coll (NY)
Wesleyan Coll (GA)
Wesleyan U (CT)
Wesley Coll (DE)
West Chester U of Pennsylvania (PA)
Western Carolina U (NC)
Western Connecticut State U (CT)
Western Illinois U (IL)
Western Kentucky U (KY)
Western Maryland Coll (MD)
Western Michigan U (MI)
Western New England Coll (MA)
Western Oregon U (OR)
Western State Coll of Colorado (CO)
Western Washington U (WA)
Westfield State Coll (MA)
West Liberty State Coll (WV)
Westminster Coll (MO)
Westminster Coll (PA)
Westminster Coll (UT)
Westmont Coll (CA)
West Texas A&M U (TX)
West Virginia State Coll (WV)
West Virginia U (WV)
West Virginia U Inst of Technology (WV)
West Virginia Wesleyan Coll (WV)
Wheaton Coll (IL)
Wheaton Coll (MA)
Wheeling Jesuit U (WV)
Whitman Coll (WA)
Whittier Coll (CA)
Whitworth Coll (WA)
Wichita State U (KS)
Widener U (PA)
Wiley Coll (TX)
Wilfrid Laurier U (ON, Canada)
Wilkes U (PA)
Willamette U (OR)
William Carey Coll (MS)
William Jewell Coll (MO)
William Paterson U of New Jersey (NJ)
William Penn U (IA)
Williams Baptist Coll (AR)
Williams Coll (MA)
William Tyndale Coll (MI)
William Woods U (MO)
Wilmington Coll (OH)
Wingate U (NC)
Winona State U (MN)
Winston-Salem State U (NC)
Winthrop U (SC)
Wisconsin Lutheran Coll (WI)
Wittenberg U (OH)
Wofford Coll (SC)
Woodbury U (CA)
Worcester Polytechnic Inst (MA)
Worcester State Coll (MA)
Wright State U (OH)
Xavier U (OH)
Xavier U of Louisiana (LA)
Yale U (CT)
Yeshiva U (NY)
York Coll (NE)
York Coll of Pennsylvania (PA)
York Coll of the City U of New York (NY)
York U (ON, Canada)
Youngstown State U (OH)

HISTORY EDUCATION

Abilene Christian U (TX)
Adams State Coll (CO)
Anderson Coll (SC)
Appalachian State U (NC)
Baylor U (TX)
Berry Coll (GA)
Bethel Coll (TN)
Bowling Green State U (OH)
Bridgewater Coll (VA)
Brigham Young U (UT)
Carroll Coll (MT)
The Catholic U of America (DC)
Central Michigan U (MI)
Central Washington U (WA)
Chadron State Coll (NE)
Christian Brothers U (TN)
Citadel, The Military Coll of South Carolina (SC)
Clearwater Christian Coll (FL)
The Coll of New Jersey (NJ)
Coll of the Ozarks (MO)
Concordia Coll (MN)
Concordia U (IL)
Concordia U (NE)
Crown Coll (MN)
Culver-Stockton Coll (MO)
Cumberland U (TN)
Dakota Wesleyan U (SD)
Dana Coll (NE)
Dominican Coll (NY)
Eastern Michigan U (MI)
East Texas Baptist U (TX)
Elmhurst Coll (IL)
Elmira Coll (NY)
Framingham State Coll (MA)
Franklin Coll of Indiana (IN)
Georgia Southern U (GA)
Hardin-Simmons U (TX)
Hastings Coll (NE)
Howard Payne U (TX)
Huntingdon Coll (AL)
Huron U (SD)
Johnson State Coll (VT)
King Coll (TN)
Liberty U (VA)
Luther Coll (IA)
Maryville Coll (TN)
McGill U (PQ, Canada)
McKendree Coll (IL)
McMurry U (TX)
Mercer U (GA)
Minot State U (ND)
Montana State U–Billings (MT)
Mount Marty Coll (SD)
Nazareth Coll of Rochester (NY)
North Carolina Central U (NC)
North Dakota State U (ND)
Northern Arizona U (AZ)
Northwest Coll (WA)
Northwest Nazarene U (ID)
Oklahoma Baptist U (OK)
Pontifical Catholic U of Puerto Rico (PR)
Rocky Mountain Coll (MT)
St. Ambrose U (IA)
Saint Xavier U (IL)
Salve Regina U (RI)
Seton Hill Coll (PA)
Southwestern Oklahoma State U (OK)
Southwest Missouri State U (MO)
Talladega Coll (AL)
Tennessee Wesleyan Coll (TN)
Texas A&M International U (TX)
Texas Lutheran U (TX)
Texas Wesleyan U (TX)
Trevecca Nazarene U (TN)
Trinity Christian Coll (IL)
Union Coll (NE)
The U of Akron (OH)
The U of Arizona (AZ)
U of Central Oklahoma (OK)
U of Delaware (DE)
U of Illinois at Chicago (IL)
The U of Iowa (IA)
Western Montana Coll of The U of Montana (MT)
U of Nebraska–Lincoln (NE)
The U of North Carolina at Charlotte (NC)
The U of North Carolina at Wilmington (NC)
U of North Texas (TX)
U of Puerto Rico, Cayey U Coll (PR)
U of Rio Grande (OH)
The U of Tennessee at Martin (TN)
U of Utah (UT)
U of Windsor (ON, Canada)
U of Wisconsin–River Falls (WI)
U of Wisconsin–Superior (WI)
Utica Coll of Syracuse U (NY)
Valley City State U (ND)
Wartburg Coll (IA)
Washington U in St. Louis (MO)
Weber State U (UT)
Wheeling Jesuit U (WV)
York Coll (NE)
York U (ON, Canada)
Youngstown State U (OH)

HISTORY OF PHILOSOPHY

Bard Coll (NY)
Bennington Coll (VT)
The Evergreen State Coll (WA)
Hampshire Coll (MA)
Harvard U (MA)
Marlboro Coll (VT)
Marquette U (WI)
St. John's Coll (NM)
Spring Arbor U (MI)
U of Regina (SK, Canada)
U of Southern California (CA)
U of Toronto (ON, Canada)

HISTORY OF SCIENCE AND TECHNOLOGY

Bard Coll (NY)
Case Western Reserve U (OH)
Cornell U (NY)
Dalhousie U (NS, Canada)
Georgia Inst of Technology (GA)
Hampshire Coll (MA)
Harvard U (MA)
Johns Hopkins U (MD)
Oregon State U (OR)
U of Chicago (IL)
U of Pennsylvania (PA)
U of Pittsburgh (PA)
U of Toronto (ON, Canada)
U of Washington (WA)
U of Wisconsin–Madison (WI)
Worcester Polytechnic Inst (MA)

HISTORY RELATED

The Colorado Coll (CO)
Marylhurst U (OR)
Mount St. Clare Coll (IA)
The Ohio State U (OH)
Ohio U (OH)
Saint Mary's U of Minnesota (MN)

HOME ECONOMICS

Abilene Christian U (TX)
Alcorn State U (MS)
Appalachian State U (NC)
Ashland U (OH)
Auburn U (AL)
Baldwin-Wallace Coll (OH)
Ball State U (IN)
Baylor U (TX)
Bennett Coll (NC)
Bluffton Coll (OH)
Bridgewater Coll (VA)
California State Polytechnic U, Pomona (CA)
California State U, Long Beach (CA)
California State U, Northridge (CA)
Campbell U (NC)
Carson-Newman Coll (TN)
Central Michigan U (MI)
Central Missouri State U (MO)
Central Washington U (WA)
Coll of St. Catherine (MN)
Coll of the Ozarks (MO)
Colorado State U (CO)
Concordia U (NE)
Delaware State U (DE)
Delta State U (MS)
East Central U (OK)
Eastern Illinois U (IL)
Eastern Kentucky U (KY)
Eastern New Mexico U (NM)
East Tennessee State U (TN)
Fairmont State Coll (WV)
Florida State U (FL)
Fontbonne U (MO)
Framingham State Coll (MA)
Freed-Hardeman U (TN)
George Fox U (OR)
Henderson State U (AR)
Idaho State U (ID)
Immaculata Coll (PA)
Indiana State U (IN)
Iowa State U of Science and Technology (IA)
Jacksonville State U (AL)
Keene State Coll (NH)
Kent State U (OH)
Lamar U (TX)
Lipscomb U (TN)
Marshall U (WV)
Marymount Coll of Fordham U (NY)
The Master's Coll and Seminary (CA)
McNeese State U (LA)
Mercyhurst Coll (PA)
Meredith Coll (NC)
Miami U (OH)
Michigan State U (MI)
Minnesota State U, Mankato (MN)
Mississippi State U (MS)
Montana State U–Bozeman (MT)
Montclair State U (NJ)
Morehead State U (KY)
Morgan State U (MD)
Mount Vernon Nazarene U (OH)
Nicholls State U (LA)
Norfolk State U (VA)
North Carolina Ag and Tech State U (NC)
North Carolina Central U (NC)
Northeastern State U (OK)
Northwestern State U of Louisiana (LA)
Northwest Missouri State U (MO)
Oakwood Coll (AL)
Ohio U (OH)
Oklahoma State U (OK)
Olivet Nazarene U (IL)
Oregon State U (OR)
Ouachita Baptist U (AR)
Pacific Union Coll (CA)
Pittsburg State U (KS)
Point Loma Nazarene U (CA)
Pontifical Catholic U of Puerto Rico (PR)
Purdue U (IN)
Queens Coll of the City U of NY (NY)
Saint Joseph Coll (CT)
Sam Houston State U (TX)
San Francisco State U (CA)
Seton Hill Coll (PA)
Shepherd Coll (WV)
South Carolina State U (SC)
Southeast Missouri State U (MO)
Southern Utah U (UT)
Southwest Texas State U (TX)
State U of NY Coll at Oneonta (NY)
Stephen F. Austin State U (TX)
Tarleton State U (TX)
Tennessee Technological U (TN)

Texas A&M U–Kingsville (TX)
Texas Southern U (TX)
Texas Tech U (TX)
Texas Woman's U (TX)
The U of Akron (OH)
The U of Alabama (AL)
U of Alberta (AB, Canada)
U of Arkansas (AR)
U of Arkansas at Pine Bluff (AR)
The U of British Columbia (BC, Canada)
U of Central Arkansas (AR)
U of Central Oklahoma (OK)
U of Hawaii at Manoa (HI)
U of Houston (TX)
U of Kentucky (KY)
U of Louisiana at Monroe (LA)
U of Manitoba (MB, Canada)
U of Maryland Eastern Shore (MD)
U of Mississippi (MS)
U of Montevallo (AL)
U of New Hampshire (NH)
U of New Mexico (NM)
U of North Alabama (AL)
The U of North Carolina at Greensboro (NC)
U of Southern Mississippi (MS)
The U of Tennessee at Chattanooga (TN)
The U of Tennessee at Martin (TN)
The U of Texas at Austin (TX)
U of the District of Columbia (DC)
U of Utah (UT)
The U of Western Ontario (ON, Canada)
U of Wisconsin–Madison (WI)
Washington State U (WA)
Wayne State Coll (NE)
Western Illinois U (IL)
West Virginia U (WV)
Youngstown State U (OH)

HOME ECONOMICS COMMUNICATIONS
Framingham State Coll (MA)

HOME ECONOMICS EDUCATION
Abilene Christian U (TX)
Appalachian State U (NC)
Ashland U (OH)
Auburn U (AL)
Baldwin-Wallace Coll (OH)
Ball State U (IN)
Berea Coll (KY)
Bluffton Coll (OH)
Bowling Green State U (OH)
Bridgewater Coll (VA)
California State U, Northridge (CA)
Campbell U (NC)
Carson-Newman Coll (TN)
Central Michigan U (MI)
Central Missouri State U (MO)
Chadron State Coll (NE)
Cheyney U of Pennsylvania (PA)
Coll of St. Catherine (MN)
Coll of the Ozarks (MO)
Colorado State U (CO)
Concordia U (NE)
Cornell U (NY)
Delta State U (MS)
East Carolina U (NC)
Eastern Kentucky U (KY)
Eastern Michigan U (MI)
Fairmont State Coll (WV)
Ferris State U (MI)
Florida International U (FL)
Florida State U (FL)
Fontbonne U (MO)
Fort Valley State U (GA)
Framingham State Coll (MA)
George Fox U (OR)
Georgia Southern U (GA)
Grambling State U (LA)
Hampton U (VA)
Henderson State U (AR)
Immaculata Coll (PA)
Indiana U of Pennsylvania (PA)
Iowa State U of Science and Technology (IA)
Jacksonville State U (AL)
Keene State Coll (NH)
Lamar U (TX)
Marymount Coll of Fordham U (NY)
Marywood U (PA)
McNeese State U (LA)
Mercyhurst Coll (PA)
Miami U (OH)
Michigan State U (MI)
Minnesota State U, Mankato (MN)
Mississippi Coll (MS)
Montclair State U (NJ)
Morehead State U (KY)
Mount Vernon Nazarene U (OH)
Murray State U (KY)
New Mexico State U (NM)
North Carolina Ag and Tech State U (NC)
North Carolina Central U (NC)
North Dakota State U (ND)
Northeastern State U (OK)
Northern Illinois U (IL)
Northwest Missouri State U (MO)
Oakwood Coll (AL)
Olivet Nazarene U (IL)
Ouachita Baptist U (AR)
Pacific Union Coll (CA)
Pittsburg State U (KS)
Pontifical Catholic U of Puerto Rico (PR)
Queens Coll of the City U of NY (NY)
Saint Joseph Coll (CT)
Sam Houston State U (TX)
Seattle Pacific U (WA)
Seton Hill Coll (PA)
South Carolina State U (SC)
South Dakota State U (SD)
Southeast Missouri State U (MO)
Southern Utah U (UT)
Southwest Missouri State U (MO)
State U of NY Coll at Oneonta (NY)
Tennessee Technological U (TN)
Texas A&M U–Kingsville (TX)
The U of Akron (OH)
U of Alberta (AB, Canada)
The U of Arizona (AZ)
U of Arkansas at Pine Bluff (AR)
The U of British Columbia (BC, Canada)
U of Central Arkansas (AR)
U of Central Oklahoma (OK)
U of Georgia (GA)
U of Hawaii at Manoa (HI)
U of Idaho (ID)
U of Illinois at Springfield (IL)
U of Maryland Eastern Shore (MD)
U of Minnesota, Twin Cities Campus (MN)
U of Montevallo (AL)
U of Nevada, Reno (NV)
U of New Mexico (NM)
U of North Texas (TX)
U of Saskatchewan (SK, Canada)
The U of Tennessee (TN)
The U of Tennessee at Martin (TN)
U of the District of Columbia (DC)
U of Utah (UT)
U of Wisconsin–Madison (WI)
U of Wisconsin–Stevens Point (WI)
U of Wisconsin–Stout (WI)
Utah State U (UT)
Washington State U (WA)
Wayne State Coll (NE)
Western Kentucky U (KY)
Western Michigan U (MI)
Winthrop U (SC)
Youngstown State U (OH)

HOME ECONOMICS RELATED
Norfolk State U (VA)
Northwestern State U of Louisiana (LA)
The U of Alabama (AL)

HORTICULTURE SCIENCE
Auburn U (AL)
Berry Coll (GA)
Brigham Young U (UT)
California Polytechnic State U, San Luis Obispo (CA)
California State Polytechnic U, Pomona (CA)
Cameron U (OK)
Christopher Newport U (VA)
Clemson U (SC)
Coll of the Ozarks (MO)
Colorado State U (CO)
Cornell U (NY)
Delaware Valley Coll (PA)
Eastern Kentucky U (KY)
Florida A&M U (FL)
Florida Southern Coll (FL)
Iowa State U of Science and Technology (IA)
Kansas State U (KS)
Michigan State U (MI)
Mississippi State U (MS)
Montana State U–Bozeman (MT)
Murray State U (KY)
Naropa U (CO)
New Mexico State U (NM)
North Carolina State U (NC)
North Dakota State U (ND)
Northwest Missouri State U (MO)
The Ohio State U (OH)
Oklahoma State U (OK)
Oregon State U (OR)
Penn State U Univ Park Campus (PA)
Purdue U (IN)
Sam Houston State U (TX)
Southeastern Louisiana U (LA)
Southeast Missouri State U (MO)
Southwest Missouri State U (MO)
State U of NY Coll of A&T at Cobleskill (NY)
Stephen F. Austin State U (TX)
Tarleton State U (TX)
Tennessee Technological U (TN)
Texas A&M U–Kingsville (TX)
Texas Tech U (TX)
Thomas Edison State Coll (NJ)
U of Arkansas (AR)
The U of British Columbia (BC, Canada)
U of Calif, Davis (CA)
U of Connecticut (CT)
U of Delaware (DE)
U of Florida (FL)
U of Guelph (ON, Canada)
U of Hawaii at Hilo (HI)
U of Hawaii at Manoa (HI)
U of Idaho (ID)
U of Illinois at Urbana–Champaign (IL)
U of Maryland, Coll Park (MD)
U of Minnesota, Crookston (MN)
U of Nebraska–Lincoln (NE)
U of New Hampshire (NH)
U of Saskatchewan (SK, Canada)
U of Vermont (VT)
U of Wisconsin–Madison (WI)
U of Wisconsin–River Falls (WI)
Utah State U (UT)
Virginia Polytechnic Inst and State U (VA)
Washington State U (WA)
West Virginia U (WV)

HORTICULTURE SERVICES
Iowa State U of Science and Technology (IA)
Nova Scotia Ag Coll (NS, Canada)
South Dakota State U (SD)
Stephen F. Austin State U (TX)
Texas A&M U (TX)
Texas Tech U (TX)
U of Georgia (GA)
U of Hawaii at Manoa (HI)
U of Vermont (VT)

HOSPITALITY MANAGEMENT
Arkansas Tech U (AR)
Bay Path Coll (MA)
Becker Coll (MA)
Belmont U (TN)
Boston U (MA)
Bowling Green State U (OH)
Central Michigan U (MI)
Champlain Coll (VT)
The Coll of Southeastern Europe, The American U of Athens(Greece)
Concord Coll (WV)
Davis & Elkins Coll (WV)
Delta State U (MS)
Eastern Michigan U (MI)
Endicott Coll (MA)
Ferris State U (MI)
Florida International U (FL)
Florida State U (FL)
Husson Coll (ME)
Indiana U–Purdue U Fort Wayne (IN)
International Business Coll, Fort Wayne (IN)
Johnson & Wales U (RI)
Johnson State Coll (VT)
Kendall Coll (IL)
Lakeland Coll (WI)
Marywood U (PA)
Mercyhurst Coll (PA)
Metropolitan State Coll of Denver (CO)
Metropolitan State U (MN)
Morgan State U (MD)
Morris Brown Coll (GA)
Mount Saint Vincent U (NS, Canada)
National American U (NM)
National American U–St. Paul Campus (MN)
North Carolina Central U (NC)
Nova Southeastern U (FL)
The Ohio State U (OH)
The Ohio State U at Lima (OH)
Penn State U Univ Park Campus (PA)
Philander Smith Coll (AR)
Robert Morris U (PA)
Rochester Inst of Technology (NY)
Roosevelt U (IL)
San Francisco State U (CA)
San Jose State U (CA)
Siena Heights U (MI)
Sojourner-Douglass Coll (MD)
Southern New Hampshire U (NH)
Southern Vermont Coll (VT)
Stephen F. Austin State U (TX)
Syracuse U (NY)
Tiffin U (OH)
Touro U International (CA)
Tuskegee U (AL)
U Coll of Cape Breton (NS, Canada)
U of Central Florida (FL)
U of Denver (CO)
U of Kentucky (KY)
U of Massachusetts Amherst (MA)
The U of Memphis (TN)
U of Nevada, Las Vegas (NV)
U of Nevada, Reno (NV)
U of New Haven (CT)
U of New Orleans (LA)
U of Prince Edward Island (PE, Canada)
U of South Carolina (SC)
Western Carolina U (NC)
Youngstown State U (OH)

HOSPITALITY/RECREATION MARKETING
Rochester Inst of Technology (NY)

HOSPITALITY/RECREATION MARKETING OPERATIONS
Champlain Coll (VT)
Methodist Coll (NC)
Tuskegee U (AL)
U Coll of Cape Breton (NS, Canada)

HOSPITALITY SERVICES MANAGEMENT RELATED
Drexel U (PA)
Indiana U–Purdue U Indianapolis (IN)
San Diego State U (CA)
U of Hawaii at Manoa (HI)
U of Louisiana at Lafayette (LA)

HOTEL AND RESTAURANT MANAGEMENT
Alliant International U (CA)
Appalachian State U (NC)
Ashland U (OH)
Auburn U (AL)
Baltimore International Coll (MD)
Barber-Scotia Coll (NC)
Becker Coll (MA)
Belmont U (TN)
Berea Coll (KY)
Bethune-Cookman Coll (FL)
Boston U (MA)
Brigham Young U–Hawaii (HI)
California State Polytechnic U, Pomona (CA)
Central Michigan U (MI)
Central Missouri State U (MO)
Central State U (OH)
Champlain Coll (VT)
Cheyney U of Pennsylvania (PA)
Chicago State U (IL)
The Coll of Southeastern Europe, The American U of Athens(Greece)
Coll of the Ozarks (MO)
Colorado State U (CO)
Concord Coll (WV)
Cornell U (NY)
Davenport U, Grand Rapids (MI)
Delaware State U (DE)
East Carolina U (NC)
East Stroudsburg U of Pennsylvania (PA)
Fairleigh Dickinson U, Florham-Madison Campus (NJ)
Fairleigh Dickinson U, Teaneck-Hackensack Campus (NJ)
Florida Metropolitan U-Fort Lauderdale Coll (FL)
Florida Southern Coll (FL)
Georgia Southern U (GA)
Georgia State U (GA)
Grambling State U (LA)
Grand Valley State U (MI)
Hampton U (VA)
Howard U (DC)
Indiana U of Pennsylvania (PA)
Inter American U of PR, Aguadilla Campus (PR)
Iowa State U of Science and Technology (IA)
James Madison U (VA)
Johnson & Wales U (RI)
Kansas State U (KS)
Kendall Coll (IL)
Keuka Coll (NY)
Lasell Coll (MA)
Lynn U (FL)
Mercyhurst Coll (PA)
Michigan State U (MI)
Morgan State U (MD)
Mount Ida Coll (MA)
Mount Saint Vincent U (NS, Canada)
National American U (NM)
National American U–Sioux Falls Branch (SD)
Newbury Coll (MA)
New England Culinary Inst (VT)
New Mexico State U (NM)
New York Inst of Technology (NY)
New York U (NY)
Niagara U (NY)
North Carolina Wesleyan Coll (NC)
North Dakota State U (ND)
Northern Arizona U (AZ)
Northwood U (MI)
Northwood U, Florida Campus (FL)
Northwood U, Texas Campus (TX)
Nova Southeastern U (FL)
Oklahoma State U (OK)
Pace U (NY)
Paul Smith's Coll of Arts and Sciences (NY)
Peirce Coll (PA)
Penn State U Univ Park Campus (PA)
Plattsburgh State U of NY (NY)
Purdue U (IN)
Purdue U Calumet (IN)
Rochester Inst of Technology (NY)
St. John's U (NY)
Saint Leo U (FL)
St. Thomas U (FL)
San Diego State U (CA)
Schiller International U (FL)
Schiller International U(Spain)
Schiller International U(United Kingdom)
Schiller International U, American Coll of Switzerland(Switzerland)
Sierra Nevada Coll (NV)
South Dakota State U (SD)
Southern New Hampshire U (NH)
Southern Oregon U (OR)
Southern Vermont Coll (VT)
Southwest Missouri State U (MO)
State U of NY Coll at Buffalo (NY)
State U of NY Coll of Technology at Delhi (NY)
Sullivan U (KY)
Texas A&M U–Kingsville (TX)
Texas Tech U (TX)
Thomas Coll (ME)
Thomas Edison State Coll (NJ)
The U of Alabama (AL)
U of Arkansas at Pine Bluff (AR)
U of Calgary (AB, Canada)
U of Central Oklahoma (OK)
U of Delaware (DE)
U of Denver (CO)
The U of Findlay (OH)
U of Guelph (ON, Canada)
U of Houston (TX)
U of Maine at Machias (ME)
U of Maryland Eastern Shore (MD)
U of Minnesota, Crookston (MN)
U of Missouri–Columbia (MO)
U of New Hampshire (NH)
U of New Haven (CT)

U of North Texas (TX)
U of San Francisco (CA)
U of Southern Mississippi (MS)
The U of Tennessee (TN)
U of the Incarnate Word (TX)
U of Victoria (BC, Canada)
U of Wisconsin–Stout (WI)
Virginia State U (VA)
Washington State U (WA)
Webber International U (FL)
Western Kentucky U (KY)
Widener U (PA)
Wiley Coll (TX)
Youngstown State U (OH)

HOTEL/MOTEL SERVICES MARKETING OPERATIONS
Champlain Coll (VT)
Lake Erie Coll (OH)
Lewis-Clark State Coll (ID)

HOUSING STUDIES
Auburn U (AL)
Florida State U (FL)
Iowa State U of Science and Technology (IA)
Ohio U (OH)
Southeast Missouri State U (MO)
Southwest Missouri State U (MO)
U of Arkansas (AR)
U of Georgia (GA)
U of Missouri–Columbia (MO)
U of Northern Iowa (IA)
Utah State U (UT)
Western Kentucky U (KY)

HUMAN ECOLOGY
California State U, Hayward (CA)
Cameron U (OK)
Coll of the Atlantic (ME)
Concordia U (QC, Canada)
Connecticut Coll (CT)
Cornell U (NY)
Emory U (GA)
The Evergreen State Coll (WA)
Goddard Coll (VT)
Kansas State U (KS)
Lambuth U (TN)
Long Island U, Southampton Coll, Friends World Program (NY)
Marymount Coll of Fordham U (NY)
Mercyhurst Coll (PA)
Morgan State U (MD)
Mount Saint Vincent U (NS, Canada)
Prescott Coll (AZ)
Regis U (CO)
Rutgers, The State U of New Jersey, New Brunswick (NJ)
State U of NY Coll at Oneonta (NY)
Sterling Coll (VT)
U of Alberta (AB, Canada)
U of Calif, Irvine (CA)
U of Calif, San Diego (CA)
U of Manitoba (MB, Canada)
U of Maryland Eastern Shore (MD)

HUMANITIES
Adelphi U (NY)
Albertus Magnus Coll (CT)
Alma Coll (MI)
Angelo State U (TX)
Antioch U McGregor (OH)
Arizona State U (AZ)
Athens State U (AL)
Atlanta Christian Coll (GA)
Augsburg Coll (MN)
Aurora U (IL)
Avila Coll (MO)
Bard Coll (NY)
Becker Coll (MA)
Belhaven Coll (MS)
Bemidji State U (MN)
Bennington Coll (VT)
Biola U (CA)
Bishop's U (PQ, Canada)
Bloomsburg U of Pennsylvania (PA)
Bluefield State Coll (WV)
Bluffton Coll (OH)
Bowling Green State U (OH)
Brigham Young U (UT)
Brock U (ON, Canada)
Bryn Athyn Coll of the New Church (PA)
Bucknell U (PA)
Burlington Coll (VT)
California State Polytechnic U, Pomona (CA)
California State U, Chico (CA)
California State U, Dominguez Hills (CA)
California State U, Monterey Bay (CA)
California State U, Northridge (CA)
California State U, Sacramento (CA)
California State U, San Bernardino (CA)
Canisius Coll (NY)
Carleton U (ON, Canada)
Carnegie Mellon U (PA)
Catawba Coll (NC)
Chaminade U of Honolulu (HI)
Charleston Southern U (SC)
Clarion U of Pennsylvania (PA)
Clarkson U (NY)
Clearwater Christian Coll (FL)
Colgate U (NY)
Coll of Mount St. Joseph (OH)
Coll of Saint Benedict (MN)
Coll of Saint Mary (NE)
The Coll of St. Scholastica (MN)
Coll of Santa Fe (NM)
Colorado Christian U (CO)
Colorado State U (CO)
Columbia Coll (MO)
Columbia International U (SC)
Concordia Coll (MN)
Concordia U (CA)
Concordia U (OR)
Concordia U Wisconsin (WI)
Daemen Coll (NY)
Dominican Coll (NY)
Dominican U of California (CA)
Dowling Coll (NY)
Drexel U (PA)
Eastern Washington U (WA)
Eckerd Coll (FL)
Edinboro U of Pennsylvania (PA)
Elmira Coll (NY)
Eugene Lang Coll, New School U (NY)
The Evergreen State Coll (WA)
Fairleigh Dickinson U, Florham-Madison Campus (NJ)
Fairleigh Dickinson U, Teaneck-Hackensack Campus (NJ)
Faulkner U (AL)
Felician Coll (NJ)
Florida Inst of Technology (FL)
Florida International U (FL)
Florida Southern Coll (FL)
Florida State U (FL)
Fort Lewis Coll (CO)
Framingham State Coll (MA)
Franciscan U of Steubenville (OH)
Freed-Hardeman U (TN)
Fresno Pacific U (CA)
Gannon U (PA)
The George Washington U (DC)
Georgian Court Coll (NJ)
Goddard Coll (VT)
Grace U (NE)
Grand Valley State U (MI)
Hampden-Sydney Coll (VA)
Hampshire Coll (MA)
Harding U (AR)
Harvard U (MA)
Hawai'i Pacific U (HI)
Hofstra U (NY)
Holy Apostles Coll and Seminary (CT)
Holy Family Coll (PA)
Holy Names Coll (CA)
Hope Coll (MI)
Houghton Coll (NY)
Huron U USA in London(United Kingdom)
Indiana State U (IN)
Indiana U Kokomo (IN)
Jacksonville U (FL)
John Carroll U (OH)
John F. Kennedy U (CA)
Johnson State Coll (VT)
Juniata Coll (PA)
Kansas State U (KS)
Kenyon Coll (OH)
Lambuth U (TN)
Lawrence Technological U (MI)
Lees-McRae Coll (NC)
LeMoyne-Owen Coll (TN)
Lesley U (MA)
Lincoln Memorial U (TN)
Lock Haven U of Pennsylvania (PA)
Long Island U, Brooklyn Campus (NY)
Long Island U, Southampton Coll, Friends World Program (NY)
Loyola Marymount U (CA)
Loyola U Chicago (IL)
Loyola U New Orleans (LA)
Lubbock Christian U (TX)
Lynn U (FL)
Macalester Coll (MN)
Maranatha Baptist Bible Coll (WI)
Marist Coll (NY)
Marlboro Coll (VT)
Marshall U (WV)
Maryville U of Saint Louis (MO)
Massachusetts Inst of Technology (MA)
McGill U (PQ, Canada)
Medaille Coll (NY)
Memorial U of Newfoundland (NF, Canada)
Mercyhurst Coll (PA)
Mesa State Coll (CO)
Messiah Coll (PA)
Michigan State U (MI)
Middlebury Coll (VT)
Midland Lutheran Coll (NE)
Midwestern State U (TX)
Milligan Coll (TN)
Minnesota State U, Mankato (MN)
Monmouth Coll (IL)
Montana State U–Northern (MT)
Montclair State U (NJ)
Mount Allison U (NB, Canada)
Mount Aloysius Coll (PA)
Mount St. Clare Coll (IA)
Mount Saint Vincent U (NS, Canada)
Muskingum Coll (OH)
New Coll of California (CA)
New York U (NY)
North Central Coll (IL)
North Dakota State U (ND)
Northern Arizona U (AZ)
North Greenville Coll (SC)
Northwest Christian Coll (OR)
Northwestern Coll (IA)
Northwestern U (IL)
Northwest Missouri State U (MO)
Notre Dame de Namur U (CA)
Nova Southeastern U (FL)
Oakland City U (IN)
The Ohio State U (OH)
Ohio Wesleyan U (OH)
Oklahoma Baptist U (OK)
Oklahoma City U (OK)
Oklahoma Panhandle State U (OK)
Pacific U (OR)
Pepperdine U, Malibu (CA)
Pfeiffer U (NC)
Plymouth State Coll (NH)
Pomona Coll (CA)
Portland State U (OR)
Prescott Coll (AZ)
Principia Coll (IL)
Providence Coll (RI)
Providence Coll and Theological Seminary (MB, Canada)
Purdue U (IN)
Purdue U Calumet (IN)
Quincy U (IL)
Redeemer U Coll (ON, Canada)
Regis U (CO)
Roberts Wesleyan Coll (NY)
Rockford Coll (IL)
Rosemont Coll (PA)
St. Gregory's U (OK)
Saint John's U (MN)
Saint Joseph Coll (CT)
Saint Joseph's U (PA)
Saint Louis U (MO)
Saint Martin's Coll (WA)
Saint Mary-of-the-Woods Coll (IN)
Saint Mary's Coll (IN)
St. Norbert Coll (WI)
Saint Peter's Coll (NJ)
St. Thomas Aquinas Coll (NY)
Samford U (AL)
Sam Houston State U (TX)
San Diego State U (CA)
San Francisco State U (CA)
San Jose State U (CA)
Sarah Lawrence Coll (NY)
Schreiner U (TX)
Seattle U (WA)
Seton Hall U (NJ)
Shawnee State U (OH)
Sheldon Jackson Coll (AK)
Shimer Coll (IL)
Shorter Coll (GA)
Siena Heights U (MI)
Sierra Nevada Coll (NV)
Simon Fraser U (BC, Canada)
Southeastern Louisiana U (LA)
Southern Methodist U (TX)
Southern New Hampshire U (NH)
Southwest Missouri State U (MO)
Spring Hill Coll (AL)
State U of NY Coll at Buffalo (NY)
State U of NY Coll at Old Westbury (NY)
State U of NY Empire State Coll (NY)
State U of NY Maritime Coll (NY)
Stephen F. Austin State U (TX)
Stetson U (FL)
Stevens Inst of Technology (NJ)
State U of NY at Stony Brook (NY)
Suffolk U (MA)
Tabor Coll (KS)
Tennessee State U (TN)
Texas Wesleyan U (TX)
Thomas Edison State Coll (NJ)
Thomas U (GA)
Tiffin U (OH)
Touro Coll (NY)
Trent U (ON, Canada)
Trinity International U (IL)
Trinity U (TX)
Trinity Western U (BC, Canada)
Union Coll (NY)
Union Inst & U (OH)
United States Air Force Academy (CO)
United States Military Academy (NY)
The U of Akron (OH)
U of Alberta (AB, Canada)
The U of Arizona (AZ)
U of Bridgeport (CT)
U of Calgary (AB, Canada)
U of Calif, Irvine (CA)
U of Calif, Riverside (CA)
U of Central Florida (FL)
U of Charleston (WV)
U of Chicago (IL)
U of Cincinnati (OH)
U of Colorado at Boulder (CO)
U of Hawaii–West Oahu (HI)
U of Houston–Clear Lake (TX)
U of Houston–Victoria (TX)
U of Illinois at Urbana–Champaign (IL)
U of Kansas (KS)
The U of Lethbridge (AB, Canada)
U of Maryland University Coll (MD)
U of Massachusetts Amherst (MA)
U of Michigan (MI)
U of Michigan–Dearborn (MI)
U of Missouri–St. Louis (MO)
U of Mobile (AL)
U of New England (ME)
U of New Hampshire (NH)
U of New Mexico (NM)
U of North Dakota (ND)
U of Northern Iowa (IA)
U of Ottawa (ON, Canada)
U of Pennsylvania (PA)
U of Pittsburgh (PA)
U of Pittsburgh at Greensburg (PA)
U of Pittsburgh at Johnstown (PA)
U of Puerto Rico, Cayey U Coll (PR)
U of Regina (SK, Canada)
U of Rio Grande (OH)
U of San Diego (CA)
U of South Florida (FL)
The U of Tennessee at Chattanooga (TN)
The U of Texas at Austin (TX)
The U of Texas at Dallas (TX)
The U of Texas at San Antonio (TX)
The U of Texas of the Permian Basin (TX)
U of the Virgin Islands (VI)
U of Toledo (OH)
U of Toronto (ON, Canada)
U of Washington (WA)
U of West Florida (FL)
U of Windsor (ON, Canada)
U of Wisconsin–Green Bay (WI)
U of Wisconsin–Parkside (WI)
U of Wyoming (WY)
Ursuline Coll (OH)
Villa Julie Coll (MD)
Virginia Wesleyan Coll (VA)
Viterbo U (WI)
Waldorf Coll (IA)
Walla Walla Coll (WA)
Warren Wilson Coll (NC)
Washington Coll (MD)
Washington State U (WA)
Wesleyan Coll (GA)
Wesleyan U (CT)
Western Baptist Coll (OR)
Western Oregon U (OR)
Western Washington U (WA)
Widener U (PA)
Willamette U (OR)
William Paterson U of New Jersey (NJ)
Wittenberg U (OH)
Wofford Coll (SC)
Worcester Polytechnic Inst (MA)
Yale U (CT)
York Coll of Pennsylvania (PA)
York U (ON, Canada)

HUMAN RESOURCES MANAGEMENT
Abilene Christian U (TX)
American International Coll (MA)
American U (DC)
Anderson Coll (SC)
Antioch U McGregor (OH)
Arcadia U (PA)
Athens State U (AL)
Auburn U (AL)
Auburn U Montgomery (AL)
Baker Coll of Owosso (MI)
Ball State U (IN)
Barton Coll (NC)
Bayamón Central U (PR)
Baylor U (TX)
Bay Path Coll (MA)
Becker Coll (MA)
Bellarmine U (KY)
Baruch Coll of the City U of NY (NY)
Birmingham-Southern Coll (AL)
Bishop's U (PQ, Canada)
Black Hills State U (SD)
Bloomfield Coll (NJ)
Bluefield Coll (VA)
Boise State U (ID)
Boston Coll (MA)
Bowling Green State U (OH)
Brescia U (KY)
Briar Cliff U (IA)
Brock U (ON, Canada)
Cabrini Coll (PA)
California Polytechnic State U, San Luis Obispo (CA)
California State Polytechnic U, Pomona (CA)
California State U, Chico (CA)
California State U, Dominguez Hills (CA)
California State U, Fresno (CA)
California State U, Hayward (CA)
California State U, Long Beach (CA)
Calvary Bible Coll and Theological Seminary (MO)
Caribbean U (PR)
Carleton U (ON, Canada)
The Catholic U of America (DC)
Central Baptist Coll (AR)
Central Michigan U (MI)
Central Missouri State U (MO)
Chestnut Hill Coll (PA)
Clarkson U (NY)
Cleary Coll (MI)
Coll of Saint Elizabeth (NJ)
The Coll of Southeastern Europe, The American U of Athens(Greece)
Colorado Christian U (CO)
Colorado Tech U (CO)
Colorado Tech U Sioux Falls Campus (SD)
Concordia U (QC, Canada)
Davenport U, Lansing (MI)
DePaul U (IL)
DeSales U (PA)
Dominican Coll (NY)
Dominican U of California (CA)
Drexel U (PA)
East Central U (OK)
Eastern Michigan U (MI)
Eastern New Mexico U (NM)
Eastern Washington U (WA)
Eckerd Coll (FL)

École des Hautes Études Commerciales de Montréal (PQ, Canada)
Excelsior Coll (NY)
Faulkner U (AL)
Florida Atlantic U (FL)
Florida International U (FL)
Florida Southern Coll (FL)
Florida State U (FL)
Framingham State Coll (MA)
Franklin U (OH)
Freed-Hardeman U (TN)
Friends U (KS)
George Fox U (OR)
The George Washington U (DC)
Georgia Southwestern State U (GA)
Georgia State U (GA)
Golden Gate U (CA)
Governors State U (IL)
Grace U (NE)
Grand Canyon U (AZ)
Grand Valley State U (MI)
Gwynedd-Mercy Coll (PA)
Harding U (AR)
Hastings Coll (NE)
Hawai'i Pacific U (HI)
Holy Names Coll (CA)
Idaho State U (ID)
Indiana Inst of Technology (IN)
Indiana State U (IN)
Indiana U of Pennsylvania (PA)
Inter American U of PR, San Germán Campus (PR)
Ithaca Coll (NY)
Judson Coll (IL)
Juniata Coll (PA)
Keystone Coll (PA)
King's Coll (PA)
Kutztown U of Pennsylvania (PA)
Lakehead U (ON, Canada)
La Salle U (PA)
Lewis U (IL)
Lincoln U (PA)
Lindenwood U (MO)
Loras Coll (IA)
Louisiana Tech U (LA)
Loyola U Chicago (IL)
Mansfield U of Pennsylvania (PA)
Marietta Coll (OH)
Marquette U (WI)
Marymount U (VA)
McGill U (PQ, Canada)
Medaille Coll (NY)
Mercyhurst Coll (PA)
Meredith Coll (NC)
Mesa State Coll (CO)
Messiah Coll (PA)
Metropolitan State U (MN)
Miami U (OH)
Michigan State U (MI)
MidAmerica Nazarene U (KS)
Millikin U (IL)
Muhlenberg Coll (PA)
National U (CA)
Nazareth Coll of Rochester (NY)
Newbury Coll (MA)
New York Inst of Technology (NY)
Niagara U (NY)
North Carolina State U (NC)
Northeastern Illinois U (IL)
Northeastern State U (OK)
Northeastern U (MA)
Notre Dame Coll (OH)
Oakland City U (IN)
Oakland U (MI)
The Ohio State U (OH)
Ohio U (OH)
Ohio Valley Coll (WV)
Oklahoma Baptist U (OK)
Oklahoma State U (OK)
Olivet Nazarene U (IL)
Our Lady of the Lake U of San Antonio (TX)
Pace U (NY)
Palm Beach Atlantic Coll (FL)
Peace Coll (NC)
Point Park Coll (PA)
Pontifical Catholic U of Puerto Rico (PR)
Portland State U (OR)
Purdue U Calumet (IN)
Quinnipiac U (CT)
Redeemer U Coll (ON, Canada)
Rider U (NJ)
Robert Morris U (PA)
Roberts Wesleyan Coll (NY)
Rockhurst U (MO)
Roosevelt U (IL)
St. Cloud State U (MN)
Saint Francis U (PA)
St. John Fisher Coll (NY)
St. Joseph's Coll, New York (NY)
St. Joseph's Coll, Suffolk Campus (NY)
Saint Leo U (FL)
Saint Louis U (MO)
Saint Mary-of-the-Woods Coll (IN)
Saint Mary's Coll of Ave Maria U (MI)
Saint Mary's U (NS, Canada)
Saint Mary's U of Minnesota (MN)
St. Mary's U of San Antonio (TX)
Samford U (AL)
Sam Houston State U (TX)
San Jose State U (CA)
Seton Hill Coll (PA)
Silver Lake Coll (WI)
Simpson Coll and Graduate School (CA)
Sojourner-Douglass Coll (MD)
Southeast Missouri State U (MO)
Southwestern Coll (KS)
Spring Arbor U (MI)
Springfield Coll (MA)
State U of NY at Oswego (NY)
Susquehanna U (PA)
Tarleton State U (TX)
Taylor U (IN)
Temple U (PA)
Tennessee Wesleyan Coll (TN)
Texas A&M U–Commerce (TX)
Texas A&M U–Texarkana (TX)
Thomas Coll (ME)
Thomas Edison State Coll (NJ)
Tiffin U (OH)
Trinity Christian Coll (IL)
Trinity International U (IL)
Troy State U Montgomery (AL)
Université de Montréal (QC, Canada)
U Coll of the Cariboo (BC, Canada)
The U of Akron (OH)
U of Alberta (AB, Canada)
The U of Arizona (AZ)
U of Baltimore (MD)
U of Central Oklahoma (OK)
The U of Findlay (OH)
U of Florida (FL)
U of Guelph (ON, Canada)
U of Hawaii at Manoa (HI)
U of Idaho (ID)
U of Indianapolis (IN)
The U of Iowa (IA)
The U of Lethbridge (AB, Canada)
U of Maryland, Coll Park (MD)
U of Maryland University Coll (MD)
U of Miami (FL)
U of Michigan–Flint (MI)
U of Minnesota, Duluth (MN)
U of Nebraska at Omaha (NE)
U of Nevada, Las Vegas (NV)
U of Nevada, Reno (NV)
U of New Haven (CT)
The U of North Carolina at Chapel Hill (NC)
U of Ottawa (ON, Canada)
U of Pennsylvania (PA)
U of Puerto Rico, Humacao U Coll (PR)
U of Saint Francis (IN)
U of St. Thomas (MN)
U of Saskatchewan (SK, Canada)
The U of Scranton (PA)
U of South Dakota (SD)
The U of Texas at San Antonio (TX)
U of Toledo (OH)
U of Waterloo (ON, Canada)
U of Windsor (ON, Canada)
U of Wisconsin–Milwaukee (WI)
U of Wisconsin–Whitewater (WI)
U System Coll for Lifelong Learning (NH)
Urbana U (OH)
Ursuline Coll (OH)
Utah State U (UT)
Valley City State U (ND)
Vanderbilt U (TN)
Virginia Polytechnic Inst and State U (VA)
Viterbo U (WI)
Washington U in St. Louis (MO)
Weber State U (UT)
Webster U (MO)
Western Illinois U (IL)
Western Michigan U (MI)
Western State Coll of Colorado (CO)
Western Washington U (WA)
Westminster Coll (UT)
Wichita State U (KS)
Wilmington Coll (DE)
Winona State U (MN)
Worcester State Coll (MA)
Xavier U (OH)
York Coll (NE)
York U (ON, Canada)

HUMAN RESOURCES MANAGEMENT RELATED

Bloomfield Coll (NJ)
Capella U (MN)
Columbia Southern U (AL)
Limestone Coll (SC)
Park U (MO)

HUMAN SERVICES

Adrian Coll (MI)
Adrian Coll (MI)
Alaska Pacific U (AK)
Albertus Magnus Coll (CT)
Albion Coll (MI)
Albion Coll (MI)
American International Coll (MA)
Anderson Coll (SC)
Antioch U McGregor (OH)
Arcadia U (PA)
Assumption Coll (MA)
Audrey Cohen Coll (NY)
Baldwin-Wallace Coll (OH)
Becker Coll (MA)
Bethel Coll (IN)
Bethel Coll (TN)
Bethel Coll (TN)
Black Hills State U (SD)
Burlington Coll (VT)
California State U, Dominguez Hills (CA)
California State U, Monterey Bay (CA)
California State U, San Bernardino (CA)
Caribbean U (PR)
Caribbean U (PR)
Carson-Newman Coll (TN)
Cazenovia Coll (NY)
Champlain Coll (VT)
Coll of Notre Dame of Maryland (MD)
Coll of St. Joseph (VT)
Coll of Saint Mary (NE)
Coll of Saint Mary (NE)
Cornell U (NY)
Dakota Wesleyan U (SD)
Dakota Wesleyan U (SD)
Delaware State U (DE)
Doane Coll (NE)
Elmira Coll (NY)
Elmira Coll (NY)
Elon U (NC)
The Evergreen State Coll (WA)
Fairmont State Coll (WV)
Finlandia U (MI)
Fitchburg State Coll (MA)
Florida Gulf Coast U (FL)
Fontbonne U (MO)
Framingham State Coll (MA)
Framingham State Coll (MA)
Friends U (KS)
Geneva Coll (PA)
The George Washington U (DC)
Grace Bible Coll (MI)
Graceland U (IA)
Grand View Coll (IA)
Grand View Coll (IA)
Hannibal-LaGrange Coll (MO)
Hannibal-LaGrange Coll (MO)
Hastings Coll (NE)
Hawai'i Pacific U (HI)
High Point U (NC)
Hilbert Coll (NY)
Holy Names Coll (CA)
Holy Names Coll (CA)
Indiana Inst of Technology (IN)
Inter American U of PR, Aguadilla Campus (PR)
Judson Coll (IL)
Kendall Coll (IL)
Kentucky Wesleyan Coll (KY)
LaGrange Coll (GA)
Lake Erie Coll (OH)
Lake Superior State U (MI)
La Roche Coll (PA)
Lasell Coll (MA)
Lenoir-Rhyne Coll (NC)
Lesley U (MA)
Lincoln U (PA)
Lindenwood U (MO)
Lindsey Wilson Coll (KY)
Mansfield U of Pennsylvania (PA)
Marian Coll of Fond du Lac (WI)
Martin Methodist Coll (TN)
Medaille Coll (NY)
Medaille Coll (NY)
Mercer U (GA)
Merrimack Coll (MA)
Mesa State Coll (CO)
Metropolitan State Coll of Denver (CO)
Metropolitan State Coll of Denver (CO)
Metropolitan State U (MN)
Midland Lutheran Coll (NE)
Millikin U (IL)
Missouri Valley Coll (MO)
Montreat Coll (NC)
Mount Olive Coll (NC)
Mount St. Clare Coll (IA)
Mount Saint Mary Coll (NY)
Mount Saint Mary Coll (NY)
National-Louis U (IL)
Northeastern U (MA)
Northern Kentucky U (KY)
Notre Dame de Namur U (CA)
Notre Dame de Namur U (CA)
Ottawa U (KS)
Pacific Oaks Coll (CA)
Park U (MO)
Pikeville Coll (KY)
Pikeville Coll (KY)
Quincy U (IL)
Quinnipiac U (CT)
Roosevelt U (IL)
St. Joseph's Coll, New York (NY)
Saint Joseph's U (PA)
Saint Leo U (FL)
Saint Mary-of-the-Woods Coll (IN)
Salem International U (WV)
Seton Hill Coll (PA)
Siena Heights U (MI)
Simmons Coll (MA)
Sinte Gleska U (SD)
Sojourner-Douglass Coll (MD)
Southwest Baptist U (MO)
Southwest Baptist U (MO)
Springfield Coll (MA)
State U of NY Empire State Coll (NY)
Suffolk U (MA)
Tennessee Wesleyan Coll (TN)
Tennessee Wesleyan Coll (TN)
Texas A&M U–Kingsville (TX)
Touro Coll (NY)
Trinity Western U (BC, Canada)
Tyndale Coll & Seminary (ON, Canada)
U of Baltimore (MD)
U of Bridgeport (CT)
U of Great Falls (MT)
U of Maine at Machias (ME)
U of Massachusetts Boston (MA)
U of Minnesota, Morris (MN)
U of Nevada, Las Vegas (NV)
U of New England (ME)
U of Oregon (OR)
U of Phoenix–Sacramento Campus (CA)
U of Rhode Island (RI)
The U of Scranton (PA)
The U of Tennessee at Chattanooga (TN)
The U of Texas–Pan American (TX)
U of Wisconsin–Oshkosh (WI)
Upper Iowa U (IA)
Villanova U (PA)
Virginia Polytechnic Inst and State U (VA)
Virginia Wesleyan Coll (VA)
Walsh U (OH)
Western Washington U (WA)
William Penn U (IA)
Wingate U (NC)

INDIVIDUAL/FAMILY DEVELOPMENT

Abilene Christian U (TX)
Antioch U McGregor (OH)
Ashland U (OH)
Auburn U (AL)
Baylor U (TX)
Boston Coll (MA)
Bowling Green State U (OH)
California State U, Hayward (CA)
California State U, Long Beach (CA)
California State U, San Bernardino (CA)
Cameron U (OK)
Christian Heritage Coll (CA)
Colorado State U (CO)
Concordia U (MI)
Cornell U (NY)
Crown Coll (MN)
East Carolina U (NC)
Eastern Michigan U (MI)
Eckerd Coll (FL)
Florida State U (FL)
Geneva Coll (PA)
Georgia Southern U (GA)
Goddard Coll (VT)
Hampshire Coll (MA)
Harvard U (MA)
Hawai'i Pacific U (HI)
Hellenic Coll (MA)
Hope International U (CA)
Indiana State U (IN)
Indiana U Bloomington (IN)
Indiana U of Pennsylvania (PA)
Kansas State U (KS)
Kent State U (OH)
Kentucky State U (KY)
Lee U (TN)
Louisiana State U and A&M Coll (LA)
Miami U (OH)
Mississippi U for Women (MS)
Mitchell Coll (CT)
Murray State U (KY)
National-Louis U (IL)
Northern Illinois U (IL)
The Ohio State U (OH)
Ohio U (OH)
Oregon State U (OR)
Pacific Oaks Coll (CA)
Penn State U Altoona Coll (PA)
Penn State U Delaware County Campus of the Commonwealth Coll (PA)
Penn State U DuBois Campus of the Commonwealth Coll (PA)
Penn State U Fayette Campus of the Commonwealth Coll (PA)
Penn State U Mont Alto Campus of the Commonwealth Coll (PA)
Penn State U Shenango Campus of the Commonwealth Coll (PA)
Penn State U Univ Park Campus (PA)
Penn State U Worthington Scranton Cmps Commonwealth Coll (PA)
Prescott Coll (AZ)
Purdue U (IN)
Radford U (VA)
St. Olaf Coll (MN)
Samford U (AL)
Sarah Lawrence Coll (NY)
Seton Hill Coll (PA)
Sojourner-Douglass Coll (MD)
South Dakota State U (SD)
Southeast Missouri State U (MO)
Southern U and A&M Coll (LA)
Southwest Missouri State U (MO)
Southwest Texas State U (TX)
State U of NY at Oswego (NY)
State U of NY Empire State Coll (NY)
Stephen F. Austin State U (TX)
Syracuse U (NY)
Texas Tech U (TX)
Texas Woman's U (TX)
Trinity Coll (DC)
The U of Alabama (AL)
The U of Arizona (AZ)
U of Arkansas (AR)
U of Calif, Davis (CA)
U of Calif, Riverside (CA)
U of Connecticut (CT)
U of Delaware (DE)
U of Georgia (GA)
U of Hawaii at Manoa (HI)
U of Houston (TX)
U of Illinois at Urbana–Champaign (IL)
U of Maine (ME)
The U of Memphis (TN)
U of Missouri–Columbia (MO)
U of Nevada, Reno (NV)
U of New England (ME)
The U of North Carolina at Charlotte (NC)

The U of North Carolina at Greensboro (NC)
U of Rhode Island (RI)
The U of Tennessee (TN)
The U of Texas at Austin (TX)
U of Utah (UT)
U of Vermont (VT)
U of Wisconsin–Stout (WI)
Utah State U (UT)
Vanderbilt U (TN)
Warner Pacific Coll (OR)
Washington State U (WA)
Wheelock Coll (MA)
Youngstown State U (OH)

INDIVIDUAL/FAMILY DEVELOPMENT RELATED
Saint Mary's U of Minnesota (MN)
U of Louisiana at Lafayette (LA)

INDUSTRIAL ARTS
Andrews U (MI)
Appalachian State U (NC)
Ball State U (IN)
Bemidji State U (MN)
Berea Coll (KY)
California State U, Fresno (CA)
Chicago State U (IL)
Coll of the Ozarks (MO)
Colorado State U (CO)
Eastern Kentucky U (KY)
Elizabeth City State U (NC)
Fairmont State Coll (WV)
Fitchburg State Coll (MA)
Florida A&M U (FL)
Fort Hays State U (KS)
Humboldt State U (CA)
Jackson State U (MS)
Keene State Coll (NH)
Lincoln U (MO)
McPherson Coll (KS)
Millersville U of Pennsylvania (PA)
Minnesota State U, Mankato (MN)
Montclair State U (NJ)
Murray State U (KY)
New Mexico Highlands U (NM)
North Carolina Ag and Tech State U (NC)
Northeastern State U (OK)
Northern State U (SD)
Ohio Northern U (OH)
Oklahoma Panhandle State U (OK)
Oklahoma State U (OK)
Pacific Union Coll (CA)
Pittsburg State U (KS)
Rhode Island Coll (RI)
St. Cloud State U (MN)
St. John Fisher Coll (NY)
San Diego State U (CA)
San Francisco State U (CA)
South Carolina State U (SC)
Southern Utah U (UT)
Southwestern Oklahoma State U (OK)
State U of NY at Oswego (NY)
State U of NY Coll at Buffalo (NY)
Sul Ross State U (TX)
Tarleton State U (TX)
Tennessee State U (TN)
Texas A&M U–Commerce (TX)
U of Alberta (AB, Canada)
U of Arkansas at Pine Bluff (AR)
The U of British Columbia (BC, Canada)
U of Maryland Eastern Shore (MD)
Western Montana Coll of The U of Montana (MT)
U of Southern Colorado (CO)
U of Southern Maine (ME)
U of the District of Columbia (DC)
U of Wisconsin–Platteville (WI)
Walla Walla Coll (WA)
Western State Coll of Colorado (CO)
William Penn U (IA)

INDUSTRIAL ARTS EDUCATION
Abilene Christian U (TX)
Alcorn State U (MS)
Black Hills State U (SD)
Brigham Young U (UT)
California State U, Los Angeles (CA)
California State U, Stanislaus (CA)
Central Connecticut State U (CT)
Central Michigan U (MI)
Central Missouri State U (MO)
Central Washington U (WA)
Chadron State Coll (NE)
Clemson U (SC)
The Coll of New Jersey (NJ)
Coll of the Ozarks (MO)
Concordia U (NE)
Eastern Michigan U (MI)
Georgia Southern U (GA)
Grambling State U (LA)
Illinois State U (IL)
Jackson State U (MS)
Kean U (NJ)
Kent State U (OH)
Middle Tennessee State U (TN)
Millersville U of Pennsylvania (PA)
Mississippi State U (MS)
Montana State U–Bozeman (MT)
Morehead State U (KY)
New York Inst of Technology (NY)
Northern Arizona U (AZ)
Northern Illinois U (IL)
The Ohio State U (OH)
Oklahoma Panhandle State U (OK)
Purdue U (IN)
Southeast Missouri State U (MO)
Southwestern Oklahoma State U (OK)
Southwest Missouri State U (MO)
Texas Southern U (TX)
Texas Wesleyan U (TX)
U of Central Arkansas (AR)
U of Georgia (GA)
U of Hawaii at Manoa (HI)
U of Idaho (ID)
U of Nebraska–Lincoln (NE)
U of Nevada, Reno (NV)
U of New Mexico (NM)
U of Northern Iowa (IA)
U of Southern Mississippi (MS)
U of Wisconsin–Stout (WI)
U of Wyoming (WY)
Utah State U (UT)
Valley City State U (ND)
Virginia Polytechnic Inst and State U (VA)
Viterbo U (WI)

INDUSTRIAL DESIGN
Academy of Art Coll (CA)
Appalachian State U (NC)
Arizona State U (AZ)
Art Center Coll of Design (CA)
The Art Inst of Colorado (CO)
The Art Inst of Fort Lauderdale (FL)
The Art Inst of Philadelphia (PA)
Auburn U (AL)
Brigham Young U (UT)
California Coll of Arts and Crafts (CA)
California State U, Long Beach (CA)
California State U, Northridge (CA)
Campbell U (NC)
Carleton U (ON, Canada)
Carnegie Mellon U (PA)
Clemson U (SC)
The Cleveland Inst of Art (OH)
Ctr for Creative Studies—Coll of Art and Design (MI)
Columbus Coll of Art and Design (OH)
Fashion Inst of Technology (NY)
Finlandia U (MI)
Georgia Inst of Technology (GA)
ITT Tech Inst, San Bernardino (CA)
ITT Tech Inst, Fort Wayne (IN)
ITT Tech Inst (UT)
Kansas City Art Inst (MO)
Kean U (NJ)
Kendall Coll of Art and Design of Ferris State U (MI)
Massachusetts Coll of Art (MA)
Metropolitan State Coll of Denver (CO)
Milwaukee Inst of Art and Design (WI)
North Carolina State U (NC)
Northern Michigan U (MI)
The Ohio State U (OH)
Parsons School of Design, New School U (NY)
Philadelphia U (PA)
Pittsburg State U (KS)
Pratt Inst (NY)
Rhode Island School of Design (RI)
Rochester Inst of Technology (NY)
San Francisco State U (CA)
San Jose State U (CA)
Savannah Coll of Art and Design (GA)
Syracuse U (NY)
Université de Montréal (QC, Canada)
U of Alberta (AB, Canada)
U of Bridgeport (CT)
U of Cincinnati (OH)
U of Illinois at Chicago (IL)
U of Illinois at Urbana–Champaign (IL)
U of Louisiana at Lafayette (LA)
U of Michigan (MI)
U of San Francisco (CA)
The U of the Arts (PA)
U of Washington (WA)
U of Wisconsin–Platteville (WI)
Virginia Polytechnic Inst and State U (VA)
Wentworth Inst of Technology (MA)
Western Michigan U (MI)
Western Washington U (WA)

INDUSTRIAL ELECTRONICS INSTALLATION/REPAIR
Lewis-Clark State Coll (ID)

INDUSTRIAL/MANUFACTURING ENGINEERING
Arizona State U (AZ)
Auburn U (AL)
Boston U (MA)
Bradley U (IL)
California Polytechnic State U, San Luis Obispo (CA)
California State Polytechnic U, Pomona (CA)
California State U, Fresno (CA)
California State U, Hayward (CA)
California State U, Northridge (CA)
Caribbean U (PR)
Central Michigan U (MI)
Central State U (OH)
Clarkson U (NY)
Clemson U (SC)
Cleveland State U (OH)
The Coll of Southeastern Europe, The American U of Athens(Greece)
Columbia U, School of Engineering & Applied Sci (NY)
Concordia U (QC, Canada)
Cornell U (NY)
Dalhousie U (NS, Canada)
Drexel U (PA)
Eastern Nazarene Coll (MA)
Elizabethtown Coll (PA)
Ferris State U (MI)
Florida A&M U (FL)
Florida State U (FL)
Georgia Inst of Technology (GA)
Grand Valley State U (MI)
Hofstra U (NY)
Iowa State U of Science and Technology (IA)
Johns Hopkins U (MD)
Kansas State U (KS)
Kent State U (OH)
Kettering U (MI)
Lamar U (TX)
Lawrence Technological U (MI)
Lehigh U (PA)
Louisiana State U and A&M Coll (LA)
Louisiana Tech U (LA)
Marquette U (WI)
McMaster U (ON, Canada)
Memorial U of Newfoundland (NF, Canada)
Mercer U (GA)
Miami U (OH)
Michigan Technological U (MI)
Midwestern State U (TX)
Milwaukee School of Engineering (WI)
Mississippi State U (MS)
Montana State U–Bozeman (MT)
Morgan State U (MD)
New Jersey Inst of Technology (NJ)
New Mexico State U (NM)
New York Inst of Technology (NY)
North Carolina Ag and Tech State U (NC)
North Carolina State U (NC)
North Dakota State U (ND)
Northeastern U (MA)
Northern Illinois U (IL)
Northern Kentucky U (KY)
Northwestern U (IL)
The Ohio State U (OH)
Ohio U (OH)
Oklahoma State U (OK)
Oregon State U (OR)
Penn State U Univ Park Campus (PA)
Polytechnic U of Puerto Rico (PR)
Purdue U (IN)
Purdue U Calumet (IN)
Rensselaer Polytechnic Inst (NY)
Robert Morris U (PA)
Rochester Inst of Technology (NY)
St. Ambrose U (IA)
St. Cloud State U (MN)
St. Mary's U of San Antonio (TX)
San Jose State U (CA)
Seattle U (WA)
South Dakota School of Mines and Technology (SD)
Southern Illinois U Edwardsville (IL)
Southwest Texas State U (TX)
Stanford U (CA)
State U of NY at Binghamton (NY)
State U of NY at Farmingdale (NY)
Tennessee State U (TN)
Tennessee Technological U (TN)
Texas A&M U (TX)
Texas A&M U–Commerce (TX)
Texas A&M U–Kingsville (TX)
Texas Tech U (TX)
Tufts U (MA)
State U of NY at Buffalo (NY)
The U of Alabama (AL)
The U of Alabama in Huntsville (AL)
The U of Arizona (AZ)
U of Arkansas (AR)
U of Calgary (AB, Canada)
U of Calif, Berkeley (CA)
U of Central Florida (FL)
U of Cincinnati (OH)
U of Connecticut (CT)
U of Florida (FL)
U of Hartford (CT)
U of Houston (TX)
U of Idaho (ID)
U of Illinois at Chicago (IL)
U of Illinois at Urbana–Champaign (IL)
The U of Iowa (IA)
U of Louisville (KY)
U of Manitoba (MB, Canada)
U of Massachusetts Amherst (MA)
The U of Memphis (TN)
U of Miami (FL)
U of Michigan (MI)
U of Michigan–Dearborn (MI)
U of Minnesota, Duluth (MN)
U of Minnesota, Twin Cities Campus (MN)
U of Missouri–Columbia (MO)
U of Nebraska–Lincoln (NE)
U of New Haven (CT)
U of New Mexico (NM)
U of Oklahoma (OK)
U of Pittsburgh (PA)
U of Regina (SK, Canada)
U of Rhode Island (RI)
U of San Diego (CA)
U of Southern California (CA)
U of Southern Colorado (CO)
U of South Florida (FL)
The U of Tennessee (TN)
The U of Tennessee at Chattanooga (TN)
The U of Texas at Arlington (TX)
The U of Texas at Dallas (TX)
The U of Texas at El Paso (TX)
The U of Texas–Pan American (TX)
U of Toledo (OH)
U of Toronto (ON, Canada)
U of Washington (WA)
U of Windsor (ON, Canada)
U of Wisconsin–Madison (WI)
U of Wisconsin–Milwaukee (WI)
U of Wisconsin–Platteville (WI)
U of Wisconsin–Stout (WI)
Virginia Polytechnic Inst and State U (VA)
Virginia State U (VA)
Washington State U (WA)
Wayne State U (MI)
Western Michigan U (MI)
Western New England Coll (MA)
West Virginia U (WV)
Wichita State U (KS)
Worcester Polytechnic Inst (MA)
Youngstown State U (OH)

INDUSTRIAL PRODUCTION TECHNOLOGIES RELATED
Chadron State Coll (NE)
East Carolina U (NC)
Georgia Southern U (GA)
Indiana State U (IN)
Pennsylvania Coll of Technology (PA)
Southwestern Coll (KS)
The U of Akron (OH)
U of Nebraska–Lincoln (NE)
U of Wisconsin–Stout (WI)
Utah State U (UT)
Wayne State U (MI)
Western Kentucky U (KY)

INDUSTRIAL RADIOLOGIC TECHNOLOGY
Alderson-Broaddus Coll (WV)
Andrews U (MI)
Armstrong Atlantic State U (GA)
Baker Coll of Owosso (MI)
Boise State U (ID)
Briar Cliff U (IA)
California State U, Northridge (CA)
Columbus State U (GA)
Concordia U Wisconsin (WI)
Francis Marion U (SC)
Friends U (KS)
Howard U (DC)
Jamestown Coll (ND)
Marian Coll of Fond du Lac (WI)
Mars Hill Coll (NC)
National-Louis U (IL)
Newman U (KS)
Oregon Inst of Technology (OR)
Saint Mary's Coll of Ave Maria U (MI)
Thomas Jefferson U (PA)
U of Arkansas for Medical Sciences (AR)
U of Maryland Eastern Shore (MD)
U of Oklahoma Health Sciences Center (OK)
U of Sioux Falls (SD)
William Carey Coll (MS)

INDUSTRIAL TECHNOLOGY
Abilene Christian U (TX)
Alcorn State U (MS)
Andrews U (MI)
Arizona State U East (AZ)
Baker Coll of Flint (MI)
Ball State U (IN)
Bemidji State U (MN)
Berea Coll (KY)
Black Hills State U (SD)
Boise State U (ID)
Bowling Green State U (OH)
Bradley U (IL)
California Polytechnic State U, San Luis Obispo (CA)
California State U, Chico (CA)
California State U, Fresno (CA)
California State U, Long Beach (CA)
California State U, Los Angeles (CA)
California U of Pennsylvania (PA)
Central Connecticut State U (CT)
Central Missouri State U (MO)
Central State U (OH)
Central Washington U (WA)
Cheyney U of Pennsylvania (PA)
Colorado State U (CO)
East Carolina U (NC)
Eastern Illinois U (IL)
Eastern Kentucky U (KY)
Eastern Michigan U (MI)
Eastern Washington U (WA)
Elizabeth City State U (NC)
Excelsior Coll (NY)
Fairmont State Coll (WV)
Ferris State U (MI)
Fitchburg State Coll (MA)
Georgia Southern U (GA)
Grambling State U (LA)
Illinois Inst of Technology (IL)
Illinois State U (IL)
Indiana State U (IN)
Indiana U–Purdue U Fort Wayne (IN)
Jackson State U (MS)
Jacksonville State U (AL)
Kean U (NJ)
Keene State Coll (NH)
Kent State U (OH)

Kent State U, Tuscarawas Campus (OH)
Lake Superior State U (MI)
Lamar U (TX)
Metropolitan State Coll of Denver (CO)
Middle Tennessee State U (TN)
Millersville U of Pennsylvania (PA)
Minnesota State U, Mankato (MN)
Minnesota State U Moorhead (MN)
Mississippi State U (MS)
Mississippi Valley State U (MS)
Montana State U–Northern (MT)
Montclair State U (NJ)
Morehead State U (KY)
Murray State U (KY)
North Carolina Ag and Tech State U (NC)
Northeastern State U (OK)
Northeastern U (MA)
Northern Illinois U (IL)
Northern Kentucky U (KY)
Northern Michigan U (MI)
Northwestern State U of Louisiana (LA)
Ohio Northern U (OH)
Ohio U (OH)
Oklahoma Panhandle State U (OK)
Oklahoma State U (OK)
Oregon Inst of Technology (OR)
Pacific Union Coll (CA)
Pennsylvania Coll of Technology (PA)
Pittsburg State U (KS)
Prairie View A&M U (TX)
Purdue U (IN)
Purdue U Calumet (IN)
Rhode Island Coll (RI)
Rochester Inst of Technology (NY)
Roger Williams U (RI)
Rowan U (NJ)
Saginaw Valley State U (MI)
Saint Mary's U of Minnesota (MN)
Sam Houston State U (TX)
San Jose State U (CA)
South Carolina State U (SC)
South Dakota State U (SD)
Southeastern Louisiana U (LA)
Southeastern Oklahoma State U (OK)
Southeast Missouri State U (MO)
Southern Arkansas U–Magnolia (AR)
Southern Illinois U Carbondale (IL)
Southern Polytechnic State U (GA)
Southwestern Coll (KS)
Southwestern Oklahoma State U (OK)
Southwest Texas State U (TX)
State U of NY at Farmingdale (NY)
State U of NY Coll at Buffalo (NY)
State U of NY Inst of Tech at Utica/Rome (NY)
Tarleton State U (TX)
Tennessee State U (TN)
Tennessee Technological U (TN)
Texas A&M U–Kingsville (TX)
Texas Southern U (TX)
Thomas Edison State Coll (NJ)
The U of Akron (OH)
U of Arkansas at Fort Smith (AR)
U of Arkansas at Pine Bluff (AR)
U of Dayton (OH)
U of Houston (TX)
U of Idaho (ID)
U of Louisiana at Lafayette (LA)
U of Nebraska–Lincoln (NE)
U of New Haven (CT)
The U of North Carolina at Charlotte (NC)
U of North Dakota (ND)
U of Northern Iowa (IA)
U of North Texas (TX)
U of Rio Grande (OH)
U of Southern Mississippi (MS)
U of Toledo (OH)
The U of West Alabama (AL)
U of West Florida (FL)
U of Wisconsin–Platteville (WI)
U of Wisconsin–Stout (WI)
Wayne State U (MI)
Weber State U (UT)
Western Carolina U (NC)
Western Illinois U (IL)
Western Kentucky U (KY)
Western Michigan U (MI)
Western Washington U (WA)
West Texas A&M U (TX)
West Virginia U Inst of Technology (WV)
William Penn U (IA)

INFORMATION SCIENCES/ SYSTEMS

Alabama State U (AL)
Albertus Magnus Coll (CT)
Albright Coll (PA)
Alfred U (NY)
Alliant International U (CA)
Alma Coll (MI)
Alvernia Coll (PA)
American Coll of Computer & Information Sciences (AL)
American International Coll (MA)
American U (DC)
Anderson U (IN)
Andrews U (MI)
Aquinas Coll (MI)
Armstrong Atlantic State U (GA)
Ashland U (OH)
Athabasca U (AB, Canada)
Athens State U (AL)
Atlantic Union Coll (MA)
Averett U (VA)
Avila Coll (MO)
Baker Coll of Cadillac (MI)
Baker Coll of Flint (MI)
Baker Coll of Jackson (MI)
Baker Coll of Muskegon (MI)
Baker Coll of Owosso (MI)
Baker Coll of Port Huron (MI)
Baker U (KS)
Baldwin-Wallace Coll (OH)
Ball State U (IN)
Barry U (FL)
Belhaven Coll (MS)
Belmont Abbey Coll (NC)
Belmont U (TN)
Bemidji State U (MN)
Benedictine U (IL)
Baruch Coll of the City U of NY (NY)
Berry Coll (GA)
Bethune-Cookman Coll (FL)
Bloomfield Coll (NJ)
Boise State U (ID)
Boston U (MA)
Bradley U (IL)
Brewton-Parker Coll (GA)
Brigham Young U–Hawaii (HI)
Brock U (ON, Canada)
Bryant Coll (RI)
Buena Vista U (IA)
California Baptist U (CA)
California Lutheran U (CA)
California State Polytechnic U, Pomona (CA)
California State U, Chico (CA)
California State U, Dominguez Hills (CA)
California State U, Fullerton (CA)
California State U, Hayward (CA)
California State U, Northridge (CA)
Cameron U (OK)
Campbellsville U (KY)
Caribbean U (PR)
Carleton U (ON, Canada)
Carlow Coll (PA)
Carnegie Mellon U (PA)
Carroll Coll (WI)
Carson-Newman Coll (TN)
Catawba Coll (NC)
Cedar Crest Coll (PA)
Cedarville U (OH)
Centenary Coll (NJ)
Central Coll (IA)
Chadron State Coll (NE)
Champlain Coll (VT)
Chapman U (CA)
Chicago State U (IL)
Chowan Coll (NC)
Christopher Newport U (VA)
Claflin U (SC)
Clarion U of Pennsylvania (PA)
Clark Atlanta U (GA)
Clarke Coll (IA)
Clayton Coll & State U (GA)
Cleary Coll (MI)
Clemson U (SC)
Cleveland State U (OH)
Coll Misericordia (PA)
Coll of Charleston (SC)
Coll of Mount St. Joseph (OH)
Coll of Notre Dame of Maryland (MD)
Coll of St. Joseph (VT)
Coll of Saint Mary (NE)
The Coll of Saint Rose (NY)
Coll of Staten Island of the City U of NY (NY)
Colorado Christian U (CO)
Colorado State U (CO)
Colorado Tech U (CO)
Colorado Tech U Denver Campus (CO)
Colorado Tech U Sioux Falls Campus (SD)
Columbia Coll (MO)
Columbia Union Coll (MD)
Columbus State U (GA)
Concord Coll (WV)
Concordia U (IL)
Concordia U (MI)
Cornell U (NY)
Cornerstone U (MI)
Culver-Stockton Coll (MO)
Dakota State U (SD)
Daniel Webster Coll (NH)
Davenport U, Grand Rapids (MI)
Davenport U, Lansing (MI)
Delaware State U (DE)
Delaware Valley Coll (PA)
Denver Tech Coll (CO)
DePaul U (IL)
DeVry Inst of Technology (NY)
DeVry U (AZ)
DeVry U, Fremont (CA)
DeVry U, Long Beach (CA)
DeVry U, Pomona (CA)
DeVry U, West Hills (CA)
DeVry U, Colorado Springs (CO)
DeVry U (FL)
DeVry U, Alpharetta (GA)
DeVry U, Decatur (GA)
DeVry U, Addison (IL)
DeVry U, Chicago (IL)
DeVry U, Tinley Park (IL)
DeVry U (MO)
DeVry U (OH)
DeVry U (TX)
DeVry U (VA)
DeVry U (WA)
Dillard U (LA)
Dominican Coll (NY)
Dominican U (IL)
Dowling Coll (NY)
Drake U (IA)
Drexel U (PA)
Eastern Kentucky U (KY)
Eastern Michigan U (MI)
Eastern Washington U (WA)
École des Hautes Études Commerciales de Montréal (PQ, Canada)
Edgewood Coll (WI)
Edward Waters Coll (FL)
Elizabeth City State U (NC)
Elmira Coll (NY)
Emmanuel Coll (GA)
Emporia State U (KS)
Excelsior Coll (NY)
Fairfield U (CT)
Faulkner U (AL)
Ferris State U (MI)
Ferrum Coll (VA)
Fitchburg State Coll (MA)
Florida A&M U (FL)
Florida Inst of Technology (FL)
Florida International U (FL)
Fontbonne U (MO)
Fordham U (NY)
Fort Hays State U (KS)
Fort Lewis Coll (CO)
Francis Marion U (SC)
Freed-Hardeman U (TN)
Gallaudet U (DC)
Georgetown Coll (KY)
Georgia Southwestern State U (GA)
Glenville State Coll (WV)
Golden Gate U (CA)
Goldey-Beacom Coll (DE)
Gonzaga U (WA)
Goshen Coll (IN)
Grambling State U (LA)
Grand Valley State U (MI)
Grand View Coll (IA)
Guilford Coll (NC)
Gwynedd-Mercy Coll (PA)
Hampton U (VA)
Hannibal-LaGrange Coll (MO)
Harris-Stowe State Coll (MO)
Harvard U (MA)
Hawai'i Pacific U (HI)
Heidelberg Coll (OH)
Herzing Coll (AL)
High Point U (NC)
Hollins U (VA)
Houston Baptist U (TX)
Howard Payne U (TX)
Howard U (DC)
Humboldt State U (CA)
Huron U (SD)
Husson Coll (ME)
Idaho State U (ID)
Illinois Coll (IL)
Illinois Inst of Technology (IL)
Illinois State U (IL)
Indiana Inst of Technology (IN)
Indiana U–Purdue U Fort Wayne (IN)
Inter American U of PR, San Germán Campus (PR)
Iona Coll (NY)
Iowa Wesleyan Coll (IA)
James Madison U (VA)
John Jay Coll of Criminal Justice, the City U of NY (NY)
Johnson & Wales U (RI)
Johnson C. Smith U (NC)
Johnson State Coll (VT)
Jones Coll (FL)
Judson Coll (AL)
Judson Coll (IL)
Kansas State U (KS)
Kansas Wesleyan U (KS)
Kendall Coll (IL)
Kennesaw State U (GA)
Kettering U (MI)
King Coll (TN)
Lakehead U (ON, Canada)
Lamar U (TX)
Lambuth U (TN)
La Salle U (PA)
Lasell Coll (MA)
Lawrence Technological U (MI)
Lees-McRae Coll (NC)
Lee U (TN)
Lehigh U (PA)
Le Moyne Coll (NY)
LeTourneau U (TX)
Limestone Coll (SC)
Lincoln U (MO)
Lipscomb U (TN)
Lock Haven U of Pennsylvania (PA)
Long Island U, Brooklyn Campus (NY)
Long Island U, C.W. Post Campus (NY)
Loyola U Chicago (IL)
Loyola U New Orleans (LA)
MacMurray Coll (IL)
Macon State Coll (GA)
Mansfield U of Pennsylvania (PA)
Marietta Coll (OH)
Marist Coll (NY)
Marquette U (WI)
Marymount Coll of Fordham U (NY)
McGill U (PQ, Canada)
McKendree Coll (IL)
Medaille Coll (NY)
Medgar Evers Coll of the City U of NY (NY)
Memorial U of Newfoundland (NF, Canada)
Mercer U (GA)
Mercy Coll (NY)
Mercyhurst Coll (PA)
Mesa State Coll (CO)
Messiah Coll (PA)
Metropolitan State U (MN)
Michigan Technological U (MI)
Midwestern State U (TX)
Minnesota State U, Mankato (MN)
Mississippi U for Women (MS)
Missouri Southern State Coll (MO)
Missouri Western State Coll (MO)
Monroe Coll, Bronx (NY)
Monroe Coll, New Rochelle (NY)
Montana State U–Northern (MT)
Montana Tech of The U of Montana (MT)
Morgan State U (MD)
Mountain State U (WV)
Mount Aloysius Coll (PA)
Mount Olive Coll (NC)
Mount Saint Vincent U (NS, Canada)
Mount Union Coll (OH)
Murray State U (KY)
National American U, Colorado Springs (CO)
National American U (NM)
National American U (SD)
National American U–St. Paul Campus (MN)
National American U–Sioux Falls Branch (SD)
The National Hispanic U (CA)
National-Louis U (IL)
National U (CA)
Nazareth Coll of Rochester (NY)
Nebraska Wesleyan U (NE)
New Jersey Inst of Technology (NJ)
Newman U (KS)
New Mexico Highlands U (NM)
New Mexico State U (NM)
New York Inst of Technology (NY)
New York U (NY)
Niagara U (NY)
North Carolina Central U (NC)
North Carolina Wesleyan Coll (NC)
Northeastern U (MA)
Northern Kentucky U (KY)
Northern Michigan U (MI)
Northland Coll (WI)
Northwest Christian Coll (OR)
Northwestern Oklahoma State U (OK)
Northwestern State U of Louisiana (LA)
Northwest Missouri State U (MO)
Norwich U (VT)
Notre Dame Coll (OH)
Nova Southeastern U (FL)
Oakland City U (IN)
Oakwood Coll (AL)
Ohio Dominican Coll (OH)
The Ohio State U (OH)
Oklahoma Baptist U (OK)
Oklahoma Christian U of Science and Arts (OK)
Oklahoma Panhandle State U (OK)
Oklahoma State U (OK)
Oklahoma Wesleyan U (OK)
Olivet Nazarene U (IL)
Oregon State U (OR)
Ottawa U (KS)
Pace U (NY)
Pacific Union Coll (CA)
Palm Beach Atlantic Coll (FL)
Peirce Coll (PA)
Penn State U Abington Coll (PA)
Penn State U Beaver Campus of the Commonwealth Coll (PA)
Penn State U Berks Cmps of Berks-Lehigh Valley Coll (PA)
Penn State U Delaware County Campus of the Commonwealth Coll (PA)
Penn State U Hazleton Campus of the Commonwealth Coll (PA)
Penn State U McKeesport Campus of the Commonwealth Coll (PA)
Penn State U New Kensington Campus of the Commonwealth Coll (PA)
Penn State U Univ Park Campus (PA)
Penn State U Wilkes-Barre Campus of the Commonwealth Coll (PA)
Pfeiffer U (NC)
Philadelphia U (PA)
Piedmont Coll (GA)
Pittsburg State U (KS)
Plymouth State Coll (NH)
Polytechnic U, Brooklyn Campus (NY)
Purdue U Calumet (IN)
Queens Coll (NC)
Quincy U (IL)
Quinnipiac U (CT)
Ramapo Coll of New Jersey (NJ)
Reinhardt Coll (GA)
Rensselaer Polytechnic Inst (NY)
Rhode Island Coll (RI)
The Richard Stockton Coll of New Jersey (NJ)
Richmond, The American International U in London(United Kingdom)
Rider U (NJ)
Rivier Coll (NH)
Roanoke Coll (VA)
Robert Morris U (PA)
Roberts Wesleyan Coll (NY)
Rochester Inst of Technology (NY)
Rockhurst U (MO)
Rocky Mountain Coll (MT)
Roger Williams U (RI)
Rowan U (NJ)

Russell Sage Coll (NY)
St. Ambrose U (IA)
St. Cloud State U (MN)
St. Francis Xavier U (NS, Canada)
St. John's U (NY)
Saint Leo U (FL)
Saint Martin's Coll (WA)
Saint Mary Coll (KS)
Saint Mary-of-the-Woods Coll (IN)
Saint Mary's Coll of Ave Maria U (MI)
Saint Mary's U of Minnesota (MN)
St. Mary's U of San Antonio (TX)
Saint Peter's Coll (NJ)
St. Thomas Aquinas Coll (NY)
St. Thomas U (FL)
Salve Regina U (RI)
San Diego State U (CA)
San Francisco State U (CA)
Siena Heights U (MI)
Simpson Coll (IA)
Slippery Rock U of Pennsylvania (PA)
South Dakota State U (SD)
Southeastern Oklahoma State U (OK)
Southeastern U (DC)
Southeast Missouri State U (MO)
Southern Nazarene U (OK)
Southern New Hampshire U (NH)
Southwest Baptist U (MO)
Southwestern Adventist U (TX)
Springfield Coll (MA)
State U of NY at Albany (NY)
State U of NY at Binghamton (NY)
State U of NY at Oswego (NY)
State U of NY Coll at Buffalo (NY)
State U of NY Coll at Fredonia (NY)
State U of NY Coll at Old Westbury (NY)
State U of NY Coll of Technology at Delhi (NY)
State U of NY Inst of Tech at Utica/Rome (NY)
Stetson U (FL)
State U of NY at Stony Brook (NY)
Strayer U (DC)
Suffolk U (MA)
Susquehanna U (PA)
Syracuse U (NY)
Tarleton State U (TX)
Taylor U (IN)
Temple U (PA)
Tennessee Technological U (TN)
Tennessee Temple U (TN)
Texas A&M International U (TX)
Texas A&M U–Commerce (TX)
Texas A&M U–Corpus Christi (TX)
Texas A&M U–Kingsville (TX)
Texas Lutheran U (TX)
Thiel Coll (PA)
Tiffin U (OH)
Towson U (MD)
Trevecca Nazarene U (TN)
Trinity Christian Coll (IL)
Tulane U (LA)
Tusculum Coll (TN)
Union Coll (NE)
Union U (TN)
United States Military Academy (NY)
Université de Sherbrooke (PQ, Canada)
U Coll of Cape Breton (NS, Canada)
U of Alberta (AB, Canada)
U of Arkansas at Little Rock (AR)
U of Baltimore (MD)
U of Bridgeport (CT)
U of Calif, Santa Cruz (CA)
U of Charleston (WV)
U of Cincinnati (OH)
U of Dayton (OH)
U of Guelph (ON, Canada)
U of Hartford (CT)
U of Houston (TX)
U of Houston–Clear Lake (TX)
U of Indianapolis (IN)
The U of Iowa (IA)
U of Mary (ND)
U of Mary Hardin-Baylor (TX)
U of Maryland, Baltimore County (MD)
U of Maryland University Coll (MD)
U of Massachusetts Lowell (MA)
U of Miami (FL)
U of Michigan–Dearborn (MI)
U of Minnesota, Crookston (MN)
U of Missouri–Kansas City (MO)
U of Missouri–Rolla (MO)
U of Mobile (AL)
The U of Montana–Missoula (MT)
U of Nebraska at Omaha (NE)
U of New Mexico (NM)
U of Northern Iowa (IA)
U of North Texas (TX)
U of Ottawa (ON, Canada)
U of Phoenix–Jacksonville Campus (FL)
U of Pittsburgh at Bradford (PA)
U of San Francisco (CA)
U of Saskatchewan (SK, Canada)
The U of Scranton (PA)
U of Sioux Falls (SD)
U of South Dakota (SD)
U of Southern Colorado (CO)
U of South Florida (FL)
The U of Tampa (FL)
The U of Tennessee at Chattanooga (TN)
The U of Texas at El Paso (TX)
The U of Texas at San Antonio (TX)
The U of Texas–Pan American (TX)
U of the District of Columbia (DC)
U of the Pacific (CA)
U of Toledo (OH)
U of Tulsa (OK)
U of Vermont (VT)
U of Washington (WA)
U of Windsor (ON, Canada)
U of Wisconsin–Green Bay (WI)
U of Wisconsin–River Falls (WI)
U of Wisconsin–Superior (WI)
U of Wyoming (WY)
Utah State U (UT)
Valdosta State U (GA)
Villa Julie Coll (MD)
Villanova U (PA)
Virginia Commonwealth U (VA)
Virginia Polytechnic Inst and State U (VA)
Viterbo U (WI)
Waldorf Coll (IA)
Wartburg Coll (IA)
Washburn U of Topeka (KS)
Washington U in St. Louis (MO)
Wayne State Coll (NE)
Wayne State U (MI)
Weber State U (UT)
Webster U (MO)
West Chester U of Pennsylvania (PA)
Western Governors U (UT)
Western International U (AZ)
Western New England Coll (MA)
Westfield State Coll (MA)
West Liberty State Coll (WV)
Westminster Coll (PA)
West Virginia Wesleyan Coll (WV)
Widener U (PA)
Wilberforce U (OH)
Wilkes U (PA)
William Jewell Coll (MO)
Wingate U (NC)
Winona State U (MN)
Woodbury U (CA)
Worcester Polytechnic Inst (MA)
Xavier U of Louisiana (LA)
York Coll of Pennsylvania (PA)
York Coll of the City U of New York (NY)
Youngstown State U (OH)

INFORMATION TECHNOLOGY

American InterContinental U, Atlanta (GA)
Bay Path Coll (MA)
Capella U (MN)
Everglades Coll (FL)
Nazareth Coll of Rochester (NY)
New Mexico Inst of Mining and Technology (NM)
Simmons Coll (MA)
U of Phoenix–Colorado Campus (CO)
U of Phoenix–Hawaii Campus (HI)
U of Phoenix–Maryland Campus (MD)
U of Phoenix–Metro Detroit Campus (MI)
U of Phoenix–New Mexico Campus (NM)
U of Phoenix–Northern California Campus (CA)
U of Phoenix–Oklahoma City Campus (OK)
U of Phoenix–Oregon Campus (OR)
U of Phoenix–Philadelphia Campus (PA)
U of Phoenix–Phoenix Campus (AZ)
U of Phoenix–Pittsburgh Campus (PA)
U of Phoenix–Puerto Rico Campus (PR)
U of Phoenix–Sacramento Campus (CA)
U of Phoenix–San Diego Campus (CA)
U of Phoenix–Southern Arizona Campus (AZ)
U of Phoenix–Southern California Campus (CA)
U of Phoenix–Southern Colorado Campus (CO)
U of Phoenix–West Michigan Campus (MI)
The U of Scranton (PA)
Virginia Coll at Birmingham (AL)
York U (ON, Canada)

INSTITUTIONAL FOOD SERVICES

Dominican U (IL)
Johnson & Wales U (RI)
Pacific Union Coll (CA)
State U of NY Coll at Oneonta (NY)

INSTITUTIONAL FOOD WORKERS

Grambling State U (LA)
Murray State U (KY)
Nicholls State U (LA)

INSTRUMENTATION TECHNOLOGY

Indiana State U (IN)
Providence Coll (RI)
U of Southern Colorado (CO)

INSURANCE MARKETING

Caribbean U (PR)

INSURANCE/RISK MANAGEMENT

Appalachian State U (NC)
Ball State U (IN)
Baylor U (TX)
Bradley U (IL)
California State Polytechnic U, Pomona (CA)
The Coll of Southeastern Europe, The American U of Athens(Greece)
Delta State U (MS)
Eastern Kentucky U (KY)
Excelsior Coll (NY)
Ferris State U (MI)
Florida International U (FL)
Florida State U (FL)
Georgia State U (GA)
Howard U (DC)
Illinois State U (IL)
Illinois Wesleyan U (IL)
Indiana State U (IN)
Mercyhurst Coll (PA)
Minnesota State U, Mankato (MN)
Mississippi State U (MS)
The Ohio State U (OH)
Olivet Coll (MI)
Penn State U Univ Park Campus (PA)
Roosevelt U (IL)
St. Cloud State U (MN)
St. John's U (NY)
Seattle U (WA)
Southwest Missouri State U (MO)
Temple U (PA)
Texas Southern U (TX)
Thomas Edison State Coll (NJ)
U of Calgary (AB, Canada)
U of Central Arkansas (AR)
U of Cincinnati (OH)
U of Connecticut (CT)
U of Florida (FL)
U of Georgia (GA)
U of Hartford (CT)
U of Louisiana at Lafayette (LA)
U of Louisiana at Monroe (LA)
The U of Memphis (TN)
U of Minnesota, Twin Cities Campus (MN)
U of Mississippi (MS)
U of North Texas (TX)
U of Pennsylvania (PA)
U of South Carolina (SC)
U of Wisconsin–Madison (WI)
Washington State U (WA)

INTERDISCIPLINARY STUDIES

Abilene Christian U (TX)
Agnes Scott Coll (GA)
Alaska Bible Coll (AK)
Albertus Magnus Coll (CT)
Albright Coll (PA)
Alfred U (NY)
Alice Lloyd Coll (KY)
American U (DC)
American U of Rome(Italy)
Amherst Coll (MA)
Angelo State U (TX)
Anna Maria Coll (MA)
Arizona State U (AZ)
Arizona State U East (AZ)
Arizona State U West (AZ)
Asbury Coll (KY)
Atlantic Baptist U (NB, Canada)
Augsburg Coll (MN)
Austin Peay State U (TN)
Baldwin-Wallace Coll (OH)
Bard Coll (NY)
Bates Coll (ME)
Baylor U (TX)
Beloit Coll (WI)
Bennett Coll (NC)
Bennington Coll (VT)
Bentley Coll (MA)
Baruch Coll of the City U of NY (NY)
Berry Coll (GA)
Bethany Coll (WV)
Bethany Coll of the Assemblies of God (CA)
Bethel Coll (TN)
Birmingham-Southern Coll (AL)
Blackburn Coll (IL)
Bloomsburg U of Pennsylvania (PA)
Bluefield Coll (VA)
Boise State U (ID)
Boston Coll (MA)
Boston U (MA)
Bowdoin Coll (ME)
Brevard Coll (NC)
Briar Cliff U (IA)
Brigham Young U–Hawaii (HI)
Brock U (ON, Canada)
Brooklyn Coll of the City U of NY (NY)
Bryn Athyn Coll of the New Church (PA)
Bucknell U (PA)
Burlington Coll (VT)
California Lutheran U (CA)
California State U, Bakersfield (CA)
California State U, Chico (CA)
California State U, Dominguez Hills (CA)
California State U, Hayward (CA)
California State U, Long Beach (CA)
California State U, Los Angeles (CA)
California State U, Monterey Bay (CA)
California State U, San Bernardino (CA)
Calvin Coll (MI)
Cameron U (OK)
Capital U (OH)
Carleton Coll (MN)
Carleton U (ON, Canada)
Carnegie Mellon U (PA)
Carson-Newman Coll (TN)
Catawba Coll (NC)
The Catholic U of America (DC)
Centenary Coll of Louisiana (LA)
Central Coll (IA)
Central Connecticut State U (CT)
Central Methodist Coll (MO)
Central Michigan U (MI)
Chadron State Coll (NE)
Christian Heritage Coll (CA)
Christopher Newport U (VA)
Clark Atlanta U (GA)
Clarkson U (NY)
Clark U (MA)
Cleveland State U (OH)
Coe Coll (IA)
Coll Misericordia (PA)
Coll of Mount Saint Vincent (NY)
The Coll of New Rochelle (NY)
Coll of Notre Dame of Maryland (MD)
The Coll of Saint Rose (NY)
Coll of the Atlantic (ME)
Coll of the Ozarks (MO)
The Coll of William and Mary (VA)
The Coll of Wooster (OH)
Columbia Coll Chicago (IL)
Concordia U (MN)
Concordia U (OR)
Concordia U (QC, Canada)
Connecticut Coll (CT)
Cornell Coll (IA)
Cornell U (NY)
Cornerstone U (MI)
Covenant Coll (GA)
Dallas Baptist U (TX)
Dana Coll (NE)
DePaul U (IL)
DePauw U (IN)
Dominican U of California (CA)
Dowling Coll (NY)
Drew U (NJ)
D'Youville Coll (NY)
Earlham Coll (IN)
Eastern Kentucky U (KY)
Eastern Michigan U (MI)
Eastern Washington U (WA)
Eckerd Coll (FL)
Elmhurst Coll (IL)
Elmira Coll (NY)
Elms Coll (MA)
Emerson Coll (MA)
Emmanuel Coll (MA)
Emory & Henry Coll (VA)
Eugene Lang Coll, New School U (NY)
The Evergreen State Coll (WA)
Felician Coll (NJ)
Florida Inst of Technology (FL)
Fordham U (NY)
Framingham State Coll (MA)
Franklin U (OH)
Freed-Hardeman U (TN)
Friends U (KS)
George Fox U (OR)
George Mason U (VA)
Georgetown U (DC)
The George Washington U (DC)
Georgia State U (GA)
Gettysburg Coll (PA)
Goddard Coll (VT)
Goucher Coll (MD)
Grand Valley State U (MI)
Grand View Coll (IA)
Greensboro Coll (NC)
Grinnell Coll (IA)
Guilford Coll (NC)
Gustavus Adolphus Coll (MN)
Hampshire Coll (MA)
Hardin-Simmons U (TX)
Harris-Stowe State Coll (MO)
Harvard U (MA)
Hastings Coll (NE)
Hawai'i Pacific U (HI)
Hendrix Coll (AR)
Hillsdale Coll (MI)
Hillsdale Free Will Baptist Coll (OK)
Hobart and William Smith Colls (NY)
Hofstra U (NY)
Hollins U (VA)
Hope Coll (MI)
Hope International U (CA)
Houston Baptist U (TX)
Huntingdon Coll (AL)
Idaho State U (ID)
Illinois Coll (IL)
Illinois Wesleyan U (IL)
Iona Coll (NY)
Iowa State U of Science and Technology (IA)
Ithaca Coll (NY)
Jacksonville U (FL)
John Brown U (AR)
John Carroll U (OH)
Johns Hopkins U (MD)
Johnson & Wales U (RI)
Jones Coll (FL)
Judson Coll (AL)
Juniata Coll (PA)
Kalamazoo Coll (MI)
Keene State Coll (NH)
Kendall Coll (IL)
Kent State U, Stark Campus (OH)
Kentucky Christian Coll (KY)
Kentucky Wesleyan Coll (KY)
Kenyon Coll (OH)

Keuka Coll (NY)
Lake Superior State U (MI)
Lamar U (TX)
Lambuth U (TN)
Lander U (SC)
Lasell Coll (MA)
Lees-McRae Coll (NC)
Lehman Coll of the City U of NY (NY)
LeTourneau U (TX)
Lewis-Clark State Coll (ID)
Liberty U (VA)
Long Island U, Brooklyn Campus (NY)
Long Island U, C.W. Post Campus (NY)
Long Island U, Southampton Coll, Friends World Program (NY)
Louisiana Coll (LA)
Loyola Coll in Maryland (MD)
Luther Coll (IA)
Lycoming Coll (PA)
Macalester Coll (MN)
Maharishi U of Management (IA)
Manchester Coll (IN)
Marlboro Coll (VT)
Marquette U (WI)
Mars Hill Coll (NC)
Martin Luther Coll (MN)
Mary Baldwin Coll (VA)
Marylhurst U (OR)
Marymount Coll of Fordham U (NY)
Maryville U of Saint Louis (MO)
Mary Washington Coll (VA)
Marywood U (PA)
Massachusetts Coll of Liberal Arts (MA)
Massachusetts Inst of Technology (MA)
McPherson Coll (KS)
Mercy Coll (NY)
Merrimack Coll (MA)
Miami U (OH)
Middle Tennessee State U (TN)
Midwestern State U (TX)
Millikin U (IL)
Mills Coll (CA)
Minneapolis Coll of Art and Design (MN)
Minnesota State U Moorhead (MN)
Molloy Coll (NY)
Monmouth U (NJ)
Montana State U–Northern (MT)
Morehouse Coll (GA)
Morningside Coll (IA)
Mountain State U (WV)
Mount Allison U (NB, Canada)
Mount Holyoke Coll (MA)
Mount Saint Mary Coll (NY)
Mount Saint Mary's Coll and Seminary (MD)
Mount Saint Vincent U (NS, Canada)
Mount Union Coll (OH)
Muskingum Coll (OH)
Naropa U (CO)
National U (CA)
Nazareth Coll of Rochester (NY)
Nebraska Wesleyan U (NE)
New Mexico Inst of Mining and Technology (NM)
New Mexico State U (NM)
New York U (NY)
Norfolk State U (VA)
North Greenville Coll (SC)
Northland Coll (WI)
Northwest Christian Coll (OR)
Northwest Coll (WA)
Northwestern U (IL)
Nova Southeastern U (FL)
Nyack Coll (NY)
Oakland City U (IN)
Oakland U (MI)
Oakwood Coll (AL)
Oberlin Coll (OH)
Oglethorpe U (GA)
Ohio Dominican Coll (OH)
Ohio U (OH)
Oklahoma Baptist U (OK)
Olivet Nazarene U (IL)
Oregon State U (OR)
Pace U (NY)
Pacific Union Coll (CA)
Penn State U Univ Park Campus (PA)
Pepperdine U, Malibu (CA)
Piedmont Coll (GA)
Pitzer Coll (CA)
Plattsburgh State U of NY (NY)
Pomona Coll (CA)
Prairie View A&M U (TX)
Prescott Coll (AZ)
Purdue U (IN)
Queens Coll of the City U of NY (NY)
Queen's U at Kingston (ON, Canada)
Quincy U (IL)
Radford U (VA)
Ramapo Coll of New Jersey (NJ)
Reformed Bible Coll (MI)
Regis Coll (MA)
Rensselaer Polytechnic Inst (NY)
Rhodes Coll (TN)
The Richard Stockton Coll of New Jersey (NJ)
Ripon Coll (WI)
Rochester Coll (MI)
Rochester Inst of Technology (NY)
Rocky Mountain Coll (MT)
Rollins Coll (FL)
Russell Sage Coll (NY)
Rutgers, The State U of New Jersey, New Brunswick (NJ)
Saginaw Valley State U (MI)
St. Andrews Presbyterian Coll (NC)
St. Bonaventure U (NY)
St. Cloud State U (MN)
St. Francis Coll (NY)
St. John Fisher Coll (NY)
St. John's Coll (MD)
Saint Joseph's U (PA)
Saint Mary Coll (KS)
Saint Mary's Coll (IN)
Saint Mary's Coll of California (CA)
St. Mary's Coll of Maryland (MD)
Saint Mary's U (NS, Canada)
St. Norbert Coll (WI)
Salem Coll (NC)
Santa Clara U (CA)
Sarah Lawrence Coll (NY)
Schiller International U (FL)
Schiller International U(France)
Schiller International U(Germany)
Schiller International U(Spain)
Schiller International U(United Kingdom)
Schiller International U, American Coll of Switzerland(Switzerland)
Seton Hill Coll (PA)
Sheldon Jackson Coll (AK)
Silver Lake Coll (WI)
Simon's Rock Coll of Bard (MA)
Smith Coll (MA)
Sonoma State U (CA)
South Dakota School of Mines and Technology (SD)
Southeastern Coll of the Assemblies of God (FL)
Southeast Missouri State U (MO)
Southern Nazarene U (OK)
Southern Oregon U (OR)
Southwest State U (MN)
Stanford U (CA)
State U of NY at Albany (NY)
State U of NY at Binghamton (NY)
State U of NY Coll at Brockport (NY)
State U of NY Coll at Fredonia (NY)
State U of NY Coll at Oneonta (NY)
State U of NY Empire State Coll (NY)
Stephen F. Austin State U (TX)
Stephens Coll (MO)
Sterling Coll (KS)
State U of NY at Stony Brook (NY)
Suffolk U (MA)
Sweet Briar Coll (VA)
Syracuse U (NY)
Tabor Coll (KS)
Tarleton State U (TX)
Taylor U, Fort Wayne Campus (IN)
Temple U (PA)
Tennessee Temple U (TN)
Tennessee Wesleyan Coll (TN)
Texas A&M U (TX)
Texas A&M U–Commerce (TX)
Texas A&M U–Corpus Christi (TX)
Texas A&M U–Texarkana (TX)
Texas Southern U (TX)
Texas Tech U (TX)
Texas Woman's U (TX)
Thomas Aquinas Coll (CA)
Tougaloo Coll (MS)
Touro Coll (NY)
Towson U (MD)
Trent U (ON, Canada)
Trinity Coll (CT)
Trinity Coll (DC)
United States Air Force Academy (CO)
United States Military Academy (NY)
Unity Coll (ME)
Université de Montréal (QC, Canada)
Université de Sherbrooke (PQ, Canada)
Université Laval (QC, Canada)
U Coll of the Fraser Valley (BC, Canada)
The U of Akron (OH)
The U of Alabama (AL)
U of Alaska Anchorage (AK)
U of Baltimore (MD)
U of Bridgeport (CT)
The U of British Columbia (BC, Canada)
U of Calif, Berkeley (CA)
U of Calif, San Diego (CA)
U of Calif, Santa Barbara (CA)
U of Chicago (IL)
U of Florida (FL)
U of Hartford (CT)
U of Hawaii at Hilo (HI)
U of Houston (TX)
U of Houston–Clear Lake (TX)
U of Illinois at Springfield (IL)
The U of Iowa (IA)
U of Judaism (CA)
U of Kentucky (KY)
U of Maine at Farmington (ME)
U of Mary (ND)
U of Maryland, Baltimore County (MD)
U of Massachusetts Amherst (MA)
U of Massachusetts Boston (MA)
U of Massachusetts Dartmouth (MA)
The U of Memphis (TN)
U of Michigan (MI)
U of Michigan–Dearborn (MI)
U of Minnesota, Crookston (MN)
U of Minnesota, Duluth (MN)
U of Missouri–Columbia (MO)
U of Missouri–Kansas City (MO)
U of Missouri–St. Louis (MO)
The U of Montana–Missoula (MT)
U of Nebraska at Omaha (NE)
U of Nevada, Las Vegas (NV)
U of New Hampshire (NH)
The U of North Carolina at Greensboro (NC)
U of Northern Colorado (CO)
U of North Texas (TX)
U of Ottawa (ON, Canada)
U of Pennsylvania (PA)
U of Pittsburgh (PA)
U of Portland (OR)
U of Puget Sound (WA)
U of Redlands (CA)
U of Rhode Island (RI)
U of Richmond (VA)
U of Rochester (NY)
U of St. Thomas (MN)
U of San Francisco (CA)
U of Sioux Falls (SD)
U of South Carolina Spartanburg (SC)
U of Southern California (CA)
U of Southern Mississippi (MS)
The U of Tennessee at Chattanooga (TN)
The U of Tennessee at Martin (TN)
The U of Texas at Arlington (TX)
The U of Texas at Dallas (TX)
The U of Texas at El Paso (TX)
The U of Texas at San Antonio (TX)
The U of Texas at Tyler (TX)
The U of Texas of the Permian Basin (TX)
The U of Texas–Pan American (TX)
U of the Incarnate Word (TX)
U of the Pacific (CA)
U of Vermont (VT)
The U of Virginia's Coll at Wise (VA)
U of Washington (WA)
U of Waterloo (ON, Canada)
U of Wisconsin–Green Bay (WI)
U of Wisconsin–Milwaukee (WI)
U of Wisconsin–Parkside (WI)
Valparaiso U (IN)
Vanderbilt U (TN)
Vanguard U of Southern California (CA)
Vassar Coll (NY)
Villa Julie Coll (MD)
Virginia Intermont Coll (VA)
Virginia Polytechnic Inst and State U (VA)
Virginia State U (VA)
Virginia Wesleyan Coll (VA)
Warren Wilson Coll (NC)
Washington and Lee U (VA)
Washington U in St. Louis (MO)
Wayne State Coll (NE)
Wayne State U (MI)
Webster U (MO)
Wesleyan Coll (GA)
Wesleyan U (CT)
Western Baptist Coll (OR)
Western Oregon U (OR)
Western Washington U (WA)
West Liberty State Coll (WV)
Westminster Coll (PA)
West Texas A&M U (TX)
West Virginia U (WV)
Wheaton Coll (MA)
William Jewell Coll (MO)
William Woods U (MO)
Wingate U (NC)
Wisconsin Lutheran Coll (WI)
Wittenberg U (OH)
Woodbury U (CA)
Worcester Polytechnic Inst (MA)
Yeshiva U (NY)
York U (ON, Canada)

INTERIOR ARCHITECTURE

Arizona State U (AZ)
Auburn U (AL)
California Coll of Arts and Crafts (CA)
Central Michigan U (MI)
Central Missouri State U (MO)
The Coll of Southeastern Europe, The American U of Athens(Greece)
Cornell U (NY)
Indiana State U (IN)
Indiana U of Pennsylvania (PA)
Kansas State U (KS)
Lawrence Technological U (MI)
Louisiana State U and A&M Coll (LA)
Louisiana Tech U (LA)
Michigan State U (MI)
Minneapolis Coll of Art and Design (MN)
Ohio U (OH)
Philadelphia U (PA)
Southwest Texas State U (TX)
Stephen F. Austin State U (TX)
Texas Tech U (TX)
U of Bridgeport (CT)
U of Hawaii at Manoa (HI)
U of Houston (TX)
U of Idaho (ID)
U of Louisiana at Lafayette (LA)
U of Nevada, Las Vegas (NV)
U of New Haven (CT)
U of Oklahoma (OK)
U of Southern Mississippi (MS)
The U of Texas at Arlington (TX)
The U of Texas at San Antonio (TX)
U of Washington (WA)
Washington State U (WA)
Woodbury U (CA)

INTERIOR DESIGN

Abilene Christian U (TX)
Academy of Art Coll (CA)
Adrian Coll (MI)
American InterContinental U (CA)
American InterContinental U, Atlanta (GA)
Anderson Coll (SC)
Appalachian State U (NC)
Arcadia U (PA)
The Art Inst of Atlanta (GA)
The Art Inst of Colorado (CO)
The Art Inst of Fort Lauderdale (FL)
The Art Inst of Philadelphia (PA)
The Art Inst of Portland (OR)
Atlanta Coll of Art (GA)
Atlantic Union Coll (MA)
Baker Coll of Flint (MI)
Baylor U (TX)
Becker Coll (MA)
Bethel Coll (IN)
Boston Architectural Center (MA)
Brenau U (GA)
Bridgewater Coll (VA)
Brigham Young U (UT)
California State U, Chico (CA)
California State U, Fresno (CA)
California State U, Long Beach (CA)
California State U, Northridge (CA)
California State U, Sacramento (CA)
Carson-Newman Coll (TN)
Cazenovia Coll (NY)
Central Missouri State U (MO)
Chaminade U of Honolulu (HI)
The Cleveland Inst of Art (OH)
Ctr for Creative Studies—Coll of Art and Design (MI)
Coll of Mount St. Joseph (OH)
Colorado State U (CO)
Columbia Coll Chicago (IL)
Columbus Coll of Art and Design (OH)
Concordia U Wisconsin (WI)
Converse Coll (SC)
Cornish Coll of the Arts (WA)
Design Inst of San Diego (CA)
Drexel U (PA)
East Carolina U (NC)
Eastern Kentucky U (KY)
Eastern Michigan U (MI)
Endicott Coll (MA)
Ferris State U (MI)
Florida International U (FL)
Florida State U (FL)
Georgia Southern U (GA)
Hampton U (VA)
Harding U (AR)
Harrington Inst of Interior Design (IL)
High Point U (NC)
Howard U (DC)
The Illinois Inst of Art (IL)
The Illinois Inst of Art-Schaumburg (IL)
Indiana U Bloomington (IN)
Indiana U–Purdue U Indianapolis (IN)
International Academy of Design & Technology (FL)
International Acad of Merchandising & Design, Ltd (IL)
Iowa State U of Science and Technology (IA)
Kansas State U (KS)
Kean U (NJ)
Kendall Coll of Art and Design of Ferris State U (MI)
Kent State U (OH)
Lamar U (TX)
Lambuth U (TN)
La Roche Coll (PA)
Longwood Coll (VA)
Maryland Inst, Coll of Art (MD)
Marylhurst U (OR)
Marymount Coll of Fordham U (NY)
Marymount U (VA)
Maryville U of Saint Louis (MO)
Mercyhurst Coll (PA)
Meredith Coll (NC)
Miami U (OH)
Middle Tennessee State U (TN)
Milwaukee Inst of Art and Design (WI)
Minnesota State U, Mankato (MN)
Mississippi Coll (MS)
Moore Coll of Art and Design (PA)
Mount Ida Coll (MA)
Mount Mary Coll (WI)
Newbury Coll (MA)
New York Inst of Technology (NY)
New York School of Interior Design (NY)
North Dakota State U (ND)
Northern Arizona U (AZ)
Northwest Missouri State U (MO)
The Ohio State U (OH)
Oklahoma Christian U of Science and Arts (OK)
Oklahoma State U (OK)
O'More Coll of Design (TN)
Oregon State U (OR)
Otis Coll of Art and Design (CA)
Pacific Union Coll (CA)
Paier Coll of Art, Inc. (CT)
Park U (MO)
Parsons School of Design, New School U (NY)
Philadelphia U (PA)
Pittsburg State U (KS)

Pratt Inst (NY)
Radford U (VA)
Rhode Island School of Design (RI)
Ringling School of Art and Design (FL)
Rochester Inst of Technology (NY)
Rocky Mountain Coll of Art & Design (CO)
Salem Coll (NC)
Samford U (AL)
Sam Houston State U (TX)
San Diego State U (CA)
San Francisco State U (CA)
San Jose State U (CA)
Savannah Coll of Art and Design (GA)
School of Visual Arts (NY)
South Dakota State U (SD)
Southern Illinois U Carbondale (IL)
Suffolk U (MA)
Syracuse U (NY)
Texas A&M U–Kingsville (TX)
Texas Christian U (TX)
The U of Akron (OH)
The U of Alabama (AL)
U of Central Oklahoma (OK)
U of Charleston (WV)
U of Cincinnati (OH)
U of Florida (FL)
U of Houston (TX)
U of Idaho (ID)
U of Kentucky (KY)
U of Louisville (KY)
U of Manitoba (MB, Canada)
U of Massachusetts Amherst (MA)
U of Michigan (MI)
U of Minnesota, Twin Cities Campus (MN)
U of Montevallo (AL)
U of Nebraska at Omaha (NE)
U of Nevada, Reno (NV)
The U of North Carolina at Greensboro (NC)
U of Northern Iowa (IA)
U of North Texas (TX)
U of Oregon (OR)
U of San Francisco (CA)
The U of Tennessee (TN)
The U of Tennessee at Martin (TN)
The U of Texas at Austin (TX)
The U of Texas at San Antonio (TX)
U of the Incarnate Word (TX)
U of Wisconsin–Madison (WI)
U of Wisconsin–Stevens Point (WI)
Ursuline Coll (OH)
Utah State U (UT)
Valdosta State U (GA)
Virginia Coll at Birmingham (AL)
Virginia Commonwealth U (VA)
Watkins Coll of Art and Design (TN)
Wayne State Coll (NE)
Wentworth Inst of Technology (MA)
Western Carolina U (NC)
Western Michigan U (MI)
William Woods U (MO)

INTERIOR ENVIRONMENTS

Lambuth U (TN)
Murray State U (KY)
Ohio U (OH)
Syracuse U (NY)
The U of Akron (OH)
U of the Incarnate Word (TX)

INTERNATIONAL AGRICULTURE

Arizona State U East (AZ)
Cornell U (NY)
Eastern Mennonite U (VA)
Iowa State U of Science and Technology (IA)
McGill U (PQ, Canada)
MidAmerica Nazarene U (KS)
Tarleton State U (TX)
U of Calif, Davis (CA)
Utah State U (UT)

INTERNATIONAL BUSINESS

Adams State Coll (CO)
Adrian Coll (MI)
Albertson Coll of Idaho (ID)
Albertus Magnus Coll (CT)
Albright Coll (PA)
Alfred U (NY)
Alliant International U (CA)
Alma Coll (MI)
Alverno Coll (WI)
American InterContinental U, Atlanta (GA)
American International Coll (MA)
American U (DC)
The American U of Paris(France)
American U of Rome(Italy)
Appalachian State U (NC)
Aquinas Coll (MI)
Arcadia U (PA)
Arizona State U West (AZ)
Arkansas State U (AR)
Assumption Coll (MA)
Auburn U (AL)
Augsburg Coll (MN)
Avila Coll (MO)
Babson Coll (MA)
Baker U (KS)
Barry U (FL)
Baylor U (TX)
Bay Path Coll (MA)
Bellarmine U (KY)
Belmont Abbey Coll (NC)
Belmont U (TN)
Benedictine U (IL)
Berkeley Coll (NJ)
Berkeley Coll, New York (NY)
Berkeley Coll, White Plains (NY)
Baruch Coll of the City U of NY (NY)
Bethany Coll (KS)
Bethel Coll (IN)
Bethune-Cookman Coll (FL)
Birmingham-Southern Coll (AL)
Bishop's U (PQ, Canada)
Boise State U (ID)
Boston U (MA)
Bowling Green State U (OH)
Bradley U (IL)
Bridgewater Coll (VA)
Bridgewater State Coll (MA)
Brigham Young U–Hawaii (HI)
Brock U (ON, Canada)
Buena Vista U (IA)
Butler U (IN)
Caldwell Coll (NJ)
California State Polytechnic U, Pomona (CA)
California State U, Dominguez Hills (CA)
California State U, Fresno (CA)
California State U, Fullerton (CA)
California State U, Long Beach (CA)
California State U, Monterey Bay (CA)
California State U, Northridge (CA)
Campbell U (NC)
Cardinal Stritch U (WI)
Carleton U (ON, Canada)
Cedarville U (OH)
Central Coll (IA)
Central Connecticut State U (CT)
Central Michigan U (MI)
Champlain Coll (VT)
Chapman U (CA)
Chatham Coll (PA)
Christopher Newport U (VA)
City U (WA)
Claremont McKenna Coll (CA)
Clarion U of Pennsylvania (PA)
Clarke Coll (IA)
Coll of Charleston (SC)
The Coll of New Jersey (NJ)
Coll of Notre Dame of Maryland (MD)
Coll of St. Catherine (MN)
The Coll of St. Scholastica (MN)
Coll of Santa Fe (NM)
The Coll of Southeastern Europe, The American U of Athens(Greece)
Coll of the Ozarks (MO)
Columbia Coll (MO)
Columbia Southern U (AL)
Concordia Coll (MN)
Concordia U (QC, Canada)
Converse Coll (SC)
Cornell Coll (IA)
Creighton U (NE)
Davenport U, Dearborn (MI)
Davenport U, Grand Rapids (MI)
Davenport U, Warren (MI)
Davis & Elkins Coll (WV)
DePaul U (IL)
Dickinson Coll (PA)
Dickinson State U (ND)
Dillard U (LA)
Dominican Coll (NY)
Dominican U (IL)
Dominican U of California (CA)
Dowling Coll (NY)
Drake U (IA)
Drexel U (PA)
Drury U (MO)
Duquesne U (PA)
D'Youville Coll (NY)
Eastern Mennonite U (VA)
Eastern Michigan U (MI)
Eckerd Coll (FL)
École des Hautes Études Commerciales de Montréal (PQ, Canada)
Elizabethtown Coll (PA)
Elmhurst Coll (IL)
Elmira Coll (NY)
Excelsior Coll (NY)
Ferris State U (MI)
Ferrum Coll (VA)
Finlandia U (MI)
Florida Atlantic U (FL)
Florida International U (FL)
Florida Metropolitan U-Fort Lauderdale Coll (FL)
Florida Southern Coll (FL)
Florida State U (FL)
Fordham U (NY)
Fort Lewis Coll (CO)
Framingham State Coll (MA)
Franklin Coll of Indiana (IN)
Franklin Coll Switzerland(Switzerland)
Fresno Pacific U (CA)
Friends U (KS)
Gannon U (PA)
Georgetown Coll (KY)
Georgetown U (DC)
The George Washington U (DC)
Georgia Southern U (GA)
Gettysburg Coll (PA)
Golden Gate U (CA)
Goldey-Beacom Coll (DE)
Gonzaga U (WA)
Grace Coll (IN)
Graceland U (IA)
Grand Canyon U (AZ)
Grand Valley State U (MI)
Green Mountain Coll (VT)
Grove City Coll (PA)
Gustavus Adolphus Coll (MN)
Hamline U (MN)
Hampshire Coll (MA)
Harding U (AR)
Hawai'i Pacific U (HI)
High Point U (NC)
Hiram Coll (OH)
Hofstra U (NY)
Holy Family Coll (PA)
Howard U (DC)
Huntingdon Coll (AL)
Husson Coll (ME)
Illinois State U (IL)
Illinois Wesleyan U (IL)
Immaculata Coll (PA)
Indiana U of Pennsylvania (PA)
Iona Coll (NY)
Iowa State U of Science and Technology (IA)
Ithaca Coll (NY)
Jacksonville U (FL)
James Madison U (VA)
John Brown U (AR)
Johnson & Wales U (RI)
Judson Coll (IL)
Juniata Coll (PA)
King Coll (TN)
King's Coll (PA)
Kutztown U of Pennsylvania (PA)
LaGrange Coll (GA)
Lake Erie Coll (OH)
Lakeland Coll (WI)
La Roche Coll (PA)
Lasell Coll (MA)
Lebanon Valley Coll (PA)
Lehigh U (PA)
Lenoir-Rhyne Coll (NC)
LeTourneau U (TX)
Lincoln U (CA)
Linfield Coll (OR)
Long Island U, C.W. Post Campus (NY)
Long Island U, Southampton Coll, Friends World Program (NY)
Loras Coll (IA)
Louisiana State U and A&M Coll (LA)
Loyola Coll in Maryland (MD)
Loyola U New Orleans (LA)
Luther Coll (IA)
Lycoming Coll (PA)
Lynn U (FL)
Maine Maritime Academy (ME)
Manhattanville Coll (NY)
Mansfield U of Pennsylvania (PA)
Marietta Coll (OH)
Marquette U (WI)
Mars Hill Coll (NC)
Marygrove Coll (MI)
Marymount Coll of Fordham U (NY)
Marymount U (VA)
Maryville Coll (TN)
Massachusetts Maritime Academy (MA)
McGill U (PQ, Canada)
McPherson Coll (KS)
Mercer U (GA)
Meredith Coll (NC)
Merrimack Coll (MA)
Messiah Coll (PA)
Metropolitan State U (MN)
Millikin U (IL)
Milwaukee School of Engineering (WI)
Minnesota State U, Mankato (MN)
Minnesota State U Moorhead (MN)
Minot State U (ND)
Missouri Southern State Coll (MO)
Montclair State U (NJ)
Moravian Coll (PA)
Mount Allison U (NB, Canada)
Mount Saint Mary Coll (NY)
Mount St. Mary's Coll (CA)
Mount Union Coll (OH)
Murray State U (KY)
Muskingum Coll (OH)
National-Louis U (IL)
Nebraska Wesleyan U (NE)
Neumann Coll (PA)
Newbury Coll (MA)
New Mexico State U (NM)
New York Inst of Technology (NY)
New York U (NY)
Niagara U (NY)
North Central Coll (IL)
Northeastern U (MA)
Northern State U (SD)
North Park U (IL)
Northwestern Coll (MN)
Northwest Missouri State U (MO)
Northwest Nazarene U (ID)
Northwood U (MI)
Northwood U, Florida Campus (FL)
Northwood U, Texas Campus (TX)
Notre Dame Coll (OH)
Notre Dame de Namur U (CA)
Ohio Dominican Coll (OH)
Ohio Northern U (OH)
The Ohio State U (OH)
Ohio U (OH)
Ohio Wesleyan U (OH)
Oklahoma Baptist U (OK)
Oklahoma City U (OK)
Oklahoma State U (OK)
Oregon State U (OR)
Otterbein Coll (OH)
Pace U (NY)
Pacific Lutheran U (WA)
Pacific Union Coll (CA)
Palm Beach Atlantic Coll (FL)
Penn State U at Erie, The Behrend Coll (PA)
Penn State U Univ Park Campus (PA)
Pepperdine U, Malibu (CA)
Philadelphia U (PA)
Plattsburgh State U of NY (NY)
Pontifical Catholic U of Puerto Rico (PR)
Quinnipiac U (CT)
Ramapo Coll of New Jersey (NJ)
Rhodes Coll (TN)
Richmond, The American International U in London(United Kingdom)
Rider U (NJ)
Rochester Inst of Technology (NY)
Roger Williams U (RI)
Rollins Coll (FL)
Roosevelt U (IL)
Sacred Heart U (CT)
St. Ambrose U (IA)
St. Andrews Presbyterian Coll (NC)
St. Bonaventure U (NY)
St. Cloud State U (MN)
St. Edward's U (TX)
Saint Francis U (PA)
St. John Fisher Coll (NY)
Saint Joseph's Coll (IN)
Saint Joseph's Coll (ME)
Saint Leo U (FL)
Saint Louis U (MO)
Saint Mary's Coll (IN)
Saint Mary's Coll of California (CA)
Saint Mary's U of Minnesota (MN)
St. Mary's U of San Antonio (TX)
St. Norbert Coll (WI)
Saint Peter's Coll (NJ)
St. Thomas U (FL)
Saint Vincent Coll (PA)
Saint Xavier U (IL)
Salem Coll (NC)
Salem International U (WV)
Samford U (AL)
Sam Houston State U (TX)
San Diego State U (CA)
San Francisco State U (CA)
San Jose State U (CA)
Savannah State U (GA)
Schiller International U (FL)
Schiller International U(France)
Schiller International U(Germany)
Schiller International U(Spain)
Schiller International U(United Kingdom)
Schiller International U, American Coll of Switzerland(Switzerland)
Seattle U (WA)
Seton Hill Coll (PA)
Shaw U (NC)
Simpson Coll (IA)
Slippery Rock U of Pennsylvania (PA)
Southern Adventist U (TN)
Southern New Hampshire U (NH)
Southwestern Adventist U (TX)
Spring Hill Coll (AL)
State U of NY at New Paltz (NY)
State U of NY Coll at Brockport (NY)
Stephen F. Austin State U (TX)
Stetson U (FL)
Strayer U (DC)
Tarleton State U (TX)
Taylor U (IN)
Taylor U, Fort Wayne Campus (IN)
Teikyo Post U (CT)
Temple U (PA)
Tennessee Technological U (TN)
Texas A&M U–Kingsville (TX)
Texas A&M U–Texarkana (TX)
Texas Christian U (TX)
Texas Tech U (TX)
Texas Wesleyan U (TX)
Thiel Coll (PA)
Thomas Coll (ME)
Thomas Edison State Coll (NJ)
Tiffin U (OH)
Touro Coll (NY)
Trinity U (TX)
The U of Akron (OH)
U of Alberta (AB, Canada)
U of Arkansas (AR)
U of Arkansas at Little Rock (AR)
U of Baltimore (MD)
U of Bridgeport (CT)
The U of British Columbia (BC, Canada)
U of Dayton (OH)
U of Denver (CO)
U of Evansville (IN)
The U of Findlay (OH)
U of Georgia (GA)
U of Hawaii at Manoa (HI)
U of Hawaii–West Oahu (HI)
U of Indianapolis (IN)
The U of Iowa (IA)
U of La Verne (CA)
The U of Lethbridge (AB, Canada)
The U of Memphis (TN)
U of Miami (FL)
U of Minnesota, Twin Cities Campus (MN)
U of Mississippi (MS)
U of Missouri–Columbia (MO)
The U of Montana–Missoula (MT)
U of Nebraska–Lincoln (NE)
U of Nevada, Las Vegas (NV)
U of Nevada, Reno (NV)
U of New Haven (CT)
The U of North Carolina at Charlotte (NC)
U of North Florida (FL)
U of Oklahoma (OK)
U of Oregon (OR)
U of Ottawa (ON, Canada)
U of Portland (OR)
U of Puget Sound (WA)

U of Rhode Island (RI)
U of Richmond (VA)
U of Rio Grande (OH)
U of Saint Francis (IN)
U of St. Thomas (MN)
U of San Francisco (CA)
The U of Scranton (PA)
U of Southern Mississippi (MS)
U of South Florida (FL)
The U of Tampa (FL)
The U of Tennessee at Martin (TN)
The U of Texas at Arlington (TX)
The U of Texas at Dallas (TX)
The U of Texas at San Antonio (TX)
The U of Texas–Pan American (TX)
U of the Incarnate Word (TX)
U of Toledo (OH)
U of Tulsa (OK)
U of Victoria (BC, Canada)
U of Washington (WA)
U of Wisconsin–La Crosse (WI)
Utica Coll of Syracuse U (NY)
Valparaiso U (IN)
Vanguard U of Southern California (CA)
Villanova U (PA)
Warren Wilson Coll (NC)
Wartburg Coll (IA)
Washington & Jefferson Coll (PA)
Washington State U (WA)
Washington U in St. Louis (MO)
Waynesburg Coll (PA)
Wayne State Coll (NE)
Webber International U (FL)
Webster U (MO)
Wesleyan Coll (GA)
Western Carolina U (NC)
Western International U (AZ)
Western New England Coll (MA)
Western State Coll of Colorado (CO)
Western Washington U (WA)
Westminster Coll (MO)
Westminster Coll (PA)
Westminster Coll (UT)
Wheeling Jesuit U (WV)
Whitworth Coll (WA)
Wichita State U (KS)
Widener U (PA)
William Jewell Coll (MO)
William Paterson U of New Jersey (NJ)
William Woods U (MO)
Wittenberg U (OH)
Wofford Coll (SC)
York Coll of Pennsylvania (PA)
York U (ON, Canada)

INTERNATIONAL BUSINESS MARKETING

American U (DC)
Eastern Michigan U (MI)
Oklahoma Baptist U (OK)
Pace U (NY)
York U (ON, Canada)

INTERNATIONAL ECONOMICS

Albertson Coll of Idaho (ID)
Albertus Magnus Coll (CT)
American U (DC)
The American U of Paris(France)
Assumption Coll (MA)
Austin Coll (TX)
Bard Coll (NY)
Bentley Coll (MA)
Brock U (ON, Canada)
Carson-Newman Coll (TN)
Carthage Coll (WI)
The Catholic U of America (DC)
Claremont McKenna Coll (CA)
Coll of St. Catherine (MN)
École des Hautes Études Commerciales de Montréal (PQ, Canada)
Framingham State Coll (MA)
Franklin Coll Switzerland(Switzerland)
Georgetown U (DC)
Gettysburg Coll (PA)
Hamline U (MN)
Hampshire Coll (MA)
Harvard U (MA)
Hastings Coll (NE)
Hiram Coll (OH)
Howard U (DC)
John Carroll U (OH)
Lawrence U (WI)
Long Island U, Southampton Coll, Friends World Program (NY)
Longwood Coll (VA)
Marlboro Coll (VT)
Middlebury Coll (VT)
Muhlenberg Coll (PA)
Ohio U (OH)
Rhodes Coll (TN)
Rockford Coll (IL)
San Diego State U (CA)
Schiller International U, American Coll of Switzerland(Switzerland)
Seattle U (WA)
State U of NY at New Paltz (NY)
State U of NY at Oswego (NY)
State U of West Georgia (GA)
Suffolk U (MA)
Taylor U (IN)
Université Laval (QC, Canada)
U of Calif, Los Angeles (CA)
U of Calif, Santa Cruz (CA)
U of Central Arkansas (AR)
U of Puget Sound (WA)
U of Richmond (VA)
Valparaiso U (IN)
Washington U in St. Louis (MO)
Westminster Coll (PA)
Youngstown State U (OH)

INTERNATIONAL FINANCE

American U (DC)
Boston U (MA)
The Catholic U of America (DC)
École des Hautes Études Commerciales de Montréal (PQ, Canada)
Franklin Coll Switzerland(Switzerland)
Rochester Inst of Technology (NY)
Washington U in St. Louis (MO)
York U (ON, Canada)

INTERNATIONAL RELATIONS

Abilene Christian U (TX)
Adrian Coll (MI)
Agnes Scott Coll (GA)
Albion Coll (MI)
Allegheny Coll (PA)
Alliant International U (CA)
Alverno Coll (WI)
American Coll of Thessaloniki(Greece)
American International Coll (MA)
American U (DC)
The American U of Paris(France)
American U of Rome(Italy)
Aquinas Coll (MI)
Arkansas Tech U (AR)
Ashland U (OH)
Assumption Coll (MA)
Augsburg Coll (MN)
Augustana Coll (SD)
Austin Coll (TX)
Azusa Pacific U (CA)
Baldwin-Wallace Coll (OH)
Bard Coll (NY)
Barry U (FL)
Baylor U (TX)
Bellarmine U (KY)
Beloit Coll (WI)
Benedictine U (IL)
Bennington Coll (VT)
Berry Coll (GA)
Bethany Coll (WV)
Bethany Coll of the Assemblies of God (CA)
Bethel Coll (MN)
Bethune-Cookman Coll (FL)
Boston U (MA)
Bowling Green State U (OH)
Bradley U (IL)
Brenau U (GA)
Bridgewater Coll (VA)
Bridgewater State Coll (MA)
Brigham Young U (UT)
Brown U (RI)
Bryant Coll (RI)
Bucknell U (PA)
Butler U (IN)
California Lutheran U (CA)
California State U, Chico (CA)
California State U, Hayward (CA)
California State U, Long Beach (CA)
California State U, Monterey Bay (CA)
Calvin Coll (MI)
Campbell U (NC)
Canisius Coll (NY)
Capital U (OH)
Carleton Coll (MN)
Carleton U (ON, Canada)
Carroll Coll (MT)
Carroll Coll (WI)
Case Western Reserve U (OH)
Catawba Coll (NC)
Cedar Crest Coll (PA)
Cedarville U (OH)
Centenary Coll (NJ)
Central Michigan U (MI)
Centre Coll (KY)
Chaminade U of Honolulu (HI)
Chatham Coll (PA)
Christopher Newport U (VA)
City Coll of the City U of NY (NY)
Claremont McKenna Coll (CA)
Clark U (MA)
Cleveland State U (OH)
Colby Coll (ME)
Colgate U (NY)
The Coll of New Jersey (NJ)
Coll of Notre Dame of Maryland (MD)
Coll of St. Catherine (MN)
Coll of Saint Elizabeth (NJ)
The Coll of St. Scholastica (MN)
Coll of Staten Island of the City U of NY (NY)
The Coll of William and Mary (VA)
The Coll of Wooster (OH)
Concordia Coll (MN)
Concordia Coll (NY)
Connecticut Coll (CT)
Cornell Coll (IA)
Cornell U (NY)
Creighton U (NE)
Dalhousie U (NS, Canada)
Denison U (OH)
DePaul U (IL)
Dickinson Coll (PA)
Doane Coll (NE)
Dominican U of California (CA)
Drake U (IA)
Duke U (NC)
Duquesne U (PA)
Earlham Coll (IN)
Eastern Washington U (WA)
Eckerd Coll (FL)
Edgewood Coll (WI)
Elmira Coll (NY)
Elms Coll (MA)
Elon U (NC)
Emory & Henry Coll (VA)
Emory U (GA)
Eugene Lang Coll, New School U (NY)
Fairfield U (CT)
Fairleigh Dickinson U, Teaneck-Hackensack Campus (NJ)
Ferrum Coll (VA)
Florida International U (FL)
Florida State U (FL)
Fordham U (NY)
Francis Marion U (SC)
Franklin Coll Switzerland(Switzerland)
Frostburg State U (MD)
Gallaudet U (DC)
Gannon U (PA)
George Fox U (OR)
George Mason U (VA)
Georgetown U (DC)
The George Washington U (DC)
Georgia Inst of Technology (GA)
Georgia Southern U (GA)
Gettysburg Coll (PA)
Gonzaga U (WA)
Gordon Coll (MA)
Goucher Coll (MD)
Graceland U (IA)
Grand Canyon U (AZ)
Grand Valley State U (MI)
Guilford Coll (NC)
Hamilton Coll (NY)
Hamline U (MN)
Hampshire Coll (MA)
Hanover Coll (IN)
Harding U (AR)
Harvard U (MA)
Hastings Coll (NE)
Hawai'i Pacific U (HI)
Heidelberg Coll (OH)
Hendrix Coll (AR)
High Point U (NC)
Hillsdale Coll (MI)
Hobart and William Smith Colls (NY)
Hollins U (VA)
Holy Names Coll (CA)
Houghton Coll (NY)
Huntingdon Coll (AL)
Huron U USA in London(United Kingdom)
Idaho State U (ID)
Illinois Coll (IL)
Illinois Wesleyan U (IL)
Immaculata Coll (PA)
Indiana U of Pennsylvania (PA)
Iona Coll (NY)
Iowa State U of Science and Technology (IA)
Jacksonville U (FL)
James Madison U (VA)
John Brown U (AR)
John Cabot U(Italy)
John Carroll U (OH)
Johns Hopkins U (MD)
Juniata Coll (PA)
Kennesaw State U (GA)
Kent State U (OH)
Kenyon Coll (OH)
Knox Coll (IL)
Lafayette Coll (PA)
Lambuth U (TN)
La Roche Coll (PA)
Lawrence U (WI)
Lees-McRae Coll (NC)
Lee U (TN)
Lehigh U (PA)
Le Moyne Coll (NY)
Lenoir-Rhyne Coll (NC)
Lewis & Clark Coll (OR)
Lincoln U (PA)
Lindenwood U (MO)
Lock Haven U of Pennsylvania (PA)
Long Island U, C.W. Post Campus (NY)
Long Island U, Southampton Coll, Friends World Program (NY)
Longwood Coll (VA)
Loras Coll (IA)
Loyola U Chicago (IL)
Luther Coll (IA)
Lycoming Coll (PA)
Lynchburg Coll (VA)
Macalester Coll (MN)
Manhattan Coll (NY)
Manhattanville Coll (NY)
Mansfield U of Pennsylvania (PA)
Marian Coll of Fond du Lac (WI)
Marlboro Coll (VT)
Marquette U (WI)
Marshall U (WV)
Mars Hill Coll (NC)
Mary Baldwin Coll (VA)
Marymount Coll of Fordham U (NY)
Marymount Manhattan Coll (NY)
Maryville Coll (TN)
Mary Washington Coll (VA)
McKendree Coll (IL)
Meredith Coll (NC)
Methodist Coll (NC)
Miami U (OH)
Michigan State U (MI)
Middlebury Coll (VT)
Middle Tennessee State U (TN)
Midwestern State U (TX)
Millikin U (IL)
Mills Coll (CA)
Minnesota State U, Mankato (MN)
Missouri Southern State Coll (MO)
Morehouse Coll (GA)
Mount Allison U (NB, Canada)
Mount Holyoke Coll (MA)
Mount Mary Coll (WI)
Mount Mercy Coll (IA)
Mount Saint Mary Coll (NY)
Mount Saint Mary's Coll and Seminary (MD)
Muhlenberg Coll (PA)
Murray State U (KY)
Muskingum Coll (OH)
Nazareth Coll of Rochester (NY)
Nebraska Wesleyan U (NE)
New Coll of Florida (FL)
New York U (NY)
Niagara U (NY)
North Central Coll (IL)
North Dakota State U (ND)
Northeastern U (MA)
Northern Arizona U (AZ)
Northern Kentucky U (KY)
Northern Michigan U (MI)
North Park U (IL)
Northwestern U (IL)
Northwest Nazarene U (ID)
Norwich U (VT)
Oakland U (MI)
Occidental Coll (CA)
Oglethorpe U (GA)
Ohio Northern U (OH)
The Ohio State U (OH)
Ohio U (OH)
Ohio Wesleyan U (OH)
Okanagan U Coll (BC, Canada)
Old Dominion U (VA)
Olivet Coll (MI)
Oral Roberts U (OK)
Oregon State U (OR)
Otterbein Coll (OH)
Pacific Lutheran U (WA)
Pacific U (OR)
Penn State U Univ Park Campus (PA)
Pepperdine U, Malibu (CA)
Pitzer Coll (CA)
Point Park Coll (PA)
Pomona Coll (CA)
Portland State U (OR)
Prairie Bible Coll (AB, Canada)
Queens Coll (NC)
Quinnipiac U (CT)
Ramapo Coll of New Jersey (NJ)
Randolph-Macon Coll (VA)
Randolph-Macon Woman's Coll (VA)
Reed Coll (OR)
Rhodes Coll (TN)
Richmond, The American International U in London(United Kingdom)
Roanoke Coll (VA)
Rockford Coll (IL)
Rockhurst U (MO)
Rocky Mountain Coll (MT)
Rollins Coll (FL)
Roosevelt U (IL)
Russell Sage Coll (NY)
Sacred Heart U (CT)
Saginaw Valley State U (MI)
Saint Augustine's Coll (NC)
St. Cloud State U (MN)
St. Edward's U (TX)
Saint Francis U (PA)
St. John Fisher Coll (NY)
Saint Joseph's Coll (IN)
Saint Joseph's U (PA)
Saint Leo U (FL)
Saint Louis U (MO)
Saint Mary's Coll of California (CA)
Saint Mary's U (NS, Canada)
St. Norbert Coll (WI)
Saint Xavier U (IL)
Salem Coll (NC)
Samford U (AL)
San Diego State U (CA)
San Francisco State U (CA)
Sarah Lawrence Coll (NY)
Schiller International U (FL)
Schiller International U(France)
Schiller International U(Germany)
Schiller International U(Spain)
Schiller International U(United Kingdom)
Schiller International U, American Coll of Switzerland(Switzerland)
Scripps Coll (CA)
Seattle U (WA)
Seton Hall U (NJ)
Seton Hill Coll (PA)
Shawnee State U (OH)
Shaw U (NC)
Simmons Coll (MA)
Simpson Coll (IA)
Southern Methodist U (TX)
Southern Nazarene U (OK)
Southern Oregon U (OR)
Southwestern Adventist U (TX)
Southwestern U (TX)
Southwest Texas State U (TX)
Spring Hill Coll (AL)
Stanford U (CA)
State U of NY at New Paltz (NY)
State U of NY at Oswego (NY)
State U of NY Coll at Brockport (NY)
State U of NY Coll at Cortland (NY)
State U of NY Coll at Geneseo (NY)
State U of NY Coll at Oneonta (NY)
State U of West Georgia (GA)
Stephens Coll (MO)
Stetson U (FL)
Stonehill Coll (MA)

Susquehanna U (PA)
Sweet Briar Coll (VA)
Syracuse U (NY)
Tabor Coll (KS)
Taylor U (IN)
Texas Christian U (TX)
Texas Lutheran U (TX)
Texas Wesleyan U (TX)
Thomas More Coll (KY)
Tiffin U (OH)
Towson U (MD)
Trent U (ON, Canada)
Trinity Coll (CT)
Trinity Coll (DC)
Trinity Western U (BC, Canada)
Tufts U (MA)
Tulane U (LA)
Union Coll (NE)
Université Laval (QC, Canada)
The U of Alabama (AL)
U of Alberta (AB, Canada)
U of Arkansas (AR)
U of Arkansas at Little Rock (AR)
U of Bridgeport (CT)
The U of British Columbia (BC, Canada)
U of Calgary (AB, Canada)
U of Calif, Davis (CA)
U of Calif, Irvine (CA)
U of Calif, Los Angeles (CA)
U of Cincinnati (OH)
U of Colorado at Boulder (CO)
U of Dayton (OH)
U of Delaware (DE)
U of Denver (CO)
U of Evansville (IN)
U of Hartford (CT)
U of Idaho (ID)
U of Indianapolis (IN)
The U of Iowa (IA)
U of Kansas (KS)
U of La Verne (CA)
U of Maine (ME)
U of Maine at Farmington (ME)
U of Maine at Presque Isle (ME)
The U of Memphis (TN)
U of Miami (FL)
U of Michigan (MI)
U of Michigan–Dearborn (MI)
U of Minnesota, Duluth (MN)
U of Minnesota, Twin Cities Campus (MN)
U of Mississippi (MS)
U of Missouri–St. Louis (MO)
U of Montevallo (AL)
U of Nebraska at Kearney (NE)
U of Nebraska at Omaha (NE)
U of Nebraska–Lincoln (NE)
U of Nevada, Reno (NV)
U of New Hampshire (NH)
U of North Florida (FL)
U of Oregon (OR)
U of Ottawa (ON, Canada)
U of Pennsylvania (PA)
U of Puget Sound (WA)
U of Redlands (CA)
U of Richmond (VA)
U of St. Thomas (MN)
U of St. Thomas (TX)
U of San Diego (CA)
U of Saskatchewan (SK, Canada)
The U of Scranton (PA)
U of South Carolina (SC)
U of Southern California (CA)
U of Southern Maine (ME)
U of Southern Mississippi (MS)
U of South Florida (FL)
The U of Tampa (FL)
The U of Tennessee at Martin (TN)
U of the Pacific (CA)
U of the South (TN)
U of Toledo (OH)
U of Toronto (ON, Canada)
U of Vermont (VT)
U of Virginia (VA)
U of Washington (WA)
U of Waterloo (ON, Canada)
U of West Florida (FL)
U of Windsor (ON, Canada)
U of Wisconsin–Madison (WI)
U of Wisconsin–Milwaukee (WI)
U of Wisconsin–Oshkosh (WI)
U of Wisconsin–Parkside (WI)
U of Wisconsin–Platteville (WI)
U of Wisconsin–Stevens Point (WI)
U of Wisconsin–Whitewater (WI)
U of Wyoming (WY)
Ursinus Coll (PA)
Utica Coll of Syracuse U (NY)
Valparaiso U (IN)
Vassar Coll (NY)
Virginia Military Inst (VA)
Virginia Polytechnic Inst and State U (VA)
Virginia Wesleyan Coll (VA)
Walsh U (OH)
Wartburg Coll (IA)
Washington Coll (MD)
Washington U in St. Louis (MO)
Wayne State U (MI)
Webster U (MO)
Wellesley Coll (MA)
Wells Coll (NY)
Wesleyan Coll (GA)
West Chester U of Pennsylvania (PA)
Western International U (AZ)
Western New England Coll (MA)
Western Oregon U (OR)
Westminster Coll (MO)
Westminster Coll (PA)
West Virginia U (WV)
West Virginia Wesleyan Coll (WV)
Wheaton Coll (IL)
Wheaton Coll (MA)
Wheeling Jesuit U (WV)
Whittier Coll (CA)
Whitworth Coll (WA)
Widener U (PA)
Wilfrid Laurier U (ON, Canada)
Wilkes U (PA)
Willamette U (OR)
William Jewell Coll (MO)
William Woods U (MO)
Wilson Coll (PA)
Winona State U (MN)
Wittenberg U (OH)
Wofford Coll (SC)
Wright State U (OH)
Xavier U (OH)
York Coll of Pennsylvania (PA)
York U (ON, Canada)

INTERNET
Bloomfield Coll (NJ)
Drexel U (PA)
Franklin U (OH)
Strayer U (DC)

INVESTMENTS AND SECURITIES
Babson Coll (MA)
Duquesne U (PA)

ISLAMIC STUDIES
American U (DC)
Brandeis U (MA)
East-West U (IL)
Hampshire Coll (MA)
Harvard U (MA)
Long Island U, Southampton Coll, Friends World Program (NY)
The Ohio State U (OH)
U of Calif, Santa Barbara (CA)
U of Michigan (MI)
The U of Texas at Austin (TX)
U of Toronto (ON, Canada)
Washington U in St. Louis (MO)
Wellesley Coll (MA)

ITALIAN
Albertus Magnus Coll (CT)
American U of Rome(Italy)
Arizona State U (AZ)
Bard Coll (NY)
Barnard Coll (NY)
Bishop's U (PQ, Canada)
Boston Coll (MA)
Boston U (MA)
Brigham Young U (UT)
Brock U (ON, Canada)
Brooklyn Coll of the City U of NY (NY)
Brown U (RI)
Bryn Mawr Coll (PA)
California State U, Northridge (CA)
Carleton U (ON, Canada)
Central Connecticut State U (CT)
City Coll of the City U of NY (NY)
Claremont McKenna Coll (CA)
Coll of the Holy Cross (MA)
Columbia Coll (NY)
Columbia U, School of General Studies (NY)
Concordia U (QC, Canada)
Connecticut Coll (CT)
Cornell U (NY)
Dartmouth Coll (NH)
DePaul U (IL)
Dickinson Coll (PA)
Dominican U (IL)
Drew U (NJ)
Duke U (NC)
Emory U (GA)
Florida International U (FL)
Florida State U (FL)
Fordham U (NY)
Georgetown U (DC)
Gonzaga U (WA)
Harvard U (MA)
Haverford Coll (PA)
Hofstra U (NY)
Hunter Coll of the City U of NY (NY)
Indiana U Bloomington (IN)
Iona Coll (NY)
Johns Hopkins U (MD)
Lake Erie Coll (OH)
La Salle U (PA)
Laurentian U (ON, Canada)
Lehman Coll of the City U of NY (NY)
Long Island U, C.W. Post Campus (NY)
Long Island U, Southampton Coll, Friends World Program (NY)
Loyola U Chicago (IL)
Marlboro Coll (VT)
McGill U (PQ, Canada)
Mercy Coll (NY)
Middlebury Coll (VT)
Montclair State U (NJ)
Mount Holyoke Coll (MA)
Nazareth Coll of Rochester (NY)
New York U (NY)
Northeastern U (MA)
Northwestern U (IL)
The Ohio State U (OH)
Penn State U Univ Park Campus (PA)
Providence Coll (RI)
Queens Coll of the City U of NY (NY)
Queen's U at Kingston (ON, Canada)
Rosemont Coll (PA)
Rutgers, The State U of New Jersey, New Brunswick (NJ)
St. John Fisher Coll (NY)
St. John's U (NY)
San Francisco State U (CA)
Santa Clara U (CA)
Sarah Lawrence Coll (NY)
Scripps Coll (CA)
Seton Hall U (NJ)
Smith Coll (MA)
Southern Connecticut State U (CT)
Stanford U (CA)
State U of NY at Albany (NY)
State U of NY at Binghamton (NY)
State U of NY at Stony Brook (NY)
Sweet Briar Coll (VA)
Syracuse U (NY)
Temple U (PA)
Trinity Coll (CT)
Tulane U (LA)
State U of NY at Buffalo (NY)
U of Alberta (AB, Canada)
The U of Arizona (AZ)
The U of British Columbia (BC, Canada)
U of Calif, Berkeley (CA)
U of Calif, Davis (CA)
U of Calif, Los Angeles (CA)
U of Calif, San Diego (CA)
U of Calif, Santa Barbara (CA)
U of Calif, Santa Cruz (CA)
U of Chicago (IL)
U of Colorado at Boulder (CO)
U of Connecticut (CT)
U of Delaware (DE)
U of Denver (CO)
U of Georgia (GA)
U of Houston (TX)
U of Illinois at Chicago (IL)
U of Illinois at Urbana–Champaign (IL)
The U of Iowa (IA)
U of Maryland, Coll Park (MD)
U of Massachusetts Amherst (MA)
U of Massachusetts Boston (MA)
U of Miami (FL)
U of Michigan (MI)
U of Minnesota, Twin Cities Campus (MN)
U of Notre Dame (IN)
U of Oregon (OR)
U of Ottawa (ON, Canada)
U of Pennsylvania (PA)
U of Pittsburgh (PA)
U of Rhode Island (RI)
The U of Scranton (PA)
U of South Carolina (SC)
U of Southern California (CA)
U of South Florida (FL)
The U of Tennessee (TN)
The U of Texas at Austin (TX)
U of Toronto (ON, Canada)
U of Victoria (BC, Canada)
U of Virginia (VA)
U of Washington (WA)
U of Windsor (ON, Canada)
U of Wisconsin–Madison (WI)
U of Wisconsin–Milwaukee (WI)
Vassar Coll (NY)
Washington U in St. Louis (MO)
Wayne State U (MI)
Wellesley Coll (MA)
Wesleyan U (CT)
Yale U (CT)
York Coll of the City U of New York (NY)
York U (ON, Canada)
Youngstown State U (OH)

ITALIAN STUDIES
Bennington Coll (VT)
Brown U (RI)
Columbia Coll (NY)
Dominican U (IL)
Lake Erie Coll (OH)
Sweet Briar Coll (VA)
U of Calif, Santa Cruz (CA)
U of Windsor (ON, Canada)
Wellesley Coll (MA)
York U (ON, Canada)

JAPANESE
Arizona State U (AZ)
Ball State U (IN)
Bates Coll (ME)
Bennington Coll (VT)
Brigham Young U (UT)
California State U, Fullerton (CA)
California State U, Long Beach (CA)
California State U, Los Angeles (CA)
Carnegie Mellon U (PA)
Claremont McKenna Coll (CA)
Colgate U (NY)
Connecticut Coll (CT)
Cornell U (NY)
Dartmouth Coll (NH)
DePaul U (IL)
Dillard U (LA)
Eastern Michigan U (MI)
The Evergreen State Coll (WA)
Georgetown U (DC)
Gustavus Adolphus Coll (MN)
Harvard U (MA)
Hobart and William Smith Colls (NY)
Indiana U Bloomington (IN)
Long Island U, Southampton Coll, Friends World Program (NY)
McMaster U (ON, Canada)
Middlebury Coll (VT)
Mount Union Coll (OH)
North Central Coll (IL)
The Ohio State U (OH)
Pacific U (OR)
Penn State U Univ Park Campus (PA)
Pomona Coll (CA)
Portland State U (OR)
Salem International U (WV)
San Diego State U (CA)
San Francisco State U (CA)
San Jose State U (CA)
Scripps Coll (CA)
Stanford U (CA)
U of Alaska Fairbanks (AK)
U of Alberta (AB, Canada)
The U of British Columbia (BC, Canada)
U of Calif, Berkeley (CA)
U of Calif, Davis (CA)
U of Calif, Los Angeles (CA)
U of Calif, San Diego (CA)
U of Calif, Santa Barbara (CA)
U of Calif, Santa Cruz (CA)
U of Chicago (IL)
U of Colorado at Boulder (CO)
The U of Findlay (OH)
U of Georgia (GA)
U of Hawaii at Hilo (HI)
U of Hawaii at Manoa (HI)
The U of Iowa (IA)
U of Kansas (KS)
U of Maryland, Coll Park (MD)
U of Massachusetts Amherst (MA)
U of Michigan (MI)
U of Minnesota, Twin Cities Campus (MN)
The U of Montana–Missoula (MT)
U of Notre Dame (IN)
U of Oregon (OR)
U of Pittsburgh (PA)
U of Rochester (NY)
The U of Scranton (PA)
U of Southern California (CA)
U of the Pacific (CA)
U of Toronto (ON, Canada)
U of Utah (UT)
U of Victoria (BC, Canada)
U of Washington (WA)
U of Windsor (ON, Canada)
U of Wisconsin–Madison (WI)
Ursinus Coll (PA)
Washington U in St. Louis (MO)
Wellesley Coll (MA)
Williams Coll (MA)
Yale U (CT)
York U (ON, Canada)

JAZZ
Aquinas Coll (MI)
Augustana Coll (IL)
Bard Coll (NY)
Bennington Coll (VT)
Berklee Coll of Music (MA)
Bowling Green State U (OH)
California Inst of the Arts (CA)
Capital U (OH)
Central State U (OH)
Chicago State U (IL)
Concordia U (QC, Canada)
DePaul U (IL)
Five Towns Coll (NY)
Florida State U (FL)
Goddard Coll (VT)
Hampshire Coll (MA)
Hampton U (VA)
Indiana U Bloomington (IN)
Ithaca Coll (NY)
Johnson State Coll (VT)
Lamar U (TX)
Long Island U, Brooklyn Campus (NY)
Long Island U, Southampton Coll, Friends World Program (NY)
Loyola U New Orleans (LA)
Manhattan School of Music (NY)
McGill U (PQ, Canada)
New England Conservatory of Music (MA)
New York U (NY)
North Carolina Central U (NC)
North Central Coll (IL)
Northwestern U (IL)
Oberlin Coll (OH)
The Ohio State U (OH)
Open Learning Agency (BC, Canada)
Roosevelt U (IL)
Rowan U (NJ)
Rutgers, The State U of New Jersey, New Brunswick (NJ)
St. Francis Xavier U (NS, Canada)
Simon's Rock Coll of Bard (MA)
Southwest Texas State U (TX)
State U of NY at New Paltz (NY)
Temple U (PA)
Texas Southern U (TX)
Université de Montréal (QC, Canada)
U of Cincinnati (OH)
U of Hartford (CT)
The U of Iowa (IA)
The U of Maine at Augusta (ME)
U of Miami (FL)
U of Michigan (MI)
U of Minnesota, Duluth (MN)
U of Nevada, Las Vegas (NV)
U of North Florida (FL)
U of North Texas (TX)
U of Rochester (NY)
U of Southern California (CA)
Virginia Union U (VA)
Webster U (MO)
Western Washington U (WA)
Westfield State Coll (MA)
William Paterson U of New Jersey (NJ)
York U (ON, Canada)

JOURNALISM

Abilene Christian U (TX)
Adams State Coll (CO)
Alabama State U (AL)
Alliant International U (CA)
American U (DC)
American U in Cairo(Egypt)
Anderson Coll (SC)
Andrews U (MI)
Angelo State U (TX)
Appalachian State U (NC)
Arizona State U (AZ)
Arkansas State U (AR)
Arkansas Tech U (AR)
Asbury Coll (KY)
Ashland U (OH)
Auburn U (AL)
Augustana Coll (SD)
Averett U (VA)
Ball State U (IN)
Barry U (FL)
Bayamón Central U (PR)
Baylor U (TX)
Belmont U (TN)
Bemidji State U (MN)
Benedict Coll (SC)
Benedictine Coll (KS)
Baruch Coll of the City U of NY (NY)
Berry Coll (GA)
Boston U (MA)
Bowling Green State U (OH)
Bradley U (IL)
Brooklyn Coll of the City U of NY (NY)
Butler U (IN)
California Polytechnic State U, San Luis Obispo (CA)
California State Polytechnic U, Pomona (CA)
California State U, Chico (CA)
California State U, Fresno (CA)
California State U, Fullerton (CA)
California State U, Hayward (CA)
California State U, Long Beach (CA)
California State U, Northridge (CA)
California State U, Sacramento (CA)
Cameron U (OK)
Campbellsville U (KY)
Campbell U (NC)
Carleton U (ON, Canada)
Carroll Coll (WI)
Carson-Newman Coll (TN)
Castleton State Coll (VT)
Central Michigan U (MI)
Central Missouri State U (MO)
Central Washington U (WA)
Chapman U (CA)
Cincinnati Bible Coll and Seminary (OH)
Coll of St. Catherine (MN)
Coll of St. Joseph (VT)
The Coll of Southeastern Europe, The American U of Athens(Greece)
Coll of the Ozarks (MO)
Colorado State U (CO)
Columbia Coll Chicago (IL)
Columbia Union Coll (MD)
Concordia Coll (MN)
Concordia U (QC, Canada)
Creighton U (NE)
Curry Coll (MA)
Davis & Elkins Coll (WV)
Delaware State U (DE)
Delta State U (MS)
Dordt Coll (IA)
Drake U (IA)
Duquesne U (PA)
Eastern Illinois U (IL)
Eastern Kentucky U (KY)
Eastern Michigan U (MI)
Eastern Nazarene Coll (MA)
Eastern Washington U (WA)
Edinboro U of Pennsylvania (PA)
Edward Waters Coll (FL)
Elon U (NC)
Emerson Coll (MA)
Evangel U (MO)
Florida A&M U (FL)
Florida Southern Coll (FL)
Fordham U (NY)
Fort Hays State U (KS)
Framingham State Coll (MA)
Franklin Coll of Indiana (IN)
Franklin Pierce Coll (NH)
The George Washington U (DC)
Georgia Coll and State U (GA)
Georgia Southern U (GA)
Georgia State U (GA)
Goddard Coll (VT)
Gonzaga U (WA)
Goshen Coll (IN)
Grace U (NE)
Grand Valley State U (MI)
Grand View Coll (IA)
Hampshire Coll (MA)
Hampton U (VA)
Harding U (AR)
Hastings Coll (NE)
Hawai'i Pacific U (HI)
Henderson State U (AR)
Hofstra U (NY)
Houston Baptist U (TX)
Howard U (DC)
Humboldt State U (CA)
Indiana State U (IN)
Indiana U Bloomington (IN)
Indiana U of Pennsylvania (PA)
Indiana U–Purdue U Indianapolis (IN)
Iona Coll (NY)
Iowa State U of Science and Technology (IA)
Ithaca Coll (NY)
Jackson State U (MS)
John Brown U (AR)
Johnson State Coll (VT)
Judson Coll (IL)
Kansas State U (KS)
Keene State Coll (NH)
Lamar U (TX)
La Salle U (PA)
Lehigh U (PA)
Lewis U (IL)
Lincoln U (MO)
Lincoln U (PA)
Lindenwood U (MO)
Lock Haven U of Pennsylvania (PA)
Long Island U, Brooklyn Campus (NY)
Long Island U, C.W. Post Campus (NY)
Long Island U, Southampton Coll, Friends World Program (NY)
Longwood Coll (VA)
Loras Coll (IA)
Louisiana Coll (LA)
Louisiana Tech U (LA)
Loyola U Chicago (IL)
Lubbock Christian U (TX)
Lynchburg Coll (VA)
Lyndon State Coll (VT)
MacMurray Coll (IL)
Malone Coll (OH)
Mansfield U of Pennsylvania (PA)
Marietta Coll (OH)
Marist Coll (NY)
Marquette U (WI)
Marshall U (WV)
Mars Hill Coll (NC)
Mary Baldwin Coll (VA)
Marymount Coll of Fordham U (NY)
Massachusetts Coll of Liberal Arts (MA)
Mercy Coll (NY)
Mercyhurst Coll (PA)
Messiah Coll (PA)
Metropolitan State Coll of Denver (CO)
Miami U (OH)
Michigan State U (MI)
Midland Lutheran Coll (NE)
Milligan Coll (TN)
Minnesota State U, Mankato (MN)
Minnesota State U Moorhead (MN)
Moravian Coll (PA)
Morris Coll (SC)
Mount St. Clare Coll (IA)
Mount Vernon Nazarene U (OH)
Multnomah Bible Coll and Biblical Seminary (OR)
Murray State U (KY)
Muskingum Coll (OH)
National U (CA)
New England Coll (NH)
New Mexico Highlands U (NM)
New Mexico State U (NM)
New York U (NY)
Norfolk State U (VA)
Northeastern State U (OK)
Northeastern U (MA)
Northern Arizona U (AZ)
Northern Illinois U (IL)
Northern Kentucky U (KY)
North Greenville Coll (SC)
Northwestern Coll (MN)
Northwestern State U of Louisiana (LA)
Northwestern U (IL)
Northwest Missouri State U (MO)
Oakland U (MI)
The Ohio State U (OH)
Ohio U (OH)
Ohio Wesleyan U (OH)
Oklahoma Baptist U (OK)
Oklahoma Christian U of Science and Arts (OK)
Oklahoma City U (OK)
Oklahoma State U (OK)
Olivet Coll (MI)
Olivet Nazarene U (IL)
Oral Roberts U (OK)
Otterbein Coll (OH)
Pace U (NY)
Pacific Lutheran U (WA)
Pacific Union Coll (CA)
Pacific U (OR)
Penn State U Univ Park Campus (PA)
Pepperdine U, Malibu (CA)
Piedmont Coll (GA)
Pittsburg State U (KS)
Point Loma Nazarene U (CA)
Point Park Coll (PA)
Purchase Coll, State U of NY (NY)
Purdue U Calumet (IN)
Queens Coll (NC)
Quincy U (IL)
Quinnipiac U (CT)
Radford U (VA)
Rider U (NJ)
Roosevelt U (IL)
Rowan U (NJ)
Rust Coll (MS)
Rutgers, The State U of New Jersey, New Brunswick (NJ)
Sacred Heart U (CT)
St. Ambrose U (IA)
St. Bonaventure U (NY)
St. Cloud State U (MN)
Saint Francis U (PA)
St. John's U (NY)
Saint Joseph's Coll (ME)
Saint Mary-of-the-Woods Coll (IN)
Saint Mary's U of Minnesota (MN)
Saint Michael's Coll (VT)
St. Thomas Aquinas Coll (NY)
St. Thomas U (NB, Canada)
Salem State Coll (MA)
Samford U (AL)
Sam Houston State U (TX)
San Diego State U (CA)
San Francisco State U (CA)
San Jose State U (CA)
Seattle U (WA)
Seton Hill Coll (PA)
Shippensburg U of Pennsylvania (PA)
Shorter Coll (GA)
Slippery Rock U of Pennsylvania (PA)
South Dakota State U (SD)
Southeast Missouri State U (MO)
Southern Adventist U (TN)
Southern Arkansas U–Magnolia (AR)
Southern Connecticut State U (CT)
Southern Illinois U Carbondale (IL)
Southern Methodist U (TX)
Southern Nazarene U (OK)
Southwestern Adventist U (TX)
Southwest Missouri State U (MO)
Southwest Texas State U (TX)
Spring Arbor U (MI)
Spring Hill Coll (AL)
State U of NY at New Paltz (NY)
State U of NY at Oswego (NY)
State U of NY Coll at Brockport (NY)
State U of NY Coll at Buffalo (NY)
Stephen F. Austin State U (TX)
Suffolk U (MA)
Susquehanna U (PA)
Syracuse U (NY)
Tabor Coll (KS)
Temple U (PA)
Tennessee Technological U (TN)
Texas A&M U (TX)
Texas A&M U–Commerce (TX)
Texas A&M U–Kingsville (TX)
Texas Christian U (TX)
Texas Southern U (TX)
Texas Tech U (TX)
Texas Wesleyan U (TX)
Thomas Edison State Coll (NJ)
Toccoa Falls Coll (GA)
Troy State U (AL)
Truman State U (MO)
Union Coll (NE)
Union U (TN)
U Coll of the Cariboo (BC, Canada)
The U of Alabama (AL)
U of Alaska Anchorage (AK)
U of Alaska Fairbanks (AK)
The U of Arizona (AZ)
U of Arkansas (AR)
U of Arkansas at Little Rock (AR)
U of Baltimore (MD)
U of Bridgeport (CT)
U of Central Arkansas (AR)
U of Central Florida (FL)
U of Central Oklahoma (OK)
U of Colorado at Boulder (CO)
U of Connecticut (CT)
U of Dayton (OH)
U of Delaware (DE)
U of Denver (CO)
The U of Findlay (OH)
U of Florida (FL)
U of Georgia (GA)
U of Hawaii at Manoa (HI)
U of Houston (TX)
U of Idaho (ID)
U of Illinois at Urbana–Champaign (IL)
The U of Iowa (IA)
U of Kansas (KS)
U of Kentucky (KY)
U of King's Coll (NS, Canada)
U of La Verne (CA)
U of Louisiana at Monroe (LA)
U of Maine (ME)
U of Maryland, Coll Park (MD)
U of Massachusetts Amherst (MA)
The U of Memphis (TN)
U of Miami (FL)
U of Michigan (MI)
U of Minnesota, Twin Cities Campus (MN)
U of Mississippi (MS)
U of Missouri–Columbia (MO)
The U of Montana–Missoula (MT)
U of Nebraska at Kearney (NE)
U of Nebraska at Omaha (NE)
U of Nevada, Reno (NV)
U of New Hampshire (NH)
U of New Mexico (NM)
The U of North Carolina at Pembroke (NC)
U of Northern Colorado (CO)
U of North Texas (TX)
U of Oklahoma (OK)
U of Oregon (OR)
U of Pittsburgh at Greensburg (PA)
U of Pittsburgh at Johnstown (PA)
U of Portland (OR)
U of Regina (SK, Canada)
U of Rhode Island (RI)
U of Richmond (VA)
U of St. Thomas (MN)
U of San Francisco (CA)
U of South Carolina (SC)
U of South Dakota (SD)
U of Southern California (CA)
U of Southern Colorado (CO)
U of Southern Indiana (IN)
U of Southern Mississippi (MS)
The U of Tennessee (TN)
The U of Tennessee at Martin (TN)
The U of Texas at Arlington (TX)
The U of Texas at Austin (TX)
The U of Texas at El Paso (TX)
The U of Texas at San Antonio (TX)
The U of Texas at Tyler (TX)
The U of Texas–Pan American (TX)
U of Toledo (OH)
U of Utah (UT)
U of Windsor (ON, Canada)
U of Wisconsin–Eau Claire (WI)
U of Wisconsin–Madison (WI)
U of Wisconsin–Milwaukee (WI)
U of Wisconsin–Oshkosh (WI)
U of Wisconsin–River Falls (WI)
U of Wisconsin–Superior (WI)
U of Wisconsin–Whitewater (WI)
U of Wyoming (WY)
Utah State U (UT)
Utica Coll of Syracuse U (NY)
Virginia Union U (VA)
Waldorf Coll (IA)
Walla Walla Coll (WA)
Wartburg Coll (IA)
Washburn U of Topeka (KS)
Washington and Lee U (VA)
Washington State U (WA)
Waynesburg Coll (PA)
Wayne State Coll (NE)
Wayne State U (MI)
Weber State U (UT)
Webster U (MO)
Western Illinois U (IL)
Western Kentucky U (KY)
Western Michigan U (MI)
Western State Coll of Colorado (CO)
Western Washington U (WA)
West Texas A&M U (TX)
West Virginia U (WV)
Whitworth Coll (WA)
Wingate U (NC)
Winona State U (MN)
Youngstown State U (OH)

JOURNALISM AND MASS COMMUNICATION RELATED

Averett U (VA)
Boston U (MA)
Central State U (OH)
City U (WA)
Duquesne U (PA)
Kent State U (OH)
Ohio U (OH)
Saint Mary's U of Minnesota (MN)
San Diego State U (CA)
U of Nebraska–Lincoln (NE)
The U of North Carolina at Asheville (NC)
U of St. Thomas (MN)
The U of Western Ontario (ON, Canada)

JUDAIC STUDIES

American U (DC)
Baltimore Hebrew U (MD)
Bard Coll (NY)
Brandeis U (MA)
Brooklyn Coll of the City U of NY (NY)
Brown U (RI)
City Coll of the City U of NY (NY)
Clark U (MA)
Cornell U (NY)
DePaul U (IL)
Dickinson Coll (PA)
Emory U (GA)
Florida Atlantic U (FL)
The George Washington U (DC)
Gratz Coll (PA)
Hamline U (MN)
Hampshire Coll (MA)
Harvard U (MA)
Hofstra U (NY)
Hunter Coll of the City U of NY (NY)
Indiana U Bloomington (IN)
Jewish Theological Seminary of America (NY)
Laura and Alvin Siegal Coll of Judaic Studies (OH)
Lehman Coll of the City U of NY (NY)
McGill U (PQ, Canada)
Mount Holyoke Coll (MA)
New York U (NY)
Oberlin Coll (OH)
The Ohio State U (OH)
Penn State U Univ Park Campus (PA)
Queens Coll of the City U of NY (NY)
Queen's U at Kingston (ON, Canada)
Rutgers, The State U of New Jersey, New Brunswick (NJ)
Scripps Coll (CA)
State U of NY at Albany (NY)
State U of NY at Binghamton (NY)
State U of NY at New Paltz (NY)
State U of NY Coll at Brockport (NY)
Temple U (PA)
Touro Coll (NY)
Trinity Coll (CT)
Tufts U (MA)
Tulane U (LA)
The U of Arizona (AZ)
U of Calif, Los Angeles (CA)
U of Calif, San Diego (CA)

U of Chicago (IL)
U of Cincinnati (OH)
U of Florida (FL)
U of Hartford (CT)
U of Judaism (CA)
U of Manitoba (MB, Canada)
U of Maryland, Coll Park (MD)
U of Massachusetts Amherst (MA)
U of Miami (FL)
U of Michigan (MI)
U of Minnesota, Twin Cities Campus (MN)
U of Missouri–Kansas City (MO)
U of Oregon (OR)
U of Pennsylvania (PA)
U of Southern California (CA)
U of Toronto (ON, Canada)
U of Washington (WA)
Vassar Coll (NY)
Washington U in St. Louis (MO)
Wellesley Coll (MA)
Yale U (CT)
Yeshiva U (NY)
York U (ON, Canada)

LABORATORY ANIMAL MEDICINE
North Carolina Ag and Tech State U (NC)
Quinnipiac U (CT)
Thomas Edison State Coll (NJ)

LABOR/PERSONNEL RELATIONS
Athabasca U (AB, Canada)
Bowling Green State U (OH)
Brock U (ON, Canada)
California State U, Dominguez Hills (CA)
Carleton U (ON, Canada)
Clarion U of Pennsylvania (PA)
Cleveland State U (OH)
Cornell U (NY)
Ferris State U (MI)
Governors State U (IL)
Grand Valley State U (MI)
Hampshire Coll (MA)
Hofstra U (NY)
Indiana U Bloomington (IN)
Indiana U Kokomo (IN)
Indiana U Northwest (IN)
Indiana U–Purdue U Fort Wayne (IN)
Indiana U–Purdue U Indianapolis (IN)
Indiana U South Bend (IN)
Indiana U Southeast (IN)
Ithaca Coll (NY)
Lakehead U (ON, Canada)
Le Moyne Coll (NY)
McGill U (PQ, Canada)
McMaster U (ON, Canada)
Memorial U of Newfoundland (NF, Canada)
Norfolk State U (VA)
Northern Kentucky U (KY)
Pace U (NY)
Penn State U Univ Park Campus (PA)
Queens Coll of the City U of NY (NY)
Rhode Island Coll (RI)
Rockhurst U (MO)
Rowan U (NJ)
Rutgers, The State U of New Jersey, New Brunswick (NJ)
Saint Francis U (PA)
Saint Joseph's U (PA)
San Francisco State U (CA)
Seton Hall U (NJ)
State U of NY Coll at Fredonia (NY)
State U of NY Coll at Old Westbury (NY)
State U of NY Coll at Potsdam (NY)
State U of NY Empire State Coll (NY)
Tennessee Technological U (TN)
Texas A&M U–Commerce (TX)
Thomas Edison State Coll (NJ)
Université de Montréal (QC, Canada)
Université Laval (QC, Canada)
U Coll of Cape Breton (NS, Canada)
U of Alberta (AB, Canada)
The U of British Columbia (BC, Canada)
The U of Iowa (IA)
U of Manitoba (MB, Canada)
U of Massachusetts Boston (MA)
U of Toronto (ON, Canada)
U of Windsor (ON, Canada)
U of Wisconsin–Madison (WI)
U of Wisconsin–Milwaukee (WI)
Wayne State U (MI)
Westminster Coll (PA)
West Virginia U Inst of Technology (WV)
Winona State U (MN)
York U (ON, Canada)

LANDSCAPE ARCHITECTURE
Arizona State U (AZ)
Auburn U (AL)
Ball State U (IN)
California Polytechnic State U, San Luis Obispo (CA)
California State Polytechnic U, Pomona (CA)
City Coll of the City U of NY (NY)
Clemson U (SC)
Coll of the Atlantic (ME)
Colorado State U (CO)
Cornell U (NY)
Delaware Valley Coll (PA)
Eastern Kentucky U (KY)
Florida A&M U (FL)
Iowa State U of Science and Technology (IA)
Kansas State U (KS)
Louisiana State U and A&M Coll (LA)
Michigan State U (MI)
Mississippi State U (MS)
North Carolina Ag and Tech State U (NC)
North Carolina State U (NC)
North Dakota State U (ND)
Northwest Missouri State U (MO)
The Ohio State U (OH)
Oklahoma State U (OK)
Penn State U Univ Park Campus (PA)
Purdue U (IN)
State U of NY Coll of Environ Sci and Forestry (NY)
Temple U (PA)
Texas A&M U (TX)
Texas Tech U (TX)
Université de Montréal (QC, Canada)
The U of Arizona (AZ)
U of Arkansas (AR)
The U of British Columbia (BC, Canada)
U of Calif, Berkeley (CA)
U of Calif, Davis (CA)
U of Connecticut (CT)
U of Florida (FL)
U of Georgia (GA)
U of Guelph (ON, Canada)
U of Hawaii at Manoa (HI)
U of Idaho (ID)
U of Illinois at Urbana–Champaign (IL)
U of Kentucky (KY)
U of Maryland, Coll Park (MD)
U of Massachusetts Amherst (MA)
U of Michigan (MI)
U of Minnesota, Twin Cities Campus (MN)
U of Nevada, Las Vegas (NV)
U of Oregon (OR)
U of Rhode Island (RI)
U of Southern California (CA)
U of Toronto (ON, Canada)
U of Washington (WA)
U of Wisconsin–Madison (WI)
Utah State U (UT)
Virginia Polytechnic Inst and State U (VA)
West Virginia U (WV)

LANDSCAPING MANAGEMENT
Andrews U (MI)
Colorado State U (CO)
Eastern Kentucky U (KY)
Mississippi State U (MS)
Oklahoma State U (OK)
Oregon State U (OR)
Penn State U Univ Park Campus (PA)
South Dakota State U (SD)
Tennessee Technological U (TN)
U of Georgia (GA)
U of Maine (ME)
The U of Tennessee at Martin (TN)
U of Vermont (VT)

LAND USE MANAGEMENT
California State U, Bakersfield (CA)
The Evergreen State Coll (WA)
Frostburg State U (MD)
Grand Valley State U (MI)
Metropolitan State Coll of Denver (CO)
Northern Michigan U (MI)
Northland Coll (WI)
State U of NY Coll of Environ Sci and Forestry (NY)
U of Alberta (AB, Canada)
U of Saskatchewan (SK, Canada)
U of Wisconsin–Platteville (WI)
U of Wisconsin–River Falls (WI)

LASER/OPTICAL TECHNOLOGY
Excelsior Coll (NY)
Oregon Inst of Technology (OR)

LATIN AMERICAN STUDIES
Adelphi U (NY)
Albright Coll (PA)
American U (DC)
Assumption Coll (MA)
Austin Coll (TX)
Ball State U (IN)
Bard Coll (NY)
Barnard Coll (NY)
Baylor U (TX)
Beloit Coll (WI)
Boston U (MA)
Bowdoin Coll (ME)
Brandeis U (MA)
Brigham Young U (UT)
Brown U (RI)
Bucknell U (PA)
California State U, Chico (CA)
California State U, Fullerton (CA)
California State U, Hayward (CA)
California State U, Los Angeles (CA)
Carleton Coll (MN)
Carleton U (ON, Canada)
Central Coll (IA)
Chapman U (CA)
City Coll of the City U of NY (NY)
Claremont McKenna Coll (CA)
Colby Coll (ME)
Colgate U (NY)
Coll of the Holy Cross (MA)
The Coll of William and Mary (VA)
The Coll of Wooster (OH)
Colorado State U (CO)
Columbia Coll (NY)
Connecticut Coll (CT)
Cornell Coll (IA)
Cornell U (NY)
Dartmouth Coll (NH)
Denison U (OH)
DePaul U (IL)
Earlham Coll (IN)
Emory U (GA)
The Evergreen State Coll (WA)
Flagler Coll (FL)
Florida State U (FL)
Fordham U (NY)
Fort Lewis Coll (CO)
The George Washington U (DC)
Gettysburg Coll (PA)
Grinnell Coll (IA)
Gustavus Adolphus Coll (MN)
Hamline U (MN)
Hampshire Coll (MA)
Hanover Coll (IN)
Harvard U (MA)
Haverford Coll (PA)
Hobart and William Smith Colls (NY)
Hofstra U (NY)
Hood Coll (MD)
Hunter Coll of the City U of NY (NY)
Illinois Wesleyan U (IL)
Indiana U Bloomington (IN)
Johns Hopkins U (MD)
Kent State U (OH)
Lake Forest Coll (IL)
Lehman Coll of the City U of NY (NY)
Lock Haven U of Pennsylvania (PA)
Long Island U, Southampton Coll, Friends World Program (NY)
Luther Coll (IA)
Macalester Coll (MN)
Marlboro Coll (VT)
Massachusetts Inst of Technology (MA)
McGill U (PQ, Canada)
McMaster U (ON, Canada)
Mount Holyoke Coll (MA)
New York U (NY)
Oakland U (MI)
Oberlin Coll (OH)
The Ohio State U (OH)
Ohio U (OH)
Penn State U Univ Park Campus (PA)
Pitzer Coll (CA)
Plattsburgh State U of NY (NY)
Pontifical Coll Josephinum (OH)
Portland State U (OR)
Prescott Coll (AZ)
Queens Coll of the City U of NY (NY)
Queen's U at Kingston (ON, Canada)
Rice U (TX)
Ripon Coll (WI)
Rollins Coll (FL)
Rutgers, The State U of New Jersey, New Brunswick (NJ)
St. Cloud State U (MN)
Samford U (AL)
San Diego State U (CA)
Sarah Lawrence Coll (NY)
Scripps Coll (CA)
Seattle Pacific U (WA)
Simon Fraser U (BC, Canada)
Simon's Rock Coll of Bard (MA)
Smith Coll (MA)
Southern Methodist U (TX)
State U of NY at Albany (NY)
State U of NY at Binghamton (NY)
State U of NY at New Paltz (NY)
State U of NY Coll at Brockport (NY)
Stetson U (FL)
Syracuse U (NY)
Temple U (PA)
Texas Christian U (TX)
Texas Tech U (TX)
Trinity U (TX)
Tulane U (LA)
United States Military Academy (NY)
The U of Alabama (AL)
U of Alberta (AB, Canada)
The U of Arizona (AZ)
The U of British Columbia (BC, Canada)
U of Calgary (AB, Canada)
U of Calif, Berkeley (CA)
U of Calif, Los Angeles (CA)
U of Calif, Riverside (CA)
U of Calif, San Diego (CA)
U of Calif, Santa Barbara (CA)
U of Calif, Santa Cruz (CA)
U of Chicago (IL)
U of Cincinnati (OH)
U of Connecticut (CT)
U of Delaware (DE)
U of Denver (CO)
U of Idaho (ID)
U of Illinois at Chicago (IL)
U of Illinois at Urbana–Champaign (IL)
The U of Iowa (IA)
U of Kansas (KS)
U of Kentucky (KY)
U of Miami (FL)
U of Michigan (MI)
U of Minnesota, Morris (MN)
U of Minnesota, Twin Cities Campus (MN)
U of Nebraska–Lincoln (NE)
U of New Mexico (NM)
The U of North Carolina at Chapel Hill (NC)
The U of North Carolina at Greensboro (NC)
U of Northern Iowa (IA)
U of Pennsylvania (PA)
U of Rhode Island (RI)
U of Richmond (VA)
U of South Carolina (SC)
The U of Texas at Austin (TX)
The U of Texas at El Paso (TX)
U of Toledo (OH)
U of Toronto (ON, Canada)
U of Vermont (VT)
U of Washington (WA)
U of Wisconsin–Eau Claire (WI)
U of Wisconsin–Madison (WI)
U of Wisconsin–Milwaukee (WI)
Vanderbilt U (TN)
Vassar Coll (NY)
Walsh U (OH)
Warren Wilson Coll (NC)
Washington Coll (MD)
Washington U in St. Louis (MO)
Wellesley Coll (MA)
Wesleyan U (CT)
Western Washington U (WA)
Yale U (CT)
York U (ON, Canada)

LATIN (ANCIENT AND MEDIEVAL)
Acadia U (NS, Canada)
Amherst Coll (MA)
Asbury Coll (KY)
Augustana Coll (IL)
Austin Coll (TX)
Ball State U (IN)
Bard Coll (NY)
Barnard Coll (NY)
Baylor U (TX)
Boston U (MA)
Bowling Green State U (OH)
Brandeis U (MA)
Brigham Young U (UT)
Brooklyn Coll of the City U of NY (NY)
Bryn Mawr Coll (PA)
Butler U (IN)
Calvin Coll (MI)
Carleton Coll (MN)
Carleton U (ON, Canada)
Carroll Coll (MT)
The Catholic U of America (DC)
Centenary Coll of Louisiana (LA)
Claremont McKenna Coll (CA)
Colgate U (NY)
The Coll of New Rochelle (NY)
The Coll of William and Mary (VA)
The Coll of Wooster (OH)
Concordia Coll (MN)
Concordia U (QC, Canada)
Cornell Coll (IA)
Cornell U (NY)
Creighton U (NE)
Dartmouth Coll (NH)
DePauw U (IN)
Dickinson Coll (PA)
Duke U (NC)
Duquesne U (PA)
Elmira Coll (NY)
Emory U (GA)
Florida State U (FL)
Fordham U (NY)
Franklin and Marshall Coll (PA)
Furman U (SC)
Gettysburg Coll (PA)
Hamilton Coll (NY)
Hampden-Sydney Coll (VA)
Harvard U (MA)
Haverford Coll (PA)
Hobart and William Smith Colls (NY)
Hope Coll (MI)
Hunter Coll of the City U of NY (NY)
Indiana U Bloomington (IN)
John Carroll U (OH)
Kent State U (OH)
Kenyon Coll (OH)
La Salle U (PA)
Lehman Coll of the City U of NY (NY)
Lenoir-Rhyne Coll (NC)
Louisiana State U and A&M Coll (LA)
Loyola Marymount U (CA)
Loyola U Chicago (IL)
Luther Coll (IA)
Macalester Coll (MN)
Marlboro Coll (VT)
Mary Washington Coll (VA)
Memorial U of Newfoundland (NF, Canada)
Mercer U (GA)
Miami U (OH)
Michigan State U (MI)
Monmouth Coll (IL)
Montclair State U (NJ)
Mount Allison U (NB, Canada)
Mount Holyoke Coll (MA)
New Coll of Florida (FL)
New York U (NY)

Oberlin Coll (OH)
Ohio U (OH)
Queens Coll of the City U of NY (NY)
Queen's U at Kingston (ON, Canada)
Randolph-Macon Coll (VA)
Randolph-Macon Woman's Coll (VA)
Rhodes Coll (TN)
Rice U (TX)
Rockford Coll (IL)
Rutgers, The State U of New Jersey, New Brunswick (NJ)
St. Bonaventure U (NY)
Saint Mary's Coll of California (CA)
St. Olaf Coll (MN)
Samford U (AL)
Santa Clara U (CA)
Sarah Lawrence Coll (NY)
Scripps Coll (CA)
Seattle Pacific U (WA)
Smith Coll (MA)
Southwest Missouri State U (MO)
State U of NY at Albany (NY)
Swarthmore Coll (PA)
Sweet Briar Coll (VA)
Syracuse U (NY)
Trent U (ON, Canada)
Tufts U (MA)
Tulane U (LA)
U of Alberta (AB, Canada)
The U of British Columbia (BC, Canada)
U of Calif, Berkeley (CA)
U of Calif, Los Angeles (CA)
U of Calif, Santa Cruz (CA)
U of Chicago (IL)
U of Delaware (DE)
U of Georgia (GA)
U of Hawaii at Manoa (HI)
U of Houston (TX)
U of Idaho (ID)
The U of Iowa (IA)
U of Maine (ME)
U of Manitoba (MB, Canada)
U of Massachusetts Boston (MA)
U of Michigan (MI)
U of Minnesota, Twin Cities Campus (MN)
The U of Montana–Missoula (MT)
U of Nebraska–Lincoln (NE)
U of New Hampshire (NH)
The U of North Carolina at Greensboro (NC)
U of Notre Dame (IN)
U of Oregon (OR)
U of Ottawa (ON, Canada)
U of Richmond (VA)
U of St. Thomas (MN)
U of Saskatchewan (SK, Canada)
The U of Scranton (PA)
U of South Dakota (SD)
U of Southern California (CA)
The U of Tennessee at Chattanooga (TN)
The U of Texas at Austin (TX)
U of the South (TN)
U of Toronto (ON, Canada)
U of Vermont (VT)
U of Victoria (BC, Canada)
U of Washington (WA)
The U of Western Ontario (ON, Canada)
U of Windsor (ON, Canada)
U of Wisconsin–Madison (WI)
U of Wisconsin–Milwaukee (WI)
Ursinus Coll (PA)
Vassar Coll (NY)
Wabash Coll (IN)
Wake Forest U (NC)
Washington U in St. Louis (MO)
Wellesley Coll (MA)
West Chester U of Pennsylvania (PA)
Western Michigan U (MI)
Westminster Coll (PA)
Wichita State U (KS)
Wilfrid Laurier U (ON, Canada)
Yale U (CT)
York U (ON, Canada)

LAW AND LEGAL STUDIES RELATED
Bethany Coll (KS)
Pennsylvania Coll of Technology (PA)
Texas Wesleyan U (TX)
U of Hawaii at Manoa (HI)
U of Miami (FL)
U of Nebraska–Lincoln (NE)
Wilson Coll (PA)

LAW ENFORCEMENT/POLICE SCIENCE
American International Coll (MA)
Becker Coll (MA)
Bemidji State U (MN)
California State U, Hayward (CA)
Carleton U (ON, Canada)
Chicago State U (IL)
Coll of the Ozarks (MO)
Defiance Coll (OH)
East Central U (OK)
Eastern Kentucky U (KY)
Fairmont State Coll (WV)
Ferris State U (MI)
George Mason U (VA)
Grambling State U (LA)
Grand Valley State U (MI)
Hannibal-LaGrange Coll (MO)
Hardin-Simmons U (TX)
Hilbert Coll (NY)
Howard U (DC)
Jackson State U (MS)
Jacksonville State U (AL)
John Jay Coll of Criminal Justice, the City U of NY (NY)
Lake Superior State U (MI)
Lamar U (TX)
Lewis-Clark State Coll (ID)
Louisiana Coll (LA)
MacMurray Coll (IL)
Memorial U of Newfoundland (NF, Canada)
Mercyhurst Coll (PA)
Metropolitan State U (MN)
Michigan State U (MI)
Minnesota State U, Mankato (MN)
Mississippi Coll (MS)
Northeastern State U (OK)
Northeastern U (MA)
Northern Michigan U (MI)
Northern State U (SD)
Northwestern Oklahoma State U (OK)
Oklahoma City U (OK)
Purdue U Calumet (IN)
Rowan U (NJ)
Saint Mary's U of Minnesota (MN)
Sam Houston State U (TX)
Southeast Missouri State U (MO)
Southwest Texas State U (TX)
State U of NY Coll of Technology at Canton (NY)
Stephen F. Austin State U (TX)
Texas A&M U–Commerce (TX)
Texas Southern U (TX)
Tiffin U (OH)
Truman State U (MO)
U of Cincinnati (OH)
U of Great Falls (MT)
U of Pittsburgh at Greensburg (PA)
U of Regina (SK, Canada)
The U of Tennessee at Chattanooga (TN)
The U of Texas at Brownsville (TX)
The U of Texas–Pan American (TX)
U of Toronto (ON, Canada)
U of Wisconsin–Milwaukee (WI)
Washburn U of Topeka (KS)
Wayne State Coll (NE)
Weber State U (UT)
West Chester U of Pennsylvania (PA)
Western Connecticut State U (CT)
Western Oregon U (OR)
Western State Coll of Colorado (CO)
Winona State U (MN)
Wright State U (OH)
York Coll of Pennsylvania (PA)
Youngstown State U (OH)

LEGAL ADMINISTRATIVE ASSISTANT
Ball State U (IN)
Davenport U, Kalamazoo (MI)
Eastern Michigan U (MI)
International Business Coll, Fort Wayne (IN)
Northwest Missouri State U (MO)
Peirce Coll (PA)
Tabor Coll (KS)
Texas A&M U–Commerce (TX)
U of West Los Angeles (CA)

LEGAL STUDIES
American U (DC)
Amherst Coll (MA)
Bay Path Coll (MA)
Becker Coll (MA)
California State U, Chico (CA)
Chapman U (CA)
Christopher Newport U (VA)
Claremont McKenna Coll (CA)
Coll of the Atlantic (ME)
Concordia U (IL)
East Central U (OK)
Elms Coll (MA)
Franciscan U of Steubenville (OH)
Gannon U (PA)
Grand Valley State U (MI)
Hamline U (MN)
Hampshire Coll (MA)
Hartford Coll for Women (CT)
Hilbert Coll (NY)
Hood Coll (MD)
John Jay Coll of Criminal Justice, the City U of NY (NY)
Kenyon Coll (OH)
Lake Superior State U (MI)
Laurentian U (ON, Canada)
Manhattanville Coll (NY)
Marymount Coll of Fordham U (NY)
Methodist Coll (NC)
Mountain State U (WV)
National U (CA)
Newbury Coll (MA)
North Carolina Wesleyan Coll (NC)
Northeastern U (MA)
Nova Southeastern U (FL)
Oberlin Coll (OH)
Park U (MO)
Pennsylvania Coll of Technology (PA)
Point Park Coll (PA)
Quinnipiac U (CT)
Ramapo Coll of New Jersey (NJ)
Rivier Coll (NH)
Roosevelt U (IL)
Sage Coll of Albany (NY)
Schreiner U (TX)
Scripps Coll (CA)
State U of NY Coll at Fredonia (NY)
Suffolk U (MA)
United States Air Force Academy (CO)
Université de Montréal (QC, Canada)
Université de Sherbrooke (PQ, Canada)
Université Laval (QC, Canada)
U of Alberta (AB, Canada)
U of Baltimore (MD)
U of Calgary (AB, Canada)
U of Calif, Berkeley (CA)
U of Calif, Santa Barbara (CA)
U of Calif, Santa Cruz (CA)
U of Evansville (IN)
U of Hartford (CT)
U of Houston–Clear Lake (TX)
U of Illinois at Springfield (IL)
U of Massachusetts Amherst (MA)
U of Massachusetts Boston (MA)
The U of Montana–Missoula (MT)
U of Pennsylvania (PA)
U of Pittsburgh (PA)
The U of Tennessee at Chattanooga (TN)
U of Tulsa (OK)
U of West Los Angeles (CA)
U of Windsor (ON, Canada)
U of Wisconsin–Superior (WI)
Valdosta State U (GA)
Villa Julie Coll (MD)
Webster U (MO)
Winona State U (MN)
York U (ON, Canada)

LIBERAL ARTS AND SCIENCES/ LIBERAL STUDIES
Abilene Christian U (TX)
Adams State Coll (CO)
Alabama State U (AL)
Alaska Pacific U (AK)
Albertus Magnus Coll (CT)
Alcorn State U (MS)
Alderson-Broaddus Coll (WV)
Alliant International U (CA)
Alma Coll (MI)
Alvernia Coll (PA)
American Coll of Thessaloniki(Greece)
American International Coll (MA)
American U (DC)
Anderson Coll (SC)
Andrews U (MI)
Angelo State U (TX)
Antioch U McGregor (OH)
Antioch U Seattle (WA)
Appalachian State U (NC)
Aquinas Coll (MI)
Arcadia U (PA)
Arkansas Baptist Coll (AR)
Armstrong Atlantic State U (GA)
Ashland U (OH)
Athabasca U (AB, Canada)
Auburn U Montgomery (AL)
Augsburg Coll (MN)
Augustana Coll (IL)
Augustana Coll (SD)
Averett U (VA)
Azusa Pacific U (CA)
Ball State U (IN)
Barry U (FL)
Bay Path Coll (MA)
Becker Coll (MA)
Bellarmine U (KY)
Bemidji State U (MN)
Benedictine Coll (KS)
Bennington Coll (VT)
Bentley Coll (MA)
Bethany Coll (WV)
Bethany Coll of the Assemblies of God (CA)
Bethany Lutheran Coll (MN)
Bethel Coll (IN)
Bethel Coll (TN)
Bethune-Cookman Coll (FL)
Bishop's U (PQ, Canada)
Blackburn Coll (IL)
Bluefield Coll (VA)
Bluffton Coll (OH)
Boise State U (ID)
Bowling Green State U (OH)
Bradley U (IL)
Brandon U (MB, Canada)
Brescia U (KY)
Brevard Coll (NC)
Brewton-Parker Coll (GA)
Brock U (ON, Canada)
Bryan Coll (TN)
Buena Vista U (IA)
Burlington Coll (VT)
Cabrini Coll (PA)
California Baptist U (CA)
California Lutheran U (CA)
California Polytechnic State U, San Luis Obispo (CA)
California State Polytechnic U, Pomona (CA)
California State U, Bakersfield (CA)
California State U, Chico (CA)
California State U, Dominguez Hills (CA)
California State U, Fresno (CA)
California State U, Fullerton (CA)
California State U, Hayward (CA)
California State U, Long Beach (CA)
California State U, Los Angeles (CA)
California State U, Monterey Bay (CA)
California State U, Northridge (CA)
California State U, Sacramento (CA)
California State U, San Bernardino (CA)
California State U, San Marcos (CA)
California State U, Stanislaus (CA)
California U of Pennsylvania (PA)
Capital U (OH)
Cardinal Stritch U (WI)
Caribbean U (PR)
Carlow Coll (PA)
Carnegie Mellon U (PA)
Carson-Newman Coll (TN)
Cascade Coll (OR)
Cazenovia Coll (NY)
Cedar Crest Coll (PA)
Centenary Coll of Louisiana (LA)
Central Christian Coll of Kansas (KS)
Chapman U (CA)
Charter Oak State Coll (CT)
Chowan Coll (NC)
Christian Heritage Coll (CA)
Clarion U of Pennsylvania (PA)
Clarkson U (NY)
Cleveland State U (OH)
Coastal Carolina U (SC)
Coe Coll (IA)
Coll Misericordia (PA)
Coll of Mount St. Joseph (OH)
Coll of Mount Saint Vincent (NY)
The Coll of New Rochelle (NY)
Coll of Notre Dame of Maryland (MD)
Coll of Saint Benedict (MN)
Coll of St. Joseph (VT)
Coll of Saint Mary (NE)
The Coll of St. Scholastica (MN)
Coll of the Atlantic (ME)
Colorado Christian U (CO)
Colorado State U (CO)
Columbia Coll (MO)
Columbia Coll Chicago (IL)
Columbia Union Coll (MD)
Columbus State U (GA)
Conception Seminary Coll (MO)
Concordia Coll (NY)
Concordia U (CA)
Concordia U (MN)
Concordia U (OR)
Concordia U Wisconsin (WI)
Coppin State Coll (MD)
Cornell Coll (IA)
Cornell U (NY)
Crichton Coll (TN)
Crown Coll (MN)
Dallas Baptist U (TX)
Defiance Coll (OH)
DeSales U (PA)
Dickinson State U (ND)
Dominican U of California (CA)
Dowling Coll (NY)
D'Youville Coll (NY)
East Carolina U (NC)
Eastern Illinois U (IL)
Eastern Kentucky U (KY)
Eastern Mennonite U (VA)
Eastern Nazarene Coll (MA)
Eastern New Mexico U (NM)
Eastern Oregon U (OR)
Eastern Washington U (WA)
Edgewood Coll (WI)
Edinboro U of Pennsylvania (PA)
Elmira Coll (NY)
Elms Coll (MA)
Emmanuel Coll (MA)
Emory U (GA)
Eugene Lang Coll, New School U (NY)
Eureka Coll (IL)
The Evergreen State Coll (WA)
Excelsior Coll (NY)
Fairleigh Dickinson U, Teaneck-Hackensack Campus (NJ)
Faulkner U (AL)
Ferrum Coll (VA)
Finlandia U (MI)
Florida Atlantic U (FL)
Florida Coll (FL)
Florida Gulf Coast U (FL)
Florida International U (FL)
Fontbonne U (MO)
Fordham U (NY)
Fort Hays State U (KS)
Fort Lewis Coll (CO)
Framingham State Coll (MA)
Francis Marion U (SC)
Franklin Pierce Coll (NH)
Freed-Hardeman U (TN)
Fresno Pacific U (CA)
Friends U (KS)
Frostburg State U (MD)
Gannon U (PA)
Gardner-Webb U (NC)
George Mason U (VA)
Georgetown U (DC)
The George Washington U (DC)
Georgia Coll and State U (GA)
Georgia State U (GA)
Gettysburg Coll (PA)
Glenville State Coll (WV)
Goddard Coll (VT)
Gonzaga U (WA)
Goshen Coll (IN)
Governors State U (IL)
Graceland U (IA)
Grace U (NE)
Grand Canyon U (AZ)
Grand Valley State U (MI)
Grand View Coll (IA)
Green Mountain Coll (VT)
Greenville Coll (IL)
Hampshire Coll (MA)
Hannibal-LaGrange Coll (MO)
Harvard U (MA)

Hastings Coll (NE)
Hawai'i Pacific U (HI)
Hobart and William Smith Colls (NY)
Hofstra U (NY)
Hollins U (VA)
Holy Family Coll (PA)
Holy Names Coll (CA)
Houghton Coll (NY)
Houston Baptist U (TX)
Howard Payne U (TX)
Humboldt State U (CA)
Huntingdon Coll (AL)
Husson Coll (ME)
Illinois Coll (IL)
Illinois State U (IL)
Illinois Wesleyan U (IL)
Iona Coll (NY)
Iowa State U of Science and Technology (IA)
Iowa Wesleyan Coll (IA)
Ithaca Coll (NY)
Jacksonville U (FL)
James Madison U (VA)
John F. Kennedy U (CA)
Johns Hopkins U (MD)
Johnson State Coll (VT)
Juniata Coll (PA)
Kansas Wesleyan U (KS)
Keene State Coll (NH)
Kendall Coll (IL)
Kent State U (OH)
Kentucky State U (KY)
Keuka Coll (NY)
Kutztown U of Pennsylvania (PA)
Lakehead U (ON, Canada)
Lamar U (TX)
La Roche Coll (PA)
La Salle U (PA)
Lasell Coll (MA)
Laurentian U (ON, Canada)
Lebanon Valley Coll (PA)
Lees-McRae Coll (NC)
Lesley U (MA)
Lewis-Clark State Coll (ID)
Lewis U (IL)
Limestone Coll (SC)
Lincoln Memorial U (TN)
Lindenwood U (MO)
Lindsey Wilson Coll (KY)
Lipscomb U (TN)
Lock Haven U of Pennsylvania (PA)
Long Island U, Brooklyn Campus (NY)
Long Island U, Southampton Coll (NY)
Long Island U, Southampton Coll, Friends World Program (NY)
Longwood Coll (VA)
Loras Coll (IA)
Louisiana Coll (LA)
Louisiana State U and A&M Coll (LA)
Lourdes Coll (OH)
Loyola Marymount U (CA)
Lubbock Christian U (TX)
Lyndon State Coll (VT)
Lynn U (FL)
MacMurray Coll (IL)
Magdalen Coll (NH)
Malaspina U-Coll (BC, Canada)
Malone Coll (OH)
Manhattan Coll (NY)
Mansfield U of Pennsylvania (PA)
Maranatha Baptist Bible Coll (WI)
Marian Coll of Fond du Lac (WI)
Marietta Coll (OH)
Mars Hill Coll (NC)
Marymount Coll of Fordham U (NY)
Marymount Manhattan Coll (NY)
Marymount U (VA)
Maryville U of Saint Louis (MO)
Mary Washington Coll (VA)
Marywood U (PA)
Massachusetts Inst of Technology (MA)
The Master's Coll and Seminary (CA)
Mayville State U (ND)
McNeese State U (LA)
Medaille Coll (NY)
Menlo Coll (CA)
Mercyhurst Coll (PA)
Mesa State Coll (CO)
Methodist Coll (NC)
Metropolitan State U (MN)
Michigan State U (MI)
Middlebury Coll (VT)
Midland Lutheran Coll (NE)
Midway Coll (KY)
Millersville U of Pennsylvania (PA)
Mills Coll (CA)
Minnesota Bible Coll (MN)
Minnesota State U, Mankato (MN)
Mississippi Coll (MS)
Mississippi State U (MS)
Missouri Valley Coll (MO)
Mitchell Coll (CT)
Monmouth Coll (IL)
Montana State U–Billings (MT)
Montana Tech of The U of Montana (MT)
Montreat Coll (NC)
Morris Coll (SC)
Mount Allison U (NB, Canada)
Mount Aloysius Coll (PA)
Mount Ida Coll (MA)
Mount Marty Coll (SD)
Mount Mercy Coll (IA)
Mount Olive Coll (NC)
Mount St. Clare Coll (IA)
Mount Saint Mary Coll (NY)
Mount Saint Vincent U (NS, Canada)
The National Hispanic U (CA)
National-Louis U (IL)
National U (CA)
Neumann Coll (PA)
New Coll of Florida (FL)
Newman U (KS)
New Mexico Inst of Mining and Technology (NM)
New Sch Bach of Arts, New Sch for Social Research (NY)
New York U (NY)
Nipissing U (ON, Canada)
North American Baptist Coll & Edmonton Baptist Sem (AB, Canada)
North Carolina State U (NC)
North Central Coll (IL)
Northeastern Illinois U (IL)
Northeastern U (MA)
Northern Arizona U (AZ)
Northern Illinois U (IL)
Northern Michigan U (MI)
Northwest Coll (WA)
Northwestern State U of Louisiana (LA)
Northwestern U (IL)
Northwest Nazarene U (ID)
Notre Dame de Namur U (CA)
Nova Southeastern U (FL)
Nyack Coll (NY)
Oakland U (MI)
Ohio U (OH)
Ohio U–Chillicothe (OH)
Ohio U–Lancaster (OH)
Ohio U–Zanesville (OH)
Ohio Valley Coll (WV)
Okanagan U Coll (BC, Canada)
Oklahoma Christian U of Science and Arts (OK)
Oklahoma City U (OK)
Olivet Coll (MI)
Olivet Nazarene U (IL)
Oral Roberts U (OK)
Oregon State U (OR)
Our Lady of the Lake U of San Antonio (TX)
Pace U (NY)
Pacific Union Coll (CA)
Pacific U (OR)
Park U (MO)
Patten Coll (CA)
Peace Coll (NC)
Penn State U Abington Coll (PA)
Penn State U Altoona Coll (PA)
Penn State U at Erie, The Behrend Coll (PA)
Penn State U Delaware County Campus of the Commonwealth Coll (PA)
Penn State U DuBois Campus of the Commonwealth Coll (PA)
Penn State U Fayette Campus of the Commonwealth Coll (PA)
Penn State U Lehigh Valley Cmps of Berks-Lehigh Valley Coll (PA)
Penn State U Univ Park Campus (PA)
Penn State U York Campus of the Commonwealth Coll (PA)
Pepperdine U, Malibu (CA)
Pittsburg State U (KS)
Point Loma Nazarene U (CA)
Point Park Coll (PA)
Polytechnic U, Brooklyn Campus (NY)
Pomona Coll (CA)
Pontifical Catholic U of Puerto Rico (PR)
Portland State U (OR)
Prescott Coll (AZ)
Principia Coll (IL)
Providence Coll (RI)
Providence Coll and Theological Seminary (MB, Canada)
Purchase Coll, State U of NY (NY)
Purdue U Calumet (IN)
Purdue U North Central (IN)
Quinnipiac U (CT)
Radford U (VA)
Randolph-Macon Woman's Coll (VA)
Redeemer U Coll (ON, Canada)
Regis U (CO)
Reinhardt Coll (GA)
Rhode Island Coll (RI)
The Richard Stockton Coll of New Jersey (NJ)
Richmond, The American International U in London(United Kingdom)
Rivier Coll (NH)
Rocky Mountain Coll (MT)
Rogers State U (OK)
Roger Williams U (RI)
Roosevelt U (IL)
Rowan U (NJ)
Sage Coll of Albany (NY)
St. Andrews Presbyterian Coll (NC)
St. Cloud State U (MN)
St. Edward's U (TX)
St. Francis Xavier U (NS, Canada)
St. Gregory's U (OK)
St. John's Coll (MD)
St. John's Coll (NM)
St. John's U (NY)
Saint Joseph Coll (CT)
Saint Joseph's Coll (ME)
St. Joseph's Coll, Suffolk Campus (NY)
Saint Joseph Seminary Coll (LA)
Saint Mary Coll (KS)
Saint Mary-of-the-Woods Coll (IN)
Saint Mary's Coll of California (CA)
St. Olaf Coll (MN)
Saint Peter's Coll (NJ)
St. Thomas U (FL)
Saint Vincent Coll (PA)
Saint Xavier U (IL)
Salem International U (WV)
Salem State Coll (MA)
Salisbury U (MD)
Salve Regina U (RI)
San Diego State U (CA)
San Francisco State U (CA)
San Jose State U (CA)
Santa Clara U (CA)
Sarah Lawrence Coll (NY)
Schreiner U (TX)
Seattle U (WA)
Seton Hall U (NJ)
Seton Hill Coll (PA)
Shaw U (NC)
Sheldon Jackson Coll (AK)
Shenandoah U (VA)
Shimer Coll (IL)
Shorter Coll (GA)
Simon Fraser U (BC, Canada)
Simpson Coll and Graduate School (CA)
Skidmore Coll (NY)
Sonoma State U (CA)
Southeast Missouri State U (MO)
Southern Connecticut State U (CT)
Southern Illinois U Carbondale (IL)
Southern Illinois U Edwardsville (IL)
Southern Oregon U (OR)
Southern Vermont Coll (VT)
Southern Virginia U (VA)
Southwestern Coll (KS)
State U of NY Coll at Cortland (NY)
State U of NY Coll at Fredonia (NY)
State U of NY Coll at Oneonta (NY)
State U of West Georgia (GA)
Stephens Coll (MO)
Suffolk U (MA)
Tarleton State U (TX)
Teikyo Post U (CT)
Tennessee State U (TN)
Texas A&M U–Commerce (TX)
Texas Christian U (TX)
Texas Tech U (TX)
Thomas Aquinas Coll (CA)
Thomas Edison State Coll (NJ)
Thomas More Coll (KY)
Thomas U (GA)
Tiffin U (OH)
Touro Coll (NY)
Trent U (ON, Canada)
Trinity Coll (DC)
Trinity International U (IL)
Trinity Western U (BC, Canada)
Tulane U (LA)
Tyndale Coll & Seminary (ON, Canada)
Union Coll (NY)
Union Inst & U (OH)
Université de Sherbrooke (PQ, Canada)
U Coll of Cape Breton (NS, Canada)
The U of Akron (OH)
U of Alaska Southeast (AK)
U of Alberta (AB, Canada)
The U of Arizona (AZ)
U of Arkansas at Little Rock (AR)
U of Baltimore (MD)
U of Bridgeport (CT)
The U of British Columbia (BC, Canada)
U of Calgary (AB, Canada)
U of Calif, Riverside (CA)
U of Central Florida (FL)
U of Central Oklahoma (OK)
U of Charleston (WV)
U of Chicago (IL)
U of Cincinnati (OH)
U of Delaware (DE)
U of Evansville (IN)
U of Georgia (GA)
U of Hawaii at Manoa (HI)
U of Idaho (ID)
U of Illinois at Springfield (IL)
U of Illinois at Urbana–Champaign (IL)
U of Indianapolis (IN)
U of Judaism (CA)
U of Kansas (KS)
U of La Verne (CA)
U of Louisville (KY)
U of Maine at Farmington (ME)
U of Maine at Fort Kent (ME)
U of Maine at Presque Isle (ME)
U of Mary (ND)
U of Maryland Eastern Shore (MD)
U of Massachusetts Dartmouth (MA)
U of Massachusetts Lowell (MA)
U of Miami (FL)
U of Michigan (MI)
U of Michigan–Dearborn (MI)
U of Michigan–Flint (MI)
U of Minnesota, Morris (MN)
U of Mississippi (MS)
U of Missouri–Columbia (MO)
U of Missouri–Kansas City (MO)
U of Missouri–St. Louis (MO)
The U of Montana–Missoula (MT)
Western Montana Coll of The U of Montana (MT)
U of Nebraska–Lincoln (NE)
U of New England (ME)
U of New Haven (CT)
U of New Mexico (NM)
The U of North Carolina at Asheville (NC)
The U of North Carolina at Chapel Hill (NC)
The U of North Carolina at Greensboro (NC)
U of Northern Iowa (IA)
U of North Florida (FL)
U of Notre Dame (IN)
U of Oregon (OR)
U of Ottawa (ON, Canada)
U of Pennsylvania (PA)
U of Pittsburgh (PA)
U of Redlands (CA)
U of Regina (SK, Canada)
U of Rhode Island (RI)
U of St. Francis (IL)
U of Saint Francis (IN)
U of St. Thomas (TX)
U of San Diego (CA)
U of San Francisco (CA)
U of Sioux Falls (SD)
U of South Carolina (SC)
U of South Carolina Aiken (SC)
U of South Dakota (SD)
U of Southern Indiana (IN)
U of South Florida (FL)
The U of Tampa (FL)
The U of Texas at Austin (TX)
The U of Texas at Brownsville (TX)
The U of Texas at Tyler (TX)
U of the Incarnate Word (TX)
U of Toledo (OH)
U of Utah (UT)
U of Victoria (BC, Canada)
U of Virginia (VA)
The U of Virginia's Coll at Wise (VA)
U of Washington (WA)
U of Waterloo (ON, Canada)
U of Wisconsin–Oshkosh (WI)
U of Wisconsin–Platteville (WI)
U of Wisconsin–River Falls (WI)
U System Coll for Lifelong Learning (NH)
Urbana U (OH)
Ursinus Coll (PA)
Utah State U (UT)
Utica Coll of Syracuse U (NY)
Valdosta State U (GA)
Valparaiso U (IN)
Villa Julie Coll (MD)
Villanova U (PA)
Virginia Intermont Coll (VA)
Virginia Wesleyan Coll (VA)
Viterbo U (WI)
Walsh U (OH)
Warner Pacific Coll (OR)
Washburn U of Topeka (KS)
Washington Coll (MD)
Washington State U (WA)
Washington U in St. Louis (MO)
Weber State U (UT)
Webster U (MO)
Wesley Coll (DE)
West Chester U of Pennsylvania (PA)
Western Baptist Coll (OR)
Western Carolina U (NC)
Western Connecticut State U (CT)
Western Illinois U (IL)
Western International U (AZ)
Western New England Coll (MA)
Western Washington U (WA)
Westfield State Coll (MA)
Westminster Choir Coll of Rider U (NJ)
Westmont Coll (CA)
West Texas A&M U (TX)
West Virginia U (WV)
Wheeling Jesuit U (WV)
Whittier Coll (CA)
Wichita State U (KS)
Wilberforce U (OH)
Wilkes U (PA)
William Carey Coll (MS)
Williams Baptist Coll (AR)
Wilmington Coll (OH)
Wingate U (NC)
Winona State U (MN)
Wittenberg U (OH)
Xavier U (OH)
York Coll (NE)
York Coll of the City U of New York (NY)
York U (ON, Canada)

LIBERAL ARTS AND STUDIES RELATED

The Colorado Coll (CO)
Duquesne U (PA)
Johns Hopkins U (MD)
Northern Arizona U (AZ)
Ohio U (OH)
Saint Anselm Coll (NH)
Troy State U Montgomery (AL)
The U of Akron (OH)
U of Louisville (KY)
U of Nebraska–Lincoln (NE)
U of Oklahoma (OK)
U of Pennsylvania (PA)
U of South Alabama (AL)
U of Utah (UT)

LIBRARY SCIENCE

Appalachian State U (NC)
Chadron State Coll (NE)
Clarion U of Pennsylvania (PA)
Concord Coll (WV)
Florida State U (FL)
Kutztown U of Pennsylvania (PA)
Lakehead U (ON, Canada)
Longwood Coll (VA)
Murray State U (KY)

Northeastern State U (OK)
Ohio Dominican Coll (OH)
St. Cloud State U (MN)
Southern Connecticut State U (CT)
Texas Woman's U (TX)
U of Hawaii at Manoa (HI)
The U of Maine at Augusta (ME)
U of Nebraska at Omaha (NE)
U of Oklahoma (OK)
U of Southern Mississippi (MS)
U of the District of Columbia (DC)

LINGUISTICS

Baylor U (TX)
Boston U (MA)
Brandeis U (MA)
Brigham Young U (UT)
Brock U (ON, Canada)
Brooklyn Coll of the City U of NY (NY)
Brown U (RI)
California State U, Dominguez Hills (CA)
California State U, Fresno (CA)
California State U, Fullerton (CA)
California State U, Northridge (CA)
Carleton U (ON, Canada)
Central Coll (IA)
City Coll of the City U of NY (NY)
Cleveland State U (OH)
The Coll of William and Mary (VA)
Columbia Coll (NY)
Concordia U (QC, Canada)
Cornell U (NY)
Crown Coll (MN)
Dalhousie U (NS, Canada)
Dartmouth Coll (NH)
Duke U (NC)
Eastern Michigan U (MI)
Florida Atlantic U (FL)
Florida State U (FL)
Georgetown U (DC)
Grinnell Coll (IA)
Hampshire Coll (MA)
Harvard U (MA)
Indiana U Bloomington (IN)
Inter American U of PR, San Germán Campus (PR)
Iowa State U of Science and Technology (IA)
Judson Coll (IL)
Lawrence U (WI)
Lehman Coll of the City U of NY (NY)
Long Island U, Southampton Coll, Friends World Program (NY)
Macalester Coll (MN)
Marlboro Coll (VT)
Massachusetts Inst of Technology (MA)
McGill U (PQ, Canada)
McMaster U (ON, Canada)
Memorial U of Newfoundland (NF, Canada)
Miami U (OH)
Michigan State U (MI)
Montclair State U (NJ)
Moody Bible Inst (IL)
Mount Saint Vincent U (NS, Canada)
New York U (NY)
Northeastern Illinois U (IL)
Northeastern U (MA)
Northwestern U (IL)
Oakland U (MI)
The Ohio State U (OH)
Ohio U (OH)
Oklahoma Wesleyan U (OK)
Pitzer Coll (CA)
Pomona Coll (CA)
Portland State U (OR)
Queens Coll of the City U of NY (NY)
Queen's U at Kingston (ON, Canada)
Reed Coll (OR)
Rice U (TX)
Rutgers, The State U of New Jersey, New Brunswick (NJ)
St. Cloud State U (MN)
San Diego State U (CA)
San Jose State U (CA)
Scripps Coll (CA)
Simon Fraser U (BC, Canada)
Southern Illinois U Carbondale (IL)
Stanford U (CA)
State U of NY at Albany (NY)
State U of NY at Binghamton (NY)
State U of NY at Oswego (NY)
State U of NY at Stony Brook (NY)
Swarthmore Coll (PA)
Syracuse U (NY)
Temple U (PA)
Trinity Western U (BC, Canada)
Tulane U (LA)
Université de Montréal (QC, Canada)
Université Laval (QC, Canada)
State U of NY at Buffalo (NY)
U of Alaska Fairbanks (AK)
U of Alberta (AB, Canada)
The U of Arizona (AZ)
The U of British Columbia (BC, Canada)
U of Calgary (AB, Canada)
U of Calif, Berkeley (CA)
U of Calif, Davis (CA)
U of Calif, Irvine (CA)
U of Calif, Los Angeles (CA)
U of Calif, Riverside (CA)
U of Calif, San Diego (CA)
U of Calif, Santa Barbara (CA)
U of Calif, Santa Cruz (CA)
U of Chicago (IL)
U of Cincinnati (OH)
U of Colorado at Boulder (CO)
U of Connecticut (CT)
U of Delaware (DE)
U of Florida (FL)
U of Georgia (GA)
U of Hawaii at Hilo (HI)
U of Hawaii at Manoa (HI)
U of Illinois at Urbana–Champaign (IL)
The U of Iowa (IA)
U of Kansas (KS)
U of Kentucky (KY)
U of King's Coll (NS, Canada)
U of Maryland, Baltimore County (MD)
U of Maryland, Coll Park (MD)
U of Massachusetts Amherst (MA)
U of Michigan (MI)
U of Minnesota, Twin Cities Campus (MN)
U of Mississippi (MS)
U of Missouri–Columbia (MO)
U of Missouri–St. Louis (MO)
The U of Montana–Missoula (MT)
U of New Hampshire (NH)
U of New Mexico (NM)
The U of North Carolina at Chapel Hill (NC)
The U of North Carolina at Greensboro (NC)
U of Northern Iowa (IA)
U of Oklahoma (OK)
U of Oregon (OR)
U of Ottawa (ON, Canada)
U of Pennsylvania (PA)
U of Pittsburgh (PA)
U of Regina (SK, Canada)
U of Rochester (NY)
U of Saskatchewan (SK, Canada)
U of Southern California (CA)
U of Southern Maine (ME)
The U of Texas at Austin (TX)
The U of Texas at El Paso (TX)
U of Toledo (OH)
U of Toronto (ON, Canada)
U of Utah (UT)
U of Victoria (BC, Canada)
U of Washington (WA)
The U of Western Ontario (ON, Canada)
U of Windsor (ON, Canada)
U of Wisconsin–Madison (WI)
U of Wisconsin–Milwaukee (WI)
Washington State U (WA)
Wayne State U (MI)
Wellesley Coll (MA)
Western Washington U (WA)
Yale U (CT)
York U (ON, Canada)

LITERATURE

Agnes Scott Coll (GA)
Alderson-Broaddus Coll (WV)
Alfred U (NY)
Alma Coll (MI)
American U (DC)
Arcadia U (PA)
Augustana Coll (IL)
Ave Maria Coll (MI)
Bard Coll (NY)
Barry U (FL)
Beloit Coll (WI)
Bennington Coll (VT)
Baruch Coll of the City U of NY (NY)
Bethel Coll (MN)
Bishop's U (PQ, Canada)
Blackburn Coll (IL)
Boise State U (ID)
Brock U (ON, Canada)
Brown U (RI)
Bryan Coll (TN)
Burlington Coll (VT)
California Inst of Technology (CA)
California State U, Dominguez Hills (CA)
California State U, Long Beach (CA)
California State U, Northridge (CA)
Capital U (OH)
Carnegie Mellon U (PA)
Carson-Newman Coll (TN)
Castleton State Coll (VT)
Cazenovia Coll (NY)
Centenary Coll of Louisiana (LA)
Chapman U (CA)
Chicago State U (IL)
Christendom Coll (VA)
Christopher Newport U (VA)
City Coll of the City U of NY (NY)
Claremont McKenna Coll (CA)
Clark U (MA)
Coe Coll (IA)
The Coll of New Rochelle (NY)
The Coll of St. Catherine (MN)
Coll of the Atlantic (ME)
Coll of the Holy Cross (MA)
Columbia Coll (SC)
Columbia U, School of General Studies (NY)
Columbus State U (GA)
Concordia U (MN)
Concordia U (NE)
Concordia U (QC, Canada)
Dalhousie U (NS, Canada)
Davis & Elkins Coll (WV)
Defiance Coll (OH)
DePaul U (IL)
Duke U (NC)
East Central U (OK)
Eastern Kentucky U (KY)
Eastern Washington U (WA)
Eckerd Coll (FL)
Elmira Coll (NY)
Emmanuel Coll (MA)
Emory U (GA)
Eugene Lang Coll, New School U (NY)
Eureka Coll (IL)
The Evergreen State Coll (WA)
Excelsior Coll (NY)
Fayetteville State U (NC)
Fitchburg State Coll (MA)
Florida State U (FL)
Fordham U (NY)
Fort Lewis Coll (CO)
Framingham State Coll (MA)
Franklin Coll Switzerland(Switzerland)
Franklin Pierce Coll (NH)
Fresno Pacific U (CA)
Friends U (KS)
Gettysburg Coll (PA)
Goddard Coll (VT)
Gonzaga U (WA)
Graceland U (IA)
Grand Canyon U (AZ)
Grand Valley State U (MI)
Grove City Coll (PA)
Hamilton Coll (NY)
Hampshire Coll (MA)
Harvard U (MA)
Hastings Coll (NE)
Hawai'i Pacific U (HI)
High Point U (NC)
Holy Family Coll (PA)
Houghton Coll (NY)
Hunter Coll of the City U of NY (NY)
Immaculata Coll (PA)
Indiana U Bloomington (IN)
Inter American U of PR, San Germán Campus (PR)
Jewish Theological Seminary of America (NY)
John Cabot U(Italy)
John Carroll U (OH)
Johns Hopkins U (MD)
Johnson State Coll (VT)
Judson Coll (IL)
Kansas Wesleyan U (KS)
Kenyon Coll (OH)
Lake Superior State U (MI)
La Salle U (PA)
Long Island U, Southampton Coll (NY)
Long Island U, Southampton Coll, Friends World Program (NY)
Lycoming Coll (PA)
Maharishi U of Management (IA)
Marist Coll (NY)
Marlboro Coll (VT)
Marymount Coll of Fordham U (NY)
Massachusetts Coll of Liberal Arts (MA)
Massachusetts Inst of Technology (MA)
Memorial U of Newfoundland (NF, Canada)
Middlebury Coll (VT)
Minnesota State U, Mankato (MN)
Montreat Coll (NC)
Morningside Coll (IA)
Mount Allison U (NB, Canada)
Mount Saint Vincent U (NS, Canada)
Mount Vernon Nazarene U (OH)
Naropa U (CO)
Nazareth Coll of Rochester (NY)
New Coll of Florida (FL)
North Central Coll (IL)
North Park U (IL)
Northwest Missouri State U (MO)
Ohio Wesleyan U (OH)
Olivet Nazarene U (IL)
Oregon State U (OR)
Otterbein Coll (OH)
Pace U (NY)
Pacific Lutheran U (WA)
Pacific U (OR)
Pitzer Coll (CA)
Prescott Coll (AZ)
Purchase Coll, State U of NY (NY)
Purdue U Calumet (IN)
Quinnipiac U (CT)
Ramapo Coll of New Jersey (NJ)
Reed Coll (OR)
Richmond, The American International U in London(United Kingdom)
Rochester Coll (MI)
Rockford Coll (IL)
Roosevelt U (IL)
Sacred Heart U (CT)
St. Edward's U (TX)
Saint Francis U (PA)
St. John's Coll (NM)
Saint Leo U (FL)
Saint Mary's Coll of California (CA)
Salem State Coll (MA)
San Francisco State U (CA)
Sarah Lawrence Coll (NY)
Schreiner U (TX)
Seton Hill Coll (PA)
Shimer Coll (IL)
Simon's Rock Coll of Bard (MA)
Skidmore Coll (NY)
Sonoma State U (CA)
Southern Connecticut State U (CT)
Southern Nazarene U (OK)
Southern Vermont Coll (VT)
Southwestern U (TX)
Southwest State U (MN)
State U of NY at Binghamton (NY)
State U of NY Coll at Brockport (NY)
State U of NY Coll at Old Westbury (NY)
Syracuse U (NY)
Taylor U (IN)
Thomas More Coll of Liberal Arts (NH)
Touro Coll (NY)
Trent U (ON, Canada)
United States Military Academy (NY)
Université de Montréal (QC, Canada)
Université Laval (QC, Canada)
The U of Akron (OH)
U of Alberta (AB, Canada)
U of Baltimore (MD)
U of Calif, Irvine (CA)
U of Calif, San Diego (CA)
U of Calif, Santa Cruz (CA)
U of Cincinnati (OH)
U of Evansville (IN)
U of Houston–Clear Lake (TX)
The U of Iowa (IA)
U of Judaism (CA)
U of Michigan (MI)
U of Missouri–St. Louis (MO)
Western Montana Coll of The U of Montana (MT)
U of New Hampshire (NH)
The U of North Carolina at Pembroke (NC)
U of North Texas (TX)
U of Ottawa (ON, Canada)
U of Pittsburgh at Greensburg (PA)
U of Pittsburgh at Johnstown (PA)
U of Redlands (CA)
The U of Texas at Dallas (TX)
U of the South (TN)
U of Toledo (OH)
U of Toronto (ON, Canada)
U of Victoria (BC, Canada)
U of Windsor (ON, Canada)
U of Wisconsin–Milwaukee (WI)
Washington U in St. Louis (MO)
Wayne State Coll (NE)
Webster U (MO)
West Chester U of Pennsylvania (PA)
Western Washington U (WA)
Westfield State Coll (MA)
Westminster Coll (MO)
West Virginia Wesleyan Coll (WV)
Wheaton Coll (MA)
Wilberforce U (OH)
William Paterson U of New Jersey (NJ)
Williams Coll (MA)
Wittenberg U (OH)
Yale U (CT)
York U (ON, Canada)

LOGISTICS/MATERIALS MANAGEMENT

Auburn U (AL)
Bowling Green State U (OH)
Central Michigan U (MI)
Duquesne U (PA)
Elmhurst Coll (IL)
Georgia Coll and State U (GA)
Georgia Southern U (GA)
Iowa State U of Science and Technology (IA)
Maine Maritime Academy (ME)
Michigan State U (MI)
Northeastern U (MA)
The Ohio State U (OH)
Park U (MO)
Penn State U Univ Park Campus (PA)
Portland State U (OR)
Robert Morris U (PA)
St. John's U (NY)
Texas A&M U (TX)
Thomas Edison State Coll (NJ)
U of Arkansas (AR)
The U of Findlay (OH)
U of Nevada, Reno (NV)
U of North Texas (TX)
The U of Tennessee (TN)
Wayne State U (MI)
Weber State U (UT)
Western Michigan U (MI)

MACHINE SHOP ASSISTANT

U Coll of Cape Breton (NS, Canada)

MAJOR APPLIANCE INSTALLATION/REPAIR

Lewis-Clark State Coll (ID)

MANAGEMENT INFORMATION SYSTEMS/BUSINESS DATA PROCESSING

Alderson-Broaddus Coll (WV)
American Coll of Thessaloniki(Greece)
American InterContinental U (CA)
American InterContinental U, Atlanta (GA)
American International Coll (MA)
American U (DC)
Angelo State U (TX)
Arcadia U (PA)
Arizona State U (AZ)
Auburn U (AL)
Auburn U Montgomery (AL)
Augsburg Coll (MN)
Augustana Coll (SD)
Aurora U (IL)
Azusa Pacific U (CA)
Babson Coll (MA)
Baker Coll of Flint (MI)

Ball State U (IN)
Barry U (FL)
Bayamón Central U (PR)
Baylor U (TX)
Bellevue U (NE)
Baruch Coll of the City U of NY (NY)
Bethel Coll (MN)
Bishop's U (PQ, Canada)
Boston Coll (MA)
Boston U (MA)
Bowling Green State U (OH)
Bradley U (IL)
Brewton-Parker Coll (GA)
Briar Cliff U (IA)
Bridgewater Coll (VA)
Bridgewater State Coll (MA)
Buena Vista U (IA)
Cabrini Coll (PA)
California Polytechnic State U, San Luis Obispo (CA)
California State U, Chico (CA)
California State U, Dominguez Hills (CA)
California State U, Fresno (CA)
California State U, Hayward (CA)
California State U, Northridge (CA)
California State U, San Bernardino (CA)
Canisius Coll (NY)
Capitol Coll (MD)
Carleton U (ON, Canada)
Carson-Newman Coll (TN)
Central Connecticut State U (CT)
Central Michigan U (MI)
Central Missouri State U (MO)
Central State U (OH)
Charleston Southern U (SC)
Chatham Coll (PA)
Chicago State U (IL)
Christian Brothers U (TN)
Clarke Coll (IA)
Clarkson U (NY)
Clayton Coll & State U (GA)
Cleary Coll (MI)
Coll Misericordia (PA)
The Coll of New Jersey (NJ)
Coll of St. Catherine (MN)
Coll of Santa Fe (NM)
Colorado Christian U (CO)
Colorado Tech U (CO)
Colorado Tech U Sioux Falls Campus (SD)
Concordia U (MN)
Concordia U (NE)
Concordia U (QC, Canada)
Creighton U (NE)
Dallas Baptist U (TX)
Dalton State Coll (GA)
Daniel Webster Coll (NH)
Davenport U, Dearborn (MI)
Delta State U (MS)
DePaul U (IL)
DeSales U (PA)
Dominican Coll (NY)
Dordt Coll (IA)
Drexel U (PA)
Duquesne U (PA)
East Carolina U (NC)
Eastern Illinois U (IL)
Eastern Michigan U (MI)
Eastern New Mexico U (NM)
Eastern U (PA)
Eastern Washington U (WA)
École des Hautes Études Commerciales de Montréal (PQ, Canada)
Elmhurst Coll (IL)
Eureka Coll (IL)
Excelsior Coll (NY)
Fairfield U (CT)
Ferris State U (MI)
Florida Atlantic U (FL)
Florida Gulf Coast U (FL)
Florida Metropolitan U-Fort Lauderdale Coll (FL)
Florida Southern Coll (FL)
Florida State U (FL)
Fontbonne U (MO)
Fordham U (NY)
Francis Marion U (SC)
Franklin U (OH)
Gannon U (PA)
Gardner-Webb U (NC)
George Fox U (OR)
Georgetown Coll (KY)
Georgia Southern U (GA)
Goldey-Beacom Coll (DE)
Governors State U (IL)
Grace Coll (IN)
Graceland U (IA)
Grand Valley State U (MI)
Grand View Coll (IA)
Greenville Coll (IL)
Hawai'i Pacific U (HI)
Henderson State U (AR)
Hilbert Coll (NY)
Husson Coll (ME)
Illinois Coll (IL)
Indiana State U (IN)
Indiana U Bloomington (IN)
Indiana U of Pennsylvania (PA)
Iona Coll (NY)
Iowa State U of Science and Technology (IA)
Jacksonville U (FL)
Jamestown Coll (ND)
Johnson State Coll (VT)
Judson Coll (IL)
Juniata Coll (PA)
Lakehead U (ON, Canada)
La Salle U (PA)
LeTourneau U (TX)
Lewis U (IL)
Lincoln U (CA)
Lindenwood U (MO)
Long Island U, C.W. Post Campus (NY)
Longwood Coll (VA)
Loras Coll (IA)
Louisiana State U and A&M Coll (LA)
Louisiana Tech U (LA)
Loyola U Chicago (IL)
Luther Coll (IA)
MacMurray Coll (IL)
Marquette U (WI)
Maryville U of Saint Louis (MO)
The Master's Coll and Seminary (CA)
Metropolitan State U (MN)
Miami U (OH)
Michigan Technological U (MI)
Middle Tennessee State U (TN)
Midland Lutheran Coll (NE)
Millikin U (IL)
Milwaukee School of Engineering (WI)
Minnesota State U Moorhead (MN)
Minot State U (ND)
Mississippi State U (MS)
Montclair State U (NJ)
Montreat Coll (NC)
Morgan State U (MD)
Morningside Coll (IA)
Mount Saint Vincent U (NS, Canada)
Murray State U (KY)
National American U (NM)
National American U (SD)
National American U–St. Paul Campus (MN)
National American U–Sioux Falls Branch (SD)
Nazareth Coll of Rochester (NY)
New Mexico Highlands U (NM)
New York Inst of Technology (NY)
New York U (NY)
Nicholls State U (LA)
North Central Coll (IL)
North Dakota State U (ND)
Northeastern U (MA)
Northern Arizona U (AZ)
Northern Kentucky U (KY)
Northern Michigan U (MI)
Northern State U (SD)
Northwestern Coll (MN)
Northwest Missouri State U (MO)
Northwood U, Florida Campus (FL)
Northwood U, Texas Campus (TX)
Oakland U (MI)
The Ohio State U (OH)
Ohio U (OH)
Oklahoma Baptist U (OK)
Oklahoma City U (OK)
Oklahoma State U (OK)
Old Dominion U (VA)
Oral Roberts U (OK)
Oregon Inst of Technology (OR)
Oregon State U (OR)
Pace U (NY)
Pacific Lutheran U (WA)
Pacific Union Coll (CA)
Park U (MO)
Penn State U at Erie, The Behrend Coll (PA)
Penn State U Harrisburg Campus of the Capital Coll (PA)
Penn State U Univ Park Campus (PA)
Peru State Coll (NE)
Philadelphia U (PA)
Point Loma Nazarene U (CA)
Radford U (VA)
Rensselaer Polytechnic Inst (NY)
Rhode Island Coll (RI)
Robert Morris U (PA)
Roberts Wesleyan Coll (NY)
Rochester Inst of Technology (NY)
Rockford Coll (IL)
Rocky Mountain Coll (MT)
Rowan U (NJ)
Saint Francis U (PA)
St. Francis Xavier U (NS, Canada)
St. John Fisher Coll (NY)
Saint Joseph's Coll (IN)
Saint Joseph's U (PA)
Saint Louis U (MO)
Saint Martin's Coll (WA)
Saint Mary's Coll (IN)
St. Norbert Coll (WI)
Salem State Coll (MA)
Salisbury U (MD)
San Jose State U (CA)
Santa Clara U (CA)
Savannah State U (GA)
Seattle U (WA)
Seton Hall U (NJ)
Seton Hill Coll (PA)
Shawnee State U (OH)
Simmons Coll (MA)
Southeastern U (DC)
Southeast Missouri State U (MO)
Southern Adventist U (TN)
Southern Illinois U Edwardsville (IL)
Southern Methodist U (TX)
Southern Nazarene U (OK)
Southern New Hampshire U (NH)
Southwestern Coll (KS)
Southwest Missouri State U (MO)
Southwest Texas State U (TX)
Spring Arbor U (MI)
Springfield Coll (MA)
State U of West Georgia (GA)
Suffolk U (MA)
Tarleton State U (TX)
Teikyo Post U (CT)
Texas A&M U–Commerce (TX)
Texas A&M U–Texarkana (TX)
Texas Tech U (TX)
Texas Wesleyan U (TX)
Thiel Coll (PA)
Thomas Coll (ME)
Tiffin U (OH)
Touro U International (CA)
Trinity Christian Coll (IL)
Tri-State U (IN)
Université de Sherbrooke (PQ, Canada)
U Coll of Cape Breton (NS, Canada)
The U of Alabama (AL)
The U of Alabama in Huntsville (AL)
U of Alaska Anchorage (AK)
U of Alberta (AB, Canada)
The U of Arizona (AZ)
The U of British Columbia (BC, Canada)
U of Calgary (AB, Canada)
U of Central Arkansas (AR)
U of Central Florida (FL)
U of Cincinnati (OH)
U of Colorado at Boulder (CO)
U of Connecticut (CT)
U of Dayton (OH)
U of Georgia (GA)
U of Hartford (CT)
U of Hawaii at Manoa (HI)
U of Houston (TX)
U of Idaho (ID)
U of Illinois at Chicago (IL)
The U of Iowa (IA)
The U of Lethbridge (AB, Canada)
U of Louisville (KY)
U of Massachusetts Dartmouth (MA)
The U of Memphis (TN)
U of Minnesota, Twin Cities Campus (MN)
U of Mississippi (MS)
U of Missouri–St. Louis (MO)
U of Montevallo (AL)
U of Nebraska at Omaha (NE)
U of Nevada, Las Vegas (NV)
U of New Orleans (LA)
U of North Alabama (AL)
The U of North Carolina at Charlotte (NC)
The U of North Carolina at Greensboro (NC)
The U of North Carolina at Wilmington (NC)
U of Northern Iowa (IA)
U of Notre Dame (IN)
U of Oklahoma (OK)
U of Ottawa (ON, Canada)
U of Pennsylvania (PA)
U of Phoenix-Atlanta Campus (GA)
U of Phoenix–Boston Campus (MA)
U of Phoenix–Colorado Campus (CO)
U of Phoenix–Dallas/Ft. Worth Campus (TX)
U of Phoenix–Fort Lauderdale Campus (FL)
U of Phoenix–Hawaii Campus (HI)
U of Phoenix–Houston Campus (TX)
U of Phoenix–Jacksonville Campus (FL)
U of Phoenix–Louisiana Campus (LA)
U of Phoenix–Maryland Campus (MD)
U of Phoenix–Metro Detroit Campus (MI)
U of Phoenix–New Mexico Campus (NM)
U of Phoenix–Northern California Campus (CA)
U of Phoenix–Ohio Campus (OH)
U of Phoenix–Oklahoma City Campus (OK)
U of Phoenix–Oregon Campus (OR)
U of Phoenix–Orlando Campus (FL)
U of Phoenix–Phoenix Campus (AZ)
U of Phoenix–Sacramento Campus (CA)
U of Phoenix–Saint Louis Campus (MO)
U of Phoenix–San Diego Campus (CA)
U of Phoenix–Southern Arizona Campus (AZ)
U of Phoenix–Southern Colorado Campus (CO)
U of Phoenix–Tampa Campus (FL)
U of Phoenix–Tulsa Campus (OK)
U of Phoenix–Utah Campus (UT)
U of Phoenix-Vancouver Campus (BC, Canada)
U of Phoenix–Washington Campus (WA)
U of Phoenix–West Michigan Campus (MI)
U of Redlands (CA)
U of Rhode Island (RI)
U of Richmond (VA)
U of St. Thomas (TX)
U of San Francisco (CA)
U of Sioux Falls (SD)
U of Southern Mississippi (MS)
The U of Tennessee at Martin (TN)
The U of Texas at Arlington (TX)
The U of Texas at Austin (TX)
The U of Texas at Dallas (TX)
The U of Texas at San Antonio (TX)
The U of Texas–Pan American (TX)
U of the Incarnate Word (TX)
U of Tulsa (OK)
U of Washington (WA)
The U of West Alabama (AL)
U of West Florida (FL)
U of Wisconsin–Eau Claire (WI)
U of Wisconsin–La Crosse (WI)
U of Wisconsin–Milwaukee (WI)
U of Wisconsin–Oshkosh (WI)
U of Wisconsin–River Falls (WI)
U of Wisconsin–Whitewater (WI)
Upper Iowa U (IA)
Ursuline Coll (OH)
Vanguard U of Southern California (CA)
Villa Julie Coll (MD)
Villanova U (PA)
Virginia Polytechnic Inst and State U (VA)
Virginia State U (VA)
Virginia Union U (VA)
Walla Walla Coll (WA)
Washington State U (WA)
Wayne State U (MI)
Weber State U (UT)
Webster U (MO)
Western Carolina U (NC)
Western Connecticut State U (CT)
Western Illinois U (IL)
Western Kentucky U (KY)
Western Michigan U (MI)
Western State Coll of Colorado (CO)
Western Washington U (WA)
Westfield State Coll (MA)
Westminster Coll (MO)
West Texas A&M U (TX)
Wichita State U (KS)
William Woods U (MO)
Wingate U (NC)
Winona State U (MN)
Winston-Salem State U (NC)
Worcester Polytechnic Inst (MA)
Wright State U (OH)
Xavier U (OH)
Yeshiva U (NY)
York U (ON, Canada)
Youngstown State U (OH)

MANAGEMENT SCIENCE

Abilene Christian U (TX)
American Military U (VA)
Arkansas Tech U (AR)
Caldwell Coll (NJ)
Capella U (MN)
Central Methodist Coll (MO)
Central Pennsylvania Coll (PA)
Clarion U of Pennsylvania (PA)
The Coll of St. Scholastica (MN)
The Coll of Southeastern Europe, The American U of Athens(Greece)
Dalhousie U (NS, Canada)
Duquesne U (PA)
Eastern U (PA)
École des Hautes Études Commerciales de Montréal (PQ, Canada)
Everglades Coll (FL)
Franklin U (OH)
Georgia Inst of Technology (GA)
Goucher Coll (MD)
Louisiana Tech U (LA)
Lourdes Coll (OH)
Maharishi U of Management (IA)
Manhattan Coll (NY)
Marymount U (VA)
McGill U (PQ, Canada)
Metropolitan State Coll of Denver (CO)
Miami U (OH)
Minnesota State U, Mankato (MN)
Northeastern U (MA)
Northwest Coll (WA)
Oakland City U (IN)
Oklahoma State U (OK)
Oral Roberts U (OK)
Prescott Coll (AZ)
Rider U (NJ)
Rockhurst U (MO)
Rutgers, The State U of New Jersey, New Brunswick (NJ)
Saint Louis U (MO)
Shippensburg U of Pennsylvania (PA)
Simon Fraser U (BC, Canada)
Southeastern Oklahoma State U (OK)
Southern Adventist U (TN)
Southern Methodist U (TX)
Southern Nazarene U (OK)
Southwestern Coll (KS)
State U of NY at Binghamton (NY)
State U of NY at Oswego (NY)
Trinity U (TX)
Tuskegee U (AL)
United States Coast Guard Academy (CT)
The U of Alabama (AL)
U of Calif, San Diego (CA)
U of Connecticut (CT)
U of Florida (FL)
U of Great Falls (MT)
The U of Iowa (IA)
U of Kentucky (KY)
U of Maryland University Coll (MD)
The U of Memphis (TN)
U of Minnesota, Morris (MN)
U of North Dakota (ND)
U of Pennsylvania (PA)
U of Phoenix-Atlanta Campus (GA)

U of Phoenix–Colorado Campus (CO)
U of Phoenix–Dallas/Ft. Worth Campus (TX)
U of Phoenix–Fort Lauderdale Campus (FL)
U of Phoenix–Hawaii Campus (HI)
U of Phoenix–Houston Campus (TX)
U of Phoenix–Jacksonville Campus (FL)
U of Phoenix–Maryland Campus (MD)
U of Phoenix–Metro Detroit Campus (MI)
U of Phoenix–New Mexico Campus (NM)
U of Phoenix–Northern California Campus (CA)
U of Phoenix–Oklahoma City Campus (OK)
U of Phoenix–Oregon Campus (OR)
U of Phoenix–Orlando Campus (FL)
U of Phoenix–Philadelphia Campus (PA)
U of Phoenix–Phoenix Campus (AZ)
U of Phoenix–Puerto Rico Campus (PR)
U of Phoenix–Sacramento Campus (CA)
U of Phoenix–Southern Colorado Campus (CO)
U of Phoenix–Tampa Campus (FL)
U of Phoenix–Tulsa Campus (OK)
U of Phoenix–Utah Campus (UT)
U of Phoenix–Washington Campus (WA)
The U of Scranton (PA)
U of South Carolina (SC)
U of South Florida (FL)
The U of Texas at San Antonio (TX)
U of the Incarnate Word (TX)
U of Washington (WA)
U of Windsor (ON, Canada)
U of Wyoming (WY)
Wake Forest U (NC)
Wheeling Jesuit U (WV)
York U (ON, Canada)

MARINE BIOLOGY
Alabama State U (AL)
Auburn U (AL)
Ball State U (IN)
Barry U (FL)
Bemidji State U (MN)
Boston U (MA)
Brown U (RI)
California State U, Long Beach (CA)
Coastal Carolina U (SC)
Coll of Charleston (SC)
Coll of the Atlantic (ME)
Dalhousie U (NS, Canada)
East Stroudsburg U of Pennsylvania (PA)
Eckerd Coll (FL)
The Evergreen State Coll (WA)
Fairleigh Dickinson U, Florham-Madison Campus (NJ)
Fairleigh Dickinson U, Teaneck-Hackensack Campus (NJ)
Florida Inst of Technology (FL)
Florida State U (FL)
Gettysburg Coll (PA)
Hampshire Coll (MA)
Hampton U (VA)
Harvard U (MA)
Hawai'i Pacific U (HI)
Hofstra U (NY)
Humboldt State U (CA)
Jacksonville State U (AL)
Juniata Coll (PA)
Long Island U, Southampton Coll (NY)
Maine Maritime Academy (ME)
McGill U (PQ, Canada)
Memorial U of Newfoundland (NF, Canada)
Mississippi State U (MS)
Missouri Southern State Coll (MO)
Nicholls State U (LA)
Northeastern U (MA)
Northern Arizona U (AZ)
Nova Southeastern U (FL)
The Richard Stockton Coll of New Jersey (NJ)
Roger Williams U (RI)
Rutgers, The State U of New Jersey, New Brunswick (NJ)
Saint Francis U (PA)
Saint Joseph's Coll (ME)
Salem State Coll (MA)
Samford U (AL)
San Diego State U (CA)
San Francisco State U (CA)
San Jose State U (CA)
Sarah Lawrence Coll (NY)
Savannah State U (GA)
Sheldon Jackson Coll (AK)
Sonoma State U (CA)
Southern Connecticut State U (CT)
Southwestern Coll (KS)
Southwest Texas State U (TX)
Spring Hill Coll (AL)
Stetson U (FL)
Suffolk U (MA)
Texas A&M U at Galveston (TX)
Troy State U (AL)
Unity Coll (ME)
The U of Alabama (AL)
U of Alaska Southeast (AK)
The U of British Columbia (BC, Canada)
U of Calif, Los Angeles (CA)
U of Calif, Santa Barbara (CA)
U of Calif, Santa Cruz (CA)
U of Connecticut (CT)
U of Guelph (ON, Canada)
U of King's Coll (NS, Canada)
U of Maine (ME)
U of Maine at Machias (ME)
U of Maryland Eastern Shore (MD)
U of Miami (FL)
U of New England (ME)
U of New Hampshire (NH)
U of New Haven (CT)
U of North Alabama (AL)
The U of North Carolina at Wilmington (NC)
U of Puerto Rico, Humacao U Coll (PR)
U of Rhode Island (RI)
U of South Carolina (SC)
U of Southern California (CA)
U of Southern Mississippi (MS)
U of the Virgin Islands (VI)
U of Victoria (BC, Canada)
The U of West Alabama (AL)
U of West Florida (FL)
U of Wisconsin–Superior (WI)
Waynesburg Coll (PA)
Western Washington U (WA)
Wittenberg U (OH)

MARINE SCIENCE
Cornell U (NY)
Dowling Coll (NY)
The Evergreen State Coll (WA)
Hampton U (VA)
Jacksonville U (FL)
Maine Maritime Academy (ME)
Massachusetts Maritime Academy (MA)
Memorial U of Newfoundland (NF, Canada)
Oregon State U (OR)
Prescott Coll (AZ)
Rider U (NJ)
Salem State Coll (MA)
State U of NY Maritime Coll (NY)
Suffolk U (MA)
Texas A&M U at Galveston (TX)
United States Coast Guard Academy (CT)
U of New Hampshire (NH)
U of San Diego (CA)
The U of Tampa (FL)

MARINE TECHNOLOGY
California Maritime Academy (CA)
Lamar U (TX)
Thomas Edison State Coll (NJ)

MARITIME SCIENCE
Coll of the Atlantic (ME)
Maine Maritime Academy (ME)
Massachusetts Maritime Academy (MA)
State U of NY Maritime Coll (NY)
Texas A&M U at Galveston (TX)
United States Merchant Marine Academy (NY)

MARKETING/DISTRIBUTION EDUCATION
Appalachian State U (NC)
Bowling Green State U (OH)
Central Michigan U (MI)
Colorado State U (CO)
East Carolina U (NC)
Eastern Michigan U (MI)
Eastern New Mexico U (NM)
Kent State U (OH)
Middle Tennessee State U (TN)
New York Inst of Technology (NY)
North Carolina State U (NC)
San Diego State U (CA)
Southern New Hampshire U (NH)
U of Georgia (GA)
U of Hawaii at Manoa (HI)
U of Nebraska–Lincoln (NE)
U of North Dakota (ND)
U of Wisconsin–Stout (WI)
Utah State U (UT)
Virginia Polytechnic Inst and State U (VA)
Western Michigan U (MI)

MARKETING MANAGEMENT AND RESEARCH RELATED
Capella U (MN)
Duquesne U (PA)
Inter American U of PR, San Germán Campus (PR)
La Roche Coll (PA)
Maryville U of Saint Louis (MO)
St. Edward's U (TX)
U of Utah (UT)
Washington U in St. Louis (MO)
Western Michigan U (MI)
Wilmington Coll (DE)

MARKETING OPERATIONS
Avila Coll (MO)
Caribbean U (PR)
Champlain Coll (VT)
Colorado Tech U Sioux Falls Campus (SD)
Dalton State Coll (GA)
Lake Erie Coll (OH)
Lambuth U (TN)
McKendree Coll (IL)
New England School of Communications (ME)
New York U (NY)
Our Lady of Holy Cross Coll (LA)
Purdue U North Central (IN)
Rochester Inst of Technology (NY)
Tuskegee U (AL)
U Coll of Cape Breton (NS, Canada)
U of Illinois at Urbana–Champaign (IL)
U of Wisconsin–Superior (WI)
York U (ON, Canada)
Youngstown State U (OH)

MARKETING OPERATIONS/ MARKETING AND DISTRIBUTION RELATED
Caribbean U (PR)
Southeast Missouri State U (MO)
Washington U in St. Louis (MO)

MARKETING RESEARCH
Ashland U (OH)
Baker Coll of Jackson (MI)
Boston U (MA)
Bowling Green State U (OH)
Carthage Coll (WI)
Concordia U (QC, Canada)
Fairleigh Dickinson U, Teaneck-Hackensack Campus (NJ)
Ithaca Coll (NY)
McGill U (PQ, Canada)
Methodist Coll (NC)
Metropolitan State Coll of Denver (CO)
Mount Saint Vincent U (NS, Canada)
Newbury Coll (MA)
Rochester Inst of Technology (NY)
Saginaw Valley State U (MI)
Southern New Hampshire U (NH)
Talladega Coll (AL)
Texas Christian U (TX)
Troy State U Montgomery (AL)
U of Great Falls (MT)
U of Houston–Clear Lake (TX)
U of Nebraska at Omaha (NE)
U of Windsor (ON, Canada)
York U (ON, Canada)

MARRIAGE/FAMILY COUNSELING
Friends U (KS)
Grace U (NE)
Oklahoma Baptist U (OK)
U of Nevada, Las Vegas (NV)
The U of North Carolina at Greensboro (NC)

MASS COMMUNICATIONS
Adrian Coll (MI)
Alabama State U (AL)
Albertus Magnus Coll (CT)
Albion Coll (MI)
Alcorn State U (MS)
Alderson-Broaddus Coll (WV)
Alfred U (NY)
Alma Coll (MI)
American International Coll (MA)
American U in Cairo(Egypt)
The American U of Paris(France)
Anderson Coll (SC)
Anderson U (IN)
Andrews U (MI)
Arcadia U (PA)
Ashland U (OH)
Atlantic Baptist U (NB, Canada)
Auburn U (AL)
Augsburg Coll (MN)
Augustana Coll (IL)
Augustana Coll (SD)
Austin Peay State U (TN)
Baker U (KS)
Baldwin-Wallace Coll (OH)
Barber-Scotia Coll (NC)
Barry U (FL)
Barton Coll (NC)
Becker Coll (MA)
Belmont U (TN)
Beloit Coll (WI)
Bemidji State U (MN)
Bennett Coll (NC)
Berry Coll (GA)
Bethel Coll (MN)
Bethune-Cookman Coll (FL)
Black Hills State U (SD)
Bloomsburg U of Pennsylvania (PA)
Bluefield Coll (VA)
Bluffton Coll (OH)
Boise State U (ID)
Boston Coll (MA)
Boston U (MA)
Bowie State U (MD)
Bowling Green State U (OH)
Brenau U (GA)
Briar Cliff U (IA)
Brock U (ON, Canada)
Bryan Coll (TN)
Buena Vista U (IA)
California Lutheran U (CA)
California State Polytechnic U, Pomona (CA)
California State U, Bakersfield (CA)
California State U, Dominguez Hills (CA)
California State U, Fresno (CA)
California State U, Hayward (CA)
California State U, Long Beach (CA)
California State U, Sacramento (CA)
California State U, San Bernardino (CA)
Calvary Bible Coll and Theological Seminary (MO)
Calvin Coll (MI)
Cameron U (OK)
Campbellsville U (KY)
Canisius Coll (NY)
Carleton U (ON, Canada)
Carnegie Mellon U (PA)
Carson-Newman Coll (TN)
Catawba Coll (NC)
Centenary Coll (NJ)
Centenary Coll of Louisiana (LA)
Central Missouri State U (MO)
Central Washington U (WA)
Chaminade U of Honolulu (HI)
Champlain Coll (VT)
Chapman U (CA)
Cheyney U of Pennsylvania (PA)
City Coll of the City U of NY (NY)
City U (WA)
Claflin U (SC)
Clark Atlanta U (GA)
Clarke Coll (IA)
Clark U (MA)
Cleveland State U (OH)
Coker Coll (SC)
Coll of Mount Saint Vincent (NY)
The Coll of New Rochelle (NY)
Coll of Notre Dame of Maryland (MD)
Coll of St. Catherine (MN)
Coll of the Ozarks (MO)
The Coll of Wooster (OH)
Colorado Christian U (CO)
Columbia Union Coll (MD)
Columbus State U (GA)
Concord Coll (WV)
Concordia Coll (MN)
Concordia U (MN)
Concordia U (NE)
Concordia U (QC, Canada)
Concordia U Wisconsin (WI)
Cornell U (NY)
Cornerstone U (MI)
Creighton U (NE)
Culver-Stockton Coll (MO)
Curry Coll (MA)
Davis & Elkins Coll (WV)
Defiance Coll (OH)
Delaware State U (DE)
Denison U (OH)
DePaul U (IL)
DePauw U (IN)
DeSales U (PA)
Dillard U (LA)
Doane Coll (NE)
Dominican U (IL)
Dordt Coll (IA)
Drake U (IA)
Drury U (MO)
East Central U (OK)
Eastern Kentucky U (KY)
Eastern Nazarene Coll (MA)
Eastern Washington U (WA)
East Tennessee State U (TN)
Edgewood Coll (WI)
Emerson Coll (MA)
Emmanuel Coll (MA)
Emory & Henry Coll (VA)
Eureka Coll (IL)
Evangel U (MO)
The Evergreen State Coll (WA)
Excelsior Coll (NY)
Fairfield U (CT)
Felician Coll (NJ)
Ferris State U (MI)
Florida A&M U (FL)
Florida State U (FL)
Fordham U (NY)
Fort Hays State U (KS)
Fort Lewis Coll (CO)
Fort Valley State U (GA)
Framingham State Coll (MA)
Francis Marion U (SC)
Franklin Pierce Coll (NH)
Freed-Hardeman U (TN)
Fresno Pacific U (CA)
Frostburg State U (MD)
Gallaudet U (DC)
Gardner-Webb U (NC)
Georgetown Coll (KY)
The George Washington U (DC)
Gonzaga U (WA)
Gordon Coll (MA)
Goshen Coll (IN)
Goucher Coll (MD)
Governors State U (IL)
Grace Coll (IN)
Grace U (NE)
Grambling State U (LA)
Grand Canyon U (AZ)
Grand Valley State U (MI)
Grand View Coll (IA)
Greenville Coll (IL)
Grove City Coll (PA)
Gustavus Adolphus Coll (MN)
Hamilton Coll (NY)
Hamline U (MN)
Hampshire Coll (MA)
Hampton U (VA)
Hannibal-LaGrange Coll (MO)
Hanover Coll (IN)
Harding U (AR)
Hardin-Simmons U (TX)
Hastings Coll (NE)
Hawai'i Pacific U (HI)
Heidelberg Coll (OH)
High Point U (NC)
Hiram Coll (OH)
Hobart and William Smith Colls (NY)

Hofstra U (NY)
Hood Coll (MD)
Houston Baptist U (TX)
Howard U (DC)
Huntington Coll (IN)
Idaho State U (ID)
Illinois Coll (IL)
Illinois State U (IL)
Indiana U Bloomington (IN)
Indiana U Northwest (IN)
Indiana U South Bend (IN)
Iona Coll (NY)
Iowa State U of Science and Technology (IA)
Iowa Wesleyan Coll (IA)
Ithaca Coll (NY)
Jackson State U (MS)
John Brown U (AR)
John Carroll U (OH)
Johnson & Wales U (RI)
Johnson C. Smith U (NC)
Judson Coll (IL)
Kansas Wesleyan U (KS)
Keene State Coll (NH)
Kentucky Mountain Bible Coll (KY)
Lake Erie Coll (OH)
Lamar U (TX)
Lambuth U (TN)
Lander U (SC)
La Salle U (PA)
Lees-McRae Coll (NC)
Lee U (TN)
Lehman Coll of the City U of NY (NY)
Lenoir-Rhyne Coll (NC)
Lewis & Clark Coll (OR)
Lewis-Clark State Coll (ID)
Lewis U (IL)
Lincoln Memorial U (TN)
Lindenwood U (MO)
Lindsey Wilson Coll (KY)
Lipscomb U (TN)
Lock Haven U of Pennsylvania (PA)
Long Island U, Brooklyn Campus (NY)
Long Island U, Southampton Coll (NY)
Long Island U, Southampton Coll, Friends World Program (NY)
Loras Coll (IA)
Louisiana Coll (LA)
Louisiana State U and A&M Coll (LA)
Louisiana State U in Shreveport (LA)
Loyola Marymount U (CA)
Lubbock Christian U (TX)
Luther Coll (IA)
Lycoming Coll (PA)
Lynchburg Coll (VA)
Lynn U (FL)
Manchester Coll (IN)
Mansfield U of Pennsylvania (PA)
Marian Coll (IN)
Marian Coll of Fond du Lac (WI)
Marist Coll (NY)
Marquette U (WI)
Mars Hill Coll (NC)
Mary Baldwin Coll (VA)
Marylhurst U (OR)
Marymount Coll of Fordham U (NY)
Marymount Manhattan Coll (NY)
Massachusetts Coll of Liberal Arts (MA)
The Master's Coll and Seminary (CA)
McKendree Coll (IL)
McNeese State U (LA)
Medaille Coll (NY)
Menlo Coll (CA)
Mercyhurst Coll (PA)
Meredith Coll (NC)
Mesa State Coll (CO)
Methodist Coll (NC)
Miami U (OH)
MidAmerica Nazarene U (KS)
Middle Tennessee State U (TN)
Midland Lutheran Coll (NE)
Midwestern State U (TX)
Minnesota State U, Mankato (MN)
Minnesota State U Moorhead (MN)
Mississippi Valley State U (MS)
Missouri Southern State Coll (MO)
Missouri Valley Coll (MO)
Monmouth Coll (IL)
Montana State U–Billings (MT)
Montana State U–Northern (MT)
Montclair State U (NJ)
Montreat Coll (NC)
Morgan State U (MD)
Morningside Coll (IA)
Morris Brown Coll (GA)
Mount Ida Coll (MA)
Mount Saint Mary Coll (NY)
Mount Union Coll (OH)
Mount Vernon Nazarene U (OH)
Muskingum Coll (OH)
Newberry Coll (SC)
Newbury Coll (MA)
New England Coll (NH)
Newman U (KS)
New Mexico Highlands U (NM)
New Mexico State U (NM)
New York U (NY)
Niagara U (NY)
Nicholls State U (LA)
Norfolk State U (VA)
North Carolina Ag and Tech State U (NC)
North Central Coll (IL)
North Dakota State U (ND)
Northeastern U (MA)
Northern Michigan U (MI)
North Greenville Coll (SC)
North Park U (IL)
Northwestern Coll (IA)
Northwestern Oklahoma State U (OK)
Northwest Missouri State U (MO)
Northwest Nazarene U (ID)
Oakwood Coll (AL)
Oglethorpe U (GA)
Ohio Northern U (OH)
Oklahoma Baptist U (OK)
Oklahoma Christian U of Science and Arts (OK)
Oklahoma City U (OK)
Oklahoma Wesleyan U (OK)
Olivet Coll (MI)
Olivet Nazarene U (IL)
Oregon State U (OR)
Ottawa U (KS)
Ouachita Baptist U (AR)
Pacific Lutheran U (WA)
Pacific Union Coll (CA)
Pacific U (OR)
Paine Coll (GA)
Pfeiffer U (NC)
Piedmont Coll (GA)
Pine Manor Coll (MA)
Pittsburg State U (KS)
Plattsburgh State U of NY (NY)
Point Loma Nazarene U (CA)
Point Park Coll (PA)
Pontifical Catholic U of Puerto Rico (PR)
Presentation Coll (SD)
Principia Coll (IL)
Purdue U Calumet (IN)
Queens Coll (NC)
Quinnipiac U (CT)
Randolph-Macon Woman's Coll (VA)
Reinhardt Coll (GA)
Rensselaer Polytechnic Inst (NY)
Rhode Island Coll (RI)
Richmond, The American International U in London(United Kingdom)
Robert Morris U (PA)
Roosevelt U (IL)
Rowan U (NJ)
Russell Sage Coll (NY)
Rutgers, The State U of New Jersey, New Brunswick (NJ)
Sacred Heart U (CT)
St. Ambrose U (IA)
St. Andrews Presbyterian Coll (NC)
St. Bonaventure U (NY)
St. Cloud State U (MN)
Saint Francis U (PA)
St. John Fisher Coll (NY)
Saint Joseph's Coll (IN)
Saint Mary Coll (KS)
Saint Mary-of-the-Woods Coll (IN)
Saint Mary's Coll of Ave Maria U (MI)
Saint Mary's Coll of California (CA)
St. Mary's U of San Antonio (TX)
St. Thomas Aquinas Coll (NY)
St. Thomas U (FL)
Salem Coll (NC)
Salem International U (WV)
Salem State Coll (MA)
San Diego State U (CA)
Savannah State U (GA)
Seattle U (WA)
Seton Hill Coll (PA)
Shaw U (NC)
Simmons Coll (MA)
Simpson Coll (IA)
Slippery Rock U of Pennsylvania (PA)
Sonoma State U (CA)
South Dakota State U (SD)
Southeast Missouri State U (MO)
Southern Adventist U (TN)
Southern Arkansas U–Magnolia (AR)
Southern Illinois U Edwardsville (IL)
Southern Nazarene U (OK)
Southern U and A&M Coll (LA)
Southern Utah U (UT)
Southern Vermont Coll (VT)
Southwestern Adventist U (TX)
Southwestern Oklahoma State U (OK)
Southwestern U (TX)
Southwest Missouri State U (MO)
Southwest Texas State U (TX)
State U of NY at Albany (NY)
State U of NY at New Paltz (NY)
State U of NY at Oswego (NY)
State U of NY Coll at Brockport (NY)
State U of NY Coll at Buffalo (NY)
State U of NY Coll at Fredonia (NY)
State U of NY Coll at Oneonta (NY)
State U of West Georgia (GA)
Stephens Coll (MO)
Stetson U (FL)
Suffolk U (MA)
Sul Ross State U (TX)
Susquehanna U (PA)
Tabor Coll (KS)
Taylor U (IN)
Temple U (PA)
Tennessee State U (TN)
Texas A&M U–Kingsville (TX)
Texas Christian U (TX)
Texas Southern U (TX)
Texas Woman's U (TX)
Towson U (MD)
Trevecca Nazarene U (TN)
Trinity Coll (DC)
Truman State U (MO)
Tulane U (LA)
Union U (TN)
Université de Montréal (QC, Canada)
Université de Sherbrooke (PQ, Canada)
Université Laval (QC, Canada)
State U of NY at Buffalo (NY)
The U of Akron (OH)
U of Alaska Anchorage (AK)
U of Baltimore (MD)
U of Bridgeport (CT)
U of Calif, Berkeley (CA)
U of Calif, San Diego (CA)
U of Charleston (WV)
U of Cincinnati (OH)
U of Colorado at Boulder (CO)
U of Dayton (OH)
U of Delaware (DE)
U of Dubuque (IA)
U of Evansville (IN)
U of Georgia (GA)
U of Illinois at Springfield (IL)
U of Illinois at Urbana–Champaign (IL)
The U of Iowa (IA)
U of Louisiana at Lafayette (LA)
U of Maine (ME)
U of Mary (ND)
U of Mary Hardin-Baylor (TX)
U of Maryland, Coll Park (MD)
U of Maryland Eastern Shore (MD)
U of Miami (FL)
U of Michigan (MI)
U of Michigan–Flint (MI)
U of Minnesota, Morris (MN)
U of Minnesota, Twin Cities Campus (MN)
U of Missouri–Columbia (MO)
U of Missouri–Kansas City (MO)
U of Missouri–St. Louis (MO)
U of Mobile (AL)
U of Montevallo (AL)
U of Nebraska at Kearney (NE)
U of Nebraska at Omaha (NE)
U of New Hampshire (NH)
U of New Mexico (NM)
The U of North Carolina at Chapel Hill (NC)
The U of North Carolina at Greensboro (NC)
The U of North Carolina at Pembroke (NC)
U of North Texas (TX)
U of Oregon (OR)
U of Ottawa (ON, Canada)
U of Pittsburgh at Bradford (PA)
U of Pittsburgh at Greensburg (PA)
U of Pittsburgh at Johnstown (PA)
U of Portland (OR)
U of Rio Grande (OH)
U of St. Francis (IL)
U of Saint Francis (IN)
U of St. Thomas (MN)
U of San Diego (CA)
U of San Francisco (CA)
U of Sioux Falls (SD)
U of South Dakota (SD)
U of Southern California (CA)
U of Southern Colorado (CO)
U of Southern Maine (ME)
The U of Tampa (FL)
The U of Tennessee at Chattanooga (TN)
The U of Texas at El Paso (TX)
The U of Texas at San Antonio (TX)
The U of Texas of the Permian Basin (TX)
The U of Texas–Pan American (TX)
U of the District of Columbia (DC)
U of the Incarnate Word (TX)
U of Toledo (OH)
U of Toronto (ON, Canada)
U of Utah (UT)
U of Windsor (ON, Canada)
U of Wisconsin–Eau Claire (WI)
U of Wisconsin–Madison (WI)
U of Wisconsin–Milwaukee (WI)
U of Wisconsin–Oshkosh (WI)
U of Wisconsin–Platteville (WI)
U of Wisconsin–Superior (WI)
U of Wisconsin–Whitewater (WI)
Upper Iowa U (IA)
Urbana U (OH)
Ursinus Coll (PA)
Valdosta State U (GA)
Vanderbilt U (TN)
Vanguard U of Southern California (CA)
Villa Julie Coll (MD)
Villanova U (PA)
Virginia Commonwealth U (VA)
Virginia State U (VA)
Waldorf Coll (IA)
Walla Walla Coll (WA)
Walsh U (OH)
Wartburg Coll (IA)
Washburn U of Topeka (KS)
Washington State U (WA)
Wayland Baptist U (TX)
Wayne State Coll (NE)
Wesley Coll (DE)
West Chester U of Pennsylvania (PA)
Western Connecticut State U (CT)
Western State Coll of Colorado (CO)
Western Washington U (WA)
Westfield State Coll (MA)
West Liberty State Coll (WV)
Westminster Coll (PA)
West Texas A&M U (TX)
West Virginia State Coll (WV)
West Virginia U (WV)
Whitworth Coll (WA)
Widener U (PA)
Wilberforce U (OH)
Wiley Coll (TX)
Wilfrid Laurier U (ON, Canada)
William Carey Coll (MS)
William Paterson U of New Jersey (NJ)
Wilmington Coll (OH)
Wilson Coll (PA)
Wingate U (NC)
Winona State U (MN)
Winston-Salem State U (NC)
Winthrop U (SC)
Worcester State Coll (MA)
Wright State U (OH)
Xavier U of Louisiana (LA)
Yeshiva U (NY)
York Coll of Pennsylvania (PA)
York U (ON, Canada)

MATERIALS ENGINEERING

Arizona State U (AZ)
Auburn U (AL)
Brown U (RI)
California Polytechnic State U, San Luis Obispo (CA)
California State Polytechnic U, Pomona (CA)
California State U, Long Beach (CA)
California State U, Northridge (CA)
Carnegie Mellon U (PA)
Case Western Reserve U (OH)
Clarkson U (NY)
Cornell U (NY)
Drexel U (PA)
Florida State U (FL)
Georgia Inst of Technology (GA)
Harvard U (MA)
Illinois Inst of Technology (IL)
Johns Hopkins U (MD)
Lehigh U (PA)
Massachusetts Inst of Technology (MA)
McMaster U (ON, Canada)
Mercyhurst Coll (PA)
Michigan Technological U (MI)
Montana Tech of The U of Montana (MT)
New Mexico Inst of Mining and Technology (NM)
New York U (NY)
North Carolina State U (NC)
Northwestern U (IL)
The Ohio State U (OH)
Purdue U (IN)
Rensselaer Polytechnic Inst (NY)
Rice U (TX)
San Jose State U (CA)
Stanford U (CA)
The U of Alabama at Birmingham (AL)
The U of British Columbia (BC, Canada)
U of Calif, Berkeley (CA)
U of Calif, Davis (CA)
U of Calif, Los Angeles (CA)
U of Connecticut (CT)
U of Florida (FL)
The U of Iowa (IA)
U of Kentucky (KY)
U of Maryland, Coll Park (MD)
U of Michigan (MI)
U of Minnesota, Twin Cities Campus (MN)
U of New Haven (CT)
U of Pennsylvania (PA)
U of Pittsburgh (PA)
The U of Tennessee (TN)
U of Toronto (ON, Canada)
U of Utah (UT)
U of Washington (WA)
The U of Western Ontario (ON, Canada)
U of Windsor (ON, Canada)
U of Wisconsin–Milwaukee (WI)
Virginia Polytechnic Inst and State U (VA)
Washington State U (WA)
Western Michigan U (MI)
Winona State U (MN)
Worcester Polytechnic Inst (MA)
Wright State U (OH)

MATERIALS SCIENCE

Alfred U (NY)
California Inst of Technology (CA)
Carnegie Mellon U (PA)
Case Western Reserve U (OH)
Clarkson U (NY)
Columbia U, School of Engineering & Applied Sci (NY)
Cornell U (NY)
Duke U (NC)
Harvard U (MA)
Johns Hopkins U (MD)
Massachusetts Inst of Technology (MA)
McMaster U (ON, Canada)
Michigan State U (MI)
Montana Tech of The U of Montana (MT)
Northwestern U (IL)
The Ohio State U (OH)
Oregon State U (OR)
Rice U (TX)
Stanford U (CA)

United States Air Force Academy (CO)
The U of Arizona (AZ)
U of Calif, Los Angeles (CA)
U of Illinois at Urbana–Champaign (IL)
U of Michigan (MI)
U of Minnesota, Twin Cities Campus (MN)
U of Toronto (ON, Canada)
U of Utah (UT)
Worcester Polytechnic Inst (MA)

MATHEMATICAL STATISTICS
American U (DC)
Appalachian State U (NC)
Barnard Coll (NY)
Baruch Coll of the City U of NY (NY)
Bowling Green State U (OH)
Brigham Young U (UT)
Brock U (ON, Canada)
California Polytechnic State U, San Luis Obispo (CA)
California State Polytechnic U, Pomona (CA)
California State U, Chico (CA)
California State U, Fullerton (CA)
California State U, Hayward (CA)
California State U, Long Beach (CA)
California State U, Northridge (CA)
Carleton U (ON, Canada)
Carnegie Mellon U (PA)
Case Western Reserve U (OH)
Central Michigan U (MI)
Cleveland State U (OH)
The Coll of New Jersey (NJ)
Colorado State U (CO)
Columbia Coll (NY)
Columbia U, School of General Studies (NY)
Concordia U (QC, Canada)
Cornell U (NY)
Dalhousie U (NS, Canada)
DePaul U (IL)
Eastern Kentucky U (KY)
Eastern Michigan U (MI)
Eastern New Mexico U (NM)
Florida International U (FL)
Florida State U (FL)
Fort Lewis Coll (CO)
Framingham State Coll (MA)
The George Washington U (DC)
Grand Valley State U (MI)
Hampshire Coll (MA)
Harvard U (MA)
Hunter Coll of the City U of NY (NY)
Iowa State U of Science and Technology (IA)
Kansas State U (KS)
Kettering U (MI)
Lehigh U (PA)
Loyola U Chicago (IL)
Luther Coll (IA)
Marquette U (WI)
McGill U (PQ, Canada)
McMaster U (ON, Canada)
Memorial U of Newfoundland (NF, Canada)
Mercyhurst Coll (PA)
Mesa State Coll (CO)
Miami U (OH)
Michigan State U (MI)
Michigan Technological U (MI)
Mills Coll (CA)
Mount Holyoke Coll (MA)
Mount Saint Vincent U (NS, Canada)
New Jersey Inst of Technology (NJ)
New York U (NY)
North Carolina State U (NC)
Northwestern U (IL)
Oakland U (MI)
Ohio Northern U (OH)
Ohio Wesleyan U (OH)
Oklahoma State U (OK)
Penn State U Univ Park Campus (PA)
Purdue U (IN)
Queen's U at Kingston (ON, Canada)
Rice U (TX)
Rochester Inst of Technology (NY)
Rutgers, The State U of New Jersey, New Brunswick (NJ)
St. Cloud State U (MN)
St. Mary's U of San Antonio (TX)
San Diego State U (CA)
San Francisco State U (CA)
San Jose State U (CA)
Sonoma State U (CA)
Southern Methodist U (TX)
State U of NY Coll at Oneonta (NY)
Stevens Inst of Technology (NJ)
Temple U (PA)
Université de Montréal (QC, Canada)
Université de Sherbrooke (PQ, Canada)
Université Laval (QC, Canada)
U Coll of the Fraser Valley (BC, Canada)
The U of Akron (OH)
U of Alaska Fairbanks (AK)
U of Alberta (AB, Canada)
The U of British Columbia (BC, Canada)
U of Calgary (AB, Canada)
U of Calif, Berkeley (CA)
U of Calif, Davis (CA)
U of Calif, Riverside (CA)
U of Calif, Santa Barbara (CA)
U of Central Florida (FL)
U of Chicago (IL)
U of Connecticut (CT)
U of Denver (CO)
U of Florida (FL)
U of Georgia (GA)
U of Guelph (ON, Canada)
U of Houston (TX)
U of Illinois at Chicago (IL)
U of Illinois at Urbana–Champaign (IL)
The U of Iowa (IA)
U of King's Coll (NS, Canada)
U of Manitoba (MB, Canada)
U of Maryland, Baltimore County (MD)
U of Michigan (MI)
U of Minnesota, Morris (MN)
U of Missouri–Columbia (MO)
U of Missouri–Kansas City (MO)
The U of Montana–Missoula (MT)
U of Nebraska at Kearney (NE)
U of Nevada, Las Vegas (NV)
U of New Hampshire (NH)
The U of North Carolina at Greensboro (NC)
U of North Florida (FL)
U of Oregon (OR)
U of Ottawa (ON, Canada)
U of Pennsylvania (PA)
U of Pittsburgh (PA)
U of Regina (SK, Canada)
U of Rochester (NY)
U of Saskatchewan (SK, Canada)
U of South Alabama (AL)
U of South Carolina (SC)
U of South Dakota (SD)
The U of Tennessee (TN)
The U of Texas at Dallas (TX)
The U of Texas at El Paso (TX)
The U of Texas at San Antonio (TX)
U of Toronto (ON, Canada)
U of Vermont (VT)
U of Victoria (BC, Canada)
U of Washington (WA)
U of Waterloo (ON, Canada)
The U of Western Ontario (ON, Canada)
U of Windsor (ON, Canada)
U of Wisconsin–Madison (WI)
U of Wisconsin–Milwaukee (WI)
U of Wyoming (WY)
Utah State U (UT)
Virginia Polytechnic Inst and State U (VA)
Washington U in St. Louis (MO)
Western Michigan U (MI)
West Virginia U (WV)
Wilfrid Laurier U (ON, Canada)
Winona State U (MN)
Xavier U of Louisiana (LA)
York U (ON, Canada)

MATHEMATICS
Abilene Christian U (TX)
Acadia U (NS, Canada)
Adams State Coll (CO)
Adelphi U (NY)
Adrian Coll (MI)
Agnes Scott Coll (GA)
Alabama State U (AL)
Albany State U (GA)
Albertson Coll of Idaho (ID)
Albertus Magnus Coll (CT)
Albion Coll (MI)
Albright Coll (PA)
Alcorn State U (MS)
Alderson-Broaddus Coll (WV)
Alfred U (NY)
Allegheny Coll (PA)
Alma Coll (MI)
Alvernia Coll (PA)
Alverno Coll (WI)
American International Coll (MA)
American U (DC)
American U in Cairo(Egypt)
Amherst Coll (MA)
Anderson Coll (SC)
Anderson U (IN)
Andrews U (MI)
Angelo State U (TX)
Appalachian State U (NC)
Aquinas Coll (MI)
Arcadia U (PA)
Arizona State U (AZ)
Arkansas State U (AR)
Arkansas Tech U (AR)
Armstrong Atlantic State U (GA)
Asbury Coll (KY)
Ashland U (OH)
Assumption Coll (MA)
Athens State U (AL)
Atlantic Union Coll (MA)
Auburn U (AL)
Auburn U Montgomery (AL)
Augsburg Coll (MN)
Augustana Coll (IL)
Augustana Coll (SD)
Augusta State U (GA)
Aurora U (IL)
Austin Coll (TX)
Austin Peay State U (TN)
Ave Maria Coll (MI)
Averett U (VA)
Avila Coll (MO)
Azusa Pacific U (CA)
Baker U (KS)
Baldwin-Wallace Coll (OH)
Ball State U (IN)
Barber-Scotia Coll (NC)
Bard Coll (NY)
Barnard Coll (NY)
Barry U (FL)
Barton Coll (NC)
Bates Coll (ME)
Baylor U (TX)
Belhaven Coll (MS)
Bellarmine U (KY)
Bellevue U (NE)
Belmont U (TN)
Beloit Coll (WI)
Bemidji State U (MN)
Benedict Coll (SC)
Benedictine Coll (KS)
Benedictine U (IL)
Bennett Coll (NC)
Bennington Coll (VT)
Bentley Coll (MA)
Berea Coll (KY)
Baruch Coll of the City U of NY (NY)
Berry Coll (GA)
Bethany Coll (KS)
Bethany Coll (WV)
Bethel Coll (IN)
Bethel Coll (KS)
Bethel Coll (MN)
Bethel Coll (TN)
Bethune-Cookman Coll (FL)
Biola U (CA)
Birmingham-Southern Coll (AL)
Bishop's U (PQ, Canada)
Blackburn Coll (IL)
Black Hills State U (SD)
Bloomsburg U of Pennsylvania (PA)
Bluefield Coll (VA)
Blue Mountain Coll (MS)
Bluffton Coll (OH)
Boise State U (ID)
Boston Coll (MA)
Boston U (MA)
Bowdoin Coll (ME)
Bowie State U (MD)
Bowling Green State U (OH)
Bradley U (IL)
Brandeis U (MA)
Brandon U (MB, Canada)
Brevard Coll (NC)
Brewton-Parker Coll (GA)
Briar Cliff U (IA)
Bridgewater Coll (VA)
Bridgewater State Coll (MA)
Brigham Young U (UT)
Brigham Young U–Hawaii (HI)
Brock U (ON, Canada)
Brooklyn Coll of the City U of NY (NY)
Brown U (RI)
Bryan Coll (TN)
Bryn Mawr Coll (PA)
Bucknell U (PA)
Buena Vista U (IA)
Butler U (IN)
Cabrini Coll (PA)
Caldwell Coll (NJ)
California Baptist U (CA)
California Inst of Technology (CA)
California Lutheran U (CA)
California Polytechnic State U, San Luis Obispo (CA)
California State Polytechnic U, Pomona (CA)
California State U, Bakersfield (CA)
California State U, Chico (CA)
California State U, Dominguez Hills (CA)
California State U, Fresno (CA)
California State U, Fullerton (CA)
California State U, Hayward (CA)
California State U, Long Beach (CA)
California State U, Los Angeles (CA)
California State U, Northridge (CA)
California State U, Sacramento (CA)
California State U, San Bernardino (CA)
California State U, San Marcos (CA)
California State U, Stanislaus (CA)
California U of Pennsylvania (PA)
Calvin Coll (MI)
Cameron U (OK)
Campbellsville U (KY)
Campbell U (NC)
Canisius Coll (NY)
Capital U (OH)
Cardinal Stritch U (WI)
Carleton Coll (MN)
Carleton U (ON, Canada)
Carlow Coll (PA)
Carnegie Mellon U (PA)
Carroll Coll (MT)
Carroll Coll (WI)
Carson-Newman Coll (TN)
Carthage Coll (WI)
Case Western Reserve U (OH)
Castleton State Coll (VT)
Catawba Coll (NC)
The Catholic U of America (DC)
Cedar Crest Coll (PA)
Cedarville U (OH)
Centenary Coll (NJ)
Centenary Coll of Louisiana (LA)
Central Coll (IA)
Central Connecticut State U (CT)
Central Methodist Coll (MO)
Central Michigan U (MI)
Central Missouri State U (MO)
Central State U (OH)
Central Washington U (WA)
Centre Coll (KY)
Chadron State Coll (NE)
Charleston Southern U (SC)
Chatham Coll (PA)
Cheyney U of Pennsylvania (PA)
Chicago State U (IL)
Chowan Coll (NC)
Christian Brothers U (TN)
Christian Heritage Coll (CA)
Christopher Newport U (VA)
Citadel, The Military Coll of South Carolina (SC)
City Coll of the City U of NY (NY)
Claflin U (SC)
Claremont McKenna Coll (CA)
Clarion U of Pennsylvania (PA)
Clark Atlanta U (GA)
Clarke Coll (IA)
Clarkson U (NY)
Clark U (MA)
Clearwater Christian Coll (FL)
Clemson U (SC)
Cleveland State U (OH)
Coe Coll (IA)
Coker Coll (SC)
Colby Coll (ME)
Colgate U (NY)
Coll Misericordia (PA)
Coll of Charleston (SC)
Coll of Mount St. Joseph (OH)
Coll of Mount Saint Vincent (NY)
The Coll of New Jersey (NJ)
The Coll of New Rochelle (NY)
Coll of Notre Dame of Maryland (MD)
Coll of Saint Benedict (MN)
Coll of St. Catherine (MN)
Coll of Saint Elizabeth (NJ)
Coll of Saint Mary (NE)
The Coll of Saint Rose (NY)
The Coll of St. Scholastica (MN)
Coll of Santa Fe (NM)
The Coll of Southeastern Europe, The American U of Athens(Greece)
Coll of Staten Island of the City U of NY (NY)
Coll of the Holy Cross (MA)
Coll of the Ozarks (MO)
Coll of the Southwest (NM)
The Coll of William and Mary (VA)
The Coll of Wooster (OH)
Colorado Christian U (CO)
The Colorado Coll (CO)
Colorado School of Mines (CO)
Colorado State U (CO)
Columbia Coll (MO)
Columbia Coll (NY)
Columbia Coll (SC)
Columbia Union Coll (MD)
Columbia U, School of General Studies (NY)
Columbus State U (GA)
Concord Coll (WV)
Concordia Coll (MN)
Concordia Coll (NY)
Concordia U (CA)
Concordia U (IL)
Concordia U (MI)
Concordia U (NE)
Concordia U (QC, Canada)
Concordia U Wisconsin (WI)
Connecticut Coll (CT)
Converse Coll (SC)
Coppin State Coll (MD)
Cornell Coll (IA)
Cornell U (NY)
Cornerstone U (MI)
Covenant Coll (GA)
Creighton U (NE)
Culver-Stockton Coll (MO)
Cumberland Coll (KY)
Cumberland U (TN)
Daemen Coll (NY)
Dakota State U (SD)
Dakota Wesleyan U (SD)
Dalhousie U (NS, Canada)
Dallas Baptist U (TX)
Dana Coll (NE)
Dartmouth Coll (NH)
Davidson Coll (NC)
Davis & Elkins Coll (WV)
Defiance Coll (OH)
Delaware State U (DE)
Delta State U (MS)
Denison U (OH)
DePaul U (IL)
DePauw U (IN)
DeSales U (PA)
Dickinson Coll (PA)
Dickinson State U (ND)
Dillard U (LA)
Doane Coll (NE)
Dominican Coll (NY)
Dominican U (IL)
Dordt Coll (IA)
Dowling Coll (NY)
Drake U (IA)
Drew U (NJ)
Drexel U (PA)
Drury U (MO)
Duke U (NC)
Duquesne U (PA)
Earlham Coll (IN)
East Carolina U (NC)
East Central U (OK)
Eastern Connecticut State U (CT)
Eastern Illinois U (IL)
Eastern Kentucky U (KY)
Eastern Mennonite U (VA)
Eastern Michigan U (MI)
Eastern Nazarene Coll (MA)
Eastern Oregon U (OR)
Eastern U (PA)
Eastern Washington U (WA)

East Stroudsburg U of Pennsylvania (PA)
East Tennessee State U (TN)
East Texas Baptist U (TX)
East-West U (IL)
Eckerd Coll (FL)
Edgewood Coll (WI)
Edinboro U of Pennsylvania (PA)
Edward Waters Coll (FL)
Elizabeth City State U (NC)
Elizabethtown Coll (PA)
Elmhurst Coll (IL)
Elmira Coll (NY)
Elms Coll (MA)
Elon U (NC)
Emmanuel Coll (MA)
Emory & Henry Coll (VA)
Emory U (GA)
Emporia State U (KS)
Erskine Coll (SC)
Eureka Coll (IL)
Evangel U (MO)
The Evergreen State Coll (WA)
Excelsior Coll (NY)
Fairfield U (CT)
Fairleigh Dickinson U, Florham-Madison Campus (NJ)
Fairleigh Dickinson U, Teaneck-Hackensack Campus (NJ)
Fairmont State Coll (WV)
Fayetteville State U (NC)
Felician Coll (NJ)
Ferris State U (MI)
Ferrum Coll (VA)
Fisk U (TN)
Fitchburg State Coll (MA)
Florida A&M U (FL)
Florida Atlantic U (FL)
Florida International U (FL)
Florida Southern Coll (FL)
Florida State U (FL)
Fontbonne U (MO)
Fordham U (NY)
Fort Hays State U (KS)
Fort Lewis Coll (CO)
Fort Valley State U (GA)
Framingham State Coll (MA)
Franciscan U of Steubenville (OH)
Francis Marion U (SC)
Franklin and Marshall Coll (PA)
Franklin Coll of Indiana (IN)
Franklin Pierce Coll (NH)
Freed-Hardeman U (TN)
Fresno Pacific U (CA)
Friends U (KS)
Frostburg State U (MD)
Furman U (SC)
Gallaudet U (DC)
Gannon U (PA)
Gardner-Webb U (NC)
George Fox U (OR)
George Mason U (VA)
Georgetown Coll (KY)
Georgetown U (DC)
The George Washington U (DC)
Georgia Coll and State U (GA)
Georgia Inst of Technology (GA)
Georgian Court Coll (NJ)
Georgia Southern U (GA)
Georgia Southwestern State U (GA)
Georgia State U (GA)
Gettysburg Coll (PA)
Gonzaga U (WA)
Gordon Coll (MA)
Goshen Coll (IN)
Goucher Coll (MD)
Grace Coll (IN)
Graceland U (IA)
Grace U (NE)
Grambling State U (LA)
Grand Canyon U (AZ)
Grand Valley State U (MI)
Greensboro Coll (NC)
Greenville Coll (IL)
Grinnell Coll (IA)
Grove City Coll (PA)
Guilford Coll (NC)
Gustavus Adolphus Coll (MN)
Gwynedd-Mercy Coll (PA)
Hamilton Coll (NY)
Hamline U (MN)
Hampden-Sydney Coll (VA)
Hampshire Coll (MA)
Hampton U (VA)
Hannibal-LaGrange Coll (MO)
Hanover Coll (IN)
Harding U (AR)
Hardin-Simmons U (TX)
Hartwick Coll (NY)
Harvard U (MA)
Harvey Mudd Coll (CA)
Hastings Coll (NE)
Haverford Coll (PA)
Heidelberg Coll (OH)
Henderson State U (AR)
Hendrix Coll (AR)
High Point U (NC)
Hillsdale Coll (MI)
Hiram Coll (OH)
Hobart and William Smith Colls (NY)
Hofstra U (NY)
Hollins U (VA)
Holy Family Coll (PA)
Hood Coll (MD)
Hope Coll (MI)
Houghton Coll (NY)
Houston Baptist U (TX)
Howard Payne U (TX)
Howard U (DC)
Humboldt State U (CA)
Hunter Coll of the City U of NY (NY)
Huntingdon Coll (AL)
Huntington Coll (IN)
Huston-Tillotson Coll (TX)
Idaho State U (ID)
Illinois Coll (IL)
Illinois State U (IL)
Illinois Wesleyan U (IL)
Immaculata Coll (PA)
Indiana State U (IN)
Indiana U Bloomington (IN)
Indiana U Kokomo (IN)
Indiana U Northwest (IN)
Indiana U of Pennsylvania (PA)
Indiana U–Purdue U Fort Wayne (IN)
Indiana U–Purdue U Indianapolis (IN)
Indiana U South Bend (IN)
Indiana U Southeast (IN)
Indiana Wesleyan U (IN)
Inter American U of PR, San Germán Campus (PR)
Iona Coll (NY)
Iowa State U of Science and Technology (IA)
Iowa Wesleyan Coll (IA)
Ithaca Coll (NY)
Jackson State U (MS)
Jacksonville State U (AL)
Jacksonville U (FL)
James Madison U (VA)
Jamestown Coll (ND)
Jarvis Christian Coll (TX)
John Brown U (AR)
John Carroll U (OH)
Johns Hopkins U (MD)
Johnson C. Smith U (NC)
Johnson State Coll (VT)
Judson Coll (AL)
Judson Coll (IL)
Juniata Coll (PA)
Kalamazoo Coll (MI)
Kansas State U (KS)
Kansas Wesleyan U (KS)
Kean U (NJ)
Keene State Coll (NH)
Kennesaw State U (GA)
Kent State U (OH)
Kentucky State U (KY)
Kentucky Wesleyan Coll (KY)
Kenyon Coll (OH)
Keuka Coll (NY)
King Coll (TN)
King's Coll (PA)
Knox Coll (IL)
Kutztown U of Pennsylvania (PA)
Lafayette Coll (PA)
LaGrange Coll (GA)
Lake Erie Coll (OH)
Lake Forest Coll (IL)
Lakehead U (ON, Canada)
Lakeland Coll (WI)
Lake Superior State U (MI)
Lamar U (TX)
Lambuth U (TN)
Lander U (SC)
La Salle U (PA)
Laurentian U (ON, Canada)
Lawrence Technological U (MI)
Lawrence U (WI)
Lebanon Valley Coll (PA)
Lees-McRae Coll (NC)
Lee U (TN)
Lehigh U (PA)
Lehman Coll of the City U of NY (NY)
Le Moyne Coll (NY)
LeMoyne-Owen Coll (TN)
Lenoir-Rhyne Coll (NC)
LeTourneau U (TX)
Lewis & Clark Coll (OR)
Lewis-Clark State Coll (ID)
Lewis U (IL)
Liberty U (VA)
Lincoln Memorial U (TN)
Lincoln U (MO)
Lincoln U (PA)
Lindenwood U (MO)
Linfield Coll (OR)
Lipscomb U (TN)
Lock Haven U of Pennsylvania (PA)
Long Island U, Brooklyn Campus (NY)
Long Island U, C.W. Post Campus (NY)
Longwood Coll (VA)
Loras Coll (IA)
Louisiana Coll (LA)
Louisiana State U and A&M Coll (LA)
Louisiana State U in Shreveport (LA)
Louisiana Tech U (LA)
Loyola Coll in Maryland (MD)
Loyola Marymount U (CA)
Loyola U Chicago (IL)
Loyola U New Orleans (LA)
Lubbock Christian U (TX)
Luther Coll (IA)
Lycoming Coll (PA)
Lynchburg Coll (VA)
Lyndon State Coll (VT)
Lyon Coll (AR)
Macalester Coll (MN)
MacMurray Coll (IL)
Maharishi U of Management (IA)
Malone Coll (OH)
Manchester Coll (IN)
Manhattan Coll (NY)
Manhattanville Coll (NY)
Mansfield U of Pennsylvania (PA)
Marian Coll (IN)
Marian Coll of Fond du Lac (WI)
Marietta Coll (OH)
Marist Coll (NY)
Marlboro Coll (VT)
Marquette U (WI)
Marshall U (WV)
Mars Hill Coll (NC)
Mary Baldwin Coll (VA)
Marygrove Coll (MI)
Marymount Coll of Fordham U (NY)
Marymount U (VA)
Maryville Coll (TN)
Maryville U of Saint Louis (MO)
Mary Washington Coll (VA)
Marywood U (PA)
Massachusetts Coll of Liberal Arts (MA)
Massachusetts Inst of Technology (MA)
The Master's Coll and Seminary (CA)
Mayville State U (ND)
McGill U (PQ, Canada)
McKendree Coll (IL)
McMaster U (ON, Canada)
McMurry U (TX)
McNeese State U (LA)
McPherson Coll (KS)
Memorial U of Newfoundland (NF, Canada)
Mercer U (GA)
Mercy Coll (NY)
Mercyhurst Coll (PA)
Meredith Coll (NC)
Merrimack Coll (MA)
Mesa State Coll (CO)
Messiah Coll (PA)
Methodist Coll (NC)
Metropolitan State Coll of Denver (CO)
Miami U (OH)
Michigan State U (MI)
Michigan Technological U (MI)
MidAmerica Nazarene U (KS)
Middlebury Coll (VT)
Middle Tennessee State U (TN)
Midland Lutheran Coll (NE)
Midwestern State U (TX)
Millersville U of Pennsylvania (PA)
Milligan Coll (TN)
Millikin U (IL)
Millsaps Coll (MS)
Mills Coll (CA)
Minnesota State U, Mankato (MN)
Minnesota State U Moorhead (MN)
Minot State U (ND)
Mississippi Coll (MS)
Mississippi State U (MS)
Mississippi U for Women (MS)
Mississippi Valley State U (MS)
Missouri Baptist Coll (MO)
Missouri Southern State Coll (MO)
Missouri Valley Coll (MO)
Missouri Western State Coll (MO)
Molloy Coll (NY)
Monmouth Coll (IL)
Monmouth U (NJ)
Montana State U–Billings (MT)
Montana State U–Bozeman (MT)
Montana Tech of The U of Montana (MT)
Montclair State U (NJ)
Montreat Coll (NC)
Moravian Coll (PA)
Morehead State U (KY)
Morehouse Coll (GA)
Morgan State U (MD)
Morningside Coll (IA)
Morris Brown Coll (GA)
Morris Coll (SC)
Mount Allison U (NB, Canada)
Mount Holyoke Coll (MA)
Mount Marty Coll (SD)
Mount Mary Coll (WI)
Mount Mercy Coll (IA)
Mount Olive Coll (NC)
Mount Saint Mary Coll (NY)
Mount St. Mary's Coll (CA)
Mount Saint Mary's Coll and Seminary (MD)
Mount Saint Vincent U (NS, Canada)
Mount Union Coll (OH)
Mount Vernon Nazarene U (OH)
Muhlenberg Coll (PA)
Murray State U (KY)
Muskingum Coll (OH)
National-Louis U (IL)
National U (CA)
Nazareth Coll of Rochester (NY)
Nebraska Wesleyan U (NE)
Newberry Coll (SC)
New Coll of Florida (FL)
New Jersey City U (NJ)
Newman U (KS)
New Mexico Highlands U (NM)
New Mexico Inst of Mining and Technology (NM)
New Mexico State U (NM)
New York U (NY)
Niagara U (NY)
Nicholls State U (LA)
Nipissing U (ON, Canada)
Norfolk State U (VA)
North Carolina Ag and Tech State U (NC)
North Carolina Central U (NC)
North Carolina State U (NC)
North Carolina Wesleyan Coll (NC)
North Central Coll (IL)
North Dakota State U (ND)
Northeastern Illinois U (IL)
Northeastern State U (OK)
Northeastern U (MA)
Northern Arizona U (AZ)
Northern Illinois U (IL)
Northern Kentucky U (KY)
Northern Michigan U (MI)
Northern State U (SD)
North Georgia Coll & State U (GA)
Northland Coll (WI)
North Park U (IL)
Northwestern Coll (IA)
Northwestern Coll (MN)
Northwestern Oklahoma State U (OK)
Northwestern State U of Louisiana (LA)
Northwestern U (IL)
Northwest Missouri State U (MO)
Northwest Nazarene U (ID)
Norwich U (VT)
Notre Dame Coll (OH)
Nyack Coll (NY)
Oakland City U (IN)
Oakland U (MI)
Oakwood Coll (AL)
Oberlin Coll (OH)
Occidental Coll (CA)
Oglethorpe U (GA)
Ohio Dominican Coll (OH)
Ohio Northern U (OH)
The Ohio State U (OH)
Ohio U (OH)
Ohio Wesleyan U (OH)
Okanagan U Coll (BC, Canada)
Oklahoma Baptist U (OK)
Oklahoma Christian U of Science and Arts (OK)
Oklahoma City U (OK)
Oklahoma Panhandle State U (OK)
Oklahoma State U (OK)
Oklahoma Wesleyan U (OK)
Old Dominion U (VA)
Olivet Coll (MI)
Olivet Nazarene U (IL)
Oral Roberts U (OK)
Oregon State U (OR)
Ottawa U (KS)
Otterbein Coll (OH)
Ouachita Baptist U (AR)
Our Lady of Holy Cross Coll (LA)
Our Lady of the Lake U of San Antonio (TX)
Pace U (NY)
Pacific Lutheran U (WA)
Pacific Union Coll (CA)
Pacific U (OR)
Paine Coll (GA)
Palm Beach Atlantic Coll (FL)
Park U (MO)
Penn State U at Erie, The Behrend Coll (PA)
Penn State U Univ Park Campus (PA)
Pepperdine U, Malibu (CA)
Peru State Coll (NE)
Pfeiffer U (NC)
Philander Smith Coll (AR)
Piedmont Coll (GA)
Pikeville Coll (KY)
Pittsburg State U (KS)
Pitzer Coll (CA)
Plattsburgh State U of NY (NY)
Plymouth State Coll (NH)
Point Loma Nazarene U (CA)
Polytechnic U, Brooklyn Campus (NY)
Pomona Coll (CA)
Pontifical Catholic U of Puerto Rico (PR)
Portland State U (OR)
Prairie View A&M U (TX)
Presbyterian Coll (SC)
Princeton U (NJ)
Principia Coll (IL)
Providence Coll (RI)
Purchase Coll, State U of NY (NY)
Purdue U (IN)
Purdue U Calumet (IN)
Queens Coll (NC)
Queens Coll of the City U of NY (NY)
Queen's U at Kingston (ON, Canada)
Quincy U (IL)
Quinnipiac U (CT)
Radford U (VA)
Ramapo Coll of New Jersey (NJ)
Randolph-Macon Coll (VA)
Randolph-Macon Woman's Coll (VA)
Redeemer U Coll (ON, Canada)
Reed Coll (OR)
Regis Coll (MA)
Regis U (CO)
Rensselaer Polytechnic Inst (NY)
Rhode Island Coll (RI)
Rhodes Coll (TN)
Rice U (TX)
The Richard Stockton Coll of New Jersey (NJ)
Richmond, The American International U in London(United Kingdom)
Rider U (NJ)
Ripon Coll (WI)
Rivier Coll (NH)
Roanoke Coll (VA)
Roberts Wesleyan Coll (NY)
Rochester Coll (MI)
Rochester Inst of Technology (NY)
Rockford Coll (IL)
Rockhurst U (MO)
Rocky Mountain Coll (MT)
Roger Williams U (RI)
Rollins Coll (FL)
Roosevelt U (IL)

Rose-Hulman Inst of Technology (IN)
Rosemont Coll (PA)
Rowan U (NJ)
Russell Sage Coll (NY)
Rust Coll (MS)
Rutgers, The State U of New Jersey, New Brunswick (NJ)
Sacred Heart U (CT)
Saginaw Valley State U (MI)
St. Ambrose U (IA)
St. Andrews Presbyterian Coll (NC)
Saint Anselm Coll (NH)
Saint Augustine's Coll (NC)
St. Bonaventure U (NY)
St. Cloud State U (MN)
St. Edward's U (TX)
St. Francis Coll (NY)
Saint Francis U (PA)
St. Francis Xavier U (NS, Canada)
St. John Fisher Coll (NY)
Saint John's U (MN)
St. John's U (NY)
Saint Joseph Coll (CT)
Saint Joseph's Coll (IN)
Saint Joseph's Coll (ME)
St. Joseph's Coll, New York (NY)
St. Joseph's Coll, Suffolk Campus (NY)
Saint Joseph's U (PA)
St. Lawrence U (NY)
Saint Louis U (MO)
Saint Martin's Coll (WA)
Saint Mary Coll (KS)
Saint Mary-of-the-Woods Coll (IN)
Saint Mary's Coll (IN)
Saint Mary's Coll of California (CA)
St. Mary's Coll of Maryland (MD)
Saint Mary's U (NS, Canada)
Saint Mary's U of Minnesota (MN)
St. Mary's U of San Antonio (TX)
Saint Michael's Coll (VT)
St. Norbert Coll (WI)
St. Olaf Coll (MN)
Saint Peter's Coll (NJ)
St. Thomas Aquinas Coll (NY)
St. Thomas U (NB, Canada)
Saint Vincent Coll (PA)
Saint Xavier U (IL)
Salem Coll (NC)
Salem International U (WV)
Salem State Coll (MA)
Salisbury U (MD)
Salve Regina U (RI)
Samford U (AL)
Sam Houston State U (TX)
San Diego State U (CA)
San Francisco State U (CA)
San Jose State U (CA)
Santa Clara U (CA)
Sarah Lawrence Coll (NY)
Savannah State U (GA)
Schreiner U (TX)
Scripps Coll (CA)
Seattle Pacific U (WA)
Seattle U (WA)
Seton Hall U (NJ)
Seton Hill Coll (PA)
Shawnee State U (OH)
Shaw U (NC)
Shenandoah U (VA)
Shepherd Coll (WV)
Shippensburg U of Pennsylvania (PA)
Shorter Coll (GA)
Siena Coll (NY)
Siena Heights U (MI)
Silver Lake Coll (WI)
Simmons Coll (MA)
Simon Fraser U (BC, Canada)
Simon's Rock Coll of Bard (MA)
Simpson Coll (IA)
Simpson Coll and Graduate School (CA)
Skidmore Coll (NY)
Slippery Rock U of Pennsylvania (PA)
Smith Coll (MA)
Sonoma State U (CA)
South Carolina State U (SC)
South Dakota School of Mines and Technology (SD)
South Dakota State U (SD)
Southeastern Louisiana U (LA)
Southeastern Oklahoma State U (OK)
Southeast Missouri State U (MO)
Southern Adventist U (TN)
Southern Arkansas U–Magnolia (AR)
Southern Connecticut State U (CT)
Southern Illinois U Carbondale (IL)
Southern Illinois U Edwardsville (IL)
Southern Methodist U (TX)
Southern Nazarene U (OK)
Southern Oregon U (OR)
Southern Polytechnic State U (GA)
Southern U and A&M Coll (LA)
Southern Utah U (UT)
Southern Wesleyan U (SC)
Southwest Baptist U (MO)
Southwestern Adventist U (TX)
Southwestern Coll (KS)
Southwestern Oklahoma State U (OK)
Southwestern U (TX)
Southwest Missouri State U (MO)
Southwest State U (MN)
Southwest Texas State U (TX)
Spelman Coll (GA)
Spring Arbor U (MI)
Springfield Coll (MA)
Spring Hill Coll (AL)
Stanford U (CA)
State U of NY at Albany (NY)
State U of NY at Binghamton (NY)
State U of NY at New Paltz (NY)
State U of NY at Oswego (NY)
State U of NY Coll at Brockport (NY)
State U of NY Coll at Buffalo (NY)
State U of NY Coll at Cortland (NY)
State U of NY Coll at Fredonia (NY)
State U of NY Coll at Geneseo (NY)
State U of NY Coll at Old Westbury (NY)
State U of NY Coll at Oneonta (NY)
State U of NY Coll at Potsdam (NY)
State U of NY Empire State Coll (NY)
State U of West Georgia (GA)
Stephen F. Austin State U (TX)
Stephens Coll (MO)
Sterling Coll (KS)
Stetson U (FL)
Stonehill Coll (MA)
State U of NY at Stony Brook (NY)
Suffolk U (MA)
Sul Ross State U (TX)
Susquehanna U (PA)
Swarthmore Coll (PA)
Sweet Briar Coll (VA)
Syracuse U (NY)
Tabor Coll (KS)
Talladega Coll (AL)
Tarleton State U (TX)
Taylor U (IN)
Temple U (PA)
Tennessee State U (TN)
Tennessee Technological U (TN)
Tennessee Wesleyan Coll (TN)
Texas A&M International U (TX)
Texas A&M U (TX)
Texas A&M U–Commerce (TX)
Texas A&M U–Corpus Christi (TX)
Texas A&M U–Kingsville (TX)
Texas A&M U–Texarkana (TX)
Texas Christian U (TX)
Texas Coll (TX)
Texas Lutheran U (TX)
Texas Southern U (TX)
Texas Tech U (TX)
Texas Wesleyan U (TX)
Texas Woman's U (TX)
Thiel Coll (PA)
Thomas Edison State Coll (NJ)
Thomas More Coll (KY)
Tougaloo Coll (MS)
Touro Coll (NY)
Towson U (MD)
Transylvania U (KY)
Trent U (ON, Canada)
Trevecca Nazarene U (TN)
Trinity Christian Coll (IL)
Trinity Coll (CT)
Trinity Coll (DC)
Trinity International U (IL)
Trinity U (TX)
Trinity Western U (BC, Canada)
Tri-State U (IN)
Troy State U (AL)
Troy State U Dothan (AL)
Troy State U Montgomery (AL)
Truman State U (MO)
Tufts U (MA)
Tulane U (LA)
Tusculum Coll (TN)
Tuskegee U (AL)
Union Coll (KY)
Union Coll (NE)
Union Coll (NY)
Union U (TN)
United States Air Force Academy (CO)
United States Military Academy (NY)
United States Naval Academy (MD)
Université de Montréal (QC, Canada)
Université de Sherbrooke (PQ, Canada)
Université Laval (QC, Canada)
State U of NY at Buffalo (NY)
U Coll of Cape Breton (NS, Canada)
U Coll of the Cariboo (BC, Canada)
U Coll of the Fraser Valley (BC, Canada)
The U of Akron (OH)
The U of Alabama (AL)
The U of Alabama at Birmingham (AL)
The U of Alabama in Huntsville (AL)
U of Alaska Anchorage (AK)
U of Alaska Fairbanks (AK)
U of Alberta (AB, Canada)
The U of Arizona (AZ)
U of Arkansas (AR)
U of Arkansas at Little Rock (AR)
U of Arkansas at Pine Bluff (AR)
U of Bridgeport (CT)
The U of British Columbia (BC, Canada)
U of Calgary (AB, Canada)
U of Calif, Berkeley (CA)
U of Calif, Davis (CA)
U of Calif, Irvine (CA)
U of Calif, Los Angeles (CA)
U of Calif, Riverside (CA)
U of Calif, San Diego (CA)
U of Calif, Santa Barbara (CA)
U of Calif, Santa Cruz (CA)
U of Central Arkansas (AR)
U of Central Florida (FL)
U of Central Oklahoma (OK)
U of Chicago (IL)
U of Cincinnati (OH)
U of Colorado at Boulder (CO)
U of Colorado at Colorado Springs (CO)
U of Colorado at Denver (CO)
U of Connecticut (CT)
U of Dallas (TX)
U of Dayton (OH)
U of Delaware (DE)
U of Denver (CO)
U of Evansville (IN)
The U of Findlay (OH)
U of Florida (FL)
U of Georgia (GA)
U of Great Falls (MT)
U of Guelph (ON, Canada)
U of Hartford (CT)
U of Hawaii at Hilo (HI)
U of Hawaii at Manoa (HI)
U of Houston (TX)
U of Houston–Victoria (TX)
U of Idaho (ID)
U of Illinois at Chicago (IL)
U of Illinois at Springfield (IL)
U of Illinois at Urbana–Champaign (IL)
U of Indianapolis (IN)
The U of Iowa (IA)
U of Kansas (KS)
U of Kentucky (KY)
U of King's Coll (NS, Canada)
U of La Verne (CA)
The U of Lethbridge (AB, Canada)
U of Louisiana at Lafayette (LA)
U of Louisiana at Monroe (LA)
U of Louisville (KY)
U of Maine (ME)
The U of Maine at Augusta (ME)
U of Maine at Farmington (ME)
U of Maine at Presque Isle (ME)
U of Manitoba (MB, Canada)
U of Mary (ND)
U of Mary Hardin-Baylor (TX)
U of Maryland, Baltimore County (MD)
U of Maryland, Coll Park (MD)
U of Maryland Eastern Shore (MD)
U of Massachusetts Amherst (MA)
U of Massachusetts Boston (MA)
U of Massachusetts Dartmouth (MA)
U of Massachusetts Lowell (MA)
The U of Memphis (TN)
U of Miami (FL)
U of Michigan (MI)
U of Michigan–Dearborn (MI)
U of Michigan–Flint (MI)
U of Minnesota, Duluth (MN)
U of Minnesota, Morris (MN)
U of Minnesota, Twin Cities Campus (MN)
U of Mississippi (MS)
U of Missouri–Columbia (MO)
U of Missouri–Kansas City (MO)
U of Missouri–St. Louis (MO)
U of Mobile (AL)
The U of Montana–Missoula (MT)
Western Montana Coll of The U of Montana (MT)
U of Montevallo (AL)
U of Nebraska at Kearney (NE)
U of Nebraska at Omaha (NE)
U of Nebraska–Lincoln (NE)
U of Nevada, Las Vegas (NV)
U of Nevada, Reno (NV)
U of New Hampshire (NH)
U of New Haven (CT)
U of New Mexico (NM)
U of New Orleans (LA)
U of North Alabama (AL)
The U of North Carolina at Asheville (NC)
The U of North Carolina at Chapel Hill (NC)
The U of North Carolina at Charlotte (NC)
The U of North Carolina at Greensboro (NC)
The U of North Carolina at Pembroke (NC)
The U of North Carolina at Wilmington (NC)
U of North Dakota (ND)
U of Northern Colorado (CO)
U of Northern Iowa (IA)
U of North Florida (FL)
U of North Texas (TX)
U of Notre Dame (IN)
U of Oklahoma (OK)
U of Oregon (OR)
U of Ottawa (ON, Canada)
U of Pennsylvania (PA)
U of Pittsburgh (PA)
U of Pittsburgh at Johnstown (PA)
U of Portland (OR)
U of Prince Edward Island (PE, Canada)
U of Puerto Rico, Cayey U Coll (PR)
U of Puget Sound (WA)
U of Redlands (CA)
U of Regina (SK, Canada)
U of Rhode Island (RI)
U of Richmond (VA)
U of Rio Grande (OH)
U of Rochester (NY)
U of St. Francis (IL)
U of St. Thomas (MN)
U of St. Thomas (TX)
U of San Diego (CA)
U of San Francisco (CA)
U of Saskatchewan (SK, Canada)
U of Science and Arts of Oklahoma (OK)
The U of Scranton (PA)
U of Sioux Falls (SD)
U of South Alabama (AL)
U of South Carolina (SC)
U of South Carolina Spartanburg (SC)
U of South Dakota (SD)
U of Southern California (CA)
U of Southern Colorado (CO)
U of Southern Indiana (IN)
U of Southern Maine (ME)
U of Southern Mississippi (MS)
U of South Florida (FL)
The U of Tampa (FL)
The U of Tennessee (TN)
The U of Tennessee at Chattanooga (TN)
The U of Tennessee at Martin (TN)
The U of Texas at Arlington (TX)
The U of Texas at Austin (TX)
The U of Texas at Brownsville (TX)
The U of Texas at Dallas (TX)
The U of Texas at El Paso (TX)
The U of Texas at San Antonio (TX)
The U of Texas at Tyler (TX)
The U of Texas of the Permian Basin (TX)
The U of Texas–Pan American (TX)
U of the District of Columbia (DC)
U of the Incarnate Word (TX)
U of the Ozarks (AR)
U of the Pacific (CA)
U of the South (TN)
U of the Virgin Islands (VI)
U of Toledo (OH)
U of Toronto (ON, Canada)
U of Tulsa (OK)
U of Utah (UT)
U of Vermont (VT)
U of Victoria (BC, Canada)
U of Virginia (VA)
The U of Virginia's Coll at Wise (VA)
U of Washington (WA)
U of Waterloo (ON, Canada)
The U of West Alabama (AL)
The U of Western Ontario (ON, Canada)
U of West Florida (FL)
U of Windsor (ON, Canada)
U of Wisconsin–Eau Claire (WI)
U of Wisconsin–Green Bay (WI)
U of Wisconsin–La Crosse (WI)
U of Wisconsin–Madison (WI)
U of Wisconsin–Milwaukee (WI)
U of Wisconsin–Oshkosh (WI)
U of Wisconsin–Parkside (WI)
U of Wisconsin–Platteville (WI)
U of Wisconsin–River Falls (WI)
U of Wisconsin–Stevens Point (WI)
U of Wisconsin–Superior (WI)
U of Wisconsin–Whitewater (WI)
U of Wyoming (WY)
Upper Iowa U (IA)
Ursinus Coll (PA)
Ursuline Coll (OH)
Utah State U (UT)
Utica Coll of Syracuse U (NY)
Valdosta State U (GA)
Valley City State U (ND)
Valparaiso U (IN)
Vanderbilt U (TN)
Vanguard U of Southern California (CA)
Vassar Coll (NY)
Villanova U (PA)
Virginia Commonwealth U (VA)
Virginia Intermont Coll (VA)
Virginia Military Inst (VA)
Virginia Polytechnic Inst and State U (VA)
Virginia State U (VA)
Virginia Union U (VA)
Virginia Wesleyan Coll (VA)
Viterbo U (WI)
Voorhees Coll (SC)
Wabash Coll (IN)
Wagner Coll (NY)
Wake Forest U (NC)
Walla Walla Coll (WA)
Walsh U (OH)
Warren Wilson Coll (NC)
Wartburg Coll (IA)
Washburn U of Topeka (KS)
Washington & Jefferson Coll (PA)
Washington and Lee U (VA)
Washington Coll (MD)
Washington State U (WA)
Washington U in St. Louis (MO)
Wayland Baptist U (TX)
Waynesburg Coll (PA)
Wayne State Coll (NE)
Wayne State U (MI)
Weber State U (UT)
Webster U (MO)
Wellesley Coll (MA)
Wells Coll (NY)
Wesleyan Coll (GA)
Wesleyan U (CT)
West Chester U of Pennsylvania (PA)
Western Baptist Coll (OR)
Western Carolina U (NC)
Western Connecticut State U (CT)
Western Illinois U (IL)
Western Kentucky U (KY)
Western Maryland Coll (MD)
Western Michigan U (MI)

Western New England Coll (MA)
Western Oregon U (OR)
Western State Coll of Colorado (CO)
Western Washington U (WA)
Westfield State Coll (MA)
West Liberty State Coll (WV)
Westminster Coll (MO)
Westminster Coll (PA)
Westminster Coll (UT)
Westmont Coll (CA)
West Texas A&M U (TX)
West Virginia State Coll (WV)
West Virginia U (WV)
West Virginia U Inst of Technology (WV)
West Virginia Wesleyan Coll (WV)
Wheaton Coll (IL)
Wheaton Coll (MA)
Wheeling Jesuit U (WV)
Whitman Coll (WA)
Whittier Coll (CA)
Whitworth Coll (WA)
Wichita State U (KS)
Widener U (PA)
Wilberforce U (OH)
Wiley Coll (TX)
Wilfrid Laurier U (ON, Canada)
Wilkes U (PA)
Willamette U (OR)
William Carey Coll (MS)
William Jewell Coll (MO)
William Paterson U of New Jersey (NJ)
Williams Coll (MA)
William Tyndale Coll (MI)
William Woods U (MO)
Wilmington Coll (OH)
Wilson Coll (PA)
Wingate U (NC)
Winona State U (MN)
Winston-Salem State U (NC)
Winthrop U (SC)
Wisconsin Lutheran Coll (WI)
Wittenberg U (OH)
Wofford Coll (SC)
Worcester Polytechnic Inst (MA)
Worcester State Coll (MA)
Wright State U (OH)
Xavier U (OH)
Xavier U of Louisiana (LA)
Yale U (CT)
Yeshiva U (NY)
York Coll of Pennsylvania (PA)
York Coll of the City U of New York (NY)
York U (ON, Canada)
Youngstown State U (OH)

MATHEMATICS/COMPUTER SCIENCE
Alfred U (NY)
Anderson U (IN)
Angelo State U (TX)
Averett U (VA)
Bethel Coll (IN)
Boston U (MA)
Brandon U (MB, Canada)
Brescia U (KY)
Brown U (RI)
Cardinal Stritch U (WI)
Carlow Coll (PA)
Central Coll (IA)
Chestnut Hill Coll (PA)
Coll of Saint Benedict (MN)
Coll of Santa Fe (NM)
The Colorado Coll (CO)
Drew U (NJ)
Eastern Illinois U (IL)
Hofstra U (NY)
Ithaca Coll (NY)
King Coll (TN)
Lake Superior State U (MI)
Long Island U, C.W. Post Campus (NY)
Loyola U Chicago (IL)
Maryville Coll (TN)
McGill U (PQ, Canada)
McMurry U (TX)
Morehead State U (KY)
Mount Allison U (NB, Canada)
Mount Saint Vincent U (NS, Canada)
Rochester Inst of Technology (NY)
Saginaw Valley State U (MI)
Saint John's U (MN)
Saint Joseph's Coll (IN)
St. Joseph's Coll, New York (NY)
Saint Mary's Coll (IN)
Saint Mary's U of Minnesota (MN)
St. Norbert Coll (WI)
San Diego State U (CA)
Southern Oregon U (OR)
Stanford U (CA)
State U of NY at Albany (NY)
State U of NY at Binghamton (NY)
Trinity Western U (BC, Canada)
The U of Akron (OH)
U of Houston–Clear Lake (TX)
U of Illinois at Chicago (IL)
U of Illinois at Urbana–Champaign (IL)
U of Oregon (OR)
U of Puerto Rico, Humacao U Coll (PR)
U of Waterloo (ON, Canada)
U of Windsor (ON, Canada)
Washington State U (WA)
Washington U in St. Louis (MO)
Yale U (CT)
York U (ON, Canada)

MATHEMATICS EDUCATION
Abilene Christian U (TX)
Adams State Coll (CO)
Alvernia Coll (PA)
Anderson Coll (SC)
Anderson U (IN)
Appalachian State U (NC)
Arkansas State U (AR)
Arkansas Tech U (AR)
Averett U (VA)
Bayamón Central U (PR)
Baylor U (TX)
Berea Coll (KY)
Berry Coll (GA)
Bethany Coll (KS)
Bethel Coll (IN)
Bethune-Cookman Coll (FL)
Bloomfield Coll (NJ)
Blue Mountain Coll (MS)
Boston U (MA)
Bowie State U (MD)
Bridgewater Coll (VA)
Brigham Young U (UT)
Brigham Young U–Hawaii (HI)
Brock U (ON, Canada)
Cabrini Coll (PA)
California State U, Chico (CA)
Canisius Coll (NY)
Caribbean U (PR)
Carroll Coll (MT)
Castleton State Coll (VT)
The Catholic U of America (DC)
Cedarville U (OH)
Central Michigan U (MI)
Central Missouri State U (MO)
Central State U (OH)
Central Washington U (WA)
Chadron State Coll (NE)
Chowan Coll (NC)
Christian Brothers U (TN)
Citadel, The Military Coll of South Carolina (SC)
Clearwater Christian Coll (FL)
Clemson U (SC)
The Coll of New Jersey (NJ)
The Coll of St. Catherine (MN)
Coll of the Ozarks (MO)
Colorado State U (CO)
Columbia Union Coll (MD)
Concordia Coll (MN)
Concordia U (IL)
Concordia U (NE)
Concordia U (OR)
Culver-Stockton Coll (MO)
Cumberland U (TN)
Daemen Coll (NY)
Dakota Wesleyan U (SD)
Dana Coll (NE)
Delta State U (MS)
Dominican Coll (NY)
Duquesne U (PA)
East Carolina U (NC)
Eastern Mennonite U (VA)
Eastern Michigan U (MI)
East Texas Baptist U (TX)
Elmhurst Coll (IL)
Elmira Coll (NY)
Elms Coll (MA)
Felician Coll (NJ)
Florida Atlantic U (FL)
Florida Inst of Technology (FL)
Florida International U (FL)
Florida State U (FL)
Franklin Coll of Indiana (IN)
Freed-Hardeman U (TN)
Geneva Coll (PA)
George Fox U (OR)
Georgia Southern U (GA)
Grace Coll (IN)
Greensboro Coll (NC)
Greenville Coll (IL)
Gustavus Adolphus Coll (MN)
Harding U (AR)
Hardin-Simmons U (TX)
Hastings Coll (NE)
Henderson State U (AR)
Hofstra U (NY)
Huntingdon Coll (AL)
Indiana U Bloomington (IN)
Indiana U Northwest (IN)
Indiana U of Pennsylvania (PA)
Indiana U–Purdue U Fort Wayne (IN)
Indiana U South Bend (IN)
Indiana U Southeast (IN)
Indiana Wesleyan U (IN)
Ithaca Coll (NY)
Jackson State U (MS)
Johnson State Coll (VT)
Judson Coll (AL)
Juniata Coll (PA)
Kennesaw State U (GA)
Keuka Coll (NY)
King Coll (TN)
La Roche Coll (PA)
Le Moyne Coll (NY)
Liberty U (VA)
Limestone Coll (SC)
Lincoln U (PA)
Long Island U, C.W. Post Campus (NY)
Louisiana State U in Shreveport (LA)
Luther Coll (IA)
Lyndon State Coll (VT)
Manhattanville Coll (NY)
Mansfield U of Pennsylvania (PA)
Marymount Coll of Fordham U (NY)
Maryville Coll (TN)
Mayville State U (ND)
McGill U (PQ, Canada)
McKendree Coll (IL)
McMurry U (TX)
Mercer U (GA)
Messiah Coll (PA)
MidAmerica Nazarene U (KS)
Millersville U of Pennsylvania (PA)
Minnesota State U Moorhead (MN)
Minot State U (ND)
Mississippi Valley State U (MS)
Molloy Coll (NY)
Montana State U–Billings (MT)
Morehead State U (KY)
Mount Marty Coll (SD)
Mount Vernon Nazarene U (OH)
Nazareth Coll of Rochester (NY)
New York Inst of Technology (NY)
New York U (NY)
Niagara U (NY)
North Carolina Central U (NC)
North Carolina State U (NC)
North Dakota State U (ND)
Northern Arizona U (AZ)
Northern Kentucky U (KY)
Northwestern Coll (MN)
Northwestern U (IL)
Northwest Nazarene U (ID)
Nova Southeastern U (FL)
Oakland City U (IN)
Ohio U (OH)
Ohio Valley Coll (WV)
Oklahoma Baptist U (OK)
Oklahoma Christian U of Science and Arts (OK)
Oral Roberts U (OK)
Pace U (NY)
Philadelphia Biblical U (PA)
Pikeville Coll (KY)
Plymouth State Coll (NH)
Point Park Coll (PA)
Pontifical Catholic U of Puerto Rico (PR)
Prescott Coll (AZ)
Queens Coll (NC)
Rivier Coll (NH)
Rocky Mountain Coll (MT)
Rust Coll (MS)
St. Ambrose U (IA)
Saint Augustine's Coll (NC)
St. John Fisher Coll (NY)
St. John's U (NY)
Saint Joseph's Coll (ME)
Saint Mary's U of Minnesota (MN)
Saint Xavier U (IL)
Salve Regina U (RI)
San Diego State U (CA)
Seattle Pacific U (WA)
Seton Hill Coll (PA)
Shaw U (NC)
Simpson Coll and Graduate School (CA)
Southeastern Coll of the Assemblies of God (FL)
Southeastern Louisiana U (LA)
Southeastern Oklahoma State U (OK)
Southeast Missouri State U (MO)
Southern Arkansas U–Magnolia (AR)
Southern Nazarene U (OK)
Southwestern Coll (KS)
Southwest Missouri State U (MO)
Southwest State U (MN)
State U of NY at Albany (NY)
State U of NY Coll at Potsdam (NY)
State U of West Georgia (GA)
Syracuse U (NY)
Talladega Coll (AL)
Tennessee Wesleyan Coll (TN)
Texas A&M International U (TX)
Texas Christian U (TX)
Texas Lutheran U (TX)
Texas Wesleyan U (TX)
Thomas Coll (ME)
Trevecca Nazarene U (TN)
Trinity Christian Coll (IL)
Tri-State U (IN)
Union Coll (NE)
The U of Arizona (AZ)
U of Calif, San Diego (CA)
U of Calif, Santa Cruz (CA)
U of Central Arkansas (AR)
U of Central Florida (FL)
U of Central Oklahoma (OK)
U of Delaware (DE)
U of Georgia (GA)
U of Great Falls (MT)
U of Hawaii at Manoa (HI)
U of Illinois at Chicago (IL)
U of Indianapolis (IN)
The U of Iowa (IA)
U of Louisiana at Monroe (LA)
U of Maine at Farmington (ME)
U of Mary (ND)
U of Maryland, Coll Park (MD)
U of Minnesota, Duluth (MN)
U of Minnesota, Twin Cities Campus (MN)
U of Mississippi (MS)
The U of Montana–Missoula (MT)
Western Montana Coll of The U of Montana (MT)
U of Nebraska–Lincoln (NE)
U of Nevada, Reno (NV)
U of New Orleans (LA)
The U of North Carolina at Charlotte (NC)
The U of North Carolina at Wilmington (NC)
U of Northern Iowa (IA)
U of North Florida (FL)
U of North Texas (TX)
U of Oklahoma (OK)
U of Puerto Rico, Cayey U Coll (PR)
U of Rio Grande (OH)
U of St. Thomas (MN)
U of Southern Colorado (CO)
U of South Florida (FL)
The U of Tennessee at Martin (TN)
U of Toledo (OH)
U of Utah (UT)
U of Vermont (VT)
U of Waterloo (ON, Canada)
U of West Florida (FL)
U of Windsor (ON, Canada)
U of Wisconsin–River Falls (WI)
U of Wisconsin–Superior (WI)
Ursuline Coll (OH)
Utah State U (UT)
Utica Coll of Syracuse U (NY)
Valley City State U (ND)
Viterbo U (WI)
Wartburg Coll (IA)
Washington U in St. Louis (MO)
Wayne State U (MI)
Western Carolina U (NC)
Westmont Coll (CA)
Wheeling Jesuit U (WV)
William Penn U (IA)
William Woods U (MO)
Winston-Salem State U (NC)
York Coll (NE)
York U (ON, Canada)
Youngstown State U (OH)

MATHEMATICS RELATED
Anderson U (IN)
Bradley U (IL)
Chestnut Hill Coll (PA)
Hofstra U (NY)
The Ohio State U (OH)
Ohio U (OH)
Seattle Pacific U (WA)
Sweet Briar Coll (VA)
The U of Akron (OH)
U of Pittsburgh (PA)
The U of Scranton (PA)
U of Wyoming (WY)

MECHANICAL DESIGN TECHNOLOGY
Bowling Green State U (OH)
Lincoln U (MO)
Pittsburg State U (KS)

MECHANICAL DRAFTING
Pennsylvania Coll of Technology (PA)
Purdue U (IN)

MECHANICAL ENGINEERING
Alfred U (NY)
American U in Cairo(Egypt)
Andrews U (MI)
Arizona State U (AZ)
Arkansas Tech U (AR)
Auburn U (AL)
Baker Coll of Flint (MI)
Baylor U (TX)
Boston U (MA)
Bradley U (IL)
Brigham Young U (UT)
Brown U (RI)
Bucknell U (PA)
California Inst of Technology (CA)
California Maritime Academy (CA)
California Polytechnic State U, San Luis Obispo (CA)
California State Polytechnic U, Pomona (CA)
California State U, Chico (CA)
California State U, Fresno (CA)
California State U, Fullerton (CA)
California State U, Long Beach (CA)
California State U, Los Angeles (CA)
California State U, Northridge (CA)
California State U, Sacramento (CA)
Calvin Coll (MI)
Carleton U (ON, Canada)
Carnegie Mellon U (PA)
Case Western Reserve U (OH)
The Catholic U of America (DC)
Cedarville U (OH)
Christian Brothers U (TN)
City Coll of the City U of NY (NY)
Clarkson U (NY)
Clemson U (SC)
Cleveland State U (OH)
The Coll of Southeastern Europe, The American U of Athens(Greece)
Colorado School of Mines (CO)
Colorado State U (CO)
Columbia U, School of Engineering & Applied Sci (NY)
Concordia U (QC, Canada)
Cooper Union for the Advancement of Science & Art (NY)
Cornell U (NY)
Dalhousie U (NS, Canada)
Delaware State U (DE)
Drexel U (PA)
Duke U (NC)
Eastern Nazarene Coll (MA)
Florida A&M U (FL)
Florida Atlantic U (FL)
Florida Inst of Technology (FL)
Florida International U (FL)
Florida State U (FL)
Frostburg State U (MD)
Gallaudet U (DC)
Gannon U (PA)
The George Washington U (DC)
Georgia Inst of Technology (GA)
Gonzaga U (WA)
Grand Valley State U (MI)

Grove City Coll (PA)
Harvard U (MA)
Henry Cogswell Coll (WA)
Hofstra U (NY)
Howard U (DC)
Illinois Inst of Technology (IL)
Indiana Inst of Technology (IN)
Indiana U–Purdue U Fort Wayne (IN)
Indiana U–Purdue U Indianapolis (IN)
Iowa State U of Science and Technology (IA)
Jacksonville U (FL)
John Brown U (AR)
Johns Hopkins U (MD)
Johnson & Wales U (RI)
Kansas State U (KS)
Kettering U (MI)
Lafayette Coll (PA)
Lakehead U (ON, Canada)
Lake Superior State U (MI)
Lamar U (TX)
Lawrence Technological U (MI)
Lehigh U (PA)
LeTourneau U (TX)
Louisiana State U and A&M Coll (LA)
Louisiana Tech U (LA)
Loyola Marymount U (CA)
Manhattan Coll (NY)
Marquette U (WI)
Massachusetts Inst of Technology (MA)
McGill U (PQ, Canada)
McMaster U (ON, Canada)
Memorial U of Newfoundland (NF, Canada)
Mercer U (GA)
Miami U (OH)
Michigan State U (MI)
Michigan Technological U (MI)
Milwaukee School of Engineering (WI)
Minnesota State U, Mankato (MN)
Mississippi State U (MS)
Montana State U–Bozeman (MT)
Montana Tech of The U of Montana (MT)
New Jersey Inst of Technology (NJ)
New Mexico Inst of Mining and Technology (NM)
New Mexico State U (NM)
New York Inst of Technology (NY)
New York U (NY)
North Carolina Ag and Tech State U (NC)
North Carolina State U (NC)
North Dakota State U (ND)
Northeastern U (MA)
Northern Arizona U (AZ)
Northern Illinois U (IL)
Northwestern U (IL)
Norwich U (VT)
Oakland U (MI)
Ohio Northern U (OH)
The Ohio State U (OH)
Ohio U (OH)
Oklahoma Christian U of Science and Arts (OK)
Oklahoma State U (OK)
Old Dominion U (VA)
Oral Roberts U (OK)
Oregon State U (OR)
Penn State U at Erie, The Behrend Coll (PA)
Penn State U Univ Park Campus (PA)
Polytechnic U, Brooklyn Campus (NY)
Polytechnic U of Puerto Rico (PR)
Portland State U (OR)
Prairie View A&M U (TX)
Princeton U (NJ)
Purdue U (IN)
Purdue U Calumet (IN)
Queen's U at Kingston (ON, Canada)
Rensselaer Polytechnic Inst (NY)
Rice U (TX)
Rochester Inst of Technology (NY)
Rose-Hulman Inst of Technology (IN)
Rowan U (NJ)
Saginaw Valley State U (MI)
St. Cloud State U (MN)
Saint Louis U (MO)
Saint Martin's Coll (WA)
San Diego State U (CA)
San Francisco State U (CA)
San Jose State U (CA)
Santa Clara U (CA)
Seattle U (WA)
South Dakota School of Mines and Technology (SD)
South Dakota State U (SD)
Southern Illinois U Carbondale (IL)
Southern Illinois U Edwardsville (IL)
Southern Methodist U (TX)
Southern U and A&M Coll (LA)
Stanford U (CA)
State U of NY at Binghamton (NY)
State U of NY Maritime Coll (NY)
Stevens Inst of Technology (NJ)
State U of NY at Stony Brook (NY)
Syracuse U (NY)
Temple U (PA)
Tennessee State U (TN)
Tennessee Technological U (TN)
Texas A&M U (TX)
Texas A&M U–Kingsville (TX)
Texas Tech U (TX)
Trinity Coll (CT)
Tri-State U (IN)
Tufts U (MA)
Tulane U (LA)
Tuskegee U (AL)
Union Coll (NY)
United States Air Force Academy (CO)
United States Coast Guard Academy (CT)
United States Military Academy (NY)
United States Naval Academy (MD)
Université de Sherbrooke (PQ, Canada)
U du Québec, École de technologie supérieure (PQ, Canada)
Université Laval (QC, Canada)
State U of NY at Buffalo (NY)
The U of Akron (OH)
The U of Alabama (AL)
The U of Alabama at Birmingham (AL)
The U of Alabama in Huntsville (AL)
U of Alaska Fairbanks (AK)
U of Alberta (AB, Canada)
The U of Arizona (AZ)
U of Arkansas (AR)
The U of British Columbia (BC, Canada)
U of Calgary (AB, Canada)
U of Calif, Berkeley (CA)
U of Calif, Davis (CA)
U of Calif, Irvine (CA)
U of Calif, Los Angeles (CA)
U of Calif, Riverside (CA)
U of Calif, San Diego (CA)
U of Calif, Santa Barbara (CA)
U of Central Florida (FL)
U of Cincinnati (OH)
U of Colorado at Boulder (CO)
U of Colorado at Colorado Springs (CO)
U of Colorado at Denver (CO)
U of Connecticut (CT)
U of Dayton (OH)
U of Delaware (DE)
U of Denver (CO)
U of Evansville (IN)
U of Florida (FL)
U of Hartford (CT)
U of Hawaii at Manoa (HI)
U of Houston (TX)
U of Idaho (ID)
U of Illinois at Chicago (IL)
U of Illinois at Urbana–Champaign (IL)
The U of Iowa (IA)
U of Kansas (KS)
U of Kentucky (KY)
U of Louisiana at Lafayette (LA)
U of Louisville (KY)
U of Maine (ME)
U of Manitoba (MB, Canada)
U of Maryland, Baltimore County (MD)
U of Maryland, Coll Park (MD)
U of Massachusetts Amherst (MA)
U of Massachusetts Dartmouth (MA)
U of Massachusetts Lowell (MA)
The U of Memphis (TN)
U of Miami (FL)
U of Michigan (MI)
U of Michigan–Dearborn (MI)
U of Minnesota, Twin Cities Campus (MN)
U of Mississippi (MS)
U of Missouri–Columbia (MO)
U of Missouri–Kansas City (MO)
U of Missouri–Rolla (MO)
U of Missouri–St. Louis (MO)
U of Nebraska–Lincoln (NE)
U of Nevada, Las Vegas (NV)
U of Nevada, Reno (NV)
U of New Hampshire (NH)
U of New Haven (CT)
U of New Mexico (NM)
U of New Orleans (LA)
The U of North Carolina at Charlotte (NC)
U of North Dakota (ND)
U of North Florida (FL)
U of Notre Dame (IN)
U of Oklahoma (OK)
U of Ottawa (ON, Canada)
U of Pennsylvania (PA)
U of Pittsburgh (PA)
U of Portland (OR)
U of Rhode Island (RI)
U of Rochester (NY)
U of St. Thomas (MN)
U of Saskatchewan (SK, Canada)
U of South Alabama (AL)
U of South Carolina (SC)
U of Southern California (CA)
U of South Florida (FL)
The U of Tennessee (TN)
The U of Tennessee at Chattanooga (TN)
The U of Texas at Arlington (TX)
The U of Texas at Austin (TX)
The U of Texas at El Paso (TX)
The U of Texas at San Antonio (TX)
The U of Texas at Tyler (TX)
The U of Texas–Pan American (TX)
U of the District of Columbia (DC)
U of the Pacific (CA)
U of Toledo (OH)
U of Toronto (ON, Canada)
U of Tulsa (OK)
U of Utah (UT)
U of Vermont (VT)
U of Victoria (BC, Canada)
U of Virginia (VA)
U of Washington (WA)
U of Waterloo (ON, Canada)
The U of Western Ontario (ON, Canada)
U of Windsor (ON, Canada)
U of Wisconsin–Madison (WI)
U of Wisconsin–Milwaukee (WI)
U of Wisconsin–Platteville (WI)
U of Wyoming (WY)
Utah State U (UT)
Valparaiso U (IN)
Vanderbilt U (TN)
Villanova U (PA)
Virginia Commonwealth U (VA)
Virginia Military Inst (VA)
Virginia Polytechnic Inst and State U (VA)
Walla Walla Coll (WA)
Washington State U (WA)
Washington U in St. Louis (MO)
Wayne State U (MI)
Western Kentucky U (KY)
Western Michigan U (MI)
Western New England Coll (MA)
West Virginia U (WV)
West Virginia U Inst of Technology (WV)
Wichita State U (KS)
Widener U (PA)
Wilkes U (PA)
William Penn U (IA)
Winona State U (MN)
Worcester Polytechnic Inst (MA)
Wright State U (OH)
Yale U (CT)
York Coll of Pennsylvania (PA)
Youngstown State U (OH)

MECHANICAL ENGINEERING TECHNOLOGIES RELATED
Indiana State U (IN)
New York Inst of Technology (NY)
Penn State U McKeesport Campus of the Commonwealth Coll (PA)

MECHANICAL ENGINEERING TECHNOLOGY
Andrews U (MI)
Arizona State U East (AZ)
Bluefield State Coll (WV)
Boise State U (ID)
British Columbia Inst of Technology (BC, Canada)
California Polytechnic State U, San Luis Obispo (CA)
California State Polytechnic U, Pomona (CA)
California State U, Sacramento (CA)
Central Connecticut State U (CT)
Central Michigan U (MI)
Central Washington U (WA)
Cleveland State U (OH)
Delaware State U (DE)
Eastern Washington U (WA)
Excelsior Coll (NY)
Fairleigh Dickinson U, Teaneck-Hackensack Campus (NJ)
Fairmont State Coll (WV)
Georgia Southern U (GA)
Indiana U–Purdue U Fort Wayne (IN)
Indiana U–Purdue U Indianapolis (IN)
Johnson & Wales U (RI)
Kansas State U (KS)
Lakehead U (ON, Canada)
Lake Superior State U (MI)
LeTourneau U (TX)
Metropolitan State Coll of Denver (CO)
Michigan Technological U (MI)
Milwaukee School of Engineering (WI)
Montana State U–Bozeman (MT)
Murray State U (KY)
New York Inst of Technology (NY)
Northeastern U (MA)
Oklahoma State U (OK)
Oregon Inst of Technology (OR)
Penn State U Berks Cmps of Berks-Lehigh Valley Coll (PA)
Penn State U Harrisburg Campus of the Capital Coll (PA)
Pittsburg State U (KS)
Point Park Coll (PA)
Purdue U Calumet (IN)
Purdue U North Central (IN)
Rochester Inst of Technology (NY)
Savannah State U (GA)
South Carolina State U (SC)
Southern Polytechnic State U (GA)
Southwest Missouri State U (MO)
State U of NY Coll at Buffalo (NY)
State U of NY Coll of Technology at Alfred (NY)
State U of NY Inst of Tech at Utica/Rome (NY)
Temple U (PA)
Texas Tech U (TX)
Thomas Edison State Coll (NJ)
The U of Akron (OH)
U of Arkansas at Little Rock (AR)
U of Cincinnati (OH)
U of Dayton (OH)
U of Hartford (CT)
U of Maine (ME)
U of Massachusetts Dartmouth (MA)
U of New Hampshire (NH)
The U of North Carolina at Charlotte (NC)
U of North Texas (TX)
U of Pittsburgh at Johnstown (PA)
U of Rio Grande (OH)
U of Southern Colorado (CO)
U of Southern Mississippi (MS)
U of Toledo (OH)
Wayne State U (MI)
Weber State U (UT)
Wentworth Inst of Technology (MA)
Youngstown State U (OH)

MEDICAL ADMINISTRATIVE ASSISTANT
Baker Coll of Auburn Hills (MI)
Ohio U (OH)
Peirce Coll (PA)
Tabor Coll (KS)

MEDICAL ASSISTANT
California State U, Dominguez Hills (CA)
International Business Coll, Fort Wayne (IN)
Jones Coll (FL)

MEDICAL BASIC SCIENCES RELATED
Fairleigh Dickinson U, Florham-Madison Campus (NJ)
Fairleigh Dickinson U, Teaneck-Hackensack Campus (NJ)
U of Hawaii at Manoa (HI)

MEDICAL CELL BIOLOGY
U of Utah (UT)

MEDICAL DIETICIAN
The Ohio State U (OH)
U of Illinois at Chicago (IL)

MEDICAL ILLUSTRATING
Alma Coll (MI)
Anna Maria Coll (MA)
Arcadia U (PA)
Clark Atlanta U (GA)
The Cleveland Inst of Art (OH)
Iowa State U of Science and Technology (IA)
Olivet Coll (MI)
Rochester Inst of Technology (NY)
Texas Woman's U (TX)
Tulane U (LA)
U of Toronto (ON, Canada)

MEDICAL LABORATORY ASSISTANT
California State U, Chico (CA)
U of Vermont (VT)

MEDICAL LABORATORY TECHNICIAN
Alabama State U (AL)
Alfred U (NY)
Andrews U (MI)
Auburn U (AL)
Barry U (FL)
Bloomsburg U of Pennsylvania (PA)
California State U, Dominguez Hills (CA)
California State U, Hayward (CA)
California State U, Northridge (CA)
California U of Pennsylvania (PA)
Columbus State U (GA)
Concordia U (NE)
DePaul U (IL)
East Central U (OK)
East Stroudsburg U of Pennsylvania (PA)
Edinboro U of Pennsylvania (PA)
Ferris State U (MI)
Gardner-Webb U (NC)
Holy Family Coll (PA)
Hunter Coll of the City U of NY (NY)
Long Island U, C.W. Post Campus (NY)
Longwood Coll (VA)
Marquette U (WI)
Massachusetts Coll of Liberal Arts (MA)
Morgan State U (MD)
Mount Saint Mary Coll (NY)
Northeastern U (MA)
Northern Michigan U (MI)
Northern State U (SD)
Northwestern Oklahoma State U (OK)
Northwest Missouri State U (MO)
Purdue U Calumet (IN)
St. Thomas Aquinas Coll (NY)
Shawnee State U (OH)
Sonoma State U (CA)
U of Alberta (AB, Canada)
The U of British Columbia (BC, Canada)
U of Mary (ND)
U of Maryland Eastern Shore (MD)
U of Missouri–Kansas City (MO)
The U of Montana–Missoula (MT)
U of New England (ME)
U of New Hampshire (NH)
The U of North Carolina at Pembroke (NC)
U of Science and Arts of Oklahoma (OK)
U of Utah (UT)
Weber State U (UT)
Winona State U (MN)

MEDICAL LABORATORY TECHNOLOGY
Auburn U (AL)
The Coll of St. Scholastica (MN)
Concordia Coll (MN)
Felician Coll (NJ)
The George Washington U (DC)
Oakland U (MI)
Quinnipiac U (CT)
Rockhurst U (MO)
Roosevelt U (IL)
Southeastern Oklahoma State U (OK)
Springfield Coll (MA)
State U of NY at Stony Brook (NY)
U of Cincinnati (OH)
U of Illinois at Springfield (IL)
U of Nevada, Las Vegas (NV)
U of New England (ME)
U of Oklahoma (OK)
U of Puerto Rico Medical Sciences Campus (PR)
U of Windsor (ON, Canada)

MEDICAL MICROBIOLOGY
Fitchburg State Coll (MA)
U of Miami (FL)
U of Wisconsin–La Crosse (WI)

MEDICAL MOLECULAR BIOLOGY
U of Hawaii at Manoa (HI)

MEDICAL NUTRITION
Edinboro U of Pennsylvania (PA)
Elmhurst Coll (IL)

MEDICAL PHARMACOLOGY AND PHARMACEUTICAL SCIENCES
Campbell U (NC)
Duquesne U (PA)
The U of Montana–Missoula (MT)
U of the Sciences in Philadelphia (PA)

MEDICAL PHYSICS/BIOPHYSICS
Laurentian U (ON, Canada)

MEDICAL RADIOLOGIC TECHNOLOGY
Arkansas State U (AR)
Averett U (VA)
Avila Coll (MO)
Bloomsburg U of Pennsylvania (PA)
British Columbia Inst of Technology (BC, Canada)
Coll Misericordia (PA)
Fairleigh Dickinson U, Florham-Madison Campus (NJ)
Fairleigh Dickinson U, Teaneck-Hackensack Campus (NJ)
Gannon U (PA)
Idaho State U (ID)
Indiana U Northwest (IN)
Indiana U–Purdue U Indianapolis (IN)
La Roche Coll (PA)
Loma Linda U (CA)
Long Island U, C.W. Post Campus (NY)
Marygrove Coll (MI)
McNeese State U (LA)
Minot State U (ND)
Mount Marty Coll (SD)
Northwestern State U of Louisiana (LA)
The Ohio State U (OH)
Oregon Health & Science U (OR)
Presentation Coll (SD)
Saint Joseph's Coll (ME)
Southern Illinois U Carbondale (IL)
Southwest Missouri State U (MO)
Southwest Texas State U (TX)
State U of New York Upstate Medical University (NY)
Thomas Edison State Coll (NJ)
The U of Alabama at Birmingham (AL)
U of Central Arkansas (AR)
U of Central Florida (FL)
U of Hartford (CT)
U of Louisiana at Monroe (LA)
U of Nebraska Medical Center (NE)
U of Nevada, Las Vegas (NV)
The U of North Carolina at Chapel Hill (NC)
U of Prince Edward Island (PE, Canada)
U of St. Francis (IL)
U of Vermont (VT)
Wayne State U (MI)
Weber State U (UT)

MEDICAL RECORDS ADMINISTRATION
Alabama State U (AL)
Arkansas Tech U (AR)
Baker Coll of Auburn Hills (MI)
Baker Coll of Flint (MI)
Carroll Coll (MT)
Chicago State U (IL)
Clark Atlanta U (GA)
Coll of Saint Mary (NE)
Dakota State U (SD)
East Carolina U (NC)
East Central U (OK)
Eastern Kentucky U (KY)
Ferris State U (MI)
Florida A&M U (FL)
Florida International U (FL)
Georgia State U (GA)
Gwynedd-Mercy Coll (PA)
Illinois State U (IL)
Indiana U Northwest (IN)
Indiana U–Purdue U Indianapolis (IN)
Jackson State U (MS)
Kean U (NJ)
Loma Linda U (CA)
Long Island U, C.W. Post Campus (NY)
Louisiana Tech U (LA)
Macon State Coll (GA)
Medical Coll of Georgia (GA)
Norfolk State U (VA)
The Ohio State U (OH)
Pace U (NY)
Regis U (CO)
Southwestern Oklahoma State U (OK)
Southwest Texas State U (TX)
Springfield Coll (MA)
State U of NY Inst of Tech at Utica/Rome (NY)
Temple U (PA)
Tennessee State U (TN)
Texas Southern U (TX)
Touro Coll (NY)
The U of Alabama at Birmingham (AL)
U of Central Florida (FL)
U of Illinois at Chicago (IL)
U of Kansas (KS)
U of Louisiana at Lafayette (LA)
U of Mississippi Medical Center (MS)
U of Pittsburgh (PA)
U of Wisconsin–Milwaukee (WI)
Western Carolina U (NC)

MEDICAL RECORDS TECHNOLOGY
Robert Morris Coll (IL)

MEDICAL TECHNOLOGY
Adams State Coll (CO)
Alcorn State U (MS)
Alderson-Broaddus Coll (WV)
Alvernia Coll (PA)
American International Coll (MA)
Anderson U (IN)
Andrews U (MI)
Angelo State U (TX)
Appalachian State U (NC)
Aquinas Coll (MI)
Arizona State U (AZ)
Arkansas State U (AR)
Arkansas Tech U (AR)
Armstrong Atlantic State U (GA)
Atlantic Union Coll (MA)
Auburn U (AL)
Augustana Coll (SD)
Augusta State U (GA)
Aurora U (IL)
Austin Peay State U (TN)
Averett U (VA)
Avila Coll (MO)
Baldwin-Wallace Coll (OH)
Ball State U (IN)
Barry U (FL)
Belmont Abbey Coll (NC)
Belmont U (TN)
Bemidji State U (MN)
Benedictine U (IL)
Bethune-Cookman Coll (FL)
Blackburn Coll (IL)
Bloomfield Coll (NJ)
Bloomsburg U of Pennsylvania (PA)
Blue Mountain Coll (MS)
Bluffton Coll (OH)
Boise State U (ID)
Boston U (MA)
Bowling Green State U (OH)
Bradley U (IL)
Brescia U (KY)
Briar Cliff U (IA)
Bridgewater Coll (VA)
Cabrini Coll (PA)
Caldwell Coll (NJ)
California State U, Dominguez Hills (CA)
California State U, Northridge (CA)
Cameron U (OK)
Campbellsville U (KY)
Canisius Coll (NY)
Carroll Coll (MT)
Carroll Coll (WI)
Carson-Newman Coll (TN)
Catawba Coll (NC)
The Catholic U of America (DC)
Cedar Crest Coll (PA)
Cedarville U (OH)
Central Connecticut State U (CT)
Central Michigan U (MI)
Central Missouri State U (MO)
Cheyney U of Pennsylvania (PA)
Clarion U of Pennsylvania (PA)
Clemson U (SC)
Coker Coll (SC)
Coll Misericordia (PA)
Coll of Mount St. Joseph (OH)
Coll of St. Catherine (MN)
Coll of Saint Elizabeth (NJ)
Coll of Saint Mary (NE)
The Coll of Saint Rose (NY)
Coll of Staten Island of the City U of NY (NY)
Coll of the Ozarks (MO)
Columbia Coll (SC)
Concord Coll (WV)
Concordia Coll (MN)
Culver-Stockton Coll (MO)
Cumberland Coll (KY)
Defiance Coll (OH)
Delta State U (MS)
DePaul U (IL)
DePauw U (IN)
DeSales U (PA)
Dominican U (IL)
Dordt Coll (IA)
East Carolina U (NC)
Eastern Illinois U (IL)
Eastern Kentucky U (KY)
Eastern Mennonite U (VA)
Eastern Michigan U (MI)
Eastern New Mexico U (NM)
Eastern Washington U (WA)
East Texas Baptist U (TX)
Eckerd Coll (FL)
Edgewood Coll (WI)
Elmhurst Coll (IL)
Elmira Coll (NY)
Elms Coll (MA)
Elon U (NC)
Emory & Henry Coll (VA)
Erskine Coll (SC)
Eureka Coll (IL)
Evangel U (MO)
Fairleigh Dickinson U, Florham-Madison Campus (NJ)
Fairleigh Dickinson U, Teaneck-Hackensack Campus (NJ)
Felician Coll (NJ)
Ferris State U (MI)
Ferrum Coll (VA)
Fitchburg State Coll (MA)
Florida Atlantic U (FL)
Florida Gulf Coast U (FL)
Fort Hays State U (KS)
Framingham State Coll (MA)
Francis Marion U (SC)
Gannon U (PA)
Gardner-Webb U (NC)
George Mason U (VA)
Georgetown Coll (KY)
The George Washington U (DC)
Georgia Southern U (GA)
Georgia State U (GA)
Graceland U (IA)
Grand Valley State U (MI)
Greensboro Coll (NC)
Gwynedd-Mercy Coll (PA)
Harding U (AR)
Hardin-Simmons U (TX)
Hartwick Coll (NY)
Henderson State U (AR)
High Point U (NC)
Houghton Coll (NY)
Houston Baptist U (TX)
Howard U (DC)
Humboldt State U (CA)
Idaho State U (ID)
Illinois Coll (IL)
Illinois State U (IL)
Illinois Wesleyan U (IL)
Indiana State U (IN)
Indiana U East (IN)
Indiana U Kokomo (IN)
Indiana U of Pennsylvania (PA)
Indiana U–Purdue U Fort Wayne (IN)
Indiana U–Purdue U Indianapolis (IN)
Indiana U Southeast (IN)
Indiana Wesleyan U (IN)
Inter American U of PR, San Germán Campus (PR)
Iona Coll (NY)
Jackson State U (MS)
Jacksonville U (FL)
Jamestown Coll (ND)
Jewish Hospital Coll of Nursing and Allied Health (MO)
John Brown U (AR)
Kansas State U (KS)
Kean U (NJ)
Kent State U (OH)
Kentucky State U (KY)
Kentucky Wesleyan Coll (KY)
Keuka Coll (NY)
King Coll (TN)
King's Coll (PA)
Kutztown U of Pennsylvania (PA)
Lake Superior State U (MI)
Lamar U (TX)
Lander U (SC)
Lebanon Valley Coll (PA)
Lee U (TN)
Lenoir-Rhyne Coll (NC)
Lewis U (IL)
Lincoln Memorial U (TN)
Lincoln U (MO)
Lindenwood U (MO)
Lock Haven U of Pennsylvania (PA)
Loma Linda U (CA)
Long Island U, Brooklyn Campus (NY)
Long Island U, C.W. Post Campus (NY)
Longwood Coll (VA)
Louisiana Coll (LA)
Louisiana State U Health Sciences Center (LA)
Louisiana Tech U (LA)
Luther Coll (IA)
Lycoming Coll (PA)
Malone Coll (OH)
Manchester Coll (IN)
Mansfield U of Pennsylvania (PA)
Marian Coll of Fond du Lac (WI)
Marist Coll (NY)
Marshall U (WV)
Mary Baldwin Coll (VA)
Marymount Coll of Fordham U (NY)
Maryville U of Saint Louis (MO)
Marywood U (PA)
Massachusetts Coll of Liberal Arts (MA)
McKendree Coll (IL)
McNeese State U (LA)
Medical Coll of Georgia (GA)
Mercy Coll (NY)
Mercyhurst Coll (PA)
Miami U (OH)
Michigan State U (MI)
Michigan Technological U (MI)
Midwestern State U (TX)
Minnesota State U, Mankato (MN)
Minnesota State U Moorhead (MN)
Minot State U (ND)
Mississippi State U (MS)
Missouri Southern State Coll (MO)
Missouri Western State Coll (MO)
Monmouth U (NJ)
Moravian Coll (PA)
Morehead State U (KY)
Morgan State U (MD)
Morningside Coll (IA)
Mount Marty Coll (SD)
Mount Mercy Coll (IA)
Mount Saint Mary Coll (NY)
Mount Vernon Nazarene U (OH)
Murray State U (KY)
Muskingum Coll (OH)
National-Louis U (IL)
New Mexico Inst of Mining and Technology (NM)
Norfolk State U (VA)
North Dakota State U (ND)
Northeastern State U (OK)
Northern Illinois U (IL)
Northern Michigan U (MI)
Northern State U (SD)
North Park U (IL)
Northwestern Coll (IA)
Northwestern State U of Louisiana (LA)
Northwest Missouri State U (MO)
Notre Dame Coll (OH)
Oakland U (MI)
Oakwood Coll (AL)
Ohio Northern U (OH)
The Ohio State U (OH)
Oklahoma Christian U of Science and Arts (OK)
Oklahoma Panhandle State U (OK)
Oklahoma State U (OK)
Old Dominion U (VA)
Olivet Nazarene U (IL)
Oregon Health & Science U (OR)
Oregon State U (OR)
Our Lady of Holy Cross Coll (LA)
Pace U (NY)
Pacific Union Coll (CA)
Peru State Coll (NE)
Pikeville Coll (KY)
Pittsburg State U (KS)
Plattsburgh State U of NY (NY)
Pontifical Catholic U of Puerto Rico (PR)
Prairie View A&M U (TX)
Purdue U (IN)
Purdue U Calumet (IN)
Quincy U (IL)
Radford U (VA)
Rhode Island Coll (RI)
Roanoke Coll (VA)
Roberts Wesleyan Coll (NY)
Rochester Inst of Technology (NY)
Roosevelt U (IL)
Rush U (IL)
Rutgers, The State U of New Jersey, New Brunswick (NJ)
Saginaw Valley State U (MI)
Saint Augustine's Coll (NC)
St. Bonaventure U (NY)
St. Cloud State U (MN)
St. Francis Coll (NY)
Saint Francis U (PA)
St. John's U (NY)
Saint Joseph Coll (CT)
Saint Joseph's Coll (IN)
Saint Leo U (FL)
Saint Mary-of-the-Woods Coll (IN)
Saint Mary's Coll (IN)
Saint Mary's U of Minnesota (MN)
St. Norbert Coll (WI)
St. Thomas Aquinas Coll (NY)
Salem Coll (NC)
Salem State Coll (MA)
Salisbury U (MD)
Salve Regina U (RI)
Sam Houston State U (TX)
Seattle U (WA)
Seton Hill Coll (PA)
Simpson Coll (IA)
Slippery Rock U of Pennsylvania (PA)
South Dakota State U (SD)
Southeastern Oklahoma State U (OK)
Southeast Missouri State U (MO)
Southern Adventist U (TN)
Southern Arkansas U–Magnolia (AR)
Southern Wesleyan U (SC)
Southwest Baptist U (MO)
Southwestern Adventist U (TX)
Southwestern Oklahoma State U (OK)
Southwest Missouri State U (MO)
Southwest Texas State U (TX)
Springfield Coll (MA)
State U of NY at Albany (NY)
State U of NY Coll at Brockport (NY)
State U of NY Coll at Fredonia (NY)

MEDICAL TOXICOLOGY

MEDICINAL/PHARMACEUTICAL CHEMISTRY

MEDIEVAL/RENAISSANCE STUDIES

MENTAL HEALTH/ REHABILITATION

MENTAL HEALTH SERVICES RELATED

METAL/JEWELRY ARTS

METALLURGICAL ENGINEERING

METALLURGICAL TECHNOLOGY

METALLURGY

MEXICAN-AMERICAN STUDIES

MICROBIOLOGY/ BACTERIOLOGY

MIDDLE EASTERN STUDIES

MIDDLE SCHOOL EDUCATION

MILITARY STUDIES

MILITARY TECHNOLOGY

MINING/MINERAL ENGINEERING

MINING/PETROLEUM TECHNOLOGIES RELATED

MINING TECHNOLOGY

MISSIONARY STUDIES

MODERN LANGUAGES

Beloit Coll (WI)
Bemidji State U (MN)
Benedictine Coll (KS)
Bennington Coll (VT)
Bishop's U (PQ, Canada)
Blue Mountain Coll (MS)
Brooklyn Coll of the City U of NY (NY)
Buena Vista U (IA)
Carleton U (ON, Canada)
Carnegie Mellon U (PA)
Carthage Coll (WI)
Chicago State U (IL)
Claremont McKenna Coll (CA)
Clark U (MA)
Coll of Mount Saint Vincent (NY)
The Coll of New Rochelle (NY)
Coll of Notre Dame of Maryland (MD)
The Coll of William and Mary (VA)
Concordia U (QC, Canada)
Converse Coll (SC)
Cornell Coll (IA)
Cornell U (NY)
Creighton U (NE)
DePaul U (IL)
Dillard U (LA)
Eastern Washington U (WA)
Eckerd Coll (FL)
Elizabethtown Coll (PA)
Elmira Coll (NY)
Fairfield U (CT)
Fordham U (NY)
Fort Lewis Coll (CO)
Framingham State Coll (MA)
Franklin Coll Switzerland(Switzerland)
Gannon U (PA)
Georgia Inst of Technology (GA)
Gettysburg Coll (PA)
Gordon Coll (MA)
Greenville Coll (IL)
Grove City Coll (PA)
Hamilton Coll (NY)
Hampton U (VA)
Harvard U (MA)
Hastings Coll (NE)
Hobart and William Smith Colls (NY)
Howard Payne U (TX)
Immaculata Coll (PA)
Iona Coll (NY)
Judson Coll (AL)
Kenyon Coll (OH)
King Coll (TN)
Lake Erie Coll (OH)
Lambuth U (TN)
La Salle U (PA)
Laurentian U (ON, Canada)
Lee U (TN)
Lenoir-Rhyne Coll (NC)
Lewis & Clark Coll (OR)
Long Island U, Brooklyn Campus (NY)
Long Island U, Southampton Coll, Friends World Program (NY)
Longwood Coll (VA)
Louisiana Coll (LA)
Luther Coll (IA)
Marian Coll of Fond du Lac (WI)
Marlboro Coll (VT)
Marymount Coll of Fordham U (NY)
Mary Washington Coll (VA)
McMaster U (ON, Canada)
Merrimack Coll (MA)
MidAmerica Nazarene U (KS)
Middlebury Coll (VT)
Minnesota State U, Mankato (MN)
Mississippi Coll (MS)
Monmouth Coll (IL)
Mount Allison U (NB, Canada)
Mount Saint Vincent U (NS, Canada)
Nazareth Coll of Rochester (NY)
North Central Coll (IL)
Northeastern U (MA)
North Park U (IL)
Oakland U (MI)
Olivet Nazarene U (IL)
Pace U (NY)
Pacific Lutheran U (WA)
Pacific U (OR)
Pomona Coll (CA)
Presbyterian Coll (SC)
Purchase Coll, State U of NY (NY)
Queens Coll of the City U of NY (NY)
Rivier Coll (NH)
St. Bonaventure U (NY)
Saint Francis U (PA)
St. Francis Xavier U (NS, Canada)
Saint Joseph Coll (CT)
St. Lawrence U (NY)
Saint Mary's Coll of California (CA)
St. Mary's Coll of Maryland (MD)
Saint Mary's U (NS, Canada)
Saint Michael's Coll (VT)
St. Thomas Aquinas Coll (NY)
Sarah Lawrence Coll (NY)
Scripps Coll (CA)
Seton Hill Coll (PA)
Slippery Rock U of Pennsylvania (PA)
Southwestern U (TX)
Stephens Coll (MO)
Suffolk U (MA)
Sweet Briar Coll (VA)
Syracuse U (NY)
Trent U (ON, Canada)
Trinity Coll (CT)
United States Military Academy (NY)
Université de Montréal (QC, Canada)
Université Laval (QC, Canada)
U of Alberta (AB, Canada)
U of Chicago (IL)
The U of Lethbridge (AB, Canada)
U of Louisiana at Lafayette (LA)
U of Maine (ME)
U of Maryland, Baltimore County (MD)
U of Missouri–St. Louis (MO)
U of New Hampshire (NH)
U of Ottawa (ON, Canada)
U of Southern Maine (ME)
U of South Florida (FL)
U of Toronto (ON, Canada)
U of Victoria (BC, Canada)
U of Windsor (ON, Canada)
Ursinus Coll (PA)
Virginia Military Inst (VA)
Walla Walla Coll (WA)
Walsh U (OH)
Washington U in St. Louis (MO)
Wayne State Coll (NE)
West Chester U of Pennsylvania (PA)
Westminster Coll (PA)
Westmont Coll (CA)
Widener U (PA)
William Carey Coll (MS)
Wilmington Coll (OH)
Winthrop U (SC)
Wittenberg U (OH)
Wright State U (OH)
York U (ON, Canada)

MOLECULAR BIOLOGY
Arizona State U (AZ)
Assumption Coll (MA)
Auburn U (AL)
Ball State U (IN)
Bard Coll (NY)
Beloit Coll (WI)
Benedictine U (IL)
Bethel Coll (MN)
Boston U (MA)
Bradley U (IL)
Bridgewater State Coll (MA)
Brigham Young U (UT)
Brown U (RI)
California Inst of Technology (CA)
California Lutheran U (CA)
California State U, Fresno (CA)
California State U, Northridge (CA)
California State U, San Marcos (CA)
Cedar Crest Coll (PA)
Centre Coll (KY)
Chestnut Hill Coll (PA)
Clarion U of Pennsylvania (PA)
Clarkson U (NY)
Clark U (MA)
Coe Coll (IA)
Colby Coll (ME)
Colgate U (NY)
The Coll of Southeastern Europe, The American U of Athens(Greece)
Concordia U (QC, Canada)
Cornell U (NY)
Dartmouth Coll (NH)
Dickinson Coll (PA)
Elms Coll (MA)
The Evergreen State Coll (WA)
Florida A&M U (FL)
Florida Inst of Technology (FL)
Fort Lewis Coll (CO)
Grove City Coll (PA)
Hamilton Coll (NY)
Hampshire Coll (MA)
Hampton U (VA)
Harvard U (MA)
Humboldt State U (CA)
Juniata Coll (PA)
Kenyon Coll (OH)
Lehigh U (PA)
Long Island U, Brooklyn Campus (NY)
Long Island U, C.W. Post Campus (NY)
Marlboro Coll (VT)
Marquette U (WI)
McGill U (PQ, Canada)
McMaster U (ON, Canada)
Meredith Coll (NC)
Middlebury Coll (VT)
Montclair State U (NJ)
Muskingum Coll (OH)
Northwestern U (IL)
Ohio Northern U (OH)
Otterbein Coll (OH)
Penn State U Univ Park Campus (PA)
Pomona Coll (CA)
Princeton U (NJ)
Rutgers, The State U of New Jersey, New Brunswick (NJ)
Salem International U (WV)
San Francisco State U (CA)
San Jose State U (CA)
Scripps Coll (CA)
Southwest Missouri State U (MO)
State U of NY at Albany (NY)
State U of NY Coll at Brockport (NY)
Stetson U (FL)
Texas A&M U (TX)
Texas Lutheran U (TX)
Texas Tech U (TX)
Towson U (MD)
Tulane U (LA)
U Coll of the Cariboo (BC, Canada)
U of Alberta (AB, Canada)
U of Calgary (AB, Canada)
U of Calif, Berkeley (CA)
U of Calif, Los Angeles (CA)
U of Calif, San Diego (CA)
U of Calif, Santa Barbara (CA)
U of Calif, Santa Cruz (CA)
U of Colorado at Boulder (CO)
U of Denver (CO)
U of Guelph (ON, Canada)
U of Idaho (ID)
U of Maine (ME)
The U of Memphis (TN)
U of Michigan (MI)
U of Minnesota, Duluth (MN)
U of New Hampshire (NH)
U of Pittsburgh (PA)
U of Richmond (VA)
U of Southern California (CA)
The U of Texas at Austin (TX)
U of Toronto (ON, Canada)
U of Vermont (VT)
U of Washington (WA)
U of Wisconsin–Madison (WI)
U of Wisconsin–Parkside (WI)
U of Wisconsin–Superior (WI)
U of Wyoming (WY)
Vanderbilt U (TN)
Wells Coll (NY)
Wesleyan U (CT)
West Chester U of Pennsylvania (PA)
Western State Coll of Colorado (CO)
Western Washington U (WA)
Westminster Coll (PA)
Whitman Coll (WA)
William Jewell Coll (MO)
Winston-Salem State U (NC)
Worcester Polytechnic Inst (MA)
Yale U (CT)
York U (ON, Canada)

MORTUARY SCIENCE
Cincinnati Coll of Mortuary Science (OH)
Gannon U (PA)
Lindenwood U (MO)
Mount Ida Coll (MA)
Point Park Coll (PA)
St. John's U (NY)
Southern Illinois U Carbondale (IL)
Thiel Coll (PA)
U of Central Oklahoma (OK)
U of Minnesota, Twin Cities Campus (MN)
U of the District of Columbia (DC)
Wayne State U (MI)

MOVEMENT THERAPY
Brock U (ON, Canada)

MULTI/INTERDISCIPLINARY STUDIES RELATED
Allegheny Coll (PA)
Austin Coll (TX)
Brandeis U (MA)
Caldwell Coll (NJ)
Coll of Saint Elizabeth (NJ)
Dartmouth Coll (NH)
Davidson Coll (NC)
Eastern Illinois U (IL)
Eastern Mennonite U (VA)
Eastern New Mexico U (NM)
East Tennessee State U (TN)
Fairleigh Dickinson U, Teaneck-Hackensack Campus (NJ)
Grace Bible Coll (MI)
Huntingdon Coll (AL)
Kent State U (OH)
Louisiana State U and A&M Coll (LA)
Marshall U (WV)
Massachusetts Coll of Liberal Arts (MA)
Mercer U (GA)
Mississippi State U (MS)
Missouri Baptist Coll (MO)
Mount St. Clare Coll (IA)
New York Inst of Technology (NY)
Norfolk State U (VA)
Nova Southeastern U (FL)
Ohio Wesleyan U (OH)
Old Dominion U (VA)
Otterbein Coll (OH)
Penn State U at Erie, The Behrend Coll (PA)
Penn State U Berks Cmps of Berks-Lehigh Valley Coll (PA)
Plymouth State Coll (NH)
Princeton U (NJ)
Rice U (TX)
St. Olaf Coll (MN)
San Diego State U (CA)
Shippensburg U of Pennsylvania (PA)
Sonoma State U (CA)
Southwest Texas State U (TX)
State U of NY Coll at Potsdam (NY)
Stephen F. Austin State U (TX)
Stonehill Coll (MA)
Texas Wesleyan U (TX)
U of Alaska Fairbanks (AK)
The U of Arizona (AZ)
U of Arkansas (AR)
U of Colorado at Boulder (CO)
U of Connecticut (CT)
U of Hawaii at Manoa (HI)
U of Idaho (ID)
U of Kentucky (KY)
U of Maryland University Coll (MD)
U of Pennsylvania (PA)
The U of Tennessee (TN)
The U of the Arts (PA)
U of Toledo (OH)
U of Wyoming (WY)
Ursuline Coll (OH)
Utah State U (UT)
Washington U in St. Louis (MO)
Western Kentucky U (KY)
West Texas A&M U (TX)
West Virginia U Inst of Technology (WV)
Wheaton Coll (IL)
Wilkes U (PA)
Yale U (CT)

MULTIMEDIA
American U (DC)
The Art Inst of Philadelphia (PA)
The Art Inst of Portland (OR)
The Art Inst of Washington (VA)
The Art Insts International Minnesota (MN)
Augusta State U (GA)
Champlain Coll (VT)
Columbia Coll Chicago (IL)
Columbus Coll of Art and Design (OH)
Eastern U (PA)
Emerson Coll (MA)
Indiana U of Pennsylvania (PA)
Long Island U, C.W. Post Campus (NY)
Maharishi U of Management (IA)
Maryland Inst, Coll of Art (MD)
Massachusetts Coll of Art (MA)
McMaster U (ON, Canada)
Minneapolis Coll of Art and Design (MN)
Platt Coll (CO)
State U of NY Coll at Fredonia (NY)
U of Calif, San Diego (CA)
U of Central Florida (FL)
U of Massachusetts Dartmouth (MA)
U of Michigan (MI)
U of Windsor (ON, Canada)

MUSEUM STUDIES
Baylor U (TX)
Beloit Coll (WI)
Coll of the Atlantic (ME)
Framingham State Coll (MA)
Jewish Theological Seminary of America (NY)
Juniata Coll (PA)
Long Island U, Southampton Coll, Friends World Program (NY)
Luther Coll (IA)
Oklahoma Baptist U (OK)
Randolph-Macon Woman's Coll (VA)
Regis Coll (MA)
Tusculum Coll (TN)
The U of Iowa (IA)
The U of North Carolina at Greensboro (NC)
U of Southern Mississippi (MS)

MUSIC
Abilene Christian U (TX)
Acadia U (NS, Canada)
Adams State Coll (CO)
Adelphi U (NY)
Adrian Coll (MI)
Agnes Scott Coll (GA)
Alabama State U (AL)
Albany State U (GA)
Albertson Coll of Idaho (ID)
Albion Coll (MI)
Albright Coll (PA)
Alderson-Broaddus Coll (WV)
Allegheny Coll (PA)
Alma Coll (MI)
Alverno Coll (WI)
American U (DC)
Amherst Coll (MA)
Anderson Coll (SC)
Andrews U (MI)
Angelo State U (TX)
Anna Maria Coll (MA)
Appalachian State U (NC)
Aquinas Coll (MI)
Arizona State U (AZ)
Arkansas State U (AR)
Arkansas Tech U (AR)
Arlington Baptist Coll (TX)
Armstrong Atlantic State U (GA)
Asbury Coll (KY)
Ashland U (OH)
Atlanta Christian Coll (GA)
Atlantic Union Coll (MA)
Augsburg Coll (MN)
Augustana Coll (IL)
Augustana Coll (SD)
Augusta State U (GA)
Austin Coll (TX)
Austin Peay State U (TN)
Averett U (VA)
Avila Coll (MO)
Azusa Pacific U (CA)
Baker U (KS)
Baldwin-Wallace Coll (OH)
Ball State U (IN)
Baptist Bible Coll (MO)
Baptist Bible Coll of Pennsylvania (PA)
Bard Coll (NY)
Barnard Coll (NY)
Bates Coll (ME)
Baylor U (TX)
Belhaven Coll (MS)
Bellarmine U (KY)
Belmont U (TN)
Beloit Coll (WI)
Bemidji State U (MN)
Benedict Coll (SC)

Benedictine Coll (KS)
Benedictine U (IL)
Bennett Coll (NC)
Bennington Coll (VT)
Berea Coll (KY)
Berklee Coll of Music (MA)
Baruch Coll of the City U of NY (NY)
Berry Coll (GA)
Bethany Coll (KS)
Bethany Coll (WV)
Bethany Lutheran Coll (MN)
Bethel Coll (IN)
Bethel Coll (KS)
Bethel Coll (MN)
Bethune-Cookman Coll (FL)
Biola U (CA)
Birmingham-Southern Coll (AL)
Bishop's U (PQ, Canada)
Blackburn Coll (IL)
Black Hills State U (SD)
Bloomsburg U of Pennsylvania (PA)
Bluefield Coll (VA)
Blue Mountain Coll (MS)
Bluffton Coll (OH)
Boise State U (ID)
Boston Coll (MA)
The Boston Conservatory (MA)
Bowdoin Coll (ME)
Bowling Green State U (OH)
Bradley U (IL)
Brandeis U (MA)
Brandon U (MB, Canada)
Brenau U (GA)
Brevard Coll (NC)
Brewton-Parker Coll (GA)
Briar Cliff U (IA)
Bridgewater Coll (VA)
Bridgewater State Coll (MA)
Briercrest Bible Coll (SK, Canada)
Brigham Young U (UT)
Brigham Young U–Hawaii (HI)
Brock U (ON, Canada)
Brooklyn Coll of the City U of NY (NY)
Brown U (RI)
Bryan Coll (TN)
Bryn Mawr Coll (PA)
Bucknell U (PA)
Buena Vista U (IA)
Butler U (IN)
Caldwell Coll (NJ)
California Baptist U (CA)
California Inst of the Arts (CA)
California Lutheran U (CA)
California Polytechnic State U, San Luis Obispo (CA)
California State Polytechnic U, Pomona (CA)
California State U, Bakersfield (CA)
California State U, Chico (CA)
California State U, Dominguez Hills (CA)
California State U, Fresno (CA)
California State U, Fullerton (CA)
California State U, Hayward (CA)
California State U, Long Beach (CA)
California State U, Los Angeles (CA)
California State U, Northridge (CA)
California State U, Sacramento (CA)
California State U, San Bernardino (CA)
California State U, Stanislaus (CA)
Calvary Bible Coll and Theological Seminary (MO)
Calvin Coll (MI)
Cameron U (OK)
Campbellsville U (KY)
Campbell U (NC)
Capital U (OH)
Cardinal Stritch U (WI)
Carleton Coll (MN)
Carleton U (ON, Canada)
Carnegie Mellon U (PA)
Carroll Coll (WI)
Carson-Newman Coll (TN)
Carthage Coll (WI)
Case Western Reserve U (OH)
Castleton State Coll (VT)
Catawba Coll (NC)
The Catholic U of America (DC)
Cedar Crest Coll (PA)
Cedarville U (OH)
Centenary Coll of Louisiana (LA)
Central Christian Coll of the Bible (MO)
Central Coll (IA)
Central Connecticut State U (CT)
Central Methodist Coll (MO)
Central Michigan U (MI)
Central Missouri State U (MO)
Central State U (OH)
Central Washington U (WA)
Centre Coll (KY)
Chadron State Coll (NE)
Chapman U (CA)
Charleston Southern U (SC)
Chatham Coll (PA)
Chestnut Hill Coll (PA)
Cheyney U of Pennsylvania (PA)
Chicago State U (IL)
Chowan Coll (NC)
Christian Heritage Coll (CA)
Christopher Newport U (VA)
City Coll of the City U of NY (NY)
Claflin U (SC)
Claremont McKenna Coll (CA)
Clark Atlanta U (GA)
Clarke Coll (IA)
Clark U (MA)
Clayton Coll & State U (GA)
Clearwater Christian Coll (FL)
Cleveland Inst of Music (OH)
Cleveland State U (OH)
Coastal Carolina U (SC)
Coe Coll (IA)
Coker Coll (SC)
Colby Coll (ME)
Colgate U (NY)
Coll of Charleston (SC)
Coll of Mount St. Joseph (OH)
The Coll of New Jersey (NJ)
Coll of Notre Dame of Maryland (MD)
Coll of Saint Benedict (MN)
Coll of St. Catherine (MN)
Coll of Saint Elizabeth (NJ)
The Coll of Saint Rose (NY)
The Coll of St. Scholastica (MN)
Coll of Santa Fe (NM)
Coll of Staten Island of the City U of NY (NY)
Coll of the Atlantic (ME)
Coll of the Holy Cross (MA)
Coll of the Ozarks (MO)
The Coll of William and Mary (VA)
The Coll of Wooster (OH)
Colorado Christian U (CO)
The Colorado Coll (CO)
Colorado State U (CO)
Columbia Coll (NY)
Columbia Coll (SC)
Columbia Coll Chicago (IL)
Columbia International U (SC)
Columbia Union Coll (MD)
Columbia U, School of General Studies (NY)
Columbus State U (GA)
Concordia Coll (MN)
Concordia Coll (NY)
Concordia U (CA)
Concordia U (IL)
Concordia U (MI)
Concordia U (MN)
Concordia U (NE)
Concordia U (QC, Canada)
Concordia U Wisconsin (WI)
Connecticut Coll (CT)
Converse Coll (SC)
Cornell Coll (IA)
Cornell U (NY)
Cornerstone U (MI)
Cornish Coll of the Arts (WA)
Covenant Coll (GA)
Creighton U (NE)
Crown Coll (MN)
Culver-Stockton Coll (MO)
Cumberland Coll (KY)
Cumberland U (TN)
The Curtis Inst of Music (PA)
Dalhousie U (NS, Canada)
Dallas Baptist U (TX)
Dana Coll (NE)
Dartmouth Coll (NH)
Davidson Coll (NC)
Davis & Elkins Coll (WV)
Delaware State U (DE)
Delta State U (MS)
Denison U (OH)
DePaul U (IL)
DePauw U (IN)
Dickinson Coll (PA)
Dickinson State U (ND)
Dillard U (LA)
Doane Coll (NE)
Dominican U of California (CA)
Dordt Coll (IA)
Dowling Coll (NY)
Drake U (IA)
Drew U (NJ)
Drexel U (PA)
Drury U (MO)
Duke U (NC)
Earlham Coll (IN)
East Central U (OK)
Eastern Illinois U (IL)
Eastern Kentucky U (KY)
Eastern Mennonite U (VA)
Eastern Michigan U (MI)
Eastern Nazarene Coll (MA)
Eastern New Mexico U (NM)
Eastern Oregon U (OR)
Eastern U (PA)
Eastern Washington U (WA)
East Tennessee State U (TN)
East Texas Baptist U (TX)
Eckerd Coll (FL)
Edgewood Coll (WI)
Edinboro U of Pennsylvania (PA)
Elizabeth City State U (NC)
Elizabethtown Coll (PA)
Elmhurst Coll (IL)
Elmira Coll (NY)
Elon U (NC)
Emmanuel Coll (GA)
Emory & Henry Coll (VA)
Emory U (GA)
Emporia State U (KS)
Erskine Coll (SC)
Eureka Coll (IL)
Evangel U (MO)
The Evergreen State Coll (WA)
Excelsior Coll (NY)
Fayetteville State U (NC)
Fisk U (TN)
Five Towns Coll (NY)
Florida A&M U (FL)
Florida Atlantic U (FL)
Florida International U (FL)
Florida Southern Coll (FL)
Florida State U (FL)
Fordham U (NY)
Fort Hays State U (KS)
Fort Lewis Coll (CO)
Franklin and Marshall Coll (PA)
Franklin Pierce Coll (NH)
Freed-Hardeman U (TN)
Fresno Pacific U (CA)
Friends U (KS)
Frostburg State U (MD)
Furman U (SC)
Gardner-Webb U (NC)
Geneva Coll (PA)
George Fox U (OR)
Georgetown Coll (KY)
The George Washington U (DC)
Georgia Coll and State U (GA)
Georgian Court Coll (NJ)
Georgia Southern U (GA)
Georgia Southwestern State U (GA)
Gettysburg Coll (PA)
Goddard Coll (VT)
Gonzaga U (WA)
Gordon Coll (MA)
Goshen Coll (IN)
Goucher Coll (MD)
Grace Bible Coll (MI)
Graceland U (IA)
Grace U (NE)
Grand Canyon U (AZ)
Grand Valley State U (MI)
Great Lakes Christian Coll (MI)
Greensboro Coll (NC)
Greenville Coll (IL)
Grinnell Coll (IA)
Guilford Coll (NC)
Gustavus Adolphus Coll (MN)
Hamilton Coll (NY)
Hamline U (MN)
Hampshire Coll (MA)
Hampton U (VA)
Hannibal-LaGrange Coll (MO)
Hanover Coll (IN)
Harding U (AR)
Hardin-Simmons U (TX)
Hartwick Coll (NY)
Harvard U (MA)
Hastings Coll (NE)
Haverford Coll (PA)
Heidelberg Coll (OH)
Henderson State U (AR)
Hendrix Coll (AR)
Hillsdale Coll (MI)
Hiram Coll (OH)
Hobart and William Smith Colls (NY)
Hofstra U (NY)
Hollins U (VA)
Holy Names Coll (CA)
Hood Coll (MD)
Hope Coll (MI)
Houghton Coll (NY)
Houston Baptist U (TX)
Howard Payne U (TX)
Howard U (DC)
Humboldt State U (CA)
Hunter Coll of the City U of NY (NY)
Huntingdon Coll (AL)
Huntington Coll (IN)
Huston-Tillotson Coll (TX)
Idaho State U (ID)
Illinois Coll (IL)
Illinois State U (IL)
Illinois Wesleyan U (IL)
Immaculata Coll (PA)
Indiana State U (IN)
Indiana U Bloomington (IN)
Indiana U of Pennsylvania (PA)
Indiana U–Purdue U Fort Wayne (IN)
Indiana U Southeast (IN)
Indiana Wesleyan U (IN)
Inter American U of PR, San Germán Campus (PR)
Iowa State U of Science and Technology (IA)
Iowa Wesleyan Coll (IA)
Ithaca Coll (NY)
Jacksonville State U (AL)
Jacksonville U (FL)
Jamestown Coll (ND)
Jarvis Christian Coll (TX)
Jewish Theological Seminary of America (NY)
John Brown U (AR)
Johns Hopkins U (MD)
Johnson State Coll (VT)
Judson Coll (AL)
Judson Coll (IL)
The Juilliard School (NY)
Kalamazoo Coll (MI)
Kansas State U (KS)
Kean U (NJ)
Keene State Coll (NH)
Kennesaw State U (GA)
Kent State U (OH)
Kentucky Christian Coll (KY)
Kenyon Coll (OH)
King Coll (TN)
The King's U Coll (AB, Canada)
Knox Coll (IL)
Kutztown U of Pennsylvania (PA)
Lafayette Coll (PA)
LaGrange Coll (GA)
Lake Erie Coll (OH)
Lake Forest Coll (IL)
Lakehead U (ON, Canada)
Lakeland Coll (WI)
Lamar U (TX)
Lambuth U (TN)
Lander U (SC)
La Salle U (PA)
Laurentian U (ON, Canada)
Lawrence U (WI)
Lebanon Valley Coll (PA)
Lee U (TN)
Lehigh U (PA)
Lehman Coll of the City U of NY (NY)
Lenoir-Rhyne Coll (NC)
Lewis & Clark Coll (OR)
Lewis U (IL)
Liberty U (VA)
Limestone Coll (SC)
Lincoln U (PA)
Lindenwood U (MO)
Linfield Coll (OR)
Lipscomb U (TN)
Lock Haven U of Pennsylvania (PA)
Long Island U, Brooklyn Campus (NY)
Long Island U, C.W. Post Campus (NY)
Long Island U, Southampton Coll, Friends World Program (NY)
Longwood Coll (VA)
Loras Coll (IA)
Louisiana Coll (LA)
Louisiana State U and A&M Coll (LA)
Louisiana Tech U (LA)
Loyola Marymount U (CA)
Loyola U Chicago (IL)
Loyola U New Orleans (LA)
Lubbock Christian U (TX)
Luther Coll (IA)
Lycoming Coll (PA)
Lynchburg Coll (VA)
Lynn U (FL)
Lyon Coll (AR)
Macalester Coll (MN)
MacMurray Coll (IL)
Malone Coll (OH)
Manchester Coll (IN)
Manhattan School of Music (NY)
Manhattanville Coll (NY)
Mannes Coll of Music, New School U (NY)
Mansfield U of Pennsylvania (PA)
Maranatha Baptist Bible Coll (WI)
Marian Coll (IN)
Marian Coll of Fond du Lac (WI)
Marietta Coll (OH)
Marlboro Coll (VT)
Mars Hill Coll (NC)
Mary Baldwin Coll (VA)
Marygrove Coll (MI)
Marylhurst U (OR)
Maryville Coll (TN)
Maryville U of Saint Louis (MO)
Mary Washington Coll (VA)
Marywood U (PA)
Massachusetts Coll of Liberal Arts (MA)
Massachusetts Inst of Technology (MA)
The Master's Coll and Seminary (CA)
McGill U (PQ, Canada)
McKendree Coll (IL)
McMaster U (ON, Canada)
McMurry U (TX)
McNeese State U (LA)
McPherson Coll (KS)
Memorial U of Newfoundland (NF, Canada)
Mercer U (GA)
Mercy Coll (NY)
Mercyhurst Coll (PA)
Meredith Coll (NC)
Mesa State Coll (CO)
Messiah Coll (PA)
Methodist Coll (NC)
Miami U (OH)
MidAmerica Nazarene U (KS)
Middlebury Coll (VT)
Middle Tennessee State U (TN)
Midland Lutheran Coll (NE)
Midwestern State U (TX)
Millersville U of Pennsylvania (PA)
Milligan Coll (TN)
Millikin U (IL)
Millsaps Coll (MS)
Mills Coll (CA)
Minnesota State U, Mankato (MN)
Minnesota State U Moorhead (MN)
Minot State U (ND)
Mississippi Coll (MS)
Mississippi Valley State U (MS)
Missouri Southern State Coll (MO)
Missouri Western State Coll (MO)
Molloy Coll (NY)
Monmouth Coll (IL)
Monmouth U (NJ)
Montana State U–Billings (MT)
Montana State U–Bozeman (MT)
Montclair State U (NJ)
Montreat Coll (NC)
Moravian Coll (PA)
Morehead State U (KY)
Morehouse Coll (GA)
Morgan State U (MD)
Morningside Coll (IA)
Morris Brown Coll (GA)
Mount Allison U (NB, Canada)
Mount Holyoke Coll (MA)
Mount Marty Coll (SD)
Mount Mary Coll (WI)
Mount Mercy Coll (IA)
Mount St. Clare Coll (IA)
Mount St. Mary's Coll (CA)
Mount Union Coll (OH)
Mount Vernon Nazarene U (OH)
Muhlenberg Coll (PA)
Multnomah Bible Coll and Biblical Seminary (OR)
Murray State U (KY)

Muskingum Coll (OH)
Naropa U (CO)
Nazareth Coll of Rochester (NY)
Nebraska Wesleyan U (NE)
Newberry Coll (SC)
New Coll of Florida (FL)
New Jersey City U (NJ)
New Mexico Highlands U (NM)
New Mexico State U (NM)
New World School of the Arts (FL)
New York U (NY)
Nicholls State U (LA)
Norfolk State U (VA)
North American Baptist Coll & Edmonton Baptist Sem (AB, Canada)
North Carolina Central U (NC)
North Carolina School of the Arts (NC)
North Central Coll (IL)
North Dakota State U (ND)
Northeastern Illinois U (IL)
Northeastern State U (OK)
Northeastern U (MA)
Northern Arizona U (AZ)
Northern Illinois U (IL)
Northern Kentucky U (KY)
Northern Michigan U (MI)
Northern State U (SD)
North Georgia Coll & State U (GA)
North Greenville Coll (SC)
Northland Coll (WI)
North Park U (IL)
Northwest Christian Coll (OR)
Northwest Coll (WA)
Northwestern Coll (IA)
Northwestern Coll (MN)
Northwestern Oklahoma State U (OK)
Northwestern State U of Louisiana (LA)
Northwestern U (IL)
Northwest Missouri State U (MO)
Northwest Nazarene U (ID)
Notre Dame de Namur U (CA)
Nyack Coll (NY)
Oak Hills Christian Coll (MN)
Oakland City U (IN)
Oakland U (MI)
Oakwood Coll (AL)
Oberlin Coll (OH)
Occidental Coll (CA)
Ohio Northern U (OH)
The Ohio State U (OH)
Ohio U (OH)
Ohio Wesleyan U (OH)
Oklahoma Baptist U (OK)
Oklahoma Christian U of Science and Arts (OK)
Oklahoma City U (OK)
Oklahoma State U (OK)
Oklahoma Wesleyan U (OK)
Olivet Nazarene U (IL)
Oral Roberts U (OK)
Oregon State U (OR)
Ottawa U (KS)
Otterbein Coll (OH)
Ouachita Baptist U (AR)
Pacific Lutheran U (WA)
Pacific Union Coll (CA)
Pacific U (OR)
Palm Beach Atlantic Coll (FL)
Peabody Conserv of Music of Johns Hopkins U (MD)
Penn State U Univ Park Campus (PA)
Pepperdine U, Malibu (CA)
Peru State Coll (NE)
Pfeiffer U (NC)
Philadelphia Biblical U (PA)
Philander Smith Coll (AR)
Piedmont Coll (GA)
Pillsbury Baptist Bible Coll (MN)
Pittsburg State U (KS)
Plattsburgh State U of NY (NY)
Plymouth State Coll (NH)
Point Loma Nazarene U (CA)
Pomona Coll (CA)
Pontifical Catholic U of Puerto Rico (PR)
Portland State U (OR)
Prairie Bible Coll (AB, Canada)
Prairie View A&M U (TX)
Presbyterian Coll (SC)
Princeton U (NJ)
Principia Coll (IL)
Providence Coll (RI)
Providence Coll and Theological Seminary (MB, Canada)
Puget Sound Christian Coll (WA)
Purchase Coll, State U of NY (NY)
Queens Coll (NC)
Queens Coll of the City U of NY (NY)
Queen's U at Kingston (ON, Canada)
Quincy U (IL)
Radford U (VA)
Randolph-Macon Coll (VA)
Randolph-Macon Woman's Coll (VA)
Redeemer U Coll (ON, Canada)
Reed Coll (OR)
Rhode Island Coll (RI)
Rhodes Coll (TN)
Rice U (TX)
Rider U (NJ)
Ripon Coll (WI)
Roanoke Coll (VA)
Roberts Wesleyan Coll (NY)
Rochester Coll (MI)
Rocky Mountain Coll (MT)
Rocky Mountain Coll (AB, Canada)
Rollins Coll (FL)
Roosevelt U (IL)
Rowan U (NJ)
Rust Coll (MS)
Rutgers, The State U of New Jersey, New Brunswick (NJ)
Saginaw Valley State U (MI)
St. Ambrose U (IA)
St. Cloud State U (MN)
St. Francis Xavier U (NS, Canada)
Saint John's U (MN)
Saint Joseph's Coll (IN)
St. Lawrence U (NY)
Saint Louis U (MO)
Saint Mary-of-the-Woods Coll (IN)
Saint Mary's Coll (IN)
Saint Mary's Coll of California (CA)
St. Mary's Coll of Maryland (MD)
Saint Mary's U of Minnesota (MN)
St. Mary's U of San Antonio (TX)
Saint Michael's Coll (VT)
St. Norbert Coll (WI)
St. Olaf Coll (MN)
Saint Vincent Coll (PA)
Saint Xavier U (IL)
Salem Coll (NC)
Salisbury U (MD)
Salve Regina U (RI)
Sam Houston State U (TX)
San Diego State U (CA)
San Francisco Conservatory of Music (CA)
San Francisco State U (CA)
San Jose Christian Coll (CA)
San Jose State U (CA)
Santa Clara U (CA)
Sarah Lawrence Coll (NY)
Savannah State U (GA)
Scripps Coll (CA)
Seattle Pacific U (WA)
Seton Hall U (NJ)
Seton Hill Coll (PA)
Shaw U (NC)
Shenandoah U (VA)
Shepherd Coll (WV)
Shorter Coll (GA)
Siena Heights U (MI)
Sierra Nevada Coll (NV)
Silver Lake Coll (WI)
Simmons Coll (MA)
Simon Fraser U (BC, Canada)
Simon's Rock Coll of Bard (MA)
Simpson Coll (IA)
Simpson Coll and Graduate School (CA)
Slippery Rock U of Pennsylvania (PA)
Smith Coll (MA)
Sonoma State U (CA)
South Dakota State U (SD)
Southeastern Bible Coll (AL)
Southeastern Oklahoma State U (OK)
Southeast Missouri State U (MO)
Southern Adventist U (TN)
Southern Illinois U Carbondale (IL)
Southern Illinois U Edwardsville (IL)
Southern Methodist U (TX)
Southern Oregon U (OR)
Southern Utah U (UT)
Southern Virginia U (VA)
Southern Wesleyan U (SC)
Southwest Baptist U (MO)
Southwestern Adventist U (TX)
Southwestern Assemblies of God U (TX)
Southwestern Coll (KS)
Southwestern Oklahoma State U (OK)
Southwestern U (TX)
Southwest Missouri State U (MO)
Southwest State U (MN)
Southwest Texas State U (TX)
Spelman Coll (GA)
Spring Arbor U (MI)
Stanford U (CA)
State U of NY at Albany (NY)
State U of NY at Binghamton (NY)
State U of NY at New Paltz (NY)
State U of NY at Oswego (NY)
State U of NY Coll at Buffalo (NY)
State U of NY Coll at Fredonia (NY)
State U of NY Coll at Geneseo (NY)
State U of NY Coll at Oneonta (NY)
State U of NY Coll at Potsdam (NY)
Steinbach Bible Coll (MB, Canada)
Stephen F. Austin State U (TX)
Sterling Coll (KS)
Stetson U (FL)
State U of NY at Stony Brook (NY)
Sul Ross State U (TX)
Susquehanna U (PA)
Swarthmore Coll (PA)
Sweet Briar Coll (VA)
Syracuse U (NY)
Tabor Coll (KS)
Talladega Coll (AL)
Tarleton State U (TX)
Taylor U (IN)
Taylor U, Fort Wayne Campus (IN)
Temple U (PA)
Tennessee State U (TN)
Tennessee Technological U (TN)
Tennessee Temple U (TN)
Tennessee Wesleyan Coll (TN)
Texas A&M U (TX)
Texas A&M U–Commerce (TX)
Texas A&M U–Corpus Christi (TX)
Texas A&M U–Kingsville (TX)
Texas Christian U (TX)
Texas Coll (TX)
Texas Lutheran U (TX)
Texas Southern U (TX)
Texas Tech U (TX)
Texas Wesleyan U (TX)
Texas Woman's U (TX)
Thomas Edison State Coll (NJ)
Thomas U (GA)
Toccoa Falls Coll (GA)
Tougaloo Coll (MS)
Towson U (MD)
Trevecca Nazarene U (TN)
Trinity Bible Coll (ND)
Trinity Christian Coll (IL)
Trinity Coll (CT)
Trinity Coll of Florida (FL)
Trinity International U (IL)
Trinity U (TX)
Trinity Western U (BC, Canada)
Truman State U (MO)
Tufts U (MA)
Tulane U (LA)
Union Coll (KY)
Union Coll (NE)
Union U (TN)
Universidad Adventista de las Antillas (PR)
Université de Montréal (QC, Canada)
Université de Sherbrooke (PQ, Canada)
Université Laval (QC, Canada)
State U of NY at Buffalo (NY)
The U of Akron (OH)
The U of Alabama (AL)
The U of Alabama at Birmingham (AL)
The U of Alabama in Huntsville (AL)
U of Alaska Anchorage (AK)
U of Alaska Fairbanks (AK)
U of Alberta (AB, Canada)
The U of Arizona (AZ)
U of Arkansas at Little Rock (AR)
U of Arkansas at Pine Bluff (AR)
U of Bridgeport (CT)
The U of British Columbia (BC, Canada)
U of Calgary (AB, Canada)
U of Calif, Berkeley (CA)
U of Calif, Davis (CA)
U of Calif, Irvine (CA)
U of Calif, Los Angeles (CA)
U of Calif, Riverside (CA)
U of Calif, San Diego (CA)
U of Calif, Santa Barbara (CA)
U of Calif, Santa Cruz (CA)
U of Central Arkansas (AR)
U of Central Oklahoma (OK)
U of Charleston (WV)
U of Chicago (IL)
U of Cincinnati (OH)
U of Colorado at Boulder (CO)
U of Colorado at Denver (CO)
U of Connecticut (CT)
U of Dayton (OH)
U of Delaware (DE)
U of Denver (CO)
U of Evansville (IN)
U of Florida (FL)
U of Georgia (GA)
U of Guelph (ON, Canada)
U of Hartford (CT)
U of Hawaii at Hilo (HI)
U of Hawaii at Manoa (HI)
U of Houston (TX)
U of Illinois at Chicago (IL)
U of Illinois at Urbana–Champaign (IL)
U of Indianapolis (IN)
The U of Iowa (IA)
U of Kansas (KS)
U of La Verne (CA)
The U of Lethbridge (AB, Canada)
U of Louisiana at Monroe (LA)
U of Louisville (KY)
U of Maine (ME)
U of Maine at Farmington (ME)
U of Manitoba (MB, Canada)
U of Mary (ND)
U of Maryland, Baltimore County (MD)
U of Maryland, Coll Park (MD)
U of Massachusetts Amherst (MA)
U of Massachusetts Boston (MA)
U of Massachusetts Dartmouth (MA)
The U of Memphis (TN)
U of Miami (FL)
U of Michigan (MI)
U of Michigan–Dearborn (MI)
U of Michigan–Flint (MI)
U of Minnesota, Duluth (MN)
U of Minnesota, Morris (MN)
U of Minnesota, Twin Cities Campus (MN)
U of Mississippi (MS)
U of Missouri–Columbia (MO)
U of Missouri–Kansas City (MO)
U of Missouri–St. Louis (MO)
U of Mobile (AL)
The U of Montana–Missoula (MT)
Western Montana Coll of The U of Montana (MT)
U of Montevallo (AL)
U of Nebraska at Kearney (NE)
U of Nebraska at Omaha (NE)
U of Nebraska–Lincoln (NE)
U of Nevada, Las Vegas (NV)
U of Nevada, Reno (NV)
U of New Hampshire (NH)
U of New Haven (CT)
U of New Orleans (LA)
U of North Alabama (AL)
The U of North Carolina at Asheville (NC)
The U of North Carolina at Chapel Hill (NC)
The U of North Carolina at Pembroke (NC)
The U of North Carolina at Wilmington (NC)
U of North Dakota (ND)
U of Northern Colorado (CO)
U of Northern Iowa (IA)
U of North Florida (FL)
U of North Texas (TX)
U of Notre Dame (IN)
U of Oklahoma (OK)
U of Oregon (OR)
U of Ottawa (ON, Canada)
U of Pennsylvania (PA)
U of Pittsburgh (PA)
U of Portland (OR)
U of Prince Edward Island (PE, Canada)
U of Puget Sound (WA)
U of Redlands (CA)
U of Regina (SK, Canada)
U of Rhode Island (RI)
U of Richmond (VA)
U of Rio Grande (OH)
U of Rochester (NY)
U of St. Thomas (MN)
U of St. Thomas (TX)
U of San Diego (CA)
U of Saskatchewan (SK, Canada)
U of Science and Arts of Oklahoma (OK)
U of Sioux Falls (SD)
U of South Alabama (AL)
U of South Carolina (SC)
U of South Dakota (SD)
U of Southern California (CA)
U of Southern Colorado (CO)
U of Southern Maine (ME)
U of Southern Mississippi (MS)
The U of Tampa (FL)
The U of Tennessee (TN)
The U of Tennessee at Chattanooga (TN)
The U of Tennessee at Martin (TN)
The U of Texas at Arlington (TX)
The U of Texas at Austin (TX)
The U of Texas at El Paso (TX)
The U of Texas at San Antonio (TX)
The U of Texas at Tyler (TX)
The U of Texas–Pan American (TX)
U of the District of Columbia (DC)
U of the Incarnate Word (TX)
U of the Ozarks (AR)
U of the Pacific (CA)
U of the South (TN)
U of Toledo (OH)
U of Toronto (ON, Canada)
U of Tulsa (OK)
U of Utah (UT)
U of Vermont (VT)
U of Victoria (BC, Canada)
U of Virginia (VA)
U of Washington (WA)
U of Waterloo (ON, Canada)
The U of Western Ontario (ON, Canada)
U of Windsor (ON, Canada)
U of Wisconsin–Eau Claire (WI)
U of Wisconsin–Green Bay (WI)
U of Wisconsin–La Crosse (WI)
U of Wisconsin–Madison (WI)
U of Wisconsin–Milwaukee (WI)
U of Wisconsin–Oshkosh (WI)
U of Wisconsin–Parkside (WI)
U of Wisconsin–Platteville (WI)
U of Wisconsin–River Falls (WI)
U of Wisconsin–Stevens Point (WI)
U of Wisconsin–Superior (WI)
U of Wisconsin–Whitewater (WI)
U of Wyoming (WY)
Upper Iowa U (IA)
Ursinus Coll (PA)
Utah State U (UT)
Valdosta State U (GA)
Valley City State U (ND)
Valparaiso U (IN)
Vanderbilt U (TN)
Vanguard U of Southern California (CA)
Vassar Coll (NY)
Virginia Polytechnic Inst and State U (VA)
Virginia Union U (VA)
Virginia Wesleyan Coll (VA)
Viterbo U (WI)
Wabash Coll (IN)
Wagner Coll (NY)
Wake Forest U (NC)
Walla Walla Coll (WA)
Warner Pacific Coll (OR)
Wartburg Coll (IA)
Washburn U of Topeka (KS)
Washington & Jefferson Coll (PA)
Washington and Lee U (VA)
Washington Bible Coll (MD)
Washington Coll (MD)
Washington State U (WA)
Washington U in St. Louis (MO)
Wayland Baptist U (TX)
Wayne State Coll (NE)
Wayne State U (MI)
Weber State U (UT)
Webster U (MO)
Wellesley Coll (MA)
Wells Coll (NY)
Wesleyan Coll (GA)
Wesleyan U (CT)

MUSICOLOGY

MUSIC (PIANO AND ORGAN PERFORMANCE)

MUSIC RELATED

MUSIC TEACHER EDUCATION

NONPROFIT/PUBLIC MANAGEMENT

NUCLEAR ENGINEERING

NUCLEAR MEDICAL TECHNOLOGY

NUCLEAR PHYSICS

NUCLEAR TECHNOLOGY

NURSERY MANAGEMENT

NURSING

NURSING ADMINISTRATION

NURSING (ADULT HEALTH)

NURSING (ANESTHETIST)

NURSING (FAMILY PRACTICE)

NURSING (MATERNAL/CHILD HEALTH)

NURSING (MIDWIFERY)

NURSING (PSYCHIATRIC/MENTAL HEALTH)

NURSING (PUBLIC HEALTH)

NURSING RELATED

NURSING SCIENCE

NURSING (SURGICAL)

NUTRITIONAL SCIENCES

NUTRITION SCIENCE

NUTRITION STUDIES

OCCUPATIONAL HEALTH/ INDUSTRIAL HYGIENE

OCCUPATIONAL SAFETY/ HEALTH TECHNOLOGY

OCCUPATIONAL THERAPY

OCCUPATIONAL THERAPY ASSISTANT

OCEAN ENGINEERING
California State U, Long Beach (CA)
Florida Atlantic U (FL)
Florida Inst of Technology (FL)
Massachusetts Inst of Technology (MA)
Memorial U of Newfoundland (NF, Canada)
Texas A&M U (TX)
Texas A&M U at Galveston (TX)
United States Naval Academy (MD)
U of Hawaii at Manoa (HI)
U of New Hampshire (NH)
U of Rhode Island (RI)
Virginia Polytechnic Inst and State U (VA)

OCEANOGRAPHY
Central Michigan U (MI)
Florida Inst of Technology (FL)
Hampshire Coll (MA)
Hawai'i Pacific U (HI)
Humboldt State U (CA)
Kutztown U of Pennsylvania (PA)
Lamar U (TX)
Maine Maritime Academy (ME)
Memorial U of Newfoundland (NF, Canada)
Millersville U of Pennsylvania (PA)
North Carolina State U (NC)
Nova Southeastern U (FL)
Rider U (NJ)
San Jose State U (CA)
Sheldon Jackson Coll (AK)
State U of NY Maritime Coll (NY)
Texas A&M U at Galveston (TX)
United States Naval Academy (MD)
The U of British Columbia (BC, Canada)
U of Hawaii at Manoa (HI)
U of Miami (FL)
U of Michigan (MI)
U of New Hampshire (NH)
U of San Diego (CA)
U of Victoria (BC, Canada)
U of Washington (WA)

OFFICE MANAGEMENT
Arkansas Tech U (AR)
Baker Coll of Flint (MI)
Berkeley Coll, New York (NY)
Berkeley Coll, White Plains (NY)
Bowling Green State U (OH)
Central Michigan U (MI)
Central Missouri State U (MO)
Central Washington U (WA)
Concordia Coll (MN)
Davenport U, Dearborn (MI)
Delta State U (MS)
Georgia Coll and State U (GA)
Indiana State U (IN)
Indiana U of Pennsylvania (PA)
Jackson State U (MS)
Mayville State U (ND)
Middle Tennessee State U (TN)
Mississippi Valley State U (MS)
Norfolk State U (VA)
Peirce Coll (PA)
Radford U (VA)
Southeastern Oklahoma State U (OK)
Southeast Missouri State U (MO)
State U of West Georgia (GA)
Stephen F. Austin State U (TX)
Tarleton State U (TX)
Texas Southern U (TX)
Texas Woman's U (TX)
U of Nebraska–Lincoln (NE)
U of North Dakota (ND)
U of South Carolina (SC)
Valley City State U (ND)
Weber State U (UT)
Youngstown State U (OH)

OPERATIONS MANAGEMENT
Appalachian State U (NC)
Auburn U (AL)
Aurora U (IL)
Baker Coll of Flint (MI)
Baylor U (TX)
Boise State U (ID)
Boston U (MA)
Bowling Green State U (OH)
California State U, Chico (CA)
California State U, Stanislaus (CA)
Central Michigan U (MI)
Central Washington U (WA)
Clarkson U (NY)
Clemson U (SC)
Concordia U (NE)
Dalton State Coll (GA)
DeVry U (AZ)
DeVry U, Fremont (CA)
DeVry U, Long Beach (CA)
DeVry U, Pomona (CA)
DeVry U, West Hills (CA)
DeVry U, Alpharetta (GA)
DeVry U, Decatur (GA)
DeVry U, Addison (IL)
DeVry U, Chicago (IL)
DeVry U, Tinley Park (IL)
DeVry U (MO)
DeVry U (OH)
DeVry U (TX)
Edinboro U of Pennsylvania (PA)
Excelsior Coll (NY)
Florida Southern Coll (FL)
Franklin U (OH)
Georgia Inst of Technology (GA)
Golden Gate U (CA)
Indiana U–Purdue U Fort Wayne (IN)
Indiana U–Purdue U Indianapolis (IN)
Kennesaw State U (GA)
Kettering U (MI)
Louisiana Tech U (LA)
Loyola U Chicago (IL)
Metropolitan State U (MN)
Miami U (OH)
Michigan State U (MI)
Michigan Technological U (MI)
Missouri Baptist Coll (MO)
National U (CA)
Northern Illinois U (IL)
The Ohio State U (OH)
Purdue U (IN)
Robert Morris U (PA)
Saginaw Valley State U (MI)
Sam Houston State U (TX)
San Jose State U (CA)
Seattle U (WA)
Southeast Missouri State U (MO)
Tennessee Technological U (TN)
Texas Southern U (TX)
Thomas Edison State Coll (NJ)
Tri-State U (IN)
The U of Arizona (AZ)
U of Delaware (DE)
U of Houston (TX)
U of Idaho (ID)
U of Indianapolis (IN)
U of Maryland, Coll Park (MD)
U of Nebraska at Kearney (NE)
U of Nebraska at Omaha (NE)
The U of North Carolina at Asheville (NC)
The U of North Carolina at Charlotte (NC)
U of North Texas (TX)
U of Pennsylvania (PA)
U of St. Francis (IL)
U of St. Thomas (MN)
U of Saskatchewan (SK, Canada)
The U of Scranton (PA)
The U of Texas at San Antonio (TX)
Utah State U (UT)
Washington U in St. Louis (MO)
Western Washington U (WA)
Worcester State Coll (MA)
Youngstown State U (OH)

OPERATIONS RESEARCH
Babson Coll (MA)
Baruch Coll of the City U of NY (NY)
Boston Coll (MA)
California State U, Fullerton (CA)
California State U, Northridge (CA)
Carleton U (ON, Canada)
Columbia U, School of Engineering & Applied Sci (NY)
Concordia U (QC, Canada)
Cornell U (NY)
DePaul U (IL)
Georgia State U (GA)
Iona Coll (NY)
Mercy Coll (NY)
Miami U (OH)
New York U (NY)
Texas A&M U (TX)
United States Air Force Academy (CO)
United States Coast Guard Academy (CT)
United States Military Academy (NY)
Université de Montréal (QC, Canada)
Université de Sherbrooke (PQ, Canada)
U of Cincinnati (OH)
U of Denver (CO)
U of Michigan–Flint (MI)
U of Waterloo (ON, Canada)
York U (ON, Canada)

OPHTHALMIC/OPTOMETRIC SERVICES
Ferris State U (MI)
Gannon U (PA)
Indiana U Bloomington (IN)
Northeastern State U (OK)
Nova Southeastern U (FL)
State U of NY at New Paltz (NY)
State U of NY Coll at Oneonta (NY)
Université de Montréal (QC, Canada)
U of Waterloo (ON, Canada)

OPHTHALMIC/OPTOMETRIC SERVICES RELATED
Concordia Coll (MN)
Tennessee Wesleyan Coll (TN)

OPTICS
Albright Coll (PA)
Rose-Hulman Inst of Technology (IN)
Saginaw Valley State U (MI)
The U of Arizona (AZ)
U of Rochester (NY)

OPTOMETRIC/OPHTHALMIC LABORATORY TECHNICIAN
Louisiana State U Health Sciences Center (LA)
Viterbo U (WI)

ORGANIZATIONAL BEHAVIOR
Anderson U (IN)
Benedictine U (IL)
Boston U (MA)
Bridgewater Coll (VA)
Brown U (RI)
California Baptist U (CA)
Carroll Coll (WI)
Denison U (OH)
Manhattan Coll (NY)
McGill U (PQ, Canada)
Memorial U of Newfoundland (NF, Canada)
Miami U (OH)
Mid-Continent Coll (KY)
Northern Kentucky U (KY)
Northwestern Coll (MN)
Northwestern U (IL)
Oakland City U (IN)
Penn State U Harrisburg Campus of the Capital Coll (PA)
Philander Smith Coll (AR)
St. Ambrose U (IA)
Seattle Pacific U (WA)
Southern Methodist U (TX)
Thomas Edison State Coll (NJ)
U Coll of Cape Breton (NS, Canada)
U of Houston (TX)
U of La Verne (CA)
U of New England (ME)
U of North Texas (TX)
U of Pennsylvania (PA)
The U of Texas at Dallas (TX)
U of the Incarnate Word (TX)
Wayne State U (MI)
York U (ON, Canada)

ORGANIZATIONAL PSYCHOLOGY
Abilene Christian U (TX)
Albright Coll (PA)
Averett U (VA)
Bridgewater State Coll (MA)
California State U, Hayward (CA)
Clarkson U (NY)
Fitchburg State Coll (MA)
Georgia Inst of Technology (GA)
Holy Family Coll (PA)
Husson Coll (ME)
Ithaca Coll (NY)
Lincoln U (PA)
Marymount U (VA)
Maryville U of Saint Louis (MO)
Middle Tennessee State U (TN)
Moravian Coll (PA)
Nebraska Wesleyan U (NE)
Point Loma Nazarene U (CA)
Saint Xavier U (IL)
Texas Wesleyan U (TX)

ORNAMENTAL HORTICULTURE
Auburn U (AL)
California Polytechnic State U, San Luis Obispo (CA)
California State Polytechnic U, Pomona (CA)
California State U, Fresno (CA)
Cornell U (NY)
Delaware Valley Coll (PA)
Eastern Kentucky U (KY)
Florida A&M U (FL)
Florida Southern Coll (FL)
Fort Valley State U (GA)
Iowa State U of Science and Technology (IA)
Long Island U, Southampton Coll, Friends World Program (NY)
Texas A&M U (TX)
U of Arkansas (AR)
U of Delaware (DE)
U of Illinois at Urbana–Champaign (IL)
The U of Tennessee (TN)
U of the District of Columbia (DC)
Utah State U (UT)

ORTHOTICS/PROSTHETICS
Florida International U (FL)
U of Texas Southwestern Medical Center at Dallas (TX)
U of Washington (WA)

PACIFIC AREA STUDIES
Brigham Young U–Hawaii (HI)
U of Hawaii at Manoa (HI)

PAINTING
Adams State Coll (CO)
American Academy of Art (IL)
Atlanta Coll of Art (GA)
Bard Coll (NY)
Barton Coll (NC)
Bellarmine U (KY)
Bethany Coll (KS)
Birmingham-Southern Coll (AL)
Boston U (MA)
Bowling Green State U (OH)
California Coll of Arts and Crafts (CA)
California State U, Hayward (CA)
California State U, Stanislaus (CA)
The Catholic U of America (DC)
The Cleveland Inst of Art (OH)
Coll of Santa Fe (NM)
Coll of Visual Arts (MN)
Colorado State U (CO)
Columbus Coll of Art and Design (OH)
Concordia U (QC, Canada)
Escuela de Artes Plasticas de Puerto Rico (PR)
Grace Coll (IN)
Harding U (AR)
Henderson State U (AR)
Indiana Wesleyan U (IN)
Kansas City Art Inst (MO)
Lewis U (IL)
Lyme Academy Coll of Fine Arts (CT)
Maharishi U of Management (IA)
Maine Coll of Art (ME)
Maryland Inst, Coll of Art (MD)
Massachusetts Coll of Art (MA)
Memorial U of Newfoundland (NF, Canada)
Memphis Coll of Art (TN)
Milwaukee Inst of Art and Design (WI)
Minneapolis Coll of Art and Design (MN)
Minnesota State U Moorhead (MN)
Northwest Nazarene U (ID)
Nova Scotia Coll of Art and Design (NS, Canada)
The Ohio State U (OH)
Ohio U (OH)
Pacific Northwest Coll of Art (OR)
Paier Coll of Art, Inc. (CT)
Rivier Coll (NH)
Rocky Mountain Coll of Art & Design (CO)
Rutgers, The State U of New Jersey, New Brunswick (NJ)
Sam Houston State U (TX)
San Diego State U (CA)
San Francisco Art Inst (CA)
Savannah Coll of Art and Design (GA)
School of Visual Arts (NY)
Seton Hill Coll (PA)
Shawnee State U (OH)
Simon's Rock Coll of Bard (MA)
State U of NY Coll at Brockport (NY)
State U of NY Coll at Potsdam (NY)
Syracuse U (NY)
Texas Woman's U (TX)
Trinity Christian Coll (IL)
U of Dallas (TX)
U of Hartford (CT)
U of Houston (TX)
U of Illinois at Urbana–Champaign (IL)
The U of Iowa (IA)
U of Kansas (KS)
U of Massachusetts Dartmouth (MA)
U of Miami (FL)
U of Michigan (MI)
U of North Texas (TX)
U of San Francisco (CA)
The U of the Arts (PA)
U of Washington (WA)
U of Windsor (ON, Canada)
Virginia Commonwealth U (VA)
Washington U in St. Louis (MO)
Webster U (MO)
York U (ON, Canada)
Youngstown State U (OH)

PALEONTOLOGY
Bowling Green State U (OH)
Long Island U, Southampton Coll, Friends World Program (NY)
Mercyhurst Coll (PA)
San Diego State U (CA)
Southeast Missouri State U (MO)
U of Alberta (AB, Canada)
U of Delaware (DE)
U of Toronto (ON, Canada)

PARALEGAL/LEGAL ASSISTANT
Anna Maria Coll (MA)
Avila Coll (MO)
Ball State U (IN)
Boston U (MA)
Brenau U (GA)
Calvary Bible Coll and Theological Seminary (MO)
Cedar Crest Coll (PA)
Champlain Coll (VT)
Coll of Mount St. Joseph (OH)
Coll of Saint Mary (NE)
Concordia U Wisconsin (WI)
Davenport U, Grand Rapids (MI)
Davenport U, Kalamazoo (MI)
David N. Myers U (OH)
Eastern Kentucky U (KY)
Elms Coll (MA)
Florida Metropolitan U-Orlando Coll, North (FL)
Florida Metropolitan U-Orlando Coll, South (FL)
Gannon U (PA)
Grand Valley State U (MI)
Hamline U (MN)
Hampton U (VA)
Hartford Coll for Women (CT)
Hilbert Coll (NY)
Howard Payne U (TX)
Husson Coll (ME)
International Business Coll, Fort Wayne (IN)
International Coll (FL)
Johnson & Wales U (RI)
Jones Coll (FL)
Lake Erie Coll (OH)
Lake Superior State U (MI)
Lasell Coll (MA)
Marist Coll (NY)
Marymount U (VA)
Maryville U of Saint Louis (MO)
Marywood U (PA)
McMurry U (TX)
Mercy Coll (NY)
Midway Coll (KY)
Minnesota State U Moorhead (MN)
Mississippi Coll (MS)
Mississippi U for Women (MS)

Morehead State U (KY)
National American U (SD)
National American U–Sioux Falls Branch (SD)
Notre Dame Coll (OH)
Nova Southeastern U (FL)
Peirce Coll (PA)
Quinnipiac U (CT)
Robert Morris Coll (IL)
Roger Williams U (RI)
Roosevelt U (IL)
St. John's U (NY)
Saint Mary-of-the-Woods Coll (IN)
Southern Illinois U Carbondale (IL)
Stephen F. Austin State U (TX)
Suffolk U (MA)
Sullivan U (KY)
Teikyo Post U (CT)
Texas Woman's U (TX)
Thomas Edison State Coll (NJ)
U of Central Florida (FL)
U of Great Falls (MT)
U of La Verne (CA)
U of Maryland University Coll (MD)
U of Nebraska at Omaha (NE)
U of Southern Mississippi (MS)
The U of Tennessee at Chattanooga (TN)
U of West Florida (FL)
U of West Los Angeles (CA)
U of Wisconsin–Superior (WI)
Valdosta State U (GA)
Villa Julie Coll (MD)
Virginia Intermont Coll (VA)
Wesley Coll (DE)
William Woods U (MO)
Winona State U (MN)

PARKS, RECREATION, LEISURE AND FITNESS STUDIES RELATED
Chadron State Coll (NE)
Culver-Stockton Coll (MO)
U of North Alabama (AL)
Utah State U (UT)

PASTORAL COUNSELING
Abilene Christian U (TX)
Alaska Bible Coll (AK)
American Christian Coll and Seminary (OK)
American Indian Coll of the Assemblies of God, Inc (AZ)
Baptist Bible Coll (MO)
Baptist Bible Coll of Pennsylvania (PA)
The Baptist Coll of Florida (FL)
Barclay Coll (KS)
Belhaven Coll (MS)
Bellarmine U (KY)
Belmont U (TN)
Bethany Bible Inst (SK, Canada)
Bethany Coll of the Assemblies of God (CA)
Biola U (CA)
Boise Bible Coll (ID)
Briercrest Bible Coll (SK, Canada)
Calvary Bible Coll and Theological Seminary (MO)
Campbellsville U (KY)
Cedarville U (OH)
Central Bible Coll (MO)
Central Christian Coll of Kansas (KS)
Christian Heritage Coll (CA)
Clearwater Christian Coll (FL)
Coll Dominicain de Philosophie et de Théologie (ON, Canada)
Coll of Mount St. Joseph (OH)
Colorado Christian U (CO)
Columbia Bible Coll (BC, Canada)
Columbia International U (SC)
Concordia U (IL)
Concordia U (MN)
Concordia U (NE)
Concordia U Wisconsin (WI)
Cornerstone U (MI)
Crown Coll (MN)
Dallas Baptist U (TX)
Dordt Coll (IA)
East Texas Baptist U (TX)
Emmanuel Coll (GA)
Eugene Bible Coll (OR)
Faith Baptist Bible Coll and Theological Seminary (IA)
Faulkner U (AL)
Fresno Pacific U (CA)
George Fox U (OR)
Global U of the Assemblies of God (MO)
God's Bible School and Coll (OH)
Grace Bible Coll (MI)
Grace Coll (IN)
Grace U (NE)
Greenville Coll (IL)
Hannibal-LaGrange Coll (MO)
Harding U (AR)
Hardin-Simmons U (TX)
Houghton Coll (NY)
Indiana Wesleyan U (IN)
John Brown U (AR)
John Wesley Coll (NC)
Kentucky Christian Coll (KY)
LaGrange Coll (GA)
Lee U (TN)
Lenoir-Rhyne Coll (NC)
LIFE Bible Coll (CA)
Malone Coll (OH)
Manhattan Christian Coll (KS)
Marylhurst U (OR)
The Master's Coll and Seminary (CA)
Mercyhurst Coll (PA)
Milligan Coll (TN)
Multnomah Bible Coll and Biblical Seminary (OR)
Nazarene Bible Coll (CO)
Nebraska Christian Coll (NE)
Newman U (KS)
North Greenville Coll (SC)
Northwest Coll (WA)
Northwestern Coll (MN)
Northwest Nazarene U (ID)
Notre Dame Coll (OH)
Nyack Coll (NY)
Oklahoma Baptist U (OK)
Oklahoma Christian U of Science and Arts (OK)
Olivet Nazarene U (IL)
Oral Roberts U (OK)
Ouachita Baptist U (AR)
Pacific Union Coll (CA)
Patten Coll (CA)
Pillsbury Baptist Bible Coll (MN)
Providence Coll (RI)
Providence Coll and Theological Seminary (MB, Canada)
Puget Sound Christian Coll (WA)
Reformed Bible Coll (MI)
Roberts Wesleyan Coll (NY)
Rochester Coll (MI)
Rocky Mountain Coll (AB, Canada)
Saint Francis U (PA)
Saint Mary-of-the-Woods Coll (IN)
Saint Mary's Coll of Ave Maria U (MI)
Saint Mary's U of Minnesota (MN)
St. Thomas U (FL)
San Jose Christian Coll (CA)
Simpson Coll and Graduate School (CA)
Southeastern Bible Coll (AL)
Southeastern Coll of the Assemblies of God (FL)
Southwestern Assemblies of God U (TX)
Southwestern Coll (AZ)
Tabor Coll (KS)
Taylor U, Fort Wayne Campus (IN)
Tennessee Temple U (TN)
Trinity Baptist Coll (FL)
Trinity Bible Coll (ND)
Trinity Coll of Florida (FL)
Tyndale Coll & Seminary (ON, Canada)
Union Coll (NE)
Universidad Adventista de las Antillas (PR)
U of Ottawa (ON, Canada)
U of St. Thomas (TX)
U of Sioux Falls (SD)
Vanguard U of Southern California (CA)
Walsh U (OH)
Warner Pacific Coll (OR)
Western Baptist Coll (OR)
Williams Baptist Coll (AR)
William Tyndale Coll (MI)

PATHOLOGY
U of Connecticut (CT)

PEACE/CONFLICT STUDIES
American U (DC)
Bethel Coll (KS)
Bluffton Coll (OH)
Chapman U (CA)
Clark U (MA)
Colgate U (NY)
Coll of Saint Benedict (MN)
Coll of the Holy Cross (MA)
DePauw U (IN)
Earlham Coll (IN)
Eastern Mennonite U (VA)
Elizabethtown Coll (PA)
Fordham U (NY)
Goddard Coll (VT)
Goshen Coll (IN)
Guilford Coll (NC)
Hampshire Coll (MA)
Haverford Coll (PA)
Juniata Coll (PA)
Kent State U (OH)
Long Island U, Southampton Coll, Friends World Program (NY)
Manchester Coll (IN)
Molloy Coll (NY)
Mount Saint Vincent U (NS, Canada)
Nebraska Wesleyan U (NE)
Northland Coll (WI)
Norwich U (VT)
Ohio Dominican Coll (OH)
The Ohio State U (OH)
Rocky Mountain Coll (MT)
Saint John's U (MN)
Salisbury U (MD)
U of Calif, Berkeley (CA)
U of Calif, Santa Cruz (CA)
The U of North Carolina at Chapel Hill (NC)
U of St. Thomas (MN)
U of Wisconsin–Milwaukee (WI)
Wayne State U (MI)
Wellesley Coll (MA)
Whitworth Coll (WA)

PERFUSION TECHNOLOGY
MCP Hahnemann U (PA)
Medical U of South Carolina (SC)
Rush U (IL)
State U of New York Upstate Medical University (NY)
Thomas Edison State Coll (NJ)

PERSONAL SERVICES MARKETING OPERATIONS
Lake Erie Coll (OH)

PETROLEUM ENGINEERING
California State Polytechnic U, Pomona (CA)
Colorado School of Mines (CO)
Louisiana State U and A&M Coll (LA)
Marietta Coll (OH)
Montana Tech of The U of Montana (MT)
New Mexico Inst of Mining and Technology (NM)
Penn State U Univ Park Campus (PA)
Stanford U (CA)
Texas A&M U (TX)
Texas A&M U–Kingsville (TX)
Texas Tech U (TX)
U of Alaska Fairbanks (AK)
U of Alberta (AB, Canada)
U of Calif, Berkeley (CA)
U of Kansas (KS)
U of Louisiana at Lafayette (LA)
U of Missouri–Rolla (MO)
U of Oklahoma (OK)
U of Regina (SK, Canada)
U of Southern California (CA)
The U of Texas at Austin (TX)
U of Toronto (ON, Canada)
U of Tulsa (OK)
West Virginia U (WV)

PETROLEUM PRODUCTS RETAILING OPERATIONS
U Coll of Cape Breton (NS, Canada)

PETROLEUM TECHNOLOGY
Mercyhurst Coll (PA)
Montana State U–Billings (MT)
Nicholls State U (LA)
U Coll of Cape Breton (NS, Canada)

PHARMACOLOGY
Belmont U (TN)
McMaster U (ON, Canada)
State U of NY at Stony Brook (NY)
U of Alberta (AB, Canada)
The U of British Columbia (BC, Canada)
U of Calif, Santa Barbara (CA)
U of Cincinnati (OH)
U of Hawaii at Manoa (HI)
U of the Sciences in Philadelphia (PA)
U of Toronto (ON, Canada)
The U of Western Ontario (ON, Canada)
U of Wisconsin–Madison (WI)

PHARMACY
Albany Coll of Pharmacy of Union U (NY)
Briar Cliff U (IA)
Butler U (IN)
Campbell U (NC)
Dalhousie U (NS, Canada)
Drake U (IA)
Eastern Nazarene Coll (MA)
Ferris State U (MI)
Florida A&M U (FL)
Howard U (DC)
Idaho State U (ID)
Long Island U, Brooklyn Campus (NY)
Longwood Coll (VA)
Mass Coll of Pharmacy and Allied Health Sciences (MA)
Memorial U of Newfoundland (NF, Canada)
North Dakota State U (ND)
Northeastern U (MA)
Ohio Northern U (OH)
The Ohio State U (OH)
Oregon State U (OR)
Purdue U (IN)
Rutgers, The State U of New Jersey, New Brunswick (NJ)
St. John's U (NY)
St. Louis Coll of Pharmacy (MO)
Saint Vincent Coll (PA)
Simmons Coll (MA)
South Dakota State U (SD)
Southwestern Oklahoma State U (OK)
Texas Southern U (TX)
Université de Montréal (QC, Canada)
Université Laval (QC, Canada)
U of Alberta (AB, Canada)
The U of British Columbia (BC, Canada)
U of Cincinnati (OH)
U of Connecticut (CT)
U of Florida (FL)
U of Georgia (GA)
U of Houston (TX)
The U of Iowa (IA)
U of Louisiana at Monroe (LA)
U of Manitoba (MB, Canada)
U of Michigan (MI)
U of Mississippi (MS)
U of Missouri–Kansas City (MO)
The U of Montana–Missoula (MT)
U of New Mexico (NM)
U of Pittsburgh (PA)
U of Puerto Rico Medical Sciences Campus (PR)
U of Rhode Island (RI)
U of Saskatchewan (SK, Canada)
The U of Texas at Austin (TX)
U of the Pacific (CA)
U of the Sciences in Philadelphia (PA)
U of Toledo (OH)
U of Toronto (ON, Canada)
U of Utah (UT)
U of Washington (WA)
U of Wisconsin–Madison (WI)
Virginia Commonwealth U (VA)
Wayne State U (MI)
West Virginia U (WV)

PHARMACY ADMINISTRATION/ PHARMACEUTICS
DeSales U (PA)
Drake U (IA)
State U of NY at Buffalo (NY)
U of the Sciences in Philadelphia (PA)

PHARMACY RELATED
Mass Coll of Pharmacy and Allied Health Sciences (MA)
U of the Sciences in Philadelphia (PA)

PHARMACY TECHNICIAN/ ASSISTANT
The U of Montana–Missoula (MT)

PHILOSOPHY
Acadia U (NS, Canada)
Adelphi U (NY)
Agnes Scott Coll (GA)
Albertson Coll of Idaho (ID)
Albion Coll (MI)
Albright Coll (PA)
Alfred U (NY)
Allegheny Coll (PA)
Alma Coll (MI)
Alvernia Coll (PA)
Alverno Coll (WI)
American International Coll (MA)
American U (DC)
American U in Cairo(Egypt)
Amherst Coll (MA)
Anderson U (IN)
Anna Maria Coll (MA)
Aquinas Coll (MI)
Arcadia U (PA)
Arizona State U (AZ)
Arkansas State U (AR)
Asbury Coll (KY)
Ashland U (OH)
Assumption Coll (MA)
Auburn U (AL)
Augsburg Coll (MN)
Augustana Coll (IL)
Augustana Coll (SD)
Aurora U (IL)
Austin Coll (TX)
Austin Peay State U (TN)
Ave Maria Coll (MI)
Azusa Pacific U (CA)
Baker U (KS)
Baldwin-Wallace Coll (OH)
Ball State U (IN)
Baltimore Hebrew U (MD)
Bard Coll (NY)
Barnard Coll (NY)
Barry U (FL)
Barton Coll (NC)
Bates Coll (ME)
Bayamón Central U (PR)
Baylor U (TX)
Belhaven Coll (MS)
Bellarmine U (KY)
Bellevue U (NE)
Belmont Abbey Coll (NC)
Belmont U (TN)
Beloit Coll (WI)
Bemidji State U (MN)
Benedict Coll (SC)
Benedictine Coll (KS)
Benedictine U (IL)
Bennington Coll (VT)
Bentley Coll (MA)
Berea Coll (KY)
Baruch Coll of the City U of NY (NY)
Berry Coll (GA)
Bethany Coll (KS)
Bethany Coll (WV)
Bethel Coll (IN)
Bethel Coll (MN)
Biola U (CA)
Birmingham-Southern Coll (AL)
Bishop's U (PQ, Canada)
Bloomfield Coll (NJ)
Bloomsburg U of Pennsylvania (PA)
Bluefield Coll (VA)
Bluffton Coll (OH)
Boise State U (ID)
Boston Coll (MA)
Boston U (MA)
Bowdoin Coll (ME)
Bowling Green State U (OH)
Bradley U (IL)
Brandeis U (MA)
Brandon U (MB, Canada)
Bridgewater State Coll (MA)
Brigham Young U (UT)
Brock U (ON, Canada)
Brooklyn Coll of the City U of NY (NY)
Brown U (RI)
Bryn Mawr Coll (PA)
Bucknell U (PA)
Buena Vista U (IA)
Butler U (IN)

Cabrini Coll (PA)
California Baptist U (CA)
California Lutheran U (CA)
California Polytechnic State U, San Luis Obispo (CA)
California State Polytechnic U, Pomona (CA)
California State U, Bakersfield (CA)
California State U, Chico (CA)
California State U, Dominguez Hills (CA)
California State U, Fresno (CA)
California State U, Fullerton (CA)
California State U, Hayward (CA)
California State U, Long Beach (CA)
California State U, Los Angeles (CA)
California State U, Northridge (CA)
California State U, Sacramento (CA)
California State U, San Bernardino (CA)
California State U, Stanislaus (CA)
California U of Pennsylvania (PA)
Calvin Coll (MI)
Canisius Coll (NY)
Capital U (OH)
Carleton Coll (MN)
Carleton U (ON, Canada)
Carlow Coll (PA)
Carnegie Mellon U (PA)
Carroll Coll (MT)
Carson-Newman Coll (TN)
Carthage Coll (WI)
Case Western Reserve U (OH)
Catawba Coll (NC)
The Catholic U of America (DC)
Cedar Crest Coll (PA)
Cedarville U (OH)
Centenary Coll of Louisiana (LA)
Central Coll (IA)
Central Connecticut State U (CT)
Central Methodist Coll (MO)
Central Michigan U (MI)
Central Washington U (WA)
Centre Coll (KY)
Chaminade U of Honolulu (HI)
Chapman U (CA)
Chatham Coll (PA)
Christendom Coll (VA)
Christopher Newport U (VA)
City Coll of the City U of NY (NY)
Claremont McKenna Coll (CA)
Clarion U of Pennsylvania (PA)
Clark Atlanta U (GA)
Clarke Coll (IA)
Clark U (MA)
Clemson U (SC)
Cleveland State U (OH)
Coastal Carolina U (SC)
Coe Coll (IA)
Colby Coll (ME)
Colgate U (NY)
Coll Dominicain de Philosophie et de Théologie (ON, Canada)
Coll Misericordia (PA)
Coll of Charleston (SC)
Coll of Mount Saint Vincent (NY)
The Coll of New Jersey (NJ)
The Coll of New Rochelle (NY)
Coll of Saint Benedict (MN)
Coll of St. Catherine (MN)
Coll of Saint Elizabeth (NJ)
The Coll of Southeastern Europe, The American U of Athens(Greece)
Coll of Staten Island of the City U of NY (NY)
Coll of the Atlantic (ME)
Coll of the Holy Cross (MA)
Coll of the Ozarks (MO)
The Coll of William and Mary (VA)
The Coll of Wooster (OH)
The Colorado Coll (CO)
Colorado State U (CO)
Columbia Coll (NY)
Columbia U, School of General Studies (NY)
Concordia Coll (MN)
Concordia U (IL)
Concordia U (QC, Canada)
Connecticut Coll (CT)
Coppin State Coll (MD)
Cornell Coll (IA)
Cornell U (NY)
Covenant Coll (GA)
Creighton U (NE)
Curry Coll (MA)
Dakota Wesleyan U (SD)
Dalhousie U (NS, Canada)
Dallas Baptist U (TX)
Dartmouth Coll (NH)
Davidson Coll (NC)
Denison U (OH)
DePaul U (IL)
DePauw U (IN)
Dickinson Coll (PA)
Doane Coll (NE)
Dominican School of Philosophy and Theology (CA)
Dominican U (IL)
Dordt Coll (IA)
Drake U (IA)
Drew U (NJ)
Drury U (MO)
Duke U (NC)
Duquesne U (PA)
D'Youville Coll (NY)
Earlham Coll (IN)
East Carolina U (NC)
Eastern Illinois U (IL)
Eastern Kentucky U (KY)
Eastern Michigan U (MI)
Eastern U (PA)
Eastern Washington U (WA)
East Stroudsburg U of Pennsylvania (PA)
East Tennessee State U (TN)
Eckerd Coll (FL)
Edinboro U of Pennsylvania (PA)
Elizabethtown Coll (PA)
Elmhurst Coll (IL)
Elmira Coll (NY)
Elon U (NC)
Emory & Henry Coll (VA)
Emory U (GA)
Erskine Coll (SC)
Eugene Lang Coll, New School U (NY)
Eureka Coll (IL)
The Evergreen State Coll (WA)
Excelsior Coll (NY)
Fairfield U (CT)
Fairleigh Dickinson U, Florham-Madison Campus (NJ)
Fairleigh Dickinson U, Teaneck-Hackensack Campus (NJ)
Felician Coll (NJ)
Ferrum Coll (VA)
Fisk U (TN)
Flagler Coll (FL)
Florida A&M U (FL)
Florida Atlantic U (FL)
Florida International U (FL)
Florida State U (FL)
Fordham U (NY)
Fort Hays State U (KS)
Fort Lewis Coll (CO)
Franciscan U of Steubenville (OH)
Franklin and Marshall Coll (PA)
Franklin Coll of Indiana (IN)
Freed-Hardeman U (TN)
Friends U (KS)
Frostburg State U (MD)
Furman U (SC)
Gallaudet U (DC)
Gannon U (PA)
Geneva Coll (PA)
George Mason U (VA)
Georgetown Coll (KY)
Georgetown U (DC)
The George Washington U (DC)
Georgia Southern U (GA)
Georgia State U (GA)
Gettysburg Coll (PA)
Goddard Coll (VT)
Gonzaga U (WA)
Gordon Coll (MA)
Goucher Coll (MD)
Grand Valley State U (MI)
Greenville Coll (IL)
Grinnell Coll (IA)
Grove City Coll (PA)
Guilford Coll (NC)
Gustavus Adolphus Coll (MN)
Hamilton Coll (NY)
Hamline U (MN)
Hampden-Sydney Coll (VA)
Hampshire Coll (MA)
Hanover Coll (IN)
Hardin-Simmons U (TX)
Hartwick Coll (NY)
Harvard U (MA)
Hastings Coll (NE)
Haverford Coll (PA)
Heidelberg Coll (OH)
Hendrix Coll (AR)
High Point U (NC)
Hillsdale Coll (MI)
Hiram Coll (OH)
Hobart and William Smith Colls (NY)
Hofstra U (NY)
Hollins U (VA)
Holy Apostles Coll and Seminary (CT)
Holy Names Coll (CA)
Hood Coll (MD)
Hope Coll (MI)
Houghton Coll (NY)
Howard Payne U (TX)
Howard U (DC)
Humboldt State U (CA)
Hunter Coll of the City U of NY (NY)
Huntington Coll (IN)
Idaho State U (ID)
Illinois Coll (IL)
Illinois State U (IL)
Illinois Wesleyan U (IL)
Indiana State U (IN)
Indiana U Bloomington (IN)
Indiana U Northwest (IN)
Indiana U of Pennsylvania (PA)
Indiana U–Purdue U Fort Wayne (IN)
Indiana U–Purdue U Indianapolis (IN)
Indiana U South Bend (IN)
Indiana U Southeast (IN)
Indiana Wesleyan U (IN)
Iona Coll (NY)
Iowa State U of Science and Technology (IA)
Ithaca Coll (NY)
Jacksonville U (FL)
James Madison U (VA)
Jamestown Coll (ND)
Jewish Theological Seminary of America (NY)
John Carroll U (OH)
Johns Hopkins U (MD)
Judson Coll (IL)
Kalamazoo Coll (MI)
Kansas State U (KS)
Kent State U (OH)
Kentucky Wesleyan Coll (KY)
Kenyon Coll (OH)
King's Coll (PA)
The King's U Coll (AB, Canada)
Knox Coll (IL)
Kutztown U of Pennsylvania (PA)
Lafayette Coll (PA)
Lake Forest Coll (IL)
Lakehead U (ON, Canada)
Lakeland Coll (WI)
La Salle U (PA)
Laurentian U (ON, Canada)
Lawrence U (WI)
Lebanon Valley Coll (PA)
Lehigh U (PA)
Lehman Coll of the City U of NY (NY)
Le Moyne Coll (NY)
Lenoir-Rhyne Coll (NC)
Lewis & Clark Coll (OR)
Lewis U (IL)
Lincoln U (MO)
Lincoln U (PA)
Linfield Coll (OR)
Lipscomb U (TN)
Lock Haven U of Pennsylvania (PA)
Long Island U, Brooklyn Campus (NY)
Long Island U, C.W. Post Campus (NY)
Long Island U, Southampton Coll, Friends World Program (NY)
Loras Coll (IA)
Louisiana Coll (LA)
Louisiana State U and A&M Coll (LA)
Loyola Coll in Maryland (MD)
Loyola Marymount U (CA)
Loyola U Chicago (IL)
Loyola U New Orleans (LA)
Luther Coll (IA)
Lycoming Coll (PA)
Lynchburg Coll (VA)
Macalester Coll (MN)
MacMurray Coll (IL)
Manchester Coll (IN)
Manhattan Coll (NY)
Manhattanville Coll (NY)
Mansfield U of Pennsylvania (PA)
Marian Coll (IN)
Marietta Coll (OH)
Marlboro Coll (VT)
Marquette U (WI)
Mary Baldwin Coll (VA)
Marymount U (VA)
Maryville U of Saint Louis (MO)
Mary Washington Coll (VA)
Massachusetts Coll of Liberal Arts (MA)
Massachusetts Inst of Technology (MA)
McGill U (PQ, Canada)
McKendree Coll (IL)
McMaster U (ON, Canada)
McMurry U (TX)
McPherson Coll (KS)
Memorial U of Newfoundland (NF, Canada)
Mercer U (GA)
Mercyhurst Coll (PA)
Merrimack Coll (MA)
Messiah Coll (PA)
Metropolitan State Coll of Denver (CO)
Metropolitan State U (MN)
Miami U (OH)
Michigan State U (MI)
Middlebury Coll (VT)
Middle Tennessee State U (TN)
Millersville U of Pennsylvania (PA)
Millikin U (IL)
Millsaps Coll (MS)
Mills Coll (CA)
Minnesota State U, Mankato (MN)
Minnesota State U Moorhead (MN)
Mississippi State U (MS)
Missouri Valley Coll (MO)
Molloy Coll (NY)
Monmouth Coll (IL)
Montana State U–Bozeman (MT)
Montclair State U (NJ)
Moravian Coll (PA)
Morehead State U (KY)
Morehouse Coll (GA)
Morgan State U (MD)
Morningside Coll (IA)
Morris Brown Coll (GA)
Mount Allison U (NB, Canada)
Mount Holyoke Coll (MA)
Mount Mary Coll (WI)
Mount St. Mary's Coll (CA)
Mount Saint Mary's Coll and Seminary (MD)
Mount Saint Vincent U (NS, Canada)
Mount Union Coll (OH)
Mount Vernon Nazarene U (OH)
Muhlenberg Coll (PA)
Murray State U (KY)
Muskingum Coll (OH)
Nazareth Coll of Rochester (NY)
Nebraska Wesleyan U (NE)
Newberry Coll (SC)
New Coll of Florida (FL)
New England Coll (NH)
New Jersey City U (NJ)
New Mexico State U (NM)
New York U (NY)
Niagara U (NY)
Nipissing U (ON, Canada)
North Carolina State U (NC)
North Carolina Wesleyan Coll (NC)
North Central Coll (IL)
Northeastern Illinois U (IL)
Northeastern U (MA)
Northern Arizona U (AZ)
Northern Illinois U (IL)
Northern Kentucky U (KY)
Northern Michigan U (MI)
Northland Coll (WI)
North Park U (IL)
Northwest Coll (WA)
Northwestern Coll (IA)
Northwestern U (IL)
Northwest Missouri State U (MO)
Northwest Nazarene U (ID)
Notre Dame de Namur U (CA)
Nyack Coll (NY)
Oakland U (MI)
Oberlin Coll (OH)
Occidental Coll (CA)
Oglethorpe U (GA)
Ohio Dominican Coll (OH)
Ohio Northern U (OH)
The Ohio State U (OH)
Ohio U (OH)
Ohio Wesleyan U (OH)
Okanagan U Coll (BC, Canada)
Oklahoma Baptist U (OK)
Oklahoma City U (OK)
Oklahoma State U (OK)
Old Dominion U (VA)
Olivet Nazarene U (IL)
Oral Roberts U (OK)
Oregon State U (OR)
Otterbein Coll (OH)
Ouachita Baptist U (AR)
Our Lady of the Lake U of San Antonio (TX)
Pacific Lutheran U (WA)
Pacific U (OR)
Paine Coll (GA)
Palm Beach Atlantic Coll (FL)
Penn State U Univ Park Campus (PA)
Pepperdine U, Malibu (CA)
Piedmont Coll (GA)
Pitzer Coll (CA)
Plattsburgh State U of NY (NY)
Plymouth State Coll (NH)
Point Loma Nazarene U (CA)
Pomona Coll (CA)
Pontifical Catholic U of Puerto Rico (PR)
Pontifical Coll Josephinum (OH)
Portland State U (OR)
Presbyterian Coll (SC)
Prescott Coll (AZ)
Princeton U (NJ)
Principia Coll (IL)
Providence Coll (RI)
Purchase Coll, State U of NY (NY)
Purdue U (IN)
Purdue U Calumet (IN)
Queens Coll (NC)
Queens Coll of the City U of NY (NY)
Queen's U at Kingston (ON, Canada)
Quincy U (IL)
Radford U (VA)
Randolph-Macon Coll (VA)
Randolph-Macon Woman's Coll (VA)
Redeemer U Coll (ON, Canada)
Reed Coll (OR)
Regis U (CO)
Rensselaer Polytechnic Inst (NY)
Rhode Island Coll (RI)
Rhodes Coll (TN)
Rice U (TX)
The Richard Stockton Coll of New Jersey (NJ)
Rider U (NJ)
Ripon Coll (WI)
Roanoke Coll (VA)
Roberts Wesleyan Coll (NY)
Rockford Coll (IL)
Rockhurst U (MO)
Rocky Mountain Coll (MT)
Roger Williams U (RI)
Rollins Coll (FL)
Roosevelt U (IL)
Rosemont Coll (PA)
Rutgers, The State U of New Jersey, New Brunswick (NJ)
Sacred Heart Major Seminary (MI)
Sacred Heart U (CT)
St. Ambrose U (IA)
St. Andrews Presbyterian Coll (NC)
Saint Anselm Coll (NH)
St. Bonaventure U (NY)
St. Charles Borromeo Seminary, Overbrook (PA)
St. Cloud State U (MN)
St. Edward's U (TX)
St. Francis Coll (NY)
Saint Francis U (PA)
St. Francis Xavier U (NS, Canada)
St. John Fisher Coll (NY)
St. John's Seminary Coll (CA)
Saint John's Seminary Coll of Liberal Arts (MA)
Saint John's U (MN)
St. John's U (NY)
Saint Joseph Coll (CT)
Saint Joseph's Coll (IN)
Saint Joseph's Coll (ME)
Saint Joseph's U (PA)
St. Lawrence U (NY)
Saint Louis U (MO)
Saint Mary's Coll (IN)
Saint Mary's Coll of Ave Maria U (MI)
Saint Mary's Coll of California (CA)
St. Mary's Coll of Maryland (MD)
Saint Mary's U (NS, Canada)

Saint Mary's U of Minnesota (MN)
St. Mary's U of San Antonio (TX)
Saint Michael's Coll (VT)
St. Norbert Coll (WI)
St. Olaf Coll (MN)
Saint Peter's Coll (NJ)
St. Thomas Aquinas Coll (NY)
St. Thomas U (NB, Canada)
Saint Vincent Coll (PA)
Saint Xavier U (IL)
Salem Coll (NC)
Salisbury U (MD)
Salve Regina U (RI)
Samford U (AL)
Sam Houston State U (TX)
San Diego State U (CA)
San Francisco State U (CA)
San Jose State U (CA)
Santa Clara U (CA)
Sarah Lawrence Coll (NY)
Schreiner U (TX)
Scripps Coll (CA)
Seattle Pacific U (WA)
Seattle U (WA)
Seton Hall U (NJ)
Shaw U (NC)
Siena Coll (NY)
Siena Heights U (MI)
Simmons Coll (MA)
Simon Fraser U (BC, Canada)
Simon's Rock Coll of Bard (MA)
Simpson Coll (IA)
Skidmore Coll (NY)
Slippery Rock U of Pennsylvania (PA)
Smith Coll (MA)
Sonoma State U (CA)
Southeast Missouri State U (MO)
Southern Connecticut State U (CT)
Southern Illinois U Carbondale (IL)
Southern Illinois U Edwardsville (IL)
Southern Methodist U (TX)
Southern Nazarene U (OK)
Southern Virginia U (VA)
Southwestern U (TX)
Southwest Missouri State U (MO)
Southwest State U (MN)
Southwest Texas State U (TX)
Spelman Coll (GA)
Spring Arbor U (MI)
Spring Hill Coll (AL)
Stanford U (CA)
State U of NY at Albany (NY)
State U of NY at Binghamton (NY)
State U of NY at New Paltz (NY)
State U of NY at Oswego (NY)
State U of NY Coll at Brockport (NY)
State U of NY Coll at Buffalo (NY)
State U of NY Coll at Cortland (NY)
State U of NY Coll at Fredonia (NY)
State U of NY Coll at Geneseo (NY)
State U of NY Coll at Old Westbury (NY)
State U of NY Coll at Oneonta (NY)
State U of NY Coll at Potsdam (NY)
State U of West Georgia (GA)
Stephens Coll (MO)
Stetson U (FL)
Stevens Inst of Technology (NJ)
Stonehill Coll (MA)
State U of NY at Stony Brook (NY)
Suffolk U (MA)
Susquehanna U (PA)
Swarthmore Coll (PA)
Sweet Briar Coll (VA)
Syracuse U (NY)
Tabor Coll (KS)
Taylor U (IN)
Temple U (PA)
Texas A&M U (TX)
Texas Christian U (TX)
Texas Lutheran U (TX)
Texas Tech U (TX)
Thiel Coll (PA)
Thomas Edison State Coll (NJ)
Thomas More Coll (KY)
Thomas More Coll of Liberal Arts (NH)
Toccoa Falls Coll (GA)
Touro Coll (NY)
Towson U (MD)
Transylvania U (KY)
Trent U (ON, Canada)
Trinity Christian Coll (IL)
Trinity Coll (CT)
Trinity International U (IL)
Trinity U (TX)
Trinity Western U (BC, Canada)
Truman State U (MO)
Tufts U (MA)
Tulane U (LA)
Tyndale Coll & Seminary (ON, Canada)
Union Coll (NY)
Union U (TN)
United States Military Academy (NY)
Université de Montréal (QC, Canada)
Université de Sherbrooke (PQ, Canada)
Université Laval (QC, Canada)
State U of NY at Buffalo (NY)
U Coll of Cape Breton (NS, Canada)
The U of Akron (OH)
The U of Alabama (AL)
The U of Alabama at Birmingham (AL)
The U of Alabama in Huntsville (AL)
U of Alaska Fairbanks (AK)
U of Alberta (AB, Canada)
The U of Arizona (AZ)
U of Arkansas (AR)
U of Arkansas at Little Rock (AR)
The U of British Columbia (BC, Canada)
U of Calgary (AB, Canada)
U of Calif, Berkeley (CA)
U of Calif, Davis (CA)
U of Calif, Irvine (CA)
U of Calif, Los Angeles (CA)
U of Calif, Riverside (CA)
U of Calif, San Diego (CA)
U of Calif, Santa Barbara (CA)
U of Calif, Santa Cruz (CA)
U of Central Arkansas (AR)
U of Central Florida (FL)
U of Central Oklahoma (OK)
U of Charleston (WV)
U of Chicago (IL)
U of Cincinnati (OH)
U of Colorado at Boulder (CO)
U of Colorado at Colorado Springs (CO)
U of Colorado at Denver (CO)
U of Connecticut (CT)
U of Dallas (TX)
U of Dayton (OH)
U of Delaware (DE)
U of Denver (CO)
U of Dubuque (IA)
U of Evansville (IN)
The U of Findlay (OH)
U of Florida (FL)
U of Georgia (GA)
U of Guelph (ON, Canada)
U of Hartford (CT)
U of Hawaii at Hilo (HI)
U of Hawaii at Manoa (HI)
U of Hawaii–West Oahu (HI)
U of Houston (TX)
U of Idaho (ID)
U of Illinois at Chicago (IL)
U of Illinois at Urbana–Champaign (IL)
U of Indianapolis (IN)
The U of Iowa (IA)
U of Kansas (KS)
U of Kentucky (KY)
U of King's Coll (NS, Canada)
U of La Verne (CA)
The U of Lethbridge (AB, Canada)
U of Louisiana at Lafayette (LA)
U of Louisville (KY)
U of Maine (ME)
U of Maine at Farmington (ME)
U of Manitoba (MB, Canada)
U of Maryland, Baltimore County (MD)
U of Maryland, Coll Park (MD)
U of Massachusetts Amherst (MA)
U of Massachusetts Boston (MA)
U of Massachusetts Dartmouth (MA)
U of Massachusetts Lowell (MA)
The U of Memphis (TN)
U of Miami (FL)
U of Michigan (MI)
U of Michigan–Dearborn (MI)
U of Michigan–Flint (MI)
U of Minnesota, Duluth (MN)
U of Minnesota, Morris (MN)
U of Minnesota, Twin Cities Campus (MN)
U of Mississippi (MS)
U of Missouri–Columbia (MO)
U of Missouri–Kansas City (MO)
U of Missouri–Rolla (MO)
U of Missouri–St. Louis (MO)
The U of Montana–Missoula (MT)
U of Nebraska at Omaha (NE)
U of Nebraska–Lincoln (NE)
U of Nevada, Las Vegas (NV)
U of Nevada, Reno (NV)
U of New Hampshire (NH)
U of New Mexico (NM)
U of New Orleans (LA)
The U of North Carolina at Asheville (NC)
The U of North Carolina at Chapel Hill (NC)
The U of North Carolina at Charlotte (NC)
The U of North Carolina at Greensboro (NC)
The U of North Carolina at Pembroke (NC)
U of North Dakota (ND)
U of Northern Colorado (CO)
U of Northern Iowa (IA)
U of North Florida (FL)
U of North Texas (TX)
U of Notre Dame (IN)
U of Oklahoma (OK)
U of Oregon (OR)
U of Ottawa (ON, Canada)
U of Pennsylvania (PA)
U of Pittsburgh (PA)
U of Portland (OR)
U of Prince Edward Island (PE, Canada)
U of Puget Sound (WA)
U of Redlands (CA)
U of Regina (SK, Canada)
U of Rhode Island (RI)
U of Richmond (VA)
U of Rochester (NY)
U of St. Thomas (MN)
U of St. Thomas (TX)
U of San Diego (CA)
U of San Francisco (CA)
U of Saskatchewan (SK, Canada)
The U of Scranton (PA)
U of Sioux Falls (SD)
U of South Alabama (AL)
U of South Carolina (SC)
U of South Dakota (SD)
U of Southern California (CA)
U of Southern Indiana (IN)
U of Southern Maine (ME)
U of Southern Mississippi (MS)
U of South Florida (FL)
The U of Tennessee (TN)
The U of Tennessee at Chattanooga (TN)
The U of Tennessee at Martin (TN)
The U of Texas at Arlington (TX)
The U of Texas at Austin (TX)
The U of Texas at El Paso (TX)
The U of Texas at San Antonio (TX)
The U of Texas–Pan American (TX)
U of the District of Columbia (DC)
U of the Incarnate Word (TX)
U of the Pacific (CA)
U of the South (TN)
U of Toledo (OH)
U of Toronto (ON, Canada)
U of Tulsa (OK)
U of Utah (UT)
U of Vermont (VT)
U of Victoria (BC, Canada)
U of Virginia (VA)
U of Washington (WA)
U of Waterloo (ON, Canada)
The U of Western Ontario (ON, Canada)
U of West Florida (FL)
U of Windsor (ON, Canada)
U of Wisconsin–Eau Claire (WI)
U of Wisconsin–Green Bay (WI)
U of Wisconsin–La Crosse (WI)
U of Wisconsin–Madison (WI)
U of Wisconsin–Milwaukee (WI)
U of Wisconsin–Oshkosh (WI)
U of Wisconsin–Parkside (WI)
U of Wisconsin–Platteville (WI)
U of Wisconsin–Stevens Point (WI)
U of Wyoming (WY)
Urbana U (OH)
Ursinus Coll (PA)
Ursuline Coll (OH)
Utah State U (UT)
Utica Coll of Syracuse U (NY)
Valdosta State U (GA)
Valparaiso U (IN)
Vanderbilt U (TN)
Vassar Coll (NY)
Villanova U (PA)
Virginia Commonwealth U (VA)
Virginia Polytechnic Inst and State U (VA)
Virginia Wesleyan Coll (VA)
Wabash Coll (IN)
Wadhams Hall Seminary-Coll (NY)
Wake Forest U (NC)
Walla Walla Coll (WA)
Walsh U (OH)
Wartburg Coll (IA)
Washburn U of Topeka (KS)
Washington & Jefferson Coll (PA)
Washington and Lee U (VA)
Washington Coll (MD)
Washington State U (WA)
Washington U in St. Louis (MO)
Wayne State U (MI)
Webster U (MO)
Wellesley Coll (MA)
Wells Coll (NY)
Wesleyan Coll (GA)
Wesleyan U (CT)
West Chester U of Pennsylvania (PA)
Western Carolina U (NC)
Western Illinois U (IL)
Western Kentucky U (KY)
Western Maryland Coll (MD)
Western Michigan U (MI)
Western Oregon U (OR)
Western Washington U (WA)
Westminster Coll (MO)
Westminster Coll (PA)
Westminster Coll (UT)
Westmont Coll (CA)
West Virginia U (WV)
West Virginia Wesleyan Coll (WV)
Wheaton Coll (IL)
Wheaton Coll (MA)
Wheeling Jesuit U (WV)
Whitman Coll (WA)
Whittier Coll (CA)
Whitworth Coll (WA)
Wichita State U (KS)
Wiley Coll (TX)
Wilfrid Laurier U (ON, Canada)
Wilkes U (PA)
Willamette U (OR)
William Jewell Coll (MO)
William Paterson U of New Jersey (NJ)
Williams Coll (MA)
Wilmington Coll (OH)
Wingate U (NC)
Winthrop U (SC)
Wittenberg U (OH)
Wofford Coll (SC)
Worcester Polytechnic Inst (MA)
Wright State U (OH)
Xavier U (OH)
Xavier U of Louisiana (LA)
Yale U (CT)
Yeshiva U (NY)
York Coll of the City U of New York (NY)
York U (ON, Canada)
Youngstown State U (OH)

PHILOSOPHY AND RELIGION RELATED

Bethune-Cookman Coll (FL)
Bridgewater Coll (VA)
Eastern Mennonite U (VA)
Graceland U (IA)
Kean U (NJ)
Kentucky Wesleyan Coll (KY)
Lyon Coll (AR)
McGill U (PQ, Canada)
Point Loma Nazarene U (CA)
Southwestern Coll (KS)
State U of NY at Oswego (NY)
Sterling Coll (KS)
Union U (TN)
The U of North Carolina at Wilmington (NC)
U of Notre Dame (IN)
U of Oklahoma (OK)
Washington U in St. Louis (MO)

PHOTOGRAPHIC TECHNOLOGY

Kent State U (OH)
Ohio U (OH)
Rochester Inst of Technology (NY)

PHOTOGRAPHY

Academy of Art Coll (CA)
Adams State Coll (CO)
Alberta Coll of Art & Design (AB, Canada)
Albertus Magnus Coll (CT)
Alfred U (NY)
American InterContinental U (CA)
American InterContinental U, Atlanta (GA)
Andrews U (MI)
Arcadia U (PA)
Arizona State U (AZ)
Art Academy of Cincinnati (OH)
Art Center Coll of Design (CA)
The Art Inst of Atlanta (GA)
The Art Inst of Boston at Lesley U (MA)
Atlanta Coll of Art (GA)
Ball State U (IN)
Bard Coll (NY)
Barry U (FL)
Barton Coll (NC)
Bennington Coll (VT)
Bowling Green State U (OH)
Brigham Young U (UT)
California Coll of Arts and Crafts (CA)
California Inst of the Arts (CA)
California State U, Fullerton (CA)
California State U, Hayward (CA)
California State U, Long Beach (CA)
California State U, Northridge (CA)
Carson-Newman Coll (TN)
Cazenovia Coll (NY)
Central Missouri State U (MO)
The Cleveland Inst of Art (OH)
Coker Coll (SC)
Ctr for Creative Studies—Coll of Art and Design (MI)
Coll of Santa Fe (NM)
Coll of Staten Island of the City U of NY (NY)
Coll of Visual Arts (MN)
Colorado State U (CO)
Columbia Coll (MO)
Columbia Coll Chicago (IL)
Columbus Coll of Art and Design (OH)
Concordia U (QC, Canada)
Corcoran Coll of Art and Design (DC)
Cornell U (NY)
Dominican U (IL)
Drexel U (PA)
The Evergreen State Coll (WA)
Fitchburg State Coll (MA)
Fordham U (NY)
Gallaudet U (DC)
Goddard Coll (VT)
Governors State U (IL)
Grand Valley State U (MI)
Hampshire Coll (MA)
Hampton U (VA)
Indiana U Bloomington (IN)
Indiana Wesleyan U (IN)
Inter American U of PR, San Germán Campus (PR)
Ithaca Coll (NY)
Kansas City Art Inst (MO)
Long Island U, C.W. Post Campus (NY)
Long Island U, Southampton Coll, Friends World Program (NY)
Louisiana Tech U (LA)
Loyola U Chicago (IL)
Maine Coll of Art (ME)
Marlboro Coll (VT)
Maryland Inst, Coll of Art (MD)
Massachusetts Coll of Art (MA)
McNeese State U (LA)
Memorial U of Newfoundland (NF, Canada)
Memphis Coll of Art (TN)
Milwaukee Inst of Art and Design (WI)
Minneapolis Coll of Art and Design (MN)
Montserrat Coll of Art (MA)
Morningside Coll (IA)
Mount Allison U (NB, Canada)
Nazareth Coll of Rochester (NY)

New England Coll (NH)
New World School of the Arts (FL)
New York U (NY)
Northern Arizona U (AZ)
Northern Michigan U (MI)
Nova Scotia Coll of Art and Design (NS, Canada)
Ohio U (OH)
Otis Coll of Art and Design (CA)
Pacific Northwest Coll of Art (OR)
Parsons School of Design, New School U (NY)
Point Park Coll (PA)
Pratt Inst (NY)
Prescott Coll (AZ)
Rhode Island School of Design (RI)
Ringling School of Art and Design (FL)
Rivier Coll (NH)
Rochester Inst of Technology (NY)
Rutgers, The State U of New Jersey, New Brunswick (NJ)
St. Edward's U (TX)
St. John's U (NY)
Saint Mary-of-the-Woods Coll (IN)
Salem State Coll (MA)
Sam Houston State U (TX)
San Francisco Art Inst (CA)
San Jose State U (CA)
Sarah Lawrence Coll (NY)
Savannah Coll of Art and Design (GA)
School of the Museum of Fine Arts (MA)
School of Visual Arts (NY)
Seattle U (WA)
Simon's Rock Coll of Bard (MA)
State U of NY at New Paltz (NY)
State U of NY Coll at Buffalo (NY)
State U of NY Coll at Potsdam (NY)
Syracuse U (NY)
Temple U (PA)
Texas A&M U–Commerce (TX)
Texas Christian U (TX)
Texas Southern U (TX)
Texas Woman's U (TX)
Thomas Edison State Coll (NJ)
Trinity Christian Coll (IL)
The U of Akron (OH)
U of Calif, Santa Cruz (CA)
U of Central Oklahoma (OK)
U of Dayton (OH)
U of Hartford (CT)
U of Houston (TX)
U of Idaho (ID)
U of Illinois at Chicago (IL)
U of Illinois at Urbana–Champaign (IL)
The U of Iowa (IA)
U of Maryland, Baltimore County (MD)
U of Massachusetts Dartmouth (MA)
U of Miami (FL)
U of Michigan (MI)
U of Missouri–St. Louis (MO)
U of Montevallo (AL)
U of North Texas (TX)
U of Ottawa (ON, Canada)
U of San Francisco (CA)
U of South Dakota (SD)
The U of Texas at Arlington (TX)
The U of the Arts (PA)
U of Washington (WA)
Virginia Commonwealth U (VA)
Virginia Intermont Coll (VA)
Washington U in St. Louis (MO)
Weber State U (UT)
Webster U (MO)
White Pines Coll (NH)
Wright State U (OH)
York U (ON, Canada)
Youngstown State U (OH)

PHYSICAL EDUCATION

Abilene Christian U (TX)
Adams State Coll (CO)
Adelphi U (NY)
Adrian Coll (MI)
Alabama State U (AL)
Albany State U (GA)
Albertson Coll of Idaho (ID)
Albion Coll (MI)
Alcorn State U (MS)
Alderson-Broaddus Coll (WV)
Alice Lloyd Coll (KY)
American U of Puerto Rico (PR)
Anderson Coll (SC)
Anderson U (IN)
Andrews U (MI)
Appalachian State U (NC)
Aquinas Coll (MI)
Arkansas State U (AR)
Arkansas Tech U (AR)
Armstrong Atlantic State U (GA)
Asbury Coll (KY)
Ashland U (OH)
Athens State U (AL)
Atlantic Union Coll (MA)
Auburn U (AL)
Augsburg Coll (MN)
Augustana Coll (IL)
Augustana Coll (SD)
Augusta State U (GA)
Aurora U (IL)
Austin Coll (TX)
Averett U (VA)
Azusa Pacific U (CA)
Baker U (KS)
Baldwin-Wallace Coll (OH)
Ball State U (IN)
Barry U (FL)
Barton Coll (NC)
Bayamón Central U (PR)
Baylor U (TX)
Bellevue U (NE)
Belmont U (TN)
Bemidji State U (MN)
Benedictine Coll (KS)
Berea Coll (KY)
Berry Coll (GA)
Bethany Coll (KS)
Bethany Coll (WV)
Bethel Coll (IN)
Bethel Coll (MN)
Bethel Coll (TN)
Bethune-Cookman Coll (FL)
Biola U (CA)
Blackburn Coll (IL)
Bluefield Coll (VA)
Blue Mountain Coll (MS)
Bluffton Coll (OH)
Boise State U (ID)
Boston U (MA)
Bowling Green State U (OH)
Brewton-Parker Coll (GA)
Briar Cliff U (IA)
Bridgewater State Coll (MA)
Brigham Young U (UT)
Brigham Young U–Hawaii (HI)
Brock U (ON, Canada)
Brooklyn Coll of the City U of NY (NY)
Bryan Coll (TN)
Buena Vista U (IA)
California Lutheran U (CA)
California Polytechnic State U, San Luis Obispo (CA)
California State Polytechnic U, Pomona (CA)
California State U, Bakersfield (CA)
California State U, Chico (CA)
California State U, Dominguez Hills (CA)
California State U, Fresno (CA)
California State U, Fullerton (CA)
California State U, Hayward (CA)
California State U, Long Beach (CA)
California State U, Los Angeles (CA)
California State U, Northridge (CA)
California State U, San Bernardino (CA)
California State U, Stanislaus (CA)
Calvin Coll (MI)
Cameron U (OK)
Campbellsville U (KY)
Campbell U (NC)
Canisius Coll (NY)
Capital U (OH)
Carroll Coll (MT)
Carroll Coll (WI)
Carson-Newman Coll (TN)
Carthage Coll (WI)
Castleton State Coll (VT)
Catawba Coll (NC)
Cedarville U (OH)
Centenary Coll of Louisiana (LA)
Central Connecticut State U (CT)
Central Methodist Coll (MO)
Central Michigan U (MI)
Central Missouri State U (MO)
Central State U (OH)
Central Washington U (WA)
Chadron State Coll (NE)
Chapman U (CA)
Charleston Southern U (SC)
Chicago State U (IL)
Chowan Coll (NC)
Christian Heritage Coll (CA)
Christopher Newport U (VA)
Citadel, The Military Coll of South Carolina (SC)
Claflin U (SC)
Clark Atlanta U (GA)
Clarke Coll (IA)
Clearwater Christian Coll (FL)
Cleveland State U (OH)
Coastal Carolina U (SC)
Coe Coll (IA)
Coker Coll (SC)
Coll of Charleston (SC)
Coll of Mount St. Joseph (OH)
Coll of Mount Saint Vincent (NY)
The Coll of New Jersey (NJ)
Coll of St. Catherine (MN)
Coll of the Ozarks (MO)
Coll of the Southwest (NM)
The Coll of William and Mary (VA)
Colorado State U (CO)
Columbus State U (GA)
Concord Coll (WV)
Concordia Coll (MN)
Concordia U (IL)
Concordia U (MI)
Concordia U (MN)
Concordia U (NE)
Concordia U (OR)
Concordia U Wisconsin (WI)
Coppin State Coll (MD)
Cornell Coll (IA)
Cornerstone U (MI)
Crown Coll (MN)
Culver-Stockton Coll (MO)
Cumberland Coll (KY)
Cumberland U (TN)
Dakota State U (SD)
Dakota Wesleyan U (SD)
Dallas Baptist U (TX)
Dana Coll (NE)
Davis & Elkins Coll (WV)
Defiance Coll (OH)
Delaware State U (DE)
Delta State U (MS)
Denison U (OH)
DePaul U (IL)
Dickinson State U (ND)
Dillard U (LA)
Doane Coll (NE)
Dordt Coll (IA)
Drury U (MO)
East Carolina U (NC)
East Central U (OK)
Eastern Connecticut State U (CT)
Eastern Illinois U (IL)
Eastern Kentucky U (KY)
Eastern Mennonite U (VA)
Eastern Michigan U (MI)
Eastern Nazarene Coll (MA)
Eastern New Mexico U (NM)
Eastern Oregon U (OR)
Eastern Washington U (WA)
East Stroudsburg U of Pennsylvania (PA)
East Texas Baptist U (TX)
Edinboro U of Pennsylvania (PA)
Edward Waters Coll (FL)
Elizabeth City State U (NC)
Elmhurst Coll (IL)
Elon U (NC)
Emporia State U (KS)
Erskine Coll (SC)
Eureka Coll (IL)
Evangel U (MO)
Fairmont State Coll (WV)
Faulkner U (AL)
Fayetteville State U (NC)
Ferrum Coll (VA)
Florida A&M U (FL)
Florida International U (FL)
Florida Southern Coll (FL)
Florida State U (FL)
Fort Hays State U (KS)
Fort Lewis Coll (CO)
Fort Valley State U (GA)
Franklin Coll of Indiana (IN)
Freed-Hardeman U (TN)
Fresno Pacific U (CA)
Friends U (KS)
Frostburg State U (MD)
Gallaudet U (DC)
Gardner-Webb U (NC)
George Fox U (OR)
George Mason U (VA)
Georgetown Coll (KY)
Georgia Coll and State U (GA)
Georgia Southern U (GA)
Georgia Southwestern State U (GA)
Georgia State U (GA)
Gettysburg Coll (PA)
Glenville State Coll (WV)
Gonzaga U (WA)
Goshen Coll (IN)
Grace Coll (IN)
Graceland U (IA)
Grambling State U (LA)
Grand Canyon U (AZ)
Grand Valley State U (MI)
Greensboro Coll (NC)
Greenville Coll (IL)
Gustavus Adolphus Coll (MN)
Hamline U (MN)
Hampton U (VA)
Hannibal-LaGrange Coll (MO)
Hanover Coll (IN)
Harding U (AR)
Hardin-Simmons U (TX)
Hastings Coll (NE)
Heidelberg Coll (OH)
Henderson State U (AR)
Hendrix Coll (AR)
High Point U (NC)
Hillsdale Coll (MI)
Hofstra U (NY)
Hope Coll (MI)
Houghton Coll (NY)
Howard Payne U (TX)
Howard U (DC)
Humboldt State U (CA)
Hunter Coll of the City U of NY (NY)
Huntingdon Coll (AL)
Huntington Coll (IN)
Huron U (SD)
Husson Coll (ME)
Huston-Tillotson Coll (TX)
Idaho State U (ID)
Illinois Coll (IL)
Illinois State U (IL)
Indiana State U (IN)
Indiana U Bloomington (IN)
Indiana U of Pennsylvania (PA)
Indiana U–Purdue U Indianapolis (IN)
Indiana Wesleyan U (IN)
Inter American U of PR, San Germán Campus (PR)
Iowa Wesleyan Coll (IA)
Ithaca Coll (NY)
Jackson State U (MS)
Jacksonville State U (AL)
Jacksonville U (FL)
Jamestown Coll (ND)
Jarvis Christian Coll (TX)
John Brown U (AR)
John Carroll U (OH)
Johnson C. Smith U (NC)
Johnson State Coll (VT)
Judson Coll (IL)
Kansas Wesleyan U (KS)
Kean U (NJ)
Keene State Coll (NH)
Kennesaw State U (GA)
Kent State U (OH)
Kentucky State U (KY)
Kentucky Wesleyan Coll (KY)
Lakehead U (ON, Canada)
Lamar U (TX)
Lambuth U (TN)
Lander U (SC)
Laurentian U (ON, Canada)
Lees-McRae Coll (NC)
Lee U (TN)
LeMoyne-Owen Coll (TN)
Lenoir-Rhyne Coll (NC)
LeTourneau U (TX)
Lewis-Clark State Coll (ID)
Lewis U (IL)
Liberty U (VA)
Limestone Coll (SC)
Lincoln Memorial U (TN)
Lincoln U (MO)
Lincoln U (PA)
Lindenwood U (MO)
Lindsey Wilson Coll (KY)
Lipscomb U (TN)
Lock Haven U of Pennsylvania (PA)
Long Island U, Brooklyn Campus (NY)
Long Island U, C.W. Post Campus (NY)
Longwood Coll (VA)
Loras Coll (IA)
Louisiana Coll (LA)
Louisiana State U and A&M Coll (LA)
Louisiana State U in Shreveport (LA)
Louisiana Tech U (LA)
Lubbock Christian U (TX)
Luther Coll (IA)
Lynchburg Coll (VA)
Lyndon State Coll (VT)
MacMurray Coll (IL)
Malone Coll (OH)
Manchester Coll (IN)
Manhattan Coll (NY)
Maranatha Baptist Bible Coll (WI)
Marian Coll (IN)
Marshall U (WV)
Mars Hill Coll (NC)
Maryville Coll (TN)
Marywood U (PA)
The Master's Coll and Seminary (CA)
Mayville State U (ND)
McGill U (PQ, Canada)
McKendree Coll (IL)
McMurry U (TX)
McNeese State U (LA)
McPherson Coll (KS)
Memorial U of Newfoundland (NF, Canada)
Meredith Coll (NC)
Mesa State Coll (CO)
Messiah Coll (PA)
Methodist Coll (NC)
Miami U (OH)
Michigan State U (MI)
MidAmerica Nazarene U (KS)
Midland Lutheran Coll (NE)
Milligan Coll (TN)
Millikin U (IL)
Minnesota State U, Mankato (MN)
Minnesota State U Moorhead (MN)
Minot State U (ND)
Mississippi State U (MS)
Mississippi U for Women (MS)
Mississippi Valley State U (MS)
Missouri Baptist Coll (MO)
Missouri Southern State Coll (MO)
Missouri Valley Coll (MO)
Monmouth Coll (IL)
Montana State U–Billings (MT)
Montana State U–Northern (MT)
Montclair State U (NJ)
Morehead State U (KY)
Morehouse Coll (GA)
Morgan State U (MD)
Mount Marty Coll (SD)
Mount Union Coll (OH)
Mount Vernon Nazarene U (OH)
Murray State U (KY)
Muskingum Coll (OH)
Nebraska Wesleyan U (NE)
Newberry Coll (SC)
New England Coll (NH)
New Mexico Highlands U (NM)
New Mexico State U (NM)
Nicholls State U (LA)
North Carolina Ag and Tech State U (NC)
North Carolina Central U (NC)
North Carolina Wesleyan Coll (NC)
North Central Coll (IL)
North Dakota State U (ND)
Northeastern Illinois U (IL)
Northeastern State U (OK)
Northeastern U (MA)
Northern Arizona U (AZ)
Northern Illinois U (IL)
Northern Kentucky U (KY)
Northern Michigan U (MI)
Northern State U (SD)
North Georgia Coll & State U (GA)
North Park U (IL)
Northwest Coll (WA)
Northwestern Coll (IA)
Northwestern Coll (MN)
Northwestern Oklahoma State U (OK)
Northwestern State U of Louisiana (LA)
Northwest Missouri State U (MO)
Northwest Nazarene U (ID)
Norwich U (VT)
Oakland City U (IN)
Oakwood Coll (AL)
Ohio Northern U (OH)
The Ohio State U (OH)
Ohio U (OH)

Ohio Valley Coll (WV)
Ohio Wesleyan U (OH)
Oklahoma Baptist U (OK)
Oklahoma Christian U of Science and Arts (OK)
Oklahoma City U (OK)
Oklahoma Panhandle State U (OK)
Oklahoma State U (OK)
Oklahoma Wesleyan U (OK)
Old Dominion U (VA)
Olivet Coll (MI)
Olivet Nazarene U (IL)
Oral Roberts U (OK)
Oregon State U (OR)
Ottawa U (KS)
Otterbein Coll (OH)
Ouachita Baptist U (AR)
Pacific Lutheran U (WA)
Pacific Union Coll (CA)
Palm Beach Atlantic Coll (FL)
Pepperdine U, Malibu (CA)
Peru State Coll (NE)
Pfeiffer U (NC)
Philadelphia Biblical U (PA)
Pittsburg State U (KS)
Plymouth State Coll (NH)
Pontifical Catholic U of Puerto Rico (PR)
Prescott Coll (AZ)
Purdue U (IN)
Queens Coll of the City U of NY (NY)
Queen's U at Kingston (ON, Canada)
Quincy U (IL)
Radford U (VA)
Reinhardt Coll (GA)
Rhode Island Coll (RI)
Rice U (TX)
Ripon Coll (WI)
Rockford Coll (IL)
Rocky Mountain Coll (MT)
Rowan U (NJ)
Saginaw Valley State U (MI)
St. Ambrose U (IA)
St. Andrews Presbyterian Coll (NC)
Saint Augustine's Coll (NC)
St. Bonaventure U (NY)
St. Cloud State U (MN)
St. Edward's U (TX)
St. Francis Coll (NY)
St. Francis Xavier U (NS, Canada)
Saint Joseph's Coll (IN)
Saint Joseph's Coll (ME)
Saint Leo U (FL)
Saint Mary's Coll of California (CA)
Salem International U (WV)
Salem State Coll (MA)
Salisbury U (MD)
Samford U (AL)
San Diego State U (CA)
San Francisco State U (CA)
San Jose State U (CA)
Seattle Pacific U (WA)
Shenandoah U (VA)
Simpson Coll (IA)
Slippery Rock U of Pennsylvania (PA)
Sonoma State U (CA)
South Carolina State U (SC)
South Dakota State U (SD)
Southeastern Bible Coll (AL)
Southeastern Louisiana U (LA)
Southeastern Oklahoma State U (OK)
Southeast Missouri State U (MO)
Southern Adventist U (TN)
Southern Arkansas U–Magnolia (AR)
Southern Connecticut State U (CT)
Southern Illinois U Carbondale (IL)
Southern Nazarene U (OK)
Southern Oregon U (OR)
Southern Utah U (UT)
Southern Wesleyan U (SC)
Southwest Baptist U (MO)
Southwestern Coll (KS)
Southwestern Oklahoma State U (OK)
Southwestern U (TX)
Southwest Missouri State U (MO)
Southwest State U (MN)
Spring Arbor U (MI)
Springfield Coll (MA)
State U of NY Coll at Brockport (NY)
State U of NY Coll at Cortland (NY)
State U of NY Coll at Potsdam (NY)
State U of West Georgia (GA)
Sterling Coll (KS)
Sul Ross State U (TX)
Syracuse U (NY)
Tabor Coll (KS)
Tarleton State U (TX)
Taylor U (IN)
Temple U (PA)
Tennessee State U (TN)
Tennessee Technological U (TN)
Tennessee Wesleyan Coll (TN)
Texas A&M International U (TX)
Texas A&M U–Commerce (TX)
Texas A&M U–Corpus Christi (TX)
Texas A&M U–Kingsville (TX)
Texas Christian U (TX)
Texas Lutheran U (TX)
Texas Southern U (TX)
Texas Wesleyan U (TX)
Towson U (MD)
Transylvania U (KY)
Trevecca Nazarene U (TN)
Trinity Christian Coll (IL)
Trinity International U (IL)
Trinity Western U (BC, Canada)
Tri-State U (IN)
Troy State U (AL)
Tusculum Coll (TN)
Union Coll (KY)
Union Coll (NE)
Union U (TN)
Université de Montréal (QC, Canada)
Université de Sherbrooke (PQ, Canada)
Université Laval (QC, Canada)
U Coll of the Fraser Valley (BC, Canada)
The U of Akron (OH)
The U of Alabama (AL)
The U of Alabama at Birmingham (AL)
U of Alaska Anchorage (AK)
U of Alberta (AB, Canada)
The U of Arizona (AZ)
U of Arkansas at Pine Bluff (AR)
U of Calif, Davis (CA)
U of Central Arkansas (AR)
U of Central Florida (FL)
U of Central Oklahoma (OK)
U of Cincinnati (OH)
U of Connecticut (CT)
U of Dayton (OH)
U of Delaware (DE)
U of Evansville (IN)
The U of Findlay (OH)
U of Florida (FL)
U of Georgia (GA)
U of Hawaii at Manoa (HI)
U of Idaho (ID)
U of Indianapolis (IN)
U of Kansas (KS)
U of Kentucky (KY)
U of La Verne (CA)
The U of Lethbridge (AB, Canada)
U of Louisiana at Lafayette (LA)
U of Louisiana at Monroe (LA)
U of Maine (ME)
U of Maine at Presque Isle (ME)
U of Manitoba (MB, Canada)
U of Mary (ND)
U of Mary Hardin-Baylor (TX)
U of Maryland, Coll Park (MD)
U of Maryland Eastern Shore (MD)
U of Massachusetts Boston (MA)
U of Miami (FL)
U of Michigan (MI)
U of Minnesota, Duluth (MN)
U of Minnesota, Twin Cities Campus (MN)
U of Missouri–Kansas City (MO)
U of Missouri–St. Louis (MO)
U of Mobile (AL)
The U of Montana–Missoula (MT)
Western Montana Coll of The U of Montana (MT)
U of Nebraska at Kearney (NE)
U of Nebraska at Omaha (NE)
U of Nebraska–Lincoln (NE)
U of Nevada, Las Vegas (NV)
U of Nevada, Reno (NV)
U of New Hampshire (NH)
U of New Mexico (NM)
U of New Orleans (LA)
The U of North Carolina at Greensboro (NC)
The U of North Carolina at Pembroke (NC)
The U of North Carolina at Wilmington (NC)
U of North Dakota (ND)
U of Northern Iowa (IA)
U of North Florida (FL)
U of North Texas (TX)
U of Ottawa (ON, Canada)
U of Pittsburgh (PA)
U of Puerto Rico, Cayey U Coll (PR)
U of Regina (SK, Canada)
U of Rhode Island (RI)
U of Richmond (VA)
U of Rio Grande (OH)
U of St. Thomas (MN)
U of San Francisco (CA)
U of Saskatchewan (SK, Canada)
U of Sioux Falls (SD)
U of South Alabama (AL)
U of South Carolina (SC)
U of South Carolina Spartanburg (SC)
U of South Dakota (SD)
U of Southern Colorado (CO)
U of Southern Indiana (IN)
U of Southern Mississippi (MS)
U of South Florida (FL)
The U of Tampa (FL)
The U of Tennessee at Chattanooga (TN)
The U of Texas–Pan American (TX)
U of the District of Columbia (DC)
U of the Incarnate Word (TX)
U of the Ozarks (AR)
U of Toledo (OH)
U of Toronto (ON, Canada)
U of Utah (UT)
U of Vermont (VT)
U of Victoria (BC, Canada)
U of Virginia (VA)
The U of West Alabama (AL)
The U of Western Ontario (ON, Canada)
U of West Florida (FL)
U of Windsor (ON, Canada)
U of Wisconsin–La Crosse (WI)
U of Wisconsin–Madison (WI)
U of Wisconsin–Oshkosh (WI)
U of Wisconsin–River Falls (WI)
U of Wisconsin–Stevens Point (WI)
U of Wisconsin–Superior (WI)
U of Wisconsin–Whitewater (WI)
U of Wyoming (WY)
Upper Iowa U (IA)
Ursinus Coll (PA)
Utah State U (UT)
Valdosta State U (GA)
Valley City State U (ND)
Valparaiso U (IN)
Vanguard U of Southern California (CA)
Virginia Intermont Coll (VA)
Virginia State U (VA)
Voorhees Coll (SC)
Walla Walla Coll (WA)
Walsh U (OH)
Warner Pacific Coll (OR)
Warner Southern Coll (FL)
Wartburg Coll (IA)
Washburn U of Topeka (KS)
Washington State U (WA)
Wayland Baptist U (TX)
Wayne State Coll (NE)
Wayne State U (MI)
Weber State U (UT)
Wesley Coll (DE)
West Chester U of Pennsylvania (PA)
Western Carolina U (NC)
Western Illinois U (IL)
Western Kentucky U (KY)
Western Michigan U (MI)
Western State Coll of Colorado (CO)
Western Washington U (WA)
Westfield State Coll (MA)
West Liberty State Coll (WV)
Westminster Coll (MO)
Westmont Coll (CA)
West Virginia State Coll (WV)
West Virginia U (WV)
West Virginia U Inst of Technology (WV)
West Virginia Wesleyan Coll (WV)
Whittier Coll (CA)
Whitworth Coll (WA)
Wichita State U (KS)
Wiley Coll (TX)
Wilfrid Laurier U (ON, Canada)
Willamette U (OR)
William Carey Coll (MS)
William Paterson U of New Jersey (NJ)
William Penn U (IA)
Williams Baptist Coll (AR)
William Woods U (MO)
Wilmington Coll (OH)
Wingate U (NC)
Winona State U (MN)
Winston-Salem State U (NC)
Winthrop U (SC)
Wright State U (OH)
Xavier U of Louisiana (LA)
York Coll (NE)
York Coll of the City U of New York (NY)
York U (ON, Canada)
Youngstown State U (OH)

PHYSICAL SCIENCES

Arkansas Tech U (AR)
Armstrong Atlantic State U (GA)
Asbury Coll (KY)
Auburn U Montgomery (AL)
Augusta State U (GA)
Bard Coll (NY)
Bemidji State U (MN)
Biola U (CA)
Black Hills State U (SD)
Bridgewater Coll (VA)
Brigham Young U–Hawaii (HI)
Brock U (ON, Canada)
California Inst of Technology (CA)
California Polytechnic State U, San Luis Obispo (CA)
California State U, Chico (CA)
California State U, Hayward (CA)
California State U, Sacramento (CA)
California State U, Stanislaus (CA)
Calvin Coll (MI)
Centenary Coll of Louisiana (LA)
Central Connecticut State U (CT)
Central Michigan U (MI)
Chowan Coll (NC)
Coe Coll (IA)
Colgate U (NY)
Colorado State U (CO)
Columbia Coll (SC)
Concordia U (IL)
Concordia U (MN)
Concordia U (NE)
Concordia U (OR)
Defiance Coll (OH)
Doane Coll (NE)
Eastern Michigan U (MI)
Eastern Washington U (WA)
East Stroudsburg U of Pennsylvania (PA)
Emporia State U (KS)
Eureka Coll (IL)
The Evergreen State Coll (WA)
Florida State U (FL)
Fordham U (NY)
Fort Hays State U (KS)
Framingham State Coll (MA)
Freed-Hardeman U (TN)
Georgia Southwestern State U (GA)
Goddard Coll (VT)
Goshen Coll (IN)
Graceland U (IA)
Grand Canyon U (AZ)
Grand Valley State U (MI)
Hampshire Coll (MA)
Hampton U (VA)
Hardin-Simmons U (TX)
Harvard U (MA)
Humboldt State U (CA)
Judson Coll (IL)
Juniata Coll (PA)
Kansas State U (KS)
Kutztown U of Pennsylvania (PA)
Lenoir-Rhyne Coll (NC)
Lincoln U (PA)
Linfield Coll (OR)
Lock Haven U of Pennsylvania (PA)
Loras Coll (IA)
Lyndon State Coll (VT)
Mansfield U of Pennsylvania (PA)
The Master's Coll and Seminary (CA)
Mayville State U (ND)
McMaster U (ON, Canada)
McPherson Coll (KS)
Mesa State Coll (CO)
Michigan State U (MI)
Michigan Technological U (MI)
Middlebury Coll (VT)
Midland Lutheran Coll (NE)
Midwestern State U (TX)
Minnesota State U, Mankato (MN)
Minot State U (ND)
Mississippi U for Women (MS)
Muhlenberg Coll (PA)
Northern Arizona U (AZ)
Northwest Missouri State U (MO)
Oklahoma Baptist U (OK)
Olivet Nazarene U (IL)
Oregon State U (OR)
Otterbein Coll (OH)
Pacific Union Coll (CA)
Penn State U at Erie, The Behrend Coll (PA)
Peru State Coll (NE)
Pittsburg State U (KS)
Radford U (VA)
Rensselaer Polytechnic Inst (NY)
Rhode Island Coll (RI)
Rowan U (NJ)
St. Cloud State U (MN)
St. Francis Xavier U (NS, Canada)
St. John's U (NY)
Saint Michael's Coll (VT)
San Diego State U (CA)
San Francisco State U (CA)
San Jose State U (CA)
Shawnee State U (OH)
Slippery Rock U of Pennsylvania (PA)
Southern Utah U (UT)
Southwest State U (MN)
Texas A&M International U (TX)
Trent U (ON, Canada)
Tri-State U (IN)
Troy State U (AL)
Troy State U Dothan (AL)
U of Alberta (AB, Canada)
U of Calif, Berkeley (CA)
U of Calif, Riverside (CA)
U of Central Arkansas (AR)
U of Dayton (OH)
U of Guelph (ON, Canada)
U of Houston–Clear Lake (TX)
U of Maryland, Coll Park (MD)
U of Michigan–Dearborn (MI)
U of Michigan–Flint (MI)
U of Missouri–St. Louis (MO)
Western Montana Coll of The U of Montana (MT)
U of North Alabama (AL)
U of Ottawa (ON, Canada)
U of Pittsburgh (PA)
U of Pittsburgh at Bradford (PA)
U of Rio Grande (OH)
U of Southern California (CA)
U of the Pacific (CA)
U of Toledo (OH)
U of Wisconsin–River Falls (WI)
U of Wisconsin–Superior (WI)
Walsh U (OH)
Warner Pacific Coll (OR)
Washington U in St. Louis (MO)
Wayland Baptist U (TX)
Wayne State Coll (NE)
Wesleyan Coll (GA)
Westfield State Coll (MA)
Wheaton Coll (IL)
Wiley Coll (TX)
William Paterson U of New Jersey (NJ)
Winona State U (MN)
Wittenberg U (OH)
York Coll of Pennsylvania (PA)
York U (ON, Canada)

PHYSICAL SCIENCES RELATED

Florida State U (FL)
Grand View Coll (IA)
Ohio U (OH)
The U of Texas at Austin (TX)

PHYSICAL SCIENCE TECHNOLOGIES RELATED

Millersville U of Pennsylvania (PA)

PHYSICAL/THEORETICAL CHEMISTRY

Michigan State U (MI)
Rice U (TX)

PHYSICAL THERAPY

Alcorn State U (MS)
Andrews U (MI)
Armstrong Atlantic State U (GA)

PHYSICAL THERAPY ASSISTANT

PHYSICIAN ASSISTANT

PHYSICS

Hunter Coll of the City U of NY (NY)
Idaho State U (ID)
Illinois Coll (IL)
Illinois Inst of Technology (IL)
Illinois State U (IL)
Illinois Wesleyan U (IL)
Immaculata Coll (PA)
Indiana State U (IN)
Indiana U Bloomington (IN)
Indiana U of Pennsylvania (PA)
Indiana U–Purdue U Fort Wayne (IN)
Indiana U–Purdue U Indianapolis (IN)
Indiana U South Bend (IN)
Iona Coll (NY)
Iowa State U of Science and Technology (IA)
Ithaca Coll (NY)
Jackson State U (MS)
Jacksonville State U (AL)
Jacksonville U (FL)
James Madison U (VA)
Jarvis Christian Coll (TX)
John Carroll U (OH)
Johns Hopkins U (MD)
Juniata Coll (PA)
Kalamazoo Coll (MI)
Kansas State U (KS)
Kansas Wesleyan U (KS)
Keene State Coll (NH)
Kent State U (OH)
Kentucky Wesleyan Coll (KY)
Kenyon Coll (OH)
Kettering U (MI)
King Coll (TN)
Knox Coll (IL)
Kutztown U of Pennsylvania (PA)
Lafayette Coll (PA)
Lake Forest Coll (IL)
Lakehead U (ON, Canada)
Lamar U (TX)
Laurentian U (ON, Canada)
Lawrence Technological U (MI)
Lawrence U (WI)
Lebanon Valley Coll (PA)
Lehigh U (PA)
Lehman Coll of the City U of NY (NY)
Le Moyne Coll (NY)
Lenoir-Rhyne Coll (NC)
Lewis & Clark Coll (OR)
Lewis U (IL)
Lincoln U (MO)
Lincoln U (PA)
Linfield Coll (OR)
Lipscomb U (TN)
Lock Haven U of Pennsylvania (PA)
Long Island U, Brooklyn Campus (NY)
Long Island U, C.W. Post Campus (NY)
Longwood Coll (VA)
Loras Coll (IA)
Louisiana Coll (LA)
Louisiana State U and A&M Coll (LA)
Louisiana State U in Shreveport (LA)
Louisiana Tech U (LA)
Loyola Coll in Maryland (MD)
Loyola Marymount U (CA)
Loyola U Chicago (IL)
Loyola U New Orleans (LA)
Luther Coll (IA)
Lycoming Coll (PA)
Lynchburg Coll (VA)
Macalester Coll (MN)
MacMurray Coll (IL)
Manchester Coll (IN)
Manhattan Coll (NY)
Mansfield U of Pennsylvania (PA)
Marietta Coll (OH)
Marlboro Coll (VT)
Marquette U (WI)
Marshall U (WV)
Mary Baldwin Coll (VA)
Mary Washington Coll (VA)
Massachusetts Coll of Liberal Arts (MA)
Massachusetts Inst of Technology (MA)
McGill U (PQ, Canada)
McMaster U (ON, Canada)
McMurry U (TX)
McNeese State U (LA)
Memorial U of Newfoundland (NF, Canada)
Mercer U (GA)
Mercyhurst Coll (PA)
Merrimack Coll (MA)
Mesa State Coll (CO)
Messiah Coll (PA)
Metropolitan State Coll of Denver (CO)
Miami U (OH)
Michigan State U (MI)
Michigan Technological U (MI)
MidAmerica Nazarene U (KS)
Middlebury Coll (VT)
Middle Tennessee State U (TN)
Midwestern State U (TX)
Millersville U of Pennsylvania (PA)
Millikin U (IL)
Millsaps Coll (MS)
Minnesota State U, Mankato (MN)
Minnesota State U Moorhead (MN)
Minot State U (ND)
Mississippi Coll (MS)
Mississippi State U (MS)
Missouri Southern State Coll (MO)
Monmouth Coll (IL)
Montana State U–Bozeman (MT)
Montclair State U (NJ)
Moravian Coll (PA)
Morehead State U (KY)
Morehouse Coll (GA)
Morgan State U (MD)
Morningside Coll (IA)
Mount Allison U (NB, Canada)
Mount Holyoke Coll (MA)
Mount Union Coll (OH)
Muhlenberg Coll (PA)
Murray State U (KY)
Muskingum Coll (OH)
Nebraska Wesleyan U (NE)
New Coll of Florida (FL)
New Jersey City U (NJ)
New Jersey Inst of Technology (NJ)
New Mexico Inst of Mining and Technology (NM)
New Mexico State U (NM)
New York Inst of Technology (NY)
New York U (NY)
Norfolk State U (VA)
North Carolina Ag and Tech State U (NC)
North Carolina Central U (NC)
North Carolina State U (NC)
North Central Coll (IL)
North Dakota State U (ND)
Northeastern Illinois U (IL)
Northeastern State U (OK)
Northeastern U (MA)
Northern Arizona U (AZ)
Northern Illinois U (IL)
Northern Kentucky U (KY)
Northern Michigan U (MI)
North Georgia Coll & State U (GA)
North Park U (IL)
Northwestern State U of Louisiana (LA)
Northwestern U (IL)
Northwest Missouri State U (MO)
Northwest Nazarene U (ID)
Norwich U (VT)
Oakland U (MI)
Oberlin Coll (OH)
Occidental Coll (CA)
Oglethorpe U (GA)
Ohio Northern U (OH)
The Ohio State U (OH)
Ohio U (OH)
Ohio Wesleyan U (OH)
Okanagan U Coll (BC, Canada)
Oklahoma Baptist U (OK)
Oklahoma City U (OK)
Oklahoma State U (OK)
Old Dominion U (VA)
Oral Roberts U (OK)
Oregon State U (OR)
Otterbein Coll (OH)
Ouachita Baptist U (AR)
Pace U (NY)
Pacific Lutheran U (WA)
Pacific Union Coll (CA)
Pacific U (OR)
Penn State U at Erie, The Behrend Coll (PA)
Penn State U Univ Park Campus (PA)
Pittsburg State U (KS)
Pitzer Coll (CA)
Plattsburgh State U of NY (NY)
Point Loma Nazarene U (CA)
Polytechnic U, Brooklyn Campus (NY)
Pomona Coll (CA)
Pontifical Catholic U of Puerto Rico (PR)
Portland State U (OR)
Prairie View A&M U (TX)
Presbyterian Coll (SC)
Princeton U (NJ)
Principia Coll (IL)
Purdue U (IN)
Purdue U Calumet (IN)
Queens Coll of the City U of NY (NY)
Queen's U at Kingston (ON, Canada)
Ramapo Coll of New Jersey (NJ)
Randolph-Macon Coll (VA)
Randolph-Macon Woman's Coll (VA)
Reed Coll (OR)
Rensselaer Polytechnic Inst (NY)
Rhode Island Coll (RI)
Rhodes Coll (TN)
Rice U (TX)
The Richard Stockton Coll of New Jersey (NJ)
Rider U (NJ)
Ripon Coll (WI)
Roanoke Coll (VA)
Roberts Wesleyan Coll (NY)
Rochester Inst of Technology (NY)
Rockhurst U (MO)
Rollins Coll (FL)
Rose-Hulman Inst of Technology (IN)
Rutgers, The State U of New Jersey, New Brunswick (NJ)
Saginaw Valley State U (MI)
St. Ambrose U (IA)
St. Bonaventure U (NY)
St. Cloud State U (MN)
St. Francis Xavier U (NS, Canada)
St. John Fisher Coll (NY)
Saint John's U (MN)
St. John's U (NY)
Saint Joseph's U (PA)
St. Lawrence U (NY)
Saint Louis U (MO)
Saint Mary's Coll of California (CA)
St. Mary's Coll of Maryland (MD)
Saint Mary's U (NS, Canada)
St. Mary's U of San Antonio (TX)
Saint Michael's Coll (VT)
St. Norbert Coll (WI)
St. Olaf Coll (MN)
Saint Peter's Coll (NJ)
Saint Vincent Coll (PA)
Salisbury U (MD)
Samford U (AL)
Sam Houston State U (TX)
San Diego State U (CA)
San Francisco State U (CA)
San Jose State U (CA)
Santa Clara U (CA)
Sarah Lawrence Coll (NY)
Scripps Coll (CA)
Seattle Pacific U (WA)
Seattle U (WA)
Seton Hall U (NJ)
Seton Hill Coll (PA)
Shaw U (NC)
Shippensburg U of Pennsylvania (PA)
Siena Coll (NY)
Simon Fraser U (BC, Canada)
Simon's Rock Coll of Bard (MA)
Skidmore Coll (NY)
Slippery Rock U of Pennsylvania (PA)
Smith Coll (MA)
Sonoma State U (CA)
South Carolina State U (SC)
South Dakota School of Mines and Technology (SD)
South Dakota State U (SD)
Southeastern Louisiana U (LA)
Southeastern Oklahoma State U (OK)
Southeast Missouri State U (MO)
Southern Adventist U (TN)
Southern Connecticut State U (CT)
Southern Illinois U Carbondale (IL)
Southern Illinois U Edwardsville (IL)
Southern Methodist U (TX)
Southern Nazarene U (OK)
Southern Oregon U (OR)
Southern Polytechnic State U (GA)
Southern U and A&M Coll (LA)
Southwestern Adventist U (TX)
Southwestern Coll (KS)
Southwestern Oklahoma State U (OK)
Southwestern U (TX)
Southwest Missouri State U (MO)
Southwest Texas State U (TX)
Spelman Coll (GA)
Stanford U (CA)
State U of NY at Albany (NY)
State U of NY at Binghamton (NY)
State U of NY at New Paltz (NY)
State U of NY at Oswego (NY)
State U of NY Coll at Brockport (NY)
State U of NY Coll at Buffalo (NY)
State U of NY Coll at Cortland (NY)
State U of NY Coll at Fredonia (NY)
State U of NY Coll at Geneseo (NY)
State U of NY Coll at Oneonta (NY)
State U of NY Coll at Potsdam (NY)
State U of West Georgia (GA)
Stephen F. Austin State U (TX)
Stetson U (FL)
Stevens Inst of Technology (NJ)
State U of NY at Stony Brook (NY)
Suffolk U (MA)
Susquehanna U (PA)
Swarthmore Coll (PA)
Sweet Briar Coll (VA)
Syracuse U (NY)
Talladega Coll (AL)
Tarleton State U (TX)
Taylor U (IN)
Temple U (PA)
Tennessee State U (TN)
Tennessee Technological U (TN)
Texas A&M U (TX)
Texas A&M U–Commerce (TX)
Texas A&M U–Kingsville (TX)
Texas Christian U (TX)
Texas Lutheran U (TX)
Texas Southern U (TX)
Texas Tech U (TX)
Thiel Coll (PA)
Thomas Edison State Coll (NJ)
Thomas More Coll (KY)
Tougaloo Coll (MS)
Towson U (MD)
Transylvania U (KY)
Trent U (ON, Canada)
Trevecca Nazarene U (TN)
Trinity Coll (CT)
Trinity U (TX)
Truman State U (MO)
Tufts U (MA)
Tulane U (LA)
Tuskegee U (AL)
Union Coll (KY)
Union Coll (NE)
Union Coll (NY)
Union U (TN)
United States Air Force Academy (CO)
United States Military Academy (NY)
United States Naval Academy (MD)
Université de Montréal (QC, Canada)
Université de Sherbrooke (PQ, Canada)
Université Laval (QC, Canada)
State U of NY at Buffalo (NY)
U Coll of the Cariboo (BC, Canada)
U Coll of the Fraser Valley (BC, Canada)
The U of Akron (OH)
The U of Alabama (AL)
The U of Alabama at Birmingham (AL)
The U of Alabama in Huntsville (AL)
U of Alaska Fairbanks (AK)
U of Alberta (AB, Canada)
The U of Arizona (AZ)
U of Arkansas (AR)
U of Arkansas at Little Rock (AR)
U of Arkansas at Pine Bluff (AR)
The U of British Columbia (BC, Canada)
U of Calgary (AB, Canada)
U of Calif, Berkeley (CA)
U of Calif, Davis (CA)
U of Calif, Irvine (CA)
U of Calif, Los Angeles (CA)
U of Calif, Riverside (CA)
U of Calif, San Diego (CA)
U of Calif, Santa Barbara (CA)
U of Calif, Santa Cruz (CA)
U of Central Arkansas (AR)
U of Central Florida (FL)
U of Central Oklahoma (OK)
U of Chicago (IL)
U of Cincinnati (OH)
U of Colorado at Boulder (CO)
U of Colorado at Colorado Springs (CO)
U of Colorado at Denver (CO)
U of Connecticut (CT)
U of Dallas (TX)
U of Dayton (OH)
U of Delaware (DE)
U of Denver (CO)
U of Evansville (IN)
U of Florida (FL)
U of Georgia (GA)
U of Guelph (ON, Canada)
U of Hartford (CT)
U of Hawaii at Hilo (HI)
U of Hawaii at Manoa (HI)
U of Houston (TX)
U of Idaho (ID)
U of Illinois at Chicago (IL)
U of Illinois at Urbana–Champaign (IL)
U of Indianapolis (IN)
The U of Iowa (IA)
U of Kansas (KS)
U of Kentucky (KY)
U of King's Coll (NS, Canada)
U of La Verne (CA)
The U of Lethbridge (AB, Canada)
U of Louisiana at Lafayette (LA)
U of Louisiana at Monroe (LA)
U of Louisville (KY)
U of Maine (ME)
U of Manitoba (MB, Canada)
U of Maryland, Baltimore County (MD)
U of Maryland, Coll Park (MD)
U of Massachusetts Amherst (MA)
U of Massachusetts Boston (MA)
U of Massachusetts Dartmouth (MA)
U of Massachusetts Lowell (MA)
The U of Memphis (TN)
U of Miami (FL)
U of Michigan (MI)
U of Michigan–Dearborn (MI)
U of Michigan–Flint (MI)
U of Minnesota, Duluth (MN)
U of Minnesota, Morris (MN)
U of Minnesota, Twin Cities Campus (MN)
U of Mississippi (MS)
U of Missouri–Columbia (MO)
U of Missouri–Kansas City (MO)
U of Missouri–Rolla (MO)
U of Missouri–St. Louis (MO)
The U of Montana–Missoula (MT)
U of Nebraska at Kearney (NE)
U of Nebraska at Omaha (NE)
U of Nebraska–Lincoln (NE)
U of Nevada, Las Vegas (NV)
U of Nevada, Reno (NV)
U of New Hampshire (NH)
U of New Mexico (NM)
U of New Orleans (LA)
U of North Alabama (AL)
The U of North Carolina at Asheville (NC)
The U of North Carolina at Chapel Hill (NC)
The U of North Carolina at Charlotte (NC)
The U of North Carolina at Greensboro (NC)
The U of North Carolina at Wilmington (NC)
U of North Dakota (ND)
U of Northern Colorado (CO)
U of Northern Iowa (IA)
U of North Florida (FL)
U of North Texas (TX)
U of Notre Dame (IN)
U of Oklahoma (OK)
U of Oregon (OR)
U of Ottawa (ON, Canada)
U of Pennsylvania (PA)
U of Pittsburgh (PA)
U of Portland (OR)
U of Prince Edward Island (PE, Canada)

PHYSICS EDUCATION

PHYSICS RELATED

PHYSIOLOGICAL PSYCHOLOGY/ PSYCHOBIOLOGY

PHYSIOLOGY

PLANT BREEDING

PLANT PATHOLOGY

PLANT PHYSIOLOGY

PLANT PROTECTION

PLANT SCIENCES

PLANT SCIENCES RELATED

PLASTICS ENGINEERING

PLASTICS TECHNOLOGY

PLAY/SCREENWRITING

POLITICAL SCIENCE

Auburn U Montgomery (AL)
Augsburg Coll (MN)
Augustana Coll (IL)
Augustana Coll (SD)
Augusta State U (GA)
Aurora U (IL)
Austin Coll (TX)
Austin Peay State U (TN)
Ave Maria Coll (MI)
Averett U (VA)
Avila Coll (MO)
Azusa Pacific U (CA)
Baker U (KS)
Baldwin-Wallace Coll (OH)
Ball State U (IN)
Barber-Scotia Coll (NC)
Bard Coll (NY)
Barnard Coll (NY)
Barry U (FL)
Barton Coll (NC)
Bates Coll (ME)
Baylor U (TX)
Bellarmine U (KY)
Bellevue U (NE)
Belmont Abbey Coll (NC)
Belmont U (TN)
Beloit Coll (WI)
Bemidji State U (MN)
Benedict Coll (SC)
Benedictine Coll (KS)
Benedictine U (IL)
Bennett Coll (NC)
Berea Coll (KY)
Baruch Coll of the City U of NY (NY)
Berry Coll (GA)
Bethany Coll (KS)
Bethany Coll (WV)
Bethel Coll (MN)
Bethune-Cookman Coll (FL)
Birmingham-Southern Coll (AL)
Bishop's U (PQ, Canada)
Blackburn Coll (IL)
Black Hills State U (SD)
Bloomfield Coll (NJ)
Bloomsburg U of Pennsylvania (PA)
Bluffton Coll (OH)
Boise State U (ID)
Boston Coll (MA)
Boston U (MA)
Bowdoin Coll (ME)
Bowie State U (MD)
Bowling Green State U (OH)
Bradley U (IL)
Brandeis U (MA)
Brandon U (MB, Canada)
Brenau U (GA)
Briar Cliff U (IA)
Bridgewater Coll (VA)
Bridgewater State Coll (MA)
Brigham Young U (UT)
Brigham Young U–Hawaii (HI)
Brock U (ON, Canada)
Brooklyn Coll of the City U of NY (NY)
Brown U (RI)
Bryn Mawr Coll (PA)
Bucknell U (PA)
Buena Vista U (IA)
Butler U (IN)
Cabrini Coll (PA)
Caldwell Coll (NJ)
California Baptist U (CA)
California Lutheran U (CA)
California Polytechnic State U, San Luis Obispo (CA)
California State Polytechnic U, Pomona (CA)
California State U, Bakersfield (CA)
California State U, Chico (CA)
California State U, Dominguez Hills (CA)
California State U, Fresno (CA)
California State U, Fullerton (CA)
California State U, Hayward (CA)
California State U, Long Beach (CA)
California State U, Los Angeles (CA)
California State U, Northridge (CA)
California State U, Sacramento (CA)
California State U, San Bernardino (CA)
California State U, San Marcos (CA)
California State U, Stanislaus (CA)
California U of Pennsylvania (PA)
Calvin Coll (MI)
Cameron U (OK)
Campbellsville U (KY)
Campbell U (NC)
Canisius Coll (NY)
Capital U (OH)
Cardinal Stritch U (WI)
Carleton Coll (MN)
Carleton U (ON, Canada)
Carnegie Mellon U (PA)
Carroll Coll (MT)
Carroll Coll (WI)
Carson-Newman Coll (TN)
Carthage Coll (WI)
Case Western Reserve U (OH)
Catawba Coll (NC)
The Catholic U of America (DC)
Cedar Crest Coll (PA)
Cedarville U (OH)
Centenary Coll (NJ)
Centenary Coll of Louisiana (LA)
Central Coll (IA)
Central Connecticut State U (CT)
Central Methodist Coll (MO)
Central Michigan U (MI)
Central Missouri State U (MO)
Central State U (OH)
Central Washington U (WA)
Centre Coll (KY)
Chaminade U of Honolulu (HI)
Chapman U (CA)
Charleston Southern U (SC)
Chatham Coll (PA)
Chestnut Hill Coll (PA)
Cheyney U of Pennsylvania (PA)
Chicago State U (IL)
Christendom Coll (VA)
Christopher Newport U (VA)
Citadel, The Military Coll of South Carolina (SC)
City Coll of the City U of NY (NY)
Claremont McKenna Coll (CA)
Clarion U of Pennsylvania (PA)
Clark Atlanta U (GA)
Clarkson U (NY)
Clark U (MA)
Clemson U (SC)
Cleveland State U (OH)
Coastal Carolina U (SC)
Coe Coll (IA)
Coker Coll (SC)
Colby Coll (ME)
Colgate U (NY)
Coll of Charleston (SC)
The Coll of New Jersey (NJ)
The Coll of New Rochelle (NY)
Coll of Notre Dame of Maryland (MD)
Coll of Saint Benedict (MN)
Coll of St. Catherine (MN)
Coll of St. Joseph (VT)
Coll of Santa Fe (NM)
The Coll of Southeastern Europe, The American U of Athens(Greece)
Coll of Staten Island of the City U of NY (NY)
Coll of the Holy Cross (MA)
Coll of the Ozarks (MO)
The Coll of William and Mary (VA)
The Coll of Wooster (OH)
Colorado Christian U (CO)
The Colorado Coll (CO)
Colorado State U (CO)
Columbia Coll (MO)
Columbia Coll (NY)
Columbia Coll (SC)
Columbia Union Coll (MD)
Columbia U, School of General Studies (NY)
Columbus State U (GA)
Concord Coll (WV)
Concordia Coll (MN)
Concordia U (CA)
Concordia U (IL)
Concordia U (QC, Canada)
Connecticut Coll (CT)
Converse Coll (SC)
Cornell Coll (IA)
Cornell U (NY)
Creighton U (NE)
Cumberland Coll (KY)
Cumberland U (TN)
Curry Coll (MA)
Daemen Coll (NY)
Dalhousie U (NS, Canada)
Dallas Baptist U (TX)
Dartmouth Coll (NH)
Davidson Coll (NC)
Davis & Elkins Coll (WV)
Delaware State U (DE)
Delta State U (MS)
Denison U (OH)
DePaul U (IL)
DePauw U (IN)
DeSales U (PA)
Dickinson Coll (PA)
Dickinson State U (ND)
Dillard U (LA)
Doane Coll (NE)
Dominican Coll (NY)
Dominican U (IL)
Dominican U of California (CA)
Dordt Coll (IA)
Dowling Coll (NY)
Drake U (IA)
Drew U (NJ)
Drury U (MO)
Duke U (NC)
Duquesne U (PA)
Earlham Coll (IN)
East Carolina U (NC)
East Central U (OK)
Eastern Connecticut State U (CT)
Eastern Illinois U (IL)
Eastern Kentucky U (KY)
Eastern Michigan U (MI)
Eastern New Mexico U (NM)
Eastern U (PA)
Eastern Washington U (WA)
East Stroudsburg U of Pennsylvania (PA)
East Tennessee State U (TN)
Eckerd Coll (FL)
Edgewood Coll (WI)
Edinboro U of Pennsylvania (PA)
Elizabeth City State U (NC)
Elizabethtown Coll (PA)
Elmhurst Coll (IL)
Elmira Coll (NY)
Elon U (NC)
Emmanuel Coll (MA)
Emory & Henry Coll (VA)
Emory U (GA)
Emporia State U (KS)
Eugene Lang Coll, New School U (NY)
Eureka Coll (IL)
Evangel U (MO)
The Evergreen State Coll (WA)
Excelsior Coll (NY)
Fairfield U (CT)
Fairleigh Dickinson U, Florham-Madison Campus (NJ)
Fairleigh Dickinson U, Teaneck-Hackensack Campus (NJ)
Fairmont State Coll (WV)
Faulkner U (AL)
Fayetteville State U (NC)
Felician Coll (NJ)
Ferrum Coll (VA)
Fisk U (TN)
Fitchburg State Coll (MA)
Flagler Coll (FL)
Florida A&M U (FL)
Florida Atlantic U (FL)
Florida International U (FL)
Florida Southern Coll (FL)
Florida State U (FL)
Fordham U (NY)
Fort Hays State U (KS)
Fort Lewis Coll (CO)
Fort Valley State U (GA)
Framingham State Coll (MA)
Franciscan U of Steubenville (OH)
Francis Marion U (SC)
Franklin and Marshall Coll (PA)
Franklin Coll of Indiana (IN)
Franklin Pierce Coll (NH)
Fresno Pacific U (CA)
Friends U (KS)
Frostburg State U (MD)
Furman U (SC)
Gannon U (PA)
Gardner-Webb U (NC)
Geneva Coll (PA)
George Mason U (VA)
Georgetown Coll (KY)
Georgetown U (DC)
The George Washington U (DC)
Georgia Coll and State U (GA)
Georgia Southern U (GA)
Georgia Southwestern State U (GA)
Georgia State U (GA)
Gettysburg Coll (PA)
Goddard Coll (VT)
Gonzaga U (WA)
Gordon Coll (MA)
Goshen Coll (IN)
Goucher Coll (MD)
Grambling State U (LA)
Grand Canyon U (AZ)
Grand Valley State U (MI)
Grand View Coll (IA)
Greensboro Coll (NC)
Greenville Coll (IL)
Grinnell Coll (IA)
Grove City Coll (PA)
Guilford Coll (NC)
Gustavus Adolphus Coll (MN)
Hamilton Coll (NY)
Hamline U (MN)
Hampden-Sydney Coll (VA)
Hampshire Coll (MA)
Hampton U (VA)
Hanover Coll (IN)
Harding U (AR)
Hardin-Simmons U (TX)
Hartwick Coll (NY)
Harvard U (MA)
Hastings Coll (NE)
Haverford Coll (PA)
Hawai'i Pacific U (HI)
Heidelberg Coll (OH)
Henderson State U (AR)
Hendrix Coll (AR)
High Point U (NC)
Hillsdale Coll (MI)
Hiram Coll (OH)
Hobart and William Smith Colls (NY)
Hofstra U (NY)
Hollins U (VA)
Hood Coll (MD)
Hope Coll (MI)
Houghton Coll (NY)
Houston Baptist U (TX)
Howard Payne U (TX)
Howard U (DC)
Humboldt State U (CA)
Hunter Coll of the City U of NY (NY)
Huntingdon Coll (AL)
Huston-Tillotson Coll (TX)
Idaho State U (ID)
Illinois Coll (IL)
Illinois Inst of Technology (IL)
Illinois State U (IL)
Illinois Wesleyan U (IL)
Indiana State U (IN)
Indiana U Bloomington (IN)
Indiana U Northwest (IN)
Indiana U of Pennsylvania (PA)
Indiana U–Purdue U Fort Wayne (IN)
Indiana U–Purdue U Indianapolis (IN)
Indiana U South Bend (IN)
Indiana U Southeast (IN)
Indiana Wesleyan U (IN)
Inter American U of PR, San Germán Campus (PR)
Iona Coll (NY)
Iowa State U of Science and Technology (IA)
Ithaca Coll (NY)
Jackson State U (MS)
Jacksonville State U (AL)
Jacksonville U (FL)
James Madison U (VA)
Jamestown Coll (ND)
Jarvis Christian Coll (TX)
John Cabot U(Italy)
John Carroll U (OH)
Johns Hopkins U (MD)
Johnson C. Smith U (NC)
Johnson State Coll (VT)
Juniata Coll (PA)
Kalamazoo Coll (MI)
Kansas State U (KS)
Kean U (NJ)
Keene State Coll (NH)
Kennesaw State U (GA)
Kent State U (OH)
Kentucky State U (KY)
Kentucky Wesleyan Coll (KY)
Kenyon Coll (OH)
King Coll (TN)
King's Coll (PA)
Knox Coll (IL)
Kutztown U of Pennsylvania (PA)
Lafayette Coll (PA)
LaGrange Coll (GA)
Lake Forest Coll (IL)
Lakehead U (ON, Canada)
Lake Superior State U (MI)
Lamar U (TX)
Lambuth U (TN)
Lander U (SC)
La Salle U (PA)
Laurentian U (ON, Canada)
Lawrence U (WI)
Lebanon Valley Coll (PA)
Lehigh U (PA)
Lehman Coll of the City U of NY (NY)
Le Moyne Coll (NY)
LeMoyne-Owen Coll (TN)
Lenoir-Rhyne Coll (NC)
Lewis & Clark Coll (OR)
Lewis U (IL)
Liberty U (VA)
Lincoln U (MO)
Lincoln U (PA)
Lindenwood U (MO)
Linfield Coll (OR)
Lipscomb U (TN)
Lock Haven U of Pennsylvania (PA)
Long Island U, Brooklyn Campus (NY)
Long Island U, C.W. Post Campus (NY)
Long Island U, Southampton Coll (NY)
Long Island U, Southampton Coll, Friends World Program (NY)
Longwood Coll (VA)
Loras Coll (IA)
Louisiana State U and A&M Coll (LA)
Louisiana State U in Shreveport (LA)
Louisiana Tech U (LA)
Loyola Coll in Maryland (MD)
Loyola Marymount U (CA)
Loyola U Chicago (IL)
Loyola U New Orleans (LA)
Luther Coll (IA)
Lycoming Coll (PA)
Lynchburg Coll (VA)
Lynn U (FL)
Lyon Coll (AR)
Macalester Coll (MN)
MacMurray Coll (IL)
Malone Coll (OH)
Manchester Coll (IN)
Manhattan Coll (NY)
Manhattanville Coll (NY)
Mansfield U of Pennsylvania (PA)
Marian Coll of Fond du Lac (WI)
Marietta Coll (OH)
Marist Coll (NY)
Marlboro Coll (VT)
Marquette U (WI)
Marshall U (WV)
Mars Hill Coll (NC)
Mary Baldwin Coll (VA)
Marygrove Coll (MI)
Marymount Coll of Fordham U (NY)
Marymount Manhattan Coll (NY)
Marymount U (VA)
Maryville Coll (TN)
Maryville U of Saint Louis (MO)
Mary Washington Coll (VA)
Massachusetts Inst of Technology (MA)
The Master's Coll and Seminary (CA)
McGill U (PQ, Canada)
McKendree Coll (IL)
McMaster U (ON, Canada)
McMurry U (TX)
McNeese State U (LA)
Medaille Coll (NY)
Memorial U of Newfoundland (NF, Canada)
Mercer U (GA)
Mercy Coll (NY)
Mercyhurst Coll (PA)
Meredith Coll (NC)
Merrimack Coll (MA)
Mesa State Coll (CO)
Messiah Coll (PA)
Methodist Coll (NC)
Metropolitan State Coll of Denver (CO)
Miami U (OH)
Michigan State U (MI)
Middlebury Coll (VT)
Middle Tennessee State U (TN)
Midwestern State U (TX)
Millersville U of Pennsylvania (PA)
Millikin U (IL)
Millsaps Coll (MS)

Minnesota State U, Mankato (MN)
Minnesota State U Moorhead (MN)
Mississippi Coll (MS)
Mississippi State U (MS)
Mississippi U for Women (MS)
Mississippi Valley State U (MS)
Missouri Southern State Coll (MO)
Missouri Valley Coll (MO)
Missouri Western State Coll (MO)
Molloy Coll (NY)
Monmouth Coll (IL)
Monmouth U (NJ)
Montana State U–Bozeman (MT)
Montclair State U (NJ)
Moravian Coll (PA)
Morehead State U (KY)
Morehouse Coll (GA)
Morgan State U (MD)
Morningside Coll (IA)
Morris Brown Coll (GA)
Morris Coll (SC)
Mount Allison U (NB, Canada)
Mount Holyoke Coll (MA)
Mount Mercy Coll (IA)
Mount Saint Mary Coll (NY)
Mount St. Mary's Coll (CA)
Mount Saint Mary's Coll and Seminary (MD)
Mount Saint Vincent U (NS, Canada)
Mount Union Coll (OH)
Muhlenberg Coll (PA)
Murray State U (KY)
Muskingum Coll (OH)
Nazareth Coll of Rochester (NY)
Nebraska Wesleyan U (NE)
Neumann Coll (PA)
Newberry Coll (SC)
New Coll of Florida (FL)
New England Coll (NH)
New Jersey City U (NJ)
New Mexico Highlands U (NM)
New Mexico State U (NM)
New York Inst of Technology (NY)
New York U (NY)
Niagara U (NY)
Nicholls State U (LA)
Norfolk State U (VA)
North Carolina Ag and Tech State U (NC)
North Carolina Central U (NC)
North Carolina State U (NC)
North Carolina Wesleyan Coll (NC)
North Central Coll (IL)
North Dakota State U (ND)
Northeastern Illinois U (IL)
Northeastern State U (OK)
Northeastern U (MA)
Northern Arizona U (AZ)
Northern Illinois U (IL)
Northern Kentucky U (KY)
Northern Michigan U (MI)
Northern State U (SD)
North Georgia Coll & State U (GA)
North Park U (IL)
Northwestern Coll (IA)
Northwestern Oklahoma State U (OK)
Northwestern State U of Louisiana (LA)
Northwestern U (IL)
Northwest Missouri State U (MO)
Northwest Nazarene U (ID)
Norwich U (VT)
Notre Dame Coll (OH)
Notre Dame de Namur U (CA)
Oakland U (MI)
Oberlin Coll (OH)
Occidental Coll (CA)
Oglethorpe U (GA)
Ohio Dominican Coll (OH)
Ohio Northern U (OH)
The Ohio State U (OH)
Ohio U (OH)
Ohio Wesleyan U (OH)
Okanagan U Coll (BC, Canada)
Oklahoma Baptist U (OK)
Oklahoma City U (OK)
Oklahoma State U (OK)
Oklahoma Wesleyan U (OK)
Old Dominion U (VA)
Oral Roberts U (OK)
Oregon State U (OR)
Ottawa U (KS)
Otterbein Coll (OH)
Ouachita Baptist U (AR)
Our Lady of the Lake U of San Antonio (TX)
Pace U (NY)
Pacific Lutheran U (WA)
Pacific Union Coll (CA)
Pacific U (OR)
Palm Beach Atlantic Coll (FL)
Park U (MO)
Penn State U at Erie, The Behrend Coll (PA)
Penn State U Univ Park Campus (PA)
Pepperdine U, Malibu (CA)
Pfeiffer U (NC)
Philander Smith Coll (AR)
Pine Manor Coll (MA)
Pittsburg State U (KS)
Pitzer Coll (CA)
Plattsburgh State U of NY (NY)
Plymouth State Coll (NH)
Point Loma Nazarene U (CA)
Point Park Coll (PA)
Pomona Coll (CA)
Pontifical Catholic U of Puerto Rico (PR)
Portland State U (OR)
Prairie View A&M U (TX)
Presbyterian Coll (SC)
Prescott Coll (AZ)
Princeton U (NJ)
Principia Coll (IL)
Providence Coll (RI)
Purchase Coll, State U of NY (NY)
Purdue U (IN)
Purdue U Calumet (IN)
Queens Coll (NC)
Queens Coll of the City U of NY (NY)
Queen's U at Kingston (ON, Canada)
Quincy U (IL)
Quinnipiac U (CT)
Radford U (VA)
Ramapo Coll of New Jersey (NJ)
Randolph-Macon Coll (VA)
Randolph-Macon Woman's Coll (VA)
Redeemer U Coll (ON, Canada)
Reed Coll (OR)
Regis Coll (MA)
Regis U (CO)
Rhode Island Coll (RI)
Rhodes Coll (TN)
Rice U (TX)
The Richard Stockton Coll of New Jersey (NJ)
Richmond, The American International U in London(United Kingdom)
Rider U (NJ)
Ripon Coll (WI)
Roanoke Coll (VA)
Rockford Coll (IL)
Rockhurst U (MO)
Rocky Mountain Coll (MT)
Roger Williams U (RI)
Rollins Coll (FL)
Roosevelt U (IL)
Rosemont Coll (PA)
Rowan U (NJ)
Russell Sage Coll (NY)
Rust Coll (MS)
Rutgers, The State U of New Jersey, New Brunswick (NJ)
Sacred Heart U (CT)
Saginaw Valley State U (MI)
St. Ambrose U (IA)
St. Andrews Presbyterian Coll (NC)
Saint Anselm Coll (NH)
Saint Augustine's Coll (NC)
St. Bonaventure U (NY)
St. Cloud State U (MN)
St. Edward's U (TX)
St. Francis Coll (NY)
Saint Francis U (PA)
St. Francis Xavier U (NS, Canada)
St. John Fisher Coll (NY)
Saint John's U (MN)
St. John's U (NY)
Saint Joseph Coll (CT)
Saint Joseph's Coll (IN)
Saint Joseph's U (PA)
St. Lawrence U (NY)
Saint Leo U (FL)
Saint Louis U (MO)
Saint Martin's Coll (WA)
Saint Mary Coll (KS)
Saint Mary's Coll (IN)
Saint Mary's Coll of California (CA)
St. Mary's Coll of Maryland (MD)
Saint Mary's U (NS, Canada)
Saint Mary's U of Minnesota (MN)
St. Mary's U of San Antonio (TX)
Saint Michael's Coll (VT)
St. Norbert Coll (WI)
St. Olaf Coll (MN)
Saint Peter's Coll (NJ)
St. Thomas U (FL)
St. Thomas U (NB, Canada)
Saint Vincent Coll (PA)
Saint Xavier U (IL)
Salem State Coll (MA)
Salisbury U (MD)
Salve Regina U (RI)
Samford U (AL)
Sam Houston State U (TX)
San Diego State U (CA)
San Francisco State U (CA)
San Jose State U (CA)
Santa Clara U (CA)
Sarah Lawrence Coll (NY)
Savannah State U (GA)
Scripps Coll (CA)
Seattle Pacific U (WA)
Seattle U (WA)
Seton Hall U (NJ)
Seton Hill Coll (PA)
Shaw U (NC)
Shepherd Coll (WV)
Shippensburg U of Pennsylvania (PA)
Siena Coll (NY)
Simmons Coll (MA)
Simon Fraser U (BC, Canada)
Simon's Rock Coll of Bard (MA)
Simpson Coll (IA)
Skidmore Coll (NY)
Slippery Rock U of Pennsylvania (PA)
Smith Coll (MA)
Sonoma State U (CA)
South Carolina State U (SC)
South Dakota State U (SD)
Southeastern Louisiana U (LA)
Southeastern Oklahoma State U (OK)
Southeast Missouri State U (MO)
Southern Arkansas U–Magnolia (AR)
Southern Connecticut State U (CT)
Southern Illinois U Carbondale (IL)
Southern Illinois U Edwardsville (IL)
Southern Methodist U (TX)
Southern Nazarene U (OK)
Southern New Hampshire U (NH)
Southern Oregon U (OR)
Southern U and A&M Coll (LA)
Southern Utah U (UT)
Southwest Baptist U (MO)
Southwestern Oklahoma State U (OK)
Southwestern U (TX)
Southwest Missouri State U (MO)
Southwest State U (MN)
Southwest Texas State U (TX)
Spelman Coll (GA)
Springfield Coll (MA)
Spring Hill Coll (AL)
Stanford U (CA)
State U of NY at Albany (NY)
State U of NY at Binghamton (NY)
State U of NY at New Paltz (NY)
State U of NY at Oswego (NY)
State U of NY Coll at Brockport (NY)
State U of NY Coll at Buffalo (NY)
State U of NY Coll at Cortland (NY)
State U of NY Coll at Fredonia (NY)
State U of NY Coll at Geneseo (NY)
State U of NY Coll at Oneonta (NY)
State U of NY Coll at Potsdam (NY)
State U of West Georgia (GA)
Stephen F. Austin State U (TX)
Stephens Coll (MO)
Stetson U (FL)
Stonehill Coll (MA)
State U of NY at Stony Brook (NY)
Suffolk U (MA)
Sul Ross State U (TX)
Susquehanna U (PA)
Swarthmore Coll (PA)
Sweet Briar Coll (VA)
Syracuse U (NY)
Tarleton State U (TX)
Taylor U (IN)
Temple U (PA)
Tennessee State U (TN)
Tennessee Technological U (TN)
Texas A&M International U (TX)
Texas A&M U (TX)
Texas A&M U–Commerce (TX)
Texas A&M U–Corpus Christi (TX)
Texas A&M U–Kingsville (TX)
Texas Christian U (TX)
Texas Coll (TX)
Texas Lutheran U (TX)
Texas Southern U (TX)
Texas Tech U (TX)
Texas Wesleyan U (TX)
Texas Woman's U (TX)
Thiel Coll (PA)
Thomas Edison State Coll (NJ)
Thomas More Coll of Liberal Arts (NH)
Thomas U (GA)
Tougaloo Coll (MS)
Touro Coll (NY)
Towson U (MD)
Transylvania U (KY)
Trent U (ON, Canada)
Trinity Coll (CT)
Trinity Coll (DC)
Trinity U (TX)
Trinity Western U (BC, Canada)
Troy State U (AL)
Troy State U Montgomery (AL)
Truman State U (MO)
Tufts U (MA)
Tulane U (LA)
Tuskegee U (AL)
Union Coll (NY)
Union U (TN)
United States Air Force Academy (CO)
United States Coast Guard Academy (CT)
United States Military Academy (NY)
United States Naval Academy (MD)
Université de Montréal (QC, Canada)
Université Laval (QC, Canada)
State U of NY at Buffalo (NY)
U Coll of Cape Breton (NS, Canada)
The U of Akron (OH)
The U of Alabama (AL)
The U of Alabama at Birmingham (AL)
The U of Alabama in Huntsville (AL)
U of Alaska Anchorage (AK)
U of Alaska Fairbanks (AK)
U of Alaska Southeast (AK)
U of Alberta (AB, Canada)
The U of Arizona (AZ)
U of Arkansas (AR)
U of Arkansas at Little Rock (AR)
U of Arkansas at Pine Bluff (AR)
U of Baltimore (MD)
The U of British Columbia (BC, Canada)
U of Calgary (AB, Canada)
U of Calif, Berkeley (CA)
U of Calif, Davis (CA)
U of Calif, Irvine (CA)
U of Calif, Los Angeles (CA)
U of Calif, Riverside (CA)
U of Calif, San Diego (CA)
U of Calif, Santa Barbara (CA)
U of Calif, Santa Cruz (CA)
U of Central Arkansas (AR)
U of Central Florida (FL)
U of Central Oklahoma (OK)
U of Charleston (WV)
U of Chicago (IL)
U of Cincinnati (OH)
U of Colorado at Boulder (CO)
U of Colorado at Colorado Springs (CO)
U of Colorado at Denver (CO)
U of Connecticut (CT)
U of Dallas (TX)
U of Dayton (OH)
U of Delaware (DE)
U of Denver (CO)
U of Evansville (IN)
The U of Findlay (OH)
U of Florida (FL)
U of Georgia (GA)
U of Great Falls (MT)
U of Guelph (ON, Canada)
U of Hartford (CT)
U of Hawaii at Hilo (HI)
U of Hawaii at Manoa (HI)
U of Hawaii–West Oahu (HI)
U of Houston (TX)
U of Idaho (ID)
U of Illinois at Chicago (IL)
U of Illinois at Springfield (IL)
U of Illinois at Urbana–Champaign (IL)
U of Indianapolis (IN)
The U of Iowa (IA)
U of Judaism (CA)
U of Kansas (KS)
U of Kentucky (KY)
U of King's Coll (NS, Canada)
U of La Verne (CA)
The U of Lethbridge (AB, Canada)
U of Louisiana at Lafayette (LA)
U of Louisiana at Monroe (LA)
U of Louisville (KY)
U of Maine (ME)
U of Maine at Farmington (ME)
U of Maine at Presque Isle (ME)
U of Manitoba (MB, Canada)
U of Mary Hardin-Baylor (TX)
U of Maryland, Baltimore County (MD)
U of Maryland, Coll Park (MD)
U of Massachusetts Amherst (MA)
U of Massachusetts Boston (MA)
U of Massachusetts Dartmouth (MA)
U of Massachusetts Lowell (MA)
The U of Memphis (TN)
U of Miami (FL)
U of Michigan (MI)
U of Michigan–Dearborn (MI)
U of Michigan–Flint (MI)
U of Minnesota, Duluth (MN)
U of Minnesota, Morris (MN)
U of Minnesota, Twin Cities Campus (MN)
U of Mississippi (MS)
U of Missouri–Columbia (MO)
U of Missouri–Kansas City (MO)
U of Missouri–St. Louis (MO)
U of Mobile (AL)
U of Montevallo (AL)
U of Nebraska at Kearney (NE)
U of Nebraska at Omaha (NE)
U of Nebraska–Lincoln (NE)
U of Nevada, Las Vegas (NV)
U of Nevada, Reno (NV)
U of New Hampshire (NH)
U of New Haven (CT)
U of New Mexico (NM)
U of New Orleans (LA)
U of North Alabama (AL)
The U of North Carolina at Asheville (NC)
The U of North Carolina at Chapel Hill (NC)
The U of North Carolina at Charlotte (NC)
The U of North Carolina at Greensboro (NC)
The U of North Carolina at Pembroke (NC)
The U of North Carolina at Wilmington (NC)
U of North Dakota (ND)
U of Northern Colorado (CO)
U of Northern Iowa (IA)
U of North Florida (FL)
U of North Texas (TX)
U of Notre Dame (IN)
U of Oklahoma (OK)
U of Oregon (OR)
U of Ottawa (ON, Canada)
U of Pennsylvania (PA)
U of Pittsburgh (PA)
U of Pittsburgh at Bradford (PA)
U of Pittsburgh at Greensburg (PA)
U of Pittsburgh at Johnstown (PA)
U of Portland (OR)
U of Prince Edward Island (PE, Canada)
U of Puget Sound (WA)
U of Redlands (CA)
U of Regina (SK, Canada)
U of Rhode Island (RI)
U of Richmond (VA)
U of Rio Grande (OH)
U of Rochester (NY)
U of St. Francis (IL)
U of St. Thomas (MN)
U of St. Thomas (TX)
U of San Diego (CA)
U of San Francisco (CA)
U of Saskatchewan (SK, Canada)
U of Science and Arts of Oklahoma (OK)

POLITICAL SCIENCE/ GOVERNMENT RELATED

POLYMER CHEMISTRY

PORTUGUESE

POULTRY SCIENCE

PRACTICAL NURSE

PRE-DENTISTRY

PRE-ENGINEERING

PRE-LAW

Hobart and William Smith Colls (NY)
Holy Family Coll (PA)
Hood Coll (MD)
Houghton Coll (NY)
Houston Baptist U (TX)
Howard Payne U (TX)
Humboldt State U (CA)
Huntingdon Coll (AL)
Huntington Coll (IN)
Illinois Coll (IL)
Illinois Wesleyan U (IL)
Immaculata Coll (PA)
Indiana U Bloomington (IN)
Indiana U–Purdue U Indianapolis (IN)
Indiana Wesleyan U (IN)
Iowa State U of Science and Technology (IA)
Iowa Wesleyan Coll (IA)
Ithaca Coll (NY)
Jackson State U (MS)
Jacksonville U (FL)
John Brown U (AR)
John Carroll U (OH)
John Jay Coll of Criminal Justice, the City U of NY (NY)
Johnson C. Smith U (NC)
Judson Coll (IL)
Juniata Coll (PA)
Kansas Wesleyan U (KS)
Kentucky Wesleyan Coll (KY)
King Coll (TN)
King's Coll (PA)
LaGrange Coll (GA)
Lake Erie Coll (OH)
Lake Forest Coll (IL)
Lakeland Coll (WI)
Lake Superior State U (MI)
Lambuth U (TN)
Lander U (SC)
Lawrence U (WI)
Lebanon Valley Coll (PA)
Lees-McRae Coll (NC)
Le Moyne Coll (NY)
Lenoir-Rhyne Coll (NC)
LeTourneau U (TX)
Lewis & Clark Coll (OR)
Lewis-Clark State Coll (ID)
Lewis U (IL)
Limestone Coll (SC)
Lincoln Memorial U (TN)
Lindenwood U (MO)
Lindsey Wilson Coll (KY)
Lipscomb U (TN)
Lock Haven U of Pennsylvania (PA)
Long Island U, Brooklyn Campus (NY)
Long Island U, C.W. Post Campus (NY)
Long Island U, Southampton Coll (NY)
Longwood Coll (VA)
Louisiana Coll (LA)
Loyola U Chicago (IL)
Lubbock Christian U (TX)
Luther Coll (IA)
Lycoming Coll (PA)
Lynchburg Coll (VA)
Lynn U (FL)
MacMurray Coll (IL)
Maharishi U of Management (IA)
Manchester Coll (IN)
Manhattanville Coll (NY)
Mansfield U of Pennsylvania (PA)
Marian Coll (IN)
Marian Coll of Fond du Lac (WI)
Marist Coll (NY)
Marlboro Coll (VT)
Marquette U (WI)
Mars Hill Coll (NC)
Marymount Coll of Fordham U (NY)
Mary Washington Coll (VA)
Massachusetts Coll of Liberal Arts (MA)
Massachusetts Inst of Technology (MA)
Mayville State U (ND)
McKendree Coll (IL)
Medaille Coll (NY)
Mercy Coll (NY)
Mercyhurst Coll (PA)
Merrimack Coll (MA)
Methodist Coll (NC)
Miami U (OH)
Middlebury Coll (VT)
Midland Lutheran Coll (NE)
Midwestern State U (TX)
Millikin U (IL)
Minnesota State U, Mankato (MN)
Minnesota State U Moorhead (MN)
Mississippi Coll (MS)
Missouri Valley Coll (MO)
Molloy Coll (NY)
Montclair State U (NJ)
Montreat Coll (NC)
Morgan State U (MD)
Morningside Coll (IA)
Mount Allison U (NB, Canada)
Mount Aloysius Coll (PA)
Mount Mary Coll (WI)
Mount Mercy Coll (IA)
Mount St. Clare Coll (IA)
Mount Saint Mary Coll (NY)
Mount St. Mary's Coll (CA)
Mount Vernon Nazarene U (OH)
Muhlenberg Coll (PA)
Muskingum Coll (OH)
Nazareth Coll of Rochester (NY)
Newberry Coll (SC)
Newbury Coll (MA)
New England Coll (NH)
Newman U (KS)
New Mexico Highlands U (NM)
New York U (NY)
Niagara U (NY)
North Central Coll (IL)
North Dakota State U (ND)
Northeastern State U (OK)
Northeastern U (MA)
Northern Arizona U (AZ)
Northern Kentucky U (KY)
Northern Michigan U (MI)
Northern State U (SD)
Northland Coll (WI)
North Park U (IL)
Northwest Coll (WA)
Northwestern Oklahoma State U (OK)
Northwest Missouri State U (MO)
Northwest Nazarene U (ID)
Notre Dame Coll (OH)
Notre Dame de Namur U (CA)
Nova Southeastern U (FL)
Oakland City U (IN)
Oakland U (MI)
Oglethorpe U (GA)
Ohio U (OH)
Ohio Wesleyan U (OH)
Oklahoma Baptist U (OK)
Oklahoma Christian U of Science and Arts (OK)
Oklahoma City U (OK)
Oklahoma State U (OK)
Oklahoma Wesleyan U (OK)
Olivet Coll (MI)
Olivet Nazarene U (IL)
Otterbein Coll (OH)
Pacific Union Coll (CA)
Palm Beach Atlantic Coll (FL)
Pepperdine U, Malibu (CA)
Peru State Coll (NE)
Pfeiffer U (NC)
Pittsburg State U (KS)
Point Park Coll (PA)
Polytechnic U, Brooklyn Campus (NY)
Pontifical Catholic U of Puerto Rico (PR)
Presbyterian Coll (SC)
Purdue U Calumet (IN)
Queens Coll (NC)
Quinnipiac U (CT)
Redeemer U Coll (ON, Canada)
Regis U (CO)
Rensselaer Polytechnic Inst (NY)
Rhode Island Coll (RI)
Ripon Coll (WI)
Rivier Coll (NH)
Roberts Wesleyan Coll (NY)
Rochester Inst of Technology (NY)
Rockford Coll (IL)
Rocky Mountain Coll (MT)
Rollins Coll (FL)
Roosevelt U (IL)
Rowan U (NJ)
Rutgers, The State U of New Jersey, New Brunswick (NJ)
St. Andrews Presbyterian Coll (NC)
Saint Anselm Coll (NH)
St. Bonaventure U (NY)
St. Cloud State U (MN)
St. Francis Coll (NY)
Saint Francis U (PA)
St. Francis Xavier U (NS, Canada)
Saint John's U (MN)
Saint Joseph Coll (CT)
St. Joseph's Coll, New York (NY)
St. Joseph's Coll, Suffolk Campus (NY)
Saint Leo U (FL)
Saint Martin's Coll (WA)
Saint Mary-of-the-Woods Coll (IN)
Saint Mary's Coll of California (CA)
Saint Michael's Coll (VT)
St. Norbert Coll (WI)
St. Thomas U (FL)
Salem State Coll (MA)
San Diego State U (CA)
Sarah Lawrence Coll (NY)
Schreiner U (TX)
Seattle Pacific U (WA)
Seton Hill Coll (PA)
Shawnee State U (OH)
Siena Coll (NY)
Siena Heights U (MI)
Simmons Coll (MA)
Simon's Rock Coll of Bard (MA)
Simpson Coll (IA)
Sonoma State U (CA)
South Carolina State U (SC)
South Dakota State U (SD)
Southern Connecticut State U (CT)
Southern Nazarene U (OK)
Southern Oregon U (OR)
Southwestern Oklahoma State U (OK)
Southwest State U (MN)
Springfield Coll (MA)
State U of NY at Binghamton (NY)
State U of NY at New Paltz (NY)
State U of NY at Oswego (NY)
State U of NY Coll at Brockport (NY)
State U of NY Coll at Buffalo (NY)
State U of NY Coll at Cortland (NY)
State U of NY Coll at Fredonia (NY)
State U of NY Coll at Geneseo (NY)
State U of NY Coll at Oneonta (NY)
State U of NY Coll of Environ Sci and Forestry (NY)
State U of West Georgia (GA)
Stephens Coll (MO)
Stetson U (FL)
Stevens Inst of Technology (NJ)
Stonehill Coll (MA)
Suffolk U (MA)
Sul Ross State U (TX)
Susquehanna U (PA)
Syracuse U (NY)
Talladega Coll (AL)
Taylor U (IN)
Taylor U, Fort Wayne Campus (IN)
Tennessee Technological U (TN)
Tennessee Wesleyan Coll (TN)
Texas A&M U–Kingsville (TX)
Texas Lutheran U (TX)
Texas Wesleyan U (TX)
Thiel Coll (PA)
Thomas More Coll (KY)
Touro Coll (NY)
Trinity Coll (DC)
Trinity U (TX)
Trinity Western U (BC, Canada)
Tri-State U (IN)
Truman State U (MO)
Tusculum Coll (TN)
Union Coll (KY)
Union U (TN)
United States Military Academy (NY)
U Coll of Cape Breton (NS, Canada)
The U of Akron (OH)
U of Alberta (AB, Canada)
U of Bridgeport (CT)
The U of British Columbia (BC, Canada)
U of Calif, Riverside (CA)
U of Cincinnati (OH)
U of Colorado at Colorado Springs (CO)
U of Dallas (TX)
U of Dayton (OH)
U of Evansville (IN)
The U of Findlay (OH)
U of Hawaii at Manoa (HI)
U of Houston (TX)
U of Illinois at Chicago (IL)
U of Indianapolis (IN)
The U of Iowa (IA)
U of La Verne (CA)
U of Louisiana at Lafayette (LA)
U of Louisiana at Monroe (LA)
U of Manitoba (MB, Canada)
U of Mary Hardin-Baylor (TX)
U of Maryland, Baltimore County (MD)
U of Maryland Eastern Shore (MD)
U of Miami (FL)
U of Minnesota, Duluth (MN)
U of Minnesota, Morris (MN)
U of Minnesota, Twin Cities Campus (MN)
U of Missouri–Rolla (MO)
U of Missouri–St. Louis (MO)
The U of Montana–Missoula (MT)
Western Montana Coll of The U of Montana (MT)
U of Montevallo (AL)
U of Nebraska at Omaha (NE)
U of New England (ME)
The U of North Carolina at Greensboro (NC)
The U of North Carolina at Pembroke (NC)
U of Ottawa (ON, Canada)
U of Pittsburgh at Greensburg (PA)
U of Pittsburgh at Johnstown (PA)
U of Portland (OR)
U of Puget Sound (WA)
U of Regina (SK, Canada)
U of Rio Grande (OH)
U of Saint Francis (IN)
U of St. Thomas (TX)
U of San Francisco (CA)
U of Saskatchewan (SK, Canada)
U of Sioux Falls (SD)
U of South Dakota (SD)
U of Southern Colorado (CO)
The U of Tampa (FL)
U of the Incarnate Word (TX)
U of Toledo (OH)
U of Toronto (ON, Canada)
U of Victoria (BC, Canada)
U of West Los Angeles (CA)
U of Windsor (ON, Canada)
U of Wisconsin–Milwaukee (WI)
U of Wisconsin–Oshkosh (WI)
U of Wisconsin–Parkside (WI)
U of Wisconsin–River Falls (WI)
U of Wisconsin–Superior (WI)
U of Wisconsin–Whitewater (WI)
Urbana U (OH)
Ursinus Coll (PA)
Ursuline Coll (OH)
Utah State U (UT)
Utica Coll of Syracuse U (NY)
Valdosta State U (GA)
Valley City State U (ND)
Vanguard U of Southern California (CA)
Villa Julie Coll (MD)
Villanova U (PA)
Virginia Intermont Coll (VA)
Virginia Wesleyan Coll (VA)
Viterbo U (WI)
Wabash Coll (IN)
Wagner Coll (NY)
Walla Walla Coll (WA)
Walsh U (OH)
Warner Pacific Coll (OR)
Warner Southern Coll (FL)
Washburn U of Topeka (KS)
Washington Coll (MD)
Washington State U (WA)
Waynesburg Coll (PA)
Webber International U (FL)
Wells Coll (NY)
West Chester U of Pennsylvania (PA)
Western Baptist Coll (OR)
Western State Coll of Colorado (CO)
Western Washington U (WA)
Westfield State Coll (MA)
West Liberty State Coll (WV)
Westminster Coll (MO)
Westminster Coll (PA)
Westmont Coll (CA)
West Virginia Wesleyan Coll (WV)
Whitworth Coll (WA)
Wiley Coll (TX)
Wilkes U (PA)
Willamette U (OR)
William Carey Coll (MS)
William Jewell Coll (MO)
William Paterson U of New Jersey (NJ)
William Penn U (IA)
Williams Baptist Coll (AR)
William Tyndale Coll (MI)
Wilmington Coll (OH)
Wingate U (NC)
Winona State U (MN)
Wittenberg U (OH)
Wofford Coll (SC)
Xavier U of Louisiana (LA)
Yeshiva U (NY)
York Coll of Pennsylvania (PA)
York U (ON, Canada)
Youngstown State U (OH)

PRE-MEDICINE

Abilene Christian U (TX)
Acadia U (NS, Canada)
Adams State Coll (CO)
Adrian Coll (MI)
Alabama State U (AL)
Albertson Coll of Idaho (ID)
Albertus Magnus Coll (CT)
Albion Coll (MI)
Albright Coll (PA)
Alderson-Broaddus Coll (WV)
Alfred U (NY)
Alice Lloyd Coll (KY)
Alma Coll (MI)
Alvernia Coll (PA)
American International Coll (MA)
American U (DC)
Anderson U (IN)
Andrews U (MI)
Appalachian State U (NC)
Aquinas Coll (MI)
Arcadia U (PA)
Ashland U (OH)
Atlantic Union Coll (MA)
Auburn U (AL)
Augsburg Coll (MN)
Augustana Coll (IL)
Augustana Coll (SD)
Averett U (VA)
Avila Coll (MO)
Baker U (KS)
Baldwin-Wallace Coll (OH)
Ball State U (IN)
Bard Coll (NY)
Barnard Coll (NY)
Barry U (FL)
Barton Coll (NC)
Baylor U (TX)
Bellarmine U (KY)
Belmont Abbey Coll (NC)
Beloit Coll (WI)
Bemidji State U (MN)
Benedict Coll (SC)
Benedictine U (IL)
Bennington Coll (VT)
Berea Coll (KY)
Berry Coll (GA)
Bethany Coll (WV)
Bethel Coll (IN)
Bethel Coll (MN)
Bethel Coll (TN)
Birmingham-Southern Coll (AL)
Blackburn Coll (IL)
Bloomfield Coll (NJ)
Blue Mountain Coll (MS)
Bluffton Coll (OH)
Boise State U (ID)
Boston Coll (MA)
Bowdoin Coll (ME)
Brandon U (MB, Canada)
Brevard Coll (NC)
Briar Cliff U (IA)
Bryan Coll (TN)
Buena Vista U (IA)
California Polytechnic State U, San Luis Obispo (CA)
California State Polytechnic U, Pomona (CA)
California State U, Chico (CA)
California State U, Dominguez Hills (CA)
California State U, Fullerton (CA)
California State U, Hayward (CA)
California State U, Northridge (CA)
Calvin Coll (MI)
Campbellsville U (KY)
Campbell U (NC)
Capital U (OH)
Cardinal Stritch U (WI)
Caribbean U (PR)
Carroll Coll (MT)
Carroll Coll (WI)
Carthage Coll (WI)
Catawba Coll (NC)
Cedar Crest Coll (PA)
Cedarville U (OH)
Centenary Coll of Louisiana (LA)
Central Missouri State U (MO)

U of Regina (SK, Canada)
U of Rio Grande (OH)
U of St. Francis (IL)
U of Saint Francis (IN)
U of St. Thomas (TX)
U of San Diego (CA)
U of San Francisco (CA)
U of Saskatchewan (SK, Canada)
U of Sioux Falls (SD)
U of South Dakota (SD)
U of Southern Colorado (CO)
The U of Tampa (FL)
The U of Tennessee at Chattanooga (TN)
The U of Tennessee at Martin (TN)
The U of Texas–Pan American (TX)
U of the Incarnate Word (TX)
U of the Ozarks (AR)
U of the Sciences in Philadelphia (PA)
U of Toledo (OH)
U of Toronto (ON, Canada)
U of Victoria (BC, Canada)
U of Windsor (ON, Canada)
U of Wisconsin–Milwaukee (WI)
U of Wisconsin–Oshkosh (WI)
U of Wisconsin–Parkside (WI)
U of Wisconsin–River Falls (WI)
Upper Iowa U (IA)
Urbana U (OH)
Ursinus Coll (PA)
Ursuline Coll (OH)
Utah State U (UT)
Utica Coll of Syracuse U (NY)
Valdosta State U (GA)
Valley City State U (ND)
Villa Julie Coll (MD)
Villanova U (PA)
Virginia Intermont Coll (VA)
Virginia Wesleyan Coll (VA)
Viterbo U (WI)
Wabash Coll (IN)
Wagner Coll (NY)
Walla Walla Coll (WA)
Walsh U (OH)
Warner Pacific Coll (OR)
Warren Wilson Coll (NC)
Washburn U of Topeka (KS)
Washington Coll (MD)
Washington State U (WA)
Washington U in St. Louis (MO)
Waynesburg Coll (PA)
Wayne State Coll (NE)
Wells Coll (NY)
West Chester U of Pennsylvania (PA)
Western Connecticut State U (CT)
Western State Coll of Colorado (CO)
Westfield State Coll (MA)
West Liberty State Coll (WV)
Westminster Coll (MO)
Westminster Coll (PA)
Westmont Coll (CA)
West Virginia State Coll (WV)
West Virginia Wesleyan Coll (WV)
Wheaton Coll (MA)
Whitworth Coll (WA)
Widener U (PA)
Wiley Coll (TX)
Wilkes U (PA)
Willamette U (OR)
William Carey Coll (MS)
William Jewell Coll (MO)
William Paterson U of New Jersey (NJ)
William Penn U (IA)
Williams Baptist Coll (AR)
Wilmington Coll (OH)
Wingate U (NC)
Winona State U (MN)
Wittenberg U (OH)
Wofford Coll (SC)
Xavier U of Louisiana (LA)
Yeshiva U (NY)
York Coll of Pennsylvania (PA)
York U (ON, Canada)
Youngstown State U (OH)

PRE-PHARMACY STUDIES

Abilene Christian U (TX)
Adams State Coll (CO)
American U (DC)
Ashland U (OH)
Barry U (FL)
Barton Coll (NC)
Bellarmine U (KY)
Belmont Abbey Coll (NC)
Blue Mountain Coll (MS)
Brevard Coll (NC)
Carroll Coll (MT)
Central Missouri State U (MO)
Christian Brothers U (TN)
Clemson U (SC)
Coll of Saint Benedict (MN)
Coll of the Ozarks (MO)
Elmhurst Coll (IL)
Florida State U (FL)
Freed-Hardeman U (TN)
Holy Family Coll (PA)
Juniata Coll (PA)
King Coll (TN)
King's Coll (PA)
Lander U (SC)
Le Moyne Coll (NY)
Long Island U, C.W. Post Campus (NY)
Mayville State U (ND)
McPherson Coll (KS)
Meredith Coll (NC)
Missouri Southern State Coll (MO)
Mount Allison U (NB, Canada)
Mount Vernon Nazarene U (OH)
Ohio U (OH)
Oklahoma Baptist U (OK)
Roberts Wesleyan Coll (NY)
Saint John's U (MN)
Saint Martin's Coll (WA)
Saint Mary-of-the-Woods Coll (IN)
Southern Nazarene U (OK)
Tennessee Wesleyan Coll (TN)
Union U (TN)
The U of Akron (OH)
U of Connecticut (CT)
U of Hawaii at Manoa (HI)
The U of Iowa (IA)
U of Mary Hardin-Baylor (TX)
U of Miami (FL)
U of Minnesota, Duluth (MN)
U of Minnesota, Morris (MN)
The U of Montana–Missoula (MT)
U of Nebraska–Lincoln (NE)
U of Nevada, Reno (NV)
U of Saskatchewan (SK, Canada)
The U of Tennessee at Martin (TN)
U of Windsor (ON, Canada)
U of Wisconsin–Parkside (WI)
U of Wisconsin–River Falls (WI)
Valley City State U (ND)
Viterbo U (WI)
Washington U in St. Louis (MO)
Westmont Coll (CA)
York U (ON, Canada)
Youngstown State U (OH)

PRE-THEOLOGY

Alma Coll (MI)
Ashland U (OH)
Atlanta Christian Coll (GA)
Blue Mountain Coll (MS)
California Christian Coll (CA)
Central Christian Coll of Kansas (KS)
Christian Brothers U (TN)
Circleville Bible Coll (OH)
Coll of Saint Benedict (MN)
Coll of Santa Fe (NM)
Columbia Bible Coll (BC, Canada)
Columbia International U (SC)
Concordia Coll (MN)
Concordia U (IL)
Concordia U (OR)
Emmaus Bible Coll (IA)
Florida State U (FL)
Geneva Coll (PA)
Grace U (NE)
Juniata Coll (PA)
Kentucky Mountain Bible Coll (KY)
Loras Coll (IA)
Loyola U Chicago (IL)
Luther Coll (IA)
Martin Luther Coll (MN)
Minnesota State U, Mankato (MN)
Moody Bible Inst (IL)
Mount Allison U (NB, Canada)
Northwest Christian Coll (OR)
Northwestern Coll (MN)
Ohio Wesleyan U (OH)
Redeemer U Coll (ON, Canada)
Reformed Bible Coll (MI)
Saint John's U (MN)
Southwestern Coll (KS)
Tennessee Wesleyan Coll (TN)
Trinity Christian Coll (IL)
U of Dallas (TX)
U of Indianapolis (IN)
U of North Texas (TX)
U of Rio Grande (OH)
Valparaiso U (IN)
Warner Southern Coll (FL)
Waynesburg Coll (PA)
Westmont Coll (CA)

PRE-VETERINARY STUDIES

Abilene Christian U (TX)
Acadia U (NS, Canada)
Adams State Coll (CO)
Adrian Coll (MI)
Albertus Magnus Coll (CT)
Albion Coll (MI)
Albright Coll (PA)
Alderson-Broaddus Coll (WV)
Alfred U (NY)
Alice Lloyd Coll (KY)
Alma Coll (MI)
American International Coll (MA)
American U (DC)
Anderson U (IN)
Andrews U (MI)
Aquinas Coll (MI)
Arcadia U (PA)
Arizona State U East (AZ)
Ashland U (OH)
Atlantic Union Coll (MA)
Auburn U (AL)
Augsburg Coll (MN)
Augustana Coll (IL)
Augustana Coll (SD)
Baker U (KS)
Baldwin-Wallace Coll (OH)
Bard Coll (NY)
Barry U (FL)
Barton Coll (NC)
Bellarmine U (KY)
Belmont Abbey Coll (NC)
Bemidji State U (MN)
Benedictine U (IL)
Bennington Coll (VT)
Berea Coll (KY)
Berry Coll (GA)
Bethany Coll (WV)
Bethel Coll (MN)
Blackburn Coll (IL)
Bloomfield Coll (NJ)
Blue Mountain Coll (MS)
Boise State U (ID)
Brandon U (MB, Canada)
Brevard Coll (NC)
Briar Cliff U (IA)
Buena Vista U (IA)
California State Polytechnic U, Pomona (CA)
California State U, Chico (CA)
California State U, Dominguez Hills (CA)
California State U, Fullerton (CA)
California State U, Hayward (CA)
California State U, Northridge (CA)
Calvin Coll (MI)
Campbellsville U (KY)
Campbell U (NC)
Capital U (OH)
Cardinal Stritch U (WI)
Carroll Coll (MT)
Carthage Coll (WI)
Catawba Coll (NC)
Cedar Crest Coll (PA)
Cedarville U (OH)
Centenary Coll of Louisiana (LA)
Central Missouri State U (MO)
Chapman U (CA)
Chicago State U (IL)
Chowan Coll (NC)
City Coll of the City U of NY (NY)
Clarkson U (NY)
Clark U (MA)
Clemson U (SC)
Cleveland State U (OH)
Coe Coll (IA)
Coll Misericordia (PA)
Coll of Notre Dame of Maryland (MD)
Coll of Saint Benedict (MN)
Coll of St. Catherine (MN)
Coll of Saint Elizabeth (NJ)
Coll of Saint Mary (NE)
Coll of Santa Fe (NM)
Coll of the Atlantic (ME)
Coll of the Ozarks (MO)
The Coll of Wooster (OH)
Colorado State U (CO)
Columbia Coll (MO)
Columbia Coll (SC)
Columbia Union Coll (MD)
Columbus State U (GA)
Concord Coll (WV)
Concordia Coll (MN)
Converse Coll (SC)
Cornell U (NY)
Cornerstone U (MI)
Cumberland U (TN)
Dakota State U (SD)
Dalhousie U (NS, Canada)
Davis & Elkins Coll (WV)
Defiance Coll (OH)
Delaware State U (DE)
Delaware Valley Coll (PA)
DeSales U (PA)
Dickinson State U (ND)
Dillard U (LA)
Dominican U (IL)
Dordt Coll (IA)
Drake U (IA)
Drury U (MO)
D'Youville Coll (NY)
East Central U (OK)
Eastern Kentucky U (KY)
Eastern Mennonite U (VA)
Eastern Oregon U (OR)
Eastern Washington U (WA)
Eckerd Coll (FL)
Edgewood Coll (WI)
Elizabethtown Coll (PA)
Elmhurst Coll (IL)
Elmira Coll (NY)
Elms Coll (MA)
Elon U (NC)
Emory & Henry Coll (VA)
Eureka Coll (IL)
Evangel U (MO)
The Evergreen State Coll (WA)
Florida Southern Coll (FL)
Florida State U (FL)
Fordham U (NY)
Fort Lewis Coll (CO)
Framingham State Coll (MA)
Francis Marion U (SC)
Franklin Pierce Coll (NH)
Freed-Hardeman U (TN)
Friends U (KS)
Furman U (SC)
Gannon U (PA)
Gardner-Webb U (NC)
Georgia Southwestern State U (GA)
Gettysburg Coll (PA)
Goshen Coll (IN)
Grand Canyon U (AZ)
Grand Valley State U (MI)
Greenville Coll (IL)
Grove City Coll (PA)
Gustavus Adolphus Coll (MN)
Gwynedd-Mercy Coll (PA)
Hamline U (MN)
Hampshire Coll (MA)
Hampton U (VA)
Harding U (AR)
Hartwick Coll (NY)
Harvard U (MA)
Hastings Coll (NE)
Haverford Coll (PA)
Heidelberg Coll (OH)
High Point U (NC)
Hillsdale Coll (MI)
Hiram Coll (OH)
Hobart and William Smith Colls (NY)
Holy Family Coll (PA)
Hood Coll (MD)
Houghton Coll (NY)
Houston Baptist U (TX)
Humboldt State U (CA)
Huntingdon Coll (AL)
Huntington Coll (IN)
Illinois Coll (IL)
Illinois Wesleyan U (IL)
Immaculata Coll (PA)
Indiana U–Purdue U Indianapolis (IN)
Indiana Wesleyan U (IN)
Iowa State U of Science and Technology (IA)
Iowa Wesleyan Coll (IA)
Jackson State U (MS)
Jacksonville U (FL)
John Brown U (AR)
John Carroll U (OH)
Juniata Coll (PA)
Kansas State U (KS)
Kansas Wesleyan U (KS)
Kentucky Wesleyan Coll (KY)
King Coll (TN)
King's Coll (PA)
LaGrange Coll (GA)
Lake Erie Coll (OH)
Lake Forest Coll (IL)
Lake Superior State U (MI)
Lander U (SC)
La Salle U (PA)
Lawrence U (WI)
Lebanon Valley Coll (PA)
Lees-McRae Coll (NC)
Le Moyne Coll (NY)
Lenoir-Rhyne Coll (NC)
LeTourneau U (TX)
Lewis & Clark Coll (OR)
Lewis U (IL)
Lincoln Memorial U (TN)
Lindenwood U (MO)
Lipscomb U (TN)
Lock Haven U of Pennsylvania (PA)
Long Island U, C.W. Post Campus (NY)
Longwood Coll (VA)
Loyola U Chicago (IL)
Lubbock Christian U (TX)
Luther Coll (IA)
Lycoming Coll (PA)
Lynchburg Coll (VA)
MacMurray Coll (IL)
Manchester Coll (IN)
Marian Coll (IN)
Marian Coll of Fond du Lac (WI)
Marist Coll (NY)
Marlboro Coll (VT)
Mars Hill Coll (NC)
Mary Washington Coll (VA)
Massachusetts Inst of Technology (MA)
Mayville State U (ND)
McKendree Coll (IL)
McPherson Coll (KS)
Mercyhurst Coll (PA)
Meredith Coll (NC)
Mesa State Coll (CO)
Methodist Coll (NC)
Miami U (OH)
Michigan Technological U (MI)
Middlebury Coll (VT)
Midland Lutheran Coll (NE)
Midwestern State U (TX)
Milligan Coll (TN)
Millikin U (IL)
Minnesota State U, Mankato (MN)
Minnesota State U Moorhead (MN)
Missouri Southern State Coll (MO)
Missouri Valley Coll (MO)
Molloy Coll (NY)
Morningside Coll (IA)
Mount Allison U (NB, Canada)
Mount Mary Coll (WI)
Mount Mercy Coll (IA)
Mount Vernon Nazarene U (OH)
Muhlenberg Coll (PA)
Muskingum Coll (OH)
Nazareth Coll of Rochester (NY)
Newberry Coll (SC)
Newman U (KS)
New Mexico Inst of Mining and Technology (NM)
Niagara U (NY)
North Central Coll (IL)
North Dakota State U (ND)
Northeastern State U (OK)
Northern Arizona U (AZ)
Northern Kentucky U (KY)
Northern Michigan U (MI)
North Georgia Coll & State U (GA)
Northland Coll (WI)
North Park U (IL)
Northwest Missouri State U (MO)
Nova Scotia Ag Coll (NS, Canada)
Nova Southeastern U (FL)
Oakland City U (IN)
Oakland U (MI)
Oglethorpe U (GA)
Ohio U (OH)
Ohio Wesleyan U (OH)
Oklahoma Baptist U (OK)
Oklahoma City U (OK)
Oklahoma State U (OK)
Oklahoma Wesleyan U (OK)
Olivet Coll (MI)
Olivet Nazarene U (IL)
Oregon State U (OR)
Otterbein Coll (OH)
Pacific Union Coll (CA)
Paine Coll (GA)
Peru State Coll (NE)
Pittsburg State U (KS)
Presbyterian Coll (SC)
Purdue U (IN)
Purdue U Calumet (IN)
Queens Coll (NC)

Quincy U (IL)
Quinnipiac U (CT)
Redeemer U Coll (ON, Canada)
Regis U (CO)
Rhode Island Coll (RI)
Ripon Coll (WI)
Rivier Coll (NH)
Roberts Wesleyan Coll (NY)
Rochester Inst of Technology (NY)
Rockford Coll (IL)
Rocky Mountain Coll (MT)
Roger Williams U (RI)
Rollins Coll (FL)
Sacred Heart U (CT)
St. Andrews Presbyterian Coll (NC)
St. Bonaventure U (NY)
St. Cloud State U (MN)
Saint Francis U (PA)
St. Francis Xavier U (NS, Canada)
Saint John's U (MN)
St. Joseph's Coll, Suffolk Campus (NY)
Saint Leo U (FL)
Saint Martin's Coll (WA)
Saint Mary-of-the-Woods Coll (IN)
Saint Mary's Coll of California (CA)
Saint Michael's Coll (VT)
St. Norbert Coll (WI)
Salem State Coll (MA)
Seton Hill Coll (PA)
Shawnee State U (OH)
Simpson Coll (IA)
Slippery Rock U of Pennsylvania (PA)
Sonoma State U (CA)
South Carolina State U (SC)
South Dakota State U (SD)
Southern Connecticut State U (CT)
Southwestern Oklahoma State U (OK)
Southwest State U (MN)
Spring Hill Coll (AL)
State U of NY at Oswego (NY)
State U of NY Coll at Brockport (NY)
State U of NY Coll at Buffalo (NY)
State U of NY Coll at Fredonia (NY)
State U of NY Coll at Geneseo (NY)
State U of NY Coll at Oneonta (NY)
State U of NY Coll of Environ Sci and Forestry (NY)
State U of West Georgia (GA)
Stephens Coll (MO)
Stetson U (FL)
Stonehill Coll (MA)
Suffolk U (MA)
Sul Ross State U (TX)
Susquehanna U (PA)
Syracuse U (NY)
Taylor U (IN)
Tennessee Technological U (TN)
Tennessee Wesleyan Coll (TN)
Texas A&M U–Kingsville (TX)
Texas Lutheran U (TX)
Thiel Coll (PA)
Trinity Christian Coll (IL)
Trinity U (TX)
Trinity Western U (BC, Canada)
Tri-State U (IN)
Troy State U (AL)
Truman State U (MO)
Tusculum Coll (TN)
Union Coll (KY)
U Coll of Cape Breton (NS, Canada)
The U of Akron (OH)
U of Alberta (AB, Canada)
The U of Arizona (AZ)
U of Bridgeport (CT)
The U of British Columbia (BC, Canada)
U of Cincinnati (OH)
U of Colorado at Colorado Springs (CO)
U of Delaware (DE)
U of Evansville (IN)
The U of Findlay (OH)
U of Houston (TX)
U of Illinois at Urbana–Champaign (IL)
U of Indianapolis (IN)
The U of Iowa (IA)
U of Maine (ME)
U of Manitoba (MB, Canada)
U of Mary Hardin-Baylor (TX)
U of Maryland, Baltimore County (MD)
U of Maryland, Coll Park (MD)
U of Massachusetts Amherst (MA)
U of Miami (FL)
U of Minnesota, Duluth (MN)
U of Minnesota, Morris (MN)
U of Minnesota, Twin Cities Campus (MN)
U of Missouri–St. Louis (MO)
Western Montana Coll of The U of Montana (MT)
U of Montevallo (AL)
U of Nebraska–Lincoln (NE)
U of Nevada, Reno (NV)
U of New England (ME)
U of New Hampshire (NH)
U of New Orleans (LA)
The U of North Carolina at Greensboro (NC)
U of Oklahoma (OK)
U of Pittsburgh at Johnstown (PA)
U of Prince Edward Island (PE, Canada)
U of Puget Sound (WA)
U of Regina (SK, Canada)
U of Rio Grande (OH)
U of St. Francis (IL)
U of Saint Francis (IN)
U of San Francisco (CA)
U of Saskatchewan (SK, Canada)
U of Sioux Falls (SD)
U of South Dakota (SD)
U of Southern Colorado (CO)
The U of Tampa (FL)
The U of Tennessee at Chattanooga (TN)
The U of Tennessee at Martin (TN)
U of the Ozarks (AR)
U of the Sciences in Philadelphia (PA)
U of Vermont (VT)
U of Victoria (BC, Canada)
U of Wisconsin–Oshkosh (WI)
U of Wisconsin–Parkside (WI)
U of Wisconsin–River Falls (WI)
Upper Iowa U (IA)
Urbana U (OH)
Ursinus Coll (PA)
Utah State U (UT)
Utica Coll of Syracuse U (NY)
Valley City State U (ND)
Villa Julie Coll (MD)
Villanova U (PA)
Virginia Intermont Coll (VA)
Virginia Wesleyan Coll (VA)
Viterbo U (WI)
Wabash Coll (IN)
Walla Walla Coll (WA)
Walsh U (OH)
Warner Pacific Coll (OR)
Warren Wilson Coll (NC)
Washington Coll (MD)
Washington U in St. Louis (MO)
Waynesburg Coll (PA)
Wayne State Coll (NE)
Wells Coll (NY)
West Chester U of Pennsylvania (PA)
Western State Coll of Colorado (CO)
Westminster Coll (MO)
Westminster Coll (PA)
Westmont Coll (CA)
West Virginia State Coll (WV)
West Virginia Wesleyan Coll (WV)
Whitworth Coll (WA)
Wilkes U (PA)
Willamette U (OR)
William Carey Coll (MS)
William Jewell Coll (MO)
Wilmington Coll (OH)
Wingate U (NC)
Winona State U (MN)
Wittenberg U (OH)
Wofford Coll (SC)
Xavier U of Louisiana (LA)
York Coll of Pennsylvania (PA)
York U (ON, Canada)
Youngstown State U (OH)

PRINTMAKING

Academy of Art Coll (CA)
Adams State Coll (CO)
Alberta Coll of Art & Design (AB, Canada)
Alfred U (NY)
Arizona State U (AZ)
Atlanta Coll of Art (GA)
Ball State U (IN)
Bennington Coll (VT)
Birmingham-Southern Coll (AL)
Bowling Green State U (OH)
California Coll of Arts and Crafts (CA)
California State U, Fullerton (CA)
California State U, Hayward (CA)
California State U, Long Beach (CA)
California State U, Stanislaus (CA)
The Cleveland Inst of Art (OH)
Coll of Santa Fe (NM)
Coll of Visual Arts (MN)
Colorado State U (CO)
Columbus Coll of Art and Design (OH)
Concordia U (QC, Canada)
Corcoran Coll of Art and Design (DC)
Emmanuel Coll (MA)
Escuela de Artes Plasticas de Puerto Rico (PR)
Framingham State Coll (MA)
Grand Valley State U (MI)
Indiana Wesleyan U (IN)
Kansas City Art Inst (MO)
Long Island U, Southampton Coll, Friends World Program (NY)
Longwood Coll (VA)
Maine Coll of Art (ME)
Maryland Inst, Coll of Art (MD)
Massachusetts Coll of Art (MA)
McNeese State U (LA)
Memorial U of Newfoundland (NF, Canada)
Memphis Coll of Art (TN)
Milwaukee Inst of Art and Design (WI)
Minneapolis Coll of Art and Design (MN)
Minnesota State U Moorhead (MN)
Mississippi U for Women (MS)
Montserrat Coll of Art (MA)
Mount Allison U (NB, Canada)
New World School of the Arts (FL)
Northern Michigan U (MI)
Nova Scotia Coll of Art and Design (NS, Canada)
The Ohio State U (OH)
Ohio U (OH)
Pacific Northwest Coll of Art (OR)
Pratt Inst (NY)
Rhode Island School of Design (RI)
Rutgers, The State U of New Jersey, New Brunswick (NJ)
School of the Art Inst of Chicago (IL)
School of the Museum of Fine Arts (MA)
Seton Hill Coll (PA)
Simon's Rock Coll of Bard (MA)
Sonoma State U (CA)
State U of NY Coll at Buffalo (NY)
State U of NY Coll at Potsdam (NY)
Syracuse U (NY)
Texas Christian U (TX)
Trinity Christian Coll (IL)
The U of Akron (OH)
U of Alberta (AB, Canada)
U of Calif, Santa Cruz (CA)
U of Dallas (TX)
U of Houston (TX)
The U of Iowa (IA)
U of Kansas (KS)
U of Massachusetts Dartmouth (MA)
U of Miami (FL)
U of Michigan (MI)
U of Missouri–St. Louis (MO)
U of Montevallo (AL)
U of North Texas (TX)
U of Oklahoma (OK)
U of Oregon (OR)
U of San Francisco (CA)
U of South Dakota (SD)
The U of Texas at El Paso (TX)
The U of the Arts (PA)
U of Washington (WA)
Washington U in St. Louis (MO)
Webster U (MO)
York U (ON, Canada)
Youngstown State U (OH)

PROFESSIONAL STUDIES

Bemidji State U (MN)
Briar Cliff U (IA)
Champlain Coll (VT)
Grand View Coll (IA)
Juniata Coll (PA)
Kent State U (OH)
Lake Erie Coll (OH)
Missouri Southern State Coll (MO)
Mount Aloysius Coll (PA)
Saint Mary-of-the-Woods Coll (IN)
Thomas Coll (ME)
U of Dubuque (IA)
The U of Memphis (TN)
U of Oklahoma (OK)
The U of Tennessee at Martin (TN)

PROTECTIVE SERVICES RELATED

Franklin U (OH)
Lewis U (IL)
Northwestern Oklahoma State U (OK)
Ohio U (OH)

PSYCHIATRIC/MENTAL HEALTH SERVICES

Franciscan U of Steubenville (OH)
MCP Hahnemann U (PA)
Pennsylvania Coll of Technology (PA)

PSYCHOLOGY

Abilene Christian U (TX)
Acadia U (NS, Canada)
Adams State Coll (CO)
Adelphi U (NY)
Adrian Coll (MI)
Agnes Scott Coll (GA)
Alabama State U (AL)
Alaska Pacific U (AK)
Albany State U (GA)
Albertson Coll of Idaho (ID)
Albertus Magnus Coll (CT)
Albion Coll (MI)
Albright Coll (PA)
Alderson-Broaddus Coll (WV)
Alfred U (NY)
Allegheny Coll (PA)
Alliant International U (CA)
Alma Coll (MI)
Alvernia Coll (PA)
Alverno Coll (WI)
American Coll of Thessaloniki(Greece)
American International Coll (MA)
American U (DC)
American U in Cairo(Egypt)
Amherst Coll (MA)
Anderson Coll (SC)
Anderson U (IN)
Andrews U (MI)
Angelo State U (TX)
Anna Maria Coll (MA)
Appalachian State U (NC)
Aquinas Coll (MI)
Arcadia U (PA)
Arizona State U (AZ)
Arizona State U East (AZ)
Arizona State U West (AZ)
Arkansas State U (AR)
Arkansas Tech U (AR)
Armstrong Atlantic State U (GA)
Asbury Coll (KY)
Ashland U (OH)
Assumption Coll (MA)
Athabasca U (AB, Canada)
Athens State U (AL)
Atlantic Baptist U (NB, Canada)
Atlantic Union Coll (MA)
Auburn U (AL)
Auburn U Montgomery (AL)
Augsburg Coll (MN)
Augustana Coll (IL)
Augustana Coll (SD)
Augusta State U (GA)
Aurora U (IL)
Austin Coll (TX)
Austin Peay State U (TN)
Avila Coll (MO)
Azusa Pacific U (CA)
Baker U (KS)
Baldwin-Wallace Coll (OH)
Ball State U (IN)
Baptist Bible Coll of Pennsylvania (PA)
Barclay Coll (KS)
Bard Coll (NY)
Barnard Coll (NY)
Barry U (FL)
Barton Coll (NC)
Bastyr U (WA)
Bates Coll (ME)
Bayamón Central U (PR)
Baylor U (TX)
Bay Path Coll (MA)
Beacon Coll and Graduate School (GA)
Becker Coll (MA)
Belhaven Coll (MS)
Bellarmine U (KY)
Bellevue U (NE)
Belmont Abbey Coll (NC)
Belmont U (TN)
Beloit Coll (WI)
Bemidji State U (MN)
Benedictine Coll (KS)
Benedictine U (IL)
Bennett Coll (NC)
Bennington Coll (VT)
Berea Coll (KY)
Baruch Coll of the City U of NY (NY)
Berry Coll (GA)
Bethany Coll (KS)
Bethany Coll (WV)
Bethany Coll of the Assemblies of God (CA)
Bethel Coll (IN)
Bethel Coll (KS)
Bethel Coll (MN)
Bethel Coll (TN)
Bethune-Cookman Coll (FL)
Biola U (CA)
Birmingham-Southern Coll (AL)
Bishop's U (PQ, Canada)
Blackburn Coll (IL)
Black Hills State U (SD)
Bloomfield Coll (NJ)
Bloomsburg U of Pennsylvania (PA)
Bluefield Coll (VA)
Blue Mountain Coll (MS)
Bluffton Coll (OH)
Boise State U (ID)
Boston Coll (MA)
Boston U (MA)
Bowdoin Coll (ME)
Bowie State U (MD)
Bowling Green State U (OH)
Bradley U (IL)
Brandeis U (MA)
Brandon U (MB, Canada)
Brenau U (GA)
Brescia U (KY)
Brewton-Parker Coll (GA)
Briar Cliff U (IA)
Bridgewater Coll (VA)
Bridgewater State Coll (MA)
Brigham Young U (UT)
Brigham Young U–Hawaii (HI)
Brock U (ON, Canada)
Brooklyn Coll of the City U of NY (NY)
Brown U (RI)
Bryan Coll (TN)
Bryant Coll (RI)
Bryn Mawr Coll (PA)
Bucknell U (PA)
Buena Vista U (IA)
Burlington Coll (VT)
Butler U (IN)
Cabrini Coll (PA)
Caldwell Coll (NJ)
California Baptist U (CA)
California Lutheran U (CA)
California Polytechnic State U, San Luis Obispo (CA)
California State Polytechnic U, Pomona (CA)
California State U, Bakersfield (CA)
California State U, Chico (CA)
California State U, Dominguez Hills (CA)
California State U, Fresno (CA)
California State U, Fullerton (CA)
California State U, Hayward (CA)
California State U, Long Beach (CA)
California State U, Los Angeles (CA)
California State U, Northridge (CA)
California State U, Sacramento (CA)
California State U, San Bernardino (CA)
California State U, San Marcos (CA)
California State U, Stanislaus (CA)
California U of Pennsylvania (PA)
Calvin Coll (MI)

Cambridge Coll (MA)
Cameron U (OK)
Campbellsville U (KY)
Campbell U (NC)
Canisius Coll (NY)
Cardinal Stritch U (WI)
Carleton Coll (MN)
Carleton U (ON, Canada)
Caribbean Ctr for Advanced Studies/ Miami Inst of Psych (FL)
Carlow Coll (PA)
Carnegie Mellon U (PA)
Carroll Coll (MT)
Carroll Coll (WI)
Carson-Newman Coll (TN)
Carthage Coll (WI)
Cascade Coll (OR)
Case Western Reserve U (OH)
Castleton State Coll (VT)
Catawba Coll (NC)
The Catholic U of America (DC)
Cazenovia Coll (NY)
Cedar Crest Coll (PA)
Cedarville U (OH)
Centenary Coll (NJ)
Centenary Coll of Louisiana (LA)
Central Coll (IA)
Central Connecticut State U (CT)
Central Methodist Coll (MO)
Central Michigan U (MI)
Central Missouri State U (MO)
Central State U (OH)
Central Washington U (WA)
Centre Coll (KY)
Chadron State Coll (NE)
Chaminade U of Honolulu (HI)
Chapman U (CA)
Charleston Southern U (SC)
Chatham Coll (PA)
Chestnut Hill Coll (PA)
Cheyney U of Pennsylvania (PA)
Chicago State U (IL)
Chowan Coll (NC)
Christian Brothers U (TN)
Christian Heritage Coll (CA)
Christopher Newport U (VA)
Cincinnati Bible Coll and Seminary (OH)
Citadel, The Military Coll of South Carolina (SC)
City Coll of the City U of NY (NY)
City U (WA)
Claremont McKenna Coll (CA)
Clarion U of Pennsylvania (PA)
Clark Atlanta U (GA)
Clarke Coll (IA)
Clarkson U (NY)
Clark U (MA)
Clearwater Christian Coll (FL)
Clemson U (SC)
Cleveland State U (OH)
Coastal Carolina U (SC)
Coe Coll (IA)
Coker Coll (SC)
Colby Coll (ME)
Colby-Sawyer Coll (NH)
Colgate U (NY)
Coll Misericordia (PA)
Coll of Charleston (SC)
Coll of Mount St. Joseph (OH)
Coll of Mount Saint Vincent (NY)
The Coll of New Jersey (NJ)
The Coll of New Rochelle (NY)
Coll of Notre Dame of Maryland (MD)
Coll of Saint Benedict (MN)
Coll of St. Catherine (MN)
Coll of Saint Elizabeth (NJ)
Coll of St. Joseph (VT)
Coll of Saint Mary (NE)
The Coll of Saint Rose (NY)
The Coll of St. Scholastica (MN)
Coll of Santa Fe (NM)
The Coll of Southeastern Europe, The American U of Athens(Greece)
Coll of Staten Island of the City U of NY (NY)
Coll of the Atlantic (ME)
Coll of the Holy Cross (MA)
Coll of the Ozarks (MO)
Coll of the Southwest (NM)
The Coll of William and Mary (VA)
The Coll of Wooster (OH)
Colorado Christian U (CO)
The Colorado Coll (CO)
Colorado State U (CO)
Columbia Coll (MO)
Columbia Coll (NY)
Columbia Coll (SC)
Columbia International U (SC)
Columbia Union Coll (MD)
Columbia U, School of General Studies (NY)
Columbus State U (GA)
Concord Coll (WV)
Concordia Coll (MN)
Concordia U (CA)
Concordia U (IL)
Concordia U (MI)
Concordia U (MN)
Concordia U (NE)
Concordia U (OR)
Concordia U (QC, Canada)
Concordia U Wisconsin (WI)
Connecticut Coll (CT)
Converse Coll (SC)
Coppin State Coll (MD)
Cornell Coll (IA)
Cornell U (NY)
Cornerstone U (MI)
Covenant Coll (GA)
Creighton U (NE)
Crichton Coll (TN)
Crown Coll (MN)
Culver-Stockton Coll (MO)
Cumberland Coll (KY)
Cumberland U (TN)
Curry Coll (MA)
Daemen Coll (NY)
Dakota Wesleyan U (SD)
Dalhousie U (NS, Canada)
Dallas Baptist U (TX)
Dana Coll (NE)
Dartmouth Coll (NH)
Davidson Coll (NC)
Davis & Elkins Coll (WV)
Defiance Coll (OH)
Delaware State U (DE)
Delta State U (MS)
Denison U (OH)
DePaul U (IL)
DePauw U (IN)
DeSales U (PA)
Dickinson Coll (PA)
Dickinson State U (ND)
Dillard U (LA)
Doane Coll (NE)
Dominican Coll (NY)
Dominican U (IL)
Dominican U of California (CA)
Dordt Coll (IA)
Dowling Coll (NY)
Drake U (IA)
Drew U (NJ)
Drexel U (PA)
Drury U (MO)
Duke U (NC)
Duquesne U (PA)
Earlham Coll (IN)
East Carolina U (NC)
East Central U (OK)
Eastern Connecticut State U (CT)
Eastern Illinois U (IL)
Eastern Kentucky U (KY)
Eastern Mennonite U (VA)
Eastern Michigan U (MI)
Eastern Nazarene Coll (MA)
Eastern New Mexico U (NM)
Eastern Oregon U (OR)
Eastern U (PA)
Eastern Washington U (WA)
East Stroudsburg U of Pennsylvania (PA)
East Tennessee State U (TN)
East Texas Baptist U (TX)
Eckerd Coll (FL)
Edgewood Coll (WI)
Edinboro U of Pennsylvania (PA)
Edward Waters Coll (FL)
Elizabeth City State U (NC)
Elizabethtown Coll (PA)
Elmhurst Coll (IL)
Elmira Coll (NY)
Elms Coll (MA)
Elon U (NC)
Emmanuel Coll (GA)
Emmanuel Coll (MA)
Emory & Henry Coll (VA)
Emory U (GA)
Emporia State U (KS)
Endicott Coll (MA)
Erskine Coll (SC)
Eugene Lang Coll, New School U (NY)
Eureka Coll (IL)
Evangel U (MO)
The Evergreen State Coll (WA)
Excelsior Coll (NY)
Fairfield U (CT)
Fairleigh Dickinson U, Florham-Madison Campus (NJ)
Fairleigh Dickinson U, Teaneck-Hackensack Campus (NJ)
Fairmont State Coll (WV)
Faulkner U (AL)
Fayetteville State U (NC)
Felician Coll (NJ)
Ferrum Coll (VA)
Fisk U (TN)
Fitchburg State Coll (MA)
Flagler Coll (FL)
Florida A&M U (FL)
Florida Atlantic U (FL)
Florida Inst of Technology (FL)
Florida International U (FL)
Florida Southern Coll (FL)
Florida State U (FL)
Fontbonne U (MO)
Fordham U (NY)
Fort Hays State U (KS)
Fort Lewis Coll (CO)
Fort Valley State U (GA)
Framingham State Coll (MA)
Franciscan U of Steubenville (OH)
Francis Marion U (SC)
Franklin and Marshall Coll (PA)
Franklin Coll of Indiana (IN)
Franklin Pierce Coll (NH)
Freed-Hardeman U (TN)
Fresno Pacific U (CA)
Friends U (KS)
Frostburg State U (MD)
Furman U (SC)
Gallaudet U (DC)
Gannon U (PA)
Gardner-Webb U (NC)
Geneva Coll (PA)
George Fox U (OR)
George Mason U (VA)
Georgetown Coll (KY)
Georgetown U (DC)
The George Washington U (DC)
Georgia Coll and State U (GA)
Georgian Court Coll (NJ)
Georgia Southern U (GA)
Georgia Southwestern State U (GA)
Georgia State U (GA)
Gettysburg Coll (PA)
Goddard Coll (VT)
Gonzaga U (WA)
Gordon Coll (MA)
Goshen Coll (IN)
Goucher Coll (MD)
Governors State U (IL)
Grace Coll (IN)
Graceland U (IA)
Grace U (NE)
Grambling State U (LA)
Grand Canyon U (AZ)
Grand Valley State U (MI)
Grand View Coll (IA)
Greensboro Coll (NC)
Greenville Coll (IL)
Grinnell Coll (IA)
Grove City Coll (PA)
Guilford Coll (NC)
Gustavus Adolphus Coll (MN)
Gwynedd-Mercy Coll (PA)
Hamilton Coll (NY)
Hamline U (MN)
Hampden-Sydney Coll (VA)
Hampshire Coll (MA)
Hampton U (VA)
Hannibal-LaGrange Coll (MO)
Hanover Coll (IN)
Harding U (AR)
Hardin-Simmons U (TX)
Hartwick Coll (NY)
Harvard U (MA)
Hastings Coll (NE)
Haverford Coll (PA)
Hawai'i Pacific U (HI)
Heidelberg Coll (OH)
Henderson State U (AR)
Hendrix Coll (AR)
High Point U (NC)
Hilbert Coll (NY)
Hillsdale Coll (MI)
Hiram Coll (OH)
Hobart and William Smith Colls (NY)
Hofstra U (NY)
Hollins U (VA)
Holy Family Coll (PA)
Holy Names Coll (CA)
Hood Coll (MD)
Hope Coll (MI)
Hope International U (CA)
Houghton Coll (NY)
Houston Baptist U (TX)
Howard Payne U (TX)
Howard U (DC)
Humboldt State U (CA)
Hunter Coll of the City U of NY (NY)
Huntingdon Coll (AL)
Huntington Coll (IN)
Huston-Tillotson Coll (TX)
Idaho State U (ID)
Illinois Coll (IL)
Illinois Inst of Technology (IL)
Illinois State U (IL)
Illinois Wesleyan U (IL)
Immaculata Coll (PA)
Indiana State U (IN)
Indiana U Bloomington (IN)
Indiana U East (IN)
Indiana U Kokomo (IN)
Indiana U Northwest (IN)
Indiana U of Pennsylvania (PA)
Indiana U–Purdue U Fort Wayne (IN)
Indiana U–Purdue U Indianapolis (IN)
Indiana U South Bend (IN)
Indiana U Southeast (IN)
Indiana Wesleyan U (IN)
Inter American U of PR, San Germán Campus (PR)
Iona Coll (NY)
Iowa State U of Science and Technology (IA)
Iowa Wesleyan Coll (IA)
Ithaca Coll (NY)
Jackson State U (MS)
Jacksonville State U (AL)
Jacksonville U (FL)
James Madison U (VA)
Jamestown Coll (ND)
John Brown U (AR)
John Carroll U (OH)
John F. Kennedy U (CA)
John Jay Coll of Criminal Justice, the City U of NY (NY)
Johns Hopkins U (MD)
Johnson C. Smith U (NC)
Johnson State Coll (VT)
John Wesley Coll (NC)
Judson Coll (AL)
Judson Coll (IL)
Juniata Coll (PA)
Kalamazoo Coll (MI)
Kansas State U (KS)
Kansas Wesleyan U (KS)
Kean U (NJ)
Keene State Coll (NH)
Kendall Coll (IL)
Kennesaw State U (GA)
Kent State U (OH)
Kentucky Christian Coll (KY)
Kentucky State U (KY)
Kentucky Wesleyan Coll (KY)
Kenyon Coll (OH)
Keuka Coll (NY)
King Coll (TN)
King's Coll (PA)
The King's U Coll (AB, Canada)
Knox Coll (IL)
Kutztown U of Pennsylvania (PA)
Lafayette Coll (PA)
LaGrange Coll (GA)
Lake Erie Coll (OH)
Lake Forest Coll (IL)
Lakehead U (ON, Canada)
Lakeland Coll (WI)
Lake Superior State U (MI)
Lamar U (TX)
Lambuth U (TN)
Lander U (SC)
La Roche Coll (PA)
La Salle U (PA)
Lasell Coll (MA)
Laurentian U (ON, Canada)
Lawrence U (WI)
Lebanon Valley Coll (PA)
Lees-McRae Coll (NC)
Lee U (TN)
Lehigh U (PA)
Lehman Coll of the City U of NY (NY)
Le Moyne Coll (NY)
Lenoir-Rhyne Coll (NC)
LeTourneau U (TX)
Lewis & Clark Coll (OR)
Lewis-Clark State Coll (ID)
Lewis U (IL)
Liberty U (VA)
Limestone Coll (SC)
Lincoln Memorial U (TN)
Lincoln U (MO)
Lincoln U (PA)
Lindenwood U (MO)
Linfield Coll (OR)
Lipscomb U (TN)
Lock Haven U of Pennsylvania (PA)
Long Island U, Brooklyn Campus (NY)
Long Island U, C.W. Post Campus (NY)
Long Island U, Southampton Coll (NY)
Long Island U, Southampton Coll, Friends World Program (NY)
Longwood Coll (VA)
Loras Coll (IA)
Louisiana Coll (LA)
Louisiana State U and A&M Coll (LA)
Louisiana State U in Shreveport (LA)
Louisiana Tech U (LA)
Lourdes Coll (OH)
Loyola Coll in Maryland (MD)
Loyola Marymount U (CA)
Loyola U Chicago (IL)
Loyola U New Orleans (LA)
Lubbock Christian U (TX)
Luther Coll (IA)
Lycoming Coll (PA)
Lynchburg Coll (VA)
Lyndon State Coll (VT)
Lynn U (FL)
Lyon Coll (AR)
Macalester Coll (MN)
MacMurray Coll (IL)
Maharishi U of Management (IA)
Malaspina U-Coll (BC, Canada)
Malone Coll (OH)
Manchester Coll (IN)
Manhattan Coll (NY)
Manhattanville Coll (NY)
Mansfield U of Pennsylvania (PA)
Marian Coll (IN)
Marian Coll of Fond du Lac (WI)
Marietta Coll (OH)
Marist Coll (NY)
Marlboro Coll (VT)
Marquette U (WI)
Marshall U (WV)
Mars Hill Coll (NC)
Mary Baldwin Coll (VA)
Marygrove Coll (MI)
Marylhurst U (OR)
Marymount Coll of Fordham U (NY)
Marymount Manhattan Coll (NY)
Marymount U (VA)
Maryville Coll (TN)
Maryville U of Saint Louis (MO)
Mary Washington Coll (VA)
Marywood U (PA)
Massachusetts Coll of Liberal Arts (MA)
McGill U (PQ, Canada)
McKendree Coll (IL)
McMaster U (ON, Canada)
McMurry U (TX)
McNeese State U (LA)
McPherson Coll (KS)
Medaille Coll (NY)
Medgar Evers Coll of the City U of NY (NY)
Memorial U of Newfoundland (NF, Canada)
Mercer U (GA)
Mercy Coll (NY)
Mercyhurst Coll (PA)
Meredith Coll (NC)
Merrimack Coll (MA)
Mesa State Coll (CO)
Messiah Coll (PA)
Methodist Coll (NC)
Metropolitan State Coll of Denver (CO)
Metropolitan State U (MN)
Miami U (OH)
Michigan State U (MI)
MidAmerica Nazarene U (KS)
Middlebury Coll (VT)
Middle Tennessee State U (TN)
Midland Lutheran Coll (NE)
Midway Coll (KY)
Midwestern State U (TX)

Millersville U of Pennsylvania (PA)
Milligan Coll (TN)
Millikin U (IL)
Millsaps Coll (MS)
Mills Coll (CA)
Minnesota State U, Mankato (MN)
Minnesota State U Moorhead (MN)
Minot State U (ND)
Mississippi Coll (MS)
Mississippi State U (MS)
Mississippi U for Women (MS)
Missouri Baptist Coll (MO)
Missouri Southern State Coll (MO)
Missouri Valley Coll (MO)
Missouri Western State Coll (MO)
Molloy Coll (NY)
Monmouth Coll (IL)
Monmouth U (NJ)
Montana State U–Billings (MT)
Montana State U–Bozeman (MT)
Montclair State U (NJ)
Moravian Coll (PA)
Morehead State U (KY)
Morehouse Coll (GA)
Morgan State U (MD)
Morningside Coll (IA)
Morris Brown Coll (GA)
Mount Allison U (NB, Canada)
Mount Aloysius Coll (PA)
Mount Holyoke Coll (MA)
Mount Mercy Coll (IA)
Mount Olive Coll (NC)
Mount St. Clare Coll (IA)
Mount Saint Mary Coll (NY)
Mount St. Mary's Coll (CA)
Mount Saint Mary's Coll and Seminary (MD)
Mount Saint Vincent U (NS, Canada)
Mount Union Coll (OH)
Mount Vernon Nazarene U (OH)
Muhlenberg Coll (PA)
Murray State U (KY)
Muskingum Coll (OH)
Naropa U (CO)
National-Louis U (IL)
National U (CA)
Nazareth Coll of Rochester (NY)
Nebraska Wesleyan U (NE)
Neumann Coll (PA)
Newberry Coll (SC)
Newbury Coll (MA)
New Coll of Florida (FL)
New England Coll (NH)
New Jersey City U (NJ)
Newman U (KS)
New Mexico Highlands U (NM)
New Mexico Inst of Mining and Technology (NM)
New Mexico State U (NM)
New York Inst of Technology (NY)
New York U (NY)
Niagara U (NY)
Nicholls State U (LA)
Nipissing U (ON, Canada)
Norfolk State U (VA)
North Carolina Ag and Tech State U (NC)
North Carolina Central U (NC)
North Carolina State U (NC)
North Carolina Wesleyan Coll (NC)
North Central Coll (IL)
North Dakota State U (ND)
Northeastern Illinois U (IL)
Northeastern State U (OK)
Northeastern U (MA)
Northern Arizona U (AZ)
Northern Illinois U (IL)
Northern Kentucky U (KY)
Northern Michigan U (MI)
Northern State U (SD)
North Georgia Coll & State U (GA)
Northland Coll (WI)
North Park U (IL)
Northwest Christian Coll (OR)
Northwest Coll (WA)
Northwestern Coll (IA)
Northwestern Coll (MN)
Northwestern Oklahoma State U (OK)
Northwestern State U of Louisiana (LA)
Northwestern U (IL)
Northwest Missouri State U (MO)
Northwest Nazarene U (ID)
Norwich U (VT)
Notre Dame Coll (OH)
Notre Dame de Namur U (CA)
Nova Southeastern U (FL)
Nyack Coll (NY)
Oak Hills Christian Coll (MN)
Oakland U (MI)
Oakwood Coll (AL)
Oberlin Coll (OH)
Occidental Coll (CA)
Oglethorpe U (GA)
Ohio Dominican Coll (OH)
Ohio Northern U (OH)
The Ohio State U (OH)
The Ohio State U at Lima (OH)
Ohio U (OH)
Ohio Valley Coll (WV)
Ohio Wesleyan U (OH)
Okanagan U Coll (BC, Canada)
Oklahoma Baptist U (OK)
Oklahoma Christian U of Science and Arts (OK)
Oklahoma City U (OK)
Oklahoma Panhandle State U (OK)
Oklahoma State U (OK)
Old Dominion U (VA)
Olivet Coll (MI)
Olivet Nazarene U (IL)
Oral Roberts U (OK)
Oregon State U (OR)
Ottawa U (KS)
Otterbein Coll (OH)
Ouachita Baptist U (AR)
Our Lady of the Lake U of San Antonio (TX)
Pace U (NY)
Pacific Lutheran U (WA)
Pacific Union Coll (CA)
Pacific U (OR)
Paine Coll (GA)
Palm Beach Atlantic Coll (FL)
Park U (MO)
Peace Coll (NC)
Penn State U at Erie, The Behrend Coll (PA)
Penn State U Harrisburg Campus of the Capital Coll (PA)
Penn State U Lehigh Valley Cmps of Berks-Lehigh Valley Coll (PA)
Penn State U Schuylkill Campus of the Capital Coll (PA)
Penn State U Univ Park Campus (PA)
Pepperdine U, Malibu (CA)
Peru State Coll (NE)
Pfeiffer U (NC)
Philadelphia U (PA)
Philander Smith Coll (AR)
Piedmont Coll (GA)
Pikeville Coll (KY)
Pine Manor Coll (MA)
Pittsburg State U (KS)
Pitzer Coll (CA)
Plattsburgh State U of NY (NY)
Plymouth State Coll (NH)
Point Loma Nazarene U (CA)
Point Park Coll (PA)
Pomona Coll (CA)
Pontifical Catholic U of Puerto Rico (PR)
Portland State U (OR)
Prairie View A&M U (TX)
Presbyterian Coll (SC)
Prescott Coll (AZ)
Princeton U (NJ)
Providence Coll (RI)
Purchase Coll, State U of NY (NY)
Purdue U (IN)
Purdue U Calumet (IN)
Queens Coll (NC)
Queens Coll of the City U of NY (NY)
Queen's U at Kingston (ON, Canada)
Quincy U (IL)
Quinnipiac U (CT)
Radford U (VA)
Ramapo Coll of New Jersey (NJ)
Randolph-Macon Coll (VA)
Randolph-Macon Woman's Coll (VA)
Redeemer U Coll (ON, Canada)
Reed Coll (OR)
Regis Coll (MA)
Regis U (CO)
Reinhardt Coll (GA)
Rensselaer Polytechnic Inst (NY)
Rhode Island Coll (RI)
Rhodes Coll (TN)
Rice U (TX)
The Richard Stockton Coll of New Jersey (NJ)
Richmond, The American International U in London(United Kingdom)
Rider U (NJ)
Ripon Coll (WI)
Rivier Coll (NH)
Roanoke Coll (VA)
Roberts Wesleyan Coll (NY)
Rochester Coll (MI)
Rochester Inst of Technology (NY)
Rockford Coll (IL)
Rockhurst U (MO)
Rocky Mountain Coll (MT)
Roger Williams U (RI)
Rollins Coll (FL)
Roosevelt U (IL)
Rosemont Coll (PA)
Rowan U (NJ)
Russell Sage Coll (NY)
Rutgers, The State U of New Jersey, New Brunswick (NJ)
Sacred Heart U (CT)
Sage Coll of Albany (NY)
Saginaw Valley State U (MI)
St. Ambrose U (IA)
St. Andrews Presbyterian Coll (NC)
Saint Anselm Coll (NH)
Saint Augustine's Coll (NC)
St. Bonaventure U (NY)
St. Cloud State U (MN)
St. Edward's U (TX)
St. Francis Coll (NY)
Saint Francis U (PA)
St. Francis Xavier U (NS, Canada)
St. John Fisher Coll (NY)
Saint John's U (MN)
St. John's U (NY)
Saint Joseph Coll (CT)
Saint Joseph's Coll (IN)
Saint Joseph's Coll (ME)
St. Joseph's Coll, New York (NY)
St. Joseph's Coll, Suffolk Campus (NY)
Saint Joseph's U (PA)
St. Lawrence U (NY)
Saint Leo U (FL)
Saint Louis U (MO)
Saint Martin's Coll (WA)
Saint Mary Coll (KS)
Saint Mary-of-the-Woods Coll (IN)
Saint Mary's Coll (IN)
Saint Mary's Coll of Ave Maria U (MI)
Saint Mary's Coll of California (CA)
St. Mary's Coll of Maryland (MD)
Saint Mary's U (NS, Canada)
Saint Mary's U of Minnesota (MN)
St. Mary's U of San Antonio (TX)
Saint Michael's Coll (VT)
St. Norbert Coll (WI)
St. Olaf Coll (MN)
Saint Peter's Coll (NJ)
St. Thomas Aquinas Coll (NY)
St. Thomas U (FL)
St. Thomas U (NB, Canada)
Saint Vincent Coll (PA)
Saint Xavier U (IL)
Salem Coll (NC)
Salem State Coll (MA)
Salisbury U (MD)
Salve Regina U (RI)
Samford U (AL)
Sam Houston State U (TX)
San Diego State U (CA)
San Francisco State U (CA)
San Jose State U (CA)
Santa Clara U (CA)
Sarah Lawrence Coll (NY)
Schiller International U(United Kingdom)
Schreiner U (TX)
Scripps Coll (CA)
Seattle Pacific U (WA)
Seattle U (WA)
Seton Hall U (NJ)
Seton Hill Coll (PA)
Shaw U (NC)
Shenandoah U (VA)
Shepherd Coll (WV)
Shippensburg U of Pennsylvania (PA)
Shorter Coll (GA)
Siena Coll (NY)
Siena Heights U (MI)
Silver Lake Coll (WI)
Simmons Coll (MA)
Simon Fraser U (BC, Canada)
Simon's Rock Coll of Bard (MA)
Simpson Coll (IA)
Simpson Coll and Graduate School (CA)
Skidmore Coll (NY)
Slippery Rock U of Pennsylvania (PA)
Smith Coll (MA)
Sojourner-Douglass Coll (MD)
Sonoma State U (CA)
South Carolina State U (SC)
South Dakota State U (SD)
Southeastern Coll of the Assemblies of God (FL)
Southeastern Louisiana U (LA)
Southeastern Oklahoma State U (OK)
Southeast Missouri State U (MO)
Southern Adventist U (TN)
Southern Arkansas U–Magnolia (AR)
Southern Connecticut State U (CT)
Southern Illinois U Carbondale (IL)
Southern Illinois U Edwardsville (IL)
Southern Methodist U (TX)
Southern Nazarene U (OK)
Southern New Hampshire U (NH)
Southern Oregon U (OR)
Southern U and A&M Coll (LA)
Southern Utah U (UT)
Southern Vermont Coll (VT)
Southern Wesleyan U (SC)
Southwest Baptist U (MO)
Southwestern Adventist U (TX)
Southwestern Coll (KS)
Southwestern Oklahoma State U (OK)
Southwestern U (TX)
Southwest Missouri State U (MO)
Southwest State U (MN)
Southwest Texas State U (TX)
Spelman Coll (GA)
Spring Arbor U (MI)
Springfield Coll (MA)
Spring Hill Coll (AL)
Stanford U (CA)
State U of NY at Albany (NY)
State U of NY at Binghamton (NY)
State U of NY at New Paltz (NY)
State U of NY at Oswego (NY)
State U of NY Coll at Brockport (NY)
State U of NY Coll at Buffalo (NY)
State U of NY Coll at Cortland (NY)
State U of NY Coll at Fredonia (NY)
State U of NY Coll at Geneseo (NY)
State U of NY Coll at Old Westbury (NY)
State U of NY Coll at Oneonta (NY)
State U of NY Coll at Potsdam (NY)
State U of NY Inst of Tech at Utica/Rome (NY)
State U of West Georgia (GA)
Stephen F. Austin State U (TX)
Stephens Coll (MO)
Stetson U (FL)
Stonehill Coll (MA)
State U of NY at Stony Brook (NY)
Suffolk U (MA)
Sul Ross State U (TX)
Susquehanna U (PA)
Swarthmore Coll (PA)
Sweet Briar Coll (VA)
Syracuse U (NY)
Tabor Coll (KS)
Talladega Coll (AL)
Tarleton State U (TX)
Taylor U (IN)
Taylor U, Fort Wayne Campus (IN)
Teikyo Post U (CT)
Temple U (PA)
Tennessee State U (TN)
Tennessee Technological U (TN)
Tennessee Temple U (TN)
Tennessee Wesleyan Coll (TN)
Texas A&M International U (TX)
Texas A&M U (TX)
Texas A&M U–Commerce (TX)
Texas A&M U–Corpus Christi (TX)
Texas A&M U–Kingsville (TX)
Texas A&M U–Texarkana (TX)
Texas Christian U (TX)
Texas Lutheran U (TX)
Texas Southern U (TX)
Texas Tech U (TX)
Texas Wesleyan U (TX)
Texas Woman's U (TX)
Thiel Coll (PA)
Thomas Coll (ME)
Thomas Edison State Coll (NJ)
Thomas More Coll (KY)
Thomas U (GA)
Tiffin U (OH)
Tougaloo Coll (MS)
Touro Coll (NY)
Towson U (MD)
Transylvania U (KY)
Trent U (ON, Canada)
Trevecca Nazarene U (TN)
Trinity Bible Coll (ND)
Trinity Christian Coll (IL)
Trinity Coll (CT)
Trinity Coll (DC)
Trinity International U (IL)
Trinity U (TX)
Trinity Western U (BC, Canada)
Tri-State U (IN)
Troy State U (AL)
Troy State U Dothan (AL)
Troy State U Montgomery (AL)
Truman State U (MO)
Tufts U (MA)
Tulane U (LA)
Tusculum Coll (TN)
Tuskegee U (AL)
Tyndale Coll & Seminary (ON, Canada)
Union Coll (KY)
Union Coll (NE)
Union Coll (NY)
Union Inst & U (OH)
Union U (TN)
United States Military Academy (NY)
Université de Montréal (QC, Canada)
Université de Sherbrooke (PQ, Canada)
Université Laval (QC, Canada)
State U of NY at Buffalo (NY)
U Coll of Cape Breton (NS, Canada)
U Coll of the Cariboo (BC, Canada)
U Coll of the Fraser Valley (BC, Canada)
The U of Akron (OH)
The U of Alabama (AL)
The U of Alabama at Birmingham (AL)
The U of Alabama in Huntsville (AL)
U of Alaska Anchorage (AK)
U of Alaska Fairbanks (AK)
U of Alberta (AB, Canada)
The U of Arizona (AZ)
U of Arkansas (AR)
U of Arkansas at Little Rock (AR)
U of Arkansas at Pine Bluff (AR)
U of Baltimore (MD)
The U of British Columbia (BC, Canada)
U of Calgary (AB, Canada)
U of Calif, Berkeley (CA)
U of Calif, Davis (CA)
U of Calif, Irvine (CA)
U of Calif, Los Angeles (CA)
U of Calif, Riverside (CA)
U of Calif, San Diego (CA)
U of Calif, Santa Barbara (CA)
U of Calif, Santa Cruz (CA)
U of Central Arkansas (AR)
U of Central Florida (FL)
U of Central Oklahoma (OK)
U of Charleston (WV)
U of Chicago (IL)
U of Cincinnati (OH)
U of Colorado at Boulder (CO)
U of Colorado at Colorado Springs (CO)
U of Colorado at Denver (CO)
U of Connecticut (CT)
U of Dallas (TX)
U of Dayton (OH)
U of Delaware (DE)
U of Denver (CO)
U of Dubuque (IA)
U of Evansville (IN)
The U of Findlay (OH)
U of Florida (FL)
U of Georgia (GA)
U of Great Falls (MT)
U of Guelph (ON, Canada)
U of Hartford (CT)
U of Hawaii at Hilo (HI)
U of Hawaii at Manoa (HI)
U of Hawaii–West Oahu (HI)

U of Houston (TX)
U of Houston–Clear Lake (TX)
U of Idaho (ID)
U of Illinois at Chicago (IL)
U of Illinois at Springfield (IL)
U of Illinois at Urbana–Champaign (IL)
U of Indianapolis (IN)
The U of Iowa (IA)
U of Judaism (CA)
U of Kansas (KS)
U of Kentucky (KY)
U of King's Coll (NS, Canada)
U of La Verne (CA)
The U of Lethbridge (AB, Canada)
U of Louisiana at Lafayette (LA)
U of Louisiana at Monroe (LA)
U of Louisville (KY)
U of Maine (ME)
U of Maine at Farmington (ME)
U of Maine at Machias (ME)
U of Manitoba (MB, Canada)
U of Mary (ND)
U of Mary Hardin-Baylor (TX)
U of Maryland, Baltimore County (MD)
U of Maryland, Coll Park (MD)
U of Maryland University Coll (MD)
U of Massachusetts Amherst (MA)
U of Massachusetts Boston (MA)
U of Massachusetts Dartmouth (MA)
U of Massachusetts Lowell (MA)
The U of Memphis (TN)
U of Miami (FL)
U of Michigan (MI)
U of Michigan–Dearborn (MI)
U of Michigan–Flint (MI)
U of Minnesota, Duluth (MN)
U of Minnesota, Morris (MN)
U of Minnesota, Twin Cities Campus (MN)
U of Mississippi (MS)
U of Missouri–Columbia (MO)
U of Missouri–Kansas City (MO)
U of Missouri–Rolla (MO)
U of Missouri–St. Louis (MO)
U of Mobile (AL)
The U of Montana–Missoula (MT)
U of Montevallo (AL)
U of Nebraska at Kearney (NE)
U of Nebraska at Omaha (NE)
U of Nebraska–Lincoln (NE)
U of Nevada, Las Vegas (NV)
U of Nevada, Reno (NV)
U of New England (ME)
U of New Hampshire (NH)
U of New Haven (CT)
U of New Mexico (NM)
U of New Orleans (LA)
U of North Alabama (AL)
The U of North Carolina at Asheville (NC)
The U of North Carolina at Chapel Hill (NC)
The U of North Carolina at Charlotte (NC)
The U of North Carolina at Greensboro (NC)
The U of North Carolina at Pembroke (NC)
The U of North Carolina at Wilmington (NC)
U of North Dakota (ND)
U of Northern Colorado (CO)
U of Northern Iowa (IA)
U of North Florida (FL)
U of North Texas (TX)
U of Notre Dame (IN)
U of Oklahoma (OK)
U of Oregon (OR)
U of Ottawa (ON, Canada)
U of Pennsylvania (PA)
U of Pittsburgh (PA)
U of Pittsburgh at Bradford (PA)
U of Pittsburgh at Greensburg (PA)
U of Pittsburgh at Johnstown (PA)
U of Portland (OR)
U of Prince Edward Island (PE, Canada)
U of Puerto Rico, Cayey U Coll (PR)
U of Puget Sound (WA)
U of Redlands (CA)
U of Regina (SK, Canada)
U of Rhode Island (RI)
U of Richmond (VA)
U of Rochester (NY)
U of St. Francis (IL)
U of Saint Francis (IN)
U of St. Thomas (MN)
U of St. Thomas (TX)
U of San Diego (CA)
U of San Francisco (CA)
U of Saskatchewan (SK, Canada)
U of Science and Arts of Oklahoma (OK)
The U of Scranton (PA)
U of Sioux Falls (SD)
U of South Alabama (AL)
U of South Carolina Aiken (SC)
U of South Carolina Spartanburg (SC)
U of South Dakota (SD)
U of Southern California (CA)
U of Southern Colorado (CO)
U of Southern Indiana (IN)
U of Southern Maine (ME)
U of Southern Mississippi (MS)
U of South Florida (FL)
The U of Tampa (FL)
The U of Tennessee (TN)
The U of Tennessee at Chattanooga (TN)
The U of Tennessee at Martin (TN)
The U of Texas at Arlington (TX)
The U of Texas at Austin (TX)
The U of Texas at Dallas (TX)
The U of Texas at El Paso (TX)
The U of Texas at San Antonio (TX)
The U of Texas at Tyler (TX)
The U of Texas of the Permian Basin (TX)
The U of Texas–Pan American (TX)
U of the District of Columbia (DC)
U of the Incarnate Word (TX)
U of the Ozarks (AR)
U of the Pacific (CA)
U of the Sciences in Philadelphia (PA)
U of the South (TN)
U of the Virgin Islands (VI)
U of Toledo (OH)
U of Toronto (ON, Canada)
U of Tulsa (OK)
U of Utah (UT)
U of Vermont (VT)
U of Victoria (BC, Canada)
U of Virginia (VA)
The U of Virginia's Coll at Wise (VA)
U of Washington (WA)
U of Waterloo (ON, Canada)
The U of West Alabama (AL)
The U of Western Ontario (ON, Canada)
U of West Florida (FL)
U of Windsor (ON, Canada)
U of Wisconsin–Eau Claire (WI)
U of Wisconsin–Green Bay (WI)
U of Wisconsin–La Crosse (WI)
U of Wisconsin–Madison (WI)
U of Wisconsin–Milwaukee (WI)
U of Wisconsin–Oshkosh (WI)
U of Wisconsin–Parkside (WI)
U of Wisconsin–Platteville (WI)
U of Wisconsin–River Falls (WI)
U of Wisconsin–Stevens Point (WI)
U of Wisconsin–Stout (WI)
U of Wisconsin–Superior (WI)
U of Wisconsin–Whitewater (WI)
U of Wyoming (WY)
Upper Iowa U (IA)
Urbana U (OH)
Ursinus Coll (PA)
Ursuline Coll (OH)
Utah State U (UT)
Utica Coll of Syracuse U (NY)
Valdosta State U (GA)
Valparaiso U (IN)
Vanderbilt U (TN)
Vanguard U of Southern California (CA)
Vassar Coll (NY)
Villa Julie Coll (MD)
Villanova U (PA)
Virginia Commonwealth U (VA)
Virginia Intermont Coll (VA)
Virginia Military Inst (VA)
Virginia Polytechnic Inst and State U (VA)
Virginia State U (VA)
Virginia Union U (VA)
Virginia Wesleyan Coll (VA)
Viterbo U (WI)
Wabash Coll (IN)
Wagner Coll (NY)
Wake Forest U (NC)
Walla Walla Coll (WA)
Walsh U (OH)
Warner Pacific Coll (OR)
Warner Southern Coll (FL)
Warren Wilson Coll (NC)
Wartburg Coll (IA)
Washburn U of Topeka (KS)
Washington & Jefferson Coll (PA)
Washington and Lee U (VA)
Washington Coll (MD)
Washington State U (WA)
Washington U in St. Louis (MO)
Wayland Baptist U (TX)
Waynesburg Coll (PA)
Wayne State Coll (NE)
Wayne State U (MI)
Weber State U (UT)
Webster U (MO)
Wellesley Coll (MA)
Wells Coll (NY)
Wesleyan Coll (GA)
Wesleyan U (CT)
Wesley Coll (DE)
West Chester U of Pennsylvania (PA)
Western Baptist Coll (OR)
Western Carolina U (NC)
Western Connecticut State U (CT)
Western Illinois U (IL)
Western Kentucky U (KY)
Western Maryland Coll (MD)
Western Michigan U (MI)
Western New England Coll (MA)
Western Oregon U (OR)
Western State Coll of Colorado (CO)
Western Washington U (WA)
Westfield State Coll (MA)
West Liberty State Coll (WV)
Westminster Coll (MO)
Westminster Coll (PA)
Westminster Coll (UT)
Westmont Coll (CA)
West Texas A&M U (TX)
West Virginia State Coll (WV)
West Virginia U (WV)
West Virginia Wesleyan Coll (WV)
Wheaton Coll (IL)
Wheaton Coll (MA)
Wheeling Jesuit U (WV)
Whitman Coll (WA)
Whittier Coll (CA)
Whitworth Coll (WA)
Wichita State U (KS)
Widener U (PA)
Wilberforce U (OH)
Wilfrid Laurier U (ON, Canada)
Wilkes U (PA)
Willamette U (OR)
William Carey Coll (MS)
William Jewell Coll (MO)
William Paterson U of New Jersey (NJ)
William Penn U (IA)
Williams Baptist Coll (AR)
Williams Coll (MA)
William Tyndale Coll (MI)
William Woods U (MO)
Wilmington Coll (OH)
Wingate U (NC)
Winona State U (MN)
Winston-Salem State U (NC)
Winthrop U (SC)
Wisconsin Lutheran Coll (WI)
Wittenberg U (OH)
Wofford Coll (SC)
Woodbury U (CA)
Worcester State Coll (MA)
Wright State U (OH)
Xavier U (OH)
Xavier U of Louisiana (LA)
Yale U (CT)
Yeshiva U (NY)
York Coll (NE)
York Coll of Pennsylvania (PA)
York Coll of the City U of New York (NY)
York U (ON, Canada)
Youngstown State U (OH)

PSYCHOLOGY RELATED

Averett U (VA)
Kean U (NJ)
Loyola U Chicago (IL)
Point Park Coll (PA)
Skidmore Coll (NY)
State U of NY at Oswego (NY)
Wilmington Coll (DE)

PUBLIC ADMINISTRATION

Abilene Christian U (TX)
Alfred U (NY)
American International Coll (MA)
Athabasca U (AB, Canada)
Auburn U (AL)
Augustana Coll (IL)
Bayamón Central U (PR)
Baylor U (TX)
Baruch Coll of the City U of NY (NY)
Blackburn Coll (IL)
Bloomfield Coll (NJ)
Boise State U (ID)
Bowling Green State U (OH)
Brock U (ON, Canada)
Buena Vista U (IA)
California State Polytechnic U, Pomona (CA)
California State U, Bakersfield (CA)
California State U, Chico (CA)
California State U, Dominguez Hills (CA)
California State U, Fresno (CA)
California State U, Fullerton (CA)
California State U, Hayward (CA)
California State U, Sacramento (CA)
California State U, San Bernardino (CA)
Calvin Coll (MI)
Campbell U (NC)
Canisius Coll (NY)
Carleton U (ON, Canada)
Carroll Coll (MT)
Cedarville U (OH)
Central Methodist Coll (MO)
Christopher Newport U (VA)
Concordia U (QC, Canada)
David N. Myers U (OH)
Doane Coll (NE)
Dominican Coll (NY)
Eastern Michigan U (MI)
Eastern Washington U (WA)
Edgewood Coll (WI)
Edward Waters Coll (FL)
Elon U (NC)
Evangel U (MO)
The Evergreen State Coll (WA)
Ferris State U (MI)
Fisk U (TN)
Florida A&M U (FL)
Florida Atlantic U (FL)
Florida International U (FL)
Fordham U (NY)
Framingham State Coll (MA)
George Mason U (VA)
Governors State U (IL)
Grambling State U (LA)
Grand Valley State U (MI)
Hamline U (MN)
Harding U (AR)
Hawai'i Pacific U (HI)
Heidelberg Coll (OH)
Henderson State U (AR)
Huntingdon Coll (AL)
Indiana U Bloomington (IN)
Indiana U Northwest (IN)
Indiana U–Purdue U Fort Wayne (IN)
Indiana U–Purdue U Indianapolis (IN)
Indiana U South Bend (IN)
Inter American U of PR, San Germán Campus (PR)
Iowa State U of Science and Technology (IA)
James Madison U (VA)
John Carroll U (OH)
John Jay Coll of Criminal Justice, the City U of NY (NY)
Johns Hopkins U (MD)
Juniata Coll (PA)
Kean U (NJ)
Kentucky State U (KY)
Kutztown U of Pennsylvania (PA)
Lakeland Coll (WI)
La Salle U (PA)
Lewis U (IL)
Lincoln U (MO)
Lindenwood U (MO)
Lipscomb U (TN)
Long Island U, Brooklyn Campus (NY)
Long Island U, C.W. Post Campus (NY)
Louisiana Coll (LA)
Marist Coll (NY)
Medgar Evers Coll of the City U of NY (NY)
Mercyhurst Coll (PA)
Metropolitan State U (MN)
Miami U (OH)
Michigan State U (MI)
Minnesota State U, Mankato (MN)
Mississippi Valley State U (MS)
Missouri Valley Coll (MO)
Northeastern U (MA)
Northern Kentucky U (KY)
Northern Michigan U (MI)
Northern State U (SD)
Northwest Missouri State U (MO)
Oakland U (MI)
Ohio Wesleyan U (OH)
Park U (MO)
Plymouth State Coll (NH)
Point Park Coll (PA)
Pontifical Catholic U of Puerto Rico (PR)
Princeton U (NJ)
Rhode Island Coll (RI)
Roger Williams U (RI)
Roosevelt U (IL)
Saginaw Valley State U (MI)
St. Ambrose U (IA)
St. Cloud State U (MN)
Saint Francis U (PA)
St. John's U (NY)
Saint Joseph's U (PA)
Saint Leo U (FL)
Saint Mary's U of Minnesota (MN)
St. Thomas U (FL)
Samford U (AL)
San Diego State U (CA)
San Jose State U (CA)
Seattle U (WA)
Seton Hill Coll (PA)
Shaw U (NC)
Shenandoah U (VA)
Shippensburg U of Pennsylvania (PA)
Siena Heights U (MI)
Slippery Rock U of Pennsylvania (PA)
Sojourner-Douglass Coll (MD)
Southeastern U (DC)
Southwest Missouri State U (MO)
Southwest State U (MN)
Southwest Texas State U (TX)
State U of NY at Albany (NY)
Stephen F. Austin State U (TX)
Stonehill Coll (MA)
Suffolk U (MA)
Talladega Coll (AL)
Tennessee State U (TN)
Texas A&M U–Kingsville (TX)
Texas Southern U (TX)
Texas Woman's U (TX)
Thomas Edison State Coll (NJ)
Union Inst & U (OH)
The U of Arizona (AZ)
U of Arkansas (AR)
U of Calif, Riverside (CA)
U of Central Arkansas (AR)
U of Central Florida (FL)
U of Denver (CO)
U of Hartford (CT)
U of Hawaii at Manoa (HI)
U of Hawaii–West Oahu (HI)
U of La Verne (CA)
The U of Lethbridge (AB, Canada)
U of Maine (ME)
The U of Maine at Augusta (ME)
U of Maine at Fort Kent (ME)
U of Manitoba (MB, Canada)
U of Massachusetts Boston (MA)
U of Michigan–Dearborn (MI)
U of Michigan–Flint (MI)
U of Mississippi (MS)
U of Missouri–St. Louis (MO)
U of Nebraska at Omaha (NE)
U of New Haven (CT)
The U of North Carolina at Pembroke (NC)
U of North Dakota (ND)
U of Northern Iowa (IA)
U of Oklahoma (OK)
U of Oregon (OR)
U of Ottawa (ON, Canada)
U of Pittsburgh (PA)
U of Regina (SK, Canada)
U of San Francisco (CA)
U of Saskatchewan (SK, Canada)
U of Southern California (CA)
The U of Tennessee (TN)
The U of Tennessee at Martin (TN)
The U of Texas at Dallas (TX)

The U of Texas–Pan American (TX)
U of the District of Columbia (DC)
U of Toronto (ON, Canada)
U of Victoria (BC, Canada)
U of Washington (WA)
The U of Western Ontario (ON, Canada)
U of Wisconsin–Green Bay (WI)
U of Wisconsin–La Crosse (WI)
U of Wisconsin–Stevens Point (WI)
U of Wisconsin–Whitewater (WI)
Upper Iowa U (IA)
Virginia State U (VA)
Wagner Coll (NY)
Washburn U of Topeka (KS)
Washington State U (WA)
Waynesburg Coll (PA)
Wayne State Coll (NE)
Wayne State U (MI)
West Chester U of Pennsylvania (PA)
Western Michigan U (MI)
Western Oregon U (OR)
Westminster Coll (MO)
West Texas A&M U (TX)
West Virginia U Inst of Technology (WV)
Winona State U (MN)
York Coll of Pennsylvania (PA)
York U (ON, Canada)
Youngstown State U (OH)

PUBLIC ADMINISTRATION AND SERVICES RELATED

Kentucky Wesleyan Coll (KY)
Ohio U (OH)
U of Phoenix–Colorado Campus (CO)
U of Phoenix–Hawaii Campus (HI)
U of Phoenix–Nevada Campus (NV)
U of Phoenix–New Mexico Campus (NM)
U of Phoenix–Northern California Campus (CA)
U of Phoenix–Phoenix Campus (AZ)
U of Phoenix–San Diego Campus (CA)
U of Phoenix–Southern Arizona Campus (AZ)
U of Phoenix–Southern California Campus (CA)
U of Phoenix–Southern Colorado Campus (CO)
U of Phoenix–Tampa Campus (FL)
U of Phoenix–Utah Campus (UT)
U of Phoenix–West Michigan Campus (MI)

PUBLIC HEALTH

Alma Coll (MI)
Boise State U (ID)
Brock U (ON, Canada)
California State U, Dominguez Hills (CA)
California State U, Long Beach (CA)
Central Michigan U (MI)
Dillard U (LA)
Eastern Kentucky U (KY)
Eastern Washington U (WA)
East Tennessee State U (TN)
Grand Valley State U (MI)
Hampshire Coll (MA)
Hunter Coll of the City U of NY (NY)
Indiana U Bloomington (IN)
Indiana U–Purdue U Indianapolis (IN)
Johns Hopkins U (MD)
Maryville U of Saint Louis (MO)
Minnesota State U, Mankato (MN)
New Mexico State U (NM)
Oregon State U (OR)
The Richard Stockton Coll of New Jersey (NJ)
Rutgers, The State U of New Jersey, New Brunswick (NJ)
St. Joseph's Coll, New York (NY)
Salem International U (WV)
Slippery Rock U of Pennsylvania (PA)
Southern Connecticut State U (CT)
Springfield Coll (MA)
Touro U International (CA)
Truman State U (MO)
Tufts U (MA)
U of Cincinnati (OH)
U of Hawaii at Manoa (HI)
U of Minnesota, Twin Cities Campus (MN)
U of Southern Mississippi (MS)
U of Washington (WA)
U of Wisconsin–Eau Claire (WI)
West Chester U of Pennsylvania (PA)
William Paterson U of New Jersey (NJ)
Winona State U (MN)
York U (ON, Canada)

PUBLIC HEALTH EDUCATION/ PROMOTION

Appalachian State U (NC)
Coastal Carolina U (SC)
Dillard U (LA)
East Carolina U (NC)
Georgia Southern U (GA)
Ithaca Coll (NY)
Laurentian U (ON, Canada)
Malone Coll (OH)
North Carolina Central U (NC)
Plymouth State Coll (NH)
St. Francis Coll (NY)
U of Northern Colorado (CO)
U of North Texas (TX)
U of St. Thomas (MN)
U of Toledo (OH)
U of Wisconsin–La Crosse (WI)
Walla Walla Coll (WA)
Western Washington U (WA)
Worcester State Coll (MA)

PUBLIC HEALTH RELATED

Florida Gulf Coast U (FL)
U of Hawaii at Manoa (HI)
U of Illinois at Urbana–Champaign (IL)
Utah State U (UT)

PUBLIC POLICY ANALYSIS

Albion Coll (MI)
Baruch Coll of the City U of NY (NY)
Bloomfield Coll (NJ)
Central Washington U (WA)
Chatham Coll (PA)
Coll of the Atlantic (ME)
The Coll of William and Mary (VA)
Columbia Coll (SC)
Concordia U (QC, Canada)
Cornell U (NY)
DePaul U (IL)
Dickinson Coll (PA)
Duke U (NC)
Eastern Washington U (WA)
Edgewood Coll (WI)
The Evergreen State Coll (WA)
The George Washington U (DC)
Georgia Inst of Technology (GA)
Grand Valley State U (MI)
Hamilton Coll (NY)
Hampden-Sydney Coll (VA)
Hampshire Coll (MA)
Harvard U (MA)
Hobart and William Smith Colls (NY)
Indiana U Bloomington (IN)
Kenyon Coll (OH)
Lincoln U (PA)
Long Island U, Southampton Coll, Friends World Program (NY)
Marymount U (VA)
Mills Coll (CA)
Muskingum Coll (OH)
New Coll of Florida (FL)
North Carolina State U (NC)
Northern Arizona U (AZ)
Northwestern U (IL)
Occidental Coll (CA)
Penn State U Harrisburg Campus of the Capital Coll (PA)
Pomona Coll (CA)
Rice U (TX)
Rochester Inst of Technology (NY)
St. Cloud State U (MN)
St. Mary's Coll of Maryland (MD)
Saint Peter's Coll (NJ)
Saint Vincent Coll (PA)
San Jose State U (CA)
Sarah Lawrence Coll (NY)
Simmons Coll (MA)
Southern Methodist U (TX)
Stanford U (CA)
State U of NY at Albany (NY)
Suffolk U (MA)
Syracuse U (NY)
Texas Southern U (TX)
Trinity Coll (CT)
United States Military Academy (NY)
U of Chicago (IL)
U of Cincinnati (OH)
U of Massachusetts Boston (MA)
U of Miami (FL)
U of Missouri–St. Louis (MO)
The U of North Carolina at Chapel Hill (NC)
U of Oregon (OR)
U of Ottawa (ON, Canada)
U of Pennsylvania (PA)
U of Rhode Island (RI)
U of Toledo (OH)
U of Wisconsin–Whitewater (WI)
Washington and Lee U (VA)
Wells Coll (NY)
Western State Coll of Colorado (CO)
York U (ON, Canada)

PUBLIC RELATIONS

Alabama State U (AL)
American U (DC)
Andrews U (MI)
Appalachian State U (NC)
Assumption Coll (MA)
Auburn U (AL)
Ball State U (IN)
Barry U (FL)
Berry Coll (GA)
Boston U (MA)
Bowling Green State U (OH)
Bradley U (IL)
Buena Vista U (IA)
Butler U (IN)
California State Polytechnic U, Pomona (CA)
California State U, Chico (CA)
California State U, Dominguez Hills (CA)
California State U, Fresno (CA)
California State U, Fullerton (CA)
California State U, Hayward (CA)
California State U, Long Beach (CA)
Cameron U (OK)
Campbell U (NC)
Capital U (OH)
Cardinal Stritch U (WI)
Carroll Coll (MT)
Carroll Coll (WI)
Central Michigan U (MI)
Central Missouri State U (MO)
Central Washington U (WA)
Champlain Coll (VT)
Chapman U (CA)
Clarke Coll (IA)
Cleveland State U (OH)
Coe Coll (IA)
The Coll of Southeastern Europe, The American U of Athens(Greece)
Coll of the Ozarks (MO)
Colorado State U (CO)
Columbia Coll Chicago (IL)
Columbus State U (GA)
Concordia Coll (MN)
Curry Coll (MA)
Defiance Coll (OH)
Doane Coll (NE)
Drake U (IA)
Eastern Kentucky U (KY)
Eastern Michigan U (MI)
Eastern Washington U (WA)
Emerson Coll (MA)
Ferris State U (MI)
Florida A&M U (FL)
Florida Southern Coll (FL)
Florida State U (FL)
Fontbonne U (MO)
Fort Hays State U (KS)
Framingham State Coll (MA)
Freed-Hardeman U (TN)
George Fox U (OR)
Georgia Southern U (GA)
Gonzaga U (WA)
Grand Valley State U (MI)
Greenville Coll (IL)
Gwynedd-Mercy Coll (PA)
Hampton U (VA)
Harding U (AR)
Hastings Coll (NE)
Hawai'i Pacific U (HI)
Heidelberg Coll (OH)
Hofstra U (NY)
Howard Payne U (TX)
Illinois State U (IL)
Indiana U Northwest (IN)
Indiana U–Purdue U Fort Wayne (IN)
Iona Coll (NY)
Ithaca Coll (NY)
John Brown U (AR)
Kent State U (OH)
Lambuth U (TN)
La Salle U (PA)
Lewis U (IL)
Lindenwood U (MO)
Lipscomb U (TN)
Lock Haven U of Pennsylvania (PA)
Long Island U, C.W. Post Campus (NY)
Long Island U, Southampton Coll, Friends World Program (NY)
Loras Coll (IA)
Malone Coll (OH)
Mansfield U of Pennsylvania (PA)
Marietta Coll (OH)
Marist Coll (NY)
Marquette U (WI)
Mary Baldwin Coll (VA)
Marylhurst U (OR)
Marywood U (PA)
The Master's Coll and Seminary (CA)
McKendree Coll (IL)
Mercyhurst Coll (PA)
Mesa State Coll (CO)
Metropolitan State Coll of Denver (CO)
MidAmerica Nazarene U (KS)
Middle Tennessee State U (TN)
Milligan Coll (TN)
Minnesota State U, Mankato (MN)
Minnesota State U Moorhead (MN)
Monmouth Coll (IL)
Montana State U–Billings (MT)
Mount Mary Coll (WI)
Mount Saint Mary Coll (NY)
Mount Saint Vincent U (NS, Canada)
Murray State U (KY)
New England Coll (NH)
North Central Coll (IL)
Northeastern U (MA)
Northern Arizona U (AZ)
Northern Michigan U (MI)
Northwestern Coll (MN)
Northwestern Oklahoma State U (OK)
Northwest Missouri State U (MO)
Northwest Nazarene U (ID)
Ohio Dominican Coll (OH)
Ohio Northern U (OH)
Ohio U (OH)
Ohio U–Zanesville (OH)
Oklahoma Baptist U (OK)
Oklahoma Christian U of Science and Arts (OK)
Oklahoma City U (OK)
Oral Roberts U (OK)
Otterbein Coll (OH)
Pacific Union Coll (CA)
Pepperdine U, Malibu (CA)
Pittsburg State U (KS)
Point Park Coll (PA)
Pontifical Catholic U of Puerto Rico (PR)
Purdue U Calumet (IN)
Queens Coll (NC)
Quincy U (IL)
Quinnipiac U (CT)
Rider U (NJ)
Rockhurst U (MO)
Roosevelt U (IL)
Rowan U (NJ)
St. Ambrose U (IA)
St. Cloud State U (MN)
Saint Francis U (PA)
Saint Louis U (MO)
Saint Mary-of-the-Woods Coll (IN)
Saint Mary's U of Minnesota (MN)
Salem State Coll (MA)
Sam Houston State U (TX)
San Diego State U (CA)
San Jose State U (CA)
Seattle U (WA)
Seton Hill Coll (PA)
Shorter Coll (GA)
Simmons Coll (MA)
Southeast Missouri State U (MO)
Southern Adventist U (TN)
Southern Methodist U (TX)
Southwest Texas State U (TX)
Spring Hill Coll (AL)
State U of NY at Oswego (NY)
State U of NY Coll at Brockport (NY)
State U of NY Coll at Buffalo (NY)
Stephens Coll (MO)
Suffolk U (MA)
Susquehanna U (PA)
Syracuse U (NY)
Tabor Coll (KS)
Taylor U, Fort Wayne Campus (IN)
Temple U (PA)
Texas Tech U (TX)
Toccoa Falls Coll (GA)
Trinity Christian Coll (IL)
Union Coll (NE)
Union U (TN)
The U of Alabama (AL)
U of Central Oklahoma (OK)
U of Dayton (OH)
U of Delaware (DE)
The U of Findlay (OH)
U of Florida (FL)
U of Georgia (GA)
U of Houston (TX)
U of Idaho (ID)
The U of Iowa (IA)
U of Louisiana at Lafayette (LA)
U of Miami (FL)
U of Nebraska at Omaha (NE)
U of Nevada, Reno (NV)
The U of North Carolina at Pembroke (NC)
U of Northern Iowa (IA)
U of North Texas (TX)
U of Oklahoma (OK)
U of Oregon (OR)
U of Ottawa (ON, Canada)
U of Pittsburgh at Bradford (PA)
U of Rio Grande (OH)
U of St. Thomas (MN)
U of Sioux Falls (SD)
U of South Carolina (SC)
U of South Dakota (SD)
U of Southern California (CA)
U of Southern Colorado (CO)
U of Southern Indiana (IN)
The U of Tennessee at Martin (TN)
The U of Texas at Arlington (TX)
The U of Texas at Austin (TX)
U of Utah (UT)
U of Wisconsin–Madison (WI)
U of Wisconsin–River Falls (WI)
Ursuline Coll (OH)
Utica Coll of Syracuse U (NY)
Valdosta State U (GA)
Walla Walla Coll (WA)
Wartburg Coll (IA)
Washington State U (WA)
Wayne State U (MI)
Weber State U (UT)
Webster U (MO)
Western Kentucky U (KY)
Western Michigan U (MI)
Westminster Coll (PA)
West Virginia Wesleyan Coll (WV)
William Woods U (MO)
Wingate U (NC)
Winona State U (MN)
Xavier U (OH)
York Coll of Pennsylvania (PA)
Youngstown State U (OH)

PUBLISHING

Benedictine U (IL)
Emerson Coll (MA)
Graceland U (IA)
Pontifical Catholic U of Puerto Rico (PR)
Rochester Inst of Technology (NY)
U of Missouri–Columbia (MO)
U of St. Thomas (MN)

PURCHASING/CONTRACTS MANAGEMENT

American U of Puerto Rico (PR)
Arizona State U (AZ)
Bloomfield Coll (NJ)
California State U, Hayward (CA)
Eastern Michigan U (MI)
Miami U (OH)
Michigan State U (MI)
Thomas Edison State Coll (NJ)
U of the District of Columbia (DC)

QUALITY CONTROL TECHNOLOGY
California State U, Long Beach (CA)
Ferris State U (MI)
Winona State U (MN)

QUANTITATIVE ECONOMICS
The Colorado Coll (CO)
Haverford Coll (PA)
San Diego State U (CA)
Southern Methodist U (TX)
State U of NY at Oswego (NY)
United States Naval Academy (MD)
Université Laval (QC, Canada)
U of Calif, San Diego (CA)
U of Guelph (ON, Canada)
U of Northern Iowa (IA)
U of Rhode Island (RI)
Youngstown State U (OH)

RABBINICAL/TALMUDIC STUDIES
Baltimore Hebrew U (MD)
Talmudical Yeshiva of Philadelphia (PA)
Université Laval (QC, Canada)

RADIOLOGICAL SCIENCE
Austin Peay State U (TN)
Boise State U (ID)
Champlain Coll (VT)
Clarion U of Pennsylvania (PA)
Clarkson Coll (NE)
Comm Hospital Roanoke Valley–Coll of Health Scis (VA)
The George Washington U (DC)
Holy Family Coll (PA)
Indiana U Northwest (IN)
Manhattan Coll (NY)
Mass Coll of Pharmacy and Allied Health Sciences (MA)
Medical Coll of Georgia (GA)
Midwestern State U (TX)
Mount Aloysius Coll (PA)
The Ohio State U (OH)
Oregon Inst of Technology (OR)
Quinnipiac U (CT)
St. Francis Coll (NY)
State U of New York Upstate Medical University (NY)
Suffolk U (MA)
U of Charleston (WV)
The U of Findlay (OH)
U of Mary (ND)
U of Michigan (MI)
U of Missouri–Columbia (MO)
U of Pittsburgh at Bradford (PA)
U of St. Francis (IL)
U of South Alabama (AL)
U of Southern Indiana (IN)

RADIO/TELEVISION BROADCASTING
Alabama State U (AL)
Appalachian State U (NC)
Arizona State U (AZ)
Arkansas State U (AR)
Ashland U (OH)
Auburn U (AL)
Barry U (FL)
Belmont U (TN)
Bemidji State U (MN)
Biola U (CA)
Boston U (MA)
Bowling Green State U (OH)
Bradley U (IL)
Brooklyn Coll of the City U of NY (NY)
Buena Vista U (IA)
California State U, Chico (CA)
California State U, Fresno (CA)
California State U, Fullerton (CA)
California State U, Long Beach (CA)
California State U, Los Angeles (CA)
California State U, Northridge (CA)
Cameron U (OK)
Campbell U (NC)
Castleton State Coll (VT)
Cedarville U (OH)
Central Michigan U (MI)
Central Missouri State U (MO)
Central State U (OH)
Central Washington U (WA)
Chicago State U (IL)
Colorado State U (CO)
Columbia Coll Chicago (IL)
Columbia Coll–Hollywood (CA)
Concordia Coll (MN)
Curry Coll (MA)
Drake U (IA)
East Central U (OK)
Eastern Kentucky U (KY)
Eastern Nazarene Coll (MA)
Eastern Washington U (WA)
Emerson Coll (MA)
Evangel U (MO)
Florida State U (FL)
Fordham U (NY)
Fort Hays State U (KS)
Franklin Pierce Coll (NH)
Freed-Hardeman U (TN)
Gallaudet U (DC)
Gannon U (PA)
Geneva Coll (PA)
George Fox U (OR)
The George Washington U (DC)
Georgia Southern U (GA)
Grace U (NE)
Grand Valley State U (MI)
Grand View Coll (IA)
Hampshire Coll (MA)
Harding U (AR)
Hastings Coll (NE)
Howard U (DC)
Indiana State U (IN)
Indiana U Bloomington (IN)
Ithaca Coll (NY)
John Brown U (AR)
Kent State U (OH)
Lamar U (TX)
La Salle U (PA)
Lindenwood U (MO)
Lock Haven U of Pennsylvania (PA)
Long Island U, Brooklyn Campus (NY)
Long Island U, C.W. Post Campus (NY)
Lyndon State Coll (VT)
Mansfield U of Pennsylvania (PA)
Marietta Coll (OH)
Marist Coll (NY)
Marywood U (PA)
The Master's Coll and Seminary (CA)
Mercy Coll (NY)
Mercyhurst Coll (PA)
Mesa State Coll (CO)
Messiah Coll (PA)
Milligan Coll (TN)
Minot State U (ND)
Murray State U (KY)
Muskingum Coll (OH)
New York Inst of Technology (NY)
New York U (NY)
Northeastern U (MA)
Northern Arizona U (AZ)
Northern Kentucky U (KY)
Northwestern Coll (MN)
Northwestern U (IL)
Northwest Missouri State U (MO)
Ohio U (OH)
Oklahoma Baptist U (OK)
Oklahoma Christian U of Science and Arts (OK)
Oklahoma City U (OK)
Olivet Coll (MI)
Olivet Nazarene U (IL)
Oral Roberts U (OK)
Otterbein Coll (OH)
Pacific Lutheran U (WA)
Pacific U (OR)
Pittsburg State U (KS)
Point Park Coll (PA)
Pontifical Catholic U of Puerto Rico (PR)
Purdue U Calumet (IN)
Quincy U (IL)
Rider U (NJ)
Rowan U (NJ)
Sacred Heart U (CT)
St. Ambrose U (IA)
St. Cloud State U (MN)
Salem International U (WV)
Sam Houston State U (TX)
San Diego State U (CA)
San Francisco State U (CA)
San Jose State U (CA)
Southeast Missouri State U (MO)
Southern Illinois U Carbondale (IL)
Southern Methodist U (TX)
Southwest State U (MN)
Spring Arbor U (MI)
Spring Hill Coll (AL)
State U of NY at New Paltz (NY)
State U of NY Coll at Brockport (NY)
State U of NY Coll at Buffalo (NY)
State U of NY Coll at Fredonia (NY)
Stephen F. Austin State U (TX)
Stephens Coll (MO)
Susquehanna U (PA)
Syracuse U (NY)
Temple U (PA)
Texas A&M U–Commerce (TX)
Texas Christian U (TX)
Texas Southern U (TX)
Texas Tech U (TX)
Texas Wesleyan U (TX)
Toccoa Falls Coll (GA)
Union U (TN)
The U of Alabama (AL)
The U of Arizona (AZ)
U of Arkansas at Little Rock (AR)
U of Calif, Los Angeles (CA)
U of Central Florida (FL)
U of Central Oklahoma (OK)
U of Cincinnati (OH)
U of Dayton (OH)
U of Florida (FL)
U of Houston (TX)
U of Idaho (ID)
The U of Iowa (IA)
U of Kansas (KS)
U of Kentucky (KY)
U of La Verne (CA)
U of Louisiana at Monroe (LA)
U of Miami (FL)
U of Mississippi (MS)
U of Missouri–Columbia (MO)
The U of Montana–Missoula (MT)
U of Montevallo (AL)
U of Nebraska at Omaha (NE)
The U of North Carolina at Greensboro (NC)
U of Northern Iowa (IA)
U of North Texas (TX)
U of Oklahoma (OK)
U of Oregon (OR)
U of San Francisco (CA)
U of Sioux Falls (SD)
U of South Dakota (SD)
U of Southern California (CA)
U of Southern Colorado (CO)
U of Southern Indiana (IN)
U of Southern Mississippi (MS)
The U of Tennessee (TN)
The U of Texas at Arlington (TX)
The U of Texas at Austin (TX)
U of Utah (UT)
U of Windsor (ON, Canada)
U of Wisconsin–Madison (WI)
U of Wisconsin–Oshkosh (WI)
U of Wisconsin–River Falls (WI)
U of Wisconsin–Superior (WI)
Valdosta State U (GA)
Vanguard U of Southern California (CA)
Walla Walla Coll (WA)
Washburn U of Topeka (KS)
Washington State U (WA)
Waynesburg Coll (PA)
Wayne State U (MI)
Weber State U (UT)
Webster U (MO)
Western Kentucky U (KY)
Western Michigan U (MI)
Western State Coll of Colorado (CO)
Westfield State Coll (MA)
Westminster Coll (PA)
William Woods U (MO)
Winona State U (MN)
Xavier U (OH)
York Coll of Pennsylvania (PA)
Youngstown State U (OH)

RADIO/TELEVISION BROADCASTING TECHNOLOGY
Asbury Coll (KY)
Eastern Michigan U (MI)
East Stroudsburg U of Pennsylvania (PA)
Emerson Coll (MA)
Hofstra U (NY)
Lewis U (IL)
New England School of Communications (ME)
Ohio U (OH)
Texas Tech U (TX)
Towson U (MD)
Trevecca Nazarene U (TN)
U of Georgia (GA)
U of Southern California (CA)

RANGE MANAGEMENT
Abilene Christian U (TX)
Angelo State U (TX)
Brigham Young U (UT)
California State U, Chico (CA)
Chadron State Coll (NE)
Colorado State U (CO)
Fort Hays State U (KS)
Humboldt State U (CA)
Montana State U–Bozeman (MT)
New Mexico State U (NM)
North Dakota State U (ND)
Oregon State U (OR)
South Dakota State U (SD)
Sul Ross State U (TX)
Tarleton State U (TX)
Texas A&M U (TX)
Texas A&M U–Kingsville (TX)
Texas Tech U (TX)
U of Alberta (AB, Canada)
U of Calif, Davis (CA)
U of Idaho (ID)
U of Nebraska–Lincoln (NE)
U of Nevada, Reno (NV)
U of Saskatchewan (SK, Canada)
U of Wyoming (WY)
Utah State U (UT)
Washington State U (WA)

READING EDUCATION
Abilene Christian U (TX)
Aquinas Coll (MI)
Baylor U (TX)
Belmont U (TN)
Boise State U (ID)
Bowling Green State U (OH)
Catawba Coll (NC)
Central Missouri State U (MO)
Chicago State U (IL)
City Coll of the City U of NY (NY)
Clarion U of Pennsylvania (PA)
Eastern Washington U (WA)
Grand Valley State U (MI)
Hardin-Simmons U (TX)
Jarvis Christian Coll (TX)
Longwood Coll (VA)
Luther Coll (IA)
Lyndon State Coll (VT)
Millersville U of Pennsylvania (PA)
Mount Saint Vincent U (NS, Canada)
Northeastern State U (OK)
Northwest Missouri State U (MO)
Ohio U (OH)
Our Lady of Holy Cross Coll (LA)
Pacific Lutheran U (WA)
St. Cloud State U (MN)
St. Mary's U of San Antonio (TX)
State U of NY Coll at Cortland (NY)
Tennessee State U (TN)
Texas A&M International U (TX)
Texas A&M U–Commerce (TX)
Texas Southern U (TX)
Texas Wesleyan U (TX)
U of Alberta (AB, Canada)
The U of British Columbia (BC, Canada)
U of Central Arkansas (AR)
U of Central Oklahoma (OK)
U of Georgia (GA)
U of Great Falls (MT)
U of Mary Hardin-Baylor (TX)
U of Missouri–St. Louis (MO)
The U of Montana–Missoula (MT)
U of New Orleans (LA)
U of Northern Iowa (IA)
U of North Texas (TX)
The U of Texas–Pan American (TX)
U of the Incarnate Word (TX)
U of Wisconsin–Superior (WI)
Upper Iowa U (IA)
Walsh U (OH)
Westfield State Coll (MA)
Wingate U (NC)
Winona State U (MN)
Wright State U (OH)
York Coll (NE)

REAL ESTATE
Angelo State U (TX)
Appalachian State U (NC)
Arizona State U (AZ)
Ball State U (IN)
Baylor U (TX)
California State Polytechnic U, Pomona (CA)
California State U, Dominguez Hills (CA)
California State U, Fresno (CA)
California State U, Hayward (CA)
California State U, Northridge (CA)
Christopher Newport U (VA)
Clarion U of Pennsylvania (PA)
Colorado State U (CO)
David N. Myers U (OH)
Eastern Kentucky U (KY)
Eastern Michigan U (MI)
Florida Atlantic U (FL)
Florida International U (FL)
Florida State U (FL)
Georgia State U (GA)
Indiana U Bloomington (IN)
Marylhurst U (OR)
Minnesota State U, Mankato (MN)
Mississippi State U (MS)
Morehead State U (KY)
New York U (NY)
The Ohio State U (OH)
Penn State U Univ Park Campus (PA)
St. Cloud State U (MN)
St. John's U (NY)
San Diego State U (CA)
San Francisco State U (CA)
Schreiner U (TX)
Southern Methodist U (TX)
State U of West Georgia (GA)
Temple U (PA)
Texas A&M U–Kingsville (TX)
Texas Christian U (TX)
Thomas Edison State Coll (NJ)
U of Central Oklahoma (OK)
U of Cincinnati (OH)
U of Connecticut (CT)
U of Denver (CO)
U of Florida (FL)
U of Georgia (GA)
U of Guelph (ON, Canada)
U of Hawaii at Manoa (HI)
The U of Memphis (TN)
U of Miami (FL)
U of Mississippi (MS)
U of Missouri–Columbia (MO)
U of Nebraska at Omaha (NE)
U of Nevada, Las Vegas (NV)
U of New Orleans (LA)
U of Northern Iowa (IA)
U of North Texas (TX)
U of Oklahoma (OK)
U of Pennsylvania (PA)
U of St. Thomas (MN)
U of South Carolina (SC)
The U of Texas at Arlington (TX)
The U of Texas at El Paso (TX)
U of Wisconsin–Madison (WI)
U of Wisconsin–Milwaukee (WI)
Washington State U (WA)
Webster U (MO)

RECREATIONAL THERAPY
Alderson-Broaddus Coll (WV)
Ashland U (OH)
Belmont Abbey Coll (NC)
California State U, Chico (CA)
California State U, Hayward (CA)
California State U, Northridge (CA)
Catawba Coll (NC)
Coll of Mount St. Joseph (OH)
Columbus State U (GA)
Concordia U (QC, Canada)
East Carolina U (NC)
Eastern Kentucky U (KY)
Eastern Washington U (WA)
Gallaudet U (DC)
Grand Valley State U (MI)
Green Mountain Coll (VT)
Hampton U (VA)
Indiana Inst of Technology (IN)
Indiana U Bloomington (IN)
Ithaca Coll (NY)
Jackson State U (MS)
Lake Superior State U (MI)
Lock Haven U of Pennsylvania (PA)
Long Island U, Southampton Coll, Friends World Program (NY)
Longwood Coll (VA)
Mars Hill Coll (NC)
Minnesota State U, Mankato (MN)
Montclair State U (NJ)
Northeastern U (MA)
Northland Coll (WI)
Northwest Missouri State U (MO)

RECREATION/LEISURE FACILITIES MANAGEMENT

RECREATION/LEISURE STUDIES

RECREATION PRODUCTS/ SERVICES MARKETING OPERATIONS

REHABILITATION/THERAPEUTIC SERVICES RELATED

REHABILITATION THERAPY

RELIGIOUS EDUCATION

RELIGIOUS MUSIC

RELIGIOUS STUDIES

Seton Hill Coll (PA)
Shawnee State U (OH)
Shorter Coll (GA)
Slippery Rock U of Pennsylvania (PA)
Southeastern Coll of the Assemblies of God (FL)
Southeastern Louisiana U (LA)
Southeastern Oklahoma State U (OK)
Southeast Missouri State U (MO)
Southern Arkansas U–Magnolia (AR)
Southern Connecticut State U (CT)
Southern Illinois U Edwardsville (IL)
Southwestern Coll (KS)
Southwestern Oklahoma State U (OK)
Southwest Missouri State U (MO)
Springfield Coll (MA)
State U of NY at Albany (NY)
State U of NY at New Paltz (NY)
State U of NY at Oswego (NY)
State U of NY Coll at Buffalo (NY)
State U of NY Coll at Cortland (NY)
State U of NY Coll at Fredonia (NY)
State U of NY Coll at Old Westbury (NY)
State U of NY Coll at Oneonta (NY)
State U of NY Coll at Potsdam (NY)
State U of NY Coll of Environ Sci and Forestry (NY)
State U of West Georgia (GA)
Syracuse U (NY)
Tabor Coll (KS)
Talladega Coll (AL)
Tarleton State U (TX)
Taylor U (IN)
Temple U (PA)
Tennessee Temple U (TN)
Texas A&M International U (TX)
Texas Christian U (TX)
Texas Wesleyan U (TX)
Trinity Christian Coll (IL)
Tri-State U (IN)
Troy State U (AL)
Troy State U Dothan (AL)
Union U (TN)
The U of Akron (OH)
U of Alberta (AB, Canada)
The U of Arizona (AZ)
The U of British Columbia (BC, Canada)
U of Central Arkansas (AR)
U of Central Florida (FL)
U of Central Oklahoma (OK)
U of Charleston (WV)
U of Dayton (OH)
U of Delaware (DE)
U of Evansville (IN)
The U of Findlay (OH)
U of Georgia (GA)
U of Great Falls (MT)
U of Hawaii at Manoa (HI)
U of Illinois at Chicago (IL)
U of Indianapolis (IN)
The U of Iowa (IA)
U of Kentucky (KY)
The U of Lethbridge (AB, Canada)
U of Louisiana at Monroe (LA)
U of Maine at Farmington (ME)
U of Maine at Presque Isle (ME)
U of Manitoba (MB, Canada)
U of Maryland, Coll Park (MD)
U of Michigan–Dearborn (MI)
U of Minnesota, Duluth (MN)
U of Minnesota, Twin Cities Campus (MN)
U of Mississippi (MS)
U of Missouri–Columbia (MO)
U of Missouri–St. Louis (MO)
The U of Montana–Missoula (MT)
Western Montana Coll of The U of Montana (MT)
U of Nebraska–Lincoln (NE)
U of Nevada, Reno (NV)
U of New England (ME)
U of New Hampshire (NH)
U of New Orleans (LA)
The U of North Carolina at Pembroke (NC)
U of North Dakota (ND)
U of Northern Iowa (IA)
U of North Florida (FL)
U of North Texas (TX)
U of Notre Dame (IN)
U of Oklahoma (OK)
U of Pittsburgh at Johnstown (PA)
U of Puerto Rico, Cayey U Coll (PR)
U of Regina (SK, Canada)
U of Rio Grande (OH)
U of Saint Francis (IN)
U of St. Thomas (MN)
U of Sioux Falls (SD)
U of South Dakota (SD)
U of Southern Colorado (CO)
U of South Florida (FL)
The U of Tennessee at Chattanooga (TN)
The U of Tennessee at Martin (TN)
U of the Ozarks (AR)
U of the Sciences in Philadelphia (PA)
U of Toledo (OH)
U of Utah (UT)
U of Vermont (VT)
U of Washington (WA)
U of West Florida (FL)
U of Windsor (ON, Canada)
U of Wisconsin–Eau Claire (WI)
U of Wisconsin–La Crosse (WI)
U of Wisconsin–Madison (WI)
U of Wisconsin–Platteville (WI)
U of Wisconsin–River Falls (WI)
U of Wisconsin–Superior (WI)
Upper Iowa U (IA)
Urbana U (OH)
Ursuline Coll (OH)
Utah State U (UT)
Valley City State U (ND)
Villa Julie Coll (MD)
Virginia Wesleyan Coll (VA)
Viterbo U (WI)
Walsh U (OH)
Warner Pacific Coll (OR)
Warner Southern Coll (FL)
Washington U in St. Louis (MO)
Wayne State Coll (NE)
Wayne State U (MI)
Weber State U (UT)
West Chester U of Pennsylvania (PA)
Western Carolina U (NC)
Western Kentucky U (KY)
Western State Coll of Colorado (CO)
Western Washington U (WA)
Westfield State Coll (MA)
West Virginia State Coll (WV)
Wheeling Jesuit U (WV)
Wichita State U (KS)
Widener U (PA)
William Penn U (IA)
William Woods U (MO)
Wilmington Coll (OH)
Wingate U (NC)
Winona State U (MN)
Wittenberg U (OH)
Wright State U (OH)
Xavier U (OH)
Xavier U of Louisiana (LA)
York Coll (NE)
York Coll of Pennsylvania (PA)
York U (ON, Canada)
Youngstown State U (OH)

SCIENCE TECHNOLOGIES RELATED

Arizona State U East (AZ)
Athens State U (AL)
Clemson U (SC)
Northern Arizona U (AZ)
U of Wisconsin–Stout (WI)

SCIENCE/TECHNOLOGY AND SOCIETY

Columbia Coll (SC)
Cornell U (NY)
Georgetown U (DC)
Georgia Inst of Technology (GA)
Grinnell Coll (IA)
James Madison U (VA)
Lehigh U (PA)
Massachusetts Inst of Technology (MA)
New Jersey Inst of Technology (NJ)
Pitzer Coll (CA)
Rensselaer Polytechnic Inst (NY)
Samford U (AL)
Scripps Coll (CA)
Slippery Rock U of Pennsylvania (PA)
Stanford U (CA)
Texas Southern U (TX)
U of Alaska Anchorage (AK)
U of Nevada, Reno (NV)
U of Windsor (ON, Canada)
Vassar Coll (NY)
Virginia Wesleyan Coll (VA)
Washington U in St. Louis (MO)
Wesleyan U (CT)
Worcester Polytechnic Inst (MA)
York U (ON, Canada)

SCULPTURE

Academy of Art Coll (CA)
Adams State Coll (CO)
Alberta Coll of Art & Design (AB, Canada)
Alfred U (NY)
Aquinas Coll (MI)
Arizona State U (AZ)
Art Academy of Cincinnati (OH)
Atlanta Coll of Art (GA)
Ball State U (IN)
Bard Coll (NY)
Bellarmine U (KY)
Bennington Coll (VT)
Bethany Coll (KS)
Birmingham-Southern Coll (AL)
Boston U (MA)
Bowling Green State U (OH)
California Coll of Arts and Crafts (CA)
California Inst of the Arts (CA)
California State U, Fullerton (CA)
California State U, Hayward (CA)
California State U, Long Beach (CA)
California State U, Northridge (CA)
California State U, Stanislaus (CA)
Carnegie Mellon U (PA)
The Catholic U of America (DC)
The Cleveland Inst of Art (OH)
Ctr for Creative Studies—Coll of Art and Design (MI)
Coll of Santa Fe (NM)
Coll of Visual Arts (MN)
Colorado State U (CO)
Columbus Coll of Art and Design (OH)
Concordia U (QC, Canada)
Corcoran Coll of Art and Design (DC)
Cornell U (NY)
DePaul U (IL)
Drake U (IA)
Eastern Kentucky U (KY)
Escuela de Artes Plasticas de Puerto Rico (PR)
Framingham State Coll (MA)
Goddard Coll (VT)
Grand Valley State U (MI)
Hampshire Coll (MA)
Indiana U Bloomington (IN)
Inter American U of PR, San Germán Campus (PR)
Kansas City Art Inst (MO)
Long Island U, Southampton Coll, Friends World Program (NY)
Longwood Coll (VA)
Lyme Academy Coll of Fine Arts (CT)
Maharishi U of Management (IA)
Maine Coll of Art (ME)
Marlboro Coll (VT)
Maryland Inst, Coll of Art (MD)
Massachusetts Coll of Art (MA)
Memorial U of Newfoundland (NF, Canada)
Memphis Coll of Art (TN)
Mercyhurst Coll (PA)
Milwaukee Inst of Art and Design (WI)
Minneapolis Coll of Art and Design (MN)
Minnesota State U, Mankato (MN)
Minnesota State U Moorhead (MN)
Montserrat Coll of Art (MA)
Moore Coll of Art and Design (PA)
Mount Allison U (NB, Canada)
New World School of the Arts (FL)
New York U (NY)
Northern Michigan U (MI)
Northwest Missouri State U (MO)
Nova Scotia Coll of Art and Design (NS, Canada)
The Ohio State U (OH)
Ohio U (OH)
Otis Coll of Art and Design (CA)
Pacific Northwest Coll of Art (OR)
Parsons School of Design, New School U (NY)
Portland State U (OR)
Pratt Inst (NY)
Rhode Island School of Design (RI)
Rochester Inst of Technology (NY)
Rocky Mountain Coll of Art & Design (CO)
Rutgers, The State U of New Jersey, New Brunswick (NJ)
San Diego State U (CA)
San Francisco Art Inst (CA)
Sarah Lawrence Coll (NY)
School of the Art Inst of Chicago (IL)
School of the Museum of Fine Arts (MA)
School of Visual Arts (NY)
Seton Hill Coll (PA)
Simon's Rock Coll of Bard (MA)
Sonoma State U (CA)
State U of NY at New Paltz (NY)
State U of NY Coll at Brockport (NY)
State U of NY Coll at Buffalo (NY)
State U of NY Coll at Potsdam (NY)
Syracuse U (NY)
Temple U (PA)
Texas A&M U–Commerce (TX)
Texas Christian U (TX)
Texas Woman's U (TX)
Trinity Christian Coll (IL)
The U of Akron (OH)
U of Alberta (AB, Canada)
U of Calif, Santa Cruz (CA)
U of Dallas (TX)
U of Evansville (IN)
U of Hartford (CT)
U of Houston (TX)
U of Illinois at Urbana–Champaign (IL)
The U of Iowa (IA)
U of Kansas (KS)
U of Massachusetts Dartmouth (MA)
U of Miami (FL)
U of Michigan (MI)
U of Montevallo (AL)
The U of North Carolina at Greensboro (NC)
U of North Texas (TX)
U of Oklahoma (OK)
U of Oregon (OR)
U of South Dakota (SD)
The U of Tennessee at Chattanooga (TN)
The U of Texas at El Paso (TX)
The U of the Arts (PA)
U of Washington (WA)
U of Windsor (ON, Canada)
U of Wisconsin–Milwaukee (WI)
Virginia Commonwealth U (VA)
Washington U in St. Louis (MO)
Webster U (MO)
Western Michigan U (MI)
Wittenberg U (OH)
York U (ON, Canada)

SECONDARY EDUCATION

Abilene Christian U (TX)
Acadia U (NS, Canada)
Adams State Coll (CO)
Adrian Coll (MI)
Alabama State U (AL)
Albion Coll (MI)
Albright Coll (PA)
Alcorn State U (MS)
Alderson-Broaddus Coll (WV)
Alfred U (NY)
Alice Lloyd Coll (KY)
Alma Coll (MI)
Alverno Coll (WI)
American International Coll (MA)
American U (DC)
Anderson Coll (SC)
Andrews U (MI)
Aquinas Coll (MI)
Arcadia U (PA)
Arizona State U (AZ)
Arizona State U West (AZ)
Arkansas Baptist Coll (AR)
Armstrong Atlantic State U (GA)
Ashland U (OH)
Assumption Coll (MA)
Athens State U (AL)
Atlantic Union Coll (MA)
Auburn U (AL)
Auburn U Montgomery (AL)
Augsburg Coll (MN)
Augustana Coll (IL)
Augustana Coll (SD)
Baldwin-Wallace Coll (OH)
Ball State U (IN)
Baptist Bible Coll of Pennsylvania (PA)
Barton Coll (NC)
Baylor U (TX)
Bellarmine U (KY)
Belmont Abbey Coll (NC)
Beloit Coll (WI)
Bemidji State U (MN)
Benedictine Coll (KS)
Benedictine U (IL)
Berea Coll (KY)
Berry Coll (GA)
Bethel Coll (MN)
Biola U (CA)
Birmingham-Southern Coll (AL)
Blackburn Coll (IL)
Bloomsburg U of Pennsylvania (PA)
Bluefield Coll (VA)
Bluffton Coll (OH)
Boise State U (ID)
Boston Coll (MA)
Bowie State U (MD)
Bowling Green State U (OH)
Brandon U (MB, Canada)
Brescia U (KY)
Brewton-Parker Coll (GA)
Briar Cliff U (IA)
Bridgewater Coll (VA)
Brigham Young U–Hawaii (HI)
Brock U (ON, Canada)
Brooklyn Coll of the City U of NY (NY)
Bryan Coll (TN)
Bucknell U (PA)
Buena Vista U (IA)
Butler U (IN)
Calvary Bible Coll and Theological Seminary (MO)
Calvin Coll (MI)
Campbellsville U (KY)
Campbell U (NC)
Canisius Coll (NY)
Capital U (OH)
Cardinal Stritch U (WI)
Caribbean U (PR)
Carroll Coll (MT)
Carson-Newman Coll (TN)
Carthage Coll (WI)
Catawba Coll (NC)
The Catholic U of America (DC)
Cedar Crest Coll (PA)
Cedarville U (OH)
Centenary Coll (NJ)
Centenary Coll of Louisiana (LA)
Central Coll (IA)
Central Methodist Coll (MO)
Central Missouri State U (MO)
Centre Coll (KY)
Chadron State Coll (NE)
Charleston Southern U (SC)
Cheyney U of Pennsylvania (PA)
Chicago State U (IL)
Christian Heritage Coll (CA)
Christopher Newport U (VA)
City Coll of the City U of NY (NY)
Clark Atlanta U (GA)
Clarke Coll (IA)
Clark U (MA)
Clearwater Christian Coll (FL)
Clemson U (SC)
Coastal Carolina U (SC)
Coe Coll (IA)
Coker Coll (SC)
Coll Misericordia (PA)
Coll of Mount Saint Vincent (NY)
The Coll of New Jersey (NJ)
The Coll of New Rochelle (NY)
Coll of Saint Benedict (MN)
Coll of St. Catherine (MN)
Coll of St. Joseph (VT)
Coll of Saint Mary (NE)
Coll of Santa Fe (NM)
Coll of the Atlantic (ME)
Coll of the Ozarks (MO)
Coll of the Southwest (NM)
Columbia Coll (MO)
Columbia Coll (SC)
Columbus State U (GA)
Concord Coll (WV)
Concordia Coll (MN)
Concordia Coll (NY)
Concordia U (CA)
Concordia U (IL)

Concordia U (MI)
Concordia U (MN)
Concordia U (NE)
Concordia U (OR)
Concordia U Wisconsin (WI)
Converse Coll (SC)
Coppin State Coll (MD)
Cornell Coll (IA)
Cornerstone U (MI)
Crichton Coll (TN)
Cumberland U (TN)
Dakota State U (SD)
Dallas Baptist U (TX)
Dana Coll (NE)
Davis & Elkins Coll (WV)
Defiance Coll (OH)
Delaware Valley Coll (PA)
Delta State U (MS)
DePaul U (IL)
DeSales U (PA)
Dickinson State U (ND)
Dillard U (LA)
Doane Coll (NE)
Dominican Coll (NY)
Dordt Coll (IA)
Dowling Coll (NY)
Drake U (IA)
Drury U (MO)
Duquesne U (PA)
D'Youville Coll (NY)
East Central U (OK)
Eastern Kentucky U (KY)
Eastern Mennonite U (VA)
Eastern Michigan U (MI)
Eastern Nazarene Coll (MA)
Eastern U (PA)
Eastern Washington U (WA)
East Stroudsburg U of Pennsylvania (PA)
East Texas Baptist U (TX)
Edward Waters Coll (FL)
Elizabeth City State U (NC)
Elizabethtown Coll (PA)
Elmhurst Coll (IL)
Elmira Coll (NY)
Elms Coll (MA)
Elon U (NC)
Emmanuel Coll (MA)
Emory U (GA)
Emporia State U (KS)
Eureka Coll (IL)
Evangel U (MO)
Fairfield U (CT)
Fairmont State Coll (WV)
Faulkner U (AL)
Ferris State U (MI)
Fitchburg State Coll (MA)
Flagler Coll (FL)
Florida Southern Coll (FL)
Florida State U (FL)
Fontbonne U (MO)
Fordham U (NY)
Fort Lewis Coll (CO)
Framingham State Coll (MA)
Franklin Pierce Coll (NH)
Freed-Hardeman U (TN)
Fresno Pacific U (CA)
Friends U (KS)
Frostburg State U (MD)
Furman U (SC)
Gallaudet U (DC)
Gannon U (PA)
Gardner-Webb U (NC)
Geneva Coll (PA)
Georgetown Coll (KY)
Georgia Southwestern State U (GA)
Gettysburg Coll (PA)
Glenville State Coll (WV)
Goddard Coll (VT)
Gonzaga U (WA)
Goshen Coll (IN)
Grace Bible Coll (MI)
Graceland U (IA)
Grace U (NE)
Grambling State U (LA)
Grand Canyon U (AZ)
Grand Valley State U (MI)
Grand View Coll (IA)
Green Mountain Coll (VT)
Greensboro Coll (NC)
Greenville Coll (IL)
Grove City Coll (PA)
Guilford Coll (NC)
Gustavus Adolphus Coll (MN)
Gwynedd-Mercy Coll (PA)
Hamline U (MN)
Hampshire Coll (MA)
Hampton U (VA)
Hannibal-LaGrange Coll (MO)
Hardin-Simmons U (TX)
Harris-Stowe State Coll (MO)
Hastings Coll (NE)
Heidelberg Coll (OH)
High Point U (NC)
Hillsdale Coll (MI)
Hiram Coll (OH)
Hobe Sound Bible Coll (FL)
Hofstra U (NY)
Holy Family Coll (PA)
Hope Coll (MI)
Houghton Coll (NY)
Houston Baptist U (TX)
Howard Payne U (TX)
Humboldt State U (CA)
Hunter Coll of the City U of NY (NY)
Huntingdon Coll (AL)
Huntington Coll (IN)
Huron U (SD)
Huston-Tillotson Coll (TX)
Idaho State U (ID)
Illinois Coll (IL)
Illinois Wesleyan U (IL)
Immaculata Coll (PA)
Indiana U Bloomington (IN)
Indiana U East (IN)
Indiana U Northwest (IN)
Indiana U of Pennsylvania (PA)
Indiana U–Purdue U Fort Wayne (IN)
Indiana U–Purdue U Indianapolis (IN)
Indiana U South Bend (IN)
Indiana U Southeast (IN)
Indiana Wesleyan U (IN)
Inter Amer U of PR, Barranquitas Campus (PR)
Inter American U of PR, San Germán Campus (PR)
Iona Coll (NY)
Iowa State U of Science and Technology (IA)
Iowa Wesleyan Coll (IA)
Ithaca Coll (NY)
Jackson State U (MS)
Jacksonville State U (AL)
Jacksonville U (FL)
Jarvis Christian Coll (TX)
John Brown U (AR)
John Carroll U (OH)
Johnson C. Smith U (NC)
Johnson State Coll (VT)
Judson Coll (AL)
Judson Coll (IL)
Juniata Coll (PA)
Kansas State U (KS)
Keene State Coll (NH)
Kennesaw State U (GA)
Kentucky State U (KY)
Kentucky Wesleyan Coll (KY)
King Coll (TN)
King's Coll (PA)
Kutztown U of Pennsylvania (PA)
LaGrange Coll (GA)
Lake Forest Coll (IL)
Lakehead U (ON, Canada)
Lakeland Coll (WI)
Lake Superior State U (MI)
Lamar U (TX)
Lambuth U (TN)
La Salle U (PA)
Lawrence U (WI)
Lebanon Valley Coll (PA)
Lee U (TN)
Le Moyne Coll (NY)
LeMoyne-Owen Coll (TN)
Lenoir-Rhyne Coll (NC)
LeTourneau U (TX)
Lewis U (IL)
Liberty U (VA)
Lincoln Christian Coll (IL)
Lincoln Memorial U (TN)
Lindenwood U (MO)
Lipscomb U (TN)
Lock Haven U of Pennsylvania (PA)
Long Island U, Brooklyn Campus (NY)
Long Island U, C.W. Post Campus (NY)
Long Island U, Southampton Coll, Friends World Program (NY)
Longwood Coll (VA)
Loras Coll (IA)
Louisiana Coll (LA)
Louisiana State U and A&M Coll (LA)
Louisiana Tech U (LA)
Lubbock Christian U (TX)
Luther Coll (IA)
Lycoming Coll (PA)
Lynchburg Coll (VA)
Lynn U (FL)
MacMurray Coll (IL)
Manchester Coll (IN)
Manhattanville Coll (NY)
Mansfield U of Pennsylvania (PA)
Maranatha Baptist Bible Coll (WI)
Marian Coll (IN)
Marian Coll of Fond du Lac (WI)
Marietta Coll (OH)
Marist Coll (NY)
Marquette U (WI)
Marshall U (WV)
Mars Hill Coll (NC)
Marymount Coll of Fordham U (NY)
Maryville U of Saint Louis (MO)
Mary Washington Coll (VA)
Marywood U (PA)
Massachusetts Coll of Liberal Arts (MA)
The Master's Coll and Seminary (CA)
McGill U (PQ, Canada)
McKendree Coll (IL)
McNeese State U (LA)
McPherson Coll (KS)
Memorial U of Newfoundland (NF, Canada)
Mercy Coll (NY)
Mercyhurst Coll (PA)
Merrimack Coll (MA)
Mesa State Coll (CO)
Methodist Coll (NC)
Miami U (OH)
Michigan Technological U (MI)
MidAmerica Nazarene U (KS)
Middlebury Coll (VT)
Midland Lutheran Coll (NE)
Midwestern State U (TX)
Milligan Coll (TN)
Minnesota State U, Mankato (MN)
Minnesota State U Moorhead (MN)
Mississippi State U (MS)
Mississippi U for Women (MS)
Missouri Southern State Coll (MO)
Missouri Valley Coll (MO)
Molloy Coll (NY)
Monmouth Coll (IL)
Monmouth U (NJ)
Montana State U–Billings (MT)
Montana State U–Bozeman (MT)
Montana State U–Northern (MT)
Montreat Coll (NC)
Moravian Coll (PA)
Morehouse Coll (GA)
Morgan State U (MD)
Morningside Coll (IA)
Morris Coll (SC)
Mount Marty Coll (SD)
Mount Mary Coll (WI)
Mount Mercy Coll (IA)
Mount St. Clare Coll (IA)
Mount Saint Mary Coll (NY)
Mount St. Mary's Coll (CA)
Mount Saint Mary's Coll and Seminary (MD)
Mount Saint Vincent U (NS, Canada)
Mount Vernon Nazarene U (OH)
Muhlenberg Coll (PA)
Muskingum Coll (OH)
Nazareth Coll of Rochester (NY)
Nebraska Christian Coll (NE)
Newberry Coll (SC)
New England Coll (NH)
Newman U (KS)
New Mexico Highlands U (NM)
New Mexico State U (NM)
New York U (NY)
Niagara U (NY)
Nicholls State U (LA)
North Carolina State U (NC)
North Carolina Wesleyan Coll (NC)
North Central Coll (IL)
North Dakota State U (ND)
Northeastern State U (OK)
Northern Michigan U (MI)
Northern State U (SD)
North Georgia Coll & State U (GA)
Northland Coll (WI)
North Park U (IL)
Northwest Coll (WA)
Northwestern Coll (IA)
Northwestern Oklahoma State U (OK)
Northwestern State U of Louisiana (LA)
Northwestern U (IL)
Northwest Missouri State U (MO)
Northwest Nazarene U (ID)
Notre Dame Coll (OH)
Notre Dame de Namur U (CA)
Nova Southeastern U (FL)
Nyack Coll (NY)
Oakland City U (IN)
Oakland U (MI)
Oglethorpe U (GA)
Ohio Dominican Coll (OH)
Ohio U (OH)
Ohio Valley Coll (WV)
Ohio Wesleyan U (OH)
Oklahoma Baptist U (OK)
Oklahoma Christian U of Science and Arts (OK)
Oklahoma City U (OK)
Oklahoma Panhandle State U (OK)
Oklahoma State U (OK)
Oklahoma Wesleyan U (OK)
Olivet Coll (MI)
Olivet Nazarene U (IL)
Otterbein Coll (OH)
Ouachita Baptist U (AR)
Our Lady of Holy Cross Coll (LA)
Pacific Lutheran U (WA)
Pacific U (OR)
Paine Coll (GA)
Palm Beach Atlantic Coll (FL)
Penn State U Univ Park Campus (PA)
Pepperdine U, Malibu (CA)
Peru State Coll (NE)
Piedmont Coll (GA)
Pillsbury Baptist Bible Coll (MN)
Pine Manor Coll (MA)
Pittsburg State U (KS)
Plattsburgh State U of NY (NY)
Point Park Coll (PA)
Pontifical Catholic U of Puerto Rico (PR)
Prescott Coll (AZ)
Principia Coll (IL)
Providence Coll (RI)
Purdue U Calumet (IN)
Queens Coll (NC)
Queens Coll of the City U of NY (NY)
Queen's U at Kingston (ON, Canada)
Reformed Bible Coll (MI)
Rhode Island Coll (RI)
Rider U (NJ)
Ripon Coll (WI)
Rivier Coll (NH)
Roberts Wesleyan Coll (NY)
Rockhurst U (MO)
Rocky Mountain Coll (MT)
Roger Williams U (RI)
Roosevelt U (IL)
Rowan U (NJ)
Sacred Heart U (CT)
St. Ambrose U (IA)
Saint Anselm Coll (NH)
St. Bonaventure U (NY)
St. Cloud State U (MN)
St. Francis Coll (NY)
Saint Francis U (PA)
St. Francis Xavier U (NS, Canada)
Saint John's U (MN)
St. John's U (NY)
Saint Joseph Coll (CT)
Saint Joseph's Coll (IN)
St. Joseph's Coll, Suffolk Campus (NY)
Saint Joseph's U (PA)
Saint Leo U (FL)
Saint Martin's Coll (WA)
Saint Mary-of-the-Woods Coll (IN)
Saint Mary's Coll of California (CA)
Saint Michael's Coll (VT)
St. Thomas Aquinas Coll (NY)
St. Thomas U (FL)
Salem International U (WV)
Salisbury U (MD)
Salve Regina U (RI)
Seton Hall U (NJ)
Seton Hill Coll (PA)
Shawnee State U (OH)
Sheldon Jackson Coll (AK)
Shepherd Coll (WV)
Shorter Coll (GA)
Siena Coll (NY)
Siena Heights U (MI)
Simmons Coll (MA)
Simpson Coll (IA)
Simpson Coll and Graduate School (CA)
Slippery Rock U of Pennsylvania (PA)
South Dakota State U (SD)
Southeastern Bible Coll (AL)
Southeastern Oklahoma State U (OK)
Southeast Missouri State U (MO)
Southern Connecticut State U (CT)
Southern Nazarene U (OK)
Southern New Hampshire U (NH)
Southern U and A&M Coll (LA)
Southern Utah U (UT)
Southwest Baptist U (MO)
Southwestern Assemblies of God U (TX)
Southwestern Coll (AZ)
Southwestern Oklahoma State U (OK)
Southwest State U (MN)
Spring Arbor U (MI)
Springfield Coll (MA)
Spring Hill Coll (AL)
State U of NY at New Paltz (NY)
State U of NY at Oswego (NY)
State U of NY Coll at Brockport (NY)
State U of NY Coll at Buffalo (NY)
State U of NY Coll at Cortland (NY)
State U of NY Coll at Fredonia (NY)
State U of NY Coll at Old Westbury (NY)
State U of NY Coll at Oneonta (NY)
State U of West Georgia (GA)
State U of NY at Stony Brook (NY)
Suffolk U (MA)
Susquehanna U (PA)
Syracuse U (NY)
Tabor Coll (KS)
Taylor U (IN)
Temple U (PA)
Tennessee Technological U (TN)
Tennessee Temple U (TN)
Tennessee Wesleyan Coll (TN)
Texas A&M U–Commerce (TX)
Texas A&M U–Kingsville (TX)
Texas Christian U (TX)
Texas Southern U (TX)
Thiel Coll (PA)
Toccoa Falls Coll (GA)
Tougaloo Coll (MS)
Trent U (ON, Canada)
Trevecca Nazarene U (TN)
Trinity Baptist Coll (FL)
Trinity Christian Coll (IL)
Trinity Coll (DC)
Trinity International U (IL)
Trinity Western U (BC, Canada)
Tri-State U (IN)
Troy State U (AL)
Troy State U Dothan (AL)
Tufts U (MA)
Tusculum Coll (TN)
Union Coll (KY)
Union Coll (NE)
Union U (TN)
Universidad Adventista de las Antillas (PR)
Université de Montréal (QC, Canada)
Université de Sherbrooke (PQ, Canada)
Université Laval (QC, Canada)
The U of Akron (OH)
The U of Alabama (AL)
The U of Alabama at Birmingham (AL)
U of Alaska Anchorage (AK)
U of Alberta (AB, Canada)
The U of Arizona (AZ)
U of Arkansas at Pine Bluff (AR)
The U of British Columbia (BC, Canada)
U of Calgary (AB, Canada)
U of Central Oklahoma (OK)
U of Cincinnati (OH)
U of Dallas (TX)
U of Dayton (OH)
U of Delaware (DE)
U of Evansville (IN)
The U of Findlay (OH)
U of Great Falls (MT)
U of Hartford (CT)
U of Hawaii at Hilo (HI)
U of Hawaii at Manoa (HI)
U of Idaho (ID)

U of Illinois at Chicago (IL)
U of Illinois at Springfield (IL)
U of Indianapolis (IN)
The U of Iowa (IA)
U of Kansas (KS)
U of La Verne (CA)
U of Louisiana at Lafayette (LA)
U of Maine (ME)
U of Maine at Farmington (ME)
U of Maine at Presque Isle (ME)
U of Manitoba (MB, Canada)
U of Mary Hardin-Baylor (TX)
U of Maryland, Coll Park (MD)
U of Miami (FL)
U of Michigan (MI)
U of Michigan–Dearborn (MI)
U of Michigan–Flint (MI)
U of Minnesota, Morris (MN)
U of Mississippi (MS)
U of Missouri–Kansas City (MO)
U of Missouri–Rolla (MO)
U of Missouri–St. Louis (MO)
U of Mobile (AL)
The U of Montana–Missoula (MT)
Western Montana Coll of The U of Montana (MT)
U of Nebraska at Omaha (NE)
U of Nevada, Las Vegas (NV)
U of New England (ME)
U of New Mexico (NM)
U of New Orleans (LA)
U of North Alabama (AL)
The U of North Carolina at Pembroke (NC)
U of North Florida (FL)
U of North Texas (TX)
U of Ottawa (ON, Canada)
U of Pittsburgh at Johnstown (PA)
U of Portland (OR)
U of Prince Edward Island (PE, Canada)
U of Puerto Rico, Cayey U Coll (PR)
U of Redlands (CA)
U of Regina (SK, Canada)
U of Rhode Island (RI)
U of Richmond (VA)
U of Rio Grande (OH)
U of Saint Francis (IN)
U of St. Thomas (MN)
U of St. Thomas (TX)
U of San Francisco (CA)
U of Saskatchewan (SK, Canada)
The U of Scranton (PA)
U of Sioux Falls (SD)
U of South Alabama (AL)
U of South Carolina Aiken (SC)
U of South Carolina Spartanburg (SC)
U of South Dakota (SD)
U of Southern Colorado (CO)
The U of Tampa (FL)
The U of Tennessee at Chattanooga (TN)
The U of Texas–Pan American (TX)
U of the Incarnate Word (TX)
U of Toledo (OH)
U of Utah (UT)
U of Vermont (VT)
U of Victoria (BC, Canada)
U of Washington (WA)
The U of Western Ontario (ON, Canada)
U of Windsor (ON, Canada)
U of Wisconsin–La Crosse (WI)
U of Wisconsin–Madison (WI)
U of Wisconsin–Milwaukee (WI)
U of Wisconsin–Oshkosh (WI)
U of Wisconsin–Platteville (WI)
U of Wisconsin–River Falls (WI)
U of Wisconsin–Stevens Point (WI)
U of Wisconsin–Whitewater (WI)
U of Wyoming (WY)
Upper Iowa U (IA)
Urbana U (OH)
Ursinus Coll (PA)
Utah State U (UT)
Utica Coll of Syracuse U (NY)
Valdosta State U (GA)
Valley City State U (ND)
Valparaiso U (IN)
Vanderbilt U (TN)
Vanguard U of Southern California (CA)
Villanova U (PA)
Virginia Intermont Coll (VA)
Virginia Wesleyan Coll (VA)
Wagner Coll (NY)
Walsh U (OH)
Warner Pacific Coll (OR)
Warren Wilson Coll (NC)
Wartburg Coll (IA)
Washington State U (WA)
Washington U in St. Louis (MO)
Waynesburg Coll (PA)
Weber State U (UT)
Webster U (MO)
Wells Coll (NY)
Wesley Coll (DE)
West Chester U of Pennsylvania (PA)
Western Baptist Coll (OR)
Western Connecticut State U (CT)
Western Oregon U (OR)
Western State Coll of Colorado (CO)
Western Washington U (WA)
Westfield State Coll (MA)
West Liberty State Coll (WV)
Westminster Coll (MO)
Westmont Coll (CA)
West Virginia State Coll (WV)
West Virginia U (WV)
West Virginia Wesleyan Coll (WV)
Wheeling Jesuit U (WV)
Whitworth Coll (WA)
Wichita State U (KS)
William Carey Coll (MS)
William Jewell Coll (MO)
William Paterson U of New Jersey (NJ)
William Penn U (IA)
William Woods U (MO)
Wilmington Coll (OH)
Wingate U (NC)
Winona State U (MN)
Wittenberg U (OH)
Wright State U (OH)
Xavier U of Louisiana (LA)
York Coll (NE)
York Coll of Pennsylvania (PA)
York U (ON, Canada)
Youngstown State U (OH)

SECRETARIAL SCIENCE

Alabama State U (AL)
Albany State U (GA)
Alcorn State U (MS)
American U of Puerto Rico (PR)
Appalachian State U (NC)
Arkansas State U (AR)
Baker Coll of Flint (MI)
Baker Coll of Muskegon (MI)
Baker Coll of Owosso (MI)
Baker Coll of Port Huron (MI)
Baptist Bible Coll (MO)
Baptist Bible Coll of Pennsylvania (PA)
Bayamón Central U (PR)
Belmont U (TN)
Benedict Coll (SC)
Bluefield State Coll (WV)
California State U, Northridge (CA)
Campbellsville U (KY)
Caribbean U (PR)
Cedarville U (OH)
Clearwater Christian Coll (FL)
Coleman Coll (CA)
Davenport U, Kalamazoo (MI)
Davenport U, Lansing (MI)
David N. Myers U (OH)
Davis & Elkins Coll (WV)
East Central U (OK)
Eastern Kentucky U (KY)
East-West U (IL)
Elizabeth City State U (NC)
Evangel U (MO)
Florida A&M U (FL)
Fort Hays State U (KS)
Fort Valley State U (GA)
Husson Coll (ME)
Inter American U of PR, Aguadilla Campus (PR)
Inter Amer U of PR, Barranquitas Campus (PR)
Inter American U of PR, San Germán Campus (PR)
International Business Coll, Fort Wayne (IN)
Jackson State U (MS)
Jones Coll (FL)
Lake Superior State U (MI)
Lamar U (TX)
Lee U (TN)
Lincoln Christian Coll (IL)
Lincoln U (MO)
Maranatha Baptist Bible Coll (WI)
Mayville State U (ND)
Mercyhurst Coll (PA)
Mesa State Coll (CO)
Midland Lutheran Coll (NE)
Montclair State U (NJ)
Morehead State U (KY)
Mount Vernon Nazarene U (OH)
Murray State U (KY)
North Carolina Ag and Tech State U (NC)
Northern State U (SD)
Northwest Missouri State U (MO)
Oakwood Coll (AL)
Pacific Union Coll (CA)
Peirce Coll (PA)
Pillsbury Baptist Bible Coll (MN)
Pontifical Catholic U of Puerto Rico (PR)
Salem State Coll (MA)
South Carolina State U (SC)
Southeast Missouri State U (MO)
Southern Adventist U (TN)
Southwestern Adventist U (TX)
Suffolk U (MA)
Sul Ross State U (TX)
Tabor Coll (KS)
Tennessee State U (TN)
Tennessee Temple U (TN)
Texas A&M U–Commerce (TX)
Texas Woman's U (TX)
Trinity Bible Coll (ND)
Universidad Adventista de las Antillas (PR)
U of Idaho (ID)
U of Maine at Machias (ME)
The U of Montana–Missoula (MT)
The U of North Carolina at Pembroke (NC)
U of Puerto Rico, Humacao U Coll (PR)
U of Puerto Rico at Ponce (PR)
U of Sioux Falls (SD)
The U of Texas–Pan American (TX)
U of Wisconsin–Superior (WI)
Utah State U (UT)
Valdosta State U (GA)
Weber State U (UT)
Wiley Coll (TX)
Winona State U (MN)
Youngstown State U (OH)

SECURITY

Ohio U (OH)
Youngstown State U (OH)

SIGN LANGUAGE INTERPRETATION

Bethel Coll (IN)
Bloomsburg U of Pennsylvania (PA)
California State U, Northridge (CA)
Columbia Coll Chicago (IL)
Converse Coll (SC)
Gallaudet U (DC)
Gardner-Webb U (NC)
Goshen Coll (IN)
Indiana U–Purdue U Indianapolis (IN)
Long Island U, Southampton Coll, Friends World Program (NY)
MacMurray Coll (IL)
Maryville Coll (TN)
Mount Aloysius Coll (PA)
Northeastern U (MA)
Ozark Christian Coll (MO)
Rochester Inst of Technology (NY)
U of Arkansas at Little Rock (AR)
U of New Mexico (NM)
The U of North Carolina at Greensboro (NC)
U of Rochester (NY)
Western Oregon U (OR)
William Woods U (MO)
York U (ON, Canada)

SLAVIC LANGUAGES

Barnard Coll (NY)
Boston Coll (MA)
Columbia Coll (NY)
Columbia U, School of General Studies (NY)
Cornell U (NY)
Duke U (NC)
Harvard U (MA)
Indiana U Bloomington (IN)
Long Island U, Southampton Coll, Friends World Program (NY)
Northwestern U (IL)
Saint Mary's Coll of Ave Maria U (MI)
Stanford U (CA)
State U of NY at Albany (NY)
U of Alberta (AB, Canada)
The U of British Columbia (BC, Canada)
U of Calif, Berkeley (CA)
U of Calif, Los Angeles (CA)
U of Calif, Santa Barbara (CA)
U of Chicago (IL)
U of Georgia (GA)
U of Illinois at Chicago (IL)
U of Manitoba (MB, Canada)
U of Ottawa (ON, Canada)
U of Pittsburgh (PA)
U of Saskatchewan (SK, Canada)
The U of Scranton (PA)
The U of Texas at Austin (TX)
U of Toronto (ON, Canada)
U of Victoria (BC, Canada)
U of Virginia (VA)
U of Washington (WA)
U of Windsor (ON, Canada)
U of Wisconsin–Madison (WI)
U of Wisconsin–Milwaukee (WI)
Wayne State U (MI)

SOCIAL/PHILOSOPHICAL FOUNDATIONS OF EDUCATION

Northwestern U (IL)
Ohio U (OH)
Texas Southern U (TX)
U of Hawaii at Manoa (HI)
Washington U in St. Louis (MO)

SOCIAL PSYCHOLOGY

Clarion U of Pennsylvania (PA)
Florida Atlantic U (FL)
Loyola U Chicago (IL)
Marymount U (VA)
Maryville U of Saint Louis (MO)
Park U (MO)
U of Calif, Santa Cruz (CA)
U of Nevada, Reno (NV)
U of Wisconsin–Superior (WI)

SOCIAL SCIENCE EDUCATION

Abilene Christian U (TX)
Alverno Coll (WI)
Arkansas State U (AR)
Baylor U (TX)
Bethune-Cookman Coll (FL)
Blue Mountain Coll (MS)
Bowling Green State U (OH)
Bridgewater Coll (VA)
California State U, Chico (CA)
Carroll Coll (MT)
Central Methodist Coll (MO)
Central Michigan U (MI)
Central Washington U (WA)
Chadron State Coll (NE)
The Coll of St. Scholastica (MN)
Coll of Santa Fe (NM)
Concordia U (IL)
Concordia U (NE)
Dana Coll (NE)
Delta State U (MS)
Eastern Illinois U (IL)
Eastern Mennonite U (VA)
Eastern Michigan U (MI)
East Stroudsburg U of Pennsylvania (PA)
Elmira Coll (NY)
Elon U (NC)
Florida Atlantic U (FL)
Florida International U (FL)
Florida State U (FL)
Grambling State U (LA)
Hastings Coll (NE)
Hope International U (CA)
Howard Payne U (TX)
Jackson State U (MS)
Johnson State Coll (VT)
Judson Coll (AL)
Kennesaw State U (GA)
Liberty U (VA)
Luther Coll (IA)
Lyndon State Coll (VT)
Mansfield U of Pennsylvania (PA)
Maryville Coll (TN)
Mayville State U (ND)
McGill U (PQ, Canada)
McKendree Coll (IL)
McMurry U (TX)
Michigan State U (MI)
Millikin U (IL)
Minot State U (ND)
Mississippi Coll (MS)
Mississippi Valley State U (MS)
Montana State U–Billings (MT)
North Dakota State U (ND)
Northern Arizona U (AZ)
Northwest Nazarene U (ID)
Oklahoma Baptist U (OK)
Pace U (NY)
Plymouth State Coll (NH)
Point Park Coll (PA)
Prescott Coll (AZ)
Rivier Coll (NH)
Rocky Mountain Coll (MT)
Rust Coll (MS)
St. Ambrose U (IA)
Saint Mary's U of Minnesota (MN)
Samford U (AL)
San Diego State U (CA)
Seattle Pacific U (WA)
Simpson Coll and Graduate School (CA)
Southern Nazarene U (OK)
Southwestern Oklahoma State U (OK)
State U of NY at Albany (NY)
Union Coll (NE)
The U of Akron (OH)
The U of Arizona (AZ)
U of Central Florida (FL)
U of Georgia (GA)
U of Great Falls (MT)
U of Hawaii at Manoa (HI)
U of Illinois at Chicago (IL)
U of Maine at Farmington (ME)
U of Mary (ND)
U of Minnesota, Twin Cities Campus (MN)
The U of Montana–Missoula (MT)
U of Nebraska–Lincoln (NE)
U of Nevada, Reno (NV)
U of Northern Iowa (IA)
U of Puerto Rico, Cayey U Coll (PR)
U of Rio Grande (OH)
U of South Florida (FL)
U of Utah (UT)
U of Vermont (VT)
U of West Florida (FL)
U of Wisconsin–River Falls (WI)
U of Wisconsin–Superior (WI)
Utica Coll of Syracuse U (NY)
Valley City State U (ND)
Warner Southern Coll (FL)
Wartburg Coll (IA)
Washington U in St. Louis (MO)
Weber State U (UT)
Westminster Coll (UT)
Westmont Coll (CA)
William Penn U (IA)
York U (ON, Canada)
Youngstown State U (OH)

SOCIAL SCIENCES

Adams State Coll (CO)
Adelphi U (NY)
Adrian Coll (MI)
Alabama State U (AL)
Albertus Magnus Coll (CT)
Alma Coll (MI)
Alvernia Coll (PA)
Alverno Coll (WI)
American International Coll (MA)
Andrews U (MI)
Angelo State U (TX)
Anna Maria Coll (MA)
Appalachian State U (NC)
Aquinas Coll (MI)
Arizona State U West (AZ)
Asbury Coll (KY)
Ashland U (OH)
Augsburg Coll (MN)
Averett U (VA)
Azusa Pacific U (CA)
Ball State U (IN)
Bard Coll (NY)
Barton Coll (NC)
Bellevue U (NE)
Bemidji State U (MN)
Benedictine Coll (KS)
Benedictine U (IL)
Bennington Coll (VT)
Berry Coll (GA)
Bethany Coll of the Assemblies of God (CA)
Bethel Coll (IN)
Bethel Coll (KS)
Biola U (CA)
Bishop's U (PQ, Canada)
Black Hills State U (SD)

Bloomsburg U of Pennsylvania (PA)
Bluefield Coll (VA)
Bluefield State Coll (WV)
Blue Mountain Coll (MS)
Bluffton Coll (OH)
Boise State U (ID)
Bowling Green State U (OH)
Brescia U (KY)
Brock U (ON, Canada)
Buena Vista U (IA)
Caldwell Coll (NJ)
California Baptist U (CA)
California Inst of Technology (CA)
California Lutheran U (CA)
California Polytechnic State U, San Luis Obispo (CA)
California State Polytechnic U, Pomona (CA)
California State U, Chico (CA)
California State U, Los Angeles (CA)
California State U, Sacramento (CA)
California State U, San Bernardino (CA)
California State U, San Marcos (CA)
California State U, Stanislaus (CA)
California U of Pennsylvania (PA)
Calvin Coll (MI)
Campbellsville U (KY)
Campbell U (NC)
Cardinal Stritch U (WI)
Carnegie Mellon U (PA)
Carroll Coll (MT)
Carthage Coll (WI)
Castleton State Coll (VT)
Cazenovia Coll (NY)
Cedarville U (OH)
Centenary Coll of Louisiana (LA)
Central Coll (IA)
Central Connecticut State U (CT)
Central Michigan U (MI)
Chaminade U of Honolulu (HI)
Chapman U (CA)
Charleston Southern U (SC)
Chestnut Hill Coll (PA)
Cheyney U of Pennsylvania (PA)
Christian Heritage Coll (CA)
Clarion U of Pennsylvania (PA)
Clark Atlanta U (GA)
Clarkson U (NY)
Cleveland State U (OH)
Colgate U (NY)
Coll of Mount Saint Vincent (NY)
Coll of Saint Benedict (MN)
Coll of St. Catherine (MN)
Coll of Saint Mary (NE)
Coll of the Southwest (NM)
Colorado State U (CO)
Concordia Coll (NY)
Concordia U (MI)
Concordia U (MN)
Concordia U (NE)
Concordia U (OR)
Concordia U (QC, Canada)
Coppin State Coll (MD)
Cumberland U (TN)
Dana Coll (NE)
Daniel Webster Coll (NH)
David N. Myers U (OH)
Davis & Elkins Coll (WV)
Defiance Coll (OH)
Delta State U (MS)
DePaul U (IL)
Dickinson State U (ND)
Doane Coll (NE)
Dominican Coll (NY)
Dominican U (IL)
Dordt Coll (IA)
Dowling Coll (NY)
Drexel U (PA)
Duquesne U (PA)
Eastern Mennonite U (VA)
Eastern Michigan U (MI)
Eastern New Mexico U (NM)
Eastern Washington U (WA)
East-West U (IL)
Edgewood Coll (WI)
Edinboro U of Pennsylvania (PA)
Edward Waters Coll (FL)
Elizabeth City State U (NC)
Elizabethtown Coll (PA)
Elmira Coll (NY)
Emporia State U (KS)
Eugene Lang Coll, New School U (NY)
Eureka Coll (IL)
Evangel U (MO)
The Evergreen State Coll (WA)
Faulkner U (AL)
Fayetteville State U (NC)
Felician Coll (NJ)
Ferrum Coll (VA)
Flagler Coll (FL)
Florida A&M U (FL)
Florida Atlantic U (FL)
Florida Southern Coll (FL)
Florida State U (FL)
Fontbonne U (MO)
Fordham U (NY)
Fort Valley State U (GA)
Framingham State Coll (MA)
Freed-Hardeman U (TN)
Fresno Pacific U (CA)
Friends U (KS)
Frostburg State U (MD)
Gardner-Webb U (NC)
Georgia Southwestern State U (GA)
Gettysburg Coll (PA)
Goddard Coll (VT)
Governors State U (IL)
Graceland U (IA)
Grand Canyon U (AZ)
Grand Valley State U (MI)
Gustavus Adolphus Coll (MN)
Hamline U (MN)
Hampshire Coll (MA)
Hampton U (VA)
Harding U (AR)
Harvard U (MA)
Hawai'i Pacific U (HI)
Hofstra U (NY)
Holy Apostles Coll and Seminary (CT)
Holy Family Coll (PA)
Hope International U (CA)
Howard Payne U (TX)
Humboldt State U (CA)
Indiana Wesleyan U (IN)
Inter American U of PR, San Germán Campus (PR)
Iona Coll (NY)
Ithaca Coll (NY)
Jackson State U (MS)
James Madison U (VA)
John Brown U (AR)
Johns Hopkins U (MD)
Johnson C. Smith U (NC)
Judson Coll (IL)
Juniata Coll (PA)
Kansas State U (KS)
Kansas Wesleyan U (KS)
Keene State Coll (NH)
Kendall Coll (IL)
Kent State U (OH)
Keuka Coll (NY)
The King's U Coll (AB, Canada)
Lake Erie Coll (OH)
Lakeland Coll (WI)
Lake Superior State U (MI)
La Salle U (PA)
Lebanon Valley Coll (PA)
Lees-McRae Coll (NC)
Lee U (TN)
LeMoyne-Owen Coll (TN)
Lesley U (MA)
Lewis-Clark State Coll (ID)
Liberty U (VA)
Lincoln U (MO)
Lock Haven U of Pennsylvania (PA)
Long Island U, Brooklyn Campus (NY)
Long Island U, Southampton Coll (NY)
Long Island U, Southampton Coll, Friends World Program (NY)
Loyola U New Orleans (LA)
Lynchburg Coll (VA)
Lyndon State Coll (VT)
Lynn U (FL)
Mansfield U of Pennsylvania (PA)
Marlboro Coll (VT)
Mars Hill Coll (NC)
Marygrove Coll (MI)
Marylhurst U (OR)
Marywood U (PA)
Mayville State U (ND)
McKendree Coll (IL)
McPherson Coll (KS)
Medaille Coll (NY)
Memorial U of Newfoundland (NF, Canada)
Mercer U (GA)
Mercyhurst Coll (PA)
Mesa State Coll (CO)
Metropolitan State U (MN)
Michigan State U (MI)
Michigan Technological U (MI)
Middlebury Coll (VT)
Midland Lutheran Coll (NE)
Mills Coll (CA)
Minnesota State U, Mankato (MN)
Minot State U (ND)
Mississippi Coll (MS)
Mississippi U for Women (MS)
Missouri Baptist Coll (MO)
Montana State U–Northern (MT)
Montreat Coll (NC)
Moravian Coll (PA)
Morehead State U (KY)
Morris Coll (SC)
Mount Holyoke Coll (MA)
Mount St. Clare Coll (IA)
Mount Saint Mary Coll (NY)
Mount St. Mary's Coll (CA)
Mount Saint Vincent U (NS, Canada)
Mount Vernon Nazarene U (OH)
Muhlenberg Coll (PA)
Muskingum Coll (OH)
National-Louis U (IL)
Nazareth Coll of Rochester (NY)
New Coll of Florida (FL)
New York Inst of Technology (NY)
New York U (NY)
Niagara U (NY)
North Carolina Ag and Tech State U (NC)
North Central Coll (IL)
North Dakota State U (ND)
Northern Arizona U (AZ)
Northern Illinois U (IL)
Northern Kentucky U (KY)
Northern Michigan U (MI)
North Georgia Coll & State U (GA)
Northland Coll (WI)
North Park U (IL)
Northwest Christian Coll (OR)
Northwest Coll (WA)
Northwestern Coll (MN)
Northwestern Oklahoma State U (OK)
Northwestern State U of Louisiana (LA)
Northwest Missouri State U (MO)
Northwest Nazarene U (ID)
Notre Dame de Namur U (CA)
Nyack Coll (NY)
Oakland City U (IN)
Oakwood Coll (AL)
Ohio Dominican Coll (OH)
The Ohio State U (OH)
Ohio U (OH)
Oklahoma Baptist U (OK)
Oklahoma Panhandle State U (OK)
Oklahoma Wesleyan U (OK)
Olivet Coll (MI)
Olivet Nazarene U (IL)
Ouachita Baptist U (AR)
Our Lady of Holy Cross Coll (LA)
Our Lady of the Lake U of San Antonio (TX)
Pace U (NY)
Pacific Union Coll (CA)
Peru State Coll (NE)
Pfeiffer U (NC)
Piedmont Coll (GA)
Pikeville Coll (KY)
Pittsburg State U (KS)
Point Loma Nazarene U (CA)
Point Park Coll (PA)
Portland State U (OR)
Presbyterian Coll (SC)
Providence Coll (RI)
Providence Coll and Theological Seminary (MB, Canada)
Puget Sound Christian Coll (WA)
Purdue U (IN)
Quinnipiac U (CT)
Radford U (VA)
Ramapo Coll of New Jersey (NJ)
Rhode Island Coll (RI)
Richmond, The American International U in London(United Kingdom)
Robert Morris U (PA)
Roberts Wesleyan Coll (NY)
Rockford Coll (IL)
Rockhurst U (MO)
Rocky Mountain Coll (AB, Canada)
Rogers State U (OK)
Roger Williams U (RI)
Roosevelt U (IL)
Rosemont Coll (PA)
St. Bonaventure U (NY)
St. Cloud State U (MN)
St. Edward's U (TX)
St. Francis Coll (NY)
St. Gregory's U (OK)
Saint John's U (MN)
St. John's U (NY)
Saint Joseph Coll (CT)
Saint Joseph's Coll (IN)
St. Joseph's Coll, New York (NY)
St. Joseph's Coll, Suffolk Campus (NY)
Saint Joseph's U (PA)
Saint Louis U (MO)
Saint Mary-of-the-Woods Coll (IN)
Saint Mary's Coll of Ave Maria U (MI)
Saint Mary's U of Minnesota (MN)
Saint Peter's Coll (NJ)
St. Thomas Aquinas Coll (NY)
Saint Xavier U (IL)
Salem State Coll (MA)
Samford U (AL)
San Diego State U (CA)
San Francisco State U (CA)
San Jose State U (CA)
Sarah Lawrence Coll (NY)
Shawnee State U (OH)
Sheldon Jackson Coll (AK)
Shimer Coll (IL)
Shorter Coll (GA)
Siena Heights U (MI)
Silver Lake Coll (WI)
Simpson Coll (IA)
Simpson Coll and Graduate School (CA)
Southern Connecticut State U (CT)
Southern Illinois U Carbondale (IL)
Southern Methodist U (TX)
Southern New Hampshire U (NH)
Southern Oregon U (OR)
Southern Utah U (UT)
Southern Wesleyan U (SC)
Southwest Baptist U (MO)
Southwestern Adventist U (TX)
Southwestern U (TX)
Spring Arbor U (MI)
Spring Hill Coll (AL)
State U of NY Coll at Old Westbury (NY)
State U of NY Empire State Coll (NY)
Stephen F. Austin State U (TX)
Stephens Coll (MO)
Stetson U (FL)
State U of NY at Stony Brook (NY)
Suffolk U (MA)
Sul Ross State U (TX)
Syracuse U (NY)
Tabor Coll (KS)
Taylor U (IN)
Texas A&M International U (TX)
Texas A&M U–Commerce (TX)
Texas Wesleyan U (TX)
Thomas Edison State Coll (NJ)
Thomas U (GA)
Tiffin U (OH)
Towson U (MD)
Trent U (ON, Canada)
Trevecca Nazarene U (TN)
Trinity International U (IL)
Trinity Western U (BC, Canada)
Tri-State U (IN)
Troy State U (AL)
Troy State U Dothan (AL)
Troy State U Montgomery (AL)
Union Coll (NE)
Union Coll (NY)
Union Inst & U (OH)
United States Air Force Academy (CO)
Université de Montréal (QC, Canada)
State U of NY at Buffalo (NY)
The U of Akron (OH)
U of Arkansas at Pine Bluff (AR)
U of Bridgeport (CT)
The U of British Columbia (BC, Canada)
U of Calif, Berkeley (CA)
U of Calif, Irvine (CA)
U of Calif, Riverside (CA)
U of Central Florida (FL)
U of Chicago (IL)
U of Cincinnati (OH)
U of Denver (CO)
The U of Findlay (OH)
U of Great Falls (MT)
U of Hawaii–West Oahu (HI)
U of Houston–Victoria (TX)
The U of Iowa (IA)
U of Kentucky (KY)
U of La Verne (CA)
The U of Lethbridge (AB, Canada)
The U of Maine at Augusta (ME)
U of Maine at Fort Kent (ME)
U of Mary (ND)
U of Maryland Eastern Shore (MD)
U of Maryland University Coll (MD)
U of Michigan (MI)
U of Michigan–Dearborn (MI)
U of Michigan–Flint (MI)
U of Minnesota, Morris (MN)
U of Missouri–St. Louis (MO)
U of Mobile (AL)
The U of Montana–Missoula (MT)
Western Montana Coll of The U of Montana (MT)
U of Montevallo (AL)
U of Nevada, Las Vegas (NV)
U of New England (ME)
U of North Dakota (ND)
U of Northern Colorado (CO)
U of North Texas (TX)
U of Ottawa (ON, Canada)
U of Pittsburgh (PA)
U of Pittsburgh at Bradford (PA)
U of Pittsburgh at Greensburg (PA)
U of Pittsburgh at Johnstown (PA)
U of Puerto Rico, Cayey U Coll (PR)
U of Regina (SK, Canada)
U of Rio Grande (OH)
U of St. Thomas (MN)
U of Sioux Falls (SD)
U of Southern Colorado (CO)
U of Southern Indiana (IN)
U of Southern Maine (ME)
U of South Florida (FL)
The U of Tampa (FL)
U of the Ozarks (AR)
U of the Pacific (CA)
U of the South (TN)
U of the Virgin Islands (VI)
U of Utah (UT)
U of Washington (WA)
U of West Florida (FL)
U of Windsor (ON, Canada)
U of Wisconsin–Madison (WI)
U of Wisconsin–Platteville (WI)
U of Wisconsin–River Falls (WI)
U of Wisconsin–Stevens Point (WI)
U of Wisconsin–Superior (WI)
U of Wyoming (WY)
Upper Iowa U (IA)
Utica Coll of Syracuse U (NY)
Valley City State U (ND)
Vanguard U of Southern California (CA)
Virginia Wesleyan Coll (VA)
Warner Pacific Coll (OR)
Warner Southern Coll (FL)
Washington State U (WA)
Washington U in St. Louis (MO)
Wayland Baptist U (TX)
Waynesburg Coll (PA)
Wayne State Coll (NE)
Webster U (MO)
Wesleyan Coll (GA)
Wesleyan U (CT)
West Chester U of Pennsylvania (PA)
Western Baptist Coll (OR)
Western Carolina U (NC)
Western Connecticut State U (CT)
Western Kentucky U (KY)
Western Oregon U (OR)
Western State Coll of Colorado (CO)
Westfield State Coll (MA)
West Liberty State Coll (WV)
Westminster Coll (UT)
Westmont Coll (CA)
West Texas A&M U (TX)
Widener U (PA)
Wiley Coll (TX)
William Carey Coll (MS)
William Paterson U of New Jersey (NJ)
William Tyndale Coll (MI)
Wilmington Coll (OH)
Wilson Coll (PA)
Wingate U (NC)
Winona State U (MN)
Winston-Salem State U (NC)
Wisconsin Lutheran Coll (WI)
Wittenberg U (OH)

Worcester Polytechnic Inst (MA)
York U (ON, Canada)
Youngstown State U (OH)

SOCIAL SCIENCES AND HISTORY RELATED

Bethel Coll (KS)
Boston U (MA)
Colby-Sawyer Coll (NH)
The Colorado Coll (CO)
Georgetown U (DC)
Marywood U (PA)
Mid-Continent Coll (KY)
Nebraska Wesleyan U (NE)
Northwestern U (IL)
Plymouth State Coll (NH)
Queens Coll of the City U of NY (NY)
Saint Mary's U of Minnesota (MN)
San Diego State U (CA)
Skidmore Coll (NY)
Towson U (MD)
The U of Alabama at Birmingham (AL)
U of Hawaii at Manoa (HI)
U of Massachusetts Amherst (MA)
U of Miami (FL)
U of Pittsburgh at Bradford (PA)

SOCIAL STUDIES EDUCATION

Abilene Christian U (TX)
Adams State Coll (CO)
Alverno Coll (WI)
Anderson U (IN)
Appalachian State U (NC)
Arkansas Tech U (AR)
Augustana Coll (SD)
Averett U (VA)
Baylor U (TX)
Bethany Coll (KS)
Bethel Coll (IN)
Bloomfield Coll (NJ)
Bloomsburg U of Pennsylvania (PA)
Boston U (MA)
Bowling Green State U (OH)
Brescia U (KY)
Bridgewater Coll (VA)
Brigham Young U (UT)
Cabrini Coll (PA)
Canisius Coll (NY)
Carlow Coll (PA)
Castleton State Coll (VT)
Cedarville U (OH)
Central Michigan U (MI)
Central Missouri State U (MO)
Central State U (OH)
Citadel, The Military Coll of South Carolina (SC)
Clarion U of Pennsylvania (PA)
Clearwater Christian Coll (FL)
Colby-Sawyer Coll (NH)
Coll of St. Catherine (MN)
Colorado State U (CO)
Concordia Coll (MN)
Concordia U (OR)
Crown Coll (MN)
Cumberland Coll (KY)
Daemen Coll (NY)
Dakota Wesleyan U (SD)
Duquesne U (PA)
East Carolina U (NC)
Eastern Michigan U (MI)
East Texas Baptist U (TX)
Edinboro U of Pennsylvania (PA)
Elmira Coll (NY)
Elon U (NC)
Erskine Coll (SC)
Franklin Coll of Indiana (IN)
George Fox U (OR)
Greensboro Coll (NC)
Greenville Coll (IL)
Gustavus Adolphus Coll (MN)
Hardin-Simmons U (TX)
Hastings Coll (NE)
Hofstra U (NY)
Holy Family Coll (PA)
Huston-Tillotson Coll (TX)
Illinois State U (IL)
Indiana State U (IN)
Indiana U Bloomington (IN)
Indiana U Northwest (IN)
Indiana U of Pennsylvania (PA)
Indiana U–Purdue U Fort Wayne (IN)
Indiana U–Purdue U Indianapolis (IN)
Indiana U South Bend (IN)
Indiana U Southeast (IN)
Indiana Wesleyan U (IN)
Ithaca Coll (NY)
Johnson State Coll (VT)
Juniata Coll (PA)
Kent State U (OH)
Kentucky State U (KY)
Keuka Coll (NY)
Le Moyne Coll (NY)
Limestone Coll (SC)
Lincoln U (PA)
Long Island U, C.W. Post Campus (NY)
Louisiana State U in Shreveport (LA)
Malone Coll (OH)
Manhattanville Coll (NY)
Mansfield U of Pennsylvania (PA)
Marymount Coll of Fordham U (NY)
McGill U (PQ, Canada)
McMurry U (TX)
Mercer U (GA)
Messiah Coll (PA)
Miami U (OH)
MidAmerica Nazarene U (KS)
Millersville U of Pennsylvania (PA)
Minnesota State U, Mankato (MN)
Minnesota State U Moorhead (MN)
Mississippi Coll (MS)
Molloy Coll (NY)
Mount Vernon Nazarene U (OH)
Nazareth Coll of Rochester (NY)
New York Inst of Technology (NY)
New York U (NY)
Niagara U (NY)
North Carolina State U (NC)
Northwestern Coll (MN)
Nova Southeastern U (FL)
Oakland City U (IN)
Ohio U (OH)
Ohio Valley Coll (WV)
Oklahoma Baptist U (OK)
Oklahoma Christian U of Science and Arts (OK)
Oral Roberts U (OK)
Pace U (NY)
Philadelphia Biblical U (PA)
Pikeville Coll (KY)
Pontifical Catholic U of Puerto Rico (PR)
Rocky Mountain Coll (MT)
Saint Augustine's Coll (NC)
St. John's U (NY)
Saint Joseph's Coll (ME)
St. Mary's U of San Antonio (TX)
St. Olaf Coll (MN)
Seton Hill Coll (PA)
Shaw U (NC)
Southeastern Coll of the Assemblies of God (FL)
Southeastern Louisiana U (LA)
Southeastern Oklahoma State U (OK)
Southeast Missouri State U (MO)
Southern Arkansas U–Magnolia (AR)
State U of NY Coll at Potsdam (NY)
State U of West Georgia (GA)
Syracuse U (NY)
Texas A&M International U (TX)
Texas Christian U (TX)
Texas Lutheran U (TX)
Texas Wesleyan U (TX)
Thomas More Coll (KY)
Tri-State U (IN)
The U of Akron (OH)
The U of Arizona (AZ)
U of Central Arkansas (AR)
U of Central Oklahoma (OK)
U of Charleston (WV)
U of Hawaii at Manoa (HI)
U of Indianapolis (IN)
The U of Iowa (IA)
U of Louisiana at Monroe (LA)
U of Maryland, Coll Park (MD)
U of Minnesota, Duluth (MN)
U of Mississippi (MS)
U of Nevada, Reno (NV)
U of New Orleans (LA)
U of Oklahoma (OK)
U of Pittsburgh at Johnstown (PA)
U of Puerto Rico, Cayey U Coll (PR)
U of St. Francis (IL)
U of St. Thomas (MN)
U of Southern Colorado (CO)
U of Toledo (OH)
U of Utah (UT)
U of Wisconsin–Eau Claire (WI)
U of Wisconsin–La Crosse (WI)
U of Wisconsin–River Falls (WI)
U of Wisconsin–Superior (WI)
Ursuline Coll (OH)
Utah State U (UT)
Utica Coll of Syracuse U (NY)
Virginia Intermont Coll (VA)
Viterbo U (WI)
Washington U in St. Louis (MO)
Wayne State U (MI)
Weber State U (UT)
Western Carolina U (NC)
Wheaton Coll (IL)
Wheeling Jesuit U (WV)
Winston-Salem State U (NC)
York U (ON, Canada)
Youngstown State U (OH)

SOCIAL WORK

Abilene Christian U (TX)
Adams State Coll (CO)
Adelphi U (NY)
Adrian Coll (MI)
Alabama State U (AL)
Albany State U (GA)
Alvernia Coll (PA)
Anderson U (IN)
Andrews U (MI)
Anna Maria Coll (MA)
Appalachian State U (NC)
Arizona State U (AZ)
Arizona State U West (AZ)
Arkansas Baptist Coll (AR)
Arkansas State U (AR)
Asbury Coll (KY)
Ashland U (OH)
Atlantic Union Coll (MA)
Auburn U (AL)
Augsburg Coll (MN)
Augustana Coll (SD)
Aurora U (IL)
Austin Peay State U (TN)
Avila Coll (MO)
Azusa Pacific U (CA)
Baldwin-Wallace Coll (OH)
Ball State U (IN)
Barton Coll (NC)
Bayamón Central U (PR)
Baylor U (TX)
Belmont U (TN)
Bemidji State U (MN)
Benedict Coll (SC)
Bennett Coll (NC)
Bethany Coll (KS)
Bethany Coll (WV)
Bethel Coll (KS)
Bethel Coll (MN)
Bloomsburg U of Pennsylvania (PA)
Bluffton Coll (OH)
Boise State U (ID)
Bowie State U (MD)
Bowling Green State U (OH)
Bradley U (IL)
Brescia U (KY)
Briar Cliff U (IA)
Bridgewater State Coll (MA)
Brigham Young U (UT)
Brigham Young U–Hawaii (HI)
Buena Vista U (IA)
Cabrini Coll (PA)
California State U, Chico (CA)
California State U, Fresno (CA)
California State U, Hayward (CA)
California State U, Long Beach (CA)
California State U, Los Angeles (CA)
California State U, Northridge (CA)
California State U, Sacramento (CA)
California State U, San Bernardino (CA)
California U of Pennsylvania (PA)
Calvin Coll (MI)
Campbellsville U (KY)
Campbell U (NC)
Capital U (OH)
Caribbean U (PR)
Carleton U (ON, Canada)
Carlow Coll (PA)
Carroll Coll (MT)
Carroll Coll (WI)
Carthage Coll (WI)
Castleton State Coll (VT)
The Catholic U of America (DC)
Cedar Crest Coll (PA)
Cedarville U (OH)
Central Christian Coll of the Bible (MO)
Central Connecticut State U (CT)
Central Michigan U (MI)
Central Missouri State U (MO)
Central State U (OH)
Chadron State Coll (NE)
Champlain Coll (VT)
Chapman U (CA)
Chatham Coll (PA)
Christopher Newport U (VA)
Clark Atlanta U (GA)
Clarke Coll (IA)
Cleveland State U (OH)
Coker Coll (SC)
Coll Misericordia (PA)
Coll of Mount St. Joseph (OH)
The Coll of New Rochelle (NY)
Coll of Saint Benedict (MN)
Coll of St. Catherine (MN)
The Coll of Saint Rose (NY)
The Coll of St. Scholastica (MN)
Coll of Staten Island of the City U of NY (NY)
Coll of the Ozarks (MO)
Colorado State U (CO)
Columbia Coll (MO)
Columbia Coll (SC)
Concord Coll (WV)
Concordia Coll (MN)
Concordia Coll (NY)
Concordia U (CA)
Concordia U (IL)
Concordia U (OR)
Concordia U Wisconsin (WI)
Coppin State Coll (MD)
Cornerstone U (MI)
Creighton U (NE)
Cumberland Coll (KY)
Daemen Coll (NY)
Dalhousie U (NS, Canada)
Dalton State Coll (GA)
Dana Coll (NE)
Defiance Coll (OH)
Delaware State U (DE)
Delta State U (MS)
DeSales U (PA)
Dickinson State U (ND)
Dillard U (LA)
Dominican Coll (NY)
Dordt Coll (IA)
D'Youville Coll (NY)
East Carolina U (NC)
East Central U (OK)
Eastern Connecticut State U (CT)
Eastern Kentucky U (KY)
Eastern Mennonite U (VA)
Eastern Michigan U (MI)
Eastern Nazarene Coll (MA)
Eastern U (PA)
Eastern Washington U (WA)
East Tennessee State U (TN)
Edinboro U of Pennsylvania (PA)
Edward Waters Coll (FL)
Elizabeth City State U (NC)
Elizabethtown Coll (PA)
Elmira Coll (NY)
Elms Coll (MA)
Evangel U (MO)
Ferris State U (MI)
Ferrum Coll (VA)
Florida A&M U (FL)
Florida Atlantic U (FL)
Florida International U (FL)
Florida State U (FL)
Fordham U (NY)
Fort Hays State U (KS)
Fort Valley State U (GA)
Franciscan U of Steubenville (OH)
Franklin Pierce Coll (NH)
Freed-Hardeman U (TN)
Fresno Pacific U (CA)
Frostburg State U (MD)
Gallaudet U (DC)
Gannon U (PA)
George Fox U (OR)
George Mason U (VA)
Georgian Court Coll (NJ)
Georgia State U (GA)
Gordon Coll (MA)
Goshen Coll (IN)
Governors State U (IL)
Grace Coll (IN)
Graceland U (IA)
Grambling State U (LA)
Grand Valley State U (MI)
Greenville Coll (IL)
Gwynedd-Mercy Coll (PA)
Hampton U (VA)
Harding U (AR)
Hardin-Simmons U (TX)
Hawai'i Pacific U (HI)
Henderson State U (AR)
Holy Family Coll (PA)
Hood Coll (MD)
Hope Coll (MI)
Hope International U (CA)
Howard Payne U (TX)
Howard U (DC)
Humboldt State U (CA)
Idaho State U (ID)
Illinois State U (IL)
Immaculata Coll (PA)
Indiana State U (IN)
Indiana U Bloomington (IN)
Indiana U East (IN)
Indiana U–Purdue U Indianapolis (IN)
Indiana Wesleyan U (IN)
Iona Coll (NY)
Iowa Wesleyan Coll (IA)
Jackson State U (MS)
Jacksonville State U (AL)
James Madison U (VA)
Johnson C. Smith U (NC)
Juniata Coll (PA)
Kansas State U (KS)
Kean U (NJ)
Kennesaw State U (GA)
Kentucky Christian Coll (KY)
Kentucky State U (KY)
Keuka Coll (NY)
Kutztown U of Pennsylvania (PA)
LaGrange Coll (GA)
Lakehead U (ON, Canada)
Lamar U (TX)
La Salle U (PA)
Laurentian U (ON, Canada)
Lehman Coll of the City U of NY (NY)
LeMoyne-Owen Coll (TN)
Lewis-Clark State Coll (ID)
Lewis U (IL)
Limestone Coll (SC)
Lincoln Memorial U (TN)
Lincoln U (PA)
Lindenwood U (MO)
Lindsey Wilson Coll (KY)
Lipscomb U (TN)
Lock Haven U of Pennsylvania (PA)
Long Island U, Brooklyn Campus (NY)
Long Island U, C.W. Post Campus (NY)
Long Island U, Southampton Coll, Friends World Program (NY)
Longwood Coll (VA)
Loras Coll (IA)
Louisiana Coll (LA)
Lourdes Coll (OH)
Loyola U Chicago (IL)
Lubbock Christian U (TX)
Luther Coll (IA)
MacMurray Coll (IL)
Malone Coll (OH)
Manchester Coll (IN)
Mansfield U of Pennsylvania (PA)
Marian Coll of Fond du Lac (WI)
Marist Coll (NY)
Marquette U (WI)
Marshall U (WV)
Mars Hill Coll (NC)
Mary Baldwin Coll (VA)
Marygrove Coll (MI)
Marymount Coll of Fordham U (NY)
Marywood U (PA)
Massachusetts Coll of Liberal Arts (MA)
McGill U (PQ, Canada)
McKendree Coll (IL)
McMaster U (ON, Canada)
Memorial U of Newfoundland (NF, Canada)
Mercy Coll (NY)
Mercyhurst Coll (PA)
Meredith Coll (NC)
Messiah Coll (PA)
Methodist Coll (NC)
Metropolitan State Coll of Denver (CO)
Metropolitan State U (MN)
Miami U (OH)
Michigan State U (MI)
Middle Tennessee State U (TN)
Midwestern State U (TX)
Millersville U of Pennsylvania (PA)
Minnesota State U, Mankato (MN)

Minnesota State U Moorhead (MN)
Minot State U (ND)
Mississippi Coll (MS)
Mississippi State U (MS)
Mississippi Valley State U (MS)
Missouri Western State Coll (MO)
Molloy Coll (NY)
Monmouth U (NJ)
Morehead State U (KY)
Morgan State U (MD)
Mountain State U (WV)
Mount Mary Coll (WI)
Mount Mercy Coll (IA)
Mount Vernon Nazarene U (OH)
Murray State U (KY)
Nazareth Coll of Rochester (NY)
Nebraska Wesleyan U (NE)
New Mexico Highlands U (NM)
New Mexico State U (NM)
New York U (NY)
Niagara U (NY)
Norfolk State U (VA)
North Carolina Ag and Tech State U (NC)
North Carolina Central U (NC)
North Carolina State U (NC)
Northeastern Illinois U (IL)
Northeastern State U (OK)
Northern Arizona U (AZ)
Northern Kentucky U (KY)
Northern Michigan U (MI)
Northwestern Coll (IA)
Northwestern Oklahoma State U (OK)
Northwestern State U of Louisiana (LA)
Northwest Nazarene U (ID)
Nyack Coll (NY)
Oakwood Coll (AL)
Oglethorpe U (GA)
Ohio Dominican Coll (OH)
The Ohio State U (OH)
Ohio U (OH)
Okanagan U Coll (BC, Canada)
Oklahoma Baptist U (OK)
Oral Roberts U (OK)
Our Lady of the Lake U of San Antonio (TX)
Pacific Lutheran U (WA)
Pacific Union Coll (CA)
Pacific U (OR)
Philadelphia Biblical U (PA)
Philander Smith Coll (AR)
Pittsburg State U (KS)
Plattsburgh State U of NY (NY)
Plymouth State Coll (NH)
Point Loma Nazarene U (CA)
Pontifical Catholic U of Puerto Rico (PR)
Prairie View A&M U (TX)
Presentation Coll (SD)
Providence Coll (RI)
Purdue U Calumet (IN)
Quincy U (IL)
Radford U (VA)
Ramapo Coll of New Jersey (NJ)
Redeemer U Coll (ON, Canada)
Reformed Bible Coll (MI)
Regis Coll (MA)
Rhode Island Coll (RI)
The Richard Stockton Coll of New Jersey (NJ)
Roberts Wesleyan Coll (NY)
Rochester Inst of Technology (NY)
Rockford Coll (IL)
Rust Coll (MS)
Sacred Heart U (CT)
Saginaw Valley State U (MI)
St. Augustine Coll (IL)
St. Cloud State U (MN)
St. Edward's U (TX)
St. Francis Coll (NY)
Saint Francis U (PA)
Saint John's U (MN)
Saint Joseph Coll (CT)
Saint Joseph's Coll (ME)
Saint Leo U (FL)
Saint Louis U (MO)
Saint Mary's Coll (IN)
St. Olaf Coll (MN)
St. Thomas U (NB, Canada)
Salem State Coll (MA)
Salisbury U (MD)
Salve Regina U (RI)
San Diego State U (CA)
San Francisco State U (CA)
San Jose State U (CA)
Savannah State U (GA)
Seattle U (WA)
Seton Hall U (NJ)
Seton Hill Coll (PA)
Shaw U (NC)
Shepherd Coll (WV)
Shippensburg U of Pennsylvania (PA)
Siena Coll (NY)
Siena Heights U (MI)
Skidmore Coll (NY)
Slippery Rock U of Pennsylvania (PA)
Sojourner-Douglass Coll (MD)
South Carolina State U (SC)
Southeastern Coll of the Assemblies of God (FL)
Southeastern Louisiana U (LA)
Southeast Missouri State U (MO)
Southern Adventist U (TN)
Southern Arkansas U–Magnolia (AR)
Southern Connecticut State U (CT)
Southern Illinois U Carbondale (IL)
Southern Illinois U Edwardsville (IL)
Southern Nazarene U (OK)
Southern U and A&M Coll (LA)
Southern Vermont Coll (VT)
Southwestern Adventist U (TX)
Southwestern Oklahoma State U (OK)
Southwest Missouri State U (MO)
Southwest State U (MN)
Southwest Texas State U (TX)
Spring Arbor U (MI)
State U of NY at Albany (NY)
State U of NY at New Paltz (NY)
State U of NY Coll at Brockport (NY)
State U of NY Coll at Buffalo (NY)
State U of NY Coll at Cortland (NY)
State U of NY Coll at Fredonia (NY)
Stephen F. Austin State U (TX)
State U of NY at Stony Brook (NY)
Suffolk U (MA)
Syracuse U (NY)
Talladega Coll (AL)
Tarleton State U (TX)
Taylor U (IN)
Taylor U, Fort Wayne Campus (IN)
Temple U (PA)
Tennessee State U (TN)
Tennessee Technological U (TN)
Texas A&M U–Commerce (TX)
Texas A&M U–Kingsville (TX)
Texas Christian U (TX)
Texas Coll (TX)
Texas Southern U (TX)
Texas Tech U (TX)
Thomas U (GA)
Troy State U (AL)
Tuskegee U (AL)
Union Coll (NE)
Union Inst & U (OH)
Union U (TN)
Université de Montréal (QC, Canada)
Université de Sherbrooke (PQ, Canada)
Université Laval (QC, Canada)
U Coll of the Cariboo (BC, Canada)
U Coll of the Fraser Valley (BC, Canada)
The U of Akron (OH)
The U of Alabama (AL)
The U of Alabama at Birmingham (AL)
U of Alaska Anchorage (AK)
U of Alaska Fairbanks (AK)
U of Arkansas (AR)
U of Arkansas at Little Rock (AR)
U of Arkansas at Pine Bluff (AR)
The U of British Columbia (BC, Canada)
U of Calgary (AB, Canada)
U of Calif, Berkeley (CA)
U of Central Florida (FL)
U of Cincinnati (OH)
The U of Findlay (OH)
U of Georgia (GA)
U of Hawaii at Manoa (HI)
U of Houston–Clear Lake (TX)
U of Illinois at Chicago (IL)
U of Illinois at Springfield (IL)
U of Indianapolis (IN)
The U of Iowa (IA)
U of Kansas (KS)
U of Kentucky (KY)
U of Louisiana at Monroe (LA)
U of Maine (ME)
U of Maine at Presque Isle (ME)
U of Manitoba (MB, Canada)
U of Mary (ND)
U of Mary Hardin-Baylor (TX)
U of Maryland, Baltimore County (MD)
U of Maryland Eastern Shore (MD)
U of Massachusetts Boston (MA)
The U of Memphis (TN)
U of Michigan–Flint (MI)
U of Mississippi (MS)
U of Missouri–Columbia (MO)
U of Missouri–St. Louis (MO)
The U of Montana–Missoula (MT)
U of Montevallo (AL)
U of Nebraska at Kearney (NE)
U of Nebraska at Omaha (NE)
U of Nevada, Las Vegas (NV)
U of Nevada, Reno (NV)
U of New Hampshire (NH)
U of North Alabama (AL)
The U of North Carolina at Charlotte (NC)
The U of North Carolina at Greensboro (NC)
The U of North Carolina at Pembroke (NC)
The U of North Carolina at Wilmington (NC)
U of North Dakota (ND)
U of Northern Iowa (IA)
U of North Texas (TX)
U of Oklahoma (OK)
U of Pittsburgh (PA)
U of Portland (OR)
U of Puerto Rico, Humacao U Coll (PR)
U of Regina (SK, Canada)
U of Rio Grande (OH)
U of St. Francis (IL)
U of Saint Francis (IN)
U of St. Thomas (MN)
U of Sioux Falls (SD)
U of South Dakota (SD)
U of Southern Colorado (CO)
U of Southern Indiana (IN)
U of Southern Maine (ME)
U of Southern Mississippi (MS)
U of South Florida (FL)
The U of Tennessee (TN)
The U of Tennessee at Chattanooga (TN)
The U of Tennessee at Martin (TN)
The U of Texas at Arlington (TX)
The U of Texas at Austin (TX)
The U of Texas at El Paso (TX)
The U of Texas–Pan American (TX)
U of the District of Columbia (DC)
U of the Virgin Islands (VI)
U of Toledo (OH)
U of Utah (UT)
U of Vermont (VT)
U of Victoria (BC, Canada)
U of Washington (WA)
U of Waterloo (ON, Canada)
The U of Western Ontario (ON, Canada)
U of West Florida (FL)
U of Windsor (ON, Canada)
U of Wisconsin–Eau Claire (WI)
U of Wisconsin–Green Bay (WI)
U of Wisconsin–Madison (WI)
U of Wisconsin–Milwaukee (WI)
U of Wisconsin–Oshkosh (WI)
U of Wisconsin–River Falls (WI)
U of Wisconsin–Superior (WI)
U of Wisconsin–Whitewater (WI)
U of Wyoming (WY)
Ursuline Coll (OH)
Utah State U (UT)
Valparaiso U (IN)
Virginia Commonwealth U (VA)
Virginia Intermont Coll (VA)
Virginia State U (VA)
Virginia Union U (VA)
Viterbo U (WI)
Walla Walla Coll (WA)
Warner Pacific Coll (OR)
Warner Southern Coll (FL)
Warren Wilson Coll (NC)
Wartburg Coll (IA)
Washburn U of Topeka (KS)
Washington State U (WA)
Wayne State U (MI)
Weber State U (UT)
West Chester U of Pennsylvania (PA)
Western Carolina U (NC)
Western Connecticut State U (CT)
Western Illinois U (IL)
Western Kentucky U (KY)
Western Maryland Coll (MD)
Western Michigan U (MI)
Western New England Coll (MA)
West Texas A&M U (TX)
West Virginia State Coll (WV)
West Virginia U (WV)
Wheelock Coll (MA)
Whittier Coll (CA)
Wichita State U (KS)
Widener U (PA)
Wiley Coll (TX)
William Woods U (MO)
Wilmington Coll (OH)
Winona State U (MN)
Winthrop U (SC)
Wright State U (OH)
Xavier U (OH)
York Coll of the City U of New York (NY)
York U (ON, Canada)
Youngstown State U (OH)

SOCIOBIOLOGY

Beloit Coll (WI)
Cornell U (NY)
Hampshire Coll (MA)
Harvard U (MA)
Long Island U, Southampton Coll, Friends World Program (NY)
Tufts U (MA)

SOCIOLOGY

Abilene Christian U (TX)
Acadia U (NS, Canada)
Adams State Coll (CO)
Adelphi U (NY)
Adrian Coll (MI)
Agnes Scott Coll (GA)
Alabama State U (AL)
Albany State U (GA)
Albertson Coll of Idaho (ID)
Albertus Magnus Coll (CT)
Albion Coll (MI)
Albright Coll (PA)
Alcorn State U (MS)
Alderson-Broaddus Coll (WV)
Alfred U (NY)
Alliant International U (CA)
Alma Coll (MI)
American International Coll (MA)
American U (DC)
American U in Cairo(Egypt)
Amherst Coll (MA)
Anderson U (IN)
Andrews U (MI)
Angelo State U (TX)
Appalachian State U (NC)
Aquinas Coll (MI)
Arcadia U (PA)
Arizona State U (AZ)
Arizona State U West (AZ)
Arkansas State U (AR)
Arkansas Tech U (AR)
Asbury Coll (KY)
Ashland U (OH)
Assumption Coll (MA)
Athabasca U (AB, Canada)
Athens State U (AL)
Atlantic Baptist U (NB, Canada)
Atlantic Union Coll (MA)
Auburn U (AL)
Auburn U Montgomery (AL)
Augsburg Coll (MN)
Augustana Coll (IL)
Augustana Coll (SD)
Augusta State U (GA)
Aurora U (IL)
Austin Coll (TX)
Austin Peay State U (TN)
Averett U (VA)
Avila Coll (MO)
Azusa Pacific U (CA)
Baker U (KS)
Baldwin-Wallace Coll (OH)
Ball State U (IN)
Barber-Scotia Coll (NC)
Bard Coll (NY)
Barnard Coll (NY)
Barry U (FL)
Bates Coll (ME)
Baylor U (TX)
Bellarmine U (KY)
Bellevue U (NE)
Belmont Abbey Coll (NC)
Belmont U (TN)
Beloit Coll (WI)
Bemidji State U (MN)
Benedict Coll (SC)
Benedictine Coll (KS)
Benedictine U (IL)
Bennett Coll (NC)
Bennington Coll (VT)
Berea Coll (KY)
Baruch Coll of the City U of NY (NY)
Berry Coll (GA)
Bethany Coll (KS)
Bethel Coll (IN)
Bethune-Cookman Coll (FL)
Biola U (CA)
Birmingham-Southern Coll (AL)
Bishop's U (PQ, Canada)
Black Hills State U (SD)
Bloomfield Coll (NJ)
Bloomsburg U of Pennsylvania (PA)
Bluefield Coll (VA)
Bluffton Coll (OH)
Boise State U (ID)
Boston Coll (MA)
Boston U (MA)
Bowdoin Coll (ME)
Bowie State U (MD)
Bowling Green State U (OH)
Bradley U (IL)
Brandeis U (MA)
Brandon U (MB, Canada)
Brewton-Parker Coll (GA)
Briar Cliff U (IA)
Bridgewater Coll (VA)
Bridgewater State Coll (MA)
Brigham Young U (UT)
Brock U (ON, Canada)
Brooklyn Coll of the City U of NY (NY)
Brown U (RI)
Bryn Mawr Coll (PA)
Bucknell U (PA)
Butler U (IN)
Cabrini Coll (PA)
Caldwell Coll (NJ)
California Lutheran U (CA)
California State Polytechnic U, Pomona (CA)
California State U, Bakersfield (CA)
California State U, Chico (CA)
California State U, Dominguez Hills (CA)
California State U, Fresno (CA)
California State U, Fullerton (CA)
California State U, Hayward (CA)
California State U, Long Beach (CA)
California State U, Los Angeles (CA)
California State U, Northridge (CA)
California State U, Sacramento (CA)
California State U, San Bernardino (CA)
California State U, San Marcos (CA)
California State U, Stanislaus (CA)
California U of Pennsylvania (PA)
Calvin Coll (MI)
Cameron U (OK)
Campbellsville U (KY)
Canisius Coll (NY)
Capital U (OH)
Cardinal Stritch U (WI)
Carleton Coll (MN)
Carleton U (ON, Canada)
Carlow Coll (PA)
Carroll Coll (MT)
Carroll Coll (WI)
Carson-Newman Coll (TN)
Carthage Coll (WI)
Case Western Reserve U (OH)
Castleton State Coll (VT)
Catawba Coll (NC)
The Catholic U of America (DC)
Cedar Crest Coll (PA)
Cedarville U (OH)
Centenary Coll (NJ)
Centenary Coll of Louisiana (LA)
Central Coll (IA)
Central Connecticut State U (CT)
Central Methodist Coll (MO)
Central Michigan U (MI)
Central Missouri State U (MO)
Central State U (OH)
Central Washington U (WA)
Centre Coll (KY)
Chadron State Coll (NE)
Chapman U (CA)
Charleston Southern U (SC)

Chestnut Hill Coll (PA)
Cheyney U of Pennsylvania (PA)
Chicago State U (IL)
Christopher Newport U (VA)
City Coll of the City U of NY (NY)
Claflin U (SC)
Clarion U of Pennsylvania (PA)
Clark Atlanta U (GA)
Clarke Coll (IA)
Clarkson U (NY)
Clark U (MA)
Clemson U (SC)
Cleveland State U (OH)
Coastal Carolina U (SC)
Coe Coll (IA)
Coker Coll (SC)
Colby Coll (ME)
Colgate U (NY)
Coll of Charleston (SC)
Coll of Mount St. Joseph (OH)
Coll of Mount Saint Vincent (NY)
The Coll of New Jersey (NJ)
The Coll of New Rochelle (NY)
Coll of Saint Benedict (MN)
Coll of St. Catherine (MN)
Coll of Saint Elizabeth (NJ)
The Coll of Saint Rose (NY)
The Coll of Southeastern Europe, The American U of Athens(Greece)
Coll of Staten Island of the City U of NY (NY)
Coll of the Holy Cross (MA)
Coll of the Ozarks (MO)
The Coll of William and Mary (VA)
The Coll of Wooster (OH)
The Colorado Coll (CO)
Colorado State U (CO)
Columbia Coll (MO)
Columbia Coll (NY)
Columbia Coll (SC)
Columbia U, School of General Studies (NY)
Columbus State U (GA)
Concord Coll (WV)
Concordia Coll (MN)
Concordia U (IL)
Concordia U (MI)
Concordia U (MN)
Concordia U (NE)
Concordia U (QC, Canada)
Connecticut Coll (CT)
Converse Coll (SC)
Cornell Coll (IA)
Cornell U (NY)
Cornerstone U (MI)
Covenant Coll (GA)
Creighton U (NE)
Culver-Stockton Coll (MO)
Cumberland U (TN)
Curry Coll (MA)
Dakota Wesleyan U (SD)
Dalhousie U (NS, Canada)
Dallas Baptist U (TX)
Dana Coll (NE)
Dartmouth Coll (NH)
Davidson Coll (NC)
Davis & Elkins Coll (WV)
Delaware State U (DE)
Denison U (OH)
DePaul U (IL)
DePauw U (IN)
Dickinson Coll (PA)
Dillard U (LA)
Doane Coll (NE)
Dominican U (IL)
Dordt Coll (IA)
Dowling Coll (NY)
Drake U (IA)
Drew U (NJ)
Drexel U (PA)
Drury U (MO)
Duke U (NC)
Duquesne U (PA)
D'Youville Coll (NY)
Earlham Coll (IN)
East Carolina U (NC)
East Central U (OK)
Eastern Connecticut State U (CT)
Eastern Illinois U (IL)
Eastern Kentucky U (KY)
Eastern Mennonite U (VA)
Eastern Michigan U (MI)
Eastern Nazarene Coll (MA)
Eastern New Mexico U (NM)
Eastern Oregon U (OR)
Eastern U (PA)
Eastern Washington U (WA)
East Stroudsburg U of Pennsylvania (PA)
East Tennessee State U (TN)
East Texas Baptist U (TX)
East-West U (IL)
Eckerd Coll (FL)
Edgewood Coll (WI)
Edinboro U of Pennsylvania (PA)
Edward Waters Coll (FL)
Elizabeth City State U (NC)
Elizabethtown Coll (PA)
Elmhurst Coll (IL)
Elmira Coll (NY)
Elms Coll (MA)
Elon U (NC)
Emmanuel Coll (MA)
Emory & Henry Coll (VA)
Emory U (GA)
Emporia State U (KS)
Eugene Lang Coll, New School U (NY)
Eureka Coll (IL)
Evangel U (MO)
The Evergreen State Coll (WA)
Excelsior Coll (NY)
Fairfield U (CT)
Fairleigh Dickinson U, Florham-Madison Campus (NJ)
Fairleigh Dickinson U, Teaneck-Hackensack Campus (NJ)
Fairmont State Coll (WV)
Fayetteville State U (NC)
Felician Coll (NJ)
Fisk U (TN)
Fitchburg State Coll (MA)
Flagler Coll (FL)
Florida A&M U (FL)
Florida Atlantic U (FL)
Florida International U (FL)
Florida Southern Coll (FL)
Florida State U (FL)
Fordham U (NY)
Fort Hays State U (KS)
Fort Lewis Coll (CO)
Fort Valley State U (GA)
Framingham State Coll (MA)
Franciscan U of Steubenville (OH)
Francis Marion U (SC)
Franklin and Marshall Coll (PA)
Franklin Coll of Indiana (IN)
Franklin Pierce Coll (NH)
Friends U (KS)
Frostburg State U (MD)
Furman U (SC)
Gallaudet U (DC)
Gardner-Webb U (NC)
Geneva Coll (PA)
George Fox U (OR)
George Mason U (VA)
Georgetown Coll (KY)
Georgetown U (DC)
The George Washington U (DC)
Georgia Coll and State U (GA)
Georgian Court Coll (NJ)
Georgia Southern U (GA)
Georgia Southwestern State U (GA)
Georgia State U (GA)
Gettysburg Coll (PA)
Goddard Coll (VT)
Gonzaga U (WA)
Gordon Coll (MA)
Goshen Coll (IN)
Goucher Coll (MD)
Grace Coll (IN)
Graceland U (IA)
Grambling State U (LA)
Grand Canyon U (AZ)
Grand Valley State U (MI)
Greensboro Coll (NC)
Greenville Coll (IL)
Grinnell Coll (IA)
Grove City Coll (PA)
Guilford Coll (NC)
Gustavus Adolphus Coll (MN)
Gwynedd-Mercy Coll (PA)
Hamilton Coll (NY)
Hamline U (MN)
Hampshire Coll (MA)
Hampton U (VA)
Hanover Coll (IN)
Hardin-Simmons U (TX)
Hartwick Coll (NY)
Harvard U (MA)
Hastings Coll (NE)
Haverford Coll (PA)
Hawai'i Pacific U (HI)
Henderson State U (AR)
Hendrix Coll (AR)
High Point U (NC)
Hillsdale Coll (MI)
Hiram Coll (OH)
Hobart and William Smith Colls (NY)
Hofstra U (NY)
Hollins U (VA)
Holy Family Coll (PA)
Holy Names Coll (CA)
Hood Coll (MD)
Hope Coll (MI)
Houghton Coll (NY)
Houston Baptist U (TX)
Howard Payne U (TX)
Howard U (DC)
Humboldt State U (CA)
Hunter Coll of the City U of NY (NY)
Huntington Coll (IN)
Huston-Tillotson Coll (TX)
Idaho State U (ID)
Illinois Coll (IL)
Illinois State U (IL)
Illinois Wesleyan U (IL)
Immaculata Coll (PA)
Indiana State U (IN)
Indiana U Bloomington (IN)
Indiana U East (IN)
Indiana U Kokomo (IN)
Indiana U Northwest (IN)
Indiana U of Pennsylvania (PA)
Indiana U–Purdue U Fort Wayne (IN)
Indiana U–Purdue U Indianapolis (IN)
Indiana U South Bend (IN)
Indiana U Southeast (IN)
Indiana Wesleyan U (IN)
Inter American U of PR, San Germán Campus (PR)
Iona Coll (NY)
Iowa State U of Science and Technology (IA)
Ithaca Coll (NY)
Jackson State U (MS)
Jacksonville State U (AL)
Jacksonville U (FL)
James Madison U (VA)
Jarvis Christian Coll (TX)
John Carroll U (OH)
Johns Hopkins U (MD)
Johnson C. Smith U (NC)
Johnson State Coll (VT)
Judson Coll (IL)
Juniata Coll (PA)
Kalamazoo Coll (MI)
Kansas State U (KS)
Kansas Wesleyan U (KS)
Kean U (NJ)
Keene State Coll (NH)
Kennesaw State U (GA)
Kent State U (OH)
Kentucky State U (KY)
Kentucky Wesleyan Coll (KY)
Kenyon Coll (OH)
Keuka Coll (NY)
King's Coll (PA)
The King's U Coll (AB, Canada)
Knox Coll (IL)
Kutztown U of Pennsylvania (PA)
Lafayette Coll (PA)
Lake Erie Coll (OH)
Lake Forest Coll (IL)
Lakehead U (ON, Canada)
Lakeland Coll (WI)
Lake Superior State U (MI)
Lamar U (TX)
Lambuth U (TN)
Lander U (SC)
La Roche Coll (PA)
La Salle U (PA)
Lasell Coll (MA)
Laurentian U (ON, Canada)
Lees-McRae Coll (NC)
Lee U (TN)
Lehigh U (PA)
Lehman Coll of the City U of NY (NY)
Le Moyne Coll (NY)
LeMoyne-Owen Coll (TN)
Lenoir-Rhyne Coll (NC)
Lewis & Clark Coll (OR)
Lewis U (IL)
Lincoln U (MO)
Lincoln U (PA)
Lindenwood U (MO)
Linfield Coll (OR)
Lock Haven U of Pennsylvania (PA)
Long Island U, Brooklyn Campus (NY)
Long Island U, C.W. Post Campus (NY)
Long Island U, Southampton Coll (NY)
Long Island U, Southampton Coll, Friends World Program (NY)
Longwood Coll (VA)
Loras Coll (IA)
Louisiana Coll (LA)
Louisiana State U and A&M Coll (LA)
Louisiana State U in Shreveport (LA)
Louisiana Tech U (LA)
Lourdes Coll (OH)
Loyola Coll in Maryland (MD)
Loyola Marymount U (CA)
Loyola U Chicago (IL)
Loyola U New Orleans (LA)
Luther Coll (IA)
Lycoming Coll (PA)
Lynchburg Coll (VA)
Macalester Coll (MN)
Malaspina U-Coll (BC, Canada)
Manchester Coll (IN)
Manhattan Coll (NY)
Manhattanville Coll (NY)
Mansfield U of Pennsylvania (PA)
Marian Coll (IN)
Marlboro Coll (VT)
Marquette U (WI)
Marshall U (WV)
Mars Hill Coll (NC)
Mary Baldwin Coll (VA)
Marymount Coll of Fordham U (NY)
Marymount Manhattan Coll (NY)
Marymount U (VA)
Maryville Coll (TN)
Maryville U of Saint Louis (MO)
Mary Washington Coll (VA)
Massachusetts Coll of Liberal Arts (MA)
McGill U (PQ, Canada)
McKendree Coll (IL)
McMaster U (ON, Canada)
McMurry U (TX)
McNeese State U (LA)
McPherson Coll (KS)
Memorial U of Newfoundland (NF, Canada)
Mercer U (GA)
Mercy Coll (NY)
Mercyhurst Coll (PA)
Meredith Coll (NC)
Merrimack Coll (MA)
Mesa State Coll (CO)
Messiah Coll (PA)
Methodist Coll (NC)
Metropolitan State Coll of Denver (CO)
Miami U (OH)
Michigan State U (MI)
MidAmerica Nazarene U (KS)
Middlebury Coll (VT)
Middle Tennessee State U (TN)
Midland Lutheran Coll (NE)
Midwestern State U (TX)
Millersville U of Pennsylvania (PA)
Milligan Coll (TN)
Millikin U (IL)
Millsaps Coll (MS)
Mills Coll (CA)
Minnesota State U, Mankato (MN)
Minnesota State U Moorhead (MN)
Minot State U (ND)
Mississippi Coll (MS)
Mississippi State U (MS)
Mississippi Valley State U (MS)
Missouri Southern State Coll (MO)
Missouri Valley Coll (MO)
Molloy Coll (NY)
Monmouth Coll (IL)
Montana State U–Billings (MT)
Montana State U–Bozeman (MT)
Montclair State U (NJ)
Moravian Coll (PA)
Morehead State U (KY)
Morehouse Coll (GA)
Morgan State U (MD)
Morris Brown Coll (GA)
Morris Coll (SC)
Mount Allison U (NB, Canada)
Mount Holyoke Coll (MA)
Mount Mercy Coll (IA)
Mount Saint Mary Coll (NY)
Mount St. Mary's Coll (CA)
Mount Saint Mary's Coll and Seminary (MD)
Mount Saint Vincent U (NS, Canada)
Mount Union Coll (OH)
Mount Vernon Nazarene U (OH)
Muhlenberg Coll (PA)
Murray State U (KY)
Muskingum Coll (OH)
Nazareth Coll of Rochester (NY)
Nebraska Wesleyan U (NE)
Newberry Coll (SC)
New Coll of Florida (FL)
New England Coll (NH)
New Jersey City U (NJ)
Newman U (KS)
New Mexico Highlands U (NM)
New Mexico State U (NM)
New York Inst of Technology (NY)
New York U (NY)
Niagara U (NY)
Nicholls State U (LA)
Nipissing U (ON, Canada)
Norfolk State U (VA)
North Carolina Ag and Tech State U (NC)
North Carolina Central U (NC)
North Carolina State U (NC)
North Carolina Wesleyan Coll (NC)
North Central Coll (IL)
North Dakota State U (ND)
Northeastern Illinois U (IL)
Northeastern State U (OK)
Northeastern U (MA)
Northern Arizona U (AZ)
Northern Illinois U (IL)
Northern Kentucky U (KY)
Northern Michigan U (MI)
Northern State U (SD)
North Georgia Coll & State U (GA)
Northland Coll (WI)
North Park U (IL)
Northwestern Coll (IA)
Northwestern Oklahoma State U (OK)
Northwestern State U of Louisiana (LA)
Northwestern U (IL)
Northwest Missouri State U (MO)
Notre Dame de Namur U (CA)
Oakland U (MI)
Oberlin Coll (OH)
Occidental Coll (CA)
Oglethorpe U (GA)
Ohio Dominican Coll (OH)
Ohio Northern U (OH)
The Ohio State U (OH)
Ohio U (OH)
Ohio Wesleyan U (OH)
Oklahoma Baptist U (OK)
Oklahoma City U (OK)
Oklahoma State U (OK)
Old Dominion U (VA)
Olivet Coll (MI)
Oregon State U (OR)
Ottawa U (KS)
Otterbein Coll (OH)
Ouachita Baptist U (AR)
Our Lady of the Lake U of San Antonio (TX)
Pacific Lutheran U (WA)
Pacific Union Coll (CA)
Pacific U (OR)
Paine Coll (GA)
Park U (MO)
Penn State U Harrisburg Campus of the Capital Coll (PA)
Penn State U Univ Park Campus (PA)
Pepperdine U, Malibu (CA)
Peru State Coll (NE)
Pfeiffer U (NC)
Philander Smith Coll (AR)
Piedmont Coll (GA)
Pikeville Coll (KY)
Pittsburg State U (KS)
Pitzer Coll (CA)
Plattsburgh State U of NY (NY)
Point Loma Nazarene U (CA)
Pomona Coll (CA)
Pontifical Catholic U of Puerto Rico (PR)
Portland State U (OR)
Prairie View A&M U (TX)
Presbyterian Coll (SC)
Prescott Coll (AZ)
Princeton U (NJ)
Principia Coll (IL)
Providence Coll (RI)

Purchase Coll, State U of NY (NY)
Purdue U (IN)
Purdue U Calumet (IN)
Queens Coll of the City U of NY (NY)
Queen's U at Kingston (ON, Canada)
Quincy U (IL)
Quinnipiac U (CT)
Radford U (VA)
Ramapo Coll of New Jersey (NJ)
Randolph-Macon Coll (VA)
Randolph-Macon Woman's Coll (VA)
Redeemer U Coll (ON, Canada)
Reed Coll (OR)
Regis Coll (MA)
Regis U (CO)
Reinhardt Coll (GA)
Rhode Island Coll (RI)
Rhodes Coll (TN)
Rice U (TX)
The Richard Stockton Coll of New Jersey (NJ)
Richmond, The American International U in London(United Kingdom)
Rider U (NJ)
Ripon Coll (WI)
Rivier Coll (NH)
Roanoke Coll (VA)
Roberts Wesleyan Coll (NY)
Rockford Coll (IL)
Rockhurst U (MO)
Rocky Mountain Coll (MT)
Rollins Coll (FL)
Roosevelt U (IL)
Rosemont Coll (PA)
Rowan U (NJ)
Russell Sage Coll (NY)
Rust Coll (MS)
Rutgers, The State U of New Jersey, New Brunswick (NJ)
Sacred Heart U (CT)
Saginaw Valley State U (MI)
St. Ambrose U (IA)
Saint Anselm Coll (NH)
Saint Augustine's Coll (NC)
St. Bonaventure U (NY)
St. Cloud State U (MN)
St. Edward's U (TX)
St. Francis Coll (NY)
Saint Francis U (PA)
St. Francis Xavier U (NS, Canada)
St. John Fisher Coll (NY)
Saint John's U (MN)
St. John's U (NY)
Saint Joseph Coll (CT)
Saint Joseph's Coll (IN)
Saint Joseph's Coll (ME)
St. Joseph's Coll, Suffolk Campus (NY)
Saint Joseph's U (PA)
St. Lawrence U (NY)
Saint Leo U (FL)
Saint Louis U (MO)
Saint Mary Coll (KS)
Saint Mary's Coll (IN)
Saint Mary's Coll of Ave Maria U (MI)
Saint Mary's Coll of California (CA)
St. Mary's Coll of Maryland (MD)
Saint Mary's U (NS, Canada)
Saint Mary's U of Minnesota (MN)
St. Mary's U of San Antonio (TX)
Saint Michael's Coll (VT)
St. Norbert Coll (WI)
St. Olaf Coll (MN)
Saint Peter's Coll (NJ)
St. Thomas U (FL)
St. Thomas U (NB, Canada)
Saint Vincent Coll (PA)
Saint Xavier U (IL)
Salem Coll (NC)
Salem State Coll (MA)
Salisbury U (MD)
Salve Regina U (RI)
Samford U (AL)
Sam Houston State U (TX)
San Diego State U (CA)
San Francisco State U (CA)
San Jose State U (CA)
Santa Clara U (CA)
Sarah Lawrence Coll (NY)
Savannah State U (GA)
Scripps Coll (CA)
Seattle Pacific U (WA)
Seattle U (WA)
Seton Hall U (NJ)
Seton Hill Coll (PA)
Shaw U (NC)
Shenandoah U (VA)
Shepherd Coll (WV)
Shippensburg U of Pennsylvania (PA)
Shorter Coll (GA)
Siena Coll (NY)
Simmons Coll (MA)
Simon Fraser U (BC, Canada)
Simpson Coll (IA)
Skidmore Coll (NY)
Slippery Rock U of Pennsylvania (PA)
Smith Coll (MA)
Sojourner-Douglass Coll (MD)
Sonoma State U (CA)
South Carolina State U (SC)
South Dakota State U (SD)
Southeastern Louisiana U (LA)
Southeastern Oklahoma State U (OK)
Southeast Missouri State U (MO)
Southern Arkansas U–Magnolia (AR)
Southern Connecticut State U (CT)
Southern Illinois U Carbondale (IL)
Southern Illinois U Edwardsville (IL)
Southern Methodist U (TX)
Southern Nazarene U (OK)
Southern Oregon U (OR)
Southern U and A&M Coll (LA)
Southern Utah U (UT)
Southwest Baptist U (MO)
Southwestern U (TX)
Southwest Missouri State U (MO)
Southwest State U (MN)
Southwest Texas State U (TX)
Spelman Coll (GA)
Spring Arbor U (MI)
Springfield Coll (MA)
Stanford U (CA)
State U of NY at Albany (NY)
State U of NY at Binghamton (NY)
State U of NY at New Paltz (NY)
State U of NY at Oswego (NY)
State U of NY Coll at Brockport (NY)
State U of NY Coll at Buffalo (NY)
State U of NY Coll at Cortland (NY)
State U of NY Coll at Fredonia (NY)
State U of NY Coll at Geneseo (NY)
State U of NY Coll at Old Westbury (NY)
State U of NY Coll at Oneonta (NY)
State U of NY Coll at Potsdam (NY)
State U of NY Inst of Tech at Utica/Rome (NY)
State U of West Georgia (GA)
Stephen F. Austin State U (TX)
Stetson U (FL)
Stonehill Coll (MA)
State U of NY at Stony Brook (NY)
Suffolk U (MA)
Susquehanna U (PA)
Swarthmore Coll (PA)
Sweet Briar Coll (VA)
Syracuse U (NY)
Tabor Coll (KS)
Talladega Coll (AL)
Tarleton State U (TX)
Taylor U (IN)
Teikyo Post U (CT)
Temple U (PA)
Tennessee State U (TN)
Tennessee Technological U (TN)
Texas A&M International U (TX)
Texas A&M U (TX)
Texas A&M U–Commerce (TX)
Texas A&M U–Corpus Christi (TX)
Texas A&M U–Kingsville (TX)
Texas Christian U (TX)
Texas Coll (TX)
Texas Lutheran U (TX)
Texas Southern U (TX)
Texas Tech U (TX)
Texas Wesleyan U (TX)
Texas Woman's U (TX)
Thiel Coll (PA)
Thomas Edison State Coll (NJ)
Thomas More Coll (KY)
Thomas U (GA)
Tougaloo Coll (MS)
Touro Coll (NY)
Towson U (MD)
Transylvania U (KY)
Trent U (ON, Canada)
Trinity Christian Coll (IL)
Trinity Coll (CT)
Trinity International U (IL)
Trinity U (TX)
Troy State U (AL)
Troy State U Dothan (AL)
Truman State U (MO)
Tufts U (MA)
Tulane U (LA)
Tuskegee U (AL)
Union Coll (NY)
Union U (TN)
Université de Montréal (QC, Canada)
Université Laval (QC, Canada)
State U of NY at Buffalo (NY)
U Coll of Cape Breton (NS, Canada)
U Coll of the Cariboo (BC, Canada)
U Coll of the Fraser Valley (BC, Canada)
The U of Akron (OH)
The U of Alabama (AL)
The U of Alabama at Birmingham (AL)
The U of Alabama in Huntsville (AL)
U of Alaska Anchorage (AK)
U of Alaska Fairbanks (AK)
U of Alberta (AB, Canada)
The U of Arizona (AZ)
U of Arkansas (AR)
U of Arkansas at Little Rock (AR)
U of Arkansas at Pine Bluff (AR)
The U of British Columbia (BC, Canada)
U of Calgary (AB, Canada)
U of Calif, Berkeley (CA)
U of Calif, Davis (CA)
U of Calif, Irvine (CA)
U of Calif, Los Angeles (CA)
U of Calif, Riverside (CA)
U of Calif, San Diego (CA)
U of Calif, Santa Barbara (CA)
U of Calif, Santa Cruz (CA)
U of Central Arkansas (AR)
U of Central Florida (FL)
U of Central Oklahoma (OK)
U of Chicago (IL)
U of Cincinnati (OH)
U of Colorado at Boulder (CO)
U of Colorado at Colorado Springs (CO)
U of Colorado at Denver (CO)
U of Connecticut (CT)
U of Dayton (OH)
U of Delaware (DE)
U of Denver (CO)
U of Dubuque (IA)
U of Evansville (IN)
The U of Findlay (OH)
U of Florida (FL)
U of Georgia (GA)
U of Great Falls (MT)
U of Guelph (ON, Canada)
U of Hartford (CT)
U of Hawaii at Hilo (HI)
U of Hawaii at Manoa (HI)
U of Hawaii–West Oahu (HI)
U of Houston (TX)
U of Houston–Clear Lake (TX)
U of Idaho (ID)
U of Illinois at Chicago (IL)
U of Illinois at Springfield (IL)
U of Illinois at Urbana–Champaign (IL)
U of Indianapolis (IN)
The U of Iowa (IA)
U of Kansas (KS)
U of Kentucky (KY)
U of King's Coll (NS, Canada)
U of La Verne (CA)
The U of Lethbridge (AB, Canada)
U of Louisiana at Lafayette (LA)
U of Louisiana at Monroe (LA)
U of Louisville (KY)
U of Maine (ME)
U of Maine at Farmington (ME)
U of Maine at Presque Isle (ME)
U of Manitoba (MB, Canada)
U of Mary Hardin-Baylor (TX)
U of Maryland, Baltimore County (MD)
U of Maryland, Coll Park (MD)
U of Maryland Eastern Shore (MD)
U of Massachusetts Amherst (MA)
U of Massachusetts Boston (MA)
U of Massachusetts Dartmouth (MA)
U of Massachusetts Lowell (MA)
The U of Memphis (TN)
U of Miami (FL)
U of Michigan (MI)
U of Michigan–Dearborn (MI)
U of Michigan–Flint (MI)
U of Minnesota, Duluth (MN)
U of Minnesota, Morris (MN)
U of Minnesota, Twin Cities Campus (MN)
U of Mississippi (MS)
U of Missouri–Columbia (MO)
U of Missouri–Kansas City (MO)
U of Missouri–St. Louis (MO)
U of Mobile (AL)
The U of Montana–Missoula (MT)
U of Montevallo (AL)
U of Nebraska at Kearney (NE)
U of Nebraska at Omaha (NE)
U of Nebraska–Lincoln (NE)
U of Nevada, Las Vegas (NV)
U of Nevada, Reno (NV)
U of New Hampshire (NH)
U of New Mexico (NM)
U of New Orleans (LA)
U of North Alabama (AL)
The U of North Carolina at Asheville (NC)
The U of North Carolina at Chapel Hill (NC)
The U of North Carolina at Charlotte (NC)
The U of North Carolina at Greensboro (NC)
The U of North Carolina at Pembroke (NC)
The U of North Carolina at Wilmington (NC)
U of North Dakota (ND)
U of Northern Colorado (CO)
U of Northern Iowa (IA)
U of North Florida (FL)
U of North Texas (TX)
U of Notre Dame (IN)
U of Oklahoma (OK)
U of Oregon (OR)
U of Ottawa (ON, Canada)
U of Pennsylvania (PA)
U of Pittsburgh (PA)
U of Pittsburgh at Bradford (PA)
U of Pittsburgh at Johnstown (PA)
U of Portland (OR)
U of Prince Edward Island (PE, Canada)
U of Puerto Rico, Cayey U Coll (PR)
U of Puget Sound (WA)
U of Redlands (CA)
U of Regina (SK, Canada)
U of Rhode Island (RI)
U of Richmond (VA)
U of Rio Grande (OH)
U of St. Thomas (MN)
U of San Diego (CA)
U of San Francisco (CA)
U of Saskatchewan (SK, Canada)
U of Science and Arts of Oklahoma (OK)
The U of Scranton (PA)
U of Sioux Falls (SD)
U of South Alabama (AL)
U of South Carolina (SC)
U of South Carolina Aiken (SC)
U of South Carolina Spartanburg (SC)
U of South Dakota (SD)
U of Southern California (CA)
U of Southern Colorado (CO)
U of Southern Indiana (IN)
U of Southern Maine (ME)
U of South Florida (FL)
The U of Tampa (FL)
The U of Tennessee (TN)
The U of Tennessee at Chattanooga (TN)
The U of Tennessee at Martin (TN)
The U of Texas at Arlington (TX)
The U of Texas at Austin (TX)
The U of Texas at Brownsville (TX)
The U of Texas at Dallas (TX)
The U of Texas at El Paso (TX)
The U of Texas at San Antonio (TX)
The U of Texas at Tyler (TX)
The U of Texas of the Permian Basin (TX)
The U of Texas–Pan American (TX)
U of the District of Columbia (DC)
U of the Incarnate Word (TX)
U of the Ozarks (AR)
U of the Pacific (CA)
U of Toledo (OH)
U of Toronto (ON, Canada)
U of Tulsa (OK)
U of Utah (UT)
U of Vermont (VT)
U of Victoria (BC, Canada)
U of Virginia (VA)
The U of Virginia's Coll at Wise (VA)
U of Washington (WA)
U of Waterloo (ON, Canada)
The U of West Alabama (AL)
The U of Western Ontario (ON, Canada)
U of West Florida (FL)
U of Windsor (ON, Canada)
U of Wisconsin–Eau Claire (WI)
U of Wisconsin–La Crosse (WI)
U of Wisconsin–Madison (WI)
U of Wisconsin–Milwaukee (WI)
U of Wisconsin–Oshkosh (WI)
U of Wisconsin–Parkside (WI)
U of Wisconsin–River Falls (WI)
U of Wisconsin–Stevens Point (WI)
U of Wisconsin–Superior (WI)
U of Wisconsin–Whitewater (WI)
U of Wyoming (WY)
Upper Iowa U (IA)
Urbana U (OH)
Ursinus Coll (PA)
Ursuline Coll (OH)
Utah State U (UT)
Utica Coll of Syracuse U (NY)
Valdosta State U (GA)
Valparaiso U (IN)
Vanderbilt U (TN)
Vanguard U of Southern California (CA)
Vassar Coll (NY)
Villanova U (PA)
Virginia Commonwealth U (VA)
Virginia Polytechnic Inst and State U (VA)
Virginia State U (VA)
Virginia Union U (VA)
Virginia Wesleyan Coll (VA)
Viterbo U (WI)
Voorhees Coll (SC)
Wagner Coll (NY)
Wake Forest U (NC)
Walla Walla Coll (WA)
Walsh U (OH)
Warren Wilson Coll (NC)
Wartburg Coll (IA)
Washburn U of Topeka (KS)
Washington & Jefferson Coll (PA)
Washington and Lee U (VA)
Washington Coll (MD)
Washington State U (WA)
Waynesburg Coll (PA)
Wayne State Coll (NE)
Wayne State U (MI)
Weber State U (UT)
Webster U (MO)
Wellesley Coll (MA)
Wells Coll (NY)
Wesleyan Coll (GA)
Wesleyan U (CT)
West Chester U of Pennsylvania (PA)
Western Carolina U (NC)
Western Connecticut State U (CT)
Western Illinois U (IL)
Western Kentucky U (KY)
Western Maryland Coll (MD)
Western Michigan U (MI)
Western New England Coll (MA)
Western Oregon U (OR)
Western State Coll of Colorado (CO)
Western Washington U (WA)
Westfield State Coll (MA)
West Liberty State Coll (WV)
Westminster Coll (MO)
Westminster Coll (PA)
Westminster Coll (UT)
Westmont Coll (CA)
West Texas A&M U (TX)
West Virginia State Coll (WV)
West Virginia U (WV)
West Virginia Wesleyan Coll (WV)
Wheaton Coll (IL)
Wheaton Coll (MA)
Whitman Coll (WA)
Whittier Coll (CA)

Whitworth Coll (WA)
Wichita State U (KS)
Widener U (PA)
Wilberforce U (OH)
Wiley Coll (TX)
Wilfrid Laurier U (ON, Canada)
Wilkes U (PA)
Willamette U (OR)
William Paterson U of New Jersey (NJ)
William Penn U (IA)
Williams Coll (MA)
Wingate U (NC)
Winona State U (MN)
Winston-Salem State U (NC)
Winthrop U (SC)
Wittenberg U (OH)
Wofford Coll (SC)
Worcester State Coll (MA)
Wright State U (OH)
Xavier U (OH)
Xavier U of Louisiana (LA)
Yale U (CT)
Yeshiva U (NY)
York Coll of Pennsylvania (PA)
York Coll of the City U of New York (NY)
York U (ON, Canada)
Youngstown State U (OH)

SOCIO-PSYCHOLOGICAL SPORTS STUDIES
Greensboro Coll (NC)
Ithaca Coll (NY)
St. John Fisher Coll (NY)
U of Minnesota, Twin Cities Campus (MN)

SOIL CONSERVATION
Ball State U (IN)
California State Polytechnic U, Pomona (CA)
Colorado State U (CO)
The Ohio State U (OH)
U of Delaware (DE)
U of New Hampshire (NH)
The U of Tennessee at Martin (TN)
U of Wisconsin–Stevens Point (WI)

SOIL SCIENCES
Colorado State U (CO)
Cornell U (NY)
McGill U (PQ, Canada)
Michigan State U (MI)
New Mexico State U (NM)
North Dakota State U (ND)
Penn State U Univ Park Campus (PA)
The U of Arizona (AZ)
The U of British Columbia (BC, Canada)
U of Delaware (DE)
U of Florida (FL)
U of Georgia (GA)
U of Hawaii at Manoa (HI)
U of Idaho (ID)
U of Maine (ME)
U of Minnesota, Twin Cities Campus (MN)
U of Nebraska–Lincoln (NE)
U of Saskatchewan (SK, Canada)
U of Vermont (VT)
U of Wisconsin–River Falls (WI)
Utah State U (UT)
Washington State U (WA)

SOLAR TECHNOLOGY
Hampshire Coll (MA)

SOLID STATE AND LOW-TEMPERATURE PHYSICS
George Mason U (VA)

SOUTH ASIAN LANGUAGES
Northwestern U (IL)
Yale U (CT)

SOUTH ASIAN STUDIES
Barnard Coll (NY)
Brown U (RI)
The Coll of Wooster (OH)
Concordia U (QC, Canada)
Gettysburg Coll (PA)
Hampshire Coll (MA)
Harvard U (MA)
Long Island U, Southampton Coll, Friends World Program (NY)
Oakland U (MI)
U of Calif, Santa Cruz (CA)
U of Chicago (IL)
U of Hawaii at Manoa (HI)
U of Manitoba (MB, Canada)
U of Michigan (MI)
U of Minnesota, Twin Cities Campus (MN)
U of Missouri–Columbia (MO)
U of Pennsylvania (PA)
U of Toronto (ON, Canada)
U of Washington (WA)
Ursinus Coll (PA)

SOUTHEAST ASIAN STUDIES
Cornell U (NY)
Hampshire Coll (MA)
Harvard U (MA)
Long Island U, Southampton Coll, Friends World Program (NY)
Middlebury Coll (VT)
Tufts U (MA)
U of Calif, Berkeley (CA)
U of Calif, Los Angeles (CA)
U of Calif, Santa Cruz (CA)
U of Chicago (IL)
U of Hawaii at Manoa (HI)
U of Michigan (MI)
U of Washington (WA)
U of Wisconsin–Madison (WI)

SPANISH
Abilene Christian U (TX)
Adams State Coll (CO)
Adelphi U (NY)
Adrian Coll (MI)
Agnes Scott Coll (GA)
Alabama State U (AL)
Albany State U (GA)
Albertson Coll of Idaho (ID)
Albertus Magnus Coll (CT)
Albion Coll (MI)
Albright Coll (PA)
Alfred U (NY)
Allegheny Coll (PA)
Alma Coll (MI)
American International Coll (MA)
American U (DC)
Amherst Coll (MA)
Anderson Coll (SC)
Anderson U (IN)
Andrews U (MI)
Angelo State U (TX)
Appalachian State U (NC)
Aquinas Coll (MI)
Arcadia U (PA)
Arizona State U (AZ)
Arizona State U West (AZ)
Arkansas State U (AR)
Arkansas Tech U (AR)
Asbury Coll (KY)
Ashland U (OH)
Assumption Coll (MA)
Atlantic Union Coll (MA)
Auburn U (AL)
Augsburg Coll (MN)
Augustana Coll (IL)
Augustana Coll (SD)
Augusta State U (GA)
Austin Coll (TX)
Austin Peay State U (TN)
Azusa Pacific U (CA)
Baker U (KS)
Baldwin-Wallace Coll (OH)
Ball State U (IN)
Bard Coll (NY)
Barnard Coll (NY)
Barry U (FL)
Bates Coll (ME)
Baylor U (TX)
Bellarmine U (KY)
Bellevue U (NE)
Belmont U (TN)
Beloit Coll (WI)
Bemidji State U (MN)
Benedictine Coll (KS)
Benedictine U (IL)
Bennington Coll (VT)
Berea Coll (KY)
Baruch Coll of the City U of NY (NY)
Berry Coll (GA)
Bethany Coll (WV)
Bethel Coll (KS)
Bethel Coll (MN)
Biola U (CA)
Birmingham-Southern Coll (AL)
Bishop's U (PQ, Canada)
Blackburn Coll (IL)
Black Hills State U (SD)
Bloomsburg U of Pennsylvania (PA)
Blue Mountain Coll (MS)
Bluffton Coll (OH)
Boise State U (ID)
Boston U (MA)
Bowdoin Coll (ME)
Bowling Green State U (OH)
Bradley U (IL)
Brandeis U (MA)
Brescia U (KY)
Briar Cliff U (IA)
Bridgewater Coll (VA)
Bridgewater State Coll (MA)
Brigham Young U (UT)
Brock U (ON, Canada)
Brooklyn Coll of the City U of NY (NY)
Brown U (RI)
Bryn Mawr Coll (PA)
Bucknell U (PA)
Buena Vista U (IA)
Butler U (IN)
Cabrini Coll (PA)
Caldwell Coll (NJ)
California Lutheran U (CA)
California State Polytechnic U, Pomona (CA)
California State U, Bakersfield (CA)
California State U, Chico (CA)
California State U, Dominguez Hills (CA)
California State U, Fresno (CA)
California State U, Fullerton (CA)
California State U, Hayward (CA)
California State U, Long Beach (CA)
California State U, Los Angeles (CA)
California State U, Northridge (CA)
California State U, Sacramento (CA)
California State U, San Bernardino (CA)
California State U, San Marcos (CA)
California State U, Stanislaus (CA)
California U of Pennsylvania (PA)
Calvin Coll (MI)
Campbell U (NC)
Canisius Coll (NY)
Capital U (OH)
Cardinal Stritch U (WI)
Carleton Coll (MN)
Carleton U (ON, Canada)
Carnegie Mellon U (PA)
Carroll Coll (MT)
Carroll Coll (WI)
Carson-Newman Coll (TN)
Carthage Coll (WI)
Case Western Reserve U (OH)
Castleton State Coll (VT)
Catawba Coll (NC)
The Catholic U of America (DC)
Cedar Crest Coll (PA)
Cedarville U (OH)
Centenary Coll of Louisiana (LA)
Central Coll (IA)
Central Connecticut State U (CT)
Central Methodist Coll (MO)
Central Michigan U (MI)
Central Missouri State U (MO)
Centre Coll (KY)
Chadron State Coll (NE)
Chapman U (CA)
Charleston Southern U (SC)
Chatham Coll (PA)
Chestnut Hill Coll (PA)
Cheyney U of Pennsylvania (PA)
Chicago State U (IL)
Christopher Newport U (VA)
Citadel, The Military Coll of South Carolina (SC)
City Coll of the City U of NY (NY)
Claremont McKenna Coll (CA)
Clarion U of Pennsylvania (PA)
Clark Atlanta U (GA)
Clarke Coll (IA)
Clark U (MA)
Cleveland State U (OH)
Coastal Carolina U (SC)
Coe Coll (IA)
Coker Coll (SC)
Colby Coll (ME)
Colgate U (NY)
Coll of Charleston (SC)
Coll of Mount Saint Vincent (NY)
The Coll of New Jersey (NJ)
The Coll of New Rochelle (NY)
Coll of Saint Benedict (MN)
Coll of St. Catherine (MN)
Coll of Saint Elizabeth (NJ)
The Coll of Saint Rose (NY)
Coll of Staten Island of the City U of NY (NY)
Coll of the Holy Cross (MA)
Coll of the Ozarks (MO)
The Coll of William and Mary (VA)
The Coll of Wooster (OH)
The Colorado Coll (CO)
Colorado State U (CO)
Columbia Coll (NY)
Columbia Coll (SC)
Columbia U, School of General Studies (NY)
Concordia Coll (MN)
Concordia U (NE)
Concordia U (QC, Canada)
Concordia U Wisconsin (WI)
Connecticut Coll (CT)
Converse Coll (SC)
Cornell Coll (IA)
Cornell U (NY)
Cornerstone U (MI)
Creighton U (NE)
Daemen Coll (NY)
Dalhousie U (NS, Canada)
Dana Coll (NE)
Dartmouth Coll (NH)
Davidson Coll (NC)
Davis & Elkins Coll (WV)
Delaware State U (DE)
Denison U (OH)
DePaul U (IL)
DePauw U (IN)
DeSales U (PA)
Dickinson Coll (PA)
Dickinson State U (ND)
Dillard U (LA)
Doane Coll (NE)
Dominican Coll (NY)
Dominican U (IL)
Dordt Coll (IA)
Drew U (NJ)
Drury U (MO)
Duke U (NC)
Duquesne U (PA)
Earlham Coll (IN)
East Carolina U (NC)
Eastern Connecticut State U (CT)
Eastern Kentucky U (KY)
Eastern Mennonite U (VA)
Eastern Michigan U (MI)
Eastern New Mexico U (NM)
Eastern U (PA)
Eastern Washington U (WA)
East Stroudsburg U of Pennsylvania (PA)
East Texas Baptist U (TX)
Eckerd Coll (FL)
Edgewood Coll (WI)
Edinboro U of Pennsylvania (PA)
Elizabethtown Coll (PA)
Elmhurst Coll (IL)
Elmira Coll (NY)
Elms Coll (MA)
Elon U (NC)
Emmanuel Coll (MA)
Emory & Henry Coll (VA)
Emory U (GA)
Erskine Coll (SC)
Evangel U (MO)
The Evergreen State Coll (WA)
Fairfield U (CT)
Fairleigh Dickinson U, Florham-Madison Campus (NJ)
Fairleigh Dickinson U, Teaneck-Hackensack Campus (NJ)
Fayetteville State U (NC)
Ferrum Coll (VA)
Fisk U (TN)
Flagler Coll (FL)
Florida A&M U (FL)
Florida Atlantic U (FL)
Florida International U (FL)
Florida Southern Coll (FL)
Florida State U (FL)
Fordham U (NY)
Fort Hays State U (KS)
Fort Lewis Coll (CO)
Framingham State Coll (MA)
Franciscan U of Steubenville (OH)
Francis Marion U (SC)
Franklin and Marshall Coll (PA)
Franklin Coll of Indiana (IN)
Fresno Pacific U (CA)
Friends U (KS)
Furman U (SC)
Gallaudet U (DC)
Gardner-Webb U (NC)
Geneva Coll (PA)
George Fox U (OR)
Georgetown Coll (KY)
Georgetown U (DC)
The George Washington U (DC)
Georgia Coll and State U (GA)
Georgian Court Coll (NJ)
Georgia Southern U (GA)
Georgia Southwestern State U (GA)
Georgia State U (GA)
Gettysburg Coll (PA)
Gonzaga U (WA)
Gordon Coll (MA)
Goshen Coll (IN)
Goucher Coll (MD)
Grace Coll (IN)
Graceland U (IA)
Grambling State U (LA)
Grand Valley State U (MI)
Greensboro Coll (NC)
Greenville Coll (IL)
Grinnell Coll (IA)
Grove City Coll (PA)
Guilford Coll (NC)
Gustavus Adolphus Coll (MN)
Hamilton Coll (NY)
Hamline U (MN)
Hampden-Sydney Coll (VA)
Hanover Coll (IN)
Harding U (AR)
Hardin-Simmons U (TX)
Hartwick Coll (NY)
Harvard U (MA)
Hastings Coll (NE)
Haverford Coll (PA)
Heidelberg Coll (OH)
Henderson State U (AR)
Hendrix Coll (AR)
High Point U (NC)
Hillsdale Coll (MI)
Hiram Coll (OH)
Hobart and William Smith Colls (NY)
Hofstra U (NY)
Hollins U (VA)
Holy Family Coll (PA)
Hood Coll (MD)
Hope Coll (MI)
Houghton Coll (NY)
Houston Baptist U (TX)
Howard Payne U (TX)
Howard U (DC)
Humboldt State U (CA)
Hunter Coll of the City U of NY (NY)
Huntingdon Coll (AL)
Idaho State U (ID)
Illinois Coll (IL)
Illinois State U (IL)
Illinois Wesleyan U (IL)
Immaculata Coll (PA)
Indiana State U (IN)
Indiana U Bloomington (IN)
Indiana U Northwest (IN)
Indiana U of Pennsylvania (PA)
Indiana U–Purdue U Fort Wayne (IN)
Indiana U–Purdue U Indianapolis (IN)
Indiana U South Bend (IN)
Indiana U Southeast (IN)
Indiana Wesleyan U (IN)
Iona Coll (NY)
Iowa State U of Science and Technology (IA)
Ithaca Coll (NY)
Jackson State U (MS)
Jacksonville State U (AL)
Jacksonville U (FL)
James Madison U (VA)
John Carroll U (OH)
Johns Hopkins U (MD)
Juniata Coll (PA)
Kalamazoo Coll (MI)
Kansas Wesleyan U (KS)
Kean U (NJ)
Keene State Coll (NH)
Kennesaw State U (GA)
Kent State U (OH)
Kenyon Coll (OH)
King Coll (TN)
King's Coll (PA)
Knox Coll (IL)
Kutztown U of Pennsylvania (PA)
Lafayette Coll (PA)
Lake Erie Coll (OH)

Lake Forest Coll (IL)
Lakeland Coll (WI)
Lamar U (TX)
Lander U (SC)
La Salle U (PA)
Laurentian U (ON, Canada)
Lawrence U (WI)
Lebanon Valley Coll (PA)
Lehigh U (PA)
Lehman Coll of the City U of NY (NY)
Le Moyne Coll (NY)
Lenoir-Rhyne Coll (NC)
Lewis & Clark Coll (OR)
Liberty U (VA)
Lincoln U (PA)
Lindenwood U (MO)
Linfield Coll (OR)
Lipscomb U (TN)
Lock Haven U of Pennsylvania (PA)
Long Island U, C.W. Post Campus (NY)
Long Island U, Southampton Coll, Friends World Program (NY)
Longwood Coll (VA)
Loras Coll (IA)
Louisiana Coll (LA)
Louisiana State U and A&M Coll (LA)
Louisiana State U in Shreveport (LA)
Louisiana Tech U (LA)
Loyola Coll in Maryland (MD)
Loyola Marymount U (CA)
Loyola U Chicago (IL)
Loyola U New Orleans (LA)
Lubbock Christian U (TX)
Luther Coll (IA)
Lycoming Coll (PA)
Lynchburg Coll (VA)
Lyon Coll (AR)
Macalester Coll (MN)
MacMurray Coll (IL)
Malone Coll (OH)
Manchester Coll (IN)
Manhattan Coll (NY)
Manhattanville Coll (NY)
Mansfield U of Pennsylvania (PA)
Marian Coll (IN)
Marian Coll of Fond du Lac (WI)
Marietta Coll (OH)
Marist Coll (NY)
Marlboro Coll (VT)
Marquette U (WI)
Mars Hill Coll (NC)
Mary Baldwin Coll (VA)
Marymount Coll of Fordham U (NY)
Maryville Coll (TN)
Mary Washington Coll (VA)
Marywood U (PA)
Massachusetts Inst of Technology (MA)
McGill U (PQ, Canada)
McMurry U (TX)
McNeese State U (LA)
McPherson Coll (KS)
Memorial U of Newfoundland (NF, Canada)
Mercer U (GA)
Mercy Coll (NY)
Mercyhurst Coll (PA)
Meredith Coll (NC)
Merrimack Coll (MA)
Messiah Coll (PA)
Methodist Coll (NC)
Metropolitan State Coll of Denver (CO)
Miami U (OH)
Michigan State U (MI)
MidAmerica Nazarene U (KS)
Middlebury Coll (VT)
Midwestern State U (TX)
Millersville U of Pennsylvania (PA)
Millikin U (IL)
Millsaps Coll (MS)
Minnesota State U, Mankato (MN)
Minnesota State U Moorhead (MN)
Minot State U (ND)
Mississippi Coll (MS)
Mississippi U for Women (MS)
Missouri Southern State Coll (MO)
Missouri Western State Coll (MO)
Molloy Coll (NY)
Monmouth Coll (IL)
Montana State U–Billings (MT)
Montclair State U (NJ)
Moravian Coll (PA)
Morehead State U (KY)
Morehouse Coll (GA)
Morningside Coll (IA)
Morris Brown Coll (GA)
Mount Allison U (NB, Canada)
Mount Holyoke Coll (MA)
Mount Mary Coll (WI)
Mount St. Mary's Coll (CA)
Mount Saint Mary's Coll and Seminary (MD)
Mount Saint Vincent U (NS, Canada)
Mount Union Coll (OH)
Mount Vernon Nazarene U (OH)
Muhlenberg Coll (PA)
Murray State U (KY)
Muskingum Coll (OH)
Nazareth Coll of Rochester (NY)
Nebraska Wesleyan U (NE)
Newberry Coll (SC)
New Coll of Florida (FL)
New Jersey City U (NJ)
New Mexico Highlands U (NM)
New York U (NY)
Niagara U (NY)
North Carolina Central U (NC)
North Carolina State U (NC)
North Central Coll (IL)
North Dakota State U (ND)
Northeastern Illinois U (IL)
Northeastern State U (OK)
Northeastern U (MA)
Northern Arizona U (AZ)
Northern Illinois U (IL)
Northern Kentucky U (KY)
Northern Michigan U (MI)
Northern State U (SD)
North Georgia Coll & State U (GA)
North Park U (IL)
Northwestern Coll (IA)
Northwestern Coll (MN)
Northwestern Oklahoma State U (OK)
Northwestern U (IL)
Northwest Missouri State U (MO)
Northwest Nazarene U (ID)
Notre Dame Coll (OH)
Oakland U (MI)
Oakwood Coll (AL)
Oberlin Coll (OH)
Occidental Coll (CA)
Ohio Northern U (OH)
The Ohio State U (OH)
Ohio U (OH)
Ohio Wesleyan U (OH)
Oklahoma Baptist U (OK)
Oklahoma Christian U of Science and Arts (OK)
Oklahoma City U (OK)
Oklahoma State U (OK)
Olivet Nazarene U (IL)
Oral Roberts U (OK)
Oregon State U (OR)
Otterbein Coll (OH)
Ouachita Baptist U (AR)
Our Lady of the Lake U of San Antonio (TX)
Pace U (NY)
Pacific Lutheran U (WA)
Pacific Union Coll (CA)
Pacific U (OR)
Park U (MO)
Peace Coll (NC)
Penn State U Univ Park Campus (PA)
Pepperdine U, Malibu (CA)
Piedmont Coll (GA)
Pittsburg State U (KS)
Pitzer Coll (CA)
Plattsburgh State U of NY (NY)
Plymouth State Coll (NH)
Point Loma Nazarene U (CA)
Pomona Coll (CA)
Pontifical Catholic U of Puerto Rico (PR)
Portland State U (OR)
Prairie View A&M U (TX)
Presbyterian Coll (SC)
Prescott Coll (AZ)
Principia Coll (IL)
Providence Coll (RI)
Purchase Coll, State U of NY (NY)
Purdue U Calumet (IN)
Queens Coll (NC)
Queens Coll of the City U of NY (NY)
Queen's U at Kingston (ON, Canada)
Quinnipiac U (CT)
Randolph-Macon Coll (VA)
Randolph-Macon Woman's Coll (VA)
Reed Coll (OR)
Regis Coll (MA)
Regis U (CO)
Rhode Island Coll (RI)
Rhodes Coll (TN)
Rice U (TX)
Rider U (NJ)
Ripon Coll (WI)
Rivier Coll (NH)
Roanoke Coll (VA)
Rockford Coll (IL)
Rockhurst U (MO)
Rollins Coll (FL)
Roosevelt U (IL)
Rosemont Coll (PA)
Rowan U (NJ)
Russell Sage Coll (NY)
Rutgers, The State U of New Jersey, New Brunswick (NJ)
Sacred Heart U (CT)
Saginaw Valley State U (MI)
St. Ambrose U (IA)
Saint Anselm Coll (NH)
Saint Augustine's Coll (NC)
St. Bonaventure U (NY)
St. Cloud State U (MN)
St. Edward's U (TX)
Saint Francis U (PA)
St. John Fisher Coll (NY)
St. John's Seminary Coll (CA)
Saint John's U (MN)
St. John's U (NY)
Saint Joseph Coll (CT)
St. Joseph's Coll, New York (NY)
Saint Joseph's U (PA)
St. Lawrence U (NY)
Saint Louis U (MO)
Saint Mary Coll (KS)
Saint Mary-of-the-Woods Coll (IN)
Saint Mary's Coll (IN)
Saint Mary's Coll of California (CA)
Saint Mary's U of Minnesota (MN)
St. Mary's U of San Antonio (TX)
Saint Michael's Coll (VT)
St. Norbert Coll (WI)
St. Olaf Coll (MN)
Saint Peter's Coll (NJ)
St. Thomas Aquinas Coll (NY)
St. Thomas U (NB, Canada)
Saint Vincent Coll (PA)
Saint Xavier U (IL)
Salem Coll (NC)
Salisbury U (MD)
Salve Regina U (RI)
Samford U (AL)
Sam Houston State U (TX)
San Diego State U (CA)
San Francisco State U (CA)
San Jose State U (CA)
Santa Clara U (CA)
Sarah Lawrence Coll (NY)
Scripps Coll (CA)
Seattle Pacific U (WA)
Seattle U (WA)
Seton Hall U (NJ)
Seton Hill Coll (PA)
Shippensburg U of Pennsylvania (PA)
Shorter Coll (GA)
Siena Coll (NY)
Siena Heights U (MI)
Simmons Coll (MA)
Simon Fraser U (BC, Canada)
Simon's Rock Coll of Bard (MA)
Simpson Coll (IA)
Skidmore Coll (NY)
Slippery Rock U of Pennsylvania (PA)
Smith Coll (MA)
Sonoma State U (CA)
South Carolina State U (SC)
South Dakota State U (SD)
Southeastern Louisiana U (LA)
Southeast Missouri State U (MO)
Southern Arkansas U–Magnolia (AR)
Southern Connecticut State U (CT)
Southern Illinois U Carbondale (IL)
Southern Methodist U (TX)
Southern Nazarene U (OK)
Southern Oregon U (OR)
Southern U and A&M Coll (LA)
Southern Utah U (UT)
Southern Virginia U (VA)
Southwest Baptist U (MO)
Southwestern U (TX)
Southwest Missouri State U (MO)
Southwest State U (MN)
Southwest Texas State U (TX)
Spelman Coll (GA)
Spring Arbor U (MI)
Spring Hill Coll (AL)
Stanford U (CA)
State U of NY at Albany (NY)
State U of NY at Binghamton (NY)
State U of NY at New Paltz (NY)
State U of NY at Oswego (NY)
State U of NY Coll at Brockport (NY)
State U of NY Coll at Buffalo (NY)
State U of NY Coll at Cortland (NY)
State U of NY Coll at Fredonia (NY)
State U of NY Coll at Geneseo (NY)
State U of NY Coll at Old Westbury (NY)
State U of NY Coll at Oneonta (NY)
State U of NY Coll at Potsdam (NY)
State U of West Georgia (GA)
Stephen F. Austin State U (TX)
Stetson U (FL)
State U of NY at Stony Brook (NY)
Suffolk U (MA)
Sul Ross State U (TX)
Susquehanna U (PA)
Swarthmore Coll (PA)
Sweet Briar Coll (VA)
Syracuse U (NY)
Talladega Coll (AL)
Tarleton State U (TX)
Taylor U (IN)
Temple U (PA)
Tennessee State U (TN)
Tennessee Technological U (TN)
Texas A&M International U (TX)
Texas A&M U (TX)
Texas A&M U–Commerce (TX)
Texas A&M U–Corpus Christi (TX)
Texas A&M U–Kingsville (TX)
Texas Christian U (TX)
Texas Lutheran U (TX)
Texas Southern U (TX)
Texas Tech U (TX)
Texas Wesleyan U (TX)
Texas Woman's U (TX)
Thiel Coll (PA)
Towson U (MD)
Transylvania U (KY)
Trent U (ON, Canada)
Trinity Christian Coll (IL)
Trinity Coll (CT)
Trinity Coll (DC)
Trinity U (TX)
Truman State U (MO)
Tufts U (MA)
Tulane U (LA)
Union Coll (NE)
Union U (TN)
United States Military Academy (NY)
Universidad Adventista de las Antillas (PR)
Université de Montréal (QC, Canada)
Université Laval (QC, Canada)
State U of NY at Buffalo (NY)
The U of Akron (OH)
The U of Alabama (AL)
The U of Alabama at Birmingham (AL)
U of Alberta (AB, Canada)
The U of Arizona (AZ)
U of Arkansas (AR)
U of Arkansas at Little Rock (AR)
The U of British Columbia (BC, Canada)
U of Calgary (AB, Canada)
U of Calif, Berkeley (CA)
U of Calif, Davis (CA)
U of Calif, Irvine (CA)
U of Calif, Los Angeles (CA)
U of Calif, Riverside (CA)
U of Calif, San Diego (CA)
U of Calif, Santa Barbara (CA)
U of Calif, Santa Cruz (CA)
U of Central Arkansas (AR)
U of Central Florida (FL)
U of Central Oklahoma (OK)
U of Chicago (IL)
U of Cincinnati (OH)
U of Colorado at Boulder (CO)
U of Colorado at Colorado Springs (CO)
U of Colorado at Denver (CO)
U of Connecticut (CT)
U of Dallas (TX)
U of Dayton (OH)
U of Delaware (DE)
U of Denver (CO)
U of Evansville (IN)
The U of Findlay (OH)
U of Florida (FL)
U of Georgia (GA)
U of Guelph (ON, Canada)
U of Hawaii at Manoa (HI)
U of Houston (TX)
U of Idaho (ID)
U of Illinois at Chicago (IL)
U of Illinois at Urbana–Champaign (IL)
U of Indianapolis (IN)
The U of Iowa (IA)
U of Kansas (KS)
U of Kentucky (KY)
U of King's Coll (NS, Canada)
U of La Verne (CA)
U of Louisiana at Monroe (LA)
U of Louisville (KY)
U of Maine (ME)
U of Manitoba (MB, Canada)
U of Mary Hardin-Baylor (TX)
U of Maryland, Baltimore County (MD)
U of Maryland, Coll Park (MD)
U of Massachusetts Amherst (MA)
U of Massachusetts Boston (MA)
U of Massachusetts Dartmouth (MA)
U of Miami (FL)
U of Michigan (MI)
U of Michigan–Dearborn (MI)
U of Michigan–Flint (MI)
U of Minnesota, Duluth (MN)
U of Minnesota, Morris (MN)
U of Minnesota, Twin Cities Campus (MN)
U of Mississippi (MS)
U of Missouri–Columbia (MO)
U of Missouri–Kansas City (MO)
U of Missouri–St. Louis (MO)
The U of Montana–Missoula (MT)
U of Montevallo (AL)
U of Nebraska at Kearney (NE)
U of Nebraska at Omaha (NE)
U of Nebraska–Lincoln (NE)
U of Nevada, Las Vegas (NV)
U of Nevada, Reno (NV)
U of New Hampshire (NH)
U of New Mexico (NM)
U of New Orleans (LA)
The U of North Carolina at Asheville (NC)
The U of North Carolina at Charlotte (NC)
The U of North Carolina at Greensboro (NC)
The U of North Carolina at Wilmington (NC)
U of North Dakota (ND)
U of Northern Colorado (CO)
U of Northern Iowa (IA)
U of North Florida (FL)
U of North Texas (TX)
U of Notre Dame (IN)
U of Oklahoma (OK)
U of Oregon (OR)
U of Ottawa (ON, Canada)
U of Pennsylvania (PA)
U of Pittsburgh (PA)
U of Portland (OR)
U of Prince Edward Island (PE, Canada)
U of Puerto Rico, Cayey U Coll (PR)
U of Puget Sound (WA)
U of Redlands (CA)
U of Rhode Island (RI)
U of Richmond (VA)
U of Rochester (NY)
U of St. Thomas (MN)
U of St. Thomas (TX)
U of San Diego (CA)
U of San Francisco (CA)
U of Saskatchewan (SK, Canada)
The U of Scranton (PA)
U of South Carolina (SC)
U of South Carolina Spartanburg (SC)
U of South Dakota (SD)
U of Southern California (CA)
U of Southern Colorado (CO)
U of Southern Indiana (IN)

U of South Florida (FL)
The U of Tampa (FL)
The U of Tennessee (TN)
The U of Tennessee at Chattanooga (TN)
The U of Tennessee at Martin (TN)
The U of Texas at Arlington (TX)
The U of Texas at Austin (TX)
The U of Texas at Brownsville (TX)
The U of Texas at El Paso (TX)
The U of Texas at San Antonio (TX)
The U of Texas at Tyler (TX)
The U of Texas of the Permian Basin (TX)
The U of Texas–Pan American (TX)
U of the District of Columbia (DC)
U of the Incarnate Word (TX)
U of the Pacific (CA)
U of the South (TN)
U of Toledo (OH)
U of Toronto (ON, Canada)
U of Tulsa (OK)
U of Utah (UT)
U of Vermont (VT)
U of Victoria (BC, Canada)
U of Virginia (VA)
The U of Virginia's Coll at Wise (VA)
U of Washington (WA)
U of Waterloo (ON, Canada)
The U of Western Ontario (ON, Canada)
U of Windsor (ON, Canada)
U of Wisconsin–Eau Claire (WI)
U of Wisconsin–Green Bay (WI)
U of Wisconsin–La Crosse (WI)
U of Wisconsin–Madison (WI)
U of Wisconsin–Milwaukee (WI)
U of Wisconsin–Oshkosh (WI)
U of Wisconsin–Parkside (WI)
U of Wisconsin–Platteville (WI)
U of Wisconsin–River Falls (WI)
U of Wisconsin–Stevens Point (WI)
U of Wisconsin–Whitewater (WI)
U of Wyoming (WY)
Ursinus Coll (PA)
Utah State U (UT)
Valdosta State U (GA)
Valley City State U (ND)
Valparaiso U (IN)
Vanderbilt U (TN)
Vanguard U of Southern California (CA)
Villanova U (PA)
Virginia Polytechnic Inst and State U (VA)
Virginia Wesleyan Coll (VA)
Viterbo U (WI)
Wabash Coll (IN)
Wagner Coll (NY)
Wake Forest U (NC)
Walla Walla Coll (WA)
Walsh U (OH)
Wartburg Coll (IA)
Washburn U of Topeka (KS)
Washington & Jefferson Coll (PA)
Washington and Lee U (VA)
Washington Coll (MD)
Washington State U (WA)
Washington U in St. Louis (MO)
Wayland Baptist U (TX)
Wayne State Coll (NE)
Wayne State U (MI)
Weber State U (UT)
Webster U (MO)
Wellesley Coll (MA)
Wells Coll (NY)
Wesleyan Coll (GA)
Wesleyan U (CT)
West Chester U of Pennsylvania (PA)
Western Carolina U (NC)
Western Connecticut State U (CT)
Western Illinois U (IL)
Western Kentucky U (KY)
Western Maryland Coll (MD)
Western Michigan U (MI)
Western Oregon U (OR)
Western State Coll of Colorado (CO)
Western Washington U (WA)
Westminster Coll (MO)
Westminster Coll (PA)
Westmont Coll (CA)
West Texas A&M U (TX)
Wheaton Coll (IL)
Wheeling Jesuit U (WV)
Whitman Coll (WA)
Whittier Coll (CA)
Whitworth Coll (WA)
Wichita State U (KS)
Widener U (PA)
Wilfrid Laurier U (ON, Canada)
Wilkes U (PA)
Willamette U (OR)
William Carey Coll (MS)
William Jewell Coll (MO)
William Paterson U of New Jersey (NJ)
Williams Coll (MA)
William Woods U (MO)
Wilmington Coll (OH)
Wingate U (NC)
Winona State U (MN)
Winston-Salem State U (NC)
Wisconsin Lutheran Coll (WI)
Wittenberg U (OH)
Wofford Coll (SC)
Worcester State Coll (MA)
Wright State U (OH)
Xavier U (OH)
Xavier U of Louisiana (LA)
Yale U (CT)
York Coll of Pennsylvania (PA)
York Coll of the City U of New York (NY)
York U (ON, Canada)
Youngstown State U (OH)

SPANISH LANGUAGE EDUCATION

Abilene Christian U (TX)
Adams State Coll (CO)
Anderson Coll (SC)
Anderson U (IN)
Arkansas State U (AR)
Bayamón Central U (PR)
Baylor U (TX)
Berea Coll (KY)
Berry Coll (GA)
Blue Mountain Coll (MS)
Bowling Green State U (OH)
Bridgewater Coll (VA)
Brigham Young U (UT)
Canisius Coll (NY)
Carroll Coll (MT)
The Catholic U of America (DC)
Cedarville U (OH)
Central Michigan U (MI)
Central Missouri State U (MO)
Chadron State Coll (NE)
The Coll of New Jersey (NJ)
Coll of St. Catherine (MN)
Colorado State U (CO)
Concordia Coll (MN)
Concordia U (NE)
Daemen Coll (NY)
Duquesne U (PA)
East Carolina U (NC)
Eastern Mennonite U (VA)
Eastern Michigan U (MI)
East Texas Baptist U (TX)
Elmhurst Coll (IL)
Elmira Coll (NY)
Flagler Coll (FL)
Framingham State Coll (MA)
Franklin Coll of Indiana (IN)
Georgia Southern U (GA)
Grace Coll (IN)
Greensboro Coll (NC)
Greenville Coll (IL)
Hardin-Simmons U (TX)
Henderson State U (AR)
Indiana U Bloomington (IN)
Indiana U Northwest (IN)
Indiana U–Purdue U Fort Wayne (IN)
Indiana U–Purdue U Indianapolis (IN)
Indiana U South Bend (IN)
Inter American U of PR, Aguadilla Campus (PR)
Ithaca Coll (NY)
Juniata Coll (PA)
Kennesaw State U (GA)
King Coll (TN)
La Roche Coll (PA)
Long Island U, C.W. Post Campus (NY)
Luther Coll (IA)
Malone Coll (OH)
Manhattanville Coll (NY)
Mansfield U of Pennsylvania (PA)
Marymount Coll of Fordham U (NY)
Maryville Coll (TN)
Messiah Coll (PA)
MidAmerica Nazarene U (KS)
Minnesota State U Moorhead (MN)
Minot State U (ND)
Missouri Western State Coll (MO)
Molloy Coll (NY)
Montana State U–Billings (MT)
Niagara U (NY)
North Carolina Central U (NC)
North Carolina State U (NC)
North Dakota State U (ND)
Northern Arizona U (AZ)
Northwest Nazarene U (ID)
Ohio U (OH)
Oklahoma Baptist U (OK)
Oral Roberts U (OK)
Pace U (NY)
St. Ambrose U (IA)
St. John's U (NY)
Saint Mary's U of Minnesota (MN)
Saint Xavier U (IL)
Salve Regina U (RI)
San Diego State U (CA)
Seton Hill Coll (PA)
Southeastern Louisiana U (LA)
Southeastern Oklahoma State U (OK)
Southern Arkansas U–Magnolia (AR)
Southern Nazarene U (OK)
Southwest Missouri State U (MO)
State U of NY at Albany (NY)
State U of NY Coll at Potsdam (NY)
Texas A&M International U (TX)
The U of Arizona (AZ)
U of Illinois at Chicago (IL)
U of Illinois at Urbana–Champaign (IL)
U of Indianapolis (IN)
The U of Iowa (IA)
U of Minnesota, Duluth (MN)
U of Nebraska–Lincoln (NE)
The U of North Carolina at Charlotte (NC)
The U of North Carolina at Wilmington (NC)
U of North Texas (TX)
U of Puerto Rico, Cayey U Coll (PR)
U of Southern Colorado (CO)
The U of Tennessee at Martin (TN)
U of Toledo (OH)
U of Utah (UT)
U of Wisconsin–River Falls (WI)
Valley City State U (ND)
Viterbo U (WI)
Washington U in St. Louis (MO)
Weber State U (UT)
Western Carolina U (NC)
Wheeling Jesuit U (WV)
Winston-Salem State U (NC)
Youngstown State U (OH)

SPECIAL EDUCATION

Abilene Christian U (TX)
Alabama State U (AL)
Albany State U (GA)
Albright Coll (PA)
Alcorn State U (MS)
Alderson-Broaddus Coll (WV)
American International Coll (MA)
American U of Puerto Rico (PR)
Anderson Coll (SC)
Aquinas Coll (MI)
Arcadia U (PA)
Arizona State U (AZ)
Arizona State U West (AZ)
Arkansas State U (AR)
Armstrong Atlantic State U (GA)
Ashland U (OH)
Athens State U (AL)
Augustana Coll (SD)
Augusta State U (GA)
Austin Peay State U (TN)
Avila Coll (MO)
Baldwin-Wallace Coll (OH)
Ball State U (IN)
Barry U (FL)
Barton Coll (NC)
Bayamón Central U (PR)
Baylor U (TX)
Bellarmine U (KY)
Belmont U (TN)
Benedictine Coll (KS)
Benedictine U (IL)
Bennett Coll (NC)
Bethel Coll (TN)
Bethune-Cookman Coll (FL)
Black Hills State U (SD)
Bloomsburg U of Pennsylvania (PA)
Bluffton Coll (OH)
Boise State U (ID)
Boston Coll (MA)
Boston U (MA)
Bowie State U (MD)
Bowling Green State U (OH)
Brenau U (GA)
Brescia U (KY)
Bridgewater Coll (VA)
Bridgewater State Coll (MA)
Brigham Young U–Hawaii (HI)
Buena Vista U (IA)
Cabrini Coll (PA)
California State U, Northridge (CA)
California U of Pennsylvania (PA)
Calvin Coll (MI)
Canisius Coll (NY)
Cardinal Stritch U (WI)
Caribbean U (PR)
Carlow Coll (PA)
Carson-Newman Coll (TN)
Carthage Coll (WI)
Cedarville U (OH)
Centenary Coll (NJ)
Central Connecticut State U (CT)
Central Missouri State U (MO)
Central State U (OH)
Central Washington U (WA)
Chadron State Coll (NE)
Cheyney U of Pennsylvania (PA)
Chicago State U (IL)
City Coll of the City U of NY (NY)
City U (WA)
Clarion U of Pennsylvania (PA)
Clarke Coll (IA)
Clearwater Christian Coll (FL)
Clemson U (SC)
Cleveland State U (OH)
Coastal Carolina U (SC)
Coll Misericordia (PA)
Coll of Charleston (SC)
Coll of Mount St. Joseph (OH)
Coll of Mount Saint Vincent (NY)
The Coll of New Jersey (NJ)
The Coll of New Rochelle (NY)
Coll of Notre Dame of Maryland (MD)
Coll of Saint Elizabeth (NJ)
Coll of St. Joseph (VT)
Coll of Saint Mary (NE)
The Coll of Saint Rose (NY)
Coll of the Southwest (NM)
Columbia Coll (SC)
Columbus State U (GA)
Concord Coll (WV)
Concordia U (NE)
Converse Coll (SC)
Coppin State Coll (MD)
Creighton U (NE)
Culver-Stockton Coll (MO)
Cumberland Coll (KY)
Cumberland U (TN)
Curry Coll (MA)
Daemen Coll (NY)
Dakota State U (SD)
Dakota Wesleyan U (SD)
Dana Coll (NE)
Defiance Coll (OH)
Delaware State U (DE)
Delta State U (MS)
Dillard U (LA)
Doane Coll (NE)
Dominican Coll (NY)
Dowling Coll (NY)
D'Youville Coll (NY)
East Central U (OK)
Eastern Illinois U (IL)
Eastern Kentucky U (KY)
Eastern Michigan U (MI)
Eastern Nazarene Coll (MA)
Eastern New Mexico U (NM)
Eastern Oregon U (OR)
Eastern Washington U (WA)
East Stroudsburg U of Pennsylvania (PA)
East Tennessee State U (TN)
Edinboro U of Pennsylvania (PA)
Elizabeth City State U (NC)
Elmhurst Coll (IL)
Elms Coll (MA)
Elon U (NC)
Erskine Coll (SC)
Evangel U (MO)
Fairmont State Coll (WV)
Felician Coll (NJ)
Fitchburg State Coll (MA)
Florida Atlantic U (FL)
Florida Gulf Coast U (FL)
Fontbonne U (MO)
Freed-Hardeman U (TN)
Furman U (SC)
Gannon U (PA)
Geneva Coll (PA)
Georgia Coll and State U (GA)
Georgian Court Coll (NJ)
Georgia Southern U (GA)
Georgia Southwestern State U (GA)
Glenville State Coll (WV)
Gonzaga U (WA)
Gordon Coll (MA)
Grambling State U (LA)
Grand Canyon U (AZ)
Grand Valley State U (MI)
Grand View Coll (IA)
Green Mountain Coll (VT)
Greensboro Coll (NC)
Greenville Coll (IL)
Gwynedd-Mercy Coll (PA)
Hampton U (VA)
Hastings Coll (NE)
Heidelberg Coll (OH)
High Point U (NC)
Holy Family Coll (PA)
Hood Coll (MD)
Houston Baptist U (TX)
Huntington Coll (IN)
Idaho State U (ID)
Illinois State U (IL)
Indiana State U (IN)
Indiana U Bloomington (IN)
Indiana U of Pennsylvania (PA)
Indiana U South Bend (IN)
Indiana U Southeast (IN)
Indiana Wesleyan U (IN)
Iona Coll (NY)
Jackson State U (MS)
Jacksonville State U (AL)
Jacksonville U (FL)
James Madison U (VA)
Jarvis Christian Coll (TX)
John Brown U (AR)
John Carroll U (OH)
Juniata Coll (PA)
Kansas Wesleyan U (KS)
Kean U (NJ)
Keene State Coll (NH)
Kent State U (OH)
Keuka Coll (NY)
King's Coll (PA)
Kutztown U of Pennsylvania (PA)
Lamar U (TX)
Lambuth U (TN)
Lander U (SC)
La Salle U (PA)
Lasell Coll (MA)
Lee U (TN)
Lesley U (MA)
Lewis-Clark State Coll (ID)
Lewis U (IL)
Liberty U (VA)
Lincoln U (MO)
Lindenwood U (MO)
Lock Haven U of Pennsylvania (PA)
Long Island U, Brooklyn Campus (NY)
Long Island U, Southampton Coll, Friends World Program (NY)
Longwood Coll (VA)
Louisiana Coll (LA)
Louisiana State U in Shreveport (LA)
Louisiana Tech U (LA)
Loyola Coll in Maryland (MD)
Loyola U Chicago (IL)
Luther Coll (IA)
Lynchburg Coll (VA)
Lyndon State Coll (VT)
MacMurray Coll (IL)
Manchester Coll (IN)
Manhattan Coll (NY)
Mansfield U of Pennsylvania (PA)
Marian Coll (IN)
Marist Coll (NY)
Marymount Coll of Fordham U (NY)
Marywood U (PA)
McGill U (PQ, Canada)
McNeese State U (LA)
McPherson Coll (KS)
Medgar Evers Coll of the City U of NY (NY)
Memorial U of Newfoundland (NF, Canada)
Mercy Coll (NY)
Mercyhurst Coll (PA)

Methodist Coll (NC)
Miami U (OH)
Michigan State U (MI)
Middle Tennessee State U (TN)
Millersville U of Pennsylvania (PA)
Minnesota State U Moorhead (MN)
Mississippi Coll (MS)
Mississippi State U (MS)
Mississippi U for Women (MS)
Missouri Southern State Coll (MO)
Missouri Valley Coll (MO)
Molloy Coll (NY)
Monmouth Coll (IL)
Monmouth U (NJ)
Montana State U–Billings (MT)
Morehead State U (KY)
Morningside Coll (IA)
Mount Marty Coll (SD)
Mount Saint Mary Coll (NY)
Mount Vernon Nazarene U (OH)
Murray State U (KY)
Muskingum Coll (OH)
Nazareth Coll of Rochester (NY)
Nebraska Wesleyan U (NE)
Newberry Coll (SC)
New England Coll (NH)
New Jersey City U (NJ)
New Mexico Highlands U (NM)
New Mexico State U (NM)
New York U (NY)
Niagara U (NY)
Nicholls State U (LA)
Norfolk State U (VA)
North Carolina Ag and Tech State U (NC)
Northeastern Illinois U (IL)
Northeastern State U (OK)
Northern Arizona U (AZ)
Northern Illinois U (IL)
Northern Kentucky U (KY)
Northern Michigan U (MI)
Northern State U (SD)
North Georgia Coll & State U (GA)
Northwest Coll (WA)
Northwestern Oklahoma State U (OK)
Northwestern State U of Louisiana (LA)
Northwest Missouri State U (MO)
Nova Southeastern U (FL)
Ohio Dominican Coll (OH)
The Ohio State U (OH)
Ohio U (OH)
Ohio Valley Coll (WV)
Oklahoma Baptist U (OK)
Oklahoma Christian U of Science and Arts (OK)
Oral Roberts U (OK)
Ouachita Baptist U (AR)
Our Lady of the Lake U of San Antonio (TX)
Pace U (NY)
Pacific Lutheran U (WA)
Pacific Oaks Coll (CA)
Penn State U Univ Park Campus (PA)
Peru State Coll (NE)
Pfeiffer U (NC)
Piedmont Coll (GA)
Plattsburgh State U of NY (NY)
Pontifical Catholic U of Puerto Rico (PR)
Presbyterian Coll (SC)
Prescott Coll (AZ)
Providence Coll (RI)
Purdue U Calumet (IN)
Quincy U (IL)
Rhode Island Coll (RI)
Rivier Coll (NH)
Rowan U (NJ)
Russell Sage Coll (NY)
Saginaw Valley State U (MI)
Saint Augustine's Coll (NC)
St. Cloud State U (MN)
St. John Fisher Coll (NY)
St. John's U (NY)
Saint Joseph Coll (CT)
St. Joseph's Coll, Suffolk Campus (NY)
Saint Leo U (FL)
Saint Martin's Coll (WA)
Saint Mary-of-the-Woods Coll (IN)
St. Thomas Aquinas Coll (NY)
Salve Regina U (RI)
Seattle Pacific U (WA)
Seton Hall U (NJ)
Seton Hill Coll (PA)
Simmons Coll (MA)
Slippery Rock U of Pennsylvania (PA)
South Carolina State U (SC)
Southeastern Louisiana U (LA)
Southeastern Oklahoma State U (OK)
Southeast Missouri State U (MO)
Southern Connecticut State U (CT)
Southern Illinois U Carbondale (IL)
Southern Illinois U Edwardsville (IL)
Southern New Hampshire U (NH)
Southern U and A&M Coll (LA)
Southern Utah U (UT)
Southern Wesleyan U (SC)
Southwestern Oklahoma State U (OK)
Southwest Missouri State U (MO)
Springfield Coll (MA)
State U of NY at New Paltz (NY)
State U of NY Coll at Buffalo (NY)
State U of NY Coll at Geneseo (NY)
State U of NY Coll at Old Westbury (NY)
State U of West Georgia (GA)
Syracuse U (NY)
Tabor Coll (KS)
Temple U (PA)
Tennessee State U (TN)
Tennessee Technological U (TN)
Texas A&M International U (TX)
Texas A&M U–Commerce (TX)
Texas Christian U (TX)
Texas Southern U (TX)
Touro Coll (NY)
Towson U (MD)
Trinity Christian Coll (IL)
Trinity Coll (DC)
Troy State U (AL)
Tufts U (MA)
Tusculum Coll (TN)
Union Coll (KY)
Union U (TN)
Université de Montréal (QC, Canada)
Université de Sherbrooke (PQ, Canada)
The U of Alabama (AL)
The U of Alabama at Birmingham (AL)
U of Alberta (AB, Canada)
The U of Arizona (AZ)
U of Arkansas (AR)
U of Arkansas at Pine Bluff (AR)
The U of British Columbia (BC, Canada)
U of Central Arkansas (AR)
U of Central Florida (FL)
U of Central Oklahoma (OK)
U of Cincinnati (OH)
U of Connecticut (CT)
U of Dayton (OH)
U of Delaware (DE)
U of Evansville (IN)
The U of Findlay (OH)
U of Florida (FL)
U of Georgia (GA)
U of Great Falls (MT)
U of Hartford (CT)
U of Hawaii at Manoa (HI)
U of Idaho (ID)
U of Illinois at Urbana–Champaign (IL)
U of Kentucky (KY)
The U of Lethbridge (AB, Canada)
U of Louisiana at Lafayette (LA)
U of Louisiana at Monroe (LA)
U of Maine at Farmington (ME)
U of Mary (ND)
U of Mary Hardin-Baylor (TX)
U of Maryland, Coll Park (MD)
U of Maryland Eastern Shore (MD)
The U of Memphis (TN)
U of Miami (FL)
U of Minnesota, Duluth (MN)
U of Mississippi (MS)
U of Missouri–St. Louis (MO)
Western Montana Coll of The U of Montana (MT)
U of Nebraska at Kearney (NE)
U of Nebraska at Omaha (NE)
U of Nevada, Las Vegas (NV)
U of Nevada, Reno (NV)
U of New Mexico (NM)
U of North Alabama (AL)
The U of North Carolina at Pembroke (NC)
U of Northern Iowa (IA)
U of North Florida (FL)
U of North Texas (TX)
U of Oklahoma (OK)
U of Ottawa (ON, Canada)
U of St. Francis (IL)
U of Saint Francis (IN)
The U of Scranton (PA)
U of South Alabama (AL)
U of South Dakota (SD)
U of Southern Mississippi (MS)
U of South Florida (FL)
The U of Tennessee (TN)
The U of Tennessee at Chattanooga (TN)
The U of Tennessee at Martin (TN)
The U of Texas at Brownsville (TX)
The U of Texas–Pan American (TX)
U of the District of Columbia (DC)
U of the Incarnate Word (TX)
U of the Pacific (CA)
U of Toledo (OH)
U of Tulsa (OK)
U of Victoria (BC, Canada)
The U of West Alabama (AL)
The U of Western Ontario (ON, Canada)
U of West Florida (FL)
U of Windsor (ON, Canada)
U of Wisconsin–Eau Claire (WI)
U of Wisconsin–Madison (WI)
U of Wisconsin–Milwaukee (WI)
U of Wisconsin–Oshkosh (WI)
U of Wisconsin–Superior (WI)
U of Wisconsin–Whitewater (WI)
U of Wyoming (WY)
Upper Iowa U (IA)
Ursuline Coll (OH)
Utah State U (UT)
Valdosta State U (GA)
Vanderbilt U (TN)
Virginia Union U (VA)
Walsh U (OH)
Warner Southern Coll (FL)
Washington State U (WA)
Waynesburg Coll (PA)
Wayne State Coll (NE)
Wayne State U (MI)
Webster U (MO)
West Chester U of Pennsylvania (PA)
Western Carolina U (NC)
Western Illinois U (IL)
Western Kentucky U (KY)
Western State Coll of Colorado (CO)
Western Washington U (WA)
Westfield State Coll (MA)
Westminster Coll (UT)
Wheelock Coll (MA)
Whitworth Coll (WA)
Widener U (PA)
Wiley Coll (TX)
William Paterson U of New Jersey (NJ)
William Penn U (IA)
William Woods U (MO)
Winona State U (MN)
Winston-Salem State U (NC)
Winthrop U (SC)
Wittenberg U (OH)
Xavier U (OH)
Xavier U of Louisiana (LA)
York Coll of Pennsylvania (PA)
York U (ON, Canada)
Youngstown State U (OH)

SPECIAL EDUCATION RELATED

Briar Cliff U (IA)
Minot State U (ND)
The U of Akron (OH)
U of Nebraska–Lincoln (NE)
U of Wyoming (WY)

SPEECH EDUCATION

Abilene Christian U (TX)
Anderson U (IN)
Arkansas Tech U (AR)
Baylor U (TX)
Bowling Green State U (OH)
Cedarville U (OH)
Central Michigan U (MI)
Central Missouri State U (MO)
Chadron State Coll (NE)
Coll of St. Catherine (MN)
Concordia U (IL)
Concordia U (NE)
Dana Coll (NE)
East Texas Baptist U (TX)
Elmira Coll (NY)
Emporia State U (KS)
Greenville Coll (IL)
Hastings Coll (NE)
Henderson State U (AR)
Howard Payne U (TX)
Indiana U Bloomington (IN)
Indiana U–Purdue U Fort Wayne (IN)
Indiana U–Purdue U Indianapolis (IN)
Kean U (NJ)
Louisiana Tech U (LA)
Malone Coll (OH)
McMurry U (TX)
Minnesota State U Moorhead (MN)
North Dakota State U (ND)
Oklahoma Baptist U (OK)
Pace U (NY)
Samford U (AL)
Southeastern Louisiana U (LA)
Southeastern Oklahoma State U (OK)
Southeast Missouri State U (MO)
Southern Nazarene U (OK)
Southwest Missouri State U (MO)
Southwest State U (MN)
Texas Wesleyan U (TX)
The U of Akron (OH)
The U of Arizona (AZ)
U of Central Arkansas (AR)
U of Indianapolis (IN)
The U of Iowa (IA)
U of Louisiana at Monroe (LA)
U of North Texas (TX)
U of Rio Grande (OH)
William Jewell Coll (MO)
Youngstown State U (OH)

SPEECH-LANGUAGE PATHOLOGY

Brigham Young U (UT)
Central Missouri State U (MO)
Duquesne U (PA)
Emerson Coll (MA)
Grambling State U (LA)
James Madison U (VA)
Loyola Coll in Maryland (MD)
Miami U (OH)
Northwestern U (IL)
Pace U (NY)
Rockhurst U (MO)
Saint Xavier U (IL)
Southeast Missouri State U (MO)
State U of West Georgia (GA)
Towson U (MD)
U of Maryland, Coll Park (MD)
U of Nebraska at Omaha (NE)
U of Nebraska–Lincoln (NE)
U of Nevada, Reno (NV)
U of Northern Colorado (CO)
U of Northern Iowa (IA)
U of Science and Arts of Oklahoma (OK)
The U of Tennessee (TN)
U of Toledo (OH)
Wayne State U (MI)
Yeshiva U (NY)

SPEECH-LANGUAGE PATHOLOGY/AUDIOLOGY

Abilene Christian U (TX)
Adelphi U (NY)
Andrews U (MI)
Appalachian State U (NC)
Arkansas State U (AR)
Auburn U (AL)
Augustana Coll (IL)
Augustana Coll (SD)
Baldwin-Wallace Coll (OH)
Ball State U (IN)
Brescia U (KY)
Brooklyn Coll of the City U of NY (NY)
Butler U (IN)
California State U, Fresno (CA)
California State U, Fullerton (CA)
California State U, Hayward (CA)
California State U, Long Beach (CA)
California State U, Northridge (CA)
California State U, Sacramento (CA)
Calvin Coll (MI)
Centenary Coll of Louisiana (LA)
Central Michigan U (MI)
Clarion U of Pennsylvania (PA)
Cleveland State U (OH)
The Coll of Wooster (OH)
Columbia Coll (SC)
Delta State U (MS)
East Carolina U (NC)
Eastern Kentucky U (KY)
Eastern New Mexico U (NM)
Eastern Washington U (WA)
East Stroudsburg U of Pennsylvania (PA)
Elmhurst Coll (IL)
Elmira Coll (NY)
Elms Coll (MA)
Emerson Coll (MA)
Florida Atlantic U (FL)
Florida State U (FL)
Fontbonne U (MO)
Fort Hays State U (KS)
Geneva Coll (PA)
The George Washington U (DC)
Governors State U (IL)
Hampton U (VA)
Hardin-Simmons U (TX)
Hofstra U (NY)
Idaho State U (ID)
Illinois State U (IL)
Indiana State U (IN)
Indiana U Bloomington (IN)
Indiana U–Purdue U Fort Wayne (IN)
Iona Coll (NY)
Ithaca Coll (NY)
Jackson State U (MS)
Kean U (NJ)
Kent State U (OH)
Lamar U (TX)
Lambuth U (TN)
La Salle U (PA)
Lehman Coll of the City U of NY (NY)
Loma Linda U (CA)
Long Island U, C.W. Post Campus (NY)
Louisiana State U and A&M Coll (LA)
Louisiana State U in Shreveport (LA)
Louisiana Tech U (LA)
Marquette U (WI)
Marymount Manhattan Coll (NY)
Marywood U (PA)
Mercy Coll (NY)
Miami U (OH)
Michigan State U (MI)
Minnesota State U, Mankato (MN)
Minnesota State U Moorhead (MN)
Mississippi U for Women (MS)
Molloy Coll (NY)
Murray State U (KY)
Nazareth Coll of Rochester (NY)
New Mexico State U (NM)
Nicholls State U (LA)
Northeastern State U (OK)
Northeastern U (MA)
Northern Michigan U (MI)
Northern State U (SD)
Northwestern U (IL)
Northwest Nazarene U (ID)
The Ohio State U (OH)
Ohio U (OH)
Old Dominion U (VA)
Otterbein Coll (OH)
Ouachita Baptist U (AR)
Our Lady of the Lake U of San Antonio (TX)
Pacific Union Coll (CA)
Penn State U Univ Park Campus (PA)
Plattsburgh State U of NY (NY)
Purdue U (IN)
Queens Coll of the City U of NY (NY)
The Richard Stockton Coll of New Jersey (NJ)
St. Cloud State U (MN)
St. John's U (NY)
San Francisco State U (CA)
San Jose State U (CA)
Shaw U (NC)
South Carolina State U (SC)
Southern Illinois U Edwardsville (IL)
Southern U and A&M Coll (LA)
Southwest Missouri State U (MO)
Southwest Texas State U (TX)
State U of NY at New Paltz (NY)
State U of NY Coll at Buffalo (NY)
State U of NY Coll at Cortland (NY)
State U of NY Coll at Fredonia (NY)
State U of NY Coll at Geneseo (NY)
Stephen F. Austin State U (TX)

Syracuse U (NY)
Temple U (PA)
Tennessee State U (TN)
Texas Christian U (TX)
Texas Woman's U (TX)
Thiel Coll (PA)
Touro Coll (NY)
Towson U (MD)
Université de Montréal (QC, Canada)
State U of NY at Buffalo (NY)
The U of Akron (OH)
The U of Alabama (AL)
U of Arkansas (AR)
U of Arkansas at Little Rock (AR)
U of Central Arkansas (AR)
U of Central Florida (FL)
U of Central Oklahoma (OK)
U of Cincinnati (OH)
U of Florida (FL)
U of Hawaii at Manoa (HI)
U of Houston (TX)
U of Illinois at Urbana–Champaign (IL)
The U of Iowa (IA)
U of Kentucky (KY)
U of Louisiana at Lafayette (LA)
U of Louisiana at Monroe (LA)
U of Minnesota, Duluth (MN)
U of Minnesota, Twin Cities Campus (MN)
U of Mississippi (MS)
The U of Montana–Missoula (MT)
U of Montevallo (AL)
U of Nebraska at Omaha (NE)
U of Nevada, Reno (NV)
U of New Hampshire (NH)
U of New Mexico (NM)
The U of North Carolina at Greensboro (NC)
U of North Dakota (ND)
U of North Texas (TX)
U of Oklahoma Health Sciences Center (OK)
U of Oregon (OR)
U of Pittsburgh (PA)
U of Puerto Rico Medical Sciences Campus (PR)
U of Redlands (CA)
U of South Alabama (AL)
U of South Dakota (SD)
U of Southern Mississippi (MS)
U of South Florida (FL)
The U of Texas at Dallas (TX)
The U of Texas at El Paso (TX)
The U of Texas–Pan American (TX)
U of the District of Columbia (DC)
U of the Pacific (CA)
U of Tulsa (OK)
U of Utah (UT)
U of Vermont (VT)
U of Virginia (VA)
U of Washington (WA)
U of Wisconsin–Milwaukee (WI)
U of Wisconsin–Oshkosh (WI)
U of Wisconsin–Stevens Point (WI)
U of Wyoming (WY)
Utah State U (UT)
Valdosta State U (GA)
Washington State U (WA)
West Chester U of Pennsylvania (PA)
Western Michigan U (MI)
Western Washington U (WA)
West Virginia U (WV)
Wichita State U (KS)
Worcester State Coll (MA)
Xavier U of Louisiana (LA)
Yeshiva U (NY)

SPEECH/RHETORICAL STUDIES

Abilene Christian U (TX)
Adams State Coll (CO)
Alabama State U (AL)
Albany State U (GA)
Alderson-Broaddus Coll (WV)
Anderson Coll (SC)
Appalachian State U (NC)
Arkansas State U (AR)
Arkansas Tech U (AR)
Asbury Coll (KY)
Ashland U (OH)
Auburn U (AL)
Augsburg Coll (MN)
Augustana Coll (IL)
Baker U (KS)
Ball State U (IN)
Bates Coll (ME)
Baylor U (TX)
Belmont U (TN)
Bemidji State U (MN)
Berry Coll (GA)
Bethel Coll (MN)
Blackburn Coll (IL)
Black Hills State U (SD)
Bloomsburg U of Pennsylvania (PA)
Blue Mountain Coll (MS)
Bluffton Coll (OH)
Bowling Green State U (OH)
Bradley U (IL)
Brooklyn Coll of the City U of NY (NY)
Buena Vista U (IA)
Butler U (IN)
California Polytechnic State U, San Luis Obispo (CA)
California State U, Chico (CA)
California State U, Fresno (CA)
California State U, Fullerton (CA)
California State U, Hayward (CA)
California State U, Long Beach (CA)
California State U, Los Angeles (CA)
California State U, Northridge (CA)
Calvin Coll (MI)
Cameron U (OK)
Capital U (OH)
Carson-Newman Coll (TN)
Carthage Coll (WI)
Cedarville U (OH)
Centenary Coll of Louisiana (LA)
Central Michigan U (MI)
Central Missouri State U (MO)
Chadron State Coll (NE)
Chapman U (CA)
Charleston Southern U (SC)
Clarion U of Pennsylvania (PA)
Clark Atlanta U (GA)
Clemson U (SC)
Coe Coll (IA)
The Coll of New Jersey (NJ)
Coll of Saint Benedict (MN)
Coll of St. Catherine (MN)
Coll of the Ozarks (MO)
The Coll of Wooster (OH)
Colorado State U (CO)
Concordia Coll (MN)
Concordia U (NE)
Cornell Coll (IA)
Cornerstone U (MI)
Creighton U (NE)
Cumberland Coll (KY)
Defiance Coll (OH)
Denison U (OH)
Dickinson State U (ND)
Dillard U (LA)
Doane Coll (NE)
Dowling Coll (NY)
Drake U (IA)
East Central U (OK)
Eastern Illinois U (IL)
Eastern Kentucky U (KY)
Eastern Michigan U (MI)
Eastern Washington U (WA)
East Stroudsburg U of Pennsylvania (PA)
East Tennessee State U (TN)
East Texas Baptist U (TX)
Emerson Coll (MA)
Evangel U (MO)
Fairmont State Coll (WV)
Fisk U (TN)
Florida Atlantic U (FL)
Friends U (KS)
Frostburg State U (MD)
Geneva Coll (PA)
George Mason U (VA)
Georgetown Coll (KY)
The George Washington U (DC)
Georgia Southern U (GA)
Georgia State U (GA)
Gonzaga U (WA)
Governors State U (IL)
Graceland U (IA)
Grand Canyon U (AZ)
Greenville Coll (IL)
Gustavus Adolphus Coll (MN)
Hannibal-LaGrange Coll (MO)
Hardin-Simmons U (TX)
Hastings Coll (NE)
Henderson State U (AR)
Hillsdale Coll (MI)
Houston Baptist U (TX)
Howard Payne U (TX)
Humboldt State U (CA)
Huntingdon Coll (AL)
Illinois Coll (IL)
Illinois State U (IL)
Indiana U Bloomington (IN)
Indiana U South Bend (IN)
Iona Coll (NY)
Iowa State U of Science and Technology (IA)
Ithaca Coll (NY)
Jackson State U (MS)
Judson Coll (IL)
Kansas Wesleyan U (KS)
Kent State U (OH)
Kutztown U of Pennsylvania (PA)
La Salle U (PA)
Lehman Coll of the City U of NY (NY)
Lewis-Clark State Coll (ID)
Lewis U (IL)
Lipscomb U (TN)
Lock Haven U of Pennsylvania (PA)
Long Island U, Brooklyn Campus (NY)
Louisiana Coll (LA)
Louisiana State U and A&M Coll (LA)
Louisiana State U in Shreveport (LA)
Louisiana Tech U (LA)
Lynchburg Coll (VA)
Manchester Coll (IN)
Mansfield U of Pennsylvania (PA)
Maranatha Baptist Bible Coll (WI)
Marietta Coll (OH)
Marquette U (WI)
Marshall U (WV)
Marymount Coll of Fordham U (NY)
The Master's Coll and Seminary (CA)
McKendree Coll (IL)
McNeese State U (LA)
Mercy Coll (NY)
Metropolitan State Coll of Denver (CO)
Miami U (OH)
Minnesota State U, Mankato (MN)
Minnesota State U Moorhead (MN)
Minot State U (ND)
Mississippi Valley State U (MS)
Missouri Valley Coll (MO)
Missouri Western State Coll (MO)
Monmouth Coll (IL)
Morehead State U (KY)
Morgan State U (MD)
Morris Brown Coll (GA)
Mount Mercy Coll (IA)
Mount Saint Mary's Coll and Seminary (MD)
Murray State U (KY)
Nebraska Wesleyan U (NE)
Newberry Coll (SC)
New England School of Communications (ME)
New Mexico State U (NM)
North Carolina Ag and Tech State U (NC)
North Central Coll (IL)
North Dakota State U (ND)
Northeastern Illinois U (IL)
Northern Arizona U (AZ)
Northern Kentucky U (KY)
Northern Michigan U (MI)
Northern State U (SD)
North Park U (IL)
Northwest Christian Coll (OR)
Northwestern Coll (IA)
Northwestern Oklahoma State U (OK)
Northwestern U (IL)
Northwest Missouri State U (MO)
Ohio Northern U (OH)
Ohio U (OH)
Oklahoma Baptist U (OK)
Oklahoma Christian U of Science and Arts (OK)
Oklahoma City U (OK)
Oklahoma State U (OK)
Old Dominion U (VA)
Olivet Nazarene U (IL)
Oregon State U (OR)
Ouachita Baptist U (AR)
Pace U (NY)
Penn State U Delaware County Campus of the Commonwealth Coll (PA)
Penn State U Univ Park Campus (PA)
Pepperdine U, Malibu (CA)
Pillsbury Baptist Bible Coll (MN)
Pittsburg State U (KS)
Point Loma Nazarene U (CA)
Portland State U (OR)
Rensselaer Polytechnic Inst (NY)
Rhode Island Coll (RI)
Rider U (NJ)
Ripon Coll (WI)
Rowan U (NJ)
St. Cloud State U (MN)
Saint John's U (MN)
St. John's U (NY)
St. Joseph's Coll, New York (NY)
St. Joseph's Coll, Suffolk Campus (NY)
St. Mary's U of San Antonio (TX)
Samford U (AL)
Sam Houston State U (TX)
San Diego State U (CA)
San Francisco State U (CA)
San Jose State U (CA)
Shippensburg U of Pennsylvania (PA)
Simpson Coll (IA)
South Dakota State U (SD)
Southeast Missouri State U (MO)
Southern Illinois U Carbondale (IL)
Southern Illinois U Edwardsville (IL)
Southern Nazarene U (OK)
Southern U and A&M Coll (LA)
Southern Utah U (UT)
Southwest Texas State U (TX)
State U of NY at Albany (NY)
State U of NY at New Paltz (NY)
State U of NY Coll at Brockport (NY)
State U of NY Coll at Cortland (NY)
State U of NY Coll at Oneonta (NY)
State U of NY Coll at Potsdam (NY)
Stephen F. Austin State U (TX)
Stetson U (FL)
Suffolk U (MA)
Susquehanna U (PA)
Syracuse U (NY)
Tarleton State U (TX)
Temple U (PA)
Texas A&M U (TX)
Texas A&M U–Kingsville (TX)
Texas Christian U (TX)
Texas Southern U (TX)
Texas Tech U (TX)
Texas Wesleyan U (TX)
Thomas More Coll (KY)
Trevecca Nazarene U (TN)
Trinity U (TX)
Troy State U (AL)
Truman State U (MO)
Union U (TN)
U Coll of Cape Breton (NS, Canada)
The U of Akron (OH)
The U of Alabama (AL)
The U of Alabama in Huntsville (AL)
U of Arkansas at Little Rock (AR)
U of Arkansas at Pine Bluff (AR)
U of Calif, Berkeley (CA)
U of Calif, Davis (CA)
U of Central Arkansas (AR)
U of Central Florida (FL)
U of Dubuque (IA)
U of Georgia (GA)
U of Hawaii at Manoa (HI)
U of Houston (TX)
U of Illinois at Chicago (IL)
U of Illinois at Urbana–Champaign (IL)
The U of Iowa (IA)
U of Kansas (KS)
U of Louisiana at Monroe (LA)
U of Michigan (MI)
U of Michigan–Dearborn (MI)
U of Minnesota, Morris (MN)
The U of Montana–Missoula (MT)
U of Montevallo (AL)
U of Nebraska at Kearney (NE)
U of Nebraska at Omaha (NE)
U of New Mexico (NM)
U of North Alabama (AL)
The U of North Carolina at Greensboro (NC)
The U of North Carolina at Wilmington (NC)
U of Pittsburgh (PA)
U of Richmond (VA)
U of Sioux Falls (SD)
U of South Dakota (SD)
U of Southern Colorado (CO)
U of South Florida (FL)
The U of Tennessee (TN)
The U of Texas at Arlington (TX)
The U of Texas at El Paso (TX)
The U of Texas at Tyler (TX)
The U of Texas of the Permian Basin (TX)
The U of Texas–Pan American (TX)
U of the Incarnate Word (TX)
U of the Virgin Islands (VI)
U of Utah (UT)
U of Washington (WA)
U of Waterloo (ON, Canada)
U of Wisconsin–La Crosse (WI)
U of Wisconsin–Platteville (WI)
U of Wisconsin–River Falls (WI)
U of Wisconsin–Superior (WI)
U of Wisconsin–Whitewater (WI)
Utah State U (UT)
Valdosta State U (GA)
Vanguard U of Southern California (CA)
Wabash Coll (IN)
Walla Walla Coll (WA)
Washburn U of Topeka (KS)
Wayne State Coll (NE)
West Chester U of Pennsylvania (PA)
Western Kentucky U (KY)
West Texas A&M U (TX)
West Virginia Wesleyan Coll (WV)
Wheaton Coll (IL)
Whitworth Coll (WA)
Willamette U (OR)
William Jewell Coll (MO)
Wingate U (NC)
Winona State U (MN)
Yeshiva U (NY)
York Coll of Pennsylvania (PA)
York Coll of the City U of New York (NY)
Youngstown State U (OH)

SPEECH/THEATER EDUCATION

Augustana Coll (SD)
Baptist Bible Coll of Pennsylvania (PA)
Bemidji State U (MN)
Boston U (MA)
Briar Cliff U (IA)
Columbus State U (GA)
Culver-Stockton Coll (MO)
Dickinson State U (ND)
Graceland U (IA)
Grambling State U (LA)
Hamline U (MN)
Hastings Coll (NE)
Idaho State U (ID)
King Coll (TN)
Lewis-Clark State Coll (ID)
Lewis U (IL)
McKendree Coll (IL)
McPherson Coll (KS)
Midland Lutheran Coll (NE)
Missouri Western State Coll (MO)
Northwestern Oklahoma State U (OK)
Oklahoma City U (OK)
St. Ambrose U (IA)
Southwest Baptist U (MO)
Southwest State U (MN)
Tennessee Temple U (TN)
U of Minnesota, Morris (MN)
U of St. Thomas (MN)
U of Windsor (ON, Canada)
Viterbo U (WI)
Wartburg Coll (IA)
William Woods U (MO)
York Coll (NE)
York U (ON, Canada)

SPEECH THERAPY

Adelphi U (NY)
Auburn U (AL)
Augustana Coll (IL)
Columbia Coll (SC)
Eastern Kentucky U (KY)
Eastern Washington U (WA)
Elms Coll (MA)
Emerson Coll (MA)
Fontbonne U (MO)
Hampton U (VA)
Indiana U Bloomington (IN)
Iona Coll (NY)
Lamar U (TX)
Lambuth U (TN)
Murray State U (KY)
Northeastern State U (OK)
Northwestern U (IL)

Ohio U (OH)
Queens Coll of the City U of NY (NY)
St. Cloud State U (MN)
Southeast Missouri State U (MO)
State U of NY at New Paltz (NY)
State U of NY Coll at Fredonia (NY)
State U of NY Coll at Geneseo (NY)
Temple U (PA)
Texas A&M U–Kingsville (TX)
Texas Southern U (TX)
The U of British Columbia (BC, Canada)
The U of Iowa (IA)
U of New Hampshire (NH)
U of Oklahoma Health Sciences Center (OK)
U of Redlands (CA)
The U of Texas–Pan American (TX)
U of Toledo (OH)
U of Wisconsin–Madison (WI)
U of Wisconsin–River Falls (WI)
West Chester U of Pennsylvania (PA)
Xavier U of Louisiana (LA)

SPORT/FITNESS ADMINISTRATION

Albertson Coll of Idaho (ID)
Alvernia Coll (PA)
American U (DC)
Anderson Coll (SC)
Arkansas Tech U (AR)
Augustana Coll (SD)
Averett U (VA)
Baldwin-Wallace Coll (OH)
Ball State U (IN)
Barber-Scotia Coll (NC)
Barry U (FL)
Barton Coll (NC)
Baylor U (TX)
Becker Coll (MA)
Belhaven Coll (MS)
Bemidji State U (MN)
Benedictine Coll (KS)
Bethany Coll (WV)
Bethel Coll (IN)
Black Hills State U (SD)
Bluffton Coll (OH)
Bowling Green State U (OH)
Brock U (ON, Canada)
Campbell U (NC)
Carroll Coll (MT)
Cazenovia Coll (NY)
Centenary Coll (NJ)
Central Methodist Coll (MO)
Central Washington U (WA)
Champlain Coll (VT)
Chowan Coll (NC)
Christopher Newport U (VA)
Colby-Sawyer Coll (NH)
Coll Misericordia (PA)
Columbia Southern U (AL)
Concordia U (MI)
Concordia U (NE)
Concordia U (OR)
Cornerstone U (MI)
Crown Coll (MN)
Daniel Webster Coll (NH)
Davis & Elkins Coll (WV)
Defiance Coll (OH)
Delaware State U (DE)
Delaware Valley Coll (PA)
DeSales U (PA)
Eastern Connecticut State U (CT)
Eastern Mennonite U (VA)
Edinboro U of Pennsylvania (PA)
Elmhurst Coll (IL)
Elon U (NC)
Endicott Coll (MA)
Erskine Coll (SC)
Faulkner U (AL)
Flagler Coll (FL)
Franklin Pierce Coll (NH)
Fresno Pacific U (CA)
Gardner-Webb U (NC)
George Fox U (OR)
Georgia Southern U (GA)
Gonzaga U (WA)
Graceland U (IA)
Greensboro Coll (NC)
Guilford Coll (NC)
Hampton U (VA)
Harding U (AR)
Hastings Coll (NE)
High Point U (NC)
Holy Family Coll (PA)
Howard Payne U (TX)
Huntingdon Coll (AL)
Husson Coll (ME)
Indiana U Bloomington (IN)
Indiana Wesleyan U (IN)
Iowa Wesleyan Coll (IA)
Ithaca Coll (NY)
Johnson State Coll (VT)
Judson Coll (IL)
Keene State Coll (NH)
Kennesaw State U (GA)
Kentucky Wesleyan Coll (KY)
Laurentian U (ON, Canada)
LeTourneau U (TX)
Liberty U (VA)
Limestone Coll (SC)
Lock Haven U of Pennsylvania (PA)
Longwood Coll (VA)
Loras Coll (IA)
Luther Coll (IA)
Lynchburg Coll (VA)
Lyndon State Coll (VT)
Lynn U (FL)
MacMurray Coll (IL)
Malone Coll (OH)
Marian Coll of Fond du Lac (WI)
Mars Hill Coll (NC)
Marymount U (VA)
Medaille Coll (NY)
Mercyhurst Coll (PA)
Meredith Coll (NC)
Methodist Coll (NC)
Miami U (OH)
MidAmerica Nazarene U (KS)
Millikin U (IL)
Minnesota State U, Mankato (MN)
Minnesota State U Moorhead (MN)
Minot State U (ND)
Mississippi U for Women (MS)
Missouri Baptist Coll (MO)
Montana State U–Billings (MT)
Montana State U–Bozeman (MT)
Montreat Coll (NC)
Morgan State U (MD)
Mount Union Coll (OH)
Mount Vernon Nazarene U (OH)
National American U (SD)
National U (CA)
Nebraska Wesleyan U (NE)
Neumann Coll (PA)
New England Coll (NH)
New York U (NY)
North Greenville Coll (SC)
Northwestern Coll (MN)
Northwest Missouri State U (MO)
Nova Southeastern U (FL)
Ohio Northern U (OH)
Ohio U (OH)
Olivet Coll (MI)
Olivet Nazarene U (IL)
Otterbein Coll (OH)
Pfeiffer U (NC)
Principia Coll (IL)
Quincy U (IL)
Reinhardt Coll (GA)
Robert Morris U (PA)
Rochester Coll (MI)
Sacred Heart U (CT)
St. Ambrose U (IA)
St. Andrews Presbyterian Coll (NC)
St. John's U (NY)
Saint Joseph's Coll (ME)
Saint Leo U (FL)
St. Thomas U (FL)
Salem International U (WV)
Salem State Coll (MA)
Seton Hall U (NJ)
Shawnee State U (OH)
Simpson Coll (IA)
Slippery Rock U of Pennsylvania (PA)
Southeast Missouri State U (MO)
Southern Adventist U (TN)
Southern Nazarene U (OK)
Southern New Hampshire U (NH)
Southern Virginia U (VA)
Southwest Baptist U (MO)
Southwestern Coll (KS)
Spring Arbor U (MI)
Springfield Coll (MA)
State U of NY Coll at Brockport (NY)
Stetson U (FL)
Taylor U (IN)
Temple U (PA)
Tennessee Wesleyan Coll (TN)
Texas Lutheran U (TX)
Texas Wesleyan U (TX)
Thomas Coll (ME)
Tiffin U (OH)
Towson U (MD)
Tri-State U (IN)
Tulane U (LA)
Tusculum Coll (TN)
Union Coll (KY)
Union Coll (NE)
Union U (TN)
U Coll of Cape Breton (NS, Canada)
U of Alberta (AB, Canada)
U of Dayton (OH)
U of Georgia (GA)
The U of Iowa (IA)
U of Louisville (KY)
U of Massachusetts Amherst (MA)
U of Michigan (MI)
U of Nebraska at Kearney (NE)
U of Nevada, Las Vegas (NV)
U of New England (ME)
U of New Haven (CT)
U of Pittsburgh at Bradford (PA)
U of Regina (SK, Canada)
U of San Francisco (CA)
U of South Carolina (SC)
The U of Tennessee (TN)
The U of Tennessee at Martin (TN)
U of the Incarnate Word (TX)
U of Tulsa (OK)
U of Victoria (BC, Canada)
U of Windsor (ON, Canada)
U of Wisconsin–La Crosse (WI)
U of Wisconsin–Parkside (WI)
Valparaiso U (IN)
Virginia Intermont Coll (VA)
Warner Southern Coll (FL)
Wartburg Coll (IA)
Washington State U (WA)
Wayne State Coll (NE)
Webber International U (FL)
Western Baptist Coll (OR)
Western Carolina U (NC)
Western New England Coll (MA)
West Virginia U (WV)
Wheeling Jesuit U (WV)
Widener U (PA)
William Penn U (IA)
Wilmington Coll (DE)
Wilmington Coll (OH)
Wingate U (NC)
Winona State U (MN)
Winston-Salem State U (NC)
Winthrop U (SC)
Xavier U (OH)
York Coll of Pennsylvania (PA)
York U (ON, Canada)
Youngstown State U (OH)

STRINGED INSTRUMENTS

Acadia U (NS, Canada)
Alma Coll (MI)
Appalachian State U (NC)
Aquinas Coll (MI)
Augustana Coll (IL)
Baldwin-Wallace Coll (OH)
Ball State U (IN)
Benedictine Coll (KS)
Bennington Coll (VT)
Berklee Coll of Music (MA)
The Boston Conservatory (MA)
Butler U (IN)
California Inst of the Arts (CA)
California State U, Fullerton (CA)
California State U, Northridge (CA)
Capital U (OH)
Centenary Coll of Louisiana (LA)
Chapman U (CA)
Cleveland Inst of Music (OH)
Columbus State U (GA)
Converse Coll (SC)
Cornish Coll of the Arts (WA)
The Curtis Inst of Music (PA)
DePaul U (IL)
Eastern Washington U (WA)
Five Towns Coll (NY)
Florida State U (FL)
Friends U (KS)
Grand Valley State U (MI)
Harding U (AR)
Hardin-Simmons U (TX)
Hastings Coll (NE)
Heidelberg Coll (OH)
Houghton Coll (NY)
Howard Payne U (TX)
Illinois Wesleyan U (IL)
Inter American U of PR, San Germán Campus (PR)
The Juilliard School (NY)
Lamar U (TX)
Lawrence U (WI)
Lindenwood U (MO)
Lipscomb U (TN)
Luther Coll (IA)
Manhattan School of Music (NY)
Mannes Coll of Music, New School U (NY)
Mars Hill Coll (NC)
Memorial U of Newfoundland (NF, Canada)
Meredith Coll (NC)
Montclair State U (NJ)
Mount Allison U (NB, Canada)
New England Conservatory of Music (MA)
New World School of the Arts (FL)
Northern Michigan U (MI)
Northwest Missouri State U (MO)
Notre Dame de Namur U (CA)
Oberlin Coll (OH)
Oklahoma City U (OK)
Olivet Nazarene U (IL)
Otterbein Coll (OH)
Palm Beach Atlantic Coll (FL)
Peabody Conserv of Music of Johns Hopkins U (MD)
Pittsburg State U (KS)
Queen's U at Kingston (ON, Canada)
Roosevelt U (IL)
San Francisco Conservatory of Music (CA)
Sarah Lawrence Coll (NY)
Seton Hill Coll (PA)
State U of NY Coll at Fredonia (NY)
Susquehanna U (PA)
Syracuse U (NY)
Temple U (PA)
The U of Akron (OH)
U of Alberta (AB, Canada)
The U of British Columbia (BC, Canada)
U of Central Oklahoma (OK)
U of Cincinnati (OH)
The U of Iowa (IA)
U of Kansas (KS)
U of Miami (FL)
U of Michigan (MI)
U of Missouri–Kansas City (MO)
U of New Hampshire (NH)
U of North Texas (TX)
U of Oklahoma (OK)
U of South Dakota (SD)
U of Southern California (CA)
The U of Tennessee at Martin (TN)
U of Washington (WA)
The U of Western Ontario (ON, Canada)
U of Wisconsin–Milwaukee (WI)
Vanderbilt U (TN)
West Chester U of Pennsylvania (PA)
Xavier U of Louisiana (LA)
Youngstown State U (OH)

STRUCTURAL ENGINEERING

Clarkson U (NY)
The Coll of Southeastern Europe, The American U of Athens(Greece)
Johnson & Wales U (RI)
Penn State U Berks Cmps of Berks-Lehigh Valley Coll (PA)
Penn State U Harrisburg Campus of the Capital Coll (PA)
U of Calif, San Diego (CA)
U of Southern California (CA)

SURVEYING

British Columbia Inst of Technology (BC, Canada)
California State Polytechnic U, Pomona (CA)
California State U, Fresno (CA)
East Tennessee State U (TN)
Ferris State U (MI)
Metropolitan State Coll of Denver (CO)
Michigan Technological U (MI)
New Mexico State U (NM)
The Ohio State U (OH)
Oregon Inst of Technology (OR)
Penn State U Wilkes-Barre Campus of the Commonwealth Coll (PA)
Polytechnic U of Puerto Rico (PR)
Purdue U (IN)
Southern Polytechnic State U (GA)
State U of NY Coll of Technology at Alfred (NY)
Texas A&M U–Corpus Christi (TX)
Thomas Edison State Coll (NJ)
Université Laval (QC, Canada)
The U of Akron (OH)
U of Alaska Anchorage (AK)
U of Arkansas at Little Rock (AR)
U of Florida (FL)
U of Maine (ME)
U of Toronto (ON, Canada)
U of Wisconsin–Madison (WI)

SYSTEM ADMINISTRATION

American Coll of Computer & Information Sciences (AL)

SYSTEM/NETWORKING/LAN/WAN MANAGEMENT

Champlain Coll (VT)

SYSTEMS ENGINEERING

Boston U (MA)
California State U, Northridge (CA)
Carleton U (ON, Canada)
Case Western Reserve U (OH)
Eastern Nazarene Coll (MA)
Florida International U (FL)
George Mason U (VA)
The George Washington U (DC)
Harvard U (MA)
Maine Maritime Academy (ME)
Missouri Tech (MO)
Montana Tech of The U of Montana (MT)
Oakland U (MI)
The Ohio State U (OH)
Ohio U (OH)
Rensselaer Polytechnic Inst (NY)
Richmond, The American International U in London(United Kingdom)
United States Military Academy (NY)
United States Naval Academy (MD)
The U of Arizona (AZ)
U of Calif, San Diego (CA)
U of Florida (FL)
The U of Memphis (TN)
U of Pennsylvania (PA)
U of Regina (SK, Canada)
U of Southern California (CA)
U of Virginia (VA)
U of Waterloo (ON, Canada)
Washington U in St. Louis (MO)

SYSTEMS SCIENCE/THEORY

Indiana U Bloomington (IN)
Marshall U (WV)
Miami U (OH)
Providence Coll (RI)
Stanford U (CA)
U of Kansas (KS)
U of Ottawa (ON, Canada)
Washington U in St. Louis (MO)
Yale U (CT)

TAXATION

California State U, Fullerton (CA)
Drexel U (PA)

TEACHER ASSISTANT/AIDE

Long Island U, Southampton Coll, Friends World Program (NY)

TEACHER EDUCATION RELATED

Boston U (MA)
U of Hawaii at Manoa (HI)
Xavier U (OH)

TEACHER EDUCATION, SPECIFIC PROGRAMS RELATED

Averett U (VA)
Bradley U (IL)
Chadron State Coll (NE)
Drexel U (PA)
Duquesne U (PA)
Franklin Coll of Indiana (IN)
Henderson State U (AR)
Hofstra U (NY)
Juniata Coll (PA)
Louisiana State U and A&M Coll (LA)
Minot State U (ND)
Northern Arizona U (AZ)
Ohio U (OH)

Old Dominion U (VA)
Plymouth State Coll (NH)
San Diego State U (CA)
Thomas More Coll (KY)
The U of Akron (OH)
The U of Arizona (AZ)
U of Central Oklahoma (OK)
U of Hawaii at Manoa (HI)
U of Kentucky (KY)
U of Louisiana at Lafayette (LA)
U of Nebraska–Lincoln (NE)
The U of North Carolina at Wilmington (NC)
U of St. Thomas (MN)
U of Toledo (OH)
Utah State U (UT)

TEACHING ENGLISH AS A SECOND LANGUAGE
Alaska Bible Coll (AK)
Bethel Coll (MN)
Bridgewater Coll (VA)
Brigham Young U–Hawaii (HI)
California State U, Northridge (CA)
Calvin Coll (MI)
Carleton U (ON, Canada)
Carroll Coll (MT)
Concordia U (QC, Canada)
Concordia U Wisconsin (WI)
Doane Coll (NE)
Elms Coll (MA)
Goshen Coll (IN)
Hawai'i Pacific U (HI)
Hobe Sound Bible Coll (FL)
Howard Payne U (TX)
Inter American U of PR, Aguadilla Campus (PR)
Inter American U of PR, San Germán Campus (PR)
John Brown U (AR)
Liberty U (VA)
Long Island U, Southampton Coll, Friends World Program (NY)
Maryville Coll (TN)
McGill U (PQ, Canada)
Mercy Coll (NY)
Moody Bible Inst (IL)
Murray State U (KY)
Northern Arizona U (AZ)
Northwest Coll (WA)
Northwestern Coll (MN)
Nyack Coll (NY)
Ohio Dominican Coll (OH)
Ohio U (OH)
Oklahoma Christian U of Science and Arts (OK)
Oklahoma Wesleyan U (OK)
Oral Roberts U (OK)
Providence Coll and Theological Seminary (MB, Canada)
Queens Coll of the City U of NY (NY)
Simmons Coll (MA)
Texas Christian U (TX)
Texas Wesleyan U (TX)
Union U (TN)
Université Laval (QC, Canada)
U of Alberta (AB, Canada)
The U of British Columbia (BC, Canada)
U of Delaware (DE)
The U of Findlay (OH)
U of Hawaii at Manoa (HI)
The U of Montana–Missoula (MT)
U of Nebraska–Lincoln (NE)
U of Northern Iowa (IA)
U of Ottawa (ON, Canada)
U of Puerto Rico, Humacao U Coll (PR)
U of Victoria (BC, Canada)
U of Washington (WA)
U of Wisconsin–Oshkosh (WI)
U of Wisconsin–River Falls (WI)
York U (ON, Canada)

TECHNICAL/BUSINESS WRITING
Alderson-Broaddus Coll (WV)
Boise State U (ID)
Bowling Green State U (OH)
Carlow Coll (PA)
Carnegie Mellon U (PA)
Carroll Coll (MT)
Cedarville U (OH)
Central Michigan U (MI)
Chicago State U (IL)
Christian Brothers U (TN)
Clarkson U (NY)
Coll of Santa Fe (NM)
Drexel U (PA)
Ferris State U (MI)
Fitchburg State Coll (MA)
Gannon U (PA)
Grand Valley State U (MI)
Iowa State U of Science and Technology (IA)
James Madison U (VA)
La Roche Coll (PA)
Lawrence Technological U (MI)
Maryville Coll (TN)
Mercyhurst Coll (PA)
Metropolitan State U (MN)
Miami U (OH)
Michigan Technological U (MI)
Montana Tech of The U of Montana (MT)
Mount Mary Coll (WI)
New Jersey Inst of Technology (NJ)
New Mexico Inst of Mining and Technology (NM)
New York Inst of Technology (NY)
Northeastern U (MA)
Northwestern Coll (MN)
Oklahoma State U (OK)
Oregon State U (OR)
Pennsylvania Coll of Technology (PA)
Polytechnic U, Brooklyn Campus (NY)
Rensselaer Polytechnic Inst (NY)
San Francisco State U (CA)
San Jose State U (CA)
Southern Polytechnic State U (GA)
Southwest Missouri State U (MO)
Tennessee Technological U (TN)
U of Arkansas at Little Rock (AR)
U of Baltimore (MD)
U of Delaware (DE)
U of Hartford (CT)
The U of Montana–Missoula (MT)
U of Victoria (BC, Canada)
U of Washington (WA)
U of Wisconsin–Stout (WI)
Weber State U (UT)
White Pines Coll (NH)
Winthrop U (SC)
Wittenberg U (OH)
Worcester Polytechnic Inst (MA)
York U (ON, Canada)
Youngstown State U (OH)

TECHNICAL EDUCATION
Bowling Green State U (OH)
Colorado State U (CO)
Idaho State U (ID)
Mississippi State U (MS)
New York Inst of Technology (NY)
The Ohio State U (OH)
San Diego State U (CA)
Texas Christian U (TX)
Université Laval (QC, Canada)
The U of Akron (OH)
U of Idaho (ID)
U of Nebraska at Kearney (NE)
U of Saskatchewan (SK, Canada)
The U of Tennessee (TN)
U of Wisconsin–Stout (WI)
Utah State U (UT)
Valley City State U (ND)
Wayne State U (MI)

TELECOMMUNICATIONS
Ball State U (IN)
Baylor U (TX)
Bowling Green State U (OH)
Butler U (IN)
California State Polytechnic U, Pomona (CA)
California State U, Hayward (CA)
California State U, Monterey Bay (CA)
Cameron U (OK)
Capitol Coll (MD)
Champlain Coll (VT)
Colorado Tech U (CO)
Columbia Coll–Hollywood (CA)
Ferris State U (MI)
Golden Gate U (CA)
Grand Valley State U (MI)
Hampshire Coll (MA)
Howard Payne U (TX)
Indiana U Bloomington (IN)
Ithaca Coll (NY)
Kean U (NJ)
Kutztown U of Pennsylvania (PA)
Marywood U (PA)
Michigan State U (MI)
Morgan State U (MD)
Murray State U (KY)
New York Inst of Technology (NY)
Ohio U (OH)
Oklahoma Baptist U (OK)
Pacific U (OR)
Penn State U Univ Park Campus (PA)
Pepperdine U, Malibu (CA)
Rochester Inst of Technology (NY)
Roosevelt U (IL)
St. John's U (NY)
Salem International U (WV)
Southern Polytechnic State U (GA)
Syracuse U (NY)
Texas Southern U (TX)
Tusculum Coll (TN)
U of Florida (FL)
U of Southern Colorado (CO)
U of Wisconsin–Platteville (WI)
Western Michigan U (MI)
Westminster Coll (PA)
Wingate U (NC)
Winona State U (MN)
Youngstown State U (OH)

TEXTILE ARTS
Academy of Art Coll (CA)
Adams State Coll (CO)
Alberta Coll of Art & Design (AB, Canada)
Bowling Green State U (OH)
California Coll of Arts and Crafts (CA)
California State U, Long Beach (CA)
California State U, Northridge (CA)
The Cleveland Inst of Art (OH)
Ctr for Creative Studies—Coll of Art and Design (MI)
Colorado State U (CO)
Concordia U (QC, Canada)
Cornell U (NY)
Finlandia U (MI)
Kansas City Art Inst (MO)
Long Island U, Southampton Coll, Friends World Program (NY)
Maryland Inst, Coll of Art (MD)
Massachusetts Coll of Art (MA)
Memphis Coll of Art (TN)
Mercyhurst Coll (PA)
Moore Coll of Art and Design (PA)
Northern Michigan U (MI)
Northwest Missouri State U (MO)
Nova Scotia Coll of Art and Design (NS, Canada)
Oregon State U (OR)
Philadelphia U (PA)
Rhode Island School of Design (RI)
Savannah Coll of Art and Design (GA)
School of the Art Inst of Chicago (IL)
Syracuse U (NY)
Texas Woman's U (TX)
U of Massachusetts Dartmouth (MA)
U of Michigan (MI)
U of North Texas (TX)
U of Oregon (OR)
U of Washington (WA)
U of Wisconsin–Milwaukee (WI)

TEXTILE SCIENCES/ ENGINEERING
Auburn U (AL)
Georgia Inst of Technology (GA)
North Carolina State U (NC)
Philadelphia U (PA)
Texas Tech U (TX)
Université de Sherbrooke (PQ, Canada)
U of Massachusetts Dartmouth (MA)

THEATER ARTS/DRAMA
Abilene Christian U (TX)
Acadia U (NS, Canada)
Adams State Coll (CO)
Adelphi U (NY)
Adrian Coll (MI)
Agnes Scott Coll (GA)
Alabama State U (AL)
Albertson Coll of Idaho (ID)
Albertus Magnus Coll (CT)
Albion Coll (MI)
Albright Coll (PA)
Alderson-Broaddus Coll (WV)
Alfred U (NY)
Allegheny Coll (PA)
Alma Coll (MI)
American U (DC)
American U in Cairo(Egypt)
Amherst Coll (MA)
Anderson Coll (SC)
Anderson U (IN)
Angelo State U (TX)
Appalachian State U (NC)
Arcadia U (PA)
Arizona State U (AZ)
Arkansas State U (AR)
Armstrong Atlantic State U (GA)
Ashland U (OH)
Auburn U (AL)
Augsburg Coll (MN)
Augustana Coll (IL)
Augustana Coll (SD)
Averett U (VA)
Avila Coll (MO)
Baker U (KS)
Baldwin-Wallace Coll (OH)
Ball State U (IN)
Bard Coll (NY)
Barnard Coll (NY)
Barry U (FL)
Barton Coll (NC)
Bates Coll (ME)
Baylor U (TX)
Belhaven Coll (MS)
Belmont U (TN)
Beloit Coll (WI)
Bemidji State U (MN)
Benedictine Coll (KS)
Bennington Coll (VT)
Berea Coll (KY)
Berry Coll (GA)
Bethany Coll (WV)
Bethany Coll of the Assemblies of God (CA)
Bethel Coll (IN)
Bethel Coll (MN)
Bethel Coll (TN)
Birmingham-Southern Coll (AL)
Bishop's U (PQ, Canada)
Bloomfield Coll (NJ)
Bloomsburg U of Pennsylvania (PA)
Bluefield Coll (VA)
Blue Mountain Coll (MS)
Boise State U (ID)
Boston Coll (MA)
The Boston Conservatory (MA)
Bowling Green State U (OH)
Bradley U (IL)
Brandeis U (MA)
Brenau U (GA)
Briar Cliff U (IA)
Bridgewater State Coll (MA)
Brigham Young U (UT)
Brock U (ON, Canada)
Brooklyn Coll of the City U of NY (NY)
Brown U (RI)
Bucknell U (PA)
Buena Vista U (IA)
Butler U (IN)
California Inst of the Arts (CA)
California Lutheran U (CA)
California State Polytechnic U, Pomona (CA)
California State U, Bakersfield (CA)
California State U, Chico (CA)
California State U, Dominguez Hills (CA)
California State U, Fresno (CA)
California State U, Fullerton (CA)
California State U, Hayward (CA)
California State U, Long Beach (CA)
California State U, Los Angeles (CA)
California State U, Monterey Bay (CA)
California State U, Northridge (CA)
California State U, Sacramento (CA)
California State U, San Bernardino (CA)
California State U, Stanislaus (CA)
California U of Pennsylvania (PA)
Calvin Coll (MI)
Cameron U (OK)
Campbell U (NC)
Cardinal Stritch U (WI)
Carleton U (ON, Canada)
Carnegie Mellon U (PA)
Carroll Coll (MT)
Carroll Coll (WI)
Carson-Newman Coll (TN)
Carthage Coll (WI)
Case Western Reserve U (OH)
Castleton State Coll (VT)
Catawba Coll (NC)
The Catholic U of America (DC)
Cedar Crest Coll (PA)
Cedarville U (OH)
Centenary Coll of Louisiana (LA)
Central Coll (IA)
Central Connecticut State U (CT)
Central Methodist Coll (MO)
Central Michigan U (MI)
Central Missouri State U (MO)
Central Washington U (WA)
Centre Coll (KY)
Chadron State Coll (NE)
Chapman U (CA)
Chatham Coll (PA)
Cheyney U of Pennsylvania (PA)
Christopher Newport U (VA)
City Coll of the City U of NY (NY)
Claremont McKenna Coll (CA)
Clarion U of Pennsylvania (PA)
Clark Atlanta U (GA)
Clarke Coll (IA)
Clark U (MA)
Cleveland State U (OH)
Coastal Carolina U (SC)
Coe Coll (IA)
Coker Coll (SC)
Colby Coll (ME)
Colgate U (NY)
Coll of Charleston (SC)
Coll of Saint Benedict (MN)
Coll of St. Catherine (MN)
Coll of Santa Fe (NM)
Coll of Staten Island of the City U of NY (NY)
Coll of the Holy Cross (MA)
Coll of the Ozarks (MO)
The Coll of William and Mary (VA)
The Coll of Wooster (OH)
Colorado Christian U (CO)
The Colorado Coll (CO)
Colorado State U (CO)
Columbia Coll (NY)
Columbia Coll Chicago (IL)
Columbia U, School of General Studies (NY)
Columbus State U (GA)
Concordia Coll (MN)
Concordia U (CA)
Concordia U (IL)
Concordia U (MN)
Concordia U (NE)
Concordia U (OR)
Concordia U (QC, Canada)
Concordia U Wisconsin (WI)
Connecticut Coll (CT)
Converse Coll (SC)
Cornell Coll (IA)
Cornell U (NY)
Cornish Coll of the Arts (WA)
Creighton U (NE)
Culver-Stockton Coll (MO)
Cumberland Coll (KY)
Cumberland U (TN)
Dakota Wesleyan U (SD)
Dalhousie U (NS, Canada)
Dartmouth Coll (NH)
Davidson Coll (NC)
Davis & Elkins Coll (WV)
Delaware State U (DE)
Denison U (OH)
DePaul U (IL)
DeSales U (PA)
Dickinson Coll (PA)
Dickinson State U (ND)
Dillard U (LA)
Doane Coll (NE)
Dominican U (IL)
Dordt Coll (IA)
Dowling Coll (NY)
Drake U (IA)
Drew U (NJ)
Drury U (MO)
Duke U (NC)
Duquesne U (PA)
Earlham Coll (IN)
East Carolina U (NC)
Eastern Illinois U (IL)
Eastern Kentucky U (KY)
Eastern Mennonite U (VA)
Eastern Michigan U (MI)
Eastern Nazarene Coll (MA)
Eastern New Mexico U (NM)
Eastern Oregon U (OR)
Eastern Washington U (WA)

THEATER ARTS/DRAMA AND STAGECRAFT RELATED

THEATER DESIGN

THEOLOGICAL STUDIES/ RELIGIOUS VOCATIONS RELATED

THEOLOGY

Wisconsin Lutheran Coll (WI)
Wittenberg U (OH)
Xavier U (OH)
Xavier U of Louisiana (LA)

THEOLOGY/MINISTRY RELATED
Brescia U (KY)
California Baptist U (CA)
Malone Coll (OH)
Northwestern Coll (MN)
Southeastern Coll of the Assemblies of God (FL)
Wheaton Coll (IL)

THEORETICAL/MATHEMATICAL PHYSICS
San Diego State U (CA)
U of Guelph (ON, Canada)
U of Saskatchewan (SK, Canada)

TOOL/DIE MAKING
Utah State U (UT)

TOURISM PROMOTION OPERATIONS
Central Connecticut State U (CT)
Champlain Coll (VT)
Eastern Michigan U (MI)
New Mexico State U (NM)
Open Learning Agency (BC, Canada)
Our Lady of Holy Cross Coll (LA)
U Coll of Cape Breton (NS, Canada)

TOURISM/TRAVEL MARKETING
Central Missouri State U (MO)
Eastern Michigan U (MI)
Johnson & Wales U (RI)
Mount Saint Vincent U (NS, Canada)
Ohio U (OH)
Rochester Inst of Technology (NY)
U Coll of the Cariboo (BC, Canada)
U of Guelph (ON, Canada)
Western Montana Coll of The U of Montana (MT)

TOXICOLOGY
Ashland U (OH)
Bloomfield Coll (NJ)
Clarkson U (NY)
Coll of Saint Elizabeth (NJ)
Eastern Michigan U (MI)
Felician Coll (NJ)
Humboldt State U (CA)
Minnesota State U, Mankato (MN)
Monmouth U (NJ)
St. John's U (NY)
Texas Southern U (TX)
U of Guelph (ON, Canada)
U of Louisiana at Monroe (LA)
U of Miami (FL)
U of the Sciences in Philadelphia (PA)
U of Toronto (ON, Canada)
The U of Western Ontario (ON, Canada)
U of Wisconsin–Madison (WI)

TRADE/INDUSTRIAL EDUCATION
Athens State U (AL)
Auburn U (AL)
Ball State U (IN)
Bemidji State U (MN)
California Polytechnic State U, San Luis Obispo (CA)
California State U, Fresno (CA)
California State U, Long Beach (CA)
California State U, Los Angeles (CA)
California State U, San Bernardino (CA)
Central Connecticut State U (CT)
Central Washington U (WA)
Colorado State U (CO)
Dakota State U (SD)
Delaware State U (DE)
Eastern Kentucky U (KY)
Florida A&M U (FL)
Florida International U (FL)
Gustavus Adolphus Coll (MN)
Indiana State U (IN)
Indiana U of Pennsylvania (PA)
Iowa State U of Science and Technology (IA)
Keene State Coll (NH)
Kent State U (OH)
Memorial U of Newfoundland (NF, Canada)
Morehead State U (KY)
Murray State U (KY)
New York Inst of Technology (NY)
Norfolk State U (VA)
North Carolina Ag and Tech State U (NC)
Northeastern State U (OK)
Northern Kentucky U (KY)
Oklahoma State U (OK)
Pittsburg State U (KS)
Prairie View A&M U (TX)
San Francisco State U (CA)
South Carolina State U (SC)
Southern Illinois U Carbondale (IL)
State U of NY at Oswego (NY)
State U of NY Coll at Buffalo (NY)
Temple U (PA)
Texas A&M U–Commerce (TX)
Texas A&M U–Corpus Christi (TX)
U of Alberta (AB, Canada)
U of Arkansas (AR)
U of Arkansas at Pine Bluff (AR)
U of Central Florida (FL)
U of Central Oklahoma (OK)
U of Hawaii at Manoa (HI)
U of Idaho (ID)
U of Louisville (KY)
U of Nebraska at Omaha (NE)
U of Nebraska–Lincoln (NE)
U of Nevada, Reno (NV)
U of New Hampshire (NH)
U of North Dakota (ND)
U of Northern Iowa (IA)
U of North Florida (FL)
U of Regina (SK, Canada)
U of Saskatchewan (SK, Canada)
U of Southern Maine (ME)
U of South Florida (FL)
U of the District of Columbia (DC)
U of the Virgin Islands (VI)
U of Toledo (OH)
U of West Florida (FL)
U of Wyoming (WY)
Valdosta State U (GA)
Virginia Polytechnic Inst and State U (VA)
Virginia State U (VA)
Wayland Baptist U (TX)
Western Illinois U (IL)
Western Kentucky U (KY)

TRANSPORTATION AND MATERIALS MOVING RELATED
Averett U (VA)

TRANSPORTATION ENGINEERING
Dowling Coll (NY)
Rensselaer Polytechnic Inst (NY)
U of Pennsylvania (PA)

TRANSPORTATION TECHNOLOGY
Auburn U (AL)
Dowling Coll (NY)
Eastern Kentucky U (KY)
Iowa State U of Science and Technology (IA)
Maine Maritime Academy (ME)
Niagara U (NY)
North Carolina Ag and Tech State U (NC)
Pacific Union Coll (CA)
San Francisco State U (CA)
State U of NY at Farmingdale (NY)
Tennessee State U (TN)
Texas A&M U at Galveston (TX)
Texas Southern U (TX)
The U of British Columbia (BC, Canada)
U of Cincinnati (OH)

TRAVEL SERVICES MARKETING OPERATIONS
Champlain Coll (VT)

TRAVEL/TOURISM MANAGEMENT
Alliant International U (CA)
American InterContinental U (CA)
American InterContinental U, Atlanta (GA)
Arkansas State U (AR)
Ball State U (IN)
Black Hills State U (SD)
Brigham Young U–Hawaii (HI)
Brock U (ON, Canada)
Champlain Coll (VT)
Coastal Carolina U (SC)
The Coll of Southeastern Europe, The American U of Athens(Greece)
Concord Coll (WV)
Davis & Elkins Coll (WV)
Dowling Coll (NY)
Eastern Kentucky U (KY)
Fort Lewis Coll (CO)
Grand Valley State U (MI)
Hawai'i Pacific U (HI)
International Business Coll, Fort Wayne (IN)
Johnson & Wales U (RI)
Johnson State Coll (VT)
Lasell Coll (MA)
Long Island U, Southampton Coll, Friends World Program (NY)
Lynn U (FL)
Malaspina U-Coll (BC, Canada)
Mansfield U of Pennsylvania (PA)
Montclair State U (NJ)
Mount Saint Vincent U (NS, Canada)
New Mexico Highlands U (NM)
New Mexico State U (NM)
New York U (NY)
Niagara U (NY)
North Carolina State U (NC)
Northeastern State U (OK)
Our Lady of Holy Cross Coll (LA)
Pontifical Catholic U of Puerto Rico (PR)
Robert Morris U (PA)
Rochester Inst of Technology (NY)
St. Cloud State U (MN)
St. Thomas U (FL)
Salem State Coll (MA)
San Diego State U (CA)
Schiller International U (FL)
Schiller International U, American Coll of Switzerland(Switzerland)
Slippery Rock U of Pennsylvania (PA)
Southern New Hampshire U (NH)
State U of NY Coll of Technology at Delhi (NY)
Sullivan U (KY)
U Coll of Cape Breton (NS, Canada)
U of Calgary (AB, Canada)
U of Maine at Machias (ME)
U of Nevada, Las Vegas (NV)
U of New Hampshire (NH)
U of New Haven (CT)
The U of Texas at San Antonio (TX)
Virginia Polytechnic Inst and State U (VA)
Webber International U (FL)
Western Michigan U (MI)
Youngstown State U (OH)

TURF MANAGEMENT
Colorado State U (CO)
The Ohio State U (OH)
Penn State U Univ Park Campus (PA)
State U of NY Coll of A&T at Cobleskill (NY)
U of Georgia (GA)
U of Maryland, Coll Park (MD)
U of Rhode Island (RI)

URBAN STUDIES
Albertus Magnus Coll (CT)
Aquinas Coll (MI)
Augsburg Coll (MN)
Barnard Coll (NY)
Baylor U (TX)
Bellevue U (NE)
Beulah Heights Bible Coll (GA)
Boston U (MA)
Brown U (RI)
Bryn Mawr Coll (PA)
California State Polytechnic U, Pomona (CA)
California State U, Northridge (CA)
Canisius Coll (NY)
Carleton U (ON, Canada)
Cleveland State U (OH)
Coll of Charleston (SC)
Coll of Mount Saint Vincent (NY)
The Coll of Wooster (OH)
Columbia Coll (NY)
Columbia U, School of General Studies (NY)
Concordia U (QC, Canada)
Connecticut Coll (CT)
Cornell U (NY)
DePaul U (IL)
Dillard U (LA)
Eastern U (PA)
Eastern Washington U (WA)
Elmhurst Coll (IL)
Eugene Lang Coll, New School U (NY)
The Evergreen State Coll (WA)
Florida International U (FL)
Fordham U (NY)
Framingham State Coll (MA)
Furman U (SC)
Georgia State U (GA)
Hamline U (MN)
Hampshire Coll (MA)
Harris-Stowe State Coll (MO)
Harvard U (MA)
Haverford Coll (PA)
Hobart and William Smith Colls (NY)
Hunter Coll of the City U of NY (NY)
Indiana U Bloomington (IN)
Iona Coll (NY)
Jackson State U (MS)
Lehigh U (PA)
Lipscomb U (TN)
Long Island U, Southampton Coll, Friends World Program (NY)
Loyola Marymount U (CA)
Macalester Coll (MN)
Manhattan Coll (NY)
McGill U (PQ, Canada)
Metropolitan State Coll of Denver (CO)
Minnesota State U, Mankato (MN)
Montclair State U (NJ)
Morehouse Coll (GA)
Mount Mercy Coll (IA)
New Coll of Florida (FL)
New Jersey City U (NJ)
New York U (NY)
Northeastern Illinois U (IL)
North Park U (IL)
Northwestern U (IL)
Oglethorpe U (GA)
Ohio Wesleyan U (OH)
Portland State U (OR)
Queens Coll of the City U of NY (NY)
Rhodes Coll (TN)
Rockford Coll (IL)
Roosevelt U (IL)
Rutgers, The State U of New Jersey, New Brunswick (NJ)
St. Cloud State U (MN)
Saint Louis U (MO)
Saint Peter's Coll (NJ)
San Diego State U (CA)
San Francisco State U (CA)
Sarah Lawrence Coll (NY)
Sojourner-Douglass Coll (MD)
Stanford U (CA)
State U of NY at Albany (NY)
State U of NY Coll at Buffalo (NY)
Taylor U, Fort Wayne Campus (IN)
Temple U (PA)
Towson U (MD)
Trinity U (TX)
Tufts U (MA)
Université de Montréal (QC, Canada)
U of Alberta (AB, Canada)
The U of British Columbia (BC, Canada)
U of Calgary (AB, Canada)
U of Calif, San Diego (CA)
U of Cincinnati (OH)
U of Connecticut (CT)
The U of Lethbridge (AB, Canada)
U of Michigan–Flint (MI)
U of Minnesota, Duluth (MN)
U of Minnesota, Twin Cities Campus (MN)
U of Missouri–Kansas City (MO)
U of Missouri–St. Louis (MO)
U of Nebraska at Omaha (NE)
The U of North Carolina at Greensboro (NC)
U of Pennsylvania (PA)
U of Pittsburgh (PA)
U of Richmond (VA)
U of San Diego (CA)
U of Saskatchewan (SK, Canada)
U of Southern California (CA)
The U of Tampa (FL)
The U of Tennessee at Chattanooga (TN)
U of the District of Columbia (DC)
U of Toledo (OH)
U of Toronto (ON, Canada)
U of Utah (UT)
The U of Western Ontario (ON, Canada)
U of Wisconsin–Green Bay (WI)
U of Wisconsin–Madison (WI)
U of Wisconsin–Milwaukee (WI)
U of Wisconsin–Oshkosh (WI)
Vanderbilt U (TN)
Vassar Coll (NY)
Virginia Commonwealth U (VA)
Virginia Polytechnic Inst and State U (VA)
Washington U in St. Louis (MO)
Wayne State U (MI)
Wittenberg U (OH)
Worcester State Coll (MA)
Wright State U (OH)
York U (ON, Canada)

VEHICLE MARKETING OPERATIONS
Northwood U, Florida Campus (FL)
Northwood U, Texas Campus (TX)

VEHICLE PARTS/ACCESSORIES MARKETING OPERATIONS
Northwood U, Florida Campus (FL)
Northwood U, Texas Campus (TX)

VETERINARIAN ASSISTANT
Michigan State U (MI)
Morehead State U (KY)
Murray State U (KY)
U of Nebraska–Lincoln (NE)

VETERINARY SCIENCES
Becker Coll (MA)
Lincoln Memorial U (TN)
Mercy Coll (NY)
Pontifical Catholic U of Puerto Rico (PR)
Université de Montréal (QC, Canada)
U of Guelph (ON, Canada)
Wagner Coll (NY)
Washington State U (WA)

VETERINARY TECHNOLOGY
Mercy Coll (NY)
Michigan State U (MI)
Mount Ida Coll (MA)
Newberry Coll (SC)
North Dakota State U (ND)
Quinnipiac U (CT)
U of Puerto Rico Medical Sciences Campus (PR)

VISUAL AND PERFORMING ARTS RELATED
Clemson U (SC)
Illinois State U (IL)
Long Island U, C.W. Post Campus (NY)
Rice U (TX)
Scripps Coll (CA)
Simon Fraser U (BC, Canada)
State U of NY Coll at Geneseo (NY)
Swarthmore Coll (PA)
The U of Akron (OH)
U of Colorado at Boulder (CO)
U of Oklahoma (OK)
The U of the Arts (PA)

VISUAL/PERFORMING ARTS
American Academy of Art (IL)
Arizona State U West (AZ)
Art Center Coll of Design (CA)
Assumption Coll (MA)
Bard Coll (NY)
Bennington Coll (VT)
Bethel Coll (KS)
Brigham Young U (UT)
Brown U (RI)
California State U, San Marcos (CA)
Cazenovia Coll (NY)
Christopher Newport U (VA)
Columbia Coll (NY)
Delta State U (MS)

WOOD SCIENCE/PAPER TECHNOLOGY

ZOOLOGY

ZOOLOGY RELATED

2001–02 Changes in Four-Year Institutions

Following is an alphabetical listing of institutions that have recently closed, merged with other institutions, or changed their name or status. In the case of a name change, the former name appears first, followed by the new name.

American Bible College and Seminary (Oklahoma City, OK); name changed to American Christian College and Seminary.

Art Institutes International at San Francisco (San Francisco, CA); name changed to The Art Institute of California-San Francisco.

Averett College (Danville, VA); name changed to Averett University.

Barat College (Lake Forest, IL); closed.

Beacon College (Columbus, GA); name changed to Beacon College and Graduate School.

Berkeley College (White Plains, NY); name changed to Berkeley College-Westchester Campus.

Boston Conservatory (Boston, MA); name changed to The Boston Conservatory.

Briar Cliff College (Sioux City, IA); name changed to Briar Cliff University.

Brigham Young University–Hawaii Campus (Laie, HI); name changed to Brigham Young University&-Hawaii.

Center for Creative Studies-College of Art and Design (Detroit, MI); name changed to College for Creative Studies.

Cleveland Chiropractic College of Kansas City (Kansas City, MO); name changed to Cleveland Chiropractic College-Kansas City Campus.

Cleveland Chiropractic College of Los Angeles (Los Angeles, CA); name changed to Cleveland Chiropractic College-Los Angeles Campus.

Cleveland College of Jewish Studies (Beachwood, OH); name changed to Laura and Alvin Siegal College of Judaic Studies.

Collége universitaire de Saint-Boniface (Saint-Boniface, MB); name changed to Collège universitaire de Saint-Boniface.

College of Notre Dame (Belmont, CA); name changed to Notre Dame de Namur University.

College of Our Lady of the Elms (Chicopee, MA); name changed to Elms College.

Concordia College (Ann Arbor, MI); name changed to Concordia University.

David N. Myers College (Cleveland, OH); name changed to David N. Myers University.

DeVry Institute of Technology (Addison, IL); name changed to DeVry University.

DeVry Institute of Technology (Alpharetta, GA); name changed to DeVry University.

DeVry Institute of Technology (Chicago, IL); name changed to DeVry University.

DeVry Institute of Technology (Columbus, OH); name changed to DeVry University.

DeVry Institute of Technology (Decatur, GA); name changed to DeVry University.

DeVry Institute of Technology (Fremont, CA); name changed to DeVry University.

DeVry Institute of Technology (Irving, TX); name changed to DeVry University.

DeVry Institute of Technology (Kansas City, MO); name changed to DeVry University.

DeVry Institute of Technology (Long Beach, CA); name changed to DeVry University.

DeVry Institute of Technology (Orlando, FL); name changed to DeVry University.

DeVry Institute of Technology (Phoenix, AZ); name changed to DeVry University.

DeVry Institute of Technology (Pomona, CA); name changed to DeVry University.

DeVry Institute of Technology (Tinley Park, IL); name changed to DeVry University.

DeVry Institute of Technology (West Hills, CA); name changed to DeVry University.

Dr. William M. Scholl College of Podiatric Medicine (Chicago, IL); name changed to Scholl College of Podiatric Medicine at Finch University of Health Sciences/The Chicago Medical School.

Eastern College (St. Davids, PA); name changed to Eastern University.

Eastern Pentecostal Bible College (Peterborough, ON); name changed to Master's College and Seminary.

École des Hautes Études Commerciales (Montréal, PQ); name changed to École des Hautes Études Commerciales de Montr&,eal.

Fairleigh Dickinson University, Florham-Madison Campus (Madison, NJ); name changed to Fairleigh Dickinson University, College at Florham.

Fairleigh Dickinson University, Teaneck–Hackensack Campus (Teaneck, NJ); name changed to Fairleigh Dickinson University, Metropolitan Campus.

Florida Metropolitan University–Fort Lauderdale College (Fort Lauderdale, FL); name changed to Florida Metropolitan University–Fort Lauderdale Campus.

Florida Metropolitan University–Orlando College, North (Orlando, FL); name changed to Florida Metropolitan University–North Orlando Campus.

Florida Metropolitan University–Orlando College, South (Orlando, FL); name changed to Florida Metropolitan University–South Orlando Campus.

Florida Metropolitan University–Tampa College (Tampa, FL); name changed to Florida Metropolitan University–Tampa Campus.

Florida Metropolitan University–Tampa College, Lakeland (Lakeland, FL); name changed to Florida Metropolitan University–Lakeland Campus.

Fontbonne College (St. Louis, MO); name changed to Fontbonne University.

Franklin Institute of Boston (Boston, MA); name changed to Benjamin Franklin Institute of Technology.

Hawaii Pacific University (Honolulu, HI); name changed to Hawai'i Pacific University.

Institute for Christian Studies (Austin, TX); name changed to Austin Graduate School of Theology.

International Academy of Merchandising & Design, Ltd. (Chicago, IL); name changed to International Academy of Design & Technology.

International Bible College (Florence, AL); name changed to Heritage Christian University.

Kendall College of Art and Design at Ferris State University (Grand Rapids, MI); name changed to Kendall College of Art and Design of Ferris State University.

Logan University of Chiropractic (Chesterfield, MO); name changed to Logan University-College of Chiropractic.

Lyme Academy of Fine Arts (Old Lyme, CT); name changed to Lyme Academy College of Fine Arts.

Marycrest International University (Davenport, IA); closed.

Marymount College (Tarrytown, NY); name changed to Marymount College of Fordham University.

Mayo School of Health-Related Sciences (Rochester, MN); name changed to Mayo School of Health Sciences.

Mount Senario College (Ladysmith, WI); closed.

Mount Vernon Nazarene College (Mount Vernon, OH); name changed to Mount Vernon Nazarene University.

Nazarene Indian Bible College (Albuquerque, NM); closed.

New College of the University of South Florida (Sarasota, FL); name changed to New College of Florida.

Notre Dame College of Ohio (South Euclid, OH); name changed to Notre Dame College.

Notre Dame College (Manchester, NH); closed.

Oklahoma Wesleyan College (Bartlesville, OK); name changed to Oklahoma Wesleyan University.

Oregon College of Art and Craft (Portland, OR); name changed to Oregon College of Art & Craft.

Oregon Health Sciences University (Portland, OR); name changed to Oregon Health & Science University.

Pace University, New York City Campus (New York, NY); name changed to Pace University.

Robert Morris College (Moon Township, PA); name changed to Robert Morris University.

Ryerson Polytechnic University (Toronto, ON); name changed to Ryerson University.

Salisbury State University (Salisbury, MD); name changed to Salisbury University.

Seton Hill College (Greensburg, PA); name changed to Seton Hill University.

South College (Montgomery, AL); name changed to South University.

South College (Savannah, GA); name changed to South University.

South College (West Palm Beach, FL); name changed to South University.

Southern Virginia College (Buena Vista, VA); name changed to Southern Virginia University.

Southwestern College of Christian Ministries (Bethany, OK); name changed to Southwestern Christian University.

Technical University of British Columbia (Surrey, BC); closed.

The College of Insurance (New York, NY); closed.

The New York College for Wholistic Health Education & Research (Syosset, NY); name changed to The New York College of Health Professions.

The Union Institute (Cincinnati, OH); name changed to Union Institute & University.

The University of Texas Medical Branch at Galveston (Galveston, TX); name changed to The University of Texas Medical Branch.

Trinity College of Nursing and Schools of Allied Health (Moline, IL); name changed to Trinity College of Nursing and Health Sciences Schools.

United States International University–Africa (Nairobi,); name changed to United States International University.

United States International University–Mexico (Mexico City,); name changed to Alliant International University–México City.

United States International University (San Diego, CA); name changed to Alliant International University.

United States Open University (Wilmington, DE); closed.

University of Maryland University College at Schw&;abisch Gm&;und (Schw&;abisch Gm&;und,); closed.

University of Mobile–Latin American Branch Campus (San Marcos,); name changed to Ave Maria College of the Americas.

University of Phoenix–Grand Rapids Campus (Grand Rapids, MI); name changed to University of Phoenix–West Michigan Campus.

University of Phoenix-Louisiana Campus (Metairie, LA); name changed to University of Phoenix–Louisiana Campus.

University of Sarasota (Sarasota, FL); name changed to Argosy University-Sarasota.

University of Sarasota, California Campus (Orange, CA); name changed to Argosy University-Orange County.

Webber College (Babson Park, FL); name changed to Webber International University.

Westark College (Fort Smith, AR); name changed to University of Arkansas at Fort Smith.

Western Maryland College (Westminster, Maryland); name changed to McDaniel College.

Western Montana College of The University of Montana (Dillon, MT); name changed to The University of Montana&-Western.

Alphabetical Listing of Colleges and Universities

This index gives the page locations of various entries for all the colleges and universities in this section. The page numbers for the college profiles with *Special Announcements* are in italic type.

Two-Year
COLLEGES

How to Use This Section

This section contains a wealth of information for anyone interested in colleges offering associate degrees, with detail on the criteria that institutions must meet to be included in this guide and information about research procedures used by Peterson's.

In addition, you'll get an overview of the various databased components of this section with explanatory material to help you interpret the data it contains.

If you have a very specific idea of what you want out of a college education, you will have an easier time compiling your list of prospective colleges. That is, if you've set your sights on majoring in broadcast journalism, you will most likely limit your search to those colleges that offer a program in that discipline. Or, if your priority is to be within easy driving distance of your home and family, only nearby colleges will make your list. By considering some of the following criteria, you will soon find that your initial list of colleges has been narrowed to a more reasonable number.

1. **Location.** For some students, staying close to home might be a priority. Or, you may know that city life is not for you; therefore, you would like to limit your search to suburban or even rural colleges. Or, if you can't live without the frenetic energy of a major urban setting, you may be destined to attend college in the city. Whatever the reason, the location of a college often plays a key role in the college selection process.

   If you know that you fit into this category, you may wish to make use of two special features in this section: the **State-by-State Summary Table** and the **College Profiles and Special Announcements.** In both cases, you can quickly turn to the state, or states, of interest to you to discover what options are available.
2. **Education Costs.** As the price tag for higher education continues to rise, cost becomes an increasingly important factor when selecting a college. Certainly it is necessary to consider your family's resources when choosing a list of schools to which you might apply. On the other hand, avoid eliminating colleges that you might otherwise consider based solely on cost. You may be able to obtain the necessary financial aid to allow you to enroll in your higher-priced college of choice. You will find detailed expense information in the individual college profiles.
3. **Programs of Study Offered.** Despite all of the other factors that might influence your selection, certainly one of the most important is whether a college offers a program in your academic area of interest. Or, conversely, if you have not selected a program at the onset, you will want to find a college with a broad enough selection to satisfy your eventual choice. An easy way to research this is by referring to **Associate Degree Programs at Two-Year Colleges** or **Associate Degree Programs at Four-Year Colleges.** In these indexes you will find the colleges that offer majors in hundreds of different disciplines. In addition, for a complete listing of majors offered at a particular institution, consult the *Majors* paragraph in the college's profile.

Beyond these major factors, you will undoubtedly uncover other criteria that will strongly influence your choice of where to attend college. Questions about a particular institution's financial resources, the diversity of its student body, the number and variety of study areas offered, or its financial aid policy may weigh heavily in the decision process. The straightforward format of the **Quick-Reference College Search Indexes** and the **College Profiles and Special Announcements** makes it easy to gather the facts on all of these points and more, providing you with the answers you need to make the most informed choice. The following paragraphs describe in detail the data that are contained within these features.

CRITERIA FOR INCLUSION

This section of *Peterson's Complete Guide to Colleges* covers accredited institutions in the United States, U.S. territories, and other countries that award the associate degree as their most popular undergraduate offering (a few also offer bachelor's, master's, or doctoral degrees). The term "two-year college" is the commonly used designation for institutions that grant the associate, since two years is the normal duration of the traditional associate degree program. However, some programs may be completed in one year, others require three years, and, of course, part-time programs may take a considerably longer period. Therefore, "two-year college" should be understood as a conventional term that accurately describes most of the institutions included in this section but which should not be taken literally in all cases. Also included are some non-degree-granting institutions, usually branch campuses of a multicampus system, that offer the equivalent of the first two years of a bachelor's degree, transferable to a bachelor's-degree-granting institution.

To be included in this section, an institution must have full accreditation or candidate-for-accreditation (preaccreditation) status granted by an institutional or specialized accrediting body recognized by the U.S. Department of Education or the Council for Higher Education Accreditation (CHEA). Recognized institutional accrediting bodies, which consider each institution as a whole, are the following: the six regional associations of schools and colleges (Middle States, New

England, North Central, Northwest, Southern, and Western), each of which is responsible for a specified portion of the United States and its territories; the Accrediting Association of Bible Colleges (AABC); the Accrediting Council for Independent Colleges and Schools (ACICS); the Accrediting Commission for Career Schools and Colleges of Technology (ACCSCT); the Distance Education and Training Council (DETC); the American Academy for Liberal Education (AALE); the Council on Occupational Education (COE); and the Transnational Association of Christian Colleges and Schools (TRACS). Program registration by the New York State Board of Regents is considered to be the equivalent of institutional accreditation, since the board requires that all programs offered by an institution meet its standards before recognition is granted.

This section also includes institutions outside the United States and its territories that are accredited by the same U.S. accrediting bodies. In addition, there are recognized specialized accrediting bodies in over forty different fields, each of which is authorized to accredit specific programs in its particular field. This can serve as the equivalent of institutional accreditation for specialized institutions that offer programs in one field only, such as schools of art, music, optometry, or theology. A full explanation of the accrediting process and complete information on recognized accrediting bodies can be found online at http://www.chea.org.

STATE-BY-STATE SUMMARY TABLE

This geographically arranged table lists colleges by name and city within the state, territory, or country in which they are located. Areas are listed in the following order: United States, U.S. territories, and other countries; the institutions in these countries are included because they are accredited by recognized U.S. accrediting bodies (see the previous **Criteria for Inclusion** section).

The table contains basic information that will enable the reader to classify each institution quickly according to broad characteristics. An asterisk (*) after an institution's name denotes that a **Special Announcement** is included in the college's profile.

Column 1 (Degrees Awarded)

C = *college transfer associate degree:* the degree awarded after a "university-parallel" program, equivalent to the first two years of a bachelor's degree.

T = *terminal associate degree:* the degree resulting from a one- to three-year program providing training for a specific occupation.

B = *bachelor's degree (baccalaureate):* the degree resulting from a liberal arts, science, professional, or preprofessional program normally lasting four years, although in some cases an accelerated program can be completed in three years.

M = *master's degree:* the first graduate (postbaccalaureate) degree in the liberal arts and sciences and certain professional fields, usually requiring one to two years of full-time study.

D = *doctoral degree (doctorate):* the highest degree awarded in research-oriented academic disciplines, usually requiring from three to six years of full-time study beyond the baccalaureate and intended as preparation for university-level teaching and research.

F = *first professional degree:* the degree required to be academically qualified to practice in certain professions, such as law and medicine, having as a prerequisite at least two years of college credit and usually requiring a total of at least six years of study including prior college-level work.

Column 2 (Institutional Control)

Private institutions are designated as one of the following:

Ind = *independent* (nonprofit)

I-R = *independent-religious:* nonprofit; sponsored by or affiliated with a particular religious group or having a nondenominational or interdenominational religious orientation.

Prop = *proprietary* (profit-making)

Public institutions are designated by the source of funding, as follows:

Fed = *federal*
St = *state*
Comm = *commonwealth* (Puerto Rico)
Terr = *territory* (U.S. territories)

RESEARCH PROCEDURES

The data contained in the college indexes and college profiles were researched between fall 2001 and spring 2002 through Peterson's Annual Survey of Undergraduate Institutions. Questionnaires were sent to the more than 1,700 colleges that meet the criteria for inclusion outlined above. All data included in this section have been submitted by officials (usually admission and financial aid officers, registrars, or institutional research personnel) at the colleges themselves. In addition, the great majority of institutions that submitted data were contacted directly by Peterson's research staff to verify unusual figures, resolve discrepancies, and obtain additional data. All usable information received in time for publication has been included. The omission of any particular item from an index or profile listing signifies either that the item is not applicable to that institution or that data were not available. Because of the comprehensive data review that takes place in Peterson's offices and because all material comes directly from college officials, we have every reason to believe that the information presented in this guide is accurate. However, check with a specific college at the time of application to verify such information as tuition and fees and application deadlines, which may have changed since publication.

Cou = *county*

Dist = *district:* an administrative unit of public education, often having boundaries different from units of local government.

City

St-L = *state and local:* "local" may refer to county, district, or city.

St-R = *state-related:* funded primarily by the state but administratively autonomous.

Column 3 (Student Body)

M = *men only* (100% of student body)

PM = *coed, primarily men*

W = *women only* (100% of student body)

PW = *coed, primarily women*

M/W = *coeducational*

Column 4 (Undergraduate Enrollment)

The figure shown represents the number of full-time and part-time students enrolled in undergraduate degree programs as of fall 2001.

Columns 5–7 (Enrollment Percentages)

Figures are shown for the percentages of the fall 2001 undergraduate enrollment made up of students attending part-time (column 5) and students 25 years of age or older (column 6). Also listed is the percentage of students in the last graduating class who completed a college-transfer associate program and went directly on to four-year colleges (column 7).

For columns 8 through 15, the following letter codes are used: Y = yes; N = no; R = recommended; S = for some.

Columns 8–10 (Admission Policies)

The information in these columns shows whether the college has an open admission policy (column 8) whereby virtually all applicants are accepted without regard to standardized test scores, grade average, or class rank; whether a high school equivalency certificate is accepted in place of a high school diploma for admission consideration (column 9); and whether a high school transcript (column 10) is required as part of the application process. In column 10, the combination of the codes R and S indicates that a high school transcript is recommended for all applicants *and* required for some.

Columns 11–12 (Financial Aid)

These columns show which colleges offer the following types of financial aid: need-based aid (column 11) and part-time jobs (column 12), including those offered through the federal government's Federal Work-Study Program.

Columns 13–15 (Services and Facilities)

These columns show which colleges offer the following: career counseling (column 13) on either an individual or group basis, job placement services (column 14) for individual students, and college-owned or -operated housing facilities (column 16) for noncommuting students.

Column 16 (Sports)

This figure indicates the number of sports that a college offers at the intramural and/or intercollegiate levels.

Column 17 (Majors)

This figure indicates the number of major fields of study in which a college offers degree programs.

COLLEGE PROFILES AND SPECIAL ANNOUNCEMENTS

Bulleted Highlights

The bulleted highlights feature important information for quick reference and comparison. The number of *possible* bulleted highlights that an ideal profile would have if all questions were answered in a timely manner are represented below. However, not every institution provides all of the information necessary to fill out every bulleted line. In such instances, the line will not appear.

First bullet

Institutional control: Private institutions are designated as independent (nonprofit), proprietary (profit-making), or inde-

THE FIVE LEVELS OF ENTRANCE DIFFICULTY

1. **Most difficult:** More than 75 percent of the current freshmen were in the top 10 percent of their high school class and scored above 1310 on the SAT I (verbal and mathematical combined) or above 29 on the ACT (composite); about 30 percent or fewer of the applicants to this class were accepted.
2. **Very difficult:** More than 50 percent of the current freshmen were in the top 10 percent of their high school class and scored above 1230 on the SAT I or above 26 on the ACT; about 60 percent or fewer of the applicants were accepted.
3. **Moderately difficult:** More than 75 percent of the current freshmen were in the top half of their high school class and scored above 1010 on the SAT I or above 18 on the ACT; about 85 percent or fewer of the applicants were accepted.
4. **Minimally difficult:** Most current freshmen were not in the top half of their high school class and scored somewhat below 1010 on the SAT I or below 18 on the ACT; up to 95 percent of the applicants were accepted.
5. **Noncompetitive:** Virtually all applicants were accepted regardless of high school rank or test scores. Many public institutions are required to admit all state residents.

pendent, with a specific religious denomination or affiliation. Nondenominational or interdenominational religious orientation is possible and would be indicated.

Public institutions are designated by the source of funding. Designations include federal, state, province, commonwealth (Puerto Rico), territory (U.S. territories), county, district (an educational administrative unit often having boundaries different from units of local government), city, state and local (local may refer to county, district, or city), or state-related (funded primarily by the state but administratively autonomous).

Religious affiliation is also noted here.

Institutional type: Each institution is classified as one of the following:

Primarily two-year college: Awards baccalaureate degrees, but the vast majority of students are enrolled in two-year programs.

Four-year college: Awards baccalaureate degrees; may also award associate degrees; does not award graduate (postbaccalaureate) degrees.

Five-year college: Awards a five-year baccalaureate in a professional field such as architecture or pharmacy; does not award graduate degrees.

Upper-level institution: Awards baccalaureate degrees, but entering students must have at least two years of previous college-level credit; may also offer graduate degrees.

Comprehensive institution: Awards baccalaureate degrees; may also award associate degrees; offers graduate degree programs, primarily at the master's, specialist's, or professional level, although one or two doctoral programs may be offered.

University: Offers four years of undergraduate work plus graduate degrees through the doctorate in more than two academic or professional fields.

Founding date: If the year an institution was chartered differs from the year when instruction actually began, the earlier date is given.

System or administrative affiliation: Any coordinate institutions or system affiliations are indicated. An institution that has separate colleges or campuses for men and women but shares facilities and courses it is termed a coordinate institution. A formal administrative grouping of institutions, either private or public, of which the college is a part, or the name of a single institution with which the college is administratively affiliated is a system.

Second bullet

Calendar: Most colleges indicate one of the following: *4-1-4, 4-4-1,* or a similar arrangement (two terms of equal length plus an abbreviated winter or spring term, with the numbers referring to months); *semesters; trimesters; quarters; 3-3* (three courses for each of three terms); *modular* (the academic year is divided into small blocks of time; course of varying lengths are assembled according to individual programs); or *standard year* (for most Canadian institutions).

Third bullet

Degree: This names the full range of levels of certificates, diplomas, and degrees, including prebaccalaureate, graduate, and professional, that are offered by this institution.

Associate degree: Normally requires at least two but fewer than four years of full-time college work or its equivalent.

Bachelor's degree (baccalaureate): Requires at least four years but not more than five years of full-time college-level work or its equivalent. This includes all bachelor's degrees in which the normal four years of work are completed in three years and bachelor's degrees conferred in a five-year cooperative (work-study plan) program. A cooperative plan provides for alternate class attendance and employment in business, industry, or government. This allows students to combine actual work experience with their college studies. *Master's degree:* Requires the successful completion of a program of study of at least the full-time equivalent of one but not more than two years of work beyond the bachelor's degree. *Doctoral degree (doctorate):* The highest degree in graduate study. The doctoral degree classification includes Doctor of Education, Doctor of Juridical Science, Doctor of Public Health, and the Doctor of Philosophy in any nonprofessional field. *First professional degree:* The first postbaccalaureate degree in one of the following fields: chiropractic (DC, DCM), dentistry (DDS, DMD), medicine (MD), optometry (OD), osteopathic medicine (DO), rabbinical and Talmudic studies (MHL, Rav), pharmacy (BPharm, PharmD), podiatry (PodD, DP, DPM), veterinary medicine (DVM), law (JD), or divinity/ministry (BD, MDiv). *First professional certificate (postdegree):* Requires completion of an organized program of study after completion of the first professional degree. Examples are refresher courses or additional units of study in a specialty or subspecialty. *Post-master's certificate:* Requires completion of an organized program of study of 24 credit hours beyond the master's degree but does not meet the requirements of academic degrees at the doctoral level.

Fourth bullet

Setting: Schools are designated as *urban* (located within a major city), *suburban* (a residential area within commuting distance of a major city), *small-town* (a small but compactly settled area not within commuting distance of a major city), or *rural* (a remote and sparsely populated area). The phrase *easy access to . . .* indicates that the campus is within an hour's drive of the nearest major metropolitan area that has a population greater than 500,000.

Fifth bullet

Endowment: The total dollar value of donations to the institution or the multicampus educational system of which the institution is a part.

Sixth bullet

Student body: An institution is coed (coeducational—admits men and women), primarily (80 percent or more) women, primarily men, women only, or men only.

Undergraduate students: Represents the number of full-time and part-time students enrolled in undergraduate degree programs as of fall 2001. The percentage of full-time undergraduates and the percentages of men and women are given.

Seventh bullet

Entrance level: See guidelines in "The Five Levels of Entrance Difficulty" explanation box.

Percent of applicants admitted: The percentage of applicants who were granted admission.

Special Announcements

These messages have been written by those colleges that wished to supplement the profile data with additional, timely, important information.

Undergraduates

For fall 2001, the number of full- and part-time undergraduate students is listed. This list provides the number of states and U.S. territories, including the District of Columbia and Puerto Rico (or, for Canadian institutions, provinces and territories), and other countries from which undergraduates come. Percentages are given of undergraduates who are from out of state; Native American, African American, and Asian American or Pacific Islander; international students; transfer students; and living on campus

Retention: The percentage of 2000 freshmen (or, for upper-level institutions, entering students) who returned for the fall 2001 term.

Freshmen

Admission: Figures are given for the number of students who applied for fall 2001 admission, the number of those who were admitted, and the number who enrolled. Freshman statistics include the average high school GPA; the percentage of freshmen who took the SAT I and received verbal and math scores above 500, above 600, and above 700, as well as the percentage of freshmen taking the ACT who received a composite score of 18 or higher.

Faculty

Total: The total number of faculty members; the percentage of full-time faculty members as of fall 2001; and the percentage of full-time faculty members who hold doctoral/first professional/terminal degrees.

Student-aculty ratio: The school's estimate of the ratio of matriculated undergraduate students to faculty members teaching undergraduate courses.

Majors

This section lists the major fields of study offered by the college.

Academic Programs

Details are given here on study options available at each college.

Accelerated degree program: Students may earn a bachelor's degree in three academic years.

Academic remediation for entering students: Instructional courses designed for students deficient in the general competencies necessary for a regular postsecondary curriculum and educational setting.

Adult/continuing education programs: Courses offered for nontraditional students who are currently working or are returning to formal education.

Advanced placement: Credit toward a degree awarded for acceptable scores on College Board Advanced Placement tests.

Cooperative (co-op) education programs: Formal arrangements with off-campus employers allowing students to combine work and study in order to gain degree-related experience, usually extending the time required to complete a degree.

Distance learning: For-credit courses that can be accessed off campus via cable television, the Internet, satellite, videotapes, correspondence course, or other media.

Double major: A program of study in which a student concurrently completes the requirements of two majors.

English as a second language (ESL): A course of study designed specifically for students whose native language is not English.

External degree programs: A program of study in which students earn credits toward a degree through a combination of independent study, college courses, proficiency examinations, and personal experience. External degree programs require minimal or no classroom attendance.

Freshmen honors college: A separate academic program for talented freshmen.

Honors programs: Any special program for very able students offering the opportunity for educational enrichment, independent study, acceleration, or some combination of these.

Independent study: Academic work, usually undertaken outside the regular classroom structure, chosen or designed by the student with the departmental approval and instructor supervision.

Internships: Any short-term, supervised work experience usually related to a student's major field, for which the student earns academic credit. The work can be full- or part-time, on or off campus, paid or unpaid.

Off-campus study: A formal arrangement with one or more domestic institutions under which students may take courses at the other institution(s) for credit.

Part-time degree program: Students may earn a degree through part-time enrollment in regular session (daytime) classes or evening, weekend, or summer classes.

Self-designed major: Program of study based on individual interests, designed by the student with the assistance of an adviser.

Services for LD students: Special help for learning-disabled students with resolvable difficulties, such as dyslexia.

Study abroad: An arrangement by which a student completes part of the academic program studying in another country. A college may operate a campus abroad or it may have a cooperative agreement with other U.S. institutions or institutions in other countries.

Summer session for credit: Summer courses through which students may make up degree work or accelerate their program.

Tutorials: Undergraduates can arrange for special in-depth academic assignments (not for remediation) working with faculty one-on-one or in small groups..

ROTC: Army, Naval, or Air Force Reserve Officers' Training Corps programs offered either on campus or at a cooperating host institution [designated by (C)].

Unusual degree programs: Nontraditional programs such as a 3-2 degree program, in which 3 years of liberal arts study is followed by two years of study in a professional field at another institution (or in a professional division of the same institution), resulting in two bachelor's degrees or a bachelor's and a master's degree.

Library

This section lists the name of the main library; the number of other libraries on campus; numbers of books, microform titles, serials, commercial online services, and audiovisual materials.

Computers on Campus

This paragraph includes the number of on-campus computer terminals and PCs available for general student use and their locations; computer purchase or lease plans; PC requirements for entering students; and campuswide computer network, e-mail, and access to computer labs, the Internet, and software.

Student Life

Housing options: The institution's policy about whether students are permitted to live off campus or are required to live on campus for a specified period; whether freshmen-only, coed, single-sex, cooperative, and disabled student housing options are available. The phrase *college housing not available* indicates that no college-owned or -operated housing facilities are provided for undergraduates and that noncommuting students must arrange for their own accommodations.

Activities and organizations: Lists information on drama-theater groups, choral groups, marching bands, student-run campus newspapers, student-run radio stations and social organizations (sororities, fraternities, eating clubs, etc.) and how many are represented on campus.

Campus security: Campus safety measures including 24-hour emergency response devices (telephones and alarms) and patrols by trained security personnel, student patrols, late-night transport-escort service, and controlled dormitory access (key, security card, etc.).

Student services:
Information provided indicates services offered to students by the college, such as legal services, health clinics, personal-psychological counseling and women's centers.

Athletics

Membership in one or more of the following athletic associations is indicated by initials.

NCAA: National Collegiate Athletic Association

NAIA: National Association of Intercollegiate Athletics

NCCAA: National Christian College Athletic Association

NSCAA: National Small College Athletic Association

NJCAA: National Junior College Athletic Association

CIAU: Canadian Interuniversity Athletic Union

The overall NCAA division in which all or most intercollegiate teams compete is designated by a roman numeral I, II, or III. All teams that do not compete in this division are listed as exceptions.

Sports offered by the college are divided into two groups: intercollegiate (**M** or **W** following the name of each sport indicates that it is offered for men or women) and intramural. An **s** in parentheses following an **M** or **W** for an intercollegiate sport indicates that athletic scholarships (or grants-in-aid) are offered for men or women in that sport, and a **c** indicates a club team as opposed to a varsity team.

Standardized Tests

The most commonly required standardized tests are ACT, SAT I, and SAT II Subject Tests, including the SAT II: Writing. These and other standardized tests may be used for selective admission, as a basis for counseling or course placement, or for both purposes. This section notes if a test is used for admission or placement and whether it is required, required for some, or recommended.

In addition to the ACT and SAT I, the following standardized entrance and placement examinations are referred to by their initials:

ABLE: Adult Basic Learning Examination
ACT ASSET: ACT Assessment of Skills for Successful Entry and Transfer
ACT PEP: ACT Proficiency Examination Program
CAT: California Achievement Tests
CELT: Comprehensive English Language Test
CPAt: Career Programs Assessment
CPT: Computerized Placement Test
DAT: Differential Aptitude Test
LSAT: Law School Admission Test
MAPS: Multiple Assessment Program Service

MCAT: Medical College Admission Test

MMPI: Minnesota Multiphasic Personality Inventory

OAT: Optometry Admission Test

PAA: Prueba de Aptitude Académica (Spanish-language version of the SAT I)

PCAT: Pharmacy College Admission Test

PSAT: Preliminary SAT

SCAT: Scholastic College Aptitude Test

SRA: Scientific Research Association (administers verbal, arithmetical, and achievement tests)

TABE: Test of Adult Basic Education

TASP: Texas Academic Skills Program

TOEFL: Test of English as a Foreign Language (for international students whose native language is not English)

WPCT: Washington Pre-College Test

Costs

Costs are given for the 2002–03 academic year or for the 2001–02 academic year if 2002–03 figures were not yet available. Annual expenses may be expressed as a comprehensive fee (including full-time tuition, mandatory fees, and college room and board) or as separate figures for full-time tuition, fees, room and board, or room only. For public institutions where tuition differs according to residence, separate figures are given for area or state residents and for nonresidents. Part-time tuition is expressed in terms of a per-unit rate (per credit, per semester hour, etc.) as specified by the institution.

The tuition structure at some institutions is complex in that freshmen and sophomores may be charged a different rate from that for juniors and seniors, a professional or vocational division may have a different fee structure from the liberal arts division of the same institution, or part-time tuition may be prorated on a sliding scale according to the number of credit hours taken. Tuition and fees may vary according to academic program, campus/location, class time (day, evening, weekend), course/credit load, course level, degree level, reciprocity agreements, and student level. Room and board charges are reported as an average for one academic year and may vary according to the board plan selected, campus/location, type of housing facility, or student level. If no college-owned or -operated housing facilities are offered, the phrase *college housing not available* will appear in the Housing section of the Student Life paragraph.

Tuition payment plans that may be offered to undergraduates include tuition prepayment, installment payments, and deferred payment. A tuition prepayment plan gives a student the option of locking in the current tuition rate for the entire term of enrollment by paying the full amount in advance rather than year by year. Colleges that offer such a prepayment plan may also help the student to arrange financing.

The availability of full or partial undergraduate tuition waivers to minority students, children of alumni, employees or their children, adult students, and senior citizens may be listed.

Financial Aid

Financial aid information presented represents aid awarded to undergraduates for the 2001–02 academic year. Figures are given for the number of undergraduates who applied for aid, the number who were judged to have need, and the number who had their need met. The number of Federal Work-Study and/or part-time jobs and average earnings are listed, as well as the number of non-need based awards that were made. Non-need based awards are college-administered scholarships for which the college determines the recipient and amount of each award. These scholarships are awarded to full-time undergraduates on the basis of merit or personal attributes without regard to need, although they many certainly be given to students who also happen to need aid. The average percent of need met, the average financial aid package awarded to undergraduates (the amount of scholarships, grants, work-study payments, or loans in the institutionally administered financial aid package divided by the number of students who received any financial aid—amounts used to pay the officially designated Expected Family Contribution (EFC), such as PLUS or other alternative loans, are excluded from the amounts reported), the average amount of need-based gift aid, and the average amount of non-need based aid are given. Average indebtedness, which is the average per-borrower indebtedness of the last graduating undergraduate class from amounts borrowed at this institution through any loan programs, excluding parent loans, is listed last.

Applying

Application and admission options include the following:

Early admission: Highly qualified students may matriculate before graduating from high school.

Early action plan: An admission plan that allows students to apply and be notified of an admission decision well in advance of the regular notification dates. If accepted, the candidate is not committed to enroll; students may reply to the offer under the college's regular reply policy.

Early decision plan: A plan that permits students to apply and be notified of an admission decision (and financial aid offer, if applicable) well in advance of the regular notification date. Applicants agree to accept an offer of admission and to withdraw their applications from other colleges. Candidates who are not accepted under early decision are automatically considered with the regular applicant pool, without prejudice.

Deferred entrance: The practice of permitting accepted students to postpone enrollment, usually for a period of one academic term or year.

Application fee: The fee required with an application is noted. This is typically nonrefundable, although under certain specified conditions it may be waived or returned.

Requirements: Other application requirements are grouped into three categories: required for all, required for some, and recommended. They may include an essay, standardized test scores, a high school transcript, a minimum high school grade point average (expressed as a number on a scale of 0 to 4.0, where 4.0 equals A, 3.0 equals B, etc.), letters of recommendation, an interview on campus or with local alumni, and, for certain types of schools or programs, special requirements such as a musical audition or an art portfolio.

Application deadlines and notification dates: Admission application deadlines and dates for notification of acceptance or rejection are given either as specific dates or as *rolling* and *continuous*. Rolling means that applications are processed as they are received, and qualified students are accepted as long as there are openings. Continuous means that applicants are notified of acceptance or rejection as applications are processed up until the date indicated or the actual beginning of classes. The application deadline and the notification date for transfers are given if they differ from the dates for freshmen. Early decision and early action application deadlines and notification dates are also indicated when relevant.

Admissions Contact

The name, title, and telephone number of the person to contact for application information are given at the end of the profile. The admission office address is listed. Toll-free telephone numbers may also be included. The admission office fax number and e-mail address, if available, are listed, provided the school wanted them printed for use by prospective students.

ASSOCIATE DEGREE PROGRAMS AT TWO- AND FOUR-YEAR COLLEGES

These indexes present hundreds of undergraduate fields of study that are currently offered most widely at two- and four-year colleges, according to the colleges' responses on *Peterson's Annual Survey of Undergraduate Institutions*. The majors appear in alphabetical order, each followed by an alphabetical list of the schools that offer an associate's-level program in that field. Liberal Arts and Studies indicates a general program with no specified major.

The terms used for the majors are those of the U.S. Department of Education Classification of Instructional Programs (CIPs). Many institutions, however, use different terms. Readers should visit http://www.petersons.com in order to contact a college and ask for its catalog to see the school's exact terminology. In addition, although the term "major" is used in this guide, some colleges may use other terms, such as "concentration," "program of study," or "field."

State-by-State Summary Table

A quick state-by-state way to compare institutions by a variety of characteristics, including enrollment, application requirements, types of financial aid available, and numbers of sports and majors offered.

State-by-State Summary Table

This index includes the names and locations of accredited two-year colleges in the United States and U.S. territories and shows institutions' responses to our 2001 Survey of Undergraduate Institutions. If an institution submitted incomplete or no data, one or more columns opposite the institution's name is blank. An asterisk after the school name denotes a *Special Announcement* following the college's profile.

Y—Yes; N—No; R—Recommended; S—For Some

Institution	Location	Degrees Awarded: Transfer Associate (C), Terminal Associate (T), Bachelor's (B), Master's (M), Doctoral (D), First Professional (F)	Institutional Control: Independent (Ind), Independent-Religious, Proprietary, Federal, State, Province, Commonwealth, Territory, County, District, City, State and Local, State-Related	Student Body: Men, Primarily Men, Women, Primarily Women, Coed	Undergraduate Enrollment Fall 2001	Percent Attending Part-Time	Percent 25 Years of Age or Older	Percent of Grads Going on to 4-Year Colleges	Open Admissions	High School Equivalency Certificate Accepted	High School Transcript Required	Need-based aid available	Part-Time Jobs Available	Career Counseling Available	Job Placement Services Available	College Housing Available	Number of Sports Offered	Number of Majors Offered
UNITED STATES																		
Alabama																		
Alabama Southern Community College	Monroeville																	
Bessemer State Technical College	Bessemer	T	St	M/W	2,087		51		N	Y	Y	Y	Y	Y	Y	N		10
Bevill State Community College	Sumiton	C,T	St	M/W	3,504		33		Y	Y	Y	Y	Y	Y	Y	N	9	12
Bishop State Community College	Mobile																	
Calhoun Community College	Decatur	C,T	St	M/W	8,372	61	45		Y	Y	S	Y	Y			N		18
Central Alabama Community College	Alexander City	C,T	St	M/W	1,609	46	52	33	Y	Y	Y	Y	Y	Y		N	5	11
Chattahoochee Valley Community College	Phenix City	C,T	St	M/W	1,891		45	18	Y	Y	Y	Y	Y	Y	Y	N	2	24
Community College of the Air Force	Maxwell Air Force Base	T	Fed	PM	373,943		63		Y		Y			Y		Y	15	51
Douglas MacArthur State Technical College	Opp	T	St	M/W	375		58		Y	Y	Y	Y	Y	Y	Y	N		12
Enterprise State Junior College	Enterprise	C,T	St	M/W	1,590	46	21		Y	Y	Y	Y	Y	Y	Y	N	7	28
Gadsden State Community College	Gadsden	C,T	St	M/W	4,729	45			Y	Y	Y	Y	Y	Y	Y	Y	7	21
George Corley Wallace State Community College	Selma	C,T	St	M/W	1,579	39	35	25	Y	Y		Y	Y	Y	Y	N	4	22
George C. Wallace Community College	Dothan																	
Harry M. Ayers State Technical College	Anniston	C,T	St	M/W	1,137	40	39		Y	Y	Y	Y	Y	Y	Y	N		11
Herzing College	Birmingham	T,B	Prop	M/W	600	34	70	20	N	Y		Y	Y	Y	Y	N		9
ITT Technical Institute	Birmingham	T,B	Prop	M/W	443				N	Y	Y	Y	Y	Y	Y	N		5
James H. Faulkner State Community College*	Bay Minette	C,T	St	M/W	3,500		23		Y	Y	Y	Y	Y	Y	Y	Y	7	13
Jefferson Davis Community College	Brewton	C,T	St	M/W	1,300		30		Y	Y	Y	Y	Y	Y		Y		19
Jefferson State Community College	Birmingham	C,T	St	M/W	5,652	63	45		Y	Y	S	Y	Y	Y	Y	N	8	24
J. F. Drake State Technical College	Huntsville	C	St	M/W	690	47	53		Y		Y		Y	Y	Y	N		7
Lawson State Community College	Birmingham	C,T	St	M/W	2,017													
Lurleen B. Wallace Junior College	Andalusia	C,T	St	M/W	834	26	27		Y	Y	Y	Y	Y	Y	Y	N	4	3
Marion Military Institute	Marion	C,T	Ind	PM	165		0	100	N	Y	Y	Y	Y	Y		Y	14	3
Northeast Alabama Community College	Rainsville	C,T	St	M/W	1,714	32	32	30	Y	Y			Y	Y	Y	N		18
Northwest-Shoals Community College	Muscle Shoals	C,T	St	M/W	3,922	43	39		Y	Y	Y	Y	Y	Y	Y	Y	8	28
Prince Institute of Professional Studies	Montgomery	T	Ind	PW	103		50			Y	Y	Y				N		3
Reid State Technical College	Evergreen	T	St	M/W	741	43	55		Y		Y	Y	Y	Y	Y	N		2
Shelton State Community College	Tuscaloosa	C,T	St	M/W	6,211													
Snead State Community College	Boaz	C,T	St	M/W	1,679	36	28	53	Y	Y	Y	Y	Y	Y	Y	Y	4	10
Southern Union State Community College	Wadley	C,T	St	M/W	4,500													
South University	Montgomery	T,B	Prop	PW	240	38	56		N	Y	Y	Y	Y	Y	Y	N		6
Trenholm State Technical College	Montgomery	T	St	M/W	663	36												
Trenholm State Technical College, Patterson Campus	Montgomery	T	St	M/W	1,800		46		Y	Y	S	Y	Y	Y	Y	N		15
Virginia College at Huntsville	Huntsville																	
Wallace State Community College	Hanceville	C,T	St	M/W	4,770	46	40	79	Y	Y	Y	Y	Y	Y	Y	Y	9	59
Alaska																		
Charter College	Anchorage	C,T,B	Prop	M/W	416				Y	Y	Y	Y		Y	Y	N		6
U of Alaska Anchorage, Kenai Peninsula College	Soldotna	C,T	St	M/W	1,911		82		Y	Y	Y	Y	Y	Y		N		7
U of Alaska Anchorage, Kodiak College	Kodiak	C,T	St	M/W	755		83		Y	Y	R	Y		Y		N		3
U of Alaska Anchorage, Matanuska-Susitna College	Palmer	C,T	St	M/W	1,594		82	25	Y	Y	Y	Y	Y	Y		N		8
U of Alaska, Prince William Sound Comm College	Valdez	C,T	St	M/W														
U of Alaska Southeast, Ketchikan Campus	Ketchikan	C,T	St-L	M/W	589		46		Y	Y	Y	Y		Y	Y	N		4
U of Alaska Southeast, Sitka Campus	Sitka	C,T	St	M/W	1,503		65	40	Y	Y	Y			Y		Y		9
Arizona																		
AIBT International Institute of the Americas	Phoenix	C,T,B	Ind	M/W	1,036		76	14	Y	Y				Y	Y	N		9
Apollo College–Phoenix, Inc.	Phoenix																	
Apollo College–Tri-City, Inc.	Mesa																	
Apollo College–Tucson, Inc.	Tucson																	
Apollo College–Westside, Inc.	Phoenix																	
Arizona Automotive Institute	Glendale	T	Prop		450		40				Y							3
Arizona Western College	Yuma	C,T	St-L	M/W	6,089	74	40		Y	Y		Y	Y	Y	Y	Y	9	43
The Art Center	Tucson	T	Priv		300													
The Bryman School	Phoenix	T	Prop	PW	1,100		30			Y	Y	Y		Y	Y	N		5
Central Arizona College	Coolidge	C,T	Cou	M/W	5,007		71		Y			Y	Y	Y	Y	Y	7	26
Chandler-Gilbert Community College	Chandler																	
Chaparral College	Tucson	C,T,B	Prop	M/W	343		60		Y	Y	Y	Y		Y	Y	N		7
Cochise College	Douglas	C,T	St-L	M/W	6,011		33		Y		R	Y	Y	Y	Y	Y	4	37
Cochise College	Sierra Vista	C,T	St-L	M/W	3,026													
Coconino Community College	Flagstaff	C,T	St	M/W	3,689													
Diné College	Tsaile	C,T	Fed	M/W	1,725		63		Y	Y	Y	Y	Y	Y	Y	Y	2	14

Y—Yes; N—No; R—Recommended; S—For Some

This index includes the names and locations of accredited two-year colleges in the United States and U.S. territories and shows institutions' responses to our 2001 Survey of Undergraduate Institutions. If an institution submitted incomplete or no data, one or more columns opposite the institution's name is blank. An asterisk after the school name denotes a *Special Announcement* following the college's profile.

College	Location	Degrees Awarded: Transfer Associate (C), Terminal Associate (T), Bachelor's (B), Master's (M), Doctoral (D), First Professional (F)	Institutional Control: Independent, Independent-Religious, Proprietary, Federal, State, Province, Commonwealth, Territory, County, District, City, State and Local, State-Related	Student Body: Men, Primarily Men, Women, Primarily Women, Coed	Undergraduate Enrollment Fall 2001	Percent Attending Part-Time	Percent 25 Years of Age or Older	Percent of Grads Going on to 4-Year Colleges	Open Admissions	High School Equivalency Certificate Accepted	High School Transcript Required	Need-based aid available	Part-Time Jobs Available	Career Counseling Available	Job Placement Services Available	College Housing Available	Number of Sports Offered	Number of Majors Offered
Eastern Arizona College	Thatcher	C,T	St-L	M/W	6,492	77	34		Y		R	Y	Y	Y		Y	9	49
Estrella Mountain Community College	Avondale	C,T	St-L	M/W	4,657				Y			Y	Y					2
Everest College	Phoenix	C,T	Prop	M/W	291		95	2	N	Y	Y	Y		Y	Y	N		4
GateWay Community College	Phoenix	C,T	St-L	M/W	9,377	90	31		Y		S	Y	Y	Y	Y	N		39
Glendale Community College	Glendale	C,T	St-L	M/W	19,775	74	45		Y		S	Y	Y	Y	Y	N	11	28
High-Tech Institute	Phoenix																	
ITT Technical Institute	Phoenix	T,B	Prop	M/W	417				N	Y		Y	Y	Y	Y	N		5
ITT Technical Institute	Tucson	T	Prop	M/W	280				N	Y	Y	Y	Y	Y	Y	N		5
Lamson College	Tempe																	
Mesa Community College	Mesa																	
Mohave Community College	Kingman	C,T	St	M/W	5,736		72		Y		S	Y	Y	Y	Y	N		23
Northland Pioneer College	Holbrook	C,T	St-L	M/W	5,374		76		Y			Y	Y	Y	Y	Y	2	32
Paradise Valley Community College	Phoenix	C,T	St-L	M/W	7,349				Y			Y	Y	Y	Y	N	5	7
The Paralegal Institute, Inc.	Phoenix	T	Prop		2,576													1
Phoenix College	Phoenix	C,T	St-L	M/W	12,296				Y			Y	Y	Y	Y	N	12	40
Pima Community College†	Tucson	C,T	St-L	M/W	28,176	73	45	15	Y			Y	Y	Y	Y	N	15	59
Pima Medical Institute	Mesa																	
Pima Medical Institute	Tucson	T	Prop		350													
The Refrigeration School	Phoenix	T	Prop	M/W	300							Y				N		1
Rio Salado College	Tempe	C,T	St-L	M/W	11,386													
Scottsdale Community College	Scottsdale	C,T	St-L	M/W	10,397		50		Y			Y	Y	Y		N	11	25
Scottsdale Culinary Institute	Scottsdale																	
South Mountain Community College	Phoenix	C,T	St-L	M/W	3,406		42	18	Y			Y	Y	Y	Y	N	8	19
Universal Technical Institute	Phoenix																	
Yavapai College	Prescott																	

Arkansas

College	Location	Degrees Awarded	Institutional Control	Student Body	Undergraduate Enrollment Fall 2001	Percent Attending Part-Time	Percent 25 Years of Age or Older	Percent of Grads Going on to 4-Year Colleges	Open Admissions	High School Equivalency Certificate Accepted	High School Transcript Required	Need-based aid available	Part-Time Jobs Available	Career Counseling Available	Job Placement Services Available	College Housing Available	Number of Sports Offered	Number of Majors Offered
Arkansas State University–Beebe	Beebe	C,T	St	M/W	3,302		38		Y	Y	Y	Y	Y	Y		Y	12	22
Arkansas State University–Mountain Home	Mountain Home	C,T	St	M/W	1,238	50	50		Y	Y	Y							9
Arkansas State University–Newport	Newport	C	St	M/W	604		38		Y	Y								
Black River Technical College	Pocahontas	C,T	St	M/W	1,243	48	53	4	Y	Y	S	Y		Y	Y	N		10
Cossatot Community College of the University of Arkansas	De Queen	C	St	M/W	814													
Crowley's Ridge College	Paragould	C,T	I-R	M/W	155				Y	Y	Y					Y	3	2
East Arkansas Community College	Forrest City	C,T	St	M/W	1,358		47	54	Y	Y	Y	Y	Y	Y	Y	N		7
Education America, Southeast College of Technology, Little Rock Campus	Little Rock																	
Garland County Community College	Hot Springs	C,T	St-L	M/W	2,300													
ITT Technical Institute	Little Rock	T	Prop	M/W	301				N	Y	Y	Y	Y	Y	Y	N		5
Mid-South Community College	West Memphis	C,T	St	M/W	996	62	44	73	Y	Y	Y	Y	Y	Y		N		8
Mississippi County Community College	Blytheville	C,T	St	M/W	1,840	43	38	10	Y	Y	R	Y	Y	Y	Y	N		9
North Arkansas College	Harrison	C,T	St-L	M/W	1,889	43	40		Y	Y	S	Y	Y	Y	Y	N	11	11
NorthWest Arkansas Community College	Bentonville	C,T	St-L	M/W	4,292		31		Y	Y	R	Y	Y	Y	Y	N	11	17
Ouachita Technical College	Malvern	C,T	St	M/W	968	57	45		Y	Y	Y	Y	Y	Y	Y	N		16
Ozarka College	Melbourne	C,T	St	M/W	858		43	52	Y	Y	Y	Y	Y	Y		N		10
Phillips Comm Coll of the U of Arkansas	Helena	C,T	St-L	M/W	2,100													
Pulaski Technical College	North Little Rock	C,T	St	M/W	4,966		55		Y	Y	Y	Y	Y	Y	Y	N		6
Rich Mountain Community College	Mena	C,T	St-L	M/W	1,005	65		75	Y	Y	Y	Y	Y	Y	Y	N		2
South Arkansas Community College	El Dorado	C	St	M/W	1,173		43		Y			Y	Y	Y	Y	N	4	10
Southeast Arkansas College	Pine Bluff	C,T	St	M/W	2,025		58		Y	Y	Y	Y	Y	Y	Y	N		14
Southern Arkansas University Tech	Camden	C,T	St	M/W	896	50	54	75	Y	Y	R,S	Y	Y	Y	Y	N	7	18
University of Arkansas at Fort Smith	Fort Smith	C,T,B	St-L	M/W	5,746	56	40	75	Y	Y	Y	Y	Y	Y	Y	N	5	23
University of Arkansas Community College at Batesville	Batesville	C,T	St	M/W	328	32	37		Y		Y	Y	Y					13
University of Arkansas Community College at Hope	Hope	C,T	St	M/W	1,137	41	38		Y		Y	Y	Y	Y	Y	N		10
University of Arkansas Community College at Morrilton	Morrilton	C,T	St	M/W	1,294		44		Y	Y	Y	Y	Y	Y	Y	N		17

California

College	Location	Degrees Awarded	Institutional Control	Student Body	Undergraduate Enrollment Fall 2001	Percent Attending Part-Time	Percent 25 Years of Age or Older	Percent of Grads Going on to 4-Year Colleges	Open Admissions	High School Equivalency Certificate Accepted	High School Transcript Required	Need-based aid available	Part-Time Jobs Available	Career Counseling Available	Job Placement Services Available	College Housing Available	Number of Sports Offered	Number of Majors Offered
Allan Hancock College	Santa Maria	C,T	St-L	M/W	12,548	78			Y	Y	Y	Y	Y	Y	Y	N	10	50
American Academy of Dramatic Arts/Hollywood†	Hollywood	C	Ind	M/W	182		15		N	Y	Y	Y	Y	Y		N		1
American River College	Sacramento	C,T	Dist	M/W	2,145	68	19		Y			Y	Y	Y	Y	N	9	68
Antelope Valley College	Lancaster	C,T	St-L	M/W	12,500		44		Y		Y	Y	Y	Y	Y	N	12	45
The Art Institute of Los Angeles	Santa Monica	C,T,B	Prop	M/W	1,429	9	15											4
Bakersfield College	Bakersfield	C,T	St-L	M/W	15,001		50		Y			Y	Y	Y	Y	N	11	77
Barstow College	Barstow	C,T	St-L	M/W	3,264		60		Y		R	Y	Y	Y	Y	N	3	17
Brooks College	Long Beach	T	Prop	M/W	1,375		3		N	Y	Y		Y	Y	Y	Y		5
Butte College	Oroville	C,T	Dist	M/W	14,724	78	53		Y		S	Y	Y	Y	Y	N	11	55
Cabrillo College	Aptos																	
California College of Technology	Sacramento																	
California Culinary Academy	San Francisco	T	Prop	M/W	813		25			Y	Y	Y	Y	Y	Y	Y		1
California Design College	Los Angeles	T	Prop	M/W	425		64	5		Y	Y	Y	Y	Y	Y	N		3
Cañada College	Redwood City	C,T	St-L	M/W	6,217		65		Y	Y			Y	Y	Y	N	5	49
Cerritos College	Norwalk	C,T	St-L	M/W	23,000		46		Y			Y	Y	Y	Y	N	13	67
Cerro Coso Community College	Ridgecrest	C,T	St	M/W	6,653	90	60		Y		R	Y	Y	Y	Y	N	5	41
Chabot College	Hayward	C,T	St	M/W	15,149		47		Y	Y	Y	Y	Y	Y	Y	N	21	90
Chaffey College	Rancho Cucamonga	C,T	Dist	M/W	18,025		47		Y			Y	Y	Y	Y	N	10	63
Citrus College	Glendora	C,T	St-L	M/W	11,159		36		Y	Y	Y	Y	Y	Y	Y	N	12	43
City College of San Francisco	San Francisco	C,T	St-L	M/W	100,544		56		Y			Y	Y	Y	Y	N	16	69
Coastline Community College	Fountain Valley	C	St-L	M/W	12,220		75		Y		R	Y	Y	Y	Y	N		1
College of Alameda	Alameda	C,T	St-L	M/W	5,500		44		Y	Y		Y	Y	Y	Y	N	6	31

This index includes the names and locations of accredited two-year colleges in the United States and U.S. territories and shows institutions' responses to our 2001 Survey of Undergraduate Institutions. If an institution submitted incomplete or no data, one or more columns opposite the institution's name is blank. An asterisk after the school name denotes a *Special Announcement* following the college's profile.

Y—Yes; N—No; R—Recommended; S—For Some

Institution	Location	Degrees Awarded: Transfer Associate (C), Terminal Associate (T), Bachelor's (B), Master's (M), Doctoral (D), First Professional (F)	Institutional Control: Independent, Independent-Religious, Proprietary, Federal, State, Province, Commonwealth, Territory, County, District, City, State and Local, State-Related	Student Body: Men, Primarily Men, Women, Primarily Women, Coed	Undergraduate Enrollment Fall 2001	Percent Attending Part-Time	Percent 25 Years of Age or Older	Percent of Grads Going on to 4-Year Colleges	Open Admissions	High School Equivalency Certificate Accepted	High School Transcript Required	Need-based aid available	Part-Time Jobs Available	Career Counseling Available	Job Placement Services Available	College Housing Available	Number of Sports Offered	Number of Majors Offered
College of Marin	Kentfield	C,T	St-L	M/W	8,365		50		Y			Y	Y	Y	Y	N	10	56
College of Oceaneering	Wilmington	C	Prop	PM	245													
College of San Mateo	San Mateo	C,T	St-L	M/W	10,872													
College of the Canyons	Santa Clarita	C,T	St-L	M/W	10,700		35		Y		R	Y	Y	Y	Y	N	10	46
College of the Desert	Palm Desert	C,T	St-L	M/W	9,794		40		Y	Y		Y	Y	Y		N	14	64
College of the Redwoods	Eureka	C,T	St-L	M/W	7,503		51		Y	Y		Y	Y	Y	Y	Y	8	29
College of the Sequoias	Visalia	C,T	St-L	M/W	10,780		46		Y		Y		Y	Y	Y	N	12	75
College of the Siskiyous*	Weed	C,T	St-L	M/W	3,127	74	61	30	Y			Y	Y	Y	Y	Y	12	46
Columbia College	Sonora																	
Compton Community College	Compton	C,T	St-L	M/W	7,900		69	25	Y			Y	Y	Y	Y	N	6	76
Contra Costa College	San Pablo																	
Copper Mountain College	Joshua Tree																	
Cosumnes River College	Sacramento																	
Crafton Hills College	Yucaipa	C,T	St-L	M/W	5,200		47		Y	Y	S	Y	Y	Y	Y	N	4	42
Cuesta College	San Luis Obispo	C,T	Dist	M/W	10,165		33		Y		Y	Y	Y	Y	Y	N	11	50
Cuyamaca College	El Cajon	C,T	St	M/W	7,423		63		Y	Y		Y	Y	Y	Y	N	6	33
Cypress College	Cypress	C,T	St-L	M/W	15,347		45		Y		R	Y	Y	Y	Y	N	11	69
De Anza College	Cupertino	C,T	St-L	M/W	24,984		52	13	Y	Y		Y	Y	Y	Y	N	13	65
Deep Springs College	Deep Springs	C	Ind	M	26		0	46	N	N	Y					Y	10	1
Diablo Valley College	Pleasant Hill	C,T	St-L	M/W	23,035		41		Y		R	Y	Y	Y	Y	N	11	15
Don Bosco College of Science and Technology	Rosemead	C,T	I-R	PM	1,208		0	85	N	Y	Y	Y	Y	Y	Y	N	8	8
D-Q University	Davis																	
East Los Angeles College	Monterey Park																	
El Camino College	Torrance																	
Empire College	Santa Rosa	T	Prop	M/W	616		66		N	Y	Y	Y		Y	Y			5
Everest College	Rancho Cucamonga																	
Evergreen Valley College	San Jose	C,T	St-L	M/W	10,000		52		Y			Y	Y	Y	Y	N	5	27
Fashion Careers of California College	San Diego	C,T	Prop	PW	100		17	0	N	Y	Y	Y	Y	Y	Y	N		2
Fashion Inst of Design & Merchandising, LA Campus†	Los Angeles	C	Prop	M/W	2,873	16	17		N	Y	Y	Y	Y	Y	Y	Y		8
Fashion Inst of Design & Merchandising, SD Campus	San Diego	C	Prop	M/W	276		10	18	N	Y	Y		Y	Y	Y			7
Fashion Inst of Design & Merchandising, SF Campus	San Francisco	C	Prop	M/W	732		20		N	Y	Y		Y	Y	Y	Y		8
Feather River Community College District	Quincy	C,T	St-L	M/W	1,200				Y		R	Y	Y	Y	Y	N	5	21
Foothill College	Los Altos Hills	C,T	St-L	M/W	18,500		67	31	Y		R	Y	Y	Y	Y	N	10	66
Foundation College	San Diego																	
Fresno City College	Fresno	C,T	Dist	M/W	30,069		7	85	Y		Y	Y	Y	Y	Y	N	16	62
Fullerton College	Fullerton	C,T	St-L	M/W	21,104		40		Y			Y	Y	Y	Y	N	10	68
Gavilan College	Gilroy	C,T	St-L	M/W			58		Y	Y		Y	Y	Y		N	9	40
Glendale Community College	Glendale	C,T	St-L	M/W			45		Y	Y	R	Y	Y	Y	Y	N	9	61
Golden West College	Huntington Beach	C,T	St-L	M/W	13,091		44	80	Y	Y	R	Y	Y	Y	Y	N	13	35
Grossmont College	El Cajon	C,T	St-L	M/W	16,175													
Hartnell College	Salinas																	
Heald College Concord	Concord																	
Heald College, School of Business	Concord																	
Heald College, School of Business	Salinas																	
Heald College, School of Business	Santa Rosa																	
Heald College, School of Business	Stockton																	
Heald College, Schools of Business and Technology	Fresno																	
Heald College, Schools of Business and Technology	Hayward	C,T	Ind	M/W	1,250		30		Y	Y	Y	Y	Y	Y	Y	N		9
Heald College, Schools of Business and Technology	Milpitas	T	Ind	M/W	1,200													
Heald College, Schools of Business and Technology	Rancho Cordova	C,T	Ind	M/W	676		20		N	Y	Y	Y	Y	Y	Y	N		5
Heald College, Schools of Business and Technology	Roseville																	
Heald College, Schools of Business and Technology	San Francisco																	
Imperial Valley College	Imperial	C,T	St-L	M/W	7,223	65		12	Y		R,S	Y	Y	Y	Y	N	6	35
Irvine Valley College	Irvine																	
ITT Technical Institute	Anaheim	T,B	Prop	M/W	691				N	Y	Y	Y	Y	Y	Y	N		5
ITT Technical Institute	Hayward	T,B	Prop		286				N		Y	Y	Y	Y	Y	N		5
ITT Technical Institute	Lathrop	T	Prop	M/W							Y					N		3
ITT Technical Institute	Oxnard	C,T,B	Prop	M/W	549				N	Y	Y	Y	Y	Y	Y	N		5
ITT Technical Institute	Rancho Cordova	T,B	Prop	M/W	533				N	Y	Y		Y	Y	Y	N		7
ITT Technical Institute	San Bernardino	T,B	Prop	M/W	862				N	Y	Y		Y	Y	Y	N		6
ITT Technical Institute	San Diego	T,B	Prop	M/W	885				N	Y	Y	Y	Y	Y	Y	N		5
ITT Technical Institute	Santa Clara	T	Prop		208				N	Y	Y			Y	Y	N		4
ITT Technical Institute	Sylmar	T,B	Prop	M/W	715				N	Y	Y	Y	Y	Y	Y	N		6
ITT Technical Institute	Torrance	T	Prop	M/W	562				N	Y	Y	Y	Y	Y	Y	N		5
ITT Technical Institute	West Covina	T,B	Prop	M/W					N	Y	Y	Y	Y	Y	Y	N		6
Lake Tahoe Community College	South Lake Tahoe	C,T	St-L	M/W	3,400		71		Y		S	Y	Y	Y	Y	N	2	27
Laney College*	Oakland	C,T	St-L	M/W	9,516													
Las Positas College	Livermore	C,T	St	M/W	8,044		50		Y	Y	R	Y	Y	Y	Y	N	7	23
Lassen Community College District	Susanville																	
Long Beach City College	Long Beach	C,T	St	M/W	28,000		50	23	Y		R	Y	Y	Y	Y	N	18	69
Los Angeles City College	Los Angeles	C,T	Dist	M/W	24,652		62		Y				Y	Y	Y	N	16	85
Los Angeles County Med Ctr Sch for Nursing	Los Angeles																	
Los Angeles Harbor College	Wilmington	C,T	St-L	M/W	7,467	75	49	18	Y		S	Y	Y	Y	Y	N	7	23
Los Angeles Mission College	Sylmar	C,T	St-L	M/W	7,617		55	8	Y			Y	Y	Y	Y	N		38
Los Angeles Pierce College	Woodland Hills	C,T	St-L	M/W	18,260		48		Y			Y	Y	Y	Y	N	16	34
Los Angeles Southwest College	Los Angeles																	
Los Angeles Trade-Technical College	Los Angeles																	
Los Angeles Valley College	Valley Glen	C,T	St-L	M/W	17,786	83												
Los Medanos College	Pittsburg																	
Maric College	San Diego	C,T	Prop	M/W	900		60			Y	Y		Y	Y	Y	N		1

This index includes the names and locations of accredited two-year colleges in the United States and U.S. territories and shows institutions' responses to our 2001 Survey of Undergraduate Institutions. If an institution submitted incomplete or no data, one or more columns opposite the institution's name is blank. An asterisk after the school name denotes a *Special Announcement* following the college's profile.

Y—Yes; N—No; R—Recommended; S—For Some

Institution	Location	Degrees Awarded (Transfer Associate (C), Terminal Associate (T), Bachelor's (B), Master's (M), Doctoral (D), First Professional (F))	Institutional Control (Independent, Independent-Religious, Proprietary, Federal, State, Province, Commonwealth, Territory, County, District, City, State and Local, State-Related)	Student Body (Men, Primarily Men, Women, Primarily Women, Coed)	Undergraduate Enrollment Fall 2001	Percent Attending Part-Time	Percent 25 Years of Age or Older	Percent of Grads Going on to 4-Year Colleges	High School Equivalency Certificate Accepted	Open Admissions	High School Transcript Required	Need-based aid available	Part-Time Jobs Available	Career Counseling Available	Job Placement Services Available	College Housing Available	Number of Sports Offered	Number of Majors Offered
Marymount College, Palos Verdes, California	Rancho Palos Verdes	C,T	I-R	M/W	790	14	20		N	Y	Y	Y	Y	Y		Y	8	1
Mendocino College	Ukiah	C,T	St-L	M/W	5,200													
Merced College	Merced	C,T	St-L	M/W	9,024		51		Y			Y	Y	Y	Y	N	14	58
Merritt College	Oakland	C,T	St-L	M/W	6,000													
MiraCosta College*	Oceanside	C,T	St	M/W	10,129	71	33	80	Y			Y	Y	Y	Y	N	4	54
Mission College	Santa Clara	C,T	St-L	M/W	10,500													
Modesto Junior College	Modesto	C,T	St-L	M/W	15,696		53		Y		R	Y	Y	Y	Y	N	15	89
Monterey Peninsula College	Monterey	C,T	St	M/W	8,000				Y			Y	Y	Y	Y	N	10	70
Moorpark College	Moorpark	C,T	Cou	M/W	14,538		42		Y	Y		Y	Y	Y	Y	N	10	38
Mt. San Antonio College	Walnut	C,T	Dist	M/W	28,329													
Mt. San Jacinto College	San Jacinto	C,T	St-L	M/W	12,288		51		Y		R	Y	Y	Y	Y	N	7	29
MTI College	Orange																	
MTI College of Business and Technology	Sacramento																	
Napa Valley College	Napa																	
Northwestern Technical College	Sacramento																	
Ohlone College	Fremont																	
Orange Coast College	Costa Mesa	C,T	St-L	M/W	24,630	67	65		Y			Y	Y	Y	Y	N	14	104
Oxnard College	Oxnard	C	St	M/W	7,594		62		Y	Y		Y	Y	Y	Y	N	6	44
Palomar College	San Marcos	C	St-L	M/W	29,715		3		Y			Y	Y	Y	Y	N	12	78
Palo Verde College	Blythe	C,T	St-L	M/W	2,903		88		Y		R	Y	Y	Y	Y	N		30
Pasadena City College	Pasadena	C,T	St-L	M/W	25,269		39		Y				Y	Y	Y	N	11	104
Pima Medical Institute	Chula Vista																	
Platt College	Cerritos	C,T	Prop		320													
Platt College†	Newport Beach	C	Ind	M/W	270		75		N	Y	Y			Y	Y	N		4
Platt College†	Ontario	C,T	Ind	M/W	284		52		N	Y				Y	Y	N		5
Platt College–Los Angeles, Inc†	Los Angeles	C,T	Prop	M/W	209		53	9	N	Y				Y	Y	N		7
Platt College San Diego*	San Diego	C	Ind	M/W	375		90		N	Y	Y					N		2
Porterville College	Porterville																	
Professional Golfers Career College	Temecula	T	Ind		120													
Queen of the Holy Rosary College	Mission San Jose	C	I-R	PW	198		100		Y	Y	Y					N		1
Reedley College	Reedley	C,T	St-L	M/W	11,305	60	39		Y	Y	Y	Y	Y	Y	Y	Y	9	39
Rio Hondo College	Whittier																	
Riverside Community College	Riverside	T	St-L	M/W	29,865	73	32		Y		Y	Y	Y	Y	Y	N	16	65
Sacramento City College	Sacramento	C,T	St-L	M/W	20,781		50		Y			Y	Y	Y	Y	N	18	49
Saddleback College	Mission Viejo																	
Salvation Army College for Officer Training	Rancho Palos Verdes																	
San Bernardino Valley College	San Bernardino	C,T	St-L	M/W			55		Y	Y		Y	Y	Y	Y	N	9	64
San Diego City College	San Diego	C,T	St-L	M/W	14,126		63		Y		S	Y	Y	Y	Y	N	16	69
San Diego Golf Academy	Vista																	
San Diego Mesa College	San Diego	C,T	St-L	M/W	21,700		51		Y			Y	Y	Y	Y	N	19	72
San Diego Miramar College	San Diego																	
San Francisco College of Mortuary Science	San Francisco																	
San Joaquin Delta College	Stockton	C	Dist	M/W	18,546		52		Y			Y	Y	Y	Y	N	17	82
San Joaquin Valley College	Visalia	T	Ind	M/W	1,844				Y	Y	Y	Y		Y	Y	N		19
San Jose City College	San Jose																	
Santa Ana College	Santa Ana	C,T	St	M/W	25,386	86	63		Y	Y			Y	Y	Y	N	13	74
Santa Barbara City College	Santa Barbara	T	St-L	M/W	14,949	64	27		Y	Y	R	Y	Y	Y	Y	N	10	79
Santa Monica College†	Santa Monica	C,T	St-L	M/W	29,077	68	25		Y	Y	Y	Y	Y	Y	Y	N	10	62
Santa Rosa Junior College	Santa Rosa	C,T	St-L	M/W	25,233													
Santiago Canyon College	Orange	C,T	St	M/W	9,742	87	50		Y	Y				Y	Y			
Sequoia Institute	Fremont	T	Prop	PM	758													3
Shasta College	Redding	C,T	St-L	M/W	10,108	64	56	16	Y		Y	Y	Y	Y	Y	Y	11	36
Sierra College	Rocklin	C,T	St	M/W	19,000				Y	Y		Y	Y	Y		Y	16	51
Silicon Valley College	Fremont																	
Silicon Valley College	San Jose	T,B	Prop	M/W	197													6
Silicon Valley College	Walnut Creek																	
Skyline College	San Bruno	C,T	St-L	M/W	8,573													
Solano Community College	Suisun																	
Southern California College of Business and Law	Brea																	
Southern California Institute of Technology	Anaheim																	
Southwestern College	Chula Vista	C,T	St-L	M/W	19,538		26		Y		S	Y	Y	Y	Y	N	10	73
Taft College	Taft	C,T	St-L	M/W	2,929	83	54		Y		S	Y	Y	Y	Y	Y	5	24
Ventura College	Ventura	C,T	St-L	M/W	11,860	70	47		Y	Y	Y	Y	Y	Y	Y	N	13	42
Victor Valley College	Victorville	C,T	St	M/W	8,111	75	40		Y			Y		Y	Y	N	11	41
Vista Community College*	Berkeley	C,T	St-L	M/W	4,500		65	90	Y		R	Y	Y	Y		N		21
Western Institute of Science & Health	Rohnert Park	T	Prop	M/W			60		Y	Y	Y	Y	Y	Y		N		3
West Hills Community College	Coalinga																	
West Los Angeles College	Culver City																	
West Valley College	Saratoga																	
Westwood College of Aviation Technology–Los Angeles†	Inglewood	C,B	Prop	PM	560				Y	Y		Y				N		2
Westwood College of Technology–Anaheim†	Anaheim	T,B	Prop	M/W	650													4
Westwood College of Technology–Inland Empire†	Upland	T,B	Prop	M/W														4
Westwood College of Technology–Los Angeles†	Los Angeles	C	Prop	M/W	496													4
Yuba College	Marysville	C,T	St-L	M/W	12,348	63												
Colorado																		
Aims Community College	Greeley	C,T	Dist	M/W	6,868		60		Y			Y	Y	Y	Y	N	2	18
Arapahoe Community College†	Littleton	C,T	St	M/W	7,076				Y			Y	Y	Y	Y	N	8	51
Bel–Rea Institute of Animal Technology	Denver	T	Prop	M/W	600		40	10	N	Y	Y	Y		Y	Y			1

This index includes the names and locations of accredited two-year colleges in the United States and U.S. territories and shows institutions' responses to our 2001 Survey of Undergraduate Institutions. If an institution submitted incomplete or no data, one or more columns opposite the institution's name is blank. An asterisk after the school name denotes a *Special Announcement* following the college's profile.

Y—Yes; N—No; R—Recommended; S—For Some

		Degrees Awarded: Transfer Associate (C), Terminal Associate (T), Bachelor's (B), Master's (M), Doctoral (D), First Professional (F)	Institutional Control: Independent, Independent-Religious, Proprietary, Federal, State, Province, Commonwealth, Territory, County, District, City, State and Local, State-Related	Student Body: Men, Primarily Men, Women, Primarily Women, Coed	Undergraduate Enrollment Fall 2001	Percent Attending Part-Time	Percent 25 Years of Age or Older	Percent of Grads Going on to 4-Year Colleges	Open Admissions	High School Equivalency Certificate Accepted	High School Transcript Required	Need-based aid available	Part-Time Jobs Available	Career Counseling Available	Job Placement Services Available	College Housing Available	Number of Sports Offered	Number of Majors Offered
Blair College	Colorado Springs	T	Prop	M/W	500				Y	Y	Y	Y	Y	Y	Y	N	1	9
Cambridge College	Aurora																	
CollegeAmerica–Denver	Denver																	
CollegeAmerica–Fort Collins	Fort Collins																	
Colorado Mountn Coll, Alpine Cmps	Steamboat Springs	C,T	Dist	M/W	1,474		23	57	Y	Y	Y	Y	Y	Y	Y	Y	5	20
Colorado Mountn Coll*†	Glenwood Springs	C,T	Dist	M/W	753		36	57	Y	Y	Y	Y	Y	Y	Y	Y	5	25
Colorado Mountn Coll, Timberline Cmps	Leadville	C,T	Dist	M/W	474		24	57	Y	Y	Y	Y	Y	Y	Y	Y	5	24
Colorado Northwestern Community College*†	Rangely	C,T	St	M/W	2,109	78	34		Y		Y	Y	Y	Y	Y	Y	11	16
Colorado School of Trades	Lakewood																	
Community College of Aurora†	Aurora	C,T	St	M/W	4,000		59	20	Y				Y	Y	Y	N		17
Community College of Denver†	Denver	C,T	St	M/W	6,509	72	51		Y			Y	Y	Y	Y	N	23	29
Denver Academy of Court Reporting	Denver																	
Denver Automotive and Diesel College	Denver																	
Front Range Community College†	Westminster	C,T	St	M/W	13,511	69	48		Y			Y	Y	Y	Y	N	1	30
Institute of Business & Medical Careers	Fort Collins																	
IntelliTec College	Colorado Springs																	
IntelliTec College	Grand Junction																	
IntelliTec Medical Institute	Colorado Springs	T	Prop	PW	361				Y	Y	Y	Y	Y	Y	Y	N		3
ITT Technical Institute	Thornton	T,B	Prop	M/W	419				N	Y	Y	Y	Y	Y	Y	N		5
Lamar Community College†	Lamar	C,T	St	M/W	1,021		43		Y	Y		Y	Y	Y		Y	7	50
Morgan Community College†	Fort Morgan	C,T	St	M/W	1,781		52		Y		Y	Y	Y	Y	Y	N		10
Northeastern Junior College†	Sterling	C,T	St	M/W	3,633	75												
Otero Junior College†	La Junta	C,T	St	M/W	1,402		52	36	Y	Y	R	Y	Y	Y	Y	Y	5	27
Parks College	Denver																	
Pikes Peak Community College†	Colorado Springs	C,T	St	M/W	9,772	69	53		Y			Y	Y	Y	Y	N	3	34
Pima Medical Institute	Denver																	
Platt College	Aurora	T,B	Prop	M/W	215				Y	Y	Y	Y		Y	Y	N		6
Pueblo Community College†	Pueblo																	
Red Rocks Community College†	Lakewood	C,T	St	M/W	7,394		53		Y			Y	Y	Y	Y	N	1	40
Trinidad State Junior College†	Trinidad	C,T	St	M/W	2,804	38	59	37	Y	Y	Y	Y	Y	Y	Y	Y	15	51
Westwood College of Aviation Technology–Denver†	Broomfield	T	Prop	M/W	628					Y		Y	Y	Y	Y	N		3
Westwood College of Technology–Denver North†	Denver	T,B	Prop	M/W	969	32	31		N	Y	S	Y	Y	Y	Y	N		16
Westwood College of Technology–Denver South†	Denver	C,B	Prop	M/W	421													7
Connecticut																		
Asnuntuck Community College	Enfield	T	St	M/W	1,723	76	58		Y	Y	Y	Y	Y	Y	Y	N		15
Briarwood College†	Southington	C,T	Prop	M/W	575		38	7	N	Y	Y	Y	Y	Y	Y	Y	4	22
Capital Community College	Hartford	C,T	St	M/W	3,129	80	61		Y	Y	R	Y	Y	Y	Y	N	4	25
Gateway Community College	New Haven	C,T	St	M/W	4,724		58	40	Y	Y	Y		Y	Y	Y	N	1	34
Gibbs College	Norwalk	T	Prop	M/W	480													
Goodwin College	East Hartford	C,T	Prop	M/W	721	28	42		Y	Y	Y			Y	Y	N		2
Housatonic Community College	Bridgeport	C,T	St	M/W	4,247		46		Y	Y	Y	Y	Y	Y	Y	N		24
International College of Hospitality Management, César Ritz*†	Washington	C,T	Prop	M/W	116		14	35	N	Y	Y	Y	Y	Y	Y	Y	4	1
Manchester Community College	Manchester	C,T	St	M/W	5,405	65	43		Y	Y	Y	Y	Y	Y		N	4	31
Middlesex Community College	Middletown	C,T	St	M/W	2,309	75												
Mitchell College†	New London	C,T,B	Ind	M/W	708	17	10	95	N	Y	Y	Y	Y	Y	Y	Y	16	21
Naugatuck Valley Community College	Waterbury	C,T	St	M/W	5,223	66	51	30	Y	Y	Y	Y	Y	Y	Y	N	3	50
Northwestern Connecticut Community-Technical Coll	Winsted	C,T	St	M/W	1,609	75	56	30	Y	Y		Y	Y	Y	Y	N		35
Norwalk Community College	Norwalk	C,T	St	M/W	5,569	70	51	41	Y	Y	Y	Y	Y	Y	Y	N		32
Quinebaug Valley Community College	Danielson	C,T	St	M/W	1,347	71												
St. Vincent's College	Bridgeport																	
Three Rivers Community College	Norwich	C,T	St	M/W	3,426		63		Y	Y	R	Y	Y	Y	Y	N	3	41
Tunxis Community College	Farmington	C,T	St	M/W	3,720	72	47		Y	Y	Y		Y	Y	Y	N		23
Delaware																		
Delaware Tech & Comm Coll, Jack F Owens Cmps	Georgetown	T	St	M/W	3,546		50		Y		Y	Y	Y	Y	Y	N	2	36
Delaware Tech & Comm Coll, Stanton/ Wilmington Cmps	Newark	T	St	M/W	1,263	44	49		Y		Y	Y	Y	Y	Y	N	5	43
Delaware Tech & Comm Coll, Terry Cmps	Dover	T	St	M/W	379	52	57		Y		Y	Y	Y	Y	Y	N		25
Florida																		
The Academy	Lakeland																	
The Art Institute of Fort Lauderdale*†	Fort Lauderdale	C,T,B	Prop	M/W	3,500		12		N	Y	Y	Y	Y	Y	Y	Y		11
ATI Career Training Center	Miami																	
ATI Career Training Center	Oakland Park																	
ATI Career Training Center Electronics Campus	Fort Lauderdale	T	Prop	M/W	350					Y		Y	Y					3
ATI Health Education Center	Miami																	
Atlantic Coast Institute	Fort Lauderdale	C,T	Prop	PW	147													
Brevard Community College	Cocoa	C,T	St	M/W	13,681		46	42	Y	Y	Y	Y	Y	Y	Y	N	9	52
Broward Community College	Fort Lauderdale																	
Central Florida Community College	Ocala	C,T	St-L	M/W	5,708		35	29	Y	Y	Y	Y	Y	Y	Y	N	5	9
Chipola Junior College	Marianna	C,T	St	M/W	1,834	52		40	Y	Y	Y	Y	Y	Y	Y		3	16
City College	Fort Lauderdale																	
College for Professional Studies	Boca Raton																	
Cooper Career Institute	West Palm Beach																	
Daytona Beach Community College	Daytona Beach	C,T	St	M/W	11,214	59	54		Y	Y	Y	Y	Y	Y	Y	N	11	95
Edison Community College	Fort Myers	C,T	St-L	M/W	9,390		70	66	Y	Y	Y	Y	Y	Y	Y	N		29

This index includes the names and locations of accredited two-year colleges in the United States and U.S. territories and shows institutions' responses to our 2001 Survey of Undergraduate Institutions. If an institution submitted incomplete or no data, one or more columns opposite the institution's name is blank. An asterisk after the school name denotes a *Special Announcement* following the college's profile.

Y—Yes; N—No; R—Recommended; S—For Some

Institution	Location	Degrees Awarded: Transfer Associate (C), Terminal Associate (T), Bachelor's (B), Master's (M), Doctoral (D), First Professional (F)	Institutional Control: Independent (Ind), Independent-Religious, Proprietary, Federal, State, Province, Commonwealth, Territory, County, District, City, State and Local, State-Related	Student Body: Men, Primarily Men, Women, Primarily Women, Coed	Undergraduate Enrollment Fall 2001	Percent Attending Part-Time	Percent 25 Years of Age or Older	Percent of Grads Going on to 4-Year Colleges	Open Admissions	High School Equivalency Certificate Accepted	High School Transcript Required	Need-based aid available	Part-Time Jobs Available	Career Counseling Available	Job Placement Services Available	College Housing Available	Number of Sports Offered	Number of Majors Offered
Education America, Tampa Technical Institute, Jacksonville Campus	Jacksonville																	
Education America, Tampa Technical Institute, Pinellas Campus	Largo																	
Education America–Tampa Tech Inst Campus	Tampa	C,B	Prop	M/W	1,138													
Florida Community College at Jacksonville	Jacksonville	C,T	St	M/W	23,425	70	47	81	Y	Y	Y		Y	Y	Y	N	11	91
Florida Computer & Business School	Miami	T	Prop	M/W	621		75		Y	Y	Y	Y	Y	Y	Y	N		5
Florida Culinary Institute	West Palm Beach	T	Prop		1,500							Y	Y					2
Florida Hospital College of Health Sciences	Orlando	C,T,B	Ind	PW	746	45			Y	Y	Y	Y		Y		Y	3	6
Florida Keys Community College	Key West																	
Florida National College	Hialeah	C,T	Prop	M/W	1,248		60		Y	Y	Y	Y	Y	Y	Y	N		33
Florida Technical College	Auburndale	C,T	Prop	M/W	185													
Florida Technical College	DeLand																	
Florida Technical College	Jacksonville	T	Prop	M/W	225				Y									2
Florida Technical College	Orlando	T	Prop	M/W	227		63		N	Y	Y	Y		Y	Y	N		10
Full Sail Real World Education	Winter Park	T	Prop	M/W	3,100		19	10	Y	Y	Y	Y		Y	Y	N		6
Gulf Coast Community College	Panama City	C,T	St	M/W	5,765	65	45	68	Y	Y	Y	Y	Y	Y		N	5	29
Herzing College	Melbourne	T	Prop	M/W	180													
Herzing College	Orlando																	
Hillsborough Community College	Tampa	C,T	St	M/W	19,436	70	34		Y	Y	Y	Y	Y	Y	Y	N	5	53
Indian River Community College	Fort Pierce	C,T	St	M/W	23,160		48	78	Y	Y	Y	Y	Y	Y	Y	N	7	85
Institute of Career Education	West Palm Beach																	
ITT Technical Institute	Fort Lauderdale	T,B	Prop	M/W	587				N	Y	Y	Y	Y	Y	Y	N		5
ITT Technical Institute	Jacksonville	T,B	Prop	M/W	455				N	Y	Y	Y	Y	Y	Y	N		5
ITT Technical Institute	Maitland	T,B	Prop	M/W	418				N	Y	Y		Y	Y	Y	N		6
ITT Technical Institute	Miami	T	Prop		461				N	Y	Y			Y	Y	N		5
ITT Technical Institute	Tampa	T,B	Prop	M/W	649				N	Y	Y		Y	Y	Y	N		6
Keiser College	Daytona Beach																	
Keiser College	Fort Lauderdale	C,T	Prop	M/W	2,850													
Keiser College	Melbourne																	
Keiser College	Sarasota																	
Keiser College	Tallahassee																	
Lake City Community College	Lake City	C,T	St	M/W	2,287	54	52	35	Y	Y	S	Y	Y	Y	Y	Y	9	19
Lake-Sumter Community College	Leesburg	C,T	St-L	M/W	2,881	70	43		Y	Y	Y	Y	Y	Y	Y	N	6	15
Manatee Community College	Bradenton	C,T	St	M/W	1,954	56	39		Y	Y	Y	Y	Y	Y	Y	N	5	96
Miami-Dade Community College*†	Miami	C,T	St-L	M/W	53,486		45	78	Y	Y		Y	Y	Y	Y	N	7	128
New England Inst of Tech & Florida Culinary Inst	West Palm Beach	C,T	Prop	M/W	1,200		40		Y	Y	Y	Y	Y	Y	Y	N		9
North Florida Community College	Madison	C,T	St	M/W	1,012													
Okaloosa-Walton Community College	Niceville	C,T	St-L	M/W	7,148	76	49		Y		Y	Y	Y	Y	Y	N	4	54
Palm Beach Community College	Lake Worth	C,T	St	M/W	23,410	72	18	90	Y	Y		Y	Y	Y	Y	Y	9	67
Pasco-Hernando Community College	New Port Richey	C,T	St	M/W	5,625	67	41	80	Y	Y	Y	Y	Y	Y	Y	N	5	17
Pensacola Junior College	Pensacola	C,T	St	M/W	6,680		50		Y	Y	Y	Y	Y	Y	Y	N	16	64
Peoples College	Kissimmee																	
Polk Community College	Winter Haven	C,T	St	M/W	6,329	72	40	50	Y	Y	Y	Y	Y	Y	Y	N	5	22
Prospect Hall School of Business	Hollywood																	
St. Johns River Community College	Palatka	C,T	St	M/W	3,459													
St. Petersburg College	St. Petersburg	C,T,B	St-L	M/W	20,734	70	45		Y	Y	Y	Y	Y	Y		N	5	46
Santa Fe Community College	Gainesville	C,T	St-L	M/W	13,225	54	29	59	Y	Y	Y	Y	Y	Y	Y	N	8	38
Seminole Community College	Sanford	C,T	St-L	M/W	10,556	62	45		Y	Y	Y	Y	Y	Y	Y	N	6	51
Southern College	Orlando																	
South Florida Community College	Avon Park																	
South University	West Palm Beach	T,B	Prop	M/W	450													
Southwest Florida College	Fort Myers	T	Ind	M/W	785													
Tallahassee Community College	Tallahassee	C,T	St-L	M/W	11,606	54	26	82	Y	Y	Y	Y	Y	Y	Y	N	15	30
Valencia Community College	Orlando	C,T	St	M/W	27,565	64												
Webster College	Holiday	T,B	Prop		250						Y	Y	Y					6
Webster College	Ocala	T	Prop	PW	375		70		Y	Y	Y	Y	Y	Y	Y	N		7
Webster Institute of Technology	Tampa	T	Priv	PW	150		35		Y	Y		Y	Y	Y	Y	N		6
Georgia																		
Abraham Baldwin Agricultural College	Tifton	C,T	St	M/W	2,857		31		Y	Y	Y	Y	Y	Y	Y	Y	9	57
Andrew College†	Cuthbert	C	I-R	M/W	379		5	96	N	Y	Y	Y	Y	Y		Y	19	39
The Art Institute of Atlanta	Atlanta	T,B	Prop	M/W	2,437	13			N	Y	S	Y	Y	Y	Y	Y	2	8
Asher School of Business	Norcross																	
Ashworth College	Norcross																	
Athens Technical College	Athens	T	St	M/W	3,200		40		Y	Y	Y		Y	Y	Y	N		28
Atlanta Metropolitan College	Atlanta	C,T	St	M/W	1,917	59	40		N	Y	Y	Y		Y	Y	N	1	43
Atlanta Technical College	Atlanta																	
Augusta Technical College	Augusta	T	St	M/W	3,711		52		N	Y	Y	Y	Y	Y	Y	N	1	10
Bainbridge College	Bainbridge	C,T	St	M/W	1,736		38	30	Y	Y		Y	Y	Y	Y	N	2	34
Bauder College	Atlanta	C	Prop	PW	715			8	N	Y	Y	Y	Y	Y	Y	Y		5
Central Georgia Technical College	Macon	C,T	St	M/W	4,955	59	55		Y	Y	Y	Y	Y	Y	Y	N		10
Chattahoochee Technical College	Marietta	T	St	M/W	5,963		52		Y	Y	R		Y	Y	Y	N		14
Coastal Georgia Community College	Brunswick	C,T	St	M/W	2,210		50			Y	Y	Y	Y	Y	Y	N	6	35
Columbus Technical College	Columbus	T	St	M/W	3,031				Y	Y	Y	Y		Y	Y	N		5
Coosa Valley Technical Institute	Rome																	
Darton College	Albany	C,T	St	M/W	3,185	57	38	75	N	Y	Y	Y	Y	Y	Y	N	10	60
DeKalb Technical College	Clarkston																	
East Georgia College	Swainsboro	C	St	M/W	1,393	45	18	86	N	Y	Y	Y	Y	Y		N	10	23

This index includes the names and locations of accredited two-year colleges in the United States and U.S. territories and shows institutions' responses to our 2001 Survey of Undergraduate Institutions. If an institution submitted incomplete or no data, one or more columns opposite the institution's name is blank. An asterisk after the school name denotes a *Special Announcement* following the college's profile.

Y—Yes; N—No; R—Recommended; S—For Some

Institution	City	Degrees Awarded: Transfer Associate (C), Terminal Associate (T), Bachelor's (B), Master's (M), Doctoral (D), First Professional (F)	Institutional Control: Independent, Independent-Religious, Proprietary, Federal, State, Province, Commonwealth, Territory, County, District, City, State and Local, State-Related	Student Body: Men, Primarily Men, Women, Primarily Women, Coed	Undergraduate Enrollment Fall 2001	Percent Attending Part-Time	Percent 25 Years of Age or Older	Percent of Grads Going on to 4-Year Colleges	Open Admissions	High School Equivalency Certificate Accepted	High School Transcript Required	Need-based aid available	Part-Time Jobs Available	Career Counseling Available	Job Placement Services Available	College Housing Available	Number of Sports Offered	Number of Majors Offered
Emory University, Oxford College	Oxford	C	I-R	M/W	601	1	0.49	99	N	Y	Y	Y	Y			Y	11	1
Flint River Technical College	Thomaston																	
Floyd College	Rome	C,T	St	M/W	2,500		35		N	Y	Y	Y	Y	Y	Y	N	8	41
Gainesville College	Gainesville																	
Georgia Military College	Milledgeville	C,T	St-L	M/W	3,465		27		N	Y	Y	Y	Y	Y		Y	9	10
Georgia Perimeter College	Decatur	C,T	St	M/W	15,372	58	36		N	N	Y	Y	Y	Y	Y	N	5	66
Gordon College	Barnesville	C,T	St	M/W	3,074		24	50	Y	Y	Y	Y	Y	Y		Y	11	25
Griffin Technical College	Griffin	C,T	St	M/W	4,383				Y	Y	Y					N		6
Gupton-Jones College of Funeral Service	Decatur	T	Ind	M/W	250		20		Y	Y	Y	Y		Y	Y	N		1
Gwinnett Technical College	Lawrenceville	T	St	M/W	3,964		80		N	Y	Y	Y	Y			N		25
Herzing College	Atlanta	T,B	Prop	M/W	375		56		N	Y	Y	Y	Y	Y	Y	N		4
Interactive College of Technology	Chamblee	T	Prop	M/W	853	2												
Middle Georgia College*	Cochran	C,T	St	M/W	2,164	35	22		N	Y	Y	Y	Y	Y	Y	Y	7	15
Middle Georgia Technical College	Warner Robbins																	
Northwestern Technical College	Rock Springs	T	St	M/W	1,500													
Ogeechee Technical College	Statesboro																	
Savannah Technical College	Savannah	T	St	M/W	3,134	53	59		Y	Y	Y	Y		Y	Y	N		11
South Georgia College	Douglas																	
Southwest Georgia Technical College	Thomasville	T	St	M/W	2,448		74		Y	Y	Y	Y	Y	Y	Y	N		11
Truett-McConnell College	Cleveland	C,T	I-R	M/W	1,747	19	11		N	Y	Y	Y	Y	Y		Y	8	5
Waycross College	Waycross	C,T	St	M/W	884		43			Y		Y	Y	Y	Y	N	8	41
West Central Technical College	Carrollton	T	St	M/W	2,620	71	13		Y	Y	Y	Y	Y	Y	Y	N		13
West Georgia Technical College	LaGrange	T	St	M/W	1,234													
Young Harris College	Young Harris	C	I-R	M/W	594	5	1	93	N	Y	Y	Y	Y	Y		Y	13	36
Hawaii																		
Hawaii Business College	Honolulu	C,T	Ind	M/W	426				Y	Y	Y		Y	Y	Y	N		6
Hawaii Community College	Hilo	C,T	St	M/W	2,181		40		Y				Y			Y		17
Hawaii Tokai International College	Honolulu	C	Ind	M/W	45		17	88	N	Y	Y	Y		Y		Y		1
Heald College, Schools of Business and Technology	Honolulu	T	Ind	M/W	1,200		35		Y	Y	Y	Y	Y	Y	Y	N		8
Honolulu Community College	Honolulu	C,T	St	M/W	4,653	62	41		Y			Y	Y	Y	Y	N		22
Kapiolani Community College	Honolulu																	
Kauai Community College	Lihue	C	St	M/W	227	35			Y		R,S	Y	Y	Y	Y	N	3	11
Leeward Community College	Pearl City																	
Maui Community College	Kahului	C,T	St	M/W	2,657	63												
TransPacific Hawaii College	Honolulu	C	Ind	PW	110													
Windward Community College	Kaneohe	C,T	St	M/W	1,446	56												
Idaho																		
American Institute of Health Technology, Inc.	Boise	C,T	Prop	PW	224	22	38				Y					N		3
Brigham Young University –Idaho	Rexburg	C,T	I-R	M/W	9,000													
College of Southern Idaho	Twin Falls	C,T	St-L	M/W	5,344		57		Y	Y	Y	Y	Y	Y	Y	Y	10	73
Eastern Idaho Technical College	Idaho Falls	T	St	M/W	601	45	48		Y	Y	Y	Y	Y	Y	Y	N		9
ITT Technical Institute	Boise	T,B	Prop	M/W	382				N	Y	Y	Y	Y	Y	Y	N		6
North Idaho College	Coeur d'Alene	C,T	St-L	M/W	4,133		31		Y	Y	S	Y	Y	Y	Y		18	68
Illinois																		
Black Hawk College	Moline	C,T	St-L	M/W	6,248	54	33		Y		Y	Y	Y	Y	Y	N	6	76
Career Colleges of Chicago	Chicago	T	Prop	PW	144	76	71		Y	Y	Y	Y		Y	Y	N		4
Carl Sandburg College	Galesburg	C,T	St-L	M/W	4,000			63	Y		Y		Y	Y	Y	N	3	21
City Colls of Chicago, Harold Washington Coll	Chicago																	
City Colls of Chicago, Harry S Truman Coll	Chicago	C,T	St-L	M/W	5,873		70		Y	Y		Y	Y	Y	Y	N	6	23
City Colls of Chicago, Kennedy-King Coll	Chicago	C,T	St-L	M/W	6,575													
City Colls of Chicago, Malcolm X Coll	Chicago	C,T	St-L	M/W	8,791	43	54	38	Y	Y	Y	Y	Y	Y	Y	N	3	26
City Colls of Chicago, Olive-Harvey Coll	Chicago	C,T	St-L	M/W	3,165													
City Colls of Chicago, Richard J Daley Coll	Chicago	C,T	St-L	M/W	5,149	69	47		Y	Y	Y	Y	Y	Y	Y	N		38
City Colls of Chicago, Wilbur Wright Coll	Chicago	C,T	St-L	M/W	6,253	71	43	28	Y	Y	Y	Y	Y	Y	Y		8	24
College of DuPage	Glen Ellyn	C,T	St-L	M/W	29,423	68	49	73	Y			Y	Y	Y	Y	N	14	69
College of Lake County	Grayslake	C,T	Dist	M/W	14,886	76	46		Y		S	Y	Y	Y	Y	N	9	36
The College of Office Technology	Chicago																	
The Cooking and Hospitality Institute of Chicago†	Chicago	C,T	Prop	M/W	950		65	10	Y	Y	R	Y	Y	Y	Y	N		1
Danville Area Community College	Danville	C,T	St-L	M/W	3,000		41		Y	Y	Y	Y	Y	Y	Y	N	7	52
Elgin Community College	Elgin	C,T	St-L	M/W	10,174													
Gem City College	Quincy	T	Prop	M/W	150		40		Y	Y		Y		Y	Y	N		11
Heartland Community College	Normal	C,T	St-L	M/W	4,558		43	94	Y		R	Y	Y	Y	Y	N		38
Highland Community College	Freeport	C,T	St-L	M/W	2,541	61	58	80	Y	Y	S	Y	Y	Y	Y	N	6	44
Illinois Central College	East Peoria																	
Illinois Eastern Comm Colls, Frontier Comm Coll	Fairfield	C,T	St-L	M/W	1,913	90	53		Y	Y	Y	Y	Y	Y	Y	N		8
Illinois Eastern Comm Colls, Lincoln Trail Coll	Robinson	C,T	St-L	M/W	1,100	49	42		Y	Y	Y	Y	Y	Y	Y	N	4	16
Illinois Eastern Comm Colls, Olney Central Coll	Olney	C,T	St-L	M/W	1,617	52	43		Y	Y	Y	Y	Y	Y	Y	N	4	13
Illinois Eastern Comm Colls, Wabash Valley Coll	Mount Carmel	C,T	St-L	M/W	2,643	77	68		Y	Y	Y	Y	Y	Y	Y	N	6	15
Illinois Valley Community College	Oglesby	C,T	Dist	M/W	4,582													
ITT Technical Institute	Burr Ridge	T	Prop	M/W	267						Y					N		4
ITT Technical Institute	Matteson	T	Prop	M/W	331				N	Y	Y	Y	Y	Y	Y	N		5
ITT Technical Institute	Mount Prospect	T,B	Prop	M/W	447				N	Y	Y	Y	Y	Y	Y	N		5
John A. Logan College	Carterville	C	St-L	M/W	5,130		54		Y	Y	Y	Y	Y	Y	Y	N	5	49
John Wood Community College	Quincy	C,T	Dist	M/W	2,111	53	41		Y	Y	Y	Y	Y	Y	Y	N	5	20

This index includes the names and locations of accredited two-year colleges in the United States and U.S. territories and shows institutions' responses to our 2001 Survey of Undergraduate Institutions. If an institution submitted incomplete or no data, one or more columns opposite the institution's name is blank. An asterisk after the school name denotes a *Special Announcement* following the college's profile.

Y—Yes; N—No; R—Recommended; S—For Some

Institution	Location	Degrees Awarded: Transfer Associate (C), Terminal Associate (T), Bachelor's (B), Master's (M), Doctoral (D), First Professional (F)	Institutional Control: Independent, Independent-Religious, Proprietary, Federal, State, Province, Commonwealth, Territory, County, District, City, State and Local, State-Related	Student Body: Men, Primarily Men, Women, Primarily Women, Coed	Undergraduate Enrollment Fall 2001	Percent Attending Part-Time	Percent 25 Years of Age or Older	Percent of Grads Going on to 4-Year Colleges	Open Admissions	High School Equivalency Certificate Accepted	High School Transcript Required	Need-based aid available	Part-Time Jobs Available	Career Counseling Available	Job Placement Services Available	College Housing Available	Number of Sports Offered	Number of Majors Offered
Joliet Junior College	Joliet	C,T	St-L	M/W	12,089	68	44	77	Y		Y	Y	Y	Y	Y	N	6	58
Kankakee Community College	Kankakee	C,T	St-L	M/W	3,000				Y	Y	Y	Y	Y	Y	Y	N	6	28
Kaskaskia College	Centralia	C	St-L	M/W	3,097	53	45		Y	Y	Y	Y	Y	Y	Y	N	4	23
Kishwaukee College	Malta	C,T	St-L	M/W	4,337		31	82	Y		Y	Y	Y	Y		N	7	28
Lake Land College	Mattoon	C,T	St-L	M/W	6,102		42		Y	Y	R	Y	Y	Y	Y	N	7	38
Lewis and Clark Community College	Godfrey	C,T	Dist	M/W	6,985		30		Y		R	Y	Y	Y	Y	N	7	30
Lexington College	Chicago	C,T	Ind	W	35		7	0	Y	Y	Y	Y		Y	Y	Y		3
Lincoln College†	Lincoln	C	Ind	M/W	650		3	89	N	Y	Y	Y	Y	Y	Y	Y	17	72
Lincoln College†	Normal	C,T,B	Ind	M/W	400		8	89	N	Y	Y	Y	Y	Y	Y	Y	13	31
Lincoln Land Community College	Springfield	C,T	Dist	M/W	6,873	65	38		Y		R	Y	Y	Y	Y	N	6	70
MacCormac College	Chicago	C,T	Ind	M/W	511													
McHenry County College	Crystal Lake	C,T	St-L	M/W	5,747	72	43		Y		Y	Y	Y	Y	Y	N	6	23
Midstate College	Peoria																	
Moraine Valley Community College	Palos Hills	C,T	St-L	M/W	14,033	62	41	83	Y	Y	Y	Y	Y		Y	N	8	31
Morrison Institute of Technology†	Morrison	C,T	Ind	PM	146	2	8		Y	Y	Y	Y	Y	Y	Y	Y	5	3
Morton College	Cicero	C,T	St-L	M/W	4,698		53		Y	Y	Y	Y	Y	Y		N	7	20
Northwestern Business College†	Chicago	C,T	Prop	M/W	1,600		21		N	Y	Y		Y	Y	Y	N		18
Oakton Community College	Des Plaines	C,T	Dist	M/W	10,000		46	60	Y	Y	Y	Y	Y	Y		N	14	37
Parkland College	Champaign	C,T	Dist	M/W	8,482	53	31		Y	Y	R	Y	Y	Y	Y	N	8	57
Prairie State College	Chicago Heights	C,T	St-L	M/W	5,188	72	50		Y		Y	Y	Y	Y	Y	N	9	24
Ravenswood Hospital Medical Center–Henry J. Kutsch College of Nursing	Chicago	T	Ind	M/W	31													
Rend Lake College	Ina	C,T	St	M/W	3,637		70		Y	Y	Y	Y	Y	Y	Y	N	8	30
Richland Community College	Decatur	C,T	Dist	M/W	3,261	68	40	37	Y	Y	Y	Y	Y	Y	Y	N		27
Rockford Business College	Rockford	T	Ind	PW	357		45		Y	Y	Y	Y	Y	Y	Y			9
Rock Valley College	Rockford	C,T	Dist	M/W														
Sanford-Brown College	Granite City																	
Sauk Valley Community College	Dixon	C,T	Dist	M/W			50		Y		R	Y	Y	Y	Y	N	5	44
Shawnee Community College	Ullin																	
Southeastern Illinois College	Harrisburg	C,T	St	M/W	3,272	56												
South Suburban College	South Holland	C,T	St-L	M/W	5,580		49	43	Y	Y	Y	Y	Y	Y	Y	N	7	40
Southwestern Illinois College	Belleville	C,T	Dist	M/W	13,923													
Spoon River College	Canton	C,T	St	M/W	1,861	53												
Springfield College in Illinois	Springfield	C	I-R	M/W	308	22												
Triton College	River Grove	C,T	St	M/W	10,672		45		Y	Y	Y	Y	Y	Y	Y	N	7	91
Waubonsee Community College	Sugar Grove	C,T	Dist	M/W	7,890	74	32	85	Y				Y	Y	Y	N	11	38
Westwood College of Technology-Chicago Du Page†	Woodridge	C	Prop	M/W														3
Westwood College of Technology–Chicago O'Hare†	Schiller Park	C	Prop	M/W	475													4
Westwood College of Technology–Chicago River Oaks†	Calumet City	C	Prop	M/W	416													4
William Rainey Harper College	Palatine	C,T	St-L	M/W														
Worsham College of Mortuary Science	Wheeling	T	Ind	M/W	150													1
Indiana																		
Ancilla College	Donaldson	C,T	I-R	M/W	504	40	8	59	Y	Y	Y	Y	Y	Y		N	7	15
College of Court Reporting	Hobart	C,T	Prop	M/W	100		60											1
Commonwealth Business College	Merrillville	T	Prop	M/W	370		40		N	Y	Y	Y	Y	Y	Y	N		6
Commonwealth Business College	Michigan City																	
Holy Cross College†	Notre Dame	C	I-R	M/W	558	5	2	85	N	Y	Y	Y	Y	Y		Y	4	1
Indiana Business College	Anderson	T	Prop	M/W	241				Y	Y	Y			Y	Y			6
Indiana Business College	Columbus	T	Prop	M/W	209				Y	Y	Y			Y	Y			11
Indiana Business College	Evansville	C,T	Prop	M/W	244				Y		Y			Y	Y			9
Indiana Business College	Fort Wayne	C,T	Prop	M/W	172				Y	Y	Y			Y	Y			6
Indiana Business College†	Indianapolis	T	Prop	M/W	818				Y	Y	Y	Y	Y	Y	Y	N		16
Indiana Business College	Lafayette	C,T	Prop	M/W	155				Y	Y	Y			Y	Y			7
Indiana Business College	Marion	T	Prop	M/W	168				Y	Y	Y			Y	Y			4
Indiana Business College	Muncie	T	Prop	M/W	282			0	Y	Y	Y	Y	Y	Y	Y	N		10
Indiana Business College	Terre Haute	C,T	Prop	M/W	282				Y	Y	Y			Y	Y			11
Indiana Business College-Medical	Indianapolis	T	Prop	M/W	354				Y	Y	Y			Y	Y			4
International Business College	Fort Wayne	T,B	Prop	PW	659				N	Y	Y			Y	Y	Y		14
International Business College	Indianapolis	T	Prop	M/W	214													
ITT Technical Institute	Fort Wayne	T,B	Prop	M/W	509				N	Y	Y	Y	Y	Y	Y	N		6
ITT Technical Institute	Indianapolis	T,B,M	Prop	M/W	798				N	Y	Y		Y	Y	Y	N		7
ITT Technical Institute	Newburgh	T,B	Prop	M/W	364				N	Y	Y	Y	Y	Y	Y	N		6
Ivy Tech State College–Bloomington	Bloomington	C,T	St	M/W	2,391	61	50				Y							13
Ivy Tech State College–Central Indiana	Indianapolis	C,T	St	M/W	7,357	73	58		Y		Y	Y	Y	Y	Y	N		30
Ivy Tech State College–Columbus	Columbus	C,T	St	M/W	1,600	74	56		Y		Y	Y	Y	Y	Y	N		18
Ivy Tech State College–Eastcentral	Muncie	C,T	St	M/W	4,052	60	51		Y		Y	Y	Y	Y	Y	N		24
Ivy Tech State College–Kokomo	Kokomo	C,T	St	M/W	2,003	71	57		Y		Y		Y	Y	Y	N		16
Ivy Tech State College–Lafayette	Lafayette	C,T	St	M/W	4,143	64	46		Y		Y	Y	Y	Y	Y	N		21
Ivy Tech State College–North Central	South Bend	C,T	St	M/W	3,784	77	64		Y		Y	Y	Y	Y	Y	N	3	26
Ivy Tech State College–Northeast	Fort Wayne	C,T	St	M/W	4,019	70	60		Y		Y	Y	Y	Y	Y	N		22
Ivy Tech State College–Northwest	Gary	C,T	St	M/W	5,146	71	58		Y		Y	Y	Y	Y	Y	N	2	23
Ivy Tech State College–Southcentral	Sellersburg	C,T	St	M/W	2,035	72	57		Y		Y	Y	Y	Y	Y	N		23
Ivy Tech State College–Southeast	Madison	C,T	St	M/W	1,495	68	57		Y		Y	Y	Y	Y	Y	N	1	11
Ivy Tech State College–Southwest	Evansville	C,T	St	M/W	4,290	73	54	1	Y		Y	Y	Y	Y	Y	N		25
Ivy Tech State College–Wabash Valley	Terre Haute	C,T	St	M/W	3,810	60	54		Y		Y	Y	Y	Y	Y	N	3	28
Ivy Tech State College–Whitewater	Richmond	C,T	St	M/W	1,469	82	59		Y		Y	Y	Y	Y	Y	N		15
Lincoln Technical Institute	Indianapolis	T	Prop	M/W	650													
Michiana College	Fort Wayne																	

This index includes the names and locations of accredited two-year colleges in the United States and U.S. territories and shows institutions' responses to our 2001 Survey of Undergraduate Institutions. If an institution submitted incomplete or no data, one or more columns opposite the institution's name is blank. An asterisk after the school name denotes a *Special Announcement* following the college's profile.

Y—Yes; N—No; R—Recommended; S—For Some

		Degrees Awarded: Transfer Associate (C), Terminal Associate (T), Bachelor's (B), Master's (M), Doctoral (D), First Professional (F)	Institutional Control: Independent, Independent-Religious, Proprietary, Federal, State, Province, Commonwealth, Territory, County, District, City, State and Local, State-Related	Student Body: Men, Primarily Men, Women, Primarily Women, Coed	Undergraduate Enrollment Fall 2001	Percent Attending Part-Time	Percent 25 Years of Age or Older	Percent of Grads Going on to 4-Year Colleges	Open Admissions	High School Equivalency Certificate Accepted	High School Transcript Required	Need-based aid available	Part-Time Jobs Available	Career Counseling Available	Job Placement Services Available	College Housing Available	Number of Sports Offered	Number of Majors Offered
Michiana College	South Bend	C,T	Prop	PW	374													
Mid-America College of Funeral Service	Jeffersonville	T	Ind	PM	94		13		Y	Y	Y	Y		Y	Y	N		1
Professional Careers Institute	Indianapolis	T	Ind	PW	469					Y	Y	Y		Y	Y			2
Sawyer College	Hammond																	
Vincennes University	Vincennes	C,T	St	M/W	4,883		22	43	Y	Y	Y	Y	Y	Y	Y	Y	17	162
Vincennes University Jasper Campus	Jasper	C,T	St	M/W	794		50		Y	Y	Y	Y	Y	Y		N		25
Iowa																		
AIB College of Business	Des Moines	T	Ind	M/W	887		24		N	Y	Y	Y	Y	Y	Y	Y	8	18
Clinton Community College	Clinton	C,T	St-L	M/W	1,217		38	59	Y		Y	Y	Y	Y	Y	N	11	14
Des Moines Area Community College	Ankeny	C,T	St-L	M/W	11,886	57	46	72	Y	Y	S	Y	Y	Y	Y	N	6	52
Ellsworth Community College	Iowa Falls	C,T	St-L	M/W	930		18	60	Y	Y	Y	Y	Y	Y	Y	Y	14	47
Hamilton College	Cedar Rapids	C,T,B	Prop	M/W	467		47		N		Y	Y	Y	Y	Y	N		12
Hawkeye Community College	Waterloo	C,T	St-L	M/W	4,456		27	62	Y	Y	Y	Y	Y	Y	Y	N	5	60
Indian Hills Community College	Ottumwa	C,T	St-L	M/W	3,926		40	45	Y	Y	S	Y	Y	Y		Y	10	25
Iowa Central Community College	Fort Dodge	C,T	St-L	M/W	4,295													
Iowa Lakes Community College	Estherville	C,T	St-L	M/W	2,711	49	18	60	Y	Y	Y	Y	Y	Y	Y	Y	13	106
Iowa Western Community College	Council Bluffs	C,T	Dist	M/W	4,299		34	67	Y	Y	Y	Y	Y	Y	Y	Y	7	57
Kaplan College	Davenport	C,T,B	Prop	M/W	745	44	60		N	Y	Y	Y	Y	Y	Y	N		8
Kirkwood Community College	Cedar Rapids	C,T	St-L	M/W	12,555	46	29		Y	Y	Y	Y	Y	Y	Y	N	10	108
Marshalltown Community College	Marshalltown	C,T	Dist	M/W	1,188		34	80	Y	Y	Y	Y	Y	Y	Y	Y	7	22
Muscatine Community College	Muscatine	C,T	St	M/W	1,129		44	45	Y		Y	Y	Y	Y	Y	N	7	15
Northeast Iowa Community College	Calmar	C,T	St-L	M/W	3,615	46	36		Y	Y	R	Y	Y	Y	Y	N	9	13
North Iowa Area Community College	Mason City	C,T	St-L	M/W	2,722	34	30	70	Y	Y	R,S	Y	Y	Y	Y	Y	11	30
Northwest Iowa Community College	Sheldon	C,T	St	M/W	897	43												
St. Luke's College of Nursing and Health Sciences	Sioux City	T	Ind	PW	107	24	21		N	Y	Y					Y		1
Scott Community College	Bettendorf	C,T	St-L	M/W	3,985		44	55	Y		Y	Y	Y	Y	Y	N	4	30
Southeastern Community College, North Campus	West Burlington																	
Southeastern Community College, South Campus	Keokuk	C,T	St-L	M/W	600				Y		R	Y	Y	Y		N	2	11
Southwestern Community College	Creston	C,T	St	M/W	1,198	45	30		Y	Y	Y	Y	Y	Y	Y	Y	6	16
Western Iowa Tech Community College	Sioux City	C,T	St	M/W	4,920	63	30		Y	Y	Y	Y	Y	Y	Y	Y	8	26
Kansas																		
Allen County Community College	Iola	C,T	St-L	M/W	2,150	63	35	60	Y	Y	Y	Y	Y	Y	Y	Y	11	69
Barton County Community College	Great Bend	C,T	St-L	M/W	4,178	74	45		Y	Y	R	Y	Y	Y	Y	Y	13	71
The Brown Mackie College	Salina	C,T	Prop	M/W	325		40	27	Y	Y	Y	Y	Y	Y	Y	N	3	7
The Brown Mackie College–Olathe Campus	Olathe	T	Prop	M/W	234		60		Y	Y	Y	Y	Y	Y	Y	N		16
Butler County Community College	El Dorado																	
Cloud County Community College	Concordia																	
Coffeyville Community College	Coffeyville	C,T	St-L	M/W	1,499		45	70	Y		Y	Y	Y	Y		Y	13	69
Colby Community College*	Colby	C,T	St-L	M/W	2,166	64	25	60	Y	Y	Y	Y	Y	Y	Y	Y	8	58
Cowley County Comm Coll and Voc-Tech School	Arkansas City	C,T	St-L	M/W	4,475		19		Y	Y	Y	Y	Y	Y		Y	8	41
Dodge City Community College	Dodge City	C,T	St-L	M/W	1,956		67	92	Y		Y	Y	Y	Y	Y	Y	11	71
Donnelly College	Kansas City	C,T	I-R	M/W	626		85	90	Y	Y	R	Y	Y	Y	Y	N		22
Education America, Topeka Technical College, Topeka Campus	Topeka																	
Fort Scott Community College	Fort Scott	C,T	St-L	M/W	1,900				Y	Y		Y	Y	Y	Y	Y	10	36
Garden City Community College	Garden City	C,T	Cou	M/W	2,047	56	37	60	Y	Y	Y	Y	Y	Y	Y	Y	13	64
Hesston College	Hesston	C,T	I-R	M/W	445	13	13		Y	Y	Y	Y	Y	Y	Y	Y	6	8
Highland Community College	Highland	C,T	St-L	M/W	2,673		31		Y	Y	Y	Y	Y	Y	Y	Y	7	69
Hutchinson Comm Coll and Area Vocational School	Hutchinson	C,T	St-L	M/W	3,733	52	37	70	Y	Y	R	Y	Y	Y	Y	Y	13	42
Independence Community College	Independence	C,T	St	M/W	1,022	52	43		Y	Y	Y	Y	Y	Y	Y	Y	8	40
Johnson County Community College	Overland Park	C,T	St-L	M/W	17,776		43		Y	Y	S	Y	Y	Y	Y	N	8	36
Kansas City Kansas Community College	Kansas City	C,T	St-L	M/W	5,240	70	46		Y	Y	Y	Y	Y	Y		N	8	44
Labette Community College	Parsons	C,T	St-L	M/W	1,354		40	30	Y	Y	R	Y	Y	Y		Y	5	33
Neosho County Community College	Chanute	C,T	St-L	M/W	1,519		58	60	Y	Y	Y	Y	Y	Y		Y	6	24
Pratt Comm Coll and Area Vocational School	Pratt	C,T	St-L	M/W	1,374	56			Y	Y	Y	Y	Y			Y	12	65
Seward County Community College	Liberal																	
Kentucky																		
Ashland Community College	Ashland	C,T	St	M/W	2,626		41	40	Y	Y	Y	Y	Y	Y		N	2	12
Beckfield College	Florence	T	Prop	M/W	275		60					Y						3
Daymar College	Owensboro	C	Prop	M/W	357	19	48		N	Y	Y	Y	Y	Y	Y	N		27
Draughons Junior College	Bowling Green	C	Prop	PW	316	45	48	0.06	Y	Y	Y	Y	Y	Y	Y	N		8
Elizabethtown Community College	Elizabethtown	C,T	St	PW	3,522		50		Y	Y	Y	Y	Y	Y	Y	N	7	12
Hazard Community College	Hazard	C	St	M/W	3,000		35		Y	Y	Y		Y	Y	Y	Y	2	13
Henderson Community College	Henderson	C,T	St	M/W	1,407		57		Y	Y	Y	Y	Y	Y	Y	N	5	19
Hopkinsville Community College	Hopkinsville	C,T	St	M/W	2,849		56		Y	Y	S	Y	Y	Y	Y	N	5	15
ITT Technical Institute	Louisville	T	Prop	PM	358				N	Y	Y		Y	Y	Y	N		5
Jefferson Community College	Louisville	C,T	St	M/W	9,227		42		Y			Y	Y	Y	Y	N		48
Louisville Technical Institute	Louisville	T	Prop	M/W	688	7	32		N	Y	Y	Y		Y	Y	Y	3	33
Madisonville Community College	Madisonville	C,T	St	M/W			42		Y	Y	Y	Y	Y	Y	Y	N	2	18
Maysville Community College	Maysville	C	St	M/W	1,393		35	38	Y	Y	Y	Y	Y	Y	Y	N		9
National College of Business & Technology	Danville	T	Prop	M/W					Y	Y	Y	Y	Y	Y	Y	N		5
National College of Business & Technology	Florence	T	Prop	M/W					Y	Y	S	Y	Y	Y	Y	N		5
National College of Business & Technology	Lexington	T	Prop	M/W					Y	Y	Y	Y	Y	Y	Y	N		5
National College of Business & Technology	Louisville	T	Prop	M/W					Y	Y	S	Y	Y	Y	Y	N		6

This index includes the names and locations of accredited two-year colleges in the United States and U.S. territories and shows institutions' responses to our 2001 Survey of Undergraduate Institutions. If an institution submitted incomplete or no data, one or more columns opposite the institution's name is blank. An asterisk after the school name denotes a *Special Announcement* following the college's profile.

Y—Yes; N—No; R—Recommended; S—For Some

Institution	City	Degrees Awarded: Transfer Associate (C), Terminal Associate (T), Bachelor's (B), Master's (M), Doctoral (D), First Professional (F)	Institutional Control: Independent (I), Independent-Religious (I-R), Proprietary (Prop), Federal, State, Province, Commonwealth, Territory, County, District, City, State and Local, State-Related	Student Body: Men, Primarily Men, Women, Primarily Women, Coed	Undergraduate Enrollment Fall 2001	Percent Attending Part-Time	Percent 25 Years of Age or Older	Percent of Grads Going on to 4-Year Colleges	Open Admissions	High School Equivalency Certificate Accepted	High School Transcript Required	Need-based aid available	Part-Time Jobs Available	Career Counseling Available	Job Placement Services Available	College Housing Available	Number of Sports Offered	Number of Majors Offered
National College of Business & Technology	Pikeville	T	Prop	M/W					Y	Y	S	Y	Y	Y	Y	N		5
National College of Business & Technology	Richmond	T	Prop	M/W					Y	Y	S	Y	Y	Y	Y	N		5
Owensboro Community College	Owensboro	C,T	St	M/W	3,362	63	32	26	Y	Y	Y	Y	Y	Y	Y	N	2	17
Paducah Community College	Paducah	C,T	St	M/W	3,322		41		Y	Y	S	Y	Y	Y	Y	N	4	10
Paducah Technical College	Paducah	T	Prop	PM	200				Y	Y	Y	Y		Y	Y	N		4
Prestonsburg Community College	Prestonsburg																	
RETS Electronic Institute	Louisville																	
RETS Medical and Business Istitute	Hopkinsville																	
St. Catharine College	St. Catharine	C,T	I-R	M/W	672		39		N	Y	S	Y	Y	Y		Y	7	49
Somerset Community College	Somerset	C,T	St	M/W	2,799				Y	Y	Y	Y	Y	Y	Y	N	3	7
Southeast Community College	Cumberland	C,T	St	M/W	2,491				Y	Y	Y	Y	Y	Y	Y		5	14
Southern Ohio College, Northern Kentucky Campus	Fort Mitchell	C,T	Prop	M/W	350		42		Y	Y	Y	Y	Y	Y	Y	N		5
Southwestern College of Business	Crestview Hills	T	Prop	PW	130													
Spencerian College	Louisville	C,T	Prop	PW	584		50				Y	Y				Y		3
Spencerian College–Lexington	Lexington	T	Prop	M/W	330		33			Y	Y	Y	Y	Y	Y	Y		4
U of Kentucky, Lexington Community College	Lexington	C,T	St	M/W	7,793	37	26		Y	Y	Y	Y	Y	Y	Y	N	11	23
Louisiana																		
Baton Rouge School of Computers	Baton Rouge																	
Bossier Parish Community College	Bossier City	C,T	St	M/W	3,964				Y	Y	Y	Y	Y	Y	Y	N	11	12
Camelot Career College	Baton Rouge																	
Cameron College	New Orleans																	
Culinary Arts Institute of Louisiana	Baton Rouge	T	Prop	M/W	60		25		Y	Y	Y	Y			Y	N		2
Delgado Community College	New Orleans	C,T	St	M/W	13,404	54	45	35	Y	Y	R,S	Y	Y	Y	Y	N	8	44
Delta College of Arts and Technology	Baton Rouge	T	Priv	PW	250													3
Delta School of Business & Technology	Lake Charles																	
Education America, Remington College, Baton Rouge Campus	Baton Rouge																	
Education America, Remington College, Lafayette Campus	Lafayette	T	Prop	M/W	472		40		N	Y	Y	Y	Y		Y	N		11
Education America, Southeast College of Technology, New Orleans Campus	Metairie	T	Prop	M/W	650				N	Y						N		8
Elaine P. Nunez Community College	Chalmette	C,T	St	M/W	1,924		54	31	Y		S	Y	Y	Y	Y	N	4	21
Herzing College	Kenner	C,T,B	Prop	M/W	220	30												
ITT Technical Institute	St. Rose	T	Prop	M/W	356						Y					N		5
Louisiana State University at Alexandria	Alexandria	C,T	St	M/W	2,715	55	41		Y	Y	Y	Y	Y	Y	Y	N	3	8
Louisiana State University at Eunice	Eunice	C,T	St	M/W	2,748		40	40	Y	Y	Y	Y	Y	Y			6	11
Louisiana Technical College–Acadian Campus	Crowley																	
Louisiana Technical College–Alexandria Campus	Alexandria																	
Louisiana Technical College–Ascension Campus	Sorrento																	
Louisiana Technical College–Avoyelles Campus	Cottonport																	
Louisiana Technical College–Bastrop Campus	Bastrop		St		241	31												
Louisiana Technical College–Baton Rouge Campus	Baton Rouge																	
Louisiana Technical College–Charles B. Coreil Campus	Ville Platte																	
Louisiana Technical College–Delta Ouachita Campus	West Monroe	C,T	St	PW	835													10
Louisiana Technical College–Evangeline Campus	St. Martinville																	
Louisiana Technical College–Florida Parishes Campus	Greensburg	T	St	M/W	233	58	35	2	Y		Y	Y		Y	Y	N		3
Louisiana Technical College–Folkes Campus	Jackson	T	St	M/W	221	29	87		Y	Y	S	Y		Y	Y	N		
Louisiana Technical College–Gulf Area Campus	Abbeville																	
Louisiana Technical College–Hammond Campus	Hammond	C,T	St	M/W	168													
Louisiana Technical College–Huey P. Long Campus	Winnfield																	
Louisiana Technical College–Jefferson Campus	Metairie																	
Louisiana Technical College–Lafayette Campus	Lafayette																	
Louisiana Technical College–LaFourche Campus	Thibodaux																	
Louisiana Technical College–Lamar Salter Campus	Leesville	T	St	M/W	535													
Louisiana Technical College–L.E. Fletcher Campus	Hourma																	
Louisiana Technical College–Mansfield Campus	Mansfield	C,T	St	M/W	200							Y						4
Louisiana Technical College–Morgan Smith Campus	Jennings																	
Louisiana Technical College–Natchitoches Campus	Natchitoches	C	St	M/W	528	66												3
Louisiana Technical College–North Central Campus	Farmerville	T	St	M/W														
Louisiana Technical College–Northeast Louisiana Campus	Winnsboro																	
Louisiana Technical College–Northwest Louisiana Campus	Minden																	
Louisiana Technical College–Oakdale Campus	Oakdale																	
Louisiana Technical College–River Parishes Campus	Reserve																	
Louisiana Technical College–Sabine Valley Campus	Many	T	St	M/W	494													
Louisiana Technical College–Shelby M. Jackson Campus	Ferriday																	
Louisiana Technical College–Shreveport-Bossier Campus	Shreveport																	
Louisiana Technical College–Sidney N. Collier Campus	New Orleans																	
Louisiana Technical College–Slidell Campus	Slidell																	
Louisiana Technical College–Sowela Campus	Lake Charles																	
Louisiana Technical College–Sullivan Campus	Bogalusa																	
Louisiana Technical College–Tallulah Campus	Tallulah																	
Louisiana Technical College–Teche Area Campus	New Iberia																	
Louisiana Technical College–T.H. Harris Campus	Opelousas																	
Louisiana Technical College–West Jefferson Campus	Harvey																	
Louisiana Technical College–Young Memorial Campus	Morgan City	T	St	M/W	850													
MedVance Institute	Baton Rouge	T	Prop	M/W	225		50		N	Y	Y	Y		Y	Y	N		1
Our Lady of the Lake College	Baton Rouge	C,T,B	I-R	M/W	1,218	71	52		Y	Y	Y	Y	Y	Y		N		8
Southern University at Shreveport	Shreveport																	

This index includes the names and locations of accredited two-year colleges in the United States and U.S. territories and shows institutions' responses to our 2001 Survey of Undergraduate Institutions. If an institution submitted incomplete or no data, one or more columns opposite the institution's name is blank. An asterisk after the school name denotes a *Special Announcement* following the college's profile.

Y—Yes; N—No; R—Recommended; S—For Some

Institution	Location	Degrees Awarded: Transfer Associate (C), Terminal Associate (T), Bachelor's (B), Master's (M), Doctoral (D), First Professional (F)	Institutional Control: Independent, Independent-Religious, Proprietary, Federal, State, Province, Commonwealth, Territory, County, District, City, State and Local, State-Related	Student Body: Men, Primarily Men, Women, Primarily Women, Coed	Undergraduate Enrollment Fall 2001	Percent Attending Part-Time	Percent 25 Years of Age or Older	Percent of Grads Going on to 4-Year Colleges	Open Admissions	High School Equivalency Certificate Accepted	High School Transcript Required	Need-based aid available	Part-Time Jobs Available	Career Counseling Available	Job Placement Services Available	College Housing Available	Number of Sports Offered	Number of Majors Offered
Maine																		
Andover College*	Portland	T	Prop	M/W	520		63	0	Y	Y	Y	Y	Y	Y	Y	Y		16
Beal College	Bangor	T	Prop	M/W	338	30												
Central Maine Medical Center School of Nursing	Lewiston	T	Ind	PW	98	74	74		N	Y	Y	Y				Y		1
Central Maine Technical College	Auburn	C,T	St	M/W	1,435	56	46		N	Y	Y	Y	Y	Y	Y	Y	13	23
Eastern Maine Technical College	Bangor	C,T	St	M/W	1,604	58	26		N	Y	Y	Y	Y	Y	Y	Y	10	20
Kennebec Valley Technical College	Fairfield	C,T	St	M/W	1,255	70	60		Y	Y	Y	Y	Y	Y	Y	N	2	37
Mid-State College*	Auburn	C	Prop	M/W	275		72		Y	Y		Y	Y	Y	Y	Y		11
Northern Maine Technical College	Presque Isle	T	St-R	M/W	784	35	45		Y	Y	Y	Y	Y	Y	Y	Y	12	22
Southern Maine Technical College	South Portland	C,T	St	M/W	2,471	56	48	10	N	Y	Y		Y	Y	Y	Y	7	46
Washington County Technical College	Calais																	
York County Technical College	Wells	C,T	St	M/W	704													
Maryland																		
Allegany College of Maryland	Cumberland	C,T	St-L	M/W	2,879	44	31	80	Y	Y	Y	Y	Y	Y	Y	N	9	41
Anne Arundel Community College	Arnold	C,T	St-L	M/W	52,088		43		Y			Y	Y	Y	Y	N	9	69
Baltimore City Community College	Baltimore	C,T	St	M/W	6,268		57		Y	Y	Y	Y	Y	Y	Y	N	3	35
Baltimore International College†	Baltimore	C,T,B	Ind	M/W	456	5	32		N	Y	Y	Y	Y	Y	Y	Y		4
Carroll Community College	Westminster	C,T	St-L	M/W	2,634	59	33		Y	Y	Y	Y	Y	Y		N		15
Cecil Community College	North East	C,T	Cou	M/W	1,448	67	37		Y		R	Y	Y	Y	Y	N	8	33
Chesapeake College	Wye Mills	C,T	St-L	M/W	2,186	72	47	45	Y	Y	Y	Y	Y	Y	Y	N	6	29
College of Southern Maryland	La Plata	C,T	St-L	M/W	6,803		60	38	Y		R	Y	Y	Y	Y	N	7	14
The Community College of Baltimore County–Catonsville Campus	Baltimore	C,T	Cou	M/W	3,372	44	36	48	Y	Y	Y	Y	Y	Y	Y	N	7	95
The Community College of Baltimore County–Dundalk Campus	Baltimore	C,T	Cou	M/W	2,622	75												
The Community College of Baltimore County–Essex Campus	Baltimore	C,T	Cou	M/W	1,701	43												
Frederick Community College	Frederick	C,T	St-L	M/W	4,558		60	39	Y			Y	Y	Y	Y	N	6	41
Garrett Community College	McHenry	C,T	St-L	M/W	700													
Hagerstown Business College	Hagerstown	T	Prop	PW	823		55		Y	Y	Y	Y	Y	Y	Y	Y		11
Hagerstown Community College	Hagerstown	C,T	Cou	M/W	2,679	63	39		Y		S	Y	Y	Y	Y	N	10	17
Harford Community College	Bel Air	C,T	St-L	M/W	5,256		43	23	Y			Y	Y	Y	Y	N	7	51
Howard Community College	Columbia	C,T	St-L	M/W	5,934		43	76	Y		S	Y	Y	Y	Y	N	8	55
Maryland College of Art and Design	Silver Spring	C,T	Ind	M/W	104	34	10	80	N	Y	Y	Y		Y		N		5
Montgomery College	Rockville	C,T	St-L	M/W	21,347	64	45									N	12	31
Prince George's Community College	Largo	C,T	Cou	M/W	12,287	74	52		Y		S	Y	Y	Y	Y	N	8	30
Wor-Wic Community College	Salisbury	C,T	St-L	M/W	2,721	73	47		Y		R		Y	Y	Y	N		18
Massachusetts																		
Baptist Bible College East	Boston	C,T,B	I-R	M/W	110		10		N	Y	Y	Y				Y		1
Bay State College*†	Boston	C,T	Ind	M/W	419	20	12		N	Y	Y	Y	Y	Y	Y	Y		17
Benjamin Franklin Institute of Technology†	Boston	C,T,B	Ind	PM	314	4	10	38	Y	Y	Y		Y	Y	Y	N	3	9
Berkshire Community College	Pittsfield	C,T	St	M/W	2,401	61	51	41	Y	Y	Y	Y	Y	Y	Y	N	5	50
Bristol Community College	Fall River	C,T	St	M/W	6,132		47	43	Y	Y	Y	Y	Y	Y	Y	N		41
Bunker Hill Community College	Boston	C,T	St	M/W	6,914	64	48	35	Y	Y	Y	Y	Y	Y	Y	N	5	31
Cape Cod Community College	West Barnstable	C,T	St	M/W	4,176	78	50	67	Y	Y	Y	Y	Y	Y	Y	N	12	41
Dean College*†	Franklin	C,T	Ind	M/W	1,402		3	90	N	Y	Y	Y	Y	Y	Y	Y	11	16
Fisher College†	Boston	C,T,B	Ind	M/W	526	2		50	N	Y	Y	Y	Y	Y	Y	Y	5	13
Greenfield Community College	Greenfield	C,T	St	M/W	2,355		46	50	Y	Y	S	Y	Y	Y	Y	N		29
Holyoke Community College	Holyoke	C,T	St	M/W	5,998		35	45	Y	Y	Y	Y	Y	Y	Y	N	6	40
ITT Technical Institute	Norwood	T	Prop	M/W	260				N	Y	Y		Y	Y	Y	N		5
ITT Technical Institute	Woburn	T	Prop	M/W	230						Y					N		5
Katharine Gibbs School	Boston	C,T	Prop	M/W														
Labouré College*	Boston	C,T	I-R	M/W	253	78	72	25	N	Y	Y	Y	Y	Y	Y	N		5
Marian Court College	Swampscott	C	I-R	PW	281		45	25	N	Y	Y	Y	Y	Y	Y	N		12
Massachusetts Bay Community College	Wellesley Hills	C,T	St	M/W	4,950	49	44		Y	Y		Y	Y	Y	Y	N	7	36
Massasoit Community College	Brockton	C,T	St	M/W	6,906		45	32	Y	Y		Y	Y	Y	Y	N	4	36
Middlesex Community College	Bedford	C,T	St	M/W	7,568	58	39		Y	Y	S	Y	Y	Y	Y	N	3	35
Mount Wachusett Community College*	Gardner	C,T	St	M/W	3,711	57	42	61	Y	Y	Y	Y	Y	Y	Y			28
Newbury College†	Brookline	C,T,B	Ind	M/W	1,689	61	34	31	N	Y	Y	Y	Y	Y	Y	Y	10	29
New England College of Finance	Boston																	
New England Institute of Art & Communications†	Brookline	C,T	Prop	M/W					N	Y								5
Northern Essex Community College*	Haverhill	C,T	St	M/W	1,450	46	51	40	Y	Y	Y	Y	Y	Y	Y	N	11	50
North Shore Community College	Danvers	C,T	St	M/W	6,100	62	48	72	Y	Y	S	Y	Y	Y	Y	N	3	42
Quincy College	Quincy	C,T	City	M/W	4,622		45		Y	Y	Y	Y	Y	Y	Y	N		41
Quinsigamond Community College	Worcester	C,T	St	M/W	6,137		45	40	Y	Y	Y	Y	Y	Y	Y	N	10	28
Roxbury Community College	Roxbury Crossing																	
Springfield Technical Community College	Springfield	C,T	St	M/W	6,257	58	35		Y	Y	Y	Y	Y	Y	Y	N	11	60
Urban College of Boston	Boston	T	Ind	PW	638	100	100	50				Y				N		3
Michigan																		
Alpena Community College	Alpena	C,T	St-L	M/W	1,932	52	55	42	Y		Y	Y	Y	Y	Y	Y	7	25
Bay de Noc Community College	Escanaba	C,T	Cou	M/W	2,200		36	60	Y	Y	Y	Y	Y	Y	Y	Y	5	27
Bay Mills Community College	Brimley																	
Davenport University	Midland	C,T,B	Ind	M/W	1,500													
Delta College	University Center	C,T	Dist	M/W	10,000				Y		R	Y	Y	Y	Y	N	10	102

This index includes the names and locations of accredited two-year colleges in the United States and U.S. territories and shows institutions' responses to our 2001 Survey of Undergraduate Institutions. If an institution submitted incomplete or no data, one or more columns opposite the institution's name is blank. An asterisk after the school name denotes a *Special Announcement* following the college's profile.

Y—Yes; N—No; R—Recommended; S—For Some

College	City	Degrees Awarded: Transfer Associate (C), Terminal Associate (T), Bachelor's (B), Master's (M), Doctoral (D), First Professional (F)	Institutional Control: Independent, Independent-Religious, Proprietary, Federal, State, Province, Commonwealth, Territory, County, District, City, State and Local, State-Related	Student Body: Men, Primarily Men, Women, Primarily Women, Coed	Undergraduate Enrollment Fall 2001	Percent Attending Part-Time	Percent 25 Years of Age or Older	Percent of Grads Going on to 4-Year Colleges	Open Admissions	High School Equivalency Certificate Accepted	High School Transcript Required	Need-based aid available	Part-Time Jobs Available	Career Counseling Available	Job Placement Services Available	College Housing Available	Number of Sports Offered	Number of Majors Offered
Glen Oaks Community College	Centreville	C,T	St-L	M/W	1,894	94	53		Y			Y	Y	Y		N	5	5
Gogebic Community College	Ironwood	C,T	St-L	M/W	1,165	56	46		Y	Y	Y	Y	Y	Y	Y	N	10	43
Grand Rapids Community College	Grand Rapids	C,T	Dist	M/W	13,483	62	30	78	Y	Y	Y	Y	Y	Y	Y	N	14	30
Henry Ford Community College	Dearborn	C,T	Dist	M/W	12,123		44		Y	Y	R	Y	Y	Y	Y	N	12	52
ITT Technical Institute	Grand Rapids	T	Prop		519				N	Y	Y			Y	Y	N		5
ITT Technical Institute	Troy	T	Prop	M/W	665				N	Y	Y	Y	Y	Y	Y	N		5
Jackson Community College	Jackson	C,T	Cou	M/W	6,457				Y	Y		Y	Y	Y	Y	N		36
Kalamazoo Valley Community College	Kalamazoo	C,T	St-L	M/W	12,500		50		Y			Y	Y	Y	Y	N	6	29
Kellogg Community College	Battle Creek	C,T	St-L	M/W	9,741		47	64	Y		S	Y	Y	Y	Y	N	5	73
Kirtland Community College	Roscommon																	
Lake Michigan College	Benton Harbor	C,T	Dist	M/W	3,478	68	56		Y	Y	Y	Y	Y	Y	Y	N	5	42
Lansing Community College	Lansing	C,T	St-L	M/W	17,358	70	53		Y		S	Y	Y	Y	Y	N	9	104
Lewis College of Business	Detroit	C,T	Ind	M/W	324				Y	Y	Y	Y	Y	Y	Y	N	1	11
Macomb Community College	Warren	C,T	Dist	M/W	21,818	72	40		Y			Y	Y	Y	Y	N	11	56
Mid Michigan Community College	Harrison	C,T	St-L	PW	2,350	79	70		Y	Y	R	Y	Y	Y	Y	N		55
Monroe County Community College	Monroe	C,T	Cou	M/W	3,800		45		Y	Y	Y		Y	Y	Y	N		43
Montcalm Community College	Sidney	C,T	St-L	M/W	1,520	76	45		Y	Y	R	Y	Y	Y	Y	N	1	23
Mott Community College	Flint	C,T	Dist	M/W	9,019	67	43		Y		Y	Y	Y	Y	Y	N	6	51
Muskegon Community College	Muskegon																	
North Central Michigan College	Petoskey	C,T	Cou	M/W	2,248		55	85	Y		Y	Y	Y	Y		Y	1	21
Northwestern Michigan College	Traverse City	C,T	St-L	M/W	4,251	61	37		Y	Y	S	Y	Y	Y	Y	Y	7	28
Oakland Community College	Bloomfield Hills	C,T	St-L	M/W	23,503	74	45		Y		R	Y	Y	Y	Y	N	8	57
St. Clair County Community College	Port Huron	C,T	St-L	M/W	4,066		38		Y	Y	Y	Y	Y	Y	Y		5	36
Schoolcraft College	Livonia	C,T	Dist	M/W	9,530	68	40		Y	Y	R,S	Y	Y	Y	Y	N	5	36
Southwestern Michigan College	Dowagiac	C,T	St-L	M/W	3,172	65	43		Y	Y	Y	Y	Y	Y	Y	N	17	27
Washtenaw Community College	Ann Arbor	C,T	St-L	M/W	11,089	78												
Wayne County Community College District	Detroit	C,T	St-L	M/W	10,000													
West Shore Community College	Scottville	C,T	Dist	M/W	1,338	66	43		Y		Y	Y	Y	Y	Y	N	8	14
Minnesota																		
Academy College	Minneapolis	C,T,B	Prop	M/W	400							Y	Y			N		10
Alexandria Technical College	Alexandria	C,T	St	M/W	2,066		24		Y	Y	Y	Y	Y	Y	Y	N	8	38
Anoka-Hennepin Technical College	Anoka	T	St	M/W	3,970		40		Y	Y	Y	Y	Y	Y	Y			26
Anoka-Ramsey Community College*	Coon Rapids	C,T	St	M/W	4,416		29		Y	Y	S	Y	Y	Y		N	11	16
Anoka-Ramsey Community College, Cambridge Campus	Cambridge	C,T	St	M/W	1,411				Y	Y	S			Y				7
Argosy University-Twin Cities†	Bloomington	T,B,M,D	Prop	PW	883		50		N	Y	Y	Y	Y	Y	Y	N		7
The Art Institutes International Minnesota	Minneapolis	T,B	Prop	M/W	948		44	3	N	Y	Y	Y	Y	Y	Y	Y		5
Bethany Lutheran College*	Mankato	C,B	I-R	M/W	420		2	87	N	Y	Y	Y	Y	Y		Y	10	8
Brown College	Mendota Heights	C,T	Prop	M/W	2,250				N	Y	Y	Y	Y	Y	Y	N		6
Central Lakes College	Brainerd	C,T	St	M/W	2,857		33		Y	Y		Y	Y	Y		N	8	10
Century Community and Technical College	White Bear Lake	C,T	St	M/W	7,396	55	32		Y		Y	Y	Y	Y		N	5	36
College of St. Catherine–Minneapolis	Minneapolis	C,T	I-R	PW	3,610	36	57		N	Y	Y	Y	Y	Y		Y		9
Dakota County Technical College	Rosemount	C,T	St	M/W	3,103	60	58		Y	Y	S			Y	Y	N	1	28
Duluth Business University	Duluth																	
Dunwoody College of Technology	Minneapolis	T	Ind	PM	1,164	4	28		N	Y	Y	Y	Y	Y	Y	N		15
Fergus Falls Community College	Fergus Falls	C,T	St	M/W	2,401	64	30	81	Y	Y	Y	Y	Y	Y	Y	Y	13	13
Fond du Lac Tribal and Community College	Cloquet																	
Globe College	Oakdale	T,B	Priv		774	56	48					Y		Y	Y			
Hennepin Technical College	Brooklyn Park	C,T	St	M/W	14,733				Y	Y	R	Y	Y			N		18
Herzing College, Minneapolis Drafting School Campus	Minneapolis	T	Prop	M/W	162		57		Y	Y	Y			Y	Y	N		3
Hibbing Community College	Hibbing	C,T	St	M/W	1,541		55	39	Y	Y	Y	Y	Y	Y	Y	Y	11	20
Inver Hills Community College	Inver Grove Heights	C,T	St	M/W	4,943		56		Y	Y	R,S	Y	Y	Y	Y	N	9	23
Itasca Community College	Grand Rapids	C,T	St	M/W	1,094		23	75	Y	Y	Y	Y	Y	Y		N	10	31
Lakeland Medical–Dental Academy	Minneapolis																	
Lake Superior College	Duluth																	
Mesabi Range Community and Technical College	Virginia	C,T	St	M/W	1,687		32	80	Y	Y		Y	Y	Y	Y	Y	13	17
Minneapolis Business College	Roseville	T	Prop	PW	322													
Minneapolis Community and Technical College	Minneapolis	C,T	St	M/W	6,984		42		Y		Y	Y	Y	Y	Y	N	3	19
Minnesota School of Business	Richfield	T,B	Prop	M/W	2,100		40		Y	Y	Y	Y		Y	Y	N		12
Minnesota State College–Southeast Technical	Winona	C,T	St	M/W	2,058		46		Y	Y	Y	Y	Y	Y	Y	N		28
Minnesota West Comm & Tech Coll-Pipestone Cmps	Pipestone	C,T	St	M/W	2,044	35	32		Y	Y	Y	Y	Y	Y	Y	N	7	5
Music Tech	Minneapolis																	
NEI College of Technology	Columbia Heights	C,T	Ind	PM	690	48	52	10	N	Y	Y	Y	Y	Y	Y	N	3	19
Normandale Community College	Bloomington																	
North Hennepin Community College	Minneapolis	C,T	St	M/W	4,452		43	56	Y		S	Y	Y	Y	Y	N	9	26
Northland Community and Technical College	Thief River Falls	C,T	St	M/W	2,152		19	76	Y	Y	Y	Y	Y	Y	Y	N	9	46
Northwest Technical College	Perham																	
Northwest Technical Institute	Eden Prairie	C,T	Prop	M/W	125		10		Y	Y	Y	Y		Y	Y	N		2
Pine Technical College	Pine City	C,T	St	M/W	1,074		45		Y	Y	Y	Y	Y	Y	Y	N		6
Rainy River Community College	International Falls	C	St	M/W	480	35	54	62	Y	Y	Y	Y	Y	Y	Y	Y	11	6
Rasmussen College Eagan	Eagan	T	Prop	PW	340	20	35		N	Y	Y	Y		Y	Y	N		9
Rasmussen College Mankato	Mankato	T	Prop	PW	313	35	40		N	Y	Y	Y	Y	Y	Y	N		34
Rasmussen College Minnetonka	Minnetonka	T	Prop	M/W	255	41	80		N	Y	Y	Y		Y	Y	N		8
Rasmussen College St. Cloud	St. Cloud	C,T	Prop	PW	387	39	42		N	Y	Y	Y	Y	Y	Y	N		9
Ridgewater College	Willmar	C,T	St	M/W	3,129		28	76	Y	Y	Y	Y	Y	Y	Y	N	9	76
Riverland Community College	Austin	C,T	St	M/W			32	55	Y	Y	Y	Y	Y	Y	Y		5	31
Rochester Community and Technical College	Rochester																	
St. Cloud Technical College	St. Cloud	T	St	M/W	3,023	37	33		Y	Y	Y	Y	Y	Y	Y	N	4	56
St. Paul Technical College	St. Paul	T	St-R	M/W	5,381	74	60		Y	Y	S	Y	Y	Y	Y	N		13

This index includes the names and locations of accredited two-year colleges in the United States and U.S. territories and shows institutions' responses to our 2001 Survey of Undergraduate Institutions. If an institution submitted incomplete or no data, one or more columns opposite the institution's name is blank. An asterisk after the school name denotes a *Special Announcement* following the college's profile.

Y—Yes; N—No; R—Recommended; S—For Some

Institution	Location	Degrees Awarded: Transfer Associate (C), Terminal Associate (T), Bachelor's (B), Master's (M), Doctoral (D), First Professional (F)	Institutional Control: Independent, Independent-Religious, Proprietary, Federal, State, Province, Commonwealth, Territory, County, District, City, State and Local, State-Related	Student Body: Men, Primarily Men, Women, Primarily Women, Coed	Undergraduate Enrollment Fall 2001	Percent Attending Part-Time	Percent 25 Years of Age or Older	Percent of Grads Going on to 4-Year Colleges	High School Equivalency Certificate Accepted	Open Admissions	High School Transcript Required	Need-based aid available	Part-Time Jobs Available	Career Counseling Available	Job Placement Services Available	College Housing Available	Number of Sports Offered	Number of Majors Offered
South Central Technical College	North Mankato																	
Vermilion Community College	Ely	C,T	St	M/W	986		10		Y	Y	Y	Y	Y	Y	Y	Y	14	77
Mississippi																		
Antonelli College	Hattiesburg																	
Antonelli College	Jackson	C,T	Prop	M/W	214													
Coahoma Community College	Clarksdale	C,T	St-L	M/W	1,400		10		Y	Y	Y		Y	Y	Y	Y	2	17
Copiah-Lincoln Community College	Wesson																	
Copiah-Lincoln Community College–Natchez Campus	Natchez	C,T	St-L	M/W	312	10	50		Y	Y	Y	Y	Y	Y		N		11
East Central Community College	Decatur	C,T	St-L	M/W	2,382		32		Y	Y	Y	Y	Y	Y		Y	8	41
East Mississippi Community College	Scooba	C,T	St-L	M/W	3,009	41			Y	Y	Y	Y	Y	Y		Y	7	36
Hinds Community College	Raymond	C,T	St-L	M/W	14,390		40		Y	Y	Y	Y	Y	Y	Y	Y	10	76
Holmes Community College	Goodman	C,T	St-L	M/W	3,252			65	Y	Y	Y	Y	Y	Y	Y	Y	10	29
Itawamba Community College	Fulton																	
Jones County Junior College	Ellisville	C,T	St-L	M/W	5,025		22		Y	Y	Y	Y	Y	Y		Y	9	31
Mary Holmes College	West Point	C	I-R	M/W	293	34												
Meridian Community College	Meridian	C,T	St-L	M/W	3,248	26	30	75	Y	Y	Y	Y	Y	Y	Y	Y	11	21
Mississippi Delta Community College	Moorhead	C,T	Dist	M/W	2,956		19		N	Y	Y	Y	Y	Y	Y	Y	9	42
Mississippi Gulf Coast Community College	Perkinston	C,T	Dist	M/W	8,944	38	0		Y	Y	Y	Y	Y	Y	Y	Y	9	46
Northeast Mississippi Community College	Booneville																	
Northwest Mississippi Community College	Senatobia	C,T	St-L	M/W	5,000				Y	Y	Y	Y	Y	Y		Y	7	48
Pearl River Community College	Poplarville																	
Southwest Mississippi Community College	Summit	C,T	St-L	M/W	1,772		31		Y	Y	Y	Y	Y	Y	Y	Y	6	38
Virginia College at Jackson	Jackson	C,T	Prop	M/W	675						Y					N		9
Wood College	Mathiston																	
Missouri																		
Blue River Community College	Blue Springs	C,T	St-L	M/W	2,294	67	33		Y	Y				Y	Y			9
Cottey College	Nevada	C	Ind	W			1	100	N	Y	Y	Y	Y	Y		Y	12	2
Crowder College	Neosho	C,T	St-L	M/W	2,012	51	23		Y	Y	Y	Y	Y	Y	Y	Y	2	34
East Central College	Union	C,T	Dist	M/W	3,462	60	46	65	Y	Y	Y	Y	Y	Y	Y	N	5	76
Electronics Institute	Kansas City																	
Hickey College*	St. Louis	T	Prop	M/W	450					Y	Y					Y		5
ITT Technical Institute	Arnold	T	Prop	M/W	484						Y					N		5
ITT Technical Institute	Earth City	T,B	Prop	M/W	600				N	Y	Y	Y	Y	Y	Y	N		6
Jefferson College	Hillsboro	C,T	St-L	M/W	3,899		35		Y	Y	Y	Y	Y	Y	Y	N	5	56
Linn State Technical College	Linn																	
Longview Community College	Lee's Summit	C,T	St-L	M/W	5,791	65	37		Y	Y		Y	Y	Y	Y	N	4	28
Maple Woods Community College	Kansas City	C,T	St-L	M/W	5,045	67	29		Y	Y		Y	Y	Y	Y	N	3	24
Metro Business College	Cape Girardeau	T,B	Priv		90													
Mineral Area College	Park Hills	C,T	Dist	M/W	2,878	48	36		Y		Y	Y	Y	Y	Y		3	34
Missouri College	St. Louis	T	Prop	PW	450		42		Y	Y		Y	Y		Y	N		1
Moberly Area Community College	Moberly	C,T	St-L	M/W	3,269	55	28		Y	Y	Y	Y	Y	Y	Y	Y	2	14
North Central Missouri College	Trenton																	
Ozarks Technical Community College	Springfield	C,T	Dist	M/W	6,343	61												
Patricia Stevens College	St. Louis	C,T	Prop	PW	170		37			Y	Y	Y		Y	Y			7
Penn Valley Community College	Kansas City	C,T	St-L	M/W	4,376	72	37		Y	Y	Y	Y	Y	Y	Y	N	1	38
Ranken Technical College	St. Louis																	
Saint Charles Community College	St. Peters	C,T	St	M/W	6,171	58	34		Y	Y	R,S	Y	Y	Y	Y	N	6	22
St. Louis Community College at Florissant Valley	St. Louis	C,T	Dist	M/W	7,365		53	26	Y	Y	Y		Y	Y	Y	N	7	48
St. Louis Community College at Forest Park	St. Louis	C,T	Dist	M/W	6,749	74												
St. Louis Community College at Meramec	Kirkwood	C,T	Dist	M/W	12,518													
Sanford-Brown College	Fenton	T	Prop	M/W	511	39	75		Y	Y	Y	Y	Y	Y	Y	N	1	7
Sanford-Brown College	Hazelwood	C,T	Prop	M/W	350				N	Y	Y	Y	Y	Y	Y		1	7
Sanford-Brown College	North Kansas City	T	Prop	M/W	300													
Sanford-Brown College	St. Charles																	
Southwest Missouri State University–West Plains	West Plains	C,T	St	M/W	1,653													
Springfield College	Springfield	T	Prop	M/W	520													
State Fair Community College	Sedalia	C,T	Dist	M/W	3,356		54		Y	Y	Y	Y	Y	Y	Y	Y	3	31
Three Rivers Community College	Poplar Bluff	C,T	St-L	M/W	2,500													
Vatterott College	St. Ann	T	Prop	M/W	600				N	Y		Y		Y	Y	N		3
Wentworth Military Academy and Junior College	Lexington	C	Ind	M/W	312	60	10	76	N	Y	Y	Y	Y	Y		Y	12	1
Montana																		
Blackfeet Community College	Browning	C,T	Ind	M/W	375		73		Y	Y	Y	Y	Y	Y	Y	N	9	7
Dawson Community College	Glendive	C,T	St-L	M/W	449	22	26	43	Y	Y	Y	Y	Y	Y	Y	Y	10	10
Dull Knife Memorial College	Lame Deer																	
Flathead Valley Community College*	Kalispell	C,T	St-L	M/W	1,867	55	42		Y	Y	Y	Y	Y	Y	Y	N	8	24
Fort Belknap College	Harlem																	
Fort Peck Community College	Poplar	C,T	Ind	M/W	370													
Helena Coll of Tech of The U of Montana	Helena	C,T	St	M/W	850				Y	Y		Y	Y	Y	Y	N	2	18
Little Big Horn College	Crow Agency																	
Miles Community College	Miles City	C,T	St-L	M/W	590	34	19	50	Y	Y	Y	Y	Y	Y	Y	Y	14	23
Montana State U Coll of Tech-Great Falls	Great Falls	C,T	St	M/W	1,251	54	57		Y	Y	Y	Y	Y	Y	Y	N		23
Salish Kootenai College	Pablo	C,T,B	Ind	M/W	1,042	47	48		Y	Y	Y	Y	Y	Y	Y	N	8	15
Stone Child College	Box Elder	C	Ind	M/W	240				Y	Y	Y		Y					5

This index includes the names and locations of accredited two-year colleges in the United States and U.S. territories and shows institutions' responses to our 2001 Survey of Undergraduate Institutions. If an institution submitted incomplete or no data, one or more columns opposite the institution's name is blank. An asterisk after the school name denotes a *Special Announcement* following the college's profile.

Y—Yes; N—No; R—Recommended; S—For Some

Institution	Location	Degrees Awarded: Transfer Associate (C), Terminal Associate (T), Bachelor's (B), Master's (M), Doctoral (D), First Professional (F)	Institutional Control: Independent, Independent-Religious, Proprietary, Federal, State, Province, Commonwealth, Territory, County, District, City, State and Local, State-Related	Student Body: Men, Primarily Men, Women, Primarily Women, Coed	Undergraduate Enrollment Fall 2001	Percent Attending Part-Time	Percent 25 Years of Age or Older	Percent of Grads Going on to 4-Year Colleges	Open Admissions	High School Equivalency Certificate Accepted	High School Transcript Required	Need-based aid available	Part-Time Jobs Available	Career Counseling Available	Job Placement Services Available	College Housing Available	Number of Sports Offered	Number of Majors Offered
Nebraska																		
Central Community College–Columbus Campus	Columbus	C,T	St-L	M/W	1,794	73	64		Y	Y	Y	Y	Y	Y	Y	Y	5	22
Central Community College–Grand Island Campus	Grand Island	C,T	St-L	M/W	2,780	80	67		Y	Y	Y	Y	Y	Y	Y	Y	3	22
Central Community College–Hastings Campus	Hastings	C,T	St-L	M/W	2,245	62	36		Y	Y	Y	Y	Y	Y	Y	Y	6	36
ITT Technical Institute	Omaha	T	Prop	M/W	341				N	Y	Y	Y	Y	Y	Y	N		5
Lincoln School of Commerce	Lincoln	C,T	Prop	M/W	494	6	38	10	Y	Y	Y	Y	Y	Y	Y	Y	3	12
Little Priest Tribal College	Winnebago																	
Metropolitan Community College*	Omaha	C,T	St-L	M/W	11,704	68	52		Y		R	Y	Y	Y	Y	N		33
Mid-Plains Community College Area	North Platte	C,T	Dist	M/W	2,823	63	48	80	Y		Y			Y		Y	4	25
Nebraska College of Business	Omaha	T	Prop	M/W	450													
Nebraska Indian Community College	Macy	C,T	Ind	M/W	299													
Northeast Community College	Norfolk	C,T	St-L	M/W	4,600	61	15	50	Y	Y	R	Y	Y	Y	Y	Y	11	69
Omaha College of Health Careers	Omaha																	
Southeast Community College, Beatrice Campus	Beatrice	C,T	Dist	M/W	987		40	80	Y	Y	Y	Y	Y	Y	Y	Y	6	24
Southeast Community College, Lincoln Campus	Lincoln	C,T	Dist	M/W	5,431	54												
Southeast Community College, Milford Campus	Milford	T	Dist	PM	936	2	20		Y	Y	Y	Y	Y	Y	Y	Y	13	29
Western Nebraska Community College	Scottsbluff	C,T	St-L	M/W	2,479		43	44	Y	Y	R	Y	Y	Y	Y	Y	7	48
Nevada																		
Career College of Northern Nevada	Reno	T	Prop	M/W	254		62		Y	Y		Y	Y	Y	Y	N		6
Community College of Southern Nevada	North Las Vegas	C	St	M/W	31,851	81	60		Y			Y	Y	Y	Y	N	6	82
Great Basin College	Elko	C,T,B	St	M/W	2,470	75	60		Y		Y	Y	Y	Y	Y		4	25
Heritage College	Las Vegas																	
ITT Technical Institute	Henderson	T	Prop	M/W	426						Y	Y	Y			N		5
Las Vegas College	Las Vegas	T	Prop	M/W	540													
Truckee Meadows Community College	Reno	C,T	St	M/W	9,697	80	54		Y			Y	Y	Y	Y	N		50
Western Nevada Community College	Carson City	C,T	St	M/W	5,117		68		Y	Y	S	Y	Y	Y	Y	N		42
New Hampshire																		
Hesser College†	Manchester	C,T,B	Prop	M/W	2,766	51	25	65	N	Y	Y	Y	Y	Y	Y	Y	8	41
McIntosh College†	Dover	C,T	Prop	M/W	1,224		65		Y	Y	Y	Y	Y	Y	Y	Y		19
New Hampshire Comm Tech Coll, Berlin/Laconia	Berlin	C,T	St	M/W	538	60			N	Y	Y	Y	Y	Y	Y	N	6	19
New Hampshire Comm Tech Coll, Manchester/Stratham	Manchester																	
New Hampshire Comm Tech Coll, Nashua/Claremont	Nashua																	
New Hampshire Technical Institute†	Concord	C	St	M/W	3,308	60	50	18		Y	Y	Y	Y	Y	Y	Y	5	30
New Jersey																		
Assumption College for Sisters	Mendham	C	I-R	W	34		50	100		Y	Y	Y		Y		N		4
Atlantic Cape Community College†	Mays Landing	C,T	Cou	M/W	5,483	60	68	14	Y		R	Y	Y	Y	Y	N	4	28
Bergen Community College*	Paramus	C,T	Cou	M/W	12,145	52	41	77	Y	Y		Y	Y	Y	Y	N	9	56
Berkeley College†	West Paterson	C,T,B	Prop	M/W	2,144	16	23		N	Y	Y	Y	Y	Y	Y	Y	7	11
Brookdale Community College*	Lincroft	C,T	Cou	M/W	11,876	51	28	72	Y	Y	Y	Y	Y	Y	Y	N	8	57
Burlington County College	Pemberton	C,T	Cou	M/W	6,467		52	60	Y	Y		Y	Y	Y	Y	N	5	55
Camden County College*	Blackwood	C,T	St-L	M/W	12,566		39		Y	Y	S	Y	Y	Y	Y	N	4	54
County College of Morris	Randolph	C,T	Cou	M/W	8,190		27	76	Y		Y	Y	Y	Y	Y	N	12	28
Cumberland County College	Vineland	C,T	St-L	M/W	465	18	50		Y	Y	Y	Y	Y	Y	Y	N	6	39
Essex County College	Newark	C,T	Cou	M/W	9,539	48	48	60	Y		Y	Y	Y	Y	Y	N	6	39
Gibbs College	Montclair																	
Gloucester County College	Sewell	C,T	Cou	M/W	4,895				Y	Y	Y	Y	Y	Y	Y	N	9	43
Hudson County Community College	Jersey City	C,T	St-L	M/W	5,285		38	13	Y		Y	Y	Y	Y	Y	N	10	16
Mercer County Community College	Trenton	C,T	St-L	M/W	8,132	64	41	64	Y		Y	Y	Y	Y	Y	N	8	51
Middlesex County College†	Edison	C,T	Cou	M/W	10,500		44		Y	Y	Y	Y	Y	Y	Y	N	11	73
Ocean County College	Toms River	C,T	Cou	M/W	7,441	52		65	Y		S	Y	Y	Y	Y	N	9	27
Passaic County Community College	Paterson	C,T	Cou	M/W	4,633	71												
Raritan Valley Community College	Somerville	C,T	Cou	M/W	5,830	64	33		Y	Y	Y	Y	Y	Y	Y	N	5	46
Salem Community College	Carneys Point	C,T	Cou	M/W	1,229	59	52		Y	Y	Y	Y	Y	Y	Y	N	4	41
Somerset Christian College	Zarephath	C	I-R	M/W	107		95	0			S					N		1
Sussex County Community College	Newton	C,T	St-L	M/W	2,479	58	41	73	Y		Y	Y	Y	Y	Y	N	4	20
Union County College	Cranford	C,T	St-L	M/W	8,950	48	50	60	Y	Y	Y	Y	Y	Y	Y	N	6	35
Warren County Community College	Washington	C,T	St-L	M/W	981		57		Y			Y	Y	Y	Y	N		13
New Mexico																		
Albuquerque Technical Vocational Institute	Albuquerque	C,T	St	M/W	18,833	70	16		Y		R	Y	Y	Y	Y	N		34
The Art Center	Albuquerque	T	Prop	M/W	275													
Clovis Community College	Clovis	C,T	St	M/W	2,767	65	42		Y	Y	Y	Y	Y	Y	Y	N	7	31
Doña Ana Branch Community College	Las Cruces	T	St-L	M/W	4,987				Y	Y	Y	Y	Y	Y	Y	Y		22
Eastern New Mexico University–Roswell	Roswell																	
Institute of American Indian Arts	Santa Fe	C	Fed	M/W	150		51		N	Y	Y	Y	Y	Y	Y	Y	11	11
ITT Technical Institute	Albuquerque	T,B	Prop		392				N	Y	Y			Y	Y	N		5
Luna Community College	Las Vegas																	
Mesa Technical College	Tucumcari	C,T	St	M/W	576		52				Y					N		14
New Mexico Junior College	Hobbs	C,T	St-L	M/W	3,200	62												
New Mexico Military Institute*†	Roswell	C	St	PM	423		0	89	N	Y	Y	Y	Y	Y		Y	17	28
New Mexico State University–Alamogordo	Alamogordo	C,T	St	M/W	1,839	63	70		Y	Y	Y	Y	Y	Y	Y	N	2	16
New Mexico State University–Carlsbad	Carlsbad	C,T	St	M/W	1,011		70		Y	Y	Y	Y	Y	Y	Y	N		17

This index includes the names and locations of accredited two-year colleges in the United States and U.S. territories and shows institutions' responses to our 2001 Survey of Undergraduate Institutions. If an institution submitted incomplete or no data, one or more columns opposite the institution's name is blank. An asterisk after the school name denotes a *Special Announcement* following the college's profile.

Y—Yes; N—No; R—Recommended; S—For Some

Institution	Location	**Degrees Awarded** Transfer Associate (C), Terminal Associate (T), Bachelor's (B), Master's (M), Doctoral (D), First Professional (F)	**Institutional Control** Independent, Independent-Religious, Proprietary, Federal, State, Province, Commonwealth, Territory, County, District, City, State and Local, State-Related	**Student Body** Men, Primarily Men, Women, Primarily Women, Coed	**Undergraduate Enrollment Fall 2001**	Percent Attending Part-Time	Percent 25 Years of Age or Older	Percent of Grads Going on to 4-Year Colleges	Open Admissions	High School Equivalency Certificate Accepted	High School Transcript Required	Need-based aid available	Part-Time Jobs Available	Career Counseling Available	Job Placement Services Available	College Housing Available	Number of Sports Offered	Number of Majors Offered
New Mexico State University–Grants	Grants	C,T	St	M/W	535													
Northern New Mexico Community College	Española	C,T	St	M/W	2,116	69	60		Y	Y	Y	Y	Y	Y	Y	Y		13
Pima Medical Institute	Albuquerque	T	Prop	M/W	400													
San Juan College	Farmington	C,T	Cou	M/W	4,558	52	48		Y	Y	Y	Y	Y	Y	Y	N	14	52
Santa Fe Community College	Santa Fe	C,T	St-L	M/W	5,056	85	58	50	Y	Y	Y	Y	Y	Y	Y	N	1	33
Southwestern Indian Polytechnic Institute	Albuquerque	C,T	Fed	M/W	730													
University of New Mexico–Gallup	Gallup	C,T,B	St	M/W	2,515		50	10	Y	Y	S	Y	Y	Y	Y	N		26
University of New Mexico–Los Alamos Branch	Los Alamos	C,T	St	M/W	948		40		Y	Y		Y	Y	Y	Y	N		14
University of New Mexico–Valencia Campus	Los Lunas	C,T	St	M/W	1,544													
New York																		
Adirondack Community College*	Queensbury	C,T	St-L	M/W	3,200		46	81	Y	Y	Y	Y	Y	Y	Y	N	13	55
American Acad McAllister Inst of Funeral Service	New York	T	Ind	M/W	130		29		Y	Y	Y	Y		Y		N		1
American Academy of Dramatic Arts†	New York	T	Ind	M/W	220		22		N	Y	R,S	Y	Y	Y	Y	N		1
The Art Institute of New York City	New York	C,T	Prop	M/W	1,300			1	Y	Y	Y	Y	Y	Y	Y	N		4
Berkeley College†	New York	C,T,B	Prop	M/W	1,666	9	29		N	Y	Y	Y	Y	Y	Y	N		8
Berkeley College-Westchester Campus†	White Plains	C,T,B	Prop	M/W	667	14	19		N	Y	Y	Y	Y	Y	Y	Y		8
Borough of Manhattan Comm Coll of City U of NY	New York	C,T	St-L	M/W	16,025		43	46	Y	Y	Y	Y	Y	Y	Y	N	4	17
Bramson ORT College	Forest Hills																	
Bronx Comm Coll of City U of NY	Bronx	C,T	St-L	M/W	6,942	38	50	56	Y	Y	Y		Y	Y	Y	N	6	27
Broome Community College	Binghamton	C,T	St-L	M/W	5,818	42	35	39	Y	Y	Y	Y	Y	Y	Y	N	11	41
Bryant & Stratton Business Inst	Albany	T	Prop	M/W	307	23	54		N	Y	Y	Y	Y	Y	Y	N		7
Bryant & Stratton Business Inst	Buffalo	T	Prop	M/W	440		49		N	Y	Y	Y	Y	Y	Y	N		8
Bryant & Stratton Business Inst	Lackawanna	C,T	Prop	M/W	256	20	33	4	N	Y	Y	Y	Y	Y	Y	N		7
Bryant & Stratton Business Inst	Rochester	T	Prop	M/W	348		54		N	Y	Y	Y	Y	Y	Y	N		12
Bryant & Stratton Business Inst	Rochester	T	Prop	M/W	202		60		N	Y	Y	Y	Y	Y	Y	N	3	10
Bryant & Stratton Business Inst	Syracuse	T	Prop	M/W	233	12												
Bryant & Stratton Business Inst, Eastern Hills Cmps	Clarence	C	Prop	M/W	116	60	55		N	Y	Y	Y	Y	Y	Y	N		7
Bryant & Stratton Business Inst	Liverpool	T	Prop	M/W	198	12			N	Y	Y	Y	Y	Y	Y	N	1	8
Cath Med Ctr of Brooklyn & Queens Sch of Nursing	Fresh Meadows																	
Cayuga County Community College	Auburn	C,T	St-L	M/W	2,739		31	61	Y	Y	Y	Y	Y	Y	Y	N	5	26
Clinton Community College	Plattsburgh	C,T	St-L	M/W	1,852	40	27		Y	Y	Y	Y	Y	Y	Y	Y	4	17
Cochran School of Nursing	Yonkers	T	Ind	PW	94		45		N	Y	Y	Y		Y		N		1
Columbia-Greene Community College	Hudson	C,T	St-L	M/W	1,624	49	41	54	Y		Y	Y	Y	Y	Y	N	12	23
Corning Community College	Corning	C,T	St-L	M/W	4,596	53	38	78	Y	Y	Y	Y	Y	Y	Y	N	15	46
Crouse Hospital School of Nursing	Syracuse	C	Ind	PW	169	49												
Dorothea Hopfer School of Nursing at The Mount Vernon Hospital	Mount Vernon																	
Dutchess Community College	Poughkeepsie	C,T	St-L	M/W	6,981		48	56	Y	Y	Y	Y	Y	Y	Y	N	10	44
Ellis Hospital School of Nursing	Schenectady	C,T	Ind	PW	69		80				Y	Y						1
Elmira Business Institute	Elmira	C,T	Priv		230													
Erie Community College, City Campus	Buffalo	C,T	St-L	M/W	2,517	29	44	29	Y	Y	Y	Y	Y	Y	Y	N	12	17
Erie Community College, North Campus	Williamsville	C,T	St-L	M/W	5,162	38	30	35	Y	Y	Y	Y	Y	Y	Y	N	12	26
Erie Community College, South Campus	Orchard Park	C,T	St-L	M/W	3,370	34	22	39	Y	Y	Y	Y	Y	Y	Y	N	12	18
Eugenio María de Hostos Comm Coll of City U of NY	Bronx	C,T	St-L	M/W	3,285	25	54	25	Y	Y	Y	Y	Y	Y	Y	N	2	15
Finger Lakes Community College†	Canandaigua	C,T	St-L	M/W	4,753		32		Y	Y	Y	Y	Y	Y	Y	N	7	49
Fiorello H LaGuardia Comm Coll of City U of NY*	Long Island City	C,T	St-L	M/W	11,427		41	50	Y	Y	Y	Y	Y	Y	Y	N	9	33
Fulton-Montgomery Community College	Johnstown	C,T	St-L	M/W	624	25	34		Y		Y	Y	Y	Y		N	9	44
Genesee Community College	Batavia	C,T	St-L	M/W	4,809	54	19	64	Y	Y	Y	Y	Y	Y	Y	Y	15	37
Helene Fuld Coll of Nursing of North General Hosp	New York	C,T	Ind	PW	296	50	96		N	Y	Y	Y		Y		N		1
Herkimer County Community College	Herkimer	C,T	St-L	M/W	2,873	30	23		Y	Y	Y	Y	Y	Y	Y	Y	13	53
Hudson Valley Community College	Troy	C,T	St-L	M/W	8,116													
Institute of Design and Construction	Brooklyn	C	Ind	PM	248		60	20		Y	Y	Y		Y	Y	N		4
Interboro Institute	New York	T	Prop	M/W	1,344		20		Y		R	Y		Y	Y	N	1	8
Island Drafting and Technical Institute	Amityville	C,T	Prop		241		25		Y	Y	R	Y		Y	Y			7
ITT Technical Institute	Albany	T	Prop	M/W	245						Y					N		4
ITT Technical Institute	Getzville	T	Prop	M/W	595						Y					N		5
ITT Technical Institute	Liverpool	T	Prop	M/W	267						Y					N		4
Jamestown Business College	Jamestown	T	Prop	M/W	298	2	50		N	Y	Y	Y		Y	Y	N	10	7
Jamestown Community College	Jamestown	C,T	St-L	M/W	4,092	53	36	72	Y	Y	Y	Y	Y	Y	Y	N	12	25
Jefferson Community College	Watertown	C,T	St-L	M/W	3,602	49	36	61	N	Y	Y	Y	Y	Y	Y	N	8	29
Katharine Gibbs School	Melville																	
Katharine Gibbs School	New York	C,T	Prop	M/W	2,717													
Kingsborough Comm Coll of City U of NY	Brooklyn	C,T	St-L	M/W	15,055	48	29	75	Y	Y	Y	Y	Y	Y	Y	N	7	36
Long Island Business Institute	Commack	C	Prop	PW	104	57	95	0	Y	Y	Y			Y	Y	N		4
Long Island College Hospital School of Nursing	Brooklyn																	
Maria College*†	Albany	C,T	Ind	M/W	659	64												
Mildred Elley	Latham	T	Priv		387							Y	Y					
Mohawk Valley Community College†	Utica	C,T	St-L	M/W	5,287		34	45	Y	Y	Y	Y	Y		Y	Y	16	73
Monroe College*	Bronx	C,T,B	Prop	M/W	3,449	14	46	26	N		Y	Y	Y	Y	Y	Y	4	10
Monroe College	New Rochelle	C,T,B	Prop	M/W	1,156	18	54	26	N		Y	Y	Y	Y	Y	Y	4	9
Monroe Community College	Rochester	C,T	St-L	M/W	16,157	51	35	52	Y	Y	Y	Y	Y	Y	Y	N	16	67
Nassau Community College	Garden City	C,T	St-L	M/W	19,712	44	15	65		Y	Y	Y	Y	Y	Y	N	17	55
New York Career Institute	New York																	
New York City Tech Coll of the City U of NY	Brooklyn	C,T,B	St-L	M/W	11,028	33	38		Y	Y	Y	Y	Y	Y	Y	N	5	29
New Ctr Coll for Wholistic Health Ed & Research†	Syosset	T,B,M	Ind	M/W	550				N	Y	Y	Y	Y	Y	Y	N		1
Niagara County Community College	Sanborn	C,T	St-L	M/W	4,915	38	31	62	Y	Y	Y	Y	Y	Y	Y	N	15	33
North Country Community College	Saranac Lake	C,T	St-L	M/W	1,217	35	39	34	Y	Y	Y	Y	Y	Y	Y	N	12	13
Olean Business Institute	Olean																	

This index includes the names and locations of accredited two-year colleges in the United States and U.S. territories and shows institutions' responses to our 2001 Survey of Undergraduate Institutions. If an institution submitted incomplete or no data, one or more columns opposite the institution's name is blank. An asterisk after the school name denotes a *Special Announcement* following the college's profile.

		Degrees Awarded (Transfer Associate (C), Terminal Associate (T), Bachelor's (B), Master's (M), Doctoral (D), First Professional (F))	Institutional Control (Independent, Independent-Religious, Proprietary, Federal, State, Province, Commonwealth, Territory, County, District, City, State and Local, State-Related)	Student Body (Men, Primarily Men, Women, Primarily Women, Coed)	Undergraduate Enrollment Fall 2001	Percent Attending Part-Time	Percent 25 Years of Age or Older	Percent of Grads Going on to 4-Year Colleges	Open Admissions	High School Equivalency Certificate Accepted	High School Transcript Required	Need-based aid available	Part-Time Jobs Available	Career Counseling Available	Job Placement Services Available	College Housing Available	Number of Sports Offered	Number of Majors Offered
									Y—Yes; N—No; R—Recommended; S—For Some									
Onondaga Community College	Syracuse	C,T	St-L	M/W	8,000		48	73	Y	Y	Y	Y	Y	Y	Y	N	8	58
Orange County Community College	Middletown	C,T	St-L	M/W	5,532	52	37	62	Y	Y	Y	Y	Y	Y	Y	N	9	41
Paul Smith's College of Arts and Sciences*	Paul Smiths	C,T,B	Ind	M/W	817	3	7		N	Y	Y		Y	Y	Y	Y	14	15
Phillips Beth Israel School of Nursing	New York	C,T	Ind	PW	91	70	56	10	N	Y	Y	Y		Y		N		1
Plaza Business Institute	Jackson Heights																	
Queensborough Comm Coll of City U of NY	Bayside	C,T	St-L	M/W	10,880	48	34	16	Y	Y	Y	Y	Y	Y	Y	N	14	21
Rochester Business Institute	Rochester	T	Prop	M/W	990		45		N	Y		Y	Y	Y	Y	N	2	5
Rockland Community College	Suffern	C,T	St-L	M/W	6,260	43	39	67	Y		Y	Y	Y	Y	Y	N	11	42
Saint Joseph's Hospital Health Center School of Nursing	Syracuse	T	Ind	PW	250	36	51			Y	Y	Y		Y	Y	Y		1
Samaritan Hospital School of Nursing	Troy	C,T	Ind		70													
Schenectady County Community College	Schenectady	C,T	St-L	M/W	3,526	50	47	74	Y	Y	Y	Y	Y	Y	Y	N	6	34
Simmons Institute of Funeral Service	Syracuse	C,T	Prop	M/W	41	29	60		Y	Y	Y	Y				N		1
State U of NY Coll of A&T at Morrisville†	Morrisville	C,T,B	St	M/W	3,130		24	44	N	Y	Y	Y	Y	Y	Y	Y	19	61
State U of NY Coll of Environ Sci & For Ranger Sch†	Wanakena	C,T	St	PM	40		20	38	N	N		Y	Y	Y	Y	Y	7	2
State U of NY Coll of Technology at Alfred	Alfred	C,T,B	St	M/W	3,041		16	83	N	Y	Y	Y	Y	Y	Y	Y	19	65
State U of NY Coll of Technology at Canton	Canton	C,T,B	St	M/W	2,223	21	30		N	Y	Y	Y	Y	Y	Y	Y	12	36
State U of NY Coll of Technology at Delhi	Delhi	C,T,B	St	M/W	2,013	8	19	81	N	Y	Y	Y	Y	Y	Y	Y	17	42
Suffolk County Community College	Selden	C,T	St-L	M/W	19,851	56	33	75	Y	Y	Y	Y	Y	Y	Y	N	11	60
Sullivan County Community College	Loch Sheldrake	C,T	St-L	M/W	1,591	40	31		Y	Y	Y	Y	Y	Y	Y	N	16	32
Taylor Business Institute	New York																	
TCI-The College for Technology	New York	T	Prop	M/W	4,319		49		N	Y	Y	Y	Y	Y	Y	N	5	6
Tompkins Cortland Community College	Dryden	C,T	St-L	M/W	2,889	39	37	60	Y		Y	Y	Y	Y	Y	Y	16	46
Trocaire College	Buffalo	C,T	Ind	PW	721		57	17	N	Y	Y	Y	Y	Y	Y			15
Ulster County Community College	Stone Ridge	C,T	St-L	M/W	2,913		40	15	Y	Y		Y	Y	Y	Y	N	7	28
Utica School of Commerce	Utica	C,T	Prop	PW	550		57		Y	Y	Y	Y	Y	Y	Y	N	3	7
Villa Maria College of Buffalo	Buffalo	C,T	I-R	M/W	423	31	38	59	N	Y	Y	Y	Y	Y	Y	N		13
The Westchester Business Institute†	White Plains	C,T	Prop	M/W	1,113	2	48		N	Y	Y	Y	Y	Y	Y	N		27
Westchester Community College	Valhalla	C,T	St-L	M/W	11,025	57	32		Y	Y	Y	Y	Y	Y	Y	N	11	53
Wood Tobe–Coburn School	New York	T	Prop	PW	467													
North Carolina																		
Alamance Community College	Graham	C,T	St	M/W	3,991	68	47	1	Y	Y	Y	Y	Y	Y	Y	N	4	33
Asheville-Buncombe Technical Community College	Asheville	C,T	St	M/W	5,448	66	47		Y	Y	Y	Y	Y	Y	Y	N	3	27
Beaufort County Community College	Washington	C,T	St	M/W	1,721		58	75	Y	Y	Y	Y	Y	Y	Y	N		22
Bladen Community College	Dublin	C,T	St-L	M/W	1,033	39	60	40	Y	Y	Y	Y	Y	Y	Y	N		9
Blue Ridge Community College	Flat Rock	C	St-L	M/W	1,907		53		Y	Y	Y	Y	Y	Y	Y	N		22
Brunswick Community College	Supply	C,T	St	M/W	978	49	41	85	Y	Y	Y	Y		Y	Y	N	4	15
Cabarrus College of Health Sciences	Concord	T,B	Ind	PW	280		59		N	Y	Y	Y	Y	Y		N		6
Caldwell Comm Coll and Tech Inst	Hudson	C,T	St	M/W	3,636	56	44		Y	Y	Y	Y	Y	Y	Y	N	3	22
Cape Fear Community College	Wilmington	C,T	St	M/W	6,051	52	38	85	Y	Y	Y	Y	Y	Y	Y	N	6	33
Carolinas College of Health Sciences	Charlotte	T	Ind	PW	314	55	40	5	N	Y	Y	Y	Y	Y	Y	N		3
Carteret Community College	Morehead City	C,T	St	M/W	1,555		53		Y	Y	Y	Y	Y	Y	Y	N	2	18
Catawba Valley Community College	Hickory	C,T	St-L	M/W	3,943	61	46		Y	Y	Y	Y	Y	Y	Y	N	2	42
Central Carolina Community College	Sanford	C,T	St-L	M/W	4,062	55	49		Y	Y	Y	Y	Y	Y	Y	N	5	29
Central Piedmont Community College	Charlotte	C,T	St-L	M/W	1,076	36	57	29	Y	Y	S	Y	Y	Y	Y	N	6	68
Cleveland Community College	Shelby	C,T	St	M/W	2,782		54	50	Y	Y	Y	Y	Y	Y	Y	N		16
Coastal Carolina Community College	Jacksonville	C,T	St-L	M/W	4,033	58	39		Y	Y	Y	Y	Y	Y	Y	N		19
College of The Albemarle	Elizabeth City																	
Craven Community College	New Bern	C,T	St	M/W	2,555		50		Y	Y	Y	Y	Y	Y	Y	N	2	19
Davidson County Community College	Lexington																	
Durham Technical Community College	Durham	C,T	St	M/W	5,283		63	45	Y	Y	Y	Y	Y	Y		N		37
Edgecombe Community College	Tarboro	C,T	St-L	M/W	2,032	64	52	60	Y	Y	Y	Y	Y	Y	Y	N	1	27
Fayetteville Technical Community College	Fayetteville	C,T	St	M/W	8,310		63		Y	Y	Y	Y	Y	Y	Y	N	3	80
Forsyth Technical Community College	Winston-Salem	C,T	St	M/W	6,246		51		Y	Y	Y	Y	Y	Y	Y	N	4	38
Gaston College	Dallas	C,T	St-L	M/W	4,250		52	42	Y	Y	S	Y	Y	Y	Y	N		22
Guilford Technical Community College	Jamestown	C,T	St-L	M/W	8,573	58	44		Y	Y	Y	Y	Y	Y	Y	N		52
Halifax Community College	Weldon	C,T	St-L	M/W	1,580				Y	Y	Y	Y	Y	Y	Y	N		16
Haywood Community College	Clyde	C,T	St-L	M/W	1,874		43		Y	Y	Y	Y	Y	Y	Y	N	6	21
Isothermal Community College	Spindale	C,T	St	M/W	1,801		49		Y	Y	Y	Y	Y	Y		N	3	34
James Sprunt Community College	Kenansville	C,T	St	M/W	1,344	58	51	68	Y	Y	Y	Y	Y	Y	Y	N	2	14
Johnston Community College	Smithfield	C,T	St	M/W	3,296	58	44		Y	Y	Y		Y	Y	Y	N	4	18
Lenoir Community College	Kinston	C,T	St	M/W	3,033				Y	Y	Y	Y	Y	Y	Y	N	4	44
Louisburg College	Louisburg	C	I-R	M/W	467		12	90	N	Y	Y	Y	Y	Y		Y	9	42
Martin Community College	Williamston	C,T	St	M/W	726	50	62	50	Y	Y	Y	Y	Y	Y	Y	N	3	20
Mayland Community College	Spruce Pine	C	St-L	M/W	1,350		48			Y	Y	Y	Y	Y	Y	N		18
McDowell Technical Community College	Marion	C,T	St	M/W	1,078													
Mitchell Community College	Statesville	C,T	St	M/W	2,160		57		Y	Y	Y	Y	Y	Y	Y	N		24
Montgomery Community College	Troy	C,T	St	M/W	702		53		Y	Y	Y	Y	Y	Y	Y	N		15
Nash Community College	Rocky Mount	C,T	St	M/W	2,184	61	43	90	Y	Y	Y	Y	Y	Y	Y	N		16
Pamlico Community College	Grantsboro	C,T	St	M/W	338		58		Y	Y	Y	Y	Y	Y	Y	N	2	11
Piedmont Community College	Roxboro	C,T	St	M/W	2,029		47	100	Y	Y	S	Y	Y	Y	Y	N	1	10
Pitt Community College	Greenville	C,T	St-L	M/W	5,600	50	37		Y	Y	Y	Y	Y	Y	Y	N	5	36
Randolph Community College	Asheboro	C,T	St	M/W	2,007	64	42		Y	Y	Y	Y	Y	Y	Y	N		23
Richmond Community College	Hamlet	C,T	St	M/W	1,465	49	55		Y	Y	Y	Y	Y	Y	Y	N		16
Roanoke-Chowan Community College	Ahoskie	C,T	St	M/W	976		48	84	Y	Y		Y	Y	Y	Y	N	2	16
Robeson Community College	Lumberton	C,T	St	M/W	2,125				Y	Y			Y	Y	Y	N		8
Rockingham Community College	Wentworth	C,T	St	M/W	2,085	53			Y	Y		Y	Y	Y	Y	N	7	32
Rowan-Cabarrus Community College	Salisbury	C,T	St	M/W	4,705		55	95	Y	Y	Y	Y	Y	Y	Y	N	1	16
Sampson Community College	Clinton	C,T	St-L	M/W	1,399		52	23	Y	Y	Y	Y	Y	Y	Y	N	2	15

This index includes the names and locations of accredited two-year colleges in the United States and U.S. territories and shows institutions' responses to our 2001 Survey of Undergraduate Institutions. If an institution submitted incomplete or no data, one or more columns opposite the institution's name is blank. An asterisk after the school name denotes a *Special Announcement* following the college's profile.

Y—Yes; N—No; R—Recommended; S—For Some

Institution	Location	Degrees Awarded: Transfer Associate (C), Terminal Associate (T), Bachelor's (B), Master's (M), Doctoral (D), First Professional (F)	Institutional Control: County, District, City, State and Local, State-Related; Federal, State, Province, Commonwealth, Territory; Independent, Independent-Religious, Proprietary	Student Body: Men, Primarily Men, Women, Primarily Women, Coed	Undergraduate Enrollment Fall 2001	Percent Attending Part-Time	Percent 25 Years of Age or Older	Percent of Grads Going on to 4-Year Colleges	Open Admissions	High School Equivalency Certificate Accepted	High School Transcript Required	Need-based aid available	Part-Time Jobs Available	Career Counseling Available	Job Placement Services Available	College Housing Available	Number of Sports Offered	Number of Majors Offered
Sandhills Community College	Pinehurst	C,T	St-L	M/W	3,174	49	44		Y	Y	Y	Y	Y	Y	Y	N		48
South College	Asheville	T	Prop	M/W	170		64		Y	Y	Y	Y	Y	Y	Y	N		6
Southeastern Baptist Theological Seminary	Wake Forest	C,T,M,D,F	I-R	M/W	397													
Southeastern Community College	Whiteville	C,T	St	M/W	1,950		45		Y	Y	Y	Y	Y	Y	Y	N	2	20
South Piedmont Community College	Polkton	C,T	St	M/W	1,875	60	62	32	Y	Y	Y	Y	Y	Y	Y			23
Southwestern Community College	Sylva	C,T	St	M/W	1,802	56	45	75	Y	Y	Y	Y	Y	Y	Y	N		29
Stanly Community College	Albemarle	C,T	St	M/W	800	57	48		Y	Y	Y	Y	Y	Y	Y	N		33
Surry Community College	Dobson	C,T	St	M/W	3,303	51	42	81	Y	Y	Y	Y	Y	Y	Y	N	4	29
Tri-County Community College	Murphy	C,T	St	M/W	1,368		65	40	Y	Y	Y	Y	Y	Y	Y	N		9
Vance-Granville Community College	Henderson	C,T	St	M/W	3,733	61	50	92	Y	Y	Y	Y	Y	Y	Y	N	2	30
Wake Technical Community College	Raleigh	C,T	St-L	M/W	10,984		56		Y	Y	Y	Y	Y	Y	Y	N		49
Wayne Community College	Goldsboro	C,T	St-L	M/W	3,162		33	25	Y	Y	Y	Y	Y	Y	Y	N	8	29
Western Piedmont Community College	Morganton	C,T	St	M/W	2,405				Y	Y	Y	Y	Y	Y	Y	N	2	26
Wilkes Community College	Wilkesboro	C,T	St	M/W	2,334	47	44	70	Y	Y	Y	Y	Y	Y	Y	N	4	22
Wilson Technical Community College	Wilson	C,T	St	M/W	1,732	56	53	80	Y	Y	Y	Y	Y	Y	Y	N		19
North Dakota																		
Bismarck State College	Bismarck	C,T	St	M/W	3,044	31	29		Y	Y	Y	Y	Y	Y	Y	Y	6	21
Cankdeska Cikana Community College	Fort Totten																	
Fort Berthold Community College	New Town	C,T	Ind	M/W	416		40	42	Y	Y		Y	Y	Y	Y	N	7	16
Lake Region State College	Devils Lake	C,T	St	M/W	1,308	72	29		Y	Y	Y	Y	Y	Y	Y	Y	8	18
Minot State University–Bottineau Campus	Bottineau	C,T	St	M/W	520	33	20	60	Y	Y	Y	Y	Y	Y	Y	Y	8	45
North Dakota State College of Science	Wahpeton	C,T	St	M/W	2,292	18	18	81	Y	Y	Y	Y	Y	Y	Y	Y	6	31
Sitting Bull College	Fort Yates	C,T	Ind	M/W	194	31	35		Y	Y	Y	Y	Y	Y		N	1	15
Turtle Mountain Community College	Belcourt																	
United Tribes Technical College	Bismarck	C,T	Fed	M/W	306	8			Y	Y	Y	Y	Y	Y	Y	Y	3	23
Williston State College	Williston	C,T	St	M/W	749	30	28	80	Y	Y	Y	Y	Y	Y	Y	Y	4	15
Ohio																		
Antonelli College	Cincinnati	T	Prop	M/W	360	40	30		Y	Y	Y	Y	Y	Y	Y	N		6
The Art Institute of Cincinnati	Cincinnati	C	Prop	M/W	66		5	0			Y					N		
Belmont Technical College	St. Clairsville	T	St	M/W	1,623		55		Y	Y		Y	Y	Y	Y	N		17
Bohecker's Business College	Ravenna																	
Bowling Green State University-Firelands Coll	Huron	C,T	St	M/W	1,487	58	43	45	Y	Y	Y	Y	Y	Y	Y	N	6	27
Bradford School	Columbus	C,T	Prop	PW	250		12		N	Y	S	Y		Y	Y	Y		9
Bryant and Stratton Coll	Parma	T	Prop	M/W	202	55	46		N	Y	Y	Y	Y	Y	Y		1	5
Bryant and Stratton Coll	Willoughby Hills	T	Prop	M/W	172	43	84	5	N		Y	Y	Y	Y	Y	N	1	4
Central Ohio Technical College	Newark	T	St	M/W	1,973	62	76		Y	Y	Y	Y	Y	Y	Y	Y	12	18
Chatfield College	St. Martin	C	I-R	PW	304	53	50	39	Y	Y	Y	Y	Y			N		4
Cincinnati College of Mortuary Science	Cincinnati	T,B	Ind	M/W	131		35		N	Y	Y	Y		Y	Y	N	4	1
Cincinnati State Technical and Community College	Cincinnati	C,T	St	M/W	7,184	62	40	31	Y	Y	Y	Y	Y	Y	Y	N	4	49
Clark State Community College	Springfield	C,T	St	M/W	2,808	65												
Cleveland Institute of Electronics	Cleveland	T	Prop	PM	3,077		85		Y	Y	Y					N		1
College of Art Advertising	Cincinnati																	
Columbus State Community College	Columbus	C,T	St	M/W	19,549		47	31	Y		R	Y	Y	Y	Y	N	9	55
Cuyahoga Community College	Cleveland	C,T	St-L	M/W	21,278	68	53		Y		S			Y	Y	N	8	32
Davis College	Toledo	T	Prop	M/W	455	64	39	10	N	Y	Y	Y	Y	Y	Y	N		15
Edison State Community College	Piqua	C,T	St	M/W	2,915		47		Y	Y	Y		Y	Y	Y	N	1	38
Education America, Remington College, Cleveland Campus	Cleveland																	
ETI Technical College	North Canton																	
ETI Technical College of Niles	Niles	T	Prop	M/W	222	16												
Gallipolis Career College	Gallipolis	T	Ind	PW	147	10			N	Y	Y			Y	Y			9
Hocking College	Nelsonville	C,T	St	M/W	6,435													
Hondros College	Westerville	T	Prop	M/W														
International College of Broadcasting	Dayton	C,T	Priv		118							Y						2
ITT Technical Institute	Dayton	T	Prop	M/W	557				N	Y	Y	Y	Y	Y	Y	N		5
ITT Technical Institute	Norwood	C	Prop	M/W	550						Y					N		5
ITT Technical Institute	Strongsville	T	Prop	M/W	516						Y					N		5
ITT Technical Institute	Youngstown	T	Prop	M/W	447				N	Y	Y	Y	Y	Y	Y	N		5
Jefferson Community College	Steubenville	C,T	St-L	M/W	1,612	50	43		Y	Y	S	Y	Y	Y	Y	N	4	26
Kent State University, Ashtabula Campus	Ashtabula																	
Kent State University, East Liverpool Campus	East Liverpool	C,T	St	M/W	585		47		Y	Y	Y	Y	Y	Y	Y	N		10
Kent State University, Geauga Campus	Burton	C,B,M	St	M/W	670	59	36		Y	Y	Y	Y	Y	Y		N	4	7
Kent State University, Salem Campus	Salem	C,T	St	M/W	1,150		47		Y	Y	Y	Y	Y	Y	Y	N	11	11
Kent State University, Stark Campus	Canton	C,B	St	M/W	3,449		33		Y	Y	Y	Y	Y	Y		N		6
Kent State University, Trumbull Campus	Warren	C,T	St	M/W	2,219		54		Y	Y	Y	Y	Y	Y	Y	N	4	16
Kent State University, Tuscarawas Campus	New Philadelphia	C,T,B	St	M/W	1,845		30		Y	Y	Y	Y	Y	Y	Y	N	2	12
Kettering College of Medical Arts	Kettering																	
Lakeland Community College	Kirtland	C,T	St-L	M/W	8,253	68	43	61	Y	Y	Y	Y	Y	Y	Y	N	8	38
Lima Technical College	Lima	C,T	St	M/W	2,894	48	13	12	Y	Y	Y	Y	Y	Y	Y	N	10	32
Lorain County Community College	Elyria	C,T	St-L	M/W	7,818	63	44	80	Y	Y	S	Y	Y	Y	Y	N	6	74
Marion Technical College	Marion	C,T	St-R	M/W	2,739		55		Y		Y		Y	Y	Y	N	8	18
Mercy College of Northwest Ohio	Toledo	C,T,B	I-R	PW	217	70												
Miami–Jacobs College	Dayton	T	Prop	M/W	408	18												
Miami University–Hamilton Campus	Hamilton	C,T,B,M	St	M/W	2,900				Y	Y	Y	Y	Y	Y	Y	N	10	9
Miami University–Middletown Campus	Middletown	C,T,B	St	M/W	2,061		28		Y	Y	Y	Y	Y	Y	Y	N	13	51
Muskingum Area Technical College	Zanesville	C,T	St-L	M/W	2,007		49	6	Y	Y	Y	Y	Y	Y	Y	N	4	27
North Central State College	Mansfield	T	St	M/W	2,760													

This index includes the names and locations of accredited two-year colleges in the United States and U.S. territories and shows institutions' responses to our 2001 Survey of Undergraduate Institutions. If an institution submitted incomplete or no data, one or more columns opposite the institution's name is blank. An asterisk after the school name denotes a *Special Announcement* following the college's profile.

Y—Yes; N—No; R—Recommended; S—For Some

Institution	Location	Degrees Awarded: Transfer Associate (C), Terminal Associate (T), Bachelor's (B), Master's (M), Doctoral (D), First Professional (F)	Institutional Control: Independent, Independent-Religious, Proprietary, Federal, State, Province, Commonwealth, Territory, County, District, City, State and Local, State-Related	Student Body: Men, Primarily Men, Women, Primarily Women, Coed	Undergraduate Enrollment Fall 2001	Percent Attending Part-Time	Percent 25 Years of Age or Older	Percent of Grads Going on to 4-Year Colleges	Open Admissions	High School Equivalency Certificate Accepted	High School Transcript Required	Need-based aid available	Part-Time Jobs Available	Career Counseling Available	Job Placement Services Available	College Housing Available	Number of Sports Offered	Number of Majors Offered
Northwest State Community College	Archbold	C,T	St	M/W	2,931	65	43		Y	Y	Y	Y	Y	Y	Y	N	4	30
Ohio Business College	Lorain	T	Ind	PW	229	13	40					Y	Y					6
Ohio Institute of Photography and Technology	Dayton																	
Ohio State U Agricultural Technical Institute	Wooster	T	St	M/W	696													
Ohio Valley Business College	East Liverpool	T	Prop	PW	116	4	47			Y	Y	Y		Y	Y	N		7
Owens Community College	Findlay	C,T	St	M/W	1,985	67												
Owens Community College	Toledo	C,T	St	M/W	14,820	73												
Professional Skills Institute	Toledo	T	Prop	M/W	174	6	60		N	Y	Y	Y		Y	Y	N		1
RETS Tech Center	Centerville	C,T	Prop	M/W	471		55	0	Y	Y	Y	Y		Y	Y	N		6
Sinclair Community College	Dayton	C,T	St-L	M/W	18,869	72	48		Y		S	Y	Y	Y	Y	N	5	89
Southeastern Business College	Chillicothe																	
Southern Ohio College, Cincinnati Campus	Cincinnati	T	Prop	M/W	766		55		Y	Y	Y	Y	Y	Y	Y	N		10
Southern Ohio College, Findlay Campus	Findlay																	
Southern Ohio College, Northeast Campus	Akron	T	Prop	M/W	387													
Southern State Community College	Hillsboro	C,T	St	M/W	2,038		47		Y	Y	Y	Y	Y	Y	Y	N	7	11
Southwestern College of Business	Cincinnati																	
Southwestern College of Business	Cincinnati																	
Southwestern College of Business	Dayton	T	Prop	M/W	340				N	Y			Y	Y	Y	N		5
Southwestern College of Business	Middletown																	
Stark State College of Technology	Canton	C,T	St-L	M/W	4,774		55		Y	Y	Y	Y	Y	Y	Y	N		49
Stautzenberger College	Toledo																	
Technology Education College	Columbus																	
Terra State Community College	Fremont	C,T	St	M/W	2,554		45		Y	Y	Y	Y	Y	Y	Y	N	7	37
Trumbull Business College	Warren	T	Prop	PW	375		51				Y	Y	Y			N		7
The University of Akron–Wayne College	Orrville	C,T	St	M/W	1,932		53	75	Y	Y	S	Y	Y	Y	Y	N	2	21
University of Cincinnati Clermont College	Batavia																	
University of Cincinnati Raymond Walters College	Cincinnati																	
University of Northwestern Ohio*	Lima	C,B	Ind	M/W	2,125	16	15	40	Y	Y	Y	Y	Y	Y	Y	Y	3	16
Virginia Marti College of Fashion and Art	Lakewood	T	Prop	M/W	208													
Washington State Community College	Marietta	C,T	St	M/W	1,911	45												
West Side Institute of Technology	Cleveland	C,T	Prop	PM	279													
Wright State University, Lake Campus	Celina																	
Oklahoma																		
Bacone College	Muskogee	C,T	I-R	M/W			50	80	Y	Y	Y	Y	Y	Y	Y	Y	10	25
Carl Albert State College	Poteau																	
Connors State College	Warner	C,T	St	M/W	1,954	42	38		Y		S	Y	Y	Y		Y	7	20
Eastern Oklahoma State College	Wilburton	C,T	St	M/W	2,026	47	31	80	Y	Y	Y	Y	Y	Y	Y	Y	10	52
Murray State College	Tishomingo	C,T	St	M/W	1,825													
Northeastern Oklahoma A&M College	Miami	C,T	St	M/W	2,000													
Northern Oklahoma College	Tonkawa	C,T	St	M/W	2,900		40		Y	Y	Y	Y	Y	Y		Y	10	17
Oklahoma City Community College	Oklahoma City	C,T	St	M/W	10,321	64	48	27	Y			Y	Y	Y	Y	N	6	44
Oklahoma State U, Oklahoma City	Oklahoma City	C,T	St	M/W	4,522		51	30	Y	Y		Y	Y	Y	Y		2	31
Oklahoma State U, Okmulgee	Okmulgee	C,T	St	M/W	2,329	26	37		Y		Y	Y	Y	Y	Y	Y	8	29
Redlands Community College	El Reno	C,T	St	M/W	2,173	67												
Rose State College	Midwest City	C,T	St-L	M/W	7,350													
Seminole State College	Seminole	C,T	St	M/W	1,965	44	35		Y		Y	Y	Y	Y		Y	6	18
Southwestern Oklahoma State University at Sayre	Sayre	C,T	St-L	M/W	488	37	36	75	Y	Y	Y	Y	Y	Y	Y	N		10
Spartan School of Aeronautics	Tulsa	T,B	Prop	PM	1,625		32	2	Y	Y	Y	Y	Y	Y	Y	N	8	7
Tulsa Community College	Tulsa	C,T	St	M/W	20,827		52	3	Y	Y	Y	Y	Y	Y	Y	N	10	161
Western Oklahoma State College	Altus	C,T	St	M/W	2,296													
Oregon																		
Blue Mountain Community College	Pendleton																	
Central Oregon Community College*	Bend	C,T	Dist	M/W	4,399	61	44	50	Y	Y	R,S	Y	Y	Y		Y	19	43
Chemeketa Community College	Salem	C,T	St-L	M/W	8,718		45		Y		S	Y	Y	Y	Y	N	5	48
Clackamas Community College	Oregon City	C,T	Dist	M/W	6,715	67	73	77	Y		R	Y	Y	Y	Y	N	10	15
Clatsop Community College	Astoria	C,T	Cou	M/W	1,796	78												
Heald College, Schools of Business and Technology	Portland																	
ITT Technical Institute	Portland	T,B	Prop	M/W	499				N	Y	Y	Y	Y	Y	Y	N		7
Lane Community College	Eugene	C,T	St-L	M/W	10,626	54	42		Y			Y	Y	Y	Y	N	15	36
Linn-Benton Community College	Albany	C,T	St-L	M/W	4,746	43	48		Y		S	Y	Y	Y	Y	N	5	52
Mt. Hood Community College	Gresham	C,T	St-L	M/W	8,771	64	56		Y		S	Y	Y	Y	Y	N	19	40
Pioneer Pacific College†	Wilsonville	C	Prop	M/W	368		78		Y	Y	Y	Y		Y	Y	N		6
Portland Community College*	Portland	C,T	St-L	M/W	46,295		55		Y			Y	Y	Y	Y	N	17	53
Rogue Community College	Grants Pass	C,T	St-L	M/W	4,496	62	56		Y			Y	Y	Y	Y	N	5	21
Southwestern Oregon Community College	Coos Bay																	
Treasure Valley Community College*	Ontario																	
Umpqua Community College	Roseburg	C,T	St-L	M/W	2,155		60	35	Y		R	Y	Y	Y	Y	N	3	53
Western Business College	Portland																	
Pennsylvania																		
Academy of Medical Arts and Business	Harrisburg	C,T	Prop	PW	197		70	0	Y	Y	Y	Y	Y	Y	Y	N		14
Allentown Business School†	Allentown	T	Prop	M/W	1,230		40		Y	Y	Y	Y	Y	Y	Y	N		9
Antonelli Institute	Erdenheim	C,T	Prop	M/W	207	2	9	0	Y	Y	Y	Y	Y	Y	Y	Y		2
The Art Institute of Philadelphia*†	Philadelphia	T,B	Prop	M/W	2,807	30	20		N	Y	Y	Y	Y	Y	Y	Y		13
The Art Institute of Pittsburgh†	Pittsburgh	C,T,B	Prop	M/W	2,500		18		N	Y	Y			Y	Y	Y		15

This index includes the names and locations of accredited two-year colleges in the United States and U.S. territories and shows institutions' responses to our 2001 Survey of Undergraduate Institutions. If an institution submitted incomplete or no data, one or more columns opposite the institution's name is blank. An asterisk after the school name denotes a *Special Announcement* following the college's profile.

Y—Yes; N—No; R—Recommended; S—For Some

Institution	Location	Degrees Awarded: Transfer Associate (C), Terminal Associate (T), Bachelor's (B), Master's (M), Doctoral (D), First Professional (F)	Institutional Control: Independent, Independent-Religious, Proprietary, Federal, State, Province, Commonwealth, Territory, County, District, City, State and Local, State-Related	Student Body: Men, Primarily Men, Women, Primarily Women, Coed	Undergraduate Enrollment Fall 2001	Percent Attending Part-Time	Percent 25 Years of Age or Older	Percent of Grads Going on to 4-Year Colleges	Open Admissions	High School Equivalency Certificate Accepted	High School Transcript Required	Need-based aid available	Part-Time Jobs Available	Career Counseling Available	Job Placement Services Available	College Housing Available	Number of Sports Offered	Number of Majors Offered
Berean Institute	Philadelphia																	
Berks Technical Institute	Wyomissing	C,T	Prop	M/W	526		25			Y	Y	Y		Y	Y	N		8
Bradford School	Pittsburgh																	
Bradley Academy for the Visual Arts†	York	T	Prop	M/W	447	13	11		N	Y	Y	Y	Y	Y	Y			13
Bucks County Community College	Newtown	C,T	Cou	M/W	8,806	64	39	90	Y	Y	S	Y	Y	Y	Y	N	11	57
Business Institute of Pennsylvania	Sharon	T	Prop	M/W	146					Y	Y	Y				N		9
Butler County Community College	Butler	C,T	Cou	M/W	3,183		40		Y	Y		Y	Y	Y	Y	N	11	49
Cambria County Area Community College	Johnstown	C,T	St-L	M/W	1,208		66		Y		R	Y	Y	Y	Y			23
Cambria-Rowe Business College	Johnstown	C,T	Prop	PW	219		30	3	N	Y	Y	Y		Y	Y	N		5
Central Pennsylvania College*	Summerdale	C,T,B	Prop	M/W	604	16	9	6	Y	Y	Y	Y	Y	Y	Y	Y	4	23
CHI Institute	Southampton	C,T	Prop	M/W	700		50		N	Y	Y	Y	Y	Y	Y	N		16
CHI Institute, RETS Campus	Broomall	T	Prop	M/W	650													
Churchman Business School	Easton	C,T	Prop	M/W	100		1	15		Y	Y	Y		Y	Y	N	1	5
Commonwealth Technical Institute	Johnstown	T	St	M/W	375													
Community College of Allegheny County†	Pittsburgh	C,T	Cou	M/W	16,999	61	48	39	Y		R	Y	Y	Y	Y	N	15	116
Community College of Beaver County	Monaca	C,T	St	M/W	2,260		56		Y		R	Y	Y	Y	Y	N	6	30
Community College of Philadelphia	Philadelphia																	
Consolidated School of Business	Lancaster	C,T	Prop	M/W	189		41		Y	Y	Y	Y		Y	Y	N		7
Consolidated School of Business	York	C,T	Prop	M/W	161		41		Y	Y	Y	Y		Y	Y	N		7
Dean Institute of Technology	Pittsburgh																	
Delaware County Community College	Media	C,T	St-L	M/W	9,467		46	70	Y	Y	Y	Y	Y	Y	Y	N	8	44
Douglas Education Center	Monessen	C,T	Prop	M/W	130		30					Y	Y					6
DuBois Business College	DuBois	T	Prop	PW	412		40		N	Y	Y	Y		Y	Y	Y	3	6
Duff's Business Institute	Pittsburgh	C,T	Prop	PW	500		40	10	N	Y		Y	Y	Y	Y	N	1	10
Education Direct	Scranton	T	Prop	M/W			80		Y	Y	Y					N		11
Electronic Institutes	Middletown	C,T	Ind	PM	50		11		N	Y	Y	Y		Y	Y	N		9
Erie Business Center, Main	Erie	T	Prop	M/W	375		38		N	Y	Y	Y	Y	Y	Y	Y		15
Erie Business Center South	New Castle	C,T	Prop	PW	98				N	Y		Y		Y	Y	N	4	10
Erie Institute of Technology	Erie	T	Prop	M/W	53													
Harcum College†	Bryn Mawr	C,T	Ind	PW	548	35	40			Y	Y	Y	Y	Y	Y	Y	6	20
Harrisburg Area Community College	Harrisburg	C,T	St-L	M/W	11,671	59	45	67	Y		Y	Y	Y	Y	Y	N	11	76
Hussian School of Art	Philadelphia	C,T,B	Prop	M/W	137		2		N	Y	Y	Y	Y	Y	Y	N		2
ICM School of Business & Medical Careers	Pittsburgh																	
Information Computer Systems Institute	Allentown	C,T	Priv		125		60											
International Academy of Design & Technology	Pittsburgh	T	Priv		954	12	70											2
ITT Technical Institute	Bensalem		Prop	M/W	48													2
ITT Technical Institute	Mechanicsburg	T	Prop	M/W	275						Y					N		4
ITT Technical Institute	Monroeville	T	Prop	M/W	516						Y					N		4
ITT Technical Institute	Pittsburgh	T	Prop	M/W	364						Y					N		4
Johnson College	Scranton	T	Ind	M/W	331	4	30		N	Y	Y	Y	Y	Y	Y	Y	8	22
Keystone College	La Plume	C,T,B	Ind	M/W	1,373	29	30	71	N	Y	Y	Y	Y	Y	Y	Y	14	31
Lackawanna College	Scranton	C,T	Ind	M/W	877													
Lansdale School of Business	North Wales																	
Laurel Business Institute	Uniontown	C,T	Prop	M/W	378				Y	Y	Y			Y	Y	N		29
Lehigh Carbon Community College	Schnecksville	C,T	St-L	M/W	4,958	66	62	23	Y		S	Y	Y	Y	Y	N	18	50
Lincoln Technical Institute	Allentown	T	Prop	M/W	600													
Lincoln Technical Institute	Philadelphia																	
Luzerne County Community College	Nanticoke	C,T	Cou	M/W	6,076		46		Y	Y	R	Y	Y	Y	Y	N	10	71
Manor College*†	Jenkintown	C,T	I-R	M/W	800		41	54	N	Y	Y	Y	Y	Y	Y	Y	3	28
McCann School of Business	Mahanoy City	C,T	Prop	M/W	297	34	51		Y	Y	Y	Y		Y	Y	N		10
Median School of Allied Health Careers	Pittsburgh	T	Prop	M/W	255													
Montgomery County Community College	Blue Bell	C,T	Cou	M/W	9,592	63	50	56	Y	Y	S	Y	Y	Y	Y	N	15	42
New Castle School of Trades	Pulaski																	
Newport Business Institute	Lower Burrell	C,T	Prop	M/W	146													
Newport Business Institute	Williamsport	T	Prop	PW	146	2	49		N	Y	Y	Y		Y	Y	N		4
Northampton County Area Community College	Bethlehem	C,T	St-L	M/W	6,216	57	39	70	Y	Y	Y	Y	Y	Y	Y	Y	12	48
Northwest Pennsylvania Technical Institute	Erie																	
Oakbridge Academy of Arts	Lower Burrell	C,T	Prop	M/W	97		28		N	Y	Y	Y		Y	Y	N		3
Orleans Technical Institute-Center City Campus	Philadelphia																	
Pace Institute	Reading	C,T	Priv	M/W	260		95					Y	Y					9
Penn Commercial Business and Technical School	Washington	C,T	Prop	M/W	268		50		Y	Y	Y	Y		Y	Y	N		7
Pennco Tech	Bristol																	
Pennsylvania College of Technology*†	Williamsport	C,T,B	St-R	M/W	5,538	20	23		Y	Y	Y	Y	Y	Y	Y	Y	17	81
Pennsylvania Institute of Culinary Arts	Pittsburgh	T	Prop	M/W	1,447		16		N	Y	Y	Y		Y	Y			2
Pennsylvania Institute of Technology	Media	C,T	Ind	M/W	335	50	47		Y	Y	Y	Y	Y	Y	Y	N	2	9
Penn State U Beaver Campus of the Commonwealth Coll	Monaca	C,T,B	St-R	M/W	752	9	5		N	Y	Y	Y	Y	Y	Y	Y	12	10
Penn State U Delaware County Campus of the Commonwealth Coll	Media	C,T,B	St-R	M/W	1,646	18	12		N	Y		Y	Y	Y	Y	N	12	10
Penn State U DuBois Campus of the Commonwealth Coll	DuBois	C,T,B	St-R	M/W	997	23	32		N	Y	Y	Y	Y	Y	Y	N	7	13
Penn State U Fayette Campus of the Commonwealth Coll	Uniontown	C,T,B	St-R	M/W	1,128	25	30		N	Y	Y	Y	Y	Y	Y	N	12	10
Penn State U Hazleton Campus of the Commonwealth Coll	Hazleton	C,T,B	St-R	M/W	1,342	7	7		N	Y	Y	Y	Y	Y	Y	Y	6	10
Penn State U McKeesport Campus of the Commonwealth Coll	McKeesport	C,T,B	St-R	M/W	941	13	7		N	Y	Y	Y	Y	Y	Y	Y	15	8
Penn State U Mont Alto Campus of the Commonwealth Coll	Mont Alto	C,T,B	St-R	M/W	1,105	25	22		N	N	Y	Y	Y	Y	Y	Y	11	10
Penn State U New Kensington Campus of the Commonwealth Coll	New Kensington	C,T,B	St-R	M/W	979	28	25		N	Y	Y	Y	Y	Y	Y	N	10	14
Penn State U Shenango Campus of the Commonwealth Coll	Sharon	C,T,B	St-R	M/W	984	41	45		N	Y	Y	Y	Y	Y	Y	N	6	11
Penn State U Wilkes-Barre Campus of the Commonwealth Coll	Lehman	C,T,B	St-R	M/W	832	22	17		N	Y	Y	Y	Y	Y	Y	N	8	9

This index includes the names and locations of accredited two-year colleges in the United States and U.S. territories and shows institutions' responses to our 2001 Survey of Undergraduate Institutions. If an institution submitted incomplete or no data, one or more columns opposite the institution's name is blank. An asterisk after the school name denotes a *Special Announcement* following the college's profile.

Y—Yes; N—No; R—Recommended; S—For Some

		Degrees Awarded Transfer Associate (C), Terminal Associate (T), Bachelor's (B), Master's (M), Doctoral (D), First Professional (F)	**Institutional Control** Independent, Independent-Religious, Proprietary, Federal, State, Province, Commonwealth, Territory, County, District, City, State and Local, State-Related	**Student Body** Men, Primarily Men, Women, Primarily Women, Coed	**Undergraduate Enrollment Fall 2001**	Percent Attending Part-Time	Percent 25 Years of Age or Older	Percent of Grads Going on to 4-Year Colleges	Open Admissions	High School Equivalency Certificate Accepted	High School Transcript Required	Need-based aid available	Part-Time Jobs Available	Career Counseling Available	Job Placement Services Available	College Housing Available	Number of Sports Offered	Number of Majors Offered
Penn State U Worthington Scranton Cmps Commonwealth Coll	Dunmore	C,T,B	St-R	M/W	1,520	23	21		N	Y	Y	Y	Y	Y	Y	N	7	9
Penn State U York Campus of the Commonwealth Coll	York	C,T,B	St-R	M/W	1,729	47	38		N	Y	Y	Y	Y	Y	Y	N	9	9
Pittsburgh Institute of Aeronautics	Pittsburgh	C	Ind	PM	397		30		Y	Y	R			Y	Y	N		3
Pittsburgh Institute of Mortuary Science, Inc	Pittsburgh	C,T	Ind	M/W	132	8	48	6	Y	Y	Y	Y		Y	Y	N		1
Pittsburgh Technical Institute	Pittsburgh	T	Prop	M/W	2,108		16		N	Y	Y	Y	Y	Y	Y	Y	3	24
Reading Area Community College	Reading	C,T	Cou	M/W	3,000		56		Y	Y		Y	Y	Y	Y	N	4	53
The Restaurant School†	Philadelphia	T,B	Prop	M/W	585		21		Y	Y	Y	Y		Y	Y	Y		2
Schuylkill Institute of Business and Technology	Pottsville	C,T	Prop	M/W	185		55					Y						4
South Hills School of Business & Technology	Altoona	C,T	Prop	M/W	99	6	54	1			Y	Y				N		4
South Hills School of Business & Technology	State College	C,T	Prop	M/W	594	10	30	2	N	Y	Y	Y		Y	Y	N		10
Thaddeus Stevens College of Technology	Lancaster	C,T	St	M/W	591		8	10	N	Y	Y	Y		Y	Y	Y	15	20
Thompson Institute	Harrisburg																	
Triangle Tech, Inc.	Pittsburgh	C,T	Prop	PM	259		35		N	Y	Y	Y	Y	Y	Y	N		6
Triangle Tech, Inc.–DuBois School	DuBois	T	Prop	M/W	339		20		N	Y	Y	Y		Y	Y	N		4
Triangle Tech, Inc.–Erie School	Erie	C,T	Prop	PM	140		65	2	N	Y	Y	Y	Y	Y	Y	N	5	4
Triangle Tech, Inc.–Greensburg Center	Greensburg	T	Prop	M/W	170	5	20		N	Y		Y	Y	Y	Y			4
Tri-State Business Institute	Erie																	
University of Pittsburgh at Titusville	Titusville	C,T	St-R	M/W	513	33		13	N	Y	Y	Y	Y	Y	Y	Y	11	5
Valley Forge Military College*†	Wayne	C	Ind	M	120		1	98	N	Y	Y	Y	Y	Y		Y	14	5
Western School of Health and Business Careers	Pittsburgh	T	Prop	M/W	600		50	18		Y	Y	Y	Y	Y	Y	N	1	10
Westmoreland County Community College	Youngwood	C,T	Cou	M/W	5,700		47		Y	Y		Y	Y	Y	Y	N	12	53
The Williamson Free School of Mechanical Trades	Media	T	Ind	M	253													
York Technical Institute	York	T	Priv		740		15		Y	Y	Y	Y	Y	Y	Y			10
Yorktowne Business Institute	York	C,T	Prop	M/W	286	34	60		N	Y	Y	Y		Y	Y	N		9
Rhode Island																		
Community College of Rhode Island	Warwick	C,T	St	M/W	16,223	66	43		Y			Y	Y	Y	Y	N	11	43
New England Institute of Technology	Warwick	C,T,B	Ind	M/W	2,430		48		Y	Y	Y	Y	Y	Y	Y	N		17
South Carolina																		
Aiken Technical College	Aiken																	
Central Carolina Technical College	Sumter	C,T	St	M/W	2,963	67	37	11	Y	Y	Y	Y	Y	Y	Y	N		16
Columbia Junior College	Columbia	T	Prop	M/W	177	25												
Denmark Technical College	Denmark	C,T	St	M/W	1,401		20		Y	Y	Y	Y	Y	Y	Y	Y	5	7
Florence-Darlington Technical College	Florence	C,T	St	M/W	3,632	44			Y		S	Y	Y	Y	Y	N		29
Forrest Junior College	Anderson	C,T	Prop	PM	225			2		Y	Y	Y	Y	Y	Y	N		1
Greenville Technical College	Greenville	C,T	St	M/W	11,500		42		Y	Y	Y	Y	Y	Y	Y	N	4	33
Horry-Georgetown Technical College	Conway	C,T	St-L	M/W	4,113	55			Y		S	Y	Y	Y	Y	N		25
ITT Technical Institute	Greenville	T	Prop		245				N	Y	Y	Y	Y		Y	N		5
Midlands Technical College	Columbia	C,T	St-L	M/W	9,874	57	40		Y	Y	R	Y	Y	Y	Y	N	4	30
Northeastern Technical College	Cheraw	C,T	St-L	M/W	967	70	54		Y	Y	Y	Y	Y	Y	Y	N		11
Orangeburg-Calhoun Technical College	Orangeburg	C,T	St-L	M/W	2,020	49	42		Y	Y	Y	Y	Y	Y	Y	N		20
Piedmont Technical College	Greenwood	C,T	St	M/W	4,544		38		Y	Y	Y	Y	Y	Y	Y	N	4	35
Spartanburg Methodist College*†	Spartanburg	C,T	I-R	M/W	635	9	4	94	N	Y	Y	Y	Y	Y	Y	Y	11	4
Spartanburg Technical College	Spartanburg	C,T	St	M/W	3,359		39		Y	Y	Y	Y	Y	Y	Y	N		24
Technical College of the Lowcountry	Beaufort																	
Tri-County Technical College	Pendleton	C,T	St	M/W	3,773		38		Y	Y		Y	Y	Y	Y	N		20
Trident Technical College	Charleston	C,T	St-L	M/W	10,461	64	47		Y	Y	S	Y	Y	Y	Y	N		40
U of South Carolina at Beaufort	Beaufort	C	St	M/W	1,070	62			Y	Y	Y	Y	Y	Y	Y	N		1
U of South Carolina at Lancaster	Lancaster	C,T	St	M/W	939		37	42	Y	Y	Y	Y	Y	Y		N	6	6
U of South Carolina Salkehatchie Regional Cmps	Allendale																	
U of South Carolina at Sumter	Sumter	C	St	M/W	1,229	37	35	68	N	Y	Y	Y	Y	Y		N	10	2
U of South Carolina at Union	Union	C	St	M/W	382		35		N	Y	Y	Y	Y			N		2
Williamsburg Technical College	Kingstree	C,T	St	PW	661	58												
York Technical College	Rock Hill	C,T	St	M/W	3,700		39		Y		S	Y	Y	Y	Y	N		27
South Dakota																		
Kilian Community College	Sioux Falls	C,T	Ind	M/W	303		52		Y	Y	Y	Y	Y	Y	Y	N		12
Lake Area Technical Institute	Watertown	T	St	M/W	1,057				N	Y	Y	Y	Y	Y	Y	N	3	27
Mitchell Technical Institute	Mitchell	C,T	Dist	M/W	868		20	2	Y	Y	Y	Y	Y	Y	Y		4	21
Sisseton-Wahpeton Community College	Sisseton	C,T	Fed	M/W	229	39												
Southeast Technical Institute	Sioux Falls	T	St	M/W	2,246	25	18		N	Y	Y	Y	Y	Y	Y	N	2	51
Western Dakota Technical Institute	Rapid City	T	St	M/W	1,052	30	33	4	Y		Y	Y	Y	Y	Y			17
Tennessee																		
American Academy of Nutrition, Coll of Nutrition	Knoxville	C,T	Prop	M/W	251		90		Y		S							1
Chattanooga State Technical Community College	Chattanooga	C,T	St	M/W	9,600		52		Y	Y	Y	Y	Y	Y	Y	N	5	63
Cleveland State Community College	Cleveland	C,T	St	M/W	3,177	46	38	30	Y	Y	Y	Y	Y	Y	Y	N	10	10
Columbia State Community College	Columbia	C,T	St	M/W	4,451		28		Y	Y	Y	Y	Y	Y	Y	N	5	33
Draughons Junior College	Clarksville	T	Prop	M/W	340				Y	Y	Y	Y	Y					14
Draughons Junior College	Nashville	C,T	Prop	M/W	600		50		Y	Y	Y	Y	Y	Y	Y	N		12
Dyersburg State Community College	Dyersburg	C,T	St	M/W	2,284	44	43		Y	Y	Y	Y	Y	Y	Y	N	3	8
Education America, Southeast College of Technology, Memphis Campus	Memphis	C,B	Prop		600													
Electronic Computer Programming College	Chattanooga	C	Prop		160		60					Y						3

This index includes the names and locations of accredited two-year colleges in the United States and U.S. territories and shows institutions' responses to our 2001 Survey of Undergraduate Institutions. If an institution submitted incomplete or no data, one or more columns opposite the institution's name is blank. An asterisk after the school name denotes a *Special Announcement* following the college's profile.

Y—Yes; N—No; R—Recommended; S—For Some

Institution	Location	Degrees Awarded: Transfer Associate (C), Terminal Associate (T), Bachelor's (B), Master's (M), Doctoral (D), First Professional (F)	Institutional Control: Independent, Independent-Religious, Proprietary, Federal, State, Province, Commonwealth, Territory, County, District, City, State and Local, State-Related	Student Body: Men, Primarily Men, Women, Primarily Women, Coed	Undergraduate Enrollment Fall 2001	Percent Attending Part-Time	Percent 25 Years of Age or Older	Percent of Grads Going on to 4-Year Colleges	Open Admissions	High School Equivalency Certificate Accepted	High School Transcript Required	Need-based aid available	Part-Time Jobs Available	Career Counseling Available	Job Placement Services Available	College Housing Available	Number of Sports Offered	Number of Majors Offered
Hiwassee College	Madisonville	C,T	I-R	M/W	393	17	8	72	N	Y	Y	Y	Y	Y		Y	8	4
ITT Technical Institute	Knoxville	T,B	Prop	M/W	475				N	Y	Y	Y	Y	Y	Y	N		5
ITT Technical Institute	Memphis	T	Prop	M/W	283				N	Y	Y	Y	Y	Y	Y	N		5
ITT Technical Institute	Nashville	T,B	Prop	M/W	560				N	Y	Y	Y	Y	Y	Y	N		5
Jackson State Community College	Jackson	C,T	St	M/W	3,933	47	37	67	Y	Y	S	Y	Y	Y	Y	N	7	11
John A. Gupton College	Nashville	C	Ind	M/W	83	28	27	8	N	Y	Y	Y		Y	Y	Y		1
MedVance Institute	Cookeville	T	Prop	PW	231		46		N	Y	Y	Y		Y	Y	N		2
Mid-America Baptist Theological Seminary	Germantown	T,M,D,F	I-R	PM	58	48	100		Y	Y	Y	Y		Y	Y			1
Miller-Motte Business College	Clarksville																	
Motlow State Community College	Tullahoma	C,T	St	M/W	3,586	46	36	76	Y	Y	Y	Y	Y	Y	Y	N	9	4
Nashville Auto Diesel College	Nashville	T	Prop	PM	1,306		5		N	Y	Y	Y	Y	Y	Y	Y		3
Nashville State Technical Institute	Nashville	T	St	M/W	7,017	74	61		Y	Y	Y	Y	Y	Y	Y	N	2	19
National College of Business & Technology	Nashville	T	Prop	M/W					Y	Y		Y	Y	Y	Y	N		4
North Central Institute	Clarksville	T	Prop	PM	134	56	50		Y	Y		Y		Y	Y	N		2
Northeast State Technical Community College	Blountville	C,T	St	M/W	4,462	49	21	90	Y	Y	Y	Y	Y	Y	Y	N	3	22
Nossi College of Art	Goodlettsville	T	Ind	M/W	250		70		N	Y		Y						2
Pellissippi State Technical Community College	Knoxville	C,T	St	M/W	7,833		40		Y	Y	Y	Y	Y	Y	Y	N	6	39
Roane State Community College	Harriman	C,T	St	M/W	5,233	46	46		Y	Y	Y	Y	Y	Y	Y	N	5	38
South College	Knoxville	C,T	Prop	PW	411		50		N	Y	Y	Y	Y	Y	Y	N		12
Southwest Tennessee Community College	Memphis	T	St	M/W	12,736	60	41		Y	Y	Y	Y	Y	Y	Y	N	2	35
Tennessee Institute of Electronics	Knoxville	C,T,B	Prop	M/W			20		Y	Y	R	Y		Y	Y	N		4
Volunteer State Community College	Gallatin	C,T	St	M/W	6,822	54	40		Y	Y	Y	Y	Y	Y	Y	N	3	11
Walters State Community College	Morristown	C,T	St	M/W	5,995		42	85	Y	Y	Y	Y	Y	Y	Y	N	3	20
Texas																		
Alvin Community College	Alvin	C,T	St-L	M/W	3,671	61	41			Y	S	Y	Y	Y	Y	N	4	33
Amarillo College	Amarillo	C,T	St-L	M/W	8,650		43	52	Y		Y	Y	Y	Y	Y	Y	3	83
Angelina College	Lufkin	C,T	St-L	M/W	4,418		33		Y	Y	Y	Y	Y	Y	Y	Y	8	60
The Art Institute of Dallas	Dallas																	
The Art Institute of Houston	Houston	C,T,B	Prop	M/W	1,679	17	31		N	Y	Y	Y	Y	Y	Y	Y	4	9
Austin Business College	Austin	T	Prop	M/W	252	20	70		Y	Y	Y	Y	Y	Y	Y			2
Austin Community College	Austin	C,T	Dist	M/W	27,548		39		Y	Y		Y	Y	Y		N	6	75
Blinn College	Brenham	C,T	St-L	M/W	12,025	42	18	55	Y	Y	Y	Y		Y	Y	Y	7	34
Border Institute of Technology	El Paso	C,T	Prop		200													
Brazosport College	Lake Jackson	C,T	St-L	M/W	4,022	73	34	22	Y	Y	S	Y		Y	Y	N	11	55
Brookhaven College	Farmers Branch																	
Cedar Valley College	Lancaster	C,T	St	M/W	3,974	72			Y	Y	R	Y	Y	Y	Y	N	3	16
Center for Advanced Legal Studies	Houston																	
Central Texas College	Killeen	C,T	St-L	M/W	15,473	82	55	11	Y	Y	Y	Y	Y	Y	Y	Y	10	48
Cisco Junior College	Cisco	C,T	St-L	M/W	2,616		45		Y	Y		Y	Y	Y		Y	7	35
Clarendon College	Clarendon	C,T	St-L	M/W	1,000													
Coastal Bend College	Beeville	C,T	Cou	M/W	3,259	54	41	72	Y	Y	Y	Y	Y	Y	Y	Y	13	67
College of the Mainland	Texas City	C,T	St-L	M/W	3,400													
Collin County Community College District	Plano	C,T	St-L	M/W	14,497	62	38		Y		Y	Y	Y	Y	Y	N	5	29
Commonwealth Institute of Funeral Service	Houston	T	Ind	M/W	123		48		N	Y	Y	Y		Y	Y	N		1
Computer Career Center	El Paso	C,T	Prop	M/W	300													
Court Reporting Institute of Dallas	Dallas	C,T	Priv	PW	600		68				Y	Y				N		1
Cy-Fair College	Houston	C,T	St-L	M/W														
Dallas Institute of Funeral Service	Dallas																	
Del Mar College	Corpus Christi	C,T	St-L	M/W	10,256		42		Y	Y	Y	Y	Y	Y	Y	N	14	86
Eastfield College	Mesquite	C,T	St-L	M/W	9,210	67	35	60	Y	Y	R	Y	Y	Y	Y	N	7	29
Education America, Dallas Campus	Garland																	
Education America, Fort Worth Campus	Fort Worth																	
Education America, Houston Campus	Houston																	
El Centro College	Dallas	C,T	Cou	M/W	4,923	68	56	30	Y	Y	S	Y	Y	Y	Y	N	3	45
El Paso Community College	El Paso	C,T	Cou	M/W	18,566	56												
Frank Phillips College	Borger																	
Galveston College	Galveston	C,T	St-L	M/W	2,255	70	45		Y	Y	S	Y	Y	Y	Y	N	5	33
Grayson County College	Denison	C,T	St-L	M/W	3,471	53	53		Y	Y		Y	Y	Y		Y	2	39
Hallmark Institute of Aeronautics	San Antonio																	
Hallmark Institute of Technology	San Antonio																	
Hill College of the Hill Junior College District	Hillsboro	C,T	Dist	M/W	2,421	60	20	40	Y	Y	Y	Y	Y	Y	Y	Y	5	87
Houston Community College System	Houston	C,T	St-L	M/W	38,175	70	54	25	Y	Y	S	Y	Y	Y	Y	N		65
Howard College	Big Spring	C,T	St-L	M/W	2,135	55	33		Y	Y	Y	Y	Y	Y	Y	Y	7	31
ITT Technical Institute	Arlington	T	Prop	M/W	475				N	Y	Y			Y	Y	N		5
ITT Technical Institute	Austin	T	Prop	M/W	644				N	Y	Y	Y	Y	Y	Y	N		5
ITT Technical Institute	Houston	T	Prop		466				N	Y	Y	Y	Y	Y	Y	N		5
ITT Technical Institute	Houston	T	Prop	M/W	567				N	Y	Y		Y	Y	Y	N		5
ITT Technical Institute	Houston	T	Prop	M/W	569				N	Y	Y		Y	Y	Y	N		5
ITT Technical Institute	Richardson	T	Prop	M/W	567				N	Y	Y	Y	Y	Y	Y	N		5
ITT Technical Institute	San Antonio	T	Prop	M/W	699				N	Y	Y	Y	Y	Y	Y	N		5
Jacksonville College	Jacksonville	C,T	I-R	M/W	259	24	12		Y	Y		Y	Y	Y		Y	4	2
KD Studio	Dallas	T	Prop	M/W	148		20	5	Y	Y	Y	Y		Y		N		1
Kilgore College	Kilgore	C,T	St-L	M/W	4,194	47	31		Y	Y	Y	Y	Y	Y	Y	Y	7	65
Kingwood College	Kingwood	C,T	St-L	M/W	5,302	66	34		Y	Y	Y	Y	Y	Y		N	1	17
Lamar Institute of Technology	Beaumont																	
Lamar State College–Orange	Orange	C,T	St	M/W	2,020		38		Y	Y	Y	Y	Y	Y		N	4	16
Lamar State College–Port Arthur	Port Arthur	C,T	St	M/W	2,497		43		Y		Y	Y	Y	Y	Y	N		31
Laredo Community College	Laredo	C,T	St-L	M/W			35		Y		Y	Y	Y	Y	Y	Y	7	29

This index includes the names and locations of accredited two-year colleges in the United States and U.S. territories and shows institutions' responses to our 2001 Survey of Undergraduate Institutions. If an institution submitted incomplete or no data, one or more columns opposite the institution's name is blank. An asterisk after the school name denotes a *Special Announcement* following the college's profile.

Y—Yes; N—No; R—Recommended; S—For Some

Institution	Location	Degrees Awarded: Transfer Associate (C), Terminal Associate (T), Bachelor's (B), Master's (M), Doctoral (D), First Professional (F)	Institutional Control: County, District, City, State and Local, State-Related; Federal, State, Province, Commonwealth, Territory; Independent, Independent-Religious, Proprietary	Student Body: Men, Primarily Men, Women, Primarily Women, Coed	Undergraduate Enrollment Fall 2001	Percent Attending Part-Time	Percent 25 Years of Age or Older	Percent of Grads Going on to 4-Year Colleges	Open Admissions	High School Equivalency Certificate Accepted	High School Transcript Required	Need-based aid available	Part-Time Jobs Available	Career Counseling Available	Job Placement Services Available	College Housing Available	Number of Sports Offered	Number of Majors Offered
Lee College	Baytown																	
Lon Morris College	Jacksonville	T	I-R	M/W			1			Y	Y	Y	Y	Y		Y	10	49
McLennan Community College	Waco	C,T	Cou	M/W	6,133		42		Y	Y	Y	Y	Y	Y	Y	N	7	26
Midland College	Midland	C,T	St-L	M/W	5,034		45		Y		Y	Y	Y	Y	Y	Y	7	67
Montgomery College	Conroe	C,T	St-L	M/W	5,312	64												
Mountain View College	Dallas	C,T	St-L	M/W	6,350		41		Y	Y	Y	Y	Y	Y	Y	N	6	16
MTI College of Business and Technology	Houston																	
MTI College of Business and Technology	Houston	T	Prop	M/W	362		40		N	Y	Y	Y	Y	Y	Y	N		2
Navarro College	Corsicana	C,T	St-L	M/W	4,411	43	35		Y	Y	Y	Y	Y	Y	Y	Y	9	56
North Central Texas College	Gainesville	C,T	Cou	M/W	5,180		33		Y	Y	Y	Y	Y	Y		Y	8	44
Northeast Texas Community College	Mount Pleasant	C,T	St-L	M/W	2,212		48		Y	Y		Y	Y	Y	Y	Y	4	16
North Harris College	Houston	C,T	St-L	M/W	9,127	74	41		Y	Y	S	Y	Y	Y	Y	N	15	41
North Lake College	Irving	C,T	Cou	M/W	8,000													
Odessa College	Odessa	C,T	St-L	M/W	4,579		36	42	Y	Y		Y	Y	Y	Y	Y	11	57
Palo Alto College	San Antonio	C,T	St-L	M/W														
Panola College	Carthage	C,T	St-L	M/W	1,424	37												
Paris Junior College	Paris	C,T	St-L	M/W	2,850													
Ranger College	Ranger	C,T	St-R	M/W	843				Y	Y		Y	Y	Y	Y	Y	8	6
Richland College	Dallas																	
St. Philip's College	San Antonio	C,T	Dist	M/W	8,326	60	47		Y	Y	Y	Y	Y	Y	Y	N	5	75
San Antonio College	San Antonio	C,T	St-L	M/W	21,853		62		Y	Y			Y	Y	Y	N	10	47
San Jacinto College Central Campus	Pasadena	C,T	St-L	M/W	10,854	61	48		Y	Y	Y	Y	Y	Y	Y	N	7	84
San Jacinto College North Campus	Houston	C,T	St-L	M/W	5,020	61	37		Y	Y	Y	Y	Y	Y	Y	N	11	65
San Jacinto College South Campus	Houston	C,T	St-L	M/W	6,269	60	42		Y	Y		Y	Y	Y	Y	N	10	38
South Plains College	Levelland	C,T	St-L	M/W	8,574		39	90	Y	Y	Y	Y	Y	Y	Y	Y	10	59
South Texas Community College	McAllen	C,T	Dist	M/W	12,469	56	35		Y	Y	Y	Y	Y	Y		N	10	26
Southwest School of Electronics	Austin																	
Southwest Texas Junior College	Uvalde																	
Tarrant County College District	Fort Worth	C,T	Cou	M/W	28,751		44	65	Y			Y	Y	Y	Y	N	6	43
Temple College	Temple	C,T	Dist	M/W	3,585	61	54		Y		S	Y	Y	Y	Y	Y	8	20
Texarkana College	Texarkana	C,T	St-L	M/W	3,875		42	25	Y	Y	Y	Y	Y	Y	Y		7	34
Texas Culinary Academy	Austin	C,T	Ind	M/W	200						Y	Y						1
Texas Southmost College	Brownsville																	
Texas State Tech Coll–Harlingen	Harlingen	C,T	St	M/W	3,846	48	31		Y	Y	Y	Y	Y	Y	Y	Y	14	45
Texas State Tech Coll– Waco/Marshall Campus	Waco	C,T	St	M/W	1,038	11	36		Y	Y	Y	Y	Y	Y	Y	Y	7	45
Texas State Tech Coll	Sweetwater	T	St	M/W	1,607	35	45		Y	Y	Y	Y	Y	Y	Y	Y	11	13
Tomball College	Tomball	C,T	St-L	M/W	8,357	65	32	77	Y	Y		Y	Y	Y		N		10
Trinity Valley Community College	Athens	C,T	St-L	M/W	4,605		48		Y	Y		Y	Y	Y	Y	Y	6	54
Tyler Junior College	Tyler	C,T	St-L	M/W	8,451	42	50		Y	Y	Y	Y	Y	Y	Y	Y	9	59
Universal Technical Institute	Houston																	
Vernon College	Vernon	C,T	St-L	M/W	2,270		47		Y	Y		Y	Y	Y	Y	Y	9	16
Victoria College	Victoria	C,T	Cou	M/W	4,010		49		Y	Y	Y	Y	Y	Y	Y	N	2	16
Wade College†	Dallas	C,T	Prop	PW	87		14		Y	Y	Y	Y	Y	Y	Y	Y		6
Weatherford College	Weatherford	C,T	St-L	M/W	3,172				Y	Y		Y	Y	Y	Y	Y	3	15
Western Technical Institute	El Paso		Priv															
Western Technical Institute	El Paso																	
Western Texas College	Snyder	C,T	St-L	M/W	1,404		39		Y	Y	Y	Y	Y	Y	Y	Y	11	22
Westwood College of Aviation Technology–Houston†	Houston	C	Prop	M/W	380													2
Westwood Institute of Technology–Fort Worth†	Euless	C	Prop	M/W														3
Wharton County Junior College	Wharton	C,T	St-L	M/W	5,281		30		Y	Y	Y	Y	Y	Y	Y	Y	2	29
Utah																		
Certified Careers Institute	Salt Lake City	T	Prop	M/W	300				Y	Y	S	Y		Y	Y	N		8
College of Eastern Utah	Price	C,T	St	M/W	2,742	38	36	60	Y	Y	R	Y	Y	Y	Y	Y	7	15
Dixie State College of Utah	St. George	C,T,B	St	M/W	7,001	55	17		Y	Y	Y	Y	Y	Y	Y	Y	8	78
ITT Technical Institute	Murray	T,B	Prop	M/W	472				N	Y	Y	Y	Y	Y	Y	N		6
LDS Business College	Salt Lake City	C,T	I-R	M/W	422	14	29		Y	Y	Y	Y		Y	Y	Y		11
Mountain West College	West Valley City	C,T	Prop	M/W	404	45	42		N	Y	Y	Y	Y	Y	Y	N		8
Salt Lake Community College	Salt Lake City	C,T	St	M/W	21,596	68												
Snow College	Ephraim	C,T	St	M/W	2,999	18		38	Y	Y	Y	Y	Y	Y		Y	12	67
Stevens-Henager College	Ogden	T	Prop	M/W	400													
Utah Career College	West Jordan																	
Utah Valley State College	Orem	C,T,B	St	M/W	20,946	54												
Vermont																		
Community College of Vermont	Waterbury	C,T	St	M/W	5,000		64		Y	Y		Y	Y	Y		N		15
Landmark College	Putney	C,T	Ind	M/W	367		6	90	N	Y	Y	Y	Y	Y		Y	10	1
New England Culinary Institute*	Montpelier	T,B	Prop	M/W	639		58	14	N	Y	Y	Y	Y	Y	Y	Y		3
Vermont Technical College*	Randolph Center	C,T,B	St	M/W	1,272	30	22	18	N	Y	Y	Y	Y	Y	Y	Y	19	25
Woodbury College	Montpelier	C,T,B	Ind	M/W	157		87		Y	Y	S	Y	Y	Y		N		4
Virginia																		
Blue Ridge Community College	Weyers Cave	C,T	St	M/W	1,090	56	36		Y	Y	S	Y	Y	Y	Y	N	2	12
Bryant and Stratton College, Richmond	Richmond	T	Prop	M/W	234	40												
Bryant and Stratton College, Virginia Beach	Virginia Beach	T,B	Prop	M/W	297	33	45		N	Y	S		Y	Y	Y	N		11
Central Virginia Community College	Lynchburg	C,T	St	M/W	4,791		42	24	Y		S	Y	Y	Y	Y	N		23
Dabney S. Lancaster Community College	Clifton Forge																	

This index includes the names and locations of accredited two-year colleges in the United States and U.S. territories and shows institutions' responses to our 2001 Survey of Undergraduate Institutions. If an institution submitted incomplete or no data, one or more columns opposite the institution's name is blank. An asterisk after the school name denotes a *Special Announcement* following the college's profile.

Y—Yes; N—No; R—Recommended; S—For Some

College	Location	Degrees Awarded: Transfer Associate (C), Terminal Associate (T), Bachelor's (B), Master's (M), Doctoral (D), First Professional (F)	Institutional Control: Independent, Independent-Religious, Proprietary, Federal, State, Province, Commonwealth, Territory, County, District, City, State and Local, State-Related	Student Body: Men, Primarily Men, Women, Primarily Women, Coed	Undergraduate Enrollment Fall 2001	Percent Attending Part-Time	Percent 25 Years of Age or Older	Percent of Grads Going on to 4-Year Colleges	Open Admissions	High School Equivalency Certificate Accepted	High School Transcript Required	Need-based aid available	Part-Time Jobs Available	Career Counseling Available	Job Placement Services Available	College Housing Available	Number of Sports Offered	Number of Majors Offered
Danville Community College	Danville	C,T	St	M/W	3,879	70	58		Y	Y	Y	Y	Y	Y	Y	N	6	9
Dominion College	Roanoke	T	Prop	M/W	197		6		N	Y	Y			Y	Y			4
Eastern Shore Community College	Melfa	C,T	St	M/W	884	79	45	90	Y	Y	Y	Y	Y	Y	Y	N	2	9
ECPI College of Technology	Newport News	T	Prop	M/W			64		N	Y	Y	Y	Y	Y	Y	N		17
ECPI College of Technology	Virginia Beach	T	Prop	M/W			72		N	Y	Y	Y	Y	Y	Y	N		20
ECPI Technical College	Richmond	T	Prop	M/W	680		50		N	Y	Y	Y	Y	Y	Y	N		19
ECPI Technical College	Roanoke	T	Prop	M/W	241		50		N	Y		Y	Y	Y	Y	N		15
Germanna Community College	Locust Grove	C,T	St	M/W	5,637		53	80	Y		S	Y	Y	Y	Y	N	7	11
ITT Technical Institute	Norfolk	T,B	Prop	M/W	381				N	Y	Y	Y	Y	Y	Y	N		5
ITT Technical Institute	Richmond	T	Prop	M/W	222						Y					N		5
John Tyler Community College	Chester	C,T	St	M/W	5,656		51		Y		R	Y	Y	Y		N	4	14
J. Sargeant Reynolds Community College	Richmond	C,T	St	M/W	11,079	76	49	75	Y	Y	Y	Y	Y	Y	Y	N	7	39
Lord Fairfax Community College	Middletown	C,T	St	M/W	4,587	74	49		Y		R	Y	Y	Y		N		21
Mountain Empire Community College	Big Stone Gap	C,T	St	M/W	2,900	55	30	90	Y	Y	Y	Y	Y	Y	Y	N	5	34
National College of Business & Technology	Bluefield	T	Prop	M/W					Y	Y		Y	Y	Y	Y	N		5
National College of Business & Technology	Bristol	T	Prop	M/W					Y	Y	Y	Y	Y	Y	Y	N		5
National College of Business & Technology	Charlottesville	T	Prop	M/W					Y	Y	S	Y	Y	Y	Y			5
National College of Business & Technology	Danville	T	Prop	M/W					Y	Y	S	Y	Y	Y	Y			5
National College of Business & Technology	Harrisonburg	T	Prop	M/W					Y	Y	S	Y	Y	Y	Y	N		5
National College of Business & Technology	Lynchburg	T	Prop	M/W			24		Y	Y	S	Y	Y	Y	Y	N		5
National College of Business & Technology	Martinsville	T	Prop	M/W					Y	Y	S	Y	Y	Y	Y	N		4
National College of Business & Technology	Salem	C,T,B	Prop	M/W					Y	Y	Y	Y	Y	Y	Y	Y		12
New River Community College	Dublin	C,T	St	M/W	3,947	55	40	68	Y		S	Y	Y	Y	Y	N	10	30
Northern Virginia Community College	Annandale	C,T	St	M/W	37,073		57		Y	Y	S	Y	Y	Y	Y	N	4	55
Patrick Henry Community College	Martinsville	C,T	St	M/W	3,024	74	58		Y	Y	Y	Y	Y	Y	Y	N	7	15
Paul D. Camp Community College	Franklin	C,T	St	M/W	1,552		55	45	Y	Y	Y	Y	Y	Y	Y	N		6
Piedmont Virginia Community College	Charlottesville	C,T	St	M/W	4,171	79	52	23	Y	Y	S	Y	Y	Y	Y	N	10	18
Rappahannock Community College	Glenns	C,T	St-R	M/W	2,615		68		Y			Y	Y	Y	Y	N	6	9
Richard Bland Coll of the Coll of William and Mary	Petersburg	C	St	M/W	1,304	42	18	68	N	Y	Y	Y	Y	Y		N	5	1
Southside Virginia Community College	Alberta	C,T	St	M/W	4,313	75	48		Y	Y	Y	Y	Y	Y	Y	N	5	14
Southwest Virginia Community College	Richlands	C,T	St	M/W	4,621		57		Y	Y	Y	Y	Y	Y	Y	N	10	18
Stratford University	Falls Church	C,T,M	Prop	M/W	851		61			Y	Y			Y	Y	N		7
Thomas Nelson Community College	Hampton	C,T	St	M/W	7,885	68			Y		Y	Y	Y	Y	Y	N	5	23
Tidewater Community College	Norfolk	C,T	St	M/W	22,091		53	65	Y			Y	Y	Y	Y	N	2	21
Virginia Highlands Community College	Abingdon	C,T	St	M/W	3,867													
Virginia Western Community College	Roanoke	C,T	St	M/W	8,311		54		Y	Y	Y	Y	Y	Y	Y	N	1	25
Wytheville Community College	Wytheville	C,T	St	M/W	2,450													
Washington																		
The Art Institute of Seattle†	Seattle	T	Prop	M/W	2,480	34	32			Y	Y	Y	Y	Y	Y	Y	2	10
Bates Technical College	Tacoma	C,T	St	M/W	16,162							Y	Y			N		26
Bellevue Community College	Bellevue	C,T	St	M/W	21,700		47		Y			Y	Y	Y	Y	N	10	19
Bellingham Technical College	Bellingham		St		3,791	81												
Big Bend Community College	Moses Lake	C,T	St	M/W	1,912	37	30		Y		S	Y	Y	Y	Y	Y	4	14
Cascadia Community College	Bothell	C	St	M/W	2,011	32										N		3
Centralia College	Centralia	C,T	St	M/W	3,823		51		Y	Y	Y	Y	Y	Y	Y	N	5	67
Clark College	Vancouver	C,T	St	M/W	9,274	59	37		Y		S	Y	Y	Y	Y	N	9	57
Clover Park Technical College	Lakewood	T	St		7,429	77	58		Y	Y	S	Y	Y	Y	Y	N		24
Columbia Basin College	Pasco	C,T	St	M/W	5,837	58												
Court Reporting Institute	Seattle																	
Crown College	Tacoma	T,B	Prop	M/W	199		59			Y	Y	Y	Y	Y	Y	N		4
Edmonds Community College	Lynnwood	C,T	St-L	M/W	7,738	58	55	25	Y			Y	Y	Y	Y	N	10	32
Everett Community College	Everett	C,T	St	M/W	7,227	56	37		Y		R	Y	Y	Y	Y	N	13	73
Grays Harbor College	Aberdeen	C,T	St	M/W	565			40	Y	Y	R	Y	Y	Y	Y	N	7	18
Green River Community College	Auburn	C,T	St	M/W	6,566		31		Y	Y	S	Y	Y	Y	Y	N	10	24
Highline Community College*	Des Moines	C,T	St	M/W	6,372	49	52		Y			Y	Y	Y	Y	N	7	48
ITT Technical Institute	Bothell	T	Prop		242				N	Y	Y			Y	Y	N		5
ITT Technical Institute	Seattle	T,B	Prop	M/W	436				N	Y	Y	Y	Y	Y	Y	N		5
ITT Technical Institute	Spokane	T	Prop	M/W	422				N	Y	Y	Y	Y	Y	Y	N		6
Lake Washington Technical College	Kirkland	T	Dist	M/W	4,934		64		Y		S	Y	Y	Y		N		19
Lower Columbia College	Longview	C,T	St	M/W	3,651	48	47	72	Y		R	Y	Y	Y	Y	N	4	44
North Seattle Community College	Seattle	C,T	St	M/W	6,340	61	55	40	Y		Y	Y	Y	Y	Y	N	7	39
Northwest Aviation College	Auburn																	
Northwest Indian College	Bellingham																	
Olympic College	Bremerton	C,T	St	M/W	5,613		49	31	Y		S	Y	Y	Y	Y	N	4	28
Peninsula College	Port Angeles	C,T	St	M/W	4,355	67	63		Y		S	Y	Y	Y	Y	Y	12	19
Pierce College	Lakewood	C,T	St	M/W	13,294		56		Y			Y	Y	Y	Y	N	5	20
Pima Medical Institute	Seattle																	
Renton Technical College	Renton	T	St	M/W	5,424													
Seattle Central Community College	Seattle	C,T	St	M/W	10,500		63		Y			Y	Y	Y		N	6	25
Shoreline Community College	Seattle	C	St	M/W	7,000		45		Y		Y	Y	Y	Y	Y	N	14	42
Skagit Valley College	Mount Vernon	C,T	St	M/W	6,174		68		Y		S	Y	Y	Y	Y	Y	12	65
South Puget Sound Community College	Olympia	C,T	St	M/W	5,678		54		Y			Y	Y	Y	Y	N	3	30
South Seattle Community College	Seattle	C	St	M/W														
Spokane Community College	Spokane	C,T	St	M/W	7,468		51		Y	Y	R	Y	Y	Y	Y	N	12	53
Spokane Falls Community College	Spokane	C,T	St	M/W	14,974		54		Y	Y	R	Y	Y	Y	Y	N	11	31
Tacoma Community College	Tacoma	C,T	St	M/W	7,299		46		Y			Y	Y	Y	Y	N	11	76
Walla Walla Community College	Walla Walla	C,T	St	M/W	6,775	55	57		Y		R	Y	Y	Y	Y	N	12	31
Wenatchee Valley College	Wenatchee																	

This index includes the names and locations of accredited two-year colleges in the United States and U.S. territories and shows institutions' responses to our 2001 Survey of Undergraduate Institutions. If an institution submitted incomplete or no data, one or more columns opposite the institution's name is blank. An asterisk after the school name denotes a *Special Announcement* following the college's profile.

Y—Yes; N—No; R—Recommended; S—For Some

		Degrees Awarded: Transfer Associate (C), Terminal Associate (T), Bachelor's (B), Master's (M), Doctoral (D), First Professional (F)	Institutional Control: Independent, Independent-Religious, Proprietary, Federal, State, Province, Commonwealth, Territory, County, District, City, State and Local, State-Related	Student Body: Men, Primarily Men, Women, Primarily Women, Coed	Undergraduate Enrollment Fall 2001	Percent Attending Part-Time	Percent 25 Years of Age or Older	Percent of Grads Going on to 4-Year Colleges	Open Admissions	High School Equivalency Certificate Accepted	High School Transcript Required	Need-based aid available	Part-Time Jobs Available	Career Counseling Available	Job Placement Services Available	College Housing Available	Number of Sports Offered	Number of Majors Offered
Whatcom Community College	Bellingham	C,T	St	M/W	3,993	44	30		Y			Y	Y	Y		N	5	14
Yakima Valley Community College	Yakima																	
West Virginia																		
Fairmont State Community & Technical College	Fairmont																	
Huntington Junior College of Business	Huntington	T	Prop	M/W	600		40		Y	Y	Y	Y		Y	Y	N		11
Mountain State College	Parkersburg	T	Prop	M/W	249				N			Y	Y					3
National Institute of Technology	Cross Lanes	C	Prop	M/W	440		30		N	Y	Y	Y	Y	Y	Y	N		2
Potomac State College of West Virginia University	Keyser	C,T	St	M/W	1,109	43												
Southern West Virginia Comm and Tech Coll	Mount Gay	C,T	St	M/W	2,520		80		Y	Y	Y	Y	Y	Y	Y	N		16
West Virginia Business College	Wheeling	T	Priv		58													
West Virginia Junior College	Charleston	T	Prop	M/W	230		40		Y	Y			Y	Y	Y	N		8
West Virginia Junior College	Morgantown																	
West Virginia Northern Community College	Wheeling	C,T	St	M/W	2,994		94	33	Y	Y	S	Y	Y	Y	Y	N	4	18
West Virginia University at Parkersburg	Parkersburg	C,T,B	St	M/W	3,340	50	42	20	Y	Y	S		Y	Y	Y	N	10	22
Wisconsin																		
Blackhawk Technical College	Janesville	C,T	Dist	M/W	2,300		60		Y	Y	Y	Y	Y	Y	Y	N		17
Bryant and Stratton College	Milwaukee	T	Prop	M/W	274	35	44	9	N	Y	Y	Y	Y	Y	Y	N		8
Chippewa Valley Technical College	Eau Claire	T	Dist	M/W	2,600		50		Y	Y	Y	Y	Y	Y	Y	N		34
College of Menominee Nation	Keshena																	
Fox Valley Technical College	Appleton																	
Gateway Technical College	Kenosha	T	St-L	M/W	6,247	81	50		Y		S	Y	Y	Y	Y	N		41
Herzing College	Madison	C,B	Prop	PM	584	12												
ITT Technical Institute	Green Bay		Prop	M/W	93													5
ITT Technical Institute	Greenfield	T,B	Prop	M/W	421				N	Y	Y	Y	Y	Y	Y	N		5
Lac Courte Oreilles Ojibwa Community College	Hayward	C,T	Fed	M/W	500		75	15	Y	Y	Y		Y	Y	Y	N	4	9
Lakeshore Technical College	Cleveland	C,T	St-L	M/W	2,886	76	55		Y	Y	S	Y	Y	Y	Y	N		21
Madison Area Technical College	Madison																	
Madison Media Institute	Madison																	
Mid-State Technical College	Wisconsin Rapids	C,T	St-L	M/W	10,737		51		Y	Y	Y		Y	Y	Y	N	5	21
Milwaukee Area Technical College	Milwaukee	C,T	Dist	M/W	60,174				Y	Y	Y	Y	Y	Y	Y	N	11	87
Moraine Park Technical College	Fond du Lac	C,T	St-L	M/W	8,943		51		Y		R	Y	Y	Y	Y	N	2	27
Nicolet Area Technical College	Rhinelander	C,T	St-L	M/W	1,415													
Northcentral Technical College	Wausau	C,T	Dist	M/W	3,609	71	65	5	Y	Y	Y	Y	Y	Y	Y	N	8	26
Northeast Wisconsin Technical College	Green Bay																	
Southwest Wisconsin Technical College	Fennimore	T	St-L	M/W	2,993		29	4	Y		Y	Y	Y	Y	Y	Y	4	31
U of Wisconsin Center–Baraboo/ Sauk County	Baraboo	C,T	St	M/W	554	41	24	80	N	Y	Y	Y	Y	Y		N	10	1
U of Wisconsin Center–Barron County	Rice Lake	C	St	M/W	575		21		N	Y	Y	Y	Y	Y		N	8	1
U of Wisconsin Center–Fond du Lac	Fond du Lac	C	St	M/W	572	38												
U of Wisconsin Center–Fox Valley	Menasha	C	St	M/W	1,782				N	Y	Y	Y	Y	Y		N	4	1
U of Wisconsin Center–Manitowoc County	Manitowoc	C	St	M/W			23	90	N	Y	Y	Y	Y	Y		N	4	1
U of Wisconsin Center–Marathon County	Wausau	C	St	M/W	1,339													
U of Wisconsin Center–Marinette County	Marinette	C	St	M/W	535		40	90	Y	Y	Y	Y	Y	Y		N	4	1
U of Wisconsin Center–Marshfield/ Wood County	Marshfield	C	St	M/W			25	98	N	Y	Y	Y	Y	Y		N	9	1
U of Wisconsin Center–Richland	Richland Center	C	St	M/W	496	36	25		N	Y	Y	Y	Y	Y		Y	11	2
U of Wisconsin Center–Rock County	Janesville	C	St	M/W	991		34		N	Y	Y	Y	Y	Y		N	5	1
U of Wisconsin Center–Sheboygan County	Sheboygan	C	St	M/W	777		31		Y	Y	Y	Y	Y	Y	Y	N	8	1
U of Wisconsin Center–Washington County	West Bend	C	St	M/W	941		16		N	Y	Y	Y	Y	Y		N	7	1
U of Wisconsin Center–Waukesha County	Waukesha	C	St	M/W	2,253	47	20	95	N	Y	Y	Y	Y	Y		N	9	1
Waukesha County Technical College	Pewaukee	T	St-L	M/W														
Western Wisconsin Technical College	La Crosse	T	Dist	M/W	5,181	59	42		Y	Y	Y	Y	Y	Y	Y	Y	3	44
Wisconsin Indianhead Technical College	Shell Lake	T	Dist	M/W	3,765		45											25
Wyoming																		
Casper College	Casper	C,T	Dist	M/W	3,853	52	45	50	Y	Y	Y	Y	Y	Y	Y	Y	18	86
Central Wyoming College	Riverton	C,T	St-L	M/W	1,544	58	47		Y	Y	R	Y	Y	Y	Y	Y	12	33
Eastern Wyoming College*	Torrington	C,T	St-L	M/W	1,278	70	33		Y	Y	R	Y	Y	Y	Y	Y	11	46
Laramie County Community College	Cheyenne	C,T	Cou	M/W	3,863	65	50	36	Y	Y	Y	Y	Y	Y	Y	Y	9	48
Northwest College	Powell	C,T	St-L	M/W	1,576	32	33		Y	Y	Y	Y	Y	Y	Y	Y	23	64
Sheridan College	Sheridan	C,T	St-L	M/W	2,730	65	35		Y	Y	R,S	Y	Y	Y	Y	Y	7	42
Western Wyoming Community College*	Rock Springs	C,T	St-L	M/W	2,612		49	35	Y	Y	Y	Y	Y	Y	Y	Y	14	60
Wyoming Technical Institute	Laramie	T	Prop	PM	774				Y	Y	Y	Y	Y	Y	Y	Y	4	1
U.S. TERRITORIES																		
American Samoa																		
American Samoa Community College	Pago Pago																	

This index includes the names and locations of accredited two-year colleges in the United States and U.S. territories and shows institutions' responses to our 2001 Survey of Undergraduate Institutions. If an institution submitted incomplete or no data, one or more columns opposite the institution's name is blank. An asterisk after the school name denotes a *Special Announcement* following the college's profile.

Y—Yes; N—No; R—Recommended; S—For Some

Institution	Location	Degrees Awarded: Transfer Associate (C), Terminal Associate (T), Bachelor's (B), Master's (M), Doctoral (D), First Professional (F)	Institutional Control: Independent, Independent-Religious, Proprietary, Federal, State, Province, Commonwealth, Territory, County, District, City, State and Local, State-Related	Student Body: Men, Primarily Men, Women, Primarily Women, Coed	Undergraduate Enrollment Fall 2001	Percent Attending Part-Time	Percent 25 Years of Age or Older	Percent of Grads Going on to 4-Year Colleges	Open Admissions	High School Equivalency Certificate Accepted	High School Transcript Required	Need-based aid available	Part-Time Jobs Available	Career Counseling Available	Job Placement Services Available	College Housing Available	Number of Sports Offered	Number of Majors Offered
Federated States of Micronesia																		
College of Micronesia–FSM	Kolonia Pohnpei																	
Guam																		
Guam Community College	Barrigada	T	Terr	M/W	1,754	78	47		Y	Y	Y	Y	Y	Y		N		30
Northern Mariana Islands																		
Northern Marianas College	Saipan																	
Puerto Rico																		
Huertas Junior College	Caguas																	
Humacao Community College	Humacao	T	Priv		403	24												
Instituto Comercial de Puerto Rico Junior College	San Juan	T	Prop	M/W	1,562	10			Y	Y	Y	Y	Y	Y	Y	N		5
Instituto Fontecha	San Juan																	
International Junior College	San Juan																	
National College of Business & Technology	Bayamon																	
Ramírez College of Business and Technology	San Juan																	
Technological College of Municipality of San Juan	San Juan	C,T	City	M/W	777	24												
U of Puerto Rico, Carolina Regional College	Carolina																	
OTHER COUNTRIES																		
Marshall Islands																		
College of the Marshall Islands	Majuro																	
Palau																		
Palau Community College	Koror	C,T	Terr	M/W	582	31	33		Y	Y	Y	Y	Y	Y	Y	Y	7	14
Switzerland																		
Schiller International University	Engelberg	C,T	Ind	M/W	60				N	Y				Y		Y	4	3

College Profiles and Special Announcements

This section contains detailed factual profiles of colleges, covering such items as background facts, enrollment figures, faculty size, admission requirements, expenses, financing, housing, student life, campus security, undergraduate majors and degrees, and whom to contact for more information. In addition, there are **Special Announcements** from college administrators about new programs or special events. The data in each of these profiles, collected from fall 2001 to spring 2002, come solely from *Peterson's Annual Survey of Undergraduate Institutions,* which was sent to deans or admission officers at each institution. The profiles are organized state by state and arranged alphabetically within those sections by the official names of the institutions.

ALABAMA

ALABAMA SOUTHERN COMMUNITY COLLEGE
Monroeville, Alabama

Admissions Contact Ms. Mandy Lanier, Admissions Coordinator, Alabama Southern Community College, PO Box 2000, Monroeville, AL 36461. *Phone:* 334-575-3156 Ext. 222. *E-mail:* mlanier@ascc.edu.

BESSEMER STATE TECHNICAL COLLEGE
Bessemer, Alabama

- **State-supported** 2-year, founded 1966, part of Alabama College System
- **Calendar** semesters
- **Degree** certificates, diplomas, and associate
- **Small-town** 60-acre campus with easy access to Birmingham
- **Endowment** $43,950
- **Coed,** 2,087 undergraduate students

Undergraduates 39% African American, 0.3% Asian American or Pacific Islander, 0.3% Hispanic American, 0.1% Native American.
Freshmen *Admission:* 1,955 applied, 1,136 admitted.
Faculty *Total:* 200, 50% full-time.
Majors Accounting; auto mechanic/technician; computer science; construction technology; drafting; electrical/electronic engineering technology; ornamental horticulture; practical nurse; retail management; secretarial science.
Academic Programs *Special study options:* academic remediation for entering students, advanced placement credit, internships, part-time degree program, services for LD students.
Computers on Campus 180 computers available on campus for general student use. Internet access available.
Student Life *Housing:* college housing not available. *Campus security:* 24-hour patrols, student patrols.
Costs (2002–03) *Tuition:* state resident $1248 full-time, $52 per credit part-time; nonresident $2496 full-time, $104 per credit part-time. *Required fees:* $192 full-time, $8 per credit.
Financial Aid In 2001, 65 Federal Work-Study jobs (averaging $3000). 5 State and other part-time jobs.
Applying *Required:* high school transcript. *Application deadlines:* 8/4 (freshmen), 8/4 (transfers). *Notification:* continuous until 8/4 (freshmen).
Admissions Contact Director of Admissions, Bessemer State Technical College, PO Box 308, Bessemer, AL 35021-0308. *Phone:* 205-428-6391. *Toll-free phone:* 800-235-5368.

BEVILL STATE COMMUNITY COLLEGE
Sumiton, Alabama

- **State-supported** 2-year, founded 1969, part of Alabama College System
- **Calendar** semesters
- **Degree** associate
- **Rural** 23-acre campus with easy access to Birmingham
- **Coed,** 3,504 undergraduate students

Undergraduates Students come from 4 states and territories.
Faculty *Total:* 195, 49% full-time. *Student/faculty ratio:* 12:1.
Majors Business administration; computer/information sciences; drafting; emergency medical technology; general studies; heating/air conditioning/refrigeration technology; liberal arts and sciences/liberal studies; medical laboratory technician; nursing; secretarial science; tool/die making; welding technology.
Academic Programs *Special study options:* academic remediation for entering students, adult/continuing education programs, advanced placement credit, cooperative education, honors programs, off-campus study, part-time degree program, services for LD students, summer session for credit.
Library 31,690 titles, 192 serial subscriptions.
Computers on Campus 65 computers available on campus for general student use.
Student Life *Housing:* college housing not available. *Activities and Organizations:* choral group, Student LPN club, Phi Beta Lambda, campus ministries. *Student Services:* personal/psychological counseling.
Athletics Member NJCAA. *Intercollegiate sports:* baseball M(s), basketball M(s)/W(s), softball W(s), volleyball W(s). *Intramural sports:* basketball M/W, football M, golf M, softball M/W, swimming M/W, table tennis M/W, tennis M/W, volleyball M/W.
Standardized Tests *Required:* ACT ASSET. *Required for some:* ACT (for placement).
Costs (2001–02) *Tuition:* area resident $1982 full-time, $56 per semester hour part-time; nonresident $3774 full-time, $112 per semester hour part-time.
Financial Aid In 2001, 85 Federal Work-Study jobs (averaging $1878).
Applying *Options:* early admission, deferred entrance. *Required:* high school transcript. *Application deadline:* rolling (freshmen), rolling (transfers).
Admissions Contact Ms. Melissa Stowe, Enrollment Supervisor, Bevill State Community College, PO Box 800, Sumiton, AL 35148. *Phone:* 205-932-3221 Ext. 5101.

BISHOP STATE COMMUNITY COLLEGE
Mobile, Alabama

Admissions Contact Dr. Terry Hazzard, Dean of Students, Bishop State Community College, 351 North Broad Street, Mobile, AL 36603-5898. *Phone:* 334-690-6419. *Toll-free phone:* 800-523-7235. *Fax:* 334-438-5403. *E-mail:* wdaniels@bscc.cc.al.us.

CALHOUN COMMUNITY COLLEGE
Decatur, Alabama

- **State-supported** 2-year, founded 1965, part of Alabama College System
- **Calendar** semesters
- **Degree** certificates and associate
- **Rural** campus
- **Coed,** 8,372 undergraduate students, 39% full-time, 57% women, 43% men

Undergraduates 3,250 full-time, 5,122 part-time. Students come from 15 states and territories, 15 other countries, 1% are from out of state, 20% African American, 2% Asian American or Pacific Islander, 1% Hispanic American, 3% Native American, 0.3% international, 3% transferred in. *Retention:* 80% of 2001 full-time freshmen returned.
Freshmen *Admission:* 4,978 applied, 4,125 admitted, 1,695 enrolled. *Test scores:* SAT verbal scores over 500: 22%; SAT math scores over 500: 28%; ACT scores over 18: 63%; SAT math scores over 600: 6%; ACT scores over 24: 12%; ACT scores over 30: 1%.
Faculty *Total:* 421, 29% full-time, 15% with terminal degrees. *Student/faculty ratio:* 20:1.
Majors Aerospace engineering technology; business administration; child care/guidance; communications related; computer/information sciences; dental assistant; drafting; electrical/power transmission installers related; electromechanical instrumentation and maintenance technologies related; emergency medical technology; general studies; graphic design/commercial art/illustration; liberal arts and sciences/liberal studies; military technology; music; nursing; paralegal/legal assistant; tool/die making.
Academic Programs *Special study options:* academic remediation for entering students, accelerated degree program, adult/continuing education programs, advanced placement credit, cooperative education, distance learning, English as a second language, independent study, part-time degree program, services for LD students, summer session for credit. *ROTC:* Army (c).
Library Brewer Library plus 2 others with 36,699 titles, 202 serial subscriptions, 23,948 audiovisual materials, an OPAC, a Web page.
Computers on Campus 160 computers available on campus for general student use.
Student Life *Housing:* college housing not available. *Activities and Organizations:* drama/theater group, student-run newspaper, choral group, Student Government Association, Black Students Alliance, Phi Theta Kappa, BACCHUS/SADD, VICA. *Campus security:* 24-hour patrols. *Student Services:* personal/psychological counseling.
Standardized Tests *Required for some:* SAT I or ACT (for placement). *Recommended:* SAT I or ACT (for placement).
Costs (2001–02) *Tuition:* state resident $2080 full-time, $60 per semester hour part-time; nonresident $4000 full-time, $120 per semester hour part-time. Full-time tuition and fees vary according to course load. Part-time tuition and fees vary according to course load. *Required fees:* $2080 full-time, $5 per semester hour. *Waivers:* senior citizens and employees or children of employees.
Financial Aid In 2001, 50 Federal Work-Study jobs (averaging $3000).
Applying *Required for some:* high school transcript. *Application deadline:* rolling (freshmen), rolling (transfers). *Notification:* continuous (freshmen).
Admissions Contact Ms. Patricia Landers, Admissions Receptionist, Calhoun Community College, PO Box 2216, 6250 Highway 31 North, Decatur, AL

35609-2216. *Phone:* 256-306-2593. *Toll-free phone:* 800-626-3628 Ext. 2594. *Fax:* 256-306-2941. *E-mail:* pml@calhoun.cc.al.us.

CENTRAL ALABAMA COMMUNITY COLLEGE
Alexander City, Alabama

- **State-supported** 2-year, founded 1965, part of Alabama College System
- **Calendar** semesters
- **Degree** certificates and associate
- **Small-town** 100-acre campus
- **Coed,** 1,609 undergraduate students, 54% full-time, 62% women, 38% men

Undergraduates 863 full-time, 746 part-time. Students come from 6 states and territories, 5 other countries.
Freshmen *Admission:* 439 enrolled.
Faculty *Total:* 193, 27% full-time. *Student/faculty ratio:* 15:1.
Majors Business administration; clothing/textiles; computer programming; computer science; drafting; electrical/electronic engineering technology; environmental technology; information sciences/systems; liberal arts and sciences/liberal studies; nursing; secretarial science.
Academic Programs *Special study options:* academic remediation for entering students, adult/continuing education programs, advanced placement credit, cooperative education, distance learning, internships, part-time degree program, services for LD students, summer session for credit.
Library Thomas D. Russell Library with 35,000 titles, 455 serial subscriptions.
Computers on Campus 70 computers available on campus for general student use. A campuswide network can be accessed from off campus. Internet access, at least one staffed computer lab available.
Student Life *Housing:* college housing not available. *Activities and Organizations:* drama/theater group, student-run radio station, choral group, Cultural Unity, Baptist Campus Ministry, Student Government Association, Phi Theta Kappa. *Campus security:* evening security. *Student Services:* personal/psychological counseling.
Athletics Member NJCAA. *Intercollegiate sports:* baseball M(s), golf M(s), softball W(s), tennis M(s)/W(s), volleyball W(s).
Standardized Tests *Required for some:* SAT I or ACT (for admission).
Costs (2001–02) *Tuition:* state resident $1600 full-time, $50 per semester hour part-time; nonresident $3200 full-time, $100 per semester hour part-time. *Required fees:* $128 full-time, $4 per semester hour. *Waivers:* senior citizens and employees or children of employees.
Applying *Options:* common application, early admission. *Required:* high school transcript. *Required for some:* 3 letters of recommendation, interview. *Application deadlines:* 9/9 (freshmen), 9/9 (transfers).
Admissions Contact Ms. Bettie Macmillan, Admission, Central Alabama Community College, PO Box 699, Alexander City, AL 35011-0699. *Phone:* 256-234-6346 Ext. 6232. *Toll-free phone:* 800-643-2657 Ext. 6232. *Fax:* 256-234-0384.

CHATTAHOOCHEE VALLEY COMMUNITY COLLEGE
Phenix City, Alabama

- **State-supported** 2-year, founded 1974
- **Calendar** semesters
- **Degree** certificates and associate
- **Small-town** 103-acre campus
- **Endowment** $40,063
- **Coed,** 1,891 undergraduate students

Undergraduates Students come from 6 states and territories, 10 other countries, 0.3% are from out of state, 34% African American, 1% Asian American or Pacific Islander, 3% Hispanic American, 0.4% Native American. *Retention:* 66% of 2001 full-time freshmen returned.
Freshmen *Admission:* 822 applied, 822 admitted.
Faculty *Total:* 98, 29% full-time, 12% with terminal degrees. *Student/faculty ratio:* 18:1.
Majors Agricultural sciences; biology; business administration; chemistry; criminal justice/law enforcement administration; data processing technology; elementary education; fire science; forestry; industrial radiologic technology; information sciences/systems; legal administrative assistant; liberal arts and sciences/liberal studies; mathematics; medical technology; music; music teacher education; nursing; physical education; physics; practical nurse; pre-engineering; secretarial science; theater arts/drama.
Academic Programs *Special study options:* academic remediation for entering students, adult/continuing education programs, advanced placement credit, distance learning, honors programs, off-campus study, part-time degree program, student-designed majors, summer session for credit.
Library Estelle Bain Owens Learning Resource Center and Library with 54,129 titles, 90 serial subscriptions, 853 audiovisual materials, a Web page.
Computers on Campus 55 computers available on campus for general student use. A campuswide network can be accessed from off campus. Internet access, at least one staffed computer lab available.
Student Life *Housing:* college housing not available. *Activities and Organizations:* drama/theater group, choral group. *Campus security:* 24-hour emergency response devices and patrols. *Student Services:* personal/psychological counseling.
Athletics Member NJCAA. *Intercollegiate sports:* baseball M(s), softball W(s).
Standardized Tests *Required for some:* SAT I or ACT (for placement).
Costs (2001–02) *Tuition:* state resident $2040 full-time, $60 per semester hour part-time; nonresident $3840 full-time, $128 per semester hour part-time. Full-time tuition and fees vary according to reciprocity agreements. Part-time tuition and fees vary according to reciprocity agreements. *Required fees:* $8 per semester hour. *Payment plan:* deferred payment. *Waivers:* senior citizens and employees or children of employees.
Financial Aid In 2001, 40 Federal Work-Study jobs (averaging $2000). 10 State and other part-time jobs (averaging $2000).
Applying *Options:* common application, early admission. *Required:* high school transcript. *Application deadline:* rolling (freshmen), rolling (transfers). *Notification:* continuous (freshmen).
Admissions Contact Ms. Rita Cherry, Admissions Clerk, Chattahoochee Valley Community College, 2602 College Drive, Phenix City, AL 36869-7928. *Phone:* 334-291-4995. *Toll-free phone:* 800-842-2822. *Fax:* 334-291-4994.

COMMUNITY COLLEGE OF THE AIR FORCE
Maxwell Air Force Base, Alabama

- **Federally supported** 2-year, founded 1972
- **Calendar** continuous
- **Degrees** certificates and associate (courses conducted at 140 branch locations worldwide for members of the U.S. Air Force)
- **Suburban** campus
- **Coed, primarily men,** 373,943 undergraduate students, 20% women, 80% men

Undergraduates Students come from 58 states and territories, 18% African American, 3% Asian American or Pacific Islander, 6% Hispanic American, 0.5% Native American.
Faculty *Total:* 6,269, 100% full-time.
Majors Aircraft mechanic/airframe; air traffic control; atmospheric sciences; auto mechanic/technician; aviation/airway science; aviation technology; biomedical engineering-related technology; cardiovascular technology; clothing/apparel/textile; communication equipment technology; construction technology; criminal justice/law enforcement administration; dental assistant; dental laboratory technician; education administration; educational media design; electrical/electronic engineering technology; environmental health; environmental science; finance; fire science; graphic design/commercial art/illustration; health services administration; hematology technology; hotel and restaurant management; human resources management; industrial technology; logistics/materials management; management information systems/business data processing; medical dietician; medical laboratory technician; medical physiology; medical radiologic technology; mental health/rehabilitation; metallurgical technology; military technology; music (general performance); nuclear medical technology; occupational safety/health technology; office management; operating room technician; optometric/ophthalmic laboratory technician; paralegal/legal assistant; pharmacy technician/assistant; physical therapy assistant; public relations; purchasing/contracts management; recreation/leisure studies; security; social work; vehicle/equipment operation.
Academic Programs *Special study options:* academic remediation for entering students, adult/continuing education programs, advanced placement credit, distance learning, independent study, internships.
Library Air Force Library Service with 5.0 million titles, 56,654 serial subscriptions, an OPAC, a Web page.
Computers on Campus Internet access available.
Student Life *Housing:* on-campus residence required for freshman year. *Options:* coed. *Campus security:* 24-hour emergency response devices and patrols. *Student Services:* health clinic, personal/psychological counseling, legal services.
Athletics *Intramural sports:* badminton M/W, baseball M, basketball M/W, bowling M/W, cross-country running M/W, football M, golf M/W, racquetball

Community College of the Air Force (continued)
M/W, softball M/W, squash M/W, table tennis M/W, tennis M/W, track and field M/W, volleyball M/W, weight lifting M/W.
Costs (2001–02) *Tuition:* Tuition, room and board, and medical and dental care are provided by the U.S. government. Each student receives a salary from which to pay for uniforms, supplies, and personal expenses. *Waivers:* minority students and adult students.
Applying *Required:* high school transcript, interview. *Application deadline:* rolling (freshmen), rolling (transfers). *Notification:* continuous (freshmen).
Admissions Contact C.M. Sgt. Ronald D. Hall, Director of Admissions/Registrar, Community College of the Air Force, 130 West Maxwell Boulevard, Maxwell Air Force Base, AL 36112-6613. *Phone:* 334-953-6436. *E-mail:* ronald.hall@maxwell.af.mil.

DOUGLAS MACARTHUR STATE TECHNICAL COLLEGE
Opp, Alabama

- **State-supported** 2-year, founded 1965
- **Calendar** semesters
- **Degree** certificates, diplomas, and associate
- **Small-town** 96-acre campus
- **Coed,** 375 undergraduate students

Undergraduates Students come from 2 states and territories.
Faculty *Total:* 27, 93% full-time.
Majors Accounting; auto mechanic/technician; carpentry; computer programming; computer science; cosmetology; drafting; electrical/electronic engineering technology; practical nurse; radio/television broadcasting; secretarial science; welding technology.
Academic Programs *Special study options:* academic remediation for entering students, cooperative education, part-time degree program, summer session for credit.
Library 3,000 titles, 15 serial subscriptions.
Computers on Campus 78 computers available on campus for general student use.
Student Life *Housing:* college housing not available.
Costs (2001–02) *Tuition:* state resident $1536 full-time, $64 per credit hour part-time; nonresident $3072 full-time, $128 per credit hour part-time.
Applying *Options:* early admission. *Required:* high school transcript. *Application deadline:* rolling (freshmen), rolling (transfers). *Notification:* continuous (freshmen).
Admissions Contact Ms. Susan Dee, Admissions Officer, Douglas MacArthur State Technical College, PO Drawer 910, Opp, AL 36467. *Phone:* 334-493-3573 Ext. 260.

ENTERPRISE STATE JUNIOR COLLEGE
Enterprise, Alabama

- **State-supported** 2-year, founded 1965, part of Alabama College System
- **Calendar** semesters
- **Degree** certificates and associate
- **Small-town** 100-acre campus
- **Coed,** 1,590 undergraduate students, 54% full-time, 64% women, 36% men

Undergraduates 866 full-time, 724 part-time. 21% African American, 3% Asian American or Pacific Islander, 4% Hispanic American, 1% Native American.
Freshmen *Admission:* 369 enrolled.
Majors Agricultural business; aircraft mechanic/airframe; auto mechanic/technician; aviation technology; biological/physical sciences; business administration; business marketing and marketing management; child care/development; computer science; criminal justice/law enforcement administration; early childhood education; education; finance; food products retailing; insurance/risk management; journalism; law enforcement/police science; legal administrative assistant; liberal arts and sciences/liberal studies; mass communications; medical administrative assistant; medical records administration; pre-engineering; real estate; recreation/leisure studies; retail management; secretarial science; social sciences.
Academic Programs *Special study options:* academic remediation for entering students, adult/continuing education programs, advanced placement credit, English as a second language, honors programs, internships, off-campus study, part-time degree program, services for LD students, summer session for credit.
Library Snuggs Hall with 45,076 titles, 349 serial subscriptions.
Computers on Campus 100 computers available on campus for general student use. At least one staffed computer lab available.
Student Life *Housing:* college housing not available. *Activities and Organizations:* student-run newspaper, choral group. *Campus security:* security personnel. *Student Services:* personal/psychological counseling, women's center.
Athletics Member NJCAA. *Intercollegiate sports:* baseball M, basketball M(s), golf M, softball W(s), tennis M(s)/W(s), volleyball W. *Intramural sports:* basketball M, football M, volleyball M/W.
Standardized Tests *Recommended:* SAT I or ACT (for placement).
Costs (2001–02) *Tuition:* state resident $1800 full-time, $60 per semester hour part-time; nonresident $3600 full-time, $120 per semester hour part-time. Part-time tuition and fees vary according to program. *Required fees:* $240 full-time, $8 per semester hour. *Waivers:* senior citizens and employees or children of employees.
Financial Aid In 2001, 50 Federal Work-Study jobs (averaging $2000).
Applying *Options:* early admission, deferred entrance. *Required:* high school transcript. *Application deadline:* rolling (freshmen), rolling (transfers). *Notification:* continuous (freshmen).
Admissions Contact Ms. Robin Wyatt, Director of Admissions, Enterprise State Junior College, PO Box 1300, Enterprise, AL 36331-1300. *Phone:* 334-347-2623 Ext. 234.

GADSDEN STATE COMMUNITY COLLEGE
Gadsden, Alabama

- **State-supported** 2-year, founded 1965, part of Alabama College System
- **Calendar** semesters
- **Degree** certificates and associate
- **Small-town** 275-acre campus with easy access to Birmingham
- **Endowment** $1.3 million
- **Coed,** 4,729 undergraduate students, 55% full-time, 56% women, 44% men

Undergraduates 2,581 full-time, 2,148 part-time. Students come from 10 states and territories, 17% African American, 0.4% Asian American or Pacific Islander, 0.6% Hispanic American, 0.4% Native American, 3% international.
Freshmen *Admission:* 1,392 applied, 1,392 admitted, 1,074 enrolled.
Faculty *Total:* 324, 48% full-time.
Majors Alcohol/drug abuse counseling; child care/guidance; civil engineering technology; computer/information sciences; court reporting; emergency medical technology; general retailing/wholesaling; general studies; heating/air conditioning/refrigeration technology; law enforcement/police science; liberal arts and sciences/liberal studies; mechanical engineering technology; medical laboratory technician; medical radiologic technology; nursing; paralegal/legal assistant; physical education; radio/television broadcasting technology; secretarial science; telecommunications; tool/die making.
Academic Programs *Special study options:* academic remediation for entering students, adult/continuing education programs, advanced placement credit, cooperative education, English as a second language, external degree program, part-time degree program, services for LD students, summer session for credit.
Library Meadows Library with 72,915 titles, 303 serial subscriptions.
Computers on Campus 200 computers available on campus for general student use. Internet access, at least one staffed computer lab available.
Student Life *Housing Options:* coed. *Activities and Organizations:* drama/theater group, student-run newspaper, radio station, choral group, Science, Math, and Engineering Club, Student Government Association, Circle K, Phi Beta Lambda, VICA. *Campus security:* 24-hour patrols. *Student Services:* women's center.
Athletics Member NJCAA. *Intercollegiate sports:* baseball M(s), basketball M(s)/W(s), cross-country running W(s), golf M(s), softball W(s), tennis M(s), volleyball W(s). *Intramural sports:* basketball M/W, volleyball M/W.
Costs (2002–03) *Tuition:* state resident $2888 full-time, $76 per credit hour part-time; nonresident $5168 full-time, $136 per credit hour part-time. *Room and board:* $2350.
Financial Aid In 2001, 95 Federal Work-Study jobs (averaging $1364).
Applying *Options:* early admission, deferred entrance. *Required:* high school transcript. *Application deadline:* rolling (freshmen), rolling (transfers).

Admissions Contact Ms. Cynthia Whisenhunt, Director of Admissions, Gadsden State Community College, Admissions, Allen Hall. *Phone:* 256-549-8210. *Toll-free phone:* 800-226-5563. *Fax:* 256-549-8205. *E-mail:* info@gadsdenstate.edu.

GEORGE CORLEY WALLACE STATE COMMUNITY COLLEGE

Selma, Alabama

- **State-supported** 2-year, founded 1966, part of Alabama College System
- **Calendar** semesters
- **Degree** certificates, diplomas, and associate
- **Small-town** campus
- **Coed,** 1,579 undergraduate students, 61% full-time, 64% women, 36% men

Undergraduates 959 full-time, 620 part-time. 55% African American, 0.3% Asian American or Pacific Islander, 0.3% Hispanic American, 0.1% Native American, 14% transferred in.

Freshmen *Admission:* 650 applied, 650 admitted, 486 enrolled.

Faculty *Total:* 93, 54% full-time, 9% with terminal degrees. *Student/faculty ratio:* 17:1.

Majors Accounting; biomedical technology; business administration; business education; computer programming; computer science; criminal justice/law enforcement administration; drafting; electrical/electronic engineering technology; fire science; industrial radiologic technology; law enforcement/police science; machine technology; medical assistant; medical laboratory technician; medical records administration; nursing; occupational therapy; physical therapy; practical nurse; respiratory therapy; welding technology.

Academic Programs *Special study options:* academic remediation for entering students, adult/continuing education programs, advanced placement credit, independent study, part-time degree program, services for LD students, summer session for credit.

Library George Corley Wallace Library with 16,598 titles, 2,240 serial subscriptions, 913 audiovisual materials, an OPAC, a Web page.

Computers on Campus 160 computers available on campus for general student use. Internet access, at least one staffed computer lab available.

Student Life *Housing:* college housing not available. *Activities and Organizations:* choral group. *Campus security:* 24-hour patrols.

Athletics Member NJCAA. *Intercollegiate sports:* baseball M(s), basketball M(s), softball W(s), tennis M(s)/W(s). *Intramural sports:* basketball M/W, softball W, tennis M/W.

Standardized Tests *Required:* ACT ASSET.

Costs (2001–02) *Tuition:* state resident $2040 full-time, $65 per semester hour part-time; nonresident $4080 full-time, $136 per semester hour part-time. Part-time tuition and fees vary according to course load. *Waivers:* minority students, senior citizens, and employees or children of employees.

Applying *Options:* common application, early admission, deferred entrance. *Application deadline:* rolling (freshmen), rolling (transfers).

Admissions Contact Dr. Lisa Hammons, Dean of Students, George Corley Wallace State Community College, 3000 Earl Goodwin Parkway, Selma, AL 36702-2530. *Phone:* 334-876-9327. *Fax:* 334-876-9300.

GEORGE C. WALLACE COMMUNITY COLLEGE

Dothan, Alabama

Admissions Contact Mrs. Brenda Barnes, Assistant Dean of Student Affairs, George C. Wallace Community College, Route 6, Box 62, Dothan, AL 36303-9234. *Phone:* 334-983-3521 Ext. 283. *Toll-free phone:* 800-821-1542.

HARRY M. AYERS STATE TECHNICAL COLLEGE

Anniston, Alabama

- **State-supported** 2-year, founded 1966
- **Calendar** semesters
- **Degree** certificates and associate
- **Small-town** 25-acre campus with easy access to Birmingham
- **Coed,** 1,137 undergraduate students, 60% full-time, 57% women, 43% men

Undergraduates 686 full-time, 451 part-time. Students come from 2 states and territories, 31% African American, 0.5% Hispanic American, 0.6% Native American.

Freshmen *Admission:* 278 admitted, 259 enrolled.

Faculty *Total:* 94, 29% full-time, 6% with terminal degrees. *Student/faculty ratio:* 18:1.

Majors Accounting; child care provider; computer science; drafting; electrical/electronic engineering technology; electrical equipment installation/repair; heating/air conditioning/refrigeration; machine shop assistant; machine technology; office management; system administration.

Academic Programs *Special study options:* advanced placement credit, part-time degree program, services for LD students.

Library Cain Learning Resource Center with 4,645 titles, 120 serial subscriptions.

Computers on Campus Internet access, at least one staffed computer lab available.

Student Life *Housing:* college housing not available. *Campus security:* late-night transport/escort service. *Student Services:* personal/psychological counseling.

Standardized Tests *Required:* ACT ASSET.

Costs (2001–02) *Tuition:* state resident $1440 full-time, $60 per credit hour part-time; nonresident $2880 full-time, $120 per credit hour part-time. Full-time tuition and fees vary according to reciprocity agreements. Part-time tuition and fees vary according to reciprocity agreements. *Required fees:* $192 full-time, $8 per credit hour. *Waivers:* senior citizens and employees or children of employees.

Financial Aid In 2001, 25 Federal Work-Study jobs (averaging $2500).

Applying *Options:* deferred entrance. *Required:* high school transcript. *Application deadline:* rolling (freshmen), rolling (transfers). *Notification:* continuous (freshmen).

Admissions Contact Mrs. Michele Conger, Director of Admissions and Records, Harry M. Ayers State Technical College, 1801 Coleman Road, Anniston, AL 36207. *Phone:* 256-835-5400. *Fax:* 256-835-5479. *E-mail:* mlonger@ayers.cc.al.us.

HERZING COLLEGE

Birmingham, Alabama

- **Proprietary** primarily 2-year, founded 1965, part of Herzing Institutes, Inc
- **Calendar** semesters
- **Degrees** diplomas, associate, and bachelor's
- **Urban** campus
- **Coed,** 600 undergraduate students, 66% full-time, 29% women, 72% men

Undergraduates 398 full-time, 202 part-time. Students come from 3 states and territories, 7 other countries, 1% are from out of state, 43% African American, 0.2% Asian American or Pacific Islander, 0.5% Hispanic American, 8% transferred in. *Retention:* 6% of 2001 full-time freshmen returned.

Freshmen *Admission:* 55 enrolled. *Average high school GPA:* 3.00.

Faculty *Total:* 27, 33% full-time, 78% with terminal degrees. *Student/faculty ratio:* 20:1.

Majors Business machine repair; business management/administrative services related; computer/information sciences; computer programming; computer science; data processing technology; electrical/electronic engineering technology; information sciences/systems; secretarial science.

Academic Programs *Special study options:* adult/continuing education programs, advanced placement credit, cooperative education, external degree program, internships, student-designed majors, summer session for credit.

Computers on Campus 125 computers available on campus for general student use. Internet access, at least one staffed computer lab available.

Student Life *Housing:* college housing not available. *Campus security:* 24-hour emergency response devices, late-night transport/escort service, security guard. *Student Services:* personal/psychological counseling, women's center.

Costs (2001–02) *Tuition:* $23,520 full-time, $250 per credit hour part-time. Full-time tuition and fees vary according to location and program. Part-time tuition and fees vary according to location and program. *Payment plan:* installment. *Waivers:* employees or children of employees.

Applying *Options:* early admission, deferred entrance. *Application deadline:* rolling (freshmen), rolling (transfers). *Notification:* continuous (freshmen).

Admissions Contact Mr. Michael A. Cates, Admissions Coordinator, Herzing College, 280 West Valley Avenue, Birmingham, AL 35209. *Phone:* 205-916-2800. *Fax:* 205-916-2807.

ITT TECHNICAL INSTITUTE

Birmingham, Alabama

- **Proprietary** primarily 2-year, founded 1994, part of ITT Educational Services, Inc

ITT Technical Institute (continued)
- **Calendar** quarters
- **Degrees** associate and bachelor's
- **Suburban** campus
- **Coed,** 443 undergraduate students

Majors Computer/information sciences related; computer programming; drafting; electrical/electronic engineering technologies related; information technology.

Student Life *Housing:* college housing not available. *Activities and Organizations:* student-run newspaper. *Campus security:* 24-hour emergency response devices.

Costs (2001–02) *Tuition:* Full-time tuition and fees vary according to program. Part-time tuition and fees vary according to program. $260—$330 per credit hour.

Applying *Options:* deferred entrance. *Application fee:* $100. *Required:* high school transcript, interview. *Recommended:* letters of recommendation. *Application deadline:* rolling (freshmen), rolling (transfers). *Notification:* continuous (freshmen).

Admissions Contact Mr. Jerome Ruffin, Director of Recruitment, ITT Technical Institute, 500 Riverhills Business Park, Birmingham, AL 35242. *Phone:* 205-991-5410. *Toll-free phone:* 800-488-7033. *Fax:* 205-991-5025.

JAMES H. FAULKNER STATE COMMUNITY COLLEGE
Bay Minette, Alabama

- **State-supported** 2-year, founded 1965, part of Alabama College System
- **Calendar** semesters
- **Degree** certificates and associate
- **Small-town** 105-acre campus
- **Coed,** 3,500 undergraduate students

Faulkner State Community College (FSCC), accredited by the Southern Association of Colleges and Schools, offers both transfer and certificate programs. The main campus is located in Bay Minette, Alabama, with branches in Fairhope and Gulf Shores, Alabama. FSCC serves the entire Gulf Coast area. For information, call 800-231-3752 (toll-free).

Undergraduates Students come from 12 states and territories, 5 other countries, 3% are from out of state, 9% live on campus.

Faculty *Total:* 152, 63% full-time. *Student/faculty ratio:* 15:1.

Majors Business administration; computer/information sciences; court reporting; dental assistant; environmental technology; general studies; graphic design/commercial art/illustration; hospitality management; landscaping management; liberal arts and sciences/liberal studies; paralegal/legal assistant; recreation/leisure facilities management; secretarial science.

Academic Programs *Special study options:* academic remediation for entering students, adult/continuing education programs, advanced placement credit, cooperative education, honors programs, internships, part-time degree program, services for LD students.

Library Austin R. Meadows Library with 53,100 titles, 200 serial subscriptions, 2,513 audiovisual materials, an OPAC.

Computers on Campus 208 computers available on campus for general student use. Internet access, at least one staffed computer lab available.

Student Life *Housing Options:* men-only, women-only. *Activities and Organizations:* drama/theater group, student-run newspaper, choral group, Student Government Association, Pow-Wow Leadership Society, Phi Theta Kappa, Association of Computational Machinery, national fraternities. *Campus security:* 24-hour patrols, controlled dormitory access. *Student Services:* personal/psychological counseling.

Athletics Member NJCAA. *Intercollegiate sports:* baseball M(s), basketball M(s)/W(s), golf M(s), softball W(s), tennis M(s)/W(s), volleyball W(s). *Intramural sports:* basketball M, racquetball M/W, tennis M/W, volleyball M/W.

Standardized Tests *Required for some:* ACT ASSET, ACT COMPASS. *Recommended:* ACT ASSET, ACT COMPASS.

Costs (2001–02) *Tuition:* state resident $1896 full-time, $79 per credit hour part-time; nonresident $3336 full-time, $137 per credit hour part-time. *Required fees:* $456 full-time, $19 per credit hour. *Room and board:* $2970. *Payment plan:* deferred payment. *Waivers:* employees or children of employees.

Applying *Options:* early admission, deferred entrance. *Required:* high school transcript. *Application deadline:* rolling (freshmen), rolling (transfers). *Notification:* continuous until 8/28 (freshmen).

Admissions Contact Ms. Peggy Duck, Director of Admissions, James H. Faulkner State Community College, 1900 Highway 31 South, Bay Minette, AL 36507. *Phone:* 334-580-2152. *Toll-free phone:* 800-231-3752. *Fax:* 334-580-2285. *E-mail:* fpugh@faulkner.cc.al.us.

JEFFERSON DAVIS COMMUNITY COLLEGE
Brewton, Alabama

- **State-supported** 2-year, founded 1965
- **Calendar** semesters
- **Degree** certificates and associate
- **Small-town** 100-acre campus
- **Coed,** 1,300 undergraduate students

Undergraduates Students come from 8 states and territories, 13% are from out of state.

Faculty *Total:* 121, 39% full-time. *Student/faculty ratio:* 11:1.

Majors Applied art; biological/physical sciences; biology; business administration; business marketing and marketing management; education; elementary education; finance; history; law enforcement/police science; liberal arts and sciences/liberal studies; medical assistant; music; nursing; physical education; political science; recreation/leisure studies; secretarial science; theater arts/drama.

Academic Programs *Special study options:* academic remediation for entering students, adult/continuing education programs, advanced placement credit, honors programs, part-time degree program, services for LD students, summer session for credit.

Library 926 titles, 330 serial subscriptions.

Computers on Campus 40 computers available on campus for general student use.

Student Life *Activities and Organizations:* drama/theater group. *Student Services:* personal/psychological counseling.

Athletics Member NJCAA.

Standardized Tests *Required:* ACT COMPASS.

Costs (2002–03) *Tuition:* state resident $1800 full-time, $60 per credit hour part-time; nonresident $3600 full-time, $120 per credit hour part-time. *Required fees:* $240 full-time, $8 per credit hour. *Room and board:* Room and board charges vary according to housing facility. *Waivers:* senior citizens and employees or children of employees.

Applying *Options:* early admission. *Required:* high school transcript. *Application deadline:* rolling (freshmen), rolling (transfers).

Admissions Contact Ms. Cynthia M. Moore, Registrar, Jefferson Davis Community College, PO Box 958, Brewton, AL 36427. *Phone:* 334-809-1590. *Fax:* 334-809-1596.

JEFFERSON STATE COMMUNITY COLLEGE
Birmingham, Alabama

- **State-supported** 2-year, founded 1965, part of Alabama College System
- **Calendar** semesters
- **Degree** certificates and associate
- **Suburban** 234-acre campus
- **Endowment** $1.3 million
- **Coed,** 5,652 undergraduate students, 37% full-time, 60% women, 40% men

Undergraduates 2,080 full-time, 3,572 part-time. Students come from 12 states and territories, 55 other countries, 1% are from out of state, 23% African American, 0.7% Asian American or Pacific Islander, 0.6% Hispanic American, 0.4% Native American, 5% international, 5% transferred in.

Freshmen *Admission:* 493 enrolled. *Average high school GPA:* 2.70.

Faculty *Total:* 335, 30% full-time, 12% with terminal degrees. *Student/faculty ratio:* 21:1.

Majors Accounting technician; agricultural business; banking; biomedical engineering-related technology; business; child care/guidance; computer/information sciences; construction technology; fire services administration; general studies; home furnishings; hospitality management; law enforcement/police science; liberal arts and sciences/liberal studies; medical laboratory technician; medical radiologic technology; mortuary science; nursing; occupational therapy assistant; physical therapy assistant; radio/television broadcasting technology; retailing operations; robotics technology; secretarial science.

Academic Programs *Special study options:* academic remediation for entering students, adult/continuing education programs, advanced placement credit, distance learning, honors programs, independent study, internships, part-time degree program, services for LD students, summer session for credit. *ROTC:* Army (c), Air Force (c).

Library James B. Allen Library plus 1 other with 84,901 titles, 240 serial subscriptions, 3,335 audiovisual materials, an OPAC.
Computers on Campus A campuswide network can be accessed from off campus. Internet access, online (class) registration, at least one staffed computer lab available.
Student Life *Housing:* college housing not available. *Activities and Organizations:* drama/theater group, student-run newspaper, radio station, choral group, Student Government Association, Phi Theta Kappa, Baptist Campus Ministries, Jefferson State Ambassadors, Students in Free Enterprise (SIFE). *Campus security:* 24-hour patrols. *Student Services:* women's center.
Athletics Member NJCAA. *Intercollegiate sports:* baseball M(s), softball W(s). *Intramural sports:* badminton M/W, basketball M/W, bowling M/W, soccer M/W, softball M/W, tennis M/W, volleyball M/W.
Standardized Tests *Required for some:* ACT ASSET, ACT COMPASS. *Recommended:* ACT (for placement).
Costs (2001–02) *Tuition:* state resident $1800 full-time, $60 per semester hour part-time; nonresident $3600 full-time, $120 per semester hour part-time. Full-time tuition and fees vary according to course load. Part-time tuition and fees vary according to course load. *Required fees:* $480 full-time, $16 per semester hour. *Waivers:* senior citizens and employees or children of employees.
Financial Aid In 2001, 189 Federal Work-Study jobs (averaging $1926).
Applying *Options:* common application, electronic application, early admission, deferred entrance. *Required for some:* high school transcript. *Application deadline:* rolling (freshmen). *Notification:* continuous (freshmen).
Admissions Contact Mr. Michael Hobbs, Director of Admissions, Advising, and Records, Jefferson State Community College, 2601 Carson Road, Birmingham, AL 35215-3098. *Phone:* 205-853-1200 Ext. 7991. *Toll-free phone:* 800-239-5900. *Fax:* 205-856-6070.

J. F. Drake State Technical College
Huntsville, Alabama

- **State-supported** 2-year, founded 1961, part of State of Alabama Department of Postsecondary Education
- **Calendar** semesters
- **Degree** certificates, diplomas, and associate
- **Urban** 6-acre campus
- **Coed,** 690 undergraduate students, 53% full-time, 41% women, 59% men

Undergraduates 369 full-time, 321 part-time. Students come from 2 states and territories, 2 other countries, 4% are from out of state, 49% African American, 0.4% Asian American or Pacific Islander, 0.6% Hispanic American, 0.4% Native American, 3% international, 37% transferred in.
Freshmen *Admission:* 275 applied, 249 admitted, 218 enrolled.
Faculty *Total:* 55, 42% full-time, 4% with terminal degrees. *Student/faculty ratio:* 20:1.
Majors Accounting; drafting; electrical/electronic engineering technology; graphic design/commercial art/illustration; information sciences/systems; machine technology; secretarial science.
Academic Programs *Special study options:* academic remediation for entering students, cooperative education, services for LD students.
Computers on Campus 145 computers available on campus for general student use. At least one staffed computer lab available.
Student Life *Housing:* college housing not available. *Activities and Organizations:* student-run newspaper, Phi Beta Lambda, Vocational Industrial Clubs of America. *Campus security:* 24-hour patrols.
Standardized Tests *Required:* ACT COMPASS.
Costs (2001–02) *Tuition:* state resident $1440 full-time, $60 per semester hour part-time; nonresident $2880 full-time, $120 per semester hour part-time. *Required fees:* $96 full-time, $4 per semester hour. *Waivers:* senior citizens and employees or children of employees.
Applying *Options:* deferred entrance. *Required:* high school transcript. *Application deadline:* rolling (freshmen).
Admissions Contact Mrs. Mary Malone, Registrar, J. F. Drake State Technical College, 3421 Meridian Street, Huntsville, AL 35811. *Phone:* 256-551-3109 Ext. 109. *E-mail:* malonem@dstc.cc.al.us.

Lawson State Community College
Birmingham, Alabama

- **State-supported** 2-year, founded 1949, part of Alabama College System
- **Calendar** semesters
- **Degree** certificates, diplomas, and associate
- **Urban** 30-acre campus
- **Coed**

Faculty *Student/faculty ratio:* 16:1.
Student Life *Campus security:* 24-hour emergency response devices and patrols, student patrols.
Athletics Member NJCAA.
Standardized Tests *Recommended:* ACT (for placement).
Costs (2002–03) *Tuition:* area resident $1632 full-time, $60 per credit part-time; state resident $3264 full-time, $60 per credit part-time; nonresident $120 per credit part-time. *Required fees:* $192 full-time, $8 per credit, $10 per term part-time.
Financial Aid In 2001, 91 Federal Work-Study jobs (averaging $3000).
Applying *Options:* common application, early admission, deferred entrance. *Required:* high school transcript.
Admissions Contact Mr. Darren C. Allen, Director of Admissions and Records, Lawson State Community College, 3060 Wilson Road, SW, Birmingham, AL 35221-1798. *Phone:* 205-929-6361. *Fax:* 205-923-7106.

Lurleen B. Wallace Junior College
Andalusia, Alabama

- **State-supported** 2-year, founded 1969, part of Alabama College System
- **Calendar** semesters
- **Degree** certificates and associate
- **Small-town** 200-acre campus
- **Coed,** 834 undergraduate students, 74% full-time, 57% women, 43% men

Undergraduates 613 full-time, 221 part-time. Students come from 6 states and territories, 1 other country, 5% are from out of state, 12% African American, 0.3% Hispanic American, 0.4% Native American, 0.1% international.
Freshmen *Admission:* 295 enrolled.
Faculty *Total:* 70, 36% full-time.
Majors Emergency medical technology; forest harvesting production technology; liberal arts and sciences/liberal studies.
Academic Programs *Special study options:* academic remediation for entering students, advanced placement credit, cooperative education, freshman honors college, part-time degree program, services for LD students, summer session for credit.
Library Lurleen B. Wallace Library with 35,278 titles, 133 serial subscriptions.
Computers on Campus 45 computers available on campus for general student use. Internet access, at least one staffed computer lab available.
Student Life *Housing:* college housing not available. *Activities and Organizations:* drama/theater group, student-run newspaper, Student Government Association, College Ambassadors, Phi Theta Kappa, Mu Alpha Theta, Christian Student Union. *Campus security:* 24-hour emergency response devices. *Student Services:* personal/psychological counseling.
Athletics Member NJCAA. *Intercollegiate sports:* baseball M(s), basketball M(s)/W(s), cross-country running M(s)/W(s), softball W(s).
Standardized Tests *Recommended:* ACT (for placement).
Costs (2001–02) *Tuition:* state resident $1632 full-time, $68 per credit hour part-time; nonresident $3264 full-time, $136 per credit hour part-time.
Applying *Options:* early admission, deferred entrance. *Required:* high school transcript. *Application deadline:* rolling (freshmen), rolling (transfers). *Notification:* continuous until 9/15 (freshmen).
Admissions Contact Mrs. Judy Hall, Director of Student Services, Lurleen B. Wallace Junior College, PO Box 1418, Andalusia, AL 36420. *Phone:* 334-222-6591 Ext. 271.

Marion Military Institute
Marion, Alabama

- **Independent** 2-year, founded 1842
- **Calendar** semesters
- **Degree** associate
- **Small-town** 130-acre campus
- **Endowment** $1.2 million
- **Coed, primarily men,** 165 undergraduate students

Undergraduates Students come from 35 states and territories, 3 other countries, 8% are from out of state, 97% live on campus.
Freshmen *Admission:* 269 applied, 226 admitted. *Average high school GPA:* 3.00.

Marion Military Institute (continued)

Faculty *Total:* 44, 91% full-time, 82% with terminal degrees. *Student/faculty ratio:* 6:1.

Majors Biological/physical sciences; engineering; liberal arts and sciences/liberal studies.

Academic Programs *Special study options:* academic remediation for entering students, off-campus study, part-time degree program. *ROTC:* Army (b), Air Force (b).

Library Baer Memorial Library with 36,000 titles, 140 serial subscriptions, 8,471 audiovisual materials.

Computers on Campus 21 computers available on campus for general student use. Internet access, at least one staffed computer lab available.

Student Life *Housing Options:* men-only, women-only. *Activities and Organizations:* drama/theater group, student-run newspaper, choral group, marching band, Swamp Foxes, White Knights, Marching Band, Drama Club, Scabbard and Blade. *Campus security:* night patrols by trained security personnel. *Student Services:* health clinic, personal/psychological counseling.

Athletics Member NJCAA. *Intercollegiate sports:* golf M/W, soccer M/W, tennis M/W. *Intramural sports:* baseball M/W, basketball M/W, football M/W, golf M/W, lacrosse M/W, racquetball M/W, soccer M/W, softball M/W, swimming M/W, table tennis M/W, tennis M/W, volleyball M/W, water polo M/W, weight lifting M/W.

Standardized Tests *Required:* SAT I or ACT (for admission).

Costs (2002–03) *Tuition:* state resident $11,430 full-time. *Required fees:* $535 full-time. *Room and board:* $3000. *Payment plan:* installment. *Waivers:* employees or children of employees.

Financial Aid In 2001, 21 Federal Work-Study jobs (averaging $339).

Applying *Options:* common application, deferred entrance. *Application fee:* $35. *Required:* high school transcript, minimum 2.0 GPA, 2 letters of recommendation. *Recommended:* interview, minimum SAT score of 920 or ACT score of 19. *Application deadlines:* 8/30 (freshmen), 8/30 (transfers).

Admissions Contact Col. Jim Carruthers, Director of Admissions, Marion Military Institute, 1101 Washington Street, Marion, AL 36756. *Phone:* 800-664-1842 Ext. 306. *Toll-free phone:* 800-664-1842 Ext. 307. *Fax:* 334-683-2383. *E-mail:* marionmilitary@zebra.net.

NORTHEAST ALABAMA COMMUNITY COLLEGE
Rainsville, Alabama

- **State-supported** 2-year, founded 1963, part of Alabama College System
- **Calendar** quarters
- **Degree** certificates and associate
- **Rural** 100-acre campus
- **Coed,** 1,714 undergraduate students, 68% full-time, 64% women, 36% men

Undergraduates 1,159 full-time, 555 part-time. Students come from 3 states and territories, 2% are from out of state, 0.9% African American, 0.4% Asian American or Pacific Islander, 0.6% Hispanic American, 7% Native American.

Freshmen *Admission:* 923 enrolled.

Faculty *Total:* 50, 60% full-time. *Student/faculty ratio:* 25:1.

Majors Biological/physical sciences; business administration; computer graphics; computer science; computer typography/composition; electrical/electronic engineering technology; emergency medical technology; finance; information sciences/systems; legal administrative assistant; liberal arts and sciences/liberal studies; medical administrative assistant; nursing; paralegal/legal assistant; pre-engineering; real estate; secretarial science; water resources.

Academic Programs *Special study options:* academic remediation for entering students, accelerated degree program, adult/continuing education programs, advanced placement credit, honors programs, part-time degree program, services for LD students, summer session for credit.

Library 45,000 titles, 142 serial subscriptions, an OPAC.

Computers on Campus 50 computers available on campus for general student use. At least one staffed computer lab available.

Student Life *Housing:* college housing not available. *Activities and Organizations:* drama/theater group, choral group, Baptist Campus Ministry, theater, SGA, Spectrum Art Club, choral group. *Campus security:* 24-hour emergency response devices and patrols, late-night transport/escort service. *Student Services:* personal/psychological counseling.

Standardized Tests *Required:* ACT ASSET, ACT COMPASS.

Costs (2001–02) *Tuition:* state resident $1920 full-time, $60 per credit part-time; nonresident $3584 full-time, $112 per credit part-time. *Waivers:* senior citizens and employees or children of employees.

Financial Aid In 2001, 40 Federal Work-Study jobs (averaging $2000).

Applying *Options:* early admission, deferred entrance. *Application deadline:* rolling (freshmen), rolling (transfers). *Notification:* continuous (freshmen).

Admissions Contact Dr. Joe Burke, Director of Admissions, Northeast Alabama Community College, PO Box 159, Rainsville, AL 35986. *Phone:* 256-638-4418 Ext. 325.

NORTHWEST-SHOALS COMMUNITY COLLEGE
Muscle Shoals, Alabama

- **State-supported** 2-year, founded 1963, part of State of Alabama Department of Postsecondary Education
- **Calendar** semesters
- **Degree** certificates, diplomas, and associate
- **Small-town** 205-acre campus
- **Coed,** 3,922 undergraduate students, 57% full-time, 58% women, 42% men

Undergraduates 2,225 full-time, 1,697 part-time. Students come from 3 states and territories, 1% are from out of state, 12% African American, 0.2% Asian American or Pacific Islander, 0.7% Hispanic American, 2% Native American, 0.1% international, 3% transferred in, 2% live on campus.

Freshmen *Admission:* 1,048 admitted, 1,048 enrolled.

Faculty *Total:* 208, 36% full-time, 5% with terminal degrees. *Student/faculty ratio:* 25:1.

Majors Accounting; agricultural education; art; business administration; computer engineering technology; computer programming; computer science; computer typography/composition; criminal justice/law enforcement administration; drafting; education; electrical/electronic engineering technology; elementary education; fire science; forestry; information sciences/systems; law enforcement/police science; liberal arts and sciences/liberal studies; medical laboratory technology; medical technology; music; nursing; pharmacy; practical nurse; pre-engineering; secretarial science; veterinary sciences; water treatment technology.

Academic Programs *Special study options:* academic remediation for entering students, accelerated degree program, adult/continuing education programs, advanced placement credit, cooperative education, honors programs, internships, part-time degree program, summer session for credit. *ROTC:* Army (c).

Library Larry W. McCoy Learning Resource Center and James Glasgow Library with 100,257 titles, 157 serial subscriptions, 1,176 audiovisual materials.

Computers on Campus 620 computers available on campus for general student use. A campuswide network can be accessed from off campus. Internet access, at least one staffed computer lab available.

Student Life *Housing Options:* coed. *Activities and Organizations:* student-run newspaper, choral group, Student Government Association, Science Club, Phi Theta Kappa, Baptist Campus Ministry, Northwest-Shoals Singers. *Campus security:* 24-hour emergency response devices and patrols. *Student Services:* personal/psychological counseling.

Athletics Member NJCAA. *Intercollegiate sports:* baseball M(s), basketball M(s)/W(s), cross-country running M(s), golf M(s), softball W(s), tennis W(s), volleyball W(s). *Intramural sports:* basketball M/W, softball M/W, table tennis M/W, tennis M/W, volleyball M/W.

Standardized Tests *Required:* ACT, ACT ASSET, or ACT COMPASS.

Costs (2002–03) *Tuition:* state resident $1920 full-time, $60 per credit hour part-time; nonresident $3840 full-time, $120 per credit hour part-time. *Required fees:* $256 full-time, $8 per credit hour. *Room and board:* room only: $1450. *Waivers:* senior citizens and employees or children of employees.

Financial Aid *Financial aid deadline:* 8/1.

Applying *Options:* common application. *Required:* high school transcript. *Application deadline:* rolling (freshmen), rolling (transfers).

Admissions Contact Dr. Karen Berryhill, Vice President of Student Development Services, Northwest-Shoals Community College, PO Box 2545, Muscle Shoals, AL 35662. *Phone:* 256-331-5261. *Toll-free phone:* 800-645-8967. *Fax:* 256-331-5366.

PRINCE INSTITUTE OF PROFESSIONAL STUDIES
Montgomery, Alabama

- **Independent** 2-year
- **Calendar** quarters
- **Degree** certificates and associate
- **Endowment** $6040
- **Coed, primarily women,** 103 undergraduate students, 74% full-time, 99% women, 1% men

Undergraduates 1% are from out of state, 14% African American, 1% Asian American or Pacific Islander.
Freshmen *Admission:* 9 applied, 9 admitted.
Faculty *Total:* 12, 58% full-time. *Student/faculty ratio:* 15:1.
Majors Business management/administrative services related; court reporting; medical transcription.
Student Life *Housing:* college housing not available. *Student Services:* personal/psychological counseling.
Costs (2002–03) *Tuition:* $4530 full-time, $1510 per term part-time. *Required fees:* $60 full-time, $60 per year. *Payment plan:* installment.
Applying *Application fee:* $90. *Required:* high school transcript, interview. *Application deadline:* 10/1 (freshmen).
Admissions Contact Ms. Hayley Mauldin, Director of Admissions, Prince Institute of Professional Studies, 7735 Atlanta Highway, Montgomery, AL 36117. *Phone:* 334-271-1670. *Toll-free phone:* 877-853-5569. *Fax:* 334-271-1671. *E-mail:* enterpips@aol.com.

REID STATE TECHNICAL COLLEGE
Evergreen, Alabama

- **State-supported** 2-year, founded 1966, part of Alabama College System
- **Calendar** semesters
- **Degree** certificates, diplomas, and associate
- **Rural** 26-acre campus
- **Coed,** 741 undergraduate students, 57% full-time, 60% women, 40% men

Undergraduates 419 full-time, 322 part-time. Students come from 2 states and territories, 1% are from out of state.
Freshmen *Admission:* 205 applied, 205 admitted, 205 enrolled.
Faculty *Total:* 44, 55% full-time, 59% with terminal degrees. *Student/faculty ratio:* 16:1.
Majors Electrical/electronic engineering technology; secretarial science.
Academic Programs *Special study options:* academic remediation for entering students, adult/continuing education programs, double majors, independent study, internships, part-time degree program, services for LD students, summer session for credit.
Library an OPAC, a Web page.
Computers on Campus 56 computers available on campus for general student use. A campuswide network can be accessed from off campus. At least one staffed computer lab available.
Student Life *Housing:* college housing not available. *Activities and Organizations:* student-run newspaper, Student Government Association. *Campus security:* 24-hour emergency response devices, day and evening security guard. *Student Services:* personal/psychological counseling.
Standardized Tests *Required:* ACT ASSET, Ability-To-Benefit Admissions Test.
Costs (2001–02) *Tuition:* state resident $1680 full-time, $56 per credit hour part-time; nonresident $3360 full-time, $112 per credit hour part-time. Full-time tuition and fees vary according to course load. Part-time tuition and fees vary according to course load. *Waivers:* senior citizens and employees or children of employees.
Financial Aid In 2001, 35 Federal Work-Study jobs (averaging $1500).
Applying *Options:* common application, early admission. *Required:* high school transcript. *Application deadline:* rolling (freshmen), rolling (transfers).
Admissions Contact Ms. Alesia Stuart, Public Relations/Marketing, Reid State Technical College, PO Box 588, Evergreen, AL 36401-0588. *Phone:* 251-578-1313 Ext. 108. *Fax:* 251-578-5355.

SHELTON STATE COMMUNITY COLLEGE
Tuscaloosa, Alabama

- **State-supported** 2-year, founded 1979
- **Calendar** semesters
- **Degree** certificates, diplomas, and associate
- **Small-town** campus with easy access to Birmingham
- **Coed**

Faculty *Student/faculty ratio:* 26:1.
Student Life *Campus security:* 24-hour emergency response devices and patrols.
Athletics Member NJCAA.
Standardized Tests *Required:* ACT ASSET.
Financial Aid In 2001, 97 Federal Work-Study jobs.
Admissions Contact Ms. Loretta Jones, Assistant to the Dean of Students, Shelton State Community College, 9500 Old Greensboro Highway, Tuscaloosa, AL 35405. *Phone:* 205-391-2236.

SNEAD STATE COMMUNITY COLLEGE
Boaz, Alabama

- **State-supported** 2-year, founded 1898, part of Alabama College System
- **Calendar** semesters
- **Degree** certificates and associate
- **Small-town** 42-acre campus with easy access to Birmingham
- **Endowment** $1.1 million
- **Coed,** 1,679 undergraduate students, 64% full-time, 62% women, 38% men

Undergraduates 1,068 full-time, 611 part-time. Students come from 3 states and territories, 2% are from out of state, 2% African American, 0.2% Asian American or Pacific Islander, 0.3% Hispanic American, 1% Native American, 8% transferred in, 2% live on campus.
Freshmen *Admission:* 599 applied, 599 admitted, 469 enrolled.
Faculty *Total:* 94, 28% full-time, 15% with terminal degrees. *Student/faculty ratio:* 26:1.
Majors Business administration; child care/guidance; computer/information sciences; data processing technology; engineering-related technology; engineering technology; general studies; liberal arts and sciences/liberal studies; multi/interdisciplinary studies related; veterinarian assistant.
Academic Programs *Special study options:* academic remediation for entering students, accelerated degree program, adult/continuing education programs, advanced placement credit, distance learning, external degree program, independent study, internships, off-campus study, part-time degree program, services for LD students, student-designed majors, summer session for credit.
Library McCain Learning Resource Center with 31,700 titles, 195 serial subscriptions, 1,340 audiovisual materials, an OPAC, a Web page.
Computers on Campus 250 computers available on campus for general student use. A campuswide network can be accessed from off campus. Internet access, at least one staffed computer lab available.
Student Life *Housing Options:* coed. *Activities and Organizations:* drama/theater group, student-run newspaper, choral group, Phi Theta Kappa, Snead Agricultural Organization, North American Veterinary Technician Association, Ambassadors, Baptist Campus Ministry. *Campus security:* 24-hour patrols, student patrols. *Student Services:* personal/psychological counseling.
Athletics Member NJCAA. *Intercollegiate sports:* baseball M(s), basketball M(s)/W(s), tennis W(s). *Intramural sports:* basketball M/W, volleyball M/W.
Standardized Tests *Required for some:* SAT I or ACT (for placement), ACT ASSET, ACT COMPASS.
Costs (2001–02) *Tuition:* state resident $1664 full-time, $52 per semester hour part-time; nonresident $3328 full-time, $104 per semester hour part-time. Full-time tuition and fees vary according to course load and reciprocity agreements. Part-time tuition and fees vary according to course load and reciprocity agreements. *Required fees:* $192 full-time, $6 per semester hour. *Room and board:* $1724; room only: $600. Room and board charges vary according to housing facility. *Waivers:* senior citizens and employees or children of employees.
Financial Aid In 2001, 40 Federal Work-Study jobs.
Applying *Options:* early admission, deferred entrance. *Required:* high school transcript. *Required for some:* interview. *Application deadlines:* 8/21 (freshmen), 8/21 (transfers). *Notification:* 8/21 (freshmen).
Admissions Contact Ms. Martha Buchanan, Director of Admissions and Records, Snead State Community College, PO Box 734, Boaz, AL 35957-0734. *Phone:* 256-593-5120 Ext. 207. *Fax:* 256-840-4122. *E-mail:* mbuchanan@snead.edu.

SOUTHERN UNION STATE COMMUNITY COLLEGE
Wadley, Alabama

- **State-supported** 2-year, founded 1922, part of Alabama College System
- **Calendar** quarters
- **Degree** certificates, diplomas, and associate
- **Rural** campus
- **Coed**

Faculty *Student/faculty ratio:* 19:1.
Student Life *Campus security:* 24-hour patrols, controlled dormitory access.

Southern Union State Community College (continued)
Athletics Member NSCAA, NJCAA.
Financial Aid In 2001, 150 Federal Work-Study jobs (averaging $1000). 35 State and other part-time jobs (averaging $1000).
Applying *Options:* common application, early admission, deferred entrance. *Required:* high school transcript.
Admissions Contact Mrs. Susan Salatto, Director of Student Development, Southern Union State Community College, PO Box 1000, Roberts Street, Wadley, AL 36276. *Phone:* 256-395-2211. *Fax:* 256-395-2215.

SOUTH UNIVERSITY
Montgomery, Alabama

- **Proprietary** primarily 2-year, founded 1887
- **Calendar** quarters
- **Degrees** associate and bachelor's
- **Urban** 1-acre campus
- **Coed, primarily women,** 240 undergraduate students, 62% full-time, 81% women, 19% men

Undergraduates 148 full-time, 92 part-time. Students come from 1 other state, 66% African American, 0.4% Asian American or Pacific Islander, 0.4% Hispanic American, 20% transferred in.
Freshmen *Admission:* 36 applied, 36 admitted, 36 enrolled.
Faculty *Total:* 28, 32% full-time, 14% with terminal degrees. *Student/faculty ratio:* 11:1.
Majors Accounting; business administration; health science; information sciences/systems; medical assistant; paralegal/legal assistant.
Academic Programs *Special study options:* academic remediation for entering students, double majors, internships, part-time degree program, summer session for credit.
Library South College Library with 5,000 titles, 43 serial subscriptions.
Computers on Campus 37 computers available on campus for general student use. Internet access, at least one staffed computer lab available.
Student Life *Housing:* college housing not available. *Campus security:* evening security guard.
Standardized Tests *Required for some:* SAT I or ACT (for admission).
Costs (2001–02) *Tuition:* $8685 full-time, $2195 per term part-time. Full-time tuition and fees vary according to course load and program. Part-time tuition and fees vary according to course load and program. *Payment plans:* installment, deferred payment. *Waivers:* employees or children of employees.
Financial Aid In 2001, 36 Federal Work-Study jobs (averaging $816).
Applying *Application fee:* $25. *Required:* high school transcript, interview. *Required for some:* 3 letters of recommendation. *Application deadline:* rolling (transfers). *Notification:* continuous (freshmen).
Admissions Contact Ms. Anna Pearson, Director of Admissions, South University, 122 Commerce Street, Montgomery, AL 36104-2538. *Phone:* 334-263-1013. *Fax:* 334-834-9559. *E-mail:* mtgfd@southuniversity.edu.

TRENHOLM STATE TECHNICAL COLLEGE
Montgomery, Alabama

- **State-supported** 2-year, founded 1963, part of Alabama College System
- **Calendar** semesters
- **Degree** certificates, diplomas, and associate
- **Suburban** 35-acre campus
- **Coed**

Student Life *Campus security:* 24-hour patrols.
Standardized Tests *Required for some:* SAT I or ACT (for admission).
Financial Aid In 2001, 92 Federal Work-Study jobs (averaging $767).
Applying *Options:* common application, deferred entrance. *Required:* high school transcript.
Admissions Contact Mr. Sam Munnerlyn, Dean of Students, Trenholm State Technical College, 1225 Air Base Blvd, PO Box 9000, Montgomery, AL 36108-3105. *Phone:* 334-240-9650. *Fax:* 334-832-9777. *E-mail:* smunnerlyn@acs.cc.al.us.

TRENHOLM STATE TECHNICAL COLLEGE, PATTERSON CAMPUS
Montgomery, Alabama

- **State-supported** 2-year, founded 1962, part of Alabama College System
- **Calendar** semesters
- **Degree** certificates, diplomas, and associate
- **Urban** 40-acre campus
- **Coed,** 1,800 undergraduate students

Undergraduates Students come from 3 states and territories.
Freshmen *Admission:* 235 applied, 235 admitted.
Faculty *Total:* 90, 78% full-time.
Majors Auto mechanic/technician; carpentry; clothing/textiles; construction technology; cosmetology; drafting; electrical/electronic engineering technology; graphic/printing equipment; heating/air conditioning/refrigeration; heavy equipment maintenance; information sciences/systems; instrumentation technology; machine technology; plumbing; welding technology.
Academic Programs *Special study options:* academic remediation for entering students, adult/continuing education programs, advanced placement credit, cooperative education, internships, part-time degree program, services for LD students, summer session for credit.
Computers on Campus 150 computers available on campus for general student use. Internet access, at least one staffed computer lab available.
Student Life *Housing:* college housing not available. *Campus security:* 24-hour emergency response devices and patrols.
Standardized Tests *Required for some:* ACT ASSET. *Recommended:* ACT (for placement).
Costs (2002–03) *Tuition:* area resident $1824 full-time, $76 per credit hour part-time; nonresident $3264 full-time, $136 per credit hour part-time.
Applying *Options:* early admission. *Required for some:* high school transcript. *Application deadline:* rolling (freshmen), rolling (transfers).
Admissions Contact Mr. David A. Jones, Dean of Student Resources, Trenholm State Technical College, Patterson Campus, 3920 Troy Highway, Montgomery, AL 36116-2699. *Phone:* 334-420-4303.

VIRGINIA COLLEGE AT HUNTSVILLE
Huntsville, Alabama

Admissions Contact Ms. Pat Foster, Director of Admissions, Virginia College at Huntsville, 2800-A Bob Wallace Avenue, Huntsville, AL 35805. *Phone:* 205-533-7387.

WALLACE STATE COMMUNITY COLLEGE
Hanceville, Alabama

- **State-supported** 2-year, founded 1966
- **Calendar** semesters
- **Degree** diplomas and associate
- **Rural** 216-acre campus with easy access to Birmingham
- **Coed,** 4,770 undergraduate students, 54% full-time, 60% women, 40% men

Undergraduates 2,555 full-time, 2,215 part-time. Students come from 15 states and territories, 6% are from out of state, 6% transferred in, 3% live on campus.
Freshmen *Admission:* 2,238 applied, 2,220 admitted, 1,002 enrolled. *Test scores:* ACT scores over 18: 72%; ACT scores over 24: 14%; ACT scores over 30: 1%.
Faculty *Total:* 339, 35% full-time.
Majors Accounting; agricultural sciences; aircraft pilot (professional); art education; auto mechanic/technician; aviation technology; business administration; business education; business marketing and marketing management; carpentry; child care/development; computer programming; computer science; construction technology; cosmetology; criminal justice/law enforcement administration; dental assistant; dental hygiene; drafting; early childhood education; education; electrical/electronic engineering technology; elementary education; emergency medical technology; engineering; farm/ranch management; fashion merchandising; finance; fire science; food products retailing; heating/air conditioning/refrigeration; horticulture science; industrial radiologic technology; interior design; labor/personnel relations; law enforcement/police science; legal administrative assistant; liberal arts and sciences/liberal studies; library science; machine technology; medical administrative assistant; medical assistant; medical laboratory technician; medical records administration; mental health/rehabilitation; music; nursing; occupational safety/health technology; occupational therapy; paralegal/legal assistant; physical therapy; postal management; poultry science; practical nurse; real estate; religious studies; respiratory therapy; secretarial science; welding technology.
Academic Programs *Special study options:* academic remediation for entering students, advanced placement credit, cooperative education, part-time degree program, summer session for credit.

Library Wallace State College Library with 41,500 titles, 425 serial subscriptions, an OPAC.
Computers on Campus 75 computers available on campus for general student use. At least one staffed computer lab available.
Student Life *Housing Options:* men-only, women-only. *Activities and Organizations:* choral group, Student Government Association, Vocational Industrial Clubs of America. *Student Services:* personal/psychological counseling.
Athletics Member NJCAA. *Intercollegiate sports:* baseball M(s), basketball M(s)/W(s), cross-country running M(s)/W(s), golf M(s), soccer M(s)/W(s), softball W(s), tennis M/W, track and field M(s)/W(s), volleyball W(s). *Intramural sports:* basketball M/W, softball M/W, tennis M/W, volleyball M/W.
Standardized Tests *Required for some:* ACT (for placement), nursing exam. *Recommended:* ACT (for placement).
Costs (2001–02) *Tuition:* state resident $52 per credit part-time; nonresident $104 per credit part-time. *Required fees:* $2 per hour. *Room and board:* room only: $1350. Room and board charges vary according to housing facility. *Waivers:* senior citizens and employees or children of employees.
Financial Aid In 2001, 70 Federal Work-Study jobs. *Financial aid deadline:* 5/1.
Applying *Options:* early admission, deferred entrance. *Required:* high school transcript. *Application deadline:* rolling (freshmen), rolling (transfers). *Notification:* continuous (freshmen).
Admissions Contact Ms. Linda Sperling, Director of Admissions, Wallace State Community College, PO Box 2000, Hanceville, AL 35077-2000. *Phone:* 256-352-8278. *Fax:* 256-352-8228.

ALASKA

CHARTER COLLEGE
Anchorage, Alaska

- **Proprietary** primarily 2-year, founded 1985
- **Calendar** quarters
- **Degrees** certificates, associate, and bachelor's
- **Urban** campus
- **Coed,** 416 undergraduate students

Faculty *Total:* 43, 23% full-time. *Student/faculty ratio:* 15:1.
Majors Accounting; business administration; business systems networking/ telecommunications; computer maintenance technology; computer science; medical assistant.
Academic Programs *Special study options:* adult/continuing education programs, internships, part-time degree program, summer session for credit.
Library Charter College Library with 1,000 titles, 50 serial subscriptions, a Web page.
Computers on Campus 85 computers available on campus for general student use. Internet access, at least one staffed computer lab available.
Student Life *Housing:* college housing not available. *Activities and Organizations:* Student Support Committee. *Campus security:* 24-hour emergency response devices.
Costs (2001–02) *Tuition:* $6705 full-time, $169 per credit hour part-time. Full-time tuition and fees vary according to course load. Part-time tuition and fees vary according to course load. *Payment plans:* installment, deferred payment.
Applying *Application fee:* $20. *Required:* high school transcript, interview. *Application deadline:* rolling (freshmen), rolling (transfers). *Notification:* continuous (freshmen).
Admissions Contact Ms. Lily Sirianni, Vice President, Charter College, 2221 East Northern Lights Boulevard, Suite 120, Anchorage, AK 99508-4157. *Phone:* 907-277-1000. *Toll-free phone:* 800-279-1008. *Fax:* 907-274-3342. *E-mail:* contact@chartercollege.org.

UNIVERSITY OF ALASKA ANCHORAGE, KENAI PENINSULA COLLEGE
Soldotna, Alaska

- **State-supported** 2-year, founded 1964, part of University of Alaska System
- **Calendar** semesters
- **Degree** certificates and associate
- **Rural** 360-acre campus
- **Endowment** $950,000
- **Coed,** 1,911 undergraduate students

Freshmen *Admission:* 91 applied, 91 admitted.
Faculty *Total:* 150, 20% full-time. *Student/faculty ratio:* 15:1.
Majors Business administration; electrical/electronic engineering technology; instrumentation technology; liberal arts and sciences/liberal studies; machine technology; petroleum technology; secretarial science.
Academic Programs *Special study options:* academic remediation for entering students, adult/continuing education programs, advanced placement credit, English as a second language, part-time degree program, services for LD students.
Library Kenai Peninsula College Library with 25,000 titles, 95 serial subscriptions.
Computers on Campus 45 computers available on campus for general student use. At least one staffed computer lab available.
Student Life *Housing:* college housing not available. *Activities and Organizations:* drama/theater group, student-run newspaper. *Campus security:* 24-hour emergency response devices. *Student Services:* personal/psychological counseling.
Costs (2001–02) *Tuition:* state resident $82 per credit part-time; nonresident $256 per credit part-time. Full-time tuition and fees vary according to class time. Part-time tuition and fees vary according to class time. *Required fees:* $10 per credit. *Payment plans:* tuition prepayment, installment, deferred payment. *Waivers:* senior citizens and employees or children of employees.
Applying *Options:* common application. *Required:* high school transcript. *Required for some:* interview. *Application deadline:* rolling (freshmen), rolling (transfers).
Admissions Contact Ms. Shelly Love, Admission and Registration Coordinator, University of Alaska Anchorage, Kenai Peninsula College, 34820 College Drive, Soldotna, AK 99669-9798. *Phone:* 907-262-0311.

UNIVERSITY OF ALASKA ANCHORAGE, KODIAK COLLEGE
Kodiak, Alaska

- **State-supported** 2-year, founded 1968, part of University of Alaska System
- **Calendar** semesters
- **Degree** certificates and associate
- **Rural** 68-acre campus
- **Coed,** 755 undergraduate students

Undergraduates Students come from 1 other state.
Freshmen *Admission:* 71 applied, 71 admitted.
Faculty *Total:* 40. *Student/faculty ratio:* 19:1.
Majors Business administration; liberal arts and sciences/liberal studies; secretarial science.
Academic Programs *Special study options:* adult/continuing education programs, advanced placement credit, double majors, part-time degree program.
Library Carolyn Floyd Library with 20,000 titles, 100 serial subscriptions.
Computers on Campus 40 computers available on campus for general student use. Internet access, at least one staffed computer lab available.
Student Life *Housing:* college housing not available.
Standardized Tests *Required:* ACT ASSET.
Costs (2002–03) *Tuition:* state resident $2130 full-time, $71 per credit part-time; nonresident $7350 full-time, $245 per credit part-time. *Required fees:* $10 full-time, $5 per term part-time. *Payment plan:* installment. *Waivers:* senior citizens and employees or children of employees.
Applying *Recommended:* high school transcript. *Application deadline:* rolling (freshmen).
Admissions Contact Ms. Karen Hamer, Registrar, University of Alaska Anchorage, Kodiak College, 117 Benny Benson Drive, Kodiak, AK 99615. *Phone:* 907-486-1235. *Fax:* 907-486-1264.

UNIVERSITY OF ALASKA ANCHORAGE, MATANUSKA-SUSITNA COLLEGE
Palmer, Alaska

- **State-supported** 2-year, founded 1958, part of University of Alaska System
- **Calendar** semesters
- **Degree** certificates and associate
- **Small-town** 950-acre campus with easy access to Anchorage
- **Coed,** 1,594 undergraduate students, 22% full-time, 68% women, 32% men

University of Alaska Anchorage, Matanuska-Susitna College (continued)

Undergraduates Students come from 10 other countries, 0.8% African American, 1% Asian American or Pacific Islander, 2% Hispanic American, 4% Native American.

Freshmen *Admission:* 107 applied, 107 admitted.

Faculty *Total:* 106, 16% full-time, 5% with terminal degrees. *Student/faculty ratio:* 11:1.

Majors Accounting; business administration; electrical/electronic engineering technology; fire science; heating/air conditioning/refrigeration; human services; liberal arts and sciences/liberal studies; secretarial science.

Academic Programs *Special study options:* academic remediation for entering students, adult/continuing education programs, advanced placement credit, cooperative education, distance learning, independent study, internships, off-campus study, part-time degree program.

Library Al Okeson Library with 40,000 titles, 200 serial subscriptions, 460 audiovisual materials, an OPAC, a Web page.

Computers on Campus 109 computers available on campus for general student use. A campuswide network can be accessed from off campus. Internet access, at least one staffed computer lab available.

Student Life *Housing:* college housing not available. *Activities and Organizations:* student-run newspaper, choral group, student government, Math Club. *Campus security:* 24-hour patrols.

Standardized Tests *Recommended:* SAT I or ACT (for placement).

Costs (2002–03) *Tuition:* state resident $1968 full-time; nonresident $6144 full-time. *Required fees:* $100 full-time.

Financial Aid In 2001, 8 Federal Work-Study jobs (averaging $3000).

Applying *Options:* common application, early admission. *Application fee:* $35. *Required:* high school transcript. *Recommended:* minimum 2.0 GPA. *Application deadline:* rolling (freshmen), rolling (transfers).

Admissions Contact Ms. Sandra Gravley, Admissions and Records Coordinator, University of Alaska Anchorage, Matanuska-Susitna College, PO Box 2889, Palmer, AK 99645-2889. *Phone:* 907-745-9712. *Fax:* 907-745-9747. *E-mail:* pamgh@uaa.alaska.edu.

UNIVERSITY OF ALASKA, PRINCE WILLIAM SOUND COMMUNITY COLLEGE

Valdez, Alaska

- **State-supported** 2-year, founded 1978, part of University of Alaska System
- **Calendar** semesters
- **Degree** certificates, diplomas, and associate
- **Small-town** campus
- **Endowment** $62,630
- **Coed**

Student Life *Campus security:* student patrols, housing manager supervision.

Standardized Tests *Required:* ACT ASSET.

Costs (2001–02) *Tuition:* state resident $1584 full-time, $66 per credit part-time; nonresident $1584 full-time, $66 per credit part-time. Full-time tuition and fees vary according to class time and course load. Part-time tuition and fees vary according to class time and course load. *Required fees:* $108 full-time, $53 per term part-time. *Room and board:* $1950. Room and board charges vary according to housing facility.

Applying *Options:* early admission. *Application fee:* $10.

Admissions Contact Mr. Nathan J. Platt, Director of Student Services, University of Alaska, Prince William Sound Community College, PO Box 97, Valdez, AK 99686-0097. *Phone:* 907-834-1631. *Toll-free phone:* 800-478-8800 Ext. 1600. *Fax:* 907-834-1661. *E-mail:* vnnjp@uaa.alaska.edu.

UNIVERSITY OF ALASKA SOUTHEAST, KETCHIKAN CAMPUS

Ketchikan, Alaska

- **State and locally supported** 2-year, founded 1954, part of University of Alaska System
- **Calendar** semesters
- **Degree** associate
- **Small-town** 51-acre campus
- **Endowment** $2.6 million
- **Coed,** 589 undergraduate students

Undergraduates Students come from 5 states and territories, 2 other countries.

Freshmen *Admission:* 68 applied, 68 admitted.

Faculty *Total:* 40, 25% full-time. *Student/faculty ratio:* 14:1.

Majors Business administration; liberal arts and sciences/liberal studies; secretarial science; travel/tourism management.

Academic Programs *Special study options:* academic remediation for entering students, adult/continuing education programs, distance learning, English as a second language, independent study, internships, off-campus study, part-time degree program, services for LD students, student-designed majors.

Library Ketchikan Campus Library with 54,000 titles, 175 serial subscriptions, an OPAC.

Computers on Campus 40 computers available on campus for general student use. Internet access, at least one staffed computer lab available.

Student Life *Housing:* college housing not available. *Activities and Organizations:* student council. *Campus security:* 24-hour emergency response devices. *Student Services:* personal/psychological counseling.

Standardized Tests *Required for some:* ACT ASSET. *Recommended:* SAT I or ACT (for placement).

Costs (2001–02) *Tuition:* state resident $1896 full-time, $79 per credit hour part-time. Full-time tuition and fees vary according to class time, course load, and reciprocity agreements. Part-time tuition and fees vary according to class time, course load, and reciprocity agreements. *Required fees:* $144 full-time, $6 per credit. *Payment plan:* deferred payment. *Waivers:* senior citizens and employees or children of employees.

Applying *Options:* early admission. *Application fee:* $35. *Required:* high school transcript. *Required for some:* essay or personal statement. *Application deadline:* rolling (freshmen).

Admissions Contact Mrs. Gail Klein, Student Services Coordinator, University of Alaska Southeast, Ketchikan Campus, 2600 7th Avenue, Ketchikan, AK 99901-5798. *Phone:* 907-228-4508. *Fax:* 907-225-3624. *E-mail:* gail.klein@uas.alaska.edu.

UNIVERSITY OF ALASKA SOUTHEAST, SITKA CAMPUS

Sitka, Alaska

- **State-supported** 2-year, founded 1962, part of University of Alaska System
- **Calendar** semesters
- **Degree** certificates, diplomas, and associate
- **Small-town** campus
- **Coed,** 1,503 undergraduate students

Undergraduates Students come from 10 states and territories, 2 other countries, 2% live on campus.

Faculty *Total:* 105. *Student/faculty ratio:* 13:1.

Majors Business administration; computer engineering technology; computer/information sciences; computer systems analysis; environmental technology; health services administration; liberal arts and sciences/liberal studies; medical assistant; water treatment technology.

Academic Programs *Special study options:* academic remediation for entering students, adult/continuing education programs, cooperative education, English as a second language, internships, off-campus study, part-time degree program, summer session for credit.

Library Stratton Library with 80,050 titles, 306 serial subscriptions, an OPAC, a Web page.

Computers on Campus 45 computers available on campus for general student use. A campuswide network can be accessed from student residence rooms and from off campus. Internet access, at least one staffed computer lab available.

Student Life *Housing Options:* coed. *Activities and Organizations:* Student Government Association, Tai Chi Club. *Campus security:* 24-hour emergency response devices.

Costs (2001–02) *Tuition:* state resident $1872 full-time, $78 per credit part-time; nonresident $5808 full-time, $242 per credit part-time. *Required fees:* $696 full-time, $348 per term part-time.

Applying *Options:* common application, early admission. *Application fee:* $35. *Required:* high school transcript, minimum 2.0 GPA. *Required for some:* essay or personal statement. *Application deadline:* rolling (freshmen), rolling (transfers). *Notification:* continuous (freshmen).

Admissions Contact Mr. Tim Schroeder, Coordinator of Student Services, University of Alaska Southeast, Sitka Campus, 1332 Seward Avenue, Sitka, AK 99835-9418. *Phone:* 907-747-7703 Ext. 9112. *Toll-free phone:* 800-478-6653. *Fax:* 907-747-7747. *E-mail:* tnkmn@acadl.alaska.edu.

ARIZONA

AIBT INTERNATIONAL INSTITUTE OF THE AMERICAS
Phoenix, Arizona

- **Independent** primarily 2-year
- **Calendar** semesters
- **Degrees** certificates, diplomas, associate, and bachelor's
- **Coed,** 1,036 undergraduate students, 100% full-time, 72% women, 28% men

Undergraduates 1,036 full-time. Students come from 7 states and territories, 2% are from out of state, 11% African American, 5% Asian American or Pacific Islander, 36% Hispanic American, 12% Native American, 2% transferred in.
Freshmen *Admission:* 1,617 applied, 1,617 admitted, 350 enrolled.
Faculty *Total:* 95, 58% full-time, 25% with terminal degrees. *Student/faculty ratio:* 11:1.
Majors Accounting related; business administration; business information/data processing related; computer/information technology services administration and management related; criminal justice/law enforcement administration; health professions and related sciences; information technology; medical assistant; medical transcription.
Academic Programs *Special study options:* accelerated degree program, adult/continuing education programs, cooperative education, distance learning, internships, summer session for credit.
Library Learning Resrouce Center with 1,974 titles, 1,750 serial subscriptions, 120 audiovisual materials, an OPAC, a Web page.
Computers on Campus 421 computers available on campus for general student use. Internet access, online (class) registration, at least one staffed computer lab available.
Student Life *Housing:* college housing not available. *Campus security:* 24-hour emergency response devices.
Costs (2002–03) *Tuition:* $7800 full-time, $260 per credit part-time. Full-time tuition and fees vary according to program. No tuition increase for student's term of enrollment. *Required fees:* $350 full-time. *Payment plan:* tuition prepayment. *Waivers:* employees or children of employees.
Applying *Options:* electronic application, early admission, deferred entrance. *Required:* interview. *Application deadline:* rolling (freshmen). *Notification:* continuous (freshmen).
Admissions Contact Mark Wright, Admission Representative, AIBT International Institute of the Americas, 6049 North 43 Avenue, Phoenix, AZ 85019. *Phone:* 888-884-2428. *Toll-free phone:* 888-884-2428 Ext. 218 (in-state); 800-793-2428 (out-of-state). *Fax:* 602-973-2572. *E-mail:* info@aibt.edu.

APOLLO COLLEGE-PHOENIX, INC.
Phoenix, Arizona

Admissions Contact Ms. Cindy Nestor, Director of Admissions, Apollo College-Phoenix, Inc., 2701 West Bethany Home Road, Phoenix, AZ 85051. *Phone:* 602-433-1333. *Toll-free phone:* 800-36-TRAIN.

APOLLO COLLEGE-TRI-CITY, INC.
Mesa, Arizona

Admissions Contact Mr. Tim Kulesha, Campus Director, Apollo College-Tri-City, Inc., 630 West Southern Avenue, Mesa, AZ 85210-5004. *Phone:* 602-831-6585. *Toll-free phone:* 800-36-TRAIN.

APOLLO COLLEGE-TUCSON, INC.
Tucson, Arizona

Admissions Contact Ms. Elaine Cue, Campus Director, Apollo College-Tucson, Inc., 3870 North Oracle Road, Tucson, AZ 85705-3227. *Phone:* 520-888-5885. *Toll-free phone:* 800-36-TRAIN.

APOLLO COLLEGE-WESTSIDE, INC.
Phoenix, Arizona

Admissions Contact Ms. Julie Citron, Director of Admissions, Apollo College-Westside, Inc., 2701 West Bethany Home Road, Phoenix, AZ 85017. *Phone:* 602-433-1333. *Toll-free phone:* 800-36-TRAIN.

ARIZONA AUTOMOTIVE INSTITUTE
Glendale, Arizona

- **Proprietary** 2-year
- **Degree** diplomas and associate
- 450 undergraduate students, 100% full-time
- 100% of applicants were admitted

Undergraduates Students come from 10 states and territories, 4% African American, 5% Asian American or Pacific Islander, 25% Hispanic American, 25% Native American, 0.9% international.
Freshmen *Admission:* 303 applied, 303 admitted.
Faculty *Total:* 15, 87% full-time.
Majors Auto mechanic/technician; automotive engineering technology; diesel engine mechanic.
Applying *Required:* high school transcript.
Admissions Contact Mark LaCara, Director of Admissions, Arizona Automotive Institute, 6829 North 46th Avenue, Glendale, AZ 85301-3597. *Phone:* 623-934-7273 Ext. 211.

ARIZONA WESTERN COLLEGE
Yuma, Arizona

- **State and locally supported** 2-year, founded 1962, part of Arizona State Community College System
- **Calendar** semesters
- **Degree** certificates and associate
- **Rural** 640-acre campus
- **Coed,** 6,089 undergraduate students, 26% full-time, 61% women, 39% men

Undergraduates 1,613 full-time, 4,476 part-time. Students come from 17 states and territories, 12% are from out of state, 3% African American, 1% Asian American or Pacific Islander, 65% Hispanic American, 1% Native American, 0.1% international, 7% live on campus.
Freshmen *Admission:* 765 applied, 765 admitted.
Faculty *Total:* 373, 28% full-time. *Student/faculty ratio:* 16:1.
Majors Agricultural business; agricultural sciences; art; auto mechanic/technician; biological/physical sciences; biology; broadcast journalism; business administration; chemistry; computer science; criminal justice/law enforcement administration; developmental/child psychology; drafting; education; electrical/electronic engineering technology; engineering technology; English; environmental science; family/consumer studies; finance; fire science; gaming/sports officiating related; geology; health science; heating/air conditioning/refrigeration; hospitality management; human services; information sciences/systems; law enforcement/police science; liberal arts and sciences/liberal studies; mathematics; music; nursing; oceanography; physical education; physics; practical nurse; pre-engineering; secretarial science; social sciences; Spanish; theater arts/drama; welding technology.
Academic Programs *Special study options:* academic remediation for entering students, adult/continuing education programs, advanced placement credit, cooperative education, distance learning, English as a second language, honors programs, independent study, part-time degree program, summer session for credit.
Library Arizona Western College Library with 698 serial subscriptions, 10,800 audiovisual materials, an OPAC, a Web page.
Computers on Campus 120 computers available on campus for general student use. A campuswide network can be accessed from off campus. Internet access, at least one staffed computer lab available.
Student Life *Housing Options:* coed. *Activities and Organizations:* drama/theater group, student-run newspaper, radio and television station, choral group, Associated Students Governing Board, MECHA, Umoja, Honors Club, UVU. *Campus security:* 24-hour emergency response devices and patrols, student patrols, late-night transport/escort service. *Student Services:* health clinic, personal/psychological counseling.
Athletics Member NJCAA. *Intercollegiate sports:* baseball M(s), basketball M(s), football M(s), soccer M(s), softball W(s), volleyball W(s). *Intramural sports:* badminton M/W, basketball M/W, football M, soccer M, softball M/W, swimming M/W, table tennis M/W, volleyball M/W.
Costs (2001–02) *Tuition:* state resident $990 full-time, $33 per credit hour part-time; nonresident $5358 full-time, $38 per credit hour part-time. Full-time tuition and fees vary according to course load. Part-time tuition and fees vary according to course load. *Room and board:* $3680. Room and board charges vary according to board plan. *Payment plan:* deferred payment. *Waivers:* senior citizens and employees or children of employees.

Arizona Western College (continued)

Applying *Options:* common application, early admission, deferred entrance. *Required for some:* minimum 3.0 GPA. *Application deadline:* rolling (freshmen), rolling (transfers).

Admissions Contact Mr. Bryan Doak, Registrar, Arizona Western College, PO Box 929, Yuma, AZ 85366. *Phone:* 928-317-7617. *Toll-free phone:* 888-293-0392. *Fax:* 928-344-7730. *E-mail:* bryan.doak@azwestern.edu.

THE ART CENTER
Tucson, Arizona

- **Private** 2-year, founded 1983
- **Degree** certificates, diplomas, and associate
- **Suburban** campus
- 300 undergraduate students

Applying *Application fee:* $25.

Admissions Contact Ms. Colleen Gimbel-Froebe, Associate Director of Admissions and Placement, The Art Center, 2525 North Country Club Road, Tucson, AZ 85716-2505. *Phone:* 520-325-0123. *Toll-free phone:* 800-827-8753. *Fax:* 520-325-5535.

THE BRYMAN SCHOOL
Phoenix, Arizona

- **Proprietary** 2-year, founded 1964
- **Calendar** continuous
- **Degree** diplomas and associate
- **Urban** campus
- **Coed, primarily women,** 1,100 undergraduate students

Undergraduates Students come from 20 states and territories, 20% are from out of state.

Majors Dental assistant; health facilities administration; medical assistant; medical radiologic technology; operating room technician.

Library Main Library plus 1 other.

Computers on Campus Internet access available.

Student Life *Housing:* college housing not available. *Campus security:* late-night transport/escort service.

Applying *Required:* high school transcript, interview. *Application deadline:* rolling (freshmen), rolling (transfers).

Admissions Contact Ms. Vicki Maurer, Admission Manager, The Bryman School, 4343 North 16th Street, Phoenix, AZ 85016-5338. *Phone:* 602-274-4300. *Toll-free phone:* 800-729-4819. *Fax:* 602-248-9087.

CENTRAL ARIZONA COLLEGE
Coolidge, Arizona

- **County-supported** 2-year, founded 1961
- **Calendar** semesters
- **Degree** certificates and associate
- **Rural** 709-acre campus with easy access to Phoenix
- **Coed,** 5,007 undergraduate students

Undergraduates Students come from 6 other countries, 4% African American, 0.6% Asian American or Pacific Islander, 28% Hispanic American, 7% Native American, 0.5% international.

Faculty *Total:* 51. *Student/faculty ratio:* 15:1.

Majors Accounting; agricultural sciences; auto mechanic/technician; business administration; business marketing and marketing management; child care/development; civil engineering technology; computer/information sciences; computer science; corrections; criminal justice/law enforcement administration; dietetics; early childhood education; emergency medical technology; engineering; health aide; hotel and restaurant management; industrial technology; legal administrative assistant; liberal arts and sciences/liberal studies; materials science; medical administrative assistant; medical transcription; nursing; practical nurse; secretarial science.

Academic Programs *Special study options:* academic remediation for entering students, adult/continuing education programs, distance learning, honors programs, independent study, part-time degree program, services for LD students, student-designed majors, summer session for credit.

Library Learning Resource Center with 99,480 titles, 494 serial subscriptions.

Computers on Campus Internet access, at least one staffed computer lab available.

Student Life *Activities and Organizations:* drama/theater group, student-run newspaper, choral group. *Campus security:* 24-hour emergency response devices and patrols. *Student Services:* personal/psychological counseling.

Athletics Member NJCAA. *Intercollegiate sports:* baseball M(s), basketball M(s)/W(s), cross-country running M(s)/W(s), equestrian sports M(s)/W(s), golf M(s), softball W(s), track and field M(s)/W(s).

Standardized Tests *Required:* ACT ASSET or ACT COMPASS.

Costs (2002–03) *Tuition:* state resident $1036 full-time, $37 per credit part-time; nonresident $5824 full-time, $208 per credit part-time. Part-time tuition and fees vary according to class time. *Required fees:* $14 full-time, $7 per term part-time. *Room and board:* $3820. Room and board charges vary according to housing facility.

Financial Aid In 2001, 58 Federal Work-Study jobs (averaging $1290).

Applying *Options:* common application, early admission, deferred entrance. *Application deadline:* rolling (freshmen), rolling (transfers). *Notification:* continuous (freshmen).

Admissions Contact Central Arizona College, 8470 North Overfield Road, Coolidge, AZ 85228. *Phone:* 520-426-4406. *Toll-free phone:* 800-237-9814. *Fax:* 520-426-4271. *E-mail:* leonor_verduzco@centralaz.edu.

CHANDLER-GILBERT COMMUNITY COLLEGE
Chandler, Arizona

Admissions Contact Ms. Ruth M. Romano, Supervisor of Admissions and Records, Chandler-Gilbert Community College, 2626 East Pecos Road, Chandler, AZ 85225-2479. *Phone:* 602-732-7319.

CHAPARRAL COLLEGE
Tucson, Arizona

- **Proprietary** primarily 2-year, founded 1972
- **Calendar** 5 five-week modules
- **Degrees** certificates, diplomas, associate, and bachelor's (bachelor's degree in business administration only)
- **Suburban** campus with easy access to Phoenix
- **Coed,** 343 undergraduate students, 100% full-time, 59% women, 41% men

Undergraduates 343 full-time. Students come from 1 other state, 3 other countries, 5% African American, 1% Asian American or Pacific Islander, 38% Hispanic American, 14% Native American.

Freshmen *Admission:* 125 enrolled.

Faculty *Total:* 29, 38% full-time, 21% with terminal degrees. *Student/faculty ratio:* 25:1.

Majors Accounting; business administration; computer installation/repair; computer systems networking/telecommunications; criminal justice studies; legal administrative assistant; secretarial science.

Academic Programs *Special study options:* academic remediation for entering students, internships, summer session for credit.

Library 6,000 titles, 65 serial subscriptions, 500 audiovisual materials, a Web page.

Computers on Campus 150 computers available on campus for general student use. Internet access, at least one staffed computer lab available.

Student Life *Housing:* college housing not available. *Activities and Organizations:* student-run newspaper. *Campus security:* 24-hour emergency response devices. *Student Services:* personal/psychological counseling.

Costs (2002–03) *Tuition:* $7590 full-time.

Applying *Options:* common application. *Application fee:* $25. *Required:* high school transcript, interview. *Required for some:* letters of recommendation. *Application deadline:* rolling (freshmen), rolling (transfers).

Admissions Contact Becki Rossini, Lead Representative, Chaparral College, 4585 E. Speedway No. 204, Tucson, AZ 85712. *Phone:* 520-327-6866. *Fax:* 520-325-0108.

COCHISE COLLEGE
Douglas, Arizona

- **State and locally supported** 2-year, founded 1962, part of Cochise College
- **Calendar** semesters
- **Degree** certificates and associate
- **Rural** 500-acre campus

■ **Coed,** 6,011 undergraduate students

Undergraduates Students come from 4 states and territories, 8 other countries, 17% live on campus.
Freshmen *Admission:* 490 applied, 490 admitted.
Faculty *Total:* 406, 25% full-time.
Majors Agricultural sciences; aircraft mechanic/airframe; aircraft pilot (professional); anthropology; art; aviation technology; behavioral sciences; biology; business administration; chemistry; computer programming; computer science; criminal justice/law enforcement administration; drafting; education; English; film studies; fire science; history; information sciences/systems; international relations; journalism; law enforcement/police science; legal administrative assistant; liberal arts and sciences/liberal studies; mass communications; medical administrative assistant; nursing; physical education; political science; pre-engineering; psychology; secretarial science; social sciences; social work; Spanish; teacher assistant/aide.
Academic Programs *Special study options:* academic remediation for entering students, accelerated degree program, cooperative education, distance learning, English as a second language, independent study, internships, part-time degree program, services for LD students, summer session for credit.
Library 42,876 titles, 182 serial subscriptions, a Web page.
Computers on Campus 84 computers available on campus for general student use. Internet access, at least one staffed computer lab available.
Student Life *Activities and Organizations:* choral group, student government, Phi Theta Kappa. *Campus security:* 24-hour emergency response devices and patrols, controlled dormitory access. *Student Services:* health clinic, personal/psychological counseling.
Athletics Member NJCAA. *Intercollegiate sports:* baseball M(s), basketball M(s)/W(s), equestrian sports M(s)/W(s), soccer W(s). *Intramural sports:* basketball M.
Standardized Tests *Recommended:* SAT I or ACT (for placement).
Costs (2002–03) *Tuition:* $33 per credit part-time; state resident $1030 full-time, $48 per credit part-time. Full-time tuition and fees vary according to class time. Part-time tuition and fees vary according to class time. *Room and board:* $3228. *Waivers:* senior citizens and employees or children of employees.
Financial Aid In 2001, 137 Federal Work-Study jobs (averaging $1070).
Applying *Options:* early admission, deferred entrance. *Recommended:* high school transcript. *Application deadline:* rolling (freshmen), rolling (transfers). *Notification:* continuous (freshmen).
Admissions Contact Ms. Pati Mapp, Admissions Counselor, Cochise College, 4190 West Highway 80, Douglas, AZ 85607-9724. *Phone:* 520-364-0336. *Toll-free phone:* 800-966-7946. *Fax:* 520-364-0236. *E-mail:* mappp@cochise.cc.az.us.

COCHISE COLLEGE
Sierra Vista, Arizona

■ **State and locally supported** 2-year, founded 1977, part of Cochise College
■ **Calendar** semesters
■ **Degree** certificates and associate
■ **Small-town** 200-acre campus with easy access to Tucson
■ **Coed**

Student Life *Campus security:* 24-hour emergency response devices and patrols.
Standardized Tests *Recommended:* SAT I or ACT (for placement).
Applying *Options:* early admission, deferred entrance. *Recommended:* high school transcript.
Admissions Contact Ms. Debbie Quick, Admissions Officer, Cochise College, 901 North Columbo, Sierra Vista, AZ 85635-2317. *Phone:* 520-515-5412. *Toll-free phone:* 800-966-7943. *Fax:* 520-515-5452. *E-mail:* quickd@cochise.cc.az.us.

COCONINO COMMUNITY COLLEGE
Flagstaff, Arizona

■ **State-supported** 2-year, founded 1991
■ **Calendar** semesters
■ **Degree** certificates and associate
■ **Small-town** 5-acre campus
■ **Endowment** $11,275
■ **Coed**

Student Life *Campus security:* 24-hour patrols.
Applying *Application fee:* $10. *Required for some:* high school transcript.
Admissions Contact Mr. Steve Miller, Director of Admissions/Registrar, Coconino Community College, 3000 North Fourth Street, Flagstaff, AZ 86003. *Phone:* 520-527-1222 Ext. 302. *Toll-free phone:* 800-350-7122. *Fax:* 520-526-1821. *E-mail:* smiller@coco.cc.az.us.

DINE COLLEGE
Tsaile, Arizona

■ **Federally supported** 2-year, founded 1968
■ **Calendar** semesters
■ **Degree** certificates and associate
■ **Rural** 1200-acre campus
■ **Endowment** $3.5 million
■ **Coed,** 1,725 undergraduate students, 48% full-time, 77% women, 23% men

Undergraduates Students come from 1 other state, 3 other countries, 8% live on campus.
Faculty *Total:* 152, 34% full-time.
Majors Art; business administration; computer science; earth sciences; elementary education; exercise sciences; health science; information sciences/systems; liberal arts and sciences/liberal studies; Native American studies; pre-engineering; secretarial science; social sciences; social work.
Academic Programs *Special study options:* academic remediation for entering students, adult/continuing education programs, off-campus study, part-time degree program, services for LD students, summer session for credit.
Library Tsaile-Navajo Community College Library plus 1 other with 50,000 titles, 329 serial subscriptions, a Web page.
Computers on Campus 262 computers available on campus for general student use. A campuswide network can be accessed from off campus. Internet access, at least one staffed computer lab available.
Student Life *Housing Options:* coed. *Activities and Organizations:* Associate Students of Navajo Community College, Bar-N-Rodeo club, Red Dawn Indian Club, Native American Church. *Campus security:* 24-hour emergency response devices and patrols, student patrols, late-night transport/escort service. *Student Services:* health clinic, personal/psychological counseling.
Athletics Member NSCAA, NJCAA. *Intercollegiate sports:* archery M/W, cross-country running M(s)/W(s).
Standardized Tests *Recommended:* SAT I and SAT II or ACT (for placement), SAT II: Writing Test (for placement).
Costs (2001–02) *One-time required fee:* $10. *Tuition:* state resident $600 full-time; nonresident $600 full-time. *Required fees:* $40 full-time, $20 per term part-time. *Room and board:* $3552; room only: $1120.
Financial Aid In 2001, 100 Federal Work-Study jobs (averaging $650).
Applying *Options:* common application, early admission. *Required:* high school transcript, Certificate of Indian Blood form for Native American Students. *Recommended:* minimum 2.0 GPA. *Application deadline:* rolling (freshmen), rolling (transfers). *Notification:* continuous (freshmen).
Admissions Contact Mrs. Louise Litzin, Registrar, Dine College, PO Box 67, Tsaile, AZ 86556. *Phone:* 520-724-6633. *Fax:* 520-724-3349. *E-mail:* louise@crystal.ncc.cc.nm.us.

EASTERN ARIZONA COLLEGE
Thatcher, Arizona

■ **State and locally supported** 2-year, founded 1888, part of Arizona State Community College System
■ **Calendar** semesters
■ **Degree** certificates and associate
■ **Small-town** campus
■ **Endowment** $723,412
■ **Coed,** 6,492 undergraduate students, 23% full-time, 58% women, 42% men

Undergraduates 1,512 full-time, 4,980 part-time. Students come from 39 states and territories, 16 other countries, 6% are from out of state, 2% African American, 1% Asian American or Pacific Islander, 19% Hispanic American, 9% Native American, 0.4% international, 5% live on campus. *Retention:* 53% of 2001 full-time freshmen returned.
Freshmen *Admission:* 644 applied, 644 admitted, 646 enrolled.
Faculty *Total:* 269, 29% full-time. *Student/faculty ratio:* 22:1.
Majors Administrative/secretarial services; agribusiness; agricultural sciences; anthropology; art; art education; auto mechanic/technician; biology; business administration; business education; business management/administrative services

Eastern Arizona College (continued)
related; chemistry; child care provider; civil engineering technology; corrections; criminal justice/law enforcement administration; data entry/microcomputer applications; drafting; elementary education; emergency medical technology; English; enterprise management; foreign languages/literatures; forestry; geology; graphic design/commercial art/illustration; health/medical preparatory programs related; health/physical education; history; industrial arts education; information sciences/systems; law enforcement/police science; liberal arts and sciences/liberal studies; machine shop assistant; mathematics; mining technology; music; nursing; physics; political science; pre-law; pre-medicine; pre-pharmacy studies; psychology; secondary education; sociology; theater arts/drama; welding technology; wildlife biology.
Academic Programs *Special study options:* academic remediation for entering students, adult/continuing education programs, advanced placement credit, cooperative education, double majors, independent study, part-time degree program, services for LD students, summer session for credit.
Library Alumni Library plus 1 other with 56,311 titles, 1,410 serial subscriptions, 4,216 audiovisual materials, an OPAC, a Web page.
Computers on Campus 527 computers available on campus for general student use. A campuswide network can be accessed from student residence rooms and from off campus. Internet access, online (class) registration, at least one staffed computer lab available.
Student Life *Housing Options:* men-only, women-only. *Activities and Organizations:* drama/theater group, choral group, marching band, Latter-Day Saints Student Association, Criminal Justice Student Association, Multicultural Council, Phi Theta Kappa, Mark Allen Dorm Club. *Campus security:* late-night transport/escort service, controlled dormitory access, 20-hour patrols by trained security personnel. *Student Services:* personal/psychological counseling.
Athletics Member NJCAA. *Intercollegiate sports:* baseball M(s), basketball M(s)/W(s), football M(s), softball W(s), volleyball W(s). *Intramural sports:* basketball M/W, racquetball M/W, swimming M/W, table tennis M/W, tennis M/W, volleyball M/W.
Standardized Tests *Recommended:* SAT I or ACT (for placement).
Costs (2002–03) *Tuition:* state resident $788 full-time, $32 per credit part-time; nonresident $4908 full-time, $57 per credit part-time. Full-time tuition and fees vary according to course load. Part-time tuition and fees vary according to course load. *Room and board:* $3580; room only: $1360. Room and board charges vary according to board plan and housing facility. *Payment plan:* deferred payment. *Waivers:* senior citizens and employees or children of employees.
Financial Aid In 2001, 228 Federal Work-Study jobs (averaging $1036). 395 State and other part-time jobs (averaging $1078).
Applying *Options:* electronic application, early admission, deferred entrance. *Recommended:* high school transcript. *Application deadline:* rolling (freshmen), rolling (transfers). *Notification:* continuous (freshmen).
Admissions Contact Eastern Arizona College, 3714 West Church Street, Thatcher, AZ 85552-0769. *Phone:* 928-428-8247. *Toll-free phone:* 800-678-3808. *Fax:* 928-428-8462. *E-mail:* admissions@eac.edu.

ESTRELLA MOUNTAIN COMMUNITY COLLEGE
Avondale, Arizona

- **State and locally supported** 2-year, part of Maricopa County Community College District System
- **Calendar** semesters
- **Degree** certificates and associate
- **Urban** campus with easy access to Phoenix
- **Coed,** 4,657 undergraduate students

Majors General studies; liberal arts and sciences/liberal studies.
Costs (2001–02) *Tuition:* state resident $1104 full-time, $46 per credit hour part-time; nonresident $4824 full-time, $114 per credit hour part-time. *Required fees:* $10 full-time, $5 per term part-time.
Admissions Contact Mr. Joe Ochap, Director of Registration, Advisement, and Enrollment, Estrella Mountain Community College, 3000 North Dysart Road, Avondale, AZ 85323-1000. *Phone:* 602-935-8808.

EVEREST COLLEGE
Phoenix, Arizona

- **Proprietary** 2-year, founded 1982
- **Calendar** six-week terms
- **Degree** certificates, diplomas, and associate
- **Urban** campus
- **Coed,** 291 undergraduate students, 100% full-time, 60% women, 40% men

Undergraduates 291 full-time. Students come from 2 states and territories, 2 other countries, 2% are from out of state, 5% African American, 2% Asian American or Pacific Islander, 14% Hispanic American, 7% Native American, 0.7% international.
Freshmen *Admission:* 291 enrolled.
Faculty *Total:* 32, 22% full-time.
Majors Accounting; computer engineering technology; paralegal/legal assistant; secretarial science.
Academic Programs *Special study options:* adult/continuing education programs, distance learning, double majors, internships, summer session for credit.
Library Academy of Business College Library with 57 serial subscriptions, a Web page.
Computers on Campus 50 computers available on campus for general student use. Internet access, at least one staffed computer lab available.
Student Life *Housing:* college housing not available. *Activities and Organizations:* Collegiate Secretaries International, Toastmasters. *Campus security:* 24-hour emergency response devices and patrols. *Student Services:* personal/psychological counseling.
Costs (2001–02) *Tuition:* Tuition varies by program.
Applying *Options:* deferred entrance. *Application fee:* $50. *Required:* high school transcript, minimum 2.0 GPA, interview. *Required for some:* essay or personal statement. *Application deadline:* rolling (freshmen). *Notification:* continuous (freshmen).
Admissions Contact Jack Rose, Director of Admissions, Everest College, 2525 West Beryl Avenue, Phoenix, AZ 85021. *Phone:* 602-942-4141. *Fax:* 602-943-0960.

GATEWAY COMMUNITY COLLEGE
Phoenix, Arizona

- **State and locally supported** 2-year, founded 1968, part of Maricopa County Community College District System
- **Calendar** semesters
- **Degree** certificates and associate
- **Urban** 20-acre campus
- **Coed,** 9,377 undergraduate students, 10% full-time, 47% women, 53% men

Undergraduates 976 full-time, 8,401 part-time. Students come from 50 states and territories, 26 other countries, 5% are from out of state.
Freshmen *Admission:* 1,482 enrolled.
Faculty *Total:* 259, 27% full-time. *Student/faculty ratio:* 25:1.
Majors Accounting; aerospace engineering technology; auto mechanic/technician; business; carpentry; computer/information sciences; computer programming (specific applications); computer programming, vendor/product certification; computer science related; construction technology; court reporting; diagnostic medical sonography; economics; education; electromechanical technology; finance; general office/clerical; general studies; health services administration; heating/air conditioning/refrigeration; heating/air conditioning/refrigeration technology; industrial technology; information technology; international business; liberal arts and sciences/liberal studies; management science; materials science; medical radiologic technology; nuclear medical technology; nursing; occupational safety/health technology; operating room technician; physical therapy assistant; plumbing; psychology; real estate; respiratory therapy; social work; system administration.
Academic Programs *Special study options:* academic remediation for entering students, adult/continuing education programs, advanced placement credit, cooperative education, English as a second language, honors programs, independent study, internships, part-time degree program, services for LD students, summer session for credit. *ROTC:* Army (c), Air Force (c).
Library Gateway Library with 50,000 titles, 300 serial subscriptions, an OPAC.
Computers on Campus 300 computers available on campus for general student use. Internet access, at least one staffed computer lab available.
Student Life *Housing:* college housing not available. *Activities and Organizations:* student-run newspaper, Associated Students, African-American Students Association, MECHA SAMO THRACE, Volunteer Committee, VA Club. *Campus security:* 24-hour emergency response devices and patrols, student patrols, late-night transport/escort service. *Student Services:* personal/psychological counseling, women's center.
Standardized Tests *Required:* ACT ASSET or ACT COMPASS.
Costs (2001–02) *Tuition:* area resident $1230 full-time, $41 per credit hour part-time; nonresident $5670 full-time, $189 per credit hour part-time. Part-time tuition and fees vary according to course load. *Required fees:* $690 full-time. *Payment plan:* deferred payment. *Waivers:* employees or children of employees.

Applying *Options:* common application, electronic application, early admission, deferred entrance. *Required for some:* high school transcript. *Application deadline:* rolling (freshmen), rolling (transfers). *Notification:* continuous (freshmen).

Admissions Contact Ms. Cathy Gibson, Director of Admissions and Records, GateWay Community College, 108 North 40th Street, Phoenix, AZ 85034. *Phone:* 602-392-5194. *Fax:* 602-392-5209. *E-mail:* cathy.gibson@gwmail.maricopa.edu.

GLENDALE COMMUNITY COLLEGE

Glendale, Arizona

- **State and locally supported** 2-year, founded 1965, part of Maricopa County Community College District System
- **Calendar** semesters
- **Degree** certificates and associate
- **Suburban** 160-acre campus with easy access to Phoenix
- **Endowment** $189,550
- **Coed,** 19,775 undergraduate students, 26% full-time, 57% women, 43% men

Undergraduates 5,149 full-time, 14,626 part-time. Students come from 49 states and territories, 63 other countries, 2% are from out of state, 30% transferred in.

Freshmen *Admission:* 891 enrolled.

Faculty *Total:* 914, 29% full-time, 69% with terminal degrees. *Student/faculty ratio:* 21:1.

Majors Accounting technician; agribusiness; architectural drafting; auto mechanic/technician; business; business administration; business systems networking/telecommunications; criminal justice/law enforcement administration; early childhood education; electrical/electronic engineering technology; emergency medical technology; engineering technology; film/video production; fire science; graphic design/commercial art/illustration; horticulture services; human services; industrial technology; landscaping management; law enforcement/police science; liberal arts and sciences/liberal studies; management information systems/business data processing; nurse assistant/aide; nursing; public relations; real estate; retail management; secretarial science.

Academic Programs *Special study options:* academic remediation for entering students, adult/continuing education programs, advanced placement credit, cooperative education, double majors, English as a second language, honors programs, internships, part-time degree program, services for LD students, summer session for credit. *ROTC:* Army (c), Air Force (c).

Library Library/Media Center plus 1 other with 75,386 titles, 393 serial subscriptions, 2,768 audiovisual materials, an OPAC, a Web page.

Computers on Campus 1500 computers available on campus for general student use. A campuswide network can be accessed from off campus. Internet access, online (class) registration, at least one staffed computer lab available.

Student Life *Housing:* college housing not available. *Activities and Organizations:* drama/theater group, student-run newspaper, choral group, marching band, LDS Student Association, Phi Theta Kappa International Honor Society, band, Glendale Association of Student Nurses, Intervarsity Christian Fellowship. *Campus security:* 24-hour patrols, student patrols, late-night transport/escort service. *Student Services:* personal/psychological counseling, legal services.

Athletics Member NJCAA. *Intercollegiate sports:* baseball M(s), basketball M(s)/W(s), cross-country running M(s)/W(s), football M(s), golf M(s), soccer M(s)/W(s), softball W(s), tennis M(s)/W(s), track and field M(s)/W(s), volleyball W(s). *Intramural sports:* golf M, racquetball M/W, softball W, tennis M/W, volleyball W.

Standardized Tests *Required for some:* ACT ASSET.

Costs (2001–02) *Tuition:* area resident $1032 full-time, $43 per credit hour part-time; nonresident $4320 full-time, $180 per credit hour part-time. *Required fees:* $10 full-time, $5 per term part-time.

Financial Aid In 2001, 350 Federal Work-Study jobs (averaging $1700).

Applying *Options:* common application, electronic application, early admission. *Required for some:* high school transcript. *Application deadlines:* 8/25 (freshmen), 8/25 (transfers). *Notification:* continuous until 8/25 (freshmen).

Admissions Contact Mrs. Mary Lou Massal, Senior Associate Dean of Student Services, Glendale Community College, 6000 West Olive Avenue, Glendale, AZ 85302. *Phone:* 623-435-3305. *Toll-free phone:* 623-845-3000. *Fax:* 623-845-3303. *E-mail:* info@gc.maricopa.edu.

HIGH-TECH INSTITUTE

Phoenix, Arizona

Admissions Contact Mr. Glen Husband, Vice President of Admissions, High-Tech Institute, 1515 East Indian School Road, Phoenix, AZ 85014-4901. *Phone:* 602-279-9700. *Fax:* 602-279-2999.

ITT TECHNICAL INSTITUTE

Tucson, Arizona

- **Proprietary** 2-year, founded 1984, part of ITT Educational Services, Inc
- **Calendar** quarters
- **Degree** associate
- **Urban** 3-acre campus
- **Coed,** 280 undergraduate students

Majors Computer/information sciences related; computer programming; drafting; electrical/electronic engineering technologies related; information technology.

Student Life *Housing:* college housing not available.

Costs (2001–02) *Tuition:* Full-time tuition and fees vary according to program. Part-time tuition and fees vary according to program. $260—$330 per credit hour.

Applying *Options:* deferred entrance. *Application fee:* $100. *Required:* high school transcript, interview. *Recommended:* letters of recommendation. *Application deadline:* rolling (freshmen), rolling (transfers). *Notification:* continuous (freshmen).

Admissions Contact Ms. Linda Lemken, Director of Recruitment, ITT Technical Institute, 1455 West River Road, Tucson, AZ 85704. *Phone:* 520-408-7488. *Toll-free phone:* 800-950-2944.

ITT TECHNICAL INSTITUTE

Phoenix, Arizona

- **Proprietary** primarily 2-year, founded 1972, part of ITT Educational Services, Inc
- **Calendar** quarters
- **Degrees** associate and bachelor's
- **Urban** 2-acre campus
- **Coed,** 417 undergraduate students

Majors Computer programming; data processing technology; design/applied arts related; drafting; electrical/electronic engineering technologies related.

Academic Programs *Special study options:* academic remediation for entering students.

Library 450 titles, 6 serial subscriptions.

Computers on Campus 100 computers available on campus for general student use. Internet access available.

Student Life *Housing:* college housing not available. *Activities and Organizations:* Student Activities Council. *Student Services:* personal/psychological counseling.

Costs (2001–02) *Tuition:* Full-time tuition and fees vary according to program. Part-time tuition and fees vary according to program. $260—$330 per credit hour.

Financial Aid In 2001, 10 Federal Work-Study jobs (averaging $4000).

Applying *Options:* deferred entrance. *Application fee:* $100. *Application deadline:* rolling (freshmen).

Admissions Contact Mr. Gene McWhorter, Director of Recruitment, ITT Technical Institute, 4837 East McDowell Road, Phoenix, AZ 85008-4292. *Phone:* 602-252-2331. *Toll-free phone:* 800-879-4881.

LAMSON COLLEGE

Tempe, Arizona

Admissions Contact Mr. William Wade, Admissions Representative, Lamson College, 1126 North Scottsdale Road, Suite 17, Tempe, AZ 85281. *Phone:* 480-898-7000. *Toll-free phone:* 800-898-7017.

MESA COMMUNITY COLLEGE

Mesa, Arizona

Admissions Contact Mr. Gordon Benson, Associate Dean of Students, Mesa Community College, 1833 West Southern Avenue, Mesa, AZ 85202-4866. *Phone:* 602-461-7478. *Fax:* 602-461-7805. *E-mail:* admissions@mc.maricopa.edu.

MOHAVE COMMUNITY COLLEGE
Kingman, Arizona

- **State-supported** 2-year, founded 1971
- **Calendar** semesters
- **Degree** certificates and associate
- **Small-town** 160-acre campus
- **Coed,** 5,736 undergraduate students

Undergraduates Students come from 9 states and territories, 10% are from out of state, 3% African American, 1% Hispanic American, 3% Native American.
Faculty *Total:* 349, 14% full-time.
Majors Accounting; art; auto mechanic/technician; business administration; business marketing and marketing management; ceramic arts; computer programming (specific applications); computer science; computer science related; English; fire science; health science; history; information technology; law enforcement/police science; liberal arts and sciences/liberal studies; mathematics; metal/jewelry arts; music; nursing; psychology; sociology; word processing.
Academic Programs *Special study options:* academic remediation for entering students, adult/continuing education programs, distance learning, English as a second language, independent study, part-time degree program, summer session for credit.
Library Mohave Community College Library with 45,849 titles, 476 serial subscriptions.
Computers on Campus 120 computers available on campus for general student use. At least one staffed computer lab available.
Student Life *Housing:* college housing not available. *Campus security:* 24-hour emergency response devices, late-night transport/escort service.
Standardized Tests *Recommended:* SAT I and SAT II or ACT (for placement).
Costs (2001–02) *Tuition:* state resident $772 full-time, $32 per credit hour part-time; nonresident $3956 full-time, $44 per credit hour part-time. Full-time tuition and fees vary according to reciprocity agreements. Part-time tuition and fees vary according to course load and reciprocity agreements. *Required fees:* $20 full-time, $10 per term part-time. *Waivers:* senior citizens and employees or children of employees.
Applying *Options:* early admission, deferred entrance. *Required for some:* high school transcript, interview. *Recommended:* minimum 2.0 GPA. *Application deadline:* rolling (freshmen), rolling (transfers). *Notification:* continuous (freshmen).
Admissions Contact Dr. Roger L. Johnson, Registrar/Director of Enrollment Services, Mohave Community College, 1971 Jagerson Avenue, Kingman, AZ 86401. *Phone:* 520-757-0847. *Fax:* 520-757-0808. *E-mail:* rogjoh@mohave.edu.

NORTHLAND PIONEER COLLEGE
Holbrook, Arizona

- **State and locally supported** 2-year, founded 1974, part of Arizona State Community College System
- **Calendar** semesters
- **Degree** certificates and associate
- **Rural** 40-acre campus
- **Endowment** $100,000
- **Coed,** 5,374 undergraduate students

Undergraduates 1% live on campus. *Retention:* 2% of 2001 full-time freshmen returned.
Freshmen *Admission:* 364 admitted.
Faculty *Total:* 397, 15% full-time. *Student/faculty ratio:* 13:1.
Majors Accounting technician; biological/physical sciences; business; business administration; business services marketing; carpentry; child care/guidance; child guidance; clothing/textiles; computer/information sciences; construction technology; corrections; cosmetology; court reporting; criminal justice studies; data processing technology; drafting; electrical/electronic engineering technology; emergency medical technology; fire science; industrial technology; legal administrative assistant; liberal arts and sciences/liberal studies; library assistant; medical assistant; medical transcription; nursing; paralegal/legal assistant; photographic technology; secretarial science; teacher assistant/aide; turf management.
Academic Programs *Special study options:* academic remediation for entering students, advanced placement credit, cooperative education, distance learning, double majors, English as a second language, freshman honors college, honors programs, independent study, internships, part-time degree program, services for LD students, summer session for credit.
Library Northland Pioneer College Library with 60,000 titles, 240 serial subscriptions, an OPAC.
Computers on Campus 200 computers available on campus for general student use. At least one staffed computer lab available.
Student Life *Housing Options:* coed. *Activities and Organizations:* drama/theater group, choral group, Spanish Club, Math Club, Hiking/Skiing Club, Native American Students. *Campus security:* evening security.
Athletics Member NJCAA. *Intercollegiate sports:* basketball M(s)/W(s), golf M(s)/W(s).
Costs (2002–03) *Tuition:* state resident $720 full-time, $30 per credit part-time; nonresident $55 per credit part-time. *Room and board:* room only: $1500.
Applying *Options:* early admission. *Application deadline:* rolling (freshmen).
Admissions Contact Ms. Dawn Edgmon, Coordinator of Admissions, Northland Pioneer College, PO Box 610, 993 Hermosa Drive, Holbrook, AZ 86025-0610. *Phone:* 520-536-6271. *Toll-free phone:* 800-266-7845 Ext. 7450. *Fax:* 520-524-7312.

PARADISE VALLEY COMMUNITY COLLEGE
Phoenix, Arizona

- **State and locally supported** 2-year, founded 1985, part of Maricopa County Community College District System
- **Calendar** semesters
- **Degree** certificates and associate
- **Urban** campus
- **Coed,** 7,349 undergraduate students

Faculty *Total:* 344, 24% full-time.
Majors Accounting; business administration; computer typography/composition; international business; liberal arts and sciences/liberal studies; occupational safety/health technology; secretarial science.
Academic Programs *Special study options:* academic remediation for entering students, adult/continuing education programs, advanced placement credit, cooperative education, distance learning, honors programs, services for LD students, summer session for credit.
Library Paradise Valley Community College Library plus 1 other with an OPAC, a Web page.
Computers on Campus 500 computers available on campus for general student use. Internet access, at least one staffed computer lab available.
Student Life *Housing:* college housing not available. *Activities and Organizations:* drama/theater group, student-run newspaper, choral group, Phi Theta Kappa, International Student Club, Recreational Outing Club, AWARE, Student Christian Association. *Campus security:* 24-hour emergency response devices, late-night transport/escort service. *Student Services:* personal/psychological counseling.
Athletics Member NJCAA. *Intercollegiate sports:* cross-country running M/W, golf M/W, soccer M, tennis M/W, track and field M/W.
Costs (2001–02) *Tuition:* area resident $1290 full-time, $43 per hour part-time; state resident $43 per hour part-time; nonresident $2040 full-time, $68 per hour part-time. Full-time tuition and fees vary according to course load. Part-time tuition and fees vary according to course load. *Waivers:* employees or children of employees.
Financial Aid In 2001, 43 Federal Work-Study jobs.
Applying *Options:* early admission. *Application deadline:* rolling (freshmen), rolling (transfers).
Admissions Contact Dr. Shirley Green, Associate Dean of Student Services, Paradise Valley Community College, 18401 North 32nd Street, Phoenix, AZ 85032-1200. *Phone:* 602-787-7020.

THE PARALEGAL INSTITUTE, INC.
Phoenix, Arizona

- **Proprietary** 2-year, founded 1974
- **Degree** diplomas and associate
- 2,576 undergraduate students
- 25% of applicants were admitted

Freshmen *Admission:* 500 applied, 125 admitted.
Faculty *Total:* 3.
Majors Paralegal/legal assistant.
Costs (2001–02) *Tuition:* Full and part-time tuition not available as this is a Distance Learning Program.
Admissions Contact Mr. John W. Morrison, President, The Paralegal Institute, Inc., 2933 West Indian School Road, Drawer 11408, Phoenix, AZ 85061-1408. *Phone:* 602-212-6501. *Toll-free phone:* 800-354-1254. *E-mail:* paralegalinst@mindspring.com.

PHOENIX COLLEGE
Phoenix, Arizona

- **State and locally supported** 2-year, founded 1920, part of Maricopa County Community College District System
- **Calendar** semesters
- **Degree** associate
- **Urban** 52-acre campus
- **Coed,** 12,296 undergraduate students

Undergraduates Students come from 42 states and territories, 67 other countries, 2% are from out of state, 6% African American, 3% Asian American or Pacific Islander, 29% Hispanic American, 4% Native American.

Faculty *Total:* 104, 100% full-time.

Majors Accounting; architectural engineering technology; art; behavioral sciences; business administration; business marketing and marketing management; civil engineering technology; computer graphics; computer/information sciences; construction technology; corrections; criminal justice studies; data processing technology; dental hygiene; drafting; emergency medical technology; fashion design/illustration; finance; fire science; food products retailing; home economics; information sciences/systems; interior design; law enforcement/police science; legal administrative assistant; liberal arts and sciences/liberal studies; management science; mass communications; mechanical design technology; medical administrative assistant; medical assistant; medical laboratory technician; medical laboratory technology; medical records administration; medical technology; nursing; paralegal/legal assistant; real estate; secretarial science; travel/tourism management.

Academic Programs *Special study options:* academic remediation for entering students, adult/continuing education programs, advanced placement credit, cooperative education, English as a second language, freshman honors college, honors programs, internships, part-time degree program, services for LD students, study abroad, summer session for credit. *ROTC:* Army (c), Air Force (c).

Library Fannin Library with 83,000 titles, 394 serial subscriptions.

Computers on Campus 250 computers available on campus for general student use. A campuswide network can be accessed from off campus. Internet access, at least one staffed computer lab available.

Student Life *Housing:* college housing not available. *Activities and Organizations:* drama/theater group, student-run newspaper, choral group, Black Student Union, NASA (Native American Club), Asian American Club, MECHA (Mexican Club). *Campus security:* 24-hour emergency response devices, student patrols, late-night transport/escort service. *Student Services:* personal/psychological counseling, women's center, legal services.

Athletics Member NJCAA. *Intercollegiate sports:* baseball M(s), basketball M(s)/W(s), cross-country running M(s)/W(s), football M(s), golf M(s)/W(s), soccer M/W, softball W(s), tennis M(s)/W(s), track and field M(s)/W(s), volleyball W(s). *Intramural sports:* skiing (cross-country) M(c)/W(c), skiing (downhill) M(c)/W(c).

Standardized Tests *Required:* ACT ASSET.

Costs (2001–02) *Tuition:* $43 per credit hour part-time; state resident $68 per credit hour part-time; nonresident $180 per credit hour part-time.

Financial Aid In 2001, 350 Federal Work-Study jobs (averaging $2800).

Applying *Options:* common application, electronic application, early admission, deferred entrance. *Application deadline:* rolling (freshmen), rolling (transfers). *Notification:* continuous (freshmen).

Admissions Contact Ms. Donna Fischer, Supervisor of Admissions and Records, Phoenix College, Phoenix, AZ 85013. *Phone:* 602-285-7500. *Fax:* 602-285-7813.

PIMA COMMUNITY COLLEGE
Tucson, Arizona

- **State and locally supported** 2-year, founded 1966, part of Arizona State Community College System
- **Calendar** semesters
- **Degree** certificates and associate
- **Urban** 428-acre campus
- **Coed,** 28,176 undergraduate students, 27% full-time, 56% women, 44% men

Undergraduates 7,730 full-time, 20,446 part-time. Students come from 32 states and territories, 68 other countries, 3% are from out of state, 4% African American, 3% Asian American or Pacific Islander, 33% Hispanic American, 4% Native American, 0.7% international, 5% transferred in.

Freshmen *Admission:* 5,807 admitted, 3,443 enrolled. *Test scores:* ACT scores over 18: 52%; ACT scores over 24: 14%; ACT scores over 30: 2%.

Faculty *Total:* 1,622, 20% full-time. *Student/faculty ratio:* 19:1.

Majors Accounting; aircraft mechanic/powerplant; anthropology; archaeology; architectural drafting; art; Asian studies; auto mechanic/technician; banking; building maintenance/management; business administration; business systems networking/ telecommunications; child care/guidance; child care provider; computer/information sciences; computer maintenance technology; computer systems analysis; construction management related; construction technology; criminal justice studies; dental hygiene; dental laboratory technician; design/visual communications; electrical/electronic engineering technology; emergency medical technology; environmental technology; fire science; general studies; gerontology; graphic design/commercial art/illustration; hospitality management; hotel and restaurant management; industrial/manufacturing engineering; international business; journalism; law enforcement/police science; liberal arts and sciences/liberal studies; machine shop assistant; medical administrative assistant; medical radiologic technology; music; Native American studies; nursing; paralegal/legal assistant; pharmacy technician/assistant; political science; protective services related; radio/television broadcasting; real estate; respiratory therapy; restaurant operations; secretarial science; sign language interpretation; sociology; speech/rhetorical studies; theater arts/drama; travel/tourism management; veterinarian assistant; welding technology.

Academic Programs *Special study options:* academic remediation for entering students, accelerated degree program, adult/continuing education programs, advanced placement credit, cooperative education, distance learning, double majors, English as a second language, freshman honors college, honors programs, independent study, internships, part-time degree program, services for LD students, student-designed majors, summer session for credit. *ROTC:* Army (c), Navy (c), Air Force (c).

Library Pima College Library with 160,492 titles, 1,340 serial subscriptions, 17,940 audiovisual materials, an OPAC, a Web page.

Computers on Campus 2500 computers available on campus for general student use. A campuswide network can be accessed from off campus. Internet access, online (class) registration, at least one staffed computer lab available.

Student Life *Housing:* college housing not available. *Activities and Organizations:* drama/theater group, student-run newspaper, choral group. *Campus security:* 24-hour emergency response devices and patrols, late-night transport/escort service. *Student Services:* personal/psychological counseling, women's center.

Athletics Member NJCAA. *Intercollegiate sports:* baseball M(s), basketball M(s)/W(s), cross-country running M(s)/W(s), football M(s), golf M(s)/W(s), soccer M(s)/W(s), softball W(s), tennis M(s)/W(s), track and field M(s)/W(s), volleyball W(s). *Intramural sports:* badminton M/W, basketball M/W, cross-country running M/W, equestrian sports M(c)/W(c), football M, golf M/W, ice hockey M(c), racquetball M/W, tennis M/W, track and field M/W, volleyball M/W, wrestling M(c).

Standardized Tests *Recommended:* SAT I or ACT (for placement).

Costs (2001–02) *Tuition:* state resident $840 full-time, $37 per credit hour part-time; nonresident $4320 full-time, $175 per credit hour part-time. Full-time tuition and fees vary according to course load. Part-time tuition and fees vary according to course load. *Required fees:* $10 full-time. *Payment plan:* deferred payment. *Waivers:* employees or children of employees.

Applying *Options:* common application, early admission. *Application fee:* $15 (non-residents). *Application deadline:* rolling (freshmen), rolling (transfers).

Admissions Contact Ms. Nancee Sorenson, Director of Enrollment Services and Registration, Pima Community College, 4905B East Broadway Boulevard, Tucson, AZ 85709-1120. *Phone:* 520-206-4640. *Fax:* 520-206-4790.

PIMA MEDICAL INSTITUTE
Tucson, Arizona

- **Proprietary** 2-year, founded 1972, part of Vocational Training Institutes, Inc
- **Calendar** modular
- **Degree** certificates and associate
- 350 undergraduate students

Admissions Contact Mr. Carlos Flores, Admissions Director, Pima Medical Institute, 3350 East Grant Road, Tucson, AZ 85716. *Phone:* 520-326-1600.

PIMA MEDICAL INSTITUTE
Mesa, Arizona

Admissions Contact Mr. Dave Brown, Associate Director of Admissions, Pima Medical Institute, 957 South Dobson Road, Mesa, AZ 85202. *Phone:* 602-345-7777.

The Refrigeration School

Phoenix, Arizona

- **Proprietary** 2-year
- **Calendar** continuous
- **Degree** certificates, diplomas, and associate
- **Urban** campus
- **Coed,** 300 undergraduate students

Majors Mechanical engineering technology.
Student Life *Housing:* college housing not available.
Costs (2001–02) *Tuition:* $5000-$15,000 per degree program.
Admissions Contact Ms. Mary Simmons, Admissions Director, The Refrigeration School, 4210 East Washington Street, Phoenix, AZ 85034-1816. *Phone:* 602-275-7133. *Fax:* 602-267-4805. *E-mail:* loney@primenet.com.

Rio Salado College

Tempe, Arizona

- **State and locally supported** 2-year, founded 1978, part of Maricopa County Community College District System
- **Calendar** semesters
- **Degree** certificates and associate
- **Urban** campus
- **Coed**

Faculty *Student/faculty ratio:* 25:1.
Student Life *Campus security:* 24-hour emergency response devices, late-night transport/escort service.
Standardized Tests *Required for some:* ACT ASSET.
Financial Aid In 2001, 1 Federal Work-Study job (averaging $700).
Applying *Options:* electronic application, early admission, deferred entrance.
Admissions Contact Mrs. Deborah Lain, Supervisor of Admissions and Records, Rio Salado College, Tampe, AZ 85281. *Phone:* 480-517-8152. *Toll-free phone:* 800-729-1197. *Fax:* 480-517-8199. *E-mail:* admission@email.rio.maricopa.

Scottsdale Community College

Scottsdale, Arizona

- **State and locally supported** 2-year, founded 1969, part of Maricopa County Community College District System
- **Calendar** semesters
- **Degree** certificates, diplomas, and associate
- **Suburban** 160-acre campus with easy access to Phoenix
- **Coed,** 10,397 undergraduate students

Undergraduates Students come from 50 states and territories, 49 other countries, 5% are from out of state, 2% African American, 3% Asian American or Pacific Islander, 7% Hispanic American, 4% Native American, 4% international.
Freshmen *Admission:* 8,865 applied, 8,865 admitted.
Faculty *Total:* 509, 28% full-time, 13% with terminal degrees.
Majors Accounting; architectural environmental design; business administration; criminal justice/law enforcement administration; culinary arts; early childhood education; electrical/electronic engineering technology; emergency medical technology; equestrian studies; fashion merchandising; finance; fire science; food products retailing; hospitality management; hotel and restaurant management; information sciences/systems; interior design; mathematics; medical administrative assistant; nursing; photography; public administration; real estate; secretarial science; theater arts/drama.
Academic Programs *Special study options:* academic remediation for entering students, adult/continuing education programs, advanced placement credit, cooperative education, English as a second language, honors programs, off-campus study, part-time degree program, services for LD students, student-designed majors, summer session for credit.
Computers on Campus 75 computers available on campus for general student use.
Student Life *Housing:* college housing not available. *Activities and Organizations:* drama/theater group, student-run newspaper, choral group. *Campus security:* 24-hour emergency response devices and patrols, student patrols, late-night transport/escort service, 24-hour automatic surveillance cameras. *Student Services:* personal/psychological counseling, women's center, legal services.
Athletics Member NJCAA. *Intercollegiate sports:* basketball M/W, cross-country running M/W, football M, golf M/W, tennis M/W, track and field M/W, volleyball W. *Intramural sports:* archery M/W, badminton M/W, basketball M/W, bowling M/W, racquetball M/W, track and field M/W, volleyball M/W.
Standardized Tests *Required for some:* ACT ASSET. *Recommended:* ACT ASSET.
Costs (2001–02) *Tuition:* area resident $1380 full-time, $46 per credit hour part-time; state resident $2130 full-time, $71 per credit hour part-time; nonresident $6330 full-time, $211 per credit hour part-time. Part-time tuition and fees vary according to course load. *Required fees:* $10 full-time. *Payment plan:* installment. *Waivers:* employees or children of employees.
Financial Aid In 2001, 125 Federal Work-Study jobs (averaging $2500). 275 State and other part-time jobs (averaging $2000). *Financial aid deadline:* 7/15.
Applying *Options:* early admission. *Application deadline:* rolling (freshmen). *Notification:* continuous (freshmen).
Admissions Contact Ms. Ruby Miller, Registrar, Scottsdale Community College, 9000 East Chaparral Road, Scottsdale, AZ 85256. *Phone:* 602-423-6128. *Fax:* 480-423-6200. *E-mail:* ruby.miller@sccmail.maricopa.edu.

Scottsdale Culinary Institute

Scottsdale, Arizona

Admissions Contact 8100 East Camelback Road, Suite 1001, Scottsdale, AZ 85251-3940. *Toll-free phone:* 800-848-2433.

South Mountain Community College

Phoenix, Arizona

- **State and locally supported** 2-year, founded 1979, part of Maricopa County Community College District System
- **Calendar** semesters
- **Degree** certificates and associate
- **Suburban** 108-acre campus
- **Coed,** 3,406 undergraduate students, 21% full-time, 60% women, 40% men

Undergraduates 2% are from out of state, 13% African American, 2% Asian American or Pacific Islander, 46% Hispanic American, 3% Native American.
Freshmen *Admission:* 260 applied, 260 admitted.
Faculty *Total:* 195, 25% full-time, 100% with terminal degrees.
Majors Art; biology; business administration; chemistry; computer typography/composition; history; home economics; information sciences/systems; liberal arts and sciences/liberal studies; mass communications; mathematics; music; physical education; physics; political science; pre-engineering; psychology; secretarial science; sociology.
Academic Programs *Special study options:* academic remediation for entering students, adult/continuing education programs, advanced placement credit, cooperative education, English as a second language, honors programs, part-time degree program, services for LD students, summer session for credit. *ROTC:* Air Force (c).
Library Learning Resource Center with 35,591 titles, 475 serial subscriptions, an OPAC.
Computers on Campus 150 computers available on campus for general student use. Internet access, at least one staffed computer lab available.
Student Life *Housing:* college housing not available. *Campus security:* late-night transport/escort service, 18-hour patrols, campus lockdown. *Student Services:* legal services.
Athletics Member NJCAA. *Intercollegiate sports:* baseball M, basketball M/W, cross-country running M/W, soccer M, softball W, tennis M/W, track and field M/W, volleyball W.
Costs (2001–02) *Tuition:* area resident $1032 full-time, $43 per credit hour part-time; state resident $68 per credit hour part-time; nonresident $4320 full-time.
Financial Aid In 2001, 50 Federal Work-Study jobs (averaging $2400). 50 State and other part-time jobs (averaging $2400).
Applying *Application deadlines:* 8/22 (freshmen), 8/22 (transfers). *Notification:* continuous until 8/22 (freshmen).
Admissions Contact Mr. Tony Bracamonte, Dean of Enrollment Services, South Mountain Community College, 7050 South 24th Street, Phoenix, AZ 85042. *Phone:* 602-243-8120. *Fax:* 602-243-8329. *E-mail:* bracamonte@smc.maricopa.edu.

Universal Technical Institute

Phoenix, Arizona

Admissions Contact 3121 West Weldon Avenue, Phoenix, AZ 85017-4599. *Toll-free phone:* 800-859-1202.

YAVAPAI COLLEGE
Prescott, Arizona

Admissions Contact Mr. Gene Carson, Admissions, Registration, and Records Manager, Yavapai College, 1100 East Sheldon Street, Prescott, AZ 86301-3297. *Phone:* 520-776-2188. *Toll-free phone:* 800-922-6787. *Fax:* 520-776-2151. *E-mail:* preg-work@yavapai.cc.az.us.

ARKANSAS

ARKANSAS STATE UNIVERSITY-BEEBE
Beebe, Arkansas

- **State-supported** 2-year, founded 1927, part of Arkansas State University System
- **Calendar** semesters
- **Degree** certificates and associate
- **Rural** 320-acre campus with easy access to Memphis
- **Coed,** 3,302 undergraduate students

Undergraduates Students come from 25 states and territories, 11 other countries, 7% African American, 1% Asian American or Pacific Islander, 1% Hispanic American, 1% Native American, 0.1% international, 12% live on campus.

Freshmen *Average high school GPA:* 2.70.

Faculty *Total:* 97, 65% full-time, 22% with terminal degrees. *Student/faculty ratio:* 25:1.

Majors Agricultural sciences; animal sciences; artificial intelligence/robotics; biology; business administration; computer engineering related; computer engineering technology; computer graphics; computer programming, vendor/product certification; computer systems networking/telecommunications; drafting; electrical/electronic engineering technology; information sciences/systems; information technology; liberal arts and sciences/liberal studies; mathematics; medical laboratory technician; nursing; physical sciences; quality control technology; social sciences; speech/rhetorical studies.

Academic Programs *Special study options:* academic remediation for entering students, adult/continuing education programs, advanced placement credit, distance learning, honors programs, part-time degree program, summer session for credit.

Library Abington Library with 90,000 titles, 500 serial subscriptions, 10 audiovisual materials.

Computers on Campus 375 computers available on campus for general student use. A campuswide network can be accessed from off campus. Internet access, at least one staffed computer lab available.

Student Life *Housing Options:* men-only, women-only. *Activities and Organizations:* drama/theater group, choral group, Student Arkansas Education Association, Art Club, Agri Club, Social Science Club, Leadership Council. *Campus security:* 24-hour emergency response devices and patrols. *Student Services:* personal/psychological counseling.

Athletics *Intramural sports:* archery M/W, badminton M/W, basketball M/W, football M/W, golf M/W, racquetball M/W, softball M/W, squash M/W, table tennis M/W, tennis M/W, track and field M/W, volleyball M/W.

Standardized Tests *Recommended:* ACT (for placement).

Costs (2001–02) *Tuition:* state resident $1680 full-time, $56 per credit hour part-time; nonresident $2760 full-time, $92 per credit hour part-time. Full-time tuition and fees vary according to course load. *Required fees:* $72 full-time, $3 per credit hour. *Room and board:* $2800. *Payment plan:* installment. *Waivers:* senior citizens.

Financial Aid In 2001, 36 Federal Work-Study jobs (averaging $1800). 112 State and other part-time jobs (averaging $750).

Applying *Options:* common application, deferred entrance. *Required:* high school transcript. *Application deadline:* rolling (freshmen). *Notification:* continuous (freshmen).

Admissions Contact Mrs. Robin Hayes, Coordinator of Enrollment, Arkansas State University-Beebe, PO Box 1000, Beebe, AR 72012-1000. *Phone:* 501-882-8280 Ext. 336. *Toll-free phone:* 800-632-9985. *Fax:* 501-882-8370. *E-mail:* rahayes@asub.arknet.edu.

ARKANSAS STATE UNIVERSITY-MOUNTAIN HOME
Mountain Home, Arkansas

- **State-supported** 2-year, part of Arkansas State University
- **Calendar** semesters
- **Degree** certificates and associate
- **Endowment** $1.5 million
- **Coed,** 1,238 undergraduate students, 50% full-time, 68% women, 32% men

Undergraduates 619 full-time, 619 part-time. Students come from 2 states and territories, 5% are from out of state, 0.3% African American, 0.7% Asian American or Pacific Islander, 0.6% Hispanic American, 0.4% Native American.

Freshmen *Admission:* 194 applied, 194 admitted.

Faculty *Total:* 58, 59% full-time, 17% with terminal degrees. *Student/faculty ratio:* 24:1.

Majors Criminal justice/law enforcement administration; emergency medical technology; hearing sciences; industrial machinery maintenance/repair; industrial technology; information sciences/systems; liberal arts and sciences/liberal studies; mortuary science; secretarial science.

Academic Programs *Special study options:* academic remediation for entering students, advanced placement credit, cooperative education, distance learning, part-time degree program, summer session for credit.

Library Norma Wood Library with 13,329 titles, 220 serial subscriptions, 1,328 audiovisual materials, an OPAC.

Computers on Campus 60 computers available on campus for general student use. A campuswide network can be accessed from off campus. Internet access, at least one staffed computer lab available.

Student Life *Activities and Organizations:* drama/theater group, choral group, Phi Theta Kappa, Circle K, Criminal Justice Club, Mortuary Science Club, Student Ambassadors.

Standardized Tests *Required:* SAT I or ACT (for placement), ACT ASSET or ACT COMPASS.

Costs (2001–02) *Tuition:* state resident $1200 full-time, $50 per credit part-time; nonresident $1824 full-time, $76 per credit part-time. Full-time tuition and fees vary according to course load. Part-time tuition and fees vary according to course load. *Required fees:* $192 full-time, $8 per credit. *Payment plan:* installment. *Waivers:* children of alumni, senior citizens, and employees or children of employees.

Applying *Required:* high school transcript. *Notification:* continuous (freshmen).

Admissions Contact Ms. Karen Heslep, Director of Marketing and Recruiting, Arkansas State University-Mountain Home, 1600 South College Street, Mountain Home, AR 72653. *Phone:* 870-508-6105. *Fax:* 870-508-6287. *E-mail:* kheslep@brook.asumh.edu.

ARKANSAS STATE UNIVERSITY-NEWPORT
Newport, Arkansas

- **State-supported** 2-year, part of Arkansas State University
- **Calendar** semesters
- **Degree** certificates, diplomas, and associate
- **Coed,** 604 undergraduate students

Undergraduates 16% African American, 2% Asian American or Pacific Islander, 2% Hispanic American, 0.8% Native American, 0.6% international.

Faculty *Total:* 50, 46% full-time. *Student/faculty ratio:* 12:1.

Academic Programs *Special study options:* academic remediation for entering students, adult/continuing education programs, English as a second language, external degree program, independent study, internships, off-campus study, services for LD students.

Standardized Tests *Required:* ACT (for admission).

Costs (2001–02) *Tuition:* state resident $1320 full-time, $55 per credit hour part-time; nonresident $2160 full-time, $90 per credit hour part-time. *Payment plan:* installment. *Waivers:* senior citizens.

Applying *Options:* common application. *Required:* interview.

Admissions Contact Ms. Tara Byrd, Registrar, Director of Admissions, Arkansas State University-Newport, 7648 Victory Boulevard, Newport, AR 72112. *Phone:* 870-512-7800. *Toll-free phone:* 800-976-1676. *Fax:* 870-512-7825. *E-mail:* tlbryd@asun.arknet.edu.

BLACK RIVER TECHNICAL COLLEGE
Pocahontas, Arkansas

- **State-supported** 2-year, founded 1972
- **Calendar** semesters
- **Degree** associate
- **Small-town** 55-acre campus
- **Coed,** 1,243 undergraduate students, 52% full-time, 56% women, 44% men

Undergraduates 652 full-time, 591 part-time. Students come from 2 states and territories.
Freshmen *Admission:* 151 enrolled. *Test scores:* ACT scores over 18: 25%; ACT scores over 24: 10%.
Faculty *Total:* 70, 43% full-time. *Student/faculty ratio:* 16:1.
Majors Aviation technology; business administration; data processing technology; dietetics; emergency medical technology; fire science; industrial technology; information sciences/systems; liberal arts and sciences/liberal studies; nursing.
Academic Programs *Special study options:* academic remediation for entering students, cooperative education, honors programs, internships, part-time degree program, services for LD students, student-designed majors, summer session for credit.
Library Black River Technical College Library with 10,000 titles, 200 serial subscriptions, an OPAC.
Computers on Campus 100 computers available on campus for general student use. At least one staffed computer lab available.
Student Life *Housing:* college housing not available. *Campus security:* night patrol.
Costs (2001–02) *Tuition:* area resident $1032 full-time, $43 per credit hour part-time; state resident $1368 full-time, $57 per credit hour part-time; nonresident $4056 full-time, $169 per credit hour part-time.
Applying *Options:* common application. *Required for some:* high school transcript, interview. *Application deadline:* rolling (freshmen), rolling (transfers).
Admissions Contact Mr. Jim Ulmer, Director of Admissions, Black River Technical College, Highway 304 East, PO Box 468, Pocahontas, AR 72455. *Phone:* 870-892-4565. *Toll-free phone:* 800-919-3086. *Fax:* 870-892-3546.

COSSATOT COMMUNITY COLLEGE OF THE UNIVERSITY OF ARKANSAS
De Queen, Arkansas

- **State-supported** 2-year, founded 1991
- **Calendar** semesters
- **Degree** certificates, diplomas, and associate
- **Rural** campus
- **Coed**

Financial Aid In 2001, 10 Federal Work-Study jobs (averaging $2500).
Applying *Recommended:* high school transcript.
Admissions Contact Ms. Kristin Bowden, Dean of Student Services, Cossatot Community College of the University of Arkansas, PO Box 960, De Queen, AR 71832. *Phone:* 870-584-4471.

CROWLEY'S RIDGE COLLEGE
Paragould, Arkansas

- **Independent** 2-year, affiliated with Church of Christ
- **Calendar** semesters
- **Degree** associate
- **Small-town** 112-acre campus
- **Coed,** 155 undergraduate students

Faculty *Total:* 23, 35% full-time. *Student/faculty ratio:* 16:1.
Majors Biblical studies; general studies.
Academic Programs *Special study options:* academic remediation for entering students, double majors, honors programs, independent study, part-time degree program.
Library Learning Center with an OPAC, a Web page.
Computers on Campus 9 computers available on campus for general student use. Internet access available.
Student Life *Housing:* on-campus residence required through sophomore year. *Options:* men-only, women-only. *Activities and Organizations:* drama/theater group, student-run newspaper, choral group.
Athletics Member NSCAA. *Intercollegiate sports:* baseball M, basketball M/W, volleyball W.
Standardized Tests *Required:* ACT, ACT ASSET.
Costs (2001–02) *Tuition:* $4200 full-time, $175 per credit hour part-time. *Required fees:* $800 full-time, $400 per term part-time. *Room only:* $3600. *Waivers:* employees or children of employees.
Applying *Options:* common application, electronic application. *Required:* high school transcript. *Required for some:* interview. *Application deadline:* rolling (freshmen).
Admissions Contact Mrs. Nancy Joneshill, Director of Admissions, Crowley's Ridge College, 100 College Drive, Paragould, AR 72450. *Phone:* 870-236-6901 Ext. 14. *Toll-free phone:* 800-264-1096. *Fax:* 870-236-7748. *E-mail:* njoneshi@crc.pioneer.paragould.ar.us.

EAST ARKANSAS COMMUNITY COLLEGE
Forrest City, Arkansas

- **State-supported** 2-year, founded 1974
- **Calendar** semesters
- **Degree** certificates and associate
- **Small-town** 40-acre campus with easy access to Memphis
- **Endowment** $28,661
- **Coed,** 1,358 undergraduate students

Undergraduates Students come from 4 states and territories.
Freshmen *Admission:* 480 applied, 480 admitted.
Faculty *Total:* 100.
Majors Business administration; computer engineering technology; criminal justice/law enforcement administration; drafting; law enforcement/police science; liberal arts and sciences/liberal studies; practical nurse.
Academic Programs *Special study options:* academic remediation for entering students, adult/continuing education programs, advanced placement credit, honors programs, part-time degree program, services for LD students, summer session for credit.
Library Learning Resource Center plus 1 other with 21,908 titles, 109 serial subscriptions.
Computers on Campus 26 computers available on campus for general student use. At least one staffed computer lab available.
Student Life *Housing:* college housing not available. *Activities and Organizations:* drama/theater group, choral group, Gamma Beta Phi, Baptist Student Union, Student Activities Committee, Lambda Alpha Epsilon. *Campus security:* 24-hour emergency response devices, 16-hour patrols by trained security personnel. *Student Services:* personal/psychological counseling.
Standardized Tests *Required for some:* ACT (for placement), ACT ASSET. *Recommended:* ACT (for placement), ACT ASSET.
Costs (2001–02) *Tuition:* area resident $988 full-time, $41 per credit hour part-time; state resident $1152 full-time, $48 per credit hour part-time; nonresident $1392 full-time, $58 per credit hour part-time. *Required fees:* $120 full-time, $5 per credit hour. *Waivers:* senior citizens.
Financial Aid In 2001, 74 Federal Work-Study jobs (averaging $1104).
Applying *Options:* early admission, deferred entrance. *Required:* high school transcript. *Application deadline:* rolling (freshmen), rolling (transfers). *Notification:* continuous (freshmen).
Admissions Contact Mrs. Sarah C. Buford, Director of Enrollment Management/Registrar, East Arkansas Community College, 1700 Newcastle Road, Forrest City, AR 72335-2204. *Phone:* 870-633-4480 Ext. 219. *Toll-free phone:* 877-797-3222.

EDUCATION AMERICA, SOUTHEAST COLLEGE OF TECHNOLOGY, LITTLE ROCK CAMPUS
Little Rock, Arkansas

Admissions Contact 8901 Kanis Road, Little Rock, AR 72205.

GARLAND COUNTY COMMUNITY COLLEGE
Hot Springs, Arkansas

- **State and locally supported** 2-year, founded 1973, part of Arkansas Department of Higher Education
- **Calendar** semesters
- **Degree** certificates, diplomas, and associate

■ **Suburban** 50-acre campus with easy access to Little Rock
■ **Endowment** $11.3 million
■ **Coed**

Faculty *Student/faculty ratio:* 18:1.
Student Life *Campus security:* 24-hour emergency response devices and patrols.
Applying *Options:* common application, early admission, deferred entrance. *Required:* high school transcript.
Admissions Contact Dr. Allen B. Moody, Director of Institutional Services/Registrar, Garland County Community College, 101 College Drive, Hot Springs, AR 71913. *Phone:* 501-760-4222. *Fax:* 501-760-4100. *E-mail:* admissions@gccc.cc.ar.us.

ITT TECHNICAL INSTITUTE
Little Rock, Arkansas

■ **Proprietary** 2-year, founded 1993, part of ITT Educational Services, Inc
■ **Calendar** quarters
■ **Degree** associate
■ **Urban** campus
■ **Coed,** 301 undergraduate students

Majors Computer/information sciences related; computer programming; drafting; electrical/electronic engineering technologies related; information technology.
Student Life *Housing:* college housing not available.
Costs (2001–02) *Tuition:* Full-time tuition and fees vary according to program. Part-time tuition and fees vary according to program. $260—$330 per credit hour.
Applying *Options:* deferred entrance. *Application fee:* $100. *Required:* high school transcript, interview. *Recommended:* letters of recommendation. *Application deadline:* rolling (freshmen), rolling (transfers).
Admissions Contact Mr. Tom Crawford, Director, ITT Technical Institute, 4520 South University, Little Rock, AR 72204. *Phone:* 501-565-5550. *Toll-free phone:* 800-359-4429.

MID-SOUTH COMMUNITY COLLEGE
West Memphis, Arkansas

■ **State-supported** 2-year, founded 1993
■ **Calendar** semesters
■ **Degree** certificates and associate
■ **Suburban** 80-acre campus with easy access to Memphis
■ **Coed,** 996 undergraduate students, 38% full-time, 67% women, 33% men

Undergraduates 378 full-time, 618 part-time. Students come from 5 states and territories, 2 other countries, 3% are from out of state, 53% African American, 0.1% Asian American or Pacific Islander, 0.7% Hispanic American, 0.1% Native American, 2% international, 2% transferred in.
Freshmen *Admission:* 30 applied, 30 admitted. *Test scores:* ACT scores over 18: 60%; ACT scores over 24: 46%.
Faculty *Total:* 66, 44% full-time. *Student/faculty ratio:* 12:1.
Majors Business information/data processing related; business marketing and marketing management; computer/information sciences; criminal justice studies; liberal arts and sciences/liberal studies; multi/interdisciplinary studies related; office management; Web/multimedia management/webmaster.
Academic Programs *Special study options:* academic remediation for entering students, adult/continuing education programs, distance learning, independent study, internships, part-time degree program, summer session for credit.
Library Mid-South Community College Library/Media Center with 7,565 titles, 92 serial subscriptions, 1,321 audiovisual materials, an OPAC, a Web page.
Computers on Campus 280 computers available on campus for general student use. A campuswide network can be accessed from off campus. Internet access, at least one staffed computer lab available.
Student Life *Housing:* college housing not available. *Activities and Organizations:* choral group, Phi Theta Kappa, Baptist Student Union. *Campus security:* 24-hour emergency response devices, security during class hours.
Standardized Tests *Required:* ACT ASSET. *Recommended:* ACT (for placement).
Costs (2002–03) *Tuition:* area resident $912 full-time, $38 per credit hour part-time; state resident $1128 full-time, $47 per credit hour part-time; nonresident $1392 full-time, $58 per credit hour part-time. Full-time tuition and fees vary according to course load and reciprocity agreements. Part-time tuition and fees vary according to course load and reciprocity agreements. *Required fees:* $72 full-time, $27 per term part-time. *Waivers:* senior citizens and employees or children of employees.
Financial Aid In 2001, 22 Federal Work-Study jobs (averaging $1678).
Applying *Options:* early admission. *Required:* high school transcript. *Required for some:* 2 letters of recommendation. *Application deadline:* rolling (freshmen), rolling (transfers). *Notification:* continuous (freshmen).
Admissions Contact Leslie Anderson, Assistant Registrar, Mid-South Community College, 2000 West Broadway, West Memphis, AR 72301. *Phone:* 870-733-6732. *Fax:* 870-733-6719. *E-mail:* landerson@midsouthcc.edu.

MISSISSIPPI COUNTY COMMUNITY COLLEGE
Blytheville, Arkansas

■ **State-supported** 2-year, founded 1975
■ **Calendar** semesters
■ **Degree** certificates and associate
■ **Rural** 80-acre campus with easy access to Memphis
■ **Coed,** 1,840 undergraduate students, 57% full-time, 71% women, 29% men

Undergraduates 1,046 full-time, 794 part-time. Students come from 5 states and territories, 18% are from out of state, 34% African American, 1% Asian American or Pacific Islander, 1% Hispanic American, 2% transferred in.
Freshmen *Admission:* 430 applied, 430 admitted, 308 enrolled.
Faculty *Total:* 98, 40% full-time, 6% with terminal degrees. *Student/faculty ratio:* 18:1.
Majors Agricultural sciences; business; child care/guidance; general studies; horticulture services; industrial machinery maintenance/repair; law enforcement/police science; metallurgical technology; nursing.
Academic Programs *Special study options:* academic remediation for entering students, adult/continuing education programs, advanced placement credit, distance learning, double majors, external degree program, part-time degree program, summer session for credit.
Library Adams/Vines Library with 14,132 titles, 165 serial subscriptions, 709 audiovisual materials, an OPAC.
Computers on Campus 280 computers available on campus for general student use. Internet access, at least one staffed computer lab available.
Student Life *Housing:* college housing not available. *Activities and Organizations:* drama/theater group, student-run newspaper, choral group, Gamma Beta Phi, Association of Childhood Education International, Nursing Club, Cultural Diversity. *Campus security:* 24-hour patrols.
Standardized Tests *Required:* ACT ASSET. *Required for some:* ACT (for placement). *Recommended:* ACT (for placement).
Costs (2001–02) *Tuition:* area resident $984 full-time, $41 per semester hour part-time; state resident $1224 full-time, $51 per semester hour part-time; nonresident $2424 full-time, $101 per semester hour part-time. *Required fees:* $68 full-time, $2 per semester hour, $2 per term part-time. *Payment plans:* installment, deferred payment. *Waivers:* senior citizens and employees or children of employees.
Financial Aid In 2001, 37 Federal Work-Study jobs (averaging $2400).
Applying *Options:* deferred entrance. *Recommended:* high school transcript. *Application deadline:* rolling (freshmen), rolling (transfers). *Notification:* continuous (freshmen).
Admissions Contact Mrs. Leslie Wells, Admissions Counselor, Mississippi County Community College, PO Box 1109, Blytheville, AR 72315. *Phone:* 870-762-1020 Ext. 1118. *Fax:* 870-763-1654. *E-mail:* goff@mccc.cc.ar.us.

NORTH ARKANSAS COLLEGE
Harrison, Arkansas

■ **State and locally supported** 2-year, founded 1974
■ **Calendar** semesters
■ **Degree** certificates and associate
■ **Small-town** 40-acre campus
■ **Endowment** $103,275
■ **Coed,** 1,889 undergraduate students, 57% full-time, 59% women, 41% men

Undergraduates 1,081 full-time, 808 part-time. Students come from 14 states and territories, 5% are from out of state, 0.3% African American, 0.5% Asian American or Pacific Islander, 1% Hispanic American, 0.9% Native American, 6% transferred in.
Freshmen *Admission:* 686 applied, 686 admitted, 496 enrolled.

North Arkansas College (continued)

Faculty *Total:* 121, 53% full-time, 7% with terminal degrees. *Student/faculty ratio:* 15:1.

Majors Agricultural sciences; business administration; electromechanical technology; emergency medical technology; general studies; liberal arts and sciences/liberal studies; medical laboratory technician; medical radiologic technology; nursing; operating room technician; secretarial science.

Academic Programs *Special study options:* academic remediation for entering students, adult/continuing education programs, advanced placement credit, distance learning, freshman honors college, honors programs, independent study, part-time degree program, services for LD students, summer session for credit.

Library North Arkansas College Library plus 1 other with 29,969 titles, 340 serial subscriptions, 2,879 audiovisual materials, an OPAC, a Web page.

Computers on Campus 200 computers available on campus for general student use. A campuswide network can be accessed from off campus. Internet access, at least one staffed computer lab available.

Student Life *Housing:* college housing not available. *Activities and Organizations:* drama/theater group, choral group, Phi Beta Lambda, Phi Theta Kappa, Student Nurses Association, Vocational Industrial Clubs, Baptist Student Union. *Campus security:* 24-hour patrols. *Student Services:* personal/psychological counseling.

Athletics Member NJCAA. *Intercollegiate sports:* baseball M, basketball M(s)/W(s), softball W. *Intramural sports:* archery M/W, badminton M/W, baseball M/W, football M/W, golf M/W, racquetball M/W, softball W, table tennis M/W, tennis M/W, volleyball M/W.

Standardized Tests *Required:* ACT (for placement), ACT ASSET, ACT COMPASS.

Costs (2001–02) *Tuition:* area resident $960 full-time, $40 per credit hour part-time; state resident $1200 full-time, $50 per credit hour part-time; nonresident $2448 full-time, $102 per credit hour part-time. Full-time tuition and fees vary according to location and reciprocity agreements. Part-time tuition and fees vary according to location and reciprocity agreements. *Required fees:* $120 full-time, $5 per credit hour. *Payment plan:* installment. *Waivers:* senior citizens and employees or children of employees.

Financial Aid In 2001, 92 Federal Work-Study jobs (averaging $1188).

Applying *Options:* deferred entrance. *Required for some:* high school transcript. *Application deadline:* rolling (freshmen), rolling (transfers). *Notification:* continuous (freshmen).

Admissions Contact Ms. Charla McDonald Jennings, Director of Admissions, North Arkansas College, 1515 Pioneer Drive, Harrison, AR 72601. *Phone:* 870-391-3221. *Toll-free phone:* 800-679-6622. *Fax:* 870-391-3339. *E-mail:* charlam@northark.edu.

NORTHWEST ARKANSAS COMMUNITY COLLEGE
Bentonville, Arkansas

- **State and locally supported** 2-year, founded 1989
- **Calendar** semesters
- **Degree** certificates and associate
- **Urban** 77-acre campus
- **Coed,** 4,292 undergraduate students, 31% full-time, 59% women, 41% men

Undergraduates Students come from 4 states and territories, 0.8% African American, 2% Asian American or Pacific Islander, 3% Hispanic American, 1% Native American.

Freshmen *Admission:* 893 applied, 893 admitted.

Faculty *Total:* 235, 28% full-time.

Majors Accounting; business administration; computer programming; criminal justice/law enforcement administration; data processing technology; drafting; education; electrical/electronic engineering technology; emergency medical technology; finance; industrial radiologic technology; liberal arts and sciences/liberal studies; nursing; occupational safety/health technology; physical therapy; respiratory therapy; secretarial science.

Academic Programs *Special study options:* academic remediation for entering students, adult/continuing education programs, advanced placement credit, cooperative education, distance learning, honors programs, independent study, internships, part-time degree program, services for LD students, summer session for credit.

Library Library Resource Center plus 1 other with 15,500 titles, 159 serial subscriptions, an OPAC.

Computers on Campus 97 computers available on campus for general student use. Internet access, at least one staffed computer lab available.

Student Life *Housing:* college housing not available. *Activities and Organizations:* drama/theater group, choral group, Student Advisory Activity Council, Gamma Beta Phi, Phi Beta Lambda, Student Nurses Association, Students in Free Enterprise. *Campus security:* 24-hour emergency response devices and patrols.

Athletics *Intramural sports:* basketball M/W, bowling M/W, football M/W, golf M, racquetball M/W, softball M/W, swimming M/W, table tennis M/W, tennis M/W, volleyball W, weight lifting M/W.

Standardized Tests *Required:* SAT I or ACT (for placement), ACT ASSET, ACT COMPASS.

Costs (2002–03) *Tuition:* area resident $1008 full-time, $46 per credit hour part-time; state resident $2016 full-time, $92 per credit hour part-time; nonresident $2520 full-time, $117 per credit hour part-time. *Required fees:* $60 full-time, $2.

Applying *Recommended:* high school transcript. *Application deadline:* rolling (freshmen). *Notification:* continuous (freshmen).

Admissions Contact Dr. Charles Mullins, Director of Admissions, NorthWest Arkansas Community College, One College Drive, Bentonville, AR 72712. *Phone:* 501-636-9222 Ext. 4231. *Fax:* 501-619-4116.

OUACHITA TECHNICAL COLLEGE
Malvern, Arkansas

- **State-supported** 2-year, founded 1972
- **Calendar** semesters
- **Degree** certificates and associate
- **Small-town** 11-acre campus
- **Coed,** 968 undergraduate students, 43% full-time, 51% women, 49% men

Undergraduates 420 full-time, 548 part-time. Students come from 2 states and territories, 0.4% are from out of state, 9% transferred in.

Freshmen *Admission:* 339 applied, 339 admitted, 189 enrolled. *Test scores:* ACT scores over 18: 53%; ACT scores over 24: 10%.

Faculty *Total:* 80, 36% full-time, 4% with terminal degrees. *Student/faculty ratio:* 13:1.

Majors Accounting; auto mechanic/technician; business administration; business marketing and marketing management; child care/guidance; computer/information sciences; industrial arts; industrial technology; legal administrative assistant; liberal arts and sciences/liberal studies; machine technology; management information systems/business data processing; medical administrative assistant; paralegal/legal assistant; practical nurse; secretarial science.

Academic Programs *Special study options:* academic remediation for entering students, accelerated degree program, advanced placement credit, cooperative education, distance learning, double majors, independent study, internships, part-time degree program, services for LD students, summer session for credit.

Library Ouachita Technical College Library/Learning Resource Center with 172 serial subscriptions, 1,039 audiovisual materials, a Web page.

Computers on Campus 125 computers available on campus for general student use. A campuswide network can be accessed from off campus. Internet access, at least one staffed computer lab available.

Student Life *Housing:* college housing not available. *Activities and Organizations:* student-run newspaper. *Campus security:* 24-hour patrols. *Student Services:* personal/psychological counseling.

Standardized Tests *Required for some:* SAT I or ACT (for placement), ACT ASSET.

Costs (2002–03) *Tuition:* area resident $1350 full-time, $45 per credit hour part-time; state resident $1350 full-time, $45 per credit hour part-time; nonresident $4050 full-time, $135 per credit hour part-time. No tuition increase for student's term of enrollment. *Required fees:* $330 full-time, $11 per credit hour. *Payment plan:* installment. *Waivers:* senior citizens and employees or children of employees.

Financial Aid In 2001, 18 Federal Work-Study jobs (averaging $2400).

Applying *Options:* electronic application, early admission, deferred entrance. *Application fee:* $20. *Required:* high school transcript. *Application deadline:* rolling (freshmen), rolling (transfers).

Admissions Contact Mr. Vaughn Kesterson, Counselor, Ouachita Technical College, PO Box 816, Malvern, AR 72104. *Phone:* 501-332-3658 Ext. 1117. *Toll-free phone:* 800-337-0266. *Fax:* 501-337-9382. *E-mail:* lindaj@otc1.otc.tcc.ar.us.

OZARKA COLLEGE
Melbourne, Arkansas

- **State-supported** 2-year, founded 1973
- **Calendar** semesters
- **Degree** certificates and associate

- **Rural** 40-acre campus
- **Coed,** 858 undergraduate students

Undergraduates Students come from 2 states and territories, 1% are from out of state.
Freshmen *Admission:* 189 applied, 189 admitted.
Faculty *Total:* 69, 35% full-time, 4% with terminal degrees. *Student/faculty ratio:* 18:1.
Majors Auto mechanic/technician; banking; business administration; criminal justice/law enforcement administration; culinary arts; information sciences/systems; liberal arts and sciences/liberal studies; medical records technology; middle school education; secretarial science.
Academic Programs *Special study options:* academic remediation for entering students, advanced placement credit, distance learning, external degree program, internships, part-time degree program, services for LD students, summer session for credit.
Library Ozarka College Library with 8,361 titles, 2,000 serial subscriptions, 1,081 audiovisual materials, an OPAC.
Computers on Campus 114 computers available on campus for general student use. A campuswide network can be accessed from off campus that provide access to check on grades—midterm and final. Internet access, online (class) registration, at least one staffed computer lab available.
Student Life *Housing:* college housing not available. *Activities and Organizations:* drama/theater group, VICA, Phi Beta Lambda, Drama Club, HOSA, Phi Theta Kappa. *Campus security:* security patrols 7 a.m. to 11 p.m. *Student Services:* personal/psychological counseling.
Standardized Tests *Required:* ACT (for placement), ACT ASSET.
Costs (2001–02) *Tuition:* state resident $1200 full-time, $50 per credit hour part-time; nonresident $4032 full-time, $168 per credit hour part-time. *Required fees:* $126 full-time, $4 per credit hour, $15 per term part-time. *Payment plan:* installment. *Waivers:* senior citizens and employees or children of employees.
Financial Aid In 2001, 50 Federal Work-Study jobs, 35 State and other part-time jobs.
Applying *Options:* deferred entrance. *Required:* high school transcript. *Required for some:* essay or personal statement, letters of recommendation, interview. *Recommended:* minimum 2.0 GPA. *Application deadlines:* 8/15 (freshmen), 8/15 (transfers).
Admissions Contact Mr. Randy Scaggs, Counselor and Recruiter, Ozarka College, PO Box 12, 218 College Drive, Melbourne, AR 72556. *Phone:* 870-368-7371. *Toll-free phone:* 800-821-4335. *Fax:* 870-368-4733. *E-mail:* rscaggs@ozarka.edu.

PHILLIPS COMMUNITY COLLEGE OF THE UNIVERSITY OF ARKANSAS
Helena, Arkansas

- **State and locally supported** 2-year, founded 1965, part of University of Arkansas System
- **Calendar** semesters
- **Degree** certificates and associate
- **Small-town** 80-acre campus with easy access to Memphis
- **Coed**

Student Life *Campus security:* 24-hour patrols.
Standardized Tests *Required:* ACT (for placement), ACT ASSET.
Applying *Options:* early admission.
Admissions Contact Mr. James R. Brasel, Vice Chancellor of Administrative Services, Phillips Community College of the University of Arkansas, PO Box 785, Helena, AR 72342-0785. *Phone:* 870-338-6474.

PULASKI TECHNICAL COLLEGE
North Little Rock, Arkansas

- **State-supported** 2-year, founded 1945
- **Calendar** semesters
- **Degree** certificates and associate
- **Urban** 40-acre campus with easy access to Little Rock
- **Coed,** 4,966 undergraduate students

Undergraduates Students come from 1 other state, 7 other countries, 37% African American.
Freshmen *Test scores:* ACT scores over 18: 48%; ACT scores over 24: 5%.
Faculty *Total:* 155. *Student/faculty ratio:* 20:1.
Majors Computer engineering technology; drafting; electromechanical technology; industrial technology; information sciences/systems; secretarial science.
Academic Programs *Special study options:* academic remediation for entering students, advanced placement credit, distance learning, part-time degree program, services for LD students, summer session for credit.
Library Library Resource Center with an OPAC.
Computers on Campus 75 computers available on campus for general student use. Internet access, at least one staffed computer lab available.
Student Life *Housing:* college housing not available. *Campus security:* security personnel 7 a.m. to 11 p.m.
Standardized Tests *Required:* ACT, ACT ASSET, or ACT COMPASS.
Costs (2002–03) *Tuition:* state resident $1680 full-time, $56 per credit hour part-time; nonresident $2400 full-time, $80 per credit hour part-time. Full-time tuition and fees vary according to course load. *Required fees:* $180 full-time, $6 per credit hour. *Payment plan:* deferred payment. *Waivers:* senior citizens and employees or children of employees.
Applying *Options:* common application. *Required:* high school transcript. *Application deadline:* rolling (freshmen).
Admissions Contact Ms. Janice Hurd, Director of Admissions and Records, Pulaski Technical College, 3000 West Scenic Drive, North Little Rock, AR 72118. *Phone:* 501-812-2233. *Fax:* 501-812-2316.

RICH MOUNTAIN COMMUNITY COLLEGE
Mena, Arkansas

- **State and locally supported** 2-year, founded 1983
- **Calendar** semesters
- **Degree** certificates and associate
- **Small-town** 40-acre campus
- **Endowment** $301,360
- **Coed,** 1,005 undergraduate students, 35% full-time, 67% women, 33% men

Undergraduates 352 full-time, 653 part-time. Students come from 2 states and territories, 2 other countries, 2% are from out of state, 7% transferred in.
Freshmen *Admission:* 182 enrolled. *Average high school GPA:* 2.81.
Faculty *Total:* 55, 35% full-time, 4% with terminal degrees. *Student/faculty ratio:* 18:1.
Majors Liberal arts and sciences/liberal studies; secretarial science.
Academic Programs *Special study options:* academic remediation for entering students, adult/continuing education programs, advanced placement credit, distance learning, double majors, English as a second language, part-time degree program, services for LD students, summer session for credit.
Library St. John Library with 13,299 titles, 81 serial subscriptions, 674 audiovisual materials, an OPAC.
Computers on Campus 88 computers available on campus for general student use. A campuswide network can be accessed from off campus. Internet access, at least one staffed computer lab available.
Student Life *Housing:* college housing not available. *Activities and Organizations:* student-run television station, SGA, Baptist Student Union, Phi Theta Kappa, Golf Club, TV and Video Club. *Campus security:* administrator on night duty. *Student Services:* personal/psychological counseling.
Costs (2002–03) *Tuition:* area resident $888 full-time, $37 per semester hour part-time; state resident $1104 full-time, $46 per semester hour part-time; nonresident $3312 full-time, $138 per semester hour part-time. *Required fees:* $48 full-time, $2 per credit hour. *Payment plan:* installment. *Waivers:* senior citizens and employees or children of employees.
Financial Aid In 2001, 12 Federal Work-Study jobs (averaging $1500).
Applying *Options:* common application, early admission. *Required:* high school transcript. *Application deadlines:* 8/25 (freshmen), 8/25 (transfers). *Notification:* continuous until 8/25 (freshmen).
Admissions Contact Dr. Steve Rook, Dean of Students, Rich Mountain Community College, 1100 College Drive, Mena, AR 71953. *Phone:* 479-394-7622 Ext. 1400.

SOUTH ARKANSAS COMMUNITY COLLEGE
El Dorado, Arkansas

- **State-supported** 2-year, founded 1975, part of Arkansas Department of Higher Education
- **Calendar** semesters
- **Degree** certificates and associate
- **Small-town** 4-acre campus

South Arkansas Community College (continued)
■ **Coed,** 1,173 undergraduate students, 100% full-time, 60% women, 40% men

Undergraduates 1,173 full-time. Students come from 2 states and territories, 3% are from out of state, 24% African American, 0.4% Asian American or Pacific Islander, 0.8% Hispanic American, 0.7% Native American.
Freshmen *Admission:* 435 enrolled.
Faculty *Total:* 88, 58% full-time. *Student/faculty ratio:* 13:1.
Majors Business; emergency medical technology; general studies; industrial technology; law enforcement/police science; management information systems/business data processing; medical laboratory technician; medical radiologic technology; physical therapy assistant; secretarial science.
Academic Programs *Special study options:* academic remediation for entering students, adult/continuing education programs, advanced placement credit, internships, part-time degree program, services for LD students, summer session for credit.
Library South Arkansas Community College Library with 22,652 titles, 223 serial subscriptions.
Computers on Campus 75 computers available on campus for general student use. Internet access, at least one staffed computer lab available.
Student Life *Housing:* college housing not available. *Activities and Organizations:* choral group. *Campus security:* security guard. *Student Services:* personal/psychological counseling.
Athletics *Intramural sports:* badminton M/W, basketball M/W, tennis M/W, volleyball M/W.
Standardized Tests *Required:* ACT ASSET. *Recommended:* SAT I or ACT (for placement).
Costs (2002–03) *Tuition:* area resident $1296 full-time, $54 per hour part-time; state resident $1560 full-time, $65 per hour part-time; nonresident $2880 full-time, $120 per hour part-time. *Required fees:* $58 full-time, $3 per hour, $50 per term part-time. *Payment plan:* installment. *Waivers:* senior citizens.
Financial Aid In 2001, 45 Federal Work-Study jobs (averaging $1300).
Applying *Options:* early admission, deferred entrance. *Application deadline:* rolling (freshmen), rolling (transfers).
Admissions Contact Mr. Dean Inman, Director of Enrollment Services, South Arkansas Community College, PO Box 7010, El Dorado, AR 71731-7010. *Phone:* 870-864-7142. *Toll-free phone:* 800-955-2289 Ext. 142. *Fax:* 870-864-7109. *E-mail:* dinman@southark.cc.ar.us.

SOUTHEAST ARKANSAS COLLEGE
Pine Bluff, Arkansas

■ **State-supported** 2-year, founded 1991
■ **Calendar** semesters
■ **Degree** certificates and associate
■ **Coed,** 2,025 undergraduate students

Faculty *Total:* 125, 36% full-time. *Student/faculty ratio:* 18:1.
Majors Auto mechanic/technician; biological technology; business; business administration; criminology; drafting; electrical/electronic engineering technology; emergency medical technology; general studies; industrial technology; operating room technician; paralegal/legal assistant; radiological science; science/technology and society.
Academic Programs *Special study options:* academic remediation for entering students, accelerated degree program, advanced placement credit, cooperative education, double majors, honors programs, independent study, internships, part-time degree program, services for LD students, summer session for credit.
Library Southeast Arkansas Technical College Library with 5,000 titles, 75 serial subscriptions.
Computers on Campus 62 computers available on campus for general student use. Internet access, at least one staffed computer lab available.
Student Life *Housing:* college housing not available. *Activities and Organizations:* choral group, Phi Beta Lambda, HOSA, Phi Theta Kappa, Student Senate. *Campus security:* student patrols. *Student Services:* personal/psychological counseling.
Standardized Tests *Required:* SAT I or ACT (for placement), ACT ASSET.
Costs (2001–02) *Tuition:* state resident $1080 full-time, $38 per credit part-time; nonresident $2160 full-time, $72 per credit part-time. *Required fees:* $210 full-time, $7 per credit.
Applying *Options:* common application, early admission. *Required:* high school transcript. *Application deadlines:* 8/21 (freshmen), 8/21 (transfers). *Notification:* continuous (freshmen).
Admissions Contact Ms. Donna R. Ryles, Coordinator of Admissions and Enrollment Management, Southeast Arkansas College, 1900 Hazel Street, Pine Bluff, AR 71603. *Phone:* 870-543-5952. *Toll-free phone:* 888-SEARK TC. *E-mail:* dryles@stc.seark.tec.ar.us.

SOUTHERN ARKANSAS UNIVERSITY TECH
Camden, Arkansas

■ **State-supported** 2-year, founded 1967, part of Arkansas Department of Higher Education
■ **Calendar** semesters
■ **Degree** certificates and associate
■ **Rural** 96-acre campus
■ **Coed,** 896 undergraduate students, 50% full-time, 53% women, 47% men

Undergraduates 444 full-time, 452 part-time. Students come from 5 states and territories, 0.9% are from out of state, 33% African American, 2% Hispanic American, 11% transferred in.
Freshmen *Admission:* 127 applied, 127 admitted, 106 enrolled. *Average high school GPA:* 2.79. *Test scores:* ACT scores over 18: 70%; ACT scores over 24: 3%.
Faculty *Total:* 60, 62% full-time, 7% with terminal degrees. *Student/faculty ratio:* 13:1.
Majors Aircraft mechanic/powerplant; business administration; child care provider; computer/information sciences related; computer maintenance technology; computer programming; computer science; drafting; educational media design; emergency medical technology; engineering technologies related; environmental technology; fire science; general studies; graphic design/commercial art/illustration; industrial machinery maintenance/repair; industrial technology; office management.
Academic Programs *Special study options:* academic remediation for entering students, adult/continuing education programs, advanced placement credit, distance learning, double majors, honors programs, independent study, internships, off-campus study, part-time degree program, summer session for credit.
Library Southern Arkansas University Tech Learning Resource Center with 14,532 titles, 153 serial subscriptions, 478 audiovisual materials, an OPAC.
Computers on Campus 190 computers available on campus for general student use. Internet access, at least one staffed computer lab available.
Student Life *Housing:* college housing not available. *Activities and Organizations:* Phi Beta Lambda, SAU Tech Ambassadors, Allied Health Student Club, computer club, Phi Theta Kappa. *Campus security:* 24-hour emergency response devices, patrols by trained security personnel. *Student Services:* personal/psychological counseling.
Athletics *Intramural sports:* basketball M/W, bowling M/W, football M/W, golf M/W, tennis M/W, volleyball M/W, weight lifting M/W.
Standardized Tests *Required:* SAT I or ACT (for placement), ACT ASSET.
Costs (2001–02) *One-time required fee:* $15. *Tuition:* state resident $1200 full-time, $50 per semester hour part-time; nonresident $1680 full-time, $70 per semester hour part-time. *Required fees:* $480 full-time, $20 per semester hour. *Waivers:* senior citizens and employees or children of employees.
Financial Aid In 2001, 20 Federal Work-Study jobs (averaging $1017). *Financial aid deadline:* 6/1.
Applying *Options:* deferred entrance. *Required for some:* high school transcript. *Recommended:* high school transcript, minimum 2.0 GPA. *Application deadline:* 8/15 (freshmen), rolling (transfers). *Notification:* continuous (freshmen).
Admissions Contact Mr. Scott Raney, Admissions Director, Southern Arkansas University Tech, PO Box 3499, East Camden, AR 71711. *Phone:* 870-574-4558. *Fax:* 870-574-4478. *E-mail:* sraney@sautech.edu.

UNIVERSITY OF ARKANSAS AT FORT SMITH
Fort Smith, Arkansas

■ **State and locally supported** primarily 2-year, founded 1928, part of University of Arkansas System
■ **Calendar** semesters
■ **Degrees** certificates, associate, and bachelor's
■ **Suburban** 108-acre campus
■ **Endowment** $27.4 million
■ **Coed,** 5,746 undergraduate students, 44% full-time, 57% women, 43% men

Undergraduates 2,541 full-time, 3,205 part-time. Students come from 22 states and territories, 3 other countries, 11% are from out of state, 4% African American, 4% Asian American or Pacific Islander, 2% Hispanic American, 3% Native American, 0.3% international, 6% transferred in. *Retention:* 55% of 2001 full-time freshmen returned.

Freshmen *Admission:* 1,921 applied, 1,921 admitted, 1,153 enrolled. *Average high school GPA:* 3.05. *Test scores:* SAT verbal scores over 500: 25%; ACT scores over 18: 72%; ACT scores over 24: 18%.
Faculty *Total:* 293, 48% full-time. *Student/faculty ratio:* 19:1.
Majors Auto mechanic/technician; business administration; cartography; dental hygiene; drafting; electrical/electronic engineering technology; emergency medical technology; environmental technology; general studies; gerontological services; graphic design/commercial art/illustration; industrial technology; liberal arts and sciences/liberal studies; machine technology; management information systems/business data processing; medical radiologic technology; multi/interdisciplinary studies related; nursing; operating room technician; paralegal/legal assistant; respiratory therapy; secretarial science; welding technology.
Academic Programs *Special study options:* academic remediation for entering students, accelerated degree program, adult/continuing education programs, advanced placement credit, cooperative education, distance learning, English as a second language, honors programs, internships, off-campus study, part-time degree program, services for LD students, summer session for credit.
Library Boreham Library with 59,101 titles, 647 serial subscriptions, 1,266 audiovisual materials, an OPAC, a Web page.
Computers on Campus 919 computers available on campus for general student use. A campuswide network can be accessed from off campus that provide access to online grade reports, online subscription databases. Internet access, online (class) registration, at least one staffed computer lab available.
Student Life *Housing:* college housing not available. *Activities and Organizations:* student-run newspaper, choral group, Student Activities Council, Phi Beta Lambda, Phi Theta Kappa, student publications, Baptist Student Union. *Campus security:* 24-hour emergency response devices and patrols, late-night transport/escort service.
Athletics Member NJCAA. *Intercollegiate sports:* baseball M(s), basketball M(s)/W(s), volleyball W(s). *Intramural sports:* basketball M/W, football M, table tennis M/W.
Standardized Tests *Required for some:* ACT ASSET, ACT COMPASS. *Recommended:* ACT (for placement).
Costs (2001–02) *Tuition:* area resident $1260 full-time, $41 per credit part-time; state resident $1590 full-time, $52 per credit part-time; nonresident $3090 full-time, $102 per credit part-time. Full-time tuition and fees vary according to class time and degree level. Part-time tuition and fees vary according to class time and degree level. *Required fees:* $30 full-time, $15 per term part-time. *Payment plan:* installment. *Waivers:* senior citizens and employees or children of employees.
Financial Aid In 2001, 110 Federal Work-Study jobs (averaging $3000). 94 State and other part-time jobs (averaging $3000).
Applying *Options:* early admission, deferred entrance. *Required:* high school transcript. *Application deadline:* rolling (freshmen), rolling (transfers).
Admissions Contact Mr. Scott McDonald, Director of Admissions and School Relations, University of Arkansas at Fort Smith, 5210 Grand Avenue, PO Box 3649, Fort Smith, AR 72913-3649. *Phone:* 501-788-7125. *Toll-free phone:* 888-512-5466. *Fax:* 501-788-7016. *E-mail:* westark@systema.westark.edu.

UNIVERSITY OF ARKANSAS COMMUNITY COLLEGE AT BATESVILLE
Batesville, Arkansas

- **State-supported** 2-year, part of University of Arkansas System
- **Calendar** semesters for day division, quarters for evening division
- **Degree** certificates and associate
- **Coed,** 328 undergraduate students, 68% full-time, 61% women, 39% men

Undergraduates 224 full-time, 104 part-time.
Freshmen *Admission:* 423 applied, 423 admitted, 328 enrolled.
Faculty *Total:* 99, 45% full-time. *Student/faculty ratio:* 13:1.
Majors Business; computer systems networking/telecommunications; criminal justice studies; data entry/microcomputer applications; early childhood education; education; emergency medical technology; industrial technology; information technology; Internet; medical office management; nursing; system/networking/LAN/WAN management.
Academic Programs *Special study options:* academic remediation for entering students, adult/continuing education programs, advanced placement credit, cooperative education, distance learning, double majors, English as a second language, external degree program, independent study, internships, off-campus study, part-time degree program, services for LD students, student-designed majors, summer session for credit.
Library University of Arkansas Community College at Batesville Library with 8,000 titles, 149 serial subscriptions, 1,500 audiovisual materials, an OPAC.
Standardized Tests *Required:* SAT I and SAT II or ACT (for placement).
Costs (2001–02) *Tuition:* area resident $840 full-time, $35 per credit part-time; state resident $1056 full-time, $44 per credit part-time; nonresident $2112 full-time, $88 per credit part-time. Full-time tuition and fees vary according to program. Part-time tuition and fees vary according to course load. *Required fees:* $202 full-time, $29 per course. *Waivers:* senior citizens and employees or children of employees.
Financial Aid In 2001, 32 Federal Work-Study jobs (averaging $781).
Applying *Options:* common application. *Required:* high school transcript, immunization records.
Admissions Contact Mr. Andy Thomas, Admissions/Recruitment Officer, University of Arkansas Community College at Batesville, PO Box 3350, Batesville, AR 72503. *Phone:* 870-793-7581. *E-mail:* uaccb@cc.ar.us.

UNIVERSITY OF ARKANSAS COMMUNITY COLLEGE AT HOPE
Hope, Arkansas

- **State-supported** 2-year, founded 1966, part of University of Arkansas System
- **Calendar** semesters
- **Degree** diplomas and associate
- **Rural** 60-acre campus
- **Coed,** 1,137 undergraduate students, 59% full-time, 66% women, 34% men

Undergraduates 675 full-time, 462 part-time. Students come from 4 states and territories.
Freshmen *Admission:* 558 applied, 558 admitted, 320 enrolled.
Faculty *Total:* 68, 54% full-time, 7% with terminal degrees.
Majors Business administration; child care provider; criminal justice/law enforcement administration; human services; industrial machinery maintenance/repair; liberal arts and sciences/liberal studies; machine shop assistant; mortuary science; respiratory therapy; trade/industrial education.
Academic Programs *Special study options:* academic remediation for entering students, accelerated degree program, English as a second language, internships, part-time degree program, summer session for credit.
Library University of Arkansas Community College at Hope Library with 5,150 titles, 250 serial subscriptions, 524 audiovisual materials, an OPAC, a Web page.
Computers on Campus Internet access, at least one staffed computer lab available.
Student Life *Housing:* college housing not available. *Activities and Organizations:* Student Government Association, Phi Theta Kappa, Phi Beta Lambda, Circle K. *Campus security:* on-campus security during class hours.
Standardized Tests *Required for some:* ACT ASSET. *Recommended:* ACT (for placement), ACT ASSET.
Costs (2001–02) *Tuition:* area resident $1196 full-time, $44 per credit part-time; state resident $1268 full-time, $47 per credit part-time; nonresident $2348 full-time, $92 per credit part-time. Part-time tuition and fees vary according to course load. *Required fees:* $140 full-time, $1 per credit. *Payment plan:* installment. *Waivers:* senior citizens and employees or children of employees.
Financial Aid In 2001, 60 Federal Work-Study jobs.
Applying *Options:* early admission. *Required:* high school transcript. *Application deadline:* rolling (freshmen), rolling (transfers).
Admissions Contact Ms. Danita Ormand, Director of Enrollment Services, University of Arkansas Community College at Hope, 71802-0140. *Phone:* 870-777-5722 Ext. 1267. *Fax:* 870-722-6630.

UNIVERSITY OF ARKANSAS COMMUNITY COLLEGE AT MORRILTON
Morrilton, Arkansas

- **State-supported** 2-year, founded 1961
- **Calendar** semesters
- **Degree** certificates and associate
- **Rural** 63-acre campus
- **Coed,** 1,294 undergraduate students

Undergraduates Students come from 1 other state, 1 other country, 7% African American, 0.5% Asian American or Pacific Islander, 1% Hispanic American, 0.7% Native American, 0.7% international.
Freshmen *Admission:* 595 applied, 595 admitted. *Average high school GPA:* 2.20.

University of Arkansas Community College at Morrilton (continued)

Faculty *Total:* 65, 62% full-time, 2% with terminal degrees. *Student/faculty ratio:* 19:1.

Majors Auto mechanic/technician; business marketing and marketing management; child care/development; computer systems networking/telecommunications; computer typography/composition; drafting; graphic design/commercial art/illustration; heating/air conditioning/refrigeration; horticulture science; information sciences/systems; liberal arts and sciences/liberal studies; machine technology; ornamental horticulture; practical nurse; secretarial science; surveying; welding technology.

Academic Programs *Special study options:* academic remediation for entering students, advanced placement credit, double majors, internships, part-time degree program, services for LD students, student-designed majors, summer session for credit.

Library Gordon Library with 6,600 titles, 76 serial subscriptions.

Computers on Campus 100 computers available on campus for general student use. At least one staffed computer lab available.

Student Life *Housing:* college housing not available. *Activities and Organizations:* Business Students' Organization, Student Activity Board, Early Childhood Development Organization, Graphic Design, Student Practical Nurses Organization. *Campus security:* 24-hour emergency response devices. *Student Services:* personal/psychological counseling.

Standardized Tests *Required:* ACT (for placement), ACT ASSET.

Costs (2001–02) *Tuition:* area resident $1488 full-time, $48 per credit hour part-time; state resident $1620 full-time, $53 per credit hour part-time; nonresident $2400 full-time, $80 per credit hour part-time. Part-time tuition and fees vary according to course load. *Required fees:* $70 full-time, $25 per term part-time. *Payment plan:* deferred payment. *Waivers:* senior citizens and employees or children of employees.

Financial Aid In 2001, 20 Federal Work-Study jobs (averaging $1000). *Financial aid deadline:* 8/5.

Applying *Options:* common application, early admission, deferred entrance. *Required:* high school transcript. *Required for some:* immunization records. *Application deadline:* rolling (freshmen), rolling (transfers). *Notification:* continuous (freshmen).

Admissions Contact Dr. Gary Gaston, Vice Chancellor for Student Services, University of Arkansas Community College at Morrilton, One Bruce Street, Morrilton, AR 72110. *Phone:* 501-977-2014. *Toll-free phone:* 800-264-1094. *Fax:* 501-354-9948.

CALIFORNIA

ALLAN HANCOCK COLLEGE

Santa Maria, California

- **State and locally supported** 2-year, founded 1920
- **Calendar** semesters
- **Degree** certificates and associate
- **Small-town** 120-acre campus
- **Endowment** $1.1 million
- **Coed,** 12,548 undergraduate students, 22% full-time, 59% women, 41% men

Undergraduates 2,777 full-time, 9,771 part-time. Students come from 27 states and territories, 12 other countries, 5% African American, 5% Asian American or Pacific Islander, 32% Hispanic American, 1% Native American, 0.2% international.

Freshmen *Admission:* 938 enrolled.

Faculty *Total:* 576, 26% full-time.

Majors Accounting; aerospace engineering; agribusiness; applied art; architectural engineering technology; art; auto mechanic/technician; biology; business administration; chemistry; civil engineering technology; computer engineering technology; computer science; cosmetology; dance; dental assistant; dietetics; early childhood education; electrical/electronic engineering technology; engineering; engineering technology; English; environmental technology; family/consumer studies; fashion design/illustration; film studies; fire science; graphic design/commercial art/illustration; heavy equipment maintenance; human services; information sciences/systems; interior design; international relations; law enforcement/police science; legal administrative assistant; liberal arts and sciences/liberal studies; machine technology; medical assistant; music; nursing; photography; physical education; physical therapy; physics; practical nurse; recreation/leisure studies; secretarial science; social sciences; Spanish; welding technology.

Academic Programs *Special study options:* adult/continuing education programs, advanced placement credit, cooperative education, distance learning, English as a second language, part-time degree program, services for LD students, study abroad, summer session for credit.

Library Learning Resources Center with 47,370 titles, 397 serial subscriptions, 2,463 audiovisual materials, an OPAC, a Web page.

Computers on Campus 200 computers available on campus for general student use. Internet access, at least one staffed computer lab available.

Student Life *Housing:* college housing not available. *Activities and Organizations:* drama/theater group, student-run newspaper, choral group, MECHA, AHC Student Club, Club Med (medical), Hancock Christian Fellowship, Vocational Industrial Clubs of America. *Campus security:* 24-hour emergency response devices and patrols, student patrols, late-night transport/escort service. *Student Services:* health clinic, personal/psychological counseling, legal services.

Athletics *Intercollegiate sports:* baseball M, basketball M/W, cross-country running M/W, football M, golf M, soccer M/W, softball W, tennis M/W, track and field M/W, volleyball W.

Standardized Tests *Required for some:* Assessment and Placement Services for Community Colleges.

Costs (2001–02) *Tuition:* state resident $0 full-time; nonresident $3216 full-time, $134 per unit part-time. Full-time tuition and fees vary according to course load and location. Part-time tuition and fees vary according to course load and location. *Required fees:* $288 full-time, $11 per unit, $12 per term part-time. *Payment plans:* installment, deferred payment.

Financial Aid In 2001, 250 Federal Work-Study jobs (averaging $3000).

Applying *Options:* early admission. *Required:* high school transcript. *Application deadline:* rolling (freshmen), rolling (transfers). *Notification:* continuous (freshmen).

Admissions Contact Ms. Norma Razo, Director of Admissions and Records, Allan Hancock College, 800 South College Drive, Santa Maria, CA 93454-6399. *Phone:* 805-922-6966 Ext. 3272. *Fax:* 805-922-3477. *E-mail:* nrazo@ahc.sbceo.k12.ca.us.

AMERICAN ACADEMY OF DRAMATIC ARTS/HOLLYWOOD

Hollywood, California

- **Independent** 2-year, founded 1974
- **Calendar** continuous
- **Degree** certificates, diplomas, and associate
- **Suburban** 4-acre campus with easy access to Los Angeles
- **Coed,** 182 undergraduate students

Undergraduates Students come from 21 states and territories, 3 other countries, 40% are from out of state.

Freshmen *Admission:* 230 applied, 182 admitted.

Faculty *Total:* 26, 31% with terminal degrees. *Student/faculty ratio:* 12:1.

Majors Theater arts/drama.

Library Bryn Morgan Library with 7,700 titles, 24 serial subscriptions, 320 audiovisual materials.

Student Life *Housing:* college housing not available. *Campus security:* 24-hour emergency response devices, 8-hour patrols by trained security personnel.

Costs (2002–03) *Tuition:* $13,700 full-time. *Required fees:* $400 full-time. *Payment plan:* installment.

Financial Aid In 2001, 15 Federal Work-Study jobs (averaging $2000).

Applying *Options:* deferred entrance. *Application fee:* $50. *Required:* essay or personal statement, high school transcript, 2 letters of recommendation, interview, audition. *Recommended:* minimum 2.0 GPA. *Application deadline:* rolling (freshmen), rolling (transfers). *Notification:* continuous (freshmen).

Admissions Contact Mr. James Wickline, Director of Admissions, American Academy of Dramatic Arts/Hollywood, 1336 North LaBrea Avenue, Hollywood, CA 90028. *Phone:* 800-222-2867. *Toll-free phone:* 800-222-2867. *E-mail:* admissions-ca@aada.org.

AMERICAN RIVER COLLEGE

Sacramento, California

- **District-supported** 2-year, founded 1955, part of Los Rios Community College District System
- **Calendar** semesters
- **Degree** certificates and associate
- **Suburban** 153-acre campus

■ **Coed,** 2,145 undergraduate students, 32% full-time, 53% women, 47% men

Undergraduates 693 full-time, 1,452 part-time. 0.2% are from out of state, 424% transferred in.
Freshmen *Admission:* 2,471 applied, 2,471 admitted, 2,145 enrolled.
Faculty *Total:* 914, 40% full-time. *Student/faculty ratio:* 34:1.
Majors Accounting; advertising; art; auto mechanic/technician; biological/physical sciences; business administration; business marketing and marketing management; carpentry; child care/development; computer engineering technology; computer graphics; computer/information systems security; computer programming; computer programming related; computer programming (specific applications); computer programming, vendor/product certification; computer science related; computer software and media applications related; computer systems networking/telecommunications; computer/technical support; construction technology; culinary arts; data entry/microcomputer applications; data processing technology; drafting; early childhood education; electrical/electronic engineering technology; engineering technology; fashion design/illustration; fashion merchandising; finance; fire science; food products retailing; food sales operations; forest harvesting production technology; gerontology; home economics education; horticulture science; hotel and restaurant management; human services; industrial arts; interior design; journalism; landscape architecture; legal administrative assistant; liberal arts and sciences/liberal studies; mathematics; medical administrative assistant; music; music business management/merchandising; natural resources management; nursing; paralegal/legal assistant; physical sciences; pre-engineering; real estate; recreation/leisure studies; respiratory therapy; retail management; secretarial science; sign language interpretation; social sciences; system administration; system/networking/LAN/WAN management; theater arts/drama; Web/multimedia management/webmaster; Web page, digital/multimedia and information resources design; welding technology.
Academic Programs *Special study options:* academic remediation for entering students, adult/continuing education programs, advanced placement credit, cooperative education, English as a second language, part-time degree program, services for LD students, summer session for credit.
Library 78,400 titles, 75 serial subscriptions.
Computers on Campus At least one staffed computer lab available.
Student Life *Housing:* college housing not available. *Activities and Organizations:* drama/theater group, student-run newspaper. *Campus security:* 24-hour emergency response devices and patrols, student patrols, late-night transport/escort service. *Student Services:* health clinic, personal/psychological counseling, women's center.
Athletics *Intercollegiate sports:* basketball M/W, cross-country running M/W, football M, golf M/W, soccer M/W, swimming M/W, tennis M/W, track and field M/W, volleyball M/W. *Intramural sports:* basketball M/W.
Standardized Tests *Required for some:* nursing exam. *Recommended:* SAT I or ACT (for placement).
Costs (2002–03) *Tuition:* state resident $0 full-time; nonresident $4104 full-time, $154 per unit part-time. *Required fees:* $332 full-time, $11 per unit, $1 per term part-time.
Financial Aid In 2001, 300 Federal Work-Study jobs (averaging $1500). 100 State and other part-time jobs (averaging $2000).
Applying *Options:* common application, early admission, deferred entrance. *Application deadline:* rolling (freshmen), rolling (transfers).
Admissions Contact Ms. Celia Esposito, Dean of Enrollment Services, American River College, 4700 College Oak Drive, Sacramento, CA 95841-4286. *Phone:* 916-484-8171. *E-mail:* recadmiss@mail.arc.losrios.cc.ca.us.

ANTELOPE VALLEY COLLEGE
Lancaster, California

■ **State and locally supported** 2-year, founded 1929, part of California Community College System
■ **Calendar** semesters
■ **Degree** certificates and associate
■ **Suburban** 160-acre campus with easy access to Los Angeles
■ **Endowment** $299,569
■ **Coed,** 12,500 undergraduate students

Undergraduates Students come from 7 states and territories, 1% are from out of state.
Freshmen *Admission:* 1,947 applied, 1,947 admitted.
Faculty *Total:* 324, 38% full-time.
Majors Aircraft mechanic/airframe; aircraft mechanic/powerplant; auto body repair; auto mechanic/technician; aviation technology; biology; business; business administration; business marketing and marketing management; child care/guidance; child guidance; clothing/textiles; computer graphics; computer/information sciences; computer programming; construction technology; consumer education; corrections; criminal justice/law enforcement administration; data processing technology; drafting; electrical/electronic engineering technology; engineering; engineering technology; family living/parenthood; film/video production; fire protection/safety technology; health/physical education; heating/air conditioning/refrigeration; interior design; law enforcement/police science; liberal arts and sciences/liberal studies; mathematics; medical administrative assistant; music; nursing; nutrition studies; ornamental horticulture; photography; physical sciences; real estate; secretarial science; teacher assistant/aide; textile arts; welding technology.
Academic Programs *Special study options:* academic remediation for entering students, adult/continuing education programs, advanced placement credit, cooperative education, English as a second language, honors programs, part-time degree program, services for LD students, study abroad, summer session for credit. *ROTC:* Air Force (c).
Library Antelope Valley College Library with 43,000 titles, 175 serial subscriptions.
Computers on Campus A campuswide network can be accessed from off campus. Internet access, at least one staffed computer lab available.
Student Life *Housing:* college housing not available. *Activities and Organizations:* drama/theater group, student-run newspaper, choral group. *Campus security:* 24-hour emergency response devices and patrols, late-night transport/escort service. *Student Services:* personal/psychological counseling.
Athletics *Intercollegiate sports:* baseball M, basketball M/W, cross-country running M/W, football M, soccer W, softball W, tennis W, track and field M/W, volleyball W. *Intramural sports:* basketball M/W, golf M/W, swimming M/W, tennis M/W, volleyball M/W, weight lifting M/W.
Costs (2001–02) *Tuition:* state resident $0 full-time; nonresident $3384 full-time, $141 per unit part-time. *Required fees:* $264 full-time, $11 per unit.
Applying *Options:* common application, early admission. *Required:* high school transcript. *Application deadline:* rolling (freshmen), rolling (transfers). *Notification:* continuous (freshmen).
Admissions Contact Dr. Margaret Ramey, Dean of Admissions and Records, Antelope Valley College, 3041 West Avenue K, Lancaster, CA 93536-5426. *Phone:* 661-722-6300 Ext. 6332.

THE ART INSTITUTE OF LOS ANGELES
Santa Monica, California

■ **Proprietary** primarily 2-year
■ **Calendar** quarters
■ **Degrees** associate and bachelor's
■ **Coed,** 1,429 undergraduate students, 91% full-time, 34% women, 66% men

Undergraduates 1,303 full-time, 126 part-time.
Freshmen *Admission:* 675 enrolled.
Faculty *Total:* 103.
Majors Culinary arts; film/video production; graphic design/commercial art/illustration; multimedia.
Costs (2001–02) *Tuition:* $16,400 full-time, $307 per credit part-time. *Required fees:* $150 full-time. *Room only:* $7688.
Admissions Contact Director of Admissions, The Art Institute of Los Angeles, 2900 31st Street, Santa Monica, CA 90405-3035. *Phone:* 310-752-4700. *Toll-free phone:* 888-646-4610.

BAKERSFIELD COLLEGE
Bakersfield, California

■ **State and locally supported** 2-year, founded 1913, part of California Community College System
■ **Calendar** semesters
■ **Degree** associate
■ **Urban** 175-acre campus
■ **Coed,** 15,001 undergraduate students

Majors Accounting; agricultural business; agricultural sciences; animal sciences; anthropology; architectural engineering technology; art; art education; auto mechanic/technician; biology; broadcast journalism; business administration; business marketing and marketing management; carpentry; chemistry; child care/development; computer science; corrections; cosmetology; criminal justice/law enforcement administration; culinary arts; data processing technology; dental hygiene; developmental/child psychology; dietetics; drafting; economics; electrical/

Bakersfield College (continued)
electronic engineering technology; emergency medical technology; engineering; English; environmental technology; family/consumer studies; finance; fire science; forestry; French; geography; geology; German; history; horticulture science; hotel and restaurant management; human services; industrial arts; industrial radiologic technology; industrial technology; information sciences/systems; interior design; journalism; law enforcement/police science; legal administrative assistant; liberal arts and sciences/liberal studies; machine technology; mathematics; music; nursing; nutrition science; ornamental horticulture; petroleum technology; philosophy; photography; physical education; physics; plumbing; political science; psychology; real estate; recreation/leisure studies; secretarial science; sociology; Spanish; speech/rhetorical studies; surveying; theater arts/drama; welding technology; wood science/paper technology.

Academic Programs *Special study options:* academic remediation for entering students, accelerated degree program, adult/continuing education programs, advanced placement credit, cooperative education, English as a second language, internships, part-time degree program, services for LD students, summer session for credit.

Library Grace Van Dyke Bird Library with 93,500 titles, 298 serial subscriptions, an OPAC, a Web page.

Computers on Campus 650 computers available on campus for general student use. Internet access, at least one staffed computer lab available.

Student Life *Housing:* college housing not available. *Activities and Organizations:* drama/theater group, student-run newspaper, radio station, choral group. *Campus security:* 24-hour patrols, late-night transport/escort service. *Student Services:* health clinic, women's center.

Athletics *Intercollegiate sports:* baseball M, basketball M/W, cross-country running M/W, football M, golf M, soccer W, softball W, tennis M/W, track and field M/W, volleyball W, wrestling M.

Costs (2001–02) *Tuition:* Full-time tuition, books, and fees dependent upon program selected.

Financial Aid In 2001, 300 Federal Work-Study jobs (averaging $2500). 15 State and other part-time jobs (averaging $2500).

Applying *Application deadline:* rolling (freshmen).

Admissions Contact Ms. Sue Vaughn, Director of Enrollment Services, Bakersfield College, 1801 Panorama Drive, Bakersfield, CA 93305-1299. *Phone:* 661-395-4301. *E-mail:* svaughn@bc.cc.ca.us.

BARSTOW COLLEGE
Barstow, California

- **State and locally supported** 2-year, founded 1959, part of California Community College System
- **Calendar** semesters
- **Degree** associate
- **Small-town** 50-acre campus
- **Coed,** 3,264 undergraduate students

Undergraduates Students come from 43 states and territories, 8 other countries.

Faculty *Total:* 127, 28% full-time. *Student/faculty ratio:* 20:1.

Majors Accounting; auto mechanic/technician; business administration; child care/development; computer science; cosmetology; drafting; early childhood education; education; electrical/electronic engineering technology; humanities; liberal arts and sciences/liberal studies; mathematics; medical assistant; physical education; secretarial science; social sciences.

Academic Programs *Special study options:* academic remediation for entering students, adult/continuing education programs, cooperative education, English as a second language, external degree program, part-time degree program, services for LD students, student-designed majors, summer session for credit.

Library Thomas Kimball Library with 38,000 titles, 110 serial subscriptions, an OPAC, a Web page.

Computers on Campus 85 computers available on campus for general student use. Internet access, at least one staffed computer lab available.

Student Life *Housing:* college housing not available. *Activities and Organizations:* drama/theater group, student-run newspaper. *Campus security:* evening security personnel. *Student Services:* personal/psychological counseling.

Athletics Member NJCAA. *Intercollegiate sports:* baseball M, basketball M, volleyball W. *Intramural sports:* basketball M.

Standardized Tests *Required:* assessment test approved by the Chancellor's office.

Costs (2001–02) *Tuition:* state resident $0 full-time; nonresident $3384 full-time, $141 per unit part-time. *Required fees:* $264 full-time, $11 per unit.

Applying *Options:* common application, early admission, deferred entrance. *Recommended:* high school transcript. *Application deadline:* rolling (freshmen), rolling (transfers).

Admissions Contact Don Low, Interim Vice President, Barstow College, 2700 Barstow Road, Barstow, CA 92311-6699. *Fax:* 760-252-1875.

BROOKS COLLEGE
Long Beach, California

- **Proprietary** 2-year, founded 1971
- **Calendar** quarters
- **Degree** associate
- **Suburban** 7-acre campus with easy access to Los Angeles
- **Coed,** 1,375 undergraduate students

Undergraduates Students come from 17 other countries, 60% live on campus.

Faculty *Total:* 95. *Student/faculty ratio:* 25:1.

Majors Clothing/textiles; fashion design/illustration; fashion merchandising; graphic design/commercial art/illustration; interior design.

Academic Programs *Special study options:* academic remediation for entering students, cooperative education, internships, services for LD students, summer session for credit.

Library 15,000 titles, 80 serial subscriptions.

Computers on Campus 50 computers available on campus for general student use. At least one staffed computer lab available.

Student Life *Activities and Organizations:* student-run newspaper. *Campus security:* 24-hour emergency response devices and patrols, controlled dormitory access. *Student Services:* personal/psychological counseling.

Applying *Options:* deferred entrance. *Required:* essay or personal statement, high school transcript, minimum 2.0 GPA, letters of recommendation, interview. *Recommended:* portfolio. *Application deadline:* rolling (freshmen), rolling (transfers). *Notification:* continuous (freshmen).

Admissions Contact Ms. Christina Varon, Director of Admissions, Brooks College, 4825 East Pacific Coast Highway, Long Beach, CA 90804-3291. *Phone:* 562-498-2441 Ext. 265. *Toll-free phone:* 800-421-3775. *Fax:* 562-597-7412. *E-mail:* info@brookscollege.edu.

BUTTE COLLEGE
Oroville, California

- **District-supported** 2-year, founded 1966, part of California Community College System
- **Calendar** semesters
- **Degree** certificates and associate
- **Rural** 900-acre campus
- **Coed,** 14,724 undergraduate students, 22% full-time, 55% women, 45% men

Undergraduates 3,295 full-time, 11,429 part-time. Students come from 19 states and territories, 25 other countries, 3% African American, 8% Asian American or Pacific Islander, 12% Hispanic American, 2% Native American, 8% international.

Freshmen *Admission:* 1,102 applied, 1,102 admitted, 1,102 enrolled.

Faculty *Total:* 617, 28% full-time, 6% with terminal degrees. *Student/faculty ratio:* 24:1.

Majors Accounting; agricultural business; agricultural economics; agricultural sciences; agronomy/crop science; animal sciences; applied art; art; auto mechanic/technician; biology; business education; business marketing and marketing management; civil engineering technology; construction technology; cosmetology; court reporting; criminal justice/law enforcement administration; data processing technology; drafting; early childhood education; electrical/electronic engineering technology; family/consumer studies; fashion design/illustration; fashion merchandising; finance; fire science; graphic design/commercial art/illustration; health science; home economics; horticulture science; landscape architecture; law enforcement/police science; legal administrative assistant; liberal arts and sciences/liberal studies; mathematics; medical administrative assistant; medical technology; music; natural resources management; nursing; ornamental horticulture; photography; physical education; physical sciences; political science; practical nurse; psychology; real estate; recreation/leisure facilities management; respiratory therapy; secretarial science; social sciences; telecommunications; travel/tourism management; welding technology.

Academic Programs *Special study options:* academic remediation for entering students, accelerated degree program, adult/continuing education programs, advanced placement credit, cooperative education, English as a second language,

honors programs, internships, part-time degree program, services for LD students, study abroad, summer session for credit.
Library 50,000 titles, 300 serial subscriptions, an OPAC.
Computers on Campus 65 computers available on campus for general student use. A campuswide network can be accessed from off campus. At least one staffed computer lab available.
Student Life *Housing:* college housing not available. *Activities and Organizations:* drama/theater group, student-run newspaper, television station. *Campus security:* 24-hour emergency response devices and patrols, student patrols. *Student Services:* health clinic, personal/psychological counseling, legal services.
Athletics *Intercollegiate sports:* baseball M, basketball M/W, cross-country running M/W, football M, golf M/W, soccer W, softball W, tennis M/W, track and field M/W, volleyball W. *Intramural sports:* equestrian sports M/W.
Costs (2001–02) *Tuition:* state resident $0 full-time; nonresident $4244 full-time, $159 per unit part-time. Part-time tuition and fees vary according to course load. *Required fees:* $428 full-time, $11 per unit, $64 per term part-time.
Applying *Options:* early admission, deferred entrance. *Required for some:* high school transcript. *Application deadline:* rolling (freshmen), rolling (transfers).
Admissions Contact Ms. Nancy Jenson, Registrar, Butte College, 3536 Butte Campus Drive, Oroville, CA 95965. *Phone:* 530-895-2361. *E-mail:* admissions@butte.cc.ca.us.

CABRILLO COLLEGE
Aptos, California

Admissions Contact Ms. Gloria Garing, Director of Admissions and Records, Cabrillo College, 6500 Soquel Drive, Aptos, CA 95003-3194. *Phone:* 831-479-6201.

CALIFORNIA COLLEGE OF TECHNOLOGY
Sacramento, California

Admissions Contact 4330 Watt Avenue, Suite 400, Sacramento, CA 95660. *Toll-free phone:* 800-955-8168.

CALIFORNIA CULINARY ACADEMY
San Francisco, California

- **Proprietary** 2-year, founded 1977
- **Calendar** continuous
- **Degree** certificates and associate
- **Urban** campus
- **Coed,** 813 undergraduate students, 100% full-time, 40% women, 60% men

Undergraduates 813 full-time. 10% are from out of state, 4% African American, 9% Asian American or Pacific Islander, 8% Hispanic American, 4% Native American, 2% international, 39% live on campus. *Retention:* 88% of 2001 full-time freshmen returned.
Freshmen *Admission:* 530 applied, 521 admitted, 150 enrolled.
Faculty *Total:* 46, 96% full-time. *Student/faculty ratio:* 16:1.
Majors Baker/pastry chef; culinary arts.
Academic Programs *Special study options:* cooperative education, services for LD students.
Library Academy Library plus 1 other with 3,000 titles, 70 serial subscriptions.
Computers on Campus 40 computers available on campus for general student use. Internet access, at least one staffed computer lab available.
Student Life *Housing Options:* coed. *Activities and Organizations:* Student Council. *Campus security:* 24-hour emergency response devices and patrols, controlled dormitory access.
Costs (2002–03) *Tuition:* $37,600 per degree program part-time.
Financial Aid In 2001, 45 Federal Work-Study jobs (averaging $3000).
Applying *Options:* common application, electronic application. *Application fee:* $65. *Required:* high school transcript, interview.
Admissions Contact Ms. Nancy Seyfert, Director of Admissions, California Culinary Academy, 625 Polk Street, San Francisco, CA 94102-3368. *Phone:* 800-229-2433 Ext. 275. *Toll-free phone:* 800-BAYCHEF. *Fax:* 415-771-2194.

CALIFORNIA DESIGN COLLEGE
Los Angeles, California

- **Proprietary** 2-year, founded 1992
- **Calendar** quarters
- **Degree** certificates and associate
- **Urban** campus
- **Endowment** $564,970
- **Coed,** 425 undergraduate students
- 81% of applicants were admitted

Undergraduates Students come from 2 states and territories, 15 other countries, 1% are from out of state.
Freshmen *Admission:* 340 applied, 275 admitted. *Average high school GPA:* 2.8.
Faculty *Total:* 16, 19% full-time. *Student/faculty ratio:* 22:1.
Majors Apparel marketing; fashion design/illustration; fashion merchandising.
Academic Programs *Special study options:* adult/continuing education programs, English as a second language, part-time degree program.
Library CDC Library with 964 titles, 10 serial subscriptions, a Web page.
Computers on Campus 11 computers available on campus for general student use. Internet access, at least one staffed computer lab available.
Student Life *Housing:* college housing not available. *Campus security:* 24-hour emergency response devices and patrols, late-night transport/escort service.
Costs (2002–03) *One-time required fee:* $150. *Tuition:* $12,450 full-time. Full-time tuition and fees vary according to course load. Part-time tuition and fees vary according to course load. *Payment plan:* installment.
Financial Aid In 2001, 50 Federal Work-Study jobs (averaging $800).
Applying *Options:* common application, deferred entrance. *Application fee:* $25. *Required:* essay or personal statement, high school transcript, interview. *Required for some:* portfolio. *Application deadline:* rolling (freshmen), rolling (transfers). *Notification:* continuous (freshmen).
Admissions Contact Mr. Allan S. Gueco, Director of Admissions, California Design College, 3440 Wilshire Boulevard, Seventh Floor, Los Angeles, CA 90010. *Phone:* 213-251-3636 Ext. 120. *Fax:* 213-385-3545. *E-mail:* sk@cdc.edu.

CANADA COLLEGE
Redwood City, California

- **State and locally supported** 2-year, founded 1968, part of San Mateo County Community College District System
- **Calendar** semesters
- **Degree** certificates and associate
- **Suburban** 131-acre campus with easy access to San Francisco and San Jose
- **Coed,** 6,217 undergraduate students

Undergraduates Students come from 32 other countries.
Faculty *Total:* 227.
Majors Accounting; anatomy; anthropology; art; art history; biological/physical sciences; biology; business administration; business machine repair; chemistry; computer engineering technology; computer programming; computer science; dance; data processing technology; drawing; early childhood education; economics; engineering; English; environmental science; exercise sciences; fashion design/illustration; French; geography; geology; German; health education; health science; history; humanities; industrial radiologic technology; information sciences/systems; interior design; journalism; liberal arts and sciences/liberal studies; mathematics; music; paralegal/legal assistant; philosophy; physical education; political science; psychology; secretarial science; sociology; Spanish; speech/rhetorical studies; theater arts/drama; travel/tourism management.
Academic Programs *Special study options:* academic remediation for entering students, accelerated degree program, adult/continuing education programs, advanced placement credit, cooperative education, English as a second language, internships, part-time degree program, services for LD students, study abroad, summer session for credit.
Library 53,417 titles, 414 serial subscriptions, an OPAC.
Computers on Campus 55 computers available on campus for general student use. At least one staffed computer lab available.
Student Life *Housing:* college housing not available. *Activities and Organizations:* drama/theater group, choral group, Latin-American club, student government, Environmental Club, athletics, Interior Design Club. *Campus security:* 12-hour patrols by trained security personnel. *Student Services:* health clinic, personal/psychological counseling.
Athletics *Intercollegiate sports:* baseball M, basketball M, soccer M/W, tennis M. *Intramural sports:* basketball M/W, soccer M, tennis M/W, volleyball M/W.
Costs (2001–02) *Tuition:* nonresident $3552 full-time, $148 per unit part-time. *Required fees:* $264 full-time, $11 per unit, $12 per term part-time.
Financial Aid In 2001, 30 Federal Work-Study jobs (averaging $4000).
Applying *Options:* early admission. *Application deadline:* rolling (freshmen), rolling (transfers).

Canada College (continued)
Admissions Contact Mr. Jose Romero, Lead Records Clerk, Canada College, 4200 Farm Hill Boulevard, Redwood City, CA 94061. *Phone:* 650-306-3395. *Fax:* 650-306-3113.

CERRITOS COLLEGE
Norwalk, California

- **State and locally supported** 2-year, founded 1956, part of California Community College System
- **Calendar** semesters
- **Degree** associate
- **Suburban** 140-acre campus with easy access to Los Angeles
- **Coed,** 23,000 undergraduate students

Undergraduates Students come from 32 other countries.
Faculty *Total:* 690, 36% full-time.
Majors Accounting; agricultural sciences; anthropology; architectural engineering technology; art; auto mechanic/technician; biology; biomedical technology; botany; business administration; business marketing and marketing management; chemistry; computer programming; computer science; cosmetology; court reporting; data processing technology; dental hygiene; drafting; early childhood education; economics; electrical/electronic engineering technology; English; fashion design/illustration; food services technology; forestry; French; geography; geology; German; history; home economics; industrial arts; industrial technology; journalism; law enforcement/police science; legal administrative assistant; liberal arts and sciences/liberal studies; machine technology; mathematics; medical administrative assistant; medical assistant; metallurgy; Mexican-American studies; music; nursing; ornamental horticulture; pharmacy; philosophy; photography; physical education; physical therapy; physics; plastics technology; political science; pre-engineering; psychology; real estate; recreation/leisure studies; secretarial science; sociology; Spanish; speech/rhetorical studies; theater arts/drama; welding technology; wildlife management; zoology.
Academic Programs *Special study options:* academic remediation for entering students, adult/continuing education programs, advanced placement credit, English as a second language, part-time degree program, services for LD students, study abroad, summer session for credit.
Library Wilford Michael Library with 74,502 titles, 396 serial subscriptions.
Computers on Campus 400 computers available on campus for general student use. A campuswide network can be accessed from off campus. Internet access available.
Student Life *Housing:* college housing not available. *Activities and Organizations:* drama/theater group, student-run newspaper, radio station. *Student Services:* health clinic, personal/psychological counseling, women's center, legal services.
Athletics Member NJCAA. *Intercollegiate sports:* baseball M, basketball M/W, cross-country running M/W, football M, golf M, soccer M, softball W, swimming M/W, tennis M/W, track and field M/W, volleyball W, water polo M, wrestling M.
Standardized Tests *Recommended:* CEPT, Nelson Denny Reading Test.
Costs (2002–03) *Tuition:* nonresident $130 per unit part-time. *Required fees:* $11 per unit, $22 per unit part-time.
Financial Aid In 2001, 180 Federal Work-Study jobs (averaging $3000). 89 State and other part-time jobs (averaging $2734).
Applying *Options:* early admission, deferred entrance. *Application deadline:* rolling (freshmen), rolling (transfers).
Admissions Contact Ms. Stephanie Murguia, Director of Admissions and Records, Cerritos College, 11110 Alondra Boulevard, Norwalk, CA 90650-6298. *Phone:* 562-860-2451. *E-mail:* rbell@cerritos.edu.

CERRO COSO COMMUNITY COLLEGE
Ridgecrest, California

- **State-supported** 2-year, founded 1973, part of Kern Community College District System
- **Calendar** semesters
- **Degree** associate
- **Small-town** 320-acre campus
- **Coed,** 6,653 undergraduate students, 10% full-time, 60% women, 40% men

Undergraduates 673 full-time, 5,980 part-time. 7% African American, 5% Asian American or Pacific Islander, 12% Hispanic American, 2% Native American. *Retention:* 54% of 2001 full-time freshmen returned.
Freshmen *Admission:* 2,048 applied, 2,048 admitted, 660 enrolled.
Faculty *Total:* 233, 22% full-time. *Student/faculty ratio:* 14:1.
Majors Art; auto mechanic/technician; biological/physical sciences; business administration; child care provider; child care services management; comparative literature; computer engineering technology; computer graphics; computer science; computer software and media applications related; criminal justice/law enforcement administration; data processing technology; drafting; early childhood education; economics; electrical/electronic engineering technology; emergency medical technology; engineering technology; English; fine/studio arts; fire science; health/physical education; history; humanities; liberal arts and sciences/liberal studies; machine technology; mathematics; music; natural resources management; physical sciences; practical nurse; pre-engineering; psychology; recreation/leisure facilities management; recreation products/services marketing operations; social sciences; Spanish; Web/multimedia management/webmaster; Web page, digital/multimedia and information resources design; welding technology.
Academic Programs *Special study options:* academic remediation for entering students, adult/continuing education programs, cooperative education, distance learning, English as a second language, honors programs, part-time degree program, services for LD students, summer session for credit.
Library Walter Stiern Memorial Library with 25,000 titles, 800 serial subscriptions, an OPAC, a Web page.
Computers on Campus 100 computers available on campus for general student use. A campuswide network can be accessed from off campus. At least one staffed computer lab available.
Student Life *Housing:* college housing not available. *Activities and Organizations:* Special Services Club, Art Club, LVN Club, Athletic Club, Drama Club. *Campus security:* patrols by trained security personnel. *Student Services:* personal/psychological counseling.
Athletics *Intercollegiate sports:* baseball M, basketball M/W, softball W, tennis W, volleyball W.
Standardized Tests *Required for some:* ACT ASSET.
Costs (2001–02) *Tuition:* state resident $0 full-time; nonresident $4020 full-time, $134 per unit part-time. *Required fees:* $330 full-time, $11 per unit. *Payment plan:* installment. *Waivers:* employees or children of employees.
Financial Aid In 2001, 50 Federal Work-Study jobs (averaging $2000).
Applying *Options:* early admission. *Recommended:* high school transcript. *Application deadline:* rolling (freshmen), rolling (transfers).
Admissions Contact Dr. Corey Marvin, Interim Vice President of Student Learning, Cerro Coso Community College, 3000 College Heights Boulevard, Ridgecrest, CA 93555-9571. *Phone:* 760-384-6201. *Fax:* 760-375-4776.

CHABOT COLLEGE
Hayward, California

- **State-supported** 2-year, founded 1961, part of California Community College System
- **Calendar** semesters
- **Degree** certificates and associate
- **Suburban** 245-acre campus with easy access to San Francisco
- **Coed,** 15,149 undergraduate students

Undergraduates Students come from 78 other countries, 2% are from out of state. *Retention:* 66% of 2001 full-time freshmen returned.
Freshmen *Admission:* 1,063 applied, 1,063 admitted.
Faculty *Total:* 516, 35% full-time. *Student/faculty ratio:* 24:1.
Majors Accounting; advertising; applied mathematics; architectural engineering technology; art; auto mechanic/technician; behavioral sciences; biological/physical sciences; biology; broadcast journalism; business administration; business economics; business education; business machine repair; chemistry; civil engineering technology; computer engineering technology; computer programming (specific applications); computer science; computer science related; computer typography/composition; corrections; criminal justice/law enforcement administration; data processing technology; dental hygiene; drawing; early childhood education; ecology; economics; education; electrical/electronic engineering technology; electromechanical technology; emergency medical technology; engineering; engineering technology; English; fashion design/illustration; fashion merchandising; finance; fine/studio arts; fire science; graphic design/commercial art/illustration; health education; history; horticulture science; humanities; human services; industrial arts; industrial technology; information sciences/systems; instrumentation technology; interdisciplinary studies; Italian; journalism; landscaping management; law enforcement/police science; legal administrative assistant; liberal arts and sciences/liberal studies; literature; mass communications; mathematical statistics; mathematics; medical assistant; medical records administration; music; natural sciences; nursing; ornamental horticulture; photography;

physical education; physics; physiology; political science; pre-engineering; psychology; radio/television broadcasting; real estate; recreation/leisure studies; retail management; secretarial science; social sciences; sociology; solar technology; Spanish; surveying; teacher assistant/aide; travel/tourism management; welding technology; women's studies; zoology.

Academic Programs *Special study options:* academic remediation for entering students, adult/continuing education programs, advanced placement credit, distance learning, double majors, English as a second language, internships, off-campus study, part-time degree program, services for LD students, student-designed majors, study abroad, summer session for credit. *ROTC:* Army (c), Air Force (c).

Library Chabot Library with 100,000 titles, 160 serial subscriptions.

Computers on Campus 100 computers available on campus for general student use. A campuswide network can be accessed from off campus. Internet access, online (class) registration, at least one staffed computer lab available.

Student Life *Housing:* college housing not available. *Activities and Organizations:* drama/theater group, student-run newspaper, radio and television station, choral group, Chinese Club, International Club, MECHA, ASCC, SCTA (Student California Teachers Association. *Campus security:* 24-hour emergency response devices, late-night transport/escort service. *Student Services:* personal/psychological counseling, legal services.

Athletics *Intercollegiate sports:* baseball M, basketball M/W, cross-country running M/W, football M, golf M, soccer M/W, softball W, swimming M/W, tennis M/W, track and field M/W, wrestling M. *Intramural sports:* archery M/W, badminton M/W, basketball M/W, bowling M/W, football M, golf M/W, gymnastics M/W, racquetball M/W, skiing (cross-country) M/W, skiing (downhill) M/W, soccer M/W, softball M/W, swimming M/W, table tennis M/W, tennis M/W, track and field M/W, volleyball M/W, weight lifting M/W.

Costs (2001–02) *Tuition:* state resident $0 full-time; nonresident $3264 full-time, $136 per unit part-time. *Required fees:* $264 full-time, $11 per unit. *Payment plan:* installment.

Applying *Options:* electronic application. *Required:* high school transcript. *Notification:* continuous (freshmen).

Admissions Contact Ms. Judy Young, Director of Admissions and Records, Chabot College, 25555 Hesperian Boulevard, Hayward, CA 94545. *Phone:* 510-723-6700. *Fax:* 510-723-7510.

CHAFFEY COLLEGE
Rancho Cucamonga, California

- **District-supported** 2-year, founded 1883, part of California Community College System
- **Calendar** semesters
- **Degree** certificates and associate
- **Suburban** 200-acre campus with easy access to Los Angeles
- **Coed,** 18,025 undergraduate students, 100% full-time, 62% women, 38% men

Undergraduates 25% are from out of state.

Faculty *Total:* 893, 23% full-time.

Majors Accounting; anthropology; art; auto mechanic/technician; biology; broadcast journalism; business administration; business education; business marketing and marketing management; ceramic arts; chemistry; child care/development; computer typography/composition; corrections; court reporting; dance; developmental/child psychology; dietetics; drafting; early childhood education; economics; electrical/electronic engineering technology; engineering; English; environmental technology; fashion design/illustration; food products retailing; French; geology; German; gerontology; history; home economics; hotel and restaurant management; humanities; industrial design; information sciences/systems; interior design; journalism; legal administrative assistant; liberal arts and sciences/liberal studies; mathematics; medical administrative assistant; medical radiologic technology; music; nursing; philosophy; photography; physical education; physical sciences; physics; political science; psychology; quality control technology; real estate; religious studies; secretarial science; social sciences; sociology; Spanish; speech/rhetorical studies; telecommunications; theater arts/drama.

Academic Programs *Special study options:* academic remediation for entering students, adult/continuing education programs, advanced placement credit, cooperative education, English as a second language, honors programs, internships, part-time degree program, services for LD students, study abroad, summer session for credit. *ROTC:* Army (c).

Library Chaffey College Library with 72,000 titles, 232 serial subscriptions.

Computers on Campus 150 computers available on campus for general student use.

Student Life *Housing:* college housing not available. *Activities and Organizations:* drama/theater group, student-run newspaper, radio station, choral group, The Associated Students of Chaffey College, Multicultural Club, Style Club. *Campus security:* 24-hour emergency response devices, late-night transport/escort service. *Student Services:* health clinic, personal/psychological counseling.

Athletics Member NJCAA. *Intercollegiate sports:* baseball M, basketball M/W, cross-country running M/W, football M, golf M/W, swimming M/W, tennis M/W, track and field M/W, volleyball W, water polo M.

Costs (2002–03) *Required fees:* $300 full-time, $11 per unit.

Financial Aid In 2001, 200 Federal Work-Study jobs.

Applying *Options:* early admission. *Application deadline:* rolling (freshmen), rolling (transfers). *Notification:* continuous (freshmen).

Admissions Contact Ms. Cecilia Carerra, Director of Admissions, Registration, and Records, Chaffey College, 5885 Haven Avenue, Rancho Cucamonga, CA 91737-3002. *Phone:* 909-941-2631.

CITRUS COLLEGE
Glendora, California

- **State and locally supported** 2-year, founded 1915, part of California Community College System
- **Calendar** semesters
- **Degree** certificates, diplomas, and associate
- **Small-town** 104-acre campus with easy access to Los Angeles
- **Coed,** 11,159 undergraduate students, 31% full-time, 57% women, 43% men

Undergraduates 6% African American, 13% Asian American or Pacific Islander, 40% Hispanic American, 0.9% Native American.

Faculty *Total:* 525, 32% full-time, 30% with terminal degrees.

Majors Art; auto mechanic/technician; behavioral sciences; biology; business administration; computer science; computer science related; cosmetology; criminal justice/law enforcement administration; dance; data processing technology; dental assistant; drafting; electrical/electronic engineering technology; engineering; engineering technology; English; French; German; health/physical education; Japanese; journalism; law enforcement/police science; liberal arts and sciences/liberal studies; library assistant; library science; mathematics; mechanical engineering technology; modern languages; music; natural sciences; photography; physical education; physical sciences; practical nurse; public administration; real estate; secretarial science; social sciences; Spanish; theater arts/drama; visual/performing arts; water resources.

Academic Programs *Special study options:* academic remediation for entering students, adult/continuing education programs, advanced placement credit, cooperative education, distance learning, English as a second language, part-time degree program, services for LD students, study abroad, summer session for credit.

Library Hayden Library plus 1 other with 45,091 titles, 125 serial subscriptions, 6,771 audiovisual materials, an OPAC, a Web page.

Computers on Campus 800 computers available on campus for general student use. At least one staffed computer lab available.

Student Life *Housing:* college housing not available. *Activities and Organizations:* drama/theater group, student-run newspaper, choral group, Student Government, AGS Honor Society, International Student Association, Cosmetology Club. *Campus security:* 24-hour patrols, student patrols, late-night transport/escort service. *Student Services:* health clinic, personal/psychological counseling, legal services.

Athletics *Intercollegiate sports:* baseball M, basketball M/W, cross-country running M/W, football M, golf M/W, soccer M/W, softball W, swimming M/W, tennis M/W, track and field M/W, volleyball W, water polo M/W.

Standardized Tests *Required for some:* ACT ASSET.

Costs (2002–03) *Tuition:* state resident $0 full-time; nonresident $4676 full-time, $143 per unit part-time. Full-time tuition and fees vary according to course load. Part-time tuition and fees vary according to course load. *Required fees:* $386 full-time, $11 per unit. *Waivers:* senior citizens.

Financial Aid In 2001, 80 Federal Work-Study jobs (averaging $2000). 40 State and other part-time jobs (averaging $2000).

Applying *Required:* high school transcript. *Application deadlines:* 8/1 (freshmen), 8/1 (transfers).

Admissions Contact Admissions and Records, Citrus College, 1000 West Foothill Boulevard, Glendora, CA 91741-1899. *Phone:* 626-914-8511. *Fax:* 626-914-8613. *E-mail:* admissions@citrus.cc.ca.us.

CITY COLLEGE OF SAN FRANCISCO
San Francisco, California

- **State and locally supported** 2-year, founded 1935, part of California Community College System

City College of San Francisco (continued)
- **Calendar** semesters
- **Degree** certificates, diplomas, and associate
- **Urban** 56-acre campus
- **Coed,** 100,544 undergraduate students

Undergraduates Students come from 51 states and territories, 71 other countries.
Faculty *Total:* 890, 89% full-time.
Majors Accounting; African-American studies; agricultural business; aircraft mechanic/airframe; art; Asian studies; atmospheric sciences; auto mechanic/technician; aviation technology; botany; broadcast journalism; business administration; business marketing and marketing management; chemical engineering technology; chemistry; civil engineering technology; computer programming; computer science; construction management; consumer services; court reporting; criminal justice/law enforcement administration; dental hygiene; developmental/child psychology; dietetics; educational media design; electrical/electronic engineering technology; English; fashion merchandising; film/video production; finance; fire science; forestry; geology; graphic/printing equipment; horticulture science; hotel and restaurant management; industrial radiologic technology; industrial technology; insurance/risk management; interior design; journalism; labor/personnel relations; landscape architecture; Latin American studies; law enforcement/police science; legal administrative assistant; library science; mathematics; mechanical engineering technology; medical records administration; music; nursing; ornamental horticulture; photography; physical therapy; practical nurse; pre-engineering; psychology; public administration; public health; real estate; recreation/leisure studies; respiratory therapy; social sciences; social work; transportation technology; wildlife management; women's studies.
Academic Programs *Special study options:* academic remediation for entering students, adult/continuing education programs, advanced placement credit, English as a second language, internships, off-campus study, part-time degree program, services for LD students, study abroad, summer session for credit. *ROTC:* Army (c).
Library Alice Statler Library with 93,518 titles, 774 serial subscriptions.
Computers on Campus At least one staffed computer lab available.
Student Life *Housing:* college housing not available. *Activities and Organizations:* drama/theater group, student-run newspaper. *Campus security:* 24-hour patrols. *Student Services:* health clinic, personal/psychological counseling, women's center.
Athletics *Intercollegiate sports:* archery W, basketball M, cross-country running M/W, fencing W, football M, golf M, gymnastics W, soccer M, swimming M, tennis M/W, track and field M/W, volleyball M/W, water polo M. *Intramural sports:* archery M/W, badminton M/W, basketball M/W, bowling M/W, fencing M/W, football M, golf M, gymnastics M/W, soccer M/W, swimming M/W, tennis M/W, track and field M/W, volleyball M/W, wrestling M.
Costs (2001–02) *Tuition:* nonresident $3900 full-time, $130 per unit part-time. *Required fees:* $330 full-time, $11 per unit.
Financial Aid In 2001, 2,000 Federal Work-Study jobs (averaging $3000). *Financial aid deadline:* 6/11.
Applying *Options:* early admission. *Application deadline:* rolling (freshmen), rolling (transfers). *Notification:* continuous (freshmen).
Admissions Contact Mr. Robert Balesteri, Dean of Admissions and Records, City College of San Francisco, 50 Phelan Avenue, San Francisco, CA 94112-1821. *Phone:* 415-239-3291. *Fax:* 415-239-3936.

COASTLINE COMMUNITY COLLEGE
Fountain Valley, California

- **State and locally supported** 2-year, founded 1976, part of Coast Community College District System
- **Calendar** semesters
- **Degree** certificates and associate
- **Urban** campus with easy access to Los Angeles
- **Coed,** 12,220 undergraduate students

Undergraduates Students come from 1 other state, 4% African American, 33% Asian American or Pacific Islander, 12% Hispanic American, 0.8% Native American, 1% international.
Faculty *Total:* 350, 14% full-time. *Student/faculty ratio:* 24:1.
Majors Liberal arts and sciences/liberal studies.
Academic Programs *Special study options:* academic remediation for entering students, adult/continuing education programs, advanced placement credit, cooperative education, distance learning, English as a second language, external degree program, internships, part-time degree program, services for LD students, summer session for credit.
Computers on Campus Internet access available.
Student Life *Housing:* college housing not available. *Campus security:* 24-hour emergency response devices. *Student Services:* health clinic.
Costs (2001–02) *Tuition:* state resident $0 full-time; nonresident $4350 full-time, $145 per unit part-time. Full-time tuition and fees vary according to course load. Part-time tuition and fees vary according to course load. *Required fees:* $350 full-time, $11 per unit, $10 per term part-time.
Applying *Options:* common application, early admission. *Recommended:* high school transcript. *Application deadline:* rolling (freshmen), rolling (transfers).
Admissions Contact Jennifer McDonald, Director of Admissions and Records, Coastline Community College, 11460 Warner Avenue, Fountain Valley, CA 92708. *Phone:* 714-241-6163. *Fax:* 714-241-6288.

COLLEGE OF ALAMEDA
Alameda, California

- **State and locally supported** 2-year, founded 1970, part of Peralta Community College District System
- **Calendar** semesters
- **Degree** certificates and associate
- **Urban** 62-acre campus with easy access to San Francisco
- **Coed,** 5,500 undergraduate students

Undergraduates Students come from 18 states and territories, 9 other countries.
Faculty *Total:* 166, 48% full-time.
Majors Accounting; African-American studies; anthropology; art; auto mechanic/technician; aviation technology; biological/physical sciences; biology; business administration; business education; business marketing and marketing management; dental hygiene; English; fashion design/illustration; fashion merchandising; general studies; geography; history; humanities; individual/family development; information sciences/systems; liberal arts and sciences/liberal studies; mathematics; Mexican-American studies; philosophy; political science; psychology; secretarial science; social sciences; sociology; Spanish.
Academic Programs *Special study options:* academic remediation for entering students, adult/continuing education programs, cooperative education, off-campus study, part-time degree program, services for LD students, summer session for credit.
Library Learning Resources Center with 40,000 titles, 200 serial subscriptions.
Computers on Campus 20 computers available on campus for general student use.
Student Life *Housing:* college housing not available. *Activities and Organizations:* student-run newspaper. *Student Services:* women's center.
Athletics *Intercollegiate sports:* basketball M/W, bowling M/W. *Intramural sports:* soccer M/W, tennis M/W, track and field M/W, volleyball M/W.
Standardized Tests *Recommended:* SAT I or ACT (for placement).
Costs (2002–03) *Tuition:* state resident $0 full-time; nonresident $175 per unit part-time. *Required fees:* $264 full-time, $11 per unit.
Financial Aid In 2001, 90 Federal Work-Study jobs (averaging $2500).
Applying *Application deadline:* rolling (freshmen), rolling (transfers).
Admissions Contact Ms. Barbara Simmons, District Admissions Officer, College of Alameda, 555 Atlantic Avenue, Alameda, CA 94501-2109. *Phone:* 510-466-7370. *E-mail:* hperdue@peralta.cc.ca.us.

COLLEGE OF MARIN
Kentfield, California

- **State and locally supported** 2-year, founded 1926, part of California Community College System
- **Calendar** semesters
- **Degree** associate
- **Small-town** 410-acre campus with easy access to San Francisco
- **Coed,** 8,365 undergraduate students

Faculty *Total:* 464, 35% full-time.
Majors Accounting; applied art; architectural engineering technology; art; auto mechanic/technician; behavioral sciences; biology; business administration; business marketing and marketing management; chemistry; computer science; corrections; court reporting; cultural studies; dance; data processing technology; dental hygiene; early childhood education; ecology; electrical/electronic engineering technology; engineering; engineering technology; fire science; French; geology; German; history; humanities; information sciences/systems; interior design; journalism; landscape architecture; landscaping management; law enforcement/

police science; liberal arts and sciences/liberal studies; machine technology; marine technology; mass communications; mathematics; medical administrative assistant; medical assistant; music; natural sciences; nursing; philosophy; physical education; physics; political science; psychology; real estate; retail management; secretarial science; sociology; Spanish; speech/rhetorical studies; theater arts/ drama.

Academic Programs *Special study options:* academic remediation for entering students, adult/continuing education programs, cooperative education, English as a second language, part-time degree program, services for LD students, summer session for credit.

Library 85,000 titles, 500 serial subscriptions.

Computers on Campus 25 computers available on campus for general student use. Internet access, at least one staffed computer lab available.

Student Life *Housing:* college housing not available. *Activities and Organizations:* drama/theater group, student-run newspaper. *Campus security:* 24-hour patrols. *Student Services:* health clinic, personal/psychological counseling.

Athletics *Intercollegiate sports:* basketball M/W, cross-country running M/W, football M/W, golf M/W, soccer M/W, swimming M/W, tennis M/W, track and field M/W, volleyball M/W, water polo M/W.

Costs (2001–02) *Tuition:* state resident $0 full-time; nonresident $4770 full-time, $159 per unit part-time. *Required fees:* $354 full-time, $11 per unit, $12 per term part-time.

Financial Aid In 2001, 100 Federal Work-Study jobs (averaging $2500).

Applying *Options:* early admission. *Application deadline:* rolling (freshmen). *Notification:* continuous (freshmen).

Admissions Contact Ms. Gina Longo, Dean of Enrollment Services, College of Marin, 835 College Avenue, Kentfield, CA 94904. *Phone:* 415-485-9417.

COLLEGE OF OCEANEERING
Wilmington, California

- **Proprietary** 2-year
- **Calendar** continuous
- **Degree** certificates and associate
- **Suburban** 5-acre campus with easy access to Los Angeles
- **Coed, primarily men**

Faculty *Student/faculty ratio:* 10:1.

Student Life *Campus security:* 24-hour emergency response devices.

Costs (2001–02) *Tuition:* $16,100 full-time. No tuition increase for student's term of enrollment. *Required fees:* $50 full-time.

Financial Aid In 2001, 30 Federal Work-Study jobs (averaging $4000).

Applying *Options:* common application, electronic application, deferred entrance. *Application fee:* $50. *Required:* essay or personal statement, high school transcript, interview, physical examination.

Admissions Contact Ms. Shirley Estep, Director of Admissions, College of Oceaneering, 272 South Fries Avenue, Wilmington, CA 90744-6399. *Phone:* 310-834-2501 Ext. 237. *Toll-free phone:* 800-432-DIVE Ext. 237. *Fax:* 310-834-7132. *E-mail:* sestep@diveco.com.

COLLEGE OF SAN MATEO
San Mateo, California

- **State and locally supported** 2-year, founded 1922, part of California Community College System
- **Calendar** semesters
- **Degree** certificates and associate
- **Suburban** 150-acre campus
- **Coed**

Student Life *Campus security:* 24-hour emergency response devices and patrols.

Standardized Tests *Required for some:* in-house placement tests.

Applying *Options:* early admission.

Admissions Contact Mr. John Mullen, Dean of Admissions and Records, College of San Mateo, 1700 West Hillsdale Boulevard, San Mateo, CA 94402-3784. *Phone:* 650-574-6594. *E-mail:* csmadmission@smcccd.cc.ca.us.

COLLEGE OF THE CANYONS
Santa Clarita, California

- **State and locally supported** 2-year, founded 1969, part of California Community College System
- **Calendar** semesters
- **Degree** certificates and associate
- **Suburban** 158-acre campus with easy access to Los Angeles
- **Coed,** 10,700 undergraduate students

Undergraduates Students come from 15 states and territories, 35 other countries, 3% are from out of state, 3% African American, 4% Asian American or Pacific Islander, 18% Hispanic American, 0.9% Native American, 0.8% international.

Faculty *Total:* 400, 44% full-time. *Student/faculty ratio:* 24:1.

Majors Accounting; art; biological/physical sciences; biology; business administration; chemistry; child care/development; computer engineering related; computer science; computer science related; criminal justice/law enforcement administration; developmental/child psychology; drafting; early childhood education; electrical/electronic engineering technology; English; film/video production; French; geography; geology; German; health science; history; hotel and restaurant management; humanities; information sciences/systems; interior design; journalism; law enforcement/police science; liberal arts and sciences/liberal studies; mathematics; natural sciences; nursing; physical education; physical sciences; political science; practical nurse; pre-engineering; psychology; quality control technology; real estate; secretarial science; social sciences; Spanish; water resources; welding technology.

Academic Programs *Special study options:* academic remediation for entering students, adult/continuing education programs, advanced placement credit, cooperative education, distance learning, double majors, English as a second language, honors programs, independent study, internships, off-campus study, part-time degree program, services for LD students, study abroad, summer session for credit.

Library College of the Canyons Library with 40,646 titles, 233 serial subscriptions, 29,955 audiovisual materials, an OPAC, a Web page.

Computers on Campus 650 computers available on campus for general student use. Internet access, at least one staffed computer lab available.

Student Life *Housing:* college housing not available. *Activities and Organizations:* drama/theater group, student-run newspaper, choral group, HITE, Phi Theta Kappa, Alpha Gamma Sigma, MECHA, Biology Club. *Campus security:* student patrols, late-night transport/escort service. *Student Services:* health clinic, personal/ psychological counseling.

Athletics *Intercollegiate sports:* baseball M, basketball M/W, cross-country running M/W, football M, golf M, soccer W, softball W, swimming M/W, track and field M/W, volleyball W.

Standardized Tests *Recommended:* SAT I or ACT (for placement).

Costs (2001–02) *Tuition:* nonresident $130 per unit part-time. *Required fees:* $328 full-time, $11 per unit, $12 per term part-time.

Applying *Options:* electronic application, early admission. *Recommended:* high school transcript. *Application deadlines:* 8/22 (freshmen), 8/22 (transfers). *Notification:* continuous until 8/22 (freshmen).

Admissions Contact Ms. Deborah Rio, Director, Admissions and Records, College of the Canyons, 26455 Rockwell Canyon Road, Santa Clara, CA 91355. *Phone:* 661-362-3280. *Toll-free phone:* 661-362-3280. *Fax:* 661-254-7996.

COLLEGE OF THE DESERT
Palm Desert, California

- **State and locally supported** 2-year, founded 1959, part of California Community College System
- **Calendar** semesters
- **Degree** certificates, diplomas, and associate
- **Small-town** 160-acre campus
- **Coed,** 9,794 undergraduate students

Undergraduates Students come from 23 states and territories, 11 other countries, 1% are from out of state.

Freshmen *Average high school GPA:* 2.72.

Faculty *Total:* 279, 31% full-time.

Majors Agricultural business; anthropology; architectural engineering technology; art; auto mechanic/technician; biology; business administration; business economics; business marketing and marketing management; chemistry; computer graphics; computer programming related; computer science; computer science related; computer/technical support; computer typography/composition; construction management; criminal justice/law enforcement administration; culinary arts; drafting; early childhood education; economics; education; engineering technology; English; environmental science; fire science; French; geography; geology; heating/air conditioning/refrigeration; history; horticulture science; interior design; Italian; journalism; law enforcement/police science; liberal arts and sciences/

College of the Desert (continued)
liberal studies; mass communications; mathematics; medical assistant; music; natural resources management; nursing; ornamental horticulture; philosophy; physical education; physics; political science; pre-engineering; psychology; real estate; recreation/leisure facilities management; recreation/leisure studies; respiratory therapy; romance languages; secretarial science; social sciences; sociology; speech/rhetorical studies; teacher assistant/aide; theater arts/drama; welding technology; word processing.

Academic Programs *Special study options:* academic remediation for entering students, adult/continuing education programs, English as a second language, honors programs, part-time degree program, services for LD students, summer session for credit.

Library College of the Desert Library with 58,000 titles, 260 serial subscriptions.

Computers on Campus 43 computers available on campus for general student use. A campuswide network can be accessed from off campus. At least one staffed computer lab available.

Student Life *Housing:* college housing not available. *Activities and Organizations:* drama/theater group, student-run newspaper, choral group, student association, International Club, African-Americans for College Education. *Campus security:* 24-hour emergency response devices, late-night transport/escort service. *Student Services:* health clinic, personal/psychological counseling.

Athletics *Intercollegiate sports:* baseball M, basketball M/W, cross-country running M/W, football M, golf M/W, soccer M, softball W, tennis M/W, track and field M/W, volleyball W. *Intramural sports:* badminton M/W, basketball M/W, fencing M/W, golf M/W, soccer M, softball M/W, swimming M/W, table tennis M/W, tennis M/W, volleyball M/W.

Costs (2001–02) *Tuition:* state resident $0 full-time; nonresident $3240 full-time, $135 per unit part-time. Full-time tuition and fees vary according to course load. *Required fees:* $332 full-time, $11 per unit, $31 per term part-time.

Financial Aid In 2001, 125 Federal Work-Study jobs (averaging $750). 50 State and other part-time jobs (averaging $750).

Applying *Options:* early admission. *Application deadline:* rolling (freshmen), rolling (transfers). *Notification:* continuous (freshmen).

Admissions Contact Ms. Kathi Westerfield, Registrar, College of the Desert, 43-500 Monterey Avenue, Palm Desert, CA 92260-9305. *Phone:* 760-773-2519. *Toll-free phone:* 760-773-2516.

COLLEGE OF THE REDWOODS
Eureka, California

- **State and locally supported** 2-year, founded 1964, part of California Community College System
- **Calendar** semesters
- **Degree** certificates and associate
- **Small-town** 322-acre campus
- **Endowment** $1.8 million
- **Coed,** 7,503 undergraduate students, 36% full-time, 60% women, 40% men

Undergraduates Students come from 52 states and territories, 2% African American, 3% Asian American or Pacific Islander, 6% Hispanic American, 8% Native American, 2% live on campus.

Freshmen *Admission:* 717 applied, 717 admitted.

Faculty *Total:* 413, 28% full-time. *Student/faculty ratio:* 13:1.

Majors Agricultural business; agronomy/crop science; architectural engineering technology; auto mechanic/technician; business administration; child care provider; computer engineering technology; computer/information sciences; computer programming; computer typography/composition; construction technology; criminal justice/law enforcement administration; dental assistant; diesel engine mechanic; drafting; early childhood education; electrical/electronic engineering technology; forestry; graphic design/commercial art/illustration; legal administrative assistant; machine technology; marine science; medical assistant; nursing; paralegal/legal assistant; real estate; secretarial science; Web page, digital/multimedia and information resources design; welding technology.

Academic Programs *Special study options:* academic remediation for entering students, adult/continuing education programs, advanced placement credit, cooperative education, distance learning, English as a second language, honors programs, off-campus study, part-time degree program, services for LD students, summer session for credit.

Library College of the Redwoods Library with 50,266 titles, 969 serial subscriptions, an OPAC.

Computers on Campus 387 computers available on campus for general student use. A campuswide network can be accessed from off campus. Internet access, at least one staffed computer lab available.

Student Life *Housing Options:* coed. *Activities and Organizations:* Associated Students College of the Redwoods, Spanish Club, Computer Information Systems Club, Math/Science Club, International Student Club. *Campus security:* 24-hour emergency response devices and patrols, late-night transport/escort service. *Student Services:* health clinic, personal/psychological counseling.

Athletics *Intercollegiate sports:* baseball M, basketball M/W, cross-country running M/W, football M, golf M, softball W, track and field M/W, volleyball W.

Costs (2001–02) *Tuition:* state resident $0 full-time; nonresident $3888 full-time, $162 per unit part-time. *Required fees:* $294 full-time, $11 per unit, $15 per term part-time. *Room and board:* $5310. Room and board charges vary according to board plan.

Financial Aid *Financial aid deadline:* 6/30.

Applying *Options:* common application, early admission. *Application deadline:* rolling (freshmen), rolling (transfers).

Admissions Contact Ms. Jean Butler, Director of Enrollment Management, College of the Redwoods, 7351 Tompkins Hill Road, Eureka, CA 95501-9300. *Phone:* 707-476-4168. *Toll-free phone:* 800-641-0400. *Fax:* 707-476-4406. *E-mail:* admissions@eureka.redwoods.cc.ca.us.

COLLEGE OF THE SEQUOIAS
Visalia, California

- **State and locally supported** 2-year, founded 1925, part of California Community College System
- **Calendar** semesters
- **Degree** certificates and associate
- **Suburban** 215-acre campus
- **Endowment** $1.2 million
- **Coed,** 10,780 undergraduate students, 37% full-time, 60% women, 40% men

Undergraduates Students come from 23 states and territories, 3% Asian American or Pacific Islander, 42% Hispanic American, 1% Native American.

Freshmen *Admission:* 2,748 applied, 2,748 admitted.

Faculty *Total:* 174. *Student/faculty ratio:* 42:1.

Majors Accounting; agricultural business; agricultural education; agricultural mechanization; agricultural sciences; animal sciences; architectural engineering technology; art; athletic training/sports medicine; auto mechanic/technician; biological/physical sciences; biology; business administration; business marketing and marketing management; carpentry; chemistry; community services; computer engineering technology; computer graphics; computer programming; computer science; computer software and media applications related; computer typography/composition; construction technology; corrections; cosmetology; criminal justice/law enforcement administration; culinary arts; cultural studies; dairy science; data warehousing/mining/database administration; developmental/child psychology; drafting; early childhood education; electrical/electronic engineering technology; engineering; English; fashion design/illustration; fashion merchandising; fire science; French; graphic design/commercial art/illustration; health education; heating/air conditioning/refrigeration; history; home economics; home economics education; horticulture science; humanities; industrial arts; information sciences/systems; interior design; journalism; law enforcement/police science; liberal arts and sciences/liberal studies; mass communications; mathematics; modern languages; music; nursing; ornamental horticulture; paralegal/legal assistant; physical education; pre-engineering; real estate; secretarial science; sign language interpretation; social sciences; sociology; Spanish; speech/rhetorical studies; theater arts/drama; Web page, digital/multimedia and information resources design; welding technology; word processing.

Academic Programs *Special study options:* academic remediation for entering students, accelerated degree program, adult/continuing education programs, advanced placement credit, cooperative education, English as a second language, freshman honors college, honors programs, internships, part-time degree program, services for LD students, study abroad, summer session for credit. *ROTC:* Air Force (c).

Library College of the Sequoias Library with 73,557 titles, 430 serial subscriptions, an OPAC, a Web page.

Computers on Campus 190 computers available on campus for general student use. A campuswide network can be accessed from off campus. At least one staffed computer lab available.

Student Life *Housing:* college housing not available. *Activities and Organizations:* drama/theater group, student-run newspaper, choral group, MECHA, Ag Club, Alpha Gamma Sigma, Paralegal Association, Sports Medicine Club. *Campus security:* 24-hour emergency response devices and patrols, student patrols, late-night transport/escort service, 18 hour patrols by trained security personnel. *Student Services:* health clinic, personal/psychological counseling, women's center.

Athletics Member NJCAA. *Intercollegiate sports:* baseball M, basketball M/W, cross-country running M/W, football M, golf M, soccer W, softball W, swimming M/W, tennis M/W, track and field M/W, volleyball W, water polo M.

Costs (2002–03) *Tuition:* state resident $0 full-time; nonresident $4230 full-time, $141 per unit part-time. Part-time tuition and fees vary according to course load. *Required fees:* $330 full-time, $11 per unit.

Applying *Options:* early admission. *Required:* high school transcript. *Application deadlines:* 8/15 (freshmen), 8/15 (transfers). *Notification:* continuous (freshmen).

Admissions Contact Mr. Don Mast, Associate Dean of Admissions/Registrar, College of the Sequoias, 915 South Mooney Boulevard, Visalia, CA 93277-2234. *Phone:* 559-737-4844. *Fax:* 559-737-4820.

COLLEGE OF THE SISKIYOUS
Weed, California

- **State and locally supported** 2-year, founded 1957, part of California Community College System
- **Calendar** semesters
- **Degree** certificates and associate
- **Rural** 260-acre campus
- **Coed,** 3,127 undergraduate students, 26% full-time, 61% women, 39% men

COS is located at the base of Mt. Shasta in northern California, 60 miles south of the Oregon border, and provides many recreational opportunities. COS offers excellent transfer and vocational programs, support services, on-campus residence halls, and athletic programs. Small class sizes and individualized instruction provide a supportive environment that encourages learning.

Undergraduates 804 full-time, 2,323 part-time. Students come from 15 states and territories, 11 other countries, 11% are from out of state, 4% African American, 4% Asian American or Pacific Islander, 6% Hispanic American, 5% Native American, 1% international, 13% transferred in, 10% live on campus.

Freshmen *Admission:* 323 applied, 323 admitted, 323 enrolled.

Faculty *Total:* 164, 32% full-time, 7% with terminal degrees. *Student/faculty ratio:* 25:1.

Majors Accounting; alcohol/drug abuse counseling; art education; biology; botany; business administration; ceramic arts; chemistry; child care provider; civil engineering technology; computer graphics; computer programming; computer programming related; computer programming (specific applications); computer science; computer/technical support; cosmetology; criminal justice/law enforcement administration; data processing technology; early childhood education; emergency medical technology; engineering; English; fine/studio arts; fire science; forestry; geology; history; home economics; law enforcement/police science; legal studies; mathematics; music; natural resources management; physical education; physical sciences; physics; psychology; secretarial science; social sciences; speech/theater education; theater arts/drama; Web page, digital/multimedia and information resources design; welding technology; wildlife management; zoology.

Academic Programs *Special study options:* academic remediation for entering students, adult/continuing education programs, advanced placement credit, cooperative education, distance learning, double majors, English as a second language, honors programs, independent study, internships, part-time degree program, services for LD students, student-designed majors, summer session for credit.

Library College of the Siskiyous Library with 34,708 titles, 148 serial subscriptions, 9,433 audiovisual materials, an OPAC, a Web page.

Computers on Campus 260 computers available on campus for general student use. A campuswide network can be accessed from off campus. Internet access, at least one staffed computer lab available.

Student Life *Housing Options:* coed, men-only. *Activities and Organizations:* drama/theater group, student-run newspaper, choral group, Associated Student Body, Latino Student Union, Phi Theta Kappa, Black Student Union, American Indian Alliance. *Campus security:* 24-hour emergency response devices, controlled dormitory access. *Student Services:* health clinic, personal/psychological counseling, women's center, legal services.

Athletics Member NJCAA. *Intercollegiate sports:* baseball M, basketball M/W, cross-country running M/W, football M, golf W, skiing (downhill) M/W, soccer W, softball W, track and field M/W, volleyball W. *Intramural sports:* basketball M/W, skiing (cross-country) M/W, skiing (downhill) M/W, soccer W, tennis M/W, volleyball W.

Costs (2001–02) *Tuition:* state resident $0 full-time; nonresident $3500 full-time, $147 per unit part-time. Full-time tuition and fees vary according to course load and reciprocity agreements. Part-time tuition and fees vary according to reciprocity agreements. *Required fees:* $350 full-time, $11 per unit. *Room and board:* $4910; room only: $2190. Room and board charges vary according to board plan.

Financial Aid In 2001, 51 Federal Work-Study jobs (averaging $1897). 30 State and other part-time jobs (averaging $2000).

Applying *Options:* early admission, deferred entrance. *Application deadline:* rolling (freshmen), rolling (transfers). *Notification:* continuous (freshmen).

Admissions Contact Ms. Christina Bruck, Recruitment and Outreach Coordinator, College of the Siskiyous, 800 College Avenue, Weed, CA 96094. *Phone:* 530-938-5847. *Toll-free phone:* 888-397-4339 Ext. 5847. *Fax:* 530-938-5367. *E-mail:* info@siskiyous.edu.

COLUMBIA COLLEGE
Sonora, California

Admissions Contact Ms. Kathy Smith, Coordinator of Admissions and Records, Columbia College, 11600 Columbia College Drive, Sonora, CA 95370. *Phone:* 209-588-5231.

COMPTON COMMUNITY COLLEGE
Compton, California

- **State and locally supported** 2-year, founded 1927, part of California Community College System
- **Calendar** semesters
- **Degree** associate
- **Urban** 83-acre campus with easy access to Los Angeles
- **Coed,** 7,900 undergraduate students

Undergraduates Students come from 4 states and territories, 25 other countries.

Freshmen *Admission:* 1,650 applied, 1,650 admitted.

Faculty *Total:* 347, 29% full-time.

Majors Accounting; African-American studies; aircraft pilot (professional); art; art education; auto mechanic/technician; behavioral sciences; biological/physical sciences; biology; business administration; chemistry; child care/development; civil engineering technology; computer engineering technology; computer programming; construction technology; criminal justice/law enforcement administration; cultural studies; dance; data processing technology; developmental/child psychology; drafting; early childhood education; economics; electrical/electronic engineering technology; emergency medical technology; engineering; English; fire science; French; German; graphic design/commercial art/illustration; graphic/printing equipment; health science; history; home economics; human services; industrial radiologic technology; information sciences/systems; jazz; journalism; law enforcement/police science; liberal arts and sciences/liberal studies; literature; machine technology; mathematics; mechanical engineering technology; Mexican-American studies; music; nuclear medical technology; nursing; nutrition science; paralegal/legal assistant; philosophy; photography; physical education; physical sciences; physics; pre-engineering; psychology; real estate; recreation/leisure facilities management; recreation/leisure studies; respiratory therapy; secretarial science; social sciences; social work; sociology; Spanish; speech/rhetorical studies; teacher assistant/aide; telecommunications; textile arts; theater arts/drama; trade/industrial education; welding technology.

Academic Programs *Special study options:* academic remediation for entering students, adult/continuing education programs, advanced placement credit, English as a second language, honors programs, part-time degree program, services for LD students, summer session for credit.

Library Compton Community College Library with 45,000 titles, 400 serial subscriptions.

Computers on Campus 30 computers available on campus for general student use.

Student Life *Housing:* college housing not available. *Activities and Organizations:* drama/theater group. *Campus security:* 24-hour patrols. *Student Services:* personal/psychological counseling.

Athletics *Intercollegiate sports:* baseball M, basketball M/W, cross-country running M/W, football M, golf M, track and field M/W. *Intramural sports:* basketball M/W.

Costs (2001–02) *Tuition:* nonresident $4230 full-time, $141 per unit part-time. *Required fees:* $330 full-time, $11 per unit, $15 per term part-time.

Financial Aid In 2001, 300 Federal Work-Study jobs (averaging $3000).

Applying *Options:* early admission. *Application deadline:* rolling (freshmen), rolling (transfers). *Notification:* continuous (freshmen).

Admissions Contact Dr. Essie French-Preston, Vice President of Student Affairs, Compton Community College, 1111 East Artesia Boulevard, Compton, CA 90221-5393. *Phone:* 310-637-2660 Ext. 2024.

CONTRA COSTA COLLEGE
San Pablo, California

Admissions Contact Mrs. Linda Ames, Lead Admissions Assistant, Contra Costa College, 2600 Mission Bell Drive, San Pablo, CA 94806-3195. *Phone:* 510-235-7800 Ext. 4211.

COPPER MOUNTAIN COLLEGE
Joshua Tree, California

Admissions Contact 6162 Rotary Way, Joshua Tree, CA 92252.

COSUMNES RIVER COLLEGE
Sacramento, California

Admissions Contact Ms. Dianna L. Moore, Supervisor of Admissions Records, Cosumnes River College, 8401 Center Parkway, Sacramento, CA 95823-5799. *Phone:* 916-688-7423. *Fax:* 916-688-7467.

CRAFTON HILLS COLLEGE
Yucaipa, California

- **State and locally supported** 2-year, founded 1972, part of California Community College System
- **Calendar** semesters
- **Degree** certificates and associate
- **Small-town** 526-acre campus with easy access to Los Angeles
- **Coed,** 5,200 undergraduate students

Undergraduates Students come from 19 states and territories, 12 other countries.
Faculty *Total:* 217, 27% full-time, 8% with terminal degrees.
Majors Accounting; anthropology; art; astronomy; biological/physical sciences; biology; business administration; business marketing and marketing management; chemistry; child care/development; child care provider; community services; computer science; criminal justice/law enforcement administration; economics; emergency medical technology; English; fire science; French; geology; history; humanities; human services; industrial radiologic technology; liberal arts and sciences/liberal studies; mathematics; medical administrative assistant; music; philosophy; physical education; physics; political science; pre-engineering; psychology; religious studies; respiratory therapy; secretarial science; sociology; Spanish; speech-language pathology; speech/rhetorical studies; theater arts/drama.
Academic Programs *Special study options:* academic remediation for entering students, adult/continuing education programs, advanced placement credit, cooperative education, distance learning, part-time degree program, services for LD students, student-designed majors, summer session for credit.
Library Crafton Hills College Library with 65,731 titles, 425 serial subscriptions.
Computers on Campus 52 computers available on campus for general student use. A campuswide network can be accessed from off campus. At least one staffed computer lab available.
Student Life *Housing:* college housing not available. *Activities and Organizations:* drama/theater group. *Campus security:* 24-hour patrols, late-night transport/escort service. *Student Services:* health clinic, personal/psychological counseling, women's center.
Athletics *Intramural sports:* golf M/W, tennis M/W, volleyball M/W, weight lifting M/W.
Standardized Tests *Required for some:* ACT, SAT, SCAT, CGP, ACT ASSET, Nelson Denny Reading Test, or ACCUPLACER.
Costs (2002–03) *One-time required fee:* $25. *Tuition:* state resident $0 full-time; nonresident $3312 full-time, $138 per unit part-time. *Required fees:* $264 full-time, $11 per credit.
Applying *Options:* common application, early admission, deferred entrance. *Required for some:* high school transcript. *Application deadline:* rolling (freshmen). *Notification:* continuous (freshmen).
Admissions Contact Crafton Hills College, 11711 Sand Canyon Road, Yucaipa, CA 92399. *Phone:* 909-389-3355. *Fax:* 909-389-9141. *E-mail:* bdavis@sbccd.cc.ca.us.

CUESTA COLLEGE
San Luis Obispo, California

- **District-supported** 2-year, founded 1964
- **Calendar** semesters
- **Degree** certificates and associate
- **Rural** 129-acre campus
- **Coed,** 10,165 undergraduate students

Undergraduates Students come from 19 other countries, 10% are from out of state.
Faculty *Total:* 401, 33% full-time, 10% with terminal degrees.
Majors Agricultural mechanization; applied art; art; artificial intelligence/robotics; arts management; auto mechanic/technician; biology; business administration; business marketing and marketing management; chemistry; child care/development; computer engineering technology; computer hardware engineering; computer science; computer systems networking/telecommunications; computer/technical support; construction technology; data processing technology; early childhood education; electrical/electronic engineering technology; engineering; family/consumer studies; fashion merchandising; geology; human services; individual/family development; industrial technology; information technology; interior design; journalism; liberal arts and sciences/liberal studies; library science; mass communications; mathematics; medical assistant; nursing; nutrition science; physical education; physics; pre-engineering; psychology; radio/television broadcasting; real estate; recreational therapy; recreation/leisure facilities management; secretarial science; system/networking/LAN/WAN management; telecommunications; Web page, digital/multimedia and information resources design; welding technology.
Academic Programs *Special study options:* academic remediation for entering students, adult/continuing education programs, advanced placement credit, cooperative education, distance learning, double majors, English as a second language, honors programs, independent study, internships, off-campus study, part-time degree program, services for LD students, study abroad, summer session for credit. *ROTC:* Army (c).
Library Cuesta College Library with 64,814 titles, 584 serial subscriptions, an OPAC, a Web page.
Computers on Campus 400 computers available on campus for general student use. A campuswide network can be accessed from off campus. At least one staffed computer lab available.
Student Life *Housing:* college housing not available. *Activities and Organizations:* drama/theater group, student-run newspaper, radio station, choral group, Associated Students of Cuesta College, Alpha Gamma Sigma, Student Nurses Association, Latina Leadership Network, MECHA. *Campus security:* 24-hour emergency response devices and patrols, late-night transport/escort service. *Student Services:* health clinic, personal/psychological counseling, legal services.
Athletics *Intercollegiate sports:* baseball M, basketball M/W, cross-country running M/W, soccer W, softball W, swimming M/W, tennis W, track and field M/W, volleyball W, water polo M/W, wrestling M.
Standardized Tests *Recommended:* Assessment and Placement Services for Community Colleges.
Costs (2001–02) *Tuition:* state resident $0 full-time; nonresident $4088 full-time, $146 per unit part-time. Full-time tuition and fees vary according to course load. Part-time tuition and fees vary according to course load. *Required fees:* $401 full-time, $11 per unit, $11 per term part-time.
Applying *Options:* common application, early admission, deferred entrance. *Required:* high school transcript. *Recommended:* essay or personal statement. *Application deadline:* rolling (freshmen), rolling (transfers). *Notification:* continuous (freshmen).
Admissions Contact Ms. Juileta Siu, Admissions Clerk, Cuesta College, PO Box 8106, Highway 1, SanLuis Obispo, CA 93403-8106. *Phone:* 805-546-3140. *Fax:* 805-546-3975.

CUYAMACA COLLEGE
El Cajon, California

- **State-supported** 2-year, founded 1978, part of Grossmont-Cuyamaca Community College District
- **Calendar** semesters
- **Degree** certificates, diplomas, and associate
- **Suburban** 165-acre campus with easy access to San Diego
- **Coed,** 7,423 undergraduate students, 24% full-time, 56% women, 44% men

Undergraduates Students come from 8 other countries, 1% are from out of state, 5% African American, 6% Asian American or Pacific Islander, 15% Hispanic American, 2% Native American, 0.8% international.

Freshmen *Admission:* 1,012 applied, 1,012 admitted.
Faculty *Total:* 342, 24% full-time.
Majors Accounting; accounting technician; auto mechanic/technician; biological/physical sciences; business; business administration; chemistry; child guidance; drafting; drawing; elementary education; English; enterprise management; environmental technology; floristry marketing; general studies; graphic design/commercial art/illustration; history; information sciences/systems; landscaping management; liberal arts and sciences/liberal studies; mechanical design technology; nursery management; occupational safety/health technology; office management; ornamental horticulture; painting; paralegal/legal assistant; physics; real estate; speech/rhetorical studies; surveying; turf management.
Academic Programs *Special study options:* academic remediation for entering students, adult/continuing education programs, advanced placement credit, cooperative education, English as a second language, part-time degree program, services for LD students, student-designed majors, study abroad, summer session for credit. *ROTC:* Army (c), Air Force (c).
Library Library plus 1 other with 32,000 titles, 125 serial subscriptions, an OPAC, a Web page.
Computers on Campus 396 computers available on campus for general student use. A campuswide network can be accessed from off campus. Internet access, at least one staffed computer lab available.
Student Life *Housing:* college housing not available. *Activities and Organizations:* student-run newspaper. *Student Services:* health clinic, personal/psychological counseling.
Athletics *Intercollegiate sports:* basketball M/W, cross-country running M/W, soccer M/W, tennis W, track and field M/W, volleyball W.
Standardized Tests *Required:* ACT ASSET.
Costs (2002–03) *Tuition:* state resident $0 full-time; nonresident $3384 full-time, $141 per unit part-time. Full-time tuition and fees vary according to course load. Part-time tuition and fees vary according to course load. *Required fees:* $298 full-time, $11 per unit, $12 per term part-time.
Financial Aid In 2001, 64 Federal Work-Study jobs (averaging $1600). 28 State and other part-time jobs (averaging $1300).
Applying *Options:* common application, early admission. *Application deadline:* rolling (freshmen), rolling (transfers).
Admissions Contact Dr. Beth Appenzeller, Associate Dean of Admissions and Records, Cuyamaca College, 900 Rancho San Diego Parkway, El Cajon, CA 92019-4304. *Phone:* 619-660-4302. *Fax:* 610-660-4399.

CYPRESS COLLEGE
Cypress, California

- **State and locally supported** 2-year, founded 1966, part of California Community College System
- **Calendar** semesters
- **Degree** certificates and associate
- **Suburban** 108-acre campus with easy access to Los Angeles
- **Coed,** 15,347 undergraduate students

Undergraduates Students come from 41 states and territories, 22 other countries, 1% are from out of state.
Faculty *Total:* 590, 39% full-time.
Majors Accounting; advertising; aircraft pilot (professional); anthropology; applied art; art; auto body repair; auto mechanic/technician; aviation management; biological/physical sciences; biology; business administration; business marketing and marketing management; chemistry; computer graphics; computer/information technology services administration and management related; computer programming related; computer programming (specific applications); computer science; computer science related; computer software and media applications related; computer systems networking/telecommunications; court reporting; culinary arts; dance; data entry/microcomputer applications; data entry/microcomputer applications related; dental assistant; dental hygiene; economics; engineering; English; flight attendant; food products retailing; geography; geology; health science; heating/air conditioning/refrigeration; history; hotel and restaurant management; human services; industrial radiologic technology; information sciences/systems; legal administrative assistant; liberal arts and sciences/liberal studies; mathematics; medical administrative assistant; medical records administration; mortuary science; music; natural sciences; nursing; philosophy; photography; physical education; physics; political science; psychiatric/mental health services; psychology; secretarial science; social sciences; sociology; speech/rhetorical studies; system administration; system/networking/LAN/WAN management; theater arts/drama; travel/tourism management; Web page, digital/multimedia and information resources design; word processing.
Academic Programs *Special study options:* academic remediation for entering students, adult/continuing education programs, advanced placement credit, cooperative education, distance learning, double majors, English as a second language, freshman honors college, honors programs, independent study, internships, off-campus study, part-time degree program, services for LD students, study abroad, summer session for credit.
Library Cypress College Library plus 1 other with 76,696 titles, 255 serial subscriptions, 1,113 audiovisual materials, an OPAC, a Web page.
Computers on Campus 500 computers available on campus for general student use. A campuswide network can be accessed from off campus. Internet access, at least one staffed computer lab available.
Student Life *Housing:* college housing not available. *Activities and Organizations:* drama/theater group, student-run newspaper, choral group, Alpha Gamma Sigma, California Student Nurses Association, Court Reporting Club, MECHA. *Campus security:* 24-hour emergency response devices. *Student Services:* health clinic, personal/psychological counseling, women's center, legal services.
Athletics *Intercollegiate sports:* baseball M, basketball M/W, golf M/W, soccer M/W, softball W, swimming M/W, tennis M/W, volleyball W, water polo M/W, wrestling M. *Intramural sports:* football M(c).
Costs (2002–03) *Tuition:* state resident $0 full-time; nonresident $4224 full-time, $141 per unit part-time. *Required fees:* $326 full-time, $11 per unit.
Financial Aid In 2001, 100 Federal Work-Study jobs (averaging $4000).
Applying *Recommended:* high school transcript. *Application deadlines:* 8/25 (freshmen), 1/25 (transfers).
Admissions Contact Mr. Dennis Doran, Cypress College, 9200 Valley View, Cypress, CA 90630. *Phone:* 714-484-7348. *Fax:* 714-484-7446. *E-mail:* info@cypress.cc.ca.us.

DE ANZA COLLEGE
Cupertino, California

- **State and locally supported** 2-year, founded 1967, part of California Community College System
- **Calendar** quarters
- **Degree** certificates, diplomas, and associate
- **Small-town** 112-acre campus with easy access to San Francisco and San Jose
- **Coed,** 24,984 undergraduate students

Undergraduates Students come from 48 states and territories, 79 other countries.
Freshmen *Admission:* 4,013 applied, 3,283 admitted. *Average high school GPA:* 2.86.
Faculty *Total:* 775, 36% full-time.
Majors Accounting; art; art history; auto mechanic/technician; behavioral sciences; biology; business administration; business machine repair; business marketing and marketing management; ceramic arts; child care/development; computer graphics; computer management; computer programming; computer science; construction technology; corrections; criminal justice/law enforcement administration; cultural studies; developmental/child psychology; drawing; economics; engineering; engineering technology; English; environmental science; film studies; graphic design/commercial art/illustration; history; humanities; industrial technology; information sciences/systems; international relations; journalism; law enforcement/police science; liberal arts and sciences/liberal studies; machine technology; mass communications; mathematics; mechanical design technology; medical assistant; music; nursing; paralegal/legal assistant; philosophy; photography; physical education; physical therapy; physics; political science; practical nurse; pre-engineering; printmaking; psychology; purchasing/contracts management; radio/television broadcasting; real estate; sculpture; secretarial science; social sciences; sociology; Spanish; speech/rhetorical studies; technical/business writing; theater arts/drama.
Academic Programs *Special study options:* academic remediation for entering students, adult/continuing education programs, advanced placement credit, cooperative education, English as a second language, external degree program, honors programs, internships, part-time degree program, services for LD students, study abroad, summer session for credit. *ROTC:* Army (c), Air Force (c).
Library A. Robert DeHart Learning Center with 80,000 titles, 927 serial subscriptions.
Computers on Campus 800 computers available on campus for general student use. A campuswide network can be accessed from off campus. At least one staffed computer lab available.
Student Life *Housing:* college housing not available. *Activities and Organizations:* drama/theater group, student-run newspaper, choral group, Student Nurses Association, Phi Theta Kappa, Automotive Club, Vietnamese Club, Filipino Club. *Campus security:* 24-hour emergency response devices, student patrols, late-night transport/escort service. *Student Services:* health clinic, personal/psychological counseling, legal services.

De Anza College (continued)

Athletics *Intercollegiate sports:* baseball M, basketball M/W, cross-country running M/W, football M, golf M/W, soccer M/W, softball W, swimming M/W, tennis M/W, track and field M/W, volleyball M/W, water polo M. *Intramural sports:* badminton M/W, basketball M, soccer M/W, swimming M/W, volleyball M/W.

Standardized Tests *Required for some:* SAT I (for placement), CPT, DTLS, DTMS.

Costs (2001–02) *Tuition:* nonresident $3204 full-time, $89 per unit part-time. *Required fees:* $286 full-time, $12 per quarter part-time.

Applying *Options:* common application, early admission. *Application fee:* $22. *Application deadline:* rolling (freshmen), rolling (transfers). *Notification:* continuous (freshmen).

Admissions Contact Ms. Kathleen Kyne, Admissions and Records, De Anza College, 21250 Stevens Creek Boulevard, Cupertino, CA 95014-5793. *Phone:* 408-864-8419. *E-mail:* webregda@mercury.fhda.edu.

DEEP SPRINGS COLLEGE
Deep Springs, California

- **Independent** 2-year, founded 1917
- **Calendar** 6 seven-week terms
- **Degree** associate
- **Rural** 3000-acre campus
- **Endowment** $11.1 million
- **Men only,** 26 undergraduate students, 100% full-time

Undergraduates 26 full-time. Students come from 14 states and territories, 3 other countries, 89% are from out of state, 4% transferred in, 100% live on campus.

Freshmen *Admission:* 13 enrolled. *Average high school GPA:* 3.80. *Test scores:* SAT verbal scores over 500: 100%; SAT math scores over 500: 100%; SAT verbal scores over 600: 100%; SAT math scores over 600: 100%; SAT verbal scores over 700: 75%; SAT math scores over 700: 75%.

Faculty *Total:* 6, 67% full-time, 83% with terminal degrees. *Student/faculty ratio:* 3:1.

Majors Liberal arts and sciences/liberal studies.

Academic Programs *Special study options:* accelerated degree program, cooperative education, freshman honors college, honors programs, independent study, internships, student-designed majors, summer session for credit.

Library Mossner Library of Deep Springs with 20,000 titles, 60 serial subscriptions, an OPAC, a Web page.

Computers on Campus 6 computers available on campus for general student use.

Student Life *Housing:* on-campus residence required through sophomore year. *Options:* men-only. *Activities and Organizations:* drama/theater group, choral group, Student Self-Government, Labor Program, Applications Committee, Review Committee, Curriculum Committee. *Student Services:* personal/psychological counseling, legal services.

Athletics *Intramural sports:* archery M, basketball M, cross-country running M, equestrian sports M, football M, riflery M, soccer M, swimming M, water polo M, weight lifting M.

Costs (2001–02) *Tuition:* All students are on full scholarship.

Applying *Options:* common application. *Required:* essay or personal statement, high school transcript, letters of recommendation, interview. *Application deadlines:* 11/15 (freshmen), 11/15 (transfers). *Notification:* 4/15 (freshmen).

Admissions Contact Dr. L. Jackson Newell, President, Deep Springs College, HC 72, Box 45001, Dyer, NV 89010-9803. *Phone:* 760-872-2000. *E-mail:* apcom@deepsprings.edu.

DIABLO VALLEY COLLEGE
Pleasant Hill, California

- **State and locally supported** 2-year, founded 1949, part of Contra Costa Community College District
- **Calendar** semesters
- **Degree** certificates and associate
- **Small-town** 100-acre campus with easy access to San Francisco
- **Coed,** 23,035 undergraduate students

Undergraduates Students come from 65 other countries, 5% African American, 18% Asian American or Pacific Islander, 11% Hispanic American, 0.7% Native American.

Faculty *Total:* 868, 32% full-time.

Majors Computer graphics; computer/information technology services administration and management related; computer programming related; computer programming (specific applications); computer programming, vendor/product certification; computer science related; computer software and media applications related; computer systems networking/telecommunications; computer/technical support; data entry/microcomputer applications; data entry/microcomputer applications related; information technology; liberal arts and sciences/liberal studies; Web page, digital/multimedia and information resources design; word processing.

Academic Programs *Special study options:* academic remediation for entering students, adult/continuing education programs, advanced placement credit, cooperative education, part-time degree program, services for LD students, student-designed majors, study abroad, summer session for credit. *ROTC:* Air Force (c).

Library 73,821 titles, 428 serial subscriptions.

Computers on Campus 450 computers available on campus for general student use. A campuswide network can be accessed from off campus. Internet access, online (class) registration, at least one staffed computer lab available.

Student Life *Housing:* college housing not available. *Activities and Organizations:* drama/theater group, student-run newspaper. *Student Services:* women's center.

Athletics *Intercollegiate sports:* basketball M/W, cross-country running M/W, football M, golf M, gymnastics W, soccer M, swimming M/W, tennis M/W, track and field M/W, volleyball W, wrestling M.

Costs (2002–03) *Tuition:* state resident $0 full-time; nonresident $3576 full-time. *Required fees:* $264 full-time, $11 per unit.

Financial Aid *Financial aid deadline:* 4/5.

Applying *Options:* early admission. *Recommended:* high school transcript. *Application deadline:* rolling (freshmen), rolling (transfers).

Admissions Contact Director of Admissions and Records, Diablo Valley College, 321 Golf Club Road, Pleasant Hill, CA 94523-1544. *Phone:* 925-685-1230 Ext. 2330.

DON BOSCO COLLEGE OF SCIENCE AND TECHNOLOGY
Rosemead, California

- **Independent** 2-year, founded 1955, affiliated with Roman Catholic Church
- **Calendar** semesters
- **Degree** associate
- **Suburban** 30-acre campus with easy access to Los Angeles
- **Coed, primarily men,** 1,208 undergraduate students

Undergraduates Students come from 1 other state.

Faculty *Total:* 80.

Majors Auto mechanic/technician; construction technology; drafting; electrical/electronic engineering technology; graphic design/commercial art/illustration; graphic/printing equipment; industrial technology; metallurgical technology.

Academic Programs *Special study options:* advanced placement credit, cooperative education, independent study.

Library 16,400 titles, 70 serial subscriptions.

Computers on Campus 100 computers available on campus for general student use. Internet access, at least one staffed computer lab available.

Student Life *Housing:* college housing not available. *Activities and Organizations:* marching band. *Campus security:* 24-hour emergency response devices. *Student Services:* personal/psychological counseling.

Athletics *Intramural sports:* baseball M, basketball M, cross-country running M, football M, golf M, soccer M, volleyball M, weight lifting M.

Standardized Tests *Required for some:* SAT I or ACT (for admission).

Costs (2001–02) *Tuition:* $5400 full-time, $100 per unit part-time. *Payment plan:* installment. *Waivers:* employees or children of employees.

Financial Aid In 2001, 2 Federal Work-Study jobs (averaging $2650).

Applying *Options:* common application. *Application fee:* $25. *Required:* high school transcript, minimum 2.0 GPA, 2 letters of recommendation. *Application deadlines:* 2/15 (freshmen), 8/1 (transfers).

Admissions Contact Mr. Tom Bauman, Director of College Admissions, Don Bosco College of Science and Technology, 1151 San Gabriel Boulevard, Rosemead, CA 91770-4299. *Phone:* 626-940-2036.

D-Q University
Davis, California

Admissions Contact Ms. Martha Amesquita, Director of Admissions and Records, D-Q University, PO Box 409, Davis, CA 95617-0409. *Phone:* 530-758-0470. *Fax:* 530-758-4891.

East Los Angeles College
Monterey Park, California

Admissions Contact Mr. Jeremy Allred, Associate Dean of Admissions, East Los Angeles College, 1301 Avenida Cesar Chavez, Monterey Park, CA 91754-6001. *Phone:* 323-265-8801. *Fax:* 323-265-8688.

El Camino College
Torrance, California

Admissions Contact Mr. William Robinson, Director of Admissions, El Camino College, 16007 Crenshaw Boulevard, Torrance, CA 90506-0001. *Phone:* 310-660-3418. *Fax:* 310-660-3818.

Empire College
Santa Rosa, California

- **Proprietary** 2-year, founded 1961
- **Calendar** continuous
- **Degree** certificates, diplomas, and associate
- **Suburban** campus with easy access to San Francisco
- **Coed,** 616 undergraduate students

Undergraduates Students come from 1 other state. *Retention:* 90% of 2001 full-time freshmen returned.
Faculty *Total:* 47, 60% full-time. *Student/faculty ratio:* 19:1.
Majors Accounting; computer/information sciences; legal administrative assistant; medical assistant; secretarial science.
Academic Programs *Special study options:* double majors.
Computers on Campus 143 computers available on campus for general student use. Internet access available.
Student Life *Campus security:* 24-hour emergency response devices.
Costs (2002–03) *Comprehensive fee:* $7810 includes full-time tuition ($6900), mandatory fees ($75), and room and board ($835).
Applying *Application fee:* $75. *Required:* high school transcript, interview. *Required for some:* essay or personal statement. *Application deadline:* rolling (freshmen), rolling (transfers).
Admissions Contact Mr. Gib Linzman, Admissions Officer, Empire College, 3035 Cleveland Avenue, Santa Rosa, CA 95403. *Phone:* 707-546-4000. *Fax:* 707-546-4058. *E-mail:* rhurd@empcol.com.

Everest College
Rancho Cucamonga, California

Admissions Contact 9616 Archibald Avenue, Suite 100, Rancho Cucamonga, CA 91730.

Evergreen Valley College
San Jose, California

- **State and locally supported** 2-year, founded 1975, part of California Community College System
- **Calendar** semesters
- **Degree** associate
- **Urban** 175-acre campus
- **Coed,** 10,000 undergraduate students

Undergraduates Students come from 23 states and territories, 11 other countries.
Majors Accounting; applied art; auto mechanic/technician; biology; business; business administration; computer graphics; computer/information sciences; criminal justice/law enforcement administration; data processing technology; desktop publishing equipment operation; drafting; electrical/electronic engineering technology; engineering; English; family/consumer studies; fashion merchandising; general studies; industrial technology; information sciences/systems; interdisciplinary studies; liberal arts and sciences/liberal studies; management information systems/business data processing; mental health/rehabilitation; nursing; paralegal/legal assistant; pre-engineering.
Academic Programs *Special study options:* academic remediation for entering students, accelerated degree program, adult/continuing education programs, advanced placement credit, cooperative education, distance learning, English as a second language, freshman honors college, honors programs, independent study, off-campus study, part-time degree program, services for LD students, summer session for credit. *ROTC:* Army (c).
Library Evergreen Valley College Library with 42,782 titles, 368 serial subscriptions.
Computers on Campus 415 computers available on campus for general student use. At least one staffed computer lab available.
Student Life *Housing:* college housing not available. *Activities and Organizations:* drama/theater group, student-run newspaper, choral group, Affirm, Edlace, Phi Theta Kappa, Vietnamese Student Association. *Campus security:* 24-hour emergency response devices, late-night transport/escort service, patrols by trained security personnel. *Student Services:* health clinic, personal/psychological counseling.
Athletics *Intramural sports:* basketball M/W, racquetball M/W, soccer M, tennis M/W, volleyball M/W.
Costs (2001–02) *Tuition:* area resident $264 full-time; nonresident $3648 full-time, $152 per unit part-time. *Required fees:* $46 full-time, $11 per unit, $1 per term part-time.
Financial Aid In 2001, 107 Federal Work-Study jobs (averaging $3000). 6 State and other part-time jobs (averaging $1500).
Applying *Options:* early admission. *Application deadline:* rolling (freshmen), rolling (transfers). *Notification:* continuous (freshmen).
Admissions Contact Kathleen Mohlberg, Director of Admissions and Records, Evergreen Valley College, 3095 Yerba Buena Road, San Jose, CA 95135-1598. *Phone:* 408-270-6423. *Fax:* 408-223-9351.

Fashion Careers of California College
San Diego, California

- **Proprietary** 2-year, founded 1979
- **Calendar** quarters
- **Degree** certificates and associate
- **Urban** campus
- **Coed, primarily women,** 100 undergraduate students, 100% full-time, 91% women, 9% men

Undergraduates 100 full-time. Students come from 10 states and territories, 4 other countries, 15% are from out of state, 8% African American, 8% Asian American or Pacific Islander, 22% Hispanic American, 1% Native American, 5% international. *Retention:* 75% of 2001 full-time freshmen returned.
Freshmen *Admission:* 17 applied, 17 admitted, 17 enrolled.
Faculty *Total:* 15. *Student/faculty ratio:* 20:1.
Majors Fashion design/illustration; fashion merchandising.
Academic Programs *Special study options:* adult/continuing education programs, cooperative education, double majors, internships.
Library Fashion Careers of California Library with 744 titles, 14 serial subscriptions, 168 audiovisual materials.
Computers on Campus 7 computers available on campus for general student use. Internet access, at least one staffed computer lab available.
Student Life *Housing:* college housing not available. *Campus security:* 24-hour emergency response devices.
Costs (2002–03) *One-time required fee:* $300. *Tuition:* $14,900 full-time. Full-time tuition and fees vary according to program. No tuition increase for student's term of enrollment. *Required fees:* $25 full-time. *Payment plans:* installment, deferred payment. *Waivers:* employees or children of employees.
Financial Aid In 2001, 10 Federal Work-Study jobs (averaging $1200).
Applying *Options:* common application, electronic application. *Application fee:* $25. *Required:* essay or personal statement, high school transcript, interview. *Application deadline:* rolling (freshmen), rolling (transfers).
Admissions Contact Ms. Lisa Paik, Admissions Representative, Fashion Careers of California College, 1923 Morena Boulevard, San Diego, CA 92110. *Phone:* 619-275-4700 Ext. 309. *Toll-free phone:* 888-FCCC999. *Fax:* 619-275-0635. *E-mail:* lisa@fashioncollege.com.

Fashion Institute of Design and Merchandising, Los Angeles Campus
Los Angeles, California

- **Proprietary** 2-year, founded 1969, part of Fashion Institute of Design and Merchandising
- **Calendar** quarters
- **Degrees** associate (also includes Costa Mesa campus)
- **Urban** campus
- **Coed,** 2,873 undergraduate students, 84% full-time, 89% women, 11% men

Undergraduates 2,416 full-time, 457 part-time. Students come from 40 states and territories, 30 other countries, 23% are from out of state, 5% African American, 18% Asian American or Pacific Islander, 20% Hispanic American, 0.4% Native American, 10% international.

Freshmen *Admission:* 750 admitted, 750 enrolled.

Faculty *Total:* 147, 19% full-time. *Student/faculty ratio:* 19:1.

Majors Apparel marketing; clothing/apparel/textile studies; design/visual communications; fashion design/illustration; fashion merchandising; graphic design/commercial art/illustration; interior design; retail management.

Academic Programs *Special study options:* academic remediation for entering students, adult/continuing education programs, advanced placement credit, cooperative education, English as a second language, internships, part-time degree program, study abroad, summer session for credit.

Library Resource and Research Center with 234 serial subscriptions, 5,899 audiovisual materials, a Web page.

Computers on Campus 74 computers available on campus for general student use. Internet access, at least one staffed computer lab available.

Student Life *Activities and Organizations:* student-run newspaper, ASID (student chapter), International Club, DECA, Association of Manufacturing Students, Honor Society. *Campus security:* 24-hour emergency response devices and patrols, late-night transport/escort service. *Student Services:* personal/psychological counseling.

Costs (2002–03) *Tuition:* $14,000 full-time, $933 per course part-time. Full-time tuition and fees vary according to program. *Required fees:* $500 full-time, $311 per unit.

Applying *Options:* common application, electronic application, deferred entrance. *Application fee:* $25. *Required:* essay or personal statement, high school transcript, 3 letters of recommendation. *Required for some:* interview, major-determined project. *Recommended:* minimum 2.0 GPA. *Application deadline:* rolling (freshmen), rolling (transfers).

Admissions Contact Ms. Susan Aronson, Director of Admissions FIDM/The Fashion Institute of Design and Merchandise, Fashion Institute of Design and Merchandising, Los Angeles Campus, 90015. *Phone:* 213-624-1200 Ext. 5400. *Toll-free phone:* 800-711-7175. *Fax:* 213-624-4799. *E-mail:* info@fidm.com.

Fashion Institute of Design and Merchandising, San Diego Campus
San Diego, California

- **Proprietary** 2-year, founded 1985, part of Fashion Institute of Design and Merchandising
- **Calendar** quarters
- **Degree** associate
- **Urban** campus
- **Coed,** 276 undergraduate students

Undergraduates Students come from 13 states and territories, 15% are from out of state.

Faculty *Total:* 23. *Student/faculty ratio:* 10:1.

Majors Apparel marketing; design/visual communications; fashion design/illustration; fashion merchandising; graphic design/commercial art/illustration; interior design; retail management.

Academic Programs *Special study options:* academic remediation for entering students, adult/continuing education programs, advanced placement credit, cooperative education, internships, part-time degree program, study abroad, summer session for credit.

Library Resource and Research Center with 2,000 titles, 100 serial subscriptions, a Web page.

Computers on Campus 9 computers available on campus for general student use. At least one staffed computer lab available.

Student Life *Activities and Organizations:* ASID (student chapter), DECA, Honor Society, Phi Theta Kappa. *Campus security:* 24-hour emergency response devices and patrols. *Student Services:* personal/psychological counseling.

Costs (2001–02) *Tuition:* $14,500 full-time. Full-time tuition and fees vary according to program. No tuition increase for student's term of enrollment. *Required fees:* $500 full-time. *Payment plans:* tuition prepayment, installment, deferred payment.

Applying *Options:* common application, electronic application, deferred entrance. *Application fee:* $25. *Required:* essay or personal statement, high school transcript, 3 letters of recommendation. *Required for some:* interview, major-determined project. *Recommended:* minimum 2.5 GPA. *Application deadline:* rolling (freshmen), rolling (transfers).

Admissions Contact Ms. Gayle Heinimann, Director of Admissions, Fashion Institute of Design and Merchandising, San Diego Campus, 1010 Second Avenue, Suite 200, San Diego, CA 92101-4903. *Phone:* 619-235-2049. *Toll-free phone:* 800-243-3436. *Fax:* 619-232-4322. *E-mail:* info@fidm.com.

Fashion Institute of Design and Merchandising, San Francisco Campus
San Francisco, California

- **Proprietary** 2-year, founded 1973, part of Fashion Institute of Design and Merchandising
- **Calendar** quarters
- **Degree** associate
- **Urban** campus
- **Coed,** 732 undergraduate students

Undergraduates Students come from 20 other countries.

Faculty *Total:* 60, 5% full-time. *Student/faculty ratio:* 10:1.

Majors Apparel marketing; clothing/apparel/textile studies; design/visual communications; fashion design/illustration; fashion merchandising; graphic design/commercial art/illustration; interior design; retail management.

Academic Programs *Special study options:* academic remediation for entering students, adult/continuing education programs, English as a second language, honors programs, internships, off-campus study, part-time degree program, study abroad, summer session for credit.

Library Resource and Research Center with 4,168 titles, 148 serial subscriptions, a Web page.

Computers on Campus 26 computers available on campus for general student use. At least one staffed computer lab available.

Student Life *Activities and Organizations:* ASID (student chapter), DECA, Visual Design Form, Honor Society. *Campus security:* 24-hour emergency response devices and patrols. *Student Services:* personal/psychological counseling.

Costs (2001–02) *Tuition:* $14,560 full-time. Full-time tuition and fees vary according to program. No tuition increase for student's term of enrollment. *Required fees:* $500 full-time. *Payment plans:* tuition prepayment, installment, deferred payment.

Applying *Options:* common application, electronic application, deferred entrance. *Application fee:* $25. *Required:* essay or personal statement, high school transcript, 3 letters of recommendation. *Required for some:* interview, major-determined project. *Recommended:* minimum 2.0 GPA. *Application deadline:* rolling (freshmen), rolling (transfers).

Admissions Contact Ms. Sheryl Bada Lamenti, Director of Admissions, Fashion Institute of Design and Merchandising, San Francisco Campus, 55 Stockton Street, San Francisco, CA 94108. *Phone:* 415-433-6691 Ext. 200. *Toll-free phone:* 800-711-7175. *Fax:* 415-296-7299. *E-mail:* info@fidm.com.

Feather River Community College District
Quincy, California

- **State and locally supported** 2-year, founded 1968, part of California Community College System
- **Calendar** semesters
- **Degree** certificates, diplomas, and associate
- **Rural** 150-acre campus
- **Coed,** 1,200 undergraduate students

Undergraduates Students come from 3 other countries.

Freshmen *Admission:* 426 applied, 426 admitted.

Faculty *Total:* 87, 29% full-time, 10% with terminal degrees. *Student/faculty ratio:* 12:1.

Majors Accounting; biology; business administration; child care/development; construction technology; criminal justice/law enforcement administration; English; environmental science; equestrian studies; forest harvesting production technology; history; law enforcement/police science; liberal arts and sciences/liberal studies; mathematics; natural sciences; practical nurse; recreation/leisure studies; secretarial science; social sciences; water resources; wildlife biology.

Academic Programs *Special study options:* academic remediation for entering students, adult/continuing education programs, advanced placement credit, cooperative education, distance learning, double majors, freshman honors college, honors programs, independent study, internships, off-campus study, part-time degree program, services for LD students, summer session for credit.

Library Joe Brennan Library plus 1 other with 16,100 titles, 116 serial subscriptions, an OPAC.

Computers on Campus 25 computers available on campus for general student use. A campuswide network can be accessed from off campus. Internet access, online (class) registration, at least one staffed computer lab available.

Student Life *Housing:* college housing not available. *Activities and Organizations:* drama/theater group, choral group. *Campus security:* student patrols.

Athletics *Intercollegiate sports:* baseball M, basketball M/W, football M, softball W, volleyball W. *Intramural sports:* basketball M/W, volleyball W.

Costs (2001–02) *Tuition:* state resident $0 full-time; nonresident $4500 full-time, $150 per unit part-time. Full-time tuition and fees vary according to reciprocity agreements. Part-time tuition and fees vary according to reciprocity agreements. *Required fees:* $382 full-time, $11 per unit, $52 per year part-time. *Payment plan:* deferred payment.

Financial Aid In 2001, 22 Federal Work-Study jobs (averaging $750). 103 State and other part-time jobs (averaging $1504).

Applying *Options:* common application, electronic application, early admission. *Recommended:* high school transcript. *Application deadline:* rolling (freshmen), rolling (transfers).

Admissions Contact Ms. Michelle Jaureguito, College Outreach and Recruitment, Feather River Community College District, 570 Golden Eagle Avenue, Quincy, CA 95971. *Phone:* 530-283-0202 Ext. 276. *Toll-free phone:* 800-442-9799 Ext. 286. *Fax:* 530-283-3757. *E-mail:* info@frcc.cc.ca.us.

FOOTHILL COLLEGE
Los Altos Hills, California

- **State and locally supported** 2-year, founded 1958, part of Foothill/DeAnza Community College District System
- **Calendar** quarters
- **Degree** certificates and associate
- **Suburban** 122-acre campus with easy access to San Jose
- **Coed,** 18,500 undergraduate students

Undergraduates Students come from 51 states and territories, 101 other countries.

Faculty *Total:* 587, 37% full-time.

Majors Accounting; American studies; anthropology; art; art history; athletic training/sports medicine; aviation technology; biological technology; biology; business administration; chemistry; child care/development; classics; communications; computer engineering technology; computer science; creative writing; cultural studies; dental assistant; dental hygiene; diagnostic medical sonography; economics; electrical/electronic engineering technology; emergency medical technology; engineering; English; fine/studio arts; French; geography; geology; German; graphic design/commercial art/illustration; history; humanities; international business; Japanese; landscape architecture; legal studies; liberal arts and sciences/liberal studies; library science; linguistics; literature; mathematics; medical radiologic technology; music; nursery management; ornamental horticulture; philosophy; photography; physical education; physician assistant; physics; political science; psychology; radiological science; radio/television broadcasting; real estate; respiratory therapy; social sciences; sociology; Spanish; speech/rhetorical studies; theater arts/drama; travel/tourism management; veterinary technology; women's studies.

Academic Programs *Special study options:* academic remediation for entering students, accelerated degree program, adult/continuing education programs, advanced placement credit, cooperative education, distance learning, English as a second language, honors programs, independent study, internships, off-campus study, part-time degree program, services for LD students, student-designed majors, study abroad, summer session for credit. *ROTC:* Army (c), Navy (c), Air Force (c).

Library Hubert H. Semans Library with 70,000 titles, 450 serial subscriptions, an OPAC, a Web page.

Computers on Campus 200 computers available on campus for general student use. A campuswide network can be accessed from off campus. Internet access, online (class) registration, at least one staffed computer lab available.

Student Life *Housing:* college housing not available. *Activities and Organizations:* drama/theater group, student-run newspaper, radio station, choral group, Alpha Gamma Sigma, student government. *Campus security:* 24-hour emergency response devices and patrols, late-night transport/escort service. *Student Services:* health clinic, personal/psychological counseling, legal services.

Athletics Member NJCAA. *Intercollegiate sports:* basketball M/W, football M, golf M/W, soccer M/W, softball W, swimming M/W, tennis M, track and field M/W, volleyball W, water polo M/W.

Costs (2002–03) *Tuition:* state resident $0 full-time; nonresident $84 per unit part-time. *Required fees:* $401 full-time, $28 per quarter hour, $28 per term part-time.

Financial Aid In 2001, 80 Federal Work-Study jobs (averaging $1300). 210 State and other part-time jobs.

Applying *Options:* electronic application. *Recommended:* high school transcript. *Application deadline:* 9/15 (freshmen), rolling (transfers). *Notification:* continuous (freshmen).

Admissions Contact Ms. Penny Johnson, Dean, Counseling and Student Services, Foothill College, 12345 El Monte Road, Los Altos Hills, CA 94022-4599. *Phone:* 650-949-7326. *Fax:* 650-949-7375.

FOUNDATION COLLEGE
San Diego, California

Admissions Contact Admissions Coordinator, Foundation College, 5353 Mission Center Road, Suite 100, San Diego, CA 92108-1306. *Phone:* 619-683-3273 Ext. 26. *E-mail:* jdurb@foundationcollege.com.

FRESNO CITY COLLEGE
Fresno, California

- **District-supported** 2-year, founded 1910, part of California Community College System
- **Calendar** semesters
- **Degree** certificates and associate
- **Urban** 103-acre campus
- **Endowment** $853,060
- **Coed,** 30,069 undergraduate students

Undergraduates Students come from 1 other state, 8% African American, 10% Asian American or Pacific Islander, 37% Hispanic American, 0.5% Native American, 0.2% international.

Freshmen *Admission:* 2,996 applied, 2,996 admitted.

Faculty *Total:* 1,617, 23% full-time. *Student/faculty ratio:* 16:1.

Majors African-American studies; alcohol/drug abuse counseling; anthropology; art; auto body repair; auto mechanic/technician; business administration; carpentry; computer typography/composition; construction management; construction technology; corrections; criminal justice/law enforcement administration; cultural studies; dental hygiene; design/visual communications; dietetics; drafting; engineering; fashion merchandising; fire science; food services technology; graphic design/commercial art/illustration; graphic/printing equipment; heating/air conditioning/refrigeration; home economics; humanities; human services; industrial arts; industrial radiologic technology; industrial technology; journalism; law enforcement/police science; legal administrative assistant; liberal arts and sciences/liberal studies; library science; machine technology; mathematics/computer science; medical administrative assistant; medical assistant; medical records administration; Mexican-American studies; music (general performance); music (piano and organ performance); music (voice and choral/opera performance); Native American studies; nursing; paralegal/legal assistant; photography; physical sciences; practical nurse; real estate; recreation/leisure studies; respiratory therapy; secretarial science; social sciences; Spanish; speech/rhetorical studies; teacher assistant/aide; theater arts/drama; theater design; women's studies.

Academic Programs *Special study options:* academic remediation for entering students, advanced placement credit, cooperative education, English as a second language, freshman honors college, honors programs, off-campus study, part-time degree program, services for LD students, study abroad, summer session for credit. *ROTC:* Army (c), Air Force (c).

Library Fresno City College Library with 67,500 titles, an OPAC, a Web page.

Computers on Campus 600 computers available on campus for general student use. Internet access, online (class) registration, at least one staffed computer lab available.

Fresno City College (continued)

Student Life *Housing:* college housing not available. *Activities and Organizations:* drama/theater group, student-run newspaper, choral group, marching band, MECHA, HMONG Club, Rotaract, Students in Free Enterprise, Latter Day Saints Student Association. *Campus security:* 24-hour emergency response devices and patrols, late-night transport/escort service. *Student Services:* health clinic, personal/psychological counseling.

Athletics Member NJCAA. *Intercollegiate sports:* baseball M(s), basketball M/W, cross-country running M(s)/W(s), football M(s), golf M(s)/W(s), soccer M(s)/W(s), softball W(s), tennis M(s)/W(s), track and field M(s)/W(s), volleyball W(s), wrestling M(s). *Intramural sports:* badminton M/W, basketball M/W, cross-country running M/W, football M, golf M/W, gymnastics M/W, soccer M/W, softball M/W, swimming M/W, table tennis M/W, tennis M/W, track and field M/W, volleyball M/W, weight lifting M/W, wrestling M.

Costs (2002–03) *Tuition:* Full-time tuition and fees vary according to location and program. Part-time tuition and fees vary according to location and program.

Applying *Options:* common application, early admission, deferred entrance. *Required:* high school transcript. *Application deadline:* rolling (freshmen), rolling (transfers). *Notification:* continuous (freshmen).

Admissions Contact Ms. Stephanie Pauhi, Office Assistant, Fresno City College, 1101 East University Avenue, Fresno, CA 93741. *Phone:* 559-442-8225. *Fax:* 559-237-4232.

FULLERTON COLLEGE

Fullerton, California

- **State and locally supported** 2-year, founded 1913, part of California Community College System
- **Calendar** semesters
- **Degree** certificates and associate
- **Suburban** 79-acre campus with easy access to Los Angeles
- **Coed,** 21,104 undergraduate students

Undergraduates Students come from 21 other countries. *Retention:* 50% of 2001 full-time freshmen returned.

Faculty *Total:* 835, 39% full-time.

Majors Accounting; agricultural sciences; anthropology; architectural engineering technology; art; astronomy; auto mechanic/technician; biology; business administration; business marketing and marketing management; carpentry; chemistry; civil engineering technology; computer science; construction technology; cosmetology; cultural studies; dance; data processing technology; developmental/child psychology; drafting; early childhood education; economics; English; environmental science; fashion design/illustration; fashion merchandising; fish/game management; forestry; geology; graphic/printing equipment; history; home economics; horticulture science; industrial arts; industrial technology; information sciences/systems; interior design; international business; journalism; land use management; Latin American studies; law enforcement/police science; legal administrative assistant; liberal arts and sciences/liberal studies; library science; mass communications; mathematics; music; oceanography; ornamental horticulture; paralegal/legal assistant; philosophy; physical education; physics; political science; psychology; purchasing/contracts management; radio/television broadcasting; real estate; recreation/leisure studies; religious studies; sociology; speech/rhetorical studies; theater arts/drama; travel/tourism management; wildlife management; zoology.

Academic Programs *Special study options:* academic remediation for entering students, adult/continuing education programs, advanced placement credit, cooperative education, English as a second language, honors programs, part-time degree program, services for LD students, study abroad, summer session for credit. *ROTC:* Army (c), Navy (c), Air Force (c).

Library William T. Boyce Library with 113,236 titles, 600 serial subscriptions.

Computers on Campus 600 computers available on campus for general student use. At least one staffed computer lab available.

Student Life *Housing:* college housing not available. *Activities and Organizations:* drama/theater group, student-run newspaper, radio station. *Student Services:* health clinic, personal/psychological counseling, women's center, legal services.

Athletics *Intercollegiate sports:* basketball M/W, cross-country running M/W, football M, golf M/W, soccer M, swimming M/W, tennis M/W, track and field M/W, volleyball W, water polo M.

Costs (2002–03) *Tuition:* nonresident $141 per unit part-time. *Required fees:* $11 per unit, $12 per term part-time.

Financial Aid In 2001, 300 Federal Work-Study jobs (averaging $4000). *Financial aid deadline:* 5/30.

Applying *Options:* early admission. *Application deadline:* rolling (freshmen), rolling (transfers).

Admissions Contact Mr. Peter Fong, Dean of Admissions and Records, Fullerton College, 321 East Chapman Avenue, Fullerton, CA 92832-2095. *Phone:* 714-992-7582. *E-mail:* gibsonc@fullcoll.edu.

GAVILAN COLLEGE

Gilroy, California

- **State and locally supported** 2-year, founded 1919, part of California Community College System
- **Calendar** semesters
- **Degree** certificates, diplomas, and associate
- **Rural** 150-acre campus with easy access to San Jose
- **Coed,** 5,925 undergraduate students

Undergraduates Students come from 6 states and territories, 11 other countries, 20% are from out of state.

Freshmen *Admission:* 6,290 admitted.

Faculty *Total:* 164, 45% full-time.

Majors Accounting; art; auto mechanic/technician; aviation technology; biological/physical sciences; biology; business administration; chemistry; child care/development; computer graphics; computer programming; computer science; computer science related; corrections; cosmetology; criminal justice/law enforcement administration; developmental/child psychology; drafting; early childhood education; English; history; information sciences/systems; information technology; journalism; law enforcement/police science; legal administrative assistant; liberal arts and sciences/liberal studies; mathematics; music; natural sciences; nursing; physical education; political science; practical nurse; pre-engineering; psychology; secretarial science; social sciences; sociology; Spanish.

Academic Programs *Special study options:* academic remediation for entering students, adult/continuing education programs, advanced placement credit, cooperative education, distance learning, English as a second language, honors programs, independent study, internships, part-time degree program, services for LD students, study abroad, summer session for credit.

Library 55,440 titles, 205 serial subscriptions.

Computers on Campus 31 computers available on campus for general student use. Internet access, at least one staffed computer lab available.

Student Life *Housing:* college housing not available. *Activities and Organizations:* drama/theater group, student-run newspaper, Student Government. *Campus security:* 24-hour emergency response devices and patrols, late-night transport/escort service. *Student Services:* health clinic, personal/psychological counseling.

Athletics *Intercollegiate sports:* baseball W, basketball M/W, football M, golf M, soccer M/W, softball W, tennis M, volleyball W, wrestling M.

Standardized Tests *Required for some:* ACT ASSET.

Costs (2001–02) *Tuition:* state resident $0 full-time; nonresident $3648 full-time, $152 per unit part-time. Full-time tuition and fees vary according to course load. Part-time tuition and fees vary according to course load. *Required fees:* $308 full-time, $11 per unit.

Applying *Application deadline:* rolling (freshmen), rolling (transfers). *Notification:* continuous (freshmen).

Admissions Contact Ms. Joy Parker, Director of Admissions, Gavilan College, 5055 Santa Teresa Boulevard, Gilroy, CA 95020. *Phone:* 408-848-4735. *Fax:* 408-846-4910.

GLENDALE COMMUNITY COLLEGE

Glendale, California

- **State and locally supported** 2-year, founded 1927, part of California Community College System
- **Calendar** semesters
- **Degree** certificates and associate
- **Urban** 119-acre campus with easy access to Los Angeles
- **Endowment** $4.1 million
- **Coed,** 17,303 undergraduate students, 21% full-time, 60% women, 40% men

Undergraduates Students come from 19 states and territories, 68 other countries, 1% are from out of state.

Freshmen *Admission:* 7,989 admitted.

Faculty *Total:* 742, 32% full-time.

Majors Accounting; aircraft mechanic/airframe; aircraft pilot (professional); applied art; art; art history; aviation management; aviation technology; biological/physical sciences; business administration; ceramic arts; child care/development; computer engineering related; computer engineering technology; computer programming related; computer programming (specific applications); computer science; computer science related; computer software and media applications related; computer/technical support; cosmetology; culinary arts; dance; data entry/microcomputer applications; data entry/microcomputer applications related; data processing technology; desktop publishing equipment operation; drafting; education; electromechanical technology; English; fashion design/illustration; finance; fire science; foreign languages/literatures; graphic design/commercial art/illustration; hotel and restaurant management; humanities; industrial technology; journalism; law enforcement/police science; legal administrative assistant; liberal arts and sciences/liberal studies; machine technology; mass communications; mathematics; medical administrative assistant; medical assistant; medical records administration; mental health/rehabilitation; music; nursing; photography; practical nurse; real estate; recreation/leisure studies; secretarial science; social sciences; speech/rhetorical studies; theater arts/drama; welding technology.

Academic Programs *Special study options:* academic remediation for entering students, adult/continuing education programs, advanced placement credit, cooperative education, distance learning, English as a second language, honors programs, independent study, internships, part-time degree program, services for LD students, study abroad, summer session for credit.

Library Glendale Community College Library with 81,177 titles, 1,200 serial subscriptions, 430 audiovisual materials, an OPAC, a Web page.

Computers on Campus 534 computers available on campus for general student use. A campuswide network can be accessed from off campus. Internet access, online (class) registration, at least one staffed computer lab available.

Student Life *Housing:* college housing not available. *Activities and Organizations:* drama/theater group, student-run newspaper, choral group, Alpha Gamma Sigma, Armenian Student Association, Korean Christian Fellowship, Theatre Guild, International Student Association. *Campus security:* student patrols, late-night transport/escort service. *Student Services:* health clinic, personal/psychological counseling.

Athletics *Intercollegiate sports:* baseball M, basketball M/W, cross-country running M/W, football M, soccer M/W, softball W, tennis M/W, track and field M/W, volleyball W.

Costs (2002–03) *Tuition:* nonresident $3428 full-time, $130 per unit part-time. Full-time tuition and fees vary according to course load. Part-time tuition and fees vary according to course load. *Required fees:* $308 full-time, $11 per unit, $44 per year part-time. *Payment plan:* deferred payment.

Financial Aid In 2001, 300 Federal Work-Study jobs (averaging $2500).

Applying *Options:* common application, electronic application, early admission, deferred entrance. *Recommended:* high school transcript. *Application deadline:* 7/1 (freshmen), rolling (transfers).

Admissions Contact Ms. Sharon Combs, Dean, Admissions and Records, Glendale Community College, 1500 North Verdugo Road, Glendale, CA 91208. *Phone:* 818-551-5115. *Fax:* 818-551-5255. *E-mail:* prosas@glendale.cc.ca.us.

GOLDEN WEST COLLEGE
Huntington Beach, California

- **State and locally supported** 2-year, founded 1966, part of Coast Community College District System
- **Calendar** semesters
- **Degree** certificates and associate
- **Suburban** 122-acre campus with easy access to Los Angeles
- **Endowment** $880,684
- **Coed,** 13,091 undergraduate students, 32% full-time, 54% women, 46% men

Undergraduates Students come from 28 other countries.

Faculty *Total:* 440, 44% full-time. *Student/faculty ratio:* 32:1.

Majors Accounting; architectural engineering technology; art; auto mechanic/technician; biological/physical sciences; biology; business administration; business marketing and marketing management; cosmetology; criminal justice/law enforcement administration; drafting; electrical/electronic engineering technology; engineering technology; graphic design/commercial art/illustration; graphic/printing equipment; humanities; journalism; law enforcement/police science; legal administrative assistant; liberal arts and sciences/liberal studies; mathematics; music; natural sciences; nursing; ornamental horticulture; physical sciences; pre-engineering; public relations; radio/television broadcasting; real estate; retail management; secretarial science; sign language interpretation; technical/business writing; telecommunications.

Academic Programs *Special study options:* academic remediation for entering students, adult/continuing education programs, advanced placement credit, cooperative education, English as a second language, external degree program, internships, part-time degree program, student-designed majors, study abroad, summer session for credit. *ROTC:* Air Force (c).

Library Golden West College Library plus 1 other with 95,000 titles, 410 serial subscriptions, an OPAC, a Web page.

Computers on Campus 680 computers available on campus for general student use. A campuswide network can be accessed from off campus. Internet access, at least one staffed computer lab available.

Student Life *Housing:* college housing not available. *Activities and Organizations:* drama/theater group, student-run newspaper, radio station, choral group. *Campus security:* 24-hour emergency response devices and patrols, late-night transport/escort service. *Student Services:* health clinic, personal/psychological counseling, legal services.

Athletics Member NJCAA. *Intercollegiate sports:* baseball M, basketball M/W, cross-country running M/W, football M, golf M/W, soccer M/W, softball W, swimming M/W, tennis M/W, track and field M/W, volleyball M/W, water polo M/W, wrestling M.

Standardized Tests *Required for some:* ACT COMPASS. *Recommended:* ACT COMPASS.

Costs (2002–03) *One-time required fee:* $3. *Tuition:* state resident $0 full-time; nonresident $3220 full-time, $132 per unit part-time. Full-time tuition and fees vary according to course load. Part-time tuition and fees vary according to course load. *Required fees:* $312 full-time, $11 per unit, $24 per term part-time. *Payment plan:* deferred payment.

Applying *Options:* early admission. *Required for some:* essay or personal statement. *Recommended:* high school transcript. *Application deadline:* rolling (freshmen), rolling (transfers). *Notification:* continuous (freshmen).

Admissions Contact Golden West College, 15744 Golden West Street, Huntington Beach, CA 92647. *Phone:* 714-892-7711 Ext. 58196.

GROSSMONT COLLEGE
El Cajon, California

- **State and locally supported** 2-year, founded 1961, part of California Community College System
- **Calendar** semesters
- **Degree** certificates and associate
- **Suburban** 135-acre campus with easy access to San Diego
- **Coed**

Student Life *Campus security:* 24-hour emergency response devices, student patrols, late-night transport/escort service.

Athletics Member NJCAA.

Standardized Tests *Recommended:* Assessment and Placement Services for Community Colleges.

Financial Aid In 2001, 229 Federal Work-Study jobs (averaging $1752).

Applying *Options:* common application, early admission.

Admissions Contact Ms. Sharon Clark, Registrar, Grossmont College, El Cajon, CA 92020-1799. *Phone:* 619-644-7170. *Fax:* 619-644-7922.

HARTNELL COLLEGE
Salinas, California

Admissions Contact Ms. Cheri Gray, Director of Admissions, Hartnell College, 156 Homestead Avenue, Salinas, CA 93901-1697. *Phone:* 831-755-6711. *Fax:* 331-759-6014.

HEALD COLLEGE CONCORD
Concord, California

Admissions Contact Ms. Laura Kalk, Administrator, Heald College Concord, 2860 Howe Road, Martinez, CA 94553-4000. *Phone:* 925-228-9000.

HEALD COLLEGE, SCHOOL OF BUSINESS
Salinas, California

Admissions Contact Mr. Steve Coffee, Director of Admissions, Heald College, School of Business, 1450 North Main Street, Salinas, CA 93906. *Phone:* 408-443-1700. *E-mail:* steve_coffee@heald.edu.

HEALD COLLEGE, SCHOOL OF BUSINESS
Stockton, California

Admissions Contact Ms. Suzanne Mutinner, Campus Director, Heald College, School of Business, 1605 East March Lane, Stockton, CA 95210. *Phone:* 209-477-1114.

Heald College, School of Business
Santa Rosa, California

Admissions Contact Mr. Gordon Kent, Admissions Counselor, Heald College, School of Business, 100 Professional Center Drive, Santa Rosa, CA 95403-3116. *Phone:* 707-525-1300.

Heald College, School of Business
Concord, California

Admissions Contact Ms. Cindi Stevens, Director of Admissions, Heald College, School of Business, 2150 John Glenn Drive, Concord, CA 94520-5618. *Phone:* 510-827-1300. *Fax:* 510-353-2898.

Heald College, Schools of Business and Technology
Rancho Cordova, California

- **Independent** 2-year, founded 1863, part of Heald Colleges
- **Calendar** quarters
- **Degree** certificates, diplomas, and associate
- **Suburban** 1-acre campus with easy access to Sacramento
- **Coed,** 676 undergraduate students

Faculty *Total:* 41.
Majors Accounting; business administration; legal administrative assistant; medical administrative assistant; secretarial science.
Academic Programs *Special study options:* academic remediation for entering students, adult/continuing education programs, internships, summer session for credit.
Library Learning Resource Center with 8,800 titles, 87 serial subscriptions, an OPAC.
Computers on Campus 225 computers available on campus for general student use. Internet access, at least one staffed computer lab available.
Student Life *Housing:* college housing not available. *Campus security:* late-night transport/escort service.
Costs (2001–02) *Tuition:* $5700 full-time. *Required fees:* $200 full-time.
Applying *Application fee:* $50. *Required:* high school transcript, interview. *Application deadlines:* 10/15 (freshmen), 10/15 (transfers). *Notification:* continuous (freshmen).
Admissions Contact Ms. Susan Sorenson, Director of Admissions, Heald College, Schools of Business and Technology, 2910 Prospect Park Drive, Rancho Cordova, CA 95670-6005. *Phone:* 916-638-1616 Ext. 2307. *Toll-free phone:* 800-499-4333. *Fax:* 916-853-8282.

Heald College, Schools of Business and Technology
Milpitas, California

- **Independent** 2-year, founded 1863, part of Heald Colleges of California
- **Calendar** quarters
- **Degree** certificates and associate
- **Small-town** 5-acre campus with easy access to San Jose
- **Coed**

Standardized Tests *Required:* CPAt.
Costs (2001–02) *Tuition:* $2520 full-time, $1890 per year part-time. No tuition increase for student's term of enrollment.
Financial Aid In 2001, 15 Federal Work-Study jobs.
Applying *Options:* common application. *Application fee:* $50. *Required:* high school transcript, minimum 2.0 GPA, interview.
Admissions Contact Dr. Lori Hart Ebert, Associate Director, Heald College, Schools of Business and Technology, 341 Great Mall Parkway, Milpitas, CA 95035. *Phone:* 408-934-4900. *Toll-free phone:* 800-967-7576. *Fax:* 408-934-7777. *E-mail:* lori_hart@heald.edu.

Heald College, Schools of Business and Technology
San Francisco, California

Admissions Contact Mr. Rod Maulis, Director of Admissions, Heald College, Schools of Business and Technology, 350 Mission Street, San Francisco, CA 94105-2206. *Phone:* 415-822-2900. *Fax:* 415-626-1404.

Heald College, Schools of Business and Technology
Hayward, California

- **Independent** 2-year, founded 1863, part of Heald Colleges of California
- **Calendar** quarters
- **Degree** certificates, diplomas, and associate
- **Urban** campus with easy access to San Francisco
- **Coed,** 1,250 undergraduate students

Faculty *Total:* 52, 81% full-time. *Student/faculty ratio:* 20:1.
Majors Accounting; computer/information technology services administration and management related; computer management; computer programming, vendor/product certification; computer science; computer science related; legal administrative assistant; medical administrative assistant; secretarial science.
Academic Programs *Special study options:* academic remediation for entering students, adult/continuing education programs, double majors, internships.
Library Learning Resource Center (LRC) plus 1 other with 22 serial subscriptions, 2 audiovisual materials.
Computers on Campus 31 computers available on campus for general student use. Internet access available.
Student Life *Housing:* college housing not available. *Campus security:* 24-hour emergency response devices and patrols. *Student Services:* personal/psychological counseling.
Costs (2001–02) *One-time required fee:* $75. *Tuition:* $11,400 full-time. Full-time tuition and fees vary according to course load. Part-time tuition and fees vary according to course load. No tuition increase for student's term of enrollment. *Payment plan:* installment.
Applying *Application fee:* $50. *Required:* high school transcript, interview. *Required for some:* essay or personal statement, letters of recommendation. *Application deadline:* rolling (freshmen).
Admissions Contact Ms. Sheryl Valente, Director of Admissions, Heald College, Schools of Business and Technology, 25500 Industrial Boulevard, Hayward, CA 94915. *Phone:* 510-783-2100. *Fax:* 510-783-3287.

Heald College, Schools of Business and Technology
Roseville, California

Admissions Contact Ms. Jennifer Melamed, Director of Admissions, Heald College, Schools of Business and Technology, Seven Sierra Gate Plaza, Roseville, CA 95678. *Phone:* 916-789-8600 Ext. 15. *Toll-free phone:* 800-669-GRAD (in-state); 800-699-GRAD (out-of-state).

Heald College, Schools of Business and Technology
Fresno, California

Admissions Contact Ms. Jeanne Smith, Director of Admissions, Heald College, Schools of Business and Technology, 255 West Bullard Avenue, Fresno, CA 93704-1706. *Phone:* 209-438-4222.

Imperial Valley College
Imperial, California

- **State and locally supported** 2-year, founded 1922, part of California Community College System
- **Calendar** semesters
- **Degree** certificates and associate
- **Rural** 160-acre campus
- **Endowment** $832,061
- **Coed,** 7,223 undergraduate students, 35% full-time, 63% women, 37% men

Undergraduates 2,513 full-time, 4,710 part-time. Students come from 12 states and territories, 3% are from out of state, 2% African American, 2% Asian American or Pacific Islander, 86% Hispanic American, 0.2% Native American.
Freshmen *Admission:* 330 enrolled.
Faculty *Total:* 272, 34% full-time.
Majors Accounting; agricultural business; agricultural mechanization; agricultural sciences; anthropology; art; auto mechanic/technician; behavioral sciences; biological/physical sciences; business administration; business marketing and

marketing management; criminal justice/law enforcement administration; early childhood education; English; fire science; French; humanities; individual/family development; information sciences/systems; journalism; liberal arts and sciences/liberal studies; mathematics; modern languages; music; nursing; physical education; physical sciences; practical nurse; pre-engineering; psychology; secretarial science; social sciences; Spanish; water resources; welding technology.

Academic Programs *Special study options:* academic remediation for entering students, accelerated degree program, adult/continuing education programs, advanced placement credit, double majors, English as a second language, part-time degree program, services for LD students, student-designed majors, summer session for credit.

Library Spencer Library with 55,875 titles, 425 serial subscriptions, 3,383 audiovisual materials, an OPAC, a Web page.

Computers on Campus 235 computers available on campus for general student use. A campuswide network can be accessed from off campus. Internet access, at least one staffed computer lab available.

Student Life *Housing:* college housing not available. *Activities and Organizations:* drama/theater group, student-run newspaper, choral group, Student Support Services club, Pre-School Mothers, Care Club, Christian Club, Nursing Club. *Campus security:* student patrols. *Student Services:* personal/psychological counseling, women's center.

Athletics *Intercollegiate sports:* baseball M, basketball M/W, soccer M/W, softball W, tennis M/W, volleyball W.

Costs (2002–03) *Tuition:* state resident $0 full-time; nonresident $4560 full-time, $152 per unit part-time. *Required fees:* $330 full-time, $11 per unit.

Financial Aid In 2001, 378 Federal Work-Study jobs (averaging $1328). 212 State and other part-time jobs (averaging $2426).

Applying *Required for some:* high school transcript. *Recommended:* high school transcript. *Application deadline:* rolling (freshmen), rolling (transfers). *Notification:* continuous (freshmen).

Admissions Contact Mrs. Sandra Standiford, Dean of Admissions, Imperial Valley College, PO Box 158, Imperial, CA 92251. *Phone:* 760-352-8320 Ext. 200.

IRVINE VALLEY COLLEGE
Irvine, California

Admissions Contact Mr. Jess Craig, Dean of Students, Irvine Valley College, 5500 Irvine Center Drive, Irvine, CA 92620-4399. *Phone:* 949-451-5410.

ITT TECHNICAL INSTITUTE
Lathrop, California

- **Proprietary** 2-year
- **Calendar** quarters
- **Degree** associate
- **Coed**

Majors Drafting; electrical/electronic engineering technology; information sciences/systems.

Student Life *Housing:* college housing not available.

Applying *Application fee:* $100. *Required:* high school transcript, interview. *Recommended:* letters of recommendation. *Application deadline:* rolling (freshmen). *Notification:* continuous (freshmen).

Admissions Contact Mr. Don Fraser, Director of Recruitment, ITT Technical Institute, 16916 South Harlan Road, Lathrop, CA 95330. *Phone:* 209-858-0077.

ITT TECHNICAL INSTITUTE
Rancho Cordova, California

- **Proprietary** primarily 2-year, founded 1954, part of ITT Educational Services, Inc
- **Calendar** quarters
- **Degrees** associate and bachelor's
- **Urban** 5-acre campus
- **Coed,** 533 undergraduate students

Majors Computer/information sciences related; computer programming; design/visual communications; drafting; electrical/electronic engineering technologies related; electromechanical instrumentation and maintenance technologies related; information technology.

Student Life *Housing:* college housing not available.

Costs (2001–02) *Tuition:* Full-time tuition and fees vary according to program. Part-time tuition and fees vary according to program. $260—$330 per credit hour.

Applying *Options:* deferred entrance. *Application fee:* $100. *Required:* high school transcript, interview. *Recommended:* letters of recommendation. *Application deadline:* rolling (freshmen), rolling (transfers). *Notification:* continuous (freshmen).

Admissions Contact Mr. Bob Menszer, Director of Recruitment, ITT Technical Institute, 10863 Gold Center Drive, Rancho Cordova, CA 95670-6034. *Phone:* 916-851-3900. *Toll-free phone:* 800-488-8466.

ITT TECHNICAL INSTITUTE
Oxnard, California

- **Proprietary** primarily 2-year, founded 1993, part of ITT Educational Services, Inc
- **Calendar** quarters
- **Degrees** associate and bachelor's
- **Urban** campus with easy access to Los Angeles
- **Coed,** 549 undergraduate students

Faculty *Total:* 22, 73% full-time.

Majors Computer programming; drafting; electrical/electronic engineering technologies related; electrical/electronic engineering technology; information technology.

Library Learning Resource Center plus 1 other with 877 titles, 71 serial subscriptions.

Computers on Campus 12 computers available on campus for general student use. Internet access, at least one staffed computer lab available.

Student Life *Housing:* college housing not available. *Campus security:* 24-hour emergency response devices and patrols.

Costs (2001–02) *Tuition:* Full-time tuition and fees vary according to program. Part-time tuition and fees vary according to program. $260—$330 per credit hour.

Applying *Options:* deferred entrance. *Application fee:* $100. *Required:* high school transcript, letters of recommendation, interview. *Recommended:* minimum 2.0 GPA. *Application deadline:* rolling (freshmen), rolling (transfers).

Admissions Contact Ms. Lorraine Bunt, Director of Recruitment, ITT Technical Institute, 2051 Solar Drive, Suite 150, Oxnard, CA 93030. *Phone:* 805-988-0143 Ext. 112. *Toll-free phone:* 800-530-1582. *Fax:* 805-988-1813.

ITT TECHNICAL INSTITUTE
Torrance, California

- **Proprietary** 2-year, founded 1987, part of ITT Educational Services, Inc
- **Calendar** quarters
- **Degree** associate
- **Urban** campus with easy access to Los Angeles
- **Coed,** 562 undergraduate students

Majors Computer/information sciences related; computer programming; drafting; electrical/electronic engineering technologies related; information technology.

Computers on Campus At least one staffed computer lab available.

Student Life *Housing:* college housing not available.

Costs (2001–02) *Tuition:* Full-time tuition and fees vary according to program. Part-time tuition and fees vary according to program. $260—$330 per credit hour.

Financial Aid In 2001, 6 Federal Work-Study jobs (averaging $4000).

Applying *Options:* deferred entrance. *Application fee:* $100. *Required:* high school transcript, interview. *Recommended:* letters of recommendation. *Application deadline:* rolling (freshmen), rolling (transfers). *Notification:* continuous (freshmen).

Admissions Contact Mr. Freddie Polk, Director of Recruitment, ITT Technical Institute, 20050 South Vermont Avenue, Torrance, CA 90502. *Phone:* 310-380-1555.

ITT TECHNICAL INSTITUTE
San Bernardino, California

- **Proprietary** primarily 2-year, founded 1987, part of ITT Educational Services, Inc
- **Calendar** quarters
- **Degrees** associate and bachelor's
- **Urban** campus with easy access to Los Angeles

ITT Technical Institute (continued)
- **Coed,** 862 undergraduate students

Majors Computer/information sciences related; computer programming; drafting; electrical/electronic engineering technologies related; industrial design; information technology.
Student Life *Housing:* college housing not available.
Costs (2001–02) *Tuition:* Full-time tuition and fees vary according to program. Part-time tuition and fees vary according to program. $260—$330 per credit hour.
Applying *Options:* deferred entrance. *Application fee:* $100. *Required:* high school transcript, interview. *Recommended:* letters of recommendation. *Application deadline:* rolling (freshmen), rolling (transfers). *Notification:* continuous (freshmen).
Admissions Contact Ms. Maria Alamat, Director of Recruitment, ITT Technical Institute, 630 E Brier Drive, San Bernardino, CA 92408. *Phone:* 909-889-3800 Ext. 11. *Toll-free phone:* 800-888-3801. *Fax:* 909-888-6970.

ITT Technical Institute
Anaheim, California

- **Proprietary** primarily 2-year, founded 1982, part of ITT Educational Services, Inc
- **Calendar** quarters
- **Degrees** associate and bachelor's
- **Suburban** 5-acre campus with easy access to Los Angeles
- **Coed,** 691 undergraduate students

Majors Computer/information sciences related; computer programming; drafting; electrical/electronic engineering technologies related; information technology.
Student Life *Housing:* college housing not available. *Activities and Organizations:* student-run newspaper.
Costs (2001–02) *Tuition:* Full-time tuition and fees vary according to program. Part-time tuition and fees vary according to program. $260—$330 per credit hour.
Applying *Options:* deferred entrance. *Application fee:* $100. *Required:* high school transcript, interview. *Recommended:* letters of recommendation. *Application deadline:* rolling (freshmen), rolling (transfers). *Notification:* continuous (freshmen).
Admissions Contact Mr. Ramon Abreu, Director of Recruitment, ITT Technical Institute, 525 North Muller Avenue, Anaheim, CA 92801. *Phone:* 714-535-3700.

ITT Technical Institute
San Diego, California

- **Proprietary** primarily 2-year, founded 1981, part of ITT Educational Services, Inc
- **Calendar** quarters
- **Degrees** associate and bachelor's
- **Suburban** campus
- **Coed,** 885 undergraduate students

Majors Computer/information sciences related; computer programming; data processing technology; drafting; electrical/electronic engineering technologies related.
Student Life *Housing:* college housing not available.
Costs (2001–02) *Tuition:* Full-time tuition and fees vary according to program. Part-time tuition and fees vary according to program. $260—$330 per credit hour.
Applying *Options:* deferred entrance. *Application fee:* $100. *Required:* high school transcript, interview. *Recommended:* letters of recommendation. *Application deadline:* rolling (freshmen), rolling (transfers). *Notification:* continuous (freshmen).
Admissions Contact Ms. Sheryl Schulgen, Director of Recruitment, ITT Technical Institute, 9680 Granite Ridge Drive, Suite 100, San Diego, CA 92123. *Phone:* 858-571-8500.

ITT Technical Institute
Sylmar, California

- **Proprietary** primarily 2-year, founded 1982, part of ITT Educational Services, Inc
- **Calendar** quarters
- **Degrees** associate and bachelor's
- **Urban** campus with easy access to Los Angeles
- **Coed,** 715 undergraduate students

Majors Computer/information sciences related; computer programming; design/applied arts related; drafting; electrical/electronic engineering technologies related; information technology.
Student Life *Housing:* college housing not available.
Costs (2001–02) *Tuition:* Full-time tuition and fees vary according to program. Part-time tuition and fees vary according to program. $260—$330 per credit hour.
Applying *Options:* deferred entrance. *Application fee:* $100. *Required:* high school transcript, interview. *Recommended:* letters of recommendation. *Application deadline:* rolling (freshmen), rolling (transfers). *Notification:* continuous (freshmen).
Admissions Contact Mr. Albert Naranjo, Director of Recruitment, ITT Technical Institute, 12669 Encinitas Avenue, Sylmar, CA 91342-3664. *Phone:* 818-364-5151. *Toll-free phone:* 800-363-2086.

ITT Technical Institute
West Covina, California

- **Proprietary** primarily 2-year, founded 1982, part of ITT Educational Services, Inc
- **Calendar** quarters
- **Degrees** associate and bachelor's
- **Suburban** 4-acre campus with easy access to Los Angeles
- **Coed**

Majors Computer/information sciences related; computer programming; drafting; electrical/electronic engineering technologies related; information technology; robotics technology.
Student Life *Housing:* college housing not available.
Costs (2001–02) *Tuition:* Full-time tuition and fees vary according to program. Part-time tuition and fees vary according to program. $260—$330 per credit hour.
Financial Aid In 2001, 20 Federal Work-Study jobs (averaging $4500).
Applying *Options:* deferred entrance. *Application fee:* $100. *Required:* high school transcript, interview. *Recommended:* letters of recommendation. *Application deadline:* rolling (freshmen), rolling (transfers). *Notification:* continuous (freshmen).
Admissions Contact Mr. John Drinkall, Director of Recruitment, ITT Technical Institute, 1530 West Cameron Avenue, West Covina, CA 91790-2711. *Phone:* 626-960-8681. *Toll-free phone:* 800-414-6522. *Fax:* 626-330-5271.

ITT Technical Institute
Hayward, California

- **Proprietary** primarily 2-year, founded 1994, part of ITT Educational Services, Inc
- **Calendar** quarters
- **Degrees** associate and bachelor's
- 286 undergraduate students

Majors Computer/information sciences related; computer programming; electrical/electronic engineering technologies related; electrical/electronic engineering technology; information technology.
Student Life *Housing:* college housing not available.
Costs (2001–02) *Tuition:* Full-time tuition and fees vary according to program. Part-time tuition and fees vary according to program. $260—$330 per credit hour.
Financial Aid In 2001, 20 Federal Work-Study jobs.
Applying *Options:* deferred entrance. *Application fee:* $100. *Required:* high school transcript, interview. *Recommended:* letters of recommendation. *Application deadline:* rolling (freshmen), rolling (transfers).
Admissions Contact Ms. Kathleen Paradis, Director of Recruitment, ITT Technical Institute, 3979 Trust Way, Hayward, CA 94545. *Phone:* 510-785-8522.

ITT Technical Institute
Santa Clara, California

- **Proprietary** 2-year, founded 1994, part of ITT Educational Services, Inc
- **Calendar** quarters
- **Degree** associate
- 208 undergraduate students

Majors Computer/information sciences related; computer programming; electrical/electronic engineering technologies related; information technology.
Student Life *Housing:* college housing not available.
Costs (2001–02) *Tuition:* Full-time tuition and fees vary according to program. Part-time tuition and fees vary according to program. $260—$330 per credit hour.
Applying *Options:* deferred entrance. *Application fee:* $100. *Required:* high school transcript, interview. *Recommended:* letters of recommendation. *Application deadline:* rolling (freshmen), rolling (transfers).
Admissions Contact Ms. Sue Schmith, Director, ITT Technical Institute, 5104 Old Ironsides Drive, Santa Clara, CA 95050. *Phone:* 408-496-0655.

LAKE TAHOE COMMUNITY COLLEGE
South Lake Tahoe, California

- **State and locally supported** 2-year, founded 1975, part of California Community College System
- **Calendar** quarters
- **Degree** associate
- **Small-town** 164-acre campus
- **Coed,** 3,400 undergraduate students

Undergraduates 0.8% African American, 3% Asian American or Pacific Islander, 8% Hispanic American, 1% Native American, 0.1% international.
Faculty *Total:* 200, 25% full-time.
Majors Accounting; art; biological/physical sciences; business administration; business marketing and marketing management; computer science; criminal justice/law enforcement administration; dance; early childhood education; finance; fire science; hotel and restaurant management; humanities; law enforcement/police science; liberal arts and sciences/liberal studies; mathematics; medical administrative assistant; medical assistant; music; natural sciences; physical education; psychology; real estate; secretarial science; social sciences; Spanish; theater arts/drama.
Academic Programs *Special study options:* academic remediation for entering students, cooperative education, double majors, English as a second language, internships, part-time degree program, services for LD students, summer session for credit.
Library Lake Tahoe Community College Library with 38,950 titles, 382 serial subscriptions, an OPAC.
Computers on Campus 135 computers available on campus for general student use. At least one staffed computer lab available.
Student Life *Housing:* college housing not available. *Activities and Organizations:* drama/theater group, choral group, Associated Student Council, Alpha Gamma Sigma, Foreign Language Club, Art Club, Performing Arts League. *Campus security:* 24-hour emergency response devices, late-night transport/escort service. *Student Services:* personal/psychological counseling.
Athletics *Intercollegiate sports:* skiing (cross-country) M/W, volleyball W.
Costs (2001–02) *Tuition:* state resident $0 full-time; nonresident $3540 full-time, $35 per credit part-time. Full-time tuition and fees vary according to location and reciprocity agreements. Part-time tuition and fees vary according to location and reciprocity agreements. *Required fees:* $327 full-time, $7 per credit.
Financial Aid In 2001, 15 Federal Work-Study jobs (averaging $1500).
Applying *Options:* early admission. *Required for some:* high school transcript. *Application deadline:* rolling (freshmen), rolling (transfers). *Notification:* continuous (freshmen).
Admissions Contact Ms. Linda M. Stevenson, Director of Admissions and Records, Lake Tahoe Community College, One College Drive, South Lake Tahoe, CA 96150-4524. *Phone:* 530-541-4660 Ext. 282. *Fax:* 530-541-7852.

LANEY COLLEGE
Oakland, California

- **State and locally supported** 2-year, founded 1953, part of Peralta Community College District System
- **Calendar** semesters
- **Degree** certificates and associate
- **Urban** campus with easy access to San Francisco
- **Coed**

Laney College, in the heart of downtown Oakland, has long been a leader in vocational and university transfer education. With dozens of degree and certificate programs, Laney is one of the premier community colleges in northern California. Diverse and vibrant, Laney is a terrific place for students to get started on their futures.

Costs (2001–02) *Tuition:* nonresident $164 per unit part-time. *Required fees:* $11 per unit.
Applying *Options:* early admission.
Admissions Contact Mrs. Barbara Simmons, District Admissions Officer, Laney College, 900 Fallon Street, Oakland, CA 94607-4893. *Phone:* 510-466-7369.

LAS POSITAS COLLEGE
Livermore, California

- **State-supported** 2-year, founded 1988, part of California Community College System
- **Calendar** semesters
- **Degree** certificates, diplomas, and associate
- **Suburban** 150-acre campus with easy access to Oakland and San Francisco
- **Coed,** 8,044 undergraduate students

Majors Accounting; auto mechanic/technician; business administration; business marketing and marketing management; computer science; drafting; early childhood education; education; electrical/electronic engineering technology; environmental science; fashion merchandising; fire science; horticulture science; industrial design; industrial radiologic technology; information sciences/systems; interior design; law enforcement/police science; liberal arts and sciences/liberal studies; occupational safety/health technology; real estate; secretarial science; welding technology.
Academic Programs *Special study options:* academic remediation for entering students, advanced placement credit, English as a second language, internships, part-time degree program, services for LD students, student-designed majors, summer session for credit.
Library Learning Resource Center.
Computers on Campus Internet access, at least one staffed computer lab available.
Student Life *Housing:* college housing not available. *Activities and Organizations:* drama/theater group, student-run newspaper, choral group. *Campus security:* 24-hour emergency response devices, late-night transport/escort service. *Student Services:* health clinic, personal/psychological counseling.
Athletics *Intercollegiate sports:* cross-country running M/W, soccer M/W. *Intramural sports:* basketball M/W, fencing M/W, racquetball M/W, soccer M/W, softball M/W, volleyball M/W.
Standardized Tests *Required:* institutional placement tests.
Costs (2002–03) *Tuition:* state resident $0 full-time; nonresident $3432 full-time, $143 per unit part-time. *Required fees:* $11 per unit.
Financial Aid In 2001, 26 Federal Work-Study jobs (averaging $1500).
Applying *Recommended:* high school transcript.
Admissions Contact Mrs. Sylvia R. Rodriguez, Director of Admissions and Records, Las Positas College, 3033 Collier Canyon Road, Livermore, CA 94550-7650. *Phone:* 925-373-4942.

LASSEN COMMUNITY COLLEGE DISTRICT
Susanville, California

Admissions Contact Mr. Chris J. Alberico, Registrar, Lassen Community College District, Highway 139, PO Box 3000, Susanville, CA 96130. *Phone:* 530-257-6181 Ext. 132.

LONG BEACH CITY COLLEGE
Long Beach, California

- **State-supported** 2-year, founded 1927, part of California Community College System
- **Calendar** semesters
- **Degree** certificates and associate
- **Urban** 40-acre campus with easy access to Los Angeles
- **Coed,** 28,000 undergraduate students

Undergraduates 20% African American, 10% Asian American or Pacific Islander, 20% Hispanic American, 1% Native American, 17% international.
Freshmen *Admission:* 5,632 applied, 5,632 admitted.
Faculty *Total:* 1,800.
Majors Accounting; advertising; aircraft pilot (professional); architectural engineering technology; art; auto mechanic/technician; aviation management; aviation technology; biology; business administration; business marketing and

Long Beach City College (continued)
marketing management; carpentry; computer programming; computer typography/composition; criminal justice/law enforcement administration; culinary arts; dance; data processing technology; developmental/child psychology; dietetics; drafting; early childhood education; electrical/electronic engineering technology; engineering; English; family/consumer studies; fashion design/illustration; fashion merchandising; film studies; fire science; food products retailing; food services technology; French; German; heating/air conditioning/refrigeration; heavy equipment maintenance; home economics; horticulture science; hotel and restaurant management; human services; industrial arts; industrial radiologic technology; industrial technology; interior design; international business; journalism; legal administrative assistant; liberal arts and sciences/liberal studies; machine technology; mathematics; medical administrative assistant; medical assistant; music; nursing; ornamental horticulture; photography; physical education; physical sciences; pre-engineering; radio/television broadcasting; real estate; retail management; secretarial science; social sciences; Spanish; speech/rhetorical studies; theater arts/drama; travel/tourism management; welding technology.

Academic Programs *Special study options:* academic remediation for entering students, adult/continuing education programs, advanced placement credit, distance learning, English as a second language, honors programs, internships, part-time degree program, services for LD students, summer session for credit.

Library Long Beach City College Library plus 1 other with 151,367 titles, 471 serial subscriptions, 3,150 audiovisual materials, an OPAC, a Web page.

Computers on Campus 200 computers available on campus for general student use. At least one staffed computer lab available.

Student Life *Housing:* college housing not available. *Activities and Organizations:* drama/theater group, student-run newspaper, radio and television station, choral group, American Criminal Justice Association, AGS Scholarship Organization, American Association of Future Firefighters, Vietnamese Club, Network Christian Fellowship. *Campus security:* 24-hour emergency response devices and patrols, student patrols, late-night transport/escort service. *Student Services:* health clinic, personal/psychological counseling, women's center, legal services.

Athletics Member NJCAA. *Intercollegiate sports:* badminton M/W, baseball M, basketball M/W, cross-country running M/W, football M, golf M/W, soccer M/W, softball W, swimming M/W, tennis M/W, track and field M/W, volleyball M/W, water polo M/W. *Intramural sports:* archery M/W, basketball M/W, bowling M/W, football M/W, golf M/W, racquetball M/W, soccer M/W, softball M/W, swimming M/W, tennis M/W, track and field M/W, volleyball M/W, weight lifting M, wrestling M.

Costs (2002–03) *Tuition:* state resident $0 full-time; nonresident $3408 full-time, $142 per unit part-time. *Required fees:* $318 full-time, $11 per unit, $27 per term part-time.

Financial Aid In 2001, 275 Federal Work-Study jobs (averaging $4400). 225 State and other part-time jobs (averaging $4400).

Applying *Options:* early admission. *Recommended:* high school transcript. *Application deadline:* rolling (freshmen).

Admissions Contact Mr. Ross Miyashiro, Dean of Admissions and Records, Long Beach City College, 4901 East Carson Boulevard, Long Beach, CA 90800. *Phone:* 562-938-4130. *Fax:* 562-938-4118.

Los Angeles City College
Los Angeles, California

- **District-supported** 2-year, founded 1929, part of Los Angeles Community College District System
- **Calendar** semesters
- **Degree** certificates and associate
- **Urban** 42-acre campus
- **Coed,** 24,652 undergraduate students

Undergraduates Students come from 52 states and territories, 36 other countries.

Faculty *Total:* 625, 32% full-time.

Majors Accounting; advertising; African-American studies; American studies; applied art; architectural engineering technology; art; biological/physical sciences; biology; broadcast journalism; business administration; business marketing and marketing management; ceramic arts; chemistry; child care/development; clothing/textiles; computer engineering technology; computer/information systems security; computer/information technology services administration and management related; computer programming; computer programming related; computer programming (specific applications); computer programming, vendor/product certification; computer science related; computer software and media applications related; computer systems networking/telecommunications; computer/technical support; corrections; criminal justice/law enforcement administration; data entry/microcomputer applications; data entry/microcomputer applications related; data processing technology; dental hygiene; developmental/child psychology; dietetics; drafting; electrical/electronic engineering technology; engineering; English; family/consumer studies; finance; food products retailing; food sciences; food services technology; French; German; history; home economics; human services; industrial radiologic technology; information technology; journalism; law enforcement/police science; legal administrative assistant; liberal arts and sciences/liberal studies; mass communications; mathematics; medical administrative assistant; mental health/rehabilitation; Mexican-American studies; music; nuclear medical technology; optometric/ophthalmic laboratory technician; photography; physics; psychology; public administration; public relations; radiological science; radio/television broadcasting; real estate; retail management; secretarial science; sociology; Spanish; speech/rhetorical studies; system administration; system/networking/LAN/WAN management; teacher assistant/aide; telecommunications; theater arts/drama; travel/tourism management; Web/multimedia management/webmaster; Web page, digital/multimedia and information resources design; word processing.

Academic Programs *Special study options:* academic remediation for entering students, adult/continuing education programs, advanced placement credit, English as a second language, honors programs, part-time degree program, services for LD students, study abroad, summer session for credit. *ROTC:* Army (c), Air Force (c).

Library 150,000 titles, 150 serial subscriptions.

Computers on Campus 200 computers available on campus for general student use. A campuswide network can be accessed from off campus that provide access to telephone registration. Internet access, online (class) registration, at least one staffed computer lab available.

Student Life *Housing:* college housing not available. *Activities and Organizations:* drama/theater group, student-run newspaper, choral group, marching band. *Campus security:* 24-hour emergency response devices and patrols, student patrols, late-night transport/escort service. *Student Services:* health clinic, personal/psychological counseling.

Athletics *Intercollegiate sports:* basketball M, cross-country running M, football M, gymnastics M, track and field M/W, volleyball M/W. *Intramural sports:* archery M/W, badminton M/W, basketball W, bowling M/W, golf M/W, gymnastics W, soccer M/W, swimming M/W, table tennis M/W, tennis M/W, weight lifting M/W, wrestling M.

Standardized Tests *Required:* in-house test.

Costs (2002–03) *Tuition:* nonresident $141 per unit part-time. *Required fees:* $11 per unit. *Payment plan:* deferred payment.

Applying *Application deadlines:* 9/5 (freshmen), 9/5 (transfers). *Notification:* continuous until 9/5 (freshmen).

Admissions Contact Elaine Geismar, Director of Student Assistance Center, Los Angeles City College, 855 North Vermont Avenue, Los Angeles, CA 90029. *Phone:* 323-953-4340. *Fax:* 323-953-4536.

Los Angeles County College of Nursing and Allied Health
Los Angeles, California

Admissions Contact Los Angeles County College of Nursing and Allied Health, 1200 N State St, Muir Hall, Rm 114, Los Angeles, CA 90033-1084.

Los Angeles Harbor College
Wilmington, California

- **State and locally supported** 2-year, founded 1949, part of Los Angeles Community College District System
- **Calendar** semesters
- **Degree** certificates and associate
- **Suburban** 80-acre campus
- **Coed,** 7,467 undergraduate students, 25% full-time, 61% women, 39% men

Undergraduates 1,867 full-time, 5,600 part-time. Students come from 14 states and territories, 16 other countries. *Retention:* 20% of 2001 full-time freshmen returned.

Freshmen *Admission:* 1,537 applied, 1,537 admitted, 2,164 enrolled. *Average high school GPA:* 2.50.

Faculty *Total:* 270, 41% full-time. *Student/faculty ratio:* 40:1.

Majors Accounting; architectural engineering technology; auto mechanic/technician; biology; business administration; computer engineering technology; data processing technology; developmental/child psychology; drafting; electrical/electronic engineering technology; electromechanical technology; engineering technology; fire science; information sciences/systems; law enforcement/police science; legal administrative assistant; liberal arts and sciences/liberal studies; medical administrative assistant; nursing; physics; pre-engineering; real estate; secretarial science.

Academic Programs *Special study options:* academic remediation for entering students, adult/continuing education programs, advanced placement credit, cooperative education, distance learning, double majors, English as a second language, external degree program, freshman honors college, honors programs, independent study, off-campus study, part-time degree program, services for LD students, study abroad, summer session for credit.

Library Harbor College Library with 82,790 titles, 302 serial subscriptions, an OPAC, a Web page.

Computers on Campus 250 computers available on campus for general student use. A campuswide network can be accessed from off campus. Internet access, online (class) registration, at least one staffed computer lab available.

Student Life *Housing:* college housing not available. *Activities and Organizations:* drama/theater group, student-run radio and television station, choral group, Alpha Gamma Sigma, Abilities Unlimited, Students in Free Enterprise, Association of Future Firefighters. *Campus security:* 24-hour emergency response devices and patrols. *Student Services:* health clinic, personal/psychological counseling, legal services.

Athletics *Intercollegiate sports:* baseball M, basketball M/W, football M, golf M, soccer M, tennis W, volleyball W.

Costs (2002–03) *Tuition:* state resident $0 full-time; nonresident $3502 full-time, $154 per unit part-time. *Required fees:* $310 full-time, $11 per unit, $24 per year part-time. *Waivers:* employees or children of employees.

Financial Aid In 2001, 105 Federal Work-Study jobs (averaging $1800).

Applying *Options:* early admission, deferred entrance. *Required for some:* essay or personal statement, high school transcript. *Application deadlines:* 9/3 (freshmen), 9/3 (transfers).

Admissions Contact Mr. David Ching, Dean of Admissions and Records, Los Angeles Harbor College, 1111 Figueroa Place, Wilmington, CA 90744-2397. *Phone:* 310-522-8318. *Fax:* 310-834-1882.

LOS ANGELES MISSION COLLEGE

Sylmar, California

- **State and locally supported** 2-year, founded 1974, part of Los Angeles Community College District System
- **Calendar** semesters
- **Degree** associate
- **Small-town** 22-acre campus with easy access to Los Angeles
- **Coed,** 7,617 undergraduate students

Undergraduates Students come from 8 other countries.

Faculty *Total:* 270, 31% full-time. *Student/faculty ratio:* 33:1.

Majors Accounting; art education; aviation technology; biology; business administration; chemistry; computer programming; consumer services; culinary arts; developmental/child psychology; economics; English; family/consumer studies; finance; French; geography; health education; history; home economics education; humanities; Italian; journalism; law enforcement/police science; liberal arts and sciences/liberal studies; mathematics; music; philosophy; physical education; physical sciences; psychology; real estate; secretarial science; social sciences; sociology; Spanish; speech/rhetorical studies; teacher assistant/aide; theater arts/drama.

Academic Programs *Special study options:* academic remediation for entering students, adult/continuing education programs, advanced placement credit, cooperative education, English as a second language, external degree program, part-time degree program, services for LD students, summer session for credit.

Library Los Angeles Mission College with 40,000 titles, 450 serial subscriptions, an OPAC, a Web page.

Computers on Campus 103 computers available on campus for general student use. Internet access, at least one staffed computer lab available.

Student Life *Housing:* college housing not available. *Activities and Organizations:* drama/theater group, student-run newspaper. *Campus security:* 24-hour emergency response devices and patrols, student patrols. *Student Services:* personal/psychological counseling, women's center.

Standardized Tests *Required:* in-house English and math placement tests.

Costs (2002–03) *Tuition:* nonresident $128 per unit part-time. *Required fees:* $132 full-time, $11 per unit.

Financial Aid In 2001, 30 Federal Work-Study jobs (averaging $3000).

Applying *Options:* early admission. *Notification:* continuous until 9/25 (freshmen).

Admissions Contact Ms. Angela Merrill, Admissions Supervisor, Los Angeles Mission College, 13356 Eldridge Avenue, Sylmar, CA 91342-3245. *Phone:* 818-364-7658.

LOS ANGELES PIERCE COLLEGE

Woodland Hills, California

- **State and locally supported** 2-year, founded 1947, part of Los Angeles Community College District System
- **Calendar** semesters
- **Degree** certificates and associate
- **Suburban** 425-acre campus with easy access to Los Angeles
- **Coed,** 18,260 undergraduate students

Undergraduates Students come from 2 states and territories, 48 other countries.

Freshmen *Admission:* 27,981 applied, 27,981 admitted.

Faculty *Total:* 800.

Majors Accounting; agricultural sciences; animal sciences; architectural engineering technology; art; auto mechanic/technician; computer engineering technology; computer programming; computer science; construction technology; data processing technology; drafting; electrical/electronic engineering technology; equestrian studies; horticulture science; industrial arts; industrial technology; journalism; landscape architecture; landscaping management; liberal arts and sciences/liberal studies; machine technology; music; nursing; ornamental horticulture; photography; plant protection; pre-engineering; quality control technology; real estate; sign language interpretation; theater arts/drama; veterinary technology; welding technology.

Academic Programs *Special study options:* academic remediation for entering students, adult/continuing education programs, advanced placement credit, cooperative education, distance learning, English as a second language, honors programs, independent study, internships, part-time degree program, services for LD students, study abroad, summer session for credit.

Library Pierce College Library plus 1 other with 106,122 titles, 395 serial subscriptions.

Computers on Campus 60 computers available on campus for general student use. At least one staffed computer lab available.

Student Life *Housing:* college housing not available. *Activities and Organizations:* drama/theater group, student-run newspaper, choral group, Alpha Gamma Sigma, Club Latino United for Education, United African-American Student Association, Hillel Club, Filipino Club. *Campus security:* 24-hour patrols, late-night transport/escort service. *Student Services:* health clinic, personal/psychological counseling, women's center.

Athletics Member NJCAA. *Intercollegiate sports:* baseball M, basketball W, football M, softball W, swimming M/W, tennis M/W, volleyball M/W, water polo M. *Intramural sports:* cross-country running M/W, equestrian sports M/W, fencing M/W, golf M/W, racquetball M/W, skiing (downhill) M/W, soccer M/W, swimming M/W, tennis M/W, volleyball M/W, weight lifting M/W.

Costs (2002–03) *Tuition:* nonresident $141 per unit part-time. *Required fees:* $11 per unit.

Financial Aid In 2001, 110 Federal Work-Study jobs (averaging $3000). 22 State and other part-time jobs (averaging $3000).

Applying *Options:* common application, electronic application, early admission. *Application deadline:* 8/20 (freshmen).

Admissions Contact Ms. Shelley L. Gerstl, Dean of Admissions and Records, Los Angeles Pierce College, 6201 Winnetka Avenue, Woodland Hills, CA 91371-0001. *Phone:* 818-719-6448.

LOS ANGELES SOUTHWEST COLLEGE

Los Angeles, California

Admissions Contact Los Angeles Southwest College, 1600 West Imperial Highway, Los Angeles, CA 90047-4810. *Phone:* 323-241-5279.

LOS ANGELES TRADE-TECHNICAL COLLEGE

Los Angeles, California

Admissions Contact Ms. Merilyn Abel, Associate Dean of Admissions and Records, Los Angeles Trade-Technical College, 400 West Washington Boulevard, Los Angeles, CA 90015-4108. *Phone:* 213-744-9420.

Los Angeles Valley College

Valley Glen, California

- **State and locally supported** 2-year, founded 1949, part of Los Angeles Community College District System
- **Calendar** semesters
- **Degree** certificates and associate
- **Suburban** 105-acre campus
- **Endowment** $120,000
- **Coed**

Faculty *Student/faculty ratio:* 35:1.

Student Life *Campus security:* 24-hour emergency response devices and patrols, student patrols, late-night transport/escort service.

Standardized Tests *Required:* ACT (for placement).

Costs (2001–02) *Tuition:* nonresident $2920 full-time, $130 per unit part-time. Full-time tuition and fees vary according to class time, class time, course load, degree level, location, and student level. Part-time tuition and fees vary according to class time, class time, course load, degree level, location, and student level. *Required fees:* $39 full-time, $11 per unit, $39 per term part-time.

Financial Aid In 2001, 55 Federal Work-Study jobs (averaging $3000).

Applying *Options:* common application, electronic application, early admission. *Recommended:* high school transcript.

Admissions Contact Ms. Yasmin Delahoussaye, Vice President of Student Services, Los Angeles Valley College, 5800 Fulton Avenue, Valley Glen, CA 91401. *Phone:* 818-947-2671. *Toll-free phone:* 818-947-2600. *Fax:* 818-785-4672.

Los Medanos College

Pittsburg, California

Admissions Contact Mrs. Gail Newman, Director of Admissions and Records, Los Medanos College, 2700 East Leland Road, Pittsburg, CA 94565-5197. *Phone:* 925-439-2181 Ext. 3250.

Maric College

San Diego, California

- **Proprietary** 2-year, founded 1976
- **Calendar** semesters
- **Degree** certificates and associate
- **Urban** 4-acre campus
- **Coed,** 900 undergraduate students

Faculty *Total:* 65, 69% full-time.

Majors Nursing.

Academic Programs *Special study options:* academic remediation for entering students, adult/continuing education programs, internships, summer session for credit.

Library Student Resource Center.

Computers on Campus 100 computers available on campus for general student use. At least one staffed computer lab available.

Student Life *Housing:* college housing not available. *Campus security:* 24-hour patrols.

Costs (2001–02) *Tuition:* $8900-$29,000 depending on degree program.

Applying *Options:* common application. *Required:* essay or personal statement, high school transcript, interview. *Notification:* continuous (freshmen).

Admissions Contact Admissions, Maric College, 3666 Kearny Villa Road, San Diego, CA 92123-1995. *Phone:* 858-654-3601.

Marymount College, Palos Verdes, California

Rancho Palos Verdes, California

- **Independent Roman Catholic** 2-year, founded 1932
- **Calendar** semesters
- **Degree** associate
- **Suburban** 26-acre campus with easy access to Los Angeles
- **Coed,** 790 undergraduate students, 86% full-time, 49% women, 51% men

Undergraduates 683 full-time, 107 part-time. Students come from 26 states and territories, 40 other countries, 48% live on campus. *Retention:* 53% of 2001 full-time freshmen returned.

Freshmen *Admission:* 1,051 applied, 783 admitted, 385 enrolled. *Average high school GPA:* 2.63. *Test scores:* SAT verbal scores over 500: 15%; SAT math scores over 500: 30%; SAT verbal scores over 600: 5%; SAT math scores over 600: 10%.

Faculty *Total:* 91, 46% full-time, 35% with terminal degrees. *Student/faculty ratio:* 16:1.

Majors Liberal arts and sciences/liberal studies.

Academic Programs *Special study options:* academic remediation for entering students, adult/continuing education programs, advanced placement credit, English as a second language, honors programs, independent study, internships, part-time degree program, services for LD students, study abroad, summer session for credit.

Library College Library plus 1 other with 42,104 titles, 328 serial subscriptions, 400 audiovisual materials, an OPAC.

Computers on Campus 60 computers available on campus for general student use. Internet access, at least one staffed computer lab available.

Student Life *Housing Options:* coed. *Activities and Organizations:* drama/theater group, student-run newspaper, choral group, Socratic Circle, Hawaii Club, Ski Club, African-American Student Union, MOVE (Marymount Opportunities for Volunteer Experiences). *Campus security:* 24-hour patrols, late-night transport/escort service, controlled dormitory access. *Student Services:* health clinic, personal/psychological counseling.

Athletics Member NJCAA. *Intercollegiate sports:* golf M/W, tennis M(s)/W(s). *Intramural sports:* archery M, basketball M/W, golf M/W, soccer M/W, softball M/W, swimming M/W, tennis M/W, volleyball M/W.

Standardized Tests *Recommended:* SAT I or ACT (for admission).

Costs (2002–03) *Comprehensive fee:* $24,400 includes full-time tuition ($16,300) and room and board ($8100). Full-time tuition and fees vary according to program. Part-time tuition: $700 per credit. Part-time tuition and fees vary according to program. *Payment plan:* installment. *Waivers:* employees or children of employees.

Financial Aid In 2001, 40 Federal Work-Study jobs (averaging $1500).

Applying *Options:* common application, electronic application, early admission. *Application fee:* $35. *Required:* high school transcript. *Required for some:* essay or personal statement, letters of recommendation, interview. *Recommended:* minimum 2.0 GPA. *Application deadlines:* 8/15 (freshmen), 8/15 (transfers). *Notification:* continuous until 9/1 (freshmen).

Admissions Contact Ms. Nina Lococo, Dean of Admission and School Relations, Marymount College, Palos Verdes, California, 30800 Palos Verdes Drive East, Rancho Palos Verdes, CA 90815. *Phone:* 310-377-5501 Ext. 182. *Fax:* 310-265-0962. *E-mail:* admissions@marymountpv.edu.

Mendocino College

Ukiah, California

- **State and locally supported** 2-year, founded 1973, part of California Community College System
- **Calendar** semesters
- **Degree** certificates and associate
- **Rural** 127-acre campus
- **Coed**

Student Life *Campus security:* late-night transport/escort service, security patrols 6 p.m. to 10 p.m.

Standardized Tests *Required for some:* CPT. *Recommended:* SAT I or ACT (for placement).

Financial Aid *Financial aid deadline:* 5/20.

Applying *Options:* early admission, deferred entrance.

Admissions Contact Ms. Kristie A. Taylor, Director of Admissions and Records, Mendocino College, PO Box 3000, Ukiah, CA 95482-0300. *Phone:* 707-468-3103. *E-mail:* ktaylor@mendocino.cc.ca.us.

Merced College

Merced, California

- **State and locally supported** 2-year, founded 1962, part of California Community College System
- **Calendar** semesters
- **Degree** associate
- **Small-town** 168-acre campus
- **Endowment** $1.0 million

■ **Coed,** 9,024 undergraduate students, 37% full-time, 60% women, 40% men

Undergraduates Students come from 30 states and territories.
Freshmen *Admission:* 421 applied.
Faculty *Total:* 421, 34% full-time.
Majors Accounting; agricultural business; agricultural sciences; agronomy/crop science; aircraft mechanic/airframe; animal sciences; applied art; art; auto mechanic/technician; biological/physical sciences; business administration; business marketing and marketing management; carpentry; computer engineering technology; computer science; construction technology; data processing technology; dental hygiene; developmental/child psychology; dietetics; early childhood education; electrical/electronic engineering technology; environmental technology; fashion design/illustration; fashion merchandising; finance; fire science; food products retailing; home economics; humanities; human services; industrial arts; industrial radiologic technology; insurance/risk management; landscape architecture; law enforcement/police science; legal administrative assistant; liberal arts and sciences/liberal studies; library science; management information systems/business data processing; mathematics; medical administrative assistant; medical assistant; music; natural sciences; nursing; ornamental horticulture; physical education; physical sciences; political science; practical nurse; pre-engineering; real estate; retail management; secretarial science; social sciences; teacher assistant/aide; theater arts/drama.
Academic Programs *Special study options:* academic remediation for entering students, adult/continuing education programs, advanced placement credit, cooperative education, English as a second language, honors programs, off-campus study, part-time degree program, services for LD students, study abroad, summer session for credit. *ROTC:* Army (c).
Library Lesher Library with 35,000 titles, 400 serial subscriptions.
Computers on Campus 400 computers available on campus for general student use.
Student Life *Housing:* college housing not available. *Activities and Organizations:* drama/theater group, student-run newspaper, choral group. *Campus security:* 24-hour patrols, late-night transport/escort service. *Student Services:* health clinic, personal/psychological counseling, women's center, legal services.
Athletics *Intercollegiate sports:* baseball M, basketball M/W, bowling M/W, cross-country running M, equestrian sports M/W, football M, golf M/W, soccer M, softball W, swimming M/W, tennis M/W, track and field M/W, volleyball W, water polo M.
Standardized Tests *Recommended:* SAT I or ACT (for placement).
Costs (2002–03) *Tuition:* nonresident $3948 full-time, $141 per unit part-time. *Required fees:* $308 full-time, $11 per unit.
Financial Aid In 2001, 543 Federal Work-Study jobs (averaging $1984). 163 State and other part-time jobs (averaging $1227).
Applying *Options:* common application, early admission. *Application deadline:* rolling (freshmen), rolling (transfers). *Notification:* continuous (freshmen).
Admissions Contact Ms. Helen Torres, Admissions Clerk, Merced College, 3600 M Street, Merced, CA 95348-2898. *Phone:* 209-384-6187.

MERRITT COLLEGE
Oakland, California

■ **State and locally supported** 2-year, founded 1953, part of Peralta Community College District System
■ **Calendar** semesters
■ **Degree** certificates and associate
■ **Urban** 130-acre campus with easy access to San Francisco
■ **Coed**

Standardized Tests *Recommended:* SAT I or ACT (for placement).
Applying *Options:* early admission, deferred entrance.
Admissions Contact Ms. Barbara Simmons, District Admissions Officer, Merritt College, 12500 Campus Drive, Oakland, CA 94619-3196. *Phone:* 510-466-7369. *E-mail:* hperdue@peralta.cc.ca.us.

MIRACOSTA COLLEGE
Oceanside, California

■ **State-supported** 2-year, founded 1934, part of California Community College System
■ **Calendar** semesters
■ **Degree** certificates, diplomas, and associate
■ **Suburban** 131-acre campus with easy access to San Diego
■ **Endowment** $894,495
■ **Coed,** 10,129 undergraduate students, 29% full-time, 59% women, 41% men

MiraCosta's campuses in Oceanside and Cardiff are minutes from the beach. MiraCosta offers a strong university transfer program, including transfer admission guarantees. Courses of special interest include music technology, multimedia, and computer science. Facilities include technology hubs at both campuses and a wellness center at the Oceanside campus.

Undergraduates 2,940 full-time, 7,189 part-time. Students come from 37 states and territories, 44 other countries, 2% are from out of state, 6% African American, 8% Asian American or Pacific Islander, 20% Hispanic American, 1% Native American, 3% international, 10% transferred in. *Retention:* 61% of 2001 full-time freshmen returned.
Freshmen *Admission:* 1,024 enrolled.
Faculty *Total:* 393, 27% full-time. *Student/faculty ratio:* 23:1.
Majors Accounting; African studies; architectural engineering technology; art; auto mechanic/technician; behavioral sciences; biology; business administration; business marketing and marketing management; chemistry; child care/guidance; computer engineering technology; consumer/homemaking education; cosmetology; criminal justice/law enforcement administration; dance; developmental/child psychology; drafting; early childhood education; economics; English; French; general studies; history; horticulture science; hotel and restaurant management; humanities; industrial technology; information sciences/systems; institutional food workers; Japanese; journalism; landscaping management; law enforcement/police science; liberal arts and sciences/liberal studies; machine technology; mathematics; music; ornamental horticulture; philosophy; physical sciences; physics; political science; practical nurse; psychology; real estate; secretarial science; social sciences; sociology; Spanish; speech/rhetorical studies; teacher assistant/aide; theater arts/drama; travel/tourism management.
Academic Programs *Special study options:* academic remediation for entering students, accelerated degree program, adult/continuing education programs, advanced placement credit, cooperative education, distance learning, double majors, English as a second language, freshman honors college, honors programs, independent study, internships, part-time degree program, services for LD students, student-designed majors, study abroad, summer session for credit.
Library MiraCosta College Library with 113,810 titles, 272 serial subscriptions, 5,340 audiovisual materials, an OPAC, a Web page.
Computers on Campus 753 computers available on campus for general student use. A campuswide network can be accessed from off campus that provide access to course listing. Internet access, at least one staffed computer lab available.
Student Life *Housing:* college housing not available. *Activities and Organizations:* drama/theater group, student-run newspaper, choral group, African-American Student Alliance, Spanish Club, Cultural Exchange Program, Phi Theta Kappa, Friends of EOPS. *Campus security:* 24-hour emergency response devices, student patrols, late-night transport/escort service, trained security personnel during class hours. *Student Services:* health clinic, personal/psychological counseling, women's center.
Athletics Member NJCAA. *Intercollegiate sports:* basketball M, cross-country running M/W, soccer W, track and field W. *Intramural sports:* soccer M/W.
Costs (2002–03) *Tuition:* state resident $0 full-time; nonresident $4020 full-time, $134 per unit part-time. Part-time tuition and fees vary according to course load. *Required fees:* $362 full-time, $11 per unit, $16 per term part-time. *Payment plan:* deferred payment.
Financial Aid In 2001, 83 Federal Work-Study jobs (averaging $1315).
Applying *Options:* early admission, deferred entrance. *Application deadline:* rolling (freshmen), rolling (transfers).
Admissions Contact Admissions and Records Assistant, MiraCosta College, One Barnard Drive, Oceanside, CA 92056. *Phone:* 760-795-6620. *Toll-free phone:* 888-201-8480. *Fax:* 760-795-6626.

MISSION COLLEGE
Santa Clara, California

■ **State and locally supported** 2-year, founded 1977, part of California Community College System
■ **Calendar** semesters
■ **Degree** certificates, diplomas, and associate
■ **Urban** 167-acre campus with easy access to San Francisco and San Jose
■ **Coed**

Faculty *Student/faculty ratio:* 20:1.
Student Life *Campus security:* 24-hour emergency response devices, late-night transport/escort service.
Standardized Tests *Recommended:* SAT I (for placement).

Mission College (continued)

Costs (2001–02) *Tuition:* state resident $0 full-time; nonresident $4270 full-time, $141 per unit part-time. Full-time tuition and fees vary according to course load. Part-time tuition and fees vary according to course load. *Required fees:* $370 full-time, $11 per unit, $53 per term part-time.

Financial Aid *Financial aid deadline:* 7/1.

Applying *Options:* common application, electronic application, early admission.

Admissions Contact Mr. R. Dan Mataragas, Vice President of Student Services, Mission College, 3000 Mission College Boulevard, Santa Clara, CA 95054-1897. *Phone:* 408-855-5195. *Fax:* 408-855-5467.

MODESTO JUNIOR COLLEGE
Modesto, California

- **State and locally supported** 2-year, founded 1921, part of Yosemite Community College District System
- **Calendar** semesters
- **Degree** certificates and associate
- **Urban** 229-acre campus
- **Endowment** $817,811
- **Coed,** 15,696 undergraduate students, 100% full-time, 59% women, 41% men

Undergraduates 3% African American, 8% Asian American or Pacific Islander, 27% Hispanic American.

Freshmen *Admission:* 9,034 applied, 9,034 admitted.

Faculty *Total:* 563, 41% full-time. *Student/faculty ratio:* 40:1.

Majors Accounting; agricultural business; agricultural mechanization; agricultural production; agricultural sciences; agronomy/crop science; animal sciences; architectural engineering technology; art; auto body repair; auto mechanic/technician; banking; behavioral sciences; biology; business administration; business marketing and marketing management; child care/development; child care provider; child care services management; clothing/apparel/textile studies; communication systems installation/repair; computer graphics; computer graphics; computer/information technology services administration and management related; computer installation/repair; computer science; construction/building inspection; construction management; corrections; criminal justice/law enforcement administration; dairy science; data entry/microcomputer applications; dental assistant; drafting/design technology; early childhood education; electrical/electronic engineering technology; electrical equipment installation/repair; emergency medical technology; engineering; English; family/consumer studies; fashion merchandising; finance; fire science; food sciences; food services technology; foreign languages/literatures; forest products technology; forestry; general office/clerical; general studies; graphic design/commercial art/illustration; graphic/printing equipment; heating/air conditioning/refrigeration; home products marketing operations; humanities; human services; industrial arts; industrial electronics installation/repair; interior design; interior environments; landscape architecture; law enforcement/police science; machine shop assistant; machine technology; management information systems/business data processing; mass communications; mathematics; medical assistant; music; nurse assistant/aide; nursery management; nursing; office management; ornamental horticulture; photography; physical education; poultry science; radio/television broadcasting; real estate; recreation/leisure facilities management; respiratory therapy; secretarial science; social sciences; speech/rhetorical studies; theater arts/drama; welding technology; word processing.

Academic Programs *Special study options:* academic remediation for entering students, adult/continuing education programs, advanced placement credit, cooperative education, distance learning, English as a second language, honors programs, independent study, part-time degree program, services for LD students, study abroad, summer session for credit.

Library Modesto Junior College Library with 69,865 titles, 4,161 audiovisual materials, an OPAC, a Web page.

Computers on Campus 95 computers available on campus for general student use. A campuswide network can be accessed from off campus. Internet access, at least one staffed computer lab available.

Student Life *Housing:* college housing not available. *Activities and Organizations:* drama/theater group, student-run newspaper, radio and television station, choral group, Young Farmers, Red Nations, Psychology Club, Alpha Gamma Sigma, MECHA. *Campus security:* 24-hour emergency response devices and patrols, late-night transport/escort service. *Student Services:* health clinic, personal/psychological counseling.

Athletics *Intercollegiate sports:* baseball M, basketball M/W, cross-country running M/W, football M, golf M, gymnastics W, soccer M/W, softball W, swimming M/W, tennis M/W, track and field M/W, volleyball W, water polo M/W, wrestling M. *Intramural sports:* basketball M/W, football M, softball W, table tennis M/W, tennis M/W, volleyball M/W.

Costs (2001–02) *Tuition:* state resident $0 full-time; nonresident $3550 full-time, $145 per credit part-time. *Required fees:* $334 full-time, $11 per credit.

Financial Aid In 2001, 136 Federal Work-Study jobs (averaging $2037). 96 State and other part-time jobs (averaging $1572).

Applying *Options:* electronic application. *Recommended:* high school transcript, interview. *Application deadline:* rolling (freshmen), rolling (transfers). *Notification:* continuous (freshmen).

Admissions Contact Ms. Susie Agostini, Dean of Matriculation, Admissions, and Records, Modesto Junior College, 435 College Avenue, Modesto, CA 95350. *Phone:* 209-575-6470. *Fax:* 209-575-6859. *E-mail:* mjc@yosemite.cc.ca.us.

MONTEREY PENINSULA COLLEGE
Monterey, California

- **State-supported** 2-year, founded 1947, part of California Community College System
- **Calendar** semesters
- **Degree** associate
- **Small-town** 87-acre campus
- **Coed,** 8,000 undergraduate students

Undergraduates Students come from 29 states and territories, 47 other countries.

Faculty *Total:* 388, 36% full-time.

Majors Accounting; anthropology; art; art history; auto mechanic/technician; biology; business administration; business marketing and marketing management; ceramic arts; chemistry; child care/development; clothing/textiles; computer engineering technology; computer science; computer typography/composition; criminal justice/law enforcement administration; cultural studies; dance; data processing technology; dental hygiene; drawing; early childhood education; economics; engineering; English; exercise sciences; family/consumer studies; fashion merchandising; fine/studio arts; fire science; fish/game management; French; geology; German; graphic design/commercial art/illustration; history; hospitality management; hotel and restaurant management; information sciences/systems; interior design; international business; law enforcement/police science; legal administrative assistant; liberal arts and sciences/liberal studies; mass communications; mathematics; medical administrative assistant; medical assistant; metal/jewelry arts; music; nursing; occupational therapy; ornamental horticulture; philosophy; photography; physical education; physical therapy; physics; political science; psychology; real estate; recreation/leisure facilities management; sculpture; secretarial science; sociology; Spanish; textile arts; theater arts/drama; wildlife management; women's studies.

Academic Programs *Special study options:* academic remediation for entering students, adult/continuing education programs, advanced placement credit, cooperative education, English as a second language, part-time degree program, services for LD students, summer session for credit.

Library Monterey Peninsula College Library with 52,000 titles, 281 serial subscriptions, 2,623 audiovisual materials, an OPAC, a Web page.

Computers on Campus 120 computers available on campus for general student use. A campuswide network can be accessed from off campus. At least one staffed computer lab available.

Student Life *Housing:* college housing not available. *Activities and Organizations:* drama/theater group, student-run newspaper, choral group. *Campus security:* 24-hour emergency response devices, late-night transport/escort service. *Student Services:* health clinic, personal/psychological counseling, women's center.

Athletics *Intercollegiate sports:* baseball M, basketball M, cross-country running M/W, football M, golf M/W, softball W, swimming M/W, tennis M/W, track and field M/W, volleyball W.

Costs (2001–02) *Tuition:* state resident $0 full-time; nonresident $3216 full-time, $134 per unit part-time. *Required fees:* $306 full-time, $11 per unit, $21 per term part-time.

Financial Aid In 2001, 167 Federal Work-Study jobs. *Financial aid deadline:* 6/30.

Applying *Options:* early admission. *Application deadline:* rolling (freshmen), rolling (transfers). *Notification:* continuous (freshmen).

Admissions Contact Dr. Sharon Coniglio, Dean of Counseling, Admissions and Records, Monterey Peninsula College, 980 Fremont Street, Monterey, CA 93940. *Phone:* 831-645-1372. *Fax:* 831-646-4015. *E-mail:* rich_montori@mpc.cc.ca.us.

MOORPARK COLLEGE

Moorpark, California

- **County-supported** 2-year, founded 1967, part of Ventura County Community College District System
- **Calendar** semesters
- **Degree** certificates and associate
- **Small-town** 121-acre campus with easy access to Los Angeles
- **Coed,** 14,538 undergraduate students

Undergraduates Students come from 45 states and territories, 2% African American, 11% Asian American or Pacific Islander, 14% Hispanic American, 0.9% Native American.

Freshmen *Admission:* 1,800 applied, 1,800 admitted.

Faculty *Total:* 422, 45% full-time.

Majors Accounting; animal sciences; anthropology; art; behavioral sciences; biology; broadcast journalism; business administration; business machine repair; business marketing and marketing management; chemistry; computer science; corrections; criminal justice/law enforcement administration; data processing technology; early childhood education; electrical/electronic engineering technology; engineering; engineering technology; fashion design/illustration; film studies; geology; graphic design/commercial art/illustration; graphic/printing equipment; information sciences/systems; journalism; laser/optical technology; law enforcement/police science; liberal arts and sciences/liberal studies; mathematics; music; natural sciences; nursing; photography; teacher assistant/aide; telecommunications; theater arts/drama; wildlife management.

Academic Programs *Special study options:* academic remediation for entering students, adult/continuing education programs, advanced placement credit, cooperative education, English as a second language, part-time degree program, services for LD students, summer session for credit.

Library 50,000 titles, 100 serial subscriptions.

Computers on Campus 80 computers available on campus for general student use. Internet access, at least one staffed computer lab available.

Student Life *Housing:* college housing not available. *Activities and Organizations:* student-run newspaper. *Campus security:* 24-hour patrols. *Student Services:* health clinic, personal/psychological counseling, women's center.

Athletics *Intercollegiate sports:* baseball M, basketball M/W, cross-country running M/W, football M, golf M/W, soccer M/W, softball W, track and field M/W, volleyball W, wrestling M.

Costs (2002–03) *Tuition:* state resident $0 full-time; nonresident $3384 full-time, $141 per unit part-time. *Required fees:* $302 full-time, $11 per unit, $19 per term part-time.

Financial Aid In 2001, 62 Federal Work-Study jobs (averaging $2200).

Applying *Options:* early admission, deferred entrance. *Application deadline:* rolling (freshmen), rolling (transfers). *Notification:* continuous (freshmen).

Admissions Contact Ms. Kathy Colborn, Registrar, Moorpark College, 7075 Campus Road, Moorpark, CA 93021-2899. *Phone:* 805-378-1415. *Fax:* 805-378-1499. *E-mail:* kroussin@vcccd.cc.ca.us.

MT. SAN ANTONIO COLLEGE

Walnut, California

- **District-supported** 2-year, founded 1946, part of California Community College System
- **Calendar** semesters
- **Degree** certificates and associate
- **Suburban** 421-acre campus with easy access to Los Angeles
- **Coed**

Student Life *Campus security:* 24-hour emergency response devices and patrols, late-night transport/escort service.

Costs (2001–02) *Tuition:* nonresident $3120 full-time, $130 per unit part-time. Full-time tuition and fees vary according to course load. Part-time tuition and fees vary according to course load. *Required fees:* $378 full-time, $11 per unit. *Room and board:* $7038.

Financial Aid In 2001, 250 Federal Work-Study jobs (averaging $1600).

Applying *Options:* early admission, deferred entrance. *Required for some:* high school transcript.

Admissions Contact Ms. Eloise Young, Director of Admissions and Records, Mt. San Antonio College, 1100 North Grand Avenue, Walnut, CA 91789-1399. *Phone:* 909-594-5611 Ext. 4415. *Toll-free phone:* 800-672-2463. *E-mail:* admissions@mtsac.edu.

MT. SAN JACINTO COLLEGE

San Jacinto, California

- **State and locally supported** 2-year, founded 1963, part of California Community College System
- **Calendar** semesters
- **Degree** certificates, diplomas, and associate
- **Suburban** 180-acre campus with easy access to San Diego
- **Endowment** $2.0 million
- **Coed,** 12,288 undergraduate students

Undergraduates Students come from 15 states and territories, 1% are from out of state.

Faculty *Total:* 421, 25% full-time. *Student/faculty ratio:* 24:1.

Majors Alcohol/drug abuse counseling; art; audio engineering; auto mechanic/technician; behavioral sciences; biological/physical sciences; business administration; computer science; computer software engineering; dance; early childhood education; engineering; fire science; gerontology; home health aide; humanities; interdisciplinary studies; law enforcement/police science; mathematics; music; nursing; paralegal/legal assistant; photography; physical education; public administration; real estate; secretarial science; social sciences; visual/performing arts.

Academic Programs *Special study options:* academic remediation for entering students, adult/continuing education programs, advanced placement credit, distance learning, double majors, English as a second language, honors programs, off-campus study, part-time degree program, services for LD students, study abroad, summer session for credit.

Library Milo P. Johnson Library plus 1 other with 28,000 titles, 330 serial subscriptions.

Computers on Campus 35 computers available on campus for general student use. At least one staffed computer lab available.

Student Life *Housing:* college housing not available. *Activities and Organizations:* drama/theater group. *Campus security:* part-time trained security personnel. *Student Services:* personal/psychological counseling.

Athletics *Intercollegiate sports:* baseball M, basketball M/W, football M, golf M, soccer W, tennis M/W, volleyball W.

Standardized Tests *Required:* Assessment and Placement Services for Community Colleges.

Costs (2001–02) *Tuition:* nonresident $131 per unit part-time. *Required fees:* $11 per unit.

Financial Aid In 2001, 109 Federal Work-Study jobs (averaging $1114). 125 State and other part-time jobs (averaging $1000).

Applying *Options:* early admission. *Recommended:* high school transcript. *Application deadline:* rolling (freshmen), rolling (transfers).

Admissions Contact Ms. Elida Gonzales, Dean of Student Services, Enrollment Services, Mt. San Jacinto College, 1499 North State Street, San Jacinto, CA 92583-2399. *Phone:* 909-487-6752 Ext. 1414. *Toll-free phone:* 800-624-5561. *Fax:* 909-654-6738. *E-mail:* egonzale@msjc.edu.

MTI COLLEGE

Orange, California

Admissions Contact 2011 West Chapman Avenue, Suite 100, Orange, CA 92868-2632.

MTI COLLEGE OF BUSINESS AND TECHNOLOGY

Sacramento, California

Admissions Contact Ms. Marilyn Arnold, Director of Admissions, MTI College of Business and Technology, 5221 Madison Avenue, Sacramento, CA 95841. *Phone:* 916-339-1500.

NAPA VALLEY COLLEGE

Napa, California

Admissions Contact Ms. Sue Nelson, Assistant Dean of Admissions and Records/International Student Advisor, Napa Valley College, 2277 Napa-Vallejo Highway, Napa, CA 94558-6236. *Phone:* 707-253-3000. *Fax:* 707-253-3064. *E-mail:* snelson@admin.nvc.cc.ca.us.

NORTHWESTERN TECHNICAL COLLEGE
Sacramento, California

Admissions Contact 1825 Bell Street, #100, Sacramento, CA 95825.

OHLONE COLLEGE
Fremont, California

Admissions Contact Mr. Ron Travenick, Director, Admissions and Records, Ohlone College, 43600 Mission Boulevard, Fremont, CA 94539-5884. *Phone:* 510-659-6107.

ORANGE COAST COLLEGE
Costa Mesa, California

- **State and locally supported** 2-year, founded 1947, part of Coast Community College District System
- **Calendar** semesters
- **Degree** certificates and associate
- **Suburban** 200-acre campus with easy access to Los Angeles
- **Endowment** $5.1 million
- **Coed,** 24,630 undergraduate students, 33% full-time, 52% women, 48% men

Undergraduates 8,122 full-time, 16,508 part-time. Students come from 52 states and territories, 76 other countries, 4% are from out of state, 3% African American, 29% Asian American or Pacific Islander, 23% Hispanic American, 0.9% Native American, 5% international. *Retention:* 74% of 2001 full-time freshmen returned.

Freshmen *Admission:* 3,457 applied, 3,457 admitted, 3,398 enrolled.

Faculty *Total:* 801, 42% full-time, 6% with terminal degrees. *Student/faculty ratio:* 20:1.

Majors Accounting; aerospace science; aircraft pilot (professional); anthropology; architectural engineering technology; art; athletic training/sports medicine; aviation technology; behavioral sciences; biology; business administration; business marketing and marketing management; cardiovascular technology; chemistry; child care provider; child care services management; communication equipment technology; computer engineering technology; computer graphics; computer graphics; computer programming; computer programming (specific applications); computer typography/composition; construction/building inspection; construction technology; culinary arts; cultural studies; dance; data entry/microcomputer applications related; data processing technology; dental hygiene; dietetics; drafting; drafting/design technology; early childhood education; economics; electrical/electronic engineering technology; electrical equipment installation/repair; electrical/power transmission installation; emergency medical technology; engineering; English; exercise sciences; family/consumer studies; fashion merchandising; film studies; film/video production; food products retailing; food sciences; food services technology; French; general retailing/wholesaling; geography; geology; German; graphic design/commercial art/illustration; health science; heating/air conditioning/refrigeration; history; home economics; horticulture science; hotel and restaurant management; humanities; individual/family development; industrial design; industrial radiologic technology; information sciences/systems; interior design; interior environments; journalism; legal administrative assistant; liberal arts and sciences/liberal studies; machine shop assistant; machine technology; marine technology; mass communications; mathematics; medical administrative assistant; medical assistant; medical technology; music; musical instrument technology; music business management/merchandising; natural sciences; nuclear medical technology; nutrition science; ornamental horticulture; philosophy; photography; physical education; physics; political science; religious studies; respiratory therapy; restaurant operations; retailing operations; sales operations; secretarial science; social sciences; sociology; Spanish; theater arts/drama; welding technology; word processing.

Academic Programs *Special study options:* academic remediation for entering students, adult/continuing education programs, advanced placement credit, cooperative education, distance learning, double majors, English as a second language, external degree program, freshman honors college, honors programs, internships, off-campus study, part-time degree program, services for LD students, student-designed majors, study abroad, summer session for credit. *ROTC:* Army (c), Air Force (c).

Library Norman E. Watson Library with 84,447 titles, 420 serial subscriptions, 2,510 audiovisual materials, an OPAC, a Web page.

Computers on Campus 1515 computers available on campus for general student use. A campuswide network can be accessed from off campus. Internet access, at least one staffed computer lab available.

Student Life *Housing:* college housing not available. *Activities and Organizations:* drama/theater group, student-run newspaper, choral group, Vietnamese Student Association, International Club, Adventurist Souls, Muslim Student Association. *Campus security:* 24-hour emergency response devices and patrols, student patrols, late-night transport/escort service. *Student Services:* health clinic, personal/psychological counseling, legal services.

Athletics *Intercollegiate sports:* baseball M, basketball M/W, bowling M(c)/W(c), crew M/W, cross-country running M/W, football M, golf M/W, soccer M/W, softball W, swimming M/W, tennis M/W, track and field M/W, volleyball M/W, water polo M/W.

Costs (2001–02) *Tuition:* state resident $0 full-time; nonresident $4050 full-time, $134 per unit part-time. *Required fees:* $410 full-time, $11 per unit.

Financial Aid In 2001, 80 Federal Work-Study jobs (averaging $3020). *Financial aid deadline:* 4/7.

Applying *Options:* common application. *Application deadline:* rolling (freshmen), rolling (transfers). *Notification:* continuous (freshmen).

Admissions Contact Ms. Nancy Kidder, Administrative Dean of Admissions and Records, Orange Coast College, 2701 Fairview Road, PO Box 5005, Costa Mesa, CA 92628-5005. *Phone:* 714-432-5788. *Fax:* 714-432-5072.

OXNARD COLLEGE
Oxnard, California

- **State-supported** 2-year, founded 1975, part of Ventura County Community College District System
- **Calendar** semesters
- **Degree** certificates and associate
- **Urban** 119-acre campus
- **Coed,** 7,594 undergraduate students, 100% full-time, 56% women, 44% men

Undergraduates Students come from 10 states and territories, 5% African American, 10% Asian American or Pacific Islander, 57% Hispanic American, 0.9% Native American.

Faculty *Total:* 349, 28% full-time. *Student/faculty ratio:* 35:1.

Majors Accounting; agricultural business; agricultural mechanization; anthropology; art education; auto mechanic/technician; behavioral sciences; biology; business administration; business marketing and marketing management; child care/development; culinary arts; dental assistant; dental hygiene; early childhood education; economics; electrical/electronic engineering technology; English; family/community studies; fashion merchandising; fire science; heating/air conditioning/refrigeration; history; home economics; hotel and restaurant management; information sciences/systems; journalism; legal studies; liberal arts and sciences/liberal studies; library science; machine technology; mathematics; mental health/rehabilitation; philosophy; physical education; radio/television broadcasting; real estate; secretarial science; sociology; Spanish; telecommunications; theater arts/drama; transportation technology; welding technology.

Academic Programs *Special study options:* academic remediation for entering students, adult/continuing education programs, advanced placement credit, English as a second language, honors programs, part-time degree program, services for LD students, summer session for credit.

Library 25,223 titles, 107 serial subscriptions.

Computers on Campus 116 computers available on campus for general student use.

Student Life *Housing:* college housing not available. *Activities and Organizations:* drama/theater group, student-run newspaper, television station, choral group. *Campus security:* 24-hour patrols. *Student Services:* health clinic, personal/psychological counseling, women's center.

Athletics *Intercollegiate sports:* baseball M, basketball M/W, cross-country running M/W, soccer M/W, track and field M/W, volleyball W.

Costs (2002–03) *Tuition:* state resident $0 full-time; nonresident $3384 full-time, $141 per unit part-time. Full-time tuition and fees vary according to course load. Part-time tuition and fees vary according to course load. *Required fees:* $286 full-time, $11 per unit, $11 per term part-time. *Payment plan:* installment.

Financial Aid In 2001, 90 Federal Work-Study jobs (averaging $2000).

Applying *Options:* early admission. *Application fee:* $10. *Application deadline:* rolling (freshmen), rolling (transfers). *Notification:* continuous (freshmen).

Admissions Contact Ms. Susan D. Brent, Registrar, Oxnard College, 4000 South Rose Avenue, Oxnard, CA 93033-6699. *Phone:* 805-986-5843. *Fax:* 805-986-5806.

PALOMAR COLLEGE
San Marcos, California

- **State and locally supported** 2-year, founded 1946, part of California Community College System
- **Calendar** semesters
- **Degree** certificates and associate
- **Suburban** 156-acre campus with easy access to San Diego
- **Coed,** 29,715 undergraduate students, 20% full-time, 53% women, 47% men

Undergraduates Students come from 50 other countries, 4% African American, 10% Asian American or Pacific Islander, 27% Hispanic American, 2% Native American, 1% international.
Freshmen *Admission:* 5,859 applied, 5,859 admitted.
Faculty *Total:* 1,210, 28% full-time. *Student/faculty ratio:* 22:1.
Majors Accounting; advertising; anthropology; applied art; archaeology; art; art education; arts management; astronomy; auto mechanic/technician; aviation management; aviation technology; biology; business administration; business education; business machine repair; business marketing and marketing management; carpentry; ceramic arts; chemistry; computer science; construction technology; criminal justice/law enforcement administration; dance; dental hygiene; developmental/child psychology; drafting; drawing; early childhood education; economics; electrical/electronic engineering technology; emergency medical technology; engineering; family/consumer studies; fashion design/illustration; fashion merchandising; film studies; fire science; food products retailing; food services technology; geology; graphic design/commercial art/illustration; graphic/printing equipment; information sciences/systems; interior design; international business; journalism; law enforcement/police science; legal administrative assistant; liberal arts and sciences/liberal studies; library science; mathematics; medical administrative assistant; medical assistant; metal/jewelry arts; music; nursing; paralegal/legal assistant; photography; physical education; plumbing; public administration; radio/television broadcasting; real estate; recreation/leisure facilities management; recreation/leisure studies; sanitation technology; secretarial science; sign language interpretation; speech/rhetorical studies; surveying; telecommunications; theater arts/drama; travel/tourism management; water resources; welding technology; women's studies; zoology.
Academic Programs *Special study options:* academic remediation for entering students, advanced placement credit, cooperative education, distance learning, English as a second language, internships, part-time degree program, services for LD students, study abroad, summer session for credit.
Library Palomar Library with 108,000 titles, an OPAC, a Web page.
Computers on Campus 922 computers available on campus for general student use. Internet access, at least one staffed computer lab available.
Student Life *Housing:* college housing not available. *Activities and Organizations:* drama/theater group, student-run newspaper, radio station, choral group, bible clubs. *Campus security:* 24-hour patrols, student patrols, late-night transport/escort service. *Student Services:* health clinic, personal/psychological counseling.
Athletics *Intercollegiate sports:* basketball M/W, football M, soccer M, swimming M/W, tennis M/W, volleyball W, water polo M, wrestling M. *Intramural sports:* basketball M/W, bowling M, golf M, skiing (downhill) M/W, soccer M, softball W, tennis M, volleyball M, water polo M, wrestling M.
Standardized Tests *Required for some:* ACT ASSET.
Costs (2002–03) *Tuition:* nonresident $4350 full-time, $145 per unit part-time. *Required fees:* $364 full-time, $10 per year part-time. *Payment plan:* deferred payment. *Waivers:* employees or children of employees.
Applying *Options:* electronic application. *Application deadline:* rolling (freshmen), rolling (transfers). *Notification:* continuous (freshmen).
Admissions Contact Mr. Herman Lee, Director of Enrollment Services, Palomar College, 1140 West Mission Road, San Marcos, CA 92069-1487. *Phone:* 760-744-1150 Ext. 2171. *Fax:* 760-744-2932. *E-mail:* admissions@palomar.edu.

PALO VERDE COLLEGE
Blythe, California

- **State and locally supported** 2-year, founded 1947, part of California Community College System
- **Calendar** semesters
- **Degree** associate
- **Small-town** 10-acre campus
- **Coed,** 2,903 undergraduate students

Undergraduates Students come from 4 states and territories, 3 other countries.
Freshmen *Admission:* 300 applied, 300 admitted.
Faculty *Total:* 129, 22% full-time. *Student/faculty ratio:* 23:1.
Majors Accounting; agricultural sciences; auto mechanic/technician; behavioral sciences; biology; business administration; business marketing and marketing management; child guidance; computer/information sciences; construction trades related; criminal justice/law enforcement administration; developmental/child psychology; early childhood education; economics; education; English; enterprise management; forestry; general studies; health science; history; interior design; law enforcement/police science; liberal arts and sciences/liberal studies; political science; pre-engineering; psychology; secretarial science; sociology; transportation and materials moving related.
Academic Programs *Special study options:* academic remediation for entering students, adult/continuing education programs, advanced placement credit, English as a second language, internships, part-time degree program, services for LD students, summer session for credit.
Library Palo Verde College Library with 21,457 titles, 165 serial subscriptions.
Computers on Campus 25 computers available on campus for general student use. At least one staffed computer lab available.
Student Life *Housing:* college housing not available. *Activities and Organizations:* drama/theater group, student-run newspaper, Extended Opportunity Program and Services club, Associated Student Body. *Campus security:* student patrols, security personnel during open hours. *Student Services:* personal/psychological counseling.
Costs (2002–03) *Tuition:* state resident $0 full-time; nonresident $3216 full-time, $134 per unit part-time. Full-time tuition and fees vary according to reciprocity agreements. Part-time tuition and fees vary according to reciprocity agreements. *Required fees:* $264 full-time, $11 per unit. *Payment plan:* installment.
Financial Aid In 2001, 30 Federal Work-Study jobs (averaging $1000).
Applying *Options:* early admission. *Recommended:* high school transcript. *Application deadline:* rolling (freshmen), rolling (transfers). *Notification:* continuous (freshmen).
Admissions Contact Ms. Sally Rivera, Dean of Student Services, Palo Verde College, 811 West Chanslorway, Blythe, CA 92225-1118. *Phone:* 760-922-6168 Ext. 220.

PASADENA CITY COLLEGE
Pasadena, California

- **State and locally supported** 2-year, founded 1924, part of California Community College System
- **Calendar** semesters
- **Degree** certificates and associate
- **Urban** 55-acre campus with easy access to Los Angeles
- **Coed,** 25,269 undergraduate students

Undergraduates Students come from 15 states and territories, 50 other countries.
Faculty *Total:* 1,296, 29% full-time. *Student/faculty ratio:* 20:1.
Majors Accounting; advertising; African-American studies; African studies; aircraft pilot (professional); anthropology; architectural engineering technology; art; art history; astronomy; auto mechanic/technician; aviation management; aviation technology; biological/physical sciences; biology; broadcast journalism; business administration; business education; business marketing and marketing management; carpentry; ceramic arts; ceramic sciences/engineering; chemistry; civil engineering technology; communication equipment technology; computer engineering technology; computer programming; computer science; computer typography/composition; construction technology; cosmetology; criminal justice/law enforcement administration; cultural studies; data processing technology; dental hygiene; developmental/child psychology; drafting; drawing; early childhood education; economics; electrical/electronic engineering technology; engineering; engineering technology; English; fashion merchandising; finance; fire science; forest harvesting production technology; French; geography; geology; German; history; human services; industrial radiologic technology; information sciences/systems; interdisciplinary studies; interior design; journalism; landscape architecture; Latin American studies; legal administrative assistant; legal studies; liberal arts and sciences/liberal studies; library science; machine technology; mass communications; mathematical statistics; mathematics; mechanical engineering technology; medical assistant; metal/jewelry arts; Mexican-American studies; modern languages; music; music therapy; nursing; occupational therapy; pharmacy; philosophy; photography; physical education; physical sciences; physics; political science; practical nurse; psychology; radio/television broadcasting; real estate; recreation/leisure studies; religious studies; secretarial science; sign language interpretation; social sciences; sociology; Spanish; speech/rhetorical studies; teacher assistant/aide; telecommunications; textile arts; theater arts/drama; travel/tourism management; veterinary sciences; welding technology.

Pasadena City College (continued)

Academic Programs *Special study options:* academic remediation for entering students, adult/continuing education programs, advanced placement credit, English as a second language, honors programs, part-time degree program, services for LD students, student-designed majors, study abroad, summer session for credit.

Library Pasadena City College Library plus 1 other with 117,660 titles, 300 serial subscriptions, an OPAC.

Computers on Campus 274 computers available on campus for general student use. At least one staffed computer lab available.

Student Life *Housing:* college housing not available. *Activities and Organizations:* drama/theater group, student-run newspaper, radio station, choral group, marching band. *Campus security:* 24-hour emergency response devices and patrols, late-night transport/escort service, cadet patrols. *Student Services:* health clinic, personal/psychological counseling, women's center.

Athletics *Intercollegiate sports:* baseball M, basketball M/W, cross-country running M/W, football M, soccer M/W, softball W, swimming M/W, tennis M/W, track and field M/W, volleyball W, water polo M.

Costs (2002–03) *Tuition:* nonresident $4350 full-time, $145 per unit part-time. *Required fees:* $35 full-time, $13 per term part-time.

Applying *Options:* early admission, deferred entrance. *Application deadline:* rolling (freshmen), rolling (transfers). *Notification:* continuous (freshmen).

Admissions Contact Ms. Carol Kaser, Supervisor of Admissions and Records, Pasadena City College, 1570 East Colorado Boulevard, Pasadena, CA 91106-2041. *Phone:* 626-585-7397. *Fax:* 626-585-7915.

PIMA MEDICAL INSTITUTE
Chula Vista, California

Admissions Contact 780 Bay Boulevard, Chula Vista, CA 91910.

PLATT COLLEGE
Newport Beach, California

- **Independent** 2-year, founded 1985
- **Calendar** continuous
- **Degree** certificates, diplomas, and associate
- **Urban** campus
- **Coed,** 270 undergraduate students

Undergraduates Students come from 12 states and territories, 5 other countries.

Faculty *Total:* 24, 33% full-time. *Student/faculty ratio:* 19:1.

Majors Computer graphics; graphic design/commercial art/illustration; information sciences/systems; information technology.

Academic Programs *Special study options:* accelerated degree program, adult/continuing education programs, summer session for credit.

Library Platt Library with 1,100 titles, 15 serial subscriptions, 100 audiovisual materials.

Computers on Campus 10 computers available on campus for general student use. Internet access, at least one staffed computer lab available.

Student Life *Housing:* college housing not available. *Campus security:* 24-hour emergency response devices.

Costs (2002–03) *Tuition:* $10,269 full-time. Full-time tuition and fees vary according to program. No tuition increase for student's term of enrollment. *Payment plans:* tuition prepayment, installment. *Waivers:* employees or children of employees.

Applying *Application fee:* $75. *Required:* essay or personal statement, high school transcript, interview.

Admissions Contact Ms. Suzanne Eckert, Admissions Coordinator, Platt College, 3901 MacArthur Boulevard, Newport Beach, CA 92660. *Phone:* 949-833-2300 Ext. 230. *Toll-free phone:* 888-866-6697 Ext. 230. *Fax:* 949-833-0269. *E-mail:* seckert@plattcollege.edu.

PLATT COLLEGE
Cerritos, California

- **Proprietary** 2-year, founded 1879
- **Calendar** continuous
- **Degree** certificates, diplomas, and associate
- **Urban** campus with easy access to Los Angeles
- 320 undergraduate students

Faculty *Student/faculty ratio:* 12:1.

Admissions Contact Ms. Ilene Holt, Dean of Student Services, Platt College, 10900 East 183rd Street, Suite 290, Cerritos, CA 90703-5342. *Phone:* 562-809-5100. *Toll-free phone:* 800-807-5288.

PLATT COLLEGE
Ontario, California

- **Independent** 2-year
- **Calendar** continuous
- **Degree** certificates, diplomas, and associate
- **Coed,** 284 undergraduate students

Undergraduates 10% African American, 6% Asian American or Pacific Islander, 32% Hispanic American, 0.6% Native American, 0.9% international.

Freshmen *Admission:* 400 applied, 388 admitted.

Faculty *Total:* 28, 25% full-time, 29% with terminal degrees.

Majors Business systems networking/ telecommunications; computer graphics; graphic design/commercial art/illustration; information technology; paralegal/legal assistant.

Academic Programs *Special study options:* academic remediation for entering students, accelerated degree program, honors programs, independent study, internships, summer session for credit.

Library Main Library-Platt College with 2,506 titles, 10 serial subscriptions, 20 audiovisual materials.

Computers on Campus 80 computers available on campus for general student use. Internet access available.

Student Life *Housing:* college housing not available.

Costs (2001–02) *Tuition:* $20,538 per degree program part-time. Full-time tuition and fees vary according to program. No tuition increase for student's term of enrollment. *Payment plans:* tuition prepayment, installment, deferred payment. *Waivers:* employees or children of employees.

Applying *Required:* essay or personal statement, interview, CPAT. *Application deadline:* rolling (freshmen), rolling (transfers). *Notification:* continuous (freshmen).

Admissions Contact Mr. David Fowler, Admissions Coordinator, Platt College, 3700 Inland Empire Boulevard, Ontario, CA 91764. *Phone:* 909-941-9410. *Toll-free phone:* 888-866-6697.

PLATT COLLEGE-LOS ANGELES, INC
Los Angeles, California

- **Proprietary** 2-year, founded 1987
- **Calendar** continuous
- **Degree** certificates, diplomas, and associate
- **Suburban** campus
- **Coed,** 209 undergraduate students

Undergraduates Students come from 18 states and territories, 15 other countries, 2% are from out of state, 5% African American, 24% Asian American or Pacific Islander, 31% Hispanic American, 3% Native American.

Freshmen *Admission:* 395 applied, 343 admitted.

Faculty *Total:* 20, 35% full-time, 90% with terminal degrees.

Majors Computer graphics; computer/information sciences; design/visual communications; graphic design/commercial art/illustration; information sciences/systems; information technology; paralegal/legal assistant.

Academic Programs *Special study options:* academic remediation for entering students, accelerated degree program, internships, summer session for credit.

Library Platt College Library with 808 titles, 20 serial subscriptions, 70 audiovisual materials.

Computers on Campus 80 computers available on campus for general student use. Internet access, at least one staffed computer lab available.

Student Life *Housing:* college housing not available. *Activities and Organizations:* Latin American Designers, Graphic Designers Mobilized for the Environment, Multimedia Club. *Campus security:* parking lot security.

Costs (2001–02) *Tuition:* $20,538 per degree program part-time. Full-time tuition and fees vary according to program. *Payment plans:* installment, deferred payment. *Waivers:* employees or children of employees.

Applying *Options:* common application. *Application fee:* $35. *Required:* interview. *Required for some:* essay or personal statement. *Application deadline:* rolling (freshmen), rolling (transfers).

Admissions Contact Ms. Arlene Aguilar, Admissions Representative, Platt College-Los Angeles, Inc, 7470 North Figueroa Street, Los Angeles, CA 90041-

1717. *Phone:* 323-258-8050. *Toll-free phone:* 888-866-6697. *Fax:* 323-258-8532. *E-mail:* ademitroff@plattcollege.edu.

PLATT COLLEGE SAN DIEGO
San Diego, California

- **Independent** 2-year, founded 1879
- **Calendar** continuous
- **Degree** certificates, diplomas, and associate
- **Suburban** campus
- **Coed,** 375 undergraduate students, 100% full-time, 100% men

Success doesn't just happen, it happens by design. Platt College San Diego offers diploma and Associate of Applied Science degree programs in graphic design, multimedia, animation, and Web design. Prospective students should visit the College's Web site (http://www.platt.edu).

Undergraduates 375 full-time. Students come from 4 states and territories, 6% African American, 12% Asian American or Pacific Islander, 22% Hispanic American, 2% Native American.
Freshmen *Admission:* 210 enrolled.
Faculty *Total:* 17, 47% full-time. *Student/faculty ratio:* 20:1.
Majors Graphic design/commercial art/illustration; multimedia.
Student Life *Housing:* college housing not available. *Student Services:* personal/psychological counseling.
Costs (2002–03) *Tuition:* $12,275 full-time. Full-time tuition, per degree program: $12,275-$16,325. *Payment plan:* installment. *Waivers:* employees or children of employees.
Applying *Required:* high school transcript, interview.
Admissions Contact Rachelle Wilson, Admissions Representative, Platt College San Diego, 6250 El Cajon Boulevard, San Diego, CA 92115-3919. *Phone:* 619-265-0107.

PORTERVILLE COLLEGE
Porterville, California

Admissions Contact Ms. Judy Pope, Director of Admissions and Records/Registrar, Porterville College, 100 East College Avenue, Porterville, CA 93257-6058. *Phone:* 559-791-2222. *Fax:* 559-791-2349.

PROFESSIONAL GOLFERS CAREER COLLEGE
Temecula, California

- **Independent** 2-year
- **Degree** associate
- 120 undergraduate students
- 84% of applicants were admitted

Freshmen *Admission:* 38 applied, 32 admitted.
Faculty *Total:* 28, 25% full-time, 4% with terminal degrees.
Costs (2001–02) *Tuition:* $9580 full-time. *Required fees:* $120 full-time.
Admissions Contact Sandi Somerville, Director of Admissions, Professional Golfers Career College, PO Box 892319, Temecula, CA 92589. *Phone:* 909-693-2963. *Toll-free phone:* 800-877-4380.

QUEEN OF THE HOLY ROSARY COLLEGE
Mission San Jose, California

- **Independent Roman Catholic** 2-year, founded 1930
- **Calendar** semesters
- **Degree** associate
- **Suburban** 37-acre campus with easy access to San Jose
- **Coed, primarily women,** 198 undergraduate students, 2% full-time, 97% women, 3% men

Faculty *Total:* 15, 7% with terminal degrees. *Student/faculty ratio:* 5:1.
Majors Religious studies.
Academic Programs *Special study options:* academic remediation for entering students, adult/continuing education programs, English as a second language, part-time degree program, summer session for credit.
Library Karcher Library with 24,937 titles, 150 serial subscriptions, 502 audiovisual materials, an OPAC.
Computers on Campus 7 computers available on campus for general student use. Internet access, at least one staffed computer lab available.
Student Life *Housing:* college housing not available. *Activities and Organizations:* choral group. *Campus security:* 24-hour emergency response devices. *Student Services:* health clinic, personal/psychological counseling.
Standardized Tests *Recommended:* SAT I (for admission).
Costs (2002–03) *One-time required fee:* $15. *Tuition:* $2500 full-time, $100 per credit part-time.
Applying *Application fee:* $15. *Required:* essay or personal statement, high school transcript, minimum 2.0 GPA. *Recommended:* minimum 3.0 GPA, interview. *Application deadlines:* 7/1 (freshmen), 7/1 (transfers).
Admissions Contact Sr. Mary Paul Mehegan, Dean of the College, Queen of the Holy Rosary College, 43326 Mission Boulevard, PO Box 3908, Mission San Jose, CA 94539. *Phone:* 510-657-2468 Ext. 322. *Fax:* 510-657-1734.

REEDLEY COLLEGE
Reedley, California

- **State and locally supported** 2-year, founded 1926, part of State Center Community College District System
- **Calendar** semesters
- **Degree** certificates, diplomas, and associate
- **Rural** 350-acre campus
- **Coed,** 11,305 undergraduate students, 40% full-time, 61% women, 39% men

Undergraduates 4,556 full-time, 6,749 part-time. Students come from 15 states and territories, 2% are from out of state, 3% African American, 5% Asian American or Pacific Islander, 42% Hispanic American, 2% Native American, 0.3% international. *Retention:* 62% of 2001 full-time freshmen returned.
Freshmen *Admission:* 1,224 applied, 1,224 admitted, 1,224 enrolled. *Average high school GPA:* 2.50.
Faculty *Total:* 542, 28% full-time. *Student/faculty ratio:* 14:1.
Majors Accounting; agricultural business; agricultural mechanization related; agricultural sciences; animal sciences; art; auto mechanic/technician; aviation technology; biology; business; child care/guidance; computer/information sciences; criminal justice/corrections related; dental assistant; English; enterprise management; fine arts and art studies related; foreign languages/literatures; general office/clerical; general studies; graphic design/commercial art/illustration; health/physical education; horticulture science; hospitality management; information sciences/systems; law enforcement/police science; liberal arts and sciences/liberal studies; machine technology; management science; mathematics; music (general performance); music (voice and choral/opera performance); natural resources management/protective services related; physical sciences; plant sciences; precision metal working related; secretarial science; social sciences; welding technology.
Academic Programs *Special study options:* academic remediation for entering students, adult/continuing education programs, advanced placement credit, cooperative education, distance learning, English as a second language, freshman honors college, honors programs, independent study, part-time degree program, services for LD students, study abroad, summer session for credit. *ROTC:* Air Force (c).
Library Reedley College Library with 36,000 titles, 217 serial subscriptions, 50 audiovisual materials, an OPAC.
Computers on Campus 303 computers available on campus for general student use. A campuswide network can be accessed from student residence rooms and from off campus. Internet access, online (class) registration, at least one staffed computer lab available.
Student Life *Housing Options:* coed. *Activities and Organizations:* drama/theater group, student-run newspaper, choral group. *Campus security:* on-campus plice department. *Student Services:* personal/psychological counseling.
Athletics *Intercollegiate sports:* baseball M, basketball M/W, football M, golf M, softball W, tennis M/W, track and field M/W, volleyball W. *Intramural sports:* basketball M/W, football M/W, swimming M/W, tennis M/W, track and field M/W, volleyball M/W.
Standardized Tests *Required for some:* CPT. *Recommended:* CPT.
Costs (2002–03) *One-time required fee:* $24. *Tuition:* state resident $0 full-time; nonresident $4230 full-time, $141 per unit part-time. Full-time tuition and fees vary according to course load. Part-time tuition and fees vary according to course load. *Required fees:* $330 full-time, $11 per unit. *Room and board:* Room and board charges vary according to board plan and housing facility. *Payment plan:* deferred payment. *Waivers:* employees or children of employees.
Financial Aid In 2001, 400 Federal Work-Study jobs (averaging $4500). 50 State and other part-time jobs (averaging $6000).
Applying *Required:* high school transcript. *Application deadline:* rolling (freshmen), rolling (transfers). *Notification:* continuous until 8/1 (freshmen).

Reedley College (continued)

Admissions Contact Ms. Leticia Alvarez, Admissions and Records Manager, Reedley College, 995 North Reed Avenue, Reedley, CA 93654. *Phone:* 559-638-0323 Ext. 3624.

RIO HONDO COLLEGE
Whittier, California

Admissions Contact Mr. Joe Rameirz, Dean of Counseling and Matriculation, Rio Hondo College, 3600 Workman Mill Road, Whittier, CA 90601-1699. *Phone:* 562-692-0921. *Fax:* 562-692-9318.

RIVERSIDE COMMUNITY COLLEGE
Riverside, California

- **State and locally supported** 2-year, founded 1916, part of California Community College System
- **Calendar** semesters
- **Degree** certificates and associate
- **Suburban** 108-acre campus with easy access to Los Angeles
- **Coed,** 29,865 undergraduate students, 27% full-time, 59% women, 41% men

Undergraduates 8,060 full-time, 21,805 part-time. Students come from 41 states and territories, 14% African American, 9% Asian American or Pacific Islander, 29% Hispanic American, 0.9% Native American.

Freshmen *Admission:* 2,528 applied, 2,528 admitted, 2,528 enrolled.

Faculty *Total:* 1,436, 23% full-time. *Student/faculty ratio:* 28:1.

Majors Accounting; agricultural business; anatomy; anthropology; architecture; art; astronomy; biological/physical sciences; botany; business administration; chemistry; child care/development; computer graphics; computer/information sciences; computer programming; computer programming related; computer systems networking/telecommunications; computer/technical support; criminal justice/law enforcement administration; culinary arts; cultural studies; dental hygiene; dietetics; early childhood education; economics; education; engineering; English; environmental science; forestry; French; geography; geology; German; health/physical education; health science; history; home economics; humanities; journalism; landscape architecture; liberal arts and sciences/liberal studies; library science; marketing research; mathematics; medical laboratory assistant; microbiology/bacteriology; music; nursing; oceanography; pharmacy; philosophy; physical sciences; physical therapy; political science; pre-law; psychology; sign language interpretation; social sciences; Spanish; speech/rhetorical studies; theater arts/drama; theology; urban studies; word processing.

Academic Programs *Special study options:* academic remediation for entering students, adult/continuing education programs, advanced placement credit, distance learning, double majors, English as a second language, internships, part-time degree program, services for LD students, study abroad, summer session for credit. *ROTC:* Army (c), Air Force (c).

Library Martin Luther King Jr. Library with 101,243 titles, 911 serial subscriptions, 5,417 audiovisual materials, an OPAC, a Web page.

Computers on Campus 200 computers available on campus for general student use. A campuswide network can be accessed from off campus. Internet access, at least one staffed computer lab available.

Student Life *Housing:* college housing not available. *Activities and Organizations:* drama/theater group, student-run newspaper, radio station, choral group, marching band, Marching Tigers Band, Wind Ensemble, Student Nurses Organization, Gospel Singers, Alpha Gamma Sigma. *Campus security:* 24-hour patrols, late-night transport/escort service. *Student Services:* health clinic, personal/psychological counseling.

Athletics *Intercollegiate sports:* baseball M, basketball M/W, cross-country running M/W, football M, golf M, soccer M/W, softball W, swimming M/W, tennis M/W, track and field M/W, volleyball W, water polo M/W. *Intramural sports:* badminton M/W, basketball M/W, bowling M/W, football M, golf M/W, racquetball M/W, soccer M/W, tennis M/W, volleyball M/W, weight lifting M/W.

Standardized Tests *Required:* Assessment and Placement Services for Community Colleges.

Costs (2001–02) *Tuition:* state resident $0 full-time; nonresident $4020 full-time, $134 per unit part-time. Full-time tuition and fees vary according to course load. Part-time tuition and fees vary according to course load. *Required fees:* $350 full-time, $11 per unit, $10 per term part-time. *Payment plan:* deferred payment.

Financial Aid In 2001, 572 Federal Work-Study jobs (averaging $3000).

Applying *Required:* high school transcript. *Application deadline:* rolling (freshmen), rolling (transfers). *Notification:* continuous (freshmen).

Admissions Contact Ms. Stephanie Murguia, Director of Admissions and Records, Riverside Community College, 4800 Magnolia Avenue, Riverside, CA 92506. *Phone:* 909-222-8615. *Fax:* 909-222-8037.

SACRAMENTO CITY COLLEGE
Sacramento, California

- **State and locally supported** 2-year, founded 1916, part of California Community College System
- **Calendar** semesters
- **Degree** certificates, diplomas, and associate
- **Urban** 60-acre campus
- **Coed,** 20,781 undergraduate students

Undergraduates Students come from 35 states and territories, 41 other countries, 13% African American, 24% Asian American or Pacific Islander, 14% Hispanic American, 2% Native American.

Faculty *Total:* 554. *Student/faculty ratio:* 30:1.

Majors Accounting; advertising; aircraft mechanic/airframe; Army R.O.T.C./military science; art; aviation technology; biological/physical sciences; business administration; computer science; cosmetology; criminal justice/law enforcement administration; cultural studies; data processing technology; dental assistant; dental hygiene; drafting; early childhood education; electrical/electronic engineering technology; engineering; family/consumer studies; graphic/printing equipment; humanities; human services; legal administrative assistant; liberal arts and sciences/liberal studies; library science; literature; mass communications; mathematics; medical administrative assistant; music; natural resources management; natural sciences; nursing; occupational therapy; physical education; physical sciences; physical therapy assistant; practical nurse; psychology; real estate; secretarial science; social sciences; social work; speech/rhetorical studies; surveying; theater arts/drama; transportation technology; women's studies.

Academic Programs *Special study options:* academic remediation for entering students, adult/continuing education programs, advanced placement credit, cooperative education, English as a second language, honors programs, off-campus study, part-time degree program, services for LD students, student-designed majors, study abroad, summer session for credit.

Library Sacramento City College Library with 68,462 titles, 415 serial subscriptions, an OPAC, a Web page.

Computers on Campus 450 computers available on campus for general student use. A campuswide network can be accessed from off campus. Internet access, at least one staffed computer lab available.

Student Life *Housing:* college housing not available. *Activities and Organizations:* drama/theater group, student-run newspaper, choral group, BOSS, African Student Alliance, Asian Pacific Club, MECHA, SMEC. *Campus security:* 24-hour emergency response devices and patrols, student patrols, late-night transport/escort service. *Student Services:* personal/psychological counseling, women's center.

Athletics *Intercollegiate sports:* baseball M, basketball M/W, cross-country running M/W, football M, golf M/W, soccer W, softball W, swimming M/W, tennis M/W, track and field M/W, volleyball W, water polo W, wrestling M. *Intramural sports:* badminton M/W, baseball M/W, basketball M/W, bowling M/W, cross-country running M/W, fencing M/W, football M/W, golf M/W, soccer M/W, softball W, swimming M/W, table tennis M/W, tennis M/W, volleyball M/W, weight lifting M/W.

Costs (2002–03) *Tuition:* nonresident $3696 full-time, $171 per unit part-time. *Required fees:* $264 full-time, $11 per unit.

Financial Aid In 2001, 168 Federal Work-Study jobs (averaging $1950).

Applying *Application deadline:* rolling (freshmen), rolling (transfers). *Notification:* continuous (freshmen).

Admissions Contact Mr. Sam T. Sandusky, Dean, Student Services, Sacramento City College, 3835 Freeport Boulevard, Sacramento, CA 95822-1386. *Phone:* 916-558-2438. *Fax:* 916-558-2190.

SADDLEBACK COLLEGE
Mission Viejo, California

Admissions Contact Admissions Office, Saddleback College, 28000 Marguerite Parkway, Mission Viejo, CA 92692-3697. *Phone:* 949-582-4555. *E-mail:* earaiza@saddleback.cc.ca.us.

Salvation Army College for Officer Training

Rancho Palos Verdes, California

Admissions Contact Capt. Edward Hill, Salvation Army College for Officer Training, 30840 Hawthorne Boulevard, Rancho Palos Verdes, CA 90275. *Phone:* 310-544-6467.

San Bernardino Valley College

San Bernardino, California

- **State and locally supported** 2-year, founded 1926, part of San Bernardino Community College District System
- **Calendar** semesters
- **Degree** certificates, diplomas, and associate
- 82-acre campus with easy access to Los Angeles
- **Coed**

Undergraduates Students come from 2 states and territories.
Faculty *Total:* 375, 47% full-time.
Majors Accounting; aerospace science; anthropology; architectural engineering technology; art; astronomy; auto mechanic/technician; biology; botany; business administration; business marketing and marketing management; chemical engineering technology; chemistry; civil engineering technology; computer engineering technology; computer science; corrections; data processing technology; dental hygiene; developmental/child psychology; drafting; economics; electrical/electronic engineering technology; English; environmental science; family/consumer studies; finance; French; geography; geology; German; graphic design/commercial art/illustration; heating/air conditioning/refrigeration; history; hotel and restaurant management; human services; interior design; journalism; law enforcement/police science; liberal arts and sciences/liberal studies; machine technology; mathematics; medical laboratory technician; mental health/rehabilitation; music; nursing; philosophy; photography; physical education; physical sciences; physics; political science; pre-engineering; psychology; radio/television broadcasting; real estate; recreation/leisure studies; religious studies; secretarial science; sociology; Spanish; telecommunications; welding technology; zoology.
Academic Programs *Special study options:* academic remediation for entering students, cooperative education, part-time degree program, services for LD students, summer session for credit.
Library 122,802 titles, 657 serial subscriptions.
Computers on Campus 180 computers available on campus for general student use. At least one staffed computer lab available.
Student Life *Housing:* college housing not available. *Activities and Organizations:* drama/theater group, student-run newspaper, radio station. *Student Services:* health clinic, personal/psychological counseling, women's center.
Athletics *Intercollegiate sports:* basketball M/W, cross-country running M/W, football M, golf M, tennis M/W, track and field M/W, volleyball W, wrestling M. *Intramural sports:* basketball M/W, soccer M/W.
Standardized Tests *Required:* CGP.
Financial Aid In 2001, 100 Federal Work-Study jobs (averaging $3000).
Applying *Application deadline:* 8/29 (freshmen).
Admissions Contact Mr. Daniel T. Angelo, Director of Admissions and Records, San Bernardino Valley College, 701 South Mt Vernon Avenue, San Bernardino, CA 92410-2748. *Phone:* 909-888-6511 Ext. 1656.

San Diego City College

San Diego, California

- **State and locally supported** 2-year, founded 1914, part of San Diego Community College District System
- **Calendar** semesters
- **Degree** certificates and associate
- **Urban** 56-acre campus
- **Coed,** 14,126 undergraduate students, 21% full-time, 51% women, 49% men

Undergraduates 19% African American, 12% Asian American or Pacific Islander, 26% Hispanic American, 1% Native American.
Faculty *Total:* 485, 33% full-time, 26% with terminal degrees. *Student/faculty ratio:* 35:1.
Majors Accounting; African-American studies; anthropology; art; auto mechanic/technician; behavioral sciences; biology; business administration; business marketing and marketing management; carpentry; computer engineering technology; consumer services; cosmetology; court reporting; data processing technology; developmental/child psychology; drafting; electrical/electronic engineering technology; emergency medical technology; engineering technology; English; environmental technology; fashion merchandising; finance; food products retailing; graphic design/commercial art/illustration; graphic/printing equipment; Hispanic-American studies; hospitality management; industrial arts; industrial technology; insurance/risk management; interior design; journalism; labor/personnel relations; Latin American studies; legal administrative assistant; liberal arts and sciences/liberal studies; machine technology; mathematics; Mexican-American studies; modern languages; music; nursing; occupational safety/health technology; paralegal/legal assistant; photography; physical education; physical sciences; political science; postal management; practical nurse; pre-engineering; psychology; radio/television broadcasting; real estate; recreation/leisure studies; robotics; secretarial science; social sciences; social work; sociology; speech/rhetorical studies; teacher assistant/aide; telecommunications; theater arts/drama; transportation technology; travel/tourism management; welding technology.
Academic Programs *Special study options:* academic remediation for entering students, adult/continuing education programs, cooperative education, distance learning, English as a second language, external degree program, honors programs, independent study, off-campus study, part-time degree program, services for LD students, student-designed majors, summer session for credit. *ROTC:* Air Force (c).
Library San Diego City College Library with 73,000 titles, 337 serial subscriptions, an OPAC.
Computers on Campus 396 computers available on campus for general student use. At least one staffed computer lab available.
Student Life *Housing:* college housing not available. *Activities and Organizations:* drama/theater group, student-run newspaper, radio station, choral group, Alpha Gamma Sigma, Association of United Latin American Students, MECHA, Afrikan Student Union, Student Nurses Association. *Campus security:* 24-hour emergency response devices and patrols, late-night transport/escort service. *Student Services:* health clinic, personal/psychological counseling.
Athletics Member NJCAA. *Intercollegiate sports:* baseball M, basketball M/W, cross-country running M/W, football M, golf M/W, soccer M/W, softball W, tennis M/W, track and field M/W, volleyball M/W. *Intramural sports:* archery M/W, badminton M/W, baseball M, basketball M/W, bowling M/W, racquetball M/W, soccer M/W, softball W, swimming M/W, tennis M/W, track and field M/W, volleyball M/W, weight lifting M/W.
Costs (2002–03) *Tuition:* state resident $0 full-time; nonresident $3900 full-time, $120 per unit part-time. Full-time tuition and fees vary according to course load. Part-time tuition and fees vary according to course load. *Required fees:* $363 full-time, $11 per unit.
Financial Aid In 2001, 100 Federal Work-Study jobs (averaging $4000).
Applying *Options:* common application, early admission. *Required for some:* high school transcript. *Application deadline:* rolling (freshmen), rolling (transfers).
Admissions Contact Ms. Lou Humphries, Supervisor of Admissions and Records, San Diego City College, 1313 Twelfth Avenue, San Diego, CA 92101-4787. *Phone:* 619-388-3474. *Fax:* 619-388-3135. *E-mail:* lhumphr@sdccd.net.

San Diego Golf Academy

Vista, California

Admissions Contact Ms. Deborah Wells, Admissions Coordinator, San Diego Golf Academy, 1910 Shadowridge Drive, Suite 111, Vista, CA 92083. *Phone:* 760-414-1501. *Toll-free phone:* 800-342-7342. *Fax:* 760-918-8949. *E-mail:* sdga@sdgagolf.com.

San Diego Mesa College

San Diego, California

- **State and locally supported** 2-year, founded 1964, part of San Diego Community College District System
- **Calendar** semesters
- **Degree** certificates, diplomas, and associate
- **Suburban** 104-acre campus
- **Coed,** 21,700 undergraduate students

Undergraduates 6% African American, 12% Asian American or Pacific Islander, 14% Hispanic American, 1% Native American.
Freshmen *Admission:* 2,152 applied, 2,152 admitted.
Faculty *Total:* 745.
Majors Accounting; African-American studies; anthropology; applied art; architectural engineering technology; architecture; art; biology; business administra-

San Diego Mesa College (continued)
tion; business computer programming; business marketing and marketing management; chemistry; child care provider; computer graphics; computer/information sciences; computer programming related; computer science; computer software and media applications related; computer systems networking/telecommunications; construction technology; data entry/microcomputer applications related; dental assistant; developmental/child psychology; electrical/electronic engineering technology; engineering; English; fashion design/illustration; fashion merchandising; fine/studio arts; food products retailing; foods/nutrition studies related; French; geography; German; hospitality/recreation marketing operations; hotel and restaurant management; hotel/motel services marketing operations; industrial radiologic technology; interior design; Italian; Italian studies; landscape architecture; legal administrative assistant; liberal arts and sciences/liberal studies; marketing operations; marketing research; mathematics; medical assistant; medical laboratory technician; medical records administration; Mexican-American studies; multimedia; music; nutrition science; physical education; physical sciences; physical therapy assistant; physics; psychology; real estate; recreation/leisure studies; Russian; secretarial science; social sciences; sociology; Spanish; speech/rhetorical studies; technical/business writing; travel services marketing operations; travel/tourism management; veterinary technology; water resources.

Academic Programs *Special study options:* academic remediation for entering students, adult/continuing education programs, English as a second language, external degree program, honors programs, independent study, part-time degree program, services for LD students, summer session for credit.

Library 84,353 titles, 657 serial subscriptions.

Computers on Campus 350 computers available on campus for general student use. Internet access, at least one staffed computer lab available.

Student Life *Housing:* college housing not available. *Activities and Organizations:* drama/theater group, student-run newspaper, choral group, Alpha Gamma Sigma, Black Students Association, MECHA, Gay and Lesbian Student Group, Vietnamese Student Association. *Campus security:* 24-hour emergency response devices and patrols, late-night transport/escort service. *Student Services:* health clinic, personal/psychological counseling.

Athletics *Intercollegiate sports:* baseball M, basketball M/W, cross-country running M/W, football M, soccer M/W, softball W, swimming M/W, tennis M/W, track and field M/W, volleyball M/W, water polo M/W. *Intramural sports:* badminton M/W, basketball M/W, bowling M/W, fencing M/W, football M, golf M/W, gymnastics M/W, racquetball M/W, skiing (downhill) M, soccer M/W, softball M/W, swimming M/W, tennis M/W, volleyball M/W, weight lifting M/W.

Standardized Tests *Recommended:* ACT (for placement).

Costs (2002–03) *Tuition:* state resident $0 full-time; nonresident $3120 full-time, $130 per unit part-time. *Required fees:* $290 full-time, $11 per unit, $13 per term part-time. *Waivers:* minority students, adult students, and senior citizens.

Financial Aid *Financial aid deadline:* 6/30.

Applying *Options:* early admission. *Notification:* continuous (freshmen).

Admissions Contact Ms. Ivonne Alvarez, Director of Admissions and Records, San Diego Mesa College, 7250 Mesa College Drive, San Diego, CA 92111. *Phone:* 619-388-2689. *Fax:* 619-388-3960.

SAN DIEGO MIRAMAR COLLEGE
San Diego, California

Admissions Contact Ms. Dana Andras, Admissions Supervisor, San Diego Miramar College, 10440 Black Mountain Road, San Diego, CA 92126-2999. *Phone:* 619-536-7854. *Fax:* 619-693-1899. *E-mail:* dandras@sdccd.cc.ca.us.

SAN FRANCISCO COLLEGE OF MORTUARY SCIENCE
San Francisco, California

Admissions Contact Ms. Shayneh West, Admissions Counselor, San Francisco College of Mortuary Science, 1598 Dolores Street, San Francisco, CA 94110-4927. *Phone:* 415-824-1313. *Fax:* 415-824-1390. *E-mail:* sfcms@ix.netcom.com.

SAN JOAQUIN DELTA COLLEGE
Stockton, California

- **District-supported** 2-year, founded 1935, part of California Community College System
- **Calendar** semesters
- **Degree** associate
- **Urban** 165-acre campus with easy access to Sacramento
- **Coed,** 18,546 undergraduate students

Undergraduates Students come from 38 other countries.

Faculty *Total:* 561, 40% full-time. *Student/faculty ratio:* 33:1.

Majors Accounting; agricultural business; agricultural mechanization; agricultural sciences; animal sciences; anthropology; art; auto mechanic/technician; behavioral sciences; biology; botany; broadcast journalism; business administration; business economics; business marketing and marketing management; carpentry; chemistry; child care/development; civil engineering technology; computer engineering technology; computer programming; computer science; construction technology; corrections; culinary arts; dance; developmental/child psychology; drafting; drawing; early childhood education; economics; electrical/electronic engineering technology; emergency medical technology; engineering; engineering design; engineering technology; English; fashion merchandising; fire science; food products retailing; food services technology; French; geology; German; graphic design/commercial art/illustration; graphic/printing equipment; health science; heating/air conditioning/refrigeration; history; home economics; humanities; industrial radiologic technology; interior design; Italian; Japanese; journalism; law enforcement/police science; liberal arts and sciences/liberal studies; literature; machine technology; mathematics; mechanical engineering technology; music; natural resources management; natural sciences; nursing; ornamental horticulture; philosophy; photography; physical education; physical sciences; political science; practical nurse; psychiatric/mental health services; psychology; public administration; religious studies; social sciences; sociology; Spanish; speech/rhetorical studies; theater arts/drama.

Academic Programs *Special study options:* academic remediation for entering students, adult/continuing education programs, advanced placement credit, cooperative education, English as a second language, honors programs, part-time degree program, services for LD students, summer session for credit.

Library Goleman Library plus 1 other with 92,398 titles, 605 serial subscriptions, an OPAC, a Web page.

Computers on Campus 400 computers available on campus for general student use. A campuswide network can be accessed from off campus. Internet access, online (class) registration, at least one staffed computer lab available.

Student Life *Housing:* college housing not available. *Activities and Organizations:* drama/theater group, student-run newspaper, radio station, choral group, Alpha Gamma Sigma, Fashion Club, International Club, Badminton Club. *Campus security:* 24-hour emergency response devices and patrols, late-night transport/escort service. *Student Services:* personal/psychological counseling, legal services.

Athletics Member NJCAA. *Intercollegiate sports:* baseball M, basketball M/W, cross-country running M/W, fencing M/W, football M, golf M/W, soccer M/W, softball W, swimming M/W, tennis M/W, track and field M/W, volleyball W, water polo M/W, wrestling M. *Intramural sports:* badminton M/W, basketball M/W, bowling M/W, soccer M/W, swimming M/W, tennis M/W, volleyball M/W, weight lifting M/W.

Standardized Tests *Recommended:* Michigan Test of English Language Proficiency.

Costs (2002–03) *Tuition:* state resident $0 full-time; nonresident $4290 full-time, $143 per unit part-time. *Required fees:* $330 full-time, $11 per unit. *Payment plan:* installment. *Waivers:* employees or children of employees.

Financial Aid In 2001, 315 Federal Work-Study jobs (averaging $3100). 210 State and other part-time jobs.

Applying *Options:* common application, electronic application, early admission. *Application deadline:* rolling (freshmen), rolling (transfers). *Notification:* continuous (freshmen).

Admissions Contact Ms. Catherine Mooney, Registrar, San Joaquin Delta College, 5151 Pacific Avenue, Stockton, CA 95207. *Phone:* 209-954-5635. *Fax:* 209-954-5769. *E-mail:* questions@sjdccd.cc.ca.us.

SAN JOAQUIN VALLEY COLLEGE
Visalia, California

- **Independent** 2-year, founded 1977
- **Calendar** continuous
- **Degree** associate
- **Small-town** campus
- **Coed,** 1,844 undergraduate students, 100% full-time, 70% women, 30% men

Undergraduates 7% African American, 5% Asian American or Pacific Islander, 45% Hispanic American, 2% Native American, 0.1% international. *Retention:* 59% of 2001 full-time freshmen returned.

Faculty *Total:* 231, 65% full-time, 3% with terminal degrees. *Student/faculty ratio:* 17:1.

Majors Aircraft mechanic/airframe; aircraft mechanic/powerplant; business; business systems networking/ telecommunications; computer/technical support;

corrections; dental assistant; dental hygiene; electrical/electronic engineering technology; heating/air conditioning/refrigeration; medical administrative assistant; medical assistant; operating room technician; pharmacy technician/assistant; practical nurse; respiratory therapy; security; travel/tourism management; veterinary technology.

Academic Programs *Special study options:* academic remediation for entering students.

Library SJVC Visalia Campus Library with 4,003 titles, 25 serial subscriptions, 75 audiovisual materials.

Computers on Campus 100 computers available on campus for general student use. At least one staffed computer lab available.

Student Life *Housing:* college housing not available. *Activities and Organizations:* Associated Student Body, Students in Free Enterprise, American Medical Technologists. *Campus security:* late-night transport/escort service, full-time security personnel.

Applying *Required:* high school transcript. *Required for some:* essay or personal statement, interview.

Admissions Contact Ms. Wendy Mendes, Vice President of Administration, San Joaquin Valley College, 8400 West Mineral King Avenue, Visalia, CA 93291. *Phone:* 559-651-2500.

San Jose City College
San Jose, California

Admissions Contact Ms. Rosalie Eskew, Director of Admissions/Registrar, San Jose City College, 2100 Moorpark Avenue, San Jose, CA 95128-2799. *Phone:* 408-288-3707.

Santa Ana College
Santa Ana, California

- **State-supported** 2-year, founded 1915, part of California Community College System
- **Calendar** semesters
- **Degree** certificates and associate
- **Urban** 58-acre campus with easy access to Los Angeles
- **Coed,** 25,386 undergraduate students, 14% full-time, 37% women, 63% men

Undergraduates 3,431 full-time, 21,955 part-time. Students come from 50 states and territories, 4% are from out of state, 3% African American, 24% Asian American or Pacific Islander, 47% Hispanic American, 0.7% Native American, 6% transferred in.

Freshmen *Admission:* 2,021 enrolled.

Faculty *Total:* 1,296, 19% full-time. *Student/faculty ratio:* 20:1.

Majors Accounting; African-American studies; anthropology; art; auto mechanic/technician; biological/physical sciences; biology; business administration; business marketing and marketing management; chemistry; communications; computer programming related; computer science; computer science related; cosmetology; criminal justice/law enforcement administration; cultural studies; dance; data entry/microcomputer applications; data entry/microcomputer applications related; diesel engine mechanic; drafting; early childhood education; economics; electrical/electronic engineering technology; engineering; engineering technology; English; entrepreneurship; environmental science; exercise sciences; family/consumer studies; fashion design/illustration; fashion merchandising; fire science; geography; geology; graphic design/commercial art/illustration; history; industrial technology; information sciences/systems; information technology; journalism; law enforcement/police science; legal studies; liberal arts and sciences/liberal studies; library science; management science; mathematics; medical assistant; Mexican-American studies; modern languages; music; nursing; nutrition science; occupational therapy; pharmacy technician/assistant; philosophy; photography; physics; political science; psychology; quality control technology; real estate; secretarial science; social sciences; sociology; telecommunications; theater arts/drama; travel/tourism management; water resources engineering; welding technology; women's studies; word processing.

Academic Programs *Special study options:* academic remediation for entering students, accelerated degree program, adult/continuing education programs, advanced placement credit, cooperative education, distance learning, English as a second language, external degree program, freshman honors college, honors programs, part-time degree program, services for LD students, study abroad, summer session for credit. *ROTC:* Air Force (c).

Library McNeally Library with 99,473 titles, 7,690 audiovisual materials.

Computers on Campus 100 computers available on campus for general student use. Internet access, at least one staffed computer lab available.

Student Life *Housing:* college housing not available. *Activities and Organizations:* drama/theater group, student-run newspaper, television station, choral group, Students of Diverse Cultures, Students United for Better Education, Phi Beta Kappa, Alpha Gamma Sigma, Puente. *Campus security:* late-night transport/escort service. *Student Services:* health clinic, personal/psychological counseling, women's center, legal services.

Athletics *Intercollegiate sports:* baseball M, basketball M/W, cross-country running M/W, football M, golf M, soccer M, softball W, swimming M, tennis M/W, track and field M/W, volleyball W, water polo M, wrestling M.

Costs (2001–02) *Tuition:* nonresident $3384 full-time, $141 per unit part-time. *Required fees:* $301 full-time, $11 per unit, $37 per term part-time.

Applying *Options:* early admission. *Application deadlines:* 8/21 (freshmen), 8/21 (transfers).

Admissions Contact Mrs. Chris Steward, Admissions Clerk, Santa Ana College, 1530 West 17th Street, Santa Ana, CA 92704. *Phone:* 714-564-6053. *Fax:* 714-564-4379.

Santa Barbara City College
Santa Barbara, California

- **State and locally supported** 2-year, founded 1908, part of California Community College System
- **Calendar** semesters
- **Degree** certificates and associate
- **Small-town** 65-acre campus
- **Coed,** 14,949 undergraduate students, 36% full-time, 51% women, 49% men

Undergraduates 5,311 full-time, 9,638 part-time. Students come from 44 states and territories, 60 other countries, 5% are from out of state, 2% African American, 5% Asian American or Pacific Islander, 22% Hispanic American, 1% Native American, 7% international, 5% transferred in.

Freshmen *Admission:* 2,276 applied, 2,276 admitted, 1,539 enrolled.

Faculty *Total:* 639, 34% full-time. *Student/faculty ratio:* 24:1.

Majors Accounting; acting/directing; African-American studies; anthropology; art history; athletic training/sports medicine; auto mechanic/technician; biology; biomedical technology; biotechnology research; business administration; business marketing and marketing management; chemistry; child care/guidance; communications; computer engineering; computer science; cosmetic services; criminal justice/law enforcement administration; culinary arts and services related; cultural studies; drafting; early childhood education; economics; electrical/electronic engineering technology; electrical equipment installation/repair; engineering; engineering-related technology; English; entrepreneurship; environmental engineering; environmental science; exercise sciences; film studies; finance; fine/studio arts; French; geography; geology; graphic design/commercial art/illustration; history; horticulture services; hotel and restaurant management; industrial/manufacturing engineering; industrial technology; information sciences/systems; information technology; institutional food services; institutional food workers; interior design; international relations; landscaping management; legal studies; liberal arts and sciences/liberal studies; marine technology; mathematics; medical radiologic technology; medical records technology; Mexican-American studies; music; Native American studies; nursing; ornamental horticulture; philosophy; physical education; physics; political science; practical nurse; psychology; real estate; recreational therapy; recreation/leisure studies; sales operations; secretarial science; sociology; Spanish; system/networking/LAN/WAN management; theater arts/drama; theater design.

Academic Programs *Special study options:* academic remediation for entering students, adult/continuing education programs, advanced placement credit, cooperative education, distance learning, double majors, English as a second language, honors programs, independent study, internships, part-time degree program, services for LD students, study abroad, summer session for credit. *ROTC:* Army (c).

Library Eli Luria Library with 105,412 titles, 2,003 serial subscriptions, 12,632 audiovisual materials, an OPAC, a Web page.

Computers on Campus 930 computers available on campus for general student use. A campuswide network can be accessed from off campus. Internet access, at least one staffed computer lab available.

Student Life *Housing:* college housing not available. *Activities and Organizations:* drama/theater group, student-run newspaper, choral group, MECHA, International-Cultural Exchange Club, Geology Club, Computer Club, Future Teachers Club. *Campus security:* 24-hour emergency response devices and patrols, late-night transport/escort service. *Student Services:* health clinic, personal/psychological counseling.

Athletics *Intercollegiate sports:* baseball M, basketball M/W, cross-country running M/W, football M, golf M/W, soccer M/W, softball W, tennis M/W, track and field M/W, volleyball M/W.

Santa Barbara City College (continued)

Standardized Tests *Recommended:* SAT I (for placement), SAT II: Subject Tests (for placement), SAT II: Writing Test (for placement), California State University EPT, UC Subject A Exam.

Costs (2002–03) *Tuition:* nonresident $4350 full-time, $145 per unit part-time. Full-time tuition and fees vary according to course load. Part-time tuition and fees vary according to course load. *Required fees:* $65 full-time, $63 per term part-time.

Applying *Options:* early admission. *Recommended:* high school transcript. *Application deadlines:* 8/18 (freshmen), 8/18 (transfers). *Notification:* continuous (freshmen).

Admissions Contact Ms. Jane Craven, Dean of Educational Programs, Santa Barbara City College, 721 Cliff Drive, Santa Barbara, CA 93109. *Phone:* 805-965-0581 Ext. 2793. *Fax:* 805-962-0497 Ext. 2220. *E-mail:* admissions@sbcc.net.

SANTA MONICA COLLEGE
Santa Monica, California

- **State and locally supported** 2-year, founded 1929, part of California Community College System
- **Calendar** semester plus optional winter and summer terms
- **Degree** certificates and associate
- **Urban** 40-acre campus with easy access to Los Angeles
- **Endowment** $4.6 million
- **Coed,** 29,077 undergraduate students, 32% full-time, 57% women, 43% men

Undergraduates 9,449 full-time, 19,628 part-time. Students come from 50 states and territories, 101 other countries, 4% are from out of state, 11% African American, 14% Asian American or Pacific Islander, 28% Hispanic American, 0.6% Native American, 16% international, 47% transferred in. *Retention:* 63% of 2001 full-time freshmen returned.

Freshmen *Admission:* 2,422 enrolled. *Average high school GPA:* 2.61.

Faculty *Total:* 1,267, 27% full-time. *Student/faculty ratio:* 26:1.

Majors Accounting; anthropology; architectural engineering technology; art; astronomy; athletic training/sports medicine; auto mechanic/technician; biology; broadcast journalism; business administration; chemistry; computer programming; computer programming (specific applications); computer science related; construction technology; cosmetology; criminal justice/law enforcement administration; cultural studies; dance; data processing technology; dental hygiene; developmental/child psychology; drafting; early childhood education; economics; electrical/electronic engineering technology; English; fashion merchandising; fire science; French; geography; geology; German; graphic design/commercial art/illustration; graphic/printing equipment; history; home economics; industrial arts; information sciences/systems; interior design; journalism; law enforcement/police science; liberal arts and sciences/liberal studies; mass communications; mathematics; music; nursing; philosophy; photography; physical education; physics; political science; pre-engineering; psychology; radio/television broadcasting; real estate; recreation/leisure studies; respiratory therapy; secretarial science; sociology; theater arts/drama; welding technology.

Academic Programs *Special study options:* academic remediation for entering students, adult/continuing education programs, advanced placement credit, cooperative education, distance learning, English as a second language, honors programs, independent study, internships, part-time degree program, services for LD students, study abroad, summer session for credit. *ROTC:* Army (c).

Library Santa Monica College Library with 138,674 titles, 459 serial subscriptions, an OPAC, a Web page.

Computers on Campus 600 computers available on campus for general student use. A campuswide network can be accessed from off campus. Internet access, at least one staffed computer lab available.

Student Life *Housing:* college housing not available. *Activities and Organizations:* drama/theater group, student-run newspaper, choral group, Club Latino United for Education, African Student Union, Gay and Lesbian Union, Alpha Gamma Sigma, International Speakers Club. *Campus security:* 24-hour emergency response devices and patrols, student patrols, late-night transport/escort service. *Student Services:* health clinic, personal/psychological counseling, women's center, legal services.

Athletics *Intercollegiate sports:* basketball M/W, cross-country running M/W, football M, soccer W, softball W, swimming M/W, tennis W, track and field M/W, volleyball M/W, water polo M/W.

Standardized Tests *Required for some:* ACT, COMPASS, ACCUPLACER.

Costs (2002–03) *Tuition:* state resident $0 full-time; nonresident $4230 full-time, $141 per unit part-time. *Required fees:* $388 full-time, $11 per unit, $29 per term part-time.

Financial Aid In 2001, 320 Federal Work-Study jobs (averaging $2500).

Applying *Options:* early admission. *Required:* high school transcript. *Application deadlines:* 8/30 (freshmen), 8/30 (transfers). *Notification:* continuous until 8/30 (freshmen).

Admissions Contact Ms. Brenda Simmons, Dean of Enrollment Services, Santa Monica College, 1900 Pico Boulevard, Santa Monica, CA 90405-1628. *Phone:* 310-434-4880.

SANTA ROSA JUNIOR COLLEGE
Santa Rosa, California

- **State and locally supported** 2-year, founded 1918, part of California Community College System
- **Calendar** semesters
- **Degree** certificates and associate
- **Urban** 93-acre campus with easy access to San Francisco
- **Endowment** $24.9 million
- **Coed**

Faculty *Student/faculty ratio:* 17:1.

Student Life *Campus security:* 24-hour emergency response devices and patrols.

Standardized Tests *Required for some:* Assessment and Placement Services for Community Colleges.

Financial Aid In 2001, 226 Federal Work-Study jobs (averaging $3269).

Applying *Options:* electronic application, early admission.

Admissions Contact Ms. Renee LoPilato, Dean of Admissions, Santa Rosa Junior College, 1501 Mendocino Avenue, Santa Rosa, CA 95401-4395. *Phone:* 707-527-4510. *Fax:* 707-527-4798. *E-mail:* lori_koches@garfield.santarosa.edu.

SANTIAGO CANYON COLLEGE
Orange, California

- **State-supported** 2-year, founded 2000, part of California Community College System
- **Calendar** semesters
- **Degree** certificates and associate
- **Coed,** 9,742 undergraduate students, 13% full-time, 41% women, 59% men

Undergraduates 1,288 full-time, 8,454 part-time.

Freshmen *Admission:* 986 applied, 986 admitted, 1,369 enrolled.

Faculty *Total:* 417, 22% full-time. *Student/faculty ratio:* 23:1.

Academic Programs *Special study options:* academic remediation for entering students, adult/continuing education programs, advanced placement credit, cooperative education, distance learning, English as a second language, external degree program, freshman honors college, honors programs, part-time degree program, services for LD students, summer session for credit.

Library Santiago Canyon College Library with 31,000 titles, 2,260 serial subscriptions, 4,082 audiovisual materials, an OPAC, a Web page.

Computers on Campus 45 computers available on campus for general student use. Internet access available.

Costs (2001–02) *Tuition:* nonresident $3384 full-time, $141 per unit part-time. *Required fees:* $301 full-time, $11 per unit, $37 per term part-time. *Payment plan:* deferred payment.

Applying *Options:* early admission. *Application deadlines:* 8/21 (freshmen), 8/21 (transfers).

Admissions Contact Denise Pennock, Admissions and Records, Santiago Canyon College, 8045 East Chapman, Orange, CA 92669. *Phone:* 714-564-4000. *Fax:* 714-564-4379.

SEQUOIA INSTITUTE
Fremont, California

- **Proprietary** 2-year, founded 1966
- **Degree** certificates, diplomas, and associate
- **Coed, primarily men,** 758 undergraduate students, 100% full-time, 9% women, 91% men

Faculty *Total:* 54, 89% full-time. *Student/faculty ratio:* 20:1.

Majors Auto mechanic/technician; automotive engineering technology; heating/air conditioning/refrigeration.

Costs (2001–02) *Tuition:* $23,375 for a 15-month program.

Admissions Contact Mr. Joseph Files, Vice President of Marketing and Admissions, Sequoia Institute, 200 Whitney Place, Fremont, CA 94539-7663. *Phone:* 510-580-5440. *Toll-free phone:* 800-248-8585.

SHASTA COLLEGE
Redding, California

- **State and locally supported** 2-year, founded 1948, part of California Community College System
- **Calendar** semesters
- **Degree** certificates and associate
- **Rural** 336-acre campus
- **Endowment** $1.3 million
- **Coed,** 10,108 undergraduate students, 36% full-time, 60% women, 40% men

Undergraduates 3,656 full-time, 6,452 part-time. 2% are from out of state.
Freshmen *Admission:* 1,280 enrolled.
Faculty *Total:* 491, 30% full-time.
Majors Accounting; agricultural business; animal sciences; art; auto mechanic/technician; aviation technology; business administration; civil engineering technology; computer management; construction technology; criminal justice/law enforcement administration; culinary arts; dental hygiene; design/visual communications; diesel engine mechanic; drafting; early childhood education; electrical/electronic engineering technology; fire science; home economics; horticulture science; journalism; legal administrative assistant; management information systems/business data processing; medical administrative assistant; medical assistant; music; natural resources management; nursing; ornamental horticulture; paralegal/legal assistant; real estate; secretarial science; speech/rhetorical studies; theater arts/drama; welding technology.
Academic Programs *Special study options:* academic remediation for entering students, adult/continuing education programs, advanced placement credit, cooperative education, distance learning, double majors, English as a second language, honors programs, internships, part-time degree program, services for LD students, summer session for credit.
Library Shasta College Learning Resource Center with 67,500 titles, 1,700 serial subscriptions, 4,859 audiovisual materials, an OPAC, a Web page.
Computers on Campus 154 computers available on campus for general student use. A campuswide network can be accessed from off campus. Internet access, at least one staffed computer lab available.
Student Life *Housing Options:* coed. *Activities and Organizations:* drama/theater group, student-run newspaper, choral group, Associated Student Body, Environmental Resource Leadership Club, Intercultural Club, Intervarsity Christian Fellowship, Music Education National Conference. *Campus security:* 24-hour emergency response devices, student patrols, late-night transport/escort service, 16-hour patrols by trained security personnel. *Student Services:* health clinic, personal/psychological counseling.
Athletics *Intercollegiate sports:* baseball M, basketball M/W, cross-country running M/W, football M, golf M/W, soccer M/W, softball W, swimming M/W, tennis M/W, track and field M/W, volleyball W. *Intramural sports:* cross-country running M/W.
Standardized Tests *Required:* Assessment and Placement Services for Community Colleges. *Recommended:* SAT I or ACT (for placement).
Costs (2002–03) *Tuition:* state resident $0 full-time; nonresident $3419 full-time, $153 per unit part-time. Full-time tuition and fees vary according to course load. *Required fees:* $319 full-time, $11 per unit. *Room and board:* Room and board charges vary according to housing facility.
Financial Aid In 2001, 1,000 Federal Work-Study jobs (averaging $2500).
Applying *Options:* common application, early admission. *Required:* high school transcript. *Application deadline:* rolling (freshmen). *Notification:* continuous (freshmen).
Admissions Contact Ms. Cassandra Ryan, Admissions and Records Office Manager, Shasta College, PO Box 496006, Redding, CA 96049-6006. *Phone:* 530-225-4841.

SIERRA COLLEGE
Rocklin, California

- **State-supported** 2-year, founded 1936, part of California Community College System
- **Calendar** semesters
- **Degree** certificates and associate
- **Rural** 327-acre campus with easy access to Sacramento
- **Coed,** 19,000 undergraduate students

Undergraduates 1% live on campus.
Freshmen *Admission:* 24,000 applied, 24,000 admitted.
Faculty *Total:* 530.
Majors Accounting; agricultural mechanization; agronomy/crop science; animal sciences; art; auto mechanic/technician; biology; business administration; business marketing and marketing management; carpentry; chemistry; computer engineering technology; computer science; construction management; construction technology; corrections; criminal justice/law enforcement administration; drafting; early childhood education; electrical/electronic engineering technology; engineering; equestrian studies; fashion merchandising; fire science; food services technology; forest harvesting production technology; forestry; geology; home economics; horticulture science; industrial arts; industrial technology; information sciences/systems; interior design; journalism; law enforcement/police science; legal administrative assistant; liberal arts and sciences/liberal studies; mass communications; medical administrative assistant; metallurgical technology; mining technology; nursing; ornamental horticulture; photography; practical nurse; real estate; secretarial science; surveying; teacher assistant/aide; welding technology.
Academic Programs *Special study options:* academic remediation for entering students, accelerated degree program, advanced placement credit, distance learning, double majors, English as a second language, independent study, internships, off-campus study, part-time degree program, services for LD students, study abroad, summer session for credit.
Library Winstead Library plus 1 other with 69,879 titles, 189 serial subscriptions, an OPAC.
Computers on Campus 430 computers available on campus for general student use. A campuswide network can be accessed from off campus. At least one staffed computer lab available.
Student Life *Housing Options:* coed. *Activities and Organizations:* drama/theater group, student-run newspaper, choral group, Drama Club, student government, Art Club, band, Aggie Club. *Campus security:* 24-hour emergency response devices and patrols, late-night transport/escort service. *Student Services:* health clinic, personal/psychological counseling.
Athletics *Intercollegiate sports:* baseball M, basketball M/W, cross-country running M/W, football M, golf M/W, skiing (cross-country) M/W, skiing (downhill) M/W, softball W, swimming M/W, tennis M/W, track and field M/W, volleyball W, water polo M/W, wrestling M. *Intramural sports:* archery M/W, badminton M/W, basketball M/W, tennis M/W, volleyball M/W.
Standardized Tests *Required:* APS. *Recommended:* ACT (for placement).
Costs (2001–02) *Tuition:* nonresident $3528 full-time, $147 per unit part-time. *Required fees:* $264 full-time, $11 per unit. *Room and board:* $5790.
Financial Aid In 2001, 150 Federal Work-Study jobs (averaging $2340).
Applying *Options:* common application, early admission. *Application deadline:* rolling (freshmen). *Notification:* continuous (freshmen).
Admissions Contact Ms. Carla Epting-Davis, Associate Dean of Student Support Services, Sierra College, 5000 Rocklin Road, Rocklin, CA 95677-3397. *Phone:* 916-789-2939. *E-mail:* jradford-harris@scmail.sierra.cc.ca.us.

SILICON VALLEY COLLEGE
Fremont, California

Admissions Contact 41350 Christy Street, Fremont, CA 94538.

SILICON VALLEY COLLEGE
Walnut Creek, California

Admissions Contact 2800 Mitchell Drive, Walnut Creek, CA 94598.

SILICON VALLEY COLLEGE
San Jose, California

- **Proprietary** primarily 2-year
- **Degrees** certificates, associate, and bachelor's
- **Coed,** 197 undergraduate students

Majors Architectural drafting; computer graphics; mechanical drafting; medical assistant; pharmacy technician/assistant; system/networking/LAN/WAN management.
Admissions Contact 6201 San Ignacio Boulevard, San Jose, CA 95119.

SKYLINE COLLEGE
San Bruno, California

- **State and locally supported** 2-year, founded 1969, part of San Mateo County Community College District System
- **Calendar** semesters
- **Degree** certificates and associate
- **Suburban** 125-acre campus with easy access to San Francisco
- **Coed**

Faculty *Student/faculty ratio:* 27:1.
Student Life *Campus security:* security guards during open hours.
Athletics Member NJCAA.
Standardized Tests *Recommended:* SAT I and SAT II or ACT (for placement).
Costs (2001–02) *Tuition:* state resident $0 full-time; nonresident $3576 full-time, $148 per unit part-time. Part-time tuition and fees vary according to location. *Required fees:* $298 full-time, $11 per unit, $17 per term part-time.
Financial Aid In 2001, 112 Federal Work-Study jobs (averaging $2400).
Applying *Required for some:* essay or personal statement, high school transcript, minimum 2.0 GPA, interview.
Admissions Contact Mr. Dennis Arreola, Dean of Admissions and Records, Skyline College, 3300 College Drive, San Bruno, CA 94066-1698. *Phone:* 650-738-4251. *E-mail:* skyadmissions@smccd.net.

SOLANO COMMUNITY COLLEGE
Suisun, California

Admissions Contact Mr. Gerald Fisher, Assistant Dean of Admissions and Records, Solano Community College, 4000 Suisun Valley Road, Suisun, CA 94585-3197. *Phone:* 707-864-7171. *E-mail:* admissions@solano.cc.ca.us.

SOUTHERN CALIFORNIA COLLEGE OF BUSINESS AND LAW
Brea, California

Admissions Contact 595 West Lambert Road, Brea, CA 92821-3909.

SOUTHERN CALIFORNIA INSTITUTE OF TECHNOLOGY
Anaheim, California

Admissions Contact Dr. Parviz Shams, President, Southern California Institute of Technology, 1900 West Crescent Avenue, Building B, Anaheim, CA 92801. *Phone:* 714-520-5552.

SOUTHWESTERN COLLEGE
Chula Vista, California

- **State and locally supported** 2-year, founded 1961, part of California Community College System
- **Calendar** semesters
- **Degree** certificates and associate
- **Suburban** 158-acre campus with easy access to San Diego
- **Endowment** $320,596
- **Coed,** 19,538 undergraduate students

Undergraduates 2% are from out of state, 5% African American, 18% Asian American or Pacific Islander, 57% Hispanic American, 0.5% Native American, 0.8% international.
Freshmen *Admission:* 6,233 applied, 6,233 admitted.
Majors Accounting; African-American studies; African studies; anthropology; architectural engineering technology; art; Asian-American studies; astronomy; auto mechanic/technician; biological/physical sciences; biology; business administration; business marketing and marketing management; chemistry; computer graphics; computer/information systems security; computer programming; computer science; computer science related; construction technology; corrections; criminal justice/law enforcement administration; dance; dental hygiene; early childhood education; economics; electrical/electronic engineering technology; elementary education; emergency medical technology; engineering; English; finance; fire science; French; general studies; geography; geology; graphic design/commercial art/illustration; history; information sciences/systems; information technology; journalism; landscape architecture; landscaping management; legal administrative assistant; liberal arts and sciences/liberal studies; literature; mathematics; Mexican-American studies; music; nursing; operating room technician; philosophy; photography; physical sciences; physics; political science; pre-engineering; psychology; public administration; real estate; recreation/leisure facilities management; secretarial science; small engine mechanic; social work; sociology; Spanish; telecommunications; theater arts/drama; travel/tourism management; Web/multimedia management/webmaster; Web page, digital/multimedia and information resources design; women's studies.
Academic Programs *Special study options:* academic remediation for entering students, adult/continuing education programs, advanced placement credit, cooperative education, English as a second language, external degree program, freshman honors college, honors programs, independent study, internships, part-time degree program, services for LD students, summer session for credit.
Library Southwestern College Library with 85,003 titles, 6,983 audiovisual materials, an OPAC, a Web page.
Computers on Campus 1300 computers available on campus for general student use. A campuswide network can be accessed from off campus. At least one staffed computer lab available.
Student Life *Housing:* college housing not available. *Activities and Organizations:* drama/theater group, student-run newspaper, choral group, MECHA, Business Club, Alpha Phi Epsilon, ABLE (disabled club), Society of Hispanic Engineers, national fraternities. *Campus security:* 24-hour emergency response devices, student patrols, late-night transport/escort service. *Student Services:* health clinic, personal/psychological counseling, women's center.
Athletics *Intercollegiate sports:* baseball M, basketball M/W, cross-country running M/W, football M, golf M, soccer M, softball W, swimming M/W, tennis M/W, track and field M/W.
Standardized Tests *Required for some:* EAT,ART,PCT,IAT,APS,CTEP,CELSA.
Costs (2001–02) *Tuition:* state resident $0 full-time; nonresident $3900 full-time, $130 per unit part-time. Full-time tuition and fees vary according to course load. *Required fees:* $364 full-time, $11 per unit, $17 per term part-time. *Payment plan:* deferred payment.
Applying *Options:* early admission. *Required for some:* high school transcript. *Application deadline:* rolling (freshmen), rolling (transfers). *Notification:* continuous (freshmen).
Admissions Contact Ms. Georgia Copeland, Director of Admissions and Records, Southwestern College, 900 Otay Lakes Road, Chula Vista, CA 91910. *Phone:* 619-482-6550.

TAFT COLLEGE
Taft, California

- **State and locally supported** 2-year, founded 1922, part of California Community College System
- **Calendar** semesters
- **Degree** certificates and associate
- **Small-town** 15-acre campus
- **Endowment** $18,000
- **Coed,** 2,929 undergraduate students, 17% full-time, 31% women, 69% men

Undergraduates 494 full-time, 2,435 part-time. Students come from 10 states and territories, 6 other countries, 4% are from out of state, 13% African American, 6% Asian American or Pacific Islander, 19% Hispanic American, 2% Native American, 26% transferred in, 6% live on campus.
Freshmen *Admission:* 210 applied, 210 admitted, 210 enrolled.
Faculty *Total:* 95, 28% full-time, 9% with terminal degrees. *Student/faculty ratio:* 18:1.
Majors Accounting; art; auto mechanic/technician; biology; business administration; computer science; criminal justice/law enforcement administration; data processing technology; dental hygiene; drafting; early childhood education; electrical/electronic engineering technology; English; general studies; industrial arts; journalism; liberal arts and sciences/liberal studies; mathematics; physical education; physical sciences; pre-engineering; recreation/leisure studies; secretarial science; social sciences.
Academic Programs *Special study options:* academic remediation for entering students, adult/continuing education programs, advanced placement credit, distance learning, independent study, part-time degree program, services for LD students, summer session for credit.
Library Taft College Library with 30,000 titles, 150 serial subscriptions, 17,000 audiovisual materials, an OPAC, a Web page.
Computers on Campus 91 computers available on campus for general student use. Internet access, online (class) registration, at least one staffed computer lab available.

Student Life *Housing Options:* coed. *Activities and Organizations:* student-run newspaper, International Club, Alpha Gamma Sigma, Rotoract Club, ASB Club. *Campus security:* controlled dormitory access, parking lot security. *Student Services:* personal/psychological counseling.

Athletics *Intercollegiate sports:* baseball M, basketball W, soccer M, softball W, volleyball W.

Costs (2002–03) *Tuition:* state resident $0 full-time; nonresident $4560 full-time, $152 per unit part-time. Full-time tuition and fees vary according to course load. Part-time tuition and fees vary according to course load. *Required fees:* $370 full-time, $11 per unit, $20 per term part-time. *Room and board:* $2720; room only: $1120. *Payment plan:* installment.

Financial Aid In 2001, 45 Federal Work-Study jobs (averaging $3000). 30 State and other part-time jobs (averaging $3000).

Applying *Options:* electronic application. *Required for some:* high school transcript. *Application deadlines:* rolling (freshmen), 8/1 (transfers).

Admissions Contact Ms. Gayle Roberts, Director of Financial Aid and Admissions, Taft College, 29 Emmons Park Drive, Taft, CA 93268. *Phone:* 661-763-7763. *Fax:* 661-763-7758. *E-mail:* cdeclue@taft.org.

VENTURA COLLEGE
Ventura, California

- **State and locally supported** 2-year, founded 1925, part of California Community College System
- **Calendar** semesters
- **Degree** certificates, diplomas, and associate
- **Suburban** 103-acre campus with easy access to Los Angeles
- **Coed,** 11,860 undergraduate students, 30% full-time, 58% women, 42% men

Undergraduates 3,587 full-time, 8,273 part-time. Students come from 25 states and territories, 11% are from out of state, 2% African American, 6% Asian American or Pacific Islander, 31% Hispanic American, 1% Native American, 1% international, 20% transferred in.

Freshmen *Admission:* 1,979 applied, 1,979 admitted, 953 enrolled.

Faculty *Total:* 574, 25% full-time. *Student/faculty ratio:* 22:1.

Majors Accounting; agricultural business; agronomy/crop science; animal sciences; architectural engineering technology; art; auto mechanic/technician; biology; business administration; ceramic arts; communications; computer/information sciences; construction technology; criminal justice/law enforcement administration; cultural studies; drafting; early childhood education; education; engineering; fashion design/illustration; food services technology; graphic design/commercial art/illustration; home economics; horticulture science; information sciences/systems; journalism; landscape architecture; liberal arts and sciences/liberal studies; machine technology; medical assistant; music; natural resources management; nursing; ornamental horticulture; photography; physical sciences; real estate; recreation/leisure studies; secretarial science; theater arts/drama; water resources; welding technology.

Academic Programs *Special study options:* academic remediation for entering students, adult/continuing education programs, advanced placement credit, English as a second language, independent study, internships, part-time degree program, services for LD students, summer session for credit.

Library Ventura College Library with 63,529 titles, 341 serial subscriptions, an OPAC, a Web page.

Computers on Campus 40 computers available on campus for general student use. Internet access, online (class) registration, at least one staffed computer lab available.

Student Life *Housing:* college housing not available. *Activities and Organizations:* drama/theater group, student-run newspaper, choral group, Pan American Student Union, MECHA, Automotive Technology Club, Campus Christian Fellowship, Asian-American Club. *Campus security:* 24-hour emergency response devices and patrols, student patrols. *Student Services:* health clinic, personal/psychological counseling, women's center.

Athletics *Intercollegiate sports:* baseball M, basketball M/W, cross-country running M/W, football M, golf M, soccer M/W, softball W, swimming M/W, tennis M/W, track and field M/W, volleyball W, water polo M/W, wrestling M.

Costs (2001–02) *Tuition:* nonresident $152 per unit part-time. *Required fees:* $11 per unit, $42 per term part-time.

Financial Aid In 2001, 70 Federal Work-Study jobs.

Applying *Required:* high school transcript.

Admissions Contact Ms. Susan Bricker, Registrar, Ventura College, 4667 Telegraph Road, Ventura, CA 93003-3899. *Phone:* 805-654-6456. *Fax:* 805-654-6466. *E-mail:* sbricker@server.vcccd.cc.ca.us.

VICTOR VALLEY COLLEGE
Victorville, California

- **State-supported** 2-year, founded 1961, part of California Community College System
- **Calendar** semesters
- **Degree** certificates and associate
- **Small-town** 280-acre campus with easy access to Los Angeles
- **Coed,** 8,111 undergraduate students, 25% full-time, 57% women, 43% men

Undergraduates 1,998 full-time, 6,113 part-time. Students come from 10 states and territories, 5 other countries, 8% African American, 4% Asian American or Pacific Islander, 23% Hispanic American, 1% Native American, 0.2% international, 6% transferred in.

Freshmen *Admission:* 1,632 applied, 1,632 admitted, 834 enrolled.

Faculty *Total:* 539, 30% full-time.

Majors Agricultural education; art; auto mechanic/technician; biological/physical sciences; biology; business; business administration; business computer programming; child care/development; child care/guidance; computer/information sciences; computer science; construction management; construction technology; early childhood education; electrical/electronic engineering technology; fire protection/safety technology; fire science; food services technology; horticulture science; humanities; information sciences/systems; law enforcement/police science; liberal arts and sciences/liberal studies; management information systems/business data processing; mathematics; music; natural sciences; nursing; ornamental horticulture; physical sciences; real estate; respiratory therapy; science technologies related; secretarial science; social sciences; teacher assistant/aide; theater arts/drama; trade/industrial education; vehicle/mobile equipment mechanics and repair related; welding technology.

Academic Programs *Special study options:* academic remediation for entering students, adult/continuing education programs, cooperative education, English as a second language, honors programs, part-time degree program, services for LD students, student-designed majors, summer session for credit. *ROTC:* Navy (c).

Library Victor Valley College Library with 41,789 titles, 534 serial subscriptions.

Computers on Campus 260 computers available on campus for general student use. At least one staffed computer lab available.

Student Life *Housing:* college housing not available. *Activities and Organizations:* drama/theater group, student-run newspaper, choral group, Black Student Union, Drama Club, rugby, Phi Theta Kappa. *Campus security:* 24-hour emergency response devices and patrols, late-night transport/escort service, part-time trained security personnel. *Student Services:* health clinic, personal/psychological counseling.

Athletics Member NCAA, NJCAA. *Intercollegiate sports:* baseball M, basketball M/W, cross-country running M/W, football M, golf M, soccer M/W, softball W, tennis M/W, track and field M/W, volleyball W, wrestling M.

Standardized Tests *Recommended:* CPT.

Costs (2001–02) *Tuition:* state resident $0 full-time; nonresident $4020 full-time, $134 per unit part-time. *Required fees:* $330 full-time, $11 per unit.

Applying *Options:* early admission. *Application deadline:* rolling (freshmen). *Notification:* continuous (freshmen).

Admissions Contact Ms. Becky Millen, Director of Admissions and Records, Victor Valley College, 18422 Bear Valley Road, Victorville, CA 92392. *Phone:* 760-245-4271 Ext. 2668. *Fax:* 760-245-9745. *E-mail:* bmillen@victor.cc.ca.us.

VISTA COMMUNITY COLLEGE
Berkeley, California

- **State and locally supported** 2-year, founded 1974
- **Calendar** semesters
- **Degree** certificates and associate
- **Urban** campus with easy access to San Francisco
- **Coed,** 4,500 undergraduate students

Just 2 blocks from the University of California, Berkeley, the energetic urban campus of Vista Community College stands on the cutting edge of community college education. University preparation and occupational training form the core of Vista's curriculum. A special arrangement allows Vista students to complete lower-division requirements in evening and Saturday classes on the University of California, Berkeley, campus. The College features model programs in American Sign Language, bioscience, and multimedia.

Undergraduates 1% are from out of state.

Faculty *Total:* 172, 19% full-time. *Student/faculty ratio:* 25:1.

Vista Community College (continued)

Majors Accounting; art; biological technology; business; business administration; computer graphics; computer/information sciences; computer/information systems security; computer science related; computer software and media applications related; creative writing; data entry/microcomputer applications related; English; English composition; fine/studio arts; general studies; liberal arts and sciences/liberal studies; medical administrative assistant; office management; Spanish; Web page, digital/multimedia and information resources design.

Academic Programs *Special study options:* academic remediation for entering students, adult/continuing education programs, English as a second language, independent study, internships, off-campus study, part-time degree program, services for LD students, student-designed majors, study abroad, summer session for credit.

Library Vista Community College Library with a Web page.

Computers on Campus 50 computers available on campus for general student use. Internet access, online (class) registration, at least one staffed computer lab available.

Student Life *Housing:* college housing not available.

Costs (2001–02) *Tuition:* state resident $0 full-time; nonresident $4920 full-time, $164 per unit part-time. Full-time tuition and fees vary according to course load. Part-time tuition and fees vary according to course load. *Required fees:* $334 full-time, $11 per unit, $2 per term part-time.

Applying *Options:* common application, electronic application, early admission, deferred entrance. *Recommended:* high school transcript. *Application deadline:* rolling (freshmen).

Admissions Contact Dr. Mario Rivas, Vice President of Student Services, Vista Community College, 2020 Milvia Street, Berkeley, CA 94704. *Phone:* 510-981-2820. *Fax:* 510-841-7333. *E-mail:* sfogarino@peralta.cc.ca.us.

WESTERN INSTITUTE OF SCIENCE & HEALTH
Rohnert Park, California

- **Proprietary** 2-year, founded 1993
- **Calendar** semesters
- **Degree** certificates and associate
- **Suburban** campus with easy access to San Francisco
- **Coed**

Undergraduates Students come from 3 states and territories, 1 other country, 5% are from out of state.

Faculty *Total:* 22, 9% full-time, 9% with terminal degrees. *Student/faculty ratio:* 8:1.

Majors Health/medical diagnostic and treatment services related; occupational therapy assistant; physical therapy assistant.

Academic Programs *Special study options:* distance learning, internships.

Computers on Campus 15 computers available on campus for general student use. Internet access available.

Student Life *Housing:* college housing not available. *Campus security:* 24-hour emergency response devices and patrols.

Costs (2001–02) *Tuition:* $7000 full-time. Full-time tuition and fees vary according to program. No tuition increase for student's term of enrollment. *Required fees:* $150 full-time.

Financial Aid In 2001, 19 Federal Work-Study jobs (averaging $1000).

Applying *Application fee:* $100. *Required:* essay or personal statement, high school transcript, minimum 2.0 GPA, 2 letters of recommendation, interview.

Admissions Contact Ms. Delores Ford, Director of Administrative and Student Services, Western Institute of Science & Health, 130 Avram Avenue, Rhonert Park, CA 94928. *Phone:* 707-664-9267 Ext. 12. *Toll-free phone:* 800-437-9474. *E-mail:* info@westerni.org.

WEST HILLS COMMUNITY COLLEGE
Coalinga, California

Admissions Contact Mrs. Darlene Georgatos, Registrar, West Hills Community College, 300 Cherry Lane, Coalinga, CA 93210-1399. *Phone:* 559-935-0801 Ext. 3217. *Toll-free phone:* 800-266-1114. *E-mail:* georgada@whccd.cc.ca.us.

WEST LOS ANGELES COLLEGE
Culver City, California

Admissions Contact Mr. Len Isaksen, Director of Admissions, West Los Angeles College, 4800 Freshman Drive, Culver City, CA 90230-3519. *Phone:* 310-287-4255.

WEST VALLEY COLLEGE
Saratoga, California

Admissions Contact Mr. Albert Moore, Admissions and Records Supervisor, West Valley College, 14000 Fruitvale Avenue, Saratoga, CA 95070-5698. *Phone:* 408-741-2533.

WESTWOOD COLLEGE OF AVIATION TECHNOLOGY-LOS ANGELES
Inglewood, California

- **Proprietary** primarily 2-year, founded 1942
- **Calendar** quarters
- **Degrees** associate and bachelor's
- **Urban** campus
- **Coed, primarily men,** 560 undergraduate students

Faculty *Total:* 31, 100% full-time.

Majors Aircraft mechanic/airframe; aircraft mechanic/powerplant.

Academic Programs *Special study options:* part-time degree program.

Computers on Campus 24 computers available on campus for general student use.

Student Life *Housing:* college housing not available.

Costs (2002–03) *Tuition:* Airframe and Powerplant: $23,538 for 17.5 month program (includes tuition, books, tools, registration fees and student insurance).

Applying *Application fee:* $75. *Application deadline:* rolling (freshmen). *Notification:* continuous (freshmen).

Admissions Contact Mr. Steve Sexton, Director of Admissions, Westwood College of Aviation Technology-Los Angeles, 8911 Aviation Boulevard, Inglewood, CA 90301-2904. *Phone:* 310-337-4444. *Toll-free phone:* 800-597-8690.

WESTWOOD COLLEGE OF TECHNOLOGY-ANAHEIM
Anaheim, California

- **Proprietary** primarily 2-year
- **Degrees** associate and bachelor's
- **Coed,** 650 undergraduate students

Faculty *Total:* 24, 79% full-time.

Majors Computer systems networking/telecommunications; design/visual communications; graphic design/commercial art/illustration; multimedia.

Costs (2002–03) *Tuition:* Standard program price $3,355 per term, lab fees and books additional, 5 terms/year, program length: associate degree = 7 terms, bachelors degree = 14 terms.

Admissions Contact Mr. Ron Milman, Director of Admissions, Westwood College of Technology-Anaheim, 2461 West La Palma Avenue, Anaheim, CA 92801. *Phone:* 714-226-9990.

WESTWOOD COLLEGE OF TECHNOLOGY-INLAND EMPIRE
Upland, California

- **Proprietary** primarily 2-year
- **Degrees** associate and bachelor's
- **Coed**

Faculty *Total:* 4.

Majors Computer systems networking/telecommunications; design/visual communications; graphic design/commercial art/illustration; multimedia.

Costs (2002–03) *Tuition:* Standard program price $3,355 per term, lab fees and books additional, 5 terms/year, program length: associate degree = 7 terms, bachelors degree = 14 terms.

Admissions Contact Ranae Ferchert, Director of Admissions, Westwood College of Technology-Inland Empire, 20 West 7th Street, Upland, CA 91786. *Phone:* 909-931-7550.

WESTWOOD COLLEGE OF TECHNOLOGY-LOS ANGELES
Los Angeles, California

- **Proprietary** 2-year
- **Degree** associate

■ **Coed,** 496 undergraduate students

Faculty *Total:* 31, 35% full-time.
Majors Computer programming; computer systems networking/telecommunications; graphic design/commercial art/illustration; multimedia.
Costs (2002–03) *Tuition:* Standard program price $3,355 per term, lab fees and books additional, 5 terms/year, program length: associate degree = 7 terms.
Admissions Contact Toheed Asghar, Director of Admissions, Westwood College of Technology-Los Angeles, 3460 Wilshire Boulevard, Suite 700, Los Angeles, CA 90010. *Phone:* 213-739-9999.

YUBA COLLEGE
Marysville, California

■ **State and locally supported** 2-year, founded 1927, part of California Community College System
■ **Calendar** semesters
■ **Degree** certificates and associate
■ **Rural** 160-acre campus with easy access to Sacramento
■ **Coed**

Student Life *Campus security:* 24-hour patrols, student patrols.
Standardized Tests *Recommended:* SAT I or ACT (for placement).
Costs (2001–02) *Tuition:* state resident $0 full-time; nonresident $4260 full-time, $153 per unit part-time. *Required fees:* $672 full-time, $11 per unit, $6 per term part-time.
Financial Aid In 2001, 290 Federal Work-Study jobs (averaging $1578). 75 State and other part-time jobs (averaging $1000).
Applying *Options:* common application, early admission, deferred entrance. *Recommended:* high school transcript.
Admissions Contact Ms. Juhree Patterson, Administrative Secretary and Foreign Student Assistant, Yuba College, 2088 North Beale Road, Marysville, CA 95901. *Phone:* 530-741-6705. *Fax:* 530-634-7709. *E-mail:* jpatters@mail2.yuba.cc.ca.us.

COLORADO

AIMS COMMUNITY COLLEGE
Greeley, Colorado

■ **District-supported** 2-year, founded 1967
■ **Calendar** quarters
■ **Degree** certificates, diplomas, and associate
■ **Urban** 185-acre campus with easy access to Denver
■ **Endowment** $71,813
■ **Coed,** 6,868 undergraduate students

Undergraduates Students come from 8 states and territories.
Faculty *Total:* 425, 26% full-time. *Student/faculty ratio:* 16:1.
Majors Accounting; agricultural mechanization; auto mechanic/technician; aviation technology; business marketing and marketing management; child care/development; criminal justice/law enforcement administration; early childhood education; electrical/electronic engineering technology; engineering technology; fire science; graphic design/commercial art/illustration; industrial radiologic technology; information sciences/systems; law enforcement/police science; liberal arts and sciences/liberal studies; secretarial science; welding technology.
Academic Programs *Special study options:* academic remediation for entering students, adult/continuing education programs, advanced placement credit, cooperative education, English as a second language, external degree program, freshman honors college, honors programs, part-time degree program, student-designed majors, summer session for credit. *ROTC:* Air Force (c).
Library Aims Community College Library with 39,129 titles, 258 serial subscriptions, an OPAC.
Computers on Campus 700 computers available on campus for general student use. A campuswide network can be accessed from off campus. Internet access, at least one staffed computer lab available.
Student Life *Housing:* college housing not available. *Activities and Organizations:* drama/theater group, student-run newspaper, radio station, choral group. *Campus security:* 24-hour emergency response devices, day and evening patrols by trained security personnel. *Student Services:* personal/psychological counseling, women's center.
Athletics *Intramural sports:* basketball M/W, volleyball M/W.
Standardized Tests *Required:* CPT.
Costs (2001–02) *Tuition:* area resident $1305 full-time, $29 per credit hour part-time; state resident $2160 full-time, $48 per credit hour part-time; nonresident $6255 full-time, $139 per credit hour part-time. *Required fees:* $360 full-time, $8 per credit hour.
Applying *Options:* early admission, deferred entrance. *Application deadline:* rolling (freshmen), rolling (transfers).
Admissions Contact Ms. Susie Gallardo, Admissions Technician, Aims Community College, Box 69, Greeley, CO 80632-0069. *Phone:* 970-330-8008 Ext. 6624. *Fax:* 970-339-6682. *E-mail:* wgreen@aims.edu.

ARAPAHOE COMMUNITY COLLEGE
Littleton, Colorado

■ **State-supported** 2-year, founded 1965, part of Community Colleges of Colorado
■ **Calendar** semesters
■ **Degree** certificates, diplomas, and associate
■ **Suburban** 52-acre campus with easy access to Denver
■ **Coed,** 7,076 undergraduate students

Undergraduates Students come from 42 states and territories, 35 other countries.
Faculty *Total:* 414, 28% full-time.
Majors Accounting; architectural engineering technology; auto mechanic/technician; biological/physical sciences; business administration; business marketing and marketing management; child care provider; child care services management; communication equipment technology; communication systems installation/repair; computer graphics; computer/information technology services administration and management related; computer programming; computer programming related; computer programming (specific applications); computer science; computer software and media applications related; computer systems networking/telecommunications; computer/technical support; construction/building inspection; construction management; criminal justice/law enforcement administration; data warehousing/mining/database administration; drafting; drafting/design technology; electrical/electronic engineering technology; emergency medical technology; engineering; environmental technology; finance; food services technology; graphic design/commercial art/illustration; information sciences/systems; law enforcement/police science; legal administrative assistant; liberal arts and sciences/liberal studies; management information systems/business data processing; mechanical design technology; medical assistant; medical laboratory technician; medical records administration; medical technology; mortuary science; nursing; paralegal/legal assistant; pharmacy; physical therapy; retail management; secretarial science; travel/tourism management; Web page, digital/multimedia and information resources design.
Academic Programs *Special study options:* academic remediation for entering students, accelerated degree program, adult/continuing education programs, advanced placement credit, cooperative education, English as a second language, honors programs, internships, off-campus study, part-time degree program, services for LD students, student-designed majors, study abroad, summer session for credit. *ROTC:* Army (c), Air Force (c).
Library Weber Center for Learning Resources plus 1 other with 45,000 titles, 441 serial subscriptions.
Computers on Campus 200 computers available on campus for general student use. A campuswide network can be accessed from off campus. Internet access, at least one staffed computer lab available.
Student Life *Housing:* college housing not available. *Activities and Organizations:* drama/theater group, student-run newspaper, choral group. *Campus security:* 24-hour emergency response devices and patrols, late-night transport/escort service. *Student Services:* personal/psychological counseling.
Athletics Member NJCAA. *Intercollegiate sports:* baseball M(s), soccer M(c), softball W(s), volleyball M(c)/W(c). *Intramural sports:* skiing (cross-country) M/W, skiing (downhill) M/W, soccer M/W, swimming M/W, tennis M/W, volleyball M/W.
Standardized Tests *Required:* CPT. *Recommended:* SAT II: Writing Test (for placement).
Costs (2002–03) *Tuition:* state resident $1400 full-time, $60 per credit hour part-time; nonresident $5000 full-time, $291 per credit hour part-time. Full-time tuition and fees vary according to location and program. Part-time tuition and fees vary according to location and program. *Payment plans:* installment, deferred payment. *Waivers:* senior citizens and employees or children of employees.
Financial Aid In 2001, 100 Federal Work-Study jobs, 200 State and other part-time jobs.
Applying *Options:* common application, early admission, deferred entrance. *Application deadline:* rolling (freshmen), rolling (transfers).

Arapahoe Community College (continued)

Admissions Contact Mr. Howard Fukaye, Admissions Specialist, Arapahoe Community College, 5900 South Santa Fe Drive, PO Box 9002, Littleton, CO 80160-9002. *Phone:* 303-797-5622. *Fax:* 303-797-5970. *E-mail:* hfukaye@arapahoe.edu.

BEL-REA INSTITUTE OF ANIMAL TECHNOLOGY
Denver, Colorado

- **Proprietary** 2-year, founded 1971
- **Calendar** quarters
- **Degree** associate
- **Suburban** 4-acre campus
- **Endowment** $16,500
- **Coed,** 600 undergraduate students

Undergraduates Students come from 25 states and territories, 3 other countries.

Freshmen *Admission:* 865 applied, 600 admitted. *Average high school GPA:* 3.00.

Faculty *Total:* 24, 79% full-time, 75% with terminal degrees. *Student/faculty ratio:* 25:1.

Majors Veterinary technology.

Academic Programs *Special study options:* academic remediation for entering students, internships.

Library 1,800 titles, 57 serial subscriptions.

Computers on Campus 4 computers available on campus for general student use. At least one staffed computer lab available.

Student Life *Activities and Organizations:* National Association of Veterinary Technicians. *Student Services:* personal/psychological counseling.

Costs (2002–03) *Comprehensive fee:* $14,750 includes full-time tuition ($8750) and room and board ($6000).

Applying *Options:* common application. *Application fee:* $100. *Required:* high school transcript, minimum 2.5 GPA. *Recommended:* interview. *Application deadline:* rolling (freshmen), rolling (transfers).

Admissions Contact Ms. Paulette Bottoms, Director, Bel-Rea Institute of Animal Technology, 1681 South Dayton Street, Denver, CO 80231-3048. *Phone:* 303-751-8700. *Toll-free phone:* 800-950-8001.

BLAIR COLLEGE
Colorado Springs, Colorado

- **Proprietary** 2-year, founded 1897, part of Corinthian Colleges, Inc
- **Calendar** quarters
- **Degree** diplomas and associate
- **Suburban** 5-acre campus with easy access to Denver
- **Coed,** 500 undergraduate students

Faculty *Total:* 28, 43% full-time. *Student/faculty ratio:* 13:1.

Majors Accounting; business administration; computer programming; computer science; medical administrative assistant; medical assistant; paralegal/legal assistant; secretarial science; travel/tourism management.

Academic Programs *Special study options:* academic remediation for entering students, cooperative education, internships, services for LD students.

Library Blair College Library with 45 serial subscriptions.

Computers on Campus 45 computers available on campus for general student use.

Student Life *Housing:* college housing not available. *Campus security:* 24-hour emergency response devices.

Athletics *Intramural sports:* bowling M/W.

Costs (2001–02) *Tuition:* $9744 full-time, $225 per credit hour part-time. *Required fees:* $100 full-time, $25 per term part-time.

Applying *Application fee:* $25. *Required:* high school transcript. *Application deadline:* rolling (freshmen), rolling (transfers). *Notification:* continuous (freshmen).

Admissions Contact Mr. Scott Prester, Director of Admissions, Blair College, 828 Wooten Road, Colorado Springs, CO 80915. *Phone:* 719-574-1082.

CAMBRIDGE COLLEGE
Aurora, Colorado

Admissions Contact 12500 East Iliff Avenue, # 100, Aurora, CO 80014.

COLLEGEAMERICA-DENVER
Denver, Colorado

Admissions Contact 1385 South Colorado Boulevard, Denver, CO 80222-1912. *Toll-free phone:* 800-97-SKILLS.

COLLEGEAMERICA-FORT COLLINS
Fort Collins, Colorado

Admissions Contact Lamar Haynes, Director, CollegeAmerica-Fort Collins, 4601 South Mason Street, Fort Collins, CO 80525-3740. *Phone:* 970-223-6060. *Toll-free phone:* 800-97-SKILLS.

COLORADO MOUNTAIN COLLEGE, ALPINE CAMPUS
Steamboat Springs, Colorado

- **District-supported** 2-year, founded 1965, part of Colorado Mountain College District System
- **Calendar** semesters
- **Degree** certificates and associate
- **Rural** 10-acre campus
- **Coed,** 1,474 undergraduate students, 35% full-time, 58% women, 42% men

Undergraduates Students come from 49 states and territories, 65% are from out of state, 0.1% African American, 0.7% Asian American or Pacific Islander, 2% Hispanic American, 0.5% Native American, 0.3% international, 44% live on campus.

Freshmen *Average high school GPA:* 2.40.

Faculty *Student/faculty ratio:* 15:1.

Majors Accounting; behavioral sciences; biological/physical sciences; biology; business administration; business marketing and marketing management; computer engineering technology; data entry/microcomputer applications related; English; fine/studio arts; geology; hospitality management; hotel and restaurant management; humanities; liberal arts and sciences/liberal studies; mathematics; physical sciences; recreation/leisure facilities management; retail management; social sciences.

Academic Programs *Special study options:* academic remediation for entering students, adult/continuing education programs, advanced placement credit, cooperative education, distance learning, independent study, internships, part-time degree program, services for LD students, study abroad, summer session for credit.

Library 17,000 titles, 192 serial subscriptions, an OPAC, a Web page.

Computers on Campus 60 computers available on campus for general student use. A campuswide network can be accessed from student residence rooms. Internet access, at least one staffed computer lab available.

Student Life *Housing:* on-campus residence required for freshman year. *Options:* coed. *Activities and Organizations:* student-run newspaper, student government, Forensics Team, Ski Club, International Club, Phi Theta Kappa. *Campus security:* 24-hour emergency response devices, controlled dormitory access. *Student Services:* health clinic, personal/psychological counseling.

Athletics *Intercollegiate sports:* skiing (cross-country) M(s)/W(s), skiing (downhill) M(s)/W(s). *Intramural sports:* basketball M/W, skiing (cross-country) M/W, skiing (downhill) M/W, soccer M/W, volleyball M/W.

Standardized Tests *Recommended:* SAT I or ACT (for placement).

Costs (2002–03) *Tuition:* area resident $948 full-time, $41 per credit part-time; state resident $1656 full-time, $69 per credit part-time; nonresident $220 per credit part-time. Full-time tuition and fees vary according to course load and program. Part-time tuition and fees vary according to course load and program. *Required fees:* $180 full-time. *Room and board:* $5700. Room and board charges vary according to board plan and housing facility. *Payment plan:* deferred payment. *Waivers:* senior citizens and employees or children of employees.

Applying *Options:* early admission, deferred entrance. *Required:* high school transcript. *Application deadline:* rolling (freshmen), rolling (transfers).

Admissions Contact Ms. Janice Bell, Admissions Assistant, Colorado Mountain College, Alpine Campus, PO Box 10001, Department PG, Glenwood Springs, CO 81602. *Phone:* 970-870-4417. *Toll-free phone:* 800-621-8559. *E-mail:* joinus@coloradomtn.edu.

COLORADO MOUNTAIN COLLEGE, SPRING VALLEY CAMPUS

Glenwood Springs, Colorado

- **District-supported** 2-year, founded 1965, part of Colorado Mountain College District System
- **Calendar** semesters
- **Degree** certificates and associate
- **Rural** 680-acre campus
- **Coed,** 753 undergraduate students, 54% full-time, 58% women, 42% men

CMC offers an outstanding liberal arts education and awards 2-year associate degrees that transfer to 4-year colleges and universities, including all Colorado schools. CMC offers programs in natural resources, outdoor leadership, ski area operations, ski and snowboard business, resort management, and culinary arts and a semester in the Rockies. CMC also offers strong programs in photography, graphic design, law enforcement, and veterinary technology.

Undergraduates Students come from 48 states and territories, 18% are from out of state, 0.5% Asian American or Pacific Islander, 5% Hispanic American, 0.8% Native American, 0.4% international, 44% live on campus.

Freshmen *Average high school GPA:* 2.40.

Faculty *Student/faculty ratio:* 15:1.

Majors Accounting; art; behavioral sciences; biological/physical sciences; biology; business administration; computer engineering technology; computer systems networking/telecommunications; computer/technical support; criminal justice/law enforcement administration; data entry/microcomputer applications related; English; graphic design/commercial art/illustration; humanities; liberal arts and sciences/liberal studies; mathematics; natural sciences; nursing; photography; practical nurse; psychology; recreational therapy; social sciences; theater arts/drama; veterinary technology.

Academic Programs *Special study options:* academic remediation for entering students, adult/continuing education programs, advanced placement credit, cooperative education, distance learning, independent study, internships, part-time degree program, services for LD students, study abroad, summer session for credit.

Library 36,000 titles, 186 serial subscriptions, an OPAC, a Web page.

Computers on Campus 65 computers available on campus for general student use. A campuswide network can be accessed from student residence rooms. Internet access, at least one staffed computer lab available.

Student Life *Housing Options:* coed. *Activities and Organizations:* drama/theater group, student-run newspaper, student government, outdoor activities, World Awareness Society, Peer Mentors, Student Activities Board. *Campus security:* 24-hour emergency response devices, controlled dormitory access. *Student Services:* personal/psychological counseling.

Athletics *Intercollegiate sports:* skiing (cross-country) M/W, skiing (downhill) M/W. *Intramural sports:* basketball M/W, skiing (cross-country) M/W, skiing (downhill) M/W, soccer M/W, volleyball M/W.

Standardized Tests *Recommended:* SAT I or ACT (for placement).

Costs (2002–03) *Tuition:* area resident $948 full-time, $41 per credit part-time; state resident $1656 full-time, $69 per credit part-time; nonresident $220 per credit part-time. Full-time tuition and fees vary according to course load and program. Part-time tuition and fees vary according to course load and program. *Required fees:* $180 full-time. *Room and board:* $5700. Room and board charges vary according to board plan and housing facility. *Waivers:* senior citizens and employees or children of employees.

Applying *Options:* early admission, deferred entrance. *Required:* high school transcript. *Application deadline:* rolling (freshmen), rolling (transfers).

Admissions Contact Ms. Tammy Recker, Admissions Assistant, Colorado Mountain College, Spring Valley Campus, PO Box 10001, Department PG, Glenwood Springs, CO 81601. *Phone:* 970-947-8276. *Toll-free phone:* 800-621-8559. *E-mail:* joinus@coloradomtn.edu.

COLORADO MOUNTAIN COLLEGE, TIMBERLINE CAMPUS

Leadville, Colorado

- **District-supported** 2-year, founded 1965, part of Colorado Mountain College District System
- **Calendar** semesters
- **Degree** certificates and associate
- **Rural** 200-acre campus
- **Endowment** $700,000
- **Coed,** 474 undergraduate students, 44% full-time, 47% women, 53% men

Undergraduates Students come from 48 states and territories, 60% are from out of state, 0.4% African American, 1% Asian American or Pacific Islander, 14% Hispanic American, 0.8% Native American, 0.4% international, 30% live on campus.

Freshmen *Average high school GPA:* 2.40.

Faculty *Student/faculty ratio:* 15:1.

Majors Accounting; art; behavioral sciences; biological/physical sciences; biology; business administration; child care/development; computer engineering technology; data entry/microcomputer applications; data entry/microcomputer applications related; early childhood education; ecology; English; environmental education; environmental science; humanities; land use management; liberal arts and sciences/liberal studies; mathematics; psychology; recreation/leisure facilities management; recreation/leisure studies; social sciences; water resources.

Academic Programs *Special study options:* academic remediation for entering students, adult/continuing education programs, advanced placement credit, cooperative education, distance learning, English as a second language, independent study, internships, part-time degree program, services for LD students, study abroad, summer session for credit.

Library 25,000 titles, 185 serial subscriptions.

Computers on Campus 30 computers available on campus for general student use. A campuswide network can be accessed from student residence rooms. Internet access, at least one staffed computer lab available.

Student Life *Housing Options:* coed. *Activities and Organizations:* Environmental Club, Outdoor Club, Student Activities Board. *Campus security:* 24-hour emergency response devices, controlled dormitory access. *Student Services:* personal/psychological counseling.

Athletics *Intercollegiate sports:* skiing (cross-country) M/W, skiing (downhill) M/W. *Intramural sports:* basketball M, skiing (cross-country) M/W, skiing (downhill) M/W, soccer M/W, volleyball M/W.

Standardized Tests *Recommended:* SAT I or ACT (for placement).

Costs (2002–03) *Tuition:* area resident $948 full-time, $41 per credit part-time; state resident $1656 full-time, $69 per credit part-time; nonresident $220 per credit part-time. Full-time tuition and fees vary according to course load and program. Part-time tuition and fees vary according to course load and program. *Required fees:* $180 full-time. *Room and board:* $5700. Room and board charges vary according to board plan and housing facility. *Payment plan:* deferred payment. *Waivers:* senior citizens and employees or children of employees.

Applying *Options:* early admission, deferred entrance. *Required:* high school transcript. *Application deadline:* rolling (freshmen), rolling (transfers).

Admissions Contact Ms. Virginia Espinoza, Admissions Assistant, Colorado Mountain College, Timberline Campus, PO Box 10001, Department PG, Glenwood Springs, CO 81602. *Phone:* 719-486-4291. *Toll-free phone:* 800-621-8559. *E-mail:* joinus@coloradomtn.edu.

COLORADO NORTHWESTERN COMMUNITY COLLEGE

Rangely, Colorado

- **State-supported** 2-year, founded 1962, part of Colorado Community College and Occupational Education System
- **Calendar** semesters
- **Degree** certificates and associate
- **Rural** 150-acre campus
- **Coed,** 2,109 undergraduate students, 22% full-time, 49% women, 51% men

Colorado Northwestern Community College (CNCC) is a 2-year, residential community college located in Rangely, among the high mesas of northwestern Colorado. CNCC also has service centers in Craig, Meeker, Hayden, and South Routt. CNCC offers 2-year AA and AS degrees in aviation technology, aviation maintenance, business information systems, criminal justice, commercial recreation, fire science, sports medicine, dental hygiene, fine arts, and natural resources, which has 17 different degree options. CNCC has outstanding residential housing, facilities, and the benefit of average classroom sizes of 13 students. The outdoor recreation opportunities are fantastic and include mountain biking, skiing, rock climbing, camping, white-water rafting, and spelunking. Students should visit the Web site (http://www.cncc.cccoes.edu) or call 800-562-1105 (toll-free) for more information or to arrange a campus visit.

Undergraduates 459 full-time, 1,650 part-time. Students come from 18 states and territories, 1 other country, 17% are from out of state, 2% transferred in, 62% live on campus. *Retention:* 55% of 2001 full-time freshmen returned.

Freshmen *Admission:* 524 admitted, 131 enrolled. *Average high school GPA:* 2.94.

Colorado Northwestern Community College (continued)
Faculty *Total:* 198, 25% full-time. *Student/faculty ratio:* 20:1.
Majors Aircraft mechanic/airframe; aircraft mechanic/powerplant; aircraft pilot (professional); child care/guidance; criminal justice/law enforcement administration; dental hygiene; enterprise management; environmental science; farm/ranch management; general studies; information technology; instrumentation technology; liberal arts and sciences/liberal studies; medical administrative assistant; paralegal/legal assistant; secretarial science.
Academic Programs *Special study options:* academic remediation for entering students, adult/continuing education programs, advanced placement credit, distance learning, double majors, independent study, internships, part-time degree program, services for LD students, student-designed majors, summer session for credit.
Library Colorado Northwestern Community College Library plus 1 other with 19,170 titles, 291 serial subscriptions.
Computers on Campus 55 computers available on campus for general student use. A campuswide network can be accessed from off campus. At least one staffed computer lab available.
Student Life *Housing:* on-campus residence required for freshman year. *Options:* coed. *Activities and Organizations:* drama/theater group, choral group, Campus Activities Board, SADHA, Aero Club, Criminal Justice Club. *Campus security:* student patrols, late-night transport/escort service. *Student Services:* personal/psychological counseling.
Athletics Member NJCAA. *Intercollegiate sports:* baseball M(s), basketball M(s)/W(s), softball W(s). *Intramural sports:* basketball M/W, football M/W, golf M/W, racquetball M/W, skiing (cross-country) M/W, skiing (downhill) M/W, softball M/W, table tennis M/W, tennis M/W, volleyball M/W.
Standardized Tests *Recommended:* ACT (for placement).
Costs (2002–03) *Tuition:* state resident $1885 full-time, $63 per semester hour part-time; nonresident $7530 full-time, $233 per semester hour part-time. *Required fees:* $170 full-time, $7 per semester hour, $10 per term part-time. *Room and board:* $4890. Room and board charges vary according to housing facility. *Payment plan:* installment. *Waivers:* senior citizens and employees or children of employees.
Financial Aid In 2001, 39 Federal Work-Study jobs (averaging $1530). 80 State and other part-time jobs (averaging $1600).
Applying *Options:* early admission, deferred entrance. *Required:* high school transcript. *Required for some:* 3 letters of recommendation, interview. *Application deadline:* rolling (freshmen), rolling (transfers).
Admissions Contact Mr. Craig Dowen, Director of Enrollment Management, Colorado Northwestern Community College, 500 Kennedy Drive, Rangely, CO 81648-3598. *Phone:* 970-675-3216. *Toll-free phone:* 800-562-1105 Ext. 220. *Fax:* 970-675-3343. *E-mail:* cjones@cncc.cc.co.us.

COLORADO SCHOOL OF TRADES
Lakewood, Colorado

Admissions Contact 1575 Hoyt Street, Lakewood, CO 80215-2996. *Toll-free phone:* 800-234-4594.

COMMUNITY COLLEGE OF AURORA
Aurora, Colorado

- **State-supported** 2-year, founded 1983
- **Calendar** semesters
- **Degree** certificates and associate
- **Suburban** campus with easy access to Denver
- **Coed,** 4,000 undergraduate students

Undergraduates Students come from 11 other countries.
Faculty *Total:* 340, 12% full-time.
Majors Accounting; auto mechanic/technician; biological/physical sciences; business administration; business marketing and marketing management; carpentry; criminal justice/law enforcement administration; early childhood education; finance; graphic design/commercial art/illustration; information sciences/systems; liberal arts and sciences/liberal studies; medical administrative assistant; medical assistant; optometric/ophthalmic laboratory technician; paralegal/legal assistant; secretarial science.
Academic Programs *Special study options:* academic remediation for entering students, adult/continuing education programs, distance learning, English as a second language, external degree program, independent study, internships, off-campus study, part-time degree program, services for LD students, summer session for credit.
Library 7,440 titles, 126 serial subscriptions, an OPAC, a Web page.
Computers on Campus 160 computers available on campus for general student use. Internet access, at least one staffed computer lab available.
Student Life *Housing:* college housing not available. *Activities and Organizations:* drama/theater group, student-run newspaper. *Campus security:* late-night transport/escort service. *Student Services:* women's center.
Standardized Tests *Recommended:* SAT I or ACT (for placement).
Costs (2002–03) *Tuition:* state resident $1905 full-time, $64 per credit hour part-time; nonresident $9413 full-time, $314 per credit hour part-time.
Applying *Options:* early admission. *Application deadline:* rolling (freshmen), rolling (transfers). *Notification:* continuous (freshmen).
Admissions Contact Mr. Bryan Doak, Director of Registrations, Records, and Admission, Community College of Aurora, 16000 East Centre Tech Parkway, Aurora, CO 80011-9036. *Phone:* 303-360-4700.

COMMUNITY COLLEGE OF DENVER
Denver, Colorado

- **State-supported** 2-year, founded 1970, part of Community Colleges of Colorado
- **Calendar** semesters
- **Degree** certificates and associate
- **Urban** 171-acre campus
- **Endowment** $599,331
- **Coed,** 6,509 undergraduate students, 28% full-time, 60% women, 40% men

Undergraduates 1,839 full-time, 4,670 part-time. Students come from 34 states and territories, 1% are from out of state, 18% African American, 6% Asian American or Pacific Islander, 28% Hispanic American, 2% Native American, 7% international, 3% transferred in.
Freshmen *Admission:* 1,140 enrolled.
Faculty *Total:* 372, 28% full-time.
Majors Accounting; business administration; computer programming; computer typography/composition; construction trades related; dental hygiene; drafting; early childhood education; electrical/electronic engineering technology; environmental technology; graphic design/commercial art/illustration; graphic/printing equipment; heating/air conditioning/refrigeration; human services; industrial radiologic technology; information sciences/systems; legal administrative assistant; liberal arts and sciences/liberal studies; medical administrative assistant; multimedia; nursing; paralegal/legal assistant; photography; postal management; radiological science; recreation/leisure studies; secretarial science; travel/tourism management; veterinary technology.
Academic Programs *Special study options:* academic remediation for entering students, adult/continuing education programs, advanced placement credit, cooperative education, distance learning, English as a second language, honors programs, independent study, internships, off-campus study, part-time degree program, services for LD students, study abroad, summer session for credit. *ROTC:* Army (c).
Library Auraria Library plus 1 other with 460,518 titles, 3,233 serial subscriptions, an OPAC, a Web page.
Computers on Campus 1142 computers available on campus for general student use. A campuswide network can be accessed from off campus. Internet access, at least one staffed computer lab available.
Student Life *Housing:* college housing not available. *Activities and Organizations:* student-run newspaper, Trio Advocates for Multicultural Students, Student Alliance for Human Services, Ad Hoc Nursing, Black Men on Campus, Auraria Fine Arts, national fraternities. *Campus security:* 24-hour emergency response devices and patrols, late-night transport/escort service. *Student Services:* health clinic, personal/psychological counseling, women's center, legal services.
Athletics *Intramural sports:* archery M/W, badminton M/W, basketball M/W, bowling M/W, cross-country running M/W, equestrian sports M/W, fencing M/W, field hockey M/W, football M/W, golf M/W, gymnastics M/W, racquetball M/W, riflery M/W, rugby M/W, skiing (cross-country) M/W, skiing (downhill) M/W, soccer M/W, swimming M/W, table tennis M/W, tennis M/W, track and field M/W, volleyball M/W, weight lifting M/W.
Standardized Tests *Recommended:* SAT I or ACT (for placement).
Costs (2001–02) *Tuition:* state resident $1441 full-time, $60 per credit part-time; nonresident $6991 full-time, $291 per credit part-time. Full-time tuition and fees vary according to location and program. Part-time tuition and fees vary according to location and program. *Required fees:* $301 full-time, $4 per credit, $65 per term part-time. *Payment plan:* deferred payment. *Waivers:* senior citizens.
Financial Aid In 2001, 95 Federal Work-Study jobs (averaging $2442). 305 State and other part-time jobs (averaging $2156).

Applying *Options:* electronic application, early admission, deferred entrance. *Recommended:* interview. *Application deadline:* rolling (freshmen), rolling (transfers).

Admissions Contact Ms. Emita Samuels, Director of Registration and Records, Community College of Denver, PO Box 173363, 1111 West Colfax Avenue, Denver, CO 80217-3363. *Phone:* 303-556-2430. *E-mail:* emita.samuels@ccd.cccoes.edu.

DENVER ACADEMY OF COURT REPORTING

Denver, Colorado

Admissions Contact Mr. Howard Brookner, Director of Admissions, Denver Academy of Court Reporting, 7290 Samuel Drive, Suite 200, Denver, CO 80221-2792. *Phone:* 303-427-5292 Ext. 14. *Toll-free phone:* 800-574-2087. *Fax:* 303-427-5383.

DENVER AUTOMOTIVE AND DIESEL COLLEGE

Denver, Colorado

Admissions Contact Mr. John Chalupa, Director of Admissions, Denver Automotive and Diesel College, 460 South Lipan Street, Denver, CO 80223-2025. *Phone:* 303-722-5724. *Toll-free phone:* 800-347-3232. *Fax:* 303-778-8264. *E-mail:* dad@mho.net.

FRONT RANGE COMMUNITY COLLEGE

Westminster, Colorado

- **State-supported** 2-year, founded 1968, part of Community Colleges of Colorado System
- **Calendar** semesters
- **Degree** certificates and associate
- **Suburban** 90-acre campus with easy access to Denver
- **Coed,** 13,511 undergraduate students, 31% full-time, 57% women, 43% men

Undergraduates 4,197 full-time, 9,314 part-time. Students come from 26 states and territories, 98 other countries, 2% are from out of state, 6% transferred in.

Freshmen *Admission:* 7,074 applied, 7,074 admitted, 3,352 enrolled.

Faculty *Total:* 789, 20% full-time, 15% with terminal degrees. *Student/faculty ratio:* 16:1.

Majors Accounting technician; animal sciences related; architectural engineering technology; athletic training/sports medicine; auto mechanic/technician; business administration; child care services management; data processing; design/visual communications; dietician assistant; drafting; electrical/electronic engineering technology; enterprise management; environmental technology; general studies; heating/air conditioning/refrigeration technology; horticulture services; industrial technology; institutional food workers related; laser/optical technology; liberal arts and sciences/liberal studies; machine shop assistant; management information systems/business data processing; nursing; respiratory therapy; science technologies related; secretarial science; sign language interpretation; welding technology; wildlife management.

Academic Programs *Special study options:* academic remediation for entering students, adult/continuing education programs, advanced placement credit, cooperative education, distance learning, double majors, English as a second language, external degree program, freshman honors college, honors programs, internships, off-campus study, part-time degree program, services for LD students, student-designed majors, study abroad, summer session for credit. *ROTC:* Army (c), Air Force (c).

Library College Hill Library with an OPAC, a Web page.

Computers on Campus 800 computers available on campus for general student use. A campuswide network can be accessed from off campus that provide access to online courses. Internet access, online (class) registration, at least one staffed computer lab available.

Student Life *Housing:* college housing not available. *Activities and Organizations:* drama/theater group, student-run newspaper, Student Government Association, Student Colorado Registry of Interpreters for the Deaf, Alpha Mu Psi, Alpha Tau Kappa, Hispanic Club. *Campus security:* 24-hour patrols, late-night transport/escort service. *Student Services:* personal/psychological counseling, women's center.

Athletics *Intramural sports:* volleyball M/W.

Costs (2001–02) *Tuition:* state resident $1802 full-time, $61 per credit part-time; nonresident $8739 full-time, $291 per credit part-time. Full-time tuition and fees vary according to course load. Part-time tuition and fees vary according to course load. *Required fees:* $183 full-time, $6 per credit, $91 per term part-time. *Payment plan:* deferred payment. *Waivers:* senior citizens and employees or children of employees.

Financial Aid In 2001, 165 Federal Work-Study jobs (averaging $1316). 277 State and other part-time jobs (averaging $1635).

Applying *Options:* common application, electronic application, early admission, deferred entrance. *Application deadline:* rolling (freshmen), rolling (transfers).

Admissions Contact Ms. Gayle Mahler, Director of Enrollment Services, Front Range Community College, 3645 West 112th Avenue, Westminster, CO 80031. *Phone:* 303-404-5471. *Fax:* 303-439-2614. *E-mail:* gayle.mahler@wc.frcc.cccoes.edu.

INSTITUTE OF BUSINESS & MEDICAL CAREERS

Fort Collins, Colorado

Admissions Contact 1609 Oakridge Drive, Suite 102, Fort Collins, CO 80525.

INTELLITEC COLLEGE

Colorado Springs, Colorado

Admissions Contact Ms. Shirley Stark, Director of Admissions, IntelliTec College, 2315 East Pikes Peak Avenue, Colorado Springs, CO 80909-6030. *Phone:* 719-632-7626. *Toll-free phone:* 800-748-2282. *Fax:* 719-632-7451.

INTELLITEC COLLEGE

Grand Junction, Colorado

Admissions Contact 772 Horizon Drive, Grand Junction, CO 81506.

INTELLITEC MEDICAL INSTITUTE

Colorado Springs, Colorado

- **Proprietary** 2-year, founded 1966
- **Calendar** clock hours
- **Degree** diplomas and associate
- **Suburban** campus
- **Coed, primarily women,** 361 undergraduate students, 100% full-time, 92% women, 8% men

Undergraduates 361 full-time. 2% are from out of state, 25% African American, 12% Hispanic American, 0.6% Native American, 2% international, 0.6% transferred in. *Retention:* 70% of 2001 full-time freshmen returned.

Freshmen *Admission:* 191 applied, 191 admitted, 191 enrolled.

Faculty *Total:* 20, 15% full-time. *Student/faculty ratio:* 14:1.

Majors Medical administrative assistant; medical assistant; medical laboratory technician.

Academic Programs *Special study options:* advanced placement credit, cooperative education, independent study, internships, part-time degree program, services for LD students.

Library Main Library plus 1 other.

Computers on Campus 40 computers available on campus for general student use. At least one staffed computer lab available.

Student Life *Housing:* college housing not available. *Activities and Organizations:* AMT.

Costs (2002–03) *Tuition:* $9570 full-time. Part-time tuition and fees vary according to program. No tuition increase for student's term of enrollment. *Payment plans:* tuition prepayment, installment. *Waivers:* employees or children of employees.

Financial Aid In 2001, 10 Federal Work-Study jobs (averaging $4000).

Applying *Options:* common application, electronic application. *Required:* high school transcript, interview. *Application deadline:* rolling (freshmen).

Admissions Contact Michelle Squibb, Admissions Representative, IntelliTec Medical Institute, 2345 North Academy Boulevard, Colorado Springs, CO 80909. *Phone:* 719-596-7400. *E-mail:* adm@intellitecmedicalinstitute.com.

ITT TECHNICAL INSTITUTE

Thornton, Colorado

- **Proprietary** primarily 2-year, founded 1984, part of ITT Educational Services, Inc

ITT Technical Institute (continued)
- **Calendar** quarters
- **Degrees** associate and bachelor's
- **Suburban** 2-acre campus with easy access to Denver
- **Coed,** 419 undergraduate students

Majors Computer/information sciences related; computer programming; drafting; electrical/electronic engineering technologies related; information technology.
Student Life *Housing:* college housing not available. *Activities and Organizations:* student-run newspaper.
Costs (2001–02) *Tuition:* Full-time tuition and fees vary according to program. Part-time tuition and fees vary according to program. $260—$330 per credit hour.
Applying *Options:* deferred entrance. *Application fee:* $100. *Required:* high school transcript, interview. *Recommended:* letters of recommendation. *Application deadline:* rolling (freshmen), rolling (transfers). *Notification:* continuous (freshmen).
Admissions Contact Mr. Richard F. Hansen, Director, ITT Technical Institute, 500 East 84th Avenue, Suite B12, Thornton, CO 80229. *Phone:* 303-288-4488. *Toll-free phone:* 800-395-4488.

LAMAR COMMUNITY COLLEGE
Lamar, Colorado

- **State-supported** 2-year, founded 1937, part of Colorado Community College and Occupational Education System
- **Calendar** semesters
- **Degree** certificates, diplomas, and associate
- **Small-town** 125-acre campus
- **Endowment** $200,000
- **Coed,** 1,021 undergraduate students

Undergraduates Students come from 25 states and territories, 12 other countries.
Freshmen *Admission:* 414 applied, 414 admitted.
Faculty *Total:* 48, 50% full-time.
Majors Accounting; agricultural business; agricultural education; agricultural sciences; agronomy/crop science; animal sciences; art; behavioral sciences; biological/physical sciences; biology; business administration; business education; business marketing and marketing management; community services; computer engineering technology; computer management; computer programming; computer science; computer typography/composition; cosmetology; criminal justice studies; data processing technology; emergency medical technology; engineering; English; equestrian studies; farm/ranch management; history; humanities; information sciences/systems; legal administrative assistant; liberal arts and sciences/liberal studies; literature; management information systems/business data processing; mass communications; mathematics; medical administrative assistant; medical office management; nursing; physical sciences; physics; practical nurse; pre-engineering; quality control technology; range management; secretarial science; social sciences; social work; teacher assistant/aide; western civilization.
Academic Programs *Special study options:* academic remediation for entering students, adult/continuing education programs, advanced placement credit, cooperative education, English as a second language, internships, part-time degree program, services for LD students, student-designed majors, summer session for credit.
Library Learning Resources Center with 27,729 titles, 172 serial subscriptions.
Computers on Campus 60 computers available on campus for general student use. Internet access, online (class) registration, at least one staffed computer lab available.
Student Life *Housing:* on-campus residence required for freshman year. *Options:* coed. *Activities and Organizations:* drama/theater group, student-run newspaper, choral group. *Campus security:* 24-hour emergency response devices and patrols, student patrols, late-night transport/escort service, controlled dormitory access. *Student Services:* health clinic, personal/psychological counseling.
Athletics Member NJCAA. *Intercollegiate sports:* baseball M(s), basketball M(s), cross-country running W, equestrian sports M/W, golf M, softball W, volleyball W(s).
Standardized Tests *Recommended:* SAT I or ACT (for placement).
Costs (2002–03) *Tuition:* state resident $1905 full-time, $64 per credit part-time; nonresident $7530 full-time, $251 per credit part-time. *Required fees:* $1506 full-time, $19 per credit. *Payment plan:* installment. *Waivers:* senior citizens and employees or children of employees.
Financial Aid In 2001, 32 Federal Work-Study jobs (averaging $1000). 89 State and other part-time jobs (averaging $1000).
Applying *Options:* common application, early admission. *Application deadlines:* 9/16 (freshmen), 9/16 (transfers).
Admissions Contact Mrs. Angela Woodward, Director of Admissions, Lamar Community College, 2401 South Main Street, Lamar, CO 81052-3999. *Phone:* 719-336-2248 Ext. 140. *Toll-free phone:* 800-968-6920. *Fax:* 719-336-2400. *E-mail:* angela.woodward@lcc.cccoes.edu.

MORGAN COMMUNITY COLLEGE
Fort Morgan, Colorado

- **State-supported** 2-year, founded 1967, part of Colorado Community College and Occupational Education System
- **Calendar** semesters
- **Degree** certificates and associate
- **Rural** 20-acre campus with easy access to Denver
- **Coed,** 1,781 undergraduate students

Undergraduates Students come from 3 states and territories, 2% are from out of state.
Freshmen *Admission:* 38 applied, 38 admitted.
Faculty *Total:* 221, 15% full-time. *Student/faculty ratio:* 9:1.
Majors Accounting; auto mechanic/technician; biological/physical sciences; business administration; business economics; business education; liberal arts and sciences/liberal studies; occupational therapy; physical therapy; secretarial science.
Academic Programs *Special study options:* academic remediation for entering students, adult/continuing education programs, advanced placement credit, internships, part-time degree program, services for LD students, summer session for credit.
Library Learning Resource Center with 13,800 titles, 80 serial subscriptions, 1,096 audiovisual materials, an OPAC, a Web page.
Computers on Campus 60 computers available on campus for general student use. A campuswide network can be accessed from off campus. Internet access, online (class) registration, at least one staffed computer lab available.
Student Life *Housing:* college housing not available. *Activities and Organizations:* student-run newspaper.
Standardized Tests *Required for some:* ACT (for placement).
Costs (2002–03) *Tuition:* state resident $1920 full-time, $64 per credit hour part-time; nonresident $314 per credit hour part-time. *Required fees:* $178 full-time, $6 per credit hour.
Financial Aid In 2001, 20 Federal Work-Study jobs (averaging $1700). 50 State and other part-time jobs (averaging $2000).
Applying *Options:* early admission, deferred entrance. *Required:* high school transcript. *Application deadline:* rolling (freshmen), rolling (transfers).
Admissions Contact Ms. Jody Brown, Student Services, Morgan Community College, Student Services, 17800 Road 20, Fort Morgan, CO 80701. *Phone:* 970-542-3156. *Toll-free phone:* 800-622-0216. *Fax:* 970-867-6608. *E-mail:* jody.brown@mcc.cccoes.edu.

NORTHEASTERN JUNIOR COLLEGE
Sterling, Colorado

- **State-supported** 2-year, founded 1941, part of Colorado Community College and Occupational Education System
- **Calendar** semesters
- **Degree** certificates and associate
- **Small-town** 65-acre campus
- **Endowment** $800,000
- **Coed**

Faculty *Student/faculty ratio:* 4:1.
Student Life *Campus security:* 24-hour emergency response devices, controlled dormitory access, night patrols by trained security personnel.
Athletics Member NJCAA.
Standardized Tests *Required for some:* SAT I or ACT (for placement). *Recommended:* ACT (for placement).
Costs (2001–02) *Tuition:* state resident $1784 full-time, $59 per credit part-time; nonresident $6759 full-time. Full-time tuition and fees vary according to course load and program. Part-time tuition and fees vary according to course load and program. *Required fees:* $580 full-time, $290 per term part-time. *Room and board:* $5949. Room and board charges vary according to board plan, housing facility, and student level. *Payment plans:* installment, deferred payment.

Applying *Options:* common application, electronic application, early admission, deferred entrance. *Required:* high school transcript.
Admissions Contact Ms. Barbara Baker, Coordinator of College Admissions, Northeastern Junior College, 100 College Drive, Sterling, CO 80751-2399. *Phone:* 970-522-6600 Ext. 652. *Toll-free phone:* 800-626-4637. *Fax:* 970-521-6801. *E-mail:* barbara.baker@njc.cccoes.edu.

OTERO JUNIOR COLLEGE
La Junta, Colorado

- **State-supported** 2-year, founded 1941, part of Colorado Community College and Occupational Education System
- **Calendar** semesters
- **Degree** certificates and associate
- **Rural** 50-acre campus
- **Coed,** 1,402 undergraduate students

Undergraduates Students come from 8 states and territories, 2 other countries, 1% are from out of state, 13% live on campus.
Faculty *Total:* 75, 43% full-time.
Majors Agricultural business; auto mechanic/technician; biological/physical sciences; biology; business administration; child care/development; computer management; data processing technology; early childhood education; education; elementary education; history; humanities; legal administrative assistant; liberal arts and sciences/liberal studies; literature; mathematics; medical administrative assistant; modern languages; nursing; physical sciences; political science; pre-engineering; psychology; secretarial science; social sciences; theater arts/drama.
Academic Programs *Special study options:* academic remediation for entering students, adult/continuing education programs, advanced placement credit, distance learning, external degree program, internships, part-time degree program, summer session for credit.
Library Wheeler Library with 35,638 titles, 300 serial subscriptions, an OPAC.
Computers on Campus 100 computers available on campus for general student use. A campuswide network can be accessed from student residence rooms. Internet access, at least one staffed computer lab available.
Student Life *Housing:* on-campus residence required for freshman year. *Options:* coed. *Activities and Organizations:* drama/theater group, student-run newspaper, choral group. *Campus security:* 24-hour patrols, late-night transport/escort service. *Student Services:* personal/psychological counseling.
Athletics Member NJCAA. *Intercollegiate sports:* baseball M(s), basketball M(s)/W(s), golf M(s)/W(s), softball W(s), volleyball W(s). *Intramural sports:* basketball M, volleyball M/W.
Standardized Tests *Recommended:* SAT I or ACT (for placement).
Costs (2002–03) *Tuition:* state resident $1524 full-time, $64 per credit part-time; nonresident $6024 full-time, $251 per credit part-time. Full-time tuition and fees vary according to reciprocity agreements. Part-time tuition and fees vary according to reciprocity agreements. *Required fees:* $170 full-time. *Room and board:* $4010. Room and board charges vary according to board plan.
Financial Aid In 2001, 30 Federal Work-Study jobs (averaging $2000). 100 State and other part-time jobs (averaging $2000).
Applying *Options:* electronic application, early admission. *Recommended:* high school transcript. *Application deadlines:* 8/30 (freshmen), 8/30 (transfers). *Notification:* continuous (freshmen).
Admissions Contact Mr. Brad Franz, Vice President for Student Services, Otero Junior College, 1802 Colorado Avenue, La Junta, CO 81050-3415. *Phone:* 719-384-6833. *Fax:* 719-384-6933. *E-mail:* j_schiro@ojc.cccoes.edu.

PARKS COLLEGE
Denver, Colorado

Admissions Contact Ms. Kelly Wingate, Director of Admissions, Parks College, 9065 Grant Street, Denver, CO 80229-4339. *Phone:* 303-457-2757.

PIKES PEAK COMMUNITY COLLEGE
Colorado Springs, Colorado

- **State-supported** 2-year, founded 1968, part of Colorado Community College and Occupational Education System
- **Calendar** semesters
- **Degree** certificates and associate
- **Urban** 287-acre campus with easy access to Denver
- **Coed,** 9,772 undergraduate students, 31% full-time, 54% women, 46% men

Undergraduates 3,059 full-time, 6,713 part-time. Students come from 38 states and territories, 19% are from out of state, 12% African American, 4% Asian American or Pacific Islander, 10% Hispanic American, 2% Native American, 0.7% international, 15% transferred in.
Freshmen *Admission:* 4,122 applied, 4,122 admitted, 1,902 enrolled.
Faculty *Total:* 662, 19% full-time.
Majors Accounting technician; architectural engineering technology; auto body repair; auto mechanic/technician; business administration; business marketing and marketing management; business systems networking/ telecommunications; child care/guidance; construction management; criminal justice/law enforcement administration; dental assistant; design/visual communications; educational media technology; electrical/electronic engineering technology; emergency medical technology; energy management technology; fire protection/safety technology; general studies; institutional food workers; interior design; liberal arts and sciences/liberal studies; machine technology; management information systems/ business data processing; medical office management; natural resources management; nursing; occupational safety/health technology; paralegal/legal assistant; psychiatric/mental health services; public administration; robotics technology; sign language interpretation; theater arts/drama; welding technology.
Academic Programs *Special study options:* academic remediation for entering students, adult/continuing education programs, advanced placement credit, cooperative education, distance learning, double majors, English as a second language, independent study, internships, part-time degree program, services for LD students, summer session for credit. *ROTC:* Army (b).
Library PPCC Learning Resources Center plus 1 other with 34,332 titles, 311 serial subscriptions, 3,832 audiovisual materials, an OPAC.
Computers on Campus 180 computers available on campus for general student use. A campuswide network can be accessed from off campus. Internet access, at least one staffed computer lab available.
Student Life *Housing:* college housing not available. *Activities and Organizations:* drama/theater group, student-run newspaper. *Campus security:* 24-hour emergency response devices and patrols, late-night transport/escort service.
Athletics *Intramural sports:* basketball M/W, soccer M, volleyball M/W.
Standardized Tests *Recommended:* SAT I or ACT (for placement).
Costs (2002–03) *Tuition:* state resident $1884 full-time, $63 per credit hour part-time; nonresident $4141 full-time, $305 per credit hour part-time. Full-time tuition and fees vary according to course load. *Required fees:* $125 full-time. *Payment plan:* deferred payment. *Waivers:* senior citizens and employees or children of employees.
Financial Aid In 2001, 107 Federal Work-Study jobs (averaging $2292). 214 State and other part-time jobs (averaging $2444).
Applying *Options:* early admission, deferred entrance. *Application deadline:* rolling (freshmen), rolling (transfers).
Admissions Contact Mr. Rick Lee, Director, Enrollment Services, Pikes Peak Community College, 5675 South Academy Boulevard, Colorado Springs, CO 80906-5498. *Phone:* 719-540-7089. *Toll-free phone:* 800-456-6847 Ext. 7113. *Fax:* 719-540-7092. *E-mail:* admissions@ppcc.cccoes.edu.

PIMA MEDICAL INSTITUTE
Denver, Colorado

Admissions Contact Admissions Office, Pima Medical Institute, 1701 West 72nd Avenue, #130, Denver, CO 80221. *Phone:* 303-426-1800.

PLATT COLLEGE
Aurora, Colorado

- **Proprietary** primarily 2-year, founded 1986
- **Calendar** quarters
- **Degrees** diplomas, associate, and bachelor's
- **Suburban** campus
- **Coed,** 215 undergraduate students, 100% full-time, 51% women, 49% men

Freshmen *Admission:* 47 applied, 47 admitted.
Faculty *Total:* 22, 64% full-time. *Student/faculty ratio:* 14:1.
Majors Advertising; computer graphics; computer/information technology services administration and management related; graphic design/commercial art/ illustration; multimedia; Web page, digital/multimedia and information resources design.
Academic Programs *Special study options:* academic remediation for entering students, advanced placement credit.
Student Life *Housing:* college housing not available.
Costs (2001–02) *Tuition:* $7560 full-time. *Required fees:* $75 full-time.

Platt College (continued)
Applying *Application fee:* $75. *Required:* high school transcript, interview. *Application deadline:* rolling (freshmen), rolling (transfers).
Admissions Contact Admissions Office, Platt College, 3100 South Parker Road, Suite 200, Aurora, CO 80014-3141. *Phone:* 303-369-5151. *E-mail:* admissions@plattcolo.com.

PUEBLO COMMUNITY COLLEGE
Pueblo, Colorado

Admissions Contact Mr. Dan Cordova, Admissions Counselor, Pueblo Community College, 900 West Orman Avenue, College Center, Room 215, Pueblo, CO 81004. *Phone:* 719-549-3017. *Fax:* 719-549-3012. *E-mail:* admissions@pcc.cccoes.edu.

RED ROCKS COMMUNITY COLLEGE
Lakewood, Colorado

- **State-supported** 2-year, founded 1969, part of Colorado Community College and Occupational Education System
- **Calendar** semesters
- **Degree** certificates and associate
- **Urban** 120-acre campus with easy access to Denver
- **Coed,** 7,394 undergraduate students

Undergraduates Students come from 27 states and territories.
Faculty *Total:* 276, 23% full-time.
Majors Accounting; art; biological/physical sciences; biology; business administration; business marketing and marketing management; carpentry; chemistry; computer engineering technology; computer programming; computer science; criminal justice/law enforcement administration; drafting; economics; electrical/electronic engineering technology; English; fire science; French; geology; German; heavy equipment maintenance; history; humanities; liberal arts and sciences/liberal studies; mass communications; mathematics; mechanical engineering technology; physics; political science; psychology; public administration; real estate; sanitation technology; secretarial science; sociology; solar technology; Spanish; surveying; water resources; welding technology.
Academic Programs *Special study options:* academic remediation for entering students, adult/continuing education programs, cooperative education, English as a second language, off-campus study, part-time degree program, study abroad, summer session for credit. *ROTC:* Army (c).
Library 45,511 titles, 304 serial subscriptions.
Computers on Campus 200 computers available on campus for general student use. Internet access, online (class) registration, at least one staffed computer lab available.
Student Life *Housing:* college housing not available. *Activities and Organizations:* drama/theater group, student-run newspaper. *Campus security:* 24-hour emergency response devices and patrols. *Student Services:* personal/psychological counseling, women's center.
Athletics *Intramural sports:* volleyball M/W.
Standardized Tests *Recommended:* ACT ASSET or ACT COMPASS.
Costs (2001–02) *Tuition:* state resident $1646 full-time; nonresident $7196 full-time. *Payment plan:* deferred payment. *Waivers:* senior citizens.
Financial Aid In 2001, 60 Federal Work-Study jobs (averaging $2155). 200 State and other part-time jobs (averaging $2039).
Applying *Options:* early admission. *Application deadline:* rolling (freshmen), rolling (transfers). *Notification:* continuous (freshmen).
Admissions Contact Mr. Bob Austin, Registrar and Director of Admissions and Records, Red Rocks Community College, 13300 West 6th Avenue, Lakewood, CO 80228-1255. *Phone:* 303-988-6160 Ext. 6360. *Fax:* 303-969-8039.

TRINIDAD STATE JUNIOR COLLEGE
Trinidad, Colorado

- **State-supported** 2-year, founded 1925, part of Colorado Community College and Occupational Education System
- **Calendar** semesters
- **Degree** certificates and associate
- **Small-town** 17-acre campus
- **Endowment** $3.2 million
- **Coed,** 2,804 undergraduate students, 62% full-time, 60% women, 40% men

Undergraduates 1,749 full-time, 1,055 part-time. Students come from 33 states and territories, 11 other countries, 2% transferred in, 30% live on campus.
Freshmen *Admission:* 410 applied, 410 admitted, 437 enrolled. *Average high school GPA:* 2.21.
Faculty *Total:* 171, 33% full-time, 8% with terminal degrees.
Majors Accounting; art education; auto mechanic/technician; biological/physical sciences; biology; business administration; business marketing and marketing management; carpentry; chemistry; civil engineering technology; computer science; computer science related; computer systems networking/telecommunications; construction technology; corrections; cosmetic services; cosmetology; data processing technology; design/visual communications; drafting; early childhood education; education; electrical/electronic engineering technology; engineering; English; farm/ranch management; forestry; graphic design/commercial art/illustration; heavy equipment maintenance; industrial technology; information sciences/systems; information technology; journalism; landscape architecture; law enforcement/police science; liberal arts and sciences/liberal studies; management information systems/business data processing; mining technology; music; natural resources management; nurse assistant/aide; nursing; occupational safety/health technology; physical education; practical nurse; pre-engineering; psychology; secretarial science; soil conservation; theater arts/drama; water treatment technology.
Academic Programs *Special study options:* academic remediation for entering students, accelerated degree program, adult/continuing education programs, advanced placement credit, cooperative education, distance learning, double majors, English as a second language, honors programs, independent study, internships, part-time degree program, services for LD students, student-designed majors, summer session for credit.
Library Frendenthal Library plus 1 other with 49,033 titles, 123 serial subscriptions, an OPAC.
Computers on Campus 125 computers available on campus for general student use. A campuswide network can be accessed from student residence rooms and from off campus. Internet access, online (class) registration, at least one staffed computer lab available.
Student Life *Housing Options:* coed, men-only, women-only. *Activities and Organizations:* drama/theater group, student-run newspaper, choral group, student association, International Club, Gunsmithing Club, Nursing Club, Cosmetology Club. *Campus security:* 24-hour emergency response devices and patrols, late-night transport/escort service.
Athletics Member NJCAA. *Intercollegiate sports:* baseball M(s), basketball M(s), cross-country running W, golf M(s)/W, volleyball W(s). *Intramural sports:* badminton M/W, basketball M, bowling M/W, cross-country running W, football M/W, riflery M/W, skiing (cross-country) M/W, skiing (downhill) M/W, softball M/W, table tennis M/W, tennis M/W, volleyball M/W, weight lifting M/W.
Standardized Tests *Required for some:* ACT (for placement), ACT ASSET, ACCUPLACER. *Recommended:* SAT I and SAT II or ACT (for placement).
Costs (2002–03) *Tuition:* state resident $1986 full-time, $63 per semester hour part-time; nonresident $6486 full-time, $224 per semester hour part-time. *Required fees:* $400 full-time, $10 per semester hour, $200 per term part-time. *Room and board:* $4700. Room and board charges vary according to board plan. *Payment plan:* installment. *Waivers:* senior citizens and employees or children of employees.
Applying *Options:* common application, electronic application, deferred entrance. *Required:* high school transcript. *Application deadline:* rolling (freshmen), rolling (transfers). *Notification:* continuous (freshmen).
Admissions Contact Mr. Rick Sciacca, Admissions Director, Trinidad State Junior College, 600 Prospect, Trinidad, CO 81082-2396. *Phone:* 719-846-5621 Ext. 5625. *Toll-free phone:* 800-621-8752. *Fax:* 719-846-5667.

WESTWOOD COLLEGE OF AVIATION TECHNOLOGY-DENVER
Broomfield, Colorado

- **Proprietary** 2-year, founded 1965
- **Calendar** continuous
- **Degree** associate
- **Suburban** 4-acre campus with easy access to Denver
- **Coed,** 628 undergraduate students

Faculty *Total:* 52, 87% full-time.
Majors Aircraft mechanic/airframe; aircraft mechanic/powerplant; aviation technology.
Library Resource Center.
Computers on Campus At least one staffed computer lab available.
Student Life *Housing:* college housing not available.

Costs (2002–03) *Tuition:* Airframe and Powerplant: $23,538 for 17.5 month program; Advanced Electronics Technology: $23,459 for 17 month program. (Includes tuition, books, tools, registration fees, and student insurance).
Financial Aid In 2001, 20 Federal Work-Study jobs.
Applying *Options:* electronic application. *Required:* interview, references, student profile. *Application deadline:* rolling (freshmen), rolling (transfers). *Notification:* continuous (freshmen).
Admissions Contact Ms. Laura Goldhammer, Director of Admissions, Westwood College of Aviation Technology-Denver, 10851 West 120th Avenue, Broomfield, CO 80021. *Phone:* 303-466-1714. *Toll-free phone:* 800-888-3995. *Fax:* 303-469-3797.

WESTWOOD COLLEGE OF TECHNOLOGY-DENVER NORTH
Denver, Colorado

- **Proprietary** primarily 2-year, founded 1953
- **Calendar** 5 terms
- **Degrees** diplomas, associate, bachelor's, and postbachelor's certificates
- **Suburban** 11-acre campus
- **Coed,** 969 undergraduate students, 68% full-time, 27% women, 73% men

Undergraduates 656 full-time, 313 part-time. Students come from 21 states and territories, 10 other countries, 14% are from out of state, 4% African American, 5% Asian American or Pacific Islander, 13% Hispanic American, 0.4% Native American, 0.1% international. *Retention:* 22% of 2001 full-time freshmen returned.
Freshmen *Admission:* 2,198 applied, 996 admitted, 555 enrolled.
Faculty *Total:* 103, 40% full-time. *Student/faculty ratio:* 11:1.
Majors Architectural drafting; auto mechanic/technician; business administration/management related; computer engineering technology; computer/information technology services administration and management related; computer programming; computer systems networking/telecommunications; design/visual communications; electrical/electronic engineering technology; graphic design/commercial art/illustration; heating/air conditioning/refrigeration; hotel and restaurant management; mechanical drafting; medical assistant; medical transcription; surveying.
Academic Programs *Special study options:* academic remediation for entering students, accelerated degree program, advanced placement credit, internships, summer session for credit.
Library DIT Library with 2,500 titles, 90 serial subscriptions.
Computers on Campus 150 computers available on campus for general student use. Internet access available.
Student Life *Housing:* college housing not available. *Activities and Organizations:* student government, Athletic Club, American Institute of Graphic Arts, Social Club. *Campus security:* 24-hour emergency response devices. *Student Services:* personal/psychological counseling.
Costs (2002–03) *Tuition:* $16,775 full-time, $2516 per term part-time. Full-time tuition and fees vary according to course load and program. Part-time tuition and fees vary according to course load and program. *Required fees:* $900 full-time, $382 per credit, $120 per term part-time. *Payment plan:* installment. *Waivers:* employees or children of employees.
Applying *Options:* deferred entrance. *Application fee:* $100. *Required for some:* high school transcript. *Recommended:* interview. *Application deadline:* rolling (freshmen), rolling (transfers). *Notification:* continuous (freshmen).
Admissions Contact Ms. Nicole Blaschko, New Student Coordinator, Westwood College of Technology-Denver North, 7350 North Broadway, Denver, CO 80221-3653. *Phone:* 303-650-5050 Ext. 329. *Toll-free phone:* 800-992-5050.

WESTWOOD COLLEGE OF TECHNOLOGY-DENVER SOUTH
Denver, Colorado

- **Proprietary** primarily 2-year
- **Degrees** associate and bachelor's
- **Coed,** 421 undergraduate students

Faculty *Total:* 38, 37% full-time.
Majors Business administration/management related; computer programming; computer systems networking/telecommunications; design/visual communications; electrical/electronic engineering technology; graphic design/commercial art/illustration; multimedia.
Costs (2002–03) *Tuition:* Standard program price $3,355 per term, lab fees and books additional, 5 terms/year, program length: associate degree = 7 terms, bachelors degree = 14 terms.
Admissions Contact Mr. Ron DeJong, Director of Admissions, Westwood College of Technology-Denver South, 3150 South Sheridan Boulevard, Denver, CO 80227. *Phone:* 303-934-1122.

CONNECTICUT

ASNUNTUCK COMMUNITY COLLEGE
Enfield, Connecticut

- **State-supported** 2-year, founded 1972, part of Connecticut Community College System
- **Calendar** semesters
- **Degree** certificates and associate
- **Small-town** 4-acre campus
- **Coed,** 1,723 undergraduate students, 24% full-time, 53% women, 47% men

Undergraduates 409 full-time, 1,314 part-time. Students come from 3 states and territories, 3% are from out of state, 3% African American, 2% Asian American or Pacific Islander, 1% Hispanic American, 0.3% Native American, 0.3% international. *Retention:* 60% of 2001 full-time freshmen returned.
Freshmen *Admission:* 663 applied, 663 admitted, 154 enrolled.
Faculty *Total:* 115, 21% full-time.
Majors Accounting; alcohol/drug abuse counseling; art; business administration; computer science; criminal justice studies; early childhood education; engineering science; food products retailing; general studies; graphic design/commercial art/illustration; human services; liberal arts and sciences/liberal studies; mass communications; secretarial science.
Academic Programs *Special study options:* academic remediation for entering students, adult/continuing education programs, advanced placement credit, distance learning, double majors, English as a second language, independent study, internships, part-time degree program, services for LD students, student-designed majors, summer session for credit.
Library ACTC Learning Resource Center with 28,500 titles, 310 serial subscriptions, an OPAC.
Computers on Campus 90 computers available on campus for general student use. A campuswide network can be accessed from off campus. Internet access, at least one staffed computer lab available.
Student Life *Housing:* college housing not available. *Activities and Organizations:* drama/theater group, student-run newspaper, Phi Theta Kappa, Drama Club, Outdoor Club, Poetry Club, Ski Club. *Campus security:* 24-hour patrols, late-night transport/escort service. *Student Services:* women's center.
Costs (2002–03) *Tuition:* state resident $1764 full-time, $74 per credit part-time; nonresident $221 per credit part-time. Full-time tuition and fees vary according to course load. Part-time tuition and fees vary according to course load. *Required fees:* $216 full-time, $47 per credit. *Waivers:* senior citizens and employees or children of employees.
Financial Aid In 2001, 20 Federal Work-Study jobs (averaging $3000). 10 State and other part-time jobs (averaging $3000).
Applying *Options:* early admission, deferred entrance. *Application fee:* $20. *Required:* high school transcript. *Application deadline:* rolling (freshmen), rolling (transfers). *Notification:* continuous (freshmen).
Admissions Contact Ms. Donna Shaw, Director of Admissions and Marketing, Asnuntuck Community College, 170 Elm Street, Enfield, CT 06082-3800. *Phone:* 860-253-3018. *Fax:* 860-253-9310.

BRIARWOOD COLLEGE
Southington, Connecticut

- **Proprietary** 2-year, founded 1966
- **Calendar** semesters
- **Degree** certificates, diplomas, and associate
- **Small-town** 32-acre campus with easy access to Boston and Hartford
- **Endowment** $27,595
- **Coed,** 575 undergraduate students

Undergraduates Students come from 11 states and territories, 7% are from out of state, 21% live on campus.

Briarwood College (continued)

Freshmen *Admission:* 627 applied, 623 admitted. *Test scores:* SAT verbal scores over 500: 16%; SAT verbal scores over 600: 3%; SAT verbal scores over 700: 3%.

Faculty *Total:* 100.

Majors Accounting; biotechnology research; business administration; child care/development; communications; criminal justice/law enforcement administration; dental assistant; dietetics; fashion merchandising; general studies; hotel and restaurant management; legal administrative assistant; medical administrative assistant; medical assistant; medical office management; medical records administration; mortuary science; occupational therapy assistant; paralegal/legal assistant; radio/television broadcasting technology; secretarial science; travel/tourism management.

Academic Programs *Special study options:* academic remediation for entering students, adult/continuing education programs, double majors, English as a second language, independent study, internships, part-time degree program, services for LD students, summer session for credit.

Library Pupillo Library with 11,500 titles, 154 serial subscriptions, 130 audiovisual materials, a Web page.

Computers on Campus 54 computers available on campus for general student use. Internet access, online (class) registration, at least one staffed computer lab available.

Student Life *Housing Options:* coed. *Activities and Organizations:* student-run radio station, student government, Yearbook Committee, Student Ambassador Club, F.A.M.E. (Fashion Merchandising Club). *Campus security:* 24-hour patrols, late-night transport/escort service. *Student Services:* personal/psychological counseling.

Athletics *Intramural sports:* basketball M, softball M/W, tennis M/W, volleyball M/W.

Standardized Tests *Required:* College Board Diagnostic Tests.

Costs (2001–02) *Tuition:* $13,100 full-time, $420 per credit hour part-time. Part-time tuition and fees vary according to course load and program. *Room only:* $2800. *Payment plan:* installment. *Waivers:* employees or children of employees.

Financial Aid In 2001, 33 Federal Work-Study jobs (averaging $600). 30 State and other part-time jobs.

Applying *Options:* common application, electronic application. *Application fee:* $25. *Required:* high school transcript. *Required for some:* essay or personal statement, letters of recommendation, interview. *Application deadline:* rolling (freshmen), rolling (transfers).

Admissions Contact Mrs. Debra LaRoche, Director of Admissions, Briarwood College, 2279 Mount Vernon Road, Southington, CT 06489. *Phone:* 860-628-4751 Ext. 25. *Toll-free phone:* 800-952-2444. *Fax:* 860-628-6444.

CAPITAL COMMUNITY COLLEGE
Hartford, Connecticut

- **State-supported** 2-year, founded 1946, part of Connecticut Community College System
- **Calendar** semesters
- **Degree** certificates and associate
- **Urban** 10-acre campus
- **Coed,** 3,129 undergraduate students, 20% full-time, 69% women, 31% men

Undergraduates 640 full-time, 2,489 part-time. Students come from 4 states and territories, 37% African American, 4% Asian American or Pacific Islander, 24% Hispanic American, 0.3% Native American, 0.3% international.

Freshmen *Admission:* 461 admitted, 461 enrolled.

Faculty *Total:* 222, 27% full-time, 7% with terminal degrees.

Majors Accounting; alcohol/drug abuse counseling; business administration; chemical engineering technology; civil engineering technology; computer engineering technology; computer/information sciences; computer science related; construction technology; data entry/microcomputer applications related; early childhood education; electrical/electronic engineering technology; emergency medical technology; fire protection/safety technology; fire services administration; information technology; liberal arts and sciences/liberal studies; mechanical engineering technology; medical assistant; medical radiologic technology; nursing; physical therapy assistant; secretarial science; social work; Web page, digital/multimedia and information resources design.

Academic Programs *Special study options:* academic remediation for entering students, accelerated degree program, adult/continuing education programs, advanced placement credit, distance learning, double majors, English as a second language, independent study, internships, part-time degree program, services for LD students, summer session for credit.

Library Arthur C. Banks, Jr. Library plus 1 other with 51,539 titles, 445 serial subscriptions, 3,231 audiovisual materials, an OPAC, a Web page.

Computers on Campus 180 computers available on campus for general student use. A campuswide network can be accessed from off campus. Internet access, at least one staffed computer lab available.

Student Life *Housing:* college housing not available. *Activities and Organizations:* choral group, Latin American Student Association, Student Senate, Senior Renewal Club, Early Childhood Club, Pre-Professional Club. *Campus security:* late-night transport/escort service, security staff during hours of operation, emergency telephones 7 a.m.—11 p.m. *Student Services:* personal/psychological counseling.

Athletics Member NJCAA. *Intercollegiate sports:* basketball M(s)/W(s). *Intramural sports:* football M, soccer M/W, softball M/W.

Standardized Tests *Required for some:* SAT I (for placement).

Costs (2001–02) *Tuition:* state resident $1908 full-time, $70 per credit hour part-time; nonresident $5460 full-time, $218 per credit hour part-time. Part-time tuition and fees vary according to course load. *Required fees:* $228 full-time, $53 per credit hour. *Waivers:* employees or children of employees.

Applying *Application fee:* $20. *Recommended:* high school transcript. *Application deadline:* rolling (freshmen), rolling (transfers). *Notification:* continuous until 9/1 (freshmen).

Admissions Contact Ms. Jackie Phillips, Director of the Welcome and Advising Center, Capital Community College, 61 Woodland Street, Hartford, CT 06105. *Phone:* 860-520-2310. *Toll-free phone:* 800-894-6126 Ext. 7829. *Fax:* 860-520-7906. *E-mail:* balldavis@ccc.commnet.edu.

GATEWAY COMMUNITY COLLEGE
New Haven, Connecticut

- **State-supported** 2-year, founded 1992, part of Connecticut Community College System
- **Calendar** semesters
- **Degree** certificates and associate
- **Urban** 5-acre campus with easy access to New York City
- **Coed,** 4,724 undergraduate students

Undergraduates Students come from 7 states and territories, 12 other countries, 0.6% are from out of state, 22% African American, 3% Asian American or Pacific Islander, 13% Hispanic American, 0.3% Native American, 1% international.

Faculty *Total:* 294, 29% full-time. *Student/faculty ratio:* 20:1.

Majors Accounting; alcohol/drug abuse counseling; auto mechanic/technician; aviation technology; biomedical technology; business administration; computer engineering related; computer engineering technology; computer graphics; computer science related; computer typography/composition; data entry/microcomputer applications; data processing technology; dietetics; early childhood education; electrical/electronic engineering technology; engineering technology; fashion merchandising; fire science; food products retailing; gerontology; hotel and restaurant management; human services; industrial radiologic technology; industrial technology; legal administrative assistant; liberal arts and sciences/liberal studies; mechanical engineering technology; medical administrative assistant; mental health/rehabilitation; nuclear medical technology; pharmacy; retail management; word processing.

Academic Programs *Special study options:* academic remediation for entering students, adult/continuing education programs, advanced placement credit, distance learning, English as a second language, external degree program, independent study, internships, off-campus study, part-time degree program, services for LD students, summer session for credit.

Library Main Library plus 1 other with 49,505 titles, 670 serial subscriptions, 9,500 audiovisual materials, an OPAC.

Computers on Campus 280 computers available on campus for general student use. A campuswide network can be accessed from off campus. Internet access, at least one staffed computer lab available.

Student Life *Housing:* college housing not available. *Campus security:* late-night transport/escort service.

Athletics Member NJCAA. *Intercollegiate sports:* basketball M/W.

Costs (2002–03) *Tuition:* state resident $1764 full-time, $74 per credit part-time; nonresident $5292 full-time, $221 per credit part-time. Full-time tuition and fees vary according to course load. Part-time tuition and fees vary according to course load. *Required fees:* $216 full-time, $47 per credit. *Payment plan:* deferred payment. *Waivers:* senior citizens.

Applying *Options:* early admission, deferred entrance. *Application fee:* $20. *Required:* high school transcript. *Required for some:* essay or personal statement, interview. *Application deadlines:* 9/1 (freshmen), 9/1 (transfers). *Notification:* continuous until 9/1 (freshmen).

Admissions Contact Ms. Catherine Surface, Director of Admissions, Gateway Community College, 60 Sargent Drive, New Haven, CT 06511. *Phone:* 203-789-7043. *Toll-free phone:* 800-390-7723. *Fax:* 203-285-2018. *E-mail:* gateway_ctc@commnet.edu.

GIBBS COLLEGE
Norwalk, Connecticut

- **Proprietary** 2-year, founded 1975, part of Career Education Corporation
- **Calendar** quarters
- **Degree** certificates and associate
- **Suburban** 2-acre campus with easy access to New York City
- **Coed**

Student Life *Campus security:* 24-hour emergency response devices.
Standardized Tests *Recommended:* SAT I or ACT (for admission).
Applying *Options:* common application, electronic application, deferred entrance. *Application fee:* $25. *Required:* high school transcript, interview. *Recommended:* essay or personal statement.
Admissions Contact Ms. Jane Pascarella, Director of Admissions, Gibbs College, 142 East Avenue, Norwalk, CT 06851-5754. *Phone:* 203-633-2301. *Toll-free phone:* 800-845-5333. *Fax:* 203-853-6402. *E-mail:* ejeffers@kgibbs.com.

GOODWIN COLLEGE
East Hartford, Connecticut

- **Proprietary** 2-year
- **Calendar** modular
- **Degree** certificates, diplomas, and associate
- **Endowment** $900,000
- **Coed,** 721 undergraduate students, 72% full-time, 51% women, 49% men

Undergraduates 519 full-time, 202 part-time. Students come from 3 states and territories, 6 other countries, 8% are from out of state, 2% transferred in.
Freshmen *Admission:* 498 applied, 345 admitted, 345 enrolled. *Average high school GPA:* 2.8.
Faculty *Total:* 35, 51% full-time, 6% with terminal degrees. *Student/faculty ratio:* 10:1.
Majors Computer/technical support; word processing.
Academic Programs *Special study options:* academic remediation for entering students, accelerated degree program, adult/continuing education programs, advanced placement credit, cooperative education, distance learning, double majors, English as a second language, external degree program, honors programs, independent study, internships, part-time degree program, services for LD students, summer session for credit.
Library Goodwin College Library with 1,100 titles, 1,200 serial subscriptions, 281 audiovisual materials, an OPAC.
Computers on Campus 220 computers available on campus for general student use. A campuswide network can be accessed from off campus. Internet access, at least one staffed computer lab available.
Student Life *Housing:* college housing not available. *Campus security:* evening security patrolman.
Standardized Tests *Recommended:* SAT I or ACT (for placement), SAT I and SAT II or ACT (for placement), SAT II: Writing Test (for placement).
Costs (2001–02) *One-time required fee:* $100. *Tuition:* $8400 full-time, $280 per credit part-time. Full-time tuition and fees vary according to course load. Part-time tuition and fees vary according to course load. No tuition increase for student's term of enrollment. *Required fees:* $290 full-time. *Payment plans:* tuition prepayment, installment, deferred payment. *Waivers:* employees or children of employees.
Applying *Options:* common application, electronic application, deferred entrance. *Application fee:* $25. *Required:* essay or personal statement, high school transcript, minimum 2.0 GPA, medical exam. *Recommended:* 2 letters of recommendation, interview. *Notification:* continuous until 8/1 (freshmen).
Admissions Contact Mr. Daniel P. Noonan, Director of Enrollment and Student Services, Goodwin College, 745 Burnside Avenue, East Hartford, CT 06108. *Phone:* 860-528-4111 Ext. 230. *Toll-free phone:* 800-889-3282 (in-state); 860-528-4111 (out-of-state). *E-mail:* dnoonan@goodwincollege.org.

HOUSATONIC COMMUNITY COLLEGE
Bridgeport, Connecticut

- **State-supported** 2-year, founded 1965, part of Connecticut Community-Technical College System
- **Calendar** semesters
- **Degree** certificates and associate
- **Urban** 4-acre campus with easy access to New York City
- **Coed,** 4,247 undergraduate students

Faculty *Total:* 227, 27% full-time.
Majors Accounting; alcohol/drug abuse counseling; art; aviation technology; business administration; child care/development; computer typography/composition; criminal justice/law enforcement administration; data processing technology; environmental science; graphic design/commercial art/illustration; humanities; human services; journalism; liberal arts and sciences/liberal studies; mathematics; medical laboratory technician; mental health/rehabilitation; nursing; physical therapy; pre-engineering; public administration; secretarial science; social sciences.
Academic Programs *Special study options:* academic remediation for entering students, adult/continuing education programs, advanced placement credit, cooperative education, double majors, English as a second language, honors programs, independent study, internships, part-time degree program, services for LD students, summer session for credit. *ROTC:* Army (c).
Library 30,000 titles, 280 serial subscriptions, an OPAC, a Web page.
Computers on Campus 200 computers available on campus for general student use. Internet access, at least one staffed computer lab available.
Student Life *Housing:* college housing not available. *Activities and Organizations:* student-run newspaper, Student Senate, Association of Latin American Students, African-American Cultural Society, Art Club. *Campus security:* 24-hour emergency response devices, late-night transport/escort service. *Student Services:* personal/psychological counseling.
Standardized Tests *Required for some:* ACCUPLACER.
Costs (2001–02) *Tuition:* state resident $1680 full-time, $70 per credit part-time; nonresident $5232 full-time, $218 per credit part-time. Part-time tuition and fees vary according to course load. *Required fees:* $208 full-time. *Waivers:* senior citizens.
Applying *Options:* common application, deferred entrance. *Application fee:* $20. *Required:* high school transcript. *Required for some:* letters of recommendation, interview. *Application deadline:* rolling (freshmen), rolling (transfers).
Admissions Contact Ms. Deloris Y. Curtis, Director of Admissions, Housatonic Community College, 900 Lafayette Boulevard, Bridgeport, CT 06604-4704. *Phone:* 203-332-5102.

INTERNATIONAL COLLEGE OF HOSPITALITY MANAGEMENT, CESAR RITZ
Washington, Connecticut

- **Proprietary** 2-year, founded 1992
- **Calendar** continuous
- **Degree** certificates and associate
- **Small-town** 27-acre campus with easy access to New York City
- **Coed,** 116 undergraduate students, 100% full-time, 59% women, 41% men

The International College of Hospitality Management, Cesar Ritz, is the only Swiss college of hospitality management in the United States. The Swiss tradition of *hôtellerie*, combined with practical experience obtained on paid internships in the best American hospitality properties, prepares students for managerial positions in the fastest-growing industry in the world.

Undergraduates 116 full-time. Students come from 6 states and territories, 34 other countries, 50% are from out of state, 6% African American, 23% Asian American or Pacific Islander, 51% international, 16% transferred in, 90% live on campus.
Freshmen *Admission:* 35 applied, 27 admitted, 27 enrolled.
Faculty *Total:* 14, 43% full-time, 7% with terminal degrees. *Student/faculty ratio:* 15:1.
Majors Hospitality management.
Academic Programs *Special study options:* academic remediation for entering students, accelerated degree program, adult/continuing education programs, advanced placement credit, cooperative education, distance learning, English as a second language, independent study, internships, part-time degree program, services for LD students, study abroad.
Library International College of Hospitality Management Library with 10,000 titles, 232 serial subscriptions, an OPAC.
Computers on Campus 23 computers available on campus for general student use. A campuswide network can be accessed from off campus. Internet access, at least one staffed computer lab available.
Student Life *Housing Options:* coed. *Activities and Organizations:* student-run newspaper, student committee, student newsletter, yearbook committee, Ritz

International College of Hospitality Management, Cesar Ritz (continued)
Guild, Student Ambassadors. *Campus security:* 24-hour emergency response devices, student patrols, late-night transport/escort service, controlled dormitory access, weekend patrols by trained security personnel. *Student Services:* health clinic, personal/psychological counseling.

Athletics *Intramural sports:* basketball M/W, soccer M/W, tennis M/W, volleyball M/W.

Standardized Tests *Recommended:* SAT I (for admission).

Costs (2002–03) *Comprehensive fee:* $18,250 includes full-time tuition ($14,000) and room and board ($4250). Part-time tuition: $600 per credit. *Payment plans:* installment, deferred payment. *Waivers:* employees or children of employees.

Applying *Options:* common application, electronic application, deferred entrance. *Application fee:* $25. *Required:* high school transcript, letters of recommendation. *Required for some:* essay or personal statement, interview. *Recommended:* interview. *Application deadline:* rolling (freshmen), rolling (transfers). *Notification:* continuous (freshmen).

Admissions Contact Ms. Jacqueline Ocholla, Enrollment Coordinator, International College of Hospitality Management, *Cesar Ritz*, 101 Wykeham Road, Washington, CT 06793-1300. *Phone:* 860-868-9555 Ext. 126. *Toll-free phone:* 800-955-0809. *Fax:* 860-868-2114. *E-mail:* admissions@ichm.cc.ct.us.

MANCHESTER COMMUNITY COLLEGE
Manchester, Connecticut

- **State-supported** 2-year, founded 1963, part of Connecticut Community College System
- **Calendar** semesters
- **Degree** certificates and associate
- **Small-town** 160-acre campus with easy access to Hartford
- **Coed,** 5,405 undergraduate students, 35% full-time, 58% women, 42% men

Undergraduates 1,872 full-time, 3,533 part-time. 13% African American, 4% Asian American or Pacific Islander, 9% Hispanic American, 0.4% Native American.

Freshmen *Admission:* 1,513 applied, 1,513 admitted, 692 enrolled.

Faculty *Total:* 268, 34% full-time. *Student/faculty ratio:* 19:1.

Majors Accounting; business administration; business marketing and marketing management; communications; criminal justice/law enforcement administration; early childhood education; engineering science; fine/studio arts; general studies; graphic design/commercial art/illustration; hotel and restaurant management; human services; industrial/manufacturing engineering; industrial technology; information sciences/systems; journalism; legal administrative assistant; liberal arts and sciences/liberal studies; management information systems/business data processing; medical administrative assistant; medical laboratory technician; music; occupational therapy assistant; operating room technician; paralegal/legal assistant; physical therapy assistant; respiratory therapy; secretarial science; social work; teacher assistant/aide; theater arts/drama.

Academic Programs *Special study options:* academic remediation for entering students, cooperative education, distance learning, double majors, English as a second language, honors programs, independent study, internships, off-campus study, part-time degree program, student-designed majors, summer session for credit. *ROTC:* Army (c).

Library 45,265 titles, 493 serial subscriptions, 2,481 audiovisual materials.

Student Life *Housing:* college housing not available. *Activities and Organizations:* drama/theater group, student-run newspaper, choral group. *Student Services:* women's center.

Athletics Member NJCAA. *Intercollegiate sports:* baseball M, basketball M/W, soccer M/W, softball W.

Standardized Tests *Required for some:* SAT I (for admission).

Costs (2002–03) *Tuition:* state resident $1764 full-time, $74 per credit hour part-time; nonresident $5292 full-time, $221 per credit hour part-time. *Required fees:* $216 full-time, $7 per credit hour.

Financial Aid In 2001, 100 Federal Work-Study jobs (averaging $2000). 25 State and other part-time jobs (averaging $2000).

Applying *Options:* deferred entrance. *Application fee:* $20. *Required:* high school transcript. *Application deadline:* rolling (freshmen), rolling (transfers).

Admissions Contact Mr. Peter Harris, Director of Admissions, Manchester Community College, PO Box 1046, Manchester, CT 06045-1046. *Phone:* 860-512-3210. *Fax:* 860-512-3221.

MIDDLESEX COMMUNITY COLLEGE
Middletown, Connecticut

- **State-supported** 2-year, founded 1966, part of Connecticut Community College System
- **Calendar** semesters
- **Degree** certificates and associate
- **Suburban** 38-acre campus with easy access to Hartford
- **Coed**

Student Life *Campus security:* 24-hour patrols.

Standardized Tests *Required:* Accuplacer.

Financial Aid In 2001, 50 Federal Work-Study jobs (averaging $5000). 2 State and other part-time jobs (averaging $5000).

Applying *Options:* early admission, deferred entrance. *Application fee:* $20. *Required:* high school transcript, CPT.

Admissions Contact Mr. Peter McCluskey, Director of Admissions, Middlesex Community College, 100 Training Hill Road, Middletown, CT 06457-4889. *Phone:* 860-343-5719. *Fax:* 860-344-7488.

MITCHELL COLLEGE
New London, Connecticut

- **Independent** primarily 2-year, founded 1938
- **Calendar** semesters
- **Degrees** associate and bachelor's
- **Suburban** 67-acre campus with easy access to Hartford and Providence
- **Endowment** $6.0 million
- **Coed,** 708 undergraduate students, 83% full-time, 51% women, 49% men

Undergraduates 588 full-time, 120 part-time. Students come from 19 states and territories, 12 other countries, 42% are from out of state, 10% African American, 1% Asian American or Pacific Islander, 5% Hispanic American, 5% Native American, 3% international, 5% transferred in, 80% live on campus.

Freshmen *Admission:* 1,024 applied, 641 admitted, 288 enrolled. *Average high school GPA:* 2.65. *Test scores:* SAT verbal scores over 500: 15%; SAT math scores over 500: 13%; ACT scores over 18: 57%; SAT verbal scores over 600: 2%; SAT math scores over 600: 2%; ACT scores over 24: 14%.

Faculty *Total:* 60, 33% full-time, 23% with terminal degrees. *Student/faculty ratio:* 12:1.

Majors Accounting; athletic training/sports medicine; biological/physical sciences; business administration; child care/development; criminal justice/law enforcement administration; developmental/child psychology; early childhood education; engineering; graphic design/commercial art/illustration; human services; individual/family development; liberal arts and sciences/liberal studies; marine biology; physical education; physical sciences; psychology; recreational therapy; recreation/leisure studies; sport/fitness administration.

Academic Programs *Special study options:* adult/continuing education programs, advanced placement credit, double majors, English as a second language, internships, part-time degree program, services for LD students, summer session for credit.

Library Mitchell College Library plus 1 other with 42,000 titles, 90 serial subscriptions, 50 audiovisual materials, an OPAC.

Computers on Campus 155 computers available on campus for general student use. A campuswide network can be accessed from student residence rooms and from off campus. Internet access, at least one staffed computer lab available.

Student Life *Housing Options:* coed, men-only, women-only. *Activities and Organizations:* drama/theater group, student-run newspaper, choral group, Multicultural Club, Business Club, student government, student newspaper, Outdoor Adventure Club. *Campus security:* 24-hour emergency response devices and patrols, student patrols, late-night transport/escort service, controlled dormitory access. *Student Services:* health clinic, personal/psychological counseling.

Athletics Member NJCAA. *Intercollegiate sports:* baseball M(s), basketball M(s)/W(s), cross-country running M/W, golf M/W, lacrosse M(s), sailing M/W, soccer M(s)/W(s), softball W(s), tennis M/W, volleyball W(s). *Intramural sports:* badminton M/W, baseball M, basketball M/W, bowling M/W, cross-country running M/W, football M/W, golf M/W, ice hockey M, sailing M/W, soccer M/W, softball M/W, table tennis M/W, tennis M/W, volleyball M/W, weight lifting M/W.

Standardized Tests *Required:* SAT I or ACT (for admission).

Costs (2001–02) *Comprehensive fee:* $23,950 includes full-time tuition ($15,600), mandatory fees ($850), and room and board ($7500). Part-time tuition: $250 per credit hour. Part-time tuition and fees vary according to course load. *Required fees:* $35 per term part-time. *Payment plan:* installment. *Waivers:* employees or children of employees.

Financial Aid *Financial aid deadline:* 3/1.

Applying *Options:* common application, electronic application, early admission, early action, deferred entrance. *Application fee:* $30. *Required:* essay or personal statement, high school transcript, minimum 2.0 GPA, letters of recommendation. *Recommended:* interview. *Application deadline:* rolling (freshmen), rolling (transfers). *Notification:* continuous until 8/30 (freshmen).

Admissions Contact Ms. Kathleen E. Neal, Director of Admissions, Mitchell College, 437 Pequot Avenue, New London, CT 06320. *Phone:* 860-701-5038. *Toll-free phone:* 800-443-2811. *Fax:* 860-444-1209. *E-mail:* admissions@mitchell.edu.

NAUGATUCK VALLEY COMMUNITY COLLEGE
Waterbury, Connecticut

- **State-supported** 2-year, founded 1992, part of Connecticut Community-Technical College System
- **Calendar** semesters
- **Degree** certificates and associate
- **Urban** 110-acre campus
- **Coed,** 5,223 undergraduate students, 34% full-time, 57% women, 43% men

Undergraduates 1,774 full-time, 3,449 part-time. 7% African American, 2% Asian American or Pacific Islander, 9% Hispanic American, 0.3% Native American, 1% international, 0.1% transferred in.

Freshmen *Admission:* 2,224 applied, 1,724 admitted, 967 enrolled.

Faculty *Total:* 180, 60% full-time, 27% with terminal degrees. *Student/faculty ratio:* 8:1.

Majors Accounting; alcohol/drug abuse counseling; American studies; auto mechanic/technician; biological/physical sciences; business administration; business marketing and marketing management; chemical engineering technology; computer/information technology services administration and management related; computer programming; computer programming (specific applications); criminal justice/law enforcement administration; drafting; early childhood education; electrical/electronic engineering technology; engineering technology; environmental science; exercise sciences; finance; fire science; food products retailing; gerontology; history; horticulture science; hospitality management; hotel and restaurant management; human services; industrial radiologic technology; industrial technology; information sciences/systems; information technology; international relations; legal administrative assistant; liberal arts and sciences/liberal studies; mathematics; mechanical engineering technology; medical administrative assistant; mental health/rehabilitation; music; natural sciences; nursing; paralegal/legal assistant; physical sciences; physical therapy assistant; pre-engineering; quality control technology; secretarial science; social work; system/networking/LAN/WAN management; word processing.

Academic Programs *Special study options:* academic remediation for entering students, accelerated degree program, adult/continuing education programs, advanced placement credit, cooperative education, English as a second language, external degree program, independent study, internships, off-campus study, part-time degree program, services for LD students, student-designed majors, study abroad, summer session for credit.

Library Max R. Traurig Learning Resource Center with 35,000 titles, 520 serial subscriptions, an OPAC, a Web page.

Computers on Campus 450 computers available on campus for general student use. Internet access, at least one staffed computer lab available.

Student Life *Housing:* college housing not available. *Activities and Organizations:* drama/theater group, student-run newspaper, choral group, Student Senate, Choral Society, Automotive Technician Club, Human Service Club, Legal Assistant Club. *Campus security:* 24-hour emergency response devices and patrols, late-night transport/escort service, security escort service. *Student Services:* health clinic, personal/psychological counseling.

Athletics Member NJCAA. *Intercollegiate sports:* baseball M, basketball M/W, softball W.

Standardized Tests *Required:* ACCUPLACER. *Required for some:* SAT I (for placement).

Costs (2002–03) *Tuition:* state resident $1980 full-time, $74 per credit part-time; nonresident $5900 full-time, $221 per credit part-time. Part-time tuition and fees vary according to class time and program.

Financial Aid In 2001, 70 Federal Work-Study jobs (averaging $1942). 16 State and other part-time jobs (averaging $1660).

Applying *Options:* deferred entrance. *Application fee:* $20. *Required:* high school transcript. *Required for some:* interview. *Application deadline:* rolling (freshmen), rolling (transfers). *Notification:* continuous (freshmen).

Admissions Contact Ms. Lucretia Sveda, Director of Enrollment Services, Naugatuck Valley Community College, Waterbury, CT 06708. *Phone:* 203-575-8016. *Fax:* 203-596-8766. *E-mail:* nv_admissions@commnet.edu.

NORTHWESTERN CONNECTICUT COMMUNITY COLLEGE
Winsted, Connecticut

- **State-supported** 2-year, founded 1965, part of Connecticut Community-Technical College System
- **Calendar** semesters
- **Degree** certificates and associate
- **Small-town** 5-acre campus with easy access to Hartford
- **Coed,** 1,609 undergraduate students, 25% full-time, 69% women, 31% men

Undergraduates 402 full-time, 1,207 part-time. Students come from 6 states and territories, 1% are from out of state, 3% African American, 0.8% Asian American or Pacific Islander, 2% Hispanic American, 0.2% Native American, 0.3% international, 8% transferred in.

Freshmen *Admission:* 354 applied, 354 admitted, 174 enrolled.

Faculty *Total:* 107, 30% full-time. *Student/faculty ratio:* 14:1.

Majors Accounting; alcohol/drug abuse counseling; art; behavioral sciences; biology; business administration; child care/development; communication equipment technology; computer engineering technology; computer graphics; computer programming; computer science; criminal justice/law enforcement administration; early childhood education; electrical/electronic engineering technology; engineering; English; graphic design/commercial art/illustration; health science; human services; information sciences/systems; law enforcement/police science; liberal arts and sciences/liberal studies; mathematics; medical assistant; paralegal/legal assistant; physical sciences; pre-engineering; recreational therapy; recreation/leisure facilities management; recreation/leisure studies; secretarial science; sign language interpretation; social sciences; veterinary technology.

Academic Programs *Special study options:* academic remediation for entering students, adult/continuing education programs, advanced placement credit, cooperative education, distance learning, double majors, English as a second language, external degree program, independent study, internships, part-time degree program, services for LD students, summer session for credit.

Library Northwestern Connecticut Community-Technical College Learning Center with 34,967 titles, 260 serial subscriptions, 1,860 audiovisual materials, an OPAC.

Computers on Campus 90 computers available on campus for general student use. A campuswide network can be accessed from off campus. Internet access, at least one staffed computer lab available.

Student Life *Housing:* college housing not available. *Activities and Organizations:* student-run newspaper, Ski Club, Student Senate, Deaf Club, Recreation Club, Early Childhood Educational Club. *Campus security:* evening security patrols.

Standardized Tests *Required:* ACCUPLACER.

Costs (2002–03) *Tuition:* state resident $1680 full-time, $70 per credit hour part-time; nonresident $5232 full-time, $218 per credit hour part-time. *Required fees:* $208 full-time, $57 per term part-time.

Financial Aid In 2001, 20 Federal Work-Study jobs (averaging $1400).

Applying *Options:* deferred entrance. *Application fee:* $20. *Application deadline:* rolling (freshmen), rolling (transfers). *Notification:* continuous until 9/1 (freshmen).

Admissions Contact Ms. Beverly Chrzan, Director of Admissions, Northwestern Connecticut Community College, Park Place East, Winsted, CT 06098-1798. *Phone:* 860-738-6329. *Fax:* 860-379-4465.

NORWALK COMMUNITY COLLEGE
Norwalk, Connecticut

- **State-supported** 2-year, founded 1961, part of Connecticut Community College System
- **Calendar** semesters
- **Degree** certificates and associate
- **Urban** 30-acre campus with easy access to New York City
- **Coed,** 5,569 undergraduate students, 30% full-time, 61% women, 39% men

Undergraduates 1,663 full-time, 3,906 part-time. Students come from 4 states and territories, 30 other countries, 1% are from out of state, 23% African American, 4% Asian American or Pacific Islander, 17% Hispanic American, 0.3% Native American, 4% international, 14% transferred in.

Freshmen *Admission:* 1,479 applied, 493 admitted, 493 enrolled.

Faculty *Total:* 349, 26% full-time. *Student/faculty ratio:* 16:1.

Majors Accounting; alcohol/drug abuse counseling; architectural engineering technology; art; business administration; business marketing and marketing management; computer programming related; computer science related; construc-

Norwalk Community College (continued)
tion technology; criminal justice/law enforcement administration; data processing technology; early childhood education; electrical/electronic engineering technology; engineering science; engineering technology; finance; fine/studio arts; fire science; general studies; graphic design/commercial art/illustration; hotel and restaurant management; human services; information sciences/systems; liberal arts and sciences/liberal studies; marketing operations; mass communications; nursing; paralegal/legal assistant; recreational therapy; recreation/leisure studies; respiratory therapy; secretarial science.

Academic Programs *Special study options:* academic remediation for entering students, adult/continuing education programs, advanced placement credit, cooperative education, distance learning, English as a second language, freshman honors college, honors programs, independent study, internships, part-time degree program, services for LD students, summer session for credit.

Library Everett I. L. Baker Library with 66,080 titles, 221 serial subscriptions, 2,988 audiovisual materials, an OPAC, a Web page.

Computers on Campus 500 computers available on campus for general student use. A campuswide network can be accessed from off campus. Internet access, online (class) registration, at least one staffed computer lab available.

Student Life *Housing:* college housing not available. *Activities and Organizations:* drama/theater group, student-run newspaper, choral group, African Culture Club, Archaeology Club, Hay Motivo Club, Art Club, Phi Theta Kappa. *Campus security:* 24-hour emergency response devices and patrols, student patrols, late-night transport/escort service, patrols by security.

Costs (2002–03) *Tuition:* state resident $1980 full-time, $121 per credit part-time; nonresident $5900 full-time, $352 per credit part-time. Full-time tuition and fees vary according to reciprocity agreements. Part-time tuition and fees vary according to course load. *Waivers:* senior citizens and employees or children of employees.

Financial Aid In 2001, 42 Federal Work-Study jobs (averaging $2581). 60 State and other part-time jobs (averaging $2046).

Applying *Options:* deferred entrance. *Application fee:* $20. *Required:* high school transcript. *Application deadline:* rolling (freshmen), rolling (transfers). *Notification:* continuous (freshmen).

Admissions Contact Ms. Danita Brown, Admissions Counselor, Norwalk Community College, 188 Richards Avenue, Norwalk, CT 06854-1655. *Phone:* 203-857-7060. *Toll-free phone:* 888-462-6282. *Fax:* 203-857-3335. *E-mail:* nccadmit@commnet.edu.

QUINEBAUG VALLEY COMMUNITY COLLEGE
Danielson, Connecticut

- **State-supported** 2-year, founded 1971, part of Connecticut Community College System
- **Calendar** semesters
- **Degree** certificates and associate
- **Rural** 60-acre campus
- **Coed**

Student Life *Campus security:* evening security guard.

Financial Aid In 2001, 20 Federal Work-Study jobs (averaging $2000). 38 State and other part-time jobs (averaging $1288).

Applying *Options:* common application, electronic application, early admission, deferred entrance. *Application fee:* $20. *Required for some:* high school transcript. *Recommended:* high school transcript.

Admissions Contact Dr. Toni Moumouris, Enrollment and Transition Counselor, Quinebaug Valley Community College, 742 Upper Maple Street, Danielson, CT 06239. *Phone:* 860-774-1130 Ext. 318. *Fax:* 860-774-7768. *E-mail:* qu_lsd@commnet.edu.

ST. VINCENT'S COLLEGE
Bridgeport, Connecticut

Admissions Contact Mr. Tracey Chavis, Associate Dean for Enrollment Management, St. Vincent's College, 2800 Main Street, Bridgeport, CT 06606-4292. *Phone:* 203-576-5578.

THREE RIVERS COMMUNITY COLLEGE
Norwich, Connecticut

- **State-supported** 2-year, founded 1963, part of Connecticut Community-Technical College System
- **Calendar** semesters
- **Degrees** certificates and associate (engineering technology programs are offered on the Thames Valley Campus; liberal arts, transfer and career programs are offered on the Mohegan Campus)
- **Small-town** 40-acre campus with easy access to Hartford
- **Coed,** 3,426 undergraduate students

Undergraduates Students come from 6 states and territories, 1% are from out of state.

Faculty *Total:* 222, 32% full-time.

Majors Accounting; alcohol/drug abuse counseling; architectural engineering technology; aviation technology; business administration; business marketing and marketing management; civil engineering technology; computer engineering technology; computer programming; computer typography/composition; corrections; criminal justice/law enforcement administration; data processing technology; drafting; early childhood education; electrical/electronic engineering technology; engineering; engineering science; engineering technology; environmental technology; fire science; food products retailing; hospitality management; hotel and restaurant management; human services; industrial technology; laser/optical technology; legal administrative assistant; liberal arts and sciences/liberal studies; mechanical engineering technology; medical administrative assistant; nuclear technology; nursing; pre-engineering; public administration; retail management; secretarial science; technical/business writing; theater arts/drama; travel/tourism management; water resources.

Academic Programs *Special study options:* academic remediation for entering students, adult/continuing education programs, advanced placement credit, cooperative education, double majors, English as a second language, external degree program, independent study, internships, part-time degree program, services for LD students, student-designed majors, study abroad, summer session for credit.

Library Three Rivers Community College Learning Resource Center plus 2 others with 53,768 titles, 549 serial subscriptions, an OPAC.

Computers on Campus 350 computers available on campus for general student use. Internet access, at least one staffed computer lab available.

Student Life *Housing:* college housing not available. *Activities and Organizations:* drama/theater group, student-run newspaper, Student Senate/Student Government Association, Theater Guild, Phi Theta Kappa, Student Nurses Association, African-American Organization, national fraternities. *Campus security:* late-night transport/escort service, 14 hour patrols by trained security personnel. *Student Services:* personal/psychological counseling.

Athletics *Intercollegiate sports:* basketball M, golf M/W. *Intramural sports:* bowling M/W.

Standardized Tests *Required:* ACCUPLACER.

Costs (2001–02) *Tuition:* state resident $1888 full-time, $70 per credit hour part-time; nonresident $5816 full-time, $218 per credit hour part-time. Full-time tuition and fees vary according to reciprocity agreements. Part-time tuition and fees vary according to course load and reciprocity agreements. *Payment plans:* installment, deferred payment. *Waivers:* senior citizens and employees or children of employees.

Financial Aid In 2001, 40 Federal Work-Study jobs (averaging $3000). 80 State and other part-time jobs (averaging $3000).

Applying *Options:* early admission, deferred entrance. *Application fee:* $20. *Required for some:* minimum 3.0 GPA. *Recommended:* high school transcript. *Application deadline:* rolling (freshmen), rolling (transfers). *Notification:* continuous (freshmen).

Admissions Contact Ms. Aida Garcia, Admissions and Recruitment Counselor, Mohegan Campus, Three Rivers Community College, Mahan Drive, Norwich, CT 06360. *Phone:* 860-383-5201. *Fax:* 860-886-0691. *E-mail:* info3rivers@sirus.commnet.edu.

TUNXIS COMMUNITY COLLEGE
Farmington, Connecticut

- **State-supported** 2-year, founded 1969, part of Connecticut Community College System
- **Calendar** semesters
- **Degree** certificates and associate
- **Suburban** 12-acre campus with easy access to Hartford
- **Coed,** 3,720 undergraduate students, 28% full-time, 62% women, 38% men

Undergraduates 1,049 full-time, 2,671 part-time. Students come from 6 states and territories, 6% African American, 2% Asian American or Pacific Islander, 9% Hispanic American, 0.3% Native American, 0.7% international.

Freshmen *Admission:* 1,605 applied, 1,605 admitted, 554 enrolled.

Faculty *Total:* 247, 23% full-time. *Student/faculty ratio:* 15:1.

Majors Accounting; alcohol/drug abuse counseling; applied art; art; business administration; business marketing and marketing management; corrections; criminal justice/law enforcement administration; data processing technology; dental hygiene; early childhood education; engineering; engineering technology; fashion merchandising; forensic technology; graphic design/commercial art/illustration; human services; information sciences/systems; legal administrative assistant; liberal arts and sciences/liberal studies; medical administrative assistant; physical therapy; secretarial science.

Academic Programs *Special study options:* academic remediation for entering students, adult/continuing education programs, English as a second language, part-time degree program, summer session for credit.

Library Tunxis Community College Library with 33,866 titles, 285 serial subscriptions, 3,571 audiovisual materials, an OPAC.

Computers on Campus 274 computers available on campus for general student use. A campuswide network can be accessed from off campus. Internet access, at least one staffed computer lab available.

Student Life *Housing:* college housing not available. *Activities and Organizations:* Phi Theta Kappa, Student American Dental Hygiene Association (SADHA), Human Services Club, student newspaper, Bible Club. *Campus security:* 24-hour patrols. *Student Services:* health clinic.

Costs (2001–02) *Tuition:* state resident $1888 full-time, $70 per credit part-time; nonresident $5816 full-time, $218 per credit part-time. Full-time tuition and fees vary according to reciprocity agreements. Part-time tuition and fees vary according to course load and reciprocity agreements. *Required fees:* $208 full-time, $57 per term part-time. *Waivers:* senior citizens and employees or children of employees.

Applying *Options:* common application, deferred entrance. *Application fee:* $20. *Required:* high school transcript. *Application deadline:* rolling (freshmen), rolling (transfers).

Admissions Contact Mr. Peter McCloskey, Director of Admissions, Tunxis Community College, 271 Scott Swamp Road, Farmington, CT 06032. *Phone:* 860-677-7701 Ext. 152. *Fax:* 860-676-8906.

DELAWARE

DELAWARE TECHNICAL & COMMUNITY COLLEGE, JACK F. OWENS CAMPUS
Georgetown, Delaware

- **State-supported** 2-year, founded 1967, part of Delaware Technical and Community College System
- **Calendar** semesters
- **Degree** certificates, diplomas, and associate
- **Small-town** 120-acre campus
- **Coed,** 3,546 undergraduate students

Undergraduates Students come from 6 states and territories, 9 other countries, 4% are from out of state, 15% African American, 1% Asian American or Pacific Islander, 3% Hispanic American, 0.8% Native American, 1% international.

Freshmen *Admission:* 1,009 applied, 1,009 admitted.

Faculty *Total:* 240, 38% full-time.

Majors Accounting; agricultural business; architectural engineering technology; auto mechanic/technician; business administration; business marketing and marketing management; carpentry; chemical engineering technology; child care/development; civil engineering technology; computer programming; construction management; criminal justice/law enforcement administration; data processing technology; drafting; electrical/electronic engineering technology; emergency medical technology; engineering; engineering technology; environmental technology; heavy equipment maintenance; hospitality management; hotel and restaurant management; human services; journalism; legal administrative assistant; medical administrative assistant; medical assistant; medical laboratory technician; medical laboratory technology; nursing; practical nurse; retail management; secretarial science; veterinary technology; welding technology.

Academic Programs *Special study options:* academic remediation for entering students, adult/continuing education programs, cooperative education, English as a second language, external degree program, internships, part-time degree program, services for LD students, student-designed majors, summer session for credit.

Library Stephen J. Betze Library plus 1 other with 72,657 titles, 514 serial subscriptions, an OPAC.

Computers on Campus 400 computers available on campus for general student use. At least one staffed computer lab available.

Student Life *Housing:* college housing not available. *Activities and Organizations:* student-run radio station, Student Government Association, Student Nursing Association, Phi Beta Kappa, Occupational Therapy Assistant Club, Physical Therapy Assistant Club. *Campus security:* 24-hour patrols, late-night transport/escort service.

Athletics Member NJCAA. *Intercollegiate sports:* baseball M(s), softball W.

Standardized Tests *Required:* CPT.

Costs (2001–02) *Tuition:* state resident $1584 full-time, $63 per credit part-time; nonresident $3960 full-time, $156 per credit part-time. *Required fees:* $69 full-time, $5 per credit. *Payment plans:* installment, deferred payment. *Waivers:* senior citizens and employees or children of employees.

Financial Aid In 2001, 250 Federal Work-Study jobs (averaging $2000).

Applying *Options:* early admission. *Application fee:* $10. *Required:* high school transcript. *Application deadline:* rolling (freshmen), rolling (transfers). *Notification:* continuous (freshmen).

Admissions Contact Claire McDonald, Admissions Counselor, Delaware Technical & Community College, Jack F. Owens Campus, PO Box 610, Georgetown, DE 19947. *Phone:* 302-856-5400.

DELAWARE TECHNICAL & COMMUNITY COLLEGE, STANTON/WILMINGTON CAMPUS
Newark, Delaware

- **State-supported** 2-year, founded 1968, part of Delaware Technical and Community College System
- **Calendar** semesters
- **Degree** certificates, diplomas, and associate
- **Coed,** 1,263 undergraduate students, 56% full-time, 53% women, 47% men

Undergraduates 703 full-time, 560 part-time. Students come from 13 states and territories, 45 other countries, 11% are from out of state.

Freshmen *Admission:* 2,019 applied, 1,448 admitted, 1,263 enrolled.

Faculty *Total:* 471, 33% full-time.

Majors Accounting; alcohol/drug abuse counseling; architectural engineering technology; banking; biomedical technology; business administration; business marketing and marketing management; chemical engineering technology; civil engineering technology; corrections; criminal justice/law enforcement administration; culinary arts; data processing technology; dental hygiene; diagnostic medical sonography; drafting; early childhood education; electrical/electronic engineering technology; emergency medical technology; engineering; exercise sciences; fire science; food services technology; gerontology; hotel and restaurant management; human services; industrial radiologic technology; industrial technology; information sciences/systems; instrumentation technology; law enforcement/police science; management information systems/business data processing; mechanical engineering technology; medical administrative assistant; nuclear medical technology; nursing; occupational safety/health technology; occupational therapy assistant; physical therapy assistant; respiratory therapy; secretarial science; sign language interpretation; transportation technology.

Academic Programs *Special study options:* academic remediation for entering students, adult/continuing education programs, cooperative education, English as a second language, external degree program, part-time degree program, services for LD students, summer session for credit.

Library 60,066 titles, 793 serial subscriptions, an OPAC.

Computers on Campus 200 computers available on campus for general student use. At least one staffed computer lab available.

Student Life *Housing:* college housing not available. *Campus security:* 24-hour patrols, late-night transport/escort service.

Athletics Member NJCAA. *Intercollegiate sports:* basketball M, soccer M, softball W, tennis M/W, volleyball M/W. *Intramural sports:* basketball M, tennis M/W.

Standardized Tests *Required:* CPT.

Costs (2001–02) *Tuition:* state resident $1584 full-time, $66 per credit part-time; nonresident $165 per credit part-time. Part-time tuition and fees vary according to course load. *Required fees:* $186 full-time, $4 per credit, $6 per term part-time. *Waivers:* senior citizens and employees or children of employees.

Applying *Options:* early admission. *Application fee:* $10. *Required:* high school transcript. *Application deadline:* rolling (freshmen), rolling (transfers). *Notification:* continuous (freshmen).

Admissions Contact Ms. Rebecca Bailey, Admissions Coordinator, Wilmington, Delaware Technical & Community College, Stanton/Wilmington Campus, 333 Shipley Street, Wilmington, DE 19713. *Phone:* 302-571-5366.

DELAWARE TECHNICAL & COMMUNITY COLLEGE, TERRY CAMPUS
Dover, Delaware

- **State-supported** 2-year, founded 1972, part of Delaware Technical and Community College System
- **Calendar** semesters
- **Degree** certificates, diplomas, and associate
- **Small-town** 70-acre campus with easy access to Philadelphia
- **Coed,** 379 undergraduate students, 48% full-time, 65% women, 35% men

Undergraduates 182 full-time, 197 part-time. Students come from 10 states and territories, 10 other countries, 3% are from out of state, 21% African American, 2% Asian American or Pacific Islander, 3% Hispanic American, 0.8% Native American, 1% international, 65% transferred in.
Freshmen *Admission:* 514 applied, 439 admitted, 379 enrolled.
Faculty *Total:* 170, 31% full-time.
Majors Accounting; aerospace science; architectural engineering technology; aviation management; aviation technology; business administration; civil engineering technology; computer engineering technology; computer programming; construction management; construction technology; corrections; criminal justice/law enforcement administration; data processing technology; drafting; early childhood education; electrical/electronic engineering technology; electromechanical technology; engineering technology; human services; industrial technology; nursing; practical nurse; secretarial science; surveying.
Academic Programs *Special study options:* academic remediation for entering students, adult/continuing education programs, cooperative education, English as a second language, internships, part-time degree program, services for LD students, summer session for credit.
Library 9,663 titles, 245 serial subscriptions, an OPAC.
Computers on Campus 125 computers available on campus for general student use. At least one staffed computer lab available.
Student Life *Housing:* college housing not available. *Activities and Organizations:* Students of Kolor, Human Services Organization, Phi Theta Kappa, Alpha Beta Gamma. *Campus security:* late-night transport/escort service.
Standardized Tests *Required:* CPT.
Costs (2001–02) *Tuition:* state resident $1584 full-time, $66 per credit part-time; nonresident $3960 full-time, $165 per credit part-time. Full-time tuition and fees vary according to course load. Part-time tuition and fees vary according to course load. *Required fees:* $186 full-time, $4 per credit, $6 per term part-time. *Payment plans:* tuition prepayment, installment, deferred payment. *Waivers:* senior citizens and employees or children of employees.
Financial Aid In 2001, 50 Federal Work-Study jobs (averaging $1500).
Applying *Options:* early admission. *Application fee:* $10. *Required:* high school transcript. *Application deadline:* rolling (freshmen), rolling (transfers).
Admissions Contact Mrs. Maria Harris, Admissions Officer, Delaware Technical & Community College, Terry Campus, 100 Campus Drive, Dover, DE 19904. *Phone:* 302-857-1020. *Fax:* 302-857-1020. *E-mail:* mharris@outland.dtcc.edu.

FLORIDA

THE ACADEMY
Lakeland, Florida

Admissions Contact 3131 Flightline Drive, Lakeland, FL 33811-2836. *Toll-free phone:* 800-532-3210.

THE ART INSTITUTE OF FORT LAUDERDALE
Fort Lauderdale, Florida

- **Proprietary** primarily 2-year, founded 1968
- **Calendar** quarters
- **Degrees** associate and bachelor's
- **Urban** campus with easy access to Miami
- **Coed,** 3,500 undergraduate students

The Art Institute of Fort Lauderdale has been showing students how to turn a passion for the visual and practical arts into a profession since 1968. The Institute offers Associate of Science degree programs in animation, broadcasting, culinary arts, fashion design, graphic design, information technology and design, multimedia and Web design, photography, and video production. Bachelor of Science degrees are offered in culinary management, digital media production, graphic design, industrial design, interior design, media arts and animation, multimedia and Web design, and visual effects and motion graphics. Faculty members are working professionals with impressive achievements in their respective fields.

Freshmen *Admission:* 3,000 applied, 2,146 admitted.
Faculty *Total:* 110. *Student/faculty ratio:* 20:1.
Majors Applied art; clothing/textiles; computer graphics; culinary arts; fashion design/illustration; film/video production; graphic design/commercial art/illustration; industrial design; interior design; photography; radio/television broadcasting.
Academic Programs *Special study options:* academic remediation for entering students, accelerated degree program, adult/continuing education programs, advanced placement credit, cooperative education, internships, off-campus study, summer session for credit.
Library 16,200 titles, 270 serial subscriptions, an OPAC, a Web page.
Computers on Campus 125 computers available on campus for general student use. Internet access, at least one staffed computer lab available.
Student Life *Housing Options:* coed. *Student Services:* personal/psychological counseling.
Standardized Tests *Recommended:* SAT I or ACT (for placement).
Costs (2001–02) *Room and board:* $4480.
Applying *Options:* common application. *Application fee:* $50. *Required:* essay or personal statement, high school transcript. *Recommended:* interview. *Application deadline:* rolling (freshmen), rolling (transfers).
Admissions Contact Ms. Eileen L. Northrop, Vice President and Director of Admissions, The Art Institute of Fort Lauderdale, 1799 Southeast 17th Street Causeway, Fort Lauderdale, FL 33316-3000. *Phone:* 954-527-1799 Ext. 420. *Toll-free phone:* 800-275-7603. *Fax:* 954-728-8637.

ATI CAREER TRAINING CENTER
Oakland Park, Florida

Admissions Contact 3501 NW 9th Avenue, Oakland Park, FL 33309-9612.

ATI CAREER TRAINING CENTER
Miami, Florida

Admissions Contact 1 NE 19th Street, Miami, FL 33132.

ATI CAREER TRAINING CENTER ELECTRONICS CAMPUS
Fort Lauderdale, Florida

- **Proprietary** 2-year
- **Calendar** quarters
- **Degree** associate
- **Suburban** campus
- **Coed,** 350 undergraduate students

Majors Drafting; electrical/electronic engineering technology; medical administrative assistant.
Admissions Contact Ms. Wendy Hopkins Goffinet, Director of Admissions, ATI Career Training Center Electronics Campus, 2880 NW 62nd Street, Fort Lauderdale, FL 33309-9731. *Phone:* 954-973-4760. *Fax:* 954-973-6422.

ATI HEALTH EDUCATION CENTER
Miami, Florida

Admissions Contact Mr. Chris Covone, Director of Admissions, ATI Health Education Center, 1395 NW 167th Street, Suite 200, Miami, FL 33169-5742. *Phone:* 305-628-1000.

ATLANTIC COAST INSTITUTE
Fort Lauderdale, Florida

- **Proprietary** 2-year, founded 1881
- **Calendar** quarters

- **Degree** certificates, diplomas, and associate
- **Suburban** campus with easy access to Miami
- **Coed, primarily women**

Faculty *Student/faculty ratio:* 12:1.
Student Life *Campus security:* 24-hour emergency response devices.
Costs (2001–02) *One-time required fee:* $35. *Tuition:* $6510 full-time. Full-time tuition and fees vary according to program. No tuition increase for student's term of enrollment. *Required fees:* $95 full-time. *Payment plans:* tuition prepayment, installment, deferred payment.
Applying *Options:* common application, electronic application, deferred entrance. *Application fee:* $95. *Required:* high school transcript, interview.
Admissions Contact Atlantic Coast Institute, 5225 West Broward Boulevard, Ft. Lauderdale, FL 33317. *Phone:* 954-581-2223 Ext. 23. *Toll-free phone:* 800-581-8292. *Fax:* 954-583-9458. *E-mail:* rhd114@aol.com.

BREVARD COMMUNITY COLLEGE
Cocoa, Florida

- **State-supported** 2-year, founded 1960, part of Florida Community College System
- **Calendar** semesters
- **Degree** certificates and associate
- **Suburban** 100-acre campus with easy access to Orlando
- **Coed,** 13,681 undergraduate students

Undergraduates Students come from 50 states and territories, 64 other countries, 8% African American, 3% Asian American or Pacific Islander, 5% Hispanic American, 0.5% Native American, 1% international.
Freshmen *Admission:* 3,553 applied, 3,553 admitted.
Faculty *Total:* 956, 24% full-time.
Majors Accounting; auto mechanic/technician; business administration; business marketing and marketing management; carpentry; child care/development; computer/information technology services administration and management related; computer programming; computer programming (specific applications); computer systems analysis; construction technology; corrections; cosmetology; court reporting; criminal justice/law enforcement administration; culinary arts; dental hygiene; developmental/child psychology; drafting; economics; electrical/electronic engineering technology; emergency medical technology; environmental science; fashion merchandising; fire science; heating/air conditioning/refrigeration; hotel and restaurant management; human resources management; industrial radiologic technology; instrumentation technology; international business; law enforcement/police science; liberal arts and sciences/liberal studies; logistics/materials management; medical administrative assistant; medical assistant; medical laboratory technician; nursing; operating room technician; paralegal/legal assistant; photography; plumbing; practical nurse; quality control technology; radio/television broadcasting; real estate; respiratory therapy; secretarial science; security; veterinary technology; water treatment technology; welding technology.
Academic Programs *Special study options:* academic remediation for entering students, accelerated degree program, adult/continuing education programs, advanced placement credit, cooperative education, distance learning, double majors, English as a second language, external degree program, honors programs, independent study, internships, part-time degree program, services for LD students, study abroad, summer session for credit. *ROTC:* Army (b), Air Force (b).
Library UCF Library with 172,610 titles, 956 serial subscriptions, an OPAC, a Web page.
Computers on Campus 125 computers available on campus for general student use. A campuswide network can be accessed from off campus. At least one staffed computer lab available.
Student Life *Housing:* college housing not available. *Activities and Organizations:* drama/theater group, student-run newspaper, choral group, Phi Theta Kappa, ROTORACT, African-American Student Union, Terraphile Society. *Campus security:* 24-hour emergency response devices and patrols, late-night transport/escort service. *Student Services:* women's center.
Athletics Member NJCAA. *Intercollegiate sports:* baseball M(s), basketball M(s)/W(s), golf M(s)/W(s), softball W(s), volleyball W(s). *Intramural sports:* cross-country running M/W, fencing M/W, soccer M/W, track and field M/W.
Standardized Tests *Required:* SAT I, ACT, or CPT.
Costs (2001–02) *Tuition:* area resident $1808 full-time, $60 per credit hour part-time; nonresident $5389 full-time, $180 per credit hour part-time. *Payment plan:* deferred payment.
Financial Aid In 2001, 200 Federal Work-Study jobs (averaging $2244). 200 State and other part-time jobs (averaging $2000).
Applying *Options:* common application, electronic application, early admission, deferred entrance. *Application fee:* $20. *Required:* high school transcript. *Application deadline:* rolling (freshmen), rolling (transfers). *Notification:* continuous (freshmen).
Admissions Contact Ms. Stephanie Burnette, Supervisor of Admissions, Brevard Community College, 1519 Clearlake Road, Cocoa, FL 32922-6597. *Phone:* 321-632-1111 Ext. 62154. *Fax:* 321-633-4565.

BROWARD COMMUNITY COLLEGE
Fort Lauderdale, Florida

Admissions Contact Mrs. Barbara Humphrey, Director of Enrollment Management/Registrar, Broward Community College, 225 East Las Olas Boulevard, Fort Lauderdale, FL 33301-2298. *Phone:* 954-761-7465.

CENTRAL FLORIDA COMMUNITY COLLEGE
Ocala, Florida

- **State and locally supported** 2-year, founded 1957, part of Florida Community College System
- **Calendar** semesters
- **Degree** certificates and associate
- **Small-town** 120-acre campus
- **Endowment** $11.8 million
- **Coed,** 5,708 undergraduate students, 37% full-time, 63% women, 37% men

Undergraduates Students come from 20 states and territories, 12% African American, 1% Asian American or Pacific Islander, 6% Hispanic American, 0.6% Native American, 0.2% international.
Faculty *Total:* 238, 46% full-time.
Majors Business administration; computer programming; criminal justice/law enforcement administration; electrical/electronic engineering technology; fire protection/safety technology; horticulture services related; industrial radiologic technology; legal administrative assistant; nursing.
Academic Programs *Special study options:* academic remediation for entering students, adult/continuing education programs, advanced placement credit, cooperative education, distance learning, English as a second language, freshman honors college, honors programs, part-time degree program, services for LD students, study abroad, summer session for credit.
Library Central Florida Community College Library plus 1 other with 54,491 titles, 367 serial subscriptions, an OPAC, a Web page.
Computers on Campus 188 computers available on campus for general student use. A campuswide network can be accessed from off campus. Internet access, at least one staffed computer lab available.
Student Life *Housing:* college housing not available. *Activities and Organizations:* drama/theater group, student-run newspaper, choral group, student government, Campus Ambassadors, Phi Theta Kappa, African-American Student Union, Student Nurses Association. *Campus security:* 24-hour patrols, student patrols, late-night transport/escort service. *Student Services:* personal/psychological counseling, women's center.
Athletics Member NJCAA. *Intercollegiate sports:* baseball M, basketball M(s)/W(s), softball W. *Intramural sports:* basketball M, swimming M/W, volleyball M/W.
Standardized Tests *Required:* SAT I, ACT, or CPT.
Costs (2001–02) *Tuition:* state resident $1547 full-time, $52 per credit hour part-time; nonresident $5737 full-time, $191 per credit hour part-time. *Required fees:* $299 full-time. *Waivers:* employees or children of employees.
Financial Aid In 2001, 71 Federal Work-Study jobs (averaging $1300).
Applying *Options:* early admission. *Application fee:* $20. *Required:* high school transcript. *Application deadlines:* 8/10 (freshmen), 8/10 (transfers). *Notification:* continuous (freshmen).
Admissions Contact Mrs. Captoria Rawls, Director of Admissions and Records, Central Florida Community College, PO Box 1388, Ocala, FL 34478-1388. *Phone:* 352-237-2111 Ext. 1319. *Fax:* 352-873-5882. *E-mail:* rawlsc@cfcc.cc.fl.us.

CHIPOLA JUNIOR COLLEGE
Marianna, Florida

- **State-supported** 2-year, founded 1947
- **Calendar** semesters
- **Degree** certificates and associate

Chipola Junior College (continued)
- **Rural** 105-acre campus
- **Coed,** 1,834 undergraduate students, 48% full-time, 59% women, 41% men

Undergraduates 878 full-time, 956 part-time. Students come from 15 states and territories, 4 other countries, 3% are from out of state, 19% African American, 0.5% Asian American or Pacific Islander, 1% Hispanic American, 1% Native American.
Freshmen *Admission:* 730 applied, 669 admitted, 236 enrolled.
Faculty *Total:* 69, 78% full-time, 12% with terminal degrees. *Student/faculty ratio:* 24:1.
Majors Accounting; agricultural sciences; agronomy/crop science; art; biological/physical sciences; business administration; computer science; computer science related; education; finance; liberal arts and sciences/liberal studies; mass communications; medical technology; nursing; pre-engineering; social work.
Academic Programs *Special study options:* academic remediation for entering students, adult/continuing education programs, advanced placement credit, distance learning, honors programs, independent study, part-time degree program, services for LD students, summer session for credit.
Library Chipola Library with 37,740 titles, 226 serial subscriptions.
Computers on Campus 80 computers available on campus for general student use. A campuswide network can be accessed from off campus. Internet access, at least one staffed computer lab available.
Student Life *Activities and Organizations:* drama/theater group, student-run newspaper, choral group, Drama/Theater Group. *Campus security:* night security personnel.
Athletics Member NJCAA. *Intercollegiate sports:* baseball M(s), basketball M(s)/W(s), softball W(s).
Standardized Tests *Required:* SAT I or ACT (for placement).
Costs (2001–02) *Tuition:* state resident $1600 full-time, $50 per semester hour part-time; nonresident $6045 full-time, $189 per semester hour part-time. Full-time tuition and fees vary according to course load. Part-time tuition and fees vary according to course load.
Applying *Options:* early admission. *Required:* high school transcript. *Application deadline:* rolling (freshmen), rolling (transfers). *Notification:* continuous (freshmen).
Admissions Contact Mrs. Annette Widner, Registrar and Admissions Director, Chipola Junior College, Marianna, FL 32446. *Phone:* 850-526-2761 Ext. 2292. *Fax:* 850-718-2287.

CITY COLLEGE
Fort Lauderdale, Florida

Admissions Contact 1401 West Cypress Creek Road, Fort Lauderdale, FL 33309.

COLLEGE FOR PROFESSIONAL STUDIES
Boca Raton, Florida

Admissions Contact Ms. Kristina Belanger, Dean, College for Professional Studies, 1801 Clint Moore Road, Suite 215, Boca Raton, FL 33487. *Phone:* 561-994-2522. *Toll-free phone:* 800-669-2555. *Fax:* 561-988-2223.

COOPER CAREER INSTITUTE
West Palm Beach, Florida

Admissions Contact Ms. Sue Middleton, Admissions Representative, Cooper Career Institute, 2247 Palm Beach Lakes Boulevard, Suite 110, West Palm Beach, FL 33409. *Phone:* 561-640-6999. *Toll-free phone:* 800-588-4401.

DAYTONA BEACH COMMUNITY COLLEGE
Daytona Beach, Florida

- **State-supported** 2-year, founded 1958, part of Florida Community College System
- **Calendar** semesters
- **Degree** certificates and associate
- **Suburban** 93-acre campus with easy access to Orlando
- **Endowment** $12.3 million
- **Coed,** 11,214 undergraduate students, 41% full-time, 60% women, 40% men

Undergraduates 4,571 full-time, 6,643 part-time. Students come from 41 states and territories, 70 other countries, 2% are from out of state, 10% African American, 2% Asian American or Pacific Islander, 6% Hispanic American, 0.4% Native American, 2% international, 8% transferred in.
Freshmen *Admission:* 1,690 enrolled.
Faculty *Total:* 956, 26% full-time, 12% with terminal degrees. *Student/faculty ratio:* 25:1.
Majors Accounting; advertising; agricultural sciences; anthropology; architectural engineering technology; art; astronomy; atmospheric sciences; auto mechanic/technician; behavioral sciences; biological/physical sciences; biology; business administration; business marketing and marketing management; chemistry; child care/development; civil engineering technology; computer engineering related; computer graphics; computer/information technology services administration and management related; computer programming; computer programming (specific applications); computer science; computer science related; computer systems networking/telecommunications; computer typography/composition; construction technology; corrections; cosmetology; court reporting; criminal justice/law enforcement administration; criminology; culinary arts; dance; drafting; early childhood education; economics; education; electrical/electronic engineering technology; emergency medical technology; engineering; English; fashion design/illustration; film/video production; finance; fire science; food products retailing; forestry; geology; graphic design/commercial art/illustration; health education; health science; heating/air conditioning/refrigeration; history; hospitality management; hotel and restaurant management; humanities; human services; industrial radiologic technology; information sciences/systems; information technology; insurance/risk management; interior design; journalism; law enforcement/police science; legal administrative assistant; liberal arts and sciences/liberal studies; marine biology; mass communications; mathematical statistics; mathematics; medical administrative assistant; medical records administration; music; nursing; nutrition science; occupational therapy; paralegal/legal assistant; philosophy; photography; physical education; physical therapy; physics; postal management; practical nurse; psychology; radio/television broadcasting; respiratory therapy; secretarial science; social sciences; sociology; telecommunications; theater arts/drama; travel/tourism management; zoology.
Academic Programs *Special study options:* academic remediation for entering students, adult/continuing education programs, advanced placement credit, cooperative education, English as a second language, honors programs, internships, part-time degree program, services for LD students, study abroad, summer session for credit. *ROTC:* Army (c), Air Force (c).
Library Mary Karl Memorial Library with 66,312 titles, 699 serial subscriptions, 3,862 audiovisual materials.
Computers on Campus 752 computers available on campus for general student use. Internet access, at least one staffed computer lab available.
Student Life *Housing:* college housing not available. *Activities and Organizations:* drama/theater group, student-run newspaper, choral group, Florida Student Nursing Association, International Club, SGA, History Club, Drama Club. *Campus security:* 24-hour patrols, late-night transport/escort service. *Student Services:* personal/psychological counseling, women's center.
Athletics Member NJCAA. *Intercollegiate sports:* basketball M(s), softball W(s). *Intramural sports:* basketball M/W, bowling M/W, fencing M/W, football M, golf M, racquetball M/W, soccer M/W, table tennis M/W, tennis M/W, volleyball M/W.
Standardized Tests *Required:* ACT ASSET, CPT. *Recommended:* SAT I and SAT II or ACT (for placement).
Costs (2001–02) *Tuition:* state resident $1573 full-time, $52 per semester hour part-time; nonresident $5851 full-time, $195 per semester hour part-time. *Required fees:* $30 full-time. *Waivers:* senior citizens and employees or children of employees.
Applying *Options:* common application, early admission, deferred entrance. *Required:* high school transcript. *Application deadline:* rolling (freshmen), rolling (transfers).
Admissions Contact Mr. Joseph Roof, Dean of Enrollment Development, Daytona Beach Community College, PO Box 2811, Daytona Beach, FL 32120-2811. *Phone:* 386-254-4414.

EDISON COMMUNITY COLLEGE
Fort Myers, Florida

- **State and locally supported** 2-year, founded 1962, part of Florida Community College System
- **Calendar** semesters
- **Degree** certificates and associate
- **Urban** 80-acre campus
- **Coed,** 9,390 undergraduate students

Undergraduates Students come from 21 states and territories, 45 other countries, 3% are from out of state.
Freshmen *Admission:* 1,034 admitted.
Faculty *Total:* 417, 22% full-time.
Majors Accounting; applied art; art; business administration; computer programming; computer programming (specific applications); computer science; criminal justice/law enforcement administration; dental hygiene; drafting; electrical/electronic engineering technology; emergency medical technology; engineering; engineering technology; finance; fire science; horticulture science; hospitality management; human services; information technology; legal studies; liberal arts and sciences/liberal studies; medical technology; music; nursing; radiological science; respiratory therapy; social sciences; system/networking/LAN/WAN management.
Academic Programs *Special study options:* academic remediation for entering students, accelerated degree program, adult/continuing education programs, advanced placement credit, cooperative education, distance learning, English as a second language, honors programs, independent study, internships, part-time degree program, services for LD students, summer session for credit.
Library Learning Resources Center with 181,085 titles, 10,297 audiovisual materials.
Computers on Campus 160 computers available on campus for general student use. A campuswide network can be accessed from off campus. Internet access, at least one staffed computer lab available.
Student Life *Housing:* college housing not available. *Activities and Organizations:* drama/theater group, choral group, Student Government Association, Phi Theta Kappa, African-American Student Association, Latin-American Student Association, national fraternities, national sororities. *Campus security:* 24-hour emergency response devices and patrols, student patrols, late-night transport/escort service.
Standardized Tests *Required:* SAT I, ACT, or CPT. *Recommended:* SAT I or ACT (for placement).
Costs (2001–02) *Tuition:* state resident $1211 full-time, $50 per credit part-time; nonresident $4511 full-time, $188 per credit part-time. *Required fees:* $10 full-time, $5 per term part-time.
Applying *Options:* early admission, deferred entrance. *Required:* high school transcript. *Application deadlines:* 8/18 (freshmen), 8/18 (transfers). *Notification:* continuous (freshmen).
Admissions Contact Ms. Pat Armstrong, Admissions Specialist, Edison Community College, PO Box 60210, Fort Myers, FL 33906-6210. *Phone:* 941-489-9121. *Toll-free phone:* 800-749-2ECC. *Fax:* 941-489-9094.

EDUCATION AMERICA, TAMPA TECHNICAL INSTITUTE, JACKSONVILLE CAMPUS
Jacksonville, Florida

Admissions Contact 7011 A.C. Skinner Parkway, Jacksonville, FL 32256.

EDUCATION AMERICA, TAMPA TECHNICAL INSTITUTE, PINELLAS CAMPUS
Largo, Florida

Admissions Contact 8550 Ulmerton Road, Largo, FL 33771. *Toll-free phone:* 888-900-2343.

EDUCATION AMERICA, TAMPA TECHNICAL INSTITUTE, TAMPA CAMPUS
Tampa, Florida

- **Proprietary** primarily 2-year, founded 1948, part of Education America Inc.
- **Calendar** quarters
- **Degrees** associate and bachelor's
- **Urban** 10-acre campus
- **Coed**

Student Life *Campus security:* late-night transport/escort service.
Financial Aid In 2001, 12 Federal Work-Study jobs (averaging $8000).
Applying *Options:* common application, deferred entrance. *Application fee:* $50. *Required:* high school transcript, interview.
Admissions Contact Ms. Kathy Miller, Director of Admissions, Education America, Tampa Technical Institute, Tampa Campus, 2410 East Busch Boulevard, Tampa, FL 33612-8410. *Phone:* 813-935-5700. *Toll-free phone:* 800-992-4850. *E-mail:* rams@ix.netcom.com.

FLORIDA COMMUNITY COLLEGE AT JACKSONVILLE
Jacksonville, Florida

- **State-supported** 2-year, founded 1963, part of Florida Community College System
- **Calendar** semesters
- **Degree** certificates, diplomas, and associate
- **Urban** 656-acre campus
- **Endowment** $3.9 million
- **Coed,** 23,425 undergraduate students, 30% full-time, 59% women, 41% men

Undergraduates 7,120 full-time, 16,305 part-time. Students come from 19 states and territories, 108 other countries, 23% are from out of state, 25% transferred in.
Freshmen *Admission:* 2,658 applied, 2,658 admitted, 2,658 enrolled. *Test scores:* SAT verbal scores over 500: 52%; SAT math scores over 500: 46%; ACT scores over 18: 92%; SAT verbal scores over 600: 9%; SAT math scores over 600: 6%; ACT scores over 24: 26%; SAT verbal scores over 700: 1%; ACT scores over 30: 3%.
Faculty *Total:* 1,134, 32% full-time, 10% with terminal degrees. *Student/faculty ratio:* 21:1.
Majors Accounting; aircraft mechanic/airframe; aircraft mechanic/powerplant; aircraft pilot (professional); alcohol/drug abuse counseling; architectural drafting; architectural engineering technology; auto body repair; auto mechanic/technician; aviation management; banking; biomedical engineering-related technology; business administration; business marketing and marketing management; child care/guidance; child care provider; child care services management; civil engineering technology; computer engineering technology; computer graphics; computer hardware engineering; computer/information sciences; computer/information systems security; computer/information technology services administration and management related; computer programming; computer programming related; computer programming (specific applications); computer programming, vendor/product certification; computer science related; computer software and media applications related; computer software engineering; computer systems analysis; computer systems networking/telecommunications; computer/technical support; construction technology; criminal justice/law enforcement administration; culinary arts; data entry/microcomputer applications; data entry/microcomputer applications related; data warehousing/mining/database administration; dental hygiene; design/visual communications; diagnostic medical sonography; dietetics; dietician assistant; drafting/design technology; electrical/electronic engineering technology; emergency medical technology; engineering-related technology; fashion merchandising; fire protection/safety technology; fire science; general office/clerical; graphic design/commercial art/illustration; hospitality management; hospitality/recreation marketing operations; hotel and restaurant management; human services; information sciences/systems; information technology; institutional food services; instrument calibration/repair; insurance/risk management; interior design; law enforcement/police science; liberal arts and sciences/liberal studies; machine shop assistant; masonry/tile setting; medical laboratory technology; medical office management; medical radiologic technology; medical records administration; nuclear technology; nursing; office management; paralegal/legal assistant; physical therapy assistant; printmaking; real estate; respiratory therapy; retailing operations; secretarial science; sign language interpretation; system/networking/LAN/WAN management; theater design; travel services marketing operations; visual and performing arts related; water treatment technology; Web/multimedia management/webmaster; Web page, digital/multimedia and information resources design; word processing.
Academic Programs *Special study options:* academic remediation for entering students, accelerated degree program, adult/continuing education programs, advanced placement credit, cooperative education, distance learning, double majors, English as a second language, honors programs, independent study, internships, off-campus study, part-time degree program, services for LD students, study abroad, summer session for credit. *ROTC:* Navy (c).
Library Main Library plus 6 others with 412,856 titles, 4,137 serial subscriptions, 15,286 audiovisual materials, an OPAC, a Web page.
Computers on Campus 2500 computers available on campus for general student use. A campuswide network can be accessed from off campus. Internet access, online (class) registration, at least one staffed computer lab available.
Student Life *Housing:* college housing not available. *Activities and Organizations:* drama/theater group, student-run newspaper, radio and television station, choral group, Phi Theta Kappa, Troupe de Kent, Foresnic Team, Brain Bowl Team, International Student Association. *Campus security:* 24-hour emergency response devices and patrols, student patrols, late-night transport/escort service. *Student Services:* personal/psychological counseling, women's center.

Florida Community College at Jacksonville (continued)

Athletics Member NJCAA. *Intercollegiate sports:* baseball M(s), basketball M(s)/W(s), softball W(s), tennis W(s), volleyball W(s). *Intramural sports:* badminton M/W, basketball M/W, bowling M/W, football M/W, golf M/W, soccer M/W, softball M/W, table tennis M/W, tennis M/W, volleyball M/W.

Costs (2001–02) *Tuition:* state resident $1544 full-time, $51 per credit hour part-time; nonresident $5759 full-time, $192 per credit hour part-time. Full-time tuition and fees vary according to course load and program. Part-time tuition and fees vary according to course load and program. *Payment plan:* deferred payment. *Waivers:* employees or children of employees.

Applying *Options:* common application, early admission, deferred entrance. *Application fee:* $15. *Required:* high school transcript. *Application deadline:* rolling (freshmen), rolling (transfers).

Admissions Contact Mr. Peter J. Biegel, District Director of Enrollment Services and Registrar, Florida Community College at Jacksonville, 501 West State Street, Jacksonville, FL 32202. *Phone:* 904-632-3131. *Fax:* 904-632-5105. *E-mail:* admissions@fccj.org.

Florida Computer & Business School

Miami, Florida

- **Proprietary** 2-year, founded 1982
- **Calendar** quarters
- **Degree** certificates, diplomas, and associate
- **Urban** campus
- **Coed,** 621 undergraduate students, 95% full-time, 20% women, 80% men

Undergraduates Students come from 2 states and territories, 3 other countries, 5% African American, 86% Hispanic American, 3% international.

Faculty *Total:* 37, 43% full-time, 51% with terminal degrees. *Student/faculty ratio:* 15:1.

Majors Computer engineering related; computer programming; computer programming (specific applications); computer science; Web/multimedia management/webmaster.

Academic Programs *Special study options:* academic remediation for entering students, independent study, part-time degree program, summer session for credit.

Library Resource Center plus 1 other with 1,200 titles, 200 serial subscriptions.

Computers on Campus 288 computers available on campus for general student use. A campuswide network can be accessed from off campus that provide access to online student information, grades, schedules. Internet access, at least one staffed computer lab available.

Student Life *Housing:* college housing not available. *Campus security:* 24-hour emergency response devices.

Costs (2001–02) *Tuition:* $6660 full-time, $185 per credit part-time. Full-time tuition and fees vary according to course load. Part-time tuition and fees vary according to course load. No tuition increase for student's term of enrollment. *Required fees:* $435 full-time, $109 per term part-time. *Payment plan:* installment. *Waivers:* employees or children of employees.

Applying *Options:* common application, deferred entrance. *Application fee:* $100. *Required:* high school transcript, interview. *Application deadline:* rolling (freshmen), rolling (transfers). *Notification:* continuous (freshmen).

Admissions Contact Mr. David Knobel, President, Florida Computer & Business School, 1321 Southwest 107 Avenue, Miami, FL 33174. *Phone:* 305-553-6065. *Fax:* 305-225-0128.

Florida Culinary Institute

West Palm Beach, Florida

- **Proprietary** 2-year
- **Degree** associate
- 1,500 undergraduate students

Faculty *Total:* 21, 100% full-time.

Majors Baker/pastry chef; culinary arts.

Costs (2001–02) *Tuition:* $21,600 per degree program part-time.

Financial Aid In 2001, 25 Federal Work-Study jobs (averaging $3385).

Admissions Contact Mr. Michael Schwam, Director of Admissions, Florida Culinary Institute, 2400 Metrocenter Boulevard, West Palm Beach, FL 33407. *Phone:* 561-842-8324 Ext. 125. *Toll-free phone:* 800-826-9986. *E-mail:* info@newenglandtech.com.

Florida Hospital College of Health Sciences

Orlando, Florida

- **Independent** primarily 2-year
- **Calendar** semesters
- **Degrees** certificates, associate, and bachelor's
- **Urban** campus
- **Endowment** $153,800
- **Coed, primarily women,** 746 undergraduate students, 55% full-time, 80% women, 20% men

Undergraduates 408 full-time, 338 part-time. 14% African American, 9% Asian American or Pacific Islander, 18% Hispanic American, 0.9% Native American, 3% international, 16% live on campus.

Freshmen *Admission:* 102 enrolled. *Test scores:* ACT scores over 18: 60%; ACT scores over 24: 10%; ACT scores over 30: 1%.

Faculty *Total:* 55, 60% full-time, 18% with terminal degrees. *Student/faculty ratio:* 15:1.

Majors Diagnostic medical sonography; medical radiologic technology; nuclear medical technology; nursing; occupational therapy assistant; radiological science.

Academic Programs *Special study options:* academic remediation for entering students, adult/continuing education programs, distance learning, honors programs, independent study, services for LD students, student-designed majors, summer session for credit.

Library Florida plus 1 other with 17,152 titles, 163 serial subscriptions, 9 audiovisual materials.

Computers on Campus 10 computers available on campus for general student use. Internet access, at least one staffed computer lab available.

Student Life *Housing Options:* coed. *Activities and Organizations:* drama/theater group, student-run newspaper, choral group. *Campus security:* 24-hour emergency response devices and patrols, late-night transport/escort service, controlled dormitory access. *Student Services:* personal/psychological counseling.

Athletics *Intramural sports:* baseball M/W, soccer M/W, volleyball M/W.

Standardized Tests *Required:* ACT (for admission).

Costs (2001–02) *Tuition:* $3840 full-time, $160 per credit part-time. Full-time tuition and fees vary according to course load, degree level, and program. Part-time tuition and fees vary according to course load and program. *Required fees:* $550 full-time, $125 per term part-time. *Room only:* $1400. Room and board charges vary according to housing facility.

Applying *Options:* common application, electronic application. *Application fee:* $20. *Required:* high school transcript, minimum 2.5 GPA, 2 letters of recommendation. *Required for some:* essay or personal statement, interview. *Application deadline:* 8/28 (freshmen).

Admissions Contact Florida Hospital College of Health Sciences, 800 Lake Estelle Drive, Orlando, FL 32803. *Phone:* 407-303-9798 Ext. 5548. *Toll-free phone:* 800-500-7747. *Fax:* 407-303-9408. *E-mail:* joe_forton@fhchs.edu.

Florida Keys Community College

Key West, Florida

Admissions Contact Ms. Cheryl A. Malsheimer, Director of Admissions and Records, Florida Keys Community College, 5901 College Road, Key West, FL 33040. *Phone:* 305-296-9081 Ext. 201. *Fax:* 305-292-5163. *E-mail:* dubois_d@popmail.firn.edu.

Florida National College

Hialeah, Florida

- **Proprietary** 2-year, founded 1982
- **Calendar** semesters
- **Degree** certificates, diplomas, and associate
- **Urban** campus with easy access to Miami
- **Coed,** 1,248 undergraduate students, 100% full-time, 71% women, 29% men

Undergraduates 1,248 full-time. Students come from 1 other state, 3% African American, 0.3% Asian American or Pacific Islander, 93% Hispanic American, 0.7% international.

Freshmen *Admission:* 423 enrolled.

Faculty *Total:* 35, 80% full-time, 29% with terminal degrees. *Student/faculty ratio:* 14:1.

Majors Accounting; business administration; computer graphics; computer/information systems security; computer programming; computer programming related; computer programming (specific applications); computer science; computer systems networking/telecommunications; computer/technical support; data entry/microcomputer applications; data entry/microcomputer applications related; data processing technology; dental hygiene; health education; hospitality management; hotel and restaurant management; legal administrative assistant; legal studies; liberal arts and sciences/liberal studies; medical administrative assistant; medical assistant; paralegal/legal assistant; secretarial science; Spanish; system administration; system/networking/LAN/WAN management; technical/business writing; tourism promotion operations; trade/industrial education; travel/tourism management; Web page, digital/multimedia and information resources design; word processing.

Academic Programs *Special study options:* academic remediation for entering students, adult/continuing education programs, cooperative education, English as a second language, services for LD students, student-designed majors, summer session for credit.

Library Hialeah Campus Library plus 2 others with 21,344 titles, 112 serial subscriptions, 1,103 audiovisual materials, an OPAC, a Web page.

Computers on Campus 132 computers available on campus for general student use. A campuswide network can be accessed from off campus. Internet access available.

Student Life *Housing:* college housing not available. *Activities and Organizations:* Student Government Association. *Campus security:* 24-hour emergency response devices.

Standardized Tests *Required:* TABE.

Costs (2001–02) *Tuition:* $7800 full-time, $260 per credit part-time. Full-time tuition and fees vary according to program. No tuition increase for student's term of enrollment. *Required fees:* $210 full-time. *Payment plan:* installment. *Waivers:* employees or children of employees.

Applying *Options:* common application, deferred entrance. *Application fee:* $100. *Required:* high school transcript. *Application deadline:* rolling (freshmen), rolling (transfers). *Notification:* continuous (freshmen).

Admissions Contact Ms. Maria C. Reguerio, Vice President, Florida National College, 4162 West 12 Avenue, Hialeah, FL 33012. *Phone:* 305-821-3333 Ext. 3. *Fax:* 305-362-0595. *E-mail:* admissions@fnc.edu.

FLORIDA TECHNICAL COLLEGE
Auburndale, Florida

- **Proprietary** 2-year
- **Calendar** quarters
- **Degree** certificates, diplomas, and associate
- **Coed,** 185 undergraduate students

Undergraduates 15% African American, 12% Hispanic American.

Freshmen *Admission:* 175 applied, 175 admitted.

Faculty *Total:* 8, 63% full-time.

Costs (2002–03) *Tuition:* Full-time tuition, ranging from 20,000 to 24,000 is dependent on program selected.

Admissions Contact Mr. Charles Owens, Admissions Office, Florida Technical College, 298 Havendale Boulevard, Auburndale, FL 33823. *Phone:* 863-967-8822.

FLORIDA TECHNICAL COLLEGE
DeLand, Florida

Admissions Contact 1450 South Woodland Boulevard, 3rd Floor, DeLand, FL 32720.

FLORIDA TECHNICAL COLLEGE
Jacksonville, Florida

- **Proprietary** 2-year
- **Calendar** quarters
- **Degree** diplomas and associate
- **Coed,** 225 undergraduate students

Freshmen *Admission:* 117 applied, 106 admitted.

Faculty *Total:* 11, 82% full-time. *Student/faculty ratio:* 19:1.

Majors Computer programming; electrical/electronic engineering technology.

Costs (2002–03) *Tuition:* $10,998 full-time. *Required fees:* $200 full-time.

Applying *Application deadline:* rolling (freshmen), rolling (transfers). *Notification:* continuous (freshmen).

Admissions Contact Mr. Bryan Gulebiam, Director of Admissions, Florida Technical College, 8711 Lone Star Road, Jacksonville, FL 32211. *Phone:* 407-678-5600.

FLORIDA TECHNICAL COLLEGE
Orlando, Florida

- **Proprietary** 2-year, founded 1982
- **Calendar** quarters
- **Degree** certificates, diplomas, and associate
- **Urban** 1-acre campus
- **Coed,** 227 undergraduate students

Undergraduates Students come from 1 other state, 1 other country, 18% African American, 5% Asian American or Pacific Islander, 18% Hispanic American, 3% international.

Freshmen *Admission:* 123 applied, 112 admitted.

Faculty *Total:* 13, 77% full-time.

Majors Architectural drafting; business systems networking/ telecommunications; civil/structural drafting; computer programming; electrical/electronic engineering technology; electrical/electronics drafting; management information systems/business data processing; mechanical drafting; medical administrative assistant; paralegal/legal assistant.

Academic Programs *Special study options:* accelerated degree program, double majors.

Library Florida Technical College Learning Resource Center.

Computers on Campus 35 computers available on campus for general student use. At least one staffed computer lab available.

Student Life *Housing:* college housing not available. *Activities and Organizations:* student-run newspaper.

Costs (2002–03) *Tuition:* $10,998 full-time. *Required fees:* $200 full-time.

Applying *Application fee:* $25. *Required:* high school transcript, interview. *Recommended:* essay or personal statement, letters of recommendation.

Admissions Contact Mr. Bryan Gulebiam, Director of Admissions, Florida Technical College, 1819 North Semoran Boulevard, Orlando, FL 32807-3546. *Phone:* 407-678-5600. *Fax:* 407-678-1149.

FULL SAIL REAL WORLD EDUCATION
Winter Park, Florida

- **Proprietary** 2-year, founded 1979
- **Calendar** modular
- **Degree** associate
- **Suburban** campus with easy access to Orlando
- **Coed,** 3,100 undergraduate students

Undergraduates Students come from 44 states and territories, 9 other countries.

Faculty *Total:* 550. *Student/faculty ratio:* 6:1.

Majors Audio engineering; computer graphics; film/video production; graphic design/commercial art/illustration; multimedia; music business management/merchandising.

Academic Programs *Special study options:* academic remediation for entering students, adult/continuing education programs, cooperative education, internships, part-time degree program, services for LD students, summer session for credit.

Library Full Sail Library with 610 titles, 31 serial subscriptions.

Computers on Campus 32 computers available on campus for general student use. A campuswide network can be accessed from off campus. Internet access, at least one staffed computer lab available.

Student Life *Housing:* college housing not available. *Activities and Organizations:* Student Chapter of Audio Engineering Society. *Campus security:* 24-hour patrols. *Student Services:* personal/psychological counseling.

Costs (2001–02) *Tuition:* $30,000 full-time, $30,000 per degree program part-time. Full-time tuition and fees vary according to program. Part-time tuition and fees vary according to program.

Applying *Options:* common application, early admission, deferred entrance. *Application fee:* $150. *Required:* high school transcript. *Application deadline:* rolling (freshmen), rolling (transfers).

Full Sail Real World Education (continued)

Admissions Contact Ms. Mary Beth Plank, Director of Admissions, Full Sail Real World Education, 3300 University Boulevard, Winter Park, FL 32792. *Phone:* 407-679-6333 Ext. 2141. *Toll-free phone:* 800-226-7625. *E-mail:* admissions@fullsail.com.

GULF COAST COMMUNITY COLLEGE
Panama City, Florida

- **State-supported** 2-year, founded 1957
- **Calendar** semesters
- **Degree** certificates and associate
- **Suburban** 80-acre campus
- **Endowment** $14.7 million
- **Coed,** 5,765 undergraduate students, 35% full-time, 58% women, 42% men

Undergraduates 1,996 full-time, 3,769 part-time. Students come from 18 states and territories, 11 other countries, 12% African American, 2% Asian American or Pacific Islander, 3% Hispanic American, 0.7% Native American, 0.7% international.

Freshmen *Admission:* 515 enrolled.

Faculty *Total:* 611, 19% full-time. *Student/faculty ratio:* 20:1.

Majors Accounting; business administration; child care provider; child guidance; civil engineering technology; computer engineering related; computer engineering technology; computer programming; computer programming (specific applications); construction technology; criminal justice/law enforcement administration; culinary arts; dental hygiene; drafting; drafting/design technology; electrical/electronic engineering technology; emergency medical technology; engineering-related technology; fire science; hospitality management; human services; industrial radiologic technology; liberal arts and sciences/liberal studies; nursing; paralegal/legal assistant; physical therapy assistant; radio/television broadcasting; respiratory therapy; secretarial science.

Academic Programs *Special study options:* academic remediation for entering students, accelerated degree program, adult/continuing education programs, advanced placement credit, cooperative education, distance learning, double majors, English as a second language, external degree program, honors programs, independent study, off-campus study, part-time degree program, services for LD students, summer session for credit.

Library Gulf Coast Community College Library with 80,000 titles, 933 serial subscriptions, 21,567 audiovisual materials, an OPAC, a Web page.

Computers on Campus 650 computers available on campus for general student use. A campuswide network can be accessed from off campus. Internet access, at least one staffed computer lab available.

Student Life *Housing:* college housing not available. *Activities and Organizations:* drama/theater group, student-run newspaper, radio station, choral group, Student Activities Board, Baptist Campus Ministry, Theater Club, Phi Theta Kappa, Muslim Student Association. *Campus security:* patrols by trained security personnel during campus hours. *Student Services:* personal/psychological counseling.

Athletics Member NJCAA. *Intercollegiate sports:* baseball M(s), basketball M(s)/W(s), softball W(s), volleyball W(s). *Intramural sports:* basketball M/W, football M, volleyball M/W.

Standardized Tests *Required:* CPT. *Recommended:* SAT I and SAT II or ACT (for placement).

Costs (2001–02) *Tuition:* state resident $1229 full-time, $51 per credit part-time; nonresident $4914 full-time, $189 per credit part-time. *Required fees:* $293 full-time. *Payment plan:* deferred payment.

Financial Aid In 2001, 75 Federal Work-Study jobs (averaging $2000). 76 State and other part-time jobs (averaging $2500).

Applying *Options:* early admission, deferred entrance. *Required:* high school transcript. *Application deadline:* rolling (freshmen), rolling (transfers). *Notification:* continuous (freshmen).

Admissions Contact Mrs. Jackie Kuczenski, Administrative Secretary of Admissions, Gulf Coast Community College, 5230 West Highway 98, Panama City, FL 32401. *Phone:* 850-769-1551 Ext. 4892. *Fax:* 850-913-3308. *E-mail:* lwolfkill@ccmail.gc.cc.fl.us.

HERZING COLLEGE
Melbourne, Florida

- **Proprietary** 2-year, founded 1980
- **Calendar** semesters
- **Degree** diplomas and associate
- **Coed**

Faculty *Student/faculty ratio:* 10:1.

Admissions Contact Ms. Darlene Wohl, Director, Herzing College, 1270 North Wickham Road, Suite 51, Melbourne, FL 32935. *Phone:* 321-255-9232.

HERZING COLLEGE
Orlando, Florida

Admissions Contact Ms. Karen Mohamad, Herzing College, 1300 North Semoran Boulevard, Suite 103, Orlando, FL 32807. *Phone:* 407-380-6315.

HILLSBOROUGH COMMUNITY COLLEGE
Tampa, Florida

- **State-supported** 2-year, founded 1968, part of Florida Community College System
- **Calendar** semesters
- **Degree** certificates and associate
- **Urban** campus
- **Endowment** $1.9 million
- **Coed,** 19,436 undergraduate students, 30% full-time, 58% women, 42% men

Undergraduates 5,742 full-time, 13,694 part-time. Students come from 68 other countries, 5% are from out of state, 17% African American, 4% Asian American or Pacific Islander, 17% Hispanic American, 0.5% Native American, 1% international, 8% transferred in. *Retention:* 48% of 2001 full-time freshmen returned.

Freshmen *Admission:* 3,442 applied, 3,442 admitted, 3,442 enrolled.

Faculty *Total:* 1,518, 18% full-time, 11% with terminal degrees. *Student/faculty ratio:* 19:1.

Majors Accounting; administrative/secretarial services; agricultural production; aquaculture operations/production management; architectural engineering technology; art; biomedical technology; business administration; business marketing and marketing management; business systems networking/ telecommunications; child care/development; computer engineering technology; computer programming; construction technology; corrections; criminal justice/law enforcement administration; dance; diagnostic medical sonography; electrical/electronic engineering technology; elementary education; emergency medical technology; environmental science; finance; fire science; graphic design/commercial art/illustration; hospitality management; hotel and restaurant management; human services; industrial radiologic technology; information sciences/systems; interior design; law enforcement/police science; legal administrative assistant; legal studies; liberal arts and sciences/liberal studies; mass communications; medical administrative assistant; multimedia; music; nuclear medical technology; nursing; occupational therapy; optometric/ophthalmic laboratory technician; ornamental horticulture; pharmacy technician/assistant; physical education; physical therapy; radiological science; radio/television broadcasting technology; respiratory therapy; secretarial science; sign language interpretation; theater arts/drama.

Academic Programs *Special study options:* academic remediation for entering students, adult/continuing education programs, advanced placement credit, cooperative education, English as a second language, honors programs, off-campus study, part-time degree program, services for LD students, summer session for credit. *ROTC:* Army (c), Air Force (c).

Library Main Library plus 4 others with 170,615 titles, 1,283 serial subscriptions, 50,000 audiovisual materials, an OPAC, a Web page.

Computers on Campus 600 computers available on campus for general student use. Internet access, at least one staffed computer lab available.

Student Life *Housing:* college housing not available. *Activities and Organizations:* drama/theater group, student-run newspaper, Student Government Association, Student Nursing Association, Phi Theta Kappa, Disabled Students Association, Radiography Club, national fraternities. *Campus security:* 24-hour emergency response devices and patrols. *Student Services:* personal/psychological counseling.

Athletics Member NJCAA. *Intercollegiate sports:* baseball M(s), basketball M(s)/W(s), softball W(s), tennis W(s), volleyball W(s).

Standardized Tests *Required for some:* CPT.

Costs (2001–02) *Tuition:* state resident $1581 full-time, $53 per credit hour part-time; nonresident $5891 full-time, $196 per credit hour part-time.

Applying *Options:* common application, early admission. *Application fee:* $20. *Required:* high school transcript. *Application deadline:* rolling (freshmen), rolling (transfers).

Admissions Contact Ms. Kathy G. Cecil, Admissions, Registration, and Records Officer, Hillsborough Community College, PO Box 31127, Tampa, FL 33631-3127. *Phone:* 813-253-7027.

INDIAN RIVER COMMUNITY COLLEGE
Fort Pierce, Florida

- **State-supported** 2-year, founded 1960, part of Florida Community College System
- **Calendar** semesters
- **Degree** certificates, diplomas, and associate
- **Small-town** 133-acre campus
- **Coed,** 23,160 undergraduate students

Undergraduates Students come from 33 states and territories, 12 other countries, 2% are from out of state.

Freshmen *Admission:* 1,149 applied, 1,149 admitted. *Test scores:* SAT verbal scores over 500: 47%; SAT math scores over 500: 43%; SAT math scores over 600: 5%; SAT math scores over 700: 5%.

Faculty *Total:* 796, 20% full-time.

Majors Accounting; agricultural business; aircraft pilot (professional); anthropology; architectural drafting; art education; auto mechanic/technician; banking; biology; business administration; business marketing and marketing management; carpentry; chemistry; child care/development; civil engineering technology; clothing/textiles; computer engineering technology; computer programming; computer science; computer typography/composition; corrections; cosmetology; criminal justice/law enforcement administration; culinary arts; dental hygiene; drafting; early childhood education; economics; education; electrical/electronic engineering technology; emergency medical technology; engineering; engineering technology; English; fashion merchandising; finance; fire science; food/nutrition; food products retailing; foreign language translation; forestry; French; heating/air conditioning/refrigeration; history; home economics; hotel and restaurant management; humanities; human services; industrial radiologic technology; information sciences/systems; interior design; journalism; law enforcement/police science; liberal arts and sciences/liberal studies; library science; marine science; mathematics; medical administrative assistant; medical laboratory technician; medical records administration; music; nursing; paralegal/legal assistant; pharmacy; philosophy; physical education; physical therapy; physical therapy assistant; physics; political science; practical nurse; pre-engineering; psychology; respiratory therapy; retail management; secretarial science; social sciences; social work; sociology; Spanish; speech/rhetorical studies; surveying; teacher assistant/aide; theater arts/drama; water resources.

Academic Programs *Special study options:* academic remediation for entering students, adult/continuing education programs, advanced placement credit, distance learning, English as a second language, independent study, part-time degree program, services for LD students, summer session for credit.

Library Charles S. Miley Learning Resource Center with 58,657 titles, 554 serial subscriptions, an OPAC.

Computers on Campus 500 computers available on campus for general student use. Internet access, at least one staffed computer lab available.

Student Life *Housing:* college housing not available. *Activities and Organizations:* drama/theater group, choral group, Phi Beta Lambda, Distributive Education Club of America, International Club, Cultural Exchange, Human Services Club. *Campus security:* 24-hour patrols. *Student Services:* health clinic, personal/psychological counseling, women's center.

Athletics Member NJCAA. *Intercollegiate sports:* baseball M(s), basketball M(s)/W(s), softball W(s), swimming M(s)/W(s), volleyball W(s). *Intramural sports:* basketball M/W, racquetball M/W, soccer M, volleyball M/W.

Standardized Tests *Required:* SAT I, ACT, or CPT.

Costs (2001–02) *Tuition:* state resident $1200 full-time, $50 per credit part-time; nonresident $4488 full-time, $187 per credit part-time.

Financial Aid In 2001, 110 Federal Work-Study jobs (averaging $1500).

Applying *Options:* early admission, deferred entrance. *Required:* high school transcript. *Application deadline:* rolling (freshmen), rolling (transfers). *Notification:* continuous (freshmen).

Admissions Contact Mrs. Linda Hays, Dean of Educational Services, Indian River Community College, 3209 Virginia Avenue, Fort Pierce, FL 34981-5596. *Phone:* 561-462-4740.

INSTITUTE OF CAREER EDUCATION
West Palm Beach, Florida

Admissions Contact Mr. Mark Proefrock, Vice President, Institute of Career Education, 1750 45th Street, West Palm Beach, FL 33407-2192. *Phone:* 561-881-0220.

ITT TECHNICAL INSTITUTE
Tampa, Florida

- **Proprietary** primarily 2-year, founded 1981, part of ITT Educational Services, Inc
- **Calendar** quarters
- **Degrees** associate and bachelor's
- **Suburban** campus with easy access to St. Petersburg
- **Coed,** 649 undergraduate students

Majors Computer/information sciences related; computer programming; design/applied arts related; drafting; electrical/electronic engineering technologies related; information technology.

Student Life *Housing:* college housing not available.

Costs (2001–02) *Tuition:* Full-time tuition and fees vary according to program. Part-time tuition and fees vary according to program. $260—$330 per credit hour.

Applying *Options:* deferred entrance. *Application fee:* $100. *Required:* high school transcript, interview. *Recommended:* letters of recommendation. *Application deadline:* rolling (freshmen), rolling (transfers). *Notification:* continuous (freshmen).

Admissions Contact Mr. Marty Baca, Director of Recruitment, ITT Technical Institute, 4809 Memorial Highway, Tampa, FL 33634-7151. *Phone:* 813-885-2244. *Toll-free phone:* 800-825-2831.

ITT TECHNICAL INSTITUTE
Fort Lauderdale, Florida

- **Proprietary** primarily 2-year, founded 1991, part of ITT Educational Services, Inc
- **Calendar** quarters
- **Degrees** associate and bachelor's
- **Suburban** campus with easy access to Miami
- **Coed,** 587 undergraduate students

Majors Computer/information sciences related; computer programming; drafting; electrical/electronic engineering technologies related; information technology.

Student Life *Housing:* college housing not available.

Costs (2001–02) *Tuition:* Full-time tuition and fees vary according to program. Part-time tuition and fees vary according to program. $260—$330 per credit hour.

Applying *Options:* deferred entrance. *Application fee:* $100. *Required:* high school transcript, interview. *Recommended:* letters of recommendation. *Application deadline:* rolling (freshmen), rolling (transfers).

Admissions Contact Mr. Bob Bixler, Director of Recruitment, ITT Technical Institute, 3401 South University Drive, Ft. Lauderdale, FL 33328-2021. *Phone:* 954-476-9300. *Toll-free phone:* 800-488-7797. *Fax:* 954-476-6889.

ITT TECHNICAL INSTITUTE
Jacksonville, Florida

- **Proprietary** primarily 2-year, founded 1991, part of ITT Educational Services, Inc
- **Calendar** quarters
- **Degrees** associate and bachelor's
- **Urban** 1-acre campus
- **Coed,** 455 undergraduate students

Majors Computer/information sciences related; computer programming; data processing technology; drafting; electrical/electronic engineering technologies related.

Student Life *Housing:* college housing not available.

Costs (2001–02) *Tuition:* Full-time tuition and fees vary according to program. Part-time tuition and fees vary according to program. $260—$330 per credit hour.

Financial Aid In 2001, 5 Federal Work-Study jobs.

Applying *Options:* deferred entrance. *Application fee:* $100. *Required:* high school transcript, interview. *Recommended:* letters of recommendation. *Application deadline:* rolling (freshmen), rolling (transfers).

Admissions Contact Mr. Del McCormick, Director of Recruitment, ITT Technical Institute, 6610-10 Youngerman Circle, Jacksonville, FL 32244. *Phone:* 904-573-9100. *Toll-free phone:* 800-318-1264.

ITT TECHNICAL INSTITUTE
Maitland, Florida

- **Proprietary** primarily 2-year, founded 1989, part of ITT Educational Services, Inc
- **Calendar** quarters
- **Degrees** associate and bachelor's
- **Suburban** 1-acre campus with easy access to Orlando
- **Coed,** 418 undergraduate students

Majors Computer/information sciences related; computer programming; drafting; electrical/electronic engineering technologies related; electrical/electronic engineering technology; information technology.

Student Life *Housing:* college housing not available. *Activities and Organizations:* student-run newspaper.

Costs (2001–02) *Tuition:* Full-time tuition and fees vary according to program. Part-time tuition and fees vary according to program. $260—$330 per credit hour.

Applying *Options:* deferred entrance. *Application fee:* $100. *Required:* high school transcript, interview. *Recommended:* letters of recommendation. *Application deadline:* rolling (freshmen), rolling (transfers). *Notification:* continuous (freshmen).

Admissions Contact Ms. Sally Mills, Director of Recruitment, ITT Technical Institute, 2600 Lake Lucien Drive, Suite 140, Maitland, FL 32751-7234. *Phone:* 407-660-2900.

ITT TECHNICAL INSTITUTE
Miami, Florida

- **Proprietary** 2-year, founded 1996, part of ITT Educational Services, Inc
- **Calendar** quarters
- **Degree** associate
- 461 undergraduate students

Majors Computer/information sciences related; computer programming; drafting; electrical/electronic engineering technologies related; information technology.

Student Life *Housing:* college housing not available.

Costs (2001–02) *Tuition:* Full-time tuition and fees vary according to program. Part-time tuition and fees vary according to program. $260—$330 per credit hour.

Applying *Options:* deferred entrance. *Application fee:* $100. *Required:* high school transcript, interview. *Recommended:* letters of recommendation. *Application deadline:* rolling (freshmen).

Admissions Contact Mr. Robert Haywood, Director, ITT Technical Institute, 7955 NW 12th Street, Miami, FL 33126. *Phone:* 305-477-3080.

KEISER COLLEGE
Fort Lauderdale, Florida

- **Proprietary** 2-year, founded 1977
- **Calendar** 3 semesters per year
- **Degrees** diplomas and associate (profile includes data from Daytona Beach, Melbourne, Sarasota, Tallahassee, and Lakeland campuses)
- **Suburban** 4-acre campus with easy access to Miami
- **Coed**

Student Life *Campus security:* security guard after 8 p.m.

Applying *Options:* deferred entrance. *Application fee:* $50. *Required:* high school transcript, minimum 2.0 GPA, interview.

Admissions Contact Mr. Brian Woods, Vice President of Enrollment Management, Keiser College, 1500 Northwest 49th Street, Fort Lauderdale, FL 33309. *Phone:* 954-776-4476.

KEISER COLLEGE
Daytona Beach, Florida

Admissions Contact Mr. Jim Wallis, Director of Admissions, Keiser College, 1800 West International Speedway, Building 3, Daytona Beach, FL 32114. *Phone:* 904-255-1707. *Toll-free phone:* 800-749-4456. *Fax:* 904-239-0955.

KEISER COLLEGE
Melbourne, Florida

Admissions Contact Ms. Susan Zeigelhofer, Director of Admissions, Keiser College, 900 South Babcock Street, Melbourne, FL 32901-1461. *Phone:* 954-776-4456. *Toll-free phone:* 800-749-4456. *E-mail:* susanz@keisercollege.cc.fl.us.

KEISER COLLEGE
Sarasota, Florida

Admissions Contact Mr. Roger Buck, Executive Director, Keiser College, 332 Sarasota Quay, Sarasota, FL 34236. *Phone:* 941-954-0954.

KEISER COLLEGE
Tallahassee, Florida

Admissions Contact Mr. Fred Teresa, Director of Admissions, Keiser College, 1700 Halstead Boulevard, Tallahassee, FL 32308. *Phone:* 850-906-9494. *Toll-free phone:* 800-749-4456. *Fax:* 850-906-9497.

LAKE CITY COMMUNITY COLLEGE
Lake City, Florida

- **State-supported** 2-year, founded 1962, part of Florida Community College System
- **Calendar** semesters
- **Degree** certificates and associate
- **Small-town** 132-acre campus with easy access to Jacksonville
- **Endowment** $3.3 million
- **Coed,** 2,287 undergraduate students, 46% full-time, 62% women, 38% men

Undergraduates 1,051 full-time, 1,236 part-time. Students come from 18 states and territories, 7 other countries, 11% African American, 1% Asian American or Pacific Islander, 1% Hispanic American, 1% Native American, 0.6% international, 2% live on campus.

Freshmen *Admission:* 1,337 applied, 1,337 admitted, 1,899 enrolled. *Test scores:* SAT verbal scores over 500: 13%; SAT math scores over 500: 15%; ACT scores over 18: 56%; SAT verbal scores over 600: 7%; SAT math scores over 600: 10%; ACT scores over 24: 14%; SAT verbal scores over 700: 2%; SAT math scores over 700: 2%; ACT scores over 30: 3%.

Faculty *Total:* 209, 29% full-time. *Student/faculty ratio:* 16:1.

Majors Business administration; computer hardware engineering; computer programming; computer programming (specific applications); computer programming, vendor/product certification; computer software engineering; criminal justice/law enforcement administration; electrical/electronic engineering technology; emergency medical technology; forest management; forest products technology; landscaping management; liberal arts and sciences/liberal studies; medical laboratory technician; nursing; physical therapy assistant; secretarial science; turf management; Web page, digital/multimedia and information resources design.

Academic Programs *Special study options:* academic remediation for entering students, adult/continuing education programs, advanced placement credit, cooperative education, distance learning, English as a second language, independent study, internships, part-time degree program, services for LD students, study abroad, summer session for credit.

Library Learning Resources Center with 42,000 titles, 180 serial subscriptions, an OPAC.

Computers on Campus 150 computers available on campus for general student use. Internet access, at least one staffed computer lab available.

Student Life *Housing Options:* coed. *Activities and Organizations:* drama/theater group, choral group, student government, Florida Turf Grass Association, Florida Student Nurses Association, Phi Theta Kappa, Multicultural Student Union. *Campus security:* 24-hour patrols.

Athletics Member NJCAA. *Intercollegiate sports:* baseball M(s), golf W(s), softball W(s). *Intramural sports:* basketball M, racquetball M/W, softball M/W, table tennis M/W, tennis M/W, volleyball M/W, weight lifting M/W.

Standardized Tests *Required:* SAT I, ACT, or CPT. *Recommended:* SAT I or ACT (for placement).

Costs (2001–02) *Tuition:* state resident $1403 full-time, $47 per semester hour part-time; nonresident $5244 full-time, $175 per semester hour part-time. Full-time tuition and fees vary according to program. Part-time tuition and fees vary according to program. *Room and board:* Room and board charges vary according to board plan.

Financial Aid In 2001, 40 Federal Work-Study jobs (averaging $975).

Applying *Options:* early admission, deferred entrance. *Application fee:* $15. *Required for some:* high school transcript. *Application deadline:* rolling (freshmen), rolling (transfers). *Notification:* continuous (freshmen).

Admissions Contact Dr. Barry Bunn, Director of Postsecondary Transition, Lake City Community College, Route 19, Box 1030, Lake City, FL 32025-8703. *Phone:* 386-754-4288. *Fax:* 386-755-1521. *E-mail:* admissions@mail.lakecity.cc.fl.us.

LAKE-SUMTER COMMUNITY COLLEGE
Leesburg, Florida

- **State and locally supported** 2-year, founded 1962, part of Florida Community College System
- **Calendar** semesters
- **Degree** certificates, diplomas, and associate
- **Rural** 110-acre campus with easy access to Orlando
- **Endowment** $2.0 million
- **Coed,** 2,881 undergraduate students, 30% full-time, 68% women, 32% men

Undergraduates 865 full-time, 2,016 part-time. Students come from 4 states and territories, 22 other countries, 2% are from out of state, 7% African American, 1% Asian American or Pacific Islander, 4% Hispanic American, 0.6% Native American, 2% international.

Freshmen *Admission:* 705 admitted, 1,005 enrolled.

Faculty *Total:* 146, 30% full-time, 7% with terminal degrees. *Student/faculty ratio:* 20:1.

Majors Business administration; computer science; computer science related; computer systems networking/telecommunications; criminal justice/law enforcement administration; emergency medical technology; finance; fire science; graphic design/commercial art/illustration; hospitality management; Internet; liberal arts and sciences/liberal studies; medical records administration; nursing; paralegal/legal assistant.

Academic Programs *Special study options:* academic remediation for entering students, adult/continuing education programs, advanced placement credit, cooperative education, distance learning, double majors, off-campus study, part-time degree program, services for LD students, summer session for credit. *ROTC:* Air Force (c).

Library Lake-Sumter Community College Library with 53,692 titles, 372 serial subscriptions, 860 audiovisual materials, an OPAC, a Web page.

Computers on Campus 335 computers available on campus for general student use. A campuswide network can be accessed from off campus. Internet access, at least one staffed computer lab available.

Student Life *Housing:* college housing not available. *Activities and Organizations:* drama/theater group, student-run newspaper, television station, choral group, Phi Theta Kappa, Baptist Collegiate Ministry, Environmental Society, Nursing Students' Association. *Campus security:* late-night transport/escort service. *Student Services:* women's center.

Athletics Member NJCAA. *Intercollegiate sports:* baseball M(s), softball W(s), volleyball W(s). *Intramural sports:* basketball M/W, golf M/W, softball M/W, volleyball M/W, weight lifting M/W.

Standardized Tests *Required:* SAT I, ACT, or CPT.

Costs (2001–02) *Tuition:* state resident $1539 full-time, $51 per semester hour part-time; nonresident $5742 full-time, $191 per semester hour part-time. Full-time tuition and fees vary according to course load. Part-time tuition and fees vary according to course load. *Required fees:* $30 full-time. *Waivers:* employees or children of employees.

Applying *Options:* early admission, deferred entrance. *Application fee:* $25. *Required:* high school transcript. *Application deadline:* rolling (freshmen), rolling (transfers). *Notification:* continuous (freshmen).

Admissions Contact Ms. Janet Osborne, Enrollment Specialist, Lake-Sumter Community College, 9501 US Highway 441, Leesburg, FL 34788-8751. *Phone:* 352-365-3601 Ext. 3601. *Fax:* 352-365-3553 Ext. 3553. *E-mail:* osbornej@lscc.cc.fl.us.

MANATEE COMMUNITY COLLEGE
Bradenton, Florida

- **State-supported** 2-year, founded 1957, part of Florida Community College System
- **Calendar** semesters
- **Degree** certificates and associate
- **Suburban** 100-acre campus with easy access to Tampa-St. Petersburg
- **Coed,** 1,954 undergraduate students, 44% full-time, 58% women, 42% men

Undergraduates 868 full-time, 1,086 part-time. Students come from 27 states and territories, 50 other countries, 3% are from out of state, 8% African American, 1% Asian American or Pacific Islander, 4% Hispanic American, 0.4% Native American, 4% international, 20% transferred in. *Retention:* 64% of 2001 full-time freshmen returned.

Freshmen *Admission:* 1,958 admitted, 1,954 enrolled.

Faculty *Total:* 417, 24% full-time. *Student/faculty ratio:* 28:1.

Majors Accounting; advertising; African-American studies; American government; American studies; art; art history; Asian studies; astronomy; biology; biology education; business; business administration; business economics; chemistry; chemistry education; child guidance; civil engineering technology; community health liaison; computer engineering technology; computer graphics; computer/information sciences; computer programming; computer programming related; computer science related; construction technology; criminal justice studies; dietetics; drafting; early childhood education; Eastern European area studies; economics; electrical/electronic engineering technology; engineering; English; English education; finance; fine/studio arts; fire science; foreign languages education; French; German; graphic design/commercial art/illustration; health education; health facilities administration; health services administration; history; home economics education; humanities; industrial arts education; information sciences/systems; jazz; journalism; Judaic studies; Latin American studies; liberal arts and sciences/liberal studies; mass communications; mathematical statistics; mathematics education; medical radiologic technology; music; music (general performance); music teacher education; music theory and composition; nursing; occupational therapy; occupational therapy assistant; paralegal/legal assistant; philosophy; physical education; physical therapy; physical therapy assistant; physician assistant; physics; physics education; pre-pharmacy studies; psychology; public administration; radiological science; radio/television broadcasting; radio/television broadcasting technology; religious studies; respiratory therapy; Russian/Slavic studies; science education; secretarial science; social psychology; social sciences; social studies education; social work; Spanish; speech/rhetorical studies; theater arts/drama; trade/industrial education; vocational rehabilitation counseling; women's studies.

Academic Programs *Special study options:* academic remediation for entering students, advanced placement credit, cooperative education, distance learning, English as a second language, honors programs, independent study, part-time degree program, services for LD students, summer session for credit.

Library Sara Harlee Library plus 1 other with 65,386 titles, 331 serial subscriptions, 14,915 audiovisual materials, an OPAC, a Web page.

Computers on Campus 600 computers available on campus for general student use. A campuswide network can be accessed from off campus. Internet access, at least one staffed computer lab available.

Student Life *Housing:* college housing not available. *Activities and Organizations:* drama/theater group, student-run newspaper, choral group, Student Government Association, Phi Theta Kappa, American Chemical Society Student Affiliate, Campus Ministry, Medical Community Club. *Campus security:* 24-hour emergency response devices and patrols, late-night transport/escort service.

Athletics Member NJCAA. *Intercollegiate sports:* baseball M(s), basketball M(s), softball W(s), volleyball W(s). *Intramural sports:* basketball M/W, softball M/W, volleyball M/W, weight lifting M/W.

Standardized Tests *Required:* SAT I or ACT (for placement), Florida Placement Test.

Costs (2002–03) *Tuition:* state resident $1600 full-time, $53 per credit hour part-time; nonresident $5900 full-time, $196 per credit hour part-time. *Waivers:* employees or children of employees.

Financial Aid In 2001, 82 Federal Work-Study jobs (averaging $2000).

Applying *Options:* early admission. *Application fee:* $20. *Required:* high school transcript. *Application deadlines:* 8/20 (freshmen), 8/20 (transfers). *Notification:* continuous (freshmen).

Admissions Contact Mrs. Karen Armstrong, Assistant Registrar, Manatee Community College, PO Box 1849, Bradenton, FL 34206. *Phone:* 941-752-5031. *Fax:* 941-727-6380.

MIAMI-DADE COMMUNITY COLLEGE
Miami, Florida

- **State and locally supported** 2-year, founded 1960, part of Florida Community College System
- **Calendar** 16-16-6-6
- **Degree** associate
- **Urban** campus
- **Endowment** $32.4 million
- **Coed,** 53,486 undergraduate students

Miami-Dade Community College offers undergraduate study in more than 150 academic areas and professions. The College is internationally recognized as an educational leader in undergraduate programs that are innovative and diverse within a multicultural, multiethnic environment. Annually, more than 128,000 credit and noncredit students are enrolled at 6 major campuses and numerous outreach centers.

Undergraduates Students come from 31 states and territories, 154 other countries, 1% are from out of state, 21% African American, 1% Asian American or Pacific Islander, 64% Hispanic American, 3% international.

Miami-Dade Community College (continued)

Freshmen *Admission:* 10,478 applied, 10,375 admitted.

Faculty *Total:* 2,046, 33% full-time, 12% with terminal degrees.

Majors Accounting; aerospace science; agricultural sciences; aircraft pilot (professional); American studies; anthropology; architectural engineering technology; art; art education; Asian studies; aviation management; aviation technology; behavioral sciences; biology; broadcast journalism; business administration; business marketing and marketing management; chemistry; child care/development; civil engineering technology; computer graphics; computer programming; computer science; construction technology; court reporting; criminal justice/law enforcement administration; dance; data processing technology; dental hygiene; drafting; drama therapy; early childhood education; economics; education; electrical/electronic engineering technology; electromechanical technology; elementary education; emergency medical technology; engineering; engineering design; engineering science; engineering technology; English; fashion design/illustration; fashion merchandising; film studies; film/video production; finance; fire science; food sciences; food services technology; forestry; French; general studies; geology; German; graphic design/commercial art/illustration; heating/air conditioning/refrigeration; history; horticulture science; hotel and restaurant management; humanities; industrial technology; information sciences/systems; instrumentation technology; interior design; international relations; Italian; jazz; journalism; landscape architecture; laser/optical technology; Latin American studies; law enforcement/police science; legal administrative assistant; legal studies; literature; management information systems/business data processing; mass communications; mathematics; medical administrative assistant; medical assistant; medical laboratory technician; medical records administration; medical technology; middle school education; mortuary science; music; music (piano and organ performance); music teacher education; natural sciences; nursing; oceanography; optometric/ophthalmic laboratory technician; ornamental horticulture; paralegal/legal assistant; pharmacy; philosophy; photography; physical education; physical sciences; physical therapy; physics; political science; Portuguese; postal management; pre-engineering; psychology; public administration; radiological science; radio/television broadcasting; recreation/leisure studies; respiratory therapy; science education; secretarial science; sign language interpretation; social sciences; social work; sociology; Spanish; speech/rhetorical studies; stringed instruments; surveying; teacher assistant/aide; theater arts/drama; travel/tourism management; veterinary sciences; wind/percussion instruments.

Academic Programs *Special study options:* academic remediation for entering students, adult/continuing education programs, advanced placement credit, cooperative education, English as a second language, honors programs, internships, part-time degree program, services for LD students, study abroad, summer session for credit. *ROTC:* Army (c), Air Force (c).

Library 331,695 titles, 1,921 serial subscriptions.

Computers on Campus 4423 computers available on campus for general student use. A campuswide network can be accessed from off campus. Internet access, at least one staffed computer lab available.

Student Life *Housing:* college housing not available. *Activities and Organizations:* drama/theater group, student-run newspaper, radio station, choral group, national fraternities, national sororities. *Campus security:* 24-hour patrols. *Student Services:* personal/psychological counseling, women's center.

Athletics Member NJCAA. *Intercollegiate sports:* baseball M(s), basketball M(s)/W(s), softball W(s), volleyball W(s). *Intramural sports:* basketball M/W, racquetball M/W, soccer M/W, softball M/W, tennis M/W, volleyball M/W.

Standardized Tests *Required:* CPT.

Costs (2001–02) *Tuition:* state resident $51 per credit part-time; nonresident $179 per credit part-time. Tuition and fees are determined by number of credits taken.

Financial Aid In 2001, 727 Federal Work-Study jobs, 200 State and other part-time jobs.

Applying *Options:* early admission, deferred entrance. *Application fee:* $20. *Application deadline:* rolling (freshmen), rolling (transfers).

Admissions Contact Mr. Samuel LaRoue, District Director of Admissions and Registration Services, Miami-Dade Community College, 300 Northeast Second Avenue, Miami, FL 33132. *Phone:* 305-237-7478. *Fax:* 305-237-7534. *E-mail:* slaroue@mdcc.edu.

NEW ENGLAND INSTITUTE OF TECHNOLOGY AT PALM BEACH
West Palm Beach, Florida

- **Proprietary** 2-year, founded 1983
- **Calendar** quarters
- **Degree** certificates, diplomas, and associate
- **Urban** 7-acre campus with easy access to Miami
- **Coed,** 1,200 undergraduate students

Freshmen *Admission:* 450 applied, 450 admitted.

Faculty *Total:* 46, 100% full-time. *Student/faculty ratio:* 25:1.

Majors Architectural drafting; auto mechanic/technician; business systems networking/ telecommunications; cosmetology; dental assistant; drafting; electrical/electronic engineering technology; food sales operations; heating/air conditioning/refrigeration; industrial electronics installation/repair; medical assistant; office management; paralegal/legal assistant.

Academic Programs *Special study options:* academic remediation for entering students, internships.

Computers on Campus 58 computers available on campus for general student use.

Student Life *Housing:* college housing not available. *Student Services:* personal/psychological counseling.

Costs (2001–02) *Tuition:* $18,000 per degree program part-time. Full-time tuition and fees vary according to program and student level. No tuition increase for student's term of enrollment. $18,000 per degree program.

Applying *Options:* early admission. *Application fee:* $150. *Required:* high school transcript. *Application deadline:* rolling (freshmen), rolling (transfers). *Notification:* continuous (freshmen).

Admissions Contact Mr. Michael Schwam, Director of Admissions, New England Institute of Technology at Palm Beach, 1126 53rd Court, West Palm Beach, FL 33407-2384. *Phone:* 561-842-8324 Ext. 125. *Toll-free phone:* 800-826-9986.

NORTH FLORIDA COMMUNITY COLLEGE
Madison, Florida

- **State-supported** 2-year, founded 1958
- **Calendar** modified semester
- **Degree** certificates and associate
- **Small-town** 109-acre campus
- **Coed**

Faculty *Student/faculty ratio:* 18:1.

Student Life *Campus security:* 24-hour emergency response devices.

Athletics Member NJCAA.

Standardized Tests *Required for some:* SAT I or ACT (for placement).

Applying *Options:* common application, early admission. *Application fee:* $20. *Required:* high school transcript, minimum 2.0 GPA.

Admissions Contact Mrs. Betty Starling, Admissions Assistant, North Florida Community College, 1000 Turner Davis Drive, Madison, FL 32340-1602. *Phone:* 850-973-1622. *Fax:* 850-973-1697.

OKALOOSA-WALTON COMMUNITY COLLEGE
Niceville, Florida

- **State and locally supported** 2-year, founded 1963, part of Florida Community College System
- **Calendar** semesters
- **Degree** certificates and associate
- **Small-town** 264-acre campus
- **Endowment** $18.4 million
- **Coed,** 7,148 undergraduate students, 24% full-time, 58% women, 42% men

Undergraduates 1,737 full-time, 5,411 part-time. Students come from 18 states and territories, 10% African American, 4% Asian American or Pacific Islander, 4% Hispanic American, 0.6% Native American, 0.3% international, 27% transferred in.

Freshmen *Admission:* 772 applied, 772 admitted, 772 enrolled.

Faculty *Total:* 295, 27% full-time, 21% with terminal degrees. *Student/faculty ratio:* 20:1.

Majors Accounting; art; atmospheric sciences; auto mechanic/technician; aviation technology; biological/physical sciences; biology; business administration; chemistry; child care/development; computer engineering related; computer programming; computer programming (specific applications); computer science; computer systems networking/telecommunications; construction technology; criminal justice/law enforcement administration; data entry/microcomputer applications; dietetics; divinity/ministry; drafting; early childhood education; education; electrical/electronic engineering technology; elementary education; engineering; fashion merchandising; finance; graphic design/commercial art/illustration; heating/air conditioning/refrigeration; home economics education; hotel and restaurant management; humanities; human resources management; information technology; interior design; law enforcement/police science; legal studies; liberal arts and sciences/liberal studies; mathematics; medical technology; modern languages; music; nursing; nutrition science; paralegal/legal assistant; physical education; physics; real estate; secretarial science; social sciences; social work; welding technology; word processing.

Academic Programs *Special study options:* academic remediation for entering students, adult/continuing education programs, advanced placement credit, distance learning, English as a second language, independent study, part-time degree program, services for LD students, summer session for credit. *ROTC:* Army (c).

Library Okaloosa-Walton Community College Learning Resource Center with 84,991 titles, 365 serial subscriptions, 10,800 audiovisual materials, an OPAC, a Web page.

Computers on Campus 643 computers available on campus for general student use. Internet access, online (class) registration, at least one staffed computer lab available.

Student Life *Housing:* college housing not available. *Activities and Organizations:* drama/theater group, choral group. *Campus security:* 24-hour patrols. *Student Services:* health clinic.

Athletics Member NJCAA. *Intercollegiate sports:* baseball M(s), basketball M(s)/W(s), softball W(s). *Intramural sports:* baseball M, basketball M/W, soccer M(c)/W(c), softball W.

Costs (2001–02) *Tuition:* state resident $1360 full-time, $43 per credit hour part-time; nonresident $5064 full-time, $167 per credit hour part-time. *Payment plans:* installment, deferred payment.

Financial Aid In 2001, 66 Federal Work-Study jobs (averaging $1500).

Applying *Options:* early admission, deferred entrance. *Required:* high school transcript. *Application deadline:* rolling (freshmen), rolling (transfers). *Notification:* continuous (freshmen).

Admissions Contact Mr. Mickey Englett, Dean of Students, Okaloosa-Walton Community College, 100 College Boulevard, Niceville, FL 32578. *Phone:* 850-729-5373. *Toll-free phone:* 850-729-5373. *Fax:* 850-729-5323. *E-mail:* registrar@owcc.net.

PALM BEACH COMMUNITY COLLEGE
Lake Worth, Florida

- **State-supported** 2-year, founded 1933, part of Florida Community College System
- **Calendar** semesters
- **Degree** certificates and associate
- **Urban** 150-acre campus with easy access to West Palm Beach
- **Endowment** $9.0 million
- **Coed,** 23,410 undergraduate students, 28% full-time, 60% women, 40% men

Undergraduates 6,579 full-time, 16,831 part-time. Students come from 44 states and territories, 63 other countries, 6% are from out of state, 10% transferred in, 2% live on campus.

Freshmen *Admission:* 2,450 applied, 2,450 admitted, 2,450 enrolled.

Faculty *Total:* 1,190, 19% full-time. *Student/faculty ratio:* 22:1.

Majors Accounting; aircraft pilot (professional); art; art history; biology; botany; business administration; business marketing and marketing management; ceramic arts; chemistry; clothing/textiles; computer programming; computer programming (specific applications); computer science; computer/technical support; construction management; criminal justice/law enforcement administration; data processing technology; dental hygiene; drafting; early childhood education; economics; education; electrical/electronic engineering technology; elementary education; English; fashion design/illustration; fashion merchandising; finance; fire science; food products retailing; graphic design/commercial art/illustration; health education; history; home economics; hotel and restaurant management; industrial radiologic technology; interior design; journalism; law enforcement/police science; legal administrative assistant; liberal arts and sciences/liberal studies; literature; mass communications; mathematics; music; nursing; nutrition science; occupational therapy; philosophy; photography; physical education; physical sciences; physical therapy; political science; pre-engineering; psychology; religious studies; secretarial science; social sciences; social work; surveying; system/networking/LAN/WAN management; theater arts/drama; Web page, digital/multimedia and information resources design; word processing; zoology.

Academic Programs *Special study options:* academic remediation for entering students, adult/continuing education programs, advanced placement credit, cooperative education, distance learning, double majors, English as a second language, freshman honors college, honors programs, independent study, internships, off-campus study, part-time degree program, services for LD students, student-designed majors, study abroad, summer session for credit.

Library Harold C. Manor Library plus 3 others with 151,000 titles, 1,474 serial subscriptions, 9,700 audiovisual materials, an OPAC, a Web page.

Computers on Campus 2000 computers available on campus for general student use. A campuswide network can be accessed from off campus. Internet access, online (class) registration, at least one staffed computer lab available.

Student Life *Housing Options:* coed, disabled students. *Activities and Organizations:* drama/theater group, student-run newspaper, choral group, student government, Phi Theta Kappa, Students for International Understanding, Black Student Union, Drama Club, national fraternities. *Campus security:* 24-hour emergency response devices and patrols. *Student Services:* health clinic, women's center.

Athletics Member NJCAA. *Intercollegiate sports:* baseball M(s), basketball M(s)/W(s), softball W(s), volleyball M(s)/W(s). *Intramural sports:* basketball M/W, bowling M/W, football M/W, racquetball M/W, soccer M, tennis M/W, volleyball M/W.

Standardized Tests *Required:* SAT I, ACT, or CPT.

Costs (2002–03) *Tuition:* state resident $1406 full-time, $50 per semester hour part-time; nonresident $5625 full-time, $187 per semester hour part-time. *Required fees:* $244 full-time, $8 per term part-time. *Room and board:* room only: $4356. *Payment plan:* tuition prepayment. *Waivers:* minority students, senior citizens, and employees or children of employees.

Applying *Options:* electronic application, early admission, deferred entrance. *Application fee:* $20. *Application deadlines:* 8/23 (freshmen), 8/23 (transfers). *Notification:* continuous until 8/23 (freshmen).

Admissions Contact Ms. Annaleah Morrow, College Registrar, Palm Beach Community College, 4200 Congress Avenue, Lake Worth, FL 33461. *Phone:* 561-868-3032. *Fax:* 561-868-3584.

PASCO-HERNANDO COMMUNITY COLLEGE
New Port Richey, Florida

- **State-supported** 2-year, founded 1972, part of Florida Community College System
- **Calendar** semesters
- **Degree** certificates, diplomas, and associate
- **Small-town** 370-acre campus with easy access to Tampa
- **Endowment** $18.0 million
- **Coed,** 5,625 undergraduate students, 33% full-time, 67% women, 33% men

Undergraduates 1,831 full-time, 3,794 part-time. Students come from 11 states and territories, 10 other countries, 1% are from out of state, 3% African American, 2% Asian American or Pacific Islander, 5% Hispanic American, 0.6% Native American, 0.8% international, 8% transferred in.

Freshmen *Admission:* 2,260 applied, 2,260 admitted, 1,215 enrolled.

Faculty *Total:* 262, 30% full-time, 18% with terminal degrees. *Student/faculty ratio:* 25:1.

Majors Business administration; business marketing and marketing management; computer programming related; computer programming (specific applications); computer systems networking/telecommunications; criminal justice/law enforcement administration; dental hygiene; drafting; emergency medical technology; human services; information technology; Internet; liberal arts and sciences/liberal studies; nursing; paralegal/legal assistant; physical therapy assistant; radiological science.

Academic Programs *Special study options:* academic remediation for entering students, accelerated degree program, adult/continuing education programs, advanced placement credit, cooperative education, distance learning, double majors, honors programs, independent study, internships, off-campus study, part-time degree program, services for LD students, summer session for credit. *ROTC:* Army (c).

Library Pottberg Library plus 2 others with 64,131 titles, 309 serial subscriptions, 6,845 audiovisual materials, an OPAC.

Computers on Campus 1170 computers available on campus for general student use. Internet access, at least one staffed computer lab available.

Student Life *Housing:* college housing not available. *Activities and Organizations:* drama/theater group, choral group, Student Government Association, Phi Theta Kappa, Phi Beta Lambda, Human Services, PHCC Cares. *Campus security:* 24-hour patrols.

Athletics Member NJCAA. *Intercollegiate sports:* baseball M(s), basketball M(s), softball W(s), tennis W(s), volleyball W(s).

Standardized Tests *Required:* CPT (preferred), SAT I, or ACT.

Costs (2001–02) *Tuition:* state resident $1504 full-time, $50 per credit part-time; nonresident $5567 full-time, $186 per credit part-time.

Financial Aid In 2001, 62 Federal Work-Study jobs (averaging $2600).

Pasco-Hernando Community College (continued)

Applying *Options:* deferred entrance. *Application fee:* $20. *Required:* high school transcript. *Application deadline:* rolling (freshmen), rolling (transfers). *Notification:* continuous (freshmen).

Admissions Contact Mr. Michael Malizia, Director of Admissions and Student Records, Pasco-Hernando Community College, 10230 Ridge Road, New Port Richey, FL 34654-5199. *Phone:* 727-816-3261. *Fax:* 727-816-3389. *E-mail:* malizim@phcc.edu.

PENSACOLA JUNIOR COLLEGE
Pensacola, Florida

- **State-supported** 2-year, founded 1948, part of Florida Community College System
- **Calendar** semesters
- **Degree** certificates, diplomas, and associate
- **Suburban** 160-acre campus
- **Coed,** 6,680 undergraduate students

Undergraduates Students come from 37 states and territories, 21 other countries, 2% are from out of state, 14% African American, 4% Asian American or Pacific Islander, 3% Hispanic American, 1% Native American.

Faculty *Total:* 747, 28% full-time.

Majors Accounting; agricultural sciences; art; art education; auto mechanic/technician; biology; business; business administration; chemical technology; chemistry; child care/development; civil engineering technology; computer science; construction technology; court reporting; criminal justice studies; criminology; culinary arts; dental hygiene; design/visual communications; dietetics; drafting; early childhood education; education; electrical/electronic engineering technology; emergency medical technology; environmental science; fire science; forest harvesting production technology; general studies; geology; graphic design/commercial art/illustration; health/physical education; health services administration; history; horticulture science; hotel and restaurant management; industrial technology; information sciences/systems; journalism; landscaping management; liberal arts and sciences/liberal studies; mathematics; medical administrative assistant; medical records administration; medical technology; music; music teacher education; natural resources conservation; nursing; ornamental horticulture; paralegal/legal assistant; philosophy; physical therapy; physical therapy assistant; physics; pre-engineering; psychology; radiological science; religious studies; respiratory therapy; secretarial science; theater arts/drama; zoology.

Academic Programs *Special study options:* academic remediation for entering students, adult/continuing education programs, advanced placement credit, cooperative education, distance learning, double majors, external degree program, honors programs, independent study, part-time degree program, services for LD students, summer session for credit. *ROTC:* Army (b).

Library Learning Resource Center plus 2 others.

Computers on Campus 1200 computers available on campus for general student use. Internet access, at least one staffed computer lab available.

Student Life *Housing:* college housing not available. *Activities and Organizations:* drama/theater group, student-run newspaper, choral group, Baptist Student Union, Campus Activities Board, Students for a Multicultural Society, International Council, Engineering Club, national fraternities, national sororities. *Campus security:* 24-hour emergency response devices and patrols, student patrols, late-night transport/escort service. *Student Services:* health clinic, personal/psychological counseling.

Athletics Member NJCAA. *Intercollegiate sports:* baseball M(s), basketball M(s)/W(s), softball W(s). *Intramural sports:* archery M/W, badminton M/W, basketball M/W, bowling M/W, cross-country running M/W, gymnastics M/W, racquetball M/W, sailing M/W, swimming M/W, tennis M/W, track and field M/W, volleyball M/W, weight lifting M/W, wrestling M.

Standardized Tests *Required:* SAT I, ACT, or CPT.

Costs (2001–02) *Tuition:* state resident $1211 full-time, $50 per credit part-time; nonresident $4508 full-time, $188 per credit part-time.

Financial Aid In 2001, 120 Federal Work-Study jobs (averaging $3000).

Applying *Options:* early admission. *Application fee:* $30. *Required:* high school transcript. *Application deadlines:* 8/30 (freshmen), 8/30 (transfers). *Notification:* continuous until 8/30 (freshmen).

Admissions Contact Coordinator of Admissions and Registration, Pensacola Junior College, 1000 College Boulevard, Pensacola, FL 32504-8998. *Phone:* 850-484-1600. *Fax:* 850-484-1829.

PEOPLES COLLEGE
Kissimmee, Florida

Admissions Contact Ms. Carolyn Huggins, Director, Peoples College, 233 Academy Drive, PO Box 421768, Kissimmee, FL 34742-1768. *Phone:* 407-847-4444 Ext. 325. *Toll-free phone:* 800-765-4732.

POLK COMMUNITY COLLEGE
Winter Haven, Florida

- **State-supported** 2-year, founded 1964, part of Florida Community College System
- **Calendar** 16-16-6-6
- **Degree** certificates and associate
- **Suburban** 88-acre campus with easy access to Orlando and Tampa
- **Endowment** $5.1 million
- **Coed,** 6,329 undergraduate students, 28% full-time, 62% women, 38% men

Undergraduates 1,755 full-time, 4,574 part-time. Students come from 25 states and territories, 57 other countries, 10% are from out of state, 13% African American, 1% Asian American or Pacific Islander, 7% Hispanic American, 0.4% Native American, 4% international.

Freshmen *Admission:* 2,150 applied, 2,150 admitted, 926 enrolled.

Faculty *Total:* 322, 32% full-time. *Student/faculty ratio:* 25:1.

Majors Accounting technician; business administration; business marketing and marketing management; child care/development; corrections; criminal justice/law enforcement administration; data processing technology; emergency medical technology; finance; fire science; information sciences/systems; law enforcement/police science; legal administrative assistant; liberal arts and sciences/liberal studies; medical administrative assistant; medical records administration; nursing; occupational therapy assistant; operating room technician; physical therapy assistant; pre-engineering; radiological science.

Academic Programs *Special study options:* academic remediation for entering students, accelerated degree program, adult/continuing education programs, advanced placement credit, cooperative education, distance learning, double majors, English as a second language, independent study, part-time degree program, services for LD students, student-designed majors, summer session for credit. *ROTC:* Army (c).

Library Polk Community College Library with 179,015 titles, 354 serial subscriptions, 4,527 audiovisual materials, an OPAC, a Web page.

Computers on Campus 171 computers available on campus for general student use. Internet access, at least one staffed computer lab available.

Student Life *Housing:* college housing not available. *Activities and Organizations:* drama/theater group, student-run newspaper, choral group. *Campus security:* 24-hour emergency response devices and patrols.

Athletics Member NJCAA. *Intercollegiate sports:* baseball M(s), basketball M(s), softball W(s), tennis W(s), volleyball W(s).

Standardized Tests *Required:* CPT.

Costs (2001–02) *Tuition:* state resident $1290 full-time, $43 per credit hour part-time; nonresident $5162 full-time, $172 per credit hour part-time. *Required fees:* $249 full-time, $8 per credit, $96 per term part-time. *Waivers:* employees or children of employees.

Financial Aid In 2001, 16 Federal Work-Study jobs (averaging $400).

Applying *Options:* early admission, deferred entrance. *Application fee:* $20. *Required:* high school transcript. *Application deadline:* rolling (freshmen), rolling (transfers). *Notification:* continuous (freshmen).

Admissions Contact Ms. Barbara Guthrie, Registrar, Polk Community College, 999 Avenue H North East, Winter Haven, FL 33881. *Phone:* 863-297-1010 Ext. 5016. *Toll-free phone:* 863-297-1000 Ext. 5016. *Fax:* 863-297-1010.

PROSPECT HALL SCHOOL OF BUSINESS
Hollywood, Florida

Admissions Contact Dr. Wedad Ashurax, Admissions Director, Prospect Hall School of Business, 2620 Hollywood Boulevard, Hollywood, FL 33020. *Phone:* 954-923-8100 Ext. 20. *Fax:* 954-923-4297. *E-mail:* info@prospect.edu.

ST. JOHNS RIVER COMMUNITY COLLEGE
Palatka, Florida

- **State-supported** 2-year, founded 1958
- **Calendar** trimesters

- **Degree** certificates, diplomas, and associate
- **Small-town** 105-acre campus with easy access to Jacksonville
- **Coed**

Student Life *Campus security:* 24-hour patrols.
Athletics Member NJCAA.
Standardized Tests *Recommended:* SAT I and SAT II or ACT (for placement).
Financial Aid In 2001, 30 Federal Work-Study jobs (averaging $2000). 40 State and other part-time jobs (averaging $2000).
Applying *Options:* common application, early admission. *Application fee:* $20. *Required:* high school transcript.
Admissions Contact Mr. O'Neal Williams, Dean of Admissions and Records, St. Johns River Community College, 5001 Saint Johns Avenue, Palatka, FL 32177-3897. *Phone:* 386-312-4032.

St. Petersburg College
St. Petersburg, Florida

- **State and locally supported** primarily 2-year, founded 1927, part of Florida Community College System
- **Calendar** semesters
- **Degrees** certificates, diplomas, associate, and bachelor's
- **Suburban** campus
- **Coed,** 20,734 undergraduate students, 30% full-time, 60% women, 40% men

Undergraduates 6,149 full-time, 14,585 part-time. Students come from 45 states and territories, 30 other countries, 4% are from out of state.
Freshmen *Admission:* 2,783 applied, 2,783 admitted, 2,783 enrolled. *Test scores:* SAT verbal scores over 500: 50%; SAT math scores over 500: 35%; SAT verbal scores over 600: 11%; SAT math scores over 600: 8%; SAT verbal scores over 700: 1%.
Faculty *Total:* 1,258, 21% full-time, 10% with terminal degrees.
Majors Accounting technician; alcohol/drug abuse counseling; architectural engineering technology; business administration; business marketing and marketing management; computer engineering technology; computer programming; computer systems networking/telecommunications; construction technology; corrections; dental hygiene; drafting/design technology; early childhood education; education; electrical/electronic engineering technology; emergency medical technology; engineering/industrial management; fire science; graphic design/commercial art/illustration; health services administration; hospitality management; human services; industrial radiologic technology; industrial technology; information sciences/systems; landscaping management; law enforcement/police science; legal administrative assistant; liberal arts and sciences/liberal studies; medical laboratory technician; medical records administration; mortuary science; natural resources management/protective services related; nursing; paralegal/legal assistant; physical therapy assistant; plastics technology; quality control technology; radiological science; respiratory therapy; sign language interpretation; telecommunications; travel/tourism management; veterinary technology; water resources; Web/multimedia management/webmaster.
Academic Programs *Special study options:* academic remediation for entering students, adult/continuing education programs, advanced placement credit, cooperative education, distance learning, English as a second language, freshman honors college, honors programs, internships, part-time degree program, services for LD students, summer session for credit.
Library M. M. Bennett Library plus 5 others with 219,799 titles, 1,346 serial subscriptions, 12,440 audiovisual materials, an OPAC, a Web page.
Computers on Campus 1060 computers available on campus for general student use. A campuswide network can be accessed from off campus. Internet access, online (class) registration, at least one staffed computer lab available.
Student Life *Housing:* college housing not available. *Activities and Organizations:* drama/theater group, student-run newspaper. *Campus security:* late-night transport/escort service. *Student Services:* women's center.
Athletics Member NJCAA. *Intercollegiate sports:* baseball M(s), basketball M(s)/W(s), softball W(s), volleyball W(s). *Intramural sports:* basketball M, bowling M/W, volleyball M/W.
Standardized Tests *Required for some:* SAT I and SAT II or ACT (for placement), SAT II: Writing Test (for placement), CPT.
Costs (2001–02) *Tuition:* state resident $1349 full-time, $45 per credit part-time; nonresident $5591 full-time, $186 per credit part-time. *Required fees:* $233 full-time, $8 per credit. *Payment plan:* deferred payment. *Waivers:* senior citizens and employees or children of employees.
Financial Aid In 2001, 350 Federal Work-Study jobs (averaging $2500).
Applying *Options:* common application, electronic application, early admission, deferred entrance. *Application fee:* $25. *Required:* high school transcript. *Application deadline:* rolling (freshmen). *Notification:* continuous (freshmen).
Admissions Contact Mr. Martyn Clay, Admissions Director/Registrar, St. Petersburg College, PO Box 13489, St. Petersburg, FL 33733-3489. *Phone:* 727-341-3322. *Fax:* 727-341-3150.

Santa Fe Community College
Gainesville, Florida

- **State and locally supported** 2-year, founded 1966, part of Florida Community College System
- **Calendar** semesters
- **Degrees** certificates and associate (offers bachelor's degrees in conjunction with Saint Leo College)
- **Suburban** 175-acre campus with easy access to Jacksonville
- **Coed,** 13,225 undergraduate students, 46% full-time, 52% women, 48% men

Undergraduates 6,100 full-time, 7,125 part-time. Students come from 45 states and territories, 81 other countries, 3% are from out of state, 11% African American, 3% Asian American or Pacific Islander, 7% Hispanic American, 0.6% Native American, 3% international, 11% transferred in. *Retention:* 61% of 2001 full-time freshmen returned.
Freshmen *Admission:* 1,609 applied, 1,609 admitted, 1,776 enrolled.
Faculty *Total:* 839, 38% full-time.
Majors Accounting; auto mechanic/technician; biomedical technology; business administration; business marketing and marketing management; child care/development; communication equipment technology; computer engineering technology; computer programming; construction technology; corrections; criminal justice/law enforcement administration; data processing technology; dental hygiene; drafting; early childhood education; education; electrical/electronic engineering technology; emergency medical technology; engineering; environmental science; fashion merchandising; finance; fire science; graphic design/commercial art/illustration; industrial radiologic technology; information sciences/systems; law enforcement/police science; legal administrative assistant; legal studies; liberal arts and sciences/liberal studies; medical administrative assistant; medical records administration; nuclear medical technology; nursing; ornamental horticulture; recreation/leisure facilities management; respiratory therapy.
Academic Programs *Special study options:* academic remediation for entering students, adult/continuing education programs, advanced placement credit, cooperative education, distance learning, English as a second language, honors programs, independent study, part-time degree program, services for LD students, student-designed majors, summer session for credit. *ROTC:* Army (c), Navy (c), Air Force (c).
Library Santa Fe Community College Library with 100,000 titles, 480 serial subscriptions, an OPAC, a Web page.
Computers on Campus 400 computers available on campus for general student use. A campuswide network can be accessed from off campus. Internet access, at least one staffed computer lab available.
Student Life *Housing:* college housing not available. *Activities and Organizations:* drama/theater group, choral group, Black Student Union, student government. *Campus security:* 24-hour emergency response devices and patrols. *Student Services:* personal/psychological counseling.
Athletics Member NJCAA. *Intercollegiate sports:* baseball M(s), basketball M(s)/W(s), softball W(s). *Intramural sports:* basketball M/W, football M, golf M, softball M/W, tennis M/W, volleyball M/W, weight lifting M/W.
Standardized Tests *Required:* SAT I, ACT, or CPT.
Costs (2001–02) *Tuition:* state resident $1514 full-time, $50 per credit part-time; nonresident $5639 full-time, $188 per credit part-time. *Waivers:* senior citizens and employees or children of employees.
Applying *Options:* early admission. *Application fee:* $30. *Required:* high school transcript. *Application deadline:* rolling (freshmen), rolling (transfers). *Notification:* continuous (freshmen).
Admissions Contact Ms. Margaret Karrh, Director of Enrollment Services, Santa Fe Community College, 3000 Northwest 83rd Street, Gainesville, FL 32606-6200. *Phone:* 352-395-5857. *Fax:* 352-395-4118. *E-mail:* information@santafe.cc.fl.us.

Seminole Community College
Sanford, Florida

- **State and locally supported** 2-year, founded 1966
- **Calendar** semesters
- **Degree** certificates, diplomas, and associate
- **Small-town** 200-acre campus with easy access to Orlando
- **Endowment** $3.5 million

Seminole Community College (continued)
■ **Coed,** 10,556 undergraduate students, 38% full-time, 54% women, 46% men

Undergraduates 3,979 full-time, 6,577 part-time. Students come from 18 states and territories, 3% are from out of state, 11% African American, 2% Asian American or Pacific Islander, 12% Hispanic American, 0.4% Native American, 5% international, 22% transferred in.
Freshmen *Admission:* 1,883 applied, 1,883 admitted, 1,883 enrolled.
Faculty *Total:* 788, 19% full-time, 10% with terminal degrees. *Student/faculty ratio:* 21:1.
Majors Accounting; architectural engineering technology; auto mechanic/technician; banking; business administration; business marketing and marketing management; child care/development; civil engineering technology; computer engineering related; computer engineering technology; computer graphics; computer hardware engineering; computer/information systems security; computer/information technology services administration and management related; computer programming; computer programming related; computer programming (specific applications); computer programming, vendor/product certification; computer science related; computer software and media applications related; computer software engineering; computer systems networking/telecommunications; computer/technical support; construction management; construction technology; criminal justice/law enforcement administration; data entry/microcomputer applications; data entry/microcomputer applications related; data processing technology; data warehousing/mining/database administration; drafting; electrical/electronic engineering technology; emergency medical technology; finance; fire science; industrial technology; information sciences/systems; information technology; interior design; liberal arts and sciences/liberal studies; nursing; paralegal/legal assistant; physical therapy; respiratory therapy; secretarial science; system administration; system/networking/LAN/WAN management; telecommunications; Web/multimedia management/webmaster; Web page, digital/multimedia and information resources design; word processing.
Academic Programs *Special study options:* academic remediation for entering students, accelerated degree program, adult/continuing education programs, advanced placement credit, cooperative education, distance learning, double majors, English as a second language, honors programs, independent study, internships, part-time degree program, services for LD students, study abroad, summer session for credit. *ROTC:* Army (b).
Library Seminole Community College Library plus 1 other with 151,617 titles, 425 serial subscriptions, 7,189 audiovisual materials, an OPAC, a Web page.
Computers on Campus 56 computers available on campus for general student use. A campuswide network can be accessed from off campus. Internet access, online (class) registration, at least one staffed computer lab available.
Student Life *Housing:* college housing not available. *Activities and Organizations:* drama/theater group, student-run newspaper, choral group, Phi Beta Lambda, Phi Theta Kappa, Student Government Association, International Student Organization. *Campus security:* 24-hour emergency response devices and patrols. *Student Services:* personal/psychological counseling.
Athletics Member NJCAA. *Intercollegiate sports:* baseball M(s), basketball M(s)/W(s), softball W(s). *Intramural sports:* basketball M/W, golf M, tennis M/W, volleyball M/W.
Standardized Tests *Required:* SAT I, ACTand Enhanced ACT, ASSET, MARS and New MAPS, or CPT.
Costs (2001–02) *Tuition:* state resident $1258 full-time, $52 per credit hour part-time; nonresident $4657 full-time, $194 per credit hour part-time. *Payment plan:* deferred payment. *Waivers:* senior citizens and employees or children of employees.
Applying *Options:* early admission, deferred entrance. *Required:* high school transcript, minimum 2.0 GPA. *Application deadline:* rolling (freshmen), rolling (transfers). *Notification:* continuous (freshmen).
Admissions Contact Ms. Pamela Palaez, Director of Admissions, Seminole Community College, 100 Weldon Boulevard, Sanford, FL 32773-6199. *Phone:* 407-328-2041. *Fax:* 407-328-2395. *E-mail:* admissions@scc-fl.edu.

SOUTHERN COLLEGE
Orlando, Florida

Admissions Contact Ms. Kristi French, Director of Admissions, Southern College, 5600 Lake Underhill Road, Orlando, FL 32807. *Phone:* 407-273-1000 Ext. 1201. *Fax:* 407-273-0492. *E-mail:* kfrench@southerncollege.org.

SOUTH FLORIDA COMMUNITY COLLEGE
Avon Park, Florida

Admissions Contact Ms. Annie Alexander-Harvey, Dean of Student Services, South Florida Community College, 600 West College Drive, Avon Park, FL 33825-9356. *Phone:* 863-453-6661 Ext. 7104.

SOUTH UNIVERSITY
West Palm Beach, Florida

■ **Proprietary** primarily 2-year, founded 1899
■ **Calendar** quarters
■ **Degrees** associate and bachelor's
■ **Suburban** 1-acre campus with easy access to Miami
■ **Coed**

Faculty *Student/faculty ratio:* 8:1.
Student Life *Campus security:* evening security personnel.
Standardized Tests *Recommended:* SAT I and SAT II or ACT (for admission).
Financial Aid In 2001, 14 Federal Work-Study jobs (averaging $1530).
Applying *Options:* common application, electronic application, early admission, deferred entrance. *Application fee:* $25. *Required:* high school transcript. *Required for some:* letters of recommendation, interview.
Admissions Contact Mr. James W. Keeley III, Director of Admissions, South University, 1760 North Congress Avenue, West Palm Beach, FL 33409. *Phone:* 561-697-9200. *Fax:* 561-697-9944. *E-mail:* socowpb@icanect.net.

SOUTHWEST FLORIDA COLLEGE
Fort Myers, Florida

■ **Independent** 2-year, founded 1940
■ **Calendar** quarters
■ **Degree** diplomas and associate
■ **Urban** campus
■ **Coed**

Student Life *Campus security:* day and evening security guards.
Standardized Tests *Required:* CPAt.
Financial Aid In 2001, 10 Federal Work-Study jobs (averaging $5000).
Applying *Options:* common application. *Recommended:* high school transcript.
Admissions Contact Ms. Carmen King, Senior Admissions Representative, Southwest Florida College, Suite 200, 1685 Medical Lane, Fort Myers, FL 33907. *Phone:* 941-939-4766.

TALLAHASSEE COMMUNITY COLLEGE
Tallahassee, Florida

■ **State and locally supported** 2-year, founded 1966, part of Florida Community College System
■ **Calendar** semesters
■ **Degree** certificates and associate
■ **Suburban** 191-acre campus
■ **Coed,** 11,606 undergraduate students, 46% full-time, 53% women, 47% men

Undergraduates 5,377 full-time, 6,229 part-time. Students come from 32 states and territories, 75 other countries, 10% are from out of state, 31% African American, 1% Asian American or Pacific Islander, 0.5% Native American, 1% international, 31% transferred in.
Freshmen *Admission:* 2,063 applied, 1,298 admitted, 1,708 enrolled.
Faculty *Total:* 467, 31% full-time, 23% with terminal degrees. *Student/faculty ratio:* 46:1.
Majors Accounting technician; business administration; business marketing and marketing management; business systems networking/ telecommunications; civil engineering technology; computer graphics; computer/information sciences; computer programming; computer programming (specific applications); construction technology; criminal justice/law enforcement administration; data processing technology; dental hygiene; early childhood education; emergency medical technology; engineering; film studies; finance; legal administrative assistant;

liberal arts and sciences/liberal studies; management information systems/business data processing; medical records technology; nursing; paralegal/legal assistant; public administration; recreation/leisure studies; respiratory therapy; secretarial science; system/networking/LAN/WAN management; word processing.

Academic Programs *Special study options:* academic remediation for entering students, accelerated degree program, adult/continuing education programs, advanced placement credit, distance learning, English as a second language, external degree program, honors programs, independent study, off-campus study, part-time degree program, services for LD students, study abroad, summer session for credit. *ROTC:* Army (c), Air Force (c).

Library Tallahassee Community College Library with 84,415 titles, 1,073 serial subscriptions, an OPAC.

Computers on Campus 170 computers available on campus for general student use. A campuswide network can be accessed from off campus. At least one staffed computer lab available.

Student Life *Housing:* college housing not available. *Activities and Organizations:* drama/theater group, student-run newspaper, choral group, Phi Theta Kappa, student government, International Student Organization, Black Student Union, Returning Adults Valuing Education. *Campus security:* 24-hour emergency response devices, late-night transport/escort service. *Student Services:* personal/psychological counseling.

Athletics Member NJCAA. *Intercollegiate sports:* baseball M(s), basketball M(s)/W(s), softball W(s). *Intramural sports:* basketball M/W, bowling M/W, cross-country running M/W, football M/W, golf M/W, racquetball M/W, soccer M/W, softball M/W, swimming M/W, table tennis M/W, tennis M/W, track and field M/W, volleyball M/W, weight lifting M/W.

Standardized Tests *Required:* Florida College Entry-Level Placement Test. *Recommended:* SAT I or ACT (for placement).

Costs (2001–02) *Tuition:* state resident $1320 full-time, $50 per credit part-time; nonresident $4882 full-time, $187 per credit part-time. Full-time tuition and fees vary according to course load. Part-time tuition and fees vary according to course load. *Required fees:* $20 full-time, $10 per term part-time. *Waivers:* employees or children of employees.

Applying *Options:* electronic application, early admission, deferred entrance. *Required:* high school transcript. *Application deadlines:* 8/1 (freshmen), 8/1 (transfers).

Admissions Contact Ms. Sharon Jefferson, Director of Enrollment Services, Tallahassee Community College, 444 Appleyard Drive, Tallahassee, FL 32304-2895. *Phone:* 850-201-8555. *Fax:* 850-201-8474. *E-mail:* enroll@mail.tallahassee.cc.fl.us.

Valencia Community College
Orlando, Florida

- **State-supported** 2-year, founded 1967, part of Florida Community College System
- **Calendar** semesters
- **Degree** certificates and associate
- **Urban** campus
- **Endowment** $14.4 million
- **Coed**

Faculty *Student/faculty ratio:* 21:1.

Student Life *Campus security:* 24-hour emergency response devices and patrols, student patrols, late-night transport/escort service.

Standardized Tests *Required:* SAT I, ACT, or CPT.

Financial Aid In 2001, 449 Federal Work-Study jobs (averaging $1467).

Applying *Options:* early admission. *Application fee:* $25. *Required:* high school transcript.

Admissions Contact Mr. Charles H. Drosin, Director of Admissions and Records, Valencia Community College, PO Box 3028, Orlando, FL 32802-3028. *Phone:* 407-299-5000 Ext. 1506.

Webster College
Holiday, Florida

- **Proprietary** primarily 2-year
- **Degrees** diplomas, associate, and bachelor's
- 250 undergraduate students
- 100% of applicants were admitted

Freshmen *Admission:* 58 applied, 58 admitted.

Faculty *Total:* 18, 33% full-time, 11% with terminal degrees. *Student/faculty ratio:* 12:1.

Majors Accounting; business administration; computer science; legal studies; medical assistant; travel/tourism management.

Computers on Campus 60 computers available on campus for general student use. At least one staffed computer lab available.

Costs (2002–03) *Tuition:* $3195 per term part-time.

Applying *Required:* high school transcript, minimum 2.0 GPA, interview. *Required for some:* essay or personal statement. *Application deadline:* rolling (freshmen), rolling (transfers).

Admissions Contact Ms. Susan L. Van Hoose, Senior Admissions Representative, Webster College, 2127 Grand Boulevard, Holiday, FL 34690. *Phone:* 727-942-0069. *Toll-free phone:* 888-729-7247. *Fax:* 813-938-5709.

Webster College
Ocala, Florida

- **Proprietary** 2-year, founded 1984
- **Calendar** quarters
- **Degree** diplomas and associate
- **Suburban** 3-acre campus with easy access to Orlando
- **Coed, primarily women,** 375 undergraduate students

Undergraduates Students come from 5 states and territories. *Retention:* 65% of 2001 full-time freshmen returned.

Freshmen *Average high school GPA:* 2.6.

Faculty *Total:* 36, 33% full-time.

Majors Accounting; business administration; data processing technology; legal administrative assistant; medical administrative assistant; medical assistant; secretarial science.

Academic Programs *Special study options:* academic remediation for entering students, adult/continuing education programs, part-time degree program, summer session for credit.

Library Webster College Library with 2,400 titles, 32 serial subscriptions.

Computers on Campus 31 computers available on campus for general student use. Internet access, at least one staffed computer lab available.

Student Life *Housing:* college housing not available. *Campus security:* 24-hour emergency response devices, late-night transport/escort service. *Student Services:* personal/psychological counseling.

Costs (2002–03) *Tuition:* $11,400 full-time, $1425 per term part-time.

Applying *Options:* deferred entrance. *Application fee:* $250. *Required:* high school transcript, minimum 2.0 GPA, interview. *Application deadline:* rolling (freshmen), rolling (transfers).

Admissions Contact Admissions Office, Webster College, 1530 SW Third Avenue, Ocala, FL 34474. *Phone:* 352-629-1941.

Webster Institute of Technology
Tampa, Florida

- **Private** 2-year, founded 1978
- **Calendar** quarters
- **Degree** diplomas and associate
- **Urban** 2-acre campus
- **Coed, primarily women,** 150 undergraduate students

Undergraduates Students come from 1 other state, 21% African American, 21% Hispanic American.

Faculty *Total:* 12, 33% full-time, 8% with terminal degrees. *Student/faculty ratio:* 12:1.

Majors Computer science; computer systems analysis; information technology; medical assistant; system/networking/LAN/WAN management; travel/tourism management.

Academic Programs *Special study options:* accelerated degree program, advanced placement credit, internships.

Library Webster Tech Library with 1,680 titles, 8 serial subscriptions, 65 audiovisual materials.

Computers on Campus 60 computers available on campus for general student use. Internet access, at least one staffed computer lab available.

Student Life *Housing:* college housing not available. *Campus security:* 24-hour emergency response devices, evening security guard. *Student Services:* personal/psychological counseling.

Costs (2001–02) *Tuition:* $8625 full-time. *Required fees:* $555 full-time.

Webster Institute of Technology (continued)

Financial Aid In 2001, 5 Federal Work-Study jobs.

Applying *Options:* electronic application. *Required:* interview.

Admissions Contact Todd A. Matthews Sr., Regional Vice President, Webster Institute of Technology, 3910 US Hwy 301 North, Suite 200, Tampa, FL 33619. *Phone:* 813-620-1446. *Toll-free phone:* 888-729-7247. *E-mail:* admissions@websterinstitute.com.

GEORGIA

ABRAHAM BALDWIN AGRICULTURAL COLLEGE
Tifton, Georgia

- **State-supported** 2-year, founded 1933, part of University System of Georgia
- **Calendar** semesters
- **Degree** certificates and associate
- **Small-town** 390-acre campus
- **Coed,** 2,857 undergraduate students

Undergraduates Students come from 13 states and territories, 18 other countries, 28% live on campus.

Freshmen *Average high school GPA:* 2.8.

Faculty *Total:* 96. *Student/faculty ratio:* 25:1.

Majors Accounting; agricultural business; agricultural economics; agricultural mechanization; agricultural sciences; animal sciences; architectural environmental design; art; biological/physical sciences; biology; business administration; business marketing and marketing management; chemistry; child care/development; computer engineering technology; computer programming; computer science; computer typography/composition; criminal justice/law enforcement administration; data processing technology; early childhood education; ecology; education; elementary education; English; farm/ranch management; fashion merchandising; fish/game management; forest harvesting production technology; forestry; history; home economics; horticulture science; hospitality management; humanities; journalism; landscaping management; law enforcement/police science; liberal arts and sciences/liberal studies; mathematics; music; nursing; ornamental horticulture; pharmacy; physical education; physical sciences; political science; poultry science; pre-engineering; psychology; recreation/leisure facilities management; secretarial science; social sciences; social work; sociology; speech/rhetorical studies; wildlife management.

Academic Programs *Special study options:* academic remediation for entering students, adult/continuing education programs, advanced placement credit, English as a second language, honors programs, internships, off-campus study, part-time degree program, services for LD students, summer session for credit.

Library Baldwin Library with 69,986 titles, 431 serial subscriptions.

Computers on Campus 158 computers available on campus for general student use. Internet access, at least one staffed computer lab available.

Student Life *Housing:* on-campus residence required for freshman year. *Options:* coed. *Activities and Organizations:* drama/theater group, student-run newspaper, radio station, choral group, Rodeo Club, Baptist Student Union, Forestry/Wildlife Club. *Campus security:* 24-hour emergency response devices and patrols, late-night transport/escort service. *Student Services:* health clinic, personal/psychological counseling.

Athletics Member NJCAA. *Intercollegiate sports:* baseball M(s), basketball M(s), softball W(s), tennis M(s)/W(s), volleyball W(s). *Intramural sports:* basketball M/W, bowling M/W, football M/W, golf M/W, soccer M/W, softball M/W, tennis M/W, volleyball M/W.

Standardized Tests *Required:* SAT I or ACT (for placement).

Costs (2001–02) *Tuition:* state resident $1234 full-time, $53 per semester hour part-time; nonresident $4936 full-time, $213 per semester hour part-time. Part-time tuition and fees vary according to course load. *Required fees:* $384 full-time, $192 per term part-time. *Room and board:* $3308. Room and board charges vary according to board plan and housing facility. *Waivers:* senior citizens and employees or children of employees.

Applying *Options:* common application, early admission, deferred entrance. *Application fee:* $5. *Required:* high school transcript. *Application deadline:* 9/24 (freshmen).

Admissions Contact Mr. Garth L. Webb Jr., Director of Admissions, Abraham Baldwin Agricultural College, 2802 Moore Highway, Tifton, GA 31794-2601. *Phone:* 229-386-3230. *Toll-free phone:* 800-733-3653. *Fax:* 912-386-7006.

ANDREW COLLEGE
Cuthbert, Georgia

- **Independent United Methodist** 2-year, founded 1854
- **Calendar** semesters
- **Degree** certificates and associate
- **Small-town** 40-acre campus
- **Endowment** $7.0 million
- **Coed,** 379 undergraduate students

Undergraduates Students come from 8 states and territories, 10 other countries, 74% live on campus.

Faculty *Total:* 36, 56% full-time. *Student/faculty ratio:* 12:1.

Majors Agricultural sciences; art; biological/physical sciences; biology; business administration; business education; chemistry; dental hygiene; divinity/ministry; education; English; forestry; health education; history; humanities; journalism; literature; mass communications; mathematics; medical technology; music; natural sciences; nursing; occupational therapy; philosophy; photography; physical education; physical therapy; physics; pre-engineering; pre-pharmacy studies; psychology; religious studies; respiratory therapy; social sciences; social work; sociology; speech/rhetorical studies; theater arts/drama.

Academic Programs *Special study options:* academic remediation for entering students, advanced placement credit, English as a second language, honors programs, part-time degree program, services for LD students, summer session for credit.

Library Pitts Library with 40,000 titles, 100 serial subscriptions.

Computers on Campus 50 computers available on campus for general student use. A campuswide network can be accessed from student residence rooms and from off campus. Internet access, online (class) registration, at least one staffed computer lab available.

Student Life *Housing:* on-campus residence required through sophomore year. *Options:* coed. *Activities and Organizations:* drama/theater group, student-run newspaper, choral group, Drama Club, Outdoor Club, International Club, BYU. *Campus security:* controlled dormitory access, night patrols by trained security personnel. *Student Services:* health clinic, personal/psychological counseling.

Athletics Member NJCAA. *Intercollegiate sports:* baseball M(s), cross-country running M(s)/W(s), soccer M(s)/W(s), softball W(s), tennis M(s)/W(s). *Intramural sports:* archery M/W, badminton M/W, basketball M/W, equestrian sports M/W, fencing M/W, football M, golf M, racquetball M/W, skiing (downhill) M/W, soccer M/W, softball M/W, swimming M/W, table tennis M/W, tennis M/W, volleyball M/W, weight lifting M/W, wrestling M.

Standardized Tests *Required:* SAT I or ACT (for admission).

Costs (2002–03) *Comprehensive fee:* $12,480 includes full-time tuition ($7620) and room and board ($4860). Part-time tuition: $345 per credit hour. *Payment plan:* installment. *Waivers:* employees or children of employees.

Financial Aid In 2001, 119 Federal Work-Study jobs (averaging $772).

Applying *Options:* early admission, deferred entrance. *Application fee:* $20. *Required:* high school transcript. *Required for some:* essay or personal statement, 1 letter of recommendation, interview. *Recommended:* minimum 2.0 GPA. *Application deadlines:* 8/15 (freshmen), 8/15 (transfers).

Admissions Contact Mr. Brad Parrish, Director of Admission and Financial Aid, Andrew College, 413 College Street, Cuthbert, GA 31740. *Phone:* 229-732-5934. *Fax:* 229-732-2176. *E-mail:* admissions@andrewcollege.edu.

THE ART INSTITUTE OF ATLANTA
Atlanta, Georgia

- **Proprietary** primarily 2-year, founded 1949, part of The Art Institutes
- **Calendar** quarters
- **Degrees** associate and bachelor's
- **Urban** 1-acre campus
- **Coed,** 2,437 undergraduate students, 87% full-time, 48% women, 52% men

Undergraduates 2,132 full-time, 305 part-time. Students come from 39 states and territories, 43 other countries, 20% are from out of state, 30% African American, 4% Asian American or Pacific Islander, 3% Hispanic American, 0.5% Native American, 4% international, 13% live on campus.

Freshmen *Admission:* 421 enrolled.

Faculty *Total:* 146, 49% full-time. *Student/faculty ratio:* 23:1.

Majors Computer graphics; culinary arts; film/video production; graphic design/commercial art/illustration; graphic/printing equipment related; interior design; multimedia; photography.

Academic Programs *Special study options:* academic remediation for entering students, adult/continuing education programs, advanced placement credit, dis-

tance learning, independent study, internships, part-time degree program, services for LD students, study abroad, summer session for credit.

Library Library with 35,872 titles, 157 serial subscriptions, 2,548 audiovisual materials, an OPAC.

Computers on Campus 282 computers available on campus for general student use. Internet access, at least one staffed computer lab available.

Student Life *Housing Options:* coed. *Activities and Organizations:* student-run newspaper, AIM (Artists in Motion), AIGA (American Institute of Graphic Artists, student chapter), The Marquee, student newspaper, ASID (American Society of Interior Designers, student chapter), SAA (Student Advisory Assembly). *Campus security:* 24-hour patrols, late-night transport/escort service, controlled dormitory access. *Student Services:* personal/psychological counseling.

Athletics *Intramural sports:* basketball M, football M/W.

Costs (2001–02) *One-time required fee:* $590. *Tuition:* $14,544 full-time, $303 per credit part-time. Full-time tuition and fees vary according to course load and program. Part-time tuition and fees vary according to course load and program. No tuition increase for student's term of enrollment. *Room only:* $5490. Room and board charges vary according to housing facility. *Payment plans:* installment, deferred payment. *Waivers:* employees or children of employees.

Financial Aid In 2001, 35 Federal Work-Study jobs (averaging $3000).

Applying *Options:* electronic application, early admission, deferred entrance. *Application fee:* $50. *Required:* essay or personal statement, minimum 2.0 GPA, interview. *Required for some:* high school transcript. *Application deadlines:* 9/29 (freshmen), 9/29 (transfers). *Notification:* continuous (freshmen).

Admissions Contact Dr. John Dietrich, Director of Admissions, The Art Institute of Atlanta, 6600 Peachtree Dunwoody Road, 100 Embassy Row, Atlanta, GA 30328. *Phone:* 770-394-8300. *Toll-free phone:* 800-275-4242. *Fax:* 770-394-0008. *E-mail:* aiaadm@aii.edu.

ASHER SCHOOL OF BUSINESS

Norcross, Georgia

Admissions Contact 4975 Jimmy Carter Boulevard, Suite 600, Norcross, GA 30093.

ASHWORTH COLLEGE

Norcross, Georgia

Admissions Contact 430 Technology Parkway, Norcross, GA 30092. *Toll-free phone:* 800-223-4542.

ATHENS TECHNICAL COLLEGE

Athens, Georgia

- **State-supported** 2-year, founded 1958, part of Georgia Department of Technical and Adult Education
- **Calendar** quarters
- **Degree** certificates, diplomas, and associate
- **Suburban** 41-acre campus with easy access to Atlanta
- **Coed,** 3,200 undergraduate students

Undergraduates Students come from 2 states and territories.

Faculty *Total:* 190, 37% full-time. *Student/faculty ratio:* 20:1.

Majors Accounting; auto mechanic/technician; biological technology; business machine repair; business marketing and marketing management; child care/development; communication equipment technology; computer programming; cosmetology; dental hygiene; drafting; electrical/electronic engineering technology; electromechanical technology; engineering technology; heating/air conditioning/refrigeration; industrial radiologic technology; machine technology; medical administrative assistant; medical assistant; medical laboratory technology; medical technology; nursing; paralegal/legal assistant; physical therapy; practical nurse; respiratory therapy; secretarial science; teacher assistant/aide.

Academic Programs *Special study options:* academic remediation for entering students, adult/continuing education programs, internships, part-time degree program, services for LD students, summer session for credit.

Library 25,000 titles, 350 serial subscriptions.

Computers on Campus 277 computers available on campus for general student use. Internet access, online (class) registration, at least one staffed computer lab available.

Student Life *Housing:* college housing not available. *Activities and Organizations:* Athens Technical Student Advisory Council, Phi Theta Kappa, Delta Epsilon Chi, Radiological Technology Society, Organized Black Students Encouraging Unity and Excellence. *Campus security:* 24-hour patrols. *Student Services:* personal/psychological counseling.

Standardized Tests *Required for some:* SAT I or ACT (for admission).

Costs (2002–03) *Tuition:* state resident $1041 full-time, $26 per quarter hour part-time; nonresident $2082 full-time, $52 per quarter hour part-time. *Required fees:* $176 full-time, $44 per term part-time.

Financial Aid In 2001, 34 Federal Work-Study jobs (averaging $3090).

Applying *Options:* early admission. *Required:* high school transcript. *Application deadline:* rolling (freshmen). *Notification:* continuous (freshmen).

Admissions Contact Mr. Lenzy Reid, Director of Admissions, Athens Technical College, 800 US Highway 29 North, Athens, GA 30601-1500. *Phone:* 706-355-5008. *Fax:* 706-369-5753.

ATLANTA METROPOLITAN COLLEGE

Atlanta, Georgia

- **State-supported** 2-year, founded 1974, part of University System of Georgia
- **Calendar** semesters
- **Degree** certificates and associate
- **Urban** 83-acre campus
- **Coed,** 1,917 undergraduate students, 41% full-time, 66% women, 34% men

Undergraduates 777 full-time, 1,140 part-time. Students come from 31 states and territories, 43 other countries, 7% are from out of state, 8% transferred in.

Freshmen *Admission:* 1,628 applied, 614 admitted, 463 enrolled. *Test scores:* SAT verbal scores over 500: 15%; SAT math scores over 500: 12%; SAT verbal scores over 600: 2%; SAT math scores over 600: 2%.

Faculty *Total:* 84, 57% full-time, 36% with terminal degrees. *Student/faculty ratio:* 23:1.

Majors Accounting; art; aviation technology; biology; business; business administration; business education; chemistry; computer/information sciences; computer/information technology services administration and management related; computer programming; computer science; criminal justice/corrections related; criminal justice/law enforcement administration; criminal justice studies; dental assistant; dental laboratory technician; drafting; early childhood education; education; engineering technology; English; foreign languages/literatures; health/physical education; history; human services; industrial arts education; legal administrative assistant; mathematics; medical assistant; medical laboratory technician; music; parks, recreation, leisure and fitness studies related; physics; political science; practical nurse; pre-engineering; psychology; recreation/leisure studies; secretarial science; social work; sociology; speech/rhetorical studies.

Academic Programs *Special study options:* academic remediation for entering students, adult/continuing education programs, cooperative education, distance learning, internships, part-time degree program, study abroad, summer session for credit.

Library Atlanta Metropolitan College Library with 45,526 titles, an OPAC, a Web page.

Computers on Campus 150 computers available on campus for general student use. A campuswide network can be accessed from off campus. Internet access, at least one staffed computer lab available.

Student Life *Housing:* college housing not available. *Activities and Organizations:* drama/theater group, student-run newspaper, choral group, International Students Club, Choir, Writing Club, Peer Student Health Educators Club, Psychology Club. *Campus security:* 24-hour emergency response devices and patrols. *Student Services:* personal/psychological counseling.

Athletics Member NJCAA. *Intercollegiate sports:* basketball M(s)/W(s).

Standardized Tests *Required:* SAT I or ACT (for admission).

Costs (2002–03) *One-time required fee:* $85. *Tuition:* state resident $1280 full-time, $53 per credit hour part-time; nonresident $5120 full-time, $213 per credit hour part-time. *Required fees:* $170 full-time, $85 per term part-time. *Waivers:* employees or children of employees.

Applying *Options:* early admission, deferred entrance. *Application fee:* $20. *Required:* high school transcript, minimum 1.9 GPA. *Application deadlines:* 7/24 (freshmen), 7/24 (transfers). *Notification:* continuous until 8/15 (freshmen).

Admissions Contact Ms. Joanne Crump, Director, Office of Admissions, Atlanta Metropolitan College, 1630 Metropolitan Parkway, Atlanta, GA 30310-4498. *Phone:* 404-756-4004 Ext. 5687. *Fax:* 404-756-4407. *E-mail:* admissions@amcmail.atlm.peachnet.edu.

ATLANTA TECHNICAL COLLEGE

Atlanta, Georgia

Admissions Contact 1560 Metropolitan Parkway, Atlanta, GA 30310.

AUGUSTA TECHNICAL COLLEGE
Augusta, Georgia

- **State-supported** 2-year, founded 1961, part of Georgia Department of Technical and Adult Education
- **Calendar** quarters
- **Degree** certificates, diplomas, and associate
- **Urban** 70-acre campus
- **Coed,** 3,711 undergraduate students, 52% full-time, 59% women, 41% men

Undergraduates Students come from 2 states and territories.
Faculty *Total:* 327, 39% full-time.
Majors Accounting; business marketing and marketing management; child care/development; computer programming; electrical/electronic engineering technology; emergency medical technology; information sciences/systems; mechanical engineering technology; respiratory therapy; secretarial science.
Academic Programs *Special study options:* academic remediation for entering students, advanced placement credit, cooperative education, distance learning, English as a second language, internships, part-time degree program, services for LD students, summer session for credit.
Library Information Technology Center with 84,220 titles, 2,031 serial subscriptions.
Computers on Campus 339 computers available on campus for general student use. A campuswide network can be accessed from off campus. Internet access, at least one staffed computer lab available.
Student Life *Housing:* college housing not available. *Activities and Organizations:* VICA, student activities, professional organizations. *Campus security:* 24-hour emergency response devices, 12-hour patrols by trained security personnel.
Athletics Member NJCAA. *Intercollegiate sports:* golf M.
Costs (2002–03) *Tuition:* state resident $25 per quarter hour part-time; nonresident $52 per quarter hour part-time. Full-time tuition and fees vary according to course load. Part-time tuition and fees vary according to course load. *Waivers:* senior citizens and employees or children of employees.
Applying *Options:* early admission, deferred entrance. *Application fee:* $15. *Required:* high school transcript. *Application deadline:* rolling (freshmen), rolling (transfers). *Notification:* continuous (freshmen).
Admissions Contact Mr. Brian Roberts, Director of Admissions and Counseling, Augusta Technical College, 3116 Deans Bridge Road, Augusta, GA 30904. *Phone:* 706-771-4031. *Fax:* 706-771-4034. *E-mail:* bcrobert@augusta.tec.ga.us.

BAINBRIDGE COLLEGE
Bainbridge, Georgia

- **State-supported** 2-year, founded 1972, part of University System of Georgia
- **Calendar** semesters
- **Degree** certificates and associate
- **Small-town** 160-acre campus
- **Coed,** 1,736 undergraduate students

Undergraduates Students come from 3 states and territories, 1% are from out of state.
Freshmen *Average high school GPA:* 2.72.
Faculty *Total:* 67, 51% full-time.
Majors Accounting; agricultural sciences; art; auto mechanic/technician; biology; business administration; business education; business marketing and marketing management; chemistry; criminal justice/law enforcement administration; data processing technology; drafting; early childhood education; education; electrical/electronic engineering technology; elementary education; English; forestry; health education; history; home economics; information sciences/systems; journalism; liberal arts and sciences/liberal studies; mathematics; nursing; political science; practical nurse; psychology; secretarial science; sociology; speech/rhetorical studies; theater arts/drama; welding technology.
Academic Programs *Special study options:* academic remediation for entering students, adult/continuing education programs, advanced placement credit, distance learning, part-time degree program, services for LD students, summer session for credit.
Library Bainbridge College Library with 35,187 titles, 668 serial subscriptions, an OPAC.
Computers on Campus 215 computers available on campus for general student use. Internet access, online (class) registration, at least one staffed computer lab available.
Student Life *Housing:* college housing not available. *Activities and Organizations:* drama/theater group, Phi Theta Kappa, Alpha Beta Gamma, Drama Club, Delta Club, Sigma Kappa Delta. *Campus security:* 24-hour patrols.
Athletics *Intramural sports:* table tennis M/W, volleyball M/W.
Standardized Tests *Required for some:* SAT I or ACT (for admission).
Costs (2001–02) *Tuition:* state resident $1404 full-time; nonresident $5244 full-time. Part-time tuition and fees vary according to course load. *Waivers:* senior citizens.
Applying *Options:* early admission, deferred entrance. *Application deadlines:* 8/1 (freshmen), 8/1 (transfers). *Notification:* continuous (freshmen).
Admissions Contact Bainbridge College, 2500 East Shotwell Street, Bainbridge 31717. *Phone:* 229-248-2504. *Fax:* 229-248-2525. *E-mail:* csnyder@catfish.bbc.peachnet.edu.

BAUDER COLLEGE
Atlanta, Georgia

- **Proprietary** 2-year, founded 1964
- **Calendar** quarters
- **Degree** associate
- **Suburban** campus
- **Coed, primarily women,** 715 undergraduate students

Undergraduates 56% African American, 2% Asian American or Pacific Islander, 2% Hispanic American, 0.4% Native American, 2% international.
Freshmen *Admission:* 600 applied, 300 admitted.
Faculty *Total:* 75, 69% full-time.
Majors Business administration; fashion design/illustration; fashion merchandising; information technology; interior design.
Academic Programs *Special study options:* academic remediation for entering students, internships, summer session for credit.
Library 4,000 titles, 65 serial subscriptions.
Computers on Campus 50 computers available on campus for general student use. Internet access, at least one staffed computer lab available.
Student Life *Activities and Organizations:* drama/theater group, student-run newspaper. *Campus security:* 24-hour emergency response devices and patrols. *Student Services:* personal/psychological counseling.
Costs (2001–02) *Tuition:* $9930 full-time, $200 per credit hour part-time. Full-time tuition and fees vary according to program. *Required fees:* $350 full-time. *Room only:* $3900. *Payment plans:* tuition prepayment, installment, deferred payment. *Waivers:* employees or children of employees.
Applying *Options:* electronic application. *Required:* essay or personal statement, high school transcript, 2 letters of recommendation, interview. *Application deadline:* rolling (freshmen), rolling (transfers). *Notification:* continuous (freshmen).
Admissions Contact Ms. Lillie Lanier, Admissions Representative, Bauder College, Phipps Plaza, 3500 Peachtree Road NE, Atlanta, GA 30326. *Phone:* 404-237-7573. *Toll-free phone:* 404-237-7573 (in-state); 800-241-3797 (out-of-state). *Fax:* 404-237-1642. *E-mail:* admissions@bauder.edu.

CENTRAL GEORGIA TECHNICAL COLLEGE
Macon, Georgia

- **State-supported** 2-year, founded 1966, part of Georgia Department of Technical and Adult Education
- **Calendar** quarters
- **Degree** certificates, diplomas, and associate
- **Suburban** 152-acre campus
- **Coed,** 4,955 undergraduate students, 41% full-time, 54% women, 46% men

Undergraduates 2,038 full-time, 2,917 part-time. Students come from 1 other state, 28% transferred in.
Freshmen *Admission:* 944 enrolled. *Average high school GPA:* 2.50.
Faculty *Total:* 387, 28% full-time, 3% with terminal degrees. *Student/faculty ratio:* 12:1.
Majors Accounting; accounting technician; business administration; child care/guidance; computer management; developmental/child psychology; human resources management; industrial technology; information sciences/systems; medical laboratory technician.
Academic Programs *Special study options:* academic remediation for entering students, cooperative education, distance learning, external degree program, internships, off-campus study, part-time degree program, services for LD students.
Computers on Campus Internet access, at least one staffed computer lab available.

Student Life *Housing:* college housing not available. *Activities and Organizations:* Skills USA/VICA, student government. *Campus security:* 24-hour patrols.
Costs (2002–03) *Tuition:* state resident $1202 full-time, $24 per credit part-time; nonresident $2040 full-time, $48 per credit part-time. Full-time tuition and fees vary according to program. Part-time tuition and fees vary according to program. *Required fees:* $60 full-time, $40 per term part-time. *Waivers:* senior citizens.
Financial Aid In 2001, 100 Federal Work-Study jobs. *Financial aid deadline:* 9/1.
Applying *Application fee:* $15. *Required:* high school transcript. *Application deadline:* 9/10 (freshmen).
Admissions Contact Ms. Amy McDonald, Director of Admissions, Central Georgia Technical College, 3300 Macon Tech Drive, Macon, GA 31206-3628. *Phone:* 912-757-3400. *Fax:* 912-757-3454. *E-mail:* info@macontech.org.

CHATTAHOOCHEE TECHNICAL COLLEGE
Marietta, Georgia

- **State-supported** 2-year, founded 1961, part of Georgia Department of Technical and Adult Education
- **Calendar** quarters
- **Degree** certificates, diplomas, and associate
- **Suburban** campus with easy access to Atlanta
- **Coed,** 5,963 undergraduate students

Faculty *Total:* 173, 34% full-time. *Student/faculty ratio:* 19:1.
Majors Accounting; auto mechanic/technician; biomedical technology; business administration; business marketing and marketing management; child care/development; computer engineering technology; computer programming; computer typography/composition; corrections; data processing technology; electrical/electronic engineering technology; electromechanical technology; law enforcement/police science.
Academic Programs *Special study options:* academic remediation for entering students, internships, part-time degree program, services for LD students, student-designed majors.
Library 10,000 titles, 194 serial subscriptions, a Web page.
Computers on Campus 200 computers available on campus for general student use. At least one staffed computer lab available.
Student Life *Housing:* college housing not available. *Activities and Organizations:* student government, Vocational Industrial Clubs of America, Institute for Electrical and Electronic Engineers, National Technical-Vocational Honor Society, Phi Beta Lambda. *Campus security:* full-time day and evening security. *Student Services:* personal/psychological counseling.
Standardized Tests *Required for some:* ACT ASSET.
Costs (2001–02) *Tuition:* area resident $728 full-time, $26 per credit hour part-time; state resident $1328 full-time, $50 per credit hour part-time; nonresident $2504 full-time, $100 per credit hour part-time. *Required fees:* $52 full-time.
Applying *Options:* early admission, deferred entrance. *Application fee:* $15. *Recommended:* high school transcript. *Application deadline:* rolling (freshmen), rolling (transfers).
Admissions Contact Ms. Nichole Kennedy, Director of the Access Center, Chattahoochee Technical College, 980 South Cobb Drive, Marietta, GA 30060. *Phone:* 770-528-4581. *Fax:* 770-528-4578.

COASTAL GEORGIA COMMUNITY COLLEGE
Brunswick, Georgia

- **State-supported** 2-year, founded 1961, part of University System of Georgia
- **Calendar** semesters
- **Degree** certificates and associate
- **Small-town** 193-acre campus with easy access to Jacksonville
- **Endowment** $78,366
- **Coed,** 2,210 undergraduate students

Undergraduates Students come from 8 states and territories, 14% are from out of state, 23% African American, 1% Asian American or Pacific Islander, 2% Hispanic American, 0.4% Native American.
Freshmen *Admission:* 644 applied, 494 admitted. *Average high school GPA:* 2.30.
Faculty *Total:* 94, 66% full-time.
Majors Agricultural business; art; biology; business administration; chemistry; computer science; criminal justice/law enforcement administration; dental hygiene; education (multiple levels); English; foreign languages/literatures; forestry; geology; health/physical education; history; liberal arts and sciences/liberal studies; mathematics; medical laboratory technician; medical radiologic technology; nursing; occupational therapy; philosophy; physical therapy; physician assistant; physics; political science; pre-dentistry; pre-engineering; pre-medicine; pre-pharmacy studies; pre-veterinary studies; psychology; recreation/leisure facilities management; respiratory therapy; sociology.
Academic Programs *Special study options:* academic remediation for entering students, adult/continuing education programs, advanced placement credit, distance learning, double majors, part-time degree program, services for LD students, study abroad, summer session for credit.
Library Clara Wood Gould Memorial Library with 535 serial subscriptions, 1,151 audiovisual materials, an OPAC.
Computers on Campus 250 computers available on campus for general student use. A campuswide network can be accessed from off campus. Internet access, at least one staffed computer lab available.
Student Life *Housing:* college housing not available. *Activities and Organizations:* student-run newspaper, Association of Nursing Students, Minority Advisement and Social Development Association, Student Government Association, Baptist Student Union, Phi Theta Kappa. *Campus security:* 24-hour patrols, late-night transport/escort service. *Student Services:* personal/psychological counseling.
Athletics Member NJCAA. *Intercollegiate sports:* basketball M(s), softball W(s). *Intramural sports:* basketball M/W, soccer M/W, swimming M/W, tennis M/W, volleyball M/W.
Standardized Tests *Required for some:* SAT I or ACT (for admission), SAT I and SAT II or ACT (for admission), SAT II: Subject Tests (for admission), SAT II: Writing Test (for admission).
Costs (2001–02) *Tuition:* state resident $1280 full-time, $53 per credit part-time; nonresident $5332 full-time, $213 per credit part-time. *Required fees:* $52 per credit. *Waivers:* senior citizens.
Financial Aid In 2001, 80 Federal Work-Study jobs (averaging $1500).
Applying *Options:* common application, electronic application, deferred entrance. *Application fee:* $20. *Required:* high school transcript, minimum 2.0 GPA, immunization records. *Application deadlines:* 8/19 (freshmen), 8/19 (transfers). *Notification:* continuous (freshmen).
Admissions Contact Dr. Mollie DeHart, Director of Admissions/Registrar, Coastal Georgia Community College, 3700 Altama Avenue, Brunswick, GA 31525. *Phone:* 912-264-7253. *Toll-free phone:* 800-675-7235. *Fax:* 912-262-3072. *E-mail:* admiss@bc900.bc.peachnet.edu.

COLUMBUS TECHNICAL COLLEGE
Columbus, Georgia

- **State-supported** 2-year, founded 1961, part of Georgia Department of Technical and Adult Education
- **Calendar** quarters
- **Degree** certificates, diplomas, and associate
- **Urban** campus with easy access to Atlanta
- **Coed,** 3,031 undergraduate students

Undergraduates Students come from 25 states and territories.
Faculty *Total:* 72.
Majors Accounting; computer engineering related; mechanical engineering technology; secretarial science; word processing.
Academic Programs *Special study options:* academic remediation for entering students, accelerated degree program, adult/continuing education programs, advanced placement credit, cooperative education, honors programs, internships, part-time degree program, services for LD students.
Library Columbus Technical College Library with 19,701 titles, 34 serial subscriptions, 559 audiovisual materials.
Computers on Campus 25 computers available on campus for general student use. A campuswide network can be accessed from off campus. Internet access, at least one staffed computer lab available.
Student Life *Housing:* college housing not available. *Campus security:* security patrols during class hours.
Standardized Tests *Required:* SAT I or ACT (for admission).
Costs (2001–02) *Tuition:* state resident $1200 full-time, $25 per credit hour part-time; nonresident $2400 full-time, $50 per credit hour part-time. Full-time tuition and fees vary according to program. Part-time tuition and fees vary according to program. *Required fees:* $75 full-time, $15 per term part-time.
Applying *Options:* common application, early admission. *Application fee:* $15. *Required:* high school transcript. *Required for some:* letters of recommendation, interview. *Notification:* continuous (freshmen).

Columbus Technical College (continued)

Admissions Contact Dr. Pamela Robinson, Director of Admissions and Registrar, Columbus Technical College, 928 Manchester Expressway, Columbus, GA 31904. *Phone:* 706-649-1858. *E-mail:* probinson@columbustech.org.

COOSA VALLEY TECHNICAL INSTITUTE
Rome, Georgia

Admissions Contact One Maurice Culberson Drive, Rome, GA 30161. *Toll-free phone:* 888-331-CVTC.

DARTON COLLEGE
Albany, Georgia

- **State-supported** 2-year, founded 1965, part of University System of Georgia
- **Calendar** semesters
- **Degree** certificates and associate
- **Suburban** 185-acre campus
- **Coed,** 3,185 undergraduate students, 43% full-time, 68% women, 32% men
- 79% of applicants were admitted

Undergraduates 1,365 full-time, 1,820 part-time. Students come from 6 other countries, 4% are from out of state, 37% African American, 1% Asian American or Pacific Islander, 1% Hispanic American, 0.2% Native American, 0.8% international, 7% transferred in.

Freshmen *Admission:* 1,316 applied, 1,044 admitted, 656 enrolled. *Average high school GPA:* 2.70.

Faculty *Total:* 317, 28% full-time. *Student/faculty ratio:* 16:1.

Majors Accounting; agricultural sciences; anthropology; art; biology; business administration; business economics; business education; business marketing and marketing management; chemistry; computer/information sciences; computer management; computer programming; computer science; corrections; criminal justice/law enforcement administration; data processing technology; dental assistant; dental hygiene; early childhood education; economics; education; elementary education; emergency medical technology; engineering technology; English; forestry; general office/clerical; health education; history; journalism; legal administrative assistant; liberal arts and sciences/liberal studies; mathematics; medical administrative assistant; medical assistant; medical laboratory technician; medical laboratory technology; medical radiologic technology; medical records administration; medical records technology; music; nursing; occupational therapy assistant; operating room technician; pharmacy technician/assistant; philosophy; physical education; physical therapy assistant; physics; political science; practical nurse; pre-engineering; psychology; respiratory therapy; secretarial science; social work; sociology; speech/rhetorical studies; theater arts/drama.

Academic Programs *Special study options:* academic remediation for entering students, accelerated degree program, adult/continuing education programs, advanced placement credit, cooperative education, distance learning, double majors, English as a second language, honors programs, independent study, part-time degree program, services for LD students, student-designed majors, study abroad, summer session for credit. *ROTC:* Army (c).

Library Weatherbee Learning Resources Center with 67,507 titles, an OPAC, a Web page.

Computers on Campus A campuswide network can be accessed from off campus. Internet access, online (class) registration, at least one staffed computer lab available.

Student Life *Housing:* college housing not available. *Activities and Organizations:* drama/theater group, student-run newspaper, choral group, Students in Free Enterprise (SIFE), Darton Ambassadors, Alpha Beta Gamma, Darton Association of Nursing Students (DANS), Delta Psi Omega. *Campus security:* 24-hour patrols, student patrols, late-night transport/escort service. *Student Services:* personal/psychological counseling, women's center.

Athletics Member NJCAA. *Intercollegiate sports:* baseball M, basketball W, golf M/W, softball W, swimming M/W, tennis M/W. *Intramural sports:* badminton M/W, basketball M/W, bowling M/W, football M, volleyball M/W.

Standardized Tests *Required for some:* SAT I or ACT (for admission), SAT II: Subject Tests (for admission).

Costs (2001–02) *Tuition:* $53 per semester hour part-time; state resident $1272 full-time; nonresident $5112 full-time, $160 per semester hour part-time. Full-time tuition and fees vary according to course load. Part-time tuition and fees vary according to course load. *Required fees:* $224 full-time, $112 per term part-time. *Payment plan:* deferred payment. *Waivers:* senior citizens and employees or children of employees.

Financial Aid In 2001, 60 Federal Work-Study jobs.

Applying *Options:* common application, electronic application, early admission. *Application fee:* $20. *Required:* high school transcript, minimum 1.8 GPA, proof of immunization. *Application deadlines:* 7/20 (freshmen), 7/20 (transfers). *Notification:* continuous until 7/27 (freshmen).

Admissions Contact Assistant Director, Admissions, Darton College, 2400 Gillionville Road, Albany, GA 31707. *Phone:* 229-430-6740. *Fax:* 229-430-2926. *E-mail:* darton@mail.dartnet.peachnet.edu.

DEKALB TECHNICAL COLLEGE
Clarkston, Georgia

Admissions Contact Ms. Tracey Axelberd, Recruiter/Admissions Specialist, DeKalb Technical College, 495 North Indian Creek Drive, Clarkston, GA 30021-2397. *Phone:* 404-297-9522 Ext. 1602. *Fax:* 404-294-4234. *E-mail:* diane@admin2.dekalb.tec.ga.us.

EAST GEORGIA COLLEGE
Swainsboro, Georgia

- **State-supported** 2-year, founded 1973, part of University System of Georgia
- **Calendar** semesters
- **Degree** associate
- **Rural** 207-acre campus
- **Endowment** $32,500
- **Coed,** 1,393 undergraduate students, 55% full-time, 58% women, 42% men

Undergraduates 763 full-time, 630 part-time. Students come from 12 states and territories, 1% are from out of state, 35% African American, 1% Asian American or Pacific Islander, 2% Hispanic American, 0.4% Native American, 0.4% transferred in.

Freshmen *Admission:* 1,242 applied, 719 admitted, 481 enrolled. *Average high school GPA:* 2.5. *Test scores:* SAT verbal scores over 500: 27%; SAT math scores over 500: 21%; SAT verbal scores over 600: 5%; SAT math scores over 600: 3%; SAT verbal scores over 700: 1%.

Faculty *Total:* 61, 54% full-time, 21% with terminal degrees. *Student/faculty ratio:* 23:1.

Majors Agricultural sciences; anthropology; art; biology; business administration; business education; chemistry; criminal justice/law enforcement administration; education; elementary education; English; geology; health education; history; home economics education; liberal arts and sciences/liberal studies; mathematics; nursing; physical education; political science; psychology; recreation/leisure studies; sociology.

Academic Programs *Special study options:* academic remediation for entering students, adult/continuing education programs, advanced placement credit, part-time degree program, services for LD students, summer session for credit.

Library East Georgia College Library with 43,780 titles, 203 serial subscriptions, an OPAC, a Web page.

Computers on Campus 90 computers available on campus for general student use. A campuswide network can be accessed from off campus. At least one staffed computer lab available.

Student Life *Housing:* college housing not available. *Activities and Organizations:* drama/theater group, student-run newspaper, choral group, Hoopee Bird, student government, yearbook, Gamma Beta Phi, Wiregrass. *Campus security:* 24-hour patrols. *Student Services:* personal/psychological counseling.

Athletics *Intramural sports:* archery M/W, badminton M/W, basketball M/W, football M/W, golf M/W, softball M/W, table tennis M/W, tennis M/W, volleyball M/W, weight lifting M/W.

Standardized Tests *Required:* SAT I or ACT (for admission). *Required for some:* SAT I or ACT (for placement).

Costs (2001–02) *Tuition:* state resident $1376 full-time, $53 per semester hour part-time; nonresident $5216 full-time, $213 per semester hour part-time. Full-time tuition and fees vary according to course load and location. Part-time tuition and fees vary according to course load and location. *Required fees:* $48 full-time, $48 per year part-time. *Waivers:* senior citizens.

Financial Aid In 2001, 47 Federal Work-Study jobs (averaging $1071). 31 State and other part-time jobs.

Applying *Options:* early admission, deferred entrance. *Application fee:* $20. *Required:* high school transcript. *Application deadline:* rolling (freshmen), rolling (transfers). *Notification:* continuous (freshmen).

Admissions Contact Ms. Valerie Bennett, Admissions Specialist, East Georgia College, 131 College Circle, Swainsboro, GA 30401-2699. *Phone:* 478-289-2019. *Fax:* 478-289-2038. *E-mail:* rlosser@mail.ega.peachnet.edu.

EMORY UNIVERSITY, OXFORD COLLEGE
Oxford, Georgia

- **Independent Methodist** 2-year, founded 1836, part of Emory University
- **Calendar** semesters
- **Degree** associate
- **Small-town** 150-acre campus with easy access to Atlanta
- **Endowment** $26.0 million
- **Coed,** 601 undergraduate students, 99% full-time, 58% women, 42% men

Undergraduates 596 full-time, 5 part-time. Students come from 36 states and territories, 7 other countries, 37% are from out of state, 14% African American, 20% Asian American or Pacific Islander, 3% Hispanic American, 0.7% Native American, 2% international, 0.5% transferred in, 95% live on campus. *Retention:* 83% of 2001 full-time freshmen returned.

Freshmen *Admission:* 1,180 applied, 890 admitted, 309 enrolled. *Average high school GPA:* 3.50. *Test scores:* SAT verbal scores over 500: 94%; SAT math scores over 500: 91%; ACT scores over 18: 97%; SAT verbal scores over 600: 50%; SAT math scores over 600: 50%; ACT scores over 24: 62%; SAT verbal scores over 700: 12%; SAT math scores over 700: 13%; ACT scores over 30: 19%.

Faculty *Total:* 55, 84% full-time, 80% with terminal degrees. *Student/faculty ratio:* 12:1.

Majors Liberal arts and sciences/liberal studies.

Academic Programs *Special study options:* advanced placement credit, distance learning, double majors, independent study, internships, services for LD students, student-designed majors, study abroad, summer session for credit.

Library Hoke O'Kelly Library with 51,638 titles, 300 serial subscriptions, 587 audiovisual materials, an OPAC, a Web page.

Computers on Campus 110 computers available on campus for general student use. A campuswide network can be accessed from student residence rooms and from off campus. Internet access, online (class) registration, at least one staffed computer lab available.

Student Life *Housing:* on-campus residence required through sophomore year. *Options:* coed, women-only. *Activities and Organizations:* drama/theater group, student-run newspaper, choral group, Residence Hall Association, intramurals/junior varsity sports, Student Government Association, Student Admissions Association, Volunteer Oxford. *Campus security:* 24-hour emergency response devices and patrols, student patrols, late-night transport/escort service, controlled dormitory access. *Student Services:* health clinic, personal/psychological counseling.

Athletics Member NJCAA. *Intercollegiate sports:* basketball M, soccer W, tennis M/W. *Intramural sports:* badminton M/W, basketball M/W, football M/W, golf M/W, soccer M/W, softball M/W, table tennis M/W, tennis M/W, volleyball M/W, water polo M/W, weight lifting M/W.

Standardized Tests *Required:* SAT I or ACT (for admission). *Required for some:* SAT II: Subject Tests (for admission).

Costs (2002–03) *Comprehensive fee:* $25,832 includes full-time tuition ($19,636), mandatory fees ($220), and room and board ($5976). Part-time tuition: $817 per credit hour. *Room and board:* College room only: $3928. Room and board charges vary according to housing facility. *Payment plans:* tuition prepayment, installment. *Waivers:* employees or children of employees.

Financial Aid In 2001, 225 Federal Work-Study jobs (averaging $1200).

Applying *Options:* common application, electronic application, early admission, deferred entrance. *Application fee:* $40. *Required:* high school transcript, 1 letter of recommendation, level of interest. *Required for some:* interview. *Recommended:* essay or personal statement, minimum 3.0 GPA, 2 letters of recommendation. *Application deadline:* rolling (freshmen), rolling (transfers). *Notification:* continuous (freshmen).

Admissions Contact Ms. Jennifer B. Taylor, Associate Dean of Admission and Financial Aid, Emory University, Oxford College, 100 Hamill Street, PO Box 1418, Oxford, GA 30054. *Phone:* 770-784-8328. *Toll-free phone:* 800-723-8328. *Fax:* 770-784-8359.

FLINT RIVER TECHNICAL COLLEGE
Thomaston, Georgia

Admissions Contact 1533 US highway 19 South, Thomaston, GA 30286. *Toll-free phone:* 800-752-9681.

FLOYD COLLEGE
Rome, Georgia

- **State-supported** 2-year, founded 1970, part of University System of Georgia
- **Calendar** semesters
- **Degree** certificates, diplomas, and associate
- **Small-town** 226-acre campus with easy access to Atlanta
- **Coed,** 2,500 undergraduate students

Undergraduates 14% are from out of state, 11% African American, 1% Asian American or Pacific Islander, 2% Hispanic American, 0.2% Native American.

Freshmen *Average high school GPA:* 2.7.

Faculty *Total:* 250, 34% full-time. *Student/faculty ratio:* 30:1.

Majors Accounting; agricultural sciences; art; auto mechanic/technician; biological/physical sciences; business administration; business marketing and marketing management; computer programming; criminal justice studies; dental hygiene; early childhood education; economics; electrical/electronic engineering technology; emergency medical technology; English; foreign languages/literatures; forestry; geology; history; horticulture science; hotel and restaurant management; human services; information sciences/systems; journalism; law enforcement/police science; liberal arts and sciences/liberal studies; medical technology; nursing; occupational therapy; paralegal/legal assistant; philosophy; physical therapy; physical therapy assistant; physician assistant; political science; psychology; radiological science; respiratory therapy; secondary education; sign language interpretation; sociology.

Academic Programs *Special study options:* academic remediation for entering students, advanced placement credit, cooperative education, distance learning, double majors, freshman honors college, honors programs, independent study, part-time degree program, services for LD students, study abroad, summer session for credit.

Library Floyd College Library plus 1 other with 48,000 titles, 350 serial subscriptions, an OPAC.

Computers on Campus A campuswide network can be accessed from off campus. Internet access, online (class) registration, at least one staffed computer lab available.

Student Life *Housing:* college housing not available. *Activities and Organizations:* student-run newspaper, choral group, Floyd Association of Nursing Students, Health, Physical Education, and Recreation Club, Black Awareness Society, Political Science Association. *Campus security:* 24-hour patrols. *Student Services:* personal/psychological counseling.

Athletics *Intramural sports:* basketball M/W, bowling M/W, football M, golf M/W, sailing M/W, table tennis M/W, tennis M/W, volleyball M/W.

Standardized Tests *Required:* SAT I or ACT (for admission).

Costs (2001–02) *Tuition:* state resident $1280 full-time, $53 per semester hour part-time; nonresident $5120 full-time, $212 per semester hour part-time. Part-time tuition and fees vary according to course load. *Required fees:* $230 full-time, $92 per term part-time. *Waivers:* senior citizens and employees or children of employees.

Financial Aid In 2001, 30 Federal Work-Study jobs (averaging $3500). *Financial aid deadline:* 7/1.

Applying *Options:* common application, electronic application, early admission, deferred entrance. *Application fee:* $20. *Required:* high school transcript, minimum 1.8 GPA. *Application deadline:* rolling (freshmen), rolling (transfers). *Notification:* continuous (freshmen).

Admissions Contact Ms. Renee L. Tumblin, Recruitment Coordinator, Floyd College, PO Box 1864, Rome, GA 30162-1864. *Phone:* 706-295-6339. *Toll-free phone:* 706-295-6339 (in-state); 800-332-2406 Ext. 6339 (out-of-state). *Fax:* 706-295-6610. *E-mail:* admitme@mail.fc.peachnet.edu.

GAINESVILLE COLLEGE
Gainesville, Georgia

Admissions Contact Dr. Susan J. Daniell, Director of Admissions, Gainesville College, PO Box 1358, Gainesville, GA 30503-1358. *Phone:* 770-718-3641. *Fax:* 770-718-3859.

GEORGIA MILITARY COLLEGE
Milledgeville, Georgia

- **State and locally supported** 2-year, founded 1879
- **Calendar** quarters
- **Degree** associate
- **Small-town** 40-acre campus
- **Coed,** 3,465 undergraduate students

Undergraduates Students come from 29 states and territories, 4 other countries.

Freshmen *Admission:* 832 applied, 828 admitted.

Georgia Military College (continued)

Faculty *Total:* 190. *Student/faculty ratio:* 20:1.

Majors Army R.O.T.C./military science; biological/physical sciences; business administration; criminal justice/law enforcement administration; engineering; fire science; liberal arts and sciences/liberal studies; mass communications; nuclear technology; pre-engineering.

Academic Programs *Special study options:* academic remediation for entering students, advanced placement credit, external degree program, off-campus study, part-time degree program, summer session for credit. *ROTC:* Army (b).

Library Sibley-Cone Library with 20,000 titles, 150 serial subscriptions.

Computers on Campus 40 computers available on campus for general student use. At least one staffed computer lab available.

Student Life *Housing:* on-campus residence required through sophomore year. *Options:* coed. *Activities and Organizations:* student-run newspaper, marching band. *Campus security:* 24-hour emergency response devices and patrols. *Student Services:* personal/psychological counseling.

Athletics Member NSCAA. *Intercollegiate sports:* football M(s), riflery M(s)/W(s). *Intramural sports:* basketball M, cross-country running M/W, football M, golf M, soccer M/W, tennis M/W, track and field M/W, volleyball M/W.

Standardized Tests *Required for some:* SAT I or ACT (for admission). *Recommended:* SAT I or ACT (for admission).

Costs (2001–02) *Comprehensive fee:* $14,360 includes full-time tuition ($10,425), mandatory fees ($335), and room and board ($3600). Part-time tuition: $80 per credit hour. *Required fees:* $50 per term part-time.

Financial Aid In 2001, 45 Federal Work-Study jobs (averaging $1034).

Applying *Options:* early admission, deferred entrance. *Application fee:* $25. *Required:* high school transcript. *Application deadline:* rolling (freshmen), rolling (transfers).

Admissions Contact Lt. Col. Thomas Webb, Director of Admissions, Georgia Military College, 201 East Greene Street, Milledgeville, GA 31061-3398. *Phone:* 478-445-2751. *Toll-free phone:* 800-342-0413.

GEORGIA PERIMETER COLLEGE
Decatur, Georgia

- **State-supported** 2-year, founded 1964, part of University System of Georgia
- **Calendar** semesters
- **Degree** certificates and associate
- **Suburban** 100-acre campus with easy access to Atlanta
- **Endowment** $136,686
- **Coed,** 15,372 undergraduate students, 42% full-time, 61% women, 39% men

Undergraduates 6,430 full-time, 8,942 part-time. Students come from 40 states and territories, 125 other countries, 7% are from out of state, 5% transferred in.

Freshmen *Admission:* 2,847 enrolled. *Average high school GPA:* 2.88.

Faculty *Total:* 783, 39% full-time. *Student/faculty ratio:* 19:1.

Majors Accounting; anthropology; applied art; art; auto mechanic/technician; behavioral sciences; biological/physical sciences; broadcast journalism; business administration; business economics; business education; business machine repair; business marketing and marketing management; chemistry; child care/development; computer engineering technology; computer/information technology services administration and management related; computer programming; computer science; data entry/microcomputer applications related; data processing technology; dental assistant; dental hygiene; early childhood education; economics; electrical/electronic engineering technologies related; elementary education; emergency medical technology; engineering; English; fashion merchandising; fire science; foreign languages/literatures related; general office/clerical; general studies; geology; health/physical education; health professions and related sciences; history; hotel and restaurant management; industrial machinery maintenance/repair; journalism; landscaping management; mathematics; mechanical engineering technology; medical assistant; medical laboratory technician; music; nursing; optometric/ophthalmic laboratory technician; philosophy; physical education; physical therapy; physics; political science/government related; pre-dentistry; pre-engineering; pre-medicine; pre-pharmacy studies; psychology; radiological science; retail management; sign language interpretation; system/networking/LAN/WAN management; theater arts/drama; Web page, digital/multimedia and information resources design.

Academic Programs *Special study options:* academic remediation for entering students, adult/continuing education programs, advanced placement credit, distance learning, English as a second language, honors programs, part-time degree program, services for LD students, study abroad, summer session for credit. *ROTC:* Army (c).

Library Georgia Perimeter College Library with 369,969 titles, 2,032 serial subscriptions, 15,500 audiovisual materials, an OPAC.

Computers on Campus A campuswide network can be accessed from off campus. At least one staffed computer lab available.

Student Life *Housing:* college housing not available. *Activities and Organizations:* drama/theater group, student-run newspaper, choral group. *Campus security:* 24-hour emergency response devices and patrols, late-night transport/escort service. *Student Services:* personal/psychological counseling.

Athletics Member NJCAA. *Intercollegiate sports:* baseball M(s), basketball M(s)/W(s), soccer M(s)/W(s), softball W(s), tennis M(s)/W(s). *Intramural sports:* basketball M.

Standardized Tests *Required:* SAT I or ACT (for admission). *Required for some:* SAT II: Subject Tests (for admission).

Costs (2002–03) *Tuition:* state resident $1280 full-time, $53 per credit hour part-time; nonresident $5120 full-time, $213 per credit hour part-time. Full-time tuition and fees vary according to course load. Part-time tuition and fees vary according to course load. *Required fees:* $230 full-time, $115 per term part-time. *Waivers:* senior citizens.

Applying *Options:* early admission. *Application fee:* $20. *Required:* high school transcript. *Application deadlines:* 7/1 (freshmen), 7/1 (transfers). *Notification:* continuous (freshmen).

Admissions Contact Georgia Perimeter College, 555 North Indian Creek Drive, Clarkston, GA 30021-2396. *Phone:* 404-299-4550. *Toll-free phone:* 888-696-2780. *Fax:* 404-299-4574.

GORDON COLLEGE
Barnesville, Georgia

- **State-supported** 2-year, founded 1852, part of University System of Georgia
- **Calendar** semesters
- **Degree** certificates and associate
- **Small-town** 125-acre campus with easy access to Atlanta
- **Endowment** $4.5 million
- **Coed,** 3,074 undergraduate students

Undergraduates Students come from 12 other countries, 23% African American, 2% Asian American or Pacific Islander, 2% Hispanic American, 0.3% Native American, 20% live on campus.

Freshmen *Admission:* 6,390 admitted. *Average high school GPA:* 2.55. *Test scores:* SAT verbal scores over 500: 33%; SAT math scores over 500: 30%; SAT verbal scores over 600: 6%; SAT math scores over 600: 6%; SAT verbal scores over 700: 1%; SAT math scores over 700: 1%.

Faculty *Total:* 139, 53% full-time. *Student/faculty ratio:* 25:1.

Majors Agricultural sciences; art; behavioral sciences; biological/physical sciences; biology; business administration; computer science; computer science related; education; English; general studies; history; information technology; journalism; mathematics; nursing; physical sciences; political science; practical nurse; psychology; recreation/leisure studies; secretarial science; sociology; Spanish; theater arts/drama.

Academic Programs *Special study options:* academic remediation for entering students, adult/continuing education programs, advanced placement credit, cooperative education, honors programs, off-campus study, part-time degree program, services for LD students, summer session for credit.

Library Hightower Library with 118,000 titles, 219 serial subscriptions, an OPAC.

Computers on Campus 75 computers available on campus for general student use. A campuswide network can be accessed from student residence rooms and from off campus. At least one staffed computer lab available.

Student Life *Housing Options:* coed. *Activities and Organizations:* drama/theater group, choral group, Explorers, Minority Advisement Program, Georgia Association of Nursing Students, Baptist Student Union, Phi Beta Lambda. *Campus security:* 24-hour patrols, late-night transport/escort service. *Student Services:* personal/psychological counseling.

Athletics Member NJCAA. *Intercollegiate sports:* baseball M(s), soccer M(s), softball W(s), tennis W(s). *Intramural sports:* badminton M/W, basketball M/W, football M/W, golf M/W, racquetball M/W, soccer M/W, softball M/W, table tennis M/W, tennis M/W, volleyball M/W.

Standardized Tests *Required:* SAT I or ACT (for admission), SAT I or ACT (for placement).

Costs (2002–03) *Tuition:* $86 per credit part-time; state resident $1512 full-time, $86 per credit part-time; nonresident $5508 full-time, $252 per credit part-time. *Required fees:* $90 part-time.

Financial Aid In 2001, 75 Federal Work-Study jobs (averaging $1850).

Applying *Options:* electronic application, early admission, deferred entrance. *Required:* high school transcript, minimum 1.8 GPA. *Application deadline:* rolling (freshmen), rolling (transfers).

Admissions Contact Terry Betkowski, Acting Director of Enrollment Services, Gordon College, 419 College Drive, Barnesville, GA 30204-1762. *Phone:* 770-358-5354. *Toll-free phone:* 800-282-6504. *Fax:* 770-358-3031. *E-mail:* gordon@eagle.gdn.peachnet.edu.

GRIFFIN TECHNICAL COLLEGE
Griffin, Georgia

- **State-supported** 2-year, founded 1965, part of Department of Technical and Adult Education
- **Calendar** quarters
- **Degree** certificates and associate
- **Small-town** 10-acre campus with easy access to Atlanta
- **Coed,** 4,383 undergraduate students

Faculty *Total:* 110, 41% full-time.
Majors Accounting; computer programming; industrial radiologic technology; industrial technology; law enforcement/police science; secretarial science.
Academic Programs *Special study options:* part-time degree program.
Library 7,500 titles, an OPAC.
Computers on Campus 80 computers available on campus for general student use. Internet access, at least one staffed computer lab available.
Student Life *Housing:* college housing not available. *Activities and Organizations:* student-run newspaper, Phi Beta Lambda, Vocational Industrial Clubs of America, student government.
Costs (2001–02) *Tuition:* state resident $661 full-time, $24 per credit hour part-time; nonresident $1324 full-time, $48 per credit hour part-time. Full-time tuition and fees vary according to course load.
Applying *Options:* early admission. *Required:* high school transcript.
Admissions Contact Ms. Christine James-Brown, Vice President of Student Services, Griffin Technical College, 501 Varsity Road, Griffin, GA 30223. *Phone:* 770-228-7371.

GUPTON-JONES COLLEGE OF FUNERAL SERVICE
Decatur, Georgia

- **Independent** 2-year, founded 1920, part of Pierce Mortuary Colleges, Inc
- **Calendar** quarters
- **Degree** associate
- **Suburban** 3-acre campus with easy access to Atlanta
- **Coed,** 250 undergraduate students

Undergraduates Students come from 14 states and territories, 2 other countries, 60% are from out of state.
Faculty *Total:* 9, 89% full-time. *Student/faculty ratio:* 30:1.
Majors Mortuary science.
Academic Programs *Special study options:* academic remediation for entering students, summer session for credit.
Library Russell Millison Library with 3,500 titles, 15 serial subscriptions.
Computers on Campus 5 computers available on campus for general student use. Internet access, at least one staffed computer lab available.
Student Life *Housing:* college housing not available. *Activities and Organizations:* national fraternities.
Applying *Options:* common application. *Application fee:* $25. *Required:* high school transcript, health certificate. *Recommended:* minimum 3.0 GPA. *Application deadline:* rolling (freshmen).
Admissions Contact Ms. Beverly Wheaton, Registrar, Gupton-Jones College of Funeral Service, 5141 Snapfinger Woods Drive, Decatur, GA 30035-4022. *Phone:* 770-593-2257. *Fax:* 770-593-1891. *E-mail:* gjcfs@mindspring.com.

GWINNETT TECHNICAL COLLEGE
Lawrenceville, Georgia

- **State-supported** 2-year, founded 1984
- **Calendar** quarters
- **Degree** certificates, diplomas, and associate
- **Suburban** 92-acre campus with easy access to Atlanta
- **Coed,** 3,964 undergraduate students

Faculty *Total:* 300.
Majors Accounting; auto mechanic/technician; business marketing and marketing management; computer programming; computer science; construction management; dental hygiene; drafting; electrical/electronic engineering technology; emergency medical technology; fashion merchandising; horticulture science; hotel and restaurant management; industrial radiologic technology; interior design; machine technology; management information systems/business data processing; medical assistant; ornamental horticulture; photography; physical therapy; respiratory therapy; secretarial science; telecommunications; travel/tourism management.
Academic Programs *Special study options:* academic remediation for entering students, adult/continuing education programs, advanced placement credit, English as a second language, part-time degree program, services for LD students, summer session for credit.
Library Gwinnett Technical Institute Media Center with 16,800 titles, 269 serial subscriptions.
Computers on Campus 264 computers available on campus for general student use. Internet access, at least one staffed computer lab available.
Student Life *Housing:* college housing not available. *Campus security:* patrols by campus police. *Student Services:* personal/psychological counseling.
Standardized Tests *Recommended:* SAT I or ACT (for admission).
Costs (2001–02) *Tuition:* $30 per credit hour part-time; state resident $1404 full-time, $98 per credit hour part-time; nonresident $2508 full-time.
Financial Aid In 2001, 20 Federal Work-Study jobs (averaging $2100).
Applying *Required:* high school transcript. *Application deadline:* 8/1 (freshmen). *Notification:* continuous (freshmen).
Admissions Contact Ms. Sandra Causey, Director of Admissions and Records, Gwinnett Technical College, PO Box 1505, Lawrenceville, GA 30046-1505. *Phone:* 770-962-7580 Ext. 246.

HERZING COLLEGE
Atlanta, Georgia

- **Proprietary** primarily 2-year, founded 1949, part of Herzing Institutes, Inc
- **Calendar** semesters
- **Degrees** certificates, diplomas, associate, and bachelor's
- **Urban** campus
- **Coed,** 375 undergraduate students

Undergraduates Students come from 5 states and territories.
Freshmen *Admission:* 279 applied, 209 admitted.
Faculty *Total:* 25. *Student/faculty ratio:* 8:1.
Majors Business administration; computer management; electrical/electronic engineering technology; information sciences/systems.
Academic Programs *Special study options:* academic remediation for entering students, English as a second language, honors programs, internships.
Library Loretta Herzing Library with 6,000 titles, 25 serial subscriptions, a Web page.
Computers on Campus 125 computers available on campus for general student use.
Student Life *Housing:* college housing not available. *Campus security:* 24-hour patrols. *Student Services:* personal/psychological counseling.
Costs (2002–03) *Tuition:* $7680 full-time, $240 per credit part-time. *Payment plan:* installment. *Waivers:* employees or children of employees.
Applying *Application fee:* $25. *Required:* high school transcript, interview. *Application deadline:* rolling (freshmen), rolling (transfers). *Notification:* continuous (freshmen).
Admissions Contact Stacy Johnston, Director of Admissions, Herzing College, 3355 Lenox Road, Suite 100, Atlanta, GA 30326. *Phone:* 404-816-4533. *Toll-free phone:* 800-573-4533. *Fax:* 404-816-5576. *E-mail:* leec@atl.herzing.edu.

INTERACTIVE COLLEGE OF TECHNOLOGY
Chamblee, Georgia

- **Proprietary** 2-year, part of Interactive Learning Systems
- **Degree** certificates, diplomas, and associate
- **Coed**

Faculty *Student/faculty ratio:* 19:1.
Costs (2001–02) *Tuition:* $5460 full-time, $230 per credit hour part-time. *Required fees:* $200 full-time. *Payment plans:* installment, deferred payment.
Applying *Application fee:* $50. *Required:* high school transcript.

Interactive College of Technology (continued)

Admissions Contact Ms. Diana Mamas, Associate Dean of Admissions, Interactive College of Technology, 5303 New Peachtree Road, Chamblee, GA 30341. *Phone:* 770-216-2960. *Toll-free phone:* 800-550-3475.

MIDDLE GEORGIA COLLEGE
Cochran, Georgia

- **State-supported** 2-year, founded 1884, part of University System of Georgia
- **Calendar** semesters
- **Degree** certificates and associate
- **Small-town** 165-acre campus
- **Endowment** $1.1 million
- **Coed,** 2,164 undergraduate students, 65% full-time, 50% women, 50% men

Middle Georgia College is a 2-year residential public college with a student population of approximately 2,200 students. Transfer programs are offered in more than 100 academic disciplines, including engineering, nursing, business, and education. Numerous clubs and organizations, as well as intercollegiate athletics for men and women, enrich student life.

Undergraduates 1,406 full-time, 758 part-time. Students come from 34 states and territories, 7% are from out of state, 29% African American, 0.9% Asian American or Pacific Islander, 0.8% Hispanic American, 0.3% Native American, 0.8% international, 14% transferred in, 32% live on campus.

Freshmen *Admission:* 1,490 applied, 1,137 admitted, 775 enrolled. *Average high school GPA:* 2.71. *Test scores:* SAT verbal scores over 500: 29%; SAT math scores over 500: 28%; ACT scores over 18: 32%; SAT verbal scores over 600: 8%; SAT math scores over 600: 9%; ACT scores over 24: 3%; SAT verbal scores over 700: 1%; SAT math scores over 700: 1%; ACT scores over 30: 1%.

Faculty *Total:* 125, 60% full-time, 27% with terminal degrees. *Student/faculty ratio:* 18:1.

Majors Business administration; computer engineering related; computer/information technology services administration and management related; computer science; computer science related; data processing technology; fashion merchandising; information sciences/systems; law enforcement/police science; liberal arts and sciences/liberal studies; nursing; occupational therapy assistant; physical therapy assistant; public administration; surveying.

Academic Programs *Special study options:* academic remediation for entering students, accelerated degree program, adult/continuing education programs, advanced placement credit, cooperative education, distance learning, honors programs, part-time degree program, services for LD students, study abroad, summer session for credit.

Library Roberts Memorial Library with 78,835 titles, 800 serial subscriptions, 5,064 audiovisual materials, an OPAC, a Web page.

Computers on Campus 350 computers available on campus for general student use. A campuswide network can be accessed from student residence rooms and from off campus. Internet access, online (class) registration, at least one staffed computer lab available.

Student Life *Housing:* on-campus residence required through sophomore year. *Options:* men-only, women-only. *Activities and Organizations:* drama/theater group, student-run newspaper, choral group, marching band, Baptist Student Union, Student Government Association, MGC Ambassadors, Encore Productions, United Voices of Praise. *Campus security:* 24-hour emergency response devices and patrols, student patrols, late-night transport/escort service, controlled dormitory access, patrols by police officers. *Student Services:* health clinic, personal/psychological counseling.

Athletics Member NJCAA. *Intercollegiate sports:* baseball M(s), basketball M(s)/W(s), softball W(s), tennis W(s). *Intramural sports:* badminton M/W, basketball M/W, football M, softball M/W, swimming M/W, tennis M/W.

Standardized Tests *Required:* SAT I or ACT (for admission). *Required for some:* SAT II: Subject Tests (for admission).

Costs (2001–02) *Tuition:* state resident $1280 full-time, $53 per credit hour part-time; nonresident $5120 full-time, $213 per credit hour part-time. Full-time tuition and fees vary according to location and program. Part-time tuition and fees vary according to course load, location, and program. *Required fees:* $462 full-time, $231 per term part-time. *Room and board:* $3454; room only: $1562. Room and board charges vary according to board plan. *Waivers:* senior citizens and employees or children of employees.

Financial Aid In 2001, 66 Federal Work-Study jobs (averaging $1277).

Applying *Options:* common application, electronic application, early admission, deferred entrance. *Application fee:* $20. *Required:* high school transcript, minimum 2.0 GPA. *Required for some:* essay or personal statement, minimum 3.5 GPA, letters of recommendation, interview. *Application deadline:* rolling (freshmen), rolling (transfers). *Notification:* continuous (freshmen).

Admissions Contact Mr. John McElveen, Vice President for Student Development, Middle Georgia College, 1100 2nd Street, SE, Cochran, GA 31014. *Phone:* 478-934-3352. *Fax:* 478-934-3049. *E-mail:* admissions@warrior.mgc.peachnet.edu.

MIDDLE GEORGIA TECHNICAL COLLEGE
Warner Robbins, Georgia

Admissions Contact 80 Cohen Walker Drive, Warner Robbins, GA 31088. *Toll-free phone:* 800-474-1031.

NORTHWESTERN TECHNICAL COLLEGE
Rock Springs, Georgia

- **State-supported** 2-year, founded 1966, part of Georgia Department of Technical and Adult Education
- **Calendar** quarters
- **Degree** certificates, diplomas, and associate
- **Rural** campus
- **Coed**

Faculty *Student/faculty ratio:* 15:1.

Standardized Tests *Required:* ACT ASSET, SAT I, or ACT.

Costs (2001–02) *Tuition:* area resident $1200 full-time; state resident $2400 full-time, $25 per hour part-time; nonresident $4800 full-time, $50 per hour part-time. Full-time tuition and fees vary according to course load. Part-time tuition and fees vary according to course load. *Required fees:* $160 full-time, $40 per term part-time.

Applying *Application fee:* $15. *Required for some:* essay or personal statement, high school transcript, letters of recommendation, interview.

Admissions Contact Mrs. Carolyn Solmon, Director of Admissions and Career Planning, Northwestern Technical College, PO Box 569, Rock Springs, GA 30739. *Phone:* 706-764-3518. *E-mail:* csolmon@northwestern.tec.ga.us.

OGEECHEE TECHNICAL COLLEGE
Statesboro, Georgia

Admissions Contact One Joe Kennedy Boulevard, Statesboro, GA 30458. *Toll-free phone:* 800-646-1316.

SAVANNAH TECHNICAL COLLEGE
Savannah, Georgia

- **State-supported** 2-year, founded 1929, part of Georgia Department of Technical and Adult Education
- **Calendar** quarters
- **Degree** certificates, diplomas, and associate
- **Urban** 15-acre campus
- **Endowment** $4.2 million
- **Coed,** 3,134 undergraduate students, 47% full-time, 62% women, 38% men

Undergraduates 1,468 full-time, 1,666 part-time. Students come from 4 states and territories, 5% are from out of state, 59% African American, 3% Asian American or Pacific Islander, 3% Hispanic American, 0.3% Native American, 3% transferred in. *Retention:* 40% of 2001 full-time freshmen returned.

Freshmen *Admission:* 1,041 enrolled.

Faculty *Total:* 201, 28% full-time. *Student/faculty ratio:* 15:1.

Majors Accounting; biomedical technology; civil engineering technology; computer programming; electrical/electronic engineering technology; electromechanical technology; fire science; information technology; instrumentation technology; operating room technician; secretarial science.

Academic Programs *Special study options:* academic remediation for entering students, advanced placement credit, English as a second language, internships, part-time degree program, services for LD students, summer session for credit.

Library Savannah Technical Institute Library plus 1 other with 265 serial subscriptions, 3,583 audiovisual materials, an OPAC, a Web page.

Computers on Campus Internet access, at least one staffed computer lab available.

Student Life *Housing:* college housing not available. *Activities and Organizations:* Phi Beta Lambda, Vocational Industrial Clubs of America (VICA).

Costs (2002–03) *Tuition:* state resident $1077 full-time, $25 per credit part-time; nonresident $1977 full-time, $50 per credit part-time.
Applying *Application fee:* $15. *Required:* high school transcript. *Notification:* continuous (freshmen).
Admissions Contact Ms. Shevon Carr, Vice President of Student Services, Savannah Technical College, 5717 White Bluff Road, Savannah, GA 31405. *Phone:* 912-303-1775. *Toll-free phone:* 800-769-6362. *Fax:* 912-303-1781. *E-mail:* vlampley@savtec.org.

SOUTH GEORGIA COLLEGE
Douglas, Georgia

Admissions Contact Dr. Randy L. Braswell, Director of Admissions, Records, and Research, South Georgia College, 100 West College Park Drive, Douglas, GA 31533-5098. *Phone:* 912-389-4200. *Toll-free phone:* 800-342-6364. *Fax:* 912-389-4392. *E-mail:* admissions@mail.sgc.peachnet.edu.

SOUTHWEST GEORGIA TECHNICAL COLLEGE
Thomasville, Georgia

- **State-supported** 2-year, founded 1963
- **Calendar** quarters
- **Degree** certificates, diplomas, and associate
- **Coed,** 2,448 undergraduate students

Undergraduates Students come from 4 states and territories, 31% African American, 0.2% Asian American or Pacific Islander, 0.4% Hispanic American, 0.6% Native American.
Freshmen *Admission:* 162 applied, 76 admitted.
Faculty *Total:* 104, 42% full-time, 1% with terminal degrees. *Student/faculty ratio:* 16:1.
Majors Accounting; agricultural mechanization; heavy equipment maintenance; hospitality services management related; information sciences/systems; medical laboratory technician; medical radiologic technology; occupational therapy assistant; physical therapy; respiratory therapy; secretarial science.
Academic Programs *Special study options:* academic remediation for entering students, cooperative education, distance learning, internships, part-time degree program.
Library Thomas Technical Institute Library plus 1 other with an OPAC.
Computers on Campus 430 computers available on campus for general student use. Internet access available.
Student Life *Housing:* college housing not available.
Standardized Tests *Required:* SAT I, ACT, or ACT ASSET.
Costs (2001–02) *Tuition:* state resident $1200 full-time, $25 per quarter hour part-time; nonresident $2400 full-time, $50 per quarter hour part-time. *Required fees:* $168 full-time, $35 per term part-time.
Applying *Options:* common application, electronic application. *Application fee:* $15. *Required:* high school transcript. *Application deadline:* 8/1 (freshmen).
Admissions Contact Ms. Lorette M. McNeil, Vice President of Student Services, Southwest Georgia Technical College, 15689 US 19 North, Thomasville, GA 31792. *Phone:* 229-225-5060. *Fax:* 229-225-4330.

TRUETT-MCCONNELL COLLEGE
Cleveland, Georgia

- **Independent Baptist** 2-year, founded 1946
- **Calendar** semesters
- **Degree** certificates and associate
- **Rural** 310-acre campus with easy access to Atlanta
- **Endowment** $7.7 million
- **Coed,** 1,747 undergraduate students, 81% full-time, 50% women, 50% men

Undergraduates 1,414 full-time, 333 part-time. Students come from 15 states and territories, 10 other countries, 2% are from out of state, 4% African American, 0.8% Asian American or Pacific Islander, 1% Hispanic American, 0.3% Native American, 0.8% international, 9% transferred in, 19% live on campus. *Retention:* 55% of 2001 full-time freshmen returned.
Freshmen *Admission:* 1,388 applied, 1,291 admitted, 553 enrolled. *Average high school GPA:* 2.86. *Test scores:* SAT verbal scores over 500: 36%; SAT math scores over 500: 36%; ACT scores over 18: 53%; SAT verbal scores over 600: 6%; SAT math scores over 600: 5%; ACT scores over 24: 7%.
Faculty *Total:* 180, 27% full-time. *Student/faculty ratio:* 17:1.
Majors Business; education; general studies; liberal arts and sciences/liberal studies; music.
Academic Programs *Special study options:* academic remediation for entering students, accelerated degree program, advanced placement credit, honors programs, part-time degree program, services for LD students, study abroad, summer session for credit.
Library Cofer Library with 36,562 titles, 343 serial subscriptions, 2,716 audiovisual materials, an OPAC.
Computers on Campus 124 computers available on campus for general student use. Internet access, at least one staffed computer lab available.
Student Life *Housing:* on-campus residence required through sophomore year. *Options:* men-only, women-only. *Activities and Organizations:* choral group, intramurals, Baptist Student Union, College Choir, Student Government Association, Fellowship of Christian Athletes (FCA). *Campus security:* 24-hour weekday patrols, 10-hour weekend patrols by trained security personnel. *Student Services:* personal/psychological counseling.
Athletics Member NJCAA. *Intercollegiate sports:* baseball M(s), basketball M(s)/W(s), cross-country running M(s)/W(s), soccer M(s)/W(s). *Intramural sports:* basketball M/W, football M/W, golf M/W, soccer M/W, tennis M/W, volleyball M/W.
Standardized Tests *Required for some:* SAT I or ACT (for admission).
Costs (2001–02) *Comprehensive fee:* $10,620 includes full-time tuition ($7100) and room and board ($3520). Part-time tuition: $240 per credit hour. *Room and board:* College room only: $1620. *Payment plan:* installment. *Waivers:* senior citizens and employees or children of employees.
Applying *Options:* early admission, deferred entrance. *Application fee:* $20. *Required:* high school transcript, minimum 2.0 GPA, minimum SAT score of 720 or ACT score of 15. *Required for some:* interview. *Application deadlines:* 8/1 (freshmen), 8/1 (transfers). *Notification:* continuous (freshmen).
Admissions Contact Mr. Ken Thomas, Associate Dean of Admissions, Truett-McConnell College, 100 Alumni Drive, Cleveland, GA 30528-9799. *Phone:* 706-865-2134 Ext. 129. *Toll-free phone:* 800-226-8621. *Fax:* 706-865-7615. *E-mail:* admissions@truett.cc.ga.us.

WAYCROSS COLLEGE
Waycross, Georgia

- **State-supported** 2-year, founded 1976, part of University System of Georgia
- **Calendar** semesters
- **Degree** associate
- **Small-town** 150-acre campus
- **Endowment** $85,583
- **Coed,** 884 undergraduate students

Undergraduates Students come from 1 other country.
Freshmen *Admission:* 381 applied, 381 admitted. *Average high school GPA:* 2.90.
Faculty *Total:* 47, 43% full-time, 26% with terminal degrees. *Student/faculty ratio:* 22:1.
Majors Accounting; agricultural sciences; auto mechanic/technician; biology; business administration; business education; chemistry; computer/information sciences; computer science; cosmetology; criminal justice/law enforcement administration; developmental/child psychology; drafting; education; electrical/electronic engineering technology; elementary education; emergency medical technology; engineering technology; English; forest harvesting production technology; forestry; health education; heavy equipment maintenance; history; liberal arts and sciences/liberal studies; machine technology; mathematics; medical laboratory technician; medical radiologic technology; medical technology; nursing; operating room technician; physical education; physical therapy; political science; psychology; radiological science; respiratory therapy; secretarial science; sociology; welding technology.
Academic Programs *Special study options:* academic remediation for entering students, adult/continuing education programs, advanced placement credit, off-campus study, part-time degree program, summer session for credit.
Library Waycross College Library with 32,461 titles, 251 serial subscriptions.
Computers on Campus 56 computers available on campus for general student use. At least one staffed computer lab available.
Student Life *Housing:* college housing not available. *Activities and Organizations:* drama/theater group, student-run newspaper, choral group, Black Student Alliance, Georgia Association of Nursing Students, Baptist Student Union, Sigma Club, Student Government Association. *Campus security:* late-night transport/escort service, security guards. *Student Services:* personal/psychological counseling.
Athletics *Intramural sports:* bowling M/W, football M/W, golf M/W, racquetball M/W, softball M/W, table tennis M/W, tennis M/W, volleyball M/W.

Waycross College (continued)

Standardized Tests *Required for some:* SAT I (for admission).

Costs (2002–03) *Tuition:* area resident $1332 full-time, $56 per credit hour part-time; state resident $56 per credit hour part-time; nonresident $222 per credit hour part-time. *Required fees:* $150 full-time, $6 per credit hour, $4 per term part-time.

Financial Aid In 2001, 20 Federal Work-Study jobs (averaging $2000).

Applying *Options:* early admission, deferred entrance. *Application deadline:* rolling (freshmen), rolling (transfers). *Notification:* continuous (freshmen).

Admissions Contact Mr. J. Porter, Director of Admissions, Financial Aid, and Student Records, Waycross College, 2001 South Georgia Parkway, Waycross, GA 31503-9248. *Phone:* 912-285-6133. *Fax:* 912-287-4909.

WEST CENTRAL TECHNICAL COLLEGE

Carrollton, Georgia

- **State-supported** 2-year, founded 1968, part of Georgia Department of Technical and Adult Education
- **Calendar** quarters
- **Degree** certificates, diplomas, and associate
- **Coed,** 2,620 undergraduate students, 29% full-time, 66% women, 34% men

Undergraduates 771 full-time, 1,849 part-time. 47% are from out of state, 23% African American, 1% Asian American or Pacific Islander, 1% Hispanic American, 0.5% Native American.

Freshmen *Admission:* 746 enrolled.

Faculty *Total:* 150, 40% full-time.

Majors Accounting; business administration; business marketing and marketing management; computer programming (specific applications); computer science related; data entry/microcomputer applications; dental hygiene; electrical/electronic engineering technology; heavy equipment maintenance; industrial radiologic technology; information sciences/systems; secretarial science; word processing.

Academic Programs *Special study options:* academic remediation for entering students, adult/continuing education programs, cooperative education, distance learning, English as a second language, external degree program, independent study, internships, off-campus study, part-time degree program, services for LD students, student-designed majors.

Library 6,265 titles, 162 serial subscriptions.

Computers on Campus 109 computers available on campus for general student use. At least one staffed computer lab available.

Student Life *Housing:* college housing not available.

Costs (2001–02) *Tuition:* $25,839 per degree program part-time. Full-time tuition and fees vary according to program. *Required fees:* $147 full-time.

Financial Aid In 2001, 40 Federal Work-Study jobs (averaging $1000).

Applying *Options:* electronic application. *Application fee:* $15. *Required:* high school transcript. *Required for some:* interview. *Application deadline:* rolling (freshmen), rolling (transfers).

Admissions Contact Mrs. Mary Aderhold, Director of Student Services, West Central Technical College, 997 South Highway 16, Carrollton, GA 30116. *Phone:* 770-836-6830. *Fax:* 770-836-6814.

WEST GEORGIA TECHNICAL COLLEGE

LaGrange, Georgia

- **State-supported** 2-year, founded 1966, part of Georgia Department of Technical and Adult Education
- **Calendar** quarters
- **Degree** certificates, diplomas, and associate
- **Endowment** $58,000
- **Coed**

Faculty *Student/faculty ratio:* 12:1.

Student Life *Campus security:* 24-hour emergency response devices.

Financial Aid In 2001, 57 Federal Work-Study jobs (averaging $854). *Financial aid deadline:* 11/27.

Applying *Application fee:* $15. *Required:* high school transcript.

Admissions Contact Ms. Tina Jackson, Admissions Coordinator/Assistant Registrar, West Georgia Technical College, 303 Fort Drive, LaGrange, GA 30240. *Phone:* 706-845-4323 Ext. 5711. *Fax:* 706-845-4340. *E-mail:* tjackson@westga.tec.ga.us.

YOUNG HARRIS COLLEGE

Young Harris, Georgia

- **Independent United Methodist** 2-year, founded 1886
- **Calendar** semesters
- **Degree** associate
- **Rural** campus
- **Endowment** $96.5 million
- **Coed,** 594 undergraduate students, 95% full-time, 53% women, 47% men

Undergraduates 565 full-time, 29 part-time. Students come from 12 states and territories, 5 other countries, 7% are from out of state, 1% African American, 0.7% Asian American or Pacific Islander, 2% Hispanic American, 0.2% Native American, 0.8% international, 3% transferred in, 90% live on campus.

Freshmen *Admission:* 958 applied, 750 admitted, 412 enrolled. *Average high school GPA:* 3.27. *Test scores:* SAT verbal scores over 500: 65%; SAT math scores over 500: 62%; ACT scores over 18: 81%; SAT verbal scores over 600: 17%; SAT math scores over 600: 16%; ACT scores over 24: 30%; SAT verbal scores over 700: 1%; SAT math scores over 700: 2%; ACT scores over 30: 2%.

Faculty *Total:* 39, 79% full-time, 56% with terminal degrees. *Student/faculty ratio:* 15:1.

Majors Agricultural sciences; art; art education; biological/physical sciences; biology; business administration; chemistry; computer science; criminal justice/law enforcement administration; education; English; French; geology; health education; history; hospitality management; international business; journalism; liberal arts and sciences/liberal studies; mathematics; medical technology; music; music related; music teacher education; natural sciences; nursing; physical therapy; physics; political science; pre-engineering; psychology; recreation/leisure studies; religious studies; sociology; Spanish; theater arts/drama.

Academic Programs *Special study options:* academic remediation for entering students, accelerated degree program, advanced placement credit, double majors, internships, part-time degree program, summer session for credit.

Library J. Lon Duckworth Library with 55,201 titles, 260 serial subscriptions, 1,850 audiovisual materials, an OPAC, a Web page.

Computers on Campus 85 computers available on campus for general student use. A campuswide network can be accessed from student residence rooms and from off campus. Internet access, at least one staffed computer lab available.

Student Life *Housing:* on-campus residence required through sophomore year. *Options:* coed, men-only, women-only. *Activities and Organizations:* drama/theater group, student-run newspaper, choral group, Wesley Fellowship, BSU, Quantrek (outdoor club), Greek organizations, intramurals. *Campus security:* 24-hour emergency response devices and patrols. *Student Services:* health clinic, personal/psychological counseling.

Athletics Member NJCAA. *Intercollegiate sports:* baseball M(s), soccer M(s)/W(s), softball W(s), tennis W(s). *Intramural sports:* badminton M/W, basketball M/W, bowling M/W, football M/W, golf M/W, skiing (downhill) M/W, softball M/W, swimming M/W, tennis M/W, volleyball M/W, weight lifting M/W.

Standardized Tests *Required:* SAT I or ACT (for admission).

Costs (2002–03) *Comprehensive fee:* $15,844 includes full-time tuition ($11,600) and room and board ($4244). Part-time tuition: $450 per hour. Part-time tuition and fees vary according to course load. No tuition increase for student's term of enrollment. *Room and board:* College room only: $1770. *Payment plan:* installment. *Waivers:* employees or children of employees.

Financial Aid In 2001, 85 Federal Work-Study jobs (averaging $1400). 221 State and other part-time jobs (averaging $1400).

Applying *Options:* electronic application, early admission, deferred entrance. *Application fee:* $30. *Required:* high school transcript, minimum 2.5 GPA. *Required for some:* letters of recommendation. *Recommended:* interview. *Application deadline:* rolling (freshmen), rolling (transfers). *Notification:* continuous (freshmen).

Admissions Contact Mr. Clinton G. Hobbs, Director of Admissions, Young Harris College, PO Box 116, Young Harris, GA 30582-0098. *Phone:* 706-379-3111 Ext. 5147. *Toll-free phone:* 800-241-3754. *Fax:* 706-379-3108. *E-mail:* admissions@yhc.edu.

HAWAII

HAWAII BUSINESS COLLEGE

Honolulu, Hawaii

- **Independent** 2-year, founded 1973
- **Calendar** quarters

■ **Degree** certificates, diplomas, and associate
■ **Urban** campus
■ **Coed,** 426 undergraduate students, 84% full-time, 71% women, 29% men

Faculty *Total:* 21. *Student/faculty ratio:* 15:1.
Majors Accounting; business administration; computer science; health/medical administrative services related; travel/tourism management; Web page, digital/multimedia and information resources design.
Academic Programs *Special study options:* academic remediation for entering students, adult/continuing education programs, advanced placement credit, cooperative education, double majors, English as a second language, external degree program, independent study, internships, part-time degree program, summer session for credit.
Library 1,000 titles, 25 serial subscriptions.
Computers on Campus Internet access available.
Student Life *Housing:* college housing not available. *Activities and Organizations:* student-run newspaper, SCA (Student Council Association), Computer Club, Polynesian Club, SIFE. *Student Services:* personal/psychological counseling.
Standardized Tests *Required:* Wonderlic Basic Skills Test.
Costs (2001–02) *Tuition:* $7200 full-time, $160 per credit part-time. Full-time tuition and fees vary according to course load and program. Part-time tuition and fees vary according to course load and program. *Required fees:* $420 full-time, $140 per term part-time. *Payment plans:* tuition prepayment, installment, deferred payment.
Applying *Options:* deferred entrance. *Application fee:* $30. *Required:* high school transcript. *Required for some:* essay or personal statement, interview. *Application deadline:* rolling (freshmen).
Admissions Contact Ms. Elizabeth K. Lyons, Director of Admissions, Hawaii Business College, 33 South King Street, Fourth Floor, Honolulu, HI 96813. *Phone:* 808-524-4014. *Fax:* 808-524-0284. *E-mail:* admin@hbc.edu.

HAWAII COMMUNITY COLLEGE
Hilo, Hawaii

■ **State-supported** 2-year, founded 1954, part of University of Hawaii System
■ **Calendar** semesters
■ **Degree** certificates, diplomas, and associate
■ **Small-town** campus
■ **Coed,** 2,181 undergraduate students, 46% full-time, 63% women, 37% men

Undergraduates Students come from 12 states and territories, 32 other countries.
Freshmen *Admission:* 1,163 applied, 1,156 admitted.
Faculty *Total:* 149, 48% full-time.
Majors Accounting; agricultural sciences; auto mechanic/technician; carpentry; criminal justice/law enforcement administration; drafting; early childhood education; electrical/electronic engineering technology; fire science; food services technology; hotel and restaurant management; liberal arts and sciences/liberal studies; mechanical engineering technology; nursing; practical nurse; secretarial science; welding technology.
Academic Programs *Special study options:* advanced placement credit, cooperative education, English as a second language, honors programs, part-time degree program, services for LD students, summer session for credit.
Library Edwin H. Mookini Library plus 1 other.
Computers on Campus 100 computers available on campus for general student use. A campuswide network can be accessed from off campus. Internet access, at least one staffed computer lab available.
Student Life *Housing Options:* coed. *Campus security:* 24-hour patrols.
Costs (2002–03) *Tuition:* state resident $1032 full-time, $43 per credit part-time; nonresident $5808 full-time, $242 per credit part-time. *Required fees:* $50 full-time, $2 per credit, $5 per term part-time.
Applying *Options:* common application, early admission. *Application deadline:* 8/1 (freshmen).
Admissions Contact Mr. David Loeding, Registrar, Hawaii Community College, 200 West Kawili Street, Hilo, HI 96720-4091. *Phone:* 808-974-7662. *E-mail:* loeding@hawaii.edu.

HAWAII TOKAI INTERNATIONAL COLLEGE
Honolulu, Hawaii

■ **Independent** 2-year, founded 1992, part of Tokai University Educational System (Japan)
■ **Calendar** quarters
■ **Degree** certificates and associate
■ **Urban** campus
■ **Coed,** 45 undergraduate students, 100% full-time, 56% women, 44% men

Undergraduates 45 full-time. Students come from 1 other state, 3 other countries, 4% Asian American or Pacific Islander, 96% international, 60% live on campus. *Retention:* 83% of 2001 full-time freshmen returned.
Freshmen *Admission:* 9 applied, 9 admitted, 6 enrolled.
Faculty *Total:* 20, 45% full-time, 20% with terminal degrees. *Student/faculty ratio:* 12:1.
Majors Liberal arts and sciences/liberal studies.
Academic Programs *Special study options:* English as a second language, summer session for credit.
Library The Learning Center with 7,000 titles, 100 serial subscriptions, 500 audiovisual materials, an OPAC, a Web page.
Computers on Campus 45 computers available on campus for general student use. A campuswide network can be accessed from student residence rooms and from off campus. Internet access, at least one staffed computer lab available.
Student Life *Housing:* on-campus residence required for freshman year. *Options:* coed. *Activities and Organizations:* student-run newspaper, Basketball Club, Hula Club, Martial Arts Club, Chinese and Japanese Culture Club, fishing. *Campus security:* 24-hour patrols.
Costs (2002–03) *Comprehensive fee:* $12,510 includes full-time tuition ($7950), mandatory fees ($300), and room and board ($4260). Part-time tuition: $300 per credit. Part-time tuition and fees vary according to course load. *Required fees:* $100 per term part-time. *Room and board:* Room and board charges vary according to board plan. *Waivers:* employees or children of employees.
Applying *Options:* deferred entrance. *Application fee:* $50. *Required:* essay or personal statement, high school transcript, interview. *Application deadline:* 9/1 (freshmen). *Notification:* continuous (freshmen).
Admissions Contact Ms. Terry Lee McCandliss, Admissions Officer, Hawaii Tokai International College, 2241 Kapiolani Boulevard, Honolulu, HI 96826. *Phone:* 808-983-4150. *E-mail:* htic@tokai.edu.

HEALD COLLEGE, SCHOOLS OF BUSINESS AND TECHNOLOGY
Honolulu, Hawaii

■ **Independent** 2-year, founded 1863, part of Heald Colleges
■ **Calendar** quarters
■ **Degree** diplomas and associate
■ **Urban** campus
■ **Coed,** 1,200 undergraduate students

Faculty *Total:* 42, 45% full-time.
Majors Accounting; business administration; electrical/electronic engineering technology; information sciences/systems; legal administrative assistant; medical administrative assistant; secretarial science; travel/tourism management.
Academic Programs *Special study options:* internships, part-time degree program, summer session for credit.
Library Learning Resource Center with 2,500 titles, 56 serial subscriptions, an OPAC.
Computers on Campus 350 computers available on campus for general student use. Internet access available.
Student Life *Housing:* college housing not available.
Standardized Tests *Required:* CPAt.
Costs (2002–03) *Tuition:* Tuition fees are dependent on program and campus selected.
Applying *Options:* early admission, deferred entrance. *Required:* high school transcript, interview. *Application deadline:* rolling (freshmen), rolling (transfers). *Notification:* continuous (freshmen).
Admissions Contact Mr. Lon Ibaraki, Director of Admissions, Heald College, Schools of Business and Technology, 1500 Kapiolani Boulevard, Honolulu, HI 96814-3797. *Phone:* 808-955-1500. *Fax:* 808-955-6964. *E-mail:* evelyn_schemmel@heald.edu.

HONOLULU COMMUNITY COLLEGE
Honolulu, Hawaii

■ **State-supported** 2-year, founded 1920, part of University of Hawaii System
■ **Calendar** semesters

Honolulu Community College (continued)
- **Degree** certificates and associate
- **Urban** 20-acre campus
- **Endowment** $472,659
- **Coed,** 4,653 undergraduate students, 38% full-time, 42% women, 58% men

Undergraduates 1,783 full-time, 2,870 part-time. Students come from 36 states and territories, 39 other countries, 4% African American, 65% Asian American or Pacific Islander, 4% Hispanic American, 0.3% Native American, 2% international, 27% transferred in.
Freshmen *Admission:* 1,436 applied, 1,353 admitted.
Faculty *Total:* 187, 57% full-time, 7% with terminal degrees. *Student/faculty ratio:* 21:1.
Majors Architectural engineering technology; auto mechanic/technician; aviation technology; carpentry; community services; cosmetology; drafting; early childhood education; electrical/electronic engineering technology; engineering technology; fashion design/illustration; fire science; food services technology; graphic design/commercial art/illustration; heating/air conditioning/refrigeration; human services; industrial arts; law enforcement/police science; liberal arts and sciences/liberal studies; marine technology; occupational safety/health technology; welding technology.
Academic Programs *Special study options:* academic remediation for entering students, accelerated degree program, advanced placement credit, cooperative education, distance learning, English as a second language, internships, part-time degree program, services for LD students, student-designed majors, summer session for credit. *ROTC:* Army (c), Air Force (c).
Library Honolulu Community College Library with 54,902 titles, 1,280 serial subscriptions, 858 audiovisual materials, an OPAC, a Web page.
Computers on Campus 120 computers available on campus for general student use. A campuswide network can be accessed from off campus. At least one staffed computer lab available.
Student Life *Housing:* college housing not available. *Activities and Organizations:* student-run newspaper. *Campus security:* 24-hour emergency response devices. *Student Services:* health clinic.
Costs (2001–02) *Tuition:* state resident $1032 full-time, $43 per semester hour part-time; nonresident $5808 full-time, $242 per semester hour part-time. *Required fees:* $20 full-time, $20 per year part-time. *Waivers:* employees or children of employees.
Financial Aid In 2001, 48 Federal Work-Study jobs (averaging $1200).
Applying *Options:* common application, early admission. *Application fee:* $25 (non-residents). *Application deadlines:* 8/15 (freshmen), 8/15 (transfers). *Notification:* continuous until 8/15 (freshmen).
Admissions Contact Admissions Office, Honolulu Community College, 874 Dillingham Boulevard, Honolulu, HI 96817. *Phone:* 808-845-9129. *E-mail:* admission@hcc.hawaii.edu.

KAPIOLANI COMMUNITY COLLEGE
Honolulu, Hawaii

Admissions Contact Ms. Cynthia Suzuki, Chief Admissions Officer, Kapiolani Community College, 4303 Diamond Head Road, Honolulu, HI 96816-4421. *Phone:* 808-734-9897. *E-mail:* cio@leahi.kcc.hawaii.edu.

KAUAI COMMUNITY COLLEGE
Lihue, Hawaii

- **State-supported** 2-year, founded 1965, part of University of Hawaii System
- **Calendar** semesters
- **Degree** certificates and associate
- **Small-town** 100-acre campus
- **Coed,** 227 undergraduate students, 65% full-time, 51% women, 49% men

Undergraduates 147 full-time, 80 part-time.
Freshmen *Admission:* 227 enrolled.
Faculty *Total:* 71, 73% full-time.
Majors Accounting; auto body repair; auto mechanic/technician; carpentry; culinary arts; early childhood education; electrical/electronic engineering technology; hospitality management; liberal arts and sciences/liberal studies; nursing; secretarial science.
Academic Programs *Special study options:* accelerated degree program, advanced placement credit, cooperative education, distance learning, English as a second language, internships, part-time degree program, services for LD students, summer session for credit.
Library S. W. Wilcox II Learning Resource Center plus 1 other with 51,875 titles, 165 serial subscriptions, 1,248 audiovisual materials, an OPAC, a Web page.
Computers on Campus 173 computers available on campus for general student use. Internet access, at least one staffed computer lab available.
Student Life *Housing:* college housing not available. *Activities and Organizations:* student-run newspaper, choral group, Food Service Club, Hui O Hana Po'okela (Hoper Club), Nursing Club, Phi Theta Kappa, Pamantasan Club. *Campus security:* student patrols, 6-hour evening patrols by trained security personnel. *Student Services:* health clinic, personal/psychological counseling.
Athletics *Intramural sports:* basketball M/W, golf M/W, tennis M/W.
Standardized Tests *Recommended:* ACT COMPASS.
Costs (2001–02) *Tuition:* state resident $1032 full-time, $43 per credit part-time; nonresident $5808 full-time, $242 per credit part-time. Part-time tuition and fees vary according to course load. *Required fees:* $10 full-time, $1 per credit. *Waivers:* minority students, senior citizens, and employees or children of employees.
Financial Aid In 2001, 10 Federal Work-Study jobs (averaging $3000). 30 State and other part-time jobs (averaging $3000).
Applying *Options:* common application, early admission. *Application fee:* $25 (non-residents). *Required for some:* high school transcript. *Recommended:* high school transcript. *Application deadlines:* 8/1 (freshmen), 8/1 (transfers). *Notification:* continuous until 8/1 (freshmen).
Admissions Contact Mr. Leighton Oride, Admissions Officer and Registrar, Kauai Community College, 3-1901 Kaumualii Highway, Lihue, HI 96766. *Phone:* 808-245-8226. *Fax:* 808-245-8297. *E-mail:* adrec@mail.kauaicc.hawaii.edu.

LEEWARD COMMUNITY COLLEGE
Pearl City, Hawaii

Admissions Contact Ms. Veda Tokashiki, Clerk, Leeward Community College, 96-045 Ala Ike, Pearl City, HI 96782-3393. *Phone:* 808-455-0217.

MAUI COMMUNITY COLLEGE
Kahului, Hawaii

- **State-supported** 2-year, founded 1967, part of University of Hawaii System
- **Calendar** semesters
- **Degree** certificates and associate
- **Rural** 77-acre campus
- **Coed**

Student Life *Campus security:* 24-hour emergency response devices and patrols.
Standardized Tests *Required:* CTBS.
Costs (2001–02) *Tuition:* state resident $1050 full-time, $43 per credit part-time; nonresident $5826 full-time, $242 per credit part-time. Part-time tuition and fees vary according to course load. *Required fees:* $18 full-time, $1 per credit, $4 per term part-time. *Room and board:* Room and board charges vary according to housing facility.
Applying *Options:* common application, electronic application, early admission. *Application fee:* $25. *Required for some:* high school transcript.
Admissions Contact Mr. Stephen Kameda, Director of Admissions and Records, Maui Community College, 310 Kaahumanu Avenue, Kahului, HI 96732. *Phone:* 808-984-3267 Ext. 517. *Toll-free phone:* 800-479-6692. *Fax:* 808-242-9618.

TRANSPACIFIC HAWAII COLLEGE
Honolulu, Hawaii

- **Independent** 2-year, founded 1977
- **Degrees** associate (majority of students are from outside of U.S. and participate in intensive ESL program in preparation for transfer to a 4-year institution)
- **Suburban** campus
- **Coed, primarily women**

Faculty *Student/faculty ratio:* 5:1.
Student Life *Campus security:* 24-hour emergency response devices.
Costs (2001–02) *One-time required fee:* $100. *Tuition:* $9750 full-time. Full-time tuition and fees vary according to program. *Required fees:* $190 full-time.

Applying *Options:* common application, electronic application, early admission, deferred entrance. *Application fee:* $50. *Required:* essay or personal statement, high school transcript. *Required for some:* letters of recommendation, interview.

Admissions Contact Ms. Loreen Toji, Assistant to the President, TransPacific Hawaii College, 5257 Kalanianaole Highway, Honolulu, HI 96821. *Phone:* 808-377-5402 Ext. 309. *Fax:* 808-373-4754. *E-mail:* admissions@transpacific.org.

WINDWARD COMMUNITY COLLEGE
Kaneohe, Hawaii

- **State-supported** 2-year, founded 1972, part of University of Hawaii System
- **Calendar** semesters
- **Degree** certificates and associate
- **Small-town** 78-acre campus with easy access to Honolulu
- **Coed**

Applying *Options:* early admission. *Application fee:* $25.

Admissions Contact Ms. Meili Castanares, Registrar, Windward Community College, Kaneohe, HI 96744. *Phone:* 808-235-7400 Ext. 432.

IDAHO

AMERICAN INSTITUTE OF HEALTH TECHNOLOGY, INC.
Boise, Idaho

- **Proprietary** 2-year, founded 1980
- **Calendar** semesters
- **Degree** certificates, diplomas, and associate
- **Coed, primarily women,** 224 undergraduate students, 78% full-time, 88% women, 13% men

Undergraduates 174 full-time, 50 part-time. Students come from 5 states and territories, 1 other country, 10% are from out of state, 2% Asian American or Pacific Islander, 6% Hispanic American, 2% Native American, 6% international, 0.9% transferred in.

Freshmen *Admission:* 47 enrolled. *Average high school GPA:* 3.10. *Test scores:* SAT verbal scores over 500: 81%; SAT math scores over 500: 76%; ACT scores over 18: 85%; SAT verbal scores over 600: 2%; SAT math scores over 600: 1%; ACT scores over 24: 3%.

Faculty *Total:* 46, 30% full-time, 93% with terminal degrees. *Student/faculty ratio:* 9:1.

Majors Dental hygiene; medical office management; occupational therapy assistant.

Student Life *Housing:* college housing not available. *Campus security:* 24-hour patrols.

Costs (2001–02) *One-time required fee:* $50. *Tuition:* $31,275 per degree program part-time. Full-time tuition and fees vary according to program. Part-time tuition and fees vary according to program. *Payment plans:* tuition prepayment, installment. *Waivers:* employees or children of employees.

Applying *Application fee:* $30. *Required:* high school transcript, 3 letters of recommendation, interview. *Application deadline:* 3/1 (freshmen). *Notification:* continuous until 9/1 (freshmen).

Admissions Contact Susanna Hancock, Admissions Counselor, American Institute of Health Technology, Inc., 1200 North Liberty, Boise, ID 83607. *Phone:* 208-377-8080 Ext. 21. *Toll-free phone:* 800-473-4365 Ext. 21. *Fax:* 208-322-7658. *E-mail:* receptionist@aiht.com.

BRIGHAM YOUNG UNIVERSITY -IDAHO
Rexburg, Idaho

- **Independent** 2-year, founded 1888, affiliated with Church of Jesus Christ of Latter-day Saints
- **Calendar** semesters
- **Degree** associate
- **Small-town** 255-acre campus
- **Coed**

Faculty *Student/faculty ratio:* 25:1.

Student Life *Campus security:* 24-hour emergency response devices and patrols, late-night transport/escort service.

Athletics Member NJCAA.

Standardized Tests *Required:* SAT I or ACT (for admission).

Applying *Options:* electronic application. *Application fee:* $25. *Required:* essay or personal statement, high school transcript, interview.

Admissions Contact Mr. Steven Davis, Assistant Director of Admissions, Brigham Young University -Idaho, 120 Kimball, Rexburg, ID 83460-1615. *Phone:* 208-356-1026. *Fax:* 208-356-1220. *E-mail:* harrisk@ricks.edu.

COLLEGE OF SOUTHERN IDAHO
Twin Falls, Idaho

- **State and locally supported** 2-year, founded 1964
- **Calendar** semesters
- **Degree** certificates, diplomas, and associate
- **Small-town** 287-acre campus
- **Endowment** $13.6 million
- **Coed,** 5,344 undergraduate students

Undergraduates Students come from 16 states and territories, 21 other countries, 5% are from out of state, 0.3% African American, 0.8% Asian American or Pacific Islander, 5% Hispanic American, 0.7% Native American, 0.6% international, 10% live on campus.

Faculty *Total:* 141, 100% full-time. *Student/faculty ratio:* 23:1.

Majors Accounting; agricultural business; agricultural sciences; anthropology; art; auto body repair; auto mechanic/technician; biology; botany; business; business administration; business marketing and marketing management; cabinet making; chemistry; child care/development; communications; computer science; criminal justice/law enforcement administration; culinary arts; dental assistant; dental hygiene; diesel engine mechanic; dietetics; drafting; education; electrical/electronic engineering technology; elementary education; engineering; English; environmental science; equestrian studies; finance; fish/game management; foreign languages/literatures; forestry; geography; geology; graphic design/commercial art/illustration; health services administration; heating/air conditioning/refrigeration; history; hotel and restaurant management; human services; law enforcement/police science; liberal arts and sciences/liberal studies; library science; mathematics; medical radiologic technology; medical technology; music; natural sciences; nursing; occupational therapy; operating room technician; photography; physical education; physical therapy; physician assistant; physics; political science; pre-pharmacy studies; psychology; public health education/promotion; range management; real estate; respiratory therapy; sociology; theater arts/drama; veterinary technology; water resources; welding technology; woodworking; zoology.

Academic Programs *Special study options:* academic remediation for entering students, adult/continuing education programs, advanced placement credit, cooperative education, distance learning, English as a second language, honors programs, internships, part-time degree program, services for LD students, summer session for credit.

Library College of Southern Idaho Library with 53,706 titles, 267 serial subscriptions, 2,270 audiovisual materials, an OPAC, a Web page.

Computers on Campus 350 computers available on campus for general student use. A campuswide network can be accessed from off campus. Internet access, online (class) registration, at least one staffed computer lab available.

Student Life *Housing Options:* coed. *Activities and Organizations:* drama/theater group, student-run newspaper, radio station, choral group, BPA, Dex, Chi Alpha (Christian Group), Vet Tech, Equine Club. *Campus security:* 24-hour emergency response devices and patrols, controlled dormitory access. *Student Services:* health clinic, personal/psychological counseling, women's center, legal services.

Athletics Member NJCAA. *Intercollegiate sports:* baseball M(s), basketball M(s)/W(s), equestrian sports M(s)/W(s), volleyball W(s). *Intramural sports:* basketball M/W, football M/W, golf M/W, racquetball M/W, soccer M/W, softball M/W, tennis M/W, volleyball M/W.

Standardized Tests *Required for some:* ACT (for admission).

Costs (2002–03) *Tuition:* state resident $1550 full-time, $78 per credit part-time; nonresident $4300 full-time, $215 per credit part-time. *Room and board:* $3200. Room and board charges vary according to board plan. *Waivers:* senior citizens and employees or children of employees.

Financial Aid In 2001, 250 Federal Work-Study jobs (averaging $1700). 100 State and other part-time jobs (averaging $1700).

Applying *Options:* common application. *Required:* high school transcript. *Required for some:* letters of recommendation, interview. *Application deadline:* rolling (freshmen), rolling (transfers).

College of Southern Idaho (continued)
Admissions Contact Dr. John S. Martin, Director of Admissions, Registration, and Records, College of Southern Idaho, PO Box 1238, Twin Falls, ID 83303. *Phone:* 208-733-9554 Ext. 2232. *Toll-free phone:* 800-680-0274. *Fax:* 208-736-3014.

EASTERN IDAHO TECHNICAL COLLEGE
Idaho Falls, Idaho

- **State-supported** 2-year, founded 1970
- **Calendar** semesters
- **Degree** certificates and associate
- **Small-town** 40-acre campus
- **Endowment** $1.3 million
- **Coed,** 601 undergraduate students, 55% full-time, 65% women, 35% men

Undergraduates 331 full-time, 270 part-time. Students come from 1 other state, 0.8% African American, 0.8% Asian American or Pacific Islander, 4% Hispanic American, 1% Native American, 32% transferred in. *Retention:* 70% of 2001 full-time freshmen returned.
Freshmen *Admission:* 542 applied, 149 admitted, 149 enrolled.
Faculty *Total:* 106, 39% full-time, 3% with terminal degrees. *Student/faculty ratio:* 13:1.
Majors Accounting; auto mechanic/technician; business marketing and marketing management; business systems networking/ telecommunications; electrical/electronic engineering technology; medical assistant; paralegal/legal assistant; secretarial science; welding technology.
Academic Programs *Special study options:* academic remediation for entering students, adult/continuing education programs, cooperative education, distance learning, internships, part-time degree program, services for LD students, summer session for credit.
Library Eastern Idaho Technical College Library plus 1 other with 7,500 titles, 50 serial subscriptions, 100 audiovisual materials, an OPAC, a Web page.
Computers on Campus 105 computers available on campus for general student use. Internet access, at least one staffed computer lab available.
Student Life *Housing:* college housing not available. *Campus security:* 24-hour patrols. *Student Services:* personal/psychological counseling.
Standardized Tests *Required:* ACT COMPASS.
Costs (2002–03) *Tuition:* state resident $1512 full-time, $68 per credit part-time; nonresident $5110 full-time, $136 per credit part-time. Full-time tuition and fees vary according to course load and reciprocity agreements. Part-time tuition and fees vary according to class time and reciprocity agreements. *Waivers:* employees or children of employees.
Financial Aid In 2001, 37 Federal Work-Study jobs (averaging $1176). 11 State and other part-time jobs (averaging $1619).
Applying *Options:* deferred entrance. *Application fee:* $10. *Required:* high school transcript, interview. *Required for some:* essay or personal statement. *Recommended:* letters of recommendation. *Application deadline:* 8/20 (freshmen).
Admissions Contact Dr. Steve Albiston, Dean of Students, Eastern Idaho Technical College, 1600 South 25th E., Idaho Falls, ID 83404. *Phone:* 208-524-3000 Ext. 3366. *Toll-free phone:* 800-662-0261 Ext. 3371. *Fax:* 208-525-7026. *E-mail:* salbisto@eitc.edu.

ITT TECHNICAL INSTITUTE
Boise, Idaho

- **Proprietary** primarily 2-year, founded 1906, part of ITT Educational Services, Inc
- **Calendar** quarters
- **Degrees** associate and bachelor's
- **Urban** 1-acre campus
- **Coed,** 382 undergraduate students

Majors Administrative/secretarial services; computer/information sciences related; computer programming; drafting; electrical/electronic engineering technologies related; information technology.
Student Life *Housing:* college housing not available.
Costs (2001–02) *Tuition:* Full-time tuition and fees vary according to program. Part-time tuition and fees vary according to program. $260—$330 per credit hour.
Financial Aid In 2001, 9 Federal Work-Study jobs (averaging $5500).
Applying *Options:* deferred entrance. *Application fee:* $100. *Required:* high school transcript, interview. *Recommended:* letters of recommendation. *Application deadline:* rolling (freshmen), rolling (transfers). *Notification:* continuous (freshmen).
Admissions Contact Mr. Bart Van Ry, Director of Recruitment, ITT Technical Institute, 12302 West Explorer Drive, Boise, ID 83713. *Phone:* 208-322-8844. *Toll-free phone:* 800-666-4888. *Fax:* 208-322-0173.

NORTH IDAHO COLLEGE
Coeur d'Alene, Idaho

- **State and locally supported** 2-year, founded 1933
- **Calendar** semesters
- **Degree** certificates and associate
- **Small-town** 42-acre campus
- **Endowment** $4.9 million
- **Coed,** 4,133 undergraduate students

Undergraduates Students come from 27 states and territories, 16 other countries, 5% are from out of state.
Freshmen *Admission:* 1,797 applied, 1,689 admitted. *Average high school GPA:* 2.81.
Faculty *Total:* 338, 43% full-time. *Student/faculty ratio:* 17:1.
Majors Agricultural sciences; anthropology; art; astronomy; athletic training/sports medicine; auto mechanic/technician; biological/physical sciences; biology; botany; business administration; business education; carpentry; chemistry; computer programming; computer science; computer science related; computer/technical support; criminal justice/law enforcement administration; culinary arts; developmental/child psychology; drafting; education; electrical/electronic engineering technology; elementary education; engineering; English; environmental health; fish/game management; forestry; French; geology; German; graphic design/commercial art/illustration; health services administration; heating/air conditioning/refrigeration; heavy equipment maintenance; history; hospitality management; human services; journalism; law enforcement/police science; legal administrative assistant; liberal arts and sciences/liberal studies; machine technology; marine technology; mass communications; mathematics; medical administrative assistant; medical technology; music; music teacher education; Native American studies; nursing; paralegal/legal assistant; physical sciences; physics; political science; practical nurse; psychology; secretarial science; social sciences; sociology; Spanish; theater arts/drama; welding technology; wildlife biology; wildlife management; zoology.
Academic Programs *Special study options:* academic remediation for entering students, accelerated degree program, adult/continuing education programs, advanced placement credit, cooperative education, distance learning, English as a second language, internships, off-campus study, part-time degree program, services for LD students, summer session for credit.
Library Molstead Library Computer Center with 60,893 titles, 751 serial subscriptions, an OPAC, a Web page.
Computers on Campus 145 computers available on campus for general student use. Internet access, at least one staffed computer lab available.
Student Life *Activities and Organizations:* drama/theater group, student-run newspaper, choral group, ski club, Fusion, Baptist student ministries, journalism club, Phi Theta Kappa. *Campus security:* 24-hour emergency response devices and patrols, late-night transport/escort service. *Student Services:* health clinic, personal/psychological counseling, women's center, legal services.
Athletics Member NJCAA. *Intercollegiate sports:* baseball M(s), basketball M(s)/W(s), cross-country running M(s)/W(s), soccer M/W, softball W(s), track and field M(s)/W(s), volleyball W(s), wrestling M(s). *Intramural sports:* basketball M/W, bowling M/W, crew M(c)/W(c), cross-country running M/W, football M/W, golf M/W, racquetball M/W, sailing M(c)/W(c), skiing (cross-country) M(c)/W(c), skiing (downhill) M(c)/W(c), soccer M(c)/W(c), softball M/W, table tennis M/W, tennis M/W, volleyball M/W.
Standardized Tests *Required for some:* ACT ASSET, ACT COMPASS. *Recommended:* SAT I or ACT (for placement), ACT ASSET, ACT COMPASS.
Costs (2002–03) *Tuition:* area resident $1544 full-time, $95 per credit part-time; state resident $2544 full-time, $158 per credit part-time; nonresident $328 per credit part-time. *Room and board:* $5400.
Financial Aid In 2001, 112 Federal Work-Study jobs (averaging $1857). 103 State and other part-time jobs (averaging $1747).
Applying *Options:* early admission, deferred entrance. *Application fee:* $15. *Required for some:* essay or personal statement, high school transcript, minimum 2.0 GPA, 3 letters of recommendation, county residency certificate.
Admissions Contact Mr. John Jensen, Director of Admissions, North Idaho College, 1000 West Garden Avenue, Coeur d'Alene, ID 83814-2199. *Phone:* 208-769-3311. *Toll-free phone:* 877-404-4536. *Fax:* 208-769-3399. *E-mail:* admit@nic.edu.

ILLINOIS

BLACK HAWK COLLEGE
Moline, Illinois

- **State and locally supported** 2-year, founded 1946, part of Black Hawk College District System
- **Calendar** semesters
- **Degree** certificates and associate
- **Suburban** 149-acre campus
- **Coed,** 6,248 undergraduate students, 46% full-time, 60% women, 40% men

Undergraduates 2,878 full-time, 3,370 part-time. Students come from 5 states and territories, 17 other countries, 2% are from out of state, 32% transferred in. *Retention:* 64% of 2001 full-time freshmen returned.
Freshmen *Admission:* 1,027 admitted, 1,278 enrolled. *Test scores:* ACT scores over 18: 59%; ACT scores over 24: 10%.
Faculty *Total:* 352, 41% full-time, 13% with terminal degrees. *Student/faculty ratio:* 19:1.
Majors Accounting; accounting technician; agricultural business; agricultural production; agricultural sciences; auto body repair; auto mechanic/technician; aviation technology; banking; biological/physical sciences; broadcast journalism; business administration; business computer programming; business marketing and marketing management; child care/development; child guidance; civil engineering technology; computer engineering technology; computer science; cosmetology; culinary arts; data processing; dental hygiene; design/visual communications; diesel engine mechanic; drafting; education; electroencephalograph technology; electromechanical technology; engineering technology; English; environmental technology; equestrian studies; executive assistant; fashion design/illustration; fashion merchandising; finance; fire services administration; heating/air conditioning/refrigeration; horticulture services; hotel and restaurant management; industrial technology; instrumentation technology; interior design; journalism; law enforcement/police science; legal administrative assistant; liberal arts and sciences/liberal studies; machine technology; mechanical design technology; mechanical drafting; mechanical engineering technology; medical administrative assistant; medical laboratory technician; medical radiologic technology; medical records administration; natural sciences; nursing; paralegal/legal assistant; physical education; physical sciences; physical therapy assistant; practical nurse; pre-engineering; public relations; radio/television broadcasting; radio/television broadcasting technology; real estate; retail management; robotics; secretarial science; sign language interpretation; speech/rhetorical studies; technical/business writing; theater arts/drama; veterinary sciences.
Academic Programs *Special study options:* academic remediation for entering students, accelerated degree program, adult/continuing education programs, advanced placement credit, cooperative education, distance learning, English as a second language, honors programs, independent study, internships, off-campus study, part-time degree program, services for LD students, study abroad, summer session for credit.
Library Quad City Campus Library plus 1 other with 65,186 titles, 1,264 serial subscriptions, 140 audiovisual materials, an OPAC, a Web page.
Computers on Campus 650 computers available on campus for general student use. A campuswide network can be accessed from off campus. Internet access, at least one staffed computer lab available.
Student Life *Housing:* college housing not available. *Activities and Organizations:* drama/theater group, student-run newspaper, television station, choral group. *Campus security:* 24-hour patrols. *Student Services:* personal/psychological counseling.
Athletics Member NJCAA. *Intercollegiate sports:* baseball M(s), basketball M(s)/W(s), golf M(s), softball W(s), track and field M/W, volleyball W(s).
Standardized Tests *Required:* ACT ASSET. *Required for some:* ACT (for placement), ACT ASSET.
Costs (2002–03) *Tuition:* area resident $1530 full-time, $51 per credit hour part-time; state resident $4200 full-time, $140 per credit hour part-time; nonresident $7770 full-time, $259 per credit hour part-time. *Required fees:* $120 full-time, $2 per credit hour. *Payment plans:* installment, deferred payment. *Waivers:* senior citizens and employees or children of employees.
Applying *Options:* early admission, deferred entrance. *Required:* high school transcript. *Application deadline:* rolling (freshmen).
Admissions Contact Ms. Rose Hernandez, Coordinator of Recruitment, Black Hawk College, 6600 34th Avenue, Moline, IL 61265-5899. *Phone:* 309-796-5342. *E-mail:* duncanr@bhc.bhc.edu.

CAREER COLLEGES OF CHICAGO
Chicago, Illinois

- **Proprietary** 2-year, founded 1950
- **Calendar** quarters
- **Degree** certificates and associate
- **Urban** campus
- **Coed, primarily women,** 144 undergraduate students, 24% full-time, 86% women, 14% men

Undergraduates 35 full-time, 109 part-time. Students come from 1 other state.
Freshmen *Admission:* 26 applied, 26 admitted, 26 enrolled.
Faculty *Total:* 19, 32% with terminal degrees. *Student/faculty ratio:* 11:1.
Majors Computer science; court reporting; legal administrative assistant; medical administrative assistant.
Academic Programs *Special study options:* advanced placement credit, internships, part-time degree program, summer session for credit.
Library Main Library plus 1 other with 1,000 titles, 10 serial subscriptions.
Computers on Campus 46 computers available on campus for general student use. Internet access, at least one staffed computer lab available.
Student Life *Housing:* college housing not available. *Campus security:* 24-hour emergency response devices, guard on duty during building hours.
Standardized Tests *Recommended:* ACT (for admission).
Costs (2001–02) *Tuition:* $12,240 full-time, $255 per quarter hour part-time. *Required fees:* $400 full-time, $40 per quarter part-time.
Financial Aid *Financial aid deadline:* 6/1.
Applying *Options:* deferred entrance. *Application fee:* $40. *Required:* high school transcript, interview. *Application deadline:* rolling (freshmen), rolling (transfers).
Admissions Contact Ms. Rosa Alvarado, Admissions Assistant, Career Colleges of Chicago, 11 East Adams Street, Chicago, IL 60603. *Phone:* 312-895-6306. *Fax:* 312-895-6301. *E-mail:* icoburn@careerchi.com.

CARL SANDBURG COLLEGE
Galesburg, Illinois

- **State and locally supported** 2-year, founded 1967, part of Illinois Community College Board
- **Calendar** semesters
- **Degree** associate
- **Small-town** 105-acre campus with easy access to Peoria
- **Coed,** 4,000 undergraduate students

Undergraduates Students come from 5 states and territories, 2 other countries.
Faculty *Total:* 208, 28% full-time. *Student/faculty ratio:* 17:1.
Majors Accounting; agricultural business; agricultural mechanization; auto mechanic/technician; business administration; business marketing and marketing management; cosmetology; criminal justice/law enforcement administration; data processing technology; developmental/child psychology; drafting; electrical/electronic engineering technology; fashion merchandising; industrial radiologic technology; law enforcement/police science; liberal arts and sciences/liberal studies; mortuary science; nursing; practical nurse; real estate; secretarial science.
Academic Programs *Special study options:* academic remediation for entering students, adult/continuing education programs, advanced placement credit, cooperative education, English as a second language, internships, part-time degree program, services for LD students, student-designed majors, summer session for credit. *ROTC:* Army (c).
Library Learning Resource Center plus 1 other with 39,900 titles, 290 serial subscriptions.
Computers on Campus 110 computers available on campus for general student use. At least one staffed computer lab available.
Student Life *Housing:* college housing not available. *Activities and Organizations:* drama/theater group, choral group. *Campus security:* 24-hour emergency response devices and patrols. *Student Services:* personal/psychological counseling.
Athletics Member NJCAA. *Intercollegiate sports:* baseball M(s), basketball M(s)/W(s), volleyball W(s).
Standardized Tests *Required:* ACT ASSET.
Costs (2001–02) *Tuition:* area resident $2412 full-time, $67 per credit hour part-time; state resident $2592 full-time, $81 per credit hour part-time; nonresident $11,736 full-time, $326 per credit hour part-time. *Payment plan:* deferred payment. *Waivers:* senior citizens and employees or children of employees.
Applying *Options:* early admission, deferred entrance. *Required:* high school transcript. *Application deadline:* rolling (freshmen), rolling (transfers).

Carl Sandburg College (continued)
Admissions Contact Ms. Carol Kreider, Director of Admissions and Records, Carl Sandburg College, 2400 Tom L. Wilson Boulevard, Galesburg, IL 61401-9576. *Phone:* 309-344-2518 Ext. 5227.

CITY COLLEGES OF CHICAGO, HAROLD WASHINGTON COLLEGE
Chicago, Illinois

Admissions Contact Mr. Terry Pendleton, Admissions Coordinator, City Colleges of Chicago, Harold Washington College, 30 East Lake Street, Chicago, IL 60601-2449. *Phone:* 312-553-6006. *Fax:* 312-553-6077.

CITY COLLEGES OF CHICAGO, HARRY S. TRUMAN COLLEGE
Chicago, Illinois

- **State and locally supported** 2-year, founded 1956, part of City Colleges of Chicago
- **Calendar** semesters
- **Degree** certificates, diplomas, and associate
- **Urban** 5-acre campus
- **Coed,** 5,873 undergraduate students

Undergraduates *Retention:* 25% of 2001 full-time freshmen returned.
Faculty *Total:* 503, 23% full-time. *Student/faculty ratio:* 61:1.
Majors Accounting; art; business administration; business marketing and marketing management; chemical engineering technology; developmental/child psychology; drafting; education; elementary education; information sciences/systems; journalism; law enforcement/police science; legal studies; liberal arts and sciences/liberal studies; medical administrative assistant; medical records administration; medical technology; modern languages; nursing; physical education; pre-engineering; speech/rhetorical studies; teacher assistant/aide.
Academic Programs *Special study options:* academic remediation for entering students, adult/continuing education programs, advanced placement credit, cooperative education, distance learning, English as a second language, honors programs, internships, part-time degree program, services for LD students, summer session for credit.
Library 59,750 titles, 250 serial subscriptions.
Computers on Campus 150 computers available on campus for general student use. Internet access, at least one staffed computer lab available.
Student Life *Housing:* college housing not available. *Activities and Organizations:* drama/theater group. *Campus security:* 24-hour patrols, late-night transport/escort service. *Student Services:* personal/psychological counseling.
Athletics Member NJCAA. *Intercollegiate sports:* baseball M, basketball M/W, tennis M/W, wrestling M. *Intramural sports:* basketball M/W, swimming M/W, tennis M/W, volleyball M/W.
Standardized Tests *Required:* ACT (for placement).
Costs (2002–03) *Tuition:* $52 per credit hour part-time; state resident $175 per credit hour part-time; nonresident $254 per credit hour part-time. *Required fees:* $75 full-time, $75 per term part-time.
Financial Aid In 2001, 150 Federal Work-Study jobs (averaging $3000).
Applying *Options:* common application, early admission, deferred entrance. *Application deadline:* rolling (freshmen), rolling (transfers). *Notification:* continuous until 9/8 (freshmen).
Admissions Contact Mrs. Kelly O'Malley, Assistant Dean, Student Services, City Colleges of Chicago, Harry S. Truman College, 1145 West Wilson Avenue, Chicago, IL 60640-5616. *Phone:* 773-907-4720. *Fax:* 773-989-6135.

CITY COLLEGES OF CHICAGO, KENNEDY-KING COLLEGE
Chicago, Illinois

- **State and locally supported** 2-year, founded 1935, part of City Colleges of Chicago
- **Calendar** semesters
- **Degree** certificates and associate
- **Urban** 18-acre campus
- **Endowment** $8.6 million
- **Coed**

Student Life *Campus security:* late-night transport/escort service.
Athletics Member NJCAA.
Standardized Tests *Recommended:* SAT I or ACT (for placement).
Financial Aid In 2001, 148 Federal Work-Study jobs (averaging $1539).
Applying *Options:* early admission, deferred entrance. *Required:* high school transcript.
Admissions Contact Ms. Joyce Collins, Clerical Supervisor for Admissions and Records, City Colleges of Chicago, Kennedy-King College, 6800 South Wentworth Avenue, Chicago, IL 60621. *Phone:* 773-602-5000 Ext. 5055. *E-mail:* w.murphy@ccc.edu.

CITY COLLEGES OF CHICAGO, MALCOLM X COLLEGE
Chicago, Illinois

- **State and locally supported** 2-year, founded 1911, part of City Colleges of Chicago
- **Calendar** semesters
- **Degree** certificates and associate
- **Urban** 20-acre campus
- **Coed,** 8,791 undergraduate students, 57% full-time, 58% women, 42% men

Undergraduates 5,037 full-time, 3,754 part-time. Students come from 1 other state, 78% African American, 4% Asian American or Pacific Islander, 11% Hispanic American, 0.8% Native American, 18% transferred in.
Freshmen *Admission:* 637 applied, 637 admitted.
Faculty *Total:* 171, 37% full-time, 16% with terminal degrees. *Student/faculty ratio:* 22:1.
Majors Accounting; art; business computer programming; child care provider; dietician assistant; elementary education; emergency medical technology; general studies; health facilities administration; liberal arts and sciences/liberal studies; medical assistant; medical laboratory technician; medical radiologic technology; mortuary science; music; nursing; operating room technician; physical education; physician assistant; pre-medicine; pre-pharmacy studies; respiratory therapy; restaurant operations; secondary education; secretarial science; teacher assistant/aide.
Academic Programs *Special study options:* academic remediation for entering students, adult/continuing education programs, advanced placement credit, cooperative education, English as a second language, honors programs, part-time degree program, services for LD students, student-designed majors, summer session for credit.
Library The Carter G. Woodson Library with 50,000 titles, 250 serial subscriptions, 300 audiovisual materials, an OPAC, a Web page.
Computers on Campus 275 computers available on campus for general student use. Internet access, at least one staffed computer lab available.
Student Life *Housing:* college housing not available. *Activities and Organizations:* student-run newspaper, Student Government Association, Phi Theta Kappa honor society, Phi Beta Lambda business organization, Chess Club, Latino Leadership Council. *Campus security:* 24-hour emergency response devices and patrols. *Student Services:* personal/psychological counseling.
Athletics Member NJCAA. *Intercollegiate sports:* basketball M/W, cross-country running M. *Intramural sports:* basketball M/W, volleyball M/W.
Standardized Tests *Required for some:* SAT I and SAT II or ACT (for placement).
Costs (2001–02) *Tuition:* area resident $1500 full-time, $50 per credit part-time; state resident $4987 full-time, $166 per credit part-time; nonresident $7292 full-time, $243 per credit part-time. *Required fees:* $190 full-time, $95 per term part-time. *Payment plan:* deferred payment. *Waivers:* senior citizens and employees or children of employees.
Financial Aid In 2001, 200 Federal Work-Study jobs (averaging $2500).
Applying *Options:* common application, early admission, deferred entrance. *Required:* high school transcript, minimum 2.0 GPA. *Required for some:* essay or personal statement, interview. *Application deadline:* rolling (freshmen), rolling (transfers).
Admissions Contact Mr. Ghingo C. Brooks, Vice President of Enrollment Management and Student Services, City Colleges of Chicago, Malcolm X

College, 1900 West Van Buren Street, Chicago, IL 60612. *Phone:* 312-850-7120. *Fax:* 312-850-7092. *E-mail:* gbrooks@ccc.edu.

City Colleges of Chicago, Olive-Harvey College
Chicago, Illinois

- **State and locally supported** 2-year, founded 1970, part of City Colleges of Chicago
- **Calendar** semesters
- **Degree** certificates and associate
- **Urban** 67-acre campus
- **Coed**

Student Life *Campus security:* 24-hour emergency response devices and patrols.
Athletics Member NJCAA.
Standardized Tests *Required:* SAT I or ACT (for placement).
Applying *Options:* common application, early admission, deferred entrance.
Admissions Contact Mrs. Ruby M. Howard, Director of Admissions/Registrar, City Colleges of Chicago, Olive-Harvey College, 10001 South Woodlawn Avenue, Chicago, IL 60628-1645. *Phone:* 773-291-6380. *Fax:* 773-291-6304.

City Colleges of Chicago, Richard J. Daley College
Chicago, Illinois

- **State and locally supported** 2-year, founded 1960, part of City Colleges of Chicago
- **Calendar** semesters
- **Degree** certificates and associate
- **Urban** 25-acre campus
- **Coed,** 5,149 undergraduate students, 31% full-time, 62% women, 38% men

Undergraduates 1,579 full-time, 3,570 part-time. Students come from 29 states and territories, 71 other countries, 36% African American, 2% Asian American or Pacific Islander, 41% Hispanic American, 0.4% Native American.
Freshmen *Admission:* 339 admitted, 339 enrolled.
Faculty *Total:* 180, 39% full-time. *Student/faculty ratio:* 26:1.
Majors Accounting; architectural engineering technology; art; aviation technology; business administration; business marketing and marketing management; child care/development; data processing technology; dental hygiene; developmental/child psychology; drafting; education; electrical/electronic engineering technology; elementary education; fire science; horticulture science; humanities; journalism; law enforcement/police science; legal studies; liberal arts and sciences/liberal studies; machine technology; mass communications; medical administrative assistant; medical technology; modern languages; music; nursing; pharmacy; photography; pre-engineering; secretarial science; social work; speech/rhetorical studies; teacher assistant/aide; telecommunications; theater arts/drama; transportation technology.
Academic Programs *Special study options:* academic remediation for entering students, adult/continuing education programs, advanced placement credit, English as a second language, honors programs, off-campus study, part-time degree program, services for LD students, summer session for credit. *ROTC:* Air Force (c).
Library Learning Resource Center plus 1 other with 53,201 titles, 275 serial subscriptions, an OPAC.
Computers on Campus 325 computers available on campus for general student use.
Student Life *Housing:* college housing not available. *Activities and Organizations:* drama/theater group, student-run newspaper, Latin Student Organization, Student Government Association, African-American Culture Club. *Campus security:* 24-hour patrols. *Student Services:* personal/psychological counseling.
Standardized Tests *Required for some:* ACT (for placement). *Recommended:* ACT (for placement).
Costs (2001–02) *Tuition:* area resident $1500 full-time, $50 per credit hour part-time; state resident $4987 full-time, $166 per credit hour part-time; nonresident $7292 full-time, $243 per credit hour part-time. *Required fees:* $250 full-time, $75 per term part-time. *Waivers:* senior citizens and employees or children of employees.
Financial Aid In 2001, 129 Federal Work-Study jobs (averaging $1871).
Applying *Options:* common application, early admission, deferred entrance. *Required:* high school transcript. *Required for some:* essay or personal statement, letters of recommendation. *Recommended:* interview. *Application deadline:* rolling (freshmen), rolling (transfers).
Admissions Contact Ms. Karla Reynolds, Registrar, City Colleges of Chicago, Richard J. Daley College, 7500 South Pulaski Road, Chicago, IL 60652-1242. *Phone:* 773-838-7599. *E-mail:* kreynolds@ccc.edu.

City Colleges of Chicago, Wilbur Wright College
Chicago, Illinois

- **State and locally supported** 2-year, founded 1934, part of City Colleges of Chicago
- **Calendar** semesters
- **Degree** certificates and associate
- **Urban** 9-acre campus
- **Coed,** 6,253 undergraduate students, 29% full-time, 60% women, 40% men

Undergraduates 1,838 full-time, 4,415 part-time.
Freshmen *Admission:* 2,450 applied, 2,450 admitted. *Average high school GPA:* 2.5.
Faculty *Total:* 231, 46% full-time. *Student/faculty ratio:* 21:1.
Majors Accounting; architectural engineering technology; art; biological/physical sciences; business administration; business marketing and marketing management; computer/information sciences; data processing technology; elementary education; English; environmental technology; gerontology; journalism; law enforcement/police science; liberal arts and sciences/liberal studies; library science; machine technology; medical radiologic technology; modern languages; music; occupational therapy; physical sciences; pre-engineering; speech/rhetorical studies.
Academic Programs *Special study options:* academic remediation for entering students, accelerated degree program, adult/continuing education programs, English as a second language, part-time degree program, summer session for credit.
Library Learning Resource Center plus 1 other with 60,000 titles, 350 serial subscriptions.
Computers on Campus 534 computers available on campus for general student use. Internet access, at least one staffed computer lab available.
Student Life *Activities and Organizations:* drama/theater group, student-run newspaper, choral group, student government, Circle K, Phi Theta Kappa, Black Student Union. *Campus security:* 24-hour emergency response devices and patrols, student patrols, late-night transport/escort service. *Student Services:* legal services.
Athletics Member NJCAA. *Intramural sports:* basketball M, cross-country running M/W, golf M/W, swimming M/W, tennis M, volleyball M/W, weight lifting M/W, wrestling M/W.
Standardized Tests *Required:* ACT (for placement).
Costs (2001–02) *Tuition:* area resident $1700 full-time, $52 per credit hour part-time; state resident $175 per credit hour part-time; nonresident $252 per credit hour part-time. Full-time tuition and fees vary according to course load. Part-time tuition and fees vary according to course load. *Required fees:* $50 per term part-time. *Waivers:* senior citizens and employees or children of employees.
Financial Aid In 2001, 67 Federal Work-Study jobs (averaging $1000).
Applying *Options:* common application, early admission, deferred entrance. *Required:* essay or personal statement, high school transcript. *Application deadline:* rolling (freshmen), rolling (transfers). *Notification:* continuous (freshmen).
Admissions Contact Ms. Amy Aiello, Assistant Dean of Student Services, City Colleges of Chicago, Wilbur Wright College, 4300 North Narragansett, Chicago, IL 60634. *Phone:* 773-481-8207.

College of DuPage
Glen Ellyn, Illinois

- **State and locally supported** 2-year, founded 1967, part of Illinois Community College Board
- **Calendar** quarters
- **Degree** certificates and associate
- **Suburban** 297-acre campus with easy access to Chicago
- **Endowment** $10.6 million
- **Coed,** 29,423 undergraduate students, 32% full-time, 57% women, 43% men

Undergraduates 9,362 full-time, 20,061 part-time. Students come from 5 states and territories, 1% are from out of state, 4% African American, 11% Asian American or Pacific Islander, 6% Hispanic American, 0.1% Native American, 7% transferred in.

College of DuPage (continued)

Freshmen *Admission:* 4,252 admitted, 4,252 enrolled.

Faculty *Total:* 1,573, 18% full-time, 12% with terminal degrees. *Student/faculty ratio:* 21:1.

Majors Accounting; alcohol/drug abuse counseling; auto mechanic/technician; baker/pastry chef; biological/physical sciences; business administration; business marketing and marketing management; buying operations; child care/development; child care provider; child care services management; communication equipment technology; communication systems installation/repair; computer installation/repair; computer typography/composition; corrections; criminal justice/law enforcement administration; culinary arts; distribution operations; drafting; electrical/electronic engineering technology; electrical equipment installation/repair; electromechanical technology; emergency medical technology; engineering; fashion design/illustration; fashion merchandising; film/video production; fire science; graphic design/commercial art/illustration; graphic/printing equipment; health services administration; heating/air conditioning/refrigeration; hospitality management; hotel and restaurant management; human services; industrial electronics installation/repair; industrial technology; interior design; landscaping management; law enforcement/police science; legal administrative assistant; liberal arts and sciences/liberal studies; library science; machine technology; marketing operations; mechanical design technology; medical records administration; nuclear medical technology; nursing; occupational therapy; occupational therapy assistant; operating room technician; ornamental horticulture; photography; physical therapy assistant; plastics technology; real estate; respiratory therapy; restaurant operations; retailing operations; sales operations; secretarial science; speech-language pathology; tourism promotion operations; transportation technology; travel services marketing operations; travel/tourism management; welding technology.

Academic Programs *Special study options:* academic remediation for entering students, accelerated degree program, adult/continuing education programs, advanced placement credit, cooperative education, distance learning, double majors, English as a second language, external degree program, honors programs, independent study, internships, off-campus study, part-time degree program, services for LD students, student-designed majors, study abroad, summer session for credit.

Library College of DuPage Library with 182,000 titles, 1,500 serial subscriptions, 81,650 audiovisual materials, an OPAC, a Web page.

Computers on Campus 2203 computers available on campus for general student use. A campuswide network can be accessed from off campus. Internet access, online (class) registration, at least one staffed computer lab available.

Student Life *Housing:* college housing not available. *Activities and Organizations:* drama/theater group, student-run newspaper, choral group, Latino Ethnic Awareness Association, The Christian Group, Phi Theta Kappa, International Students Organization, Muslim Student Association. *Campus security:* 24-hour emergency response devices and patrols, student patrols, late-night transport/escort service. *Student Services:* health clinic, personal/psychological counseling.

Athletics Member NJCAA. *Intercollegiate sports:* baseball M, basketball M/W, football M, golf M, soccer M/W, softball W, swimming M/W, tennis M/W, track and field M/W, volleyball W. *Intramural sports:* basketball M/W, bowling M/W, golf M/W, ice hockey M(c), racquetball M/W, soccer M/W, softball M/W, swimming M/W, tennis M/W, volleyball M/W, weight lifting M/W.

Standardized Tests *Recommended:* ACT (for placement).

Costs (2001–02) *One-time required fee:* $10. *Tuition:* area resident $1776 full-time, $37 per quarter hour part-time; state resident $5760 full-time, $120 per quarter hour part-time; nonresident $7824 full-time, $163 per quarter hour part-time. Full-time tuition and fees vary according to course load and program. Part-time tuition and fees vary according to course load and program. *Required fees:* $185 full-time, $37 per quarter hour. *Payment plan:* deferred payment. *Waivers:* senior citizens and employees or children of employees.

Applying *Options:* early admission, deferred entrance. *Application fee:* $10. *Application deadline:* rolling (freshmen), rolling (transfers). *Notification:* continuous (freshmen).

Admissions Contact Mrs. Christine A. Legner, Coordinator of Admission Services, College of DuPage, SRC 2046, 425 Fawell Boulevard, Glen Ellyn, IL 60137-6599. *Phone:* 630-942-2442. *Fax:* 630-790-2686. *E-mail:* protis@cdnet.cod.edu.

COLLEGE OF LAKE COUNTY
Grayslake, Illinois

- **District-supported** 2-year, founded 1967, part of Illinois Community College Board
- **Calendar** semesters
- **Degree** certificates and associate
- **Suburban** 232-acre campus with easy access to Chicago and Milwaukee
- **Coed,** 14,886 undergraduate students, 24% full-time, 54% women, 46% men

Undergraduates 3,518 full-time, 11,368 part-time. Students come from 2 states and territories, 40 other countries, 2% are from out of state, 10% African American, 5% Asian American or Pacific Islander, 13% Hispanic American, 0.5% Native American, 3% international, 2% transferred in. *Retention:* 67% of 2001 full-time freshmen returned.

Freshmen *Admission:* 4,022 applied, 4,022 admitted, 1,908 enrolled.

Faculty *Total:* 977, 16% full-time, 7% with terminal degrees. *Student/faculty ratio:* 19:1.

Majors Accounting; aerospace engineering technology; alcohol/drug abuse counseling; architectural drafting; auto mechanic/technician; business administration; chemical technology; civil engineering technology; computer programming; computer systems networking/telecommunications; construction technology; data processing; dental hygiene; early childhood education; electrical/electronic engineering technology; engineering; fire protection/safety technology; food systems administration; heating/air conditioning/refrigeration; heavy equipment maintenance; industrial electronics installation/repair; industrial machinery maintenance/repair; landscaping management; law enforcement/police science; library assistant; machine shop assistant; mechanical engineering technology; medical laboratory technician; medical radiologic technology; medical records technology; music teacher education; nursing; ornamental horticulture; secretarial science; social work; technical/business writing.

Academic Programs *Special study options:* academic remediation for entering students, adult/continuing education programs, advanced placement credit, cooperative education, distance learning, double majors, English as a second language, honors programs, independent study, internships, off-campus study, part-time degree program, services for LD students, student-designed majors, study abroad, summer session for credit.

Library College of Lake County Library with 120,642 titles, 904 serial subscriptions, 8,028 audiovisual materials, an OPAC, a Web page.

Computers on Campus 1000 computers available on campus for general student use. A campuswide network can be accessed from off campus. At least one staffed computer lab available.

Student Life *Housing:* college housing not available. *Activities and Organizations:* drama/theater group, student-run newspaper, radio station, choral group, Latino Club, Black Student Union, International Student Council, Phi Theta Kappa, Campus Crusade. *Campus security:* 24-hour emergency response devices and patrols, late-night transport/escort service. *Student Services:* health clinic, personal/psychological counseling.

Athletics Member NJCAA. *Intercollegiate sports:* baseball M(s), basketball M(s)/W(s), cross-country running M(s)/W(s), golf M(s), soccer M(s)/W(s), softball W(s), tennis M(s)/W(s), volleyball W(s), wrestling M(s). *Intramural sports:* golf M/W.

Standardized Tests *Recommended:* SAT I or ACT (for placement).

Costs (2001–02) *Tuition:* area resident $1500 full-time, $50 per credit hour part-time; state resident $5310 full-time, $177 per credit hour part-time; nonresident $7440 full-time, $248 per credit hour part-time. *Required fees:* $150 full-time, $5 per credit hour. *Payment plan:* installment. *Waivers:* senior citizens and employees or children of employees.

Financial Aid In 2001, 95 Federal Work-Study jobs (averaging $1100).

Applying *Options:* common application, electronic application, early admission, deferred entrance. *Required for some:* high school transcript, interview. *Application deadline:* rolling (freshmen), rolling (transfers). *Notification:* continuous (freshmen).

Admissions Contact Ms. Karen Hlavin, Director of Admissions, College of Lake County, 19351 West Washington Street, Grayslake, IL 60030-1198. *Phone:* 847-543-2384. *Fax:* 847-223-1017. *E-mail:* terryspets@clc.cc.il.us.

THE COLLEGE OF OFFICE TECHNOLOGY
Chicago, Illinois

Admissions Contact 1514-20 West Division Street, Second Floor, Chicago, IL 60622.

THE COOKING AND HOSPITALITY INSTITUTE OF CHICAGO
Chicago, Illinois

- **Proprietary** 2-year, founded 1983, part of Career Education Corporation
- **Calendar** continuous
- **Degree** associate

- **Urban** campus
- **Endowment** $35,000
- **Coed,** 950 undergraduate students

Undergraduates Students come from 25 states and territories, 15 other countries, 25% are from out of state.
Freshmen *Admission:* 300 applied, 300 admitted. *Test scores:* ACT scores over 18: 75%; ACT scores over 24: 15%.
Faculty *Total:* 50, 80% full-time. *Student/faculty ratio:* 20:1.
Majors Culinary arts.
Academic Programs *Special study options:* academic remediation for entering students, accelerated degree program, adult/continuing education programs, advanced placement credit, cooperative education, double majors, services for LD students, summer session for credit.
Library Learning Resource Center plus 1 other with 5,000 titles, 100 serial subscriptions, 200 audiovisual materials.
Computers on Campus 25 computers available on campus for general student use. A campuswide network can be accessed from off campus. Internet access, at least one staffed computer lab available.
Student Life *Housing:* college housing not available. *Activities and Organizations:* student-run newspaper, The Student Board, Culinary Competition Club, Recipe Development Association, The Cellar Club, Pastry Display Club.
Standardized Tests *Recommended:* SAT I or ACT (for placement).
Costs (2002–03) *Tuition:* $16,000 full-time, $625 per credit part-time. No tuition increase for student's term of enrollment. *Required fees:* $1200 full-time. *Payment plans:* tuition prepayment, installment.
Financial Aid In 2001, 10 Federal Work-Study jobs.
Applying *Options:* common application, electronic application, deferred entrance. *Application fee:* $150. *Recommended:* essay or personal statement, high school transcript, interview.
Admissions Contact Caryn Jilly, Director of High School Admissions, The Cooking and Hospitality Institute of Chicago, 361 West Chestnut, Chicago, IL 60610. *Phone:* 312-873-2036. *Toll-free phone:* 877-828-7772 (in-state); 312-944-0882 (out-of-state). *Fax:* 312-944-8557. *E-mail:* chic@chicnet.org.

DANVILLE AREA COMMUNITY COLLEGE
Danville, Illinois

- **State and locally supported** 2-year, founded 1946, part of Illinois Community College Board
- **Calendar** semesters
- **Degree** certificates and associate
- **Small-town** 50-acre campus
- **Endowment** $978,329
- **Coed,** 3,000 undergraduate students

Undergraduates Students come from 4 states and territories, 1% are from out of state, 10% African American, 0.7% Asian American or Pacific Islander, 3% Hispanic American, 0.1% Native American.
Faculty *Total:* 121, 41% full-time, 5% with terminal degrees. *Student/faculty ratio:* 20:1.
Majors Accounting; agricultural business; agricultural sciences; alcohol/drug abuse counseling; art; auto mechanic/technician; biological/physical sciences; biology; business administration; business marketing and marketing management; child care/development; computer programming; criminal justice/law enforcement administration; data processing technology; drafting; early childhood education; education; electrical/electronic engineering technology; elementary education; engineering; English; history; horticulture science; humanities; human services; industrial radiologic technology; industrial technology; information sciences/systems; journalism; landscaping management; law enforcement/police science; legal administrative assistant; liberal arts and sciences/liberal studies; mathematics; mechanical engineering technology; medical administrative assistant; nursing; occupational therapy; ornamental horticulture; philosophy; physical education; physical therapy; practical nurse; pre-engineering; psychology; real estate; respiratory therapy; social sciences; social work; teacher assistant/aide; travel/tourism management; welding technology.
Academic Programs *Special study options:* academic remediation for entering students, adult/continuing education programs, advanced placement credit, cooperative education, distance learning, double majors, English as a second language, independent study, internships, part-time degree program, services for LD students, summer session for credit.
Library Learning Resources Center with 50,000 titles, 2,487 audiovisual materials, an OPAC.
Computers on Campus 332 computers available on campus for general student use. A campuswide network can be accessed from off campus. Internet access, at least one staffed computer lab available.
Student Life *Housing:* college housing not available. *Activities and Organizations:* choral group, choral group. *Campus security:* 24-hour patrols. *Student Services:* personal/psychological counseling.
Athletics Member NJCAA. *Intercollegiate sports:* baseball M(s), basketball M(s)/W(s), cross-country running M(s), softball W(s), track and field M(s)/W(s), volleyball W(s). *Intramural sports:* basketball M/W, cross-country running M, racquetball M/W.
Standardized Tests *Required for some:* ACT ASSET.
Costs (2001–02) *Tuition:* area resident $1200 full-time, $50 per credit hour part-time; state resident $4800 full-time, $200 per credit hour part-time; nonresident $4800 full-time, $200 per credit hour part-time. *Required fees:* $24 full-time, $1 per credit hour. *Payment plan:* deferred payment. *Waivers:* senior citizens and employees or children of employees.
Financial Aid In 2001, 90 Federal Work-Study jobs (averaging $4000). 100 State and other part-time jobs (averaging $4000).
Applying *Options:* early admission, deferred entrance. *Required:* high school transcript. *Application deadline:* rolling (freshmen), rolling (transfers).
Admissions Contact Ms. Stacy L. Ehmen, Director of Admissions of Records/Registrar, Danville Area Community College, 2000 East Main Street, Danville, IL 61832-5199. *Phone:* 217-443-8800. *Fax:* 217-443-8560. *E-mail:* sehmen@dacc.cc.il.us.

ELGIN COMMUNITY COLLEGE
Elgin, Illinois

- **State and locally supported** 2-year, founded 1949, part of Illinois Community College Board
- **Calendar** semesters
- **Degree** certificates, diplomas, and associate
- **Suburban** 145-acre campus with easy access to Chicago
- **Coed**

Faculty *Student/faculty ratio:* 18:1.
Student Life *Campus security:* 24-hour patrols.
Athletics Member NJCAA.
Standardized Tests *Recommended:* ACT (for placement).
Costs (2001–02) *Tuition:* area resident $1560 full-time, $52 per credit hour part-time; state resident $6908 full-time, $230 per credit hour part-time; nonresident $8361 full-time, $279 per credit hour part-time. *Required fees:* $15 full-time, $1 per credit hour.
Applying *Options:* early admission. *Application fee:* $15.
Admissions Contact Mr. Russ Fahrner, Dean of Student Services, Elgin Community College, 1700 Spartan Drive, Elgin, IL 60123-7193. *Phone:* 847-214-7226. *E-mail:* admissions@mail.elgin.cc.il.us.

GEM CITY COLLEGE
Quincy, Illinois

- **Proprietary** 2-year, founded 1870
- **Calendar** quarters
- **Degree** diplomas and associate
- **Small-town** campus
- **Coed,** 150 undergraduate students

Undergraduates Students come from 10 states and territories, 1 other country.
Freshmen *Admission:* 65 applied, 65 admitted.
Faculty *Total:* 7, 71% full-time.
Majors Accounting; business administration; computer science; cosmetology; information sciences/systems; legal administrative assistant; medical administrative assistant; medical assistant; metal/jewelry arts; paralegal/legal assistant; secretarial science.
Academic Programs *Special study options:* academic remediation for entering students, adult/continuing education programs, internships, part-time degree program, summer session for credit.
Library 2,700 titles, 40 serial subscriptions.
Computers on Campus 40 computers available on campus for general student use. At least one staffed computer lab available.
Student Life *Housing:* college housing not available. *Student Services:* personal/psychological counseling.
Costs (2001–02) *Tuition:* $8400 full-time.

Gem City College (continued)

Applying *Options:* early admission, deferred entrance. *Application fee:* $25. *Application deadline:* rolling (freshmen), rolling (transfers).

Admissions Contact Admissions Director, Gem City College, PO Box 179, Quincy, IL 62306-0179. *Phone:* 217-222-0391.

HEARTLAND COMMUNITY COLLEGE

Normal, Illinois

- **State and locally supported** 2-year, founded 1990, part of Illinois Community College Board
- **Calendar** semesters
- **Degree** certificates and associate
- **Urban** campus
- **Coed,** 4,558 undergraduate students, 35% full-time, 54% women, 46% men

Undergraduates Students come from 4 states and territories, 2 other countries, 1% are from out of state, 8% African American, 2% Asian American or Pacific Islander, 2% Hispanic American, 0.4% Native American, 0.1% international. *Retention:* 55% of 2001 full-time freshmen returned.

Freshmen *Admission:* 1,711 applied, 1,711 admitted.

Faculty *Total:* 252, 24% full-time. *Student/faculty ratio:* 21:1.

Majors Biological/physical sciences; business administration; business systems networking/ telecommunications; child care/development; child care provider; computer engineering technology; computer/information sciences; computer programming; computer programming (specific applications); computer programming, vendor/product certification; computer science; computer science related; computer systems networking/telecommunications; computer/technical support; corrections; data entry/microcomputer applications; data entry/microcomputer applications related; drafting; early childhood education; electrical/electronic engineering technology; engineering; heating/air conditioning/refrigeration; industrial machinery maintenance/repair; industrial technology; information sciences/systems; information technology; insurance marketing; liberal arts and sciences/liberal studies; machine technology; management information systems/business data processing; mechanical design technology; nursing; practical nurse; quality control technology; secretarial science; system/networking/LAN/WAN management; Web page, digital/multimedia and information resources design; welding technology.

Academic Programs *Special study options:* academic remediation for entering students, adult/continuing education programs, advanced placement credit, cooperative education, distance learning, double majors, independent study, internships, part-time degree program, services for LD students, study abroad, summer session for credit. *ROTC:* Army (c).

Library Heartland Community College Library with 2,600 titles, 110 serial subscriptions, 2,100 audiovisual materials, a Web page.

Computers on Campus 400 computers available on campus for general student use. Internet access, at least one staffed computer lab available.

Student Life *Housing:* college housing not available. *Activities and Organizations:* drama/theater group, student-run newspaper, choral group, Environmental Club, Early Childhood Club, student government, Nursing Club, Phi Theta Kappa. *Campus security:* 24-hour emergency response devices and patrols. *Student Services:* personal/psychological counseling.

Standardized Tests *Recommended:* SAT I (for placement), ACT (for placement).

Costs (2001–02) *Tuition:* area resident $1440 full-time, $48 per credit part-time; state resident $6136 full-time, $205 per credit part-time; nonresident $8283 full-time, $276 per credit part-time. *Waivers:* minority students, senior citizens, and employees or children of employees.

Applying *Recommended:* high school transcript. *Application deadline:* rolling (freshmen), rolling (transfers).

Admissions Contact Ms. Christine Riley, Director of Advisement and Enrollment Services, Heartland Community College, 1500 West Raab Road, Normal, IL 61761. *Phone:* 309-268-8000. *Fax:* 309-268-7992. *E-mail:* angie.robinson@hcc.cc.il.us.

HIGHLAND COMMUNITY COLLEGE

Freeport, Illinois

- **State and locally supported** 2-year, founded 1962, part of Illinois Community College Board
- **Calendar** semesters
- **Degree** certificates and associate
- **Rural** 240-acre campus
- **Endowment** $6.8 million
- **Coed,** 2,541 undergraduate students, 39% full-time, 64% women, 36% men

Undergraduates 1,000 full-time, 1,541 part-time. Students come from 8 states and territories, 2% are from out of state, 8% African American, 0.8% Asian American or Pacific Islander, 0.9% Hispanic American, 0.3% Native American, 0.2% international. *Retention:* 65% of 2001 full-time freshmen returned.

Freshmen *Admission:* 362 applied, 362 admitted.

Faculty *Total:* 188, 27% full-time, 3% with terminal degrees. *Student/faculty ratio:* 19:1.

Majors Accounting; agricultural business; agricultural mechanization; art; auto mechanic/technician; biological/physical sciences; business administration; business marketing and marketing management; chemistry; child care/development; child care provider; child care services management; computer programming (specific applications); computer science; computer science related; computer/technical support; data processing technology; drafting; drafting/design technology; early childhood education; education; electrical/electronic engineering technology; engineering; engineering science; engineering technology; geology; graphic design/commercial art/illustration; history; human services; liberal arts and sciences/liberal studies; mathematics; mechanical engineering technology; music teacher education; nursing; physical sciences; physics; political science; pre-engineering; psychology; secretarial science; sociology; speech/theater education; theater arts/drama.

Academic Programs *Special study options:* academic remediation for entering students, adult/continuing education programs, advanced placement credit, distance learning, English as a second language, external degree program, independent study, internships, part-time degree program, services for LD students, student-designed majors, summer session for credit.

Library Highland Library plus 1 other with 47,000 titles, 3,980 serial subscriptions, 2,776 audiovisual materials, an OPAC, a Web page.

Computers on Campus 200 computers available on campus for general student use. Internet access, at least one staffed computer lab available.

Student Life *Housing:* college housing not available. *Activities and Organizations:* drama/theater group, student-run newspaper, choral group, Phi Theta Kappa, Royal Scots, Prairie Wind, intramurals, Collegiate Choir. *Campus security:* 24-hour patrols. *Student Services:* personal/psychological counseling.

Athletics Member NJCAA. *Intercollegiate sports:* baseball M(s)/W(s), basketball M(s)/W(s), golf M(s)/W(s), softball W(s), volleyball W(s). *Intramural sports:* basketball M/W, racquetball M/W, volleyball M/W.

Standardized Tests *Required for some:* ACT (for placement). *Recommended:* ACT (for placement).

Costs (2001–02) *Tuition:* area resident $1500 full-time, $50 per credit hour part-time; state resident $4808 full-time, $160 per credit hour part-time; nonresident $6096 full-time, $203 per credit hour part-time. Full-time tuition and fees vary according to course load and reciprocity agreements. Part-time tuition and fees vary according to course load and reciprocity agreements. *Required fees:* $40 full-time, $10 per term part-time. *Payment plan:* deferred payment. *Waivers:* senior citizens and employees or children of employees.

Applying *Options:* early admission, deferred entrance. *Required for some:* high school transcript. *Application deadline:* rolling (freshmen), rolling (transfers).

Admissions Contact Mr. Karl Richards, Dean of Enrollment Services, Highland Community College, 2998 West Pearl City Road, Freeport, IL 61032. *Phone:* 815-235-6121 Ext. 3486. *Fax:* 815-235-6130.

ILLINOIS CENTRAL COLLEGE

East Peoria, Illinois

Admissions Contact Mrs. Joanne Bannon-Gray, Director of Enrollment Management, Illinois Central College, One College Drive, East Peoria, IL 61635-0001. *Phone:* 309-694-5354. *Toll-free phone:* 800-422-2293. *Fax:* 309-694-5450.

ILLINOIS EASTERN COMMUNITY COLLEGES, FRONTIER COMMUNITY COLLEGE

Fairfield, Illinois

- **State and locally supported** 2-year, founded 1976, part of Illinois Eastern Community College System
- **Calendar** semesters
- **Degree** certificates and associate
- **Rural** 8-acre campus
- **Coed,** 1,913 undergraduate students, 10% full-time, 66% women, 34% men

Undergraduates 192 full-time, 1,721 part-time.
Freshmen *Admission:* 74 admitted, 74 enrolled.
Faculty *Total:* 141, 3% full-time. *Student/faculty ratio:* 38:1.
Majors Biological/physical sciences; computer/information sciences; information sciences/systems; liberal arts and sciences/liberal studies; nursing; quality control technology; secretarial science; teacher assistant/aide.
Academic Programs *Special study options:* academic remediation for entering students, adult/continuing education programs, advanced placement credit, cooperative education, distance learning, double majors, English as a second language, external degree program, independent study, part-time degree program, services for LD students, student-designed majors, summer session for credit.
Library 14,551 titles, 109 serial subscriptions, 1,552 audiovisual materials.
Computers on Campus 42 computers available on campus for general student use. At least one staffed computer lab available.
Student Life *Housing:* college housing not available.
Standardized Tests *Required:* SAT I or ACT (for placement), ACT ASSET.
Costs (2001–02) *Tuition:* area resident $1354 full-time, $40 per credit hour part-time; state resident $5692 full-time, $176 per credit hour part-time; nonresident $7035 full-time, $218 per credit hour part-time. *Required fees:* $74 full-time, $2 per credit hour. *Waivers:* senior citizens and employees or children of employees.
Applying *Options:* early admission, deferred entrance. *Application fee:* $10. *Required:* high school transcript. *Application deadline:* rolling (freshmen), rolling (transfers). *Notification:* continuous (freshmen).
Admissions Contact Mrs. Suzanne Brooks, Coordinator of Registration and Records, Illinois Eastern Community Colleges, Frontier Community College, 2 Frontier Drive, Fairfield, IL 62837. *Phone:* 618-842-3711 Ext. 4111.

ILLINOIS EASTERN COMMUNITY COLLEGES, LINCOLN TRAIL COLLEGE
Robinson, Illinois

- **State and locally supported** 2-year, founded 1969, part of Illinois Eastern Community College System
- **Calendar** semesters
- **Degree** certificates and associate
- **Rural** 120-acre campus
- **Coed,** 1,100 undergraduate students, 51% full-time, 44% women, 56% men

Undergraduates 557 full-time, 543 part-time. 12% African American, 1% Asian American or Pacific Islander, 3% Hispanic American, 0.1% Native American, 0.1% international.
Freshmen *Admission:* 381 admitted, 381 enrolled.
Faculty *Total:* 81, 43% full-time. *Student/faculty ratio:* 38:1.
Majors Biology; computer/information sciences; computer programming; computer systems analysis; data processing; data processing technology; drafting; education; finance; food services technology; heating/air conditioning/refrigeration; industrial technology; liberal arts and sciences/liberal studies; quality control technology; secretarial science; telecommunications.
Academic Programs *Special study options:* academic remediation for entering students, adult/continuing education programs, advanced placement credit, cooperative education, distance learning, double majors, English as a second language, external degree program, independent study, internships, part-time degree program, services for LD students, student-designed majors, summer session for credit.
Library Eagleton Learning Resource Center with 24,352 titles, 89 serial subscriptions, 1,317 audiovisual materials.
Computers on Campus 96 computers available on campus for general student use. At least one staffed computer lab available.
Student Life *Housing:* college housing not available. *Activities and Organizations:* drama/theater group, choral group, national fraternities. *Student Services:* personal/psychological counseling.
Athletics Member NJCAA. *Intercollegiate sports:* baseball M(s), basketball M(s)/W(s), softball W(s), volleyball W(s). *Intramural sports:* baseball M, basketball M, softball W, volleyball M/W.
Standardized Tests *Required:* SAT I or ACT (for placement), ACT ASSET.
Costs (2001–02) *Tuition:* area resident $1354 full-time, $40 per credit hour part-time; state resident $5692 full-time, $176 per credit hour part-time; nonresident $7035 full-time, $218 per credit hour part-time. *Required fees:* $74 full-time, $2 per credit hour. *Waivers:* senior citizens and employees or children of employees.
Applying *Options:* early admission, deferred entrance. *Application fee:* $10. *Required:* high school transcript. *Application deadline:* rolling (freshmen), rolling (transfers). *Notification:* continuous (freshmen).
Admissions Contact Ms. Becky Mikeworth, Director of Admissions, Illinois Eastern Community Colleges, Lincoln Trail College, 11220 State Highway 1, Robinson, IL 62454. *Phone:* 618-544-8657 Ext. 1137.

ILLINOIS EASTERN COMMUNITY COLLEGES, OLNEY CENTRAL COLLEGE
Olney, Illinois

- **State and locally supported** 2-year, founded 1962, part of Illinois Eastern Community College System
- **Calendar** semesters
- **Degree** certificates and associate
- **Rural** 128-acre campus
- **Coed,** 1,617 undergraduate students, 48% full-time, 58% women, 42% men

Undergraduates 769 full-time, 848 part-time. 0.6% African American, 0.5% Asian American or Pacific Islander, 0.3% Hispanic American, 0.2% Native American, 0.8% international.
Freshmen *Admission:* 229 admitted, 229 enrolled.
Faculty *Total:* 83, 49% full-time.
Majors Accounting; auto body repair; auto mechanic/technician; computer/information sciences; heavy equipment maintenance; industrial radiologic technology; law enforcement/police science; liberal arts and sciences/liberal studies; medical administrative assistant; metallurgical technology; nursing; practical nurse; secretarial science.
Academic Programs *Special study options:* academic remediation for entering students, adult/continuing education programs, advanced placement credit, cooperative education, distance learning, double majors, English as a second language, external degree program, independent study, internships, part-time degree program, services for LD students, student-designed majors, summer session for credit.
Library Anderson Learning Resources Center with 26,994 titles, 88 serial subscriptions.
Computers on Campus 125 computers available on campus for general student use. At least one staffed computer lab available.
Student Life *Housing:* college housing not available. *Activities and Organizations:* drama/theater group, student-run newspaper, choral group. *Student Services:* personal/psychological counseling, women's center.
Athletics Member NJCAA. *Intercollegiate sports:* baseball M(s), basketball M(s)/W(s), softball W(s), volleyball W(s). *Intramural sports:* baseball M, basketball M/W, softball W.
Standardized Tests *Required:* SAT I or ACT (for placement), ACT ASSET.
Costs (2001–02) *Tuition:* area resident $1354 full-time, $40 per credit hour part-time; state resident $5692 full-time, $176 per credit hour part-time; nonresident $7035 full-time, $218 per credit hour part-time. *Required fees:* $74 full-time, $2 per credit hour. *Waivers:* senior citizens and employees or children of employees.
Applying *Options:* early admission, deferred entrance. *Application fee:* $10. *Required:* high school transcript. *Application deadline:* rolling (freshmen), rolling (transfers). *Notification:* continuous (freshmen).
Admissions Contact Mrs. Chris Webber, Assistant Dean for Student Services, Illinois Eastern Community Colleges, Olney Central College, 305 North West Street, Olney, IL 62450. *Phone:* 618-395-7777 Ext. 2005.

ILLINOIS EASTERN COMMUNITY COLLEGES, WABASH VALLEY COLLEGE
Mount Carmel, Illinois

- **State and locally supported** 2-year, founded 1960, part of Illinois Eastern Community College System
- **Calendar** semesters
- **Degree** certificates and associate
- **Rural** 40-acre campus
- **Coed,** 2,643 undergraduate students, 23% full-time, 46% women, 54% men

Undergraduates 606 full-time, 2,037 part-time. 2% African American, 0.9% Asian American or Pacific Islander, 0.9% Hispanic American, 0.3% Native American.
Freshmen *Admission:* 597 admitted, 597 enrolled.
Faculty *Total:* 78, 50% full-time. *Student/faculty ratio:* 38:1.
Majors Agricultural business; agricultural mechanization; business administration; child care/development; computer/information sciences; court reporting;

Illinois Eastern Community Colleges, Wabash Valley College (continued)
electrical/electronic engineering technology; industrial technology; liberal arts and sciences/liberal studies; machine technology; mining technology; radio/television broadcasting; secretarial science; social work; transportation technology.
Academic Programs *Special study options:* academic remediation for entering students, adult/continuing education programs, advanced placement credit, cooperative education, distance learning, double majors, English as a second language, external degree program, independent study, internships, part-time degree program, services for LD students, student-designed majors, summer session for credit.
Library Bauer Media Center with 30,813 titles, 252 serial subscriptions, 1,294 audiovisual materials.
Computers on Campus 100 computers available on campus for general student use. At least one staffed computer lab available.
Student Life *Housing:* college housing not available. *Activities and Organizations:* drama/theater group, student-run newspaper, radio and television station, choral group.
Athletics Member NJCAA. *Intercollegiate sports:* baseball M(s), basketball M(s)/W(s), softball W(s), tennis M, volleyball W(s). *Intramural sports:* baseball M, basketball M/W, cross-country running M/W, softball W, volleyball M/W.
Standardized Tests *Required:* SAT I or ACT (for placement), ACT ASSET.
Costs (2001–02) *Tuition:* area resident $1354 full-time, $40 per credit hour part-time; state resident $5692 full-time, $176 per credit hour part-time; nonresident $7035 full-time, $218 per credit hour part-time. *Required fees:* $74 full-time, $2 per credit hour. *Waivers:* senior citizens and employees or children of employees.
Applying *Options:* early admission, deferred entrance. *Application fee:* $10. *Required:* high school transcript. *Application deadline:* rolling (freshmen), rolling (transfers). *Notification:* continuous (freshmen).
Admissions Contact Mrs. Diana Spear, Assistant Dean for Student Services, Illinois Eastern Community Colleges, Wabash Valley College, 2200 College Drive, Mt. Carmel, IL 62863. *Phone:* 618-262-8641 Ext. 3101.

Illinois Valley Community College
Oglesby, Illinois

- **District-supported** 2-year, founded 1924, part of Illinois Community College Board
- **Calendar** semesters
- **Degree** associate
- **Rural** 410-acre campus with easy access to Chicago
- **Coed**

Student Life *Campus security:* 24-hour patrols.
Standardized Tests *Recommended:* ACT (for placement).
Costs (2001–02) *Tuition:* area resident $1500 full-time, $50 per semester hour part-time; state resident $5441 full-time, $181 per semester hour part-time; nonresident $6720 full-time, $224 per semester hour part-time. *Required fees:* $217 full-time, $7 per semester hour, $3 per term part-time.
Financial Aid In 2001, 84 Federal Work-Study jobs (averaging $1028).
Applying *Options:* early admission, deferred entrance. *Required:* high school transcript.
Admissions Contact Ms. Kelly Conrad, Director of Admissions and Records, Illinois Valley Community College, 815 North Orlando Smith Avenue, Oglesby, IL 61348-9692. *Phone:* 815-224-2720 Ext. 437.

ITT Technical Institute
Burr Ridge, Illinois

- **Proprietary** 2-year
- **Calendar** quarters
- **Degree** associate
- **Coed,** 267 undergraduate students

Majors Computer/information sciences related; computer programming; electrical/electronic engineering technologies related; information technology.
Student Life *Housing:* college housing not available.
Costs (2001–02) *Tuition:* Full-time tuition and fees vary according to program. Part-time tuition and fees vary according to program. $260—$330 per credit hour.
Applying *Application fee:* $100. *Required:* high school transcript, interview. *Recommended:* letters of recommendation. *Application deadline:* rolling (freshmen). *Notification:* continuous (freshmen).
Admissions Contact Ms. Joan Malatesta, Director, ITT Technical Institute, 7040 High Grove Boulevard, Burr Ridge, IL 60521. *Phone:* 630-455-6470.

ITT Technical Institute
Mount Prospect, Illinois

- **Proprietary** primarily 2-year, founded 1986, part of ITT Educational Services, Inc
- **Calendar** quarters
- **Degrees** associate and bachelor's
- **Suburban** 1-acre campus with easy access to Chicago
- **Coed,** 447 undergraduate students

Majors Computer/information sciences related; drafting; electrical/electronic engineering technologies related; electrical/electronic engineering technology; information technology.
Student Life *Housing:* college housing not available.
Costs (2001–02) *Tuition:* Full-time tuition and fees vary according to program. Part-time tuition and fees vary according to program. $260—$330 per credit hour.
Applying *Options:* deferred entrance. *Application fee:* $100. *Required:* high school transcript, interview. *Recommended:* letters of recommendation. *Application deadline:* rolling (freshmen), rolling (transfers). *Notification:* continuous (freshmen).
Admissions Contact Mr. Ernest Lloyd, Director of Recruitment, ITT Technical Institute, 375 West Higgins Road, Hoffman Estates, IL 60195. *Phone:* 847-519-9300 Ext. 11.

ITT Technical Institute
Matteson, Illinois

- **Proprietary** 2-year, founded 1993, part of ITT Educational Services, Inc
- **Calendar** quarters
- **Degree** associate
- **Suburban** campus with easy access to Chicago
- **Coed,** 331 undergraduate students

Majors Computer/information sciences related; computer programming; drafting; electrical/electronic engineering technologies related; information technology.
Student Life *Housing:* college housing not available.
Costs (2001–02) *Tuition:* Full-time tuition and fees vary according to program. Part-time tuition and fees vary according to program. $260—$330 per credit hour.
Financial Aid In 2001, 6 Federal Work-Study jobs (averaging $4000).
Applying *Options:* deferred entrance. *Application fee:* $100. *Required:* high school transcript, interview. *Recommended:* letters of recommendation. *Application deadline:* rolling (freshmen), rolling (transfers).
Admissions Contact Ms. Lillian Williams-McClain, Director, ITT Technical Institute, 6000 Holiday Plaza Drive, Matteson, IL 60443. *Phone:* 708-747-2571.

John A. Logan College
Carterville, Illinois

- **State and locally supported** 2-year, founded 1967, part of Illinois Community College Board
- **Calendar** semesters
- **Degree** certificates and associate
- **Rural** 160-acre campus
- **Endowment** $19,000
- **Coed,** 5,130 undergraduate students

Undergraduates Students come from 2 states and territories, 2 other countries.
Faculty *Total:* 43, 53% full-time, 2% with terminal degrees.
Majors Accounting; agricultural sciences; art; art education; auto mechanic/technician; biology; business administration; business education; business marketing and marketing management; chemistry; computer science; cosmetology; criminal justice/law enforcement administration; data processing technology; dental hygiene; drafting; early childhood education; education; electrical/electronic engineering technology; elementary education; emergency medical technology; English; fashion merchandising; finance; heating/air conditioning/refrigeration; history; humanities; information sciences/systems; journalism; legal administrative assistant; liberal arts and sciences/liberal studies; machine technology; mathematics; medical laboratory technician; medical records administration; nursing; occupational therapy; physical education; physics; political science;

practical nurse; pre-engineering; psychology; retail management; sign language interpretation; social work; teacher assistant/aide; travel/tourism management; welding technology.

Academic Programs *Special study options:* academic remediation for entering students, adult/continuing education programs, advanced placement credit, cooperative education, distance learning, internships, off-campus study, part-time degree program, services for LD students, study abroad, summer session for credit. *ROTC:* Army (c), Air Force (c).

Library Learning Resource Center with 33,306 titles, 298 serial subscriptions, a Web page.

Computers on Campus 150 computers available on campus for general student use. Internet access, at least one staffed computer lab available.

Student Life *Housing:* college housing not available. *Activities and Organizations:* drama/theater group, student-run newspaper, choral group. *Campus security:* 24-hour emergency response devices and patrols.

Athletics Member NJCAA. *Intercollegiate sports:* baseball M, basketball M/W, golf M/W, softball W, volleyball W.

Standardized Tests *Required:* ACT ASSET. *Recommended:* SAT I or ACT (for placement).

Costs (2001–02) *Tuition:* area resident $1380 full-time, $46 per semester hour part-time; state resident $4257 full-time, $142 per semester hour part-time; nonresident $6413 full-time, $214 per semester hour part-time. *Waivers:* senior citizens and employees or children of employees.

Applying *Options:* electronic application, early admission. *Required:* high school transcript. *Application deadlines:* 8/25 (freshmen), 8/25 (transfers). *Notification:* continuous (freshmen).

Admissions Contact Mr. Terry Crain, Associate Dean of Student Services, John A. Logan College, 700 Logan College Road, Carterville, IL 62918-9900. *Phone:* 618-985-3741 Ext. 8382. *Fax:* 618-985-4433. *E-mail:* terry.crain@jal.cc.il.us.

JOHN WOOD COMMUNITY COLLEGE
Quincy, Illinois

- **District-supported** 2-year, founded 1974, part of Illinois Community College Board
- **Calendar** semesters
- **Degree** certificates and associate
- **Small-town** campus
- **Coed,** 2,111 undergraduate students, 47% full-time, 65% women, 35% men

Undergraduates 998 full-time, 1,113 part-time. Students come from 3 states and territories, 3 other countries, 9% are from out of state, 4% African American, 0.6% Asian American or Pacific Islander, 0.9% Hispanic American, 0.3% Native American, 0.4% international, 4% transferred in.

Freshmen *Admission:* 450 applied, 450 admitted, 456 enrolled. *Test scores:* ACT scores over 18: 71%; ACT scores over 24: 17%; ACT scores over 30: 1%.

Faculty *Total:* 176, 28% full-time. *Student/faculty ratio:* 15:1.

Majors Agricultural business; agricultural production; biological/physical sciences; business administration; business computer programming; child guidance; electrical/electronic engineering technology; fire protection/safety technology; fire science; horticulture services; hotel and restaurant management; law enforcement/police science; legal administrative assistant; liberal arts and sciences/liberal studies; medical administrative assistant; medical laboratory technician; medical radiologic technology; nursing; radio/television broadcasting technology; secretarial science.

Academic Programs *Special study options:* academic remediation for entering students, adult/continuing education programs, advanced placement credit, cooperative education, distance learning, English as a second language, external degree program, independent study, internships, off-campus study, part-time degree program, services for LD students, student-designed majors, study abroad, summer session for credit.

Library 18,000 titles, 160 serial subscriptions, 2,200 audiovisual materials, an OPAC, a Web page.

Computers on Campus 200 computers available on campus for general student use. Internet access, at least one staffed computer lab available.

Student Life *Housing:* college housing not available. *Activities and Organizations:* choral group. *Campus security:* 24-hour emergency response devices, late-night transport/escort service.

Athletics Member NJCAA. *Intercollegiate sports:* baseball M(s), basketball M(s)/W(s), golf M(s), softball W(s), volleyball W(s). *Intramural sports:* basketball M/W, volleyball M/W.

Standardized Tests *Required:* ACT ASSET, ACT COMPASS. *Recommended:* SAT I or ACT (for placement).

Costs (2002–03) *Tuition:* area resident $1890 full-time, $63 per credit hour part-time; state resident $4890 full-time, $163 per credit hour part-time; nonresident $4890 full-time, $163 per credit hour part-time. *Required fees:* $90 full-time, $3 per credit hour. *Payment plan:* installment. *Waivers:* senior citizens and employees or children of employees.

Applying *Options:* common application, early admission. *Required:* high school transcript. *Application deadline:* rolling (freshmen), rolling (transfers). *Notification:* continuous (freshmen).

Admissions Contact Mr. Mark C. McNett, Director of Admissions, John Wood Community College, 1301 South 48th Street, Quincy, IL 62305-8736. *Phone:* 217-224-6500 Ext. 4339. *Fax:* 217-224-4208. *E-mail:* admissions@jwcc.edu.

JOLIET JUNIOR COLLEGE
Joliet, Illinois

- **State and locally supported** 2-year, founded 1901, part of Illinois Community College Board
- **Calendar** semesters
- **Degree** certificates, diplomas, and associate
- **Suburban** campus with easy access to Chicago
- **Coed,** 12,089 undergraduate students, 32% full-time, 59% women, 41% men

Undergraduates 3,874 full-time, 8,215 part-time. Students come from 8 states and territories, 8% are from out of state, 8% African American, 2% Asian American or Pacific Islander, 7% Hispanic American, 0.2% Native American, 0.2% international, 2% transferred in.

Freshmen *Admission:* 3,836 applied, 3,836 admitted, 2,005 enrolled. *Test scores:* ACT scores over 18: 61%; ACT scores over 24: 17%; ACT scores over 30: 1%.

Faculty *Total:* 597, 31% full-time, 7% with terminal degrees. *Student/faculty ratio:* 12:1.

Majors Accounting; agricultural business; art; auto mechanic/technician; biology; business administration; business economics; business marketing and marketing management; chemistry; child care/guidance; computer/information sciences; computer programming; computer programming (specific applications); computer/technical support; construction technology; corrections; culinary arts; data processing; ecology; education; electrical/electronic engineering technology; electrical/electronics drafting; English; fashion merchandising; finance; fire science; food products retailing; forestry; geography; history; horticulture science; hotel and restaurant management; industrial technology; interior design; landscaping management; law enforcement/police science; liberal arts and sciences/liberal studies; mathematics; mechanical design technology; medical technology; music; natural resources conservation; nuclear technology; nursing; physical education; physics; physiology; political science; pre-engineering; psychology; real estate; secretarial science; sociology; teacher assistant/aide; theater arts/drama; veterinarian assistant; Web page, digital/multimedia and information resources design; zoology.

Academic Programs *Special study options:* academic remediation for entering students, adult/continuing education programs, advanced placement credit, distance learning, English as a second language, honors programs, independent study, internships, part-time degree program, services for LD students, summer session for credit.

Library Learning Resource Center with 60,364 titles, 360 serial subscriptions, an OPAC.

Computers on Campus A campuswide network can be accessed from off campus. Internet access, at least one staffed computer lab available.

Student Life *Housing:* college housing not available. *Activities and Organizations:* drama/theater group, student-run newspaper, choral group, Phi Theta Kappa, JC Players, Nursing Student Association, Student Agricultural Association, Intervarsity Christian Fellowship, national fraternities. *Campus security:* 24-hour emergency response devices and patrols, student patrols, late-night transport/escort service. *Student Services:* personal/psychological counseling, women's center.

Athletics Member NJCAA. *Intercollegiate sports:* basketball M/W, football M, golf M, softball W, tennis M/W, volleyball W.

Standardized Tests *Required for some:* ACT (for placement). *Recommended:* SAT I or ACT (for placement).

Costs (2002–03) *One-time required fee:* $210. *Tuition:* area resident $1470 full-time, $49 per credit hour part-time; state resident $5337 full-time, $178 per credit hour part-time; nonresident $7474 full-time, $222 per credit hour part-time. *Required fees:* $7 per credit hour. *Payment plan:* deferred payment. *Waivers:* employees or children of employees.

Financial Aid In 2001, 96 Federal Work-Study jobs (averaging $1168). 254 State and other part-time jobs (averaging $1778).

Joliet Junior College (continued)

Applying *Options:* early admission, deferred entrance. *Required:* high school transcript. *Application deadline:* rolling (freshmen), rolling (transfers).

Admissions Contact Dr. Denis Wright, Vice President of Academic Affairs, Joliet Junior College, 1215 Houbolt Road, Joliet, IL 60431. *Phone:* 815-280-2236.

KANKAKEE COMMUNITY COLLEGE
Kankakee, Illinois

- **State and locally supported** 2-year, founded 1966, part of Illinois Community College Board
- **Calendar** semesters
- **Degrees** certificates and associate (also offers continuing education program with significant enrollment not reflected in profile)
- **Small-town** 178-acre campus with easy access to Chicago
- **Coed,** 3,000 undergraduate students

Faculty *Total:* 162, 36% full-time.

Majors Accounting; auto mechanic/technician; aviation technology; biological/physical sciences; business; business marketing and marketing management; child care/development; criminal justice/law enforcement administration; drafting; electrical/electronic engineering technology; elementary education; emergency medical technology; engineering; fine/studio arts; heating/air conditioning/refrigeration; industrial radiologic technology; information sciences/systems; law enforcement/police science; liberal arts and sciences/liberal studies; machine technology; medical laboratory technician; nursing; physical therapy assistant; psychology; real estate; respiratory therapy; secretarial science; welding technology.

Academic Programs *Special study options:* academic remediation for entering students, adult/continuing education programs, advanced placement credit, cooperative education, honors programs, internships, off-campus study, part-time degree program, services for LD students, student-designed majors, study abroad, summer session for credit.

Library 41,000 titles, 420 serial subscriptions, an OPAC.

Computers on Campus 120 computers available on campus for general student use. Internet access, at least one staffed computer lab available.

Student Life *Housing:* college housing not available. *Campus security:* 24-hour patrols.

Athletics Member NJCAA. *Intercollegiate sports:* baseball M(s), basketball M(s)/W(s), softball W(s), volleyball W(s). *Intramural sports:* basketball M, football M/W, golf M/W, volleyball M/W.

Standardized Tests *Required for some:* ACT ASSET. *Recommended:* ACT ASSET.

Costs (2001–02) *Tuition:* area resident $1245 full-time, $42 per semester hour part-time; state resident $2886 full-time, $96 per semester hour part-time; nonresident $7506 full-time, $313 per semester hour part-time. *Required fees:* $75 full-time.

Financial Aid In 2001, 89 Federal Work-Study jobs (averaging $850). *Financial aid deadline:* 10/1.

Applying *Options:* early admission. *Required:* high school transcript. *Application deadline:* rolling (freshmen), rolling (transfers). *Notification:* continuous (freshmen).

Admissions Contact Mr. Thomas D. Dolliger, Director of Admissions and Registration, Kankakee Community College, Box 888, Kankakee, IL 60901. *Phone:* 815-933-0242.

KASKASKIA COLLEGE
Centralia, Illinois

- **State and locally supported** 2-year, founded 1966, part of Illinois Community College Board
- **Calendar** semesters
- **Degree** certificates and associate
- **Rural** 195-acre campus with easy access to St. Louis
- **Coed,** 3,097 undergraduate students, 47% full-time, 59% women, 41% men

Undergraduates 1,461 full-time, 1,636 part-time. Students come from 3 states and territories, 1 other country, 8% African American, 0.6% Asian American or Pacific Islander, 1% Hispanic American, 0.5% Native American, 0.1% international, 39% transferred in.

Freshmen *Admission:* 494 applied, 494 admitted, 799 enrolled.

Faculty *Total:* 194, 32% full-time, 5% with terminal degrees. *Student/faculty ratio:* 19:1.

Majors Accounting; agricultural business; aircraft pilot (professional); auto body repair; auto mechanic/technician; biological/physical sciences; business administration; child care provider; data processing; drafting; electrical/electronic engineering technology; executive assistant; heavy equipment maintenance; industrial machinery maintenance/repair; law enforcement/police science; liberal arts and sciences/liberal studies; management information systems/business data processing; medical radiologic technology; nursing; physical therapy assistant; respiratory therapy; restaurant operations; welding technology.

Academic Programs *Special study options:* academic remediation for entering students, adult/continuing education programs, cooperative education, distance learning, independent study, internships, off-campus study, part-time degree program, services for LD students, study abroad, summer session for credit. *ROTC:* Army (b).

Library Kaskaskia College Library with 27,426 titles, 119 serial subscriptions, an OPAC, a Web page.

Computers on Campus 285 computers available on campus for general student use. Internet access, at least one staffed computer lab available.

Student Life *Housing:* college housing not available. *Activities and Organizations:* drama/theater group, student-run newspaper, choral group, Student Nurse Association, Cosmetology Club, Phi Beta Lambda, Students in Free Enterprise. *Campus security:* 24-hour patrols, late-night transport/escort service. *Student Services:* personal/psychological counseling.

Athletics Member NJCAA. *Intercollegiate sports:* baseball M(s), basketball M(s)/W(s), softball W(s), volleyball W(s).

Standardized Tests *Required for some:* ACT (for placement). *Recommended:* ACT (for admission), ACT (for placement).

Costs (2002–03) *Tuition:* area resident $1376 full-time, $43 per credit part-time; state resident $4288 full-time, $101 per credit part-time; nonresident $7296 full-time, $252 per credit part-time. Full-time tuition and fees vary according to location. Part-time tuition and fees vary according to location. *Required fees:* $160 full-time, $5 per credit. *Payment plan:* installment. *Waivers:* senior citizens and employees or children of employees.

Applying *Options:* common application, early admission, deferred entrance. *Required:* high school transcript. *Required for some:* interview. *Application deadline:* rolling (freshmen), rolling (transfers). *Notification:* continuous (freshmen).

Admissions Contact Ms. Jan Ripperda, Admissions and Records Officer, Kaskaskia College, 27210 College Road, Centralia, IL 62801. *Phone:* 618-545-3041. *Toll-free phone:* 800-642-0859. *Fax:* 618-532-1135.

KISHWAUKEE COLLEGE
Malta, Illinois

- **State and locally supported** 2-year, founded 1967, part of Illinois Community College Board
- **Calendar** semesters
- **Degree** certificates and associate
- **Rural** 120-acre campus with easy access to Chicago
- **Endowment** $1.5 million
- **Coed,** 4,337 undergraduate students

Undergraduates Students come from 5 states and territories, 0.1% are from out of state, 13% African American, 4% Asian American or Pacific Islander, 9% Hispanic American, 0.4% Native American, 0.1% international.

Faculty *Total:* 210, 35% full-time, 7% with terminal degrees. *Student/faculty ratio:* 15:1.

Majors Agricultural business; agricultural mechanization; agricultural production; art; art education; auto body repair; auto mechanic/technician; business administration; business computer programming; child care/guidance; computer programming related; computer science related; engineering; greenhouse management; horticulture services; industrial design; landscaping management; law enforcement/police science; liberal arts and sciences/liberal studies; medical radiologic technology; nursing; operations management; ornamental horticulture; quality control technology; secretarial science; tool/die making; turf management; word processing.

Academic Programs *Special study options:* academic remediation for entering students, adult/continuing education programs, advanced placement credit, distance learning, double majors, English as a second language, external degree program, independent study, internships, off-campus study, part-time degree program, services for LD students, study abroad, summer session for credit. *ROTC:* Army (c).

Library Learning Resource Center with 40,835 titles, 248 serial subscriptions, 2,551 audiovisual materials, an OPAC, a Web page.

Computers on Campus 520 computers available on campus for general student use. Internet access, online (class) registration, at least one staffed computer lab available.
Student Life *Housing:* college housing not available. *Activities and Organizations:* drama/theater group, student-run newspaper, choral group, student association, Black Student Union, Horticulture Club, Student Nurses Association, International Club. *Campus security:* 24-hour patrols. *Student Services:* health clinic, personal/psychological counseling.
Athletics Member NJCAA. *Intercollegiate sports:* baseball M(s), basketball M(s)/W(s), golf M(s), soccer M(s), softball W(s), tennis W(s), volleyball W(s). *Intramural sports:* basketball M/W, volleyball W.
Standardized Tests *Required for some:* ACT, SAT I, or in-house placement test.
Costs (2001–02) *Tuition:* area resident $1470 full-time, $49 per credit part-time; state resident $4846 full-time, $201 per credit part-time; nonresident $5759 full-time, $240 per credit part-time. Full-time tuition and fees vary according to reciprocity agreements. Part-time tuition and fees vary according to reciprocity agreements. *Required fees:* $68 full-time, $2 per credit, $10 per term part-time. *Payment plan:* deferred payment. *Waivers:* senior citizens and employees or children of employees.
Financial Aid In 2001, 92 Federal Work-Study jobs (averaging $961). 65 State and other part-time jobs (averaging $881).
Applying *Options:* common application, early admission, deferred entrance. *Required:* high school transcript. *Required for some:* minimum 2.0 GPA. *Application deadline:* rolling (freshmen), rolling (transfers). *Notification:* continuous (freshmen).
Admissions Contact Ms. Sally Misciasci, Admission Analyst, Kishwaukee College, 21193 Malta Road, Malta, IL 60150-9699. *Phone:* 815-825-2086 Ext. 400. *Fax:* 815-825-2306.

LAKE LAND COLLEGE
Mattoon, Illinois

- **State and locally supported** 2-year, founded 1966, part of Illinois Community College Board
- **Calendar** semesters
- **Degree** certificates and associate
- **Rural** 304-acre campus
- **Endowment** $1.6 million
- **Coed,** 6,102 undergraduate students, 44% full-time, 45% women, 55% men

Undergraduates Students come from 5 other countries, 12% African American, 0.4% Asian American or Pacific Islander, 3% Hispanic American, 0.4% Native American, 0.5% international.
Freshmen *Admission:* 890 applied, 890 admitted.
Faculty *Total:* 197, 70% full-time, 3% with terminal degrees.
Majors Accounting technician; agricultural business; agricultural mechanization; agricultural production; architectural engineering technology; auto mechanic/technician; biological/physical sciences; business administration; business computer programming; business marketing and marketing management; child care/guidance; civil engineering technology; computer programming (specific applications); computer systems networking/telecommunications; corrections; dental hygiene; desktop publishing equipment operation; drafting; electrical/electronic engineering technology; electromechanical technology; executive assistant; general studies; graphic/printing equipment; human services; industrial technology; information technology; law enforcement/police science; legal administrative assistant; liberal arts and sciences/liberal studies; medical administrative assistant; nursing; office management; physical therapy assistant; printing press operation; radio/television broadcasting; secretarial science; social work; telecommunications.
Academic Programs *Special study options:* academic remediation for entering students, adult/continuing education programs, cooperative education, distance learning, English as a second language, external degree program, honors programs, internships, part-time degree program, services for LD students, summer session for credit.
Library Virgil H. Judge Learning Resource Center with 29,012 titles, 244 serial subscriptions, 1,938 audiovisual materials, an OPAC.
Computers on Campus 100 computers available on campus for general student use. Internet access, online (class) registration, at least one staffed computer lab available.
Student Life *Housing:* college housing not available. *Activities and Organizations:* student-run newspaper, radio station, choral group, Agriculture Production and Management Club, Cosmetology Club, Agriculture Transfer Club, Phi Theta Kappa, Civil Engineering Technology Club. *Campus security:* 24-hour patrols. *Student Services:* personal/psychological counseling.
Athletics Member NJCAA. *Intercollegiate sports:* baseball M(s), basketball M(s)/W(s), softball W(s), tennis M(s), volleyball W(s). *Intramural sports:* basketball M/W, bowling M/W, golf M/W, softball M/W, volleyball M/W.
Standardized Tests *Required for some:* ACT (for placement). *Recommended:* ACT (for placement).
Costs (2001–02) *Tuition:* area resident $1290 full-time, $43 per credit hour part-time; state resident $2702 full-time, $90 per credit hour part-time; nonresident $6735 full-time, $225 per credit hour part-time. Full-time tuition and fees vary according to reciprocity agreements. Part-time tuition and fees vary according to reciprocity agreements. *Required fees:* $324 full-time, $11 per credit hour. *Payment plan:* deferred payment. *Waivers:* senior citizens and employees or children of employees.
Financial Aid In 2001, 120 Federal Work-Study jobs (averaging $1400).
Applying *Options:* common application, electronic application, early admission. *Application fee:* $10. *Required for some:* letters of recommendation. *Recommended:* high school transcript. *Application deadline:* rolling (freshmen), rolling (transfers). *Notification:* continuous (freshmen).
Admissions Contact Mrs. Linda Von Behren, Dean of Admission Services, Lake Land College, 5001 Lake Land Boulevard, Mattoon, IL 61938-9366. *Phone:* 217-234-5254. *Toll-free phone:* 800-252-4121.

LEWIS AND CLARK COMMUNITY COLLEGE
Godfrey, Illinois

- **District-supported** 2-year, founded 1970, part of Illinois Community College Board
- **Calendar** semesters
- **Degree** certificates and associate
- **Small-town** 275-acre campus with easy access to St. Louis
- **Coed,** 6,985 undergraduate students, 27% full-time, 58% women, 42% men

Undergraduates Students come from 2 states and territories, 2 other countries, 1% are from out of state, 6% African American, 0.4% Asian American or Pacific Islander, 0.8% Hispanic American, 0.3% Native American, 0.4% international.
Faculty *Total:* 382, 21% full-time.
Majors Accounting; agricultural business; agricultural sciences; art; auto mechanic/technician; biological/physical sciences; biology; business administration; child care/development; computer programming; criminal justice/law enforcement administration; data processing technology; dental hygiene; drafting; early childhood education; fire science; hotel and restaurant management; legal administrative assistant; liberal arts and sciences/liberal studies; library science; machine technology; medical administrative assistant; medical laboratory technician; music; nursing; occupational therapy assistant; pre-engineering; radio/television broadcasting; secretarial science; teacher assistant/aide.
Academic Programs *Special study options:* academic remediation for entering students, adult/continuing education programs, advanced placement credit, cooperative education, distance learning, double majors, English as a second language, independent study, internships, off-campus study, part-time degree program, services for LD students, summer session for credit. *ROTC:* Army (b).
Library Reid Memorial with 30,000 titles, 300 serial subscriptions, 500 audiovisual materials, an OPAC, a Web page.
Computers on Campus 350 computers available on campus for general student use. Internet access, at least one staffed computer lab available.
Student Life *Housing:* college housing not available. *Activities and Organizations:* student-run newspaper, radio station, choral group, Phi Beta Lambda, Data Processing Club, Nursing Club, Clinical Laboratory Technicians Club, Music Club. *Campus security:* 24-hour emergency response devices and patrols. *Student Services:* health clinic, personal/psychological counseling.
Athletics Member NJCAA. *Intercollegiate sports:* baseball M, basketball M/W(s), golf M, soccer M(s)/W, softball W, tennis M(s)/W(s), volleyball W(s).
Costs (2002–03) *Tuition:* area resident $1560 full-time, $52 per credit hour part-time; state resident $6437 full-time, $215 per credit hour part-time; nonresident $9776 full-time, $326 per credit hour part-time. *Required fees:* $180 full-time. *Payment plans:* installment, deferred payment. *Waivers:* senior citizens and employees or children of employees.
Applying *Options:* early admission, deferred entrance. *Required for some:* interview. *Recommended:* high school transcript. *Application deadline:* rolling (freshmen), rolling (transfers). *Notification:* continuous (freshmen).
Admissions Contact Ms. Peggy Hudson, Director of Enrollment Center for Admissions Services, Lewis and Clark Community College, Enrollment Center, 5800 Godfrey Road, Godfrey, IL 62035. *Phone:* 618-468-5100. *Toll-free phone:* 800-500-LCCC. *Fax:* 618-467-2310.

LEXINGTON COLLEGE
Chicago, Illinois

- **Independent** 2-year, founded 1977
- **Calendar** semesters
- **Degree** associate
- **Urban** campus
- **Endowment** $11,000
- **Women only,** 35 undergraduate students

Undergraduates Students come from 7 states and territories, 2 other countries, 21% are from out of state, 28% live on campus.
Freshmen *Average high school GPA:* 2.5.
Faculty *Total:* 14, 14% full-time. *Student/faculty ratio:* 5:1.
Majors Culinary arts; hospitality management; hotel and restaurant management.
Academic Programs *Special study options:* academic remediation for entering students, adult/continuing education programs, cooperative education, internships, part-time degree program.
Library Lexington College Library with 2,000 titles, 40 serial subscriptions.
Computers on Campus 6 computers available on campus for general student use. At least one staffed computer lab available.
Student Life *Campus security:* 24-hour emergency response devices and patrols, patrols by municipal security personnel. *Student Services:* health clinic, personal/psychological counseling, women's center.
Costs (2001–02) *Tuition:* $9100 full-time, $400 per credit hour part-time. Part-time tuition and fees vary according to course load. *Required fees:* $250 full-time, $75 per term part-time. *Room only:* Room and board charges vary according to housing facility. *Payment plan:* installment.
Financial Aid *Financial aid deadline:* 10/1.
Applying *Required:* essay or personal statement, high school transcript. *Required for some:* 2 letters of recommendation. *Recommended:* minimum 2.0 GPA, interview. *Application deadline:* rolling (freshmen), rolling (transfers).
Admissions Contact Mrs. Carol Starks, Director of Admissions, Lexington College, 310 South Peoria Street, Chicago, IL 60607-3534. *Phone:* 312-226-6294. *Fax:* 773-779-7450.

LINCOLN COLLEGE
Lincoln, Illinois

- **Independent** 2-year, founded 1865
- **Calendar** semesters
- **Degree** associate
- **Small-town** 42-acre campus
- **Endowment** $14.0 million
- **Coed,** 650 undergraduate students

Undergraduates Students come from 15 states and territories, 5 other countries, 9% are from out of state, 90% live on campus.
Freshmen *Admission:* 650 applied, 493 admitted. *Average high school GPA:* 2.77. *Test scores:* ACT scores over 18: 33%; ACT scores over 24: 9%.
Faculty *Total:* 57, 60% full-time. *Student/faculty ratio:* 13:1.
Majors Accounting; applied art; applied mathematics; art education; art history; behavioral sciences; biological/physical sciences; biology; botany; broadcast journalism; business administration; business economics; business education; business marketing and marketing management; ceramic arts; chemistry; computer programming; computer science; computer typography/composition; corrections; cosmetology; creative writing; criminal justice/law enforcement administration; criminology; dance; data processing technology; developmental/child psychology; drawing; early childhood education; earth sciences; economics; education; elementary education; English; fine/studio arts; geography; graphic design/commercial art/illustration; history; humanities; individual/family development; jazz; journalism; law enforcement/police science; liberal arts and sciences/liberal studies; marine biology; mass communications; mathematical statistics; mathematics; middle school education; music; music business management/merchandising; music history; music (piano and organ performance); music (voice and choral/opera performance); nursing; nutrition science; painting; philosophy; photography; physical education; physical sciences; political science; practical nurse; psychology; radio/television broadcasting; religious education; sociology; Spanish; theater arts/drama; travel/tourism management; western civilization; zoology.
Academic Programs *Special study options:* academic remediation for entering students, accelerated degree program, freshman honors college, honors programs, independent study, part-time degree program, summer session for credit.
Library McKinstry Library with 42,500 titles, 380 serial subscriptions, an OPAC, a Web page.
Computers on Campus 72 computers available on campus for general student use. Internet access, at least one staffed computer lab available.
Student Life *Housing:* on-campus residence required through sophomore year. *Options:* men-only, women-only. *Activities and Organizations:* drama/theater group, student-run newspaper, radio station, choral group, Admissions Ambassadors, Phi Beta Kappa, Connections, SHOS, Spanish Club. *Campus security:* 24-hour emergency response devices and patrols, controlled dormitory access. *Student Services:* health clinic.
Athletics Member NJCAA. *Intercollegiate sports:* baseball M(s), basketball M(s)/W(s), golf M(s)/W(s), soccer M(s)/W(s), softball W(s), swimming M(s)/W(s), tennis M/W, volleyball W(s), wrestling M(s). *Intramural sports:* basketball M/W, bowling M/W, equestrian sports M/W, football M, golf M/W, racquetball M/W, soccer M, softball M/W, swimming M/W, table tennis M/W, track and field M/W, volleyball M/W, water polo M/W, weight lifting M/W, wrestling M.
Standardized Tests *Required:* SAT I or ACT (for admission).
Costs (2002–03) *Comprehensive fee:* $17,485 includes full-time tuition ($11,700), mandatory fees ($885), and room and board ($4900). No tuition increase for student's term of enrollment. *Room and board:* College room only: $1700. Room and board charges vary according to housing facility. *Payment plans:* installment, deferred payment. *Waivers:* employees or children of employees.
Financial Aid In 2001, 175 Federal Work-Study jobs (averaging $700).
Applying *Options:* early admission, deferred entrance. *Application fee:* $25. *Required:* high school transcript. *Required for some:* 1 letter of recommendation. *Recommended:* interview. *Application deadline:* rolling (freshmen), rolling (transfers).
Admissions Contact Ms. Stacy Rachel, Director of Enrollment Management, Lincoln College, 300 Keokuk Street, Lincoln, IL 62656-1699. *Phone:* 800-569-0556. *Toll-free phone:* 800-569-0556. *Fax:* 217-732-7715. *E-mail:* information@lincolncollege.com.

LINCOLN COLLEGE
Normal, Illinois

- **Independent** primarily 2-year, founded 1865
- **Calendar** semesters
- **Degrees** certificates, associate, and bachelor's
- **Suburban** 10-acre campus
- **Coed,** 400 undergraduate students

Undergraduates Students come from 6 states and territories, 3 other countries, 6% are from out of state, 13% African American, 2% Asian American or Pacific Islander, 2% Hispanic American, 0.3% Native American, 1% international, 40% live on campus.
Freshmen *Average high school GPA:* 2.40. *Test scores:* ACT scores over 18: 80%; ACT scores over 24: 15%.
Faculty *Total:* 35, 14% full-time, 14% with terminal degrees. *Student/faculty ratio:* 14:1.
Majors Accounting; applied art; art education; behavioral sciences; business administration; business education; business marketing and marketing management; computer graphics; computer management; computer programming; computer science; computer typography/composition; corrections; data processing technology; drawing; economics; education; graphic design/commercial art/illustration; humanities; information sciences/systems; legal administrative assistant; liberal arts and sciences/liberal studies; medical administrative assistant; nursing; paralegal/legal assistant; philosophy; physical education; practical nurse; psychology; social sciences; travel/tourism management.
Academic Programs *Special study options:* academic remediation for entering students, adult/continuing education programs, cooperative education, honors programs, internships, part-time degree program, summer session for credit.
Library Milner Library plus 1 other with an OPAC, a Web page.
Computers on Campus 100 computers available on campus for general student use. A campuswide network can be accessed from student residence rooms and from off campus. Internet access, at least one staffed computer lab available.
Student Life *Housing:* on-campus residence required for freshman year. *Options:* coed. *Activities and Organizations:* Phi Theta Kappa, Student Ambassadors, student activities. *Campus security:* 24-hour emergency response devices and patrols, student patrols, late-night transport/escort service, controlled dormitory access. *Student Services:* health clinic.
Athletics Member NJCAA. *Intercollegiate sports:* baseball M, basketball M/W, golf M/W, soccer M/W, softball W, swimming M/W, volleyball W, wrestling M. *Intramural sports:* bowling M/W, football M, ice hockey M, lacrosse M, tennis M/W.

Standardized Tests *Required for some:* SAT I or ACT (for admission).
Costs (2002–03) *Comprehensive fee:* $17,200 includes full-time tuition ($11,700), mandatory fees ($500), and room and board ($5000). Full-time tuition and fees vary according to program. Part-time tuition and fees vary according to course load. No tuition increase for student's term of enrollment. *Room and board:* Room and board charges vary according to board plan. *Payment plan:* installment. *Waivers:* employees or children of employees.
Applying *Options:* deferred entrance. *Application fee:* $25. *Required:* high school transcript, interview. *Required for some:* 2 letters of recommendation. *Application deadline:* rolling (freshmen), rolling (transfers).
Admissions Contact Mr. Joe Hendrix, Director of Admissions, Lincoln College, 715 West Raab Road, Normal, IL 61761. *Phone:* 800-569-0558. *Toll-free phone:* 800-569-0558. *Fax:* 309-454-5652. *E-mail:* admissions@lincoln.mclean.il.us.

LINCOLN LAND COMMUNITY COLLEGE
Springfield, Illinois

- **District-supported** 2-year, founded 1967, part of Illinois Community College Board
- **Calendar** semesters
- **Degree** certificates and associate
- **Suburban** 441-acre campus with easy access to St. Louis
- **Coed,** 6,873 undergraduate students, 35% full-time, 59% women, 41% men

Undergraduates 2,422 full-time, 4,451 part-time. Students come from 6 states and territories, 4 other countries, 5% African American, 0.9% Asian American or Pacific Islander, 0.9% Hispanic American, 0.2% Native American, 0.3% international.
Freshmen *Admission:* 6,883 applied, 6,883 admitted, 1,677 enrolled.
Faculty *Total:* 341, 35% full-time. *Student/faculty ratio:* 17:1.
Majors Accounting; agricultural business; agricultural mechanization; agricultural sciences; aircraft mechanic/airframe; aircraft mechanic/powerplant; anthropology; architectural drafting; art; auto mechanic/technician; aviation management; behavioral sciences; biological/physical sciences; biology; business administration; business marketing and marketing management; chemistry; child care/development; child guidance; computer programming; computer science; construction technology; corrections; criminal justice/law enforcement administration; data processing technology; economics; education; elementary education; English; family/community studies; fire science; food products retailing; French; geography; geology; history; humanities; industrial radiologic technology; Italian; journalism; law enforcement/police science; liberal arts and sciences/liberal studies; literature; mathematics; middle school education; music; nursing; occupational therapy assistant; philosophy; physical education; physical therapy assistant; physics; political science; pre-dentistry; pre-engineering; pre-law; pre-medicine; pre-pharmacy studies; pre-veterinary studies; psychology; real estate; respiratory therapy; secretarial science; social work; sociology; speech/rhetorical studies; teacher assistant/aide; theater arts/drama; welding technology; women's studies.
Academic Programs *Special study options:* academic remediation for entering students, accelerated degree program, adult/continuing education programs, advanced placement credit, distance learning, English as a second language, external degree program, honors programs, independent study, internships, off-campus study, part-time degree program, services for LD students, study abroad, summer session for credit.
Library Learning Resource Center plus 1 other with 72,956 titles, 438 serial subscriptions, an OPAC.
Computers on Campus 130 computers available on campus for general student use. Internet access, at least one staffed computer lab available.
Student Life *Housing:* college housing not available. *Activities and Organizations:* drama/theater group, student-run newspaper, choral group, Student Senate, Phi Theta Kappa, Model Illinois Government, student newspaper, Madrigals. *Campus security:* 24-hour emergency response devices and patrols, late-night transport/escort service. *Student Services:* health clinic, personal/psychological counseling, women's center.
Athletics Member NJCAA. *Intercollegiate sports:* baseball M(s), basketball M(s)/W(s), soccer M(s), softball W(s), volleyball W(s). *Intramural sports:* basketball M/W, tennis M/W.
Standardized Tests *Required for some:* SAT I or ACT (for admission).
Costs (2001–02) *Tuition:* area resident $1260 full-time; state resident $4214 full-time; nonresident $15,352 full-time.
Applying *Options:* common application, early admission, deferred entrance. *Recommended:* high school transcript. *Application deadline:* rolling (freshmen), rolling (transfers). *Notification:* continuous (freshmen).
Admissions Contact Mr. Ron Gregoire, Director of Admissions, Lincoln Land Community College, 5250 Shepherd Road, PO Box 19256, Springfield, IL 62794-9256. *Phone:* 217-786-2243. *Toll-free phone:* 800-727-4161 Ext. 298. *Fax:* 217-786-2492. *E-mail:* rgregoir@cabin.llcc.cc.il.us.

MACCORMAC COLLEGE
Chicago, Illinois

- **Independent** 2-year, founded 1904
- **Calendar** quarters
- **Degree** certificates, diplomas, and associate
- **Urban** 8-acre campus
- **Coed**

Faculty *Student/faculty ratio:* 15:1.
Student Life *Campus security:* late-night transport/escort service.
Standardized Tests *Required:* ACT (for admission). *Recommended:* SAT I (for admission).
Costs (2002–03) *Tuition:* $4500 full-time, $195 per semester hour part-time.
Applying *Options:* common application, deferred entrance. *Application fee:* $20. *Required:* high school transcript. *Recommended:* interview.
Admissions Contact Mr. Milton Kobus, Dean of Enrollment Management, MacCormac College, 506 South Wabash Avenue, Chicago, IL 60605-1667. *Phone:* 312-922-1884 Ext. 210. *Fax:* 630-941-0937.

MCHENRY COUNTY COLLEGE
Crystal Lake, Illinois

- **State and locally supported** 2-year, founded 1967, part of Illinois Community College Board
- **Calendar** semesters
- **Degree** certificates and associate
- **Suburban** 109-acre campus with easy access to Chicago
- **Coed,** 5,747 undergraduate students, 28% full-time, 58% women, 42% men

Undergraduates 1,597 full-time, 4,150 part-time. Students come from 2 states and territories, 11 other countries, 1% are from out of state, 0.5% African American, 1% Asian American or Pacific Islander, 11% Hispanic American, 0.2% Native American, 0.4% international, 6% transferred in.
Freshmen *Admission:* 749 enrolled.
Faculty *Total:* 275, 32% full-time, 11% with terminal degrees. *Student/faculty ratio:* 19:1.
Majors Accounting technician; art; auto mechanic/technician; biological/physical sciences; business administration; business computer programming; child care/guidance; child care provider; electrical/electronic engineering technology; emergency medical technology; engineering; fire science; general retailing/wholesaling; general studies; horticulture services; law enforcement/police science; liberal arts and sciences/liberal studies; mechanical engineering technology; music; operations management; real estate; sales operations; secretarial science.
Academic Programs *Special study options:* academic remediation for entering students, adult/continuing education programs, advanced placement credit, cooperative education, distance learning, English as a second language, honors programs, independent study, internships, part-time degree program, services for LD students, study abroad, summer session for credit.
Library McHenry County College Library with 36,885 titles, 341 serial subscriptions, 2,580 audiovisual materials, an OPAC, a Web page.
Computers on Campus 100 computers available on campus for general student use. Internet access, at least one staffed computer lab available.
Student Life *Housing:* college housing not available. *Activities and Organizations:* drama/theater group, student-run newspaper, choral group, Campus Life Union Board, International Club, Music Club, Voices, Scots' Christian Fellowship. *Campus security:* 24-hour emergency response devices and patrols, late-night transport/escort service. *Student Services:* personal/psychological counseling.
Athletics Member NJCAA. *Intercollegiate sports:* baseball M(s), basketball M(s)/W(s), soccer M(s), softball W(s), tennis M(s)/W(s), volleyball W(s).
Costs (2002–03) *Tuition:* area resident $1470 full-time, $49 per credit part-time; state resident $7349 full-time, $245 per credit part-time; nonresident $8607 full-time, $287 per credit part-time. Full-time tuition and fees vary according to course load. Part-time tuition and fees vary according to course load. *Required fees:* $254 full-time, $8 per credit, $7 per term part-time. *Payment plans:* installment, deferred payment. *Waivers:* senior citizens and employees or children of employees.

McHenry County College (continued)

Financial Aid In 2001, 40 Federal Work-Study jobs, 50 State and other part-time jobs.

Applying *Options:* early admission, deferred entrance. *Required:* high school transcript. *Application deadline:* rolling (freshmen), rolling (transfers). *Notification:* continuous (freshmen).

Admissions Contact Ms. Sue Grenwis, Admissions Processor, McHenry County College, 8900 US Highway 14, Crystal Lake, IL 60012-2761. *Phone:* 815-455-8530. *Fax:* 815-455-3766.

MIDSTATE COLLEGE
Peoria, Illinois

Admissions Contact Ms. Meredith Bunch, Director of Enrollment Management, Midstate College, 411 West Northmoor Road, Peoria, IL 61614. *Phone:* 309-692-4092. *Fax:* 309-692-3893.

MORAINE VALLEY COMMUNITY COLLEGE
Palos Hills, Illinois

- **State and locally supported** 2-year, founded 1967, part of Illinois Community College Board
- **Calendar** semesters
- **Degree** certificates and associate
- **Suburban** 294-acre campus with easy access to Chicago
- **Endowment** $11.7 million
- **Coed,** 14,033 undergraduate students, 38% full-time, 57% women, 43% men

Undergraduates 5,304 full-time, 8,729 part-time. Students come from 2 states and territories, 37 other countries, 7% African American, 2% Asian American or Pacific Islander, 6% Hispanic American, 0.3% Native American, 1% international, 1% transferred in. *Retention:* 67% of 2001 full-time freshmen returned.

Freshmen *Admission:* 2,328 applied, 2,328 admitted, 3,239 enrolled. *Test scores:* ACT scores over 18: 71%; ACT scores over 24: 13%; ACT scores over 30: 1%.

Faculty *Total:* 786, 22% full-time. *Student/faculty ratio:* 22:1.

Majors Auto mechanic/technician; biological/physical sciences; business administration; business computer programming; business systems networking/ telecommunications; child care/guidance; child care provider; culinary arts; design/ visual communications; enterprise management; fire protection/safety technology; human resources management; industrial machinery maintenance/repair; instrumentation technology; law enforcement/police science; liberal arts and sciences/ liberal studies; mechanical engineering technology; medical laboratory technician; medical radiologic technology; medical records technology; nursing; quality control technology; recreational therapy; recreation/leisure facilities management; respiratory therapy; restaurant operations; retailing operations; sales operations; secretarial science; tourism/travel marketing; travel services marketing operations.

Academic Programs *Special study options:* academic remediation for entering students, accelerated degree program, adult/continuing education programs, advanced placement credit, cooperative education, distance learning, double majors, English as a second language, independent study, internships, off-campus study, part-time degree program, services for LD students, study abroad, summer session for credit.

Library Robert E. Turner Learning Resources Center/Library plus 1 other with 65,163 titles, 898 serial subscriptions, 14,242 audiovisual materials, an OPAC, a Web page.

Computers on Campus 775 computers available on campus for general student use. A campuswide network can be accessed from off campus. Internet access, online (class) registration, at least one staffed computer lab available.

Student Life *Housing:* college housing not available. *Activities and Organizations:* drama/theater group, student-run newspaper, choral group, student newspaper, Speech Team, Alliance of Latin American Students, Phi Theta Kappa, Arab Student Union. *Campus security:* 24-hour emergency response devices and patrols, late-night transport/escort service, safety and security programs. *Student Services:* personal/psychological counseling, women's center.

Athletics Member NJCAA. *Intercollegiate sports:* baseball M(s), basketball M(s)/W(s), golf M(s), soccer M(s)/W(s), softball W(s), tennis W(s), volleyball W(s). *Intramural sports:* badminton M/W, basketball M/W, softball W, volleyball M/W.

Standardized Tests *Required:* ACT COMPASS. *Required for some:* ACT (for placement). *Recommended:* ACT (for placement).

Costs (2001–02) *Tuition:* area resident $1470 full-time, $49 per credit hour part-time; state resident $5700 full-time, $190 per credit hour part-time; nonresident $6600 full-time, $220 per credit hour part-time. *Required fees:* $150 full-time, $5 per credit hour. *Payment plans:* installment, deferred payment. *Waivers:* senior citizens and employees or children of employees.

Financial Aid In 2001, 89 Federal Work-Study jobs (averaging $1900).

Applying *Options:* electronic application, early admission, deferred entrance. *Required:* high school transcript. *Required for some:* minimum 2.0 GPA. *Recommended:* minimum 2.0 GPA. *Application deadline:* rolling (freshmen), rolling (transfers). *Notification:* continuous (freshmen).

Admissions Contact Ms. Wendy Manser, Dean of Enrollment Services, Moraine Valley Community College, 10900 South 88th Avenue, Palos Hills, IL 60465-0937. *Phone:* 708-974-5346. *Fax:* 708-974-0681. *E-mail:* manser@morainevalley.edu.

MORRISON INSTITUTE OF TECHNOLOGY
Morrison, Illinois

- **Independent** 2-year, founded 1973
- **Calendar** semesters
- **Degree** associate
- **Small-town** 17-acre campus
- **Coed, primarily men,** 146 undergraduate students, 98% full-time, 7% women, 93% men

Undergraduates 143 full-time, 3 part-time. Students come from 5 states and territories, 6% are from out of state, 8% transferred in, 69% live on campus.

Freshmen *Admission:* 78 applied, 74 admitted, 74 enrolled. *Average high school GPA:* 2.3. *Test scores:* ACT scores over 18: 72%; ACT scores over 24: 10%; ACT scores over 30: 2%.

Faculty *Total:* 10. *Student/faculty ratio:* 14:1.

Majors Construction technology; engineering technology; mechanical drafting.

Academic Programs *Special study options:* double majors, part-time degree program.

Library Milikan Library with 7,946 titles, 39 serial subscriptions, a Web page.

Computers on Campus 60 computers available on campus for general student use. A campuswide network can be accessed from student residence rooms. Internet access, at least one staffed computer lab available.

Student Life *Housing:* on-campus residence required for freshman year. *Options:* coed. *Campus security:* late-night transport/escort service, controlled dormitory access.

Athletics *Intramural sports:* basketball M, bowling M/W, softball M/W, table tennis M/W, volleyball M/W.

Standardized Tests *Recommended:* SAT I or ACT (for admission).

Costs (2001–02) *Tuition:* $9050 full-time, $377 per semester hour part-time. *Required fees:* $125 full-time, $125 per term part-time. *Room only:* $1600. *Payment plans:* installment, deferred payment. *Waivers:* children of alumni.

Financial Aid In 2001, 25 Federal Work-Study jobs (averaging $2000).

Applying *Options:* common application, deferred entrance. *Application fee:* $100. *Required:* high school transcript, proof of immunization. *Recommended:* interview. *Application deadline:* rolling (freshmen). *Notification:* continuous until 9/1 (freshmen).

Admissions Contact Ms. Jane Haan, Admission Secretary, Morrison Institute of Technology, 701 Portland Avenue, Morrison, IL 61270. *Phone:* 815-772-7218. *Fax:* 815-772-7584. *E-mail:* admissions@morrison.tec.il.us.

MORTON COLLEGE
Cicero, Illinois

- **State and locally supported** 2-year, founded 1924, part of Illinois Community College Board
- **Calendar** semesters
- **Degree** certificates and associate
- **Suburban** 25-acre campus with easy access to Chicago
- **Coed,** 4,698 undergraduate students

Undergraduates Students come from 2 states and territories, 2% African American, 2% Asian American or Pacific Islander, 64% Hispanic American, 0.1% Native American.

Faculty *Total:* 191, 25% full-time.

Majors Accounting; art; auto mechanic/technician; biological/physical sciences; business administration; business marketing and marketing management; data processing technology; drafting; finance; fine/studio arts; heating/air conditioning/refrigeration; law enforcement/police science; legal administrative assistant; liberal arts and sciences/liberal studies; medical administrative assistant; music; nursing; physical therapy; real estate; secretarial science.

Academic Programs *Special study options:* academic remediation for entering students, adult/continuing education programs, advanced placement credit, English as a second language, internships, part-time degree program, services for LD students, student-designed majors, summer session for credit.

Library Learning Resource Center with 40,972 titles, 327 serial subscriptions.

Computers on Campus 150 computers available on campus for general student use. At least one staffed computer lab available.

Student Life *Housing:* college housing not available. *Activities and Organizations:* drama/theater group, student-run newspaper, choral group, Hispanic Heritage Club, Program Board, Student Senate, Law Enforcement Association, Nursing Club. *Campus security:* 24-hour patrols, security cameras.

Athletics Member NJCAA. *Intercollegiate sports:* baseball M(s), basketball M(s)/W(s), cross-country running M(s)/W(s), soccer M, softball W(s), volleyball W(s). *Intramural sports:* basketball M/W, cross-country running M/W, volleyball M/W, weight lifting M/W.

Costs (2002–03) *Tuition:* area resident $1488 full-time, $48 per credit part-time; state resident $4639 full-time, $150 per credit part-time; nonresident $5963 full-time, $192 per credit part-time. *Payment plan:* deferred payment. *Waivers:* employees or children of employees.

Financial Aid In 2001, 15 Federal Work-Study jobs (averaging $2000).

Applying *Application fee:* $10. *Required:* high school transcript. *Application deadline:* rolling (freshmen), rolling (transfers).

Admissions Contact Ms. Jill Caccamo-Beer, Director of Enrollment Management, Morton College, 3801 South Central Avenue, Cicero, IL 60804. *Phone:* 708-656-8000 Ext. 400. *Fax:* 708-656-9592 Ext. 344. *E-mail:* enroll@morton.cc.il.us.

NORTHWESTERN BUSINESS COLLEGE
Chicago, Illinois

- **Proprietary** 2-year, founded 1902
- **Calendar** quarters
- **Degree** associate
- **Urban** 3-acre campus
- **Coed,** 1,600 undergraduate students

Undergraduates Students come from 4 other countries.

Freshmen *Admission:* 900 applied, 564 admitted.

Faculty *Total:* 45, 49% full-time.

Majors Accounting; advertising; business administration; business marketing and marketing management; computer programming; computer programming (specific applications); computer science; data processing technology; fashion merchandising; hospitality management; legal administrative assistant; medical administrative assistant; medical assistant; paralegal/legal assistant; public relations; secretarial science; travel/tourism management; Web page, digital/multimedia and information resources design.

Academic Programs *Special study options:* academic remediation for entering students, internships, part-time degree program, summer session for credit.

Library Edward G. Schumacher Memorial Library with 2,000 titles, 20 serial subscriptions.

Computers on Campus 69 computers available on campus for general student use. At least one staffed computer lab available.

Student Life *Housing:* college housing not available.

Costs (2002–03) *Tuition:* $12,240 full-time, $255 per credit hour part-time. Full-time tuition and fees vary according to course load and program. Part-time tuition and fees vary according to course load and program. *Required fees:* $180 full-time.

Applying *Application fee:* $25. *Required:* high school transcript. *Application deadline:* rolling (freshmen).

Admissions Contact Mr. Mark Sliz, Director of Admissions, Northwestern Business College, 4839 North Milwaukee Avenue, Chicago, IL 60630. *Phone:* 773-481-3730. *Toll-free phone:* 800-396-5613. *Fax:* 773-481-3738.

OAKTON COMMUNITY COLLEGE
Des Plaines, Illinois

- **District-supported** 2-year, founded 1969, part of Illinois Community College Board
- **Calendar** semesters
- **Degree** certificates and associate
- **Suburban** 193-acre campus with easy access to Chicago
- **Coed,** 10,000 undergraduate students

Undergraduates Students come from 1 other state.

Faculty *Total:* 659, 23% full-time. *Student/faculty ratio:* 25:1.

Majors Accounting; architectural engineering technology; art; auto mechanic/technician; biological/physical sciences; business administration; business marketing and marketing management; computer graphics; computer programming; computer programming (specific applications); computer science; computer science related; computer/technical support; construction management; early childhood education; electrical/electronic engineering technology; finance; fire science; food products retailing; graphic design/commercial art/illustration; heating/air conditioning/refrigeration technology; hotel and restaurant management; information sciences/systems; international business; law enforcement/police science; liberal arts and sciences/liberal studies; machine technology; management science; mechanical design technology; medical laboratory technician; medical records administration; music; nursing; physical therapy; pre-engineering; real estate; secretarial science.

Academic Programs *Special study options:* academic remediation for entering students, adult/continuing education programs, advanced placement credit, distance learning, English as a second language, honors programs, independent study, part-time degree program, services for LD students, study abroad, summer session for credit.

Library Oakton Community College Library plus 1 other with 92,000 titles, 586 serial subscriptions, 10,500 audiovisual materials, an OPAC, a Web page.

Computers on Campus 750 computers available on campus for general student use. A campuswide network can be accessed from off campus. At least one staffed computer lab available.

Student Life *Housing:* college housing not available. *Activities and Organizations:* drama/theater group, student-run newspaper, choral group, board of student affairs, college program board, Phi Theta Kappa, honors student organization, Occurrence (student newspaper). *Campus security:* 24-hour emergency response devices and patrols, student patrols, late-night transport/escort service. *Student Services:* health clinic, personal/psychological counseling.

Athletics Member NJCAA. *Intercollegiate sports:* baseball M, basketball M/W, cross-country running M/W, golf M, soccer M, softball W, tennis M/W, track and field M/W, volleyball W, wrestling M. *Intramural sports:* badminton M/W, basketball M/W, bowling M/W, football M, soccer M, table tennis M/W, volleyball M/W, wrestling M.

Standardized Tests *Recommended:* ACT (for placement).

Costs (2002–03) *Tuition:* area resident $1620 full-time, $54 per credit hour part-time; state resident $4860 full-time, $62 per credit hour part-time; nonresident $6480 full-time, $216 per credit hour part-time. *Payment plan:* installment. *Waivers:* senior citizens and employees or children of employees.

Financial Aid In 2001, 15 Federal Work-Study jobs (averaging $3500). 200 State and other part-time jobs (averaging $3200).

Applying *Application fee:* $25. *Required:* high school transcript. *Required for some:* interview. *Application deadline:* rolling (freshmen), rolling (transfers). *Notification:* continuous (freshmen).

Admissions Contact Mr. Dale Cohen, Admissions Specialist, Oakton Community College, 1600 East Golf Road, Des Plaines, IL 60016. *Phone:* 847-635-1703. *Fax:* 847-635-1890. *E-mail:* dcohen@oakton.edu.

PARKLAND COLLEGE
Champaign, Illinois

- **District-supported** 2-year, founded 1967, part of Illinois Community College Board
- **Calendar** semesters
- **Degree** certificates and associate
- **Suburban** 233-acre campus
- **Coed,** 8,482 undergraduate students, 47% full-time, 55% women, 45% men

Undergraduates 3,961 full-time, 4,521 part-time. 1% are from out of state, 11% African American, 4% Asian American or Pacific Islander, 2% Hispanic American, 0.3% Native American, 4% international, 4% transferred in.

Freshmen *Admission:* 2,588 applied, 2,329 admitted, 2,105 enrolled. *Test scores:* ACT scores over 18: 71%; ACT scores over 24: 22%; ACT scores over 30: 1%.

Faculty *Total:* 485, 35% full-time, 11% with terminal degrees. *Student/faculty ratio:* 17:1.

Majors Accounting technician; advertising; agricultural business; agricultural mechanization; art; art education; auto body repair; auto mechanic/technician; biological/physical sciences; biomedical engineering-related technology; busi-

Parkland College (continued)
ness administration; business computer programming; business systems networking/telecommunications; child care provider; computer graphics; computer graphics; computer/information sciences; computer/information technology services administration and management related; computer programming; computer programming (specific applications); computer programming, vendor/product certification; computer science; computer software and media applications related; computer systems networking/telecommunications; computer/technical support; construction management; criminal justice studies; data entry/microcomputer applications; data processing; dental hygiene; design/visual communications; desktop publishing equipment operation; electroencephalograph technology; engineering science; equestrian studies; general studies; human services; industrial technology; information sciences/systems; landscaping management; liberal arts and sciences/liberal studies; marketing/distribution education; medical radiologic technology; music (general performance); music teacher education; nursing; occupational therapy assistant; radio/television broadcasting; radio/television broadcasting technology; respiratory therapy; retail management; secretarial science; speech-language pathology; system administration; system/networking/LAN/WAN management; veterinarian assistant; Web page, digital/multimedia and information resources design.

Academic Programs *Special study options:* academic remediation for entering students, adult/continuing education programs, advanced placement credit, cooperative education, distance learning, double majors, English as a second language, honors programs, independent study, internships, off-campus study, part-time degree program, services for LD students, study abroad, summer session for credit. *ROTC:* Army (c), Navy (c), Air Force (c).

Library Parkland College Library with 230,823 titles, 926 serial subscriptions, 8,141 audiovisual materials, an OPAC, a Web page.

Computers on Campus 600 computers available on campus for general student use. Internet access, online (class) registration, at least one staffed computer lab available.

Student Life *Housing:* college housing not available. *Activities and Organizations:* drama/theater group, student-run newspaper, radio and television station, choral group. *Campus security:* 24-hour emergency response devices and patrols, late-night transport/escort service. *Student Services:* personal/psychological counseling, women's center.

Athletics Member NJCAA. *Intercollegiate sports:* baseball M(s), basketball M(s)/W(s), golf M(s), soccer M/W, softball W(s), tennis M(s)/W(s), volleyball W(s). *Intramural sports:* basketball M/W, bowling M/W, softball M/W, tennis M/W, volleyball M/W.

Costs (2002–03) *Tuition:* area resident $1620 full-time, $54 per credit hour part-time; state resident $6000 full-time, $200 per credit hour part-time; nonresident $7350 full-time, $245 per credit hour part-time. *Payment plan:* installment. *Waivers:* senior citizens and employees or children of employees.

Applying *Recommended:* high school transcript. *Application deadline:* rolling (freshmen), rolling (transfers). *Notification:* continuous (freshmen).

Admissions Contact Admissions Representative, Parkland College, 2400 West Bradley Avenue, Champaign, IL 61821. *Phone:* 217-351-2482. *Toll-free phone:* 800-346-8089. *Fax:* 217-351-7640.

PRAIRIE STATE COLLEGE
Chicago Heights, Illinois

- **State and locally supported** 2-year, founded 1958, part of Illinois Community College Board
- **Calendar** semesters
- **Degree** certificates and associate
- **Suburban** 68-acre campus with easy access to Chicago
- **Endowment** $750,000
- **Coed,** 5,188 undergraduate students, 28% full-time, 60% women, 40% men

Undergraduates 1,445 full-time, 3,743 part-time. Students come from 4 states and territories, 4% are from out of state, 33% African American, 1% Asian American or Pacific Islander, 8% Hispanic American, 0.5% Native American, 0.4% transferred in.

Freshmen *Admission:* 1,065 applied, 1,065 admitted, 1,065 enrolled.

Faculty *Total:* 315, 24% full-time, 8% with terminal degrees. *Student/faculty ratio:* 17:1.

Majors Alcohol/drug abuse counseling; auto body repair; auto mechanic/technician; child guidance; computer graphics; computer/information sciences; criminal justice/law enforcement administration; dental hygiene; electrical/electronic engineering technology; executive assistant; finance; fire science; human resources management; industrial technology; interior design; liberal arts and sciences/liberal studies; logistics/materials management; management science; mechanical design technology; mental health/rehabilitation; nursing; photography; teacher assistant/aide; tool/die making.

Academic Programs *Special study options:* academic remediation for entering students, adult/continuing education programs, advanced placement credit, distance learning, English as a second language, honors programs, internships, part-time degree program, services for LD students, student-designed majors, summer session for credit.

Library Learning Resource Center with 45,000 titles, 515 serial subscriptions, 4,000 audiovisual materials, an OPAC.

Computers on Campus 300 computers available on campus for general student use. Internet access, at least one staffed computer lab available.

Student Life *Housing:* college housing not available. *Activities and Organizations:* drama/theater group, student-run newspaper, choral group, Phi Theta Kappa, Black Student Union, Student Government Association, student newspaper, Mental Health Club. *Campus security:* 24-hour emergency response devices and patrols, student patrols, late-night transport/escort service. *Student Services:* personal/psychological counseling.

Athletics Member NJCAA. *Intercollegiate sports:* baseball M(s), basketball M(s)/W(s), football M(s), golf M(s)/W(s), soccer M/W, softball M/W(s), tennis W(s). *Intramural sports:* basketball M/W, soccer M/W, softball W, table tennis M/W, volleyball W.

Standardized Tests *Required for some:* ACT COMPASS.

Costs (2001–02) *Tuition:* $60 per credit hour part-time; state resident $200 per credit hour part-time; nonresident $207 per credit hour part-time. *Required fees:* $10 per term part-time.

Financial Aid In 2001, 60 Federal Work-Study jobs (averaging $1200).

Applying *Options:* common application, deferred entrance. *Application fee:* $10. *Required:* high school transcript. *Application deadline:* rolling (freshmen), rolling (transfers).

Admissions Contact Mary Welsh, Director of Admissions, Records and Registration, Prairie State College, 202 South Halsted Street, Chicago Heights, IL 60411. *Phone:* 708-709-3513. *Toll-free phone:* 708-709-3516. *E-mail:* webmaster@prairie.cc.il.us.

RAVENSWOOD HOSPITAL MEDICAL CENTER-HENRY J. KUTSCH COLLEGE OF NURSING
Chicago, Illinois

- **Independent** 2-year
- **Calendar** semesters
- **Degree** associate
- **Coed**

Admissions Contact Mrs. Kimberly Quinn, Dean of Admissions, Ravenswood Hospital Medical Center-Henry J. Kutsch College of Nursing, 2318 West Irving Park Road, Chicago, IL 60618. *Phone:* 773-866-6965.

REND LAKE COLLEGE
Ina, Illinois

- **State-supported** 2-year, founded 1967, part of Illinois Community College Board
- **Calendar** semesters
- **Degree** certificates and associate
- **Rural** 350-acre campus
- **Endowment** $1.7 million
- **Coed,** 3,637 undergraduate students, 35% full-time, 55% women, 45% men

Undergraduates Students come from 2 states and territories, 1% are from out of state, 2% African American, 0.5% Asian American or Pacific Islander, 0.5% Hispanic American, 0.2% Native American.

Faculty *Total:* 147, 41% full-time, 3% with terminal degrees. *Student/faculty ratio:* 15:1.

Majors Agricultural business; agricultural mechanization; agricultural production; architectural drafting; art; auto mechanic/technician; automotive engineering technology; biological/physical sciences; business administration; business computer programming; child care provider; computer engineering technology; culinary arts; diesel engine mechanic; engineering; fire services administration; graphic design/commercial art/illustration; heavy equipment maintenance; horticulture services; industrial machinery maintenance/repair; industrial technology; law enforcement/police science; liberal arts and sciences/liberal studies; medical administrative assistant; medical laboratory technician; medical records technology; mining technology; nursing; occupational therapy assistant; secretarial science.

Academic Programs *Special study options:* academic remediation for entering students, adult/continuing education programs, advanced placement credit, cooperative education, distance learning, double majors, English as a second language, honors programs, independent study, internships, off-campus study, part-time degree program, services for LD students, summer session for credit.
Library Learning Resource Center plus 1 other with 31,300 titles, 283 serial subscriptions, 64,000 audiovisual materials, an OPAC, a Web page.
Computers on Campus 325 computers available on campus for general student use. A campuswide network can be accessed from off campus that provide access to online registration for online courses. Internet access, at least one staffed computer lab available.
Student Life *Housing:* college housing not available. *Activities and Organizations:* drama/theater group, student-run newspaper, choral group, Student Senate, Psi Beta, Phi Theta Kappa, Student Ambassadors. *Campus security:* 24-hour emergency response devices and patrols, late-night transport/escort service.
Athletics Member NJCAA. *Intercollegiate sports:* baseball M(s), basketball M(s)/W(s), cross-country running M(s), golf M(s)/W(s), softball W(s), tennis M(s)/W(s), volleyball W(s). *Intramural sports:* basketball M, table tennis M/W, volleyball M/W.
Standardized Tests *Required:* SAT I or ACT (for placement), ACT ASSET, ACT COMPASS.
Costs (2002–03) *Tuition:* area resident $1536 full-time, $48 per credit hour part-time; state resident $2352 full-time, $74 per credit hour part-time; nonresident $4800 full-time, $150 per credit hour part-time.
Financial Aid In 2001, 133 Federal Work-Study jobs (averaging $1000). 174 State and other part-time jobs (averaging $940).
Applying *Options:* early admission, deferred entrance. *Required:* high school transcript. *Application deadlines:* 8/19 (freshmen), 8/19 (transfers).
Admissions Contact Ann Bullock, Director, Counseling, Rend Lake College, 468 North Ken Gray Parkway, Ina, IL 62846-9801. *Phone:* 618-437-5321 Ext. 205. *Toll-free phone:* 618-437-5321 Ext. 230. *Fax:* 618-437-5677. *E-mail:* admis@rlc.cc.il.us.

Richland Community College
Decatur, Illinois

- **District-supported** 2-year, founded 1971, part of Illinois Community College Board
- **Calendar** semesters
- **Degree** certificates and associate
- **Small-town** 117-acre campus
- **Endowment** $3.8 million
- **Coed,** 3,261 undergraduate students, 32% full-time, 63% women, 37% men

Undergraduates 1,048 full-time, 2,213 part-time. Students come from 1 other state, 13% African American, 0.7% Asian American or Pacific Islander, 1% Hispanic American, 0.2% Native American, 42% transferred in. *Retention:* 53% of 2001 full-time freshmen returned.
Freshmen *Admission:* 738 applied, 738 admitted, 607 enrolled.
Faculty *Total:* 227, 27% full-time, 5% with terminal degrees. *Student/faculty ratio:* 17:1.
Majors Accounting; agricultural business; auto mechanic/technician; biological/physical sciences; business administration; child care/development; computer graphics; computer programming (specific applications); computer science related; construction technology; data entry/microcomputer applications; data entry/microcomputer applications related; drafting; electrical/electronic engineering technology; fire science; food services technology; industrial technology; information sciences/systems; insurance/risk management; law enforcement/police science; legal administrative assistant; liberal arts and sciences/liberal studies; medical administrative assistant; nursing; pre-engineering; secretarial science; word processing.
Academic Programs *Special study options:* academic remediation for entering students, adult/continuing education programs, advanced placement credit, distance learning, English as a second language, freshman honors college, honors programs, part-time degree program, services for LD students, student-designed majors, summer session for credit.
Library Kitty Lindsay Library with 39,452 titles, 275 serial subscriptions, 2,910 audiovisual materials, an OPAC, a Web page.
Computers on Campus 150 computers available on campus for general student use. Internet access, online (class) registration, at least one staffed computer lab available.
Student Life *Housing:* college housing not available. *Activities and Organizations:* student-run newspaper, Student Senate, Forensics Club, Drama Club, Black Student Association, Student Activities Board. *Campus security:* 24-hour emergency response devices and patrols.
Standardized Tests *Required for some:* ACT (for placement).
Costs (2002–03) *Tuition:* area resident $1530 full-time, $51 per semester hour part-time; state resident $5300 full-time, $176 per semester hour part-time; nonresident $8850 full-time, $295 per semester hour part-time. *Required fees:* $3 per semester hour. *Payment plan:* installment. *Waivers:* senior citizens and employees or children of employees.
Financial Aid In 2001, 43 Federal Work-Study jobs (averaging $1339). 129 State and other part-time jobs (averaging $578).
Applying *Options:* early admission. *Required:* high school transcript. *Application deadline:* rolling (freshmen), rolling (transfers).
Admissions Contact Mr. D. Michael Beube, Dean of Admissions and Records, Richland Community College, One College Park, Decatur, IL 62521. *Phone:* 217-875-7200 Ext. 286. *Fax:* 217-875-7783.

Rockford Business College
Rockford, Illinois

- **Independent** 2-year, founded 1862
- **Calendar** quarters
- **Degree** certificates, diplomas, and associate
- **Urban** campus with easy access to Chicago
- **Coed, primarily women,** 357 undergraduate students, 38% full-time, 85% women, 15% men

Undergraduates Students come from 6 states and territories, 1% are from out of state.
Freshmen *Admission:* 95 applied, 95 admitted.
Faculty *Total:* 23, 35% full-time. *Student/faculty ratio:* 15:1.
Majors Accounting; business administration; business marketing and marketing management; computer/information sciences; executive assistant; legal administrative assistant; medical assistant; medical transcription; paralegal/legal assistant.
Academic Programs *Special study options:* academic remediation for entering students, cooperative education, distance learning, double majors, English as a second language, honors programs, independent study, internships, part-time degree program, services for LD students, summer session for credit.
Computers on Campus 65 computers available on campus for general student use. Internet access, at least one staffed computer lab available.
Student Life *Activities and Organizations:* student-run newspaper, International Students Club. *Campus security:* 24-hour patrols, late-night transport/escort service. *Student Services:* personal/psychological counseling.
Costs (2001–02) *Tuition:* $12,120 full-time, $485 per course part-time. *Required fees:* $435 full-time, $15 per course, $30 per course part-time.
Applying *Options:* common application, electronic application, early admission, early decision. *Application fee:* $50. *Required:* high school transcript, interview. *Required for some:* essay or personal statement. *Application deadlines:* 9/4 (freshmen), 9/4 (transfers). *Early decision:* 3/4.
Admissions Contact Ms. Jane Emerson, Director of Admissions, Rockford Business College, 730 North Church Street, Rockford, IL 61103. *Phone:* 815-965-8616 Ext. 16. *Fax:* 815-965-0360. *E-mail:* kbirbc@aol.com.

Rock Valley College
Rockford, Illinois

- **District-supported** 2-year, founded 1964, part of Illinois Community College Board
- **Calendar** semesters
- **Degree** certificates and associate
- **Suburban** 217-acre campus with easy access to Chicago
- **Coed**

Student Life *Campus security:* 24-hour emergency response devices and patrols, late-night transport/escort service.
Athletics Member NJCAA.
Standardized Tests *Required for some:* ACT (for placement). *Recommended:* ACT (for placement).
Costs (2001–02) *Tuition:* area resident $1056 full-time, $44 per credit hour part-time; state resident $4704 full-time, $196 per credit hour part-time; nonresident $7032 full-time, $293 per credit hour part-time. *Required fees:* $174 full-time, $7 per credit hour, $3 per term part-time.
Financial Aid In 2001, 120 Federal Work-Study jobs (averaging $1800).
Applying *Options:* early admission. *Required:* high school transcript.

Rock Valley College (continued)
Admissions Contact Ms. Lisa Allman, Coordinator of Admissions and Records, Rock Valley College, 3301 North Mulford Road, Rockford, IL 61114-5699. *Phone:* 815-654-5527. *Fax:* 815-654-5568. *E-mail:* adad1pl@rvcux1.rvc.cc.il.us.

SANFORD-BROWN COLLEGE
Granite City, Illinois

Admissions Contact 3237 West Chain of Rocks Road, Granite City, IL 62040.

SAUK VALLEY COMMUNITY COLLEGE
Dixon, Illinois

- **District-supported** 2-year, founded 1965, part of Illinois Community College Board
- **Calendar** semesters
- **Degree** certificates and associate
- **Rural** 165-acre campus
- **Coed,** 2,688 undergraduate students, 39% full-time, 57% women, 43% men

Undergraduates 2% African American, 0.8% Asian American or Pacific Islander, 6% Hispanic American, 0.3% Native American.
Freshmen *Admission:* 1,400 applied, 1,400 admitted.
Faculty *Total:* 152, 41% full-time.
Majors Accounting; anthropology; art; biology; business administration; business marketing and marketing management; chemistry; child care/development; computer engineering related; computer science related; corrections; criminal justice/law enforcement administration; data processing technology; drafting; economics; education; electrical/electronic engineering technology; elementary education; English; French; heating/air conditioning/refrigeration; history; human services; industrial radiologic technology; information technology; law enforcement/police science; liberal arts and sciences/liberal studies; mathematics; mechanical design technology; medical laboratory technician; mental health/rehabilitation; music; nursing; philosophy; physical education; physics; political science; pre-engineering; psychology; secretarial science; sociology; Spanish; speech/rhetorical studies; theater arts/drama.
Academic Programs *Special study options:* academic remediation for entering students, accelerated degree program, adult/continuing education programs, cooperative education, distance learning, English as a second language, honors programs, independent study, internships, off-campus study, part-time degree program, services for LD students, student-designed majors.
Library Learning Resource Center plus 1 other with 55,000 titles, 268 serial subscriptions.
Computers on Campus 100 computers available on campus for general student use. Internet access, at least one staffed computer lab available.
Student Life *Housing:* college housing not available. *Activities and Organizations:* drama/theater group, choral group. *Campus security:* 24-hour emergency response devices and patrols, late-night transport/escort service. *Student Services:* personal/psychological counseling.
Athletics Member NJCAA. *Intercollegiate sports:* baseball M(s), basketball M(s)/W(s), softball W, tennis M(s)/W(s), volleyball W(s). *Intramural sports:* basketball M/W.
Standardized Tests *Required:* ACT ASSET, Nelson Denny Reading Test.
Costs (2001–02) *Tuition:* area resident $1530 full-time, $51 per semester hour part-time; state resident $6360 full-time, $212 per semester hour part-time; nonresident $7980 full-time, $266 per semester hour part-time. *Waivers:* senior citizens and employees or children of employees.
Financial Aid In 2001, 150 Federal Work-Study jobs (averaging $3000).
Applying *Options:* early admission, deferred entrance. *Recommended:* high school transcript. *Application deadline:* rolling (freshmen), rolling (transfers). *Notification:* continuous (freshmen).
Admissions Contact Ms. Pamela Clodfelter, Director of Admissions, Records, and Placement, Sauk Valley Community College, 173 Illinois Route 2, Dixon, IL 61021. *Phone:* 815-288-5511 Ext. 310. *Fax:* 815-288-3190.

SHAWNEE COMMUNITY COLLEGE
Ullin, Illinois

Admissions Contact Mr. James Dumas, Dean of Student Services, Shawnee Community College, 8364 Shawnee College Road, Ullin, IL 62992-9725. *Phone:* 618-634-2242 Ext. 245. *Toll-free phone:* 800-481-2242. *Fax:* 618-634-9028.

SOUTHEASTERN ILLINOIS COLLEGE
Harrisburg, Illinois

- **State-supported** 2-year, founded 1960, part of Illinois Community College Board
- **Calendar** semesters
- **Degree** certificates and associate
- **Rural** 140-acre campus
- **Coed**

Faculty *Student/faculty ratio:* 26:1.
Student Life *Campus security:* student patrols, evening security guard.
Athletics Member NJCAA.
Standardized Tests *Required:* ACT ASSET. *Recommended:* ACT (for placement).
Financial Aid In 2001, 393 Federal Work-Study jobs (averaging $1448). 46 State and other part-time jobs (averaging $969).
Applying *Options:* electronic application, early admission, deferred entrance. *Required:* high school transcript.
Admissions Contact Dr. Dana Keating, Registrar, Southeastern Illinois College, 3575 College Road, Harrisburg, IL 62946-4925. *Phone:* 618-252-5400 Ext. 2440.

SOUTH SUBURBAN COLLEGE
South Holland, Illinois

- **State and locally supported** 2-year, founded 1927, part of Illinois Community College Board
- **Calendar** semesters
- **Degree** certificates and associate
- **Suburban** campus with easy access to Chicago
- **Coed,** 5,580 undergraduate students, 32% full-time, 69% women, 31% men

Undergraduates Students come from 1 other state, 52% African American, 1% Asian American or Pacific Islander, 8% Hispanic American, 0.4% Native American, 0.4% international.
Freshmen *Admission:* 851 applied, 851 admitted. *Average high school GPA:* 2.33.
Faculty *Total:* 329, 36% full-time. *Student/faculty ratio:* 17:1.
Majors Accounting; advertising; architectural engineering technology; biomedical technology; business marketing and marketing management; chemistry; child care/development; construction technology; court reporting; criminal justice/law enforcement administration; data processing technology; drafting; early childhood education; electrical/electronic engineering technology; elementary education; entrepreneurship; fashion merchandising; finance; fine/studio arts; fire science; graphic design/commercial art/illustration; graphic/printing equipment; human services; industrial radiologic technology; industrial technology; information sciences/systems; law enforcement/police science; liberal arts and sciences/liberal studies; machine technology; management information systems/business data processing; mathematics; mechanical design technology; mental health/rehabilitation; nursing; occupational therapy assistant; paralegal/legal assistant; pre-engineering; retail management; secretarial science; teacher assistant/aide.
Academic Programs *Special study options:* academic remediation for entering students, adult/continuing education programs, advanced placement credit, cooperative education, double majors, English as a second language, honors programs, independent study, internships, off-campus study, part-time degree program, services for LD students, study abroad, summer session for credit.
Library South Suburban College Library plus 2 others with 38,845 titles, 403 serial subscriptions, an OPAC, a Web page.
Computers on Campus 250 computers available on campus for general student use. A campuswide network can be accessed from off campus. Internet access, online (class) registration, at least one staffed computer lab available.
Student Life *Housing:* college housing not available. *Activities and Organizations:* drama/theater group, student-run newspaper, choral group, Returning Adult Organization, Business Professionals, Disabled Students Organization, O.T. Organization, PAC Rats. *Campus security:* 24-hour emergency response devices and patrols. *Student Services:* personal/psychological counseling.
Athletics Member NJCAA. *Intercollegiate sports:* baseball M, basketball M/W, cross-country running M/W, softball W, volleyball W. *Intramural sports:* baseball M, basketball M/W, bowling M/W, cross-country running M/W, soccer M, softball W, volleyball W.
Standardized Tests *Required:* ACT ASSET.

Costs (2002–03) *Tuition:* area resident $1320 full-time, $55 per credit hour part-time; state resident $5280 full-time, $61 per credit hour part-time; nonresident $5760 full-time, $240 per credit hour part-time. *Required fees:* $212 full-time, $8 per credit hour.
Financial Aid In 2001, 98 Federal Work-Study jobs (averaging $1500).
Applying *Options:* early admission, deferred entrance. *Required:* high school transcript. *Required for some:* essay or personal statement, interview. *Recommended:* minimum 2.0 GPA. *Application deadline:* rolling (freshmen), rolling (transfers). *Notification:* continuous (freshmen).
Admissions Contact Ms. Jane Stocker, Director of Admissions and Records, South Suburban College, 15800 South State Street, South Holland, IL 60473-1270. *Phone:* 708-596-2000.

SOUTHWESTERN ILLINOIS COLLEGE
Belleville, Illinois

- **District-supported** 2-year, founded 1946, part of Illinois Community College Board
- **Calendar** semesters
- **Degree** certificates, diplomas, and associate
- **Suburban** 150-acre campus with easy access to St. Louis
- **Endowment** $3.1 million
- **Coed**

Faculty *Student/faculty ratio:* 16:1.
Student Life *Campus security:* 24-hour emergency response devices and patrols, student patrols, late-night transport/escort service.
Athletics Member NJCAA.
Standardized Tests *Required for some:* ACT ASSET or ACT COMPASS.
Applying *Options:* early admission, deferred entrance. *Application fee:* $10. *Required:* high school transcript.
Admissions Contact Ms. Michelle Birk, Assistant Director of Admission, Southwestern Illinois College, 2500 Carlyle Road, Belleville, IL 62221-5899. *Phone:* 618-235-2700 Ext. 5400. *Toll-free phone:* 800-222-5131. *Fax:* 618-277-0631.

SPOON RIVER COLLEGE
Canton, Illinois

- **State-supported** 2-year, founded 1959, part of Illinois Community College Board
- **Calendar** semesters
- **Degree** certificates and associate
- **Rural** 160-acre campus
- **Endowment** $267,036
- **Coed**

Faculty *Student/faculty ratio:* 14:1.
Student Life *Campus security:* 24-hour emergency response devices.
Athletics Member NJCAA.
Standardized Tests *Required for some:* nursing exam, ACT ASSET. *Recommended:* SAT I or ACT (for placement).
Costs (2001–02) *Tuition:* area resident $1600 full-time, $50 per semester hour part-time; state resident $2400 full-time, $75 per semester hour part-time; nonresident $4000 full-time, $125 per semester hour part-time. Full-time tuition and fees vary according to course load. Part-time tuition and fees vary according to course load. *Required fees:* $224 full-time, $7 per semester hour.
Applying *Options:* early admission. *Required:* high school transcript.
Admissions Contact Ms. Sharon Wrenn, Dean of Student Services, Spoon River College, 23235 North County 22, Canton, IL 61520-9801. *Phone:* 309-649-6305. *Toll-free phone:* 800-334-7337. *Fax:* 309-649-6235. *E-mail:* info@src.cc.il.us.

SPRINGFIELD COLLEGE IN ILLINOIS
Springfield, Illinois

- **Independent** 2-year, founded 1929, affiliated with Roman Catholic Church
- **Calendar** semesters
- **Degree** associate
- **Urban** 8-acre campus
- **Endowment** $519,554
- **Coed**

Faculty *Student/faculty ratio:* 10:1.
Student Life *Campus security:* 24-hour emergency response devices.
Athletics Member NJCAA.
Standardized Tests *Required:* ACT (for admission).
Costs (2001–02) *Tuition:* $6480 full-time, $270 per credit hour part-time. *Required fees:* $105 full-time, $80 per term part-time. *Room only:* $2700.
Financial Aid In 2001, 33 Federal Work-Study jobs (averaging $2000).
Applying *Options:* common application. *Application fee:* $15. *Required:* high school transcript. *Required for some:* interview. *Recommended:* minimum 2.0 GPA.
Admissions Contact Ms. Kim Fontana, Director of Admissions, Springfield College in Illinois, 1500 North Fifth Street, Springfield, IL 62702-2694. *Phone:* 217-525-1420 Ext. 241. *Toll-free phone:* 800-635-7289. *Fax:* 217-525-1497.

TRITON COLLEGE
River Grove, Illinois

- **State-supported** 2-year, founded 1964, part of Illinois Community College Board
- **Calendar** semesters
- **Degree** certificates and associate
- **Suburban** 100-acre campus with easy access to Chicago
- **Coed,** 10,672 undergraduate students

Undergraduates Students come from 26 other countries, 1% are from out of state, 21% African American, 4% Asian American or Pacific Islander, 16% Hispanic American, 0.3% Native American.
Freshmen *Admission:* 2,214 applied, 2,214 admitted.
Faculty *Total:* 579, 23% full-time.
Majors Accounting; alcohol/drug abuse counseling; anthropology; architectural engineering technology; art; auto mechanic/technician; baker/pastry chef; biological/physical sciences; biology; business administration; business marketing and marketing management; chemistry; child care provider; computer engineering technology; computer graphics; computer graphics; computer/information systems security; computer programming related; computer science; computer software and media applications related; computer systems networking/telecommunications; computer/technical support; computer typography/composition; construction management; construction technology; court reporting; criminal justice/law enforcement administration; culinary arts; data processing technology; drafting; early childhood education; economics; education; electrical/electronic engineering technology; engineering design; engineering-related technology; engineering technology; English; fashion merchandising; fire science; French; geography; geology; graphic design/commercial art/illustration; graphic/printing equipment; heating/air conditioning/refrigeration; history; hospitality management; hotel and restaurant management; industrial technology; information sciences/systems; interdisciplinary studies; interior design; international business; Italian; journalism; landscape architecture; landscaping management; law enforcement/police science; legal administrative assistant; liberal arts and sciences/liberal studies; machine technology; management information systems/business data processing; mass communications; mathematics; music; nuclear medical technology; nursing; ophthalmic medical technology; opticianry; optometric/ophthalmic laboratory technician; ornamental horticulture; philosophy; physics; political science; practical nurse; psychology; radiological science; real estate; respiratory therapy; retail management; secretarial science; social sciences; Spanish; speech/rhetorical studies; system/networking/LAN/WAN management; theater arts/drama; transportation technology; Web/multimedia management/webmaster; Web page, digital/multimedia and information resources design; welding technology.
Academic Programs *Special study options:* academic remediation for entering students, adult/continuing education programs, advanced placement credit, cooperative education, distance learning, English as a second language, freshman honors college, honors programs, internships, part-time degree program, student-designed majors, summer session for credit.
Library Learning Resource Center with 70,859 titles, 1,247 serial subscriptions.
Computers on Campus 350 computers available on campus for general student use. At least one staffed computer lab available.
Student Life *Housing:* college housing not available. *Activities and Organizations:* drama/theater group, student-run newspaper, radio station, choral group, student government, Program Board. *Campus security:* 24-hour emergency response devices and patrols. *Student Services:* health clinic, personal/psychological counseling.
Athletics Member NJCAA. *Intercollegiate sports:* baseball M, basketball M/W, soccer M, softball W, swimming W, volleyball W, wrestling M.
Standardized Tests *Recommended:* SAT I or ACT (for placement).

Triton College (continued)

Costs (2002–03) *Tuition:* area resident $1536 full-time, $48 per credit hour part-time; state resident $5443 full-time, $170 per credit hour part-time; nonresident $8289 full-time, $259 per credit hour part-time. Full-time tuition and fees vary according to course load. Part-time tuition and fees vary according to course load. *Required fees:* $230 full-time, $6 per credit hour, $45 per term part-time. *Payment plan:* installment. *Waivers:* senior citizens and employees or children of employees.

Financial Aid In 2001, 250 Federal Work-Study jobs (averaging $2000).

Applying *Options:* deferred entrance. *Required:* high school transcript. *Application deadline:* rolling (freshmen), rolling (transfers).

Admissions Contact Ms. Gail Fuller, Director of Admission and Records, Triton College, 2000 Fifth Avenue, River Grove, IL 60171. *Phone:* 708-456-0300 Ext. 3397. *E-mail:* gfuller@triton.cc.il.us.

WAUBONSEE COMMUNITY COLLEGE

Sugar Grove, Illinois

- **District-supported** 2-year, founded 1966, part of Illinois Community College Board
- **Calendar** semesters
- **Degree** certificates and associate
- **Rural** 243-acre campus with easy access to Chicago
- **Coed,** 7,890 undergraduate students, 26% full-time, 55% women, 45% men

Undergraduates 2,070 full-time, 5,820 part-time. Students come from 1 other state, 6% African American, 2% Asian American or Pacific Islander, 15% Hispanic American, 0.8% Native American, 0.1% international, 2% transferred in.

Freshmen *Admission:* 1,223 applied, 1,223 admitted, 1,223 enrolled.

Faculty *Total:* 692, 10% full-time, 3% with terminal degrees. *Student/faculty ratio:* 16:1.

Majors Accounting technician; art; art education; auto mechanic/technician; banking; biological/physical sciences; business administration; business computer programming; child care provider; communications; computer/information sciences; data processing; design/visual communications; early childhood education; electrical/electronic engineering technology; engineering; enterprise management; executive assistant; fire protection/safety technology; general studies; heating/air conditioning/refrigeration; industrial machinery maintenance/repair; industrial technology; law enforcement/police science; liberal arts and sciences/liberal studies; logistics/materials management; mass communications; music; music teacher education; nursing; operations management; quality control technology; retailing operations; robotics technology; secretarial science; sign language interpretation; social work; travel services marketing operations.

Academic Programs *Special study options:* academic remediation for entering students, advanced placement credit, distance learning, honors programs, independent study, part-time degree program, services for LD students, study abroad, summer session for credit. *ROTC:* Army (c).

Library Learning Resource Center with 57,157 titles, 495 serial subscriptions, 18,958 audiovisual materials, an OPAC, a Web page.

Computers on Campus 139 computers available on campus for general student use. Internet access, at least one staffed computer lab available.

Student Life *Housing:* college housing not available. *Activities and Organizations:* drama/theater group, student-run newspaper, television station, choral group, Phi Theta Kappa, VICA, Alpha Sigma Lamda, Latinos Unidos, Christian Fellowship. *Campus security:* 24-hour emergency response devices and patrols, late-night transport/escort service.

Athletics Member NJCAA. *Intercollegiate sports:* baseball M, basketball M(s)/W(s), cross-country running M(s)/W(s), golf M(s), soccer M(s), softball W(s), tennis M(s)/W(s), volleyball W(s), wrestling M(s). *Intramural sports:* basketball M/W, bowling M/W, golf M/W, table tennis M/W, volleyball M/W.

Costs (2002–03) *Tuition:* area resident $1568 full-time, $49 per semester hour part-time; state resident $6172 full-time, $193 per semester hour part-time; nonresident $7457 full-time, $234 per semester hour part-time. Full-time tuition and fees vary according to course load. Part-time tuition and fees vary according to course load. *Required fees:* $36 full-time, $49 per semester hour. *Payment plans:* installment, deferred payment. *Waivers:* senior citizens and employees or children of employees.

Financial Aid In 2001, 23 Federal Work-Study jobs (averaging $1000).

Applying *Application fee:* $10. *Application deadline:* rolling (freshmen), rolling (transfers).

Admissions Contact Ms. Mary Perkins, Recruitment and Retention Manager, Waubonsee Community College, Route 47 at Waubonsee Drive, Sugar Grove, IL 60554. *Phone:* 630-466-7900 Ext. 2938. *Fax:* 630-466-4964. *E-mail:* recruitment@waubonsee.edu.

WESTWOOD COLLEGE OF TECHNOLOGY-CHICAGO DU PAGE

Woodridge, Illinois

- **Proprietary** 2-year
- **Degree** associate
- **Coed**

Majors Computer systems networking/telecommunications; graphic design/commercial art/illustration; multimedia.

Costs (2002–03) *Tuition:* Standard program price $3,355 per term, lab fees and books additional, 5 terms/year, program length: associate degree = 7 terms.

Admissions Contact Kris Simonich, Director of Admissions, Westwood College of Technology-Chicago Du Page, 7155 Janes Avenue, Woodridge, IL 60517. *Phone:* 630-434-8244.

WESTWOOD COLLEGE OF TECHNOLOGY-CHICAGO O'HARE

Schiller Park, Illinois

- **Proprietary** 2-year
- **Degree** associate
- **Coed,** 475 undergraduate students

Faculty *Total:* 30, 17% full-time.

Majors Computer programming; computer systems networking/telecommunications; graphic design/commercial art/illustration; multimedia.

Costs (2002–03) *Tuition:* Standard program price $3,355 per term, lab fees and books additional, 5 terms/year, program length: associate degree = 7 terms.

Admissions Contact Ms. Cathy Selig, Director of Admissions, Westwood College of Technology-Chicago O'Hare, 4825 North Scott Street, Suite 100, Schiller Park, IL 60176. *Phone:* 847-928-0200.

WESTWOOD COLLEGE OF TECHNOLOGY-CHICAGO RIVER OAKS

Calumet City, Illinois

- **Proprietary** 2-year
- **Degree** associate
- **Coed,** 416 undergraduate students

Faculty *Total:* 20, 20% full-time.

Majors Computer programming; computer systems networking/telecommunications; graphic design/commercial art/illustration; multimedia.

Costs (2002–03) *Tuition:* Standard program price $3,355 per term, lab fees and books additional, 5 terms/year, program length: associate degree = 7 terms.

Admissions Contact Mr. Gus Pyroulis, Director of Admissions, Westwood College of Technology-Chicago River Oaks, 80 River Oaks Drive, Suite D-49, Calumet City, IL 60409. *Phone:* 708-832-1988.

WILLIAM RAINEY HARPER COLLEGE

Palatine, Illinois

- **State and locally supported** 2-year, founded 1965, part of Illinois Community College Board
- **Calendar** semesters
- **Degree** certificates and associate
- **Suburban** 200-acre campus with easy access to Chicago
- **Endowment** $2.9 million
- **Coed**

Student Life *Campus security:* 24-hour emergency response devices and patrols, late-night transport/escort service.

Athletics Member NJCAA.

Standardized Tests *Required for some:* SAT I or ACT (for placement).

Financial Aid In 2001, 85 Federal Work-Study jobs (averaging $1210).

Applying *Options:* early admission, deferred entrance. *Application fee:* $25. *Required:* high school transcript. *Required for some:* minimum 2.0 GPA.

Admissions Contact Ms. Debbie Michelini, Student Recruitment Coordinator, William Rainey Harper College, 1200 West Algonquin Road, Palatine, IL 60067. *Phone:* 847-925-6247. *Fax:* 847-925-6044. *E-mail:* info@harper.cc.il.us.

Worsham College of Mortuary Science
Wheeling, Illinois

- **Independent** 2-year
- **Degree** associate
- **Coed,** 150 undergraduate students
- 100% of applicants were admitted

Undergraduates 20% African American, 10% Asian American or Pacific Islander, 10% Hispanic American.
Freshmen *Admission:* 70 applied, 70 admitted.
Faculty *Total:* 12. *Student/faculty ratio:* 17:1.
Majors Mortuary science.
Costs (2001–02) *Tuition:* $11,100 full-time. *Required fees:* $90 full-time.
Admissions Contact Ms. Stephanie Kann, President, Worsham College of Mortuary Science, 495 Northgate Parkway, Wheeling, IL 60090-2646. *Phone:* 847-808-8444.

INDIANA

Ancilla College
Donaldson, Indiana

- **Independent Roman Catholic** 2-year, founded 1937
- **Calendar** 4-4-1
- **Degree** certificates and associate
- **Rural** 63-acre campus with easy access to Chicago
- **Endowment** $94,963
- **Coed,** 504 undergraduate students, 60% full-time, 65% women, 35% men

Undergraduates 303 full-time, 201 part-time. Students come from 3 states and territories, 4 other countries, 1% are from out of state, 3% African American, 2% Asian American or Pacific Islander, 3% Hispanic American, 1% Native American, 0.6% international, 7% transferred in. *Retention:* 45% of 2001 full-time freshmen returned.
Freshmen *Admission:* 395 applied, 226 admitted, 191 enrolled. *Average high school GPA:* 2.40. *Test scores:* SAT verbal scores over 500: 6%; SAT math scores over 500: 15%; ACT scores over 18: 53%; ACT scores over 24: 6%.
Faculty *Total:* 51, 18% full-time, 14% with terminal degrees. *Student/faculty ratio:* 17:1.
Majors Administrative/secretarial services; biology; business administration; chemistry; computer programming; computer software and media applications related; computer systems networking/telecommunications; criminal justice/law enforcement administration; elementary education; fine arts and art studies related; health/medical preparatory programs related; humanities; liberal arts and sciences/liberal studies; mathematics; social sciences.
Academic Programs *Special study options:* academic remediation for entering students, adult/continuing education programs, advanced placement credit, cooperative education, double majors, independent study, part-time degree program, summer session for credit.
Library Ball Library with 28,456 titles, 188 serial subscriptions, 1,357 audiovisual materials, an OPAC.
Computers on Campus 56 computers available on campus for general student use. Internet access, at least one staffed computer lab available.
Student Life *Housing:* college housing not available. *Activities and Organizations:* student-run newspaper, Student Senate, Scripta Literary Magazine, Ancilla student ambassadors. *Campus security:* 24-hour patrols, late-night transport/escort service. *Student Services:* personal/psychological counseling.
Athletics Member NJCAA. *Intercollegiate sports:* baseball M(s), basketball M(s)/W(s), cross-country running M(s)/W(s), golf M(s), soccer M(s)/W(s), softball W(s), tennis M(s)/W(s).
Standardized Tests *Recommended:* SAT I or ACT (for admission).
Costs (2001–02) *Tuition:* $6000 full-time, $200 per semester hour part-time. Full-time tuition and fees vary according to course load. Part-time tuition and fees vary according to course load. *Required fees:* $200 full-time, $50 per term part-time. *Payment plan:* deferred payment. *Waivers:* employees or children of employees.
Financial Aid In 2001, 28 Federal Work-Study jobs (averaging $1820). 16 State and other part-time jobs (averaging $1000). *Financial aid deadline:* 3/1.
Applying *Options:* common application, electronic application. *Application fee:* $25. *Required:* high school transcript. *Recommended:* interview. *Application deadline:* rolling (freshmen), rolling (transfers).
Admissions Contact Mr. Steve Olson, Executive Director of Enrollment Management, Ancilla College, 9601 Union Road, Donaldson, IN 46513. *Phone:* 574-936-8898 Ext. 350. *Toll-free phone:* 866-262-4552 Ext. 350. *Fax:* 574-935-1773. *E-mail:* admissions@ancilla.edu.

College of Court Reporting
Hobart, Indiana

- **Proprietary** 2-year
- **Degree** certificates, diplomas, and associate
- **Coed,** 100 undergraduate students
- 91% of applicants were admitted

Undergraduates Students come from 3 states and territories, 5% are from out of state.
Freshmen *Admission:* 22 applied, 20 admitted.
Faculty *Total:* 16, 50% full-time. *Student/faculty ratio:* 8:1.
Majors Court reporting.
Costs (2001–02) *Tuition:* $4560 full-time, $190 per credit part-time. *Required fees:* $150 full-time.
Admissions Contact Ms. Stacy Drohoskie, Director of Admissions, College of Court Reporting, 111 West Tenth Street, Suite 111, Hobart, IN 46342. *Phone:* 219-942-1459. *Fax:* 219-942-1631. *E-mail:* dmiller@ccredu.com.

Commonwealth Business College
Merrillville, Indiana

- **Proprietary** 2-year, founded 1890, part of Commonwealth Business College, Inc
- **Calendar** quarters
- **Degree** certificates and associate
- **Small-town** 2-acre campus with easy access to Chicago
- **Coed,** 370 undergraduate students

Faculty *Total:* 12, 25% full-time.
Majors Accounting; business administration; information sciences/systems; management information systems/business data processing; medical assistant; paralegal/legal assistant.
Academic Programs *Special study options:* adult/continuing education programs, internships, part-time degree program, student-designed majors, summer session for credit.
Computers on Campus 45 computers available on campus for general student use. At least one staffed computer lab available.
Student Life *Housing:* college housing not available. *Campus security:* 24-hour emergency response devices.
Standardized Tests *Required:* ACT ASSET.
Costs (2001–02) *Tuition:* $148 per credit hour part-time.
Financial Aid In 2001, 2 Federal Work-Study jobs.
Applying *Options:* common application, early admission, deferred entrance. *Application fee:* $20. *Required:* high school transcript. *Application deadline:* rolling (freshmen), rolling (transfers). *Notification:* continuous (freshmen).
Admissions Contact Ms. Sheryl Elston, Director of Admissions, Commonwealth Business College, 1000 East 80th Place, Suite 101, N, Merrillville, IN 46410. *Phone:* 219-769-3321. *Fax:* 219-738-1076.

Commonwealth Business College
Michigan City, Indiana

Admissions Contact Ms. Sheryl Belle, Director of Admissions, Commonwealth Business College, 325 East US Highway 20, Michigan City, IN 46360. *Phone:* 219-769-3321.

Holy Cross College
Notre Dame, Indiana

- **Independent Roman Catholic** 2-year, founded 1966
- **Calendar** semesters
- **Degree** associate
- **Urban** 150-acre campus
- **Coed,** 558 undergraduate students, 95% full-time, 39% women, 61% men

Holy Cross College (continued)

Undergraduates 528 full-time, 30 part-time. Students come from 32 states and territories, 46% are from out of state, 3% African American, 1% Asian American or Pacific Islander, 6% Hispanic American, 0.5% Native American, 2% international, 6% transferred in, 50% live on campus.

Freshmen *Admission:* 471 applied, 442 admitted, 304 enrolled.

Faculty *Total:* 42, 60% full-time, 29% with terminal degrees. *Student/faculty ratio:* 17:1.

Majors Liberal arts and sciences/liberal studies.

Academic Programs *Special study options:* academic remediation for entering students, advanced placement credit, English as a second language, off-campus study, part-time degree program, summer session for credit. *ROTC:* Army (c), Air Force (c).

Library Holy Cross Library with 15,000 titles, 160 serial subscriptions, an OPAC.

Computers on Campus 60 computers available on campus for general student use. A campuswide network can be accessed from student residence rooms and from off campus. Internet access, at least one staffed computer lab available.

Student Life *Housing Options:* coed. *Activities and Organizations:* drama/theater group, student-run newspaper, choral group, Student Advisory Committee, Campus Ministry, Volunteers in Support of Admissions, Intramural Athletics. *Campus security:* 24-hour emergency response devices, 24-hour patrols by trained personnel on certain days. *Student Services:* personal/psychological counseling.

Athletics *Intramural sports:* basketball M/W, football M/W, golf M/W, volleyball M/W.

Standardized Tests *Required:* SAT I or ACT (for admission).

Costs (2001–02) *Comprehensive fee:* $15,050 includes full-time tuition ($8500), mandatory fees ($250), and room and board ($6300). Part-time tuition: $295 per credit hour. Part-time tuition and fees vary according to course load. *Required fees:* $125 per term part-time. *Room and board:* Room and board charges vary according to housing facility. *Payment plan:* installment. *Waivers:* employees or children of employees.

Financial Aid In 2001, 44 Federal Work-Study jobs (averaging $857).

Applying *Options:* common application, electronic application, deferred entrance. *Application fee:* $50. *Required:* essay or personal statement, high school transcript, minimum 2.0 GPA. *Recommended:* interview. *Application deadline:* rolling (freshmen), rolling (transfers).

Admissions Contact Mr. Vincent M. Duke, Director of Admissions, Holy Cross College, PO Box 308, Notre Dame, IN 46556. *Phone:* 574-239-8400 Ext. 407. *Fax:* 574-233-7427. *E-mail:* vduke@hcc-nd.edu.

INDIANA BUSINESS COLLEGE
Anderson, Indiana

- **Proprietary** 2-year, founded 1902
- **Calendar** quarters
- **Degree** certificates, diplomas, and associate
- **Coed,** 241 undergraduate students

Undergraduates Students come from 4 states and territories.

Faculty *Student/faculty ratio:* 20:1.

Majors Accounting; business administration; business computer programming; health professions and related sciences; medical radiologic technology; secretarial science.

Academic Programs *Special study options:* adult/continuing education programs, cooperative education, double majors, internships, part-time degree program.

Computers on Campus Internet access, online (class) registration available.

Costs (2001–02) *Tuition:* $126 per credit hour part-time. Full-time tuition and fees vary according to program. Part-time tuition and fees vary according to program. *Payment plan:* installment.

Applying *Options:* electronic application, early decision, early action. *Application fee:* $30. *Required:* high school transcript, minimum 2.0 GPA, interview. *Application deadline:* rolling (freshmen), rolling (transfers). *Notification:* continuous (freshmen).

Admissions Contact Ms. Charlene Stacy, Executive Director, Indiana Business College, 140 East 53rd Street, Anderson, IN 46013. *Phone:* 765-644-7514. *Toll-free phone:* 800-IBC-GRAD. *Fax:* 765-644-5724.

INDIANA BUSINESS COLLEGE
Columbus, Indiana

- **Proprietary** 2-year
- **Calendar** quarters
- **Degree** certificates, diplomas, and associate
- **Coed,** 209 undergraduate students

Undergraduates Students come from 4 states and territories.

Faculty *Student/faculty ratio:* 20:1.

Majors Accounting; business administration; business administration/management related; business computer programming; business information/data processing related; computer/information sciences related; health professions and related sciences; information technology; medical assistant; medical radiologic technology; secretarial science.

Academic Programs *Special study options:* adult/continuing education programs, cooperative education, double majors, internships, part-time degree program.

Computers on Campus Internet access, online (class) registration available.

Costs (2001–02) *Tuition:* $126 per credit hour part-time. Full-time tuition and fees vary according to program. Part-time tuition and fees vary according to program. *Payment plan:* installment.

Applying *Options:* electronic application, early decision, early action. *Application fee:* $30. *Required:* high school transcript, minimum 2.0 GPA, interview. *Application deadline:* rolling (freshmen), rolling (transfers). *Notification:* continuous (freshmen).

Admissions Contact Mr. Gary McGee, Regional Director, Indiana Business College, 2222 Poshard Drive, Columbus, IN 47203. *Phone:* 812-379-9000. *Toll-free phone:* 800-IBC-GRAD. *Fax:* 812-375-0414.

INDIANA BUSINESS COLLEGE
Lafayette, Indiana

- **Proprietary** 2-year
- **Calendar** quarters
- **Degree** certificates and associate
- **Coed,** 155 undergraduate students

Undergraduates Students come from 4 states and territories.

Faculty *Student/faculty ratio:* 20:1.

Majors Accounting; business administration; business administration/management related; business information/data processing related; computer/information sciences related; information technology; secretarial science.

Academic Programs *Special study options:* adult/continuing education programs, cooperative education, double majors, internships, part-time degree program.

Computers on Campus Internet access, online (class) registration available.

Costs (2001–02) *Tuition:* $126 per credit hour part-time. Full-time tuition and fees vary according to program. Part-time tuition and fees vary according to program. *Payment plan:* installment.

Applying *Options:* electronic application, early decision, early action. *Application fee:* $30. *Required:* high school transcript, minimum 2.0 GPA, interview. *Application deadline:* rolling (freshmen), rolling (transfers). *Notification:* continuous (freshmen).

Admissions Contact Mr. Greg Reger, Executive Director, Indiana Business College, 2 Executive Drive, Lafayette, IN 47905. *Phone:* 765-447-9550. *Toll-free phone:* 800-IBC-GRAD. *Fax:* 765-447-0868.

INDIANA BUSINESS COLLEGE
Terre Haute, Indiana

- **Proprietary** 2-year, founded 1902
- **Calendar** quarters
- **Degree** certificates and associate
- **Coed,** 282 undergraduate students

Undergraduates Students come from 4 states and territories.

Faculty *Student/faculty ratio:* 20:1.

Majors Accounting; business administration; business administration/management related; business computer programming; business information/data processing related; computer/information sciences related; health professions and related sciences; information technology; medical assistant; medical radiologic technology; secretarial science.

Academic Programs *Special study options:* adult/continuing education programs, cooperative education, double majors, internships, part-time degree program.

Computers on Campus Internet access, online (class) registration available.

Costs (2001–02) *Tuition:* $126 per credit hour part-time. Full-time tuition and fees vary according to program. Part-time tuition and fees vary according to program. *Payment plan:* installment.
Applying *Options:* electronic application, early decision, early action. *Application fee:* $30. *Required:* high school transcript, minimum 2.0 GPA, interview. *Application deadline:* rolling (freshmen), rolling (transfers). *Notification:* continuous (freshmen).
Admissions Contact Ms. Laura Hale, Executive Director, Indiana Business College, 3175 South Third Place, Terre Haute, IN 47802. *Phone:* 812-234-2361. *Toll-free phone:* 800-IBC-GRAD. *Fax:* 812-234-2361.

INDIANA BUSINESS COLLEGE
Fort Wayne, Indiana

- **Proprietary** 2-year
- **Calendar** quarters
- **Degree** certificates and associate
- **Coed,** 172 undergraduate students

Undergraduates Students come from 4 states and territories.
Faculty *Student/faculty ratio:* 20:1.
Majors Accounting; business administration; health professions and related sciences; medical assistant; medical radiologic technology; secretarial science.
Academic Programs *Special study options:* adult/continuing education programs, cooperative education, double majors, internships, part-time degree program.
Computers on Campus Internet access, online (class) registration available.
Costs (2001–02) *Tuition:* $126 per credit hour part-time. Full-time tuition and fees vary according to program. Part-time tuition and fees vary according to program. *Payment plan:* installment.
Applying *Options:* electronic application, early decision, early action. *Application fee:* $30. *Required:* high school transcript, minimum 2.0 GPA, interview. *Application deadline:* rolling (freshmen), rolling (transfers). *Notification:* continuous (freshmen).
Admissions Contact Ms. Janet Hein, Executive Director, Indiana Business College, 6413 North Clinton Street, Fort Wayne, IN 46825. *Phone:* 219-471-7667. *Toll-free phone:* 800-IBC-GRAD. *Fax:* 219-471-6918.

INDIANA BUSINESS COLLEGE
Marion, Indiana

- **Proprietary** 2-year
- **Calendar** quarters
- **Degree** certificates, diplomas, and associate
- **Coed,** 168 undergraduate students

Undergraduates Students come from 4 states and territories.
Faculty *Student/faculty ratio:* 20:1.
Majors Accounting; business administration; medical radiologic technology; secretarial science.
Academic Programs *Special study options:* adult/continuing education programs, cooperative education, double majors, internships, part-time degree program.
Computers on Campus Internet access, online (class) registration available.
Costs (2001–02) *Tuition:* $126 per credit hour part-time. Full-time tuition and fees vary according to program. Part-time tuition and fees vary according to program. *Payment plan:* installment.
Applying *Options:* electronic application, early decision, early action. *Application fee:* $30. *Required:* high school transcript, minimum 2.0 GPA, interview. *Application deadline:* rolling (freshmen), rolling (transfers). *Notification:* continuous (freshmen).
Admissions Contact Ms. Rebecca Cox, Executive Director, Indiana Business College, 830 North Miller Avenue, Marion, IN 46952. *Phone:* 765-662-7497. *Toll-free phone:* 800-IBC-GRAD. *Fax:* 765-651-6421.

INDIANA BUSINESS COLLEGE
Evansville, Indiana

- **Proprietary** 2-year
- **Calendar** quarters
- **Degree** certificates and associate
- **Coed,** 244 undergraduate students

Undergraduates Students come from 4 states and territories.
Faculty *Student/faculty ratio:* 20:1.
Majors Accounting; business administration; business computer programming; computer programming; health professions and related sciences; information technology; medical assistant; medical radiologic technology; secretarial science.
Academic Programs *Special study options:* adult/continuing education programs, cooperative education, double majors, internships, part-time degree program.
Computers on Campus Internet access, online (class) registration available.
Costs (2001–02) *Tuition:* $126 per credit hour part-time. Full-time tuition and fees vary according to program. Part-time tuition and fees vary according to program. *Payment plan:* installment.
Applying *Options:* electronic application, early decision, early action. *Application fee:* $30. *Required:* high school transcript, minimum 2.0 GPA, interview. *Application deadline:* rolling (freshmen), rolling (transfers). *Notification:* continuous (freshmen).
Admissions Contact Ms. Janelle Roberts, Associate Director of Admissions, Indiana Business College, 4601 Theater Drive, Evansville, IN 47715. *Phone:* 812-476-6000. *Toll-free phone:* 800-IBC-GRAD. *Fax:* 812-471-8576.

INDIANA BUSINESS COLLEGE
Indianapolis, Indiana

- **Proprietary** 2-year, founded 1902
- **Calendar** quarters
- **Degree** certificates, diplomas, and associate
- **Urban** 1-acre campus
- **Coed,** 818 undergraduate students

Undergraduates Students come from 4 states and territories.
Faculty *Student/faculty ratio:* 20:1.
Majors Accounting; business administration; business administration/management related; business computer programming; business information/data processing related; computer/information sciences; computer/information sciences related; computer programming; fashion merchandising; information technology; legal administrative assistant; medical administrative assistant; medical assistant; medical records technology; secretarial science; travel/tourism management.
Academic Programs *Special study options:* adult/continuing education programs, cooperative education, double majors, internships, part-time degree program, summer session for credit.
Computers on Campus Internet access, online (class) registration available.
Student Life *Housing:* college housing not available. *Activities and Organizations:* Student Advisory Board, Student Ambassadors, Phi Beta Lambda. *Campus security:* 24-hour patrols. *Student Services:* personal/psychological counseling.
Costs (2001–02) *Tuition:* $126 per credit hour part-time. Full-time tuition and fees vary according to program. Part-time tuition and fees vary according to program. *Payment plan:* installment.
Applying *Options:* electronic application, early decision, early action. *Application fee:* $30. *Required:* high school transcript, minimum 2.0 GPA, interview. *Application deadline:* rolling (freshmen), rolling (transfers). *Notification:* continuous (freshmen).
Admissions Contact Mr. Jason Konesco, Assistant Executive Director, Indiana Business College, 802 North Meridian Street, Indianapolis, IN 46204. *Phone:* 317-264-5656. *Toll-free phone:* 800-999-9229. *Fax:* 317-634-0471.

INDIANA BUSINESS COLLEGE
Muncie, Indiana

- **Proprietary** 2-year
- **Calendar** quarters
- **Degree** certificates, diplomas, and associate
- **Coed,** 282 undergraduate students

Undergraduates Students come from 4 states and territories.
Faculty *Student/faculty ratio:* 20:1.
Majors Accounting; business administration; business administration/management related; business computer programming; business information/data processing related; computer/information sciences related; information technology; medical records technology; secretarial science; travel/tourism management.
Academic Programs *Special study options:* cooperative education, double majors, external degree program, internships, part-time degree program.
Computers on Campus Internet access, online (class) registration available.

Indiana Business College (continued)

Student Life *Housing:* college housing not available. *Activities and Organizations:* Phi Beta Lambda, national fraternities, national sororities.

Costs (2001–02) *Tuition:* $126 per credit hour part-time. Full-time tuition and fees vary according to program. Part-time tuition and fees vary according to program. *Payment plan:* installment.

Applying *Options:* electronic application, early decision, early action. *Application fee:* $30. *Required:* high school transcript, minimum 2.0 GPA, interview. *Application deadline:* rolling (freshmen), rolling (transfers). *Notification:* continuous (freshmen).

Admissions Contact Mr. Gregory Bond, Executive Director, Indiana Business College, 411 West Riggin Road, Muncie, IN 47303. *Phone:* 765-288-8681. *Toll-free phone:* 800-IBC-GRAD. *Fax:* 765-288-8797.

INDIANA BUSINESS COLLEGE-MEDICAL
Indianapolis, Indiana

- **Proprietary** 2-year
- **Calendar** quarters
- **Degree** certificates, diplomas, and associate
- **Coed,** 354 undergraduate students

Undergraduates Students come from 4 states and territories.

Faculty *Student/faculty ratio:* 20:1.

Majors Health/physical education/fitness related; health professions and related sciences; medical assistant; medical radiologic technology.

Academic Programs *Special study options:* adult/continuing education programs, cooperative education, double majors, internships, part-time degree program.

Computers on Campus Internet access, online (class) registration available.

Costs (2001–02) *Tuition:* $126 per credit hour part-time. Full-time tuition and fees vary according to program. Part-time tuition and fees vary according to program. *Payment plan:* installment.

Applying *Options:* electronic application, early decision, early action. *Application fee:* $30. *Required:* high school transcript, minimum 2.0 GPA, interview. *Application deadline:* rolling (freshmen), rolling (transfers). *Notification:* continuous (freshmen).

Admissions Contact Ms. Pam Soladine-Davis, Regional Director, Indiana Business College-Medical, 8150 Brookville Road, Indianapolis, IN 46239. *Phone:* 317-375-8000. *Toll-free phone:* 800-IBC-GRAD.

INTERNATIONAL BUSINESS COLLEGE
Fort Wayne, Indiana

- **Proprietary** primarily 2-year, founded 1889, part of Bradford Schools, Inc
- **Calendar** semesters
- **Degrees** diplomas, associate, and bachelor's
- **Suburban** 2-acre campus
- **Coed, primarily women,** 659 undergraduate students

Freshmen *Admission:* 1,053 applied, 1,011 admitted.

Faculty *Total:* 44, 25% full-time. *Student/faculty ratio:* 24:1.

Majors Accounting; business administration; computer engineering technology; computer programming; engineering/industrial management; finance; graphic design/commercial art/illustration; hospitality management; legal administrative assistant; medical assistant; paralegal/legal assistant; retail management; secretarial science; travel/tourism management.

Academic Programs *Special study options:* adult/continuing education programs, independent study, internships, part-time degree program.

Library 2,100 titles, 100 serial subscriptions.

Computers on Campus 150 computers available on campus for general student use. At least one staffed computer lab available.

Student Life *Activities and Organizations:* Student Senate, Collegiate Secretarial Institute, Accounting Club. *Campus security:* controlled dormitory access.

Costs (2001–02) *Tuition:* $9200 full-time. No tuition increase for student's term of enrollment. *Room only:* $3900.

Applying *Options:* deferred entrance. *Application fee:* $50. *Required:* high school transcript. *Application deadline:* 9/3 (freshmen).

Admissions Contact Mr. Steve Kinzer, School Director, International Business College, 3811 Illinois Road, Fort Wayne, IN 46804. *Phone:* 219-459-4513. *Toll-free phone:* 800-589-6363. *Fax:* 219-436-1896.

INTERNATIONAL BUSINESS COLLEGE
Indianapolis, Indiana

- **Proprietary** 2-year
- **Calendar** semesters
- **Degree** diplomas and associate
- **Coed**

Admissions Contact Ms. Kathy Chiudioni, Director of Admissions, International Business College, 7205 Shadeland Station, Indianapolis, IN 46256. *Phone:* 317-213-2320.

ITT TECHNICAL INSTITUTE
Newburgh, Indiana

- **Proprietary** primarily 2-year, founded 1966, part of ITT Educational Services, Inc
- **Calendar** quarters
- **Degrees** associate and bachelor's
- **Coed,** 364 undergraduate students

Majors Computer/information sciences related; computer programming; drafting; electrical/electronic engineering technologies related; information technology; robotics technology.

Student Life *Housing:* college housing not available.

Costs (2001–02) *Tuition:* Full-time tuition and fees vary according to program. Part-time tuition and fees vary according to program. $260—$330 per credit hour.

Financial Aid *Financial aid deadline:* 3/1.

Applying *Options:* deferred entrance. *Application fee:* $100. *Required:* high school transcript, interview. *Recommended:* letters of recommendation. *Application deadline:* rolling (freshmen), rolling (transfers). *Notification:* continuous (freshmen).

Admissions Contact Mr. Jim Smolinski, Director of Recruitment, ITT Technical Institute, 10999 Stahl Road, Newburgh, IN 47630-7430. *Phone:* 812-858-1600.

ITT TECHNICAL INSTITUTE
Fort Wayne, Indiana

- **Proprietary** primarily 2-year, founded 1967, part of ITT Educational Services, Inc
- **Calendar** quarters
- **Degrees** associate and bachelor's
- **Coed,** 509 undergraduate students

Majors Computer/information sciences related; computer programming; drafting; industrial design; information technology; robotics technology.

Student Life *Housing:* college housing not available.

Costs (2001–02) *Tuition:* Full-time tuition and fees vary according to program. Part-time tuition and fees vary according to program. $260—$330 per credit hour.

Applying *Options:* deferred entrance. *Application fee:* $100. *Required:* high school transcript, interview. *Recommended:* letters of recommendation. *Application deadline:* rolling (freshmen), rolling (transfers). *Notification:* continuous (freshmen).

Admissions Contact Mr. Jack Young, Director of Recruitment, ITT Technical Institute, 4919 Coldwater Road, Fort Wayne, IN 46825-5532. *Phone:* 260-484-4107 Ext. 244. *Toll-free phone:* 800-866-4488.

ITT TECHNICAL INSTITUTE
Indianapolis, Indiana

- **Proprietary** founded 1966, part of ITT Educational Services, Inc
- **Calendar** quarters
- **Degrees** diplomas, associate, bachelor's, and master's
- **Suburban** 10-acre campus
- **Coed,** 798 undergraduate students

Majors Computer/information sciences related; computer programming; design/applied arts related; drafting; electrical/electronic engineering technologies related; information technology; robotics technology.

Student Life *Housing:* college housing not available. *Activities and Organizations:* student-run newspaper.

Costs (2001–02) *Tuition:* Full-time tuition and fees vary according to program. Part-time tuition and fees vary according to program. $260—$330 per credit hour.
Applying *Options:* deferred entrance. *Application fee:* $100. *Required:* high school transcript, interview. *Recommended:* letters of recommendation. *Application deadline:* rolling (freshmen), rolling (transfers). *Notification:* continuous (freshmen).
Admissions Contact Mr. Byron Ratclife, Director of Recruitment, ITT Technical Institute, 9511 Angola Court, Indianapolis, IN 46268-1119. *Phone:* 317-875-8640. *Toll-free phone:* 800-937-4488. *Fax:* 317-875-8641.

IVY TECH STATE COLLEGE-BLOOMINGTON
Bloomington, Indiana

- **State-supported** 2-year, founded 2001, part of Ivy Tech State College System
- **Calendar** semesters
- **Degree** associate
- **Endowment** $5.0 million
- **Coed,** 2,391 undergraduate students, 39% full-time, 61% women, 39% men
- 100% of applicants were admitted

Undergraduates 937 full-time, 1,454 part-time. 3% African American, 0.6% Asian American or Pacific Islander, 1% Hispanic American, 0.7% Native American, 0.5% international, 8% transferred in.
Freshmen *Admission:* 750 applied, 750 admitted, 432 enrolled.
Faculty *Total:* 186, 18% full-time.
Majors Accounting technician; building maintenance/management; business administration; child care/guidance; computer/information sciences; drafting; electrical/electronic engineering technology; executive assistant; industrial machinery maintenance/repair; machine technology; nursing; stationary energy sources installation; tool/die making.
Student Life *Activities and Organizations:* Student Government, Phi Theta Kappa. *Campus security:* late-night transport/escort service.
Standardized Tests *Required:* ACT ASSET.
Costs (2002–03) *Tuition:* state resident $2214 full-time, $74 per credit part-time; nonresident $4463 full-time, $149 per credit part-time. Full-time tuition and fees vary according to course load and reciprocity agreements. Part-time tuition and fees vary according to course load and reciprocity agreements. *Required fees:* $50 full-time, $25 per term part-time. *Payment plan:* installment. *Waivers:* employees or children of employees.
Applying *Required:* high school transcript. *Required for some:* interview. *Application deadline:* rolling (freshmen), rolling (transfers). *Notification:* continuous (freshmen).
Admissions Contact Mr. Neil Frederick, Assistant Director of Admissions, Ivy Tech State College-Bloomington, 3116 Canterbury Court, Bloomington, IN 47404. *Phone:* 812-332-1559 Ext. 4118. *E-mail:* nfrederi@ivytech.edu.

IVY TECH STATE COLLEGE-CENTRAL INDIANA
Indianapolis, Indiana

- **State-supported** 2-year, founded 1963, part of Ivy Tech State College System
- **Calendar** semesters
- **Degree** associate
- **Urban** 10-acre campus
- **Endowment** $5.0 million
- **Coed,** 7,357 undergraduate students, 27% full-time, 54% women, 46% men

Undergraduates 1,982 full-time, 5,375 part-time. 25% African American, 0.8% Asian American or Pacific Islander, 2% Hispanic American, 0.4% Native American, 0.3% international, 4% transferred in.
Freshmen *Admission:* 2,359 applied, 2,359 admitted, 1,079 enrolled.
Faculty *Total:* 386, 25% full-time.
Majors Accounting; accounting technician; auto mechanic/technician; building maintenance/management; business administration; cabinet making; carpentry; child guidance; computer/information sciences; design/visual communications; drafting; electrical/electronic engineering technology; executive assistant; industrial machinery maintenance/repair; machine shop assistant; machine technology; masonry/tile setting; medical assistant; medical radiologic technology; nursing; occupational safety/health technology; occupational therapy assistant; operating room technician; paralegal/legal assistant; plumbing; psychiatric/mental health services; respiratory therapy; sheet metal working; stationary energy sources installation; tool/die making.
Academic Programs *Special study options:* academic remediation for entering students, adult/continuing education programs, advanced placement credit, distance learning, English as a second language, internships, part-time degree program, services for LD students, summer session for credit.
Library 7,808 titles, 300 serial subscriptions, 11,154 audiovisual materials, an OPAC, a Web page.
Computers on Campus 340 computers available on campus for general student use. Internet access, online (class) registration, at least one staffed computer lab available.
Student Life *Housing:* college housing not available. *Activities and Organizations:* student-run newspaper, Student Government, Phi Theta Kappa, Alumni Association, Administrative Office Assistants Club, Radiology Club. *Campus security:* 24-hour emergency response devices and patrols, late-night transport/escort service. *Student Services:* personal/psychological counseling.
Standardized Tests *Required:* ACT ASSET.
Costs (2002–03) *Tuition:* state resident $2214 full-time, $74 per credit part-time; nonresident $4463 full-time, $149 per credit part-time. Full-time tuition and fees vary according to course load. Part-time tuition and fees vary according to course load. *Required fees:* $50 full-time, $25 per term part-time. *Payment plan:* installment. *Waivers:* senior citizens and employees or children of employees.
Financial Aid *Financial aid deadline:* 3/1.
Applying *Options:* early admission, deferred entrance. *Required:* high school transcript. *Required for some:* interview. *Application deadline:* rolling (freshmen), rolling (transfers). *Notification:* continuous (freshmen).
Admissions Contact Ms. Sonia Dickerson, Director of Admissions, Ivy Tech State College-Central Indiana, One West 26th Street, Indianapolis, IN 46208-4777. *Phone:* 317-921-4882 Ext. 4612. *Toll-free phone:* 800-732-1470. *Fax:* 317-921-4753. *E-mail:* sdickers@ivytech.edu.

IVY TECH STATE COLLEGE-COLUMBUS
Columbus, Indiana

- **State-supported** 2-year, founded 1963, part of Ivy Tech State College System
- **Calendar** semesters
- **Degree** associate
- **Small-town** campus with easy access to Indianapolis
- **Endowment** $5.0 million
- **Coed,** 1,600 undergraduate students, 26% full-time, 63% women, 37% men

Undergraduates 418 full-time, 1,182 part-time. 2% African American, 0.3% Asian American or Pacific Islander, 0.5% Hispanic American, 0.6% Native American, 0.4% international, 2% transferred in.
Freshmen *Admission:* 533 applied, 533 admitted, 213 enrolled.
Faculty *Total:* 139, 21% full-time.
Majors Accounting; accounting technician; auto mechanic/technician; building maintenance/management; business administration; child care/guidance; computer/information sciences; design/visual communications; drafting; electrical/electronic engineering technology; executive assistant; industrial machinery maintenance/repair; machine technology; masonry/tile setting; medical assistant; robotics technology; stationary energy sources installation; tool/die making.
Academic Programs *Special study options:* academic remediation for entering students, adult/continuing education programs, advanced placement credit, distance learning, internships, part-time degree program, services for LD students, summer session for credit.
Library 5,868 titles, 164 serial subscriptions, 927 audiovisual materials, an OPAC, a Web page.
Computers on Campus 160 computers available on campus for general student use. Internet access, online (class) registration, at least one staffed computer lab available.
Student Life *Housing:* college housing not available. *Activities and Organizations:* Student Government, Phi Theta Kappa, LPN Club. *Campus security:* late-night transport/escort service, trained evening security personnel, escort service.
Standardized Tests *Required:* ACT ASSET.
Costs (2002–03) *Tuition:* state resident $2214 full-time, $74 per credit part-time; nonresident $4463 full-time, $149 per credit part-time. Full-time tuition and fees vary according to course load. Part-time tuition and fees vary according to course load. *Required fees:* $50 full-time, $25 per term part-time. *Payment plan:* installment. *Waivers:* senior citizens and employees or children of employees.
Financial Aid In 2001, 23 Federal Work-Study jobs (averaging $1500). 3 State and other part-time jobs (averaging $1000).
Applying *Options:* early admission, deferred entrance. *Required:* high school transcript. *Required for some:* interview. *Application deadline:* rolling (freshmen), rolling (transfers). *Notification:* continuous (freshmen).

Ivy Tech State College-Columbus (continued)

Admissions Contact Ms. Lisa Morris, Director of Admissions, Ivy Tech State College-Columbus, 4475 Central Avenue, Columbus, IN 47203-1868. *Phone:* 812-372-9925 Ext. 129. *Toll-free phone:* 800-922-4838. *Fax:* 812-372-9925. *E-mail:* lmorris@ivytech.edu.

IVY TECH STATE COLLEGE-EASTCENTRAL

Muncie, Indiana

- **State-supported** 2-year, founded 1968, part of Ivy Tech State College System
- **Calendar** semesters
- **Degree** associate
- **Suburban** 15-acre campus with easy access to Indianapolis
- **Endowment** $5.0 million
- **Coed,** 4,052 undergraduate students, 40% full-time, 61% women, 39% men

Undergraduates 1,602 full-time, 2,450 part-time. 8% African American, 0.4% Asian American or Pacific Islander, 1% Hispanic American, 0.4% Native American, 2% transferred in.

Freshmen *Admission:* 1,439 applied, 1,439 admitted, 920 enrolled.

Faculty *Total:* 276, 21% full-time.

Majors Accounting technician; auto mechanic/technician; building maintenance/management; business administration; carpentry; child care/guidance; computer/information sciences; drafting; electrical/electronic engineering technology; executive assistant; industrial machinery maintenance/repair; machine technology; masonry/tile setting; medical assistant; medical radiologic technology; nursing; operating room technician; paralegal/legal assistant; physical therapy assistant; plumbing; psychiatric/mental health services; robotics technology; stationary energy sources installation; tool/die making.

Academic Programs *Special study options:* academic remediation for entering students, adult/continuing education programs, advanced placement credit, distance learning, internships, part-time degree program, services for LD students.

Library 3,081 titles, 250 serial subscriptions, 5,317 audiovisual materials, an OPAC, a Web page.

Computers on Campus 357 computers available on campus for general student use. A campuswide network can be accessed from off campus. Internet access, online (class) registration, at least one staffed computer lab available.

Student Life *Housing:* college housing not available. *Activities and Organizations:* Business Professionals of America, Skills USA-VICA, Student Government, Phi Theta Kappa, Alumni Association.

Standardized Tests *Required:* ACT ASSET.

Costs (2002–03) *Tuition:* state resident $2214 full-time, $74 per credit part-time; nonresident $4463 full-time, $149 per credit part-time. Full-time tuition and fees vary according to course load. Part-time tuition and fees vary according to course load. *Required fees:* $50 full-time, $25 per term part-time. *Payment plan:* installment. *Waivers:* senior citizens and employees or children of employees.

Applying *Options:* early admission, deferred entrance. *Required:* high school transcript. *Required for some:* interview. *Application deadline:* rolling (freshmen), rolling (transfers). *Notification:* continuous (freshmen).

Admissions Contact Ms. Gail Chesterfield, Dean of Student Affairs, Ivy Tech State College-Eastcentral, 4301 S Cowan Road, Muncie, IN 47302-9448. *Phone:* 765-289-2291 Ext. 391. *Toll-free phone:* 800-589-8324. *Fax:* 765-289-2291 Ext. 502. *E-mail:* gchester@ivytech.edu.

IVY TECH STATE COLLEGE-KOKOMO

Kokomo, Indiana

- **State-supported** 2-year, founded 1968, part of Ivy Tech State College System
- **Calendar** semesters
- **Degree** associate
- **Small-town** 20-acre campus with easy access to Indianapolis
- **Endowment** $5.0 million
- **Coed,** 2,003 undergraduate students, 29% full-time, 57% women, 43% men

Undergraduates 581 full-time, 1,422 part-time. 4% African American, 0.4% Asian American or Pacific Islander, 2% Hispanic American, 1% Native American, 0.3% international, 4% transferred in.

Freshmen *Admission:* 550 applied, 550 admitted, 296 enrolled.

Faculty *Total:* 161, 24% full-time.

Majors Accounting; accounting technician; auto mechanic/technician; building maintenance/management; business administration; child care/guidance; computer/information sciences; drafting; electrical/electronic engineering technology; emergency medical technology; executive assistant; industrial machinery maintenance/repair; machine technology; medical assistant; stationary energy sources installation; tool/die making.

Academic Programs *Special study options:* academic remediation for entering students, adult/continuing education programs, advanced placement credit, distance learning, internships, part-time degree program, services for LD students, summer session for credit.

Library 3,015 titles, 85 serial subscriptions, 1,123 audiovisual materials, an OPAC, a Web page.

Computers on Campus 348 computers available on campus for general student use. A campuswide network can be accessed from off campus. Internet access, online (class) registration, at least one staffed computer lab available.

Student Life *Housing:* college housing not available. *Activities and Organizations:* Student Government, Alumni Association, Collegiate Secretaries International, Licensed Practical Nursing Club, Phi Theta Kappa. *Campus security:* 24-hour emergency response devices, late-night transport/escort service. *Student Services:* personal/psychological counseling.

Standardized Tests *Required:* ACT ASSET.

Costs (2002–03) *Tuition:* state resident $2214 full-time, $74 per credit part-time; nonresident $4463 full-time, $149 per credit part-time. Full-time tuition and fees vary according to course load. Part-time tuition and fees vary according to course load. *Required fees:* $50 full-time, $25 per term part-time. *Payment plan:* installment. *Waivers:* senior citizens and employees or children of employees.

Financial Aid In 2001, 15 Federal Work-Study jobs (averaging $3360).

Applying *Options:* early admission. *Required:* high school transcript. *Required for some:* interview. *Application deadline:* rolling (freshmen), rolling (transfers). *Notification:* continuous (freshmen).

Admissions Contact Alayne Cook, Assistant Director of Admissions, Ivy Tech State College-Kokomo, 1815 E. Morgan Street, Kokomo, IN 46903-1373. *Phone:* 765-459-0561 Ext. 318. *Toll-free phone:* 800-459-0561. *Fax:* 765-454-5111. *E-mail:* acook@ivytech.edu.

IVY TECH STATE COLLEGE-LAFAYETTE

Lafayette, Indiana

- **State-supported** 2-year, founded 1968, part of Ivy Tech State College System
- **Calendar** semesters
- **Degree** certificates and associate
- **Suburban** campus with easy access to Indianapolis
- **Endowment** $5.0 million
- **Coed,** 4,143 undergraduate students, 36% full-time, 48% women, 52% men

Undergraduates 1,499 full-time, 2,644 part-time. 3% African American, 0.7% Asian American or Pacific Islander, 3% Hispanic American, 0.4% Native American, 1% international, 7% transferred in.

Freshmen *Admission:* 1,167 applied, 1,167 admitted, 558 enrolled.

Faculty *Total:* 197, 24% full-time.

Majors Accounting technician; auto mechanic/technician; building maintenance/management; business administration; carpentry; child care/guidance; computer/information sciences; drafting; electrical/electronic engineering technology; executive assistant; industrial machinery maintenance/repair; industrial technology; machine technology; masonry/tile setting; medical assistant; nursing; operating room technician; robotics technology; sheet metal working; stationary energy sources installation; tool/die making.

Academic Programs *Special study options:* academic remediation for entering students, advanced placement credit, distance learning, internships, part-time degree program, services for LD students, summer session for credit.

Library 4,310 titles, 217 serial subscriptions, 1,946 audiovisual materials, an OPAC, a Web page.

Computers on Campus 203 computers available on campus for general student use. Internet access, online (class) registration, at least one staffed computer lab available.

Student Life *Housing:* college housing not available. *Activities and Organizations:* student-run newspaper, Student Government, Phi Theta Kappa, LPN Club, Accounting Club, Student Computer Technology Association. *Student Services:* personal/psychological counseling.

Standardized Tests *Required:* ACT ASSET.

Costs (2002–03) *Tuition:* state resident $2214 full-time, $74 per credit part-time; nonresident $4463 full-time, $149 per credit part-time. Full-time tuition and fees vary according to course load. Part-time tuition and fees vary according to course load. *Required fees:* $50 full-time, $25 per term part-time. *Payment plan:* installment. *Waivers:* senior citizens and employees or children of employees.

Applying *Required:* high school transcript. *Required for some:* interview. *Application deadline:* rolling (freshmen), rolling (transfers). *Notification:* continuous (freshmen).

Admissions Contact Ms. Judy Dopplefeld, Director of Admissions, Ivy Tech State College-Lafayette, 3101 South Creagy Lane, PO Box 6299, Lafayette, IN 47903. *Phone:* 765-772-9100 Ext. 116. *Toll-free phone:* 800-669-4882. *Fax:* 765-772-9214. *E-mail:* jdopplef@ivytech.edu.

IVY TECH STATE COLLEGE-NORTH CENTRAL

South Bend, Indiana

- **State-supported** 2-year, founded 1968, part of Ivy Tech State College System
- **Calendar** semesters
- **Degree** certificates and associate
- **Suburban** 4-acre campus
- **Endowment** $5.0 million
- **Coed,** 3,784 undergraduate students, 23% full-time, 54% women, 46% men

Undergraduates 865 full-time, 2,919 part-time. 1% are from out of state, 12% African American, 0.6% Asian American or Pacific Islander, 3% Hispanic American, 0.8% Native American, 2% international, 2% transferred in.

Freshmen *Admission:* 1,368 applied, 1,368 admitted, 770 enrolled.

Faculty *Total:* 276, 20% full-time.

Majors Accounting; accounting technician; auto mechanic/technician; business administration; cabinet making; carpentry; child care/guidance; computer/information sciences; design/visual communications; drafting; educational media technology; electrical/electronic engineering technology; executive assistant; heavy equipment maintenance; industrial machinery maintenance/repair; interior design; machine technology; masonry/tile setting; medical assistant; medical laboratory technician; nursing; plumbing; robotics technology; sheet metal working; stationary energy sources installation; tool/die making.

Academic Programs *Special study options:* academic remediation for entering students, adult/continuing education programs, advanced placement credit, distance learning, internships, part-time degree program, services for LD students, summer session for credit.

Library 1,565 titles, 109 serial subscriptions, 1,106 audiovisual materials, an OPAC, a Web page.

Computers on Campus 102 computers available on campus for general student use. Internet access, online (class) registration, at least one staffed computer lab available.

Student Life *Housing:* college housing not available. *Activities and Organizations:* Phi Theta Kappa, Student Government, LPN Club, Alumni Association. *Campus security:* 24-hour emergency response devices and patrols, late-night transport/escort service, security during open hours. *Student Services:* personal/psychological counseling, women's center.

Athletics *Intramural sports:* basketball M, softball M/W, volleyball W.

Standardized Tests *Required:* ACT ASSET.

Costs (2002–03) *Tuition:* state resident $2214 full-time, $74 per credit part-time; nonresident $4463 full-time, $149 per credit part-time. Full-time tuition and fees vary according to course load. Part-time tuition and fees vary according to course load. *Required fees:* $50 full-time, $25 per term part-time. *Payment plan:* installment. *Waivers:* senior citizens and employees or children of employees.

Financial Aid In 2001, 40 Federal Work-Study jobs (averaging $2600).

Applying *Options:* early admission, deferred entrance. *Required:* high school transcript. *Required for some:* interview. *Application deadline:* rolling (freshmen), rolling (transfers). *Notification:* continuous (freshmen).

Admissions Contact Ivy Tech State College-North Central, 220 Dean Johnson Parkway, South Bend, IN 46601-3415. *Phone:* 219-289-7001 Ext. 423. *Fax:* 219-236-7165.

IVY TECH STATE COLLEGE-NORTHEAST

Fort Wayne, Indiana

- **State-supported** 2-year, founded 1969, part of Ivy Tech State College System
- **Calendar** semesters
- **Degree** certificates and associate
- **Urban** 22-acre campus
- **Endowment** $5.0 million
- **Coed,** 4,019 undergraduate students, 30% full-time, 57% women, 43% men

Undergraduates 1,194 full-time, 2,825 part-time. 1% are from out of state, 14% African American, 0.7% Asian American or Pacific Islander, 2% Hispanic American, 0.3% Native American, 0.9% international, 1% transferred in.

Freshmen *Admission:* 1,086 applied, 1,086 admitted, 513 enrolled.

Faculty *Total:* 337, 20% full-time.

Majors Accounting technician; auto mechanic/technician; building maintenance/management; business administration; child care/guidance; computer/information sciences; drafting; electrical/electronic engineering technology; executive assistant; industrial machinery maintenance/repair; machine technology; masonry/tile setting; medical assistant; occupational safety/health technology; paralegal/legal assistant; plumbing; psychiatric/mental health services; respiratory therapy; robotics technology; sheet metal working; stationary energy sources installation; tool/die making.

Academic Programs *Special study options:* academic remediation for entering students, adult/continuing education programs, advanced placement credit, distance learning, English as a second language, internships, part-time degree program, services for LD students, summer session for credit.

Library 13,148 titles, 190 serial subscriptions, 2,280 audiovisual materials, an OPAC, a Web page.

Computers on Campus 158 computers available on campus for general student use. Internet access, online (class) registration, at least one staffed computer lab available.

Student Life *Housing:* college housing not available. *Activities and Organizations:* Student Government, LPN Club, Phi Theta Kappa. *Campus security:* 24-hour emergency response devices and patrols, late-night transport/escort service.

Standardized Tests *Required:* ACT ASSET.

Costs (2002–03) *Tuition:* state resident $2214 full-time, $74 per credit part-time; nonresident $4463 full-time, $149 per credit part-time. Full-time tuition and fees vary according to course load. Part-time tuition and fees vary according to course load. *Required fees:* $50 full-time, $25 per term part-time. *Payment plan:* installment. *Waivers:* senior citizens and employees or children of employees.

Applying *Options:* early admission. *Required:* high school transcript. *Required for some:* interview. *Application deadline:* rolling (freshmen), rolling (transfers). *Notification:* continuous (freshmen).

Admissions Contact Mr. Steve Scheer, Director of Admissions, Ivy Tech State College-Northeast, 3800 N. Anthony Boulevard, Ft. Wayne, IN 46805-1489. *Phone:* 219-482-9171 Ext. 4221. *Toll-free phone:* 800-859-4882. *Fax:* 219-480-4177. *E-mail:* sscheer@ivytech.edu.

IVY TECH STATE COLLEGE-NORTHWEST

Gary, Indiana

- **State-supported** 2-year, founded 1963, part of Ivy Tech State College System
- **Calendar** semesters
- **Degree** certificates and associate
- **Urban** 13-acre campus with easy access to Chicago
- **Endowment** $5.0 million
- **Coed,** 5,146 undergraduate students, 29% full-time, 49% women, 51% men

Undergraduates 1,472 full-time, 3,674 part-time. 25% African American, 0.4% Asian American or Pacific Islander, 9% Hispanic American, 0.4% Native American, 0.2% international, 4% transferred in.

Freshmen *Admission:* 1,250 applied, 1,250 admitted, 763 enrolled.

Faculty *Total:* 305, 27% full-time.

Majors Accounting technician; auto mechanic/technician; building maintenance/management; business administration; cabinet making; carpentry; child care/guidance; computer/information sciences; drafting; electrical/electronic engineering technology; executive assistant; machine technology; masonry/tile setting; medical assistant; nursing; occupational safety/health technology; operating room technician; paralegal/legal assistant; physical therapy assistant; plumbing; respiratory therapy; sheet metal working; tool/die making.

Academic Programs *Special study options:* academic remediation for entering students, adult/continuing education programs, advanced placement credit, distance learning, internships, part-time degree program, services for LD students, summer session for credit.

Library 5,138 titles, 265 serial subscriptions, 3,984 audiovisual materials, an OPAC, a Web page.

Computers on Campus 150 computers available on campus for general student use. Internet access, online (class) registration, at least one staffed computer lab available.

Student Life *Housing:* college housing not available. *Activities and Organizations:* Phi Theta Kappa, LPN Club, Computer Club, Student Government, Alumni Association. *Campus security:* 24-hour emergency response devices, late-night transport/escort service.

Athletics *Intramural sports:* basketball M, softball M.

Ivy Tech State College-Northwest (continued)

Standardized Tests *Required:* ACT ASSET.

Costs (2002–03) *Tuition:* state resident $2214 full-time, $74 per credit part-time; nonresident $4463 full-time, $149 per credit part-time. Full-time tuition and fees vary according to course load. Part-time tuition and fees vary according to course load. *Required fees:* $50 full-time, $25 per term part-time. *Payment plan:* installment. *Waivers:* senior citizens and employees or children of employees.

Applying *Options:* deferred entrance. *Required:* high school transcript. *Required for some:* interview. *Application deadline:* rolling (freshmen), rolling (transfers). *Notification:* continuous (freshmen).

Admissions Contact Ivy Tech State College-Northwest, 1440 East 35th Avenue, Gary, IN 46409-1499. *Phone:* 219-981-1111 Ext. 273. *Toll-free phone:* 800-843-4882. *Fax:* 219-981-4415. *E-mail:* tlewis@ivytech.edu.

IVY TECH STATE COLLEGE-SOUTHCENTRAL

Sellersburg, Indiana

- **State-supported** 2-year, founded 1968, part of Ivy Tech State College System
- **Calendar** semesters
- **Degree** associate
- **Small-town** 63-acre campus with easy access to Louisville
- **Endowment** $5.0 million
- **Coed,** 2,035 undergraduate students, 28% full-time, 60% women, 40% men

Undergraduates 570 full-time, 1,465 part-time. 9% are from out of state, 4% African American, 0.5% Asian American or Pacific Islander, 1% Hispanic American, 0.2% Native American, 5% transferred in.

Freshmen *Admission:* 739 applied, 739 admitted, 333 enrolled.

Faculty *Total:* 146, 25% full-time.

Majors Accounting technician; auto mechanic/technician; building maintenance/management; business administration; cabinet making; carpentry; child care/guidance; computer/information sciences; design/visual communications; drafting; electrical/electronic engineering technology; executive assistant; industrial machinery maintenance/repair; machine technology; masonry/tile setting; medical assistant; nursing; plumbing; psychiatric/mental health services; robotics technology; sheet metal working; stationary energy sources installation; tool/die making.

Academic Programs *Special study options:* academic remediation for entering students, adult/continuing education programs, advanced placement credit, distance learning, internships, part-time degree program, services for LD students, summer session for credit.

Library 2,265 titles, 125 serial subscriptions, 1,500 audiovisual materials, an OPAC, a Web page.

Computers on Campus 73 computers available on campus for general student use. Internet access, online (class) registration, at least one staffed computer lab available.

Student Life *Housing:* college housing not available. *Activities and Organizations:* Phi Theta Kappa, Practical Nursing Club, Medical Assistant Club, Accounting Club, Student Government. *Campus security:* late-night transport/escort service.

Standardized Tests *Required:* ACT ASSET.

Costs (2002–03) *Tuition:* state resident $2214 full-time, $74 per credit part-time; nonresident $4463 full-time, $149 per credit part-time. Full-time tuition and fees vary according to course load and reciprocity agreements. Part-time tuition and fees vary according to course load and reciprocity agreements. *Required fees:* $50 full-time, $25 per term part-time. *Payment plan:* installment. *Waivers:* senior citizens and employees or children of employees.

Financial Aid In 2001, 20 Federal Work-Study jobs (averaging $3500). 2 State and other part-time jobs (averaging $3000).

Applying *Options:* early admission, deferred entrance. *Required:* high school transcript. *Required for some:* interview. *Application deadline:* rolling (freshmen), rolling (transfers). *Notification:* continuous (freshmen).

Admissions Contact Mr. Randy G. Emily, Director of Admissions, Ivy Tech State College-Southcentral, 8204 Highway 311, Sellersburg, IN 47172-1897. *Phone:* 812-246-3301 Ext. 4137. *Toll-free phone:* 800-321-9021. *Fax:* 812-246-9905. *E-mail:* remily@ivytech.edu.

IVY TECH STATE COLLEGE-SOUTHEAST

Madison, Indiana

- **State-supported** 2-year, founded 1963, part of Ivy Tech State College System
- **Calendar** semesters
- **Degree** associate
- **Small-town** 5-acre campus with easy access to Louisville
- **Endowment** $5.0 million
- **Coed,** 1,495 undergraduate students, 32% full-time, 70% women, 30% men

Undergraduates 477 full-time, 1,018 part-time. 5% are from out of state, 1% African American, 0.3% Asian American or Pacific Islander, 0.5% Hispanic American, 0.3% Native American, 0.1% international, 0.4% transferred in.

Freshmen *Admission:* 354 applied, 354 admitted, 252 enrolled.

Faculty *Total:* 134, 22% full-time.

Majors Accounting; accounting technician; business administration; child care/guidance; computer/information sciences; electrical/electronic engineering technology; executive assistant; industrial machinery maintenance/repair; medical assistant; nursing; robotics technology.

Academic Programs *Special study options:* academic remediation for entering students, advanced placement credit, distance learning, internships, part-time degree program, services for LD students, summer session for credit.

Library 6,034 titles, 150 serial subscriptions, 1,500 audiovisual materials, an OPAC, a Web page.

Computers on Campus 76 computers available on campus for general student use. Internet access, online (class) registration, at least one staffed computer lab available.

Student Life *Housing:* college housing not available. *Activities and Organizations:* Student Government, Phi Theta Kappa, LPU Club. *Campus security:* 24-hour emergency response devices.

Athletics *Intramural sports:* basketball M.

Standardized Tests *Required:* ACT ASSET.

Costs (2002–03) *Tuition:* state resident $2214 full-time, $74 per credit part-time; nonresident $4463 full-time, $149 per credit part-time. Full-time tuition and fees vary according to course load and reciprocity agreements. Part-time tuition and fees vary according to course load and reciprocity agreements. *Required fees:* $50 full-time, $25 per term part-time. *Payment plan:* installment. *Waivers:* senior citizens and employees or children of employees.

Applying *Required:* high school transcript. *Required for some:* interview. *Application deadline:* rolling (freshmen), rolling (transfers). *Notification:* continuous (freshmen).

Admissions Contact Ms. Cindy Hutcherson, Assistant Director of Admission/Career Counselor, Ivy Tech State College-Southeast, 590 Ivy Tech Drive, Madison, IN 47250-1881. *Phone:* 812-265-2580 Ext. 4142. *Toll-free phone:* 800-403-2190. *Fax:* 812-265-4028. *E-mail:* chutcher@ivytech.edu.

IVY TECH STATE COLLEGE-SOUTHWEST

Evansville, Indiana

- **State-supported** 2-year, founded 1963, part of Ivy Tech State College System
- **Calendar** semesters
- **Degree** associate
- **Suburban** 15-acre campus
- **Endowment** $5.0 million
- **Coed,** 4,290 undergraduate students, 27% full-time, 53% women, 47% men

Undergraduates 1,143 full-time, 3,147 part-time. 3% are from out of state, 6% African American, 0.5% Asian American or Pacific Islander, 0.6% Hispanic American, 0.7% Native American, 0.1% international, 3% transferred in.

Freshmen *Admission:* 1,083 applied, 1,083 admitted, 540 enrolled.

Faculty *Total:* 223, 28% full-time.

Majors Accounting technician; auto mechanic/technician; building maintenance/management; business administration; cabinet making; carpentry; child care/guidance; computer/information sciences; design/visual communications; drafting; electrical/electronic engineering technology; emergency medical technology; executive assistant; industrial machinery maintenance/repair; interior design; machine technology; masonry/tile setting; medical assistant; nursing; operating room technician; plumbing; robotics technology; sheet metal working; stationary energy sources installation; tool/die making.

Academic Programs *Special study options:* academic remediation for entering students, advanced placement credit, distance learning, internships, part-time degree program, services for LD students, summer session for credit.

Library 4,620 titles, 200 serial subscriptions, 2,000 audiovisual materials, an OPAC, a Web page.

Computers on Campus 275 computers available on campus for general student use. Internet access, online (class) registration, at least one staffed computer lab available.

Student Life *Housing:* college housing not available. *Activities and Organizations:* Student Government, Phi Theta Kappa, LPN Club, National Association of Industrial Technology, Design Club. *Campus security:* late-night transport/escort service.

Standardized Tests *Required:* ACT ASSET.
Costs (2002–03) *Tuition:* state resident $2214 full-time, $74 per credit part-time; nonresident $4463 full-time, $149 per credit part-time. Full-time tuition and fees vary according to course load and reciprocity agreements. Part-time tuition and fees vary according to course load and reciprocity agreements. *Required fees:* $50 full-time, $25 per term part-time. *Payment plan:* installment. *Waivers:* senior citizens and employees or children of employees.
Financial Aid In 2001, 103 Federal Work-Study jobs (averaging $3240).
Applying *Options:* early admission, deferred entrance. *Required:* high school transcript. *Required for some:* interview. *Application deadline:* rolling (freshmen), rolling (transfers). *Notification:* continuous (freshmen).
Admissions Contact Director of Admissions, Ivy Tech State College-Southwest, 3501 First Avenue, Evansville, IN 47710-3398. *Phone:* 812-426-2865. *Fax:* 812-429-1483.

Ivy Tech State College-Wabash Valley
Terre Haute, Indiana

- **State-supported** 2-year, founded 1966, part of Ivy Tech State College System
- **Calendar** semesters
- **Degree** associate
- **Suburban** 55-acre campus with easy access to Indianapolis
- **Endowment** $5.0 million
- **Coed,** 3,810 undergraduate students, 40% full-time, 51% women, 49% men

Undergraduates 1,508 full-time, 2,302 part-time. 3% are from out of state, 4% African American, 0.3% Asian American or Pacific Islander, 0.8% Hispanic American, 0.8% Native American, 0.1% international.
Freshmen *Admission:* 1,251 applied, 1,251 admitted, 700 enrolled.
Faculty *Total:* 227, 27% full-time.
Majors Accounting technician; aircraft mechanic/airframe; auto mechanic/technician; building maintenance/management; business administration; carpentry; child care/guidance; computer/information sciences; design/visual communications; drafting; electrical/electronic engineering technology; emergency medical technology; executive assistant; industrial machinery maintenance/repair; industrial technology; machine technology; masonry/tile setting; medical assistant; medical laboratory technician; medical radiologic technology; occupational safety/health technology; operating room technician; plumbing; psychiatric/mental health services; robotics technology; sheet metal working; stationary energy sources installation; tool/die making.
Academic Programs *Special study options:* academic remediation for entering students, adult/continuing education programs, advanced placement credit, distance learning, internships, part-time degree program, services for LD students, summer session for credit.
Library 817 titles, 82 serial subscriptions, 432 audiovisual materials, an OPAC, a Web page.
Computers on Campus 220 computers available on campus for general student use. Internet access, online (class) registration, at least one staffed computer lab available.
Student Life *Housing:* college housing not available. *Activities and Organizations:* Student Government, Phi Theta Kappa, LPN Club, National Association of Industrial Technology. *Campus security:* 24-hour emergency response devices. *Student Services:* personal/psychological counseling, women's center.
Athletics *Intramural sports:* basketball M/W, bowling M/W, softball M/W.
Standardized Tests *Required:* ACT ASSET.
Costs (2002–03) *Tuition:* state resident $2214 full-time, $74 per credit part-time; nonresident $4463 full-time, $149 per credit part-time. Full-time tuition and fees vary according to course load. Part-time tuition and fees vary according to course load. *Required fees:* $50 full-time, $25 per term part-time. *Payment plan:* installment. *Waivers:* senior citizens and employees or children of employees.
Applying *Options:* early admission, deferred entrance. *Required:* high school transcript. *Required for some:* interview. *Application deadline:* rolling (freshmen), rolling (transfers). *Notification:* continuous (freshmen).
Admissions Contact Mr. Michael Fisher, Director of Admissions, Ivy Tech State College-Wabash Valley, 7777 U.S. Highway 41 South, Terre Haute, IN 47802-4898. *Phone:* 812-299-1121 Ext. 262. *Toll-free phone:* 800-377-4882. *Fax:* 812-299-5723. *E-mail:* mfisher@ivytech.edu.

Ivy Tech State College-Whitewater
Richmond, Indiana

- **State-supported** 2-year, founded 1963, part of Ivy Tech State College System
- **Calendar** semesters
- **Degree** associate
- **Small-town** 23-acre campus with easy access to Indianapolis
- **Endowment** $5.0 million
- **Coed,** 1,469 undergraduate students, 18% full-time, 70% women, 30% men

Undergraduates 258 full-time, 1,211 part-time. 1% are from out of state, 4% African American, 0.2% Asian American or Pacific Islander, 0.3% Hispanic American, 1% Native American, 0.1% international, 0.9% transferred in.
Freshmen *Admission:* 328 applied, 328 admitted, 167 enrolled.
Faculty *Total:* 131, 18% full-time.
Majors Accounting technician; auto mechanic/technician; building maintenance/management; business administration; child care/guidance; computer/information sciences; electrical/electronic engineering technology; executive assistant; industrial machinery maintenance/repair; machine technology; medical assistant; nursing; robotics technology; stationary energy sources installation; tool/die making.
Academic Programs *Special study options:* academic remediation for entering students, adult/continuing education programs, advanced placement credit, distance learning, internships, part-time degree program, services for LD students, summer session for credit.
Computers on Campus 200 computers available on campus for general student use. Internet access, online (class) registration, at least one staffed computer lab available.
Student Life *Housing:* college housing not available. *Activities and Organizations:* Student Government, Phi Theta Kappa, LPN Club, CATS 2000, Business Professionals of America. *Campus security:* 24-hour emergency response devices, late-night transport/escort service. *Student Services:* personal/psychological counseling.
Standardized Tests *Required:* ACT ASSET.
Costs (2002–03) *Tuition:* state resident $2214 full-time, $74 per credit part-time; nonresident $4463 full-time, $149 per credit part-time. Full-time tuition and fees vary according to course load. Part-time tuition and fees vary according to course load. *Required fees:* $50 full-time, $25 per term part-time. *Payment plan:* installment. *Waivers:* senior citizens and employees or children of employees.
Financial Aid In 2001, 10 Federal Work-Study jobs (averaging $2800). 1 State and other part-time jobs (averaging $1200).
Applying *Options:* early admission. *Required:* high school transcript. *Required for some:* interview. *Application deadline:* rolling (freshmen), rolling (transfers). *Notification:* continuous (freshmen).
Admissions Contact Mr. Jeff Plasterer, Director of Admissions, Ivy Tech State College-Whitewater, 2325 Chester Boulevard, Richmond, IN 47374-1298. *Phone:* 765-966-2656 Ext. 335. *Toll-free phone:* 800-659-4562. *Fax:* 765-962-8741. *E-mail:* jplaster@ivytech.edu.

Lincoln Technical Institute
Indianapolis, Indiana

- **Proprietary** 2-year, founded 1946, part of Lincoln Technical Institute, Inc
- **Calendar** modular
- **Degree** certificates and associate
- **Urban** campus
- **Coed**

Applying *Required:* high school transcript, interview.
Admissions Contact Ms. Cindy Ryan, Director of Admissions, Lincoln Technical Institute, 1201 Stadium Drive, Indianapolis, IN 46202-2194. *Phone:* 317-632-5553. *Toll-free phone:* 800-554-4465.

Michiana College
Fort Wayne, Indiana

Admissions Contact 4422 East State Boulevard, Fort Wayne, IN 46815.

Michiana College
South Bend, Indiana

- **Proprietary** 2-year, founded 1882
- **Calendar** quarters
- **Degree** certificates, diplomas, and associate
- **Urban** 5-acre campus with easy access to Chicago
- **Coed, primarily women**

Faculty *Student/faculty ratio:* 11:1.

Michiana College (continued)
Student Life *Campus security:* 24-hour emergency response devices.
Applying *Options:* common application, deferred entrance. *Application fee:* $20. *Required:* essay or personal statement, high school transcript, interview. *Required for some:* minimum 2.0 GPA, 2 letters of recommendation.
Admissions Contact Ms. Rita Harvey, Admissions Representative; High School, Michiana College, 1030 East Jefferson Boulevard, South Bend, IN 46617-3123. *Phone:* 219-237-0774. *Toll-free phone:* 800-743-2447. *Fax:* 219-237-3585. *E-mail:* mcsb@michianacollege.com.

MID-AMERICA COLLEGE OF FUNERAL SERVICE
Jeffersonville, Indiana

- **Independent** 2-year, founded 1905
- **Calendar** quarters
- **Degree** associate
- **Small-town** 3-acre campus with easy access to Louisville
- **Coed, primarily men,** 94 undergraduate students

Undergraduates Students come from 6 states and territories.
Faculty *Total:* 7, 86% full-time. *Student/faculty ratio:* 13:1.
Majors Mortuary science.
Academic Programs *Special study options:* academic remediation for entering students.
Library 1,500 titles, 20 serial subscriptions.
Computers on Campus 15 computers available on campus for general student use. Internet access, at least one staffed computer lab available.
Student Life *Housing:* college housing not available.
Costs (2001–02) *Tuition:* $8000 full-time.
Applying *Options:* deferred entrance. *Application fee:* $25. *Required:* high school transcript. *Application deadline:* rolling (freshmen).
Admissions Contact Mr. Richard Nelson, Dean of Students, Mid-America College of Funeral Service, 3111 Hamburg Pike, Jeffersonville, IN 47130-9630. *Phone:* 812-288-8878. *Toll-free phone:* 800-221-6158. *E-mail:* macfs@mindspring.com.

PROFESSIONAL CAREERS INSTITUTE
Indianapolis, Indiana

- **Independent** 2-year
- **Degree** certificates and associate
- **Coed, primarily women,** 469 undergraduate students, 100% full-time, 90% women, 10% men

Freshmen *Admission:* 107 applied, 71 admitted. *Average high school GPA:* 2.00.
Faculty *Total:* 39, 74% full-time. *Student/faculty ratio:* 12:1.
Majors Computer programming (specific applications); computer software and media applications related.
Academic Programs *Special study options:* internships, part-time degree program.
Computers on Campus 25 computers available on campus for general student use. Internet access available.
Costs (2002–03) *Tuition:* $7350 full-time. No tuition increase for student's term of enrollment. *Required fees:* $150 full-time. *Payment plan:* installment. *Waivers:* employees or children of employees.
Applying *Options:* common application. *Application fee:* $100. *Required:* essay or personal statement, high school transcript, minimum 1.7 GPA, 2 letters of recommendation. *Required for some:* interview, CPAt, health exam, keyboard test.
Admissions Contact Ms. Paulette M. Clay, Director of Admissions, Professional Careers Institute, 7302 Woodland Drive, Indianapolis, IN 46217. *Phone:* 317-299-6001 Ext. 320. *E-mail:* lilgeneral9@hotmail.com.

SAWYER COLLEGE
Hammond, Indiana

Admissions Contact 6040 Hohman Avenue, Hammond, IN 46320.

VINCENNES UNIVERSITY
Vincennes, Indiana

- **State-supported** 2-year, founded 1801
- **Calendar** semesters
- **Degree** certificates and associate
- **Small-town** 100-acre campus
- **Coed,** 4,883 undergraduate students, 86% full-time, 40% women, 60% men

Undergraduates Students come from 25 states and territories, 34 other countries, 3% are from out of state, 8% African American, 0.5% Asian American or Pacific Islander, 0.8% Hispanic American, 0.2% Native American, 2% international, 50% live on campus.
Freshmen *Admission:* 2,500 applied, 2,400 admitted. *Average high school GPA:* 2.50.
Faculty *Total:* 383, 99% full-time. *Student/faculty ratio:* 20:1.
Majors Accounting; advertising; agricultural business; agricultural extension; agricultural mechanization; aircraft mechanic/airframe; aircraft pilot (professional); alcohol/drug abuse counseling; anthropology; architectural engineering technology; art; art education; artificial intelligence/robotics; athletic training/sports medicine; auto mechanic/technician; aviation technology; baker/pastry chef; behavioral sciences; biology; broadcast journalism; business administration; business education; business marketing and marketing management; chemistry; child care/development; child care provider; child care services management; civil engineering technology; communication equipment technology; communications; computer engineering related; computer engineering technology; computer graphics; computer hardware engineering; computer/information technology services administration and management related; computer programming; computer programming related; computer programming (specific applications); computer programming, vendor/product certification; computer science; computer science related; computer software and media applications related; computer software engineering; computer systems networking/telecommunications; computer/technical support; construction/building inspection; construction technology; corrections; cosmetology; criminal justice/law enforcement administration; culinary arts; data entry/microcomputer applications; data entry/microcomputer applications related; dental hygiene; dietetics; drafting; drafting/design technology; early childhood education; earth sciences; education; education (K-12); electrical/electronic engineering technology; elementary education; engineering; engineering-related technology; engineering technology; English; environmental health; environmental science; exercise sciences; family/consumer studies; fashion design/illustration; fashion merchandising; fire science; food sciences; forestry; French; geography; geology; German; graphic design/commercial art/illustration; graphic/printing equipment; heavy equipment maintenance; history; home economics; home economics communications; horticulture science; hospitality/recreation marketing operations; hotel and restaurant management; hotel/motel services marketing operations; industrial design; industrial electronics installation/repair; industrial machinery maintenance/repair; information sciences/systems; information technology; interior design; interior environments; international business; journalism; landscape architecture; laser/optical technology; law enforcement/police science; legal administrative assistant; liberal arts and sciences/liberal studies; machine shop assistant; machine technology; management information systems/business data processing; marketing operations; mass communications; mathematics; mechanical engineering technology; medical administrative assistant; medical assistant; medical laboratory technician; medical laboratory technology; medical records administration; medical technology; middle school education; mortuary science; music; music teacher education; natural resources conservation; natural resources management; nuclear medical technology; nursing; occupational therapy; paralegal/legal assistant; pharmacy; physical education; physical therapy; physics; political science; practical nurse; pre-engineering; psychology; public administration; public relations; radio/television broadcasting; recreational therapy; recreation/leisure studies; recreation products/services marketing operations; respiratory therapy; restaurant operations; robotics; science education; secretarial science; sign language interpretation; social sciences; social work; sociology; Spanish; speech/theater education; sport/fitness administration; surveying; system administration; system/networking/LAN/WAN management; theater arts/drama; veterinary sciences; Web/multimedia management/webmaster; Web page, digital/multimedia and information resources design; welding technology; word processing.
Academic Programs *Special study options:* academic remediation for entering students, adult/continuing education programs, advanced placement credit, cooperative education, distance learning, double majors, English as a second language, external degree program, freshman honors college, honors programs, independent study, internships, off-campus study, part-time degree program, services for LD students, student-designed majors, summer session for credit. *ROTC:* Army (c), Navy (c), Air Force (c).
Library Shake Learning Resource Center plus 1 other with 100,000 titles, 560 serial subscriptions, an OPAC, a Web page.
Computers on Campus 600 computers available on campus for general student use. A campuswide network can be accessed from student residence rooms and from off campus. Internet access, at least one staffed computer lab available.

Student Life *Housing:* on-campus residence required for freshman year. *Options:* coed, men-only, women-only, disabled students. *Activities and Organizations:* drama/theater group, student-run newspaper, radio and television station, choral group, Student Senate, Student Alumni Corporation, Intramurals, Law Enforcement Association, Campus Christian Fellowship, national fraternities, national sororities. *Campus security:* 24-hour emergency response devices and patrols, student patrols, late-night transport/escort service, controlled dormitory access, surveillance cameras. *Student Services:* health clinic, personal/psychological counseling.

Athletics Member NJCAA. *Intercollegiate sports:* baseball M(s), basketball M(s)/W(s), bowling M(s)/W(s), cross-country running M(s)/W(s), soccer M/W, swimming M(s)/W(s), tennis M(s), track and field M(s)/W(s), volleyball W(s). *Intramural sports:* archery M/W, badminton M/W, basketball M/W, bowling M/W, cross-country running M/W, gymnastics M/W, racquetball M/W, skiing (downhill) M/W, soccer M/W, softball M/W, swimming M/W, tennis M/W, track and field M/W, volleyball M/W, weight lifting M/W, wrestling M.

Standardized Tests *Required for some:* SAT I or ACT (for admission). *Recommended:* SAT I or ACT (for admission).

Costs (2001–02) *Tuition:* state resident $2501 full-time, $83 per credit part-time; nonresident $6240 full-time, $208 per credit part-time. Full-time tuition and fees vary according to reciprocity agreements. Part-time tuition and fees vary according to course load and reciprocity agreements. *Required fees:* $100 full-time. *Room and board:* $4726. Room and board charges vary according to board plan and housing facility. *Payment plan:* installment. *Waivers:* senior citizens and employees or children of employees.

Financial Aid In 2001, 200 Federal Work-Study jobs (averaging $1800).

Applying *Options:* common application, electronic application, early admission. *Application fee:* $20. *Required:* high school transcript. *Required for some:* interview. *Application deadline:* rolling (freshmen), rolling (transfers). *Notification:* continuous until 8/1 (freshmen).

Admissions Contact Ms. Anne M. Skuce, Director of Admissions, Vincennes University, 1002 North First Street, Vincennes, IN 47591. *Phone:* 812-888-4313. *Toll-free phone:* 800-742-9198. *Fax:* 812-888-5707. *E-mail:* vuadmit@indian.vinu.edu.

VINCENNES UNIVERSITY JASPER CAMPUS
Jasper, Indiana

- **State-supported** 2-year, founded 1970, part of Vincennes University
- **Calendar** semesters
- **Degree** certificates and associate
- **Small-town** 120-acre campus
- **Coed,** 794 undergraduate students, 42% full-time, 74% women, 26% men

Undergraduates Students come from 1 other state, 1 other country, 0.1% African American, 0.1% Asian American or Pacific Islander, 0.3% Hispanic American, 0.1% international.

Freshmen *Admission:* 290 applied, 265 admitted.

Faculty *Total:* 53, 40% full-time. *Student/faculty ratio:* 15:1.

Majors Accounting; behavioral sciences; business administration; business education; computer programming; computer programming related; computer systems networking/telecommunications; drafting/design technology; education; education (K-12); elementary education; finance; furniture design; industrial technology; law enforcement/police science; legal administrative assistant; liberal arts and sciences/liberal studies; management information systems/business data processing; medical administrative assistant; psychology; secretarial science; social sciences; social work; sociology; word processing.

Academic Programs *Special study options:* academic remediation for entering students, adult/continuing education programs, advanced placement credit, distance learning, part-time degree program, summer session for credit.

Library Vincennes University Jasper Library with 14,000 titles, 180 serial subscriptions, an OPAC.

Computers on Campus 105 computers available on campus for general student use. A campuswide network can be accessed from off campus. Internet access available.

Student Life *Housing:* college housing not available. *Activities and Organizations:* student-run newspaper. *Student Services:* personal/psychological counseling.

Standardized Tests *Required:* institutional placement test. *Required for some:* SAT I or ACT (for placement). *Recommended:* SAT I or ACT (for placement).

Costs (2001–02) *Tuition:* state resident $2000 full-time, $83 per credit hour part-time; nonresident $4992 full-time, $208 per credit hour part-time. Full-time tuition and fees vary according to program. Part-time tuition and fees vary according to program. *Required fees:* $100 full-time, $50 per term part-time. *Payment plan:* installment. *Waivers:* senior citizens.

Applying *Application fee:* $20. *Required:* high school transcript. *Application deadline:* rolling (freshmen), rolling (transfers).

Admissions Contact Ms. LouAnn Gilbert, Director, Vincennes University Jasper Campus, Jasper, IN 47546. *Phone:* 812-482-3030. *Toll-free phone:* 800-809-VUJC. *Fax:* 812-481-5960. *E-mail:* lgilbert@indian.vinu.edu.

IOWA

AIB COLLEGE OF BUSINESS
Des Moines, Iowa

- **Independent** 2-year, founded 1921
- **Calendar** continuous
- **Degree** diplomas and associate
- **Urban** 20-acre campus
- **Coed,** 887 undergraduate students

Undergraduates Students come from 5 states and territories, 5% are from out of state, 48% live on campus.

Freshmen *Admission:* 488 applied, 437 admitted.

Faculty *Total:* 60, 38% full-time.

Majors Accounting; business administration; business marketing and marketing management; computer management; computer programming (specific applications); computer software and media applications related; computer systems networking/telecommunications; court reporting; data entry/microcomputer applications related; finance; hotel/motel services marketing operations; legal administrative assistant; medical administrative assistant; secretarial science; system/networking/LAN/WAN management; tourism promotion operations; travel services marketing operations; travel/tourism management.

Academic Programs *Special study options:* academic remediation for entering students, accelerated degree program, adult/continuing education programs, double majors, internships, part-time degree program, summer session for credit.

Library 5,400 titles, 185 serial subscriptions.

Computers on Campus 188 computers available on campus for general student use. A campuswide network can be accessed from student residence rooms and from off campus. Internet access, at least one staffed computer lab available.

Student Life *Housing:* on-campus residence required through sophomore year. *Options:* coed. *Activities and Organizations:* Business Management Association, Institute of Management Accountants, International Associaton of Administrative Professionals, Association of Information Technology Professionals, Student Court Reporters Association, national fraternities, national sororities. *Campus security:* 24-hour emergency response devices, late-night transport/escort service, controlled dormitory access, video security. *Student Services:* personal/psychological counseling.

Athletics *Intramural sports:* badminton M/W, basketball M/W, bowling M/W, football M/W, golf M/W, softball M/W, table tennis M/W, volleyball M/W.

Standardized Tests *Recommended:* ACT (for admission).

Costs (2002–03) *One-time required fee:* $23. *Tuition:* $7740 full-time, $215 per credit hour part-time. Full-time tuition and fees vary according to class time, course load, and program. Part-time tuition and fees vary according to class time, course load, and program. No tuition increase for student's term of enrollment. *Room only:* $2175. Room and board charges vary according to housing facility. *Payment plan:* installment. *Waivers:* children of alumni and employees or children of employees.

Financial Aid In 2001, 129 Federal Work-Study jobs (averaging $761). 100 State and other part-time jobs (averaging $548).

Applying *Application fee:* $25. *Required:* high school transcript. *Recommended:* interview. *Application deadline:* rolling (freshmen), rolling (transfers).

Admissions Contact Ms. Gail Cline, Director of Admissions, AIB College of Business, Keith Fenton Administration Building, 2500 Fleur Drive, Des Moines, IA 50321-1799. *Phone:* 515-246-5356. *Toll-free phone:* 800-444-1921. *Fax:* 515-244-6773. *E-mail:* clineg@aib.edu.

CLINTON COMMUNITY COLLEGE
Clinton, Iowa

- **State and locally supported** 2-year, founded 1946, part of Eastern Iowa Community College District
- **Calendar** semesters
- **Degree** certificates, diplomas, and associate
- **Small-town** 20-acre campus

Clinton Community College (continued)

■ **Coed,** 1,217 undergraduate students

Undergraduates Students come from 9 states and territories, 9% are from out of state.

Freshmen *Test scores:* ACT scores over 18: 70%; ACT scores over 24: 21%.

Faculty *Total:* 75, 47% full-time.

Majors Architectural drafting; business administration; business computer facilities operation; electrical/electronic engineering technology; emergency medical technology; environmental technology; graphic/printing equipment; liberal arts and sciences/liberal studies; machine technology; nursing; occupational safety/health technology; pharmacy technician/assistant; practical nurse; secretarial science.

Academic Programs *Special study options:* academic remediation for entering students, adult/continuing education programs, advanced placement credit, cooperative education, distance learning, double majors, English as a second language, independent study, internships, part-time degree program, services for LD students, study abroad, summer session for credit.

Library Clinton Community College Library with 18,701 titles, 155 serial subscriptions, an OPAC.

Computers on Campus 37 computers available on campus for general student use. A campuswide network can be accessed from off campus. Internet access, at least one staffed computer lab available.

Student Life *Housing:* college housing not available. *Activities and Organizations:* drama/theater group. *Student Services:* personal/psychological counseling.

Athletics Member NJCAA. *Intercollegiate sports:* baseball M(s), basketball M(s), softball W(s), volleyball W(s). *Intramural sports:* basketball M, bowling M/W, football M/W, golf M/W, racquetball M/W, skiing (downhill) M/W, tennis M/W, volleyball M/W, weight lifting M/W.

Standardized Tests *Required:* DTMS and DTLS or ACT.

Costs (2001–02) *Tuition:* state resident $2160 full-time, $72 per credit hour part-time; nonresident $3240 full-time, $108 per credit hour part-time. *Payment plan:* installment.

Applying *Options:* early admission, deferred entrance. *Required:* high school transcript. *Application deadline:* rolling (freshmen), rolling (transfers). *Notification:* continuous (freshmen).

Admissions Contact Ms. Susan Carmody, Assistant Dean of Student Development, Clinton Community College, 1000 Lincoln Boulevard, Clinton, IA 52732-6299. *Phone:* 563-244-7000.

DES MOINES AREA COMMUNITY COLLEGE

Ankeny, Iowa

■ **State and locally supported** 2-year, founded 1966, part of Iowa Area Community Colleges System
■ **Calendar** semesters
■ **Degrees** certificates, diplomas, and associate (profile also includes information from the Boone, Carroll, Des Moines, and Newton campuses)
■ **Small-town** 362-acre campus
■ **Coed,** 11,886 undergraduate students, 43% full-time, 56% women, 44% men

Undergraduates 5,085 full-time, 6,801 part-time. Students come from 21 states and territories, 16 other countries, 4% transferred in.

Freshmen *Admission:* 4,376 admitted, 4,258 enrolled.

Faculty *Total:* 270, 98% full-time.

Majors Accounting; agricultural business; auto mechanic/technician; biological technology; business administration; business marketing and marketing management; carpentry; child care/development; civil engineering technology; computer engineering technology; computer programming; computer programming (specific applications); corrections; criminal justice/law enforcement administration; culinary arts; data processing technology; dental hygiene; drafting; education; electrical/electronic engineering technology; fashion merchandising; fire science; food products retailing; graphic design/commercial art/illustration; graphic/printing equipment; health services administration; heating/air conditioning/refrigeration; heavy equipment maintenance; horticulture science; hospitality management; hotel and restaurant management; human services; law enforcement/police science; legal administrative assistant; liberal arts and sciences/liberal studies; machine technology; medical administrative assistant; medical assistant; medical laboratory technician; nursing; paralegal/legal assistant; practical nurse; quality control technology; respiratory therapy; retail management; robotics; safety/security technology; secretarial science; social work; teacher assistant/aide; telecommunications; welding technology.

Academic Programs *Special study options:* academic remediation for entering students, adult/continuing education programs, advanced placement credit, cooperative education, English as a second language, honors programs, off-campus study, part-time degree program, services for LD students, student-designed majors, summer session for credit.

Library Main Library plus 3 others with 56,857 titles, 570 serial subscriptions, a Web page.

Computers on Campus 700 computers available on campus for general student use. Internet access, at least one staffed computer lab available.

Student Life *Housing:* college housing not available. *Activities and Organizations:* drama/theater group, student-run newspaper, choral group. *Campus security:* 24-hour emergency response devices and patrols, late-night transport/escort service. *Student Services:* health clinic, personal/psychological counseling.

Athletics Member NJCAA. *Intercollegiate sports:* basketball M(s)/W(s), golf M/W, softball W. *Intramural sports:* basketball M/W, football M/W, golf M/W, soccer M/W, volleyball M/W.

Standardized Tests *Required:* ACT COMPASS. *Recommended:* ACT (for placement).

Costs (2001–02) *Tuition:* state resident $2010 full-time, $67 per hour part-time; nonresident $4020 full-time, $134 per hour part-time. *Required fees:* $192 full-time. *Payment plan:* installment. *Waivers:* senior citizens.

Financial Aid In 2001, 228 Federal Work-Study jobs (averaging $922).

Applying *Options:* early admission, deferred entrance. *Required for some:* high school transcript. *Application deadline:* rolling (freshmen), rolling (transfers).

Admissions Contact Mr. Keith Knowles, Director of Enrollment Management, Des Moines Area Community College, 2006 South Ankeny Boulevard, Ankeny, IA 50021-8995. *Phone:* 515-964-6216. *Toll-free phone:* 800-362-2127.

ELLSWORTH COMMUNITY COLLEGE

Iowa Falls, Iowa

■ **State and locally supported** 2-year, founded 1890, part of Iowa Valley Community College District System
■ **Calendar** semesters
■ **Degree** diplomas and associate
■ **Small-town** 10-acre campus
■ **Endowment** $2.3 million
■ **Coed,** 930 undergraduate students, 67% full-time, 55% women, 45% men

Undergraduates Students come from 18 states and territories, 4 other countries, 9% are from out of state, 8% African American, 0.3% Asian American or Pacific Islander, 4% Hispanic American, 2% international, 38% live on campus.

Freshmen *Admission:* 610 applied, 570 admitted. *Average high school GPA:* 2.55. *Test scores:* ACT scores over 18: 66%; ACT scores over 24: 15%; ACT scores over 30: 2%.

Faculty *Total:* 63, 52% full-time, 3% with terminal degrees. *Student/faculty ratio:* 17:1.

Majors Accounting; agricultural business; art; art education; biological/physical sciences; biological technology; biology; business administration; business marketing and marketing management; child care/development; computer science related; computer systems networking/telecommunications; corrections; criminal justice/law enforcement administration; data entry/microcomputer applications; data processing technology; developmental/child psychology; early childhood education; economics; education; environmental technology; equestrian studies; fashion merchandising; history; human services; interior design; legal administrative assistant; liberal arts and sciences/liberal studies; mathematics; medical administrative assistant; medical laboratory technology; medical technology; natural resources conservation; nursing; physical education; physical sciences; political science; pre-engineering; psychology; retailing operations; retail management; secretarial science; social work; sociology; teacher assistant/aide; trade/industrial education; wildlife biology.

Academic Programs *Special study options:* academic remediation for entering students, adult/continuing education programs, advanced placement credit, cooperative education, distance learning, honors programs, internships, part-time degree program, services for LD students, student-designed majors, summer session for credit.

Library Osgood Learning Resource Center with 25,500 titles, 300 serial subscriptions.

Computers on Campus 80 computers available on campus for general student use. A campuswide network can be accessed from off campus. Internet access, at least one staffed computer lab available.

Student Life *Housing:* on-campus residence required for freshman year. *Options:* men-only, women-only, disabled students. *Activities and Organizations:* drama/theater group, student-run newspaper, choral group, Agriculture-Science Club, Biotechnology Club, International Clun, Criminal Justice Club, Rodeo Club. *Campus security:* 24-hour emergency response devices and patrols. *Student Services:* personal/psychological counseling.

Athletics Member NJCAA. *Intercollegiate sports:* baseball M(s), basketball M(s)/W(s), football M(s), golf M/W, softball W(s), volleyball W(s), wrestling M(s). *Intramural sports:* baseball M, basketball M/W, bowling M/W, equestrian sports M/W, football M/W, racquetball M/W, rugby M, softball M/W, swimming M/W, volleyball W, water polo M/W, weight lifting M/W.
Standardized Tests *Required for some:* ACT (for placement). *Recommended:* ACT (for placement).
Costs (2001–02) *Tuition:* state resident $2368 full-time, $74 per semester hour part-time; nonresident $4736 full-time, $148 per semester hour part-time. Part-time tuition and fees vary according to course load. *Required fees:* $704 full-time, $22 per semester hour. *Room and board:* $3550. Room and board charges vary according to board plan. *Payment plan:* installment. *Waivers:* senior citizens.
Financial Aid In 2001, 95 Federal Work-Study jobs (averaging $1200). 40 State and other part-time jobs (averaging $1200).
Applying *Options:* electronic application, early admission, deferred entrance. *Required:* high school transcript. *Application deadlines:* rolling (freshmen), 8/1 (out-of-state freshmen), rolling (transfers). *Notification:* continuous (freshmen).
Admissions Contact Mr. Philip Rusley, Director of Admissions/Registrar, Ellsworth Community College, 1100 College Avenue, Iowa Falls, IA 50126-1199. *Phone:* 641-648-4611. *Toll-free phone:* 800-ECC-9235.

HAMILTON COLLEGE
Cedar Rapids, Iowa

- **Proprietary** primarily 2-year, founded 1900
- **Calendar** quarters
- **Degrees** certificates, diplomas, associate, and bachelor's (branch locations in Des Moines, Mason City with significant enrollment reflected in profile)
- **Suburban** 4-acre campus
- **Coed,** 467 undergraduate students

Undergraduates Students come from 1 other state.
Freshmen *Admission:* 394 applied, 394 admitted.
Faculty *Total:* 20, 30% full-time. *Student/faculty ratio:* 25:1.
Majors Accounting; business administration; computer programming; data processing technology; general studies; information sciences/systems; legal administrative assistant; management science; medical administrative assistant; medical assistant; secretarial science; travel/tourism management.
Academic Programs *Special study options:* academic remediation for entering students, adult/continuing education programs, cooperative education, distance learning, internships, part-time degree program.
Library Hamilton College Library with 5,500 titles, 40 serial subscriptions, an OPAC, a Web page.
Computers on Campus 50 computers available on campus for general student use. A campuswide network can be accessed from off campus. Internet access, at least one staffed computer lab available.
Student Life *Housing:* college housing not available. *Activities and Organizations:* student-run newspaper, Phi Beta Lambda, Travel Club, Student Senate. *Campus security:* 24-hour emergency response devices.
Costs (2001–02) *Tuition:* $10,368 full-time, $324 per quarter hour part-time. *Payment plans:* tuition prepayment, installment.
Financial Aid In 2001, 121 Federal Work-Study jobs, 3 State and other part-time jobs (averaging $1885).
Applying *Options:* common application, early admission, deferred entrance. *Application fee:* $25. *Required:* high school transcript, minimum 2.0 GPA, interview. *Application deadline:* rolling (freshmen).
Admissions Contact Ms. Bonnie Flyte, Director of Admissions, Hamilton College, 1924 D Street SW, Cedar Rapids, IA 52404. *Phone:* 563-355-3500. *Toll-free phone:* 800-728-0481. *Fax:* 319-363-3812.

HAWKEYE COMMUNITY COLLEGE
Waterloo, Iowa

- **State and locally supported** 2-year, founded 1966
- **Calendar** semesters
- **Degree** certificates, diplomas, and associate
- **Rural** 320-acre campus
- **Coed,** 4,456 undergraduate students

Undergraduates Students come from 17 states and territories, 11 other countries, 2% are from out of state, 7% African American, 0.8% Asian American or Pacific Islander, 1% Hispanic American, 0.4% Native American, 1% international.
Freshmen *Admission:* 2,480 applied, 1,790 admitted. *Average high school GPA:* 2.93. *Test scores:* ACT scores over 18: 66%; ACT scores over 24: 6%.
Faculty *Total:* 235. *Student/faculty ratio:* 21:1.
Majors Accounting; agricultural business; agricultural mechanization; agronomy/crop science; aircraft mechanic/airframe; animal sciences; architectural engineering technology; auto body repair; auto mechanic/technician; aviation technology; biology; business; business administration; business computer facilities operation; business marketing and marketing management; child care/development; civil engineering technology; computer engineering technology; computer systems networking/telecommunications; computer/technical support; corrections; criminal justice/law enforcement administration; data entry/microcomputer applications related; dental hygiene; drafting; education; emergency medical technology; engineering technology; farm/ranch management; fire science; food sciences; graphic design/commercial art/illustration; heating/air conditioning/refrigeration; heavy equipment maintenance; horticulture science; information technology; interdisciplinary studies; interior design; law enforcement/police science; liberal arts and sciences/liberal studies; machine technology; mechanical design technology; mechanical engineering technology; medical administrative assistant; medical laboratory technician; natural resources management; nursing; ornamental horticulture; photography; practical nurse; recreation/leisure facilities management; respiratory therapy; secretarial science; surveying; system/networking/LAN/WAN management; tool/die making; Web/multimedia management/webmaster; Web page, digital/multimedia and information resources design; welding technology; word processing.
Academic Programs *Special study options:* academic remediation for entering students, adult/continuing education programs, advanced placement credit, distance learning, English as a second language, external degree program, part-time degree program, services for LD students, summer session for credit. *ROTC:* Army (c).
Library Hawkeye Community College Library with 25,382 titles, 518 serial subscriptions, 1,928 audiovisual materials, an OPAC, a Web page.
Computers on Campus 276 computers available on campus for general student use. Internet access, online (class) registration, at least one staffed computer lab available.
Student Life *Housing:* college housing not available. *Activities and Organizations:* Student Senate, Phi Theta Kappa, Environmental Conservation Club/Ag Club, Law Enforcement/ Criminal Justice, Fashion Merchandising. *Campus security:* 24-hour patrols. *Student Services:* personal/psychological counseling, women's center.
Athletics *Intramural sports:* basketball M/W, bowling M/W, golf M/W, soccer M/W, volleyball M/W.
Standardized Tests *Required:* ACT ASSET, ACT COMPASS. *Required for some:* SAT I or ACT (for placement). *Recommended:* SAT I or ACT (for placement).
Costs (2001–02) *Tuition:* area resident $2280 full-time, $76 per credit part-time; nonresident $4560 full-time, $152 per credit part-time. *Required fees:* $300 full-time, $10 per credit. *Payment plan:* installment. *Waivers:* employees or children of employees.
Applying *Options:* electronic application, early action, deferred entrance. *Required:* high school transcript. *Application deadline:* rolling (freshmen), rolling (transfers). *Notification:* continuous (freshmen).
Admissions Contact Miss Molly Quinn, Admissions Coordinator, Hawkeye Community College, PO Box 8015, Waterloo, IA 50704-8015. *Phone:* 319-296-4000 Ext. 1206. *Toll-free phone:* 800-670-4769. *Fax:* 319-296-2505. *E-mail:* admision@hawkeye.cc.ia.us.

INDIAN HILLS COMMUNITY COLLEGE
Ottumwa, Iowa

- **State and locally supported** 2-year, founded 1966, part of Iowa Area Community Colleges System
- **Calendar** quarters
- **Degree** certificates, diplomas, and associate
- **Small-town** 400-acre campus
- **Coed,** 3,926 undergraduate students

Undergraduates Students come from 16 states and territories, 7 other countries, 7% are from out of state, 15% live on campus.
Freshmen *Admission:* 2,477 applied, 2,477 admitted.
Faculty *Total:* 148, 86% full-time.
Majors Agricultural mechanization; aircraft pilot (professional); auto mechanic/technician; aviation technology; biological technology; business administration; child care/development; computer engineering technology; computer programming; criminal justice/law enforcement administration; drafting; electrical/

Indian Hills Community College (continued)
electronic engineering technology; food services technology; health services administration; heavy equipment maintenance; horticulture science; industrial radiologic technology; laser/optical technology; liberal arts and sciences/liberal studies; machine technology; medical records administration; nursing; physical therapy; practical nurse; robotics.

Academic Programs *Special study options:* academic remediation for entering students, adult/continuing education programs, cooperative education, English as a second language, honors programs, internships, part-time degree program, services for LD students, student-designed majors, summer session for credit.

Library Indian Hills Community College Library plus 2 others with 53,073 titles, 350 serial subscriptions, an OPAC, a Web page.

Computers on Campus 150 computers available on campus for general student use. At least one staffed computer lab available.

Student Life *Housing Options:* coed. *Activities and Organizations:* drama/theater group, Student Senate, Warriors Club. *Campus security:* 24-hour emergency response devices and patrols. *Student Services:* personal/psychological counseling, women's center.

Athletics Member NJCAA. *Intercollegiate sports:* baseball M(s), basketball M(s), golf M(s), softball W(s), volleyball W(s). *Intramural sports:* basketball M/W, fencing M/W, football M/W, racquetball M/W, riflery M/W, tennis M/W, volleyball M/W.

Standardized Tests *Required:* ACT ASSET. *Required for some:* ACT (for placement).

Costs (2001–02) *Tuition:* state resident $2070 full-time, $69 per credit hour part-time; nonresident $3120 full-time, $104 per credit hour part-time. *Room and board:* $1820; room only: $1050. Room and board charges vary according to board plan and housing facility.

Financial Aid In 2001, 123 Federal Work-Study jobs (averaging $742). 62 State and other part-time jobs (averaging $823).

Applying *Options:* common application, early admission. *Required for some:* high school transcript. *Application deadline:* rolling (freshmen), rolling (transfers).

Admissions Contact Mrs. Jane Sapp, Admissions Officer, Indian Hills Community College, 525 Grandview Avenue, Building #1, Ottumwa, IA 52501-1398. *Phone:* 641-683-5155. *Toll-free phone:* 800-726-2585.

IOWA CENTRAL COMMUNITY COLLEGE
Fort Dodge, Iowa

- **State and locally supported** 2-year, founded 1966, part of Iowa Department of Education Division of Community Colleges
- **Calendar** semesters
- **Degree** certificates, diplomas, and associate
- **Small-town** 110-acre campus
- **Coed**

Faculty *Student/faculty ratio:* 18:1.

Student Life *Campus security:* 24-hour emergency response devices and patrols, student patrols, late-night transport/escort service, controlled dormitory access.

Athletics Member NJCAA.

Standardized Tests *Required:* SAT I or ACT (for placement), ACT ASSET or ACT COMPASS.

Applying *Options:* early admission, deferred entrance. *Required:* high school transcript.

Admissions Contact Ms. Patty Harrison, Director of Admissions, Iowa Central Community College, 330 Avenue M, Ft. Dodge, IA 50501. *Phone:* 515-576-0099 Ext. 2414. *Toll-free phone:* 800-362-2793. *Fax:* 515-576-7724. *E-mail:* admis@duke.iccc.cc.ia.us.

IOWA LAKES COMMUNITY COLLEGE
Estherville, Iowa

- **State and locally supported** 2-year, founded 1967, part of Iowa Area Community Colleges System
- **Calendar** semesters
- **Degree** certificates, diplomas, and associate
- **Small-town** 20-acre campus
- **Endowment** $63,000
- **Coed,** 2,711 undergraduate students, 51% full-time, 56% women, 44% men

Undergraduates 1,383 full-time, 1,328 part-time. Students come from 4 states and territories, 5% are from out of state, 10% live on campus.

Freshmen *Admission:* 905 enrolled.

Faculty *Total:* 123, 67% full-time. *Student/faculty ratio:* 15:1.

Majors Accounting; agricultural business; agricultural economics; agricultural education; agricultural mechanization; agricultural sciences; agronomy/crop science; aircraft pilot (professional); applied art; architectural environmental design; art; art education; art history; astronomy; auto mechanic/technician; aviation management; behavioral sciences; biological/physical sciences; biology; botany; broadcast journalism; business administration; business machine repair; business marketing and marketing management; carpentry; ceramic arts; chemistry; child care/development; computer programming; computer science; computer science related; construction technology; corrections; criminal justice/law enforcement administration; data processing technology; developmental/child psychology; drafting; drawing; early childhood education; earth sciences; ecology; economics; education; elementary education; energy management technology; English; environmental education; environmental science; environmental technology; fashion merchandising; finance; fine/studio arts; fish/game management; geology; graphic design/commercial art/illustration; graphic/printing equipment; health services administration; history; hotel and restaurant management; humanities; information technology; jazz; journalism; law enforcement/police science; legal administrative assistant; legal studies; liberal arts and sciences/liberal studies; literature; mass communications; mathematics; medical administrative assistant; medical assistant; medical laboratory technology; music; music (piano and organ performance); music teacher education; music (voice and choral/opera performance); natural resources conservation; natural sciences; nursing; paralegal/legal assistant; pharmacy; philosophy; photography; physical education; physical sciences; political science; pre-engineering; psychology; radio/television broadcasting; real estate; recreation/leisure studies; rehabilitation therapy; retail management; science education; secretarial science; social sciences; social work; sociology; speech/rhetorical studies; travel/tourism management; water resources; welding technology; wildlife biology; wildlife management; wind/percussion instruments.

Academic Programs *Special study options:* academic remediation for entering students, accelerated degree program, adult/continuing education programs, advanced placement credit, cooperative education, distance learning, honors programs, independent study, internships, part-time degree program, services for LD students, study abroad, summer session for credit.

Library Iowa Lakes Community College Library plus 2 others with 25,861 titles, 178 serial subscriptions, an OPAC.

Computers on Campus 750 computers available on campus for general student use. Internet access, at least one staffed computer lab available.

Student Life *Housing Options:* coed. *Activities and Organizations:* drama/theater group, student-run newspaper, radio and television station, choral group, Criminal Justice Club, Ecology Club, Nursing Club, Student Senate, Aviation Club. *Campus security:* 24-hour emergency response devices, student patrols. *Student Services:* personal/psychological counseling, women's center.

Athletics Member NJCAA. *Intercollegiate sports:* baseball M(s), basketball M(s)/W(s), golf M(s), softball W(s), volleyball W(s), weight lifting M/W, wrestling M. *Intramural sports:* basketball M/W, football M/W, golf M, racquetball M/W, skiing (cross-country) M/W, skiing (downhill) M/W, softball M/W, table tennis M/W, tennis M/W, volleyball M/W, weight lifting M/W.

Standardized Tests *Required for some:* ACT (for admission).

Costs (2001–02) *Tuition:* state resident $2336 full-time, $73 per semester hour part-time; nonresident $2400 full-time, $75 per semester hour part-time. Full-time tuition and fees vary according to course load. Part-time tuition and fees vary according to course load. *Required fees:* $432 full-time, $5 per credit, $12 per term part-time. *Room and board:* $6660; room only: $3600. Room and board charges vary according to board plan and housing facility. *Payment plan:* installment. *Waivers:* employees or children of employees.

Financial Aid In 2001, 210 Federal Work-Study jobs (averaging $800). 45 State and other part-time jobs (averaging $1000).

Applying *Options:* deferred entrance. *Required:* high school transcript. *Required for some:* letters of recommendation, interview. *Application deadline:* rolling (freshmen), rolling (transfers).

Admissions Contact Ms. Julie Carlson, Dean of Enrollment Management, Iowa Lakes Community College, 300 South 18th Street, Estherville, IA 51334. *Phone:* 712-362-2604. *Toll-free phone:* 800-521-5054. *Fax:* 712-362-3969. *E-mail:* info@ilcc.cc.ia.us.

IOWA WESTERN COMMUNITY COLLEGE
Council Bluffs, Iowa

- **District-supported** 2-year, founded 1966, part of Iowa Department of Education Division of Community Colleges
- **Calendar** semesters
- **Degree** certificates, diplomas, and associate

- **Suburban** 282-acre campus with easy access to Omaha
- **Coed,** 4,299 undergraduate students, 50% full-time, 56% women, 44% men

Undergraduates Students come from 27 states and territories, 10 other countries, 2% African American, 1% Asian American or Pacific Islander, 1% Hispanic American, 0.6% Native American, 2% international, 19% live on campus.

Faculty *Total:* 222, 51% full-time.

Majors Accounting; agricultural animal husbandry/production management; agricultural business; alcohol/drug abuse counseling; architectural engineering technology; auto mechanic/technician; aviation technology; business administration; business marketing and marketing management; child care/development; child care provider; child care services management; civil engineering technology; computer programming; computer programming related; computer programming (specific applications); computer/technical support; construction/building inspection; criminal justice/law enforcement administration; culinary arts; data entry/microcomputer applications; dental hygiene; electrical/electronic engineering technology; electrical equipment installation/repair; engineering-related technology; farm/ranch management; fashion merchandising; fire science; food products retailing; food sales operations; food services technology; graphic design/commercial art/illustration; hotel and restaurant management; hotel/motel services marketing operations; human services; industrial design; international business; journalism; law enforcement/police science; legal administrative assistant; liberal arts and sciences/liberal studies; machine technology; marketing operations; mechanical design technology; mechanical engineering technology; medical administrative assistant; medical assistant; nursing; paralegal/legal assistant; practical nurse; retail management; sales operations; secretarial science; sign language interpretation; speech/theater education; word processing.

Academic Programs *Special study options:* academic remediation for entering students, adult/continuing education programs, cooperative education, distance learning, English as a second language, independent study, internships, part-time degree program, services for LD students, summer session for credit. *ROTC:* Army (c), Air Force (c).

Library 59,200 titles, 207 serial subscriptions, an OPAC.

Computers on Campus 263 computers available on campus for general student use. A campuswide network can be accessed from off campus. Internet access, at least one staffed computer lab available.

Student Life *Housing Options:* coed. *Activities and Organizations:* drama/theater group, student-run newspaper, radio and television station, choral group, Student Senate, Health Occupations Student Association, Volunteer Institute Program, Data Processing Student Association, Phi Theta Kappa. *Campus security:* 24-hour patrols, late-night transport/escort service. *Student Services:* personal/psychological counseling.

Athletics Member NJCAA. *Intercollegiate sports:* baseball M(s), basketball M(s)/W(s), softball W(s), volleyball W(s). *Intramural sports:* baseball M, basketball M/W, football M/W, golf M/W, tennis M/W, volleyball M/W.

Standardized Tests *Required:* ACT ASSET or ACT COMPASS.

Costs (2001–02) *One-time required fee:* $20. *Tuition:* state resident $2310 full-time, $80 per credit part-time; nonresident $3465 full-time, $116 per credit part-time. Full-time tuition and fees vary according to course load. *Required fees:* $270 full-time, $9 per credit. *Room and board:* $3700. Room and board charges vary according to board plan. *Payment plan:* installment. *Waivers:* senior citizens and employees or children of employees.

Applying *Options:* early admission, deferred entrance. *Required:* high school transcript. *Application deadline:* rolling (freshmen), rolling (transfers).

Admissions Contact Mrs. Tammy Young, Director of Admissions, Iowa Western Community College, 2700 College Road, Box 4-C, Council Bluffs, IA 51502. *Phone:* 712-325-3288. *Toll-free phone:* 800-432-5852. *Fax:* 712-325-3720. *E-mail:* tyoung@iwcc.cc.ia.us.

KAPLAN COLLEGE
Davenport, Iowa

- **Proprietary** primarily 2-year, founded 1937, part of Quest Education Corporation
- **Calendar** quarters
- **Degrees** diplomas, associate, and bachelor's
- **Suburban** campus
- **Coed,** 745 undergraduate students, 56% full-time, 63% women, 37% men

Undergraduates 420 full-time, 325 part-time. Students come from 2 states and territories, 29% are from out of state, 10% transferred in.

Freshmen *Admission:* 368 enrolled.

Faculty *Total:* 35, 40% full-time.

Majors Accounting; business administration; business systems networking/telecommunications; computer/information sciences; computer programming; court reporting; medical assistant; medical transcription; travel/tourism management; Web page design.

Academic Programs *Special study options:* academic remediation for entering students, adult/continuing education programs, distance learning, internships, part-time degree program, summer session for credit.

Library American Institute of Commerce Library with 7,000 titles, 120 serial subscriptions.

Computers on Campus 75 computers available on campus for general student use. Internet access, at least one staffed computer lab available.

Student Life *Housing:* college housing not available. *Activities and Organizations:* student-run radio station. *Student Services:* personal/psychological counseling.

Costs (2001–02) *Tuition:* $203 per credit part-time.

Applying *Options:* early admission, deferred entrance. *Application fee:* $25. *Required:* high school transcript, interview. *Required for some:* essay or personal statement. *Application deadline:* rolling (freshmen), rolling (transfers).

Admissions Contact Ms. Bonnie Flyte, Director of Admissions, Kaplan College, 1801 East Kimberly Road, Suite 1, Davenport, IA 52807-2095. *Phone:* 563-355-3500. *Toll-free phone:* 800-747-1035.

KIRKWOOD COMMUNITY COLLEGE
Cedar Rapids, Iowa

- **State and locally supported** 2-year, founded 1966, part of Iowa Department of Education Division of Community Colleges
- **Calendar** semesters
- **Degree** certificates, diplomas, and associate
- **Suburban** 320-acre campus
- **Endowment** $4.4 million
- **Coed,** 12,555 undergraduate students, 54% full-time, 54% women, 46% men

Undergraduates 6,726 full-time, 5,829 part-time. Students come from 15 states and territories, 85 other countries, 2% are from out of state, 2% African American, 2% Asian American or Pacific Islander, 2% Hispanic American, 2% Native American, 2% international, 10% transferred in.

Freshmen *Admission:* 3,699 admitted. *Test scores:* ACT scores over 18: 60%; ACT scores over 24: 16%; ACT scores over 30: 1%.

Faculty *Total:* 669, 33% full-time. *Student/faculty ratio:* 23:1.

Majors Accounting; agricultural business; agricultural education; agricultural sciences; agronomy/crop science; animal sciences; applied art; art; art education; auto mechanic/technician; biological/physical sciences; biological technology; biology; broadcast journalism; business administration; business education; business marketing and marketing management; ceramic arts; child care/development; communication equipment technology; computer programming; computer science; construction technology; corrections; criminal justice/law enforcement administration; culinary arts; data processing technology; developmental/child psychology; drafting; early childhood education; education; electrical/electronic engineering technology; electromechanical technology; elementary education; engineering; English; equestrian studies; farm/ranch management; fashion design/illustration; fashion merchandising; finance; fire science; fish/game management; food products retailing; food sales operations; food services technology; forestry; French; graphic/printing equipment; heating/air conditioning/refrigeration; history; horticulture science; hotel and restaurant management; humanities; human services; industrial technology; interior design; international business; jazz; journalism; landscape architecture; law enforcement/police science; legal administrative assistant; legal studies; liberal arts and sciences/liberal studies; management information systems/business data processing; mass communications; mathematics; mechanical design technology; mechanical engineering technology; medical administrative assistant; medical assistant; medical records administration; music; music (voice and choral/opera performance); natural resources conservation; nursing; occupational therapy; ornamental horticulture; paralegal/legal assistant; physical education; political science; practical nurse; pre-engineering; psychology; public relations; radio/television broadcasting; recreation/leisure facilities management; recreation/leisure studies; respiratory therapy; retail management; robotics; sanitation technology; secretarial science; social sciences; social work; sociology; Spanish; teacher assistant/aide; telecommunications; theater arts/drama; veterinary sciences; veterinary technology; water resources; welding technology; wildlife biology; wildlife management; wind/percussion instruments.

Academic Programs *Special study options:* academic remediation for entering students, accelerated degree program, adult/continuing education programs, advanced placement credit, cooperative education, distance learning, English as a

Kirkwood Community College (continued)
second language, external degree program, honors programs, internships, off-campus study, part-time degree program, services for LD students, student-designed majors, summer session for credit.
Library Library with 60,622 titles, 565 serial subscriptions, 3,677 audiovisual materials, an OPAC.
Computers on Campus 1000 computers available on campus for general student use. Internet access, online (class) registration, at least one staffed computer lab available.
Student Life *Housing:* college housing not available. *Activities and Organizations:* drama/theater group, student-run newspaper, choral group. *Campus security:* 24-hour patrols. *Student Services:* health clinic, personal/psychological counseling, legal services.
Athletics Member NJCAA. *Intercollegiate sports:* baseball M(s), basketball M(s)/W(s), golf M(s), soccer M/W, softball W(s), volleyball W(s). *Intramural sports:* basketball M/W, football M/W, golf M/W, racquetball M/W, soccer M/W, softball W, tennis M/W, volleyball M/W, weight lifting M/W.
Standardized Tests *Required:* ACT (for placement), ACT COMPASS.
Costs (2001–02) *Tuition:* state resident $2190 full-time, $73 per semester hour part-time; nonresident $4380 full-time, $146 per semester hour part-time.
Applying *Options:* electronic application, early admission. *Required:* high school transcript. *Application deadline:* rolling (freshmen), rolling (transfers). *Notification:* continuous (freshmen).
Admissions Contact Mr. Doug Bannon, Director of Admissions, Kirkwood Community College, PO Box 2068, Cedar Rapids, IA 52406-2068. *Phone:* 319-398-5517. *Toll-free phone:* 800-332-2055. *E-mail:* dbannon@kirkwood.cc.ia.us.

MARSHALLTOWN COMMUNITY COLLEGE
Marshalltown, Iowa

- **District-supported** 2-year, founded 1927, part of Iowa Valley Community College District System
- **Calendar** semesters
- **Degree** certificates, diplomas, and associate
- **Small-town** 200-acre campus
- **Endowment** $1.6 million
- **Coed,** 1,188 undergraduate students

Undergraduates Students come from 3 states and territories, 6 other countries, 1% are from out of state, 1% African American, 2% Asian American or Pacific Islander, 1% Hispanic American, 2% Native American, 8% live on campus.
Faculty *Total:* 107, 36% full-time. *Student/faculty ratio:* 29:1.
Majors Accounting; biological/physical sciences; business administration; business marketing and marketing management; child care/development; community services; computer science; dental hygiene; drafting; economics; electrical/electronic engineering technology; heavy equipment maintenance; industrial radiologic technology; liberal arts and sciences/liberal studies; machine technology; mental health/rehabilitation; nursing; operating room technician; political science; practical nurse; pre-engineering; secretarial science.
Academic Programs *Special study options:* academic remediation for entering students, adult/continuing education programs, advanced placement credit, cooperative education, internships, part-time degree program, services for LD students, student-designed majors, summer session for credit. *ROTC:* Air Force (c).
Library Learning Resource Center with 39,348 titles, 216 serial subscriptions.
Computers on Campus 250 computers available on campus for general student use. At least one staffed computer lab available.
Student Life *Housing Options:* coed. *Activities and Organizations:* drama/theater group, student-run newspaper, radio and television station, choral group, Student Activities Council, Student Senate, College Community Connection, SAMS, International Student Association. *Student Services:* personal/psychological counseling.
Athletics Member NJCAA. *Intercollegiate sports:* baseball M(s), basketball M(s)/W(s), golf M/W, soccer M(s), softball W(s), volleyball W(s). *Intramural sports:* racquetball M/W, volleyball W.
Standardized Tests *Recommended:* ACT (for placement).
Costs (2001–02) *Tuition:* state resident $2292 full-time; nonresident $3216 full-time, $134 per credit hour part-time. Full-time tuition and fees vary according to program. Part-time tuition and fees vary according to program. *Required fees:* $22 per credit hour. *Room and board:* $2600. *Payment plan:* installment. *Waivers:* senior citizens.
Financial Aid In 2001, 28 Federal Work-Study jobs (averaging $1800).
Applying *Options:* early admission. *Required:* high school transcript. *Application deadline:* rolling (freshmen), rolling (transfers). *Notification:* continuous (freshmen).
Admissions Contact Mrs. Deana Trawny, Director of Admissions, Marshalltown Community College, 37005 14th Street, Marshalltown, IA 50158. *Phone:* 641-752-7106 Ext. 391. *Toll-free phone:* 866-622-4748 Ext. 216.

MUSCATINE COMMUNITY COLLEGE
Muscatine, Iowa

- **State-supported** 2-year, founded 1929, part of Eastern Iowa Community College District
- **Calendar** semesters
- **Degree** certificates, diplomas, and associate
- **Small-town** 25-acre campus
- **Coed,** 1,129 undergraduate students

Undergraduates Students come from 6 states and territories, 5% are from out of state.
Freshmen *Admission:* 461 applied, 461 admitted. *Test scores:* ACT scores over 18: 80%; ACT scores over 24: 24%; ACT scores over 30: 1%.
Faculty *Total:* 95, 38% full-time.
Majors Accounting; agricultural production; agricultural supplies; business administration; business computer facilities operation; child care/guidance; emergency medical technology; environmental technology; liberal arts and sciences/liberal studies; machine technology; natural resources conservation; occupational safety/health technology; pharmacy technician/assistant; practical nurse; secretarial science.
Academic Programs *Special study options:* academic remediation for entering students, adult/continuing education programs, advanced placement credit, cooperative education, distance learning, double majors, English as a second language, honors programs, independent study, internships, part-time degree program, services for LD students, study abroad, summer session for credit.
Library Muscatine Community College Library with 19,588 titles, 176 serial subscriptions, an OPAC.
Computers on Campus 57 computers available on campus for general student use. A campuswide network can be accessed from off campus. At least one staffed computer lab available.
Student Life *Housing:* college housing not available. *Activities and Organizations:* drama/theater group, student-run newspaper, choral group. *Student Services:* personal/psychological counseling.
Athletics Member NJCAA. *Intercollegiate sports:* baseball M(s), basketball M(s), softball W(s), volleyball W(s). *Intramural sports:* table tennis M/W, tennis M/W, water polo M/W.
Standardized Tests *Required:* ACT or DTLS, DTMS.
Costs (2001–02) *Tuition:* state resident $2160 full-time, $72 per credit hour part-time; nonresident $3240 full-time, $108 per credit hour part-time. *Payment plan:* installment.
Applying *Options:* early admission, deferred entrance. *Required:* high school transcript. *Application deadline:* rolling (freshmen), rolling (transfers). *Notification:* continuous (freshmen).
Admissions Contact Ms. Katie Watson, Admissions Coordinator, Muscatine Community College, 152 Colorado Street, Muscatine, IA 52761-5396. *Phone:* 319-288-6000. *Toll-free phone:* 800-351-4669.

NORTHEAST IOWA COMMUNITY COLLEGE
Calmar, Iowa

- **State and locally supported** 2-year, founded 1966, part of Iowa Area Community Colleges System
- **Calendar** semesters
- **Degree** certificates, diplomas, and associate
- **Small-town** 210-acre campus
- **Coed,** 3,615 undergraduate students, 54% full-time, 63% women, 37% men

Undergraduates 1,965 full-time, 1,650 part-time. Students come from 5 states and territories, 5 other countries, 3% are from out of state.
Freshmen *Admission:* 2,522 applied, 1,904 admitted, 1,365 enrolled.
Faculty *Total:* 168, 67% full-time, 11% with terminal degrees. *Student/faculty ratio:* 16:1.
Majors Accounting; agricultural business; business marketing and marketing management; computer engineering technology; construction technology; dairy science; electrical/electronic engineering technology; liberal arts and sciences/liberal studies; mechanical design technology; medical laboratory technician; medical records administration; nursing; trade/industrial education.

Academic Programs *Special study options:* academic remediation for entering students, adult/continuing education programs, cooperative education, distance learning, double majors, English as a second language, independent study, internships, off-campus study, services for LD students, student-designed majors, study abroad, summer session for credit.
Library Wilder Resource Center plus 1 other with 18,634 titles, 302 serial subscriptions, an OPAC.
Computers on Campus 4000 computers available on campus for general student use. A campuswide network can be accessed from off campus. Internet access, at least one staffed computer lab available.
Student Life *Housing:* college housing not available. *Campus security:* security personnel on week nights. *Student Services:* personal/psychological counseling.
Athletics *Intramural sports:* basketball M/W, bowling M/W, football M/W, golf M/W, skiing (cross-country) M/W, skiing (downhill) M/W, swimming M/W, tennis M/W, volleyball M/W.
Standardized Tests *Required:* ACT ASSET. *Required for some:* ACT (for placement).
Costs (2001–02) *Tuition:* area resident $2250 full-time, $78 per credit part-time; state resident $78 per credit part-time. *Required fees:* $384 full-time, $12 per credit. *Payment plan:* deferred payment. *Waivers:* employees or children of employees.
Financial Aid In 2001, 131 Federal Work-Study jobs (averaging $810). 70 State and other part-time jobs (averaging $900).
Applying *Recommended:* high school transcript. *Application deadline:* rolling (freshmen), rolling (transfers). *Notification:* continuous (freshmen).
Admissions Contact Ms. Martha Keune, Admissions Representative, Northeast Iowa Community College, PO Box 400, Calmar, IA 52132. *Phone:* 563-562-3263 Ext. 307. *Toll-free phone:* 800-728-CALMAR. *E-mail:* keunem@nicc.cc.ia.us.

NORTH IOWA AREA COMMUNITY COLLEGE
Mason City, Iowa

- **State and locally supported** 2-year, founded 1918, part of Iowa Area Community Colleges System
- **Calendar** semesters
- **Degree** certificates, diplomas, and associate
- **Rural** 320-acre campus
- **Coed,** 2,722 undergraduate students, 66% full-time, 52% women, 48% men

Undergraduates 1,790 full-time, 932 part-time. Students come from 25 states and territories, 2% are from out of state, 3% African American, 0.8% Asian American or Pacific Islander, 2% Hispanic American, 0.2% Native American, 63% transferred in, 15% live on campus.
Freshmen *Admission:* 2,283 applied, 2,283 admitted, 930 enrolled. *Average high school GPA:* 2.64. *Test scores:* ACT scores over 18: 68%; ACT scores over 24: 15%.
Faculty *Total:* 231, 40% full-time.
Majors Accounting; accounting technician; agricultural economics; agricultural production; agricultural supplies; auto mechanic/technician; business administration; business marketing and marketing management; business systems networking/telecommunications; electrical/electronic engineering technology; emergency medical technology; fashion merchandising; heating/air conditioning/refrigeration; information technology; law enforcement/police science; legal administrative assistant; liberal arts and sciences/liberal studies; mechanical design technology; medical administrative assistant; medical assistant; medical laboratory technician; nursing; physical therapy assistant; practical nurse; retail management; robotics; secretarial science; sport/fitness administration; tool/die making; welding technology.
Academic Programs *Special study options:* academic remediation for entering students, advanced placement credit, cooperative education, distance learning, double majors, English as a second language, external degree program, honors programs, independent study, internships, off-campus study, part-time degree program, services for LD students, student-designed majors, summer session for credit.
Library North Iowa Area Community College Library with 49,287 titles, 377 serial subscriptions, 14,548 audiovisual materials, an OPAC, a Web page.
Computers on Campus 365 computers available on campus for general student use. A campuswide network can be accessed from off campus. Internet access, at least one staffed computer lab available.
Student Life *Housing:* on-campus residence required for freshman year. *Options:* coed. *Activities and Organizations:* drama/theater group, student-run newspaper, choral group, Student Senate, school newspaper, intramurals, choral groups, band/orchestra. *Campus security:* 24-hour emergency response devices, late-night transport/escort service, controlled dormitory access, 12-hour patrols by trained security personnel. *Student Services:* health clinic, personal/psychological counseling.
Athletics Member NJCAA. *Intercollegiate sports:* baseball M(s), basketball M(s)/W(s), football M(s), golf M(s)/W(s), soccer M(s)/W(s), softball W(s), volleyball W(s). *Intramural sports:* basketball M/W, bowling M/W, football M, soccer M/W, softball W, table tennis M/W, tennis M/W, volleyball M/W, weight lifting M/W.
Standardized Tests *Required for some:* ACT (for placement). *Recommended:* ACT (for placement), ACT COMPASS.
Costs (2001–02) *Tuition:* state resident $2243 full-time, $75 per semester hour part-time; nonresident $3300 full-time, $110 per semester hour part-time. Full-time tuition and fees vary according to course load. Part-time tuition and fees vary according to course load. *Required fees:* $283 full-time, $9 per semester hour, $9 per term part-time. *Room and board:* $3450. Room and board charges vary according to board plan. *Payment plan:* installment. *Waivers:* employees or children of employees.
Financial Aid In 2001, 125 Federal Work-Study jobs (averaging $2000).
Applying *Options:* common application, electronic application. *Required for some:* high school transcript. *Recommended:* high school transcript. *Application deadline:* rolling (freshmen), rolling (transfers). *Notification:* continuous (freshmen).
Admissions Contact Ms. Rachel McGuire, Director of Admissions, North Iowa Area Community College, 500 College Drive, Mason City, IA 50401. *Phone:* 641-422-4104. *Toll-free phone:* 888-GO NIACC Ext. 4245. *Fax:* 641-422-4385. *E-mail:* request@niacc.cc.ia.us.

NORTHWEST IOWA COMMUNITY COLLEGE
Sheldon, Iowa

- **State-supported** 2-year, founded 1966, part of Iowa Department of Education Division of Community Colleges
- **Calendar** semesters
- **Degree** certificates, diplomas, and associate
- **Small-town** 263-acre campus with easy access to Sioux City
- **Coed**

Faculty *Student/faculty ratio:* 12:1.
Student Life *Campus security:* 24-hour emergency response devices.
Standardized Tests *Required:* ACT ASSET.
Financial Aid In 2001, 55 Federal Work-Study jobs (averaging $800).
Applying *Options:* common application. *Application fee:* $10. *Required:* high school transcript.
Admissions Contact Ms. Bonnie Brands, Director of Admissions, Northwest Iowa Community College, 603 West Park Street, Sheldon, IA 51201-1046. *Phone:* 712-324-5061 Ext. 124. *Toll-free phone:* 800-352-4907. *Fax:* 712-324-4136.

ST. LUKE'S COLLEGE OF NURSING AND HEALTH SCIENCES
Sioux City, Iowa

- **Independent** 2-year, part of St., Luke's Regional Medical Center
- **Degree** certificates and associate
- **Endowment** $920,575
- **Coed, primarily women,** 107 undergraduate students, 76% full-time, 93% women, 7% men
- 56% of applicants were admitted

Undergraduates 81 full-time, 26 part-time. Students come from 10 states and territories, 21% are from out of state, 0.9% African American, 0.9% Asian American or Pacific Islander, 0.9% Native American, 11% transferred in, 34% live on campus.
Freshmen *Admission:* 126 applied, 70 admitted, 22 enrolled. *Average high school GPA:* 3.21. *Test scores:* ACT scores over 18: 85%; ACT scores over 24: 20%; ACT scores over 30: 3%.
Faculty *Total:* 20, 60% full-time, 35% with terminal degrees. *Student/faculty ratio:* 7:1.
Majors Nursing.
Academic Programs *Special study options:* advanced placement credit, cooperative education, internships, part-time degree program, summer session for credit.

St. Luke's College of Nursing and Health Sciences (continued)

Library St. Luke's Media Services Library plus 1 other with 115 serial subscriptions, 1,800 audiovisual materials, an OPAC, a Web page.

Computers on Campus 10 computers available on campus for general student use. Internet access, at least one staffed computer lab available.

Student Life *Housing Options:* coed. *Campus security:* 24-hour emergency response devices and patrols. *Student Services:* health clinic, personal/psychological counseling.

Standardized Tests *Required:* ACT (for admission).

Costs (2002–03) *One-time required fee:* $75. *Comprehensive fee:* $13,262 includes full-time tuition ($9180), mandatory fees ($526), and room and board ($3556). Full-time tuition and fees vary according to course load and program. Part-time tuition: $225 per credit hour. Part-time tuition and fees vary according to course load and program. *Room and board:* College room only: $2356. Room and board charges vary according to board plan. *Payment plan:* installment. *Waivers:* employees or children of employees.

Applying *Options:* common application. *Application fee:* $25. *Required:* essay or personal statement, high school transcript, minimum 2.50 GPA. *Application deadline:* 8/1 (freshmen). *Notification:* 8/1 (freshmen).

Admissions Contact Sherry McCarthy, Admissions Coordinator, St. Luke's College of Nursing and Health Sciences, 2720 Stone Park Boulevard, 27th and Douglas, Sioux City, IA 51104. *Phone:* 712-279-3149. *Toll-free phone:* 800-352-4660 Ext. 3149. *E-mail:* mccartsj@stlukes.org.

SCOTT COMMUNITY COLLEGE
Bettendorf, Iowa

- **State and locally supported** 2-year, founded 1966, part of Eastern Iowa Community College District
- **Calendar** semesters
- **Degree** certificates, diplomas, and associate
- **Urban** campus
- **Coed,** 3,985 undergraduate students

Undergraduates Students come from 36 states and territories, 19 other countries, 9% are from out of state.

Freshmen *Test scores:* ACT scores over 18: 68%; ACT scores over 24: 17%.

Faculty *Total:* 235, 36% full-time.

Majors Accounting; aircraft pilot (professional); auto body repair; auto mechanic/technician; business administration; child care/guidance; computer/information sciences; culinary arts; diesel engine mechanic; electroencephalograph technology; emergency medical technology; environmental technology; equestrian studies; heating/air conditioning/refrigeration; interior design; law enforcement/police science; liberal arts and sciences/liberal studies; machine technology; medical laboratory technician; medical radiologic technology; nursing; occupational safety/health technology; occupational therapy assistant; pharmacy technician/assistant; physical therapy; practical nurse; radio/television broadcasting technology; respiratory therapy; secretarial science; sign language interpretation.

Academic Programs *Special study options:* academic remediation for entering students, adult/continuing education programs, advanced placement credit, cooperative education, distance learning, double majors, English as a second language, honors programs, independent study, internships, off-campus study, part-time degree program, services for LD students, study abroad, summer session for credit.

Library Scott Community College Library with 22,700 titles, 183 serial subscriptions, an OPAC.

Computers on Campus 200 computers available on campus for general student use. A campuswide network can be accessed from off campus. At least one staffed computer lab available.

Student Life *Housing:* college housing not available. *Activities and Organizations:* drama/theater group, student government, Campus Activities Board. *Campus security:* 24-hour emergency response devices. *Student Services:* personal/psychological counseling.

Athletics Member NJCAA. *Intercollegiate sports:* baseball M(s), basketball M(s), softball W(s), volleyball W(s).

Standardized Tests *Required:* ACT (for placement), or College Board Diagnostic Tests.

Costs (2001–02) *Tuition:* state resident $2160 full-time, $72 per credit hour part-time; nonresident $3240 full-time, $108 per credit hour part-time.

Applying *Options:* early admission, deferred entrance. *Required:* high school transcript. *Application deadline:* rolling (freshmen), rolling (transfers). *Notification:* continuous (freshmen).

Admissions Contact Mr. Scott Kashmarek, Executive Director of Marketing and Enrollment Management, Scott Community College, 500 Belmont Road, Bettendorf, IA 52722-6804. *Phone:* 563-441-4005. *Toll-free phone:* 800-462-3255.

SOUTHEASTERN COMMUNITY COLLEGE, NORTH CAMPUS
West Burlington, Iowa

Admissions Contact Ms. Stacy White, Admissions, Southeastern Community College, North Campus, 1015 South Gear Avenue, PO Box 180, West Burlington, IA 52655-0180. *Phone:* 319-752-2731 Ext. 8137. *Toll-free phone:* 866-722-4692. *E-mail:* admoff@secc.cc.ia.us.

SOUTHEASTERN COMMUNITY COLLEGE, SOUTH CAMPUS
Keokuk, Iowa

- **State and locally supported** 2-year, founded 1967, part of Iowa Department of Education Division of Community Colleges
- **Calendar** semesters
- **Degree** certificates, diplomas, and associate
- **Small-town** 3-acre campus
- **Coed,** 600 undergraduate students

Faculty *Total:* 25, 72% full-time.

Majors Alcohol/drug abuse counseling; business administration; cosmetology; criminal justice studies; emergency medical technology; information sciences/systems; liberal arts and sciences/liberal studies; medical administrative assistant; nursing; practical nurse; secretarial science.

Academic Programs *Special study options:* academic remediation for entering students, advanced placement credit, distance learning, independent study, off-campus study, part-time degree program, services for LD students, summer session for credit.

Library Fred Karre Memorial Library with 10,000 titles, 70 serial subscriptions, an OPAC.

Computers on Campus 80 computers available on campus for general student use. A campuswide network can be accessed from off campus. Internet access, at least one staffed computer lab available.

Student Life *Housing:* college housing not available. *Activities and Organizations:* drama/theater group, student-run newspaper, choral group, Business Professionals of America, Art Club, Student Nurses Association, Computer Club, Student Board. *Student Services:* personal/psychological counseling.

Athletics *Intramural sports:* basketball M, volleyball M/W.

Standardized Tests *Required:* ACT ASSET.

Costs (2001–02) *Tuition:* state resident $2280 full-time, $76 per credit hour part-time; nonresident $2693 full-time, $90 per credit hour part-time. *Payment plan:* deferred payment. *Waivers:* employees or children of employees.

Applying *Options:* electronic application, early admission, deferred entrance. *Recommended:* high school transcript. *Application deadline:* rolling (freshmen), rolling (transfers).

Admissions Contact Kari Bevans, Admissions Coordinator, Southeastern Community College, South Campus, PO Box 6007, 335 Messenger Road, Keokuk, IA 52632. *Phone:* 319-524-3221 Ext. 8416. *Toll-free phone:* 866-722-4692 Ext. 8416. *Fax:* 319-524-8621. *E-mail:* sadmoff@secc.cc.ia.us.

SOUTHWESTERN COMMUNITY COLLEGE
Creston, Iowa

- **State-supported** 2-year, founded 1966, part of Iowa Department of Education Division of Community Colleges
- **Calendar** semesters
- **Degree** diplomas and associate
- **Rural** 420-acre campus
- **Endowment** $318,170
- **Coed,** 1,198 undergraduate students, 55% full-time, 58% women, 42% men

Undergraduates 660 full-time, 538 part-time. Students come from 11 states and territories, 3 other countries, 4% are from out of state, 6% transferred in, 5% live on campus.

Freshmen *Admission:* 749 applied, 672 admitted, 311 enrolled. *Average high school GPA:* 2.83. *Test scores:* ACT scores over 18: 65%; ACT scores over 24: 14%; ACT scores over 30: 1%.
Faculty *Total:* 84, 55% full-time. *Student/faculty ratio:* 14:1.
Majors Accounting; agricultural business; auto body repair; auto mechanic/technician; business administration; business marketing and marketing management; carpentry; computer programming; drafting; electromechanical technology; liberal arts and sciences/liberal studies; music; nursing; practical nurse; retail management; secretarial science.
Academic Programs *Special study options:* academic remediation for entering students, adult/continuing education programs, advanced placement credit, cooperative education, independent study, internships, part-time degree program, services for LD students, student-designed majors, summer session for credit.
Library Learning Resources Center with 14,382 titles, 170 serial subscriptions, 925 audiovisual materials, an OPAC, a Web page.
Computers on Campus 115 computers available on campus for general student use. A campuswide network can be accessed from off campus. At least one staffed computer lab available.
Student Life *Housing Options:* men-only, women-only. *Activities and Organizations:* student-run newspaper, choral group. *Campus security:* 24-hour emergency response devices and patrols, controlled dormitory access. *Student Services:* personal/psychological counseling.
Athletics Member NJCAA. *Intercollegiate sports:* baseball M(s), basketball M(s)/W(s), softball W(s), volleyball W(s). *Intramural sports:* basketball M/W, bowling M/W, table tennis M/W, volleyball M/W.
Standardized Tests *Required:* ACT (for placement), ACT ASSET.
Costs (2002–03) *Tuition:* state resident $2464 full-time, $77 per credit part-time; nonresident $3465 full-time, $116 per credit part-time. *Required fees:* $384 full-time, $12 per hour. *Room and board:* $3200. *Payment plan:* installment.
Financial Aid In 2001, 79 Federal Work-Study jobs (averaging $3000). 145 State and other part-time jobs (averaging $2000).
Applying *Options:* common application, early admission. *Required:* high school transcript. *Application deadlines:* 9/5 (freshmen), 9/5 (transfers). *Notification:* continuous (freshmen).
Admissions Contact Ms. Terri Higgins, Director of Admissions, Southwestern Community College, 1501 West Townline Street. *Phone:* 641-782-7081 Ext. 431. *Toll-free phone:* 800-247-4023. *Fax:* 641-782-3312. *E-mail:* t_higgins@swcc.cc.ia.us.

Western Iowa Tech Community College
Sioux City, Iowa

- **State-supported** 2-year, founded 1966, part of Iowa Department of Education Division of Community Colleges
- **Calendar** semesters
- **Degree** certificates, diplomas, and associate
- **Urban** 143-acre campus
- **Endowment** $337,763
- **Coed,** 4,920 undergraduate students, 37% full-time, 54% women, 46% men

Undergraduates 1,834 full-time, 3,086 part-time. Students come from 11 states and territories, 9% are from out of state, 2% African American, 2% Asian American or Pacific Islander, 4% Hispanic American, 1% Native American, 0.7% transferred in, 3% live on campus.
Freshmen *Admission:* 1,984 admitted, 1,984 enrolled. *Average high school GPA:* 2.68.
Faculty *Total:* 253, 36% full-time, 7% with terminal degrees. *Student/faculty ratio:* 20:1.
Majors Agricultural supplies; architectural engineering technology; auto body repair; auto mechanic/technician; biomedical engineering-related technology; business administration; business computer programming; child care services management; computer typography/composition; criminal justice/law enforcement administration; diesel engine mechanic; electrical/electronic engineering technology; emergency medical technology; executive assistant; heating/air conditioning/refrigeration; legal administrative assistant; liberal arts and sciences/liberal studies; machine technology; medical administrative assistant; medical laboratory technician; nurse assistant/aide; nursing; occupational therapy assistant; physical therapy assistant; tool/die making; turf management.
Academic Programs *Special study options:* academic remediation for entering students, adult/continuing education programs, distance learning, double majors, English as a second language, external degree program, honors programs, independent study, internships, off-campus study, part-time degree program, services for LD students, summer session for credit.
Library Western Iowa Tech Community College Library Services with 25,696 titles, 1,886 serial subscriptions, 3,456 audiovisual materials, an OPAC.
Computers on Campus 640 computers available on campus for general student use. A campuswide network can be accessed from student residence rooms and from off campus. Internet access, at least one staffed computer lab available.
Student Life *Housing Options:* coed. *Activities and Organizations:* Student Senate. *Campus security:* 24-hour emergency response devices and patrols. *Student Services:* health clinic, personal/psychological counseling.
Athletics *Intramural sports:* basketball M/W, bowling M/W, football M/W, golf M/W, skiing (downhill) M/W, softball W, volleyball M/W, weight lifting M/W.
Standardized Tests *Required:* CPT.
Costs (2001–02) *Tuition:* state resident $2220 full-time, $74 per credit hour part-time; nonresident $3390 full-time, $133 per credit hour part-time. *Required fees:* $360 full-time, $12 per credit hour. *Room and board:* room only: $2075.
Financial Aid In 2001, 102 Federal Work-Study jobs (averaging $1628).
Applying *Options:* common application, deferred entrance. *Application fee:* $10. *Required:* high school transcript. *Application deadline:* rolling (freshmen). *Notification:* continuous (freshmen).
Admissions Contact Lora Vanderzwaag, Director of Admissions, Western Iowa Tech Community College, 4647 Stone Avenue, Sioux City, IA 51102-5199. *Phone:* 712-274-6400. *Toll-free phone:* 800-352-4649. *Fax:* 712-274-6412. *E-mail:* vanderl@witcc.com.

KANSAS

Allen County Community College
Iola, Kansas

- **State and locally supported** 2-year, founded 1923, part of Kansas State Board of Regents
- **Calendar** semesters
- **Degree** certificates and associate
- **Small-town** 88-acre campus
- **Endowment** $2.7 million
- **Coed,** 2,150 undergraduate students, 37% full-time, 60% women, 40% men

Undergraduates 787 full-time, 1,363 part-time. Students come from 17 states and territories, 16 other countries, 4% are from out of state, 4% African American, 0.3% Asian American or Pacific Islander, 3% Hispanic American, 0.8% Native American, 3% international, 80% transferred in, 10% live on campus.
Freshmen *Admission:* 893 applied, 893 admitted, 520 enrolled. *Average high school GPA:* 2.98. *Test scores:* ACT scores over 18: 64%; ACT scores over 24: 14%; ACT scores over 30: 2%.
Faculty *Total:* 32. *Student/faculty ratio:* 17:1.
Majors Accounting; agricultural production; architecture; art; athletic training/sports medicine; banking; biology; business; business administration; business education; business systems networking/ telecommunications; chemistry; child care/development; computer science; criminal justice/law enforcement administration; data processing technology; drafting; economics; electrical/electronic engineering technology; electrical engineering; elementary education; emergency medical technology; engineering; engineering technology; English composition; equestrian studies; farm/ranch management; foreign language translation; forestry; general studies; geography; health aide; health facilities administration; health/physical education; history; home economics; home health aide; humanities; industrial arts; industrial arts education; industrial technology; information sciences/systems; journalism; library science; mathematics; mortuary science; music; nuclear technology; nurse assistant/aide; philosophy; physical therapy; physics; political science; postal management; pre-dentistry; pre-law; pre-medicine; pre-pharmacy studies; pre-veterinary studies; psychology; recreation/leisure facilities management; religious studies; secondary education; secretarial science; social work; sociology; speech/rhetorical studies; theater arts/drama; wood science/paper technology.
Academic Programs *Special study options:* academic remediation for entering students, adult/continuing education programs, cooperative education, part-time degree program, services for LD students, student-designed majors, summer session for credit.
Library Learning Resource Center with 49,416 titles, 159 serial subscriptions, an OPAC.
Computers on Campus 65 computers available on campus for general student use. Internet access, at least one staffed computer lab available.
Student Life *Housing:* on-campus residence required through sophomore year. *Options:* coed. *Activities and Organizations:* drama/theater group, student-run newspaper, choral group, intramurals, Student Senate, Biology Club, student

Allen County Community College (continued)
newspaper, Phi Theta Kappa. *Campus security:* controlled dormitory access. *Student Services:* personal/psychological counseling.

Athletics Member NJCAA. *Intercollegiate sports:* baseball M(s), basketball M(s)/W(s), cross-country running M(s)/W(s), golf M(s), soccer M(s)/W(s), softball W(s), track and field M(s)/W(s), volleyball W(s). *Intramural sports:* basketball M/W, football M/W, soccer M/W, softball M/W, table tennis M/W, tennis M/W, volleyball M/W.

Standardized Tests *Recommended:* ACT (for placement).

Costs (2002–03) *Tuition:* state resident $992 full-time, $31 per credit hour part-time; nonresident $992 full-time, $31 per credit hour part-time. *Required fees:* $736 full-time, $23 per credit hour. *Room and board:* $3250; room only: $2250. Room and board charges vary according to housing facility. *Waivers:* senior citizens and employees or children of employees.

Financial Aid In 2001, 25 Federal Work-Study jobs (averaging $1650). 80 State and other part-time jobs (averaging $1650).

Applying *Options:* common application, early admission, deferred entrance. *Required:* high school transcript. *Application deadlines:* 8/24 (freshmen), 8/24 (transfers). *Notification:* continuous (freshmen).

Admissions Contact Mr. Jason Kegler, Director of Admissions, Allen County Community College, 1801 North Cottonwood, Iola, KS 66749. *Phone:* 316-365-5116 Ext. 267. *E-mail:* kegler@allencc.net.

BARTON COUNTY COMMUNITY COLLEGE
Great Bend, Kansas

- **State and locally supported** 2-year, founded 1969, part of Kansas Board of Regents
- **Calendar** semesters
- **Degree** certificates and associate
- **Rural** 140-acre campus
- **Endowment** $4.4 million
- **Coed,** 4,178 undergraduate students, 26% full-time, 50% women, 50% men

Undergraduates 1,084 full-time, 3,094 part-time. Students come from 39 states and territories, 6% are from out of state, 16% African American, 2% Asian American or Pacific Islander, 7% Hispanic American, 0.8% Native American, 7% transferred in, 8% live on campus.

Freshmen *Admission:* 710 applied, 710 admitted, 1,373 enrolled.

Faculty *Total:* 203, 36% full-time. *Student/faculty ratio:* 22:1.

Majors Agricultural sciences; anthropology; applied art; art; athletic training/sports medicine; auto mechanic/technician; biology; business administration; chemistry; child care/development; child care services management; computer graphics; computer/information technology services administration and management related; computer programming related; computer science; computer software and media applications related; computer systems networking/telecommunications; computer/technical support; criminal justice/law enforcement administration; cytotechnology; data entry/microcomputer applications; data entry/microcomputer applications related; dietician assistant; drafting; economics; education; electrical/electronic engineering technology; emergency medical technology; English; fashion merchandising; fire science; forestry; geology; health science; history; home economics; humanities; information sciences/systems; information technology; interior design; journalism; law enforcement/police science; liberal arts and sciences/liberal studies; mathematics; medical administrative assistant; medical laboratory technician; medical records administration; music; nursing; petroleum technology; pharmacy; philosophy; physical education; physical sciences; physical therapy; physician assistant; physics; political science; pre-engineering; psychology; public administration; respiratory therapy; secretarial science; social work; sociology; sport/fitness administration; system administration; theater arts/drama; Web page, digital/multimedia and information resources design; welding technology; word processing.

Academic Programs *Special study options:* academic remediation for entering students, accelerated degree program, adult/continuing education programs, advanced placement credit, cooperative education, distance learning, English as a second language, external degree program, honors programs, independent study, internships, part-time degree program, services for LD students, student-designed majors, summer session for credit.

Library Barton County Community College Library with 28,000 titles, 213 serial subscriptions, 535 audiovisual materials, an OPAC, a Web page.

Computers on Campus 186 computers available on campus for general student use. A campuswide network can be accessed from student residence rooms and from off campus. Internet access, at least one staffed computer lab available.

Student Life *Housing:* on-campus residence required for freshman year. *Options:* coed, disabled students. *Activities and Organizations:* drama/theater group, student-run newspaper, choral group, Danceline, Business Professionals, Psychology Club, Agriculture Club, Cougarettes. *Campus security:* 24-hour emergency response devices and patrols. *Student Services:* health clinic, personal/psychological counseling.

Athletics Member NJCAA. *Intercollegiate sports:* baseball M(s), basketball M(s)/W(s), cross-country running M(s)/W(s), golf M(s), soccer M(s)/W(s), softball W(s), tennis M(s)/W(s), track and field M(s)/W(s), volleyball W(s). *Intramural sports:* basketball M/W, bowling M/W, football M/W, golf M/W, swimming M/W, table tennis M/W, tennis M/W, track and field M/W, volleyball M/W.

Standardized Tests *Required:* ACT ASSET. *Recommended:* ACT (for placement).

Costs (2001–02) *Tuition:* state resident $896 full-time, $28 per credit hour part-time; nonresident $896 full-time, $28 per credit hour part-time. Full-time tuition and fees vary according to student level. *Required fees:* $576 full-time, $18 per credit hour. *Room and board:* $2904. Room and board charges vary according to board plan and housing facility. *Payment plan:* installment. *Waivers:* senior citizens and employees or children of employees.

Financial Aid In 2001, 102 Federal Work-Study jobs (averaging $2400).

Applying *Options:* common application, electronic application, early admission. *Recommended:* high school transcript. *Application deadline:* rolling (freshmen), rolling (transfers).

Admissions Contact Mrs. Cari Ringwald, Director of Marketing, Barton County Community College, 245 Northeast 30th Road, Great Bend, KS 67530. *Phone:* 620-792-9241. *Toll-free phone:* 800-722-6842. *Fax:* 620-786-1160. *E-mail:* ringwaldc@barton.cc.ks.us.

THE BROWN MACKIE COLLEGE
Salina, Kansas

- **Proprietary** 2-year, founded 1892
- **Calendar** modular
- **Degree** certificates, diplomas, and associate
- **Small-town** 10-acre campus with easy access to Wichita
- **Coed,** 325 undergraduate students, 100% full-time, 60% women, 40% men

Undergraduates 325 full-time. Students come from 10 states and territories, 2 other countries, 24% are from out of state.

Freshmen *Admission:* 140 applied, 137 admitted, 73 enrolled.

Faculty *Total:* 15, 40% full-time, 13% with terminal degrees. *Student/faculty ratio:* 22:1.

Majors Accounting; business administration; computer/information sciences; criminal justice/law enforcement administration; medical office management; medical transcription; paralegal/legal assistant.

Academic Programs *Special study options:* academic remediation for entering students, adult/continuing education programs, advanced placement credit, cooperative education, double majors, independent study, services for LD students, summer session for credit.

Library Irene Carlson Memorial Library plus 1 other with 6,824 titles, 41 serial subscriptions, an OPAC, a Web page.

Computers on Campus 75 computers available on campus for general student use. Internet access, at least one staffed computer lab available.

Student Life *Housing:* college housing not available. *Activities and Organizations:* student-run newspaper, Student Senate, Athletic Booster Club.

Athletics Member NJCAA. *Intercollegiate sports:* baseball M, basketball M/W, softball W.

Standardized Tests *Required:* ACT ASSET.

Costs (2002–03) *Tuition:* $5400 full-time, $225 per semester hour part-time. Full-time tuition and fees vary according to course load. *Required fees:* $384 full-time, $16 per semester hour. *Payment plan:* installment. *Waivers:* employees or children of employees.

Financial Aid In 2001, 10 Federal Work-Study jobs (averaging $1500).

Applying *Options:* common application, deferred entrance. *Application fee:* $20. *Required:* high school transcript, interview. *Application deadline:* rolling (freshmen). *Notification:* continuous (freshmen).

Admissions Contact Ms. Diann Heath, Director of Admissions, The Brown Mackie College, 2106 South 9th Street, Salina, KS 67401. *Phone:* 785-825-5422 Ext. 17. *Toll-free phone:* 800-365-0433. *Fax:* 785-827-7623.

The Brown Mackie College-Olathe Campus
Olathe, Kansas

- **Proprietary** 2-year, founded 1892, part of The Brown Mackie College
- **Calendar** semesters
- **Degree** certificates, diplomas, and associate
- **Suburban** campus with easy access to Kansas City
- **Coed,** 234 undergraduate students, 100% full-time, 67% women, 33% men

Undergraduates Students come from 2 states and territories, 35% are from out of state, 20% African American, 2% Asian American or Pacific Islander, 5% Hispanic American, 2% Native American.

Freshmen *Admission:* 144 applied, 115 admitted.

Faculty *Total:* 20, 30% full-time, 25% with terminal degrees. *Student/faculty ratio:* 12:1.

Majors Accounting; business administration; computer programming related; computer/technical support; computer typography/composition; data entry/microcomputer applications; data entry/microcomputer applications related; dental hygiene; health unit coordination; health unit management; information technology; medical administrative assistant; medical assistant; medical records administration; paralegal/legal assistant; system/networking/LAN/WAN management.

Academic Programs *Special study options:* academic remediation for entering students, adult/continuing education programs, summer session for credit.

Library The Brown Mackie College Library plus 1 other with 4,500 titles, 48 serial subscriptions, an OPAC, a Web page.

Computers on Campus 86 computers available on campus for general student use. Internet access, at least one staffed computer lab available.

Student Life *Housing:* college housing not available. *Activities and Organizations:* Coffee Club (Service and social organization). *Campus security:* 24-hour emergency response devices. *Student Services:* personal/psychological counseling.

Standardized Tests *Required:* ACT ASSET.

Costs (2001–02) *Tuition:* $5400 full-time. *Required fees:* $384 full-time. *Waivers:* employees or children of employees.

Applying *Options:* deferred entrance. *Application fee:* $20. *Required:* high school transcript, interview. *Recommended:* essay or personal statement, minimum 2.0 GPA. *Application deadline:* rolling (freshmen), rolling (transfers). *Notification:* continuous (freshmen).

Admissions Contact Ms. Jacquelyn Johnson, Director of Admissions, The Brown Mackie College-Olathe Campus, 100 East Santa Fe, Suite 300, Olathe, KS 66061. *Phone:* 913-768-1900. *Fax:* 913-768-0555. *E-mail:* jjohnson@amedcts.com.

Butler County Community College
El Dorado, Kansas

Admissions Contact Mr. Paul Kyle, Director of Enrollment Management, Butler County Community College, 901 South Haverhill Road, El Dorado, KS 67042-3280. *Phone:* 316-321-2222 Ext. 163.

Cloud County Community College
Concordia, Kansas

Admissions Contact Ms. Tina Thayer, Director of Admissions, Cloud County Community College, 2221 Campus Drive, PO Box 1002, Concordia, KS 66901-1002. *Phone:* 785-243-1435 Ext. 209. *Toll-free phone:* 800-729-5101. *E-mail:* thayer@mg.cloudccc.cc.ks.us.

Coffeyville Community College
Coffeyville, Kansas

- **State and locally supported** 2-year, founded 1923, part of Kansas Board of Regents
- **Calendar** semesters
- **Degree** certificates and associate
- **Small-town** 39-acre campus with easy access to Tulsa
- **Endowment** $2.3 million
- **Coed,** 1,499 undergraduate students

Undergraduates Students come from 16 states and territories, 14 other countries, 7% are from out of state, 9% African American, 0.3% Asian American or Pacific Islander, 1% Hispanic American, 2% Native American, 3% international, 27% live on campus.

Freshmen *Admission:* 1,010 applied, 1,010 admitted. *Average high school GPA:* 2.72. *Test scores:* ACT scores over 18: 54%; ACT scores over 24: 14%.

Faculty *Total:* 85, 60% full-time. *Student/faculty ratio:* 22:1.

Majors Accounting; agricultural business; agricultural economics; agricultural education; agricultural mechanization; agricultural sciences; animal sciences; applied art; art; athletic training/sports medicine; auto mechanic/technician; behavioral sciences; biological/physical sciences; biology; botany; broadcast journalism; business administration; business education; business machine repair; business marketing and marketing management; carpentry; chemistry; communication equipment technology; computer/information sciences; computer programming; computer science; construction technology; drafting; drawing; economics; education; elementary education; emergency medical technology; engineering; English; history; home economics; horticulture science; humanities; industrial technology; information sciences/systems; journalism; legal administrative assistant; liberal arts and sciences/liberal studies; machine technology; mass communications; mathematics; mechanical engineering technology; medical administrative assistant; music; music teacher education; music (voice and choral/opera performance); nursing; occupational therapy; physical education; political science; practical nurse; pre-engineering; psychology; radio/television broadcasting; retail management; secretarial science; social sciences; social work; sociology; telecommunications; theater arts/drama; welding technology; wind/percussion instruments.

Academic Programs *Special study options:* academic remediation for entering students, adult/continuing education programs, cooperative education, distance learning, double majors, English as a second language, freshman honors college, honors programs, internships, part-time degree program, services for LD students, student-designed majors, summer session for credit.

Library Russell H. Graham Learning Resource Center plus 1 other with 28,356 titles, 247 serial subscriptions, 1,415 audiovisual materials, an OPAC, a Web page.

Computers on Campus 75 computers available on campus for general student use. A campuswide network can be accessed from off campus. Internet access, at least one staffed computer lab available.

Student Life *Housing Options:* coed. *Activities and Organizations:* drama/theater group, student-run television station, choral group, marching band, Student Government Association, Phi Theta Kappa, Delta Psi Omega, Delta Epsilon Chi, Agriculture Club. *Campus security:* 24-hour patrols, late-night transport/escort service. *Student Services:* health clinic, personal/psychological counseling, women's center.

Athletics Member NJCAA. *Intercollegiate sports:* baseball M(s), basketball M(s)/W(s), cross-country running M(s)/W(s), football M(s), golf M(s), softball W(s), track and field M(s)/W(s), volleyball W(s). *Intramural sports:* basketball M/W, bowling M/W, soccer M/W, table tennis M/W, tennis M/W, volleyball M/W, weight lifting M.

Standardized Tests *Required:* ACT (for placement), ACT ASSET.

Costs (2002–03) *Tuition:* area resident $1184 full-time, $37 per credit hour part-time; state resident $1184 full-time, $37 per credit hour part-time; nonresident $87 per credit hour part-time. Full-time tuition and fees vary according to reciprocity agreements. Part-time tuition and fees vary according to reciprocity agreements. *Required fees:* $576 full-time, $18 per credit hour. *Room and board:* $3200. Room and board charges vary according to board plan. *Payment plan:* installment. *Waivers:* senior citizens and employees or children of employees.

Financial Aid In 2001, 120 Federal Work-Study jobs (averaging $1000).

Applying *Options:* common application, early admission, deferred entrance. *Required:* high school transcript. *Application deadline:* rolling (freshmen), rolling (transfers). *Notification:* continuous (freshmen).

Admissions Contact Ms. Kim Lay, Coordinator/Advisor of Enrollment Services, Coffeyville Community College, 400 West 11th, Coffeyville, KS 67337. *Phone:* 620-252-7155. *Fax:* 620-252-7098. *E-mail:* be_a_raven@raven.ccc.cc.ks.us.

Colby Community College
Colby, Kansas

- **State and locally supported** 2-year, founded 1964
- **Calendar** semesters
- **Degree** certificates, diplomas, and associate
- **Small-town** 80-acre campus
- **Endowment** $1.4 million
- **Coed,** 2,166 undergraduate students, 36% full-time, 66% women, 34% men

Colby Community College (continued)

Colby Community College offers 2-year career programs in veterinary technology, physical therapist assistant studies, nursing, office technology, mid-management, dental hygiene, and radio/television; transfer curricula in health, education, arts and letters, behavioral science, business, mass communications, and math/science; preprofessional options in law and medicine; baccalaureate programs in general education and elementary education through area universities; and a College-owned farm operated by agriculture students.

Undergraduates 781 full-time, 1,385 part-time. Students come from 30 states and territories, 6 other countries, 25% are from out of state, 2% African American, 0.3% Asian American or Pacific Islander, 3% Hispanic American, 0.3% Native American, 4% international, 30% live on campus.

Freshmen *Admission:* 750 applied, 750 admitted, 358 enrolled. *Average high school GPA:* 3.2.

Faculty *Total:* 53, 94% full-time, 28% with terminal degrees. *Student/faculty ratio:* 15:1.

Majors Accounting; agricultural business; agricultural economics; agricultural education; agricultural sciences; agronomy/crop science; animal sciences; behavioral sciences; biological/physical sciences; biology; broadcast journalism; business administration; business economics; business education; business marketing and marketing management; chemistry; child care/development; computer science; computer science related; criminal justice/law enforcement administration; dental hygiene; early childhood education; earth sciences; education; English; farm/ranch management; forestry; graphic design/commercial art/illustration; history; home economics; humanities; journalism; liberal arts and sciences/liberal studies; library science; mass communications; mathematics; music; music teacher education; nursing; nutrition science; pharmacy; physical education; physical therapy; physical therapy assistant; political science; practical nurse; pre-engineering; psychology; radio/television broadcasting; range management; science education; social work; sociology; theater arts/drama; veterinary sciences; veterinary technology; wildlife biology; zoology.

Academic Programs *Special study options:* academic remediation for entering students, adult/continuing education programs, advanced placement credit, cooperative education, distance learning, internships, part-time degree program, services for LD students, student-designed majors, summer session for credit.

Library Davis Library with 32,000 titles, 350 serial subscriptions, an OPAC.

Computers on Campus 110 computers available on campus for general student use. Internet access, at least one staffed computer lab available.

Student Life *Housing Options:* men-only, women-only. *Activities and Organizations:* drama/theater group, student-run newspaper, radio and television station, choral group, KSNEA, Physical Therapist Assistants Club, Block and Bridle, SVTA, COPNS. *Campus security:* 24-hour emergency response devices and patrols. *Student Services:* health clinic, personal/psychological counseling.

Athletics Member NJCAA. *Intercollegiate sports:* baseball M(s), basketball M(s)/W(s), cross-country running M(s)/W(s), equestrian sports M/W, softball W(s), track and field M(s)/W(s), volleyball W(s), wrestling M(s). *Intramural sports:* basketball M/W, softball M/W, volleyball M/W.

Standardized Tests *Required:* ACT ASSET.

Costs (2001–02) *Tuition:* state resident $1056 full-time, $33 per semester hour part-time; nonresident $2272 full-time, $71 per semester hour part-time. Part-time tuition and fees vary according to location. *Required fees:* $384 full-time, $12 per semester hour. *Room and board:* $3136. Room and board charges vary according to board plan and student level. *Payment plan:* deferred payment. *Waivers:* senior citizens and employees or children of employees.

Financial Aid In 2001, 95 Federal Work-Study jobs (averaging $1500). 30 State and other part-time jobs (averaging $2000).

Applying *Options:* early admission, deferred entrance. *Application fee:* $10. *Required:* high school transcript. *Application deadline:* rolling (freshmen), rolling (transfers). *Notification:* continuous (freshmen).

Admissions Contact Mr. Skip Sharp, Director of Admissions, Colby Community College, 1255 South Range, Colby, KS 67701-4099. *Phone:* 785-462-4690 Ext. 200. *Toll-free phone:* 888-634-9350 Ext. 690. *Fax:* 785-462-4691. *E-mail:* leasa@colbycc.org.

COWLEY COUNTY COMMUNITY COLLEGE AND AREA VOCATIONAL-TECHNICAL SCHOOL

Arkansas City, Kansas

- **State and locally supported** 2-year, founded 1922, part of Kansas State Board of Education
- **Calendar** semesters
- **Degree** certificates, diplomas, and associate
- **Small-town** 19-acre campus
- **Endowment** $1.2 million
- **Coed,** 4,475 undergraduate students

Undergraduates Students come from 16 states and territories, 12 other countries, 4% are from out of state, 7% live on campus.

Faculty *Total:* 216, 23% full-time.

Majors Accounting; agricultural mechanization; agricultural sciences; agronomy/crop science; aircraft mechanic/airframe; art; auto mechanic/technician; business administration; business marketing and marketing management; chemistry; child care/development; computer graphics; corrections; cosmetology; criminal justice/law enforcement administration; drafting; education; elementary education; emergency medical technology; engineering technology; family/consumer studies; farm/ranch management; hotel and restaurant management; industrial arts; industrial radiologic technology; journalism; law enforcement/police science; liberal arts and sciences/liberal studies; machine technology; music; physical education; physical therapy; pre-engineering; recreation/leisure studies; religious studies; retail management; secretarial science; sign language interpretation; social work; theater arts/drama; welding technology.

Academic Programs *Special study options:* academic remediation for entering students, accelerated degree program, adult/continuing education programs, advanced placement credit, cooperative education, distance learning, external degree program, independent study, part-time degree program, student-designed majors, summer session for credit.

Library Renn Memorial Library with 26,000 titles, 100 serial subscriptions.

Computers on Campus 53 computers available on campus for general student use. Internet access, at least one staffed computer lab available.

Student Life *Housing Options:* coed, men-only, women-only. *Activities and Organizations:* drama/theater group, student-run newspaper, choral group, Volunteer Club, Peers Advocating for Wellness, Phi Theta Kappa, Student Government Association, Phi Beta Lambda. *Campus security:* student patrols, late-night transport/escort service, residence hall entrances are locked at night. *Student Services:* health clinic.

Athletics Member NJCAA. *Intercollegiate sports:* baseball M(s), basketball M(s)/W(s), golf M(s), softball W(s), tennis M(s)/W(s), volleyball W(s). *Intramural sports:* basketball M/W, bowling M/W, softball M/W, table tennis M/W, tennis M/W, volleyball M/W.

Standardized Tests *Required for some:* ACT ASSET, ACCUPLACER. *Recommended:* ACT (for placement).

Costs (2001–02) *Tuition:* state resident $1050 full-time, $35 per credit hour part-time; nonresident $2136 full-time, $89 per credit hour part-time. Full-time tuition and fees vary according to reciprocity agreements. Part-time tuition and fees vary according to reciprocity agreements. Oklahoma residents, $1,632 full time; of $68 per credit hour. *Required fees:* $480 full-time, $18 per credit hour. *Room and board:* Room and board charges vary according to board plan. *Payment plan:* installment. *Waivers:* employees or children of employees.

Financial Aid In 2001, 50 Federal Work-Study jobs (averaging $1500). 75 State and other part-time jobs (averaging $2000).

Applying *Options:* early admission, deferred entrance. *Required:* high school transcript. *Application deadline:* rolling (freshmen), rolling (transfers).

Admissions Contact Ms. Sue Saia, Associate Dean of Admissions, Cowley County Community College and Area Vocational-Technical School, 125 South Second, PO Box 1147, Arkansas City, KS 67005-1147. *Phone:* 620-441-5245. *Toll-free phone:* 800-593-CCCC. *Fax:* 620-441-5350. *E-mail:* admissions@cowley.cc.ks.us.

DODGE CITY COMMUNITY COLLEGE

Dodge City, Kansas

- **State and locally supported** 2-year, founded 1935, part of Kansas State Board of Education
- **Calendar** semesters
- **Degree** certificates and associate
- **Small-town** 143-acre campus
- **Coed,** 1,956 undergraduate students

Undergraduates Students come from 20 states and territories, 5 other countries, 20% live on campus.

Faculty *Total:* 163, 34% full-time.

Majors Accounting; agricultural business; agricultural economics; agricultural mechanization; agronomy/crop science; animal sciences; art; athletic training/sports medicine; auto mechanic/technician; behavioral sciences; biological/physical sciences; biology; broadcast journalism; business administration; business marketing and marketing management; chemistry; child care/development; communication equipment technology; computer programming; computer science;

construction technology; cosmetology; criminal justice/law enforcement administration; data processing technology; education; electrical/electronic engineering technology; elementary education; engineering; engineering technology; English; equestrian studies; farm/ranch management; finance; fire science; forestry; history; humanities; industrial arts; industrial technology; information sciences/systems; journalism; legal administrative assistant; liberal arts and sciences/liberal studies; mass communications; mathematics; medical administrative assistant; medical records administration; medical technology; music; music teacher education; nursing; physical education; physical sciences; physical therapy; physics; political science; practical nurse; pre-engineering; pre-pharmacy studies; psychology; radio/television broadcasting; real estate; respiratory therapy; secretarial science; social sciences; social work; speech/rhetorical studies; theater arts/drama; water resources; welding technology; wildlife biology.

Academic Programs *Special study options:* academic remediation for entering students, adult/continuing education programs, advanced placement credit, cooperative education, English as a second language, external degree program, internships, part-time degree program, student-designed majors, summer session for credit.

Library Learning Resource Center with 30,000 titles, 225 serial subscriptions.

Computers on Campus 125 computers available on campus for general student use. Internet access, at least one staffed computer lab available.

Student Life *Housing Options:* coed. *Activities and Organizations:* drama/theater group, student-run newspaper, radio station, choral group. *Student Services:* health clinic, personal/psychological counseling.

Athletics Member NJCAA. *Intercollegiate sports:* baseball M(s), basketball M(s)/W(s), cross-country running M(s)/W(s), equestrian sports M/W, football M(s), golf M(s), softball W(s), volleyball W(s). *Intramural sports:* basketball M/W, bowling M/W, football M, golf M, racquetball M/W, volleyball M/W, weight lifting M/W.

Standardized Tests *Required:* ACT ASSET. *Recommended:* SAT I and SAT II or ACT (for placement).

Costs (2001–02) *Tuition:* state resident $792 full-time, $33 per credit part-time; nonresident $1080 full-time, $45 per credit part-time. *Required fees:* $408 full-time, $17 per credit.

Applying *Options:* common application, early admission, deferred entrance. *Required:* high school transcript. *Application deadline:* rolling (freshmen), rolling (transfers). *Notification:* continuous (freshmen).

Admissions Contact Corbin Strobel, Director of Admissions, Placement, Testing and Student Services Marketing, Dodge City Community College, 2501 North 14th Avenue, Dodge City, KS 67801-2399. *Phone:* 316-225-1321. *Toll-free phone:* 800-742-9519. *Fax:* 316-225-0918. *E-mail:* admin@dccc.dodge-city.cc.ks.us.

DONNELLY COLLEGE
Kansas City, Kansas

- **Independent Roman Catholic** 2-year, founded 1949
- **Calendar** semesters
- **Degree** certificates and associate
- **Urban** 4-acre campus
- **Endowment** $5.0 million
- **Coed,** 626 undergraduate students

Undergraduates Students come from 15 states and territories, 39 other countries, 12% are from out of state, 32% African American, 5% Asian American or Pacific Islander, 24% Hispanic American, 0.4% Native American, 20% international.

Faculty *Total:* 46, 28% full-time, 15% with terminal degrees. *Student/faculty ratio:* 10:1.

Majors Accounting; biological/physical sciences; business administration; computer programming related; computer science; computer science related; data entry/microcomputer applications related; data processing technology; drafting; early childhood education; education; engineering; English; health education; history; liberal arts and sciences/liberal studies; mathematics; nursing; philosophy; physical therapy; political science; psychology.

Academic Programs *Special study options:* academic remediation for entering students, double majors, English as a second language, external degree program, internships, part-time degree program, services for LD students, summer session for credit.

Library Trant Memorial Library with 30,000 titles, 130 serial subscriptions, an OPAC, a Web page.

Computers on Campus 30 computers available on campus for general student use. A campuswide network can be accessed from off campus. Internet access, at least one staffed computer lab available.

Student Life *Housing:* college housing not available. *Campus security:* 24-hour emergency response devices. *Student Services:* personal/psychological counseling.

Costs (2001–02) *Tuition:* $3570 full-time, $137 per credit part-time. *Waivers:* senior citizens and employees or children of employees.

Applying *Options:* early admission, deferred entrance. *Recommended:* high school transcript. *Application deadline:* rolling (freshmen), rolling (transfers).

Admissions Contact Sr. Mary Agnes Patterson, Vice President, Donnelly College, 603 North 13th Street, Kansas City, KS 66102. *Phone:* 913-621-8700. *Fax:* 913-621-0354.

EDUCATION AMERICA, TOPEKA TECHNICAL COLLEGE, TOPEKA CAMPUS
Topeka, Kansas

Admissions Contact 1620 N.W. Gage Boulevard, Topeka, KS 66618.

FORT SCOTT COMMUNITY COLLEGE
Fort Scott, Kansas

- **State and locally supported** 2-year, founded 1919
- **Calendar** semesters
- **Degree** certificates and associate
- **Small-town** 147-acre campus
- **Coed,** 1,900 undergraduate students

Undergraduates Students come from 24 states and territories, 7 other countries, 9% live on campus.

Faculty *Total:* 173, 31% full-time. *Student/faculty ratio:* 28:1.

Majors Accounting; agricultural business; agricultural economics; agricultural education; agricultural mechanization; agricultural sciences; agronomy/crop science; animal sciences; architectural engineering technology; athletic training/sports medicine; business administration; computer science; cosmetology; criminal justice/law enforcement administration; drafting; education; electrical/electronic engineering technology; emergency medical technology; graphic design/commercial art/illustration; industrial arts; legal administrative assistant; liberal arts and sciences/liberal studies; medical administrative assistant; medical technology; music; nursing; photography; physical sciences; public policy analysis; quality control technology; retail management; secretarial science; teacher assistant/aide; transportation technology; water resources; welding technology.

Academic Programs *Special study options:* academic remediation for entering students, adult/continuing education programs, advanced placement credit, cooperative education, distance learning, English as a second language, external degree program, independent study, internships, part-time degree program, services for LD students, student-designed majors, study abroad, summer session for credit. *ROTC:* Army (c).

Library Learning Resource Center with 25,308 titles, 124 serial subscriptions, an OPAC.

Computers on Campus 95 computers available on campus for general student use. Internet access, at least one staffed computer lab available.

Student Life *Housing Options:* coed. *Activities and Organizations:* drama/theater group, choral group, marching band, Aggie Club, Student Nurses Association, student government, Soccer Club, Phi Theta Kappa. *Campus security:* controlled dormitory access, evening security from 9 pm to 6am. *Student Services:* personal/psychological counseling.

Athletics Member NJCAA. *Intercollegiate sports:* baseball M(s), basketball M(s)/W(s), football M(s), softball W(s), volleyball W(s). *Intramural sports:* basketball M/W, racquetball M/W, soccer M/W, softball M/W, table tennis M/W, tennis M/W, volleyball M/W, weight lifting M/W.

Standardized Tests *Required:* ACT ASSET. *Required for some:* ACT (for placement).

Costs (2001–02) *Tuition:* state resident $1500 full-time, $50 per semester hour part-time; nonresident $3180 full-time, $106 per semester hour part-time. *Required fees:* $150 full-time.

Applying *Options:* early admission, deferred entrance. *Application deadlines:* 8/15 (freshmen), 8/15 (transfers).

Admissions Contact Mrs. Mert Barrows, Director of Admissions, Fort Scott Community College, 2108 South Horton, Fort Scott, KS 66701. *Phone:* 316-223-2700 Ext. 353. *Toll-free phone:* 800-874-3722 Ext. 87 (in-state); 800-874-3722 (out-of-state). *E-mail:* mertb@fsccax.ftscott.cc.ks.us.

GARDEN CITY COMMUNITY COLLEGE

Garden City, Kansas

- **County-supported** 2-year, founded 1919, part of Kansas Board of Regents
- **Calendar** semesters
- **Degree** certificates and associate
- **Rural** 12-acre campus
- **Endowment** $3.6 million
- **Coed,** 2,047 undergraduate students, 44% full-time, 57% women, 43% men

Undergraduates 905 full-time, 1,142 part-time. Students come from 32 states and territories, 8 other countries, 8% are from out of state, 12% live on campus. *Retention:* 78% of 2001 full-time freshmen returned.

Freshmen *Admission:* 1,061 applied, 1,061 admitted, 435 enrolled. *Average high school GPA:* 2.4.

Faculty *Total:* 157, 44% full-time, 6% with terminal degrees. *Student/faculty ratio:* 17:1.

Majors Accounting; agricultural business; agricultural economics; agricultural mechanization; agricultural mechanization related; agricultural sciences; athletic training/sports medicine; auto mechanic/technician; biological/physical sciences; business administration; business marketing and marketing management; business systems networking/ telecommunications; ceramic arts; child care/ development; computer engineering technology; computer graphics; computer programming; computer science; cosmetology; criminal justice/law enforcement administration; developmental/child psychology; drafting; education; electrical/ electronic engineering technology; elementary education; emergency medical technology; engineering; engineering technology; English; family/community studies; farm/ranch management; fashion design/illustration; fashion merchandising; fine/studio arts; graphic design/commercial art/illustration; health/physical education/fitness related; home economics; humanities; industrial arts; industrial technology; information sciences/systems; interior design; journalism; law enforcement/police science; legal administrative assistant; liberal arts and sciences/ liberal studies; mathematics; mechanical design technology; mechanical engineering technology; metal/jewelry arts; music; nursing; physical education; pre-engineering; retailing operations; retail management; secretarial science; social sciences; sociology; speech/rhetorical studies; teacher assistant/aide; theater arts/drama; trade/industrial education; welding technology.

Academic Programs *Special study options:* academic remediation for entering students, adult/continuing education programs, advanced placement credit, distance learning, English as a second language, external degree program, part-time degree program, services for LD students, student-designed majors, summer session for credit.

Library Saffell Library with 43,987 titles, 116 serial subscriptions, 303 audiovisual materials, an OPAC, a Web page.

Computers on Campus 150 computers available on campus for general student use. A campuswide network can be accessed from student residence rooms. Internet access, at least one staffed computer lab available.

Student Life *Housing Options:* coed. *Activities and Organizations:* drama/ theater group, student-run newspaper, choral group, student government, Hispanic American Leadership Organization, Business Professionals of America, Criminal Justice Organization, Phi Theta Kappa. *Campus security:* 24-hour emergency response devices and patrols, student patrols, late-night transport/ escort service, controlled dormitory access. *Student Services:* health clinic, personal/psychological counseling.

Athletics Member NJCAA. *Intercollegiate sports:* baseball M(s), basketball M(s)/W(s), cross-country running M(s)/W(s), football M(s), softball W(s), track and field M(s)/W(s), volleyball W(s). *Intramural sports:* archery M/W, basketball M/W, bowling M/W, football M/W, golf M/W, racquetball M/W, table tennis M/W, tennis M/W, track and field M/W, volleyball M/W.

Standardized Tests *Recommended:* ACT (for admission).

Costs (2002–03) *Tuition:* state resident $1088 full-time, $34 per credit hour part-time; nonresident $65 per credit hour part-time. Full-time tuition and fees vary according to course load. Part-time tuition and fees vary according to course load. *Required fees:* $512 full-time, $16 per credit hour. *Room and board:* $3800. Room and board charges vary according to housing facility. *Payment plans:* installment, deferred payment. *Waivers:* senior citizens and employees or children of employees.

Financial Aid In 2001, 75 Federal Work-Study jobs (averaging $1500). 75 State and other part-time jobs (averaging $1500).

Applying *Options:* deferred entrance. *Required:* high school transcript. *Application deadline:* rolling (freshmen), rolling (transfers).

Admissions Contact Ms. Nikki Geier, Director of Admissions, Garden City Community College, 801 Campus Drive, Garden City, KS 67846-6399. *Phone:* 620-276-7611 Ext. 531. *E-mail:* ngeier@gccc.cc.ks.us.

HESSTON COLLEGE

Hesston, Kansas

- **Independent Mennonite** 2-year, founded 1909
- **Calendar** semesters
- **Degree** associate
- **Small-town** 50-acre campus with easy access to Wichita
- **Endowment** $7.6 million
- **Coed,** 445 undergraduate students, 87% full-time, 47% women, 53% men

Undergraduates 389 full-time, 56 part-time. Students come from 23 states and territories, 15 other countries, 32% are from out of state, 3% African American, 1% Asian American or Pacific Islander, 2% Hispanic American, 12% international, 11% transferred in, 71% live on campus. *Retention:* 80% of 2001 full-time freshmen returned.

Freshmen *Admission:* 471 applied, 471 admitted, 169 enrolled. *Average high school GPA:* 3.22. *Test scores:* SAT verbal scores over 500: 54%; SAT math scores over 500: 62%; ACT scores over 18: 87%; SAT verbal scores over 600: 15%; SAT math scores over 600: 20%; ACT scores over 24: 47%; SAT math scores over 700: 5%; ACT scores over 30: 9%.

Faculty *Total:* 51, 73% full-time, 20% with terminal degrees. *Student/faculty ratio:* 11:1.

Majors Aviation technology; biblical studies; business administration; computer/ information technology services administration and management related; early childhood education; liberal arts and sciences/liberal studies; nursing; pastoral counseling.

Academic Programs *Special study options:* academic remediation for entering students, advanced placement credit, cooperative education, double majors, English as a second language, independent study, internships, part-time degree program, services for LD students, summer session for credit.

Library Mary Miller Library with 35,000 titles, 234 serial subscriptions, 2,409 audiovisual materials, an OPAC, a Web page.

Computers on Campus 67 computers available on campus for general student use. A campuswide network can be accessed from student residence rooms and from off campus. Internet access, at least one staffed computer lab available.

Student Life *Housing:* on-campus residence required through sophomore year. *Options:* men-only, women-only. *Activities and Organizations:* drama/theater group, student-run newspaper, choral group. *Campus security:* 24-hour emergency response devices. *Student Services:* personal/psychological counseling.

Athletics Member NJCAA. *Intercollegiate sports:* baseball M(s), basketball M(s)/W(s), soccer M(s), softball W, tennis M/W, volleyball W(s). *Intramural sports:* basketball M/W, soccer M/W, softball W, tennis M/W, volleyball M/W.

Costs (2002–03) *Comprehensive fee:* $18,218 includes full-time tuition ($12,938), mandatory fees ($220), and room and board ($5060). Part-time tuition: $540 per hour. Part-time tuition and fees vary according to course load. *Required fees:* $55 per term part-time. *Payment plan:* installment. *Waivers:* senior citizens and employees or children of employees.

Financial Aid In 2001, 120 Federal Work-Study jobs (averaging $800).

Applying *Options:* early admission, deferred entrance. *Application fee:* $15. *Required:* high school transcript, letters of recommendation. *Required for some:* interview. *Application deadline:* rolling (freshmen), rolling (transfers).

Admissions Contact Mr. Clark Roth, Vice President for Admissions, Hesston College, Box 3000, Hesston, KS 67062. *Phone:* 620-327-8222. *Toll-free phone:* 800-995-2757. *Fax:* 620-327-8300. *E-mail:* admissions@hesston.edu.

HIGHLAND COMMUNITY COLLEGE

Highland, Kansas

- **State and locally supported** 2-year, founded 1858, part of Kansas Community College System
- **Calendar** semesters
- **Degree** certificates and associate
- **Rural** 20-acre campus
- **Coed,** 2,673 undergraduate students

Undergraduates Students come from 9 states and territories.

Faculty *Total:* 226, 15% full-time.

Majors Accounting; advertising; agricultural business; agricultural economics; agricultural education; agricultural sciences; agronomy/crop science; animal sciences; art; athletic training/sports medicine; auto mechanic/technician; biology; business administration; business education; carpentry; chemistry; computer science; construction technology; criminal justice/law enforcement administration; cytotechnology; dairy science; data processing technology; dental hygiene; drafting; education; emergency medical technology; English; farm/ranch management; fashion design/illustration; food sciences; forestry; geology; graphic design/commercial art/illustration; health education; history; home economics; industrial arts; industrial radiologic technology; information sciences/systems; journalism; law enforcement/police science; legal administrative assistant; liberal arts and sciences/liberal studies; library science; mathematics; medical administrative assistant; medical records administration; medical technology; mortuary science; music; natural resources conservation; nursing; occupational therapy; pharmacy; physical education; physical sciences; physical therapy; political science; pre-engineering; psychology; respiratory therapy; secretarial science; social work; sociology; telecommunications; textile arts; theater arts/drama; theology; veterinary sciences.

Academic Programs *Special study options:* academic remediation for entering students, adult/continuing education programs, advanced placement credit, cooperative education, internships, off-campus study, part-time degree program, services for LD students, student-designed majors, summer session for credit. *ROTC:* Army (c).

Library 30,000 titles, 268 serial subscriptions.

Computers on Campus 94 computers available on campus for general student use. At least one staffed computer lab available.

Student Life *Housing Options:* coed. *Activities and Organizations:* drama/theater group, student-run newspaper.

Athletics Member NJCAA. *Intercollegiate sports:* basketball M(s)/W(s), cross-country running M(s)/W(s), football M(s), golf M(s), track and field M(s)/W(s), volleyball W(s). *Intramural sports:* basketball M/W, cross-country running M/W, football M, golf M, tennis M/W, track and field M/W, volleyball M/W.

Standardized Tests *Required:* ACT ASSET. *Recommended:* ACT (for placement).

Costs (2001–02) *Tuition:* area resident $720 full-time, $30 per credit hour part-time; state resident $792 full-time, $33 per credit hour part-time; nonresident $2088 full-time, $87 per credit hour part-time. *Required fees:* $648 full-time, $27 per credit hour. *Room and board:* $3340. Room and board charges vary according to board plan and housing facility.

Financial Aid In 2001, 100 Federal Work-Study jobs (averaging $2000). 20 State and other part-time jobs (averaging $1000).

Applying *Options:* early admission. *Required:* high school transcript. *Application deadlines:* 8/20 (freshmen), 8/20 (transfers). *Notification:* continuous (freshmen).

Admissions Contact Mr. David Reist, Dean of Student Services, Highland Community College, 606 West Main Street, Highland, KS 66035. *Phone:* 785-442-6020. *Fax:* 785-442-6100. *E-mail:* dreist@highland.cc.ks.us.

HUTCHINSON COMMUNITY COLLEGE AND AREA VOCATIONAL SCHOOL

Hutchinson, Kansas

- **State and locally supported** 2-year, founded 1928, part of Kansas Board of Regents
- **Calendar** semesters
- **Degree** certificates and associate
- **Small-town** 47-acre campus
- **Endowment** $3.1 million
- **Coed,** 3,733 undergraduate students, 48% full-time, 57% women, 43% men

Undergraduates 1,798 full-time, 1,935 part-time. Students come from 23 states and territories, 17 other countries, 2% are from out of state, 5% African American, 0.7% Asian American or Pacific Islander, 5% Hispanic American, 1% Native American, 0.6% international, 12% transferred in, 10% live on campus. *Retention:* 62% of 2001 full-time freshmen returned.

Freshmen *Admission:* 1,607 applied, 1,607 admitted, 1,236 enrolled. *Average high school GPA:* 2.83. *Test scores:* ACT scores over 18: 69%; ACT scores over 24: 20%; ACT scores over 30: 1%.

Faculty *Total:* 287, 36% full-time, 6% with terminal degrees. *Student/faculty ratio:* 14:1.

Majors Agricultural business; agricultural mechanization; agricultural sciences; auto body repair; auto mechanic/technician; biology; business; carpentry; communication equipment technology; communications; computer/information sciences; drafting; education; educational media technology; electrical equipment installation/repair; emergency medical technology; engineering; English; farm/ranch management; financial services marketing; fire science; foreign languages/literatures; general retailing/wholesaling; graphic/printing equipment; home economics; industrial technology; law enforcement/police science; liberal arts and sciences/liberal studies; machine technology; management information systems/business data processing; mathematics; medical radiologic technology; medical records technology; nursing; paralegal/legal assistant; physical sciences; psychology; radio/television broadcasting; secretarial science; social sciences; visual/performing arts; welding technology.

Academic Programs *Special study options:* academic remediation for entering students, adult/continuing education programs, advanced placement credit, cooperative education, distance learning, double majors, English as a second language, honors programs, independent study, internships, part-time degree program, services for LD students, student-designed majors, summer session for credit. *ROTC:* Army (c).

Library John F. Kennedy Library plus 1 other with 43,487 titles, 258 serial subscriptions, 2,746 audiovisual materials, an OPAC, a Web page.

Computers on Campus 438 computers available on campus for general student use. A campuswide network can be accessed from off campus. Internet access, at least one staffed computer lab available.

Student Life *Housing Options:* men-only, women-only. *Activities and Organizations:* drama/theater group, student-run newspaper, choral group, Student Government Association, Black Cultural Society, Hispanic-American Leadership Organization, Hutchinson Christian Fellowship, Campus Crusade for Christ. *Campus security:* 24-hour emergency response devices and patrols, student patrols, late-night transport/escort service, controlled dormitory access. *Student Services:* health clinic, personal/psychological counseling.

Athletics Member NJCAA. *Intercollegiate sports:* baseball M(s), basketball M(s)/W(s), cross-country running M(s)/W(s), football M(s), golf M(s), softball W(s), tennis M(s)/W(s), track and field M(s)/W(s), volleyball W(s). *Intramural sports:* badminton M/W, basketball M/W, bowling M/W, football M/W, racquetball M/W, soccer M/W, tennis M/W, track and field M/W, volleyball M/W.

Standardized Tests *Required for some:* ACT (for placement), ACT ASSET, ACT COMPASS, ACCUPLACER. *Recommended:* ACT (for placement).

Costs (2001–02) *Tuition:* state resident $1184 full-time, $37 per credit hour part-time; nonresident $2784 full-time, $87 per credit hour part-time. *Required fees:* $384 full-time, $12 per credit hour. *Room and board:* $3364. Room and board charges vary according to board plan. *Payment plan:* deferred payment. *Waivers:* senior citizens and employees or children of employees.

Financial Aid In 2001, 45 Federal Work-Study jobs (averaging $2040).

Applying *Options:* electronic application, early admission, deferred entrance. *Required for some:* interview. *Recommended:* high school transcript. *Application deadline:* rolling (freshmen), rolling (transfers).

Admissions Contact Ms. Lori Bair, Director of Admissions, Hutchinson Community College and Area Vocational School, 1300 North Plum, Hutchinson, KS 67501. *Phone:* 620-665-3536. *Toll-free phone:* 800-289-3501. *Fax:* 620-665-3301. *E-mail:* bairl@hutchcc.edu.

INDEPENDENCE COMMUNITY COLLEGE

Independence, Kansas

- **State-supported** 2-year, founded 1925, part of Kansas State Board of Education
- **Calendar** semesters
- **Degree** certificates and associate
- **Small-town** 68-acre campus
- **Coed,** 1,022 undergraduate students, 48% full-time, 61% women, 39% men

Undergraduates 494 full-time, 528 part-time. Students come from 16 states and territories, 19 other countries, 8% are from out of state, 9% African American, 0.3% Asian American or Pacific Islander, 3% Hispanic American, 2% Native American, 4% international, 10% live on campus.

Freshmen *Admission:* 731 enrolled.

Faculty *Total:* 49, 63% full-time, 12% with terminal degrees.

Majors Accounting; art education; athletic training/sports medicine; biological/physical sciences; biology; business administration; business education; chemistry; child care/development; civil engineering technology; cosmetology; data processing technology; drafting; early childhood education; electrical/electronic engineering technology; elementary education; emergency medical technology; engineering; engineering technology; English; finance; French; history; humanities; liberal arts and sciences/liberal studies; mathematics; modern languages; music; music business management/merchandising; music teacher education; natural sciences; physical education; physical sciences; political science; pre-engineering; psychology; science education; secretarial science; sociology; Spanish.

Academic Programs *Special study options:* academic remediation for entering students, adult/continuing education programs, advanced placement credit, cooperative education, English as a second language, internships, part-time degree program, student-designed majors, summer session for credit.

Library Independence Community College Library plus 1 other with 32,372 titles, 166 serial subscriptions.

Independence Community College (continued)

Computers on Campus 75 computers available on campus for general student use. A campuswide network can be accessed from off campus. Internet access, at least one staffed computer lab available.

Student Life *Activities and Organizations:* drama/theater group, student-run newspaper, choral group, Student Senate, Phi Theta Kappa, Student Ambassadors, Campus Christians, multicultural student organization. *Campus security:* night patrol. *Student Services:* personal/psychological counseling.

Athletics Member NJCAA. *Intercollegiate sports:* baseball M(s), basketball M(s)/W(s), football M(s), golf M(s), softball W, tennis M(s)/W(s), track and field M(s)/W(s), volleyball W(s). *Intramural sports:* basketball M/W.

Standardized Tests *Recommended:* SAT I or ACT (for placement).

Costs (2001–02) *Tuition:* state resident $44 per semester hour part-time; nonresident $49 per semester hour part-time. *Room and board:* $3600. *Payment plans:* installment, deferred payment. *Waivers:* adult students, senior citizens, and employees or children of employees.

Financial Aid In 2001, 85 Federal Work-Study jobs (averaging $900).

Applying *Options:* common application, early admission. *Required:* high school transcript. *Application deadline:* rolling (freshmen), rolling (transfers).

Admissions Contact Miss Dixie Schierlman, Dean of Student Services, Independence Community College, PO Box 708, Independence, KS 67301. *Phone:* 620-331-4100. *Toll-free phone:* 800-842-6063. *Fax:* 620-331-5344. *E-mail:* admissions@indycc.net.

JOHNSON COUNTY COMMUNITY COLLEGE
Overland Park, Kansas

- **State and locally supported** 2-year, founded 1967, part of Kansas State Board of Education
- **Calendar** semesters
- **Degree** certificates and associate
- **Suburban** 220-acre campus with easy access to Kansas City
- **Endowment** $4.4 million
- **Coed,** 17,776 undergraduate students

Undergraduates Students come from 26 states and territories, 36 other countries, 5% are from out of state.

Faculty *Total:* 797, 37% full-time. *Student/faculty ratio:* 19:1.

Majors Accounting technician; aircraft mechanic/airframe; auto mechanic/technician; business administration; business computer programming; business systems networking/ telecommunications; chemical technology; civil engineering technology; cosmetology; dental hygiene; drafting; education; electrical/power transmission installation; emergency medical technology; entrepreneurship; fire services administration; graphic design/commercial art/illustration; heating/air conditioning/refrigeration technology; hospitality management; hotel and restaurant management; law enforcement/police science; liberal arts and sciences/liberal studies; machine technology; medical records technology; nurse assistant/aide; nursing; occupational therapy assistant; paralegal/legal assistant; physical therapy assistant; practical nurse; respiratory therapy; retailing operations; secretarial science; sign language interpretation; travel/tourism management; veterinary technology.

Academic Programs *Special study options:* academic remediation for entering students, adult/continuing education programs, advanced placement credit, cooperative education, distance learning, double majors, English as a second language, honors programs, independent study, internships, off-campus study, part-time degree program, services for LD students, student-designed majors, summer session for credit.

Library Johnson County Community College Library with 89,400 titles, 708 serial subscriptions, 4,770 audiovisual materials, an OPAC, a Web page.

Computers on Campus 800 computers available on campus for general student use. A campuswide network can be accessed from off campus. Internet access, online (class) registration, at least one staffed computer lab available.

Student Life *Housing:* college housing not available. *Activities and Organizations:* drama/theater group, student-run newspaper. *Campus security:* 24-hour emergency response devices and patrols, late-night transport/escort service.

Athletics Member NJCAA. *Intercollegiate sports:* baseball M(s), basketball M(s)/W(s), cross-country running M(s)/W(s), soccer M(s), softball W(s), tennis M(s)/W(s), track and field M(s)/W(s), volleyball W(s). *Intramural sports:* basketball M/W, soccer M, tennis M/W, volleyball M/W.

Standardized Tests *Required for some:* ACT (for placement), ACT ASSET.

Costs (2001–02) *Tuition:* area resident $1392 full-time, $58 per credit hour part-time; state resident $1752 full-time, $73 per credit hour part-time; nonresident $3336 full-time, $139 per credit hour part-time.

Financial Aid In 2001, 85 Federal Work-Study jobs (averaging $4000).

Applying *Options:* early admission. *Application fee:* $10. *Required for some:* high school transcript. *Application deadline:* rolling (freshmen), rolling (transfers). *Notification:* continuous (freshmen).

Admissions Contact Dr. Charles J. Carlsen, President, Johnson County Community College, 12345 College Boulevard, Overland Park, KS 66210-1299. *Phone:* 913-469-8500 Ext. 3806.

KANSAS CITY KANSAS COMMUNITY COLLEGE
Kansas City, Kansas

- **State and locally supported** 2-year, founded 1923
- **Calendar** semesters
- **Degree** certificates, diplomas, and associate
- **Urban** 148-acre campus
- **Endowment** $5.0 million
- **Coed,** 5,240 undergraduate students, 30% full-time, 64% women, 36% men

Undergraduates 1,574 full-time, 3,666 part-time. Students come from 14 states and territories, 15 other countries, 3% are from out of state, 26% African American, 2% Asian American or Pacific Islander, 6% Hispanic American, 0.7% Native American, 1% international, 4% transferred in.

Freshmen *Admission:* 749 admitted, 749 enrolled.

Faculty *Total:* 347, 33% full-time. *Student/faculty ratio:* 15:1.

Majors Accounting; alcohol/drug abuse counseling; biology; business; business administration; business marketing and marketing management; chemistry; child care/guidance; computer/information sciences; computer/information technology services administration and management related; computer programming related; computer programming (specific applications); computer science related; computer/technical support; corrections; data processing technology; data warehousing/mining/database administration; drafting; electrical/electronic engineering technology; elementary education; emergency medical technology; engineering; environmental technology; fire science; journalism; law enforcement/police science; liberal arts and sciences/liberal studies; mathematics; mortuary science; nursing; occupational therapy assistant; paralegal/legal assistant; physical education; physical therapy assistant; physics; respiratory therapy; robotics; secretarial science; telecommunications; theater arts/drama; visual/performing arts; Web/multimedia management/webmaster; Web page, digital/multimedia and information resources design; women's studies.

Academic Programs *Special study options:* academic remediation for entering students, accelerated degree program, adult/continuing education programs, advanced placement credit, cooperative education, distance learning, double majors, English as a second language, external degree program, freshman honors college, honors programs, independent study, internships, off-campus study, part-time degree program, services for LD students, student-designed majors, summer session for credit.

Library Kansas City Kansas Community College Library with 65,000 titles, 400 serial subscriptions, 22,000 audiovisual materials, an OPAC, a Web page.

Computers on Campus 500 computers available on campus for general student use. Internet access, at least one staffed computer lab available.

Student Life *Housing:* college housing not available. *Activities and Organizations:* drama/theater group, student-run newspaper, television station, choral group, Student Senate, Phi Theta Kappa, Sigma Phi Sigma, International Student Association, Student Nurses Association. *Campus security:* 24-hour emergency response devices and patrols, student patrols, late-night transport/escort service. *Student Services:* health clinic, personal/psychological counseling, women's center.

Athletics Member NJCAA. *Intercollegiate sports:* baseball M(s), basketball M(s)/W(s), cross-country running M(s)/W(s), golf M(s), soccer M(s), softball W(s), track and field M(s)/W(s), volleyball W(s).

Standardized Tests *Required:* ACCUPLACER.

Costs (2001–02) *Tuition:* state resident $1036 full-time, $37 per credit hour part-time; nonresident $3108 full-time, $111 per credit hour part-time. *Required fees:* $224 full-time, $8 per credit hour. *Payment plan:* installment. *Waivers:* employees or children of employees.

Financial Aid In 2001, 125 Federal Work-Study jobs (averaging $3000).

Applying *Options:* common application, electronic application, early admission, deferred entrance. *Required:* high school transcript. *Application deadline:* rolling (freshmen), rolling (transfers). *Notification:* continuous (freshmen).

Admissions Contact Ms. Sherri Neff, Assistant Director of Admissions, Kansas City Kansas Community College, 7250 State Avenue, Kansas City, KS 66112. *Phone:* 913-288-7201. *Fax:* 913-288-7646. *E-mail:* admiss@toto.net.

Labette Community College

Parsons, Kansas

- **State and locally supported** 2-year, founded 1923, part of Kansas State Board of Education
- **Calendar** semesters
- **Degree** certificates and associate
- **Small-town** 4-acre campus
- **Coed,** 1,354 undergraduate students

Undergraduates Students come from 7 states and territories, 4 other countries.
Faculty *Total:* 208, 15% full-time.
Majors Accounting; art; behavioral sciences; biology; business administration; chemistry; child care/development; computer science; criminal justice/law enforcement administration; data processing technology; drafting; early childhood education; education; elementary education; English; fire science; graphic design/commercial art/illustration; heating/air conditioning/refrigeration; history; industrial radiologic technology; industrial technology; law enforcement/police science; legal administrative assistant; liberal arts and sciences/liberal studies; mathematics; medical administrative assistant; music; nursing; physical education; pre-engineering; respiratory therapy; secretarial science; social sciences.
Academic Programs *Special study options:* academic remediation for entering students, accelerated degree program, adult/continuing education programs, advanced placement credit, cooperative education, distance learning, double majors, independent study, internships, off-campus study, part-time degree program, services for LD students, summer session for credit. *ROTC:* Army (c).
Library Labette Community College Library with 26,000 titles, 235 serial subscriptions, 542 audiovisual materials, an OPAC, a Web page.
Computers on Campus 66 computers available on campus for general student use. At least one staffed computer lab available.
Student Life *Housing Options:* coed. *Activities and Organizations:* choral group, Adult Women Who Are Returning to Education (AWARE), Phi Beta Lambda. *Student Services:* personal/psychological counseling.
Athletics Member NJCAA. *Intercollegiate sports:* baseball M(s), basketball M(s)/W(s), tennis W(s), volleyball W(s), wrestling M(s).
Standardized Tests *Required:* ACT COMPASS. *Recommended:* ACT (for placement).
Costs (2002–03) *Tuition:* area resident $1110 full-time, $38 per hour part-time; state resident $1110 full-time, $38 per hour part-time; nonresident $2730 full-time, $93 per hour part-time. *Required fees:* $450 full-time, $16 per hour. *Room and board:* $3040.
Financial Aid In 2001, 17 Federal Work-Study jobs (averaging $1172).
Applying *Options:* early admission. *Required for some:* letters of recommendation, interview. *Recommended:* high school transcript. *Application deadline:* rolling (freshmen), rolling (transfers). *Notification:* continuous (freshmen).
Admissions Contact Dr. Wayne Hatcher, Dean of Student Services, Labette Community College, 200 South 14th Street, Parsons, KS 67357. *Phone:* 620-421-6700 Ext. 1264. *Toll-free phone:* 888-LABETTE. *E-mail:* chrisb@labette.cc.ks.us/.

Neosho County Community College

Chanute, Kansas

- **State and locally supported** 2-year, founded 1936, part of Kansas State Board of Education
- **Calendar** semesters
- **Degree** certificates and associate
- **Small-town** 50-acre campus
- **Endowment** $370,000
- **Coed,** 1,519 undergraduate students

Undergraduates Students come from 15 states and territories, 3 other countries, 5% live on campus.
Freshmen *Average high school GPA:* 3.2.
Faculty *Total:* 96.
Majors Accounting; athletic training/sports medicine; biological/physical sciences; business administration; business machine repair; business marketing and marketing management; carpentry; computer science; construction technology; criminal justice/law enforcement administration; electrical/electronic engineering technology; finance; information sciences/systems; law enforcement/police science; liberal arts and sciences/liberal studies; materials science; nursing; physical sciences; practical nurse; pre-engineering; secretarial science; teacher assistant/aide; trade/industrial education; welding technology.
Academic Programs *Special study options:* academic remediation for entering students, adult/continuing education programs, advanced placement credit, part-time degree program, services for LD students, student-designed majors, summer session for credit.
Library Chapman Library with 33,000 titles, 200 serial subscriptions.
Computers on Campus 100 computers available on campus for general student use. At least one staffed computer lab available.
Student Life *Housing:* on-campus residence required for freshman year. *Options:* coed. *Activities and Organizations:* drama/theater group, student-run newspaper, choral group, Business Club, Science Club, Student Nurses Association, Fellowship of Christian Athletes, Nontraditional Student Organization. *Campus security:* controlled dormitory access. *Student Services:* personal/psychological counseling.
Athletics Member NJCAA. *Intercollegiate sports:* baseball M(s), basketball M(s)/W(s), cross-country running M(s)/W(s), softball W(s), track and field M(s), volleyball W(s). *Intramural sports:* basketball M/W, cross-country running M/W, softball M/W, track and field M/W, volleyball M/W.
Standardized Tests *Required:* ACT (for placement).
Costs (2001–02) *Tuition:* state resident $1088 full-time, $34 per credit part-time; nonresident $1536 full-time, $48 per credit part-time.
Financial Aid In 2001, 45 Federal Work-Study jobs (averaging $800).
Applying *Options:* common application, early admission. *Required:* high school transcript. *Application deadlines:* 9/15 (freshmen), 9/15 (transfers). *Notification:* continuous (freshmen).
Admissions Contact Penny Galemore, Assistant Registrar, Neosho County Community College, 800 West 14th Street, Chanute, KS 66720-2699. *Phone:* 316-431-2820. *Toll-free phone:* 800-729-6222. *Fax:* 316-431-6222.

Pratt Community College and Area Vocational School

Pratt, Kansas

- **State and locally supported** 2-year, founded 1938, part of Kansas Board of Regents
- **Calendar** semesters
- **Degree** certificates and associate
- **Rural** 80-acre campus with easy access to Wichita
- **Coed,** 1,374 undergraduate students, 44% full-time, 50% women, 50% men

Undergraduates 603 full-time, 771 part-time. Students come from 17 states and territories, 3 other countries.
Freshmen *Admission:* 935 applied, 935 admitted, 222 enrolled.
Faculty *Total:* 96, 48% full-time, 8% with terminal degrees. *Student/faculty ratio:* 13:1.
Majors Accounting; agricultural animal husbandry/production management; agricultural business; agricultural economics; agricultural education; agricultural mechanization; agricultural sciences; animal sciences; applied art; art; art education; athletic training/sports medicine; auto mechanic/technician; biological/physical sciences; biology; broadcast journalism; business administration; business education; business marketing and marketing management; chemistry; child care/development; computer systems networking/telecommunications; computer/technical support; computer typography/composition; counselor education/guidance; data entry/microcomputer applications; data entry/microcomputer applications related; early childhood education; education; education (K-12); elementary education; energy management technology; English; farm/ranch management; fine/studio arts; fish/game management; graphic design/commercial art/illustration; health education; history; home economics; humanities; human services; industrial arts; liberal arts and sciences/liberal studies; literature; mass communications; mathematics; music; nursing; physical education; physical sciences; pre-engineering; professional studies; psychology; secretarial science; social sciences; social work; sociology; speech/rhetorical studies; speech/theater education; trade/industrial education; welding technology; wildlife biology; wildlife management; word processing.
Academic Programs *Special study options:* academic remediation for entering students, adult/continuing education programs, advanced placement credit, cooperative education, internships, part-time degree program, summer session for credit.
Library 26,000 titles, 250 serial subscriptions, a Web page.
Computers on Campus 100 computers available on campus for general student use. A campuswide network can be accessed from off campus. Internet access, at least one staffed computer lab available.
Student Life *Housing:* on-campus residence required through sophomore year. *Options:* coed, men-only, women-only. *Activities and Organizations:* drama/

Pratt Community College and Area Vocational School (continued)
theater group, student-run newspaper, choral group, Phi Theta Kappa, Student Senate, Baptist Student Union, Block and Bridle, Business Professionals Club. *Campus security:* 24-hour patrols, late-night transport/escort service, controlled dormitory access. *Student Services:* health clinic, personal/psychological counseling.

Athletics Member NJCAA. *Intercollegiate sports:* baseball M(s), basketball M(s)/W(s), cross-country running M(s)/W(s), golf M(s)/W(s), softball W(s), tennis M(s)/W(s), track and field M(s)/W(s), volleyball W(s). *Intramural sports:* badminton M/W, basketball M/W, bowling M/W, softball M/W, table tennis M/W, volleyball M/W, weight lifting M/W.

Standardized Tests *Recommended:* ACT (for placement).

Costs (2002–03) *Tuition:* state resident $992 full-time, $31 per credit hour part-time; nonresident $992 full-time, $31 per credit hour part-time. Full-time tuition and fees vary according to course load. Part-time tuition and fees vary according to course load. *Required fees:* $640 full-time, $20 per credit hour. *Room and board:* $3288. Room and board charges vary according to board plan and housing facility. *Waivers:* employees or children of employees.

Financial Aid In 2001, 83 Federal Work-Study jobs (averaging $800). 47 State and other part-time jobs (averaging $800).

Applying *Options:* common application, early admission. *Required:* high school transcript. *Application deadline:* rolling (freshmen), rolling (transfers).

Admissions Contact Ms. Mary Bolyard, Administrative Assistant, Pratt Community College and Area Vocational School, 348 NE State Road, Pratt, KS 67124. *Phone:* 620-672-5641 Ext. 217. *Toll-free phone:* 800-794-3091. *Fax:* 620-672-5288. *E-mail:* lynnp@pcc.cc.ks.us.

SEWARD COUNTY COMMUNITY COLLEGE
Liberal, Kansas

Admissions Contact Mr. Jon Armstrong, Director of Admissions, Seward County Community College, PO Box 1137, Liberal, KS 67905-1137. *Phone:* 316-624-1951 Ext. 713. *Toll-free phone:* 800-373-9951 Ext. 710. *Fax:* 316-629-2725. *E-mail:* admit@sccc.cc.ks.us.

KENTUCKY

ASHLAND COMMUNITY COLLEGE
Ashland, Kentucky

- **State-supported** 2-year, founded 1937, part of Kentucky Community and Technical College System
- **Calendar** semesters
- **Degree** associate
- **Small-town** 47-acre campus
- **Endowment** $870,926
- **Coed,** 2,626 undergraduate students

Undergraduates Students come from 6 states and territories, 10% are from out of state.

Freshmen *Admission:* 478 applied, 478 admitted. *Average high school GPA:* 2.89.

Faculty *Total:* 85, 61% full-time. *Student/faculty ratio:* 20:1.

Majors Accounting; business administration; engineering technology; information sciences/systems; law enforcement/police science; liberal arts and sciences/liberal studies; management information systems/business data processing; nursing; physical therapy assistant; real estate; respiratory therapy; secretarial science.

Academic Programs *Special study options:* academic remediation for entering students, adult/continuing education programs, advanced placement credit, cooperative education, distance learning, honors programs, internships, off-campus study, part-time degree program, services for LD students, summer session for credit.

Library Joseph and Sylvia Mansbach Memorial Library with 41,379 titles, 391 serial subscriptions, an OPAC.

Computers on Campus 150 computers available on campus for general student use. A campuswide network can be accessed from off campus. Internet access, at least one staffed computer lab available.

Student Life *Housing:* college housing not available. *Activities and Organizations:* drama/theater group, student-run newspaper, choral group, Phi Theta Kappa, Phi Beta Lambda, Kentucky Association of Nursing Students, Baptist Student Union/Students for Christ, Circle K. *Campus security:* 24-hour emergency response devices and patrols, late-night transport/escort service, electronic surveillance of bookstore and business office. *Student Services:* personal/psychological counseling.

Athletics *Intramural sports:* fencing M/W, tennis M/W.

Standardized Tests *Required:* ACT COMPASS. *Recommended:* ACT (for placement).

Costs (2001–02) *Tuition:* state resident $1932 full-time, $64 per credit hour part-time; nonresident $5796 full-time, $192 per credit hour part-time. *Payment plan:* installment. *Waivers:* employees or children of employees.

Financial Aid In 2001, 12 Federal Work-Study jobs (averaging $2500). 1 State and other part-time jobs (averaging $1000).

Applying *Options:* common application, early admission, deferred entrance. *Required:* high school transcript. *Application deadlines:* 8/20 (freshmen), 8/20 (transfers).

Admissions Contact Mrs. Willy McCullough, Dean of Students, Ashland Community College, 1400 College Drive, Ashland, KY 41101. *Phone:* 606-326-2068 Ext. 2. *Toll-free phone:* 800-370-7191. *Fax:* 606-326-2192. *E-mail:* willie.mccullough@kctcs.net.

BECKFIELD COLLEGE
Florence, Kentucky

- **Proprietary** 2-year
- **Calendar** quarters
- **Degree** certificates, diplomas, and associate
- **Coed,** 275 undergraduate students, 100% full-time, 33% women, 67% men

Undergraduates 275 full-time.

Freshmen *Admission:* 72 applied, 275 enrolled.

Faculty *Total:* 26, 15% full-time. *Student/faculty ratio:* 17:1.

Majors Business systems networking/ telecommunications; computer maintenance technology; paralegal/legal assistant.

Costs (2002–03) *Tuition:* $8820 full-time. *Required fees:* $9620 full-time.

Admissions Contact Mr. Ken Leeds, Director of Admissions, Beckfield College, PO Box 143, 8095 Connector Drive, Florence, KY 41022-0143. *Phone:* 859-371-9393.

DAYMAR COLLEGE
Owensboro, Kentucky

- **Proprietary** 2-year, founded 1963
- **Calendar** quarters
- **Degree** certificates, diplomas, and associate
- **Small-town** 1-acre campus
- **Coed,** 357 undergraduate students, 81% full-time, 77% women, 23% men

Undergraduates 288 full-time, 69 part-time. Students come from 2 states and territories, 15% are from out of state, 2% African American, 0.6% Hispanic American.

Freshmen *Admission:* 130 applied, 77 admitted. *Average high school GPA:* 2.95.

Faculty *Total:* 26, 38% full-time, 15% with terminal degrees. *Student/faculty ratio:* 9:1.

Majors Business administration; communication systems installation/repair; computer engineering related; computer graphics; computer hardware engineering; computer/information systems security; computer/information technology services administration and management related; computer installation/repair; computer programming related; computer programming (specific applications); computer programming, vendor/product certification; computer science; computer software and media applications related; computer software engineering; computer systems networking/telecommunications; computer/technical support; data entry/microcomputer applications; data entry/microcomputer applications related; data warehousing/mining/database administration; medical office management; paralegal/legal assistant; secretarial science; system administration; system/networking/LAN/WAN management; Web/multimedia management/webmaster; Web page, digital/multimedia and information resources design; word processing.

Academic Programs *Special study options:* academic remediation for entering students, accelerated degree program, adult/continuing education programs, advanced placement credit, cooperative education, double majors, independent study, internships, part-time degree program, summer session for credit.

Library Learning Resource Center with 3,215 titles, 67 serial subscriptions, 77 audiovisual materials, a Web page.

Computers on Campus 103 computers available on campus for general student use. A campuswide network can be accessed from off campus. Internet access, at least one staffed computer lab available.
Student Life *Housing:* college housing not available. *Activities and Organizations:* student-run newspaper. *Campus security:* 24-hour emergency response devices. *Student Services:* personal/psychological counseling.
Standardized Tests *Required for some:* SAT I or ACT (for admission).
Costs (2001–02) *One-time required fee:* $75. *Tuition:* $5400 full-time, $175 per credit hour part-time. Part-time tuition and fees vary according to course load. *Required fees:* $685 full-time, $60 per course. *Payment plans:* tuition prepayment, installment. *Waivers:* senior citizens and employees or children of employees.
Financial Aid In 2001, 12 Federal Work-Study jobs (averaging $6500).
Applying *Options:* deferred entrance. *Application fee:* $20. *Required:* high school transcript, interview. *Application deadline:* rolling (freshmen), rolling (transfers).
Admissions Contact Mary Ellen Downey, Director of Admissions, Daymar College, 3361 Buckland Square, P.O. Box 22150, Owensboro, KY 42303. *Phone:* 270-926-4040. *Toll-free phone:* 800-960-4090. *Fax:* 270-685-4090. *E-mail:* info@daymarcollege.com.

DRAUGHONS JUNIOR COLLEGE
Bowling Green, Kentucky

- **Proprietary** 2-year, founded 1989
- **Calendar** semesters
- **Degree** diplomas and associate
- **Suburban** campus
- **Coed, primarily women,** 316 undergraduate students, 55% full-time, 89% women, 11% men

Undergraduates 175 full-time, 141 part-time. Students come from 2 states and territories, 1% are from out of state, 17% African American, 0.6% Asian American or Pacific Islander, 0.3% Hispanic American, 9% transferred in.
Freshmen *Admission:* 110 applied, 110 admitted, 98 enrolled. *Average high school GPA:* 3.00.
Faculty *Total:* 25, 36% full-time, 4% with terminal degrees. *Student/faculty ratio:* 10:1.
Majors Accounting; business administration; information sciences/systems; information technology; legal administrative assistant; medical assistant; medical records administration; secretarial science.
Academic Programs *Special study options:* adult/continuing education programs, internships, part-time degree program.
Library Draughons Junior College Library with 5,000 titles, 30 serial subscriptions, 75 audiovisual materials, a Web page.
Computers on Campus 35 computers available on campus for general student use. Online (class) registration, at least one staffed computer lab available.
Student Life *Housing:* college housing not available. *Activities and Organizations:* student-run newspaper, Student Council. *Campus security:* 24-hour emergency response devices. *Student Services:* personal/psychological counseling.
Standardized Tests *Recommended:* SAT I or ACT (for placement).
Costs (2001–02) *Tuition:* Full-time tuition and fees vary according to course load. Part-time tuition and fees vary according to course load. Contact school as tuition varies according to program. *Payment plan:* installment. *Waivers:* employees or children of employees.
Financial Aid In 2001, 3 Federal Work-Study jobs (averaging $1500).
Applying *Options:* common application. *Application fee:* $20. *Required:* high school transcript.
Admissions Contact Ms. Kathy Elson, Admissions Director, Draughons Junior College, 2424 Airway Court, Bowling Green, KY 42103. *Phone:* 270-843-6750. *Fax:* 270-843-6976.

ELIZABETHTOWN COMMUNITY COLLEGE
Elizabethtown, Kentucky

- **State-supported** 2-year, founded 1964, part of Kentucky Community and Technical College System
- **Calendar** semesters
- **Degree** associate
- **Small-town** 40-acre campus with easy access to Louisville
- **Coed, primarily women,** 3,522 undergraduate students, 44% full-time, 68% women, 32% men

Undergraduates Students come from 10 states and territories, 11% African American, 2% Asian American or Pacific Islander, 3% Hispanic American, 1% Native American.
Majors Biological/physical sciences; business administration; child guidance; dental hygiene; finance; information sciences/systems; law enforcement/police science; liberal arts and sciences/liberal studies; nursing; quality control technology; real estate; secretarial science.
Academic Programs *Special study options:* academic remediation for entering students, adult/continuing education programs, advanced placement credit, cooperative education, external degree program, internships, off-campus study, part-time degree program, services for LD students, summer session for credit.
Library Elizabethtown Community College Media Center with 35,175 titles, 240 serial subscriptions, an OPAC.
Computers on Campus 70 computers available on campus for general student use. Internet access, at least one staffed computer lab available.
Student Life *Housing:* college housing not available. *Activities and Organizations:* drama/theater group, student-run newspaper, choral group, Baptist Student Union, Kentucky Association of Nursing Students. *Campus security:* late night security.
Athletics *Intramural sports:* basketball M/W, football M, golf M, soccer M, table tennis M/W, tennis M/W, volleyball M/W.
Standardized Tests *Required for some:* ACT (for admission).
Costs (2001–02) *Tuition:* state resident $1450 full-time, $61 per credit part-time; nonresident $4350 full-time, $183 per credit part-time.
Financial Aid In 2001, 30 Federal Work-Study jobs (averaging $1000).
Applying *Options:* common application, early admission. *Required:* essay or personal statement, high school transcript. *Application deadline:* rolling (freshmen), rolling (transfers). *Notification:* continuous (freshmen).
Admissions Contact Dale Buckles, Director, Elizabethtown Community College, 600 College Street Road, Elizabethtown, KY 42701-3081. *Phone:* 270-769-2371 Ext. 231.

HAZARD COMMUNITY COLLEGE
Hazard, Kentucky

- **State-supported** 2-year, founded 1968, part of Kentucky Community and Technical College System
- **Calendar** semesters
- **Degree** associate
- **Rural** 34-acre campus
- **Coed,** 3,000 undergraduate students

Undergraduates Students come from 3 states and territories, 5% are from out of state.
Faculty *Total:* 160, 63% full-time.
Majors Business administration; computer typography/composition; data processing technology; early childhood education; forest harvesting production technology; information sciences/systems; liberal arts and sciences/liberal studies; management science; medical laboratory technician; medical radiologic technology; nursing; physical therapy assistant; secretarial science.
Academic Programs *Special study options:* academic remediation for entering students, adult/continuing education programs, honors programs, part-time degree program, summer session for credit.
Library 36,550 titles, 160 serial subscriptions.
Computers on Campus 28 computers available on campus for general student use.
Student Life *Housing Options:* coed. *Activities and Organizations:* drama/theater group, choral group. *Campus security:* late-night transport/escort service. *Student Services:* personal/psychological counseling.
Athletics *Intercollegiate sports:* basketball M, softball W.
Standardized Tests *Required:* ACT (for placement).
Costs (2001–02) *Tuition:* state resident $1450 full-time, $61 per credit hour part-time; nonresident $4350 full-time, $183 per credit hour part-time. Part-time tuition and fees vary according to course load.
Applying *Options:* common application, early admission. *Required:* high school transcript. *Application deadline:* rolling (freshmen), rolling (transfers). *Notification:* continuous (freshmen).
Admissions Contact Mr. Steve Jones, Director of Admissions, Hazard Community College, 1 Community College Drive, Hazard, KY 41701-2403. *Phone:* 606-436-5721 Ext. 8076.

HENDERSON COMMUNITY COLLEGE
Henderson, Kentucky

- **State-supported** 2-year, founded 1963, part of Kentucky Community and Technical College System
- **Calendar** semesters
- **Degree** associate
- **Small-town** 120-acre campus
- **Coed,** 1,407 undergraduate students

Undergraduates Students come from 12 states and territories, 1% are from out of state.
Freshmen *Admission:* 1,251 applied, 1,251 admitted.
Faculty *Total:* 101, 48% full-time. *Student/faculty ratio:* 13:1.
Majors Business administration; computer/information technology services administration and management related; computer programming related; computer programming (specific applications); computer programming, vendor/product certification; computer science related; computer systems networking/telecommunications; data entry/microcomputer applications; data entry/microcomputer applications related; data processing technology; electrical/electronic engineering technology; engineering technology; human services; information technology; mass communications; medical technology; nursing; secretarial science; word processing.
Academic Programs *Special study options:* academic remediation for entering students, accelerated degree program, adult/continuing education programs, advanced placement credit, cooperative education, distance learning, double majors, English as a second language, external degree program, independent study, internships, off-campus study, part-time degree program, summer session for credit.
Library Hartfield Learning Resource Center plus 1 other with 30,206 titles, 231 serial subscriptions, 1,053 audiovisual materials, an OPAC, a Web page.
Computers on Campus 200 computers available on campus for general student use. Internet access available.
Student Life *Housing:* college housing not available. *Activities and Organizations:* drama/theater group, student-run radio station. *Campus security:* 24-hour emergency response devices. *Student Services:* personal/psychological counseling.
Athletics *Intramural sports:* basketball M, football M, golf M, softball M/W, table tennis M/W.
Standardized Tests *Required:* ACT (for admission).
Costs (2001–02) *Tuition:* area resident $1230 full-time, $48 per credit hour part-time; state resident $1450 full-time, $61 per credit hour part-time; nonresident $4350 full-time, $183 per credit hour part-time. *Payment plan:* deferred payment. *Waivers:* senior citizens.
Applying *Options:* common application. *Required:* high school transcript. *Required for some:* essay or personal statement, letters of recommendation, interview. *Application deadlines:* 9/1 (freshmen), 9/1 (transfers).
Admissions Contact Ms. Teresa Hamiton, Admissions Counselor, Henderson Community College, 2660 South Green Street, Henderson, KY 42420-4623. *Phone:* 270-827-1867 Ext. 354.

HOPKINSVILLE COMMUNITY COLLEGE
Hopkinsville, Kentucky

- **State-supported** 2-year, founded 1965, part of Kentucky Community and Technical College System
- **Calendar** semesters
- **Degree** certificates, diplomas, and associate
- **Small-town** 70-acre campus with easy access to Nashville
- **Endowment** $2.5 million
- **Coed,** 2,849 undergraduate students, 37% full-time, 63% women, 37% men

Undergraduates Students come from 12 states and territories, 10% are from out of state, 25% African American, 1% Asian American or Pacific Islander, 4% Hispanic American, 0.8% Native American.
Freshmen *Test scores:* ACT scores over 18: 50%; ACT scores over 24: 11%.
Faculty *Total:* 166, 42% full-time, 5% with terminal degrees. *Student/faculty ratio:* 22:1.
Majors Agricultural animal husbandry/production management; business administration; child care services management; early childhood education; electrical/electronic engineering technology; finance; human services; industrial technology; law enforcement/police science; liberal arts and sciences/liberal studies; management information systems/business data processing; mental health/rehabilitation; nursing; secretarial science.
Academic Programs *Special study options:* academic remediation for entering students, adult/continuing education programs, advanced placement credit, distance learning, honors programs, independent study, part-time degree program, summer session for credit.
Library HCC Library plus 1 other with 43,542 titles, 232 serial subscriptions.
Computers on Campus 110 computers available on campus for general student use. A campuswide network can be accessed from off campus. Internet access, at least one staffed computer lab available.
Student Life *Housing:* college housing not available. *Activities and Organizations:* student-run newspaper, television station, Baptist Student Union, Circle K, Minority Student Union, Donovan Scholars, Nursing Club. *Campus security:* 24-hour emergency response devices, late-night transport/escort service.
Athletics *Intramural sports:* basketball M, football M, golf M, table tennis M/W, volleyball M/W.
Standardized Tests *Required:* ACT (for placement), ACT or ACT COMPASS.
Costs (2001–02) *Tuition:* state resident $1450 full-time, $61 per credit hour part-time; nonresident $4350 full-time, $183 per credit hour part-time. *Payment plan:* installment. *Waivers:* senior citizens and employees or children of employees.
Financial Aid In 2001, 30 Federal Work-Study jobs (averaging $1500). *Financial aid deadline:* 6/30.
Applying *Options:* common application, early admission, deferred entrance. *Required for some:* high school transcript, interview. *Application deadline:* rolling (freshmen), rolling (transfers). *Notification:* continuous (freshmen).
Admissions Contact Ms. Ruth Ann Rettie, Registrar, Hopkinsville Community College, PO Box 2100, Hopkinsville, KY 42241-2100. *Phone:* 270-886-3921 Ext. 6197. *E-mail:* admit.record@kctcs.net.

ITT TECHNICAL INSTITUTE
Louisville, Kentucky

- **Proprietary** 2-year, founded 1993, part of ITT Educational Services, Inc
- **Calendar** quarters
- **Degree** associate
- **Suburban** campus
- **Coed, primarily men,** 358 undergraduate students

Majors Computer/information sciences related; computer programming; drafting; electrical/electronic engineering technologies related; information technology.
Student Life *Housing:* college housing not available.
Costs (2001–02) *Tuition:* Full-time tuition and fees vary according to program. Part-time tuition and fees vary according to program. $260—$330 per credit hour.
Applying *Options:* deferred entrance. *Application fee:* $100. *Required:* high school transcript, interview. *Recommended:* letters of recommendation. *Application deadline:* rolling (freshmen), rolling (transfers).
Admissions Contact Mr. Chuck Taylor, Director of Recruitment, ITT Technical Institute, 10509 Timberwood Circle, Suite 100, Louisville, KY 40223. *Phone:* 502-327-7424.

JEFFERSON COMMUNITY COLLEGE
Louisville, Kentucky

- **State-supported** 2-year, founded 1968, part of Kentucky Community and Technical College System
- **Calendar** semesters
- **Degree** certificates and associate
- **Urban** 10-acre campus
- **Coed,** 9,227 undergraduate students

Undergraduates Students come from 24 states and territories, 4 other countries, 3% are from out of state.
Freshmen *Admission:* 7,772 applied, 2,509 admitted.
Faculty *Total:* 463, 45% full-time.
Majors Accounting; applied mathematics; art; art education; auto mechanic/technician; biology; business administration; business education; chemical engineering technology; chemistry; child care/development; civil engineering technology; computer programming; computer science; culinary arts; data processing technology; early childhood education; economics; education; electrical/electronic engineering technology; elementary education; English; fire science; forestry; French; geography; graphic design/commercial art/illustration; history; home economics; home economics education; horticulture science; liberal arts and sciences/liberal studies; mass communications; mathematical statistics; mathemat-

s; mechanical engineering technology; mental health/rehabilitation; music teacher education; nursing; philosophy; physical therapy; political science; real estate; respiratory therapy; social work; sociology; Spanish; zoology.

Academic Programs *Special study options:* academic remediation for entering students, adult/continuing education programs, advanced placement credit, cooperative education, distance learning, English as a second language, external degree program, honors programs, independent study, internships, off-campus study, part-time degree program, services for LD students, summer session for credit. *ROTC:* Army (c).

Library John T. Smith Learning Resource Center with 76,578 titles, 391 serial subscriptions, 15,103 audiovisual materials, an OPAC, a Web page.

Computers on Campus 895 computers available on campus for general student use. A campuswide network can be accessed from off campus. Internet access, at least one staffed computer lab available.

Student Life *Housing:* college housing not available. *Activities and Organizations:* drama/theater group, student-run newspaper. *Campus security:* 24-hour emergency response devices and patrols, late-night transport/escort service. *Student Services:* personal/psychological counseling.

Standardized Tests *Required:* ACT (for placement).

Costs (2002–03) *Tuition:* state resident $768 full-time, $64 per credit hour part-time; nonresident $2304 full-time, $192 per credit hour part-time. *Payment plans:* installment, deferred payment. *Waivers:* senior citizens.

Financial Aid In 2001, 500 Federal Work-Study jobs (averaging $1500).

Applying *Options:* early admission. *Application deadline:* rolling (freshmen), rolling (transfers). *Notification:* continuous (freshmen).

Admissions Contact Maryetta Fisher, Dean of Student Affairs, Jefferson Community College, Jefferson Community College-Office of Admissions, 109 East Broadway, Louisville, KY 40202. *Phone:* 502-213-2136. *Toll-free phone:* 502-213-4000. *Fax:* 502-213-2540.

LOUISVILLE TECHNICAL INSTITUTE
Louisville, Kentucky

- **Proprietary** 2-year, founded 1961, part of Sullivan Colleges System
- **Calendar** quarters
- **Degree** certificates, diplomas, and associate
- **Suburban** 10-acre campus
- **Coed,** 688 undergraduate students, 93% full-time, 37% women, 63% men

Undergraduates 641 full-time, 47 part-time. Students come from 6 states and territories, 17% are from out of state, 7% African American, 0.3% Hispanic American, 3% international, 10% transferred in, 6% live on campus.

Freshmen *Admission:* 287 applied, 135 admitted. *Average high school GPA:* 2.17.

Faculty *Total:* 55, 42% full-time. *Student/faculty ratio:* 10:1.

Majors Architectural drafting; architectural engineering technology; artificial intelligence/robotics; business systems networking/ telecommunications; computer engineering technology; computer graphics; computer graphics; computer hardware engineering; computer/information sciences; computer installation/repair; computer maintenance technology; computer programming, vendor/product certification; computer systems networking/telecommunications; computer/technical support; desktop publishing equipment operation; drafting; drafting/design technology; electrical/electronic engineering technology; electrical equipment installation/repair; engineering-related technology; engineering technology; industrial machinery maintenance/repair; information technology; interior design; interior environments; marine technology; mechanical design technology; mechanical drafting; mechanical engineering technology; robotics; robotics technology; system administration; Web page, digital/multimedia and information resources design.

Academic Programs *Special study options:* academic remediation for entering students, accelerated degree program, adult/continuing education programs, cooperative education, internships, part-time degree program, services for LD students, summer session for credit.

Library Louisville Tech Library plus 1 other with 3,463 titles, 96 serial subscriptions, 242 audiovisual materials, an OPAC.

Computers on Campus 193 computers available on campus for general student use. A campuswide network can be accessed from off campus. Internet access, at least one staffed computer lab available.

Student Life *Housing Options:* men-only, women-only. *Activities and Organizations:* student-run newspaper, ASID, IIDA, ADDA, Robotics International. *Campus security:* late-night transport/escort service.

Athletics *Intramural sports:* basketball M, bowling M/W, softball M.

Costs (2001–02) *Tuition:* $10,980 full-time, $225 per credit hour part-time. Full-time tuition and fees vary according to program. Part-time tuition and fees vary according to program. No tuition increase for student's term of enrollment. *Required fees:* $395 full-time, $18 per credit hour. *Room only:* $3375. *Payment plans:* tuition prepayment, installment. *Waivers:* employees or children of employees.

Applying *Options:* deferred entrance. *Application fee:* $90. *Required:* high school transcript, minimum 2.0 GPA, interview. *Application deadline:* rolling (freshmen), rolling (transfers).

Admissions Contact Mr. David Ritz, Director of Admissions, Louisville Technical Institute, 3901 Atkinson Square Drive, Louisville, KY 40218. *Phone:* 502-456-6509. *Toll-free phone:* 800-884-6528. *E-mail:* dritz@louisvilletech.com.

MADISONVILLE COMMUNITY COLLEGE
Madisonville, Kentucky

- **State-supported** 2-year, founded 1968, part of Kentucky Community and Technical College System
- **Calendar** semesters
- **Degree** certificates, diplomas, and associate
- **Small-town** 150-acre campus
- **Endowment** $3.1 million
- **Coed**

Undergraduates 0.2% are from out of state.

Faculty *Total:* 184, 52% full-time, 8% with terminal degrees.

Majors Accounting; accounting technician; banking; biomedical technology; business administration; computer maintenance technology; electrical/electronic engineering technology; information sciences/systems; law enforcement/police science; mechanical engineering technology; nursing; occupational therapy assistant; physical therapy assistant; radiological science; real estate; respiratory therapy; retail management; secretarial science.

Academic Programs *Special study options:* academic remediation for entering students, adult/continuing education programs, advanced placement credit, cooperative education, distance learning, external degree program, independent study, internships, off-campus study, part-time degree program, services for LD students, summer session for credit.

Library Loman C. Trover Library plus 1 other with 26,793 titles, 227 serial subscriptions, 1,688 audiovisual materials, an OPAC, a Web page.

Computers on Campus 35 computers available on campus for general student use. A campuswide network can be accessed from off campus. Internet access, at least one staffed computer lab available.

Student Life *Housing:* college housing not available. *Activities and Organizations:* drama/theater group, student-run newspaper, choral group, student government, Baptist Student Union, Socratic Society, Student Ambassadors, Academic Team. *Campus security:* 24-hour emergency response devices, late-night transport/escort service, evening patrols. *Student Services:* personal/psychological counseling.

Athletics *Intramural sports:* basketball M/W, volleyball M/W.

Standardized Tests *Required:* ACT (for placement), ACT ASSET.

Costs (2001–02) *Tuition:* $10,570 full-time.

Financial Aid In 2001, 50 Federal Work-Study jobs (averaging $2100). 15 State and other part-time jobs (averaging $1600).

Applying *Options:* electronic application, early admission, deferred entrance. *Required:* high school transcript. *Application deadline:* rolling (freshmen), rolling (transfers). *Notification:* continuous (freshmen).

Admissions Contact Jay Parent, Registrar, Madisonville Community College, 2000 College Drive, Madisonville, KY 42431-9185. *Phone:* 270-821-2250. *Fax:* 502-821-1555. *E-mail:* dmcox@pop.uky.edu.

MAYSVILLE COMMUNITY COLLEGE
Maysville, Kentucky

- **State-supported** 2-year, founded 1967, part of Kentucky Community and Technical College System
- **Calendar** semesters
- **Degree** certificates, diplomas, and associate
- **Rural** 120-acre campus
- **Coed,** 1,393 undergraduate students

Undergraduates Students come from 2 states and territories, 5% are from out of state, 3% African American, 0.1% Asian American or Pacific Islander, 0.1% Hispanic American, 1% Native American.

Freshmen *Admission:* 758 applied, 758 admitted. *Average high school GPA:* 2.50. *Test scores:* ACT scores over 18: 52%; ACT scores over 24: 15%; ACT scores over 30: 6%.

Maysville Community College (continued)

Faculty *Total:* 128, 34% full-time.

Majors Accounting; business administration; business marketing and marketing management; electrical/electronic engineering technology; electromechanical technology; liberal arts and sciences/liberal studies; nursing; respiratory therapy; secretarial science.

Academic Programs *Special study options:* academic remediation for entering students, adult/continuing education programs, advanced placement credit, cooperative education, distance learning, external degree program, independent study, internships, off-campus study, part-time degree program, services for LD students, summer session for credit.

Library Finch Library with 30,398 titles, 288 serial subscriptions, an OPAC, a Web page.

Computers on Campus 37 computers available on campus for general student use. A campuswide network can be accessed from off campus. Internet access, at least one staffed computer lab available.

Student Life *Housing:* college housing not available. *Activities and Organizations:* student-run television station, Student Government Association, Math and Science Club, Retail Marketing Club, Student Education Association. *Campus security:* student patrols, evening parking lot security. *Student Services:* personal/psychological counseling.

Standardized Tests *Required for some:* ACT (for placement).

Costs (2001–02) *Tuition:* state resident $1450 full-time, $61 per credit hour part-time; nonresident $4350 full-time, $183 per credit hour part-time. Part-time tuition and fees vary according to course load. *Payment plan:* deferred payment. *Waivers:* senior citizens and employees or children of employees.

Financial Aid In 2001, 30 Federal Work-Study jobs (averaging $1500).

Applying *Options:* early admission. *Required:* high school transcript. *Application deadline:* rolling (freshmen), rolling (transfers). *Notification:* continuous (freshmen).

Admissions Contact Ms. Patricia K. Massie, Registrar/Admissions Officer, Maysville Community College, 1755 US 68, Maysville, KY 41056. *Phone:* 606-759-7141 Ext. 184. *Fax:* 606-759-5818 Ext. 184. *E-mail:* patee.massie@kctcs.net.

NATIONAL COLLEGE OF BUSINESS & TECHNOLOGY
Lexington, Kentucky

- **Proprietary** 2-year, founded 1947, part of National College of Business and Technology
- **Calendar** quarters
- **Degree** diplomas and associate
- **Urban** campus
- **Coed**

Faculty *Total:* 24, 4% full-time. *Student/faculty ratio:* 10:1.

Majors Accounting; business administration; computer science related; radio/television broadcasting; secretarial science.

Academic Programs *Special study options:* advanced placement credit, double majors, honors programs, internships, part-time degree program, summer session for credit.

Computers on Campus 30 computers available on campus for general student use. Internet access, at least one staffed computer lab available.

Student Life *Housing:* college housing not available. *Student Services:* personal/psychological counseling.

Costs (2002–03) *Tuition:* $5013 full-time, $148 per credit hour part-time. Full-time tuition and fees vary according to course load. Part-time tuition and fees vary according to course load. *Required fees:* $45 full-time, $15 per term part-time. *Payment plans:* installment, deferred payment. *Waivers:* employees or children of employees.

Financial Aid In 2001, 6 Federal Work-Study jobs.

Applying *Options:* electronic application. *Application fee:* $30. *Required:* high school transcript. *Application deadline:* rolling (freshmen), rolling (transfers).

Admissions Contact Ms. Carolyn Howard, Campus Director, National College of Business & Technology, 628 East Main Street, Lexington, KY 40508-2312. *Phone:* 859-266-0401. *Toll-free phone:* 800-664-1886. *Fax:* 859-233-3054. *E-mail:* market@educorp.edu.

NATIONAL COLLEGE OF BUSINESS & TECHNOLOGY
Danville, Kentucky

- **Proprietary** 2-year, founded 1962, part of National College of Business and Technology
- **Calendar** quarters
- **Degree** diplomas and associate
- **Coed**

Faculty *Total:* 24. *Student/faculty ratio:* 10:1.

Majors Accounting; business administration; computer science related; medical assistant; secretarial science.

Academic Programs *Special study options:* advanced placement credit, double majors, honors programs, internships, part-time degree program, services for LD students, summer session for credit.

Computers on Campus 30 computers available on campus for general student use. Internet access, at least one staffed computer lab available.

Student Life *Housing:* college housing not available.

Costs (2002–03) *Tuition:* $5013 full-time, $148 per credit hour part-time. Full-time tuition and fees vary according to course load. Part-time tuition and fees vary according to course load. *Required fees:* $45 full-time, $15 per term part-time. *Payment plans:* installment, deferred payment. *Waivers:* employees or children of employees.

Financial Aid In 2001, 1 Federal Work-Study job.

Applying *Options:* common application, electronic application. *Application fee:* $30. *Required:* high school transcript. *Application deadline:* rolling (freshmen), rolling (transfers).

Admissions Contact Mr. Steve Hardin, Campus Director, National College of Business & Technology, 115 East Lexington Avenue, Danville, KY 40422. *Phone:* 859-236-6991. *Toll-free phone:* 800-664-1886. *Fax:* 859-236-1063. *E-mail:* adm@educorp.edu.

NATIONAL COLLEGE OF BUSINESS & TECHNOLOGY
Florence, Kentucky

- **Proprietary** 2-year, founded 1941, part of National College of Business and Technology
- **Calendar** quarters
- **Degree** diplomas and associate
- **Suburban** campus
- **Coed**

Faculty *Total:* 16, 13% full-time. *Student/faculty ratio:* 10:1.

Majors Accounting; business administration; computer science related; medical assistant; secretarial science.

Academic Programs *Special study options:* advanced placement credit, double majors, honors programs, internships, part-time degree program, services for LD students, summer session for credit.

Computers on Campus 30 computers available on campus for general student use. Internet access, at least one staffed computer lab available.

Student Life *Housing:* college housing not available. *Campus security:* 24-hour emergency response devices.

Costs (2002–03) *Tuition:* $5013 full-time, $148 per credit hour part-time. Full-time tuition and fees vary according to course load. Part-time tuition and fees vary according to course load. *Required fees:* $45 full-time, $15 per term part-time. *Payment plans:* installment, deferred payment. *Waivers:* employees or children of employees.

Financial Aid In 2001, 3 Federal Work-Study jobs.

Applying *Options:* electronic application. *Application fee:* $30. *Required for some:* high school transcript. *Recommended:* interview. *Application deadline:* rolling (freshmen), rolling (transfers).

Admissions Contact Ms. Vicky Barnes, Campus Director, National College of Business & Technology, 7627 Ewing Boulevard, Florence, KY 41042. *Phone:* 859-525-6510. *Toll-free phone:* 800-664-1886. *Fax:* 859-525-8961. *E-mail:* adm@educorp.edu.

NATIONAL COLLEGE OF BUSINESS & TECHNOLOGY
Louisville, Kentucky

- **Proprietary** 2-year, founded 1990, part of National College of Business and Technology
- **Calendar** quarters
- **Degree** diplomas and associate
- **Coed**

Faculty *Total:* 22, 45% full-time. *Student/faculty ratio:* 10:1.
Majors Accounting; business administration; computer science related; health services administration; medical assistant; secretarial science.
Academic Programs *Special study options:* advanced placement credit, double majors, honors programs, internships, part-time degree program, services for LD students, summer session for credit.
Computers on Campus 55 computers available on campus for general student use. Internet access, at least one staffed computer lab available.
Student Life *Housing:* college housing not available.
Costs (2002–03) *Tuition:* $5013 full-time, $148 per credit hour part-time. Full-time tuition and fees vary according to course load. Part-time tuition and fees vary according to course load. *Required fees:* $45 full-time, $15 per term part-time. *Payment plans:* installment, deferred payment. *Waivers:* employees or children of employees.
Financial Aid In 2001, 2 Federal Work-Study jobs.
Applying *Options:* electronic application. *Application fee:* $30. *Required for some:* high school transcript. *Recommended:* interview. *Application deadline:* rolling (freshmen), rolling (transfers). *Notification:* continuous (freshmen).
Admissions Contact Mr. Bob Boutell, Campus Director, National College of Business & Technology, 3950 Dixie Highway, Louisville, KY 40216. *Phone:* 502-447-7634. *Toll-free phone:* 800-664-1886. *Fax:* 502-447-7665. *E-mail:* adm@educorp.edu.

NATIONAL COLLEGE OF BUSINESS & TECHNOLOGY
Pikeville, Kentucky

- **Proprietary** 2-year, founded 1976, part of National College of Business and Technology
- **Calendar** quarters
- **Degree** diplomas and associate
- **Rural** campus
- **Coed**

Faculty *Total:* 12, 17% full-time. *Student/faculty ratio:* 10:1.
Majors Accounting; business administration; computer science related; medical assistant; secretarial science.
Academic Programs *Special study options:* advanced placement credit, double majors, honors programs, internships, part-time degree program, services for LD students, summer session for credit.
Computers on Campus 24 computers available on campus for general student use. Internet access, at least one staffed computer lab available.
Student Life *Housing:* college housing not available.
Costs (2002–03) *Tuition:* $5013 full-time, $148 per credit hour part-time. Full-time tuition and fees vary according to course load. Part-time tuition and fees vary according to course load. *Required fees:* $45 full-time, $15 per term part-time. *Payment plans:* installment, deferred payment. *Waivers:* employees or children of employees.
Financial Aid In 2001, 4 Federal Work-Study jobs.
Applying *Application fee:* $30. *Required for some:* high school transcript. *Recommended:* interview. *Application deadline:* rolling (freshmen), rolling (transfers).
Admissions Contact Ms. Tina Adkins, Campus Director, National College of Business & Technology, 288 South Mayo Trail, Suite 2, Pikeville, KY 41501. *Phone:* 540-986-1800. *Toll-free phone:* 800-664-1886. *Fax:* 606-437-4952. *E-mail:* adm@educorp.edu.

NATIONAL COLLEGE OF BUSINESS & TECHNOLOGY
Richmond, Kentucky

- **Proprietary** 2-year, founded 1951, part of National College of Business and Technology
- **Calendar** quarters
- **Degree** diplomas and associate
- **Suburban** campus
- **Coed**

Faculty *Total:* 15, 20% full-time. *Student/faculty ratio:* 10:1.
Majors Accounting; business administration; computer science related; medical assistant; secretarial science.
Academic Programs *Special study options:* advanced placement credit, double majors, honors programs, internships, part-time degree program, summer session for credit.
Computers on Campus 20 computers available on campus for general student use. Internet access, at least one staffed computer lab available.
Student Life *Housing:* college housing not available.
Costs (2002–03) *Tuition:* $5013 full-time, $148 per credit hour part-time. Full-time tuition and fees vary according to course load. Part-time tuition and fees vary according to course load. *Required fees:* $45 full-time, $15 per term part-time. *Payment plans:* installment, deferred payment. *Waivers:* employees or children of employees.
Financial Aid In 2001, 1 Federal Work-Study job.
Applying *Options:* electronic application. *Application fee:* $30. *Required for some:* high school transcript. *Recommended:* interview. *Application deadline:* rolling (freshmen), rolling (transfers).
Admissions Contact Ms. Keeley Gadd, Campus Director, National College of Business & Technology, 139 Killarney Lane, Richmond, KY 40475. *Phone:* 859-623-8956. *Toll-free phone:* 800-664-1886. *Fax:* 606-624-5544. *E-mail:* adm@educorp.edu.

OWENSBORO COMMUNITY COLLEGE
Owensboro, Kentucky

- **State-supported** 2-year, founded 1986, part of Kentucky Community and Technical College System
- **Calendar** semesters
- **Degree** certificates and associate
- **Suburban** 102-acre campus
- **Coed,** 3,362 undergraduate students, 37% full-time, 67% women, 33% men

Undergraduates 1,239 full-time, 2,123 part-time. Students come from 6 states and territories, 3 other countries, 4% are from out of state, 4% African American, 0.4% Asian American or Pacific Islander, 0.5% Hispanic American, 0.2% Native American, 0.2% international, 3% transferred in. *Retention:* 58% of 2001 full-time freshmen returned.
Freshmen *Admission:* 604 applied, 604 admitted, 481 enrolled. *Test scores:* ACT scores over 18: 68%; ACT scores over 24: 13%.
Faculty *Total:* 138, 39% full-time, 14% with terminal degrees. *Student/faculty ratio:* 18:1.
Majors Agricultural sciences; business administration; computer/information sciences; computer/information technology services administration and management related; data entry/microcomputer applications; early childhood education; electrical/electronic engineering technology; executive assistant; human services; information technology; law enforcement/police science; liberal arts and sciences/liberal studies; medical radiologic technology; nursing; social work; system/networking/LAN/WAN management; word processing.
Academic Programs *Special study options:* academic remediation for entering students, adult/continuing education programs, advanced placement credit, cooperative education, distance learning, double majors, external degree program, honors programs, internships, off-campus study, part-time degree program, study abroad, summer session for credit.
Library Learning Resource Center with 18,200 titles, 80 serial subscriptions, an OPAC, a Web page.
Computers on Campus 90 computers available on campus for general student use. Internet access, at least one staffed computer lab available.
Student Life *Housing:* college housing not available. *Activities and Organizations:* drama/theater group, student-run newspaper, radio and television station, choral group, student government, Psychology Club, Nursing Club. *Campus security:* 24-hour emergency response devices, late-night transport/escort service.
Athletics *Intramural sports:* basketball M, softball M/W.
Standardized Tests *Required:* ACT (for placement). *Required for some:* ACT COMPASS.
Costs (2001–02) *Tuition:* state resident $1450 full-time, $61 per credit hour part-time; nonresident $4350 full-time, $183 per credit hour part-time. Full-time tuition and fees vary according to reciprocity agreements. Part-time tuition and fees vary according to course load and reciprocity agreements. *Required fees:*

Owensboro Community College (continued)
$120 full-time, $10 per term part-time. *Payment plan:* installment. *Waivers:* senior citizens and employees or children of employees.
Financial Aid In 2001, 50 Federal Work-Study jobs (averaging $2478). *Financial aid deadline:* 4/1.
Applying *Required:* high school transcript. *Application deadline:* rolling (freshmen), rolling (transfers). *Notification:* continuous (freshmen).
Admissions Contact Ms. Barbara Tipmore, Admissions Counselor, Owensboro Community College, 4800 New Hartford Road, Owensboro, KY 42303. *Phone:* 270-686-4400 Ext. 463. *Toll-free phone:* 877-734-0694 Ext. 412 (in-state); 877-734-0694 (out-of-state).

PADUCAH COMMUNITY COLLEGE
Paducah, Kentucky

- **State-supported** 2-year, founded 1932, part of University of Kentucky Community College System
- **Calendar** semesters
- **Degree** associate
- **Small-town** 117-acre campus
- **Coed,** 3,322 undergraduate students

Undergraduates Students come from 12 states and territories.
Freshmen *Admission:* 505 applied, 505 admitted.
Faculty *Total:* 151, 51% full-time. *Student/faculty ratio:* 15:1.
Majors Accounting; business administration; electrical/electronic engineering technology; industrial radiologic technology; information sciences/systems; mass communications; nursing; physical therapy; retail management; secretarial science.
Academic Programs *Special study options:* academic remediation for entering students, adult/continuing education programs, cooperative education, honors programs, internships, part-time degree program, services for LD students, summer session for credit.
Library Paducah Community College Library with 31,339 titles, 152 serial subscriptions, an OPAC, a Web page.
Computers on Campus 160 computers available on campus for general student use. At least one staffed computer lab available.
Student Life *Housing:* college housing not available. *Activities and Organizations:* drama/theater group, student-run newspaper, choral group. *Campus security:* 14-hour patrols by trained security personnel. *Student Services:* women's center.
Athletics *Intramural sports:* basketball M/W, golf M/W, soccer M/W, volleyball M/W.
Standardized Tests *Required for some:* ACT (for placement).
Costs (2001–02) *Tuition:* state resident $1920 full-time, $64 per credit hour part-time; nonresident $5760 full-time, $192 per credit hour part-time. Part-time tuition and fees vary according to course load. *Payment plan:* deferred payment. *Waivers:* senior citizens and employees or children of employees.
Financial Aid In 2001, 50 Federal Work-Study jobs (averaging $1650).
Applying *Options:* early admission. *Required for some:* high school transcript. *Application deadline:* rolling (freshmen), rolling (transfers).
Admissions Contact Mr. Jerry Anderson, Admissions Counselor, Paducah Community College, PO Box 7380, Paducah, KY 42002-7380. *Phone:* 270-554-9200.

PADUCAH TECHNICAL COLLEGE
Paducah, Kentucky

- **Proprietary** 2-year, founded 1964
- **Calendar** trimesters
- **Degree** diplomas and associate
- **Small-town** campus
- **Coed, primarily men,** 200 undergraduate students

Undergraduates Students come from 4 states and territories, 48% are from out of state.
Freshmen *Admission:* 82 applied, 82 admitted.
Faculty *Total:* 12, 67% full-time. *Student/faculty ratio:* 20:1.
Majors Communication equipment technology; computer engineering technology; electrical/electronic engineering technology; industrial technology.
Academic Programs *Special study options:* cooperative education, summer session for credit.
Computers on Campus 17 computers available on campus for general student use.
Student Life *Housing:* college housing not available.
Costs (2001–02) *Tuition:* $18,975 per degree program part-time. No tuition increase for student's term of enrollment. *Payment plans:* installment, deferred payment.
Applying *Options:* deferred entrance. *Required:* high school transcript. *Application deadline:* rolling (freshmen), rolling (transfers).
Admissions Contact Mr. Arnold Harris, Director of Admissions, Paducah Technical College, 509 South 30th Street, PO Box 8252, Paducah, KY 42001. *Phone:* 502-444-9676. *Toll-free phone:* 800-995-4438.

PRESTONSBURG COMMUNITY COLLEGE
Prestonsburg, Kentucky

Admissions Contact Ms. Gia Rae Potter, Director of Admissions/Registrar, Prestonsburg Community College, One Bert T Combs Drive, Prestonsburg, KY 41653-1815. *Phone:* 606-886-3863 Ext. 220. *Fax:* 606-886-6943. *E-mail:* gia@pop.uky.edu.

RETS ELECTRONIC INSTITUTE
Louisville, Kentucky

Admissions Contact Mr. Terry Queeno, Director of Admissions, RETS Electronic Institute, 300 High rise Drive, Louisville, KY 40213. *Phone:* 502-968-7191. *Toll-free phone:* 800-999-7387. *Fax:* 502-968-1727.

RETS MEDICAL AND BUSINESS ISTITUTE
Hopkinsville, Kentucky

Admissions Contact Ms. Connie Pickhaver, Admissions Coordinator, RETS Medical and Business Istitute, 4001 Fort Campbell Boulevard, Hopkinsville, KY 42240-4962. *Phone:* 610-353-7630. *Toll-free phone:* 800-359-4753.

ST. CATHARINE COLLEGE
St. Catharine, Kentucky

- **Independent Roman Catholic** 2-year, founded 1931
- **Calendar** semesters
- **Degree** certificates and associate
- **Rural** 643-acre campus with easy access to Louisville
- **Endowment** $300,000
- **Coed,** 672 undergraduate students

Undergraduates Students come from 6 other countries, 9% African American, 1% Asian American or Pacific Islander, 0.2% Hispanic American, 0.4% Native American, 2% international, 19% live on campus.
Freshmen *Admission:* 394 applied, 216 admitted.
Faculty *Total:* 38, 61% full-time. *Student/faculty ratio:* 15:1.
Majors Accounting; agricultural business; agricultural sciences; animal sciences; art; art education; art history; biblical studies; biological/physical sciences; biology; business administration; business economics; business education; business machine repair; ceramic arts; chemistry; computer engineering technology; criminal justice/law enforcement administration; dance; early childhood education; education; elementary education; environmental science; farm/ranch management; health education; history; horticulture science; humanities; information sciences/systems; insurance/risk management; Japanese; journalism; landscape architecture; landscaping management; land use management; legal administrative assistant; liberal arts and sciences/liberal studies; mathematics; medical administrative assistant; music; music (piano and organ performance); nursing; physical education; range management; secretarial science; social sciences; social work; sociology; Spanish.
Academic Programs *Special study options:* academic remediation for entering students, advanced placement credit, cooperative education, internships, part-time degree program, services for LD students, summer session for credit.
Library St. Catharine College Library with 22,000 titles, 37 serial subscriptions.
Computers on Campus 60 computers available on campus for general student use. At least one staffed computer lab available.
Student Life *Housing Options:* coed. *Activities and Organizations:* drama/theater group, student-run newspaper, choral group, African-American Club,

nternational Club, student government, Phi Theta Kappa. *Campus security:* 24-hour emergency response devices, night security guard. *Student Services:* ersonal/psychological counseling.

thletics Member NJCAA. *Intercollegiate sports:* baseball M(s)/W(s), basketall M(s)/W(s), softball W(s). *Intramural sports:* archery M/W, badminton M/W, ennis M/W, volleyball M/W.

tandardized Tests *Required:* ACT (for admission).

osts (2001–02) *Comprehensive fee:* $12,000 includes full-time tuition ($7000), nandatory fees ($180), and room and board ($4820). Part-time tuition: $230 per redit hour.

inancial Aid In 2001, 45 Federal Work-Study jobs (averaging $1000).

pplying *Options:* early admission. *Application fee:* $15. *Required:* minimum ACT score of 12. *Required for some:* high school transcript. *Application deadline:* olling (freshmen), rolling (transfers).

dmissions Contact Director of Admissions, St. Catharine College, 2735 Bardstown Road, St. Catharine, KY 40061-9499. *Phone:* 859-336-5082. *Toll-free phone:* 800-599-2000 (in-state); 800-949-5727 (out-of-state). *Fax:* 859-336-031.

SOMERSET COMMUNITY COLLEGE
omerset, Kentucky

- **State-supported** 2-year, founded 1965, part of Kentucky Community and Technical College System
- **Calendar** semesters
- **Degree** associate
- **Small-town** 70-acre campus
- **Coed,** 2,799 undergraduate students, 60% full-time, 69% women, 31% men

ndergraduates Students come from 6 states and territories, 1% African American, 0.4% Asian American or Pacific Islander, 0.4% Hispanic American, .9% Native American. *Retention:* 41% of 2001 full-time freshmen returned.

reshmen *Admission:* 1,633 applied, 1,633 admitted. *Test scores:* ACT scores ver 18: 57%; ACT scores over 24: 9%; ACT scores over 30: 1%.

aculty *Total:* 193, 36% full-time. *Student/faculty ratio:* 25:1.

Majors Accounting; business administration; information sciences/systems; nedical laboratory technician; nursing; physical therapy assistant; secretarial science.

cademic Programs *Special study options:* academic remediation for entering tudents, adult/continuing education programs, advanced placement credit, cooprative education, distance learning, double majors, independent study, internhips, part-time degree program, services for LD students, summer session for redit.

ibrary Strunk Learning Resources Center with 45,724 titles, 250 serial ubscriptions, 4,394 audiovisual materials, an OPAC, a Web page.

omputers on Campus 267 computers available on campus for general tudent use. A campuswide network can be accessed from off campus. Internet ccess, at least one staffed computer lab available.

tudent Life *Housing:* college housing not available. *Activities and Organizations:* drama/theater group, student-run newspaper, choral group, Student Government Association, Students in Free Enterprise, Phi Beta Lambda, Phi Theta Kappa.

thletics *Intramural sports:* basketball M/W, football M/W, softball M/W.

tandardized Tests *Required:* ACT (for placement). *Required for some:* ACT COMPASS.

osts (2001–02) *Tuition:* state resident $1450 full-time, $61 per credit hour art-time; nonresident $4350 full-time, $183 per credit hour part-time.

inancial Aid In 2001, 40 Federal Work-Study jobs (averaging $2500). 25 State nd other part-time jobs (averaging $2500).

pplying *Options:* common application, early admission. *Required:* high school ranscript. *Application deadlines:* 8/31 (freshmen), 8/31 (transfers). *Notification:* ontinuous (freshmen).

dmissions Contact Mr. Sean Ayers, Director of Admissions, Somerset Community College, 808 Monticello Street, Somerset, KY 42501. *Phone:* 606-79-8501 Ext. 3219. *Toll-free phone:* 877-629-9722.

SOUTHEAST COMMUNITY COLLEGE
umberland, Kentucky

- **State-supported** 2-year, founded 1960, part of Kentucky Community and Technical College System
- **Calendar** semesters
- **Degree** diplomas and associate
- **Small-town** 150-acre campus
- **Endowment** $1.8 million
- **Coed,** 2,491 undergraduate students, 62% full-time, 66% women, 34% men

Faculty *Total:* 119, 56% full-time, 12% with terminal degrees. *Student/faculty ratio:* 20:1.

Majors Business administration; computer engineering technology; computer/information technology services administration and management related; data processing technology; information technology; law enforcement/police science; liberal arts and sciences/liberal studies; management information systems/business data processing; medical laboratory technician; medical radiologic technology; nursing; physical therapy assistant; respiratory therapy; secretarial science.

Academic Programs *Special study options:* academic remediation for entering students, accelerated degree program, adult/continuing education programs, advanced placement credit, distance learning, internships, part-time degree program, summer session for credit.

Library Gertrude Dale Library with 25,921 titles, 200 serial subscriptions, an OPAC, a Web page.

Computers on Campus 46 computers available on campus for general student use. A campuswide network can be accessed from off campus that provide access to online admissions. Internet access, at least one staffed computer lab available.

Student Life *Activities and Organizations:* drama/theater group, student-run newspaper, choral group, Professional Business Leaders, Student Government Association, Phi Theta Kappa, Black Student Union, Nursing Club.

Athletics *Intramural sports:* basketball M/W, football M/W, golf M/W, table tennis M/W, volleyball M/W.

Costs (2001–02) *Tuition:* state resident $61 per credit hour part-time; nonresident $183 per credit hour part-time. Full-time tuition and fees vary according to course load. Part-time tuition and fees vary according to course load. *Waivers:* senior citizens.

Financial Aid In 2001, 90 Federal Work-Study jobs (averaging $635).

Applying *Required:* high school transcript. *Application deadline:* 8/20 (freshmen). *Notification:* continuous until 9/3 (freshmen).

Admissions Contact Mr. Charles W. Sellars, Dean of Student Affairs, Southeast Community College, 700 College Road, Cumberland, KY 40823-1099. *Phone:* 606-589-2145 Ext. 2003. *Toll-free phone:* 888-274-SECC Ext. 2108. *Fax:* 606-589-5435. *E-mail:* red.sellars@kctcs.net.

SOUTHERN OHIO COLLEGE, NORTHERN KENTUCKY CAMPUS
Fort Mitchell, Kentucky

- **Proprietary** 2-year, founded 1927, part of American Education Centers, Inc
- **Calendar** quarters
- **Degree** certificates, diplomas, and associate
- **Suburban** 5-acre campus with easy access to Cincinnati
- **Coed,** 350 undergraduate students

Undergraduates Students come from 3 states and territories, 1 other country.

Faculty *Total:* 19. *Student/faculty ratio:* 15:1.

Majors Accounting technician; business administration; computer science; information sciences/systems; medical assistant.

Academic Programs *Special study options:* academic remediation for entering students, adult/continuing education programs, internships, part-time degree program, summer session for credit.

Library 1,500 titles, 50 serial subscriptions.

Computers on Campus 50 computers available on campus for general student use. Internet access, at least one staffed computer lab available.

Student Life *Housing:* college housing not available. *Campus security:* 24-hour emergency response devices, late-night transport/escort service. *Student Services:* personal/psychological counseling.

Applying *Options:* common application, early admission, deferred entrance. *Application fee:* $50. *Required:* high school transcript, interview. *Application deadline:* rolling (freshmen), rolling (transfers).

Admissions Contact Terry Focht, Director of Admissions, Southern Ohio College, Northern Kentucky Campus, 309 Buttermilk Pike, Fort Mitchell, KY 41017-2191. *Phone:* 859-341-5627.

SOUTHWESTERN COLLEGE OF BUSINESS
Crestview Hills, Kentucky

- **Proprietary** 2-year, founded 1978
- **Calendar** quarters

Southwestern College of Business (continued)
- **Degree** certificates, diplomas, and associate
- **Suburban** campus with easy access to Cincinnati
- **Coed, primarily women**

Applying *Options:* common application, early admission.
Admissions Contact Mr. Bruce Budesheim, Admissions Director, Southwestern College of Business, 2929 South Dixie Highway, Crestview Hills, KY 41017. *Phone:* 859-341-6633. *Fax:* 859-341-6749.

SPENCERIAN COLLEGE
Louisville, Kentucky

- **Proprietary** 2-year, founded 1892
- **Calendar** quarters
- **Degree** certificates, diplomas, and associate
- **Urban** campus
- **Coed, primarily women,** 584 undergraduate students, 100% full-time, 93% women, 7% men

Undergraduates 584 full-time. Students come from 2 states and territories, 13% are from out of state, 16% African American, 0.9% Asian American or Pacific Islander, 1% Hispanic American, 0.7% Native American, 2% transferred in.
Freshmen *Admission:* 250 admitted.
Faculty *Total:* 73, 23% full-time. *Student/faculty ratio:* 7:1.
Majors Accounting; business administration; medical office management.
Student Life *Housing Options:* coed. *Activities and Organizations:* student-run newspaper, Spencerian Business Leaders. *Campus security:* 24-hour emergency response devices. *Student Services:* personal/psychological counseling.
Costs (2002–03) *Tuition:* $10,770 full-time, $180 per credit hour part-time. *Required fees:* $625 full-time, $150 per term part-time. *Room only:* $3530.
Applying *Application fee:* $80. *Required:* high school transcript. *Required for some:* essay or personal statement, interview.
Admissions Contact Terri D. Thomas, Director of Admissions, Spencerian College, 4627 Dixie Highway, Louisville, KY 40216. *Phone:* 502-447-1000 Ext. 211. *Toll-free phone:* 800-264-1799.

SPENCERIAN COLLEGE-LEXINGTON
Lexington, Kentucky

- **Proprietary** 2-year, part of Sullivan Colleges System
- **Calendar** quarters
- **Degree** certificates, diplomas, and associate
- **Urban** campus with easy access to Louisville
- **Coed,** 330 undergraduate students

Undergraduates Students come from 1 other state, 1 other country, 6% African American, 0.4% Hispanic American, 0.4% Native American, 0.4% international, 7% live on campus.
Freshmen *Admission:* 80 applied, 80 admitted. *Test scores:* ACT scores over 18: 85%; ACT scores over 24: 15%.
Faculty *Total:* 43, 37% full-time.
Majors Architectural drafting; computer graphics; electrical/electronic engineering technology; mechanical drafting.
Academic Programs *Special study options:* academic remediation for entering students, cooperative education, services for LD students, summer session for credit.
Library Spencerian College Library with 450 titles, 30 serial subscriptions, 25 audiovisual materials.
Computers on Campus 14 computers available on campus for general student use. A campuswide network can be accessed from off campus. Internet access, at least one staffed computer lab available.
Student Life *Housing Options:* men-only, women-only. *Activities and Organizations:* student-run newspaper. *Campus security:* 24-hour emergency response devices.
Costs (2001–02) *Comprehensive fee:* $12,590 includes full-time tuition ($9270), mandatory fees ($350), and room and board ($2970). Part-time tuition: $230 per credit hour. *Required fees:* $30 per credit hour.
Applying *Options:* common application. *Application fee:* $90. *Required:* high school transcript, interview. *Application deadline:* rolling (freshmen).
Admissions Contact Ms. Georgia Mullins, Admissions Representative, Spencerian College-Lexington, 2355 Harrodsburg Road, Lexington, KY 40504. *Phone:* 800-456-3253 Ext. 8010. *Toll-free phone:* 800-456-3253. *Fax:* 859-224-7744. *E-mail:* admissions@spencerian.edu.

UNIVERSITY OF KENTUCKY, LEXINGTON COMMUNITY COLLEGE
Lexington, Kentucky

- **State-supported** 2-year, founded 1965
- **Calendar** semesters
- **Degree** associate
- **Urban** 10-acre campus
- **Coed,** 7,793 undergraduate students, 63% full-time, 55% women, 45% men

Undergraduates 4,910 full-time, 2,883 part-time. Students come from 36 states and territories, 54 other countries, 5% are from out of state, 10% transferred in.
Freshmen *Admission:* 5,828 applied, 5,828 admitted, 1,049 enrolled. *Test scores:* ACT scores over 18: 60%; ACT scores over 24: 5%; ACT scores over 30: 1%.
Faculty *Total:* 393, 42% full-time. *Student/faculty ratio:* 17:1.
Majors Accounting; accounting technician; architectural drafting; architectural engineering technology; business administration; computer programming related; computer systems networking/telecommunications; data entry/microcomputer applications; dental hygiene; dental laboratory technician; executive assistant; industrial radiologic technology; information sciences/systems; liberal arts and sciences/liberal studies; mechanical engineering technology; medical radiologic technology; nuclear medical technology; nursing; real estate; respiratory therapy; secretarial science; system/networking/LAN/WAN management; word processing.
Academic Programs *Special study options:* academic remediation for entering students, accelerated degree program, adult/continuing education programs, advanced placement credit, cooperative education, distance learning, part-time degree program, services for LD students, summer session for credit. *ROTC:* Army (c), Air Force (c).
Library Lexington Community College Library with 27,000 titles, 193 serial subscriptions, an OPAC, a Web page.
Computers on Campus 80 computers available on campus for general student use. At least one staffed computer lab available.
Student Life *Housing:* college housing not available. *Activities and Organizations:* choral group, Baptist Student Union, Unity, KANS, Veterans Union, Athena. *Campus security:* 24-hour emergency response devices and patrols, late-night transport/escort service. *Student Services:* health clinic, personal/psychological counseling.
Athletics *Intramural sports:* basketball M/W, football M/W, golf M/W, racquetball M/W, soccer M/W, swimming M/W, tennis M/W, track and field M/W, volleyball M/W, water polo M/W, wrestling M.
Standardized Tests *Required:* SAT I or ACT (for placement).
Costs (2002–03) *Tuition:* area resident $876 full-time, $73 per credit hour part-time; state resident $876 full-time, $73 per credit hour part-time; nonresident $2904 full-time, $242 per credit hour part-time. Part-time tuition and fees vary according to course load. *Required fees:* $495 full-time, $13 per term part-time. *Waivers:* senior citizens and employees or children of employees.
Applying *Options:* early admission. *Required:* high school transcript. *Application deadlines:* 8/1 (freshmen), 8/1 (transfers).
Admissions Contact Mrs. Shelbie Hugle, Director of Admission Services, University of Kentucky, Lexington Community College, 200 Oswald Building, Cooper Drive, Lexington, KY 40506-0235. *Phone:* 859-257-4872 Ext. 4197. *E-mail:* kmwarfl@ukcc.uky.edu.

LOUISIANA

BATON ROUGE SCHOOL OF COMPUTERS
Baton Rouge, Louisiana

Admissions Contact 9255 Interline Avenue, Baton Rouge, LA 70809-1971.

BOSSIER PARISH COMMUNITY COLLEGE
Bossier City, Louisiana

- **State-supported** 2-year, founded 1967, part of University of Louisiana System

- **Calendar** semesters
- **Degree** certificates and associate
- **Urban** 64-acre campus
- **Coed,** 3,964 undergraduate students

Undergraduates Students come from 2 other countries.
Freshmen *Admission:* 879 applied, 879 admitted.
Faculty *Total:* 185, 54% full-time.
Majors Business administration; corrections; drafting; electrical/electronic engineering technology; emergency medical technology; information sciences/systems; law enforcement/police science; liberal arts and sciences/liberal studies; medical assistant; physical therapy; respiratory therapy; telecommunications.
Academic Programs *Special study options:* academic remediation for entering students, adult/continuing education programs, advanced placement credit, distance learning, double majors, part-time degree program, services for LD students, summer session for credit.
Library Bossier Parish Community College Library with 29,600 titles, 384 serial subscriptions, an OPAC.
Computers on Campus 83 computers available on campus for general student use. At least one staffed computer lab available.
Student Life *Housing:* college housing not available. *Activities and Organizations:* drama/theater group, student-run newspaper, choral group, Student Government Association, Cavalier Players Drama Club, Data Processing Management Association. *Campus security:* student patrols. *Student Services:* personal/psychological counseling.
Athletics Member NJCAA. *Intercollegiate sports:* baseball M(s), basketball M(s), golf M(s), softball W(s), tennis W(s). *Intramural sports:* badminton M/W, bowling M/W, football M, racquetball M, softball M, table tennis M/W, volleyball M/W.
Standardized Tests *Required:* ACT (for placement).
Costs (2001–02) *Tuition:* state resident $1360 full-time, $386 per term part-time; nonresident $3500 full-time, $856 per term part-time. *Payment plan:* deferred payment. *Waivers:* minority students and employees or children of employees.
Financial Aid In 2001, 41 Federal Work-Study jobs (averaging $1500).
Applying *Options:* early admission. *Application fee:* $15. *Required:* high school transcript. *Application deadlines:* 8/10 (freshmen), 8/10 (transfers).
Admissions Contact Ms. Ann Jampole, Admissions Officer, Bossier Parish Community College, 2719 Airline Drive North, Bossier City, LA 71111-5801. *Phone:* 318-746-9851 Ext. 215. *Fax:* 318-742-8664.

Camelot Career College
Baton Rouge, Louisiana

Admissions Contact 2742 Wooddale Boulevard, Baton Rouge, LA 70805.

Cameron College
New Orleans, Louisiana

Admissions Contact 2740 Canal Street, New Orleans, LA 70119.

Culinary Arts Institute of Louisiana
Baton Rouge, Louisiana

- **Proprietary** 2-year, founded 1988
- **Calendar** continuous
- **Degree** associate
- **Urban** 1-acre campus
- **Coed,** 60 undergraduate students, 100% full-time, 17% women, 83% men

Undergraduates Students come from 1 other country, 75% are from out of state, 17% African American, 3% Hispanic American, 8% Native American.
Faculty *Total:* 5, 80% full-time, 20% with terminal degrees. *Student/faculty ratio:* 15:1.
Majors Culinary arts; hotel and restaurant management.
Academic Programs *Special study options:* accelerated degree program, adult/continuing education programs, cooperative education.
Library Culinary Arts Institute Library with 300 titles, 45 serial subscriptions, 10 audiovisual materials.
Computers on Campus 2 computers available on campus for general student use. Internet access, online (class) registration available.
Student Life *Housing:* college housing not available. *Campus security:* 24-hour emergency response devices. *Student Services:* personal/psychological counseling.
Costs (2001–02) *Tuition:* $18,910 per degree program part-time.
Applying *Options:* common application, electronic application, deferred entrance. *Application fee:* $50. *Required:* essay or personal statement, high school transcript, 2 letters of recommendation, interview. *Application deadline:* rolling (freshmen), rolling (transfers). *Notification:* continuous (freshmen).
Admissions Contact Ms. Maureen Harrington, Director of Admissions, Culinary Arts Institute of Louisiana, 427 Lafayette Street, Baton Rouge, LA 70802. *Phone:* 225-343-6233. *Toll-free phone:* 800-927-0839. *Fax:* 225-336-4880. *E-mail:* school@caila.com.

Delgado Community College
New Orleans, Louisiana

- **State-supported** 2-year, founded 1921, part of Louisiana Community and Technical college System
- **Calendar** semesters
- **Degree** certificates and associate
- **Urban** 57-acre campus
- **Endowment** $1.0 million
- **Coed,** 13,404 undergraduate students, 46% full-time, 67% women, 33% men

Undergraduates 6,198 full-time, 7,206 part-time. Students come from 30 states and territories, 2% are from out of state, 41% African American, 2% Asian American or Pacific Islander, 5% Hispanic American, 0.9% Native American.
Freshmen *Admission:* 1,804 applied, 1,804 admitted.
Faculty *Total:* 643, 55% full-time. *Student/faculty ratio:* 20:1.
Majors Accounting; architectural engineering technology; auto mechanic/technician; biological/physical sciences; biomedical engineering-related technology; building maintenance/management; business administration; civil engineering technology; communications related; computer engineering technology; computer installation/repair; construction management; data processing technology; dental hygiene; dental laboratory technician; dietetics; drafting; early childhood education; electrical/electronic engineering technology; electrical equipment installation/repair; emergency medical technology; fine/studio arts; fire protection/safety technology; general studies; graphic design/commercial art/illustration; horticulture services; hospitality management; institutional food workers; interior architecture; law enforcement/police science; machine shop assistant; machine technology; medical laboratory technician; medical radiologic technology; medical records technology; mortuary science; music; nursing; occupational safety/health technology; occupational therapy assistant; physical therapy assistant; respiratory therapy; secretarial science; sign language interpretation.
Academic Programs *Special study options:* academic remediation for entering students, advanced placement credit, cooperative education, distance learning, English as a second language, honors programs, off-campus study, part-time degree program, services for LD students, student-designed majors, summer session for credit. *ROTC:* Army (c), Air Force (c).
Library Moss Memorial Library with 110,000 titles, 1,299 serial subscriptions, an OPAC, a Web page.
Computers on Campus 950 computers available on campus for general student use. A campuswide network can be accessed from off campus. Internet access, at least one staffed computer lab available.
Student Life *Housing:* college housing not available. *Activities and Organizations:* drama/theater group, student-run newspaper, choral group, student government, Circle K, International Club, Phi Theta Kappa, Lambda Phi Nu. *Campus security:* 24-hour patrols, student patrols. *Student Services:* health clinic, personal/psychological counseling.
Athletics Member NJCAA. *Intercollegiate sports:* baseball M(s), basketball M(s)/W(s), track and field W. *Intramural sports:* football M, golf M, soccer M, tennis M/W, volleyball M/W.
Standardized Tests *Required for some:* ACT (for placement). *Recommended:* ACT (for placement).
Costs (2002–03) *Tuition:* state resident $1404 full-time, $408 per term part-time; nonresident $4384 full-time, $1238 per term part-time. Part-time tuition and fees vary according to course load. *Required fees:* $170 full-time, $5 per credit, $10 per term part-time. *Payment plan:* deferred payment. *Waivers:* children of alumni, senior citizens, and employees or children of employees.
Financial Aid In 2001, 308 Federal Work-Study jobs (averaging $1375).
Applying *Application fee:* $15. *Required for some:* high school transcript. *Recommended:* high school transcript, proof of immunization. *Application deadline:* rolling (freshmen), rolling (transfers).

Delgado Community College (continued)
Admissions Contact Ms. Gwen Boute, Director of Admissions, Delgado Community College, 615 City Park Avenue, New Orleans, LA 70119. *Phone:* 504-483-4004. *Fax:* 504-483-1895. *E-mail:* enroll@dcc.edu.

DELTA COLLEGE OF ARTS AND TECHNOLOGY
Baton Rouge, Louisiana

- **Private** 2-year
- **Degree** certificates, diplomas, and associate
- **Coed, primarily women,** 250 undergraduate students

Faculty *Total:* 20, 75% full-time.
Majors Graphic design/commercial art/illustration; management information systems/business data processing; medical assistant.
Costs (2001–02) *Tuition:* $12,895 full-time.
Applying *Application fee:* $100.
Admissions Contact Ms. Georgia Thompson, Admissions Director, Delta College of Arts and Technology, 7380 Exchange Place, Baton Rouge, LA 70806-3851. *Phone:* 225-928-7770. *Fax:* 225-927-9096.

DELTA SCHOOL OF BUSINESS & TECHNOLOGY
Lake Charles, Louisiana

Admissions Contact 517 Broad Street, Lake Charles, LA 70601.

EDUCATION AMERICA, REMINGTON COLLEGE, BATON ROUGE CAMPUS
Baton Rouge, Louisiana

Admissions Contact 1900 North Lobdell, Baton Rouge, LA 70806.

EDUCATION AMERICA, REMINGTON COLLEGE, LAFAYETTE CAMPUS
Lafayette, Louisiana

- **Proprietary** 2-year, founded 1940, part of Education America Inc
- **Calendar** continuous
- **Degree** associate
- **Urban** 4-acre campus
- **Coed,** 472 undergraduate students, 100% full-time, 65% women, 35% men

Undergraduates 27% African American, 0.4% Asian American or Pacific Islander, 2% Hispanic American.
Faculty *Total:* 36, 50% full-time. *Student/faculty ratio:* 15:1.
Majors Business administration; computer programming; computer programming related; computer systems analysis; computer systems networking/ telecommunications; computer/technical support; data entry/microcomputer applications related; electrical/electronic engineering technology; medical assistant; paralegal/legal assistant; Web page, digital/multimedia and information resources design.
Academic Programs *Special study options:* honors programs, independent study.
Library Remington College Library with 15,435 titles, 85 serial subscriptions, 182 audiovisual materials, an OPAC.
Computers on Campus 120 computers available on campus for general student use. A campuswide network can be accessed from off campus. Internet access, at least one staffed computer lab available.
Student Life *Housing:* college housing not available. *Campus security:* 24-hour emergency response devices.
Costs (2001–02) *Comprehensive fee:* $24,885 includes full-time tuition ($9600). No tuition increase for student's term of enrollment. *Payment plans:* tuition prepayment, installment. *Waivers:* employees or children of employees.
Applying *Options:* early admission, deferred entrance. *Application fee:* $50. *Required:* high school transcript, interview.
Admissions Contact Ms. Cheryl Powers Lokey, Director of Marketing, Education America, Remington College, Lafayette Campus, 303 Rue Louis XIV, Lafayette, LA 70508. *Phone:* 337-981-9010. *Toll-free phone:* 800-736-2687. *Fax:* 337-983-7130.

EDUCATION AMERICA, SOUTHEAST COLLEGE OF TECHNOLOGY, NEW ORLEANS CAMPUS
Metairie, Louisiana

- **Proprietary** 2-year
- **Calendar** quarters
- **Degree** associate
- **Coed,** 650 undergraduate students

Majors Business systems networking/ telecommunications; computer graphic computer hardware engineering; computer/information sciences; computer pro gramming related; data entry/microcomputer applications related; engineerin technology; system/networking/LAN/WAN management.
Student Life *Housing:* college housing not available.
Costs (2001–02) *Tuition:* $25,839 per degree program part-time. Full-tim tuition and fees vary according to program.
Applying *Application fee:* $50. *Application deadline:* rolling (freshmen), rollir (transfers). *Notification:* continuous (freshmen).
Admissions Contact Benny Montalbano, Director of Recruitment, Educatic America, Southeast College of Technology, New Orleans Campus, 321 Veterar Memorial Boulevard, Metairie, LA 70005. *Phone:* 504-831-8889. *Fax:* 504-83 6803.

ELAINE P. NUNEZ COMMUNITY COLLEGE
Chalmette, Louisiana

- **State-supported** 2-year, founded 1992, part of Louisiana Community ar Technical Colleges System
- **Calendar** semesters
- **Degree** certificates and associate
- **Suburban** 20-acre campus with easy access to New Orleans
- **Endowment** $510,000
- **Coed,** 1,924 undergraduate students

Undergraduates Students come from 6 states and territories, 20% Afric American, 2% Asian American or Pacific Islander, 3% Hispanic American, 1 Native American.
Freshmen *Admission:* 422 applied, 422 admitted. *Average high school GP* 2.5.
Faculty *Total:* 103, 44% full-time. *Student/faculty ratio:* 16:1.
Majors Accounting; computer engineering technology; computer/informatic technology services administration and management related; computer scienc computer science related; computer/technical support; drafting; early childho education; electrical/electronic engineering technology; emergency medical tec nology; environmental technology; heating/air conditioning/refrigeration; infc mation sciences/systems; institutional food workers; laser/optical technolog liberal arts and sciences/liberal studies; medical records administration; paraleg legal assistant; plastics technology; practical nurse; secretarial science.
Academic Programs *Special study options:* academic remediation for enteri students, adult/continuing education programs, advanced placement credit, coo erative education, distance learning, double majors, freshman honors colleg internships, off-campus study, part-time degree program, services for LD st dents, student-designed majors, summer session for credit.
Library Nunez Community College Library with 36,720 titles, 9,356 seri subscriptions, 1,226 audiovisual materials, an OPAC, a Web page.
Computers on Campus 100 computers available on campus for gener student use. At least one staffed computer lab available.
Student Life *Housing:* college housing not available. *Activities and Organiz tions:* drama/theater group, student-run newspaper, choral group, Nunez Enviro mental Team, national fraternities. *Campus security:* 24-hour emergency respon devices, late-night transport/escort service. *Student Services:* persona psychological counseling.
Athletics *Intramural sports:* basketball M, football M/W, softball M/W, volle ball M/W.
Standardized Tests *Required for some:* ACT COMPASS or ACT ASSE *Recommended:* ACT (for placement).
Costs (2001–02) *Tuition:* state resident $1226 full-time, $380 per te part-time; nonresident $3746 full-time, $1070 per term part-time. Full-tin tuition and fees vary according to course load. Part-time tuition and fees va according to course load. *Required fees:* $134 full-time, $5 per credit, $7 per ter part-time. *Payment plan:* deferred payment. *Waivers:* senior citizens and emplo ees or children of employees.
Financial Aid In 2001, 68 Federal Work-Study jobs (averaging $1545).

Applying *Options:* early admission. *Application fee:* $10. *Required for some:* high school transcript, letters of recommendation. *Recommended:* minimum 2.0 GPA. *Application deadlines:* 8/1 (freshmen), 8/1 (transfers).

Admissions Contact Ms. Donna Clark, Dean of Student Affairs, Elaine P. Nunez Community College, 3710 Paris Road, Chalmette, LA 70043. *Phone:* 504-680-2457. *Fax:* 504-278-7353.

HERZING COLLEGE
Kenner, Louisiana

- **Proprietary** primarily 2-year, founded 1996
- **Calendar** semesters
- **Degrees** diplomas, associate, and bachelor's
- **Coed,** 220 undergraduate students, 70% full-time, 38% women, 62% men

Undergraduates 153 full-time, 67 part-time.

Freshmen *Admission:* 240 applied, 220 admitted, 89 enrolled.

Faculty *Total:* 20, 25% full-time, 20% with terminal degrees. *Student/faculty ratio:* 17:1.

Majors Business administration; computer programming; computer systems networking/telecommunications; paralegal/legal assistant; Web page design.

Costs (2002–03) *Tuition:* $1040 per course part-time.

Admissions Contact Genny Bordelon, Director of Admissions, Herzing College, 2400 Veterans Boulevard, Kenner, LA 70062. *Phone:* 504-733-0074.

ITT TECHNICAL INSTITUTE
St. Rose, Louisiana

- **Proprietary** 2-year
- **Calendar** quarters
- **Degree** associate
- **Coed,** 356 undergraduate students

Majors Computer/information sciences related; computer programming; drafting; electrical/electronic engineering technologies related; information technology.

Student Life *Housing:* college housing not available.

Costs (2001–02) *Tuition:* Full-time tuition and fees vary according to program. Part-time tuition and fees vary according to program. $260—$330 per credit hour.

Applying *Application fee:* $100. *Required:* high school transcript, interview. *Recommended:* letters of recommendation. *Application deadline:* rolling (freshmen). *Notification:* continuous (freshmen).

Admissions Contact Ms. Brenda Nash, Director of Recruitment, ITT Technical Institute, 140 James Drive East, St. Rose, LA 70087. *Phone:* 504-463-0338.

LOUISIANA STATE UNIVERSITY AT ALEXANDRIA
Alexandria, Louisiana

- **State-supported** 2-year, founded 1960, part of Louisiana State University System
- **Calendar** semesters
- **Degree** certificates and associate
- **Rural** 3114-acre campus
- **Endowment** $307,086
- **Coed,** 2,715 undergraduate students, 45% full-time, 74% women, 26% men

Undergraduates 1,216 full-time, 1,499 part-time. Students come from 13 states and territories, 1 other country, 0.8% are from out of state, 19% African American, 0.4% Asian American or Pacific Islander, 1% Hispanic American, 1% Native American, 7% transferred in.

Freshmen *Admission:* 1,280 applied, 1,245 admitted, 616 enrolled. *Test scores:* ACT scores over 18: 59%; ACT scores over 24: 11%.

Faculty *Total:* 131, 53% full-time, 27% with terminal degrees. *Student/faculty ratio:* 19:1.

Majors Biological/physical sciences; business administration; criminal justice studies; data processing technology; liberal arts and sciences/liberal studies; medical laboratory technician; nursing; paralegal/legal assistant.

Academic Programs *Special study options:* academic remediation for entering students, adult/continuing education programs, advanced placement credit, part-time degree program, summer session for credit.

Library James C. Bolton Library with 153,194 titles, 367 serial subscriptions, an OPAC.

Computers on Campus 100 computers available on campus for general student use. A campuswide network can be accessed from off campus. Internet access, at least one staffed computer lab available.

Student Life *Housing:* college housing not available. *Activities and Organizations:* drama/theater group, student-run newspaper, Pentecostal Student Fellowship, Baptist Collegiate Ministries, Catholic Student Center, Student Government Association, Gamma Beta Phi. *Campus security:* 24-hour patrols. *Student Services:* personal/psychological counseling.

Athletics *Intramural sports:* basketball M/W, football M/W, volleyball M/W.

Standardized Tests *Recommended:* ACT (for placement).

Costs (2002–03) *Tuition:* area resident $1288 full-time, $52 per credit hour part-time; nonresident $3706 full-time, $153 per credit hour part-time. *Required fees:* $150 full-time, $3 per credit hour, $39 per term part-time.

Financial Aid In 2001, 53 Federal Work-Study jobs (averaging $1226). 76 State and other part-time jobs (averaging $1261).

Applying *Options:* early admission. *Application fee:* $20. *Required:* high school transcript. *Required for some:* essay or personal statement, minimum 2.0 GPA, 3 letters of recommendation, interview. *Application deadline:* rolling (freshmen), rolling (transfers). *Notification:* continuous (freshmen).

Admissions Contact Ms. Shelly Kieffer, Recruiter/Admissions Counselor, Louisiana State University at Alexandria, 8100 Highway 71 South, Alexandria, LA 71302-9121. *Phone:* 318-473-6508. *Toll-free phone:* 888-473-6417. *Fax:* 318-473-6418. *E-mail:* skieffer@pobox.lsua.edu.

LOUISIANA STATE UNIVERSITY AT EUNICE
Eunice, Louisiana

- **State-supported** 2-year, founded 1967, part of Louisiana State University System
- **Calendar** semesters
- **Degree** certificates and associate
- **Small-town** 199-acre campus
- **Coed,** 2,748 undergraduate students

Undergraduates Students come from 4 states and territories, 0.4% are from out of state, 22% African American, 0.1% Asian American or Pacific Islander, 0.4% Hispanic American, 0.7% Native American.

Freshmen *Admission:* 1,753 applied, 1,734 admitted. *Test scores:* ACT scores over 18: 76%; ACT scores over 24: 22%; ACT scores over 30: 2%.

Faculty *Total:* 108, 33% with terminal degrees.

Majors Business administration; computer programming; criminal justice studies; fire science; general studies; law enforcement/police science; nursing; paralegal/legal assistant; radiological science; respiratory therapy; secretarial science.

Academic Programs *Special study options:* academic remediation for entering students, adult/continuing education programs, advanced placement credit, cooperative education, distance learning, honors programs, part-time degree program, services for LD students, summer session for credit.

Library Arnold LeDoux Library with 100,000 titles, 253 serial subscriptions, an OPAC.

Computers on Campus 160 computers available on campus for general student use.

Student Life *Activities and Organizations:* student-run newspaper, Student Government Association, Students in Free Enterprise, Criminal Justice Society, Student Nurses Association, Phi Theta Kappa. *Campus security:* 24-hour emergency response devices and patrols. *Student Services:* personal/psychological counseling.

Athletics Member NJCAA. *Intercollegiate sports:* baseball M, basketball W. *Intramural sports:* basketball M/W, football M, softball M/W, tennis M/W, volleyball M/W.

Standardized Tests *Required for some:* ACT (for placement). *Recommended:* ACT (for placement).

Costs (2002–03) *Tuition:* state resident $1456 full-time, $61 per credit part-time; nonresident $4456 full-time, $125 per credit part-time. *Room and board:* room only: $4200.

Financial Aid In 2001, 66 Federal Work-Study jobs (averaging $1525). 124 State and other part-time jobs (averaging $1234).

Applying *Options:* common application, early admission. *Application fee:* $10. *Required:* high school transcript. *Application deadlines:* 8/7 (freshmen), 8/7 (transfers).

Admissions Contact Ms. Gracie Guillory, Director of Financial Aid, Louisiana State University at Eunice, PO Box 1129, Eunice, LA 70535-1129. *Phone:* 337-550-1282. *Toll-free phone:* 888-367-5783. *Fax:* 337-550-1306.

LOUISIANA TECHNICAL COLLEGE-ACADIAN CAMPUS

Crowley, Louisiana

Admissions Contact 1933 West Hutchinson Avenue, Crowley, LA 70526.

LOUISIANA TECHNICAL COLLEGE-ALEXANDRIA CAMPUS

Alexandria, Louisiana

Admissions Contact 4311 South MacArthur, Alexandria, LA 71307-5698.

LOUISIANA TECHNICAL COLLEGE-ASCENSION CAMPUS

Sorrento, Louisiana

Admissions Contact 9697 Airline Highway, Sorrento, LA 70778-3007.

LOUISIANA TECHNICAL COLLEGE-AVOYELLES CAMPUS

Cottonport, Louisiana

Admissions Contact 508 Choupique Street, Cottonport, LA 71327.

LOUISIANA TECHNICAL COLLEGE-BASTROP CAMPUS

Bastrop, Louisiana

- **State-supported** 2-year, part of Louisiana Community and Technical College System
- **Degree** certificates and diplomas
- 241 undergraduate students, 69% full-time

Faculty *Student/faculty ratio:* 15:1.
Applying *Application fee:* $5.
Admissions Contact Ms. Vickye Branton, Student Personnel Services Officer, Louisiana Technical College-Bastrop Campus, PO Box 1120, Bastrop, LA 71220. *Phone:* 318-283-0836. *Fax:* 318-283-0871. *E-mail:* vbranton@lctcs.state.la.us.

LOUISIANA TECHNICAL COLLEGE-BATON ROUGE CAMPUS

Baton Rouge, Louisiana

Admissions Contact 3250 North Acadian Thruway East, Baton Rouge, LA 70805.

LOUISIANA TECHNICAL COLLEGE-CHARLES B. COREIL CAMPUS

Ville Platte, Louisiana

Admissions Contact 1124 Vocational Drive, PO Box 296, Ville Platte, LA 70586-0296.

LOUISIANA TECHNICAL COLLEGE-DELTA OUACHITA CAMPUS

West Monroe, Louisiana

- **State-supported** 2-year
- **Degree** certificates, diplomas, and associate
- **Coed, primarily women,** 835 undergraduate students

Majors Accounting technician; auto body repair; auto mechanic/technician; computer science; culinary arts; diesel engine mechanic; drafting; heating/air conditioning/refrigeration; machine technology; welding technology.

Student Life *Activities and Organizations:* National Vocational Technical Honor Society. *Campus security:* 24-hour emergency response devices.
Costs (2002–03) *Tuition:* state resident $578 full-time, $19 per credit hour part-time.
Admissions Contact Ms. Jo Ann Deal, Student Services Officer, Louisiana Technical College-Delta Ouachita Campus, 609 Vocational Parkway, West, Ouachita Industrial Park, West Monroe, LA 71292-9064. *Phone:* 318-397-6144.

LOUISIANA TECHNICAL COLLEGE-EVANGELINE CAMPUS

St. Martinville, Louisiana

Admissions Contact Mr. Joe Reiser, Student Personnel Services Officer, Louisiana Technical College-Evangeline Campus, 600 South Martin Luther King Drive, St. Martinville, LA 70582. *Phone:* 337-394-6466. *Fax:* 337-394-3965.

LOUISIANA TECHNICAL COLLEGE-FLORIDA PARISHES CAMPUS

Greensburg, Louisiana

- **State-supported** 2-year, part of Louisiana Community and Technical College System
- **Degree** certificates, diplomas, and associate
- **Coed,** 233 undergraduate students, 42% full-time, 48% women, 52% men
- 72% of applicants were admitted

Undergraduates 98 full-time, 135 part-time. Students come from 2 states and territories, 5% are from out of state, 3% transferred in.
Freshmen *Admission:* 36 applied, 26 admitted, 26 enrolled.
Faculty *Total:* 9, 78% full-time, 56% with terminal degrees. *Student/faculty ratio:* 15:1.
Majors Accounting; computer software and media applications related; information sciences/systems.
Academic Programs *Special study options:* academic remediation for entering students, adult/continuing education programs, advanced placement credit, cooperative education, internships, services for LD students.
Computers on Campus 10 computers available on campus for general student use. At least one staffed computer lab available.
Student Life *Housing:* college housing not available. *Activities and Organizations:* student-run newspaper. *Campus security:* 24-hour emergency response devices. *Student Services:* personal/psychological counseling.
Applying *Required:* high school transcript, TABE. *Required for some:* essay or personal statement, letters of recommendation, interview. *Notification:* continuous (freshmen).
Admissions Contact Ms. Sharon G. Hornsby, Interim Campus Dean, Louisiana Technical College-Florida Parishes Campus, Student Services, PO Box 1300, 100 College Street, Greensburg, LA 70441. *Phone:* 225-222-4251. *Toll-free phone:* 800-827-9750. *Fax:* 225-222-6064. *E-mail:* shornsby@lctcs.state.la.us.

LOUISIANA TECHNICAL COLLEGE-FOLKES CAMPUS

Jackson, Louisiana

- **State-supported** 2-year, part of Louisiana Community and Technical College System (LCTCS)
- **Degree** certificates, diplomas, and associate
- **Coed,** 221 undergraduate students, 71% full-time, 29% women, 71% men
- 100% of applicants were admitted

Undergraduates 158 full-time, 63 part-time. Students come from 1 other state, 62% African American, 0.5% Hispanic American, 0.9% Native American.
Freshmen *Admission:* 221 applied, 221 admitted, 221 enrolled.
Faculty *Total:* 14, 100% full-time, 14% with terminal degrees. *Student/faculty ratio:* 7:1.
Majors Auto mechanic/technician; business administration; emergency medical technology; practical nurse; welding technology.
Academic Programs *Special study options:* academic remediation for entering students, adult/continuing education programs, advanced placement credit, cooperative education, internships, services for LD students.

Computers on Campus 5 computers available on campus for general student use. At least one staffed computer lab available.
Student Life *Housing:* college housing not available. *Student Services:* personal/psychological counseling.
Costs (2001–02) *Tuition:* state resident $780 full-time, $98 per term part-time; nonresident $1560 full-time, $195 per term part-time. Full-time tuition and fees vary according to course load and program. Part-time tuition and fees vary according to class time, course load, and program.
Applying *Application fee:* $5. *Required:* TABE. *Required for some:* high school transcript. *Recommended:* interview.
Admissions Contact Ms. Dildred S. Womack, Student Personnel Officer, Louisiana Technical College-Folkes Campus, 3337 Highway 10, PO Box 808, Jackson, LA 70748-0808. *Phone:* 225-634-2636. *Fax:* 225-634-4225. *E-mail:* dwomack@lctcs.state.la.us.

LOUISIANA TECHNICAL COLLEGE-GULF AREA CAMPUS
Abbeville, Louisiana

Admissions Contact Mr. Ray E. Lavergne, Director, Louisiana Technical College-Gulf Area Campus, 1115 Clover Street, Abbeville, LA 70510. *Phone:* 337-893-4984.

LOUISIANA TECHNICAL COLLEGE-HAMMOND CAMPUS
Hammond, Louisiana

- **State-supported** 2-year
- **Degree** certificates, diplomas, and associate
- **Coed**

Admissions Contact Mrs. Eddy Anne Ouder, Student Services Officer, Louisiana Technical College-Hammond Campus, 111 Pride Avenue, Hammond, LA 70401. *Phone:* 504-543-4120. *Toll-free phone:* 800-469-0238.

LOUISIANA TECHNICAL COLLEGE-HUEY P. LONG CAMPUS
Winnfield, Louisiana

Admissions Contact 303 South Jones Street, Winnfield, LA 71483.

LOUISIANA TECHNICAL COLLEGE-JEFFERSON CAMPUS
Metairie, Louisiana

Admissions Contact 5200 Blaire Drive, Metairie, LA 70001.

LOUISIANA TECHNICAL COLLEGE-LAFAYETTE CAMPUS
Lafayette, Louisiana

Admissions Contact 1101 Bertrand Drive, Lafayette, LA 70502-4909.

LOUISIANA TECHNICAL COLLEGE-LAFOURCHE CAMPUS
Thibodaux, Louisiana

Admissions Contact 1425 Tiger Drive, Thibodaux, LA 70302-1831.

LOUISIANA TECHNICAL COLLEGE-LAMAR SALTER CAMPUS
Leesville, Louisiana

- **State-supported** 2-year
- **Degree** certificates, diplomas, and associate
- **Coed**

Admissions Contact Mr. Alan Dunbar, Student Program Coordinator, Louisiana Technical College-Lamar Salter Campus, 15014 Lake Charles Highway, Leesville, LA 71446. *Phone:* 337-537-3135. *E-mail:* adunbar@lctcs.state.la.us.

LOUISIANA TECHNICAL COLLEGE-L.E. FLETCHER CAMPUS
Hourma, Louisiana

Admissions Contact 310 St. Charles Street, Hourma, LA 70361-5033.

LOUISIANA TECHNICAL COLLEGE-MANSFIELD CAMPUS
Mansfield, Louisiana

- **State-supported** 2-year
- **Degree** certificates, diplomas, and associate
- **Coed,** 200 undergraduate students

Faculty *Total:* 10. *Student/faculty ratio:* 10:1.
Majors Heating/air conditioning/refrigeration; nurse assistant/aide; practical nurse; welding technology.
Costs (2001–02) *Tuition:* area resident $390 full-time; state resident $780 full-time, $18 per credit hour part-time; nonresident $36 per credit hour part-time. *Required fees:* $20 full-time, $10 per term part-time.
Admissions Contact Ms. Hilda Rives, Student Personnel Services Officer, Louisiana Technical College-Mansfield Campus, 943 Oxford Road, PO Box 1236, Mansfield, LA 71052. *Phone:* 318-872-2243. *Fax:* 318-872-4249.

LOUISIANA TECHNICAL COLLEGE-MORGAN SMITH CAMPUS
Jennings, Louisiana

Admissions Contact 1230 North Main Street, Jennings, LA 70546-1327.

LOUISIANA TECHNICAL COLLEGE-NATCHITOCHES CAMPUS
Natchitoches, Louisiana

- **State-supported** 2-year
- **Degree** certificates, diplomas, and associate
- **Coed,** 528 undergraduate students, 34% full-time, 53% women, 47% men
- 100% of applicants were admitted

Undergraduates 182 full-time, 346 part-time. 38% African American, 0.8% Hispanic American, 2% Native American.
Freshmen *Admission:* 182 applied, 182 admitted.
Faculty *Total:* 17, 94% full-time, 59% with terminal degrees. *Student/faculty ratio:* 15:1.
Majors Accounting technician; early childhood education; management information systems/business data processing.
Costs (2002–03) *Tuition:* area resident $520 full-time; state resident $520 full-time; nonresident $1040 full-time. *Required fees:* $965 full-time.
Admissions Contact Ms. Carol Hebert, Student Personnel Services Officer, Louisiana Technical College-Natchitoches Campus, 6587 Highway 1, Bypass, Natchitoches, LA 71457. *Phone:* 318-357-7007.

LOUISIANA TECHNICAL COLLEGE-NORTH CENTRAL CAMPUS
Farmerville, Louisiana

- **State-supported** 2-year
- **Degree** certificates, diplomas, and associate
- **Coed**

Faculty *Student/faculty ratio:* 16:1.
Applying *Required for some:* high school transcript. *Recommended:* interview.

Louisiana Technical College-North Central Campus (continued)

Admissions Contact Ms. Donna C. Sewell, Assistant Director/Student Personnel Services Officer, Louisiana Technical College-North Central Campus, PO Box 548, Farmerville, LA 71241. *Phone:* 318-368-3179. *Fax:* 318-368-9180. *E-mail:* dsewell@lctcs.state.la.us.

LOUISIANA TECHNICAL COLLEGE-NORTHEAST LOUISIANA CAMPUS
Winnsboro, Louisiana

Admissions Contact 1710 Warren Street, Winnsboro, LA 71295.

LOUISIANA TECHNICAL COLLEGE-NORTHWEST LOUISIANA CAMPUS
Minden, Louisiana

Admissions Contact Ms. Helen Deville, Student Services Officer, Louisiana Technical College-Northwest Louisiana Campus, 814 Constable Street, Minden, LA 71058-0835. *Phone:* 318-371-3035.

LOUISIANA TECHNICAL COLLEGE-OAKDALE CAMPUS
Oakdale, Louisiana

Admissions Contact Old Pelican Highway, Oakdale, LA 71463.

LOUISIANA TECHNICAL COLLEGE-RIVER PARISHES CAMPUS
Reserve, Louisiana

Admissions Contact PO Drawer AQ, Reserve, LA 70084.

LOUISIANA TECHNICAL COLLEGE-SABINE VALLEY CAMPUS
Many, Louisiana

- **State-supported** 2-year
- **Degree** certificates, diplomas, and associate
- **Coed**

Admissions Contact Mr. Barry Goss, Student Personnel Services Officer, Louisiana Technical College-Sabine Valley Campus, 1255 Fisher Road, Many, LA 71449. *Phone:* 318-256-4101.

LOUISIANA TECHNICAL COLLEGE-SHELBY M. JACKSON CAMPUS
Ferriday, Louisiana

Admissions Contact PO Box 1465, Ferriday, LA 71334.

LOUISIANA TECHNICAL COLLEGE-SHREVEPORT-BOSSIER CAMPUS
Shreveport, Louisiana

Admissions Contact 2010 North Market Street, Shreveport, LA 71137-8527.

LOUISIANA TECHNICAL COLLEGE-SIDNEY N. COLLIER CAMPUS
New Orleans, Louisiana

Admissions Contact Ms. Linda Eubanks, Student Personnel Services Officer, Louisiana Technical College-Sidney N. Collier Campus, 3727 Louisa Street, New Orleans, LA 70126. *Phone:* 504-942-8333 Ext. 137.

LOUISIANA TECHNICAL COLLEGE-SLIDELL CAMPUS
Slidell, Louisiana

Admissions Contact 1000 Canulette Road, Slidell, LA 70459-0827.

LOUISIANA TECHNICAL COLLEGE-SOWELA CAMPUS
Lake Charles, Louisiana

Admissions Contact 3820 J. Bennett Johnston Avenue, Lake Charles, LA 70616-6950.

LOUISIANA TECHNICAL COLLEGE-SULLIVAN CAMPUS
Bogalusa, Louisiana

Admissions Contact 1710 Sullivan Drive, Bogalusa, LA 70427.

LOUISIANA TECHNICAL COLLEGE-TALLULAH CAMPUS
Tallulah, Louisiana

Admissions Contact Old Highway 65 South, Tallulah, LA 71284-1740.

LOUISIANA TECHNICAL COLLEGE-TECHE AREA CAMPUS
New Iberia, Louisiana

Admissions Contact PO Box 11057, New Iberia, LA 70562-1057.

LOUISIANA TECHNICAL COLLEGE-T.H. HARRIS CAMPUS
Opelousas, Louisiana

Admissions Contact 332 East South Street, Opelousas, LA 70570.

LOUISIANA TECHNICAL COLLEGE-WEST JEFFERSON CAMPUS
Harvey, Louisiana

Admissions Contact 475 Manhattan Boulevard, Harvey, LA 70058.

LOUISIANA TECHNICAL COLLEGE-YOUNG MEMORIAL CAMPUS
Morgan City, Louisiana

- **State-supported** 2-year
- **Degree** certificates, diplomas, and associate
- **Coed**

Admissions Contact Ms. Melanie Henry, Student Personnel Officer, Louisiana Technical College-Young Memorial Campus, 900 Youngs Road, Morgan City, LA 70381. *Phone:* 504-380-2436.

MEDVANCE INSTITUTE
Baton Rouge, Louisiana

- **Proprietary** 2-year, founded 1970
- **Calendar** quarters
- **Degree** diplomas and associate
- **Urban** 4-acre campus
- **Coed,** 225 undergraduate students

Undergraduates Students come from 1 other state.
Faculty *Total:* 10. *Student/faculty ratio:* 22:1.
Majors Medical laboratory technician.
Academic Programs *Special study options:* internships.
Computers on Campus 10 computers available on campus for general student use. At least one staffed computer lab available.
Student Life *Housing:* college housing not available.
Costs (2001–02) *Tuition:* $5770 per degree program part-time. Tuition costs vary depending on degree program. *Required fees:* $25 full-time.
Applying *Options:* common application. *Application fee:* $100. *Required:* high school transcript, interview. *Recommended:* minimum 2.0 GPA, 2 letters of recommendation. *Application deadline:* rolling (freshmen), rolling (transfers). *Notification:* continuous (freshmen).
Admissions Contact Ms. Sheri Caraccioli, Director, MedVance Institute, 4173 Government Street, Baton Rouge, LA 70806. *Phone:* 225-248-1015. *Fax:* 225-343-5426.

OUR LADY OF THE LAKE COLLEGE
Baton Rouge, Louisiana

- **Independent Roman Catholic** primarily 2-year, founded 1990
- **Calendar** semesters
- **Degrees** certificates, associate, and bachelor's
- **Suburban** 5-acre campus with easy access to New Orleans
- **Coed,** 1,218 undergraduate students, 29% full-time, 88% women, 12% men

Undergraduates 358 full-time, 860 part-time. Students come from 3 states and territories, 1% are from out of state, 20% African American, 0.4% Asian American or Pacific Islander, 1% Hispanic American, 1% Native American. *Retention:* 62% of 2001 full-time freshmen returned.
Freshmen *Admission:* 211 applied, 210 admitted, 193 enrolled. *Average high school GPA:* 3.0. *Test scores:* ACT scores over 18: 72%; ACT scores over 24: 14%; ACT scores over 30: 1%.
Faculty *Total:* 113, 47% full-time, 54% with terminal degrees. *Student/faculty ratio:* 19:1.
Majors Emergency medical technology; general studies; humanities; industrial radiologic technology; medical laboratory technician; nursing; operating room technician; physical therapy assistant.
Academic Programs *Special study options:* academic remediation for entering students, advanced placement credit, services for LD students, summer session for credit.
Library Learning Resource Center plus 1 other with 12,409 titles, 328 serial subscriptions, an OPAC.
Computers on Campus 52 computers available on campus for general student use. Internet access, at least one staffed computer lab available.
Student Life *Housing:* college housing not available. *Activities and Organizations:* Student Government Association, Cultural Arts Association, Christian Fellowship Association, Mathematics/Science Association. *Campus security:* 24-hour patrols. *Student Services:* health clinic, personal/psychological counseling.
Standardized Tests *Required for some:* SAT I or ACT (for admission).
Costs (2001–02) *Tuition:* area resident $6080 full-time, $190 per semester hour part-time. *Required fees:* $600 full-time.
Applying *Options:* common application. *Application fee:* $25. *Required:* high school transcript, minimum 2.0 GPA. *Application deadline:* rolling (freshmen), rolling (transfers).
Admissions Contact Mr. Mark Wetmore, Director of Admissions, Our Lady of the Lake College, 5345 Brittany Drive, Baton Rouge, LA 70808. *Phone:* 225-768-1718. *Toll-free phone:* 877-242-3509. *E-mail:* admission@ololcollege.edu.

SOUTHERN UNIVERSITY AT SHREVEPORT
Shreveport, Louisiana

Admissions Contact Ms. Juanita Johnson, Acting Admissions Records Technician, Southern University at Shreveport, 3050 Martin Luther King, Jr. Drive, Shreveport, LA 71107. *Phone:* 318-674-3342. *Toll-free phone:* 800-458-1472 Ext. 342.

MAINE

ANDOVER COLLEGE
Portland, Maine

- **Proprietary** 2-year, founded 1966
- **Calendar** modular
- **Degree** certificates and associate
- **Urban** 2-acre campus
- **Coed,** 520 undergraduate students, 100% full-time, 78% women, 23% men

Associate degrees offered in 16 to 22 months in accounting, business administration, computer technology, criminal justice, early childhood education, legal studies, medical assisting, office administration, and travel and tourism. Facilities include 5 computer labs with Internet access and Academic Assistance Center. Internships and placement services are offered, and the average employment rate for graduates is 95%.

Undergraduates 520 full-time. Students come from 5 states and territories, 6 other countries.
Freshmen *Admission:* 203 applied, 203 admitted, 61 enrolled.
Faculty *Total:* 37, 35% full-time. *Student/faculty ratio:* 18:1.
Majors Accounting; business administration; computer/information technology services administration and management related; computer management; computer programming; computer science; criminal justice/law enforcement administration; early childhood education; legal administrative assistant; medical administrative assistant; medical assistant; medical records administration; paralegal/legal assistant; secretarial science; system administration; Web/multimedia management/webmaster.
Academic Programs *Special study options:* academic remediation for entering students, adult/continuing education programs, cooperative education, independent study, internships, part-time degree program, summer session for credit.
Library Andover Library with 6,000 titles, 106 serial subscriptions, 59 audiovisual materials.
Computers on Campus 100 computers available on campus for general student use. Internet access, at least one staffed computer lab available.
Student Life *Activities and Organizations:* Student Advisors, Andover Computer, Student Advisors Group, Andover Student Medical Assistants, C.O.P.S. *Campus security:* 24-hour emergency response devices. *Student Services:* personal/psychological counseling.
Costs (2002–03) *Comprehensive fee:* $12,436 includes full-time tuition ($5400), mandatory fees ($900), and room and board ($6136). *Room and board:* College room only: $3600. *Waivers:* employees or children of employees.
Financial Aid In 2001, 25 Federal Work-Study jobs (averaging $3000).
Applying *Options:* common application, early admission, deferred entrance. *Application fee:* $25. *Required:* high school transcript. *Recommended:* interview. *Application deadline:* rolling (freshmen), rolling (transfers).
Admissions Contact Mr. David Blessing, Director of Admissions, Andover College, 901 Washington Avenue, Portland, ME 04103-2791. *Phone:* 207-774-6126 Ext. 242. *Toll-free phone:* 800-639-3110 Ext. 403. *Fax:* 207-774-1715. *E-mail:* enroll@andovercollege.com.

BEAL COLLEGE
Bangor, Maine

- **Proprietary** 2-year, founded 1891
- **Calendar** modular
- **Degree** certificates, diplomas, and associate
- **Small-town** 4-acre campus
- **Coed**

Faculty *Student/faculty ratio:* 14:1.
Applying *Options:* deferred entrance. *Application fee:* $25. *Required:* high school transcript. *Recommended:* interview.
Admissions Contact Ms. Susan Palmer, Admissions Assistant, Beal College, 629 Main Street, Bangor, ME 04401. *Phone:* 207-947-4591. *Toll-free phone:* 800-660-7351. *Fax:* 207-947-0208.

CENTRAL MAINE MEDICAL CENTER SCHOOL OF NURSING
Lewiston, Maine

- **Independent** 2-year, founded 1891
- **Calendar** semesters

Central Maine Medical Center School of Nursing (continued)
- **Degree** certificates and associate
- **Urban** campus
- **Endowment** $184,938
- **Coed, primarily women,** 98 undergraduate students, 26% full-time, 90% women, 10% men

Undergraduates 25 full-time, 73 part-time. Students come from 2 states and territories, 2% are from out of state, 1% African American, 3% Hispanic American, 5% live on campus.
Freshmen *Admission:* 3 enrolled. *Average high school GPA:* 3.30. *Test scores:* SAT verbal scores over 500: 34%.
Faculty *Total:* 10, 80% full-time, 20% with terminal degrees. *Student/faculty ratio:* 8:1.
Majors Nursing.
Academic Programs *Special study options:* advanced placement credit, off-campus study.
Library Gerrish True Health Sciences Library with 1,975 titles, 339 serial subscriptions, an OPAC, a Web page.
Computers on Campus 10 computers available on campus for general student use. At least one staffed computer lab available.
Student Life *Housing Options:* coed. *Activities and Organizations:* Student Communication Council, student government, Student Nurses Association. *Campus security:* 24-hour emergency response devices and patrols, late-night transport/escort service, controlled dormitory access. *Student Services:* health clinic, personal/psychological counseling.
Standardized Tests *Required:* SAT I (for admission).
Costs (2001–02) *Tuition:* $2310 full-time, $110 per credit part-time. *Required fees:* $935 full-time, $20 per term part-time. *Room only:* $1500.
Applying *Application fee:* $20. *Required:* essay or personal statement, high school transcript, 2 letters of recommendation. *Application deadline:* 6/1 (freshmen).
Admissions Contact Mrs. Kathleen C. Jacques, Registrar, Central Maine Medical Center School of Nursing, 70 Middle Street, Lewiston, ME 04240-0305. *Phone:* 207-795-2858. *Fax:* 207-795-2849. *E-mail:* jacqueka@cmhc.org.

CENTRAL MAINE TECHNICAL COLLEGE
Auburn, Maine

- **State-supported** 2-year, founded 1964, part of Maine Technical College System
- **Calendar** semesters
- **Degree** certificates, diplomas, and associate
- **Small-town** 135-acre campus
- **Coed,** 1,435 undergraduate students, 44% full-time, 45% women, 55% men

Undergraduates 625 full-time, 810 part-time. Students come from 5 states and territories, 0.5% African American, 0.5% Asian American or Pacific Islander, 1% Hispanic American, 1% Native American, 5% transferred in, 11% live on campus. *Retention:* 77% of 2001 full-time freshmen returned.
Freshmen *Admission:* 858 applied, 446 admitted, 464 enrolled.
Faculty *Total:* 135, 39% full-time, 1% with terminal degrees. *Student/faculty ratio:* 11:1.
Majors Accounting; architecture; auto mechanic/technician; business administration; civil engineering technology; computer science; construction technology; early childhood education; electromechanical technology; general studies; graphic design/commercial art/illustration; graphic/printing equipment; hospitality management; industrial radiologic technology; machine technology; mechanical design technology; medical administrative assistant; medical laboratory technician; medical laboratory technology; nursing; occupational safety/health technology; secretarial science; telecommunications.
Academic Programs *Special study options:* academic remediation for entering students, adult/continuing education programs, advanced placement credit, cooperative education, internships, part-time degree program, services for LD students, summer session for credit.
Library Central Maine Technical College Library with 15,000 titles, 240 serial subscriptions, a Web page.
Computers on Campus 150 computers available on campus for general student use. Internet access, at least one staffed computer lab available.
Student Life *Housing Options:* coed, men-only, women-only. *Activities and Organizations:* drama/theater group, student-run television station, Student Senate, Drama Club, Outing Club, intramural sports, Phi Theta Kappa. *Campus security:* 24-hour emergency response devices, controlled dormitory access, night patrols by police. *Student Services:* health clinic, personal/psychological counseling.
Athletics Member NSCAA. *Intercollegiate sports:* baseball M, basketball M/W, soccer M/W, softball W, volleyball M/W. *Intramural sports:* baseball M, basketball M/W, bowling M/W, cross-country running M/W, field hockey M/W, golf M/W, ice hockey M/W, skiing (cross-country) M/W, skiing (downhill) M/W, soccer M/W, softball M/W, swimming M/W, volleyball M/W.
Standardized Tests *Required for some:* ACCUPLACER. *Recommended:* SAT I (for placement).
Costs (2002–03) *Tuition:* area resident $2176 full-time, $68 per credit part-time; state resident $3264 full-time, $102 per credit part-time; nonresident $4768 full-time, $149 per credit part-time. No tuition increase for student's term of enrollment. *Required fees:* $690 full-time. *Room and board:* $4175; room only: $1000. *Payment plans:* tuition prepayment, installment. *Waivers:* children of alumni, senior citizens, and employees or children of employees.
Financial Aid In 2001, 170 Federal Work-Study jobs (averaging $1000).
Applying *Options:* deferred entrance. *Application fee:* $20. *Required:* essay or personal statement, high school transcript. *Required for some:* 2 letters of recommendation, interview. *Recommended:* minimum 2.0 GPA. *Application deadline:* rolling (freshmen), rolling (transfers). *Notification:* continuous (freshmen).
Admissions Contact Mr. Walter Clark, Director of Admissions, Central Maine Technical College, 1250 Turner Street, Auburn, ME 04210-6498. *Phone:* 207-755-5334 Ext. 334. *Toll-free phone:* 800-891-2002 Ext. 273. *Fax:* 207-755-5490. *E-mail:* enroll@cmtc.net.

EASTERN MAINE TECHNICAL COLLEGE
Bangor, Maine

- **State-supported** 2-year, founded 1966, part of Maine Technical College System
- **Calendar** semesters
- **Degree** certificates, diplomas, and associate
- **Small-town** 72-acre campus
- **Endowment** $1.5 million
- **Coed,** 1,604 undergraduate students, 42% full-time, 50% women, 50% men

Undergraduates 671 full-time, 933 part-time. Students come from 4 states and territories, 1% are from out of state, 0.5% African American, 0.3% Asian American or Pacific Islander, 0.2% Hispanic American, 2% Native American, 20% live on campus.
Freshmen *Admission:* 1,407 applied, 705 admitted, 383 enrolled.
Faculty *Total:* 142, 38% full-time, 6% with terminal degrees. *Student/faculty ratio:* 11:1.
Majors Auto mechanic/technician; banking; business administration; carpentry; computer maintenance technology; construction technology; culinary arts; drafting/design technology; early childhood education; electrical/electronic engineering technology; general studies; heating/air conditioning/refrigeration; heavy equipment maintenance; machine technology; medical laboratory technician; nursing; practical nurse; radiological science; secretarial science; welding technology.
Academic Programs *Special study options:* academic remediation for entering students, adult/continuing education programs, advanced placement credit, part-time degree program, summer session for credit.
Library Eastern Maine Technical College Library plus 1 other with 17,554 titles, 159 serial subscriptions, an OPAC, a Web page.
Computers on Campus 85 computers available on campus for general student use. A campuswide network can be accessed from off campus. Internet access, at least one staffed computer lab available.
Student Life *Housing Options:* coed. *Activities and Organizations:* student-run newspaper, Student Senate, Phi Theta Kappa, Senior Council, Resident's Council, Associated General Contractors Student Chapter. *Campus security:* late-night transport/escort service, controlled dormitory access. *Student Services:* health clinic, personal/psychological counseling.
Athletics Member NSCAA. *Intercollegiate sports:* basketball M, soccer M/W. *Intramural sports:* badminton M/W, basketball M/W, bowling M/W, ice hockey M(c)/W(c), skiing (cross-country) M/W, skiing (downhill) M/W, soccer M/W, table tennis M/W, volleyball M/W, weight lifting M/W.
Standardized Tests *Required for some:* SAT I (for admission).
Costs (2001–02) *Tuition:* state resident $2448 full-time, $68 per credit part-time; nonresident $5364 full-time, $149 per credit part-time. *Room and board:* $4052. Room and board charges vary according to board plan. *Waivers:* employees or children of employees.
Financial Aid In 2001, 100 Federal Work-Study jobs (averaging $1000).
Applying *Options:* deferred entrance. *Application fee:* $20. *Required:* essay or personal statement, high school transcript, letters of recommendation. *Required for some:* interview. *Recommended:* minimum 2.0 GPA. *Application deadline:* rolling (freshmen). *Notification:* continuous (freshmen).

Admissions Contact Ms. Elizabeth Russell, Director of Admissions, Eastern Maine Technical College, 354 Hogan Road, Bangor, ME 04401. *Phone:* 207-941-4680. *Toll-free phone:* 800-286-9357. *Fax:* 207-941-4683. *E-mail:* admissions@emtc.org.

KENNEBEC VALLEY TECHNICAL COLLEGE
Fairfield, Maine

- **State-supported** 2-year, founded 1970, part of Maine Technical College System
- **Calendar** semesters
- **Degree** certificates, diplomas, and associate
- **Small-town** 58-acre campus
- **Coed,** 1,255 undergraduate students, 30% full-time, 59% women, 41% men

Undergraduates 381 full-time, 874 part-time. Students come from 3 states and territories, 0.2% African American, 0.4% Asian American or Pacific Islander, 0.5% Hispanic American, 0.9% Native American.

Freshmen *Admission:* 841 applied, 505 admitted, 199 enrolled.

Faculty *Total:* 103, 41% full-time. *Student/faculty ratio:* 28:1.

Majors Accounting; biology; business administration; business marketing and marketing management; child care provider; child care services management; communication systems installation/repair; computer/information technology services administration and management related; computer installation/repair; computer management; computer programming related; computer software and media applications related; computer systems networking/telecommunications; culinary arts; data warehousing/mining/database administration; drafting/design technology; education; electrical equipment installation/repair; emergency medical technology; executive assistant; general studies; industrial electronics installation/repair; industrial machinery maintenance/repair; legal administrative assistant; liberal arts and sciences/liberal studies; machine technology; marketing operations; medical assistant; medical records administration; nursing; occupational therapy assistant; physical therapy assistant; respiratory therapy; secretarial science; Web/multimedia management/webmaster; Web page, digital/multimedia and information resources design; wood science/paper technology.

Academic Programs *Special study options:* academic remediation for entering students, accelerated degree program, adult/continuing education programs, advanced placement credit, distance learning, double majors, external degree program, independent study, internships, part-time degree program, services for LD students, summer session for credit.

Library KVTC Library and Information Technology Center with 16,537 titles, 3,340 serial subscriptions, 1,260 audiovisual materials, an OPAC, a Web page.

Computers on Campus 87 computers available on campus for general student use. Internet access, at least one staffed computer lab available.

Student Life *Housing:* college housing not available. *Activities and Organizations:* Vocational Industrial Clubs of America (VICA) Skills USA, Student Senate, Phi Theta Kappa, Glee Club. *Campus security:* Evening security patrol. *Student Services:* personal/psychological counseling.

Athletics *Intramural sports:* archery M, volleyball M/W.

Costs (2002–03) *Tuition:* state resident $2040 full-time, $68 per credit hour part-time; nonresident $4470 full-time, $149 per credit hour part-time. *Waivers:* senior citizens and employees or children of employees.

Financial Aid In 2001, 43 Federal Work-Study jobs (averaging $605).

Applying *Options:* electronic application, deferred entrance. *Application fee:* $20. *Required:* essay or personal statement, high school transcript. *Required for some:* letters of recommendation, interview. *Application deadline:* rolling (freshmen), rolling (transfers). *Notification:* continuous (freshmen).

Admissions Contact Mr. Jim Bourgoin, Director of Recruitment, Kennebec Valley Technical College, 92 Western Avenue, Fairfield, ME 04937-1367. *Phone:* 207-453-5035. *Toll-free phone:* 800-528-5882 Ext. 5131 (in-state); 207-453-5131 (out-of-state). *Fax:* 207-453-5011. *E-mail:* admissions@kvtc.net.

MID-STATE COLLEGE
Auburn, Maine

- **Proprietary** 2-year, founded 1867
- **Calendar** modular
- **Degree** certificates and associate
- **Suburban** 20-acre campus
- **Coed,** 275 undergraduate students

The small college in central Maine that means business, Mid-State has an atmosphere of close cooperation between students and staff and faculty members. In small classes at each of the two campuses in Augusta and Auburn, students receive the benefit of personal attention. Mid-State offers an accelerated yet flexible program of study in a series of six 8-week sessions with both day and evening classes. Its open admission policy attracts a diverse student body that enhances the learning environment.

Undergraduates Students come from 1 other state, 1 other country, 1% live on campus.

Freshmen *Admission:* 66 applied, 66 admitted.

Faculty *Total:* 24, 42% full-time.

Majors Accounting; business administration; computer systems analysis; hospitality management; information sciences/systems; legal administrative assistant; medical administrative assistant; medical assistant; office management; secretarial science; travel/tourism management.

Academic Programs *Special study options:* academic remediation for entering students, accelerated degree program, adult/continuing education programs, advanced placement credit, cooperative education, double majors, internships, part-time degree program, summer session for credit.

Library 3,000 titles, 75 serial subscriptions.

Computers on Campus 65 computers available on campus for general student use. Internet access, at least one staffed computer lab available.

Student Life *Housing Options:* coed. *Activities and Organizations:* student-run newspaper, student newspaper, yearbook, student government, Collegiate Secretaries International. *Campus security:* 24-hour emergency response devices. *Student Services:* personal/psychological counseling.

Costs (2002–03) *Tuition:* $4680 full-time, $390 per course part-time. Full-time tuition and fees vary according to course load and program. Part-time tuition and fees vary according to course load and program. *Required fees:* $100 full-time. *Payment plans:* installment, deferred payment. *Waivers:* employees or children of employees.

Financial Aid In 2001, 5 Federal Work-Study jobs.

Applying *Options:* early admission, deferred entrance. *Application fee:* $25. *Application deadline:* rolling (freshmen), rolling (transfers).

Admissions Contact Ms. Wendy Berube-Gamache, Director of Admissions, Mid-State College, 88 East Hardscrabble Road, Auburn, ME 04210-8888. *Phone:* 207-783-1478. *Toll-free phone:* 800-950-8686. *E-mail:* info@midstatecollege.com.

NORTHERN MAINE TECHNICAL COLLEGE
Presque Isle, Maine

- **State-related** 2-year, founded 1963, part of Maine Technical College System
- **Calendar** semesters
- **Degree** certificates, diplomas, and associate
- **Small-town** 86-acre campus
- **Coed,** 784 undergraduate students, 65% full-time, 47% women, 53% men

Undergraduates 508 full-time, 276 part-time. Students come from 5 states and territories, 1 other country, 0.8% African American, 0.6% Asian American or Pacific Islander, 0.3% Hispanic American, 5% Native American, 4% international, 28% live on campus.

Freshmen *Admission:* 656 applied, 551 admitted, 260 enrolled.

Faculty *Total:* 76, 61% full-time.

Majors Accounting; agricultural business; auto mechanic/technician; business administration; carpentry; computer engineering technology; computer programming; data processing technology; drafting; early childhood education; electrical/electronic engineering technology; emergency medical technology; heating/air conditioning/refrigeration; heavy equipment maintenance; industrial arts; instrumentation technology; legal administrative assistant; medical administrative assistant; nursing; plumbing; practical nurse; secretarial science.

Academic Programs *Special study options:* academic remediation for entering students, adult/continuing education programs, advanced placement credit, cooperative education, double majors, independent study, internships, off-campus study, part-time degree program, services for LD students, summer session for credit.

Library Northern Maine Technical College Library with 11,200 titles, 233 serial subscriptions, 250 audiovisual materials, an OPAC, a Web page.

Computers on Campus A campuswide network can be accessed from student residence rooms and from off campus. Internet access, at least one staffed computer lab available.

Student Life *Housing Options:* coed. *Campus security:* 24-hour patrols. *Student Services:* health clinic, personal/psychological counseling.

Athletics Member NSCAA. *Intercollegiate sports:* basketball M/W, golf M/W, ice hockey M/W, soccer M/W. *Intramural sports:* archery M/W, basketball M/W, football M/W, golf M, racquetball M/W, soccer M, softball M/W, table tennis M/W, tennis M/W, volleyball M/W, weight lifting M/W.

Northern Maine Technical College (continued)

Standardized Tests *Required:* Assessment and Placement Services for Community Colleges.

Costs (2002–03) *Tuition:* state resident $2040 full-time, $68 per credit part-time; nonresident $149 per credit part-time. Full-time tuition and fees vary according to course load and program. Part-time tuition and fees vary according to course load and program. *Required fees:* $200 full-time, $3 per credit, $40 per term part-time. *Room and board:* $3800; room only: $1500. Room and board charges vary according to board plan and housing facility. *Payment plan:* installment. *Waivers:* senior citizens and employees or children of employees.

Financial Aid In 2001, 55 Federal Work-Study jobs (averaging $3000).

Applying *Options:* common application, electronic application, early admission. *Application fee:* $20. *Required:* high school transcript. *Required for some:* letters of recommendation. *Recommended:* essay or personal statement, minimum 2.0 GPA. *Application deadline:* rolling (freshmen).

Admissions Contact Ms. Nancy Gagnon, Admissions Secretary, Northern Maine Technical College, 33 Edgemont Drive, Presque Isle, ME 04769-2016. *Phone:* 207-768-2785. *Toll-free phone:* 800-535-6682. *Fax:* 207-768-2831. *E-mail:* wcasavant@nmtc.net.

SOUTHERN MAINE TECHNICAL COLLEGE
South Portland, Maine

- **State-supported** 2-year, founded 1946, part of Maine Technical College System
- **Calendar** semesters
- **Degree** certificates, diplomas, and associate
- **Suburban** 65-acre campus
- **Endowment** $608,532
- **Coed,** 2,471 undergraduate students, 44% full-time, 46% women, 54% men

Undergraduates 1,086 full-time, 1,385 part-time. Students come from 10 states and territories, 7% are from out of state, 1% African American, 1% Asian American or Pacific Islander, 0.6% Hispanic American, 1% Native American, 0.5% international, 10% live on campus.

Freshmen *Admission:* 2,386 applied, 949 admitted, 488 enrolled.

Faculty *Total:* 202, 50% full-time. *Student/faculty ratio:* 11:1.

Majors Agronomy/crop science; architectural engineering technology; auto mechanic/technician; botany; business administration; business machine repair; cardiovascular technology; carpentry; child care/development; communication equipment technology; computer engineering technology; computer management; construction technology; criminal justice/law enforcement administration; culinary arts; dietetics; drafting; early childhood education; electrical/electronic engineering technology; engineering design; environmental technology; film/video production; fire science; food products retailing; food services technology; general studies; heating/air conditioning/refrigeration; horticulture science; hospitality management; hotel and restaurant management; industrial radiologic technology; information sciences/systems; landscaping management; law enforcement/police science; liberal arts and sciences/liberal studies; machine technology; management information systems/business data processing; marine biology; medical assistant; nursing; oceanography; operating room technician; plumbing; practical nurse; radiological science; respiratory therapy.

Academic Programs *Special study options:* academic remediation for entering students, advanced placement credit, cooperative education, distance learning, double majors, English as a second language, internships, off-campus study, part-time degree program, services for LD students, study abroad, summer session for credit.

Library Southern Maine Technical College Library with 15,000 titles, 350 serial subscriptions.

Computers on Campus 200 computers available on campus for general student use. A campuswide network can be accessed from student residence rooms and from off campus. Internet access, at least one staffed computer lab available.

Student Life *Housing Options:* coed. *Activities and Organizations:* drama/theater group, student-run newspaper, choral group, SEA Club, student government, Phi Theta Kappa, VICA. *Campus security:* 24-hour emergency response devices, student patrols, late-night transport/escort service. *Student Services:* health clinic, personal/psychological counseling, women's center.

Athletics Member NSCAA. *Intercollegiate sports:* baseball M, basketball M, golf M/W, soccer M/W, softball W, volleyball M/W. *Intramural sports:* basketball M/W, football M/W, golf M/W, soccer M/W, volleyball M/W.

Standardized Tests *Required for some:* SAT I (for admission).

Costs (2001–02) *Tuition:* state resident $2040 full-time, $68 per credit part-time; nonresident $4470 full-time, $149 per credit part-time. Full-time tuition and fees vary according to course load and reciprocity agreements. Part-time tuition and fees vary according to course load and reciprocity agreements. *Required fees:* $500 full-time, $20 per credit. *Room and board:* $4200. Room and board charges vary according to board plan, housing facility, and location. *Payment plan:* installment. *Waivers:* senior citizens and employees or children of employees.

Financial Aid In 2001, 130 Federal Work-Study jobs (averaging $1500).

Applying *Application fee:* $20. *Required:* essay or personal statement, high school transcript. *Required for some:* letters of recommendation, interview. *Recommended:* minimum 2.0 GPA. *Application deadline:* rolling (freshmen), rolling (transfers). *Notification:* continuous (freshmen).

Admissions Contact Mr. Robert A. Weimont, Director of Admissions, Southern Maine Technical College, Admissions, 2 Fort Road, South Portland, ME 04106. *Phone:* 207-767-9520. *Toll-free phone:* 877-282-2182 Ext. 520. *Fax:* 207-767-9671. *E-mail:* adms@smtc.net.

WASHINGTON COUNTY TECHNICAL COLLEGE
Calais, Maine

Admissions Contact Ms. Pauli Caruncho, Director of Admissions/Assistant Dean of Students, Washington County Technical College, RR#1, Box 22C River Road, Calais, ME 04619. *Phone:* 207-454-1010. *Toll-free phone:* 800-210-6932 Ext. 41049. *Fax:* 207-454-1026.

YORK COUNTY TECHNICAL COLLEGE
Wells, Maine

- **State-supported** 2-year, founded 1994, part of Maine Technical College System
- **Calendar** semesters
- **Degree** certificates and associate
- **Small-town** 84-acre campus with easy access to Boston
- **Coed**

Faculty *Student/faculty ratio:* 13:1.

Student Life *Campus security:* 24-hour emergency response devices.

Standardized Tests *Recommended:* SAT I (for placement).

Costs (2001–02) *Tuition:* state resident $2040 full-time, $68 per credit part-time; nonresident $4470 full-time, $149 per credit part-time. Full-time tuition and fees vary according to course load, program, and reciprocity agreements. Part-time tuition and fees vary according to course load, program, and reciprocity agreements. *Required fees:* $1010 full-time.

Financial Aid In 2001, 15 Federal Work-Study jobs (averaging $1000).

Applying *Application fee:* $20. *Required:* essay or personal statement, high school transcript.

Admissions Contact Ms. Leisa Grass, Director of Admissions, York County Technical College, 112 College Drive, Wells, ME 04090. *Phone:* 207-646-9282 Ext. 305. *Toll-free phone:* 800-580-3820 Ext. 304. *Fax:* 207-641-0837. *E-mail:* admissions@yctc.net.

MARYLAND

ALLEGANY COLLEGE OF MARYLAND
Cumberland, Maryland

- **State and locally supported** 2-year, founded 1961, part of Maryland State Community Colleges System
- **Calendar** semesters
- **Degree** certificates and associate
- **Small-town** 311-acre campus
- **Endowment** $5.2 million
- **Coed,** 2,879 undergraduate students, 56% full-time, 66% women, 34% men

Undergraduates 1,605 full-time, 1,274 part-time. Students come from 21 states and territories, 47% are from out of state, 5% African American, 0.4% Asian American or Pacific Islander, 0.8% Hispanic American, 0.2% Native American, 3% transferred in.

Freshmen *Admission:* 1,064 applied, 1,057 admitted, 733 enrolled. *Average high school GPA:* 2.84. *Test scores:* ACT scores over 18: 61%; ACT scores over 24: 10%.

Faculty *Total:* 215, 47% full-time. *Student/faculty ratio:* 15:1.

Majors Accounting; art; auto mechanic/technician; biology; business administration; business education; chemistry; communication equipment technology; computer engineering technology; computer programming; computer science; criminal justice/law enforcement administration; culinary arts; data processing technology; dental hygiene; education; engineering; food products retailing; forest harvesting production technology; forestry; hotel and restaurant management; human services; industrial radiologic technology; legal administrative assistant; liberal arts and sciences/liberal studies; mass communications; medical administrative assistant; medical laboratory technician; nursing; occupational therapy; paralegal/legal assistant; personal/miscellaneous services; physical therapy assistant; psychology; radio/television broadcasting; recreation/leisure studies; respiratory therapy; secretarial science; social sciences; social work; sociology.

Academic Programs *Special study options:* academic remediation for entering students, adult/continuing education programs, advanced placement credit, distance learning, double majors, honors programs, independent study, internships, part-time degree program, summer session for credit. *ROTC:* Army (c).

Library Allegany College Library with 51,999 titles, 404 serial subscriptions, 4,209 audiovisual materials, an OPAC, a Web page.

Computers on Campus 600 computers available on campus for general student use. Internet access, at least one staffed computer lab available.

Student Life *Housing:* college housing not available. *Activities and Organizations:* choral group, SAHDA, Honors Club, EMT Club, Forestry Club. *Campus security:* 24-hour patrols, late-night transport/escort service. *Student Services:* personal/psychological counseling, women's center.

Athletics Member NJCAA. *Intercollegiate sports:* baseball M, basketball M/W, soccer M/W, tennis M/W. *Intramural sports:* archery M/W, badminton M/W, baseball M/W, basketball M/W, bowling M/W, racquetball M/W, tennis M/W, volleyball M/W.

Standardized Tests *Required for some:* ACT (for admission).

Costs (2001–02) *Tuition:* area resident $2550 full-time, $85 per credit part-time; state resident $5010 full-time, $167 per credit part-time; nonresident $5130 full-time, $171 per credit part-time. Full-time tuition and fees vary according to course load and location. Part-time tuition and fees vary according to course load and location. *Required fees:* $170 full-time, $5 per credit, $30 per term part-time. *Payment plan:* deferred payment. *Waivers:* senior citizens and employees or children of employees.

Applying *Options:* electronic application, early admission. *Required:* high school transcript. *Application deadline:* rolling (freshmen), rolling (transfers).

Admissions Contact Ms. Cathy Nolan, Director of Admissions and Registration, Allegany College of Maryland, 12401 Willowbrook Road, SE, Cumberland, MD 21502. *Phone:* 301-784-5000 Ext. 5202. *Fax:* 301-784-5220. *E-mail:* cnolan@ac.cc.md.us.

ANNE ARUNDEL COMMUNITY COLLEGE
Arnold, Maryland

- **State and locally supported** 2-year, founded 1961
- **Calendar** semesters
- **Degree** certificates and associate
- **Suburban** 230-acre campus with easy access to Baltimore and Washington, DC
- **Coed,** 52,088 undergraduate students

Undergraduates Students come from 12 states and territories, 19 other countries, 0.8% are from out of state.

Faculty *Total:* 773, 29% full-time. *Student/faculty ratio:* 19:1.

Majors Accounting; American studies; applied art; architectural engineering technology; art; astronomy; behavioral sciences; biological/physical sciences; biology; botany; broadcast journalism; business administration; business economics; business marketing and marketing management; chemistry; communication equipment technology; computer engineering technology; computer management; computer programming; computer science; computer science related; computer/technical support; corrections; criminal justice/law enforcement administration; data entry/microcomputer applications; data processing technology; early childhood education; economics; education; electrical/electronic engineering technology; elementary education; emergency medical technology; engineering technology; English; environmental science; European studies; film/video production; food services technology; health education; horticulture science; hotel and restaurant management; humanities; human services; industrial radiologic technology; industrial technology; information sciences/systems; landscape architecture; law enforcement/police science; liberal arts and sciences/liberal studies; marine science; mass communications; mathematics; mechanical engineering technology; medical assistant; medical technology; mental health/rehabilitation; music; nursing; paralegal/legal assistant; photography; physical education; public administration; public policy analysis; real estate; retail management; secretarial science; social sciences; system administration; telecommunications.

Academic Programs *Special study options:* academic remediation for entering students, accelerated degree program, adult/continuing education programs, advanced placement credit, cooperative education, distance learning, English as a second language, freshman honors college, honors programs, independent study, internships, part-time degree program, services for LD students, summer session for credit. *ROTC:* Army (c), Air Force (c).

Library Andrew G. Truxal Library with 140,405 titles, 527 serial subscriptions.

Computers on Campus 250 computers available on campus for general student use. A campuswide network can be accessed from off campus. At least one staffed computer lab available.

Student Life *Housing:* college housing not available. *Activities and Organizations:* drama/theater group, student-run newspaper, choral group, Drama Club, student association, Black Student Union, International Student Association, Chemistry Club. *Campus security:* 24-hour emergency response devices and patrols, student patrols, late-night transport/escort service. *Student Services:* health clinic, personal/psychological counseling.

Athletics Member NJCAA. *Intercollegiate sports:* baseball M(s), basketball M(s)/W(s), cross-country running M(s)/W(s), lacrosse M(s)/W(s), soccer M(s)/W(s), softball W(s), tennis M(s), volleyball W. *Intramural sports:* basketball M/W, soccer M/W, softball M/W, table tennis M/W, tennis M/W, volleyball M/W.

Standardized Tests *Recommended:* SAT I or ACT (for placement).

Costs (2002–03) *Tuition:* area resident $1488 full-time, $62 per credit hour part-time; state resident $2760 full-time, $115 per credit hour part-time; nonresident $4896 full-time, $204 per credit hour part-time. *Required fees:* $112 full-time, $3 per credit, $20 per term part-time.

Financial Aid In 2001, 104 Federal Work-Study jobs (averaging $1900). 55 State and other part-time jobs (averaging $1740).

Applying *Options:* early admission, deferred entrance. *Application deadline:* rolling (freshmen), rolling (transfers).

Admissions Contact Mr. Thomas McGinn, Director of Admissions, Anne Arundel Community College, 101 College Parkway, Arnold, MD 21012-1895. *Phone:* 410-541-2240. *Fax:* 410-541-2245. *E-mail:* lfadelman@mail.aacc.cc.md.us.

BALTIMORE CITY COMMUNITY COLLEGE
Baltimore, Maryland

- **State-supported** 2-year, founded 1947
- **Calendar** semesters
- **Degree** certificates and associate
- **Urban** 19-acre campus
- **Endowment** $139,215
- **Coed,** 6,268 undergraduate students

Undergraduates Students come from 4 states and territories, 1% are from out of state.

Freshmen *Admission:* 1,380 applied.

Faculty *Total:* 123. *Student/faculty ratio:* 22:1.

Majors Accounting; biological/physical sciences; business administration; business marketing and marketing management; computer graphics; computer science; computer/technical support; corrections; data processing technology; dental hygiene; dietetics; drafting; early childhood education; electrical/electronic engineering technology; emergency medical technology; engineering; fashion design/illustration; fashion merchandising; gerontology; graphic design/commercial art/illustration; hospitality management; human services; information sciences/systems; law enforcement/police science; legal administrative assistant; liberal arts and sciences/liberal studies; medical administrative assistant; medical records administration; nursing; operating room technician; paralegal/legal assistant; physical therapy; respiratory therapy; secretarial science; word processing.

Academic Programs *Special study options:* academic remediation for entering students, adult/continuing education programs, advanced placement credit, cooperative education, distance learning, double majors, English as a second language, honors programs, internships, part-time degree program, services for LD students, study abroad, summer session for credit.

Library Bard Library with 72,413 titles, 150 serial subscriptions, 1,074 audiovisual materials, an OPAC, a Web page.

Computers on Campus Internet access, at least one staffed computer lab available.

Student Life *Housing:* college housing not available. *Activities and Organizations:* student-run newspaper, radio station, choral group. *Student Services:* health clinic, personal/psychological counseling.

Athletics *Intercollegiate sports:* basketball M/W, cross-country running M/W, track and field M/W.

Baltimore City Community College (continued)

Standardized Tests *Recommended:* SAT I and SAT II or ACT (for placement), SAT II: Subject Tests (for placement), SAT II: Writing Test (for placement).

Costs (2001–02) *Tuition:* $60 per hour part-time; state resident $1440 full-time, $150 per hour part-time; nonresident $3600 full-time. *Required fees:* $96 full-time, $4 per hour. *Payment plan:* deferred payment. *Waivers:* employees or children of employees.

Financial Aid In 2001, 331 Federal Work-Study jobs (averaging $1879).

Applying *Options:* common application, early admission, deferred entrance. *Application fee:* $10. *Required:* high school transcript. *Recommended:* interview. *Application deadlines:* 8/9 (freshmen), 8/9 (transfers). *Notification:* continuous (freshmen).

Admissions Contact Mrs. Scheherazade Forman, Admissions Coordinator, Baltimore City Community College, 2901 Liberty Heights Avenue, Baltimore, MD 21215. *Phone:* 410-462-8300. *Toll-free phone:* 888-203-1261 Ext. 8300. *Fax:* 410-462-7677. *E-mail:* sforman@bccc.state.md.us.

BALTIMORE INTERNATIONAL COLLEGE
Baltimore, Maryland

- **Independent** primarily 2-year, founded 1972
- **Calendar** semesters
- **Degrees** certificates, associate, and bachelor's
- **Urban** 6-acre campus with easy access to Washington, DC
- **Endowment** $704,390
- **Coed,** 456 undergraduate students, 95% full-time, 46% women, 54% men

Undergraduates 435 full-time, 21 part-time. Students come from 22 states and territories, 4 other countries, 44% African American, 0.9% Asian American or Pacific Islander, 5% Hispanic American, 0.2% Native American, 0.9% international, 7% transferred in, 24% live on campus.

Freshmen *Admission:* 463 applied, 228 admitted, 140 enrolled. *Average high school GPA:* 2.50.

Faculty *Total:* 34, 53% full-time, 24% with terminal degrees. *Student/faculty ratio:* 21:1.

Majors Business administration; culinary arts; hospitality management; hotel and restaurant management.

Academic Programs *Special study options:* academic remediation for entering students, accelerated degree program, adult/continuing education programs, advanced placement credit, cooperative education, double majors, honors programs, internships, off-campus study, study abroad.

Library George A. Piendak Library with 13,000 titles, 200 serial subscriptions, 1,000 audiovisual materials.

Computers on Campus 35 computers available on campus for general student use. A campuswide network can be accessed from off campus. Internet access, at least one staffed computer lab available.

Student Life *Housing:* on-campus residence required for freshman year. *Options:* coed. *Activities and Organizations:* student-run newspaper, American Culinary Federation, Beta Iota Kappa. *Campus security:* late-night transport/escort service, controlled dormitory access. *Student Services:* health clinic, personal/psychological counseling.

Standardized Tests *Required for some:* SAT I or ACT (for admission).

Costs (2002–03) *Comprehensive fee:* $22,562 includes full-time tuition ($12,742), mandatory fees ($4196), and room and board ($5624). Part-time tuition: $378 per credit hour. *Room and board:* Room and board charges vary according to housing facility. *Payment plans:* tuition prepayment, installment. *Waivers:* employees or children of employees.

Applying *Options:* common application, electronic application, deferred entrance. *Application fee:* $35. *Required:* high school transcript. *Recommended:* interview. *Application deadline:* rolling (freshmen), rolling (transfers). *Notification:* continuous until 8/15 (freshmen).

Admissions Contact Ms. Lori Makowski, Director of Admissions, Baltimore International College, Commerce Exchange, 17 Commerce Street, Baltimore, MD 21202-3230. *Phone:* 410-752-4710 Ext. 125. *Toll-free phone:* 800-624-9926 Ext. 120. *Fax:* 410-752-3730. *E-mail:* admissions@bic.edu.

CARROLL COMMUNITY COLLEGE
Westminster, Maryland

- **State and locally supported** 2-year, founded 1993, part of Maryland Higher Education Commission
- **Calendar** semesters
- **Degree** certificates and associate
- **Small-town** 80-acre campus with easy access to Baltimore
- **Coed,** 2,634 undergraduate students, 41% full-time, 63% women, 37% men

Undergraduates 1,086 full-time, 1,548 part-time. Students come from 2 states and territories, 1% are from out of state, 3% African American, 1% Asian American or Pacific Islander, 1% Hispanic American, 0.5% Native American.

Freshmen *Admission:* 667 applied, 667 admitted, 671 enrolled.

Faculty *Total:* 163, 28% full-time.

Majors Accounting; business administration; computer graphics; computer/information sciences; data processing technology; early childhood education; education (multiple levels); general studies; health science; human services; liberal arts and sciences/liberal studies; mechanical design technology; music; nursing; physical therapy assistant.

Academic Programs *Special study options:* academic remediation for entering students, advanced placement credit, distance learning, English as a second language, honors programs, independent study, internships, part-time degree program, services for LD students, summer session for credit.

Library Random House Learning Resources Center with 37,000 titles, 269 serial subscriptions, 2,127 audiovisual materials, an OPAC, a Web page.

Computers on Campus 200 computers available on campus for general student use. Internet access, at least one staffed computer lab available.

Student Life *Housing:* college housing not available. *Activities and Organizations:* drama/theater group, student-run newspaper, choral group, Student Government Organization, Carroll Community Chorus, Programming Board. *Campus security:* late-night transport/escort service. *Student Services:* personal/psychological counseling.

Standardized Tests *Recommended:* SAT I or ACT (for placement).

Costs (2001–02) *Tuition:* area resident $1800 full-time, $75 per credit part-time; state resident $3072 full-time, $128 per credit part-time; nonresident $4680 full-time, $195 per credit part-time. Full-time tuition and fees vary according to course load. Part-time tuition and fees vary according to course load. *Required fees:* $13 per credit. *Payment plan:* deferred payment. *Waivers:* senior citizens and employees or children of employees.

Financial Aid In 2001, 23 Federal Work-Study jobs (averaging $1561).

Applying *Options:* early admission. *Required:* high school transcript. *Application deadline:* rolling (freshmen), rolling (transfers). *Notification:* continuous (freshmen).

Admissions Contact Ms. Edie Hemingway, Coordinator of Admissions, Carroll Community College, 1601 Washington Road, Westminster, MD 21157. *Phone:* 410-386-8430. *Toll-free phone:* 888-221-9748. *Fax:* 410-386-8446. *E-mail:* ehemingway@carroll.cc.md.us.

CECIL COMMUNITY COLLEGE
North East, Maryland

- **County-supported** 2-year, founded 1968
- **Calendar** semesters
- **Degree** certificates, diplomas, and associate
- **Rural** 100-acre campus with easy access to Baltimore
- **Coed,** 1,448 undergraduate students, 33% full-time, 65% women, 35% men

Undergraduates 478 full-time, 970 part-time. Students come from 3 states and territories, 9% are from out of state, 6% African American, 0.8% Asian American or Pacific Islander, 1% Hispanic American, 0.6% Native American, 1% international, 4% transferred in. *Retention:* 55% of 2001 full-time freshmen returned.

Freshmen *Admission:* 663 applied, 663 admitted, 347 enrolled.

Faculty *Total:* 178, 21% full-time, 7% with terminal degrees. *Student/faculty ratio:* 12:1.

Majors Accounting; art; biology; business administration; business marketing and marketing management; carpentry; computer engineering technology; computer graphics; computer graphics; computer programming; construction technology; criminal justice/law enforcement administration; data processing technology; early childhood education; education; education (K-12); electrical/electronic engineering technology; elementary education; information sciences/systems; information technology; law enforcement/police science; liberal arts and sciences/liberal studies; mathematics; medical laboratory technology; nursing; photography; physical sciences; physics; plumbing; robotics; secretarial science; water resources; welding technology.

Academic Programs *Special study options:* academic remediation for entering students, adult/continuing education programs, advanced placement credit, cooperative education, distance learning, double majors, English as a second language, independent study, internships, part-time degree program, services for LD students, summer session for credit.

Library Cecil County Veteran's Memorial Library with 32,277 titles, 174 serial subscriptions, 1,041 audiovisual materials, an OPAC, a Web page.

Computers on Campus 63 computers available on campus for general student use. A campuswide network can be accessed from off campus. Internet access, at least one staffed computer lab available.

Student Life *Housing:* college housing not available. *Activities and Organizations:* drama/theater group, student-run newspaper, student government, Non-traditional Student Organization, Student Nurses Association, student newspaper, national fraternities. *Campus security:* late-night transport/escort service. *Student Services:* personal/psychological counseling, women's center.

Athletics Member NJCAA. *Intercollegiate sports:* baseball M, basketball M(s)/W(s), field hockey W, softball W, volleyball W(s). *Intramural sports:* basketball M/W, bowling M/W, soccer M, tennis M/W, volleyball M/W.

Costs (2001–02) *One-time required fee:* $25. *Tuition:* area resident $1950 full-time, $65 per credit part-time; state resident $4650 full-time, $155 per credit part-time; nonresident $6000 full-time, $200 per credit part-time. Full-time tuition and fees vary according to reciprocity agreements. *Required fees:* $193 full-time, $5 per credit, $25 per term part-time. *Payment plan:* installment. *Waivers:* children of alumni and employees or children of employees.

Financial Aid In 2001, 44 Federal Work-Study jobs (averaging $694).

Applying *Options:* common application, early admission, deferred entrance. *Application fee:* $25. *Recommended:* high school transcript. *Application deadline:* rolling (freshmen), rolling (transfers). *Notification:* continuous (freshmen).

Admissions Contact Ms. Sandra S. Rajaski, Registrar, Cecil Community College, One Seahawk Drive. *Phone:* 410-287-1004 Ext. 567. *Fax:* 410-287-1026. *E-mail:* srajaski@cecil.cc.md.us.

CHESAPEAKE COLLEGE
Wye Mills, Maryland

- **State and locally supported** 2-year, founded 1965
- **Calendar** semesters
- **Degree** certificates and associate
- **Rural** 170-acre campus with easy access to Baltimore and Washington, DC
- **Endowment** $933,349
- **Coed,** 2,186 undergraduate students, 28% full-time, 71% women, 29% men

Undergraduates 613 full-time, 1,573 part-time. Students come from 2 states and territories, 0.2% are from out of state, 19% African American, 0.9% Asian American or Pacific Islander, 0.7% Hispanic American, 0.3% Native American, 0.3% international, 5% transferred in.

Freshmen *Admission:* 388 applied, 352 enrolled. *Average high school GPA:* 2.75.

Faculty *Total:* 166, 30% full-time. *Student/faculty ratio:* 14:1.

Majors Accounting; architectural engineering technology; art; biological/physical sciences; business administration; computer engineering technology; computer programming; computer science; corrections; criminal justice/law enforcement administration; data processing technology; early childhood education; electrical/electronic engineering technology; elementary education; health education; humanities; human services; legal administrative assistant; liberal arts and sciences/liberal studies; mathematics; medical administrative assistant; medical radiologic technology; music; physical education; physical sciences; recreation/leisure studies; secretarial science; social sciences; sociology.

Academic Programs *Special study options:* academic remediation for entering students, adult/continuing education programs, advanced placement credit, cooperative education, distance learning, English as a second language, honors programs, independent study, internships, part-time degree program, services for LD students, student-designed majors, summer session for credit.

Library Learning Resource Center plus 1 other with 41,966 titles, 548 serial subscriptions, 4,015 audiovisual materials, an OPAC, a Web page.

Computers on Campus 350 computers available on campus for general student use. A campuswide network can be accessed from off campus. Internet access, at least one staffed computer lab available.

Student Life *Housing:* college housing not available. *Activities and Organizations:* drama/theater group, choral group, student government action teams, Phi Theta Kappa, UHURU, Chesapeake Players. *Campus security:* 24-hour patrols. *Student Services:* personal/psychological counseling, women's center.

Athletics Member NJCAA. *Intercollegiate sports:* baseball M, basketball M/W, soccer M/W, softball W, tennis M/W, volleyball W. *Intramural sports:* soccer M/W, volleyball M/W.

Costs (2001–02) *Tuition:* area resident $1560 full-time, $65 per credit hour part-time; state resident $2256 full-time, $94 per credit hour part-time; nonresident $3096 full-time, $129 per credit hour part-time. Full-time tuition and fees vary according to location. Part-time tuition and fees vary according to location. *Required fees:* $330 full-time, $10 per credit. *Payment plans:* installment, deferred payment. *Waivers:* senior citizens and employees or children of employees.

Financial Aid In 2001, 35 Federal Work-Study jobs (averaging $1879).

Applying *Options:* early admission, deferred entrance. *Required:* high school transcript. *Application deadline:* rolling (freshmen), rolling (transfers). *Notification:* continuous (freshmen).

Admissions Contact Ms. Kathy Petrichenko, Director of Admissions, Chesapeake College, PO Box 8, Wye Mills, MD 21679. *Phone:* 410-822-5400 Ext. 257. *Fax:* 410-827-9466.

COLLEGE OF SOUTHERN MARYLAND
La Plata, Maryland

- **State and locally supported** 2-year, founded 1958
- **Calendar** semesters
- **Degree** certificates and associate
- **Rural** 175-acre campus with easy access to Washington, DC
- **Coed,** 6,803 undergraduate students

Undergraduates Students come from 3 states and territories, 1% are from out of state.

Freshmen *Admission:* 3,016 applied, 3,016 admitted.

Faculty *Total:* 389, 24% full-time. *Student/faculty ratio:* 20:1.

Majors Accounting; business administration; computer programming; early childhood education; education; electrical/electronic engineering technology; elementary education; engineering; human services; information sciences/systems; liberal arts and sciences/liberal studies; nursing; paralegal/legal assistant; practical nurse.

Academic Programs *Special study options:* academic remediation for entering students, accelerated degree program, adult/continuing education programs, advanced placement credit, cooperative education, distance learning, internships, part-time degree program, services for LD students, summer session for credit.

Library Charles County Community College Library with 32,848 titles, 571 serial subscriptions.

Computers on Campus 130 computers available on campus for general student use. Internet access, at least one staffed computer lab available.

Student Life *Housing:* college housing not available. *Activities and Organizations:* drama/theater group, student-run newspaper, choral group, Spanish Club, Nursing Student Association, Science Club, Black Student Union, BACCHUS. *Campus security:* 24-hour emergency response devices and patrols. *Student Services:* personal/psychological counseling, women's center.

Athletics Member NJCAA. *Intercollegiate sports:* baseball M, basketball M, golf M/W, soccer M/W, softball W, tennis M/W, volleyball W.

Standardized Tests *Required for some:* ACT (for admission).

Costs (2001–02) *Tuition:* area resident $2160 full-time; state resident $4176 full-time; nonresident $5558 full-time. *Required fees:* $360 full-time.

Applying *Options:* early admission, deferred entrance. *Recommended:* high school transcript. *Application deadline:* rolling (freshmen), rolling (transfers). *Notification:* continuous (freshmen).

Admissions Contact Ms. Charlotte Hill, Admissions Coordinator, College of Southern Maryland, PO Box 910, La Plata, MD 20646-0910. *Phone:* 301-934-2251 Ext. 7044. *Fax:* 301-934-5255.

THE COMMUNITY COLLEGE OF BALTIMORE COUNTY-CATONSVILLE CAMPUS
Baltimore, Maryland

- **County-supported** 2-year, founded 1957
- **Calendar** semesters
- **Degree** certificates, diplomas, and associate
- **Suburban** 137-acre campus with easy access to Baltimore
- **Coed,** 3,372 undergraduate students, 56% full-time, 55% women, 45% men

Undergraduates 1,903 full-time, 1,469 part-time. 3% are from out of state, 25% African American, 4% Asian American or Pacific Islander, 2% Hispanic American, 0.4% Native American, 3% international.

Freshmen *Admission:* 3,372 enrolled.

Faculty *Total:* 965, 37% full-time.

Majors Accounting; aircraft pilot (professional); air traffic control; applied art; architectural engineering technology; art; auto mechanic/technician; biological/physical sciences; business administration; business marketing and marketing management; chemical engineering technology; child care provider; civil engineering technology; computer engineering related; computer engineering technology; computer graphics; computer graphics; computer hardware engineering;

The Community College of Baltimore County-Catonsville Campus (continued)
computer/information technology services administration and management related; computer management; computer programming; computer programming related; computer programming (specific applications); computer programming, vendor/product certification; computer science; computer science related; computer software and media applications related; computer software engineering; computer systems networking/telecommunications; computer/technical support; construction/building inspection; construction management; construction technology; corrections; criminal justice/law enforcement administration; data entry/microcomputer applications; data entry/microcomputer applications related; data processing technology; data warehousing/mining/database administration; distribution operations; drafting; drafting/design technology; early childhood education; education; electrical/electronic engineering technology; electrical equipment installation/repair; elementary education; engineering; engineering design; engineering-related technology; engineering technology; fine/studio arts; fire science; graphic design/commercial art/illustration; graphic/printing equipment; industrial machinery maintenance/repair; industrial technology; information sciences/systems; information technology; interior design; international business; landscape architecture; law enforcement/police science; legal administrative assistant; legal studies; liberal arts and sciences/liberal studies; machine technology; marketing operations; mass communications; medical administrative assistant; medical laboratory technician; mental health/rehabilitation; mortuary science; music; nursing; occupational safety/health technology; occupational therapy; photography; pre-engineering; quality control technology; radio/television broadcasting; real estate; recreational therapy; recreation/leisure studies; secretarial science; sign language interpretation; social sciences; surveying; system/networking/LAN/WAN management; theater arts/drama; transportation technology; Web/multimedia management/webmaster; Web page, digital/multimedia and information resources design; word processing; zoology.

Academic Programs *Special study options:* academic remediation for entering students, adult/continuing education programs, English as a second language, honors programs, internships, off-campus study, part-time degree program, services for LD students, summer session for credit.

Library Library/Educational Communications and Technology Center with 103,000 titles, 720 serial subscriptions, an OPAC, a Web page.

Computers on Campus 200 computers available on campus for general student use. A campuswide network can be accessed from off campus. Internet access, online (class) registration, at least one staffed computer lab available.

Student Life *Housing:* college housing not available. *Activities and Organizations:* drama/theater group, student-run newspaper, radio station, choral group, SGA, special events, Social Committee, Dance Express, WCCN (radio station). *Campus security:* 24-hour emergency response devices and patrols, late-night transport/escort service. *Student Services:* personal/psychological counseling.

Athletics Member NJCAA. *Intercollegiate sports:* baseball M, basketball M(s)/W(s), lacrosse M(s)/W(s), soccer M(s)/W(s), softball W(s), tennis M(s)/W(s), volleyball W(s).

Standardized Tests *Required for some:* SAT I or ACT (for placement), CGP.

Costs (2001–02) *Tuition:* area resident $2040 full-time, $68 per credit hour part-time; state resident $3630 full-time, $121 per credit hour part-time; nonresident $5280 full-time, $176 per credit hour part-time. *Required fees:* $316 full-time, $10 per credit, $10 per term part-time. *Payment plan:* deferred payment. *Waivers:* senior citizens and employees or children of employees.

Applying *Options:* common application, electronic application. *Application fee:* $15. *Required:* high school transcript. *Application deadline:* rolling (freshmen), rolling (transfers).

Admissions Contact Ms. Diane Marie Drake, Director of Admissions, The Community College of Baltimore County-Catonsville Campus, 800 South Rolling Road, Baltimore, MD 21228. *Phone:* 410-455-4304. *Fax:* 410-719-6546.

THE COMMUNITY COLLEGE OF BALTIMORE COUNTY-DUNDALK CAMPUS

Baltimore, Maryland

- **County-supported** 2-year, founded 1970, part of The Community College of Baltimore County
- **Calendar** semesters
- **Degree** certificates and associate
- **Urban** 60-acre campus
- **Coed**

Faculty *Student/faculty ratio:* 18:1.

Student Life *Campus security:* 24-hour emergency response devices and patrols, late-night transport/escort service.

Athletics Member NJCAA.

Standardized Tests *Required:* ACCUPLACER.

Applying *Options:* early admission. *Application fee:* $15. *Required:* high school transcript.

Admissions Contact Ms. Danielle Brookhart, Director of Admissions, The Community College of Baltimore County-Dundalk Campus, 7200 Sollers Point Road, Baltimore, MD 21222. *Phone:* 410-285-9661.

THE COMMUNITY COLLEGE OF BALTIMORE COUNTY-ESSEX CAMPUS

Baltimore, Maryland

- **County-supported** 2-year, founded 1957, part of The Community College of Baltimore County
- **Calendar** semesters
- **Degree** certificates and associate
- **Suburban** 150-acre campus with easy access to Washington, DC
- **Coed**

Student Life *Campus security:* 24-hour emergency response devices and patrols, late-night transport/escort service.

Athletics Member NJCAA.

Applying *Application fee:* $15.

Admissions Contact Ms. Marcia Amaimo, Interim Director, Admissions and Financial Aid, The Community College of Baltimore County-Essex Campus, 7201 Rossville Boulevard, Baltimore, MD 21237-3899. *Phone:* 410-780-6774. *Toll-free phone:* 800-832-0262.

FREDERICK COMMUNITY COLLEGE

Frederick, Maryland

- **State and locally supported** 2-year, founded 1957
- **Calendar** semesters
- **Degree** certificates and associate
- **Small-town** 125-acre campus with easy access to Baltimore and Washington, DC
- **Coed,** 4,558 undergraduate students

Undergraduates Students come from 9 states and territories, 1% are from out of state.

Freshmen *Admission:* 917 applied, 917 admitted.

Faculty *Total:* 240, 38% full-time.

Majors Accounting; agricultural business; agricultural sciences; art; aviation technology; biology; business administration; business marketing and marketing management; chemistry; child care/development; computer engineering technology; construction management; criminal justice/law enforcement administration; data processing technology; drafting; early childhood education; education; electrical/electronic engineering technology; elementary education; engineering; English; finance; human services; international business; legal administrative assistant; liberal arts and sciences/liberal studies; mass communications; mathematics; medical administrative assistant; medical laboratory technology; music teacher education; nursing; paralegal/legal assistant; physical education; physical sciences; psychology; recreation/leisure facilities management; recreation/leisure studies; respiratory therapy; secretarial science; wildlife management.

Academic Programs *Special study options:* academic remediation for entering students, adult/continuing education programs, advanced placement credit, cooperative education, distance learning, honors programs, independent study, off-campus study, part-time degree program, services for LD students, summer session for credit. *ROTC:* Army (c).

Library 50,000 titles, 300 serial subscriptions.

Computers on Campus Internet access, at least one staffed computer lab available.

Student Life *Housing:* college housing not available. *Activities and Organizations:* drama/theater group, student-run newspaper. *Campus security:* 24-hour emergency response devices and patrols. *Student Services:* personal/psychological counseling.

Athletics Member NJCAA. *Intercollegiate sports:* baseball M, basketball M/W, golf M/W, soccer M, softball W, volleyball W.

Costs (2001–02) *Tuition:* area resident $1848 full-time, $77 per credit hour part-time; state resident $4008 full-time, $167 per credit hour part-time; nonresident $5544 full-time, $231 per credit hour part-time. Part-time tuition and fees vary according to course load. *Required fees:* $264 full-time, $10 per credit hour, $17 per term part-time.

Financial Aid In 2001, 25 Federal Work-Study jobs (averaging $1368). 14 State and other part-time jobs (averaging $2715).

Applying *Options:* early admission, deferred entrance. *Application deadlines:* 9/1 (freshmen), 9/1 (transfers). *Notification:* continuous (freshmen).

Admissions Contact Ms. Sandra Smith, Associate Vice President of Enrollment Services, Frederick Community College, 7932 Opossumtown Pike, Frederick, MD 21702-2097. *Phone:* 301-846-2430. *Fax:* 301-624-2799.

GARRETT COMMUNITY COLLEGE
McHenry, Maryland

- **State and locally supported** 2-year, founded 1966
- **Calendar** semesters
- **Degree** certificates and associate
- **Rural** 62-acre campus
- **Endowment** $500,000
- **Coed**

Athletics Member NJCAA.

Standardized Tests *Recommended:* SAT I or ACT (for placement).

Financial Aid In 2001, 55 Federal Work-Study jobs (averaging $1018). 75 State and other part-time jobs (averaging $954).

Applying *Options:* common application, early admission, deferred entrance. *Required:* high school transcript, interview. *Recommended:* minimum 2.0 GPA.

Admissions Contact Ms. Darlene Reed, Administrative Assistant, Admissions, Garrett Community College, 687 Mosser Road, PO Box 151, McHenry, MD 21541-0151. *Phone:* 301-387-3010. *E-mail:* admission@garrett.ncin.com.

HAGERSTOWN BUSINESS COLLEGE
Hagerstown, Maryland

- **Proprietary** 2-year, founded 1938
- **Calendar** trimesters
- **Degree** certificates and associate
- **Small-town** 8-acre campus with easy access to Baltimore and Washington, DC
- **Coed, primarily women,** 823 undergraduate students

Undergraduates Students come from 5 states and territories, 63% are from out of state, 3% live on campus.

Faculty *Total:* 23, 26% full-time.

Majors Accounting; business administration; business marketing and marketing management; data processing technology; information sciences/systems; legal administrative assistant; medical administrative assistant; medical assistant; medical records administration; paralegal/legal assistant; secretarial science.

Academic Programs *Special study options:* academic remediation for entering students, adult/continuing education programs, double majors, internships, part-time degree program.

Library 6,418 titles, 91 serial subscriptions.

Computers on Campus 86 computers available on campus for general student use. Internet access available.

Student Life *Housing Options:* coed. *Activities and Organizations:* Phi Beta Lambda, Association of Legal Students, Health Information Technology Students Organization, Student Government Association, Caduceus Club. *Campus security:* 24-hour emergency response devices. *Student Services:* personal/psychological counseling.

Standardized Tests *Required:* Assessment and Placement Services for Community Colleges.

Costs (2002–03) *Tuition:* Full-time tuition and fees vary according to program. Part-time tuition and fees vary according to program.

Financial Aid In 2001, 21 Federal Work-Study jobs (averaging $1343).

Applying *Options:* early admission, deferred entrance. *Application fee:* $25. *Required:* high school transcript. *Application deadline:* rolling (freshmen), rolling (transfers).

Admissions Contact Mr. Tom Brooks, Director of Admissions, Hagerstown Business College, 18618 Crestwood Drive, Hagerstown, MD 21742-2797. *Phone:* 301-739-2670. *Toll-free phone:* 800-422-2670. *Fax:* 301-791-7661.

HAGERSTOWN COMMUNITY COLLEGE
Hagerstown, Maryland

- **County-supported** 2-year, founded 1946
- **Calendar** semesters
- **Degree** certificates and associate
- **Suburban** 187-acre campus with easy access to Baltimore and Washington, DC
- **Coed,** 2,679 undergraduate students, 37% full-time, 60% women, 40% men

Undergraduates 992 full-time, 1,687 part-time. Students come from 7 states and territories, 23% are from out of state, 6% African American, 1% Asian American or Pacific Islander, 2% Hispanic American, 0.6% Native American, 8% transferred in.

Freshmen *Admission:* 1,426 applied, 1,426 admitted, 619 enrolled.

Faculty *Total:* 180, 33% full-time. *Student/faculty ratio:* 14:1.

Majors Accounting technician; business; business administration; child care/guidance; computer/information sciences; education; electromechanical technology; emergency medical technology; engineering; law enforcement/police science; liberal arts and sciences/liberal studies; liberal arts and studies related; management information systems/business data processing; mechanical engineering technology; medical radiologic technology; nursing; psychiatric/mental health services.

Academic Programs *Special study options:* academic remediation for entering students, accelerated degree program, adult/continuing education programs, advanced placement credit, cooperative education, distance learning, honors programs, independent study, internships, off-campus study, part-time degree program, services for LD students, student-designed majors, summer session for credit.

Library William Brish Library with 45,705 titles, 228 serial subscriptions, 1,585 audiovisual materials, an OPAC, a Web page.

Computers on Campus 400 computers available on campus for general student use. A campuswide network can be accessed from off campus. Internet access, at least one staffed computer lab available.

Student Life *Housing:* college housing not available. *Activities and Organizations:* drama/theater group, student-run newspaper, choral group, Phi Theta Kappa, Robinwood Players, Association of Nursing Students, Theta Lambda Upsilon, Art Club. *Campus security:* 24-hour patrols. *Student Services:* health clinic, personal/psychological counseling.

Athletics Member NJCAA. *Intercollegiate sports:* baseball M(s), basketball M(s)/W(s), cross-country running M(s)/W(s), golf M/W, soccer M(s)/W(s), softball W(s), tennis M/W, track and field M(s)/W(s), volleyball W(s). *Intramural sports:* baseball M, basketball M/W, soccer M/W, softball W, table tennis M/W, tennis M/W, volleyball M/W.

Standardized Tests *Required for some:* SAT I or ACT (for admission).

Costs (2001–02) *Tuition:* area resident $2220 full-time, $74 per credit hour part-time; state resident $3570 full-time, $119 per credit hour part-time; nonresident $4470 full-time, $156 per credit hour part-time. *Required fees:* $220 full-time, $7 per credit. *Payment plan:* installment. *Waivers:* senior citizens and employees or children of employees.

Financial Aid In 2001, 27 Federal Work-Study jobs (averaging $2955).

Applying *Options:* common application, early admission, deferred entrance. *Required for some:* high school transcript. *Application deadline:* rolling (freshmen), rolling (transfers). *Notification:* continuous (freshmen).

Admissions Contact Ms. Jacqueline Baldwin, Director of Enrollment Management, Hagerstown Community College, 11400 Robinwood Drive, Hagerstown, MD 21742-6590. *Phone:* 301-790-2800 Ext. 238. *Fax:* 301-739-0737. *E-mail:* baldwinj@hcc.cc.md.us.

HARFORD COMMUNITY COLLEGE
Bel Air, Maryland

- **State and locally supported** 2-year, founded 1957
- **Calendar** semesters
- **Degree** certificates, diplomas, and associate
- **Small-town** 212-acre campus with easy access to Baltimore
- **Endowment** $2.6 million
- **Coed,** 5,256 undergraduate students

Undergraduates Students come from 5 states and territories, 4 other countries, 1% are from out of state.

Faculty *Total:* 323, 23% full-time. *Student/faculty ratio:* 24:1.

Majors Accounting; art; audio engineering; auto mechanic/technician; behavioral sciences; biological/physical sciences; biology; broadcast journalism; business administration; business marketing and marketing management; chemistry; child care/development; computer/information sciences; computer science; criminal justice/law enforcement administration; drafting; early childhood education; education; electrical/electronic engineering technology; elementary education; engineering; English; environmental science; environmental technology; graphic

Harford Community College (continued)
design/commercial art/illustration; health education; history; hospitality management; humanities; individual/family development; information sciences/systems; interior design; liberal arts and sciences/liberal studies; mass communications; mathematics; medical assistant; medical laboratory technician; medical laboratory technology; music; nursing; paralegal/legal assistant; philosophy; photography; physics; political science; psychology; public relations; retail management; secretarial science; social sciences; sociology.

Academic Programs *Special study options:* academic remediation for entering students, adult/continuing education programs, advanced placement credit, cooperative education, English as a second language, internships, part-time degree program, services for LD students, student-designed majors, summer session for credit.

Library Learning Resources Center with 74,731 titles, 422 serial subscriptions, 6,700 audiovisual materials, an OPAC, a Web page.

Computers on Campus 267 computers available on campus for general student use. A campuswide network can be accessed from off campus. Internet access, at least one staffed computer lab available.

Student Life *Housing:* college housing not available. *Activities and Organizations:* student-run newspaper, radio station, Student Association, Paralegal Club, Multi-National Students Association, Student Nurses Association, Video Club. *Campus security:* 24-hour patrols, late-night transport/escort service. *Student Services:* personal/psychological counseling.

Athletics Member NJCAA. *Intercollegiate sports:* baseball M(s), basketball M/W(s), field hockey W(s), lacrosse M/W(s), soccer M, softball W(s), tennis M/W(s). *Intramural sports:* lacrosse W(c).

Costs (2001–02) *Tuition:* area resident $1950 full-time, $65 per credit hour part-time; state resident $3900 full-time, $130 per credit hour part-time; nonresident $5850 full-time, $195 per credit hour part-time. Full-time tuition and fees vary according to course load. *Waivers:* employees or children of employees.

Financial Aid In 2001, 55 Federal Work-Study jobs (averaging $1800). *Financial aid deadline:* 5/15.

Applying *Options:* early admission, deferred entrance. *Application deadline:* rolling (freshmen), rolling (transfers).

Admissions Contact Ms. Donna Youngberg, Admissions Advisor, Harford Community College, 401 Thomas Run Road, Bel Air, MD 21015-1698. *Phone:* 410-836-4220. *Fax:* 410-836-4363.

HOWARD COMMUNITY COLLEGE
Columbia, Maryland

- **State and locally supported** 2-year, founded 1966
- **Calendar** semesters
- **Degree** certificates and associate
- **Suburban** 122-acre campus with easy access to Baltimore and Washington, DC
- **Endowment** $2.0 million
- **Coed,** 5,934 undergraduate students

Undergraduates Students come from 4 states and territories, 1% are from out of state.

Faculty *Total:* 369, 25% full-time, 10% with terminal degrees. *Student/faculty ratio:* 16:1.

Majors Accounting; alcohol/drug abuse counseling; applied art; architecture; art; biological/physical sciences; biomedical technology; biotechnology research; business administration; cardiovascular technology; child care/development; computer graphics; computer/information technology services administration and management related; computer science; computer science related; computer systems networking/telecommunications; criminal justice/law enforcement administration; data entry/microcomputer applications; early childhood education; electrical/electronic engineering technology; elementary education; emergency medical technology; engineering; environmental science; fashion merchandising; financial planning; general studies; health education; information sciences/systems; information technology; legal administrative assistant; liberal arts and sciences/liberal studies; medical administrative assistant; medical technology; music; nuclear medical technology; nursing; office management; ophthalmic/optometric services; photography; physical sciences; practical nurse; pre-dentistry; pre-medicine; pre-pharmacy studies; pre-veterinary studies; psychology; retail management; secondary education; secretarial science; social sciences; sport/fitness administration; telecommunications; theater arts/drama; theater design.

Academic Programs *Special study options:* academic remediation for entering students, adult/continuing education programs, advanced placement credit, cooperative education, distance learning, double majors, English as a second language, honors programs, off-campus study, part-time degree program, services for LD students, summer session for credit.

Library Howard Community College Library with 40,380 titles, 1,201 serial subscriptions, 6,253 audiovisual materials, an OPAC, a Web page.

Computers on Campus 750 computers available on campus for general student use. Internet access, online (class) registration, at least one staffed computer lab available.

Student Life *Housing:* college housing not available. *Activities and Organizations:* drama/theater group, student-run newspaper, choral group, Secretarial Club, Nursing Club, Black Leadership Organization, student newspaper, Student Government Association. *Campus security:* 24-hour emergency response devices and patrols, late-night transport/escort service. *Student Services:* personal/psychological counseling.

Athletics Member NJCAA. *Intercollegiate sports:* basketball M/W, cross-country running M/W, lacrosse M, soccer M/W, tennis M/W, track and field M/W, volleyball W. *Intramural sports:* basketball M/W, lacrosse M, softball W.

Standardized Tests *Required for some:* SAT I or ACT (for admission).

Costs (2001–02) *Tuition:* area resident $2430 full-time, $86 per credit part-time; state resident $5340 full-time, $178 per credit part-time; nonresident $6690 full-time, $223 per credit part-time.

Applying *Options:* electronic application, early admission, deferred entrance. *Application fee:* $15. *Required for some:* essay or personal statement, high school transcript, minimum 3.0 GPA, 2 letters of recommendation, interview. *Application deadline:* rolling (freshmen), rolling (transfers). *Notification:* continuous (freshmen).

Admissions Contact Mr. John Kvach, Assistant Director of Admissions, Howard Community College, 10901 Little Patuxent Parkway, Columbia, MD 21044-3197. *Phone:* 410-772-4856. *Fax:* 410-772-4589. *E-mail:* mamiller@howardcc.edu.

MARYLAND COLLEGE OF ART AND DESIGN
Silver Spring, Maryland

- **Independent** 2-year, founded 1957
- **Calendar** semesters
- **Degree** certificates and associate
- **Suburban** 4-acre campus with easy access to Washington, DC and Baltimore
- **Endowment** $350,000
- **Coed,** 104 undergraduate students, 66% full-time, 60% women, 40% men

Undergraduates 69 full-time, 35 part-time. Students come from 3 states and territories, 3 other countries, 16% are from out of state, 30% African American, 6% Asian American or Pacific Islander, 2% Hispanic American, 4% international, 8% transferred in.

Freshmen *Admission:* 105 applied, 59 admitted, 36 enrolled. *Average high school GPA:* 2.6.

Faculty *Total:* 26, 19% full-time, 31% with terminal degrees. *Student/faculty ratio:* 9:1.

Majors Applied art; art; computer graphics; fine/studio arts; graphic design/commercial art/illustration.

Academic Programs *Special study options:* accelerated degree program, advanced placement credit, double majors, English as a second language, independent study, internships, part-time degree program, summer session for credit.

Library Maryland College of Art and Design Library with 11,500 titles, 35 serial subscriptions, 60 audiovisual materials.

Computers on Campus 20 computers available on campus for general student use. At least one staffed computer lab available.

Student Life *Housing:* college housing not available. *Activities and Organizations:* student-run newspaper. *Campus security:* 24-hour emergency response devices. *Student Services:* personal/psychological counseling.

Costs (2001–02) *Tuition:* $9900 full-time, $415 per credit hour part-time. Full-time tuition and fees vary according to course load. Part-time tuition and fees vary according to course load. *Required fees:* $475 full-time, $415 per credit hour. *Payment plans:* installment, deferred payment. *Waivers:* employees or children of employees.

Financial Aid *Financial aid deadline:* 7/30.

Applying *Options:* deferred entrance. *Application fee:* $35. *Required:* high school transcript, minimum 2.3 GPA, letters of recommendation, interview, portfolio.

Admissions Contact Ms. Maggie Noss, Director of Admissions and Assistant Dean, Maryland College of Art and Design, 10500 Georgia Avenue, Silver Spring, MD 20902-4111. *Phone:* 301-649-4454 Ext. 307. *Toll-free phone:* 888-543-MCAD. *Fax:* 301-649-2940. *E-mail:* admissions@mcadmd.org.

MONTGOMERY COLLEGE
Rockville, Maryland

- **State and locally supported** 2-year
- **Calendar** semesters
- **Degree** certificates and associate
- **Coed,** 21,347 undergraduate students, 36% full-time, 57% women, 43% men

Undergraduates 7,624 full-time, 13,723 part-time. Students come from 169 other countries, 2% are from out of state.

Freshmen *Admission:* 2,688 applied, 2,688 admitted, 2,179 enrolled.

Faculty *Total:* 1,140, 38% full-time, 23% with terminal degrees. *Student/faculty ratio:* 20:1.

Majors Accounting technician; architectural drafting; auto mechanic/technician; business; business administration; child care/guidance; civil engineering technology; commercial photography; computer/information sciences; computer maintenance technology; construction management; diagnostic medical sonography; education; electrical/electronic engineering technology; electromechanical technology; engineering; fire protection/safety technology; general studies; graphic design/commercial art/illustration; graphic/printing equipment; horticulture services; hotel and restaurant management; law enforcement/police science; liberal arts and sciences/liberal studies; management information systems/business data processing; medical radiologic technology; medical records technology; nursing; paralegal/legal assistant; physical therapy assistant; psychiatric/mental health services.

Student Life *Housing:* college housing not available. *Activities and Organizations:* drama/theater group, student-run newspaper, radio station, choral group. *Campus security:* 24-hour emergency response devices and patrols, late-night transport/escort service. *Student Services:* personal/psychological counseling, women's center.

Athletics Member NJCAA. *Intercollegiate sports:* baseball M/W, basketball M/W, cross-country running M/W, football M, golf M, soccer M/W, swimming M/W, tennis M/W, track and field M/W, volleyball W. *Intramural sports:* baseball M/W, basketball M/W, bowling M/W, cross-country running M/W, fencing M/W, football M/W, golf M/W, soccer M/W, swimming M/W, tennis M/W, volleyball M/W.

Costs (2001–02) *Tuition:* area resident $2664 full-time, $74 per credit part-time; state resident $5508 full-time, $153 per credit part-time; nonresident $7200 full-time, $200 per credit part-time. *Required fees:* $168 full-time, $7 per credit. *Payment plan:* installment. *Waivers:* senior citizens and employees or children of employees.

Applying *Options:* common application. *Application fee:* $25. *Application deadline:* rolling (freshmen), rolling (transfers).

Admissions Contact Mr. Sherman Helberg, Acting Director of Admissions and Enrollment, Montgomery College, 51 Mannakee Street, Rockville, MD 20850. *Phone:* 301-279-5034.

PRINCE GEORGE'S COMMUNITY COLLEGE
Largo, Maryland

- **County-supported** 2-year, founded 1958
- **Calendar** semesters
- **Degree** certificates and associate
- **Suburban** 150-acre campus with easy access to Washington, DC
- **Coed,** 12,287 undergraduate students, 26% full-time, 66% women, 34% men

Undergraduates 3,144 full-time, 9,143 part-time. Students come from 20 states and territories, 97 other countries, 3% are from out of state, 11% transferred in. *Retention:* 58% of 2001 full-time freshmen returned.

Freshmen *Admission:* 1,773 applied, 1,773 admitted, 1,429 enrolled.

Faculty *Total:* 646, 37% full-time, 46% with terminal degrees. *Student/faculty ratio:* 16:1.

Majors Accounting; aerospace engineering; business administration; business education; business marketing and marketing management; computer engineering technology; computer management; computer programming; computer science; computer typography/composition; criminal justice/law enforcement administration; drafting; early childhood education; education; electrical/electronic engineering technology; elementary education; emergency medical technology; engineering; forensic technology; health education; information sciences/systems; liberal arts and sciences/liberal studies; medical office management; medical records administration; nuclear medical technology; nursing; paralegal/legal assistant; physical education; radiological science; respiratory therapy.

Academic Programs *Special study options:* academic remediation for entering students, adult/continuing education programs, advanced placement credit, cooperative education, distance learning, English as a second language, external degree program, honors programs, part-time degree program, services for LD students, summer session for credit. *ROTC:* Army (c).

Library Accokeek Hall with 24,251 titles, 750 serial subscriptions, 1,664 audiovisual materials, an OPAC.

Computers on Campus 450 computers available on campus for general student use. A campuswide network can be accessed from off campus. Internet access, at least one staffed computer lab available.

Student Life *Housing:* college housing not available. *Activities and Organizations:* drama/theater group, student-run newspaper, choral group, Crusaders for Christ, Student Program Board, Union of Black Scholars, International Student Groups. *Campus security:* 24-hour emergency response devices and patrols, late-night transport/escort service. *Student Services:* health clinic, personal/psychological counseling.

Athletics Member NJCAA. *Intercollegiate sports:* baseball M, basketball M/W, bowling M/W, golf M, soccer M/W, softball W, tennis M/W, volleyball W. *Intramural sports:* basketball M/W, tennis M/W, volleyball W.

Standardized Tests *Required for some:* ACCUPLACER, Michigan Test of English Language Proficiency.

Costs (2002–03) *Tuition:* area resident $2250 full-time, $75 per credit part-time; state resident $4200 full-time, $140 per credit part-time; nonresident $6660 full-time, $222 per credit part-time. Full-time tuition and fees vary according to program and reciprocity agreements. Part-time tuition and fees vary according to program and reciprocity agreements. *Required fees:* $592 full-time, $20 per credit, $45 per term part-time. *Payment plan:* installment. *Waivers:* senior citizens and employees or children of employees.

Financial Aid In 2001, 58 Federal Work-Study jobs (averaging $1800).

Applying *Options:* early admission. *Required for some:* high school transcript. *Recommended:* minimum 2.0 GPA. *Application deadline:* rolling (freshmen), rolling (transfers). *Notification:* continuous (freshmen).

Admissions Contact Ms. Vera Bagley, Director of Admissions and Records, Prince George's Community College, 301 Largo Road, Largo, MD 20774-2199. *Phone:* 301-322-0801. *Fax:* 301-322-0119.

WOR-WIC COMMUNITY COLLEGE
Salisbury, Maryland

- **State and locally supported** 2-year, founded 1976, part of Maryland State Community Colleges System
- **Calendar** semesters
- **Degree** certificates and associate
- **Small-town** campus
- **Endowment** $1.8 million
- **Coed,** 2,721 undergraduate students, 27% full-time, 67% women, 33% men

Undergraduates 734 full-time, 1,987 part-time. Students come from 7 states and territories, 2% are from out of state, 23% African American, 1% Asian American or Pacific Islander, 0.7% Hispanic American, 0.6% Native American, 7% transferred in.

Freshmen *Admission:* 834 applied, 834 admitted, 549 enrolled.

Faculty *Total:* 147, 31% full-time, 9% with terminal degrees. *Student/faculty ratio:* 18:1.

Majors Accounting technician; alcohol/drug abuse counseling; banking; business; business administration; child care/guidance; computer science; electrical/electronic engineering technology; elementary education; general studies; hotel and restaurant management; industrial technology; law enforcement/police science; management information systems/business data processing; medical radiologic technology; nursing; secondary education; secretarial science.

Academic Programs *Special study options:* academic remediation for entering students, accelerated degree program, adult/continuing education programs, advanced placement credit, distance learning, double majors, English as a second language, honors programs, independent study, internships, off-campus study, part-time degree program, services for LD students, summer session for credit.

Library Electronic Media Center plus 1 other with 4 serial subscriptions, 272 audiovisual materials, a Web page.

Computers on Campus 400 computers available on campus for general student use. A campuswide network can be accessed from off campus. Internet access, at least one staffed computer lab available.

Student Life *Housing:* college housing not available. *Activities and Organizations:* drama/theater group, student-run newspaper, Student Government Association, Arts Club, Bioneer Club, Computer Club, student newspaper. *Campus security:* 24-hour emergency response devices, late-night transport/escort service, patrols by trained security personnel 9 a.m. to midnight. *Student Services:* personal/psychological counseling.

Wor-Wic Community College (continued)

Standardized Tests *Required for some:* ACT (for admission).

Costs (2002–03) *Tuition:* area resident $1440 full-time, $60 per credit hour part-time; state resident $3576 full-time, $149 per credit hour part-time; nonresident $4224 full-time, $176 per credit hour part-time. *Required fees:* $48 full-time, $1 per credit hour, $12 per term part-time. *Payment plan:* deferred payment. *Waivers:* senior citizens and employees or children of employees.

Applying *Options:* deferred entrance. *Recommended:* high school transcript. *Application deadline:* rolling (freshmen), rolling (transfers).

Admissions Contact Mr. Richard Webster, Director of Admissions, Wor-Wic Community College, 32000 Campus Drive, Salisbury, MD 21804. *Phone:* 410-334-2895. *Fax:* 410-334-2954. *E-mail:* rwebster@worwic.edu.

MASSACHUSETTS

BAPTIST BIBLE COLLEGE EAST
Boston, Massachusetts

- **Independent Baptist** primarily 2-year, founded 1976
- **Calendar** semesters
- **Degrees** certificates, diplomas, associate, and bachelor's
- **Suburban** 8-acre campus with easy access to Providence
- **Coed,** 110 undergraduate students

Undergraduates Students come from 14 states and territories, 2 other countries, 60% are from out of state, 65% live on campus.

Faculty *Total:* 10, 50% full-time.

Majors Biblical studies.

Academic Programs *Special study options:* academic remediation for entering students, honors programs, internships, part-time degree program, summer session for credit.

Library BBC East Library.

Computers on Campus 9 computers available on campus for general student use. Internet access, at least one staffed computer lab available.

Student Life *Activities and Organizations:* drama/theater group, student-run newspaper, choral group. *Campus security:* 24-hour emergency response devices, student patrols. *Student Services:* personal/psychological counseling.

Standardized Tests *Required:* SAT I or ACT (for admission).

Costs (2001–02) *Comprehensive fee:* $8470 includes full-time tuition ($3350), mandatory fees ($980), and room and board ($4140). Part-time tuition: $150 per credit hour. *Required fees:* $50 per credit hour.

Applying *Options:* common application. *Application fee:* $25. *Required:* essay or personal statement, high school transcript, letters of recommendation. *Recommended:* interview. *Application deadline:* rolling (freshmen), rolling (transfers).

Admissions Contact Mr. James Thomasson, Director of Admissions and Records, Baptist Bible College East, 950 Metropolitan Avenue, Boston, MA 02136. *Phone:* 617-364-3510. *Toll-free phone:* 888-235-2014. *Fax:* 617-364-0723.

BAY STATE COLLEGE
Boston, Massachusetts

- **Independent** 2-year, founded 1946
- **Calendar** semesters
- **Degree** associate
- **Urban** campus
- **Coed,** 419 undergraduate students, 80% full-time, 73% women, 27% men

Bay State College, a private 2-year college, is ideally located in Boston's Back Bay. Bay State graduates earn an associate degree that prepares them for successful careers in business, early childhood education, fashion, health, legal studies, and travel. Students should visit the Web site (www.baystate.edu) or e-mail (admissions@baystate.edu) or call (800-81-LEARN) the admissions office to learn more about Bay State College.

Undergraduates 335 full-time, 84 part-time. Students come from 11 states and territories, 11 other countries, 11% are from out of state, 39% transferred in, 21% live on campus.

Freshmen *Admission:* 843 applied, 791 admitted, 280 enrolled. *Average high school GPA:* 2.00.

Faculty *Total:* 66, 29% full-time.

Majors Accounting; business administration; early childhood education; fashion design/illustration; fashion merchandising; hospitality management; hotel and restaurant management; legal administrative assistant; legal studies; liberal arts and sciences/liberal studies; medical administrative assistant; medical assistant; occupational therapy; physical therapy; retail management; secretarial science; travel/tourism management.

Academic Programs *Special study options:* academic remediation for entering students, adult/continuing education programs, advanced placement credit, cooperative education, English as a second language, independent study, internships, part-time degree program.

Library Bay State College Library with 4,490 titles, 262 serial subscriptions, 471 audiovisual materials, an OPAC.

Computers on Campus 55 computers available on campus for general student use. At least one staffed computer lab available.

Student Life *Housing Options:* coed, women-only. *Activities and Organizations:* Activities Club, Hospitality Travel Association, Fashion Club, Early Childhood Education Club, Student Medical Assisting Society. *Campus security:* late-night transport/escort service, controlled dormitory access, 14-hour patrols by trained security personnel. *Student Services:* personal/psychological counseling.

Costs (2002–03) *Comprehensive fee:* $22,100 includes full-time tuition ($13,300), mandatory fees ($300), and room and board ($8500). Full-time tuition and fees vary according to class time and program. Part-time tuition: $1310 per course. Part-time tuition and fees vary according to class time and program. *Payment plan:* installment. *Waivers:* employees or children of employees.

Financial Aid In 2001, 20 Federal Work-Study jobs (averaging $2600).

Applying *Options:* common application, early admission. *Application fee:* $25. *Required:* essay or personal statement, high school transcript. *Recommended:* minimum 2.0 GPA, interview. *Application deadline:* rolling (freshmen), rolling (transfers).

Admissions Contact Ms. Pam Notemyer-Rogers, Director of Admissions, Bay State College, 122 Commonwealth Avenue, Boston, MA 02116. *Phone:* 617-236-8006. *Toll-free phone:* 800-81-LEARN. *Fax:* 617-536-1735. *E-mail:* admissions@baystate.edu.

BENJAMIN FRANKLIN INSTITUTE OF TECHNOLOGY
Boston, Massachusetts

- **Independent** primarily 2-year, founded 1908
- **Calendar** semesters
- **Degrees** certificates, associate, and bachelor's
- **Urban** 3-acre campus
- **Endowment** $8.0 million
- **Coed, primarily men,** 314 undergraduate students, 96% full-time, 11% women, 89% men

Undergraduates 303 full-time, 11 part-time. Students come from 12 states and territories, 8% are from out of state, 33% African American, 14% Asian American or Pacific Islander, 15% Hispanic American, 2% Native American, 2% international, 1% transferred in.

Freshmen *Admission:* 574 applied, 153 enrolled. *Average high school GPA:* 2.70.

Faculty *Total:* 41, 78% full-time. *Student/faculty ratio:* 11:1.

Majors Auto mechanic/technician; automotive engineering technology; computer engineering technology; computer science; drafting; electrical/electronic engineering technology; electrical/power transmission installation; engineering technology; mechanical engineering technology.

Academic Programs *Special study options:* academic remediation for entering students, adult/continuing education programs, advanced placement credit, English as a second language, internships, part-time degree program, summer session for credit.

Library Lufkin Memorial Library with 10,000 titles, 90 serial subscriptions, an OPAC.

Computers on Campus 100 computers available on campus for general student use. Internet access, at least one staffed computer lab available.

Student Life *Housing:* college housing not available. *Activities and Organizations:* Society of Manufacturing Engineers, student government, Yearbook Committee, athletics, Institute of Electrical and electronic Engineers (IEEE). *Campus security:* 24-hour emergency response devices, student patrols.

Athletics *Intramural sports:* basketball M, soccer M, volleyball M/W.

Standardized Tests *Recommended:* SAT I or ACT (for admission).

Costs (2002–03) *Tuition:* $11,150 full-time, $465 per credit part-time. *Required fees:* $265 full-time. *Payment plan:* installment. *Waivers:* employees or children of employees.
Applying *Options:* common application, electronic application, deferred entrance. *Application fee:* $20. *Required:* high school transcript. *Recommended:* essay or personal statement, minimum 2.0 GPA, letters of recommendation, interview. *Application deadlines:* 8/15 (freshmen), 8/15 (transfers).
Admissions Contact Wildolfo Arvelo, Dean of Enrollment Services, Benjamin Franklin Institute of Technology, 41 Berkeley Street, Boston, MA 02116-6296. *Phone:* 617-423-4630 Ext. 122. *Fax:* 617-482-3706. *E-mail:* fibadm@fib.edu.

BERKSHIRE COMMUNITY COLLEGE
Pittsfield, Massachusetts

- **State-supported** 2-year, founded 1960, part of Massachusetts Public Higher Education System
- **Calendar** semesters
- **Degree** certificates and associate
- **Suburban** 100-acre campus
- **Endowment** $38,339
- **Coed,** 2,401 undergraduate students, 39% full-time, 62% women, 38% men

Undergraduates 944 full-time, 1,457 part-time. Students come from 6 states and territories, 19 other countries, 4% are from out of state, 3% African American, 1% Asian American or Pacific Islander, 3% Hispanic American, 0.3% Native American, 2% international, 17% transferred in. *Retention:* 68% of 2001 full-time freshmen returned.
Freshmen *Admission:* 585 applied, 585 admitted, 431 enrolled.
Faculty *Total:* 167, 40% full-time, 82% with terminal degrees. *Student/faculty ratio:* 14:1.
Majors Accounting; animal sciences; art; biology; biomedical technology; business administration; business marketing and marketing management; computer engineering related; computer/information technology services administration and management related; computer programming related; computer programming (specific applications); computer science; criminal justice/law enforcement administration; culinary arts; data entry/microcomputer applications; data processing technology; dental assistant; drawing; early childhood education; ecology; electrical/electronic engineering technology; engineering; engineering technology; environmental science; environmental technology; finance; fine/studio arts; fire science; hospitality management; hotel and restaurant management; human services; information sciences/systems; law enforcement/police science; liberal arts and sciences/liberal studies; medical assistant; music (general performance); natural resources conservation; nursing; operating room technician; peace/conflict studies; physical education; physical therapy; physical therapy assistant; practical nurse; pre-engineering; respiratory therapy; secretarial science; theater arts/drama; travel/tourism management; veterinarian assistant.
Academic Programs *Special study options:* academic remediation for entering students, adult/continuing education programs, advanced placement credit, distance learning, double majors, English as a second language, honors programs, independent study, internships, off-campus study, part-time degree program, services for LD students, summer session for credit.
Library Jonathan Edwards Library with 67,419 titles, 341 serial subscriptions, 3,247 audiovisual materials, an OPAC, a Web page.
Computers on Campus 218 computers available on campus for general student use. A campuswide network can be accessed from off campus. Internet access, at least one staffed computer lab available.
Student Life *Housing:* college housing not available. *Activities and Organizations:* drama/theater group, choral group, Mass PIRG, Student Nurse Organization, Student Senate, Diversity Club, LPN Organization. *Campus security:* 24-hour emergency response devices and patrols. *Student Services:* health clinic, personal/psychological counseling.
Athletics Member NJCAA. *Intercollegiate sports:* basketball M/W, cross-country running M/W, soccer M/W. *Intramural sports:* basketball M/W, tennis M/W, volleyball M/W.
Standardized Tests *Required:* ACCUPLACER.
Costs (2001–02) *Tuition:* state resident $780 full-time, $26 per credit part-time; nonresident $7350 full-time, $245 per credit part-time. Full-time tuition and fees vary according to class time, course load, and reciprocity agreements. Part-time tuition and fees vary according to class time, course load, and reciprocity agreements. *Required fees:* $1965 full-time, $66 per credit. *Payment plan:* installment. *Waivers:* senior citizens and employees or children of employees.
Financial Aid In 2001, 72 Federal Work-Study jobs (averaging $1600).
Applying *Options:* common application, early admission, deferred entrance. *Application fee:* $10. *Required:* high school transcript. *Recommended:* interview. *Application deadline:* rolling (freshmen), rolling (transfers). *Notification:* continuous (freshmen).
Admissions Contact Ms. Margo J. Handschu, Admissions Counselor, Berkshire Community College, 1350 West Street, Pittsfield, MA 01201-5786. *Phone:* 413-499-4660 Ext. 425. *Toll-free phone:* 800-456-3253. *Fax:* 413-496-9511. *E-mail:* admissions@cc.berkshire.org.

BRISTOL COMMUNITY COLLEGE
Fall River, Massachusetts

- **State-supported** 2-year, founded 1965
- **Calendar** semesters
- **Degree** certificates and associate
- **Urban** 105-acre campus with easy access to Boston
- **Coed,** 6,132 undergraduate students

Undergraduates Students come from 4 states and territories, 14 other countries, 10% are from out of state, 5% African American, 1% Asian American or Pacific Islander, 2% Hispanic American, 0.4% Native American, 0.6% international.
Freshmen *Admission:* 3,088 applied, 2,590 admitted.
Faculty *Total:* 279, 38% full-time. *Student/faculty ratio:* 22:1.
Majors Accounting; applied art; art; business administration; business education; business marketing and marketing management; child care/development; civil engineering technology; computer engineering technology; computer graphics; computer/information sciences; computer/information technology services administration and management related; computer programming; computer programming (specific applications); computer systems networking/telecommunications; computer typography/composition; criminal justice/law enforcement administration; dental hygiene; electrical/electronic engineering technology; electromechanical technology; elementary education; engineering; environmental science; fire science; general studies; human services; information technology; legal administrative assistant; liberal arts and sciences/liberal studies; mass communications; mathematics; mechanical engineering technology; medical administrative assistant; medical laboratory technician; medical records administration; nursing; occupational therapy; retail management; secretarial science; Web/multimedia management/webmaster.
Academic Programs *Special study options:* academic remediation for entering students, adult/continuing education programs, cooperative education, distance learning, English as a second language, honors programs, independent study, internships, off-campus study, part-time degree program, services for LD students, student-designed majors, summer session for credit.
Library Learning Resources Center with 65,000 titles, 380 serial subscriptions, an OPAC, a Web page.
Computers on Campus 150 computers available on campus for general student use. A campuswide network can be accessed from off campus. Internet access, at least one staffed computer lab available.
Student Life *Housing:* college housing not available. *Activities and Organizations:* drama/theater group, student-run newspaper. *Campus security:* 24-hour emergency response devices and patrols, student patrols, late-night transport/escort service. *Student Services:* health clinic, personal/psychological counseling, women's center.
Standardized Tests *Required for some:* SAT I (for admission).
Costs (2001–02) *Tuition:* state resident $864 full-time, $24 per credit part-time; nonresident $6672 full-time, $224 per credit part-time. Full-time tuition and fees vary according to course load. Part-time tuition and fees vary according to course load. *Required fees:* $1728 full-time, $48 per credit. *Payment plan:* installment. *Waivers:* senior citizens and employees or children of employees.
Financial Aid In 2001, 195 Federal Work-Study jobs (averaging $1431). 72 State and other part-time jobs (averaging $1408).
Applying *Options:* common application. *Application fee:* $10. *Required:* high school transcript. *Notification:* continuous (freshmen).
Admissions Contact Mr. Rodney S. Clark, Director of Admissions, Bristol Community College, 777 Elsbree Street, Hudnall Administration Building, Fall River, MA 02720. *Phone:* 508-678-2811 Ext. 2516. *Fax:* 508-730-3265. *E-mail:* rclark@bristol.mass.edu.

BUNKER HILL COMMUNITY COLLEGE
Boston, Massachusetts

- **State-supported** 2-year, founded 1973
- **Calendar** semesters

Bunker Hill Community College (continued)
- **Degree** certificates and associate
- **Urban** 21-acre campus
- **Endowment** $1.4 million
- **Coed,** 6,914 undergraduate students, 36% full-time, 59% women, 41% men

Undergraduates 2,492 full-time, 4,422 part-time. Students come from 11 states and territories, 78 other countries, 1% are from out of state, 3% transferred in.

Freshmen *Admission:* 3,267 applied, 2,492 admitted, 1,426 enrolled.

Faculty *Total:* 373, 31% full-time. *Student/faculty ratio:* 17:1.

Majors Accounting; administrative/secretarial services; biological technology; business administration; computer/information sciences related; computer programming; computer science; corrections; criminal justice/law enforcement administration; culinary arts; design/visual communications; diagnostic medical sonography; education; education related; electrical/electronic engineering technology; fire protection/safety technology; fire science; general office/clerical; health/medical diagnostic and treatment services related; health/medical laboratory technologies related; hotel and restaurant management; human services; law enforcement/police science; liberal arts and sciences/liberal studies; medical laboratory assistant; medical radiologic technology; nursing; operating room technician; pharmacy technician/assistant; psychiatric/mental health services; radio/television broadcasting technology; secretarial science.

Academic Programs *Special study options:* academic remediation for entering students, adult/continuing education programs, advanced placement credit, cooperative education, distance learning, English as a second language, external degree program, honors programs, independent study, internships, off-campus study, part-time degree program, services for LD students, study abroad, summer session for credit.

Library Bunker Hill Community College Library with 56,615 titles, 320 serial subscriptions, an OPAC.

Computers on Campus 225 computers available on campus for general student use. A campuswide network can be accessed from off campus. Internet access, at least one staffed computer lab available.

Student Life *Housing:* college housing not available. *Activities and Organizations:* drama/theater group, student-run newspaper, radio station, African-American Cultural Society, Asian-Pacific Students Association, Arab Students Association, Hospitality Club, Radio Station, national fraternities. *Campus security:* 24-hour emergency response devices and patrols, late-night transport/escort service. *Student Services:* health clinic, personal/psychological counseling.

Athletics Member NJCAA. *Intercollegiate sports:* baseball M, basketball M/W, soccer M/W, softball W. *Intramural sports:* table tennis M/W.

Standardized Tests *Required for some:* nursing exam.

Costs (2002–03) *Tuition:* state resident $720 full-time, $24 per credit part-time; nonresident $7350 full-time, $230 per credit part-time. *Required fees:* $1680 full-time, $56 per credit. *Payment plan:* installment. *Waivers:* minority students, senior citizens, and employees or children of employees.

Financial Aid In 2001, 103 Federal Work-Study jobs (averaging $2500).

Applying *Options:* common application, deferred entrance. *Application fee:* $25 (non-residents). *Required:* high school transcript. *Application deadline:* rolling (freshmen), rolling (transfers). *Notification:* continuous (freshmen).

Admissions Contact Ms. Susan Donnelly, Director of Admissions and Transfer Counseling, Bunker Hill Community College, 250 New Rutherford Avenue, Boston, MA 02129. *Phone:* 617-228-2284. *Fax:* 617-228-2082.

CAPE COD COMMUNITY COLLEGE
West Barnstable, Massachusetts

- **State-supported** 2-year, founded 1961, part of Massachusetts Public Higher Education System
- **Calendar** semesters
- **Degree** certificates and associate
- **Rural** 120-acre campus with easy access to Boston
- **Endowment** $3.8 million
- **Coed,** 4,176 undergraduate students, 22% full-time, 65% women, 35% men

Undergraduates 904 full-time, 3,272 part-time. Students come from 24 states and territories, 5 other countries, 1% are from out of state, 3% African American, 0.7% Asian American or Pacific Islander, 2% Hispanic American, 1% Native American, 0.8% international, 8% transferred in.

Freshmen *Admission:* 1,233 applied, 1,166 admitted, 679 enrolled.

Faculty *Total:* 331, 24% full-time, 24% with terminal degrees. *Student/faculty ratio:* 18:1.

Majors Accounting; art; biological/physical sciences; business administration; computer graphics; computer science; computer science related; computer systems networking/telecommunications; criminal justice/law enforcement administration; dental hygiene; early childhood education; education; environmental science; environmental technology; executive assistant; fire science; history; hotel and restaurant management; information sciences/systems; information technology; legal administrative assistant; liberal arts and sciences/liberal studies; management science; mass communications; mathematics; medical administrative assistant; modern languages; music; nursing; paralegal/legal assistant; philosophy; physical education; physical therapy assistant; pre-engineering; psychology; recreation/leisure studies; secretarial science; system administration; theater arts/drama; Web/multimedia management/webmaster; Web page, digital/multimedia and information resources design.

Academic Programs *Special study options:* academic remediation for entering students, adult/continuing education programs, advanced placement credit, cooperative education, distance learning, English as a second language, independent study, internships, off-campus study, part-time degree program, services for LD students, study abroad, summer session for credit.

Library Cape Cod Community College Learning Resource Center with 54,342 titles, 705 serial subscriptions, 6,107 audiovisual materials, an OPAC.

Computers on Campus 240 computers available on campus for general student use. A campuswide network can be accessed from off campus. Internet access, at least one staffed computer lab available.

Student Life *Housing:* college housing not available. *Activities and Organizations:* drama/theater group, student-run newspaper, radio station, choral group, Innkeepers Club, Phi Theta Kappa, Student Senate, Learning Disabilities Support Group, Ethnic Diversity. *Campus security:* 24-hour patrols. *Student Services:* health clinic, personal/psychological counseling, women's center.

Athletics *Intramural sports:* badminton M/W, baseball M, basketball M/W, crew M/W, racquetball M/W, sailing M/W, skiing (downhill) M/W, soccer M, softball M/W, tennis M/W, volleyball M/W, weight lifting M/W.

Costs (2001–02) *One-time required fee:* $30. *Tuition:* state resident $720 full-time, $24 per credit hour part-time; nonresident $6900 full-time, $230 per credit hour part-time. Full-time tuition and fees vary according to program. Part-time tuition and fees vary according to program. *Required fees:* $2040 full-time, $68 per credit hour. *Payment plans:* installment, deferred payment. *Waivers:* senior citizens and employees or children of employees.

Financial Aid In 2001, 60 Federal Work-Study jobs (averaging $1161).

Applying *Options:* deferred entrance. *Application fee:* $35 (non-residents). *Required:* high school transcript. *Required for some:* essay or personal statement, letters of recommendation. *Application deadlines:* 8/10 (freshmen), 8/10 (transfers). *Notification:* continuous (freshmen).

Admissions Contact Ms. Susan Kline-Symington, Director of Admissions, Cape Cod Community College, 2240 Iyanough Road, West Barnstable, MA 02668-1599. *Phone:* 508-362-2131 Ext. 4311. *Toll-free phone:* 877-846-3672. *Fax:* 508-375-4089. *E-mail:* info@capecod.mass.edu.

DEAN COLLEGE
Franklin, Massachusetts

- **Independent** 2-year, founded 1865
- **Calendar** semesters
- **Degree** certificates and associate
- **Small-town** 100-acre campus with easy access to Boston and Providence
- **Endowment** $13.8 million
- **Coed,** 1,402 undergraduate students

Dean College offers a Bachelor of Arts (BA) degree in dance. The program includes the disciplines of tap, ballet, modern, and modern jazz dance within a broad liberal arts environment. The BA program is appropriate for students interested in teaching, arts management, movement therapy, dance journalism, and performance.

Undergraduates Students come from 25 states and territories, 14 other countries, 42% are from out of state, 6% African American, 0.9% Asian American or Pacific Islander, 3% Hispanic American, 6% international, 90% live on campus.

Freshmen *Admission:* 1,937 applied, 1,432 admitted. *Average high school GPA:* 2.20. *Test scores:* SAT verbal scores over 500: 22%; SAT math scores over 500: 20%; ACT scores over 18: 74%; SAT verbal scores over 600: 4%; SAT math scores over 600: 3%; ACT scores over 24: 10%; SAT verbal scores over 700: 1%.

Majors Athletic training/sports medicine; business administration; child care/development; communications; criminal justice/law enforcement administration; dance; health/physical education; humanities; law enforcement/police science; liberal arts and sciences/liberal studies; mathematics/computer science; physical education; social sciences; social work; sport/fitness administration; theater arts/drama.

Academic Programs *Special study options:* academic remediation for entering students, accelerated degree program, adult/continuing education programs, advanced placement credit, English as a second language, freshman honors college, honors programs, independent study, internships, off-campus study, part-time degree program, services for LD students, student-designed majors, summer session for credit.

Library E. Ross Anderson Library with 54,000 titles, 350 serial subscriptions.

Computers on Campus 150 computers available on campus for general student use. A campuswide network can be accessed from student residence rooms. At least one staffed computer lab available.

Student Life *Housing:* on-campus residence required through sophomore year. *Options:* coed. *Activities and Organizations:* drama/theater group, student-run newspaper, radio station, choral group, Emerging Leaders, College Success Staff, Student Ambassadors, student government, Phi Theta Kappa. *Campus security:* 24-hour emergency response devices and patrols, late-night transport/escort service, controlled dormitory access. *Student Services:* health clinic, personal/psychological counseling.

Athletics Member NJCAA. *Intercollegiate sports:* baseball M(s), basketball M(s)/W(s), football M(s), golf M, lacrosse M(s), soccer M(s)/W(s), softball W(s), tennis M(s), volleyball W(s). *Intramural sports:* basketball M, football M, golf M, lacrosse M, skiing (cross-country) M/W, skiing (downhill) M/W, tennis M/W, volleyball M/W.

Standardized Tests *Recommended:* SAT I or ACT (for admission).

Costs (2002–03) *Tuition:* $17,360 full-time. Full-time tuition and fees vary according to program. Part-time tuition and fees vary according to program. No tuition increase for student's term of enrollment. *Required fees:* $1750 full-time. *Room only:* $8360. *Payment plan:* installment. *Waivers:* senior citizens and employees or children of employees.

Applying *Options:* common application, electronic application, deferred entrance. *Application fee:* $35. *Required:* essay or personal statement, high school transcript, letters of recommendation. *Recommended:* minimum 2.0 GPA, interview. *Application deadline:* rolling (freshmen), rolling (transfers). *Notification:* continuous (freshmen).

Admissions Contact Mr. Jay Leindecker, Vice President for Enrollment Services, Dean College, 99 Main Street, Franklin, MA 02038-1994. *Phone:* 508-541-1508. *Toll-free phone:* 800-852-7702. *Fax:* 508-541-8726. *E-mail:* admissions@dean.edu.

FISHER COLLEGE
Boston, Massachusetts

- **Independent** primarily 2-year, founded 1903
- **Calendar** semesters
- **Degrees** certificates, associate, and bachelor's
- **Urban** 3-acre campus
- **Endowment** $14.7 million
- **Coed,** 526 undergraduate students, 98% full-time, 69% women, 31% men

Undergraduates 516 full-time, 10 part-time. 21% African American, 4% Asian American or Pacific Islander, 10% Hispanic American, 0.2% Native American, 17% international, 18% transferred in, 50% live on campus.

Freshmen *Admission:* 1,046 applied, 594 admitted, 168 enrolled.

Faculty *Total:* 55, 44% full-time, 24% with terminal degrees. *Student/faculty ratio:* 18:1.

Majors Accounting; business administration; data processing technology; early childhood education; fashion design/illustration; fashion merchandising; hospitality management; humanities; liberal arts and sciences/liberal studies; office management; paralegal/legal assistant; psychology; travel/tourism management.

Academic Programs *Special study options:* academic remediation for entering students, adult/continuing education programs, advanced placement credit, English as a second language, internships, off-campus study, part-time degree program, summer session for credit.

Library Fisher College Library plus 1 other with 30,000 titles, 160 serial subscriptions, an OPAC.

Computers on Campus 112 computers available on campus for general student use. A campuswide network can be accessed from off campus. Internet access, at least one staffed computer lab available.

Student Life *Housing Options:* coed, women-only. *Activities and Organizations:* drama/theater group, choral group, Drama Club, student government, Student Activity Club, Intercultural Club. *Campus security:* 24-hour emergency response devices and patrols, controlled dormitory access. *Student Services:* health clinic, personal/psychological counseling, women's center.

Athletics Member NAIA. *Intercollegiate sports:* baseball M, basketball M/W, soccer M/W, softball W, volleyball W.

Costs (2002–03) *Comprehensive fee:* $23,100 includes full-time tuition ($13,800), mandatory fees ($1400), and room and board ($7900). Part-time tuition and fees vary according to class time, course load, and program.

Applying *Options:* deferred entrance. *Application fee:* $25. *Required:* high school transcript. *Required for some:* essay or personal statement, letters of recommendation, interview. *Recommended:* minimum 2.0 GPA. *Application deadline:* rolling (freshmen), rolling (transfers). *Notification:* continuous (freshmen).

Admissions Contact Ms. Marietta Baier, Associate Director Admissions, Fisher College, 118 Beacon Street, Boston, MA 02116. *Phone:* 617-236-8800 Ext. 818. *Toll-free phone:* 800-821-3050 (in-state); 800-446-1226 (out-of-state). *Fax:* 617-236-5473. *E-mail:* admissions@fisher.edu.

GREENFIELD COMMUNITY COLLEGE
Greenfield, Massachusetts

- **State-supported** 2-year, founded 1962
- **Calendar** semesters
- **Degree** certificates and associate
- **Small-town** 100-acre campus
- **Coed,** 2,355 undergraduate students

Undergraduates Students come from 8 states and territories, 7 other countries. *Retention:* 55% of 2001 full-time freshmen returned.

Freshmen *Admission:* 787 applied, 779 admitted.

Faculty *Total:* 185, 32% full-time. *Student/faculty ratio:* 14:1.

Majors Accounting; American studies; art; behavioral sciences; biological/physical sciences; business administration; business marketing and marketing management; computer programming; criminal justice/law enforcement administration; early childhood education; education; engineering science; fire science; food sciences; graphic design/commercial art/illustration; human ecology; humanities; human services; industrial technology; information sciences/systems; liberal arts and sciences/liberal studies; mass communications; mathematics; natural resources management; nursing; photography; pre-engineering; recreation/leisure studies; secretarial science.

Academic Programs *Special study options:* academic remediation for entering students, adult/continuing education programs, advanced placement credit, cooperative education, distance learning, English as a second language, honors programs, independent study, part-time degree program, services for LD students, summer session for credit.

Library Greenfield Community College Library with 52,690 titles, 356 serial subscriptions.

Computers on Campus 115 computers available on campus for general student use. Internet access, at least one staffed computer lab available.

Student Life *Housing:* college housing not available. *Activities and Organizations:* drama/theater group, choral group. *Campus security:* 24-hour emergency response devices and patrols, late-night transport/escort service. *Student Services:* health clinic, personal/psychological counseling, women's center.

Costs (2001–02) *Tuition:* state resident $624 full-time, $26 per credit part-time; nonresident $247 per credit part-time. *Required fees:* $1406 full-time, $74 per credit.

Applying *Options:* early admission. *Application fee:* $35 (non-residents). *Required for some:* high school transcript, interview. *Application deadline:* rolling (freshmen), rolling (transfers).

Admissions Contact Mr. Herbert Hentz, Assistant Director of Admission, Greenfield Community College, 1 College Drive, Greenfield, MA 01301-9739. *Phone:* 413-775-1000. *E-mail:* admission@gcc.mass.edu.

HOLYOKE COMMUNITY COLLEGE
Holyoke, Massachusetts

- **State-supported** 2-year, founded 1946, part of Massachusetts Public Higher Education System
- **Calendar** semesters
- **Degree** certificates and associate
- **Suburban** 135-acre campus
- **Coed,** 5,998 undergraduate students

Undergraduates Students come from 7 states and territories, 11 other countries.

Faculty *Total:* 300. *Student/faculty ratio:* 18:1.

Majors Accounting; American studies; biology; business administration; business education; chemistry; computer typography/composition; early childhood

Holyoke Community College (continued)
education; elementary education; engineering science; environmental science; film/video production; fine/studio arts; graphic design/commercial art/illustration; home economics; hospitality management; hotel and restaurant management; human services; information sciences/systems; law enforcement/police science; legal administrative assistant; liberal arts and sciences/liberal studies; mass communications; medical records administration; medical technology; music; nursing; nutrition science; photography; physics; pre-engineering; radiological science; retail management; secretarial science; sport/fitness administration; theater arts/drama; travel/tourism management; veterinary sciences; veterinary technology; visual/performing arts.

Academic Programs *Special study options:* academic remediation for entering students, adult/continuing education programs, advanced placement credit, cooperative education, English as a second language, honors programs, internships, off-campus study, part-time degree program, services for LD students, student-designed majors, study abroad, summer session for credit. *ROTC:* Army (c), Air Force (c).

Library Elaine Marieb Library with 68,965 titles, 459 serial subscriptions.

Computers on Campus 275 computers available on campus for general student use. Internet access, at least one staffed computer lab available.

Student Life *Housing:* college housing not available. *Activities and Organizations:* drama/theater group, student-run newspaper, radio station, choral group, Drama Club, Music Club, Student Advisory Board. *Campus security:* 24-hour emergency response devices and patrols, student patrols, late-night transport/escort service. *Student Services:* health clinic, personal/psychological counseling, women's center.

Athletics Member NJCAA. *Intercollegiate sports:* baseball M, basketball M, skiing (downhill) M(c)/W(c), soccer M/W, softball W, tennis M/W.

Standardized Tests *Required for some:* Assessment and Placement Services for Community Colleges, Health Occupations Exam.

Costs (2001–02) *Tuition:* state resident $576 full-time, $24 per credit part-time; nonresident $5520 full-time, $230 per credit part-time. *Required fees:* $1200 full-time, $46 per credit, $12 per term part-time.

Applying *Options:* early admission, deferred entrance. *Application fee:* $10. *Required:* high school transcript. *Recommended:* interview. *Application deadline:* rolling (freshmen), rolling (transfers). *Notification:* continuous (freshmen).

Admissions Contact Ms. Joan Mikalson, Director of Admissions, Holyoke Community College, 303 Homestead Avenue, Holyoke, MA 01040-1099. *Phone:* 413-552-2850.

ITT Technical Institute
Woburn, Massachusetts

- **Proprietary** 2-year
- **Calendar** quarters
- **Degree** associate
- **Coed,** 230 undergraduate students

Majors Computer/information sciences related; computer programming; drafting; electrical/electronic engineering technologies related; information technology.

Student Life *Housing:* college housing not available.

Costs (2001–02) *Tuition:* Full-time tuition and fees vary according to program. Part-time tuition and fees vary according to program. $260—$330 per credit hour.

Applying *Application fee:* $100. *Required:* high school transcript, interview. *Recommended:* letters of recommendation. *Application deadline:* rolling (freshmen). *Notification:* continuous (freshmen).

Admissions Contact Mr. Arthur Banester, Director of Recruitment, ITT Technical Institute, 10 Forbes Road, Woburn, MA 01801. *Phone:* 781-937-8324.

ITT Technical Institute
Norwood, Massachusetts

- **Proprietary** 2-year, founded 1990, part of ITT Educational Services, Inc
- **Calendar** quarters
- **Degree** associate
- **Suburban** campus with easy access to Boston
- **Coed,** 260 undergraduate students

Majors Computer/information sciences related; computer programming; drafting; electrical/electronic engineering technologies related; information technology.

Student Life *Housing:* college housing not available.

Costs (2001–02) *Tuition:* Full-time tuition and fees vary according to program. Part-time tuition and fees vary according to program. $260—$330 per credit hour.

Applying *Options:* deferred entrance. *Application fee:* $100. *Required:* high school transcript, interview. *Recommended:* letters of recommendation. *Application deadline:* rolling (freshmen), rolling (transfers). *Notification:* continuous (freshmen).

Admissions Contact Mr. Jared Caywood, Director of Recruitment, ITT Technical Institute, 333 Providence Highway, Norwood, MA 02062. *Phone:* 781-278-7200. *Toll-free phone:* 800-879-8324.

Katharine Gibbs School
Boston, Massachusetts

- **Proprietary** 2-year, founded 1917, part of Career Education Corporation
- **Calendar** quarters
- **Degree** certificates and associate
- **Urban** campus
- **Coed**

Applying *Application fee:* $25. *Required:* high school transcript.

Admissions Contact Mr. Robert A. Andriola, Director of Admissions, Katharine Gibbs School, 126 Newbury Street, Boston, MA 02116-2904. *Phone:* 617-578-7150. *Toll-free phone:* 800-6SKILLS. *Fax:* 617-262-2610.

Laboure College
Boston, Massachusetts

- **Independent Roman Catholic** 2-year, founded 1971
- **Calendar** semesters
- **Degree** certificates and associate
- **Urban** campus
- **Endowment** $616,697
- **Coed,** 253 undergraduate students, 22% full-time, 93% women, 7% men

Laboure's programs in health care are supported by its affiliations with more than 75 Boston-area health-care institutions. Each program offers career education and general education courses. The student-faculty ratio is 11:1. Opportunities for full- and part-time study, day or evening, and certificate programs are available. In 2000, all graduates who elected to work found employment in their respective fields upon graduation.

Undergraduates 56 full-time, 197 part-time. Students come from 3 states and territories, 1 other country, 0.1% are from out of state, 35% African American, 3% Asian American or Pacific Islander, 3% Hispanic American, 0.8% Native American, 0.8% international, 33% transferred in. *Retention:* 62% of 2001 full-time freshmen returned.

Freshmen *Admission:* 88 applied, 19 admitted, 15 enrolled.

Faculty *Total:* 39, 64% full-time, 13% with terminal degrees. *Student/faculty ratio:* 7:1.

Majors Dietetics; industrial radiologic technology; medical records administration; medical technology; nursing.

Academic Programs *Special study options:* academic remediation for entering students, accelerated degree program, adult/continuing education programs, independent study, part-time degree program, services for LD students, summer session for credit.

Library Helen Stubblefield Law Library with 10,975 titles, 155 serial subscriptions, 650 audiovisual materials, an OPAC.

Computers on Campus 20 computers available on campus for general student use. At least one staffed computer lab available.

Student Life *Housing:* college housing not available. *Activities and Organizations:* Student Government Association, college yearbook, interpreters, peer advisors. *Campus security:* 24-hour emergency response devices. *Student Services:* health clinic, personal/psychological counseling.

Costs (2001–02) *Tuition:* $9130 full-time, $360 per credit part-time. Full-time tuition and fees vary according to course load. Part-time tuition and fees vary according to course load. *Required fees:* $20 full-time, $10 per term part-time. *Payment plan:* installment.

Financial Aid In 2001, 10 Federal Work-Study jobs (averaging $1000).

Applying *Options:* deferred entrance. *Application fee:* $25. *Required:* high school transcript, letters of recommendation. *Recommended:* interview. *Application deadline:* rolling (freshmen), rolling (transfers).

Admissions Contact Ms. Linda Brierley, Director of Admissions, Laboure College, 2120 Dorchester Avenue, Boston, MA 02124-5698. *Phone:* 617-296-8300 Ext. 4015. *Fax:* 617-296-7947. *E-mail:* admit@labourecollege.org.

MARIAN COURT COLLEGE
Swampscott, Massachusetts

- **Independent Roman Catholic** 2-year, founded 1964
- **Calendar** semesters
- **Degree** certificates and associate
- **Suburban** 6-acre campus with easy access to Boston
- **Coed, primarily women,** 281 undergraduate students, 69% full-time, 93% women, 7% men

Undergraduates Students come from 1 other state, 5 other countries.
Freshmen *Admission:* 136 applied, 132 admitted. *Average high school GPA:* 2.4.
Faculty *Total:* 25, 28% full-time. *Student/faculty ratio:* 10:1.
Majors Accounting; business administration; criminal justice studies; data processing technology; hospitality management; human resources management; legal administrative assistant; liberal arts and sciences/liberal studies; medical administrative assistant; medical technology; secretarial science; travel/tourism management.
Academic Programs *Special study options:* academic remediation for entering students, adult/continuing education programs, advanced placement credit, honors programs, independent study, internships, off-campus study, part-time degree program, summer session for credit.
Library Lindsay Library with 5,006 titles, 122 serial subscriptions, an OPAC.
Computers on Campus 43 computers available on campus for general student use. Internet access, at least one staffed computer lab available.
Student Life *Housing:* college housing not available. *Activities and Organizations:* choral group, Travel Club, student government, Yearbook Committee, Theater Club. *Campus security:* well-lit parking lots. *Student Services:* personal/psychological counseling.
Costs (2002–03) *Tuition:* $9760 full-time. *Required fees:* $600 full-time.
Financial Aid In 2001, 14 Federal Work-Study jobs (averaging $780).
Applying *Options:* common application, electronic application, deferred entrance. *Required:* essay or personal statement, high school transcript, minimum 2.0 GPA, 2 letters of recommendation, interview. *Application deadline:* rolling (freshmen), rolling (transfers).
Admissions Contact Mrs. Lisa Emerson Parker, Director of Admissions, Marian Court College, 35 Little's Point Road, Swampscott, MA 01907-2840. *Phone:* 781-595-6768 Ext. 139. *Fax:* 781-595-3560. *E-mail:* marianct@shore.net.

MASSACHUSETTS BAY COMMUNITY COLLEGE
Wellesley Hills, Massachusetts

- **State-supported** 2-year, founded 1961
- **Calendar** semesters
- **Degree** certificates and associate
- **Suburban** 84-acre campus with easy access to Boston
- **Endowment** $3.7 million
- **Coed,** 4,950 undergraduate students, 51% full-time, 58% women, 42% men

Undergraduates 2,532 full-time, 2,418 part-time. Students come from 5 states and territories, 48 other countries, 2% are from out of state, 8% transferred in.
Freshmen *Admission:* 2,413 applied, 2,413 admitted, 1,153 enrolled.
Faculty *Total:* 304, 29% full-time. *Student/faculty ratio:* 21:1.
Majors Accounting; automotive engineering technology; biological/physical sciences; biological technology; business; business administration; chemical technology; child care/guidance; communications; computer engineering technology; computer/information sciences; computer science; court reporting; criminal justice/law enforcement administration; drafting; engineering technology; environmental technology; forensic technology; general studies; hospitality management; human services; information sciences/systems; international relations; laser/optical technology; liberal arts and sciences/liberal studies; marine biology; mechanical engineering technology; medical radiologic technology; nursing; occupational therapy assistant; paralegal/legal assistant; physical therapy assistant; respiratory therapy; social sciences; telecommunications; theater arts/drama.
Academic Programs *Special study options:* academic remediation for entering students, adult/continuing education programs, advanced placement credit, cooperative education, distance learning, English as a second language, honors programs, internships, part-time degree program, services for LD students, summer session for credit.
Library Perkins Library with 47,038 titles, 540 serial subscriptions, 4,500 audiovisual materials, an OPAC, a Web page.
Computers on Campus 400 computers available on campus for general student use. A campuswide network can be accessed from off campus. Internet access, at least one staffed computer lab available.
Student Life *Housing:* college housing not available. *Activities and Organizations:* drama/theater group, student-run newspaper, Student Government Association, Latino Student Organization, New World Society Club, Mass Bay Players, Student Occupational Therapy Association. *Campus security:* 24-hour emergency response devices and patrols. *Student Services:* health clinic, personal/psychological counseling.
Athletics Member NJCAA. *Intercollegiate sports:* baseball M, basketball M/W, cross-country running M/W, golf M/W, soccer M, tennis M/W. *Intramural sports:* ice hockey M, soccer M/W.
Costs (2002–03) *Tuition:* state resident $720 full-time, $41 per credit part-time; nonresident $6900 full-time, $230 per credit part-time. Full-time tuition and fees vary according to program and reciprocity agreements. Part-time tuition and fees vary according to class time, program, and reciprocity agreements. *Required fees:* $1170 full-time, $48 per credit. *Payment plan:* installment. *Waivers:* senior citizens and employees or children of employees.
Applying *Options:* common application, electronic application, early admission. *Application fee:* $35 (non-residents). *Application deadline:* rolling (freshmen), rolling (transfers). *Notification:* continuous (freshmen).
Admissions Contact Ms. Donna Raposa, Director for Admissions, Massachusetts Bay Community College, 50 Oakland Street, Wellesley Hills, MA 02481. *Phone:* 781-239-2501. *Fax:* 781-239-2525. *E-mail:* mbccinfo@mbcc.mass.edu.

MASSASOIT COMMUNITY COLLEGE
Brockton, Massachusetts

- **State-supported** 2-year, founded 1966
- **Calendar** semesters
- **Degree** certificates and associate
- **Suburban** campus with easy access to Boston
- **Coed,** 6,906 undergraduate students

Undergraduates Students come from 7 states and territories, 3 other countries, 1% are from out of state.
Freshmen *Admission:* 2,300 applied, 2,300 admitted.
Faculty *Total:* 440, 32% full-time.
Majors Accounting; architectural engineering technology; auto mechanic/technician; biological/physical sciences; business administration; business marketing and marketing management; child care/development; civil engineering technology; computer programming related; computer/technical support; culinary arts; data entry/microcomputer applications; dental hygiene; diesel engine mechanic; electrical/electronic engineering technology; electromechanical technology; executive assistant; fire science; graphic design/commercial art/illustration; heating/air conditioning/refrigeration; hospitality management; hotel and restaurant management; human services; information sciences/systems; law enforcement/police science; legal administrative assistant; liberal arts and sciences/liberal studies; medical assistant; medical radiologic technology; nursing; operations management; physical therapy assistant; respiratory therapy; secretarial science; travel/tourism management; word processing.
Academic Programs *Special study options:* academic remediation for entering students, accelerated degree program, adult/continuing education programs, cooperative education, distance learning, English as a second language, internships, off-campus study, part-time degree program, services for LD students, summer session for credit.
Library 75,000 titles, 396 serial subscriptions.
Computers on Campus 350 computers available on campus for general student use. At least one staffed computer lab available.
Student Life *Housing:* college housing not available. *Activities and Organizations:* drama/theater group, student-run newspaper, radio station, Drama Club, student newspaper, Phi Theta Kappa, International Student Association, Student Senate. *Campus security:* 24-hour patrols. *Student Services:* health clinic, personal/psychological counseling, women's center.
Athletics Member NJCAA. *Intercollegiate sports:* baseball M, basketball M/W, soccer M/W, softball W. *Intramural sports:* basketball M/W.
Costs (2001–02) *Tuition:* state resident $720 full-time, $24 per credit part-time; nonresident $6900 full-time, $230 per credit part-time. *Required fees:* $1230 full-time, $615 per term part-time. *Waivers:* senior citizens and employees or children of employees.
Applying *Application deadline:* rolling (freshmen), rolling (transfers). *Notification:* continuous (freshmen).
Admissions Contact Ms. Roberta Noodell, Director of Admissions, Massasoit Community College, 1 Massasoit Boulevard, Brockton, MA 02302-3996. *Phone:* 508-588-9100 Ext. 1410. *Toll-free phone:* 800-CAREERS.

MIDDLESEX COMMUNITY COLLEGE
Bedford, Massachusetts

- **State-supported** 2-year, founded 1970, part of Massachusetts Public Higher Education System
- **Calendar** semesters
- **Degree** certificates and associate
- **Suburban** 200-acre campus with easy access to Boston
- **Endowment** $1.1 million
- **Coed,** 7,568 undergraduate students, 42% full-time, 58% women, 42% men

Undergraduates 3,186 full-time, 4,382 part-time. Students come from 5 states and territories, 5% are from out of state, 8% transferred in.
Freshmen *Admission:* 3,359 applied, 3,123 admitted, 1,873 enrolled.
Faculty *Total:* 468, 27% full-time.
Majors Accounting; art; auto mechanic/technician; biomedical technology; business administration; business communications; business marketing and marketing management; computer engineering technology; computer science; criminal justice/law enforcement administration; dental assistant; dental hygiene; dental laboratory technician; drafting; early childhood education; electrical/electronic engineering technology; fashion merchandising; fire science; general studies; graphic design/commercial art/illustration; hospitality/recreation marketing; hotel and restaurant management; liberal arts and sciences/liberal studies; mass communications; medical assistant; medical laboratory technician; mental health/rehabilitation; nursing; office management; paralegal/legal assistant; pre-engineering; radiological science; retail management; telecommunications; theater arts/drama.
Academic Programs *Special study options:* academic remediation for entering students, accelerated degree program, adult/continuing education programs, advanced placement credit, cooperative education, distance learning, English as a second language, honors programs, independent study, internships, off-campus study, part-time degree program, services for LD students, study abroad, summer session for credit. *ROTC:* Air Force (c).
Library Main Library plus 1 other with 52,960 titles, 538 serial subscriptions, an OPAC, a Web page.
Computers on Campus 325 computers available on campus for general student use. A campuswide network can be accessed from off campus that provide access to word processing; graphics programs. Internet access, online (class) registration, at least one staffed computer lab available.
Student Life *Housing:* college housing not available. *Activities and Organizations:* drama/theater group, student-run newspaper, Mental Health Club, International Club, Early Childhood Education Club, Student Union Government Association, Student Activities Board. *Campus security:* 24-hour emergency response devices and patrols. *Student Services:* health clinic, personal/psychological counseling, legal services.
Athletics *Intramural sports:* basketball M/W, table tennis M/W, volleyball M/W.
Costs (2001–02) *Tuition:* state resident $576 full-time, $24 per credit part-time; nonresident $5520 full-time, $230 per credit part-time. *Required fees:* $1442 full-time, $58 per credit, $25 per term part-time.
Financial Aid In 2001, 52 Federal Work-Study jobs (averaging $1802).
Applying *Options:* common application, electronic application, early admission. *Required for some:* essay or personal statement, high school transcript, 3 letters of recommendation, interview. *Application deadline:* rolling (freshmen), rolling (transfers). *Notification:* continuous (freshmen).
Admissions Contact Ms. Darcy Orellana, Associate Dean, Admissions and Recruitment, Middlesex Community College, 33 Kearney Square, Lowell, MA 01852. *Phone:* 978-656-3207. *Toll-free phone:* 800-818-3434. *Fax:* 978-656-3322. *E-mail:* middlesex@middlesex.cc.ma.us.

MOUNT WACHUSETT COMMUNITY COLLEGE
Gardner, Massachusetts

- **State-supported** 2-year, founded 1963, part of Massachusetts Public Higher Education System
- **Calendar** semesters
- **Degree** certificates and associate
- **Small-town** 270-acre campus with easy access to Boston
- **Endowment** $950,380
- **Coed,** 3,711 undergraduate students, 43% full-time, 61% women, 39% men

MWCC offers a solid academic foundation for students, whether they're continuing their studies in 4-year colleges or entering the careers of their choice, with unparalleled affordability and transferability, residential housing at nearby Fitchburg State College, and financial aid programs. The main campus is located on 269 scenic acres in Gardner, Massachusetts. Web site: http://www.mwcc.mass.edu.

Undergraduates 1,605 full-time, 2,106 part-time. Students come from 9 states and territories, 18 other countries, 5% are from out of state, 3% African American, 2% Asian American or Pacific Islander, 6% Hispanic American, 0.2% Native American, 2% international, 11% transferred in. *Retention:* 50% of 2001 full-time freshmen returned.
Freshmen *Admission:* 3,136 applied, 2,881 admitted, 1,455 enrolled.
Faculty *Total:* 257, 28% full-time. *Student/faculty ratio:* 15:1.
Majors Accounting; art; auto mechanic/technician; broadcast journalism; business administration; computer graphics; computer maintenance technology; criminal justice/law enforcement administration; electrical/electronic engineering technology; environmental science; exercise sciences; fine/studio arts; fire science; general studies; human services; industrial/manufacturing engineering; industrial technology; information sciences/systems; liberal arts and sciences/liberal studies; management information systems/business data processing; medical assistant; nursing; paralegal/legal assistant; physical therapy; plastics technology; sign language interpretation; speech therapy; telecommunications.
Academic Programs *Special study options:* academic remediation for entering students, adult/continuing education programs, advanced placement credit, cooperative education, distance learning, English as a second language, honors programs, independent study, internships, part-time degree program, services for LD students, summer session for credit. *ROTC:* Army (c), Navy (c), Air Force (c).
Library Mount Wachusett Community College Library with 56,344 titles, 535 serial subscriptions, 2,612 audiovisual materials, an OPAC, a Web page.
Computers on Campus 340 computers available on campus for general student use. Internet access, at least one staffed computer lab available.
Student Life *Activities and Organizations:* drama/theater group, choral group, Sophomore Nursing Club, Freshman Nursing Club, Alpha Beta Gamma, Physical Therapist Assistant Club, Multicultural Club. *Campus security:* 24-hour emergency response devices and patrols. *Student Services:* health clinic, personal/psychological counseling, women's center.
Costs (2001–02) *Tuition:* state resident $750 full-time, $25 per credit part-time; nonresident $6900 full-time, $230 per credit part-time. Full-time tuition and fees vary according to reciprocity agreements. Part-time tuition and fees vary according to course load and reciprocity agreements. *Required fees:* $2280 full-time, $71 per credit, $75 per term part-time. *Payment plan:* installment. *Waivers:* senior citizens and employees or children of employees.
Applying *Options:* common application, early admission. *Application fee:* $10. *Required:* high school transcript. *Required for some:* essay or personal statement, 2 letters of recommendation. *Application deadline:* rolling (freshmen), rolling (transfers). *Notification:* continuous (freshmen).
Admissions Contact Ms. Karen Schedin, Director of Admission Services, Mount Wachusett Community College, 444 Green Street, Gardner, MA 01440-1000. *Phone:* 978-632-6600 Ext. 252. *Fax:* 978-630-9554. *E-mail:* admissions@mwcc.mass.edu.

NEWBURY COLLEGE
Brookline, Massachusetts

- **Independent** primarily 2-year, founded 1962
- **Calendar** semesters
- **Degrees** certificates, associate, and bachelor's
- **Suburban** 10-acre campus with easy access to Boston
- **Endowment** $4.5 million
- **Coed,** 1,689 undergraduate students, 39% full-time, 64% women, 36% men

Undergraduates 654 full-time, 1,035 part-time. Students come from 22 states and territories, 41 other countries, 34% are from out of state, 11% African American, 4% Asian American or Pacific Islander, 5% Hispanic American, 6% international, 35% live on campus. *Retention:* 80% of 2001 full-time freshmen returned.
Freshmen *Admission:* 964 applied, 850 admitted, 340 enrolled. *Average high school GPA:* 2.70. *Test scores:* SAT verbal scores over 500: 28%; SAT math scores over 500: 28%; ACT scores over 18: 75%; SAT verbal scores over 600: 9%; SAT math scores over 600: 6%; ACT scores over 24: 25%; SAT verbal scores over 700: 1%; SAT math scores over 700: 1%.
Faculty *Total:* 89, 39% full-time. *Student/faculty ratio:* 16:1.
Majors Accounting; business administration; business marketing and marketing management; computer programming; computer science; criminal justice/law enforcement administration; culinary arts; culinary arts and services related; fashion merchandising; finance; food products retailing; graphic design/commercial art/illustration; health services administration; hotel and restaurant management; humanities; human resources management; interior design; international busi-

ness; legal studies; marketing research; mass communications; paralegal/legal assistant; pre-law; psychology; radio/television broadcasting; retail management; social sciences; sociology; travel/tourism management.
Academic Programs *Special study options:* academic remediation for entering students, accelerated degree program, adult/continuing education programs, advanced placement credit, cooperative education, double majors, English as a second language, freshman honors college, honors programs, independent study, internships, off-campus study, part-time degree program, services for LD students, study abroad, summer session for credit.
Library Newbury College Library plus 1 other with 32,459 titles, 1,109 serial subscriptions, an OPAC.
Computers on Campus 75 computers available on campus for general student use. A campuswide network can be accessed from off campus. At least one staffed computer lab available.
Student Life *Housing Options:* coed, women-only. *Activities and Organizations:* student-run newspaper, radio station, student government, Newbury College Programming Board, Inn Keepers Club, Speech and Debate Team, International Student Organization. *Campus security:* 24-hour emergency response devices and patrols, late-night transport/escort service, controlled dormitory access. *Student Services:* personal/psychological counseling.
Athletics Member NCAA. All Division III. *Intercollegiate sports:* basketball M/W, cross-country running M/W, golf M/W, soccer M, softball W, tennis M/W, volleyball M/W. *Intramural sports:* basketball M/W, football M/W, softball W, swimming M/W, volleyball M/W, weight lifting M/W.
Standardized Tests *Required for some:* SAT I or ACT (for admission). *Recommended:* SAT I or ACT (for admission).
Costs (2001–02) *One-time required fee:* $300. *Comprehensive fee:* $21,700 includes full-time tuition ($13,650), mandatory fees ($650), and room and board ($7400). Full-time tuition and fees vary according to class time, course load, and program. Part-time tuition: $195 per credit. Part-time tuition and fees vary according to class time, course load, and program. *Room and board:* Room and board charges vary according to board plan. *Payment plan:* installment. *Waivers:* employees or children of employees.
Applying *Options:* electronic application, early admission, early action, deferred entrance. *Application fee:* $50. *Required:* essay or personal statement, high school transcript, letters of recommendation. *Recommended:* minimum 2.0 GPA, interview. *Application deadline:* 3/1 (freshmen), rolling (transfers). *Notification:* 4/1 (freshmen), 1/1 (early action).
Admissions Contact Ms. Jacqueline Giordano, Dean of Admission, Newbury College, 129 Fisher Avenue, Brookline, MA 02445-5796. *Phone:* 617-730-7007. *Toll-free phone:* 800-NEWBURY. *Fax:* 617-731-9618. *E-mail:* info@newbury.edu.

NEW ENGLAND COLLEGE OF FINANCE
Boston, Massachusetts

Admissions Contact Ms. Judith Marley, Vice President and Director of Academic Affairs, New England College of Finance, 1 Lincoln Plaza, Boston, MA 02111-2645. *Phone:* 617-951-2350 Ext. 227. *Toll-free phone:* 888-696-NECF. *Fax:* 617-951-2533.

NEW ENGLAND INSTITUTE OF ART & COMMUNICATIONS
Brookline, Massachusetts

- **Proprietary** 2-year
- **Calendar** semesters
- **Degree** associate
- **Coed**

Faculty *Total:* 101, 25% full-time.
Majors Communications; graphic design/commercial art/illustration; multimedia; music business management/merchandising; radio/television broadcasting technology.
Costs (2002–03) *Tuition:* $15,300 full-time, $510 per credit part-time. Full-time tuition and fees vary according to class time. *Required fees:* $250 full-time, $125 per term part-time.
Applying *Application fee:* $20. *Required:* interview. *Application deadline:* rolling (freshmen), rolling (transfers). *Notification:* continuous (freshmen).
Admissions Contact Ms. Elizabeth Allen, Dean of Admissions, New England Institute of Art & Communications, 10 Brookline Place West, Brookline, MA 02445. *Phone:* 617-739-1700 Ext. 4404.

NORTHERN ESSEX COMMUNITY COLLEGE
Haverhill, Massachusetts

- **State-supported** 2-year, founded 1960
- **Calendar** semesters
- **Degree** certificates and associate
- **Suburban** 106-acre campus with easy access to Boston
- **Endowment** $1.6 million
- **Coed,** 1,450 undergraduate students, 54% full-time, 58% women, 42% men

Public, open admissions college offering more than 80 degree and certificate programs in liberal arts, human service, health, business, biotech, engineering, and computer technologies. Outstanding program in deaf studies, sign language interpreting. Students can prepare for a career or begin a bachelor's degree through joint admissions opportunities and transfer agreements with 4-year colleges and universities.

Undergraduates 777 full-time, 673 part-time. Students come from 4 states and territories, 16% are from out of state, 3% African American, 2% Asian American or Pacific Islander, 21% Hispanic American, 0.2% Native American, 0.5% international, 17% transferred in. *Retention:* 58% of 2001 full-time freshmen returned.
Freshmen *Admission:* 3,549 applied, 3,428 admitted, 1,450 enrolled.
Faculty *Total:* 486, 19% full-time. *Student/faculty ratio:* 22:1.
Majors Accounting; biological/physical sciences; business administration; business education; business marketing and marketing management; civil engineering technology; computer engineering technology; computer graphics; computer/information sciences; computer programming; computer programming related; computer programming (specific applications); computer science; computer typography/composition; criminal justice/law enforcement administration; dance; data processing technology; early childhood education; education; electrical/electronic engineering technology; engineering science; finance; graphic design/commercial art/illustration; history; hotel and restaurant management; industrial radiologic technology; international relations; journalism; liberal arts and sciences/liberal studies; machine technology; materials science; medical administrative assistant; medical records administration; mental health/rehabilitation; music; nursing; paralegal/legal assistant; physical education; political science; real estate; recreation/leisure studies; respiratory therapy; secretarial science; sign language interpretation; theater arts/drama; travel/tourism management; Web/multimedia management/webmaster; Web page, digital/multimedia and information resources design; women's studies; word processing.
Academic Programs *Special study options:* academic remediation for entering students, adult/continuing education programs, advanced placement credit, cooperative education, distance learning, double majors, English as a second language, freshman honors college, honors programs, independent study, internships, off-campus study, part-time degree program, services for LD students, study abroad, summer session for credit. *ROTC:* Air Force (c).
Library Bentley Library with 61,120 titles, 598 serial subscriptions, an OPAC.
Computers on Campus 250 computers available on campus for general student use. A campuswide network can be accessed from off campus. At least one staffed computer lab available.
Student Life *Housing:* college housing not available. *Activities and Organizations:* drama/theater group, student-run newspaper. *Campus security:* 24-hour emergency response devices and patrols. *Student Services:* health clinic, personal/psychological counseling, women's center.
Athletics Member NJCAA. *Intercollegiate sports:* baseball M, basketball M/W, golf M/W, soccer M/W, softball W. *Intramural sports:* basketball M/W, cross-country running M/W, football M/W, golf M/W, racquetball M/W, skiing (cross-country) M/W, skiing (downhill) M/W, weight lifting M/W.
Costs (2001–02) *Tuition:* state resident $2280 full-time, $76 per credit part-time; nonresident $9150 full-time, $305 per credit part-time. Full-time tuition and fees vary according to degree level. Part-time tuition and fees vary according to degree level. *Payment plan:* installment. *Waivers:* employees or children of employees.
Financial Aid In 2001, 125 Federal Work-Study jobs (averaging $2500).
Applying *Options:* early admission. *Required:* high school transcript. *Application deadline:* rolling (freshmen), rolling (transfers). *Notification:* continuous (freshmen).

Northern Essex Community College (continued)

Admissions Contact Ms. Kathleen Borruso, Systems Analyst, Northern Essex Community College, 100 Elliott Street, Haverhill, MA 01830. *Phone:* 978-556-3605. *Toll-free phone:* 800-NECC-123. *Fax:* 978-556-3155. *E-mail:* ssullivan@necc.mass.edu.

NORTH SHORE COMMUNITY COLLEGE
Danvers, Massachusetts

- **State-supported** 2-year, founded 1965
- **Calendar** semesters
- **Degree** certificates and associate
- **Suburban** campus with easy access to Boston
- **Coed,** 6,100 undergraduate students, 38% full-time, 61% women, 39% men

Undergraduates 2,319 full-time, 3,781 part-time. Students come from 3 states and territories, 1% are from out of state, 7% African American, 3% Asian American or Pacific Islander, 11% Hispanic American, 0.5% Native American, 9% transferred in.

Freshmen *Admission:* 2,575 applied, 1,113 admitted, 1,391 enrolled.

Faculty *Total:* 441, 30% full-time. *Student/faculty ratio:* 25:1.

Majors Accounting; aircraft pilot (professional); alcohol/drug abuse counseling; biological technology; business administration; business computer programming; business marketing and marketing management; child care/development; computer engineering technology; computer graphics; computer programming; computer science; computer science related; criminal justice/law enforcement administration; culinary arts; data entry/microcomputer applications; early childhood education; engineering science; fire science; forestry; gerontology; health science; horticulture services; hospitality management; information sciences/systems; interdisciplinary studies; landscaping management; legal administrative assistant; liberal arts and sciences/liberal studies; medical administrative assistant; medical radiologic technology; mental health/rehabilitation; nursing; nutrition science; occupational therapy; paralegal/legal assistant; physical therapy assistant; pre-engineering; respiratory therapy; secretarial science; travel/tourism management; veterinary technology.

Academic Programs *Special study options:* academic remediation for entering students, adult/continuing education programs, advanced placement credit, cooperative education, distance learning, English as a second language, honors programs, independent study, internships, part-time degree program, services for LD students, summer session for credit.

Library Learning Resource Center plus 2 others with 75,000 titles, 606 serial subscriptions, 4,890 audiovisual materials, an OPAC.

Computers on Campus 300 computers available on campus for general student use. Internet access, online (class) registration, at least one staffed computer lab available.

Student Life *Housing:* college housing not available. *Activities and Organizations:* drama/theater group, student-run newspaper, Program Council, student government, performing arts, student newspaper, Phi Theta Kappa. *Campus security:* 24-hour emergency response devices and patrols, late-night transport/escort service. *Student Services:* health clinic, personal/psychological counseling, women's center.

Athletics Member NJCAA. *Intercollegiate sports:* baseball M, basketball M/W, softball W.

Standardized Tests *Required for some:* nursing exam.

Costs (2001–02) *Tuition:* state resident $600 full-time, $25 per credit part-time; nonresident $5952 full-time, $248 per credit part-time. Full-time tuition and fees vary according to reciprocity agreements. Part-time tuition and fees vary according to reciprocity agreements. *Required fees:* $1392 full-time, $58 per credit. *Payment plan:* installment. *Waivers:* senior citizens and employees or children of employees.

Applying *Options:* early admission. *Required for some:* high school transcript, minimum 2.0 GPA, interview. *Application deadline:* rolling (freshmen), rolling (transfers). *Notification:* continuous (freshmen).

Admissions Contact Dr. Joanne Light, Director of Admissions, North Shore Community College, PO Box 3340, Danvers, MA 01923. *Phone:* 978-762-4000 Ext. 4337. *Fax:* 978-762-4015. *E-mail:* enroll@nscc.ma.us.

QUINCY COLLEGE
Quincy, Massachusetts

- **City-supported** 2-year, founded 1958
- **Calendar** semesters
- **Degree** certificates and associate
- **Suburban** 2-acre campus with easy access to Boston
- **Endowment** $112,021
- **Coed,** 4,622 undergraduate students

Undergraduates Students come from 11 states and territories, 15% African American, 13% Asian American or Pacific Islander, 2% Hispanic American, 0.1% Native American.

Freshmen *Admission:* 2,480 applied, 2,480 admitted.

Faculty *Total:* 423, 9% full-time.

Majors Accounting; behavioral sciences; biological/physical sciences; broadcast journalism; business administration; business marketing and marketing management; computer graphics; computer management; computer programming; computer science; criminal justice/law enforcement administration; data processing technology; early childhood education; emergency medical technology; English; environmental science; fire science; food products retailing; hospitality management; hotel and restaurant management; humanities; information sciences/systems; labor/personnel relations; law enforcement/police science; legal administrative assistant; liberal arts and sciences/liberal studies; mass communications; mathematics; medical administrative assistant; nursing; operating room technician; paralegal/legal assistant; physical sciences; political science; practical nurse; psychology; retail management; secretarial science; social sciences; sociology; travel/tourism management.

Academic Programs *Special study options:* academic remediation for entering students, adult/continuing education programs, advanced placement credit, English as a second language, internships, part-time degree program, summer session for credit.

Library Anselmo Library plus 1 other with 30,000 titles, 305 serial subscriptions.

Computers on Campus 130 computers available on campus for general student use. At least one staffed computer lab available.

Student Life *Housing:* college housing not available. *Activities and Organizations:* Student Government Association, Phi Theta Kappa, campus newspaper. *Campus security:* 24-hour emergency response devices and patrols.

Standardized Tests *Required:* CPT.

Costs (2002–03) *Tuition:* Allied Health Programs' tuition is $4028 for full time and $2678 for part-time students. For other programs, contact the College directly for tuition and fees. *Required fees:* $20 full-time.

Applying *Options:* common application, early admission, deferred entrance. *Application fee:* $20. *Required:* high school transcript. *Application deadline:* rolling (freshmen), rolling (transfers).

Admissions Contact Ms. Kristen Caputo, Assistant Director of Admissions, Quincy College, 34 Coddington Street, Quincy, MA 02169. *Phone:* 617-984-1704. *Toll-free phone:* 800-698-1700. *Fax:* 617-984-1669. *E-mail:* kcaputo@quincycollege.com.

QUINSIGAMOND COMMUNITY COLLEGE
Worcester, Massachusetts

- **State-supported** 2-year, founded 1963
- **Calendar** semesters
- **Degree** certificates and associate
- **Urban** 57-acre campus with easy access to Boston
- **Coed,** 6,137 undergraduate students

Undergraduates Students come from 3 states and territories, 13 other countries.

Faculty *Total:* 370, 29% full-time.

Majors Accounting; art; auto mechanic/technician; business administration; computer maintenance technology; computer programming; criminal justice/law enforcement administration; data processing technology; dental hygiene; early childhood education; electrical/electronic engineering technology; emergency medical technology; fire science; general studies; graphic design/commercial art/illustration; hotel and restaurant management; human services; information sciences/systems; liberal arts and sciences/liberal studies; medical radiologic technology; nursing; occupational therapy; occupational therapy assistant; pre-engineering; respiratory therapy; retail management; secretarial science; travel/tourism management.

Academic Programs *Special study options:* academic remediation for entering students, accelerated degree program, adult/continuing education programs, advanced placement credit, cooperative education, double majors, English as a second language, internships, off-campus study, part-time degree program, services for LD students, summer session for credit. *ROTC:* Army (c).

Library Quinsigamond Library plus 1 other with 54,000 titles, 310 serial subscriptions, 230 audiovisual materials, an OPAC.

Computers on Campus 200 computers available on campus for general student use. A campuswide network can be accessed from off campus. At least one staffed computer lab available.

Student Life *Housing:* college housing not available. *Activities and Organizations:* student-run newspaper, Phi Theta Kappa, Nursing Club, Rad Tech Club, Gay Straight Alliance, Criminal Justice Club. *Campus security:* 24-hour emergency response devices and patrols, late-night transport/escort service. *Student Services:* health clinic, personal/psychological counseling, women's center.

Athletics Member NJCAA. *Intercollegiate sports:* baseball M, basketball M/W. *Intramural sports:* archery M/W, badminton M/W, basketball M/W, cross-country running M/W, skiing (cross-country) M/W, skiing (downhill) M/W, swimming M/W, tennis M/W, volleyball M/W.

Costs (2001–02) *Tuition:* state resident $720 full-time, $24 per credit part-time; nonresident $6900 full-time, $230 per credit part-time. *Required fees:* $1530 full-time, $51 per credit. *Payment plan:* installment. *Waivers:* senior citizens and employees or children of employees.

Financial Aid In 2001, 70 Federal Work-Study jobs (averaging $2200).

Applying *Options:* common application. *Application fee:* $10. *Required:* high school transcript. *Required for some:* interview. *Application deadline:* rolling (freshmen), rolling (transfers). *Notification:* continuous until 8/15 (freshmen).

Admissions Contact Mr. Ronald C. Smith, Director of Admissions, Quinsigamond Community College, 670 West Boylston Street, Worcester, MA 01606-2092. *Phone:* 508-854-4262. *Fax:* 508-854-4357. *E-mail:* qccadm@qcc.mass.edu.

ROXBURY COMMUNITY COLLEGE
Roxbury Crossing, Massachusetts

Admissions Contact Dr. Rudolph Jones, Associate Dean of Enrollment Management, Roxbury Community College, 1234 Columbus Avenue, Roxbury Crossing, MA 02120-3400. *Phone:* 617-541-5310. *Fax:* 617-427-5316.

SPRINGFIELD TECHNICAL COMMUNITY COLLEGE
Springfield, Massachusetts

- **State-supported** 2-year, founded 1967
- **Calendar** semesters
- **Degree** certificates and associate
- **Urban** 34-acre campus
- **Coed,** 6,257 undergraduate students, 42% full-time, 52% women, 48% men

Undergraduates 2,635 full-time, 3,622 part-time. Students come from 6 states and territories, 21 other countries, 2% are from out of state, 9% African American, 2% Asian American or Pacific Islander, 10% Hispanic American, 0.9% Native American, 0.3% international.

Freshmen *Admission:* 2,630 applied, 1,246 admitted, 1,354 enrolled.

Faculty *Total:* 396, 45% full-time. *Student/faculty ratio:* 18:1.

Majors Accounting; architectural engineering technology; automotive engineering technology; biology; biomedical engineering-related technology; biotechnology research; business; business administration; business marketing and marketing management; chemistry; civil engineering technology; communications technologies related; computer engineering technology; computer/information sciences related; computer science; cosmetology; court reporting; data processing technology; dental hygiene; desktop publishing equipment operation; diagnostic medical sonography; early childhood education; electrical/electronic engineering technologies related; electrical/electronic engineering technology; electromechanical technology; elementary education; engineering; enterprise management; finance; fine/studio arts; fire science; general studies; graphic design/commercial art/illustration; graphic/printing equipment; health aide; heating/air conditioning/refrigeration; heating/air conditioning/refrigeration technology; landscaping management; laser/optical technology; law enforcement/police science; legal administrative assistant; liberal arts and sciences/liberal studies; logistics/materials management; mathematics; mechanical drafting; mechanical engineering technology; medical administrative assistant; medical assistant; medical laboratory technician; medical radiologic technology; nuclear medical technology; nursing; occupational therapy assistant; operating room technician; physical therapy assistant; quality control technology; rehabilitation/therapeutic services related; respiratory therapy; secretarial science; water treatment technology.

Academic Programs *Special study options:* academic remediation for entering students, adult/continuing education programs, advanced placement credit, cooperative education, distance learning, English as a second language, honors programs, independent study, internships, off-campus study, part-time degree program, services for LD students, summer session for credit.

Library Springfield Technical Community College Library with 63,724 titles, 443 serial subscriptions, 3,651 audiovisual materials, an OPAC, a Web page.

Computers on Campus 415 computers available on campus for general student use. A campuswide network can be accessed from off campus. Internet access, at least one staffed computer lab available.

Student Life *Housing:* college housing not available. *Activities and Organizations:* drama/theater group, student-run television station, Phi Theta Kappa honor society, Landscape Club, Dental Hygiene Club, Clinical Lab Club, Physical Therapist Assistant Club. *Campus security:* 24-hour emergency response devices and patrols, late-night transport/escort service. *Student Services:* health clinic, personal/psychological counseling.

Athletics Member NJCAA. *Intercollegiate sports:* baseball M, basketball M/W, golf M/W, soccer M/W, softball W, tennis M/W, wrestling M. *Intramural sports:* basketball M/W, cross-country running M/W, golf M/W, skiing (cross-country) M/W, softball M/W, volleyball M/W, weight lifting M/W.

Standardized Tests *Required for some:* SAT I (for admission).

Costs (2001–02) *Tuition:* state resident $750 full-time, $25 per credit part-time; nonresident $6900 full-time, $234 per credit part-time. *Required fees:* $1630 full-time, $49 per credit, $77 per term part-time.

Applying *Application fee:* $10. *Required:* high school transcript. *Required for some:* interview. *Application deadline:* rolling (freshmen), rolling (transfers).

Admissions Contact Ms. Andrea Lucy-Allen, Director of Admissions, Springfield Technical Community College, 1 Armory Square, Springfield, MA 01105-1296. *Phone:* 413-781-7822 Ext. 4380. *E-mail:* admissions@stccadm.stcc.mass.edu.

URBAN COLLEGE OF BOSTON
Boston, Massachusetts

- **Independent** 2-year, founded 1993
- **Degree** certificates and associate
- **Coed, primarily women,** 638 undergraduate students, 94% women, 6% men

Undergraduates 638 part-time. Students come from 1 other state, 47% African American, 5% Asian American or Pacific Islander, 31% Hispanic American, 1% Native American.

Freshmen *Admission:* 30 enrolled.

Faculty *Total:* 21, 14% full-time, 29% with terminal degrees. *Student/faculty ratio:* 20:1.

Majors Early childhood education; human services; liberal arts and sciences/liberal studies.

Student Life *Housing:* college housing not available.

Costs (2001–02) *Tuition:* $100 per credit part-time. *Payment plan:* installment.

Applying *Application fee:* $10.

Admissions Contact Mr. Henry J. Johnson, Coordinator of Enrollment Services, Urban College of Boston, 178 Tremont Street, Boston, MA 02111-1093. *Phone:* 617-292-4723 Ext. 357. *Fax:* 617-423-4758.

MICHIGAN

ALPENA COMMUNITY COLLEGE
Alpena, Michigan

- **State and locally supported** 2-year, founded 1952
- **Calendar** semesters
- **Degree** certificates and associate
- **Small-town** 700-acre campus
- **Endowment** $2.6 million
- **Coed,** 1,932 undergraduate students, 48% full-time, 57% women, 43% men

Undergraduates 932 full-time, 1,000 part-time. Students come from 3 states and territories, 3 other countries, 1% African American, 0.4% Asian American or Pacific Islander, 0.4% Hispanic American, 0.2% Native American, 5% transferred in, 3% live on campus.

Freshmen *Admission:* 1,282 applied, 1,282 admitted, 813 enrolled. *Average high school GPA:* 2.7.

Faculty *Total:* 123, 43% full-time, 3% with terminal degrees. *Student/faculty ratio:* 17:1.

Majors Accounting; auto mechanic/technician; biology; business administration; business systems networking/ telecommunications; chemical engineering technology; chemistry; civil engineering technology; computer/information technology services administration and management related; corrections; data pro-

Alpena Community College (continued)
cessing technology; drafting; drafting/design technology; electrical/electronic engineering technology; English; graphic design/commercial art/illustration; law enforcement/police science; liberal arts and sciences/liberal studies; machine technology; mathematics; nursing; office management; practical nurse; pre-engineering; secretarial science.
Academic Programs *Special study options:* academic remediation for entering students, advanced placement credit, distance learning, double majors, internships, part-time degree program, services for LD students, summer session for credit.
Library Stephen Fletcher Library with 29,000 titles, 183 serial subscriptions, an OPAC, a Web page.
Computers on Campus 65 computers available on campus for general student use. A campuswide network can be accessed from off campus. Internet access, at least one staffed computer lab available.
Student Life *Housing Options:* men-only, women-only. *Activities and Organizations:* drama/theater group, student-run newspaper, Nursing Association, Student Senate, Phi Theta Kappa, Lumberjack Newspaper, Law Enforcement Club. *Campus security:* 24-hour emergency response devices. *Student Services:* personal/psychological counseling, women's center.
Athletics Member NJCAA. *Intercollegiate sports:* basketball M(s)/W(s), golf M, softball W(s), volleyball W(s). *Intramural sports:* basketball M/W, bowling M/W, football M, riflery M/W, softball M/W, volleyball M/W.
Standardized Tests *Required:* ACT ASSET.
Costs (2001–02) *Tuition:* area resident $1740 full-time, $58 per contact hour part-time; state resident $2580 full-time, $86 per contact hour part-time; nonresident $3450 full-time, $115 per contact hour part-time. *Required fees:* $400 full-time, $13 per contact hour, $10 per term part-time. *Waivers:* senior citizens and employees or children of employees.
Financial Aid In 2001, 100 Federal Work-Study jobs (averaging $800). 20 State and other part-time jobs (averaging $800).
Applying *Options:* early admission, deferred entrance. *Required:* high school transcript. *Application deadline:* rolling (freshmen), rolling (transfers). *Notification:* continuous (freshmen).
Admissions Contact Mr. Mike Kollien, Admissions Technician, Alpena Community College, 666 Johnson Street, Alpena, MI 49707-1495. *Phone:* 989-358-7339. *Toll-free phone:* 888-468-6222. *Fax:* 989-358-7561.

BAY DE NOC COMMUNITY COLLEGE
Escanaba, Michigan

- **County-supported** 2-year, founded 1963, part of Michigan Department of Education
- **Calendar** semesters
- **Degree** certificates and associate
- **Rural** 150-acre campus
- **Endowment** $2.1 million
- **Coed,** 2,200 undergraduate students

Undergraduates Students come from 2 states and territories, 1 other country, 1% are from out of state.
Freshmen *Average high school GPA:* 2.89.
Faculty *Total:* 172, 53% full-time.
Majors Accounting; accounting technician; auto mechanic/technician; business; business administration; business marketing and marketing management; child care/guidance; community health liaison; criminal justice/law enforcement administration; drafting; electrical/electronic engineering technology; environmental technology; human services; information sciences/systems; law enforcement/police science; liberal arts and sciences/liberal studies; machine technology; medical administrative assistant; nursing; practical nurse; pre-engineering; sanitation technology; secretarial science; social work; water resources; water treatment technology; wood science/paper technology.
Academic Programs *Special study options:* academic remediation for entering students, adult/continuing education programs, cooperative education, internships, part-time degree program, summer session for credit.
Library Learning Resources Center plus 1 other with 30,000 titles, 200 serial subscriptions.
Computers on Campus 200 computers available on campus for general student use. A campuswide network can be accessed from off campus. Internet access, online (class) registration, at least one staffed computer lab available.
Student Life *Activities and Organizations:* student-run newspaper. *Campus security:* evening housing security personnel.
Athletics *Intramural sports:* basketball M/W, skiing (cross-country) M/W, skiing (downhill) M/W, tennis M/W, volleyball M/W.
Standardized Tests *Required:* ACT ASSET.
Costs (2001–02) *Tuition:* area resident $1987 full-time, $58 per contact hour part-time; state resident $2600 full-time, $81 per contact hour part-time; nonresident $4100 full-time, $128 per contact hour part-time. Full-time tuition and fees vary according to course load. Part-time tuition and fees vary according to course load. *Required fees:* $197 full-time, $5 per contact hour, $25 per term part-time. *Room and board:* room only: $1600. *Waivers:* senior citizens and employees or children of employees.
Financial Aid In 2001, 80 Federal Work-Study jobs (averaging $2500). 40 State and other part-time jobs (averaging $2500).
Applying *Options:* early admission. *Required:* high school transcript. *Application deadlines:* 8/15 (freshmen), 8/15 (transfers). *Notification:* continuous (freshmen).
Admissions Contact Ms. Gloria Seney, Interim Vice President, Bay de Noc Community College, Student Center, Escanaba, MI 49829-2511. *Phone:* 906-786-5802 Ext. 148. *Fax:* 906-786-8515. *E-mail:* wallbern@baydenoc.cc.mi.us.

BAY MILLS COMMUNITY COLLEGE
Brimley, Michigan

Admissions Contact Ms. Elaine Lehre, Admissions Officer, Bay Mills Community College, 12214 West Lakeshore Drive, Brimley, MI 49715. *Phone:* 906-248-3354. *Fax:* 906-248-3351.

DAVENPORT UNIVERSITY
Midland, Michigan

- **Independent** primarily 2-year, founded 1907, part of Davenport Educational System
- **Calendar** semesters
- **Degrees** certificates, associate, and bachelor's
- **Urban** campus
- **Coed**

Student Life *Campus security:* 24-hour emergency response devices.
Standardized Tests *Required:* ACT ASSET.
Applying *Options:* early admission, deferred entrance. *Application fee:* $20. *Required:* high school transcript.
Admissions Contact Davenport University, 3555 East Patrick Road, Midland, MI 48642. *Toll-free phone:* 800-968-4860. *Fax:* 517-752-3453.

DELTA COLLEGE
University Center, Michigan

- **District-supported** 2-year, founded 1961
- **Calendar** semesters
- **Degree** certificates and associate
- **Rural** 640-acre campus
- **Coed,** 10,000 undergraduate students

Freshmen *Admission:* 5,572 applied, 5,572 admitted.
Faculty *Total:* 400, 50% full-time.
Majors Accounting; agricultural business; agricultural mechanization; agricultural sciences; applied art; architectural engineering technology; art education; auto mechanic/technician; aviation technology; biology; broadcast journalism; business administration; business education; business marketing and marketing management; carpentry; chemical engineering technology; chemistry; child care/development; clothing/apparel/textile; computer graphics; computer management; computer programming; computer programming related; computer science; computer science related; computer software and media applications related; construction management; construction technology; corrections; criminal justice/law enforcement administration; data entry/microcomputer applications; data entry/microcomputer applications related; data processing; data processing technology; dental assistant; dental hygiene; dietetics; drafting; elementary education; emergency medical technology; engineering; engineering technology; English; environmental science; executive assistant; fashion merchandising; finance; fire science; forestry; general office/clerical; geology; graphic/printing equipment; heating/air conditioning/refrigeration; heating/air conditioning/refrigeration technology; home economics; industrial arts; industrial radiologic technology; information sciences/systems; information technology; interior design; journalism; law enforcement/police science; legal administrative assistant; legal studies; liberal arts and sciences/liberal studies; machine technology; mechanical design technology; mechanical engineering technology; medical administrative assis-

tant; medical assistant; mortuary science; music; music teacher education; natural resources management; nursing; office management; operating room technician; paralegal/legal assistant; physical therapy; physical therapy assistant; physician assistant; plumbing; practical nurse; pre-engineering; pre-pharmacy studies; psychology; quality control technology; radiological science; radio/television broadcasting; real estate; respiratory therapy; retail management; secretarial science; social work; teacher assistant/aide; theater arts/drama; water resources; water treatment technology; Web/multimedia management/webmaster; Web page, digital/multimedia and information resources design; welding technology; word processing.

Academic Programs *Special study options:* academic remediation for entering students, adult/continuing education programs, advanced placement credit, cooperative education, distance learning, double majors, English as a second language, external degree program, freshman honors college, honors programs, independent study, internships, off-campus study, part-time degree program, services for LD students, student-designed majors, summer session for credit.

Library Library Learning Information Center with 98,100 titles, 740 serial subscriptions, an OPAC, a Web page.

Computers on Campus 550 computers available on campus for general student use. A campuswide network can be accessed from off campus. Internet access, online (class) registration, at least one staffed computer lab available.

Student Life *Housing:* college housing not available. *Activities and Organizations:* student-run newspaper, radio and television station, Intramural activities, Student Senate, Phi Theta Kappa, Intervarsity Christian Fellowship, DECA. *Campus security:* 24-hour emergency response devices and patrols, student patrols, late-night transport/escort service. *Student Services:* health clinic, personal/psychological counseling.

Athletics Member NJCAA. *Intercollegiate sports:* basketball M(s)/W(s), cross-country running M/W, soccer M(s), softball W(s), volleyball W(s). *Intramural sports:* baseball M, basketball M/W, cross-country running M/W, football M, racquetball M/W, soccer M/W, table tennis M/W, tennis M/W, volleyball M/W.

Standardized Tests *Required:* ACT COMPASS or ACT ASSET. *Recommended:* ACT (for placement).

Costs (2001–02) *Tuition:* area resident $1474 full-time, $61 per credit hour part-time; state resident $2160 full-time, $84 per credit hour part-time; nonresident $3120 full-time, $120 per credit hour part-time. Full-time tuition and fees vary according to course load. Part-time tuition and fees vary according to course load. *Required fees:* $50 full-time, $25 per term part-time. *Waivers:* senior citizens and employees or children of employees.

Financial Aid In 2001, 136 Federal Work-Study jobs (averaging $1545). 152 State and other part-time jobs.

Applying *Options:* common application, early admission, deferred entrance. *Application fee:* $10. *Recommended:* high school transcript. *Application deadline:* rolling (freshmen), rolling (transfers).

Admissions Contact Mr. Duff Zube, Director of Admissions, Delta College, 1961 Delta Road, University Center, MI 48710. *Phone:* 989-686-9449. *Fax:* 517-667-2202. *E-mail:* admit@alpha.delta.edu.

GLEN OAKS COMMUNITY COLLEGE

Centreville, Michigan

- **State and locally supported** 2-year, founded 1965, part of Michigan Department of Career Development
- **Calendar** semesters
- **Degree** certificates and associate
- **Rural** 300-acre campus
- **Coed,** 1,894 undergraduate students, 6% full-time, 60% women, 40% men

Undergraduates 112 full-time, 1,782 part-time. Students come from 3 states and territories.

Freshmen *Admission:* 255 enrolled.

Faculty *Total:* 108, 26% full-time. *Student/faculty ratio:* 13:1.

Majors Auto mechanic/technician; biological/physical sciences; business administration; liberal arts and sciences/liberal studies; nursing.

Academic Programs *Special study options:* academic remediation for entering students, adult/continuing education programs, advanced placement credit, distance learning, internships, part-time degree program, services for LD students, summer session for credit.

Library E. J. Shaheen Library with 37,087 titles, 347 serial subscriptions, an OPAC.

Computers on Campus 50 computers available on campus for general student use. Internet access, at least one staffed computer lab available.

Student Life *Housing:* college housing not available. *Activities and Organizations:* student government, choir, band, Phi Theta Kappa. *Campus security:* 24-hour emergency response devices. *Student Services:* personal/psychological counseling.

Athletics Member NJCAA. *Intercollegiate sports:* baseball M(s), basketball M(s)/W(s), tennis W(s), volleyball W(s). *Intramural sports:* baseball M, basketball M/W, table tennis M/W, tennis W.

Standardized Tests *Required:* ACT ASSET.

Costs (2002–03) *Tuition:* area resident $1710 full-time, $54 per contact hour part-time; state resident $2070 full-time, $66 per contact hour part-time; nonresident $2580 full-time, $83 per contact hour part-time. *Required fees:* $213 full-time, $7 per contact hour.

Financial Aid In 2001, 70 Federal Work-Study jobs (averaging $1100). 38 State and other part-time jobs (averaging $1200).

Applying *Application deadline:* rolling (freshmen), rolling (transfers).

Admissions Contact Ms. Beverly M. Andrews, Director of Admissions/Registrar, Glen Oaks Community College, 62249 Shimmel Road, Centreville, MI 49032-9719. *Phone:* 616-467-9945 Ext. 248. *Toll-free phone:* 888-994-7818. *Fax:* 616-467-9068. *E-mail:* webmaster@glenoaks.cc.mi.us.

GOGEBIC COMMUNITY COLLEGE

Ironwood, Michigan

- **State and locally supported** 2-year, founded 1932, part of Michigan Department of Education
- **Calendar** semesters
- **Degree** certificates and associate
- **Small-town** 195-acre campus
- **Endowment** $675,000
- **Coed,** 1,165 undergraduate students, 44% full-time, 63% women, 37% men

Undergraduates 513 full-time, 652 part-time. Students come from 6 states and territories, 3 other countries, 17% are from out of state, 0.2% African American, 0.5% Asian American or Pacific Islander, 2% Hispanic American, 4% Native American, 0.3% international, 3% transferred in.

Freshmen *Admission:* 321 enrolled.

Faculty *Total:* 91, 34% full-time. *Student/faculty ratio:* 13:1.

Majors Accounting; auto mechanic/technician; biology; business administration; business computer programming; carpentry; child care/development; child care/guidance; computer engineering technology; computer graphics; computer/information technology services administration and management related; computer science; computer typography/composition; construction management; construction technology; corrections; criminal justice/law enforcement administration; data processing; data processing technology; drafting; early childhood education; education; engineering; forestry sciences; graphic design/commercial art/illustration; graphic/printing equipment; humanities; information technology; legal administrative assistant; liberal arts and sciences/liberal studies; mathematics; medical administrative assistant; medical records administration; nursing; office management; practical nurse; psychology; secretarial science; social sciences; social work; sociology; system/networking/LAN/WAN management; word processing.

Academic Programs *Special study options:* academic remediation for entering students, adult/continuing education programs, advanced placement credit, cooperative education, distance learning, honors programs, internships, part-time degree program, services for LD students, summer session for credit.

Library Alex D. Chisholm Learning Resources Center with 26,000 titles, 220 serial subscriptions, an OPAC, a Web page.

Computers on Campus 210 computers available on campus for general student use. Internet access, at least one staffed computer lab available.

Student Life *Housing:* college housing not available. *Activities and Organizations:* drama/theater group, choral group, Drama Club, Student Senate, Phi Theta Kappa, intramural sports. *Student Services:* personal/psychological counseling.

Athletics Member NJCAA. *Intercollegiate sports:* basketball M(s)/W(s). *Intramural sports:* basketball M/W, bowling M/W, football M/W, golf M/W, skiing (cross-country) M/W, skiing (downhill) M/W, softball M/W, tennis M/W, track and field M/W, volleyball M/W.

Costs (2001–02) *Tuition:* area resident $1519 full-time, $49 per credit part-time; state resident $2139 full-time, $67 per credit part-time; nonresident $2852 full-time, $92 per credit part-time. Full-time tuition and fees vary according to location and reciprocity agreements. Part-time tuition and fees vary according to course load, location, and reciprocity agreements. *Required fees:* $220 full-time, $5 per credit hour. *Waivers:* senior citizens and employees or children of employees.

Financial Aid In 2001, 100 Federal Work-Study jobs (averaging $1600). 100 State and other part-time jobs (averaging $1600).

Gogebic Community College (continued)

Applying *Options:* electronic application, early admission, deferred entrance. *Application fee:* $5. *Required:* high school transcript. *Application deadlines:* rolling (freshmen), 8/15 (out-of-state freshmen), 8/15 (transfers). *Notification:* continuous (freshmen).

Admissions Contact Ms. Jeanne Graham, Director of Admissions, Gogebic Community College, E-4946 Jackson Road, Ironwood, MI 49938. *Phone:* 906-932-4231 Ext. 306. *Toll-free phone:* 800-682-5910 Ext. 207. *Fax:* 906-932-0229. *E-mail:* nancyg@admin1.gogebic.cc.mi.us.

GRAND RAPIDS COMMUNITY COLLEGE
Grand Rapids, Michigan

- **District-supported** 2-year, founded 1914, part of Michigan Department of Education
- **Calendar** semesters
- **Degree** certificates and associate
- **Urban** 35-acre campus
- **Endowment** $12.9 million
- **Coed,** 13,483 undergraduate students, 38% full-time, 49% women, 51% men

Undergraduates 5,144 full-time, 8,339 part-time. Students come from 31 states and territories, 35 other countries, 1% are from out of state, 9% African American, 3% Asian American or Pacific Islander, 4% Hispanic American, 0.9% Native American, 1% international. *Retention:* 55% of 2001 full-time freshmen returned.

Freshmen *Admission:* 4,552 applied, 3,811 admitted, 2,931 enrolled. *Average high school GPA:* 2.73.

Faculty *Total:* 511, 50% full-time. *Student/faculty ratio:* 23:1.

Majors Architectural engineering technology; art; auto mechanic/technician; business administration; computer engineering technology; computer programming; computer science; corrections; criminal justice/law enforcement administration; culinary arts; dental hygiene; drafting; electrical/electronic engineering technology; fashion merchandising; forestry; geology; heating/air conditioning/refrigeration; industrial technology; law enforcement/police science; legal administrative assistant; liberal arts and sciences/liberal studies; mass communications; medical administrative assistant; music; nursing; plastics technology; practical nurse; quality control technology; secretarial science; welding technology.

Academic Programs *Special study options:* academic remediation for entering students, adult/continuing education programs, advanced placement credit, cooperative education, distance learning, English as a second language, off-campus study, part-time degree program, services for LD students, study abroad, summer session for credit.

Library Arthur Andrews Memorial Library plus 1 other with 56,250 titles, 620 serial subscriptions, an OPAC, a Web page.

Computers on Campus 600 computers available on campus for general student use. A campuswide network can be accessed from off campus. Internet access, at least one staffed computer lab available.

Student Life *Housing:* college housing not available. *Activities and Organizations:* drama/theater group, student-run newspaper, choral group, marching band, Student Congress, Phi Theta Kappa, Hispanic Student Organization, Asian Student Organization, Service Learning Advisory Board. *Campus security:* 24-hour emergency response devices, late-night transport/escort service. *Student Services:* personal/psychological counseling.

Athletics Member NJCAA. *Intercollegiate sports:* baseball M/W(s), basketball M(s)/W(s), football M(s), golf M(s), softball W(s), swimming M(s)/W(s), tennis M(s)/W(s), track and field M(s), volleyball W(s), wrestling M(s). *Intramural sports:* badminton M/W, basketball M/W, skiing (cross-country) M/W, skiing (downhill) M/W, soccer M/W, swimming M/W, tennis M/W, volleyball M/W.

Standardized Tests *Recommended:* SAT I or ACT (for admission).

Costs (2002–03) *Tuition:* area resident $1476 full-time, $62 per credit hour part-time; state resident $2160 full-time, $90 per credit hour part-time; nonresident $2640 full-time, $110 per credit hour part-time. Part-time tuition and fees vary according to course load. *Required fees:* $100 full-time, $50 per term part-time. *Waivers:* employees or children of employees.

Financial Aid In 2001, 219 Federal Work-Study jobs (averaging $1421). 89 State and other part-time jobs (averaging $958).

Applying *Options:* early admission, deferred entrance. *Application fee:* $20. *Required:* high school transcript. *Application deadline:* 8/30 (freshmen). *Notification:* continuous (freshmen).

Admissions Contact Ms. Diane Defelice Patrick, Director of Admissions, Grand Rapids Community College, 143 Bostwick Avenue, NE, Grand Rapids, MI 49503-3201. *Phone:* 616-234-4100. *Fax:* 616-234-4005. *E-mail:* dpatrick@grcc.edu.

HENRY FORD COMMUNITY COLLEGE
Dearborn, Michigan

- **District-supported** 2-year, founded 1938
- **Calendar** semesters
- **Degree** certificates and associate
- **Suburban** 75-acre campus with easy access to Detroit
- **Coed,** 12,123 undergraduate students

Undergraduates Students come from 3 states and territories, 17% African American, 2% Asian American or Pacific Islander, 3% Hispanic American, 0.8% Native American, 0.2% international.

Faculty *Total:* 770, 29% full-time.

Majors Accounting; applied art; art; auto mechanic/technician; business administration; business machine repair; business marketing and marketing management; ceramic arts; computer/information sciences; computer science; construction technology; corrections; criminal justice/law enforcement administration; culinary arts; dance; data processing technology; drafting; drawing; electrical/electronic engineering technology; emergency medical technology; energy management technology; exercise sciences; fire science; food products retailing; food services technology; graphic design/commercial art/illustration; heating/air conditioning/refrigeration; hospitality management; hotel and restaurant management; industrial radiologic technology; industrial technology; information sciences/systems; instrumentation technology; interior design; law enforcement/police science; legal administrative assistant; liberal arts and sciences/liberal studies; mass communications; materials science; medical administrative assistant; medical assistant; medical records administration; nursing; paralegal/legal assistant; pre-engineering; quality control technology; real estate; respiratory therapy; robotics; secretarial science; theater arts/drama; transportation technology.

Academic Programs *Special study options:* academic remediation for entering students, adult/continuing education programs, advanced placement credit, cooperative education, freshman honors college, honors programs, internships, part-time degree program, services for LD students, summer session for credit.

Library Eshleman Library with 80,000 titles, 650 serial subscriptions, an OPAC, a Web page.

Computers on Campus 250 computers available on campus for general student use. A campuswide network can be accessed from off campus. Internet access, at least one staffed computer lab available.

Student Life *Housing:* college housing not available. *Activities and Organizations:* drama/theater group, student-run newspaper, radio station, choral group, Phi Theta Kappa, Student Nurses, Future Teachers, ASAD (American Students of African Descent), Intervarsity Christian Fellowship. *Campus security:* 24-hour emergency response devices and patrols, late-night transport/escort service. *Student Services:* personal/psychological counseling, women's center.

Athletics Member NJCAA. *Intercollegiate sports:* baseball M(s), basketball M(s)/W(s), golf M(s), softball W(s), tennis W(s), track and field M(s), volleyball W(s). *Intramural sports:* badminton M/W, basketball M/W, bowling M/W, racquetball M/W, sailing M/W, softball W, tennis M/W, volleyball M/W, weight lifting M/W.

Standardized Tests *Recommended:* ACT (for placement).

Costs (2001–02) *Tuition:* state resident $1704 full-time, $57 per credit hour part-time; nonresident $2896 full-time, $98 per credit hour part-time. No tuition increase for student's term of enrollment. *Required fees:* $9 per credit hour. *Payment plan:* deferred payment. *Waivers:* senior citizens and employees or children of employees.

Applying *Options:* early admission, deferred entrance. *Application fee:* $30. *Recommended:* high school transcript. *Application deadline:* rolling (freshmen), rolling (transfers). *Notification:* continuous (freshmen).

Admissions Contact Ms. Dorothy A. Murphy, Coordinator of Recruitment, Henry Ford Community College, 5101 Evergreen Road, Dearborn, MI 48128-1495. *Phone:* 313-845-9766. *E-mail:* dorothy@mail.henryford.cc.mi.us.

ITT TECHNICAL INSTITUTE
Grand Rapids, Michigan

- **Proprietary** 2-year, part of ITT Educational Services, Inc
- **Calendar** quarters
- **Degree** associate
- 519 undergraduate students

Majors Computer/information sciences related; computer programming; drafting; electrical/electronic engineering technologies related; information technology.

Student Life *Housing:* college housing not available.

Costs (2001–02) *Tuition:* Full-time tuition and fees vary according to program. Part-time tuition and fees vary according to program. $260—$330 per credit hour.
Applying *Options:* deferred entrance. *Application fee:* $100. *Required:* high school transcript, interview. *Recommended:* letters of recommendation. *Application deadline:* rolling (freshmen), rolling (transfers). *Notification:* continuous (freshmen).
Admissions Contact Mr. Todd Peuler, Director of Recruitment, ITT Technical Institute, 4020 Sparks Drive SE, Grand Rapids, MI 49546. *Phone:* 616-956-1060. *Toll-free phone:* 800-632-4676.

ITT TECHNICAL INSTITUTE
Troy, Michigan

- **Proprietary** 2-year, founded 1987, part of ITT Educational Services, Inc
- **Calendar** quarters
- **Degree** associate
- **Coed,** 665 undergraduate students

Majors Computer/information sciences related; computer programming; drafting; electrical/electronic engineering technologies related; information technology.
Student Life *Housing:* college housing not available.
Costs (2001–02) *Tuition:* Full-time tuition and fees vary according to program. Part-time tuition and fees vary according to program. $260—$330 per credit hour.
Applying *Options:* deferred entrance. *Application fee:* $100. *Required:* high school transcript, interview. *Recommended:* letters of recommendation. *Application deadline:* rolling (freshmen), rolling (transfers). *Notification:* continuous (freshmen).
Admissions Contact Mr. Steve Goddard, Director of Education, ITT Technical Institute, 1522 East Big Beaver Road, Troy, MI 48083-1905. *Phone:* 248-524-1800. *Toll-free phone:* 800-832-6817.

JACKSON COMMUNITY COLLEGE
Jackson, Michigan

- **County-supported** 2-year, founded 1928, part of Michigan Department of Education
- **Calendar** semesters
- **Degree** associate
- **Suburban** 580-acre campus with easy access to Detroit
- **Coed,** 6,457 undergraduate students

Undergraduates 1% are from out of state.
Faculty *Total:* 363, 26% full-time, 11% with terminal degrees.
Majors Accounting; aircraft pilot (professional); auto mechanic/technician; aviation technology; business; business administration; business marketing and marketing management; business services marketing; computer graphics; computer hardware engineering; computer programming; computer programming (specific applications); corrections; criminal justice/law enforcement administration; data entry/microcomputer applications; data processing technology; diagnostic medical sonography; drafting; electrical/electronic engineering technology; emergency medical technology; environmental technology; finance; industrial radiologic technology; industrial technology; law enforcement/police science; liberal arts and sciences/liberal studies; machine technology; medical administrative assistant; medical assistant; medical technology; nursing; practical nurse; robotics; secretarial science; system/networking/LAN/WAN management; Web page, digital/multimedia and information resources design.
Academic Programs *Special study options:* academic remediation for entering students, adult/continuing education programs, advanced placement credit, cooperative education, distance learning, external degree program, honors programs, internships, part-time degree program, services for LD students, summer session for credit.
Library Atkinson Learning Resources Center plus 1 other with 66,000 titles, 300 serial subscriptions, 4,600 audiovisual materials, an OPAC, a Web page.
Computers on Campus 338 computers available on campus for general student use. A campuswide network can be accessed from off campus. Internet access, online (class) registration, at least one staffed computer lab available.
Student Life *Housing:* college housing not available. *Activities and Organizations:* drama/theater group, student-run newspaper, choral group. *Campus security:* 24-hour patrols. *Student Services:* personal/psychological counseling.
Standardized Tests *Recommended:* ACT (for placement).
Costs (2001–02) *Tuition:* area resident $1822 full-time; state resident $2408 full-time; nonresident $2709 full-time. *Required fees:* $95 full-time. *Payment plan:* deferred payment. *Waivers:* employees or children of employees.
Financial Aid In 2001, 77 Federal Work-Study jobs (averaging $1074). 47 State and other part-time jobs (averaging $1168).
Applying *Options:* electronic application, early admission. *Application deadline:* rolling (freshmen), rolling (transfers). *Notification:* continuous (freshmen).
Admissions Contact Ms. Jodi Hines, Recruiter, Jackson Community College, Jackson, MI 49201. *Phone:* 517-787-0800 Ext. 8499. *Toll-free phone:* 888-JCC-REGI.

KALAMAZOO VALLEY COMMUNITY COLLEGE
Kalamazoo, Michigan

- **State and locally supported** 2-year, founded 1966
- **Calendar** semesters
- **Degree** certificates and associate
- **Suburban** 187-acre campus
- **Coed,** 12,500 undergraduate students

Undergraduates Students come from 3 states and territories, 46 other countries, 1% are from out of state.
Faculty *Total:* 110, 100% full-time.
Majors Accounting technician; auto mechanic/technician; business administration; business marketing and marketing management; chemical technology; computer programming; dental hygiene; drafting; electrical/electronic engineering technology; elementary education; emergency medical technology; executive assistant; fire science; graphic design/commercial art/illustration; health science; heating/air conditioning/refrigeration technology; law enforcement/police science; legal administrative assistant; liberal arts and sciences/liberal studies; machine technology; management information systems/business data processing; mechanical engineering technology; medical administrative assistant; medical assistant; nursing; plastics technology; pre-engineering; respiratory therapy; welding technology.
Academic Programs *Special study options:* academic remediation for entering students, advanced placement credit, cooperative education, distance learning, English as a second language, honors programs, independent study, internships, off-campus study, part-time degree program, services for LD students, student-designed majors, summer session for credit. *ROTC:* Army (c).
Library Kalamazoo Valley Community College Library with 88,791 titles, 420 serial subscriptions, an OPAC, a Web page.
Computers on Campus 1000 computers available on campus for general student use. A campuswide network can be accessed from off campus. Internet access, at least one staffed computer lab available.
Student Life *Housing:* college housing not available. *Activities and Organizations:* student-run newspaper, choral group. *Campus security:* 24-hour emergency response devices and patrols, late-night transport/escort service. *Student Services:* personal/psychological counseling, women's center.
Athletics Member NJCAA. *Intercollegiate sports:* baseball M(s), basketball M(s)/W(s), golf M, softball W(s), tennis M(s)/W(s), volleyball W(s). *Intramural sports:* basketball M/W.
Standardized Tests *Recommended:* ACT (for placement).
Costs (2001–02) *Tuition:* area resident $1473 full-time, $48 per credit hour part-time; state resident $1986 full-time, $83 per credit hour part-time; nonresident $3635 full-time, $117 per credit hour part-time. *Payment plan:* installment. *Waivers:* senior citizens and employees or children of employees.
Financial Aid In 2001, 56 Federal Work-Study jobs (averaging $1609). 17 State and other part-time jobs (averaging $980).
Applying *Options:* early admission, deferred entrance. *Application deadline:* rolling (freshmen), rolling (transfers). *Notification:* continuous (freshmen).
Admissions Contact Mr. Roger Miller, Director of Financial Aid, Kalamazoo Valley Community College, PO Box 4070, Kalamazoo, MI 49003-4070. *Phone:* 616-372-5340. *Fax:* 616-372-5161. *E-mail:* admissions@kvcc.edu.

KELLOGG COMMUNITY COLLEGE
Battle Creek, Michigan

- **State and locally supported** 2-year, founded 1956, part of Michigan Department of Education
- **Calendar** semesters
- **Degree** certificates and associate
- **Urban** 120-acre campus
- **Endowment** $91,005
- **Coed,** 9,741 undergraduate students

Undergraduates Students come from 3 states and territories, 11 other countries, 1% are from out of state. *Retention:* 35% of 2001 full-time freshmen returned.

Kellogg Community College (continued)

Freshmen *Admission:* 3,447 applied, 3,447 admitted. *Test scores:* ACT scores over 18: 52%; ACT scores over 24: 21%; ACT scores over 30: 4%.

Faculty *Total:* 356, 25% full-time, 6% with terminal degrees. *Student/faculty ratio:* 7:1.

Majors Accounting; accounting technician; anthropology; art; art education; biology; business administration; chemical technology; chemistry; communications; computer engineering technology; computer graphics; computer programming; computer programming (specific applications); computer software and media applications related; corrections; criminal justice studies; data entry/microcomputer applications related; dental hygiene; drafting; early childhood education; elementary education; emergency medical technology; engineering; English; executive assistant; fire protection/safety technology; general studies; graphic design/commercial art/illustration; heating/air conditioning/refrigeration; history; human services; industrial arts education; industrial technology; international relations; journalism; law enforcement/police science; legal administrative assistant; liberal arts and sciences/liberal studies; machine technology; mathematics; medical administrative assistant; medical laboratory technician; medical radiologic technology; music; nursing; paralegal/legal assistant; philosophy; physical education; physical therapy assistant; physics; plastics technology; plumbing; political science; practical nurse; pre-law; pre-medicine; pre-pharmacy studies; pre-theology; pre-veterinary studies; psychology; public relations; radio/television broadcasting technology; robotics technology; secondary education; secretarial science; sheet metal working; social work; sociology; special education; theater arts/drama; welding technology; word processing.

Academic Programs *Special study options:* academic remediation for entering students, accelerated degree program, adult/continuing education programs, advanced placement credit, distance learning, double majors, freshman honors college, honors programs, independent study, internships, off-campus study, part-time degree program, services for LD students, summer session for credit.

Library Emory W. Morris Learning Resource Center with 42,131 titles, 172 serial subscriptions, 4,145 audiovisual materials, an OPAC, a Web page.

Computers on Campus 550 computers available on campus for general student use. A campuswide network can be accessed from off campus. At least one staffed computer lab available.

Student Life *Housing:* college housing not available. *Activities and Organizations:* drama/theater group, student-run newspaper, choral group, Tech Club, Phi Theta Kappa, Student Nurses Association, Crude Arts Club, Art League. *Campus security:* 24-hour emergency response devices and patrols, late-night transport/escort service. *Student Services:* personal/psychological counseling.

Athletics Member NJCAA. *Intercollegiate sports:* baseball M(s), basketball M(s)/W(s), soccer M, softball W(s), volleyball W(s).

Standardized Tests *Required for some:* SAT I or ACT (for admission).

Costs (2002–03) *Tuition:* area resident $1793 full-time, $60 per credit hour part-time; state resident $2813 full-time, $94 per credit hour part-time; nonresident $4253 full-time, $142 per credit hour part-time. Full-time tuition and fees vary according to reciprocity agreements. Part-time tuition and fees vary according to reciprocity agreements. *Payment plan:* deferred payment. *Waivers:* senior citizens and employees or children of employees.

Financial Aid In 2001, 23 Federal Work-Study jobs (averaging $3087). 22 State and other part-time jobs (averaging $1955).

Applying *Options:* common application, early admission, deferred entrance. *Required for some:* high school transcript, minimum 2.0 GPA. *Application deadline:* 8/30 (freshmen), rolling (transfers). *Notification:* continuous (freshmen).

Admissions Contact Mrs. Connie Speers, Director of Admissions, Kellogg Community College, 450 North Avenue, Battle Creek, MI 49017. *Phone:* 616-965-3931 Ext. 2622. *Fax:* 616-965-4133.

KIRTLAND COMMUNITY COLLEGE
Roscommon, Michigan

Admissions Contact Ms. Stacey Thompson, Registrar, Kirtland Community College, 10775 North St Helen Road, Roscommon, MI 48653-9699. *Phone:* 517-275-5121 Ext. 248.

LAKE MICHIGAN COLLEGE
Benton Harbor, Michigan

- **District-supported** 2-year, founded 1946, part of Michigan Department of Education
- **Calendar** semesters
- **Degree** certificates and associate
- **Small-town** 260-acre campus
- **Coed,** 3,478 undergraduate students, 32% full-time, 56% women, 44% men

Undergraduates 1,109 full-time, 2,369 part-time. Students come from 5 states and territories, 2% are from out of state. *Retention:* 39% of 2001 full-time freshmen returned.

Freshmen *Admission:* 420 enrolled. *Average high school GPA:* 2.62.

Faculty *Total:* 213, 29% full-time, 15% with terminal degrees.

Majors Accounting technician; art; biology; business administration; business marketing and marketing management; chemistry; computer/information sciences; corrections; data processing technology; dental assistant; drafting; education; electrical/electronic engineering technology; electromechanical technology; English; exercise sciences; finance; geography; geology; health/physical education; history; hospitality management; industrial technology; law enforcement/police science; legal administrative assistant; liberal arts and sciences/liberal studies; machine technology; mathematics; medical administrative assistant; medical radiologic technology; music; nuclear technology; nursing; occupational therapy assistant; philosophy; political science; practical nurse; pre-engineering; psychology; sociology; teacher assistant/aide; theater arts/drama.

Academic Programs *Special study options:* academic remediation for entering students, adult/continuing education programs, honors programs, part-time degree program, student-designed majors, summer session for credit.

Library Lake Michigan College Library with 79,000 titles, 280 serial subscriptions.

Computers on Campus 124 computers available on campus for general student use.

Student Life *Housing:* college housing not available. *Activities and Organizations:* drama/theater group, student-run newspaper, Hospitality Club, International Club, Pride Club II, DECA. *Student Services:* personal/psychological counseling, women's center.

Athletics Member NJCAA. *Intercollegiate sports:* baseball M(s), basketball M(s)/W(s), golf M(s), softball W(s), volleyball W(s).

Standardized Tests *Required:* ACT ASSET. *Recommended:* ACT (for placement).

Costs (2001–02) *Tuition:* $51 per credit hour part-time. *Required fees:* $264 full-time, $11 per credit hour.

Applying *Options:* common application, early admission, deferred entrance. *Required:* high school transcript. *Required for some:* interview. *Application deadline:* rolling (freshmen), rolling (transfers). *Notification:* continuous (freshmen).

Admissions Contact Mrs. Linda Steinberger, Manager of Admissions, Lake Michigan College, 2755 East Napier, Benton Harbor, MI 49022-1899. *Phone:* 616-927-8100 Ext. 5205. *Toll-free phone:* 800-252-1LMC. *E-mail:* stein@raptor.lmc.cc.mi.us.

LANSING COMMUNITY COLLEGE
Lansing, Michigan

- **State and locally supported** 2-year, founded 1957, part of Michigan Department of Education
- **Calendar** semesters
- **Degree** certificates and associate
- **Urban** 28-acre campus
- **Endowment** $3.5 million
- **Coed,** 17,358 undergraduate students, 30% full-time, 56% women, 44% men

Undergraduates 5,211 full-time, 12,147 part-time. Students come from 14 states and territories, 69 other countries, 1% are from out of state, 8% African American, 3% Asian American or Pacific Islander, 4% Hispanic American, 1% Native American, 3% international.

Freshmen *Admission:* 2,522 applied, 2,522 admitted, 2,522 enrolled.

Faculty *Total:* 800, 27% full-time.

Majors Accounting; aircraft pilot (professional); architectural engineering technology; art; auto mechanic/technician; aviation technology; biological/physical sciences; biological technology; biology; broadcast journalism; business administration; business marketing and marketing management; carpentry; chemical engineering technology; chemistry; child care/development; civil engineering technology; computer engineering technology; computer graphics; computer management; computer programming; computer typography/composition; construction technology; corrections; court reporting; criminal justice/law enforcement administration; dance; dental hygiene; developmental/child psychology; diagnostic medical sonography; drafting; early childhood education; education; electrical/electronic engineering technology; electromechanical technology; elementary education; emergency medical technology; engineering; engineering technology; English; film studies; film/video production; finance; fine/studio arts; fire science; food products retailing; geography; geology; gerontology; graphic design/commercial art/illustration; heating/air conditioning/refrigeration; heavy equipment maintenance; horticulture science; hospitality management; hotel and restaurant management; human resources management; human services; industrial technology; information sciences/systems; international business; journalism; labor/personnel relations; landscape architecture; law enforcement/police science; legal administrative assistant; liberal arts and sciences/liberal studies; machine technology; management information systems/business data processing; mass communications; mathematics; mechanical design technology; mechanical engineering technology; medical assistant; medical radiologic technology; medical technology; music; music (voice and choral/opera performance); nursing; operating room technician; paralegal/legal assistant; philosophy; photography; physical education; practical nurse; pre-engineering; public administration; public relations; quality control technology; radio/television broadcasting; real estate; religious studies; respiratory therapy; retail management; secretarial science; sign language interpretation; social work; speech/rhetorical studies; surveying; teacher assistant/aide; telecommunications; theater arts/drama; travel/tourism management; veterinary technology; welding technology.

Academic Programs *Special study options:* academic remediation for entering students, adult/continuing education programs, advanced placement credit, cooperative education, distance learning, double majors, English as a second language, external degree program, honors programs, independent study, internships, part-time degree program, services for LD students, study abroad, summer session for credit. *ROTC:* Army (c), Air Force (c).

Library Abel Sykes Technology and Learning Center plus 1 other with 98,125 titles, 600 serial subscriptions, 11,653 audiovisual materials, an OPAC, a Web page.

Computers on Campus 1146 computers available on campus for general student use. A campuswide network can be accessed from off campus. At least one staffed computer lab available.

Student Life *Housing:* college housing not available. *Activities and Organizations:* drama/theater group, student-run newspaper, radio station, choral group, Student Marketing, Legal Assistants Club, Student Nursing Club, Phi Theta Kappa, Student Advising Club, national fraternities, national sororities. *Campus security:* 24-hour emergency response devices and patrols, student patrols, late-night transport/escort service. *Student Services:* personal/psychological counseling, women's center.

Athletics Member NJCAA. *Intercollegiate sports:* basketball M(s)/W(s), cross-country running M(s)/W(s), golf M(s), track and field M(s)/W(s), volleyball W(s). *Intramural sports:* baseball M, basketball M/W, cross-country running M/W, ice hockey M, soccer M/W, softball W, track and field M/W, volleyball W.

Standardized Tests *Required for some:* SAT I or ACT (for placement).

Costs (2001–02) *Tuition:* area resident $1200 full-time, $50 per credit part-time; state resident $1896 full-time, $79 per credit part-time; nonresident $2592 full-time, $108 per credit part-time. Part-time tuition and fees vary according to course load. *Required fees:* $40 full-time, $20 per term part-time. *Payment plan:* installment. *Waivers:* senior citizens and employees or children of employees.

Financial Aid In 2001, 159 Federal Work-Study jobs (averaging $2477). 61 State and other part-time jobs (averaging $2260).

Applying *Options:* common application, electronic application, early admission, deferred entrance. *Required for some:* essay or personal statement, high school transcript, 2 letters of recommendation, interview. *Application deadline:* rolling (freshmen), rolling (transfers).

Admissions Contact John Hearns, Director of Admissions, Lansing Community College, PO Box 40010, Lansing, MI 48901-7210. *Phone:* 517-483-9942. *Toll-free phone:* 800-644-4LCC. *Fax:* 517-483-9668. *E-mail:* jhearns@lcc.edu.

LEWIS COLLEGE OF BUSINESS
Detroit, Michigan

- **Independent** 2-year, founded 1929
- **Calendar** semesters
- **Degree** associate
- **Urban** 11-acre campus
- **Coed,** 324 undergraduate students

Faculty *Total:* 36, 25% full-time.

Majors Accounting; business administration; computer management; computer programming; computer science; data processing technology; information sciences/systems; legal administrative assistant; liberal arts and sciences/liberal studies; medical administrative assistant; secretarial science.

Academic Programs *Special study options:* academic remediation for entering students, cooperative education, part-time degree program, summer session for credit.

Library Main Library plus 1 other with 3,355 titles, 90 serial subscriptions.

Computers on Campus 54 computers available on campus for general student use. At least one staffed computer lab available.

Student Life *Housing:* college housing not available. *Activities and Organizations:* student-run newspaper, Sister to Sister, Brother to Brother, The Voice, Student Government Association, Business Club, national sororities. *Campus security:* parking lot security. *Student Services:* personal/psychological counseling.

Athletics *Intercollegiate sports:* basketball M.

Costs (2001–02) *Tuition:* $265 per credit part-time.

Financial Aid In 2001, 80 Federal Work-Study jobs (averaging $2000). 40 State and other part-time jobs (averaging $1500).

Applying *Options:* common application, early admission, deferred entrance. *Application fee:* $15. *Required:* high school transcript. *Application deadlines:* rolling (freshmen), 8/1 (transfers). *Notification:* continuous until 8/30 (freshmen).

Admissions Contact Ms. Frances Ambrose, Admissions Secretary, Lewis College of Business, 17370 Meyers Road, Detroit, MI 48235-1423. *Phone:* 313-862-6300.

MACOMB COMMUNITY COLLEGE
Warren, Michigan

- **District-supported** 2-year, founded 1954
- **Calendar** semesters
- **Degree** certificates and associate
- **Suburban** 384-acre campus with easy access to Detroit
- **Endowment** $8.0 million
- **Coed,** 21,818 undergraduate students, 28% full-time, 52% women, 48% men

Undergraduates 6,139 full-time, 15,679 part-time. Students come from 2 states and territories, 13% are from out of state, 5% African American, 3% Asian American or Pacific Islander, 1% Hispanic American, 0.8% Native American, 1% international, 27% transferred in.

Freshmen *Admission:* 2,353 enrolled.

Faculty *Total:* 864, 25% full-time. *Student/faculty ratio:* 28:1.

Majors Accounting; architectural engineering technology; auto mechanic/technician; aviation technology; behavioral sciences; business administration; business marketing and marketing management; child care/development; civil engineering technology; communication equipment technology; communications; computer engineering technology; computer typography/composition; construction technology; criminal justice/law enforcement administration; culinary arts; drafting; early childhood education; electrical/electronic engineering technology; electromechanical technology; emergency medical technology; energy management technology; engineering design; finance; fire science; graphic design/commercial art/illustration; graphic/printing equipment; heating/air conditioning/refrigeration; information sciences/systems; international relations; labor/personnel relations; law enforcement/police science; legal administrative assistant; legal studies; liberal arts and sciences/liberal studies; machine technology; materials science; mechanical design technology; medical administrative assistant; mental health/rehabilitation; metallurgical technology; nursing; paralegal/legal assistant; photography; physical therapy; plastics technology; plumbing; pre-engineering; quality control technology; respiratory therapy; robotics; safety/security technology; secretarial science; surveying; veterinary sciences; welding technology.

Academic Programs *Special study options:* academic remediation for entering students, adult/continuing education programs, advanced placement credit, cooperative education, English as a second language, honors programs, internships, off-campus study, part-time degree program, services for LD students, student-designed majors, summer session for credit.

Library 136,447 titles, 590 serial subscriptions, an OPAC.

Computers on Campus 1800 computers available on campus for general student use. A campuswide network can be accessed from off campus. At least one staffed computer lab available.

Student Life *Housing:* college housing not available. *Activities and Organizations:* drama/theater group, Phi Beta Kappa, Adventure Unlimited, Alpha Rho Rho, SADD. *Campus security:* 24-hour emergency response devices and patrols, late-night transport/escort service, security phones in parking lots, surveillance cameras. *Student Services:* health clinic, personal/psychological counseling.

Athletics Member NJCAA. *Intercollegiate sports:* baseball M(s), basketball M(s), cross-country running M(s)/W(s), soccer M(s), softball W(s), track and field M(s)/W(s), volleyball W(s). *Intramural sports:* baseball M, basketball M, bowling M/W, cross-country running M/W, football M/W, skiing (cross-country) M/W, skiing (downhill) M/W, volleyball M/W.

Standardized Tests *Required for some:* ACT ASSET, ACT COMPASS.

Costs (2001–02) *Tuition:* area resident $1736 full-time, $56 per semester hour part-time; state resident $2604 full-time, $84 per semester hour part-time;

Macomb Community College (continued)
nonresident $3069 full-time, $99 per semester hour part-time. Full-time tuition and fees vary according to course load. Part-time tuition and fees vary according to course load. *Required fees:* $15 per term part-time. *Waivers:* senior citizens and employees or children of employees.

Financial Aid In 2001, 100 Federal Work-Study jobs (averaging $2549).

Applying *Options:* common application, early admission, deferred entrance. *Application fee:* $15. *Application deadline:* rolling (freshmen), rolling (transfers).

Admissions Contact Mr. Richard P. Stevens, Coordinator of Admissions and Assessment, Macomb Community College, G312, 14500 East 12 Mile Road, Warren, MI 48088-3896. *Phone:* 586-445-7230. *Fax:* 586-445-7140.

MID MICHIGAN COMMUNITY COLLEGE
Harrison, Michigan

- **State and locally supported** 2-year, founded 1965, part of Michigan Department of Education
- **Calendar** semesters
- **Degree** certificates and associate
- **Rural** 560-acre campus
- **Coed, primarily women,** 2,350 undergraduate students, 21% full-time, 63% women, 37% men

Undergraduates 491 full-time, 1,859 part-time. Students come from 7 states and territories, 1% African American, 0.5% Asian American or Pacific Islander, 1% Hispanic American, 0.9% Native American, 0.1% international.

Freshmen *Admission:* 382 enrolled. *Average high school GPA:* 2.59. *Test scores:* ACT scores over 18: 72%; ACT scores over 24: 12%; ACT scores over 30: 2%.

Faculty *Total:* 80, 63% full-time. *Student/faculty ratio:* 15:1.

Majors Accounting; art; auto mechanic/technician; biochemical technology; biological/physical sciences; biological technology; biology; business administration; business marketing and marketing management; chemistry; child care/development; child care provider; computer graphics; computer science; corrections; criminal justice/law enforcement administration; drafting; education (K-12); elementary education; emergency medical technology; engineering-related technology; engineering technologies related; enterprise management; environmental science; finance; fire science; fish/game management; general studies; graphic design/commercial art/illustration; heating/air conditioning/refrigeration; hospitality management; hospitality/recreation marketing operations; industrial radiologic technology; information sciences/systems; legal administrative assistant; liberal arts and sciences/liberal studies; machine technology; mathematics; medical administrative assistant; medical assistant; medical transcription; nursing; ophthalmic/optometric services related; pharmacy; physical therapy; practical nurse; pre-engineering; psychology; secondary education; secretarial science; sociology; speech/rhetorical studies; speech/theater education; theater arts/drama; welding technology.

Academic Programs *Special study options:* academic remediation for entering students, adult/continuing education programs, advanced placement credit, honors programs, internships, part-time degree program, services for LD students, summer session for credit.

Library Charles A. Amble Library with 29,450 titles, 200 serial subscriptions.

Computers on Campus 150 computers available on campus for general student use. At least one staffed computer lab available.

Student Life *Housing:* college housing not available. *Activities and Organizations:* drama/theater group, student-run newspaper, choral group, Commission of Student Activities Services, Phi Theta Kappa, Karate Club, Volley Ball Club, Ski Club. *Campus security:* 24-hour emergency response devices.

Standardized Tests *Recommended:* ACT (for admission).

Costs (2001–02) *Tuition:* area resident $1350 full-time, $56 per credit part-time; state resident $2232 full-time, $93 per credit part-time; nonresident $3264 full-time, $136 per credit part-time. Full-time tuition and fees vary according to course load. Part-time tuition and fees vary according to course load. *Required fees:* $50 full-time, $20 per year part-time. *Payment plan:* installment. *Waivers:* senior citizens.

Financial Aid In 2001, 50 Federal Work-Study jobs (averaging $3600). 50 State and other part-time jobs (averaging $3600).

Applying *Options:* early admission. *Required for some:* interview. *Recommended:* high school transcript. *Application deadline:* rolling (freshmen), rolling (transfers). *Notification:* continuous (freshmen).

Admissions Contact Ms. Brenda Mather, Admissions Specialist, Mid Michigan Community College, 1375 South Clare Avenue, Harrison, MI 48625. *Phone:* 989-386-6661. *Fax:* 989-386-6613.

MONROE COUNTY COMMUNITY COLLEGE
Monroe, Michigan

- **County-supported** 2-year, founded 1964, part of Michigan Department of Education
- **Calendar** semesters
- **Degree** certificates and associate
- **Small-town** 150-acre campus with easy access to Detroit and Toledo
- **Coed,** 3,800 undergraduate students

Undergraduates Students come from 3 states and territories, 1 other country, 4% are from out of state, 1% African American, 0.6% Asian American or Pacific Islander, 1% Hispanic American, 0.6% Native American, 0.1% international.

Freshmen *Average high school GPA:* 2.5.

Faculty *Total:* 201, 27% full-time.

Majors Accounting; architectural engineering technology; art; biology; business administration; business marketing and marketing management; child care/development; computer engineering technology; computer graphics; computer programming (specific applications); computer science related; criminal justice studies; culinary arts; data processing technology; drafting; electrical/electronic engineering technology; elementary education; English; finance; industrial technology; information technology; journalism; law enforcement/police science; legal administrative assistant; liberal arts and sciences/liberal studies; mass communications; mathematics; medical administrative assistant; medical technology; mortuary science; nursing; physical therapy; pre-engineering; psychology; respiratory therapy; secretarial science; social work; speech/rhetorical studies; veterinary sciences; Web/multimedia management/webmaster; Web page, digital/multimedia and information resources design; welding technology; word processing.

Academic Programs *Special study options:* academic remediation for entering students, advanced placement credit, independent study, part-time degree program, services for LD students, summer session for credit.

Library Campbell Learning Resource Center with 47,352 titles, 321 serial subscriptions, an OPAC.

Computers on Campus 140 computers available on campus for general student use. At least one staffed computer lab available.

Student Life *Housing:* college housing not available. *Activities and Organizations:* drama/theater group, student-run newspaper, choral group, student government, Society of Auto Engineers, Oasis, Nursing Students Organization. *Campus security:* police patrols during open hours.

Standardized Tests *Required for some:* ACT (for admission). *Recommended:* ACT (for admission).

Costs (2001–02) *Tuition:* area resident $1320 full-time; state resident $2136 full-time; nonresident $2304 full-time. *Required fees:* $48 full-time. *Waivers:* senior citizens and employees or children of employees.

Applying *Options:* early admission, deferred entrance. *Required:* high school transcript. *Application deadline:* rolling (freshmen), rolling (transfers). *Notification:* continuous (freshmen).

Admissions Contact Ms. Julie Billmaier, Director of Admissions and Guidance, Monroe County Community College, 1555 South Raisinville Road, Monroe, MI 48161-9047. *Phone:* 734-384-4261. *Toll-free phone:* 877-YES MCCC. *Fax:* 734-242-9711.

MONTCALM COMMUNITY COLLEGE
Sidney, Michigan

- **State and locally supported** 2-year, founded 1965, part of Michigan Department of Education
- **Calendar** semesters
- **Degree** certificates and associate
- **Rural** 248-acre campus with easy access to Grand Rapids
- **Endowment** $3.7 million
- **Coed,** 1,520 undergraduate students, 24% full-time, 64% women, 36% men

Undergraduates 372 full-time, 1,148 part-time. Students come from 1 other state, 0.3% African American, 0.5% Asian American or Pacific Islander, 0.9% Hispanic American, 0.9% Native American, 4% transferred in.

Freshmen *Admission:* 313 applied, 313 admitted, 221 enrolled. *Average high school GPA:* 2.66. *Test scores:* ACT scores over 18: 62%; ACT scores over 24: 16%; ACT scores over 30: 2%.

Faculty *Total:* 92, 29% full-time, 10% with terminal degrees. *Student/faculty ratio:* 16:1.

Majors Accounting; business administration; child care/guidance; child care provider; computer installation/repair; corrections; cosmetology; criminal justice/

law enforcement administration; data processing technology; drafting; electrical/electronic engineering technology; emergency medical technology; enterprise management; executive assistant; industrial radiologic technology; industrial technology; liberal arts and sciences/liberal studies; management information systems/business data processing; medical administrative assistant; medical radiologic technology; nursing; plastics technology; secretarial science.

Academic Programs *Special study options:* academic remediation for entering students, adult/continuing education programs, advanced placement credit, cooperative education, distance learning, double majors, independent study, internships, off-campus study, part-time degree program, services for LD students, summer session for credit.

Library Montcalm Community College Library with 29,848 titles, 3,670 serial subscriptions, 580 audiovisual materials, an OPAC, a Web page.

Computers on Campus 450 computers available on campus for general student use. Internet access, at least one staffed computer lab available.

Student Life *Housing:* college housing not available. *Activities and Organizations:* drama/theater group, student-run newspaper, choral group, Nursing Club, Sports club, Phi Theta Kappa, Business Club. *Student Services:* personal/psychological counseling.

Athletics *Intramural sports:* volleyball M/W.

Standardized Tests *Required:* ACT ASSET, ACT COMPASS. *Recommended:* ACT (for placement).

Costs (2001–02) *Tuition:* area resident $1533 full-time, $58 per credit hour part-time; state resident $2351 full-time, $84 per credit hour part-time; nonresident $3000 full-time, $107 per credit hour part-time. Full-time tuition and fees vary according to course load. Part-time tuition and fees vary according to course load. *Required fees:* $154 full-time, $6 per credit hour. *Payment plan:* installment. *Waivers:* senior citizens and employees or children of employees.

Financial Aid In 2001, 57 Federal Work-Study jobs (averaging $2000).

Applying *Options:* early admission, deferred entrance. *Recommended:* high school transcript. *Application deadline:* rolling (freshmen), rolling (transfers). *Notification:* continuous (freshmen).

Admissions Contact Ms. Kathie Lofts, Director of Admissions, Montcalm Community College, 2800 College Drive, Sidney, MI 48885. *Phone:* 989-328-1250. *Toll-free phone:* 877-328-2111. *Fax:* 989-328-2950. *E-mail:* admissions@montcalm.cc.mi.us.

MOTT COMMUNITY COLLEGE
Flint, Michigan

- **District-supported** 2-year, founded 1923, part of Michigan Department of Education
- **Calendar** semesters
- **Degree** certificates and associate
- **Urban** 20-acre campus with easy access to Detroit
- **Endowment** $33.0 million
- **Coed,** 9,019 undergraduate students, 33% full-time, 61% women, 39% men

Undergraduates 2,932 full-time, 6,087 part-time. Students come from 11 states and territories, 0.3% are from out of state, 3% transferred in.

Freshmen *Admission:* 1,478 applied, 1,478 admitted, 1,478 enrolled.

Faculty *Total:* 437, 35% full-time, 9% with terminal degrees. *Student/faculty ratio:* 20:1.

Majors Accounting technician; architectural engineering technology; auto body repair; auto mechanic/technician; business; business administration; business marketing and marketing management; child care and guidance related; child care provider; communications technologies related; community health liaison; computer/information sciences; computer/information sciences related; culinary arts; data processing; dental assistant; dental hygiene; drafting; electrical/electronic engineering technology; emergency medical technology; engineering technologies related; enterprise management; fire protection/safety technology; general studies; gerontological services; graphic design/commercial art/illustration; health/medical laboratory technologies related; heating/air conditioning/refrigeration technology; institutional food services; instrumentation technology; international business; law enforcement/police science; legal administrative assistant; liberal arts and sciences/liberal studies; management information systems/business data processing; mechanical drafting; mechanical engineering technology; medical administrative assistant; medical radiologic technology; nursing; occupational therapy assistant; office management; photography; physical therapy assistant; practical nurse; precision production trades related; quality control technology; respiratory therapy; robotics technology; secretarial science; sign language interpretation.

Academic Programs *Special study options:* academic remediation for entering students, accelerated degree program, adult/continuing education programs, advanced placement credit, cooperative education, distance learning, double majors, English as a second language, honors programs, independent study, internships, part-time degree program, services for LD students, student-designed majors, summer session for credit.

Library Charles Stewart Mott Library with 118,404 titles, 354 serial subscriptions, an OPAC, a Web page.

Computers on Campus 617 computers available on campus for general student use. A campuswide network can be accessed from off campus. Internet access, online (class) registration, at least one staffed computer lab available.

Student Life *Housing:* college housing not available. *Activities and Organizations:* student-run newspaper, choral group, Criminal Justice Association, Phi Theta Kappa, Dental Assisting Club, Connoisseur's Club, Social Work Club. *Campus security:* 24-hour emergency response devices and patrols, student patrols, late-night transport/escort service. *Student Services:* health clinic, personal/psychological counseling.

Athletics Member NJCAA. *Intercollegiate sports:* baseball M(s), basketball M(s)/W(s), cross-country running M(s)/W(s), golf M(s), softball W(s), volleyball W(s).

Standardized Tests *Required:* Michigan Test of English Language Proficiency, CPT. *Recommended:* SAT I or ACT (for placement).

Costs (2002–03) *Tuition:* area resident $2200 full-time, $68 per contact hour part-time; state resident $3175 full-time, $91 per contact hour part-time; nonresident $4235 full-time, $121 per contact hour part-time. *Required fees:* $132 full-time, $44 per term part-time.

Financial Aid In 2001, 300 Federal Work-Study jobs (averaging $1000). 300 State and other part-time jobs (averaging $1000).

Applying *Options:* electronic application, early admission, deferred entrance. *Required:* high school transcript. *Application deadlines:* 8/31 (freshmen), 8/31 (transfers).

Admissions Contact Mr. Marc Payne, Executive Director of Admissions, Mott Community College, 1401 East Court Street, Flint, MI 48503. *Phone:* 810-762-0316. *Toll-free phone:* 800-852-8614. *Fax:* 810-762-0292. *E-mail:* admissions@mcc.edu.

MUSKEGON COMMUNITY COLLEGE
Muskegon, Michigan

Admissions Contact Ms. Lynda Schwartz, Admissions Coordinator, Muskegon Community College, 221 South Quarterline Road, Muskegon, MI 49442-1493. *Phone:* 231-773-9131 Ext. 366.

NORTH CENTRAL MICHIGAN COLLEGE
Petoskey, Michigan

- **County-supported** 2-year, founded 1958, part of Michigan Department of Education
- **Calendar** semesters
- **Degree** certificates and associate
- **Small-town** 270-acre campus
- **Coed,** 2,248 undergraduate students

Undergraduates Students come from 4 states and territories, 3% live on campus.

Freshmen *Admission:* 424 applied, 424 admitted.

Faculty *Total:* 133, 23% full-time. *Student/faculty ratio:* 17:1.

Majors Accounting; business administration; business marketing and marketing management; child guidance; computer programming; computer science related; computer systems networking/telecommunications; criminal justice/law enforcement administration; data processing technology; drafting; emergency medical technology; engineering technology; finance; information technology; law enforcement/police science; legal administrative assistant; liberal arts and sciences/liberal studies; nursing; paralegal/legal assistant; pre-engineering; secretarial science.

Academic Programs *Special study options:* academic remediation for entering students, advanced placement credit, cooperative education, distance learning, double majors, independent study, internships, part-time degree program, services for LD students, summer session for credit.

Library North Central Michigan College Library with 29,249 titles, 325 serial subscriptions, an OPAC, a Web page.

Computers on Campus 133 computers available on campus for general student use. Internet access, online (class) registration, at least one staffed computer lab available.

North Central Michigan College (continued)

Student Life *Housing Options:* coed. *Activities and Organizations:* choral group. *Campus security:* 24-hour emergency response devices. *Student Services:* personal/psychological counseling.

Athletics *Intramural sports:* basketball M/W.

Standardized Tests *Required:* ACT (for placement).

Costs (2002–03) *Tuition:* area resident $1560 full-time, $52 per credit part-time; state resident $2370 full-time, $79 per credit part-time; nonresident $97 per credit part-time. Part-time tuition and fees vary according to course load. *Required fees:* $150 full-time. *Room and board:* room only: $2000. *Payment plans:* installment, deferred payment. *Waivers:* senior citizens and employees or children of employees.

Financial Aid In 2001, 25 Federal Work-Study jobs (averaging $2400). 20 State and other part-time jobs (averaging $2400).

Applying *Required:* high school transcript. *Application deadline:* rolling (freshmen), rolling (transfers). *Notification:* continuous (freshmen).

Admissions Contact Julieanne Tobin, Director of Enrollment Management, North Central Michigan College, 1515 Howard Street, Petoskey, MI 49770-8717. *Phone:* 231-439-6511. *Toll-free phone:* 888-298-6605. *E-mail:* advisor@ncmc.cc.mi.us.

NORTHWESTERN MICHIGAN COLLEGE
Traverse City, Michigan

- **State and locally supported** 2-year, founded 1951
- **Calendar** semesters
- **Degree** certificates and associate
- **Small-town** 180-acre campus
- **Coed,** 4,251 undergraduate students, 39% full-time, 58% women, 42% men

Undergraduates 1,660 full-time, 2,591 part-time. Students come from 19 states and territories, 2% are from out of state, 0.4% African American, 0.8% Asian American or Pacific Islander, 1% Hispanic American, 3% Native American, 12% transferred in, 10% live on campus.

Freshmen *Admission:* 2,281 applied, 2,187 admitted, 980 enrolled.

Faculty *Total:* 88, 100% full-time, 98% with terminal degrees. *Student/faculty ratio:* 26:1.

Majors Accounting technician; agricultural production related; aircraft pilot (professional); auto mechanic/technician; business administration; business management/administrative services related; business marketing and marketing management; business services marketing; child care/guidance; culinary arts; data processing; dental assistant; drafting/design technology; electrical/electronic engineering technology; graphic design/commercial art/illustration; industrial technology; landscaping management; law enforcement/police science; legal administrative assistant; liberal arts and sciences/liberal studies; machine shop assistant; management information systems/business data processing; marine science; maritime science; nursing; paralegal/legal assistant; turf management; water transportation related.

Academic Programs *Special study options:* academic remediation for entering students, adult/continuing education programs, advanced placement credit, cooperative education, distance learning, honors programs, independent study, internships, part-time degree program, services for LD students, summer session for credit.

Library Mark and Helen Osterlin Library plus 1 other with 97,458 titles, 9,820 serial subscriptions, 3,000 audiovisual materials, an OPAC, a Web page.

Computers on Campus 625 computers available on campus for general student use. A campuswide network can be accessed from student residence rooms and from off campus. Internet access, online (class) registration, at least one staffed computer lab available.

Student Life *Housing Options:* coed, men-only, women-only. *Activities and Organizations:* drama/theater group, student-run newspaper, radio station, choral group, Residence Hall Council, honors fraternity, student newspaper, student magazine, student radio station. *Campus security:* 24-hour emergency response devices and patrols, late-night transport/escort service, controlled dormitory access, well-lit campus. *Student Services:* health clinic, personal/psychological counseling.

Athletics *Intramural sports:* basketball M/W, football M/W, golf M/W, sailing M(c)/W(c), skiing (downhill) M(c)/W(c), softball M/W, volleyball M/W.

Standardized Tests *Required:* ACT COMPASS. *Required for some:* ACT (for placement). *Recommended:* ACT (for placement).

Costs (2002–03) *Tuition:* area resident $1856 full-time, $58 per credit part-time; state resident $3232 full-time, $101 per credit part-time; nonresident $4032 full-time, $126 per credit part-time. Full-time tuition and fees vary according to location. Part-time tuition and fees vary according to course load and location. *Required fees:* $139 full-time, $9 per credit, $96 per term part-time. *Room and board:* $5350. Room and board charges vary according to board plan and housing facility. *Payment plans:* installment, deferred payment. *Waivers:* employees or children of employees.

Financial Aid In 2001, 55 Federal Work-Study jobs (averaging $1612).

Applying *Options:* common application, early admission, deferred entrance. *Application fee:* $15. *Required for some:* high school transcript. *Recommended:* minimum 2.0 GPA. *Application deadline:* rolling (freshmen), rolling (transfers). *Notification:* continuous until 8/28 (freshmen).

Admissions Contact Ms. Carol Taberski, Interim Director of Admission, Northwestern Michigan College, Traverse City, MI 49686. *Phone:* 231-995-1058. *Toll-free phone:* 800-748-0566. *Fax:* 616-955-1339. *E-mail:* welcome@nmc.edu.

OAKLAND COMMUNITY COLLEGE
Bloomfield Hills, Michigan

- **State and locally supported** 2-year, founded 1964, part of Michigan Department of Education
- **Calendar** semesters
- **Degree** certificates and associate
- **Suburban** 540-acre campus with easy access to Detroit
- **Endowment** $18.9 million
- **Coed,** 23,503 undergraduate students, 26% full-time, 60% women, 40% men

Undergraduates 6,117 full-time, 17,386 part-time. Students come from 71 other countries, 15% African American, 3% Asian American or Pacific Islander, 2% Hispanic American, 0.7% Native American, 11% international, 11% transferred in.

Freshmen *Admission:* 2,514 applied, 2,514 admitted, 2,514 enrolled.

Faculty *Total:* 845, 32% full-time. *Student/faculty ratio:* 28:1.

Majors Accounting; architecture; auto mechanic/technician; aviation management; business information/data processing related; ceramic arts; child care/guidance; computer/information sciences; cosmetology; court reporting; criminal justice/corrections related; criminal justice/law enforcement administration; culinary arts; dental hygiene; diagnostic medical sonography; electrical/electronic engineering technology; emergency medical technology; enterprise management; environmental control technologies related; exercise sciences; fine arts and art studies related; fire science; food systems administration; health/medical diagnostic and treatment services related; health/medical laboratory technologies related; health/physical education/fitness related; health professions and related sciences; health services administration; heating/air conditioning/refrigeration technology; hotel and restaurant management; industrial technology; interior design; international business; landscape architecture; library assistant; machine technology; management science; marketing management and research related; medical assistant; medical radiologic technology; medical transcription; mental health services related; nuclear medical technology; nursing; office management; operating room technician; ornamental horticulture; paralegal/legal assistant; pharmacy technician/assistant; photography; practical nurse; pre-engineering; respiratory therapy; retail management; robotics technology; sport/fitness administration; welding technology.

Academic Programs *Special study options:* academic remediation for entering students, adult/continuing education programs, advanced placement credit, cooperative education, distance learning, double majors, English as a second language, internships, off-campus study, part-time degree program, services for LD students, study abroad, summer session for credit.

Library Main Library plus 5 others with 248,494 titles, 3,880 serial subscriptions, 7,529 audiovisual materials, an OPAC, a Web page.

Computers on Campus 1500 computers available on campus for general student use. A campuswide network can be accessed from off campus. Internet access, at least one staffed computer lab available.

Student Life *Housing:* college housing not available. *Activities and Organizations:* drama/theater group, student-run newspaper, radio station, Phi Theta Kappa, International Student Organization, Organizations related to student majors. *Campus security:* 24-hour emergency response devices, late-night transport/escort service. *Student Services:* personal/psychological counseling, women's center.

Athletics Member NJCAA. *Intercollegiate sports:* basketball M(s)/W(s), cross-country running M(s)/W(s), golf M(s), soccer M, softball W(s), tennis W(s), volleyball W(s). *Intramural sports:* basketball M/W, cross-country running M/W, golf M/W, racquetball M/W, tennis M/W, volleyball M/W.

Standardized Tests *Required:* ACT ASSET.

Costs (2001–02) *Tuition:* area resident $1559 full-time, $50 per credit hour part-time; state resident $2641 full-time, $85 per credit hour part-time; nonresident $3705 full-time, $120 per credit hour part-time. Full-time tuition and fees vary according to program. Part-time tuition and fees vary according to program. *Required fees:* $241 full-time, $25 per term part-time. *Waivers:* senior citizens and employees or children of employees.

Financial Aid In 2001, 135 Federal Work-Study jobs (averaging $2800). 70 State and other part-time jobs (averaging $2800).

Applying *Options:* early admission, deferred entrance. *Recommended:* high school transcript. *Application deadline:* rolling (freshmen), rolling (transfers). *Notification:* continuous (freshmen).

Admissions Contact Dr. Maurice H. McCall, Registrar and Director of Enrollment Services, Oakland Community College, 2480 Opdyke Road, Bloomfield Hills, MI 48304-2266. *Phone:* 248-341-2186.

ST. CLAIR COUNTY COMMUNITY COLLEGE

Port Huron, Michigan

- **State and locally supported** 2-year, founded 1923, part of Michigan Department of Education
- **Calendar** semesters
- **Degree** certificates and associate
- **Small-town** 22-acre campus with easy access to Detroit
- **Endowment** $2.5 million
- **Coed,** 4,066 undergraduate students, 39% full-time, 62% women, 38% men

Undergraduates Students come from 6 other countries, 0.1% are from out of state, 2% African American, 0.4% Asian American or Pacific Islander, 2% Hispanic American, 0.6% Native American, 0.7% international.

Freshmen *Admission:* 1,319 applied, 1,319 admitted.

Faculty *Total:* 276, 29% full-time, 4% with terminal degrees.

Majors Accounting; advertising; agricultural business; agricultural mechanization; agricultural sciences; architectural engineering technology; art; biological/physical sciences; broadcast journalism; business administration; business marketing and marketing management; child care/development; computer typography/composition; corrections; criminal justice/law enforcement administration; drafting; electrical/electronic engineering technology; fire science; graphic design/commercial art/illustration; horticulture science; industrial technology; information sciences/systems; journalism; legal administrative assistant; liberal arts and sciences/liberal studies; machine technology; mass communications; medical administrative assistant; mental health/rehabilitation; nursing; pharmacy; plastics technology; quality control technology; robotics; secretarial science; welding technology.

Academic Programs *Special study options:* academic remediation for entering students, accelerated degree program, adult/continuing education programs, advanced placement credit, cooperative education, distance learning, double majors, honors programs, independent study, internships, part-time degree program, services for LD students, student-designed majors, summer session for credit.

Library Learning Resources Center with 59,134 titles, 610 serial subscriptions, 4,311 audiovisual materials, an OPAC.

Computers on Campus 450 computers available on campus for general student use. Internet access, at least one staffed computer lab available.

Student Life *Activities and Organizations:* drama/theater group, student-run newspaper, radio station, choral group, ADN Nursing Club, LPN Nursing Club, Phi Theta Kappa, DECA, student government. *Campus security:* patrols by security until 10 p.m. *Student Services:* personal/psychological counseling.

Athletics Member NJCAA. *Intercollegiate sports:* baseball M(s), basketball M(s)/W(s), golf M, softball W(s), volleyball W(s).

Standardized Tests *Recommended:* ACT (for placement).

Costs (2002–03) *Tuition:* area resident $2128 full-time; state resident $3120 full-time; nonresident $4144 full-time. *Required fees:* $58 full-time. *Payment plan:* deferred payment. *Waivers:* senior citizens and employees or children of employees.

Applying *Options:* early admission. *Required:* high school transcript. *Application deadline:* rolling (freshmen), rolling (transfers).

Admissions Contact Mrs. Michelle K. Mueller, Director of Enrollment Services, St. Clair County Community College, 323 Erie Street, PO Box 5015, PO Box 5015, Port Huron, MI 48061-5015. *Phone:* 810-989-5500. *Toll-free phone:* 800-553-2427. *Fax:* 810-984-4730. *E-mail:* enrollment@stclair.cc.mi.us.

SCHOOLCRAFT COLLEGE

Livonia, Michigan

- **District-supported** 2-year, founded 1961, part of Michigan Department of Career Development
- **Calendar** semesters
- **Degree** certificates and associate
- **Suburban** 183-acre campus with easy access to Detroit
- **Endowment** $8.9 million
- **Coed,** 9,530 undergraduate students, 32% full-time, 58% women, 42% men

Undergraduates 3,040 full-time, 6,490 part-time. Students come from 4 states and territories, 7% African American, 3% Asian American or Pacific Islander, 2% Hispanic American, 0.6% Native American, 14% transferred in.

Freshmen *Admission:* 2,624 applied, 2,624 admitted, 1,494 enrolled. *Average high school GPA:* 3.29.

Faculty *Total:* 406, 26% full-time. *Student/faculty ratio:* 24:1.

Majors Accounting; biomedical engineering-related technology; business administration; business marketing and marketing management; child care/guidance; computer maintenance technology; computer programming; corrections; culinary arts; data processing technology; drafting; education; electrical/electronic engineering technology; electromechanical technology; emergency medical technology; engineering; enterprise management; environmental technology; fire science; graphic design/commercial art/illustration; industrial technology; laser/optical technology; law enforcement/police science; liberal arts and sciences/liberal studies; mechanical engineering technology; medical laboratory technology; medical records technology; metallurgical technology; metallurgy; music teacher education; nursing; occupational therapy assistant; radio/television broadcasting technology; robotics technology; secretarial science; welding technology.

Academic Programs *Special study options:* academic remediation for entering students, accelerated degree program, adult/continuing education programs, advanced placement credit, cooperative education, distance learning, part-time degree program, services for LD students, summer session for credit.

Library Bradner Library plus 1 other with 96,216 titles, 634 serial subscriptions, an OPAC.

Computers on Campus 775 computers available on campus for general student use. A campuswide network can be accessed from off campus. At least one staffed computer lab available.

Student Life *Housing:* college housing not available. *Activities and Organizations:* drama/theater group, student-run newspaper, choral group, Student Activities Board, Ski Club, student newspaper, Music Club, Phi Theta Kappa, national fraternities. *Campus security:* 24-hour emergency response devices and patrols, late-night transport/escort service. *Student Services:* health clinic, women's center, legal services.

Athletics Member NJCAA. *Intercollegiate sports:* basketball M(s)/W(s), cross-country running W(s), golf M(s)/W(s), soccer M(s)/W(s), volleyball W(s).

Standardized Tests *Required:* ACT, ACT ASSET, or CPT.

Costs (2001–02) *Tuition:* area resident $1650 full-time, $55 per credit hour part-time; state resident $3460 full-time, $82 per credit hour part-time; nonresident $3660 full-time, $122 per credit hour part-time. *Required fees:* $110 full-time, $2 per credit hour, $25 per term part-time. *Waivers:* senior citizens and employees or children of employees.

Financial Aid In 2001, 42 Federal Work-Study jobs (averaging $1722).

Applying *Options:* early admission, deferred entrance. *Required for some:* high school transcript. *Recommended:* high school transcript. *Application deadline:* rolling (freshmen), rolling (transfers).

Admissions Contact Ms. Julieanne Ray Tobin, Director of Enrollment Management, Schoolcraft College, 18600 Haggerty Road, Livonia, MI 48152-2696. *Phone:* 734-462-4426. *Fax:* 734-462-4553.

SOUTHWESTERN MICHIGAN COLLEGE

Dowagiac, Michigan

- **State and locally supported** 2-year, founded 1964, part of Michigan Department of Education
- **Calendar** 4-4-2-2
- **Degree** certificates and associate
- **Rural** 240-acre campus
- **Endowment** $6.4 million
- **Coed,** 3,172 undergraduate students, 35% full-time, 65% women, 35% men

Undergraduates 1,109 full-time, 2,063 part-time. Students come from 3 states and territories, 19 other countries, 12% are from out of state, 8% African American, 0.5% Asian American or Pacific Islander, 4% Hispanic American, 1% Native American, 2% international, 40% transferred in.

Freshmen *Admission:* 536 applied, 536 admitted, 536 enrolled.

Faculty *Total:* 193, 26% full-time, 11% with terminal degrees. *Student/faculty ratio:* 16:1.

Majors Accounting technician; aircraft mechanic/airframe; auto mechanic/technician; business administration; business management/administrative ser-

Southwestern Michigan College (continued)
vices related; child care/guidance; computer programming; computer science related; data entry/microcomputer applications related; drafting; electrical/electronic engineering technologies related; engineering technology; general retailing/wholesaling related; general studies; graphic/printing equipment; health professions and related sciences; industrial equipment maintenance and repair related; industrial machinery maintenance/repair; liberal arts and sciences/liberal studies; liberal arts and studies related; machine shop assistant; mechanics and repair related; nursing; paralegal/legal assistant; precision production trades related; secretarial science; welding technology.

Academic Programs *Special study options:* academic remediation for entering students, accelerated degree program, adult/continuing education programs, advanced placement credit, cooperative education, distance learning, double majors, English as a second language, honors programs, independent study, internships, part-time degree program, services for LD students, student-designed majors, summer session for credit.

Library Fred L. Mathews Library with 38,000 titles, 1,100 serial subscriptions, 1,750 audiovisual materials, an OPAC, a Web page.

Computers on Campus 355 computers available on campus for general student use. Internet access available.

Student Life *Housing:* college housing not available. *Activities and Organizations:* drama/theater group, student-run newspaper, television station, choral group, Phi Theta Kappa. *Campus security:* 24-hour emergency response devices, evening police patrols.

Athletics *Intramural sports:* archery M/W, badminton M/W, basketball M/W, bowling M/W, cross-country running M/W, field hockey M/W, football M/W, golf M/W, racquetball M/W, skiing (cross-country) M/W, skiing (downhill) M/W, soccer M/W, softball M/W, tennis M/W, track and field M/W, volleyball M/W, weight lifting M/W.

Standardized Tests *Recommended:* SAT I or ACT (for placement).

Costs (2001–02) *Tuition:* area resident $1581 full-time, $51 per credit hour part-time; state resident $1798 full-time, $58 per credit hour part-time; nonresident $2403 full-time, $78 per credit hour part-time. *Required fees:* $310 full-time, $10 per credit hour. *Payment plan:* installment. *Waivers:* senior citizens and employees or children of employees.

Applying *Options:* electronic application, deferred entrance. *Required:* high school transcript. *Required for some:* letters of recommendation, interview. *Application deadline:* rolling (freshmen), rolling (transfers). *Notification:* continuous until 9/10 (freshmen).

Admissions Contact Mrs. Carol A. Churchill, Vice President for Student Services, Southwestern Michigan College, 58900 Cherry Grove Road, Dowagiac, MI 49047. *Phone:* 616-782-1000 Ext. 1307. *Toll-free phone:* 800-456-8675 Ext. 1304. *Fax:* 616-782-1331. *E-mail:* cchurch@smc.cc.mi.us.

WASHTENAW COMMUNITY COLLEGE
Ann Arbor, Michigan

- **State and locally supported** 2-year, founded 1965
- **Calendar** semesters
- **Degree** certificates and associate
- **Suburban** 235-acre campus with easy access to Detroit
- **Endowment** $3.5 million
- **Coed**

Faculty *Student/faculty ratio:* 15:1.

Student Life *Campus security:* 24-hour emergency response devices and patrols, late-night transport/escort service.

Standardized Tests *Recommended:* SAT I or ACT (for admission), SAT I or ACT (for placement).

Financial Aid In 2001, 120 Federal Work-Study jobs (averaging $4100).

Applying *Options:* common application, electronic application, early admission, deferred entrance. *Required for some:* high school transcript.

Admissions Contact Mr. Bradley D. Hoth, Admissions Representative, Washtenaw Community College, 4800 East Huron River Drive, PO Box D-1, Ann Arbor, MI 48106. *Phone:* 734-973-3676. *Fax:* 734-677-5408.

WAYNE COUNTY COMMUNITY COLLEGE DISTRICT
Detroit, Michigan

- **State and locally supported** 2-year, founded 1967
- **Calendar** semesters
- **Degree** certificates and associate
- **Urban** campus
- **Coed**

Faculty *Student/faculty ratio:* 48:1.

Student Life *Campus security:* 24-hour emergency response devices.

Athletics Member NJCAA.

Standardized Tests *Required:* ACT ASSET.

Financial Aid In 2001, 239 Federal Work-Study jobs (averaging $2360). 147 State and other part-time jobs (averaging $1200).

Applying *Options:* common application, early admission, deferred entrance. *Application fee:* $10.

Admissions Contact Office of Enrollment Management, Wayne County Community College District, 801 West Fort Street, Detroit, MI 48226-9975. *Phone:* 313-496-2539. *Fax:* 313-961-2791. *E-mail:* caafjh@wccc.edu.

WEST SHORE COMMUNITY COLLEGE
Scottville, Michigan

- **District-supported** 2-year, founded 1967, part of Michigan Department of Education
- **Calendar** semesters
- **Degree** certificates and associate
- **Rural** 375-acre campus
- **Endowment** $291,972
- **Coed,** 1,338 undergraduate students, 34% full-time, 59% women, 41% men

Undergraduates 461 full-time, 877 part-time. Students come from 3 states and territories, 1% are from out of state, 5% transferred in.

Freshmen *Admission:* 323 applied, 323 admitted, 275 enrolled. *Average high school GPA:* 2.94.

Faculty *Total:* 55, 45% full-time.

Majors Accounting; business marketing and marketing management; corrections; data entry/microcomputer applications related; data processing technology; electrical/electronic engineering technology; emergency medical technology; information technology; law enforcement/police science; liberal arts and sciences/liberal studies; machine technology; nursing; practical nurse; welding technology.

Academic Programs *Special study options:* academic remediation for entering students, adult/continuing education programs, advanced placement credit, cooperative education, distance learning, independent study, internships, off-campus study, part-time degree program, services for LD students, student-designed majors, summer session for credit.

Library West Shore Library plus 1 other with 2,500 titles, 150 serial subscriptions, 1,100 audiovisual materials, an OPAC, a Web page.

Computers on Campus 185 computers available on campus for general student use. A campuswide network can be accessed from off campus that provide access to e-mail. At least one staffed computer lab available.

Student Life *Housing:* college housing not available. *Activities and Organizations:* drama/theater group, student-run newspaper, choral group, Art Club, Student Senate, Phi Theta Kappa, Science Club, Law Enforcement Club. *Campus security:* 24-hour emergency response devices and patrols. *Student Services:* personal/psychological counseling.

Athletics *Intramural sports:* basketball M/W, football M/W, racquetball M/W, softball M/W, swimming M/W, table tennis M/W, volleyball M/W, weight lifting M/W.

Standardized Tests *Required for some:* ACT ASSET. *Recommended:* ACT (for placement).

Costs (2002–03) *Tuition:* $59 per credit part-time; state resident $1755 full-time, $91 per credit part-time; nonresident $2730 full-time, $114 per credit part-time. *Required fees:* $78 full-time, $32 per term part-time. *Payment plan:* deferred payment. *Waivers:* senior citizens and employees or children of employees.

Applying *Options:* common application, early admission, deferred entrance. *Application fee:* $10. *Required:* high school transcript. *Application deadline:* rolling (freshmen), rolling (transfers). *Notification:* continuous (freshmen).

Admissions Contact Mr. Tom Bell, Director of Admissions, West Shore Community College, PO Box 277, 3000 North Stiles Road, Scottville, MI 49454-0277. *Phone:* 231-845-6211 Ext. 3117. *Fax:* 231-845-3944. *E-mail:* admissions@westshore.cc.mi.us.

MINNESOTA

ACADEMY COLLEGE
Minneapolis, Minnesota

- **Proprietary** primarily 2-year
- **Calendar** quarters
- **Degrees** certificates, associate, and bachelor's
- **Urban** campus
- **Coed,** 400 undergraduate students

Majors Accounting; aircraft pilot (professional); aviation management; business administration; business systems networking/ telecommunications; computer graphics; computer/information sciences; computer programming; graphic design/commercial art/illustration; Web page design.

Student Life *Housing:* college housing not available.

Costs (2001–02) *Tuition:* Full-time tuition and fees vary according to program. Part-time tuition and fees vary according to program. Tuition varies according to academic program within a range of $210 to $320 per credit.

Admissions Contact Ms. Lynn Smasal, Director of Admissions, Academy College, 3050 Metro Drive, Minneaplois, MN 55425. *Phone:* 952-851-0066. *Toll-free phone:* 800-292-9149. *Fax:* 952-851-0094. *E-mail:* info@academycollege.edu.

ALEXANDRIA TECHNICAL COLLEGE
Alexandria, Minnesota

- **State-supported** 2-year, founded 1961, part of Minnesota State Colleges and Universities System
- **Calendar** semesters
- **Degree** certificates, diplomas, and associate
- **Small-town** 40-acre campus
- **Coed,** 2,066 undergraduate students, 79% full-time, 40% women, 60% men

Undergraduates Students come from 21 states and territories, 6% are from out of state, 0.1% African American, 0.2% Asian American or Pacific Islander, 0.3% Hispanic American, 0.4% Native American.

Freshmen *Admission:* 1,784 applied, 1,356 admitted.

Faculty *Total:* 100, 94% full-time, 1% with terminal degrees. *Student/faculty ratio:* 20:1.

Majors Accounting; apparel marketing; banking; business administration; business computer programming; business marketing and marketing management; business systems networking/ telecommunications; carpentry; cartography; child care/guidance; communication systems installation/repair; data processing; diesel engine mechanic; enterprise management; farm/ranch management; general office/ clerical; graphic design/commercial art/illustration; hotel and restaurant management; hydraulic technology; industrial technology; interior design; law enforcement/ police science; legal administrative assistant; machine technology; management information systems/business data processing; mechanical drafting; medical administrative assistant; medical laboratory technician; office management; operations management; practical nurse; receptionist; retailing operations; secretarial science; social work; stationary energy sources installation; tool/die making; welding technology.

Academic Programs *Special study options:* academic remediation for entering students, advanced placement credit, distance learning, double majors, internships, part-time degree program, services for LD students.

Library Learning Resource Center with 7,182 titles, 104 serial subscriptions, 649 audiovisual materials, an OPAC.

Computers on Campus 1200 computers available on campus for general student use. A campuswide network can be accessed from off campus. Internet access, online (class) registration, at least one staffed computer lab available.

Student Life *Housing:* college housing not available. *Activities and Organizations:* student-run newspaper, VICA Skills USA (Vocational Industrial Clubs of America), RPA (Business Professionals of America), DECA (Delta Epsilon Club), STAT (Student Technology and Access Team), Student Senate. *Campus security:* 24-hour patrols, late-night transport/escort service, security cameras inside and outside. *Student Services:* personal/psychological counseling.

Athletics *Intercollegiate sports:* basketball M, volleyball M/W. *Intramural sports:* basketball M, bowling M/W, football M, golf M, ice hockey M, softball M/W, tennis M/W, volleyball M/W.

Standardized Tests *Required:* ACT COMPASS.

Costs (2002–03) *Tuition:* state resident $2780 full-time, $87 per credit part-time; nonresident $5560 full-time, $174 per credit part-time. Full-time tuition and fees vary according to reciprocity agreements. Part-time tuition and fees vary according to reciprocity agreements. *Required fees:* $232 full-time, $7 per credit. *Payment plan:* deferred payment. *Waivers:* senior citizens and employees or children of employees.

Applying *Options:* common application, electronic application, early admission. *Application fee:* $20. *Required:* high school transcript, interview. *Required for some:* letters of recommendation. *Application deadline:* rolling (freshmen).

Admissions Contact Dr. David Trites, Student Services Chairperson, Alexandria Technical College, 1601 Jefferson Street, Alexandria, MN 56308. *Phone:* 320-762-0221 Ext. 4415. *Toll-free phone:* 888-234-1222. *Fax:* 320-762-4430. *E-mail:* jillk@alx.tec.mn.us.

ANOKA-HENNEPIN TECHNICAL COLLEGE
Anoka, Minnesota

- **State-supported** 2-year, founded 1967, part of Minnesota State Colleges and Universities System
- **Calendar** semesters
- **Degree** certificates, diplomas, and associate
- **Small-town** campus with easy access to Minneapolis-St. Paul
- **Coed,** 3,970 undergraduate students
- 80% of applicants were admitted

Undergraduates 2% African American, 0.6% Asian American or Pacific Islander, 0.5% Hispanic American, 0.4% Native American.

Freshmen *Admission:* 1,040 applied, 830 admitted.

Faculty *Total:* 112, 69% full-time. *Student/faculty ratio:* 16:1.

Majors Accounting; aircraft pilot (private); air traffic control; architectural drafting; auto mechanic/technician; child care/guidance; computer graphics; computer/information technology services administration and management related; computer programming related; computer programming (specific applications); computer software and media applications related; computer systems networking/ telecommunications; data entry/microcomputer applications; data entry/ microcomputer applications related; data warehousing/mining/database administration; electrical/electronic engineering technology; horticulture services; information technology; mechanical drafting; medical administrative assistant; occupational therapy assistant; physical therapy assistant; system administration; system/ networking/LAN/WAN management; Web/multimedia management/webmaster; Web page, digital/multimedia and information resources design.

Academic Programs *Special study options:* academic remediation for entering students, advanced placement credit, cooperative education, distance learning, double majors, internships, part-time degree program, services for LD students.

Computers on Campus 100 computers available on campus for general student use. Internet access, online (class) registration, at least one staffed computer lab available.

Student Life *Campus security:* late-night transport/escort service. *Student Services:* personal/psychological counseling, women's center.

Costs (2002–03) *Tuition:* area resident $2747 full-time; state resident $104 per credit part-time; nonresident $209 per credit part-time. *Required fees:* $384 full-time.

Financial Aid In 2001, 60 Federal Work-Study jobs (averaging $1500). 60 State and other part-time jobs (averaging $1500).

Applying *Options:* common application, electronic application, deferred entrance. *Application fee:* $20. *Required:* high school transcript. *Required for some:* interview.

Admissions Contact Anoka-Hennepin Technical College, 1355 West Highway 10, Anoka, MN 55303. *Phone:* 763-576-4746. *Toll-free phone:* 800-247-5588 Ext. 4850. *Fax:* 763-576-4756. *E-mail:* info@ank.tec.mn.us.

ANOKA-RAMSEY COMMUNITY COLLEGE
Coon Rapids, Minnesota

- **State-supported** 2-year, founded 1965, part of Minnesota State Colleges and Universities System
- **Calendar** semesters
- **Degree** certificates and associate
- **Suburban** 100-acre campus with easy access to Minneapolis-St. Paul
- **Coed,** 4,416 undergraduate students, 45% full-time, 64% women, 36% men

The College has two beautiful campuses in Cambridge and Coon Rapids, just north of the Minneapolis/St. Paul metropolitan area. Surrounded by wild prairie grasses and the Rum River, Cambridge Campus is in a growing rural area and offers convenient block scheduling. Overlooking the Mississippi River, Coon Rapids Campus is located in a suburban area easily accessible to

Anoka-Ramsey Community College (continued)
the metropolitan area. Both campuses feature low cost, small classes, and personal attention. Studies include four-year transfer options and two-year career programs.

Undergraduates 2% are from out of state, 2% African American, 2% Asian American or Pacific Islander, 1% Hispanic American, 0.5% Native American.
Freshmen *Admission:* 2,301 applied, 2,301 admitted.
Faculty *Total:* 250, 60% full-time. *Student/faculty ratio:* 28:1.
Majors Accounting; business administration; business marketing and marketing management; computer systems networking/telecommunications; data entry/microcomputer applications; data entry/microcomputer applications related; information sciences/systems; legal administrative assistant; liberal arts and sciences/liberal studies; medical administrative assistant; nursing; physical therapy assistant; pre-engineering; secretarial science; system/networking/LAN/WAN management; word processing.
Academic Programs *Special study options:* academic remediation for entering students, accelerated degree program, advanced placement credit, cooperative education, honors programs, independent study, internships, off-campus study, part-time degree program, services for LD students, study abroad, summer session for credit. *ROTC:* Army (c), Navy (c), Air Force (c).
Library Main Library plus 1 other with 41,000 titles, 250 serial subscriptions, an OPAC, a Web page.
Computers on Campus 200 computers available on campus for general student use. A campuswide network can be accessed from off campus. At least one staffed computer lab available.
Student Life *Housing:* college housing not available. *Activities and Organizations:* drama/theater group, student-run newspaper, choral group, Phi Theta Kappa, Student Senate, student newspaper, International Student Club, Intervarsity Christian Fellowship. *Campus security:* 24-hour emergency response devices and patrols, late-night transport/escort service. *Student Services:* personal/psychological counseling.
Athletics Member NJCAA. *Intercollegiate sports:* baseball M, basketball M/W, volleyball W. *Intramural sports:* badminton M/W, basketball M/W, bowling M/W, football M/W, golf M/W, ice hockey M/W, soccer M/W, softball M/W, tennis M/W, volleyball M/W.
Costs (2002–03) *One-time required fee:* $5. *Tuition:* state resident $2300 full-time; nonresident $4284 full-time. Full-time tuition and fees vary according to program and reciprocity agreements. Part-time tuition and fees vary according to course load, program, and reciprocity agreements. *Waivers:* senior citizens and employees or children of employees.
Financial Aid In 2001, 500 Federal Work-Study jobs (averaging $5000). 500 State and other part-time jobs (averaging $5000).
Applying *Options:* common application, early admission, deferred entrance. *Application fee:* $20. *Required for some:* high school transcript. *Application deadline:* rolling (freshmen), rolling (transfers). *Notification:* continuous (freshmen).
Admissions Contact Mr. Tom Duval, Admissions Counselor, Anoka-Ramsey Community College, 11200 Mississippi Boulevard NW, Coon Rapids, MN 55433. *Phone:* 763-422-3458. *Fax:* 763-422-3636. *E-mail:* mcvarypa@an.cc.mn.us.

ANOKA-RAMSEY COMMUNITY COLLEGE, CAMBRIDGE CAMPUS
Cambridge, Minnesota

- **State-supported** 2-year, part of Minnesota State Colleges and Universities System
- **Calendar** semesters
- **Degree** certificates and associate
- **Coed,** 1,411 undergraduate students

Undergraduates 1% African American, 0.6% Asian American or Pacific Islander, 0.8% Hispanic American, 0.7% Native American.
Freshmen *Admission:* 407 applied, 407 admitted.
Faculty *Total:* 67, 25% full-time. *Student/faculty ratio:* 25:1.
Majors Accounting technician; biomedical technology; business administration; computer systems networking/telecommunications; nursing; physical therapy assistant; pre-engineering.
Academic Programs *Special study options:* academic remediation for entering students, accelerated degree program, advanced placement credit, cooperative education, honors programs, independent study, internships, off-campus study, part-time degree program, services for LD students, study abroad, summer session for credit.
Library Main Library plus 1 other.
Computers on Campus 75 computers available on campus for general student use. A campuswide network can be accessed from off campus. Internet access, online (class) registration, at least one staffed computer lab available.
Costs (2001–02) *Tuition:* state resident $79 per credit part-time; nonresident $158 per credit part-time. Full-time tuition and fees vary according to course load. Part-time tuition and fees vary according to course load. *Required fees:* $13 per credit. *Waivers:* senior citizens and employees or children of employees.
Applying *Options:* common application, early admission, deferred entrance. *Application fee:* $20. *Required for some:* high school transcript. *Application deadline:* rolling (freshmen), rolling (transfers). *Notification:* continuous (freshmen).
Admissions Contact Ms. Judy Gall, Admissions/Records, Anoka-Ramsey Community College, Cambridge Campus, 300 Polk Street South, Cambridge, MN 55008. *Phone:* 763-689-7027. *Fax:* 763-689-7050. *E-mail:* judy.gall@cc.cc.mn.us.

ARGOSY UNIVERSITY-TWIN CITIES
Bloomington, Minnesota

- **Proprietary** primarily 2-year, founded 1961, part of Argosy Education Group
- **Calendar** quarters
- **Degrees** associate, bachelor's, master's, and doctoral
- **Suburban** 4-acre campus with easy access to Minneapolis-St. Paul
- **Coed, primarily women,** 883 undergraduate students

Undergraduates Students come from 10 states and territories, 2 other countries, 5% are from out of state.
Faculty *Total:* 89, 39% full-time. *Student/faculty ratio:* 16:1.
Majors Dental assistant; diagnostic medical sonography; medical assistant; medical laboratory technician; medical laboratory technology; medical radiologic technology; veterinary technology.
Academic Programs *Special study options:* academic remediation for entering students, double majors, internships, part-time degree program, services for LD students, summer session for credit.
Library MIM/MSPP Library with 2,000 titles, 15 serial subscriptions, an OPAC, a Web page.
Computers on Campus 50 computers available on campus for general student use. At least one staffed computer lab available.
Student Life *Housing:* college housing not available. *Campus security:* 24-hour emergency response devices, late-night transport/escort service.
Standardized Tests *Required:* SAT I or ACT (for admission).
Costs (2002–03) *Tuition:* $10,350 full-time, $345 per semester hour part-time. Full-time tuition and fees vary according to course load and program. *Required fees:* $350 full-time, $40 per credit. *Payment plans:* installment, deferred payment. *Waivers:* employees or children of employees.
Financial Aid In 2001, 20 State and other part-time jobs (averaging $1500).
Applying *Options:* common application, electronic application, deferred entrance. *Application fee:* $25. *Required:* high school transcript, interview. *Required for some:* essay or personal statement, letters of recommendation. *Application deadline:* rolling (freshmen), rolling (transfers).
Admissions Contact Ms. O. Jeanne Stoneking, Director of Admissions, Argosy University-Twin Cities, 5503 Green Valley Drive, Bloomington, MN 55437-1003. *Phone:* 952-844-0064. *Toll-free phone:* 888-844-2004. *Fax:* 952-844-0472. *E-mail:* info@medicalinstitute.org.

THE ART INSTITUTES INTERNATIONAL MINNESOTA
Minneapolis, Minnesota

- **Proprietary** primarily 2-year, founded 1964, part of The Art Institute
- **Calendar** quarters
- **Degrees** certificates, associate, and bachelor's
- **Urban** campus
- **Coed,** 948 undergraduate students

Undergraduates Students come from 27 states and territories, 8 other countries, 1% African American, 2% Asian American or Pacific Islander, 0.8% Hispanic American, 0.4% Native American, 13% live on campus.
Freshmen *Admission:* 572 applied, 316 admitted. *Average high school GPA:* 2.53.
Faculty *Total:* 57, 44% full-time. *Student/faculty ratio:* 20:1.

Majors Computer graphics; culinary arts; graphic design/commercial art/illustration; interior design; multimedia.
Academic Programs *Special study options:* academic remediation for entering students, advanced placement credit, cooperative education, internships, part-time degree program, services for LD students, summer session for credit.
Library Learning Resource Center with 1,450 titles, 25 serial subscriptions.
Computers on Campus 75 computers available on campus for general student use. Internet access, at least one staffed computer lab available.
Student Life *Housing Options:* coed. *Campus security:* security personnel during hours of operation. *Student Services:* personal/psychological counseling.
Standardized Tests *Recommended:* ACT (for admission).
Costs (2001–02) *One-time required fee:* $100. *Tuition:* $19,136 full-time, $299 per credit part-time. Full-time tuition and fees vary according to program. No tuition increase for student's term of enrollment. *Room only:* $5220. Room and board charges vary according to housing facility. *Payment plan:* installment. *Waivers:* employees or children of employees.
Applying *Options:* common application, electronic application, deferred entrance. *Application fee:* $50. *Required:* essay or personal statement, high school transcript, interview. *Application deadline:* rolling (freshmen), rolling (transfers).
Admissions Contact Mr. Jeff Marcus, Director of Admissions, The Art Institutes International Minnesota, 15 South 9th Street, Minneapolis, MN 55402. *Phone:* 612-332-3361 Ext. 120. *Toll-free phone:* 800-777-3643. *Fax:* 612-332-3934. *E-mail:* kozela@aii.edu.

BETHANY LUTHERAN COLLEGE
Mankato, Minnesota

- **Independent Lutheran** primarily 2-year, founded 1927
- **Calendar** semesters
- **Degrees** associate and bachelor's
- **Small-town** 50-acre campus with easy access to Minneapolis-St. Paul
- **Endowment** $21.7 million
- **Coed,** 420 undergraduate students, 100% full-time, 52% women, 48% men

Bethany Lutheran College (www.blc.edu) is a private, coeducational, residential, liberal arts, Christian college. Associate in Arts or Bachelor of Arts degrees are currently offered. Four-year programs are now offered in art, biology, business administration, chemistry, church music, communication, music, and liberal arts (with 14 concentrations).

Undergraduates 420 full-time. Students come from 22 states and territories, 11 other countries, 26% are from out of state, 2% African American, 1% Asian American or Pacific Islander, 1% Hispanic American, 0.2% Native American, 4% international, 3% transferred in, 88% live on campus. *Retention:* 83% of 2001 full-time freshmen returned.
Freshmen *Admission:* 296 applied, 267 admitted, 185 enrolled. *Average high school GPA:* 3.20. *Test scores:* ACT scores over 18: 87%; ACT scores over 24: 32%; ACT scores over 30: 1%.
Faculty *Total:* 65, 49% full-time, 23% with terminal degrees. *Student/faculty ratio:* 9:1.
Majors Art; biology; business administration; chemistry; communications; liberal arts and sciences/liberal studies; music; religious music.
Academic Programs *Special study options:* academic remediation for entering students, advanced placement credit, honors programs, services for LD students. *ROTC:* Army (c).
Library Memorial Library plus 1 other with 52,000 titles, 275 serial subscriptions, 2,652 audiovisual materials, an OPAC, a Web page.
Computers on Campus 40 computers available on campus for general student use. A campuswide network can be accessed from student residence rooms and from off campus. Internet access, at least one staffed computer lab available.
Student Life *Housing:* on-campus residence required through sophomore year. *Options:* men-only, women-only. *Activities and Organizations:* drama/theater group, student-run newspaper, television station, choral group, Student Senate, Paul Vluisaker Center, Phi Theta Kappa, AAL the Lutheran Brotherhood Branch, Lutherans for Life. *Campus security:* 24-hour emergency response devices and patrols, late-night transport/escort service, controlled dormitory access. *Student Services:* personal/psychological counseling.
Athletics Member NJCAA. *Intercollegiate sports:* baseball M, basketball M(s)/W(s), cross-country running M(s)/W(s), golf M(s)/W(s), soccer M(s)/W(s), softball W(s), tennis M(s)/W(s), volleyball W(s). *Intramural sports:* basketball M/W, football M/W, racquetball M/W, soccer M/W, softball M/W, volleyball M/W.
Standardized Tests *Required:* SAT I or ACT (for admission).
Costs (2002–03) *One-time required fee:* $50. *Comprehensive fee:* $17,208 includes full-time tuition ($12,260), mandatory fees ($260), and room and board ($4688). *Room and board:* College room only: $1718.
Financial Aid In 2001, 65 Federal Work-Study jobs (averaging $566). 199 State and other part-time jobs (averaging $556). *Financial aid deadline:* 7/15.
Applying *Options:* common application, electronic application. *Application fee:* $20. *Required:* essay or personal statement, high school transcript, minimum 2.0 GPA. *Required for some:* interview. *Recommended:* minimum 3.0 GPA, interview. *Application deadline:* 7/15 (freshmen), rolling (transfers).
Admissions Contact Mr. Donald Westphal, Dean of Admissions, Bethany Lutheran College, 700 Luther Drive, Mankato, MN 56001. *Phone:* 507-344-7320. *Toll-free phone:* 800-944-3066. *Fax:* 507-344-7376. *E-mail:* admiss@blc.edu.

BROWN COLLEGE
Mendota Heights, Minnesota

- **Proprietary** 2-year, founded 1946, part of Career Education Corporation
- **Calendar** quarters
- **Degree** certificates and associate
- **Suburban** 20-acre campus with easy access to Minneapolis-St. Paul
- **Coed,** 2,250 undergraduate students

Undergraduates Students come from 15 states and territories.
Faculty *Total:* 140, 32% full-time. *Student/faculty ratio:* 20:1.
Majors Advertising; broadcast journalism; business systems networking/ telecommunications; computer programming; electrical/electronic engineering technology; information sciences/systems.
Academic Programs *Special study options:* academic remediation for entering students, internships, part-time degree program, summer session for credit.
Library Career Resource Center with 768 titles, 33 serial subscriptions.
Computers on Campus 60 computers available on campus for general student use.
Student Life *Housing:* college housing not available. *Activities and Organizations:* Student Senate. *Campus security:* 24-hour emergency response devices, student patrols, late-night transport/escort service.
Costs (2001–02) *Tuition:* $23,000 per degree program part-time. *Required fees:* $50 full-time.
Financial Aid In 2001, 20 Federal Work-Study jobs (averaging $2000).
Applying *Options:* deferred entrance. *Application fee:* $50. *Required:* high school transcript, interview. *Required for some:* minimum 2.0 GPA. *Recommended:* letters of recommendation. *Application deadline:* rolling (freshmen), rolling (transfers).
Admissions Contact Ms. Dawn Bravo, Director of Admissions, Brown College, 1440 Northland Drive, Mendota Heights, MN 55120. *Phone:* 651-905-3400. *Toll-free phone:* 800-6BROWN6. *Fax:* 651-905-3510.

CENTRAL LAKES COLLEGE
Brainerd, Minnesota

- **State-supported** 2-year, founded 1938, part of Minnesota State Colleges and Universities System
- **Calendar** semesters
- **Degree** certificates, diplomas, and associate
- **Small-town** 1-acre campus
- **Coed,** 2,857 undergraduate students, 65% full-time, 52% women, 48% men

Undergraduates Students come from 10 states and territories, 1 other country, 0.3% are from out of state.
Faculty *Total:* 140. *Student/faculty ratio:* 30:1.
Majors Accounting; business administration; business marketing and marketing management; developmental/child psychology; horticulture science; legal administrative assistant; liberal arts and sciences/liberal studies; medical administrative assistant; nursing; secretarial science.
Academic Programs *Special study options:* academic remediation for entering students, advanced placement credit, external degree program, off-campus study, part-time degree program, summer session for credit.
Library Learning Resource Center with 16,052 titles, 286 serial subscriptions, an OPAC.
Computers on Campus 100 computers available on campus for general student use. Internet access, at least one staffed computer lab available.
Student Life *Housing:* college housing not available. *Activities and Organizations:* drama/theater group, student-run newspaper, choral group. *Campus security:* late-night transport/escort service.

Central Lakes College (continued)
Athletics Member NJCAA. *Intercollegiate sports:* baseball M, basketball M/W, football M, softball W, tennis M/W, volleyball W. *Intramural sports:* basketball M/W, bowling M/W, football M, golf M/W, softball M/W, tennis M/W, volleyball M/W.
Standardized Tests *Recommended:* ACT (for placement).
Costs (2001–02) *Tuition:* area resident $1211 full-time, $89 per credit part-time; nonresident $167 per credit part-time. *Required fees:* $13.
Applying *Options:* deferred entrance. *Application fee:* $20. *Application deadline:* rolling (freshmen), rolling (transfers).
Admissions Contact Charlotte Daniels, Director of Admissions, Central Lakes College, 501 West College Drive, Brainerd, MN 56401-3904. *Phone:* 218-828-2525. *Toll-free phone:* 800-933-0346 Ext. 2586. *E-mail:* dscearcy@gwmail.clc.mnscu.edu.

CENTURY COMMUNITY AND TECHNICAL COLLEGE
White Bear Lake, Minnesota

- **State-supported** 2-year, founded 1970, part of Minnesota State Colleges and Universities System
- **Calendar** semesters
- **Degree** certificates, diplomas, and associate
- **Suburban** 150-acre campus with easy access to Minneapolis-St. Paul
- **Endowment** $500,000
- **Coed,** 7,396 undergraduate students, 45% full-time, 57% women, 43% men

Undergraduates 3,308 full-time, 4,088 part-time. Students come from 45 other countries, 4% African American, 5% Asian American or Pacific Islander, 2% Hispanic American, 0.8% Native American, 0.8% international, 15% transferred in. *Retention:* 83% of 2001 full-time freshmen returned.
Freshmen *Admission:* 3,070 applied, 3,070 admitted, 2,447 enrolled.
Faculty *Total:* 279, 57% full-time. *Student/faculty ratio:* 23:1.
Majors Accounting; alcohol/drug abuse counseling; auto body repair; auto mechanic/technician; business administration; computer engineering technology; cosmetology; dental assistant; dental hygiene; dental laboratory technician; diesel engine mechanic; educational media technology; emergency medical technology; environmental science; fashion merchandising; general retailing/wholesaling; heating/air conditioning/refrigeration; industrial technology; interior design; law enforcement/police science; legal administrative assistant; liberal arts and sciences/liberal studies; machine technology; management information systems/business data processing; medical administrative assistant; medical assistant; medical radiologic technology; music business management/merchandising; nursing; orthotics/prosthetics; pharmacy technician/assistant; quality control technology; sales operations; secretarial science; small engine mechanic; social work.
Academic Programs *Special study options:* academic remediation for entering students, adult/continuing education programs, advanced placement credit, distance learning, double majors, English as a second language, honors programs, internships, part-time degree program, services for LD students, summer session for credit. *ROTC:* Air Force (c).
Library Century College Main Library plus 1 other with 56,867 titles, 486 serial subscriptions, 3,569 audiovisual materials, an OPAC, a Web page.
Computers on Campus 450 computers available on campus for general student use. A campuswide network can be accessed from off campus. Internet access, online (class) registration, at least one staffed computer lab available.
Student Life *Housing:* college housing not available. *Activities and Organizations:* drama/theater group, student-run newspaper, choral group, Student Senate, Phi Theta Kappa, Dental Assistants Club, Creative Arts Alliance, Christian Club. *Campus security:* late-night transport/escort service, day patrols. *Student Services:* personal/psychological counseling, women's center.
Athletics *Intramural sports:* badminton M/W, basketball M/W, golf M/W, soccer M/W, softball M/W.
Costs (2001–02) *Tuition:* state resident $2294 full-time, $76 per credit part-time; nonresident $153 per credit part-time. *Required fees:* $302 full-time, $10 per credit.
Financial Aid In 2001, 70 Federal Work-Study jobs (averaging $1673). 83 State and other part-time jobs (averaging $1528).
Applying *Application fee:* $20. *Required:* high school transcript. *Application deadline:* rolling (freshmen), rolling (transfers).
Admissions Contact Ms. Christine Paulos, Admissions Director, Century Community and Technical College, 3300 Century Avenue North, White Bear Lake, MN 55110. *Phone:* 651-779-2619. *Toll-free phone:* 800-228-1978. *Fax:* 651-779-5810.

COLLEGE OF ST. CATHERINE-MINNEAPOLIS
Minneapolis, Minnesota

- **Independent Roman Catholic** 2-year, founded 1964
- **Calendar** semesters
- **Degree** certificates and associate
- **Urban** 1-acre campus
- **Coed, primarily women,** 3,610 undergraduate students, 64% full-time, 97% women, 3% men

Undergraduates 2,303 full-time, 1,307 part-time. Students come from 18 states and territories, 6% are from out of state, 6% African American, 5% Asian American or Pacific Islander, 2% Hispanic American, 0.7% Native American, 2% international, 8% transferred in, 9% live on campus.
Freshmen *Admission:* 814 applied, 671 admitted, 369 enrolled. *Average high school GPA:* 3.39.
Faculty *Total:* 443, 42% full-time, 52% with terminal degrees. *Student/faculty ratio:* 10:1.
Majors Diagnostic medical sonography; liberal arts and sciences/liberal studies; medical radiologic technology; medical records administration; medical technology; nursing; occupational therapy assistant; physical therapy assistant; respiratory therapy.
Academic Programs *Special study options:* academic remediation for entering students, adult/continuing education programs, independent study, internships, part-time degree program, services for LD students, summer session for credit.
Library Minneapolis Campus Library with 2,727 audiovisual materials, an OPAC.
Computers on Campus 40 computers available on campus for general student use. A campuswide network can be accessed from student residence rooms and from off campus. Internet access, at least one staffed computer lab available.
Student Life *Housing Options:* coed. *Activities and Organizations:* Christian Healthcare Fellowship, Occupational Therapy Club, Student Nurses Association. *Campus security:* 24-hour emergency response devices and patrols, late-night transport/escort service, controlled dormitory access. *Student Services:* health clinic, personal/psychological counseling.
Standardized Tests *Recommended:* ACT (for placement).
Costs (2002–03) *Comprehensive fee:* $23,532 includes full-time tuition ($18,240), mandatory fees ($122), and room and board ($5170). Part-time tuition: $570 per credit. *Required fees:* $61 per term part-time. *Room and board:* College room only: $2920.
Applying *Options:* deferred entrance. *Application fee:* $20. *Required:* essay or personal statement, high school transcript, 2 letters of recommendation. *Required for some:* minimum 3.0 GPA. *Recommended:* minimum 2.0 GPA, interview. *Application deadline:* rolling (freshmen), rolling (transfers). *Notification:* continuous (freshmen).
Admissions Contact Mr. Cal Mosley, Assistant to the President for Admission, College of St. Catherine-Minneapolis, Minneapolis, MN 55454-1494. *Phone:* 651-690-8600. *Fax:* 651-690-8119. *E-mail:* career-info@stkate.edu.

DAKOTA COUNTY TECHNICAL COLLEGE
Rosemount, Minnesota

- **State-supported** 2-year, founded 1970, part of Minnesota State Colleges and Universities System
- **Calendar** semesters
- **Degree** certificates, diplomas, and associate
- **Endowment** $700,000
- **Coed,** 3,103 undergraduate students, 40% full-time, 44% women, 56% men

Undergraduates 1,236 full-time, 1,867 part-time. Students come from 8 states and territories, 21 other countries, 3% are from out of state, 9% transferred in. *Retention:* 83% of 2001 full-time freshmen returned.
Freshmen *Admission:* 1,388 applied, 1,166 admitted, 1,143 enrolled.
Faculty *Total:* 199, 43% full-time, 80% with terminal degrees. *Student/faculty ratio:* 18:1.
Majors Child care provider; child care services management; communication systems installation/repair; computer graphics; computer/information systems security; computer programming related; computer programming (specific applications); computer programming, vendor/product certification; computer software and media applications related; computer systems networking/telecommunications; data entry/microcomputer applications; data entry/microcomputer applications related; data warehousing/mining/database administration; drafting/design technology; electrical equipment installation/repair; engineering-related technology; furniture design; health unit coordination; industrial machinery maintenance/repair; interior environments; machine shop assistant; marketing

operations; system administration; travel services marketing operations; vehicle parts/accessories marketing operations; Web/multimedia management/webmaster; Web page, digital/multimedia and information resources design; word processing.
Academic Programs *Special study options:* academic remediation for entering students, cooperative education, distance learning, double majors, English as a second language, independent study, internships, part-time degree program, services for LD students, summer session for credit.
Library DCTC Library with 15,693 titles, 258 serial subscriptions, 1,164 audiovisual materials, an OPAC, a Web page.
Computers on Campus 100 computers available on campus for general student use. A campuswide network can be accessed from off campus. Internet access, online (class) registration, at least one staffed computer lab available.
Student Life *Housing:* college housing not available. *Activities and Organizations:* student-run newspaper. *Campus security:* 24-hour emergency response devices, late-night transport/escort service. *Student Services:* health clinic, personal/psychological counseling.
Athletics Member NJCAA. *Intercollegiate sports:* wrestling M.
Standardized Tests *Required for some:* Accuplacer/computerized placement test.
Costs (2001–02) *Tuition:* state resident $2618 full-time, $82 per semester hour part-time; nonresident $5235 full-time, $169 per semester hour part-time. *Required fees:* $488 full-time, $15 per semester hour. *Payment plans:* installment, deferred payment. *Waivers:* senior citizens and employees or children of employees.
Applying *Options:* common application, electronic application. *Application fee:* $20. *Required for some:* high school transcript, letters of recommendation. *Recommended:* interview.
Admissions Contact Patrick Lair, Admissions Director, Dakota County Technical College, Office of Admissions, Dakota County Technical College, 1300 145th Street East, Rosemount, MN 55068. *Phone:* 651-423-8399. *Toll-free phone:* 877-YES-DCTC Ext. 302 (in-state); 877-YES-DCTC (out-of-state). *Fax:* 651-423-8775. *E-mail:* admissions@dctc.mnscu.edu.

DULUTH BUSINESS UNIVERSITY
Duluth, Minnesota

Admissions Contact 412 West Superior Street, Duluth, MN 55802. *Toll-free phone:* 800-777-8406.

DUNWOODY COLLEGE OF TECHNOLOGY
Minneapolis, Minnesota

- **Independent** 2-year, founded 1914
- **Calendar** quarters
- **Degree** diplomas and associate
- **Urban** 12-acre campus
- **Endowment** $31.2 million
- **Coed, primarily men,** 1,164 undergraduate students, 96% full-time, 10% women, 90% men

Undergraduates 1,112 full-time, 52 part-time. Students come from 12 states and territories, 3 other countries, 5% are from out of state, 7% African American, 2% Asian American or Pacific Islander, 1% Hispanic American, 1% Native American, 0.3% international, 11% transferred in. *Retention:* 80% of 2001 full-time freshmen returned.
Freshmen *Admission:* 586 applied, 431 admitted, 316 enrolled. *Average high school GPA:* 2.54.
Faculty *Total:* 63, 83% full-time, 5% with terminal degrees. *Student/faculty ratio:* 21:1.
Majors Architectural drafting; auto body repair; auto mechanic/technician; business computer programming; computer/information sciences; electrical/electronic engineering technology; electrical/power transmission installation; engineering design; graphic/printing equipment; heating/air conditioning/refrigeration; heating/air conditioning/refrigeration technology; industrial technology; major appliance installation/repair; tool/die making; welding technology.
Academic Programs *Special study options:* academic remediation for entering students, English as a second language, independent study, internships, summer session for credit.
Library Learning Resource Center with 8,000 titles, 115 serial subscriptions, 250 audiovisual materials, an OPAC.
Computers on Campus 300 computers available on campus for general student use. A campuswide network can be accessed from off campus. Internet access, at least one staffed computer lab available.
Student Life *Housing:* college housing not available. *Campus security:* 24-hour emergency response devices, late-night transport/escort service. *Student Services:* personal/psychological counseling.
Costs (2001–02) *Tuition:* $7500 full-time. Full-time tuition and fees vary according to course load and program. Part-time tuition is $94 per credit for lecture courses; $234 per credit for lab courses. *Required fees:* $189 full-time. *Waivers:* employees or children of employees.
Financial Aid In 2001, 20 Federal Work-Study jobs (averaging $3000). 20 State and other part-time jobs (averaging $3000).
Applying *Options:* electronic application, early admission, deferred entrance. *Application fee:* $50. *Required:* high school transcript, interview, institutional entrance test. *Application deadline:* rolling (freshmen). *Notification:* continuous (freshmen).
Admissions Contact Ms. Yun-bok Christenson, Records Coordinator, Dunwoody College of Technology, 818 Dunwoody Boulevard, Minneapolis, MN 55403. *Phone:* 612-374-5800 Ext. 2019. *Toll-free phone:* 800-292-4625. *Fax:* 612-374-4128. *E-mail:* aylreb@dunwoody.tec.mn.us.

FERGUS FALLS COMMUNITY COLLEGE
Fergus Falls, Minnesota

- **State-supported** 2-year, founded 1960, part of Minnesota State Colleges and Universities System
- **Calendar** semesters
- **Degree** certificates, diplomas, and associate
- **Rural** 146-acre campus
- **Endowment** $1.1 million
- **Coed,** 2,401 undergraduate students, 36% full-time, 65% women, 35% men

Undergraduates 874 full-time, 1,527 part-time. Students come from 7 states and territories, 2 other countries, 4% are from out of state, 1% African American, 0.2% Asian American or Pacific Islander, 0.4% Hispanic American, 0.2% Native American, 3% transferred in, 22% live on campus. *Retention:* 49% of 2001 full-time freshmen returned.
Freshmen *Admission:* 623 applied, 623 admitted.
Faculty *Total:* 94, 44% full-time, 7% with terminal degrees. *Student/faculty ratio:* 18:1.
Majors Biological/physical sciences; business administration; business marketing and marketing management; law enforcement/police science; legal administrative assistant; liberal arts and sciences/liberal studies; medical administrative assistant; medical laboratory technician; medical laboratory technology; nursing; practical nurse; pre-engineering; secretarial science.
Academic Programs *Special study options:* academic remediation for entering students, advanced placement credit, off-campus study, part-time degree program, services for LD students, summer session for credit.
Library Fergus Falls Community College Library with 27,000 titles, 136 serial subscriptions, an OPAC.
Computers on Campus 80 computers available on campus for general student use. Internet access, at least one staffed computer lab available.
Student Life *Housing Options:* coed. *Activities and Organizations:* drama/theater group, student-run newspaper, choral group, Student Senate, Students In Free Enterprise, Phi Theta Kappa. *Campus security:* late-night transport/escort service, security for special events. *Student Services:* personal/psychological counseling, women's center.
Athletics Member NJCAA. *Intercollegiate sports:* baseball M, basketball M/W, football M, golf M/W, softball W, volleyball W. *Intramural sports:* badminton M/W, basketball M, bowling M/W, football M/W, golf M/W, skiing (cross-country) M/W, skiing (downhill) M/W, softball M/W, table tennis M/W, tennis M/W, volleyball M/W, weight lifting M/W.
Standardized Tests *Recommended:* ACT (for placement).
Costs (2002–03) *Tuition:* state resident $2856 full-time, $107 per credit part-time; nonresident $5712 full-time, $214 per credit part-time. Full-time tuition and fees vary according to course load, location, and reciprocity agreements. Part-time tuition and fees vary according to course load, location, and reciprocity agreements. *Required fees:* $549 full-time, $18 per credit. *Room and board:* room only: $2500. Room and board charges vary according to housing facility. *Waivers:* employees or children of employees.
Financial Aid In 2001, 80 Federal Work-Study jobs (averaging $1800). 80 State and other part-time jobs (averaging $1800).
Applying *Options:* common application, early admission, deferred entrance. *Application fee:* $20. *Required:* high school transcript. *Application deadline:* rolling (freshmen), rolling (transfers). *Notification:* continuous (freshmen).

Fergus Falls Community College (continued)

Admissions Contact Ms. Carrie Brimhall, Director of Enrollment Management, Fergus Falls Community College, 1414 College Way, Fergus Falls, MN 56537-1009. *Phone:* 218-739-7425. *Toll-free phone:* 877-450-3322 Ext. 7425. *Fax:* 218-739-7475.

FOND DU LAC TRIBAL AND COMMUNITY COLLEGE

Cloquet, Minnesota

Admissions Contact Ms. Patricia Maciewski, Admissions Representative, Fond du Lac Tribal and Community College, 2101 14th Street, Cloquet, MN 55720. *Phone:* 218-879-0808. *Toll-free phone:* 800-657-3712. *Fax:* 218-879-0814. *E-mail:* admissions@ezigaa.fdl.cc.mn.us.

GLOBE COLLEGE

Oakdale, Minnesota

- **Private** primarily 2-year, founded 1885
- **Calendar** quarters
- **Degrees** diplomas, associate, and bachelor's
- 774 undergraduate students, 44% full-time

Undergraduates 342 full-time, 432 part-time. 77% are from out of state.
Freshmen *Admission:* 159 enrolled.
Faculty *Total:* 63, 32% full-time, 11% with terminal degrees. *Student/faculty ratio:* 15:1.
Academic Programs *Special study options:* academic remediation for entering students, adult/continuing education programs, advanced placement credit, distance learning, external degree program, independent study, internships, part-time degree program.
Computers on Campus 180 computers available on campus for general student use. Internet access, online (class) registration, at least one staffed computer lab available.
Costs (2002–03) *Comprehensive fee:* $22,785 includes full-time tuition ($11,700), mandatory fees ($150), and room and board ($10,935). Part-time tuition: $260 per credit. *Required fees:* $10 per credit. *Payment plan:* installment. *Waivers:* employees or children of employees.
Admissions Contact Mr. Mike Hughes, Director of Admissions, Globe College, 7166 10th Street North, Oakdale, MN 55128. *Phone:* 651-730-5100 Ext. 315. *Fax:* 651-730-5151. *E-mail:* admissions@globecollege.com.

HENNEPIN TECHNICAL COLLEGE

Brooklyn Park, Minnesota

- **State-supported** 2-year, founded 1972, part of Minnesota State Colleges and Universities System
- **Calendar** semesters
- **Degree** certificates, diplomas, and associate
- **Urban** 100-acre campus with easy access to Minneapolis-St. Paul
- **Coed,** 14,733 undergraduate students

Faculty *Total:* 368, 41% full-time. *Student/faculty ratio:* 20:1.
Majors Architectural drafting; auto mechanic/technician; business systems networking/ telecommunications; carpentry; child guidance; computer programming; dental assistant; desktop publishing equipment operation; electrical/ electronic engineering technology; fire science; hydraulic technology; legal administrative assistant; machine technology; mechanical design technology; medical administrative assistant; photography; plastics technology; publishing.
Academic Programs *Special study options:* academic remediation for entering students, advanced placement credit, cooperative education, distance learning, double majors, English as a second language, independent study, internships, services for LD students.
Student Life *Housing:* college housing not available. *Campus security:* late-night transport/escort service, security service. *Student Services:* personal/ psychological counseling, women's center.
Costs (2001–02) *Tuition:* state resident $2816 full-time, $88 per credit part-time; nonresident $5632 full-time, $176 per credit part-time. Full-time tuition and fees vary according to course load and reciprocity agreements. Part-time tuition and fees vary according to course load and reciprocity agreements. *Required fees:* $6 per term part-time. *Waivers:* senior citizens and employees or children of employees.
Applying *Application fee:* $20. *Recommended:* high school transcript, interview. *Application deadline:* rolling (freshmen), rolling (transfers). *Notification:* continuous (freshmen).
Admissions Contact Mrs. Joy Bodin, Director of Admissions, Hennepin Technical College, 9000 Brooklyn Boulevard, Brooklyn Park, MN 55445. *Phone:* 763-550-3181. *Fax:* 763-550-2119.

HERZING COLLEGE, MINNEAPOLIS DRAFTING SCHOOL CAMPUS

Minneapolis, Minnesota

- **Proprietary** 2-year, part of Herzing College
- **Calendar** semesters
- **Degree** certificates and associate
- **Coed,** 162 undergraduate students, 100% full-time, 21% women, 79% men

Undergraduates 162 full-time. Students come from 5 states and territories, 1% are from out of state, 6% African American, 1% Asian American or Pacific Islander, 2% Hispanic American, 2% Native American.
Faculty *Total:* 12, 58% full-time, 25% with terminal degrees. *Student/faculty ratio:* 7:1.
Majors Business systems networking/ telecommunications; computer/ information sciences; computer systems networking/telecommunications.
Academic Programs *Special study options:* adult/continuing education programs, part-time degree program.
Library Main Library plus 1 other.
Computers on Campus 50 computers available on campus for general student use. Internet access, at least one staffed computer lab available.
Student Life *Housing:* college housing not available.
Costs (2001–02) *Tuition:* $14,720 full-time, $230 per credit part-time. Full-time tuition and fees vary according to course load. Part-time tuition and fees vary according to course load. *Payment plan:* installment. *Waivers:* employees or children of employees.
Applying *Required:* high school transcript, interview.
Admissions Contact Jeannie Noveen, Admissions Representative, Herzing College, Minneapolis Drafting School Campus, 5700 West Broadway, Minneapolis, MN 55428. *Phone:* 763-535-3000. *Toll-free phone:* 800-878-DRAW. *Fax:* 763-535-9205. *E-mail:* jeanne@mplsdrafting.com.

HIBBING COMMUNITY COLLEGE

Hibbing, Minnesota

- **State-supported** 2-year, founded 1916, part of Minnesota State Colleges and Universities System
- **Calendar** semesters
- **Degree** certificates, diplomas, and associate
- **Small-town** 100-acre campus
- **Coed,** 1,541 undergraduate students, 70% full-time, 46% women, 54% men

Undergraduates Students come from 20 states and territories, 11% are from out of state, 0.6% African American, 0.1% Asian American or Pacific Islander, 0.1% Hispanic American, 1% Native American, 0.1% international, 10% live on campus.
Faculty *Total:* 82, 80% full-time, 2% with terminal degrees. *Student/faculty ratio:* 17:1.
Majors Business administration; computer/information sciences; computer installation/repair; computer systems networking/telecommunications; culinary arts; dental assistant; drafting; drafting/design technology; educational media technology; institutional food services; law enforcement/police science; legal administrative assistant; liberal arts and sciences/liberal studies; medical administrative assistant; medical laboratory technician; nursing; pre-engineering; sales operations; secretarial science; Web page, digital/multimedia and information resources design.
Academic Programs *Special study options:* academic remediation for entering students, adult/continuing education programs, advanced placement credit, cooperative education, distance learning, internships, off-campus study, part-time degree program, services for LD students, study abroad, summer session for credit.
Library Hibbing Community College Library with 19,536 titles, 190 serial subscriptions, a Web page.
Computers on Campus 150 computers available on campus for general student use. A campuswide network can be accessed from off campus. At least one staffed computer lab available.

Student Life *Activities and Organizations:* drama/theater group, student-run newspaper, choral group, Phi Theta Kappa, Performing Music Ensembles Club, Student Senate, Engineering Club, VICA. *Campus security:* late-night transport/escort service. *Student Services:* personal/psychological counseling.
Athletics Member NJCAA. *Intercollegiate sports:* baseball M, basketball M/W, football M, golf M/W, softball W, volleyball W. *Intramural sports:* basketball M/W, bowling M/W, field hockey M/W, football W, golf M/W, skiing (cross-country) M/W, skiing (downhill) M/W, tennis M/W, volleyball M/W.
Standardized Tests *Recommended:* SAT I or ACT (for placement).
Costs (2001–02) *Tuition:* state resident $2632 full-time, $77 per credit part-time; nonresident $4867 full-time, $153 per credit part-time. Full-time tuition and fees vary according to course load and reciprocity agreements. Part-time tuition and fees vary according to course load and reciprocity agreements. *Required fees:* $13 per credit. *Payment plan:* installment. *Waivers:* senior citizens and employees or children of employees.
Applying *Options:* common application, early admission, deferred entrance. *Application fee:* $20. *Required:* high school transcript. *Application deadline:* rolling (freshmen), rolling (transfers). *Notification:* continuous (freshmen).
Admissions Contact Ms. Shelly Corradi, Admissions, Hibbing Community College, 1515 East 25th Street, Hibbing, MN 55746. *Phone:* 218-262-7207. *Toll-free phone:* 800-224-4HCC. *Fax:* 218-262-6717. *E-mail:* admissions@hcc.mnscu.edu.

INVER HILLS COMMUNITY COLLEGE
Inver Grove Heights, Minnesota

- **State-supported** 2-year, founded 1969, part of Minnesota State Colleges and Universities System
- **Calendar** semesters
- **Degree** certificates and associate
- **Suburban** 100-acre campus with easy access to Minneapolis-St. Paul
- **Coed,** 4,943 undergraduate students, 34% full-time, 69% women, 31% men

Undergraduates Students come from 13 states and territories, 3% African American, 2% Asian American or Pacific Islander, 2% Hispanic American, 0.6% Native American.
Freshmen *Admission:* 1,410 applied, 1,216 admitted.
Faculty *Total:* 220, 45% full-time.
Majors Accounting; aircraft pilot (professional); air traffic control; aviation management; business administration; business marketing and marketing management; computer programming (specific applications); computer programming, vendor/product certification; computer/technical support; construction management; construction technology; criminal justice studies; emergency medical technology; health services administration; human services; law enforcement/police science; legal administrative assistant; liberal arts and sciences/liberal studies; medical administrative assistant; nursing; paralegal/legal assistant; secretarial science; system/networking/LAN/WAN management.
Academic Programs *Special study options:* academic remediation for entering students, advanced placement credit, cooperative education, English as a second language, external degree program, honors programs, independent study, internships, off-campus study, part-time degree program, services for LD students, summer session for credit.
Library 42,073 titles, 300 serial subscriptions, an OPAC, a Web page.
Computers on Campus 250 computers available on campus for general student use. At least one staffed computer lab available.
Student Life *Housing:* college housing not available. *Activities and Organizations:* drama/theater group, student-run newspaper, choral group, PTK, Black Student Union, Student Senate, Biology Club. *Campus security:* late-night transport/escort service, evening police patrol. *Student Services:* health clinic, personal/psychological counseling.
Athletics *Intramural sports:* basketball M/W, football M/W, golf M/W, ice hockey M/W, skiing (cross-country) M/W, soccer M/W, tennis M/W, volleyball M/W, weight lifting M/W.
Costs (2001–02) *Tuition:* state resident $2885 full-time, $96 per credit part-time; nonresident $5357 full-time, $179 per credit part-time. Full-time tuition and fees vary according to course load and reciprocity agreements. Part-time tuition and fees vary according to course load and reciprocity agreements. *Payment plan:* deferred payment. *Waivers:* senior citizens and employees or children of employees.
Financial Aid In 2001, 60 Federal Work-Study jobs (averaging $2000). 90 State and other part-time jobs (averaging $2000).
Applying *Application fee:* $20. *Required for some:* high school transcript. *Recommended:* high school transcript. *Application deadline:* rolling (freshmen), rolling (transfers). *Notification:* continuous (freshmen).
Admissions Contact Ms. Susan Merkling, Admissions, Inver Hills Community College, 2500 East 80th Street, Inver Grove Heights, MN 55076-3224. *Phone:* 651-450-8501. *Fax:* 651-450-8677. *E-mail:* shandwe@inverhills.mnscu.edu.

ITASCA COMMUNITY COLLEGE
Grand Rapids, Minnesota

- **State-supported** 2-year, founded 1922, part of Minnesota State Colleges and Universities System
- **Calendar** semesters
- **Degree** certificates, diplomas, and associate
- **Rural** 24-acre campus
- **Coed,** 1,094 undergraduate students, 73% full-time, 55% women, 45% men

Undergraduates Students come from 8 states and territories, 2 other countries, 5% are from out of state, 0.3% African American, 0.4% Asian American or Pacific Islander, 0.6% Hispanic American, 3% Native American. *Retention:* 57% of 2001 full-time freshmen returned.
Freshmen *Admission:* 573 applied, 573 admitted. *Average high school GPA:* 2.78.
Faculty *Total:* 83, 52% full-time, 4% with terminal degrees. *Student/faculty ratio:* 14:1.
Majors Accounting; business administration; computer engineering related; computer engineering technology; computer/technical support; data entry/microcomputer applications; data entry/microcomputer applications related; education (K-12); engineering; engineering design; engineering science; engineering technology; environmental science; fish/game management; forest harvesting production technology; forestry; human services; information sciences/systems; information technology; liberal arts and sciences/liberal studies; medical administrative assistant; Native American studies; natural resources management; practical nurse; pre-engineering; secretarial science; system/networking/LAN/WAN management; Web/multimedia management/webmaster; Web page, digital/multimedia and information resources design; wildlife management; word processing.
Academic Programs *Special study options:* academic remediation for entering students, adult/continuing education programs, advanced placement credit, cooperative education, double majors, independent study, internships, off-campus study, part-time degree program, services for LD students, summer session for credit.
Library Itasca Community College Library plus 1 other with 23,307 titles, 293 serial subscriptions, 2,856 audiovisual materials, an OPAC.
Computers on Campus 120 computers available on campus for general student use. Internet access, online (class) registration, at least one staffed computer lab available.
Student Life *Housing:* college housing not available. *Activities and Organizations:* drama/theater group, choral group, student association, Circle K, Student Ambassadors, Minority Student Club, Theater Club. *Campus security:* student patrols, late-night transport/escort service, evening patrols by trained security personnel.
Athletics Member NJCAA. *Intercollegiate sports:* baseball M, basketball M/W, football M, softball W, volleyball W, wrestling M. *Intramural sports:* basketball M, bowling M/W, golf W, soccer M/W, softball M/W, table tennis M/W, volleyball M/W.
Costs (2001–02) *Tuition:* state resident $2558 full-time, $80 per credit part-time; nonresident $5117 full-time, $160 per credit part-time. *Required fees:* $472 full-time, $15 per credit. *Payment plans:* installment, deferred payment. *Waivers:* senior citizens and employees or children of employees.
Financial Aid In 2001, 95 Federal Work-Study jobs (averaging $1284). 163 State and other part-time jobs (averaging $1214).
Applying *Options:* common application, electronic application. *Application fee:* $20. *Required:* high school transcript. *Required for some:* essay or personal statement. *Application deadline:* rolling (freshmen), rolling (transfers). *Notification:* continuous (freshmen).
Admissions Contact Ms. Candace Perry, Director of Enrollment Services, Itasca Community College, 1851 East Highway 169, Grand Rapids, MN 55744. *Phone:* 218-327-4464. *Toll-free phone:* 800-996-6422 Ext. 4464. *Fax:* 218-327-4350. *E-mail:* iccinfo@it.cc.mn.us.

LAKELAND MEDICAL-DENTAL ACADEMY
Minneapolis, Minnesota

Admissions Contact Mr. James Decker, Director of Admissions, Lakeland Medical-Dental Academy, 1402 West Lake Street, Minneapolis, MN 55408-2682. *Phone:* 612-827-5656.

LAKE SUPERIOR COLLEGE
Duluth, Minnesota

Admissions Contact Ms. Kathy Tanski, Lake Superior College, 2101 Trinity Road, Duluth, MN 55811. *Phone:* 218-733-7617. *Toll-free phone:* 800-432-2884. *Fax:* 218-733-5945. *E-mail:* admissions@lsc.admin.

MESABI RANGE COMMUNITY AND TECHNICAL COLLEGE
Virginia, Minnesota

- **State-supported** 2-year, founded 1918, part of Minnesota State Colleges and Universities System
- **Calendar** semesters
- **Degree** certificates, diplomas, and associate
- **Small-town** 30-acre campus
- **Coed,** 1,687 undergraduate students, 63% full-time, 47% women, 53% men

Undergraduates Students come from 6 states and territories, 2% African American, 0.3% Asian American or Pacific Islander, 0.3% Hispanic American, 2% Native American, 0.4% international, 10% live on campus.

Faculty *Total:* 67, 73% full-time. *Student/faculty ratio:* 20:1.

Majors Alcohol/drug abuse counseling; business; business systems networking/telecommunications; computer graphics; computer/information technology services administration and management related; computer programming related; computer programming (specific applications); computer software and media applications related; electrical equipment installation/repair; human services; information technology; instrumentation technology; liberal arts and sciences/liberal studies; pre-engineering; secretarial science; Web page, digital/multimedia and information resources design.

Academic Programs *Special study options:* academic remediation for entering students, adult/continuing education programs, advanced placement credit, cooperative education, internships, off-campus study, part-time degree program, services for LD students, student-designed majors, summer session for credit.

Library Mesabi Library with 23,000 titles, 167 serial subscriptions.

Computers on Campus 120 computers available on campus for general student use. At least one staffed computer lab available.

Student Life *Housing Options:* coed. *Activities and Organizations:* drama/theater group, choral group, Student Senate, Human Services Club, Native Amercian Club, Student Life Club, Black Awareness Club. *Campus security:* late-night transport/escort service. *Student Services:* personal/psychological counseling.

Athletics Member NJCAA. *Intercollegiate sports:* baseball M, basketball M/W, football M, softball W, volleyball W. *Intramural sports:* badminton M/W, basketball M/W, bowling M/W, field hockey M/W, football M/W, golf M/W, ice hockey M/W, skiing (cross-country) M/W, skiing (downhill) M/W, tennis M/W, volleyball M/W.

Standardized Tests *Recommended:* ACT (for placement).

Costs (2001–02) *Tuition:* state resident $2826 full-time, $80 per credit part-time; nonresident $2826 full-time, $80 per credit part-time. Full-time tuition and fees vary according to reciprocity agreements. Part-time tuition and fees vary according to reciprocity agreements. *Required fees:* $14 per credit. *Room and board:* room only: $2310. *Waivers:* senior citizens and employees or children of employees.

Financial Aid In 2001, 209 Federal Work-Study jobs (averaging $1725). 100 State and other part-time jobs (averaging $2100).

Applying *Options:* common application, early admission, deferred entrance. *Application fee:* $20. *Application deadline:* rolling (freshmen), rolling (transfers). *Notification:* continuous (freshmen).

Admissions Contact Ms. Brenda K. Gerlach, Director of Enrollment Services, Mesabi Range Community and Technical College, 1001 Chestnut Street West, Virginia, MN 55792. *Phone:* 218-749-0314. *Toll-free phone:* 800-657-3860. *Fax:* 218-749-0313.

MINNEAPOLIS BUSINESS COLLEGE
Roseville, Minnesota

- **Proprietary** 2-year, founded 1874
- **Degree** diplomas and associate
- **Coed, primarily women**
- 91% of applicants were admitted

Faculty *Student/faculty ratio:* 30:1.

Student Life *Campus security:* 24-hour emergency response devices.

Applying *Application fee:* $50.

Admissions Contact Mr. David Whitman, President, Minneapolis Business College, 1711 West County Road B, Roseville, MN 55113. *Phone:* 651-604-4118. *Toll-free phone:* 800-279-5200. *Fax:* 651-636-8185.

MINNEAPOLIS COMMUNITY AND TECHNICAL COLLEGE
Minneapolis, Minnesota

- **State-supported** 2-year, founded 1965, part of Minnesota State Colleges and Universities System
- **Calendar** semesters
- **Degree** certificates, diplomas, and associate
- **Urban** 4-acre campus
- **Endowment** $20,525
- **Coed,** 6,984 undergraduate students

Undergraduates Students come from 48 states and territories, 37 other countries, 6% are from out of state, 20% African American, 5% Asian American or Pacific Islander, 2% Hispanic American, 1% Native American, 3% international. *Retention:* 48% of 2001 full-time freshmen returned.

Freshmen *Admission:* 4,119 applied, 4,016 admitted.

Majors Accounting technician; alcohol/drug abuse counseling; business; business administration; child guidance; computer programming; computer science related; criminal justice studies; culinary arts; film/video production; graphic design/commercial art/illustration; human services; law enforcement/police science; legal administrative assistant; liberal arts and sciences/liberal studies; nursing; secretarial science; Web/multimedia management/webmaster; Web page, digital/multimedia and information resources design.

Academic Programs *Special study options:* academic remediation for entering students, adult/continuing education programs, advanced placement credit, distance learning, English as a second language, honors programs, independent study, internships, off-campus study, part-time degree program, services for LD students, student-designed majors, summer session for credit.

Library Minneapolis Community and Technical College Library with 42,000 titles, 400 serial subscriptions, an OPAC.

Computers on Campus 150 computers available on campus for general student use. Internet access, online (class) registration, at least one staffed computer lab available.

Student Life *Housing:* college housing not available. *Activities and Organizations:* drama/theater group, student-run newspaper, choral group, Student Senate, National Vocational-Technical Honor Society, Phi Theta Kappa, Association of Black Collegiates, Soccer Club. *Campus security:* 24-hour emergency response devices, late-night transport/escort service. *Student Services:* personal/psychological counseling, women's center.

Athletics Member NJCAA. *Intercollegiate sports:* basketball M/W, golf M/W. *Intramural sports:* soccer M(c)/W(c).

Costs (2001–02) *Tuition:* state resident $2760 full-time, $92 per credit part-time; nonresident $5243 full-time, $175 per credit part-time. Full-time tuition and fees vary according to program and reciprocity agreements. Part-time tuition and fees vary according to program and reciprocity agreements. *Payment plan:* installment. *Waivers:* senior citizens and employees or children of employees.

Financial Aid In 2001, 432 Federal Work-Study jobs (averaging $4800). 1,600 State and other part-time jobs (averaging $4800).

Applying *Options:* early admission, deferred entrance. *Application fee:* $20. *Required:* high school transcript. *Application deadline:* 8/31 (freshmen), rolling (transfers). *Notification:* continuous (freshmen).

Admissions Contact Treka McMillian, Admission Representative, Minneapolis Community and Technical College, 1501 Hennepin Avenue, Minneapolis, MN 55403. *Phone:* 612-359-1325. *Toll-free phone:* 800-247-0911. *Fax:* 612-359-1357.

MINNESOTA SCHOOL OF BUSINESS
Richfield, Minnesota

- **Proprietary** primarily 2-year, founded 1877
- **Calendar** quarters
- **Degrees** certificates, diplomas, associate, and bachelor's
- **Urban** 3-acre campus with easy access to Minneapolis-St. Paul
- **Coed,** 2,100 undergraduate students

Undergraduates Students come from 5 states and territories.

Faculty *Student/faculty ratio:* 12:1.
Majors Accounting; business administration; computer graphics; dental assistant; exercise sciences; information sciences/systems; medical assistant; medical office management; office management; paralegal/legal assistant; systems engineering; veterinarian assistant.
Academic Programs *Special study options:* academic remediation for entering students, accelerated degree program, adult/continuing education programs, cooperative education, distance learning, internships.
Library Main Library plus 1 other with 3,000 titles, 5 serial subscriptions, an OPAC, a Web page.
Computers on Campus 150 computers available on campus for general student use. A campuswide network can be accessed from off campus. Internet access, online (class) registration, at least one staffed computer lab available.
Student Life *Housing:* college housing not available.
Costs (2002–03) *Tuition:* $260 per credit part-time.
Applying *Options:* common application. *Application fee:* $50. *Required:* high school transcript, interview. *Required for some:* essay or personal statement. *Application deadline:* rolling (freshmen).
Admissions Contact Mr. Roger Kuhl, Director of Marketing, Minnesota School of Business, 1401 West 76th Street, Richfield, MN 55430. *Phone:* 612-861-2000 Ext. 712. *Toll-free phone:* 800-752-4223. *Fax:* 612-861-5548. *E-mail:* rkuhl@msbcollege.com.

Minnesota State College-Southeast Technical
Winona, Minnesota

- **State-supported** 2-year, founded 1992, part of Minnesota State Colleges and Universities System
- **Calendar** semesters
- **Degree** certificates, diplomas, and associate
- **Small-town** campus with easy access to Minneapolis-St. Paul
- **Endowment** $110,000
- **Coed,** 2,058 undergraduate students

Undergraduates Students come from 20 states and territories, 6 other countries.
Freshmen *Average high school GPA:* 2.56.
Faculty *Total:* 84, 64% full-time.
Majors Accounting; auto mechanic/technician; aviation technology; business machine repair; business marketing and marketing management; carpentry; child care/development; computer engineering technology; computer programming; computer typography/composition; cosmetology; drafting; early childhood education; electrical/electronic engineering technology; emergency medical technology; heating/air conditioning/refrigeration; industrial technology; legal administrative assistant; machine technology; mechanical design technology; medical administrative assistant; musical instrument technology; nursing; practical nurse; retail management; secretarial science; stringed instruments; welding technology.
Academic Programs *Special study options:* academic remediation for entering students, English as a second language, internships, part-time degree program, services for LD students.
Library Learning Resource Center plus 1 other with 8,000 titles, 150 serial subscriptions, an OPAC, a Web page.
Computers on Campus 50 computers available on campus for general student use. A campuswide network can be accessed from off campus. Internet access, at least one staffed computer lab available.
Student Life *Housing:* college housing not available. *Activities and Organizations:* Student Senate. *Campus security:* 24-hour emergency response devices, late-night transport/escort service.
Costs (2001–02) *Tuition:* state resident $89 per credit hour part-time; nonresident $179 per credit hour part-time. Full-time tuition and fees vary according to reciprocity agreements. Part-time tuition and fees vary according to reciprocity agreements. Full-time tuition and fees vary with number of credits. *Required fees:* $10 per credit hour.
Financial Aid In 2001, 65 Federal Work-Study jobs (averaging $2500). 65 State and other part-time jobs (averaging $2500).
Applying *Application fee:* $20. *Required:* high school transcript. *Application deadline:* rolling (freshmen), rolling (transfers).
Admissions Contact Ms. Christine Humble, Student Services Specialist, Minnesota State College-Southeast Technical, PO Box 409, Winona, MN 55987. *Phone:* 507-453-2732. *Toll-free phone:* 800-372-8164. *Fax:* 507-453-2715. *E-mail:* EnrollmentServices@southeasttech.mnscu.edu.

Minnesota West Community and Technical College
Pipestone, Minnesota

- **State-supported** 2-year, founded 1967, part of Minnesota State Colleges and Universities System
- **Calendar** semesters
- **Degrees** certificates, diplomas, and associate (Profile contains information from Canby, Granite Falls, Jackson, and Worthington campuses)
- **Rural** 100-acre campus
- **Coed,** 2,044 undergraduate students, 65% full-time, 49% women, 51% men

Undergraduates 1,333 full-time, 711 part-time. Students come from 17 states and territories, 8 other countries, 2% are from out of state, 0.8% African American, 1% Asian American or Pacific Islander, 1% Hispanic American, 0.7% Native American, 1% international, 12% transferred in. *Retention:* 63% of 2001 full-time freshmen returned.
Freshmen *Admission:* 718 enrolled. *Average high school GPA:* 2.71.
Faculty *Total:* 127, 80% full-time. *Student/faculty ratio:* 15:1.
Majors Accounting; medical administrative assistant; medical assistant; medical laboratory technician; secretarial science.
Academic Programs *Special study options:* academic remediation for entering students, advanced placement credit, cooperative education, distance learning, double majors, English as a second language, external degree program, honors programs, independent study, internships, part-time degree program, services for LD students, summer session for credit.
Library Minnesota West Library with an OPAC.
Computers on Campus Internet access, online (class) registration, at least one staffed computer lab available.
Student Life *Housing:* college housing not available. *Student Services:* personal/psychological counseling.
Athletics Member NJCAA. *Intercollegiate sports:* baseball M, basketball M/W, football M, golf M/W, softball W, volleyball M/W, wrestling M. *Intramural sports:* softball M/W, volleyball M/W.
Costs (2001–02) *Tuition:* state resident $2730 full-time, $83 per credit part-time; nonresident $5460 full-time, $166 per credit part-time. *Required fees:* $248 full-time, $8 per credit. *Payment plan:* installment. *Waivers:* senior citizens and employees or children of employees.
Applying *Options:* common application, electronic application. *Application fee:* $20. *Required:* high school transcript. *Application deadline:* rolling (freshmen), rolling (transfers).
Admissions Contact Larry Schemmel, Vice President of Student and Administrative Services, Minnesota West Community and Technical College, 1314 North Hiawatha Avenue, Pipestone, MN 56164. *Phone:* 507-825-6800 Ext. 6804. *Toll-free phone:* 800-658-2330. *Fax:* 507-825-4656. *E-mail:* garyg@ps.mnwest.mnscu.edu.

Music Tech
Minneapolis, Minnesota

Admissions Contact Ms. Debbie Sandridge, Director of Admissions, Music Tech, 304 Washington Avenue North, Minneapolis, MN 55401-1315. *Phone:* 651-291-0177. *Toll-free phone:* 800-594-9500.

NEI College of Technology
Columbia Heights, Minnesota

- **Independent** 2-year, founded 1930
- **Calendar** quarters
- **Degree** certificates, diplomas, and associate
- **Suburban** 8-acre campus with easy access to Minneapolis-St. Paul
- **Coed, primarily men,** 690 undergraduate students, 52% full-time, 19% women, 81% men

Undergraduates 359 full-time, 331 part-time. Students come from 5 states and territories, 1% are from out of state, 5% African American, 6% Asian American or Pacific Islander, 2% Hispanic American, 1% Native American, 0.8% international, 10% transferred in.
Freshmen *Admission:* 152 applied, 133 admitted, 93 enrolled.
Faculty *Total:* 34, 65% full-time, 44% with terminal degrees. *Student/faculty ratio:* 19:1.
Majors Aviation technology; communication equipment technology; computer engineering technology; computer/information sciences; computer/information

NEI College of Technology (continued)
technology services administration and management related; computer programming (specific applications); computer science related; computer systems networking/telecommunications; computer/technical support; electrical/electronic engineering technology; electromechanical technology; industrial technology; information sciences/systems; information technology; liberal arts and sciences/liberal studies; management information systems/business data processing; radio/television broadcasting; system/networking/LAN/WAN management; telecommunications.

Academic Programs *Special study options:* academic remediation for entering students, adult/continuing education programs, cooperative education, honors programs, internships, part-time degree program.

Library Larson Library with 1,378 titles, 60 serial subscriptions.

Computers on Campus 184 computers available on campus for general student use. A campuswide network can be accessed from off campus. Internet access, at least one staffed computer lab available.

Student Life *Housing:* college housing not available. *Activities and Organizations:* student association. *Campus security:* 24-hour emergency response devices, late-night transport/escort service.

Athletics *Intramural sports:* basketball M/W, tennis M/W, volleyball M/W.

Costs (2001–02) *Tuition:* $10,470 full-time, $4380 per term part-time. Full-time tuition and fees vary according to course load. Part-time tuition and fees vary according to course load. No tuition increase for student's term of enrollment. *Payment plans:* installment, deferred payment. *Waivers:* employees or children of employees.

Financial Aid In 2001, 6 Federal Work-Study jobs.

Applying *Application fee:* $75. *Required:* essay or personal statement, high school transcript, letters of recommendation, interview. *Application deadline:* rolling (freshmen).

Admissions Contact Mr. Michael Olsen, Admissions Representative, NEI College of Technology, 825 41st Avenue, NE, Columbia Heights, MN 55421-2974. *Phone:* 763-782-7330. *Toll-free phone:* 800-777-7634. *Fax:* 763-782-7329. *E-mail:* michael.olsen@neicollege.org.

NORMANDALE COMMUNITY COLLEGE
Bloomington, Minnesota

Admissions Contact Information Center, Normandale Community College, 9700 France Avenue South, Bloomington, MN 55431. *Phone:* 952-832-6320. *Toll-free phone:* 866-880-8740. *Fax:* 952-832-6571. *E-mail:* information@nr.cc.mn.us.

NORTH HENNEPIN COMMUNITY COLLEGE
Minneapolis, Minnesota

- **State-supported** 2-year, founded 1966, part of Minnesota State Colleges and Universities System
- **Calendar** semesters
- **Degree** certificates and associate
- **Suburban** 80-acre campus
- **Endowment** $230,000
- **Coed,** 4,452 undergraduate students

Undergraduates Students come from 9 states and territories, 35 other countries, 3% are from out of state.

Faculty *Total:* 200, 60% full-time. *Student/faculty ratio:* 28:1.

Majors Accounting; architectural drafting; auto mechanic/technician; business administration; business marketing and marketing management; cardiovascular technology; construction management; electrical/electronic engineering technology; fire science; graphic design/commercial art/illustration; hydraulic technology; industrial technology; law enforcement/police science; liberal arts and sciences/liberal studies; management information systems/business data processing; materials science; mechanical drafting; medical laboratory technician; medical radiologic technology; medical records technology; nursing; paralegal/legal assistant; pre-engineering; retail management; secretarial science; transportation technology.

Academic Programs *Special study options:* academic remediation for entering students, accelerated degree program, adult/continuing education programs, advanced placement credit, distance learning, English as a second language, honors programs, off-campus study, part-time degree program, services for LD students, study abroad, summer session for credit. *ROTC:* Air Force (c).

Library Main Library plus 1 other with 35,000 titles, 250 serial subscriptions, an OPAC, a Web page.

Computers on Campus 200 computers available on campus for general student use. Internet access, at least one staffed computer lab available.

Student Life *Housing:* college housing not available. *Activities and Organizations:* drama/theater group, student-run newspaper, choral group. *Campus security:* 24-hour patrols, late-night transport/escort service. *Student Services:* personal/psychological counseling.

Athletics Member NJCAA. *Intercollegiate sports:* baseball M, softball W. *Intramural sports:* basketball M/W, bowling M/W, football M, golf M/W, soccer M, tennis M/W, volleyball M/W.

Costs (2001–02) *Tuition:* state resident $2324 full-time, $97 per credit part-time; nonresident $4008 full-time, $167 per credit part-time.

Applying *Options:* early admission, deferred entrance. *Application fee:* $20. *Required for some:* high school transcript. *Application deadline:* rolling (freshmen), rolling (transfers). *Notification:* continuous (freshmen).

Admissions Contact Mr. Tom Wavrin, Registrar, North Hennepin Community College, 7411 85th Avenue North, Minneapolis, MN 55445-2231. *Phone:* 763-424-0713.

NORTHLAND COMMUNITY AND TECHNICAL COLLEGE
Thief River Falls, Minnesota

- **State-supported** 2-year, founded 1965, part of Minnesota State Colleges and Universities System
- **Calendar** semesters
- **Degree** diplomas and associate
- **Rural** campus
- **Coed,** 2,152 undergraduate students, 43% full-time, 39% women, 61% men

Undergraduates Students come from 26 states and territories, 4 other countries, 7% are from out of state, 0.8% African American, 0.6% Hispanic American, 0.9% Native American, 0.6% international. *Retention:* 56% of 2001 full-time freshmen returned.

Freshmen *Admission:* 668 applied, 668 admitted.

Faculty *Total:* 89, 65% full-time, 9% with terminal degrees. *Student/faculty ratio:* 23:1.

Majors Accounting; aerospace science; architectural engineering technology; athletic training/sports medicine; auto mechanic/technician; aviation management; aviation technology; broadcast journalism; business administration; business marketing and marketing management; child care/development; child care provider; computer graphics; computer science; computer science related; computer software and media applications related; computer systems networking/telecommunications; computer/technical support; cosmetology; criminal justice/law enforcement administration; criminology; data entry/microcomputer applications; data entry/microcomputer applications related; data warehousing/mining/database administration; drafting; electrical/electronic engineering technology; farm/ranch management; industrial electronics installation/repair; information technology; international business; law enforcement/police science; legal administrative assistant; legal studies; liberal arts and sciences/liberal studies; mass communications; nursing; paralegal/legal assistant; practical nurse; radio/television broadcasting; retail management; secretarial science; system/networking/LAN/WAN management; Web/multimedia management/webmaster; Web page, digital/multimedia and information resources design; welding technology; word processing.

Academic Programs *Special study options:* academic remediation for entering students, adult/continuing education programs, advanced placement credit, distance learning, internships, off-campus study, part-time degree program, services for LD students, summer session for credit.

Library Northland College Library.

Computers on Campus 312 computers available on campus for general student use. A campuswide network can be accessed from student residence rooms and from off campus. Internet access, online (class) registration, at least one staffed computer lab available.

Student Life *Housing:* college housing not available. *Activities and Organizations:* drama/theater group, student-run newspaper, radio station, choral group, Law Enforcement Club, All-Nations Club, Environmental CLub, PAMA, VICA. *Campus security:* student patrols, late-night transport/escort service. *Student Services:* personal/psychological counseling, women's center.

Athletics Member NJCAA. *Intercollegiate sports:* baseball M, basketball M/W, football M, golf M(s)/W(s), softball W, volleyball W. *Intramural sports:* basketball M/W, bowling M/W, golf M/W, racquetball M/W, softball M/W, tennis M/W, volleyball M/W.

Standardized Tests *Recommended:* SAT I or ACT (for placement).

Costs (2001–02) *Tuition:* state resident $2656 full-time, $83 per semester hour part-time; nonresident $5312 full-time, $166 per semester hour part-time. Full-time tuition and fees vary according to course load and reciprocity agreements. Part-time tuition and fees vary according to course load and reciprocity agreements. *Required fees:* $434 full-time, $14 per semester hour. *Payment plans:* installment, deferred payment. *Waivers:* senior citizens and employees or children of employees.

Financial Aid In 2001, 75 Federal Work-Study jobs (averaging $2500). 40 State and other part-time jobs (averaging $2500).

Applying *Options:* common application, early admission, deferred entrance. *Application fee:* $20. *Required:* high school transcript. *Application deadlines:* 9/1 (freshmen), 9/1 (transfers). *Notification:* continuous (freshmen).

Admissions Contact Mr. Eugene Klinke, Director of Enrollment Management, Northland Community and Technical College, 1101 Highway #1 East, Thief River Falls, MN 56701. *Phone:* 218-681-0862. *Toll-free phone:* 800-628-9918 Ext. 0862. *Fax:* 218-681-0774. *E-mail:* eklinke@nctc.mnscu.edu.

NORTHWEST TECHNICAL COLLEGE
Perham, Minnesota

Admissions Contact Admission Office, Northwest Technical College, 905 Grant Avenue, SE, Bemidji, MN 56601. *Phone:* 218-755-4270. *Toll-free phone:* 877-598-8523.

NORTHWEST TECHNICAL INSTITUTE
Eden Prairie, Minnesota

- **Proprietary** 2-year, founded 1957
- **Calendar** semesters
- **Degree** associate
- **Suburban** 2-acre campus with easy access to Minneapolis-St. Paul
- **Coed,** 125 undergraduate students

Undergraduates Students come from 4 states and territories, 25% are from out of state.

Freshmen *Admission:* 50 applied, 50 admitted. *Average high school GPA:* 3.0.

Faculty *Total:* 10, 100% full-time. *Student/faculty ratio:* 12:1.

Majors Architectural drafting; mechanical drafting.

Academic Programs *Special study options:* honors programs, independent study.

Library 565 titles, 4 serial subscriptions.

Computers on Campus 120 computers available on campus for general student use. At least one staffed computer lab available.

Student Life *Housing:* college housing not available. *Campus security:* late-night transport/escort service.

Costs (2001–02) *Tuition:* $12,240 full-time.

Applying *Application fee:* $25. *Required:* high school transcript, interview. *Application deadline:* rolling (freshmen), rolling (transfers). *Notification:* continuous (freshmen).

Admissions Contact Mr. John Hartman, Career Consultant, Northwest Technical Institute, 11995 Singletree Lane, Eden Prairie, MN 55344-5351. *Phone:* 952-944-0080. *Toll-free phone:* 800-443-4223. *Fax:* 952-944-9274. *E-mail:* info@nw-ti.com.

PINE TECHNICAL COLLEGE
Pine City, Minnesota

- **State-supported** 2-year, founded 1965, part of Minnesota State Colleges and Universities System
- **Calendar** semesters
- **Degree** certificates, diplomas, and associate
- **Small-town** 6-acre campus with easy access to Minneapolis-St. Paul
- **Coed,** 1,074 undergraduate students, 100% full-time, 61% women, 39% men

Undergraduates 1,074 full-time. Students come from 5 states and territories, 10% are from out of state, 2% transferred in.

Freshmen *Admission:* 1,074 enrolled.

Faculty *Total:* 65, 34% full-time. *Student/faculty ratio:* 16:1.

Majors Auto mechanic/technician; business education; human services; machine technology; safety/security technology; secretarial science.

Academic Programs *Special study options:* academic remediation for entering students, advanced placement credit, distance learning, independent study, internships, part-time degree program, services for LD students, summer session for credit.

Library Media Center plus 1 other with 6,000 titles, 30 serial subscriptions, an OPAC, a Web page.

Computers on Campus 150 computers available on campus for general student use. A campuswide network can be accessed from off campus. Internet access, online (class) registration, at least one staffed computer lab available.

Student Life *Housing:* college housing not available. *Campus security:* late-night transport/escort service. *Student Services:* personal/psychological counseling, women's center.

Standardized Tests *Required:* ASAP.

Costs (2002–03) *Tuition:* state resident $2880 full-time, $90 per semester hour part-time; nonresident $5760 full-time, $180 per semester hour part-time. *Required fees:* $448 full-time, $14 per semester hour.

Financial Aid In 2001, 6 Federal Work-Study jobs (averaging $2000). 10 State and other part-time jobs.

Applying *Options:* early admission. *Application fee:* $20. *Required:* high school transcript. *Required for some:* letters of recommendation. *Application deadline:* rolling (freshmen), rolling (transfers).

Admissions Contact Mr. Phil Schroeder, Dean, Student Affairs, Pine Technical College, 1000 Fourth Street, Pine City, MN 55063. *Phone:* 320-629-5100. *Toll-free phone:* 800-521-7463.

RAINY RIVER COMMUNITY COLLEGE
International Falls, Minnesota

- **State-supported** 2-year, founded 1967, part of Minnesota State Colleges and Universities System
- **Calendar** semesters
- **Degree** certificates, diplomas, and associate
- **Small-town** 80-acre campus
- **Coed,** 480 undergraduate students, 65% full-time, 65% women, 35% men

Undergraduates 312 full-time, 168 part-time. Students come from 8 states and territories, 1 other country, 7% African American, 0.6% Asian American or Pacific Islander, 2% Hispanic American, 5% Native American, 2% transferred in, 10% live on campus.

Freshmen *Admission:* 334 applied, 334 admitted, 480 enrolled.

Faculty *Total:* 37, 68% full-time.

Majors Biological/physical sciences; business administration; liberal arts and sciences/liberal studies; pre-engineering; real estate; secretarial science.

Academic Programs *Special study options:* academic remediation for entering students, adult/continuing education programs, advanced placement credit, cooperative education, English as a second language, honors programs, independent study, internships, part-time degree program, services for LD students, summer session for credit.

Library Rainy River Community College Library with 20,000 titles, an OPAC.

Computers on Campus 70 computers available on campus for general student use. A campuswide network can be accessed from off campus. Internet access, at least one staffed computer lab available.

Student Life *Housing Options:* coed, disabled students. *Activities and Organizations:* drama/theater group, Anishinaabe Student Coalition, Student Senate, Black Student Association. *Campus security:* 24-hour emergency response devices, late-night transport/escort service, controlled dormitory access. *Student Services:* personal/psychological counseling.

Athletics Member NJCAA. *Intercollegiate sports:* basketball M/W, softball W, volleyball W. *Intramural sports:* archery M/W, badminton M/W, bowling M/W, skiing (cross-country) M/W, skiing (downhill) M/W, swimming M/W, tennis M/W, volleyball M/W, weight lifting M/W.

Standardized Tests *Required:* Academic Skills Assessment Program. *Recommended:* ACT (for placement).

Costs (2001–02) *Tuition:* area resident $1247 full-time, $78 per credit part-time; state resident $1247 full-time, $78 per credit part-time; nonresident $1247 full-time. *Required fees:* $269 full-time, $17 per credit. *Room and board:* $3440; room only: $2190.

Financial Aid In 2001, 110 Federal Work-Study jobs (averaging $2000). 55 State and other part-time jobs.

Applying *Options:* common application, early admission, deferred entrance. *Application fee:* $20. *Required:* high school transcript. *Application deadline:* rolling (freshmen), rolling (transfers). *Notification:* continuous (freshmen).

Admissions Contact Ms. Tara Fierke-Kleppe, Director of Enrollment Management, Rainy River Community College, 1501 Highway 71, International Falls, MN 56649. *Phone:* 218-285-7722 Ext. 213. *Toll-free phone:* 800-456-3996. *Fax:* 218-285-2239. *E-mail:* djohnson@rrcc.mnscu.edu.

RASMUSSEN COLLEGE EAGAN
Eagan, Minnesota

- **Proprietary** 2-year, founded 1904, part of Rasmussen College System
- **Calendar** quarters
- **Degree** certificates, diplomas, and associate
- **Suburban** 10-acre campus with easy access to Minneapolis-St. Paul
- **Coed, primarily women,** 340 undergraduate students, 80% full-time, 75% women, 25% men

Undergraduates 273 full-time, 67 part-time. Students come from 3 states and territories, 5 other countries, 6% African American, 4% Asian American or Pacific Islander, 3% Hispanic American, 0.3% Native American, 3% international. *Retention:* 64% of 2001 full-time freshmen returned.

Freshmen *Admission:* 109 enrolled.

Faculty *Total:* 40, 25% full-time. *Student/faculty ratio:* 12:1.

Majors Accounting; business administration; child care/development; computer typography/composition; court reporting; hotel and restaurant management; medical administrative assistant; medical records administration; travel/tourism management.

Academic Programs *Special study options:* academic remediation for entering students, adult/continuing education programs, internships, part-time degree program.

Computers on Campus Internet access, at least one staffed computer lab available.

Student Life *Housing:* college housing not available. *Activities and Organizations:* student-run newspaper, Student Senate, community league softball. *Campus security:* safety and security programs.

Costs (2002–03) *Tuition:* $14,700 full-time, $245 per credit part-time. Full-time tuition and fees vary according to program. Part-time tuition and fees vary according to program. *Waivers:* employees or children of employees.

Applying *Options:* common application. *Application fee:* $60. *Required:* high school transcript, minimum 2.0 GPA, interview. *Application deadline:* rolling (freshmen), rolling (transfers).

Admissions Contact Ms. Jacinda Miller, Admissions Coordinator, Rasmussen College Eagan, 3500 Federal Drive, Eagan, MN 55122-1346. *Phone:* 651-687-9000. *Toll-free phone:* 651-687-0507 (in-state); 800-852-6367 (out-of-state). *E-mail:* admission@rasmussen.edu.

RASMUSSEN COLLEGE MANKATO
Mankato, Minnesota

- **Proprietary** 2-year, founded 1904, part of Rasmussen College System
- **Calendar** quarters
- **Degree** certificates, diplomas, and associate
- **Suburban** campus with easy access to Minneapolis-St. Paul
- **Coed, primarily women,** 313 undergraduate students, 65% full-time, 79% women, 21% men

Undergraduates 205 full-time, 108 part-time. 0.6% Asian American or Pacific Islander, 2% Hispanic American. *Retention:* 72% of 2001 full-time freshmen returned.

Freshmen *Admission:* 151 enrolled.

Faculty *Total:* 39, 26% full-time. *Student/faculty ratio:* 18:1.

Majors Accounting; business administration; business marketing and marketing management; business systems networking/ telecommunications; child care/ development; child care provider; child care services management; computer graphics; computer software and media applications related; computer systems networking/telecommunications; computer/technical support; computer typography/ composition; data entry/microcomputer applications; data entry/microcomputer applications related; data processing technology; health unit coordination; hospitality management; hotel and restaurant management; hotel/motel services marketing operations; legal administrative assistant; legal studies; medical administrative assistant; medical assistant; medical records administration; paralegal/ legal assistant; restaurant operations; secretarial science; system administration; system/networking/LAN/WAN management; tourism promotion operations; travel services marketing operations; travel/tourism management; Web page, digital/ multimedia and information resources design; word processing.

Academic Programs *Special study options:* academic remediation for entering students, advanced placement credit, cooperative education, internships, part-time degree program, services for LD students, summer session for credit.

Library Media Center with 1,000 titles, 3 serial subscriptions.

Computers on Campus 70 computers available on campus for general student use. Internet access, at least one staffed computer lab available.

Student Life *Housing:* college housing not available. *Activities and Organizations:* student-run newspaper, Student Senate, Student Ambassadors, Student Life. *Campus security:* limited access to buildings after hours.

Costs (2002–03) *Tuition:* $14,700 full-time, $245 per credit part-time. Full-time tuition and fees vary according to program. Part-time tuition and fees vary according to program. *Payment plan:* tuition prepayment. *Waivers:* employees or children of employees.

Financial Aid In 2001, 3 Federal Work-Study jobs, 3 State and other part-time jobs.

Applying *Options:* common application, deferred entrance. *Application fee:* $60. *Required:* high school transcript, minimum 2.0 GPA, interview.

Admissions Contact Ms. Kathy Clifford, Admissions Representative, Rasmussen College Mankato, 501 Holly Lane, Mankato, MN 56001-6803. *Phone:* 507-625-6556. *Toll-free phone:* 800-657-6767. *E-mail:* rascoll@ic.mankato.mn.us.

RASMUSSEN COLLEGE MINNETONKA
Minnetonka, Minnesota

- **Proprietary** 2-year, founded 1904, part of Rasmussen College System
- **Calendar** quarters
- **Degree** certificates, diplomas, and associate
- **Suburban** 2-acre campus with easy access to Minneapolis-St. Paul
- **Coed,** 255 undergraduate students, 59% full-time, 82% women, 18% men

Undergraduates 151 full-time, 104 part-time. Students come from 1 other state, 3 other countries.

Freshmen *Admission:* 113 enrolled. *Average high school GPA:* 3.1.

Faculty *Total:* 27, 37% full-time, 48% with terminal degrees. *Student/faculty ratio:* 9:1.

Majors Accounting; business administration; business marketing and marketing management; child care/development; court reporting; legal administrative assistant; medical administrative assistant; secretarial science.

Academic Programs *Special study options:* academic remediation for entering students, internships, part-time degree program, summer session for credit.

Library 3,400 titles, 10 serial subscriptions.

Computers on Campus 300 computers available on campus for general student use. Internet access, at least one staffed computer lab available.

Student Life *Housing:* college housing not available. *Campus security:* late-night transport/escort service.

Costs (2002–03) *Tuition:* $245 per credit part-time.

Applying *Options:* early admission, deferred entrance. *Required:* high school transcript, interview. *Application deadline:* rolling (freshmen), rolling (transfers).

Admissions Contact Mr. Ethan Campbell, Admissions Coordinator, Rasmussen College Minnetonka, 12450 Wayzata Boulevard, Suite 315, Minnetonka, MN 55305-1928. *Phone:* 612-545-2000. *Toll-free phone:* 800-852-0929.

RASMUSSEN COLLEGE ST. CLOUD
St. Cloud, Minnesota

- **Proprietary** 2-year, founded 1904, part of Rasmussen College System
- **Calendar** quarters
- **Degree** certificates, diplomas, and associate
- **Urban** campus with easy access to Minneapolis-St. Paul
- **Coed, primarily women,** 387 undergraduate students, 61% full-time, 74% women, 26% men

Undergraduates 237 full-time, 150 part-time. 1% African American, 0.3% Asian American or Pacific Islander, 1% Hispanic American, 0.8% Native American. *Retention:* 49% of 2001 full-time freshmen returned.

Freshmen *Admission:* 195 enrolled.

Faculty *Total:* 33, 27% full-time. *Student/faculty ratio:* 9:1.

Majors Accounting; business administration; business marketing and marketing management; court reporting; legal administrative assistant; medical administrative assistant; medical records administration; secretarial science; travel/tourism management.

Academic Programs *Special study options:* adult/continuing education programs, internships, part-time degree program, student-designed majors, summer session for credit.

Library 494 titles.

Computers on Campus 75 computers available on campus for general student use. Internet access, at least one staffed computer lab available.

Student Life *Housing:* college housing not available. *Activities and Organizations:* student-run newspaper, Student Senate.

Costs (2002–03) *Tuition:* $14,700 full-time, $245 per credit part-time. Full-time tuition and fees vary according to course load. Part-time tuition and fees vary according to course load. *Payment plan:* installment. *Waivers:* employees or children of employees.
Financial Aid In 2001, 34 Federal Work-Study jobs (averaging $866). 51 State and other part-time jobs (averaging $700).
Applying *Options:* common application, early admission, deferred entrance. *Application fee:* $60. *Required:* high school transcript, minimum 2.0 GPA, interview. *Application deadline:* rolling (freshmen), rolling (transfers).
Admissions Contact Ms. Susan Hammerstrom, Director of Enrollment Management, Rasmussen College St. Cloud, 226 Park Avenue South, St. Cloud, MN 56301-3713. *Phone:* 320-251-3305. *Toll-free phone:* 800-852-0460.

RIDGEWATER COLLEGE
Willmar, Minnesota

- **State-supported** 2-year, founded 1961, part of Minnesota State Colleges and Universities System
- **Calendar** semesters
- **Degree** certificates, diplomas, and associate
- **Small-town** 83-acre campus
- **Coed,** 3,129 undergraduate students, 73% full-time, 52% women, 48% men

Undergraduates Students come from 12 states and territories, 5 other countries, 2% are from out of state.
Faculty *Total:* 229, 64% full-time. *Student/faculty ratio:* 19:1.
Majors Accounting; agricultural animal husbandry/production management; agricultural business; agricultural mechanization; alcohol/drug abuse counseling; applied art; art; audio engineering; biological/physical sciences; broadcast journalism; business administration; child care/development; community services; computer engineering technology; computer graphics; computer/information technology services administration and management related; computer installation/repair; computer management; computer programming (specific applications); computer science related; computer systems networking/telecommunications; criminal justice/law enforcement administration; data processing technology; developmental/child psychology; drafting; drafting/design technology; electrical/electronic engineering technology; electrical equipment installation/repair; engineering; family/community studies; farm/ranch management; gerontology; health unit management; history; humanities; human services; industrial radiologic technology; information sciences/systems; instrument calibration/repair; interdisciplinary studies; journalism; law enforcement/police science; legal administrative assistant; liberal arts and sciences/liberal studies; machine shop assistant; marketing operations; mass communications; mathematics; medical administrative assistant; medical records administration; mental health/rehabilitation; metallurgical technology; music; nursing; photography; physical education; physical sciences; practical nurse; pre-engineering; psychology; quality control technology; real estate; retail management; secretarial science; social work; sociology; speech/rhetorical studies; system administration; system/networking/LAN/WAN management; teacher assistant/aide; theater arts/drama; travel/tourism management; veterinary technology; Web/multimedia management/webmaster; Web page, digital/multimedia and information resources design.
Academic Programs *Special study options:* academic remediation for entering students, accelerated degree program, adult/continuing education programs, advanced placement credit, cooperative education, distance learning, English as a second language, internships, off-campus study, part-time degree program, services for LD students, student-designed majors, summer session for credit.
Library 30,000 titles, 401 serial subscriptions, an OPAC, a Web page.
Computers on Campus 215 computers available on campus for general student use. A campuswide network can be accessed from off campus. Internet access, online (class) registration, at least one staffed computer lab available.
Student Life *Housing:* college housing not available. *Activities and Organizations:* drama/theater group, student-run newspaper, choral group, Student Senate, Ski Club, Nontraditional Students Club, BACCHUS, Creative Writers, Unlimited. *Campus security:* late-night transport/escort service. *Student Services:* personal/psychological counseling, women's center.
Athletics Member NJCAA. *Intercollegiate sports:* baseball M, basketball M/W, football M, softball W, tennis M/W, volleyball W, wrestling M. *Intramural sports:* basketball M/W, football M, golf M/W, softball M/W, weight lifting M/W.
Costs (2001–02) *Tuition:* state resident $2433 full-time, $81 per semester hour part-time; nonresident $4866 full-time, $162 per semester hour part-time. Full-time tuition and fees vary according to program and reciprocity agreements. Part-time tuition and fees vary according to program and reciprocity agreements. *Required fees:* $450 full-time, $15 per semester hour. *Payment plan:* deferred payment. *Waivers:* senior citizens and employees or children of employees.
Financial Aid In 2001, 350 Federal Work-Study jobs (averaging $3000). 133 State and other part-time jobs (averaging $2400).
Applying *Options:* early admission, deferred entrance. *Application fee:* $20. *Required:* high school transcript. *Required for some:* letters of recommendation, interview.
Admissions Contact Ms. Linda Barron, Admissions Assistant, Ridgewater College, PO Box 1097, Willmar, MN 56201-1097. *Phone:* 320-231-2906 Ext. 2906. *Toll-free phone:* 800-722-1151 Ext. 2906. *Fax:* 320-231-7677. *E-mail:* cthompso@ridgewater.mnscu.edu.

RIVERLAND COMMUNITY COLLEGE
Austin, Minnesota

- **State-supported** 2-year, founded 1940, part of Minnesota State Colleges and Universities System
- **Calendar** semesters
- **Degree** certificates, diplomas, and associate
- **Small-town** 187-acre campus with easy access to Minneapolis-St. Paul
- **Coed,** 3,175 undergraduate students, 49% full-time, 51% women, 49% men

Undergraduates Students come from 5 states and territories, 0.8% African American, 0.9% Asian American or Pacific Islander, 2% Hispanic American, 0.1% Native American.
Freshmen *Admission:* 900 admitted. *Average high school GPA:* 3.08.
Faculty *Total:* 158, 64% full-time. *Student/faculty ratio:* 20:1.
Majors Auto body repair; business administration; computer/information systems security; computer installation/repair; computer programming (specific applications); computer programming, vendor/product certification; computer software and media applications related; computer systems networking/telecommunications; computer/technical support; corrections; data entry/microcomputer applications; data entry/microcomputer applications related; diesel engine mechanic; electrical equipment installation/repair; health unit coordination; human services; industrial machinery maintenance/repair; law enforcement/police science; legal administrative assistant; liberal arts and sciences/liberal studies; machine shop assistant; medical administrative assistant; medical radiologic technology; nursing; occupational therapy assistant; physical therapy assistant; secretarial science; Web/multimedia management/webmaster; Web page, digital/multimedia and information resources design; word processing.
Academic Programs *Special study options:* academic remediation for entering students, adult/continuing education programs, advanced placement credit, English as a second language, internships, off-campus study, part-time degree program, services for LD students, study abroad, summer session for credit.
Library Riverland Community College Library plus 2 others with 33,500 titles, 278 serial subscriptions, an OPAC.
Computers on Campus 175 computers available on campus for general student use. A campuswide network can be accessed from student residence rooms. At least one staffed computer lab available.
Student Life *Activities and Organizations:* drama/theater group, student-run newspaper, choral group, College Choir, student newspaper, Student Activities Board, Phi Theta Kappa, Theater Club. *Campus security:* late-night transport/escort service. *Student Services:* personal/psychological counseling, women's center.
Athletics Member NJCAA. *Intercollegiate sports:* baseball M, basketball M/W, softball W, tennis M/W, volleyball W. *Intramural sports:* basketball M.
Standardized Tests *Required:* Academic Skills Assessment Program. *Recommended:* ACT (for placement).
Costs (2001–02) *Tuition:* state resident $2378 full-time; nonresident $5076 full-time. Full-time tuition and fees vary according to reciprocity agreements. Part-time tuition and fees vary according to reciprocity agreements. *Required fees:* $416 full-time. *Room and board:* room only: $2565. *Payment plan:* deferred payment. *Waivers:* adult students, senior citizens, and employees or children of employees.
Applying *Options:* early admission. *Application fee:* $20. *Required:* high school transcript. *Application deadline:* rolling (freshmen), rolling (transfers).
Admissions Contact Sharon Jahnke, Admission Secretary, Riverland Community College, 1900 8th Avenue NW, Austin, MN 55912. *Phone:* 507-433-0820. *Toll-free phone:* 800-247-5039. *Fax:* 507-433-0515. *E-mail:* duang@river.cc.mn.us.

ROCHESTER COMMUNITY AND TECHNICAL COLLEGE

Rochester, Minnesota

Admissions Contact Mr. Troy Tynsky, Director of Admissions, Rochester Community and Technical College, 851 30th Avenue, SE, Rochester, MN 55904-4999. *Phone:* 507-280-3509. *Fax:* 507-285-7496.

ST. CLOUD TECHNICAL COLLEGE

St. Cloud, Minnesota

- **State-supported** 2-year, founded 1948, part of Minnesota State Colleges and Universities System
- **Calendar** semesters
- **Degree** certificates, diplomas, and associate
- **Urban** 35-acre campus with easy access to Minneapolis-St. Paul
- **Coed,** 3,023 undergraduate students, 63% full-time, 47% women, 53% men

Undergraduates 1,902 full-time, 1,121 part-time. Students come from 5 states and territories, 10 other countries, 3% are from out of state, 0.7% African American, 1% Asian American or Pacific Islander, 0.3% Hispanic American, 0.6% Native American, 0.6% international, 10% transferred in.

Freshmen *Admission:* 2,942 applied, 1,417 admitted, 795 enrolled.

Faculty *Total:* 147, 71% full-time.

Majors Accounting; accounting technician; advertising; architectural drafting; architectural engineering technology; auto body repair; auto mechanic/technician; banking; business administration; business computer facilities operation; business computer programming; business marketing and marketing management; business systems networking/ telecommunications; carpentry; child care/development; child care/guidance; civil engineering technology; computer programming; computer programming related; computer/technical support; computer typography/composition; construction technology; culinary arts; dental assistant; dental hygiene; diagnostic medical sonography; diesel engine mechanic; early childhood education; electrical/electronic engineering technology; electrical/power transmission installation; emergency medical technology; finance; general retailing/wholesaling; graphic design/commercial art/illustration; graphic/printing equipment; heating/air conditioning/refrigeration; heating/air conditioning/refrigeration technology; information technology; instrumentation technology; legal administrative assistant; machine technology; mechanical design technology; mechanical drafting; medical administrative assistant; medical office management; office management; operating room technician; optometric/ophthalmic laboratory technician; plumbing; practical nurse; retail management; secretarial science; teacher assistant/aide; water treatment technology; welding technology; word processing.

Academic Programs *Special study options:* academic remediation for entering students, adult/continuing education programs, cooperative education, internships, part-time degree program, services for LD students, summer session for credit.

Library Learning Resource Center with 10,000 titles, 600 serial subscriptions, an OPAC.

Computers on Campus 350 computers available on campus for general student use. Internet access, online (class) registration, at least one staffed computer lab available.

Student Life *Housing:* college housing not available. *Activities and Organizations:* student-run newspaper, Student Senate, Distributive Education Club of America, Business Professionals of America, Child and Adult Care Education, Central Minnesota Builders Association. *Campus security:* late-night transport/escort service. *Student Services:* personal/psychological counseling, women's center.

Athletics *Intercollegiate sports:* basketball M/W, golf M/W, softball M/W, volleyball M/W.

Standardized Tests *Required:* ACT ASSET.

Costs (2001–02) *Tuition:* state resident $2340 full-time, $85 per credit part-time; nonresident $4680 full-time, $156 per credit part-time. Full-time tuition and fees vary according to reciprocity agreements. Part-time tuition and fees vary according to reciprocity agreements. *Required fees:* $211 full-time, $7 per credit. *Payment plan:* installment. *Waivers:* senior citizens and employees or children of employees.

Applying *Options:* early admission, deferred entrance. *Application fee:* $20. *Required:* high school transcript. *Recommended:* interview. *Application deadline:* 8/16 (freshmen). *Notification:* continuous until 8/24 (freshmen).

Admissions Contact Ms. Jodi Elness, Admissions Office, St. Cloud Technical College, 1540 Northway Drive, St. Cloud, MN 56303. *Phone:* 320-654-5089. *Toll-free phone:* 800-222-1009. *Fax:* 320-654-5981. *E-mail:* jme@cloud.tec.mn.us.

ST. PAUL TECHNICAL COLLEGE

St. Paul, Minnesota

- **State-related** 2-year, founded 1919, part of Minnesota State Colleges and Universities System
- **Calendar** semesters
- **Degree** certificates, diplomas, and associate
- **Urban** campus
- **Coed,** 5,381 undergraduate students, 26% full-time, 38% women, 62% men

Undergraduates 1,395 full-time, 3,986 part-time. 4% transferred in.

Freshmen *Admission:* 1,290 applied, 1,309 enrolled.

Faculty *Total:* 287, 34% full-time, 45% with terminal degrees.

Majors Accounting; child care/development; civil engineering technology; computer programming; electrical/electronic engineering technology; human resources management; industrial technology; international business; medical administrative assistant; medical laboratory technician; respiratory therapy; secretarial science; sign language interpretation.

Academic Programs *Special study options:* academic remediation for entering students, adult/continuing education programs, English as a second language, internships, services for LD students.

Library St. Paul Technical College Library with 12,000 titles, 110 serial subscriptions, 260 audiovisual materials, an OPAC.

Computers on Campus Internet access, at least one staffed computer lab available.

Student Life *Housing:* college housing not available. *Activities and Organizations:* Student Senate. *Campus security:* late-night transport/escort service. *Student Services:* personal/psychological counseling, women's center.

Standardized Tests *Required:* CPT, ACCUPLACER.

Costs (2001–02) *Tuition:* state resident $2325 full-time, $78 per credit part-time; nonresident $4650 full-time, $155 per credit part-time. *Required fees:* $234 full-time.

Financial Aid In 2001, 48 Federal Work-Study jobs (averaging $2500). 94 State and other part-time jobs (averaging $2500).

Applying *Options:* early admission. *Application fee:* $20. *Required for some:* high school transcript, interview. *Application deadline:* rolling (freshmen).

Admissions Contact Ms. Lisa Netzley, Admissions Counselor, St. Paul Technical College, 235 Marshall Avenue, St. Paul, MN 55102-1800. *Phone:* 651-221-1333. *Toll-free phone:* 800-227-6029. *Fax:* 651-221-1416. *E-mail:* admiss@stp.tec.mn.us.

SOUTH CENTRAL TECHNICAL COLLEGE

North Mankato, Minnesota

Admissions Contact Mr. David Johnson, Dean of Student Affairs, South Central Technical College, 1920 Lee Boulevard, North Mankato, MN 56003. *Phone:* 507-389-7231.

VERMILION COMMUNITY COLLEGE

Ely, Minnesota

- **State-supported** 2-year, founded 1922, part of Minnesota State Colleges and Universities System
- **Calendar** semesters
- **Degree** associate
- **Rural** 5-acre campus
- **Coed,** 986 undergraduate students, 70% full-time, 41% women, 59% men

Undergraduates Students come from 13 states and territories, 3 other countries, 50% live on campus.

Freshmen *Average high school GPA:* 2.8.

Faculty *Total:* 102, 31% full-time.

Majors Accounting; agricultural business; agricultural economics; agricultural education; agronomy/crop science; aircraft pilot (professional); architectural engineering technology; art; art education; art history; aviation/airway science; aviation management; biological/physical sciences; biology; business administration; business economics; chemistry; computer engineering technology; computer management; computer science; criminal justice/law enforcement administration; criminal justice studies; data processing technology; drawing; early childhood education; earth sciences; ecology; economics; education; elementary education; engineering; environmental education; environmental science; environmental technology; finance; fish/game management; food products retailing; forest harvesting production technology; forest management; forestry; forestry sciences;

geography; health education; history; home economics; human ecology; industrial arts; industrial technology; interdisciplinary studies; land use management; law enforcement/police science; liberal arts and sciences/liberal studies; mass communications; mathematics; medical administrative assistant; medical records administration; music; natural resources conservation; natural resources management; physical education; physical sciences; physics; political science; pre-engineering; psychology; range management; recreation/leisure facilities management; recreation/leisure studies; science education; sociology; soil conservation; speech/rhetorical studies; theater arts/drama; water resources; water treatment technology; wildlife biology; wildlife management.

Academic Programs *Special study options:* academic remediation for entering students, adult/continuing education programs, advanced placement credit, cooperative education, honors programs, internships, off-campus study, part-time degree program, services for LD students, summer session for credit.

Library Vermilion Community College Library with 19,500 titles, 100 serial subscriptions, an OPAC.

Computers on Campus 60 computers available on campus for general student use. A campuswide network can be accessed from student residence rooms and from off campus. At least one staffed computer lab available.

Student Life *Housing:* on-campus residence required for freshman year. *Options:* coed. *Activities and Organizations:* Student Life Committee, student government, Drama Club. *Campus security:* student patrols, late-night transport/escort service, controlled dormitory access. *Student Services:* personal/psychological counseling, women's center.

Athletics Member NJCAA. *Intercollegiate sports:* baseball M, basketball M/W, cross-country running M/W, football M, golf M/W, softball W, volleyball W. *Intramural sports:* basketball M/W, bowling M/W, cross-country running M/W, football M, golf M/W, ice hockey M, skiing (cross-country) M/W, skiing (downhill) M/W, softball M/W, tennis M/W, volleyball M/W, weight lifting M/W, wrestling M.

Standardized Tests *Recommended:* SAT I and SAT II or ACT (for placement).

Costs (2001–02) *Tuition:* state resident $2880 full-time, $96 per credit part-time; nonresident $5320 full-time, $177 per credit part-time. Full-time tuition and fees vary according to reciprocity agreements. Part-time tuition and fees vary according to reciprocity agreements. *Room and board:* $3960; room only: $2510.

Financial Aid In 2001, 210 Federal Work-Study jobs (averaging $1800). 50 State and other part-time jobs (averaging $1800).

Applying *Options:* common application, early admission, deferred entrance. *Application fee:* $20. *Required:* high school transcript. *Application deadline:* rolling (freshmen), rolling (transfers). *Notification:* continuous (freshmen).

Admissions Contact Mr. Doug Furnstahl, Director of Enrollment Services, Vermilion Community College, 1900 East Camp Street, Ely, MN 55731-1996. *Phone:* 218-365-7224. *Toll-free phone:* 800-657-3608.

MISSISSIPPI

ANTONELLI COLLEGE
Hattiesburg, Mississippi

Admissions Contact 1500 North 31st Avenue, Hattiesburg, MS 39401.

ANTONELLI COLLEGE
Jackson, Mississippi

- **Proprietary** 2-year
- **Calendar** quarters
- **Degree** diplomas and associate
- **Coed**

Admissions Contact Ms. Kim Perry, Senior Admissions Officer, Antonelli College, 480 East Woodrow Wilson Drive, Jackson, MS 39216. *Phone:* 601-362-9991.

COAHOMA COMMUNITY COLLEGE
Clarksdale, Mississippi

- **State and locally supported** 2-year, founded 1949, part of Mississippi State Board for Community and Junior Colleges
- **Calendar** semesters
- **Degree** certificates and associate
- **Small-town** 29-acre campus with easy access to Memphis
- **Coed,** 1,400 undergraduate students

Undergraduates Students come from 8 states and territories.

Faculty *Total:* 55, 55% full-time.

Majors Accounting; art; biology; business administration; chemistry; computer science; criminal justice/law enforcement administration; early childhood education; elementary education; English; health education; liberal arts and sciences/liberal studies; medical technology; radio/television broadcasting; secretarial science; social work; sport/fitness administration.

Academic Programs *Special study options:* adult/continuing education programs, part-time degree program.

Library Dickerson-Johnson Library.

Computers on Campus 25 computers available on campus for general student use. Internet access available.

Student Life *Activities and Organizations:* drama/theater group, student-run newspaper, choral group, marching band, Student Government Association, VICA, Phi Theta Kappa Honor Society. *Campus security:* 24-hour patrols. *Student Services:* health clinic, personal/psychological counseling.

Athletics Member NJCAA. *Intercollegiate sports:* basketball M(s)/W(s), track and field M(s).

Standardized Tests *Required:* SAT I or ACT (for placement).

Costs (2001–02) *Tuition:* state resident $1300 full-time, $78 per credit hour part-time; nonresident $3200 full-time, $142 per credit hour part-time. *Required fees:* $60 full-time, $30 per term. *Room and board:* $2844. *Payment plan:* installment. *Waivers:* employees or children of employees.

Applying *Options:* common application. *Required:* high school transcript. *Application deadline:* rolling (freshmen), rolling (transfers). *Notification:* continuous (freshmen).

Admissions Contact Mrs. Wanda Holmes, Director of Admissions and Records, Coahoma Community College, Route 1, PO Box 616, Clarksdale, MS 38614-9799. *Phone:* 662-621-4205. *Toll-free phone:* 800-844-1222.

COPIAH-LINCOLN COMMUNITY COLLEGE
Wesson, Mississippi

Admissions Contact Dr. Michael McInnis, Registrar, Copiah-Lincoln Community College, PO Box 371, Wesson, MS 39191-0457. *Phone:* 601-643-8307.

COPIAH-LINCOLN COMMUNITY COLLEGE-NATCHEZ CAMPUS
Natchez, Mississippi

- **State and locally supported** 2-year, founded 1972, part of Mississippi State Board for Community and Junior Colleges
- **Calendar** semesters
- **Degree** certificates and associate
- **Small-town** 24-acre campus
- **Coed,** 312 undergraduate students, 90% full-time, 65% women, 35% men

Undergraduates 280 full-time, 32 part-time. Students come from 4 states and territories.

Freshmen *Admission:* 312 applied, 312 admitted, 312 enrolled.

Faculty *Total:* 45, 47% full-time, 100% with terminal degrees. *Student/faculty ratio:* 20:1.

Majors Business marketing and marketing management; elementary education; forestry; general studies; home economics; hotel and restaurant management; instrumentation technology; liberal arts and sciences/liberal studies; political science; respiratory therapy; secretarial science.

Academic Programs *Special study options:* academic remediation for entering students, adult/continuing education programs, advanced placement credit, distance learning, internships, part-time degree program, student-designed majors, summer session for credit.

Library Willie Mae Dunn Library with 19,000 titles, 112 serial subscriptions, 700 audiovisual materials, an OPAC, a Web page.

Computers on Campus 175 computers available on campus for general student use. A campuswide network can be accessed from off campus. Internet access, at least one staffed computer lab available.

Student Life *Housing:* college housing not available. *Activities and Organizations:* student-run newspaper, student newspaper. *Campus security:* 24-hour patrols.

Athletics Member NJCAA.

Standardized Tests *Required for some:* ACT (for admission).

Copiah-Lincoln Community College-Natchez Campus (continued)

Costs (2002–03) *Tuition:* area resident $1400 full-time, $85 per semester hour part-time; state resident $1400 full-time, $85 per semester hour part-time; nonresident $3000 full-time, $145 per semester hour part-time. *Required fees:* $105 full-time, $5 per semester hour. *Room and board:* $3000.

Financial Aid In 2001, 150 Federal Work-Study jobs.

Applying *Options:* early admission. *Required:* high school transcript. *Application deadline:* rolling (freshmen), rolling (transfers). *Notification:* continuous (freshmen).

Admissions Contact Mrs. Gwen S. McCalip, Director of Admissions and Records, Copiah-Lincoln Community College-Natchez Campus, 11 Co-Lin Circle, Natchez, MS 39120. *Phone:* 601-442-9111 Ext. 224. *Fax:* 601-446-1222. *E-mail:* gwen.mccalip@colin.cc.ms.us.

EAST CENTRAL COMMUNITY COLLEGE
Decatur, Mississippi

- **State and locally supported** 2-year, founded 1928, part of Mississippi State Board for Community and Junior Colleges
- **Calendar** semesters
- **Degree** certificates and associate
- **Rural** 200-acre campus
- **Coed,** 2,382 undergraduate students

Undergraduates Students come from 9 states and territories, 2% are from out of state, 27% live on campus.

Faculty *Total:* 144, 55% full-time.

Majors Accounting; art; art education; behavioral sciences; biological/physical sciences; biology; business administration; carpentry; chemistry; computer science; cosmetology; data processing technology; drafting; drawing; early childhood education; economics; education; electrical/electronic engineering technology; elementary education; engineering; English; health education; history; journalism; liberal arts and sciences/liberal studies; library science; literature; mathematics; medical records administration; music; music teacher education; nursing; occupational therapy; pharmacy; physical sciences; physical therapy; political science; pre-engineering; psychology; science education; social sciences.

Academic Programs *Special study options:* academic remediation for entering students, adult/continuing education programs, advanced placement credit, honors programs, part-time degree program, services for LD students, summer session for credit.

Library Burton Library.

Computers on Campus 80 computers available on campus for general student use. A campuswide network can be accessed from off campus. At least one staffed computer lab available.

Student Life *Housing Options:* men-only, women-only. *Activities and Organizations:* drama/theater group, student-run newspaper, choral group, marching band. *Campus security:* 24-hour patrols. *Student Services:* health clinic, personal/psychological counseling.

Athletics Member NJCAA. *Intercollegiate sports:* baseball M, basketball M(s)/W(s), football M(s), golf M(s)/W, softball W(s), tennis M/W. *Intramural sports:* basketball M/W, football M/W, table tennis M/W, volleyball M/W.

Standardized Tests *Required:* ACT (for placement).

Costs (2002–03) *Tuition:* area resident $1400 full-time, $65 per hour part-time; nonresident $1400 full-time. *Room and board:* $2540; room only: $910. *Waivers:* senior citizens and employees or children of employees.

Financial Aid In 2001, 86 Federal Work-Study jobs (averaging $850). 30 State and other part-time jobs (averaging $1090).

Applying *Options:* common application, early admission. *Required:* high school transcript. *Application deadline:* rolling (freshmen). *Notification:* continuous (freshmen).

Admissions Contact Mrs. Donna Luke, Director of Admissions, Records, and Research, East Central Community College, PO Box 129, Decatur, MS 39327-0129. *Phone:* 601-635-2111 Ext. 206. *Toll-free phone:* 877-462-3222. *Fax:* 601-635-2150.

EAST MISSISSIPPI COMMUNITY COLLEGE
Scooba, Mississippi

- **State and locally supported** 2-year, founded 1927, part of Mississippi State Board for Community and Junior Colleges
- **Calendar** semesters
- **Degree** certificates and associate
- **Rural** 25-acre campus
- **Endowment** $114,880
- **Coed,** 3,009 undergraduate students, 59% full-time, 57% women, 43% men

Undergraduates 1,786 full-time, 1,223 part-time. 4% are from out of state, 25% live on campus.

Freshmen *Admission:* 411 enrolled. *Test scores:* ACT scores over 18: 32%; ACT scores over 24: 5%; ACT scores over 30: 1%.

Faculty *Total:* 188, 45% full-time.

Majors Accounting; art; auto mechanic/technician; banking; biological/physical sciences; business administration; business education; computer programming; computer science; cosmetology; criminal justice/law enforcement administration; drafting; economics; education; electrical/electronic engineering technology; elementary education; English; fire science; forest harvesting production technology; general office/clerical; health education; history; hotel and restaurant management; instrumentation technology; liberal arts and sciences/liberal studies; mathematics; mortuary science; music; optometric/ophthalmic laboratory technician; pre-engineering; psychology; reading education; real estate; secretarial science; social sciences; sociology.

Academic Programs *Special study options:* academic remediation for entering students, adult/continuing education programs, advanced placement credit, cooperative education, distance learning, honors programs, part-time degree program, services for LD students, summer session for credit.

Library Tubb-May Library with 26,731 titles, 116 serial subscriptions, 3,371 audiovisual materials, an OPAC, a Web page.

Computers on Campus 100 computers available on campus for general student use. A campuswide network can be accessed from off campus. Internet access available.

Student Life *Housing Options:* men-only, women-only. *Activities and Organizations:* drama/theater group, student-run newspaper, choral group, marching band. *Campus security:* 24-hour emergency response devices and patrols. *Student Services:* personal/psychological counseling.

Athletics Member NJCAA. *Intercollegiate sports:* baseball M(s), basketball M(s)/W(s), football M(s), golf M(s), softball W(s). *Intramural sports:* basketball M/W, football M, golf M, gymnastics M/W, tennis M/W.

Standardized Tests *Required:* ACT required for students under age 21.

Costs (2001–02) *Tuition:* state resident $1100 full-time, $70 per semester hour part-time; nonresident $2850 full-time, $74 per semester hour part-time. *Required fees:* $160 full-time, $30 per term part-time. *Room and board:* $2210. Room and board charges vary according to board plan. *Payment plan:* installment. *Waivers:* employees or children of employees.

Financial Aid In 2001, 120 Federal Work-Study jobs (averaging $1200).

Applying *Options:* common application, electronic application, deferred entrance. *Required:* high school transcript. *Application deadline:* rolling (freshmen), rolling (transfers).

Admissions Contact Ms. Melinda Sciple, Admissions Officer, East Mississippi Community College, PO Box 158, Scooba, MS 39358-0158. *Phone:* 662-476-8442 Ext. 221.

HINDS COMMUNITY COLLEGE
Raymond, Mississippi

- **State and locally supported** 2-year, founded 1917, part of Mississippi State Board for Community and Junior Colleges
- **Calendar** semesters
- **Degree** certificates, diplomas, and associate
- **Small-town** 671-acre campus
- **Endowment** $948,556
- **Coed,** 14,390 undergraduate students

Undergraduates Students come from 16 states and territories, 1 other country, 3% are from out of state, 15% live on campus.

Freshmen *Average high school GPA:* 2.7.

Faculty *Total:* 905, 42% full-time, 8% with terminal degrees. *Student/faculty ratio:* 17:1.

Majors Accounting; agricultural business; agricultural economics; agricultural education; agricultural mechanization; agronomy/crop science; art; aviation technology; biology; business administration; business marketing and marketing management; carpentry; child care/development; civil engineering technology; clothing/textiles; computer graphics; computer programming; computer programming related; computer science; computer science related; computer/technical support; criminal justice/law enforcement administration; data entry/microcomputer applications; data entry/microcomputer applications related; data processing technology; dental hygiene; developmental/child psychology; dietetics; drafting;

economics; electrical/electronic engineering technology; emergency medical technology; English; fashion design/illustration; finance; food products retailing; food services technology; graphic design/commercial art/illustration; graphic/printing equipment; home economics; hotel and restaurant management; humanities; industrial arts; industrial radiologic technology; information technology; journalism; landscaping management; law enforcement/police science; liberal arts and sciences/liberal studies; machine technology; mass communications; mathematics; medical laboratory technician; medical records administration; music; nursing; operating room technician; paralegal/legal assistant; political science; postal management; practical nurse; pre-engineering; psychology; public administration; real estate; respiratory therapy; secretarial science; social sciences; sociology; system administration; system/networking/LAN/WAN management; telecommunications; theater arts/drama; veterinary sciences; veterinary technology; welding technology.

Academic Programs *Special study options:* academic remediation for entering students, accelerated degree program, adult/continuing education programs, advanced placement credit, cooperative education, distance learning, double majors, freshman honors college, honors programs, independent study, part-time degree program, services for LD students, summer session for credit. *ROTC:* Army (c).

Library McLendon Library with 165,260 titles, 1,178 serial subscriptions, an OPAC.

Computers on Campus 55 computers available on campus for general student use. Internet access, online (class) registration, at least one staffed computer lab available.

Student Life *Housing Options:* men-only, women-only. *Activities and Organizations:* drama/theater group, student-run newspaper, choral group, marching band, Phi Theta Kappa, Baptist Student Union, Residence Hall Association, Hi-Steppers Dance Team, band. *Campus security:* 24-hour emergency response devices and patrols, controlled dormitory access. *Student Services:* personal/psychological counseling, women's center.

Athletics Member NJCAA. *Intercollegiate sports:* baseball M(s), basketball M(s)/W(s), cross-country running M(s), football M(s), golf M(s), soccer M(s), softball W(s), tennis M(s)/W(s), track and field M(s). *Intramural sports:* basketball M/W, football M/W, softball M/W, volleyball M/W.

Standardized Tests *Required for some:* SAT I and SAT II or ACT (for admission).

Costs (2001–02) *Tuition:* area resident $1120 full-time, $60 per credit part-time; nonresident $3326 full-time, $140 per credit part-time. Full-time tuition and fees vary according to course load. Part-time tuition and fees vary according to course load. *Required fees:* $50 full-time. *Room and board:* $2160. Room and board charges vary according to board plan. *Payment plan:* deferred payment. *Waivers:* senior citizens and employees or children of employees.

Financial Aid In 2001, 300 Federal Work-Study jobs (averaging $1250). 200 State and other part-time jobs (averaging $1000).

Applying *Options:* common application, early admission. *Required:* high school transcript. *Application deadline:* rolling (freshmen), rolling (transfers). *Notification:* continuous (freshmen).

Admissions Contact Mr. Jay Allen, Director of Admissions and Records, Hinds Community College, PO Box 1100, Raymond, MS 39154-1100. *Phone:* 601-857-3280. *Toll-free phone:* 800-HINDSCC. *Fax:* 601-857-3539.

HOLMES COMMUNITY COLLEGE
Goodman, Mississippi

- **State and locally supported** 2-year, founded 1928, part of Mississippi State Board for Community and Junior Colleges
- **Calendar** semesters
- **Degree** certificates and associate
- **Small-town** 196-acre campus
- **Endowment** $2.1 million
- **Coed,** 3,252 undergraduate students

Undergraduates Students come from 13 states and territories, 1 other country, 20% live on campus.

Freshmen *Admission:* 1,925 admitted.

Faculty *Total:* 125, 80% full-time. *Student/faculty ratio:* 18:1.

Majors Agricultural sciences; biology; business administration; business education; child care/development; computer science; computer science related; computer/technical support; data processing technology; drafting; elementary education; engineering; finance; forestry; liberal arts and sciences/liberal studies; medical records administration; medical technology; music teacher education; nursing; pharmacy; physical therapy; radio/television broadcasting; respiratory therapy; science education; secretarial science; social work; system/networking/LAN/WAN management; veterinary sciences; wildlife biology.

Academic Programs *Special study options:* academic remediation for entering students, adult/continuing education programs, advanced placement credit, cooperative education, distance learning, services for LD students, summer session for credit.

Library McMorrough Library plus 2 others with 53,000 titles, 550 serial subscriptions, an OPAC.

Computers on Campus 150 computers available on campus for general student use. A campuswide network can be accessed from off campus. Internet access, online (class) registration, at least one staffed computer lab available.

Student Life *Activities and Organizations:* drama/theater group, student-run newspaper, choral group, marching band, Student Government Association, Drama/Theater Club, Baptist Student Union, FCA, Vocational Industrial Clubs of America. *Campus security:* 24-hour emergency response devices and patrols. *Student Services:* personal/psychological counseling.

Athletics Member NJCAA. *Intercollegiate sports:* baseball M(s), basketball M(s)/W, cross-country running M/W, football M(s), golf M(s)/W(s), soccer M(s)/W(s), softball W(s), tennis M(s)/W(s), track and field M(s)/W(s). *Intramural sports:* basketball M/W, football M/W, softball M/W, volleyball M/W.

Standardized Tests *Required:* ACT (for placement).

Costs (2002–03) *Tuition:* area resident $1428 full-time, $65 per semester hour part-time. Part-time tuition and fees vary according to course load. *Required fees:* $260 full-time, $10 per term part-time. *Room and board:* $1100; room only: $800. *Payment plan:* installment. *Waivers:* employees or children of employees.

Financial Aid In 2001, 160 Federal Work-Study jobs (averaging $700).

Applying *Options:* early admission. *Required:* high school transcript. *Application deadline:* rolling (freshmen), rolling (transfers). *Notification:* continuous (freshmen).

Admissions Contact Mr. Gene Richardson, Director of Admissions and Records, Holmes Community College, PO Box 369, Goodman, MS 39079-0369. *Phone:* 601-472-2312 Ext. 23.

ITAWAMBA COMMUNITY COLLEGE
Fulton, Mississippi

Admissions Contact Mr. Max Munn, Director of Recruiting, Itawamba Community College, 602 West Hill Street, Fulton, MS 38843. *Phone:* 601-862-8252.

JONES COUNTY JUNIOR COLLEGE
Ellisville, Mississippi

- **State and locally supported** 2-year, founded 1928, part of Mississippi State Board for Community and Junior Colleges
- **Calendar** semesters
- **Degree** certificates and associate
- **Small-town** 360-acre campus
- **Coed,** 5,025 undergraduate students

Undergraduates Students come from 9 states and territories, 19% African American, 1% Native American, 20% live on campus.

Faculty *Total:* 175.

Majors Accounting; agricultural sciences; applied art; art education; biological/physical sciences; biology; business administration; chemistry; child care/development; data processing technology; drafting; economics; education; electrical/electronic engineering technology; emergency medical technology; engineering science; English; forest harvesting production technology; home economics; home economics education; horticulture science; law enforcement/police science; mathematics; music; music teacher education; music (voice and choral/opera performance); nursing; physical education; physical sciences; practical nurse; science education.

Academic Programs *Special study options:* academic remediation for entering students, advanced placement credit, cooperative education, distance learning, honors programs, part-time degree program, summer session for credit. *ROTC:* Army (c), Air Force (c).

Library Memorial Library with 62,349 titles, 654 serial subscriptions.

Computers on Campus 600 computers available on campus for general student use. Internet access, at least one staffed computer lab available.

Student Life *Housing Options:* men-only, women-only. *Activities and Organizations:* drama/theater group, student-run newspaper, choral group, marching band, student government. *Campus security:* 24-hour patrols. *Student Services:* health clinic, personal/psychological counseling.

Athletics Member NJCAA. *Intercollegiate sports:* baseball M, basketball M(s)/W(s), football M(s), golf M, soccer M/W, softball W, tennis M/W, track and field M. *Intramural sports:* basketball M/W, tennis M/W, volleyball M/W.

Jones County Junior College (continued)

Standardized Tests *Required:* SAT I or ACT (for admission).

Costs (2001–02) *Tuition:* state resident $1048 full-time, $60 per semester hour part-time; nonresident $2948 full-time, $144 per semester hour part-time. *Required fees:* $90 full-time, $45 per term part-time. *Room and board:* $2472.

Applying *Options:* common application, early admission. *Required:* high school transcript. *Application deadlines:* 8/25 (freshmen), 8/25 (transfers). *Notification:* continuous (freshmen).

Admissions Contact Mrs. Dianne Speed, Director of Admissions, Jones County Junior College, 900 South Court Street, Ellisville, MS 39437. *Phone:* 601-477-4025. *Fax:* 601-477-4258.

MARY HOLMES COLLEGE
West Point, Mississippi

- **Independent Presbyterian** 2-year, founded 1892
- **Calendar** semesters
- **Degree** certificates and associate
- **Rural** 192-acre campus
- **Coed**
- 24% of applicants were admitted

Athletics Member NJCAA.

Costs (2001–02) *Comprehensive fee:* $7990 includes full-time tuition ($4000), mandatory fees ($100), and room and board ($3890). Part-time tuition: $134 per credit hour. *Room and board:* College room only: $1890.

Applying *Options:* early admission. *Required:* high school transcript, 2 letters of recommendation.

Admissions Contact Dr. August Milton, Vice President Student Affairs, Mary Holmes College, Highway 50 West, PO Drawer 1257, West Point, MS 39773-1257. *Phone:* 662-494-6820 Ext. 3138. *Toll-free phone:* 800-634-2749. *Fax:* 662-494-1881.

MERIDIAN COMMUNITY COLLEGE
Meridian, Mississippi

- **State and locally supported** 2-year, founded 1937, part of Mississippi State Board for Community and Junior Colleges
- **Calendar** semesters
- **Degree** certificates and associate
- **Small-town** 62-acre campus
- **Coed,** 3,248 undergraduate students, 74% full-time, 69% women, 31% men

Undergraduates 2,401 full-time, 847 part-time. Students come from 16 states and territories, 3% are from out of state, 12% live on campus.

Freshmen *Admission:* 748 applied, 748 admitted.

Faculty *Total:* 250, 56% full-time, 3% with terminal degrees.

Majors Athletic training/sports medicine; broadcast journalism; business marketing and marketing management; computer engineering technology; computer graphics; dental hygiene; drafting; electrical/electronic engineering technology; emergency medical technology; fire science; horticulture science; hotel and restaurant management; machine technology; medical laboratory technician; medical radiologic technology; medical records administration; nursing; physical therapy; respiratory therapy; secretarial science; telecommunications.

Academic Programs *Special study options:* academic remediation for entering students, adult/continuing education programs, advanced placement credit, cooperative education, part-time degree program, services for LD students, summer session for credit.

Library L.O. Todd Library with 50,000 titles, 600 serial subscriptions.

Computers on Campus 123 computers available on campus for general student use.

Student Life *Housing Options:* coed, men-only, women-only. *Activities and Organizations:* drama/theater group, student-run newspaper, radio station, choral group, Phi Theta Kappa, Vocational Industrial Clubs of America, Health Occupations Students of America, Organization of Student Nurses, Distributive Education Clubs of America. *Campus security:* 24-hour patrols, student patrols. *Student Services:* health clinic, personal/psychological counseling.

Athletics Member NJCAA. *Intercollegiate sports:* baseball M(s), basketball M(s)/W(s), cross-country running M(s)/W(s), golf M(s), soccer M(s), softball W(s), tennis M(s)/W(s), track and field M(s)/W(s). *Intramural sports:* basketball M/W, bowling M/W, cross-country running M/W, swimming M/W, tennis M/W, volleyball M/W.

Standardized Tests *Required:* SAT I or ACT (for placement). *Recommended:* ACCUPLACER.

Costs (2002–03) *Tuition:* area resident $600 full-time; state resident $65 per hour part-time; nonresident $1320 full-time, $132 per hour part-time. *Required fees:* $51 full-time, $27 per hour. *Room and board:* $1575; room only: $875.

Financial Aid In 2001, 100 Federal Work-Study jobs (averaging $1100).

Applying *Options:* early admission. *Required:* high school transcript, minimum 2.0 GPA. *Required for some:* essay or personal statement. *Application deadline:* rolling (freshmen), rolling (transfers).

Admissions Contact Ms. Mary Faye Wilson, Director of Admissions, Meridian Community College, 910 Highway 19 North, Meridian, MS 39307. *Phone:* 601-484-8621. *Toll-free phone:* 800-622-8731. *E-mail:* dwalton@mcc.cc.ms.us.

MISSISSIPPI DELTA COMMUNITY COLLEGE
Moorhead, Mississippi

- **District-supported** 2-year, founded 1926, part of Mississippi State Board for Community and Junior Colleges
- **Calendar** semesters
- **Degree** certificates, diplomas, and associate
- **Small-town** 425-acre campus
- **Coed,** 2,956 undergraduate students

Undergraduates Students come from 6 states and territories, 25% live on campus.

Freshmen *Admission:* 909 applied, 909 admitted. *Test scores:* ACT scores over 18: 35%; ACT scores over 24: 5%.

Faculty *Total:* 130, 69% full-time.

Majors Accounting; advertising; agricultural business; agricultural economics; American studies; applied art; architectural engineering technology; art education; behavioral sciences; biology; business machine repair; civil engineering technology; computer engineering technology; criminal justice/law enforcement administration; developmental/child psychology; economics; education; electrical/electronic engineering technology; elementary education; English; geography; graphic/printing equipment; health education; history; home economics; horticulture science; liberal arts and sciences/liberal studies; management information systems/business data processing; masonry/tile setting; mathematics; medical laboratory technician; medical radiologic technology; medical records administration; music; music teacher education; nursing; physical education; political science; science education; secretarial science; social work; theater arts/drama.

Academic Programs *Special study options:* academic remediation for entering students, adult/continuing education programs, advanced placement credit, part-time degree program, summer session for credit.

Library Stanny Sanders Library with 33,020 titles, 250 serial subscriptions, an OPAC.

Computers on Campus 80 computers available on campus for general student use. Internet access, at least one staffed computer lab available.

Student Life *Activities and Organizations:* drama/theater group, student-run newspaper, choral group, marching band. *Campus security:* 24-hour emergency response devices and patrols, late-night transport/escort service. *Student Services:* personal/psychological counseling.

Athletics Member NJCAA. *Intercollegiate sports:* baseball M(s), basketball M(s)/W(s), football M(s), golf M(s), soccer M, tennis M/W, track and field M. *Intramural sports:* badminton M/W, basketball M/W, football M/W, golf M/W, tennis M/W, track and field M/W, volleyball M/W.

Standardized Tests *Required for some:* ACT (for admission).

Costs (2001–02) *Tuition:* state resident $1250 full-time, $60 per semester hour part-time; nonresident $2054 full-time, $60 per semester hour part-time. Full-time tuition and fees vary according to course load and program. Part-time tuition and fees vary according to course load and program. *Room and board:* $1690. *Payment plans:* installment, deferred payment.

Applying *Options:* deferred entrance. *Required:* high school transcript. *Application deadlines:* 7/27 (freshmen), 7/27 (transfers).

Admissions Contact Mr. Joseph F. Ray Jr., Dean of Admissions, Mississippi Delta Community College, PO Box 668, Moorhead, MS 38761-0668. *Phone:* 662-246-6308.

MISSISSIPPI GULF COAST COMMUNITY COLLEGE
Perkinston, Mississippi

- **District-supported** 2-year, founded 1911, part of Mississippi State Board for Community and Junior Colleges

- **Calendar** semesters
- **Degree** certificates, diplomas, and associate
- **Small-town** 600-acre campus with easy access to New Orleans
- **Endowment** $3.1 million
- **Coed,** 8,944 undergraduate students, 62% full-time, 60% women, 40% men

Undergraduates 5,543 full-time, 3,401 part-time. Students come from 15 states and territories, 4% are from out of state, 7% live on campus. *Retention:* 55% of 2001 full-time freshmen returned.
Freshmen *Admission:* 2,723 applied, 2,723 admitted, 2,607 enrolled.
Faculty *Total:* 348, 85% full-time.
Majors Accounting; advertising; agricultural business; art; art education; auto mechanic/technician; biological/physical sciences; business administration; business education; business marketing and marketing management; chemical engineering technology; computer engineering technology; computer graphics; computer programming related; computer science; computer science related; computer systems networking/telecommunications; court reporting; criminal justice/law enforcement administration; data entry/microcomputer applications; data entry/microcomputer applications related; drafting; early childhood education; education; electrical/electronic engineering technology; elementary education; emergency medical technology; fashion merchandising; finance; horticulture science; hotel and restaurant management; human services; industrial radiologic technology; information technology; law enforcement/police science; liberal arts and sciences/liberal studies; medical laboratory technician; nursing; ornamental horticulture; paralegal/legal assistant; postal management; pre-engineering; respiratory therapy; secretarial science; welding technology; word processing.
Academic Programs *Special study options:* academic remediation for entering students, adult/continuing education programs, advanced placement credit, cooperative education, distance learning, English as a second language, honors programs, internships, part-time degree program, services for LD students, summer session for credit.
Library Main Library plus 3 others with 100,472 titles, 933 serial subscriptions, an OPAC.
Computers on Campus 435 computers available on campus for general student use. A campuswide network can be accessed from student residence rooms. At least one staffed computer lab available.
Student Life *Housing Options:* men-only, women-only. *Activities and Organizations:* drama/theater group, student-run newspaper, choral group, marching band, VICA, SIFE, Student Government Association. *Campus security:* 24-hour emergency response devices and patrols. *Student Services:* personal/psychological counseling, women's center.
Athletics Member NJCAA. *Intercollegiate sports:* baseball M(s), basketball M(s)/W(s), football M(s), golf M(s), soccer M(s)/W(s), softball W(s), tennis M(s)/W(s), track and field M(s). *Intramural sports:* basketball M/W, football M, soccer M/W, softball M/W, volleyball M/W.
Standardized Tests *Required for some:* ACT (for placement).
Costs (2002–03) *Tuition:* state resident $1090 full-time, $65 per semester hour part-time; nonresident $2936 full-time, $142 per semester hour part-time. *Required fees:* $142 full-time. *Room and board:* $1960; room only: $770. Room and board charges vary according to board plan. *Payment plan:* installment. *Waivers:* senior citizens and employees or children of employees.
Applying *Options:* common application, electronic application, early admission. *Required:* high school transcript. *Application deadline:* rolling (freshmen), rolling (transfers). *Notification:* continuous (freshmen).
Admissions Contact Ms. Michell e Sekul, Director of Admissions, Mississippi Gulf Coast Community College, PO Box 548, Perkinston, MS 39573. *Phone:* 601-928-6264. *Toll-free phone:* 601-928-6345. *E-mail:* ann.provis@mgccc.cc.ms.uc.

NORTHEAST MISSISSIPPI COMMUNITY COLLEGE
Booneville, Mississippi

Admissions Contact Mr. Ronnie Sweeney, Director of Admissions and Records, Northeast Mississippi Community College, 101 Cunningham Boulevard, Booneville, MS 38829. *Phone:* 662-728-7751 Ext. 239. *Toll-free phone:* 800-555-2154.

NORTHWEST MISSISSIPPI COMMUNITY COLLEGE
Senatobia, Mississippi

- **State and locally supported** 2-year, founded 1927, part of Mississippi State Board for Community and Junior Colleges
- **Calendar** semesters
- **Degree** associate
- **Rural** 75-acre campus with easy access to Memphis
- **Coed,** 5,000 undergraduate students

Freshmen *Admission:* 2,000 applied, 2,000 admitted.
Faculty *Total:* 200. *Student/faculty ratio:* 20:1.
Majors Accounting; agricultural business; agricultural economics; agricultural mechanization; agricultural sciences; animal sciences; art; business administration; business computer programming; civil engineering technology; computer/information sciences; computer programming; court reporting; dairy science; data processing technology; drafting; education; electrical/electronic engineering technology; elementary education; fashion merchandising; graphic design/commercial art/illustration; heating/air conditioning/refrigeration; heating/air conditioning/refrigeration technology; home economics education; hotel and restaurant management; journalism; liberal arts and sciences/liberal studies; machine technology; marketing/distribution education; mathematics education; medical administrative assistant; music teacher education; nursing; nutrition science; office management; paralegal/legal assistant; physical education; plant sciences; poultry science; practical nurse; radio/television broadcasting; radio/television broadcasting technology; respiratory therapy; science education; social science education; social studies education; speech education; telecommunications.
Academic Programs *Special study options:* academic remediation for entering students, adult/continuing education programs, honors programs, part-time degree program, services for LD students, summer session for credit. *ROTC:* Air Force (b).
Library R. C. Pugh Library with 38,000 titles, 325 serial subscriptions.
Computers on Campus 50 computers available on campus for general student use.
Student Life *Activities and Organizations:* drama/theater group, student-run newspaper, radio station, choral group, marching band. *Campus security:* 24-hour emergency response devices, late-night transport/escort service, controlled dormitory access. *Student Services:* health clinic.
Athletics Member NJCAA. *Intercollegiate sports:* baseball M, basketball M(s)/W(s), equestrian sports M(s)/W(s), football M(s), golf M, softball W(s), tennis M(s)/W(s). *Intramural sports:* basketball M/W, football M.
Standardized Tests *Required:* ACT (for placement).
Costs (2001–02) *Tuition:* area resident $1200 full-time, $55 per semester hour part-time; nonresident $2000 full-time, $100 per semester hour part-time. *Room and board:* $2200. Room and board charges vary according to board plan, gender, and housing facility. *Waivers:* employees or children of employees.
Applying *Options:* common application, early admission, deferred entrance. *Required:* high school transcript. *Application deadlines:* 9/7 (freshmen), 9/7 (transfers). *Notification:* continuous (freshmen).
Admissions Contact Ms. Deanna Ferguson, Director of Admissions and Recruiting, Northwest Mississippi Community College, 4975 Highway 51 North, Senatobia, MS 38668-1701. *Phone:* 662-562-3222.

PEARL RIVER COMMUNITY COLLEGE
Poplarville, Mississippi

Admissions Contact Mr. J. Dow Ford, Director of Admissions, Pearl River Community College, 101 Highway 11 North, Poplarville, MS 39470. *Phone:* 601-795-6801 Ext. 216. *E-mail:* jdowford@teclink.net.

SOUTHWEST MISSISSIPPI COMMUNITY COLLEGE
Summit, Mississippi

- **State and locally supported** 2-year, founded 1918, part of Mississippi State Board for Community and Junior Colleges
- **Calendar** semesters
- **Degree** certificates and associate
- **Rural** 701-acre campus
- **Coed,** 1,772 undergraduate students, 82% full-time, 64% women, 36% men

Undergraduates Students come from 6 states and territories, 10% are from out of state, 42% African American, 0.1% Hispanic American, 35% live on campus.
Faculty *Total:* 94, 87% full-time, 6% with terminal degrees. *Student/faculty ratio:* 25:1.
Majors Accounting; advertising; auto mechanic/technician; biological/physical sciences; biology; business administration; business education; business marketing and marketing management; carpentry; chemistry; computer programming

Southwest Mississippi Community College (continued)
related; computer science; construction technology; cosmetology; education; electrical/electronic engineering technology; elementary education; emergency medical technology; engineering; English; fashion merchandising; finance; health science; history; humanities; information technology; legal administrative assistant; liberal arts and sciences/liberal studies; machine technology; music; music teacher education; nursing; physical education; physical sciences; secretarial science; social sciences; system/networking/LAN/WAN management; welding technology.

Academic Programs *Special study options:* academic remediation for entering students, adult/continuing education programs, distance learning, part-time degree program, summer session for credit.

Library Library Learning Resources Center (LLRC) with 34,000 titles, 150 serial subscriptions, an OPAC.

Computers on Campus 300 computers available on campus for general student use. A campuswide network can be accessed from off campus. Internet access, online (class) registration, at least one staffed computer lab available.

Student Life *Activities and Organizations:* student-run newspaper, choral group, marching band. *Campus security:* 24-hour patrols.

Athletics Member NJCAA. *Intercollegiate sports:* baseball M, basketball M(s)/W(s), football M(s), golf M, softball W, tennis M/W. *Intramural sports:* basketball M/W.

Standardized Tests *Required for some:* ACT (for placement).

Costs (2001–02) *Tuition:* area resident $1150 full-time; state resident $1170 full-time, $60 per semester hour part-time; nonresident $2950 full-time, $135 per semester hour part-time. *Required fees:* $50 full-time, $25 per term part-time. *Room and board:* $1900. *Waivers:* senior citizens.

Financial Aid In 2001, 85 Federal Work-Study jobs (averaging $698). 6 State and other part-time jobs (averaging $550).

Applying *Required:* high school transcript. *Application deadlines:* 8/1 (freshmen), 8/1 (transfers).

Admissions Contact Mr. R. Glenn Shoemake, Director of Admissions, Southwest Mississippi Community College, College Drive, Summit, MS 39666. *Phone:* 601-276-2000. *Fax:* 601-276-3888.

VIRGINIA COLLEGE AT JACKSON
Jackson, Mississippi

- **Proprietary** 2-year
- **Calendar** quarters
- **Degree** diplomas and associate
- **Coed,** 500 undergraduate students

Faculty *Total:* 45. *Student/faculty ratio:* 11:1.

Majors Accounting related; administrative/secretarial services; computer systems networking/telecommunications; educational media technology; human resources management; medical assistant; medical office management; medical records administration; secretarial science.

Student Life *Housing:* college housing not available. *Campus security:* 24-hour patrols.

Costs (2001–02) *Payment plan:* installment.

Applying *Application fee:* $100.

Admissions Contact 5360 I-55 North, Jackson, MS 39211.

WOOD COLLEGE
Mathiston, Mississippi

Admissions Contact Mrs. Teressa Hooper, Director of Admissions, Wood College, PO Box 289, Mathiston, MS 39752-0289. *Phone:* 601-263-5352 Ext. 35. *Fax:* 601-263-8064.

MISSOURI

BLUE RIVER COMMUNITY COLLEGE
Blue Springs, Missouri

- **State and locally supported** 2-year, part of Metropolitan Community Colleges System
- **Calendar** semesters
- **Degree** certificates and associate
- **Endowment** $759,956
- **Coed,** 2,294 undergraduate students, 33% full-time, 61% women, 39% men

Undergraduates 759 full-time, 1,535 part-time. Students come from 1 other state, 1 other country, 0.5% transferred in. *Retention:* 39% of 2001 full-time freshmen returned.

Freshmen *Admission:* 326 applied, 326 admitted, 326 enrolled.

Faculty *Total:* 258, 12% full-time. *Student/faculty ratio:* 22:1.

Majors Accounting technician; business administration; computer science; computer science related; drafting; information sciences/systems; law enforcement/police science; liberal arts and sciences/liberal studies; secretarial science.

Academic Programs *Special study options:* academic remediation for entering students, accelerated degree program, adult/continuing education programs, advanced placement credit, cooperative education, distance learning, English as a second language, honors programs, internships, off-campus study, part-time degree program, services for LD students, summer session for credit.

Library Blue River Community College Library with 3,157 serial subscriptions, 463 audiovisual materials, an OPAC.

Computers on Campus 543 computers available on campus for general student use. A campuswide network can be accessed from off campus. Internet access, at least one staffed computer lab available.

Standardized Tests *Required:* ACT ASSET. *Recommended:* ACT (for placement).

Costs (2002–03) *Tuition:* area resident $1590 full-time, $53 per hour part-time; state resident $2790 full-time, $93 per hour part-time; nonresident $3900 full-time, $130 per hour part-time. Full-time tuition and fees vary according to class time and program. Part-time tuition and fees vary according to class time and program. *Required fees:* $150 full-time, $5 per hour. *Payment plan:* installment. *Waivers:* senior citizens and employees or children of employees.

Applying *Options:* early admission, deferred entrance. *Application deadline:* rolling (freshmen), rolling (transfers).

Admissions Contact Jon Burke, Dean of Campus Services, Blue River Community College, 1501 West Jefferson Street, Blue Spring, MO 64015. *Phone:* 816-655-6118. *Fax:* 816-655-6014.

COTTEY COLLEGE
Nevada, Missouri

- **Independent** 2-year, founded 1884
- **Calendar** semesters
- **Degree** associate
- **Small-town** 51-acre campus
- **Endowment** $67.4 million
- **Women only,** 320 undergraduate students, 100% full-time

Undergraduates Students come from 42 states and territories, 15 other countries, 78% are from out of state, 4% African American, 2% Asian American or Pacific Islander, 4% Hispanic American, 0.3% Native American, 10% international, 98% live on campus. *Retention:* 88% of 2001 full-time freshmen returned.

Freshmen *Average high school GPA:* 3.33. *Test scores:* SAT verbal scores over 500: 49%; SAT math scores over 500: 31%; ACT scores over 18: 92%; SAT verbal scores over 600: 13%; SAT math scores over 600: 9%; ACT scores over 24: 43%; ACT scores over 30: 2%.

Faculty *Total:* 40, 88% full-time, 63% with terminal degrees. *Student/faculty ratio:* 9:1.

Majors Biological/physical sciences; liberal arts and sciences/liberal studies.

Academic Programs *Special study options:* advanced placement credit, part-time degree program.

Library Blanche Skiff Ross Memorial Library with 54,200 titles, 246 serial subscriptions, an OPAC.

Computers on Campus 50 computers available on campus for general student use. Internet access, at least one staffed computer lab available.

Student Life *Housing:* on-campus residence required through sophomore year. *Options:* women-only. *Activities and Organizations:* drama/theater group, student-run newspaper, choral group, International Friendship Circle, Cottey Intramural Association, Ozarks Explorers Club, Intervarsity Club, Golden Keys. *Campus security:* 24-hour emergency response devices and patrols, late-night transport/escort service, controlled dormitory access. *Student Services:* health clinic, personal/psychological counseling.

Athletics Member NJCAA. *Intercollegiate sports:* basketball W. *Intramural sports:* badminton W, basketball W, fencing W, field hockey W, golf W, soccer W, softball W, swimming W, tennis W, volleyball W, water polo W, weight lifting W.

Standardized Tests *Required:* SAT I or ACT (for admission).

Costs (2002–03) *Comprehensive fee:* $14,630 includes full-time tuition ($9600), mandatory fees ($430), and room and board ($4600). Part-time tuition: $400 per credit hour. *Required fees:* $150 per term part-time.
Financial Aid In 2001, 26 Federal Work-Study jobs (averaging $1500). 127 State and other part-time jobs (averaging $1500).
Applying *Options:* electronic application, early admission, deferred entrance. *Application fee:* $20. *Required:* essay or personal statement, high school transcript, 1 letter of recommendation. *Recommended:* minimum 2.6 GPA, interview. *Application deadline:* rolling (freshmen), rolling (transfers).
Admissions Contact Ms. Marjorie J. Cooke, Dean of Enrollment Management, Cottey College, 1000 West Austin, Nevada, MO 64772. *Phone:* 417-667-8181. *Toll-free phone:* 888-526-8839. *Fax:* 417-667-8103. *E-mail:* enrollmgt@cottey.edu.

CROWDER COLLEGE
Neosho, Missouri

- **State and locally supported** 2-year, founded 1963, part of Missouri Coordinating Board for Higher Education
- **Calendar** semesters
- **Degree** certificates and associate
- **Rural** 608-acre campus
- **Coed,** 2,012 undergraduate students, 49% full-time, 60% women, 40% men

Undergraduates 984 full-time, 1,028 part-time. Students come from 16 states and territories, 6 other countries, 5% are from out of state, 0.5% African American, 0.4% Asian American or Pacific Islander, 2% Hispanic American, 2% Native American, 0.7% international, 3% transferred in, 10% live on campus.
Freshmen *Admission:* 774 applied, 774 admitted, 360 enrolled.
Faculty *Total:* 168, 40% full-time.
Majors Agribusiness; art; biology; business administration; computer systems networking/telecommunications; construction technology; data processing; drafting; education; electrical/electronic engineering technology; elementary education; environmental health; environmental technology; executive assistant; farm/ranch management; fire science; general studies; industrial technology; legal administrative assistant; liberal arts and sciences/liberal studies; mass communications; mathematics; mathematics/computer science; medical administrative assistant; music; nursing; physical education; physical sciences; poultry science; pre-engineering; psychology; public relations; secretarial science; theater arts/drama.
Academic Programs *Special study options:* academic remediation for entering students, adult/continuing education programs, advanced placement credit, cooperative education, English as a second language, freshman honors college, honors programs, internships, part-time degree program, study abroad, summer session for credit.
Library Crowder College Learning Resources Center with 32,093 titles, 307 serial subscriptions, 4,789 audiovisual materials, an OPAC, a Web page.
Computers on Campus 261 computers available on campus for general student use. At least one staffed computer lab available.
Student Life *Housing Options:* men-only, women-only. *Activities and Organizations:* drama/theater group, student-run newspaper, choral group, Phi Beta Lambda, Students in Free Enterprise, Baptist Student Union, Student Senate, Student Ambassadors. *Campus security:* 12-hour patrols by trained security personnel. *Student Services:* personal/psychological counseling.
Athletics Member NJCAA. *Intercollegiate sports:* baseball M(s), basketball W(s).
Standardized Tests *Required:* ACT COMPASS.
Costs (2001–02) *Tuition:* area resident $1380 full-time, $46 per semester hour part-time; state resident $1980 full-time, $66 per semester hour part-time; nonresident $2610 full-time, $87 per semester hour part-time. *Required fees:* $180 full-time, $6 per semester hour. *Room and board:* $2700. *Payment plan:* installment. *Waivers:* senior citizens and employees or children of employees.
Financial Aid In 2001, 150 Federal Work-Study jobs (averaging $1000).
Applying *Options:* early admission, deferred entrance. *Application fee:* $25. *Required:* high school transcript. *Application deadline:* rolling (freshmen), rolling (transfers).
Admissions Contact Heidi Gilligan, Admissions Coordinator, Crowder College, 601 Laclede, Neosho, MO 64850. *Phone:* 417-451-3223 Ext. 5466. *Toll-free phone:* 417-455-5709. *Fax:* 417-455-5731.

EAST CENTRAL COLLEGE
Union, Missouri

- **District-supported** 2-year, founded 1959, part of Missouri Coordinating Board for Higher Education
- **Calendar** semesters
- **Degree** certificates and associate
- **Rural** 207-acre campus with easy access to St. Louis
- **Endowment** $1.8 million
- **Coed,** 3,462 undergraduate students, 40% full-time, 60% women, 40% men

Undergraduates 1,375 full-time, 2,087 part-time. Students come from 4 states and territories, 0.3% are from out of state, 5% transferred in.
Freshmen *Admission:* 709 enrolled. *Test scores:* ACT scores over 18: 74%; ACT scores over 24: 18%; ACT scores over 30: 4%.
Faculty *Total:* 172, 35% full-time, 12% with terminal degrees. *Student/faculty ratio:* 17:1.
Majors Accounting; anthropology; archaeology; art; auto mechanic/technician; biology; botany; business administration; business marketing and marketing management; chemistry; computer programming; computer science; construction technology; criminal justice/law enforcement administration; data processing technology; design/visual communications; drafting; ecology; economics; education; electrical/electronic engineering technology; elementary education; emergency medical technology; English; fire science; fish/game management; food products retailing; forestry; French; geography; geology; German; graphic design/commercial art/illustration; heating/air conditioning/refrigeration; history; home economics; horticulture science; hospitality management; hotel and restaurant management; humanities; industrial technology; information sciences/systems; interior design; journalism; law enforcement/police science; legal administrative assistant; liberal arts and sciences/liberal studies; library science; machine technology; management information systems/business data processing; mass communications; mathematics; medical administrative assistant; modern languages; music; nursing; pharmacy; philosophy; physical education; physics; political science; pre-engineering; psychology; public administration; recreation/leisure studies; religious studies; secretarial science; social work; sociology; Spanish; speech/rhetorical studies; theater arts/drama; travel/tourism management; welding technology; wildlife management; zoology.
Academic Programs *Special study options:* academic remediation for entering students, adult/continuing education programs, advanced placement credit, distance learning, English as a second language, honors programs, internships, part-time degree program, study abroad, summer session for credit.
Library East Central College Library with 34,355 titles, 313 serial subscriptions, 675 audiovisual materials, an OPAC, a Web page.
Computers on Campus 358 computers available on campus for general student use. A campuswide network can be accessed from off campus. Internet access, at least one staffed computer lab available.
Student Life *Housing:* college housing not available. *Activities and Organizations:* drama/theater group, student-run newspaper, choral group, student government, Phi Theta Kappa, Amnesty International, Multicultural Club. *Campus security:* 24-hour emergency response devices, late-night transport/escort service.
Athletics Member NJCAA. *Intercollegiate sports:* basketball M(s), soccer M(s), softball W(s), volleyball W(s). *Intramural sports:* basketball M, table tennis M/W, volleyball M/W.
Standardized Tests *Required:* ACT ASSET, ACT COMPASS. *Recommended:* ACT (for placement).
Costs (2001–02) *Tuition:* area resident $1212 full-time, $51 per semester hour part-time; state resident $1644 full-time, $69 per semester hour part-time; nonresident $2388 full-time, $100 per semester hour part-time. Full-time tuition and fees vary according to course load. Part-time tuition and fees vary according to course load. *Required fees:* $192 full-time, $8 per semester hour. *Payment plan:* installment. *Waivers:* senior citizens and employees or children of employees.
Financial Aid In 2001, 35 Federal Work-Study jobs (averaging $1500). 35 State and other part-time jobs (averaging $1500).
Applying *Options:* common application, early admission, deferred entrance. *Required:* high school transcript. *Application deadline:* rolling (freshmen), rolling (transfers).
Admissions Contact Mrs. Karen Wieda, Registrar, East Central College, PO Box 529, Union, MO 63084. *Phone:* 636-583-5195 Ext. 2220. *Fax:* 636-583-1897. *E-mail:* wiedaks@ecmail.ecc.cc.mo.us.

ELECTRONICS INSTITUTE
Kansas City, Missouri

Admissions Contact 15329 Kensington Avenue, Kansas City, MO 64147-1212.

HICKEY COLLEGE
St. Louis, Missouri

- **Proprietary** 2-year, founded 1933
- **Calendar** semesters
- **Degree** diplomas and associate
- **Suburban** campus
- **Coed,** 450 undergraduate students

Diploma and associate degree programs. Founded 1933. Eight to 16 month programs include accounting, administrative assistant studies, computer applications specialist studies, computer applications and programming, graphic design, legal administrative assistant studies, and paralegal studies. Tuition and fees vary by program. Financial assistance for those who qualify. Housing available. Accredited member, ACICS. Call 314-434-2212 or 800-777-1544 (toll-free) for more information.

Faculty *Total:* 17, 71% full-time. *Student/faculty ratio:* 30:1.
Majors Accounting technician; computer programming; executive assistant; legal administrative assistant; paralegal/legal assistant.
Academic Programs *Special study options:* accelerated degree program.
Computers on Campus 109 computers available on campus for general student use.
Costs (2002–03) *Tuition:* $9420 full-time. *Room only:* $4360.
Applying *Application fee:* $50. *Required:* high school transcript, interview. *Application deadline:* rolling (freshmen), rolling (transfers).
Admissions Contact Michelle Hayes, Director of Admissions, Hickey College, 940 West Port Plaza Drive, St. Louis, MO 63146. *Phone:* 314-434-2212 Ext. 137. *Toll-free phone:* 800-777-1544. *Fax:* 314-434-1974.

ITT TECHNICAL INSTITUTE
Arnold, Missouri

- **Proprietary** 2-year
- **Calendar** quarters
- **Degree** associate
- **Coed,** 484 undergraduate students

Majors Computer/information sciences related; computer programming; drafting; electrical/electronic engineering technologies related; information technology.
Student Life *Housing:* college housing not available.
Costs (2001–02) *Tuition:* Full-time tuition and fees vary according to program. Part-time tuition and fees vary according to program. $260—$330 per credit hour.
Applying *Application fee:* $100. *Required:* high school transcript, interview. *Recommended:* letters of recommendation. *Application deadline:* rolling (freshmen). *Notification:* continuous (freshmen).
Admissions Contact Mr. Charles Boyd, Director of Recruitment, ITT Technical Institute, 1930 Meyer Drury Drive, Arnold, MO 63010. *Phone:* 636-464-6600. *Toll-free phone:* 888-488-1082.

ITT TECHNICAL INSTITUTE
Earth City, Missouri

- **Proprietary** primarily 2-year, founded 1936, part of ITT Educational Services, Inc
- **Calendar** quarters
- **Degrees** associate and bachelor's
- **Suburban** 2-acre campus with easy access to St. Louis
- **Coed,** 600 undergraduate students

Majors Computer/information sciences related; computer programming; drafting; electrical/electronic engineering technologies related; information sciences/systems; information technology.
Student Life *Housing:* college housing not available.
Costs (2001–02) *Tuition:* Full-time tuition and fees vary according to program. Part-time tuition and fees vary according to program. $260—$330 per credit hour.
Applying *Options:* common application, deferred entrance. *Application fee:* $100. *Required:* high school transcript, interview. *Recommended:* letters of recommendation. *Application deadline:* rolling (freshmen), rolling (transfers). *Notification:* continuous (freshmen).
Admissions Contact Ms. Karen Finkenkeller, Director, ITT Technical Institute, 13505 Lakefront Drive, Earth City, MO 63045. *Phone:* 314-298-7800. *Toll-free phone:* 800-235-5488. *Fax:* 314-298-0559.

JEFFERSON COLLEGE
Hillsboro, Missouri

- **State and locally supported** 2-year, founded 1963, part of Missouri Coordinating Board for Higher Education
- **Calendar** semesters
- **Degree** certificates and associate
- **Rural** 480-acre campus with easy access to St. Louis
- **Endowment** $656,648
- **Coed,** 3,899 undergraduate students, 52% full-time, 58% women, 42% men

Undergraduates Students come from 2 states and territories, 8 other countries, 1% are from out of state, 0.8% African American, 0.3% Asian American or Pacific Islander, 0.6% Hispanic American, 0.5% Native American, 0.6% international.
Freshmen *Admission:* 2,162 applied, 2,162 admitted. *Average high school GPA:* 2.83. *Test scores:* ACT scores over 18: 71%; ACT scores over 24: 17%; ACT scores over 30: 1%.
Faculty *Total:* 228, 39% full-time, 4% with terminal degrees. *Student/faculty ratio:* 19:1.
Majors Accounting; architectural engineering technology; art; auto mechanic/technician; biological/physical sciences; business administration; business education; business marketing and marketing management; child care/development; civil engineering technology; computer/information sciences; computer programming; criminal justice/law enforcement administration; data processing technology; drafting; early childhood education; education; electrical/electronic engineering technology; elementary education; emergency medical technology; English; fire science; forestry; geography; heating/air conditioning/refrigeration; history; hotel and restaurant management; information sciences/systems; interdisciplinary studies; journalism; legal administrative assistant; liberal arts and sciences/liberal studies; machine technology; mathematics; mechanical design technology; medical administrative assistant; music; nursing; physical education; physical sciences; political science; practical nurse; pre-engineering; psychology; public administration; retail management; robotics; secretarial science; social work; sociology; Spanish; speech/rhetorical studies; telecommunications; theater arts/drama; veterinary technology; welding technology.
Academic Programs *Special study options:* academic remediation for entering students, adult/continuing education programs, advanced placement credit, freshman honors college, honors programs, internships, part-time degree program, services for LD students, summer session for credit.
Library Jefferson College Library plus 1 other with 58,000 titles, 497 serial subscriptions, an OPAC.
Computers on Campus 350 computers available on campus for general student use. Internet access, at least one staffed computer lab available.
Student Life *Housing:* college housing not available. *Activities and Organizations:* drama/theater group, student-run newspaper, choral group, Student Senate, first and second-level nursing associations, Baptist Student Union, Phi Beta Lambda, Phi Theta Kappa. *Campus security:* 24-hour patrols, late-night transport/escort service.
Athletics Member NJCAA. *Intercollegiate sports:* baseball M(s), basketball W(s), tennis M(s), volleyball W(s). *Intramural sports:* basketball M/W, swimming M/W, volleyball M/W.
Standardized Tests *Required:* ACT or ACT ASSET.
Costs (2001–02) *Tuition:* area resident $1410 full-time, $47 per credit hour part-time; state resident $2100 full-time, $70 per credit hour part-time; nonresident $2820 full-time, $94 per credit hour part-time. Full-time tuition and fees vary according to course load, degree level, and program. Part-time tuition and fees vary according to course load, degree level, and program. *Required fees:* $210 full-time, $7 per semester hour. *Room and board:* Room and board charges vary according to housing facility. *Payment plan:* deferred payment. *Waivers:* senior citizens and employees or children of employees.
Financial Aid In 2001, 90 Federal Work-Study jobs (averaging $1000).
Applying *Options:* early admission. *Application fee:* $20. *Required:* high school transcript. *Application deadline:* rolling (freshmen), rolling (transfers).
Admissions Contact Ms. Deborah Below, Director of Admissions and Financial Aid, Jefferson College, 1000 Viking Drive, Hillsboro, MO 63050. *Phone:* 636-797-3000 Ext. 218. *Fax:* 636-789-5103. *E-mail:* kgosnell@jeffco.edu.

LINN STATE TECHNICAL COLLEGE
Linn, Missouri

Admissions Contact Linn State Technical College, One Technology Drive, Linn, MO 65051-9606. *Toll-free phone:* 800-743-TECH.

LONGVIEW COMMUNITY COLLEGE
Lee's Summit, Missouri

- **State and locally supported** 2-year, founded 1969, part of Metropolitan Community Colleges System
- **Calendar** semesters
- **Degree** certificates and associate
- **Suburban** 147-acre campus with easy access to Kansas City
- **Endowment** $759,956
- **Coed,** 5,791 undergraduate students, 35% full-time, 58% women, 42% men

Undergraduates 2,036 full-time, 3,755 part-time. Students come from 8 states and territories, 6 other countries, 1% are from out of state, 13% African American, 1% Asian American or Pacific Islander, 2% Hispanic American, 0.8% Native American, 0.2% international. *Retention:* 37% of 2001 full-time freshmen returned.
Freshmen *Admission:* 1,173 applied, 1,173 admitted, 610 enrolled.
Faculty *Total:* 341, 24% full-time. *Student/faculty ratio:* 22:1.
Majors Accounting; agricultural mechanization; auto mechanic/technician; biological/physical sciences; biology; business administration; business marketing and marketing management; chemistry; computer programming; computer science; computer science related; computer typography/composition; corrections; criminal justice/law enforcement administration; data processing technology; drafting; electrical/electronic engineering technology; engineering; heavy equipment maintenance; human services; law enforcement/police science; legal administrative assistant; liberal arts and sciences/liberal studies; medical administrative assistant; postal management; pre-engineering; quality control technology; secretarial science.
Academic Programs *Special study options:* academic remediation for entering students, accelerated degree program, adult/continuing education programs, advanced placement credit, cooperative education, distance learning, English as a second language, honors programs, internships, off-campus study, part-time degree program, services for LD students, summer session for credit.
Library Longview Community College Library with 6,567 serial subscriptions, 451 audiovisual materials, an OPAC.
Computers on Campus 543 computers available on campus for general student use. A campuswide network can be accessed from off campus. Internet access, at least one staffed computer lab available.
Student Life *Housing:* college housing not available. *Activities and Organizations:* drama/theater group, student-run newspaper, choral group, student newspaper, student government, Phi Theta Kappa, Longview Mighty Voices Choir, Longview Broadcasting Network, national fraternities. *Campus security:* 24-hour patrols. *Student Services:* personal/psychological counseling.
Athletics Member NJCAA. *Intercollegiate sports:* baseball M(s), volleyball W(s). *Intramural sports:* basketball M/W, swimming M/W, volleyball M/W.
Standardized Tests *Required:* ACT ASSET. *Recommended:* ACT (for placement).
Costs (2002–03) *Tuition:* area resident $1590 full-time, $53 per hour part-time; state resident $2790 full-time, $93 per hour part-time; nonresident $3900 full-time, $130 per hour part-time. Full-time tuition and fees vary according to course load and program. Part-time tuition and fees vary according to course load and program. *Required fees:* $150 full-time, $5 per hour. *Payment plan:* installment. *Waivers:* senior citizens and employees or children of employees.
Financial Aid In 2001, 34 Federal Work-Study jobs.
Applying *Options:* early admission, deferred entrance. *Application deadline:* rolling (freshmen), rolling (transfers).
Admissions Contact Ms. Janet Cline, Dean of Student Services, Longview Community College, 500 Southwest Longview Road, Lee's Summit, MO 64081-2105. *Phone:* 816-672-2247. *Fax:* 816-672-2040.

MAPLE WOODS COMMUNITY COLLEGE
Kansas City, Missouri

- **State and locally supported** 2-year, founded 1969, part of Metropolitan Community Colleges System
- **Calendar** semesters
- **Degree** certificates and associate
- **Suburban** 205-acre campus
- **Endowment** $759,956
- **Coed,** 5,045 undergraduate students, 33% full-time, 56% women, 44% men

Undergraduates 1,685 full-time, 3,360 part-time. Students come from 18 states and territories, 12 other countries, 1% are from out of state, 3% African American, 1% Asian American or Pacific Islander, 2% Hispanic American, 0.5% Native American, 0.2% international, 0.6% transferred in. *Retention:* 37% of 2001 full-time freshmen returned.
Freshmen *Admission:* 804 applied, 804 admitted, 804 enrolled.
Faculty *Total:* 380, 17% full-time. *Student/faculty ratio:* 23:1.
Majors Accounting; aviation technology; biological/physical sciences; biology; business administration; business marketing and marketing management; chemistry; computer programming; computer science; computer science related; criminal justice/law enforcement administration; data processing technology; electrical/electronic engineering technology; heating/air conditioning/refrigeration; law enforcement/police science; legal administrative assistant; liberal arts and sciences/liberal studies; machine shop assistant; machine technology; medical administrative assistant; pre-engineering; secretarial science; travel/tourism management; veterinary technology.
Academic Programs *Special study options:* academic remediation for entering students, accelerated degree program, adult/continuing education programs, advanced placement credit, cooperative education, distance learning, English as a second language, honors programs, internships, off-campus study, part-time degree program, services for LD students, summer session for credit.
Library Maple Woods Community College Library with 1,873 serial subscriptions, 2,900 audiovisual materials, an OPAC.
Computers on Campus 398 computers available on campus for general student use. A campuswide network can be accessed from off campus. Internet access, at least one staffed computer lab available.
Student Life *Housing:* college housing not available. *Activities and Organizations:* drama/theater group, student-run newspaper, choral group, Student Activities Council, Art Club, Friends of All Cultures, Phi Theta Kappa, Engineering Club, national fraternities. *Campus security:* 24-hour patrols, late-night transport/escort service. *Student Services:* personal/psychological counseling.
Athletics Member NJCAA. *Intercollegiate sports:* baseball M(s). *Intramural sports:* softball M/W, volleyball M/W.
Standardized Tests *Required:* ACT ASSET.
Costs (2002–03) *Tuition:* area resident $1590 full-time, $53 per hour part-time; state resident $2790 full-time, $93 per hour part-time; nonresident $3900 full-time, $130 per hour part-time. *Required fees:* $150 full-time, $5 per credit hour. *Payment plan:* installment. *Waivers:* senior citizens and employees or children of employees.
Financial Aid In 2001, 28 Federal Work-Study jobs.
Applying *Options:* early admission, deferred entrance. *Application deadline:* rolling (freshmen), rolling (transfers). *Notification:* continuous (freshmen).
Admissions Contact Ms. Dawn Hatterman, Registrar, Maple Woods Community College, 2601 Northeast Barry Road, Kansas City, MO 64156-1299. *Phone:* 816-437-3108. *Fax:* 816-437-3351.

METRO BUSINESS COLLEGE
Cape Girardeau, Missouri

- **Private** primarily 2-year
- **Calendar** quarters
- **Degrees** certificates, diplomas, associate, and bachelor's
- 90 undergraduate students

Admissions Contact Mr. Ken Hovis, Admissions Director, Metro Business College, 1732 North Kings Highway, Cape Girardeau, MO 63701. *Phone:* 573-334-9181.

MINERAL AREA COLLEGE
Park Hills, Missouri

- **District-supported** 2-year, founded 1922, part of Missouri Coordinating Board for Higher Education
- **Calendar** semesters
- **Degree** certificates and associate
- **Rural** 240-acre campus with easy access to St. Louis
- **Endowment** $1.3 million
- **Coed,** 2,878 undergraduate students, 52% full-time, 68% women, 32% men

Undergraduates 1,496 full-time, 1,382 part-time. Students come from 11 states and territories, 7 other countries, 1% are from out of state, 1% African American, 0.3% Asian American or Pacific Islander, 0.4% Hispanic American, 0.4% Native American, 0.6% international, 3% transferred in.
Freshmen *Admission:* 647 applied, 647 admitted, 647 enrolled. *Average high school GPA:* 2.90. *Test scores:* ACT scores over 18: 67%; ACT scores over 24: 10%; ACT scores over 30: 1%.
Faculty *Total:* 168, 43% full-time, 7% with terminal degrees. *Student/faculty ratio:* 20:1.

Mineral Area College (continued)

Majors Accounting; agribusiness; banking; business administration; business marketing and marketing management; child care provider; computer management; computer programming; construction technology; corrections; drafting/design technology; electrical/electronic engineering technology; fire science; graphic design/commercial art/illustration; health services administration; horticulture services; hospitality services management related; industrial technology; law enforcement/police science; liberal arts and sciences/liberal studies; mass communications; medical laboratory technician; medical radiologic technology; medical technology; nurse assistant/aide; nursing; occupational safety/health technology; operations management; practical nurse; radio/television broadcasting technology; recreation/leisure studies; secretarial science; system/networking/LAN/WAN management; travel/tourism management.

Academic Programs *Special study options:* academic remediation for entering students, distance learning, honors programs, internships, off-campus study, part-time degree program, services for LD students, summer session for credit.

Library C. H. Cozen Learning Resource Center with 30,540 titles, 341 serial subscriptions, 5,034 audiovisual materials, an OPAC.

Computers on Campus 226 computers available on campus for general student use. A campuswide network can be accessed from student residence rooms and from off campus. Internet access, at least one staffed computer lab available.

Student Life *Housing Options:* coed. *Activities and Organizations:* drama/theater group, choral group, Student Senate, Phi Theta Kappa, Psi Beta, MAC Ambassadors, Phi Beta Lambda. *Campus security:* 24-hour patrols. *Student Services:* personal/psychological counseling.

Athletics Member NJCAA. *Intercollegiate sports:* baseball M(s), basketball M(s)/W(s), volleyball W(s).

Standardized Tests *Required:* ACT (for placement).

Costs (2002–03) *Tuition:* area resident $1410 full-time, $47 per credit part-time; state resident $2070 full-time, $66 per credit part-time; nonresident $2610 full-time, $87 per credit part-time. *Required fees:* $180 full-time, $6 per credit. *Room and board:* room only: $3159. *Payment plans:* installment, deferred payment. *Waivers:* senior citizens and employees or children of employees.

Financial Aid In 2001, 65 Federal Work-Study jobs (averaging $3708).

Applying *Options:* electronic application, early admission. *Required:* high school transcript. *Application deadline:* rolling (freshmen), rolling (transfers).

Admissions Contact Mrs. Linda Huffman, Registrar, Mineral Area College, PO Box 1000, Park Hills, MO 63601-1000. *Phone:* 573-518-2130. *Toll-free phone:* 573-518-2206. *Fax:* 573-518-2166. *E-mail:* jsheets@mail.mac.cc.mo.us.

MISSOURI COLLEGE
St. Louis, Missouri

- **Proprietary** 2-year, founded 1963
- **Degree** diplomas and associate
- **Coed, primarily women,** 450 undergraduate students, 100% full-time, 90% women, 10% men

Undergraduates Students come from 4 states and territories, 30% African American, 0.9% Asian American or Pacific Islander, 1% Hispanic American.

Freshmen *Average high school GPA:* 3.00.

Faculty *Total:* 54, 65% full-time. *Student/faculty ratio:* 20:1.

Majors Business.

Computers on Campus 60 computers available on campus for general student use. Internet access, at least one staffed computer lab available.

Student Life *Housing:* college housing not available.

Costs (2001–02) *Tuition:* state resident $8145 full-time. *Payment plan:* installment. *Waivers:* employees or children of employees.

Financial Aid In 2001, 12 Federal Work-Study jobs (averaging $1000).

Applying *Application fee:* $100. *Required:* essay or personal statement, interview. *Application deadline:* rolling (freshmen).

Admissions Contact Mr. Doug Brinker, Admissions Director, Missouri College, 10121 Manchester Road, St. Louis, MO 63122-1583. *Phone:* 314-821-7700.

MOBERLY AREA COMMUNITY COLLEGE
Moberly, Missouri

- **State and locally supported** 2-year, founded 1927
- **Calendar** semesters
- **Degree** certificates and associate
- **Small-town** 32-acre campus
- **Endowment** $636,271
- **Coed,** 3,269 undergraduate students, 45% full-time, 64% women, 36% men

Undergraduates 1,465 full-time, 1,804 part-time. Students come from 18 states and territories, 5 other countries, 1% are from out of state, 6% African American, 0.8% Asian American or Pacific Islander, 1% Hispanic American, 0.2% Native American, 0.3% international, 4% transferred in, 1% live on campus. *Retention:* 57% of 2001 full-time freshmen returned.

Freshmen *Admission:* 711 admitted, 711 enrolled. *Test scores:* ACT scores over 18: 63%; ACT scores over 24: 9%.

Faculty *Total:* 210, 24% full-time, 13% with terminal degrees. *Student/faculty ratio:* 20:1.

Majors Accounting technician; business marketing and marketing management; child guidance; computer/information sciences; drafting; electrical/electronic engineering technology; graphic/printing equipment; industrial technology; law enforcement/police science; liberal arts and sciences/liberal studies; nursing; pre-engineering; secretarial science; welding technology.

Academic Programs *Special study options:* academic remediation for entering students, adult/continuing education programs, advanced placement credit, cooperative education, distance learning, internships, part-time degree program, services for LD students, study abroad, summer session for credit.

Library Kate Stamper Wilhite Library with 29,307 titles, 239 serial subscriptions, 1,161 audiovisual materials, an OPAC, a Web page.

Computers on Campus 440 computers available on campus for general student use. A campuswide network can be accessed from off campus. Internet access, at least one staffed computer lab available.

Student Life *Housing Options:* men-only, women-only. *Activities and Organizations:* drama/theater group, student-run newspaper, choral group, Phi Theta Kappa, Student Nurses Association, Child Care, Delta Epsilon Chi, Brother Ox. *Campus security:* student patrols, extensive surveillance.

Athletics Member NJCAA. *Intercollegiate sports:* basketball M(s)/W(s). *Intramural sports:* basketball M/W, volleyball M/W.

Standardized Tests *Required for some:* ACT (for placement), ACT ASSET. *Recommended:* ACT (for placement), ACT ASSET.

Costs (2001–02) *Tuition:* area resident $1290 full-time, $43 per credit hour part-time; state resident $2070 full-time, $69 per credit hour part-time; nonresident $3480 full-time, $116 per credit hour part-time. Part-time tuition and fees vary according to course load. *Required fees:* $160 full-time, $20 per term part-time. *Room and board:* room only: $1400. *Payment plans:* installment, deferred payment. *Waivers:* senior citizens and employees or children of employees.

Financial Aid In 2001, 43 Federal Work-Study jobs.

Applying *Options:* electronic application. *Required:* high school transcript. *Application deadline:* rolling (freshmen), rolling (transfers). *Notification:* continuous until 9/1 (freshmen).

Admissions Contact Dr. James Grant, Dean of Student Services, Moberly Area Community College, 101 College Avenue, Moberly, MO 65270-1304. *Phone:* 660-263-4110 Ext. 235. *Toll-free phone:* 800-622-2070. *Fax:* 660-263-6252. *E-mail:* info@macc.edu.

NORTH CENTRAL MISSOURI COLLEGE
Trenton, Missouri

Admissions Contact Ms. Kelly Krohn, Director of Admissions, North Central Missouri College, 1301 Main Street, Trenton, MO 64683. *Phone:* 660-359-3948 Ext. 401. *Toll-free phone:* 800-880-6180 Ext. 401. *E-mail:* kkrohn@mail.ncmc.cc.mo.us.

OZARKS TECHNICAL COMMUNITY COLLEGE
Springfield, Missouri

- **District-supported** 2-year, founded 1990, part of Missouri Coordinating Board for Higher Education
- **Calendar** semesters
- **Degree** certificates, diplomas, and associate
- **Urban** 20-acre campus
- **Endowment** $3867
- **Coed**

Student Life *Campus security:* 24-hour emergency response devices.

Standardized Tests *Required:* ACT ASSET, ACT COMPASS.

Applying *Options:* common application, early admission. *Required:* high school transcript.

Admissions Contact Mr. Bruce Renner, Dean of Admissions and Financial Aid, Ozarks Technical Community College, PO Box 5958, Srpingfield, MO 65801. *Phone:* 417-895-7130. *Fax:* 417-895-7161.

PATRICIA STEVENS COLLEGE
St. Louis, Missouri

- **Proprietary** 2-year, founded 1947
- **Calendar** quarters
- **Degree** diplomas and associate
- **Urban** campus
- **Coed, primarily women,** 170 undergraduate students

Undergraduates Students come from 4 states and territories, 42% are from out of state, 44% African American, 0.6% Asian American or Pacific Islander, 0.6% Hispanic American.
Freshmen *Average high school GPA:* 2.50.
Faculty *Total:* 32, 16% full-time, 3% with terminal degrees. *Student/faculty ratio:* 9:1.
Majors Business; fashion merchandising; interior design; medical office management; paralegal/legal assistant; retailing operations; travel/tourism management.
Academic Programs *Special study options:* academic remediation for entering students, adult/continuing education programs, advanced placement credit, cooperative education, honors programs, independent study, internships, part-time degree program, summer session for credit.
Computers on Campus 35 computers available on campus for general student use. Internet access, at least one staffed computer lab available.
Student Life *Campus security:* 24-hour emergency response devices and patrols. *Student Services:* personal/psychological counseling.
Costs (2001–02) *Tuition:* $8992 full-time, $160 per credit hour part-time. Part-time tuition and fees vary according to class time and course load. No tuition increase for student's term of enrollment. *Payment plan:* deferred payment.
Applying *Options:* deferred entrance. *Required:* high school transcript, interview. *Recommended:* essay or personal statement, letters of recommendation. *Application deadline:* rolling (freshmen).
Admissions Contact Mr. John Willmon, Director of Admissions, Patricia Stevens College, 330 North Fourth Street, Suite 306, St. Louis, MO 63102. *Phone:* 314-421-0949 Ext. 12. *Toll-free phone:* 800-871-0949. *Fax:* 314-421-0304.

PENN VALLEY COMMUNITY COLLEGE
Kansas City, Missouri

- **State and locally supported** 2-year, founded 1969, part of Metropolitan Community Colleges System
- **Calendar** semesters
- **Degree** certificates and associate
- **Urban** 25-acre campus
- **Endowment** $759,956
- **Coed,** 4,376 undergraduate students, 28% full-time, 70% women, 30% men

Undergraduates 1,221 full-time, 3,155 part-time. Students come from 3 states and territories, 51 other countries, 3% are from out of state, 33% African American, 3% Asian American or Pacific Islander, 5% Hispanic American, 0.8% Native American, 4% international, 1% transferred in. *Retention:* 36% of 2001 full-time freshmen returned.
Freshmen *Admission:* 585 applied, 585 admitted, 585 enrolled.
Faculty *Total:* 397, 25% full-time. *Student/faculty ratio:* 16:1.
Majors Accounting; biological/physical sciences; biology; business administration; business marketing and marketing management; chemistry; child care provider; computer science; computer science related; corrections; criminal justice/law enforcement administration; culinary arts; data processing technology; early childhood education; electrical/electronic engineering technology; emergency medical technology; engineering; fashion design/illustration; fashion merchandising; fire science; food products retailing; graphic design/commercial art/illustration; heating/air conditioning/refrigeration; home economics; hotel and restaurant management; industrial radiologic technology; law enforcement/police science; legal administrative assistant; liberal arts and sciences/liberal studies; medical administrative assistant; medical records administration; nursing; occupational therapy; ophthalmic medical technology; paralegal/legal assistant; physical therapy; respiratory therapy; secretarial science.
Academic Programs *Special study options:* academic remediation for entering students, accelerated degree program, adult/continuing education programs, advanced placement credit, cooperative education, distance learning, English as a second language, honors programs, internships, off-campus study, part-time degree program, services for LD students, summer session for credit.
Library Penn Valley Community College Library with 5,606 serial subscriptions, 24 audiovisual materials, an OPAC.
Computers on Campus 749 computers available on campus for general student use. A campuswide network can be accessed from off campus. Internet access, at least one staffed computer lab available.
Student Life *Housing:* college housing not available. *Activities and Organizations:* drama/theater group, student-run newspaper, choral group, Black Student Association, Los Americanos, Phi Theta Kappa, Fashion Club, national fraternities. *Campus security:* 24-hour patrols. *Student Services:* personal/psychological counseling.
Athletics Member NJCAA. *Intercollegiate sports:* basketball M(s).
Standardized Tests *Required:* ACT ASSET.
Costs (2002–03) *Tuition:* area resident $1590 full-time, $53 per hour part-time; state resident $2790 full-time, $93 per hour part-time; nonresident $3900 full-time, $130 per hour part-time. *Required fees:* $150 full-time, $5 per hour. *Payment plan:* installment. *Waivers:* senior citizens and employees or children of employees.
Financial Aid In 2001, 34 Federal Work-Study jobs.
Applying *Options:* common application, early admission. *Required:* high school transcript. *Application deadline:* rolling (freshmen), rolling (transfers).
Admissions Contact Mrs. Carroll O'Neal, Registrar, Penn Valley Community College, 3201 Southwest Trafficway, Kansas City, MO 64111. *Phone:* 816-759-4101. *Fax:* 816-759-4478.

RANKEN TECHNICAL COLLEGE
St. Louis, Missouri

Admissions Contact Dean of Students, Ranken Technical College, 4431 Finney Avenue, St. Louis, MO 63113. *Phone:* 314-371-0233 Ext. 4808. *Fax:* 314-371-0241. *E-mail:* feeller@ranken.org.

SAINT CHARLES COMMUNITY COLLEGE
St. Peters, Missouri

- **State-supported** 2-year, founded 1986, part of Missouri Coordinating Board for Higher Education
- **Calendar** semesters
- **Degree** certificates and associate
- **Small-town** 135-acre campus with easy access to St. Louis
- **Endowment** $6.7 million
- **Coed,** 6,171 undergraduate students, 42% full-time, 62% women, 38% men

Undergraduates 2,566 full-time, 3,605 part-time. 3% African American, 0.9% Asian American or Pacific Islander, 1% Hispanic American, 0.4% Native American, 0.2% international, 6% transferred in.
Freshmen *Admission:* 1,621 applied, 1,621 admitted, 979 enrolled.
Faculty *Total:* 359, 19% full-time, 5% with terminal degrees. *Student/faculty ratio:* 22:1.
Majors Accounting; business administration; business marketing and marketing management; child care/development; computer programming related; computer programming (specific applications); computer science; computer systems networking/telecommunications; criminal justice/law enforcement administration; drafting; graphic design/commercial art/illustration; human services; law enforcement/police science; liberal arts and sciences/liberal studies; medical records administration; medical transcription; nursing; occupational therapy; office management; pre-engineering; secretarial science; Web/multimedia management/webmaster.
Academic Programs *Special study options:* academic remediation for entering students, adult/continuing education programs, advanced placement credit, distance learning, double majors, English as a second language, independent study, internships, part-time degree program, services for LD students, summer session for credit.
Library Learning Resource Center with 47,852 titles, 3,900 serial subscriptions, 5,913 audiovisual materials, an OPAC, a Web page.
Computers on Campus 279 computers available on campus for general student use. A campuswide network can be accessed from off campus. At least one staffed computer lab available.
Student Life *Housing:* college housing not available. *Activities and Organizations:* drama/theater group, student-run newspaper, choral group, Phi Theta Kappa, SCCCC Roller Hockey Club, Student Senate, Criminal Justice Student

Saint Charles Community College (continued)
Organization, Human Services Student Organization. *Campus security:* 24-hour emergency response devices and patrols, late-night transport/escort service. *Student Services:* personal/psychological counseling.
Athletics Member NJCAA. *Intercollegiate sports:* baseball M(s), softball W(s). *Intramural sports:* basketball M/W, football M, soccer M/W, softball M/W, volleyball M/W.
Standardized Tests *Required:* ACT COMPASS. *Recommended:* ACT (for placement).
Costs (2002–03) *Tuition:* area resident $1440 full-time, $48 per semester hour part-time; state resident $2040 full-time, $68 per semester hour part-time; nonresident $3090 full-time, $103 per semester hour part-time. *Required fees:* $150 full-time, $5 per semester hour. *Waivers:* senior citizens and employees or children of employees.
Financial Aid In 2001, 21 Federal Work-Study jobs (averaging $1848).
Applying *Options:* common application, early admission, deferred entrance. *Required for some:* high school transcript. *Recommended:* high school transcript. *Application deadline:* rolling (freshmen), rolling (transfers). *Notification:* continuous (freshmen).
Admissions Contact Ms. Kathy Brockgreitens, Director of Admissions/Registrar, Saint Charles Community College, 4601 Mid Rivers Mall Drive, St. Peters, MO 63376-0975. *Phone:* 636-922-8229. *Fax:* 636-922-8236. *E-mail:* regist@stchas.edu.

ST. LOUIS COMMUNITY COLLEGE AT FLORISSANT VALLEY

St. Louis, Missouri

- **District-supported** 2-year, founded 1963, part of St. Louis Community College System
- **Calendar** semesters
- **Degree** certificates and associate
- **Suburban** 108-acre campus
- **Coed,** 7,365 undergraduate students

Undergraduates Students come from 31 other countries.
Freshmen *Admission:* 1,275 applied, 1,275 admitted.
Faculty *Total:* 353, 37% full-time.
Majors Accounting; art; broadcast journalism; business administration; chemical engineering technology; child care/development; civil engineering technology; computer engineering technology; computer programming; computer science; construction technology; corrections; criminal justice/law enforcement administration; data processing technology; dietetics; electrical/electronic engineering technology; elementary education; emergency medical technology; engineering; engineering science; engineering technology; fashion merchandising; film/video production; finance; fire science; food products retailing; food sciences; food services technology; graphic design/commercial art/illustration; human services; information sciences/systems; journalism; law enforcement/police science; legal studies; liberal arts and sciences/liberal studies; mass communications; mathematics; mechanical engineering technology; music; nursing; photography; pre-engineering; radio/television broadcasting; real estate; secretarial science; sign language interpretation; telecommunications; theater arts/drama.
Academic Programs *Special study options:* academic remediation for entering students, adult/continuing education programs, advanced placement credit, cooperative education, English as a second language, honors programs, part-time degree program, services for LD students, study abroad, summer session for credit. *ROTC:* Army (c).
Library 90,021 titles, 655 serial subscriptions.
Computers on Campus 470 computers available on campus for general student use. At least one staffed computer lab available.
Student Life *Housing:* college housing not available. *Activities and Organizations:* drama/theater group, student-run newspaper, radio station, Phi Theta Kappa, Student Nurses Association, Women in New Goals, Florissant Valley Association of the Deaf, Student Government Association, national fraternities, national sororities. *Campus security:* 24-hour emergency response devices and patrols, late-night transport/escort service. *Student Services:* health clinic, personal/psychological counseling.
Athletics Member NAIA, NJCAA. *Intercollegiate sports:* baseball M, basketball M(s)/W(s), cross-country running M(s)/W(s), soccer M(s)/W(s), softball W(s), track and field M(s)/W(s), volleyball W(s). *Intramural sports:* volleyball W.
Standardized Tests *Recommended:* SAT I or ACT (for placement).
Costs (2002–03) *Tuition:* area resident $1792 full-time, $56 per credit hour part-time; state resident $2336 full-time, $73 per credit hour part-time; nonresident $3296 full-time, $103 per credit hour part-time. *Waivers:* senior citizens and employees or children of employees.
Applying *Options:* electronic application, early admission. *Required:* high school transcript. *Application deadlines:* 8/19 (freshmen), 8/19 (transfers). *Notification:* continuous (freshmen).
Admissions Contact Mr. Mitchell Egeston, Manager of Admissions and Registration, St. Louis Community College at Florissant Valley, 3400 Pershall Road, St. Louis, MO 63135-1499. *Phone:* 314-595-4245. *Fax:* 314-595-2224.

ST. LOUIS COMMUNITY COLLEGE AT FOREST PARK

St. Louis, Missouri

- **District-supported** 2-year, founded 1962, part of St. Louis Community College System
- **Calendar** semesters
- **Degree** associate
- **Suburban** 34-acre campus
- **Coed**

Faculty *Student/faculty ratio:* 19:1.
Student Life *Campus security:* 24-hour patrols.
Athletics Member NJCAA.
Financial Aid In 2001, 165 Federal Work-Study jobs (averaging $3000).
Applying *Options:* electronic application, early admission. *Required:* high school transcript.
Admissions Contact Mr. Glenn Marshall, Coordinator of Enrollment Services, St. Louis Community College at Forest Park, 5600 Oakland Avenue, St. Louis, MO 63110. *Phone:* 314-644-9125. *Fax:* 314-644-9375.

ST. LOUIS COMMUNITY COLLEGE AT MERAMEC

Kirkwood, Missouri

- **District-supported** 2-year, founded 1963, part of St. Louis Community College System
- **Calendar** semesters
- **Degree** certificates and associate
- **Suburban** 80-acre campus with easy access to St. Louis
- **Coed**

Student Life *Campus security:* 24-hour emergency response devices and patrols.
Athletics Member NJCAA.
Standardized Tests *Required for some:* Michigan Test of English Language Proficiency.
Applying *Options:* early admission, deferred entrance. *Required for some:* high school transcript, interview.
Admissions Contact Mr. Mike Cundiff, Coordinator of Admissions, St. Louis Community College at Meramec, 11333 Big Bend Boulevard, Kirkwood, MO 63122-5720. *Phone:* 314-984-7608. *Fax:* 314-984-7051.

SANFORD-BROWN COLLEGE

Fenton, Missouri

- **Proprietary** 2-year, founded 1868
- **Calendar** quarters
- **Degree** certificates, diplomas, and associate
- **Suburban** 6-acre campus with easy access to St. Louis
- **Coed,** 511 undergraduate students, 61% full-time, 42% women, 58% men

Undergraduates 311 full-time, 200 part-time. Students come from 2 states and territories, 8% are from out of state.
Freshmen *Admission:* 203 enrolled.
Faculty *Total:* 28, 46% full-time.
Majors Accounting; computer programming (specific applications); computer programming, vendor/product certification; computer science; paralegal/legal assistant; radiological science; respiratory therapy.
Academic Programs *Special study options:* adult/continuing education programs, internships, services for LD students.
Library Learning Resource Center.

Computers on Campus 40 computers available on campus for general student use. Internet access, at least one staffed computer lab available.
Student Life *Housing:* college housing not available. *Activities and Organizations:* Paralegal Club, peer advisors, student council, Accounting Club, student ambassadors. *Campus security:* late-night transport/escort service, trained security personnel from 7:30 p.m. to 10:30 p.m. *Student Services:* personal/psychological counseling.
Athletics *Intercollegiate sports:* basketball M.
Costs (2001–02) *Tuition:* $19,350 per degree program part-time. Full-time tuition and fees vary according to program. *Payment plans:* tuition prepayment, installment, deferred payment. *Waivers:* employees or children of employees.
Applying *Options:* common application, deferred entrance. *Application fee:* $25. *Required:* high school transcript, interview.
Admissions Contact Mr. Todd Lush, Director of Admissions, Sanford-Brown College, 1203 Smizer Mill Road, Fenton, MO 63026. *Phone:* 636-349-4900 Ext. 102. *Toll-free phone:* 800-456-7222. *Fax:* 636-349-9170.

SANFORD-BROWN COLLEGE
Hazelwood, Missouri

- **Proprietary** 2-year, founded 1868
- **Calendar** quarters
- **Degree** diplomas and associate
- 1-acre campus with easy access to St. Louis
- **Coed,** 350 undergraduate students

Undergraduates Students come from 3 other countries.
Majors Accounting; business administration; computer programming; health education; paralegal/legal assistant; physical therapy; secretarial science.
Academic Programs *Special study options:* academic remediation for entering students, adult/continuing education programs, internships, part-time degree program, services for LD students.
Library Learning Resource Center.
Computers on Campus 32 computers available on campus for general student use. At least one staffed computer lab available.
Student Life *Activities and Organizations:* Paralegal Club, peer advisors, student council, Accounting Club. *Campus security:* 24-hour emergency response devices and patrols. *Student Services:* personal/psychological counseling.
Athletics *Intercollegiate sports:* basketball M.
Costs (2002–03) *Tuition:* $3490 full-time, $285 per credit hour part-time. Full-time tuition and fees vary according to program. Part-time tuition and fees vary according to program. *Payment plans:* installment, deferred payment. *Waivers:* employees or children of employees.
Applying *Options:* common application, deferred entrance. *Required:* high school transcript, interview. *Application deadline:* rolling (freshmen).
Admissions Contact Mr. Kenneth Thomas, Director of Admissions, Sanford-Brown College, 75 Village Square, Hazelwood, MO 63042. *Phone:* 314-731-5200 Ext. 201.

SANFORD-BROWN COLLEGE
North Kansas City, Missouri

- **Proprietary** 2-year, founded 1992
- **Calendar** quarters
- **Degree** certificates, diplomas, and associate
- **Suburban** campus
- **Coed**

Student Life *Campus security:* 24-hour patrols.
Applying *Options:* common application, deferred entrance.
Admissions Contact Ms. Rose Steptoe, Director of Admissions, Sanford-Brown College, 520 East 19th Avenue, North Kansas City, MO 64116. *Phone:* 816-472-7400. *Toll-free phone:* 800-456-7222.

SANFORD-BROWN COLLEGE
St. Charles, Missouri

Admissions Contact Mr. William Jones, Director of Admissions, Sanford-Brown College, 3555 Franks Drive, St. Charles, MO 63301. *Phone:* 636-949-2620. *Toll-free phone:* 800-456-7222.

SOUTHWEST MISSOURI STATE UNIVERSITY-WEST PLAINS
West Plains, Missouri

- **State-supported** 2-year, founded 1963, part of Southwest Missouri State University
- **Calendar** semesters
- **Degree** certificates and associate
- **Small-town** 11-acre campus
- **Endowment** $448,596
- **Coed**

Faculty *Student/faculty ratio:* 18:1.
Student Life *Campus security:* late-night transport/escort service, controlled dormitory access.
Athletics Member NJCAA.
Standardized Tests *Required for some:* ACT (for placement).
Costs (2001–02) *Tuition:* state resident $2280 full-time, $76 per credit hour part-time; nonresident $4560 full-time, $152 per credit hour part-time. Full-time tuition and fees vary according to course load. Part-time tuition and fees vary according to course load. *Required fees:* $140 full-time, $76 per credit hour, $70 per term part-time. *Room and board:* $4280.
Financial Aid In 2001, 63 Federal Work-Study jobs (averaging $2000).
Applying *Application fee:* $15. *Required for some:* high school transcript.
Admissions Contact Ms. Melissa Jett, Admissions Assistant, Southwest Missouri State University-West Plains, 128 Garfield, West Plains, MO 65775. *Phone:* 417-255-7955. *Fax:* 417-255-7223. *E-mail:* admissions@wp.smsu.edu.

SPRINGFIELD COLLEGE
Springfield, Missouri

- **Proprietary** 2-year, founded 1976, part of Corinthian Colleges, Inc
- **Calendar** quarters
- **Degree** associate
- **Urban** 2-acre campus
- **Coed**

Financial Aid In 2001, 20 Federal Work-Study jobs (averaging $3708).
Applying *Options:* deferred entrance. *Application fee:* $25. *Required:* high school transcript, interview.
Admissions Contact Ms. Melissa Barnard, Director of Admissions, Springfield College, 1010 West Sunshine, Springfield, MO 65807-2488. *Phone:* 417-864-7220. *Toll-free phone:* 800-864-5697 (in-state); 800-475-2669 (out-of-state).

STATE FAIR COMMUNITY COLLEGE
Sedalia, Missouri

- **District-supported** 2-year, founded 1966, part of Missouri Coordinating Board for Higher Education
- **Calendar** semesters
- **Degree** certificates and associate
- **Small-town** 128-acre campus
- **Coed,** 3,356 undergraduate students

Undergraduates Students come from 16 states and territories, 8 other countries, 8% African American, 1% Asian American or Pacific Islander, 2% Hispanic American, 0.5% Native American.
Freshmen *Admission:* 952 admitted.
Faculty *Total:* 171, 28% full-time.
Majors Accounting; agricultural business; agricultural mechanization; agricultural sciences; art; auto mechanic/technician; business administration; business marketing and marketing management; computer engineering technology; computer programming (specific applications); computer science related; computer systems networking/telecommunications; construction technology; court reporting; criminal justice/law enforcement administration; electrical/electronic engineering technology; finance; food products retailing; horticulture science; industrial technology; information sciences/systems; legal administrative assistant; liberal arts and sciences/liberal studies; machine technology; mass communications; medical administrative assistant; medical records administration; nursing; practical nurse; secretarial science; welding technology.
Academic Programs *Special study options:* academic remediation for entering students, accelerated degree program, adult/continuing education programs,

State Fair Community College (continued)
advanced placement credit, distance learning, internships, off-campus study, part-time degree program, services for LD students, summer session for credit.
Library Learning Resources Center with 36,000 titles, 100 serial subscriptions.
Computers on Campus 218 computers available on campus for general student use. A campuswide network can be accessed from off campus. Internet access, at least one staffed computer lab available.
Student Life *Housing Options:* coed, men-only, women-only. *Activities and Organizations:* drama/theater group, choral group. *Campus security:* security during evening class hours.
Athletics Member NJCAA. *Intercollegiate sports:* basketball M(s)/W(s), soccer M(s), volleyball W.
Standardized Tests *Required for some:* ACT (for placement), ACT ASSET, COMPASS.
Costs (2002–03) *Tuition:* area resident $1392 full-time, $58 per semester hour part-time; state resident $2040 full-time, $85 per semester hour part-time; nonresident $3312 full-time, $138 per semester hour part-time. *Room and board:* room only: $2100. *Waivers:* senior citizens and employees or children of employees.
Financial Aid In 2001, 50 Federal Work-Study jobs (averaging $1000).
Applying *Options:* early admission. *Required:* high school transcript. *Application deadline:* rolling (freshmen), rolling (transfers).
Admissions Contact Mr. Ronald L. Gerstbauer, Dean of Student Services, State Fair Community College, 3201 West 16th, Sedalia, MO 65301. *Phone:* 660-530-5800 Ext. 292. *Toll-free phone:* 877-311-SFCC Ext. 217 (in-state); 877-311-SFCC (out-of-state). *Fax:* 660-530-5546.

THREE RIVERS COMMUNITY COLLEGE
Poplar Bluff, Missouri

- **State and locally supported** 2-year, founded 1966, part of Missouri Coordinating Board for Higher Education
- **Calendar** semesters
- **Degree** certificates and associate
- **Rural** 70-acre campus
- **Coed**

Faculty *Student/faculty ratio:* 18:1.
Student Life *Campus security:* 24-hour patrols.
Athletics Member NJCAA.
Standardized Tests *Recommended:* ACT (for placement), ACT ASSET.
Applying *Options:* early admission. *Application fee:* $20. *Required:* high school transcript.
Admissions Contact Ms. Vida L. Stanard, Director, Three Rivers Community College, 2080 Three Rivers Boulevard, Poplar Bluff, MO 63901. *Phone:* 573-840-9600. *Toll-free phone:* 877-TRY-TRCC Ext. 605 (in-state); 573-840-9604 (out-of-state). *E-mail:* vstanard@trcc.cc.mo.us.

VATTEROTT COLLEGE
St. Ann, Missouri

- **Proprietary** 2-year, founded 1969
- **Calendar** continuous
- **Degree** diplomas and associate
- **Suburban** campus with easy access to St. Louis
- **Coed,** 600 undergraduate students

Majors Computer programming; electrical/electronic engineering technology; heating/air conditioning/refrigeration technology.
Library Main Library plus 7 others with a Web page.
Computers on Campus 240 computers available on campus for general student use. Internet access, at least one staffed computer lab available.
Student Life *Housing:* college housing not available.
Costs (2001–02) *Tuition:* Full time tuition: $18,300 to $28,400 per degree program. *Payment plans:* installment, deferred payment.
Applying *Options:* common application.
Admissions Contact Ms. Michelle Tinsley, Co-Director of Admissions, Vatterott College, 3925 Industrial Drive, St. Ann, MO 63074-1807. *Phone:* 314-843-4200. *Toll-free phone:* 800-345-6018. *Fax:* 314-428-5956.

WENTWORTH MILITARY ACADEMY AND JUNIOR COLLEGE
Lexington, Missouri

- **Independent** 2-year, founded 1880
- **Calendar** semesters
- **Degree** associate
- **Small-town** 130-acre campus with easy access to Kansas City
- **Coed,** 312 undergraduate students, 40% full-time, 54% women, 46% men

Undergraduates 124 full-time, 188 part-time. Students come from 22 states and territories, 4 other countries, 18% are from out of state, 7% African American, 8% Asian American or Pacific Islander, 3% Hispanic American, 2% Native American, 0.6% international, 0.3% transferred in. *Retention:* 71% of 2001 full-time freshmen returned.
Freshmen *Admission:* 110 applied, 51 admitted, 57 enrolled. *Test scores:* SAT verbal scores over 500: 33%; SAT math scores over 500: 73%; SAT math scores over 600: 33%.
Faculty *Total:* 32, 22% full-time. *Student/faculty ratio:* 9:1.
Majors Liberal arts and sciences/liberal studies.
Academic Programs *Special study options:* academic remediation for entering students, adult/continuing education programs, advanced placement credit, English as a second language, part-time degree program, student-designed majors, summer session for credit. *ROTC:* Army (b).
Library Sellers-Coombs Library with 18,890 titles, 49 serial subscriptions, 919 audiovisual materials, a Web page.
Computers on Campus 35 computers available on campus for general student use. Internet access, at least one staffed computer lab available.
Student Life *Housing:* on-campus residence required through sophomore year. *Options:* men-only, women-only. *Activities and Organizations:* drama/theater group, student-run newspaper, choral group, marching band, national fraternities. *Campus security:* 24-hour emergency response devices and patrols. *Student Services:* health clinic, personal/psychological counseling.
Athletics Member NJCAA. *Intercollegiate sports:* cross-country running M, track and field M/W. *Intramural sports:* archery M/W, basketball M/W, racquetball M/W, riflery M/W, soccer W, swimming M/W, table tennis M, tennis M/W, track and field M/W, volleyball M/W, weight lifting M/W.
Standardized Tests *Recommended:* SAT I or ACT (for admission).
Costs (2002–03) *One-time required fee:* $2010. *Comprehensive fee:* $17,410 includes full-time tuition ($10,815), mandatory fees ($2015), and room and board ($4580). Part-time tuition: $95 per credit. *Room and board:* College room only: $2060. *Payment plans:* installment, deferred payment. *Waivers:* employees or children of employees.
Applying *Options:* common application. *Application fee:* $100. *Required:* high school transcript. *Application deadline:* rolling (freshmen), rolling (transfers).
Admissions Contact Maj. Todd Kitchen, Dean of Admissions, Wentworth Military Academy and Junior College, 1880 Washington Avenue, Lexington, MO 64067. *Phone:* 660-259-2221. *Fax:* 660-259-2677. *E-mail:* admissions@wma1880.org.

MONTANA

BLACKFEET COMMUNITY COLLEGE
Browning, Montana

- **Independent** 2-year, founded 1974
- **Calendar** quarters
- **Degree** certificates, diplomas, and associate
- **Small-town** 5-acre campus
- **Coed,** 375 undergraduate students

Freshmen *Admission:* 83 admitted.
Faculty *Total:* 50, 60% full-time.
Majors Business administration; early childhood education; human services; liberal arts and sciences/liberal studies; Native American studies; secretarial science; teacher assistant/aide.
Academic Programs *Special study options:* academic remediation for entering students, adult/continuing education programs, off-campus study, part-time degree program.
Library 10,000 titles, 175 serial subscriptions.

Computers on Campus 55 computers available on campus for general student use. At least one staffed computer lab available.
Student Life *Housing:* college housing not available. *Student Services:* health clinic, personal/psychological counseling.
Athletics *Intramural sports:* basketball M/W, cross-country running M/W, racquetball M/W, skiing (cross-country) M/W, skiing (downhill) M/W, swimming M/W, tennis M/W, volleyball M/W, weight lifting M/W.
Costs (2002–03) *Tuition:* area resident $1650 full-time, $55 per credit part-time; state resident $55 per credit part-time; nonresident $55 per credit part-time. *Required fees:* $350 full-time, $36 per credit, $175 per semester part-time.
Financial Aid In 2001, 10 Federal Work-Study jobs (averaging $2316).
Applying *Options:* early admission. *Required:* high school transcript. *Application deadline:* rolling (freshmen), rolling (transfers). *Notification:* continuous (freshmen).
Admissions Contact Ms. Deana McNabb, Registrar and Admissions Officer, Blackfeet Community College, PO Box 819, Browning, MT 59417-0819. *Phone:* 406-338-5421 Ext. 243. *Fax:* 406-338-7808.

DAWSON COMMUNITY COLLEGE
Glendive, Montana

- **State and locally supported** 2-year, founded 1940, part of Montana University System
- **Calendar** semesters
- **Degree** certificates and associate
- **Rural** 300-acre campus
- **Endowment** $344,944
- **Coed,** 449 undergraduate students, 78% full-time, 55% women, 45% men

Undergraduates 350 full-time, 99 part-time. Students come from 10 states and territories, 1 other country, 8% transferred in, 19% live on campus.
Freshmen *Admission:* 219 applied, 219 admitted, 150 enrolled. *Test scores:* ACT scores over 18: 67%; ACT scores over 24: 17%.
Faculty *Total:* 49, 43% full-time. *Student/faculty ratio:* 16:1.
Majors Agricultural business; alcohol/drug abuse counseling; auto mechanic/technician; business; child care/guidance; clinical/medical social work; computer/information sciences; law enforcement/police science; liberal arts and sciences/liberal studies; secretarial science.
Academic Programs *Special study options:* academic remediation for entering students, adult/continuing education programs, independent study, internships, part-time degree program, services for LD students, summer session for credit.
Library Jane Carey Memorial Library with 18,870 titles, 1,112 audiovisual materials, an OPAC, a Web page.
Computers on Campus 70 computers available on campus for general student use. A campuswide network can be accessed from student residence rooms and from off campus. Internet access, at least one staffed computer lab available.
Student Life *Housing Options:* coed. *Activities and Organizations:* drama/theater group, choral group, Human Services Club, Law Enforcement Club, Associated Student Body, VICA, United Badlands Indian Club. *Campus security:* 24-hour emergency response devices.
Athletics Member NJCAA. *Intercollegiate sports:* baseball M, basketball M(s)/W(s), equestrian sports M(s)/W(s), softball W. *Intramural sports:* basketball M/W, bowling M/W, golf M/W, racquetball M/W, softball M/W, table tennis M/W, tennis M/W, volleyball M/W.
Standardized Tests *Required for some:* ACT (for placement). *Recommended:* ACT (for placement).
Costs (2001–02) *Tuition:* area resident $1544 full-time, $64 per credit part-time; state resident $2179 full-time, $91 per credit part-time; nonresident $4843 full-time, $202 per credit part-time. Full-time tuition and fees vary according to reciprocity agreements. Part-time tuition and fees vary according to reciprocity agreements. *Room and board:* room only: $1651. *Payment plan:* installment. *Waivers:* senior citizens and employees or children of employees.
Financial Aid In 2001, 45 Federal Work-Study jobs (averaging $1200). 17 State and other part-time jobs (averaging $1200).
Applying *Options:* deferred entrance. *Application fee:* $30. *Required:* high school transcript. *Application deadline:* rolling (freshmen), rolling (transfers). *Notification:* continuous (freshmen).
Admissions Contact Ms. Jolene Myers, Director of Admissions and Financial Aid, Dawson Community College, Box 421, Glendive, MT 59330-0421. *Phone:* 406-377-3396 Ext. 28. *Toll-free phone:* 800-821-8320. *Fax:* 406-377-8132.

DULL KNIFE MEMORIAL COLLEGE
Lame Deer, Montana

Admissions Contact Mr. William L. Wertman, Registrar and Director of Admissions, Dull Knife Memorial College, PO Box 98, Lame Deer, MT 59043-0098. *Phone:* 406-477-6215.

FLATHEAD VALLEY COMMUNITY COLLEGE
Kalispell, Montana

- **State and locally supported** 2-year, founded 1967
- **Calendar** semesters
- **Degree** certificates and associate
- **Small-town** 40-acre campus
- **Endowment** $737,839
- **Coed,** 1,867 undergraduate students, 45% full-time, 64% women, 36% men

Established in 1967, FVCC is an accredited, comprehensive community college located at the foot of the Rockies and just minutes from Glacier National Park, 2 major ski resorts, and the Bob Marshall Wilderness. The architectural award-winning, handicapped-accessible campus serves more than 1,800 students in 24 academic transfer and 16 occupational programs.

Undergraduates 833 full-time, 1,034 part-time. Students come from 17 states and territories, 2 other countries, 2% are from out of state, 4% transferred in.
Freshmen *Admission:* 397 applied, 397 admitted, 290 enrolled.
Faculty *Total:* 168, 23% full-time. *Student/faculty ratio:* 14:1.
Majors Accounting; business administration; computer engineering technology; computer/information technology services administration and management related; computer typography/composition; construction technology; criminal justice/law enforcement administration; data entry/microcomputer applications; developmental/child psychology; forest harvesting production technology; forest products technology; hotel and restaurant management; hotel/motel services marketing operations; human services; liberal arts and sciences/liberal studies; medical administrative assistant; medical assistant; metal/jewelry arts; secretarial science; surveying; Web/multimedia management/webmaster; wildlife management; word processing.
Academic Programs *Special study options:* academic remediation for entering students, adult/continuing education programs, advanced placement credit, distance learning, double majors, independent study, internships, part-time degree program, services for LD students, summer session for credit.
Library Flathead Valley Community College Library with 19,038 titles, 125 serial subscriptions, 444 audiovisual materials, an OPAC, a Web page.
Computers on Campus 132 computers available on campus for general student use. Internet access, at least one staffed computer lab available.
Student Life *Housing:* college housing not available. *Activities and Organizations:* drama/theater group, student-run newspaper, Forestry Club, Pi-Ta Club. *Student Services:* personal/psychological counseling.
Athletics Member NJCAA. *Intercollegiate sports:* cross-country running M/W, soccer M/W. *Intramural sports:* basketball M/W, football M/W, racquetball M/W, soccer M/W, tennis M/W, volleyball M/W, weight lifting M/W.
Costs (2001–02) *Tuition:* area resident $1835 full-time, $44 per credit part-time; state resident $2626 full-time, $73 per credit part-time; nonresident $5685 full-time, $187 per credit part-time. Full-time tuition and fees vary according to course load. Part-time tuition and fees vary according to course load. *Payment plan:* deferred payment. *Waivers:* senior citizens and employees or children of employees.
Financial Aid In 2001, 63 Federal Work-Study jobs (averaging $900). 50 State and other part-time jobs (averaging $900).
Applying *Options:* early admission, deferred entrance. *Application fee:* $15. *Required:* high school transcript. *Application deadline:* rolling (freshmen), rolling (transfers).
Admissions Contact Ms. Marlene C. Stoltz, Admissions/Graduation Coordinator, Flathead Valley Community College, 777 Grandview Avenue, Kalispell, MT 59901-2622. *Phone:* 406-756-3846. *Toll-free phone:* 800-313-3822. *Fax:* 406-756-3965. *E-mail:* vlorenz@fvcc.cc.mt.us.

FORT BELKNAP COLLEGE
Harlem, Montana

Admissions Contact Ms. Michele Lewis, Registrar and Admissions Officer, Fort Belknap College, PO Box 159, Harlem, MT 59526-0159. *Phone:* 406-353-2607 Ext. 219.

Fort Peck Community College

Poplar, Montana

- **Independent** 2-year, founded 1978
- **Calendar** semesters
- **Degree** certificates and associate
- **Small-town** campus
- **Coed**

Standardized Tests *Required:* ACT ASSET.

Applying *Options:* electronic application, early admission. *Application fee:* $15.

Admissions Contact Mr. Robert McAnally, Dean of Students, Fort Peck Community College, PO Box 398, Poplar, MT 59255-0398. *Phone:* 406-768-5553.

Helena College of Technology of The University of Montana

Helena, Montana

- **State-supported** 2-year, founded 1939, part of Montana University System
- **Calendar** semesters
- **Degree** certificates and associate
- **Small-town** campus
- **Coed,** 850 undergraduate students

Faculty *Total:* 80, 63% full-time. *Student/faculty ratio:* 18:1.

Majors Accounting technician; agricultural mechanization; aircraft mechanic/airframe; auto mechanic/technician; carpentry; computer programming; data processing; diesel engine mechanic; electrical/electronic engineering technology; executive assistant; fire science; general office/clerical; general studies; legal administrative assistant; machine technology; medical administrative assistant; practical nurse; welding technology.

Academic Programs *Special study options:* academic remediation for entering students, adult/continuing education programs, part-time degree program, services for LD students, summer session for credit.

Library 2,500 titles, 30 serial subscriptions.

Computers on Campus 45 computers available on campus for general student use. Internet access, at least one staffed computer lab available.

Student Life *Housing:* college housing not available. *Activities and Organizations:* Student Senate.

Athletics *Intramural sports:* basketball M/W, volleyball M/W.

Standardized Tests *Required:* ACT ASSET.

Costs (2001–02) *Tuition:* state resident $1200 full-time, $135 per credit part-time; nonresident $3000 full-time, $278 per credit part-time.

Financial Aid In 2001, 60 Federal Work-Study jobs (averaging $1500). 15 State and other part-time jobs (averaging $1500).

Applying *Options:* early admission, deferred entrance. *Application fee:* $30. *Application deadline:* rolling (freshmen), rolling (transfers).

Admissions Contact Ms. Vicky Lorenz, Director of Admissions, Helena College of Technology of The University of Montana, 1115 North Roberts Street, Helena, MT 59601. *Phone:* 406-444-6800. *Toll-free phone:* 800-241-4882. *Fax:* 406-444-6892. *E-mail:* awalstad@selway.umt.edu.

Little Big Horn College

Crow Agency, Montana

Admissions Contact Ms. Ann Bullis, Dean of Student Services, Little Big Horn College, Box 370, Crow Agency, MT 59022-0370. *Phone:* 406-638-2228 Ext. 50.

Miles Community College

Miles City, Montana

- **State and locally supported** 2-year, founded 1939, part of Montana University System
- **Calendar** semesters
- **Degree** certificates and associate
- **Small-town** 8-acre campus
- **Endowment** $2.7 million
- **Coed,** 590 undergraduate students, 66% full-time, 61% women, 39% men

Undergraduates 388 full-time, 202 part-time. Students come from 6 states and territories, 5% are from out of state, 0.8% African American, 0.4% Asian American or Pacific Islander, 0.6% Hispanic American, 1% Native American, 0.4% international, 9% transferred in, 20% live on campus.

Freshmen *Admission:* 205 applied, 205 admitted, 176 enrolled. *Average high school GPA:* 2.73.

Faculty *Total:* 40, 68% full-time. *Student/faculty ratio:* 14:1.

Majors Agricultural mechanization; auto mechanic/technician; building maintenance/management; business administration; business marketing and marketing management; carpentry; computer engineering technology; computer graphics; computer management; construction technology; electrical/electronic engineering technology; electrical equipment installation/repair; energy management technology; fire science; graphic design/commercial art/illustration; human services; information technology; liberal arts and sciences/liberal studies; medical administrative assistant; nursing; retail management; secretarial science; telecommunications.

Academic Programs *Special study options:* academic remediation for entering students, accelerated degree program, adult/continuing education programs, advanced placement credit, cooperative education, distance learning, double majors, English as a second language, independent study, internships, off-campus study, part-time degree program, services for LD students, summer session for credit.

Library Library Resource Center with 17,563 titles, 310 serial subscriptions, 174 audiovisual materials, an OPAC, a Web page.

Computers on Campus 165 computers available on campus for general student use. A campuswide network can be accessed from off campus. Internet access, at least one staffed computer lab available.

Student Life *Housing Options:* coed. *Activities and Organizations:* drama/theater group, student-run newspaper, choral group, Campus Ministry, Multicultural club, Student Nurses Association, Vocational Industrial Club, Western Club. *Campus security:* 24-hour emergency response devices. *Student Services:* personal/psychological counseling.

Athletics Member NJCAA. *Intercollegiate sports:* basketball M(s)/W(s), golf M/W. *Intramural sports:* basketball M/W, bowling M/W, cross-country running M/W, golf M/W, ice hockey M/W, racquetball M/W, soccer M/W, softball M/W, swimming M/W, table tennis M/W, tennis M/W, track and field M/W, volleyball M/W, weight lifting M/W.

Standardized Tests *Required for some:* SAT I or ACT (for placement). *Recommended:* SAT I or ACT (for placement).

Costs (2002–03) *Tuition:* area resident $975 full-time, $37 per credit part-time; state resident $1350 full-time, $62 per credit part-time; nonresident $4650 full-time, $127 per credit part-time. *Required fees:* $840 full-time, $28 per credit. *Room and board:* $3600. Room and board charges vary according to board plan, housing facility, and location. *Payment plans:* installment, deferred payment. *Waivers:* senior citizens and employees or children of employees.

Financial Aid In 2001, 35 Federal Work-Study jobs (averaging $1000). 28 State and other part-time jobs (averaging $1000).

Applying *Options:* common application, early admission, deferred entrance. *Application fee:* $40. *Required:* high school transcript. *Application deadline:* rolling (freshmen), rolling (transfers).

Admissions Contact Admissions Counselor, Miles Community College, 2715 Dickinson, Miles City, MT 59301-4799. *Phone:* 406-234-3513. *Toll-free phone:* 800-541-9281. *Fax:* 406-234-3599.

Montana State University-Great Falls College of Technology

Great Falls, Montana

- **State-supported** 2-year, founded 1969, part of Montana University System
- **Calendar** semesters
- **Degree** certificates and associate
- **Urban** 35-acre campus
- **Coed,** 1,251 undergraduate students, 46% full-time, 71% women, 29% men

Undergraduates 570 full-time, 681 part-time. Students come from 9 states and territories, 1% are from out of state, 14% transferred in.

Freshmen *Admission:* 519 applied, 519 admitted, 387 enrolled.

Faculty *Total:* 83, 48% full-time. *Student/faculty ratio:* 15:1.

Majors Accounting; auto body repair; biological technology; business; computer management; computer systems networking/telecommunications; dental assistant; dental hygiene; drafting/design technology; emergency medical technology; fire science; interior design; legal administrative assistant; medical administrative assistant; medical assistant; medical records administration; medical records technology; medical transcription; physical therapy assistant; practical nurse; respiratory therapy; secretarial science; Web page, digital/multimedia and information resources design.

Academic Programs *Special study options:* academic remediation for entering students, adult/continuing education programs, advanced placement credit, distance learning, double majors, independent study, internships, off-campus study, part-time degree program, services for LD students, summer session for credit.

Library Montana State University College of Technology—Great Falls Library with 4,000 titles, 200 serial subscriptions, an OPAC, a Web page.

Computers on Campus 150 computers available on campus for general student use. A campuswide network can be accessed from off campus. Internet access, online (class) registration, at least one staffed computer lab available.

Student Life *Housing:* college housing not available. *Activities and Organizations:* student-run newspaper. *Campus security:* 24-hour emergency response devices.

Standardized Tests *Required:* SAT I, ACT, or ACT ASSET.

Costs (2001–02) *Tuition:* state resident $2185 full-time, $74 per credit part-time; nonresident $5812 full-time, $215 per credit part-time. Full-time tuition and fees vary according to course load and program. Part-time tuition and fees vary according to course load and program. *Required fees:* $201 full-time, $22 per credit, $30 per term part-time. *Payment plans:* installment, deferred payment. *Waivers:* minority students, senior citizens, and employees or children of employees.

Financial Aid In 2001, 25 Federal Work-Study jobs (averaging $2000). 10 State and other part-time jobs (averaging $2000).

Applying *Options:* deferred entrance. *Application fee:* $30. *Required:* high school transcript, proof of immunization. *Required for some:* essay or personal statement, 3 letters of recommendation. *Application deadline:* rolling (freshmen).

Admissions Contact Mr. David Farrington, Director of Admissions and Records, Montana State University-Great Falls College of Technology, 2100 16th Avenue South, Great Falls, MT 59405. *Phone:* 406-771-4300. *Toll-free phone:* 800-446-2698. *Fax:* 406-771-4317. *E-mail:* information@msugf.edu.

SALISH KOOTENAI COLLEGE
Pablo, Montana

- **Independent** primarily 2-year, founded 1977
- **Calendar** quarters
- **Degrees** certificates, associate, and bachelor's
- **Rural** 4-acre campus
- **Coed,** 1,042 undergraduate students, 53% full-time, 57% women, 43% men

Undergraduates 554 full-time, 488 part-time. Students come from 3 states and territories.

Freshmen *Admission:* 300 applied, 150 admitted, 77 enrolled.

Faculty *Total:* 92, 54% full-time.

Majors Carpentry; child care/development; computer science; dental hygiene; early childhood education; environmental science; forest harvesting production technology; forestry; human services; liberal arts and sciences/liberal studies; Native American studies; natural resources management; natural sciences; nursing; secretarial science.

Academic Programs *Special study options:* academic remediation for entering students, adult/continuing education programs, cooperative education, off-campus study, part-time degree program, services for LD students, summer session for credit.

Library 24,000 titles, 200 serial subscriptions.

Computers on Campus 30 computers available on campus for general student use. Internet access available.

Student Life *Housing:* college housing not available. *Activities and Organizations:* drama/theater group. *Student Services:* personal/psychological counseling.

Athletics *Intramural sports:* baseball M/W, basketball M/W, skiing (cross-country) M/W, skiing (downhill) M/W, softball M/W, tennis M/W, volleyball M/W, weight lifting M/W.

Standardized Tests *Required:* ACT (for placement), TABE.

Costs (2002–03) *Tuition:* area resident $2088 full-time, $58 per credit part-time; state resident $2556 full-time, $90 per credit part-time; nonresident $243 per credit part-time. Full-time tuition and fees vary according to reciprocity agreements. Part-time tuition and fees vary according to reciprocity agreements. *Required fees:* $687 full-time. *Payment plan:* installment. *Waivers:* minority students, adult students, senior citizens, and employees or children of employees.

Financial Aid In 2001, 78 Federal Work-Study jobs (averaging $1277).

Applying *Options:* deferred entrance. *Required:* high school transcript, proof of immunization, tribal enrollment. *Application deadline:* rolling (freshmen), rolling (transfers). *Notification:* continuous (freshmen).

Admissions Contact Ms. Jackie Moran, Admissions Officer, Salish Kootenai College, PO 117, Highway 93, Pablo, MT 59855. *Phone:* 406-675-4800 Ext. 265. *Fax:* 406-675-4801. *E-mail:* jackie_moran@skc.edu.

STONE CHILD COLLEGE
Box Elder, Montana

- **Independent** 2-year, founded 1984
- **Calendar** semesters
- **Degree** certificates and associate
- **Rural** campus
- **Coed,** 240 undergraduate students

Freshmen *Admission:* 11 applied, 11 admitted.

Faculty *Total:* 22, 45% full-time.

Majors Business administration; computer science; human services; liberal arts and sciences/liberal studies; secretarial science.

Computers on Campus 42 computers available on campus for general student use. Internet access, at least one staffed computer lab available.

Costs (2002–03) *Tuition:* area resident $1680 full-time, $60 per credit part-time. *Required fees:* $270 full-time. *Room and board:* $4110.

Applying *Required:* high school transcript.

Admissions Contact Mr. Ted Whitford, Director of Admissions/Registrar, Stone Child College, RR1, Box 1082, Box Elder, MT 59521. *Phone:* 406-395-4313 Ext. 110. *Fax:* 406-395-4836. *E-mail:* uanet337@quest.ocsc.montana.edu.

NEBRASKA

CENTRAL COMMUNITY COLLEGE-COLUMBUS CAMPUS
Columbus, Nebraska

- **State and locally supported** 2-year, founded 1968, part of Central Community College
- **Calendar** semesters
- **Degree** certificates, diplomas, and associate
- **Small-town** 90-acre campus
- **Coed,** 1,794 undergraduate students, 27% full-time, 57% women, 43% men

Undergraduates 492 full-time, 1,302 part-time. Students come from 41 states and territories, 4% are from out of state, 0.6% African American, 0.8% Asian American or Pacific Islander, 3% Hispanic American, 0.3% Native American, 0.1% international, 17% live on campus.

Freshmen *Admission:* 142 admitted, 137 enrolled.

Faculty *Total:* 91, 41% full-time, 5% with terminal degrees. *Student/faculty ratio:* 15:1.

Majors Accounting; agricultural business; auto mechanic/technician; business administration; business marketing and marketing management; computer/information sciences; computer programming (specific applications); drafting; electrical/electronic engineering technology; electromechanical technology; graphic design/commercial art/illustration; home economics; industrial technology; information technology; liberal arts and sciences/liberal studies; machine technology; practical nurse; quality control technology; secretarial science; system/networking/LAN/WAN management; Web/multimedia management/webmaster; welding technology.

Academic Programs *Special study options:* academic remediation for entering students, accelerated degree program, adult/continuing education programs, advanced placement credit, cooperative education, distance learning, English as a second language, external degree program, independent study, internships, off-campus study, part-time degree program, services for LD students, student-designed majors, summer session for credit.

Library Learning Resources Center with 27,098 titles, 155 serial subscriptions, 3,020 audiovisual materials, an OPAC.

Computers on Campus 100 computers available on campus for general student use. A campuswide network can be accessed from student residence rooms and from off campus. Internet access, at least one staffed computer lab available.

Student Life *Housing Options:* coed. *Activities and Organizations:* choral group, Phi Theta Kappa, Drama Club, Art Club, Cantari, Chorale. *Campus security:* late-night transport/escort service, controlled dormitory access, night security. *Student Services:* personal/psychological counseling, women's center.

Central Community College-Columbus Campus (continued)

Athletics Member NJCAA. *Intercollegiate sports:* basketball M(s), volleyball W(s). *Intramural sports:* basketball M/W, football M, softball M/W, table tennis M/W, volleyball M/W.

Standardized Tests *Required for some:* SAT I or ACT (for placement), ACT ASSET.

Costs (2002–03) *Tuition:* state resident $1104 full-time, $46 per credit part-time; nonresident $1656 full-time, $69 per credit part-time. *Required fees:* $96 full-time, $4 per credit. *Room and board:* $3120. *Payment plan:* deferred payment. *Waivers:* employees or children of employees.

Applying *Options:* common application, electronic application, early admission, deferred entrance. *Required:* high school transcript. *Required for some:* 3 letters of recommendation, interview. *Application deadline:* rolling (freshmen), rolling (transfers). *Notification:* continuous (freshmen).

Admissions Contact Ms. Mary Young, Records Coordinator, Central Community College-Columbus Campus, PO Box 1027, Columbus, NE 68602-1027. *Phone:* 402-564-7132 Ext. 278. *Toll-free phone:* 800-642-1083. *E-mail:* myoung@cccneb.edu.

CENTRAL COMMUNITY COLLEGE-GRAND ISLAND CAMPUS

Grand Island, Nebraska

- **State and locally supported** 2-year, founded 1976, part of Central Community College
- **Calendar** semesters
- **Degree** certificates, diplomas, and associate
- **Small-town** 64-acre campus
- **Coed,** 2,780 undergraduate students, 20% full-time, 68% women, 32% men

Undergraduates 543 full-time, 2,237 part-time. Students come from 41 states and territories, 2 other countries, 4% are from out of state, 0.5% African American, 1% Asian American or Pacific Islander, 5% Hispanic American, 0.3% Native American.

Freshmen *Admission:* 182 admitted, 171 enrolled.

Faculty *Total:* 114, 37% full-time, 4% with terminal degrees. *Student/faculty ratio:* 15:1.

Majors Accounting; auto mechanic/technician; business administration; child care/development; clinical/medical social work; computer/information sciences; computer programming (specific applications); criminal justice studies; data processing technology; drafting; electrical/electronic engineering technology; heating/air conditioning/refrigeration; industrial technology; information technology; liberal arts and sciences/liberal studies; nursing; paralegal/legal assistant; practical nurse; secretarial science; system/networking/LAN/WAN management; Web/multimedia management/webmaster; welding technology.

Academic Programs *Special study options:* academic remediation for entering students, accelerated degree program, adult/continuing education programs, advanced placement credit, cooperative education, distance learning, English as a second language, external degree program, independent study, internships, off-campus study, part-time degree program, services for LD students, student-designed majors, summer session for credit.

Library Central Community College-Grand Island Campus Library with 4,274 titles, 78 serial subscriptions, 670 audiovisual materials, an OPAC, a Web page.

Computers on Campus 156 computers available on campus for general student use. A campuswide network can be accessed from off campus. Internet access, at least one staffed computer lab available.

Student Life *Housing Options:* coed. *Activities and Organizations:* Mid-Nebraska Users of Computers, Student Activities Organization, intramurals. *Student Services:* personal/psychological counseling.

Athletics *Intramural sports:* bowling M/W, table tennis M/W, volleyball M/W.

Standardized Tests *Required for some:* SAT I or ACT (for placement), ACT ASSET.

Costs (2002–03) *Tuition:* state resident $1104 full-time, $46 per credit part-time; nonresident $1656 full-time, $69 per credit part-time. *Required fees:* $96 full-time, $4 per credit. *Payment plan:* deferred payment. *Waivers:* employees or children of employees.

Financial Aid In 2001, 146 Federal Work-Study jobs (averaging $1200). 30 State and other part-time jobs (averaging $1000).

Applying *Options:* common application, electronic application, early admission, deferred entrance. *Required:* high school transcript. *Required for some:* 3 letters of recommendation, interview. *Application deadline:* rolling (freshmen), rolling (transfers). *Notification:* continuous (freshmen).

Admissions Contact Ms. Angie Pacheco, Admissions Director, Central Community College-Grand Island Campus, PO Box 4903, Grand Island, NE 68802-4903. *Phone:* 308-398-7406 Ext. 406. *Toll-free phone:* 800-652-9177. *Fax:* 308-398-7399. *E-mail:* apacheco@cccneb.edu.

CENTRAL COMMUNITY COLLEGE-HASTINGS CAMPUS

Hastings, Nebraska

- **State and locally supported** 2-year, founded 1966, part of Central Community College
- **Calendar** semesters
- **Degree** certificates, diplomas, and associate
- **Small-town** 600-acre campus
- **Coed,** 2,245 undergraduate students, 38% full-time, 56% women, 44% men

Undergraduates 852 full-time, 1,393 part-time. Students come from 41 states and territories, 4% are from out of state, 0.3% African American, 0.8% Asian American or Pacific Islander, 3% Hispanic American, 0.3% Native American, 26% live on campus.

Freshmen *Admission:* 289 enrolled.

Faculty *Total:* 91, 67% full-time, 4% with terminal degrees. *Student/faculty ratio:* 15:1.

Majors Accounting; agricultural business; auto body repair; auto mechanic/technician; business administration; child care/development; clinical/medical social work; computer/information sciences; computer programming (specific applications); construction technology; dental assistant; dental hygiene; diesel engine mechanic; drafting; electrical/electronic engineering technology; graphic design/commercial art/illustration; graphic/printing equipment; health facilities administration; heating/air conditioning/refrigeration; horticulture services; hospitality management; hotel and restaurant management; industrial technology; information technology; liberal arts and sciences/liberal studies; machine technology; mass communications; medical administrative assistant; medical assistant; medical records technology; radio/television broadcasting technology; secretarial science; system/networking/LAN/WAN management; vehicle/petroleum products marketing; Web/multimedia management/webmaster; welding technology.

Academic Programs *Special study options:* academic remediation for entering students, accelerated degree program, adult/continuing education programs, advanced placement credit, cooperative education, distance learning, English as a second language, external degree program, independent study, internships, off-campus study, part-time degree program, services for LD students, student-designed majors, summer session for credit.

Library Nuckolls Library with 4,112 titles, 53 serial subscriptions, an OPAC.

Computers on Campus 190 computers available on campus for general student use. A campuswide network can be accessed from student residence rooms and from off campus. At least one staffed computer lab available.

Student Life *Housing Options:* coed. *Activities and Organizations:* student-run radio station, Student Senate, Central Dormitory Council, Judicial Board, Seeds and Soils, Young Farmers and Ranchers. *Campus security:* 24-hour patrols, controlled dormitory access. *Student Services:* personal/psychological counseling, women's center.

Athletics *Intramural sports:* basketball M/W, bowling M/W, golf M/W, softball M/W, volleyball M/W, weight lifting M/W.

Standardized Tests *Required for some:* SAT I or ACT (for placement), ACT ASSET.

Costs (2002–03) *Tuition:* state resident $1104 full-time, $46 per credit part-time; nonresident $1656 full-time, $69 per credit part-time. *Required fees:* $96 full-time, $4 per credit. *Room and board:* $3120. *Payment plan:* deferred payment. *Waivers:* employees or children of employees.

Financial Aid In 2001, 70 Federal Work-Study jobs (averaging $1200). 12 State and other part-time jobs (averaging $1250).

Applying *Options:* common application, electronic application, early admission, deferred entrance. *Required:* high school transcript. *Required for some:* 3 letters of recommendation, interview. *Application deadline:* rolling (freshmen), rolling (transfers). *Notification:* continuous (freshmen).

Admissions Contact Mr. Robert Glenn, Admissions and Recruiting Director, Central Community College-Hastings Campus, PO Box 1024, Hastings, NE 68902-1024. *Phone:* 402-461-2428. *Toll-free phone:* 800-742-7872. *E-mail:* bglenn@cccneb.edu.

ITT TECHNICAL INSTITUTE

Omaha, Nebraska

- **Proprietary** 2-year, founded 1991, part of ITT Educational Services, Inc
- **Calendar** quarters

- **Degree** associate
- **Urban** 1-acre campus
- **Coed,** 341 undergraduate students

Majors Computer/information sciences related; computer programming; drafting; electrical/electronic engineering technologies related; information technology.
Student Life *Housing:* college housing not available.
Costs (2001–02) *Tuition:* Full-time tuition and fees vary according to program. Part-time tuition and fees vary according to program. $260—$330 per credit hour.
Financial Aid In 2001, 3 Federal Work-Study jobs.
Applying *Options:* deferred entrance. *Application fee:* $100. *Required:* high school transcript, interview. *Recommended:* letters of recommendation. *Application deadline:* rolling (freshmen), rolling (transfers).
Admissions Contact Mr. Andrew Bossaller, Director of Recruitment, ITT Technical Institute, 9814 M Street, Omaha, NE 68127-2056. *Phone:* 402-331-2900. *Toll-free phone:* 800-677-9260.

LINCOLN SCHOOL OF COMMERCE
Lincoln, Nebraska

- **Proprietary** 2-year, founded 1884, part of Quest Education Corporation
- **Calendar** quarters
- **Degree** certificates, diplomas, and associate
- **Urban** 5-acre campus with easy access to Omaha
- **Coed,** 494 undergraduate students, 94% full-time, 55% women, 45% men

Undergraduates 464 full-time, 30 part-time. Students come from 3 states and territories, 1% are from out of state, 4% African American, 0.9% Asian American or Pacific Islander, 2% Hispanic American.
Freshmen *Admission:* 442 enrolled.
Faculty *Total:* 36, 36% full-time, 8% with terminal degrees. *Student/faculty ratio:* 19:1.
Majors Accounting; business administration; computer programming; computer programming related; information sciences/systems; information technology; legal administrative assistant; medical administrative assistant; medical assistant; paralegal/legal assistant; secretarial science; travel/tourism management; word processing.
Academic Programs *Special study options:* accelerated degree program, adult/continuing education programs, cooperative education, double majors, independent study, internships, services for LD students, summer session for credit.
Library Lincoln School of Commerce Library with 7,500 titles, 1,872 serial subscriptions, 300 audiovisual materials, an OPAC.
Computers on Campus 99 computers available on campus for general student use. Internet access, at least one staffed computer lab available.
Student Life *Housing Options:* coed. *Activities and Organizations:* Travel Club, Secretarial Club, Business Club, Court Reporting Club, Legal Assistant Club. *Campus security:* late-night transport/escort service.
Athletics *Intramural sports:* basketball M/W, softball M/W, volleyball M/W.
Costs (2002–03) *Tuition:* $9000 full-time. No tuition increase for student's term of enrollment. *Required fees:* $25 full-time. *Room only:* $1875. *Payment plan:* installment.
Applying *Options:* early admission. *Application fee:* $25. *Required:* essay or personal statement, high school transcript, letters of recommendation, interview. *Application deadline:* rolling (freshmen), rolling (transfers). *Notification:* continuous (freshmen).
Admissions Contact Mr. Todd J. Lardenoit, Director of Admissions, Lincoln School of Commerce, 1821 K Street, Lincoln, NE 68508. *Phone:* 402-474-5315. *Toll-free phone:* 800-742-7738. *Fax:* 402-474-5302. *E-mail:* lsc@ix.netcom.com.

LITTLE PRIEST TRIBAL COLLEGE
Winnebago, Nebraska

Admissions Contact PO Box 270, Winnebago, NE 68071.

METROPOLITAN COMMUNITY COLLEGE
Omaha, Nebraska

- **State and locally supported** 2-year, founded 1974, part of Nebraska Coordinating Commission for Postsecondary Education
- **Calendar** quarters
- **Degree** certificates, diplomas, and associate
- **Urban** 172-acre campus
- **Endowment** $1.1 million
- **Coed,** 11,704 undergraduate students, 32% full-time, 56% women, 44% men

Metropolitan Community College offers the advantages of a comprehensive, multicampus institution with small-college friendliness. Located in Omaha, Nebraska, Metro provides personalized services and high-quality programs in business administration, computer and office technologies, food arts, industrial and construction technologies, nursing and allied health, social sciences and services, and visual and electronic technologies as well as academic transfer programs. Many courses are offered through distance learning. Students can visit the College's Web site at http://www.mccneb.edu.

Undergraduates 3,719 full-time, 7,985 part-time. Students come from 32 states and territories, 3% are from out of state, 16% transferred in. *Retention:* 34% of 2001 full-time freshmen returned.
Freshmen *Admission:* 990 applied, 990 admitted, 990 enrolled.
Faculty *Total:* 664, 27% full-time. *Student/faculty ratio:* 15:1.
Majors Accounting; architectural engineering technology; auto mechanic/technician; business administration; child care/development; civil engineering technology; computer programming; construction technology; culinary arts; drafting; early childhood education; electrical/electronic engineering technology; graphic design/commercial art/illustration; graphic/printing equipment; heating/air conditioning/refrigeration; heavy equipment maintenance; human services; interior design; law enforcement/police science; legal administrative assistant; legal studies; liberal arts and sciences/liberal studies; mental health/rehabilitation; nursing; operating room technician; ornamental horticulture; paralegal/legal assistant; photography; practical nurse; pre-engineering; respiratory therapy; secretarial science; welding technology.
Academic Programs *Special study options:* academic remediation for entering students, adult/continuing education programs, advanced placement credit, cooperative education, distance learning, English as a second language, independent study, internships, part-time degree program, services for LD students, summer session for credit. *ROTC:* Army (c).
Library Main Library plus 2 others with 46,512 titles, 896 serial subscriptions, 7,156 audiovisual materials, an OPAC, a Web page.
Computers on Campus 1300 computers available on campus for general student use. A campuswide network can be accessed from off campus that provide access to on-line classes, e-mail. Internet access, online (class) registration, at least one staffed computer lab available.
Student Life *Housing:* college housing not available. *Campus security:* 24-hour emergency response devices and patrols, late-night transport/escort service, security on duty 9 pm to 6 am. *Student Services:* personal/psychological counseling.
Standardized Tests *Recommended:* ACT (for placement), ACT ASSET or ACT COMPASS.
Costs (2002–03) *Tuition:* state resident $1328 full-time, $30 per credit hour part-time; nonresident $1665 full-time, $37 per credit hour part-time. *Required fees:* $135 full-time, $3 per quarter hour. *Payment plan:* deferred payment. *Waivers:* senior citizens and employees or children of employees.
Financial Aid In 2001, 180 Federal Work-Study jobs (averaging $1100).
Applying *Options:* early admission. *Recommended:* high school transcript. *Application deadline:* rolling (freshmen), rolling (transfers). *Notification:* continuous (freshmen).
Admissions Contact Ms. Arlene Jordan, Director of Enrollment Management, Metropolitan Community College, PO Box 3777, Omaha, NE 68103-0777. *Phone:* 402-457-2563. *Toll-free phone:* 800-228-9553. *Fax:* 402-457-2564.

MID-PLAINS COMMUNITY COLLEGE AREA
North Platte, Nebraska

- **District-supported** 2-year
- **Calendar** semesters
- **Degree** certificates, diplomas, and associate
- **Endowment** $4.0 million
- **Coed,** 2,823 undergraduate students, 37% full-time, 56% women, 44% men

Undergraduates 1,031 full-time, 1,792 part-time. Students come from 15 states and territories, 2% African American, 0.4% Asian American or Pacific Islander, 3% Hispanic American, 0.6% Native American, 8% live on campus.
Freshmen *Admission:* 893 applied, 681 admitted, 412 enrolled.
Faculty *Total:* 193, 34% full-time, 6% with terminal degrees. *Student/faculty ratio:* 18:1.
Majors Accounting; auto mechanic/technician; business administration; business education; carpentry; computer programming; construction technology;

Mid-Plains Community College Area (continued)
criminal justice/law enforcement administration; dental hygiene; early childhood education; electrical/electronic engineering technology; emergency medical technology; English; fire science; heating/air conditioning/refrigeration; industrial radiologic technology; liberal arts and sciences/liberal studies; machine technology; medical administrative assistant; medical laboratory technician; nursing; practical nurse; respiratory therapy; secretarial science; welding technology.

Academic Programs *Special study options:* academic remediation for entering students, adult/continuing education programs, advanced placement credit, cooperative education, distance learning, independent study, internships, part-time degree program, summer session for credit.

Library McDonald-Belton L R C plus 1 other with 54,465 titles, 373 serial subscriptions, 5,726 audiovisual materials.

Computers on Campus 300 computers available on campus for general student use. A campuswide network can be accessed from off campus. Internet access, at least one staffed computer lab available.

Student Life *Housing Options:* coed. *Activities and Organizations:* drama/theater group, student-run newspaper, choral group, Student Senate, Phi Theta Kappa, Phi Beta Lamda, SEAN. *Campus security:* patrols by trained security personnel.

Athletics Member NJCAA. *Intercollegiate sports:* basketball M(s)/W(s), golf M(s), softball W(s), volleyball W(s). *Intramural sports:* basketball M/W, softball W, volleyball W.

Standardized Tests *Required:* ACT COMPASS. *Recommended:* ACT (for placement).

Costs (2001–02) *Tuition:* state resident $1440 full-time, $48 per semester hour part-time; nonresident $1470 full-time, $49 per semester hour part-time. *Room and board:* $2900. Room and board charges vary according to housing facility and location. *Payment plan:* installment. *Waivers:* senior citizens and employees or children of employees.

Applying *Required:* high school transcript. *Application deadline:* rolling (freshmen), rolling (transfers). *Notification:* continuous (freshmen).

Admissions Contact Ms. Mary Schriefer, Advisor, Mid-Plains Community College Area, 1101 Halligan Drive, North Platte, NE 69101. *Phone:* 308-535-3710. *Toll-free phone:* 800-658-4308 (in-state); 800-658-4348 (out-of-state). *Fax:* 308-634-2522.

NEBRASKA COLLEGE OF BUSINESS
Omaha, Nebraska

- **Proprietary** 2-year, founded 1891, part of Educational Medical, Inc
- **Calendar** 5 10-week terms
- **Degree** certificates, diplomas, and associate
- **Urban** 3-acre campus
- **Coed**

Student Life *Campus security:* 24-hour emergency response devices.

Applying *Options:* early admission, deferred entrance. *Application fee:* $50. *Required:* high school transcript, interview.

Admissions Contact Mr. Gary Lafe, Director of Admissions, Nebraska College of Business, 3350 North 90 Street, Omaha, NE 68134. *Phone:* 402-572-8500. *Toll-free phone:* 800-642-1456. *Fax:* 402-573-1341.

NEBRASKA INDIAN COMMUNITY COLLEGE
Macy, Nebraska

- **Independent** 2-year, founded 1979
- **Calendar** semesters
- **Degree** certificates and associate
- **Rural** 2-acre campus
- **Coed**

Applying *Options:* early admission, deferred entrance. *Application fee:* $10. *Required:* high school transcript, certificate of tribal enrollment.

Admissions Contact Mr. Ernest Ricehill, Registrar, Nebraska Indian Community College, PO Box 428, Macy, NE 68039-0428. *Phone:* 402-837-5078 Ext. 109. *Fax:* 402-878-2522.

NORTHEAST COMMUNITY COLLEGE
Norfolk, Nebraska

- **State and locally supported** 2-year, founded 1973, part of Nebraska Coordinating Commission for Postsecondary Education
- **Calendar** semesters
- **Degree** certificates, diplomas, and associate
- **Small-town** 205-acre campus
- **Endowment** $1.2 million
- **Coed,** 4,600 undergraduate students, 39% full-time, 46% women, 54% men

Undergraduates 1,805 full-time, 2,795 part-time. Students come from 21 states and territories, 7% are from out of state, 0.8% African American, 0.2% Asian American or Pacific Islander, 1% Hispanic American, 1% Native American, 0.4% international, 2% transferred in, 15% live on campus.

Freshmen *Admission:* 797 admitted, 787 enrolled.

Faculty *Total:* 210, 48% full-time. *Student/faculty ratio:* 20:1.

Majors Accounting; agricultural business; agricultural mechanization; agricultural production; agricultural sciences; agronomy/crop science; art; art education; audio engineering; auto body repair; auto mechanic/technician; biological/physical sciences; biology; broadcast journalism; business administration; business education; business marketing and marketing management; carpentry; chemistry; child care/development; computer programming; computer programming (specific applications); construction technology; corrections; criminal justice/law enforcement administration; data processing technology; diesel engine mechanic; drafting; education; electrical/electronic engineering technology; electrical/power transmission installation; electromechanical technology; elementary education; engineering; English; farm/ranch management; health/physical education; heating/air conditioning/refrigeration; horticulture science; journalism; landscaping management; law enforcement/police science; legal administrative assistant; liberal arts and sciences/liberal studies; mass communications; mathematics; medical administrative assistant; music; music business management/merchandising; music (general performance); music teacher education; nursery management; nursing; operating room technician; paralegal/legal assistant; physical education; physical therapy; physics; practical nurse; public administration; radio/television broadcasting; real estate; secretarial science; social sciences; speech/rhetorical studies; theater arts/drama; turf management; veterinary technology; welding technology.

Academic Programs *Special study options:* academic remediation for entering students, accelerated degree program, adult/continuing education programs, advanced placement credit, cooperative education, distance learning, English as a second language, honors programs, independent study, internships, off-campus study, part-time degree program, services for LD students, summer session for credit.

Library Resource Center plus 1 other with 27,592 titles, 3,025 serial subscriptions, 1,298 audiovisual materials, an OPAC, a Web page.

Computers on Campus 300 computers available on campus for general student use. Internet access, at least one staffed computer lab available.

Student Life *Housing Options:* coed, disabled students. *Activities and Organizations:* drama/theater group, student-run newspaper, radio and television station, choral group, Phi Theta Kappa, Young Farmers and Ranchers, Block and Bridle Club, Building Construction Club, Diesel Club. *Campus security:* 24-hour patrols, controlled dormitory access. *Student Services:* health clinic, personal/psychological counseling.

Athletics Member NJCAA. *Intercollegiate sports:* basketball M(s)/W(s), golf M(s)/W(s), volleyball W(s). *Intramural sports:* basketball M/W, bowling M/W, football M, skiing (cross-country) M/W, soccer M/W, softball M/W, tennis M/W, weight lifting M/W, wrestling M.

Standardized Tests *Required:* ACT,ASSET. *Required for some:* ACT (for placement).

Costs (2001–02) *Tuition:* state resident $1350 full-time, $45 per hour part-time; nonresident $1695 full-time, $56 per hour part-time. *Required fees:* $188 full-time, $6 per hour. *Room and board:* $3260; room only: $1762. Room and board charges vary according to housing facility. *Waivers:* employees or children of employees.

Financial Aid In 2001, 65 Federal Work-Study jobs (averaging $1700).

Applying *Options:* early admission. *Recommended:* high school transcript. *Application deadline:* rolling (freshmen), rolling (transfers). *Notification:* continuous (freshmen).

Admissions Contact Mr. Chris Lahm, Dean of Enrollment Management, Northeast Community College, PO Box 469, Norfolk, NE 68702-0469. *Phone:* 402-844-7258. *Toll-free phone:* 800-348-9033 Ext. 7258. *Fax:* 402-844-7400. *E-mail:* admission@northeastcollege.com.

OMAHA COLLEGE OF HEALTH CAREERS
Omaha, Nebraska

Admissions Contact Mr. William J. Stuckey, Admissions Director, Omaha College of Health Careers, 225 North 80th Street, Omaha, NE 68114. *Phone:* 402-392-1300. *Toll-free phone:* 800-865-8628. *E-mail:* ochc1@aol.com.

SOUTHEAST COMMUNITY COLLEGE, BEATRICE CAMPUS

Beatrice, Nebraska

- **District-supported** 2-year, founded 1976, part of Southeast Community College System
- **Calendar** semesters
- **Degree** certificates, diplomas, and associate
- **Small-town** 640-acre campus
- **Coed,** 987 undergraduate students

Undergraduates Students come from 9 states and territories, 7 other countries, 3% are from out of state, 22% live on campus.

Freshmen *Admission:* 600 applied, 600 admitted.

Faculty *Total:* 85, 76% full-time.

Majors Accounting; agricultural business; agricultural mechanization; agricultural sciences; agronomy/crop science; animal sciences; art; biological/physical sciences; biological technology; biology; broadcast journalism; business administration; computer science; education; elementary education; finance; journalism; legal administrative assistant; liberal arts and sciences/liberal studies; medical administrative assistant; physical sciences; practical nurse; secretarial science; soil conservation.

Academic Programs *Special study options:* academic remediation for entering students, adult/continuing education programs, advanced placement credit, cooperative education, distance learning, internships, off-campus study, part-time degree program, services for LD students, summer session for credit.

Library Learning Resource Center with 13,287 titles, 225 serial subscriptions, 1,681 audiovisual materials, an OPAC.

Computers on Campus 75 computers available on campus for general student use. At least one staffed computer lab available.

Student Life *Housing Options:* coed. *Activities and Organizations:* drama/theater group, student-run newspaper, radio station, choral group, Student Senate, Agricultural Club, Residence Hall Association, Licensed Practical Association of Nebraska, International Student Association. *Campus security:* controlled dormitory access, evening security. *Student Services:* personal/psychological counseling.

Athletics Member NJCAA. *Intercollegiate sports:* basketball M(s)/W(s), golf M(s), volleyball W(s). *Intramural sports:* archery M, softball M/W, table tennis M/W.

Standardized Tests *Recommended:* SAT I or ACT (for admission).

Costs (2001–02) *Tuition:* state resident $1080 full-time, $45 per credit hour part-time; nonresident $1260 full-time, $53 per credit hour part-time. *Required fees:* $84 full-time, $4 per credit hour. *Room and board:* room only: $2280.

Applying *Options:* common application, electronic application, early admission, deferred entrance. *Required:* high school transcript. *Recommended:* minimum 2.0 GPA. *Application deadline:* rolling (freshmen), rolling (transfers).

Admissions Contact Maryann Harms, Admissions Technician, Southeast Community College, Beatrice Campus, 4771 W. Scott Road, Beatrice, NE 68310-7042. *Phone:* 800-233-5027 Ext. 214. *Toll-free phone:* 800-233-5027 Ext. 214.

SOUTHEAST COMMUNITY COLLEGE, LINCOLN CAMPUS

Lincoln, Nebraska

- **District-supported** 2-year, founded 1973, part of Southeast Community College System
- **Calendar** quarters
- **Degree** certificates, diplomas, and associate
- **Suburban** 115-acre campus with easy access to Omaha
- **Coed**

Faculty *Student/faculty ratio:* 15:1.

Student Life *Campus security:* late-night transport/escort service.

Standardized Tests *Recommended:* SAT I or ACT (for admission).

Applying *Options:* early admission, deferred entrance. *Required:* high school transcript.

Admissions Contact Ms. Pat Frakes, Admissions Representative, Southeast Community College, Lincoln Campus, 8800 "O" Street, Lincoln, NE 68520. *Phone:* 402-437-2600 Ext. 2600. *Toll-free phone:* 800-642-4075 Ext. 2600.

SOUTHEAST COMMUNITY COLLEGE, MILFORD CAMPUS

Milford, Nebraska

- **District-supported** 2-year, founded 1941, part of Southeast Community College System
- **Calendar** quarters
- **Degree** diplomas and associate
- **Small-town** 50-acre campus with easy access to Omaha
- **Coed, primarily men,** 936 undergraduate students, 98% full-time, 6% women, 94% men

Undergraduates 913 full-time, 23 part-time. 33% live on campus.

Freshmen *Admission:* 355 enrolled.

Faculty *Total:* 89, 97% full-time. *Student/faculty ratio:* 20:1.

Majors Architectural engineering technology; auto mechanic/technician; carpentry; civil engineering technology; computer engineering technology; computer/information sciences; computer programming; construction technology; data processing technology; drafting; electrical/electronic engineering technology; electromechanical technology; graphic design/commercial art/illustration; heating/air conditioning/refrigeration; industrial arts; industrial design; industrial technology; machine technology; mechanical design technology; mechanical engineering technology; metallurgical technology; metallurgy; plastics technology; plumbing; quality control technology; solar technology; surveying; transportation technology; welding technology.

Academic Programs *Special study options:* academic remediation for entering students, cooperative education, distance learning, internships, services for LD students.

Library Milford Campus Learning Resource Center with 10,000 titles, 300 serial subscriptions.

Computers on Campus 72 computers available on campus for general student use. At least one staffed computer lab available.

Student Life *Housing Options:* men-only, women-only, disabled students. *Campus security:* 24-hour patrols, late-night transport/escort service.

Athletics *Intramural sports:* archery M/W, basketball M/W, bowling M/W, football M, golf M/W, racquetball M/W, softball M/W, swimming M/W, table tennis M/W, tennis M/W, volleyball M/W, weight lifting M/W, wrestling M.

Standardized Tests *Recommended:* SAT I (for admission), ACT (for admission).

Costs (2002–03) *Tuition:* state resident $1701 full-time; nonresident $1971 full-time. Full-time tuition and fees vary according to reciprocity agreements. Part-time tuition and fees vary according to reciprocity agreements. *Required fees:* $36 full-time, $32 per quarter hour. *Room and board:* $2544. *Waivers:* minority students, adult students, senior citizens, and employees or children of employees.

Applying *Options:* common application. *Required:* high school transcript. *Application deadline:* rolling (freshmen), rolling (transfers). *Notification:* continuous (freshmen).

Admissions Contact Mr. Larry E. Meyer, Dean of Students, Southeast Community College, Milford Campus, 600 State Street, Milford, NE 68405. *Phone:* 402-761-2131 Ext. 8270. *Toll-free phone:* 800-933-7223 Ext. 8243. *Fax:* 402-761-2324. *E-mail:* lmeyer@sccm.cc.ne.us.

WESTERN NEBRASKA COMMUNITY COLLEGE

Scottsbluff, Nebraska

- **State and locally supported** 2-year, founded 1926, part of Western Community College Area System
- **Calendar** semesters
- **Degree** certificates, diplomas, and associate
- **Rural** 20-acre campus
- **Coed,** 2,479 undergraduate students

Undergraduates Students come from 18 states and territories, 10% are from out of state, 5% live on campus.

Freshmen *Admission:* 613 applied, 613 admitted. *Average high school GPA:* 2.17. *Test scores:* ACT scores over 18: 59%; ACT scores over 24: 17%; ACT scores over 30: 2%.

Faculty *Total:* 358, 18% full-time.

Majors Agricultural sciences; anthropology; art; art education; biology; business administration; chemistry; community psychology; computer/information sciences; criminal justice studies; dietetics; drama/dance education; early childhood education; ecology; economics; elementary education; English; forest management; French; general studies; geography; German; health/physical edu-

Western Nebraska Community College (continued)
cation; history; information technology; interdisciplinary studies; journalism; liberal arts and sciences/liberal studies; mathematics; medical technology; music teacher education; nursing; physical therapy; physical therapy assistant; physics; political science; pre-dentistry; pre-engineering; pre-law; pre-medicine; pre-pharmacy studies; pre-veterinary studies; psychology; radiological science; secondary education; social work; sociology; Spanish.

Academic Programs *Special study options:* academic remediation for entering students, accelerated degree program, adult/continuing education programs, advanced placement credit, cooperative education, distance learning, independent study, internships, part-time degree program, services for LD students, summer session for credit.

Library Western Nebraska Community College Library with 34,539 titles, 2,631 serial subscriptions, 2,631 audiovisual materials, an OPAC.

Computers on Campus 355 computers available on campus for general student use. A campuswide network can be accessed from off campus. Internet access, at least one staffed computer lab available.

Student Life *Housing Options:* coed. *Activities and Organizations:* drama/theater group, student-run newspaper, choral group, Choices, Phi Theta Kappa, student government, SEAN, national sororities. *Campus security:* 24-hour emergency response devices and patrols, late-night transport/escort service, controlled dormitory access, patrols by trained security personnel from 12:30 a.m. to 6 a.m. *Student Services:* personal/psychological counseling.

Athletics Member NJCAA. *Intercollegiate sports:* basketball M(s)/W(s), volleyball W(s). *Intramural sports:* basketball M/W, bowling M/W, football M/W, table tennis M/W, tennis M/W, volleyball M/W, weight lifting M/W.

Standardized Tests *Required:* ACT ASSET. *Recommended:* SAT I and SAT II or ACT (for placement).

Costs (2001–02) *Tuition:* state resident $1365 full-time, $46 per semester hour part-time; nonresident $1605 full-time, $54 per semester hour part-time. Full-time tuition and fees vary according to course load. Part-time tuition and fees vary according to course load. *Required fees:* $195 full-time, $7 per semester hour. *Room and board:* $3300. Room and board charges vary according to board plan. *Payment plan:* installment. *Waivers:* senior citizens and employees or children of employees.

Financial Aid In 2001, 65 Federal Work-Study jobs (averaging $1500).

Applying *Options:* common application, electronic application. *Recommended:* high school transcript. *Application deadline:* rolling (freshmen), rolling (transfers). *Notification:* continuous until 8/21 (freshmen).

Admissions Contact Ms. Shannon Smith, Admissions and Recruitment Director, Western Nebraska Community College, 1601 East 27th Street, Scottsbluff, NE 69361. *Phone:* 308-635-6015. *Toll-free phone:* 800-348-4435. *Fax:* 308-635-6100. *E-mail:* rhovey@wncc.net.

NEVADA

CAREER COLLEGE OF NORTHERN NEVADA
Reno, Nevada

- **Proprietary** 2-year, founded 1984
- **Calendar** six-week terms
- **Degree** diplomas and associate
- **Small-town** 1-acre campus
- **Coed,** 254 undergraduate students, 100% full-time, 59% women, 41% men

Undergraduates 254 full-time. Students come from 2 states and territories, 5% are from out of state, 7% African American, 8% Asian American or Pacific Islander, 11% Hispanic American, 3% Native American.

Freshmen *Admission:* 172 enrolled.

Faculty *Total:* 22, 45% full-time, 23% with terminal degrees. *Student/faculty ratio:* 12:1.

Majors Business administration; computer/information sciences; data processing technology; electrical/electronic engineering technology; management information systems/business data processing; medical assistant.

Academic Programs *Special study options:* academic remediation for entering students, accelerated degree program, cooperative education, double majors, internships, summer session for credit.

Library 380 titles, 7 serial subscriptions.

Computers on Campus 52 computers available on campus for general student use. Internet access, at least one staffed computer lab available.

Student Life *Housing:* college housing not available. *Activities and Organizations:* student-run newspaper. *Campus security:* 24-hour emergency response devices.

Costs (2002–03) *Tuition:* $5400 full-time. Full-time tuition and fees vary according to course load and program. Part-time tuition and fees vary according to course load and program. No tuition increase for student's term of enrollment. *Required fees:* $79 full-time. *Payment plan:* installment. *Waivers:* employees or children of employees.

Financial Aid In 2001, 6 Federal Work-Study jobs (averaging $3000).

Applying *Application fee:* $25. *Application deadline:* rolling (freshmen), rolling (transfers). *Notification:* continuous (freshmen).

Admissions Contact Mr. Gary Rentel, Director of Admissions, Career College of Northern Nevada, 1195-A Corporate Boulevard, Reno, NV 89502. *Phone:* 775-856-2266. *Fax:* 775-856-0935. *E-mail:* admissions@ccnn4u.com.

COMMUNITY COLLEGE OF SOUTHERN NEVADA
North Las Vegas, Nevada

- **State-supported** 2-year, founded 1971, part of University and Community College System of Nevada
- **Calendar** semesters
- **Degree** certificates and associate
- **Suburban** 89-acre campus with easy access to Las Vegas
- **Endowment** $2.6 million
- **Coed,** 31,851 undergraduate students, 19% full-time, 55% women, 45% men

Undergraduates 6,114 full-time, 25,737 part-time. Students come from 55 states and territories, 13 other countries, 2% are from out of state, 10% African American, 9% Asian American or Pacific Islander, 15% Hispanic American, 1% Native American, 0.2% international, 0.9% transferred in.

Freshmen *Admission:* 2,418 applied, 2,418 admitted, 2,418 enrolled.

Faculty *Total:* 2,223, 17% full-time.

Majors Accounting; anthropology; art; auto mechanic/technician; behavioral sciences; biological/physical sciences; biology; business administration; business marketing and marketing management; chemistry; child care/development; computer engineering technology; computer programming; computer science; computer typography/composition; construction management; construction technology; corrections; criminal justice/law enforcement administration; culinary arts; data processing technology; dental hygiene; drafting; early childhood education; economics; electrical/electronic engineering technology; emergency medical technology; English; environmental science; finance; fire science; food products retailing; food services technology; graphic design/commercial art/illustration; graphic/printing equipment; heating/air conditioning/refrigeration; heavy equipment maintenance; history; horticulture science; hospitality management; hotel and restaurant management; industrial radiologic technology; information sciences/systems; landscaping management; law enforcement/police science; legal administrative assistant; liberal arts and sciences/liberal studies; literature; mass communications; mathematics; mechanical design technology; mechanical engineering technology; medical administrative assistant; medical assistant; medical laboratory technician; medical records administration; medical technology; music; nursing; occupational therapy; ornamental horticulture; paralegal/legal assistant; pharmacy; photography; practical nurse; radiological science; radio/television broadcasting; real estate; recreation/leisure studies; respiratory therapy; retail management; science education; secretarial science; sign language interpretation; social sciences; sociology; surveying; teacher assistant/aide; theater arts/drama; veterinary technology; welding technology; wildlife management.

Academic Programs *Special study options:* academic remediation for entering students, accelerated degree program, adult/continuing education programs, advanced placement credit, cooperative education, distance learning, double majors, English as a second language, honors programs, independent study, internships, part-time degree program, services for LD students, summer session for credit. *ROTC:* Army (b).

Library Learning Assistance Center with 100,000 titles, 500 serial subscriptions, 5,400 audiovisual materials, an OPAC, a Web page.

Computers on Campus 500 computers available on campus for general student use. A campuswide network can be accessed from off campus. Internet access, online (class) registration, at least one staffed computer lab available.

Student Life *Housing:* college housing not available. *Activities and Organizations:* drama/theater group, student-run newspaper, choral group, Culinary Club, Art Club, Black Student Association, Student Organization of Latinos, Student Nurses Club. *Campus security:* 24-hour emergency response devices and patrols. *Student Services:* health clinic, personal/psychological counseling, women's center, legal services.

Athletics Member NJCAA. *Intercollegiate sports:* baseball M. *Intramural sports:* basketball M/W, bowling M/W, racquetball M/W, tennis M/W, weight lifting M/W.
Costs (2002–03) *Tuition:* state resident $1494 full-time, $46 per credit part-time; nonresident $5924 full-time, $94 per credit part-time. Full-time tuition and fees vary according to course load, program, and reciprocity agreements. Part-time tuition and fees vary according to course load, program, and reciprocity agreements. *Payment plan:* deferred payment. *Waivers:* senior citizens and employees or children of employees.
Applying *Options:* early admission. *Application fee:* $5. *Required:* student data form. *Application deadline:* rolling (freshmen).
Admissions Contact Mr. Arlie J. Stops, Associate Vice President for Admissions and Records, Community College of Southern Nevada, 3200 East Cheyenne Avenue, North Las Vegas, NV 89030-4296. *Phone:* 702-651-4060. *Toll-free phone:* 800-492-5728. *Fax:* 702-643-1474. *E-mail:* stops@ccsn.nevada.edu.

Great Basin College
Elko, Nevada

- **State-supported** primarily 2-year, founded 1967, part of University and Community College System of Nevada
- **Calendar** semesters
- **Degrees** certificates, associate, and bachelor's
- **Rural** 58-acre campus
- **Endowment** $150,000
- **Coed,** 2,470 undergraduate students, 25% full-time, 69% women, 31% men

Undergraduates 622 full-time, 1,848 part-time.
Freshmen *Admission:* 325 enrolled.
Faculty *Total:* 213, 21% full-time. *Student/faculty ratio:* 18:1.
Majors Anthropology; art; business; business administration; chemistry; criminal justice studies; data processing technology; diesel engine mechanic; early childhood education; electrical/electronic engineering technology; elementary education; English; environmental science; geology; history; industrial technology; interdisciplinary studies; mathematics; nursing; office management; operations management; physics; psychology; sociology; welding technology.
Academic Programs *Special study options:* academic remediation for entering students, adult/continuing education programs, cooperative education, distance learning, English as a second language, external degree program, independent study, part-time degree program, services for LD students, summer session for credit.
Library Learning Resources Center with 27,521 titles, 250 serial subscriptions, an OPAC.
Computers on Campus 95 computers available on campus for general student use. A campuswide network can be accessed from off campus. Internet access, online (class) registration, at least one staffed computer lab available.
Student Life *Activities and Organizations:* drama/theater group, choral group. *Campus security:* evening patrols by trained security personnel. *Student Services:* personal/psychological counseling.
Athletics *Intramural sports:* badminton M/W, basketball M/W, volleyball M/W, weight lifting M/W.
Standardized Tests *Recommended:* SAT I or ACT (for placement).
Costs (2002–03) *Tuition:* state resident $50 per credit part-time; nonresident $73 per credit part-time. Part-time tuition and fees vary according to course load. *Payment plans:* tuition prepayment, deferred payment. *Waivers:* senior citizens and employees or children of employees.
Financial Aid In 2001, 35 Federal Work-Study jobs (averaging $1000).
Applying *Options:* common application, electronic application, early admission, deferred entrance. *Application fee:* $5. *Required:* high school transcript. *Application deadline:* rolling (freshmen), rolling (transfers). *Notification:* continuous (freshmen).
Admissions Contact Ms. Julie Byrnes, Director of Enrollment Management, Great Basin College, 1500 College Parkway, Elko, NV 89801-3348. *Phone:* 775-753-2271. *Fax:* 775-753-2311. *E-mail:* stdsvc@gbcnv.edu.

Heritage College
Las Vegas, Nevada

Admissions Contact 3305 Spring Mountain Road, Suite 7, Las Vegas, NV 89102.

ITT Technical Institute
Henderson, Nevada

- **Proprietary** 2-year
- **Degree** associate
- **Coed,** 426 undergraduate students

Majors Computer/information sciences related; computer programming; drafting; electrical/electronic engineering technologies related; information technology.
Student Life *Housing:* college housing not available.
Costs (2001–02) *Tuition:* Full-time tuition and fees vary according to program. Part-time tuition and fees vary according to program. $260—$330 per credit hour.
Financial Aid In 2001, 6 Federal Work-Study jobs (averaging $5000).
Applying *Application fee:* $100. *Required:* high school transcript, interview. *Recommended:* letters of recommendation. *Application deadline:* rolling (freshmen). *Notification:* continuous (freshmen).
Admissions Contact Mr. Donn Nimmer, Director of Recruitment, ITT Technical Institute, 168 North Gibson Road, Henderson, NV 89014. *Phone:* 702-558-5404.

Las Vegas College
Las Vegas, Nevada

- **Proprietary** 2-year, founded 1979, part of Corinthian Colleges, Inc
- **Calendar** quarters
- **Degree** certificates, diplomas, and associate
- **Urban** campus
- **Coed**

Faculty *Student/faculty ratio:* 12:1.
Standardized Tests *Required:* CPAt.
Applying *Options:* common application. *Required:* high school transcript, interview.
Admissions Contact Mr. Bill Holl, Director of Admissions, Las Vegas College, 4100 West Flamingo Road, Suite 2100, Las Vegas, NV 89103-3926. *Phone:* 702-368-6200. *Toll-free phone:* 800-903-3101. *Fax:* 702-368-6464. *E-mail:* mmiloro@cci.edu.

Truckee Meadows Community College
Reno, Nevada

- **State-supported** 2-year, founded 1971, part of University and Community College System of Nevada
- **Calendar** semesters
- **Degree** certificates and associate
- **Suburban** 63-acre campus
- **Endowment** $5.6 million
- **Coed,** 9,697 undergraduate students, 20% full-time, 55% women, 45% men

Undergraduates 1,963 full-time, 7,734 part-time. Students come from 12 states and territories, 3 other countries, 2% African American, 6% Asian American or Pacific Islander, 9% Hispanic American, 2% Native American, 2% international.
Freshmen *Admission:* 865 enrolled.
Faculty *Total:* 480, 30% full-time. *Student/faculty ratio:* 31:1.
Majors Accounting; alcohol/drug abuse counseling; architectural engineering technology; auto mechanic/technician; business administration; business marketing and marketing management; carpentry; child care/development; computer engineering technology; computer programming; computer programming related; construction technology; corrections; criminal justice/law enforcement administration; culinary arts; data processing technology; dental assistant; dental hygiene; dietician assistant; drafting; drafting/design technology; early childhood education; education (K-12); electrical/electronic engineering technology; elementary education; engineering technology; environmental biology; environmental science; fire science; graphic design/commercial art/illustration; heating/air conditioning/refrigeration; hospitality management; industrial radiologic technology; information sciences/systems; landscape architecture; law enforcement/police science; legal administrative assistant; liberal arts and sciences/liberal studies; medical administrative assistant; mental health/rehabilitation; military studies; nursing; plumbing; radiological science; real estate; safety/security technology; secondary education; secretarial science; solar technology; welding technology.
Academic Programs *Special study options:* academic remediation for entering students, adult/continuing education programs, advanced placement credit, coop-

Truckee Meadows Community College (continued)
erative education, distance learning, English as a second language, internships, part-time degree program, services for LD students, summer session for credit. *ROTC:* Army (c).

Library Elizabeth Storm Library plus 1 other with 42,110 titles, 816 serial subscriptions, an OPAC, a Web page.

Computers on Campus A campuswide network can be accessed from off campus. Internet access, online (class) registration, at least one staffed computer lab available.

Student Life *Housing:* college housing not available. *Activities and Organizations:* drama/theater group, student-run newspaper, choral group, Associated Students of Truckee Meadows, Phi Theta Kappa, International Students, Latino Student Organization, Asian and Pacific Islander Student Association. *Campus security:* 24-hour emergency response devices and patrols, late-night transport/escort service. *Student Services:* health clinic, personal/psychological counseling.

Standardized Tests *Recommended:* SAT I or ACT (for placement).

Costs (2001–02) *Tuition:* state resident $1152 full-time, $48 per credit part-time; nonresident $5442 full-time, $70 per credit part-time. *Payment plan:* deferred payment. *Waivers:* senior citizens.

Financial Aid In 2001, 81 Federal Work-Study jobs, 26 State and other part-time jobs.

Applying *Options:* early admission, deferred entrance. *Application fee:* $10. *Application deadline:* rolling (freshmen), rolling (transfers).

Admissions Contact Mr. Dave Harbeck, Director of Admissions and Records, Truckee Meadows Community College, Mail Station #15, 7000 Dandini Boulevard, MS RDMT 319, Reno, NV 89512-3901. *Phone:* 775-674-7623.

WESTERN NEVADA COMMUNITY COLLEGE
Carson City, Nevada

- **State-supported** 2-year, founded 1971, part of University and Community College System of Nevada
- **Calendar** semesters
- **Degree** certificates, diplomas, and associate
- **Small-town** 200-acre campus
- **Endowment** $101,000
- **Coed,** 5,117 undergraduate students, 13% full-time, 60% women, 40% men

Undergraduates 3% are from out of state.

Freshmen *Admission:* 277 applied, 277 admitted.

Faculty *Total:* 354, 23% full-time.

Majors Accounting; accounting technician; auto mechanic/technician; biology; business; business administration; business marketing and marketing management; carpentry; child care/guidance; computer/information sciences; computer programming; construction management; corrections; criminal justice/law enforcement administration; data processing; drafting; electrical/electronic engineering technology; electrical/power transmission installation; engineering; environmental science; fire protection/safety technology; general studies; heating/air conditioning/refrigeration; industrial technology; law enforcement/police science; liberal arts and sciences/liberal studies; machine technology; management information systems/business data processing; management science; masonry/tile setting; mathematics; medical laboratory technician; nursing; paralegal/legal assistant; physical sciences; plumbing; real estate; recreation/leisure facilities management; secretarial science; sheet metal working; vehicle/equipment operation; welding technology.

Academic Programs *Special study options:* academic remediation for entering students, adult/continuing education programs, advanced placement credit, cooperative education, distance learning, English as a second language, honors programs, independent study, internships, part-time degree program, services for LD students, summer session for credit.

Library Western Nevada Community College Library and Media Services plus 2 others with 35,712 titles, 199 serial subscriptions, 22,723 audiovisual materials, an OPAC, a Web page.

Computers on Campus 266 computers available on campus for general student use. Internet access, at least one staffed computer lab available.

Student Life *Housing:* college housing not available. *Activities and Organizations:* drama/theater group, choral group, Phi Theta Kappa, writers group, Infinity Society, Golf Club, Physics and Engineering Club. *Campus security:* late-night transport/escort service. *Student Services:* personal/psychological counseling.

Standardized Tests *Recommended:* SAT I or ACT (for placement).

Financial Aid In 2001, 30 Federal Work-Study jobs (averaging $4500). 60 State and other part-time jobs (averaging $4500).

Applying *Options:* early admission. *Application fee:* $5. *Required for some:* high school transcript. *Application deadline:* rolling (freshmen), rolling (transfers).

Admissions Contact Ms. Connie Capurro, Dean of Student Services/Registrar, Western Nevada Community College, 2201 West College Parkway, Carson City, NV 89703-7399. *Phone:* 775-445-3277. *Toll-free phone:* 800-748-5690. *Fax:* 775-887-3141. *E-mail:* wncc_aro@pogonip.scs.unr.edu.

NEW HAMPSHIRE

HESSER COLLEGE
Manchester, New Hampshire

- **Proprietary** primarily 2-year, founded 1900, part of Quest Education Corporation
- **Calendar** semesters
- **Degrees** certificates, diplomas, associate, and bachelor's (also offers a graduate law program with Massachusetts School of Law at Andover)
- **Urban** 1-acre campus with easy access to Boston
- **Coed,** 2,766 undergraduate students, 49% full-time, 65% women, 35% men

Undergraduates 1,363 full-time, 1,403 part-time. Students come from 12 states and territories, 2% African American, 0.9% Asian American or Pacific Islander, 4% Hispanic American, 0.1% Native American, 0.1% international, 50% live on campus.

Freshmen *Admission:* 1,725 applied, 1,562 admitted, 620 enrolled. *Average high school GPA:* 2.3.

Faculty *Total:* 164, 18% full-time, 2% with terminal degrees. *Student/faculty ratio:* 18:1.

Majors Accounting; broadcast journalism; business administration; business marketing and marketing management; business services marketing; child care/guidance; computer engineering technology; computer/information sciences; computer management; computer programming; computer science; computer systems analysis; computer typography/composition; corrections; criminal justice/law enforcement administration; criminal justice studies; early childhood education; entrepreneurship; fashion design/illustration; fashion merchandising; graphic design/commercial art/illustration; hotel and restaurant management; human services; information sciences/systems; interior design; law enforcement/police science; liberal arts and sciences/liberal studies; management information systems/business data processing; mass communications; medical administrative assistant; medical assistant; paralegal/legal assistant; physical therapy assistant; psychology; radio/television broadcasting; retail management; secretarial science; security; social work; sport/fitness administration; travel/tourism management.

Academic Programs *Special study options:* accelerated degree program, adult/continuing education programs, advanced placement credit, cooperative education, internships, part-time degree program, student-designed majors, summer session for credit.

Library Kenneth W. Galeucia Memorial Library with 38,000 titles, 200 serial subscriptions, an OPAC, a Web page.

Computers on Campus 60 computers available on campus for general student use. Internet access, at least one staffed computer lab available.

Student Life *Housing Options:* coed. *Activities and Organizations:* student-run radio and television station, student government, Ski Club, Amnesty International, yearbook, student ambassador. *Campus security:* 24-hour emergency response devices and patrols, student patrols, late-night transport/escort service, controlled dormitory access. *Student Services:* health clinic, personal/psychological counseling.

Athletics *Intercollegiate sports:* basketball M(s)/W(s), soccer M(s), softball W(s), volleyball M(s)/W(s). *Intramural sports:* basketball M/W, bowling M/W, skiing (downhill) M/W, softball M/W, table tennis M/W, volleyball M/W, weight lifting M/W.

Costs (2001–02) *Comprehensive fee:* $16,210 includes full-time tuition ($9800), mandatory fees ($410), and room and board ($6000). Full-time tuition and fees vary according to class time, course load, and program. Part-time tuition: $359 per credit. Part-time tuition and fees vary according to class time and program. *Required fees:* $205 per term part-time. *Room and board:* Room and board charges vary according to board plan. *Payment plans:* installment, deferred payment. *Waivers:* employees or children of employees.

Financial Aid In 2001, 700 Federal Work-Study jobs (averaging $1000).

Applying *Options:* common application, electronic application, deferred entrance. *Application fee:* $10. *Required:* high school transcript, interview. *Required for some:* letters of recommendation. *Recommended:* minimum 2.0 GPA. *Application deadline:* rolling (freshmen), rolling (transfers). *Notification:* continuous (freshmen).

Admissions Contact Hesser College, 3 Sundial Avenue, Manchester, NH 03103. *Phone:* 603-668-6660 Ext. 2101. *Toll-free phone:* 800-526-9231 Ext. 2110. *E-mail:* admissions@hesser.edu.

McIntosh College
Dover, New Hampshire

- **Proprietary** 2-year, founded 1896
- **Calendar** modular
- **Degree** certificates and associate
- **Small-town** 11-acre campus with easy access to Boston
- **Coed,** 1,224 undergraduate students

Undergraduates Students come from 20 states and territories, 8 other countries, 10% are from out of state.
Freshmen *Admission:* 665 applied, 326 admitted. *Average high school GPA:* 2.78.
Faculty *Total:* 66, 62% full-time. *Student/faculty ratio:* 25:1.
Majors Accounting; business administration; computer/information sciences; computer management; computer science; computer systems analysis; criminal justice/law enforcement administration; culinary arts; early childhood education; entrepreneurship; information sciences/systems; legal administrative assistant; medical administrative assistant; medical assistant; office management; paralegal/legal assistant; secretarial science; telecommunications; travel/tourism management.
Academic Programs *Special study options:* accelerated degree program, adult/continuing education programs, advanced placement credit, cooperative education, double majors, internships, part-time degree program, services for LD students, summer session for credit.
Library McIntosh College Library with 11,000 titles, 130 serial subscriptions.
Computers on Campus 150 computers available on campus for general student use. Internet access, online (class) registration, at least one staffed computer lab available.
Student Life *Housing Options:* coed. *Activities and Organizations:* drama/theater group, Student Activities Committee, Drama Club, Business Club, Culture Club, Collegiate Secretaries International. *Campus security:* 24-hour emergency response devices and patrols, student patrols, controlled dormitory access. *Student Services:* personal/psychological counseling.
Standardized Tests *Recommended:* SAT II: Writing Test (for placement).
Costs (2002–03) *Comprehensive fee:* $32,700 includes full-time tuition ($24,000), mandatory fees ($300), and room and board ($8400). Part-time tuition: $200 per credit.
Applying *Options:* common application, electronic application, early admission, deferred entrance. *Application fee:* $15. *Required:* high school transcript. *Recommended:* interview. *Application deadline:* rolling (freshmen). *Notification:* continuous (freshmen).
Admissions Contact Ms. Lisa Masse, Director of Admissions, McIntosh College, 23 Cataract Avenue, Dover, NH 03820-3990. *Phone:* 603-742-1234. *Toll-free phone:* 800-McINTOSH. *Fax:* 603-743-0060. *E-mail:* admissions@mcintosh.dover.nh.us.

New Hampshire Community Technical College, Berlin/Laconia
Berlin, New Hampshire

- **State-supported** 2-year, founded 1966, part of New Hampshire Community Technical College System
- **Calendar** semesters
- **Degree** certificates, diplomas, and associate
- **Rural** 325-acre campus
- **Coed,** 538 undergraduate students, 40% full-time, 66% women, 34% men

Undergraduates 216 full-time, 322 part-time. Students come from 6 states and territories, 6% are from out of state, 8% transferred in.
Freshmen *Admission:* 305 applied, 268 admitted, 253 enrolled.
Faculty *Total:* 79, 37% full-time.
Majors Accounting; auto mechanic/technician; business administration; cartography; computer engineering technology; computer/information sciences; culinary arts; diesel engine mechanic; early childhood education; environmental science; forestry; general studies; human services; industrial technology; liberal arts and sciences/liberal studies; nursing; secretarial science; surveying; water treatment technology.
Academic Programs *Special study options:* academic remediation for entering students, adult/continuing education programs, advanced placement credit, distance learning, double majors, external degree program, independent study, internships, part-time degree program, services for LD students, summer session for credit.
Library Fortier Library with 10,000 titles, 160 serial subscriptions, 50 audiovisual materials, an OPAC.
Computers on Campus 65 computers available on campus for general student use. A campuswide network can be accessed from off campus. Internet access, at least one staffed computer lab available.
Student Life *Housing:* college housing not available. *Activities and Organizations:* student-run newspaper, Student Senate. *Student Services:* personal/psychological counseling, women's center.
Athletics Member NSCAA. *Intercollegiate sports:* basketball M/W, ice hockey M/W, soccer M/W. *Intramural sports:* basketball M/W, bowling M/W, ice hockey M/W, skiing (cross-country) M/W, volleyball M/W.
Costs (2001–02) *Tuition:* state resident $120 per credit part-time; nonresident $276 per credit part-time. Full-time tuition and fees vary according to course load, program, and reciprocity agreements. Part-time tuition and fees vary according to class time and reciprocity agreements. *Required fees:* $2 per credit. *Payment plan:* deferred payment. *Waivers:* senior citizens and employees or children of employees.
Applying *Application fee:* $10. *Required:* high school transcript. *Application deadline:* rolling (freshmen), rolling (transfers). *Notification:* continuous (freshmen).
Admissions Contact Ms. Kathleen M. Tremblay, Vice President of Student Affairs, New Hampshire Community Technical College, Berlin/Laconia, 2020 Riverside Drive, Berlin, NH 03570-3717. *Phone:* 603-752-1113 Ext. 1004. *Toll-free phone:* 800-445-4525. *Fax:* 603-752-6335. *E-mail:* berlin4u@tec.nh.us.

New Hampshire Community Technical College, Manchester/Stratham
Manchester, New Hampshire

Admissions Contact Ms. Patricia Shay, Director of Admissions and Enrollment Management, New Hampshire Community Technical College, Manchester/Stratham, 1066 Front Street, Manchester, NH 03102-8518. *Phone:* 603-668-6706 Ext. 208.

New Hampshire Community Technical College, Nashua/Claremont
Nashua, New Hampshire

Admissions Contact Mr. Arthur Harris, Provost, New Hampshire Community Technical College, Nashua/Claremont, 505 Amherst Street, Nashua, NH 03061-2052. *Phone:* 603-882-6923. *Fax:* 603-882-8690. *E-mail:* nashua@tec.nh.us.

New Hampshire Technical Institute
Concord, New Hampshire

- **State-supported** 2-year, founded 1964, part of New Hampshire Community Technical College System
- **Calendar** semesters
- **Degree** certificates, diplomas, and associate
- **Small-town** 225-acre campus with easy access to Boston
- **Coed,** 3,308 undergraduate students, 40% full-time, 58% women, 42% men

Undergraduates 1,316 full-time, 1,992 part-time. Students come from 12 states and territories, 24 other countries, 2% are from out of state, 23% live on campus.
Freshmen *Admission:* 1,916 applied, 1,430 admitted, 654 enrolled. *Average high school GPA:* 2.5.
Faculty *Total:* 146, 66% full-time, 8% with terminal degrees. *Student/faculty ratio:* 12:1.
Majors Accounting; alcohol/drug abuse counseling; architectural engineering technology; business administration; business marketing and marketing management; computer engineering technology; computer/information sciences; computer programming (specific applications); computer systems networking/telecommunications; criminal justice/law enforcement administration; dental assistant; dental hygiene; diagnostic medical sonography; early childhood education; electrical/electronic engineering technology; emergency medical technol-

New Hampshire Technical Institute (continued)
ogy; engineering technology; general studies; hotel and restaurant management; human resources management; human services; liberal arts and sciences/liberal studies; mechanical engineering technology; mental health/rehabilitation; nursing; paralegal/legal assistant; real estate; sport/fitness administration; teacher assistant/aide; travel/tourism management.

Academic Programs *Special study options:* academic remediation for entering students, adult/continuing education programs, advanced placement credit, distance learning, double majors, English as a second language, external degree program, part-time degree program, services for LD students, summer session for credit.

Library Farnum Library plus 1 other with 32,000 titles, 500 serial subscriptions, 1,000 audiovisual materials, an OPAC, a Web page.

Computers on Campus 160 computers available on campus for general student use. Internet access, at least one staffed computer lab available.

Student Life *Housing Options:* coed. *Activities and Organizations:* drama/theater group, Phi Theta Kappa, Student Senate, Student Nurses Assistant, Criminal Justice Club, Outing Club. *Campus security:* 24-hour patrols, late-night transport/escort service, controlled dormitory access. *Student Services:* health clinic, personal/psychological counseling.

Athletics Member NSCAA. *Intercollegiate sports:* baseball M, basketball M/W, soccer M/W, softball W, volleyball M/W. *Intramural sports:* softball W, volleyball M/W.

Standardized Tests *Recommended:* SAT I or ACT (for admission).

Costs (2001–02) *Tuition:* state resident $120 per credit hour part-time; nonresident $276 per credit hour part-time. Full-time tuition and fees vary according to class time, program, and reciprocity agreements. Part-time tuition and fees vary according to class time, program, and reciprocity agreements. *Required fees:* $11 per credit hour. *Room and board:* $4960. *Payment plan:* installment. *Waivers:* senior citizens and employees or children of employees.

Financial Aid In 2001, 70 Federal Work-Study jobs (averaging $1000).

Applying *Options:* electronic application. *Application fee:* $10. *Required:* high school transcript. *Required for some:* essay or personal statement, letters of recommendation, interview. *Recommended:* minimum 2.0 GPA. *Application deadline:* rolling (freshmen), rolling (transfers). *Notification:* continuous (freshmen).

Admissions Contact Mr. Francis P. Meyer, Director of Admissions, New Hampshire Technical Institute, 11 Institute Drive, Concord, NH 03301-7412. *Phone:* 603-271-7131. *Toll-free phone:* 800-247-0179. *Fax:* 603-271-7139. *E-mail:* nhtiadm@tec.nh.us.

NEW JERSEY

ASSUMPTION COLLEGE FOR SISTERS
Mendham, New Jersey

- **Independent Roman Catholic** 2-year, founded 1953
- **Calendar** semesters
- **Degree** certificates, diplomas, and associate
- **Rural** 112-acre campus with easy access to New York City
- **Women only,** 34 undergraduate students, 21% full-time

Undergraduates Students come from 2 states and territories, 7% are from out of state, 71% African American, 29% Asian American or Pacific Islander.

Faculty *Total:* 14, 43% full-time. *Student/faculty ratio:* 3:1.

Majors Computer science related; liberal arts and sciences/liberal studies; theology; word processing.

Academic Programs *Special study options:* academic remediation for entering students, advanced placement credit, English as a second language, part-time degree program, services for LD students, summer session for credit.

Library Assumption College for Sisters Library with 28,400 titles, 91 serial subscriptions, 3,834 audiovisual materials.

Computers on Campus 10 computers available on campus for general student use. Internet access, at least one staffed computer lab available.

Student Life *Housing:* college housing not available. *Activities and Organizations:* choral group.

Standardized Tests *Recommended:* SAT I or ACT (for placement).

Costs (2001–02) *Tuition:* $2400 full-time, $100 per credit part-time. *Payment plan:* installment.

Applying *Options:* deferred entrance. *Required:* high school transcript, 1 letter of recommendation, interview, intention of studying for Roman Catholic sisterhood. *Application deadline:* rolling (freshmen), rolling (transfers).

Admissions Contact Sr. Mary Theresa Wojcicki, Registrar and Academic Dean, Assumption College for Sisters, 350 Bernardsville Road, Mendham, NJ 07945-0800. *Phone:* 973-543-6528 Ext. 228. *Fax:* 973-543-9459.

ATLANTIC CAPE COMMUNITY COLLEGE
Mays Landing, New Jersey

- **County-supported** 2-year, founded 1964
- **Calendar** semesters
- **Degree** certificates, diplomas, and associate
- **Small-town** 546-acre campus with easy access to Philadelphia
- **Endowment** $576,000
- **Coed,** 5,483 undergraduate students, 40% full-time, 63% women, 37% men

Undergraduates 2,182 full-time, 3,301 part-time. Students come from 2 states and territories, 35 other countries, 1% are from out of state, 16% African American, 8% Asian American or Pacific Islander, 8% Hispanic American, 0.3% Native American, 1% international, 4% transferred in.

Freshmen *Admission:* 1,816 enrolled.

Faculty *Total:* 504, 14% full-time, 2% with terminal degrees. *Student/faculty ratio:* 15:1.

Majors Accounting; biology; business administration; chemistry; child care/development; computer programming; corrections; culinary arts; education; fine/studio arts; history; hospitality management; humanities; law enforcement/police science; liberal arts and sciences/liberal studies; literature; marine science; mathematics; nursing; occupational therapy assistant; paralegal/legal assistant; physical therapy assistant; psychology; respiratory therapy; social sciences; social work; sociology; travel/tourism management.

Academic Programs *Special study options:* academic remediation for entering students, adult/continuing education programs, advanced placement credit, cooperative education, distance learning, double majors, English as a second language, independent study, internships, part-time degree program, services for LD students, summer session for credit.

Library William Spangler Library with 76,500 titles, 500 audiovisual materials, an OPAC, a Web page.

Computers on Campus 1100 computers available on campus for general student use. A campuswide network can be accessed from off campus. At least one staffed computer lab available.

Student Life *Housing:* college housing not available. *Activities and Organizations:* drama/theater group, student-run newspaper, radio station, Culinary Student Association, Phi Theta Kappa, History/Government Club, Student Nurses Club, Occupational Therapy Club. *Campus security:* 24-hour emergency response devices and patrols. *Student Services:* personal/psychological counseling.

Athletics Member NJCAA. *Intercollegiate sports:* archery M/W, basketball M, golf M/W. *Intramural sports:* basketball M/W, soccer M.

Standardized Tests *Recommended:* SAT I (for placement).

Costs (2001–02) *Tuition:* area resident $1809 full-time, $60 per credit part-time; state resident $3618 full-time, $121 per credit part-time; nonresident $6306 full-time, $210 per credit part-time. Full-time tuition and fees vary according to program. Part-time tuition and fees vary according to program. *Required fees:* $270 full-time, $10 per credit, $13 per term part-time. *Payment plans:* installment, deferred payment. *Waivers:* senior citizens and employees or children of employees.

Financial Aid In 2001, 80 Federal Work-Study jobs (averaging $1000).

Applying *Options:* common application, early admission, deferred entrance. *Application fee:* $35. *Recommended:* high school transcript. *Application deadlines:* 7/1 (freshmen), 7/1 (transfers).

Admissions Contact Mrs. Linda McLeod, College Recruiter, Atlantic Cape Community College, Mays Landing, NJ 08330-2699. *Phone:* 609-343-5000 Ext. 5009. *Fax:* 609-343-4921. *E-mail:* accadmit@atlantic.edu.

BERGEN COMMUNITY COLLEGE
Paramus, New Jersey

- **County-supported** 2-year, founded 1965
- **Calendar** semesters
- **Degree** certificates and associate
- **Suburban** 167-acre campus with easy access to New York City
- **Coed,** 12,145 undergraduate students, 48% full-time, 56% women, 44% men

Bergen Community College offers 3 types of degree programs in more than 70 fields of study and one-year certificate programs. Students can earn an AA, AS, or AAS degree. Programs for international students and services for students with learning disabilities are available.

Undergraduates 5,773 full-time, 6,372 part-time. Students come from 90 other countries, 6% African American, 10% Asian American or Pacific Islander, 21% Hispanic American, 0.2% Native American, 7% international.
Freshmen *Admission:* 4,201 applied, 2,384 admitted, 2,042 enrolled.
Faculty *Total:* 653, 36% full-time, 20% with terminal degrees. *Student/faculty ratio:* 18:1.
Majors Accounting; art; auto mechanic/technician; biology; broadcast journalism; business administration; chemistry; computer engineering technology; computer programming; computer science; computer typography/composition; criminal justice/law enforcement administration; dance; dental hygiene; drafting; early childhood education; economics; education; electrical/electronic engineering technology; engineering science; exercise sciences; finance; food products retailing; graphic design/commercial art/illustration; health science; history; hotel and restaurant management; industrial radiologic technology; industrial technology; legal administrative assistant; liberal arts and sciences/liberal studies; literature; mass communications; mathematics; medical administrative assistant; medical assistant; medical laboratory technician; music; nursing; ornamental horticulture; paralegal/legal assistant; philosophy; photography; physics; political science; psychology; real estate; recreation/leisure studies; respiratory therapy; retail management; secretarial science; sociology; theater arts/drama; travel/tourism management; veterinary technology; women's studies.
Academic Programs *Special study options:* academic remediation for entering students, adult/continuing education programs, cooperative education, English as a second language, honors programs, internships, part-time degree program, services for LD students, study abroad, summer session for credit.
Library Sidney Silverman Library and Learning Resources Center plus 1 other with 142,746 titles, 846 serial subscriptions, an OPAC.
Computers on Campus 225 computers available on campus for general student use. At least one staffed computer lab available.
Student Life *Housing:* college housing not available. *Activities and Organizations:* drama/theater group, student-run newspaper, choral group. *Campus security:* 24-hour patrols. *Student Services:* health clinic, personal/psychological counseling.
Athletics Member NJCAA. *Intercollegiate sports:* baseball M, basketball M, cross-country running M/W, soccer M, softball W, track and field M/W, volleyball W, wrestling M. *Intramural sports:* basketball M, tennis M, volleyball M/W.
Costs (2001–02) *Tuition:* area resident $1714 full-time, $71 per credit part-time; state resident $3552 full-time, $148 per credit part-time; nonresident $3792 full-time, $158 per credit part-time. Full-time tuition and fees vary according to course load. Part-time tuition and fees vary according to course load. *Required fees:* $335 full-time, $14 per credit. *Waivers:* senior citizens and employees or children of employees.
Financial Aid In 2001, 140 Federal Work-Study jobs (averaging $2000).
Applying *Application fee:* $20. *Application deadlines:* 7/31 (freshmen), 7/31 (transfers). *Notification:* continuous (freshmen).
Admissions Contact Ms. Maxine Lisboa, Director of Admissions and Recruitment, Bergen Community College, 400 Paramus Road, Paramus, NJ 07652-1595. *Phone:* 201-612-5482. *Fax:* 201-444-7036.

BERKELEY COLLEGE
West Paterson, New Jersey

- **Proprietary** primarily 2-year, founded 1931
- **Calendar** quarters
- **Degrees** certificates, associate, and bachelor's
- **Suburban** 16-acre campus with easy access to New York City
- **Coed,** 2,144 undergraduate students, 84% full-time, 78% women, 22% men

Undergraduates 1,811 full-time, 333 part-time. Students come from 6 states and territories, 18 other countries, 3% are from out of state, 17% African American, 3% Asian American or Pacific Islander, 33% Hispanic American, 0.4% Native American, 1% international, 12% transferred in, 1% live on campus.
Freshmen *Admission:* 736 enrolled. *Average high school GPA:* 2.7.
Faculty *Total:* 118, 50% full-time. *Student/faculty ratio:* 24:1.
Majors Accounting; business; business administration; business marketing and marketing management; computer management; fashion merchandising; interior design; international business; paralegal/legal assistant; system administration; Web page design.
Academic Programs *Special study options:* academic remediation for entering students, adult/continuing education programs, advanced placement credit, cooperative education, English as a second language, internships, off-campus study, part-time degree program, study abroad, summer session for credit.
Library Walter A. Brower Library with 49,584 titles, 224 serial subscriptions, 2,659 audiovisual materials, an OPAC, a Web page.
Computers on Campus 300 computers available on campus for general student use. A campuswide network can be accessed from student residence rooms and from off campus. At least one staffed computer lab available.
Student Life *Housing Options:* coed. *Activities and Organizations:* student-run newspaper, Student Government Association, Athletics Club, Paralegal Student Association, International Club, Fashion and Marketing Club. *Campus security:* 24-hour emergency response devices, controlled dormitory access, security patrols. *Student Services:* personal/psychological counseling.
Athletics *Intramural sports:* basketball M/W, bowling M/W, football M/W, soccer M/W, softball M/W, tennis M/W, volleyball M/W.
Costs (2002–03) *One-time required fee:* $50. *Comprehensive fee:* $22,440 includes full-time tuition ($13,950), mandatory fees ($390), and room and board ($8100). Part-time tuition: $360 per credit. Part-time tuition and fees vary according to class time. *Required fees:* $60 per term part-time. *Room and board:* Room and board charges vary according to housing facility. *Payment plan:* installment. *Waivers:* employees or children of employees.
Financial Aid In 2001, 150 Federal Work-Study jobs (averaging $1200).
Applying *Options:* electronic application, deferred entrance. *Application fee:* $40. *Required:* high school transcript. *Recommended:* interview. *Application deadline:* rolling (freshmen), rolling (transfers).
Admissions Contact Ms. Carol Allen, Director of High School Admissions, Berkeley College, 44 Rifle Camp Road, West Paterson, NJ 07424-3353. *Phone:* 973-278-5400 Ext. 210. *Toll-free phone:* 800-446-5400. *E-mail:* admissions@berkeleycollege.edu.

BROOKDALE COMMUNITY COLLEGE
Lincroft, New Jersey

- **County-supported** 2-year, founded 1967, part of New Jersey Commission on Higher Education
- **Calendar** semesters
- **Degree** certificates and associate
- **Small-town** 221-acre campus with easy access to New York City
- **Coed,** 11,876 undergraduate students, 49% full-time, 57% women, 43% men

There are more than 12,000 students who attend classes at Brookdale's 250-acre campus in suburban Monmouth County, New Jersey. Here are a few reasons why they chose Brookdale: high-quality education at an affordable cost, extensive choice of curriculum, excellent transferability to 4-year colleges, and small classes with teachers who love to teach.

Undergraduates 5,811 full-time, 6,065 part-time. Students come from 6 states and territories, 50 other countries, 0.1% are from out of state, 10% African American, 4% Asian American or Pacific Islander, 6% Hispanic American, 0.1% Native American, 1% international, 5% transferred in.
Freshmen *Admission:* 3,913 applied, 3,913 admitted, 2,613 enrolled.
Faculty *Total:* 624, 35% full-time. *Student/faculty ratio:* 22:1.
Majors Accounting; architecture; art; audio engineering; auto mechanic/technician; biological/physical sciences; business administration; business marketing and marketing management; chemistry; computer engineering technology; computer programming; criminal justice/law enforcement administration; culinary arts; design/visual communications; desktop publishing equipment operation; drafting; early childhood education; education; educational media technology; electrical/electronic engineering technology; engineering; English; fashion merchandising; food products retailing; graphic design/commercial art/illustration; humanities; human services; interior design; international relations; journalism; liberal arts and sciences/liberal studies; library science; mass communications; mathematics; mechanical drafting; medical laboratory technician; modern languages; multi/interdisciplinary studies related; music; nursing; paralegal/legal assistant; photography; physics; political science; psychology; public relations; radiological science; radio/television broadcasting technology; respiratory therapy; secretarial science; social sciences; social work; sociology; speech/rhetorical studies; telecommunications; theater arts/drama; visual/performing arts.
Academic Programs *Special study options:* academic remediation for entering students, adult/continuing education programs, advanced placement credit, cooperative education, distance learning, English as a second language, honors programs, independent study, internships, part-time degree program, services for LD students, study abroad, summer session for credit. *ROTC:* Army (c), Air Force (c).
Library Brookdale Community College Library with 150,000 titles, 709 serial subscriptions, 33,000 audiovisual materials, an OPAC.
Computers on Campus 1100 computers available on campus for general student use. A campuswide network can be accessed from off campus. Internet access, online (class) registration, at least one staffed computer lab available.

Brookdale Community College (continued)

Student Life *Housing:* college housing not available. *Activities and Organizations:* drama/theater group, student-run newspaper, radio station, Circle K, SAGE, Outdoor Club. *Campus security:* 24-hour emergency response devices and patrols. *Student Services:* personal/psychological counseling, women's center.

Athletics Member NJCAA. *Intercollegiate sports:* baseball M, basketball M/W, cross-country running M/W, golf M, soccer M/W, softball W, tennis M/W. *Intramural sports:* basketball M/W, volleyball M/W.

Standardized Tests *Required for some:* ACCUPLACER.

Costs (2001–02) *Tuition:* area resident $1872 full-time, $78 per credit part-time; state resident $3744 full-time, $156 per credit part-time; nonresident $6600 full-time, $275 per credit part-time. Full-time tuition and fees vary according to course load. *Required fees:* $374 full-time, $16 per credit. *Payment plans:* installment, deferred payment. *Waivers:* senior citizens and employees or children of employees.

Applying *Options:* early admission, deferred entrance. *Application fee:* $25. *Required:* high school transcript. *Application deadline:* rolling (freshmen), rolling (transfers). *Notification:* continuous (freshmen).

Admissions Contact Kim Heuser-Schuck, Registrar, Brookdale Community College, 765 Newman Springs Road, Lincroft, NJ 07738. *Phone:* 732-224-2268. *Fax:* 732-576-1643.

BURLINGTON COUNTY COLLEGE
Pemberton, New Jersey

- **County-supported** 2-year, founded 1966, part of New Jersey Commission on Higher Education
- **Calendar** semesters
- **Degree** certificates and associate
- **Suburban** 225-acre campus with easy access to Philadelphia
- **Coed,** 6,467 undergraduate students, 44% full-time, 59% women, 41% men

Undergraduates Students come from 2 states and territories, 12 other countries, 1% are from out of state, 19% African American, 4% Asian American or Pacific Islander, 5% Hispanic American, 0.3% Native American.

Freshmen *Admission:* 2,206 applied, 2,206 admitted.

Faculty *Total:* 371, 17% full-time. *Student/faculty ratio:* 25:1.

Majors Accounting; applied art; architectural engineering technology; art; art therapy; auto mechanic/technician; biological/physical sciences; biology; business administration; business education; chemical engineering technology; chemistry; civil engineering technology; communication equipment technology; computer graphics; computer programming; computer science; computer science related; criminal justice/law enforcement administration; data processing technology; drafting; early childhood education; ecology; electrical/electronic engineering technology; elementary education; engineering; English; environmental science; fashion design/illustration; finance; fire science; food products retailing; food services technology; graphic design/commercial art/illustration; history; hotel and restaurant management; industrial radiologic technology; information technology; journalism; law enforcement/police science; legal administrative assistant; liberal arts and sciences/liberal studies; medical assistant; medical laboratory technology; music; nursing; philosophy; physics; political science; pre-engineering; psychology; secretarial science; sociology; surveying; theater arts/drama.

Academic Programs *Special study options:* academic remediation for entering students, adult/continuing education programs, advanced placement credit, cooperative education, distance learning, double majors, English as a second language, honors programs, independent study, internships, part-time degree program, services for LD students, summer session for credit.

Library Burlington County College Library plus 1 other with 92,400 titles, 1,750 serial subscriptions, 11,600 audiovisual materials, an OPAC, a Web page.

Computers on Campus 500 computers available on campus for general student use. A campuswide network can be accessed from off campus. Internet access, at least one staffed computer lab available.

Student Life *Housing:* college housing not available. *Activities and Organizations:* drama/theater group, student-run radio station. *Campus security:* 24-hour emergency response devices and patrols, late-night transport/escort service. *Student Services:* personal/psychological counseling.

Athletics Member NJCAA. *Intercollegiate sports:* baseball M, basketball M, soccer M/W, softball W, tennis M/W.

Standardized Tests *Required:* New Jersey Basic Skills Exam.

Costs (2001–02) *Tuition:* area resident $1572 full-time, $60 per credit hour part-time; state resident $1800 full-time, $75 per credit hour part-time; nonresident $3360 full-time, $140 per credit hour part-time. *Required fees:* $228 full-time, $10 per credit hour. *Payment plans:* installment, deferred payment. *Waivers:* senior citizens and employees or children of employees.

Financial Aid In 2001, 62 Federal Work-Study jobs (averaging $1000).

Applying *Options:* common application, electronic application, early admission, deferred entrance. *Application fee:* $15. *Application deadline:* rolling (freshmen), rolling (transfers). *Notification:* continuous (freshmen).

Admissions Contact Ms. Elva DeJesus-Lopez, Admissions Coordinator, Burlington County College, Route 530, Pemberton, NJ 08068. *Phone:* 609-894-9311 Ext. 7282.

CAMDEN COUNTY COLLEGE
Blackwood, New Jersey

- **State and locally supported** 2-year, founded 1967, part of New Jersey Commission on Higher Education
- **Calendar** semesters
- **Degree** certificates and associate
- **Suburban** 320-acre campus with easy access to Philadelphia
- **Coed,** 12,566 undergraduate students

New Jersey's largest community college enrolls more than 12,000 students in more than 100 degree and certificate programs at locations in Blackwood, Camden, and Cherry Hill. In addition to credit programs in allied health, education, business, technology, and liberal arts/sciences, the College offers customized training, professional and personal development courses, and cultural programming.

Undergraduates Students come from 2 states and territories, 21 other countries.

Freshmen *Admission:* 6,977 applied, 6,977 admitted.

Faculty *Total:* 717, 17% full-time. *Student/faculty ratio:* 23:1.

Majors Accounting; animal sciences; applied art; art; auto mechanic/technician; business administration; business marketing and marketing management; computer engineering technology; computer graphics; computer/information technology services administration and management related; computer programming; computer programming related; computer programming (specific applications); computer science related; computer typography/composition; criminal justice/law enforcement administration; data entry/microcomputer applications; data entry/microcomputer applications related; data processing technology; dental hygiene; dietetics; early childhood education; electrical/electronic engineering technology; engineering science; environmental science; exercise sciences; finance; fire science; food products retailing; forestry; gerontology; human services; information technology; laser/optical technology; liberal arts and sciences/liberal studies; mass communications; mechanical engineering technology; medical laboratory technician; medical laboratory technology; medical radiologic technology; nursing; nutrition science; occupational safety/health technology; real estate; recreation/leisure studies; respiratory therapy; robotics; secretarial science; system administration; system/networking/LAN/WAN management; theater arts/drama; Web/multimedia management/webmaster; Web page, digital/multimedia and information resources design; word processing.

Academic Programs *Special study options:* academic remediation for entering students, adult/continuing education programs, cooperative education, distance learning, double majors, English as a second language, external degree program, freshman honors college, honors programs, independent study, internships, off-campus study, part-time degree program, services for LD students, study abroad, summer session for credit.

Library Learning Resource Center with 91,366 titles, 449 serial subscriptions, 2,038 audiovisual materials, an OPAC.

Computers on Campus 700 computers available on campus for general student use. Internet access, at least one staffed computer lab available.

Student Life *Housing:* college housing not available. *Activities and Organizations:* drama/theater group, student-run radio station, choral group, Phi Theta Kappa, Circle K, Laser Club, Math Club, Chess Club. *Campus security:* 24-hour emergency response devices.

Athletics Member NJCAA. *Intercollegiate sports:* baseball M, basketball M/W, soccer M/W, softball W. *Intramural sports:* baseball M, basketball M/W, soccer M/W, softball W.

Costs (2001–02) *Tuition:* area resident $1440 full-time, $60 per credit part-time; state resident $1512 full-time, $63 per credit part-time; nonresident $1512 full-time, $63 per credit part-time. *Waivers:* senior citizens and employees or children of employees.

Financial Aid In 2001, 117 Federal Work-Study jobs (averaging $1126).

Applying *Options:* common application, early admission. *Required for some:* high school transcript. *Application deadline:* rolling (freshmen), rolling (transfers).

Admissions Contact Ms. Jacqueline Balwin, Director of Student Records and Registration, Camden County College, PO Box 200, Blackwood, NJ 08012-0200. *Phone:* 856-227-7200 Ext. 4200. *Toll-free phone:* 888-228-2466.

COUNTY COLLEGE OF MORRIS
Randolph, New Jersey

- **County-supported** 2-year, founded 1966, part of New Jersey Commission on Higher Education
- **Calendar** semesters
- **Degree** certificates and associate
- **Suburban** 218-acre campus with easy access to New York City
- **Endowment** $1.3 million
- **Coed,** 8,190 undergraduate students

Undergraduates Students come from 4 states and territories, 0.3% are from out of state, 4% African American, 7% Asian American or Pacific Islander, 10% Hispanic American, 0.3% Native American.

Freshmen *Admission:* 3,315 applied, 3,315 admitted. *Test scores:* SAT verbal scores over 500: 34%; SAT math scores over 500: 38%; SAT verbal scores over 600: 6%; SAT math scores over 600: 6%; SAT verbal scores over 700: 1%; SAT math scores over 700: 1%.

Faculty *Total:* 495. *Student/faculty ratio:* 18:1.

Majors Agricultural business; aircraft pilot (professional); applied art; biological technology; business administration; chemical technology; early childhood education; educational media technology; electrical/electronic engineering technology; engineering science; engineering technology; exercise sciences; graphic design/commercial art/illustration; hotel and restaurant management; interdisciplinary studies; law enforcement/police science; liberal arts and sciences/liberal studies; management information systems/business data processing; mechanical engineering technology; medical laboratory technician; nursing; photographic technology; public administration; radio/television broadcasting technology; recreation/leisure facilities management; respiratory therapy; secretarial science; veterinarian assistant.

Academic Programs *Special study options:* academic remediation for entering students, adult/continuing education programs, advanced placement credit, cooperative education, distance learning, English as a second language, honors programs, internships, part-time degree program, services for LD students, summer session for credit.

Library Matsen Learning Resource Center with 102,550 titles, 819 serial subscriptions, an OPAC, a Web page.

Computers on Campus 51 computers available on campus for general student use. A campuswide network can be accessed from off campus. Internet access, online (class) registration, at least one staffed computer lab available.

Student Life *Housing:* college housing not available. *Activities and Organizations:* drama/theater group, student-run newspaper, radio station, choral group, Student Government Association, Student Activities Programming Board, Black Student Union, United Latino Organization, student newspaper. *Campus security:* 24-hour emergency response devices and patrols, late-night transport/escort service. *Student Services:* health clinic, personal/psychological counseling, women's center.

Athletics Member NJCAA. *Intercollegiate sports:* baseball M(s), basketball M(s)/W(s), golf M/W, ice hockey M(s), soccer M, softball W(s), tennis M/W. *Intramural sports:* badminton M/W, basketball M/W, football M, soccer W, softball W, tennis M/W, volleyball M/W, weight lifting M/W, wrestling M/W.

Standardized Tests *Required:* New Jersey Basic Skills Exam. *Required for some:* SAT I or ACT (for placement).

Costs (2001–02) *Tuition:* area resident $1880 full-time, $68 per credit part-time; state resident $3496 full-time, $136 per credit part-time; nonresident $4696 full-time, $186 per credit part-time. *Required fees:* $240 full-time, $10 per credit. *Waivers:* senior citizens and employees or children of employees.

Financial Aid In 2001, 125 Federal Work-Study jobs (averaging $1000).

Applying *Options:* common application, early admission. *Application fee:* $25. *Required:* high school transcript. *Required for some:* letters of recommendation. *Notification:* continuous (freshmen).

Admissions Contact Mr. James McCarthy, Director of Admissions, County College of Morris, 214 Center Grove Road, Randolph, NJ 07869-2086. *Phone:* 973-328-5100. *Toll-free phone:* 888-226-8001. *Fax:* 973-328-1282. *E-mail:* admiss@ccm.edu.

CUMBERLAND COUNTY COLLEGE
Vineland, New Jersey

- **State and locally supported** 2-year, founded 1963, part of New Jersey Commission on Higher Education
- **Calendar** semesters
- **Degree** certificates and associate
- **Small-town** 100-acre campus with easy access to Philadelphia
- **Coed,** 465 undergraduate students, 82% full-time, 54% women, 46% men

Undergraduates 382 full-time, 83 part-time. Students come from 1 other state, 6 other countries, 18% African American, 1% Asian American or Pacific Islander, 15% Hispanic American, 1% Native American, 22% transferred in.

Freshmen *Admission:* 1,773 applied, 1,773 admitted, 465 enrolled.

Faculty *Total:* 178, 22% full-time, 7% with terminal degrees. *Student/faculty ratio:* 19:1.

Majors Accounting; agricultural business; agricultural sciences; aviation technology; biological/physical sciences; broadcast journalism; business administration; business marketing and marketing management; community services; computer science; computer systems networking/telecommunications; computer typography/composition; corrections; drafting; early childhood education; education; elementary/middle/secondary education administration; engineering; film/video production; fine/studio arts; horticulture science; hospitality/recreation marketing operations; human resources management; industrial radiologic technology; industrial technology; information sciences/systems; law enforcement/police science; legal administrative assistant; liberal arts and sciences/liberal studies; mathematics; nursing; ornamental horticulture; plastics technology; pre-engineering; robotics; secretarial science; social work; system administration; theater arts/drama.

Academic Programs *Special study options:* academic remediation for entering students, adult/continuing education programs, advanced placement credit, cooperative education, distance learning, double majors, English as a second language, honors programs, part-time degree program, services for LD students, summer session for credit.

Library 51,000 titles, 213 serial subscriptions, 480 audiovisual materials, an OPAC, a Web page.

Computers on Campus 275 computers available on campus for general student use. Internet access, at least one staffed computer lab available.

Student Life *Housing:* college housing not available. *Activities and Organizations:* drama/theater group, student-run newspaper, choral group, Student Activities Board, Student Senate. *Campus security:* 24-hour emergency response devices, late-night transport/escort service. *Student Services:* personal/psychological counseling.

Athletics Member NJCAA. *Intercollegiate sports:* baseball M, basketball M/W, softball W, track and field M. *Intramural sports:* fencing M/W, soccer M.

Costs (2001–02) *Tuition:* area resident $1680 full-time, $70 per credit part-time; state resident $3360 full-time, $140 per credit part-time; nonresident $6720 full-time, $280 per credit part-time. Full-time tuition and fees vary according to course load. Part-time tuition and fees vary according to course load. *Required fees:* $361 full-time, $14 per credit. *Payment plan:* deferred payment. *Waivers:* senior citizens and employees or children of employees.

Financial Aid In 2001, 82 Federal Work-Study jobs (averaging $600). 59 State and other part-time jobs (averaging $700).

Applying *Options:* early admission, deferred entrance. *Application fee:* $25. *Required:* high school transcript. *Application deadline:* rolling (freshmen), rolling (transfers). *Notification:* continuous (freshmen).

Admissions Contact Ms. Maud Fried-Goodnight, Executive Director of Enrollment Services, Cumberland County College, College Drive, Vineland, NJ 08362-1500. *Phone:* 856-691-8600 Ext. 228.

ESSEX COUNTY COLLEGE
Newark, New Jersey

- **County-supported** 2-year, founded 1966, part of New Jersey Commission on Higher Education
- **Calendar** semesters
- **Degree** certificates and associate
- **Urban** 22-acre campus with easy access to New York City
- **Coed,** 9,539 undergraduate students, 52% full-time, 65% women, 35% men

Undergraduates 4,924 full-time, 4,615 part-time. Students come from 15 states and territories, 85 other countries, 50% African American, 3% Asian American or Pacific Islander, 17% Hispanic American, 0.1% Native American, 8% international, 2% transferred in. *Retention:* 57% of 2001 full-time freshmen returned.

Freshmen *Admission:* 3,700 applied, 2,594 admitted, 2,135 enrolled.

Faculty *Total:* 514, 30% full-time. *Student/faculty ratio:* 28:1.

Majors Accounting; architectural engineering technology; art; biology; business administration; business education; chemical engineering technology; chem-

Essex County College (continued)

istry; computer programming; computer science; criminal justice/law enforcement administration; data processing technology; dental hygiene; early childhood education; education; electrical/electronic engineering technology; elementary education; emergency medical technology; engineering; engineering technology; fire science; health services administration; hotel and restaurant management; human services; industrial radiologic technology; information sciences/systems; laser/optical technology; law enforcement/police science; liberal arts and sciences/liberal studies; mathematics; medical administrative assistant; music; music teacher education; nursing; physical education; physical therapy; pre-engineering; secretarial science; social sciences.

Academic Programs *Special study options:* academic remediation for entering students, accelerated degree program, adult/continuing education programs, advanced placement credit, cooperative education, distance learning, double majors, English as a second language, independent study, internships, off-campus study, part-time degree program, services for LD students, summer session for credit. *ROTC:* Army (c).

Library Martin Luther King, Jr. Library with 91,000 titles, 639 serial subscriptions, 3,618 audiovisual materials, an OPAC, a Web page.

Computers on Campus 450 computers available on campus for general student use. A campuswide network can be accessed from off campus. Internet access, at least one staffed computer lab available.

Student Life *Housing:* college housing not available. *Activities and Organizations:* drama/theater group, student-run newspaper, choral group, Fashion Entertainment Board, Phi Theta Kappa, Latin Student Union, DECA, Black Student Association. *Campus security:* 24-hour emergency response devices and patrols. *Student Services:* health clinic, personal/psychological counseling, women's center.

Athletics Member NJCAA. *Intercollegiate sports:* basketball M(s)/W(s), cross-country running M(s)/W(s), soccer M, track and field M/W. *Intramural sports:* table tennis M, weight lifting M.

Standardized Tests *Required:* ACCUPLACER, COMPANION.

Costs (2001–02) *Tuition:* area resident $2205 full-time, $74 per credit hour part-time; state resident $4410 full-time, $147 per credit hour part-time; nonresident $4410 full-time, $147 per credit hour part-time. *Required fees:* $375 full-time, $12 per credit hour. *Payment plan:* installment. *Waivers:* employees or children of employees.

Financial Aid In 2001, 250 Federal Work-Study jobs (averaging $2880).

Applying *Options:* deferred entrance. *Application fee:* $20. *Required:* high school transcript. *Application deadline:* 8/15 (freshmen), rolling (transfers). *Notification:* continuous (freshmen).

Admissions Contact Director of Admissions, Essex County College, 303 University Avenue, Newark, NJ 07102. *Phone:* 973-877-3119. *Fax:* 973-623-6449.

GIBBS COLLEGE
Montclair, New Jersey

Admissions Contact Mr. Dave Dahlke, Director of Admissions, Gibbs College, 33 Plymouth Street, Montclair, NJ 07042-2699. *Phone:* 973-744-6962.

GLOUCESTER COUNTY COLLEGE
Sewell, New Jersey

- **County-supported** 2-year, founded 1967, part of New Jersey Commission on Higher Education
- **Calendar** semesters
- **Degree** certificates and associate
- **Rural** 270-acre campus with easy access to Philadelphia
- **Coed,** 4,895 undergraduate students

Faculty *Total:* 220, 31% full-time.

Majors Accounting; accounting technician; auto mechanic/technician; biology; business administration; business marketing and marketing management; chemical engineering technology; chemistry; civil engineering technology; communications; computer graphics; computer science; data processing technology; diagnostic medical sonography; drafting; education; engineering science; English; environmental technology; exercise sciences; finance; fine/studio arts; food sales operations; health/physical education; history; individual/family development; information sciences/systems; law enforcement/police science; legal administrative assistant; legal studies; liberal arts and sciences/liberal studies; mathematics; medical administrative assistant; nuclear medical technology; nursing; paralegal/legal assistant; political science; psychology; respiratory therapy; retail management; social sciences; sociology; theater arts/drama.

Academic Programs *Special study options:* academic remediation for entering students, advanced placement credit, cooperative education, distance learning, part-time degree program, services for LD students, summer session for credit.

Library Gloucester County College Library with 55,710 titles, 875 serial subscriptions, 13,407 audiovisual materials, an OPAC.

Computers on Campus 120 computers available on campus for general student use. Internet access, online (class) registration, at least one staffed computer lab available.

Student Life *Housing:* college housing not available. *Activities and Organizations:* drama/theater group, student-run newspaper, radio station, choral group, Student Activities Board, student government, Accounting Club, Student Nurses Club, student newspaper. *Campus security:* 24-hour emergency response devices and patrols, late-night transport/escort service. *Student Services:* health clinic, personal/psychological counseling, women's center.

Athletics Member NJCAA. *Intercollegiate sports:* baseball M, basketball M/W, cross-country running M/W, soccer M/W, softball W, tennis M/W, track and field M/W, wrestling M. *Intramural sports:* volleyball M/W.

Standardized Tests *Required for some:* SAT I or ACT (for admission).

Costs (2001–02) *Tuition:* area resident $2000 full-time, $63 per credit hour part-time; state resident $2032 full-time, $64 per credit hour part-time; nonresident $8000 full-time, $250 per credit hour part-time. *Required fees:* $528 full-time, $17 per credit hour. *Waivers:* senior citizens and employees or children of employees.

Financial Aid *Financial aid deadline:* 6/1.

Applying *Options:* electronic application, deferred entrance. *Application fee:* $10. *Required:* high school transcript. *Application deadline:* rolling (freshmen), rolling (transfers).

Admissions Contact Ms. Carol L. Lange, Admissions and Recruitment Coordinator, Gloucester County College, Sewell, NJ 08080. *Phone:* 856-468-5000. *Fax:* 856-468-8498.

HUDSON COUNTY COMMUNITY COLLEGE
Jersey City, New Jersey

- **State and locally supported** 2-year, founded 1974, part of New Jersey Commission on Higher Education
- **Calendar** semesters
- **Degree** certificates, diplomas, and associate
- **Urban** campus with easy access to New York City
- **Endowment** $10,000
- **Coed,** 5,285 undergraduate students

Undergraduates Students come from 2 states and territories, 1% are from out of state.

Freshmen *Admission:* 2,191 applied, 2,191 admitted.

Faculty *Total:* 297, 22% full-time.

Majors Accounting; business administration; child care/development; computer engineering technology; computer science; criminal justice studies; culinary arts; data processing technology; electrical/electronic engineering technology; engineering science; human services; liberal arts and sciences/liberal studies; medical assistant; medical records technology; nursing; paralegal/legal assistant.

Academic Programs *Special study options:* academic remediation for entering students, adult/continuing education programs, advanced placement credit, distance learning, double majors, English as a second language, independent study, internships, off-campus study, part-time degree program, services for LD students, summer session for credit.

Library Hudson County Community College Library/Learning Resources Center with 17,000 titles, 251 serial subscriptions, 500 audiovisual materials.

Computers on Campus 367 computers available on campus for general student use. At least one staffed computer lab available.

Student Life *Housing:* college housing not available. *Activities and Organizations:* drama/theater group, student-run newspaper, choral group, Psychology Club, Hispanos Unidos Pura El Progreso, International Student Organization, Drama Society. *Campus security:* 24-hour emergency response devices. *Student Services:* personal/psychological counseling.

Athletics *Intercollegiate sports:* baseball M, basketball M/W, soccer M, softball W, volleyball W. *Intramural sports:* basketball M/W, bowling M/W, football M, golf M, sailing M/W, skiing (downhill) M/W, soccer M, volleyball M/W.

Standardized Tests *Required:* ACCUPLACER.

Costs (2001–02) *Tuition:* area resident $1542 full-time, $64 per credit part-time; state resident $3084 full-time, $129 per credit part-time; nonresident $4626 full-time, $193 per credit part-time. Full-time tuition and fees vary according to course load. Part-time tuition and fees vary according to course load. *Required* *fees:* $706 full-time, $28 per credit. *Payment plan:* deferred payment. *Waivers:* senior citizens and employees or children of employees.

Financial Aid In 2001, 102 Federal Work-Study jobs (averaging $3000).

Applying *Application fee:* $15. *Required:* high school transcript. *Application deadlines:* 9/1 (freshmen), 9/1 (transfers). *Notification:* continuous until 9/1 (freshmen).

Admissions Contact Mr. Robert Martin, Director of Admissions, Hudson County Community College, 162 Sip Avenue, Jersey City, NJ 07306. *Phone:* 201-714-2115. *Fax:* 201-714-2136. *E-mail:* rkahrmann@mail.hudson.cc.nj.us.

MERCER COUNTY COMMUNITY COLLEGE

Trenton, New Jersey

- **State and locally supported** 2-year, founded 1966
- **Calendar** semesters
- **Degree** certificates and associate
- **Suburban** 292-acre campus with easy access to New York City and Philadelphia
- **Coed,** 8,132 undergraduate students, 36% full-time, 54% women, 46% men

Undergraduates 2,887 full-time, 5,245 part-time. Students come from 5 states and territories, 7% are from out of state, 23% African American, 6% Asian American or Pacific Islander, 8% Hispanic American, 0.2% Native American, 5% transferred in.

Freshmen *Admission:* 2,118 applied, 2,118 admitted, 1,701 enrolled.

Faculty *Total:* 423, 27% full-time. *Student/faculty ratio:* 21:1.

Majors Accounting; aircraft pilot (professional); architectural engineering technology; art; art history; automotive engineering technology; aviation management; biological technology; biology; business administration; business systems networking/ telecommunications; ceramic arts; chemistry; civil engineering technology; community services; computer graphics; computer science; corrections; culinary arts; dance; electrical/electronic engineering technology; engineering science; fire science; flight attendant; graphic design/commercial art/illustration; health science; heating/air conditioning/refrigeration technology; hotel and restaurant management; humanities; law enforcement/police science; liberal arts and sciences/liberal studies; management information systems/business data processing; mass communications; mathematics; medical laboratory technician; medical radiologic technology; mortuary science; music; nursing; ornamental horticulture; paralegal/legal assistant; photography; physical therapy assistant; physics; plant sciences; radio/television broadcasting technology; respiratory therapy; sculpture; secretarial science; teacher assistant/aide; theater arts/drama.

Academic Programs *Special study options:* academic remediation for entering students, accelerated degree program, adult/continuing education programs, advanced placement credit, cooperative education, distance learning, double majors, English as a second language, external degree program, independent study, internships, part-time degree program, services for LD students, student-designed majors, summer session for credit. *ROTC:* Army (c), Air Force (c).

Library Mercer County Community College Library plus 1 other with 57,317 titles, 8,934 audiovisual materials, an OPAC, a Web page.

Computers on Campus A campuswide network can be accessed from off campus. At least one staffed computer lab available.

Student Life *Housing:* college housing not available. *Activities and Organizations:* drama/theater group, student-run newspaper, radio station, choral group, Student Government Association, student radio station, African-American Student Organization, Student Activities Board, Phi Theta Kappa. *Campus security:* 24-hour emergency response devices and patrols. *Student Services:* personal/ psychological counseling.

Athletics Member NJCAA. *Intercollegiate sports:* baseball M, basketball M(s)/W(s), soccer M(s)/W(s), softball W, tennis M/W, track and field M/W. *Intramural sports:* basketball M/W, skiing (downhill) M/W, softball M/W, volleyball M/W.

Standardized Tests *Required:* New Jersey Basic Skills Exam. *Recommended:* SAT I (for placement).

Costs (2002–03) *Tuition:* area resident $1716 full-time, $72 per credit part-time; state resident $2328 full-time, $97 per credit part-time; nonresident $3888 full-time, $162 per credit part-time. *Required fees:* $234 full-time, $9 per credit, $15 per credit part-time.

Applying *Options:* common application, electronic application, deferred entrance. *Required:* high school transcript. *Recommended:* interview. *Application deadline:* rolling (freshmen), rolling (transfers). *Notification:* continuous (freshmen).

Admissions Contact Assistant Director of Admissions, Mercer County Community College, 1200 Old Trenton Road, PO Box B, Trenton, NJ 08690-1004. *Phone:* 609-586-4800 Ext. 3286. *Toll-free phone:* 800-392-MCCC. *Fax:* 609-586-6944. *E-mail:* admiss@mccc.edu.

MIDDLESEX COUNTY COLLEGE

Edison, New Jersey

- **County-supported** 2-year, founded 1964
- **Calendar** semesters
- **Degree** associate
- **Suburban** 200-acre campus with easy access to New York City
- **Coed,** 10,500 undergraduate students

Undergraduates Students come from 4 states and territories.

Freshmen *Admission:* 5,561 applied.

Faculty *Total:* 552, 37% full-time. *Student/faculty ratio:* 21:1.

Majors Accounting; advertising; applied art; art; auto mechanic/technician; biological/physical sciences; biological technology; biology; business administration; business marketing and marketing management; business systems networking/ telecommunications; chemistry; child care/development; civil engineering technology; computer engineering technology; computer graphics; computer programming; computer science; construction technology; corrections; criminal justice/law enforcement administration; culinary arts; dance; dental hygiene; dietetics; drafting; early childhood education; education; electrical/ electronic engineering technology; engineering; engineering science; engineering technology; English; fashion design/illustration; fashion merchandising; finance; fine/studio arts; fire science; food products retailing; general studies; graphic design/commercial art/illustration; heating/air conditioning/refrigeration; history; hospitality management; hotel and restaurant management; industrial technology; information sciences/systems; journalism; law enforcement/police science; legal administrative assistant; mathematics; mechanical engineering technology; medical laboratory technician; modern languages; music; nursing; paralegal/legal assistant; photography; physical education; physical sciences; physics; political science; psychology; radiological science; respiratory therapy; retail management; secretarial science; social sciences; sociology; surveying; teacher assistant/ aide; theater arts/drama; transportation technology.

Academic Programs *Special study options:* academic remediation for entering students, adult/continuing education programs, advanced placement credit, cooperative education, English as a second language, internships, part-time degree program, services for LD students, study abroad, summer session for credit. *ROTC:* Army (c), Air Force (c).

Library 82,015 titles, 727 serial subscriptions.

Computers on Campus A campuswide network can be accessed from off campus. Internet access, at least one staffed computer lab available.

Student Life *Housing:* college housing not available. *Activities and Organizations:* drama/theater group, student-run newspaper, radio station, choral group. *Campus security:* 24-hour emergency response devices and patrols. *Student Services:* health clinic, personal/psychological counseling.

Athletics Member NJCAA. *Intercollegiate sports:* baseball M, basketball M(s)/W(s), cross-country running M/W(s), field hockey W, soccer M/W, softball W(s), tennis M/W, track and field M/W, wrestling M(s). *Intramural sports:* bowling M/W, gymnastics M/W, tennis M/W.

Costs (2002–03) *Tuition:* $70 per credit part-time; state resident $1680 full-time, $140 per credit part-time; nonresident $3360 full-time. *Required fees:* $360 full-time, $15 per credit.

Financial Aid In 2001, 69 Federal Work-Study jobs (averaging $3350).

Applying *Options:* early admission, deferred entrance. *Application fee:* $25. *Required:* high school transcript. *Application deadline:* rolling (freshmen), rolling (transfers). *Notification:* continuous (freshmen).

Admissions Contact Mr. Peter W. Rice, Director of Admissions and Recruitment, Middlesex County College, 2600 Woodbridge Avenue, PO Box 3050, Edison, NJ 08818-3050. *Phone:* 732-906-4243.

OCEAN COUNTY COLLEGE

Toms River, New Jersey

- **County-supported** 2-year, founded 1964, part of New Jersey Commission on Higher Education
- **Calendar** semesters
- **Degree** certificates, diplomas, and associate
- **Small-town** 275-acre campus with easy access to Philadelphia
- **Coed,** 7,441 undergraduate students, 48% full-time, 60% women, 40% men

Undergraduates 3,555 full-time, 3,886 part-time. Students come from 6 other countries.

Freshmen *Admission:* 1,345 applied, 1,345 admitted, 1,598 enrolled.

Faculty *Total:* 371, 32% full-time.

Majors Accounting; business; business administration; child care/guidance; civil engineering technology; communication equipment technology; computer/

Ocean County College (continued)
information sciences; computer programming; construction technology; electrical/electronic engineering technology; engineering; fire protection/safety technology; general studies; graphic design/commercial art/illustration; health science; information sciences/systems; journalism; law enforcement/police science; liberal arts and sciences/liberal studies; medical assistant; medical laboratory technician; nursing; paralegal/legal assistant; real estate; secretarial science; social work; teacher assistant/aide.

Academic Programs *Special study options:* academic remediation for entering students, accelerated degree program, adult/continuing education programs, advanced placement credit, cooperative education, distance learning, English as a second language, freshman honors college, honors programs, part-time degree program, services for LD students, study abroad, summer session for credit.

Library Ocean County College Library with 74,215 titles, 428 serial subscriptions.

Computers on Campus 100 computers available on campus for general student use. Internet access, at least one staffed computer lab available.

Student Life *Housing:* college housing not available. *Activities and Organizations:* drama/theater group, student-run newspaper, radio station, choral group. *Campus security:* 24-hour emergency response devices and patrols, late-night transport/escort service. *Student Services:* health clinic, personal/psychological counseling.

Athletics Member NJCAA. *Intercollegiate sports:* baseball M, basketball M/W, golf M/W, soccer M/W, softball W, swimming M/W, tennis M/W. *Intramural sports:* basketball M/W, cross-country running M, tennis M/W, volleyball M/W.

Costs (2002–03) *Tuition:* $84 per credit part-time; state resident $98 per credit part-time; nonresident $151 per credit part-time. *Required fees:* $11 per credit.

Financial Aid *Financial aid deadline:* 4/15.

Applying *Options:* early admission, deferred entrance. *Application fee:* $15. *Required for some:* high school transcript, minimum 3.0 GPA. *Application deadline:* rolling (freshmen), rolling (transfers). *Notification:* continuous (freshmen).

Admissions Contact Mr. Carey Trevisan, Director of Admissions and Records, Ocean County College, College Drive, PO Box 2001, Toms River, NJ 08754-2001. *Phone:* 732-255-0304 Ext. 2016.

PASSAIC COUNTY COMMUNITY COLLEGE

Paterson, New Jersey

- **County-supported** 2-year, founded 1968
- **Calendar** semesters
- **Degree** certificates and associate
- **Urban** 6-acre campus with easy access to New York City
- **Endowment** $78,695
- **Coed**

Student Life *Campus security:* late-night transport/escort service.

Athletics Member NJCAA.

Standardized Tests *Required:* New Jersey Basic Skills Exam.

Financial Aid In 2001, 100 Federal Work-Study jobs (averaging $3000).

Applying *Options:* early admission, deferred entrance. *Application fee:* $15.

Admissions Contact Office of Admissions, Passaic County Community College, One College Boulevard, Patterson, NJ 07505. *Phone:* 973-684-6304.

RARITAN VALLEY COMMUNITY COLLEGE

Somerville, New Jersey

- **County-supported** 2-year, founded 1965
- **Calendar** semesters
- **Degree** certificates and associate
- **Small-town** 225-acre campus with easy access to New York City and Philadelphia
- **Coed,** 5,830 undergraduate students, 36% full-time, 58% women, 42% men

Undergraduates 2,075 full-time, 3,755 part-time. 0.5% are from out of state, 8% African American, 5% Asian American or Pacific Islander, 7% Hispanic American, 0.2% Native American, 3% international. *Retention:* 56% of 2001 full-time freshmen returned.

Freshmen *Admission:* 705 applied, 705 admitted.

Faculty *Total:* 356, 29% full-time.

Majors Accounting; auto mechanic/technician; aviation/airway science; biology; business administration; business marketing and marketing management; chemistry; computer programming; computer science; construction technology; criminal justice/law enforcement administration; data processing technology; diesel engine mechanic; early childhood education; education; electrical/electronic engineering technology; electromechanical technology; elementary education; engineering; environmental science; food sales operations; graphic design/commercial art/illustration; heating/air conditioning/refrigeration; hotel and restaurant management; human services; industrial technology; information sciences/systems; international business; liberal arts and sciences/liberal studies; management information systems/business data processing; mathematics; mechanical design technology; multimedia; music; nursing; optometric/ophthalmic laboratory technician; paralegal/legal assistant; real estate; respiratory therapy; retail management; robotics; secretarial science; social sciences; theater arts/drama; travel/tourism management; visual/performing arts.

Academic Programs *Special study options:* academic remediation for entering students, adult/continuing education programs, advanced placement credit, cooperative education, honors programs, internships, off-campus study, part-time degree program, services for LD students, summer session for credit. *ROTC:* Air Force (c).

Library Evelyn S. Field Learning Resources Center with 84,150 titles, 325 serial subscriptions.

Computers on Campus 120 computers available on campus for general student use. Internet access, at least one staffed computer lab available.

Student Life *Housing:* college housing not available. *Activities and Organizations:* drama/theater group, student-run newspaper, radio station, choral group, International Club, The Latin Pride Club, Student Nurses Association, The Record (student newspaper), Christian Fellowship Club. *Campus security:* 24-hour emergency response devices and patrols, 24-hour outdoor surveillance cameras. *Student Services:* health clinic, personal/psychological counseling.

Athletics Member NJCAA. *Intercollegiate sports:* baseball M, basketball M/W, soccer M, softball W. *Intramural sports:* golf M/W.

Costs (2001–02) *Tuition:* state resident $1860 full-time, $62 per credit part-time; nonresident $1860 full-time, $62 per credit part-time. *Required fees:* $470 full-time, $13 per credit, $40 per term part-time.

Financial Aid In 2001, 12 Federal Work-Study jobs (averaging $1000).

Applying *Options:* early admission. *Application fee:* $25. *Required:* high school transcript. *Application deadline:* rolling (freshmen), rolling (transfers).

Admissions Contact Dr. Maxwell Stevens, Dean of Academic and Student Affairs, Raritan Valley Community College, PO Box 3300, Somerville, NJ 08876-1265. *Phone:* 908-526-1200 Ext. 8802. *Fax:* 908-704-3442.

SALEM COMMUNITY COLLEGE

Carneys Point, New Jersey

- **County-supported** 2-year, founded 1972, part of New Jersey Commission on Higher Education
- **Calendar** semesters
- **Degree** certificates and associate
- **Suburban** 20-acre campus with easy access to Philadelphia
- **Coed,** 1,229 undergraduate students, 41% full-time, 60% women, 40% men

Undergraduates 498 full-time, 731 part-time. Students come from 6 states and territories, 7% are from out of state, 3% transferred in.

Freshmen *Admission:* 659 applied, 480 admitted, 209 enrolled. *Test scores:* SAT verbal scores over 500: 24%; SAT math scores over 500: 18%; SAT verbal scores over 600: 3%; SAT math scores over 600: 5%.

Faculty *Total:* 69, 36% full-time. *Student/faculty ratio:* 22:1.

Majors Accounting; biological/physical sciences; biology; business administration; business marketing and marketing management; chemistry; community services; computer engineering technology; computer systems networking/telecommunications; criminal justice/law enforcement administration; early childhood education; education; electrical/electronic engineering technology; English; health/physical education; heating/air conditioning/refrigeration; history; humanities; human resources management; industrial technology; information sciences/systems; instrumentation technology; journalism; legal administrative assistant; liberal arts and sciences/liberal studies; management information systems/business data processing; mass communications; mathematics; medical administrative assistant; medical assistant; nuclear technology; nursing; occupational safety/health technology; physics; political science; public administration; retail management; secretarial science; social sciences; sociology; Web/multimedia management/webmaster.

Academic Programs *Special study options:* academic remediation for entering students, adult/continuing education programs, advanced placement credit, cooperative education, distance learning, double majors, English as a second language, independent study, off-campus study, part-time degree program, services for LD students, summer session for credit.

Library Michael S. Cettei Memorial Library with 28,951 titles, 240 serial subscriptions, an OPAC.
Computers on Campus 200 computers available on campus for general student use. A campuswide network can be accessed from off campus. Internet access, online (class) registration, at least one staffed computer lab available.
Student Life *Housing:* college housing not available. *Activities and Organizations:* drama/theater group, choral group, Drama Club, Science Club, Multicultural Exchange Club. *Campus security:* 24-hour emergency response devices and patrols, late-night transport/escort service. *Student Services:* personal/psychological counseling, women's center.
Athletics Member NJCAA. *Intercollegiate sports:* baseball M(s), basketball M(s)/W(s), softball W(s), tennis M(s)/W(s).
Standardized Tests *Required:* New Jersey Basic Skills Exam.
Costs (2002–03) *Tuition:* area resident $1668 full-time, $70 per credit part-time; state resident $80 per credit part-time; nonresident $1920 full-time, $80 per credit part-time. Full-time tuition and fees vary according to course load. Part-time tuition and fees vary according to course load. *Required fees:* $568 full-time, $22 per credit, $25 per term part-time. *Payment plans:* installment, deferred payment. *Waivers:* senior citizens and employees or children of employees.
Financial Aid In 2001, 63 Federal Work-Study jobs (averaging $550).
Applying *Options:* early admission, deferred entrance. *Application fee:* $20. *Required:* essay or personal statement, high school transcript. *Application deadline:* rolling (freshmen), rolling (transfers). *Notification:* continuous (freshmen).
Admissions Contact Mr. Jeffrey Huckel, Coordinator of Admissions, Salem Community College, 460 Hollywood Avenue, Carney's Point, NJ 08069. *Phone:* 856-351-2698. *Fax:* 856-299-9193. *E-mail:* sccinfo@willie.salem.cc.nj.us.

SOMERSET CHRISTIAN COLLEGE
Zarephath, New Jersey

- **Independent religious** 2-year, founded 1908
- **Calendar** semesters
- **Degree** associate
- **Coed,** 107 undergraduate students
- 91% of applicants were admitted

Undergraduates Students come from 3 states and territories, 29% African American, 2% Asian American or Pacific Islander, 5% Hispanic American. *Retention:* 13% of 2001 full-time freshmen returned.
Freshmen *Admission:* 54 applied, 49 admitted.
Faculty *Total:* 8, 38% full-time, 50% with terminal degrees. *Student/faculty ratio:* 8:1.
Majors Biblical studies.
Student Life *Housing:* college housing not available. *Activities and Organizations:* student-run newspaper, radio station, Nursing Home Visitation. *Student Services:* personal/psychological counseling.
Standardized Tests *Required for some:* SAT I or ACT (for admission).
Costs (2002–03) *Tuition:* $3360 full-time, $140 per credit part-time. *Required fees:* $100 full-time, $50 per term part-time. *Payment plan:* installment.
Applying *Application fee:* $20. *Required:* essay or personal statement, letters of recommendation. *Required for some:* high school transcript, minimum 2.5 GPA, interview. *Application deadlines:* 8/26 (freshmen), 8/26 (transfers). *Notification:* continuous (freshmen).
Admissions Contact Ms. Cheryl L. Burdick, Director of Admissions, Somerset Christian College, 10 Liberty Square, Zarephath, NJ 08890. *Phone:* 732-356-1595. *Toll-free phone:* 800-234-9305. *Fax:* 732-356-4846. *E-mail:* info@somerset.edu.

SUSSEX COUNTY COMMUNITY COLLEGE
Newton, New Jersey

- **State and locally supported** 2-year, founded 1981, part of New Jersey Commission on Higher Education
- **Calendar** 4-1-4
- **Degree** certificates and associate
- **Small-town** 130-acre campus with easy access to New York City
- **Endowment** $259,296
- **Coed,** 2,479 undergraduate students, 42% full-time, 62% women, 38% men

Undergraduates 1,050 full-time, 1,429 part-time. Students come from 3 states and territories, 11% are from out of state, 2% African American, 1% Asian American or Pacific Islander, 3% Hispanic American, 0.3% Native American, 0.1% international.
Freshmen *Admission:* 726 applied, 726 admitted, 424 enrolled.
Faculty *Total:* 185, 20% full-time, 15% with terminal degrees. *Student/faculty ratio:* 18:1.
Majors Accounting; automotive engineering technology; biological/physical sciences; broadcast journalism; business administration; computer/information sciences; criminal justice/corrections related; English; environmental science; fine/studio arts; fire protection related; graphic design/commercial art/illustration; health science; human services; journalism; liberal arts and sciences/liberal studies; paralegal/legal assistant; respiratory therapy; retail management; secretarial science; veterinarian assistant.
Academic Programs *Special study options:* academic remediation for entering students, advanced placement credit, English as a second language, internships, part-time degree program, services for LD students, summer session for credit.
Library Sussex County Community College Library with 40,000 titles, 222 serial subscriptions.
Computers on Campus Internet access, at least one staffed computer lab available.
Student Life *Housing:* college housing not available. *Activities and Organizations:* drama/theater group, student-run newspaper, choral group, Student Government Association, "The College Hill" (newspaper), Human Services Club, Arts Club, Returning Adult Support Group. *Campus security:* late-night transport/escort service, trained security personnel. *Student Services:* personal/psychological counseling, women's center.
Athletics Member NJCAA. *Intercollegiate sports:* baseball M, basketball M, soccer M/W, softball W.
Costs (2002–03) *Tuition:* area resident $1980 full-time, $66 per credit part-time; state resident $2970 full-time, $99 per credit part-time; nonresident $3960 full-time, $132 per credit part-time. *Required fees:* $458 full-time, $9 per credit, $15 per term part-time. *Payment plan:* installment. *Waivers:* senior citizens and employees or children of employees.
Financial Aid In 2001, 39 Federal Work-Study jobs (averaging $846).
Applying *Application fee:* $15. *Required:* high school transcript. *Application deadline:* rolling (freshmen), rolling (transfers). *Notification:* continuous (freshmen).
Admissions Contact Mr. Harold H. Damato, Dean of Student Services, Sussex County Community College, 1 College Hill, Newton, NJ 07860. *Phone:* 973-300-2218. *E-mail:* hdamato@sussex.cc.nj.us.

UNION COUNTY COLLEGE
Cranford, New Jersey

- **State and locally supported** 2-year, founded 1933, part of New Jersey Commission on Higher Education
- **Calendar** semesters
- **Degree** certificates, diplomas, and associate
- **Suburban** 48-acre campus with easy access to New York City
- **Endowment** $2.3 million
- **Coed,** 8,950 undergraduate students, 52% full-time, 68% women, 32% men

Undergraduates 4,654 full-time, 4,296 part-time. Students come from 8 states and territories, 83 other countries, 1% are from out of state, 22% African American, 4% Asian American or Pacific Islander, 26% Hispanic American, 0.3% Native American, 2% international, 6% transferred in. *Retention:* 79% of 2001 full-time freshmen returned.
Freshmen *Admission:* 5,118 applied, 5,055 admitted, 1,719 enrolled. *Test scores:* SAT verbal scores over 500: 21%; SAT math scores over 500: 19%; SAT verbal scores over 600: 4%; SAT math scores over 600: 3%; SAT verbal scores over 700: 1%.
Faculty *Total:* 383, 47% full-time, 21% with terminal degrees. *Student/faculty ratio:* 23:1.
Majors Accounting technician; biology; business; business administration; business services marketing; chemistry; civil engineering technology; communications; dental hygiene; electromechanical technology; engineering; fire protection/safety technology; foreign language translation; gerontology; health/medical diagnostic and treatment services related; hotel and restaurant management; industrial technology; information sciences/systems; law enforcement/police science; liberal arts and sciences/liberal studies; management information systems/business data processing; mechanical engineering technology; medical assistant; medical laboratory technician; medical radiologic technology; nuclear medical technology; nursing; occupational therapy assistant; physical sciences; physical therapy assistant; practical nurse; rehabilitation/therapeutic services related; respiratory therapy; secretarial science; sign language interpretation.
Academic Programs *Special study options:* academic remediation for entering students, accelerated degree program, adult/continuing education programs,

Union County College (continued)
advanced placement credit, distance learning, English as a second language, honors programs, internships, off-campus study, part-time degree program, services for LD students, student-designed majors, summer session for credit. *ROTC:* Air Force (c).
Library MacKay Library plus 2 others with 119,261 titles, 1,939 serial subscriptions, 1,989 audiovisual materials, an OPAC.
Computers on Campus 442 computers available on campus for general student use. A campuswide network can be accessed from off campus. Internet access, at least one staffed computer lab available.
Student Life *Housing:* college housing not available. *Activities and Organizations:* drama/theater group, student-run newspaper, radio and television station, SIGN, Spanish Club, Black Students Heritage Organization, Student Government Organization, International Cultural Exchange Students. *Campus security:* 24-hour emergency response devices and patrols, late-night transport/escort service. *Student Services:* personal/psychological counseling.
Athletics Member NJCAA. *Intercollegiate sports:* baseball M, basketball M/W, golf M/W, soccer M, softball W. *Intramural sports:* tennis M/W.
Standardized Tests *Required for some:* SAT I (for placement). *Recommended:* SAT I (for placement).
Costs (2002–03) *Tuition:* area resident $2219 full-time, $73 per credit part-time; state resident $3971 full-time, $146 per credit part-time; nonresident $3971 full-time, $146 per credit part-time. Full-time tuition and fees vary according to program. Part-time tuition and fees vary according to program. *Required fees:* $467 full-time, $19 per credit. *Payment plan:* deferred payment. *Waivers:* senior citizens and employees or children of employees.
Financial Aid In 2001, 150 Federal Work-Study jobs (averaging $1700).
Applying *Options:* early admission, deferred entrance. *Application fee:* $25. *Required:* high school transcript. *Required for some:* interview. *Application deadline:* rolling (freshmen), rolling (transfers). *Notification:* continuous (freshmen).
Admissions Contact Ms. Jo Ann Davis, Director of Admissions, Records, and Registration, Union County College, 1033 Springfield Avenue, Cranford, NJ 07016. *Phone:* 908-709-7127. *Fax:* 908-709-7125.

Warren County Community College
Washington, New Jersey

- **State and locally supported** 2-year, founded 1981, part of New Jersey Commission on Higher Education
- **Calendar** semesters
- **Degree** certificates and associate
- **Rural** 77-acre campus
- **Coed,** 981 undergraduate students

Undergraduates Students come from 4 states and territories. *Retention:* 56% of 2001 full-time freshmen returned.
Freshmen *Admission:* 426 applied, 426 admitted.
Faculty *Total:* 81, 22% full-time, 16% with terminal degrees. *Student/faculty ratio:* 13:1.
Majors Accounting; biology; business administration; criminal justice/law enforcement administration; data processing technology; education; environmental science; fine/studio arts; information sciences/systems; liberal arts and sciences/liberal studies; paralegal/legal assistant; secretarial science; social sciences.
Academic Programs *Special study options:* academic remediation for entering students, advanced placement credit, cooperative education, distance learning, double majors, English as a second language, independent study, internships, off-campus study, part-time degree program, services for LD students, summer session for credit.
Library 23,143 titles, 375 serial subscriptions, 1,300 audiovisual materials.
Computers on Campus 85 computers available on campus for general student use. A campuswide network can be accessed from off campus. Internet access, at least one staffed computer lab available.
Student Life *Housing:* college housing not available. *Activities and Organizations:* drama/theater group, student-run newspaper, national fraternities. *Campus security:* evening and weekend security.
Standardized Tests *Required:* New Jersey Basic Skills Exam.
Costs (2002–03) *Tuition:* area resident $1608 full-time, $67 per credit part-time; state resident $3216 full-time, $134 per credit part-time; nonresident $201 per credit part-time. *Required fees:* $204 full-time, $9 per credit.
Financial Aid In 2001, 20 Federal Work-Study jobs (averaging $2000).
Applying *Options:* early admission, deferred entrance. *Application fee:* $15. *Application deadline:* rolling (freshmen), rolling (transfers).
Admissions Contact Admissions Advisor, Warren County Community College, 475 Route 57 West, Washington, NJ 07882-9605. *Phone:* 908-835-2300. *Fax:* 908-689-5824.

NEW MEXICO

Albuquerque Technical Vocational Institute
Albuquerque, New Mexico

- **State-supported** 2-year, founded 1965
- **Calendar** trimesters
- **Degree** certificates and associate
- **Urban** 60-acre campus
- **Endowment** $1.3 million
- **Coed,** 18,833 undergraduate students, 30% full-time, 58% women, 42% men

Undergraduates 5,655 full-time, 13,178 part-time. Students come from 46 states and territories, 2% are from out of state, 3% African American, 2% Asian American or Pacific Islander, 41% Hispanic American, 8% Native American, 0.1% international, 6% transferred in. *Retention:* 49% of 2001 full-time freshmen returned.
Freshmen *Admission:* 3,236 applied, 3,236 admitted, 2,353 enrolled.
Faculty *Total:* 798, 38% full-time. *Student/faculty ratio:* 22:1.
Majors Accounting; architectural drafting; banking; business administration; cardiovascular technology; child care/guidance; computer systems analysis; construction management related; construction trades related; cosmetology; court reporting; criminal justice studies; culinary arts; data processing technology; diagnostic medical sonography; electrical/electronic engineering technology; electrical/electronics drafting; elementary education; engineering; environmental engineering; fire protection/safety technology; hospitality management; industrial technology; information sciences/systems; international business; laser/optical technology; liberal arts and sciences/liberal studies; medical laboratory technician; medical records administration; nursing; paralegal/legal assistant; respiratory therapy; secretarial science; vehicle/mobile equipment mechanics and repair related.
Academic Programs *Special study options:* academic remediation for entering students, adult/continuing education programs, advanced placement credit, cooperative education, distance learning, double majors, English as a second language, internships, part-time degree program, services for LD students, summer session for credit.
Library Main Campus Library plus 2 others with 41,103 titles, an OPAC, a Web page.
Computers on Campus A campuswide network can be accessed from off campus. Internet access, at least one staffed computer lab available.
Student Life *Housing:* college housing not available. *Activities and Organizations:* student-run newspaper, Phi Theta Kappa, student government, Hispanic Club, TVI Times (student newspaper). *Campus security:* 24-hour patrols, student patrols, late-night transport/escort service. *Student Services:* health clinic, personal/psychological counseling.
Costs (2001–02) *Tuition:* state resident $1246 full-time, $35 per credit hour part-time; nonresident $3456 full-time, $96 per credit hour part-time. Full-time tuition and fees vary according to course load and program. Part-time tuition and fees vary according to course load and program. *Required fees:* $67 full-time, $22 per term part-time. *Payment plan:* installment. *Waivers:* senior citizens and employees or children of employees.
Financial Aid In 2001, 145 Federal Work-Study jobs (averaging $6000). 210 State and other part-time jobs (averaging $6000). *Financial aid deadline:* 6/30.
Applying *Options:* deferred entrance. *Recommended:* high school transcript. *Application deadline:* rolling (freshmen), rolling (transfers).
Admissions Contact Ms. Jane Campbell, Director of Enrollment Services, Albuquerque Technical Vocational Institute, 535 Buena Vista, SE, Albuquerque, NM 87106-4096. *Phone:* 505-224-3210. *Fax:* 505-224-4740.

The Art Center
Albuquerque, New Mexico

- **Proprietary** 2-year, founded 1989
- **Calendar** quarters
- **Degree** certificates, diplomas, and associate
- **Coed**

Applying *Application fee:* $25.
Admissions Contact Ms. Colleen Gimbel-Froebe, Associate Director of Admissions and Placement, The Art Center, 5041 Indian School Road, NE, Suite 100, Albuquerque, NM 87110. *Phone:* 520-325-0123. *Toll-free phone:* 800-827-8753. *Fax:* 520-325-5535.

CLOVIS COMMUNITY COLLEGE
Clovis, New Mexico

- **State-supported** 2-year, founded 1990
- **Calendar** semesters
- **Degree** certificates and associate
- **Small-town** 25-acre campus
- **Endowment** $462,587
- **Coed,** 2,767 undergraduate students, 35% full-time, 66% women, 34% men

Undergraduates 967 full-time, 1,800 part-time. Students come from 9 states and territories, 11 other countries, 12% are from out of state. *Retention:* 36% of 2001 full-time freshmen returned.
Freshmen *Admission:* 181 enrolled.
Faculty *Total:* 222, 26% full-time.
Majors Accounting; auto mechanic/technician; bilingual/bicultural education; business administration; carpentry; computer typography/composition; corrections; cosmetology; electrical/electronic engineering technology; electromechanical technology; executive assistant; finance; fine/studio arts; graphic design/commercial art/illustration; health/physical education; heating/air conditioning/refrigeration; law enforcement/police science; legal administrative assistant; liberal arts and sciences/liberal studies; library assistant; management information systems/business data processing; mathematics; medical administrative assistant; medical radiologic technology; nursing; paralegal/legal assistant; physical sciences; psychology; secretarial science; teacher assistant/aide; technical/business writing.
Academic Programs *Special study options:* academic remediation for entering students, cooperative education, distance learning, double majors, English as a second language, independent study, internships, part-time degree program, services for LD students, summer session for credit.
Library Clovis Community College Library and Learning Resources Center with 46,000 titles, 330 serial subscriptions, 2,500 audiovisual materials, an OPAC.
Computers on Campus 280 computers available on campus for general student use. Internet access, at least one staffed computer lab available.
Student Life *Housing:* college housing not available. *Activities and Organizations:* Student Senate, Student Nursing Association, Black Advisory Council, Hispanic Advisory Council, student ambassadors. *Campus security:* student patrols, late-night transport/escort service.
Athletics *Intramural sports:* basketball M/W, cross-country running M/W, football M/W, racquetball M/W, soccer M/W, tennis M/W, volleyball M/W.
Standardized Tests *Required for some:* TABE, ACCUPLACER. *Recommended:* TABE, ACCUPLACER.
Costs (2002–03) *Tuition:* area resident $592 full-time, $43 per credit hour part-time; state resident $640 full-time, $45 per credit hour part-time; nonresident $880 full-time, $45 per credit hour part-time. *Required fees:* $20 full-time, $10 per term part-time. *Payment plans:* installment, deferred payment. *Waivers:* senior citizens.
Applying *Options:* common application. *Required:* high school transcript.
Admissions Contact Ms. Nicole Striegel, Director of Admissions, Registrar, Clovis Community College, 417 Schepps Boulevard, Clovis, NM 88101-8381. *Phone:* 505-769-4021. *E-mail:* admissions@clovis.cc.nm.us.

DONA ANA BRANCH COMMUNITY COLLEGE
Las Cruces, New Mexico

- **State and locally supported** 2-year, founded 1973, part of New Mexico State University System
- **Calendar** semesters
- **Degree** certificates and associate
- **Urban** 15-acre campus with easy access to Ciudad Juarez and El Paso
- **Coed,** 4,987 undergraduate students

Faculty *Total:* 324, 26% full-time.
Majors Architectural engineering technology; auto mechanic/technician; business administration; computer engineering technology; computer typography/composition; drafting; electrical/electronic engineering technology; emergency medical technology; fashion merchandising; finance; fire science; heating/air conditioning/refrigeration; hospitality management; industrial radiologic technology; library science; nursing; paralegal/legal assistant; respiratory therapy; retail management; secretarial science; water resources; welding technology.
Academic Programs *Special study options:* academic remediation for entering students, adult/continuing education programs, advanced placement credit, cooperative education, English as a second language, freshman honors college, honors programs, internships, part-time degree program, services for LD students, summer session for credit. *ROTC:* Army (c), Air Force (c).
Library Library/Media Center with 17,140 titles, 213 serial subscriptions, an OPAC.
Computers on Campus 433 computers available on campus for general student use. A campuswide network can be accessed from off campus. Internet access, online (class) registration, at least one staffed computer lab available.
Student Life *Housing Options:* coed. *Activities and Organizations:* drama/theater group, student-run newspaper, radio station, choral group, marching band. *Campus security:* 24-hour emergency response devices and patrols, late-night transport/escort service. *Student Services:* health clinic, personal/psychological counseling, women's center, legal services.
Standardized Tests *Recommended:* ACT, ACT ASSET, or ACT COMPASS.
Costs (2001–02) *Tuition:* area resident $888 full-time, $37 per credit hour part-time; state resident $1008 full-time, $42 per credit hour part-time; nonresident $2304 full-time, $96 per credit hour part-time. Room and board are provided by the New Mexico State University. *Required fees:* $15 full-time. *Room and board:* Room and board charges vary according to board plan and housing facility. *Payment plan:* installment. *Waivers:* senior citizens.
Financial Aid *Financial aid deadline:* 6/30.
Applying *Options:* deferred entrance. *Application fee:* $15. *Required:* high school transcript. *Required for some:* letters of recommendation. *Application deadline:* rolling (freshmen).
Admissions Contact Admissions Counselor, Dona Ana Branch Community College, MSC-3DA, Box 30001, Las Cruces, NM 88003-8001. *Phone:* 505-527-7532. *Toll-free phone:* 800-903-7503. *Fax:* 505-527-7515.

EASTERN NEW MEXICO UNIVERSITY-ROSWELL
Roswell, New Mexico

Admissions Contact Mr. James Mares, Assistant Director, Eastern New Mexico University-Roswell, PO Box 6000, Roswell, NM 88202-6000. *Phone:* 505-624-7149. *Toll-free phone:* 800-243-6687. *Fax:* 505-624-7144.

INSTITUTE OF AMERICAN INDIAN ARTS
Santa Fe, New Mexico

- **Federally supported** 2-year, founded 1962
- **Calendar** semesters
- **Degree** associate
- **Urban** 100-acre campus
- **Endowment** $4.0 million
- **Coed,** 150 undergraduate students

Undergraduates Students come from 29 states and territories, 3 other countries.
Freshmen *Admission:* 151 applied, 50 admitted.
Faculty *Total:* 28, 43% full-time. *Student/faculty ratio:* 9:1.
Majors Art; ceramic arts; creative writing; drawing; fine/studio arts; metal/jewelry arts; museum studies; photography; printmaking; sculpture; textile arts.
Academic Programs *Special study options:* academic remediation for entering students, internships, off-campus study.
Library Fogelson Library with 15,200 titles, 60 serial subscriptions.
Computers on Campus 20 computers available on campus for general student use. Internet access, at least one staffed computer lab available.
Student Life *Housing Options:* coed. *Activities and Organizations:* drama/theater group, student-run newspaper, Powwow Club, Museum Club, Ski Club, Spring Break Club. *Campus security:* 24-hour patrols, late-night transport/escort service. *Student Services:* personal/psychological counseling.
Athletics *Intramural sports:* archery M/W, basketball M/W, bowling M/W, cross-country running M/W, skiing (cross-country) M/W, skiing (downhill) M/W, swimming M/W, table tennis M/W, tennis M/W, track and field M/W, volleyball M/W.
Standardized Tests *Recommended:* ACT (for placement).
Costs (2001–02) *Comprehensive fee:* $7136 includes full-time tuition ($2400), mandatory fees ($200), and room and board ($4536). Part-time tuition: $100 per credit hour.

Institute of American Indian Arts (continued)

Applying *Options:* deferred entrance. *Required:* high school transcript, minimum 2.0 GPA, 3 letters of recommendation. *Recommended:* interview. *Application deadlines:* 4/15 (freshmen), 4/15 (transfers). *Notification:* continuous until 7/1 (freshmen).

Admissions Contact Mr. Ramus Suina, Director of Admissions, Institute of American Indian Arts, 83 Avan Nu Po Road, Santa Fe, NM 87508. *Phone:* 505-424-2328.

ITT Technical Institute
Albuquerque, New Mexico

- **Proprietary** primarily 2-year, founded 1989, part of ITT Educational Services, Inc
- **Calendar** quarters
- **Degrees** associate and bachelor's
- 392 undergraduate students

Majors Computer/information sciences related; computer programming; drafting; electrical/electronic engineering technologies related; information technology.

Student Life *Housing:* college housing not available.

Costs (2001–02) *Tuition:* Full-time tuition and fees vary according to program. Part-time tuition and fees vary according to program. $260—$330 per credit hour.

Applying *Options:* deferred entrance. *Application fee:* $100. *Required:* high school transcript, interview. *Recommended:* letters of recommendation. *Application deadline:* rolling (freshmen), rolling (transfers). *Notification:* continuous (freshmen).

Admissions Contact Mr. John Crooks, Director of Recruitment, ITT Technical Institute, 5100 Masthead Street NE, Albuquerque, NM 87109-4366. *Phone:* 505-828-1114. *Toll-free phone:* 800-636-1114.

Luna Community College
Las Vegas, New Mexico

Admissions Contact PO Box 1510, Las Vegas, NM 87701.

Mesa Technical College
Tucumcari, New Mexico

- **State-supported** 2-year, founded 1979
- **Degree** certificates, diplomas, and associate
- **Endowment** $16,000
- **Coed,** 576 undergraduate students

Undergraduates Students come from 10 states and territories, 5% are from out of state.

Faculty *Total:* 35, 34% full-time. *Student/faculty ratio:* 10:1.

Majors Animal sciences; auto mechanic/technician; business administration; communications; diesel engine mechanic; elementary education; geology; history; human resources management; information sciences/systems; metal/jewelry arts; paleontology; public administration; social work.

Student Life *Housing:* college housing not available. *Activities and Organizations:* Student Senate, Chi Alpha, Phi Theta Kappa, SHOE, Natural Sciences Club. *Campus security:* 24-hour emergency response devices.

Standardized Tests *Required:* ACT COMPASS.

Costs (2002–03) *Tuition:* area resident $840 full-time, $28 per credit part-time; state resident $840 full-time, $28 per credit part-time; nonresident $45 per credit part-time. *Required fees:* $130 full-time, $3 per credit, $20 per semester part-time.

Applying *Required:* high school transcript. *Application deadline:* rolling (freshmen), rolling (transfers).

Admissions Contact Mr. Ken Brashear, Director of Enrollment Management, Mesa Technical College, 911 South Tenth Street, Tucumcari, NM 88401. *Phone:* 505-461-4413.

New Mexico Junior College
Hobbs, New Mexico

- **State and locally supported** 2-year, founded 1965, part of New Mexico Commission on Higher Education
- **Calendar** semesters
- **Degree** certificates and associate
- **Small-town** 185-acre campus
- **Coed**

Faculty *Student/faculty ratio:* 19:1.

Student Life *Campus security:* 24-hour emergency response devices and patrols, late-night transport/escort service, controlled dormitory access.

Athletics Member NJCAA.

Standardized Tests *Recommended:* ACT (for placement).

Applying *Options:* early admission, deferred entrance.

Admissions Contact Mr. Robert Bensing, Dean of Admissions and Records, New Mexico Junior College, 5317 Lovington Highway, Hobbs, NM 88240-9123. *Phone:* 505-392-5092. *Fax:* 505-392-0322. *E-mail:* rbensing@nmjc.cc.nm.us.

New Mexico Military Institute
Roswell, New Mexico

- **State-supported** 2-year, founded 1891, part of New Mexico Commission on Higher Education
- **Calendar** semesters
- **Degree** associate
- **Small-town** 42-acre campus
- **Endowment** $243.6 million
- **Coed, primarily men,** 423 undergraduate students

Excellence is a process achieved in stages, sustained through effort, accentuated by detail, and celebrated by all. At NMMI, excellence is a universal goal. For more than 100 years, NMMI has built a community and a world-class institute of higher learning based on shared values and disciplined behavior, which fosters the highest standards of achievement in its cadets.

Undergraduates Students come from 42 states and territories, 10 other countries, 58% are from out of state, 100% live on campus.

Freshmen *Admission:* 507 applied, 249 admitted. *Test scores:* ACT scores over 18: 87%; ACT scores over 24: 23%; ACT scores over 30: 1%.

Faculty *Total:* 61. *Student/faculty ratio:* 18:1.

Majors Accounting; Army R.O.T.C./military science; art; biological/physical sciences; biology; business administration; chemistry; civil engineering technology; computer programming; computer science; criminal justice/law enforcement administration; economics; engineering; English; finance; French; German; history; humanities; law enforcement/police science; liberal arts and sciences/liberal studies; mathematics; physical education; physics; pre-engineering; social sciences; Spanish; sport/fitness administration.

Academic Programs *Special study options:* academic remediation for entering students, advanced placement credit, English as a second language, summer session for credit. *ROTC:* Army (b).

Library Paul Horgan Library plus 2 others with 65,000 titles, 200 serial subscriptions, an OPAC.

Computers on Campus 700 computers available on campus for general student use. A campuswide network can be accessed from student residence rooms and from off campus. Internet access, at least one staffed computer lab available.

Student Life *Housing:* on-campus residence required through sophomore year. *Options:* coed. *Activities and Organizations:* drama/theater group, student-run newspaper, television station, choral group, marching band, band, chorus, drill teams, Officer's Club. *Campus security:* 24-hour emergency response devices and patrols, controlled dormitory access. *Student Services:* health clinic, personal/psychological counseling.

Athletics Member NJCAA. *Intercollegiate sports:* baseball M(s), basketball M(s), fencing M/W, football M(s), golf M(s), riflery M/W, tennis M(s)/W(s), track and field M(s)/W(s). *Intramural sports:* basketball M/W, bowling M/W, cross-country running M/W, fencing M/W, football M, golf M/W, racquetball M/W, riflery M/W, skiing (cross-country) M/W, skiing (downhill) M/W, soccer M/W, swimming M/W, tennis M/W, track and field M/W, volleyball M/W, weight lifting M/W.

Standardized Tests *Required:* SAT I or ACT (for admission).

Costs (2001–02) *Tuition:* state resident $1050 full-time; nonresident $3250 full-time. *Required fees:* $1081 full-time. *Room and board:* $3104. *Payment plan:* deferred payment.

Financial Aid In 2001, 16 Federal Work-Study jobs (averaging $338). 5 State and other part-time jobs (averaging $350).

Applying *Options:* early admission, deferred entrance. *Application fee:* $60. *Required:* high school transcript, minimum 2.0 GPA. *Application deadlines:* 8/1 (freshmen), 8/1 (transfers). *Notification:* continuous (freshmen).

Admissions Contact Lt. Col. Craig C. Collins, Director of Admissions, New Mexico Military Institute, 101 West College Boulevard, Roswell, NM 88201-

5173. *Phone:* 505-624-8051. *Toll-free phone:* 800-421-5376. *Fax:* 505-624-8058. *E-mail:* admissions@yogi.nmmi.cc.nm.us.

NEW MEXICO STATE UNIVERSITY-ALAMOGORDO
Alamogordo, New Mexico

- **State-supported** 2-year, founded 1958, part of New Mexico State University System
- **Calendar** semesters
- **Degree** certificates and associate
- **Small-town** 540-acre campus
- **Coed,** 1,839 undergraduate students, 37% full-time, 64% women, 36% men

Undergraduates 684 full-time, 1,155 part-time. Students come from 5 other countries, 14% transferred in.
Freshmen *Admission:* 330 applied, 330 admitted, 330 enrolled.
Faculty *Total:* 77, 71% full-time.
Majors Business; criminal justice studies; data processing technology; education; electrical/electronic engineering technology; engineering; fire science; general office/clerical; graphic design/commercial art/illustration; liberal arts and sciences/liberal studies; medical laboratory technician; nursing; paralegal/legal assistant; secretarial science; social work; teacher assistant/aide.
Academic Programs *Special study options:* academic remediation for entering students, adult/continuing education programs, advanced placement credit, distance learning, English as a second language, honors programs, internships, off-campus study, part-time degree program, services for LD students, student-designed majors, summer session for credit.
Library David H. Townsend Library with 39,000 titles, 350 serial subscriptions, an OPAC, a Web page.
Computers on Campus 200 computers available on campus for general student use. A campuswide network can be accessed from off campus. Internet access, online (class) registration, at least one staffed computer lab available.
Student Life *Housing:* college housing not available. *Activities and Organizations:* drama/theater group, choral group, Social Science Club, Phi Theta Kappa, Student/NEA, Christian Fellowship, Epsilon Tau Sigma. *Campus security:* 24-hour emergency response devices. *Student Services:* personal/psychological counseling.
Athletics *Intramural sports:* basketball M/W, volleyball M/W.
Costs (2002–03) *Tuition:* area resident $912 full-time, $38 per credit hour part-time; state resident $1032 full-time, $43 per credit hour part-time; nonresident $2352 full-time, $98 per credit hour part-time. *Payment plans:* installment, deferred payment. *Waivers:* senior citizens and employees or children of employees.
Financial Aid In 2001, 10 Federal Work-Study jobs (averaging $3300). 60 State and other part-time jobs (averaging $3300). *Financial aid deadline:* 5/1.
Applying *Options:* common application, electronic application, early admission, deferred entrance. *Application fee:* $15. *Required:* high school transcript, minimum 2.0 GPA. *Application deadline:* rolling (freshmen), rolling (transfers). *Notification:* continuous (freshmen).
Admissions Contact Ms. Maureen Scott, Coordinator of Admissions and Records, New Mexico State University-Alamogordo, 2400 North Scenic Drive, Alamogordo, NM 88311-0477. *Phone:* 505-439-3700. *E-mail:* advisor@nmsua.nmsu.edu.

NEW MEXICO STATE UNIVERSITY-CARLSBAD
Carlsbad, New Mexico

- **State-supported** 2-year, founded 1950, part of New Mexico State University System
- **Calendar** semesters
- **Degree** certificates and associate
- **Small-town** 40-acre campus
- **Coed,** 1,011 undergraduate students

Undergraduates Students come from 6 states and territories, 1 other country.
Freshmen *Admission:* 1,011 applied, 1,011 admitted.
Faculty *Total:* 73, 33% full-time, 8% with terminal degrees. *Student/faculty ratio:* 23:1.
Majors Agricultural sciences; business administration; computer science; criminal justice/law enforcement administration; education; electrical/electronic engineering technology; engineering technology; environmental technology; fire science; industrial technology; information sciences/systems; liberal arts and sciences/liberal studies; nursing; paralegal/legal assistant; secretarial science; social work; welding technology.
Academic Programs *Special study options:* academic remediation for entering students, adult/continuing education programs, advanced placement credit, cooperative education, distance learning, double majors, English as a second language, honors programs, independent study, internships, part-time degree program, services for LD students, student-designed majors, summer session for credit.
Library Library/Media Center.
Computers on Campus 300 computers available on campus for general student use. Internet access, online (class) registration, at least one staffed computer lab available.
Student Life *Housing:* college housing not available. *Activities and Organizations:* drama/theater group, Student Nurses Association, Alpha Sigma Phi (criminal justice), Phi Theta Kappa, Associated Students. *Campus security:* 24-hour emergency response devices.
Standardized Tests *Required for some:* ACT (for placement). *Recommended:* ACT (for placement).
Costs (2002–03) *Tuition:* area resident $840 full-time, $35 per credit part-time; state resident $960 full-time, $40 per credit part-time; nonresident $2208 full-time, $92 per credit part-time. Full-time tuition and fees vary according to course load. Part-time tuition and fees vary according to course load. *Payment plan:* deferred payment. *Waivers:* senior citizens and employees or children of employees.
Applying *Options:* electronic application, early admission, deferred entrance. *Application fee:* $15. *Required:* high school transcript. *Application deadline:* rolling (freshmen), rolling (transfers). *Notification:* continuous (freshmen).
Admissions Contact Ms. Everal Shannon, Records Specialist, New Mexico State University-Carlsbad, 1500 University Drive, Carlsbad, NM 88220-3509. *Phone:* 505-234-9222. *Fax:* 505-885-4951. *E-mail:* mcleary@nmsu.edu.

NEW MEXICO STATE UNIVERSITY-GRANTS
Grants, New Mexico

- **State-supported** 2-year, founded 1968, part of New Mexico State University System
- **Calendar** semesters
- **Degree** certificates and associate
- **Small-town** campus
- **Coed**

Financial Aid In 2001, 3 Federal Work-Study jobs (averaging $1800). 6 State and other part-time jobs (averaging $1500).
Applying *Options:* common application, early admission. *Application fee:* $15. *Required:* high school transcript.
Admissions Contact Office of Admissions, New Mexico State University-Grants, 1500 3rd Street, Grants, NM 87020-2025. *Phone:* 505-287-7981. *E-mail:* bmontoya@grants.nmsu.edu.

NORTHERN NEW MEXICO COMMUNITY COLLEGE
Espanola, New Mexico

- **State-supported** 2-year, founded 1909, part of New Mexico Commission on Higher Education
- **Calendar** semesters
- **Degree** certificates and associate
- **Rural** 35-acre campus
- **Endowment** $829,791
- **Coed,** 2,116 undergraduate students, 31% full-time, 61% women, 39% men

Undergraduates 654 full-time, 1,462 part-time. Students come from 5 states and territories, 1% are from out of state, 0.8% African American, 0.2% Asian American or Pacific Islander, 79% Hispanic American, 9% Native American, 16% transferred in, 1% live on campus.
Freshmen *Admission:* 320 applied, 320 admitted, 140 enrolled. *Average high school GPA:* 2.63.
Faculty *Total:* 253, 18% full-time, 8% with terminal degrees.
Majors Biotechnology research; business; computer/information sciences; criminal justice studies; electrical/electronic engineering technology; elementary education; environmental science; fine/studio arts; human services; industrial/manufacturing engineering; industrial radiologic technology; library assistant; medical radiologic technology.

Northern New Mexico Community College (continued)

Academic Programs *Special study options:* academic remediation for entering students, advanced placement credit, distance learning, part-time degree program, services for LD students, summer session for credit.

Library Northern New Mexico Community College Library with 18,065 titles, 222 serial subscriptions.

Computers on Campus 12 computers available on campus for general student use. A campuswide network can be accessed from off campus. Internet access, at least one staffed computer lab available.

Student Life *Housing Options:* coed. *Activities and Organizations:* nursing organization, radiography organization, AISES, Aikido, Phi Theta Kappa. *Campus security:* 24-hour emergency response devices and patrols.

Costs (2002–03) *Tuition:* state resident $648 full-time, $27 per credit hour part-time; nonresident $1416 full-time, $59 per credit part-time. *Required fees:* $46 full-time, $2 per credit hour. *Room and board:* $2928; room only: $1200.

Financial Aid In 2001, 150 Federal Work-Study jobs (averaging $3000). 140 State and other part-time jobs (averaging $3000).

Applying *Options:* early admission, deferred entrance. *Required:* high school transcript. *Application deadline:* rolling (freshmen), rolling (transfers).

Admissions Contact Mr. Mike L. Costello, Registrar, Northern New Mexico Community College, 921 Paseo de Onate, Espanola, NM 87532. *Phone:* 505-747-2193. *Fax:* 505-747-2180. *E-mail:* tina@nnm.cc.nm.us.

PIMA MEDICAL INSTITUTE
Albuquerque, New Mexico

- **Proprietary** 2-year, founded 1985, part of Vocational Training Institutes, Inc
- **Calendar** modular
- **Degree** certificates and associate
- **Urban** campus
- **Coed**

Financial Aid In 2001, 6 Federal Work-Study jobs.

Applying *Required:* interview. *Required for some:* high school transcript.

Admissions Contact Ms. Martha Garcia, Admissions Office, Pima Medical Institute, 2201 San Pedro NE, Building 3, Suite 100, Albuquerque, NM 87110. *Phone:* 505-881-1234 Ext. 105.

SAN JUAN COLLEGE
Farmington, New Mexico

- **County-supported** 2-year, founded 1958, part of New Mexico Commission on Higher Education
- **Calendar** semesters
- **Degree** certificates and associate
- **Small-town** 698-acre campus
- **Endowment** $1.2 million
- **Coed,** 4,558 undergraduate students, 48% full-time, 61% women, 39% men

Undergraduates 2,195 full-time, 2,363 part-time. 2% transferred in.

Freshmen *Admission:* 674 enrolled.

Faculty *Total:* 277, 32% full-time. *Student/faculty ratio:* 18:1.

Majors Accounting technician; aircraft pilot (professional); anthropology; art; auto body repair; auto mechanic/technician; banking; biology; business administration; carpentry; chemistry; communications; computer science; criminal justice studies; diesel engine mechanic; drafting; early childhood education; economics; education; engineering; English; fire protection/safety technology; foreign languages/literatures; general studies; geology; graphic design/commercial art/illustration; history; human services; information sciences/systems; instrumentation technology; law enforcement/police science; mathematics; medical records technology; music; nursing; paralegal/legal assistant; philosophy; physical sciences; physical therapy assistant; physics; political science; pre-medicine; psychology; public administration; real estate; recreation/leisure studies; secretarial science; social work; sociology; theater arts/drama; water treatment technology; welding technology.

Academic Programs *Special study options:* academic remediation for entering students, adult/continuing education programs, advanced placement credit, cooperative education, distance learning, English as a second language, honors programs, independent study, internships, part-time degree program, services for LD students, summer session for credit.

Library San Juan College Library with 51,473 titles, 1,779 audiovisual materials, an OPAC.

Computers on Campus A campuswide network can be accessed from off campus. Internet access, at least one staffed computer lab available.

Student Life *Housing:* college housing not available. *Activities and Organizations:* drama/theater group, student-run newspaper, radio station, choral group, national fraternities, national sororities. *Campus security:* 24-hour patrols, late-night transport/escort service. *Student Services:* personal/psychological counseling.

Athletics *Intramural sports:* archery M/W, badminton M/W, basketball M/W, bowling M/W, cross-country running M/W, football M/W, golf M/W, racquetball M/W, skiing (cross-country) M/W, skiing (downhill) M/W, soccer M/W, table tennis M/W, tennis M/W, volleyball M/W.

Standardized Tests *Required:* CPT.

Costs (2001–02) *Tuition:* state resident $360 full-time, $15 per credit hour part-time; nonresident $600 full-time, $25 per credit hour part-time. *Payment plan:* tuition prepayment.

Financial Aid In 2001, 100 Federal Work-Study jobs (averaging $1800).

Applying *Options:* early admission, deferred entrance. *Application fee:* $10. *Required:* high school transcript. *Application deadline:* rolling (freshmen), rolling (transfers). *Notification:* continuous (freshmen).

Admissions Contact Mr. Gary Golden, Vice President for Student Affairs, San Juan College, 4601 College Boulevard, Farmington, NM 87402. *Phone:* 505-599-0318. *Fax:* 505-599-0385. *E-mail:* ratliff@sjc.cc.nm.us.

SANTA FE COMMUNITY COLLEGE
Santa Fe, New Mexico

- **State and locally supported** 2-year, founded 1983
- **Calendar** semesters
- **Degree** certificates and associate
- **Suburban** 366-acre campus
- **Coed,** 5,056 undergraduate students, 15% full-time, 65% women, 35% men

Undergraduates 745 full-time, 4,311 part-time. Students come from 49 states and territories, 6 other countries, 7% are from out of state, 0.8% African American, 1% Asian American or Pacific Islander, 57% Hispanic American, 4% Native American, 0.9% international, 14% transferred in. *Retention:* 50% of 2001 full-time freshmen returned.

Freshmen *Admission:* 93 enrolled.

Faculty *Total:* 373, 18% full-time. *Student/faculty ratio:* 14:1.

Majors Accounting; area studies; art; biology; business administration; computer/information sciences; computer science related; construction technology; criminal justice studies; culinary arts; dance; design/visual communications; drafting; early childhood education; electrical/electronic engineering technology; engineering; enterprise management; general studies; health/physical education; hotel and restaurant management; interior design; natural resources management/protective services related; nursing; paralegal/legal assistant; physical sciences; radio/television broadcasting technology; recreation/leisure studies; secretarial science; sign language interpretation; social work; Spanish; surveying; visual and performing arts related.

Academic Programs *Special study options:* academic remediation for entering students, adult/continuing education programs, advanced placement credit, cooperative education, distance learning, double majors, English as a second language, external degree program, honors programs, independent study, internships, part-time degree program, services for LD students, summer session for credit.

Library Learning Resource Center with 48,000 titles, 280 serial subscriptions, 2,000 audiovisual materials, an OPAC, a Web page.

Computers on Campus 225 computers available on campus for general student use. A campuswide network can be accessed from off campus. Internet access, online (class) registration, at least one staffed computer lab available.

Student Life *Housing:* college housing not available. *Activities and Organizations:* student-run radio station, choral group, Student Nurses Association, Native American Student Association, Service Learning Club, MECHA (Movimiento Estudiantil Chicano de Aztlan), Phi Theta Kappa. *Campus security:* 24-hour emergency response devices and patrols, late-night transport/escort service. *Student Services:* personal/psychological counseling, women's center.

Athletics *Intramural sports:* volleyball M.

Costs (2001–02) *Tuition:* area resident $612 full-time, $26 per credit hour part-time; state resident $804 full-time, $34 per credit hour part-time; nonresident $1464 full-time, $61 per credit hour part-time. *Required fees:* $82 full-time, $3 per credit hour, $5 per credit hour part-time. *Payment plan:* deferred payment. *Waivers:* senior citizens and employees or children of employees.

Applying *Options:* early admission, deferred entrance. *Required:* high school transcript. *Application deadline:* rolling (freshmen), rolling (transfers).

Admissions Contact Ms. Jennifer Nollette, Admissions Counselor, Santa Fe Community College, 6401 Richards Avenue, Santa Fe, NM 87505. *Phone:* 505-428-1410. *Fax:* 505-428-1237.

SOUTHWESTERN INDIAN POLYTECHNIC INSTITUTE
Albuquerque, New Mexico

- **Federally supported** 2-year, founded 1971
- **Calendar** trimesters
- **Degree** certificates and associate
- **Suburban** 174-acre campus
- **Coed**

Faculty *Student/faculty ratio:* 15:1.
Student Life *Campus security:* 24-hour emergency response devices, late-night transport/escort service.
Athletics Member NJCAA.
Standardized Tests *Required:* TABE or ACT COMPASS.
Financial Aid In 2001, 28 Federal Work-Study jobs, 43 State and other part-time jobs.
Applying *Options:* common application. *Required:* high school transcript, Certificate of Indian Blood form.
Admissions Contact Recruitment Officer, Southwestern Indian Polytechnic Institute, PO Box 10146, Albuquerque, NM 87120-3103. *Phone:* 505-897-5348. *Toll-free phone:* 800-586-7474. *Fax:* 505-346-2320.

UNIVERSITY OF NEW MEXICO-GALLUP
Gallup, New Mexico

- **State-supported** primarily 2-year, founded 1968, part of New Mexico Commission on Higher Education
- **Calendar** semesters
- **Degrees** certificates, diplomas, associate, and bachelor's
- **Small-town** 80-acre campus
- **Coed,** 2,515 undergraduate students

Undergraduates Students come from 10 states and territories, 4 other countries.
Freshmen *Average high school GPA:* 2.25.
Faculty *Total:* 159, 47% full-time. *Student/faculty ratio:* 25:1.
Majors Accounting; art; auto mechanic/technician; business administration; business marketing and marketing management; communications; community services; construction technology; corrections; cosmetology; criminal justice/law enforcement administration; early childhood education; education; elementary education; enterprise management; general studies; graphic/printing equipment; health education; liberal arts and sciences/liberal studies; medical laboratory technician; nursing; paralegal/legal assistant; physical education; physical sciences; secretarial science; welding technology.
Academic Programs *Special study options:* academic remediation for entering students, adult/continuing education programs, advanced placement credit, cooperative education, honors programs, internships, part-time degree program, services for LD students, student-designed majors, summer session for credit.
Library Zollinger Library plus 1 other with 36,172 titles, 354 serial subscriptions.
Computers on Campus 300 computers available on campus for general student use. Internet access, at least one staffed computer lab available.
Student Life *Housing:* college housing not available. *Activities and Organizations:* student-run newspaper. *Campus security:* late-night transport/escort service.
Standardized Tests *Required for some:* SAT I (for admission), ACT (for admission).
Costs (2001–02) *Tuition:* state resident $1200 full-time, $40 per hour part-time; nonresident $1848 full-time.
Applying *Options:* early admission. *Application fee:* $15. *Required for some:* high school transcript. *Application deadline:* rolling (freshmen), rolling (transfers). *Notification:* continuous (freshmen).
Admissions Contact Ms. Pearl A. Morris, Admissions Representative, University of New Mexico-Gallup, 200 College Road, Gallup, NM 87301-5603. *Phone:* 505-863-7576. *Fax:* 505-863-7610. *E-mail:* pmorris@gallup.unm.edu.

UNIVERSITY OF NEW MEXICO-LOS ALAMOS BRANCH
Los Alamos, New Mexico

- **State-supported** 2-year, founded 1980, part of New Mexico Commission on Higher Education
- **Calendar** semesters
- **Degree** certificates and associate
- **Small-town** 5-acre campus
- **Coed,** 948 undergraduate students

Undergraduates Students come from 12 states and territories, 3 other countries.
Freshmen *Admission:* 215 applied, 215 admitted.
Faculty *Total:* 96.
Majors Accounting; applied art; biological/physical sciences; business administration; computer engineering technology; computer programming; computer science; electrical/electronic engineering technology; engineering; environmental science; fine/studio arts; liberal arts and sciences/liberal studies; pre-engineering; secretarial science.
Academic Programs *Special study options:* academic remediation for entering students, adult/continuing education programs, advanced placement credit, cooperative education, English as a second language, internships, off-campus study, part-time degree program, services for LD students, summer session for credit.
Library 10,000 titles, 160 serial subscriptions.
Computers on Campus 60 computers available on campus for general student use. At least one staffed computer lab available.
Student Life *Housing:* college housing not available. *Activities and Organizations:* student-run newspaper, choral group.
Standardized Tests *Required for some:* SAT I or ACT (for placement).
Costs (2002–03) *Tuition:* area resident $792 full-time, $33 per hour part-time; state resident $792 full-time, $33 per hour part-time; nonresident $95 per hour part-time. *Required fees:* $96 full-time, $13 per hour. *Room and board:* room only: $385.
Financial Aid In 2001, 15 Federal Work-Study jobs (averaging $5000). 10 State and other part-time jobs (averaging $7000).
Applying *Options:* early admission, deferred entrance. *Application fee:* $15. *Application deadlines:* 8/12 (freshmen), 8/12 (transfers). *Notification:* continuous (freshmen).
Admissions Contact Ms. Anna Mae Apodaca, Associate Campus Director for Student Services, University of New Mexico-Los Alamos Branch, 4000 University Drive, Los Alamos, NM 87544-2233. *Phone:* 505-661-4692.

UNIVERSITY OF NEW MEXICO-VALENCIA CAMPUS
Los Lunas, New Mexico

- **State-supported** 2-year, founded 1981, part of New Mexico Commission on Higher Education
- **Calendar** semesters
- **Degree** certificates and associate
- **Small-town** campus with easy access to Albuquerque
- **Coed**

Student Life *Campus security:* 24-hour emergency response devices and patrols, late-night transport/escort service.
Standardized Tests *Required for some:* SAT I or ACT (for placement), ACT COMPASS. *Recommended:* ACT COMPASS.
Financial Aid *Financial aid deadline:* 3/1.
Applying *Options:* early admission, deferred entrance. *Application fee:* $15. *Required for some:* minimum 2.0 GPA. *Recommended:* high school transcript.
Admissions Contact Ms. Lucy Sanchez, Registrar, University of New Mexico-Valencia Campus, 280 La Entrada, Los Lunas, NM 87031-7633. *Phone:* 505-925-8580. *Fax:* 505-925-8563.

NEW YORK

ADIRONDACK COMMUNITY COLLEGE
Queensbury, New York

- **State and locally supported** 2-year, founded 1960, part of State University of New York System

Adirondack Community College (continued)
- **Calendar** semesters
- **Degree** certificates and associate
- **Small-town** 141-acre campus
- **Endowment** $1.0 million
- **Coed,** 3,200 undergraduate students

Located in the Lake George-Saratoga Springs resort area. Most popular programs: business administration, communications and media arts, computer science, criminal justice, data processing, engineering science, food service, information technology, liberal arts and science, mechanical technology/ design and drafting, music, nursing, radio and television broadcasting, travel and tourism. Individualized attention, personalized academic advisement, award-winning freshman experience program, college survival program, writing center, math lab, academic computing center, athletics and activities programs. Small classes, high-quality faculty, low cost, financial aid available.

Undergraduates Students come from 5 states and territories, 5 other countries, 2% are from out of state.
Freshmen *Admission:* 1,328 applied, 1,211 admitted. *Average high school GPA:* 2.40.
Faculty *Total:* 244, 41% full-time. *Student/faculty ratio:* 20:1.
Majors Accounting; banking; behavioral sciences; biological/physical sciences; biology; broadcast journalism; business administration; business marketing and marketing management; business systems networking/ telecommunications; computer graphics; computer science; computer science related; computer systems networking/telecommunications; corrections; criminal justice/law enforcement administration; culinary arts; data processing; data processing technology; drafting; electrical/electronic engineering technology; engineering; engineering science; executive assistant; finance; food services technology; general studies; history; hospitality management; humanities; information sciences/systems; information technology; law enforcement/police science; liberal arts and sciences/ liberal studies; mass communications; mathematics; mathematics/computer science; mechanical design technology; mechanical drafting; mechanical engineering technology; medical administrative assistant; medical records administration; music; nursing; occupational therapy assistant; photography; physical therapy assistant; pre-engineering; radio/television broadcasting; receptionist; secretarial science; social sciences; system/networking/LAN/WAN management; travel/ tourism management; Web page, digital/multimedia and information resources design; word processing.
Academic Programs *Special study options:* academic remediation for entering students, accelerated degree program, adult/continuing education programs, advanced placement credit, cooperative education, double majors, external degree program, independent study, internships, part-time degree program, services for LD students, study abroad, summer session for credit.
Library Adirondack Community College Library with 65,000 titles, 391 serial subscriptions, an OPAC, a Web page.
Computers on Campus 250 computers available on campus for general student use. At least one staffed computer lab available.
Student Life *Housing:* college housing not available. *Activities and Organizations:* drama/theater group, student-run radio station, choral group, New Horizons, Broadcasting Club, Humanities Club, College Activity Board, Ski and Adventure Club. *Campus security:* late-night transport/escort service, patrols by trained security personnel 8 a.m. to 10 p.m. *Student Services:* personal/ psychological counseling.
Athletics Member NJCAA. *Intercollegiate sports:* baseball M, basketball M/W, bowling M/W, golf M, skiing (cross-country) M(c)/W(c), skiing (downhill) M(c)/W(c), soccer M/W, softball W, tennis M/W, volleyball W. *Intramural sports:* badminton M/W, basketball M/W, football M/W, skiing (downhill) M/W, softball M/W, tennis M/W, volleyball M/W, weight lifting M/W.
Standardized Tests *Recommended:* SAT I or ACT (for placement).
Costs (2001–02) *One-time required fee:* $35. *Tuition:* state resident $2400 full-time, $97 per credit hour part-time; nonresident $4800 full-time, $194 per credit hour part-time. Part-time tuition and fees vary according to course load. *Required fees:* $176 full-time, $4 per credit hour. *Payment plan:* installment. *Waivers:* senior citizens and employees or children of employees.
Financial Aid In 2001, 98 Federal Work-Study jobs (averaging $462).
Applying *Options:* early admission, deferred entrance. *Application fee:* $30. *Required:* high school transcript. *Required for some:* minimum 2.0 GPA. *Application deadlines:* 8/15 (freshmen), 8/15 (transfers). *Notification:* continuous until 9/1 (freshmen).
Admissions Contact Mrs. Sarah Jane Linehan, Director of Enrollment Management, Adirondack Community College, 640 Bay Road, Queensbury, NY 12804. *Phone:* 518-743-2264. *Fax:* 518-743-2317. *E-mail:* info@acc.sunyacc.edu.

American Academy McAllister Institute of Funeral Service
New York, New York

- **Independent** 2-year, founded 1926
- **Calendar** semesters
- **Degree** diplomas and associate
- **Urban** campus
- **Coed,** 130 undergraduate students, 100% full-time, 58% women, 42% men

Undergraduates 130 full-time. Students come from 9 states and territories, 4 other countries, 26% are from out of state, 44% African American, 5% Hispanic American, 7% international, 36% transferred in.
Freshmen *Admission:* 47 enrolled.
Faculty *Total:* 18, 11% with terminal degrees. *Student/faculty ratio:* 25:1.
Majors Mortuary science.
Library American Academy MacAllister Institute Library with 1,672 titles, 78 serial subscriptions, 165 audiovisual materials.
Computers on Campus 12 computers available on campus for general student use.
Student Life *Housing:* college housing not available.
Costs (2002–03) *One-time required fee:* $160. *Tuition:* No tuition increase for student's term of enrollment. *Required fees:* $640 full-time. *Waivers:* employees or children of employees.
Applying *Options:* early admission, deferred entrance. *Application fee:* $35. *Required:* high school transcript, 2 letters of recommendation. *Recommended:* interview. *Application deadlines:* rolling (freshmen), 8/30 (transfers). *Notification:* continuous until 8/15 (freshmen).
Admissions Contact Mr. Norman Provost, Registrar, American Academy McAllister Institute of Funeral Service, 450 West 56th Street, New York, NY 10019-3602. *Phone:* 212-757-1190. *Fax:* 212-765-5923.

American Academy of Dramatic Arts
New York, New York

- **Independent** 2-year, founded 1884
- **Calendar** continuous
- **Degree** certificates and associate
- **Urban** campus
- **Endowment** $5.6 million
- **Coed,** 220 undergraduate students, 100% full-time, 60% women, 40% men

Undergraduates 220 full-time. Students come from 20 states and territories, 16 other countries, 82% are from out of state.
Freshmen *Admission:* 630 applied, 138 admitted, 138 enrolled. *Average high school GPA:* 2.80.
Faculty *Total:* 31, 39% full-time. *Student/faculty ratio:* 16:1.
Majors Theater arts/drama.
Library Academy/CBS Library with 7,467 titles, 24 serial subscriptions, 570 audiovisual materials.
Computers on Campus 2 computers available on campus for general student use. Internet access available.
Student Life *Housing:* college housing not available. *Campus security:* 24-hour emergency response devices and patrols, trained security personnel during hours of operation.
Costs (2002–03) *Tuition:* $13,700 full-time. *Required fees:* $400 full-time. *Payment plan:* installment.
Financial Aid In 2001, 40 Federal Work-Study jobs (averaging $2000). 10 State and other part-time jobs (averaging $2000). *Financial aid deadline:* 5/15.
Applying *Options:* deferred entrance. *Application fee:* $50. *Required:* essay or personal statement, 2 letters of recommendation, interview, audition. *Required for some:* high school transcript. *Recommended:* high school transcript, minimum 2.0 GPA. *Application deadline:* rolling (freshmen), rolling (transfers). *Notification:* continuous (freshmen).
Admissions Contact Ms. Karen Higginbotham, Director of Admissions, American Academy of Dramatic Arts, 120 Madison Avenue, New York, NY 10016. *Phone:* 800-463—990. *Toll-free phone:* 800-463-8990. *Fax:* 212-696-1284. *E-mail:* admissions_ny@aada.org.

The Art Institute of New York City
New York, New York

- **Proprietary** 2-year, founded 1980, part of Educational Management Corporation

- **Calendar** continuous
- **Degree** certificates, diplomas, and associate
- **Coed,** 1,300 undergraduate students
- 100% of applicants were admitted

Undergraduates Students come from 3 states and territories, 25% are from out of state.
Freshmen *Admission:* 156 applied, 156 admitted. *Average high school GPA:* 2.5.
Faculty *Total:* 55, 73% full-time. *Student/faculty ratio:* 22:1.
Majors Baker/pastry chef; culinary arts; design/visual communications; hotel and restaurant management.
Academic Programs *Special study options:* advanced placement credit, cooperative education, internships.
Computers on Campus 20 computers available on campus for general student use. At least one staffed computer lab available.
Student Life *Housing:* college housing not available.
Costs (2001–02) *Tuition:* Full time tuition: $13,209-$34,809 per degree program.
Applying *Options:* common application. *Application fee:* $50. *Required:* high school transcript, interview. *Required for some:* essay or personal statement.
Admissions Contact Mr. Alfred Parcells, Director of Admissions, The Art Institute of New York City, 75 Varick Street, 16th Floor, New York, NY 10013. *Phone:* 212-226-5500 Ext. 348. *Toll-free phone:* 800-654-2433. *Fax:* 212-966-0706.

BERKELEY COLLEGE
New York, New York

- **Proprietary** primarily 2-year, founded 1936
- **Calendar** quarters
- **Degrees** certificates, associate, and bachelor's
- **Urban** campus
- **Coed,** 1,666 undergraduate students, 91% full-time, 71% women, 29% men

Undergraduates 1,512 full-time, 154 part-time. Students come from 10 states and territories, 58 other countries, 8% are from out of state, 30% African American, 6% Asian American or Pacific Islander, 31% Hispanic American, 0.2% Native American, 13% international, 13% transferred in.
Freshmen *Admission:* 1,295 applied, 1,123 admitted, 432 enrolled. *Average high school GPA:* 2.7.
Faculty *Total:* 110, 37% full-time. *Student/faculty ratio:* 24:1.
Majors Accounting; business; business administration; business marketing and marketing management; fashion merchandising; international business; office management; paralegal/legal assistant.
Academic Programs *Special study options:* academic remediation for entering students, adult/continuing education programs, advanced placement credit, cooperative education, distance learning, English as a second language, internships, off-campus study, part-time degree program, study abroad, summer session for credit.
Library 13,164 titles, 138 serial subscriptions, 949 audiovisual materials, an OPAC, a Web page.
Computers on Campus 200 computers available on campus for general student use. A campuswide network can be accessed from off campus. Internet access, at least one staffed computer lab available.
Student Life *Housing:* college housing not available. *Activities and Organizations:* student-run newspaper, student government, International Club, Paralegal Club, Accounting Club. *Campus security:* 24-hour emergency response devices. *Student Services:* personal/psychological counseling.
Costs (2002–03) *One-time required fee:* $50. *Tuition:* $13,950 full-time, $360 per credit part-time. *Required fees:* $390 full-time, $60 per term part-time. *Payment plan:* installment. *Waivers:* employees or children of employees.
Financial Aid In 2001, 120 Federal Work-Study jobs (averaging $1500).
Applying *Options:* electronic application, deferred entrance. *Application fee:* $40. *Required:* high school transcript. *Recommended:* interview. *Application deadline:* rolling (freshmen), rolling (transfers).
Admissions Contact Mr. Stuart Siegman, Director, High School Admissions, Berkeley College, 3 East 43rd Street, New York, NY 10017. *Phone:* 212-986-4343 Ext. 123. *Toll-free phone:* 800-446-5400. *Fax:* 212-818-1079. *E-mail:* admissions@berkeleycollege.edu.

BERKELEY COLLEGE-WESTCHESTER CAMPUS
White Plains, New York

- **Proprietary** primarily 2-year, founded 1945
- **Calendar** quarters
- **Degrees** certificates, associate, and bachelor's
- **Suburban** 10-acre campus with easy access to New York City
- **Coed,** 667 undergraduate students, 86% full-time, 71% women, 29% men

Undergraduates 574 full-time, 93 part-time. Students come from 11 states and territories, 26 other countries, 15% are from out of state, 25% African American, 3% Asian American or Pacific Islander, 23% Hispanic American, 0.2% Native American, 5% international, 13% transferred in, 10% live on campus.
Freshmen *Admission:* 517 applied, 453 admitted, 247 enrolled. *Average high school GPA:* 2.7.
Faculty *Total:* 42, 40% full-time. *Student/faculty ratio:* 24:1.
Majors Accounting; business; business administration; business marketing and marketing management; fashion merchandising; international business; office management; paralegal/legal assistant.
Academic Programs *Special study options:* academic remediation for entering students, adult/continuing education programs, advanced placement credit, cooperative education, distance learning, English as a second language, internships, off-campus study, part-time degree program, services for LD students, study abroad, summer session for credit.
Library 9,526 titles, 66 serial subscriptions, 777 audiovisual materials, an OPAC, a Web page.
Computers on Campus 175 computers available on campus for general student use. A campuswide network can be accessed from off campus. Internet access, at least one staffed computer lab available.
Student Life *Housing Options:* coed. *Activities and Organizations:* student-run newspaper, student government, Paralegal Club, Fashion Club, Phi Theta Kappa. *Campus security:* monitored entrance with front desk security guard. *Student Services:* personal/psychological counseling.
Costs (2002–03) *One-time required fee:* $50. *Tuition:* $13,950 full-time, $360 per credit part-time. *Required fees:* $390 full-time, $60 per term part-time. *Room only:* $6000. Room and board charges vary according to board plan. *Payment plan:* installment. *Waivers:* employees or children of employees.
Financial Aid In 2001, 40 Federal Work-Study jobs (averaging $1100).
Applying *Options:* electronic application, deferred entrance. *Application fee:* $40. *Required:* high school transcript. *Recommended:* interview. *Application deadline:* rolling (freshmen), rolling (transfers).
Admissions Contact Mr. David Bertrone, Director of High School Admissions, Berkeley College-Westchester Campus, 99 Church Street, White Plains, NY 10601. *Phone:* 914-694-1122 Ext. 3110. *Toll-free phone:* 800-446-5400. *Fax:* 914-328-9469. *E-mail:* wpcampus@berkeleycollege.edu.

BOROUGH OF MANHATTAN COMMUNITY COLLEGE OF THE CITY UNIVERSITY OF NEW YORK
New York, New York

- **State and locally supported** 2-year, founded 1963, part of City University of New York System
- **Calendar** semesters
- **Degree** certificates and associate
- **Urban** 5-acre campus
- **Endowment** $8000
- **Coed,** 16,025 undergraduate students

Undergraduates Students come from 3 states and territories, 80 other countries, 0.5% are from out of state.
Freshmen *Admission:* 3,525 applied, 3,485 admitted. *Average high school GPA:* 2.01. *Test scores:* SAT verbal scores over 500: 12%; SAT math scores over 500: 10%; SAT verbal scores over 600: 2%; SAT math scores over 600: 2%; SAT verbal scores over 700: 1%; SAT math scores over 700: 1%.
Faculty *Total:* 1,006, 71% full-time. *Student/faculty ratio:* 22:1.
Majors Accounting; biological/physical sciences; business administration; business marketing and marketing management; child care/development; computer programming; data processing technology; early childhood education; emergency medical technology; engineering science; health science; human services; liberal arts and sciences/liberal studies; mathematics; nursing; respiratory therapy; secretarial science.
Academic Programs *Special study options:* academic remediation for entering students, adult/continuing education programs, advanced placement credit, coop-

Borough of Manhattan Community College of the City University of New York (continued)

erative education, distance learning, English as a second language, honors programs, independent study, internships, off-campus study, part-time degree program, services for LD students, study abroad, summer session for credit.

Library A. Philip Randolph Library with 89,531 titles, 733 serial subscriptions, 1,103 audiovisual materials, an OPAC, a Web page.

Computers on Campus Internet access, at least one staffed computer lab available.

Student Life *Housing:* college housing not available. *Activities and Organizations:* drama/theater group, student-run newspaper, choral group, Caribbean Students Association, Dominican Students Association, When One Voice is Not Enough (WOVINE), Students of Indian Descent Association, Asian Society. *Campus security:* 24-hour patrols. *Student Services:* health clinic, personal/psychological counseling, women's center.

Athletics Member NJCAA. *Intercollegiate sports:* baseball M, basketball M/W, soccer M. *Intramural sports:* basketball M/W, soccer M, volleyball M/W.

Costs (2001–02) *Tuition:* state resident $2500 full-time, $105 per credit part-time; nonresident $3076 full-time, $130 per credit part-time. *Payment plan:* installment. *Waivers:* senior citizens and employees or children of employees.

Applying *Options:* deferred entrance. *Application fee:* $40. *Required:* high school transcript. *Application deadline:* rolling (freshmen), rolling (transfers). *Notification:* continuous (freshmen).

Admissions Contact Mr. Eugenio Barrios, Director of Admissions, Borough of Manhattan Community College of the City University of New York, 199 Chambers Street, Room S-742, New York, NY 10007. *Phone:* 212-220-1265. *Fax:* 212-346-8110. *E-mail:* bmadmrpre@cunyum.cuny.edu.

BRAMSON ORT COLLEGE
Forest Hills, New York

Admissions Contact Admissions Office, Bramson ORT College, 69-30 Austin Street, Forest Hills, NY 11375-4239. *Phone:* 718-261-5800.

BRONX COMMUNITY COLLEGE OF THE CITY UNIVERSITY OF NEW YORK
Bronx, New York

- **State and locally supported** 2-year, founded 1959, part of City University of New York System
- **Calendar** semesters
- **Degree** certificates and associate
- **Urban** 50-acre campus
- **Coed,** 6,942 undergraduate students, 62% full-time, 66% women, 34% men

Undergraduates 4,332 full-time, 2,610 part-time. Students come from 10 states and territories, 80 other countries, 4% are from out of state, 38% African American, 2% Asian American or Pacific Islander, 53% Hispanic American, 0.3% Native American, 3% international, 5% transferred in. *Retention:* 60% of 2001 full-time freshmen returned.

Freshmen *Admission:* 1,131 enrolled.

Faculty *Total:* 662, 32% full-time.

Majors Accounting; African-American studies; art; biology; business administration; business education; business marketing and marketing management; chemistry; child care/development; computer science; data processing technology; electrical/electronic engineering technology; history; human services; international relations; liberal arts and sciences/liberal studies; mathematics; medical administrative assistant; medical laboratory technician; music; nuclear medical technology; nursing; ornamental horticulture; paralegal/legal assistant; pre-engineering; psychology; secretarial science.

Academic Programs *Special study options:* academic remediation for entering students, adult/continuing education programs, advanced placement credit, cooperative education, part-time degree program, summer session for credit.

Library 75,000 titles, 800 serial subscriptions.

Computers on Campus 300 computers available on campus for general student use.

Student Life *Housing:* college housing not available. *Activities and Organizations:* drama/theater group, student-run newspaper, radio station, choral group. *Campus security:* 24-hour patrols. *Student Services:* personal/psychological counseling.

Athletics Member NJCAA. *Intercollegiate sports:* basketball M/W, soccer M, tennis M/W, track and field M/W, volleyball W, wrestling M. *Intramural sports:* basketball M/W, soccer M, tennis M/W, track and field M/W, volleyball W, wrestling M.

Costs (2001–02) *Tuition:* state resident $2500 full-time, $105 per credit part-time; nonresident $3076 full-time, $135 per credit part-time. *Required fees:* $110 full-time.

Applying *Application fee:* $40. *Required:* high school transcript. *Application deadline:* rolling (freshmen), rolling (transfers). *Notification:* continuous (freshmen).

Admissions Contact Ms. Alba N. Cancetty, Admissions Officer, Bronx Community College of the City University of New York, University Avenue & West 181st Street, Bronx, NY 10453. *Phone:* 718-289-5888.

BROOME COMMUNITY COLLEGE
Binghamton, New York

- **State and locally supported** 2-year, founded 1946, part of State University of New York System
- **Calendar** semesters
- **Degree** certificates and associate
- **Suburban** 223-acre campus
- **Coed,** 5,818 undergraduate students, 58% full-time, 57% women, 43% men

Undergraduates 3,395 full-time, 2,423 part-time. Students come from 29 states and territories, 28 other countries, 0.9% African American, 0.3% Asian American or Pacific Islander, 0.4% Hispanic American, 0.1% Native American, 3% international, 4% transferred in.

Freshmen *Admission:* 1,222 enrolled.

Faculty *Total:* 145. *Student/faculty ratio:* 16:1.

Majors Accounting; banking; business administration; business marketing and marketing management; chemical engineering technology; civil engineering technology; computer/information sciences; computer programming (specific applications); computer science; computer science related; computer systems networking/telecommunications; computer/technical support; criminal justice/law enforcement administration; data entry/microcomputer applications; data processing technology; dental hygiene; early childhood education; electrical/electronic engineering technology; emergency medical technology; engineering science; executive assistant; fire science; hotel and restaurant management; human services; information technology; international business; liberal arts and sciences/liberal studies; marketing operations; mechanical engineering technology; medical assistant; medical laboratory technician; medical radiologic technology; medical records administration; nursing; occupational safety/health technology; paralegal/legal assistant; physical therapy assistant; secretarial science; telecommunications; Web page, digital/multimedia and information resources design; word processing.

Academic Programs *Special study options:* academic remediation for entering students, adult/continuing education programs, advanced placement credit, distance learning, English as a second language, external degree program, off-campus study, part-time degree program, services for LD students, student-designed majors, study abroad, summer session for credit.

Library Cecil C. Tyrrell Learning Resources Center plus 1 other with 67,098 titles, 520 serial subscriptions, an OPAC, a Web page.

Computers on Campus 400 computers available on campus for general student use. A campuswide network can be accessed from off campus. Internet access, at least one staffed computer lab available.

Student Life *Housing:* college housing not available. *Activities and Organizations:* student-run newspaper, choral group, Broome Early Childhood Organization, Differentially Disabled Student Association, Ecology Club, Phi Theta Kappa, Criminal Justice Club. *Campus security:* 24-hour emergency response devices and patrols. *Student Services:* health clinic, personal/psychological counseling.

Athletics Member NJCAA. *Intercollegiate sports:* baseball M/W, basketball M/W, cross-country running M/W, ice hockey M/W, lacrosse M/W, soccer M/W, softball W, tennis M/W, volleyball W. *Intramural sports:* baseball M/W, basketball M/W, bowling M/W, cross-country running M/W, skiing (downhill) M/W, tennis M/W, volleyball M/W.

Standardized Tests *Required for some:* ACT ASSET.

Costs (2001–02) *One-time required fee:* $40. *Tuition:* state resident $2438 full-time, $102 per credit hour part-time; nonresident $4876 full-time, $204 per credit hour part-time. *Required fees:* $160 full-time, $5 per credit hour, $25 per term part-time. *Payment plan:* installment. *Waivers:* senior citizens and employees or children of employees.

Financial Aid In 2001, 248 Federal Work-Study jobs (averaging $813).

Applying *Options:* electronic application, early admission. *Required:* high school transcript. *Application deadline:* rolling (freshmen), rolling (transfers). *Notification:* continuous (freshmen).

Admissions Contact Mr. Anthony Fiorelli, Director of Admissions, Broome Community College, PO Box 1017, Upper Front Street, Binghamton, NY 13902. *Phone:* 607-778-5001. *E-mail:* admissions@sunybroome.edu.

BRYANT AND STRATTON BUSINESS INSTITUTE
Albany, New York

- **Proprietary** 2-year, founded 1857, part of Bryant and Stratton Business Institute, Inc
- **Calendar** semesters
- **Degree** diplomas and associate
- **Suburban** campus
- **Coed,** 307 undergraduate students, 77% full-time, 67% women, 33% men

Undergraduates 236 full-time, 71 part-time. Students come from 1 other state, 29% African American, 3% Asian American or Pacific Islander, 6% Hispanic American, 1% Native American.
Freshmen *Admission:* 85 applied, 71 admitted, 76 enrolled.
Faculty *Total:* 40, 20% full-time, 13% with terminal degrees. *Student/faculty ratio:* 7:1.
Majors Accounting; business administration; information sciences/systems; information technology; medical assistant; paralegal/legal assistant; secretarial science.
Academic Programs *Special study options:* academic remediation for entering students, distance learning, double majors, independent study, internships, part-time degree program, services for LD students, summer session for credit.
Library Resource Center with 1,418 titles, 41 serial subscriptions, 125 audiovisual materials, an OPAC.
Computers on Campus 103 computers available on campus for general student use. Internet access, at least one staffed computer lab available.
Student Life *Housing:* college housing not available. *Activities and Organizations:* student-run newspaper. *Campus security:* 24-hour emergency response devices. *Student Services:* personal/psychological counseling.
Standardized Tests *Recommended:* SAT I or ACT (for admission).
Costs (2002–03) *Tuition:* $9900 full-time, $330 per credit hour part-time. Full-time tuition and fees vary according to course load. Part-time tuition and fees vary according to course load. *Required fees:* $200 full-time, $100 per term part-time. *Payment plan:* installment. *Waivers:* employees or children of employees.
Applying *Options:* deferred entrance. *Application fee:* $25. *Required:* high school transcript, interview. *Required for some:* letters of recommendation. *Application deadline:* rolling (freshmen), rolling (transfers).
Admissions Contact Bryant and Stratton Business Institute, 1259 Central Avenue, Albany, NY 12205. *Phone:* 518-437-1802 Ext. 205. *Fax:* 518-437-1048.

BRYANT AND STRATTON BUSINESS INSTITUTE
Rochester, New York

- **Proprietary** 2-year, founded 1973, part of Bryant and Stratton Business Institute, Inc
- **Calendar** semesters
- **Degree** diplomas and associate
- **Urban** campus
- **Coed,** 202 undergraduate students

Undergraduates Students come from 4 states and territories, 14% African American, 2% Asian American or Pacific Islander, 5% Hispanic American.
Freshmen *Admission:* 69 applied, 69 admitted.
Faculty *Total:* 39, 26% full-time.
Majors Accounting; business administration; computer programming; hotel and restaurant management; information sciences/systems; information technology; legal administrative assistant; medical administrative assistant; medical assistant; secretarial science.
Academic Programs *Special study options:* academic remediation for entering students, adult/continuing education programs, distance learning, double majors, independent study, internships, part-time degree program, services for LD students, summer session for credit.
Library Campus Library with 250 titles, 27 serial subscriptions.
Computers on Campus 195 computers available on campus for general student use. Internet access, at least one staffed computer lab available.
Student Life *Housing:* college housing not available. *Activities and Organizations:* student-run newspaper, BASSA, SAMS Club. *Campus security:* 24-hour emergency response devices, late-night transport/escort service. *Student Services:* personal/psychological counseling.
Athletics *Intramural sports:* bowling M/W, softball M/W, volleyball M/W.
Standardized Tests *Recommended:* SAT I or ACT (for admission).
Costs (2001–02) *Tuition:* $9472 full-time, $296 per credit hour part-time. Full-time tuition and fees vary according to course load. Part-time tuition and fees vary according to course load. *Required fees:* $100 full-time. *Payment plan:* installment. *Waivers:* employees or children of employees.
Financial Aid In 2001, 40 Federal Work-Study jobs (averaging $600).
Applying *Options:* electronic application, deferred entrance. *Application fee:* $25. *Required:* essay or personal statement, high school transcript, interview. *Required for some:* letters of recommendation. *Recommended:* minimum 2.0 GPA. *Application deadline:* rolling (freshmen), rolling (transfers). *Notification:* continuous (freshmen).
Admissions Contact Ms. Maria Scalise, Director of Admissions, Bryant and Stratton Business Institute, 150 Bellwood Drive, Greece Campus, Rochester, NY 14600. *Phone:* 716-720-0660.

BRYANT AND STRATTON BUSINESS INSTITUTE
Lackawanna, New York

- **Proprietary** 2-year, founded 1989, part of Bryant and Stratton Business Institute, Inc
- **Calendar** semesters
- **Degree** diplomas and associate
- **Small-town** campus with easy access to Buffalo
- **Coed,** 256 undergraduate students, 80% full-time, 67% women, 33% men

Undergraduates 204 full-time, 52 part-time. Students come from 1 other state, 1 other country, 5% African American, 0.4% Asian American or Pacific Islander, 4% Hispanic American, 0.4% Native American, 7% transferred in.
Freshmen *Admission:* 93 enrolled. *Average high school GPA:* 2.70. *Test scores:* SAT verbal scores over 500: 14%; SAT math scores over 500: 14%; SAT verbal scores over 600: 10%; SAT math scores over 600: 10%.
Faculty *Total:* 32, 16% full-time, 3% with terminal degrees. *Student/faculty ratio:* 13:1.
Majors Accounting; business administration; hotel and restaurant management; information sciences/systems; legal administrative assistant; medical administrative assistant; secretarial science.
Academic Programs *Special study options:* academic remediation for entering students, cooperative education, distance learning, independent study, internships, part-time degree program, summer session for credit.
Library Southtowns Library with 1,402 titles, 42 serial subscriptions, 128 audiovisual materials, a Web page.
Computers on Campus 94 computers available on campus for general student use. Internet access, at least one staffed computer lab available.
Student Life *Housing:* college housing not available. *Activities and Organizations:* student-run newspaper, Accounting/Business Club, Administrative Professionals Club, Micro Club, Honor Society, student newsletter. *Campus security:* 24-hour emergency response devices, late-night transport/escort service. *Student Services:* personal/psychological counseling.
Standardized Tests *Recommended:* SAT I or ACT (for admission).
Costs (2002–03) *One-time required fee:* $25. *Tuition:* $9900 full-time, $330 per semester hour part-time. Full-time tuition and fees vary according to course load. Part-time tuition and fees vary according to course load. *Required fees:* $200 full-time, $100 per term part-time. *Payment plan:* installment. *Waivers:* employees or children of employees.
Applying *Options:* common application, electronic application, deferred entrance. *Application fee:* $25. *Required:* essay or personal statement, high school transcript, interview. *Required for some:* letters of recommendation. *Recommended:* minimum 2.0 GPA. *Application deadline:* rolling (freshmen), rolling (transfers).
Admissions Contact Bryant and Stratton Business Institute, 1214 Abbott Road, Lackawanna, NY 14218. *Phone:* 716-884-9120. *Fax:* 716-821-9343.

BRYANT AND STRATTON BUSINESS INSTITUTE
Rochester, New York

- **Proprietary** 2-year, founded 1985, part of Bryant and Stratton Business Institute, Inc
- **Calendar** semesters
- **Degree** diplomas and associate
- **Suburban** 1-acre campus
- **Coed,** 348 undergraduate students

Undergraduates Students come from 1 other state.

Bryant and Stratton Business Institute (continued)

Freshmen *Admission:* 133 applied, 133 admitted.

Faculty *Total:* 57, 18% full-time.

Majors Accounting; business administration; computer programming; electrical/electronic engineering technology; graphic design/commercial art/illustration; information sciences/systems; information technology; medical administrative assistant; medical assistant; paralegal/legal assistant; secretarial science; travel/tourism management.

Academic Programs *Special study options:* academic remediation for entering students, adult/continuing education programs, distance learning, double majors, independent study, internships, part-time degree program, services for LD students, summer session for credit.

Library Campus Library with 1,600 titles, 38 serial subscriptions.

Computers on Campus 162 computers available on campus for general student use. Internet access, at least one staffed computer lab available.

Student Life *Housing:* college housing not available. *Activities and Organizations:* student-run newspaper. *Campus security:* late-night transport/escort service. *Student Services:* personal/psychological counseling.

Standardized Tests *Recommended:* SAT I or ACT (for admission).

Costs (2001–02) *Tuition:* $9472 full-time, $296 per credit hour part-time. Full-time tuition and fees vary according to course load. Part-time tuition and fees vary according to course load. *Required fees:* $100 full-time. *Payment plan:* installment. *Waivers:* employees or children of employees.

Financial Aid In 2001, 44 Federal Work-Study jobs (averaging $630).

Applying *Options:* electronic application, deferred entrance. *Application fee:* $25. *Required:* essay or personal statement, high school transcript, interview. *Required for some:* letters of recommendation. *Recommended:* minimum 2.0 GPA. *Application deadline:* rolling (freshmen), rolling (transfers). *Notification:* continuous (freshmen).

Admissions Contact Ms. Maria Scalise, Director of Admissions, Bryant and Stratton Business Institute, 1225 Jefferson Road, Henrietta Campus, Rochester, NY 14623. *Phone:* 716-720-0660. *Fax:* 716-292-6015.

BRYANT AND STRATTON BUSINESS INSTITUTE
Buffalo, New York

- **Proprietary** 2-year, founded 1854, part of Bryant and Stratton Business Institute, Inc
- **Calendar** semesters
- **Degree** diplomas and associate
- **Urban** 2-acre campus
- **Coed,** 440 undergraduate students

Undergraduates Students come from 1 other state, 1 other country, 56% African American, 0.6% Asian American or Pacific Islander, 5% Hispanic American, 0.9% Native American.

Freshmen *Admission:* 205 applied, 168 admitted.

Faculty *Total:* 46, 20% full-time, 2% with terminal degrees. *Student/faculty ratio:* 10:1.

Majors Accounting; business administration; computer programming; information sciences/systems; information technology; legal administrative assistant; medical administrative assistant; medical assistant; secretarial science.

Academic Programs *Special study options:* academic remediation for entering students, adult/continuing education programs, distance learning, double majors, independent study, internships, part-time degree program, summer session for credit.

Library Learning Center/Library with 2,903 titles, 155 serial subscriptions, 252 audiovisual materials.

Computers on Campus 145 computers available on campus for general student use. Internet access, at least one staffed computer lab available.

Student Life *Housing:* college housing not available. *Activities and Organizations:* student-run newspaper, Med-Assisting Club, Secretarial Club, Accounting/Business Club.

Standardized Tests *Recommended:* SAT I or ACT (for admission).

Costs (2002–03) *Tuition:* $9900 full-time, $330 per semester hour part-time. Full-time tuition and fees vary according to course load. Part-time tuition and fees vary according to course load. *Required fees:* $200 full-time, $100 per semester hour. *Payment plan:* installment. *Waivers:* employees or children of employees.

Applying *Options:* common application, electronic application, deferred entrance. *Application fee:* $25. *Required:* high school transcript, interview. *Required for some:* letters of recommendation. *Recommended:* minimum 2.0 GPA. *Application deadline:* rolling (freshmen), rolling (transfers).

Admissions Contact Bryant and Stratton Business Institute, 465 Main Street, Buffalo, NY 14203. *Phone:* 716-884-9120. *Fax:* 716-884-0091.

BRYANT AND STRATTON BUSINESS INSTITUTE
Syracuse, New York

- **Proprietary** 2-year, founded 1854, part of Bryant and Stratton Business Institute, Inc
- **Calendar** semesters
- **Degree** diplomas and associate
- **Urban** campus
- **Coed**

Faculty *Student/faculty ratio:* 15:1.

Student Life *Campus security:* 24-hour emergency response devices, controlled dormitory access.

Athletics Member NJCAA.

Standardized Tests *Recommended:* SAT I or ACT (for admission).

Applying *Application fee:* $25. *Required:* essay or personal statement, high school transcript, interview, entrance, placement evaluations. *Required for some:* letters of recommendation. *Recommended:* minimum 2.0 GPA.

Admissions Contact Mrs. Amy Graham, Associate Director of Admissions, Bryant and Stratton Business Institute, 953 James Street, Syracuse, NY 13203-2502. *Phone:* 315-472-6603 Ext. 247.

BRYANT AND STRATTON BUSINESS INSTITUTE, AMHERST CAMPUS
Clarence, New York

- **Proprietary** 2-year, founded 1977, part of Bryant and Stratton Business Institute, Inc
- **Calendar** semesters
- **Degree** diplomas and associate
- **Suburban** 12-acre campus with easy access to Buffalo
- **Coed,** 116 undergraduate students, 40% full-time, 56% women, 44% men

Undergraduates 46 full-time, 70 part-time. 6% African American, 1% Asian American or Pacific Islander, 2% Hispanic American, 1% Native American.

Freshmen *Admission:* 143 applied, 116 admitted, 116 enrolled.

Faculty *Total:* 39, 21% full-time. *Student/faculty ratio:* 12:1.

Majors Accounting; business; electrical/electronic engineering technology; graphic design/commercial art/illustration; information sciences/systems; paralegal/legal assistant; secretarial science.

Academic Programs *Special study options:* academic remediation for entering students, adult/continuing education programs, cooperative education, independent study, internships, part-time degree program, summer session for credit.

Library Library Resource Center with 4,500 titles, 15 serial subscriptions, 150 audiovisual materials, an OPAC.

Computers on Campus 125 computers available on campus for general student use. Internet access, at least one staffed computer lab available.

Student Life *Housing:* college housing not available. *Activities and Organizations:* student-run newspaper, choral group, Phi Beta Lambda, Student Government Association, Information Technology Club, Ambassadors.

Standardized Tests *Recommended:* SAT I or ACT (for admission).

Costs (2002–03) *One-time required fee:* $25. *Tuition:* $9900 full-time, $330 per semester hour part-time. Full-time tuition and fees vary according to course load. Part-time tuition and fees vary according to course load. *Required fees:* $200 full-time, $100 per term part-time. *Payment plan:* installment. *Waivers:* employees or children of employees.

Applying *Options:* common application, deferred entrance. *Application fee:* $25. *Required:* high school transcript, entrance evaluation, placement evaluation. *Required for some:* essay or personal statement, interview. *Application deadline:* rolling (freshmen), rolling (transfers).

Admissions Contact Mr. Paul Richardson, Director of Admissions, Bryant and Stratton Business Institute, Amherst Campus, Audobon Business Centre, 40 Hazelwood Drive, Amherst, NY 14228. *Phone:* 716-691-0012 Ext. 204. *Fax:* 716-691-6716. *E-mail:* pvrichardson@bryantstratton.edu.

BRYANT AND STRATTON BUSINESS INSTITUTE, NORTH CAMPUS
Liverpool, New York

- **Proprietary** 2-year, founded 1983, part of Bryant and Stratton Business Institute, Inc
- **Calendar** semesters

- **Degree** diplomas and associate
- **Rural** 1-acre campus with easy access to Syracuse
- **Coed,** 198 undergraduate students, 88% full-time, 74% women, 26% men

Undergraduates 175 full-time, 23 part-time. Students come from 1 other country, 4% African American, 3% Hispanic American, 0.5% international.

Freshmen *Admission:* 103 applied, 103 admitted, 76 enrolled. *Average high school GPA:* 3.0.

Faculty *Total:* 30, 23% full-time, 3% with terminal degrees. *Student/faculty ratio:* 14:1.

Majors Accounting; business administration; electrical/electronic engineering technology; information sciences/systems; information technology; legal administrative assistant; paralegal/legal assistant; secretarial science.

Academic Programs *Special study options:* academic remediation for entering students, adult/continuing education programs, advanced placement credit, cooperative education, distance learning, double majors, independent study, internships, part-time degree program, services for LD students, summer session for credit.

Library Resource Center plus 1 other with 1,936 titles, 13 serial subscriptions, 85 audiovisual materials, an OPAC.

Computers on Campus 73 computers available on campus for general student use. Internet access, at least one staffed computer lab available.

Student Life *Housing:* college housing not available. *Activities and Organizations:* Institute of Managerial Accountants, Students Helping Santa, Computer Club, Bryant & Stratton Business Club (BSBC), Alpha Beta Gamma, national fraternities. *Campus security:* 24-hour emergency response devices. *Student Services:* personal/psychological counseling.

Athletics Member NJCAA. *Intercollegiate sports:* soccer M/W.

Costs (2002–03) *One-time required fee:* $25. *Tuition:* $9900 full-time, $330 per semester hour part-time. Full-time tuition and fees vary according to course load. Part-time tuition and fees vary according to course load. *Required fees:* $200 full-time, $100 per term part-time. *Payment plan:* installment. *Waivers:* employees or children of employees.

Applying *Options:* deferred entrance. *Application fee:* $25. *Required:* high school transcript, interview, entrance evaluation and placement evaluation. *Required for some:* letters of recommendation. *Recommended:* minimum 2.0 GPA. *Application deadline:* rolling (freshmen), rolling (transfers). *Notification:* continuous (freshmen).

Admissions Contact Ms. Heather Macnik, Director of Admissions, Bryant and Stratton Business Institute, North Campus, 8687 Carling Road, Liverpool, NY 13090-1315. *Phone:* 315-652-6500. *Fax:* 315-652-5500.

Catholic Medical Center of Brooklyn and Queens School of Nursing

Fresh Meadows, New York

Admissions Contact Ms. Mary E. Rohan, Director of Admissions, Catholic Medical Center of Brooklyn and Queens School of Nursing, 175-05 Horace Harding Expressway, Fresh Meadows, NY 11365. *Phone:* 718-357-0500 Ext. 125. *Fax:* 718-357-4683 Ext. 125.

Cayuga County Community College

Auburn, New York

- **State and locally supported** 2-year, founded 1953, part of State University of New York System
- **Calendar** semesters
- **Degree** certificates and associate
- **Small-town** 50-acre campus with easy access to Rochester and Syracuse
- **Endowment** $7.4 million
- **Coed,** 2,739 undergraduate students, 54% full-time, 58% women, 42% men

Undergraduates Students come from 9 states and territories, 3 other countries, 1% are from out of state, 3% African American, 0.5% Asian American or Pacific Islander, 1% Hispanic American, 0.8% Native American, 0.2% international.

Freshmen *Admission:* 945 applied, 860 admitted. *Test scores:* SAT verbal scores over 500: 33%; SAT math scores over 500: 47%; SAT verbal scores over 600: 5%; SAT math scores over 600: 9%; SAT verbal scores over 700: 1%; SAT math scores over 700: 1%.

Faculty *Total:* 162, 33% full-time, 15% with terminal degrees.

Majors Accounting; business administration; business marketing and marketing management; computer/information sciences; computer/information technology services administration and management related; computer management; computer programming; computer science; computer science related; corrections; criminal justice/law enforcement administration; data processing technology; drafting; early childhood education; electrical/electronic engineering technology; humanities; information sciences/systems; law enforcement/police science; liberal arts and sciences/liberal studies; mathematics; mechanical design technology; nursing; radio/television broadcasting; radio/television broadcasting technology; retail management; telecommunications.

Academic Programs *Special study options:* academic remediation for entering students, accelerated degree program, adult/continuing education programs, advanced placement credit, distance learning, double majors, honors programs, independent study, internships, part-time degree program, services for LD students, study abroad, summer session for credit.

Library Norman F. Bourke Memorial Library with 82,205 titles, 527 serial subscriptions, 8,930 audiovisual materials, an OPAC, a Web page.

Computers on Campus 240 computers available on campus for general student use. A campuswide network can be accessed from off campus. Internet access, at least one staffed computer lab available.

Student Life *Housing:* college housing not available. *Activities and Organizations:* drama/theater group, student-run newspaper, radio and television station, choral group, Student Government Association, Student Activities Board, Radio and Television Guild, honors and business fraternities, Phi Beta Lambda. *Campus security:* security from 8 a.m. to 9 p.m. *Student Services:* health clinic, personal/psychological counseling.

Athletics Member NJCAA. *Intercollegiate sports:* basketball M/W, lacrosse W, soccer M. *Intramural sports:* basketball M, racquetball M/W, soccer M/W, volleyball M/W.

Standardized Tests *Required for some:* ACT ASSET. *Recommended:* SAT I or ACT (for placement).

Costs (2001–02) *Tuition:* state resident $2600 full-time, $95 per credit hour part-time; nonresident $5200 full-time, $190 per credit hour part-time. *Required fees:* $378 full-time, $10 per credit hour. *Payment plan:* installment. *Waivers:* employees or children of employees.

Applying *Options:* early admission, deferred entrance. *Required:* high school transcript, interview. *Application deadline:* rolling (freshmen), rolling (transfers). *Notification:* continuous (freshmen).

Admissions Contact Mr. Dick Landers, Interim Director of Admissions, Cayuga County Community College, 197 Franklin Street, Auburn, NY 13021-3099. *Phone:* 315-255-1743 Ext. 244.

Clinton Community College

Plattsburgh, New York

- **State and locally supported** 2-year, founded 1969, part of State University of New York System
- **Calendar** semesters
- **Degree** certificates and associate
- **Small-town** 100-acre campus
- **Endowment** $1.0 million
- **Coed,** 1,852 undergraduate students, 60% full-time, 59% women, 41% men

Undergraduates 1,103 full-time, 749 part-time. Students come from 5 states and territories, 8 other countries, 1% are from out of state, 4% African American, 0.4% Asian American or Pacific Islander, 0.7% Hispanic American, 0.5% Native American, 2% international, 7% transferred in, 6% live on campus.

Freshmen *Admission:* 1,266 applied, 664 admitted, 320 enrolled. *Average high school GPA:* 2.50.

Faculty *Total:* 128, 36% full-time, 9% with terminal degrees. *Student/faculty ratio:* 18:1.

Majors Accounting; biological/physical sciences; business administration; community services; computer/information technology services administration and management related; criminal justice/law enforcement administration; electrical/electronic engineering technology; humanities; industrial technology; law enforcement/police science; liberal arts and sciences/liberal studies; medical laboratory technician; nursing; physical education; retail management; secretarial science; social sciences.

Academic Programs *Special study options:* academic remediation for entering students, adult/continuing education programs, advanced placement credit, cooperative education, distance learning, English as a second language, external degree program, independent study, internships, off-campus study, part-time degree program, services for LD students, student-designed majors, summer session for credit.

Library Clinton Community College Learning Resource Center plus 1 other with 50,000 titles, 282 serial subscriptions, an OPAC, a Web page.

Clinton Community College (continued)

Computers on Campus 250 computers available on campus for general student use. A campuswide network can be accessed from off campus. Internet access, at least one staffed computer lab available.

Student Life *Housing Options:* coed, disabled students. *Activities and Organizations:* drama/theater group, student-run newspaper, choral group, Criminal Justice Club, Business Club, Tomorrow's New Teachers, Ski Club, Nursing Club. *Campus security:* 24-hour emergency response devices, late-night transport/escort service, controlled dormitory access, security during class hours. *Student Services:* health clinic, personal/psychological counseling.

Athletics Member NJCAA. *Intercollegiate sports:* baseball M, basketball M/W, soccer M/W, softball W.

Standardized Tests *Recommended:* SAT I or ACT (for placement).

Costs (2001–02) *Tuition:* state resident $2400 full-time, $100 per credit hour part-time; nonresident $4800 full-time, $200 per credit hour part-time. *Required fees:* $128 full-time, $2 per credit hour. *Room and board:* $2000; room only: $1600. Room and board charges vary according to board plan. *Payment plan:* deferred payment. *Waivers:* senior citizens and employees or children of employees.

Financial Aid In 2001, 45 Federal Work-Study jobs (averaging $1150).

Applying *Options:* electronic application, early admission, deferred entrance. *Required:* high school transcript. *Required for some:* essay or personal statement, minimum 2.5 GPA, 3 letters of recommendation, interview. *Application deadlines:* 8/22 (freshmen), 8/26 (transfers). *Notification:* continuous (freshmen).

Admissions Contact Mr. Robert C. Wood, Associate Dean for Enrollment Management, Clinton Community College, 136 Clinton Point Drive, Plattsburgh, NY 12901. *Phone:* 518-562-4170. *Toll-free phone:* 800-552-1160. *Fax:* 518-562-4158. *E-mail:* cccadm@clintoncc.suny.edu.

COCHRAN SCHOOL OF NURSING
Yonkers, New York

- **Independent** 2-year, founded 1894
- **Calendar** semesters
- **Degree** associate
- **Urban** campus with easy access to New York City
- **Coed, primarily women,** 94 undergraduate students

Undergraduates 34% African American, 3% Asian American or Pacific Islander, 9% Hispanic American. *Retention:* 75% of 2001 full-time freshmen returned.

Faculty *Total:* 17, 59% full-time. *Student/faculty ratio:* 7:1.

Majors Nursing.

Academic Programs *Special study options:* advanced placement credit, part-time degree program.

Library Cochran School of Nursing Library with 4,314 titles, 115 serial subscriptions, 500 audiovisual materials, an OPAC.

Computers on Campus 6 computers available on campus for general student use. Internet access, at least one staffed computer lab available.

Student Life *Housing:* college housing not available. *Campus security:* 24-hour emergency response devices and patrols, late-night transport/escort service. *Student Services:* health clinic, personal/psychological counseling.

Standardized Tests *Required for some:* SAT I (for admission).

Costs (2001–02) *One-time required fee:* $50. *Tuition:* $9560 full-time, $270 per credit part-time. Full-time tuition and fees vary according to course load and student level. Part-time tuition and fees vary according to course load and student level. *Required fees:* $900 full-time. *Payment plans:* installment, deferred payment.

Applying *Options:* deferred entrance. *Application fee:* $25. *Required:* essay or personal statement, high school transcript, interview. *Application deadline:* rolling (freshmen). *Notification:* continuous (freshmen).

Admissions Contact Ms. Carol Cataldi, Registrar, Cochran School of Nursing, Yonkers, NY 10701. *Phone:* 914-964-4296.

COLUMBIA-GREENE COMMUNITY COLLEGE
Hudson, New York

- **State and locally supported** 2-year, founded 1969, part of State University of New York System
- **Calendar** semesters
- **Degree** certificates and associate
- **Rural** 143-acre campus
- **Endowment** $450,000
- **Coed,** 1,624 undergraduate students, 51% full-time, 64% women, 36% men

Undergraduates 825 full-time, 799 part-time. Students come from 5 states and territories, 5 other countries, 1% are from out of state, 5% transferred in. *Retention:* 65% of 2001 full-time freshmen returned.

Freshmen *Admission:* 581 applied, 470 admitted, 491 enrolled.

Faculty *Total:* 106, 44% full-time. *Student/faculty ratio:* 16:1.

Majors Accounting; art; auto mechanic/technician; biological/physical sciences; business administration; computer graphics; computer science; computer science related; computer systems networking/telecommunications; criminal justice/law enforcement administration; data processing technology; exercise sciences; humanities; human services; information sciences/systems; interdisciplinary studies; liberal arts and sciences/liberal studies; mathematics; nursing; real estate; secretarial science; social sciences; Web/multimedia management/webmaster.

Academic Programs *Special study options:* academic remediation for entering students, adult/continuing education programs, advanced placement credit, distance learning, honors programs, internships, part-time degree program, services for LD students, student-designed majors, summer session for credit.

Library 52,484 titles, 627 serial subscriptions, an OPAC, a Web page.

Computers on Campus 150 computers available on campus for general student use. A campuswide network can be accessed from off campus. Internet access, at least one staffed computer lab available.

Student Life *Housing:* college housing not available. *Activities and Organizations:* drama/theater group, student-run radio station, choral group, student council/government, Student Ambassadors, Nursing Club. *Campus security:* 24-hour patrols, late-night transport/escort service.

Athletics Member NJCAA. *Intercollegiate sports:* baseball M, basketball M, bowling M/W, soccer M/W, softball W. *Intramural sports:* archery M/W, badminton M/W, baseball M, basketball M/W, bowling M/W, fencing M/W, soccer M/W, table tennis M/W, tennis M/W, volleyball M/W, weight lifting M/W.

Standardized Tests *Required:* College Qualifying Test. *Recommended:* SAT I or ACT (for placement).

Costs (2001–02) *Tuition:* state resident $2400 full-time, $100 per credit hour part-time; nonresident $4800 full-time, $200 per credit hour part-time. *Required fees:* $140 full-time, $9 per credit hour. *Payment plans:* installment, deferred payment. *Waivers:* senior citizens and employees or children of employees.

Applying *Options:* early admission, deferred entrance. *Application fee:* $30. *Required:* high school transcript. *Required for some:* interview. *Application deadline:* rolling (freshmen), rolling (transfers). *Notification:* continuous (freshmen).

Admissions Contact Mrs. Patricia Hallenbeck, Director of Admissions/Registrar, Columbia-Greene Community College, 4400 Route 23, Hudson, NY 12534-0327. *Phone:* 518-828-4181 Ext. 5513. *Fax:* 518-828-8543. *E-mail:* hallenbeck@vaxa.cis.sunycgcc.edu.

CORNING COMMUNITY COLLEGE
Corning, New York

- **State and locally supported** 2-year, founded 1956, part of State University of New York System
- **Calendar** semesters
- **Degree** certificates and associate
- **Rural** 275-acre campus
- **Endowment** $1.2 million
- **Coed,** 4,596 undergraduate students, 47% full-time, 57% women, 43% men

Undergraduates 2,183 full-time, 2,413 part-time. Students come from 10 states and territories, 3 other countries, 5% are from out of state, 3% African American, 0.9% Asian American or Pacific Islander, 0.7% Hispanic American, 0.4% Native American, 0.1% international, 4% transferred in.

Freshmen *Admission:* 1,338 applied, 1,212 admitted, 1,145 enrolled. *Average high school GPA:* 2.80.

Faculty *Total:* 260, 41% full-time, 7% with terminal degrees. *Student/faculty ratio:* 19:1.

Majors Accounting; alcohol/drug abuse counseling; auto mechanic/technician; automotive engineering technology; biological/physical sciences; business administration; business systems networking/ telecommunications; chemical technology; child care provider; computer graphics; computer/information sciences; computer/information technology services administration and management related; computer maintenance technology; computer programming; computer programming related; computer science; computer science related; computer systems networking/telecommunications; criminal justice/corrections related; criminal justice/law enforcement administration; drafting/design technology; education related; electrical/electronic engineering technology; elementary education; emergency medical technology; enterprise management; fire science; general studies; health/physical education; humanities; human services; industrial technology; information technology; liberal arts and sciences/liberal studies; machine shop assistant; machine technology; mathematics; mechanical engineering technology; nursing; optics; paralegal/legal assistant; pre-engineering; secretarial science; social sciences; travel/tourism management; word processing.

Academic Programs *Special study options:* academic remediation for entering students, accelerated degree program, advanced placement credit, distance learning, double majors, honors programs, independent study, internships, part-time degree program, services for LD students, student-designed majors, summer session for credit. *ROTC:* Army (c), Navy (c), Air Force (c).

Library Arthur A. Houghton, Jr. Library with 71,233 titles, 2,500 serial subscriptions, 4,290 audiovisual materials, an OPAC, a Web page.

Computers on Campus 350 computers available on campus for general student use. A campuswide network can be accessed from off campus that provide access to email, Internet courses. Internet access, at least one staffed computer lab available.

Student Life *Housing:* college housing not available. *Activities and Organizations:* drama/theater group, student-run newspaper, radio station, choral group, student association, WCEB, Two-Bit Players, Phi Theta Kappa, Nursing Society. *Campus security:* 24-hour emergency response devices and patrols, late-night transport/escort service. *Student Services:* health clinic, personal/psychological counseling.

Athletics Member NJCAA. *Intercollegiate sports:* basketball M/W, cross-country running M/W, soccer M/W, softball W, volleyball W, wrestling M. *Intramural sports:* archery M/W, badminton M/W, basketball M/W, bowling M/W, cross-country running M/W, golf M/W, skiing (cross-country) M/W, soccer M/W, swimming M/W, table tennis M/W, tennis M/W, volleyball M/W, weight lifting M/W.

Costs (2001–02) *Tuition:* state resident $2574 full-time, $107 per credit part-time; nonresident $5148 full-time, $214 per credit part-time. Full-time tuition and fees vary according to program. Part-time tuition and fees vary according to course load and program. *Required fees:* $286 full-time, $75 per term part-time. *Payment plan:* installment. *Waivers:* senior citizens and employees or children of employees.

Financial Aid In 2001, 196 Federal Work-Study jobs (averaging $716).

Applying *Options:* electronic application, early admission. *Application fee:* $25. *Required:* high school transcript. *Required for some:* interview. *Application deadline:* rolling (freshmen), rolling (transfers). *Notification:* continuous (freshmen).

Admissions Contact Ms. Donna A. Hastings, Coordinator of Administrative Services/Admissions, Corning Community College, 1 Academic Drive, Corning, NY 14830. *Phone:* 607-962-9220. *Toll-free phone:* 800-358-7171 Ext. 220. *Fax:* 607-962-9520. *E-mail:* admissions@corning-cc.edu.

Crouse Hospital School of Nursing
Syracuse, New York

- **Independent** 2-year, founded 1913
- **Degree** associate
- **Coed, primarily women**
- 62% of applicants were admitted

Student Life *Campus security:* 24-hour emergency response devices and patrols, late-night transport/escort service, controlled dormitory access.

Standardized Tests *Recommended:* SAT I or ACT (for admission).

Financial Aid In 2001, 18 Federal Work-Study jobs (averaging $880).

Applying *Options:* deferred entrance. *Application fee:* $20. *Required:* essay or personal statement, high school transcript, minimum 2.5 GPA, 3 letters of recommendation, interview.

Admissions Contact Ms. Karen Van Sise, Enrollment Management Coordinator, Crouse Hospital School of Nursing, 736 Irving Avenue, Syracuse, NY 13210. *Phone:* 315-470-7858. *Fax:* 315-470-7925.

Dorothea Hopfer School of Nursing at The Mount Vernon Hospital
Mount Vernon, New York

Admissions Contact 53 Valentine Street, Mount Vernon, NY 10550.

Dutchess Community College
Poughkeepsie, New York

- **State and locally supported** 2-year, founded 1957, part of State University of New York System
- **Calendar** semesters
- **Degree** certificates and associate
- **Suburban** 130-acre campus with easy access to New York City
- **Coed,** 6,981 undergraduate students

Freshmen *Admission:* 1,030 applied, 1,012 admitted. *Average high school GPA:* 2.5.

Faculty *Total:* 396.

Majors Accounting; architectural engineering technology; biological/physical sciences; business administration; business machine repair; child care/development; child guidance; communications; computer/information sciences; computer science; construction technology; criminal justice/law enforcement administration; criminal justice studies; dietetics; early childhood education; electrical/electronic engineering technology; electrical engineering; electromechanical technology; elementary education; emergency medical technology; engineering science; food products retailing; graphic design/commercial art/illustration; humanities; information sciences/systems; liberal arts and sciences/liberal studies; mass communications; mathematics; medical assistant; medical laboratory technician; mental health/rehabilitation; nursing; nutrition science; paralegal/legal assistant; physical therapy assistant; psychiatric/mental health services; recreation/leisure studies; retail management; robotics; science education; secretarial science; social sciences; telecommunications; travel/tourism management.

Academic Programs *Special study options:* academic remediation for entering students, adult/continuing education programs, advanced placement credit, English as a second language, freshman honors college, honors programs, internships, off-campus study, part-time degree program, summer session for credit.

Library Dutchess Library with 103,272 titles, 540 serial subscriptions, an OPAC, a Web page.

Computers on Campus 50 computers available on campus for general student use. A campuswide network can be accessed from off campus. Internet access, at least one staffed computer lab available.

Student Life *Housing:* college housing not available. *Activities and Organizations:* drama/theater group, student-run newspaper, radio station, choral group. *Campus security:* 24-hour emergency response devices and patrols, late-night transport/escort service. *Student Services:* health clinic, personal/psychological counseling.

Athletics Member NJCAA. *Intercollegiate sports:* baseball M, basketball M/W, bowling M/W, golf M, soccer M/W, softball W, tennis M/W, volleyball W. *Intramural sports:* badminton M/W, basketball M/W, football M, soccer M/W, tennis M/W, volleyball M/W.

Costs (2001–02) *Tuition:* state resident $2300 full-time, $89 per credit hour part-time; nonresident $4600 full-time, $178 per credit hour part-time. *Required fees:* $120 full-time, $13 per term part-time. *Waivers:* employees or children of employees.

Financial Aid In 2001, 500 Federal Work-Study jobs (averaging $1500).

Applying *Options:* early admission, deferred entrance. *Required:* high school transcript. *Application deadline:* rolling (freshmen), rolling (transfers). *Notification:* continuous (freshmen).

Admissions Contact Ms. Rita Banner, Director of Admissions, Dutchess Community College, 53 Pendell Road, Poughkeepsie, NY 12601. *Phone:* 845-431-8010. *Toll-free phone:* 800-763-3933. *E-mail:* banner@sunydutchess.edu.

Ellis Hospital School of Nursing
Schenectady, New York

- **Independent** 2-year
- **Degree** associate
- **Coed, primarily women,** 69 undergraduate students, 51% full-time, 97% women, 3% men
- 50% of applicants were admitted

Undergraduates 3% African American, 1% Asian American or Pacific Islander, 1% Hispanic American.

Freshmen *Admission:* 101 applied, 50 admitted.

Faculty *Total:* 9, 100% full-time, 100% with terminal degrees. *Student/faculty ratio:* 8:1.

Majors Nursing.

Standardized Tests *Recommended:* SAT I (for admission).

Costs (2001–02) *Tuition:* $4000 full-time, $140 per credit part-time. *Required fees:* $80 full-time. *Payment plan:* installment.

Ellis Hospital School of Nursing (continued)

Applying *Required:* essay or personal statement, high school transcript, 3 letters of recommendation. *Application deadline:* rolling (freshmen), rolling (transfers).

Admissions Contact Ellis Hospital School of Nursing, 1101 Nott Street, Schenectady, NY 12308. *Phone:* 518-243-4471.

ELMIRA BUSINESS INSTITUTE
Elmira, New York

- **Private** 2-year, founded 1858
- **Degree** certificates and associate
- 230 undergraduate students

Admissions Contact Ms. Lisa Roan, Admissions Coordinator, Elmira Business Institute, 303 North Main Street, Elmira, NY 14901. *Phone:* 800-843-1812.

ERIE COMMUNITY COLLEGE, CITY CAMPUS
Buffalo, New York

- **State and locally supported** 2-year, founded 1971, part of State University of New York System
- **Calendar** 4-1-4
- **Degree** certificates, diplomas, and associate
- **Urban** 1-acre campus
- **Coed,** 2,517 undergraduate students, 71% full-time, 62% women, 38% men

Undergraduates 1,793 full-time, 724 part-time. Students come from 11 states and territories, 2 other countries, 0.6% are from out of state, 41% African American, 2% Asian American or Pacific Islander, 8% Hispanic American, 1% Native American, 0.1% international, 5% transferred in.

Freshmen *Admission:* 1,175 applied, 893 admitted, 564 enrolled. *Test scores:* SAT verbal scores over 500: 31%; SAT math scores over 500: 29%; SAT verbal scores over 600: 4%; SAT math scores over 600: 3%.

Faculty *Total:* 181, 52% full-time. *Student/faculty ratio:* 14:1.

Majors Alcohol/drug abuse counseling; building maintenance/management; business administration; child care/guidance; community health liaison; criminal justice/law enforcement administration; culinary arts; hotel and restaurant management; humanities; industrial production technologies related; information sciences/systems; liberal arts and sciences/liberal studies; medical radiologic technology; nursing; office management; paralegal/legal assistant; secretarial science.

Academic Programs *Special study options:* academic remediation for entering students, adult/continuing education programs, advanced placement credit, cooperative education, distance learning, double majors, English as a second language, honors programs, independent study, internships, part-time degree program, services for LD students, student-designed majors, study abroad, summer session for credit. *ROTC:* Army (c).

Library Leon E. Butler Library with 18,780 titles, 263 serial subscriptions, 2,422 audiovisual materials, an OPAC, a Web page.

Computers on Campus 341 computers available on campus for general student use. A campuswide network can be accessed from off campus. Internet access, at least one staffed computer lab available.

Student Life *Housing:* college housing not available. *Activities and Organizations:* student-run newspaper, Alpha Beta Gamma, Anthropology Club, Black Student Union, Business Club, Campus Ministry Club. *Campus security:* 24-hour emergency response devices and patrols, late-night transport/escort service. *Student Services:* health clinic, personal/psychological counseling, women's center.

Athletics Member NJCAA. *Intercollegiate sports:* baseball M, basketball M/W, bowling M/W, cross-country running M/W, football M, golf M/W, ice hockey M, soccer M/W, softball W, swimming M/W, track and field M/W, volleyball W.

Standardized Tests *Required:* ACT ASSET. *Recommended:* SAT I (for placement), SAT II: Subject Tests (for placement).

Costs (2001–02) *Tuition:* area resident $2475 full-time, $99 per credit hour part-time; state resident $4950 full-time, $198 per credit hour part-time; nonresident $4950 full-time, $198 per credit hour part-time. *Required fees:* $180 full-time, $5 per credit hour. *Payment plans:* installment, deferred payment. *Waivers:* senior citizens.

Applying *Options:* common application, electronic application. *Required:* high school transcript. *Required for some:* interview. *Application deadline:* rolling (freshmen), rolling (transfers). *Notification:* continuous (freshmen).

Admissions Contact Ms. Petrina Hill-Cheatom, Director of Admissions, Erie Community College, City Campus, 121 Ellicott Street, Buffalo, NY 14203-2698. *Phone:* 716-851-1588. *Fax:* 716-851-1129.

ERIE COMMUNITY COLLEGE, NORTH CAMPUS
Williamsville, New York

- **State and locally supported** 2-year, founded 1946, part of State University of New York System
- **Calendar** 4-1-4
- **Degree** certificates, diplomas, and associate
- **Suburban** 20-acre campus with easy access to Buffalo
- **Coed,** 5,162 undergraduate students, 62% full-time, 49% women, 51% men

Undergraduates 3,182 full-time, 1,980 part-time. Students come from 16 states and territories, 22 other countries, 0.6% are from out of state, 11% African American, 2% Asian American or Pacific Islander, 2% Hispanic American, 0.5% Native American, 2% international, 6% transferred in.

Freshmen *Admission:* 1,706 applied, 1,586 admitted, 1,124 enrolled. *Test scores:* SAT verbal scores over 500: 27%; SAT math scores over 500: 35%; SAT verbal scores over 600: 4%; SAT math scores over 600: 5%.

Faculty *Total:* 352, 41% full-time. *Student/faculty ratio:* 14:1.

Majors Business administration; chemical technology; civil engineering technology; computer/information sciences; construction trades related; criminal justice/law enforcement administration; dental hygiene; dietician assistant; electrical/electronic engineering technology; engineering; humanities; information sciences/systems; law enforcement/police science; liberal arts and sciences/liberal studies; machine shop assistant; mechanical engineering technology; medical laboratory technician; medical office management; medical records technology; nursing; occupational therapy assistant; office management; opticianry; respiratory therapy; restaurant operations; secretarial science.

Academic Programs *Special study options:* academic remediation for entering students, adult/continuing education programs, advanced placement credit, cooperative education, distance learning, double majors, English as a second language, honors programs, independent study, internships, part-time degree program, services for LD students, student-designed majors, study abroad, summer session for credit. *ROTC:* Army (c).

Library Richard R. Dry Memorial Library with 61,760 titles, 389 serial subscriptions, 7,284 audiovisual materials, an OPAC, a Web page.

Computers on Campus 457 computers available on campus for general student use. A campuswide network can be accessed from off campus. Internet access, online (class) registration available.

Student Life *Housing:* college housing not available. *Activities and Organizations:* student-run newspaper, APWA (American Public Works Association), Dental Hygiene Club, Environmental Awareness Club, Flame and Ice, Future Teachers. *Campus security:* 24-hour emergency response devices and patrols, late-night transport/escort service. *Student Services:* health clinic, personal/psychological counseling, women's center.

Athletics Member NJCAA. *Intercollegiate sports:* baseball M, basketball M/W, bowling M/W, cross-country running M/W, football M, golf M/W, ice hockey M, soccer M/W, softball W, swimming M/W, track and field M/W, volleyball W.

Standardized Tests *Required:* ACT ASSET. *Recommended:* SAT I (for placement), SAT II: Subject Tests (for placement).

Costs (2001–02) *Tuition:* area resident $2475 full-time, $99 per credit hour part-time; state resident $4950 full-time, $198 per credit hour part-time; nonresident $4950 full-time, $198 per credit hour part-time. *Required fees:* $180 full-time, $5 per credit hour. *Payment plans:* installment, deferred payment. *Waivers:* senior citizens.

Applying *Options:* common application, electronic application. *Required:* high school transcript. *Required for some:* interview. *Application deadline:* rolling (freshmen), rolling (transfers). *Notification:* continuous (freshmen).

Admissions Contact Ms. Petrina Hill-Cheatom, Director of Admissions, Erie Community College, North Campus, 6205 Main Street, Williamsville, NY 14221-7095. *Phone:* 716-851-1588. *Fax:* 716-851-1429.

ERIE COMMUNITY COLLEGE, SOUTH CAMPUS
Orchard Park, New York

- **State and locally supported** 2-year, founded 1974, part of State University of New York System
- **Calendar** 4-1-4
- **Degree** certificates, diplomas, and associate
- **Suburban** 20-acre campus with easy access to Buffalo
- **Coed,** 3,370 undergraduate students, 66% full-time, 44% women, 56% men

Undergraduates 2,215 full-time, 1,155 part-time. Students come from 9 states and territories, 3 other countries, 0.7% are from out of state, 3% African American, 0.6% Asian American or Pacific Islander, 1% Hispanic American, 1% Native American, 0.1% international, 4% transferred in.

Freshmen *Admission:* 1,142 applied, 1,099 admitted, 877 enrolled. *Test scores:* SAT verbal scores over 500: 31%; SAT math scores over 500: 35%; SAT verbal scores over 600: 3%; SAT math scores over 600: 3%.

Faculty *Total:* 223, 44% full-time. *Student/faculty ratio:* 14:1.

Majors Architectural engineering technology; auto body repair; auto mechanic/technician; biomedical engineering-related technology; business administration; communications; communication systems installation/repair; computer maintenance technology; dental laboratory technician; fire services administration; graphic/printing equipment; humanities; information sciences/systems; liberal arts and sciences/liberal studies; mechanical drafting; office management; recreation/leisure facilities management; secretarial science.

Academic Programs *Special study options:* academic remediation for entering students, adult/continuing education programs, advanced placement credit, cooperative education, distance learning, double majors, English as a second language, honors programs, independent study, internships, part-time degree program, services for LD students, student-designed majors, study abroad, summer session for credit. *ROTC:* Army (c).

Library 50,263 titles, 321 serial subscriptions, 2,025 audiovisual materials, an OPAC, a Web page.

Computers on Campus 434 computers available on campus for general student use. A campuswide network can be accessed from off campus. Internet access, at least one staffed computer lab available.

Student Life *Housing:* college housing not available. *Activities and Organizations:* student-run newspaper, radio station, Habitat for Humanity, Honors Society, Phi Theta Kappa, Photo Club, Recreation Leadership Club. *Campus security:* 24-hour emergency response devices and patrols, late-night transport/escort service. *Student Services:* health clinic, personal/psychological counseling, women's center.

Athletics Member NJCAA. *Intercollegiate sports:* baseball M, basketball M/W, bowling M/W, cross-country running M/W, football M, golf M/W, ice hockey M, soccer M/W, softball W, swimming M/W, track and field M/W, volleyball W.

Standardized Tests *Required:* ACT ASSET. *Recommended:* SAT I (for placement), SAT II: Subject Tests (for placement).

Costs (2001–02) *Tuition:* area resident $2475 full-time, $99 per credit hour part-time; state resident $4950 full-time, $198 per credit hour part-time; nonresident $4950 full-time, $198 per credit hour part-time. *Required fees:* $180 full-time, $5 per credit hour. *Payment plans:* installment, deferred payment. *Waivers:* senior citizens.

Applying *Options:* common application, electronic application. *Required:* high school transcript. *Required for some:* interview. *Application deadline:* rolling (freshmen), rolling (transfers). *Notification:* continuous (freshmen).

Admissions Contact Ms. Petrina Hill-Cheatom, Director of Admissions, Erie Community College, South Campus, 4041 Southwestern Boulevard, Orchard Park, NY 14127-2199. *Phone:* 716-851-1588. *Fax:* 716-851-1629.

Eugenio Maria de Hostos Community College of the City University of New York

Bronx, New York

- **State and locally supported** 2-year, founded 1968, part of City University of New York System
- **Calendar** semesters
- **Degree** certificates and associate
- **Urban** 8-acre campus
- **Endowment** $157,966
- **Coed,** 3,285 undergraduate students, 75% full-time, 77% women, 23% men

Undergraduates 2,456 full-time, 829 part-time. Students come from 2 states and territories, 36 other countries, 1% are from out of state, 22% African American, 3% Asian American or Pacific Islander, 65% Hispanic American, 0.1% Native American, 4% international, 9% transferred in. *Retention:* 59% of 2001 full-time freshmen returned.

Freshmen *Admission:* 2,139 applied, 2,139 admitted, 542 enrolled. *Average high school GPA:* 1.86. *Test scores:* SAT verbal scores over 500: 10%.

Faculty *Total:* 304, 49% full-time, 36% with terminal degrees. *Student/faculty ratio:* 14:1.

Majors Accounting; business administration; data entry/microcomputer applications related; data processing technology; dental hygiene; early childhood education; gerontology; liberal arts and sciences/liberal studies; medical administrative assistant; medical laboratory technician; medical radiologic technology; nursing; paralegal/legal assistant; public administration; secretarial science.

Academic Programs *Special study options:* academic remediation for entering students, adult/continuing education programs, distance learning, double majors, English as a second language, internships, part-time degree program, services for LD students, summer session for credit.

Library Hostos Community College Library with 43,928 titles, 355 serial subscriptions, 705 audiovisual materials, an OPAC.

Computers on Campus 550 computers available on campus for general student use. A campuswide network can be accessed from off campus. Internet access, online (class) registration, at least one staffed computer lab available.

Student Life *Housing:* college housing not available. *Activities and Organizations:* student-run newspaper, television station, Dominican Association, Puerto Rican Student Organization, Student Government Association, Black Student Union, Veterans Club. *Campus security:* 24-hour emergency response devices and patrols, late-night transport/escort service. *Student Services:* health clinic, personal/psychological counseling, women's center, legal services.

Athletics *Intramural sports:* basketball M/W, volleyball M/W.

Standardized Tests *Required:* in-house tests.

Costs (2002–03) *Tuition:* state resident $2500 full-time, $105 per credit part-time; nonresident $3076 full-time, $130 per credit part-time. *Required fees:* $172 full-time, $86 per term part-time. *Payment plans:* installment, deferred payment. *Waivers:* senior citizens and employees or children of employees.

Financial Aid In 2001, 1,890 Federal Work-Study jobs (averaging $1997).

Applying *Options:* common application. *Application fee:* $40. *Required:* high school transcript. *Application deadline:* rolling (freshmen), rolling (transfers). *Notification:* continuous until 2/15 (freshmen).

Admissions Contact Ms. Nydia R. Edgecombe, Director of Admissions, Eugenio Maria de Hostos Community College of the City University of New York, 120 149th Street, Room D-210, Bronx, NY 10451. *Phone:* 718-518-4406. *Fax:* 718-518-4256. *E-mail:* admissions2@hostos.cuny.edu.

Finger Lakes Community College

Canandaigua, New York

- **State and locally supported** 2-year, founded 1965, part of State University of New York System
- **Calendar** semesters
- **Degree** certificates and associate
- **Small-town** 300-acre campus with easy access to Rochester
- **Coed,** 4,753 undergraduate students

Undergraduates Students come from 6 states and territories, 3 other countries, 1% are from out of state.

Freshmen *Admission:* 2,987 applied, 2,750 admitted.

Faculty *Total:* 258, 41% full-time. *Student/faculty ratio:* 19:1.

Majors Accounting; alcohol/drug abuse counseling; architectural engineering technology; banking; biological/physical sciences; biological technology; biology; broadcast journalism; business administration; business marketing and marketing management; chemistry; computer/information sciences; computer science; criminal justice/law enforcement administration; data processing technology; drafting; early childhood education; engineering science; environmental science; fine/studio arts; fish/game management; graphic design/commercial art/illustration; hotel and restaurant management; humanities; human services; law enforcement/police science; liberal arts and sciences/liberal studies; mass communications; mathematics; mechanical engineering technology; music; natural resources conservation; natural resources management; natural resources protective services; nursing; ornamental horticulture; paralegal/legal assistant; physical education; physics; political science; pre-engineering; psychology; recreation/leisure facilities management; retail management; secretarial science; social sciences; sociology; theater arts/drama; travel/tourism management.

Academic Programs *Special study options:* academic remediation for entering students, advanced placement credit, distance learning, English as a second language, honors programs, internships, off-campus study, part-time degree program, services for LD students, summer session for credit. *ROTC:* Army (c), Navy (c).

Library Charles Meder Library with 73,305 titles, 464 serial subscriptions, an OPAC.

Computers on Campus 425 computers available on campus for general student use. A campuswide network can be accessed from off campus. Internet access, at least one staffed computer lab available.

Student Life *Housing:* college housing not available. *Activities and Organizations:* drama/theater group, student-run newspaper, radio station, choral group, national fraternities, national sororities. *Campus security:* 24-hour emergency response devices and patrols, late-night transport/escort service. *Student Services:* health clinic, personal/psychological counseling, legal services.

Finger Lakes Community College (continued)

Athletics Member NJCAA. *Intercollegiate sports:* baseball M, basketball M/W, cross-country running M/W, lacrosse M/W, soccer M/W. *Intramural sports:* basketball M/W, tennis M/W, volleyball M/W.

Standardized Tests *Recommended:* SAT I or ACT (for placement).

Costs (2001–02) *Tuition:* state resident $2430 full-time, $93 per credit hour part-time; nonresident $4860 full-time, $186 per credit hour part-time. *Required fees:* $170 full-time, $10 per credit hour. *Payment plan:* installment. *Waivers:* senior citizens and employees or children of employees.

Financial Aid In 2001, 150 Federal Work-Study jobs (averaging $1550). 150 State and other part-time jobs (averaging $1500).

Applying *Options:* electronic application, early admission, deferred entrance. *Required:* high school transcript. *Recommended:* interview. *Application deadline:* rolling (freshmen), rolling (transfers). *Notification:* continuous until 8/31 (freshmen).

Admissions Contact Ms. Bonnie B. Ritts, Director of Admissions, Finger Lakes Community College, 4355 Lake Shore Drive, Canandaigua, NY 14424-8395. *Phone:* 716-394-3500 Ext. 7278. *Fax:* 716-394-5005. *E-mail:* admissions@flcc.edu.

FIORELLO H. LAGUARDIA COMMUNITY COLLEGE OF THE CITY UNIVERSITY OF NEW YORK

Long Island City, New York

- **State and locally supported** 2-year, founded 1970, part of City University of New York System
- **Calendar** modified semester
- **Degree** certificates and associate
- **Urban** 6-acre campus
- **Coed,** 11,427 undergraduate students

Fiorello H. LaGuardia Community College, a branch of CUNY, is a dynamic community of teachers and learners. Founded in 1971, the College supports the principles of open access and equal opportunity for all. The College fosters innovative classroom teaching, strong support services for students, and professional development opportunities for faculty members. Its 30 degree programs and 2 professional certificates meet the needs of students who want to transfer to 4-year colleges as well as those who seek immediate employment.

Undergraduates Students come from 140 other countries, 0.1% are from out of state, 17% African American, 11% Asian American or Pacific Islander, 35% Hispanic American, 0.3% Native American, 11% international. *Retention:* 65% of 2001 full-time freshmen returned.

Freshmen *Admission:* 2,940 applied, 2,549 admitted. *Average high school GPA:* 2.10.

Faculty *Total:* 790, 31% full-time.

Majors Accounting; business administration; computer engineering technology; computer programming; computer programming related; computer programming (specific applications); computer programming, vendor/product certification; computer science; computer science related; computer systems networking/telecommunications; data entry/microcomputer applications; dietetics; early childhood education; education; emergency medical technology; fine/studio arts; food products retailing; gerontology; human services; information sciences/systems; legal administrative assistant; liberal arts and sciences/liberal studies; mental health/rehabilitation; mortuary science; nursing; occupational therapy; paralegal/legal assistant; photography; physical therapy; secretarial science; system/networking/LAN/WAN management; travel/tourism management; veterinary technology.

Academic Programs *Special study options:* academic remediation for entering students, adult/continuing education programs, advanced placement credit, cooperative education, double majors, English as a second language, honors programs, independent study, internships, off-campus study, part-time degree program, services for LD students, student-designed majors, study abroad.

Library Fiorello H. LaGuardia Community College Library Media Resources Center plus 1 other with 92,744 titles, 760 serial subscriptions, 3,921 audiovisual materials, an OPAC.

Computers on Campus 900 computers available on campus for general student use. A campuswide network can be accessed from off campus. At least one staffed computer lab available.

Student Life *Housing:* college housing not available. *Activities and Organizations:* drama/theater group, student-run newspaper, radio station, Latinos Unidos Club, Bangladesh Club, Dominican Club, Law Club. *Campus security:* 24-hour patrols. *Student Services:* health clinic, personal/psychological counseling, women's center.

Athletics *Intramural sports:* basketball M/W, football M/W, golf M/W, soccer M/W, swimming M/W, table tennis M/W, tennis M/W, volleyball M/W, weight lifting M/W.

Standardized Tests *Recommended:* SAT I or ACT (for placement).

Costs (2001–02) *Tuition:* area resident $2500 full-time, $105 per unit part-time; nonresident $130 per unit part-time. Full-time tuition and fees vary according to course load. Part-time tuition and fees vary according to course load. *Required fees:* $122 full-time, $36 per term part-time. *Payment plans:* installment, deferred payment. *Waivers:* senior citizens.

Financial Aid In 2001, 1,724 Federal Work-Study jobs (averaging $1019).

Applying *Options:* electronic application, early admission, deferred entrance. *Application fee:* $40. *Required:* high school transcript. *Application deadline:* rolling (freshmen), rolling (transfers). *Notification:* continuous (freshmen).

Admissions Contact Ms. LaVora Desvigne, Director of Admissions, Fiorello H. LaGuardia Community College of the City University of New York, RM-147, 31-10 Thomson Avenue, Long Island City, NY 11101. *Phone:* 718-482-7206. *Fax:* 718-482-5112. *E-mail:* admissions@lagcc.cuny.edu.

FULTON-MONTGOMERY COMMUNITY COLLEGE

Johnstown, New York

- **State and locally supported** 2-year, founded 1964, part of State University of New York System
- **Calendar** semesters
- **Degree** certificates and associate
- **Rural** 195-acre campus
- **Endowment** $328,000
- **Coed,** 624 undergraduate students, 75% full-time, 59% women, 41% men

Undergraduates 466 full-time, 158 part-time. Students come from 3 states and territories, 20 other countries, 2% African American, 0.6% Asian American or Pacific Islander, 4% Hispanic American, 0.5% Native American, 5% international, 11% transferred in.

Freshmen *Admission:* 1,088 applied, 1,088 admitted, 624 enrolled.

Faculty *Total:* 132, 38% full-time. *Student/faculty ratio:* 21:1.

Majors Accounting; art; auto mechanic/technician; behavioral sciences; biological/physical sciences; biology; business administration; carpentry; computer engineering technology; computer science; computer typography/composition; construction technology; criminal justice/law enforcement administration; data processing technology; developmental/child psychology; early childhood education; electrical/electronic engineering technology; elementary education; engineering science; English; environmental science; finance; fine/studio arts; graphic design/commercial art/illustration; graphic/printing equipment; health education; history; humanities; human services; information sciences/systems; legal administrative assistant; liberal arts and sciences/liberal studies; mass communications; mathematics; medical administrative assistant; natural resources conservation; nursing; physical education; physical sciences; psychology; secretarial science; social sciences; teacher assistant/aide; theater arts/drama.

Academic Programs *Special study options:* academic remediation for entering students, accelerated degree program, adult/continuing education programs, advanced placement credit, cooperative education, distance learning, double majors, English as a second language, external degree program, honors programs, independent study, internships, off-campus study, part-time degree program, services for LD students, student-designed majors, study abroad, summer session for credit. *ROTC:* Army (c), Air Force (c).

Library Evans Library with 53,485 titles, 167 serial subscriptions, 1,114 audiovisual materials, an OPAC, a Web page.

Computers on Campus 250 computers available on campus for general student use. A campuswide network can be accessed from off campus. Internet access, at least one staffed computer lab available.

Student Life *Housing:* college housing not available. *Activities and Organizations:* drama/theater group, student-run newspaper, choral group, Business Students Association, Criminal Justice Club, WAU (We Are United), Ski Club. *Campus security:* weekend and night security. *Student Services:* personal/psychological counseling.

Athletics Member NJCAA. *Intercollegiate sports:* baseball M, basketball M/W, soccer M/W, softball W, volleyball W. *Intramural sports:* baseball M, basketball M/W, fencing M(c)/W(c), golf M(c)/W(c), skiing (cross-country) M(c)/W(c), skiing (downhill) M(c)/W(c), volleyball M/W.

Costs (2001–02) *Tuition:* state resident $2380 full-time, $99 per credit part-time; nonresident $4760 full-time, $198 per credit part-time. Full-time tuition and fees vary according to program. Part-time tuition and fees vary according to course load and program. *Required fees:* $136 full-time, $2 per credit, $38 per term part-time. *Payment plans:* installment, deferred payment. *Waivers:* senior citizens and employees or children of employees.

Financial Aid In 2001, 87 Federal Work-Study jobs (averaging $1000).

Applying *Options:* common application, electronic application, early admission, deferred entrance. *Required:* high school transcript. *Application deadlines:* 9/10 (freshmen), 9/10 (transfers). *Notification:* continuous (freshmen).

Admissions Contact Ms. Diane Czechowicz, Associate Dean for Enrollment Management, Fulton-Montgomery Community College, 2805 State Highway 67, Johnstown, NY 12095-3790. *Phone:* 518-762-4651 Ext. 8301. *Fax:* 518-762-4334. *E-mail:* geninfo@fmcc.suny.edu.

GENESEE COMMUNITY COLLEGE

Batavia, New York

- **State and locally supported** 2-year, founded 1966, part of State University of New York System
- **Calendar** semesters
- **Degree** certificates and associate
- **Small-town** 256-acre campus with easy access to Buffalo
- **Endowment** $890,901
- **Coed,** 4,809 undergraduate students, 46% full-time, 63% women, 37% men

Undergraduates 2,225 full-time, 2,584 part-time. Students come from 13 states and territories, 23 other countries, 1% are from out of state, 4% African American, 0.6% Asian American or Pacific Islander, 1% Hispanic American, 0.6% Native American, 2% international, 7% transferred in.

Freshmen *Admission:* 2,649 applied, 2,649 admitted, 711 enrolled.

Faculty *Total:* 333, 18% full-time. *Student/faculty ratio:* 17:1.

Majors Accounting; alcohol/drug abuse counseling; business administration; business marketing and marketing management; computer engineering technology; computer graphics; computer science related; computer software and media applications related; criminal justice/law enforcement administration; drafting; early childhood education; education; electrical/electronic engineering technology; elementary education; engineering science; fashion merchandising; gerontology; graphic design/commercial art/illustration; hotel and restaurant management; human services; information sciences/systems; liberal arts and sciences/liberal studies; mass communications; mathematics; medical laboratory technician; nursing; occupational therapy; paralegal/legal assistant; physical education; physical therapy; psychology; respiratory therapy; retail management; secretarial science; system/networking/LAN/WAN management; theater arts/drama; travel/tourism management.

Academic Programs *Special study options:* academic remediation for entering students, adult/continuing education programs, advanced placement credit, cooperative education, distance learning, honors programs, independent study, internships, part-time degree program, services for LD students, summer session for credit. *ROTC:* Army (c).

Library Alfred O'Connell Library with 78,273 titles, 332 serial subscriptions, 4,729 audiovisual materials, an OPAC, a Web page.

Computers on Campus 408 computers available on campus for general student use. A campuswide network can be accessed from off campus that provide access to applications software. Internet access, at least one staffed computer lab available.

Student Life *Activities and Organizations:* drama/theater group, student-run newspaper, radio station, choral group, Student Government Association, Phi Theta Kappa, DECA, Student Activities Council, Forum Players. *Campus security:* 24-hour emergency response devices and patrols, late-night transport/escort service. *Student Services:* health clinic, personal/psychological counseling.

Athletics Member NJCAA. *Intercollegiate sports:* baseball M, basketball M(s)/W(s), cross-country running M/W, soccer M/W(s), softball W, swimming M/W, volleyball M/W(s). *Intramural sports:* badminton M/W, basketball M/W, football M/W, golf M/W, soccer M/W, softball M/W, swimming M/W, table tennis M/W, tennis M/W, track and field M/W, volleyball M/W, water polo M/W, weight lifting M/W.

Standardized Tests *Required:* ACT ASSET, ACT COMPASS.

Costs (2001–02) *Tuition:* state resident $2500 full-time, $97 per credit hour part-time; nonresident $2850 full-time, $106 per credit hour part-time. Full-time tuition and fees vary according to program. Part-time tuition and fees vary according to course load and program. *Required fees:* $272 full-time, $2 per credit, $8 per term part-time. *Room and board:* $4750; room only: $2995. *Waivers:* senior citizens and employees or children of employees.

Financial Aid In 2001, 115 Federal Work-Study jobs (averaging $1400). *Financial aid deadline:* 5/1.

Applying *Options:* common application, electronic application, early admission. *Required:* high school transcript. *Required for some:* 1 letter of recommendation. *Application deadline:* rolling (freshmen), rolling (transfers). *Notification:* continuous (freshmen).

Admissions Contact Mrs. Tanya Lane-Martin, Director of Admissions, Genesee Community College, 1 College Road, Batavia, NY 14020. *Phone:* 585-343-0055 Ext. 6413. *Toll-free phone:* 800-CALL GCC. *Fax:* 585-345-6810.

HELENE FULD COLLEGE OF NURSING OF NORTH GENERAL HOSPITAL

New York, New York

- **Independent** 2-year, founded 1945
- **Calendar** quarters
- **Degrees** associate (program only open to licensed practical nurses)
- **Urban** campus
- **Coed, primarily women,** 296 undergraduate students, 50% full-time, 90% women, 10% men

Undergraduates 149 full-time, 147 part-time. Students come from 3 states and territories, 3% are from out of state, 85% African American, 4% Asian American or Pacific Islander, 7% Hispanic American, 20% transferred in.

Freshmen *Admission:* 16 applied, 16 admitted, 16 enrolled.

Faculty *Total:* 26, 38% full-time, 12% with terminal degrees. *Student/faculty ratio:* 13:1.

Majors Nursing.

Academic Programs *Special study options:* accelerated degree program, part-time degree program, summer session for credit.

Library 6,200 titles, 82 serial subscriptions, 131 audiovisual materials.

Computers on Campus 24 computers available on campus for general student use. Internet access, at least one staffed computer lab available.

Student Life *Housing:* college housing not available. *Campus security:* security guard during open hours. *Student Services:* personal/psychological counseling.

Costs (2002–03) *One-time required fee:* $325. *Tuition:* $11,520 full-time, $196 per quarter hour part-time. *Required fees:* $280 full-time, $35 per term part-time.

Applying *Options:* deferred entrance. *Application fee:* $50. *Required:* essay or personal statement, high school transcript, 1 letter of recommendation, interview, must be Licensed Practical Nurse. *Application deadline:* rolling (freshmen), rolling (transfers).

Admissions Contact Mrs. Gladys Pineda, Student Services, Helene Fuld College of Nursing of North General Hospital, 1879 Madison Avenue, New York, NY 10035. *Phone:* 212-423-2768.

HERKIMER COUNTY COMMUNITY COLLEGE

Herkimer, New York

- **State and locally supported** 2-year, founded 1966, part of State University of New York System
- **Calendar** semesters
- **Degree** certificates and associate
- **Small-town** 500-acre campus with easy access to Syracuse
- **Endowment** $1.7 million
- **Coed,** 2,873 undergraduate students, 70% full-time, 57% women, 43% men

Undergraduates 2,002 full-time, 871 part-time. Students come from 23 states and territories, 17 other countries, 2% are from out of state, 5% transferred in, 25% live on campus.

Freshmen *Admission:* 2,796 applied, 2,796 admitted, 849 enrolled. *Test scores:* SAT verbal scores over 500: 30%; SAT math scores over 500: 31%; SAT verbal scores over 600: 5%; SAT math scores over 600: 3%; SAT verbal scores over 700: 1%.

Faculty *Total:* 128, 62% full-time, 9% with terminal degrees. *Student/faculty ratio:* 24:1.

Majors Accounting; art; arts management; biological/physical sciences; biology; broadcast journalism; building maintenance/management; business administration; business marketing and marketing management; chemistry; child care/development; child care provider; communication systems installation/repair; computer/information sciences related; computer installation/repair; computer programming; computer programming related; computer science; computer science related; computer systems networking/telecommunications; construction management; construction technology; corrections; criminal justice/law enforcement administration; data entry/microcomputer applications; data entry/

Herkimer County Community College (continued)
microcomputer applications related; early childhood education; English; fashion merchandising; health services administration; humanities; human resources management; human services; information sciences/systems; law enforcement/police science; liberal arts and sciences/liberal studies; mathematics; medical administrative assistant; occupational therapy; paralegal/legal assistant; photography; physical education; physical therapy; purchasing/contracts management; radio/television broadcasting; sport/fitness administration; system/networking/LAN/WAN management; technical/business writing; telecommunications; tourism promotion operations; travel services marketing operations; travel/tourism management.

Academic Programs *Special study options:* academic remediation for entering students, adult/continuing education programs, advanced placement credit, English as a second language, honors programs, internships, part-time degree program, services for LD students, summer session for credit.

Library Herkimer County Community College Library with 62,484 titles, 315 serial subscriptions, an OPAC.

Computers on Campus 222 computers available on campus for general student use. A campuswide network can be accessed from off campus. At least one staffed computer lab available.

Student Life *Housing Options:* coed. *Activities and Organizations:* drama/theater group, student-run newspaper, radio and television station, Criminal Justice Club, Travel Club, Student Senate, Physical Therapy Club. *Campus security:* 24-hour emergency response devices and patrols. *Student Services:* personal/psychological counseling.

Athletics Member NJCAA. *Intercollegiate sports:* baseball M, basketball M/W, bowling M/W, cross-country running M/W, field hockey W, golf M/W, lacrosse M, soccer M/W, softball W, swimming M/W, tennis M/W, track and field M/W, volleyball W. *Intramural sports:* baseball M, basketball M/W, lacrosse M, soccer M/W, softball W, swimming M/W, tennis M/W, volleyball M/W.

Standardized Tests *Recommended:* SAT I or ACT (for placement).

Costs (2002–03) *Tuition:* state resident $2400 full-time, $80 per credit hour part-time; nonresident $4200 full-time, $145 per credit hour part-time. Full-time tuition and fees vary according to course load and student level. Part-time tuition and fees vary according to course load. *Required fees:* $284 full-time, $11 per term part-time. *Room and board:* $5200; room only: $5100. Room and board charges vary according to board plan. *Payment plans:* installment, deferred payment. *Waivers:* employees or children of employees.

Financial Aid In 2001, 150 Federal Work-Study jobs (averaging $700).

Applying *Options:* common application, early admission. *Required:* high school transcript. *Application deadlines:* 8/20 (freshmen), 8/20 (transfers). *Notification:* continuous (freshmen).

Admissions Contact Mr. Philip G. Hubbard, Associate Dean for Enrollment Management and Marketing, Herkimer County Community College, Herkimer, NY 13350. *Phone:* 315-866-0300 Ext. 278. *Toll-free phone:* 888-464-4222 Ext. 278. *Fax:* 315-866-7253. *E-mail:* admission@hccc.suny.edu.

HUDSON VALLEY COMMUNITY COLLEGE
Troy, New York

- **State and locally supported** 2-year, founded 1953, part of State University of New York System
- **Calendar** semesters
- **Degree** certificates and associate
- **Suburban** 135-acre campus
- **Coed**

Student Life *Campus security:* 24-hour emergency response devices and patrols, late-night transport/escort service.

Athletics Member NJCAA.

Standardized Tests *Required for some:* SAT I or ACT (for placement). *Recommended:* SAT I or ACT (for placement).

Financial Aid In 2001, 100 Federal Work-Study jobs (averaging $2000).

Applying *Options:* early admission, deferred entrance. *Application fee:* $25. *Required:* high school transcript.

Admissions Contact Ms. MaryClaire Bauer, Director of Admissions, Hudson Valley Community College, 80 Vandenburgh Avenue, Troy, NY 12180-6096. *Phone:* 518-629-4603. *E-mail:* panzajul@hvcc.edu.

INSTITUTE OF DESIGN AND CONSTRUCTION
Brooklyn, New York

- **Independent** 2-year, founded 1947
- **Calendar** semesters
- **Degree** associate
- **Urban** campus
- **Coed, primarily men,** 248 undergraduate students

Undergraduates Students come from 3 states and territories, 4 other countries, 3% are from out of state, 38% African American, 9% Asian American or Pacific Islander, 19% Hispanic American, 2% international.

Freshmen *Admission:* 80 applied, 74 admitted.

Faculty *Total:* 32.

Majors Architectural engineering technology; construction technology; drafting; interior architecture.

Academic Programs *Special study options:* academic remediation for entering students, adult/continuing education programs, advanced placement credit, cooperative education, part-time degree program, summer session for credit.

Computers on Campus 17 computers available on campus for general student use.

Student Life *Housing:* college housing not available. *Student Services:* personal/psychological counseling.

Costs (2001–02) *Tuition:* $5400 full-time, $180 per credit part-time. *Required fees:* $50 full-time, $25 per term part-time.

Applying *Options:* common application. *Application fee:* $30. *Required:* high school transcript. *Recommended:* interview. *Application deadline:* rolling (freshmen). *Notification:* continuous until 9/30 (freshmen).

Admissions Contact Mr. Kevin Giannetti, Director of Admissions, Institute of Design and Construction, 141 Willoughby Street, Brooklyn, NY 11201-5317. *Phone:* 718-855-3661. *Fax:* 718-852-5889.

INTERBORO INSTITUTE
New York, New York

- **Proprietary** 2-year, founded 1888
- **Calendar** semesters
- **Degree** associate
- **Urban** campus
- **Coed,** 1,344 undergraduate students

Undergraduates Students come from 10 other countries.

Freshmen *Admission:* 1,429 applied, 659 admitted.

Faculty *Total:* 59, 42% full-time. *Student/faculty ratio:* 37:1.

Majors Accounting; business administration; legal administrative assistant; medical administrative assistant; optometric/ophthalmic laboratory technician; paralegal/legal assistant; safety/security technology; secretarial science.

Academic Programs *Special study options:* academic remediation for entering students, accelerated degree program, adult/continuing education programs, advanced placement credit, cooperative education, independent study, internships, summer session for credit.

Library Interboro Library with 5,986 titles, 98 serial subscriptions, an OPAC, a Web page.

Computers on Campus 78 computers available on campus for general student use. A campuswide network can be accessed from off campus. Internet access, at least one staffed computer lab available.

Student Life *Housing:* college housing not available. *Activities and Organizations:* student-run newspaper, OPT Society. *Campus security:* student patrols. *Student Services:* personal/psychological counseling.

Athletics *Intramural sports:* baseball M/W.

Standardized Tests *Required for some:* CPAt.

Costs (2001–02) *Tuition:* $7800 full-time, $325 per credit part-time. *Required fees:* $25 full-time.

Applying *Options:* deferred entrance. *Application fee:* $28. *Required:* essay or personal statement, interview. *Recommended:* high school transcript. *Application deadline:* rolling (freshmen), rolling (transfers). *Notification:* continuous (freshmen).

Admissions Contact Ms. Cheryl Ryan, Director of Admissions, Interboro Institute, 450 West 56th Street, New York, NY 10019-3602. *Phone:* 212-399-0091 Ext. 151. *Fax:* 212-765-5772. *E-mail:* ryan@interboro.com.

ISLAND DRAFTING AND TECHNICAL INSTITUTE
Amityville, New York

- **Proprietary** 2-year, founded 1957
- **Degree** certificates, diplomas, and associate
- 241 undergraduate students, 100% full-time

Undergraduates 241 full-time. Students come from 1 other state, 14% African American, 3% Asian American or Pacific Islander, 17% Hispanic American.
Freshmen *Admission:* 141 applied, 104 admitted, 104 enrolled. *Average high school GPA:* 3.50.
Faculty *Total:* 28, 29% full-time, 4% with terminal degrees. *Student/faculty ratio:* 15:1.
Majors Architectural drafting; computer/information systems security; computer maintenance technology; computer systems networking/telecommunications; computer/technical support; mechanical drafting; system/networking/LAN/WAN management.
Academic Programs *Special study options:* accelerated degree program, adult/continuing education programs, summer session for credit.
Costs (2002–03) *Tuition:* $9450 full-time, $335 per credit part-time. *Required fees:* $350 full-time, $18 per credit.
Applying *Options:* early admission. *Required:* interview. *Recommended:* high school transcript. *Notification:* continuous (freshmen).
Admissions Contact Mr. Gary Weiller, Island Drafting and Technical Institute, 128 Broadway, Amityville, NY 11701. *Phone:* 631-691-8733. *Fax:* 631-691-8738. *E-mail:* info@islanddrafting.com.

ITT Technical Institute
Albany, New York

- **Proprietary** 2-year
- **Calendar** quarters
- **Degree** associate
- **Coed,** 245 undergraduate students

Majors Computer/information sciences related; computer programming; electrical/electronic engineering technologies related; information technology.
Student Life *Housing:* college housing not available.
Costs (2001–02) *Tuition:* Full-time tuition and fees vary according to program. Part-time tuition and fees vary according to program. $260—$330 per credit hour.
Applying *Application fee:* $100. *Required:* high school transcript, interview. *Recommended:* letters of recommendation. *Application deadline:* rolling (freshmen). *Notification:* continuous (freshmen).
Admissions Contact Mr. Bob Barton, Director of Recruitment, ITT Technical Institute, 13 Airline Drive, Albany, NY 12205. *Phone:* 518-452-9300.

ITT Technical Institute
Liverpool, New York

- **Proprietary** 2-year
- **Calendar** semesters
- **Degree** associate
- **Coed,** 267 undergraduate students

Majors Computer/information sciences related; computer programming; electrical/electronic engineering technologies related; information technology.
Student Life *Housing:* college housing not available.
Costs (2001–02) *Tuition:* Full-time tuition and fees vary according to program. Part-time tuition and fees vary according to program. $260—$330 per credit hour.
Applying *Application fee:* $100. *Required:* high school transcript, interview. *Recommended:* letters of recommendation. *Application deadline:* rolling (freshmen). *Notification:* continuous (freshmen).
Admissions Contact Terry Riesel, Director of Recruitment, ITT Technical Institute, 235 Greenfield Parkway, Liverpool, NY 13088. *Phone:* 315-461-8000.

ITT Technical Institute
Getzville, New York

- **Proprietary** 2-year
- **Degree** associate
- **Coed,** 595 undergraduate students

Majors Computer/information sciences related; computer programming; drafting; electrical/electronic engineering technologies related; information technology.
Student Life *Housing:* college housing not available.
Costs (2001–02) *Tuition:* Full-time tuition and fees vary according to program. Part-time tuition and fees vary according to program. $260—$330 per credit hour.
Applying *Application fee:* $100. *Required:* high school transcript, interview. *Recommended:* letters of recommendation. *Application deadline:* rolling (freshmen). *Notification:* continuous (freshmen).
Admissions Contact Ms. Suzanne Noel, Director of Recruitment, ITT Technical Institute, 2295 Millersport Highway, Getzville, NY 14068. *Phone:* 716-689-2200. *Toll-free phone:* 800-469-7593.

Jamestown Business College
Jamestown, New York

- **Proprietary** 2-year, founded 1886
- **Calendar** quarters
- **Degree** certificates and associate
- **Small-town** 1-acre campus
- **Coed,** 298 undergraduate students, 98% full-time, 79% women, 21% men

Undergraduates 292 full-time, 6 part-time. Students come from 2 states and territories, 10% are from out of state, 2% African American, 1% Asian American or Pacific Islander, 6% Hispanic American, 1% Native American, 16% transferred in.
Freshmen *Admission:* 140 applied, 137 admitted, 90 enrolled. *Average high school GPA:* 3.0.
Faculty *Total:* 16, 38% full-time. *Student/faculty ratio:* 24:1.
Majors Accounting; business administration; business marketing and marketing management; computer/information sciences; legal administrative assistant; medical administrative assistant; secretarial science.
Academic Programs *Special study options:* academic remediation for entering students, advanced placement credit, double majors, internships, part-time degree program, summer session for credit.
Library James Prendergast Library with 279,270 titles, 372 serial subscriptions, an OPAC, a Web page.
Computers on Campus 106 computers available on campus for general student use. A campuswide network can be accessed from off campus. Internet access, at least one staffed computer lab available.
Student Life *Housing:* college housing not available. *Campus security:* 24-hour emergency response devices.
Athletics *Intramural sports:* basketball M(c)/W(c), bowling M(c)/W(c), racquetball M(c)/W(c), skiing (cross-country) M(c)/W(c), skiing (downhill) M(c)/W(c), softball M(c)/W(c), swimming M(c)/W(c), table tennis M(c)/W(c), volleyball M(c)/W(c), weight lifting M(c)/W(c).
Costs (2001–02) *Tuition:* $7200 full-time, $1200 per course part-time. *Required fees:* $360 full-time, $120 per term part-time. *Payment plan:* installment. *Waivers:* employees or children of employees.
Applying *Application fee:* $25. *Required:* essay or personal statement, high school transcript, interview. *Application deadline:* rolling (freshmen), rolling (transfers).
Admissions Contact Ms. Brenda Salemme, Director of Admissions and Placement, Jamestown Business College, 7 Fairmount Avenue, Jamestown, NY 14701. *Phone:* 716-664-5100. *Fax:* 716-664-3144. *E-mail:* admissions@jbcny.org.

Jamestown Community College
Jamestown, New York

- **State and locally supported** 2-year, founded 1950, part of State University of New York System
- **Calendar** semesters
- **Degree** certificates and associate
- **Small-town** 107-acre campus
- **Endowment** $3.3 million
- **Coed,** 4,092 undergraduate students, 47% full-time, 57% women, 43% men

Undergraduates 1,910 full-time, 2,182 part-time. 8% are from out of state, 2% African American, 0.7% Asian American or Pacific Islander, 2% Hispanic American, 0.9% Native American.
Freshmen *Admission:* 1,395 applied, 1,217 admitted, 1,020 enrolled.
Faculty *Total:* 266, 28% full-time. *Student/faculty ratio:* 16:1.
Majors Accounting; biological/physical sciences; business administration; computer engineering technology; computer programming (specific applications); computer science; computer science related; criminal justice/law enforcement administration; electrical/electronic engineering technology; engineering science; fine/studio arts; humanities; human services; information sciences/systems; information technology; law enforcement/police science; liberal arts and sciences/

Jamestown Community College (continued)
liberal studies; mass communications; mathematics; mechanical engineering technology; music; nursing; occupational therapy assistant; pre-engineering; social sciences.

Academic Programs *Special study options:* academic remediation for entering students, adult/continuing education programs, advanced placement credit, cooperative education, distance learning, double majors, English as a second language, honors programs, independent study, internships, off-campus study, part-time degree program, services for LD students, student-designed majors, study abroad, summer session for credit.

Library Hultquist Library plus 1 other with 79,510 titles, 585 serial subscriptions, 7,126 audiovisual materials, an OPAC, a Web page.

Computers on Campus 400 computers available on campus for general student use. A campuswide network can be accessed from off campus. At least one staffed computer lab available.

Student Life *Housing:* college housing not available. *Activities and Organizations:* drama/theater group, student-run newspaper, radio station, choral group, Nursing Club, Criminal Justice Club, Earth Awareness, Student Advisory Board, Intervarsity Christian Fellowship. *Student Services:* health clinic, personal/psychological counseling.

Athletics Member NJCAA. *Intercollegiate sports:* baseball M, basketball M(s)/W(s), cross-country running M/W, golf M/W, soccer M/W(s), softball W(s), swimming M/W, volleyball W. *Intramural sports:* basketball M/W, bowling M/W, football M/W, table tennis M/W, tennis M/W, volleyball M/W.

Standardized Tests *Required:* ACT ASSET.

Costs (2002–03) *Tuition:* $113 per credit hour part-time; state resident $2700 full-time, $113 per credit hour part-time; nonresident $5400 full-time, $204 per credit hour part-time. *Required fees:* $350 full-time. *Payment plans:* installment, deferred payment. *Waivers:* senior citizens and employees or children of employees.

Financial Aid In 2001, 100 Federal Work-Study jobs (averaging $1000). 120 State and other part-time jobs (averaging $1000).

Applying *Options:* early admission, deferred entrance. *Application fee:* $30. *Required:* high school transcript. *Required for some:* essay or personal statement. *Application deadline:* rolling (freshmen), rolling (transfers). *Notification:* continuous (freshmen).

Admissions Contact Ms. Wendy Martenson, Coordinator of Admissions and Recruitment, Jamestown Community College, 525 Falconer Street, PO Box 20, Jamestown, NY 14702-0020. *Phone:* 716-665-5220 Ext. 2240. *Toll-free phone:* 800-388-8557. *E-mail:* admissions@mail.sunyjcc.edu.

JEFFERSON COMMUNITY COLLEGE
Watertown, New York

- **State and locally supported** 2-year, founded 1961, part of State University of New York System
- **Calendar** semesters
- **Degree** certificates and associate
- **Small-town** 90-acre campus with easy access to Syracuse
- **Endowment** $1.9 million
- **Coed,** 3,602 undergraduate students, 51% full-time, 57% women, 43% men

Undergraduates 1,824 full-time, 1,778 part-time. Students come from 7 states and territories, 3 other countries, 1% are from out of state, 7% transferred in.

Freshmen *Admission:* 604 enrolled. *Test scores:* SAT verbal scores over 500: 25%; SAT math scores over 500: 28%; ACT scores over 18: 70%; SAT verbal scores over 600: 3%; SAT math scores over 600: 5%; ACT scores over 24: 8%.

Faculty *Total:* 189, 39% full-time. *Student/faculty ratio:* 17:1.

Majors Accounting; biological technology; business administration; business marketing and marketing management; chemical technology; computer science; computer systems networking/telecommunications; computer typography/composition; criminal justice/law enforcement administration; early childhood education; engineering science; forest harvesting production technology; hospitality management; hotel and restaurant management; humanities; human services; information sciences/systems; interdisciplinary studies; liberal arts and sciences/liberal studies; mathematics; medical administrative assistant; medical laboratory technology; natural sciences; nursing; paralegal/legal assistant; pre-engineering; retail management; secretarial science; travel/tourism management.

Academic Programs *Special study options:* academic remediation for entering students, advanced placement credit, cooperative education, distance learning, double majors, honors programs, independent study, internships, part-time degree program, services for LD students, student-designed majors, summer session for credit.

Library Melvil Dewey Library with 58,612 titles, 322 serial subscriptions, 3,329 audiovisual materials, an OPAC, a Web page.

Computers on Campus 290 computers available on campus for general student use. Internet access, at least one staffed computer lab available.

Student Life *Housing:* college housing not available. *Activities and Organizations:* drama/theater group, student-run newspaper, choral group, Student Nursing Association, newspaper, The Melting Pot, Paralegal Club, Criminal Justice Club. *Campus security:* 24-hour emergency response devices and patrols. *Student Services:* health clinic, personal/psychological counseling.

Athletics Member NJCAA. *Intercollegiate sports:* baseball M, basketball M/W, golf M/W, lacrosse M, soccer M/W, softball W, volleyball W. *Intramural sports:* badminton M/W, basketball M/W, soccer M/W, softball M/W, volleyball M/W.

Standardized Tests *Recommended:* SAT I or ACT (for admission).

Costs (2001–02) *Tuition:* $91 per credit hour part-time; state resident $2372 full-time, $91 per credit hour part-time; nonresident $3302 full-time, $130 per credit hour part-time. *Required fees:* $211 full-time. *Payment plan:* installment. *Waivers:* senior citizens.

Financial Aid In 2001, 125 Federal Work-Study jobs (averaging $1200). 50 State and other part-time jobs (averaging $1000).

Applying *Options:* early admission, deferred entrance. *Required:* high school transcript. *Required for some:* letters of recommendation, interview. *Application deadline:* 9/6 (freshmen), rolling (transfers). *Notification:* continuous (freshmen).

Admissions Contact Ms. Rosanne N. Weir, Director of Admissions, Jefferson Community College, 1220 Coffeen Street, Watertown, NY 13601. *Phone:* 315-786-2277. *Fax:* 315-786-2459. *E-mail:* admissions@ccmgate.sunyjefferson.edu.

KATHARINE GIBBS SCHOOL
New York, New York

- **Proprietary** 2-year, founded 1918, part of Career Education Corporation
- **Calendar** quarters
- **Degree** certificates and associate
- **Urban** campus
- **Coed**

Faculty *Student/faculty ratio:* 20:1.

Standardized Tests *Recommended:* SAT I (for admission).

Costs (2001–02) *Tuition:* $12,000 full-time. No tuition increase for student's term of enrollment. *Required fees:* $120 full-time.

Applying *Options:* deferred entrance. *Application fee:* $50. *Required:* essay or personal statement, high school transcript, interview.

Admissions Contact Stacey Fischer, Admissions Director, Katharine Gibbs School, 50 West 40th Street, New York, NY 10018. *Phone:* 212-867-9300.

KATHARINE GIBBS SCHOOL
Melville, New York

Admissions Contact Mr. Louis A. Cassano, Director of Admissions, Katharine Gibbs School, 320 South Service Road, Melville, NY 11747-3785. *Phone:* 516-293-2460. *Fax:* 516-293-2709.

KINGSBOROUGH COMMUNITY COLLEGE OF THE CITY UNIVERSITY OF NEW YORK
Brooklyn, New York

- **State and locally supported** 2-year, founded 1963, part of City University of New York System
- **Calendar** semesters
- **Degree** associate
- **Urban** 67-acre campus with easy access to New York City
- **Coed,** 15,055 undergraduate students, 52% full-time, 59% women, 41% men

Undergraduates 7,757 full-time, 7,298 part-time. 4% are from out of state, 32% African American, 9% Asian American or Pacific Islander, 15% Hispanic American, 0.2% Native American, 7% international, 8% transferred in.

Freshmen *Admission:* 2,045 enrolled. *Average high school GPA:* 1.93. *Test scores:* SAT verbal scores over 500: 9%; SAT math scores over 500: 13%; SAT verbal scores over 600: 1%; SAT math scores over 600: 1%.

Faculty *Total:* 752, 31% full-time, 37% with terminal degrees. *Student/faculty ratio:* 25:1.

Majors Accounting; applied art; art; biology; business administration; business marketing and marketing management; chemistry; child care services management; community health liaison; computer/information sciences; computer science; early childhood education; education; elementary education; engineering science; environmental health; fashion merchandising; graphic design/commercial art/illustration; health/physical education/fitness related; human services; journalism; labor/personnel relations; liberal arts and sciences/liberal studies; marine technology; mathematics; mental health/rehabilitation; music; nursing; physical therapy; physical therapy assistant; physics; recreation/leisure studies; secretarial science; sport/fitness administration; theater arts/drama; travel/tourism management.

Academic Programs *Special study options:* academic remediation for entering students, adult/continuing education programs, advanced placement credit, English as a second language, honors programs, internships, off-campus study, part-time degree program, services for LD students, student-designed majors, summer session for credit.

Library Robert J. Kibbee Library with 135,412 titles, 493 serial subscriptions, an OPAC.

Computers on Campus 400 computers available on campus for general student use. Internet access, at least one staffed computer lab available.

Student Life *Housing:* college housing not available. *Activities and Organizations:* drama/theater group, student-run newspaper, radio station, Peer Advisors, Caribbean Club, DECA. *Campus security:* 24-hour emergency response devices and patrols. *Student Services:* health clinic, personal/psychological counseling, women's center.

Athletics Member NJCAA. *Intercollegiate sports:* baseball M, basketball M/W, soccer M, softball W, tennis M, volleyball W. *Intramural sports:* baseball M, basketball M/W, soccer M, softball W, tennis M/W, track and field M/W, volleyball W.

Costs (2001–02) *Tuition:* state resident $2500 full-time, $105 per credit part-time; nonresident $3076 full-time, $130 per credit part-time. Full-time tuition and fees vary according to program. Part-time tuition and fees vary according to program. *Required fees:* $100 full-time, $25 per term part-time. *Payment plan:* installment. *Waivers:* senior citizens and employees or children of employees.

Applying *Options:* common application. *Application fee:* $40. *Required:* high school transcript. *Application deadline:* rolling (freshmen), rolling (transfers).

Admissions Contact Mr. Robert Ingenito, Director of Development and Recruitment, Kingsborough Community College of the City University of New York, 2001 Oriental Blvd, Manhattan Beach, Brooklyn, NY 11235. *Phone:* 718-368-5800. *E-mail:* adminfo@kbcc.cuny.edu.

LONG ISLAND BUSINESS INSTITUTE

Commack, New York

- **Proprietary** 2-year, founded 1968
- **Calendar** trimesters
- **Degree** certificates, diplomas, and associate
- **Suburban** campus with easy access to New York City
- **Coed, primarily women,** 104 undergraduate students, 43% full-time, 100% women

Undergraduates 45 full-time, 59 part-time. Students come from 1 other state, 15% African American, 7% Hispanic American.

Freshmen *Admission:* 39 applied, 39 admitted, 39 enrolled.

Faculty *Total:* 21, 29% full-time. *Student/faculty ratio:* 15:1.

Majors Accounting; business administration; court reporting; secretarial science.

Academic Programs *Special study options:* academic remediation for entering students, adult/continuing education programs, advanced placement credit, independent study, internships, part-time degree program, summer session for credit.

Library Mendon W. Smith Memorial Library with 1,484 titles, 15 serial subscriptions, 184 audiovisual materials, an OPAC.

Computers on Campus 77 computers available on campus for general student use. Internet access, at least one staffed computer lab available.

Student Life *Housing:* college housing not available. *Campus security:* 24-hour emergency response devices. *Student Services:* personal/psychological counseling.

Standardized Tests *Required:* CPAt.

Costs (2001–02) *Tuition:* $8500 full-time, $275 per credit part-time. Full-time tuition and fees vary according to course load, degree level, and program. Part-time tuition and fees vary according to course load, degree level, and program. *Required fees:* $50 full-time, $50 per year part-time. *Payment plan:* installment.

Applying *Application fee:* $50. *Required:* essay or personal statement, high school transcript, interview. *Application deadline:* rolling (freshmen), rolling (transfers).

Admissions Contact Robbie Woliver, Admissions Counselor, Long Island Business Institute, 6500 Jericho Turnpike, Commack, NY 11725. *Phone:* 631-499-7100. *Fax:* 631-499-7114.

LONG ISLAND COLLEGE HOSPITAL SCHOOL OF NURSING

Brooklyn, New York

Admissions Contact Ms. Barbara J. Evans, Admissions Assistant, Long Island College Hospital School of Nursing, 397 Hicks Street, Brooklyn, NY 11201-5940. *Phone:* 718-780-1898. *Fax:* 718-780-1936.

MARIA COLLEGE

Albany, New York

- **Independent** 2-year, founded 1958
- **Calendar** semesters
- **Degree** certificates and associate
- **Urban** 9-acre campus
- **Coed**

Clinical facilities for nursing, physical therapist studies, and occupational therapy assistant studies majors are among the institutional leaders. Laboratory school for education majors is among the finest in the Capital District. Liberal arts, early childhood education, and business majors are highly transferable. Also offered are associate degrees in computer information systems and legal assistant studies. One-year certificate programs include legal assistant studies, bereavement studies, complementary therapy, and gerontology.

Faculty *Student/faculty ratio:* 8:1.

Student Life *Campus security:* late-night transport/escort service.

Standardized Tests *Required:* SAT I or ACT (for admission).

Financial Aid In 2001, 43 Federal Work-Study jobs (averaging $1000).

Applying *Options:* early admission. *Application fee:* $25. *Required:* essay or personal statement, high school transcript, minimum 2.0 GPA, 1 letter of recommendation, interview.

Admissions Contact Ms. Laurie A. Gilmore, Director of Admissions, Maria College, 700 New Scotland Avenue, Albany, NY 12208. *Phone:* 518-438-3111 Ext. 17. *Fax:* 518-453-1366. *E-mail:* admissions@mariacollege.org.

MILDRED ELLEY

Latham, New York

- **Private** 2-year
- **Degree** certificates, diplomas, and associate
- 387 undergraduate students
- 100% of applicants were admitted

Freshmen *Admission:* 158 applied, 158 admitted.

Faculty *Total:* 43, 28% full-time. *Student/faculty ratio:* 20:1.

Majors Business administration; information technology; medical assistant; paralegal/legal assistant.

Costs (2002–03) *Tuition:* $3720 full-time. *Required fees:* $150 full-time.

Admissions Contact Laura Barber, Director of Admission, Mildred Elley, 800 New Louden Road, Latham, NY 12110. *Phone:* 518-786-3171. *Toll-free phone:* 800-622-6327.

MOHAWK VALLEY COMMUNITY COLLEGE

Utica, New York

- **State and locally supported** 2-year, founded 1946, part of State University of New York System
- **Calendar** semesters
- **Degree** certificates and associate
- **Suburban** 80-acre campus
- **Endowment** $2.5 million
- **Coed,** 5,287 undergraduate students

Undergraduates Students come from 14 states and territories, 21 other countries, 1% are from out of state, 5% African American, 1% Asian American or Pacific Islander, 2% Hispanic American, 0.6% Native American, 2% international, 6% live on campus.

Freshmen *Admission:* 2,987 applied, 2,718 admitted.

Faculty *Total:* 273, 52% full-time. *Student/faculty ratio:* 18:1.

Majors Accounting; advertising; aircraft mechanic/airframe; alcohol/drug abuse counseling; art; biological/physical sciences; biology; business administration;

Mohawk Valley Community College (continued)
business marketing and marketing management; chemical engineering technology; chemistry; child care/development; civil engineering technology; communication equipment technology; community services; computer graphics; computer programming; computer programming (specific applications); computer science; computer science related; computer systems networking/telecommunications; computer typography/composition; criminal justice/law enforcement administration; data processing technology; dietetics; drafting; electrical/electronic engineering technology; engineering; engineering science; environmental science; finance; fine/studio arts; food products retailing; food services technology; graphic design/commercial art/illustration; graphic/printing equipment; heating/air conditioning/refrigeration; hospitality management; hotel and restaurant management; humanities; human services; industrial radiologic technology; industrial technology; information sciences/systems; insurance/risk management; international business; international relations; legal administrative assistant; liberal arts and sciences/liberal studies; machine technology; mathematics; mechanical design technology; mechanical engineering technology; medical administrative assistant; medical laboratory technology; medical records administration; mental health/rehabilitation; metallurgical technology; nursing; nutrition science; physical education; physics; pre-engineering; recreation/leisure facilities management; recreation/leisure studies; respiratory therapy; retail management; secretarial science; social sciences; surveying; telecommunications; welding technology; word processing.

Academic Programs *Special study options:* academic remediation for entering students, adult/continuing education programs, advanced placement credit, English as a second language, internships, off-campus study, part-time degree program, services for LD students, summer session for credit. *ROTC:* Army (c).

Library Mohawk Valley Community College Library plus 2 others with 91,000 titles, 925 serial subscriptions, an OPAC, a Web page.

Computers on Campus 380 computers available on campus for general student use. A campuswide network can be accessed from off campus. Internet access, online (class) registration, at least one staffed computer lab available.

Student Life *Housing Options:* coed. *Activities and Organizations:* drama/theater group, student-run newspaper, radio station, choral group, Drama Club, Student Congress, Returning Adult Student Association, Black Student Union, Program Board. *Campus security:* 24-hour emergency response devices and patrols, late-night transport/escort service, controlled dormitory access. *Student Services:* health clinic, personal/psychological counseling.

Athletics Member NJCAA. *Intercollegiate sports:* baseball M, basketball M/W, bowling M/W, cross-country running M/W, golf M/W, ice hockey M, lacrosse M, soccer M/W, softball W, tennis M/W, track and field M/W, volleyball W, wrestling M. *Intramural sports:* basketball M/W, cross-country running M/W, football M, racquetball M/W, softball M, swimming M/W.

Costs (2002–03) *Tuition:* area resident $2500 full-time, $95 per credit hour part-time; state resident $95 per credit hour part-time; nonresident $190 per credit hour part-time. Part-time tuition and fees vary according to course load. *Required fees:* $140 full-time, $1 per credit hour. *Room and board:* $5685. Room and board charges vary according to board plan. *Payment plans:* installment, deferred payment. *Waivers:* employees or children of employees.

Applying *Options:* electronic application, early admission, deferred entrance. *Required:* high school transcript. *Application deadline:* rolling (freshmen), rolling (transfers).

Admissions Contact Mrs. Sandra Fiebiger, Electronic Data Processing Clerk, Admissions, Mohawk Valley Community College, 1101 Sherman Drive, Utica, NY 13501. *Phone:* 315-792-5640. *Toll-free phone:* 800-SEE-MVCC. *E-mail:* admissions@mvcc.edu.

MONROE COLLEGE
Bronx, New York

- **Proprietary** primarily 2-year, founded 1933
- **Calendar** trimesters
- **Degrees** associate and bachelor's
- **Urban** campus
- **Coed,** 3,449 undergraduate students, 86% full-time, 72% women, 28% men

Monroe, New York's business technology college, is a private, coeducational institution that offers associate and bachelor's (2+2) degrees, with New York City and Westchester County campuses. Programs encompass a variety of majors that develop the student's career. Monroe's dynamic faculty members and strong support services foster professional development opportunities for students.

Undergraduates 2,974 full-time, 475 part-time. Students come from 4 states and territories, 8 other countries, 1% are from out of state, 46% African American, 2% Asian American or Pacific Islander, 45% Hispanic American, 0.1% Native American, 0.9% international, 4% transferred in. *Retention:* 45% of 2001 full-time freshmen returned.

Freshmen *Admission:* 1,281 applied, 885 admitted, 672 enrolled.

Faculty *Total:* 149, 44% full-time, 17% with terminal degrees. *Student/faculty ratio:* 29:1.

Majors Accounting; business; business administration; computer science; computer typography/composition; hospitality management; information sciences/systems; medical records administration; medical records technology; secretarial science.

Academic Programs *Special study options:* academic remediation for entering students, adult/continuing education programs, cooperative education, English as a second language, internships, part-time degree program, summer session for credit.

Library Main Library plus 1 other with 28,000 titles, 301 serial subscriptions, an OPAC, a Web page.

Computers on Campus 541 computers available on campus for general student use. Internet access, at least one staffed computer lab available.

Student Life *Activities and Organizations:* drama/theater group, student-run newspaper. *Campus security:* late-night transport/escort service. *Student Services:* personal/psychological counseling.

Athletics Member NJCAA. *Intercollegiate sports:* basketball M/W, soccer M/W. *Intramural sports:* basketball M/W, bowling M/W, soccer M/W, volleyball M/W.

Standardized Tests *Required:* ACT ASSET.

Costs (2001–02) *Comprehensive fee:* $16,640 includes full-time tuition ($7440), mandatory fees ($400), and room and board ($8800). Part-time tuition: $930 per course. *Required fees:* $100 per term part-time. *Room and board:* College room only: $4480. *Payment plans:* installment, deferred payment.

Financial Aid In 2001, 125 Federal Work-Study jobs (averaging $4000).

Applying *Options:* early admission, deferred entrance. *Application fee:* $25. *Required:* high school transcript, interview. *Application deadlines:* 8/26 (freshmen), 8/26 (transfers). *Notification:* continuous until 9/3 (freshmen).

Admissions Contact Lauren Rosenthal, Director of Admissions, Monroe College, Monroe College Way, 2501 Jerome Avenue, Bronx, NY 10468. *Phone:* 718-933-6700 Ext. 536. *Toll-free phone:* 800-55MONROE.

MONROE COLLEGE
New Rochelle, New York

- **Proprietary** primarily 2-year, founded 1983
- **Calendar** trimesters
- **Degrees** associate and bachelor's
- **Urban** campus with easy access to New York City
- **Coed,** 1,156 undergraduate students, 82% full-time, 67% women, 33% men

Undergraduates 948 full-time, 208 part-time. Students come from 4 states and territories, 8 other countries, 1% are from out of state, 56% African American, 1% Asian American or Pacific Islander, 17% Hispanic American, 0.1% Native American, 7% international, 7% transferred in, 5% live on campus. *Retention:* 60% of 2001 full-time freshmen returned.

Freshmen *Admission:* 689 applied, 476 admitted, 343 enrolled.

Faculty *Total:* 54, 39% full-time, 9% with terminal degrees. *Student/faculty ratio:* 32:1.

Majors Accounting; business; business administration; computer science; computer typography/composition; hospitality management; information sciences/systems; medical records technology; secretarial science.

Academic Programs *Special study options:* academic remediation for entering students, adult/continuing education programs, cooperative education, English as a second language, internships, part-time degree program, summer session for credit.

Library Main Library plus 1 other with 8,400 titles, 211 serial subscriptions.

Computers on Campus 214 computers available on campus for general student use. At least one staffed computer lab available.

Student Life *Housing Options:* coed. *Activities and Organizations:* drama/theater group, student-run newspaper. *Campus security:* late-night transport/escort service. *Student Services:* personal/psychological counseling.

Athletics Member NJCAA. *Intercollegiate sports:* basketball M/W, soccer M/W. *Intramural sports:* basketball M/W, bowling M/W, soccer M/W, volleyball M/W.

Standardized Tests *Required:* ACT ASSET.

Costs (2001–02) *Comprehensive fee:* $16,640 includes full-time tuition ($7440), mandatory fees ($400), and room and board ($8800). Part-time tuition: $930 per course. *Required fees:* $100 per term part-time. *Room and board:* College room only: $4480. Room and board charges vary according to board plan. *Payment plans:* installment, deferred payment.

Financial Aid In 2001, 50 Federal Work-Study jobs (averaging $4000).

Applying *Options:* common application, electronic application, early admission, deferred entrance. *Application fee:* $25. *Required:* high school transcript, interview. *Application deadlines:* 8/26 (freshmen), 8/26 (transfers). *Notification:* continuous until 9/3 (freshmen).

Admissions Contact Ms. Lisa Scorca, High School Admissions, Monroe College, Monroe College Way, 2468 Jerome Avenue, Bronx, NY 10468. *Phone:* 914-632-5400 Ext. 407. *Toll-free phone:* 800-55-monroe.

MONROE COMMUNITY COLLEGE

Rochester, New York

- **State and locally supported** 2-year, founded 1961, part of State University of New York System
- **Calendar** semesters
- **Degree** certificates and associate
- **Suburban** 314-acre campus with easy access to Buffalo
- **Endowment** $3.6 million
- **Coed,** 16,157 undergraduate students, 49% full-time, 55% women, 45% men

Undergraduates 7,929 full-time, 8,228 part-time. Students come from 1 other state, 45 other countries, 6% transferred in.

Freshmen *Admission:* 9,806 applied, 7,783 admitted, 3,175 enrolled.

Faculty *Total:* 1,082, 26% full-time, 4% with terminal degrees. *Student/faculty ratio:* 20:1.

Majors Accounting; art; auto mechanic/technician; behavioral sciences; biological/physical sciences; biological technology; biology; business administration; business marketing and marketing management; chemical engineering technology; chemistry; civil engineering technology; computer engineering related; computer engineering technology; computer science; computer science related; computer/technical support; construction technology; corrections; criminal justice/law enforcement administration; data processing technology; dental hygiene; electrical/electronic engineering technology; engineering science; environmental science; fashion design/illustration; fashion merchandising; fire science; food products retailing; food services technology; forestry; graphic design/commercial art/illustration; graphic/printing equipment; heating/air conditioning/refrigeration; history; hotel and restaurant management; human ecology; human services; industrial radiologic technology; industrial technology; information sciences/systems; information technology; instrumentation technology; interior design; international business; landscape architecture; laser/optical technology; law enforcement/police science; legal administrative assistant; liberal arts and sciences/liberal studies; mass communications; mathematics; mechanical engineering technology; medical records administration; music; nursing; physical education; physics; political science; pre-pharmacy studies; quality control technology; recreation/leisure studies; retail management; secretarial science; social sciences; telecommunications; travel/tourism management.

Academic Programs *Special study options:* academic remediation for entering students, accelerated degree program, adult/continuing education programs, advanced placement credit, cooperative education, English as a second language, honors programs, internships, off-campus study, part-time degree program, services for LD students, summer session for credit. *ROTC:* Army (c), Air Force (c).

Library LeRoy V. Good Library plus 1 other with 110,748 titles, 745 serial subscriptions, 4,100 audiovisual materials, an OPAC.

Computers on Campus 150 computers available on campus for general student use. A campuswide network can be accessed from off campus. Internet access, online (class) registration, at least one staffed computer lab available.

Student Life *Housing:* college housing not available. *Activities and Organizations:* drama/theater group, student-run newspaper, radio station, choral group, student newspaper, Phi Theta Kappa, student government. *Campus security:* 24-hour emergency response devices, late-night transport/escort service. *Student Services:* health clinic, personal/psychological counseling.

Athletics Member NJCAA. *Intercollegiate sports:* baseball M(s), basketball M(s)/W(s), golf M, ice hockey M(s), lacrosse M(s), soccer M(s)/W(s), softball W, swimming M(s)/W(s), tennis M/W, volleyball W. *Intramural sports:* archery M/W, basketball M/W, bowling M/W, cross-country running M/W, lacrosse W, racquetball M/W, rugby M, skiing (cross-country) M/W, soccer M/W, softball M/W, swimming M/W, tennis M/W, volleyball M/W.

Costs (2002–03) *Tuition:* state resident $2500 full-time, $105 per credit hour part-time; nonresident $5000 full-time, $210 per credit hour part-time. Part-time tuition and fees vary according to course load. *Payment plan:* installment. *Waivers:* senior citizens and employees or children of employees.

Applying *Options:* electronic application, early admission. *Application fee:* $20. *Required:* high school transcript. *Application deadline:* rolling (freshmen), rolling (transfers). *Notification:* continuous (freshmen).

Admissions Contact Mr. Anthony Felicetti, Associate Vice President, Enrollment Management, Monroe Community College, 1000 East Henrietta Road, Rochester, NY 14623-5780. *Phone:* 716-292-2000 Ext. 2221. *Toll-free phone:* 716-292-2200. *Fax:* 716-427-2749.

NASSAU COMMUNITY COLLEGE

Garden City, New York

- **State and locally supported** 2-year, founded 1959, part of State University of New York System
- **Calendar** semesters
- **Degree** certificates and associate
- **Suburban** 225-acre campus with easy access to New York City
- **Coed,** 19,712 undergraduate students, 56% full-time, 55% women, 45% men

Undergraduates 11,007 full-time, 8,705 part-time. Students come from 99 other countries, 8% transferred in.

Freshmen *Admission:* 4,915 enrolled.

Faculty *Total:* 1,341, 42% full-time, 28% with terminal degrees. *Student/faculty ratio:* 20:1.

Majors Accounting; accounting technician; African-American studies; art; business administration; business marketing and marketing management; business systems networking/ telecommunications; civil engineering technology; communications; computer graphics; computer/information sciences; computer science; computer science related; criminal justice/law enforcement administration; criminal justice studies; dance; data processing technology; design/visual communications; early childhood education; engineering; enterprise management; fashion design/illustration; fashion merchandising; general retailing/wholesaling; general studies; graphic design/commercial art/illustration; health science; hotel and restaurant management; instrumentation technology; insurance/risk management; interior design; legal administrative assistant; liberal arts and sciences/liberal studies; management information systems/business data processing; mass communications; mathematics; medical administrative assistant; medical laboratory technician; medical radiologic technology; mortuary science; music (general performance); nursing; operating room technician; paralegal/legal assistant; photography; physical therapy assistant; real estate; rehabilitation therapy; respiratory therapy; secretarial science; security; theater arts/drama; theater design; transportation technology; visual/performing arts.

Academic Programs *Special study options:* academic remediation for entering students, adult/continuing education programs, advanced placement credit, cooperative education, distance learning, English as a second language, honors programs, internships, off-campus study, part-time degree program, services for LD students, summer session for credit. *ROTC:* Army (c).

Library A. Holly Patterson Library with 171,938 titles, 753 serial subscriptions, 55,514 audiovisual materials, an OPAC, a Web page.

Computers on Campus 700 computers available on campus for general student use. A campuswide network can be accessed from off campus. At least one staffed computer lab available.

Student Life *Housing:* college housing not available. *Activities and Organizations:* drama/theater group, student-run newspaper, radio station, choral group, Student Organization of Latinos, Student Government Association, Programming Board, Caribbean Student Organization, NYPIRG. *Campus security:* 24-hour emergency response devices and patrols, late-night transport/escort service. *Student Services:* health clinic, personal/psychological counseling, women's center.

Athletics Member NJCAA. *Intercollegiate sports:* baseball M, basketball M/W, bowling M/W, cross-country running M/W, equestrian sports M/W, football M, golf M/W, lacrosse M, soccer M/W, softball W, tennis M/W, track and field M/W, volleyball M/W, wrestling M. *Intramural sports:* badminton M/W, basketball M/W, cross-country running M/W, football M, lacrosse M/W, racquetball M/W, soccer M/W, softball M/W, table tennis M/W, tennis M/W, volleyball M/W.

Standardized Tests *Recommended:* SAT I or ACT (for admission).

Costs (2001–02) *Tuition:* state resident $2400 full-time, $100 per credit part-time; nonresident $4800 full-time, $200 per credit part-time. *Required fees:* $120 full-time.

Financial Aid In 2001, 328 Federal Work-Study jobs (averaging $3000).

Applying *Options:* deferred entrance. *Application fee:* $20. *Required:* high school transcript. *Required for some:* minimum 3.0 GPA, interview. *Recommended:* minimum 2.0 GPA. *Application deadlines:* 8/1 (freshmen), 8/1 (transfers). *Notification:* continuous (freshmen).

Nassau Community College (continued)
Admissions Contact Mr. Bernard Iantosca, Director of Admissions, Nassau Community College, 1 Education Drive, Garden City, NY 11530-6793. *Phone:* 516-572-7210.

NEW YORK CAREER INSTITUTE
New York, New York

Admissions Contact Mr. Alfred Odom, Director of Admissions, New York Career Institute, 15 Park Row, 4th Floor, New York, NY 10038-2301. *Phone:* 212-962-0002.

NEW YORK CITY TECHNICAL COLLEGE OF THE CITY UNIVERSITY OF NEW YORK
Brooklyn, New York

- **State and locally supported** primarily 2-year, founded 1946, part of City University of New York System
- **Calendar** semesters
- **Degrees** certificates, associate, and bachelor's
- **Urban** campus
- **Endowment** $11.6 million
- **Coed,** 11,028 undergraduate students, 67% full-time, 50% women, 50% men

Undergraduates 7,407 full-time, 3,621 part-time. Students come from 6 states and territories, 108 other countries, 4% transferred in.
Freshmen *Admission:* 4,211 applied, 3,657 admitted, 2,472 enrolled. *Average high school GPA:* 2.00.
Faculty *Total:* 989, 27% full-time, 21% with terminal degrees. *Student/faculty ratio:* 25:1.
Majors Accounting; architectural drafting; business marketing and marketing management; chemical technology; civil engineering technology; computer science; construction technology; data processing technology; dental hygiene; dental laboratory technician; drafting; electrical/electronic engineering technology; electromechanical technology; fashion merchandising; graphic design/commercial art/illustration; heating/air conditioning/refrigeration; hospitality management; human services; information sciences/systems; liberal arts and sciences/liberal studies; mechanical engineering technology; medical radiologic technology; nursing; optometric/ophthalmic laboratory technician; paralegal/legal assistant; technical education; telecommunications; theater design; trade/industrial education.
Academic Programs *Special study options:* academic remediation for entering students, advanced placement credit, distance learning, English as a second language, freshman honors college, honors programs, independent study, internships, off-campus study, part-time degree program, services for LD students, student-designed majors, study abroad, summer session for credit. *ROTC:* Air Force (c).
Library Ursula C. Schwerin Library with 177,569 titles, 630 serial subscriptions, an OPAC, a Web page.
Computers on Campus 500 computers available on campus for general student use. A campuswide network can be accessed from off campus. Internet access, at least one staffed computer lab available.
Student Life *Housing:* college housing not available. *Activities and Organizations:* drama/theater group, student-run newspaper, choral group, IBO, NUTREX, Human Services, Seekers Christian Fellowship Gospel Choir. *Campus security:* 24-hour emergency response devices and patrols. *Student Services:* health clinic, personal/psychological counseling, women's center.
Athletics Member NCAA. All Division III. *Intercollegiate sports:* basketball M/W, cross-country running M/W, soccer M, track and field M/W, volleyball M/W. *Intramural sports:* basketball M/W, volleyball M/W.
Costs (2002–03) *Tuition:* area resident $3319 full-time, $135 per credit hour part-time; state resident $3319 full-time, $135 per credit hour part-time; nonresident $6919 full-time, $325 per credit hour part-time. *Required fees:* $119 full-time, $60 per term part-time.
Applying *Application fee:* $40. *Required:* high school transcript. *Application deadline:* rolling (freshmen), rolling (transfers).
Admissions Contact Mr. Joseph Lento, Director of Admissions, New York City Technical College of the City University of New York, 300 Jay Street, Brooklyn, NY 11201-2983. *Phone:* 718-260-5500. *E-mail:* jlento@nyctc.cuny.edu.

THE NEW YORK COLLEGE OF HEALTH PROFESSIONS
Syosset, New York

- **Independent** founded 1981
- **Calendar** trimesters
- **Degrees** diplomas, associate, incidental bachelor's, and master's
- **Suburban** campus with easy access to New York City
- **Coed,** 550 undergraduate students

Faculty *Total:* 20.
Majors Acupuncture/oriental medicine.
Academic Programs *Special study options:* accelerated degree program, adult/continuing education programs, advanced placement credit, double majors, part-time degree program.
Library James and Lenore Jacobson Library at the New Center with 4,600 titles, 100 serial subscriptions, an OPAC.
Computers on Campus 3 computers available on campus for general student use. At least one staffed computer lab available.
Student Life *Housing:* college housing not available. *Campus security:* 24-hour patrols, security guard during certain evening and weekend hours. *Student Services:* health clinic, personal/psychological counseling.
Costs (2002–03) *Tuition:* $6600 full-time, $275 per credit part-time. *Payment plan:* installment. *Waivers:* employees or children of employees.
Financial Aid In 2001, 15 Federal Work-Study jobs.
Applying *Options:* common application, deferred entrance. *Application fee:* $85. *Required:* essay or personal statement, high school transcript, minimum 2.0 GPA, 3 letters of recommendation, interview. *Application deadline:* rolling (freshmen), rolling (transfers). *Notification:* continuous (freshmen).
Admissions Contact Mr. Joe Bubenas, Dean of Admissions, The New York College of Health Professions, 6801 Jericho Turnpike, Syosset, NY 11791. *Phone:* 800-922-7337. *Toll-free phone:* 800-922-7337.

NIAGARA COUNTY COMMUNITY COLLEGE
Sanborn, New York

- **State and locally supported** 2-year, founded 1962, part of State University of New York System
- **Calendar** semesters
- **Degree** certificates and associate
- **Rural** 287-acre campus with easy access to Buffalo
- **Endowment** $2.2 million
- **Coed,** 4,915 undergraduate students, 62% full-time, 58% women, 42% men

Undergraduates 3,041 full-time, 1,874 part-time. Students come from 18 other countries, 1% are from out of state, 4% African American, 0.5% Asian American or Pacific Islander, 0.7% Hispanic American, 1% Native American, 0.7% international, 9% transferred in.
Freshmen *Admission:* 1,799 applied, 1,799 admitted, 1,156 enrolled. *Average high school GPA:* 2.48.
Faculty *Total:* 283, 44% full-time, 10% with terminal degrees. *Student/faculty ratio:* 18:1.
Majors Accounting; animal sciences; biochemical technology; biological/physical sciences; business administration; computer science; criminal justice/law enforcement administration; culinary arts; drafting; electrical/electronic engineering technology; electroencephalograph technology; fine/studio arts; general studies; humanities; human services; information sciences/systems; liberal arts and sciences/liberal studies; mass communications; mathematics; mechanical design technology; medical assistant; music; nursing; occupational health/industrial hygiene; operating room technician; physical education; physical therapy assistant; radiological science; retail management; secretarial science; social sciences; telecommunications; theater arts/drama.
Academic Programs *Special study options:* academic remediation for entering students, adult/continuing education programs, advanced placement credit, cooperative education, double majors, honors programs, independent study, internships, off-campus study, part-time degree program, services for LD students, student-designed majors, study abroad, summer session for credit. *ROTC:* Army (c).
Library Library Learning Center with 74,473 titles, 564 serial subscriptions, 6,579 audiovisual materials, an OPAC, a Web page.
Computers on Campus 322 computers available on campus for general student use. Internet access, at least one staffed computer lab available.
Student Life *Housing:* college housing not available. *Activities and Organizations:* drama/theater group, student-run newspaper, radio station, choral group,

student radio station, Student Nurses Association, Phi Theta Kappa, Alpha Beta Gamma, Physical Education Club. *Campus security:* student patrols, late-night transport/escort service, emergency telephones. *Student Services:* health clinic, personal/psychological counseling.

Athletics Member NJCAA. *Intercollegiate sports:* baseball M, basketball M(s)/W, golf M/W, soccer M/W, softball W, volleyball W, wrestling M(s). *Intramural sports:* badminton M/W, basketball M/W, bowling M/W, racquetball M/W, skiing (cross-country) M(c)/W(c), squash M/W, swimming M/W, table tennis M/W, tennis M/W, volleyball M/W.

Costs (2002–03) *Tuition:* state resident $2600 full-time, $105 per credit hour part-time; nonresident $3900 full-time, $158 per credit hour part-time. Full-time tuition and fees vary according to program. Part-time tuition and fees vary according to program. *Required fees:* $185 full-time, $15 per term part-time.

Financial Aid In 2001, 155 Federal Work-Study jobs (averaging $1100).

Applying *Options:* electronic application, early admission. *Required:* high school transcript. *Required for some:* minimum 2.0 GPA. *Notification:* continuous until 8/31 (freshmen).

Admissions Contact Mr. Thomas Quatroche, Director of Enrollment Services, Niagara County Community College, 3111 Saunders Settlement Road, Sanborn, NY 14132. *Phone:* 716-614-6201. *Fax:* 716-614-6820. *E-mail:* admissions@niagaracc.suny.edu.

NORTH COUNTRY COMMUNITY COLLEGE
Saranac Lake, New York

- **State and locally supported** 2-year, founded 1967, part of State University of New York System
- **Calendar** semesters
- **Degree** certificates and associate
- **Rural** 100-acre campus
- **Coed,** 1,217 undergraduate students, 65% full-time, 68% women, 32% men

Undergraduates 792 full-time, 425 part-time. Students come from 9 states and territories, 4 other countries, 2% are from out of state, 1% African American, 0.5% Asian American or Pacific Islander, 0.9% Hispanic American, 3% Native American, 0.5% international, 8% transferred in.

Freshmen *Admission:* 652 applied, 622 admitted, 339 enrolled. *Test scores:* SAT verbal scores over 500: 31%; SAT math scores over 500: 28%; ACT scores over 18: 54%; SAT verbal scores over 600: 5%; SAT math scores over 600: 7%; SAT verbal scores over 700: 1%; SAT math scores over 700: 1%.

Faculty *Total:* 107, 32% full-time, 14% with terminal degrees. *Student/faculty ratio:* 16:1.

Majors Biological/physical sciences; business administration; criminal justice studies; exercise sciences; general office/clerical; interdisciplinary studies; liberal arts and sciences/liberal studies; mathematics; medical radiologic technology; mental health/rehabilitation; nursing; recreation/leisure facilities management; retail management.

Academic Programs *Special study options:* academic remediation for entering students, advanced placement credit, distance learning, double majors, internships, part-time degree program, services for LD students, student-designed majors, summer session for credit.

Library North Country Community College Library with 57,153 titles, 168 serial subscriptions, 1,226 audiovisual materials.

Computers on Campus 125 computers available on campus for general student use. Internet access, at least one staffed computer lab available.

Student Life *Housing:* college housing not available. *Activities and Organizations:* drama/theater group, student-run newspaper, Student Government Association, Wilderness Recreation Club, Nursing Club, Radiology Club, Criminal Justice Club. *Student Services:* personal/psychological counseling.

Athletics Member NJCAA. *Intercollegiate sports:* basketball M, ice hockey M, soccer M/W, softball W. *Intramural sports:* archery M/W, badminton M/W, basketball M/W, bowling M/W, football M/W, soccer M/W, softball M/W, swimming M/W, tennis M/W, volleyball M/W, weight lifting M/W.

Standardized Tests *Recommended:* SAT I or ACT (for admission).

Costs (2001–02) *One-time required fee:* $35. *Tuition:* state resident $2500 full-time, $110 per credit part-time; nonresident $5000 full-time, $220 per credit part-time. *Required fees:* $350 full-time, $10 per credit. *Payment plan:* installment. *Waivers:* employees or children of employees.

Financial Aid In 2001, 79 Federal Work-Study jobs (averaging $1880). 28 State and other part-time jobs (averaging $1605).

Applying *Options:* electronic application, early admission, early decision, deferred entrance. *Required:* high school transcript. *Recommended:* essay or personal statement, 1 letter of recommendation, interview. *Application deadline:* rolling (freshmen), rolling (transfers). *Early decision:* 11/15. *Notification:* continuous (freshmen), 12/15 (early decision).

Admissions Contact Enrollment Management Assistant, North Country Community College, 20 Winona Avenue, PO Box 89, Saranac Lake, NY 12983-0089. *Phone:* 518-891-2915 Ext. 233. *Toll-free phone:* 888-TRY-NCCC Ext. 233. *Fax:* 518-891-2915 Ext. 214. *E-mail:* info@nccc.edu.

OLEAN BUSINESS INSTITUTE
Olean, New York

Admissions Contact Mr. Patrick McCarthy, Director, Olean Business Institute, 301 North Union Street, Olean, NY 14760-2691. *Phone:* 716-372-7978. *Fax:* 716-372-2120.

ONONDAGA COMMUNITY COLLEGE
Syracuse, New York

- **State and locally supported** 2-year, founded 1962, part of State University of New York System
- **Calendar** semesters
- **Degree** certificates, diplomas, and associate
- **Suburban** 180-acre campus
- **Coed,** 8,000 undergraduate students

Undergraduates Students come from 9 states and territories, 34 other countries, 1% are from out of state.

Freshmen *Admission:* 3,581 applied, 2,726 admitted.

Faculty *Total:* 457, 35% full-time. *Student/faculty ratio:* 16:1.

Majors Accounting; architectural engineering technology; art; auto mechanic/technician; biological/physical sciences; business administration; chemical engineering technology; computer engineering related; computer engineering technology; computer/information technology services administration and management related; computer programming (specific applications); computer science; computer science related; computer systems networking/telecommunications; computer/technical support; computer typography/composition; construction technology; criminal justice/law enforcement administration; culinary arts; data entry/microcomputer applications; data entry/microcomputer applications related; data processing technology; dental hygiene; drafting; early childhood education; electrical/electronic engineering technology; engineering science; finance; fire science; food products retailing; graphic design/commercial art/illustration; hotel and restaurant management; humanities; human services; information sciences/systems; information technology; insurance/risk management; interior design; labor/personnel relations; landscape architecture; liberal arts and sciences/liberal studies; machine technology; mathematics; mechanical engineering technology; medical records administration; music; nursing; photography; physical therapy; quality control technology; radio/television broadcasting; recreation/leisure studies; respiratory therapy; secretarial science; system/networking/LAN/WAN management; telecommunications; Web/multimedia management/webmaster; Web page, digital/multimedia and information resources design.

Academic Programs *Special study options:* academic remediation for entering students, accelerated degree program, adult/continuing education programs, advanced placement credit, cooperative education, English as a second language, external degree program, honors programs, internships, part-time degree program, services for LD students, study abroad, summer session for credit. *ROTC:* Army (c), Air Force (c).

Library Sidney B. Coulter Library with 96,611 titles, 802 serial subscriptions, an OPAC, a Web page.

Computers on Campus 525 computers available on campus for general student use. A campuswide network can be accessed from off campus. Internet access, at least one staffed computer lab available.

Student Life *Housing:* college housing not available. *Activities and Organizations:* student-run newspaper, radio station, choral group, Jamal, Music Club, Photo Club, Outing Club, Veterans Club. *Campus security:* 24-hour patrols. *Student Services:* health clinic, personal/psychological counseling.

Athletics Member NJCAA. *Intercollegiate sports:* baseball M(s), basketball M/W, cross-country running M/W, lacrosse M, soccer M, softball W, tennis M/W, volleyball W. *Intramural sports:* basketball M/W, tennis M/W, volleyball W.

Standardized Tests *Required:* TSWE. *Recommended:* SAT I and SAT II or ACT (for placement).

Costs (2001–02) *Tuition:* $98 per credit part-time; state resident $196 per credit part-time; nonresident $294 per credit part-time. *Required fees:* $60 per term part-time. *Payment plan:* deferred payment. *Waivers:* senior citizens and employees or children of employees.

Financial Aid In 2001, 142 Federal Work-Study jobs (averaging $1260). *Financial aid deadline:* 6/30.

Onondaga Community College (continued)

Applying *Options:* common application, electronic application, early admission, deferred entrance. *Application fee:* $30. *Required:* high school transcript. *Required for some:* minimum 2.0 GPA, interview. *Recommended:* 1 letter of recommendation. *Application deadlines:* 9/1 (freshmen), 9/1 (transfers). *Notification:* continuous (freshmen).

Admissions Contact Mr. Monty R. Flynn, Director of Admissions, Onondaga Community College, 4941 Onondaga Road, Syracuse, NY 13215. *Phone:* 315-498-2201. *Fax:* 315-498-2107. *E-mail:* admissions@sunyocc.edu.

ORANGE COUNTY COMMUNITY COLLEGE

Middletown, New York

- **State and locally supported** 2-year, founded 1950, part of State University of New York System
- **Calendar** semesters
- **Degree** certificates and associate
- **Suburban** 37-acre campus with easy access to New York City
- **Coed,** 5,532 undergraduate students, 48% full-time, 63% women, 37% men

Undergraduates 2,680 full-time, 2,852 part-time. Students come from 19 states and territories, 1% are from out of state, 8% African American, 2% Asian American or Pacific Islander, 11% Hispanic American, 0.4% Native American, 0.1% international, 3% transferred in.

Freshmen *Admission:* 2,002 applied, 2,002 admitted, 1,675 enrolled. *Average high school GPA:* 2.25.

Faculty *Total:* 322, 41% full-time. *Student/faculty ratio:* 15:1.

Majors Accounting; architectural engineering technology; biological/physical sciences; biology; business administration; business marketing and marketing management; child care/development; computer engineering related; computer engineering technology; computer/information sciences; computer programming; computer science; computer science related; construction technology; criminal justice/law enforcement administration; data entry/microcomputer applications; data processing technology; dental hygiene; drafting; electrical/electronic engineering technology; elementary education; engineering science; exercise sciences; finance; humanities; industrial radiologic technology; information sciences/systems; information technology; law enforcement/police science; liberal arts and sciences/liberal studies; medical laboratory technician; mental health/rehabilitation; nursing; occupational therapy; physical sciences; physical therapy; real estate; recreation/leisure studies; retail management; secretarial science; word processing.

Academic Programs *Special study options:* academic remediation for entering students, accelerated degree program, adult/continuing education programs, English as a second language, external degree program, honors programs, internships, part-time degree program, services for LD students, summer session for credit.

Library Learning Resource Center with 98,628 titles, 370 serial subscriptions, 225 audiovisual materials, an OPAC, a Web page.

Computers on Campus 200 computers available on campus for general student use. Internet access, at least one staffed computer lab available.

Student Life *Housing:* college housing not available. *Activities and Organizations:* drama/theater group, student-run newspaper, radio station, choral group, Phi Theta Kappa, Masters of the Elements, Computer Club, Agassiz Society, Apprentice Players. *Campus security:* 24-hour emergency response devices, late-night transport/escort service. *Student Services:* health clinic, personal/psychological counseling.

Athletics Member NJCAA. *Intercollegiate sports:* baseball M(s), basketball M(s)/W(s), soccer M(s)/W(s), softball W(s), tennis M(s)/W(s), volleyball W. *Intramural sports:* basketball M/W, field hockey M, football M, racquetball M/W, soccer M/W, tennis M/W, volleyball M/W.

Costs (2001–02) *Tuition:* state resident $2360 full-time, $96 per credit part-time; nonresident $4720 full-time, $192 per credit part-time. *Required fees:* $85 full-time, $4 per credit. *Payment plan:* installment. *Waivers:* senior citizens and employees or children of employees.

Financial Aid In 2001, 70 Federal Work-Study jobs (averaging $2000). 25 State and other part-time jobs (averaging $2000).

Applying *Options:* common application, early admission, deferred entrance. *Application fee:* $25. *Required:* high school transcript. *Application deadlines:* 8/1 (freshmen), 8/1 (transfers). *Notification:* continuous (freshmen).

Admissions Contact Ms. Margot St. Lawrence, Director of Admissions, Orange County Community College, 115 South Street, Middletown, NY 10940. *Phone:* 914-341-4030. *E-mail:* admssns@sunyorange.edu.

PAUL SMITH'S COLLEGE OF ARTS AND SCIENCES

Paul Smiths, New York

- **Independent** primarily 2-year, founded 1937
- **Calendar** semesters
- **Degrees** certificates, associate, and bachelor's
- **Rural** 14,200-acre campus
- **Endowment** $11.8 million
- **Coed,** 817 undergraduate students, 97% full-time, 30% women, 70% men

Paul Smith's College offers 2- and 4-year degree programs in culinary arts, hotel management, fish and wildlife, ecology and the environment, forestry, recreation, surveying, business, and liberal arts. The 14,200-acre campus is located in the heart of the Adirondack Park in upstate New York. Students should call 800-421-2605 or visit the Web site at www.paulsmiths.edu for more information.

Undergraduates 794 full-time, 23 part-time. Students come from 29 states and territories, 11 other countries, 40% are from out of state, 4% African American, 0.6% Asian American or Pacific Islander, 2% Hispanic American, 1% Native American, 1% international, 9% transferred in, 95% live on campus. *Retention:* 63% of 2001 full-time freshmen returned.

Freshmen *Admission:* 1,173 applied, 933 admitted, 330 enrolled. *Test scores:* SAT verbal scores over 500: 39%; SAT math scores over 500: 33%; ACT scores over 18: 59%; SAT verbal scores over 600: 6%; SAT math scores over 600: 8%; ACT scores over 24: 7%; SAT verbal scores over 700: 1%.

Faculty *Total:* 65, 98% full-time, 18% with terminal degrees. *Student/faculty ratio:* 13:1.

Majors American studies; business administration; culinary arts; ecology; environmental science; forest harvesting production technology; forestry; hospitality management; hotel and restaurant management; liberal arts and sciences/liberal studies; natural resources management; recreation/leisure facilities management; surveying; technical/business writing; travel/tourism management.

Academic Programs *Special study options:* academic remediation for entering students, adult/continuing education programs, advanced placement credit, cooperative education, double majors, English as a second language, honors programs, internships, services for LD students, student-designed majors, study abroad, summer session for credit.

Library Frank C. Cubley Library with 56,000 titles, 504 serial subscriptions, an OPAC, a Web page.

Computers on Campus 65 computers available on campus for general student use. A campuswide network can be accessed from student residence rooms and from off campus. Internet access, at least one staffed computer lab available.

Student Life *Housing:* on-campus residence required through sophomore year. *Options:* coed. *Activities and Organizations:* drama/theater group, student-run newspaper, radio station, Forestry Club, Adirondack Experience Club, student radio station, Emergency Wilderness Response Team, Junior American Culinary. *Campus security:* 24-hour emergency response devices and patrols, late-night transport/escort service. *Student Services:* health clinic, personal/psychological counseling.

Athletics Member NJCAA. *Intercollegiate sports:* basketball M(s)/W(s), ice hockey M(s), skiing (downhill) M(s)/W(s), soccer M(s)/W(s). *Intramural sports:* basketball M/W, cross-country running M(c)/W(c), football M, golf M, ice hockey M(c), riflery M(c)/W(c), rugby M(c), soccer M/W, softball M/W, swimming M/W, table tennis M/W, tennis M/W, volleyball M/W.

Standardized Tests *Required:* SAT I or ACT (for admission).

Costs (2002–03) *Comprehensive fee:* $21,060 includes full-time tuition ($14,200), mandatory fees ($700), and room and board ($6160). Full-time tuition and fees vary according to program. Part-time tuition: $320 per credit hour. Part-time tuition and fees vary according to course load and program. No tuition increase for student's term of enrollment. *Room and board:* College room only: $3080. Room and board charges vary according to board plan. *Payment plan:* installment. *Waivers:* employees or children of employees.

Applying *Options:* common application, electronic application, early admission, deferred entrance. *Application fee:* $30. *Required:* essay or personal statement, high school transcript, 1 letter of recommendation. *Required for some:* interview. *Application deadline:* rolling (freshmen), rolling (transfers).

Admissions Contact Mr. Douglas Zander, Vice President for Enrollment and Campus Life, Paul Smith's College of Arts and Sciences, PO Box 265, Paul Smiths, NY 12970-0265. *Phone:* 518-327-6227 Ext. 6230. *Toll-free phone:* 800-421-2605. *Fax:* 518-327-6016.

Phillips Beth Israel School of Nursing
New York, New York

- **Independent** 2-year, founded 1904
- **Calendar** semesters
- **Degree** associate
- **Urban** campus
- **Endowment** $995,000
- **Coed, primarily women,** 91 undergraduate students, 30% full-time, 91% women, 9% men

Undergraduates 27 full-time, 64 part-time. Students come from 8 states and territories, 5 other countries, 10% are from out of state, 33% African American, 15% Asian American or Pacific Islander, 12% Hispanic American, 5% international, 66% transferred in.
Freshmen *Admission:* 55 applied, 4 admitted, 5 enrolled. *Average high school GPA:* 2.90. *Test scores:* SAT verbal scores over 500: 25%; SAT math scores over 500: 30%; SAT verbal scores over 600: 10%; SAT math scores over 600: 10%; SAT verbal scores over 700: 5%; SAT math scores over 700: 5%.
Faculty *Total:* 11, 91% full-time, 18% with terminal degrees. *Student/faculty ratio:* 6:1.
Majors Nursing.
Academic Programs *Special study options:* accelerated degree program, advanced placement credit, off-campus study, part-time degree program.
Library Phillips Health Science Library with 600 serial subscriptions, an OPAC.
Computers on Campus 15 computers available on campus for general student use. Internet access, at least one staffed computer lab available.
Student Life *Housing:* college housing not available. *Activities and Organizations:* student-run newspaper, choral group, Student Government Organization, National Student Nurses Association. *Campus security:* 24-hour emergency response devices. *Student Services:* health clinic, personal/psychological counseling.
Standardized Tests *Recommended:* SAT I (for admission).
Costs (2002–03) *Tuition:* $9840 full-time, $240 per credit part-time. Full-time tuition and fees vary according to class time and student level. Part-time tuition and fees vary according to student level. *Required fees:* $1780 full-time. *Payment plan:* installment. *Waivers:* employees or children of employees.
Financial Aid *Financial aid deadline:* 6/1.
Applying *Options:* deferred entrance. *Application fee:* $35. *Required:* essay or personal statement, high school transcript, minimum 2.0 GPA, 2 letters of recommendation, interview. *Recommended:* minimum 2.5 GPA. *Application deadlines:* 5/1 (freshmen), 5/1 (transfers). *Notification:* continuous (freshmen).
Admissions Contact Mrs. Bernice Pass-Stern, Director of Student Services, Phillips Beth Israel School of Nursing, 310 East 22nd Street, 9th Floor, New York, NY 10010-5702. *Phone:* 212-614-6108. *Fax:* 212-614-6109. *E-mail:* bstern@bethisraelny.org.

Plaza Business Institute
Jackson Heights, New York

Admissions Contact Mr. Michael Talarico, Director of Admissions, Plaza Business Institute, 74-09 37th Avenue, Jackson Heights, NY 11372-6300. *Phone:* 718-779-1430.

Queensborough Community College of the City University of New York
Bayside, New York

- **State and locally supported** 2-year, founded 1958, part of City University of New York System
- **Calendar** semesters
- **Degree** certificates and associate
- **Urban** 34-acre campus with easy access to New York City
- **Endowment** $1.0 million
- **Coed,** 10,880 undergraduate students, 52% full-time, 58% women, 42% men

Undergraduates 5,616 full-time, 5,264 part-time. Students come from 1 other state, 132 other countries, 1% are from out of state, 27% African American, 21% Asian American or Pacific Islander, 21% Hispanic American, 0.2% Native American, 2% international, 5% transferred in.
Freshmen *Admission:* 3,731 applied, 3,731 admitted, 2,142 enrolled. *Average high school GPA:* 1.98. *Test scores:* SAT verbal scores over 500: 12%; SAT math scores over 500: 17%; SAT verbal scores over 600: 1%; SAT math scores over 600: 2%.
Faculty *Total:* 756, 32% full-time, 21% with terminal degrees. *Student/faculty ratio:* 18:1.
Majors Accounting; architectural environmental design; business administration; business management/administrative services related; communications related; computer engineering technology; electrical/electronic engineering technology; engineering science; environmental health; fine/studio arts; health science; information sciences/systems; information technology; laser/optical technology; liberal arts and sciences/liberal studies; mechanical engineering technology; medical laboratory technician; musical instrument technology; nursing; telecommunications; visual/performing arts.
Academic Programs *Special study options:* academic remediation for entering students, adult/continuing education programs, advanced placement credit, cooperative education, English as a second language, honors programs, internships, part-time degree program, services for LD students, student-designed majors, summer session for credit.
Library The Kurt R. Schmeller with 140,000 titles, 600 serial subscriptions.
Computers on Campus 1001 computers available on campus for general student use. Internet access, online (class) registration, at least one staffed computer lab available.
Student Life *Housing:* college housing not available. *Activities and Organizations:* drama/theater group, student-run newspaper, radio station, choral group, Student Orientation Leaders, Student Nurses Association, Newman Club, Accounting Club, Flip Culture Society. *Campus security:* 24-hour patrols, late-night transport/escort service. *Student Services:* health clinic, personal/psychological counseling.
Athletics Member NJCAA. *Intercollegiate sports:* baseball M, basketball M/W, cross-country running M/W, soccer M, softball W, tennis M/W, track and field M/W, volleyball M/W. *Intramural sports:* archery M/W, badminton M/W, basketball M/W, fencing M/W, soccer M/W, softball M/W, swimming M/W, table tennis M/W, tennis M/W, track and field M/W, volleyball M/W, weight lifting M/W.
Costs (2001–02) *Tuition:* state resident $2500 full-time, $105 per credit part-time; nonresident $3076 full-time, $130 per credit part-time. Part-time tuition and fees vary according to class time. *Required fees:* $116 full-time, $23 per term part-time.
Applying *Options:* common application, electronic application, deferred entrance. *Application fee:* $40. *Required:* high school transcript. *Application deadline:* rolling (freshmen), rolling (transfers). *Notification:* continuous (freshmen).
Admissions Contact Mr. Guy Hildebrandt, Director of Registration, Queensborough Community College of the City University of New York, 222-05 56th Avenue, Bayside, NY 11364. *Phone:* 718-631-6307. *Fax:* 718-281-5189.

Rochester Business Institute
Rochester, New York

- **Proprietary** 2-year, founded 1863, part of Corinthian Colleges, Inc
- **Calendar** quarters
- **Degree** certificates, diplomas, and associate
- **Suburban** 2-acre campus
- **Coed,** 990 undergraduate students

Undergraduates Students come from 2 states and territories, 2 other countries.
Faculty *Total:* 63, 19% full-time. *Student/faculty ratio:* 16:1.
Majors Accounting; business administration; computer programming; data processing technology; management information systems/business data processing.
Academic Programs *Special study options:* academic remediation for entering students, adult/continuing education programs, advanced placement credit, double majors, summer session for credit.
Library Rochester Business Institute Library with 4,800 titles, 60 serial subscriptions, an OPAC.
Computers on Campus 70 computers available on campus for general student use. Internet access available.
Student Life *Housing:* college housing not available.
Athletics *Intramural sports:* basketball M, softball M/W.
Costs (2001–02) *Tuition:* $189 per credit hour part-time. Tuition and fees, from $16,000 to $20,000, vary with program selected.
Applying *Options:* early admission, deferred entrance. *Application fee:* $50. *Required:* interview. *Application deadline:* rolling (freshmen), rolling (transfers). *Notification:* continuous (freshmen).
Admissions Contact Ms. Deanna Pfluke, Director of Admissions, Rochester Business Institute, 1630 Portland Avenue, Rochester, NY 14621. *Phone:* 716-266-0430. *Fax:* 716-266-8243. *E-mail:* csilvio@cci.edu.

ROCKLAND COMMUNITY COLLEGE
Suffern, New York

- **State and locally supported** 2-year, founded 1959, part of State University of New York System
- **Calendar** semesters
- **Degree** associate
- **Suburban** 150-acre campus with easy access to New York City
- **Coed,** 6,260 undergraduate students, 57% full-time, 57% women, 43% men

Undergraduates 3,596 full-time, 2,664 part-time. Students come from 4 states and territories, 25 other countries, 4% are from out of state, 18% African American, 7% Asian American or Pacific Islander, 10% Hispanic American, 0.3% Native American, 4% international, 9% transferred in.

Freshmen *Admission:* 2,062 applied, 2,062 admitted, 1,505 enrolled.

Faculty *Total:* 359, 35% full-time.

Majors Accounting; advertising; applied art; art; auto mechanic/technician; biological/physical sciences; business administration; business marketing and marketing management; business systems networking/ telecommunications; computer graphics; computer/information technology services administration and management related; computer programming; computer programming related; computer programming (specific applications); computer science related; criminal justice/law enforcement administration; culinary arts; data processing technology; developmental/child psychology; dietetics; drafting; electrical/electronic engineering technology; emergency medical technology; finance; fine/studio arts; fire science; graphic design/commercial art/illustration; hospitality management; human services; liberal arts and sciences/liberal studies; mass communications; mathematics; medical records administration; nursing; occupational therapy; photography; respiratory therapy; secretarial science; system/networking/LAN/WAN management; theater arts/drama; travel/tourism management.

Academic Programs *Special study options:* academic remediation for entering students, adult/continuing education programs, advanced placement credit, cooperative education, English as a second language, external degree program, honors programs, internships, part-time degree program, services for LD students, student-designed majors, study abroad, summer session for credit. *ROTC:* Navy (b), Air Force (b).

Library Rockland Community College Library with 122,194 titles, 541 serial subscriptions, an OPAC.

Computers on Campus 177 computers available on campus for general student use. Internet access, at least one staffed computer lab available.

Student Life *Housing:* college housing not available. *Activities and Organizations:* drama/theater group, student-run newspaper, radio station, Hospitality Club, Student Senate, Student Ambassadors, Student Nurses, Latino Club. *Campus security:* 24-hour emergency response devices and patrols, student patrols, late-night transport/escort service. *Student Services:* personal/psychological counseling, legal services.

Athletics Member NJCAA. *Intercollegiate sports:* baseball M(s), basketball M/W, bowling M/W, golf M(s), soccer M/W, softball W, tennis M/W, volleyball W. *Intramural sports:* basketball M/W, bowling M/W, field hockey M/W, football M/W, golf M, racquetball M/W, soccer M/W, softball M/W, tennis M/W, volleyball M/W.

Standardized Tests *Recommended:* SAT I or ACT (for placement).

Costs (2001–02) *Tuition:* state resident $2400 full-time, $100 per credit part-time; nonresident $4800 full-time, $200 per credit part-time. *Required fees:* $79 full-time, $3 per credit. *Payment plan:* deferred payment. *Waivers:* senior citizens and employees or children of employees.

Applying *Options:* early admission, deferred entrance. *Application fee:* $25. *Required:* high school transcript. *Application deadline:* rolling (freshmen), rolling (transfers).

Admissions Contact Ms. Lorraine Glynn, Coordinator of Admissions and Recruitment, Rockland Community College, 145 College Road, Suffern, NY 10901-3699. *Phone:* 845-574-4237. *Toll-free phone:* 800-722-7666. *Fax:* 845-574-4433. *E-mail:* info@sunyrockland.edu.

SAINT JOSEPH'S HOSPITAL HEALTH CENTER SCHOOL OF NURSING
Syracuse, New York

- **Independent** 2-year
- **Degree** associate
- **Coed, primarily women,** 250 undergraduate students, 64% full-time, 91% women, 9% men

Undergraduates 159 full-time, 91 part-time. Students come from 2 states and territories, 2% African American, 0.8% Asian American or Pacific Islander, 2% Hispanic American, 2% Native American, 44% transferred in, 25% live on campus.

Freshmen *Admission:* 35 applied, 21 admitted, 14 enrolled. *Test scores:* SAT verbal scores over 500: 56%; SAT math scores over 500: 50%.

Faculty *Total:* 29, 55% full-time. *Student/faculty ratio:* 9:1.

Majors Nursing.

Academic Programs *Special study options:* academic remediation for entering students, adult/continuing education programs, advanced placement credit, cooperative education, internships, part-time degree program, services for LD students.

Library St. Joseph's Hospital Health Center School of Nursing Library with 4,500 titles, 230 serial subscriptions, 500 audiovisual materials, an OPAC.

Computers on Campus 30 computers available on campus for general student use. Internet access, at least one staffed computer lab available.

Student Life *Housing Options:* coed. *Activities and Organizations:* New York State Student Nurse's Association, Syracuse Area Black Nurses Association, Student Body Organization. *Campus security:* 24-hour patrols. *Student Services:* health clinic, personal/psychological counseling, legal services.

Standardized Tests *Required:* SAT I or ACT (for admission).

Costs (2001–02) *One-time required fee:* $125. *Tuition:* $225 per credit hour part-time. Full-time tuition and fees vary according to class time. Part-time tuition and fees vary according to class time and location. Tuition data reflects courses taken at Onondaga Community College. *Required fees:* $780 full-time, $390 per term part-time. *Room only:* $2800. Room and board charges vary according to housing facility. *Payment plan:* installment.

Applying *Options:* deferred entrance. *Application fee:* $30. *Required:* essay or personal statement, high school transcript, minimum 3.0 GPA, 4 letters of recommendation, interview.

Admissions Contact Ms. JoAnne Kiggins, Admission and Recruitment Coordinator, Saint Joseph's Hospital Health Center School of Nursing, 206 Prospect Avenue, Syracuse, NY 13203. *Phone:* 315-448-5040.

SAMARITAN HOSPITAL SCHOOL OF NURSING
Troy, New York

- **Independent** 2-year
- **Degree** diplomas and associate
- 70 undergraduate students
- 38% of applicants were admitted

Admissions Contact Linda Gallagher, Student Services Coordinator, Samaritan Hospital School of Nursing, 2215 Burdett Avenue, Troy, NY 12180. *Phone:* 518-271-3734. *E-mail:* gallagherl@nehealth.com.

SCHENECTADY COUNTY COMMUNITY COLLEGE
Schenectady, New York

- **State and locally supported** 2-year, founded 1968, part of State University of New York System
- **Calendar** semesters
- **Degree** certificates, diplomas, and associate
- **Urban** 50-acre campus
- **Coed,** 3,526 undergraduate students, 50% full-time, 57% women, 43% men

Undergraduates 1,765 full-time, 1,761 part-time. 11% transferred in.

Freshmen *Admission:* 1,662 applied, 1,461 admitted, 437 enrolled.

Faculty *Total:* 195, 33% full-time. *Student/faculty ratio:* 21:1.

Majors Accounting; aviation management; biological/physical sciences; business administration; chemical engineering technology; computer/information sciences; computer/information technology services administration and management related; computer programming related; computer science; computer science related; criminal justice/law enforcement administration; culinary arts; education; electrical/electronic engineering technology; fire science; hotel and restaurant management; humanities; human services; industrial technology; information technology; liberal arts and sciences/liberal studies; materials science; mathematics; music; music business management/merchandising; paralegal/legal assistant; plastics technology; quality control technology; secretarial science; social sciences; telecommunications; theater arts/drama; travel/tourism management; word processing.

Academic Programs *Special study options:* academic remediation for entering students, adult/continuing education programs, advanced placement credit, dis-

tance learning, double majors, English as a second language, honors programs, internships, off-campus study, part-time degree program, services for LD students, summer session for credit. *ROTC:* Army (c), Navy (c), Air Force (c).

Library Begley Library with 80,667 titles, 659 serial subscriptions, 2,808 audiovisual materials, an OPAC, a Web page.

Computers on Campus 400 computers available on campus for general student use. Internet access, at least one staffed computer lab available.

Student Life *Housing:* college housing not available. *Activities and Organizations:* drama/theater group, choral group, Black and Latino Student Alliance, Culinary Arts Club, Student Government Association, Spanish Club, Rhythms Literary Magazine. *Campus security:* 24-hour emergency response devices and patrols, late-night transport/escort service. *Student Services:* personal/psychological counseling.

Athletics Member NJCAA. *Intercollegiate sports:* baseball M, basketball M/W, bowling M/W, softball W. *Intramural sports:* soccer M/W, volleyball M/W.

Standardized Tests *Recommended:* SAT I or ACT (for placement).

Costs (2001–02) *Tuition:* state resident $2340 full-time, $96 per credit hour part-time; nonresident $4680 full-time, $192 per credit hour part-time. *Required fees:* $115 full-time, $5 per credit hour, $5 per credit hour part-time.

Financial Aid In 2001, 100 Federal Work-Study jobs (averaging $1900).

Applying *Options:* early admission, deferred entrance. *Required:* high school transcript. *Application deadline:* rolling (freshmen), rolling (transfers). *Notification:* continuous (freshmen).

Admissions Contact Mr. David Sampson, Director of Admissions, Schenectady County Community College, 78 Washington Avenue, Schenectady, NY 12305-2294. *Phone:* 518-381-1370. *E-mail:* dinellre@gw.sunysccc.edu.

SIMMONS INSTITUTE OF FUNERAL SERVICE

Syracuse, New York

- **Proprietary** 2-year, founded 1900
- **Calendar** semesters
- **Degree** associate
- **Urban** 1-acre campus
- **Coed,** 41 undergraduate students, 71% full-time, 37% women, 63% men

Undergraduates 29 full-time, 12 part-time. Students come from 3 states and territories, 1 other country, 14% are from out of state, 10% African American, 2% international, 54% transferred in.

Freshmen *Admission:* 5 enrolled.

Faculty *Total:* 8, 25% full-time, 38% with terminal degrees.

Majors Mortuary science.

Academic Programs *Special study options:* advanced placement credit, part-time degree program.

Library Simmons Library with 1,326 titles, 52 serial subscriptions.

Computers on Campus 18 computers available on campus for general student use. Internet access, at least one staffed computer lab available.

Student Life *Housing:* college housing not available. *Activities and Organizations:* Sigma Phi Sigma. *Campus security:* 24-hour emergency response devices.

Costs (2001–02) *One-time required fee:* $100. *Tuition:* $9090 full-time, $383 per credit part-time. *Payment plan:* installment.

Applying *Application fee:* $50. *Required:* essay or personal statement, high school transcript, interview. *Application deadlines:* 6/30 (freshmen), 6/30 (transfers). *Notification:* 7/30 (freshmen).

Admissions Contact Ms. Vera Wightman, Director of Admissions, Simmons Institute of Funeral Service, 1828 South Avenue, Syracuse, NY 13207. *Phone:* 315-475-5142. *Toll-free phone:* 800-727-3536. *Fax:* 315-477-3817. *E-mail:* vwightman6@aol.com.

STATE UNIVERSITY OF NEW YORK COLLEGE OF AGRICULTURE AND TECHNOLOGY AT MORRISVILLE

Morrisville, New York

- **State-supported** primarily 2-year, founded 1908, part of State University of New York System
- **Calendar** semesters
- **Degrees** certificates, associate, and bachelor's
- **Rural** 740-acre campus with easy access to Syracuse
- **Endowment** $363,621
- **Coed,** 3,130 undergraduate students

Undergraduates Students come from 14 states and territories, 11 other countries, 1% are from out of state, 17% African American, 1% Asian American or Pacific Islander, 5% Hispanic American, 1% Native American, 2% international, 60% live on campus.

Freshmen *Admission:* 3,732 applied, 3,031 admitted.

Faculty *Total:* 174, 59% full-time. *Student/faculty ratio:* 14:1.

Majors Accounting; agricultural business; agricultural mechanization; agricultural sciences; agronomy/crop science; animal sciences; architectural engineering technology; auto mechanic/technician; biological technology; biology; business administration; business marketing and marketing management; chemistry; computer engineering technology; computer programming; computer science; computer typography/composition; construction technology; dairy science; data processing technology; dietetics; drafting; electrical/electronic engineering technology; engineering; engineering science; engineering technology; environmental science; equestrian studies; fish/game management; food products retailing; food services technology; forest harvesting production technology; forestry; horticulture science; hospitality management; hotel and restaurant management; humanities; information sciences/systems; journalism; landscape architecture; landscaping management; legal administrative assistant; liberal arts and sciences/liberal studies; mathematics; mechanical engineering technology; medical administrative assistant; medical laboratory technician; natural resources conservation; natural resources management; nursing; nutrition science; physics; plastics technology; pre-engineering; recreation/leisure facilities management; secretarial science; social sciences; technical/business writing; travel/tourism management; wildlife management; wood science/paper technology.

Academic Programs *Special study options:* academic remediation for entering students, adult/continuing education programs, advanced placement credit, distance learning, double majors, honors programs, independent study, internships, off-campus study, part-time degree program, services for LD students, student-designed majors, study abroad, summer session for credit.

Library SUNY Morrisville Library plus 1 other with 99,258 titles, 568 serial subscriptions, an OPAC, a Web page.

Computers on Campus 90 computers available on campus for general student use. A campuswide network can be accessed from student residence rooms and from off campus that provide access to various software applications. At least one staffed computer lab available.

Student Life *Housing:* on-campus residence required for freshman year. *Options:* coed. *Activities and Organizations:* drama/theater group, student-run newspaper, radio station, choral group, African Student Union Black Alliance, Student Government Organization, Agriculture Club, Latino-American Student Association, WCVM (student radio station). *Campus security:* 24-hour emergency response devices and patrols, late-night transport/escort service, controlled dormitory access. *Student Services:* health clinic, personal/psychological counseling.

Athletics Member NJCAA. *Intercollegiate sports:* baseball M, basketball M/W, cross-country running M/W, equestrian sports M/W, field hockey W, football M, golf M, ice hockey M, lacrosse M/W, skiing (downhill) M/W, soccer M/W, softball W, swimming M/W, tennis W, track and field M/W, volleyball W, wrestling M. *Intramural sports:* basketball M/W, riflery M/W, skiing (cross-country) M/W, soccer M/W, softball M/W, tennis M/W, volleyball M/W.

Standardized Tests *Recommended:* SAT I and SAT II or ACT (for admission).

Costs (2002–03) *Tuition:* state resident $3200 full-time, $128 per credit hour part-time; nonresident $5000 full-time, $208 per credit hour part-time. Full-time tuition and fees vary according to degree level and student level. Part-time tuition and fees vary according to course load. *Required fees:* $1100 full-time, $25 per credit hour. *Room and board:* $6030; room only: $3310. Room and board charges vary according to board plan and housing facility. *Payment plan:* deferred payment. *Waivers:* children of alumni and employees or children of employees.

Financial Aid In 2001, 300 Federal Work-Study jobs (averaging $1500).

Applying *Options:* electronic application, early admission, deferred entrance. *Application fee:* $30. *Required:* high school transcript. *Required for some:* essay or personal statement, letters of recommendation. *Recommended:* minimum 2.0 GPA, letters of recommendation, interview. *Application deadline:* rolling (freshmen), rolling (transfers). *Notification:* continuous (freshmen).

Admissions Contact Mr. Paul Rose, Associate Dean of Enrollment Management, State University of New York College of Agriculture and Technology at

State University of New York College of Agriculture and Technology at Morrisville (continued)
Morrisville, Box 901, Morrisville, NY 13408. *Phone:* 315-684-6046. *Toll-free phone:* 800-258-0111. *Fax:* 315-684-6116. *E-mail:* admissions@morrisville.edu.

STATE UNIVERSITY OF NEW YORK COLLEGE OF ENVIRONMENTAL SCIENCE & FORESTRY, RANGER SCHOOL

Wanakena, New York

- **State-supported** 2-year, founded 1912, part of State University of New York System
- **Calendar** semesters
- **Degrees** associate (students must apply one year prior to enrollment)
- **Rural** 2800-acre campus
- **Endowment** $500,000
- **Coed, primarily men,** 40 undergraduate students, 100% full-time, 13% women, 88% men

Undergraduates 40 full-time. Students come from 4 states and territories, 6% are from out of state, 100% transferred in, 100% live on campus.

Freshmen *Admission:* 83 applied, 51 admitted.

Faculty *Total:* 6, 83% full-time. *Student/faculty ratio:* 7:1.

Majors Forest harvesting production technology; surveying.

Academic Programs *Special study options:* advanced placement credit, distance learning.

Library Ranger School Library with 5,000 titles, 60 serial subscriptions, an OPAC.

Computers on Campus 20 computers available on campus for general student use. Internet access available.

Student Life *Housing Options:* coed. *Student Services:* health clinic, personal/psychological counseling, legal services.

Athletics *Intramural sports:* basketball M/W, ice hockey M/W, skiing (cross-country) M/W, skiing (downhill) M/W, softball M/W, volleyball M/W, weight lifting M/W.

Standardized Tests *Required:* SAT I or ACT (for admission).

Costs (2002–03) *Tuition:* state resident $3200 full-time; nonresident $8300 full-time. *Required fees:* $283 full-time. *Room and board:* $6850.

Financial Aid In 2001, 30 Federal Work-Study jobs (averaging $1096). 15 State and other part-time jobs (averaging $1000).

Applying *Options:* electronic application, deferred entrance. *Application fee:* $30. *Application deadline:* rolling (freshmen), rolling (transfers).

Admissions Contact Director of Admissions, State University of New York College of Environmental Science & Forestry, Ranger School, Bray 106, Syracuse, NY 13210-2779. *Phone:* 315-470-6600. *Toll-free phone:* 800-777-7373. *Fax:* 315-470-6933. *E-mail:* esfinfo@mailbox.syr.edu.

STATE UNIVERSITY OF NEW YORK COLLEGE OF TECHNOLOGY AT ALFRED

Alfred, New York

- **State-supported** primarily 2-year, founded 1908, part of State University of New York System
- **Calendar** semesters
- **Degrees** certificates, associate, and bachelor's
- **Rural** 175-acre campus
- **Endowment** $3.2 million
- **Coed,** 3,041 undergraduate students, 90% full-time, 33% women, 67% men

Undergraduates Students come from 6 states and territories, 4 other countries, 1% are from out of state, 6% African American, 1% Asian American or Pacific Islander, 2% Hispanic American, 0.8% Native American, 1% international, 70% live on campus. *Retention:* 96% of 2001 full-time freshmen returned.

Freshmen *Admission:* 3,979 applied, 2,843 admitted. *Average high school GPA:* 3.10.

Faculty *Total:* 184, 72% full-time, 10% with terminal degrees. *Student/faculty ratio:* 20:1.

Majors Accounting; agricultural business; agricultural sciences; animal sciences; architectural engineering technology; auto body repair; auto mechanic/technician; biological/physical sciences; biological technology; business administration; business marketing and marketing management; carpentry; civil engineering technology; computer engineering technology; computer graphics; computer graphics; computer hardware engineering; computer/information sciences; computer/information technology services administration and management related; computer installation/repair; computer science; computer/technical support; computer typography/composition; construction engineering; construction technology; court reporting; culinary arts; dairy science; data processing technology; drafting; drafting/design technology; electrical/electronic engineering technology; electrical equipment installation/repair; electromechanical technology; engineering science; entrepreneurship; environmental science; finance; heating/air conditioning/refrigeration; heavy equipment maintenance; horticulture science; humanities; human services; industrial electronics installation/repair; landscaping management; liberal arts and sciences/liberal studies; machine technology; masonry/tile setting; mathematics; mechanical design technology; mechanical engineering technology; medical assistant; medical records administration; nursing; ornamental horticulture; plumbing; restaurant operations; social sciences; sport/fitness administration; surveying; system administration; system/networking/LAN/WAN management; veterinary sciences; welding technology.

Academic Programs *Special study options:* academic remediation for entering students, adult/continuing education programs, advanced placement credit, distance learning, external degree program, honors programs, independent study, off-campus study, part-time degree program, services for LD students, student-designed majors, summer session for credit. *ROTC:* Army (c).

Library Walter C. Hinkle Memorial Library plus 1 other with 72,295 titles, 729 serial subscriptions, an OPAC.

Computers on Campus 1600 computers available on campus for general student use. A campuswide network can be accessed from student residence rooms and from off campus. Internet access, online (class) registration, at least one staffed computer lab available.

Student Life *Housing Options:* coed, disabled students. *Activities and Organizations:* drama/theater group, student-run newspaper, radio station, choral group, Outdoor Activity Club, BACCHUS, Sondai Society, Drama Club, choir. *Campus security:* 24-hour emergency response devices and patrols, late-night transport/escort service, residence hall entrance guards. *Student Services:* health clinic, personal/psychological counseling.

Athletics Member NJCAA. *Intercollegiate sports:* baseball M, basketball M(s)/W(s), cross-country running M(s)/W(s), football M(s), lacrosse M(s), soccer M(s)/W(s), softball W(s), swimming M/W, track and field M(s)/W(s), volleyball W, wrestling M. *Intramural sports:* basketball M/W, bowling M/W, cross-country running M/W, football M, golf M/W, lacrosse M/W, racquetball M/W, rugby M/W, skiing (cross-country) M/W, soccer M/W, softball M/W, table tennis M/W, tennis M/W, volleyball M/W, water polo M/W.

Standardized Tests *Recommended:* SAT I or ACT (for admission).

Costs (2001–02) *Tuition:* state resident $3200 full-time, $137 per credit hour part-time; nonresident $5000 full-time, $346 per credit hour part-time. Full-time tuition and fees vary according to degree level and program. Part-time tuition and fees vary according to course load, degree level, and program. *Required fees:* $790 full-time. *Room and board:* $5358. Room and board charges vary according to board plan and housing facility. *Payment plan:* installment. *Waivers:* employees or children of employees.

Financial Aid In 2001, 350 Federal Work-Study jobs (averaging $1000).

Applying *Options:* common application, electronic application, deferred entrance. *Application fee:* $30. *Required:* high school transcript. *Required for some:* minimum 2.0 GPA. *Recommended:* essay or personal statement, letters of recommendation, interview. *Application deadline:* rolling (freshmen), rolling (transfers). *Notification:* continuous (freshmen).

Admissions Contact Ms. Deborah J. Goodrich, Director of Admissions, State University of New York College of Technology at Alfred, Huntington Administration Building, Alfred, NY 14802. *Phone:* 607-587-4215. *Toll-free phone:* 800-4-ALFRED. *Fax:* 607-587-4299. *E-mail:* admissions@alfredstate.edu.

STATE UNIVERSITY OF NEW YORK COLLEGE OF TECHNOLOGY AT CANTON

Canton, New York

- **State-supported** primarily 2-year, founded 1906, part of State University of New York System
- **Calendar** semesters
- **Degrees** certificates, associate, and bachelor's
- **Small-town** 555-acre campus
- **Endowment** $5.0 million
- **Coed,** 2,223 undergraduate students, 79% full-time, 48% women, 52% men

Undergraduates 1,749 full-time, 474 part-time. Students come from 18 states and territories, 5 other countries, 3% are from out of state, 9% African American,

0.5% Asian American or Pacific Islander, 3% Hispanic American, 2% Native American, 0.4% international, 8% transferred in, 48% live on campus.

Freshmen *Admission:* 1,778 applied, 1,611 admitted, 746 enrolled.

Faculty *Total:* 114, 73% full-time. *Student/faculty ratio:* 20:1.

Majors Accounting; auto mechanic/technician; biological/physical sciences; business administration; business economics; carpentry; civil engineering technology; construction technology; corrections; criminal justice/law enforcement administration; early childhood education; electrical/electronic engineering technology; engineering science; engineering technology; environmental science; forest harvesting production technology; heating/air conditioning/refrigeration; humanities; industrial technology; information sciences/systems; interdisciplinary studies; landscape architecture; law enforcement/police science; liberal arts and sciences/liberal studies; mechanical engineering technology; medical laboratory technician; mortuary science; nursing; occupational therapy assistant; office management; physical therapy assistant; plumbing; recreational therapy; social sciences; veterinary technology; wood science/paper technology.

Academic Programs *Special study options:* academic remediation for entering students, adult/continuing education programs, advanced placement credit, distance learning, internships, off-campus study, part-time degree program, services for LD students, student-designed majors, summer session for credit. *ROTC:* Army (c), Air Force (c).

Library Southworth Library with 71,200 titles, 397 serial subscriptions, 2,042 audiovisual materials, an OPAC, a Web page.

Computers on Campus 300 computers available on campus for general student use. Internet access, at least one staffed computer lab available.

Student Life *Housing:* on-campus residence required through sophomore year. *Options:* coed, men-only, women-only. *Activities and Organizations:* drama/theater group, student-run newspaper, radio station, choral group, Karate Club, Automotive Club, Outing Club, WATC-Radio, Afro-Latin Society, national fraternities, national sororities. *Campus security:* 24-hour emergency response devices and patrols, late-night transport/escort service, controlled dormitory access. *Student Services:* health clinic, personal/psychological counseling.

Athletics Member NJCAA. *Intercollegiate sports:* basketball M/W, bowling M/W, football M, golf M/W, ice hockey M, lacrosse M, soccer M/W, softball W, volleyball W. *Intramural sports:* badminton M/W, basketball M/W, golf M/W, skiing (cross-country) M/W, soccer M/W, softball M/W, tennis M/W, volleyball M/W.

Costs (2002–03) *Tuition:* $128 per credit hour part-time; state resident $3200 full-time, $210 per credit hour part-time; nonresident $5000 full-time. Full-time tuition and fees vary according to degree level, location, and program. Part-time tuition and fees vary according to degree level, location, and program. *Required fees:* $805 full-time, $33 per credit hour. *Room and board:* $6490. Room and board charges vary according to housing facility. *Payment plans:* installment, deferred payment. *Waivers:* employees or children of employees.

Applying *Options:* electronic application, early admission, deferred entrance. *Application fee:* $30. *Required:* high school transcript. *Required for some:* interview. *Recommended:* minimum 2.0 GPA. *Application deadline:* rolling (freshmen), rolling (transfers). *Notification:* continuous (freshmen).

Admissions Contact Mr. David M. Gerlach, Dean of Enrollment Management, State University of New York College of Technology at Canton, Canton, NY 13617. *Phone:* 315-386-7123. *Toll-free phone:* 800-388-7123. *Fax:* 315-386-7929. *E-mail:* williama@scanva.canton.edu.

STATE UNIVERSITY OF NEW YORK COLLEGE OF TECHNOLOGY AT DELHI

Delhi, New York

- **State-supported** primarily 2-year, founded 1913, part of State University of New York System
- **Calendar** semesters
- **Degrees** certificates, associate, and bachelor's
- **Small-town** 1100-acre campus
- **Endowment** $1.2 million
- **Coed,** 2,013 undergraduate students, 92% full-time, 43% women, 57% men

Undergraduates 1,857 full-time, 156 part-time. Students come from 7 states and territories, 3 other countries, 2% are from out of state, 10% African American, 1% Asian American or Pacific Islander, 6% Hispanic American, 0.7% Native American, 0.2% international, 8% transferred in, 61% live on campus.

Freshmen *Admission:* 3,126 applied, 2,013 enrolled. *Average high school GPA:* 2.8.

Faculty *Total:* 140, 73% full-time. *Student/faculty ratio:* 16:1.

Majors Accounting; architectural engineering technology; business administration; business marketing and marketing management; carpentry; computer/information technology services administration and management related; construction management; construction technology; culinary arts; drafting; drafting/design technology; electrical/power transmission installation; engineering-related technology; engineering science; forestry; general studies; health/physical education; heating/air conditioning/refrigeration; heating/air conditioning/refrigeration technology; horticulture science; hotel and restaurant management; hotel/motel services marketing operations; humanities; information sciences/systems; laboratory animal medicine; landscape architecture; landscaping management; masonry/tile setting; mathematics; nursing; physical education; plumbing; recreation/leisure facilities management; recreation/leisure studies; restaurant operations; social sciences; travel/tourism management; turf management; veterinary technology; Web page, digital/multimedia and information resources design; welding technology; woodworking.

Academic Programs *Special study options:* academic remediation for entering students, adult/continuing education programs, advanced placement credit, distance learning, English as a second language, honors programs, internships, part-time degree program, services for LD students, student-designed majors, summer session for credit.

Library Resnick Library with 47,909 titles, 384 serial subscriptions, an OPAC.

Computers on Campus 350 computers available on campus for general student use. A campuswide network can be accessed from off campus. Internet access, online (class) registration, at least one staffed computer lab available.

Student Life *Housing:* on-campus residence required through sophomore year. *Options:* coed. *Activities and Organizations:* drama/theater group, student-run newspaper, radio station, Latin American Student Organization, Hotel Sales Management Association, student radio station, Phi Theta Kappa, Student Programming Board, national fraternities. *Campus security:* 24-hour emergency response devices and patrols. *Student Services:* health clinic, personal/psychological counseling, legal services.

Athletics Member NAIA, NJCAA. *Intercollegiate sports:* basketball M/W, cross-country running M/W, golf M/W, lacrosse M, soccer M/W, softball W, swimming M/W, tennis M/W, track and field M/W, volleyball W, wrestling M. *Intramural sports:* basketball M/W, bowling M/W, cross-country running M/W, football M/W, golf M/W, racquetball M/W, skiing (cross-country) M/W, skiing (downhill) M/W, swimming M/W, tennis M/W, volleyball M/W, weight lifting M/W.

Costs (2001–02) *Tuition:* state resident $3200 full-time, $137 per credit hour part-time; nonresident $5000 full-time, $210 per credit hour part-time. Full-time tuition and fees vary according to degree level. Part-time tuition and fees vary according to degree level. *Required fees:* $735 full-time, $29 per credit hour. *Room and board:* $5790; room only: $3190. Room and board charges vary according to board plan and location. *Payment plan:* installment.

Financial Aid In 2001, 150 Federal Work-Study jobs (averaging $1050).

Applying *Options:* electronic application, early admission, deferred entrance. *Application fee:* $30. *Required:* high school transcript. *Required for some:* minimum 2.0 GPA. *Application deadline:* rolling (freshmen), rolling (transfers). *Notification:* continuous (freshmen).

Admissions Contact State University of New York College of Technology at Delhi, Delhi, NY 13753. *Phone:* 607-746-4558. *Toll-free phone:* 800-96-DELHI. *Fax:* 607-746-4104.

SUFFOLK COUNTY COMMUNITY COLLEGE

Selden, New York

- **State and locally supported** 2-year, founded 1959, part of State University of New York System
- **Calendar** semesters
- **Degree** certificates, diplomas, and associate
- **Small-town** 500-acre campus with easy access to New York City
- **Coed,** 19,851 undergraduate students, 44% full-time, 60% women, 40% men

Undergraduates 8,758 full-time, 11,093 part-time. Students come from 14 states and territories, 1% are from out of state, 3% transferred in.

Freshmen *Admission:* 6,095 applied, 5,507 admitted, 6,699 enrolled. *Average high school GPA:* 2.5. *Test scores:* SAT verbal scores over 500: 36%; SAT math scores over 500: 38%; ACT scores over 18: 30%; SAT verbal scores over 600: 8%; SAT math scores over 600: 8%; ACT scores over 24: 4%; SAT verbal scores over 700: 1%.

Faculty *Total:* 1,162, 27% full-time. *Student/faculty ratio:* 18:1.

Majors Accounting; alcohol/drug abuse counseling; art; auto mechanic/technician; biological/physical sciences; biology; business administration; business marketing and marketing management; chemistry; child care/development; civil engineering technology; communication systems installation/repair; community services; computer engineering technology; computer programming; com-

Suffolk County Community College (continued)
puter science; computer/technical support; construction technology; criminal justice/law enforcement administration; culinary arts; data processing technology; dietetics; drafting; early childhood education; electrical/electronic engineering technology; engineering; engineering science; English; graphic design/commercial art/illustration; horticulture science; humanities; human services; industrial technology; information sciences/systems; information technology; insurance/risk management; interior design; journalism; law enforcement/police science; liberal arts and sciences/liberal studies; mathematics; mechanical engineering technology; medical assistant; medical technology; music; nursing; opticianry; paralegal/legal assistant; photographic technology; physical therapy; real estate; recreational therapy; recreation/leisure studies; retail management; sign language interpretation; social sciences; telecommunications; theater arts/drama; veterinary sciences; women's studies.

Academic Programs *Special study options:* academic remediation for entering students, adult/continuing education programs, advanced placement credit, cooperative education, distance learning, English as a second language, honors programs, independent study, internships, off-campus study, part-time degree program, services for LD students, summer session for credit. *ROTC:* Army (c).

Library 659 serial subscriptions, an OPAC, a Web page.

Computers on Campus At least one staffed computer lab available.

Student Life *Housing:* college housing not available. *Activities and Organizations:* drama/theater group, student-run newspaper, choral group. *Campus security:* 24-hour emergency response devices and patrols. *Student Services:* health clinic, personal/psychological counseling, women's center.

Athletics Member NJCAA. *Intercollegiate sports:* baseball M, basketball M/W, cross-country running M/W, golf M/W, gymnastics M/W, lacrosse M, sailing M/W, soccer M, softball W, tennis M/W, volleyball W.

Standardized Tests *Required for some:* SAT I or ACT (for placement). *Recommended:* SAT I or ACT (for placement).

Costs (2001–02) *Tuition:* area resident $2430 full-time, $103 per credit part-time; state resident $4860 full-time, $206 per credit part-time; nonresident $4860 full-time, $206 per credit part-time. Part-time tuition and fees vary according to course load. *Required fees:* $344 full-time. *Payment plan:* installment. *Waivers:* employees or children of employees.

Applying *Options:* deferred entrance. *Application fee:* $30. *Required:* high school transcript. *Application deadline:* rolling (freshmen), rolling (transfers). *Notification:* continuous (freshmen).

Admissions Contact Ms. Kate Rowe, Executive Director of Admissions and Enrollment Management, Suffolk County Community College, 533 College Road, Selden, NY 11784-2899. *Phone:* 631-451-4000. *Fax:* 631-451-4415.

SULLIVAN COUNTY COMMUNITY COLLEGE
Loch Sheldrake, New York

- **State and locally supported** 2-year, founded 1962, part of State University of New York System
- **Calendar** 4-1-4
- **Degree** certificates and associate
- **Rural** 405-acre campus
- **Endowment** $1.2 million
- **Coed,** 1,591 undergraduate students, 60% full-time, 61% women, 39% men

Undergraduates 957 full-time, 634 part-time. Students come from 7 states and territories, 9 other countries, 1% are from out of state, 18% African American, 2% Asian American or Pacific Islander, 10% Hispanic American, 0.3% Native American, 0.9% international, 4% transferred in.

Freshmen *Admission:* 1,327 applied, 1,174 admitted, 643 enrolled.

Faculty *Total:* 108, 44% full-time.

Majors Accounting; alcohol/drug abuse counseling; baker/pastry chef; business administration; business marketing and marketing management; computer graphics; computer programming (specific applications); corrections; culinary arts; data entry/microcomputer applications; early childhood education; electrical/electronic engineering technology; elementary education; engineering science; environmental science; graphic design/commercial art/illustration; hospitality management; human services; information sciences/systems; liberal arts and sciences/liberal studies; mathematics; nursing; paralegal/legal assistant; photography; radio/television broadcasting; retail management; secretarial science; sport/fitness administration; surveying; travel/tourism management; Web/multimedia management/webmaster.

Academic Programs *Special study options:* academic remediation for entering students, adult/continuing education programs, advanced placement credit, distance learning, double majors, honors programs, internships, part-time degree program, services for LD students, summer session for credit.

Library Hermann Memorial Library with 65,699 titles, 400 serial subscriptions, 4,928 audiovisual materials, an OPAC, a Web page.

Computers on Campus 205 computers available on campus for general student use. Internet access, online (class) registration, at least one staffed computer lab available.

Student Life *Housing:* college housing not available. *Activities and Organizations:* student-run radio station, Science Alliance, Black Student Union, Drama Club, Baking Club, Honor Society. *Campus security:* 24-hour emergency response devices and patrols. *Student Services:* health clinic, personal/psychological counseling, legal services.

Athletics Member NJCAA. *Intercollegiate sports:* basketball M, cross-country running M/W, golf M, softball W, volleyball W. *Intramural sports:* badminton M/W, basketball M/W, bowling M/W, cross-country running M/W, equestrian sports M/W, football M, golf M/W, racquetball M/W, skiing (downhill) M/W, soccer M/W, softball M/W, table tennis M/W, tennis M/W, track and field M/W, volleyball M/W, weight lifting M/W.

Standardized Tests *Recommended:* SAT I or ACT (for placement).

Costs (2001–02) *Tuition:* state resident $2500 full-time, $90 per credit part-time; nonresident $5000 full-time, $180 per credit part-time. Full-time tuition and fees vary according to program. Part-time tuition and fees vary according to program. *Required fees:* $156 full-time, $5 per credit. *Payment plan:* deferred payment. *Waivers:* senior citizens.

Financial Aid In 2001, 105 Federal Work-Study jobs (averaging $800). 57 State and other part-time jobs (averaging $841).

Applying *Options:* common application, electronic application, early admission, deferred entrance. *Required:* high school transcript. *Application deadline:* rolling (freshmen), rolling (transfers). *Notification:* continuous (freshmen).

Admissions Contact Mr. Daniel Baldo, Director of Admissions and Registration Services, Sullivan County Community College, 112 College Road, Loch Sheldrake, NY 12759. *Phone:* 914-434-5750 Ext. 4287. *Toll-free phone:* 800-577-5243. *Fax:* 914-434-4806. *E-mail:* dbaldo@sullivan.suny.edu.

TAYLOR BUSINESS INSTITUTE
New York, New York

Admissions Contact Mr. Orlando Mangual, Director of Admissions, Taylor Business Institute, 269 West 40th Street, New York, NY 10018. *Phone:* 212-302-4000.

TCI-THE COLLEGE FOR TECHNOLOGY
New York, New York

- **Proprietary** 2-year, founded 1909
- **Calendar** semesters
- **Degree** certificates, diplomas, and associate
- **Urban** campus
- **Coed,** 4,319 undergraduate students

Undergraduates Students come from 3 states and territories, 102 other countries, 35% African American, 9% Asian American or Pacific Islander, 40% Hispanic American.

Freshmen *Admission:* 2,138 applied, 1,681 admitted.

Faculty *Total:* 215, 42% full-time. *Student/faculty ratio:* 31:1.

Majors Accounting; computer engineering technology; construction technology; electrical/electronic engineering technology; heating/air conditioning/refrigeration technology; secretarial science.

Academic Programs *Special study options:* academic remediation for entering students, adult/continuing education programs, advanced placement credit, cooperative education, double majors, English as a second language, independent study, internships, part-time degree program, services for LD students, summer session for credit.

Library Technical Career Institutes Library plus 1 other with 8,000 titles, 120 serial subscriptions, an OPAC.

Computers on Campus 490 computers available on campus for general student use. At least one staffed computer lab available.

Student Life *Housing:* college housing not available. *Activities and Organizations:* drama/theater group, student-run radio station, choral group, Dare to Dream, ASHRAE, student government, IEEE. *Campus security:* 24-hour patrols. *Student Services:* personal/psychological counseling.

Athletics Member NJCAA. *Intercollegiate sports:* basketball M, bowling W, soccer M(c), softball M(c). *Intramural sports:* table tennis M(c).

Standardized Tests *Required:* ACCUPLACER.

Costs (2001–02) *Tuition:* $7200 full-time, $300 per credit part-time. *Required fees:* $355 full-time, $355 per term part-time.
Financial Aid In 2001, 380 Federal Work-Study jobs (averaging $1697).
Applying *Options:* common application, deferred entrance. *Required:* essay or personal statement, high school transcript, interview. *Application deadline:* rolling (freshmen), rolling (transfers). *Notification:* continuous (freshmen).
Admissions Contact Mr. Larry Stieglitz, Vice President for Admissions, TCI-The College for Technology, 320 West 31st Street, New York, NY 10001-2705. *Phone:* 212-594-4000 Ext. 437. *Fax:* 212-629-3937. *E-mail:* admissions@tciedu.com.

TOMPKINS CORTLAND COMMUNITY COLLEGE
Dryden, New York

- **State and locally supported** 2-year, founded 1968, part of State University of New York System
- **Calendar** semesters
- **Degree** certificates and associate
- **Rural** 250-acre campus with easy access to Syracuse
- **Endowment** $2.0 million
- **Coed,** 2,889 undergraduate students, 61% full-time, 62% women, 38% men

Undergraduates 1,750 full-time, 1,139 part-time. Students come from 22 states and territories, 43 other countries, 1% are from out of state, 5% African American, 2% Asian American or Pacific Islander, 2% Hispanic American, 0.5% Native American, 5% international, 11% transferred in, 4% live on campus.
Freshmen *Admission:* 632 enrolled. *Average high school GPA:* 2.87.
Faculty *Total:* 213, 29% full-time, 5% with terminal degrees. *Student/faculty ratio:* 19:1.
Majors Accounting; alcohol/drug abuse counseling; aviation/airway science; biological/physical sciences; business administration; business marketing and marketing management; child care/development; child care provider; computer graphics; computer graphics; computer hardware engineering; computer/information systems security; computer/information technology services administration and management related; computer programming related; computer science; computer science related; computer software engineering; computer/technical support; construction technology; criminal justice/law enforcement administration; data entry/microcomputer applications; early childhood education; electrical/electronic engineering technology; engineering science; environmental science; graphic design/commercial art/illustration; hotel and restaurant management; humanities; human services; information sciences/systems; international business; liberal arts and sciences/liberal studies; mass communications; mathematics; nursing; paralegal/legal assistant; radio/television broadcasting; recreation/leisure studies; secretarial science; social sciences; sport/fitness administration; system administration; travel services marketing operations; travel/tourism management; Web page, digital/multimedia and information resources design; women's studies.
Academic Programs *Special study options:* academic remediation for entering students, adult/continuing education programs, advanced placement credit, cooperative education, English as a second language, honors programs, internships, off-campus study, part-time degree program, services for LD students, summer session for credit. *ROTC:* Army (c).
Library Gerald A. Barry Memorial Library with 50,630 titles, 489 serial subscriptions, an OPAC, a Web page.
Computers on Campus 350 computers available on campus for general student use. A campuswide network can be accessed from student residence rooms. Internet access, online (class) registration, at least one staffed computer lab available.
Student Life *Housing Options:* coed. *Activities and Organizations:* drama/theater group, Art Works, Accounting Club, Nurse's Association. *Campus security:* 24-hour emergency response devices and patrols. *Student Services:* personal/psychological counseling.
Athletics Member NJCAA. *Intercollegiate sports:* basketball M/W, golf M/W, soccer M/W, softball W, tennis W, volleyball W, wrestling M. *Intramural sports:* badminton M/W, basketball M/W, bowling M/W, football M/W, golf M/W, lacrosse M/W, racquetball M/W, skiing (cross-country) M/W, soccer M/W, softball M/W, swimming M/W, table tennis M/W, tennis M/W, volleyball M/W, water polo M/W.
Standardized Tests *Required for some:* SAT I or ACT (for placement). *Recommended:* ACT (for placement).
Costs (2002–03) *One-time required fee:* $59. *Tuition:* state resident $2680 full-time, $104 per credit part-time; nonresident $5360 full-time, $204 per credit part-time. Part-time tuition and fees vary according to course load. *Required fees:* $320 full-time, $10 per credit. *Room and board:* room only: $3600. Room and board charges vary according to housing facility. *Payment plans:* installment, deferred payment. *Waivers:* senior citizens and employees or children of employees.
Financial Aid In 2001, 135 Federal Work-Study jobs (averaging $1001). 130 State and other part-time jobs (averaging $831).
Applying *Options:* early admission, deferred entrance. *Application fee:* $15. *Required:* high school transcript. *Application deadline:* rolling (freshmen), rolling (transfers). *Notification:* continuous (freshmen).
Admissions Contact Mr. Craig Tucker, Director of Admissions, Tompkins Cortland Community College, 170 North Street, PO Box 139, Dryden, NY 13053-0139. *Phone:* 607-844-8222 Ext. 4225. *Toll-free phone:* 888-567-8211. *Fax:* 607-844-6538. *E-mail:* admissions@sunytcccc.edu.

TROCAIRE COLLEGE
Buffalo, New York

- **Independent** 2-year, founded 1958
- **Calendar** semesters
- **Degree** certificates and associate
- **Urban** 1-acre campus
- **Endowment** $4.2 million
- **Coed, primarily women,** 721 undergraduate students

Undergraduates Students come from 1 other state, 4 other countries.
Freshmen *Admission:* 474 applied, 443 admitted. *Test scores:* SAT verbal scores over 500: 37%; SAT math scores over 500: 32%; ACT scores over 18: 67%.
Faculty *Total:* 102, 31% full-time. *Student/faculty ratio:* 12:1.
Majors Business administration; business marketing and marketing management; early childhood education; environmental science; hotel and restaurant management; industrial radiologic technology; legal administrative assistant; liberal arts and sciences/liberal studies; medical administrative assistant; medical assistant; medical records administration; nursing; operating room technician; radiological science; secretarial science.
Academic Programs *Special study options:* academic remediation for entering students, adult/continuing education programs, advanced placement credit, external degree program, independent study, internships, off-campus study, part-time degree program, services for LD students, summer session for credit.
Library The Rachel R. Savarino Library with 15,403 titles, 93 serial subscriptions, an OPAC, a Web page.
Computers on Campus 55 computers available on campus for general student use. Internet access, at least one staffed computer lab available.
Student Life *Activities and Organizations:* student-run newspaper, Student Government Association, student newspaper, Environmental Club, Ski Club, national fraternities. *Campus security:* 24-hour emergency response devices and patrols, late-night transport/escort service. *Student Services:* health clinic, personal/psychological counseling.
Standardized Tests *Required for some:* SAT I or ACT (for admission).
Costs (2001–02) *Tuition:* $8900 full-time, $290 per credit hour part-time. Dormitory space is available on the Houghton College Satellite Campus for full time female students attending Trocaire College. *Required fees:* $100 full-time, $50 per term part-time. *Room only:* $3150.
Financial Aid In 2001, 30 Federal Work-Study jobs (averaging $1500).
Applying *Options:* deferred entrance. *Application fee:* $25. *Required:* high school transcript. *Recommended:* interview. *Application deadline:* rolling (freshmen), rolling (transfers).
Admissions Contact Mrs. Theresa Horner, Associate Director of Admissions, Trocaire College, 360 Choate Avenue, Buffalo, NY 14220. *Phone:* 716-826-1200 Ext. 1259. *Fax:* 716-828-6107. *E-mail:* info@trocaire.edu.

ULSTER COUNTY COMMUNITY COLLEGE
Stone Ridge, New York

- **State and locally supported** 2-year, founded 1961, part of State University of New York System
- **Calendar** semesters
- **Degree** certificates, diplomas, and associate
- **Rural** 165-acre campus
- **Endowment** $2.4 million
- **Coed,** 2,913 undergraduate students

Undergraduates Students come from 3 states and territories, 1 other country. *Retention:* 65% of 2001 full-time freshmen returned.
Faculty *Total:* 194, 32% full-time. *Student/faculty ratio:* 15:1.

Ulster County Community College (continued)

Majors Accounting; biological/physical sciences; business administration; business marketing and marketing management; community services; computer science; criminal justice/law enforcement administration; data processing technology; drafting; elementary education; engineering; engineering technology; environmental technology; graphic design/commercial art/illustration; humanities; human services; industrial technology; information sciences/systems; journalism; liberal arts and sciences/liberal studies; mass communications; mathematics; nursing; physical sciences; recreation/leisure studies; retail management; secretarial science; social sciences.

Academic Programs *Special study options:* academic remediation for entering students, adult/continuing education programs, advanced placement credit, cooperative education, distance learning, double majors, English as a second language, honors programs, independent study, internships, off-campus study, part-time degree program, services for LD students, student-designed majors, summer session for credit.

Library McDonald Dewitt Library with 70,758 titles, 481 serial subscriptions, 3,880 audiovisual materials, an OPAC, a Web page.

Computers on Campus 250 computers available on campus for general student use. Internet access, at least one staffed computer lab available.

Student Life *Housing:* college housing not available. *Activities and Organizations:* drama/theater group, student-run newspaper, radio station, choral group, Ski Club, Basic Club, Biology Club, Nursing Club. *Campus security:* 24-hour emergency response devices and patrols. *Student Services:* health clinic, personal/psychological counseling.

Athletics Member NJCAA. *Intercollegiate sports:* baseball M, basketball M/W, golf M/W, soccer M, softball W, tennis M/W, volleyball W. *Intramural sports:* baseball M, basketball M, volleyball M/W.

Standardized Tests *Required for some:* ACT ASSET, ACT COMPASS.

Costs (2002–03) *Tuition:* $93 per credit part-time; state resident $2600 full-time, $186 per credit part-time; nonresident $5200 full-time, $186 per credit part-time. *Required fees:* $135 full-time.

Financial Aid In 2001, 125 Federal Work-Study jobs (averaging $1000).

Applying *Options:* early admission, deferred entrance. *Application deadline:* rolling (freshmen), rolling (transfers). *Notification:* continuous (freshmen).

Admissions Contact Admissions Office, Ulster County Community College, Stone Ridge, NY 12484. *Phone:* 914-687-5022. *Toll-free phone:* 800-724-0833. *Fax:* 914-687-5083. *E-mail:* reqinfo@sunyulster.edu.

UTICA SCHOOL OF COMMERCE
Utica, New York

- **Proprietary** 2-year, founded 1896
- **Calendar** quarters
- **Degree** certificates, diplomas, and associate
- **Urban** 2-acre campus
- **Endowment** $21,000
- **Coed, primarily women,** 550 undergraduate students

Undergraduates Students come from 1 other state, 2% African American, 0.6% Asian American or Pacific Islander, 1% Hispanic American.

Freshmen *Average high school GPA:* 2.80.

Faculty *Total:* 92. *Student/faculty ratio:* 15:1.

Majors Accounting; business administration; business marketing and marketing management; computer typography/composition; data processing technology; information sciences/systems; secretarial science.

Academic Programs *Special study options:* academic remediation for entering students, accelerated degree program, adult/continuing education programs, advanced placement credit, honors programs, independent study, internships, part-time degree program, services for LD students, summer session for credit.

Library Utica School of Commerce Library plus 3 others with 2,000 titles, 135 serial subscriptions, an OPAC, a Web page.

Computers on Campus 212 computers available on campus for general student use. Internet access, at least one staffed computer lab available.

Student Life *Housing:* college housing not available. *Activities and Organizations:* student-run newspaper. *Campus security:* security during class hours.

Athletics *Intramural sports:* bowling M/W, swimming M/W, table tennis M/W.

Costs (2001–02) *Tuition:* $8700 full-time, $245 per credit hour part-time. *Required fees:* $288 full-time, $8 per credit hour.

Financial Aid In 2001, 40 Federal Work-Study jobs (averaging $2000).

Applying *Options:* electronic application, early admission, deferred entrance. *Application fee:* $20. *Required:* high school transcript, interview. *Recommended:* essay or personal statement, letters of recommendation. *Application deadline:* rolling (freshmen), rolling (transfers).

Admissions Contact Mr. Philip M. Williams, President, Utica School of Commerce, 201 Bleecker Street, Utica, NY 13501. *Phone:* 315-733-2307. *Toll-free phone:* 800-321-4USC. *Fax:* 315-733-9281. *E-mail:* tfinch@uscny.com.

VILLA MARIA COLLEGE OF BUFFALO
Buffalo, New York

- **Independent** 2-year, founded 1960, affiliated with Roman Catholic Church
- **Calendar** semesters
- **Degree** certificates and associate
- **Suburban** 9-acre campus
- **Endowment** $625,361
- **Coed,** 423 undergraduate students, 69% full-time, 72% women, 28% men

Undergraduates 292 full-time, 131 part-time. Students come from 1 other state, 20% African American, 0.8% Asian American or Pacific Islander, 0.8% Hispanic American, 0.3% Native American, 12% transferred in. *Retention:* 50% of 2001 full-time freshmen returned.

Freshmen *Admission:* 271 applied, 235 admitted, 119 enrolled. *Average high school GPA:* 2.00. *Test scores:* SAT verbal scores over 500: 33%; SAT math scores over 500: 25%; SAT verbal scores over 600: 3%; SAT math scores over 600: 3%.

Faculty *Total:* 83, 33% full-time, 17% with terminal degrees. *Student/faculty ratio:* 7:1.

Majors Business administration; computer management; early childhood education; education; graphic design/commercial art/illustration; health science; interior design; liberal arts and sciences/liberal studies; music; music business management/merchandising; photography; physical therapy assistant; secretarial science.

Academic Programs *Special study options:* academic remediation for entering students, advanced placement credit, cooperative education, double majors, independent study, internships, off-campus study, part-time degree program, services for LD students, study abroad, summer session for credit.

Library Villa Maria College Library with 40,000 titles, 200 serial subscriptions, 5,000 audiovisual materials, an OPAC, a Web page.

Computers on Campus 68 computers available on campus for general student use. A campuswide network can be accessed from off campus. Internet access, at least one staffed computer lab available.

Student Life *Housing:* college housing not available. *Activities and Organizations:* drama/theater group, student-run newspaper, radio station, choral group, Design and Beyond, Teachers Love Children, Multicultural Club, Phi Theta Kappa, Helping Adults New Dreams Succeed. *Campus security:* late-night transport/escort service. *Student Services:* health clinic, personal/psychological counseling.

Standardized Tests *Recommended:* SAT I or ACT (for admission).

Costs (2001–02) *Tuition:* $8800 full-time, $290 per credit part-time. Full-time tuition and fees vary according to course load and program. Part-time tuition and fees vary according to program. *Payment plans:* installment, deferred payment. *Waivers:* senior citizens and employees or children of employees.

Financial Aid In 2001, 48 Federal Work-Study jobs (averaging $869).

Applying *Options:* deferred entrance. *Application fee:* $30. *Required:* high school transcript, interview, writing sample. *Application deadline:* rolling (freshmen), rolling (transfers). *Notification:* continuous (freshmen).

Admissions Contact Ms. Cathy Oddo, Director of Admissions, Villa Maria College of Buffalo, Villa Maria College, 240 Pine Ridge Road, Buffalo, NY 14225-3999. *Phone:* 716-896-0700 Ext. 339. *Fax:* 716-896-0705. *E-mail:* admissions@villa.edu.

THE WESTCHESTER BUSINESS INSTITUTE
White Plains, New York

- **Proprietary** 2-year, founded 1915
- **Calendar** quarters
- **Degree** certificates and associate
- **Suburban** campus with easy access to New York City
- **Coed,** 1,113 undergraduate students, 98% full-time, 50% women, 50% men

Undergraduates 1,091 full-time, 22 part-time. Students come from 3 states and territories, 4 other countries, 6% are from out of state, 23% African American, 2% Asian American or Pacific Islander, 27% Hispanic American, 0.2% Native American, 0.2% international, 6% transferred in.

Freshmen *Admission:* 490 applied, 373 admitted, 228 enrolled.

Faculty *Total:* 74, 34% full-time, 3% with terminal degrees. *Student/faculty ratio:* 20:1.

Majors Accounting; business administration; business marketing and marketing management; computer graphics; computer/information technology services administration and management related; computer programming; computer programming related; computer programming (specific applications); computer programming, vendor/product certification; computer science related; computer software and media applications related; computer systems networking/telecommunications; computer/technical support; computer typography/composition; data entry/microcomputer applications; data entry/microcomputer applications related; data processing technology; information sciences/systems; information technology; management information systems/business data processing; medical administrative assistant; secretarial science; system administration; system/networking/LAN/WAN management; Web/multimedia management/webmaster; Web page, digital/multimedia and information resources design; word processing.

Academic Programs *Special study options:* academic remediation for entering students, accelerated degree program, adult/continuing education programs, cooperative education, double majors, honors programs, internships, part-time degree program, summer session for credit.

Library Westchester Business Institute Resource Center.

Computers on Campus 214 computers available on campus for general student use. Internet access, at least one staffed computer lab available.

Student Life *Housing:* college housing not available.

Standardized Tests *Recommended:* SAT I (for admission).

Costs (2002–03) *Tuition:* $14,025 full-time, $445 per credit part-time. Full-time tuition and fees vary according to course load and program. Part-time tuition and fees vary according to course load and program. *Required fees:* $690 full-time. *Payment plan:* installment. *Waivers:* employees or children of employees.

Applying *Options:* common application, electronic application, deferred entrance. *Application fee:* $30. *Required:* high school transcript, interview. *Required for some:* essay or personal statement. *Application deadline:* rolling (freshmen), rolling (transfers).

Admissions Contact Mr. Dale T. Smith, Vice President, The Westchester Business Institute, 325 Central Avenue, P.O. Box 710, White Plains, NY 10602. *Phone:* 914-948-4442 Ext. 311. *Toll-free phone:* 800-333-4924 Ext. 318. *Fax:* 914-948-5441. *E-mail:* admissions@wbi.org.

WESTCHESTER COMMUNITY COLLEGE
Valhalla, New York

- **State and locally supported** 2-year, founded 1946, part of State University of New York System
- **Calendar** semesters
- **Degree** certificates and associate
- **Suburban** 218-acre campus with easy access to New York City
- **Endowment** $6.4 million
- **Coed,** 11,025 undergraduate students, 43% full-time, 57% women, 43% men

Undergraduates 4,780 full-time, 6,245 part-time. Students come from 13 states and territories, 51 other countries, 0.5% are from out of state, 19% African American, 5% Asian American or Pacific Islander, 17% Hispanic American, 1% Native American, 3% international, 7% transferred in. *Retention:* 61% of 2001 full-time freshmen returned.

Freshmen *Admission:* 4,462 applied, 4,462 admitted, 2,139 enrolled.

Faculty *Total:* 674, 24% full-time. *Student/faculty ratio:* 16:1.

Majors Accounting; alcohol/drug abuse counseling; applied art; auto mechanic/technician; biological/physical sciences; business administration; business marketing and marketing management; chemical engineering technology; child care/development; child care provider; civil engineering technology; computer/information sciences; computer science; computer science related; computer systems networking/telecommunications; corrections; criminal justice/law enforcement administration; culinary arts; dance; data processing technology; dietetics; electrical/electronic engineering technology; emergency medical technology; engineering science; engineering technology; environmental technology; finance; fine/studio arts; food products retailing; food services technology; hotel and restaurant management; humanities; human services; industrial radiologic technology; information sciences/systems; international business; law enforcement/police science; legal administrative assistant; liberal arts and sciences/liberal studies; mass communications; mechanical engineering technology; medical laboratory technician; medical technology; nursing; paralegal/legal assistant; public administration; respiratory therapy; retail management; secretarial science; social sciences; tourism promotion operations; travel/tourism management.

Academic Programs *Special study options:* academic remediation for entering students, adult/continuing education programs, cooperative education, distance learning, English as a second language, honors programs, independent study, internships, off-campus study, part-time degree program, services for LD students, student-designed majors, summer session for credit.

Library Harold L. Drimmer Library with 96,419 titles, 531 serial subscriptions, 5,163 audiovisual materials, an OPAC, a Web page.

Computers on Campus 720 computers available on campus for general student use. Internet access, at least one staffed computer lab available.

Student Life *Housing:* college housing not available. *Activities and Organizations:* drama/theater group, student-run newspaper, radio station, choral group, Student Senate, African Culture Club, Italian Club, International Friendship Club, Alpha Beta Gamma. *Campus security:* 24-hour emergency response devices and patrols, late-night transport/escort service. *Student Services:* health clinic, personal/psychological counseling, women's center.

Athletics Member NJCAA. *Intercollegiate sports:* baseball M, basketball M/W, bowling M/W, golf M, soccer M, softball W, volleyball W. *Intramural sports:* badminton M/W, basketball M/W, softball M/W, swimming M/W, tennis M/W, volleyball M/W, weight lifting M/W.

Standardized Tests *Recommended:* SAT I or ACT (for placement).

Costs (2001–02) *Tuition:* state resident $2350 full-time, $98 per credit part-time; nonresident $5875 full-time, $245 per credit part-time. *Required fees:* $303 full-time, $131 per year part-time. *Payment plan:* deferred payment. *Waivers:* employees or children of employees.

Financial Aid In 2001, 100 Federal Work-Study jobs (averaging $1000).

Applying *Options:* electronic application, early admission. *Application fee:* $25. *Required:* high school transcript. *Recommended:* interview. *Application deadline:* rolling (freshmen), rolling (transfers). *Notification:* continuous until 2/2 (freshmen).

Admissions Contact Ms. Terri Weisel, Director of Admissions, Westchester Community College, 75 Grasslands Road, Administration Building, Valhalla, NY 10595-1698. *Phone:* 914-785-6735. *E-mail:* admissions@sunywcc.edu.

WOOD TOBE-COBURN SCHOOL
New York, New York

- **Proprietary** 2-year, founded 1879, part of Bradford Schools, Inc
- **Calendar** semesters
- **Degree** diplomas and associate
- **Urban** campus
- **Coed, primarily women**

Student Life *Campus security:* 24-hour emergency response devices and patrols.

Costs (2001–02) *Tuition:* $11,200 full-time. Full-time tuition and fees vary according to program.

Applying *Required:* high school transcript, interview.

Admissions Contact Ms. Sandra L. Wendland, Director of Admissions, Wood Tobe-Coburn School, 8 East 40th Street, New York, NY 10016. *Phone:* 212-686-9040 Ext. 103. *Fax:* 212-686-9171.

NORTH CAROLINA

ALAMANCE COMMUNITY COLLEGE
Graham, North Carolina

- **State-supported** 2-year, founded 1959, part of North Carolina Community College System
- **Calendar** semesters
- **Degree** certificates, diplomas, and associate
- **Small-town** 48-acre campus
- **Endowment** $2.0 million
- **Coed,** 3,991 undergraduate students, 32% full-time, 63% women, 37% men

Undergraduates 1,259 full-time, 2,732 part-time. Students come from 23 states and territories, 3 other countries, 1% are from out of state, 21% African American, 0.9% Asian American or Pacific Islander, 2% Hispanic American, 0.2% Native American, 1% international.

Freshmen *Admission:* 1,200 applied, 630 admitted, 630 enrolled.

Faculty *Total:* 226, 36% full-time, 7% with terminal degrees. *Student/faculty ratio:* 16:1.

Majors Accounting technician; animal sciences; auto mechanic/technician; banking; biotechnology research; business administration; carpentry; computer

Alamance Community College (continued)
programming; criminal justice studies; culinary arts; early childhood education; electrical/electronic engineering technology; electromechanical technology; executive assistant; general office/clerical; general retailing/wholesaling; graphic design/ commercial art/illustration; heating/air conditioning/refrigeration technology; horticulture services; information sciences/systems; legal administrative assistant; liberal arts and sciences/liberal studies; machine technology; mechanical engineering technology; medical administrative assistant; medical assistant; medical laboratory technician; nursing; operations management; real estate; social work; teacher assistant/aide; welding technology.
Academic Programs *Special study options:* academic remediation for entering students, adult/continuing education programs, cooperative education, distance learning, double majors, English as a second language, independent study, off-campus study, part-time degree program, services for LD students, summer session for credit.
Library Learning Resources Center with 22,114 titles, 185 serial subscriptions, 3,033 audiovisual materials, an OPAC, a Web page.
Computers on Campus At least one staffed computer lab available.
Student Life *Housing:* college housing not available. *Campus security:* 24-hour emergency response devices and patrols, student patrols, late-night transport/ escort service. *Student Services:* personal/psychological counseling.
Athletics *Intramural sports:* basketball M/W, bowling M/W, tennis M/W, volleyball M/W.
Standardized Tests *Recommended:* SAT I or ACT (for placement).
Costs (2001–02) *Tuition:* state resident $1022 full-time, $32 per credit hour part-time; nonresident $5574 full-time, $173 per credit hour part-time. Part-time tuition and fees vary according to course load. *Required fees:* $30 full-time, $5 per term part-time. *Waivers:* senior citizens.
Financial Aid In 2001, 80 Federal Work-Study jobs (averaging $3000).
Applying *Options:* common application, deferred entrance. *Required:* high school transcript. *Application deadline:* rolling (freshmen), rolling (transfers). *Notification:* continuous (freshmen).
Admissions Contact Ms. Suzanne Mintz, Coordinator of Admissions and Records, Alamance Community College, Jimmy Kerr Road, Graham, NC 27253-8000. *Phone:* 336-578-2002 Ext. 4138. *Fax:* 336-578-1987. *E-mail:* admissions@alamance.cc.nc.us.

ASHEVILLE-BUNCOMBE TECHNICAL COMMUNITY COLLEGE
Asheville, North Carolina

- **State-supported** 2-year, founded 1959, part of North Carolina Community College System
- **Calendar** semesters
- **Degree** certificates, diplomas, and associate
- **Urban** 126-acre campus
- **Endowment** $98,442
- **Coed,** 5,448 undergraduate students, 34% full-time, 54% women, 46% men

Undergraduates 1,866 full-time, 3,582 part-time. 2% are from out of state, 4% transferred in. *Retention:* 10% of 2001 full-time freshmen returned.
Freshmen *Admission:* 2,792 applied, 2,792 admitted, 552 enrolled.
Faculty *Total:* 567, 21% full-time, 5% with terminal degrees.
Majors Accounting technician; auto mechanic/technician; business administration; business systems networking/ telecommunications; child care/guidance; civil engineering technology; computer programming; culinary arts; dental hygiene; emergency medical technology; executive assistant; general retailing/wholesaling; heating/air conditioning/refrigeration; hotel and restaurant management; institutional food workers; law enforcement/police science; liberal arts and sciences/ liberal studies; machine technology; mechanical design technology; mechanical engineering technology; medical laboratory technician; medical radiologic technology; nursing; operations management; social work; surveying; tool/die making.
Academic Programs *Special study options:* academic remediation for entering students, adult/continuing education programs, advanced placement credit, cooperative education, distance learning, double majors, independent study, internships, part-time degree program, services for LD students, summer session for credit.
Library Holly Learning Resources Center with 37,439 titles, 195 serial subscriptions, an OPAC.
Computers on Campus 414 computers available on campus for general student use. A campuswide network can be accessed from off campus. Internet access, at least one staffed computer lab available.
Student Life *Housing:* college housing not available. *Activities and Organizations:* student-run newspaper, Student Government Association, Phi Beta Lambda. *Campus security:* 24-hour emergency response devices and patrols. *Student Services:* personal/psychological counseling.
Athletics *Intramural sports:* basketball M/W, softball M/W, volleyball M/W.
Standardized Tests *Required:* CPT, SAT I, or ACT.
Costs (2001–02) *Tuition:* area resident $885 full-time, $31 per semester hour part-time; state resident $885 full-time, $31 per semester hour part-time; nonresident $4746 full-time, $170 per semester hour part-time. Full-time tuition and fees vary according to course load and program. Part-time tuition and fees vary according to course load and program. *Required fees:* $22 full-time, $31 per semester hour. *Payment plan:* installment. *Waivers:* senior citizens.
Financial Aid In 2001, 25 Federal Work-Study jobs (averaging $1400).
Applying *Options:* deferred entrance. *Required:* high school transcript. *Required for some:* letters of recommendation, interview. *Application deadline:* rolling (freshmen), rolling (transfers). *Notification:* continuous (freshmen).
Admissions Contact Ms. Martha B. McLean, Director of Enrollment Management, Asheville-Buncombe Technical Community College, 340 Victoria Road, Asheville, NC 28801. *Phone:* 828-254-1921 Ext. 147. *Fax:* 828-251-6718. *E-mail:* admissions@asheville.cc.nc.us.

BEAUFORT COUNTY COMMUNITY COLLEGE
Washington, North Carolina

- **State-supported** 2-year, founded 1967, part of North Carolina Community College System
- **Calendar** semesters
- **Degree** certificates, diplomas, and associate
- **Rural** 67-acre campus
- **Coed,** 1,721 undergraduate students

Undergraduates 1% are from out of state, 33% African American.
Faculty *Total:* 136, 43% full-time, 2% with terminal degrees.
Majors Accounting; agricultural mechanization; auto mechanic/technician; business administration; computer programming; computer systems networking/ telecommunications; drafting; drafting/design technology; early childhood education; electrical/electronic engineering technology; environmental science; human resources management; information sciences/systems; law enforcement/police science; liberal arts and sciences/liberal studies; medical administrative assistant; medical laboratory technician; medical office management; nursing; secretarial science; social work; welding technology.
Academic Programs *Special study options:* academic remediation for entering students, advanced placement credit, cooperative education, distance learning, part-time degree program, services for LD students, summer session for credit.
Library Beaufort Community College Library with 25,734 titles, 214 serial subscriptions, an OPAC, a Web page.
Computers on Campus 60 computers available on campus for general student use. A campuswide network can be accessed from off campus. Internet access, at least one staffed computer lab available.
Student Life *Housing:* college housing not available. *Activities and Organizations:* Student Government Association, Data Processing Management Association, Gama Beta Phi, Phi Beta Lambda. *Campus security:* 24-hour emergency response devices and patrols, late-night transport/escort service. *Student Services:* personal/psychological counseling.
Costs (2001–02) *Tuition:* state resident $992 full-time, $31 per hour part-time; nonresident $5544 full-time, $173 per hour part-time. Part-time tuition and fees vary according to course load. *Required fees:* $28 full-time, $1 per hour. *Waivers:* senior citizens and employees or children of employees.
Financial Aid In 2001, 21 Federal Work-Study jobs (averaging $1600). *Financial aid deadline:* 7/15.
Applying *Options:* early admission, deferred entrance. *Required:* high school transcript. *Required for some:* essay or personal statement, letters of recommendation, interview. *Application deadline:* rolling (freshmen), rolling (transfers). *Notification:* continuous (freshmen).
Admissions Contact Mr. Gary Burbage, Director of Admissions, Beaufort County Community College, PO Box 1069, 5337 US Highway 264 East, Washington, NC 27889-1069. *Phone:* 252-940-6233. *Fax:* 252-946-0271. *E-mail:* garyb@email.beaufort.cc.nc.us.

BLADEN COMMUNITY COLLEGE
Dublin, North Carolina

- **State and locally supported** 2-year, founded 1967, part of North Carolina Community College System

■ **Calendar** semesters
■ **Degree** certificates, diplomas, and associate
■ **Rural** 45-acre campus
■ **Endowment** $60,000
■ **Coed,** 1,033 undergraduate students, 61% full-time, 77% women, 23% men

Undergraduates 635 full-time, 398 part-time. Students come from 1 other state, 43% African American, 0.2% Asian American or Pacific Islander, 1% Hispanic American, 8% Native American, 5% transferred in. *Retention:* 35% of 2001 full-time freshmen returned.
Freshmen *Admission:* 228 enrolled. *Average high school GPA:* 2.6.
Faculty *Total:* 92, 32% full-time, 4% with terminal degrees. *Student/faculty ratio:* 15:1.
Majors Business administration; computer programming; computer programming (specific applications); electrical/electronic engineering technology; general studies; information technology; law enforcement/police science; liberal arts and sciences/liberal studies; secretarial science.
Academic Programs *Special study options:* academic remediation for entering students, adult/continuing education programs, advanced placement credit, distance learning, double majors, independent study, part-time degree program, services for LD students, summer session for credit.
Library 18,230 titles, 125 serial subscriptions, 20,000 audiovisual materials, an OPAC, a Web page.
Computers on Campus 150 computers available on campus for general student use. A campuswide network can be accessed from off campus. Internet access, at least one staffed computer lab available.
Student Life *Housing:* college housing not available. *Campus security:* 14-hour patrols. *Student Services:* personal/psychological counseling.
Standardized Tests *Required:* ACT COMPASS.
Costs (2001–02) *Tuition:* area resident $992 full-time; state resident $31 per semester hour part-time; nonresident $5544 full-time, $173 per semester hour part-time. *Required fees:* $38 full-time, $19 per term part-time.
Financial Aid In 2001, 30 Federal Work-Study jobs (averaging $1200).
Applying *Options:* common application, electronic application, deferred entrance. *Required:* high school transcript, interview. *Recommended:* minimum 2.0 GPA. *Application deadlines:* 8/1 (freshmen), 8/1 (transfers). *Notification:* continuous until 8/15 (freshmen).
Admissions Contact Ms. Yvonne Willoughby, Admissions Secretary, Bladen Community College, PO Box 266, Dublin, NC 28332. *Phone:* 910-862-2164 Ext. 214. *Toll-free phone:* 910-862-2164 Ext. 214. *Fax:* 910-862-7424. *E-mail:* ywilloughby@bladen.cc.nc.us.

BLUE RIDGE COMMUNITY COLLEGE
Flat Rock, North Carolina

■ **State and locally supported** 2-year, founded 1969, part of North Carolina Community College System
■ **Calendar** semesters
■ **Degree** certificates, diplomas, and associate
■ **Small-town** 109-acre campus
■ **Endowment** $51,500
■ **Coed,** 1,907 undergraduate students, 35% full-time, 62% women, 38% men

Undergraduates Students come from 18 states and territories, 14 other countries, 2% are from out of state, 4% African American, 0.4% Asian American or Pacific Islander, 2% Hispanic American, 0.6% Native American, 2% international.
Freshmen *Admission:* 996 applied, 801 admitted.
Faculty *Total:* 225, 26% full-time, 7% with terminal degrees.
Majors Art; business administration; business marketing and marketing management; computer programming; computer programming related; cosmetology; drafting; early childhood education; electrical/electronic engineering technology; environmental technology; horticulture science; industrial technology; information sciences/systems; liberal arts and sciences/liberal studies; machine technology; mechanical engineering technology; nursing; operating room technician; secretarial science; sign language interpretation; system/networking/LAN/WAN management; travel/tourism management.
Academic Programs *Special study options:* academic remediation for entering students, adult/continuing education programs, advanced placement credit, cooperative education, distance learning, double majors, English as a second language, internships, part-time degree program, services for LD students, summer session for credit.
Library Blue Ridge Community College Library plus 1 other with 47,655 titles, 3,875 serial subscriptions, 1,692 audiovisual materials, an OPAC.
Computers on Campus 225 computers available on campus for general student use. Internet access available.
Student Life *Housing:* college housing not available. *Activities and Organizations:* drama/theater group, student-run newspaper, Student Government Association, Phi Theta Kappa, Spanish club, Rotaract. *Campus security:* sheriff's deputy during class hours. *Student Services:* personal/psychological counseling.
Costs (2001–02) *One-time required fee:* $15. *Tuition:* state resident $992 full-time, $31 per credit hour part-time; nonresident $5544 full-time, $173 per credit hour part-time. Full-time tuition and fees vary according to course load and program. Part-time tuition and fees vary according to course load and program. *Required fees:* $27 full-time, $11 per term part-time. *Waivers:* senior citizens and employees or children of employees.
Financial Aid In 2001, 35 Federal Work-Study jobs (averaging $1920). 34 State and other part-time jobs (averaging $1920).
Applying *Options:* common application, early admission. *Required:* high school transcript. *Application deadline:* rolling (freshmen), rolling (transfers). *Notification:* continuous (freshmen).
Admissions Contact Ms. Sarah Jones, Registrar, Blue Ridge Community College, College Drive, Flat Rock, NC 28731. *Phone:* 828-694-1810. *E-mail:* sarahj@blueridge.cc.nc.us.

BRUNSWICK COMMUNITY COLLEGE
Supply, North Carolina

■ **State-supported** 2-year, founded 1979, part of North Carolina Community College System
■ **Calendar** semesters
■ **Degree** certificates, diplomas, and associate
■ **Rural** 179-acre campus
■ **Endowment** $944,888
■ **Coed,** 978 undergraduate students, 51% full-time, 69% women, 31% men

Undergraduates 496 full-time, 482 part-time. Students come from 4 states and territories, 1% are from out of state, 24% African American, 0.3% Asian American or Pacific Islander, 0.6% Hispanic American, 0.7% Native American, 0.1% international, 4% transferred in.
Freshmen *Admission:* 286 admitted, 267 enrolled.
Faculty *Total:* 90, 30% full-time, 11% with terminal degrees.
Majors Aquaculture operations/production management; business administration; child care provider; computer/information technology services administration and management related; computer programming; computer programming related; electrical/electronic engineering technology; engineering-related technology; fishing sciences; industrial technology; liberal arts and sciences/liberal studies; medical records administration; secretarial science; teacher assistant/aide; turf management.
Academic Programs *Special study options:* academic remediation for entering students, advanced placement credit, cooperative education, distance learning, English as a second language, independent study, internships, part-time degree program, services for LD students, summer session for credit.
Library Brunswick Community College Library plus 1 other with 16,700 titles, 105 serial subscriptions, 1,500 audiovisual materials, an OPAC, a Web page.
Computers on Campus 128 computers available on campus for general student use. Internet access, at least one staffed computer lab available.
Student Life *Housing:* college housing not available. *Activities and Organizations:* Student Government Association, Phi Theta Kappa Honor Society, National Vocational/Technical Honor Society. *Campus security:* late-night transport/escort service, campus police. *Student Services:* personal/psychological counseling.
Athletics Member NJCAA. *Intercollegiate sports:* basketball M, golf M, softball W. *Intramural sports:* volleyball M/W.
Standardized Tests *Required:* ACT ASSET.
Costs (2002–03) *Tuition:* state resident $868 full-time, $31 per semester hour part-time; nonresident $4851 full-time, $173 per semester hour part-time. Part-time tuition and fees vary according to course load. *Required fees:* $41 full-time, $20 per semester part-time. *Payment plan:* deferred payment. *Waivers:* senior citizens and employees or children of employees.
Applying *Required:* high school transcript. *Required for some:* letters of recommendation, interview. *Application deadline:* rolling (freshmen), rolling (transfers). *Notification:* continuous (freshmen).
Admissions Contact Ms. Julie Olsen, Admissions Counselor/Recruiter, Brunswick Community College, PO Box 30, Supply, NC 28462. *Phone:* 910-755-7324. *Toll-free phone:* 800-754-1050 Ext. 324. *Fax:* 910-754-9609. *E-mail:* olsenj@brunswick.cc.nc.us.

CABARRUS COLLEGE OF HEALTH SCIENCES
Concord, North Carolina

- **Independent** primarily 2-year, founded 1942
- **Calendar** semesters
- **Degrees** certificates, diplomas, associate, and bachelor's
- **Small-town** 5-acre campus with easy access to Charlotte
- **Coed, primarily women,** 280 undergraduate students, 58% full-time, 94% women, 6% men

Undergraduates Students come from 2 states and territories, 2% are from out of state, 13% African American, 0.5% Asian American or Pacific Islander, 2% Hispanic American.

Freshmen *Admission:* 40 applied, 35 admitted. *Average high school GPA:* 3.37. *Test scores:* SAT verbal scores over 500: 41%; SAT math scores over 500: 47%.

Faculty *Total:* 43, 37% full-time, 9% with terminal degrees. *Student/faculty ratio:* 9:1.

Majors Health services administration; medical assistant; nurse assistant/aide; nursing; occupational therapy assistant; operating room technician.

Academic Programs *Special study options:* advanced placement credit, distance learning, double majors, independent study, part-time degree program.

Library Northeast Medical Center Library with 7,676 titles, 2,127 serial subscriptions, 923 audiovisual materials.

Computers on Campus 30 computers available on campus for general student use. A campuswide network can be accessed from off campus. Internet access, at least one staffed computer lab available.

Student Life *Housing:* college housing not available. *Activities and Organizations:* student-run newspaper, Student Nurse Association, Christian Student Union, student government, Honor Society, Allied Health Student Association. *Campus security:* 24-hour emergency response devices and patrols. *Student Services:* health clinic, personal/psychological counseling.

Standardized Tests *Required:* SAT I or ACT (for admission).

Costs (2001–02) *Tuition:* $6535 full-time, $170 per credit hour part-time. Full-time tuition and fees vary according to course load and student level. Part-time tuition and fees vary according to course load and student level. *Required fees:* $500 full-time, $250 per term part-time. *Payment plan:* deferred payment.

Financial Aid In 2001, 20 Federal Work-Study jobs.

Applying *Application fee:* $35. *Required:* essay or personal statement, high school transcript, minimum 2.0 GPA, 2 letters of recommendation. *Required for some:* interview. *Recommended:* minimum 3.0 GPA. *Application deadlines:* 3/1 (freshmen), 3/1 (transfers). *Notification:* 4/15 (freshmen).

Admissions Contact Ms. Deborah D. Bowman, Director of Admissions, Cabarrus College of Health Sciences, 431 Copperfield Boulevard, NE, Concord, NC 28025-2405. *Phone:* 704-783-1616. *Fax:* 704-783-1764. *E-mail:* dbowman@northeastmedical.org.

CALDWELL COMMUNITY COLLEGE AND TECHNICAL INSTITUTE
Hudson, North Carolina

- **State-supported** 2-year, founded 1964, part of North Carolina Community College System
- **Calendar** semesters
- **Degree** certificates, diplomas, and associate
- **Small-town** 50-acre campus
- **Coed,** 3,636 undergraduate students, 44% full-time, 56% women, 44% men

Undergraduates 1,617 full-time, 2,019 part-time. Students come from 24 states and territories, 2 other countries, 5% African American, 0.7% Asian American or Pacific Islander, 0.9% Hispanic American, 0.3% Native American, 0.2% international, 9% transferred in.

Freshmen *Admission:* 846 applied, 846 admitted, 610 enrolled.

Faculty *Total:* 401, 24% full-time, 6% with terminal degrees. *Student/faculty ratio:* 8:1.

Majors Accounting; aviation technology; biological/physical sciences; biomedical technology; business administration; computer programming (specific applications); data processing technology; drafting; electrical/electronic engineering technology; industrial technology; information technology; liberal arts and sciences/liberal studies; medical administrative assistant; medical radiologic technology; music; nuclear medical technology; nursing; occupational therapy; paralegal/legal assistant; physical therapy; pre-engineering; secretarial science.

Academic Programs *Special study options:* academic remediation for entering students, adult/continuing education programs, advanced placement credit, cooperative education, distance learning, double majors, independent study, part-time degree program, services for LD students, summer session for credit.

Library Broyhill Center for Learning Resources with 50,770 titles, 251 serial subscriptions, 5,352 audiovisual materials, an OPAC, a Web page.

Computers on Campus 750 computers available on campus for general student use. A campuswide network can be accessed from off campus. Internet access, online (class) registration, at least one staffed computer lab available.

Student Life *Housing:* college housing not available. *Activities and Organizations:* drama/theater group, choral group. *Campus security:* trained security personnel during open hours.

Athletics Member NJCAA. *Intercollegiate sports:* basketball M, volleyball W. *Intramural sports:* basketball M/W, tennis M/W.

Standardized Tests *Required:* CPT.

Costs (2001–02) *Tuition:* state resident $992 full-time, $31 per credit hour part-time; nonresident $5544 full-time, $277 per credit hour part-time. Part-time tuition and fees vary according to course load. *Required fees:* $32 full-time, $8 per term part-time. *Waivers:* senior citizens.

Financial Aid In 2001, 40 Federal Work-Study jobs (averaging $960).

Applying *Options:* early admission. *Required:* high school transcript. *Application deadline:* rolling (freshmen), rolling (transfers). *Notification:* continuous (freshmen).

Admissions Contact Mrs. Janice Van Osdol, Director of Admissions, Caldwell Community College and Technical Institute, 2855 Hickory Boulevard, Hudson, NC 28638. *Phone:* 828-726-2703. *Fax:* 828-726-2709.

CAPE FEAR COMMUNITY COLLEGE
Wilmington, North Carolina

- **State-supported** 2-year, founded 1959, part of North Carolina Community College System
- **Calendar** semesters
- **Degree** certificates, diplomas, and associate
- **Urban** 7-acre campus
- **Endowment** $2.0 million
- **Coed,** 6,051 undergraduate students, 48% full-time, 55% women, 45% men

Undergraduates 2,901 full-time, 3,150 part-time. Students come from 37 states and territories, 5% are from out of state, 14% African American, 0.9% Asian American or Pacific Islander, 2% Hispanic American, 0.8% Native American, 0.2% international.

Freshmen *Admission:* 4,104 applied, 3,007 admitted, 1,352 enrolled.

Faculty *Total:* 536, 34% full-time, 6% with terminal degrees. *Student/faculty ratio:* 13:1.

Majors Accounting technician; architectural engineering technology; auto mechanic/technician; business administration; business systems analysis/design; child care services management; computer maintenance technology; dental hygiene; diagnostic medical sonography; drafting/design technology; electrical/electronic engineering technology; electrical equipment installation/repair; engineering/industrial management; environmental science; executive assistant; hotel and restaurant management; industrial production technologies related; institutional food workers; instrumentation technology; interior design; landscaping management; law enforcement/police science; liberal arts and sciences/liberal studies; machine shop assistant; marine maintenance; marine technology; mechanical engineering technology; medical radiologic technology; nursing; occupational therapy assistant; paralegal/legal assistant; speech-language pathology; welding technology.

Academic Programs *Special study options:* academic remediation for entering students, adult/continuing education programs, cooperative education, distance learning, part-time degree program, services for LD students.

Library Cape Fear Community College Library with 707 serial subscriptions, 5,126 audiovisual materials, an OPAC, a Web page.

Computers on Campus 80 computers available on campus for general student use. A campuswide network can be accessed from off campus. At least one staffed computer lab available.

Student Life *Housing:* college housing not available. *Activities and Organizations:* student-run newspaper, choral group. *Campus security:* 24-hour emergency response devices, late-night transport/escort service, 14-hour patrols by trained security personnel. *Student Services:* personal/psychological counseling.

Athletics Member NJCAA. *Intercollegiate sports:* basketball M, golf M, softball M/W, tennis M/W, volleyball M/W. *Intramural sports:* soccer M.

Standardized Tests *Required:* ACT ASSET.

Costs (2001–02) *Tuition:* state resident $992 full-time, $31 per semester hour part-time; nonresident $5544 full-time, $173 per semester hour part-time. Part-time tuition and fees vary according to course load. *Required fees:* $38 full-time. *Waivers:* senior citizens and employees or children of employees.

Financial Aid In 2001, 50 Federal Work-Study jobs.
Applying *Options:* electronic application, early admission, deferred entrance. *Required:* high school transcript. *Application deadline:* rolling (freshmen), rolling (transfers). *Notification:* continuous (freshmen).
Admissions Contact Mr. Chris Zingelmann, Director of Enrollment Management, Cape Fear Community College, 411 North Front Street, Wilmington, NC 28401-3993. *Phone:* 910-251-5154. *Fax:* 910-251-5180. *E-mail:* contactlink@cfcc.net.

CAROLINAS COLLEGE OF HEALTH SCIENCES
Charlotte, North Carolina

- **Independent** 2-year, founded 1990, part of Carolinas Healthcare System
- **Calendar** semesters
- **Degree** certificates, diplomas, and associate
- **Urban** 3-acre campus
- **Coed, primarily women,** 314 undergraduate students, 45% full-time, 95% women, 5% men

Undergraduates 141 full-time, 173 part-time. Students come from 5 states and territories, 7% are from out of state, 15% African American, 1% Asian American or Pacific Islander, 1% Native American.
Freshmen *Admission:* 331 applied, 190 admitted, 129 enrolled. *Average high school GPA:* 2.93. *Test scores:* SAT verbal scores over 500: 63%; SAT math scores over 500: 53%; SAT verbal scores over 600: 3%; SAT math scores over 600: 3%.
Faculty *Total:* 26, 54% full-time. *Student/faculty ratio:* 12:1.
Majors Medical radiologic technology; nursing; radiological science.
Academic Programs *Special study options:* advanced placement credit, cooperative education, internships.
Library AHEC Library with 9,810 titles, 503 serial subscriptions, an OPAC.
Computers on Campus 36 computers available on campus for general student use. Internet access, at least one staffed computer lab available.
Student Life *Housing:* college housing not available. *Activities and Organizations:* Student Government Association. *Campus security:* 24-hour emergency response devices and patrols, student patrols, late-night transport/escort service. *Student Services:* health clinic, personal/psychological counseling, legal services.
Standardized Tests *Required:* SAT I or ACT (for admission).
Costs (2002–03) *Tuition:* $5550 full-time, $150 per credit part-time. Full-time tuition and fees vary according to course load and program. Part-time tuition and fees vary according to course load and program. *Required fees:* $200 full-time, $100 per term part-time. *Payment plan:* installment. *Waivers:* employees or children of employees.
Applying *Options:* early admission, early decision. *Application fee:* $35. *Required:* high school transcript. *Required for some:* letters of recommendation, interview. *Recommended:* minimum 2.0 GPA. *Application deadline:* 2/7 (freshmen). *Early decision:* 12/6. *Notification:* 3/15 (freshmen), 1/15 (early decision).
Admissions Contact Ms. Kim Wagner, Admissions Officer, Carolinas College of Health Sciences, PO Box 32861, Charlotte, NC 28232-2861. *Phone:* 704-355-5043. *Fax:* 704-355-5967. *E-mail:* cchsinformation@carolinashealthcare.org.

CARTERET COMMUNITY COLLEGE
Morehead City, North Carolina

- **State-supported** 2-year, founded 1963, part of North Carolina Community College System
- **Calendar** semesters
- **Degree** certificates, diplomas, and associate
- **Small-town** 25-acre campus
- **Coed,** 1,555 undergraduate students, 41% full-time, 66% women, 34% men

Undergraduates Students come from 22 states and territories, 11% African American, 0.9% Asian American or Pacific Islander, 1% Hispanic American, 0.5% Native American.
Faculty *Total:* 93, 44% full-time.
Majors Business administration; computer engineering technology; computer software and media applications related; computer systems networking/telecommunications; criminal justice/law enforcement administration; industrial radiologic technology; information technology; interior design; legal administrative assistant; liberal arts and sciences/liberal studies; medical assistant; paralegal/legal assistant; photography; practical nurse; recreational therapy; respiratory therapy; secretarial science; teacher assistant/aide.
Academic Programs *Special study options:* academic remediation for entering students, adult/continuing education programs, cooperative education, distance learning, double majors, internships, part-time degree program, services for LD students, summer session for credit.
Library Michael J. Smith Learning Resource Center with 21,000 titles, 165 serial subscriptions.
Computers on Campus 150 computers available on campus for general student use. Internet access, at least one staffed computer lab available.
Student Life *Housing:* college housing not available. *Activities and Organizations:* student-run newspaper.
Athletics *Intercollegiate sports:* softball M/W, volleyball M/W.
Standardized Tests *Recommended:* SAT I (for placement).
Costs (2001–02) *Tuition:* state resident $1271 full-time, $31 per semester hour part-time; nonresident $6939 full-time, $169 per semester hour part-time. Full-time tuition and fees vary according to course load. Part-time tuition and fees vary according to course load. *Required fees:* $32 full-time. *Waivers:* senior citizens.
Financial Aid In 2001, 40 Federal Work-Study jobs (averaging $750).
Applying *Options:* common application, electronic application, early admission. *Required:* high school transcript. *Application deadline:* rolling (freshmen), rolling (transfers). *Notification:* continuous (freshmen).
Admissions Contact Mr. Rick Hill, Director of Student Enrollment Resources, Carteret Community College, 3505 Arendell Street, Morehead City, NC 28557-2989. *Phone:* 252-222-6153 Ext. 6153. *Fax:* 252-222-6265. *E-mail:* mhw@carteret.cc.nc.us.

CATAWBA VALLEY COMMUNITY COLLEGE
Hickory, North Carolina

- **State and locally supported** 2-year, founded 1960, part of North Carolina Community College System
- **Calendar** semesters
- **Degree** certificates, diplomas, and associate
- **Small-town** 50-acre campus with easy access to Charlotte
- **Endowment** $591,181
- **Coed,** 3,943 undergraduate students, 39% full-time, 56% women, 44% men

Undergraduates 1,524 full-time, 2,419 part-time. Students come from 3 states and territories, 2 other countries, 1% are from out of state, 24% transferred in.
Freshmen *Admission:* 575 enrolled. *Average high school GPA:* 2.76.
Faculty *Total:* 443, 23% full-time, 1% with terminal degrees. *Student/faculty ratio:* 11:1.
Majors Accounting technician; architectural engineering technology; auto mechanic/technician; banking; business administration; business management/administrative services related; business marketing and marketing management; business systems networking/ telecommunications; computer engineering related; computer engineering technology; computer programming; computer programming (specific applications); computer science; criminology; data processing technology; dental hygiene; electrical/electronic engineering technology; emergency medical technology; engineering technologies related; fire protection/safety technology; furniture design; graphic design/commercial art/illustration; health/medical administrative services related; industrial technology; information technology; law enforcement/police science; liberal arts and sciences/liberal studies; mechanical engineering technology; medical radiologic technology; medical records technology; mortuary science; nursing; operations management; paralegal/legal assistant; photographic technology; photography; real estate; respiratory therapy; retailing operations; secretarial science; speech-language pathology; teacher assistant/aide.
Academic Programs *Special study options:* academic remediation for entering students, adult/continuing education programs, advanced placement credit, cooperative education, distance learning, double majors, English as a second language, independent study, part-time degree program, services for LD students, student-designed majors, summer session for credit.
Library Learning Resource Center with 46,000 titles, 274 serial subscriptions, 3,644 audiovisual materials, an OPAC.
Computers on Campus 1144 computers available on campus for general student use. A campuswide network can be accessed from off campus. Internet access, at least one staffed computer lab available.
Student Life *Housing:* college housing not available. *Activities and Organizations:* student-run newspaper, choral group, NCANS (Nursing), Phi Theta Kappa, Catawba Valley Outing Club, Respiratory Care Club, Rotoract. *Campus security:* 24-hour patrols. *Student Services:* personal/psychological counseling.
Athletics Member NJCAA. *Intercollegiate sports:* golf M(s), volleyball W.
Standardized Tests *Required:* ACT ASSET.
Costs (2001–02) *Tuition:* state resident $992 full-time, $31 per semester hour part-time; nonresident $5544 full-time, $173 per semester hour part-time. Full-time tuition and fees vary according to course load. Part-time tuition and fees vary according to course load. *Required fees:* $24 full-time, $1 per semester hour, $1 per term part-time. *Waivers:* senior citizens and employees or children of employees.

Catawba Valley Community College (continued)

Applying *Options:* common application, early admission, deferred entrance. *Required:* high school transcript. *Application deadline:* rolling (freshmen), rolling (transfers). *Notification:* continuous (freshmen).

Admissions Contact Mrs. Caroline Farmer, Director of Admissions and Records, Catawba Valley Community College, 2550 Highway 70 SE, Hickory, NC 28602-9699. *Phone:* 828-327-7000 Ext. 4218. *Fax:* 828-327-7000 Ext. 4224. *E-mail:* cfarmer@cvcc.cc.nc.us.

CENTRAL CAROLINA COMMUNITY COLLEGE
Sanford, North Carolina

- **State and locally supported** 2-year, founded 1962, part of North Carolina Community College System
- **Calendar** semesters
- **Degree** certificates, diplomas, and associate
- **Small-town** 41-acre campus
- **Endowment** $570,246
- **Coed,** 4,062 undergraduate students, 45% full-time, 60% women, 40% men

Undergraduates 1,808 full-time, 2,254 part-time. Students come from 17 states and territories, 5 other countries, 24% transferred in.

Freshmen *Admission:* 2,876 applied, 2,696 admitted, 999 enrolled.

Faculty *Total:* 426, 34% full-time, 4% with terminal degrees.

Majors Accounting; auto mechanic/technician; business administration; business marketing and marketing management; business systems networking/ telecommunications; computer/information technology services administration and management related; computer programming; computer programming (specific applications); criminal justice/law enforcement administration; drafting; early childhood education; electrical/electronic engineering technology; information sciences/systems; information technology; instrumentation technology; laser/ optical technology; legal administrative assistant; liberal arts and sciences/liberal studies; medical administrative assistant; medical assistant; nursing; operations management; paralegal/legal assistant; quality control technology; radio/television broadcasting; secretarial science; social work; telecommunications; veterinary technology.

Academic Programs *Special study options:* academic remediation for entering students, adult/continuing education programs, advanced placement credit, distance learning, double majors, English as a second language, independent study, internships, part-time degree program, services for LD students, summer session for credit.

Library Library/Learning Resources Center plus 2 others with 54,195 titles, 294 serial subscriptions, an OPAC, a Web page.

Computers on Campus 100 computers available on campus for general student use. Internet access, at least one staffed computer lab available.

Student Life *Housing:* college housing not available. *Activities and Organizations:* student-run radio station. *Campus security:* patrols by trained security personnel during operating hours. *Student Services:* personal/psychological counseling.

Athletics *Intercollegiate sports:* basketball M/W, golf M/W, softball M/W, volleyball M/W. *Intramural sports:* bowling M/W, golf M/W, softball M/W, volleyball M/W.

Costs (2001–02) *Tuition:* state resident $1309 full-time, $31 per semester hour part-time; nonresident $6141 full-time, $173 per semester hour part-time. *Required fees:* $38 full-time, $9 per term part-time. *Waivers:* senior citizens and employees or children of employees.

Financial Aid In 2001, 57 Federal Work-Study jobs (averaging $1299). *Financial aid deadline:* 5/4.

Applying *Options:* electronic application, early admission, deferred entrance. *Required:* high school transcript. *Application deadline:* rolling (freshmen), rolling (transfers). *Notification:* continuous (freshmen).

Admissions Contact Mr. Tom Graves, Dean of Student Services, Central Carolina Community College, Sanford, NC 27330. *Phone:* 919-718-7436. *Toll-free phone:* 800-682-8353 Ext. 7300. *Fax:* 919-718-7380. *E-mail:* tgraves@cccc.edu.

CENTRAL PIEDMONT COMMUNITY COLLEGE
Charlotte, North Carolina

- **State and locally supported** 2-year, founded 1963, part of North Carolina Community College System
- **Calendar** semesters
- **Degree** certificates, diplomas, and associate
- **Urban** 37-acre campus
- **Endowment** $10.1 million
- **Coed,** 1,076 undergraduate students, 64% full-time, 53% women, 47% men

Undergraduates 688 full-time, 388 part-time. Students come from 22 states and territories, 1% are from out of state.

Freshmen *Admission:* 1,076 enrolled.

Faculty *Total:* 1,312, 24% full-time.

Majors Accounting; advertising; applied art; architectural engineering technology; art; auto mechanic/technician; biology; business administration; business machine repair; business marketing and marketing management; child care/ development; civil engineering technology; computer engineering technology; computer programming; computer science; criminal justice/law enforcement administration; culinary arts; dance; data processing technology; dental hygiene; drafting; early childhood education; electrical/electronic engineering technology; electromechanical technology; engineering technology; environmental technology; fashion merchandising; finance; fire science; food products retailing; food sciences; food services technology; graphic design/commercial art/illustration; graphic/printing equipment; health services administration; horticulture science; hospitality management; hotel and restaurant management; human services; industrial technology; insurance/risk management; interior design; law enforcement/ police science; legal administrative assistant; liberal arts and sciences/liberal studies; machine technology; mechanical engineering technology; medical administrative assistant; medical assistant; medical laboratory technician; medical records administration; medical technology; music; nursing; paralegal/legal assistant; physical therapy; postal management; practical nurse; real estate; respiratory therapy; retail management; secretarial science; sign language interpretation; social work; surveying; transportation technology; travel/tourism management; welding technology.

Academic Programs *Special study options:* academic remediation for entering students, adult/continuing education programs, advanced placement credit, cooperative education, distance learning, English as a second language, honors programs, off-campus study, part-time degree program, services for LD students, student-designed majors, summer session for credit.

Library Hagemyer Learning Center plus 2 others with 98,125 titles, 689 serial subscriptions, 18,027 audiovisual materials, an OPAC, a Web page.

Computers on Campus A campuswide network can be accessed from off campus. At least one staffed computer lab available.

Student Life *Housing:* college housing not available. *Activities and Organizations:* drama/theater group, student-run newspaper, choral group, Phi Theta Kappa, Black Students Organization, Students for Environmental Sanity, Sierra Club, Nursing club. *Campus security:* 24-hour emergency response devices and patrols. *Student Services:* personal/psychological counseling.

Athletics Member NJCAA. *Intercollegiate sports:* basketball M/W, fencing M/W. *Intramural sports:* basketball M/W, fencing M/W, soccer M, softball M/W, tennis M/W, volleyball W.

Standardized Tests *Required for some:* Nelson Denny Reading Test or CPT.

Costs (2001–02) *Tuition:* state resident $992 full-time, $31 per credit hour part-time; nonresident $5544 full-time, $173 per credit hour part-time. Part-time tuition and fees vary according to course load. *Required fees:* $38 full-time, $10 per term part-time. *Waivers:* senior citizens and employees or children of employees.

Financial Aid In 2001, 125 Federal Work-Study jobs.

Applying *Options:* common application. *Required for some:* high school transcript. *Application deadline:* rolling (freshmen), rolling (transfers). *Notification:* continuous (freshmen).

Admissions Contact Ms. Linda McComb, Director of Admission, Registration, and Records, Central Piedmont Community College, PO Box 35009, Charlotte, NC 28235-5009. *Phone:* 704-330-6784.

CLEVELAND COMMUNITY COLLEGE
Shelby, North Carolina

- **State-supported** 2-year, founded 1965, part of North Carolina Community College System
- **Calendar** semesters
- **Degree** certificates, diplomas, and associate
- **Small-town** 43-acre campus with easy access to Charlotte
- **Endowment** $450,000
- **Coed,** 2,782 undergraduate students

Undergraduates Students come from 2 states and territories, 1 other country, 1% are from out of state, 21% African American, 0.7% Asian American or Pacific Islander, 0.4% Hispanic American, 0.3% Native American, 0.1% international.

Freshmen *Average high school GPA:* 2.42.

Faculty *Total:* 62.
Majors Accounting; biological/physical sciences; business administration; communication equipment technology; computer engineering technology; computer programming (specific applications); criminal justice/law enforcement administration; data entry/microcomputer applications; electrical/electronic engineering technology; fashion merchandising; industrial radiologic technology; information technology; liberal arts and sciences/liberal studies; medical administrative assistant; secretarial science; system/networking/LAN/WAN management.
Academic Programs *Special study options:* academic remediation for entering students, adult/continuing education programs, advanced placement credit, distance learning, double majors, English as a second language, independent study, part-time degree program, summer session for credit.
Library Cleveland Community College Library with 29,438 titles, 276 serial subscriptions, 3,619 audiovisual materials, an OPAC, a Web page.
Computers on Campus 300 computers available on campus for general student use. Internet access, at least one staffed computer lab available.
Student Life *Housing:* college housing not available. *Activities and Organizations:* student-run television station, choral group, Gamma Beta Phi Honor Society, Student Government Association, Lamplighters, Mu Epsilon Delta, Black Awareness Club. *Campus security:* security personnel during open hours. *Student Services:* personal/psychological counseling.
Standardized Tests *Required for some:* SAT I and SAT II or ACT (for placement).
Costs (2001–02) *Tuition:* state resident $992 full-time, $31 per semester hour part-time; nonresident $5544 full-time, $173 per semester hour part-time. Full-time tuition and fees vary according to course load. Part-time tuition and fees vary according to course load. *Required fees:* $38 full-time, $10 per term.
Financial Aid In 2001, 18 Federal Work-Study jobs.
Applying *Options:* common application, electronic application, deferred entrance. *Required:* high school transcript. *Application deadline:* rolling (freshmen), rolling (transfers). *Notification:* continuous (freshmen).
Admissions Contact Mr. Alan Price, Director of Admissions, Cleveland Community College, 137 South Post Road, Shelby, NC 28152. *Phone:* 704-484-4073. *Fax:* 704-484-5305.

COASTAL CAROLINA COMMUNITY COLLEGE
Jacksonville, North Carolina

- **State and locally supported** 2-year, founded 1964, part of North Carolina Community College System
- **Calendar** semesters
- **Degree** certificates, diplomas, and associate
- **Small-town** 98-acre campus
- **Endowment** $1.3 million
- **Coed,** 4,033 undergraduate students, 42% full-time, 61% women, 39% men

Undergraduates 1,708 full-time, 2,325 part-time. Students come from 52 states and territories, 32 other countries, 38% are from out of state, 20% African American, 2% Asian American or Pacific Islander, 9% Hispanic American, 0.8% Native American, 2% international, 29% transferred in.
Freshmen *Admission:* 2,453 applied, 1,615 admitted, 1,019 enrolled.
Faculty *Total:* 253, 45% full-time, 9% with terminal degrees. *Student/faculty ratio:* 16:1.
Majors Accounting; architectural engineering technology; business administration; business computer programming; business systems analysis/design; business systems networking/ telecommunications; child care provider; computer/information technology services administration and management related; criminal justice/law enforcement administration; dental hygiene; emergency medical technology; executive assistant; fire science; liberal arts and sciences/liberal studies; medical administrative assistant; medical laboratory technician; nursing; operating room technician; paralegal/legal assistant.
Academic Programs *Special study options:* academic remediation for entering students, adult/continuing education programs, advanced placement credit, distance learning, double majors, English as a second language, independent study, internships, part-time degree program, services for LD students, summer session for credit.
Library Learning Resources Center with 42,425 titles, 271 serial subscriptions, 8,003 audiovisual materials, an OPAC.
Computers on Campus 646 computers available on campus for general student use. A campuswide network can be accessed from off campus. Internet access, at least one staffed computer lab available.
Student Life *Housing:* college housing not available. *Activities and Organizations:* drama/theater group, SHELL (environmental group), SPYS (social sciences group), student government, Star of Life, Association of Nursing Students. *Campus security:* 24-hour emergency response devices and patrols, late-night transport/escort service. *Student Services:* personal/psychological counseling.
Standardized Tests *Required:* ACT ASSET.
Costs (2001–02) *Tuition:* state resident $992 full-time, $31 per semester hour part-time; nonresident $5544 full-time, $173 per semester hour part-time. Full-time tuition and fees vary according to course load. Part-time tuition and fees vary according to course load. *Required fees:* $30 full-time, $5 per term part-time. *Payment plans:* installment, deferred payment. *Waivers:* senior citizens.
Applying *Options:* deferred entrance. *Required:* high school transcript. *Required for some:* 2 letters of recommendation, interview. *Application deadline:* rolling (freshmen), rolling (transfers). *Notification:* continuous (freshmen).
Admissions Contact Mr. Jerry W. Snead, Director of Admissions, Coastal Carolina Community College, 444 Western Boulevard, Jacksonville, NC 28546. *Phone:* 910-938-6246. *Toll-free phone:* 910-938-6394. *Fax:* 910-455-2767.

COLLEGE OF THE ALBEMARLE
Elizabeth City, North Carolina

Admissions Contact Mr. Kenny Krentz, Assistant Dean of Admissions, College of The Albemarle, PO Box 2327, Elizabeth City, NC 27909-2327. *Phone:* 252-335-0821 Ext. 2220. *Fax:* 252-335-2011.

CRAVEN COMMUNITY COLLEGE
New Bern, North Carolina

- **State-supported** 2-year, founded 1965, part of North Carolina Community College System
- **Calendar** semesters
- **Degree** certificates, diplomas, and associate
- **Suburban** 100-acre campus
- **Endowment** $576,211
- **Coed,** 2,555 undergraduate students

Undergraduates Students come from 25 states and territories, 2 other countries, 17% are from out of state, 26% African American, 2% Asian American or Pacific Islander, 3% Hispanic American, 1% Native American, 0.2% international.
Faculty *Total:* 166, 38% full-time. *Student/faculty ratio:* 14:1.
Majors Accounting; auto mechanic/technician; business administration; business computer programming; business systems networking/ telecommunications; child care/guidance; criminal justice/law enforcement administration; electrical/electronic engineering technology; electromechanical technology; executive assistant; general retailing/wholesaling; heating/air conditioning/refrigeration; legal administrative assistant; liberal arts and sciences/liberal studies; management information systems/business data processing; mechanical engineering technology; medical administrative assistant; nursing; tool/die making.
Academic Programs *Special study options:* academic remediation for entering students, adult/continuing education programs, advanced placement credit, cooperative education, distance learning, double majors, independent study, internships, part-time degree program, services for LD students, student-designed majors, summer session for credit.
Library R. C. Godwin Memorial Library with 21,000 titles, 301 serial subscriptions, an OPAC.
Computers on Campus 350 computers available on campus for general student use. Internet access, at least one staffed computer lab available.
Student Life *Housing:* college housing not available. *Activities and Organizations:* drama/theater group, choral group, Accounting Club, Alumni Association, Association of Information Technology Professionals, Criminal Justice Society, Phi Theta Kappa. *Campus security:* 24-hour patrols. *Student Services:* personal/psychological counseling.
Athletics Member NJCAA. *Intercollegiate sports:* basketball M, softball M/W.
Standardized Tests *Recommended:* SAT I or ACT (for placement).
Costs (2002–03) *Tuition:* area resident $496 full-time, $31 per credit part-time; state resident $496 full-time, $31 per credit part-time; nonresident $2772 full-time, $173 per credit part-time. *Required fees:* $28 full-time, $7 per term part-time.
Financial Aid In 2001, 52 Federal Work-Study jobs (averaging $1377).
Applying *Required:* high school transcript, interview. *Application deadline:* rolling (freshmen), rolling (transfers).
Admissions Contact Ms. Millicent Fulford, Recruiter, Craven Community College, 800 College Court, New Bern, NC 28562-4984. *Phone:* 252-638-7232. *Fax:* 252-638-4649.

DAVIDSON COUNTY COMMUNITY COLLEGE
Lexington, North Carolina

Admissions Contact Mr. Rick Travis, Director, Career Services, Davidson County Community College, PO Box 1287, Lexington, NC 27293-1287. *Phone:* 336-249-8186 Ext. 224. *Fax:* 336-249-0379.

DURHAM TECHNICAL COMMUNITY COLLEGE
Durham, North Carolina

- **State-supported** 2-year, founded 1961, part of North Carolina Community College System
- **Calendar** semesters
- **Degree** certificates, diplomas, and associate
- **Urban** campus
- **Coed,** 5,283 undergraduate students

Undergraduates Students come from 50 states and territories, 1% are from out of state, 41% African American, 2% Asian American or Pacific Islander, 1% Hispanic American, 0.4% Native American, 8% international.
Faculty *Total:* 514, 22% full-time. *Student/faculty ratio:* 15:1.
Majors Accounting; architectural engineering technology; auto mechanic/technician; business administration; child care/development; computer programming; computer programming related; computer typography/composition; criminal justice/law enforcement administration; data processing technology; dental hygiene; early childhood education; electrical/electronic engineering technology; fire science; general studies; information sciences/systems; information technology; laser/optical technology; law enforcement/police science; liberal arts and sciences/liberal studies; machine technology; medical administrative assistant; medical records administration; nursing; occupational safety/health technology; occupational therapy; operating room technician; operations management; optometric/ophthalmic laboratory technician; paralegal/legal assistant; pharmacy; practical nurse; real estate; respiratory therapy; secretarial science; system/networking/LAN/WAN management; teacher assistant/aide.
Academic Programs *Special study options:* academic remediation for entering students, accelerated degree program, adult/continuing education programs, advanced placement credit, cooperative education, distance learning, English as a second language, internships, off-campus study, part-time degree program, services for LD students, student-designed majors, summer session for credit.
Library Educational Resource Center with 36,388 titles, 1,348 audiovisual materials, an OPAC.
Computers on Campus 664 computers available on campus for general student use. A campuswide network can be accessed from off campus. Internet access, at least one staffed computer lab available.
Student Life *Housing:* college housing not available. *Activities and Organizations:* drama/theater group, Amigos Unidos, Gamma Beta Phi, Student Senate, Student Nurses Association, Practical Nurses Students Club. *Campus security:* 24-hour patrols, late-night transport/escort service. *Student Services:* personal/psychological counseling.
Standardized Tests *Required:* ACT ASSET or ACT COMPASS.
Costs (2001–02) *Tuition:* state resident $880 full-time, $28 per credit hour part-time; nonresident $5432 full-time, $170 per credit hour part-time. Full-time tuition and fees vary according to course load. *Required fees:* $24 full-time, $12 per term part-time. *Waivers:* senior citizens and employees or children of employees.
Financial Aid In 2001, 35 Federal Work-Study jobs (averaging $2000).
Applying *Options:* deferred entrance. *Required:* high school transcript. *Recommended:* interview. *Application deadlines:* 8/4 (freshmen), 8/4 (transfers). *Notification:* continuous (freshmen).
Admissions Contact Mr. Claire Boatwright, Director of Admissions, Durham Technical Community College, 1637 Lawson Street, Durham, NC 27703. *Phone:* 919-686-3619. *Toll-free phone:* 919-686-3333.

EDGECOMBE COMMUNITY COLLEGE
Tarboro, North Carolina

- **State and locally supported** 2-year, founded 1968, part of North Carolina Community College System
- **Calendar** semesters
- **Degree** certificates, diplomas, and associate
- **Small-town** 90-acre campus
- **Endowment** $1.6 million
- **Coed,** 2,032 undergraduate students, 36% full-time, 73% women, 27% men

Undergraduates 729 full-time, 1,303 part-time. Students come from 1 other state, 3 other countries, 1% are from out of state, 61% African American, 0.3% Asian American or Pacific Islander, 0.9% Hispanic American, 0.5% Native American, 0.1% international, 3% transferred in. *Retention:* 37% of 2001 full-time freshmen returned.
Freshmen *Admission:* 353 applied, 292 admitted, 265 enrolled.
Faculty *Total:* 218, 30% full-time, 3% with terminal degrees. *Student/faculty ratio:* 16:1.
Majors Accounting; biological/physical sciences; business administration; computer engineering technology; computer programming; criminal justice/law enforcement administration; data entry/microcomputer applications; data entry/microcomputer applications related; data processing technology; early childhood education; electrical/electronic engineering technology; engineering; information technology; liberal arts and sciences/liberal studies; mechanical design technology; mechanical engineering technology; medical assistant; medical records administration; nursing; operating room technician; radiological science; real estate; respiratory therapy; secretarial science; social work; system/networking/LAN/WAN management; word processing.
Academic Programs *Special study options:* academic remediation for entering students, adult/continuing education programs, advanced placement credit, cooperative education, distance learning, double majors, English as a second language, independent study, off-campus study, part-time degree program, services for LD students, summer session for credit.
Library 35,417 titles, 176 serial subscriptions, 2,111 audiovisual materials, an OPAC, a Web page.
Computers on Campus 135 computers available on campus for general student use. At least one staffed computer lab available.
Student Life *Housing:* college housing not available.
Athletics *Intramural sports:* basketball M.
Standardized Tests *Recommended:* SAT I or ACT (for placement), MAPS.
Costs (2001–02) *Tuition:* state resident $992 full-time, $31 per semester hour part-time; nonresident $5544 full-time, $173 per semester hour part-time. Part-time tuition and fees vary according to course load. *Required fees:* $24 full-time, $1 per semester hour. *Payment plan:* installment. *Waivers:* senior citizens and employees or children of employees.
Financial Aid In 2001, 45 Federal Work-Study jobs (averaging $800).
Applying *Options:* common application, electronic application. *Required:* high school transcript, minimum 2.0 GPA. *Required for some:* letters of recommendation. *Application deadline:* rolling (freshmen), rolling (transfers). *Notification:* continuous (freshmen).
Admissions Contact Mr. Thomas B. Anderson, Vice President of Student Services, Edgecombe Community College, 2009 West Wilson Street, Tarboro, NC 27886-9399. *Phone:* 252-823-5166 Ext. 242. *Fax:* 252-823-6817.

FAYETTEVILLE TECHNICAL COMMUNITY COLLEGE
Fayetteville, North Carolina

- **State-supported** 2-year, founded 1961, part of North Carolina Community College System
- **Calendar** semesters
- **Degree** certificates, diplomas, and associate
- **Suburban** 112-acre campus with easy access to Raleigh
- **Endowment** $39,050
- **Coed,** 8,310 undergraduate students

Undergraduates Students come from 47 states and territories, 3 other countries, 27% are from out of state, 38% African American, 2% Asian American or Pacific Islander, 8% Hispanic American, 2% Native American.
Freshmen *Admission:* 4,742 applied.
Faculty *Total:* 790, 34% full-time. *Student/faculty ratio:* 20:1.
Majors Accounting; advertising; architectural engineering technology; auto body repair; auto mechanic/technician; business administration; business marketing and marketing management; business systems networking/ telecommunications; cabinet making; carpentry; child care provider; child care services management; civil engineering technology; communication systems installation/repair; computer engineering related; computer graphics; computer/information sciences; computer programming; computer programming related; computer programming (specific applications); computer science related; computer software and media applications related; computer systems networking/telecommunications; computer/technical support; cosmetology; criminal justice studies; culinary arts and services related; data entry/microcomputer applications; data processing; dental assistant; dental hygiene; early childhood education;

electrical/electronic engineering technology; electrical engineering; emergency medical technology; engineering-related technology; finance; food services technology; general studies; graphic design/commercial art/illustration; heating/air conditioning/refrigeration; horticulture science; horticulture services; hospitality services management related; human resources management related; industrial machinery maintenance/repair; industrial technology; information sciences/systems; information technology; liberal arts and sciences/liberal studies; machine technology; management information systems/business data processing; management science; marketing operations; masonry/tile setting; medical anatomy; medical laboratory technology; medical office management; medical records technology; mortuary science; nursing; operating room technician; paralegal/legal assistant; pharmacy technician/assistant; physical therapy assistant; plumbing; postal management; practical nurse; public administration; radiological science; recreation/leisure studies; respiratory therapy; speech-language pathology; surveying; system/networking/LAN/WAN management; tool/die making; Web/multimedia management/webmaster; Web page, digital/multimedia and information resources design; welding technology; word processing.

Academic Programs *Special study options:* academic remediation for entering students, adult/continuing education programs, advanced placement credit, cooperative education, distance learning, English as a second language, independent study, part-time degree program, summer session for credit.

Library Paul H. Thompson Library with 61,585 titles, 398 serial subscriptions, 10,725 audiovisual materials, an OPAC, a Web page.

Computers on Campus 400 computers available on campus for general student use. A campuswide network can be accessed from off campus. Internet access, at least one staffed computer lab available.

Student Life *Housing:* college housing not available. *Activities and Organizations:* Criminal Justice Association, Early Childhood Club, Phi Beta Lambda, Student Nurses Club, Data Processing Management Association. *Campus security:* 24-hour emergency response devices and patrols, late-night transport/escort service. *Student Services:* health clinic, personal/psychological counseling.

Athletics *Intramural sports:* basketball M/W, table tennis M/W, volleyball M/W.

Standardized Tests *Required:* ACT COMPASS.

Costs (2001–02) *Tuition:* state resident $868 full-time, $31 per semester hour part-time; nonresident $4850 full-time, $173 per semester hour part-time. *Required fees:* $19 full-time, $9 per term part-time. *Payment plan:* deferred payment. *Waivers:* senior citizens and employees or children of employees.

Financial Aid In 2001, 75 Federal Work-Study jobs (averaging $2000). *Financial aid deadline:* 6/1.

Applying *Options:* electronic application. *Required:* high school transcript. *Application deadline:* rolling (freshmen), rolling (transfers). *Notification:* continuous (freshmen).

Admissions Contact Mr. Donald W. LaHuffman, Director of Admissions, Fayetteville Technical Community College, PO Box 35236, Fayetteville, NC 28303. *Phone:* 910-678-8274. *Fax:* 910-678-8407. *E-mail:* lahuffmd@ftccmail.faytech.cc.nc.us.

FORSYTH TECHNICAL COMMUNITY COLLEGE
Winston-Salem, North Carolina

- **State-supported** 2-year, founded 1964, part of North Carolina Community College System
- **Calendar** semesters
- **Degree** certificates, diplomas, and associate
- **Suburban** 38-acre campus
- **Coed,** 6,246 undergraduate students

Undergraduates Students come from 10 states and territories, 24% African American, 1% Asian American or Pacific Islander, 1% Hispanic American, 0.5% Native American, 0.7% international.

Faculty *Total:* 664, 30% full-time.

Majors Accounting; architectural engineering technology; auto mechanic/technician; business administration; business marketing and marketing management; carpentry; child care/development; computer engineering technology; computer science; construction technology; criminal justice/law enforcement administration; data processing technology; drafting; early childhood education; electrical/electronic engineering technology; electromechanical technology; engineering technology; finance; graphic design/commercial art/illustration; graphic/printing equipment; heating/air conditioning/refrigeration; horticulture science; industrial radiologic technology; industrial technology; law enforcement/police science; machine technology; mechanical design technology; medical assistant; mortuary science; nuclear medical technology; nursing; ornamental horticulture; paralegal/legal assistant; plumbing; real estate; respiratory therapy; secretarial science; welding technology.

Academic Programs *Special study options:* academic remediation for entering students, adult/continuing education programs, English as a second language, part-time degree program, services for LD students, summer session for credit.

Library Forsyth Technical Community College Library plus 1 other with 41,606 titles, 358 serial subscriptions.

Computers on Campus 450 computers available on campus for general student use. At least one staffed computer lab available.

Student Life *Housing:* college housing not available. *Activities and Organizations:* student-run newspaper. *Campus security:* 24-hour patrols. *Student Services:* personal/psychological counseling.

Athletics *Intramural sports:* basketball M/W, bowling M/W, softball W, volleyball M/W.

Standardized Tests *Required:* Assessment and Placement Services for Community Colleges. *Recommended:* SAT I or ACT (for placement).

Costs (2001–02) *Tuition:* state resident $882 full-time, $32 per semester hour part-time; nonresident $4732 full-time, $169 per semester hour part-time. *Required fees:* $18 full-time, $9 per term part-time. *Waivers:* senior citizens.

Financial Aid In 2001, 60 Federal Work-Study jobs (averaging $1233).

Applying *Required:* high school transcript. *Application deadlines:* 8/25 (freshmen), 9/1 (transfers). *Notification:* continuous until 8/25 (freshmen).

Admissions Contact Mr. Michael Harp, Associate Dean of Enrollment Management, Forsyth Technical Community College, 2100 Silas Creek Parkway, Winston-Salem, NC 27103-5197. *Phone:* 336-734-7253. *Fax:* 336-761-2098. *E-mail:* infoftcc@forsyth.cc.nc.us.

GASTON COLLEGE
Dallas, North Carolina

- **State and locally supported** 2-year, founded 1963, part of North Carolina Community College System
- **Calendar** semesters
- **Degree** certificates, diplomas, and associate
- **Small-town** 166-acre campus with easy access to Charlotte
- **Endowment** $716,546
- **Coed,** 4,250 undergraduate students

Undergraduates Students come from 10 states and territories.

Freshmen *Average high school GPA:* 2.6.

Faculty *Total:* 195, 42% full-time. *Student/faculty ratio:* 28:1.

Majors Accounting; architectural engineering technology; art; auto mechanic/technician; business administration; civil engineering technology; computer programming; criminal justice/law enforcement administration; data processing technology; dietetics; early childhood education; electrical/electronic engineering technology; fire science; information sciences/systems; mechanical drafting; mechanical engineering technology; medical assistant; medical office management; nursing; operations management; paralegal/legal assistant; veterinary technology.

Academic Programs *Special study options:* academic remediation for entering students, adult/continuing education programs, advanced placement credit, cooperative education, English as a second language, off-campus study, part-time degree program, services for LD students, summer session for credit.

Library Gaston College Library with 49,434 titles, 561 serial subscriptions, 3,343 audiovisual materials, an OPAC.

Computers on Campus Internet access, online (class) registration, at least one staffed computer lab available.

Student Life *Housing:* college housing not available. *Activities and Organizations:* student-run radio station, Student Government Association. *Campus security:* 24-hour patrols.

Standardized Tests *Required:* ACT ASSET. *Required for some:* ACT (for placement).

Costs (2001–02) *Tuition:* state resident $770 full-time, $28 per credit hour part-time; nonresident $4753 full-time, $170 per credit hour part-time. *Required fees:* $20 full-time, $1 per credit hour, $6 per term part-time. *Payment plan:* deferred payment. *Waivers:* senior citizens and employees or children of employees.

Applying *Required for some:* high school transcript. *Application deadline:* rolling (freshmen), rolling (transfers). *Notification:* continuous (freshmen).

Admissions Contact Ms. Alice D. Hopper, Admissions Specialist, Gaston College, 201 Highway 321 South, Dallas, NC 28034. *Phone:* 704-922-6214.

GUILFORD TECHNICAL COMMUNITY COLLEGE
Jamestown, North Carolina

- **State and locally supported** 2-year, founded 1958, part of North Carolina Community College System
- **Calendar** semesters
- **Degree** certificates, diplomas, and associate
- **Suburban** 158-acre campus
- **Coed,** 8,573 undergraduate students, 42% full-time, 54% women, 46% men

Undergraduates 3,599 full-time, 4,974 part-time. Students come from 21 states and territories, 29% African American, 3% Asian American or Pacific Islander, 2% Hispanic American, 0.7% Native American.

Freshmen *Admission:* 8,054 applied, 8,054 admitted, 2,588 enrolled.

Faculty *Total:* 808, 25% full-time.

Majors Accounting; administrative/secretarial services; aircraft pilot (professional); architectural engineering technology; auto mechanic/technician; aviation management; aviation technology; biological/physical sciences; biological technology; business administration; chemistry related; civil engineering technology; computer/information technology services administration and management related; computer programming; computer systems networking/telecommunications; construction management related; cosmetology; criminal justice/law enforcement administration; culinary arts; dental hygiene; drafting/design technology; early childhood education; education related; electrical/electronic engineering technology; electrical equipment installation/repair; emergency medical technology; film/video production; fire science; graphic design/commercial art/illustration; heating/air conditioning/refrigeration; heavy equipment maintenance; human services; industrial arts; industrial machinery maintenance/repair; industrial technology; information sciences/systems; Internet; law enforcement/police science; liberal arts and sciences/liberal studies; machine technology; medical assistant; medical laboratory technician; nursing; occupational therapy assistant; operating room technician; paralegal/legal assistant; physical therapy assistant; respiratory therapy; speech-language pathology; surveying; theater arts/drama; turf management.

Academic Programs *Special study options:* academic remediation for entering students, adult/continuing education programs, advanced placement credit, cooperative education, distance learning, English as a second language, external degree program, independent study, internships, off-campus study, part-time degree program, services for LD students, student-designed majors, summer session for credit. *ROTC:* Army (c), Air Force (c).

Library M. W. Bell Library plus 2 others with 74,958 titles, 381 serial subscriptions, 7,286 audiovisual materials, an OPAC, a Web page.

Computers on Campus 90 computers available on campus for general student use. A campuswide network can be accessed from off campus. Internet access, at least one staffed computer lab available.

Student Life *Housing:* college housing not available. *Activities and Organizations:* drama/theater group.

Standardized Tests *Required:* ACT COMPASS.

Costs (2001–02) *Tuition:* state resident $992 full-time, $31 per semester hour part-time; nonresident $5568 full-time, $174 per semester hour part-time. Part-time tuition and fees vary according to course load. *Required fees:* $43 full-time. *Payment plan:* installment. *Waivers:* senior citizens and employees or children of employees.

Financial Aid In 2001, 61 Federal Work-Study jobs (averaging $2191).

Applying *Options:* early admission, deferred entrance. *Required:* high school transcript. *Required for some:* interview. *Application deadline:* rolling (freshmen), rolling (transfers). *Notification:* continuous (freshmen).

Admissions Contact Ms. Jean Groome, Director of Admissions, Guilford Technical Community College, PO Box 309, Jamestown, NC 27282. *Phone:* 336-334-4822 Ext. 2396. *E-mail:* knighte@gtcc.cc.nc.us.

HALIFAX COMMUNITY COLLEGE
Weldon, North Carolina

- **State and locally supported** 2-year, founded 1967, part of North Carolina Community College System
- **Calendar** semesters
- **Degree** certificates, diplomas, and associate
- **Rural** 109-acre campus
- **Coed,** 1,580 undergraduate students

Undergraduates Students come from 2 states and territories.

Faculty *Total:* 147, 44% full-time.

Majors Art education; business administration; business education; business marketing and marketing management; corrections; education; graphic design/commercial art/illustration; industrial technology; interior design; law enforcement/police science; liberal arts and sciences/liberal studies; medical administrative assistant; medical laboratory technician; nursing; secretarial science; social work.

Academic Programs *Special study options:* academic remediation for entering students, adult/continuing education programs, cooperative education, part-time degree program, summer session for credit.

Library Halifax Community College Library with 26,527 titles, 122 serial subscriptions.

Computers on Campus 100 computers available on campus for general student use. At least one staffed computer lab available.

Student Life *Housing:* college housing not available. *Campus security:* 12-hour patrols by trained security personnel.

Costs (2001–02) *Tuition:* state resident $880 full-time, $28 per credit hour part-time; nonresident $4753 full-time, $170 per credit hour part-time. *Required fees:* $22 full-time.

Applying *Options:* deferred entrance. *Required:* high school transcript. *Application deadline:* rolling (freshmen), rolling (transfers). *Notification:* continuous (freshmen).

Admissions Contact Mrs. Scottie Dickens, Director of Admissions, Halifax Community College, PO Drawer 809, Weldon, NC 27890-0809. *Phone:* 252-536-2551 Ext. 220.

HAYWOOD COMMUNITY COLLEGE
Clyde, North Carolina

- **State and locally supported** 2-year, founded 1964, part of North Carolina Community College System
- **Calendar** semesters
- **Degree** certificates, diplomas, and associate
- **Rural** 85-acre campus
- **Coed,** 1,874 undergraduate students

Undergraduates Students come from 7 states and territories, 1% are from out of state.

Freshmen *Admission:* 859 applied, 717 admitted.

Faculty *Total:* 190, 31% full-time, 3% with terminal degrees.

Majors Business administration; ceramic arts; cosmetology; craft/folk art; criminal justice/law enforcement administration; education; fish/game management; forest harvesting production technology; horticulture science; industrial arts; industrial technology; information sciences/systems; liberal arts and sciences/liberal studies; machine technology; management information systems/business data processing; medical assistant; metal/jewelry arts; nursing; textile arts; wildlife management; wood science/paper technology.

Academic Programs *Special study options:* academic remediation for entering students, adult/continuing education programs, advanced placement credit, cooperative education, distance learning, double majors, English as a second language, independent study, internships, part-time degree program, services for LD students.

Library Freedlander Learning Resource Center with 26,788 titles, 167 serial subscriptions.

Computers on Campus 10 computers available on campus for general student use. Internet access available.

Student Life *Housing:* college housing not available. *Activities and Organizations:* Student Government Association, Phi Theta Kappa, Phi Beta Lambda, Outdoor Club, Cosmetology Club. *Campus security:* 24-hour patrols. *Student Services:* personal/psychological counseling.

Athletics *Intramural sports:* basketball M/W, bowling M/W, football M/W, golf M/W, softball M/W, volleyball M/W.

Costs (2001–02) *Tuition:* state resident $992 full-time, $31 per credit part-time; nonresident $5544 full-time, $173 per credit part-time. Part-time tuition and fees vary according to course load. *Required fees:* $14 full-time, $8 per credit. *Waivers:* senior citizens and employees or children of employees.

Financial Aid In 2001, 20 Federal Work-Study jobs (averaging $1200).

Applying *Required:* high school transcript. *Required for some:* interview. *Application deadline:* rolling (freshmen), rolling (transfers).

Admissions Contact Ms. Debbie Rowland, Director of Admissions, Haywood Community College, 185 Freedlander Drive, Clyde, NC 28721-9453. *Phone:* 828-627-4505. *Fax:* 828-627-4513. *E-mail:* drowland@haywood.cc.nc.us.

ISOTHERMAL COMMUNITY COLLEGE
Spindale, North Carolina

- **State-supported** 2-year, founded 1965, part of North Carolina Community College System

- **Calendar** semesters
- **Degree** certificates, diplomas, and associate
- **Rural** 120-acre campus
- **Coed,** 1,801 undergraduate students

Undergraduates Students come from 40 states and territories, 3 other countries.
Faculty *Total:* 92, 55% full-time.
Majors Auto mechanic/technician; biological/physical sciences; broadcast journalism; business administration; business education; business marketing and marketing management; computer programming; computer science; cosmetology; criminal justice/law enforcement administration; drafting; early childhood education; education; electrical/electronic engineering technology; elementary education; graphic design/commercial art/illustration; insurance/risk management; law enforcement/police science; liberal arts and sciences/liberal studies; machine technology; mechanical design technology; mechanical engineering technology; music; pharmacy; plastics technology; practical nurse; pre-engineering; radio/television broadcasting; real estate; secretarial science; teacher assistant/aide; trade/industrial education; veterinary sciences; welding technology.
Academic Programs *Special study options:* academic remediation for entering students, adult/continuing education programs, advanced placement credit, cooperative education, English as a second language, external degree program, honors programs, part-time degree program, services for LD students, student-designed majors, summer session for credit.
Library 35,200 titles, 289 serial subscriptions, an OPAC, a Web page.
Computers on Campus Internet access, at least one staffed computer lab available.
Student Life *Housing:* college housing not available. *Activities and Organizations:* student-run newspaper, radio station, choral group. *Student Services:* personal/psychological counseling.
Athletics *Intramural sports:* basketball M/W, football M/W, volleyball M/W.
Standardized Tests *Required:* ACT ASSET.
Costs (2001–02) *Tuition:* area resident $1020 full-time, $31 per credit part-time; nonresident $5572 full-time, $173 per credit part-time.
Financial Aid In 2001, 21 Federal Work-Study jobs. *Financial aid deadline:* 6/1.
Applying *Options:* early admission, deferred entrance. *Required:* high school transcript. *Application deadline:* rolling (freshmen), rolling (transfers). *Notification:* continuous (freshmen).
Admissions Contact Ms. Betty Gabriel, Director of Counseling, Isothermal Community College, PO Box 804, Spindale, NC 28160-0804. *Phone:* 828-286-3636 Ext. 243. *Fax:* 828-286-8109. *E-mail:* smonday@isothermal.cc.nc.us.

JAMES SPRUNT COMMUNITY COLLEGE
Kenansville, North Carolina

- **State-supported** 2-year, founded 1964, part of North Carolina Community College System
- **Calendar** semesters
- **Degree** certificates, diplomas, and associate
- **Rural** 51-acre campus
- **Endowment** $16,587
- **Coed,** 1,344 undergraduate students, 42% full-time, 69% women, 31% men

Undergraduates 561 full-time, 783 part-time. Students come from 3 states and territories, 1% are from out of state, 44% African American, 0.4% Asian American or Pacific Islander, 1% Hispanic American, 0.4% Native American, 0.5% international, 5% transferred in.
Freshmen *Admission:* 311 applied, 267 admitted, 184 enrolled.
Faculty *Total:* 163, 37% full-time, 5% with terminal degrees. *Student/faculty ratio:* 21:1.
Majors Accounting; agribusiness; animal sciences; business administration; business systems analysis/design; cosmetology; early childhood education; graphic design/commercial art/illustration; law enforcement/police science; liberal arts and sciences/liberal studies; medical assistant; medical records technology; nursing; secretarial science.
Academic Programs *Special study options:* academic remediation for entering students, accelerated degree program, adult/continuing education programs, advanced placement credit, cooperative education, distance learning, double majors, English as a second language, external degree program, independent study, internships, part-time degree program, summer session for credit.
Library James Sprunt Community College Library with 23,433 titles, 230 serial subscriptions, 1,392 audiovisual materials, an OPAC.
Computers on Campus A campuswide network can be accessed from off campus. Internet access, at least one staffed computer lab available.
Student Life *Housing:* college housing not available. *Activities and Organizations:* student-run newspaper, Student Nurses Association, Art Club, Alumni Association, National Technical-Vocational Honor Society, Phi Theta Kappa. *Campus security:* trained security personnel. *Student Services:* personal/psychological counseling.
Athletics *Intercollegiate sports:* softball W, volleyball M/W.
Standardized Tests *Required:* ACT ASSET.
Costs (2001–02) *Tuition:* state resident $992 full-time, $31 per semester hour part-time; nonresident $5544 full-time, $173 per semester hour part-time. Part-time tuition and fees vary according to course load. *Required fees:* $38 full-time. *Waivers:* senior citizens and employees or children of employees.
Financial Aid In 2001, 55 Federal Work-Study jobs (averaging $1650).
Applying *Options:* common application, early admission, deferred entrance. *Required:* high school transcript. *Application deadline:* rolling (freshmen), rolling (transfers). *Notification:* continuous (freshmen).
Admissions Contact Rita B. Brown, Director of Admissions and Records, James Sprunt Community College, Highway 11 South, 133 James Sprunt Drive. *Phone:* 910-296-2500. *Fax:* 910-296-1222. *E-mail:* rbrown@jscc.cc.nc.us.

JOHNSTON COMMUNITY COLLEGE
Smithfield, North Carolina

- **State-supported** 2-year, founded 1969, part of North Carolina Community College System
- **Calendar** semesters
- **Degree** certificates, diplomas, and associate
- **Rural** 100-acre campus
- **Coed,** 3,296 undergraduate students, 42% full-time, 63% women, 37% men

Undergraduates 1,377 full-time, 1,919 part-time. Students come from 26 states and territories. *Retention:* 70% of 2001 full-time freshmen returned.
Freshmen *Admission:* 800 applied, 617 admitted, 1,053 enrolled.
Faculty *Total:* 306, 38% full-time, 100% with terminal degrees.
Majors Accounting technician; business administration; computer programming; diesel engine mechanic; early childhood education; electrical/electronic engineering technology; graphic design/commercial art/illustration; heating/air conditioning/refrigeration; law enforcement/police science; liberal arts and sciences/liberal studies; machine technology; medical administrative assistant; medical assistant; medical radiologic technology; nursing; operations management; paralegal/legal assistant; secretarial science.
Academic Programs *Special study options:* academic remediation for entering students, adult/continuing education programs, advanced placement credit, distance learning, honors programs, independent study, part-time degree program, services for LD students, summer session for credit.
Library Johnston Community College Library plus 1 other with 33,322 titles, 445 serial subscriptions, 3,976 audiovisual materials, an OPAC, a Web page.
Computers on Campus 186 computers available on campus for general student use.
Student Life *Housing:* college housing not available. *Campus security:* 24-hour patrols. *Student Services:* personal/psychological counseling.
Athletics *Intercollegiate sports:* golf M/W, softball M/W, volleyball M/W. *Intramural sports:* basketball M/W.
Standardized Tests *Required for some:* CGP.
Costs (2001–02) *Tuition:* state resident $868 full-time, $31 per credit hour part-time; nonresident $4889 full-time, $173 per credit hour part-time. Full-time tuition and fees vary according to course load. Part-time tuition and fees vary according to course load. *Required fees:* $38 full-time, $19 per term part-time. *Waivers:* senior citizens and employees or children of employees.
Applying *Options:* early admission. *Required:* high school transcript. *Application deadline:* rolling (freshmen), rolling (transfers). *Notification:* continuous (freshmen).
Admissions Contact Dr. Lawrence Rouse, Dean of Students Services, Johnston Community College, PO Box 2350, Smithfield, NC 27577-2350. *Phone:* 919-209-2048. *Fax:* 919-989-7862.

LENOIR COMMUNITY COLLEGE
Kinston, North Carolina

- **State-supported** 2-year, founded 1960, part of North Carolina Community College System
- **Calendar** semesters
- **Degree** certificates, diplomas, and associate
- **Small-town** 86-acre campus

Lenoir Community College (continued)
■ **Coed,** 3,033 undergraduate students

Undergraduates 45% African American.
Faculty *Total:* 80.
Majors Accounting; agricultural business; agricultural sciences; aircraft pilot (professional); art; aviation management; aviation technology; business administration; business marketing and marketing management; computer programming; cosmetology; court reporting; criminal justice/law enforcement administration; drafting; electrical/electronic engineering technology; elementary education; finance; fire science; food services technology; graphic design/commercial art/illustration; graphic/printing equipment; heavy equipment maintenance; horticulture science; industrial technology; instrumentation technology; insurance/risk management; landscape architecture; law enforcement/police science; legal administrative assistant; liberal arts and sciences/liberal studies; library science; mechanical design technology; medical administrative assistant; medical assistant; mental health/rehabilitation; nursing; ornamental horticulture; postal management; pre-engineering; retail management; secretarial science; trade/industrial education; water resources; welding technology.
Academic Programs *Special study options:* academic remediation for entering students, adult/continuing education programs, advanced placement credit, cooperative education, English as a second language, part-time degree program, summer session for credit.
Library Learning Resources Center plus 1 other with 55,053 titles, 381 serial subscriptions.
Computers on Campus 116 computers available on campus for general student use. At least one staffed computer lab available.
Student Life *Housing:* college housing not available. *Activities and Organizations:* student-run newspaper, choral group, Student Government Association, Automotive Club, Electronics Club, Drafting Club, Cosmetology Club. *Campus security:* 24-hour emergency response devices and patrols, student patrols. *Student Services:* personal/psychological counseling.
Athletics Member NJCAA. *Intercollegiate sports:* baseball M, basketball M(s), softball W. *Intramural sports:* basketball M, softball W, volleyball M/W.
Standardized Tests *Required:* Assessment and Placement Services for Community Colleges. *Recommended:* SAT I or ACT (for placement).
Costs (2001–02) *Tuition:* state resident $744 full-time, $31 per credit hour part-time; nonresident $4158 full-time, $175 per credit hour part-time. *Required fees:* $19 full-time, $5 per term part-time.
Applying *Options:* early admission. *Required:* high school transcript. *Application deadline:* rolling (freshmen), rolling (transfers). *Notification:* continuous (freshmen).
Admissions Contact Ms. Tammy Buck, Director of Enrollment Management, Lenoir Community College, PO Box 188, Kinston, NC 28502-0188. *Phone:* 252-527-6223 Ext. 309.

LOUISBURG COLLEGE
Louisburg, North Carolina

■ **Independent United Methodist** 2-year, founded 1787
■ **Calendar** semesters
■ **Degree** associate
■ **Small-town** 75-acre campus with easy access to Raleigh
■ **Endowment** $6.8 million
■ **Coed,** 467 undergraduate students

Undergraduates Students come from 21 states and territories, 4 other countries, 19% are from out of state, 90% live on campus. *Retention:* 44% of 2001 full-time freshmen returned.
Freshmen *Admission:* 763 applied, 758 admitted. *Average high school GPA:* 2.32. *Test scores:* SAT verbal scores over 500: 20%; SAT math scores over 500: 18%; ACT scores over 18: 100%; SAT verbal scores over 600: 2%; SAT math scores over 600: 2%; ACT scores over 24: 100%.
Faculty *Total:* 45, 67% full-time. *Student/faculty ratio:* 15:1.
Majors Athletic training/sports medicine; biological/physical sciences; biology; biology education; business; business administration; business education; chemistry; chemistry education; computer science; dance; economics; education (multiple levels); elementary education; English; English education; health/physical education; history; information sciences/systems; liberal arts and sciences/liberal studies; management science; marketing/distribution education; mathematics; mathematics education; medical technology; nursing; occupational therapy; physical therapy; physics; political science; pre-engineering; pre-law; pre-medicine; pre-pharmacy studies; pre-veterinary studies; psychology; social science education; social work; sociology; special education; speech/rhetorical studies; sport/fitness administration.
Academic Programs *Special study options:* academic remediation for entering students, adult/continuing education programs, advanced placement credit, English as a second language, part-time degree program, services for LD students, summer session for credit.
Library Robbins Library with 64,000 titles, 150 serial subscriptions.
Computers on Campus 30 computers available on campus for general student use. A campuswide network can be accessed from student residence rooms and from off campus. Internet access, at least one staffed computer lab available.
Student Life *Housing:* on-campus residence required through sophomore year. *Options:* men-only, women-only. *Activities and Organizations:* drama/theater group, student-run newspaper, radio station, choral group, Student Government Association, Workers Actively Volunteering Energetic Services, Drama Club, Christian Life Council, Ecological Concerns Club. *Campus security:* 24-hour emergency response devices and patrols, controlled dormitory access. *Student Services:* health clinic, personal/psychological counseling.
Athletics Member NJCAA. *Intercollegiate sports:* baseball M(s), basketball M(s)/W(s), golf M/W, soccer M(s)/W(s), softball W(s). *Intramural sports:* basketball M/W, football M/W, soccer M/W, softball M/W, table tennis M/W, tennis M, volleyball M/W.
Standardized Tests *Required:* SAT I or ACT (for admission).
Costs (2002–03) *Comprehensive fee:* $16,550 includes full-time tuition ($9200), mandatory fees ($1250), and room and board ($6100). Part-time tuition: $383 per hour. *Room and board:* Room and board charges vary according to housing facility. *Payment plan:* installment. *Waivers:* employees or children of employees.
Applying *Options:* common application, deferred entrance. *Application fee:* $25. *Required:* high school transcript. *Required for some:* letters of recommendation, interview. *Application deadline:* rolling (freshmen), rolling (transfers). *Notification:* continuous (freshmen).
Admissions Contact Yancy Gulley, Director of Admissions, Louisburg College, 501 North Main Street, Louisburg, NC 27549-2399. *Phone:* 919-497-3228. *Toll-free phone:* 800-775-0208. *Fax:* 919-496-1788. *E-mail:* admissions@earthlink.net.

MARTIN COMMUNITY COLLEGE
Williamston, North Carolina

■ **State-supported** 2-year, founded 1968, part of North Carolina Community College System
■ **Calendar** semesters
■ **Degree** certificates, diplomas, and associate
■ **Rural** 65-acre campus
■ **Endowment** $31,051
■ **Coed,** 726 undergraduate students, 50% full-time, 75% women, 25% men

Undergraduates 362 full-time, 364 part-time. Students come from 4 states and territories, 1 other country, 1% are from out of state, 52% African American, 0.4% Asian American or Pacific Islander, 0.4% Hispanic American, 0.1% Native American, 0.3% international, 13% transferred in.
Freshmen *Admission:* 170 enrolled. *Average high school GPA:* 2.13.
Faculty *Total:* 56, 52% full-time. *Student/faculty ratio:* 13:1.
Majors Accounting; auto mechanic/technician; business administration; business information/data processing related; cosmetology; dietician assistant; electrical/power transmission installers related; electromechanical technology; equestrian studies; general studies; heating/air conditioning/refrigeration; heating/air conditioning/refrigeration technology; information sciences/systems; liberal arts and sciences/liberal studies; liberal arts and studies related; management information systems/business data processing; medical administrative assistant; medical assistant; physical therapy assistant; secretarial science.
Academic Programs *Special study options:* academic remediation for entering students, advanced placement credit, distance learning, English as a second language, internships, part-time degree program, services for LD students, summer session for credit.
Library Martin Community College Learning Resources Center with 34,717 titles, 234 serial subscriptions, 3,586 audiovisual materials, an OPAC.
Computers on Campus 215 computers available on campus for general student use. A campuswide network can be accessed from off campus. At least one staffed computer lab available.
Student Life *Housing:* college housing not available. *Activities and Organizations:* Phi Theta Kappa, Student Government Association, Alpha Beta Gamma, Physical Therapy Club, Equine Club. *Campus security:* 24-hour emergency response devices, part-time patrols by trained security personnel. *Student Services:* personal/psychological counseling.
Athletics *Intramural sports:* softball M/W, table tennis M/W, volleyball M/W.
Standardized Tests *Required for some:* ACT COMPASS.

Costs (2001–02) *Tuition:* state resident $992 full-time, $31 per credit part-time; nonresident $5544 full-time, $173 per credit part-time. Full-time tuition and fees vary according to program. Part-time tuition and fees vary according to course load and program. *Required fees:* $38 full-time. *Waivers:* senior citizens and employees or children of employees.
Financial Aid In 2001, 30 Federal Work-Study jobs (averaging $1200).
Applying *Required:* high school transcript. *Required for some:* interview. *Application deadline:* rolling (freshmen), rolling (transfers). *Notification:* continuous until 8/17 (freshmen).
Admissions Contact Ms. Lena Murdock, Registrar and Admissions Officer, Martin Community College, 1161 Kehukee Park Road, Williamston, NC 27892. *Phone:* 252-792-1521 Ext. 243. *Fax:* 252-792-0826.

MAYLAND COMMUNITY COLLEGE
Spruce Pine, North Carolina

- **State and locally supported** 2-year, founded 1971, part of North Carolina Community College System
- **Calendar** semesters
- **Degree** certificates, diplomas, and associate
- **Rural** 38-acre campus
- **Coed**, 1,350 undergraduate students

Undergraduates Students come from 3 states and territories.
Freshmen *Admission:* 355 applied, 310 admitted.
Faculty *Total:* 65. *Student/faculty ratio:* 23:1.
Majors Accounting; architectural engineering technology; business administration; computer programming; criminal justice/law enforcement administration; early childhood education; electrical/electronic engineering technology; finance; horticulture science; information technology; law enforcement/police science; liberal arts and sciences/liberal studies; medical administrative assistant; nursing; postal management; real estate; secretarial science; travel/tourism management.
Academic Programs *Special study options:* academic remediation for entering students, adult/continuing education programs, advanced placement credit, part-time degree program, services for LD students, summer session for credit.
Library Learning Resources Center plus 1 other with 19,238 titles, 290 serial subscriptions, 1,820 audiovisual materials, an OPAC, a Web page.
Computers on Campus 200 computers available on campus for general student use. Internet access, at least one staffed computer lab available.
Student Life *Housing:* college housing not available. *Student Services:* personal/psychological counseling.
Costs (2001–02) *Tuition:* state resident $744 full-time, $31 per credit part-time; nonresident $4158 full-time, $173 per credit part-time. Full-time tuition and fees vary according to course load. Part-time tuition and fees vary according to course load. *Required fees:* $28 full-time, $28 per year part-time.
Financial Aid In 2001, 20 Federal Work-Study jobs (averaging $1350).
Applying *Options:* common application, deferred entrance. *Required:* high school transcript. *Application deadline:* rolling (freshmen), rolling (transfers). *Notification:* continuous (freshmen).
Admissions Contact Ms. Paula Crowder, Admissions Retention, Mayland Community College, PO Box 547, Spruce Pine, NC 28777. *Phone:* 828-765-7351. *E-mail:* mayland@cc.nc.us.

McDOWELL TECHNICAL COMMUNITY COLLEGE
Marion, North Carolina

- **State-supported** 2-year, founded 1964, part of North Carolina Community College System
- **Calendar** semesters
- **Degree** certificates, diplomas, and associate
- **Rural** 31-acre campus
- **Coed**

Student Life *Campus security:* 24-hour emergency response devices.
Standardized Tests *Required for some:* CPT.
Financial Aid In 2001, 15 Federal Work-Study jobs (averaging $1075).
Applying *Options:* common application, early admission, deferred entrance. *Required for some:* high school transcript.
Admissions Contact Mr. Jim L. Biddix, Dean of Students, McDowell Technical Community College, Route 1, Box 170, Marion, NC 28752-9724. *Phone:* 828-652-6021 Ext. 620. *Fax:* 828-652-1014.

MITCHELL COMMUNITY COLLEGE
Statesville, North Carolina

- **State-supported** 2-year, founded 1852, part of North Carolina Community College System
- **Calendar** semesters
- **Degree** certificates, diplomas, and associate
- **Small-town** 8-acre campus with easy access to Charlotte
- **Coed**, 2,160 undergraduate students

Undergraduates Students come from 5 states and territories, 1 other country, 0.1% are from out of state.
Freshmen *Admission:* 382 applied, 382 admitted.
Faculty *Total:* 135, 44% full-time. *Student/faculty ratio:* 14:1.
Majors Accounting; art; biological/physical sciences; business administration; child care/development; computer science; criminal justice/law enforcement administration; data processing technology; drafting; early childhood education; electrical/electronic engineering technology; elementary education; engineering; human services; industrial technology; liberal arts and sciences/liberal studies; machine technology; mathematics; medical assistant; nursing; physical education; psychology; secretarial science; social work.
Academic Programs *Special study options:* academic remediation for entering students, adult/continuing education programs, advanced placement credit, distance learning, English as a second language, part-time degree program, services for LD students, summer session for credit. *ROTC:* Army (c).
Library Main Library plus 1 other with 37,760 titles, 218 serial subscriptions, 2,225 audiovisual materials, an OPAC.
Computers on Campus 40 computers available on campus for general student use. At least one staffed computer lab available.
Student Life *Housing:* college housing not available. *Activities and Organizations:* choral group, Circle K, Phi Beta Lambda, Medical Assisting Club, Ebony Kinship. *Campus security:* day and evening security guards. *Student Services:* personal/psychological counseling.
Costs (2001–02) *Tuition:* state resident $992 full-time, $21 per hour part-time; nonresident $5544 full-time, $173 per hour part-time. *Required fees:* $30 full-time, $15 per term part-time.
Financial Aid In 2001, 30 Federal Work-Study jobs.
Applying *Required:* high school transcript. *Application deadline:* rolling (freshmen), rolling (transfers). *Notification:* continuous (freshmen).
Admissions Contact Mr. Doug Rhoney, Counselor, Mitchell Community College, 500 West Broad, Statesville, NC 28677-5293. *Phone:* 704-878-3280. *Fax:* 704-878-0872.

MONTGOMERY COMMUNITY COLLEGE
Troy, North Carolina

- **State-supported** 2-year, founded 1967, part of North Carolina Community College System
- **Calendar** semesters
- **Degree** certificates, diplomas, and associate
- **Rural** 159-acre campus
- **Endowment** $13,000
- **Coed**, 702 undergraduate students

Undergraduates Students come from 8 states and territories, 1% are from out of state, 23% African American, 2% Asian American or Pacific Islander, 2% Hispanic American, 0.7% Native American, 0.2% international.
Freshmen *Admission:* 150 applied, 135 admitted.
Faculty *Total:* 56, 54% full-time.
Majors Accounting; auto mechanic/technician; business administration; ceramic arts; child care/guidance; child care services management; electrical/electronic engineering technology; emergency medical technology; forest harvesting production technology; forest products technology; law enforcement/police science; liberal arts and sciences/liberal studies; management information systems/business data processing; medical assistant; secretarial science.
Academic Programs *Special study options:* academic remediation for entering students, cooperative education, distance learning, double majors, English as a second language, part-time degree program, services for LD students, summer session for credit.
Library 14,248 titles, 143 serial subscriptions, an OPAC, a Web page.
Computers on Campus 80 computers available on campus for general student use. Internet access, at least one staffed computer lab available.
Student Life *Housing:* college housing not available. *Activities and Organizations:* Gunsmithing Club, Student Government Association, Literary Club, Forestry Club. *Student Services:* personal/psychological counseling.

Montgomery Community College (continued)

Standardized Tests *Required:* ACT ASSET or ACT COMPASS.

Costs (2001–02) *Tuition:* state resident $992 full-time, $31 per semester hour part-time; nonresident $5544 full-time, $173 per semester hour part-time. Full-time tuition and fees vary according to course load and program. Part-time tuition and fees vary according to course load and program. *Required fees:* $25 full-time, $25 per year part-time. *Waivers:* senior citizens.

Financial Aid In 2001, 24 Federal Work-Study jobs (averaging $1244).

Applying *Options:* electronic application, early admission, deferred entrance. *Required:* high school transcript. *Application deadline:* rolling (freshmen), rolling (transfers). *Notification:* continuous (freshmen).

Admissions Contact Ms. Stacey Hilliard, Admissions Officer, Montgomery Community College, 1011 Page Street, Troy, NC 27371. *Phone:* 910-576-6222 Ext. 264. *Toll-free phone:* 800-839-6222. *E-mail:* hilliars@mcc.montgomery.cc.nc.us.

NASH COMMUNITY COLLEGE
Rocky Mount, North Carolina

- **State-supported** 2-year, founded 1967, part of North Carolina Community College System
- **Calendar** semesters
- **Degree** certificates, diplomas, and associate
- **Rural** 69-acre campus
- **Endowment** $147,220
- **Coed,** 2,184 undergraduate students, 39% full-time, 64% women, 36% men

Undergraduates 857 full-time, 1,327 part-time. Students come from 3 states and territories, 31% African American, 0.8% Asian American or Pacific Islander, 0.8% Hispanic American, 3% Native American, 0.1% international, 1% transferred in.

Freshmen *Admission:* 363 applied, 363 admitted, 363 enrolled.

Faculty *Total:* 120, 58% full-time, 96% with terminal degrees. *Student/faculty ratio:* 22:1.

Majors Accounting; architectural engineering technology; business administration; business marketing and marketing management; cosmetology; early childhood education; electrical/electronic engineering technology; information technology; law enforcement/police science; legal administrative assistant; liberal arts and sciences/liberal studies; medical administrative assistant; nursing; physical therapy; secretarial science; teacher assistant/aide.

Academic Programs *Special study options:* academic remediation for entering students, adult/continuing education programs, advanced placement credit, distance learning, double majors, English as a second language, independent study, part-time degree program, services for LD students, summer session for credit.

Library Nash Community College Library plus 1 other with 34,000 titles, 110 serial subscriptions, an OPAC.

Computers on Campus 110 computers available on campus for general student use. Internet access, at least one staffed computer lab available.

Student Life *Housing:* college housing not available. *Activities and Organizations:* student-run newspaper, Student Government Association, Gamma, Phi Beta Lambda, Student Nurses Organization/Physical Therapist Assistant Club, Criminal Justice Club. *Campus security:* 24-hour emergency response devices, late-night transport/escort service.

Standardized Tests *Required for some:* SAT I or ACT (for admission), SAT I and SAT II or ACT (for admission).

Costs (2001–02) *Tuition:* state resident $992 full-time, $31 per semester hour part-time; nonresident $5544 full-time, $173 per semester hour part-time. *Required fees:* $32 full-time, $1 per semester hour.

Applying *Options:* common application, deferred entrance. *Required:* high school transcript. *Recommended:* interview. *Application deadline:* rolling (freshmen), rolling (transfers). *Notification:* continuous (freshmen).

Admissions Contact Ms. Mary Blount, Admissions Officer, Nash Community College, PO Box 7488, Rocky Mount, NC 27804-0488. *Phone:* 252-443-4011 Ext. 300. *Fax:* 252-443-0828.

PAMLICO COMMUNITY COLLEGE
Grantsboro, North Carolina

- **State-supported** 2-year, founded 1963, part of North Carolina Community College System
- **Calendar** semesters
- **Degree** certificates, diplomas, and associate
- **Rural** 44-acre campus
- **Coed,** 338 undergraduate students

Faculty *Total:* 10, 60% full-time.

Majors Accounting; auto mechanic/technician; business administration; computer engineering technology; electrical/electronic engineering technology; environmental science; liberal arts and sciences/liberal studies; medical assistant; medical laboratory technician; neuroscience; secretarial science.

Academic Programs *Special study options:* academic remediation for entering students, adult/continuing education programs, cooperative education, part-time degree program, services for LD students, summer session for credit.

Library Pamlico Community College Library plus 1 other with 19,500 titles, 202 serial subscriptions.

Computers on Campus 68 computers available on campus for general student use. Internet access available.

Student Life *Housing:* college housing not available. *Activities and Organizations:* student-run newspaper. *Campus security:* evening security guard. *Student Services:* personal/psychological counseling.

Athletics *Intramural sports:* softball M/W, volleyball M/W.

Standardized Tests *Required:* ACT ASSET.

Costs (2001–02) *Tuition:* $31 per semester hour part-time; state resident $31 per semester hour part-time; nonresident $173 per semester hour part-time.

Financial Aid In 2001, 11 Federal Work-Study jobs (averaging $6874).

Applying *Options:* early admission, deferred entrance. *Required:* high school transcript. *Application deadline:* rolling (freshmen), rolling (transfers). *Notification:* continuous (freshmen).

Admissions Contact Mr. John T. Jones, Dean of Student Services, Pamlico Community College, PO Box 185, Grantsboro, NC 28529-0185. *Phone:* 252-249-1851 Ext. 28. *Fax:* 252-249-2377. *E-mail:* jjones@pamlicocommunitycollege.cc.nc.us.

PIEDMONT COMMUNITY COLLEGE
Roxboro, North Carolina

- **State-supported** 2-year, founded 1970, part of North Carolina Community College System
- **Calendar** semesters
- **Degree** certificates, diplomas, and associate
- **Small-town** 178-acre campus
- **Endowment** $1.8 million
- **Coed,** 2,029 undergraduate students

Undergraduates Students come from 10 states and territories, 2 other countries, 1% are from out of state. *Retention:* 37% of 2001 full-time freshmen returned.

Freshmen *Admission:* 743 admitted.

Faculty *Total:* 108, 61% full-time. *Student/faculty ratio:* 28:1.

Majors Accounting; business administration; computer engineering technology; computer graphics; criminal justice/law enforcement administration; electrical/electronic engineering technology; film/video production; liberal arts and sciences/liberal studies; medical administrative assistant; nursing; social sciences.

Academic Programs *Special study options:* academic remediation for entering students, adult/continuing education programs, advanced placement credit, cooperative education, English as a second language, off-campus study, part-time degree program, summer session for credit.

Library Learning Resource Center with 24,166 titles, 278 serial subscriptions.

Computers on Campus 75 computers available on campus for general student use. Internet access, at least one staffed computer lab available.

Student Life *Housing:* college housing not available. *Campus security:* security guard during certain evening and weekend hours. *Student Services:* personal/psychological counseling.

Athletics *Intramural sports:* volleyball M/W.

Standardized Tests *Required:* ACT ASSET.

Costs (2001–02) *Tuition:* state resident $992 full-time, $31 per credit hour part-time; nonresident $5544 full-time, $173 per credit hour part-time. *Required fees:* $70 full-time.

Financial Aid In 2001, 30 Federal Work-Study jobs (averaging $1500).

Applying *Options:* early admission, deferred entrance. *Required for some:* high school transcript. *Application deadline:* rolling (freshmen), rolling (transfers). *Notification:* continuous until 9/29 (freshmen).

Admissions Contact Ms. Sheila Williamson, Director of Admissions, Piedmont Community College, PO Box 1197, 1715 College Drive, Roxboro, NC 27573. *Phone:* 336-599-1181 Ext. 219. *Fax:* 336-598-9283 Ext. 218.

PITT COMMUNITY COLLEGE
Greenville, North Carolina

- **State and locally supported** 2-year, founded 1961, part of North Carolina Community College System
- **Calendar** semesters
- **Degree** certificates, diplomas, and associate
- **Small-town** 172-acre campus
- **Endowment** $182,825
- **Coed,** 5,600 undergraduate students, 50% full-time, 58% women, 43% men

Undergraduates 2,811 full-time, 2,789 part-time. Students come from 10 states and territories, 1% are from out of state, 29% African American, 0.7% Asian American or Pacific Islander, 0.9% Hispanic American, 0.4% Native American, 1% international, 10% transferred in. *Retention:* 46% of 2001 full-time freshmen returned.

Freshmen *Admission:* 799 applied, 799 admitted, 799 enrolled.

Faculty *Total:* 406, 32% full-time, 4% with terminal degrees. *Student/faculty ratio:* 30:1.

Majors Accounting; architectural engineering technology; business administration; business computer programming; business systems analysis/design; business systems networking/ telecommunications; child care/guidance; child care services management; construction trades related; diagnostic medical sonography; electrical/electronic engineering technology; electromechanical technology; engineering/industrial management; environmental control technologies related; general retailing/wholesaling; graphic design/commercial art/illustration; health professions and related sciences; industrial technology; law enforcement/police science; liberal arts and sciences/liberal studies; machine shop assistant; machine technology; medical administrative assistant; medical assistant; medical radiologic technology; medical records technology; mental health services related; nuclear medical technology; nursing; occupational therapy assistant; operations management; paralegal/legal assistant; psychiatric/mental health services; respiratory therapy; retailing operations; secretarial science.

Academic Programs *Special study options:* academic remediation for entering students, adult/continuing education programs, advanced placement credit, cooperative education, distance learning, double majors, English as a second language, external degree program, independent study, internships, part-time degree program, services for LD students, summer session for credit. *ROTC:* Army (b).

Library Learning Resources Center with 43,390 titles, 436 serial subscriptions, 5,358 audiovisual materials, an OPAC, a Web page.

Computers on Campus 60 computers available on campus for general student use. A campuswide network can be accessed from off campus. Internet access, online (class) registration available.

Student Life *Housing:* college housing not available. *Campus security:* 24-hour patrols, student patrols, late-night transport/escort service. *Student Services:* personal/psychological counseling.

Athletics Member NJCAA. *Intercollegiate sports:* baseball M(s), golf M(s)/W(s), volleyball W(s). *Intramural sports:* basketball M/W, softball W, volleyball M/W.

Standardized Tests *Required:* ACT ASSET or ACT COMPASS.

Costs (2001–02) *Tuition:* state resident $992 full-time, $31 per semester hour part-time; nonresident $5544 full-time, $173 per semester hour part-time. Part-time tuition and fees vary according to course load and program. *Required fees:* $40 full-time, $10 per term part-time. *Waivers:* senior citizens and employees or children of employees.

Financial Aid In 2001, 79 Federal Work-Study jobs (averaging $1022).

Applying *Options:* electronic application, deferred entrance. *Required:* high school transcript. *Application deadline:* rolling (freshmen), rolling (transfers).

Admissions Contact Ms. Mary Tate, Director of Counseling, Pitt Community College, PO Drawer 7007, 1986 Pitt Tech Road, Greenville, NC 27835-7007. *Phone:* 252-321-4217. *Fax:* 252-321-4612. *E-mail:* pittadm@pcc.pitt.cc.nc.us.

RANDOLPH COMMUNITY COLLEGE
Asheboro, North Carolina

- **State-supported** 2-year, founded 1962, part of North Carolina Community College System
- **Calendar** semesters
- **Degree** certificates, diplomas, and associate
- **Small-town** 27-acre campus
- **Endowment** $3.6 million
- **Coed,** 2,007 undergraduate students, 36% full-time, 66% women, 34% men

Undergraduates 725 full-time, 1,282 part-time. Students come from 5 states and territories, 1 other country, 1% are from out of state, 8% African American, 0.9% Asian American or Pacific Islander, 2% Hispanic American, 0.9% Native American, 22% transferred in.

Freshmen *Admission:* 782 applied, 782 admitted, 407 enrolled.

Faculty *Total:* 164, 30% full-time. *Student/faculty ratio:* 23:1.

Majors Accounting technician; architectural history; auto mechanic/technician; business administration; business systems analysis/design; commercial photography; electromechanical technology; executive assistant; fine/studio arts; graphic design/commercial art/illustration; graphic/printing equipment; information technology; interior design; law enforcement/police science; liberal arts and sciences/liberal studies; machine technology; nursing; photographic technology; photography; plastics technology; speech-language pathology; system administration; welding technology.

Academic Programs *Special study options:* academic remediation for entering students, adult/continuing education programs, advanced placement credit, cooperative education, distance learning, double majors, English as a second language, honors programs, internships, off-campus study, part-time degree program, services for LD students, summer session for credit.

Library R. Alton Cox Learning Resources Center with 36,000 titles, 287 serial subscriptions, 5,745 audiovisual materials, an OPAC, a Web page.

Computers on Campus 125 computers available on campus for general student use. Internet access, at least one staffed computer lab available.

Student Life *Housing:* college housing not available. *Activities and Organizations:* student-run newspaper, Student Government Association. *Campus security:* security officer during open hours. *Student Services:* personal/psychological counseling.

Standardized Tests *Required for some:* ACT ASSET or ACT COMPASS.

Costs (2001–02) *Tuition:* state resident $1128 full-time, $31 per semester hour part-time; nonresident $6960 full-time, $173 per semester hour part-time. Part-time tuition and fees vary according to course load. *Required fees:* $40 full-time, $1 per semester hour. *Waivers:* senior citizens and employees or children of employees.

Applying *Options:* common application, deferred entrance. *Required:* high school transcript. *Application deadline:* rolling (freshmen), rolling (transfers). *Notification:* continuous (freshmen).

Admissions Contact Mrs. Carol M. Elmore, Registrar, Randolph Community College, PO Box 1009, Asheboro, NC 27204-1009. *Phone:* 336-633-0213. *Fax:* 336-629-4695. *E-mail:* info@randolph.cc.nc.us.

RICHMOND COMMUNITY COLLEGE
Hamlet, North Carolina

- **State-supported** 2-year, founded 1964, part of North Carolina Community College System
- **Calendar** semesters
- **Degree** diplomas and associate
- **Rural** 163-acre campus
- **Coed,** 1,465 undergraduate students, 51% full-time, 71% women, 29% men

Undergraduates 754 full-time, 711 part-time. Students come from 3 states and territories, 25% African American, 1% Asian American or Pacific Islander, 1% Hispanic American, 9% Native American, 7% transferred in.

Freshmen *Admission:* 122 enrolled.

Faculty *Total:* 100.

Majors Accounting; business administration; business systems analysis/design; child care/guidance; computer engineering technology; criminal justice/law enforcement administration; electrical/electronic engineering technology; human services; industrial production technologies related; Internet; liberal arts and sciences/liberal studies; machine technology; mechanical engineering technology; medical assistant; nursing; secretarial science.

Academic Programs *Special study options:* academic remediation for entering students, adult/continuing education programs, advanced placement credit, cooperative education, distance learning, double majors, English as a second language, independent study, internships, part-time degree program, student-designed majors, summer session for credit.

Library Richmond Community College Library plus 1 other with 26,576 titles, 262 serial subscriptions, 1,573 audiovisual materials, an OPAC.

Computers on Campus 250 computers available on campus for general student use. A campuswide network can be accessed from off campus. Internet access, at least one staffed computer lab available.

Student Life *Housing:* college housing not available. *Activities and Organizations:* Criminal Justice Club, Human Services Club, Native American Club. *Campus security:* 24-hour emergency response devices, security guard during evening hours. *Student Services:* personal/psychological counseling.

Richmond Community College (continued)

Costs (2001–02) *Tuition:* state resident $744 full-time, $31 per credit hour part-time; nonresident $4158 full-time, $173 per credit hour part-time. Full-time tuition and fees vary according to course load. Part-time tuition and fees vary according to course load. *Required fees:* $38 full-time, $12 per term. *Payment plan:* deferred payment. *Waivers:* senior citizens and employees or children of employees.

Financial Aid In 2001, 35 Federal Work-Study jobs (averaging $1400).

Applying *Options:* deferred entrance. *Required:* high school transcript. *Application deadline:* rolling (freshmen), rolling (transfers). *Notification:* continuous until 8/1 (freshmen).

Admissions Contact Ms. Teri P. Jacobs, Director of Admissions/Registrar, Richmond Community College, PO Box 1189, Hamlet, NC 28345. *Phone:* 910-582-7113. *Fax:* 910-582-7102.

ROANOKE-CHOWAN COMMUNITY COLLEGE

Ahoskie, North Carolina

- **State-supported** 2-year, founded 1967, part of North Carolina Community College System
- **Calendar** semesters
- **Degree** certificates, diplomas, and associate
- **Rural** 39-acre campus
- **Endowment** $125,000
- **Coed,** 976 undergraduate students

Undergraduates 61% African American, 0.3% Native American.

Freshmen *Average high school GPA:* 2.60.

Faculty *Total:* 98, 38% full-time, 2% with terminal degrees.

Majors Architectural engineering technology; auto mechanic/technician; business administration; computer programming; construction technology; cosmetology; criminal justice/law enforcement administration; early childhood education; education; electrical/electronic engineering technology; environmental technology; heating/air conditioning/refrigeration; liberal arts and sciences/liberal studies; nursing; secretarial science; welding technology.

Academic Programs *Special study options:* academic remediation for entering students, adult/continuing education programs, cooperative education, distance learning, part-time degree program, summer session for credit.

Library 29,268 titles, 207 serial subscriptions, an OPAC, a Web page.

Computers on Campus 90 computers available on campus for general student use. Internet access available.

Student Life *Housing:* college housing not available.

Athletics *Intramural sports:* basketball M/W, volleyball M/W.

Standardized Tests *Required:* ACT ASSET.

Costs (2001–02) *Tuition:* state resident $1029 full-time, $31 per semester hour part-time; nonresident $5580 full-time, $173 per semester hour part-time. Part-time tuition and fees vary according to course load. *Required fees:* $34 full-time, $10 per semester hour.

Financial Aid In 2001, 40 Federal Work-Study jobs (averaging $1100).

Applying *Options:* early admission. *Required for some:* interview. *Application deadline:* rolling (freshmen), rolling (transfers). *Notification:* continuous (freshmen).

Admissions Contact Miss Sandra Copeland, Director of Admissions, Roanoke-Chowan Community College, 109 Community College Road, Ahoskie, NC 27910. *Phone:* 252-862-1225.

ROBESON COMMUNITY COLLEGE

Lumberton, North Carolina

- **State-supported** 2-year, founded 1965, part of North Carolina Community College System
- **Calendar** semesters
- **Degree** associate
- **Small-town** 78-acre campus
- **Coed,** 2,125 undergraduate students

Faculty *Total:* 114, 39% full-time.

Majors Business administration; computer/information sciences; criminal justice/law enforcement administration; early childhood education; food services technology; nursing; respiratory therapy; secretarial science.

Academic Programs *Special study options:* adult/continuing education programs, services for LD students.

Library 39,000 titles, 225 serial subscriptions.

Computers on Campus 100 computers available on campus for general student use. A campuswide network can be accessed from off campus. Internet access, at least one staffed computer lab available.

Student Life *Housing:* college housing not available. *Student Services:* personal/psychological counseling.

Standardized Tests *Required:* ACT ASSET, ACT COMPASS.

Costs (2001–02) *Tuition:* state resident $660 full-time, $28 per credit hour part-time; nonresident $4074 full-time, $170 per credit hour part-time. *Required fees:* $28 full-time, $9 per term part-time.

Applying *Options:* early admission. *Application deadline:* rolling (freshmen), rolling (transfers). *Notification:* continuous (freshmen).

Admissions Contact Ms. Judy Revels, Director of Admissions, Robeson Community College, Highway 301 North, PO Box 1420, Lumberton, NC 28359-1420. *Phone:* 910-738-7101 Ext. 251.

ROCKINGHAM COMMUNITY COLLEGE

Wentworth, North Carolina

- **State-supported** 2-year, founded 1964, part of North Carolina Community College System
- **Calendar** semesters
- **Degree** certificates, diplomas, and associate
- **Rural** 257-acre campus
- **Coed,** 2,085 undergraduate students, 47% full-time, 62% women, 38% men

Undergraduates 980 full-time, 1,105 part-time. Students come from 7 states and territories, 1 other country, 20% African American, 0.2% Asian American or Pacific Islander, 0.9% Hispanic American, 0.7% Native American, 2% international.

Freshmen *Admission:* 489 enrolled.

Faculty *Total:* 123, 51% full-time, 5% with terminal degrees. *Student/faculty ratio:* 16:1.

Majors Accounting; art; biological/physical sciences; business administration; business machine repair; carpentry; child care/development; construction technology; consumer services; cosmetology; criminal justice/law enforcement administration; electromechanical technology; heating/air conditioning/refrigeration; horticulture science; human resources management; industrial arts; information sciences/systems; labor/personnel relations; law enforcement/police science; legal administrative assistant; liberal arts and sciences/liberal studies; medical administrative assistant; medical assistant; nursing; occupational therapy assistant; paralegal/legal assistant; physical therapy assistant; practical nurse; respiratory therapy; secretarial science; teacher assistant/aide; travel/tourism management.

Academic Programs *Special study options:* academic remediation for entering students, adult/continuing education programs, advanced placement credit, cooperative education, part-time degree program, student-designed majors, summer session for credit.

Library Gerald B. James Library with 35,000 titles, 374 serial subscriptions, 3,990 audiovisual materials, an OPAC, a Web page.

Computers on Campus 150 computers available on campus for general student use. Internet access, at least one staffed computer lab available.

Student Life *Housing:* college housing not available. *Activities and Organizations:* student-run newspaper, Phi Theta Kappa, Cultural Diversity Club, Paralegal Club. *Campus security:* late-night transport/escort service. *Student Services:* personal/psychological counseling.

Athletics Member NJCAA. *Intercollegiate sports:* basketball M/W, soccer M/W. *Intramural sports:* archery M/W, badminton M/W, basketball M/W, table tennis M/W, tennis M/W, volleyball M/W.

Standardized Tests *Required for some:* CGP.

Costs (2001–02) *Tuition:* state resident $992 full-time, $31 per credit hour part-time; nonresident $5544 full-time, $173 per credit hour part-time. *Required fees:* $37 full-time, $9 per credit hour. *Waivers:* senior citizens.

Financial Aid In 2001, 37 Federal Work-Study jobs (averaging $2300).

Applying *Options:* early admission, deferred entrance. *Application deadline:* rolling (freshmen), rolling (transfers). *Notification:* continuous (freshmen).

Admissions Contact Dr. LaCheata Hall, Director of Enrollment Management, Rockingham Community College, PO Box 38, Wentworth, NC 27375-0038. *Phone:* 336-342-4261 Ext. 2117.

ROWAN-CABARRUS COMMUNITY COLLEGE

Salisbury, North Carolina

- **State-supported** 2-year, founded 1963, part of North Carolina Community College System

- **Calendar** semesters
- **Degree** diplomas and associate
- **Small-town** 100-acre campus
- **Coed,** 4,705 undergraduate students

Undergraduates Students come from 2 other countries.
Freshmen *Admission:* 1,505 applied, 1,505 admitted. *Average high school GPA:* 2.90.
Faculty *Total:* 302, 35% full-time.
Majors Accounting; auto mechanic/technician; biomedical technology; business administration; criminal justice/law enforcement administration; early childhood education; electrical/electronic engineering technology; industrial technology; information sciences/systems; liberal arts and sciences/liberal studies; mechanical drafting; medical laboratory technology; medical records technology; nursing; paralegal/legal assistant; radiological science.
Academic Programs *Special study options:* academic remediation for entering students, adult/continuing education programs, advanced placement credit, cooperative education, English as a second language, internships, part-time degree program, services for LD students, summer session for credit.
Library Learning Resource Center with 23,005 titles, 313 serial subscriptions.
Computers on Campus 200 computers available on campus for general student use. At least one staffed computer lab available.
Student Life *Housing:* college housing not available. *Campus security:* on-campus security during operating hours. *Student Services:* personal/psychological counseling.
Athletics *Intramural sports:* basketball M/W.
Standardized Tests *Required:* ACT ASSET.
Costs (2002–03) *Tuition:* area resident $992 full-time; state resident $70 per credit part-time; nonresident $140 per credit part-time. *Required fees:* $32 full-time.
Applying *Required:* high school transcript. *Application deadline:* rolling (freshmen), rolling (transfers).
Admissions Contact Mr. Kenneth C. Hayes, Director of Admissions and Recruitment, Rowan-Cabarrus Community College, PO Box 1595, Salisbury, NC 28145-1595. *Phone:* 704-637-0760 Ext. 212. *Fax:* 704-633-6804.

SAMPSON COMMUNITY COLLEGE
Clinton, North Carolina

- **State and locally supported** 2-year, founded 1965, part of North Carolina Community College System
- **Calendar** semesters
- **Degree** certificates, diplomas, and associate
- **Rural** 55-acre campus
- **Coed,** 1,399 undergraduate students

Undergraduates Students come from 4 states and territories, 1% are from out of state, 35% African American, 2% Native American.
Freshmen *Admission:* 647 applied, 647 admitted.
Faculty *Total:* 102, 44% full-time, 3% with terminal degrees. *Student/faculty ratio:* 20:1.
Majors Accounting; business administration; computer/information sciences; computer programming; criminal justice/law enforcement administration; horticulture science; industrial technology; information technology; liberal arts and sciences/liberal studies; nursing; poultry science; practical nurse; secretarial science; system/networking/LAN/WAN management; word processing.
Academic Programs *Special study options:* academic remediation for entering students, adult/continuing education programs, advanced placement credit, cooperative education, independent study, internships, part-time degree program, services for LD students, summer session for credit.
Library Sampson Community College Library with 25,000 titles, 250 serial subscriptions, an OPAC, a Web page.
Computers on Campus 78 computers available on campus for general student use. At least one staffed computer lab available.
Student Life *Housing:* college housing not available. *Activities and Organizations:* Student Government Association, Criminal Justice Club, Nursing Student Association, Cosmetology Alliance Club, Phi Beta Lambda. *Campus security:* local police patrol. *Student Services:* personal/psychological counseling.
Athletics *Intramural sports:* basketball M, volleyball M/W.
Standardized Tests *Required:* ACT ASSET.
Costs (2002–03) *Tuition:* state resident $992 full-time, $31 per credit part-time; nonresident $173 per credit part-time. *Required fees:* $36 full-time, $36 per term part-time.
Financial Aid In 2001, 37 Federal Work-Study jobs (averaging $1280). 8 State and other part-time jobs (averaging $400).
Applying *Options:* common application, deferred entrance. *Required:* high school transcript, interview. *Recommended:* minimum 2.0 GPA. *Application deadline:* rolling (freshmen), rolling (transfers). *Notification:* continuous (freshmen).
Admissions Contact Mr. William R. Jordan, Director of Admissions, Sampson Community College, PO Box 318, Clinton, NC 28329. *Phone:* 910-592-8084 Ext. 2022. *Fax:* 910-592-8048. *E-mail:* bjordan@sampson.cc.nc.us.

SANDHILLS COMMUNITY COLLEGE
Pinehurst, North Carolina

- **State and locally supported** 2-year, founded 1963, part of North Carolina Community College System
- **Calendar** semesters
- **Degree** certificates, diplomas, and associate
- **Small-town** 230-acre campus
- **Endowment** $4.1 million
- **Coed,** 3,174 undergraduate students, 51% full-time, 65% women, 35% men

Undergraduates 1,626 full-time, 1,548 part-time. Students come from 42 states and territories, 23 other countries, 1% are from out of state, 24% African American, 0.4% Asian American or Pacific Islander, 1% Hispanic American, 7% Native American, 1% international, 20% transferred in.
Freshmen *Admission:* 2,022 applied, 2,022 admitted, 572 enrolled.
Faculty *Total:* 232, 45% full-time, 6% with terminal degrees. *Student/faculty ratio:* 15:1.
Majors Accounting; alcohol/drug abuse counseling; architectural engineering technology; art; art education; auto mechanic/technician; biological/physical sciences; business administration; business management/administrative services related; child care/development; civil engineering technology; computer engineering related; computer engineering technology; computer/information technology services administration and management related; computer programming; computer programming (specific applications); cosmetology; criminal justice/law enforcement administration; culinary arts; early childhood education; fine/studio arts; gerontology; hotel and restaurant management; human services; information sciences/systems; landscaping management; law enforcement/police science; liberal arts and sciences/liberal studies; mathematics; medical administrative assistant; medical laboratory technician; mental health/rehabilitation; music; music teacher education; nurse assistant/aide; nursing; operating room technician; practical nurse; pre-engineering; radiological science; respiratory therapy; science education; secretarial science; surveying; system/networking/LAN/WAN management; teacher assistant/aide; turf management; Web/multimedia management/webmaster.
Academic Programs *Special study options:* academic remediation for entering students, advanced placement credit, cooperative education, distance learning, double majors, honors programs, independent study, internships, part-time degree program, services for LD students, summer session for credit.
Library Boyd Library with 74,551 titles, 350 serial subscriptions, 2,237 audiovisual materials, an OPAC.
Computers on Campus 300 computers available on campus for general student use. A campuswide network can be accessed from off campus. Internet access, at least one staffed computer lab available.
Student Life *Housing:* college housing not available. *Activities and Organizations:* student-run newspaper, choral group, Student Government Association, Minority Students for Academic and Cultural Enrichment, Circle K. *Campus security:* 24-hour emergency response devices, security on duty until 12 a.m. *Student Services:* personal/psychological counseling.
Standardized Tests *Required:* ACT ASSETor ACT COMPASS.
Costs (2001–02) *Tuition:* area resident $992 full-time; state resident $1020 full-time, $31 per semester hour part-time; nonresident $5544 full-time, $173 per semester hour part-time. Full-time tuition and fees vary according to course load. Part-time tuition and fees vary according to course load. *Required fees:* $28 full-time, $14 per term part-time. *Waivers:* senior citizens and employees or children of employees.
Financial Aid In 2001, 59 Federal Work-Study jobs (averaging $1750).
Applying *Options:* common application, deferred entrance. *Required:* high school transcript. *Application deadline:* rolling (freshmen), rolling (transfers). *Notification:* continuous (freshmen).
Admissions Contact Ms. Beverly Offutt, Admissions Coordinator, Sandhills Community College, 3395 Airport Road, Pinehurst, NC 28374. *Phone:* 910-692-6185 Ext. 729. *Toll-free phone:* 800-338-3944. *Fax:* 910-692-5076. *E-mail:* offuttb@email.sandhills.cc.nc.us.

SOUTH COLLEGE
Asheville, North Carolina

- **Proprietary** 2-year, founded 1905
- **Calendar** quarters
- **Degree** certificates and associate
- **Urban** 8-acre campus
- **Coed,** 170 undergraduate students

Undergraduates Students come from 2 states and territories.
Freshmen *Admission:* 28 applied, 28 admitted.
Faculty *Total:* 20, 25% full-time, 15% with terminal degrees. *Student/faculty ratio:* 9:1.
Majors Accounting; business administration; computer/information sciences; medical assistant; office management; paralegal/legal assistant.
Academic Programs *Special study options:* adult/continuing education programs, cooperative education, double majors, independent study, internships, part-time degree program, summer session for credit.
Library Hilde V. Kopf with 4,550 titles, 37 serial subscriptions.
Computers on Campus 28 computers available on campus for general student use. Internet access, at least one staffed computer lab available.
Student Life *Housing:* college housing not available. *Activities and Organizations:* C-Med, C-Cap, C-Com. *Campus security:* night security.
Costs (2001–02) *Tuition:* $8400 full-time, $1300 per course part-time. Part-time tuition and fees vary according to course load. *Required fees:* $40 full-time, $40 per year part-time. *Payment plan:* installment. *Waivers:* employees or children of employees.
Applying *Options:* deferred entrance. *Application fee:* $40. *Required:* high school transcript. *Application deadline:* rolling (freshmen), rolling (transfers).
Admissions Contact Steve Strong, Director of Admissions, South College, 1567 Patton Avenue, Asheville, NC 28806. *Phone:* 828-252-2486. *Fax:* 828-252-8558. *E-mail:* ccdean@ioa.com.

SOUTHEASTERN BAPTIST THEOLOGICAL SEMINARY
Wake Forest, North Carolina

- **Independent Southern Baptist** founded 1950
- **Calendar** semesters
- **Degrees** certificates, associate, master's, doctoral, and first professional
- **Small-town** 450-acre campus with easy access to Raleigh
- **Coed**

Student Life *Campus security:* 24-hour emergency response devices and patrols, late-night transport/escort service.
Applying *Options:* common application. *Application fee:* $25. *Required:* 3 letters of recommendation. *Required for some:* interview.
Admissions Contact Mr. L. Russ Bush III, Vice President for Academic Affairs/Dean of Faculty, Southeastern Baptist Theological Seminary, PO Box 1889, Wake Forest, NC 27588-1889. *Phone:* 919-556-3101 Ext. 249. *Toll-free phone:* 800-284-6317. *E-mail:* awallen@msn.com.

SOUTHEASTERN COMMUNITY COLLEGE
Whiteville, North Carolina

- **State-supported** 2-year, founded 1964, part of North Carolina Community College System
- **Calendar** semesters
- **Degree** certificates, diplomas, and associate
- **Rural** 106-acre campus
- **Coed,** 1,950 undergraduate students

Undergraduates Students come from 2 states and territories, 10 other countries, 1% are from out of state.
Freshmen *Admission:* 970 applied, 970 admitted.
Faculty *Total:* 145, 36% full-time.
Majors Art; biological/physical sciences; business administration; computer engineering technology; cosmetology; criminal justice/law enforcement administration; early childhood education; electrical/electronic engineering technology; environmental science; forest harvesting production technology; industrial technology; liberal arts and sciences/liberal studies; medical laboratory technician; music; nursing; recreation/leisure facilities management; recreation/leisure studies; secretarial science; teacher assistant/aide; welding technology.
Academic Programs *Special study options:* academic remediation for entering students, adult/continuing education programs, advanced placement credit, cooperative education, distance learning, double majors, English as a second language, honors programs, independent study, internships, part-time degree program, services for LD students, summer session for credit.
Library Southeastern Community College Library with 50,297 titles, 192 serial subscriptions, an OPAC.
Computers on Campus 80 computers available on campus for general student use. Internet access, at least one staffed computer lab available.
Student Life *Housing:* college housing not available. *Activities and Organizations:* drama/theater group, choral group, Student Government Association, Forestry Club, Nursing Club, Environmental Club. *Campus security:* 24-hour emergency response devices. *Student Services:* personal/psychological counseling.
Athletics Member NJCAA. *Intercollegiate sports:* baseball M(s), volleyball W(s).
Standardized Tests *Required:* ACT ASSET, ACT COMPASS.
Costs (2001–02) *Tuition:* $31 per credit hour part-time; state resident $996 full-time, $173 per credit hour part-time; nonresident $3119 full-time. *Required fees:* $60 full-time.
Applying *Options:* common application, electronic application, early admission, deferred entrance. *Required:* high school transcript. *Application deadline:* rolling (freshmen), rolling (transfers).
Admissions Contact Ms. Linda Nelms, Coordinator of Student Records, Southeastern Community College, PO Box 151, Whiteville, NC 28472. *Phone:* 910-642-7141 Ext. 264. *Fax:* 910-642-5658. *E-mail:* jfowler@mail.southeast.cc.nc.us.

SOUTH PIEDMONT COMMUNITY COLLEGE
Polkton, North Carolina

- **State-supported** 2-year, founded 1962, part of North Carolina Community College System
- **Calendar** semesters
- **Degree** certificates, diplomas, and associate
- **Rural** 56-acre campus with easy access to Charlotte
- **Endowment** $27,818
- **Coed,** 1,875 undergraduate students, 40% full-time, 64% women, 36% men

Undergraduates 746 full-time, 1,129 part-time. Students come from 3 states and territories, 1% are from out of state, 50% African American, 0.5% Asian American or Pacific Islander, 0.9% Hispanic American, 0.6% Native American, 0.3% international, 22% transferred in.
Freshmen *Admission:* 740 applied, 618 admitted, 265 enrolled.
Faculty *Total:* 146, 32% full-time. *Student/faculty ratio:* 17:1.
Majors Accounting technician; auto mechanic/technician; business administration; business computer programming; business systems analysis/design; business systems networking/ telecommunications; drafting; electrical/electronic engineering technology; electromechanical technology; executive assistant; graphic design/commercial art/illustration; heating/air conditioning/refrigeration technology; law enforcement/police science; legal administrative assistant; liberal arts and sciences/liberal studies; machine technology; mechanical engineering technology; medical administrative assistant; medical assistant; medical records technology; operations management; paralegal/legal assistant; psychiatric/mental health services; social work.
Academic Programs *Special study options:* academic remediation for entering students, accelerated degree program, adult/continuing education programs, cooperative education, English as a second language, independent study, internships, off-campus study, part-time degree program, services for LD students, summer session for credit.
Library Martin Learning Resource Center with 18,917 titles, 170 serial subscriptions, an OPAC.
Computers on Campus 150 computers available on campus for general student use. A campuswide network can be accessed from off campus. Internet access, at least one staffed computer lab available.
Student Life *Activities and Organizations:* choral group, student association, Phi Beta Lambda, Phi Theta Kappa, Social Services Club, Criminal Justice Club. *Campus security:* 24-hour emergency response devices and patrols, evening security. *Student Services:* personal/psychological counseling, women's center.
Standardized Tests *Required for some:* CAT, CPT. *Recommended:* CAT, CPT.
Costs (2002–03) *Tuition:* state resident $880 full-time, $28 per credit part-time; nonresident $5432 full-time, $170 per credit part-time. *Required fees:* $18 full-time. *Room and board:* $2175.
Financial Aid In 2001, 25 Federal Work-Study jobs (averaging $1500).

Applying *Options:* electronic application, early admission, deferred entrance. *Required:* high school transcript. *Application deadline:* rolling (freshmen), rolling (transfers). *Notification:* continuous (freshmen).

Admissions Contact Ms. Jeania Martin, Admissions Coordinator, South Piedmont Community College, PO Box 126, Polkton, NC 28135. *Phone:* 704-272-7635. *Toll-free phone:* 800-766-0319. *Fax:* 704-272-8904. *E-mail:* j-martin@spcc.cc.nc.us.

SOUTHWESTERN COMMUNITY COLLEGE
Sylva, North Carolina

- **State-supported** 2-year, founded 1964, part of North Carolina Community College System
- **Calendar** semesters
- **Degree** certificates, diplomas, and associate
- **Small-town** 55-acre campus
- **Coed,** 1,802 undergraduate students, 44% full-time, 62% women, 38% men

Undergraduates 794 full-time, 1,008 part-time. Students come from 8 states and territories, 1 other country, 1% are from out of state, 5% transferred in.

Freshmen *Admission:* 315 enrolled. *Average high school GPA:* 2.90. *Test scores:* SAT verbal scores over 500: 5%; SAT math scores over 500: 5%; ACT scores over 18: 20%.

Faculty *Total:* 229, 24% full-time, 7% with terminal degrees. *Student/faculty ratio:* 12:1.

Majors Accounting; alcohol/drug abuse counseling; auto mechanic/technician; business administration; business marketing and marketing management; child care/development; computer engineering technology; cosmetology; culinary arts; electrical/electronic engineering technology; electrocardiograph technology; emergency medical technology; environmental science; graphic design/commercial art/illustration; information sciences/systems; law enforcement/police science; liberal arts and sciences/liberal studies; medical laboratory technician; medical radiologic technology; medical records administration; mental health/rehabilitation; nursing; occupational therapy; paralegal/legal assistant; physical therapy; respiratory therapy; secretarial science; speech-language pathology; trade/industrial education.

Academic Programs *Special study options:* academic remediation for entering students, adult/continuing education programs, cooperative education, distance learning, double majors, English as a second language, independent study, off-campus study, part-time degree program, services for LD students, summer session for credit.

Library Learning Resources Center with 27,428 titles, 257 serial subscriptions, 18,410 audiovisual materials, an OPAC.

Computers on Campus 400 computers available on campus for general student use. A campuswide network can be accessed from off campus. Internet access, at least one staffed computer lab available.

Student Life *Housing:* college housing not available. *Activities and Organizations:* Electronics Club, Native American Society, Occupational Therapy Assistant Club, TREC, Information Systems Club. *Student Services:* personal/psychological counseling.

Standardized Tests *Recommended:* SAT I or ACT (for admission).

Costs (2002–03) *Tuition:* state resident $992 full-time, $31 per credit hour part-time; nonresident $5544 full-time, $173 per credit hour part-time. Part-time tuition and fees vary according to course load. *Required fees:* $32 full-time, $1 per credit hour. *Payment plan:* deferred payment. *Waivers:* senior citizens.

Financial Aid In 2001, 65 Federal Work-Study jobs (averaging $800).

Applying *Options:* common application, early admission, deferred entrance. *Required:* high school transcript. *Required for some:* minimum 2.0 GPA, letters of recommendation, interview. *Application deadline:* rolling (freshmen), rolling (transfers). *Notification:* continuous (freshmen).

Admissions Contact Ms. Myrna Campbell, Director of Admissions, Southwestern Community College, 447 College Drive, Sylva, NC 28779. *Phone:* 828-586-4091 Ext. 253. *Fax:* 828-586-4093 Ext. 293. *E-mail:* myrna@southwest.cc.nc.us.

STANLY COMMUNITY COLLEGE
Albemarle, North Carolina

- **State-supported** 2-year, founded 1971, part of North Carolina Community College System
- **Calendar** semesters
- **Degree** certificates, diplomas, and associate
- **Small-town** 150-acre campus with easy access to Charlotte
- **Coed,** 800 undergraduate students, 44% full-time, 73% women, 27% men

Undergraduates 348 full-time, 452 part-time. Students come from 13 states and territories, 3 other countries, 3% are from out of state, 3% transferred in.

Freshmen *Admission:* 642 applied, 642 admitted, 570 enrolled.

Faculty *Total:* 106, 50% full-time. *Student/faculty ratio:* 9:1.

Majors Accounting technician; auto body repair; biomedical engineering-related technology; business administration; business computer programming; business systems networking/ telecommunications; child care/guidance; computer hardware engineering; computer/information technology services administration and management related; computer maintenance technology; computer programming related; computer programming (specific applications); computer/technical support; cosmetology; electrical/electronic engineering technology; executive assistant; human services; industrial technology; information sciences/systems; law enforcement/police science; legal administrative assistant; mechanical drafting; medical administrative assistant; medical assistant; nursing; occupational therapy assistant; physical therapy assistant; respiratory therapy; system administration; system/networking/LAN/WAN management; Web/multimedia management/webmaster; Web page, digital/multimedia and information resources design; word processing.

Academic Programs *Special study options:* academic remediation for entering students, adult/continuing education programs, advanced placement credit, cooperative education, distance learning, double majors, English as a second language, independent study, internships, part-time degree program, services for LD students, summer session for credit.

Library 23,966 titles, 200 serial subscriptions, 2,500 audiovisual materials, an OPAC, a Web page.

Computers on Campus 100 computers available on campus for general student use. Internet access, at least one staffed computer lab available.

Student Life *Housing:* college housing not available. *Activities and Organizations:* student-run newspaper, television station. *Student Services:* personal/psychological counseling.

Standardized Tests *Required:* ACT ASSET. *Recommended:* SAT I (for placement).

Costs (2001–02) *Tuition:* state resident $992 full-time, $31 per credit hour part-time; nonresident $5544 full-time, $173 per credit hour part-time. *Waivers:* senior citizens.

Financial Aid In 2001, 20 Federal Work-Study jobs (averaging $1800).

Applying *Options:* early admission, deferred entrance. *Required:* high school transcript. *Application deadline:* rolling (freshmen), rolling (transfers). *Notification:* continuous (freshmen).

Admissions Contact Mr. Ronnie Hinson, Director of Admissions and Placement, Stanly Community College, 141 College Drive, Albemarle, NC 28001. *Phone:* 704-982-0121 Ext. 233. *Fax:* 704-982-0819. *E-mail:* parksdf@stanly.cc.nc.us.

SURRY COMMUNITY COLLEGE
Dobson, North Carolina

- **State-supported** 2-year, founded 1965, part of North Carolina Community College System
- **Calendar** semesters
- **Degree** certificates, diplomas, and associate
- **Rural** 100-acre campus
- **Coed,** 3,303 undergraduate students, 49% full-time, 61% women, 39% men

Undergraduates 1,616 full-time, 1,687 part-time. Students come from 3 states and territories, 4% are from out of state, 5% African American, 0.3% Asian American or Pacific Islander, 2% Hispanic American, 0.3% Native American, 0.2% international, 3% transferred in.

Freshmen *Admission:* 709 enrolled.

Faculty *Total:* 83. *Student/faculty ratio:* 27:1.

Majors Accounting; advertising; agricultural business; auto mechanic/technician; business administration; child care provider; computer engineering related; computer engineering technology; computer programming; computer programming related; computer systems networking/telecommunications; construction technology; cosmetology; criminal justice/law enforcement administration; drafting; electrical/electronic engineering technology; graphic design/commercial art/illustration; heating/air conditioning/refrigeration; horticulture science; information sciences/systems; information technology; liberal arts and sciences/liberal studies; machine technology; medical administrative assistant; nursing; paralegal/legal assistant; poultry science; practical nurse; secretarial science.

Academic Programs *Special study options:* academic remediation for entering students, adult/continuing education programs, advanced placement credit, coop-

Surry Community College (continued)
erative education, distance learning, English as a second language, independent study, internships, off-campus study, part-time degree program, summer session for credit.
Library Resource Center with 47,526 titles, 362 serial subscriptions, 3,233 audiovisual materials, an OPAC, a Web page.
Computers on Campus 200 computers available on campus for general student use. Internet access, at least one staffed computer lab available.
Student Life *Housing:* college housing not available. *Activities and Organizations:* drama/theater group, student-run radio station, choral group, Student Government Association, Phi Beta Lambda, Phi Theta Kappa, BSU. *Campus security:* security guard during day and evening hours.
Athletics Member NJCAA. *Intercollegiate sports:* baseball M, basketball M. *Intramural sports:* basketball M/W, softball M/W, volleyball M/W.
Standardized Tests *Required:* CPT.
Costs (2001–02) *Tuition:* state resident $992 full-time, $31 per semester hour part-time; nonresident $5544 full-time, $173 per semester hour part-time. *Required fees:* $28 full-time, $2 per semester hour. *Waivers:* senior citizens.
Financial Aid In 2001, 35 Federal Work-Study jobs (averaging $2800).
Applying *Options:* electronic application, early admission, deferred entrance. *Required:* high school transcript.
Admissions Contact Mr. Michael McHone, Vice President of Student Services, Surry Community College, PO Box 304, Dobson, NC 27017-0304. *Phone:* 336-386-8121 Ext. 238. *Fax:* 336-386-8951. *E-mail:* mchonem@surry.cc.nc.us.

TRI-COUNTY COMMUNITY COLLEGE
Murphy, North Carolina

- **State-supported** 2-year, founded 1964, part of North Carolina Community College System
- **Calendar** semesters
- **Degree** certificates, diplomas, and associate
- **Rural** 40-acre campus
- **Coed,** 1,368 undergraduate students

Undergraduates Students come from 8 states and territories, 3% are from out of state.
Freshmen *Admission:* 546 applied, 546 admitted.
Faculty *Total:* 80, 58% full-time, 5% with terminal degrees. *Student/faculty ratio:* 21:1.
Majors Accounting; auto mechanic/technician; business administration; computer management; electrical/electronic engineering technology; liberal arts and sciences/liberal studies; medical assistant; nursing; secretarial science.
Academic Programs *Special study options:* academic remediation for entering students, adult/continuing education programs, distance learning, double majors, part-time degree program, services for LD students, summer session for credit.
Library 16,224 titles, 306 serial subscriptions.
Computers on Campus 33 computers available on campus for general student use. Internet access available.
Student Life *Housing:* college housing not available. *Activities and Organizations:* student-run newspaper. *Student Services:* personal/psychological counseling.
Standardized Tests *Required for some:* Assessment and Placement Services for Community Colleges. *Recommended:* SAT I (for placement).
Costs (2002–03) *Tuition:* area resident $1012 full-time, $31 per semester hour part-time; state resident $1012 full-time, $31 per semester hour part-time; nonresident $2722 full-time, $173 per semester hour part-time. *Required fees:* $21 full-time, $10 per term part-time.
Financial Aid In 2001, 11 Federal Work-Study jobs.
Applying *Required:* high school transcript. *Application deadline:* rolling (freshmen), rolling (transfers). *Notification:* continuous (freshmen).
Admissions Contact Mr. Jason Chambers, Director of Admissions, Tri-County Community College, 4600 East US 64, Murphy, NC 28906-7919. *Phone:* 828-837-6810 Ext. 225.

VANCE-GRANVILLE COMMUNITY COLLEGE
Henderson, North Carolina

- **State-supported** 2-year, founded 1969, part of North Carolina Community College System
- **Calendar** semesters
- **Degree** certificates, diplomas, and associate
- **Rural** 83-acre campus with easy access to Raleigh
- **Endowment** $2.3 million
- **Coed,** 3,733 undergraduate students, 39% full-time, 61% women, 39% men

Undergraduates 1,474 full-time, 2,259 part-time. Students come from 10 states and territories, 15 other countries, 2% are from out of state, 2% transferred in.
Freshmen *Admission:* 1,765 applied, 1,765 admitted, 587 enrolled. *Average high school GPA:* 2.5.
Faculty *Total:* 317, 40% full-time, 6% with terminal degrees. *Student/faculty ratio:* 9:1.
Majors Accounting; auto mechanic/technician; business administration; carpentry; child care/development; computer engineering technology; construction technology; corrections; cosmetology; criminal justice/law enforcement administration; data processing technology; early childhood education; education; electrical/electronic engineering technology; elementary education; heating/air conditioning/refrigeration; human services; industrial radiologic technology; industrial technology; law enforcement/police science; legal administrative assistant; liberal arts and sciences/liberal studies; medical administrative assistant; medical assistant; nursing; practical nurse; recreation/leisure studies; secretarial science; teacher assistant/aide; welding technology.
Academic Programs *Special study options:* academic remediation for entering students, accelerated degree program, adult/continuing education programs, advanced placement credit, cooperative education, English as a second language, internships, part-time degree program, services for LD students, summer session for credit.
Library Vance-Granville Community College Learning Resource Center plus 1 other with 38,720 titles, 317 serial subscriptions, an OPAC, a Web page.
Computers on Campus 184 computers available on campus for general student use. A campuswide network can be accessed from off campus. Internet access, at least one staffed computer lab available.
Student Life *Housing:* college housing not available. *Activities and Organizations:* drama/theater group, Vocational Club, Phi Theta Kappa, Computer Club, Criminal Justice Club, Business Club. *Campus security:* 24-hour emergency response devices and patrols. *Student Services:* personal/psychological counseling.
Athletics *Intramural sports:* basketball M/W, volleyball M/W.
Standardized Tests *Required for some:* ACT (for placement), nursing exam, Health Occupations Exam.
Costs (2001–02) *Tuition:* state resident $744 full-time, $31 per credit hour part-time; nonresident $4158 full-time, $173 per credit hour part-time. *Required fees:* $19 full-time, $14 per term part-time.
Financial Aid In 2001, 38 Federal Work-Study jobs (averaging $1750).
Applying *Options:* common application, early admission, deferred entrance. *Required:* high school transcript. *Application deadline:* rolling (freshmen), rolling (transfers). *Notification:* continuous (freshmen).
Admissions Contact Ms. Brenda W. Beck, Admissions Officer, Vance-Granville Community College, PO Box 917, State Road 1126, Henderson, NC 27536. *Phone:* 252-492-2061 Ext. 267. *Fax:* 252-430-0460.

WAKE TECHNICAL COMMUNITY COLLEGE
Raleigh, North Carolina

- **State and locally supported** 2-year, founded 1958, part of North Carolina Community College System
- **Calendar** semesters
- **Degree** certificates, diplomas, and associate
- **Suburban** 79-acre campus
- **Coed,** 10,984 undergraduate students

Undergraduates Students come from 15 states and territories, 41 other countries.
Freshmen *Admission:* 8,361 applied, 5,527 admitted. *Test scores:* SAT verbal scores over 500: 33%; SAT math scores over 500: 41%; ACT scores over 18: 60%; SAT verbal scores over 600: 7%; SAT math scores over 600: 13%; ACT scores over 24: 14%; ACT scores over 30: 3%.
Faculty *Total:* 895, 30% full-time, 5% with terminal degrees. *Student/faculty ratio:* 11:1.
Majors Accounting; architectural engineering technology; business administration; business systems networking/ telecommunications; civil engineering technology; computer engineering technology; computer graphics; computer graphics; computer/information sciences; computer programming; computer programming (specific applications); computer systems networking/telecommunications; computer/technical support; criminal justice/law enforcement administration; culinary arts;

early childhood education; electrical/electronic engineering technology; electrical/power transmission installation; electromechanical technology; emergency medical technology; environmental technology; general studies; heavy equipment maintenance; hotel and restaurant management; human resources management; industrial technology; instrumentation technology; landscape architecture; law enforcement/police science; legal administrative assistant; liberal arts and sciences/liberal studies; machine technology; mechanical drafting; mechanical engineering technology; medical administrative assistant; medical laboratory technician; medical radiologic technology; nursing; pharmacy technician/assistant; plastics technology; pre-engineering; robotics; surveying; system administration; telecommunications; tool/die making; Web/multimedia management/webmaster; Web page, digital/multimedia and information resources design; word processing.

Academic Programs *Special study options:* academic remediation for entering students, adult/continuing education programs, advanced placement credit, cooperative education, double majors, English as a second language, part-time degree program, services for LD students, summer session for credit.

Library Bruce M. Howell Library plus 1 other with 70,617 titles, 474 serial subscriptions, 6,141 audiovisual materials, an OPAC, a Web page.

Computers on Campus 23 computers available on campus for general student use. Internet access, at least one staffed computer lab available.

Student Life *Housing:* college housing not available. *Activities and Organizations:* drama/theater group, student-run newspaper, choral group, Science Club, History Club, Drama Club, Amateur Radio Club, Design and Garden Club. *Campus security:* 24-hour patrols. *Student Services:* personal/psychological counseling.

Standardized Tests *Required:* ACT ASSET or ACT COMPASS. *Recommended:* SAT I or ACT (for placement).

Costs (2001–02) *Tuition:* state resident $992 full-time, $31 per credit hour part-time; nonresident $5544 full-time, $173 per credit hour part-time. Part-time tuition and fees vary according to class time and location. *Required fees:* $16 full-time. *Waivers:* senior citizens and employees or children of employees.

Financial Aid In 2001, 35 Federal Work-Study jobs (averaging $2000). 15 State and other part-time jobs (averaging $2000).

Applying *Options:* common application, electronic application, early admission. *Required:* high school transcript. *Application deadline:* rolling (freshmen), rolling (transfers).

Admissions Contact Ms. Susan Bloomfield, Director of Admissions, Wake Technical Community College, 9101 Fayetteville Road, Raleigh, NC 27603-5696. *Phone:* 919-662-3357. *Fax:* 919-662-3529. *E-mail:* reirelan@gwmail.wake.tec.nc.us.

WAYNE COMMUNITY COLLEGE
Goldsboro, North Carolina

- **State and locally supported** 2-year, founded 1957, part of North Carolina Community College System
- **Calendar** semesters
- **Degree** certificates, diplomas, and associate
- **Small-town** 125-acre campus
- **Endowment** $45,924
- **Coed,** 3,162 undergraduate students

Undergraduates Students come from 47 states and territories, 3 other countries, 16% are from out of state, 28% African American, 1% Asian American or Pacific Islander, 2% Hispanic American, 0.6% Native American, 0.2% international.

Faculty *Total:* 215, 43% full-time, 3% with terminal degrees. *Student/faculty ratio:* 18:1.

Majors Accounting technician; agribusiness; agricultural production; auto mechanic/technician; aviation technology; biological/physical sciences; business administration; business systems analysis/design; clinical/medical social work; dental hygiene; electrical/electronic engineering technology; electromechanical technology; executive assistant; forest harvesting production technology; law enforcement/police science; legal administrative assistant; liberal arts and sciences/liberal studies; machine technology; mechanical engineering technology; medical administrative assistant; medical assistant; medical office management; nursing; poultry science; psychiatric/mental health services; recreation/leisure facilities management; rehabilitation therapy; retailing operations; turf management.

Academic Programs *Special study options:* academic remediation for entering students, adult/continuing education programs, advanced placement credit, cooperative education, distance learning, double majors, English as a second language, part-time degree program, services for LD students, summer session for credit.

Library Wayne Community College Library with 42,133 titles, 427 serial subscriptions, 5,840 audiovisual materials, an OPAC, a Web page.

Computers on Campus 56 computers available on campus for general student use. A campuswide network can be accessed from off campus. Internet access, at least one staffed computer lab available.

Student Life *Housing:* college housing not available. *Activities and Organizations:* student-run newspaper, choral group, Student Government Association, Phi Beta Lambda, Agriculture Club, Multicultural Association for Enrichment, Student American Dental Hygienist Association, national fraternities. *Campus security:* 24-hour emergency response devices and patrols, student patrols. *Student Services:* health clinic, personal/psychological counseling.

Athletics *Intramural sports:* basketball M/W, bowling M/W, football M/W, golf M/W, softball M/W, table tennis M/W, tennis M/W, volleyball M/W.

Standardized Tests *Required:* ACT ASSET.

Costs (2001–02) *Tuition:* state resident $992 full-time, $31 per credit hour part-time; nonresident $5544 full-time, $173 per credit hour part-time. *Required fees:* $32 full-time, $8 per term part-time.

Financial Aid In 2001, 100 Federal Work-Study jobs (averaging $2000).

Applying *Options:* deferred entrance. *Required:* high school transcript, interview. *Application deadline:* rolling (freshmen), rolling (transfers). *Notification:* continuous (freshmen).

Admissions Contact Ms. Susan Mooring Sasser, Director of Admissions and Records, Wayne Community College, PO Box 8002, Goldsboro, NC 27533-8002. *Phone:* 919-735-5151 Ext. 216. *Fax:* 919-736-3204. *E-mail:* msm@wcc.wayne.cc.nc.us.

WESTERN PIEDMONT COMMUNITY COLLEGE
Morganton, North Carolina

- **State-supported** 2-year, founded 1964, part of North Carolina Community College System
- **Calendar** semesters
- **Degree** certificates, diplomas, and associate
- **Small-town** 130-acre campus
- **Coed,** 2,405 undergraduate students

Undergraduates Students come from 5 states and territories.

Freshmen *Admission:* 545 admitted.

Faculty *Total:* 133, 45% full-time.

Majors Accounting; art; business administration; business marketing and marketing management; civil engineering technology; computer engineering technology; computer programming; criminal justice/law enforcement administration; drafting; electrical/electronic engineering technology; finance; horticulture science; industrial arts; industrial technology; interior design; law enforcement/police science; legal administrative assistant; liberal arts and sciences/liberal studies; medical administrative assistant; medical assistant; medical laboratory technician; nursing; paralegal/legal assistant; pre-engineering; recreational therapy; secretarial science.

Academic Programs *Special study options:* academic remediation for entering students, adult/continuing education programs, advanced placement credit, cooperative education, part-time degree program, summer session for credit.

Library 31,195 titles, 200 serial subscriptions.

Computers on Campus 60 computers available on campus for general student use.

Student Life *Housing:* college housing not available. *Activities and Organizations:* drama/theater group, student-run newspaper. *Student Services:* personal/psychological counseling, women's center.

Athletics *Intramural sports:* basketball M, volleyball M/W.

Standardized Tests *Required:* ACT ASSET.

Costs (2001–02) *Tuition:* state resident $1000 full-time, $31 per credit part-time; nonresident $6000 full-time, $173 per credit part-time. *Required fees:* $24 full-time, $12 per term.

Financial Aid In 2001, 21 Federal Work-Study jobs (averaging $2014).

Applying *Required:* high school transcript. *Application deadline:* rolling (freshmen), rolling (transfers). *Notification:* continuous (freshmen).

Admissions Contact Mr. Jim Reed, Director of Admissions, Western Piedmont Community College, 1001 Burkemont Avenue, Morganton, NC 28655-4511. *Phone:* 828-438-6051.

WILKES COMMUNITY COLLEGE
Wilkesboro, North Carolina

- **State-supported** 2-year, founded 1965, part of North Carolina Community College System

Wilkes Community College (continued)
- **Calendar** semesters
- **Degree** certificates, diplomas, and associate
- **Small-town** 140-acre campus
- **Endowment** $2.6 million
- **Coed,** 2,334 undergraduate students, 53% full-time, 64% women, 36% men

Undergraduates 1,228 full-time, 1,106 part-time. Students come from 4 states and territories, 2 other countries, 1% are from out of state, 4% African American, 0.3% Asian American or Pacific Islander, 1% Hispanic American, 0.4% Native American, 0.1% international, 4% transferred in. *Retention:* 54% of 2001 full-time freshmen returned.
Freshmen *Admission:* 1,154 applied, 1,154 admitted, 706 enrolled.
Faculty *Total:* 305, 23% full-time, 6% with terminal degrees. *Student/faculty ratio:* 8:1.
Majors Accounting technician; architectural engineering technology; auto mechanic/technician; business administration; business computer programming; business systems analysis/design; business systems networking/ telecommunications; child care/guidance; child care services management; construction management related; diesel engine mechanic; electrical/electronic engineering technology; electromechanical technology; executive assistant; horticulture services; hotel and restaurant management; institutional food workers; law enforcement/police science; liberal arts and sciences/liberal studies; medical assistant; nursing; psychiatric/mental health services; radio/television broadcasting technology; speech-language pathology.
Academic Programs *Special study options:* academic remediation for entering students, accelerated degree program, adult/continuing education programs, advanced placement credit, cooperative education, distance learning, double majors, freshman honors college, honors programs, independent study, internships, part-time degree program, services for LD students, summer session for credit.
Library Learning Resources Center with 51,628 titles, 120 serial subscriptions, 10,639 audiovisual materials, an OPAC, a Web page.
Computers on Campus 235 computers available on campus for general student use. Internet access, at least one staffed computer lab available.
Student Life *Housing:* college housing not available. *Activities and Organizations:* drama/theater group, student-run newspaper, radio station, choral group, Student Government Association, Phi Theta Kappa, Phi Beta Lambda, Rotaract, Baptist Student Union. *Campus security:* 24-hour emergency response devices, student patrols, late-night transport/escort service. *Student Services:* personal/psychological counseling.
Athletics Member NJCAA. *Intercollegiate sports:* baseball M, basketball M/W, volleyball M/W. *Intramural sports:* basketball M/W, table tennis M/W, volleyball M/W.
Standardized Tests *Required:* ACT COMPASS.
Costs (2001–02) *Tuition:* state resident $992 full-time, $31 per credit hour part-time; nonresident $5544 full-time, $173 per credit hour part-time. Full-time tuition and fees vary according to course load. Part-time tuition and fees vary according to course load. *Required fees:* $38 full-time, $38 per year part-time. *Waivers:* senior citizens and employees or children of employees.
Financial Aid In 2001, 50 Federal Work-Study jobs (averaging $1800).
Applying *Options:* electronic application, deferred entrance. *Required:* high school transcript. *Application deadline:* rolling (freshmen), rolling (transfers). *Notification:* continuous (freshmen).
Admissions Contact Mr. Mac Warren, Director of Admissions, Wilkes Community College, PO Box 120, Wilkesboro, NC 28697. *Phone:* 336-838-6141. *Fax:* 336-838-6547. *E-mail:* warrenm@wilkes.cc.nc.us.

Wilson Technical Community College
Wilson, North Carolina

- **State-supported** 2-year, founded 1958, part of North Carolina Community College System
- **Calendar** semesters
- **Degree** certificates, diplomas, and associate
- **Small-town** 35-acre campus
- **Endowment** $914,000
- **Coed,** 1,732 undergraduate students, 44% full-time, 66% women, 34% men

Undergraduates 756 full-time, 976 part-time. Students come from 4 states and territories, 4% are from out of state, 14% transferred in.
Freshmen *Admission:* 758 applied, 491 admitted, 271 enrolled.
Faculty *Total:* 99, 56% full-time, 1% with terminal degrees. *Student/faculty ratio:* 15:1.
Majors Accounting; business administration; computer programming; criminal justice/law enforcement administration; early childhood education; electrical/electronic engineering technology; emergency medical technology; fire science; foreign language translation; general studies; industrial technology; information sciences/systems; liberal arts and sciences/liberal studies; mechanical engineering technology; nursing; paralegal/legal assistant; secretarial science; sign language interpretation; tool/die making.
Academic Programs *Special study options:* academic remediation for entering students, advanced placement credit, cooperative education, distance learning, double majors, English as a second language, independent study, internships, part-time degree program, services for LD students, summer session for credit.
Library 33,746 titles, 1,271 serial subscriptions, 2 audiovisual materials, an OPAC.
Computers on Campus 350 computers available on campus for general student use. Internet access, at least one staffed computer lab available.
Student Life *Housing:* college housing not available. *Campus security:* 11-hour patrols by trained security personnel. *Student Services:* personal/psychological counseling.
Standardized Tests *Required:* ACT COMPASS.
Costs (2001–02) *Tuition:* state resident $868 full-time, $31 per credit hour part-time; nonresident $4851 full-time, $173 per credit hour part-time. *Waivers:* senior citizens and employees or children of employees.
Financial Aid In 2001, 50 Federal Work-Study jobs (averaging $1650).
Applying *Options:* deferred entrance. *Required:* high school transcript, interview. *Application deadline:* rolling (freshmen), rolling (transfers). *Notification:* continuous (freshmen).
Admissions Contact Ms. Denise Askew, Dean of Student Services, Wilson Technical Community College, PO Box 4305, Wilson, NC 27893. *Phone:* 252-246-1275. *Fax:* 252-246-1285. *E-mail:* bpage@email.wilsontech.cc.nc.us.

NORTH DAKOTA

Bismarck State College
Bismarck, North Dakota

- **State-supported** 2-year, founded 1939, part of North Dakota University System
- **Calendar** semesters
- **Degree** certificates, diplomas, and associate
- **Suburban** 100-acre campus
- **Coed,** 3,044 undergraduate students, 69% full-time, 51% women, 49% men

Undergraduates 2,112 full-time, 932 part-time. Students come from 20 states and territories, 7 other countries, 8% are from out of state, 0.7% African American, 0.5% Asian American or Pacific Islander, 0.4% Hispanic American, 3% Native American, 0.2% international, 12% transferred in, 8% live on campus.
Freshmen *Admission:* 1,892 applied, 1,892 admitted, 1,009 enrolled.
Faculty *Total:* 193, 51% full-time, 11% with terminal degrees. *Student/faculty ratio:* 19:1.
Majors Agricultural business; auto body repair; auto mechanic/technician; business; business systems networking/ telecommunications; carpentry; electrical equipment installation/repair; electrical/power transmission installers related; energy management technology; general office/clerical; graphic design/commercial art/illustration; heating/air conditioning/refrigeration; hotel and restaurant management; industrial technology; legal administrative assistant; liberal arts and sciences/liberal studies; medical administrative assistant; medical laboratory technician; operating room technician; secretarial science; welding technology.
Academic Programs *Special study options:* academic remediation for entering students, adult/continuing education programs, advanced placement credit, cooperative education, distance learning, part-time degree program, summer session for credit. *ROTC:* Army (c), Air Force (c).
Library Bismarck State College Library with 53,750 titles, 467 serial subscriptions, 2,749 audiovisual materials, an OPAC, a Web page.
Computers on Campus 420 computers available on campus for general student use. A campuswide network can be accessed from student residence rooms and from off campus. Internet access, online (class) registration, at least one staffed computer lab available.
Student Life *Housing Options:* men-only, women-only. *Activities and Organizations:* drama/theater group, student-run newspaper, choral group, Psychology Club, Drama Club, SADD, Business Club. *Campus security:* 24-hour emergency response devices and patrols, controlled dormitory access.

Athletics Member NJCAA. *Intercollegiate sports:* baseball M, basketball M(s)/W(s), golf M/W, tennis M/W, volleyball W(s). *Intramural sports:* basketball M, softball M, volleyball M/W.
Standardized Tests *Required:* SAT I or ACT (for admission), ACT (for placement). *Required for some:* SAT II: Writing Test (for placement).
Costs (2001–02) *Tuition:* state resident $1965 full-time, $66 per credit part-time; nonresident $5247 full-time, $175 per credit part-time. Full-time tuition and fees vary according to reciprocity agreements. Part-time tuition and fees vary according to reciprocity agreements. *Required fees:* $351 full-time, $14 per credit. *Room and board:* $2998; room only: $1138. Room and board charges vary according to board plan, gender, and housing facility. *Payment plan:* installment. *Waivers:* minority students and employees or children of employees.
Financial Aid In 2001, 86 Federal Work-Study jobs (averaging $1519).
Applying *Application fee:* $25. *Required:* high school transcript. *Application deadlines:* rolling (freshmen), 8/1 (transfers). *Notification:* continuous (freshmen).
Admissions Contact Ms. Karla Gabriel, Director of Admissions, Bismarck State College, PO Box 5587, Bismarck, ND 58506-5587. *Phone:* 701-224-5426. *Toll-free phone:* 800-445-5073 Ext. 45429 (in-state); 800-445-5073 (out-of-state). *Fax:* 701-224-5643. *E-mail:* gabriel@gwmail.nodak.edu.

CANKDESKA CIKANA COMMUNITY COLLEGE
Fort Totten, North Dakota

Admissions Contact Ms. Heather Lawrence, Registrar, Cankdeska Cikana Community College, PO Box 269, Fort Totten, ND 58335-0269. *Phone:* 701-766-4415.

FORT BERTHOLD COMMUNITY COLLEGE
New Town, North Dakota

- **Independent** 2-year, founded 1973
- **Calendar** semesters
- **Degree** certificates and associate
- **Small-town** campus
- **Coed,** 416 undergraduate students

Faculty *Total:* 42, 29% full-time.
Majors Accounting; biological/physical sciences; business administration; business marketing and marketing management; construction technology; early childhood education; environmental science; farm/ranch management; human services; information sciences/systems; liberal arts and sciences/liberal studies; mathematics; medical records administration; practical nurse; public administration; secretarial science.
Academic Programs *Special study options:* academic remediation for entering students, cooperative education, internships, off-campus study, part-time degree program, summer session for credit.
Library 10,000 titles, 300 serial subscriptions.
Computers on Campus 100 computers available on campus for general student use. Internet access available.
Student Life *Housing:* college housing not available. *Activities and Organizations:* drama/theater group, student-run newspaper. *Student Services:* health clinic, personal/psychological counseling, legal services.
Athletics *Intercollegiate sports:* basketball M/W, cross-country running M/W. *Intramural sports:* basketball M/W, football M/W, golf M/W, softball M/W, volleyball M/W, weight lifting M/W.
Costs (2001–02) *Tuition:* state resident $1920 full-time. *Required fees:* $190 full-time.
Financial Aid In 2001, 11 Federal Work-Study jobs (averaging $1200).
Applying *Options:* common application, deferred entrance. *Application fee:* $10. *Application deadline:* rolling (freshmen).
Admissions Contact Mr. Russell Mason Jr., Registrar and Admissions Director, Fort Berthold Community College, PO Box 490, New Town, ND 58763-0490. *Phone:* 701-627-3665. *Fax:* 701-627-3609. *E-mail:* rmason@nt1.fort.berthold.cc.nd.us.

LAKE REGION STATE COLLEGE
Devils Lake, North Dakota

- **State-supported** 2-year, founded 1941, part of North Dakota University System
- **Calendar** semesters
- **Degree** certificates, diplomas, and associate
- **Small-town** 15-acre campus
- **Endowment** $2.8 million
- **Coed,** 1,308 undergraduate students, 28% full-time, 52% women, 48% men

Undergraduates 364 full-time, 944 part-time. Students come from 8 states and territories, 5 other countries, 2% African American, 0.5% Asian American or Pacific Islander, 2% Hispanic American, 7% Native American, 1% international, 5% transferred in, 30% live on campus.
Freshmen *Admission:* 199 applied, 168 admitted, 168 enrolled.
Faculty *Total:* 96, 26% full-time, 4% with terminal degrees. *Student/faculty ratio:* 16:1.
Majors Accounting; agricultural business; agricultural production; auto mechanic/technician; aviation technology; business administration; business services marketing; child care/guidance; computer/information sciences; diesel engine mechanic; information technology; law enforcement/police science; liberal arts and sciences/liberal studies; management information systems/business data processing; nurse assistant/aide; office management; paralegal/legal assistant; secretarial science.
Academic Programs *Special study options:* academic remediation for entering students, adult/continuing education programs, cooperative education, distance learning, double majors, English as a second language, freshman honors college, honors programs, internships, part-time degree program, summer session for credit.
Library Paul Hoghaug Library plus 1 other with 40,000 titles, 500 serial subscriptions, 8,000 audiovisual materials, an OPAC.
Computers on Campus 225 computers available on campus for general student use. Internet access, at least one staffed computer lab available.
Student Life *Housing Options:* men-only, women-only. *Activities and Organizations:* drama/theater group, DECA, Drama, SOTA (Students Other than Average), Student Senate, Computer Club. *Campus security:* 24-hour emergency response devices, controlled dormitory access. *Student Services:* personal/psychological counseling.
Athletics Member NJCAA. *Intercollegiate sports:* basketball M(s)/W(s), volleyball W(s). *Intramural sports:* basketball M/W, bowling M, football M/W, golf M/W, ice hockey M/W, softball M/W, table tennis M/W, volleyball M/W.
Standardized Tests *Required:* ACT (for admission).
Costs (2002–03) *Tuition:* $72 per credit part-time; state resident $1732 full-time, $90 per credit part-time; nonresident $4624 full-time, $193 per credit part-time. Full-time tuition and fees vary according to location and reciprocity agreements. Part-time tuition and fees vary according to location and reciprocity agreements. *Required fees:* $510 full-time, $16 per credit. *Room and board:* $3250. Room and board charges vary according to board plan and housing facility. *Waivers:* minority students, senior citizens, and employees or children of employees.
Applying *Options:* common application, electronic application. *Application fee:* $25. *Required:* high school transcript. *Application deadline:* rolling (freshmen), rolling (transfers). *Notification:* continuous (freshmen).
Admissions Contact Ms. Denise Anderson, Administrative Assistant, Lake Region State College, 1801 College Drive North, Devils Lake, ND 58301. *Phone:* 701-662-1514. *Toll-free phone:* 800-443-1313 Ext. 514. *Fax:* 701-662-1570. *E-mail:* goulding@lrsc.nodak.edu.

MINOT STATE UNIVERSITY-BOTTINEAU CAMPUS
Bottineau, North Dakota

- **State-supported** 2-year, founded 1906, part of North Dakota University System
- **Calendar** semesters
- **Degree** certificates, diplomas, and associate
- **Rural** 35-acre campus
- **Endowment** $1.0 million
- **Coed,** 520 undergraduate students, 67% full-time, 52% women, 48% men

Undergraduates 349 full-time, 171 part-time. Students come from 21 states and territories, 1 other country, 10% are from out of state, 2% African American, 0.6% Asian American or Pacific Islander, 0.8% Hispanic American, 6% Native American, 7% international, 7% transferred in, 45% live on campus.
Freshmen *Admission:* 349 applied, 349 admitted, 169 enrolled.
Faculty *Total:* 44, 59% full-time, 7% with terminal degrees. *Student/faculty ratio:* 11:1.
Majors Accounting technician; art; biological/physical sciences; biology; business administration; business education; business marketing and marketing management; chemistry; computer engineering related; computer engineering tech-

Minot State University-Bottineau Campus (continued)
nology; computer/information sciences; computer systems networking/telecommunications; education; executive assistant; fish/game management; forestry; general office/clerical; greenhouse management; history; home economics; horticulture science; horticulture services; information sciences/systems; information technology; landscape architecture; liberal arts and sciences/liberal studies; mathematics; medical administrative assistant; medical assistant; medical office management; music; natural sciences; ornamental horticulture; physical education; receptionist; recreation/leisure facilities management; secretarial science; system administration; system/networking/LAN/WAN management; turf management; water resources; Web/multimedia management/webmaster; Web page, digital/multimedia and information resources design; wildlife biology; wildlife management.

Academic Programs *Special study options:* academic remediation for entering students, cooperative education, distance learning, double majors, internships, off-campus study, part-time degree program, services for LD students, summer session for credit.

Library Minot State University-Bottineau Library plus 1 other with 45,000 titles, 250 serial subscriptions, 800 audiovisual materials, an OPAC, a Web page.

Computers on Campus 60 computers available on campus for general student use. A campuswide network can be accessed from off campus. Internet access, at least one staffed computer lab available.

Student Life *Housing:* on-campus residence required through sophomore year. *Options:* coed, men-only, women-only. *Activities and Organizations:* drama/theater group, choral group, Student Senate, Wildlife Club, Paul Bunyan Club, Horticulture Club, DECA. *Campus security:* controlled dormitory access. *Student Services:* personal/psychological counseling.

Athletics Member NJCAA. *Intercollegiate sports:* baseball M, basketball M(s)/W(s), ice hockey M(s), volleyball W(s). *Intramural sports:* archery M/W, badminton M/W, basketball M/W, skiing (downhill) M/W, softball M/W, volleyball M/W.

Costs (2001–02) *Tuition:* state resident $1682 full-time, $70 per credit part-time; nonresident $4491 full-time, $187 per credit part-time. Full-time tuition and fees vary according to location and reciprocity agreements. Part-time tuition and fees vary according to location and reciprocity agreements. *Required fees:* $407 full-time, $17 per credit. *Room and board:* $2914. *Waivers:* minority students.

Financial Aid In 2001, 50 Federal Work-Study jobs (averaging $1100).

Applying *Options:* common application, electronic application, early admission, deferred entrance. *Application fee:* $35. *Required:* high school transcript. *Application deadline:* rolling (freshmen), rolling (transfers).

Admissions Contact Ms. Lena Throlson, Admissions Counselor, Minot State University-Bottineau Campus, 105 Simrall Boulevard, Bottineau, ND 58318. *Phone:* 701-228-5426 Ext. 426. *Toll-free phone:* 800-542-6866. *Fax:* 701-228-5499. *E-mail:* bergpla@misu.nodak.edu.

NORTH DAKOTA STATE COLLEGE OF SCIENCE
Wahpeton, North Dakota

- **State-supported** 2-year, founded 1903, part of North Dakota University System
- **Calendar** semesters
- **Degree** certificates, diplomas, and associate
- **Rural** 125-acre campus
- **Endowment** $4000
- **Coed,** 2,292 undergraduate students, 82% full-time, 34% women, 66% men

Undergraduates 1,873 full-time, 419 part-time. Students come from 21 states and territories, 8 other countries, 27% are from out of state, 2% African American, 0.3% Asian American or Pacific Islander, 0.8% Hispanic American, 2% Native American, 1% international, 9% transferred in, 56% live on campus.

Freshmen *Admission:* 970 applied, 970 admitted, 793 enrolled. *Average high school GPA:* 2.73. *Test scores:* ACT scores over 18: 58%; ACT scores over 24: 10%.

Faculty *Total:* 140, 91% full-time, 1% with terminal degrees. *Student/faculty ratio:* 15:1.

Majors Agricultural business related; agricultural mechanization; agricultural production; agricultural supplies; architectural engineering technology; auto body repair; auto mechanic/technician; business; business computer programming; civil engineering technology; construction technology; dental hygiene; diesel engine mechanic; electrical/electronic engineering technology; heating/air conditioning/refrigeration; heating/air conditioning/refrigeration technology; industrial electronics installation/repair; industrial technology; institutional food services; liberal arts and sciences/liberal studies; machine shop assistant; medical records technology; occupational therapy assistant; pharmacy technician/assistant; practical nurse; psychiatric/mental health services; secretarial science; small engine mechanic; technical education; vehicle/mobile equipment mechanics and repair related; welding technology.

Academic Programs *Special study options:* academic remediation for entering students, accelerated degree program, adult/continuing education programs, advanced placement credit, cooperative education, distance learning, English as a second language, internships, part-time degree program, services for LD students, student-designed majors, summer session for credit.

Library Mildred Johnson Library with 124,508 titles, 852 serial subscriptions, 4,178 audiovisual materials, an OPAC, a Web page.

Computers on Campus 450 computers available on campus for general student use. A campuswide network can be accessed from student residence rooms and from off campus. Internet access, at least one staffed computer lab available.

Student Life *Housing:* on-campus residence required for freshman year. *Options:* coed, men-only, women-only. *Activities and Organizations:* drama/theater group, choral group, marching band, Student Health Advisory Club, Drama Club, Intervarsity Christian Fellowship, Cultural Diversity, Habitat for Humanity. *Campus security:* 24-hour emergency response devices and patrols, student patrols, late-night transport/escort service, controlled dormitory access. *Student Services:* health clinic, personal/psychological counseling, legal services.

Athletics Member NJCAA. *Intercollegiate sports:* basketball M(s)/W(s), football M(s), track and field M(s)/W(s), volleyball W(s). *Intramural sports:* basketball M/W, football M, racquetball M/W, softball M/W, volleyball M/W.

Standardized Tests *Required:* ACT (for placement).

Costs (2001–02) *Tuition:* state resident $1682 full-time, $70 per credit part-time; nonresident $4491 full-time, $187 per credit part-time. Full-time tuition and fees vary according to reciprocity agreements. Part-time tuition and fees vary according to reciprocity agreements. *Required fees:* $256 full-time, $11 per credit. *Room and board:* $3765; room only: $1120. Room and board charges vary according to board plan and housing facility. *Payment plans:* installment, deferred payment. *Waivers:* employees or children of employees.

Financial Aid In 2001, 90 Federal Work-Study jobs (averaging $1500).

Applying *Options:* common application, electronic application, early admission. *Application fee:* $35. *Required:* high school transcript. *Application deadline:* rolling (freshmen), rolling (transfers). *Notification:* continuous (freshmen).

Admissions Contact Mr. Keath Borchert, Director of Enrollment Services, North Dakota State College of Science, 800 North 6th Street, Wahpeton, ND 58076. *Phone:* 701-671-2189 Ext. 2189. *Toll-free phone:* 800-342-4325 Ext. 2202. *Fax:* 701-671-2332. *E-mail:* keath_borchert@ndscs.nodak.edu.

SITTING BULL COLLEGE
Fort Yates, North Dakota

- **Independent** 2-year, founded 1973
- **Calendar** semesters
- **Degree** certificates and associate
- **Rural** campus
- **Endowment** $541,000
- **Coed,** 194 undergraduate students, 69% full-time, 75% women, 25% men

Undergraduates 134 full-time, 60 part-time. Students come from 2 states and territories.

Freshmen *Admission:* 63 applied, 63 admitted, 26 enrolled. *Average high school GPA:* 2.5.

Faculty *Total:* 32, 50% full-time, 9% with terminal degrees. *Student/faculty ratio:* 6:1.

Majors Agribusiness; business administration; business marketing and marketing management; carpentry; child care/guidance; education; environmental science; farm/ranch management; general office/clerical; human services; liberal arts and sciences/liberal studies; Native American studies; secretarial science; social work; teacher assistant/aide.

Academic Programs *Special study options:* academic remediation for entering students, adult/continuing education programs, off-campus study, part-time degree program.

Library Sitting Bull College Library with 10,000 titles, 130 serial subscriptions, an OPAC.

Computers on Campus 16 computers available on campus for general student use. At least one staffed computer lab available.

Student Life *Housing:* college housing not available. *Activities and Organizations:* student-run newspaper, student government, Future Teachers, Ikce Oyate Culture Club, Phi Beta Lambda, Ski Club. *Student Services:* personal/psychological counseling.

Athletics *Intercollegiate sports:* basketball M/W. *Intramural sports:* basketball M/W.

Standardized Tests *Required:* TABE.
Costs (2002–03) *Tuition:* $2400 full-time, $80 per credit part-time. Full-time tuition and fees vary according to program. Part-time tuition and fees vary according to program. *Waivers:* senior citizens.
Financial Aid In 2001, 20 Federal Work-Study jobs (averaging $2000).
Applying *Options:* early admission. *Required:* high school transcript, medical questionnaire. *Application deadlines:* 9/6 (freshmen), 9/6 (transfers). *Notification:* continuous (freshmen).
Admissions Contact Ms. Melody Silk, Director of Registration and Admissions, Sitting Bull College, 1341 92nd Street, Fort Yates, ND 58538-9701. *Phone:* 701-854-3864.

TURTLE MOUNTAIN COMMUNITY COLLEGE
Belcourt, North Dakota

Admissions Contact Ms. Joni LaFontaine, Admissions/Records Officer, Turtle Mountain Community College, Box 340, Belcourt, ND 58316-0340. *Phone:* 701-477-5605 Ext. 217. *Fax:* 701-477-8967.

UNITED TRIBES TECHNICAL COLLEGE
Bismarck, North Dakota

- **Federally supported** 2-year, founded 1969
- **Calendar** 1-4-4
- **Degree** certificates and associate
- **Small-town** 105-acre campus
- **Coed,** 306 undergraduate students, 92% full-time, 58% women, 42% men

Undergraduates 281 full-time, 25 part-time. 0.7% African American, 0.3% Hispanic American, 90% Native American.
Freshmen *Admission:* 96 applied, 96 admitted.
Faculty *Total:* 37, 100% full-time. *Student/faculty ratio:* 8:1.
Majors Auto mechanic/technician; business administration; business systems networking/ telecommunications; carpentry; child care provider; computer systems analysis; criminal justice/law enforcement administration; developmental/ child psychology; dietetics; early childhood education; enterprise management; fine arts and art studies related; general office/clerical; hospitality management; hotel and restaurant management; human services; law and legal studies related; law enforcement/police science; medical records administration; medical records technology; nursing; practical nurse; welding technology.
Academic Programs *Special study options:* academic remediation for entering students, cooperative education, honors programs, internships, part-time degree program, summer session for credit.
Library United Tribes Technical College Library plus 1 other with 6,000 titles, 86 serial subscriptions, an OPAC, a Web page.
Computers on Campus 210 computers available on campus for general student use. At least one staffed computer lab available.
Student Life *Housing Options:* men-only, women-only. *Activities and Organizations:* student-run newspaper. *Campus security:* 24-hour emergency response devices and patrols. *Student Services:* personal/psychological counseling.
Athletics Member NJCAA. *Intercollegiate sports:* basketball M, cross-country running M/W. *Intramural sports:* basketball M, volleyball M/W.
Standardized Tests *Recommended:* TABE (Test of Adult Basic Education).
Costs (2001–02) *Comprehensive fee:* $5830 includes full-time tuition ($2100), mandatory fees ($730), and room and board ($3000). Part-time tuition: $88 per credit. No tuition increase for student's term of enrollment. *Room and board:* Room and board charges vary according to housing facility. *Payment plan:* installment.
Applying *Required:* high school transcript. *Application deadline:* rolling (freshmen), rolling (transfers).
Admissions Contact Vivian Gillett, Director of Admissions, United Tribes Technical College, 3315 University Drive, Bismarck, ND 58504. *Phone:* 701-255-3285 Ext. 334. *Fax:* 701-530-0640. *E-mail:* ndvivian@hotmail.com.

WILLISTON STATE COLLEGE
Williston, North Dakota

- **State-supported** 2-year, founded 1957, part of North Dakota University System
- **Calendar** semesters
- **Degree** certificates, diplomas, and associate
- **Small-town** 80-acre campus
- **Endowment** $51,950
- **Coed,** 749 undergraduate students, 70% full-time, 65% women, 35% men

Undergraduates 526 full-time, 223 part-time. Students come from 12 states and territories, 2 other countries, 13% are from out of state, 0.3% African American, 0.5% Hispanic American, 8% Native American, 1% international, 53% transferred in, 13% live on campus.
Freshmen *Admission:* 343 enrolled.
Faculty *Total:* 44, 57% full-time. *Student/faculty ratio:* 14:1.
Majors Accounting technician; agricultural sciences; auto mechanic/technician; business marketing and marketing management; computer/information sciences related; data processing technology; diesel engine mechanic; enterprise management related; liberal arts and sciences/liberal studies; medical records technology; medical transcription; multi/interdisciplinary studies related; physical therapy assistant; practical nurse; secretarial science.
Academic Programs *Special study options:* academic remediation for entering students, advanced placement credit, cooperative education, distance learning, double majors, English as a second language, independent study, internships, off-campus study, part-time degree program, services for LD students, student-designed majors, summer session for credit.
Library Williston State College Library with 16,218 titles, 214 serial subscriptions, 475 audiovisual materials, an OPAC, a Web page.
Computers on Campus 150 computers available on campus for general student use. A campuswide network can be accessed from student residence rooms and from off campus. Internet access, at least one staffed computer lab available.
Student Life *Housing Options:* coed, men-only, women-only, cooperative. *Activities and Organizations:* drama/theater group, student-run newspaper, choral group, PTK, PBL, Student Senate, VICA, Student Nurses, national sororities. *Campus security:* controlled dormitory access. *Student Services:* personal/ psychological counseling.
Athletics Member NJCAA. *Intercollegiate sports:* baseball M(s), basketball M(s)/W(s), golf M/W, volleyball W(s). *Intramural sports:* basketball M/W, volleyball M/W.
Standardized Tests *Required for some:* ACT (for placement).
Costs (2002–03) *Tuition:* state resident $1966 full-time; nonresident $4776 full-time. *Room and board:* $1897; room only: $997. Room and board charges vary according to board plan and housing facility. *Payment plan:* installment.
Financial Aid In 2001, 40 Federal Work-Study jobs (averaging $1500). 15 State and other part-time jobs (averaging $1000).
Applying *Options:* electronic application, early admission, deferred entrance. *Application fee:* $35. *Required:* high school transcript. *Application deadline:* rolling (freshmen), rolling (transfers). *Notification:* continuous (freshmen).
Admissions Contact Ms. Jan Solem, Director for Admission and Records, Williston State College, PO Box 1326, Williston, ND 58802-1326. *Phone:* 701-774-4554. *Toll-free phone:* 888-863-9455. *Fax:* 701-774-4554. *E-mail:* wsc.admission@wsc.nodak.edu.

OHIO

ANTONELLI COLLEGE
Cincinnati, Ohio

- **Proprietary** 2-year, founded 1947
- **Calendar** quarters
- **Degree** diplomas and associate
- **Urban** campus
- **Coed,** 360 undergraduate students, 60% full-time, 75% women, 25% men

Undergraduates 216 full-time, 144 part-time. Students come from 6 states and territories, 20% are from out of state, 9% African American, 2% Asian American or Pacific Islander, 0.6% Hispanic American, 1% Native American, 6% transferred in.
Freshmen *Admission:* 183 applied, 118 admitted, 118 enrolled.
Faculty *Total:* 34, 44% full-time. *Student/faculty ratio:* 10:1.
Majors Business systems networking/ telecommunications; computer/ information sciences; graphic design/commercial art/illustration; interior design; photography; Web/multimedia management/webmaster.
Academic Programs *Special study options:* honors programs, internships, part-time degree program, summer session for credit.
Library Main Library plus 1 other with 2,000 titles, 30 serial subscriptions.
Computers on Campus 46 computers available on campus for general student use. Internet access, at least one staffed computer lab available.

Antonelli College (continued)
Student Life *Housing:* college housing not available. *Campus security:* 24-hour emergency response devices, security personnel while classes are in session. *Student Services:* personal/psychological counseling.
Costs (2002–03) *Tuition:* $9585 full-time, $270 per credit hour part-time. Full-time tuition and fees vary according to program. Part-time tuition and fees vary according to course load and program. *Required fees:* $990 full-time, $330 per term part-time. *Payment plan:* installment.
Applying *Options:* early admission, deferred entrance. *Application fee:* $75. *Required:* high school transcript, interview. *Required for some:* art portfolio. *Application deadline:* rolling (freshmen), rolling (transfers).
Admissions Contact Ms. Clara Smith, Director of Student Services, Antonelli College, 124 East Seventh Street, Cincinnati, OH 45202. *Phone:* 513-241-4338. *Toll-free phone:* 800-505-4338. *Fax:* 513-241-9396. *E-mail:* tess@antonellic.com.

THE ART INSTITUTE OF CINCINNATI
Cincinnati, Ohio

- **Proprietary** 2-year
- **Degree** associate
- **Coed,** 66 undergraduate students, 100% full-time, 42% women, 58% men
- 100% of applicants were admitted

Undergraduates 66 full-time. 4% African American, 8% transferred in.
Freshmen *Admission:* 55 applied, 55 admitted, 50 enrolled. *Average high school GPA:* 3.40.
Faculty *Total:* 4, 100% full-time. *Student/faculty ratio:* 20:1.
Student Life *Housing:* college housing not available. *Campus security:* 24-hour emergency response devices.
Costs (2002–03) *Tuition:* $13,196 full-time. *Required fees:* $2260 full-time.
Applying *Required:* high school transcript, letters of recommendation, interview, portfolio. *Application deadline:* 9/10 (freshmen).
Admissions Contact Ms. Cyndi Mendell, Admissions, The Art Institute of Cincinnati, 1171 East Kemper Road, Cincinnati, OH 45246. *Phone:* 513-751-1206. *E-mail:* acacollege@fuse.net.

BELMONT TECHNICAL COLLEGE
St. Clairsville, Ohio

- **State-supported** 2-year, founded 1971, part of Ohio Board of Regents
- **Calendar** quarters
- **Degree** diplomas and associate
- **Rural** 55-acre campus
- **Coed,** 1,623 undergraduate students, 63% full-time, 56% women, 44% men

Undergraduates Students come from 10 states and territories, 3% are from out of state.
Faculty *Total:* 101, 41% full-time.
Majors Accounting; architectural history; business administration; civil engineering technology; computer engineering technology; computer programming; corrections; electrical/electronic engineering technology; electromechanical technology; emergency medical technology; heating/air conditioning/refrigeration; medical assistant; mental health/rehabilitation; nursing; practical nurse; secretarial science; welding technology.
Academic Programs *Special study options:* academic remediation for entering students, distance learning, independent study, part-time degree program, summer session for credit.
Library 5,612 titles, 217 serial subscriptions.
Computers on Campus 85 computers available on campus for general student use. Internet access, at least one staffed computer lab available.
Student Life *Housing:* college housing not available. *Student Services:* personal/psychological counseling.
Standardized Tests *Required:* ACT COMPASS.
Costs (2002–03) *Tuition:* state resident $2340 full-time, $52 per credit hour part-time; nonresident $3825 full-time, $85 per credit hour part-time. Full-time tuition and fees vary according to reciprocity agreements. Part-time tuition and fees vary according to reciprocity agreements. *Required fees:* $450 full-time, $10 per credit hour. *Waivers:* senior citizens and employees or children of employees.
Applying *Options:* early admission. *Application deadline:* rolling (freshmen).
Admissions Contact Mr. Thomas J. Tarowsky, Dean of Student Success, Belmont Technical College, 120 Fox Shannon Place, St. Clairsville, OH 43950-9735. *Phone:* 740-695-9500 Ext. 1064. *Toll-free phone:* 800-423-1188. *E-mail:* ttarowsk@belmont.tech.oh.us.

BOHECKER'S BUSINESS COLLEGE
Ravenna, Ohio

Admissions Contact 326 East Main Street, Ravenna, OH 44266.

BOWLING GREEN STATE UNIVERSITY-FIRELANDS COLLEGE
Huron, Ohio

- **State-supported** 2-year, founded 1968, part of Bowling Green State University System
- **Calendar** semesters
- **Degrees** certificates and associate (also offers some upper-level and graduate courses)
- **Rural** 216-acre campus with easy access to Cleveland and Toledo
- **Endowment** $861,499
- **Coed,** 1,487 undergraduate students, 42% full-time, 63% women, 37% men

Undergraduates 624 full-time, 863 part-time. Students come from 1 other state, 7% African American, 0.4% Asian American or Pacific Islander, 2% Hispanic American, 0.4% Native American, 7% transferred in. *Retention:* 61% of 2001 full-time freshmen returned.
Freshmen *Admission:* 368 applied, 344 admitted, 290 enrolled. *Average high school GPA:* 2.66. *Test scores:* SAT verbal scores over 500: 33%; SAT math scores over 500: 56%; ACT scores over 18: 72%; SAT verbal scores over 600: 11%; ACT scores over 24: 11%.
Faculty *Total:* 80, 40% full-time, 44% with terminal degrees. *Student/faculty ratio:* 20:1.
Majors Accounting; biological/physical sciences; business administration; computer engineering technology; computer/information technology services administration and management related; computer programming; computer systems networking/telecommunications; computer/technical support; criminal justice/law enforcement administration; education; electrical/electronic engineering technology; elementary education; humanities; human services; industrial technology; information technology; interdisciplinary studies; liberal arts and sciences/liberal studies; mechanical design technology; medical records administration; nursing; pre-engineering; quality control technology; respiratory therapy; retail management; secretarial science; social sciences.
Academic Programs *Special study options:* academic remediation for entering students, adult/continuing education programs, advanced placement credit, distance learning, double majors, independent study, internships, off-campus study, part-time degree program, services for LD students, student-designed majors, summer session for credit. *ROTC:* Army (c), Air Force (c).
Library Learning Resources Center with 30,036 titles, 224 serial subscriptions, an OPAC, a Web page.
Computers on Campus 250 computers available on campus for general student use. A campuswide network can be accessed from off campus. Internet access, at least one staffed computer lab available.
Student Life *Housing:* college housing not available. *Activities and Organizations:* drama/theater group, Speech Activities Organization, Allied Health club, student government, Intramural Club, Campus Fellowship. *Campus security:* 24-hour emergency response devices, late-night transport/escort service, patrols by trained security personnel.
Athletics *Intramural sports:* basketball M/W, football M/W, skiing (downhill) M(c)/W(c), softball M/W, volleyball M/W, weight lifting M(c)/W(c).
Standardized Tests *Required for some:* SAT I or ACT (for placement).
Costs (2001–02) *Tuition:* state resident $3044 full-time, $149 per credit hour part-time; nonresident $9296 full-time, $448 per credit hour part-time. *Required fees:* $142 full-time, $8 per credit hour, $8 per term part-time. *Payment plan:* installment. *Waivers:* employees or children of employees.
Applying *Options:* electronic application, early admission, deferred entrance. *Application fee:* $35. *Required:* high school transcript. *Application deadlines:* 8/15 (freshmen), 8/15 (transfers). *Notification:* continuous until 8/15 (freshmen).
Admissions Contact Ms. Debralee Divers, Director of Admissions and Financial Aid, Bowling Green State University-Firelands College, One University Drive, Huron, OH 44839. *Phone:* 419-433-5560. *Toll-free phone:* 800-322-4787. *E-mail:* divers@bgnet.bgsu.edu.

BRADFORD SCHOOL
Columbus, Ohio

- **Proprietary** 2-year, founded 1911
- **Calendar** semesters

■ **Degree** diplomas and associate
■ **Suburban** campus
■ **Coed, primarily women,** 250 undergraduate students, 100% full-time, 72% women, 28% men

Undergraduates 250 full-time. Students come from 1 other state, 22% African American, 2% Asian American or Pacific Islander, 0.4% Hispanic American, 2% transferred in, 44% live on campus.
Freshmen *Admission:* 547 applied, 489 admitted, 196 enrolled. *Average high school GPA:* 2.8.
Faculty *Total:* 11, 45% full-time, 64% with terminal degrees. *Student/faculty ratio:* 25:1.
Majors Accounting; computer programming; computer programming related; graphic design/commercial art/illustration; legal administrative assistant; medical assistant; paralegal/legal assistant; secretarial science; travel/tourism management.
Academic Programs *Special study options:* adult/continuing education programs, cooperative education, internships.
Library Resource Center with 50 titles, 15 serial subscriptions, 100 audiovisual materials, an OPAC.
Computers on Campus 102 computers available on campus for general student use. Internet access available.
Student Life *Housing Options:* coed, women-only, disabled students. *Activities and Organizations:* International Association of Administrative Professionals. *Campus security:* 24-hour patrols.
Costs (2002–03) *Tuition:* $9960 full-time. No tuition increase for student's term of enrollment. *Room only:* $4520. *Payment plan:* installment. *Waivers:* employees or children of employees.
Applying *Options:* common application, electronic application. *Application fee:* $50. *Required for some:* high school transcript, interview. *Application deadline:* rolling (freshmen), rolling (transfers).
Admissions Contact Ms. Raeann Lee, Director of Admissions, Bradford School, 2469 Stelzer Road, Columbus, OH 43219. *Phone:* 614-416-6200. *Toll-free phone:* 800-678-7981. *Fax:* 614-416-6210.

BRYANT AND STRATTON COLLEGE
Willoughby Hills, Ohio

■ **Proprietary** 2-year, founded 1987, part of Bryant and Stratton Business Institute, Inc
■ **Calendar** semesters
■ **Degree** diplomas and associate
■ **Suburban** campus with easy access to Cleveland
■ **Coed,** 172 undergraduate students, 57% full-time, 69% women, 31% men

Undergraduates 98 full-time, 74 part-time. 66% African American, 0.6% Asian American or Pacific Islander, 1% transferred in. *Retention:* 33% of 2001 full-time freshmen returned.
Freshmen *Admission:* 95 applied, 95 admitted, 85 enrolled. *Average high school GPA:* 2.00. *Test scores:* ACT scores over 18: 20%.
Faculty *Total:* 28, 11% full-time, 21% with terminal degrees. *Student/faculty ratio:* 10:1.
Majors Accounting; business administration; information technology; secretarial science.
Academic Programs *Special study options:* academic remediation for entering students, advanced placement credit, distance learning, double majors, independent study, internships, part-time degree program, summer session for credit.
Library Main Library plus 1 other with 1,500 titles, 19 serial subscriptions, an OPAC.
Computers on Campus 90 computers available on campus for general student use. Internet access available.
Student Life *Housing:* college housing not available. *Activities and Organizations:* student-run newspaper, choral group, Student Council, Professional Secretaries International, Accounting Club, Information Technology Organization, Ambassador Society. *Campus security:* 24-hour emergency response devices, late-night transport/escort service. *Student Services:* personal/psychological counseling.
Athletics Member NJCAA. *Intercollegiate sports:* soccer M(s)/W(s).
Standardized Tests *Recommended:* SAT I or ACT (for admission).
Costs (2002–03) *Tuition:* $9900 full-time, $330 per semester hour part-time. Full-time tuition and fees vary according to course load. Part-time tuition and fees vary according to course load. *Required fees:* $200 full-time, $100 per term part-time. *Payment plan:* installment. *Waivers:* employees or children of employees.
Applying *Options:* deferred entrance. *Application fee:* $25. *Required:* essay or personal statement, high school transcript, interview, entrance evaluation and placement evaluation. *Required for some:* letters of recommendation. *Recommended:* minimum 2.0 GPA. *Application deadline:* rolling (freshmen), rolling (transfers).
Admissions Contact Mr. James Pettit, Director of Admissions, Bryant and Stratton College, 27557 Chardon Road, Willoughby Hills, OH 44092. *Phone:* 440-944-6800. *Fax:* 440-944-9260. *E-mail:* jwpettit@bryantstratton.edu.

BRYANT AND STRATTON COLLEGE
Parma, Ohio

■ **Proprietary** 2-year, founded 1981, part of Bryant and Stratton Business Institute, Inc
■ **Calendar** semesters
■ **Degree** certificates, diplomas, and associate
■ **Suburban** 4-acre campus with easy access to Cleveland
■ **Coed,** 202 undergraduate students, 45% full-time, 67% women, 33% men

Undergraduates 90 full-time, 112 part-time. Students come from 1 other state, 11% African American, 1% Asian American or Pacific Islander, 6% Hispanic American.
Freshmen *Admission:* 84 applied, 73 admitted, 73 enrolled. *Average high school GPA:* 2.68.
Faculty *Total:* 25, 20% full-time. *Student/faculty ratio:* 10:1.
Majors Accounting; business administration; information technology; medical assistant; secretarial science.
Academic Programs *Special study options:* academic remediation for entering students, cooperative education, distance learning, double majors, independent study, internships, part-time degree program, summer session for credit.
Library Main Library plus 1 other with 1,500 titles, 20 serial subscriptions, an OPAC.
Computers on Campus 96 computers available on campus for general student use. Internet access available.
Student Life *Activities and Organizations:* student-run newspaper, Business Management Association, International Association of Administrative Professionals, Health Careers Club, Information Technology Club, Student Council. *Campus security:* 24-hour emergency response devices. *Student Services:* personal/psychological counseling.
Athletics *Intramural sports:* softball M/W.
Standardized Tests *Recommended:* SAT I or ACT (for admission).
Costs (2002–03) *One-time required fee:* $25. *Tuition:* $9900 full-time, $330 per semester hour part-time. Full-time tuition and fees vary according to course load. Part-time tuition and fees vary according to course load. *Required fees:* $200 full-time, $100 per term part-time. *Payment plan:* installment. *Waivers:* employees or children of employees.
Applying *Options:* deferred entrance. *Application fee:* $25. *Required:* essay or personal statement, high school transcript, interview. *Required for some:* letters of recommendation. *Recommended:* minimum 2.0 GPA. *Application deadline:* rolling (freshmen), rolling (transfers).
Admissions Contact Mrs. Lisa Mason, Campus Director, Bryant and Stratton College, 12955 Snow Road, Parma, OH 44130. *Phone:* 216-265-3151 Ext. 225. *Toll-free phone:* 800-327-3151. *Fax:* 216-265-0325. *E-mail:* bswhite@bryantstratton.edu.

CENTRAL OHIO TECHNICAL COLLEGE
Newark, Ohio

■ **State-supported** 2-year, founded 1971, part of Ohio Board of Regents
■ **Calendar** quarters
■ **Degree** certificates and associate
■ **Small-town** 155-acre campus with easy access to Columbus
■ **Coed,** 1,973 undergraduate students, 38% full-time, 67% women, 33% men

Undergraduates 755 full-time, 1,218 part-time. Students come from 3 states and territories, 1 other country, 1% are from out of state, 7% transferred in, 1% live on campus.
Freshmen *Admission:* 911 applied, 911 admitted, 305 enrolled.
Faculty *Total:* 139, 33% full-time. *Student/faculty ratio:* 36:1.
Majors Accounting; business administration; computer programming; corrections; criminal justice/law enforcement administration; diagnostic medical sonography; drafting; early childhood education; electrical/electronic engineering technology; electromechanical technology; human services; industrial technol-

Central Ohio Technical College (continued)
ogy; law enforcement/police science; mechanical engineering technology; medical radiologic technology; nursing; physical therapy assistant; secretarial science.
Academic Programs *Special study options:* academic remediation for entering students, accelerated degree program, adult/continuing education programs, advanced placement credit, cooperative education, double majors, English as a second language, internships, off-campus study, part-time degree program, services for LD students, summer session for credit.
Library Newark Campus Library with 45,000 titles, 500 serial subscriptions, an OPAC.
Computers on Campus 300 computers available on campus for general student use. A campuswide network can be accessed from off campus. Internet access, at least one staffed computer lab available.
Student Life *Housing Options:* coed. *Activities and Organizations:* drama/theater group, choral group, Student Senate, Phi Theta Kappa, Student Nurses Organization, Campus Chorus, Physical Therapy Assistants Organization. *Campus security:* 24-hour emergency response devices, student patrols, late-night transport/escort service. *Student Services:* personal/psychological counseling.
Athletics *Intercollegiate sports:* baseball M, basketball M/W, golf M/W, soccer M, softball W, tennis M/W, volleyball M/W. *Intramural sports:* baseball M, basketball M/W, bowling M/W, football M, golf M/W, skiing (downhill) M/W, soccer M, softball W, table tennis M/W, tennis M/W, volleyball M/W, weight lifting M/W.
Standardized Tests *Required:* ACT ASSET or ACT COMPASS.
Costs (2002–03) *Tuition:* state resident $2754 full-time, $70 per credit part-time; nonresident $4914 full-time, $130 per credit part-time. *Required fees:* $216 full-time, $6 per credit. *Room and board:* room only: $1215.
Applying *Options:* common application, electronic application, early admission, deferred entrance. *Application fee:* $15. *Required:* high school transcript. *Application deadline:* rolling (freshmen), rolling (transfers).
Admissions Contact Admissions Representative, Central Ohio Technical College, 1179 University Drive, Newark, OH 43055-1767. *Phone:* 740-366-9222. *Toll-free phone:* 800-9NEWARK. *Fax:* 740-366-5047. *E-mail:* lnelson@bigvax.newark.ohio-state.edu.

CHATFIELD COLLEGE
St. Martin, Ohio

- **Independent** 2-year, founded 1970, affiliated with Roman Catholic Church
- **Calendar** semesters
- **Degree** associate
- **Rural** 200-acre campus with easy access to Cincinnati and Dayton
- **Endowment** $700,000
- **Coed, primarily women,** 304 undergraduate students, 47% full-time, 80% women, 20% men

Undergraduates 142 full-time, 162 part-time. Students come from 1 other state, 12% African American, 0.7% Hispanic American, 0.3% Native American, 5% transferred in.
Freshmen *Admission:* 129 applied, 129 admitted, 90 enrolled.
Faculty *Total:* 42, 7% full-time, 7% with terminal degrees. *Student/faculty ratio:* 12:1.
Majors Business administration; early childhood education; human services; liberal arts and sciences/liberal studies.
Academic Programs *Special study options:* academic remediation for entering students, adult/continuing education programs, advanced placement credit, internships, off-campus study, part-time degree program, summer session for credit.
Library Chatfield College Library with 15,000 titles, 30 serial subscriptions, an OPAC.
Computers on Campus 16 computers available on campus for general student use. A campuswide network can be accessed from off campus. Internet access, at least one staffed computer lab available.
Student Life *Housing:* college housing not available. *Activities and Organizations:* drama/theater group, student-run newspaper. *Campus security:* 12-hour night patrols by security. *Student Services:* personal/psychological counseling.
Costs (2001–02) *Tuition:* $6240 full-time, $205 per credit hour part-time. Full-time tuition and fees vary according to location. Part-time tuition and fees vary according to location. *Required fees:* $90 full-time, $30 per term part-time. *Payment plan:* installment. *Waivers:* senior citizens and employees or children of employees.
Financial Aid In 2001, 8 Federal Work-Study jobs (averaging $800). 2 State and other part-time jobs (averaging $600). *Financial aid deadline:* 8/6.
Applying *Options:* common application, early admission, deferred entrance. *Application fee:* $10. *Required:* high school transcript. *Application deadline:* rolling (freshmen), rolling (transfers). *Notification:* continuous (freshmen).
Admissions Contact Ms. Julie Burdick, Director of Admissions, Chatfield College, St. Martin, OH 45118. *Phone:* 513-875-3344. *Fax:* 513-875-3912.

CINCINNATI COLLEGE OF MORTUARY SCIENCE
Cincinnati, Ohio

- **Independent** primarily 2-year, founded 1882
- **Calendar** quarters
- **Degrees** associate and bachelor's
- **Urban** 10-acre campus
- **Coed,** 131 undergraduate students, 100% full-time, 37% women, 63% men

Undergraduates 131 full-time. Students come from 15 states and territories, 10% African American, 56% transferred in.
Freshmen *Admission:* 12 enrolled.
Faculty *Total:* 12, 58% full-time. *Student/faculty ratio:* 5:1.
Majors Mortuary science.
Academic Programs *Special study options:* academic remediation for entering students, adult/continuing education programs, advanced placement credit, summer session for credit.
Library 5,000 titles, 30 serial subscriptions, a Web page.
Computers on Campus 16 computers available on campus for general student use. At least one staffed computer lab available.
Student Life *Housing:* college housing not available.
Athletics *Intramural sports:* basketball M/W, bowling M/W, football M/W, softball M/W.
Costs (2001–02) *Tuition:* $12,780 full-time, $142 per credit part-time. Full-time tuition and fees vary according to course load. *Required fees:* $25 full-time. *Waivers:* employees or children of employees.
Applying *Options:* deferred entrance. *Application fee:* $25. *Required:* high school transcript. *Recommended:* letters of recommendation. *Application deadline:* rolling (freshmen), rolling (transfers).
Admissions Contact Ms. Pat Leon, Director of Financial Aid, Cincinnati College of Mortuary Science, 645 West North Bend Road, Cincinnati, OH 45224-1462. *Phone:* 513-761-2020. *Fax:* 513-761-3333.

CINCINNATI STATE TECHNICAL AND COMMUNITY COLLEGE
Cincinnati, Ohio

- **State-supported** 2-year, founded 1966, part of Ohio Board of Regents
- **Calendar** 5 ten-week terms
- **Degree** certificates and associate
- **Urban** 46-acre campus
- **Endowment** $750,000
- **Coed,** 7,184 undergraduate students, 38% full-time, 55% women, 45% men

Undergraduates 2,719 full-time, 4,465 part-time. Students come from 6 states and territories, 49 other countries.
Freshmen *Admission:* 8,406 applied, 7,079 admitted, 666 enrolled.
Faculty *Total:* 804, 22% full-time, 5% with terminal degrees. *Student/faculty ratio:* 15:1.
Majors Accounting; aerospace engineering technology; architectural engineering technology; biological technology; biomedical engineering-related technology; business administration; business computer programming; business marketing and marketing management; civil engineering technology; computer engineering technology; culinary arts; dietetics; electrical/electronic engineering technology; electromechanical technology; emergency medical technology; engineering; environmental technology; executive assistant; financial planning; fire science; general studies; graphic design/commercial art/illustration; health/physical education; heating/air conditioning/refrigeration technology; hotel and restaurant management; industrial technology; information sciences/systems; international business; landscaping management; laser/optical technology; liberal arts and sciences/liberal studies; management information systems/business data processing; mechanical engineering technology; medical assistant; medical laboratory technician; medical records administration; nursing; occupational therapy assistant; office management; operating room technician; plastics technology; purchasing/contracts management; radio/television broadcasting technology; real estate; respiratory therapy; sign language interpretation; technical/business writing; telecommunications; turf management.
Academic Programs *Special study options:* academic remediation for entering students, advanced placement credit, cooperative education, distance learning, double majors, English as a second language, internships, off-campus study,

part-time degree program, services for LD students, student-designed majors, summer session for credit. *ROTC:* Army (c), Air Force (c).
Library Johnnie Mae Berry Library with 26,431 titles, 400 serial subscriptions, an OPAC, a Web page.
Computers on Campus 750 computers available on campus for general student use. A campuswide network can be accessed from off campus. Internet access, at least one staffed computer lab available.
Student Life *Housing:* college housing not available. *Activities and Organizations:* drama/theater group, student-run newspaper, student government, United African American Association (UAAA), national fraternities. *Campus security:* 24-hour emergency response devices and patrols, late-night transport/escort service. *Student Services:* personal/psychological counseling.
Athletics Member NJCAA. *Intercollegiate sports:* baseball M, basketball M/W, golf M/W, soccer M. *Intramural sports:* soccer M.
Standardized Tests *Required:* ACT COMPASS.
Costs (2002–03) *Tuition:* state resident $3575 full-time, $65 per credit hour part-time; nonresident $7150 full-time, $130 per credit hour part-time. Full-time tuition and fees vary according to reciprocity agreements. Part-time tuition and fees vary according to reciprocity agreements. *Waivers:* senior citizens and employees or children of employees.
Financial Aid In 2001, 71 Federal Work-Study jobs (averaging $3500).
Applying *Required:* high school transcript. *Application deadline:* rolling (freshmen), rolling (transfers).
Admissions Contact Ms. Gabriele Boeckermann, Director of Admission, Cincinnati State Technical and Community College, 3520 Central Parkway, Cincinnati, OH 45223-2690. *Phone:* 513-569-1550. *Fax:* 513-569-1562. *E-mail:* adm@cinstate.cc.oh.us.

CLARK STATE COMMUNITY COLLEGE
Springfield, Ohio

- **State-supported** 2-year, founded 1962, part of Ohio Board of Regents
- **Calendar** quarters
- **Degree** certificates and associate
- **Suburban** 60-acre campus with easy access to Columbus and Dayton
- **Coed**

Faculty *Student/faculty ratio:* 13:1.
Student Life *Campus security:* late-night transport/escort service.
Athletics Member NJCAA.
Standardized Tests *Required for some:* SAT I or ACT (for placement). *Recommended:* SAT I or ACT (for placement).
Applying *Options:* common application, electronic application, early admission, deferred entrance. *Application fee:* $15. *Required:* high school transcript.
Admissions Contact Mr. Todd Jones, Director of Admissions, Clark State Community College, PO Box 570, Springfield, OH 45501-0570. *Phone:* 937-328-6027. *Fax:* 937-328-3853. *E-mail:* admissions@clark.cc.oh.us.

CLEVELAND INSTITUTE OF ELECTRONICS
Cleveland, Ohio

- **Proprietary** 2-year, founded 1934
- **Calendar** continuous
- **Degrees** associate (offers only external degree programs conducted through home study)
- **Coed, primarily men,** 3,077 undergraduate students

Undergraduates Students come from 52 states and territories, 70 other countries, 97% are from out of state.
Faculty *Total:* 5, 80% full-time.
Majors Electrical/electronic engineering technology.
Academic Programs *Special study options:* adult/continuing education programs, external degree program, part-time degree program.
Library 5,000 titles, 38 serial subscriptions.
Student Life *Housing:* college housing not available.
Costs (2002–03) *Tuition:* $1645 per term part-time.
Applying *Options:* common application, electronic application, early admission. *Required:* high school transcript. *Application deadline:* rolling (freshmen), rolling (transfers). *Notification:* continuous (freshmen).
Admissions Contact Ms. Andrea Stokes, Registrar, Cleveland Institute of Electronics, 1776 East 17th Street, Cleveland, OH 44114. *Phone:* 216-781-9400. *Toll-free phone:* 800-243-6446. *Fax:* 216-781-0331. *E-mail:* instruct@ciewc.edu.

COLLEGE OF ART ADVERTISING
Cincinnati, Ohio

Admissions Contact 4343 Bridgetown Road, Cincinnati, OH 45211-4427.

COLUMBUS STATE COMMUNITY COLLEGE
Columbus, Ohio

- **State-supported** 2-year, founded 1963, part of Ohio Board of Regents
- **Calendar** quarters
- **Degree** certificates and associate
- **Urban** 75-acre campus
- **Coed,** 19,549 undergraduate students

Undergraduates 2% are from out of state, 20% African American, 3% Asian American or Pacific Islander, 1% Hispanic American, 0.6% Native American, 1% international.
Freshmen *Average high school GPA:* 2.50.
Faculty *Total:* 966, 23% full-time.
Majors Accounting; aircraft mechanic/airframe; alcohol/drug abuse counseling; architectural engineering technology; auto mechanic/technician; aviation technology; business administration; business marketing and marketing management; child care/development; civil engineering technology; computer engineering technology; computer programming; construction management; corrections; culinary arts; dental hygiene; dental laboratory technician; dietetics; early childhood education; electrical/electronic engineering technology; electromechanical technology; emergency medical technology; environmental technology; finance; food services technology; gerontology; graphic design/commercial art/illustration; heating/air conditioning/refrigeration; hotel and restaurant management; human resources management; industrial radiologic technology; landscape architecture; law enforcement/police science; legal administrative assistant; liberal arts and sciences/liberal studies; logistics/materials management; mechanical engineering technology; medical administrative assistant; medical laboratory technician; medical records administration; medical technology; mental health/rehabilitation; nursing; operating room technician; paralegal/legal assistant; purchasing/contracts management; quality control technology; real estate; respiratory therapy; retail management; secretarial science; sign language interpretation; sport/fitness administration; technical/business writing; veterinary technology.
Academic Programs *Special study options:* academic remediation for entering students, adult/continuing education programs, advanced placement credit, cooperative education, distance learning, English as a second language, honors programs, internships, off-campus study, part-time degree program, services for LD students, student-designed majors, summer session for credit. *ROTC:* Army (b), Air Force (c).
Library Educational Resource Center plus 1 other with 27,102 titles, 489 serial subscriptions, 30,538 audiovisual materials, an OPAC, a Web page.
Computers on Campus 960 computers available on campus for general student use. A campuswide network can be accessed from off campus. At least one staffed computer lab available.
Student Life *Housing:* college housing not available. *Activities and Organizations:* choral group, Phi Theta Kappa, Alpha Xi Tau, African-American Women's Support Group, Society of Manufacturing Engineers, Student Organization for Legal Assistants. *Campus security:* 24-hour emergency response devices and patrols, late-night transport/escort service. *Student Services:* health clinic, personal/psychological counseling.
Athletics Member NJCAA. *Intercollegiate sports:* baseball M, basketball M(s)/W(s), cross-country running M/W, equestrian sports M/W, golf M, soccer M, softball W, volleyball W. *Intramural sports:* basketball M/W, volleyball M/W, weight lifting M/W.
Standardized Tests *Required:* ACT COMPASS.
Costs (2001–02) *One-time required fee:* $35. *Tuition:* state resident $2196 full-time, $61 per credit hour part-time; nonresident $4824 full-time, $134 per credit hour part-time. Full-time tuition and fees vary according to course load. Part-time tuition and fees vary according to course load. *Waivers:* senior citizens and employees or children of employees.
Financial Aid In 2001, 133 Federal Work-Study jobs (averaging $1500).
Applying *Options:* common application, early admission, deferred entrance. *Application fee:* $10. *Recommended:* high school transcript. *Application deadline:* rolling (freshmen), rolling (transfers). *Notification:* continuous (freshmen).
Admissions Contact Mr. Kenneth Conner, Chief Admissions Officer, Columbus State Community College, 550 East Spring Street. *Phone:* 614-287-2669 Ext. 3669. *Toll-free phone:* 800-621-6407 Ext. 2669. *Fax:* 614-287-6019.

CUYAHOGA COMMUNITY COLLEGE
Cleveland, Ohio

- **State and locally supported** 2-year, founded 1963
- **Calendar** semesters
- **Degree** certificates and associate
- **Coed,** 21,278 undergraduate students, 32% full-time, 64% women, 36% men

Undergraduates 6,837 full-time, 14,441 part-time. Students come from 14 states and territories, 2% are from out of state, 32% African American, 2% Asian American or Pacific Islander, 3% Hispanic American, 0.5% Native American, 3% international, 3% transferred in. *Retention:* 41% of 2001 full-time freshmen returned.
Freshmen *Admission:* 6,781 applied, 6,781 admitted, 2,818 enrolled.
Faculty *Total:* 1,036, 30% full-time, 12% with terminal degrees. *Student/faculty ratio:* 18:1.
Majors Accounting; auto mechanic/technician; aviation technology; business administration; business marketing and marketing management; buying operations; computer engineering technology; computer typography/composition; court reporting; early childhood education; engineering-related technology; finance; fire science; graphic design/commercial art/illustration; industrial radiologic technology; law enforcement/police science; liberal arts and sciences/liberal studies; marketing operations; medical technology; nursing; operating room technician; opticianry; paralegal/legal assistant; photography; physician assistant; real estate; respiratory therapy; restaurant operations; safety/security technology; sales operations; secretarial science; veterinary technology.
Academic Programs *Special study options:* adult/continuing education programs, advanced placement credit, cooperative education, distance learning, English as a second language, external degree program, independent study, part-time degree program, services for LD students, summer session for credit.
Library 177,767 titles, 1,135 serial subscriptions, an OPAC, a Web page.
Computers on Campus 1275 computers available on campus for general student use. A campuswide network can be accessed from off campus. Internet access, at least one staffed computer lab available.
Student Life *Housing:* college housing not available. *Activities and Organizations:* drama/theater group, student-run newspaper, choral group, Student Senate, Student Nursing Organization, Business Focus, Phi Theta Kappa. *Campus security:* 24-hour emergency response devices and patrols, late-night transport/escort service. *Student Services:* health clinic, personal/psychological counseling.
Athletics Member NJCAA. *Intercollegiate sports:* baseball M(s), basketball M(s), cross-country running M(s)/W(s), soccer M(s), softball W(s). *Intramural sports:* basketball M, tennis M/W, track and field M/W, volleyball M/W.
Costs (2001–02) *Tuition:* area resident $1857 full-time, $62 per credit hour part-time; state resident $2468 full-time, $82 per credit hour part-time; nonresident $5090 full-time, $170 per credit hour part-time. *Payment plans:* installment, deferred payment. *Waivers:* senior citizens and employees or children of employees.
Applying *Options:* early admission, deferred entrance. *Required for some:* high school transcript. *Application deadline:* rolling (freshmen), rolling (transfers). *Notification:* continuous (freshmen).
Admissions Contact Dr. Sammie Tyrce-Cox, Director of Admissions and Records, Cuyahoga Community College, 2900 Community College Avenue, Cleveland, OH 44115. *Phone:* 216-987-4030. *Fax:* 216-696-2567.

DAVIS COLLEGE
Toledo, Ohio

- **Proprietary** 2-year, founded 1858
- **Calendar** quarters
- **Degree** certificates, diplomas, and associate
- **Urban** 1-acre campus with easy access to Detroit
- **Coed,** 455 undergraduate students, 36% full-time, 77% women, 23% men

Undergraduates 165 full-time, 290 part-time. Students come from 2 states and territories, 6% are from out of state, 21% African American, 0.2% Asian American or Pacific Islander, 0.9% Hispanic American, 15% transferred in.
Freshmen *Admission:* 104 applied, 104 admitted, 99 enrolled. *Average high school GPA:* 2.8.
Faculty *Total:* 29, 52% full-time, 3% with terminal degrees. *Student/faculty ratio:* 13:1.
Majors Accounting; business administration; computer systems networking/telecommunications; data processing technology; fashion merchandising; graphic design/commercial art/illustration; information technology; interior design; legal administrative assistant; medical administrative assistant; medical assistant; secretarial science; system/networking/LAN/WAN management; travel/tourism management; Web page, digital/multimedia and information resources design.
Academic Programs *Special study options:* academic remediation for entering students, adult/continuing education programs, advanced placement credit, internships, part-time degree program, summer session for credit.
Library Davis College Resource Center with 3,621 titles, 134 serial subscriptions, 352 audiovisual materials.
Computers on Campus 85 computers available on campus for general student use. Internet access, at least one staffed computer lab available.
Student Life *Housing:* college housing not available. *Activities and Organizations:* Student Advisory Board. *Campus security:* 24-hour emergency response devices, security cameras for parking lot. *Student Services:* personal/psychological counseling.
Costs (2001–02) *Tuition:* $7056 full-time, $196 per credit hour part-time. *Required fees:* $60 full-time. *Payment plan:* installment. *Waivers:* employees or children of employees.
Applying *Options:* common application, electronic application, early admission, deferred entrance. *Application fee:* $30. *Required:* high school transcript, interview. *Application deadline:* rolling (freshmen), rolling (transfers). *Notification:* continuous (freshmen).
Admissions Contact Ms. Dana Stern, Senior Career Coordinator, Davis College, 4747 Monroe Street, Toledo, OH 43623-4307. *Phone:* 419-473-2700. *Toll-free phone:* 800-477-7021. *Fax:* 419-473-2472. *E-mail:* dstern@daviscollege.com.

EDISON STATE COMMUNITY COLLEGE
Piqua, Ohio

- **State-supported** 2-year, founded 1973, part of Ohio Board of Regents
- **Calendar** semesters
- **Degree** certificates and associate
- **Small-town** 130-acre campus with easy access to Cincinnati and Dayton
- **Coed,** 2,915 undergraduate students

Undergraduates Students come from 2 states and territories.
Faculty *Total:* 298, 14% full-time.
Majors Accounting; advertising; art; business administration; business marketing and marketing management; computer engineering technology; computer graphics; computer programming; computer science; criminal justice/law enforcement administration; data processing technology; drafting; early childhood education; electrical/electronic engineering technology; elementary education; engineering; engineering design; engineering technology; English; finance; graphic design/commercial art/illustration; human resources management; human services; industrial technology; law enforcement/police science; legal studies; liberal arts and sciences/liberal studies; mathematics; mechanical design technology; medical administrative assistant; medical records administration; nursing; paralegal/legal assistant; pre-engineering; quality control technology; real estate; retail management; secretarial science.
Academic Programs *Special study options:* academic remediation for entering students, accelerated degree program, adult/continuing education programs, advanced placement credit, distance learning, double majors, independent study, internships, off-campus study, part-time degree program, services for LD students, student-designed majors, summer session for credit. *ROTC:* Army (c), Air Force (c).
Library Edison Community College Library with 29,851 titles, 542 serial subscriptions, 2,424 audiovisual materials, an OPAC, a Web page.
Computers on Campus 251 computers available on campus for general student use. A campuswide network can be accessed from off campus. Internet access, at least one staffed computer lab available.
Student Life *Housing:* college housing not available. *Activities and Organizations:* drama/theater group. *Campus security:* late-night transport/escort service, 18-hour patrols by trained security personnel. *Student Services:* personal/psychological counseling.
Athletics Member NJCAA. *Intercollegiate sports:* basketball M/W.
Standardized Tests *Required for some:* SAT I (for placement), ACT COMPASS. *Recommended:* ACT COMPASS.
Costs (2002–03) *Tuition:* state resident $1380 full-time, $92 per credit hour part-time; nonresident $2520 full-time, $168 per credit hour part-time. *Payment plan:* deferred payment. *Waivers:* senior citizens and employees or children of employees.
Applying *Options:* early admission, deferred entrance. *Application fee:* $15. *Required:* high school transcript. *Application deadline:* rolling (freshmen), rolling (transfers).

Admissions Contact Ms. Beth Iams Culbertson, Director of Admissions, Edison State Community College, 1973 Edison Drive, Piqua, OH 45356-9253. *Phone:* 937-778-8600 Ext. 317. *Toll-free phone:* 800-922-3722. *E-mail:* info@edison.cc.oh.us.

EDUCATION AMERICA, REMINGTON COLLEGE, CLEVELAND CAMPUS
Cleveland, Ohio

Admissions Contact 14445 Broadway Avenue, Cleveland, OH 44125.

ETI TECHNICAL COLLEGE
North Canton, Ohio

Admissions Contact Mr. Peter Perkowski, School Director, ETI Technical College, 1320 West Maple Street, NW, North Canton, OH 44720-2854. *Phone:* 330-494-1214.

ETI TECHNICAL COLLEGE OF NILES
Niles, Ohio

- **Proprietary** 2-year, founded 1989
- **Calendar** semesters
- **Degree** diplomas and associate
- **Small-town** campus with easy access to Cleveland and Pittsburgh
- **Coed**

Faculty *Student/faculty ratio:* 15:1.
Student Life *Campus security:* 24-hour emergency response devices.
Standardized Tests *Recommended:* SAT I (for admission), ACT (for admission).
Applying *Options:* common application, early admission, deferred entrance. *Application fee:* $50. *Required:* high school transcript, interview.
Admissions Contact Ms. Diane Marstellar, Director of Admissions, ETI Technical College of Niles, 2076 Youngstown-Warren Road, Niles, OH 44446-4398. *Phone:* 330-652-9919. *Fax:* 330-652-4399.

GALLIPOLIS CAREER COLLEGE
Gallipolis, Ohio

- **Independent** 2-year, founded 1962
- **Calendar** quarters
- **Degree** certificates, diplomas, and associate
- **Coed, primarily women,** 147 undergraduate students, 90% full-time, 84% women, 16% men

Undergraduates 132 full-time, 15 part-time. Students come from 2 states and territories, 4% African American.
Freshmen *Admission:* 41 applied, 41 admitted, 41 enrolled.
Faculty *Total:* 17. *Student/faculty ratio:* 8:1.
Majors Accounting; business; business administration; computer science; computer software and media applications related; computer/technical support; data entry/microcomputer applications; medical administrative assistant; secretarial science.
Academic Programs *Special study options:* academic remediation for entering students, adult/continuing education programs, double majors, independent study, internships, part-time degree program, summer session for credit.
Library Gallipolis Career College Library with 94 audiovisual materials.
Computers on Campus 28 computers available on campus for general student use. Internet access, at least one staffed computer lab available.
Costs (2001–02) *Tuition:* $7200 full-time, $150 per credit part-time. Full-time tuition and fees vary according to course load and program. Part-time tuition and fees vary according to course load and program. No tuition increase for student's term of enrollment. *Payment plans:* installment, deferred payment. *Waivers:* employees or children of employees.
Applying *Application fee:* $50. *Required:* high school transcript, interview. *Application deadline:* rolling (freshmen), rolling (transfers).
Admissions Contact Mr. Jack Henson, Director of Admissions, Gallipolis Career College, 1176 Jackson Pike, Suite 312, Gallipolis, OH 45631. *Phone:* 740-446-4367 Ext. 12. *Toll-free phone:* 800-214-0452. *E-mail:* admissions@gallipoliscareercollege.com.

HOCKING COLLEGE
Nelsonville, Ohio

- **State-supported** 2-year, founded 1968, part of Ohio Board of Regents
- **Calendar** quarters
- **Degree** certificates, diplomas, and associate
- **Rural** 1600-acre campus with easy access to Columbus
- **Endowment** $2.3 million
- **Coed**

Student Life *Campus security:* 24-hour emergency response devices and patrols, student patrols, late-night transport/escort service.
Standardized Tests *Required for some:* nursing exam. *Recommended:* SAT I or ACT (for placement).
Financial Aid In 2001, 125 Federal Work-Study jobs (averaging $1700). 225 State and other part-time jobs (averaging $1700).
Applying *Options:* electronic application. *Application fee:* $15. *Required:* high school transcript.
Admissions Contact Ms. Lyn Hull, Director of Admissions, Hocking College, 3301 Hocking Parkway, Nelsonville, OH 45764-9588. *Phone:* 740-753-3591 Ext. 2803. *Toll-free phone:* 800-282-4163. *Fax:* 740-753-1452. *E-mail:* admissions@hocking.edu.

HONDROS COLLEGE
Westerville, Ohio

- **Proprietary** 2-year
- **Calendar** quarters
- **Degree** certificates and associate
- **Coed**

Student Life *Campus security:* 24-hour emergency response devices.
Admissions Contact Ms. Kimberly Bennett, Manager of Academic Affairs, Hondros College, 4140 Executive Parkway, Westerville, OH 43081. *Phone:* 614-508-7244. *Toll-free phone:* 800-783-0095. *Fax:* 614-508-7279. *E-mail:* hondras@hondras.com.

INTERNATIONAL COLLEGE OF BROADCASTING
Dayton, Ohio

- **Private** 2-year
- **Degree** diplomas and associate
- 118 undergraduate students

Faculty *Total:* 12, 50% full-time.
Majors Audio engineering; radio/television broadcasting.
Admissions Contact Chuck Oesterle, Director of Admissions, International College of Broadcasting, 6 South Smithville Road, Dayton, OH 45431. *Phone:* 937-258-8251. *Fax:* 937-258-8714. *E-mail:* micicb@aol.com.

ITT TECHNICAL INSTITUTE
Norwood, Ohio

- **Proprietary** 2-year
- **Calendar** quarters
- **Degree** associate
- **Coed,** 550 undergraduate students

Majors Computer/information sciences related; computer programming; drafting; electrical/electronic engineering technologies related; information technology.
Student Life *Housing:* college housing not available.
Costs (2001–02) *Tuition:* Full-time tuition and fees vary according to program. Part-time tuition and fees vary according to program. $260—$330 per credit hour.
Applying *Application fee:* $100. *Required:* high school transcript, interview. *Recommended:* letters of recommendation. *Application deadline:* rolling (freshmen). *Notification:* continuous (freshmen).
Admissions Contact Mr. Mike Thompson, Director, ITT Technical Institute, 4750 Wesley Avenue, Norwood, OH 45212. *Phone:* 513-531-8300. *Toll-free phone:* 800-314-8324.

ITT TECHNICAL INSTITUTE
Strongsville, Ohio

- **Proprietary** 2-year
- **Calendar** quarters
- **Degree** associate
- **Coed,** 516 undergraduate students

Majors Computer/information sciences related; computer programming; drafting; electrical/electronic engineering technologies related; information technology.

Student Life *Housing:* college housing not available.

Costs (2001–02) *Tuition:* Full-time tuition and fees vary according to program. Part-time tuition and fees vary according to program. $260—$330 per credit hour.

Applying *Application fee:* $100. *Required:* high school transcript, interview. *Recommended:* letters of recommendation. *Application deadline:* rolling (freshmen). *Notification:* continuous (freshmen).

Admissions Contact Mr. James Tussing, Director of Recruitment, ITT Technical Institute, 14955 Sprague Road, Strongsville, OH 44136. *Phone:* 440-234-9091. *Toll-free phone:* 800-331-1488.

ITT TECHNICAL INSTITUTE
Dayton, Ohio

- **Proprietary** 2-year, founded 1935, part of ITT Educational Services, Inc
- **Calendar** quarters
- **Degree** associate
- **Suburban** 7-acre campus
- **Coed,** 557 undergraduate students

Majors Computer/information sciences related; computer programming; drafting; electrical/electronic engineering technologies related; information technology.

Student Life *Housing:* college housing not available.

Costs (2001–02) *Tuition:* Full-time tuition and fees vary according to program. Part-time tuition and fees vary according to program. $260—$330 per credit hour.

Applying *Options:* deferred entrance. *Application fee:* $100. *Required:* high school transcript, interview. *Recommended:* letters of recommendation. *Application deadline:* rolling (freshmen), rolling (transfers). *Notification:* continuous (freshmen).

Admissions Contact Mr. Walter Hosea, Director of Recruitment, ITT Technical Institute, 3325 Stop 8 Road, Dayton, OH 45414-3425. *Phone:* 937-454-2267.

ITT TECHNICAL INSTITUTE
Youngstown, Ohio

- **Proprietary** 2-year, founded 1967, part of ITT Educational Services, Inc
- **Calendar** quarters
- **Degree** associate
- **Suburban** campus with easy access to Cleveland and Pittsburgh
- **Coed,** 447 undergraduate students

Majors Computer/information sciences related; computer programming; drafting; electrical/electronic engineering technologies related; information technology.

Student Life *Housing:* college housing not available. *Activities and Organizations:* student-run newspaper.

Costs (2001–02) *Tuition:* Full-time tuition and fees vary according to program. Part-time tuition and fees vary according to program. $260—$330 per credit hour.

Financial Aid In 2001, 5 Federal Work-Study jobs (averaging $3979).

Applying *Options:* common application, deferred entrance. *Application fee:* $100. *Required:* high school transcript, interview. *Recommended:* letters of recommendation. *Application deadline:* rolling (freshmen), rolling (transfers). *Notification:* continuous (freshmen).

Admissions Contact Mr. Tom Flynn, Director of Recruitment, ITT Technical Institute, 1030 North Meridian Road, Youngstown, OH 44509-4098. *Phone:* 330-270-1600. *Toll-free phone:* 800-832-5001. *Fax:* 330-270-8333.

JEFFERSON COMMUNITY COLLEGE
Steubenville, Ohio

- **State and locally supported** 2-year, founded 1966, part of Ohio Board of Regents
- **Calendar** semesters
- **Degree** certificates and associate
- **Small-town** 83-acre campus with easy access to Pittsburgh
- **Endowment** $197,077
- **Coed,** 1,612 undergraduate students, 50% full-time, 60% women, 40% men

Undergraduates 810 full-time, 802 part-time. Students come from 3 states and territories, 16% are from out of state, 4% African American, 0.6% Asian American or Pacific Islander, 0.4% Hispanic American, 0.1% Native American, 0.1% international, 30% transferred in.

Freshmen *Admission:* 774 applied, 774 admitted, 402 enrolled. *Average high school GPA:* 2.53.

Faculty *Total:* 124, 28% full-time, 6% with terminal degrees. *Student/faculty ratio:* 16:1.

Majors Accounting; business administration; child care services management; computer engineering related; corrections; data processing technology; dental assistant; developmental/child psychology; drafting; drafting/design technology; electrical/electronic engineering technology; emergency medical technology; finance; food products retailing; industrial radiologic technology; industrial technology; law enforcement/police science; legal administrative assistant; mechanical engineering technology; medical administrative assistant; medical assistant; practical nurse; real estate; respiratory therapy; retail management; secretarial science.

Academic Programs *Special study options:* academic remediation for entering students, adult/continuing education programs, internships, off-campus study, part-time degree program, services for LD students, summer session for credit.

Library Jefferson Community College Library with 12,000 titles, 180 serial subscriptions, 246 audiovisual materials, an OPAC.

Computers on Campus 250 computers available on campus for general student use. At least one staffed computer lab available.

Student Life *Housing:* college housing not available. *Activities and Organizations:* Student Senate, SADD, AITP (Association for Information Technology Professionals), American Drafting and Design Association, Writers Club. *Campus security:* student patrols.

Athletics *Intramural sports:* basketball M/W, softball M/W, tennis M/W, volleyball M/W.

Standardized Tests *Required for some:* SAT I or ACT (for admission), SAT I and SAT II or ACT (for admission).

Costs (2001–02) *Tuition:* area resident $1890 full-time, $63 per credit hour part-time; state resident $2040 full-time, $68 per credit hour part-time; nonresident $2700 full-time, $90 per credit hour part-time. Full-time tuition and fees vary according to reciprocity agreements. Part-time tuition and fees vary according to reciprocity agreements. *Payment plan:* deferred payment. *Waivers:* senior citizens and employees or children of employees.

Applying *Options:* early admission, deferred entrance. *Application fee:* $20. *Required for some:* high school transcript. *Application deadlines:* 8/20 (freshmen), 8/20 (transfers). *Notification:* continuous until 8/20 (freshmen).

Admissions Contact Mr. Chuck Mascellino, Director of Admissions, Jefferson Community College, 4000 Sunset Boulevard, Steubenville, OH 43952. *Phone:* 740-264-5591 Ext. 142. *Toll-free phone:* 800-68-COLLEGE Ext. 142. *Fax:* 740-266-2944.

KENT STATE UNIVERSITY, ASHTABULA CAMPUS
Ashtabula, Ohio

Admissions Contact Ms. Kelly Sanford, Admissions Counselor, Kent State University, Ashtabula Campus, 3325 West 13th Street, Ashtabula, OH 44004-2299. *Phone:* 440-964-4217. *E-mail:* robinson@ashtabula.kent.edu.

KENT STATE UNIVERSITY, EAST LIVERPOOL CAMPUS
East Liverpool, Ohio

- **State-supported** 2-year, founded 1967, part of Kent State University System
- **Calendar** semesters
- **Degrees** certificates and associate (also offers some upper-level and graduate courses)
- **Small-town** 4-acre campus with easy access to Pittsburgh
- **Coed,** 585 undergraduate students

Undergraduates Students come from 3 states and territories, 6% are from out of state.

Freshmen *Admission:* 125 applied, 100 admitted. *Average high school GPA:* 3.18.
Faculty *Total:* 75, 27% full-time. *Student/faculty ratio:* 15:1.
Majors Accounting; business administration; computer engineering technology; computer science related; criminal justice/law enforcement administration; legal administrative assistant; liberal arts and sciences/liberal studies; nursing; occupational therapy; physical therapy.
Academic Programs *Special study options:* academic remediation for entering students, accelerated degree program, adult/continuing education programs, advanced placement credit, distance learning, internships, part-time degree program, services for LD students, student-designed majors, summer session for credit. *ROTC:* Army (c), Navy (c), Air Force (c).
Library East Liverpool Campus Library with 31,320 titles, 135 serial subscriptions, an OPAC, a Web page.
Computers on Campus 72 computers available on campus for general student use. At least one staffed computer lab available.
Student Life *Housing:* college housing not available. *Activities and Organizations:* student-run newspaper, Student Senate, Student Nurses Association, Alpha Beta Gamma, Occupational Therapist Assistant Club, Physical Therapist Assistant Club. *Campus security:* student patrols, late-night transport/escort service.
Standardized Tests *Recommended:* ACT (for placement).
Costs (2001–02) *Tuition:* state resident $3674 full-time, $167 per credit part-time; nonresident $9630 full-time, $438 per credit part-time. *Payment plans:* installment, deferred payment. *Waivers:* senior citizens and employees or children of employees.
Applying *Options:* early admission, deferred entrance. *Application fee:* $30. *Required:* high school transcript. *Application deadline:* rolling (freshmen), rolling (transfers). *Notification:* continuous until 9/1 (freshmen).
Admissions Contact Mrs. Jamie Kenneally, Director of Enrollment Management and Student Services, Kent State University, East Liverpool Campus, 400 East Fourth Street, East Liverpool, OH 43920. *Phone:* 330-382-7414. *Fax:* 330-385-6348. *E-mail:* admissions@kenteliv.kent.edu.

KENT STATE UNIVERSITY, GEAUGA CAMPUS

Burton, Ohio

- **State-supported** founded 1964, part of Kent State University System
- **Calendar** semesters
- **Degrees** associate, bachelor's, and master's
- **Rural** 87-acre campus with easy access to Cleveland
- **Coed,** 670 undergraduate students, 41% full-time, 54% women, 46% men

Undergraduates 274 full-time, 396 part-time. Students come from 3 states and territories, 2 other countries, 4% African American, 0.5% Asian American or Pacific Islander, 0.5% Hispanic American, 0.5% international, 0.3% transferred in. *Retention:* 53% of 2001 full-time freshmen returned.
Freshmen *Admission:* 274 applied, 274 admitted, 192 enrolled. *Test scores:* SAT verbal scores over 500: 50%; SAT math scores over 500: 43%; ACT scores over 18: 63%; SAT verbal scores over 600: 14%; SAT math scores over 600: 7%; ACT scores over 24: 17%.
Faculty *Total:* 55, 13% full-time, 7% with terminal degrees. *Student/faculty ratio:* 16:1.
Majors Accounting; business administration; computer engineering technology; computer programming; horticulture services; industrial technology; liberal arts and sciences/liberal studies.
Academic Programs *Special study options:* academic remediation for entering students, adult/continuing education programs, advanced placement credit, distance learning, double majors, internships, part-time degree program, services for LD students, student-designed majors, summer session for credit. *ROTC:* Army (c), Air Force (c).
Library Kent State University Library with 8,300 titles, 6,600 serial subscriptions, an OPAC, a Web page.
Computers on Campus 50 computers available on campus for general student use. Internet access, at least one staffed computer lab available.
Student Life *Housing:* college housing not available. *Activities and Organizations:* student-run newspaper, Computer Club, Student Senate, Accounting Club, student newspaper. *Campus security:* 24-hour emergency response devices.
Athletics *Intramural sports:* basketball M/W, skiing (downhill) M/W, table tennis M/W, volleyball M/W.
Standardized Tests *Recommended:* ACT (for placement).
Costs (2001–02) *Tuition:* state resident $3052 full-time, $139 per hour part-time; nonresident $8540 full-time, $389 per hour part-time. *Required fees:* $216 full-time. *Payment plan:* installment. *Waivers:* senior citizens and employees or children of employees.
Applying *Options:* early admission, deferred entrance. *Application fee:* $30. *Required:* high school transcript, interview. *Recommended:* minimum 2.0 GPA. *Application deadline:* rolling (freshmen), rolling (transfers).
Admissions Contact Ms. Betty Landrus, Admissions and Records Secretary, Kent State University, Geauga Campus, 14111 Clandon Stroy Road, Burton, OH 44021. *Phone:* 440-834-4187. *Fax:* 440-834-8846. *E-mail:* cbaker@geauga.kent.edu.

KENT STATE UNIVERSITY, SALEM CAMPUS

Salem, Ohio

- **State-supported** 2-year, founded 1966, part of Kent State University System
- **Calendar** semesters
- **Degrees** associate (also offers some upper-level and graduate courses)
- **Rural** 98-acre campus
- **Coed,** 1,150 undergraduate students

Undergraduates Students come from 2 states and territories.
Freshmen *Admission:* 410 applied, 317 admitted. *Average high school GPA:* 2.73.
Faculty *Total:* 93, 40% full-time.
Majors Accounting; business administration; computer/information sciences; early childhood education; environmental science; horticulture science; human services; industrial technology; liberal arts and sciences/liberal studies; medical radiologic technology; secretarial science.
Academic Programs *Special study options:* academic remediation for entering students, adult/continuing education programs, advanced placement credit, distance learning, freshman honors college, honors programs, internships, part-time degree program, services for LD students, summer session for credit. *ROTC:* Army (c), Air Force (c).
Library 19,000 titles, 163 serial subscriptions, 158 audiovisual materials, an OPAC, a Web page.
Computers on Campus 100 computers available on campus for general student use. Internet access, online (class) registration, at least one staffed computer lab available.
Student Life *Housing:* college housing not available. *Activities and Organizations:* drama/theater group, student government, NEXUS, Ski Club, Art Club, Drama Club. *Campus security:* late-night transport/escort service. *Student Services:* personal/psychological counseling, women's center.
Athletics *Intramural sports:* badminton M/W, basketball M/W, bowling M/W, football M/W, golf M/W, racquetball M/W, skiing (downhill) M/W, softball M/W, table tennis M/W, tennis M/W, volleyball M/W.
Standardized Tests *Required for some:* ACT (for admission), SAT I or ACT (for placement). *Recommended:* SAT I or ACT (for placement).
Costs (2001–02) *Tuition:* state resident $3160 full-time, $147 per credit hour part-time; nonresident $7320 full-time, $293 per credit hour part-time. Full-time tuition and fees vary according to class time. Part-time tuition and fees vary according to class time. *Payment plans:* tuition prepayment, installment, deferred payment. *Waivers:* employees or children of employees.
Applying *Options:* early admission, deferred entrance. *Application fee:* $30. *Required:* high school transcript. *Required for some:* essay or personal statement, minimum X GPA, letters of recommendation. *Application deadline:* rolling (freshmen), rolling (transfers).
Admissions Contact Ms. Malinda Shean, Admissions Secretary, Kent State University, Salem Campus, 2491 State Route 45 South, Salem, OH 44460-9412. *Phone:* 330-332-0361 Ext. 74208.

KENT STATE UNIVERSITY, STARK CAMPUS

Canton, Ohio

- **State-supported** primarily 2-year, founded 1967, part of Kent State University System
- **Calendar** semesters
- **Degrees** associate and bachelor's (also offers some graduate courses)
- **Suburban** 200-acre campus with easy access to Cleveland
- **Coed,** 3,449 undergraduate students

Undergraduates Students come from 2 states and territories.
Freshmen *Admission:* 631 applied, 631 admitted. *Average high school GPA:* 2.70.
Majors Art; biological/physical sciences; business administration; education; interdisciplinary studies; liberal arts and sciences/liberal studies.

Kent State University, Stark Campus (continued)

Academic Programs *Special study options:* academic remediation for entering students, adult/continuing education programs, advanced placement credit, English as a second language, freshman honors college, honors programs, internships, off-campus study, part-time degree program, services for LD students, student-designed majors, summer session for credit. *ROTC:* Army (c), Air Force (c).

Library Kent State University Library with 72,807 titles, 313 serial subscriptions, an OPAC, a Web page.

Computers on Campus 76 computers available on campus for general student use. A campuswide network can be accessed from off campus. Internet access, at least one staffed computer lab available.

Student Life *Housing:* college housing not available. *Activities and Organizations:* drama/theater group, choral group, Psychology Club, Pan African Student Alliance, Criminal Justice Society, Women's Studies, History Club. *Campus security:* 24-hour emergency response devices, late-night transport/escort service.

Standardized Tests *Required for some:* SAT I or ACT (for admission).

Costs (2001–02) *Tuition:* state resident $3344 full-time, $152 per credit part-time; nonresident $8832 full-time, $402 per credit part-time. No tuition increase for student's term of enrollment. *Payment plan:* installment. *Waivers:* senior citizens and employees or children of employees.

Applying *Options:* early admission, deferred entrance. *Application fee:* $30. *Required:* high school transcript. *Required for some:* interview. *Application deadline:* rolling (freshmen), rolling (transfers).

Admissions Contact Ms. Deborah Ann Phillipp, Acting Director of Admissions, Kent State University, Stark Campus, 6000 Frank Avenue NW, Canton, OH 44720-7599. *Phone:* 330-499-9600 Ext. 53259. *Fax:* 330-499-0301. *E-mail:* dphillipp@stark.kent.edu.

KENT STATE UNIVERSITY, TRUMBULL CAMPUS
Warren, Ohio

- **State-supported** 2-year, founded 1954, part of Kent State University System
- **Calendar** semesters
- **Degrees** certificates and associate (also offers some upper-level and graduate courses)
- **Suburban** 200-acre campus with easy access to Cleveland
- **Endowment** $1.1 million
- **Coed,** 2,219 undergraduate students

Undergraduates Students come from 4 states and territories.

Faculty *Total:* 155, 52% full-time.

Majors Accounting; auto mechanic/technician; business administration; business marketing and marketing management; computer engineering technology; criminal justice/law enforcement administration; electrical/electronic engineering technology; engineering; environmental technology; finance; industrial technology; liberal arts and sciences/liberal studies; mechanical engineering technology; real estate; secretarial science; travel/tourism management.

Academic Programs *Special study options:* academic remediation for entering students, adult/continuing education programs, advanced placement credit, cooperative education, distance learning, freshman honors college, honors programs, independent study, internships, part-time degree program, services for LD students, student-designed majors, summer session for credit. *ROTC:* Army (c), Air Force (c).

Library Trumbull Campus Library with 65,951 titles, 759 serial subscriptions, an OPAC, a Web page.

Computers on Campus 300 computers available on campus for general student use. Internet access, at least one staffed computer lab available.

Student Life *Housing:* college housing not available. *Activities and Organizations:* drama/theater group, student-run newspaper, Student Senate, Trumbull Environmental Club, Union Activities Board, Gamemasters, Kent Christian Fellowship. *Campus security:* 24-hour emergency response devices, late-night transport/escort service, patrols by trained security personnel during open hours.

Athletics *Intramural sports:* basketball M/W, bowling M/W, skiing (downhill) M/W, volleyball M/W.

Standardized Tests *Required:* ACT COMPASS. *Required for some:* SAT I or ACT (for placement).

Costs (2001–02) *Tuition:* state resident $3344 full-time, $152 per credit hour part-time; nonresident $8832 full-time, $402 per credit hour part-time. Full-time tuition and fees vary according to course load. Part-time tuition and fees vary according to course load. No tuition increase for student's term of enrollment. *Payment plan:* installment. *Waivers:* senior citizens and employees or children of employees.

Financial Aid In 2001, 25 Federal Work-Study jobs (averaging $1500).

Applying *Options:* early admission, deferred entrance. *Application fee:* $30. *Required:* high school transcript. *Application deadline:* 7/30 (freshmen), rolling (transfers). *Notification:* continuous until 8/30 (freshmen).

Admissions Contact Ms. Kerrianne Aulet, Admissions Specialist, Kent State University, Trumbull Campus, 4314 Mahoning Avenue, NW, Warren, OH 44483-1998. *Phone:* 330-847-0571 Ext. 2367. *E-mail:* info@lyceum.trumbull.kent.edu.

KENT STATE UNIVERSITY, TUSCARAWAS CAMPUS
New Philadelphia, Ohio

- **State-supported** primarily 2-year, founded 1962, part of Kent State University System
- **Calendar** semesters
- **Degrees** certificates, diplomas, associate, and bachelor's (also offers some upper-level and graduate courses)
- **Small-town** 172-acre campus with easy access to Cleveland
- **Endowment** $3.0 million
- **Coed,** 1,845 undergraduate students, 51% full-time, 63% women, 37% men

Undergraduates Students come from 2 states and territories, 1 other country, 1% African American, 0.5% Asian American or Pacific Islander, 0.3% Hispanic American, 0.3% Native American, 0.3% international.

Freshmen *Average high school GPA:* 2.76.

Faculty *Total:* 147, 29% full-time, 21% with terminal degrees. *Student/faculty ratio:* 17:1.

Majors Accounting; business administration; computer engineering technology; electrical/electronic engineering technology; engineering technology; environmental science; industrial technology; law enforcement/police science; liberal arts and sciences/liberal studies; mechanical engineering technology; nursing; secretarial science.

Academic Programs *Special study options:* academic remediation for entering students, accelerated degree program, adult/continuing education programs, advanced placement credit, distance learning, double majors, freshman honors college, honors programs, internships, part-time degree program, services for LD students, student-designed majors, summer session for credit. *ROTC:* Army (c), Air Force (c).

Library Tuscarawas Campus Library with 58,946 titles, 400 serial subscriptions, 520 audiovisual materials, an OPAC, a Web page.

Computers on Campus 161 computers available on campus for general student use. A campuswide network can be accessed from off campus. Internet access, online (class) registration, at least one staffed computer lab available.

Student Life *Housing:* college housing not available. *Activities and Organizations:* choral group, Society of Mechanical Engineers, IEEE, Imagineers, Criminal Justice Club, The Way.

Athletics *Intramural sports:* basketball M/W, volleyball M/W.

Standardized Tests *Required for some:* SAT I or ACT (for placement).

Costs (2001–02) *Tuition:* state resident $3184 full-time, $145 per semester hour part-time; nonresident $8672 full-time. Full-time tuition and fees vary according to class time. Part-time tuition and fees vary according to class time. *Payment plan:* installment. *Waivers:* employees or children of employees.

Applying *Options:* common application, early admission, deferred entrance. *Application fee:* $30. *Required:* high school transcript. *Application deadlines:* 9/1 (freshmen), 9/1 (transfers). *Notification:* continuous (freshmen).

Admissions Contact Ms. Denise L. Testa, Director of Admissions, Kent State University, Tuscarawas Campus, 330 University Drive, NE, New Philadelphia, OH 44663-9403. *Phone:* 330-339-3391 Ext. 47425. *Fax:* 330-339-3321.

KETTERING COLLEGE OF MEDICAL ARTS
Kettering, Ohio

Admissions Contact Mr. David Lofthouse, Director of Enrollment Services, Kettering College of Medical Arts, 3737 Southern Boulevard, Kettering, OH 45429-1299. *Phone:* 937-296-7228. *Toll-free phone:* 800-433-5262. *Fax:* 937-296-4238.

LAKELAND COMMUNITY COLLEGE
Kirtland, Ohio

- **State and locally supported** 2-year, founded 1967, part of Ohio Board of Regents

- **Calendar** semesters
- **Degree** certificates and associate
- **Suburban** 380-acre campus with easy access to Cleveland
- **Endowment** $1.4 million
- **Coed,** 8,253 undergraduate students, 32% full-time, 57% women, 43% men

Undergraduates 2,664 full-time, 5,589 part-time. Students come from 5 states and territories, 31 other countries, 1% are from out of state.

Freshmen *Admission:* 1,098 applied, 1,098 admitted, 1,022 enrolled.

Faculty *Total:* 611, 19% full-time, 14% with terminal degrees. *Student/faculty ratio:* 17:1.

Majors Accounting; biological/physical sciences; biotechnology research; business administration; civil engineering technology; computer graphics; computer programming related; computer programming (specific applications); computer systems networking/telecommunications; corrections; criminal justice/law enforcement administration; dental hygiene; early childhood education; electrical/electronic engineering technology; engineering technology; fire science; graphic design/commercial art/illustration; hospitality management; human services; industrial technology; information sciences/systems; law enforcement/police science; liberal arts and sciences/liberal studies; machine technology; mechanical engineering technology; medical laboratory technician; nursing; optometric/ophthalmic laboratory technician; paralegal/legal assistant; radiological science; respiratory therapy; safety/security technology; secretarial science; system administration; system/networking/LAN/WAN management; travel/tourism management; Web/multimedia management/webmaster; Web page, digital/multimedia and information resources design.

Academic Programs *Special study options:* academic remediation for entering students, adult/continuing education programs, advanced placement credit, cooperative education, distance learning, external degree program, internships, part-time degree program, services for LD students, summer session for credit.

Library Lakeland Community College Library with 70,874 titles, 2,205 serial subscriptions, 3,453 audiovisual materials, an OPAC, a Web page.

Computers on Campus 500 computers available on campus for general student use. A campuswide network can be accessed from off campus. Online (class) registration, at least one staffed computer lab available.

Student Life *Housing:* college housing not available. *Activities and Organizations:* drama/theater group, student-run newspaper, radio station, choral group, Campus Activities Board, Gamers Guild, Computers Users Group, Veterans Group, Aikido Club. *Campus security:* 24-hour emergency response devices and patrols, student patrols, late-night transport/escort service. *Student Services:* health clinic, personal/psychological counseling, women's center.

Athletics Member NJCAA. *Intercollegiate sports:* baseball M(s), basketball M(s)/W(s), golf M(s)/W(s), soccer M(s), softball W(s), volleyball W(s). *Intramural sports:* basketball M/W, racquetball M/W, volleyball M/W, wrestling M.

Standardized Tests *Required for some:* SAT I or ACT (for placement), ACT ASSET or ACT COMPASS. *Recommended:* SAT I or ACT (for placement).

Costs (2001–02) *Tuition:* area resident $1781 full-time, $59 per credit hour part-time; state resident $2239 full-time, $75 per credit hour part-time; nonresident $5070 full-time, $169 per credit hour part-time. Full-time tuition and fees vary according to course load. Part-time tuition and fees vary according to course load. *Required fees:* $265 full-time, $8 per credit hour, $14 per term part-time. *Payment plan:* installment. *Waivers:* senior citizens and employees or children of employees.

Applying *Options:* common application, electronic application, early admission, deferred entrance. *Application fee:* $15. *Required:* high school transcript. *Application deadlines:* 9/1 (freshmen), 9/1 (transfers). *Notification:* continuous until 9/1 (freshmen).

Admissions Contact Ms. Tracey Cooper, Director for Admissions/Registrar, Lakeland Community College, 7700 Clocktower Drive, Kirtland, OH 44094. *Phone:* 440-953-7230. *Toll-free phone:* 800-589-8520. *Fax:* 440-975-4330. *E-mail:* tcooper@lakeland.cc.oh.us.

LIMA TECHNICAL COLLEGE
Lima, Ohio

- **State-supported** 2-year, founded 1971
- **Calendar** quarters
- **Degree** certificates and associate
- **Rural** 565-acre campus
- **Endowment** $939,309
- **Coed,** 2,894 undergraduate students, 52% full-time, 68% women, 32% men

Undergraduates 1,503 full-time, 1,391 part-time. Students come from 6 states and territories, 1 other country, 0.6% are from out of state, 7% African American, 0.7% Asian American or Pacific Islander, 2% Hispanic American, 0.2% Native American, 0.3% transferred in.

Freshmen *Admission:* 863 applied, 863 admitted, 592 enrolled. *Average high school GPA:* 2.65.

Faculty *Total:* 222, 33% full-time, 8% with terminal degrees. *Student/faculty ratio:* 20:1.

Majors Accounting; business administration; business marketing and marketing management; child care/development; computer graphics; computer programming; corrections; dental hygiene; dietetics; drafting; electrical/electronic engineering technology; emergency medical technology; engineering technology; fashion merchandising; finance; human services; industrial radiologic technology; industrial technology; information sciences/systems; law enforcement/police science; legal administrative assistant; mechanical design technology; mechanical engineering technology; medical administrative assistant; nursing; paralegal/legal assistant; physical therapy; quality control technology; respiratory therapy; retail management; robotics; secretarial science.

Academic Programs *Special study options:* academic remediation for entering students, adult/continuing education programs, advanced placement credit, cooperative education, distance learning, independent study, internships, part-time degree program, services for LD students, student-designed majors, summer session for credit.

Library Ohio State Library with 80,000 titles, an OPAC.

Computers on Campus 150 computers available on campus for general student use. A campuswide network can be accessed from off campus. Internet access, at least one staffed computer lab available.

Student Life *Housing:* college housing not available. *Activities and Organizations:* drama/theater group, student-run newspaper, choral group, Student Senate, Social Activities Board, Ski Club, Society of Manufacturing Engineers, Psychology Club. *Campus security:* student patrols, late-night transport/escort service.

Athletics *Intercollegiate sports:* baseball M, basketball M/W, golf M, softball W, tennis M/W, volleyball W. *Intramural sports:* basketball M/W, football M/W, golf M/W, skiing (cross-country) M/W, skiing (downhill) M/W, tennis M/W, volleyball M/W, weight lifting M.

Standardized Tests *Required for some:* ACT (for placement).

Costs (2002–03) *Tuition:* state resident $72 per credit hour part-time; nonresident $2592 full-time, $144 per credit hour part-time. Full-time tuition and fees vary according to course load. *Required fees:* $65 full-time, $20 per term part-time. *Payment plan:* deferred payment. *Waivers:* senior citizens and employees or children of employees.

Financial Aid In 2001, 110 Federal Work-Study jobs (averaging $1000).

Applying *Options:* common application, early admission, deferred entrance. *Application fee:* $25. *Required:* high school transcript. *Application deadline:* rolling (freshmen), rolling (transfers). *Notification:* continuous until 9/22 (freshmen).

Admissions Contact Mr. Scot Lingrell, Director, Student Advising and Development, Lima Technical College, 4240 Campus Drive, Lima, OH 45804-3597. *Phone:* 419-995-8050. *Toll-free phone:* 419-995-8000. *Fax:* 419-995-8098. *E-mail:* lingrels@ltc.tec.oh.us.

LORAIN COUNTY COMMUNITY COLLEGE
Elyria, Ohio

- **State and locally supported** 2-year, founded 1963, part of Ohio Board of Regents
- **Calendar** semesters
- **Degree** certificates and associate
- **Suburban** 480-acre campus with easy access to Cleveland
- **Coed,** 7,818 undergraduate students, 37% full-time, 65% women, 35% men

Undergraduates 2,858 full-time, 4,960 part-time. Students come from 10 states and territories, 9 other countries, 8% African American, 0.9% Asian American or Pacific Islander, 7% Hispanic American, 0.4% Native American, 0.6% international, 4% transferred in.

Freshmen *Admission:* 3,381 applied, 2,506 admitted, 1,200 enrolled.

Faculty *Total:* 538, 20% full-time. *Student/faculty ratio:* 20:1.

Majors Accounting; art; athletic training/sports medicine; biological/physical sciences; biology; business administration; business marketing and marketing management; chemistry; civil engineering technology; computer engineering technology; computer maintenance technology; computer programming; computer programming related; computer programming (specific applications); computer programming, vendor/product certification; computer science; computer science related; computer systems networking/telecommunications; corrections; cosmetic services; cosmetic services related; data entry/microcomputer applications; data entry/microcomputer applications related; diagnostic medical sonography; drafting; early childhood education; education; electrical/electronic engineering technology; elementary education; engineering; engineering technol-

Lorain County Community College (continued)
ogy; finance; fire science; history; human services; industrial radiologic technology; industrial technology; information sciences/systems; information technology; journalism; law enforcement/police science; liberal arts and sciences/liberal studies; machine technology; mass communications; mathematics; mechanical design technology; medical laboratory technician; music; nuclear medical technology; nursing; operating room technician; personal/miscellaneous services; pharmacy; physical education; physical therapy assistant; physics; plastics technology; political science; pre-engineering; psychology; quality control technology; real estate; retail management; robotics; secretarial science; social sciences; social work; sociology; sport/fitness administration; theater arts/drama; travel/tourism management; urban studies; veterinary sciences; word processing.

Academic Programs *Special study options:* academic remediation for entering students, adult/continuing education programs, advanced placement credit, cooperative education, distance learning, English as a second language, honors programs, independent study, part-time degree program, services for LD students, student-designed majors, summer session for credit.

Library Learning Resource Center with 198,984 titles, 3,289 audiovisual materials, an OPAC.

Computers on Campus 400 computers available on campus for general student use. A campuswide network can be accessed from off campus. Internet access, online (class) registration, at least one staffed computer lab available.

Student Life *Housing:* college housing not available. *Activities and Organizations:* drama/theater group, student-run newspaper, radio station, choral group. *Campus security:* 24-hour emergency response devices and patrols, late-night transport/escort service. *Student Services:* health clinic, personal/psychological counseling, women's center, legal services.

Athletics *Intramural sports:* archery M/W, basketball M/W, softball M/W, volleyball M/W, weight lifting M/W, wrestling M.

Standardized Tests *Required for some:* Michigan English Language Assessment Battery, ACT ASSET, ACT COMPASS. *Recommended:* SAT I or ACT (for placement).

Costs (2002–03) *Tuition:* area resident $2038 full-time, $78 per credit hour part-time; state resident $2457 full-time, $95 per credit hour part-time; nonresident $5005 full-time, $193 per credit hour part-time. *Required fees:* $91 full-time, $4 per credit hour. *Payment plans:* installment, deferred payment. *Waivers:* senior citizens and employees or children of employees.

Financial Aid In 2001, 64 Federal Work-Study jobs.

Applying *Options:* early admission, deferred entrance. *Required for some:* high school transcript. *Application deadline:* rolling (freshmen), rolling (transfers). *Notification:* continuous (freshmen).

Admissions Contact Ms. Dione Somervile, Director of Enrollment Services, Lorain County Community College, 1005 Abbe Road, North, Elyria, OH 44035. *Phone:* 440-366-7566. *Toll-free phone:* 800-995-5222 Ext. 4032. *Fax:* 440-365-6519.

MARION TECHNICAL COLLEGE
Marion, Ohio

- **State-related** 2-year, founded 1971, part of Ohio Board of Regents
- **Calendar** quarters
- **Degree** certificates and associate
- **Small-town** 180-acre campus with easy access to Columbus
- **Coed,** 2,739 undergraduate students, 28% full-time, 57% women, 43% men

Undergraduates Students come from 4 states and territories.

Freshmen *Admission:* 692 admitted.

Faculty *Total:* 105, 34% full-time. *Student/faculty ratio:* 18:1.

Majors Accounting; business administration; business marketing and marketing management; data processing technology; drafting; electrical/electronic engineering technology; engineering technology; finance; human services; industrial radiologic technology; industrial technology; mechanical engineering technology; medical administrative assistant; medical laboratory technician; nursing; paralegal/legal assistant; physical therapy assistant; secretarial science.

Academic Programs *Special study options:* academic remediation for entering students, adult/continuing education programs, cooperative education, distance learning, internships, part-time degree program, services for LD students, student-designed majors, summer session for credit.

Library Marion Campus Library with 38,000 titles, 200 serial subscriptions, an OPAC.

Computers on Campus 270 computers available on campus for general student use. At least one staffed computer lab available.

Student Life *Housing:* college housing not available. *Activities and Organizations:* Student Ambassadors. *Campus security:* 24-hour emergency response devices.

Athletics *Intramural sports:* basketball M/W, football M, golf M, rugby M, skiing (cross-country) M/W, skiing (downhill) M/W, tennis M/W, volleyball M/W.

Standardized Tests *Required for some:* ACT (for placement).

Costs (2002–03) *Tuition:* state resident $2844 full-time, $79 per credit hour part-time; nonresident $4392 full-time, $122 per credit hour part-time.

Applying *Options:* early admission, deferred entrance. *Application fee:* $20. *Required:* high school transcript. *Application deadline:* rolling (freshmen), rolling (transfers). *Notification:* continuous (freshmen).

Admissions Contact Mr. Joel O. Liles, Director of Admissions and Career Services, Marion Technical College, 1467 Mt. Vernon Avenue, Marion, OH 43302. *Phone:* 740-389-4636 Ext. 249. *E-mail:* enroll@mtc.tec.oh.us.

MERCY COLLEGE OF NORTHWEST OHIO
Toledo, Ohio

- **Independent** primarily 2-year, founded 1993, affiliated with Roman Catholic Church
- **Calendar** semesters
- **Degrees** certificates, associate, and bachelor's
- **Urban** campus with easy access to Detroit
- **Endowment** $2.5 million
- **Coed, primarily women**

Faculty *Student/faculty ratio:* 6:1.

Student Life *Campus security:* 24-hour emergency response devices and patrols, late-night transport/escort service, controlled dormitory access.

Standardized Tests *Required for some:* SAT I or ACT (for admission).

Costs (2001–02) *One-time required fee:* $60. *Tuition:* $5668 full-time, $218 per semester hour part-time. Full-time tuition and fees vary according to course load and program. Part-time tuition and fees vary according to course load. *Required fees:* $147 full-time, $50 per term part-time. *Room only:* $1740. Room and board charges vary according to location. *Payment plans:* installment, deferred payment.

Financial Aid In 2001, 18 Federal Work-Study jobs.

Applying *Application fee:* $25. *Required:* high school transcript. *Required for some:* minimum 2.3 GPA.

Admissions Contact Diana Hernandez, Data Research Coordinator, Mercy College of Northwest Ohio, 2221 Madison Avenue, Toledo, OH 43624-1197. *Phone:* 419-251-1313. *Toll-free phone:* 888-80-Mercy. *Fax:* 419-251-1462.

MIAMI-JACOBS COLLEGE
Dayton, Ohio

- **Proprietary** 2-year, founded 1860
- **Calendar** quarters
- **Degree** certificates, diplomas, and associate
- **Small-town** campus
- **Coed**

Student Life *Campus security:* late-night transport/escort service.

Standardized Tests *Required for some:* ACT (for admission). *Recommended:* SAT I or ACT (for admission).

Applying *Options:* early admission, deferred entrance. *Application fee:* $50. *Required:* essay or personal statement, high school transcript, interview. *Recommended:* letters of recommendation.

Admissions Contact Ms. Susan Cooper, Associate Director of Admissions, Miami-Jacobs College, 400 East Second Street, PO Box 1433. *Phone:* 937-461-5174.

MIAMI UNIVERSITY-HAMILTON CAMPUS
Hamilton, Ohio

- **State-supported** founded 1968, part of Miami University System
- **Calendar** semesters
- **Degrees** certificates, associate, bachelor's, and master's (degrees awarded by Miami University main campus)
- **Suburban** 78-acre campus with easy access to Cincinnati
- **Coed,** 2,900 undergraduate students, 44% full-time, 57% women, 43% men

Undergraduates 5% African American, 1% Asian American or Pacific Islander, 0.8% Hispanic American, 0.4% Native American, 1% international.

Faculty *Total:* 207, 40% full-time. *Student/faculty ratio:* 16:1.
Majors Accounting technician; computer engineering technology; data processing technology; early childhood education; electrical/electronic engineering technology; engineering technology; liberal arts and sciences/liberal studies; mechanical engineering technology; nursing.
Academic Programs *Special study options:* academic remediation for entering students, adult/continuing education programs, advanced placement credit, cooperative education, internships, part-time degree program, services for LD students, student-designed majors, study abroad, summer session for credit. *ROTC:* Navy (c), Air Force (c).
Library Rentschler Library with 68,000 titles, 400 serial subscriptions, an OPAC, a Web page.
Computers on Campus 150 computers available on campus for general student use. A campuswide network can be accessed from off campus. Internet access, online (class) registration, at least one staffed computer lab available.
Student Life *Housing:* college housing not available. *Activities and Organizations:* drama/theater group, student-run newspaper, choral group, student government, Campus Activities Committee, Organization for Wiser Learners, Community Empowerment Committee, Minority Action Committee. *Campus security:* 24-hour emergency response devices and patrols, late-night transport/escort service. *Student Services:* personal/psychological counseling.
Athletics *Intercollegiate sports:* baseball M, basketball M/W, golf M, tennis M/W, volleyball W. *Intramural sports:* basketball M/W, bowling M/W, skiing (cross-country) M/W, soccer M/W, softball M/W, tennis M/W, volleyball M/W, weight lifting M/W.
Standardized Tests *Required for some:* SAT I or ACT (for placement).
Costs (2001–02) *Tuition:* state resident $2812 full-time, $117 per credit part-time; nonresident $10,486 full-time, $437 per credit part-time. Full-time tuition and fees vary according to class time. Part-time tuition and fees vary according to class time. *Required fees:* $328 full-time, $12 per credit, $15 per term part-time. *Payment plan:* installment. *Waivers:* employees or children of employees.
Applying *Application fee:* $25. *Required:* high school transcript. *Application deadline:* rolling (freshmen), rolling (transfers). *Notification:* continuous (freshmen).
Admissions Contact Ms. Triana Adlon, Director of Admission and Financial Aid, Miami University-Hamilton Campus, 1601 Peck Boulevard, Hamilton, OH 45011-3399. *Phone:* 513-785-3111.

MIAMI UNIVERSITY-MIDDLETOWN CAMPUS
Middletown, Ohio

- **State-supported** primarily 2-year, founded 1966, part of Miami University System
- **Calendar** semesters
- **Degrees** certificates, diplomas, associate, and bachelor's (also offers up to 2 years of most bachelor's degree programs offered at Miami University main campus)
- **Small-town** 141-acre campus with easy access to Cincinnati and Dayton
- **Endowment** $779,742
- **Coed,** 2,061 undergraduate students

Undergraduates Students come from 1 other country, 1% are from out of state. *Retention:* 65% of 2001 full-time freshmen returned.
Freshmen *Admission:* 763 applied, 731 admitted. *Test scores:* SAT verbal scores over 500: 49%; SAT math scores over 500: 49%; ACT scores over 18: 73%; SAT verbal scores over 600: 12%; SAT math scores over 600: 7%; ACT scores over 24: 16%; SAT verbal scores over 700: 1%; ACT scores over 30: 1%.
Faculty *Total:* 158, 53% full-time. *Student/faculty ratio:* 13:1.
Majors Accounting; anthropology; art; biological/physical sciences; botany; business; business administration; business economics; business marketing and marketing management; chemical engineering technology; chemistry; communications; computer engineering technology; computer/information sciences; computer science; early childhood education; economics; education; electrical/electronic engineering technology; electromechanical technology; elementary education; engineering; engineering technology; English; geography; history; industrial technology; information sciences/systems; interdisciplinary studies; legal administrative assistant; liberal arts and sciences/liberal studies; management information systems/business data processing; mass communications; mathematics; mechanical engineering technology; medical administrative assistant; nursing; office management; philosophy; physics; political science; pre-engineering; psychology; real estate; secretarial science; social sciences; social work; sociology; Spanish; systems science/theory; zoology.
Academic Programs *Special study options:* academic remediation for entering students, adult/continuing education programs, advanced placement credit, cooperative education, distance learning, double majors, independent study, internships, off-campus study, part-time degree program, services for LD students, student-designed majors, study abroad, summer session for credit. *ROTC:* Air Force (c).
Library Gardner-Harvey Library with 540 serial subscriptions, 4,857 audiovisual materials, an OPAC, a Web page.
Computers on Campus 180 computers available on campus for general student use. A campuswide network can be accessed from off campus. Internet access, online (class) registration, at least one staffed computer lab available.
Student Life *Housing:* college housing not available. *Activities and Organizations:* drama/theater group, student-run newspaper, radio station, choral group, student radio station, SEAL (Save Every Animal by Learning), Student Advisory Council, Model United Nations, Program Board. *Campus security:* 24-hour patrols, late-night transport/escort service. *Student Services:* personal/psychological counseling, women's center.
Athletics *Intercollegiate sports:* baseball M(c), basketball M(c)/W(c), golf M(c)/W(c), tennis M(c)/W(c), volleyball W(c). *Intramural sports:* basketball W, football M/W, golf M/W, racquetball M/W, skiing (cross-country) M/W, skiing (downhill) M/W, soccer M/W, softball M/W, table tennis M/W, tennis M/W, volleyball M/W, weight lifting M/W.
Standardized Tests *Recommended:* SAT I or ACT (for placement).
Costs (2001–02) *Tuition:* state resident $3300 full-time, $146 per credit part-time; nonresident $420 per credit part-time. Full-time tuition and fees vary according to location and student level. Part-time tuition and fees vary according to location and student level. *Required fees:* $165 full-time. *Payment plan:* installment. *Waivers:* senior citizens and employees or children of employees.
Applying *Options:* electronic application, early admission, deferred entrance. *Application fee:* $25. *Required:* high school transcript. *Application deadline:* rolling (freshmen), rolling (transfers). *Notification:* continuous (freshmen).
Admissions Contact Mrs. Mary Lu Flynn, Director of Enrollment Services, Miami University-Middletown Campus, 4200 East University Boulevard, Middletown, OH 45042. *Phone:* 513-727-3216. *Toll-free phone:* 800-622-2262. *Fax:* 513-727-3223. *E-mail:* flynnml@muohio.edu.

MUSKINGUM AREA TECHNICAL COLLEGE
Zanesville, Ohio

- **State and locally supported** 2-year, founded 1969
- **Calendar** quarters
- **Degree** certificates and associate
- **Small-town** 170-acre campus with easy access to Columbus
- **Coed,** 2,007 undergraduate students

Undergraduates Students come from 1 other state, 2 other countries, 0.2% are from out of state.
Freshmen *Admission:* 722 applied, 593 admitted.
Faculty *Total:* 116, 43% full-time. *Student/faculty ratio:* 18:1.
Majors Accounting; business administration; business marketing and marketing management; child care provider; computer programming (specific applications); criminal justice/law enforcement administration; culinary arts; data entry/microcomputer applications; drafting/design technology; electrical/electronic engineering technology; environmental science; human resources management; industrial radiologic technology; industrial technology; medical assistant; medical laboratory assistant; mental health/rehabilitation; natural resources management; occupational therapy; paralegal/legal assistant; physical therapy assistant; recreation/leisure facilities management; recreation/leisure studies; secretarial science; social work; travel/tourism management; Web page, digital/multimedia and information resources design.
Academic Programs *Special study options:* academic remediation for entering students, adult/continuing education programs, cooperative education, honors programs, internships, off-campus study, part-time degree program, services for LD students, student-designed majors, summer session for credit.
Computers on Campus 110 computers available on campus for general student use. At least one staffed computer lab available.
Student Life *Housing:* college housing not available. *Activities and Organizations:* student-run newspaper. *Student Services:* personal/psychological counseling.
Athletics *Intercollegiate sports:* baseball M/W, basketball M/W, golf M/W. *Intramural sports:* basketball M/W, golf M/W, volleyball M/W.
Standardized Tests *Recommended:* SAT I or ACT (for admission).
Costs (2001–02) *Tuition:* area resident $2970 full-time; state resident $66 per credit hour part-time; nonresident $5220 full-time, $116 per credit hour part-time. *Payment plan:* installment. *Waivers:* children of alumni and senior citizens.
Financial Aid In 2001, 65 Federal Work-Study jobs (averaging $2010).

Muskingum Area Technical College (continued)

Applying *Options:* early admission. *Required:* high school transcript. *Required for some:* letters of recommendation, interview. *Application deadline:* rolling (freshmen), rolling (transfers). *Notification:* continuous (freshmen).

Admissions Contact Mr. Paul Young, Director of Admissions, Muskingum Area Technical College, 1555 Newark Road, Zanesville, OH 43701-2626. *Phone:* 740-454-2501 Ext. 1225. *Toll-free phone:* 800-686-TECH Ext. 1225.

NORTH CENTRAL STATE COLLEGE
Mansfield, Ohio

- **State-supported** 2-year, founded 1961, part of Ohio Board of Regents
- **Calendar** quarters
- **Degree** certificates and associate
- **Suburban** 600-acre campus with easy access to Cleveland and Columbus
- **Endowment** $648,638
- **Coed**

Student Life *Campus security:* 24-hour emergency response devices and patrols, late-night transport/escort service.

Standardized Tests *Required:* ACT COMPASS. *Required for some:* ACT (for placement).

Applying *Options:* early admission, deferred entrance. *Required for some:* high school transcript.

Admissions Contact Ms. Stevi Bowler, Admission Secretary, North Central State College, PO Box 698, Mansfield, OH 44901-0698. *Phone:* 419-755-4888. *Toll-free phone:* 888-755-4899.

NORTHWEST STATE COMMUNITY COLLEGE
Archbold, Ohio

- **State-supported** 2-year, founded 1968, part of Ohio Board of Regents
- **Calendar** semesters
- **Degree** certificates and associate
- **Rural** 80-acre campus with easy access to Toledo
- **Endowment** $393,161
- **Coed,** 2,931 undergraduate students, 35% full-time, 51% women, 49% men

Undergraduates 1,017 full-time, 1,914 part-time. Students come from 5 states and territories, 2 other countries, 2% are from out of state, 0.9% African American, 0.3% Asian American or Pacific Islander, 5% Hispanic American, 0.3% Native American, 6% transferred in.

Freshmen *Admission:* 844 applied, 844 admitted, 619 enrolled. *Average high school GPA:* 2.89. *Test scores:* ACT scores over 18: 82%; ACT scores over 24: 25%.

Faculty *Total:* 163, 25% full-time, 6% with terminal degrees. *Student/faculty ratio:* 16:1.

Majors Accounting; business; business administration; business marketing and marketing management; child care/development; computer programming; corrections; criminal justice/law enforcement administration; criminal justice studies; data processing; design/visual communications; education; electrical/electronic engineering technology; engineering/industrial management; executive assistant; individual/family development related; industrial technology; law enforcement/police science; legal administrative assistant; machine technology; mechanical engineering; mechanical engineering technology; medical administrative assistant; nursing; paralegal/legal assistant; plastics technology; precision metal working related; sheet metal working; social work; tool/die making.

Academic Programs *Special study options:* academic remediation for entering students, adult/continuing education programs, advanced placement credit, cooperative education, external degree program, independent study, internships, off-campus study, part-time degree program, services for LD students, student-designed majors, summer session for credit.

Library Northwest State Community College Library with 18,256 titles, 1,680 serial subscriptions, 1,728 audiovisual materials, an OPAC, a Web page.

Computers on Campus 240 computers available on campus for general student use. Internet access, at least one staffed computer lab available.

Student Life *Housing:* college housing not available. *Activities and Organizations:* Student Body Organization, Phi Theta Kappa, Campus Crusade for Christ. *Campus security:* evening security patrols. *Student Services:* personal/psychological counseling.

Athletics *Intramural sports:* basketball M/W, bowling M/W, table tennis M/W, volleyball M/W.

Costs (2001–02) *Tuition:* state resident $2820 full-time, $100 per credit part-time; nonresident $5640 full-time, $199 per credit part-time. Full-time tuition and fees vary according to course load. Part-time tuition and fees vary according to course load. *Required fees:* $180 full-time, $10 per term part-time. *Payment plan:* deferred payment. *Waivers:* senior citizens and employees or children of employees.

Financial Aid In 2001, 37 Federal Work-Study jobs (averaging $927).

Applying *Options:* common application, early admission, deferred entrance. *Application fee:* $20. *Required:* high school transcript. *Application deadline:* rolling (freshmen), rolling (transfers).

Admissions Contact Mr. Dennis Gable, Dean of Student Services, Northwest State Community College, 22600 State Route 34, Archbold, OH 43502-9542. *Phone:* 419-267-5511 Ext. 318. *Fax:* 419-267-5604. *E-mail:* admissions@nscc.cc.oh.us.

OHIO BUSINESS COLLEGE
Lorain, Ohio

- **Independent** 2-year
- **Calendar** quarters
- **Degree** diplomas and associate
- **Coed, primarily women,** 229 undergraduate students, 87% full-time, 89% women, 11% men

Undergraduates 199 full-time, 30 part-time.

Freshmen *Admission:* 163 enrolled.

Faculty *Total:* 14, 21% full-time, 14% with terminal degrees. *Student/faculty ratio:* 15:1.

Majors Accounting; business administration; computer/information sciences; legal administrative assistant; medical administrative assistant; secretarial science.

Costs (2002–03) *Tuition:* $6960 full-time, $145 per credit hour part-time. *Required fees:* $300 full-time.

Admissions Contact Jim Unger, Admissions Manager, Ohio Business College, 1907 North Ridge Road, Lorain, OH 44055. *Toll-free phone:* 888-514-3126.

OHIO INSTITUTE OF PHOTOGRAPHY AND TECHNOLOGY
Dayton, Ohio

Admissions Contact Ms. Fran Heaston, Director of Admissions, Ohio Institute of Photography and Technology, 2029 Edgefield Road, Dayton, OH 45439-1917. *Phone:* 937-294-6155. *Toll-free phone:* 800-932-9698. *Fax:* 937-294-2259.

THE OHIO STATE UNIVERSITY AGRICULTURAL TECHNICAL INSTITUTE
Wooster, Ohio

- **State-supported** 2-year, founded 1971, part of Ohio State University
- **Calendar** quarters
- **Degree** associate
- **Small-town** 136-acre campus with easy access to Cleveland and Columbus
- **Coed**

Student Life *Campus security:* 24-hour emergency response devices and patrols.

Standardized Tests *Required for some:* SAT I or ACT (for admission).

Applying *Options:* early admission. *Application fee:* $30. *Required:* high school transcript.

Admissions Contact Ms. Veronica Thomas, Admissions Coordinator, The Ohio State University Agricultural Technical Institute, 1328 Dover Road, Wooster, OH 44691. *Phone:* 330-264-3911. *Toll-free phone:* 800-647-8283.

OHIO VALLEY BUSINESS COLLEGE
East Liverpool, Ohio

- **Proprietary** 2-year, founded 1886
- **Calendar** semesters
- **Degree** diplomas and associate
- **Small-town** campus with easy access to Pittsburgh
- **Coed, primarily women,** 116 undergraduate students, 96% full-time, 95% women, 5% men

Undergraduates 111 full-time, 5 part-time. Students come from 3 states and territories, 12% are from out of state, 3% African American, 11% transferred in.
Freshmen *Admission:* 30 enrolled. *Average high school GPA:* 2.5.
Faculty *Total:* 11, 45% full-time. *Student/faculty ratio:* 18:1.
Majors Accounting; data processing technology; dental assistant; executive assistant; information technology; medical administrative assistant; medical assistant.
Academic Programs *Special study options:* internships, part-time degree program, summer session for credit.
Computers on Campus Internet access, at least one staffed computer lab available.
Student Life *Housing:* college housing not available. *Student Services:* personal/psychological counseling.
Applying *Application fee:* $75. *Required:* high school transcript, interview. *Application deadline:* rolling (freshmen).
Admissions Contact Ms. Cheryl Jones, Admissions Representative, Ohio Valley Business College, East Liverpool, OH 43920. *Phone:* 330-385-1070.

OWENS COMMUNITY COLLEGE
Toledo, Ohio

- **State-supported** 2-year, founded 1966, part of Owens Community College System
- **Calendar** semesters
- **Degree** certificates and associate
- **Suburban** 100-acre campus
- **Coed**

Faculty *Student/faculty ratio:* 19:1.
Student Life *Campus security:* 24-hour emergency response devices and patrols, student patrols.
Athletics Member NJCAA.
Standardized Tests *Required for some:* SAT I or ACT (for placement). *Recommended:* SAT I or ACT (for placement), ACT ASSET.
Financial Aid In 2001, 100 Federal Work-Study jobs (averaging $3200).
Applying *Options:* common application, early admission. *Required:* high school transcript. *Required for some:* minimum 2.0 GPA. *Recommended:* essay or personal statement, letters of recommendation, interview.
Admissions Contact Mr. Jim Welling, Admissions Coordinator, Owens Community College, PO Box 10000, Toledo, OH 43699-1947. *Phone:* 419-661-7225. *Toll-free phone:* 800-GO-OWENS. *Fax:* 419-661-7607.

OWENS COMMUNITY COLLEGE
Findlay, Ohio

- **State-supported** 2-year, founded 1983, part of Owens Community College System
- **Calendar** semesters
- **Degree** certificates and associate
- **Suburban** 4-acre campus with easy access to Toledo
- **Coed**

Faculty *Student/faculty ratio:* 19:1.
Student Life *Campus security:* 24-hour emergency response devices and patrols, student patrols, late-night transport/escort service.
Athletics Member NJCAA.
Standardized Tests *Required for some:* ACT (for placement). *Recommended:* ACT (for placement), ACT ASSET.
Financial Aid In 2001, 20 Federal Work-Study jobs (averaging $3200).
Applying *Options:* common application, early admission, deferred entrance. *Required:* high school transcript. *Required for some:* minimum 2.0 GPA. *Recommended:* essay or personal statement, letters of recommendation, interview.
Admissions Contact Mr. Gary Ulrich, Student Services Representative, Owens Community College, 300 Davis Street, Findlay, OH 45840. *Phone:* 419-423-3500 Ext. 3539. *Toll-free phone:* 800-FINDLAY. *Fax:* 419-423-0246 Ext. 250.

PROFESSIONAL SKILLS INSTITUTE
Toledo, Ohio

- **Proprietary** 2-year, founded 1984
- **Calendar** quarters
- **Degree** certificates, diplomas, and associate
- **Urban** 2-acre campus with easy access to Detroit
- **Coed,** 174 undergraduate students, 94% full-time, 78% women, 22% men

Undergraduates 164 full-time, 10 part-time. Students come from 5 states and territories.
Freshmen *Admission:* 57 applied, 53 admitted. *Average high school GPA:* 3.11.
Faculty *Total:* 9, 56% full-time. *Student/faculty ratio:* 19:1.
Majors Physical therapy assistant.
Academic Programs *Special study options:* internships, off-campus study, part-time degree program, services for LD students.
Library Professional Skills Institute Library plus 1 other with 2,200 titles, 50 serial subscriptions, an OPAC.
Computers on Campus 28 computers available on campus for general student use. Internet access, at least one staffed computer lab available.
Student Life *Housing:* college housing not available. *Campus security:* 24-hour emergency response devices, camera, alarm system. *Student Services:* health clinic.
Costs (2002–03) *Tuition:* $6600 full-time, $84 per quarter hour part-time. *Required fees:* $325 full-time.
Applying *Required:* high school transcript, minimum 2.0 GPA, letters of recommendation, interview. *Notification:* 9/15 (freshmen).
Admissions Contact Ms. Hope Finch, Director of Marketing, Professional Skills Institute, 20 Arco Drive, Toledo, OH 43607. *Phone:* 419-531-9610. *Fax:* 419-531-4732.

RETS TECH CENTER
Centerville, Ohio

- **Proprietary** 2-year, founded 1953
- **Calendar** semesters
- **Degree** diplomas and associate
- **Suburban** 4-acre campus with easy access to Dayton
- **Coed,** 471 undergraduate students, 100% full-time, 52% women, 48% men

Undergraduates 471 full-time. Students come from 6 states and territories, 1% are from out of state, 1% transferred in.
Freshmen *Admission:* 390 enrolled.
Faculty *Total:* 65, 25% full-time, 17% with terminal degrees. *Student/faculty ratio:* 18:1.
Majors Computer engineering technology; computer programming; computer science; electrical/electronic engineering technology; medical assistant; paralegal/legal assistant.
Academic Programs *Special study options:* advanced placement credit, internships, summer session for credit.
Library RETS Library with 1,600 titles, 26 serial subscriptions.
Computers on Campus 164 computers available on campus for general student use. A campuswide network can be accessed from off campus. Internet access, at least one staffed computer lab available.
Student Life *Housing:* college housing not available. *Campus security:* 24-hour emergency response devices. *Student Services:* personal/psychological counseling.
Standardized Tests *Required:* programming aptitude tests.
Costs (2001–02) *One-time required fee:* $250. *Tuition:* $6795 full-time. No tuition increase for student's term of enrollment. *Required fees:* $255 full-time. *Payment plan:* installment.
Applying *Options:* early admission, deferred entrance. *Required:* high school transcript, interview. *Application deadline:* rolling (freshmen), rolling (transfers).
Admissions Contact Mr. Rich Elkin, Director of Admissions, RETS Tech Center, 555 East Alex Bell Road, Centerville, OH 45459-2712. *Phone:* 937-433-3410. *Toll-free phone:* 800-837-7387. *Fax:* 937-435-6516. *E-mail:* rets@erinet.com.

SINCLAIR COMMUNITY COLLEGE
Dayton, Ohio

- **State and locally supported** 2-year, founded 1887, part of Ohio Board of Regents
- **Calendar** quarters
- **Degree** certificates and associate
- **Urban** 50-acre campus with easy access to Cincinnati
- **Endowment** $16.1 million
- **Coed,** 18,869 undergraduate students, 28% full-time, 57% women, 43% men

Sinclair Community College (continued)

Undergraduates 5,225 full-time, 13,644 part-time. Students come from 20 states and territories, 1% are from out of state, 18% African American, 2% Asian American or Pacific Islander, 1% Hispanic American, 0.4% Native American, 18% transferred in.

Freshmen *Admission:* 6,271 applied, 6,271 admitted, 2,453 enrolled.

Faculty *Total:* 974, 45% full-time. *Student/faculty ratio:* 27:1.

Majors Accounting; African studies; applied art; architectural engineering technology; art; auto mechanic/technician; aviation management; business administration; business marketing and marketing management; child care/development; civil engineering technology; computer engineering related; computer graphics; computer hardware engineering; computer/information sciences; computer/information technology services administration and management related; computer programming related; computer programming (specific applications); computer programming, vendor/product certification; computer science related; computer software engineering; computer systems networking/telecommunications; corrections; criminal justice/law enforcement administration; culinary arts; dance; data entry/microcomputer applications; data entry/microcomputer applications related; dental hygiene; dietetics; drafting; early childhood education; education; electrical/electronic engineering technology; electromechanical technology; emergency medical technology; engineering; finance; fine/studio arts; fire science; food products retailing; gerontology; graphic design/commercial art/illustration; graphic/printing equipment; hotel and restaurant management; human services; industrial radiologic technology; industrial technology; information sciences/systems; information technology; interior design; labor/personnel relations; law enforcement/police science; legal administrative assistant; liberal arts and sciences/liberal studies; logistics/materials management; machine technology; mass communications; mechanical engineering technology; medical administrative assistant; medical assistant; medical records administration; mental health/rehabilitation; music; nursing; nutrition science; occupational therapy; operating room technician; paralegal/legal assistant; physical education; physical therapy; plastics technology; public administration; quality control technology; radiological science; real estate; respiratory therapy; retail management; robotics; secretarial science; sign language interpretation; surveying; system administration; system/networking/LAN/WAN management; theater arts/drama; transportation technology; travel/tourism management; Web/multimedia management/webmaster; word processing.

Academic Programs *Special study options:* academic remediation for entering students, adult/continuing education programs, cooperative education, distance learning, English as a second language, external degree program, honors programs, independent study, internships, off-campus study, part-time degree program, services for LD students, student-designed majors, summer session for credit. *ROTC:* Army (c), Air Force (c).

Library Learning Resources Center with 145,858 titles, 573 serial subscriptions, 8,606 audiovisual materials, an OPAC, a Web page.

Computers on Campus 700 computers available on campus for general student use. A campuswide network can be accessed from off campus. Internet access, at least one staffed computer lab available.

Student Life *Housing:* college housing not available. *Activities and Organizations:* drama/theater group, student-run newspaper, choral group, African-American Men of the Future, Ohio Fellows, Phi Theta Kappa, student government, student newspaper. *Campus security:* 24-hour emergency response devices and patrols, student patrols, late-night transport/escort service. *Student Services:* personal/psychological counseling.

Athletics Member NJCAA. *Intercollegiate sports:* baseball M(s), basketball M(s)/W(s), golf M(s)/W, tennis M(s)/W(s), volleyball W(s).

Standardized Tests *Required for some:* ACT COMPASS.

Costs (2001–02) *Tuition:* area resident $1440 full-time, $32 per credit part-time; state resident $2340 full-time, $52 per credit part-time; nonresident $3870 full-time, $86 per credit part-time. *Waivers:* senior citizens.

Applying *Options:* electronic application, early admission, deferred entrance. *Application fee:* $10. *Required for some:* high school transcript, interview. *Application deadline:* rolling (freshmen), rolling (transfers). *Notification:* continuous (freshmen).

Admissions Contact Ms. Sara P. Smith, Director and Systems Manager, Outreach Services, Sinclair Community College, 444 West Third Street, Dayton, OH 45402-1460. *Phone:* 937-512-3060. *Toll-free phone:* 800-315-3000. *Fax:* 937-512-2393.

SOUTHEASTERN BUSINESS COLLEGE
Chillicothe, Ohio

Admissions Contact 1855 Western Avenue, Chillicothe, OH 45601-1038.

SOUTHERN OHIO COLLEGE, CINCINNATI CAMPUS
Cincinnati, Ohio

- **Proprietary** 2-year, founded 1927, part of American Education Centers, Inc
- **Calendar** quarters
- **Degree** certificates, diplomas, and associate
- **Suburban** 3-acre campus
- **Coed,** 766 undergraduate students, 100% full-time, 53% women, 47% men

Undergraduates 766 full-time. Students come from 3 states and territories, 1% are from out of state, 35% African American, 2% Asian American or Pacific Islander, 2% Hispanic American, 0.4% Native American.

Freshmen *Admission:* 211 enrolled.

Faculty *Total:* 46, 26% full-time. *Student/faculty ratio:* 16:1.

Majors Accounting; audio engineering; business administration; computer graphics; computer science; computer science related; laser/optical technology; medical administrative assistant; medical assistant; secretarial science.

Academic Programs *Special study options:* academic remediation for entering students, adult/continuing education programs, advanced placement credit, internships, summer session for credit.

Library 8,747 titles, 80 serial subscriptions, 437 audiovisual materials.

Computers on Campus 125 computers available on campus for general student use.

Student Life *Housing:* college housing not available. *Campus security:* 24-hour emergency response devices, night security guard on-campus.

Costs (2001–02) *Tuition:* $5616 full-time, $156 per credit hour part-time. Full-time tuition and fees vary according to course load and program. *Required fees:* $360 full-time, $10 per credit hour. *Payment plan:* installment.

Financial Aid In 2001, 4 Federal Work-Study jobs.

Applying *Options:* common application, early admission, deferred entrance. *Application fee:* $20. *Required:* high school transcript, interview. *Application deadline:* rolling (freshmen), rolling (transfers).

Admissions Contact Ms. Cherie McNeel, Director of Admissions, Southern Ohio College, Cincinnati Campus, 1011 Glendale-Milford Road, Cincinnati, OH 45215. *Phone:* 513-771-2424. *Fax:* 513-771-3413.

SOUTHERN OHIO COLLEGE, FINDLAY CAMPUS
Findlay, Ohio

Admissions Contact Ms. Annarose Browning, Director of Admissions, Southern Ohio College, Findlay Campus, 1637 Tiffin Avenue, Findlay, OH 45840. *Phone:* 419-423-2211. *Toll-free phone:* 800-842-3687. *Fax:* 419-423-0725. *E-mail:* stautfin@ohio.tds.net.

SOUTHERN OHIO COLLEGE, NORTHEAST CAMPUS
Akron, Ohio

- **Proprietary** 2-year, founded 1968
- **Calendar** quarters
- **Degree** certificates, diplomas, and associate
- **Suburban** 3-acre campus with easy access to Cleveland
- **Coed**

Student Life *Campus security:* late-night transport/escort service.

Standardized Tests *Required:* CCAP. *Recommended:* SAT I or ACT (for placement).

Applying *Options:* early admission, deferred entrance. *Application fee:* $20. *Recommended:* minimum 2.0 GPA.

Admissions Contact Mr. David Marinelli, Director of Admissions, Southern Ohio College, Northeast Campus, 2791 Mogadore Road, Akron, OH 44312-1596. *Phone:* 330-733-8766.

SOUTHERN STATE COMMUNITY COLLEGE
Hillsboro, Ohio

- **State-supported** 2-year, founded 1975
- **Calendar** quarters
- **Degree** certificates and associate
- **Rural** 60-acre campus

- **Endowment** $61,195
- **Coed,** 2,038 undergraduate students, 54% full-time, 72% women, 28% men

Undergraduates Students come from 1 other state, 3 other countries.
Freshmen *Admission:* 635 applied, 635 admitted.
Faculty *Total:* 109, 39% full-time, 6% with terminal degrees. *Student/faculty ratio:* 17:1.
Majors Accounting technician; agricultural production; business; business computer programming; drafting; early childhood education; executive assistant; liberal arts and sciences/liberal studies; medical assistant; nursing; real estate.
Academic Programs *Special study options:* academic remediation for entering students, advanced placement credit, cooperative education, double majors, independent study, internships, off-campus study, part-time degree program, services for LD students, student-designed majors, summer session for credit.
Library Learning Resources Center plus 2 others with 62,300 titles, 1,075 serial subscriptions, 2,577 audiovisual materials, an OPAC, a Web page.
Computers on Campus 200 computers available on campus for general student use. A campuswide network can be accessed from off campus. Internet access, at least one staffed computer lab available.
Student Life *Housing:* college housing not available. *Activities and Organizations:* drama/theater group, choral group, Student Leadership, Student Nurses Association, Drama Club, Association of Medical Assistants, Phi Theta Kappa, national fraternities. *Student Services:* personal/psychological counseling.
Athletics Member NJCAA. *Intercollegiate sports:* basketball M(s)/W(s), soccer M(s), softball W(s), volleyball W(s). *Intramural sports:* basketball M/W, bowling M/W, football M/W, softball M/W, table tennis M/W, volleyball M/W.
Standardized Tests *Required for some:* ACT (for placement). *Recommended:* ACT (for placement).
Costs (2002–03) *Tuition:* state resident $2925 full-time, $75 per credit hour part-time; nonresident $5715 full-time, $147 per credit hour part-time. Full-time tuition and fees vary according to course load. Part-time tuition and fees vary according to course load. *Payment plan:* deferred payment. *Waivers:* senior citizens and employees or children of employees.
Applying *Options:* common application, early admission, deferred entrance. *Application fee:* $15. *Required:* high school transcript. *Application deadline:* rolling (freshmen), rolling (transfers). *Notification:* continuous (freshmen).
Admissions Contact Ms. Nicole Roades, Coordinator of Enrollment Services, Southern State Community College, 100 Hobart Drive, Hillsboro, OH 45133-9487. *Phone:* 937-393-3431 Ext. 2622. *Toll-free phone:* 800-628-7722. *Fax:* 937-393-9370. *E-mail:* khollida@soucc.southern.cc.oh.us.

SOUTHWESTERN COLLEGE OF BUSINESS
Cincinnati, Ohio

Admissions Contact Mr. Greg Petree, Director of Admissions, Southwestern College of Business, 9910 Princeton-Glendale Road, Cincinnati, OH 45246-1122. *Phone:* 513-874-0432.

SOUTHWESTERN COLLEGE OF BUSINESS
Cincinnati, Ohio

Admissions Contact Ms. Betty Streber, Director of Admissions, Southwestern College of Business, 632 Vine Street, Suite 200, Cincinnati, OH 45202-4304. *Phone:* 513-421-3212.

SOUTHWESTERN COLLEGE OF BUSINESS
Dayton, Ohio

- **Proprietary** 2-year, founded 1972
- **Calendar** quarters
- **Degree** certificates, diplomas, and associate
- **Urban** campus
- **Coed,** 340 undergraduate students, 100% full-time, 80% women, 20% men

Undergraduates 340 full-time. *Retention:* 60% of 2001 full-time freshmen returned.
Freshmen *Admission:* 125 applied, 61 admitted, 61 enrolled.
Faculty *Total:* 15, 20% full-time. *Student/faculty ratio:* 15:1.
Majors Accounting; business administration; computer science; medical assistant; secretarial science.
Academic Programs *Special study options:* academic remediation for entering students, cooperative education, external degree program, summer session for credit.
Computers on Campus 30 computers available on campus for general student use.
Student Life *Housing:* college housing not available. *Student Services:* personal/psychological counseling.
Costs (2002–03) *Tuition:* $184 per quarter hour part-time. Tuition dependent on program selected with a range of $4,050 to $6450. *Required fees:* $360 full-time, $67 per quarter hour.
Applying *Options:* deferred entrance. *Application deadline:* rolling (freshmen), rolling (transfers). *Notification:* continuous (freshmen).
Admissions Contact Ms. Cathy Riehle, Director of Admissions, Southwestern College of Business, 225 West First Street, Dayton, OH 45402-3003. *Phone:* 937-224-0061 Ext. 17.

SOUTHWESTERN COLLEGE OF BUSINESS
Middletown, Ohio

Admissions Contact Jenny Martin, Admissions Director, Southwestern College of Business, 631 South Breiel Boulevard, Middletown, OH 45044-5113. *Phone:* 937-746-6633.

STARK STATE COLLEGE OF TECHNOLOGY
Canton, Ohio

- **State and locally supported** 2-year, founded 1970, part of Ohio Board of Regents
- **Calendar** semesters
- **Degree** certificates and associate
- **Suburban** 97-acre campus with easy access to Cleveland
- **Coed,** 4,774 undergraduate students

Undergraduates Students come from 4 states and territories.
Freshmen *Admission:* 1,431 applied, 1,431 admitted.
Faculty *Total:* 340, 33% full-time, 30% with terminal degrees. *Student/faculty ratio:* 20:1.
Majors Accounting; architectural engineering technology; auto mechanic/technician; biomedical technology; business administration; business marketing and marketing management; child care/development; civil engineering technology; computer engineering related; computer hardware engineering; computer/information technology services administration and management related; computer programming; computer programming related; computer programming (specific applications); computer programming, vendor/product certification; computer science related; computer software and media applications related; computer software engineering; computer systems networking/telecommunications; computer/technical support; court reporting; data entry/microcomputer applications; data entry/microcomputer applications related; dental hygiene; drafting; environmental science; finance; fire science; food services technology; human services; industrial technology; information technology; international business; legal administrative assistant; mechanical engineering technology; medical assistant; medical laboratory technician; medical records administration; nursing; occupational therapy; operations management; physical therapy; respiratory therapy; retail management; secretarial science; surveying; Web/multimedia management/webmaster; Web page, digital/multimedia and information resources design; word processing.
Academic Programs *Special study options:* academic remediation for entering students, adult/continuing education programs, cooperative education, external degree program, independent study, off-campus study, part-time degree program, student-designed majors, summer session for credit.
Library Learning Resource Center with 70,000 titles, 425 serial subscriptions, an OPAC.
Computers on Campus 450 computers available on campus for general student use. A campuswide network can be accessed from off campus. At least one staffed computer lab available.
Student Life *Housing:* college housing not available. *Activities and Organizations:* student-run newspaper. *Campus security:* 24-hour emergency response devices, late-night transport/escort service. *Student Services:* personal/psychological counseling.
Standardized Tests *Recommended:* SAT I or ACT (for placement).
Costs (2002–03) *Tuition:* area resident $2910 full-time, $97 per credit hour part-time; nonresident $3810 full-time, $127 per credit hour part-time. *Required fees:* $100 full-time, $11 per credit hour. *Payment plan:* installment. *Waivers:* senior citizens.

Stark State College of Technology (continued)

Applying *Options:* early admission, deferred entrance. *Application fee:* $35. *Required:* high school transcript. *Application deadline:* rolling (freshmen), rolling (transfers).

Admissions Contact Mr. Wallace Hoffer, Dean of Student Services, Stark State College of Technology, 6200 Frank Road, N.W., Canton, OH 44720. *Phone:* 330-966-5450. *Toll-free phone:* 800-797-8275. *Fax:* 330-497-6313.

STAUTZENBERGER COLLEGE
Toledo, Ohio

Admissions Contact 5355 Southwyck Boulevard, Toledo, OH 43614. *Toll-free phone:* 800-552-5099.

TECHNOLOGY EDUCATION COLLEGE
Columbus, Ohio

Admissions Contact 288 South Hamilton Road, Columbus, OH 43213-2087. *Toll-free phone:* 800-838-3233.

TERRA STATE COMMUNITY COLLEGE
Fremont, Ohio

- **State-supported** 2-year, founded 1968, part of Ohio Board of Regents
- **Calendar** quarters
- **Degree** certificates and associate
- **Small-town** 100-acre campus with easy access to Toledo
- **Coed,** 2,554 undergraduate students

Undergraduates Students come from 4 states and territories, 0.1% are from out of state. *Retention:* 41% of 2001 full-time freshmen returned.

Freshmen *Admission:* 614 applied, 614 admitted.

Faculty *Total:* 139, 32% full-time. *Student/faculty ratio:* 34:1.

Majors Accounting; architectural engineering technology; auto mechanic/technician; automotive engineering technology; banking; business administration; business marketing and marketing management; chemistry; computer/information sciences; early childhood education; electromechanical technology; engineering; engineering technology; English; enterprise management; finance; general office/clerical; general studies; graphic design/commercial art/illustration; heating/air conditioning/refrigeration; heating/air conditioning/refrigeration technology; industrial technology; information sciences/systems; law enforcement/police science; mathematics; mechanical engineering technology; medical administrative assistant; plastics technology; psychology; quality control technology; robotics technology; secretarial science; sign language interpretation; social work; technical/business writing; tool/die making; welding technology.

Academic Programs *Special study options:* academic remediation for entering students, accelerated degree program, adult/continuing education programs, distance learning, double majors, honors programs, independent study, internships, part-time degree program, services for LD students, student-designed majors, summer session for credit.

Library Learning Resource Center with 19,279 titles, 376 serial subscriptions, 2,144 audiovisual materials, an OPAC, a Web page.

Computers on Campus 250 computers available on campus for general student use. A campuswide network can be accessed from off campus. Internet access, online (class) registration, at least one staffed computer lab available.

Student Life *Housing:* college housing not available. *Activities and Organizations:* choral group, Phi Theta Kappa, Student Activities Club, Society of Plastic Engineers, Koinonia, Student Senate, national fraternities. *Campus security:* 24-hour emergency response devices, late-night transport/escort service. *Student Services:* personal/psychological counseling.

Athletics Member NJCAA. *Intercollegiate sports:* golf M, volleyball W(s). *Intramural sports:* basketball M/W, bowling M/W, football M, golf M/W, softball M/W, table tennis M/W, volleyball M/W.

Standardized Tests *Required:* ACT COMPASS. *Recommended:* SAT I or ACT (for placement).

Costs (2002–03) *Tuition:* state resident $1824 full-time, $57 per credit part-time; nonresident $4384 full-time, $137 per credit part-time. Full-time tuition and fees vary according to course load. Part-time tuition and fees vary according to course load. *Required fees:* $288 full-time, $6 per credit. *Payment plans:* installment, deferred payment. *Waivers:* senior citizens and employees or children of employees.

Applying *Options:* electronic application, early admission, deferred entrance. *Required:* high school transcript. *Application deadline:* rolling (freshmen), rolling (transfers).

Admissions Contact Mr. Dale Stearns, Dean of Student Services, Terra State Community College, 2830 Napoleon Road, Fremont, OH 43420. *Phone:* 419-334-8400 Ext. 347. *Toll-free phone:* 800-334-3886. *Fax:* 419-334-9035. *E-mail:* cbork@terra.cc.oh.us.

TRUMBULL BUSINESS COLLEGE
Warren, Ohio

- **Proprietary** 2-year, founded 1972
- **Degree** diplomas and associate
- **Coed, primarily women,** 375 undergraduate students, 85% full-time, 84% women, 16% men
- 100% of applicants were admitted

Undergraduates Students come from 2 states and territories, 1% are from out of state, 21% African American, 0.3% Asian American or Pacific Islander, 2% Hispanic American.

Freshmen *Admission:* 106 applied, 106 admitted.

Faculty *Total:* 13, 69% full-time. *Student/faculty ratio:* 28:1.

Majors Accounting; computer/information technology services administration and management related; legal administrative assistant; management information systems/business data processing; medical administrative assistant; secretarial science; word processing.

Student Life *Housing:* college housing not available. *Activities and Organizations:* student-run newspaper, Student Senate, MADD/SADD.

Costs (2001–02) *Tuition:* $7280 full-time, $140 per credit hour part-time. Full-time tuition and fees vary according to program. Part-time tuition and fees vary according to program. No tuition increase for student's term of enrollment. *Required fees:* $70 full-time. *Payment plan:* installment.

Financial Aid In 2001, 7 Federal Work-Study jobs. *Financial aid deadline:* 9/30.

Applying *Application fee:* $70. *Required:* high school transcript, interview. *Application deadline:* rolling (freshmen). *Notification:* continuous until 10/1 (freshmen).

Admissions Contact Admissions Office, Trumbull Business College, 3200 Ridge Road, Warren, OH 44484. *Phone:* 330-369-3200. *E-mail:* admissions@tbc-trumbullbusiness.com.

THE UNIVERSITY OF AKRON-WAYNE COLLEGE
Orrville, Ohio

- **State-supported** 2-year, founded 1972, part of The University of Akron
- **Calendar** semesters
- **Degree** certificates and associate
- **Rural** 157-acre campus
- **Coed,** 1,932 undergraduate students

Undergraduates Students come from 1 other state.

Freshmen *Admission:* 415 applied, 415 admitted. *Average high school GPA:* 2.79. *Test scores:* ACT scores over 18: 70%; ACT scores over 24: 18%; ACT scores over 30: 1%.

Faculty *Total:* 155, 19% full-time. *Student/faculty ratio:* 14:1.

Majors Accounting; accounting technician; business administration; business systems networking/ telecommunications; computer science; data processing; data processing technology; engineering; environmental health; executive assistant; general studies; interdisciplinary studies; legal administrative assistant; liberal arts and sciences/liberal studies; management information systems/business data processing; medical administrative assistant; medical office management; occupational safety/health technology; office management; secretarial science; social work.

Academic Programs *Special study options:* academic remediation for entering students, adult/continuing education programs, advanced placement credit, cooperative education, distance learning, double majors, English as a second language, honors programs, independent study, internships, off-campus study, part-time degree program, services for LD students, summer session for credit. *ROTC:* Army (c), Air Force (c).

Library Wayne College Library with 23,450 titles, 472 serial subscriptions, an OPAC.

Computers on Campus 240 computers available on campus for general student use. A campuswide network can be accessed from off campus. Internet access, online (class) registration, at least one staffed computer lab available.

Student Life *Housing:* college housing not available. *Campus security:* late-night transport/escort service. *Student Services:* personal/psychological counseling.
Athletics *Intercollegiate sports:* basketball M/W, volleyball W. *Intramural sports:* basketball M/W, volleyball M/W.
Standardized Tests *Required for some:* SAT I or ACT (for admission). *Recommended:* SAT I or ACT (for admission).
Costs (2002–03) *Tuition:* area resident $1964 full-time; state resident $4182 full-time, $209 per credit part-time; nonresident $458 per credit part-time. Full-time tuition and fees vary according to course load. Part-time tuition and fees vary according to course load. *Payment plan:* installment. *Waivers:* minority students, adult students, senior citizens, and employees or children of employees.
Financial Aid In 2001, 8 Federal Work-Study jobs (averaging $2200).
Applying *Options:* common application, electronic application, early admission, deferred entrance. *Application fee:* $30. *Required for some:* high school transcript. *Application deadlines:* 8/28 (freshmen), 8/28 (transfers). *Notification:* continuous until 8/28 (freshmen).
Admissions Contact Ms. Alicia Broadus, Admissions Student Services Office, The University of Akron-Wayne College, 1901 Smucker Road, Orrville, OH 44667. *Phone:* 800-221-8308 Ext. 8901. *Toll-free phone:* 800-221-8308 Ext. 8900.

UNIVERSITY OF CINCINNATI CLERMONT COLLEGE
Batavia, Ohio

Admissions Contact Ms. Tanya Bohart, Admissions Assistant, University of Cincinnati Clermont College, 4200 Clermont College Drive, Batavia, OH 45103-1785. *Phone:* 513-732-5202. *E-mail:* tanya.bohart@uc.edu.

UNIVERSITY OF CINCINNATI RAYMOND WALTERS COLLEGE
Cincinnati, Ohio

Admissions Contact Ms. Julie Martin, Enrollment Services Counselor, University of Cincinnati Raymond Walters College, 9555 Plainfield Road, Cincinnati, OH 45236-1007. *Phone:* 513-745-5700.

UNIVERSITY OF NORTHWESTERN OHIO
Lima, Ohio

- **Independent** primarily 2-year, founded 1920
- **Calendar** quarters
- **Degrees** diplomas, associate, and bachelor's
- **Small-town** 35-acre campus with easy access to Dayton and Toledo
- **Coed,** 2,125 undergraduate students, 84% full-time, 29% women, 71% men

The University of Northwestern Ohio (UNOH) is a private, nonprofit university established in 1920. Located in Lima, Ohio, UNOH has a population of 2,600 students and offers associate degrees in automotive, high performance, deisel, agriculture, alternative feuls, and HVAC/R. Associate degrees are awarded in the College of Business for accounting, business, computers and medical, as well as various other majors.

Undergraduates 1,784 full-time, 341 part-time. Students come from 23 states and territories, 15% are from out of state, 1% African American, 0.1% Hispanic American, 3% transferred in, 45% live on campus.
Freshmen *Admission:* 3,000 applied, 2,800 admitted, 1,481 enrolled. *Average high school GPA:* 2.5.
Faculty *Total:* 92, 71% full-time, 10% with terminal degrees. *Student/faculty ratio:* 25:1.
Majors Accounting; agricultural business; auto mechanic/technician; business administration; business marketing and marketing management; computer programming; diesel engine mechanic; health services administration; heating/air conditioning/refrigeration; legal administrative assistant; medical administrative assistant; medical assistant; paralegal/legal assistant; pharmacy technician/assistant; secretarial science; travel/tourism management.
Academic Programs *Special study options:* academic remediation for entering students, adult/continuing education programs, advanced placement credit, cooperative education, distance learning, double majors, part-time degree program, summer session for credit.
Library Northwestern College Library with 8,857 titles, 117 serial subscriptions, 10 audiovisual materials.
Computers on Campus 86 computers available on campus for general student use. A campuswide network can be accessed from off campus. Internet access, at least one staffed computer lab available.
Student Life *Housing Options:* men-only, women-only, disabled students. *Activities and Organizations:* student-run newspaper, Students in Free Enterprise. *Campus security:* 24-hour emergency response devices and patrols, late-night transport/escort service. *Student Services:* personal/psychological counseling.
Athletics *Intramural sports:* basketball M, bowling M/W, volleyball M/W.
Costs (2001–02) *Tuition:* $8880 full-time, $160 per credit part-time. Full-time tuition and fees vary according to course load and program. Part-time tuition and fees vary according to course load and program. No tuition increase for student's term of enrollment. *Room only:* $3040. *Payment plan:* installment. *Waivers:* employees or children of employees.
Financial Aid In 2001, 31 Federal Work-Study jobs (averaging $1405).
Applying *Options:* electronic application, early admission, deferred entrance. *Application fee:* $50. *Required:* high school transcript. *Application deadline:* rolling (freshmen), rolling (transfers).
Admissions Contact Mr. Dan Klopp, Vice President for Enrollment Management, University of Northwestern Ohio, 1441 North Cable Road, Lima, OH 45805-1498. *Phone:* 419-227-3141. *Fax:* 419-229-6926. *E-mail:* info@nc.edu.

VIRGINIA MARTI COLLEGE OF FASHION AND ART
Lakewood, Ohio

- **Proprietary** 2-year, founded 1966
- **Calendar** quarters
- **Degree** diplomas and associate
- **Urban** campus with easy access to Cleveland
- **Coed**

Student Life *Campus security:* 24-hour emergency response devices.
Applying *Options:* early admission, deferred entrance. *Application fee:* $20. *Required:* minimum 2.0 GPA, interview.
Admissions Contact Linda Smityh, Director of Admissions, Virginia Marti College of Fashion and Art, 11724 Detroit Avenue, PO Box 580, Lakewood, OH 44107-3002. *Phone:* 216-221-8584. *E-mail:* dmarti@vmarti.com.

WASHINGTON STATE COMMUNITY COLLEGE
Marietta, Ohio

- **State-supported** 2-year, founded 1971, part of Ohio Board of Regents
- **Calendar** quarters
- **Degree** certificates and associate
- **Small-town** campus
- **Coed**

Standardized Tests *Required:* ACT ASSET.
Financial Aid In 2001, 50 Federal Work-Study jobs (averaging $2040).
Applying *Options:* early admission, deferred entrance. *Required for some:* high school transcript. *Recommended:* high school transcript.
Admissions Contact Ms. Rebecca Peroni, Director of Admissions, Washington State Community College, 710 Colegate Drive, Marietta, OH 45750-9225. *Phone:* 740-374-8716. *Fax:* 740-376-0257.

WEST SIDE INSTITUTE OF TECHNOLOGY
Cleveland, Ohio

- **Proprietary** 2-year, founded 1958
- **Calendar** quarters
- **Degree** associate
- **Urban** 4-acre campus
- **Coed, primarily men**

Financial Aid In 2001, 5 Federal Work-Study jobs (averaging $1000).
Applying *Options:* deferred entrance.
Admissions Contact Ms. Carol L. Swaney, Director of Admissions, West Side Institute of Technology, 9801 Walford Avenue, Cleveland, OH 44102-4797. *Phone:* 216-651-1656.

Wright State University, Lake Campus
Celina, Ohio

Admissions Contact Mrs. B.J. Hobler, Student Services Officer, Wright State University, Lake Campus, 7600 State Route 703, Celina, OH 45822-2921. *Phone:* 419-586-0324. *Toll-free phone:* 800-237-1477.

OKLAHOMA

Bacone College
Muskogee, Oklahoma

- **Independent** 2-year, founded 1880, affiliated with American Baptist Churches in the U.S.A.
- **Calendar** semesters
- **Degree** certificates, diplomas, and associate
- **Small-town** 160-acre campus with easy access to Tulsa
- **Coed**

Undergraduates Students come from 29 states and territories, 5% are from out of state.
Majors Accounting; alcohol/drug abuse counseling; art; business administration; business education; computer science; education; general studies; history; home economics; horticulture science; humanities; journalism; liberal arts and sciences/liberal studies; mass communications; mathematics; medical radiologic technology; Native American studies; natural resources management; nursing; political science; pre-theology; secretarial science; sociology; theater arts/drama.
Academic Programs *Special study options:* academic remediation for entering students, adult/continuing education programs, advanced placement credit, cooperative education, part-time degree program, services for LD students, student-designed majors, summer session for credit.
Library Bacone College Library with 33,250 titles, 147 serial subscriptions.
Computers on Campus 46 computers available on campus for general student use. A campuswide network can be accessed from off campus. Internet access, at least one staffed computer lab available.
Student Life *Housing Options:* men-only, women-only. *Activities and Organizations:* drama/theater group, student-run newspaper, Native American Club, Phi Beta Kappa, Christian Nurses Fellowship. *Campus security:* controlled dormitory access, 8-hour patrols by trained security personnel. *Student Services:* health clinic, personal/psychological counseling.
Athletics Member NJCAA. *Intercollegiate sports:* baseball M(s), basketball M(s)/W(s), softball M/W(s). *Intramural sports:* badminton M/W, basketball M/W, football M/W, golf M/W, racquetball M/W, softball M/W, table tennis M/W, tennis M/W, volleyball M/W.
Standardized Tests *Required:* SAT I or ACT (for placement).
Costs (2002–03) *Comprehensive fee:* $13,080 includes full-time tuition ($7900), mandatory fees ($180), and room and board ($5000). Part-time tuition: $285 per credit hour. Part-time tuition and fees vary according to course load. *Required fees:* $90 per term part-time. *Payment plan:* installment. *Waivers:* employees or children of employees.
Applying *Options:* common application, early admission, deferred entrance. *Required:* high school transcript. *Application deadline:* rolling (freshmen), rolling (transfers). *Notification:* continuous (freshmen).
Admissions Contact Ms. Jean Kay, Administrative Assistant, Bacone College, 2299 Old Bacone Road, Muskogee, OK 74403-1597. *Phone:* 918-683-4581 Ext. 7340. *Toll-free phone:* 888-682-5514 Ext. 7340. *Fax:* 918-682-5514. *E-mail:* admissionsoffice@bacone.edu.

Carl Albert State College
Poteau, Oklahoma

Admissions Contact Mrs. Lynda Hooper, Director of Admissions, Carl Albert State College, 1507 South McKenna, Poteau, OK 74953-5208. *Phone:* 918-647-1300. *Fax:* 918-647-1306. *E-mail:* lhooper@casc.cc.ok.us.

Connors State College
Warner, Oklahoma

- **State-supported** 2-year, founded 1908, part of Oklahoma State Regents for Higher Education
- **Calendar** semesters
- **Degree** certificates, diplomas, and associate
- **Rural** 1658-acre campus
- **Endowment** $30,000
- **Coed,** 1,954 undergraduate students, 58% full-time, 67% women, 33% men

Undergraduates 1,125 full-time, 829 part-time. Students come from 14 states and territories, 4% are from out of state, 9% African American, 0.4% Asian American or Pacific Islander, 1% Hispanic American, 26% Native American, 0.1% international, 7% transferred in, 12% live on campus.
Freshmen *Admission:* 1,230 applied, 1,230 admitted, 1,044 enrolled. *Average high school GPA:* 2.95.
Faculty *Total:* 109, 50% full-time, 5% with terminal degrees. *Student/faculty ratio:* 21:1.
Majors Accounting; animal sciences; biology; business administration; chemistry; child care/development; computer science; developmental/child psychology; education; engineering; general studies; home economics; journalism; law enforcement/police science; mathematics; nursing; psychology; social work; sociology; zoology.
Academic Programs *Special study options:* academic remediation for entering students, accelerated degree program, adult/continuing education programs, advanced placement credit, internships, part-time degree program, summer session for credit.
Library Carl Westbrook Library with 63,728 titles, 319 serial subscriptions, an OPAC.
Computers on Campus 206 computers available on campus for general student use. At least one staffed computer lab available.
Student Life *Housing Options:* men-only, women-only. *Activities and Organizations:* drama/theater group, student-run newspaper, Aggie Club, CD Club, Twilight Angels, McClarren Club, Library Club. *Campus security:* late-night transport/escort service, trained security personnel. *Student Services:* health clinic.
Athletics Member NJCAA. *Intercollegiate sports:* baseball M(s), basketball M(s)/W(s), softball W(s), tennis M/W. *Intramural sports:* basketball M/W, football M/W, golf M/W, softball W, tennis M/W, volleyball M/W.
Standardized Tests *Required for some:* SAT I or ACT (for placement), CPT.
Costs (2001–02) *Tuition:* state resident $1298 full-time, $33 per credit hour part-time; nonresident $3323 full-time, $68 per credit hour part-time. Full-time tuition and fees vary according to course load. *Required fees:* $388 full-time, $43 per credit hour, $73 per term part-time. *Room and board:* $2340; room only: $900. Room and board charges vary according to board plan. *Waivers:* senior citizens and employees or children of employees.
Financial Aid In 2001, 100 Federal Work-Study jobs (averaging $800).
Applying *Options:* early admission, deferred entrance. *Required for some:* high school transcript. *Application deadline:* rolling (freshmen), rolling (transfers).
Admissions Contact Mr. John A. Turnbull, Director of Admissions/Registrar, Connors State College, Route 1 Box 1000 College Road, Warner, OK 74469. *Phone:* 918-463-6233 Ext. 6233. *Toll-free phone:* 918-463-2931 Ext. 6241.

Eastern Oklahoma State College
Wilburton, Oklahoma

- **State-supported** 2-year, founded 1908, part of Oklahoma State Regents for Higher Education
- **Calendar** semesters
- **Degree** certificates and associate
- **Rural** 4000-acre campus
- **Coed,** 2,026 undergraduate students, 53% full-time, 64% women, 36% men

Undergraduates 1,072 full-time, 954 part-time. Students come from 8 states and territories, 2 other countries, 20% live on campus.
Freshmen *Admission:* 807 applied, 807 admitted.
Faculty *Total:* 51, 96% full-time.
Majors Accounting; agricultural business; agricultural economics; agricultural education; agronomy/crop science; animal sciences; art; art education; biology; business administration; business education; business marketing and marketing management; chemistry; computer engineering technology; computer science; corrections; criminal justice/law enforcement administration; economics; education; electrical/electronic engineering technology; elementary education; English; environmental science; farm/ranch management; fashion merchandising; forest harvesting production technology; forestry; history; horticulture science; industrial arts; journalism; legal administrative assistant; mathematics; medical assistant; medical laboratory technician; medical technology; music; nursing; physical education; physical sciences; political science; pre-engineering; psychology;

range management; science education; secretarial science; sociology; speech/rhetorical studies; surveying; theater arts/drama; veterinary sciences; wildlife management.

Academic Programs *Special study options:* academic remediation for entering students, adult/continuing education programs, advanced placement credit, cooperative education, double majors, honors programs, internships, off-campus study, part-time degree program, summer session for credit.

Library Bill H. Hill Library with 41,639 titles, 220 serial subscriptions, an OPAC.

Computers on Campus 250 computers available on campus for general student use. A campuswide network can be accessed from off campus. Internet access, at least one staffed computer lab available.

Student Life *Housing:* on-campus residence required through sophomore year. *Options:* men-only, women-only. *Activities and Organizations:* drama/theater group, student-run newspaper, choral group, Student Senate, Aggie Club, Phi Beta Lambda, Psycho Club. *Student Services:* personal/psychological counseling.

Athletics Member NJCAA. *Intercollegiate sports:* baseball M(s), basketball M(s)/W(s), softball W(s). *Intramural sports:* baseball M/W, basketball M/W, football M/W, golf M/W, soccer M/W, softball M/W, swimming M/W, tennis M/W, track and field M/W, volleyball M/W.

Standardized Tests *Required:* ACT (for placement).

Costs (2001–02) *Tuition:* state resident $1200 full-time, $34 per credit hour part-time; nonresident $2900 full-time, $74 per credit hour part-time. Full-time tuition and fees vary according to course load and location. Part-time tuition and fees vary according to course load and location. *Required fees:* $500 full-time, $18 per credit hour. *Room and board:* $2600. Room and board charges vary according to board plan and housing facility. *Payment plan:* deferred payment. *Waivers:* employees or children of employees.

Applying *Options:* common application, early admission, deferred entrance. *Application fee:* $25. *Required:* high school transcript. *Application deadline:* rolling (freshmen), rolling (transfers).

Admissions Contact Leah Miller, Director of Admissions, Eastern Oklahoma State College, 1301 West Main, Wilburton, OK 74578-4999. *Phone:* 918-465-4417 Ext. 240. *Fax:* 918-465-2431. *E-mail:* edavis@eosc.cc.ok.us.

MURRAY STATE COLLEGE
Tishomingo, Oklahoma

- **State-supported** 2-year, founded 1908, part of Oklahoma State Regents for Higher Education
- **Calendar** semesters
- **Degree** associate
- **Rural** 120-acre campus
- **Coed**

Student Life *Campus security:* 24-hour patrols.

Athletics Member NJCAA.

Standardized Tests *Required:* ACT (for placement).

Financial Aid In 2001, 70 Federal Work-Study jobs (averaging $1648). 30 State and other part-time jobs (averaging $1648).

Applying *Options:* common application, early admission, deferred entrance. *Required:* high school transcript.

Admissions Contact Mrs. Ann Beck, Registrar and Director of Admissions, Murray State College, 1Murray Campus, Tishomingo, OK 73460. *Phone:* 580-371-2371 Ext. 171. *Fax:* 580-371-9844.

NORTHEASTERN OKLAHOMA AGRICULTURAL AND MECHANICAL COLLEGE
Miami, Oklahoma

- **State-supported** 2-year, founded 1919, part of Oklahoma State Regents for Higher Education
- **Calendar** semesters
- **Degree** associate
- **Small-town** 340-acre campus
- **Coed**

Student Life *Campus security:* 24-hour patrols.

Athletics Member NJCAA.

Standardized Tests *Required:* ACT (for placement).

Financial Aid In 2001, 100 Federal Work-Study jobs (averaging $2500). 100 State and other part-time jobs (averaging $1000).

Applying *Options:* early admission. *Required:* high school transcript.

Admissions Contact Ms. Linda Burns, Director of Admissions, Northeastern Oklahoma Agricultural and Mechanical College, 200 I Street, NE, Miami, OK 74354-6434. *Phone:* 918-540-6212. *Toll-free phone:* 800-234-4727.

NORTHERN OKLAHOMA COLLEGE
Tonkawa, Oklahoma

- **State-supported** 2-year, founded 1901, part of Oklahoma State Regents for Higher Education
- **Calendar** semesters
- **Degree** associate
- **Rural** 10-acre campus
- **Coed,** 2,900 undergraduate students

Undergraduates Students come from 4 other countries, 20% live on campus.

Faculty *Total:* 80, 56% full-time.

Majors Accounting; agricultural business; biological/physical sciences; broadcast journalism; business administration; computer science; construction technology; criminal justice/law enforcement administration; drafting; elementary education; engineering; graphic design/commercial art/illustration; graphic/printing equipment; information sciences/systems; liberal arts and sciences/liberal studies; nursing; secretarial science.

Academic Programs *Special study options:* academic remediation for entering students, adult/continuing education programs, advanced placement credit, part-time degree program, services for LD students, summer session for credit.

Library Vineyard Library with 34,458 titles, 211 serial subscriptions.

Computers on Campus 150 computers available on campus for general student use. Internet access, at least one staffed computer lab available.

Student Life *Housing:* on-campus residence required through sophomore year. *Activities and Organizations:* drama/theater group, student-run newspaper, radio station, choral group, Phi Theta Kappa, Law Enforcement Club, Fellowship of Christian Athletes, Student Nurses Association, Young Republicans. *Campus security:* 24-hour emergency response devices and patrols. *Student Services:* health clinic, personal/psychological counseling.

Athletics Member NJCAA. *Intercollegiate sports:* baseball W(s), basketball M(s)/W(s). *Intramural sports:* badminton M/W, basketball M/W, football M/W, golf M/W, racquetball M/W, softball M/W, tennis M/W, volleyball M/W, water polo M/W.

Standardized Tests *Required:* ACT (for placement).

Costs (2001–02) *Tuition:* state resident $1105 full-time, $44 per credit hour part-time; nonresident $2885 full-time, $118 per credit hour part-time. *Room and board:* $1060.

Financial Aid In 2001, 73 Federal Work-Study jobs (averaging $1900). 240 State and other part-time jobs (averaging $1050).

Applying *Options:* common application, early admission. *Application fee:* $25. *Required:* high school transcript. *Application deadline:* rolling (freshmen).

Admissions Contact Ms. Sheri Snyder, Director of College Relations, Northern Oklahoma College, 1220 East Grand Avenue, PO Box 310, Tonkawa, OK 74653-0310. *Phone:* 580-628-6290. *Toll-free phone:* 800-429-5715.

OKLAHOMA CITY COMMUNITY COLLEGE
Oklahoma City, Oklahoma

- **State-supported** 2-year, founded 1969, part of Oklahoma State Regents for Higher Education
- **Calendar** semesters
- **Degree** certificates and associate
- **Urban** 143-acre campus
- **Endowment** $91,544
- **Coed,** 10,321 undergraduate students, 36% full-time, 57% women, 43% men

Undergraduates 3,730 full-time, 6,591 part-time. Students come from 3 states and territories, 16 other countries, 8% African American, 7% Asian American or Pacific Islander, 5% Hispanic American, 6% Native American, 1% international, 6% transferred in.

Freshmen *Admission:* 1,366 applied, 1,359 admitted, 1,282 enrolled. *Test scores:* ACT scores over 18: 68%; ACT scores over 24: 15%.

Faculty *Total:* 427, 26% full-time, 11% with terminal degrees. *Student/faculty ratio:* 21:1.

Majors Accounting; aircraft mechanic/airframe; applied art; area studies related; art; auto mechanic/technician; aviation technology; biology; biomedical technology; broadcast journalism; business administration; chemistry; child care/

Oklahoma City Community College (continued)
development; computer engineering technology; computer science; drafting; electrical/electronic engineering technology; emergency medical technology; finance; fine/studio arts; gerontology; graphic design/commercial art/illustration; history; humanities; insurance/risk management; liberal arts and sciences/liberal studies; literature; mass communications; mathematics; medical records administration; modern languages; music; nursing; occupational therapy; operating room technician; orthoptics; physical therapy; physics; political science; pre-engineering; psychology; respiratory therapy; sociology; theater arts/drama.

Academic Programs *Special study options:* academic remediation for entering students, accelerated degree program, advanced placement credit, cooperative education, English as a second language, external degree program, honors programs, part-time degree program, student-designed majors, summer session for credit.

Library 53,000 titles, 450 serial subscriptions, an OPAC.

Computers on Campus 190 computers available on campus for general student use. A campuswide network can be accessed from off campus. Internet access, at least one staffed computer lab available.

Student Life *Housing:* college housing not available. *Activities and Organizations:* drama/theater group, student-run newspaper, choral group, Phi Theta Kappa, College Republicans, Future Teachers, Hispanic Organization to Promote Education, Student Activities Board. *Campus security:* 24-hour emergency response devices and patrols, late-night transport/escort service. *Student Services:* personal/psychological counseling.

Athletics *Intramural sports:* basketball M/W, bowling M/W, football M, soccer M/W, softball M/W, swimming M/W.

Standardized Tests *Required for some:* ACT (for placement), ACT COMPASS.

Costs (2001–02) *Tuition:* state resident $1011 full-time, $48 per credit hour part-time; nonresident $3218 full-time, $121 per credit hour part-time. *Required fees:* $423 full-time. *Payment plan:* installment. *Waivers:* senior citizens and employees or children of employees.

Financial Aid In 2001, 280 Federal Work-Study jobs (averaging $2670).

Applying *Options:* early admission, deferred entrance. *Application fee:* $25. *Application deadline:* rolling (freshmen), rolling (transfers).

Admissions Contact Ms. Gloria Cardenas-Barton, Dean of Admissions/Registrar, Oklahoma City Community College, 7777 South May Avenue, Oklahoma City, OK 73159. *Phone:* 405-682-7515. *E-mail:* sedwards@okccc.edu.

OKLAHOMA STATE UNIVERSITY, OKLAHOMA CITY

Oklahoma City, Oklahoma

- **State-supported** 2-year, founded 1961, part of Oklahoma State University
- **Calendar** semesters
- **Degree** certificates and associate
- **Urban** 80-acre campus
- **Coed,** 4,522 undergraduate students

Undergraduates Students come from 18 states and territories, 15 other countries, 1% are from out of state.

Freshmen *Average high school GPA:* 2.44.

Faculty *Total:* 241, 26% full-time, 9% with terminal degrees. *Student/faculty ratio:* 18:1.

Majors Accounting; alcohol/drug abuse counseling; architectural engineering technology; business administration; civil engineering technology; computer engineering technology; computer programming; computer science; construction management; construction technology; data processing technology; drafting; electrical/electronic engineering technology; engineering; engineering technology; environmental technology; fire science; heating/air conditioning/refrigeration; horticulture science; industrial design; industrial technology; instrumentation technology; international business; labor/personnel relations; landscape architecture; law enforcement/police science; nursing; quality control technology; sign language interpretation; surveying; technical/business writing.

Academic Programs *Special study options:* academic remediation for entering students, advanced placement credit, distance learning, double majors, honors programs, independent study, part-time degree program, services for LD students, summer session for credit.

Library Oklahoma State University-Oklahoma City Campus with 11,973 titles, 244 serial subscriptions, an OPAC, a Web page.

Computers on Campus 75 computers available on campus for general student use. A campuswide network can be accessed from off campus. Internet access, at least one staffed computer lab available.

Student Life *Activities and Organizations:* Phi Theta Kappa, Deaf/Hearing Social Club, American Criminal Justice Association, Horticulture Club, Vet-Tech. *Campus security:* 24-hour patrols, late-night transport/escort service.

Athletics *Intramural sports:* basketball M/W, volleyball M/W.

Standardized Tests *Required for some:* SAT I or ACT (for placement), ACT COMPASS.

Costs (2001–02) *Tuition:* state resident $1900 full-time, $61 per credit hour part-time; nonresident $4500 full-time, $149 per credit hour part-time. *Room and board:* $3500.

Financial Aid In 2001, 57 Federal Work-Study jobs (averaging $1000).

Applying *Options:* early admission. *Application deadline:* rolling (freshmen), rolling (transfers). *Notification:* continuous (freshmen).

Admissions Contact Ms. Sherry Overton, Interim Director of Admissions, Oklahoma State University, Oklahoma City, 900 North Portland Avenue, Oklahoma City, OK 73107. *Phone:* 405-945-3287. *Fax:* 405-945-3277.

OKLAHOMA STATE UNIVERSITY, OKMULGEE

Okmulgee, Oklahoma

- **State-supported** 2-year, founded 1946, part of Oklahoma State University
- **Calendar** trimesters
- **Degree** associate
- **Small-town** 160-acre campus with easy access to Tulsa
- **Coed,** 2,329 undergraduate students, 74% full-time, 40% women, 60% men

Undergraduates 1,717 full-time, 612 part-time. Students come from 22 states and territories, 3 other countries, 25% live on campus.

Freshmen *Admission:* 825 enrolled.

Faculty *Total:* 129, 100% full-time, 3% with terminal degrees.

Majors Accounting; architectural engineering technology; auto mechanic/technician; aviation technology; business administration; business marketing and marketing management; computer graphics; construction technology; culinary arts; dietetics; drafting; electrical/electronic engineering technology; food products retailing; food services technology; graphic design/commercial art/illustration; graphic/printing equipment; heating/air conditioning/refrigeration; heavy equipment maintenance; hospitality management; industrial technology; information sciences/systems; legal administrative assistant; machine technology; medical administrative assistant; metal/jewelry arts; photography; plumbing; robotics; secretarial science.

Academic Programs *Special study options:* academic remediation for entering students, adult/continuing education programs, advanced placement credit, internships, part-time degree program, services for LD students, summer session for credit.

Library Learning Resource Center with 9,965 titles, 484 serial subscriptions, an OPAC, a Web page.

Computers on Campus 360 computers available on campus for general student use. At least one staffed computer lab available.

Student Life *Housing:* on-campus residence required for freshman year. *Options:* coed. *Activities and Organizations:* drama/theater group, Student Senate, Junior Ambassadors, Phi Theta Kappa, departmental clubs, Drama Club. *Campus security:* 24-hour emergency response devices and patrols, late-night transport/escort service, controlled dormitory access. *Student Services:* health clinic, personal/psychological counseling.

Athletics *Intramural sports:* basketball M/W, bowling M/W, football M, golf M, racquetball M/W, softball M/W, table tennis M/W, volleyball M/W.

Standardized Tests *Required:* SAT I or ACT (for placement).

Costs (2002–03) *Tuition:* $50 per credit hour part-time; state resident $750 full-time, $50 per credit hour part-time; nonresident $7830 full-time, $143 per credit hour part-time. *Required fees:* $307 full-time, $31 per credit hour. *Waivers:* senior citizens and employees or children of employees.

Applying *Options:* common application, deferred entrance. *Required:* high school transcript. *Application deadline:* rolling (freshmen), rolling (transfers).

Admissions Contact Kelly Hildebrant, Director of Admissions, Oklahoma State University, Okmulgee, 1801 East Fourth Street, Okmulgee, OK 74447-3901. *Phone:* 918-293-5298. *Toll-free phone:* 800-722-4401. *Fax:* 918-293-4650. *E-mail:* francie@okway.okstate.edu.

REDLANDS COMMUNITY COLLEGE

El Reno, Oklahoma

- **State-supported** 2-year, founded 1938, part of Oklahoma State Regents for Higher Education
- **Calendar** semesters

- **Degree** certificates and associate
- **Suburban** 55-acre campus with easy access to Oklahoma City
- **Coed**

Faculty *Student/faculty ratio:* 17:1.
Student Life *Campus security:* 24-hour patrols.
Athletics Member NJCAA.
Standardized Tests *Required:* ACT (for placement).
Financial Aid In 2001, 25 Federal Work-Study jobs (averaging $2000). 70 State and other part-time jobs (averaging $2000).
Applying *Options:* common application, electronic application, early admission, deferred entrance. *Required:* high school transcript.
Admissions Contact Dr. Roger French, Vice President for Student Services, Redlands Community College, El Reno, OK 73036. *Phone:* 405-262-2552 Ext. 2422. *E-mail:* frenchr@redlands.cc.net.

ROSE STATE COLLEGE
Midwest City, Oklahoma

- **State and locally supported** 2-year, founded 1968, part of Oklahoma State Regents for Higher Education
- **Calendar** semesters
- **Degree** certificates and associate
- **Suburban** 110-acre campus with easy access to Oklahoma City
- **Coed**

Student Life *Campus security:* 24-hour patrols.
Athletics Member NJCAA.
Standardized Tests *Required:* SAT I, ACT, or ACT COMPASS.
Financial Aid In 2001, 150 Federal Work-Study jobs (averaging $4000).
Applying *Options:* common application, electronic application, early admission, deferred entrance. *Application fee:* $15. *Required:* high school transcript.
Admissions Contact Ms. Evelyn K. Hutchings, Registrar and Director of Admissions, Rose State College, 6420 Southeast 15th Street, Midwest City, OK 73110-2799. *Phone:* 405-733-7673. *Fax:* 405-736-0309. *E-mail:* ekhutchings@ms.rose.cc.ok.us.

SEMINOLE STATE COLLEGE
Seminole, Oklahoma

- **State-supported** 2-year, founded 1931, part of Oklahoma State Regents for Higher Education
- **Calendar** semesters
- **Degree** diplomas and associate
- **Small-town** 40-acre campus with easy access to Oklahoma City
- **Coed,** 1,965 undergraduate students, 56% full-time, 66% women, 34% men

Undergraduates 1,101 full-time, 864 part-time. Students come from 13 states and territories, 5 other countries, 2% are from out of state, 5% African American, 0.6% Asian American or Pacific Islander, 2% Hispanic American, 22% Native American, 1% international, 8% live on campus.
Freshmen *Admission:* 400 applied, 400 admitted, 480 enrolled. *Test scores:* ACT scores over 18: 61%; ACT scores over 24: 16%; ACT scores over 30: 1%.
Faculty *Total:* 93, 48% full-time, 9% with terminal degrees. *Student/faculty ratio:* 22:1.
Majors Accounting; art; behavioral sciences; biology; business administration; computer science; elementary education; English; law enforcement/police science; liberal arts and sciences/liberal studies; mathematics; medical laboratory technician; nursing; physical education; physical sciences; pre-engineering; secretarial science; social sciences.
Academic Programs *Special study options:* academic remediation for entering students, accelerated degree program, adult/continuing education programs, advanced placement credit, cooperative education, distance learning, honors programs, independent study, off-campus study, part-time degree program, services for LD students, summer session for credit.
Library Boren Library with 27,507 titles, 200 serial subscriptions, an OPAC.
Computers on Campus 100 computers available on campus for general student use. A campuswide network can be accessed from off campus. Internet access, at least one staffed computer lab available.
Student Life *Housing Options:* coed. *Activities and Organizations:* student-run newspaper, choral group, Student Government Association, Native American Student Association, Psi Beta Honor Society, Student Nurses Association, Phi Theta Kappa. *Campus security:* 24-hour patrols. *Student Services:* personal/psychological counseling.
Athletics Member NJCAA. *Intercollegiate sports:* baseball M(s), basketball M(s)/W(s), golf M(s)/W(s), softball W(s), tennis M(s)/W(s), volleyball W(s).
Standardized Tests *Required:* SAT I, ACT, or ACT COMPASS.
Costs (2001–02) *One-time required fee:* $15. *Tuition:* state resident $1011 full-time, $34 per credit hour part-time; nonresident $3219 full-time, $107 per credit hour part-time. Full-time tuition and fees vary according to course load. Part-time tuition and fees vary according to course load. *Required fees:* $546 full-time, $18 per credit hour. *Room and board:* $3700. Room and board charges vary according to housing facility. *Payment plan:* installment. *Waivers:* senior citizens and employees or children of employees.
Applying *Options:* common application, early admission, deferred entrance. *Application fee:* $15. *Required:* high school transcript. *Application deadline:* rolling (freshmen), rolling (transfers). *Notification:* continuous (freshmen).
Admissions Contact Ms. Katherine Benton, Director of Enrollment Management, Seminole State College, PO Box 351, Seminole, OK 74818-0351. *Phone:* 405-382-9272. *E-mail:* benton_k@ssc.cc.ok.us.

SOUTHWESTERN OKLAHOMA STATE UNIVERSITY AT SAYRE
Sayre, Oklahoma

- **State and locally supported** 2-year, founded 1938, part of Southwestern Oklahoma State University
- **Calendar** semesters
- **Degree** diplomas and associate
- **Rural** 6-acre campus
- **Coed,** 488 undergraduate students, 63% full-time, 70% women, 30% men

Undergraduates 309 full-time, 179 part-time. Students come from 2 states and territories, 6% are from out of state.
Freshmen *Admission:* 118 enrolled.
Faculty *Total:* 18, 78% full-time.
Majors Business administration; computer science; corrections; criminal justice studies; general studies; medical laboratory technician; medical radiologic technology; nursing; occupational therapy assistant; physical therapy assistant.
Academic Programs *Special study options:* academic remediation for entering students, adult/continuing education programs, advanced placement credit, cooperative education, distance learning, independent study, part-time degree program, services for LD students, summer session for credit.
Library Oscar McMahan Library with 9,975 titles, 45 serial subscriptions, an OPAC, a Web page.
Computers on Campus 100 computers available on campus for general student use. Internet access, at least one staffed computer lab available.
Student Life *Housing:* college housing not available.
Standardized Tests *Required for some:* ACT (for admission).
Costs (2001–02) *Tuition:* state resident $1704 full-time, $71 per credit hour part-time; nonresident $1704 full-time, $71 per credit hour part-time.
Applying *Options:* common application, early admission, deferred entrance. *Application fee:* $15. *Required:* high school transcript. *Application deadline:* rolling (freshmen), rolling (transfers).
Admissions Contact Ms. Kim Seymour, Registrar, Southwestern Oklahoma State University at Sayre, 409 East Mississippi Street, Sayre, OK 73662-1236. *Phone:* 580-928-5533 Ext. 101.

SPARTAN SCHOOL OF AERONAUTICS
Tulsa, Oklahoma

- **Proprietary** primarily 2-year, founded 1928, part of National Education Centers, Inc
- **Calendar** quarters
- **Degrees** certificates, associate, and bachelor's
- **Urban** 26-acre campus
- **Coed, primarily men,** 1,625 undergraduate students, 100% full-time, 4% women, 96% men

Undergraduates Students come from 52 states and territories, 40 other countries, 15% are from out of state, 12% African American, 0.8% Asian American or Pacific Islander, 13% Hispanic American, 2% Native American, 12% international.
Freshmen *Average high school GPA:* 2.5.
Faculty *Total:* 150, 80% full-time.
Majors Aerospace science; aircraft pilot (professional); aviation technology; communication equipment technology; electrical/electronic engineering technology; instrumentation technology; quality control technology.

Spartan School of Aeronautics (continued)

Academic Programs *Special study options:* academic remediation for entering students, advanced placement credit, English as a second language.

Library 18,000 titles, 160 serial subscriptions.

Computers on Campus 75 computers available on campus for general student use. At least one staffed computer lab available.

Student Life *Housing:* college housing not available. *Activities and Organizations:* Student Executive Association.

Athletics *Intercollegiate sports:* softball W. *Intramural sports:* archery M(c), basketball M, bowling M(c)/W, football M, golf M, soccer M, volleyball M.

Standardized Tests *Required:* ACT ASSET.

Costs (2001–02) *Tuition:* $9750 full-time.

Financial Aid In 2001, 1 Federal Work-Study job (averaging $6740).

Applying *Options:* deferred entrance. *Application fee:* $100. *Required:* high school transcript. *Recommended:* interview. *Application deadline:* rolling (freshmen), rolling (transfers).

Admissions Contact Mr. John Buck, Vice President of Marketing, Spartan School of Aeronautics, 8820 East Pine Street, PO Box 582833, Tulsa, OK 74158-2833. *Phone:* 918-836-6886.

TULSA COMMUNITY COLLEGE

Tulsa, Oklahoma

- **State-supported** 2-year, founded 1968, part of Oklahoma State Regents for Higher Education
- **Calendar** semesters
- **Degree** certificates and associate
- **Urban** 160-acre campus
- **Coed,** 20,827 undergraduate students

Undergraduates Students come from 16 states and territories, 75 other countries, 8% African American, 2% Asian American or Pacific Islander, 3% Hispanic American, 6% Native American.

Freshmen *Average high school GPA:* 2.84.

Faculty *Total:* 1,094, 23% full-time. *Student/faculty ratio:* 20:1.

Majors Accounting; advertising; aerospace science; agricultural sciences; aircraft mechanic/airframe; American studies; architecture; art; astronomy; auto mechanic/technician; aviation/airway science; aviation technology; behavioral sciences; biology; biomedical technology; botany; business administration; business education; business marketing and marketing management; chemistry; child care/development; child care/guidance; child guidance; civil engineering technology; computer graphics; computer hardware engineering; computer/information systems security; computer/information technology services administration and management related; computer programming related; computer programming (specific applications); computer programming, vendor/product certification; computer science; computer science related; computer software and media applications related; computer software engineering; computer systems networking/telecommunications; computer/technical support; construction technology; corrections; creative writing; criminal justice/law enforcement administration; data entry/microcomputer applications; data entry/microcomputer applications related; data warehousing/mining/database administration; dental assistant; dental hygiene; desktop publishing equipment operation; drafting; early childhood education; earth sciences; ecology; economics; education; electrical/electronic engineering technology; elementary education; elementary/middle/secondary education administration; emergency medical technology; engineering; English; environmental technology; fashion design/illustration; fire protection/safety technology; fire science; forestry; French; geography; geology; German; health education; health science; heating/air conditioning/refrigeration; history; horticulture science; horticulture services; hotel and restaurant management; humanities; human resources management; human services; industrial radiologic technology; industrial technology; information sciences/systems; information technology; insurance marketing; insurance/risk management; interior design; international business; international relations; Italian; Japanese; journalism; labor/personnel relations; landscape architecture; landscaping management; Latin (ancient and medieval); law enforcement/police science; legal administrative assistant; legal studies; liberal arts and sciences/liberal studies; library science; management science; mass communications; materials science; mathematics; mechanical engineering technology; medical administrative assistant; medical assistant; medical laboratory technician; medical records administration; music; music teacher education; nursing; occupational safety/health technology; occupational therapy; occupational therapy assistant; oceanography; operating room technician; ornamental horticulture; paralegal/legal assistant; petroleum technology; philosophy; physical education; physical sciences; physical therapy; physician assistant; physics; plant protection; political science; pre-dentistry; pre-engineering; pre-medicine; pre-pharmacy studies; pre-veterinary studies; psychology; purchasing/contracts management; quality control technology; radiological science; radio/television broadcasting; recreational therapy; religious studies; respiratory therapy; robotics; Russian; safety/security technology; secretarial science; sign language interpretation; social sciences; social work; sociology; Spanish; speech/rhetorical studies; surveying; system administration; system/networking/LAN/WAN management; telecommunications; theater arts/drama; travel/tourism management; veterinary technology; Web/multimedia management/webmaster; Web page, digital/multimedia and information resources design; word processing; zoology.

Academic Programs *Special study options:* academic remediation for entering students, accelerated degree program, adult/continuing education programs, advanced placement credit, cooperative education, English as a second language, external degree program, freshman honors college, honors programs, internships, part-time degree program, services for LD students, summer session for credit.

Library Learning Resource Center plus 1 other with 110,000 titles, 987 serial subscriptions, a Web page.

Computers on Campus 1000 computers available on campus for general student use. A campuswide network can be accessed from off campus. Internet access, online (class) registration, at least one staffed computer lab available.

Student Life *Housing:* college housing not available. *Activities and Organizations:* drama/theater group, student-run newspaper. *Campus security:* 24-hour emergency response devices and patrols, student patrols, late-night transport/escort service. *Student Services:* health clinic, personal/psychological counseling, women's center.

Athletics *Intramural sports:* basketball M/W, bowling M/W, cross-country running M/W, football M/W, golf M/W, racquetball M/W, soccer M/W, tennis M/W, track and field M/W, volleyball M/W.

Standardized Tests *Required:* SAT I or ACT (for placement), CPT.

Costs (2001–02) *Tuition:* state resident $1026 full-time, $34 per credit hour part-time; nonresident $109 per credit hour part-time. *Required fees:* $586 full-time. *Waivers:* children of alumni, adult students, senior citizens, and employees or children of employees.

Applying *Options:* common application, early admission. *Application fee:* $15. *Required:* high school transcript. *Application deadline:* rolling (freshmen), rolling (transfers).

Admissions Contact Ms. Leanne Brewer, Director of Admissions and Records, Tulsa Community College, 6111 East Skelly Drive, Tulsa, OK 74135. *Phone:* 918-595-7811. *E-mail:* lbrewe@tulsa.cc.ok.us.

WESTERN OKLAHOMA STATE COLLEGE

Altus, Oklahoma

- **State-supported** 2-year, founded 1926, part of Oklahoma State Regents for Higher Education
- **Calendar** semesters
- **Degree** certificates and associate
- **Rural** 142-acre campus
- **Endowment** $2.5 million
- **Coed**

Faculty *Student/faculty ratio:* 20:1.

Student Life *Campus security:* 24-hour emergency response devices.

Athletics Member NJCAA.

Standardized Tests *Required for some:* ACT (for admission).

Costs (2001–02) *Tuition:* state resident $1484 full-time, $45 per credit hour part-time; nonresident $3690 full-time, $123 per credit hour part-time. Full-time tuition and fees vary according to course load. Part-time tuition and fees vary according to course load. *Room and board:* $1600.

Financial Aid In 2001, 85 Federal Work-Study jobs (averaging $1978).

Applying *Options:* electronic application, early admission. *Application fee:* $15. *Required:* high school transcript.

Admissions Contact Mr. Larry W. Paxton, Director of Admissions/Registrar, Western Oklahoma State College, 2801 North Main Street, Altus, OK 73521-1397. *Phone:* 580-477-7720. *Fax:* 580-477-7723. *E-mail:* lwpaxton@western.cc.ok.us.

OREGON

BLUE MOUNTAIN COMMUNITY COLLEGE
Pendleton, Oregon

Admissions Contact Ms. Dana M. Young, Dean of Students and Enrollment Services, Blue Mountain Community College, PO Box 100, Pendleton, OR 97801. *Phone:* 541-278-5752. *Fax:* 541-278-5871. *E-mail:* onlineinquiry@bmcc.cd.or.us.

CENTRAL OREGON COMMUNITY COLLEGE
Bend, Oregon

- **District-supported** 2-year, founded 1949, part of Oregon Community College Association
- **Calendar** quarters
- **Degree** certificates and associate
- **Small-town** 193-acre campus
- **Coed,** 4,399 undergraduate students, 39% full-time, 56% women, 44% men

Located in Bend, Oregon, Central Oregon Community College (COCC) offers more than 50 certificate and degree options, affordable tuition, outstanding faculty from the region, and access to more than 15 bachelor degree programs through Oregon State University's Cascades campus. COCC also features small class sizes, on-campus housing, intramural sports, and exceptional outdoor recreation opportunities.

Undergraduates 1,701 full-time, 2,698 part-time. Students come from 7 states and territories, 5 other countries, 1% are from out of state, 0.4% African American, 1% Asian American or Pacific Islander, 3% Hispanic American, 3% Native American, 0.4% international, 11% transferred in, 3% live on campus.

Freshmen *Admission:* 841 applied, 841 admitted, 841 enrolled.

Faculty *Total:* 264, 36% full-time. *Student/faculty ratio:* 18:1.

Majors Accounting; art; auto mechanic/technician; biological/physical sciences; business administration; business machine repair; business marketing and marketing management; cabinet making; cartography; computer science; computer science related; criminal justice/law enforcement administration; culinary arts; dental assistant; drafting; drafting/design technology; education; emergency medical technology; exercise sciences; fire science; fish/game management; forest products technology; forestry; hospitality management; hospitality/recreation marketing operations; hotel and restaurant management; humanities; industrial technology; landscaping management; liberal arts and sciences/liberal studies; mathematics; medical assistant; medical records technology; nursing; physical sciences; practical nurse; pre-engineering; secretarial science; social sciences; sport/fitness administration; tourism promotion operations; turf management; welding technology.

Academic Programs *Special study options:* academic remediation for entering students, adult/continuing education programs, advanced placement credit, cooperative education, distance learning, double majors, English as a second language, independent study, internships, part-time degree program, services for LD students, student-designed majors, study abroad, summer session for credit.

Library COCC Library plus 1 other with 58,294 titles, 1,356 serial subscriptions, 3,339 audiovisual materials, an OPAC, a Web page.

Computers on Campus 335 computers available on campus for general student use. A campuswide network can be accessed from student residence rooms and from off campus that provide access to e-mail. At least one staffed computer lab available.

Student Life *Housing Options:* coed. *Activities and Organizations:* drama/theater group, student-run newspaper, choral group, student government, club sports, Phi Theta Kappa, DEC, Science Learning Center. *Campus security:* 24-hour emergency response devices and patrols, late-night transport/escort service. *Student Services:* health clinic, personal/psychological counseling.

Athletics *Intercollegiate sports:* baseball M(c)/W(c), basketball M(c)/W(c), bowling M(c)/W(c), golf M(c)/W(c), skiing (cross-country) M(c)/W(c), soccer M(c)/W(c), softball M(c)/W(c), swimming M(c)/W(c), tennis M(c)/W(c), track and field M(c)/W(c), volleyball M(c)/W(c), weight lifting M(c)/W(c). *Intramural sports:* badminton M/W, basketball M/W, cross-country running M/W, equestrian sports M/W, football M, golf M/W, racquetball M/W, skiing (downhill) M/W, soccer M/W, softball M/W, table tennis M/W, tennis M/W, track and field M/W, volleyball M/W, weight lifting M/W.

Standardized Tests *Required:* ACT ASSET.

Costs (2001–02) *Tuition:* area resident $2025 full-time, $45 per credit part-time; state resident $2205 full-time, $57 per credit part-time; nonresident $3660 full-time, $154 per credit part-time. Full-time tuition and fees vary according to program and reciprocity agreements. Part-time tuition and fees vary according to reciprocity agreements. *Required fees:* $68 full-time, $2 per credit. *Room and board:* $5300. *Payment plan:* installment. *Waivers:* senior citizens and employees or children of employees.

Financial Aid In 2001, 200 Federal Work-Study jobs (averaging $800).

Applying *Options:* common application. *Required for some:* high school transcript, minimum 2.0 GPA. *Recommended:* high school transcript. *Application deadline:* rolling (freshmen), rolling (transfers). *Notification:* continuous (freshmen).

Admissions Contact Ms. Helen Pruitt, Associate Director of Enrollment Services, Central Oregon Community College, 2600 NW College Way, Bend, OR 97701-5998. *Phone:* 541-383-7261. *Fax:* 541-383-7506. *E-mail:* welcome@cocc.edu.

CHEMEKETA COMMUNITY COLLEGE
Salem, Oregon

- **State and locally supported** 2-year, founded 1955
- **Calendar** quarters
- **Degree** certificates, diplomas, and associate
- **Urban** 72-acre campus with easy access to Portland
- **Coed,** 8,718 undergraduate students

Undergraduates Students come from 5 states and territories, 25 other countries, 1% are from out of state, 0.8% African American, 3% Asian American or Pacific Islander, 8% Hispanic American, 2% Native American.

Faculty *Total:* 632, 36% full-time. *Student/faculty ratio:* 18:1.

Majors Accounting; agricultural education; art education; auto mechanic/technician; business administration; civil engineering technology; computer engineering technology; computer programming; computer science; construction technology; criminal justice/law enforcement administration; dental hygiene; drafting; early childhood education; economics; education; electrical/electronic engineering technology; emergency medical technology; engineering; English; finance; fire science; forest harvesting production technology; forestry; graphic/printing equipment; health education; health services administration; hospitality management; hotel and restaurant management; humanities; human services; industrial technology; liberal arts and sciences/liberal studies; mathematics; mechanical design technology; medical administrative assistant; medical assistant; medical records administration; nursing; physical education; political science; practical nurse; real estate; science education; secretarial science; social sciences; teacher assistant/aide; welding technology.

Academic Programs *Special study options:* academic remediation for entering students, adult/continuing education programs, advanced placement credit, cooperative education, distance learning, double majors, English as a second language, independent study, internships, part-time degree program, services for LD students, summer session for credit.

Library Chemeketa Community College Library plus 1 other with 801 audiovisual materials, an OPAC, a Web page.

Computers on Campus A campuswide network can be accessed from off campus. Internet access, at least one staffed computer lab available.

Student Life *Housing:* college housing not available. *Activities and Organizations:* drama/theater group, student-run newspaper, choral group, Health Occupations Students of America, International Conference of Building Officials, ski club, Christian Fellowship. *Campus security:* 24-hour emergency response devices and patrols, late-night transport/escort service. *Student Services:* personal/psychological counseling, women's center.

Athletics *Intercollegiate sports:* baseball M(s), basketball M(s)/W(s), cross-country running M(s)/W(s), track and field M(s)/W(s), volleyball W(s).

Standardized Tests *Required for some:* ACT ASSET.

Costs (2001–02) *Tuition:* state resident $1755 full-time, $39 per credit hour part-time; nonresident $3195 full-time, $155 per credit hour part-time. Full-time tuition and fees vary according to program. Part-time tuition and fees vary according to program. *Payment plan:* installment. *Waivers:* senior citizens and employees or children of employees.

Financial Aid In 2001, 442 Federal Work-Study jobs (averaging $800).

Applying *Options:* deferred entrance. *Required for some:* high school transcript. *Application deadline:* rolling (freshmen), rolling (transfers). *Notification:* continuous (freshmen).

Admissions Contact Ms. Carolyn Brownell, Admissions Specialist, Chemeketa Community College, 4000 Lancaster Drive, NE, Salem, OR 97305-7070. *Phone:* 503-399-5006. *Toll-free phone:* 503-399-5001. *Fax:* 503-399-3918. *E-mail:* broc@chemeketa.edu.

CLACKAMAS COMMUNITY COLLEGE
Oregon City, Oregon

- **District-supported** 2-year, founded 1966
- **Calendar** quarters
- **Degree** certificates, diplomas, and associate
- **Suburban** 175-acre campus with easy access to Portland
- **Endowment** $5.6 million
- **Coed,** 6,715 undergraduate students, 33% full-time, 49% women, 51% men

Undergraduates 2,238 full-time, 4,477 part-time. Students come from 38 states and territories, 16 other countries, 7% are from out of state, 2% African American, 3% Asian American or Pacific Islander, 4% Hispanic American, 1% Native American, 0.1% international, 32% transferred in.
Freshmen *Admission:* 1,302 enrolled.
Faculty *Total:* 582, 28% full-time. *Student/faculty ratio:* 12:1.
Majors Accounting; auto body repair; auto mechanic/technician; community services; computer maintenance technology; corrections; drafting; general studies; law enforcement/police science; liberal arts and sciences/liberal studies; machine technology; nursing; office management; ornamental horticulture; water treatment technology.
Academic Programs *Special study options:* academic remediation for entering students, accelerated degree program, adult/continuing education programs, advanced placement credit, cooperative education, distance learning, double majors, English as a second language, honors programs, independent study, internships, part-time degree program, services for LD students, study abroad, summer session for credit. *ROTC:* Air Force (c).
Library Dye Learning Resource Center plus 1 other with 92,519 titles, 274 serial subscriptions, 1,141 audiovisual materials, an OPAC, a Web page.
Computers on Campus 500 computers available on campus for general student use. At least one staffed computer lab available.
Student Life *Housing:* college housing not available. *Activities and Organizations:* drama/theater group, student-run newspaper, choral group, Ski Club, Spanish Club, Phi Theta Kappa, Horticulture Club, Speech Club, national fraternities. *Campus security:* 24-hour emergency response devices and patrols, student patrols, late-night transport/escort service. *Student Services:* personal/psychological counseling, women's center.
Athletics Member NJCAA. *Intercollegiate sports:* baseball M(s), basketball M(s)/W(s), cross-country running M(s)/W(s), softball W(s), track and field M(s)/W(s), volleyball W(s), wrestling M(s). *Intramural sports:* basketball M/W, football M, soccer M/W, tennis M/W.
Standardized Tests *Required:* Assessment and Placement Services for Community Colleges. *Recommended:* SAT I or ACT (for placement).
Costs (2001–02) *Tuition:* state resident $1590 full-time, $40 per credit hour part-time; nonresident $5040 full-time, $137 per credit hour part-time. Full-time tuition and fees vary according to course load and reciprocity agreements. Part-time tuition and fees vary according to course load and reciprocity agreements. No tuition increase for student's term of enrollment. *Required fees:* $180 full-time, $4 per credit hour. *Payment plan:* deferred payment. *Waivers:* senior citizens and employees or children of employees.
Financial Aid In 2001, 253 Federal Work-Study jobs (averaging $876).
Applying *Options:* early admission. *Recommended:* high school transcript. *Application deadline:* rolling (freshmen), rolling (transfers).
Admissions Contact Ms. Cheryl Hollatz-Wisely, Director, Clackamas Community College, 19600 South Molalla Avenue, Oregon City, OR 97045. *Phone:* 503-657-6958 Ext. 2861. *Fax:* 503-722-5864. *E-mail:* cherylhw@clackamas.cc.or.us.

CLATSOP COMMUNITY COLLEGE
Astoria, Oregon

- **County-supported** 2-year, founded 1958
- **Calendar** quarters
- **Degree** certificates and associate
- **Small-town** 20-acre campus
- **Endowment** $2.0 million
- **Coed**

Student Life *Campus security:* 24-hour emergency response devices, late-night transport/escort service.
Costs (2001–02) *Tuition:* state resident $1440 full-time, $40 per credit part-time; nonresident $3600 full-time, $100 per credit part-time. *Required fees:* $72 full-time, $2 per credit.
Financial Aid In 2001, 220 Federal Work-Study jobs (averaging $2175).
Applying *Options:* early admission. *Recommended:* high school transcript.
Admissions Contact Steve Rogers, Admissions Coordinator, Clatsop Community College, 1653 Jerome, Astoria, OR 97103-3698. *Phone:* 503-338-2325. *Toll-free phone:* 866-252-8767. *Fax:* 503-325-5738. *E-mail:* admissions@clatsop.cc.or.us.

HEALD COLLEGE, SCHOOLS OF BUSINESS AND TECHNOLOGY
Portland, Oregon

Admissions Contact 625 SW Broadway, 2nd Floor, Portland, OR 97205.

ITT TECHNICAL INSTITUTE
Portland, Oregon

- **Proprietary** primarily 2-year, founded 1971, part of ITT Educational Services, Inc
- **Calendar** quarters
- **Degrees** associate and bachelor's
- **Urban** 4-acre campus
- **Coed,** 499 undergraduate students

Majors Computer/information sciences related; computer programming; design/applied arts related; drafting; electrical/electronic engineering technologies related; information technology; robotics technology.
Student Life *Housing:* college housing not available. *Activities and Organizations:* student-run newspaper.
Costs (2001–02) *Tuition:* Full-time tuition and fees vary according to program. Part-time tuition and fees vary according to program. $260—$330 per credit hour.
Applying *Options:* deferred entrance. *Application fee:* $100. *Required:* high school transcript, interview. *Recommended:* letters of recommendation. *Application deadline:* rolling (freshmen), rolling (transfers). *Notification:* continuous (freshmen).
Admissions Contact Mr. Cliff Custer, Director of Recruitment, ITT Technical Institute, 6035 Northeast 78th Court, Portland, OR 97218-2854. *Phone:* 503-255-6500 Ext. 314. *Toll-free phone:* 800-234-5488.

LANE COMMUNITY COLLEGE
Eugene, Oregon

- **State and locally supported** 2-year, founded 1964
- **Calendar** quarters
- **Degree** certificates and associate
- **Suburban** 240-acre campus
- **Endowment** $6.0 million
- **Coed,** 10,626 undergraduate students, 46% full-time, 55% women, 45% men

Undergraduates 4,855 full-time, 5,771 part-time. Students come from 28 states and territories, 27 other countries.
Freshmen *Admission:* 1,308 enrolled.
Faculty *Total:* 605, 47% full-time. *Student/faculty ratio:* 20:1.
Majors Accounting; agricultural mechanization; aircraft pilot (professional); alcohol/drug abuse counseling; auto mechanic/technician; aviation technology; broadcast journalism; business administration; child care/development; community services; computer engineering technology; computer programming; construction technology; criminal justice/law enforcement administration; culinary arts; dental hygiene; drafting; early childhood education; electrical/electronic engineering technology; energy management technology; film/video production; food products retailing; food services technology; graphic design/commercial art/illustration; heating/air conditioning/refrigeration; heavy equipment maintenance; hospitality management; hotel and restaurant management; industrial technology; liberal arts and sciences/liberal studies; nursing; radio/television broadcasting; real estate; respiratory therapy; secretarial science; welding technology.
Academic Programs *Special study options:* academic remediation for entering students, adult/continuing education programs, advanced placement credit, English as a second language, internships, part-time degree program, services for LD students, summer session for credit.
Library Lane Community College Library plus 1 other with 67,051 titles, 513 serial subscriptions, an OPAC, a Web page.
Computers on Campus 1600 computers available on campus for general student use. At least one staffed computer lab available.

Student Life *Housing:* college housing not available. *Activities and Organizations:* drama/theater group, student-run newspaper, radio and television station, choral group, Associated Students of Lane, Multicultural Club, Native American Club, Lane Writing Club, Forensics Club. *Campus security:* 24-hour emergency response devices and patrols, student patrols, late-night transport/escort service. *Student Services:* health clinic, personal/psychological counseling, women's center, legal services.

Athletics *Intercollegiate sports:* baseball M(s), basketball M(s)/W(s), cross-country running M(s)/W(s), track and field M(s)/W(s), volleyball W(s). *Intramural sports:* badminton M/W, basketball M/W, bowling M/W, football M/W, golf M/W, skiing (cross-country) M/W, skiing (downhill) M/W, soccer M/W, softball M/W, tennis M/W, volleyball M, weight lifting M/W.

Costs (2001–02) *Tuition:* state resident $1368 full-time, $38 per credit hour part-time; nonresident $4428 full-time, $123 per credit hour part-time. *Required fees:* $58 full-time, $29 per term part-time. *Payment plan:* installment. *Waivers:* senior citizens and employees or children of employees.

Financial Aid In 2001, 451 Federal Work-Study jobs (averaging $1284).

Applying *Options:* common application, early admission. *Application deadline:* rolling (freshmen), rolling (transfers). *Notification:* continuous (freshmen).

Admissions Contact Ms. Helen Garrett, Director of Admissions/Registrar, Lane Community College, 4000 East 30th Avenue, Eugene, OR 97405-0640. *Phone:* 541-747-4501 Ext. 2686. *E-mail:* williamss@lanecc.edu.

LINN-BENTON COMMUNITY COLLEGE
Albany, Oregon

- **State and locally supported** 2-year, founded 1966
- **Calendar** quarters
- **Degree** certificates and associate
- **Small-town** 104-acre campus
- **Endowment** $2.4 million
- **Coed,** 4,746 undergraduate students, 57% full-time, 52% women, 48% men

Undergraduates 2,727 full-time, 2,019 part-time. Students come from 12 other countries, 1% African American, 3% Asian American or Pacific Islander, 3% Hispanic American, 2% Native American, 0.7% international.

Freshmen *Admission:* 2,771 applied, 2,497 admitted, 876 enrolled.

Faculty *Total:* 501, 35% full-time.

Majors Accounting; agricultural business; agricultural education; agricultural sciences; animal sciences; art; auto mechanic/technician; biological/physical sciences; biology; business administration; chemistry; child care/development; computer graphics; computer programming; computer science; computer/technical support; criminal justice/law enforcement administration; culinary arts; culinary arts and services related; dairy science; diesel engine mechanic; drafting; economics; education; electrical/electronic engineering technology; elementary education; English; equestrian studies; graphic design/commercial art/illustration; graphic/printing equipment related; home economics; horticulture science; industrial technology; journalism; legal administrative assistant; liberal arts and sciences/liberal studies; machine technology; mathematics; medical administrative assistant; medical assistant; metallurgical technology; nursing; photography; physics; pre-engineering; restaurant operations; secretarial science; teacher assistant/aide; technical/business writing; theater arts/drama; water treatment technology; welding technology.

Academic Programs *Special study options:* academic remediation for entering students, adult/continuing education programs, advanced placement credit, cooperative education, distance learning, English as a second language, internships, part-time degree program, services for LD students, summer session for credit. *ROTC:* Army (c), Air Force (c).

Library Linn-Benton Community College Library with 35,480 titles, 179 serial subscriptions, 6,756 audiovisual materials, an OPAC, a Web page.

Computers on Campus 500 computers available on campus for general student use. A campuswide network can be accessed from off campus. Internet access, at least one staffed computer lab available.

Student Life *Housing:* college housing not available. *Activities and Organizations:* drama/theater group, student-run newspaper, choral group, EBOP Club, Multicultural Club, Campus Family Co-op, Horticulture Club, Collegiate Secretary Club. *Campus security:* 24-hour emergency response devices and patrols, student patrols, late-night transport/escort service. *Student Services:* health clinic, personal/psychological counseling.

Athletics *Intercollegiate sports:* baseball M(s), basketball M(s)/W(s), volleyball W(s). *Intramural sports:* basketball M/W, table tennis M/W, tennis M/W.

Standardized Tests *Required:* CPT.

Costs (2002–03) *Tuition:* state resident $1845 full-time, $41 per credit part-time; nonresident $5760 full-time, $128 per credit part-time. Full-time tuition and fees vary according to course load. *Payment plan:* installment. *Waivers:* senior citizens and employees or children of employees.

Financial Aid In 2001, 290 Federal Work-Study jobs (averaging $1800).

Applying *Options:* deferred entrance. *Application fee:* $20. *Required for some:* high school transcript. *Application deadline:* rolling (freshmen), rolling (transfers).

Admissions Contact Ms. Christine Baker, Outreach Coordinator, Linn-Benton Community College, 6500 Pacific Boulevard SW, Albany, OR 97321. *Phone:* 541-917-4813. *E-mail:* amissions@linnbenton.edu.

MT. HOOD COMMUNITY COLLEGE
Gresham, Oregon

- **State and locally supported** 2-year, founded 1966
- **Calendar** quarters
- **Degree** certificates, diplomas, and associate
- **Suburban** 212-acre campus with easy access to Portland
- **Coed,** 8,771 undergraduate students, 36% full-time, 56% women, 44% men

Undergraduates 3,178 full-time, 5,593 part-time. Students come from 16 states and territories, 6 other countries.

Freshmen *Admission:* 2,441 enrolled.

Faculty *Total:* 638, 27% full-time. *Student/faculty ratio:* 25:1.

Majors Accounting; architectural engineering technology; auto mechanic/technician; aviation technology; broadcast journalism; business administration; business education; business marketing and marketing management; civil engineering technology; computer engineering technology; cosmetology; dental hygiene; early childhood education; electrical/electronic engineering technology; environmental health; fire science; fish/game management; food sciences; forest harvesting production technology; graphic design/commercial art/illustration; horticulture science; hospitality management; industrial technology; journalism; legal administrative assistant; liberal arts and sciences/liberal studies; mechanical engineering technology; medical administrative assistant; medical assistant; mental health/rehabilitation; mortuary science; nursing; occupational therapy; operating room technician; ornamental horticulture; physical therapy; radio/television broadcasting; respiratory therapy; secretarial science; travel/tourism management.

Academic Programs *Special study options:* academic remediation for entering students, adult/continuing education programs, advanced placement credit, cooperative education, English as a second language, internships, part-time degree program, services for LD students, study abroad, summer session for credit.

Library Library Resource Center with 64,000 titles, 412 serial subscriptions.

Computers on Campus 100 computers available on campus for general student use. Internet access, at least one staffed computer lab available.

Student Life *Housing:* college housing not available. *Activities and Organizations:* drama/theater group, student-run newspaper, radio and television station, choral group. *Campus security:* 24-hour emergency response devices and patrols, student patrols, late-night transport/escort service. *Student Services:* health clinic, personal/psychological counseling, women's center.

Athletics *Intercollegiate sports:* baseball M, basketball M(s)/W(s), cross-country running M(s)/W(s), softball W, track and field M(s)/W(s), volleyball W(s). *Intramural sports:* archery M/W, badminton M, basketball M/W, bowling M/W, cross-country running M/W, fencing M/W, field hockey M/W, football M/W, golf M, racquetball M/W, skiing (cross-country) M/W, skiing (downhill) M/W, soccer M/W, swimming M/W, tennis M/W, track and field M/W, volleyball M/W.

Standardized Tests *Required for some:* CPT.

Costs (2002–03) *Tuition:* area resident $582 full-time, $49 per credit part-time; nonresident $1890 full-time, $158 per credit part-time.

Financial Aid In 2001, 202 Federal Work-Study jobs (averaging $1240).

Applying *Options:* early admission, deferred entrance. *Required for some:* high school transcript, minimum 2.0 GPA. *Application deadline:* rolling (freshmen), rolling (transfers). *Notification:* continuous (freshmen).

Admissions Contact Dr. Craig Kolins, Associate Vice President of Enrollment Services, Mt. Hood Community College, 26000 Southeast Stark Street, Gresham, OR 97030-3300. *Phone:* 503-491-7265.

PIONEER PACIFIC COLLEGE
Wilsonville, Oregon

- **Proprietary** 2-year, founded 1981
- **Calendar** semesters
- **Degree** diplomas and associate

Pioneer Pacific College (continued)
■ **Suburban** campus with easy access to Portland
■ **Coed,** 368 undergraduate students, 100% full-time, 55% women, 45% men

Undergraduates 368 full-time. Students come from 2 states and territories, 4% are from out of state, 3% African American, 5% Asian American or Pacific Islander, 5% Hispanic American, 3% Native American, 28% transferred in.
Freshmen *Admission:* 162 applied, 162 admitted, 46 enrolled.
Faculty *Total:* 29, 79% full-time. *Student/faculty ratio:* 15:1.
Majors Computer systems networking/telecommunications; information sciences/systems; law enforcement/police science; medical assistant; paralegal/legal assistant; Web/multimedia management/webmaster.
Academic Programs *Special study options:* accelerated degree program.
Library 2,000 titles.
Computers on Campus 150 computers available on campus for general student use. Internet access available.
Student Life *Housing:* college housing not available. *Activities and Organizations:* Phi Beta Lambda.
Costs (2002–03) *One-time required fee:* $150. *Tuition:* $6480 full-time, $144 per credit hour part-time. Full-time tuition and fees vary according to program. No tuition increase for student's term of enrollment. *Required fees:* $150 full-time. *Payment plans:* installment, deferred payment. *Waivers:* employees or children of employees.
Applying *Application fee:* $50. *Required:* high school transcript, interview. *Application deadline:* rolling (freshmen).
Admissions Contact Mr. John Christensen, Admissions Officer, Pioneer Pacific College, 27501 Southwest Parkway Avenue, Wilsonville, OR 97070. *Phone:* 503-682-3903. *Fax:* 503-682-1514. *E-mail:* inquiries@pioneerpacificcollege.com.

PORTLAND COMMUNITY COLLEGE
Portland, Oregon

■ **State and locally supported** 2-year, founded 1961
■ **Calendar** quarters
■ **Degree** certificates, diplomas, and associate
■ **Urban** 400-acre campus
■ **Coed,** 46,295 undergraduate students

Portland Community College provides lower-division college transfer courses, 2-year associate degree programs, career training, and adult education courses. Low tuition, an extensive class schedule, and convenient locations combined with high-quality instruction are among its trademarks. For admissions information, contact 503-977-4519 or visit the Web site (http://www.pcc.edu).

Undergraduates 7% African American, 15% Asian American or Pacific Islander, 18% Hispanic American, 2% Native American, 1% international.
Freshmen *Admission:* 13,022 applied, 13,022 admitted.
Faculty *Total:* 1,385, 27% full-time. *Student/faculty ratio:* 25:1.
Majors Accounting; auto mechanic/technician; aviation/airway science; aviation technology; biological/physical sciences; biological technology; business administration; business marketing and marketing management; carpentry; child care/development; civil engineering technology; computer engineering technology; computer programming; construction technology; criminal justice/law enforcement administration; dental hygiene; dietetics; drafting; educational media design; electrical/electronic engineering technology; elementary education; engineering; engineering technology; family/consumer studies; fire science; gerontology; graphic design/commercial art/illustration; home economics; industrial design; industrial radiologic technology; information sciences/systems; landscape architecture; laser/optical technology; legal administrative assistant; liberal arts and sciences/liberal studies; library science; machine technology; mechanical engineering technology; medical administrative assistant; medical assistant; medical laboratory technician; medical laboratory technology; medical records administration; nursing; optometric/ophthalmic laboratory technician; paralegal/legal assistant; physical sciences; pre-engineering; real estate; secretarial science; sign language interpretation; trade/industrial education; welding technology.
Academic Programs *Special study options:* academic remediation for entering students, adult/continuing education programs, advanced placement credit, cooperative education, distance learning, double majors, English as a second language, external degree program, independent study, internships, off-campus study, part-time degree program, services for LD students, study abroad, summer session for credit.
Library Main Library plus 4 others with 83,355 titles, 815 serial subscriptions, an OPAC, a Web page.
Computers on Campus 410 computers available on campus for general student use. A campuswide network can be accessed from off campus. Internet access, online (class) registration, at least one staffed computer lab available.
Student Life *Housing:* college housing not available. *Activities and Organizations:* drama/theater group, student-run newspaper, television station, choral group. *Campus security:* 24-hour emergency response devices and patrols, late-night transport/escort service. *Student Services:* personal/psychological counseling, women's center.
Athletics Member NJCAA. *Intercollegiate sports:* basketball M(s)/W(s). *Intramural sports:* archery M/W, badminton M/W, baseball M, basketball M/W, bowling M/W, cross-country running M/W, racquetball M/W, skiing (cross-country) M/W, skiing (downhill) M/W, soccer M/W, softball W, swimming M/W, table tennis M/W, track and field M/W, volleyball M/W, weight lifting M/W, wrestling M.
Costs (2001–02) *Tuition:* state resident $1958 full-time, $40 per credit hour part-time; nonresident $7088 full-time, $155 per credit hour part-time. *Required fees:* $4 per credit hour. *Payment plan:* deferred payment. *Waivers:* senior citizens and employees or children of employees.
Applying *Application deadline:* rolling (freshmen).
Admissions Contact Mr. Dennis Bailey-Fougnier, Coordinator of Admissions, Portland Community College, PO Box 19000. *Phone:* 503-977-4519. *Fax:* 503-977-4740. *E-mail:* admissions@pcc.edu.

ROGUE COMMUNITY COLLEGE
Grants Pass, Oregon

■ **State and locally supported** 2-year, founded 1970
■ **Calendar** quarters
■ **Degree** certificates, diplomas, and associate
■ **Rural** 90-acre campus
■ **Coed,** 4,496 undergraduate students, 38% full-time, 58% women, 42% men

Undergraduates 1,718 full-time, 2,778 part-time. Students come from 3 states and territories.
Freshmen *Admission:* 524 enrolled.
Faculty *Total:* 505, 20% full-time. *Student/faculty ratio:* 19:1.
Majors Accounting; alcohol/drug abuse counseling; art history; auto mechanic/technician; biological/physical sciences; business administration; child care/development; computer science; criminal justice/law enforcement administration; electrical/electronic engineering technology; fire science; heavy equipment maintenance; humanities; human services; industrial technology; liberal arts and sciences/liberal studies; mathematics; nursing; respiratory therapy; secretarial science; social sciences; welding technology.
Academic Programs *Special study options:* academic remediation for entering students, adult/continuing education programs, advanced placement credit, cooperative education, English as a second language, internships, part-time degree program, services for LD students, summer session for credit.
Library Rogue Community College Library with 33,000 titles, 275 serial subscriptions, an OPAC.
Computers on Campus 96 computers available on campus for general student use. Internet access, at least one staffed computer lab available.
Student Life *Housing:* college housing not available. *Activities and Organizations:* drama/theater group, student-run newspaper, choral group. *Campus security:* 24-hour patrols, late-night transport/escort service. *Student Services:* personal/psychological counseling, women's center.
Athletics *Intramural sports:* badminton M/W, basketball M/W, skiing (cross-country) M/W, tennis M/W, volleyball M/W.
Standardized Tests *Required:* ACT ASSET.
Costs (2002–03) *Tuition:* area resident $1764 full-time, $49 per credit hour part-time; state resident $1764 full-time, $49 per credit hour part-time; nonresident $2124 full-time, $59 per credit hour part-time. *Required fees:* $637 full-time, $2 per credit hour.
Applying *Options:* early admission. *Application deadline:* rolling (freshmen), rolling (transfers).
Admissions Contact Claudia Sullivan, Director of Admissions, Rogue Community College, 3345 Redwood Highway, Grants Pass, OR 97527-9298. *Phone:* 541-956-7176 Ext. 301. *E-mail:* ebunton@rogue.cc.or.us.

SOUTHWESTERN OREGON COMMUNITY COLLEGE
Coos Bay, Oregon

Admissions Contact Ms. Joanna F. Blount, Registrar and Associate Dean of Student Services, Southwestern Oregon Community College, 1988 Newmark Avenue, Coos Bay, OR 97420-2912. *Phone:* 541-888-7339.

TREASURE VALLEY COMMUNITY COLLEGE
Ontario, Oregon

The College is located in the western Treasure Valley city of Ontario, Oregon, just 55 miles west of Boise, the capital and largest city in Idaho. Mountains surround the city on all sides and the area provides an abundance of outdoor activities, such as hiking, skiing, and boating. Small classes, low cost, and high-quality university transfer and vocational programs are highlights. On-campus housing is available and international students are welcome.

Admissions Contact Mr. Ron Kulm, Director of Admissions and Student Services, Treasure Valley Community College, 650 College Boulevard, Ontario, OR 97914-3423. *Phone:* 541-889-6493 Ext. 232.

UMPQUA COMMUNITY COLLEGE
Roseburg, Oregon

- **State and locally supported** 2-year, founded 1964
- **Calendar** quarters
- **Degree** certificates and associate
- **Rural** 100-acre campus
- **Endowment** $2.9 million
- **Coed,** 2,155 undergraduate students, 43% full-time, 56% women, 44% men

Undergraduates Students come from 5 states and territories, 12 other countries, 1% are from out of state.

Majors Accounting; agricultural sciences; anthropology; art; art education; art history; auto mechanic/technician; behavioral sciences; biological/physical sciences; biology; business administration; business marketing and marketing management; chemistry; child care/development; civil engineering technology; computer engineering technology; computer science; cosmetology; criminal justice/law enforcement administration; desktop publishing equipment operation; early childhood education; economics; education; electrical/electronic engineering technology; elementary education; emergency medical technology; engineering; English; fire science; forestry; health education; history; humanities; human resources management; journalism; legal administrative assistant; liberal arts and sciences/liberal studies; mathematics; medical administrative assistant; music; music teacher education; natural sciences; nursing; physical education; physical sciences; political science; pre-engineering; psychology; secretarial science; social sciences; social work; sociology; theater arts/drama.

Academic Programs *Special study options:* academic remediation for entering students, accelerated degree program, adult/continuing education programs, advanced placement credit, cooperative education, distance learning, English as a second language, honors programs, part-time degree program, services for LD students, student-designed majors, summer session for credit.

Library Umpqua Community College Library with 41,000 titles, 350 serial subscriptions, an OPAC, a Web page.

Computers on Campus 300 computers available on campus for general student use. Internet access, at least one staffed computer lab available.

Student Life *Housing:* college housing not available. *Activities and Organizations:* drama/theater group, student-run newspaper, choral group, Phi Theta Kappa, computer club, Phi Beta Lambda, nursing club, Umpqua Accounting Associates. *Student Services:* personal/psychological counseling.

Athletics *Intercollegiate sports:* basketball M(s)/W(s), soccer M(s), volleyball W(s). *Intramural sports:* basketball M/W, soccer M.

Costs (2001–02) *Tuition:* state resident $2016 full-time, $42 per credit part-time; nonresident $5280 full-time, $110 per credit part-time. *Payment plan:* deferred payment. *Waivers:* senior citizens and employees or children of employees.

Financial Aid In 2001, 100 Federal Work-Study jobs (averaging $1800).

Applying *Options:* early admission, deferred entrance. *Recommended:* high school transcript. *Application deadline:* rolling (freshmen), rolling (transfers).

Admissions Contact Dr. Larry Shipley, Director of Admissions and Records, Umpqua Community College, PO Box 967, Roseburg, OR 97470-0226. *Phone:* 541-440-4616. *Fax:* 541-440-4612. *E-mail:* shiplel@umpqua.cc.or.us.

WESTERN BUSINESS COLLEGE
Portland, Oregon

Admissions Contact 425 Southwest Washington, Portland, OR 97204.

PENNSYLVANIA

ACADEMY OF MEDICAL ARTS AND BUSINESS
Harrisburg, Pennsylvania

- **Proprietary** 2-year, founded 1980
- **Calendar** 15 week terms
- **Degree** diplomas and associate
- **Suburban** 8-acre campus
- **Coed, primarily women,** 197 undergraduate students, 100% full-time, 86% women, 14% men

Undergraduates Students come from 1 other state, 19% African American, 0.6% Asian American or Pacific Islander, 6% Hispanic American. *Retention:* 74% of 2001 full-time freshmen returned.

Faculty *Total:* 21, 33% full-time, 29% with terminal degrees. *Student/faculty ratio:* 20:1.

Majors Child care provider; child care services management; computer programming related; computer programming (specific applications); computer programming, vendor/product certification; data entry/microcomputer applications; data entry/microcomputer applications related; data processing technology; dental assistant; medical administrative assistant; medical assistant; medical office management; paralegal/legal assistant; word processing.

Academic Programs *Special study options:* advanced placement credit, internships.

Library Resource Center with 1,620 titles, 30 serial subscriptions, 30 audiovisual materials, an OPAC.

Computers on Campus 75 computers available on campus for general student use. Internet access, at least one staffed computer lab available.

Student Life *Housing:* college housing not available. *Activities and Organizations:* student-run newspaper.

Costs (2001–02) *Tuition:* $7600 full-time. Full-time tuition and fees vary according to student level. *Required fees:* $750 full-time. *Payment plan:* installment.

Applying *Options:* common application. *Application fee:* $150. *Required:* high school transcript, interview. *Application deadline:* rolling (freshmen), rolling (transfers).

Admissions Contact Mr. Gary Kay, Director of Admissions, Academy of Medical Arts and Business, 2301 Academy Drive, Harrisburg, PA 17112. *Phone:* 717-545-4747. *Toll-free phone:* 800-400-3322. *Fax:* 717-901-9090. *E-mail:* info@acadcampus.com.

ALLENTOWN BUSINESS SCHOOL
Allentown, Pennsylvania

- **Proprietary** 2-year, founded 1869, part of Career Education Corporation
- **Calendar** quarters
- **Degree** diplomas and associate
- **Urban** campus with easy access to Philadelphia
- **Coed,** 1,230 undergraduate students

Undergraduates Students come from 2 states and territories, 1% are from out of state.

Freshmen *Admission:* 453 applied, 453 admitted. *Average high school GPA:* 2.00.

Faculty *Total:* 65, 54% full-time. *Student/faculty ratio:* 26:1.

Majors Accounting; business administration; business marketing and marketing management; graphic design/commercial art/illustration; information sciences/systems; legal administrative assistant; medical administrative assistant; secretarial science; travel/tourism management.

Academic Programs *Special study options:* academic remediation for entering students, adult/continuing education programs, advanced placement credit, cooperative education, independent study, internships, services for LD students.

Library Main Library plus 1 other.

Computers on Campus 100 computers available on campus for general student use. Internet access, at least one staffed computer lab available.

Allentown Business School (continued)
Student Life *Housing:* college housing not available. *Activities and Organizations:* Student Government, Travel Club. *Campus security:* evening security guard.
Costs (2001–02) *Tuition:* $18,600 per degree program part-time. Full-time tuition and fees vary according to course load and program. Part-time tuition and fees vary according to course load. No tuition increase for student's term of enrollment. *Payment plans:* installment, deferred payment. *Waivers:* employees or children of employees.
Financial Aid In 2001, 15 Federal Work-Study jobs (averaging $1500).
Applying *Options:* common application, deferred entrance. *Application fee:* $60. *Required:* high school transcript. *Application deadline:* rolling (freshmen), rolling (transfers). *Notification:* continuous (freshmen).
Admissions Contact Janine Muschlitz, Director of High School Admissions, Allentown Business School, Allentown, PA 18103. *Phone:* 610-791-5100 Ext. 226. *Toll-free phone:* 800-227-9109. *Fax:* 610-791-7810.

ANTONELLI INSTITUTE
Erdenheim, Pennsylvania

- **Proprietary** 2-year, founded 1938
- **Calendar** semesters
- **Degree** associate
- **Suburban** 15-acre campus with easy access to Philadelphia
- **Coed,** 207 undergraduate students, 98% full-time, 63% women, 37% men

Undergraduates 203 full-time, 4 part-time. Students come from 6 states and territories, 21% are from out of state, 5% African American, 0.5% Asian American or Pacific Islander, 4% Hispanic American, 40% live on campus.
Freshmen *Admission:* 213 applied, 149 admitted, 107 enrolled. *Average high school GPA:* 2.60.
Faculty *Total:* 20, 90% full-time. *Student/faculty ratio:* 10:1.
Majors Graphic design/commercial art/illustration; photography.
Academic Programs *Special study options:* adult/continuing education programs, part-time degree program, services for LD students.
Library Antonelli Institute Library with 4,000 titles, 50 audiovisual materials.
Computers on Campus 28 computers available on campus for general student use. At least one staffed computer lab available.
Student Life *Housing Options:* coed. *Campus security:* 24-hour emergency response devices. *Student Services:* personal/psychological counseling.
Costs (2001–02) *Tuition:* $13,600 full-time, $450 per credit part-time. Full-time tuition and fees vary according to class time and program. Part-time tuition and fees vary according to class time and program. *Room only:* $4800. *Payment plan:* installment. *Waivers:* employees or children of employees.
Financial Aid In 2001, 3 Federal Work-Study jobs (averaging $2000).
Applying *Options:* common application, deferred entrance. *Application fee:* $25. *Required:* high school transcript, interview. *Recommended:* 1 letter of recommendation. *Application deadlines:* 9/1 (freshmen), 9/1 (transfers).
Admissions Contact Mr. Anthony Detore, Director of Admissions, Antonelli Institute, 300 Montgomery Avenue, Erdenheim, PA 19038. *Phone:* 215-836-2222. *Toll-free phone:* 800-722-7871. *Fax:* 215-836-2794.

THE ART INSTITUTE OF PHILADELPHIA
Philadelphia, Pennsylvania

- **Proprietary** primarily 2-year, founded 1966, part of The Art Institutes
- **Calendar** quarters
- **Degrees** associate and bachelor's
- **Urban** campus
- **Coed,** 2,807 undergraduate students, 70% full-time, 41% women, 59% men

The Art Institute of Philadelphia is one of the Art Institutes, a system of 24 schools nationwide that provide an important source of design, media arts, fashion, and culinary professionals. The parent company of the Art Institutes, Education Management Corp. (EDMC), is among the largest providers of proprietary postsecondary education in the US, offering bachelor's, associate, and nondegree programs. The company has provided career-oriented education programs for more than 35 years. Its schools have graduated more than 100,000 students.

Undergraduates 1,975 full-time, 832 part-time. Students come from 30 states and territories, 25 other countries, 23% African American, 6% Asian American or Pacific Islander, 7% Hispanic American, 1% Native American, 2% international, 0.4% transferred in, 26% live on campus.
Freshmen *Admission:* 2,065 applied, 1,158 admitted, 778 enrolled. *Average high school GPA:* 2.7. *Test scores:* SAT verbal scores over 500: 54%; SAT math scores over 500: 54%; ACT scores over 18: 3%; SAT verbal scores over 600: 24%; SAT math scores over 600: 24%; ACT scores over 24: 1%; SAT verbal scores over 700: 1%; SAT math scores over 700: 1%.
Faculty *Total:* 230, 33% full-time. *Student/faculty ratio:* 20:1.
Majors Applied art; art; culinary arts; fashion design/illustration; fashion merchandising; film/video and photographic arts related; film/video production; graphic design/commercial art/illustration; industrial design; interior design; multimedia; photography; visual and performing arts related.
Academic Programs *Special study options:* academic remediation for entering students, adult/continuing education programs, advanced placement credit, cooperative education, internships, off-campus study, part-time degree program, services for LD students, summer session for credit.
Library The Art Institute of Philadelphia Library with 19,200 titles, 150 serial subscriptions, 2,000 audiovisual materials, an OPAC.
Computers on Campus 368 computers available on campus for general student use. Internet access, at least one staffed computer lab available.
Student Life *Housing Options:* coed, disabled students. *Activities and Organizations:* student-run newspaper. *Campus security:* controlled dormitory access. *Student Services:* personal/psychological counseling.
Standardized Tests *Recommended:* SAT I or ACT (for placement).
Costs (2001–02) *One-time required fee:* $100. *Tuition:* $14,625 full-time, $325 per credit hour part-time. Full-time tuition and fees vary according to course load and program. Part-time tuition and fees vary according to course load and program. No tuition increase for student's term of enrollment. *Room only:* $7472. Room and board charges vary according to housing facility. *Payment plans:* installment, deferred payment. *Waivers:* employees or children of employees.
Applying *Options:* common application, deferred entrance. *Application fee:* $50. *Required:* essay or personal statement, high school transcript, interview. *Recommended:* minimum 2.0 GPA, letters of recommendation. *Application deadline:* rolling (freshmen), rolling (transfers). *Notification:* continuous (freshmen).
Admissions Contact Mr. Tim Howard, Director of Admissions, The Art Institute of Philadelphia, 1622 Chestnut Street, Philadelphia, PA 19103. *Phone:* 215-567-7080 Ext. 6337. *Toll-free phone:* 800-275-2474. *Fax:* 215-405-6399.

THE ART INSTITUTE OF PITTSBURGH
Pittsburgh, Pennsylvania

- **Proprietary** primarily 2-year, founded 1921, part of The Art Institutes International
- **Calendar** quarters
- **Degrees** diplomas, associate, and bachelor's
- **Urban** campus
- **Coed,** 2,500 undergraduate students

Undergraduates Students come from 42 states and territories, 20 other countries, 40% are from out of state, 29% live on campus.
Freshmen *Admission:* 1,230 applied, 689 admitted. *Average high school GPA:* 2.57. *Test scores:* SAT verbal scores over 500: 49%; SAT math scores over 500: 39%; ACT scores over 18: 50%; SAT verbal scores over 600: 13%; SAT math scores over 600: 8%; SAT verbal scores over 700: 1%.
Faculty *Total:* 120, 71% full-time. *Student/faculty ratio:* 20:1.
Majors Advertising; applied art; architectural environmental design; audio engineering; communication equipment technology; computer graphics; drafting; film/video production; graphic design/commercial art/illustration; industrial arts; industrial design; interior design; metal/jewelry arts; photography; radio/television broadcasting.
Academic Programs *Special study options:* academic remediation for entering students, adult/continuing education programs, advanced placement credit, English as a second language, internships, part-time degree program, services for LD students, student-designed majors, summer session for credit.
Library Student Resource Center with 6,997 titles, 199 serial subscriptions.
Computers on Campus 240 computers available on campus for general student use. Internet access, at least one staffed computer lab available.
Student Life *Housing Options:* coed. *Activities and Organizations:* drama/theater group, student-run newspaper, radio station, American Society of Interior Designers, The Cel Group, AIPIK, Production Monsters, Video Visions. *Campus security:* 24-hour emergency response devices and patrols, controlled dormitory access. *Student Services:* personal/psychological counseling.
Standardized Tests *Required:* ACT ASSET. *Recommended:* SAT I or ACT (for placement).

Costs (2002–03) *Comprehensive fee:* $19,470 includes full-time tuition ($14,670) and room and board ($4800). Full-time tuition and fees vary according to course load. Part-time tuition: $326 per credit. Part-time tuition and fees vary according to course load. *Room and board:* Room and board charges vary according to board plan and housing facility. *Payment plans:* installment, deferred payment. *Waivers:* employees or children of employees.
Applying *Options:* common application, deferred entrance. *Application fee:* $50. *Required:* essay or personal statement, high school transcript, minimum 2.0 GPA. *Recommended:* interview. *Application deadline:* rolling (freshmen), rolling (transfers). *Notification:* continuous (freshmen).
Admissions Contact Ms. Elaine Cook-Bartoli, Director of Admissions, The Art Institute of Pittsburgh, 420 Boulevard of the Allies, Pittsburgh, PA 15219. *Phone:* 412-291-6220. *Toll-free phone:* 800-275-2470. *Fax:* 412-263-6667. *E-mail:* admissions@aii.edu.

Berean Institute
Philadelphia, Pennsylvania

Admissions Contact Mr. John Spruill, Director of Admission, Berean Institute, 1901 West Girard Avenue, Philadelphia, PA 19130-1599. *Phone:* 215-763-4833 Ext. 104.

Berks Technical Institute
Wyomissing, Pennsylvania

- **Proprietary** 2-year, founded 1977, part of ForeFront Education, Inc
- **Calendar** semesters
- **Degree** diplomas and associate
- **Small-town** 8-acre campus
- **Coed,** 526 undergraduate students

Undergraduates Students come from 1 other state, 4% African American, 2% Asian American or Pacific Islander, 9% Hispanic American, 1% Native American.
Freshmen *Admission:* 172 admitted.
Faculty *Total:* 53, 79% full-time.
Majors Computer graphics; computer programming; computer programming related; computer science related; drafting; information technology; medical assistant; system/networking/LAN/WAN management.
Academic Programs *Special study options:* advanced placement credit, part-time degree program.
Library Learning Resource Center with 450 titles, 12 serial subscriptions.
Computers on Campus 8 computers available on campus for general student use. Internet access, online (class) registration, at least one staffed computer lab available.
Student Life *Housing:* college housing not available. *Campus security:* 24-hour emergency response devices.
Costs (2002–03) *Tuition:* $8584 full-time. *Required fees:* $240 full-time.
Applying *Options:* early admission. *Application fee:* $50. *Required:* high school transcript, letters of recommendation, interview.
Admissions Contact Mrs. Jean Vokes, Director of Admissions, Berks Technical Institute, 2205 Ridgewood Road, Wyomissing, PA 19610-1168. *Phone:* 610-372-1722. *Toll-free phone:* 800-284-4672 (in-state); 800-821-4662 (out-of-state).

Bradford School
Pittsburgh, Pennsylvania

Admissions Contact 707 Grant Street, Gulf Tower, Pittsburgh, PA 15219.

Bradley Academy for the Visual Arts
York, Pennsylvania

- **Proprietary** 2-year, founded 1952
- **Calendar** quarters
- **Degree** associate
- **Suburban** 7-acre campus with easy access to Baltimore
- **Coed,** 447 undergraduate students, 87% full-time, 55% women, 45% men

Undergraduates 387 full-time, 60 part-time. Students come from 9 states and territories, 2 other countries, 16% are from out of state, 2% African American, 1% Asian American or Pacific Islander, 3% Hispanic American, 0.4% international, 6% transferred in.
Freshmen *Admission:* 344 applied, 316 admitted, 176 enrolled. *Average high school GPA:* 2.80. *Test scores:* SAT verbal scores over 500: 40%; SAT verbal scores over 600: 8%; SAT verbal scores over 700: 1%.
Faculty *Total:* 48, 31% full-time, 6% with terminal degrees. *Student/faculty ratio:* 15:1.
Majors Advertising; art; clothing/textiles; computer graphics; computer graphics; design/visual communications; electrical/electronic engineering technology; fashion merchandising; graphic design/commercial art/illustration; interior design; interior environments; Web/multimedia management/webmaster; Web page, digital/multimedia and information resources design.
Academic Programs *Special study options:* academic remediation for entering students, adult/continuing education programs, internships, part-time degree program, summer session for credit.
Library Bradley Academy Library with 1,900 titles, 70 serial subscriptions, an OPAC, a Web page.
Computers on Campus 175 computers available on campus for general student use. A campuswide network can be accessed from off campus. Internet access, at least one staffed computer lab available.
Student Life *Activities and Organizations:* student-run newspaper, ASID, Delta Epsilon Chi, AIGA. *Student Services:* personal/psychological counseling.
Standardized Tests *Recommended:* SAT I or ACT (for admission).
Costs (2002–03) *Tuition:* $12,780 full-time, $355 per credit part-time. No tuition increase for student's term of enrollment. *Payment plans:* tuition prepayment, installment. *Waivers:* employees or children of employees.
Financial Aid In 2001, 21 Federal Work-Study jobs (averaging $600).
Applying *Options:* deferred entrance. *Application fee:* $25. *Required:* essay or personal statement, high school transcript, 2 letters of recommendation, interview. *Required for some:* minimum 2.5 GPA, portfolio. *Recommended:* minimum 2.5 GPA. *Application deadline:* rolling (freshmen), rolling (transfers).
Admissions Contact Gene Herman, Director of Admissions, Bradley Academy for the Visual Arts, 1409 Williams Road, York, PA 17402. *Phone:* 717-755-2711. *Toll-free phone:* 800-864-7725. *Fax:* 717-840-1951. *E-mail:* info@bradleyacademy.net.

Bucks County Community College
Newtown, Pennsylvania

- **County-supported** 2-year, founded 1964
- **Calendar** semesters
- **Degree** certificates and associate
- **Small-town** 200-acre campus with easy access to Philadelphia
- **Coed,** 8,806 undergraduate students, 36% full-time, 58% women, 42% men

Undergraduates 3,190 full-time, 5,616 part-time. Students come from 2 states and territories, 38 other countries, 1% are from out of state, 3% African American, 3% Asian American or Pacific Islander, 2% Hispanic American, 0.2% Native American, 0.4% international, 4% transferred in. *Retention:* 46% of 2001 full-time freshmen returned.
Freshmen *Admission:* 3,259 applied, 3,226 admitted.
Faculty *Total:* 577, 25% full-time. *Student/faculty ratio:* 19:1.
Majors Accounting; American studies; architectural history; art; banking; biology; business administration; business marketing and marketing management; chemistry; computer engineering technology; computer/information sciences; computer/information technology services administration and management related; computer programming; computer programming related; computer programming (specific applications); computer science; computer science related; corrections; criminal justice/law enforcement administration; culinary arts; data processing technology; early childhood education; education; electrical/electronic engineering technology; engineering; enterprise management; environmental science; film/video production; graphic design/commercial art/illustration; health education; health science; hospitality management; hotel and restaurant management; humanities; information sciences/systems; information technology; journalism; law enforcement/police science; liberal arts and sciences/liberal studies; mass communications; mathematics; medical assistant; music; nursing; paralegal/legal assistant; physical education; psychology; radio/television broadcasting; retail management; secretarial science; social sciences; social work; sport/fitness administration; teacher assistant/aide; theater arts/drama; visual/performing arts; woodworking.
Academic Programs *Special study options:* academic remediation for entering students, adult/continuing education programs, advanced placement credit, cooperative education, distance learning, English as a second language, external degree program, independent study, internships, part-time degree program, services for LD students, student-designed majors, summer session for credit.
Library Bucks County Community College Library with 185,377 titles, 491 serial subscriptions, 5,546 audiovisual materials, an OPAC, a Web page.

Bucks County Community College (continued)

Computers on Campus 800 computers available on campus for general student use. A campuswide network can be accessed from off campus that provide access to e-mail. Internet access, online (class) registration, at least one staffed computer lab available.

Student Life *Housing:* college housing not available. *Activities and Organizations:* drama/theater group, student-run newspaper, radio station, choral group, Phi Theta Kappa, Students in Free Enterprise, student council, The Centurion (Student newspaper). *Campus security:* 24-hour emergency response devices and patrols, late-night transport/escort service. *Student Services:* personal/psychological counseling.

Athletics Member NJCAA. *Intercollegiate sports:* baseball M, basketball M/W, equestrian sports M/W, golf M/W, soccer M/W, tennis M/W, volleyball W. *Intramural sports:* basketball M/W, bowling M/W, skiing (cross-country) M/W, skiing (downhill) M/W, softball M/W, volleyball M/W.

Costs (2001–02) *Tuition:* area resident $2280 full-time, $76 per credit part-time; state resident $4860 full-time, $152 per credit part-time; nonresident $7440 full-time, $228 per credit part-time. Full-time tuition and fees vary according to course load and reciprocity agreements. Part-time tuition and fees vary according to course load and reciprocity agreements. *Required fees:* $229 full-time, $64 per year part-time. *Payment plan:* installment. *Waivers:* senior citizens and employees or children of employees.

Financial Aid In 2001, 150 Federal Work-Study jobs (averaging $3000). 60 State and other part-time jobs (averaging $1000).

Applying *Options:* electronic application, early admission. *Application fee:* $30. *Required for some:* essay or personal statement, high school transcript, interview. *Application deadlines:* 5/1 (freshmen), 5/1 (transfers). *Notification:* 8/25 (freshmen).

Admissions Contact Mrs. Amy Gontkof, Assistant Director of Admissions, Bucks County Community College, 275 Swamp Road, Newtown, PA 18940. *Phone:* 215-968-8119 Ext. 8119. *Fax:* 215-968-8110. *E-mail:* gleasonj@bucks.edu.

BUSINESS INSTITUTE OF PENNSYLVANIA
Sharon, Pennsylvania

- **Proprietary** 2-year, founded 1926
- **Calendar** quarters
- **Degree** certificates, diplomas, and associate
- **Small-town** 2-acre campus
- **Coed,** 146 undergraduate students, 100% full-time, 79% women, 21% men
- 57% of applicants were admitted

Freshmen *Admission:* 96 applied, 55 admitted.

Faculty *Total:* 13, 69% full-time, 77% with terminal degrees. *Student/faculty ratio:* 13:1.

Majors Business administration; computer programming; data processing; executive assistant; legal administrative assistant; medical administrative assistant; medical assistant; medical records administration; secretarial science.

Student Life *Housing:* college housing not available.

Standardized Tests *Required:* ACT (for admission).

Costs (2002–03) *Tuition:* $6300 full-time, $175 per credit part-time. *Required fees:* $475 full-time.

Applying *Required:* high school transcript, interview.

Admissions Contact Mr. Richard P. McMahon, President, Business Institute of Pennsylvania, 335 Boyd Drive, Sharon, PA 16146. *Phone:* 724-983-0700. *Toll-free phone:* 800-289-2069. *Fax:* 724-983-8355.

BUTLER COUNTY COMMUNITY COLLEGE
Butler, Pennsylvania

- **County-supported** 2-year, founded 1965
- **Calendar** semesters
- **Degree** certificates, diplomas, and associate
- **Rural** 300-acre campus with easy access to Pittsburgh
- **Coed,** 3,183 undergraduate students

Undergraduates Students come from 8 states and territories, 1 other country, 1% are from out of state, 1% African American, 0.3% Asian American or Pacific Islander, 0.4% Hispanic American, 0.1% Native American.

Freshmen *Admission:* 1,805 applied, 1,805 admitted.

Faculty *Total:* 198, 34% full-time. *Student/faculty ratio:* 19:1.

Majors Accounting; architectural drafting; architectural engineering technology; biology; business administration; business marketing and marketing management; civil engineering technology; computer/information sciences; computer programming; criminology; dietetics; drafting; early childhood education; education; electrical/electronic engineering technology; elementary education; emergency medical technology; English; executive assistant; exercise sciences; food services technology; general office/clerical; general studies; graphic design/commercial art/illustration; hospitality management; humanities; instrumentation technology; law enforcement/police science; legal administrative assistant; liberal arts and sciences/liberal studies; machine technology; mass communications; mathematics; mechanical design technology; mechanical drafting; medical administrative assistant; medical assistant; nursing; physical education; physical sciences; physical therapy assistant; pre-engineering; psychology; quality control technology; recreational therapy; recreation/leisure facilities management; secretarial science; sport/fitness administration; travel/tourism management.

Academic Programs *Special study options:* academic remediation for entering students, adult/continuing education programs, advanced placement credit, cooperative education, English as a second language, internships, part-time degree program, services for LD students, summer session for credit.

Library John A. Beck, Jr. Library with 70,000 titles, 305 serial subscriptions.

Computers on Campus 350 computers available on campus for general student use. Internet access, at least one staffed computer lab available.

Student Life *Housing:* college housing not available. *Activities and Organizations:* drama/theater group, student-run newspaper, choral group, student government, Ski Club, Drama Club, Outdoor Recreation Club. *Campus security:* 24-hour emergency response devices, late-night transport/escort service. *Student Services:* personal/psychological counseling.

Athletics Member NJCAA. *Intercollegiate sports:* baseball M, basketball M, golf M/W, softball W, volleyball W. *Intramural sports:* badminton M/W, basketball M/W, racquetball M/W, soccer M/W, softball M, table tennis M/W, tennis M/W, volleyball M/W, weight lifting M/W.

Standardized Tests *Required:* ACT ASSET.

Costs (2002–03) *Tuition:* area resident $1680 full-time, $61 per credit part-time; state resident $3144 full-time, $122 per credit part-time; nonresident $4604 full-time, $183 per credit part-time. *Required fees:* $216 full-time, $9 per credit. *Waivers:* senior citizens and employees or children of employees.

Financial Aid In 2001, 65 Federal Work-Study jobs (averaging $1545).

Applying *Options:* common application, early admission, deferred entrance. *Application fee:* $15. *Application deadlines:* 8/15 (freshmen), 8/15 (transfers). *Notification:* continuous until 8/15 (freshmen).

Admissions Contact Mr. William L. Miller, Director of Admissions, Butler County Community College, College Drive, PO Box 1203, Butler, PA 16003-1203. *Phone:* 724-287-8711 Ext. 344. *Toll-free phone:* 888-826-2829. *Fax:* 724-287-4961.

CAMBRIA COUNTY AREA COMMUNITY COLLEGE
Johnstown, Pennsylvania

- **State and locally supported** 2-year
- **Degree** certificates, diplomas, and associate
- **Coed,** 1,208 undergraduate students

Freshmen *Admission:* 415 applied, 415 admitted.

Faculty *Total:* 140, 14% full-time. *Student/faculty ratio:* 14:1.

Majors Accounting; banking; computer/information sciences; computer/information technology services administration and management related; computer programming; computer programming related; computer programming (specific applications); computer/technical support; construction technology; court reporting; electrical/electronic engineering technology; environmental technology; geography; health services administration; heating/air conditioning/refrigeration technology; hospitality management; human services; industrial technology; liberal arts and sciences/liberal studies; retail management; system administration; system/networking/LAN/WAN management; Web/multimedia management/webmaster.

Academic Programs *Special study options:* academic remediation for entering students, adult/continuing education programs, advanced placement credit, cooperative education, distance learning, honors programs, independent study, internships, part-time degree program, services for LD students.

Library Cambria County Area Community College Main Library plus 3 others with an OPAC.

Computers on Campus 100 computers available on campus for general student use. Internet access, at least one staffed computer lab available.

Costs (2001–02) *Tuition:* area resident $1800 full-time, $51 per credit part-time; state resident $3600 full-time, $102 per credit part-time; nonresident $204 per credit part-time. *Required fees:* $15 full-time, $10 per credit, $10 per term part-time. *Payment plan:* installment.
Financial Aid In 2001, 25 Federal Work-Study jobs (averaging $2500).
Applying *Options:* common application. *Application fee:* $20. *Recommended:* high school transcript, interview. *Application deadline:* 8/20 (freshmen).
Admissions Contact Mr. Jeff Maul, Admissions Officer, Cambria County Area Community College, PO Box 68, Johnstown, PA 15907. *Phone:* 814-255-8805. *Fax:* 814-262-3220. *E-mail:* jmaul@mail.ccacc.cc.pa.us.

CAMBRIA-ROWE BUSINESS COLLEGE
Johnstown, Pennsylvania

- **Proprietary** 2-year, founded 1891
- **Calendar** quarters
- **Degree** diplomas and associate
- **Small-town** campus with easy access to Pittsburgh
- **Coed, primarily women,** 219 undergraduate students, 100% full-time, 90% women, 10% men

Undergraduates 219 full-time. Students come from 1 other state, 1% African American, 5% transferred in.
Freshmen *Admission:* 122 enrolled.
Faculty *Total:* 11, 100% full-time. *Student/faculty ratio:* 20:1.
Majors Accounting; business administration; legal administrative assistant; medical administrative assistant; secretarial science.
Academic Programs *Special study options:* accelerated degree program, adult/continuing education programs, advanced placement credit, part-time degree program, summer session for credit.
Computers on Campus 105 computers available on campus for general student use.
Student Life *Housing:* college housing not available.
Costs (2002–03) *One-time required fee:* $25. *Tuition:* $6000 full-time, $175 per credit part-time. *Required fees:* $600 full-time. *Payment plan:* installment.
Financial Aid *Financial aid deadline:* 8/1.
Applying *Options:* common application, electronic application, early admission. *Application fee:* $15. *Required:* high school transcript. *Recommended:* minimum 2.0 GPA, interview. *Application deadline:* rolling (freshmen). *Notification:* continuous (freshmen).
Admissions Contact Ms. Amanda C. Swincinski, Director of Admissions, Cambria-Rowe Business College, 221 Central Avenue, Johnstown, PA 15902-2494. *Phone:* 814-536-5168. *Fax:* 814-536-5160. *E-mail:* admissions@crbc.net.

CENTRAL PENNSYLVANIA COLLEGE
Summerdale, Pennsylvania

- **Proprietary** primarily 2-year, founded 1922
- **Calendar** quarters
- **Degrees** associate and bachelor's
- **Small-town** 30-acre campus
- **Coed,** 604 undergraduate students, 84% full-time, 67% women, 33% men

Central Penn is a private, coeducational institution offering students associate degrees in the business, communications, legal, medical, and information technology fields. The College also offers a bachelor's degree in business administration, featuring concentrations in e-business, finance, management, and marketing. Central Penn focuses on a fast-track career education that provides students with the experience employers seek through hands-on learning and internships.

Undergraduates 506 full-time, 98 part-time. Students come from 7 states and territories, 1% are from out of state, 5% African American, 2% Asian American or Pacific Islander, 2% Hispanic American, 1% Native American, 6% transferred in, 51% live on campus.
Freshmen *Admission:* 696 applied, 235 admitted, 188 enrolled.
Faculty *Total:* 58, 43% full-time, 14% with terminal degrees. *Student/faculty ratio:* 14:1.
Majors Accounting; accounting related; business administration; business marketing and marketing management; child care/development; computer programming related; criminal justice/law enforcement administration; entrepreneurship; executive assistant; finance; hotel and restaurant management; information sciences/systems; legal administrative assistant; management science; mass communications; medical administrative assistant; medical assistant; optometric/ophthalmic laboratory technician; paralegal/legal assistant; physical therapy assistant; retail management; travel/tourism management; Web/multimedia management/webmaster.
Academic Programs *Special study options:* academic remediation for entering students, advanced placement credit, double majors, independent study, internships, part-time degree program, summer session for credit.
Library Learning Resource Center with 6,122 titles, 94 serial subscriptions, 1,404 audiovisual materials, an OPAC.
Computers on Campus 120 computers available on campus for general student use. Internet access, at least one staffed computer lab available.
Student Life *Housing Options:* coed. *Activities and Organizations:* student-run newspaper, choral group, Campus Christian Fellowship, College Council, Student Ambassadors, Phi Beta Lambda, Travel Club. *Campus security:* 24-hour emergency response devices and patrols. *Student Services:* personal/psychological counseling.
Athletics *Intercollegiate sports:* basketball M, cross-country running M/W, golf M/W, volleyball W. *Intramural sports:* volleyball M/W.
Costs (2002–03) *One-time required fee:* $75. *Tuition:* $9330 full-time, $249 per credit part-time. Full-time tuition and fees vary according to program. Part-time tuition and fees vary according to course load and program. *Required fees:* $525 full-time, $175 per term part-time. *Room only:* $4550. Room and board charges vary according to housing facility. *Payment plan:* deferred payment. *Waivers:* employees or children of employees.
Financial Aid In 2001, 50 Federal Work-Study jobs (averaging $500).
Applying *Options:* electronic application. *Required:* high school transcript, interview. *Required for some:* minimum 2.0 GPA. *Application deadlines:* 9/20 (freshmen), 9/20 (transfers). *Notification:* continuous (freshmen).
Admissions Contact Jennifer Verhagen, Director of Admissions, Central Pennsylvania College, Central Pennsylvania College, Summerdale, PA 17093. *Phone:* 717-728-2213. *Toll-free phone:* 800-759-2727. *Fax:* 717-732-5254.

CHI INSTITUTE
Southampton, Pennsylvania

- **Proprietary** 2-year, founded 1981, part of Quest Education
- **Calendar** quarters
- **Degree** certificates, diplomas, and associate
- **Suburban** 6-acre campus with easy access to Philadelphia
- **Coed,** 700 undergraduate students, 57% full-time, 36% women, 64% men

Undergraduates Students come from 3 states and territories, 2 other countries, 22% are from out of state, 8% African American, 3% Asian American or Pacific Islander, 7% Hispanic American, 0.8% international.
Freshmen *Admission:* 650 applied, 560 admitted. *Average high school GPA:* 2.5.
Faculty *Total:* 65, 69% full-time. *Student/faculty ratio:* 20:1.
Majors Business computer facilities operation; business computer programming; computer engineering technology; computer graphics; computer programming; computer systems networking/telecommunications; computer typography/composition; electrical/electronic engineering technology; graphic design/commercial art/illustration; heating/air conditioning/refrigeration; medical administrative assistant; medical assistant; medical records administration; medical technology; system administration; telecommunications.
Academic Programs *Special study options:* academic remediation for entering students, adult/continuing education programs.
Library 2,500 titles, 25 serial subscriptions.
Computers on Campus 70 computers available on campus for general student use.
Student Life *Housing:* college housing not available. *Activities and Organizations:* student-run newspaper. *Student Services:* personal/psychological counseling.
Costs (2001–02) *Tuition:* $10,500 full-time, $21,000 per degree program part-time. Full-time tuition and fees vary according to program. No tuition increase for student's term of enrollment. *Required fees:* $100 full-time. *Payment plans:* tuition prepayment, installment. *Waivers:* employees or children of employees.
Financial Aid In 2001, 30 Federal Work-Study jobs (averaging $2050).
Applying *Options:* common application, deferred entrance. *Required:* high school transcript, interview. *Application deadline:* rolling (freshmen), rolling (transfers).
Admissions Contact Mr. Michael T. Sante, Director of Admissions, CHI Institute, 520 Street Road, Southampton, PA 18966. *Phone:* 215-357-5100. *Toll-free phone:* 800-336-7696.

CHI Institute, RETS Campus
Broomall, Pennsylvania

- **Proprietary** 2-year, founded 1958
- **Calendar** quarters
- **Degree** diplomas and associate
- **Small-town** 10-acre campus with easy access to Philadelphia
- **Coed**

Applying *Options:* deferred entrance. *Application fee:* $100. *Required:* high school transcript.

Admissions Contact Mr. Stuart Kahn, Director of Admissions, CHI Institute, RETS Campus, 1991 Lawrence Road, Suite 42, Broomall, PA 19008. *Phone:* 610-353-7630.

Churchman Business School
Easton, Pennsylvania

- **Proprietary** 2-year, founded 1911
- **Calendar** trimesters
- **Degree** diplomas and associate
- **Small-town** campus with easy access to Allentown and Bethlehem
- **Coed,** 100 undergraduate students

Undergraduates Students come from 2 states and territories.

Freshmen *Admission:* 61 applied, 61 admitted.

Faculty *Total:* 6.

Majors Accounting; business administration; legal administrative assistant; medical administrative assistant; secretarial science.

Academic Programs *Special study options:* adult/continuing education programs, part-time degree program.

Library Charles W. Churchman Sr. Library with 7 serial subscriptions, 2 audiovisual materials.

Computers on Campus 36 computers available on campus for general student use. Internet access, at least one staffed computer lab available.

Student Life *Housing:* college housing not available. *Campus security:* 24-hour emergency response devices.

Athletics *Intramural sports:* table tennis M/W.

Costs (2001–02) *Tuition:* $6885 full-time, $129 per credit part-time. Full-time tuition and fees vary according to class time. Part-time tuition and fees vary according to class time. *Required fees:* $790 full-time, $220 per term part-time. *Payment plan:* installment.

Applying *Options:* common application. *Application fee:* $25. *Required:* high school transcript. *Recommended:* interview. *Application deadline:* rolling (freshmen), rolling (transfers). *Notification:* continuous until 7/30 (freshmen).

Admissions Contact Ellis Plowman, Executive Director, Churchman Business School, 355 Spring Garden Street, Easton, PA 18042. *Phone:* 610-258-5345. *Fax:* 610-258-8086. *E-mail:* cbs4u@enter.net.

Commonwealth Technical Institute
Johnstown, Pennsylvania

- **State-supported** 2-year
- **Calendar** trimesters
- **Degree** certificates, diplomas, and associate
- **Coed**

Financial Aid In 2001, 20 Federal Work-Study jobs.

Admissions Contact Mr. Albert Hromulak, Director of Admissions, Commonwealth Technical Institute, 727 Goucher Street, Johnstown, PA 15905-3092. *Phone:* 814-255-8200 Ext. 8237. *Toll-free phone:* 800-762-4211 Ext. 8237.

Community College of Allegheny County
Pittsburgh, Pennsylvania

- **County-supported** 2-year, founded 1966
- **Calendar** semesters
- **Degree** certificates, diplomas, and associate
- **Urban** 242-acre campus
- **Coed,** 16,999 undergraduate students, 39% full-time, 53% women, 47% men

Undergraduates 6,609 full-time, 10,390 part-time. Students come from 7 states and territories, 47 other countries, 2% are from out of state, 14% African American, 1% Asian American or Pacific Islander, 0.6% Hispanic American, 1% Native American, 0.4% international.

Freshmen *Admission:* 9,152 applied, 9,078 admitted, 2,684 enrolled.

Faculty *Total:* 2,017, 13% full-time, 5% with terminal degrees. *Student/faculty ratio:* 7:1.

Majors Accounting technician; aircraft pilot (professional); alcohol/drug abuse counseling; architectural drafting; art; athletic training/sports medicine; automotive engineering technology; aviation management; banking; biology; building maintenance/management; business administration; business machine repair; business marketing and marketing management; business systems networking/telecommunications; carpentry; chemical technology; chemistry; child care and guidance related; child care/development; child care provider; civil engineering technology; civil/structural drafting; communications technologies related; community health liaison; computer engineering technology; computer maintenance technology; construction technology; construction trades related; corrections; cosmetic services related; court reporting; culinary arts; custodial services related; data processing; diagnostic medical sonography; dietician assistant; drafting; drafting related; electrical/electronic engineering technology; electroencephalograph technology; energy management technology; engineering technologies related; English; enterprise management; environmental technology; fire protection/safety technology; foreign languages/literatures; general studies; graphic design/commercial art/illustration; greenhouse management; health/physical education; health professions and related sciences; health unit coordination; heating/air conditioning/refrigeration; horticulture services; hotel and restaurant management; humanities; human resources management; industrial technology; institutional food services; insurance/risk management; journalism; landscaping management; law enforcement/police science; legal administrative assistant; liberal arts and sciences/liberal studies; machine shop assistant; management information systems/business data processing; mathematics; mechanical design technology; mechanical drafting; medical administrative assistant; medical assistant; medical laboratory technician; medical radiologic technology; medical records technology; music; nuclear medical technology; nurse assistant/aide; nursery management; nursing; nursing (surgical); occupational therapy assistant; office management; operating room technician; ornamental horticulture; paralegal/legal assistant; pharmacy technician/assistant; physical therapy assistant; physics; practical nurse; psychiatric/mental health services; psychology; quality control technology; real estate; recreational therapy; respiratory therapy; restaurant operations; retailing operations; robotics technology; science technologies related; secretarial science; sheet metal working; sign language interpretation; social sciences; social work; sociology; solar technology; teacher education related; teacher education, specific programs related; theater arts/drama; tourism promotion operations; turf management; visual and performing arts related; welding technology.

Academic Programs *Special study options:* academic remediation for entering students, accelerated degree program, advanced placement credit, cooperative education, distance learning, double majors, English as a second language, honors programs, independent study, internships, off-campus study, part-time degree program, services for LD students, study abroad, summer session for credit.

Library Community College of Allegheny County Library plus 4 others with 210,859 titles, 1,390 serial subscriptions, 12,413 audiovisual materials, an OPAC, a Web page.

Computers on Campus 2350 computers available on campus for general student use. A campuswide network can be accessed from off campus. Internet access, at least one staffed computer lab available.

Student Life *Housing:* college housing not available. *Activities and Organizations:* drama/theater group, student-run newspaper, choral group, Phi Theta Kappa. *Campus security:* 24-hour emergency response devices and patrols, late-night transport/escort service. *Student Services:* health clinic, personal/psychological counseling, women's center.

Athletics Member NJCAA. *Intercollegiate sports:* baseball M, basketball M/W, bowling M/W, golf M/W, ice hockey M, softball W, table tennis M/W, tennis M/W, volleyball W. *Intramural sports:* badminton M/W, basketball M/W, bowling M/W, cross-country running M/W, football M, golf M/W, lacrosse M, racquetball M/W, softball M/W, table tennis M/W, tennis M/W, volleyball M/W, weight lifting M/W.

Costs (2001–02) *One-time required fee:* $25. *Tuition:* area resident $1781 full-time, $68 per credit part-time; state resident $3491 full-time, $136 per credit part-time; nonresident $5201 full-time, $204 per credit part-time. Full-time tuition and fees vary according to course load and program. Part-time tuition and fees vary according to course load and program. *Required fees:* $149 full-time, $6 per credit. *Payment plan:* deferred payment. *Waivers:* employees or children of employees.

Applying *Options:* deferred entrance. *Recommended:* high school transcript. *Application deadline:* rolling (freshmen), rolling (transfers). *Notification:* continuous (freshmen).
Admissions Contact Community College of Allegheny County, 800 Allegheny Avenue, Pittsburgh, PA 15233.

COMMUNITY COLLEGE OF BEAVER COUNTY
Monaca, Pennsylvania

- **State-supported** 2-year, founded 1966
- **Calendar** semesters
- **Degree** certificates, diplomas, and associate
- **Small-town** 75-acre campus with easy access to Pittsburgh
- **Coed,** 2,260 undergraduate students

Undergraduates Students come from 7 states and territories, 2 other countries, 3% are from out of state, 7% African American, 0.6% Asian American or Pacific Islander, 0.7% Hispanic American, 0.5% Native American, 0.3% international.
Freshmen *Admission:* 920 applied, 920 admitted.
Faculty *Total:* 106, 45% full-time.
Majors Accounting; aerospace science; aircraft pilot (professional); air traffic control; architectural engineering technology; aviation technology; biology; business administration; business marketing and marketing management; communication equipment technology; computer/information sciences; computer programming; computer typography/composition; criminal justice/law enforcement administration; culinary arts; data processing technology; drafting; education; electrical/electronic engineering technology; industrial arts; information sciences/systems; law enforcement/police science; liberal arts and sciences/liberal studies; medical administrative assistant; medical laboratory technician; nursing; practical nurse; public relations; secretarial science; telecommunications.
Academic Programs *Special study options:* academic remediation for entering students, adult/continuing education programs, advanced placement credit, cooperative education, distance learning, double majors, independent study, internships, off-campus study, part-time degree program, services for LD students, summer session for credit.
Library Community College of Beaver County Library with 52,857 titles, 300 serial subscriptions.
Computers on Campus Internet access, at least one staffed computer lab available.
Student Life *Housing:* college housing not available. *Campus security:* 24-hour emergency response devices and patrols, late-night transport/escort service.
Athletics Member NJCAA. *Intercollegiate sports:* baseball M, basketball M, softball W, tennis M/W, volleyball W. *Intramural sports:* basketball M, table tennis M/W, volleyball M/W.
Standardized Tests *Required:* ACT ASSET, ACT, or nursing exam depending on program.
Costs (2001–02) *Tuition:* area resident $1846 full-time, $71 per credit part-time; state resident $3952 full-time, $152 per credit part-time; nonresident $6058 full-time, $233 per credit part-time. *Required fees:* $156 full-time, $6 per credit. *Payment plan:* deferred payment. *Waivers:* senior citizens.
Financial Aid In 2001, 80 Federal Work-Study jobs (averaging $1575).
Applying *Options:* early admission. *Application fee:* $25. *Recommended:* high school transcript, interview. *Application deadline:* rolling (freshmen), rolling (transfers). *Notification:* continuous (freshmen).
Admissions Contact Mr. Scott F. Ensworth, Dean of Enrollment, Community College of Beaver County, One Campus Drive, Monaca, PA 15061-2588. *Phone:* 724-775-8561 Ext. 330. *Toll-free phone:* 800-335-0222. *Fax:* 724-775-4055.

COMMUNITY COLLEGE OF PHILADELPHIA
Philadelphia, Pennsylvania

Admissions Contact Mr. Gordon K. Holly, Director of Admissions and Recruitment, Community College of Philadelphia, 1700 Spring Garden Street, Philadelphia, PA 19130-3991. *Phone:* 215-751-8230.

CONSOLIDATED SCHOOL OF BUSINESS
Lancaster, Pennsylvania

- **Proprietary** 2-year, founded 1986
- **Calendar** continuous
- **Degree** diplomas and associate
- **Suburban** campus with easy access to Philadelphia
- **Coed,** 189 undergraduate students

Undergraduates 8% African American, 12% Hispanic American.
Freshmen *Average high school GPA:* 2.6.
Faculty *Total:* 21, 71% full-time. *Student/faculty ratio:* 15:1.
Majors Accounting; business administration; health services administration; legal administrative assistant; medical administrative assistant; office management; travel/tourism management.
Academic Programs *Special study options:* accelerated degree program, honors programs, independent study, internships, part-time degree program, services for LD students, student-designed majors.
Computers on Campus 120 computers available on campus for general student use. Internet access, at least one staffed computer lab available.
Student Life *Housing:* college housing not available. *Activities and Organizations:* Community Service Club.
Standardized Tests *Required:* TABE.
Costs (2001–02) *One-time required fee:* $100. *Tuition:* $8400 full-time. No tuition increase for student's term of enrollment. *Payment plans:* installment, deferred payment.
Applying *Options:* common application. *Application fee:* $25. *Required:* high school transcript, interview. *Application deadline:* rolling (freshmen), rolling (transfers).
Admissions Contact Ms. Millie Liberatore, Director of Admission, Consolidated School of Business, 2124 Ambassador Circle, Lancaster, PA 17603. *Phone:* 717-764-9550. *Toll-free phone:* 800-541-8298. *Fax:* 717-394-6213. *E-mail:* admissions@csb.edu.

CONSOLIDATED SCHOOL OF BUSINESS
York, Pennsylvania

- **Proprietary** 2-year, founded 1981
- **Calendar** continuous
- **Degree** diplomas and associate
- **Suburban** 6-acre campus with easy access to Baltimore
- **Coed,** 161 undergraduate students

Undergraduates 2% African American, 3% Hispanic American, 0.6% Native American.
Freshmen *Average high school GPA:* 2.8.
Faculty *Total:* 23, 83% full-time. *Student/faculty ratio:* 15:1.
Majors Accounting; business administration; health services administration; legal administrative assistant; medical administrative assistant; office management; travel/tourism management.
Academic Programs *Special study options:* accelerated degree program, honors programs, independent study, internships, part-time degree program, services for LD students, student-designed majors.
Computers on Campus 210 computers available on campus for general student use. Internet access, at least one staffed computer lab available.
Student Life *Housing:* college housing not available. *Activities and Organizations:* Community Service Club.
Standardized Tests *Required:* TABE.
Costs (2001–02) *One-time required fee:* $100. *Tuition:* $8400 full-time. No tuition increase for student's term of enrollment. *Payment plans:* installment, deferred payment.
Applying *Options:* common application. *Application fee:* $25. *Required:* high school transcript, interview. *Application deadline:* rolling (freshmen), rolling (transfers).
Admissions Contact Ms. Millie Liberatore, Director of Admissions, Consolidated School of Business, 1605 Clugston Road, York, PA 17404. *Phone:* 717-764-9550. *Toll-free phone:* 800-520-0691. *Fax:* 717-764-9469. *E-mail:* admissions@csb.edu.

DEAN INSTITUTE OF TECHNOLOGY
Pittsburgh, Pennsylvania

Admissions Contact Mr. Burt Wolfe, Admissions Director, Dean Institute of Technology, 1501 West Liberty Avenue, Pittsburgh, PA 15226-1103. *Phone:* 412-531-4433. *Fax:* 412-531-4435.

DELAWARE COUNTY COMMUNITY COLLEGE
Media, Pennsylvania

- **State and locally supported** 2-year, founded 1967
- **Calendar** semesters

Delaware County Community College (continued)

- **Degree** certificates and associate
- **Suburban** 125-acre campus with easy access to Philadelphia
- **Coed,** 9,467 undergraduate students

Undergraduates Students come from 43 other countries, 1% are from out of state, 12% African American, 4% Asian American or Pacific Islander, 1% Hispanic American, 0.1% Native American, 2% international.

Faculty *Total:* 629, 19% full-time. *Student/faculty ratio:* 21:1.

Majors Accounting technician; anthropology; architectural engineering technology; banking; biological/physical sciences; biomedical engineering-related technology; business administration; business computer facilities operation; business computer programming; business systems networking/ telecommunications; communications; computer graphics; computer/information sciences; computer programming related; computer science related; computer systems networking/ telecommunications; construction technology; drafting; early childhood education; education (multiple levels); electrical/electronic engineering technology; engineering; enterprise management; fire protection/safety technology; general retailing/ wholesaling; general studies; graphic design/commercial art/illustration; hotel and restaurant management; information sciences/systems; journalism; law enforcement/police science; liberal arts and sciences/liberal studies; management information systems/business data processing; mechanical engineering technology; medical assistant; nursing; office management; operating room technician; paralegal/legal assistant; psychology; respiratory therapy; sociology; teacher assistant/aide; Web page, digital/multimedia and information resources design.

Academic Programs *Special study options:* academic remediation for entering students, adult/continuing education programs, advanced placement credit, cooperative education, distance learning, double majors, English as a second language, independent study, internships, part-time degree program, services for LD students, student-designed majors, summer session for credit.

Library Delaware County Community College Library with 56,229 titles, 480 serial subscriptions, an OPAC, a Web page.

Computers on Campus 1200 computers available on campus for general student use. A campuswide network can be accessed from off campus. Internet access, online (class) registration, at least one staffed computer lab available.

Student Life *Housing:* college housing not available. *Activities and Organizations:* drama/theater group, student-run radio station, choral group, student government, student radio station, Phi Theta Kappa. *Campus security:* 24-hour emergency response devices and patrols, late-night transport/escort service. *Student Services:* health clinic, personal/psychological counseling.

Athletics Member NJCAA. *Intercollegiate sports:* baseball M, basketball M/W, soccer M, softball W, tennis M/W, volleyball M/W. *Intramural sports:* basketball M/W, bowling M(c)/W(c), cross-country running M(c)/W(c), soccer W(c), tennis M/W, volleyball M/W.

Costs (2001–02) *Tuition:* area resident $1584 full-time, $66 per credit hour part-time; state resident $3192 full-time, $133 per credit hour part-time; nonresident $4800 full-time, $200 per credit hour part-time. Full-time tuition and fees vary according to course load and program. Part-time tuition and fees vary according to course load and program. *Required fees:* $234 full-time, $9 per credit hour, $15 per term part-time. *Payment plan:* deferred payment. *Waivers:* senior citizens and employees or children of employees.

Applying *Options:* early admission, deferred entrance. *Application fee:* $20. *Required:* high school transcript. *Application deadline:* rolling (freshmen), rolling (transfers). *Notification:* continuous (freshmen).

Admissions Contact Ms. Hope Lentine, Director of Admissions, Delaware County Community College, Admissions Office, 901 South Media Line Road, Media, PA 19063-1094. *Phone:* 610-359-5333. *Toll-free phone:* 800-872-1102 (in-state); 800-543-0146 (out-of-state). *Fax:* 610-359-5343. *E-mail:* admiss@dcccnet.dccc.edu.

DOUGLAS EDUCATION CENTER

Monessen, Pennsylvania

- **Proprietary** 2-year
- **Degree** certificates, diplomas, and associate
- **Coed,** 130 undergraduate students
- 91% of applicants were admitted

Freshmen *Admission:* 32 applied, 29 admitted.

Faculty *Total:* 12, 75% full-time. *Student/faculty ratio:* 10:1.

Majors Business administration; design/visual communications; medical administrative assistant; medical assistant; medical office management; secretarial science.

Costs (2002–03) *Tuition:* Part-time tuition and fees vary according to course load and degree level. Tuition varies by program; average two-year program is $12,400.

Financial Aid In 2001, 5 Federal Work-Study jobs (averaging $2500).

Admissions Contact Ms. Linda Gambattista, Director of Admissions, Douglas Education Center, 130 Seventh Street, Monessen, PA 15062. *Phone:* 724-684-3684.

DUBOIS BUSINESS COLLEGE

DuBois, Pennsylvania

- **Proprietary** 2-year, founded 1885
- **Calendar** quarters
- **Degree** diplomas and associate
- **Rural** 4-acre campus
- **Coed, primarily women,** 412 undergraduate students, 100% full-time, 80% women, 20% men

Undergraduates Students come from 1 other country, 10% are from out of state, 0.2% African American, 0.5% Asian American or Pacific Islander, 0.5% Hispanic American, 7% live on campus.

Freshmen *Admission:* 210 applied, 117 admitted. *Average high school GPA:* 2.5.

Faculty *Total:* 30, 77% full-time. *Student/faculty ratio:* 14:1.

Majors Accounting; computer management; data processing; legal administrative assistant; medical administrative assistant; secretarial science.

Academic Programs *Special study options:* academic remediation for entering students, accelerated degree program, double majors, part-time degree program, summer session for credit.

Library DuBois Business College Main Campus Library with 2,100 titles, 10 serial subscriptions, a Web page.

Computers on Campus 110 computers available on campus for general student use. Internet access, at least one staffed computer lab available.

Student Life *Housing Options:* coed. *Activities and Organizations:* student-run newspaper, student association, Bible study, national fraternities, national sororities. *Campus security:* late-night transport/escort service, controlled dormitory access. *Student Services:* personal/psychological counseling.

Athletics *Intramural sports:* badminton M/W, basketball M/W, volleyball M/W.

Costs (2002–03) *Tuition:* $6300 full-time, $150 per credit part-time. *Required fees:* $325 full-time, $50 per term. *Room only:* $2250. *Payment plan:* installment. *Waivers:* senior citizens and employees or children of employees.

Applying *Options:* common application, electronic application, deferred entrance. *Application fee:* $25. *Required:* high school transcript, interview. *Recommended:* letters of recommendation. *Application deadline:* rolling (freshmen), rolling (transfers). *Notification:* continuous (freshmen).

Admissions Contact Mr. Larry Kenawell, Admissions Director, DuBois Business College, 1 Beaver Drive, DuBois, PA 15801-2401. *Phone:* 814-371-6920. *Toll-free phone:* 800-692-6213.

DUFF'S BUSINESS INSTITUTE

Pittsburgh, Pennsylvania

- **Proprietary** 2-year, founded 1840, part of Phillips Colleges, Inc
- **Calendar** quarters
- **Degree** diplomas and associate
- **Urban** campus
- **Coed, primarily women,** 500 undergraduate students

Undergraduates Students come from 3 states and territories.

Freshmen *Average high school GPA:* 2.2.

Faculty *Total:* 28, 36% full-time.

Majors Accounting; business administration; computer programming; court reporting; fashion merchandising; legal administrative assistant; medical administrative assistant; medical assistant; paralegal/legal assistant; secretarial science.

Academic Programs *Special study options:* academic remediation for entering students, adult/continuing education programs, advanced placement credit, cooperative education, internships, part-time degree program, summer session for credit.

Library Main Library plus 1 other with 7,500 titles, 30 serial subscriptions.

Computers on Campus 80 computers available on campus for general student use.

Student Life *Housing:* college housing not available. *Campus security:* 24-hour emergency response devices. *Student Services:* personal/psychological counseling.

Athletics *Intramural sports:* basketball M/W.
Costs (2001–02) *Tuition:* $202 per credit part-time. *Required fees:* $15 per quarter hour.
Financial Aid In 2001, 40 Federal Work-Study jobs.
Applying *Options:* deferred entrance. *Application fee:* $25. *Application deadline:* rolling (freshmen), rolling (transfers).
Admissions Contact Mr. Dick Moore, Director of Admissions, Duff's Business Institute, 110 Ninth Street, Pittsburgh, PA 15222-3618. *Phone:* 412-261-4520 Ext. 212. *Toll-free phone:* 800-222-DUFF.

EDUCATION DIRECT
Scranton, Pennsylvania

- **Proprietary** 2-year, founded 1975
- **Calendar** semesters
- **Degrees** associate (offers only external degree programs conducted through home study)
- **Coed**

Undergraduates Students come from 52 states and territories, 15 other countries.
Majors Accounting; business administration; business marketing and marketing management; civil engineering technology; computer science; computer science related; electrical/electronic engineering technology; finance; hospitality management; industrial technology; mechanical engineering technology.
Academic Programs *Special study options:* academic remediation for entering students, adult/continuing education programs, distance learning, external degree program, honors programs, independent study, part-time degree program, summer session for credit.
Student Life *Housing:* college housing not available.
Costs (2001–02) *Tuition:* $3166 per degree program part-time. Part-time tuition and fees vary according to program. *Payment plan:* installment.
Applying *Options:* common application. *Required:* high school transcript. *Application deadline:* rolling (freshmen), rolling (transfers).
Admissions Contact Ms. Connie Dempsey, Director of Compliance and Academic Affairs, Education Direct, 925 Oak Street, Scranton, PA 18515. *Phone:* 570-342-7701 Ext. 4692. *Toll-free phone:* 800-233-4191.

ELECTRONIC INSTITUTES
Middletown, Pennsylvania

- **Independent** 2-year, founded 1959
- **Calendar** trimesters
- **Degree** associate
- **Small-town** campus with easy access to Baltimore and Philadelphia
- **Coed, primarily men,** 50 undergraduate students

Undergraduates 1% African American, 2% Hispanic American.
Freshmen *Admission:* 50 applied, 50 admitted.
Faculty *Total:* 5, 100% full-time. *Student/faculty ratio:* 10:1.
Majors Computer engineering related; computer engineering technology; computer hardware engineering; computer software engineering; computer systems networking/telecommunications; computer/technical support; electrical/electronic engineering technology; system administration; system/networking/LAN/WAN management.
Academic Programs *Special study options:* academic remediation for entering students, internships.
Computers on Campus 45 computers available on campus for general student use. Internet access, at least one staffed computer lab available.
Student Life *Housing:* college housing not available. *Student Services:* personal/psychological counseling.
Costs (2002–03) *Tuition:* $8500 full-time. *Required fees:* $150 full-time.
Applying *Options:* deferred entrance. *Required:* high school transcript, interview. *Application deadline:* rolling (freshmen), rolling (transfers).
Admissions Contact Mr. Tom Bogush, Chief Admissions Officer and School President, Electronic Institutes, 19 Jamesway Plaza, Middletown, PA 17057. *Phone:* 717-944-2731. *Toll-free phone:* 800-884-2731. *Fax:* 717-944-2734. *E-mail:* einet@epix.net.

ERIE BUSINESS CENTER, MAIN
Erie, Pennsylvania

- **Proprietary** 2-year, founded 1884
- **Calendar** trimesters
- **Degree** diplomas and associate
- **Urban** 1-acre campus with easy access to Cleveland and Buffalo
- **Coed,** 375 undergraduate students

Undergraduates Students come from 3 states and territories, 2% are from out of state, 35% live on campus.
Faculty *Total:* 52, 25% full-time. *Student/faculty ratio:* 15:1.
Majors Business administration; business marketing and marketing management; computer programming related; computer science; computer systems networking/telecommunications; equestrian studies; information sciences/systems; legal administrative assistant; medical administrative assistant; medical assistant; medical transcription; paralegal/legal assistant; secretarial science; travel/tourism management; Web page, digital/multimedia and information resources design.
Academic Programs *Special study options:* adult/continuing education programs, advanced placement credit, double majors, independent study, internships, part-time degree program, summer session for credit.
Library EBC Blackmer Library with 3,035 titles, 84 serial subscriptions, an OPAC.
Computers on Campus 96 computers available on campus for general student use. A campuswide network can be accessed from off campus. Internet access, at least one staffed computer lab available.
Student Life *Housing Options:* coed. *Activities and Organizations:* drama/theater group, student-run newspaper, student council, Newspaper Club, Computer Club, Drama Club, Billiard Club. *Campus security:* 24-hour emergency response devices, security guard. *Student Services:* personal/psychological counseling.
Costs (2001–02) *One-time required fee:* $125. *Tuition:* $4992 full-time, $208 per credit part-time. *Required fees:* $424 full-time, $36 per credit, $20 per term part-time.
Financial Aid In 2001, 15 Federal Work-Study jobs (averaging $600).
Applying *Options:* common application, deferred entrance. *Application fee:* $25. *Required:* essay or personal statement, high school transcript, interview. *Application deadline:* rolling (freshmen), rolling (transfers). *Notification:* continuous (freshmen).
Admissions Contact Ms. Amy Tevis, Director of Admissions, Erie Business Center, Main, 246 West Ninth Street, Erie, PA 16501-1392. *Phone:* 814-456-7504 Ext. 12. *Toll-free phone:* 800-352-ERIE Ext. 12 (in-state); 800-352-ERIE (out-of-state). *Fax:* 814-456-4882. *E-mail:* tevisa@eriebc.com.

ERIE BUSINESS CENTER SOUTH
New Castle, Pennsylvania

- **Proprietary** 2-year, founded 1894
- **Calendar** quarters
- **Degree** diplomas and associate
- **Small-town** 1-acre campus with easy access to Pittsburgh
- **Coed, primarily women,** 98 undergraduate students, 100% full-time, 83% women, 17% men

Undergraduates 8% African American. *Retention:* 80% of 2001 full-time freshmen returned.
Freshmen *Admission:* 45 applied, 34 admitted.
Faculty *Total:* 6, 50% full-time. *Student/faculty ratio:* 12:1.
Majors Accounting; advertising; business administration; business marketing and marketing management; computer science; legal administrative assistant; medical administrative assistant; medical records administration; secretarial science; travel/tourism management.
Academic Programs *Special study options:* academic remediation for entering students, adult/continuing education programs, internships, part-time degree program.
Library 1,725 titles, 20 serial subscriptions.
Computers on Campus 26 computers available on campus for general student use. Internet access, at least one staffed computer lab available.
Student Life *Housing:* college housing not available. *Activities and Organizations:* student government, Business Club, Medical Club, Travel Club, Ambassadors Club. *Campus security:* 24-hour patrols. *Student Services:* personal/psychological counseling.
Athletics *Intramural sports:* basketball M/W, bowling M/W, softball M/W, volleyball M/W.
Standardized Tests *Recommended:* SAT I and SAT II or ACT (for admission).
Costs (2001–02) *Tuition:* $4240 full-time, $424 per course part-time. *Required fees:* $250 full-time, $120 per term part-time.
Applying *Options:* common application, deferred entrance. *Application deadline:* rolling (freshmen), rolling (transfers).

Erie Business Center South (continued)

Admissions Contact Ms. Rose Hall, Admissions Representative, Erie Business Center South, 700 Moravia Street, New Castle, PA 16101-3950. *Phone:* 724-658-3595.

ERIE INSTITUTE OF TECHNOLOGY
Erie, Pennsylvania

- **Proprietary** 2-year
- **Calendar** 4 3-month terms
- **Degree** diplomas and associate
- **Coed**

Faculty *Student/faculty ratio:* 15:1.
Financial Aid *Financial aid deadline:* 8/1.
Admissions Contact Mr. Dan Albaugh, Director of Admissions, Erie Institute of Technology, 2221 Peninsula Drive, Erie, PA 16506-2954. *Phone:* 814-838-2711.

HARCUM COLLEGE
Bryn Mawr, Pennsylvania

- **Independent** 2-year, founded 1915
- **Calendar** semesters
- **Degree** certificates and associate
- **Suburban** 12-acre campus with easy access to Philadelphia
- **Endowment** $9.0 million
- **Coed, primarily women,** 548 undergraduate students, 65% full-time, 92% women, 8% men

Undergraduates 357 full-time, 191 part-time. Students come from 8 states and territories, 6 other countries, 10% are from out of state, 21% African American, 3% Asian American or Pacific Islander, 3% Hispanic American, 0.8% Native American, 2% international, 46% transferred in, 23% live on campus. *Retention:* 90% of 2001 full-time freshmen returned.
Freshmen *Admission:* 361 applied, 207 admitted, 109 enrolled. *Average high school GPA:* 2.38. *Test scores:* SAT verbal scores over 500: 27%; SAT math scores over 500: 16%; SAT verbal scores over 600: 5%; SAT math scores over 600: 1%.
Faculty *Total:* 102, 26% full-time. *Student/faculty ratio:* 9:1.
Majors Animal sciences; business administration; child care/development; dental assistant; dental hygiene; early childhood education; fashion design/illustration; fashion merchandising; health/medical diagnostic and treatment services related; health science; information sciences/systems; interdisciplinary studies; interior design; liberal arts and sciences/liberal studies; medical laboratory technician; occupational therapy assistant; physical therapy assistant; psychology; retail management; veterinary technology.
Academic Programs *Special study options:* academic remediation for entering students, adult/continuing education programs, advanced placement credit, distance learning, double majors, English as a second language, honors programs, independent study, internships, off-campus study, part-time degree program, services for LD students, summer session for credit.
Library Main Library plus 1 other with 37,000 titles, 335 serial subscriptions.
Computers on Campus 65 computers available on campus for general student use. Internet access, at least one staffed computer lab available.
Student Life *Housing Options:* coed, women-only. *Activities and Organizations:* student-run newspaper, choral group, OATS (Organization for Animal Tech Students), Student Association of Dental Hygienist of America, Ebony Club, Dental Assisting Club, FLA International Club. *Campus security:* 24-hour emergency response devices and patrols, controlled dormitory access. *Student Services:* health clinic, personal/psychological counseling, women's center.
Athletics *Intramural sports:* badminton W, basketball W, soccer W, softball W, tennis W, volleyball W.
Standardized Tests *Required:* SAT I or ACT (for admission).
Costs (2001–02) *One-time required fee:* $100. *Comprehensive fee:* $17,600 includes full-time tuition ($11,350) and room and board ($6250). Part-time tuition: $378 per credit. *Payment plan:* installment. *Waivers:* senior citizens and employees or children of employees.
Financial Aid In 2001, 88 Federal Work-Study jobs (averaging $1500).
Applying *Options:* common application, electronic application, early admission, deferred entrance. *Required:* essay or personal statement, high school transcript, letters of recommendation. *Recommended:* interview. *Application deadline:* rolling (freshmen), rolling (transfers). *Notification:* continuous (freshmen).
Admissions Contact Ms. Sandra Feather, Dean, Harcum College, 750 Montgomery Avenue, Bedford Hall, Bryn Mawr, PA 19010-3476. *Phone:* 610-526-6105 Ext. 6050. *Toll-free phone:* 800-345-2600. *Fax:* 610-526-6147. *E-mail:* enroll@harcum.edu.

HARRISBURG AREA COMMUNITY COLLEGE
Harrisburg, Pennsylvania

- **State and locally supported** 2-year, founded 1964
- **Calendar** semesters
- **Degree** certificates, diplomas, and associate
- **Urban** 212-acre campus
- **Endowment** $27.0 million
- **Coed,** 11,671 undergraduate students, 41% full-time, 62% women, 38% men

Undergraduates 4,781 full-time, 6,890 part-time. Students come from 6 states and territories, 15 other countries, 1% are from out of state, 8% African American, 3% Asian American or Pacific Islander, 3% Hispanic American, 0.3% Native American, 1% international, 32% transferred in.
Freshmen *Admission:* 6,404 applied, 6,276 admitted, 2,148 enrolled.
Faculty *Total:* 743, 27% full-time, 4% with terminal degrees. *Student/faculty ratio:* 18:1.
Majors Accounting; actuarial science; architectural engineering technology; architecture; art; auto mechanic/technician; automotive engineering technology; banking; biology; business; business administration; business education; business marketing and marketing management; business systems networking/ telecommunications; cardiovascular technology; chemistry; civil engineering technology; computer/information sciences; computer/information sciences related; computer installation/repair; construction technology; criminal justice/law enforcement administration; culinary arts; dental hygiene; design/visual communications; dietetics; early childhood education; education; electrical/electronic engineering technology; elementary education; emergency medical technology; engineering; engineering technology; environmental science; fire science; general retailing/wholesaling; graphic design/commercial art/illustration; health facilities administration; hotel and restaurant management; human services; industrial machinery maintenance/repair; institutional food workers; international relations; journalism; law enforcement/police science; legal administrative assistant; liberal arts and sciences/liberal studies; management information systems/business data processing; management science; mass communications; mathematics; mechanical engineering technology; medical laboratory technician; medical radiologic technology; medical records administration; music; nuclear medical technology; nursing; nutrition studies; opticianry; paralegal/legal assistant; pharmacy technician/assistant; photography; physical education; physical sciences; psychology; real estate; respiratory therapy; retail management; science education; secretarial science; social sciences; social work; theater arts/drama; tourism/travel marketing; travel/tourism management.
Academic Programs *Special study options:* academic remediation for entering students, adult/continuing education programs, advanced placement credit, cooperative education, English as a second language, honors programs, internships, part-time degree program, services for LD students, student-designed majors, study abroad, summer session for credit. *ROTC:* Army (b).
Library McCormick Library with 105,077 titles, 701 serial subscriptions, 16,335 audiovisual materials.
Computers on Campus 275 computers available on campus for general student use.
Student Life *Housing:* college housing not available. *Activities and Organizations:* drama/theater group, student-run newspaper, radio station. *Campus security:* 24-hour emergency response devices and patrols, late-night transport/escort service. *Student Services:* personal/psychological counseling.
Athletics *Intercollegiate sports:* basketball M, tennis M/W, volleyball W. *Intramural sports:* basketball M/W, football M/W, golf M/W, racquetball M/W, skiing (downhill) M/W, soccer M, softball M/W, squash M/W, swimming M/W, tennis M/W, volleyball M/W.
Standardized Tests *Required for some:* ACT (for placement).
Costs (2001–02) *One-time required fee:* $25. *Tuition:* area resident $2115 full-time, $71 per credit hour part-time; state resident $4230 full-time, $141 per credit hour part-time; nonresident $6345 full-time, $212 per credit hour part-time. *Required fees:* $210 full-time, $5 per credit hour.
Applying *Options:* early admission. *Application fee:* $25. *Required:* high school transcript. *Application deadline:* rolling (freshmen), rolling (transfers).
Admissions Contact Mrs. Vanita Cowan, Administrative Clerk, Admissions, Harrisburg Area Community College, 1 HACC Drive, Harrisburg, PA 17110-2999. *Phone:* 717-780-2406. *Toll-free phone:* 800-ABC-HACC.

HUSSIAN SCHOOL OF ART
Philadelphia, Pennsylvania

- **Proprietary** primarily 2-year, founded 1946
- **Calendar** semesters
- **Degrees** associate and bachelor's
- **Urban** 1-acre campus
- **Coed,** 137 undergraduate students, 100% full-time, 31% women, 69% men

Undergraduates Students come from 4 states and territories, 1 other country, 45% are from out of state. *Retention:* 90% of 2001 full-time freshmen returned.
Freshmen *Admission:* 103 applied, 64 admitted. *Average high school GPA:* 2.7.
Faculty *Total:* 28, 11% full-time, 18% with terminal degrees. *Student/faculty ratio:* 18:1.
Majors Advertising; graphic design/commercial art/illustration.
Academic Programs *Special study options:* cooperative education, internships, part-time degree program.
Library Main Library plus 1 other with 8,000 titles, 10 serial subscriptions.
Computers on Campus 25 computers available on campus for general student use. Internet access, at least one staffed computer lab available.
Student Life *Housing:* college housing not available. *Campus security:* security guard during open hours.
Costs (2002–03) *Tuition:* $8400 full-time, $271 per credit part-time. *Required fees:* $240 full-time, $11 per contact hour. *Payment plan:* installment.
Financial Aid *Financial aid deadline:* 8/1.
Applying *Options:* common application, deferred entrance. *Application fee:* $25. *Required:* high school transcript, interview, art portfolio. *Application deadline:* rolling (freshmen), rolling (transfers). *Notification:* continuous (freshmen).
Admissions Contact Ms. Lynne Wartman, Director of Admissions, Hussian School of Art, 1118 Market Street, Philadelphia, PA 19107. *Phone:* 215-981-0900. *Fax:* 215-864-9115. *E-mail:* hussian@pond.com.

ICM SCHOOL OF BUSINESS & MEDICAL CAREERS
Pittsburgh, Pennsylvania

Admissions Contact Mr. Mike Miller, Director of Admissions, ICM School of Business & Medical Careers, 10 Wood Street, Pittsburgh, PA 15222. *Phone:* 412-261-2647. *Toll-free phone:* 800-441-5222. *E-mail:* icm@citynet.com.

INFORMATION COMPUTER SYSTEMS INSTITUTE
Allentown, Pennsylvania

- **Private** 2-year, founded 1978
- **Degree** certificates and associate
- 125 undergraduate students

Faculty *Total:* 10.
Costs (2001–02) *Tuition:* Tuition and fees are dependent upon program selected.
Admissions Contact Bill Barber, Director, Information Computer Systems Institute, 2201 Hangar Place, Allentown, PA 18103-9504. *Phone:* 610-264-8029.

INTERNATIONAL ACADEMY OF DESIGN & TECHNOLOGY
Pittsburgh, Pennsylvania

- **Private** 2-year
- **Degree** associate
- 954 undergraduate students, 88% full-time
- 100% of applicants were admitted

Undergraduates 840 full-time, 114 part-time. 1% are from out of state.
Freshmen *Admission:* 174 applied, 174 admitted, 174 enrolled. *Average high school GPA:* 2.96.
Faculty *Total:* 45, 51% full-time. *Student/faculty ratio:* 15:1.
Majors Culinary arts; management information systems/business data processing.
Costs (2002–03) *Tuition:* $23,000 full-time, $186 per credit part-time. *Required fees:* $4200 full-time.
Applying *Application fee:* $50.
Admissions Contact Ms. Debbie Love, Chief Admissions Officer, International Academy of Design & Technology, 555 Grant Street, Pittsburgh, PA 15219. *Phone:* 412-391-4197. *Toll-free phone:* 800-447-8324.

ITT TECHNICAL INSTITUTE
Mechanicsburg, Pennsylvania

- **Proprietary** 2-year
- **Calendar** quarters
- **Degree** associate
- **Coed,** 275 undergraduate students

Majors Computer/information sciences related; drafting; electrical/electronic engineering technologies related; information technology.
Student Life *Housing:* college housing not available.
Costs (2001–02) *Tuition:* Full-time tuition and fees vary according to program. Part-time tuition and fees vary according to program. $260—$330 per credit hour.
Applying *Application fee:* $100. *Required:* high school transcript, interview. *Recommended:* letters of recommendation. *Application deadline:* rolling (freshmen). *Notification:* continuous (freshmen).
Admissions Contact Mr. Dick Gooding, Director of Recruitment, ITT Technical Institute, 5020 Louise Drive, Mechanicsburg, PA 17055. *Phone:* 717-691-9263. *Toll-free phone:* 800-847-4756.

ITT TECHNICAL INSTITUTE
Monroeville, Pennsylvania

- **Proprietary** 2-year
- **Calendar** quarters
- **Degree** associate
- **Coed,** 516 undergraduate students

Majors Computer/information sciences related; drafting; electrical/electronic engineering technologies related; information technology.
Student Life *Housing:* college housing not available.
Costs (2001–02) *Tuition:* Full-time tuition and fees vary according to program. Part-time tuition and fees vary according to program. $260—$330 per credit hour.
Applying *Application fee:* $100. *Required:* high school transcript, interview. *Recommended:* letters of recommendation. *Application deadline:* rolling (freshmen). *Notification:* continuous (freshmen).
Admissions Contact Mr. John Hawthorne, Director of Recruitment, ITT Technical Institute, 105 Mall Boulevard, Monroeville, PA 15146. *Phone:* 412-856-5920. *Toll-free phone:* 800-856-5920.

ITT TECHNICAL INSTITUTE
Pittsburgh, Pennsylvania

- **Proprietary** 2-year
- **Calendar** quarters
- **Degree** associate
- **Coed,** 364 undergraduate students

Majors Computer/information sciences related; drafting; electrical/electronic engineering technologies related; information technology.
Student Life *Housing:* college housing not available.
Costs (2001–02) *Tuition:* Full-time tuition and fees vary according to program. Part-time tuition and fees vary according to program. $260—$330 per credit hour.
Applying *Application fee:* $100. *Required:* high school transcript, interview. *Recommended:* letters of recommendation. *Application deadline:* rolling (freshmen). *Notification:* continuous (freshmen).
Admissions Contact Mr. Jeff DeFilippo, Director of Recruitment, ITT Technical Institute, 8 Parkway Center, Pittsburgh, PA 15220. *Phone:* 412-937-9150. *Toll-free phone:* 800-353-8324.

ITT TECHNICAL INSTITUTE
Bensalem, Pennsylvania

- **Proprietary** 2-year, founded 2000
- **Calendar** quarters
- **Coed,** 48 undergraduate students

Majors Computer/information sciences related; information technology.

ITT Technical Institute (continued)
Costs (2001–02) *Tuition:* Full-time tuition and fees vary according to program. Part-time tuition and fees vary according to program. $260—$330 per credit hour.
Admissions Contact Mr. Rodney Amadori, ITT Technical Institute, 3330 Tillman Drive, Bensalem, PA 19020. *Phone:* 215-244-8871. *Toll-free phone:* 866-488-8324.

JOHNSON COLLEGE
Scranton, Pennsylvania

- **Independent** 2-year, founded 1912
- **Calendar** semesters
- **Degree** associate
- **Urban** 65-acre campus
- **Coed,** 331 undergraduate students, 96% full-time, 18% women, 82% men

Undergraduates 318 full-time, 13 part-time. Students come from 4 states and territories, 10% are from out of state, 1% African American, 0.3% Asian American or Pacific Islander, 0.9% Hispanic American, 17% transferred in, 17% live on campus.
Freshmen *Admission:* 249 applied, 165 admitted, 135 enrolled. *Average high school GPA:* 2.95. *Test scores:* SAT verbal scores over 500: 22%; SAT math scores over 500: 26%; SAT verbal scores over 600: 1%; SAT math scores over 600: 1%.
Faculty *Total:* 29, 59% full-time, 14% with terminal degrees. *Student/faculty ratio:* 17:1.
Majors Architectural engineering technology; auto mechanic/technician; biomedical technology; cabinet making; carpentry; computer systems networking/telecommunications; construction/building inspection; construction technology; diesel engine mechanic; drafting; drafting/design technology; electrical/electronic engineering technology; electrical equipment installation/repair; electromechanical technology; engineering-related technology; industrial electronics installation/repair; industrial machinery maintenance/repair; information technology; machine shop assistant; machine technology; system/networking/LAN/WAN management; veterinarian assistant.
Academic Programs *Special study options:* academic remediation for entering students, adult/continuing education programs, internships, part-time degree program, services for LD students, summer session for credit.
Library Johnson Technical Institute Library with 4,473 titles, 118 serial subscriptions, an OPAC, a Web page.
Computers on Campus 75 computers available on campus for general student use. Internet access, at least one staffed computer lab available.
Student Life *Housing Options:* coed. *Activities and Organizations:* student government, Social Force Club, trade/technical/clinical clubs. *Campus security:* 24-hour emergency response devices. *Student Services:* personal/psychological counseling.
Athletics *Intercollegiate sports:* basketball M/W, bowling M/W, cross-country running M/W, golf M/W. *Intramural sports:* basketball M/W, skiing (downhill) M/W, softball M/W, table tennis M/W, volleyball M/W.
Standardized Tests *Required for some:* SAT I (for admission). *Recommended:* SAT I (for admission).
Costs (2002–03) *Tuition:* $9175 full-time, $290 per credit part-time. Full-time tuition and fees vary according to program. Part-time tuition and fees vary according to program. No tuition increase for student's term of enrollment. *Required fees:* $375 full-time. *Room only:* $2800. Room and board charges vary according to housing facility. *Payment plan:* installment.
Financial Aid In 2001, 40 Federal Work-Study jobs (averaging $800).
Applying *Options:* common application, electronic application, deferred entrance. *Application fee:* $30. *Required:* essay or personal statement, high school transcript, letters of recommendation, interview. *Application deadline:* rolling (freshmen), rolling (transfers). *Notification:* 8/15 (freshmen).
Admissions Contact Melissa Turlip, Acting Director of Enrollment Management, Johnson College, 3427 N. Main Avenue, Scranton, PA 18508. *Phone:* 570-342-6404 Ext. 122. *Toll-free phone:* 800-2-WE-WORK Ext. 125. *Fax:* 570-348-2181. *E-mail:* admit@epix.net.

KEYSTONE COLLEGE
La Plume, Pennsylvania

- **Independent** primarily 2-year, founded 1868
- **Calendar** semesters
- **Degrees** certificates, associate, and bachelor's
- **Rural** 270-acre campus
- **Endowment** $12.0 million
- **Coed,** 1,373 undergraduate students, 71% full-time, 60% women, 40% men

Undergraduates 968 full-time, 405 part-time. Students come from 14 states and territories, 11 other countries, 13% are from out of state, 5% African American, 0.2% Asian American or Pacific Islander, 2% Hispanic American, 0.3% Native American, 1% international, 10% transferred in, 48% live on campus.
Freshmen *Admission:* 1,030 applied, 822 admitted, 398 enrolled. *Test scores:* SAT verbal scores over 500: 24%; SAT math scores over 500: 17%; SAT verbal scores over 600: 4%; SAT math scores over 600: 3%; SAT math scores over 700: 1%.
Faculty *Total:* 179, 31% full-time, 18% with terminal degrees. *Student/faculty ratio:* 11:1.
Majors Accounting; art; biology; business; business administration; business computer programming; business systems networking/ telecommunications; communications; computer programming; criminal justice/law enforcement administration; criminal justice studies; culinary arts; data processing technology; early childhood education; education (K-12); environmental science; forestry; hotel and restaurant management; human resources management; human services; landscape architecture; liberal arts and sciences/liberal studies; medical radiologic technology; occupational therapy; physical therapy; physical therapy assistant; recreation/leisure facilities management; restaurant operations; sport/fitness administration; wildlife biology; wildlife management.
Academic Programs *Special study options:* academic remediation for entering students, adult/continuing education programs, advanced placement credit, cooperative education, English as a second language, independent study, internships, part-time degree program, services for LD students, student-designed majors, summer session for credit. *ROTC:* Army (c), Air Force (c).
Library Miller Library with 47,900 titles, 292 serial subscriptions, 37,395 audiovisual materials, an OPAC, a Web page.
Computers on Campus 80 computers available on campus for general student use. A campuswide network can be accessed from student residence rooms. Internet access, at least one staffed computer lab available.
Student Life *Housing Options:* coed, women-only, disabled students. *Activities and Organizations:* drama/theater group, student-run newspaper, radio station, choral group, Campus Activity Board, Student Senate, Art Society, Inter-Hall Council, Commuter Council. *Campus security:* 24-hour emergency response devices and patrols, student patrols, late-night transport/escort service, controlled dormitory access. *Student Services:* health clinic, personal/psychological counseling, women's center.
Athletics Member NJCAA. *Intercollegiate sports:* baseball M, basketball M/W, cross-country running M/W, golf M/W, soccer M/W, softball W, tennis M/W, volleyball W. *Intramural sports:* badminton M/W, basketball M/W, bowling M/W, football M/W, lacrosse M/W, soccer M/W, softball M/W, table tennis M/W, tennis M/W, volleyball M/W, weight lifting M/W.
Standardized Tests *Required for some:* SAT I or ACT (for admission). *Recommended:* SAT I or ACT (for admission).
Costs (2001–02) *One-time required fee:* $175. *Comprehensive fee:* $19,021 includes full-time tuition ($11,820), mandatory fees ($801), and room and board ($6400). Part-time tuition: $285 per credit. *Required fees:* $40 per term part-time. *Payment plans:* installment, deferred payment. *Waivers:* children of alumni and employees or children of employees.
Financial Aid In 2001, 310 Federal Work-Study jobs (averaging $1165). 481 State and other part-time jobs (averaging $1146).
Applying *Options:* common application, electronic application, early admission, deferred entrance. *Application fee:* $25. *Required:* high school transcript. *Required for some:* interview. *Recommended:* essay or personal statement, minimum 2.0 GPA, 2 letters of recommendation, interview. *Application deadline:* rolling (freshmen), rolling (transfers).
Admissions Contact Ms. Sarah Keating, Director of Admissions, Keystone College, One College Green, La Plume, PA 18440-1099. *Phone:* 570-945-5141 Ext. 2403. *Toll-free phone:* 877-4COLLEGE Ext. 1. *Fax:* 570-945-7916. *E-mail:* admissns@keystone.edu.

LACKAWANNA COLLEGE
Scranton, Pennsylvania

- **Independent** 2-year, founded 1894
- **Calendar** semesters
- **Degree** certificates, diplomas, and associate
- **Urban** 4-acre campus
- **Coed**

Faculty *Student/faculty ratio:* 17:1.

Student Life *Campus security:* 24-hour emergency response devices, late-night transport/escort service, patrols by college liaison staff.
Athletics Member NJCAA.
Standardized Tests *Recommended:* SAT I or ACT (for placement).
Financial Aid In 2001, 63 Federal Work-Study jobs (averaging $872). *Financial aid deadline:* 5/1.
Applying *Options:* early admission, deferred entrance. *Application fee:* $30. *Required:* high school transcript, interview.
Admissions Contact Ms. Stacie Fagerlin, Administrative Assistant/Admissions, Lackawanna College, 501 Vine Street, Scranton, PA 18509. *Phone:* 570-961-7843. *Toll-free phone:* 877-346-3552 (in-state); 570-458-2050 (out-of-state). *Fax:* 570-961-7858. *E-mail:* dudam@ljc.edu.

LANSDALE SCHOOL OF BUSINESS
North Wales, Pennsylvania

Admissions Contact Ms. Maryann H. Johnson, Director of Admissions, Lansdale School of Business, 201 Church Road, North Wales, PA 19454-4148. *Phone:* 215-699-5700 Ext. 115. *Fax:* 215-699-8770.

LAUREL BUSINESS INSTITUTE
Uniontown, Pennsylvania

- **Proprietary** 2-year, founded 1985
- **Calendar** trimesters
- **Degree** certificates, diplomas, and associate
- **Small-town** campus with easy access to Pittsburgh
- **Coed,** 378 undergraduate students
- 66% of applicants were admitted

Undergraduates Students come from 2 states and territories, 9% African American, 0.3% Hispanic American. *Retention:* 87% of 2001 full-time freshmen returned.
Freshmen *Admission:* 328 applied, 217 admitted. *Average high school GPA:* 2.75.
Faculty *Total:* 30, 70% full-time, 100% with terminal degrees. *Student/faculty ratio:* 14:1.
Majors Accounting; banking; business administration; child guidance; computer/information systems security; computer/information technology services administration and management related; computer management; computer science related; computer software and media applications related; computer systems networking/telecommunications; computer/technical support; data entry/microcomputer applications; data entry/microcomputer applications related; data processing; executive assistant; general office/clerical; home health aide; information technology; insurance/risk management; legal administrative assistant; medical administrative assistant; medical assistant; medical transcription; retail management; secretarial science; system administration; system/networking/LAN/WAN management; Web page, digital/multimedia and information resources design; word processing.
Academic Programs *Special study options:* academic remediation for entering students, adult/continuing education programs, advanced placement credit, cooperative education, double majors, freshman honors college, honors programs, internships, part-time degree program, services for LD students.
Computers on Campus 75 computers available on campus for general student use. A campuswide network can be accessed from off campus. Internet access, at least one staffed computer lab available.
Student Life *Housing:* college housing not available. *Activities and Organizations:* student-run newspaper. *Student Services:* personal/psychological counseling.
Standardized Tests *Required:* Wide Range Achievement Test, Wonderlic aptitude test.
Costs (2001–02) *Tuition:* $12,375 full-time, $2475 per term part-time. Part-time tuition and fees vary according to program. *Required fees:* $300 full-time. *Waivers:* employees or children of employees.
Applying *Options:* common application, electronic application, deferred entrance. *Application fee:* $25. *Required:* high school transcript, interview. *Application deadline:* rolling (freshmen).
Admissions Contact Mr. William Paul Guappone, Director of Admission, Laurel Business Institute, 11-15 Penn Street, PO Box 877, Uniontown, PA 15401. *Phone:* 724-439-4900. *Fax:* 724-439-3607. *E-mail:* wguappone@laurelbusiness.net.

LEHIGH CARBON COMMUNITY COLLEGE
Schnecksville, Pennsylvania

- **State and locally supported** 2-year, founded 1967
- **Calendar** semesters
- **Degree** certificates, diplomas, and associate
- **Suburban** 153-acre campus with easy access to Philadelphia
- **Endowment** $500,000
- **Coed,** 4,958 undergraduate students, 34% full-time, 60% women, 40% men

Undergraduates 1,665 full-time, 3,293 part-time. Students come from 3 states and territories, 6 other countries, 1% are from out of state, 4% African American, 3% Asian American or Pacific Islander, 7% Hispanic American, 0.2% Native American, 0.3% international, 12% transferred in.
Freshmen *Admission:* 3,044 applied, 2,766 admitted, 1,746 enrolled.
Faculty *Total:* 314, 22% full-time, 6% with terminal degrees. *Student/faculty ratio:* 18:1.
Majors Accounting technician; aircraft pilot (professional); art; aviation management; aviation technology; business administration; child care/guidance; child care provider; computer engineering technology; construction technology; criminal justice/law enforcement administration; drafting; early childhood education; education; electrical/electronic engineering technology; electrical engineering; engineering; executive assistant; gerontological services; graphic design/commercial art/illustration; health unit coordination; heating/air conditioning/refrigeration; hotel and restaurant management; humanities; industrial technology; information sciences/systems; law enforcement/police science; legal administrative assistant; liberal arts and sciences/liberal studies; machine shop assistant; mathematics; mechanical engineering technology; medical assistant; medical laboratory technician; medical records technology; nursing; occupational therapy assistant; operations management; paralegal/legal assistant; physical therapy assistant; practical nurse; precision metal working related; real estate; respiratory therapy; secretarial science; social sciences; special education; tourism promotion operations; tourism/travel marketing; veterinarian assistant.
Academic Programs *Special study options:* academic remediation for entering students, adult/continuing education programs, advanced placement credit, cooperative education, distance learning, English as a second language, independent study, internships, part-time degree program, services for LD students, summer session for credit. *ROTC:* Army (c).
Library Learning Resource Center with 98,065 titles, 553 serial subscriptions, 3,963 audiovisual materials, an OPAC, a Web page.
Computers on Campus 210 computers available on campus for general student use. At least one staffed computer lab available.
Student Life *Housing:* college housing not available. *Activities and Organizations:* student-run newspaper, radio station, Phi Theta Kappa, STEP Student Association, student radio station, student government, College Activity Board. *Campus security:* 24-hour emergency response devices and patrols, student patrols, late-night transport/escort service. *Student Services:* personal/psychological counseling.
Athletics Member NJCAA. *Intercollegiate sports:* baseball M/W, basketball M/W, golf M/W, soccer M, softball W, volleyball W. *Intramural sports:* archery M/W, badminton M/W, baseball M, basketball M/W, bowling M/W, field hockey W, football M/W, golf M/W, racquetball M/W, skiing (downhill) M/W, soccer M/W, softball M/W, swimming M/W, table tennis M/W, tennis M/W, track and field M, volleyball M/W, weight lifting M/W.
Standardized Tests *Required for some:* ACT or ACT COMPASS.
Costs (2001–02) *Tuition:* area resident $2325 full-time, $67 per credit hour part-time; state resident $4650 full-time, $134 per credit hour part-time; nonresident $6915 full-time, $201 per credit hour part-time. Full-time tuition and fees vary according to course load. Part-time tuition and fees vary according to course load. *Required fees:* $315 full-time, $11 per credit hour. *Payment plan:* installment. *Waivers:* employees or children of employees.
Financial Aid In 2001, 65 Federal Work-Study jobs (averaging $2200).
Applying *Application fee:* $25. *Required for some:* essay or personal statement, high school transcript, interview. *Application deadline:* rolling (freshmen), rolling (transfers). *Notification:* continuous (freshmen).
Admissions Contact Mr. David Solove, Director of Recruitment and Admissions, Lehigh Carbon Community College, 4525 Education Park Drive, Schnecksville, PA 18078-2598. *Phone:* 610-799-1575. *Fax:* 610-799-1527. *E-mail:* admis@lex.lccc.edu.

LINCOLN TECHNICAL INSTITUTE
Allentown, Pennsylvania

- **Proprietary** 2-year, founded 1949, part of Lincoln Technical Institute, Inc
- **Calendar** semesters

Lincoln Technical Institute (continued)
- **Degree** diplomas and associate
- **Suburban** 10-acre campus with easy access to Philadelphia
- **Coed**

Applying *Options:* common application, early admission. *Application fee:* $100. *Required:* high school transcript, interview. *Recommended:* letters of recommendation.
Admissions Contact Admissions Office, Lincoln Technical Institute, 5151 Tilghman Street, Allentown, PA 18104-3298. *Phone:* 610-398-5301.

LINCOLN TECHNICAL INSTITUTE
Philadelphia, Pennsylvania

Admissions Contact Ms. Ivone Mangaul, Director of Admissions, Lincoln Technical Institute, 9191 Torresdale Avenue, Philadelphia, PA 19136-1595. *Phone:* 215-335-0800. *Toll-free phone:* 800-238-8381.

LUZERNE COUNTY COMMUNITY COLLEGE
Nanticoke, Pennsylvania

- **County-supported** 2-year, founded 1966
- **Calendar** semesters
- **Degree** certificates, diplomas, and associate
- **Suburban** 122-acre campus with easy access to Philadelphia
- **Coed,** 6,076 undergraduate students, 42% full-time, 57% women, 43% men

Undergraduates Students come from 1 other state, 1 other country, 2% African American, 1% Asian American or Pacific Islander, 1% Hispanic American, 0.2% Native American, 0.1% international.
Freshmen *Admission:* 2,507 applied, 1,758 admitted.
Faculty *Total:* 461, 30% full-time. *Student/faculty ratio:* 19:1.
Majors Accounting; aircraft pilot (professional); architectural engineering technology; auto mechanic/technician; aviation management; baker/pastry chef; banking; biological/physical sciences; building maintenance/management; business administration; child care provider; computer graphics; computer graphics; computer/information sciences; computer maintenance technology; computer programming related; computer science; computer science related; computer systems networking/telecommunications; criminal justice/law enforcement administration; culinary arts; data entry/microcomputer applications; data processing technology; dental assistant; dental hygiene; drafting; drafting/design technology; drawing; early childhood education; education; electrical/electronic engineering technology; electrical/power transmission installation; emergency medical technology; engineering-related technology; executive assistant; fire science; food services technology; general studies; graphic design/commercial art/illustration; graphic/printing equipment; health/physical education; health services administration; heating/air conditioning/refrigeration; horticulture science; hotel and restaurant management; hotel/motel services marketing operations; humanities; human services; international business; journalism; liberal arts and sciences/ liberal studies; mathematics; mechanical design technology; medical administrative assistant; mortuary science; nursing; operating room technician; ophthalmic/ optometric services; painting; paralegal/legal assistant; photography; plumbing; pre-pharmacy studies; radio/television broadcasting technology; real estate; respiratory therapy; secretarial science; social sciences; travel services marketing operations; travel/tourism management.
Academic Programs *Special study options:* academic remediation for entering students, accelerated degree program, advanced placement credit, distance learning, external degree program, internships, part-time degree program, services for LD students, summer session for credit. *ROTC:* Air Force (c).
Library Learning Resources Center plus 1 other with 60,000 titles, 744 serial subscriptions, 3,000 audiovisual materials, an OPAC, a Web page.
Computers on Campus 150 computers available on campus for general student use. Internet access, at least one staffed computer lab available.
Student Life *Housing:* college housing not available. *Activities and Organizations:* student-run newspaper, radio and television station, student government, Circle K, Nursing Forum, Science Club, SADAH. *Campus security:* 24-hour patrols.
Athletics Member NJCAA. *Intercollegiate sports:* baseball M, basketball M/W, cross-country running M/W, golf M/W, soccer M/W, softball W, volleyball W. *Intramural sports:* badminton M/W, basketball M/W, bowling M/W, softball M/W, tennis M/W, volleyball M/W.
Standardized Tests *Recommended:* ACCUPLACER.
Costs (2002–03) *Tuition:* area resident $2010 full-time, $67 per credit part-time; state resident $4020 full-time, $134 per credit part-time; nonresident $6030 full-time, $201 per credit part-time. *Required fees:* $270 full-time, $9 per credit. *Waivers:* senior citizens and employees or children of employees.
Applying *Options:* early admission, deferred entrance. *Application fee:* $25. *Recommended:* high school transcript. *Application deadline:* rolling (freshmen), rolling (transfers).
Admissions Contact Mr. Francis Curry, Director of Admissions, Luzerne County Community College, 1333 South Prospect Street, Nanticoke, PA 18634. *Phone:* 570-740-0200 Ext. 343. *Toll-free phone:* 800-377-5222 Ext. 337. *Fax:* 570-740-0238. *E-mail:* admissions@luzerne.edu.

MANOR COLLEGE
Jenkintown, Pennsylvania

- **Independent Byzantine Catholic** 2-year, founded 1947
- **Calendar** semesters
- **Degrees** certificates, diplomas, associate, and postbachelor's certificates
- **Small-town** 35-acre campus with easy access to Philadelphia
- **Coed,** 800 undergraduate students

Manor College, located in Jenkintown, a suburb of Philadelphia, offers associate degree and transfer programs in the allied health, business, and liberal arts fields. Areas of study include accounting; allied health; business administration; early child care/human services; dental hygiene; expanded functions dental assisting; health-care management; medical, legal, and administrative science and technology; paralegal studies; psychology; and veterinary technology.

Undergraduates Students come from 5 states and territories, 8 other countries, 7% are from out of state.
Freshmen *Admission:* 934 applied, 472 admitted. *Average high school GPA:* 2.85. *Test scores:* SAT verbal scores over 500: 19%; SAT math scores over 500: 14%; SAT verbal scores over 600: 3%; SAT math scores over 600: 2%; SAT verbal scores over 700: 1%.
Faculty *Total:* 100, 22% full-time, 70% with terminal degrees. *Student/faculty ratio:* 11:1.
Majors Accounting; animal sciences; biological/physical sciences; business administration; child care/development; computer science; computer science related; computer/technical support; cytotechnology; dental hygiene; early childhood education; education; elementary education; health science; human services; international business; laboratory animal medicine; legal administrative assistant; liberal arts and sciences/liberal studies; medical administrative assistant; medical laboratory technician; occupational therapy; paralegal/legal assistant; physical therapy; psychology; secretarial science; veterinary sciences; veterinary technology.
Academic Programs *Special study options:* academic remediation for entering students, adult/continuing education programs, advanced placement credit, distance learning, double majors, English as a second language, honors programs, independent study, internships, part-time degree program, summer session for credit.
Library Basileiad Library with 42,000 titles, 225 serial subscriptions, 300 audiovisual materials, an OPAC, a Web page.
Computers on Campus 35 computers available on campus for general student use. A campuswide network can be accessed from student residence rooms. Internet access, at least one staffed computer lab available.
Student Life *Housing Options:* coed. *Activities and Organizations:* choral group. *Campus security:* 24-hour emergency response devices and patrols. *Student Services:* personal/psychological counseling.
Athletics *Intercollegiate sports:* basketball M(s)/W(s), soccer M(s)/W(s), volleyball W(s). *Intramural sports:* basketball M/W, soccer M/W, volleyball W.
Standardized Tests *Required:* SAT I or ACT (for admission).
Costs (2001–02) *Comprehensive fee:* $13,420 includes full-time tuition ($8520), mandatory fees ($300), and room and board ($4600). Part-time tuition: $205 per credit. Part-time tuition and fees vary according to course load. *Waivers:* employees or children of employees.
Financial Aid *Financial aid deadline:* 9/30.
Applying *Options:* electronic application, deferred entrance. *Application fee:* $20. *Required:* high school transcript, interview. *Application deadline:* rolling (freshmen), rolling (transfers). *Notification:* continuous (freshmen).
Admissions Contact Ms. I. Jerry Czenstuch, Dean of Admissions, Manor College, 700 Fox Chase Road, Jenkintown, PA 19046. *Phone:* 215-884-2216. *Fax:* 215-576-6564. *E-mail:* ftadmiss@manor.edu.

McCann School of Business
Mahanoy City, Pennsylvania

- **Proprietary** 2-year, founded 1897
- **Calendar** quarters
- **Degree** certificates, diplomas, and associate
- **Small-town** campus
- **Coed,** 297 undergraduate students, 66% full-time, 76% women, 24% men

Undergraduates 195 full-time, 102 part-time. Students come from 1 other state, 3% African American, 1% Asian American or Pacific Islander, 2% Hispanic American, 10% transferred in.

Freshmen *Admission:* 297 enrolled. *Average high school GPA:* 3.14.

Faculty *Total:* 77, 35% full-time. *Student/faculty ratio:* 12:1.

Majors Accounting; business administration; business marketing and marketing management; computer programming (specific applications); computer science; computer science related; medical office management; paralegal/legal assistant; secretarial science; system/networking/LAN/WAN management.

Academic Programs *Special study options:* advanced placement credit, double majors, independent study, internships, part-time degree program, summer session for credit.

Library 1,850 titles, 26 serial subscriptions.

Computers on Campus 150 computers available on campus for general student use. Internet access, at least one staffed computer lab available.

Student Life *Housing:* college housing not available. *Activities and Organizations:* student council, Circle K, American Marketing Association.

Costs (2002–03) *Tuition:* $7020 full-time, $156 per credit part-time. *Waivers:* employees or children of employees.

Applying *Options:* common application, electronic application. *Application fee:* $30. *Required:* high school transcript, minimum 2.0 GPA, interview. *Application deadline:* rolling (freshmen), rolling (transfers).

Admissions Contact Ms. Rachel M. Schoffstall, Director, Pottsville Campus, McCann School of Business, 47 South Main Street, Mahanoy City, PA 17948. *Phone:* 570-622-7622.

Median School of Allied Health Careers
Pittsburgh, Pennsylvania

- **Proprietary** 2-year, founded 1958
- **Calendar** quarters
- **Degree** diplomas and associate
- **Urban** campus
- **Coed**

Student Life *Campus security:* security during class hours.

Costs (2001–02) *Tuition:* $8200 full-time, $3065 per term part-time. Full-time tuition and fees vary according to program. No tuition increase for student's term of enrollment. *Required fees:* $400 full-time.

Financial Aid In 2001, 15 Federal Work-Study jobs.

Applying *Options:* deferred entrance. *Application fee:* $75. *Required:* essay or personal statement, high school transcript, interview. *Recommended:* minimum 2.0 GPA.

Admissions Contact Ms. Anna Bartolini, Admission Coordinator, Median School of Allied Health Careers, 125 7th Street, Pittsburgh, PA 15222-3400. *Phone:* 412-391-7021. *Toll-free phone:* 800-570-0693. *Fax:* 412-232-4348. *E-mail:* median@sgi.net.

Montgomery County Community College
Blue Bell, Pennsylvania

- **County-supported** 2-year, founded 1964
- **Calendar** semesters
- **Degree** certificates and associate
- **Suburban** 186-acre campus with easy access to Philadelphia
- **Coed,** 9,592 undergraduate students, 37% full-time, 57% women, 43% men

Undergraduates 3,554 full-time, 6,038 part-time. Students come from 5 states and territories, 0.1% are from out of state, 8% African American, 6% Asian American or Pacific Islander, 2% Hispanic American, 0.3% Native American, 1% international. *Retention:* 15% of 2001 full-time freshmen returned.

Freshmen *Admission:* 2,990 enrolled.

Faculty *Total:* 552, 24% full-time. *Student/faculty ratio:* 22:1.

Majors Accounting; accounting technician; art; biology; business; business administration; business marketing and marketing management; business systems networking/ telecommunications; child care/guidance; communications; computer/ information sciences; computer maintenance technology; computer programming; data processing; dental hygiene; drafting; electromechanical technology; elementary education; engineering science; engineering technology; environmental technology; graphic design/commercial art/illustration; hospitality/ recreation marketing operations; hotel and restaurant management; hotel/motel services marketing operations; humanities; information sciences/systems; law enforcement/police science; liberal arts and sciences/liberal studies; management information systems/business data processing; marketing operations; mathematics; mechanical engineering technology; medical laboratory technician; nursing; physical education; physical sciences; psychiatric/mental health services; real estate; retailing operations; secretarial science; social sciences.

Academic Programs *Special study options:* academic remediation for entering students, adult/continuing education programs, advanced placement credit, distance learning, English as a second language, honors programs, independent study, internships, part-time degree program, services for LD students, student-designed majors, summer session for credit.

Library Learning Resource Center with 175,574 titles, 431 serial subscriptions, 17,436 audiovisual materials, an OPAC, a Web page.

Computers on Campus 500 computers available on campus for general student use. A campuswide network can be accessed from off campus. Internet access, at least one staffed computer lab available.

Student Life *Housing:* college housing not available. *Activities and Organizations:* student-run newspaper, radio station, choral group, student government, Meridians Non-traditional Age Club, student radio station. *Campus security:* 24-hour emergency response devices and patrols, late-night transport/escort service. *Student Services:* health clinic, personal/psychological counseling.

Athletics *Intercollegiate sports:* baseball M. *Intramural sports:* archery M, badminton M, basketball M/W, bowling M/W, cross-country running M/W, field hockey W, football M, golf M, racquetball M/W, soccer M/W, softball W, table tennis M/W, tennis M/W, volleyball M/W.

Standardized Tests *Recommended:* SAT I or ACT (for placement).

Costs (2001–02) *Tuition:* area resident $2250 full-time, $75 per credit part-time; state resident $4500 full-time, $150 per credit part-time; nonresident $6750 full-time, $225 per credit part-time. *Required fees:* $210 full-time, $7 per credit. *Payment plan:* deferred payment. *Waivers:* senior citizens and employees or children of employees.

Financial Aid In 2001, 58 Federal Work-Study jobs (averaging $2121).

Applying *Options:* early admission, deferred entrance. *Application fee:* $20. *Required for some:* high school transcript, interview. *Application deadline:* rolling (freshmen), rolling (transfers). *Notification:* continuous (freshmen).

Admissions Contact Mr. Joe Rodriguez, Director of Admissions and Records (Interim), Montgomery County Community College, 340 DeKalb Pike, Blue Bell, PA 19422-0796. *Phone:* 215-641-6550. *Fax:* 215-653-0585. *E-mail:* admrec@admin.mc3.edu.

New Castle School of Trades
Pulaski, Pennsylvania

Admissions Contact New Castle Youngstown Road, Route 422 RD1, Pulaski, PA 16143-9721.

Newport Business Institute
Lower Burrell, Pennsylvania

- **Proprietary** 2-year, founded 1895
- **Calendar** quarters
- **Degree** certificates, diplomas, and associate
- **Small-town** 4-acre campus with easy access to Pittsburgh
- **Coed**

Faculty *Student/faculty ratio:* 16:1.

Student Life *Campus security:* security system.

Applying *Options:* common application, early admission. *Application fee:* $25. *Required:* high school transcript.

Admissions Contact Ms. Jan Schoeneberger, Director of Admissions, Newport Business Institute, Lower Burrell, PA 15068. *Phone:* 724-339-7542. *Toll-free phone:* 800-752-7695. *Fax:* 724-339-2950.

NEWPORT BUSINESS INSTITUTE
Williamsport, Pennsylvania

- **Proprietary** 2-year, founded 1955
- **Calendar** quarters
- **Degree** associate
- **Small-town** campus
- **Coed, primarily women,** 146 undergraduate students, 98% full-time, 97% women, 3% men

Undergraduates 143 full-time, 3 part-time. Students come from 1 other state.
Freshmen *Admission:* 63 applied, 63 admitted, 43 enrolled.
Faculty *Total:* 6, 100% full-time. *Student/faculty ratio:* 20:1.
Majors Business administration; legal administrative assistant; medical administrative assistant; secretarial science.
Academic Programs *Special study options:* internships, part-time degree program, summer session for credit.
Computers on Campus 60 computers available on campus for general student use. Internet access, at least one staffed computer lab available.
Student Life *Housing:* college housing not available. *Activities and Organizations:* Student Council, FBLA.
Costs (2001–02) *One-time required fee:* $50. *Tuition:* $6900 full-time, $575 per course part-time. *Required fees:* $400 full-time. *Payment plan:* installment. *Waivers:* employees or children of employees.
Financial Aid *Financial aid deadline:* 8/1.
Applying *Options:* deferred entrance. *Application fee:* $25. *Required:* high school transcript. *Application deadline:* rolling (freshmen), rolling (transfers).
Admissions Contact Mr. Joshua Stewart, Admissions Representative, Newport Business Institute, 941 West Third Street, Williamsport, PA 17701-5855. *Phone:* 570-326-2869. *Toll-free phone:* 800-962-6971. *Fax:* 570-326-2136.

NORTHAMPTON COUNTY AREA COMMUNITY COLLEGE
Bethlehem, Pennsylvania

- **State and locally supported** 2-year, founded 1967
- **Calendar** semesters
- **Degree** certificates, diplomas, and associate
- **Suburban** 165-acre campus with easy access to Philadelphia
- **Endowment** $10.8 million
- **Coed,** 6,216 undergraduate students, 43% full-time, 60% women, 40% men

Undergraduates 2,700 full-time, 3,516 part-time. Students come from 20 states and territories, 32 other countries, 3% are from out of state, 4% African American, 2% Asian American or Pacific Islander, 6% Hispanic American, 0.2% Native American, 2% international, 32% transferred in, 4% live on campus.
Freshmen *Admission:* 2,510 applied, 2,446 admitted, 2,104 enrolled.
Faculty *Total:* 329, 25% full-time, 15% with terminal degrees. *Student/faculty ratio:* 24:1.
Majors Accounting technician; acting/directing; architectural engineering technology; automotive engineering technology; banking; biology; business; business administration; chemical technology; chemistry; child care/guidance; computer/information sciences; computer installation/repair; criminal justice/law enforcement administration; data processing technology; dental hygiene; drafting; electrical/electronic engineering technologies related; electrical/electronic engineering technology; electromechanical technology; engineering; executive assistant; fine/studio arts; fire services administration; general studies; graphic design/commercial art/illustration; hotel and restaurant management; interior architecture; journalism; legal administrative assistant; liberal arts and sciences/liberal studies; liberal arts and studies related; mathematics; medical administrative assistant; medical radiologic technology; mortuary science; nursing; occupational health/industrial hygiene; paralegal/legal assistant; physics; quality control technology; radio/television broadcasting technology; social work; special education; sport/fitness administration; teacher education related; travel services marketing operations; veterinarian assistant.
Academic Programs *Special study options:* academic remediation for entering students, accelerated degree program, adult/continuing education programs, advanced placement credit, cooperative education, distance learning, English as a second language, internships, part-time degree program, services for LD students, student-designed majors, study abroad, summer session for credit.
Library Learning Resources Center with 51,103 titles, 376 serial subscriptions, 2,708 audiovisual materials, an OPAC.
Computers on Campus 950 computers available on campus for general student use. Internet access, online (class) registration, at least one staffed computer lab available.
Student Life *Housing Options:* coed. *Activities and Organizations:* drama/theater group, student-run newspaper, radio station, choral group, Phi Theta Kappa, Nursing Student Organization, NAVTA (Veterinary Technology Club), Criminal Justice, Student American Dental Hygiene Association. *Campus security:* 24-hour emergency response devices and patrols, controlled dormitory access. *Student Services:* health clinic, personal/psychological counseling.
Athletics *Intercollegiate sports:* baseball M, basketball M/W, bowling M/W, golf M/W, ice hockey M/W, soccer M, softball W, tennis M/W, volleyball M/W. *Intramural sports:* basketball M/W, bowling M/W, football M/W, golf M/W, racquetball M/W, soccer M/W, table tennis M/W.
Standardized Tests *Required for some:* ACT (for placement).
Costs (2001–02) *Tuition:* area resident $1980 full-time, $66 per credit hour part-time; state resident $3960 full-time, $132 per credit hour part-time; nonresident $5940 full-time, $198 per credit hour part-time. *Required fees:* $510 full-time, $17 per credit hour. *Room and board:* $5084; room only: $2944. Room and board charges vary according to board plan and housing facility. *Payment plans:* installment, deferred payment. *Waivers:* senior citizens and employees or children of employees.
Financial Aid In 2001, 200 Federal Work-Study jobs (averaging $2095). 70 State and other part-time jobs (averaging $2000).
Applying *Options:* electronic application. *Application fee:* $25. *Required:* high school transcript. *Required for some:* interview, art evaluation for communication design, fine arts programs; audition required for theatre program. *Application deadline:* rolling (freshmen), rolling (transfers). *Notification:* continuous (freshmen).
Admissions Contact Ms. Carolyn H. Holmfelt, Director of Admissions, Northampton County Area Community College, 3835 Green Pond Road, Bethlehem, PA 18020-7599. *Phone:* 610-861-5500. *Fax:* 610-861-5551. *E-mail:* adminfo@northampton.edu.

NORTHWEST PENNSYLVANIA TECHNICAL INSTITUTE
Erie, Pennsylvania

Admissions Contact 150 East Front Street, Suite 200, Erie, PA 16507.

OAKBRIDGE ACADEMY OF ARTS
Lower Burrell, Pennsylvania

- **Proprietary** 2-year, founded 1972
- **Calendar** quarters
- **Degree** associate
- **Small-town** 2-acre campus with easy access to Pittsburgh
- **Coed,** 97 undergraduate students, 100% full-time, 63% women, 37% men
- 88% of applicants were admitted

Undergraduates 97 full-time. Students come from 4 states and territories, 2% Asian American or Pacific Islander, 1% Hispanic American, 1% Native American, 6% transferred in. *Retention:* 82% of 2001 full-time freshmen returned.
Freshmen *Admission:* 73 applied, 64 admitted, 43 enrolled. *Average high school GPA:* 2.30.
Faculty *Total:* 8, 75% full-time. *Student/faculty ratio:* 11:1.
Majors Commercial photography; computer graphics; graphic design/commercial art/illustration.
Academic Programs *Special study options:* academic remediation for entering students, advanced placement credit, internships.
Library Robert J. Mullen Memorial Library plus 1 other with 3,000 titles, 15 serial subscriptions, 80 audiovisual materials, a Web page.
Computers on Campus 40 computers available on campus for general student use. Internet access, at least one staffed computer lab available.
Student Life *Housing:* college housing not available. *Campus security:* 24-hour emergency response devices.
Costs (2002–03) *Tuition:* $7800 full-time, $700 per course part-time. Full-time tuition and fees vary according to course load and program. Part-time tuition and fees vary according to course load and program. *Required fees:* $200 full-time. *Payment plan:* installment. *Waivers:* employees or children of employees.
Applying *Options:* common application, electronic application. *Required:* high school transcript, portfolio. *Application deadline:* 8/31 (freshmen).

Admissions Contact Jan Schoeneberger, Admissions Representative, Oakbridge Academy of Arts, 1250 Greensburg Road, Lower Burrell, PA 15068. *Phone:* 724-335-5336. *Toll-free phone:* 800-734-5601. *Fax:* 724-335-3367. *E-mail:* oakbridge1@aol.com.

ORLEANS TECHNICAL INSTITUTE-CENTER CITY CAMPUS
Philadelphia, Pennsylvania

Admissions Contact 1845 Walnut Street, Suite 700, Philadelphia, PA 19103-4707.

PACE INSTITUTE
Reading, Pennsylvania

- **Private** 2-year
- **Degree** diplomas and associate
- **Coed,** 260 undergraduate students, 77% full-time, 56% women, 44% men
- 91% of applicants were admitted

Freshmen *Admission:* 70 applied, 64 admitted.
Faculty *Total:* 13, 38% full-time, 8% with terminal degrees. *Student/faculty ratio:* 9:1.
Majors Accounting; business administration; business systems networking/telecommunications; computer programming; fashion merchandising; medical assistant; paralegal/legal assistant; secretarial science; travel/tourism management.
Costs (2002–03) *Tuition:* $2362 per term part-time. Tuition dependent on program selected, ranging from 4,725 to 15,300. *Required fees:* $1080 full-time, $540 per term.
Admissions Contact Ms. Barbara Tizek, Director of Admissions, Pace Institute, 606 Court Street, Reading, PA 19601. *Phone:* 610-375-1212.

PENN COMMERCIAL BUSINESS AND TECHNICAL SCHOOL
Washington, Pennsylvania

- **Proprietary** 2-year, founded 1929
- **Calendar** quarters
- **Degree** certificates, diplomas, and associate
- **Small-town** 1-acre campus with easy access to Pittsburgh
- **Coed,** 268 undergraduate students, 100% full-time, 60% women, 40% men

Undergraduates 268 full-time. Students come from 3 states and territories.
Freshmen *Admission:* 104 enrolled. *Average high school GPA:* 2.8.
Faculty *Total:* 28, 39% full-time. *Student/faculty ratio:* 16:1.
Majors Business administration; drafting; legal administrative assistant; medical administrative assistant; medical assistant; paralegal/legal assistant; secretarial science.
Academic Programs *Special study options:* academic remediation for entering students, summer session for credit.
Library 400 titles, 10 serial subscriptions.
Computers on Campus 60 computers available on campus for general student use. At least one staffed computer lab available.
Student Life *Housing:* college housing not available. *Activities and Organizations:* student-run newspaper.
Costs (2002–03) *Tuition:* $450 per credit part-time. Full-time tuition and fees vary according to program. Tuition varies, $9,000 to $19,000, depending on program. *Payment plan:* installment.
Financial Aid *Financial aid deadline:* 8/1.
Applying *Options:* early admission, deferred entrance. *Application fee:* $25. *Required:* high school transcript. *Application deadline:* rolling (freshmen), rolling (transfers). *Notification:* continuous (freshmen).
Admissions Contact Mr. Michael John Joyce, Director of Admissions, Penn Commercial Business and Technical School, 82 South Main Street, Washington, PA 15301-6822. *Phone:* 724-222-5330 Ext. 1.

PENNCO TECH
Bristol, Pennsylvania

Admissions Contact Mr. Glenn Slater, Director of Admissions, Pennco Tech, 3815 Otter Street, Bristol, PA 19007-3696. *Phone:* 215-824-3200. *E-mail:* admissions@penncotech.com.

PENNSYLVANIA COLLEGE OF TECHNOLOGY
Williamsport, Pennsylvania

- **State-related** primarily 2-year, founded 1965
- **Calendar** semesters
- **Degrees** certificates, associate, and bachelor's
- **Small-town** 927-acre campus
- **Endowment** $597,980
- **Coed,** 5,538 undergraduate students, 80% full-time, 34% women, 66% men

Pennsylvania College of Technology is a special-mission affiliate of The Pennsylvania State University and Pennsylvania's premier technical college. Committed to applied technology education, Penn College offers partnerships with business and industry that are a key ingredient of its success in placing graduates (90 percent overall, 100 percent in many majors). Unique bachelor and associate degrees focus on applied technology and combine hands-on experience with theory and management education related to the student's field of study.

Undergraduates 4,449 full-time, 1,089 part-time. Students come from 32 states and territories, 16 other countries, 6% are from out of state, 2% African American, 0.9% Asian American or Pacific Islander, 0.7% Hispanic American, 0.5% Native American, 0.6% international, 2% transferred in, 19% live on campus.
Freshmen *Admission:* 4,351 applied, 2,567 admitted, 1,571 enrolled.
Faculty *Total:* 411, 64% full-time. *Student/faculty ratio:* 18:1.
Majors Accounting; accounting technician; aerospace engineering technology; aircraft mechanic/powerplant; architectural engineering technology; auto body repair; automotive engineering technology; baker/pastry chef; banking; biology; biomedical engineering-related technology; broadcast journalism; business administration; business administration/management related; business computer programming; business systems analysis/design; business systems networking/telecommunications; child care/guidance; civil engineering technology; computer/information sciences; computer/information sciences related; computer maintenance technology; construction technology; culinary arts; data processing; dental hygiene; diesel engine mechanic; dietician assistant; drafting; drafting related; electrical/electronic engineering technologies related; electrical/electronic engineering technology; emergency medical technology; engineering science; environmental control technologies related; environmental technology; forest harvesting production technology; general studies; graphic design/commercial art/illustration; graphic/printing equipment; health/medical administrative services related; health/medical diagnostic and treatment services related; health/physical education/fitness related; health professions and related sciences; heating/air conditioning/refrigeration technology; heavy equipment maintenance; industrial electronics installation/repair; industrial machinery maintenance/repair; industrial production technologies related; industrial technology; institutional food workers; instrumentation technology; laser/optical technology; law and legal studies related; legal studies; liberal arts and sciences/liberal studies; lithography; masonry/tile setting; mass communications; mechanical drafting; medical administrative assistant; medical radiologic technology; mental health services related; nursery management; nursing; nursing (adult health); occupational therapy assistant; ornamental horticulture; paralegal/legal assistant; physical sciences; plastics technology; practical nurse; psychiatric/mental health services; quality control technology; secretarial science; surveying; teacher education, specific programs related; technical/business writing; tool/die making; travel/tourism management; vehicle/mobile equipment mechanics and repair related.
Academic Programs *Special study options:* academic remediation for entering students, advanced placement credit, cooperative education, distance learning, double majors, English as a second language, independent study, internships, off-campus study, part-time degree program, services for LD students, student-designed majors, summer session for credit. *ROTC:* Army (c).
Library Penn College Library plus 1 other with 64,462 titles, 6,985 audiovisual materials, an OPAC, a Web page.
Computers on Campus A campuswide network can be accessed from student residence rooms and from off campus. At least one staffed computer lab available.
Student Life *Housing Options:* coed. *Activities and Organizations:* student-run newspaper, radio station, Student Government Association, Resident Hall Association (RHA), Wildcats Event Board (WEB), Phi Beta Lambda, Early Educators. *Campus security:* 24-hour emergency response devices and patrols, late-night transport/escort service. *Student Services:* personal/psychological counseling, women's center.
Athletics *Intercollegiate sports:* archery M/W, baseball M, basketball M/W, bowling M/W, cross-country running M/W, golf M/W, soccer M/W, softball W, tennis M/W, volleyball W. *Intramural sports:* archery M/W, badminton M/W,

Pennsylvania College of Technology (continued)
basketball M/W, bowling M/W, football M/W, golf M/W, lacrosse M/W, racquetball M/W, soccer M/W, softball M/W, table tennis M/W, tennis M/W, volleyball M/W, weight lifting M/W, wrestling M.

Costs (2001–02) *Tuition:* state resident $7860 full-time, $262 per credit part-time; nonresident $9960 full-time, $332 per credit part-time. Full-time tuition and fees vary according to course load. Part-time tuition and fees vary according to course load. *Required fees:* $750 full-time. *Room and board:* $5000; room only: $3600. Room and board charges vary according to board plan and location. *Payment plan:* deferred payment. *Waivers:* employees or children of employees.

Financial Aid In 2001, 335 Federal Work-Study jobs (averaging $1305).

Applying *Options:* electronic application, early admission, deferred entrance. *Application fee:* $50. *Required:* high school transcript. *Application deadline:* rolling (freshmen), rolling (transfers).

Admissions Contact Mr. Chester D. Schuman, Director of Admissions, Pennsylvania College of Technology, One College Avenue, DIF #119, Williamsport, PA 17701. *Phone:* 570-327-4761. *Toll-free phone:* 800-367-9222. *Fax:* 570-321-5551. *E-mail:* cschuman@pct.edu.

PENNSYLVANIA INSTITUTE OF CULINARY ARTS
Pittsburgh, Pennsylvania

- **Proprietary** 2-year, founded 1986
- **Calendar** semesters
- **Degree** associate
- **Coed,** 1,447 undergraduate students, 100% full-time, 41% women, 59% men

Undergraduates 1,447 full-time. Students come from 23 states and territories, 2 other countries, 62% are from out of state.

Freshmen *Admission:* 1,447 enrolled.

Faculty *Total:* 46, 100% full-time. *Student/faculty ratio:* 18:1.

Majors Culinary arts; hotel and restaurant management.

Academic Programs *Special study options:* academic remediation for entering students, double majors, internships.

Library Learning Resource Center with 6,000 titles, 73 serial subscriptions, 3 audiovisual materials, a Web page.

Computers on Campus 90 computers available on campus for general student use. A campuswide network can be accessed from off campus. Internet access, at least one staffed computer lab available.

Costs (2002–03) *Comprehensive fee:* $21,766 includes full-time tuition ($15,000), mandatory fees ($200), and room and board ($6566). No tuition increase for student's term of enrollment. *Room and board:* College room only: $4118. *Waivers:* employees or children of employees.

Applying *Options:* electronic application. *Application fee:* $50. *Required:* essay or personal statement, high school transcript, interview.

Admissions Contact Ms. Sharon Vito, Enrollment Manager, Pennsylvania Institute of Culinary Arts, 717 Liberty Avenue, Pittsburgh, PA 15222-3500. *Phone:* 412-566-2433 Ext. 4727. *Toll-free phone:* 800-432-2433. *Fax:* 412-566-2434. *E-mail:* info@paculinary.com.

PENNSYLVANIA INSTITUTE OF TECHNOLOGY
Media, Pennsylvania

- **Independent** 2-year, founded 1953
- **Calendar** semesters
- **Degree** certificates and associate
- **Small-town** 12-acre campus with easy access to Philadelphia
- **Coed,** 335 undergraduate students, 50% full-time, 34% women, 66% men

Undergraduates 167 full-time, 168 part-time. Students come from 3 states and territories, 31% African American, 2% Asian American or Pacific Islander, 3% Hispanic American, 0.3% Native American. *Retention:* 52% of 2001 full-time freshmen returned.

Freshmen *Admission:* 244 applied, 148 admitted, 135 enrolled.

Faculty *Total:* 25, 40% full-time, 4% with terminal degrees. *Student/faculty ratio:* 13:1.

Majors Architectural engineering technology; business administration; electrical/electronic engineering technology; engineering-related technology; general office/clerical; mechanical engineering technologies related; mechanical engineering technology; medical office management; Web page, digital/multimedia and information resources design.

Academic Programs *Special study options:* academic remediation for entering students, adult/continuing education programs, advanced placement credit, cooperative education, part-time degree program, summer session for credit.

Library Pennsylvania Institute of Technology Library/Learning Resource Center with 16,500 titles, 217 serial subscriptions, an OPAC, a Web page.

Computers on Campus 85 computers available on campus for general student use. At least one staffed computer lab available.

Student Life *Housing:* college housing not available. *Campus security:* 24-hour emergency response devices. *Student Services:* personal/psychological counseling.

Athletics *Intramural sports:* basketball M/W, volleyball M/W.

Standardized Tests *Recommended:* SAT I or ACT (for placement).

Costs (2001–02) *Tuition:* $8250 full-time, $275 per credit part-time. Part-time tuition and fees vary according to course load. *Required fees:* $120 full-time, $5 per credit. *Payment plan:* installment. *Waivers:* employees or children of employees.

Financial Aid In 2001, 15 Federal Work-Study jobs (averaging $1025). *Financial aid deadline:* 5/1.

Applying *Options:* common application, electronic application, deferred entrance. *Application fee:* $25. *Required:* high school transcript, interview. *Required for some:* 2 letters of recommendation. *Recommended:* essay or personal statement. *Application deadline:* 8/1 (freshmen), rolling (transfers). *Notification:* continuous until 9/1 (freshmen).

Admissions Contact Matthew Kadlubowski, Director of Admissions, Pennsylvania Institute of Technology, 800 Manchester Avenue, Media, PA 19063-4036. *Phone:* 610-892-1550 Ext. 1553. *Toll-free phone:* 800-422-0025. *Fax:* 610-892-1510. *E-mail:* info@pit.edu.

THE PENNSYLVANIA STATE UNIVERSITY BEAVER CAMPUS OF THE COMMONWEALTH COLLEGE
Monaca, Pennsylvania

- **State-related** primarily 2-year, founded 1964, part of Pennsylvania State University
- **Calendar** semesters
- **Degrees** associate and bachelor's (also offers up to 2 years of most bachelor's degree programs offered at University Park campus)
- **Small-town** 90-acre campus with easy access to Pittsburgh
- **Coed,** 752 undergraduate students, 91% full-time, 35% women, 65% men

Undergraduates 687 full-time, 65 part-time. 6% are from out of state, 5% African American, 1% Asian American or Pacific Islander, 1% Hispanic American, 3% transferred in, 35% live on campus. *Retention:* 71% of 2001 full-time freshmen returned.

Freshmen *Admission:* 581 applied, 541 admitted, 283 enrolled. *Average high school GPA:* 2.92. *Test scores:* SAT verbal scores over 500: 50%; SAT math scores over 500: 50%; SAT verbal scores over 600: 8%; SAT math scores over 600: 12%; SAT math scores over 700: 2%.

Faculty *Total:* 69, 52% full-time. *Student/faculty ratio:* 15:1.

Majors Agricultural business; biological/physical sciences; biomedical engineering-related technology; business; business administration; electrical/electronic engineering technology; hotel and restaurant management; information sciences/systems; liberal arts and sciences/liberal studies; mechanical engineering technology.

Academic Programs *Special study options:* academic remediation for entering students, adult/continuing education programs, advanced placement credit, distance learning, double majors, English as a second language, honors programs, independent study, internships, services for LD students, student-designed majors, summer session for credit.

Library 38,493 titles, 245 serial subscriptions, 6,587 audiovisual materials.

Computers on Campus 106 computers available on campus for general student use. A campuswide network can be accessed from student residence rooms and from off campus. Internet access, online (class) registration, at least one staffed computer lab available.

Student Life *Housing Options:* coed. *Activities and Organizations:* drama/theater group, student-run newspaper, radio station. *Campus security:* 24-hour patrols, controlled dormitory access.

Athletics Member NJCAA. *Intercollegiate sports:* baseball M, golf M/W, softball W, volleyball W. *Intramural sports:* basketball M/W, bowling M/W, fencing M/W, golf M/W, ice hockey M/W, racquetball M/W, skiing (downhill) M/W, tennis M/W, track and field M/W, volleyball M/W.

Standardized Tests *Required:* SAT I or ACT (for admission).

Costs (2001–02) *Tuition:* state resident $6832 full-time, $276 per credit part-time; nonresident $10,574 full-time, $442 per credit part-time. Full-time tuition and fees vary according to class time, location, program, and student level. Part-time tuition and fees vary according to class time, course load, location, program, and student level. *Required fees:* $342 full-time, $57 per credit. *Room and board:* $5300; room only: $2680. Room and board charges vary according to board plan and housing facility. *Payment plan:* deferred payment. *Waivers:* senior citizens and employees or children of employees.

Financial Aid In 2001, 41 Federal Work-Study jobs (averaging $868).

Applying *Options:* electronic application, early admission, deferred entrance. *Application fee:* $50. *Required:* high school transcript. *Application deadline:* rolling (freshmen), rolling (transfers). *Notification:* continuous (freshmen).

Admissions Contact Ms. Trish Head, The Pennsylvania State University Beaver Campus of the Commonwealth College, 100 University Drive, Monaca, PA 15061-2799. *Phone:* 724-773-3800. *Fax:* 724-773-3658. *E-mail:* admissions@psu.edu.

The Pennsylvania State University Delaware County Campus of the Commonwealth College

Media, Pennsylvania

- **State-related** primarily 2-year, founded 1966, part of Pennsylvania State University
- **Calendar** semesters
- **Degrees** associate and bachelor's (also offers up to 2 years of most bachelor's degree programs offered at University Park campus)
- **Small-town** 87-acre campus with easy access to Philadelphia
- **Coed,** 1,646 undergraduate students, 82% full-time, 48% women, 52% men

Undergraduates 1,345 full-time, 301 part-time. 4% are from out of state, 11% African American, 7% Asian American or Pacific Islander, 2% Hispanic American, 0.9% international, 4% transferred in. *Retention:* 70% of 2001 full-time freshmen returned.

Freshmen *Admission:* 1,298 applied, 1,100 admitted, 439 enrolled. *Average high school GPA:* 2.85. *Test scores:* SAT verbal scores over 500: 34%; SAT math scores over 500: 38%; SAT verbal scores over 600: 8%; SAT math scores over 600: 12%; SAT verbal scores over 700: 1%; SAT math scores over 700: 1%.

Faculty *Total:* 119, 55% full-time. *Student/faculty ratio:* 17:1.

Majors Agricultural business; American studies; business; business administration; elementary education; English; individual/family development; information sciences/systems; liberal arts and sciences/liberal studies; speech/rhetorical studies.

Academic Programs *Special study options:* academic remediation for entering students, adult/continuing education programs, advanced placement credit, distance learning, double majors, English as a second language, honors programs, independent study, internships, services for LD students, student-designed majors, study abroad, summer session for credit. *ROTC:* Army (c).

Library 51,495 titles, 176 serial subscriptions, 3,226 audiovisual materials.

Computers on Campus 180 computers available on campus for general student use. A campuswide network can be accessed from off campus. Internet access, online (class) registration, at least one staffed computer lab available.

Student Life *Housing:* college housing not available. *Activities and Organizations:* drama/theater group, student-run newspaper. *Campus security:* late-night transport/escort service, part-time trained security personnel.

Athletics Member NJCAA. *Intercollegiate sports:* baseball M, basketball M/W, soccer M, tennis M/W, volleyball W. *Intramural sports:* basketball M/W, bowling M/W, golf M/W, ice hockey M/W, racquetball M/W, riflery M/W, skiing (downhill) M/W, soccer M/W, softball W, tennis M/W, volleyball M/W.

Standardized Tests *Required:* SAT I or ACT (for admission).

Costs (2001–02) *Tuition:* state resident $6832 full-time, $276 per credit part-time; nonresident $10,574 full-time, $442 per credit part-time. Full-time tuition and fees vary according to class time, location, program, and student level. Part-time tuition and fees vary according to class time, course load, location, program, and student level. *Required fees:* $332 full-time, $56 per credit. *Waivers:* senior citizens and employees or children of employees.

Financial Aid In 2001, 26 Federal Work-Study jobs (averaging $997).

Applying *Options:* electronic application, early admission, deferred entrance. *Application fee:* $50. *Application deadline:* rolling (freshmen), rolling (transfers). *Notification:* continuous (freshmen).

Admissions Contact Ms. Deborah Erie, The Pennsylvania State University Delaware County Campus of the Commonwealth College, 25 Yearsley Mill Road, Media, PA 19063-5596. *Phone:* 610-892-1200. *Fax:* 610-892-1200. *E-mail:* admissions@psu.edu.

The Pennsylvania State University DuBois Campus of the Commonwealth College

DuBois, Pennsylvania

- **State-related** primarily 2-year, founded 1935, part of Pennsylvania State University
- **Calendar** semesters
- **Degrees** associate and bachelor's (also offers up to 2 years of most bachelor's degree programs offered at University Park campus)
- **Small-town** 13-acre campus
- **Coed,** 997 undergraduate students, 77% full-time, 50% women, 50% men

Undergraduates 769 full-time, 228 part-time. 7% are from out of state, 0.7% African American, 0.5% Asian American or Pacific Islander, 0.1% Hispanic American, 0.1% Native American, 0.1% international, 2% transferred in. *Retention:* 70% of 2001 full-time freshmen returned.

Freshmen *Admission:* 396 applied, 377 admitted, 252 enrolled. *Average high school GPA:* 2.77. *Test scores:* SAT verbal scores over 500: 37%; SAT math scores over 500: 45%; SAT verbal scores over 600: 11%; SAT math scores over 600: 8%.

Faculty *Total:* 89, 55% full-time, 40% with terminal degrees. *Student/faculty ratio:* 14:1.

Majors Agricultural business; biological/physical sciences; business; business administration; electrical/electronic engineering technology; individual/family development; industrial technology; information sciences/systems; liberal arts and sciences/liberal studies; mechanical engineering technology; occupational therapy assistant; physical therapy assistant; wildlife management.

Academic Programs *Special study options:* academic remediation for entering students, adult/continuing education programs, advanced placement credit, distance learning, double majors, honors programs, independent study, internships, services for LD students, student-designed majors, summer session for credit. *ROTC:* Army (c), Navy (c), Air Force (c).

Library 38,966 titles, 1,146 serial subscriptions.

Computers on Campus 126 computers available on campus for general student use. A campuswide network can be accessed from off campus. Internet access, online (class) registration, at least one staffed computer lab available.

Student Life *Housing:* college housing not available. *Activities and Organizations:* student-run newspaper, choral group.

Athletics Member NJCAA. *Intercollegiate sports:* cross-country running M/W, golf M/W, volleyball W. *Intramural sports:* badminton M/W, basketball M, football M, tennis M/W, volleyball M/W.

Standardized Tests *Required:* SAT I or ACT (for admission).

Costs (2001–02) *Tuition:* state resident $6832 full-time, $276 per credit part-time; nonresident $10,574 full-time, $442 per credit part-time. Full-time tuition and fees vary according to class time, location, program, and student level. Part-time tuition and fees vary according to class time, course load, location, program, and student level. *Required fees:* $322 full-time, $54 per credit. *Payment plan:* installment. *Waivers:* employees or children of employees.

Financial Aid In 2001, 65 Federal Work-Study jobs (averaging $1048). 1 State and other part-time jobs (averaging $986).

Applying *Options:* electronic application, early admission, deferred entrance. *Application fee:* $50. *Required:* high school transcript. *Application deadline:* rolling (freshmen), rolling (transfers). *Notification:* continuous (freshmen).

Admissions Contact Undergraduate Admissions Office, The Pennsylvania State University DuBois Campus of the Commonwealth College, 101 Hiller, College Place, DuBois, PA 15801. *Phone:* 814-865-5471. *Fax:* 814-375-4784. *E-mail:* smc200@psu.edu.

The Pennsylvania State University Fayette Campus of the Commonwealth College

Uniontown, Pennsylvania

- **State-related** primarily 2-year, founded 1934, part of Pennsylvania State University
- **Calendar** semesters
- **Degrees** associate and bachelor's (also offers up to 2 years of most bachelor's degree programs offered at University Park campus)
- **Small-town** 193-acre campus
- **Coed,** 1,128 undergraduate students, 75% full-time, 55% women, 45% men

The Pennsylvania State University Fayette Campus of the Commonwealth College (continued)

Undergraduates 842 full-time, 286 part-time. 1% are from out of state, 4% African American, 0.5% Asian American or Pacific Islander, 0.4% Hispanic American, 0.4% Native American, 3% transferred in. *Retention:* 80% of 2001 full-time freshmen returned.

Freshmen *Admission:* 313 applied, 286 admitted, 190 enrolled. *Average high school GPA:* 2.93. *Test scores:* SAT verbal scores over 500: 38%; SAT math scores over 500: 35%; SAT verbal scores over 600: 6%; SAT math scores over 600: 9%; SAT verbal scores over 700: 1%; SAT math scores over 700: 1%.

Faculty *Total:* 93, 57% full-time. *Student/faculty ratio:* 14:1.

Majors Agricultural business; architectural engineering technology; business; business administration; criminal justice studies; electrical/electronic engineering technology; individual/family development; information sciences/systems; liberal arts and sciences/liberal studies; nursing.

Academic Programs *Special study options:* academic remediation for entering students, adult/continuing education programs, advanced placement credit, distance learning, double majors, honors programs, independent study, internships, services for LD students, student-designed majors, summer session for credit.

Library 49,620 titles, 170 serial subscriptions, 5,912 audiovisual materials.

Computers on Campus 103 computers available on campus for general student use. A campuswide network can be accessed from off campus. Internet access, online (class) registration, at least one staffed computer lab available.

Student Life *Housing:* college housing not available. *Activities and Organizations:* drama/theater group, student-run newspaper. *Campus security:* student patrols, 8-hour patrols by trained security personnel.

Athletics Member NJCAA. *Intercollegiate sports:* baseball M, basketball M, softball W, volleyball W. *Intramural sports:* badminton M/W, basketball M/W, fencing M/W, football M/W, racquetball M/W, skiing (downhill) M/W, soccer M/W, tennis M/W, track and field M/W, volleyball M/W.

Standardized Tests *Required:* SAT I or ACT (for admission).

Costs (2001–02) *Tuition:* state resident $6832 full-time, $276 per credit part-time; nonresident $10,574 full-time, $442 per credit part-time. Full-time tuition and fees vary according to class time, location, program, and student level. Part-time tuition and fees vary according to class time, course load, location, program, and student level. *Required fees:* $322 full-time, $54 per credit. *Payment plan:* deferred payment. *Waivers:* senior citizens and employees or children of employees.

Financial Aid In 2001, 60 Federal Work-Study jobs (averaging $1239).

Applying *Options:* electronic application, early admission, deferred entrance. *Application fee:* $50. *Required:* high school transcript. *Application deadline:* rolling (freshmen), rolling (transfers). *Notification:* continuous (freshmen).

Admissions Contact Undergraduate Admissions Office, The Pennsylvania State University Fayette Campus of the Commonwealth College, 108 Williams Building, Uniontown, PA 15401. *Phone:* 814-865-5471. *Fax:* 724-430-4175. *E-mail:* admissions@psu.edu.

THE PENNSYLVANIA STATE UNIVERSITY HAZLETON CAMPUS OF THE COMMONWEALTH COLLEGE

Hazleton, Pennsylvania

- **State-related** primarily 2-year, founded 1934, part of Pennsylvania State University
- **Calendar** semesters
- **Degrees** associate and bachelor's (also offers up to 2 years of most bachelor's degree programs offered at University Park campus)
- **Small-town** 92-acre campus
- **Coed,** 1,342 undergraduate students, 93% full-time, 43% women, 57% men

Undergraduates 1,247 full-time, 95 part-time. 14% are from out of state, 2% African American, 4% Asian American or Pacific Islander, 3% Hispanic American, 0.6% international, 3% transferred in, 34% live on campus. *Retention:* 84% of 2001 full-time freshmen returned.

Freshmen *Admission:* 1,211 applied, 1,122 admitted, 535 enrolled. *Average high school GPA:* 2.92. *Test scores:* SAT verbal scores over 500: 43%; SAT math scores over 500: 50%; SAT verbal scores over 600: 7%; SAT math scores over 600: 10%.

Faculty *Total:* 98, 56% full-time. *Student/faculty ratio:* 19:1.

Majors Agricultural business; business; business administration; electrical/electronic engineering technology; industrial technology; information sciences/systems; liberal arts and sciences/liberal studies; mechanical engineering technology; medical laboratory technician; physical therapy assistant.

Academic Programs *Special study options:* academic remediation for entering students, adult/continuing education programs, advanced placement credit, distance learning, double majors, honors programs, independent study, internships, services for LD students, student-designed majors, summer session for credit. *ROTC:* Army (b).

Library 77,995 titles, 283 serial subscriptions, 6,590 audiovisual materials.

Computers on Campus 131 computers available on campus for general student use. A campuswide network can be accessed from student residence rooms and from off campus. Internet access, online (class) registration, at least one staffed computer lab available.

Student Life *Housing Options:* coed. *Activities and Organizations:* drama/theater group, student-run newspaper, radio station, choral group. *Campus security:* 24-hour patrols, late-night transport/escort service, controlled dormitory access.

Athletics Member NJCAA. *Intercollegiate sports:* baseball M, basketball M, soccer M, softball W, tennis M/W, volleyball M/W. *Intramural sports:* basketball M/W, soccer M/W, volleyball M/W.

Standardized Tests *Required:* SAT I or ACT (for admission).

Costs (2001–02) *Tuition:* state resident $6832 full-time, $276 per credit part-time; nonresident $10,574 full-time, $442 per credit part-time. Full-time tuition and fees vary according to class time, location, program, and student level. Part-time tuition and fees vary according to class time, course load, location, program, and student level. *Required fees:* $332 full-time, $56 per credit. *Room and board:* $5300; room only: $2680. Room and board charges vary according to board plan and housing facility. *Payment plan:* deferred payment. *Waivers:* senior citizens and employees or children of employees.

Financial Aid In 2001, 115 Federal Work-Study jobs (averaging $1220).

Applying *Options:* common application, electronic application, early admission, deferred entrance. *Application fee:* $50. *Required:* high school transcript. *Application deadline:* rolling (freshmen), rolling (transfers). *Notification:* continuous (freshmen).

Admissions Contact Undergraduate Admissions Office, The Pennsylvania State University Hazleton Campus of the Commonwealth College, 101 Administration Building, Hazleton, PA 18201. *Phone:* 814-865-5471. *Fax:* 570-450-3182. *E-mail:* admissions@psu.edu.

THE PENNSYLVANIA STATE UNIVERSITY MCKEESPORT CAMPUS OF THE COMMONWEALTH COLLEGE

McKeesport, Pennsylvania

- **State-related** primarily 2-year, founded 1947, part of Pennsylvania State University
- **Calendar** semesters
- **Degrees** associate and bachelor's (also offers up to 2 years of most bachelor's degree programs offered at University Park campus)
- **Small-town** 40-acre campus with easy access to Pittsburgh
- **Coed,** 941 undergraduate students, 87% full-time, 39% women, 61% men

Undergraduates 822 full-time, 119 part-time. 7% are from out of state, 13% African American, 2% Asian American or Pacific Islander, 1% Hispanic American, 0.1% Native American, 0.4% international, 4% transferred in, 19% live on campus. *Retention:* 83% of 2001 full-time freshmen returned.

Freshmen *Admission:* 678 applied, 640 admitted, 342 enrolled. *Average high school GPA:* 2.82. *Test scores:* SAT verbal scores over 500: 35%; SAT math scores over 500: 42%; SAT verbal scores over 600: 5%; SAT math scores over 600: 10%; SAT verbal scores over 700: 1%; SAT math scores over 700: 1%.

Faculty *Total:* 79, 46% full-time. *Student/faculty ratio:* 17:1.

Majors Agricultural business; biological/physical sciences; business; business administration; information sciences/systems; liberal arts and sciences/liberal studies; mechanical engineering technologies related; mechanical engineering technology.

Academic Programs *Special study options:* academic remediation for entering students, adult/continuing education programs, advanced placement credit, distance learning, double majors, honors programs, independent study, internships, services for LD students, student-designed majors, summer session for credit. *ROTC:* Air Force (c).

Library 38,254 titles, 213 serial subscriptions, 4,046 audiovisual materials.

Computers on Campus 167 computers available on campus for general student use. A campuswide network can be accessed from student residence rooms and from off campus. Internet access, online (class) registration, at least one staffed computer lab available.

Student Life *Housing Options:* coed. *Activities and Organizations:* drama/theater group, student-run newspaper, radio station. *Campus security:* 24-hour patrols, controlled dormitory access.

Athletics Member NJCAA. *Intercollegiate sports:* baseball M, basketball M, softball W, volleyball W. *Intramural sports:* basketball M/W, bowling M/W, fencing M/W, football M/W, golf M/W, ice hockey M, racquetball M/W, skiing (downhill) M/W, soccer M, softball M/W, swimming M/W, tennis M/W, track and field M/W, volleyball M/W.

Standardized Tests *Required:* SAT I or ACT (for admission).

Costs (2001–02) *Tuition:* state resident $6832 full-time, $276 per credit part-time; nonresident $10,574 full-time, $442 per credit part-time. Full-time tuition and fees vary according to class time, location, program, and student level. Part-time tuition and fees vary according to class time, course load, location, program, and student level. *Required fees:* $322 full-time, $54 per credit. *Room and board:* $5300; room only: $2680. Room and board charges vary according to board plan and housing facility. *Payment plan:* deferred payment. *Waivers:* senior citizens and employees or children of employees.

Financial Aid In 2001, 45 Federal Work-Study jobs (averaging $1180).

Applying *Options:* electronic application, early admission, deferred entrance. *Application fee:* $50. *Required:* high school transcript. *Application deadline:* rolling (freshmen), rolling (transfers). *Notification:* continuous (freshmen).

Admissions Contact Undergraduate Admissions Office, The Pennsylvania State University McKeesport Campus of the Commonwealth College, 400 University Drive, McKeesport, PA 15132-7698. *Phone:* 814-865-5471. *Toll-free phone:* 800-248-5466. *Fax:* 412-675-9056. *E-mail:* dam7@psu.edu.

The Pennsylvania State University Mont Alto Campus of the Commonwealth College

Mont Alto, Pennsylvania

- **State-related** primarily 2-year, founded 1929, part of Pennsylvania State University
- **Calendar** semesters
- **Degrees** associate and bachelor's (also offers up to 2 years of most bachelor's degree programs offered at University Park campus)
- **Small-town** 62-acre campus
- **Coed,** 1,105 undergraduate students, 75% full-time, 55% women, 45% men

Undergraduates 825 full-time, 280 part-time. 15% are from out of state, 9% African American, 4% Asian American or Pacific Islander, 3% Hispanic American, 0.1% Native American, 0.2% international, 4% transferred in, 40% live on campus. *Retention:* 74% of 2001 full-time freshmen returned.

Freshmen *Admission:* 697 applied, 590 admitted, 348 enrolled. *Average high school GPA:* 2.77. *Test scores:* SAT verbal scores over 500: 37%; SAT math scores over 500: 40%; SAT verbal scores over 600: 9%; SAT math scores over 600: 11%; SAT verbal scores over 700: 1%.

Faculty *Total:* 95, 61% full-time. *Student/faculty ratio:* 13:1.

Majors Agricultural business; business; business administration; forest harvesting production technology; individual/family development; information sciences/systems; liberal arts and sciences/liberal studies; nursing; occupational therapy; physical therapy assistant.

Academic Programs *Special study options:* academic remediation for entering students, adult/continuing education programs, advanced placement credit, distance learning, double majors, honors programs, independent study, internships, services for LD students, student-designed majors, summer session for credit. *ROTC:* Army (c).

Library 34,596 titles, 252 serial subscriptions, 1,947 audiovisual materials.

Computers on Campus 182 computers available on campus for general student use. A campuswide network can be accessed from student residence rooms and from off campus. Internet access, online (class) registration, at least one staffed computer lab available.

Student Life *Housing Options:* coed. *Activities and Organizations:* student-run radio station. *Campus security:* 24-hour patrols, controlled dormitory access.

Athletics Member NJCAA. *Intercollegiate sports:* baseball M, basketball M/W, cross-country running M/W, golf M/W, soccer M/W, softball W, tennis M/W, volleyball W. *Intramural sports:* badminton M/W, basketball M/W, racquetball M/W, skiing (downhill) M/W, soccer M/W, softball W, volleyball M/W.

Standardized Tests *Required:* SAT I or ACT (for admission).

Costs (2001–02) *Tuition:* state resident $6832 full-time, $276 per credit part-time; nonresident $10,574 full-time, $442 per credit part-time. Full-time tuition and fees vary according to class time, location, and program. Part-time tuition and fees vary according to class time, course load, location, and program. *Required fees:* $332 full-time, $56 per credit. *Room and board:* $5300; room only: $2680. Room and board charges vary according to board plan and housing facility. *Payment plan:* deferred payment. *Waivers:* senior citizens and employees or children of employees.

Financial Aid In 2001, 69 Federal Work-Study jobs (averaging $966).

Applying *Options:* electronic application, early admission. *Application fee:* $50. *Required:* high school transcript. *Application deadline:* rolling (freshmen), rolling (transfers). *Notification:* continuous (freshmen).

Admissions Contact Ms. Shawn Wiley, The Pennsylvania State University Mont Alto Campus of the Commonwealth College, 1 Campus Drive, Mont Alto, PA 17237-9703. *Phone:* 717-749-6130. *Fax:* 717-749-6132. *E-mail:* admissions@psu.edu.

The Pennsylvania State University New Kensington Campus of the Commonwealth College

New Kensington, Pennsylvania

- **State-related** primarily 2-year, founded 1958, part of Pennsylvania State University
- **Calendar** semesters
- **Degrees** associate and bachelor's (also offers up to 2 years of most bachelor's degree programs offered at University Park campus)
- **Small-town** 71-acre campus with easy access to Pittsburgh
- **Coed,** 979 undergraduate students, 72% full-time, 38% women, 62% men

Undergraduates 708 full-time, 271 part-time. 2% are from out of state, 3% African American, 1% Asian American or Pacific Islander, 0.4% Hispanic American, 4% transferred in. *Retention:* 78% of 2001 full-time freshmen returned.

Freshmen *Admission:* 437 applied, 408 admitted, 244 enrolled. *Average high school GPA:* 2.87. *Test scores:* SAT verbal scores over 500: 50%; SAT math scores over 500: 48%; SAT verbal scores over 600: 11%; SAT math scores over 600: 14%; SAT math scores over 700: 1%.

Faculty *Total:* 98, 39% full-time. *Student/faculty ratio:* 14:1.

Majors Agricultural business; biological/physical sciences; biomedical engineering-related technology; business; business administration; computer engineering technology; electrical/electronic engineering technology; electromechanical technology; individual/family development; information sciences/systems; liberal arts and sciences/liberal studies; mechanical engineering technology; medical laboratory technician; nursing.

Academic Programs *Special study options:* academic remediation for entering students, adult/continuing education programs, advanced placement credit, distance learning, double majors, honors programs, independent study, internships, services for LD students, student-designed majors, summer session for credit.

Library 27,427 titles, 195 serial subscriptions, 4,086 audiovisual materials.

Computers on Campus 264 computers available on campus for general student use. A campuswide network can be accessed from off campus. Internet access, online (class) registration, at least one staffed computer lab available.

Student Life *Housing:* college housing not available. *Activities and Organizations:* drama/theater group, student-run newspaper, choral group. *Campus security:* part-time trained security personnel.

Athletics Member NJCAA. *Intercollegiate sports:* baseball M, basketball M, cross-country running M/W, golf M/W, softball W, volleyball W. *Intramural sports:* badminton M/W, basketball M/W, football M/W, racquetball M/W, soccer M/W, softball W, volleyball M/W.

Standardized Tests *Required:* SAT I or ACT (for admission).

Costs (2001–02) *Tuition:* state resident $6832 full-time, $276 per credit part-time; nonresident $10,574 full-time, $442 per credit part-time. Full-time tuition and fees vary according to class time, location, program, and student level. Part-time tuition and fees vary according to class time, course load, location, program, and student level. *Required fees:* $332 full-time, $56 per credit. *Payment plan:* deferred payment. *Waivers:* senior citizens and employees or children of employees.

Financial Aid In 2001, 38 Federal Work-Study jobs (averaging $1191).

Applying *Options:* electronic application, early admission, deferred entrance. *Application fee:* $50. *Required:* high school transcript. *Application deadline:* rolling (freshmen), rolling (transfers). *Notification:* continuous (freshmen).

Admissions Contact Undergraduate Admissions Office, The Pennsylvania State University New Kensington Campus of the Commonwealth College, 3550 7th Street Road, New Kensington, PA 15068-1798. *Phone:* 814-865-7641. *Toll-free phone:* 888-968-PAWS. *Fax:* 724-334-6111. *E-mail:* nkadmissions@psu.edu.

The Pennsylvania State University Shenango Campus of the Commonwealth College
Sharon, Pennsylvania

- **State-related** primarily 2-year, founded 1965, part of Pennsylvania State University
- **Calendar** semesters
- **Degrees** associate and bachelor's (also offers up to 2 years of most bachelor's degree programs offered at University Park campus)
- **Small-town** 14-acre campus
- **Coed,** 984 undergraduate students, 59% full-time, 60% women, 40% men

Undergraduates 577 full-time, 407 part-time. 11% are from out of state, 6% African American, 0.4% Asian American or Pacific Islander, 2% Hispanic American, 0.3% Native American, 2% transferred in. *Retention:* 64% of 2001 full-time freshmen returned.

Freshmen *Admission:* 280 applied, 263 admitted, 170 enrolled. *Average high school GPA:* 2.79. *Test scores:* SAT verbal scores over 500: 27%; SAT math scores over 500: 36%; SAT verbal scores over 600: 5%; SAT math scores over 600: 5%; SAT verbal scores over 700: 1%.

Faculty *Total:* 94, 34% full-time. *Student/faculty ratio:* 14:1.

Majors Agricultural business; biological/physical sciences; business; business administration; individual/family development; information sciences/systems; liberal arts and sciences/liberal studies; mechanical engineering technology; nursing; occupational therapy; physical therapy assistant.

Academic Programs *Special study options:* academic remediation for entering students, adult/continuing education programs, advanced placement credit, distance learning, double majors, honors programs, independent study, internships, services for LD students, student-designed majors, summer session for credit.

Library 23,263 titles, 168 serial subscriptions, 1,953 audiovisual materials.

Computers on Campus 102 computers available on campus for general student use. A campuswide network can be accessed from off campus. Internet access, online (class) registration, at least one staffed computer lab available.

Student Life *Housing:* college housing not available. *Campus security:* part-time trained security personnel.

Athletics *Intramural sports:* basketball M/W, bowling M/W, golf M/W, racquetball M/W, tennis M/W, volleyball M/W.

Standardized Tests *Required:* SAT I or ACT (for admission).

Costs (2001–02) *Tuition:* state resident $6832 full-time, $276 per credit part-time; nonresident $10,574 full-time, $442 per credit part-time. Full-time tuition and fees vary according to class time, location, program, and student level. Part-time tuition and fees vary according to class time, course load, location, program, and student level. *Required fees:* $332 full-time, $56 per credit. *Payment plan:* deferred payment. *Waivers:* senior citizens and employees or children of employees.

Financial Aid In 2001, 24 Federal Work-Study jobs (averaging $1166).

Applying *Options:* electronic application, early admission, deferred entrance. *Application fee:* $50. *Required:* high school transcript. *Application deadline:* rolling (freshmen), rolling (transfers). *Notification:* continuous (freshmen).

Admissions Contact Undergraduate Admissions Office, The Pennsylvania State University Shenango Campus of the Commonwealth College, 147 Shenango Avenue, Sharon, PA 16146. *Phone:* 814-865-5471. *E-mail:* admissions@psu.edu.

The Pennsylvania State University Wilkes-Barre Campus of the Commonwealth College
Lehman, Pennsylvania

- **State-related** primarily 2-year, founded 1916, part of Pennsylvania State University
- **Calendar** semesters
- **Degrees** associate and bachelor's (also offers up to 2 years of most bachelor's degree programs offered at University Park campus)
- **Rural** 58-acre campus
- **Coed,** 832 undergraduate students, 78% full-time, 35% women, 65% men

Undergraduates 651 full-time, 181 part-time. 4% are from out of state, 1% African American, 3% Asian American or Pacific Islander, 0.6% Hispanic American, 0.3% international, 4% transferred in. *Retention:* 85% of 2001 full-time freshmen returned.

Freshmen *Admission:* 550 applied, 506 admitted, 244 enrolled. *Average high school GPA:* 2.88. *Test scores:* SAT verbal scores over 500: 45%; SAT math scores over 500: 49%; SAT verbal scores over 600: 7%; SAT math scores over 600: 11%.

Faculty *Total:* 94, 39% full-time. *Student/faculty ratio:* 13:1.

Majors Agricultural business; biomedical engineering-related technology; business; business administration; electrical/electronic engineering technology; information sciences/systems; liberal arts and sciences/liberal studies; mechanical engineering technologies related; surveying.

Academic Programs *Special study options:* academic remediation for entering students, adult/continuing education programs, advanced placement credit, distance learning, double majors, honors programs, independent study, internships, services for LD students, student-designed majors, summer session for credit. *ROTC:* Air Force (c).

Library 32,882 titles, 205 serial subscriptions, 1,963 audiovisual materials.

Computers on Campus 137 computers available on campus for general student use. A campuswide network can be accessed from off campus. Internet access, online (class) registration, at least one staffed computer lab available.

Student Life *Housing:* college housing not available. *Activities and Organizations:* student-run newspaper, radio station. *Campus security:* part-time trained security personnel.

Athletics Member NJCAA. *Intercollegiate sports:* baseball M, basketball M, cross-country running M/W, golf M/W, soccer M/W, softball W, volleyball W. *Intramural sports:* basketball M/W, skiing (downhill) M/W, volleyball M/W.

Standardized Tests *Required:* SAT I or ACT (for admission).

Costs (2001–02) *Tuition:* state resident $6832 full-time, $276 per credit part-time; nonresident $10,574 full-time, $442 per credit part-time. Full-time tuition and fees vary according to class time, location, program, and student level. Part-time tuition and fees vary according to class time, course load, location, program, and student level. *Required fees:* $342 full-time, $57 per credit. *Payment plan:* deferred payment. *Waivers:* senior citizens and employees or children of employees.

Financial Aid In 2001, 28 Federal Work-Study jobs (averaging $953).

Applying *Options:* electronic application, early admission, deferred entrance. *Application fee:* $50. *Required:* high school transcript. *Application deadline:* rolling (freshmen), rolling (transfers). *Notification:* continuous (freshmen).

Admissions Contact Undergraduate Admissions Office, The Pennsylvania State University Wilkes-Barre Campus of the Commonwealth College, PO Box PSU, Lehman, PA 18627-0217. *Phone:* 814-865-5471. *Fax:* 570-675-8308. *E-mail:* admissions@psu.edu.

The Pennsylvania State University Worthington Scranton Campus of the Commonwealth College
Dunmore, Pennsylvania

- **State-related** primarily 2-year, founded 1923, part of Pennsylvania State University
- **Calendar** semesters
- **Degrees** associate and bachelor's (also offers up to 2 years of most bachelor's degree programs offered at University Park campus)
- **Small-town** 43-acre campus
- **Coed,** 1,520 undergraduate students, 77% full-time, 49% women, 51% men

Undergraduates 1,175 full-time, 345 part-time. 2% are from out of state, 1% African American, 1% Asian American or Pacific Islander, 1% Hispanic American, 0.1% international, 5% transferred in. *Retention:* 73% of 2001 full-time freshmen returned.

Freshmen *Admission:* 657 applied, 557 admitted, 285 enrolled. *Average high school GPA:* 2.82. *Test scores:* SAT verbal scores over 500: 35%; SAT math scores over 500: 40%; SAT verbal scores over 600: 9%; SAT math scores over 600: 6%.

Faculty *Total:* 117, 55% full-time. *Student/faculty ratio:* 16:1.

Majors Agricultural business; architectural engineering technology; business; business administration; individual/family development; information sciences/systems; liberal arts and sciences/liberal studies; nursing; occupational therapy.

Academic Programs *Special study options:* academic remediation for entering students, adult/continuing education programs, advanced placement credit, distance learning, double majors, honors programs, independent study, internships, services for LD students, student-designed majors, summer session for credit.

Library 47,563 titles, 204 serial subscriptions, 2,985 audiovisual materials.

Computers on Campus 104 computers available on campus for general student use. A campuswide network can be accessed from off campus. Internet access, online (class) registration, at least one staffed computer lab available.

Student Life *Housing:* college housing not available. *Activities and Organizations:* drama/theater group, student-run newspaper. *Campus security:* part-time trained security personnel.

Athletics Member NJCAA. *Intercollegiate sports:* baseball M, basketball M, cross-country running M/W, soccer M, softball W, volleyball W. *Intramural sports:* basketball M/W, soccer M/W, softball W, tennis M/W, volleyball M/W.

Standardized Tests *Required:* SAT I or ACT (for admission).

Costs (2001–02) *Tuition:* state resident $6832 full-time, $276 per credit part-time; nonresident $10,574 full-time, $442 per credit part-time. Full-time tuition and fees vary according to class time, location, program, and student level. Part-time tuition and fees vary according to class time, course load, location, program, and student level. *Required fees:* $322 full-time, $54 per credit. *Payment plan:* deferred payment. *Waivers:* senior citizens and employees or children of employees.

Financial Aid In 2001, 24 Federal Work-Study jobs (averaging $957).

Applying *Options:* electronic application, early admission, deferred entrance. *Application fee:* $50. *Required:* high school transcript. *Application deadline:* rolling (freshmen), rolling (transfers). *Notification:* continuous (freshmen).

Admissions Contact Undergraduate Admissions Office, The Pennsylvania State University Worthington Scranton Campus of the Commonwealth College, 120 Ridge View Drive, Dunmore, PA 18512-1699. *Phone:* 814-865-5471. *Fax:* 570-963-2535. *E-mail:* admissions@psu.edu.

THE PENNSYLVANIA STATE UNIVERSITY YORK CAMPUS OF THE COMMONWEALTH COLLEGE
York, Pennsylvania

- **State-related** primarily 2-year, founded 1926, part of Pennsylvania State University
- **Calendar** semesters
- **Degrees** associate and bachelor's (also offers up to 2 years of most bachelor's degree programs offered at University Park campus)
- **Suburban** 52-acre campus
- **Coed,** 1,729 undergraduate students, 53% full-time, 44% women, 56% men

Undergraduates 909 full-time, 820 part-time. 3% are from out of state, 3% African American, 6% Asian American or Pacific Islander, 3% Hispanic American, 0.2% Native American, 0.3% international, 3% transferred in. *Retention:* 69% of 2001 full-time freshmen returned.

Freshmen *Admission:* 672 applied, 609 admitted, 312 enrolled. *Average high school GPA:* 2.78. *Test scores:* SAT verbal scores over 500: 43%; SAT math scores over 500: 47%; SAT verbal scores over 600: 11%; SAT math scores over 600: 14%; SAT verbal scores over 700: 1%; SAT math scores over 700: 2%.

Faculty *Total:* 130, 48% full-time. *Student/faculty ratio:* 15:1.

Majors Agricultural business; business; business administration; electrical/electronic engineering technology; engineering; industrial technology; information sciences/systems; liberal arts and sciences/liberal studies; mechanical engineering technology.

Academic Programs *Special study options:* academic remediation for entering students, adult/continuing education programs, advanced placement credit, distance learning, double majors, English as a second language, honors programs, independent study, internships, services for LD students, student-designed majors, study abroad, summer session for credit.

Library 44,007 titles, 245 serial subscriptions, 2,977 audiovisual materials.

Computers on Campus 155 computers available on campus for general student use. A campuswide network can be accessed from off campus. Internet access, online (class) registration, at least one staffed computer lab available.

Student Life *Housing:* college housing not available. *Activities and Organizations:* student-run newspaper. *Campus security:* part-time trained security personnel.

Athletics Member NJCAA. *Intercollegiate sports:* basketball M/W, cross-country running M/W, soccer M, tennis M/W, volleyball W. *Intramural sports:* archery M/W, basketball M/W, football M, soccer M/W, softball M/W, table tennis M/W, tennis M/W, volleyball M/W.

Standardized Tests *Required:* SAT I or ACT (for admission).

Costs (2001–02) *Tuition:* state resident $6832 full-time, $276 per credit part-time; nonresident $10,574 full-time, $442 per credit part-time. Full-time tuition and fees vary according to class time, location, program, and student level. Part-time tuition and fees vary according to class time, course load, location, program, and student level. *Required fees:* $322 full-time, $54 per credit. *Payment plan:* deferred payment. *Waivers:* senior citizens and employees or children of employees.

Financial Aid In 2001, 39 Federal Work-Study jobs (averaging $960).

Applying *Options:* electronic application, early admission, deferred entrance. *Application fee:* $50. *Required:* high school transcript. *Application deadline:* rolling (freshmen), rolling (transfers). *Notification:* continuous (freshmen).

Admissions Contact Undergraduate Admissions Office, The Pennsylvania State University York Campus of the Commonwealth College, 18 Student Center, York, PA 17403. *Phone:* 814-865-5471. *Fax:* 717-771-4062. *E-mail:* admissions@psu.edu.

PITTSBURGH INSTITUTE OF AERONAUTICS
Pittsburgh, Pennsylvania

- **Independent** 2-year, founded 1929
- **Calendar** quarters
- **Degree** associate
- **Suburban** campus
- **Coed, primarily men,** 397 undergraduate students, 100% full-time, 3% women, 97% men

Undergraduates 397 full-time. Students come from 12 states and territories, 4 other countries, 35% are from out of state, 1% African American, 0.3% Asian American or Pacific Islander, 5% international.

Freshmen *Admission:* 124 applied, 114 admitted, 110 enrolled.

Faculty *Total:* 23, 91% full-time. *Student/faculty ratio:* 17:1.

Majors Aircraft mechanic/airframe; aviation technology; electrical/electronic engineering technology.

Academic Programs *Special study options:* academic remediation for entering students, advanced placement credit.

Library Technical Library with 15,000 titles, 35 serial subscriptions.

Computers on Campus 30 computers available on campus for general student use. Internet access, at least one staffed computer lab available.

Student Life *Housing:* college housing not available. *Student Services:* personal/psychological counseling.

Costs (2002–03) *Tuition:* $8631 full-time. *Payment plans:* tuition prepayment, installment. *Waivers:* employees or children of employees.

Applying *Options:* deferred entrance. *Application fee:* $150. *Recommended:* high school transcript, interview. *Application deadline:* rolling (freshmen), rolling (transfers). *Notification:* continuous (freshmen).

Admissions Contact Mr. Robert F. Leonard, Director of Admissions, Pittsburgh Institute of Aeronautics, PO Box 10897, Pittsburgh, PA 15236. *Phone:* 412-462-9011. *Toll-free phone:* 800-444-1440. *Fax:* 412-466-0513. *E-mail:* admissions@piainfo.org.

PITTSBURGH INSTITUTE OF MORTUARY SCIENCE, INCORPORATED
Pittsburgh, Pennsylvania

- **Independent** 2-year, founded 1939
- **Calendar** trimesters
- **Degree** diplomas and associate
- **Urban** campus
- **Coed,** 132 undergraduate students, 92% full-time, 43% women, 57% men

Undergraduates 121 full-time, 11 part-time. Students come from 10 states and territories, 23% are from out of state, 14% African American, 0.8% Hispanic American.

Freshmen *Admission:* 65 enrolled.

Faculty *Total:* 16, 25% full-time, 19% with terminal degrees. *Student/faculty ratio:* 13:1.

Majors Mortuary science.

Academic Programs *Special study options:* academic remediation for entering students, adult/continuing education programs, cooperative education, internships, part-time degree program, services for LD students.

Library William J. Musmanno Memorial Library with 2,167 titles, 48 serial subscriptions, a Web page.

Computers on Campus 10 computers available on campus for general student use. At least one staffed computer lab available.

Student Life *Housing:* college housing not available. *Campus security:* 24-hour emergency response devices.

Costs (2001–02) *One-time required fee:* $30. *Tuition:* $9600 full-time, $250 per credit part-time. Full-time tuition and fees vary according to course load. Part-time tuition and fees vary according to course load. *Required fees:* $70 full-time. *Payment plan:* installment.

Pittsburgh Institute of Mortuary Science, Incorporated (continued)

Applying *Application fee:* $40. *Required:* high school transcript. *Application deadline:* rolling (freshmen), rolling (transfers). *Notification:* continuous (freshmen).

Admissions Contact Ms. Karen S. Rocco, Registrar, Pittsburgh Institute of Mortuary Science, Incorporated, 5808 Baum Boulevard, Pittsburgh, PA 15206-3706. *Phone:* 412-362-8500 Ext. 101. *Toll-free phone:* 800-933-5808. *Fax:* 412-362-1684. *E-mail:* pims5808@aol.com.

PITTSBURGH TECHNICAL INSTITUTE
Pittsburgh, Pennsylvania

- **Proprietary** 2-year, founded 1946
- **Calendar** quarters
- **Degrees** diplomas and associate (also offers courses at 1 branch campus with significant enrollment reflected in profile)
- **Urban** campus
- **Coed,** 2,108 undergraduate students, 100% full-time, 27% women, 73% men

Undergraduates 2,108 full-time. Students come from 15 states and territories, 17% are from out of state, 2% African American, 0.2% Asian American or Pacific Islander, 0.5% Hispanic American, 0.1% Native American, 20% live on campus. *Retention:* 82% of 2001 full-time freshmen returned.

Freshmen *Admission:* 2,037 applied, 1,892 admitted, 985 enrolled.

Faculty *Total:* 96, 84% full-time, 1% with terminal degrees. *Student/faculty ratio:* 26:1.

Majors Accounting; business administration; computer graphics; computer graphics; computer/information sciences; computer/information technology services administration and management related; computer programming related; computer programming (specific applications); computer systems networking/telecommunications; computer/technical support; drafting; drafting/design technology; electrical/electronic engineering technology; electrical equipment installation/repair; graphic design/commercial art/illustration; hotel and restaurant management; hotel/motel services marketing operations; marketing operations; sales operations; system/networking/LAN/WAN management; tourism/travel marketing; travel services marketing operations; Web/multimedia management/webmaster; Web page, digital/multimedia and information resources design.

Academic Programs *Special study options:* cooperative education, internships.

Library Learning Resources Center with 2,010 titles, 70 serial subscriptions, 300 audiovisual materials, an OPAC.

Computers on Campus 484 computers available on campus for general student use. Internet access, at least one staffed computer lab available.

Student Life *Housing Options:* coed. *Activities and Organizations:* student-run newspaper, Student Activities Club. *Campus security:* 24-hour emergency response devices, electronically operated building access after hours. *Student Services:* personal/psychological counseling.

Athletics *Intramural sports:* basketball M/W, softball M/W, volleyball M/W.

Applying *Options:* common application, deferred entrance. *Required:* high school transcript, interview. *Application deadline:* rolling (freshmen), rolling (transfers).

Admissions Contact Ms. Laurel Patterson, Admissions Systems Manager, Pittsburgh Technical Institute, 1111 McKee Road, Oakdale, PA 15071. *Phone:* 412-809-5353. *Toll-free phone:* 800-784-9675. *Fax:* 412-809-5351. *E-mail:* info@pti-tec.com.

READING AREA COMMUNITY COLLEGE
Reading, Pennsylvania

- **County-supported** 2-year, founded 1971
- **Calendar** 3 10-week terms
- **Degree** associate
- **Urban** campus with easy access to Philadelphia
- **Endowment** $745,770
- **Coed,** 3,000 undergraduate students

Undergraduates Students come from 10 other countries.

Freshmen *Admission:* 1,427 applied, 1,427 admitted.

Majors Accounting; aircraft pilot (professional); behavioral sciences; biology; business administration; business education; business marketing and marketing management; chemistry; child care/development; communication equipment technology; computer programming; computer science; culinary arts; data processing technology; early childhood education; education; electrical/electronic engineering technology; elementary education; engineering; engineering science; engineering technology; finance; humanities; human resources management; human services; industrial radiologic technology; industrial technology; information sciences/systems; legal administrative assistant; legal studies; liberal arts and sciences/liberal studies; machine technology; mechanical engineering technology; medical administrative assistant; medical laboratory technician; medical laboratory technology; medical records administration; medical technology; mental health/rehabilitation; nursing; political science; practical nurse; pre-engineering; pre-pharmacy studies; psychology; public administration; respiratory therapy; retail management; secretarial science; social sciences; social work; telecommunications; travel/tourism management; veterinary sciences.

Academic Programs *Special study options:* academic remediation for entering students, adult/continuing education programs, cooperative education, English as a second language, external degree program, part-time degree program, services for LD students, student-designed majors, summer session for credit.

Library Yocum Library with 25,541 titles, 284 serial subscriptions, an OPAC, a Web page.

Computers on Campus 80 computers available on campus for general student use. At least one staffed computer lab available.

Student Life *Housing:* college housing not available. *Activities and Organizations:* student-run newspaper. *Campus security:* 24-hour patrols. *Student Services:* personal/psychological counseling, women's center.

Athletics *Intercollegiate sports:* basketball M, soccer M, volleyball W. *Intramural sports:* cross-country running M/W.

Costs (2001–02) *Tuition:* $59 per credit part-time; state resident $118 per credit part-time; nonresident $176 per credit part-time.

Financial Aid In 2001, 100 Federal Work-Study jobs (averaging $3300). 5 State and other part-time jobs (averaging $3300).

Applying *Options:* electronic application, early admission, deferred entrance. *Application fee:* $20. *Application deadline:* rolling (freshmen), rolling (transfers).

Admissions Contact Mr. Nick Wernicki, Director of Admissions, Reading Area Community College, PO Box 1706, Reading, PA 19603-1706. *Phone:* 610-607-6224 Ext. 5100. *Toll-free phone:* 800-626-1665. *Fax:* 610-375-8255.

THE RESTAURANT SCHOOL
Philadelphia, Pennsylvania

- **Proprietary** primarily 2-year, founded 1974
- **Calendar** semesters
- **Degrees** associate and bachelor's
- **Urban** 2-acre campus
- **Coed,** 585 undergraduate students

Undergraduates Students come from 10 states and territories, 5 other countries, 57% are from out of state, 20% live on campus.

Freshmen *Average high school GPA:* 2.65.

Faculty *Total:* 27, 78% full-time, 37% with terminal degrees. *Student/faculty ratio:* 25:1.

Majors Baker/pastry chef; culinary arts; hotel and restaurant management.

Academic Programs *Special study options:* academic remediation for entering students, internships, part-time degree program.

Library Alumni Resource Center with 5,000 titles, 200 serial subscriptions.

Computers on Campus 24 computers available on campus for general student use. Internet access, at least one staffed computer lab available.

Student Life *Housing Options:* coed. *Activities and Organizations:* student-run newspaper, Community Action Society, Les Gastronome, Culinary Salon, Tastevin, Pastry Club.

Standardized Tests *Recommended:* SAT I or ACT (for admission).

Costs (2002–03) *Tuition:* Full-time tuition and fees vary according to program.

Applying *Options:* common application, early admission, early decision, deferred entrance. *Application fee:* $50. *Required:* essay or personal statement, high school transcript, 2 letters of recommendation, interview. *Required for some:* entrance exam. *Recommended:* minimum 2.0 GPA. *Application deadline:* rolling (freshmen).

Admissions Contact Mr. Karl D. Becker, Director of Admissions, The Restaurant School, 4207 Walnut Street, Philadelphia, PA 19104. *Phone:* 215-222-4200 Ext. 3011. *Toll-free phone:* 877-925-6884 Ext. 3011. *Fax:* 215-222-4219. *E-mail:* info@therestaurantschool.com.

Schuylkill Institute of Business and Technology
Pottsville, Pennsylvania

- **Proprietary** 2-year
- **Calendar** quarters
- **Degree** diplomas and associate
- **Coed,** 185 undergraduate students

Freshmen *Admission:* 46 applied, 46 admitted.
Faculty *Total:* 23, 83% full-time. *Student/faculty ratio:* 14:1.
Majors Business systems networking/ telecommunications; computer programming; drafting; graphic design/commercial art/illustration.
Costs (2002–03) *Tuition:* $7000 full-time. *Required fees:* $250 full-time.
Admissions Contact Terry O'Keefe, Director of Admissions, Schuylkill Institute of Business and Technology, 171 Red Horse Road, Pottsville, PA 17901. *Phone:* 570-622-4835.

South Hills School of Business & Technology
State College, Pennsylvania

- **Proprietary** 2-year, founded 1970
- **Calendar** trimesters
- **Degree** certificates, diplomas, and associate
- **Small-town** 6-acre campus
- **Coed,** 594 undergraduate students, 90% full-time, 67% women, 33% men

Undergraduates 535 full-time, 59 part-time. Students come from 1 other state, 0.2% Hispanic American, 26% transferred in. *Retention:* 83% of 2001 full-time freshmen returned.
Freshmen *Admission:* 578 applied, 528 admitted, 354 enrolled. *Average high school GPA:* 2.75.
Faculty *Total:* 47, 53% full-time, 4% with terminal degrees. *Student/faculty ratio:* 17:1.
Majors Accounting; business; business marketing and marketing management; computer/information sciences; diagnostic medical sonography; industrial technology; legal administrative assistant; medical administrative assistant; medical records technology; secretarial science.
Academic Programs *Special study options:* accelerated degree program, advanced placement credit, cooperative education, double majors, independent study, internships, part-time degree program.
Computers on Campus 300 computers available on campus for general student use. Internet access available.
Student Life *Housing:* college housing not available. *Activities and Organizations:* Phi Beta Lambda, South Hills Executives, Student Forum, yearbook. *Student Services:* personal/psychological counseling.
Costs (2002–03) *Tuition:* $9480 full-time, $192 per credit part-time. Full-time tuition and fees vary according to program. Part-time tuition and fees vary according to program. *Required fees:* $75 full-time, $25 per term part-time. *Waivers:* employees or children of employees.
Applying *Options:* electronic application. *Application fee:* $25. *Required:* high school transcript, minimum 1.5 GPA, interview. *Required for some:* essay or personal statement, 2 letters of recommendation. *Recommended:* minimum 3.0 GPA. *Application deadline:* 9/1 (freshmen).
Admissions Contact Diane M. Brown, Director of Admissions, South Hills School of Business & Technology, 480 Waupelani Drive, State College, PA 16801-4516. *Phone:* 814-234-7755. *Toll-free phone:* 888-282-7427. *Fax:* 814-234-0926. *E-mail:* admissions@southhills.edu.

South Hills School of Business & Technology
Atloona, Pennsylvania

- **Proprietary** 2-year
- **Calendar** trimesters
- **Degree** diplomas and associate
- **Coed,** 99 undergraduate students, 94% full-time, 77% women, 23% men
- 85% of applicants were admitted

Undergraduates 93 full-time, 6 part-time. Students come from 1 other state, 1% transferred in.
Freshmen *Admission:* 111 applied, 94 admitted, 80 enrolled. *Average high school GPA:* 2.50.
Faculty *Total:* 7, 100% full-time. *Student/faculty ratio:* 14:1.
Majors Accounting; business marketing and marketing management; legal administrative assistant; medical administrative assistant.
Student Life *Housing:* college housing not available.
Costs (2002–03) *Tuition:* $9480 full-time, $192 per credit part-time. Full-time tuition and fees vary according to program. Part-time tuition and fees vary according to program. *Required fees:* $75 full-time. *Payment plan:* installment. *Waivers:* employees or children of employees.
Applying *Application fee:* $25. *Required:* high school transcript, minimum 1.5 GPA, interview. *Required for some:* essay or personal statement. *Recommended:* minimum 3.0 GPA. *Application deadline:* 9/1 (freshmen).
Admissions Contact Marianne Beyer, Director, South Hills School of Business & Technology, 508 58th Street, Altoona, PA 16602. *Phone:* 814-944-6134. *Fax:* 814-944-4684. *E-mail:* admissions@southhills.edu.

Thaddeus Stevens College of Technology
Lancaster, Pennsylvania

- **State-supported** 2-year, founded 1905
- **Calendar** semesters
- **Degree** associate
- **Urban** 33-acre campus with easy access to Philadelphia
- **Coed,** 591 undergraduate students, 100% full-time, 8% women, 92% men

Undergraduates Students come from 1 other state, 17% African American, 1% Asian American or Pacific Islander, 7% Hispanic American, 0.7% Native American, 48% live on campus. *Retention:* 60% of 2001 full-time freshmen returned.
Freshmen *Admission:* 896 applied, 388 admitted. *Average high school GPA:* 2.52.
Faculty *Total:* 48, 94% full-time. *Student/faculty ratio:* 12:1.
Majors Architectural engineering technology; auto mechanic/technician; carpentry; computer programming, vendor/product certification; construction technology; data entry/microcomputer applications; drafting; electrical/electronic engineering technology; graphic/printing equipment; heating/air conditioning/refrigeration; industrial arts; information sciences/systems; legal administrative assistant; machine technology; mechanical design technology; plumbing; system administration; system/networking/LAN/WAN management; Web page, digital/multimedia and information resources design; word processing.
Academic Programs *Special study options:* academic remediation for entering students, internships, services for LD students.
Library K.W. Schuler Learning Resources Center with 26,000 titles, 450 serial subscriptions, an OPAC, a Web page.
Computers on Campus 100 computers available on campus for general student use. At least one staffed computer lab available.
Student Life *Housing Options:* coed, men-only. *Activities and Organizations:* student-run newspaper, Tech Phi Tech. *Campus security:* 24-hour emergency response devices. *Student Services:* health clinic, personal/psychological counseling, women's center.
Athletics Member NJCAA. *Intercollegiate sports:* basketball M, cross-country running M, football M, golf M, track and field M, wrestling M. *Intramural sports:* archery M/W, baseball M, basketball M, bowling M/W, cross-country running M/W, football M, golf M, soccer M/W, softball M, table tennis M, tennis M/W, track and field M, volleyball M/W, weight lifting M/W, wrestling M/W.
Costs (2001–02) *Tuition:* state resident $4640 full-time. *Required fees:* $30 full-time. *Room and board:* $4416. *Payment plan:* installment.
Financial Aid *Financial aid deadline:* 5/1.
Applying *Options:* common application, electronic application, deferred entrance. *Application fee:* $25. *Required:* essay or personal statement, high school transcript, minimum 2.0 GPA, letters of recommendation. *Required for some:* interview. *Application deadlines:* 6/30 (freshmen), 6/30 (transfers). *Notification:* continuous until 7/15 (freshmen).
Admissions Contact Ms. Erin Kate Nelsen, Director of Enrollment, Thaddeus Stevens College of Technology, Enrollment Services, 750 East King Street,

Thaddeus Stevens College of Technology (continued)
Lancaster, PA 17602-3198. *Phone:* 717-299-7772. *Toll-free phone:* 800-842-3832. *Fax:* 717-391-6929. *E-mail:* nelsen@stevenstech.org.

THOMPSON INSTITUTE
Harrisburg, Pennsylvania

Admissions Contact Mr. Thomas Bogush, Admissions Director, Thompson Institute, 5650 Derry Street, Harrisburg, PA 17111-3518. *Phone:* 717-564-4112. *Toll-free phone:* 800-272-4632. *Fax:* 717-564-3779.

TRIANGLE TECH, INC.
Pittsburgh, Pennsylvania

- **Proprietary** 2-year, founded 1944, part of Triangle Tech, Inc
- **Calendar** semesters
- **Degree** diplomas and associate
- **Urban** 5-acre campus
- **Coed, primarily men,** 259 undergraduate students, 100% full-time, 3% women, 97% men

Undergraduates 259 full-time. Students come from 3 states and territories, 6% are from out of state, 12% African American, 0.4% Asian American or Pacific Islander.
Freshmen *Admission:* 136 applied, 112 admitted, 107 enrolled. *Average high school GPA:* 2.00.
Faculty *Total:* 28, 86% full-time. *Student/faculty ratio:* 10:1.
Majors Architectural engineering technology; carpentry; drafting; electrical/electronic engineering technology; heating/air conditioning/refrigeration; mechanical design technology.
Academic Programs *Special study options:* academic remediation for entering students, advanced placement credit.
Library 2,000 titles, 30 serial subscriptions.
Computers on Campus 50 computers available on campus for general student use. A campuswide network can be accessed from off campus. Internet access, at least one staffed computer lab available.
Student Life *Housing:* college housing not available. *Activities and Organizations:* student council. *Campus security:* 16-hour patrols by trained security personnel.
Costs (2002–03) *Tuition:* $9210 full-time, $261 per credit part-time.
Financial Aid In 2001, 16 Federal Work-Study jobs (averaging $1500). *Financial aid deadline:* 7/1.
Applying *Options:* early admission, deferred entrance. *Required:* high school transcript, minimum 2.0 GPA, interview. *Application deadline:* rolling (freshmen), rolling (transfers).
Admissions Contact Mr. John A. Mazzarese, Vice President, Triangle Tech, Inc., 1940 Perrysville Avenue, Pittsburgh, PA 15214. *Phone:* 412-359-1000 Ext. 7174. *Toll-free phone:* 800-874-8324. *Fax:* 412-359-1012. *E-mail:* info@triangle-tech.com.

TRIANGLE TECH, INC.-DUBOIS SCHOOL
DuBois, Pennsylvania

- **Proprietary** 2-year, founded 1944, part of Triangle Tech, Inc
- **Calendar** semesters
- **Degree** associate
- **Small-town** 5-acre campus
- **Coed,** 339 undergraduate students, 100% full-time, 8% women, 92% men

Undergraduates 339 full-time. Students come from 3 states and territories, 1% are from out of state, 0.3% African American.
Freshmen *Admission:* 216 applied, 208 admitted, 208 enrolled. *Average high school GPA:* 2.00.
Faculty *Total:* 23, 100% full-time. *Student/faculty ratio:* 15:1.
Majors Carpentry; drafting; electrical/electronic engineering technology; welding technology.
Academic Programs *Special study options:* academic remediation for entering students, advanced placement credit, off-campus study.
Library 1,200 titles, 15 serial subscriptions.
Computers on Campus 40 computers available on campus for general student use. A campuswide network can be accessed from off campus. At least one staffed computer lab available.
Student Life *Housing:* college housing not available.
Costs (2001–02) *Tuition:* $9210 full-time. Full-time tuition and fees vary according to program. *Required fees:* $133 full-time. *Payment plan:* installment. *Waivers:* employees or children of employees.
Applying *Options:* deferred entrance. *Required:* high school transcript, minimum 2.0 GPA, interview. *Application deadline:* rolling (freshmen), rolling (transfers).
Admissions Contact Mr. John Conway, Director of Admissions, Triangle Tech, Inc.-DuBois School, PO Box 551, DuBois, PA 15801-0551. *Phone:* 412-359-1000. *Toll-free phone:* 800-874-8324. *Fax:* 814-371-9227.

TRIANGLE TECH, INC.-ERIE SCHOOL
Erie, Pennsylvania

- **Proprietary** 2-year, founded 1976, part of Triangle Tech, Inc
- **Calendar** semesters
- **Degree** associate
- **Urban** 1-acre campus
- **Coed, primarily men,** 140 undergraduate students, 100% full-time, 11% women, 89% men

Undergraduates 140 full-time. Students come from 3 states and territories, 10% are from out of state, 7% African American, 1% Asian American or Pacific Islander, 1% Hispanic American, 105% transferred in.
Freshmen *Admission:* 96 applied, 96 admitted, 96 enrolled.
Faculty *Total:* 12, 100% full-time. *Student/faculty ratio:* 12:1.
Majors Architectural engineering technology; drafting; electrical/electronic engineering technology; mechanical design technology.
Academic Programs *Special study options:* academic remediation for entering students, advanced placement credit, services for LD students.
Library 1,000 titles, 15 serial subscriptions.
Computers on Campus 50 computers available on campus for general student use. At least one staffed computer lab available.
Student Life *Housing:* college housing not available. *Campus security:* 24-hour emergency response devices.
Athletics *Intramural sports:* basketball M(c)/W(c), bowling M(c)/W(c), football M(c)/W(c), golf M(c)/W(c), skiing (downhill) M(c)/W(c).
Costs (2001–02) *Tuition:* $18,420 full-time. *Required fees:* $200 full-time.
Financial Aid In 2001, 5 Federal Work-Study jobs (averaging $2000).
Applying *Options:* deferred entrance. *Required:* high school transcript, minimum 2.0 GPA, interview. *Application deadline:* rolling (freshmen), rolling (transfers).
Admissions Contact Jennifer Provost, Admissions Representative, Triangle Tech, Inc.-Erie School, 2000 Liberty St., Erie, PA 16502. *Phone:* 814-453-6016. *Toll-free phone:* 800-874-8324 (in-state); 800-TRI-TECH (out-of-state). *Fax:* 814-454-2818. *E-mail:* pfitzgerald@triangle-tech.com.

TRIANGLE TECH, INC.-GREENSBURG CENTER
Greensburg, Pennsylvania

- **Proprietary** 2-year, founded 1944, part of Triangle Tech, Inc
- **Calendar** semesters
- **Degree** certificates, diplomas, and associate
- **Small-town** campus with easy access to Pittsburgh
- **Coed,** 170 undergraduate students, 95% full-time, 4% women, 96% men

Undergraduates 162 full-time, 8 part-time. Students come from 4 states and territories, 1 other country, 1% African American. *Retention:* 74% of 2001 full-time freshmen returned.
Freshmen *Admission:* 74 enrolled. *Average high school GPA:* 2.57.
Faculty *Total:* 16, 88% full-time. *Student/faculty ratio:* 11:1.
Majors Architectural engineering technology; drafting; heating/air conditioning/refrigeration; mechanical design technology.
Academic Programs *Special study options:* academic remediation for entering students, adult/continuing education programs, summer session for credit.
Library 330 titles, 8 serial subscriptions.
Computers on Campus 40 computers available on campus for general student use. A campuswide network can be accessed from off campus. Internet access, at least one staffed computer lab available.
Student Life *Student Services:* personal/psychological counseling.
Standardized Tests *Required:* in-house placement test.

Costs (2002–03) *Comprehensive fee:* $15,317 includes full-time tuition ($9763), mandatory fees ($266), and room and board ($5288).
Financial Aid In 2001, 5 Federal Work-Study jobs (averaging $2000).
Applying *Options:* deferred entrance. *Application deadline:* rolling (freshmen), rolling (transfers).
Admissions Contact Mr. John A. Mazzarese, Corporate Director of Admissions, Triangle Tech, Inc.-Greensburg Center, 222 East Pittsburgh Street, Suite A, Greensburg, PA 15601-3304. *Phone:* 412-359-1000.

TRI-STATE BUSINESS INSTITUTE
Erie, Pennsylvania

Admissions Contact 5757 West 26th Street, Erie, PA 16506.

UNIVERSITY OF PITTSBURGH AT TITUSVILLE
Titusville, Pennsylvania

- **State-related** 2-year, founded 1963, part of University of Pittsburgh System
- **Calendar** trimesters
- **Degree** certificates and associate
- **Small-town** 10-acre campus
- **Endowment** $42,312
- **Coed,** 513 undergraduate students, 67% full-time, 62% women, 38% men

Undergraduates 345 full-time, 168 part-time. Students come from 8 states and territories, 3% are from out of state, 13% African American, 2% Asian American or Pacific Islander, 0.4% Hispanic American, 1% Native American, 6% transferred in, 47% live on campus.
Freshmen *Admission:* 4,236 applied, 4,197 admitted, 193 enrolled. *Average high school GPA:* 2.70. *Test scores:* SAT verbal scores over 500: 32%; SAT math scores over 500: 29%; ACT scores over 18: 50%; SAT verbal scores over 600: 7%; SAT math scores over 600: 3%.
Faculty *Total:* 55, 38% full-time, 31% with terminal degrees. *Student/faculty ratio:* 10:1.
Majors Accounting; business administration; liberal arts and sciences/liberal studies; natural sciences; physical therapy assistant.
Academic Programs *Special study options:* academic remediation for entering students, advanced placement credit, cooperative education, independent study, internships, part-time degree program, student-designed majors, summer session for credit.
Library Haskell Memorial Library with 47,754 titles, 613 audiovisual materials, an OPAC.
Computers on Campus 60 computers available on campus for general student use. A campuswide network can be accessed from student residence rooms and from off campus. Internet access, at least one staffed computer lab available.
Student Life *Housing:* on-campus residence required through sophomore year. *Options:* coed. *Activities and Organizations:* drama/theater group, choral group, Phi Theta Kappa, weight club, SAB, SIFE. *Campus security:* 24-hour emergency response devices, controlled dormitory access. *Student Services:* health clinic, personal/psychological counseling.
Athletics *Intercollegiate sports:* basketball M, volleyball W. *Intramural sports:* badminton M/W, basketball M/W, bowling M/W, football M/W, golf M/W, racquetball M/W, softball M/W, table tennis M/W, tennis M/W, volleyball M/W, weight lifting M/W.
Standardized Tests *Required:* SAT I or ACT (for admission). *Recommended:* SAT I (for admission).
Costs (2001–02) *Tuition:* state resident $6370 full-time, $213 per credit part-time; nonresident $13,992 full-time, $462 per credit part-time. *Required fees:* $600 full-time, $53 per term part-time. *Room and board:* $5950. Room and board charges vary according to board plan. *Payment plan:* installment. *Waivers:* employees or children of employees.
Financial Aid In 2001, 50 Federal Work-Study jobs (averaging $1500).
Applying *Options:* deferred entrance. *Application fee:* $35. *Required:* high school transcript, minimum 2.0 GPA. *Required for some:* essay or personal statement, 1 letter of recommendation. *Recommended:* interview. *Application deadline:* rolling (freshmen), rolling (transfers). *Notification:* 11/1 (freshmen).
Admissions Contact Mr. John R. Mumford, Vice President for Enrollment Management, University of Pittsburgh at Titusville, PO Box 287, Titusville, PA 16354. *Phone:* 814-827-4409. *Toll-free phone:* 888-878-0462. *Fax:* 814-827-4448. *E-mail:* uptadm@pitt.edu.

VALLEY FORGE MILITARY COLLEGE
Wayne, Pennsylvania

- **Independent** 2-year, founded 1928
- **Calendar** 4-1-4
- **Degree** associate
- **Suburban** 119-acre campus with easy access to Philadelphia
- **Endowment** $7.2 million
- **Men only,** 120 undergraduate students, 100% full-time

The College's primary goal is to prepare young men to transfer to and succeed at the 4-year college or university of their choice. For more than 95% of the graduates, that goal is achieved through challenging academic programs, a structured environment that builds confidence and character and fosters academic success, and personal transfer counseling and transfer agreements with major universities. The only 2-year Army ROTC commissioning program in the Northeast US, with full tuition scholarships for qualified applicants.

Undergraduates 120 full-time. Students come from 27 states and territories, 22 other countries, 64% are from out of state, 18% transferred in, 100% live on campus.
Freshmen *Admission:* 196 applied, 184 admitted, 120 enrolled. *Average high school GPA:* 2.00. *Test scores:* SAT verbal scores over 500: 49%; SAT math scores over 500: 51%; ACT scores over 18: 71%; SAT verbal scores over 600: 23%; SAT math scores over 600: 30%; ACT scores over 24: 48%; SAT verbal scores over 700: 4%; SAT math scores over 700: 4%; ACT scores over 30: 7%.
Faculty *Total:* 25, 56% full-time. *Student/faculty ratio:* 10:1.
Majors Biological/physical sciences; business administration; criminal justice/law enforcement administration; engineering; liberal arts and sciences/liberal studies.
Academic Programs *Special study options:* academic remediation for entering students, advanced placement credit, English as a second language. *ROTC:* Army (b), Air Force (c).
Library Baker Library with 75,830 titles, 189 serial subscriptions, 326 audiovisual materials, an OPAC.
Computers on Campus 44 computers available on campus for general student use. A campuswide network can be accessed from student residence rooms and from off campus. Internet access, at least one staffed computer lab available.
Student Life *Housing:* on-campus residence required through sophomore year. *Options:* men-only. *Activities and Organizations:* drama/theater group, student-run newspaper, choral group, marching band, Rotoract, Young Republicans, Phi Theta Kappa, business club, criminal justice club, national fraternities. *Campus security:* 24-hour patrols, student patrols. *Student Services:* health clinic, personal/psychological counseling.
Athletics *Intercollegiate sports:* basketball M(s), cross-country running M, equestrian sports M, football M(s), golf M, lacrosse M, riflery M, soccer M(s), tennis M, wrestling M. *Intramural sports:* basketball M, football M, rugby M, soccer M, volleyball M, water polo M, weight lifting M.
Standardized Tests *Required:* SAT I or ACT (for admission).
Costs (2002–03) *Comprehensive fee:* $24,950 includes full-time tuition ($14,900), mandatory fees ($950), and room and board ($9100). *Payment plans:* installment, deferred payment. *Waivers:* employees or children of employees.
Financial Aid In 2001, 20 Federal Work-Study jobs (averaging $1000).
Applying *Options:* common application, early admission, deferred entrance. *Application fee:* $25. *Required:* high school transcript, guidance counselor/teacher evaluation form. *Recommended:* minimum 2.0 GPA, interview. *Application deadline:* 8/2 (freshmen), rolling (transfers). *Notification:* continuous (freshmen).
Admissions Contact Maj. Kelly M. DeShane, Associate Director for College Enrollment, Valley Forge Military College, 1001 Eagle Road, Wayne, PA 19087-3695. *Phone:* 610-989-1300. *Toll-free phone:* 800-234-8362. *Fax:* 610-688-1545. *E-mail:* kdeshane@vfmac.edu.

WESTERN SCHOOL OF HEALTH AND BUSINESS CAREERS
Pittsburgh, Pennsylvania

- **Proprietary** 2-year, founded 1980
- **Calendar** continuous
- **Degree** associate
- **Urban** campus
- **Coed,** 600 undergraduate students

Undergraduates Students come from 6 states and territories, 2 other countries, 2% are from out of state.

Western School of Health and Business Careers (continued)

Freshmen *Average high school GPA:* 2.50. *Test scores:* SAT verbal scores over 500: 5%; SAT math scores over 500: 3%.

Faculty *Total:* 23, 91% full-time. *Student/faculty ratio:* 20:1.

Majors Child care/guidance; diagnostic medical sonography; medical assistant; medical laboratory technician; medical radiologic technology; operating room technician; paralegal/legal assistant; pharmacy technician/assistant; respiratory therapy; veterinary technology.

Academic Programs *Special study options:* academic remediation for entering students, accelerated degree program, adult/continuing education programs, advanced placement credit, cooperative education, English as a second language, internships, services for LD students.

Library Campus Library with 1,687 titles, 1,403 serial subscriptions.

Computers on Campus Internet access, at least one staffed computer lab available.

Student Life *Housing:* college housing not available. *Activities and Organizations:* basketball, newspaper. *Campus security:* 24-hour emergency response devices, 14-hour security patrols Monday through Friday.

Athletics *Intramural sports:* basketball M.

Standardized Tests *Recommended:* SAT I or ACT (for admission), SAT II: Subject Tests (for admission).

Applying *Options:* common application, electronic application, early admission, deferred entrance. *Required:* high school transcript, interview. *Required for some:* letters of recommendation.

Admissions Contact Mr. Bruce E. Jones, Director of Admission, Western School of Health and Business Careers, 421 Seventh Avenue, Pittsburgh, PA 15219. *Phone:* 412-281-7083 Ext. 114. *Toll-free phone:* 800-333-6607. *Fax:* 412-281-0319. *E-mail:* adm@westernschool.com.

WESTMORELAND COUNTY COMMUNITY COLLEGE

Youngwood, Pennsylvania

- **County-supported** 2-year, founded 1970
- **Calendar** semesters
- **Degree** certificates, diplomas, and associate
- **Rural** 85-acre campus with easy access to Pittsburgh
- **Coed,** 5,700 undergraduate students

Undergraduates Students come from 5 states and territories.

Freshmen *Admission:* 1,931 applied, 1,931 admitted.

Faculty *Total:* 410, 20% full-time. *Student/faculty ratio:* 17:1.

Majors Accounting; architectural engineering technology; business administration; business marketing and marketing management; child care/development; computer engineering technology; computer graphics; computer/information sciences; computer science; criminal justice/law enforcement administration; culinary arts; data processing technology; dental hygiene; dietetics; drafting; electrical/electronic engineering technology; engineering; environmental technology; fashion design/illustration; fashion merchandising; finance; fire science; food products retailing; graphic design/commercial art/illustration; graphic/printing equipment; health education; heating/air conditioning/refrigeration; horticulture science; hospitality management; hotel and restaurant management; human services; information sciences/systems; law enforcement/police science; legal administrative assistant; liberal arts and sciences/liberal studies; mechanical design technology; mechanical engineering technology; medical administrative assistant; medical records administration; nuclear technology; nursing; optometric/ophthalmic laboratory technician; paralegal/legal assistant; photography; practical nurse; public administration; publishing; real estate; retail management; robotics; secretarial science; travel/tourism management; welding technology.

Academic Programs *Special study options:* academic remediation for entering students, adult/continuing education programs, advanced placement credit, cooperative education, distance learning, double majors, English as a second language, honors programs, internships, off-campus study, part-time degree program, services for LD students, summer session for credit.

Library 34,522 titles, 643 serial subscriptions.

Computers on Campus 600 computers available on campus for general student use. Internet access, at least one staffed computer lab available.

Student Life *Housing:* college housing not available. *Activities and Organizations:* student-run newspaper, radio station, choral group. *Campus security:* 24-hour emergency response devices and patrols. *Student Services:* personal/psychological counseling.

Athletics Member NJCAA. *Intercollegiate sports:* baseball M, golf M/W, softball W, tennis M/W, volleyball W. *Intramural sports:* basketball M/W, bowling M/W, football M/W, racquetball M/W, skiing (downhill) M/W, softball M/W, table tennis M/W, volleyball M/W, weight lifting M/W.

Standardized Tests *Required:* ACT ASSET.

Costs (2001–02) *Tuition:* $52 per credit part-time; state resident $1560 full-time, $104 per credit part-time; nonresident $3210 full-time, $156 per credit part-time. *Required fees:* $60 full-time, $2 per credit. *Waivers:* senior citizens and employees or children of employees.

Applying *Options:* early admission. *Application deadline:* rolling (freshmen), rolling (transfers). *Notification:* continuous (freshmen).

Admissions Contact Ms. Susan Kuhn, Admissions Coordinator, Westmoreland County Community College, 400 Armbrust Road, Youngwood, PA 15697. *Phone:* 724-925-4064. *Toll-free phone:* 800-262-2103. *Fax:* 724-925-1150. *E-mail:* admission@wccc.westmoreland.cc.pa.us.

THE WILLIAMSON FREE SCHOOL OF MECHANICAL TRADES

Media, Pennsylvania

- **Independent** 2-year, founded 1888
- **Calendar** semesters
- **Degree** diplomas and associate
- **Small-town** 240-acre campus with easy access to Philadelphia
- **Men only**

Faculty *Student/faculty ratio:* 14:1.

Student Life *Campus security:* evening patrols, gate security.

Athletics Member NJCAA.

Applying *Required:* essay or personal statement, high school transcript, minimum 2.0 GPA, 3 letters of recommendation, interview.

Admissions Contact Mr. Edward D. Bailey, Director of Enrollments, The Williamson Free School of Mechanical Trades, 106 South New Middletown Road, Media, PA 19063. *Phone:* 610-566-1776 Ext. 235. *Toll-free phone:* 610-566-1776 Ext. 235. *E-mail:* wiltech@libertynet.org.

YORK TECHNICAL INSTITUTE

York, Pennsylvania

- **Private** 2-year
- **Degree** diplomas and associate
- 740 undergraduate students, 100% full-time

Undergraduates 740 full-time. Students come from 5 states and territories, 10% are from out of state.

Freshmen *Admission:* 740 enrolled.

Faculty *Total:* 52, 100% full-time. *Student/faculty ratio:* 25:1.

Majors Artificial intelligence/robotics; computer/information systems security; computer/information technology services administration and management related; computer science related; computer systems networking/telecommunications; computer/technical support; information technology; system administration; system/networking/LAN/WAN management; Web page, digital/multimedia and information resources design.

Academic Programs *Special study options:* academic remediation for entering students, advanced placement credit, cooperative education, internships.

Computers on Campus 250 computers available on campus for general student use. Internet access, at least one staffed computer lab available.

Costs (2001–02) *Tuition:* $11,360 full-time. Full-time tuition and fees vary according to program. No tuition increase for student's term of enrollment. *Payment plans:* tuition prepayment, installment. *Waivers:* employees or children of employees.

Financial Aid In 2001, 67 Federal Work-Study jobs (averaging $1740).

Applying *Required:* high school transcript, minimum 2.0 GPA, interview. *Required for some:* essay or personal statement.

Admissions Contact Ms. Sharon Mulligan, Associate Director of Admissions, York Technical Institute, 1405 Williams Road, York, PA 17402. *Phone:* 717-757-1100 Ext. 318. *Toll-free phone:* 800-229-9675 (in-state); 800-227-9675 (out-of-state). *E-mail:* crb@yhi.edu.

YORKTOWNE BUSINESS INSTITUTE

York, Pennsylvania

- **Proprietary** 2-year, founded 1976
- **Calendar** semesters

- **Degree** diplomas and associate
- **Small-town** 1-acre campus with easy access to Baltimore
- **Coed,** 286 undergraduate students, 66% full-time, 74% women, 26% men

Undergraduates 189 full-time, 97 part-time. Students come from 2 states and territories, 10% are from out of state.
Freshmen *Admission:* 160 applied, 142 admitted, 119 enrolled.
Faculty *Total:* 20, 75% with terminal degrees. *Student/faculty ratio:* 14:1.
Majors Accounting; business; culinary arts; executive assistant; hospitality management; management information systems/business data processing; medical administrative assistant; medical assistant; secretarial science.
Academic Programs *Special study options:* adult/continuing education programs, double majors, independent study, internships, part-time degree program.
Computers on Campus 100 computers available on campus for general student use. Internet access, at least one staffed computer lab available.
Student Life *Housing:* college housing not available.
Applying *Application fee:* $50. *Required:* high school transcript, interview. *Required for some:* admissions test. *Application deadline:* rolling (freshmen), rolling (transfers).
Admissions Contact Bonnie Gillespie, Director, Yorktowne Business Institute, West Seventh Avenue, York, PA 17404. *Phone:* 717-846-5000 Ext. 124. *Toll-free phone:* 800-840-1004. *Fax:* 717-848-4584. *E-mail:* info@ybi.edu.

RHODE ISLAND

COMMUNITY COLLEGE OF RHODE ISLAND
Warwick, Rhode Island

- **State-supported** 2-year, founded 1964
- **Calendar** semesters
- **Degree** certificates and associate
- **Suburban** 205-acre campus with easy access to Boston
- **Endowment** $946,394
- **Coed,** 16,223 undergraduate students, 34% full-time, 62% women, 38% men

Undergraduates 5,463 full-time, 10,760 part-time. Students come from 15 states and territories, 15 other countries, 7% are from out of state, 7% African American, 3% Asian American or Pacific Islander, 10% Hispanic American, 0.6% Native American, 0.1% international, 4% transferred in. *Retention:* 64% of 2001 full-time freshmen returned.
Freshmen *Admission:* 5,293 applied, 5,165 admitted, 3,158 enrolled.
Faculty *Total:* 730, 40% full-time.
Majors Accounting; alcohol/drug abuse counseling; art; banking; biological/physical sciences; business; business administration; business marketing and marketing management; chemical technology; computer engineering technology; computer programming; dental hygiene; early childhood education; electrical/electronic engineering technology; engineering; fashion merchandising; fire science; general retailing/wholesaling; general studies; gerontological services; instrumentation technology; labor/personnel relations; law enforcement/police science; legal administrative assistant; liberal arts and sciences/liberal studies; medical administrative assistant; medical laboratory technician; medical radiologic technology; music; nursing; occupational therapy assistant; paralegal/legal assistant; physical therapy assistant; psychiatric/mental health services; rehabilitation/therapeutic services related; respiratory therapy; retailing operations; secretarial science; social work; special education; theater arts/drama; theater design; urban studies.
Academic Programs *Special study options:* academic remediation for entering students, adult/continuing education programs, advanced placement credit, cooperative education, English as a second language, external degree program, honors programs, internships, off-campus study, part-time degree program, services for LD students, study abroad, summer session for credit. *ROTC:* Army (c).
Library Community College of Rhode Island Learning Resources Center with 98,140 titles, 817 serial subscriptions, 20,231 audiovisual materials, an OPAC, a Web page.
Computers on Campus 285 computers available on campus for general student use. A campuswide network can be accessed from off campus that provide access to e-mail. Internet access, at least one staffed computer lab available.
Student Life *Housing:* college housing not available. *Activities and Organizations:* drama/theater group, choral group, Distributive Education Clubs of America, theater group, ABLE, Phi Theta Kappa. *Campus security:* 24-hour emergency response devices and patrols. *Student Services:* health clinic, personal/psychological counseling.
Athletics Member NJCAA. *Intercollegiate sports:* baseball M, basketball M(s)/W(s), cross-country running M/W, golf M/W, ice hockey M/W, soccer M(s)/W(s), softball W(s), swimming M/W, tennis M/W, track and field M/W, volleyball W(s).
Costs (2001–02) *Tuition:* state resident $1664 full-time, $77 per credit part-time; nonresident $4884 full-time, $230 per credit part-time. Part-time tuition and fees vary according to course load. *Required fees:* $190 full-time, $36 per term part-time. *Payment plan:* deferred payment. *Waivers:* senior citizens and employees or children of employees.
Financial Aid In 2001, 500 Federal Work-Study jobs (averaging $2500). 70 State and other part-time jobs (averaging $2000).
Applying *Options:* deferred entrance. *Application fee:* $20. *Application deadline:* rolling (freshmen), rolling (transfers).
Admissions Contact Ms. Donnamarie Allen, Senior Admission Officer/Financial Aid Officer, Community College of Rhode Island, 400 East Avenue, Warwick, RI 02886. *Phone:* 401-333-7080. *Fax:* 401-825-2394. *E-mail:* webadmission@ccri.cc.ri.us.

NEW ENGLAND INSTITUTE OF TECHNOLOGY
Warwick, Rhode Island

- **Independent** primarily 2-year, founded 1940
- **Calendar** quarters
- **Degrees** associate and bachelor's
- **Suburban** 10-acre campus with easy access to Boston
- **Coed,** 2,430 undergraduate students

Undergraduates Students come from 8 states and territories, 22 other countries, 5% African American, 2% Asian American or Pacific Islander, 5% Hispanic American, 0.6% Native American, 1% international.
Faculty *Total:* 397, 24% full-time.
Majors Architectural engineering technology; auto mechanic/technician; business administration; computer/information sciences; computer maintenance technology; construction technology; electrical/electronic engineering technology; electrical engineering; heating/air conditioning/refrigeration; industrial technology; interior design; marine maintenance; medical assistant; occupational therapy assistant; operating room technician; plumbing; radio/television broadcasting technology.
Academic Programs *Special study options:* academic remediation for entering students, adult/continuing education programs, advanced placement credit, distance learning, English as a second language, internships, part-time degree program, services for LD students, summer session for credit.
Library Learning Resources Center with 34,829 titles, 1,000 serial subscriptions, an OPAC.
Computers on Campus 325 computers available on campus for general student use. Internet access, at least one staffed computer lab available.
Student Life *Housing:* college housing not available. *Campus security:* security personnel during open hours. *Student Services:* personal/psychological counseling.
Costs (2002–03) *Tuition:* $11,850 full-time. *Required fees:* $1280 full-time.
Applying *Options:* early admission, deferred entrance. *Application fee:* $25. *Required:* high school transcript, interview. *Application deadline:* rolling (freshmen), rolling (transfers).
Admissions Contact Mr. Michael Kwiatkowski, Director of Admissions, New England Institute of Technology, 2500 Post Road, Warwick, RI 02886-2266. *Phone:* 401-739-5000. *E-mail:* neit@ids.net.

SOUTH CAROLINA

AIKEN TECHNICAL COLLEGE
Aiken, South Carolina

Admissions Contact Mr. Dennis Harville, Director of Admissions and Records, Aiken Technical College, PO Drawer 696, Aiken, SC 29802-0696. *Phone:* 803-593-9231. *E-mail:* harden@aik.tec.sc.us.

CENTRAL CAROLINA TECHNICAL COLLEGE
Sumter, South Carolina

- **State-supported** 2-year, founded 1963, part of South Carolina State Board for Technical and Comprehensive Education

Central Carolina Technical College (continued)

- **Calendar** semesters
- **Degree** certificates, diplomas, and associate
- **Small-town** 29-acre campus
- **Coed,** 2,963 undergraduate students, 33% full-time, 67% women, 33% men

Undergraduates 974 full-time, 1,989 part-time. Students come from 1 other state, 1% are from out of state, 0.7% transferred in.
Freshmen *Admission:* 313 enrolled. *Test scores:* SAT verbal scores over 500: 24%; SAT math scores over 500: 22%; ACT scores over 18: 40%; SAT verbal scores over 600: 10%; SAT math scores over 600: 3%; ACT scores over 24: 3%.
Faculty *Total:* 142, 42% full-time. *Student/faculty ratio:* 21:1.
Majors Accounting; business administration; child care services management; civil engineering technology; criminal justice studies; data processing technology; environmental control technologies related; industrial electronics installation/repair; liberal arts and sciences/liberal studies; marketing operations; mechanical drafting; multi/interdisciplinary studies related; natural resources management; nursing; paralegal/legal assistant; secretarial science.
Academic Programs *Special study options:* academic remediation for entering students, adult/continuing education programs, advanced placement credit, cooperative education, distance learning, external degree program, independent study, internships, off-campus study, part-time degree program, student-designed majors, summer session for credit.
Library Central Carolina Technical College Library with 20,356 titles, 245 serial subscriptions, 1,317 audiovisual materials, an OPAC, a Web page.
Computers on Campus 350 computers available on campus for general student use. A campuswide network can be accessed from off campus that provide access to course registration, student account and grade information. Internet access, online (class) registration, at least one staffed computer lab available.
Student Life *Housing:* college housing not available. *Activities and Organizations:* Creative Arts Society, Phi Theta Kappa, Computer Club, National Student Nurses Association (local chapter), Natural Resources Management Club. *Campus security:* 24-hour emergency response devices. *Student Services:* personal/psychological counseling.
Standardized Tests *Required:* ACT COMPASS. *Required for some:* SAT I or ACT (for placement).
Costs (2001–02) *Tuition:* area resident $1700 full-time, $71 per credit hour part-time; state resident $2032 full-time, $85 per credit hour part-time; nonresident $3844 full-time, $161 per credit hour part-time. Full-time tuition and fees vary according to course load. *Payment plan:* installment. *Waivers:* senior citizens and employees or children of employees.
Applying *Options:* electronic application. *Application fee:* $25. *Required:* high school transcript. *Application deadline:* rolling (freshmen), rolling (transfers).
Admissions Contact Admissions and Counseling Office, Central Carolina Technical College, 506 North Guignard Drive, Sumter, SC 29150. *Phone:* 803-778-1961 Ext. 455. *Toll-free phone:* 800-221-8711 Ext. 455 (in-state); 803-778-1961 Ext. 455 (out-of-state). *Fax:* 803-778-6696. *E-mail:* colmanjh@cctc6.sum.tec.sc.us.

COLUMBIA JUNIOR COLLEGE
Columbia, South Carolina

- **Proprietary** 2-year, founded 1935
- **Calendar** quarters
- **Degree** certificates and associate
- **Urban** 2-acre campus
- **Coed**

Faculty *Student/faculty ratio:* 9:1.
Student Life *Campus security:* 24-hour emergency response devices.
Standardized Tests *Required:* SAT I or ACT (for admission).
Applying *Options:* deferred entrance. *Application fee:* $25. *Required:* high school transcript, interview, admissions test.
Admissions Contact Chief Admission Officer, Columbia Junior College, 3810 Main Street, Columbia, SC 29203-6443. *Phone:* 803-799-9082.

DENMARK TECHNICAL COLLEGE
Denmark, South Carolina

- **State-supported** 2-year, founded 1948, part of South Carolina State Board for Technical and Comprehensive Education
- **Calendar** semesters
- **Degree** certificates, diplomas, and associate
- **Rural** 53-acre campus
- **Coed,** 1,401 undergraduate students

Undergraduates Students come from 8 states and territories.
Freshmen *Admission:* 825 applied, 825 admitted.
Faculty *Total:* 59, 58% full-time. *Student/faculty ratio:* 19:1.
Majors Auto mechanic/technician; business administration; computer/information sciences; criminal justice/law enforcement administration; engineering technology; human services; secretarial science.
Academic Programs *Special study options:* academic remediation for entering students, adult/continuing education programs, advanced placement credit, cooperative education, internships, off-campus study, part-time degree program, summer session for credit. *ROTC:* Army (c).
Library Denmark Technical College Learning Resources Center with 15,437 titles, 200 serial subscriptions.
Computers on Campus 105 computers available on campus for general student use. At least one staffed computer lab available.
Student Life *Activities and Organizations:* student-run newspaper, choral group, Phi Beta Lambda, Gospel Choir, Drama Club, national fraternities, national sororities. *Campus security:* 24-hour patrols. *Student Services:* health clinic, personal/psychological counseling.
Athletics *Intercollegiate sports:* baseball M, basketball M/W, softball W. *Intramural sports:* basketball M/W, tennis M/W, volleyball M/W.
Standardized Tests *Required:* ACT ASSET.
Costs (2001–02) *Tuition:* state resident $1704 full-time, $71 per credit hour part-time; nonresident $3408 full-time, $142 per credit hour part-time. *Room and board:* $3096; room only: $1422. *Payment plan:* tuition prepayment. *Waivers:* senior citizens.
Financial Aid In 2001, 250 Federal Work-Study jobs (averaging $1200).
Applying *Options:* early admission, deferred entrance. *Application fee:* $10. *Required:* high school transcript. *Application deadline:* rolling (freshmen), rolling (transfers).
Admissions Contact Mrs. Michelle McDowell, Director of Admission and Records, Denmark Technical College, Solomon Blatt Boulevard, Box 327, Denmark, SC 29042-0327. *Phone:* 803-793-5176. *Fax:* 803-793-5942.

FLORENCE-DARLINGTON TECHNICAL COLLEGE
Florence, South Carolina

- **State-supported** 2-year, founded 1963, part of South Carolina State Board for Technical and Comprehensive Education
- **Calendar** semesters
- **Degree** certificates, diplomas, and associate
- **Small-town** 100-acre campus with easy access to Columbia
- **Endowment** $1000
- **Coed,** 3,632 undergraduate students, 56% full-time, 69% women, 31% men

Undergraduates 2,017 full-time, 1,615 part-time. Students come from 4 states and territories, 3 other countries, 3% transferred in.
Freshmen *Admission:* 737 enrolled.
Faculty *Total:* 305, 38% full-time, 6% with terminal degrees. *Student/faculty ratio:* 17:1.
Majors Accounting; auto mechanic/technician; biological/physical sciences; business administration; business marketing and marketing management; chemical engineering technology; civil engineering technology; computer engineering technology; criminal justice/law enforcement administration; dental hygiene; drafting; electrical/electronic engineering technology; electromechanical technology; engineering technology; heating/air conditioning/refrigeration; human services; industrial radiologic technology; liberal arts and sciences/liberal studies; machine technology; medical laboratory technician; medical records administration; mortuary science; nursing; occupational therapy; paralegal/legal assistant; physical therapy; respiratory therapy; secretarial science; trade/industrial education.
Academic Programs *Special study options:* academic remediation for entering students, adult/continuing education programs, advanced placement credit, English as a second language, internships, part-time degree program, study abroad, summer session for credit. *ROTC:* Army (c).
Library Florence-Darlington Technical College Library with 34,814 titles, 286 serial subscriptions.
Computers on Campus 220 computers available on campus for general student use. A campuswide network can be accessed from off campus. Internet access, at least one staffed computer lab available.
Student Life *Housing:* college housing not available. *Activities and Organizations:* student-run newspaper, choral group, International Club, FDTC Outreach

Choir, Student Ambassadors. *Campus security:* 24-hour emergency response devices and patrols, late-night transport/escort service. *Student Services:* personal/psychological counseling.

Standardized Tests *Required for some:* SAT I or ACT (for admission).

Costs (2002–03) *Tuition:* area resident $1782 full-time, $75 per credit hour part-time; state resident $2044 full-time, $86 per credit hour part-time; nonresident $3878 full-time, $162 per credit hour part-time. *Required fees:* $100 full-time, $50 per term part-time. *Waivers:* senior citizens and employees or children of employees.

Financial Aid In 2001, 95 Federal Work-Study jobs (averaging $2500).

Applying *Options:* common application, deferred entrance. *Application fee:* $15. *Required for some:* high school transcript. *Application deadlines:* 8/1 (freshmen), 8/1 (transfers).

Admissions Contact Ms. Perry T. Kirven, Director of Enrollment Services, Florence-Darlington Technical College, PO Box 100548, Florence, SC 29501-0548. *Phone:* 843-661-8153. *Fax:* 843-661-8041. *E-mail:* kirvenp@flo.tec.sc.us.

FORREST JUNIOR COLLEGE
Anderson, South Carolina

- **Proprietary** 2-year, founded 1946
- **Calendar** quarters
- **Degree** certificates, diplomas, and associate
- **Small-town** 3-acre campus
- **Coed, primarily men,** 225 undergraduate students

Faculty *Total:* 18, 22% full-time. *Student/faculty ratio:* 16:1.

Majors Business administration.

Academic Programs *Special study options:* accelerated degree program, advanced placement credit, cooperative education, distance learning, double majors, English as a second language, freshman honors college, internships, part-time degree program, summer session for credit.

Library Forrest Junior College Library plus 1 other with an OPAC.

Computers on Campus A campuswide network can be accessed from off campus. Internet access, online (class) registration, at least one staffed computer lab available.

Student Life *Housing:* college housing not available. *Campus security:* late-night transport/escort service. *Student Services:* health clinic, legal services.

Costs (2001–02) *Tuition:* $3420 full-time, $95 per quarter hour part-time. Full-time tuition and fees vary according to course load. *Payment plan:* installment.

Financial Aid In 2001, 7 Federal Work-Study jobs.

Applying *Options:* deferred entrance. *Application fee:* $20. *Required:* essay or personal statement, high school transcript, letters of recommendation, interview.

Admissions Contact Ms. Janie Turmon, Admissions Representative, Forrest Junior College, 601 East River Street, Anderson, SC 29624. *Phone:* 864-225-7653 Ext. 206. *Fax:* 864-261-7471. *E-mail:* fjc@carol.net.

GREENVILLE TECHNICAL COLLEGE
Greenville, South Carolina

- **State-supported** 2-year, founded 1962, part of South Carolina State Board for Technical and Comprehensive Education
- **Calendar** semesters
- **Degree** certificates, diplomas, and associate
- **Urban** 407-acre campus
- **Coed,** 11,500 undergraduate students

Undergraduates Students come from 6 other countries.

Faculty *Total:* 478, 52% full-time.

Majors Accounting; aircraft mechanic/airframe; architectural engineering technology; auto mechanic/technician; aviation technology; business administration; business marketing and marketing management; computer programming; construction technology; criminal justice/law enforcement administration; dental hygiene; drafting; electrical/electronic engineering technology; emergency medical technology; fire science; food products retailing; health science; heating/air conditioning/refrigeration; hospitality management; industrial radiologic technology; industrial technology; law enforcement/police science; liberal arts and sciences/liberal studies; machine technology; materials science; mechanical engineering technology; medical laboratory technician; nursing; paralegal/legal assistant; physical therapy; pre-engineering; respiratory therapy; secretarial science.

Academic Programs *Special study options:* academic remediation for entering students, adult/continuing education programs, advanced placement credit, cooperative education, part-time degree program, summer session for credit.

Library Verne Smith Library/Technical Resource Center with 49,500 titles, 658 serial subscriptions.

Computers on Campus 830 computers available on campus for general student use. At least one staffed computer lab available.

Student Life *Housing:* college housing not available. *Activities and Organizations:* Student Government Association, Phi Theta Kappa, Student Nurses Association, Christians on Campus, International and Friends Organization. *Campus security:* 24-hour emergency response devices and patrols, student patrols, late-night transport/escort service.

Athletics *Intramural sports:* basketball M/W, bowling M/W, tennis M/W, volleyball M/W.

Costs (2001–02) *Tuition:* area resident $1700 full-time, $71 per credit hour part-time; state resident $1850 full-time, $78 per credit hour part-time; nonresident $3750 full-time, $157 per credit hour part-time. Full-time tuition and fees vary according to course load. Part-time tuition and fees vary according to course load. *Required fees:* $50 full-time, $25 per term part-time. *Waivers:* minority students, senior citizens, and employees or children of employees.

Financial Aid In 2001, 120 Federal Work-Study jobs (averaging $2670).

Applying *Options:* early admission, deferred entrance. *Application fee:* $25. *Required:* high school transcript. *Application deadline:* rolling (freshmen), rolling (transfers). *Notification:* continuous until 8/20 (freshmen).

Admissions Contact Martha S. White, Director of Admissions, Greenville Technical College, PO Box 5616, Greenville, SC 29606-5616. *Phone:* 864-250-8109. *Toll-free phone:* 800-922-1183 (in-state); 800-723-0673 (out-of-state). *Fax:* 864-250-8534.

HORRY-GEORGETOWN TECHNICAL COLLEGE
Conway, South Carolina

- **State and locally supported** 2-year, founded 1966, part of South Carolina State Board for Technical and Comprehensive Education
- **Calendar** semesters
- **Degree** certificates, diplomas, and associate
- **Small-town** campus
- **Endowment** $2.4 million
- **Coed,** 4,113 undergraduate students, 45% full-time, 61% women, 39% men

Undergraduates 1,836 full-time, 2,277 part-time. Students come from 10 states and territories, 22 other countries. *Retention:* 51% of 2001 full-time freshmen returned.

Freshmen *Admission:* 2,683 applied, 1,858 admitted, 665 enrolled. *Average high school GPA:* 2.50.

Faculty *Total:* 267, 39% full-time. *Student/faculty ratio:* 18:1.

Majors Agricultural sciences; business administration; civil engineering technology; computer engineering technology; computer/information technology services administration and management related; computer programming (specific applications); criminal justice/law enforcement administration; culinary arts; data entry/microcomputer applications; electrical/electronic engineering technology; forest harvesting production technology; heating/air conditioning/refrigeration; hotel and restaurant management; industrial radiologic technology; landscaping management; machine technology; nursing; paralegal/legal assistant; practical nurse; pre-engineering; recreation/leisure facilities management; secretarial science; Web/multimedia management/webmaster; Web page, digital/multimedia and information resources design; word processing.

Academic Programs *Special study options:* academic remediation for entering students, adult/continuing education programs, advanced placement credit, cooperative education, internships, part-time degree program, services for LD students, summer session for credit.

Library Conway Campus Learning Resource Center plus 2 others with a Web page.

Computers on Campus 300 computers available on campus for general student use. A campuswide network can be accessed from off campus. Internet access, at least one staffed computer lab available.

Student Life *Housing:* college housing not available. *Student Services:* personal/psychological counseling.

Standardized Tests *Required:* CPT.

Costs (2002–03) *Tuition:* area resident $1782 full-time; state resident $2574 full-time; nonresident $4104 full-time. *Required fees:* $144 full-time.

Applying *Options:* early admission. *Application fee:* $15. *Required for some:* high school transcript. *Application deadline:* rolling (freshmen), rolling (transfers). *Notification:* continuous (freshmen).

Admissions Contact Ms. Teresa Hilburn, Director of Admissions, Horry-Georgetown Technical College, 2050 Highway 501 East, PO Box 261966, Conway, SC 29528-6066. *Phone:* 843-349-5238. *Fax:* 843-234-2213. *E-mail:* jackson@hor.tec.sc.us.

ITT TECHNICAL INSTITUTE
Greenville, South Carolina

- **Proprietary** 2-year, founded 1992, part of ITT Educational Services, Inc
- **Calendar** quarters
- **Degree** associate
- 245 undergraduate students

Majors Computer/information sciences related; computer programming; drafting; electrical/electronic engineering technologies related; information technology.
Student Life *Housing:* college housing not available.
Costs (2001–02) *Tuition:* Full-time tuition and fees vary according to program. Part-time tuition and fees vary according to program. $260—$330 per credit hour.
Financial Aid In 2001, 3 Federal Work-Study jobs, 1 State and other part-time jobs (averaging $4000).
Applying *Options:* deferred entrance. *Application fee:* $100. *Required:* high school transcript, interview. *Recommended:* letters of recommendation. *Application deadline:* rolling (freshmen), rolling (transfers).
Admissions Contact Mr. Rod Kruse, ITT Technical Institute, One Marcus Drive, Building 4, Greenville, SC 29615-4818. *Phone:* 864-288-0777 Ext. 21. *Toll-free phone:* 800-932-4488. *Fax:* 864-297-0053.

MIDLANDS TECHNICAL COLLEGE
Columbia, South Carolina

- **State and locally supported** 2-year, founded 1974, part of South Carolina State Board for Technical and Comprehensive Education
- **Calendar** semesters
- **Degree** certificates, diplomas, and associate
- **Suburban** 113-acre campus
- **Endowment** $2.3 million
- **Coed,** 9,874 undergraduate students, 43% full-time, 60% women, 40% men

Undergraduates 4,283 full-time, 5,591 part-time. Students come from 21 states and territories, 1% are from out of state, 32% African American, 1% Asian American or Pacific Islander, 2% Hispanic American, 0.4% Native American, 0.5% international.
Freshmen *Admission:* 1,812 admitted, 1,812 enrolled.
Faculty *Total:* 630, 35% full-time, 100% with terminal degrees. *Student/faculty ratio:* 20:1.
Majors Accounting; architectural engineering technology; auto mechanic/technician; business administration; business marketing and marketing management; civil engineering technology; court reporting; criminal justice/law enforcement administration; data processing technology; dental hygiene; electrical/electronic engineering technology; engineering technology; graphic design/commercial art/illustration; heating/air conditioning/refrigeration; legal studies; liberal arts and sciences/liberal studies; machine technology; mechanical drafting; mechanical engineering technology; medical administrative assistant; medical laboratory technician; medical radiologic technology; medical records administration; nursing; pharmacy technician/assistant; physical therapy assistant; respiratory therapy; secretarial science; social work; telecommunications.
Academic Programs *Special study options:* academic remediation for entering students, adult/continuing education programs, advanced placement credit, cooperative education, distance learning, double majors, English as a second language, internships, part-time degree program, services for LD students, student-designed majors, summer session for credit.
Library 77,000 titles, 488 serial subscriptions.
Computers on Campus 125 computers available on campus for general student use. A campuswide network can be accessed from off campus. Internet access, at least one staffed computer lab available.
Student Life *Housing:* college housing not available. *Activities and Organizations:* student-run newspaper. *Campus security:* 24-hour emergency response devices and patrols. *Student Services:* personal/psychological counseling, women's center.
Athletics *Intramural sports:* basketball M, football M, softball M/W, volleyball M/W.
Standardized Tests *Recommended:* SAT I or ACT (for admission).
Costs (2001–02) *Tuition:* area resident $1800 full-time, $71 per hour part-time; state resident $2226 full-time, $89 per hour part-time; nonresident $5200 full-time, $213 per hour part-time. *Required fees:* $50 per term part-time. *Waivers:* senior citizens and employees or children of employees.
Financial Aid In 2001, 217 Federal Work-Study jobs (averaging $3000).
Applying *Options:* common application, early admission, deferred entrance. *Application fee:* $25. *Recommended:* high school transcript. *Application deadline:* 7/20 (freshmen), rolling (transfers). *Notification:* continuous (freshmen).
Admissions Contact Mr. Richard Tinneny, Director of Admissions, Midlands Technical College, PO Box 2408, Columbia, SC 29202. *Phone:* 803-738-8324. *Fax:* 803-738-7840.

NORTHEASTERN TECHNICAL COLLEGE
Cheraw, South Carolina

- **State and locally supported** 2-year, founded 1967, part of South Carolina State Board for Technical and Comprehensive Education
- **Calendar** semesters
- **Degree** certificates, diplomas, and associate
- **Rural** 59-acre campus
- **Coed,** 967 undergraduate students, 30% full-time, 66% women, 34% men

Undergraduates 288 full-time, 679 part-time. Students come from 2 states and territories, 1% are from out of state, 39% African American, 0.4% Asian American or Pacific Islander, 0.1% Hispanic American, 2% Native American, 4% transferred in.
Freshmen *Admission:* 224 enrolled.
Faculty *Total:* 72, 40% full-time.
Majors Accounting; business administration; business marketing and marketing management; computer programming; computer science; data processing technology; electrical/electronic engineering technology; liberal arts and sciences/liberal studies; machine technology; mechanical design technology; secretarial science.
Academic Programs *Special study options:* academic remediation for entering students, adult/continuing education programs, advanced placement credit, part-time degree program, summer session for credit.
Library Northeastern Technical College Library with 18,072 titles, 132 serial subscriptions, 255 audiovisual materials, an OPAC, a Web page.
Computers on Campus 125 computers available on campus for general student use. A campuswide network can be accessed from off campus. Internet access, at least one staffed computer lab available.
Student Life *Housing:* college housing not available. *Campus security:* 24-hour emergency response devices. *Student Services:* personal/psychological counseling.
Standardized Tests *Required for some:* SAT I (for admission).
Costs (2002–03) *Tuition:* area resident $1782 full-time, $75 per credit hour part-time; state resident $1920 full-time, $80 per credit hour part-time; nonresident $3600 full-time, $150 per credit hour part-time. *Required fees:* $146 full-time, $12 per credit hour, $4 part-time.
Financial Aid In 2001, 25 Federal Work-Study jobs (averaging $2700).
Applying *Options:* early admission. *Application fee:* $13. *Required:* high school transcript, interview. *Application deadline:* rolling (freshmen), rolling (transfers).
Admissions Contact Mrs. Mary Newton, Dean of Students, Northeastern Technical College, PO Drawer 1007, Cheraw, SC 29520-1007. *Phone:* 843-921-6935. *Fax:* 843-537-6148. *E-mail:* mpace@netc.chm.tec.sc.us.

ORANGEBURG-CALHOUN TECHNICAL COLLEGE
Orangeburg, South Carolina

- **State and locally supported** 2-year, founded 1968, part of State Board for Technical and Comprehensive Education, South Carolina
- **Calendar** semesters
- **Degree** certificates, diplomas, and associate
- **Small-town** 100-acre campus with easy access to Columbia
- **Endowment** $2.1 million
- **Coed,** 2,020 undergraduate students, 51% full-time, 73% women, 27% men

Undergraduates 1,039 full-time, 981 part-time. Students come from 5 states and territories, 3 other countries, 5% transferred in.
Freshmen *Admission:* 496 enrolled.
Faculty *Total:* 112, 63% full-time, 2% with terminal degrees.
Majors Accounting; auto mechanic/technician; business; computer programming related; criminal justice studies; data processing technology; early childhood education; electrical/electronic engineering technology; instrumentation technology; liberal arts and sciences/liberal studies; machine technology; mechanical drafting; mechanical engineering technology; medical laboratory assistant; medical laboratory technician; medical radiologic technology; nursing; paralegal/legal assistant; respiratory therapy; secretarial science.

Academic Programs *Special study options:* academic remediation for entering students, adult/continuing education programs, advanced placement credit, cooperative education, distance learning, independent study, internships, part-time degree program, services for LD students, summer session for credit.
Library Gressette Learning Center with 30,288 titles, 361 serial subscriptions, 2,076 audiovisual materials, an OPAC.
Computers on Campus 361 computers available on campus for general student use. A campuswide network can be accessed from off campus. Internet access available.
Student Life *Housing:* college housing not available. *Activities and Organizations:* Student Advisory Council. *Campus security:* 24-hour emergency response devices and patrols. *Student Services:* personal/psychological counseling, women's center.
Standardized Tests *Required for some:* ACT ASSET. *Recommended:* SAT I and SAT II or ACT (for placement).
Costs (2001–02) *One-time required fee:* $15. *Tuition:* area resident $1296 full-time, $54 per semester hour part-time; state resident $1608 full-time, $67 per semester hour part-time; nonresident $3408 full-time, $142 per semester hour part-time. *Required fees:* $15 full-time. *Waivers:* senior citizens and employees or children of employees.
Applying *Options:* common application, early admission. *Application fee:* $15. *Required:* high school transcript. *Application deadline:* rolling (freshmen), rolling (transfers). *Notification:* continuous (freshmen).
Admissions Contact Ms. Bobbie Felder, Dean of Students, Orangeburg-Calhoun Technical College, 3250 St. Matthews Road, Highway 601, Orangeburg, SC 29118. *Phone:* 803-535-1218. *Toll-free phone:* 800-813-6519. *Fax:* 803-535-1388. *E-mail:* stoudenmire@org.tec.sc.us.

PIEDMONT TECHNICAL COLLEGE
Greenwood, South Carolina

- **State-supported** 2-year, founded 1966, part of South Carolina State Board for Technical and Comprehensive Education
- **Calendar** semesters
- **Degree** certificates, diplomas, and associate
- **Small-town** 60-acre campus
- **Endowment** $1.1 million
- **Coed,** 4,544 undergraduate students

Undergraduates Students come from 2 states and territories, 5 other countries, 1% are from out of state.
Freshmen *Admission:* 890 applied, 890 admitted.
Faculty *Total:* 233, 44% full-time. *Student/faculty ratio:* 18:1.
Majors Accounting; auto mechanic/technician; biological/physical sciences; business; business administration; business marketing and marketing management; carpentry; child care/development; computer programming; construction management; construction technology; criminal justice/law enforcement administration; criminal justice studies; data processing technology; drafting; electrical/electronic engineering technology; engineering; engineering design; engineering technology; graphic design/commercial art/illustration; heating/air conditioning/refrigeration; human services; legal administrative assistant; liberal arts and sciences/liberal studies; machine technology; mechanical drafting; mechanical engineering technology; medical administrative assistant; medical radiologic technology; mortuary science; nursing; office management; respiratory therapy; secretarial science; social work.
Academic Programs *Special study options:* academic remediation for entering students, adult/continuing education programs, advanced placement credit, cooperative education, distance learning, independent study, internships, part-time degree program, services for LD students, summer session for credit.
Library Piedmont Technical College Library with 27,497 titles, 345 serial subscriptions, 1,501 audiovisual materials, an OPAC, a Web page.
Computers on Campus 320 computers available on campus for general student use. A campuswide network can be accessed from off campus. Internet access, at least one staffed computer lab available.
Student Life *Housing:* college housing not available. *Activities and Organizations:* choral group, National Honor Society, Career Peers (student volunteers), Student Nurses Association, Psychology Club, Ebony Club. *Campus security:* 24-hour emergency response devices and patrols, late-night transport/escort service. *Student Services:* personal/psychological counseling, women's center.
Athletics *Intramural sports:* basketball M/W, football M/W, softball M/W, volleyball M/W.
Standardized Tests *Required:* ACT ACCESS, ACT COMPASS. *Recommended:* SAT I (for placement).
Costs (2001–02) *Tuition:* area resident $1512 full-time, $63 per credit part-time; state resident $1704 full-time, $71 per credit part-time. Full-time tuition and fees vary according to course load. Part-time tuition and fees vary according to course load. *Waivers:* senior citizens and employees or children of employees.
Applying *Options:* electronic application, early admission, deferred entrance. *Required:* high school transcript. *Recommended:* interview. *Application deadline:* rolling (freshmen), rolling (transfers). *Notification:* continuous until 8/20 (freshmen).
Admissions Contact Mr. Steve Coleman, Director of Admissions, Piedmont Technical College, PO Box 1467, Emerald Road, Greenwood, SC 29648. *Phone:* 864-941-8373. *Toll-free phone:* 800-868-5528. *E-mail:* coleman_s@piedmont.tec.sc.us.

SPARTANBURG METHODIST COLLEGE
Spartanburg, South Carolina

- **Independent Methodist** 2-year, founded 1911
- **Calendar** semesters
- **Degree** associate
- **Urban** 111-acre campus with easy access to Charlotte
- **Endowment** $13.0 million
- **Coed,** 635 undergraduate students, 91% full-time, 52% women, 48% men

Spartanburg Methodist College (SMC) is the only private, 2-year, residential, liberal arts, coeducational college in South Carolina. Located in Spartanburg, South Carolina, the College offers the Associate in Arts, the Associate in Science, the Associate in Criminal Justice, and the Associate in Information Management degrees. SMC offers a caring, nurturing environment that promotes success, with more than 90 percent of its graduates continuing their education.

Undergraduates 580 full-time, 55 part-time. Students come from 12 states and territories, 8 other countries, 10% are from out of state, 30% African American, 0.9% Asian American or Pacific Islander, 1% Hispanic American, 0.9% Native American, 3% international, 8% transferred in, 65% live on campus. *Retention:* 69% of 2001 full-time freshmen returned.
Freshmen *Admission:* 849 applied, 643 admitted, 366 enrolled. *Average high school GPA:* 2.98. *Test scores:* SAT verbal scores over 500: 17%; SAT math scores over 500: 15%; ACT scores over 18: 36%.
Faculty *Total:* 41, 49% full-time, 27% with terminal degrees. *Student/faculty ratio:* 18:1.
Majors Criminal justice/law enforcement administration; information technology; liberal arts and sciences/liberal studies; secretarial science.
Academic Programs *Special study options:* academic remediation for entering students, advanced placement credit, English as a second language, honors programs, independent study, part-time degree program, services for LD students, summer session for credit. *ROTC:* Army (c).
Library Marie Blair Burgess Learning Resource Center with 40,000 titles, 500 serial subscriptions, 3,000 audiovisual materials.
Computers on Campus 47 computers available on campus for general student use. A campuswide network can be accessed from student residence rooms and from off campus. Internet access, at least one staffed computer lab available.
Student Life *Housing:* on-campus residence required through sophomore year. *Options:* coed, men-only, women-only. *Activities and Organizations:* drama/theater group, student-run newspaper, choral group, College Christian Movement, Alpha Phi Omega, Campus Union, Fellowship of Christian Athletes, Kappa Sigma Alpha. *Campus security:* 24-hour emergency response devices and patrols, student patrols, late-night transport/escort service, controlled dormitory access. *Student Services:* health clinic, personal/psychological counseling.
Athletics Member NJCAA. *Intercollegiate sports:* baseball M(s), basketball M(s)/W(s), cross-country running M(s)/W(s), golf M(s)/W(s), soccer M(s)/W(s), softball W(s), tennis W(s), volleyball W(s). *Intramural sports:* basketball M/W, football M/W, golf M/W, racquetball M/W, soccer M/W, softball M/W, table tennis M/W, tennis M/W, volleyball M/W.
Standardized Tests *Required:* SAT I or ACT (for admission).
Costs (2001–02) *One-time required fee:* $150. *Comprehensive fee:* $12,250 includes full-time tuition ($7840) and room and board ($4410). Part-time tuition: $210 per credit. *Payment plan:* installment. *Waivers:* senior citizens and employees or children of employees.
Financial Aid In 2001, 77 Federal Work-Study jobs (averaging $1600). 82 State and other part-time jobs (averaging $1600). *Financial aid deadline:* 8/25.
Applying *Options:* common application, electronic application, deferred entrance. *Application fee:* $20. *Required:* high school transcript, minimum 2.0 GPA, rank in top 75% of high school class. *Required for some:* essay or personal statement, letters of recommendation, interview. *Recommended:* interview. *Application deadline:* rolling (freshmen), rolling (transfers). *Notification:* continuous (freshmen).

Spartanburg Methodist College (continued)

Admissions Contact Mr. Daniel L. Philbeck, Dean of Admissions and Financial Aid, Spartanburg Methodist College, Spartanburg, SC 29301. *Phone:* 864-587-4223. *Toll-free phone:* 800-772-7286. *Fax:* 864-587-4355. *E-mail:* admiss@smcsc.edu.

SPARTANBURG TECHNICAL COLLEGE
Spartanburg, South Carolina

- **State-supported** 2-year, founded 1961, part of South Carolina State Board for Technical and Comprehensive Education
- **Calendar** semesters
- **Degree** certificates, diplomas, and associate
- **Suburban** 104-acre campus
- **Coed,** 3,359 undergraduate students

Undergraduates Students come from 7 states and territories, 2% are from out of state, 21% African American, 1% Asian American or Pacific Islander, 3% Hispanic American.

Faculty *Total:* 99.

Majors Accounting; architectural engineering technology; auto mechanic/technician; biological/physical sciences; business administration; business marketing and marketing management; civil engineering technology; computer/information sciences; drafting; electrical/electronic engineering technology; engineering technology; heating/air conditioning/refrigeration; horticulture science; liberal arts and sciences/liberal studies; machine technology; mechanical engineering technology; medical administrative assistant; medical laboratory technician; medical radiologic technology; respiratory therapy; robotics technology; secretarial science; sign language interpretation; trade/industrial education.

Academic Programs *Special study options:* academic remediation for entering students, adult/continuing education programs, advanced placement credit, cooperative education, part-time degree program, services for LD students, summer session for credit.

Library Spartanburg Technical College Library with 36,000 titles, 400 serial subscriptions, an OPAC, a Web page.

Computers on Campus 360 computers available on campus for general student use. A campuswide network can be accessed from off campus. At least one staffed computer lab available.

Student Life *Housing:* college housing not available. *Activities and Organizations:* drama/theater group, student-run newspaper. *Campus security:* 24-hour patrols. *Student Services:* personal/psychological counseling, women's center.

Standardized Tests *Required:* ACT ASSET, ACT COMPASS.

Costs (2001–02) *Tuition:* area resident $1700 full-time, $71 per semester hour part-time; state resident $2120 full-time, $89 per semester hour part-time; nonresident $3900 full-time, $163 per semester hour part-time. *Waivers:* senior citizens.

Applying *Options:* early admission. *Required:* high school transcript. *Application deadline:* rolling (freshmen), rolling (transfers). *Notification:* continuous (freshmen).

Admissions Contact Ms. Celia Bauss, Dean of Enrollment Management, Spartanburg Technical College, PO Box 4386, Spartanburg, SC 29305. *Phone:* 864-591-3800. *Toll-free phone:* 800-922-3679. *Fax:* 864-591-3916.

TECHNICAL COLLEGE OF THE LOWCOUNTRY
Beaufort, South Carolina

Admissions Contact Mr. Les Brediger, Director of Admissions, Technical College of the Lowcountry, 921 Ribaut Road, PO Box 1288, Beaufort, SC 29901-1288. *Phone:* 843-525-8207.

TRI-COUNTY TECHNICAL COLLEGE
Pendleton, South Carolina

- **State-supported** 2-year, founded 1962, part of South Carolina State Board for Technical and Comprehensive Education
- **Calendar** semesters
- **Degree** certificates, diplomas, and associate
- **Rural** 100-acre campus
- **Coed,** 3,773 undergraduate students

Undergraduates Students come from 3 states and territories, 7 other countries, 11% African American, 0.8% Asian American or Pacific Islander, 0.8% Hispanic American, 0.3% Native American, 2% international.

Faculty *Total:* 400, 55% full-time. *Student/faculty ratio:* 25:1.

Majors Accounting; business administration; clothing/textiles; computer programming; criminal justice/law enforcement administration; data processing technology; drafting; electrical/electronic engineering technology; electromechanical technology; health science; heating/air conditioning/refrigeration; liberal arts and sciences/liberal studies; machine technology; medical assistant; medical laboratory technician; nursing; quality control technology; radio/television broadcasting; secretarial science; veterinary technology.

Academic Programs *Special study options:* academic remediation for entering students, adult/continuing education programs, advanced placement credit, cooperative education, English as a second language, internships, part-time degree program, summer session for credit. *ROTC:* Army (c), Air Force (c).

Library Tri-County Technical College Library with 34,513 titles, 356 serial subscriptions, an OPAC, a Web page.

Computers on Campus 600 computers available on campus for general student use. Internet access, at least one staffed computer lab available.

Student Life *Housing:* college housing not available. *Activities and Organizations:* student-run newspaper. *Campus security:* 24-hour emergency response devices and patrols.

Standardized Tests *Required for some:* SAT I (for placement), National League of Nursing Exam.

Costs (2001–02) *Tuition:* area resident $1700 full-time, $71 per hour part-time; state resident $2040 full-time, $85 per hour part-time; nonresident $229 per hour part-time. *Waivers:* senior citizens.

Applying *Options:* early admission. *Application deadline:* rolling (freshmen), rolling (transfers). *Notification:* continuous (freshmen).

Admissions Contact Ms. Rachael Campbell, Coordinator of Admission, Tri-County Technical College, PO Box 587, Highway 76, Pendleton, SC 29670-0587. *Phone:* 864-646-8641 Ext. 2199. *Fax:* 864-646-8256. *E-mail:* admstaff@tricty.tricounty.tec.sc.us.

TRIDENT TECHNICAL COLLEGE
Charleston, South Carolina

- **State and locally supported** 2-year, founded 1964, part of South Carolina State Board for Technical and Comprehensive Education
- **Calendar** semesters
- **Degree** certificates, diplomas, and associate
- **Urban** campus
- **Coed,** 10,461 undergraduate students, 36% full-time, 62% women, 38% men

Undergraduates 3,804 full-time, 6,657 part-time. 1% are from out of state, 30% African American, 2% Asian American or Pacific Islander, 2% Hispanic American, 0.5% Native American.

Freshmen *Admission:* 1,456 enrolled.

Faculty *Total:* 510, 51% full-time.

Majors Accounting; aircraft mechanic/airframe; auto mechanic/technician; biological/physical sciences; broadcast journalism; business administration; business marketing and marketing management; child care provider; civil engineering technology; computer engineering technology; computer graphics; computer/information technology services administration and management related; computer programming (specific applications); computer systems networking/telecommunications; criminal justice/law enforcement administration; culinary arts; dental hygiene; electrical/electronic engineering technology; engineering-related technology; graphic design/commercial art/illustration; horticulture science; hotel and restaurant management; human services; industrial technology; legal studies; liberal arts and sciences/liberal studies; machine technology; mechanical engineering technology; medical administrative assistant; medical laboratory technician; nursing; occupational therapy; paralegal/legal assistant; physical therapy; respiratory therapy; secretarial science; telecommunications; veterinary technology; Web/multimedia management/webmaster; Web page, digital/multimedia and information resources design.

Academic Programs *Special study options:* academic remediation for entering students, advanced placement credit, cooperative education, English as a second language, part-time degree program, services for LD students, summer session for credit.

Library Learning Resources Center plus 3 others with 68,462 titles, 868 serial subscriptions.

Computers on Campus 500 computers available on campus for general student use. At least one staffed computer lab available.

Student Life *Housing:* college housing not available. *Activities and Organizations:* student-run newspaper. *Campus security:* 24-hour emergency response devices and patrols, late-night transport/escort service. *Student Services:* personal/psychological counseling.

Standardized Tests *Required:* SAT I, ACT, or in-house test.
Costs (2002–03) *Tuition:* area resident $1700 full-time, $71 per credit hour part-time; state resident $1926 full-time, $81 per credit hour part-time; nonresident $4072 full-time, $170 per credit hour part-time. Full-time tuition and fees vary according to course load. Part-time tuition and fees vary according to course load. *Required fees:* $50 full-time, $5 per unit. *Waivers:* senior citizens.
Applying *Options:* common application, early admission. *Required for some:* high school transcript. *Application deadlines:* 8/5 (freshmen), 8/5 (transfers). *Notification:* continuous (freshmen).
Admissions Contact Ms. Mary Stewart, Admissions Coordinator, Trident Technical College, 7000 Rivers Avenue, Charleston, SC 29423-8067. *Phone:* 843-574-6383.

University of South Carolina Beaufort
Beaufort, South Carolina

- **State-supported** 2-year, founded 1959, part of University of South Carolina System
- **Calendar** semesters
- **Degrees** associate (offers courses for bachelor's degrees awarded by other University of South Carolina system schools)
- **Small-town** 5-acre campus
- **Coed,** 1,070 undergraduate students, 38% full-time, 65% women, 35% men

Undergraduates 403 full-time, 667 part-time. 17% African American, 2% Asian American or Pacific Islander, 3% Hispanic American, 0.9% Native American, 5% international.
Freshmen *Admission:* 248 applied, 248 admitted, 146 enrolled.
Faculty *Total:* 64, 38% full-time. *Student/faculty ratio:* 17:1.
Majors Liberal arts and sciences/liberal studies.
Academic Programs *Special study options:* academic remediation for entering students, adult/continuing education programs, advanced placement credit, freshman honors college, honors programs, independent study, off-campus study, part-time degree program, services for LD students, study abroad, summer session for credit.
Library University of South Carolina at Beaufort Library with 50,000 titles, 395 serial subscriptions, an OPAC, a Web page.
Computers on Campus 85 computers available on campus for general student use. A campuswide network can be accessed from off campus. Online (class) registration, at least one staffed computer lab available.
Student Life *Housing:* college housing not available. *Activities and Organizations:* drama/theater group, Student Government Association, Gamma Beta Phi, Black Student Organization, Business Club, Environmental Awareness Club. *Campus security:* 24-hour emergency response devices, evening security service.
Standardized Tests *Required:* SAT I or ACT (for admission).
Costs (2001–02) *Tuition:* state resident $2310 full-time, $100 per hour part-time; nonresident $5888 full-time, $247 per hour part-time. *Required fees:* $4 per hour. *Waivers:* senior citizens.
Financial Aid In 2001, 30 Federal Work-Study jobs (averaging $3000).
Applying *Options:* deferred entrance. *Application fee:* $40. *Required:* high school transcript. *Recommended:* minimum 2.0 GPA. *Application deadline:* rolling (freshmen), rolling (transfers).
Admissions Contact Ms. Anita Folsom, Director of Admissions, University of South Carolina Beaufort, 801 Carteret Street, Beaufort, SC 29902. *Phone:* 843-521-4101 Ext. 4101. *Fax:* 843-521-4194. *E-mail:* ibfrt41@vm.sc.edu.

University of South Carolina Lancaster
Lancaster, South Carolina

- **State-supported** 2-year, founded 1959, part of University of South Carolina System
- **Calendar** semesters
- **Degree** associate
- **Small-town** 17-acre campus with easy access to Charlotte
- **Coed,** 939 undergraduate students

Undergraduates Students come from 3 states and territories, 1 other country.
Freshmen *Admission:* 302 applied, 296 admitted. *Average high school GPA:* 2.5.
Faculty *Total:* 47, 49% full-time.
Majors Biological/physical sciences; business administration; criminal justice/law enforcement administration; liberal arts and sciences/liberal studies; nursing; secretarial science.
Academic Programs *Special study options:* academic remediation for entering students, adult/continuing education programs, advanced placement credit, honors programs, part-time degree program.
Library Medford Library with 68,192 titles, 454 serial subscriptions.
Computers on Campus 25 computers available on campus for general student use.
Student Life *Housing:* college housing not available. *Activities and Organizations:* student-run newspaper, choral group. *Student Services:* personal/psychological counseling, women's center.
Athletics *Intercollegiate sports:* basketball M/W. *Intramural sports:* racquetball M/W, soccer M/W, tennis M/W, volleyball M/W, weight lifting M.
Standardized Tests *Required:* SAT I or ACT (for placement).
Costs (2001–02) *Tuition:* state resident $1155 full-time, $100 per hour part-time; nonresident $2944 full-time, $247 per hour part-time. *Required fees:* $100 full-time, $4 per hour part-time.
Applying *Options:* common application, early admission. *Application fee:* $35. *Required:* high school transcript. *Application deadline:* rolling (freshmen), rolling (transfers). *Notification:* continuous (freshmen).
Admissions Contact Ms. Rebecca D. Parker, Director of Admissions, University of South Carolina Lancaster, PO Box 889, Lancaster, SC 29721-0889. *Phone:* 803-313-7471 Ext. 7073. *E-mail:* bparker@gwm.sc.edu.

University of South Carolina Salkehatchie
Allendale, South Carolina

Admissions Contact Ms. Jane T. Brewer, Associate Dean for Student Services, University of South Carolina Salkehatchie, PO Box 617, Allendale, SC 29810-0617. *Phone:* 803-584-3446. *Toll-free phone:* 800-922-5500.

University of South Carolina Sumter
Sumter, South Carolina

- **State-supported** 2-year, founded 1966, part of University of South Carolina System
- **Calendar** semesters
- **Degree** associate
- **Urban** 46-acre campus
- **Endowment** $1.5 million
- **Coed,** 1,229 undergraduate students, 63% full-time, 63% women, 37% men

Undergraduates 771 full-time, 458 part-time. Students come from 2 states and territories, 8 other countries, 1% are from out of state, 26% African American, 2% Asian American or Pacific Islander, 2% Hispanic American, 0.4% Native American, 26% transferred in. *Retention:* 68% of 2001 full-time freshmen returned.
Freshmen *Admission:* 462 applied, 289 admitted, 199 enrolled. *Average high school GPA:* 2.94. *Test scores:* ACT scores over 18: 67%; ACT scores over 24: 7%; ACT scores over 30: 1%.
Faculty *Total:* 67, 60% full-time, 60% with terminal degrees. *Student/faculty ratio:* 17:1.
Majors Interdisciplinary studies; liberal arts and sciences/liberal studies.
Academic Programs *Special study options:* adult/continuing education programs, advanced placement credit, distance learning, English as a second language, freshman honors college, honors programs, independent study, off-campus study, part-time degree program, services for LD students, summer session for credit. *ROTC:* Army (c), Air Force (c).
Library University of South Carolina at Sumter Library with 48,000 titles, 250 serial subscriptions, an OPAC, a Web page.
Computers on Campus 260 computers available on campus for general student use. A campuswide network can be accessed from off campus. Internet access, online (class) registration, at least one staffed computer lab available.
Student Life *Housing:* college housing not available. *Activities and Organizations:* drama/theater group, choral group, Association of African-American Students, Baptist Student Union, Student Education Association, Gamecock Ambassadors, Environmental. *Campus security:* late-night transport/escort service. *Student Services:* personal/psychological counseling.
Athletics Member NSCAA. *Intramural sports:* badminton M/W, basketball M/W, bowling M/W, football M, gymnastics M/W, racquetball M/W, soccer M, softball M/W, table tennis M/W, volleyball M/W.
Standardized Tests *Required:* SAT I or ACT (for admission).
Costs (2001–02) *Tuition:* state resident $2410 full-time, $104 per semester hour part-time; nonresident $5985 full-time, $251 per semester hour part-time.

University of South Carolina Sumter (continued)
Full-time tuition and fees vary according to reciprocity agreements. Part-time tuition and fees vary according to reciprocity agreements. *Payment plan:* deferred payment. *Waivers:* senior citizens and employees or children of employees.

Financial Aid In 2001, 30 Federal Work-Study jobs (averaging $1884).

Applying *Options:* electronic application. *Application fee:* $45. *Required:* high school transcript, minimum 2.0 GPA. *Application deadline:* 8/6 (freshmen), rolling (transfers).

Admissions Contact Dr. Robert Ferrell, Director of Admissions, University of South Carolina Sumter, 200 Miller Road, Sumter, SC 29150-2498. *Phone:* 803-938-3762. *Fax:* 803-938-3901. *E-mail:* bobf@usc.sumter.edu.

UNIVERSITY OF SOUTH CAROLINA UNION
Union, South Carolina

- **State-supported** 2-year, founded 1965, part of University of South Carolina System
- **Calendar** semesters
- **Degree** associate
- **Small-town** campus with easy access to Charlotte
- **Coed,** 382 undergraduate students

Undergraduates Students come from 2 states and territories.

Freshmen *Admission:* 263 applied, 260 admitted. *Test scores:* SAT verbal scores over 500: 15%; SAT math scores over 500: 18%.

Faculty *Total:* 25, 52% full-time.

Majors Biological/physical sciences; liberal arts and sciences/liberal studies.

Academic Programs *Special study options:* part-time degree program.

Computers on Campus 30 computers available on campus for general student use. A campuswide network can be accessed from off campus.

Student Life *Housing:* college housing not available. *Activities and Organizations:* drama/theater group, student-run newspaper, choral group.

Standardized Tests *Required:* SAT I or ACT (for admission).

Costs (2001–02) *Tuition:* state resident $2310 full-time, $100 per credit hour part-time; nonresident $5888 full-time, $247 per credit hour part-time. *Required fees:* $100 full-time, $4 per credit hour. *Payment plan:* deferred payment.

Financial Aid In 2001, 23 Federal Work-Study jobs (averaging $2200).

Applying *Application fee:* $25. *Required:* high school transcript. *Application deadline:* rolling (freshmen).

Admissions Contact Mr. Terry E. Young, Director of Enrollment Services, University of South Carolina Union, PO Drawer 729, Union, SC 29379-0729. *Phone:* 864-429-8728.

WILLIAMSBURG TECHNICAL COLLEGE
Kingstree, South Carolina

- **State-supported** 2-year, founded 1969, part of South Carolina State Board for Technical and Comprehensive Education
- **Calendar** semesters
- **Degree** certificates, diplomas, and associate
- **Rural** 41-acre campus
- **Endowment** $52,987
- **Coed, primarily women**

Faculty *Student/faculty ratio:* 13:1.

Student Life *Campus security:* late-night transport/escort service.

Standardized Tests *Required:* ACT COMPASS, ACT ASSET. *Recommended:* SAT I or ACT (for placement).

Costs (2001–02) *Tuition:* state resident $1080 full-time, $45 per semester hour part-time; nonresident $2880 full-time. Full-time tuition and fees vary according to course load. Part-time tuition and fees vary according to course load. *Required fees:* $20 full-time, $10 per term part-time.

Financial Aid In 2001, 22 Federal Work-Study jobs (averaging $2800).

Applying *Options:* common application, early admission, deferred entrance. *Application fee:* $10. *Required:* high school transcript.

Admissions Contact Ms. Elaine M. Hanna, Director of Admissions, Williamsburg Technical College, 601 Martin Luther King, Jr. Avenue, Kingstree, SC 29556-4197. *Phone:* 843-355-4110 Ext. 4162. *Toll-free phone:* 800-768-2021 Ext. 4162. *Fax:* 843-355-4269 Ext. 4162. *E-mail:* admissions@wil.tec.sc.us.

YORK TECHNICAL COLLEGE
Rock Hill, South Carolina

- **State-supported** 2-year, founded 1961, part of South Carolina State Board for Technical and Comprehensive Education
- **Calendar** semesters
- **Degree** certificates, diplomas, and associate
- **Small-town** 110-acre campus with easy access to Charlotte
- **Coed,** 3,700 undergraduate students

Undergraduates 28% African American, 1% Asian American or Pacific Islander, 1% Hispanic American, 2% Native American, 0.1% international.

Faculty *Total:* 218, 44% full-time.

Majors Accounting; auto mechanic/technician; business administration; child care provider; child care services management; computer engineering related; computer engineering technology; computer/information technology services administration and management related; data processing technology; dental hygiene; drafting/design technology; electrical/electronic engineering technology; electrical equipment installation/repair; engineering-related technology; forest products technology; heating/air conditioning/refrigeration; industrial electronics installation/repair; industrial machinery maintenance/repair; liberal arts and sciences/liberal studies; machine technology; mechanical drafting; mechanical engineering technology; medical laboratory technician; medical radiologic technology; nursing; secretarial science; welding technology.

Academic Programs *Special study options:* academic remediation for entering students, adult/continuing education programs, advanced placement credit, cooperative education, distance learning, honors programs, internships, off-campus study, part-time degree program, services for LD students, summer session for credit.

Library Anne Springs Close Library with 26,947 titles, 475 serial subscriptions, 1,813 audiovisual materials, an OPAC, a Web page.

Computers on Campus 250 computers available on campus for general student use. Internet access, at least one staffed computer lab available.

Student Life *Housing:* college housing not available. *Activities and Organizations:* Jacobin Society, Phi Theta Kappa, Student Government Association, Phi Beta Lambda, Student Activities Board. *Campus security:* 24-hour patrols. *Student Services:* personal/psychological counseling.

Costs (2001–02) *Tuition:* area resident $1700 full-time, $71 per credit hour part-time; state resident $2040 full-time, $85 per credit hour part-time; nonresident $5088 full-time, $212 per credit hour part-time. *Required fees:* $20 full-time, $10 per term part-time. *Payment plan:* installment. *Waivers:* senior citizens.

Applying *Options:* electronic application. *Required for some:* high school transcript. *Recommended:* interview. *Application deadline:* rolling (freshmen), rolling (transfers). *Notification:* continuous (freshmen).

Admissions Contact Mr. Kenny Aldridge, Admissions Department Manager, York Technical College, 452 South Anderson Road, Rock Hill, SC 29730. *Phone:* 803-327-8008. *Toll-free phone:* 800-922-8324. *Fax:* 803-981-7237. *E-mail:* aldridge@york.tec.sc.us.

SOUTH DAKOTA

KILIAN COMMUNITY COLLEGE
Sioux Falls, South Dakota

- **Independent** 2-year, founded 1977
- **Calendar** trimesters
- **Degree** certificates and associate
- **Urban** 1-acre campus
- **Endowment** $1587
- **Coed,** 303 undergraduate students

Undergraduates Students come from 3 states and territories, 6% are from out of state.

Faculty *Total:* 70, 7% full-time.

Majors Accounting; business administration; child care/guidance; computer engineering technology; computer science; computer typography/composition; criminal justice/law enforcement administration; human services; interdisciplinary studies; legal administrative assistant; medical administrative assistant; secretarial science.

Academic Programs *Special study options:* academic remediation for entering students, cooperative education, double majors, independent study, internships, part-time degree program, services for LD students, summer session for credit.

Library University of Sioux Falls Mears Library with 78,000 titles, 395 serial subscriptions, an OPAC, a Web page.
Computers on Campus 37 computers available on campus for general student use. Internet access, at least one staffed computer lab available.
Student Life *Housing:* college housing not available. *Campus security:* late-night transport/escort service.
Standardized Tests *Required for some:* ACT ASSET.
Costs (2001–02) *One-time required fee:* $25. *Tuition:* $3960 full-time, $165 per credit part-time. *Required fees:* $90 full-time, $45 per term part-time.
Financial Aid In 2001, 28 Federal Work-Study jobs (averaging $1120).
Applying *Options:* early admission, deferred entrance. *Application fee:* $25. *Required:* high school transcript. *Application deadline:* rolling (freshmen), rolling (transfers).
Admissions Contact Ms. Jennifer Fischer, Kilian Community College, 224 North Phillips Avenue, Sioux Falls, SD 57104-6014. *Phone:* 605-336-1711. *Toll-free phone:* 800-888-1147. *Fax:* 605-336-2606. *E-mail:* info@kcc.cc.sd.us.

LAKE AREA TECHNICAL INSTITUTE
Watertown, South Dakota

- **State-supported** 2-year, founded 1964
- **Calendar** semesters
- **Degree** diplomas and associate
- **Small-town** 16-acre campus
- **Coed,** 1,057 undergraduate students

Freshmen *Admission:* 517 admitted.
Faculty *Total:* 65. *Student/faculty ratio:* 15:1.
Majors Accounting; agricultural business; auto mechanic/technician; aviation technology; biological technology; business marketing and marketing management; carpentry; computer programming; computer programming related; computer programming (specific applications); computer systems networking/telecommunications; cosmetology; data entry/microcomputer applications related; dental assistant; drafting; electrical/electronic engineering technology; finance; information technology; machine technology; medical assistant; medical laboratory technician; occupational therapy assistant; physical therapy assistant; practical nurse; system administration; Web/multimedia management/webmaster; welding technology.
Academic Programs *Special study options:* academic remediation for entering students, internships, services for LD students.
Library Leonard H. Timmerman Library plus 1 other with 5,000 titles, 128 serial subscriptions.
Computers on Campus 650 computers available on campus for general student use. A campuswide network can be accessed from off campus. Internet access, online (class) registration, at least one staffed computer lab available.
Student Life *Housing:* college housing not available. *Activities and Organizations:* PBL, VICA, Rodeo Club.
Athletics *Intramural sports:* basketball M/W, softball M/W, volleyball M/W.
Standardized Tests *Required:* ACT (for admission).
Costs (2002–03) *Tuition:* area resident $2088 full-time, $58 per credit part-time. Full-time tuition and fees vary according to program. *Required fees:* $936 full-time, $24 per credit. *Payment plan:* installment.
Financial Aid In 2001, 100 Federal Work-Study jobs (averaging $1200).
Applying *Options:* electronic application. *Application fee:* $15. *Required:* high school transcript. *Required for some:* essay or personal statement, 3 letters of recommendation, interview.
Admissions Contact Ms. Debra Shephard, Assistant Director, Lake Area Technical Institute, 230 11th Street Northeast, Watertown, SD 57201. *Phone:* 605-882-5284. *Toll-free phone:* 800-657-4344. *E-mail:* latiinfo@lati.tec.sd.us.

MITCHELL TECHNICAL INSTITUTE
Mitchell, South Dakota

- **District-supported** 2-year, founded 1968
- **Calendar** semesters
- **Degree** diplomas and associate
- **Rural** 6-acre campus
- **Coed,** 868 undergraduate students

Undergraduates Students come from 16 states and territories, 2 other countries.
Faculty *Total:* 60, 80% full-time. *Student/faculty ratio:* 16:1.
Majors Accounting; agricultural business; agricultural production; carpentry; computer/information sciences; computer maintenance technology; computer systems networking/telecommunications; computer/technical support; culinary arts; drafting; electrical/electronic engineering technology; electrical/power transmission installation; farm/ranch management; heating/air conditioning/refrigeration; information sciences/systems; medical administrative assistant; medical assistant; medical laboratory technician; radiological science; secretarial science; telecommunications.
Academic Programs *Special study options:* academic remediation for entering students, advanced placement credit, cooperative education, distance learning, internships, services for LD students, summer session for credit.
Library Instructional Services Center with 100 serial subscriptions, an OPAC.
Computers on Campus 110 computers available on campus for general student use. Internet access, at least one staffed computer lab available.
Student Life *Activities and Organizations:* Student Senate, Vocational Industrial Clubs of America, Phi Beta Lambda, Post-Secondary Agricultural Students, AWARE. *Student Services:* personal/psychological counseling, women's center.
Athletics *Intercollegiate sports:* equestrian sports M/W. *Intramural sports:* basketball M/W, softball M/W, volleyball M/W.
Standardized Tests *Recommended:* ACT (for admission).
Costs (2001–02) *Tuition:* area resident $2100 full-time, $56 per credit hour part-time. *Required fees:* $2400 full-time. *Room and board:* $3000. *Payment plan:* installment. *Waivers:* employees or children of employees.
Financial Aid In 2001, 56 Federal Work-Study jobs (averaging $1600).
Applying *Options:* electronic application. *Application fee:* $25. *Required:* high school transcript. *Required for some:* essay or personal statement, interview. *Recommended:* minimum 2.0 GPA. *Application deadline:* rolling (freshmen), rolling (transfers). *Notification:* continuous (freshmen).
Admissions Contact Mr. Tim Edwards, Admissions Representative, Mitchell Technical Institute, 821 North Capital, Mitchell, SD 57301. *Phone:* 605-995-3025. *Toll-free phone:* 800-952-0042. *Fax:* 605-996-3299. *E-mail:* questions@mti.tec.sd.us.

SISSETON-WAHPETON COMMUNITY COLLEGE
Sisseton, South Dakota

- **Federally supported** 2-year, founded 1979
- **Calendar** semesters
- **Degree** certificates and associate
- **Rural** 2-acre campus
- **Endowment** $253,820
- **Coed**

Faculty *Student/faculty ratio:* 10:1.
Student Life *Campus security:* 24-hour emergency response devices.
Standardized Tests *Required:* Assessment and Placement Services for Community Colleges.
Costs (2001–02) *Tuition:* $96 per credit part-time; state resident $1152 full-time; nonresident $1152 full-time. *Required fees:* $310 full-time, $155 per credit.
Financial Aid In 2001, 5 Federal Work-Study jobs (averaging $1200).
Applying *Options:* common application, deferred entrance. *Required:* high school transcript. *Recommended:* minimum 2.0 GPA, letters of recommendation, interview.
Admissions Contact Ms. Darlene Redday, Director of Admissions, Sisseton-Wahpeton Community College, Old Agency Box 689, Sisseton, SD 57262. *Phone:* 605-698-3966.

SOUTHEAST TECHNICAL INSTITUTE
Sioux Falls, South Dakota

- **State-supported** 2-year, founded 1968
- **Calendar** semesters
- **Degree** certificates, diplomas, and associate
- **Urban** 169-acre campus
- **Endowment** $145,000
- **Coed,** 2,246 undergraduate students, 75% full-time, 45% women, 55% men

Undergraduates 1,676 full-time, 570 part-time. Students come from 6 states and territories, 21% are from out of state, 0.3% African American, 0.3% Asian American or Pacific Islander, 0.4% Hispanic American, 0.8% Native American.
Freshmen *Admission:* 1,667 applied, 1,009 admitted, 630 enrolled. *Average high school GPA:* 2.76.

Southeast Technical Institute (continued)

Faculty *Total:* 182, 38% full-time, 3% with terminal degrees. *Student/faculty ratio:* 13:1.

Majors Accounting; architectural engineering technology; artificial intelligence/robotics; auto body repair; auto mechanic/technician; biomedical engineering-related technology; business administration; business marketing and marketing management; cardiovascular technology; civil engineering technology; computer graphics; computer/information technology services administration and management related; computer maintenance technology; computer programming; computer programming related; computer programming (specific applications); computer programming, vendor/product certification; computer science related; computer software and media applications related; computer software engineering; computer systems networking/telecommunications; computer/technical support; diesel engine mechanic; drafting; electrical/electronic engineering technology; electromechanical technology; engineering technology; finance; graphic design/commercial art/illustration; graphic/printing equipment; health unit coordination; heating/air conditioning/refrigeration; horticulture science; industrial technology; information sciences/systems; information technology; laser/optical technology; machine technology; mechanical engineering technology; medical laboratory technician; medical transcription; nuclear medical technology; nursing related; operating room technician; sign language interpretation; surveying; system administration; system/networking/LAN/WAN management; turf management; Web/multimedia management/webmaster; Web page, digital/multimedia and information resources design.

Academic Programs *Special study options:* academic remediation for entering students, accelerated degree program, advanced placement credit, distance learning, double majors, independent study, internships, part-time degree program, services for LD students, summer session for credit.

Library Southeast Library with 10,643 titles, 158 serial subscriptions, 182 audiovisual materials, an OPAC.

Computers on Campus 400 computers available on campus for general student use. Internet access, at least one staffed computer lab available.

Student Life *Housing:* college housing not available. *Activities and Organizations:* VICA, ICON, PBL, American Landscape Contractors Association, Silent Tones. *Campus security:* 24-hour emergency response devices and patrols. *Student Services:* personal/psychological counseling.

Athletics *Intramural sports:* basketball M/W, volleyball M/W.

Standardized Tests *Recommended:* ACT (for admission).

Costs (2002–03) *Tuition:* state resident $1824 full-time, $57 per credit part-time; nonresident $1824 full-time, $57 per credit part-time. Full-time tuition and fees vary according to program. Part-time tuition and fees vary according to program. *Required fees:* $1163 full-time, $36 per credit. *Payment plan:* installment.

Applying *Required:* high school transcript, minimum 2.0 GPA. *Required for some:* interview. *Application deadline:* rolling (freshmen), rolling (transfers). *Notification:* continuous (freshmen).

Admissions Contact Mr. Darrell Borgen, Career Counselor, Southeast Technical Institute, 2320 North Career Avenue, Sioux Falls, SD 57107. *Phone:* 605-367-7624 Ext. 219. *Toll-free phone:* 800-247-0789. *Fax:* 605-367-8305. *E-mail:* darrell.bergen@southeasttech.com.

WESTERN DAKOTA TECHNICAL INSTITUTE

Rapid City, South Dakota

- **State-supported** 2-year, founded 1968
- **Calendar** semesters
- **Degree** certificates, diplomas, and associate
- **Small-town** 5-acre campus
- **Coed,** 1,052 undergraduate students, 70% full-time, 44% women, 56% men

Undergraduates 734 full-time, 318 part-time. Students come from 20 states and territories, 13% are from out of state, 0.3% African American, 0.9% Asian American or Pacific Islander, 1% Hispanic American, 8% Native American, 12% transferred in. *Retention:* 52% of 2001 full-time freshmen returned.

Freshmen *Admission:* 468 applied, 412 admitted, 269 enrolled.

Faculty *Total:* 84, 68% full-time, 5% with terminal degrees. *Student/faculty ratio:* 15:1.

Majors Agricultural animal husbandry/production management; agricultural business; auto mechanic/technician; business administration; computer installation/repair; computer/technical support; drafting; drafting/design technology; electrical/electronic engineering technology; electrical equipment installation/repair; farm/ranch management; industrial electronics installation/repair; law enforcement/police science; machine shop assistant; marketing operations; medical transcription; paralegal/legal assistant.

Academic Programs *Special study options:* academic remediation for entering students, advanced placement credit, independent study, internships, part-time degree program, services for LD students, summer session for credit.

Library Western Dakota Technical Institute Library with 10,000 titles, 40 serial subscriptions, 170 audiovisual materials, an OPAC.

Computers on Campus 140 computers available on campus for general student use. Internet access, at least one staffed computer lab available.

Student Life *Activities and Organizations:* student council, Intercollegiate Rodeo. *Student Services:* personal/psychological counseling, women's center.

Standardized Tests *Required:* TABE/NET for nursing applicants; HOBET for other medical programs. *Recommended:* ACT (for placement).

Costs (2001–02) *One-time required fee:* $65. *Tuition:* area resident $2016 full-time, $56 per credit hour part-time. Full-time tuition and fees vary according to program. Part-time tuition and fees vary according to program. *Required fees:* $1182 full-time, $33 per credit hour. *Payment plan:* deferred payment. *Waivers:* employees or children of employees.

Applying *Options:* common application, electronic application. *Application fee:* $10. *Required:* essay or personal statement, high school transcript. *Required for some:* letters of recommendation, interview. *Recommended:* minimum 2.0 GPA. *Application deadlines:* 8/1 (freshmen), 8/1 (transfers). *Notification:* continuous until 8/15 (freshmen).

Admissions Contact Janell Oberlander, Admissions Coordinator, Western Dakota Technical Institute, 800 Mickelson Drive, Rapid City, SD 57703. *Phone:* 605-394-4034 Ext. 113. *Toll-free phone:* 800-544-8765. *E-mail:* joberlander@wdti.tec.sd.us.

TENNESSEE

AMERICAN ACADEMY OF NUTRITION, COLLEGE OF NUTRITION

Knoxville, Tennessee

- **Proprietary** 2-year, founded 1984
- **Calendar** continuous
- **Degrees** certificates, diplomas, and associate (offers only external degree programs conducted through home study)
- **Suburban** campus
- **Coed,** 251 undergraduate students

Undergraduates Students come from 49 states and territories, 15 other countries.

Freshmen *Admission:* 73 applied, 73 admitted.

Faculty *Total:* 6, 33% full-time. *Student/faculty ratio:* 30:1.

Majors Nutrition science.

Academic Programs *Special study options:* academic remediation for entering students, adult/continuing education programs, distance learning, external degree program, independent study, part-time degree program, student-designed majors, summer session for credit.

Costs (2001–02) *Tuition:* $2990 full-time, $345 per quarter hour part-time. *Payment plan:* installment.

Applying *Options:* common application, electronic application, deferred entrance. *Required for some:* high school transcript, interview. *Recommended:* minimum 2.0 GPA. *Application deadline:* rolling (freshmen). *Notification:* continuous (freshmen).

Admissions Contact Jennifer Green, Faculty, American Academy of Nutrition, College of Nutrition, 1204-D Kenesaw Avenue, Knoxville, TN 37919. *Phone:* 865-524-8079. *Toll-free phone:* 800-290-4226. *Fax:* 865-524-8339. *E-mail:* aantn@aol.com.

CHATTANOOGA STATE TECHNICAL COMMUNITY COLLEGE

Chattanooga, Tennessee

- **State-supported** 2-year, founded 1965, part of Tennessee Board of Regents
- **Calendar** semesters
- **Degree** certificates, diplomas, and associate
- **Urban** 100-acre campus
- **Coed,** 9,600 undergraduate students

Undergraduates Students come from 5 states and territories, 12 other countries.
Faculty *Total:* 626, 32% full-time. *Student/faculty ratio:* 22:1.
Majors Accounting; advertising; aircraft pilot (professional); applied art; auto mechanic/technician; aviation management; aviation technology; biology; broadcast journalism; business administration; chemical engineering technology; chemistry; child care/development; civil engineering technology; computer engineering technology; computer programming; computer science; criminal justice/law enforcement administration; data processing technology; dental hygiene; drafting; early childhood education; electrical/electronic engineering technology; emergency medical technology; energy management technology; engineering design; environmental technology; finance; fire science; fish/game management; food services technology; forest harvesting production technology; forestry; graphic design/commercial art/illustration; graphic/printing equipment; heating/air conditioning/refrigeration; hotel and restaurant management; industrial radiologic technology; information sciences/systems; instrumentation technology; legal administrative assistant; liberal arts and sciences/liberal studies; machine technology; mass communications; mechanical design technology; mechanical engineering technology; medical administrative assistant; medical records administration; nuclear medical technology; nuclear technology; nursing; occupational therapy; physical therapy; radio/television broadcasting; respiratory therapy; retail management; robotics; secretarial science; sign language interpretation; surveying; transportation technology; welding technology; wildlife management.
Academic Programs *Special study options:* academic remediation for entering students, accelerated degree program, adult/continuing education programs, advanced placement credit, cooperative education, distance learning, English as a second language, honors programs, independent study, internships, part-time degree program, services for LD students, summer session for credit.
Library Augusta R. Kolwyck Library with 73,334 titles, 803 serial subscriptions, an OPAC, a Web page.
Computers on Campus 500 computers available on campus for general student use. A campuswide network can be accessed from off campus. Internet access, at least one staffed computer lab available.
Student Life *Housing:* college housing not available. *Activities and Organizations:* student-run newspaper, radio station, choral group, Black Student Association, Adult Connections, Human Services Specialists, Student Government Association, Student Nurses Association. *Campus security:* 24-hour emergency response devices and patrols, late-night transport/escort service. *Student Services:* personal/psychological counseling, women's center.
Athletics Member NJCAA. *Intercollegiate sports:* baseball M(s), basketball M(s)/W(s), soccer M(c)/W(c), softball W(s), tennis M(c)/W(c). *Intramural sports:* softball W.
Standardized Tests *Required for some:* SAT I or ACT (for placement).
Costs (2001–02) *Tuition:* state resident $1649 full-time, $64 per credit hour part-time; nonresident $6107 full-time, $193 per credit hour part-time. *Required fees:* $5 per credit hour, $18 per term part-time.
Financial Aid In 2001, 377 Federal Work-Study jobs (averaging $652).
Applying *Options:* early admission, deferred entrance. *Application fee:* $10. *Required:* high school transcript. *Application deadline:* rolling (freshmen), rolling (transfers). *Notification:* continuous (freshmen).
Admissions Contact Ms. Diane Norris, Director of Admissions, Chattanooga State Technical Community College, 4501 Amnicola Highway, Chattanooga, TN 37406-1097. *Phone:* 423-697-4422 Ext. 3107. *Fax:* 423-697-4709. *E-mail:* admsis@cstcc.cc.tn.us.

CLEVELAND STATE COMMUNITY COLLEGE
Cleveland, Tennessee

- **State-supported** 2-year, founded 1967, part of Tennessee Board of Regents
- **Calendar** semesters
- **Degree** certificates and associate
- **Small-town** 105-acre campus
- **Endowment** $3.7 million
- **Coed,** 3,177 undergraduate students, 54% full-time, 57% women, 43% men

Undergraduates 1,708 full-time, 1,469 part-time. Students come from 7 states and territories, 8 other countries, 1% are from out of state, 6% African American, 0.8% Asian American or Pacific Islander, 1% Hispanic American, 0.6% Native American, 0.3% international, 4% transferred in.
Freshmen *Admission:* 857 applied, 600 admitted, 600 enrolled. *Average high school GPA:* 2.8.
Faculty *Total:* 184, 40% full-time, 18% with terminal degrees. *Student/faculty ratio:* 18:1.
Majors Business administration; community services; early childhood education; industrial arts; industrial technology; liberal arts and sciences/liberal studies; nursing; occupational therapy assistant; paralegal/legal assistant; secretarial science.
Academic Programs *Special study options:* academic remediation for entering students, adult/continuing education programs, advanced placement credit, cooperative education, distance learning, double majors, English as a second language, external degree program, honors programs, independent study, internships, off-campus study, part-time degree program, services for LD students, summer session for credit.
Library Cleveland State Community College Library with 65,185 titles, 395 serial subscriptions, 9,038 audiovisual materials, an OPAC, a Web page.
Computers on Campus 300 computers available on campus for general student use. A campuswide network can be accessed from off campus. Internet access, online (class) registration, at least one staffed computer lab available.
Student Life *Housing:* college housing not available. *Activities and Organizations:* student-run newspaper, television station, choral group, Student Senate, International Association of Administration Professionals, Phi Theta Kappa, Student Nursing Association, Legal Assistant Association. *Campus security:* 24-hour emergency response devices and patrols, late-night transport/escort service. *Student Services:* personal/psychological counseling.
Athletics Member NJCAA. *Intercollegiate sports:* baseball M(s), basketball M(s)/W(s), softball W(s). *Intramural sports:* archery M/W, badminton M/W, basketball M/W, bowling M/W, golf M/W, softball M/W, table tennis M/W, tennis M/W, volleyball M/W.
Standardized Tests *Required for some:* ACT (for placement).
Costs (2001–02) *Tuition:* state resident $1635 full-time, $64 per semester hour part-time; nonresident $6093 full-time, $257 per semester hour part-time. Part-time tuition and fees vary according to course load. *Required fees:* $147 full-time, $5 per semester hour. *Payment plan:* deferred payment. *Waivers:* senior citizens and employees or children of employees.
Financial Aid In 2001, 67 Federal Work-Study jobs (averaging $804).
Applying *Options:* early admission, deferred entrance. *Application fee:* $5. *Required:* high school transcript. *Application deadline:* rolling (freshmen), rolling (transfers). *Notification:* continuous (freshmen).
Admissions Contact Ms. Midge Burnette, Director of Admissions and Recruitment, Cleveland State Community College, 3535 Adkisson Drive, Cleveland, TN 37320-3570. *Phone:* 423-478-6208. *Toll-free phone:* 800-604-2722. *Fax:* 423-478-6255. *E-mail:* mburnette@clscc.cc.tn.us.

COLUMBIA STATE COMMUNITY COLLEGE
Columbia, Tennessee

- **State-supported** 2-year, founded 1966
- **Calendar** semesters
- **Degree** certificates and associate
- **Small-town** 179-acre campus with easy access to Nashville
- **Endowment** $707,627
- **Coed,** 4,451 undergraduate students

Undergraduates Students come from 6 states and territories, 2 other countries, 7% African American, 1% Hispanic American.
Faculty *Total:* 285, 35% full-time.
Majors Accounting; agricultural business; art; biology; business; chemistry; dental hygiene; early childhood education; economics; electrical/electronic engineering technology; elementary education; geography; history; industrial radiologic technology; information sciences/systems; liberal arts and sciences/liberal studies; mass communications; mathematics; medical laboratory technician; music; nursing; pharmacy; physical education; physical therapy; physics; political science; pre-engineering; psychology; respiratory therapy; secretarial science; sociology; speech/rhetorical studies; veterinary technology.
Academic Programs *Special study options:* academic remediation for entering students, adult/continuing education programs, advanced placement credit, double majors, honors programs, part-time degree program, services for LD students, summer session for credit.
Library John W. Finney Memorial Learning Resources Center with 61,200 titles, 460 serial subscriptions, an OPAC.
Computers on Campus 260 computers available on campus for general student use. A campuswide network can be accessed from off campus. Internet access, at least one staffed computer lab available.
Student Life *Housing:* college housing not available. *Activities and Organizations:* drama/theater group, Student Government Association, Student Tennessee Education Association, Circle K, Gamma Beta Phi, Students in Free Enterprise. *Campus security:* 24-hour patrols. *Student Services:* health clinic, personal/psychological counseling.

Columbia State Community College (continued)

Athletics Member NJCAA. *Intercollegiate sports:* baseball M(s), basketball M(s)/W(s), softball W(s). *Intramural sports:* basketball M/W, softball M/W, table tennis M/W, volleyball M/W.
Standardized Tests *Required for some:* SAT I or ACT (for placement).
Financial Aid In 2001, 50 Federal Work-Study jobs (averaging $1250).
Applying *Options:* early admission. *Application fee:* $5. *Required:* high school transcript. *Application deadline:* rolling (freshmen), rolling (transfers).
Admissions Contact Mr. Joey Scruggs, Coordinator of Recruitment, Columbia State Community College, PO Box 1315, Columbia, TN 38402-1315. *Phone:* 931-540-2540. *Fax:* 931-540-2535. *E-mail:* scruggs@coscc.cc.tn.us.

DRAUGHONS JUNIOR COLLEGE
Nashville, Tennessee

- **Proprietary** 2-year, founded 1884
- **Calendar** semesters
- **Degree** associate
- **Suburban** 5-acre campus
- **Coed,** 600 undergraduate students

Undergraduates Students come from 5 other countries.
Faculty *Total:* 55, 45% full-time.
Majors Accounting; broadcast journalism; business administration; computer programming; computer science; fashion merchandising; information sciences/systems; legal studies; medical assistant; medical records administration; radio/television broadcasting; secretarial science.
Academic Programs *Special study options:* academic remediation for entering students, internships, part-time degree program, summer session for credit.
Library 3,250 titles, 20 serial subscriptions, a Web page.
Computers on Campus 75 computers available on campus for general student use. Internet access, at least one staffed computer lab available.
Student Life *Housing:* college housing not available. *Activities and Organizations:* student-run newspaper. *Campus security:* 24-hour emergency response devices. *Student Services:* personal/psychological counseling.
Costs (2002–03) *Tuition:* Contact school as tuition and fees vary according to program.
Financial Aid In 2001, 30 Federal Work-Study jobs (averaging $2000).
Applying *Options:* deferred entrance. *Application fee:* $20. *Required:* high school transcript. *Application deadline:* rolling (freshmen), rolling (transfers). *Notification:* continuous (freshmen).
Admissions Contact Admissions Office, Draughons Junior College, 340 Plus Park, Nashville, TN 37217. *Phone:* 615-361-7555. *Fax:* 615-367-2736.

DRAUGHONS JUNIOR COLLEGE
Clarksville, Tennessee

- **Proprietary** 2-year, founded 1987
- **Calendar** semesters
- **Degree** associate
- **Coed,** 340 undergraduate students

Faculty *Total:* 26.
Majors Accounting; business administration; computer programming; computer science; criminal justice studies; fashion merchandising; information sciences/systems; legal administrative assistant; medical assistant; medical records administration; pharmacy technician/assistant; radio/television broadcasting; retailing operations; secretarial science.
Academic Programs *Special study options:* part-time degree program.
Costs (2002–03) *Tuition:* Contact school as tuition and fees varies according to program.
Financial Aid In 2001, 20 Federal Work-Study jobs (averaging $1000).
Applying *Required:* high school transcript, interview. *Application deadline:* rolling (freshmen), rolling (transfers). *Notification:* continuous (freshmen).
Admissions Contact Admissions Office, Draughons Junior College, 1860 Wilma Rudolph Boulevard, Clarksville, TN 37040. *Fax:* 931-552-3624.

DYERSBURG STATE COMMUNITY COLLEGE
Dyersburg, Tennessee

- **State-supported** 2-year, founded 1969, part of Tennessee Board of Regents
- **Calendar** semesters
- **Degree** certificates and associate
- **Small-town** 100-acre campus with easy access to Memphis
- **Endowment** $3.7 million
- **Coed,** 2,284 undergraduate students, 56% full-time, 70% women, 30% men

Undergraduates 1,283 full-time, 1,001 part-time. Students come from 6 states and territories, 2% are from out of state, 19% African American, 0.4% Asian American or Pacific Islander, 1% Hispanic American, 0.6% Native American, 0.1% international, 6% transferred in.
Freshmen *Admission:* 902 applied, 900 admitted, 560 enrolled. *Average high school GPA:* 2.64. *Test scores:* ACT scores over 18: 53%; ACT scores over 24: 6%.
Faculty *Total:* 179, 29% full-time.
Majors Business administration; child care/development; computer/information technology services administration and management related; electrical/electronic engineering technology; law enforcement/police science; liberal arts and sciences/liberal studies; medical records technology; nursing.
Academic Programs *Special study options:* academic remediation for entering students, adult/continuing education programs, advanced placement credit, distance learning, double majors, honors programs, independent study, part-time degree program, summer session for credit.
Library Learning Resource Center with 43,007 titles, 165 serial subscriptions, a Web page.
Computers on Campus 195 computers available on campus for general student use. A campuswide network can be accessed from off campus. At least one staffed computer lab available.
Student Life *Housing:* college housing not available. *Activities and Organizations:* drama/theater group, student-run newspaper, choral group, student government, Phi Theta Kappa, Minority Association for Successful Students, Video Club, Psychology Club. *Campus security:* 24-hour patrols. *Student Services:* personal/psychological counseling.
Athletics Member NJCAA. *Intercollegiate sports:* basketball M(s)/W(s), softball W. *Intramural sports:* basketball M/W, softball W, volleyball M/W.
Standardized Tests *Required for some:* ACT (for placement).
Costs (2001–02) *Tuition:* state resident $1488 full-time, $64 per semester hour part-time; nonresident $5946 full-time, $257 per semester hour part-time. Part-time tuition and fees vary according to course load. *Required fees:* $141 full-time, $55 per term part-time. *Waivers:* senior citizens and employees or children of employees.
Financial Aid In 2001, 99 Federal Work-Study jobs (averaging $1020). 93 State and other part-time jobs (averaging $879).
Applying *Options:* common application, early admission. *Application fee:* $10. *Required:* high school transcript. *Application deadline:* rolling (freshmen), rolling (transfers). *Notification:* continuous (freshmen).
Admissions Contact Mr. J. Dan Gullett, Director of Admissions and Records, Dyersburg State Community College, 1510 Lake Road, Dyersburg, TN 38024. *Phone:* 731-286-3327. *Fax:* 731-286-3325. *E-mail:* gulett@dscc.edu.

EDUCATION AMERICA, SOUTHEAST COLLEGE OF TECHNOLOGY, MEMPHIS CAMPUS
Memphis, Tennessee

- **Proprietary** primarily 2-year
- **Calendar** quarters
- **Degrees** associate and bachelor's
- 600 undergraduate students, 100% full-time
- 71% of applicants were admitted

Admissions Contact David Cunningham, Director of Academics, Education America, Southeast College of Technology, Memphis Campus, 2731 Nonconnah Boulevard, Suite 160, Memphis, TN 38132-2131. *Phone:* 901-291-4234.

ELECTRONIC COMPUTER PROGRAMMING COLLEGE
Chattanooga, Tennessee

- **Proprietary** 2-year
- **Degree** associate
- 160 undergraduate students
- 45% of applicants were admitted

Undergraduates 33% African American.
Freshmen *Admission:* 100 applied, 45 admitted.

Faculty *Total:* 15, 80% full-time, 13% with terminal degrees. *Student/faculty ratio:* 20:1.
Majors Computer maintenance technology; data processing; medical records technology.
Costs (2001–02) *Tuition:* $6720 full-time. *Required fees:* $75 full-time.
Admissions Contact Toney McFadden, Admission Director, Electronic Computer Programming College, 3805 Brainerd Road, Chattanooga, TN 37411-3798. *Phone:* 423-624-0077.

HIWASSEE COLLEGE
Madisonville, Tennessee

- **Independent Methodist** 2-year, founded 1849
- **Calendar** semesters
- **Degree** associate
- **Rural** 410-acre campus
- **Endowment** $5.1 million
- **Coed,** 393 undergraduate students, 83% full-time, 55% women, 45% men

Undergraduates 325 full-time, 68 part-time. Students come from 11 states and territories, 8 other countries, 8% are from out of state, 9% African American, 0.5% Asian American or Pacific Islander, 2% Hispanic American, 0.3% Native American, 4% international, 6% transferred in, 40% live on campus. *Retention:* 45% of 2001 full-time freshmen returned.
Freshmen *Admission:* 596 applied, 440 admitted, 171 enrolled. *Average high school GPA:* 2.83. *Test scores:* SAT verbal scores over 500: 28%; SAT math scores over 500: 32%; ACT scores over 18: 49%; SAT verbal scores over 600: 5%; ACT scores over 24: 10%; ACT scores over 30: 2%.
Faculty *Total:* 35, 60% full-time, 40% with terminal degrees. *Student/faculty ratio:* 14:1.
Majors Agricultural business related; forestry sciences related; hospitality services management related; liberal arts and sciences/liberal studies.
Academic Programs *Special study options:* academic remediation for entering students, adult/continuing education programs, advanced placement credit, double majors, English as a second language, honors programs, part-time degree program, summer session for credit.
Library Hardwick-Johnston Memorial Library with 40,000 titles, 250 serial subscriptions, a Web page.
Computers on Campus 61 computers available on campus for general student use. A campuswide network can be accessed from student residence rooms and from off campus. Internet access, at least one staffed computer lab available.
Student Life *Housing:* on-campus residence required through sophomore year. *Options:* men-only, women-only. *Activities and Organizations:* drama/theater group, student-run newspaper, choral group, Baptist Student Union, Christian Student Movement, Future Farmers of America, Theatre Hiwassee, Student Government Association. *Campus security:* 24-hour emergency response devices, controlled dormitory access, late night security. *Student Services:* health clinic, personal/psychological counseling.
Athletics Member NJCAA. *Intercollegiate sports:* baseball M(s), basketball M(s)/W(s), soccer M(s)/W(s), softball W(s). *Intramural sports:* basketball M/W, football M/W, table tennis M/W, tennis M/W, volleyball M/W.
Standardized Tests *Required:* SAT I or ACT (for admission).
Costs (2002–03) *Comprehensive fee:* $11,400 includes full-time tuition ($7000) and room and board ($4400). Part-time tuition: $292 per credit. Part-time tuition and fees vary according to class time. *Payment plan:* installment. *Waivers:* adult students, senior citizens, and employees or children of employees.
Financial Aid In 2001, 150 Federal Work-Study jobs (averaging $750).
Applying *Options:* common application, electronic application, early admission, deferred entrance. *Required:* high school transcript, minimum 2.25 GPA. *Required for some:* 2 letters of recommendation, interview. *Application deadline:* rolling (freshmen), rolling (transfers).
Admissions Contact Kasey Abart, Director of Admission, Hiwassee College, 225 Hiwassee College Drive, Madisonville, TN 37354. *Phone:* 423-420-1891. *Toll-free phone:* 800-356-2187. *Fax:* 423-442-8521. *E-mail:* enroll@hiwassee.edu.

ITT TECHNICAL INSTITUTE
Memphis, Tennessee

- **Proprietary** 2-year, founded 1994, part of ITT Educational Services, Inc
- **Calendar** quarters
- **Degree** associate
- **Suburban** 1-acre campus
- **Coed,** 283 undergraduate students

Majors Computer/information sciences related; computer programming; drafting; electrical/electronic engineering technologies related; information technology.
Student Life *Housing:* college housing not available. *Activities and Organizations:* student-run newspaper.
Costs (2001–02) *Tuition:* Full-time tuition and fees vary according to program. Part-time tuition and fees vary according to program. $260—$330 per credit hour.
Applying *Options:* deferred entrance. *Application fee:* $100. *Required:* high school transcript, interview. *Recommended:* letters of recommendation. *Application deadline:* rolling (freshmen), rolling (transfers). *Notification:* continuous (freshmen).
Admissions Contact Ms. Melinda Jo Catron, Director, ITT Technical Institute, 1255 Lynnfield Road, Memphis, TN 38119. *Phone:* 901-762-0556 Ext. 101.

ITT TECHNICAL INSTITUTE
Nashville, Tennessee

- **Proprietary** primarily 2-year, founded 1984, part of ITT Educational Services, Inc
- **Calendar** quarters
- **Degrees** associate and bachelor's
- **Urban** 21-acre campus
- **Coed,** 560 undergraduate students

Majors Computer/information sciences related; computer programming; drafting; electrical/electronic engineering technologies related; information technology.
Student Life *Housing:* college housing not available.
Costs (2001–02) *Tuition:* Full-time tuition and fees vary according to program. Part-time tuition and fees vary according to program. $260—$330 per credit hour.
Applying *Options:* deferred entrance. *Application fee:* $100. *Required:* high school transcript, interview. *Recommended:* letters of recommendation. *Application deadline:* rolling (freshmen), rolling (transfers). *Notification:* continuous (freshmen).
Admissions Contact Mr. Ronald Binkley, Director of Recruitment, ITT Technical Institute, 441 Donnelson Pike, Nashville, TN 37214. *Phone:* 615-889-8700. *Toll-free phone:* 800-331-8386. *Fax:* 615-872-7209.

ITT TECHNICAL INSTITUTE
Knoxville, Tennessee

- **Proprietary** primarily 2-year, founded 1988, part of ITT Educational Services, Inc
- **Calendar** quarters
- **Degrees** associate and bachelor's
- **Suburban** 5-acre campus
- **Coed,** 475 undergraduate students

Majors Computer/information sciences related; computer programming; drafting; electrical/electronic engineering technologies related; information technology.
Student Life *Housing:* college housing not available.
Costs (2001–02) *Tuition:* Full-time tuition and fees vary according to program. Part-time tuition and fees vary according to program. $260—$330 per credit hour.
Applying *Options:* deferred entrance. *Application fee:* $100. *Required:* high school transcript, interview. *Recommended:* letters of recommendation. *Application deadline:* rolling (freshmen), rolling (transfers). *Notification:* continuous (freshmen).
Admissions Contact Mr. Mike Burke, Director of Recruitment, ITT Technical Institute, 10208 Technology Drive, Knoxville, TN 37932. *Phone:* 865-671-2800. *Toll-free phone:* 800-671-2801.

JACKSON STATE COMMUNITY COLLEGE
Jackson, Tennessee

- **State-supported** 2-year, founded 1967, part of Tennessee Board of Regents
- **Calendar** semesters
- **Degree** certificates and associate
- **Small-town** 104-acre campus
- **Endowment** $391,323

Jackson State Community College (continued)
■ **Coed,** 3,933 undergraduate students, 53% full-time, 64% women, 36% men

Undergraduates 2,070 full-time, 1,863 part-time. Students come from 6 states and territories, 0.4% are from out of state, 20% transferred in. *Retention:* 59% of 2001 full-time freshmen returned.
Freshmen *Admission:* 1,036 applied, 1,036 admitted, 802 enrolled. *Average high school GPA:* 2.73. *Test scores:* ACT scores over 18: 59%; ACT scores over 24: 11%.
Faculty *Total:* 221, 47% full-time, 8% with terminal degrees. *Student/faculty ratio:* 18:1.
Majors Agronomy/crop science; business administration; computer science; electromechanical technology; industrial technology; liberal arts and sciences/liberal studies; medical technology; nursing; physical therapy; radiological science; respiratory therapy.
Academic Programs *Special study options:* academic remediation for entering students, adult/continuing education programs, advanced placement credit, cooperative education, distance learning, honors programs, part-time degree program, summer session for credit.
Library Jackson State Community College Library with 63,639 titles, 300 serial subscriptions, 1,264 audiovisual materials, an OPAC, a Web page.
Computers on Campus 60 computers available on campus for general student use. A campuswide network can be accessed from off campus. Internet access, online (class) registration, at least one staffed computer lab available.
Student Life *Housing:* college housing not available. *Activities and Organizations:* student-run newspaper, choral group. *Campus security:* 24-hour patrols. *Student Services:* health clinic, personal/psychological counseling.
Athletics Member NJCAA. *Intercollegiate sports:* baseball M(s), basketball M(s)/W(s), softball W(s). *Intramural sports:* basketball M/W, football M, golf M, tennis M/W, volleyball W.
Standardized Tests *Required for some:* SAT I or ACT (for placement).
Costs (2001–02) *Tuition:* state resident $1488 full-time, $64 per semester hour part-time; nonresident $5946 full-time, $257 per semester hour part-time. Full-time tuition and fees vary according to course load. Part-time tuition and fees vary according to course load. *Required fees:* $151 full-time, $5 per semester hour, $13 per term part-time. *Payment plan:* deferred payment. *Waivers:* minority students, senior citizens, and employees or children of employees.
Financial Aid In 2001, 50 Federal Work-Study jobs (averaging $2000).
Applying *Options:* electronic application, early admission, deferred entrance. *Application fee:* $5. *Required for some:* high school transcript. *Application deadline:* 8/22 (freshmen), rolling (transfers). *Notification:* continuous (freshmen).
Admissions Contact Ms. Monica Ray, Director of Admissions and Records, Jackson State Community College, 2046 North Parkway, Jackson, TN 38301. *Phone:* 731-425-2644. *Toll-free phone:* 800-355-5722 Ext. 644. *Fax:* 731-425-9559. *E-mail:* mray@jscc.edu.

JOHN A. GUPTON COLLEGE
Nashville, Tennessee

- **Independent** 2-year, founded 1946
- **Calendar** semesters
- **Degree** associate
- **Urban** 1-acre campus
- **Endowment** $53,170
- **Coed,** 83 undergraduate students, 72% full-time, 25% women, 75% men

Undergraduates 60 full-time, 23 part-time. Students come from 9 states and territories, 23% are from out of state, 24% African American, 13% transferred in.
Freshmen *Admission:* 92 applied, 48 admitted, 39 enrolled.
Faculty *Total:* 17, 6% full-time. *Student/faculty ratio:* 15:1.
Majors Mortuary science.
Academic Programs *Special study options:* part-time degree program.
Library Memorial Library with 4,000 titles, 54 serial subscriptions, a Web page.
Computers on Campus 6 computers available on campus for general student use. At least one staffed computer lab available.
Student Life *Housing Options:* coed. *Campus security:* controlled dormitory access, day patrols.
Standardized Tests *Required:* ACT (for admission).
Costs (2001–02) *Tuition:* $4785 full-time, $145 per semester hour part-time. *Required fees:* $467 full-time, $109 per term part-time. *Room only:* $3400. Room and board charges vary according to housing facility. *Payment plan:* installment.
Financial Aid *Financial aid deadline:* 6/1.
Applying *Options:* common application, deferred entrance. *Application fee:* $20. *Required:* essay or personal statement, high school transcript, 2 letters of recommendation, health forms. *Application deadline:* rolling (freshmen), rolling (transfers).
Admissions Contact Ms. Lisa Bolin, Registrar, John A. Gupton College, 1616 Church Street, Nashville, TN 37203. *Phone:* 615-327-3927. *Toll-free phone:* 615-327-3927. *E-mail:* spann@guptoncollege.com.

MEDVANCE INSTITUTE
Cookeville, Tennessee

- **Proprietary** 2-year, founded 1970
- **Calendar** quarters
- **Degree** certificates, diplomas, and associate
- **Small-town** 4-acre campus
- **Coed, primarily women,** 231 undergraduate students, 100% full-time, 97% women, 3% men

Undergraduates Students come from 4 states and territories, 10% are from out of state.
Freshmen *Average high school GPA:* 2.00.
Faculty *Total:* 8, 100% full-time. *Student/faculty ratio:* 15:1.
Majors Medical laboratory technician; secretarial science.
Academic Programs *Special study options:* internships.
Computers on Campus 40 computers available on campus for general student use. Internet access, at least one staffed computer lab available.
Student Life *Housing:* college housing not available.
Costs (2001–02) *Tuition:* $8925 full-time. Full-time tuition and fees vary according to program. *Payment plans:* tuition prepayment, installment. *Waivers:* employees or children of employees.
Applying *Options:* common application. *Required:* high school transcript, interview. *Recommended:* minimum 2.0 GPA, 2 letters of recommendation. *Application deadline:* rolling (freshmen), rolling (transfers). *Notification:* continuous (freshmen).
Admissions Contact Ms. Sharon Mellott, Director of Admissions, MedVance Institute, 1065 East 10th Street, Cookeville, TN 38501-1907. *Phone:* 931-526-3660. *Toll-free phone:* 800-259-3659 (in-state); 800-256-9085 (out-of-state). *Fax:* 931-372-2603. *E-mail:* briddell@medvance.org.

MID-AMERICA BAPTIST THEOLOGICAL SEMINARY
Germantown, Tennessee

- **Independent Southern Baptist** founded 1972
- **Calendar** semesters
- **Degrees** associate, master's, doctoral, and first professional
- **Suburban** campus with easy access to Memphis
- **Endowment** $3.6 million
- **Coed, primarily men,** 58 undergraduate students, 52% full-time, 100% men

Undergraduates 30 full-time, 28 part-time. Students come from 26 states and territories, 3% African American.
Faculty *Total:* 25. *Student/faculty ratio:* 14:1.
Majors Theology.
Academic Programs *Special study options:* summer session for credit.
Library Ora Byram Allison Memorial Library with 119,000 titles, 931 serial subscriptions, an OPAC, a Web page.
Computers on Campus 10 computers available on campus for general student use. At least one staffed computer lab available.
Student Life *Campus security:* 24-hour emergency response devices.
Costs (2001–02) *Tuition:* $1600 full-time. Full-time tuition and fees vary according to course load. Part-time tuition and fees vary according to course load.
Applying *Options:* common application. *Application fee:* $25. *Required:* high school transcript, 2 letters of recommendation. *Application deadline:* 8/7 (freshmen).
Admissions Contact Miss Cindy Estes, Admissions Counselor, Mid-America Baptist Theological Seminary, 2216 Germantown Road South, Germantown, TN 38138. *Phone:* 901-751-8453 Ext. 3066. *Fax:* 901-751-8454. *E-mail:* info@mabts.edu.

MILLER-MOTTE BUSINESS COLLEGE
Clarksville, Tennessee

Admissions Contact 1820 Business Park Drive, Clarksville, TN 37040.

Motlow State Community College
Tullahoma, Tennessee

- **State-supported** 2-year, founded 1969, part of Tennessee Board of Regents
- **Calendar** semesters
- **Degree** certificates and associate
- **Small-town** 187-acre campus with easy access to Nashville
- **Endowment** $2.6 million
- **Coed,** 3,586 undergraduate students, 54% full-time, 64% women, 36% men

Undergraduates 1,951 full-time, 1,635 part-time. Students come from 6 states and territories, 7 other countries, 0.1% are from out of state, 9% African American, 0.7% Asian American or Pacific Islander, 0.9% Hispanic American, 0.3% Native American, 0.3% international, 6% transferred in. *Retention:* 60% of 2001 full-time freshmen returned.

Freshmen *Admission:* 1,299 applied, 1,267 admitted, 853 enrolled. *Average high school GPA:* 2.81. *Test scores:* ACT scores over 18: 55%; ACT scores over 24: 11%; ACT scores over 30: 1%.

Faculty *Total:* 216, 39% full-time, 13% with terminal degrees. *Student/faculty ratio:* 17:1.

Majors Business administration; early childhood education; industrial arts; liberal arts and sciences/liberal studies; nursing.

Academic Programs *Special study options:* academic remediation for entering students, adult/continuing education programs, advanced placement credit, cooperative education, distance learning, double majors, honors programs, independent study, off-campus study, part-time degree program, services for LD students, summer session for credit.

Library Crouch Library with 56,240 titles, 3,188 audiovisual materials, an OPAC, a Web page.

Computers on Campus 500 computers available on campus for general student use. A campuswide network can be accessed from off campus. Internet access, online (class) registration, at least one staffed computer lab available.

Student Life *Housing:* college housing not available. *Activities and Organizations:* drama/theater group, student-run newspaper, choral group, Photography Club, Psychology Club, Student Government Association, Outing Club, Baptist Student Union. *Campus security:* 24-hour patrols, late-night transport/escort service. *Student Services:* health clinic, personal/psychological counseling.

Athletics Member NJCAA. *Intercollegiate sports:* baseball M, basketball M(s)/W(s), softball W(s). *Intramural sports:* archery M/W, badminton M/W, basketball M/W, bowling M/W, golf M/W, tennis M/W, volleyball M/W.

Standardized Tests *Required for some:* SAT I or ACT (for placement).

Costs (2001–02) *Tuition:* state resident $1488 full-time, $64 per credit part-time; nonresident $5946 full-time, $257 per credit part-time. Full-time tuition and fees vary according to course load and program. Part-time tuition and fees vary according to program. *Required fees:* $147 full-time, $147 per term part-time. *Payment plan:* deferred payment. *Waivers:* senior citizens and employees or children of employees.

Financial Aid In 2001, 60 Federal Work-Study jobs (averaging $1150).

Applying *Options:* electronic application, early admission, deferred entrance. *Application fee:* $10. *Required:* high school transcript. *Application deadline:* rolling (freshmen), rolling (transfers). *Notification:* continuous (freshmen).

Admissions Contact Wendi Patton, Director of New Student Admissions, Motlow State Community College, PO Box 8500, Lynchburg, TN 37352. *Phone:* 931-393-1764. *Toll-free phone:* 800-654-4877. *Fax:* 931-393-1681. *E-mail:* wfruehauf@mscc.cc.tn.us.

Nashville Auto Diesel College
Nashville, Tennessee

- **Proprietary** 2-year, founded 1919
- **Calendar** continuous
- **Degree** diplomas and associate
- **Urban** 13-acre campus
- **Coed, primarily men,** 1,306 undergraduate students, 100% full-time, 0% women, 100% men

Undergraduates 1,306 full-time. Students come from 50 states and territories, 60 other countries, 83% are from out of state, 21% live on campus.

Freshmen *Admission:* 2,924 applied, 2,602 admitted, 95 enrolled.

Faculty *Total:* 69. *Student/faculty ratio:* 25:1.

Majors Auto body repair; auto mechanic/technician; diesel engine mechanic.

Academic Programs *Special study options:* advanced placement credit, cooperative education, honors programs.

Library NADC Library with 1,309 titles, 69 serial subscriptions.

Computers on Campus 40 computers available on campus for general student use. Internet access, at least one staffed computer lab available.

Student Life *Housing Options:* men-only. *Campus security:* 24-hour emergency response devices and patrols.

Costs (2002–03) *Tuition:* $15,500 full-time. Full-time tuition and fees vary according to degree level and program. No tuition increase for student's term of enrollment. *Room only:* $2640. Room and board charges vary according to housing facility. *Payment plan:* installment.

Applying *Options:* deferred entrance. *Application fee:* $100. *Required:* high school transcript, interview. *Application deadline:* rolling (freshmen).

Admissions Contact Ms. Peggie Robertson, Director of Admissions, Nashville Auto Diesel College, 1524 Gallatin Road, Nashville, TN 37206. *Phone:* 615-226-3990 Ext. 8465. *Toll-free phone:* 800-228-NADC. *Fax:* 615-262-8466. *E-mail:* wpruitt@nadcedu.com.

Nashville State Technical Institute
Nashville, Tennessee

- **State-supported** 2-year, founded 1970, part of Tennessee Board of Regents
- **Calendar** semesters
- **Degree** certificates and associate
- **Urban** 60-acre campus
- **Coed,** 7,017 undergraduate students, 26% full-time, 53% women, 47% men

Undergraduates 1,802 full-time, 5,215 part-time. Students come from 29 states and territories, 56 other countries, 5% are from out of state, 30% African American, 5% Asian American or Pacific Islander, 1% Hispanic American, 0.3% Native American, 3% international, 3% transferred in.

Freshmen *Admission:* 980 applied, 726 admitted, 726 enrolled.

Faculty *Total:* 431, 29% full-time, 5% with terminal degrees. *Student/faculty ratio:* 16:1.

Majors Accounting; architectural engineering technology; auto mechanic/technician; business administration; business systems networking/ telecommunications; civil engineering technology; computer engineering technology; culinary arts; early childhood education; electrical/electronic engineering technology; graphic design/commercial art/illustration; industrial/manufacturing engineering; industrial technology; information sciences/systems; law enforcement/police science; occupational therapy; photography; secretarial science; sign language interpretation.

Academic Programs *Special study options:* academic remediation for entering students, adult/continuing education programs, advanced placement credit, cooperative education, distance learning, off-campus study, part-time degree program, services for LD students, summer session for credit.

Library 38,502 titles, 275 serial subscriptions, an OPAC, a Web page.

Computers on Campus 518 computers available on campus for general student use. A campuswide network can be accessed from off campus.

Student Life *Housing:* college housing not available. *Activities and Organizations:* student-run newspaper, Data Processing Management Association, Occupational Therapy Club, Phi Theta Kappa, Student Government Association, Black Student Association. *Campus security:* 24-hour emergency response devices and patrols, late-night transport/escort service. *Student Services:* personal/psychological counseling.

Athletics *Intramural sports:* table tennis M/W, volleyball M/W.

Standardized Tests *Required for some:* SAT I or ACT (for placement).

Costs (2001–02) *Tuition:* state resident $1488 full-time, $64 per semester hour part-time; nonresident $5946 full-time, $257 per semester hour part-time. Part-time tuition and fees vary according to course load. *Required fees:* $125 full-time, $5 per semester hour. *Payment plan:* deferred payment. *Waivers:* senior citizens and employees or children of employees.

Financial Aid In 2001, 66 Federal Work-Study jobs (averaging $806). 97 State and other part-time jobs (averaging $917).

Applying *Options:* electronic application, deferred entrance. *Application fee:* $5. *Required:* high school transcript. *Application deadline:* rolling (freshmen), rolling (transfers). *Notification:* continuous (freshmen).

Admissions Contact Mrs. Nancy Jewell, Assistant Director of Admissions, Nashville State Technical Institute, 120 White Bridge Road, Nashville, TN 37209. *Phone:* 615-353-3214. *Toll-free phone:* 800-272-7363. *Fax:* 615-353-3243. *E-mail:* jewell_n@nsti.tec.tn.us.

NATIONAL COLLEGE OF BUSINESS & TECHNOLOGY
Nashville, Tennessee

- **Proprietary** 2-year, founded 1915, part of National College of Business and Technology
- **Calendar** quarters
- **Degree** diplomas and associate
- **Urban** 1-acre campus
- **Coed**

Faculty *Total:* 25, 12% full-time. *Student/faculty ratio:* 10:1.
Majors Business administration; computer science related; medical assistant; secretarial science.
Academic Programs *Special study options:* double majors, honors programs, part-time degree program, services for LD students, summer session for credit.
Computers on Campus 35 computers available on campus for general student use. Internet access, at least one staffed computer lab available.
Student Life *Housing:* college housing not available.
Costs (2002–03) *Tuition:* $5013 full-time, $148 per credit hour part-time. Full-time tuition and fees vary according to course load. Part-time tuition and fees vary according to course load. *Required fees:* $45 full-time, $15 per term part-time. *Payment plans:* installment, deferred payment. *Waivers:* employees or children of employees.
Financial Aid In 2001, 3 Federal Work-Study jobs.
Applying *Options:* electronic application. *Application fee:* $30. *Recommended:* interview. *Application deadline:* rolling (freshmen), rolling (transfers). *Notification:* continuous (freshmen).
Admissions Contact Mr. Robert Leonard, Campus Director, National College of Business & Technology, 3748 Nolensville Pike, Nashville, TN 37211. *Phone:* 615-333-3344. *Toll-free phone:* 800-664-1886. *Fax:* 615-333-3429. *E-mail:* adm@educorp.edu.

NORTH CENTRAL INSTITUTE
Clarksville, Tennessee

- **Proprietary** 2-year, founded 1988
- **Degree** associate
- **Coed, primarily men,** 134 undergraduate students, 44% full-time, 15% women, 85% men

Undergraduates 59 full-time, 75 part-time. Students come from 50 states and territories, 95% are from out of state, 10% African American, 4% Asian American or Pacific Islander, 6% Hispanic American, 3% Native American.
Freshmen *Admission:* 5 applied, 5 admitted, 31 enrolled.
Faculty *Total:* 37, 14% full-time. *Student/faculty ratio:* 10:1.
Majors Aircraft mechanic/airframe; aircraft mechanic/powerplant.
Academic Programs *Special study options:* advanced placement credit, external degree program, independent study, part-time degree program, summer session for credit.
Library Media Resource Center plus 1 other with 200 titles, 12 serial subscriptions, 20 audiovisual materials.
Student Life *Housing:* college housing not available. *Activities and Organizations:* Alpha Eta Rho (aviation fraternity). *Campus security:* 24-hour emergency response devices. *Student Services:* personal/psychological counseling.
Costs (2001–02) *One-time required fee:* $225. *Tuition:* $60 per semester hour part-time. Full-time tuition and fees vary according to course load and program. Part-time tuition and fees vary according to course load and program. *Required fees:* $180 per course. *Payment plan:* deferred payment. *Waivers:* employees or children of employees.
Applying *Options:* common application, electronic application, early admission. *Application fee:* $35.
Admissions Contact Ms. Sue Daniels, Dean of Student Services, North Central Institute, 168 Jack Miller Boulevard, Clarksville, TN 37042. *Phone:* 931-431-9700. *Fax:* 931-431-9771. *E-mail:* admissions@nci.edu.

NORTHEAST STATE TECHNICAL COMMUNITY COLLEGE
Blountville, Tennessee

- **State-supported** 2-year, founded 1966, part of Tennessee Board of Regents
- **Calendar** semesters
- **Degree** certificates and associate
- **Small-town** 100-acre campus
- **Endowment** $2.1 million
- **Coed,** 4,462 undergraduate students, 51% full-time, 53% women, 47% men

Undergraduates 2,258 full-time, 2,204 part-time. Students come from 3 states and territories, 3% are from out of state, 6% transferred in.
Freshmen *Admission:* 1,959 applied, 1,959 admitted, 793 enrolled. *Average high school GPA:* 2.51. *Test scores:* ACT scores over 18: 48%; ACT scores over 24: 7%.
Faculty *Total:* 236, 37% full-time, 12% with terminal degrees. *Student/faculty ratio:* 21:1.
Majors Accounting; auto mechanic/technician; business administration; cardiovascular technology; chemistry; computer programming; computer programming related; computer systems networking/telecommunications; data processing technology; drafting; early childhood education; electrical/electronic engineering technology; emergency medical technology; engineering technology; industrial technology; instrumentation technology; liberal arts and sciences/liberal studies; machine technology; medical assistant; operating room technician; secretarial science; welding technology.
Academic Programs *Special study options:* academic remediation for entering students, advanced placement credit, cooperative education, distance learning, honors programs, part-time degree program, services for LD students, summer session for credit.
Library Main Library plus 1 other with 31,467 titles, 436 serial subscriptions, 10,739 audiovisual materials, an OPAC, a Web page.
Computers on Campus 700 computers available on campus for general student use. A campuswide network can be accessed from off campus. At least one staffed computer lab available.
Student Life *Housing:* college housing not available. *Activities and Organizations:* drama/theater group, Phi Theta Kappa, Student Government Association, Student Tennessee Education Association, Students in Free Enterprise, Student Ambassadors. *Campus security:* 24-hour patrols, late-night transport/escort service. *Student Services:* health clinic, personal/psychological counseling.
Athletics *Intramural sports:* basketball M/W, golf M/W, volleyball M/W.
Standardized Tests *Required:* SAT I or ACT (for placement).
Costs (2001–02) *Tuition:* state resident $1488 full-time, $64 per credit part-time; nonresident $5973 full-time, $257 per credit part-time. Part-time tuition and fees vary according to course load. *Required fees:* $160 full-time, $8 per credit, $18 per term part-time. *Waivers:* senior citizens and employees or children of employees.
Financial Aid In 2001, 109 Federal Work-Study jobs (averaging $1318). 35 State and other part-time jobs (averaging $61425).
Applying *Application fee:* $10. *Required:* high school transcript, minimum 2.0 GPA. *Application deadline:* rolling (freshmen), rolling (transfers). *Notification:* continuous (freshmen).
Admissions Contact Dr. Jon P. Harr, Dean of Admissions and Records, Northeast State Technical Community College, PO Box 246, Blountville, TN 37617. *Phone:* 423-323-0231. *Toll-free phone:* 800-836-7822. *Fax:* 423-323-0215. *E-mail:* jpharr@nstcc.edu.

NOSSI COLLEGE OF ART
Goodlettsville, Tennessee

- **Independent** 2-year
- **Calendar** semesters
- **Degree** associate
- **Coed,** 250 undergraduate students, 100% full-time, 30% women, 70% men

Faculty *Total:* 29, 14% full-time. *Student/faculty ratio:* 17:1.
Majors Graphic design/commercial art/illustration; photography.
Costs (2001–02) *Tuition:* $8775 full-time. *Required fees:* $100 full-time.
Applying *Required:* portfolio.
Admissions Contact Ms. Mary Alexander, Admissions Director, Nossi College of Art, 907 Rivergate Parkway, Goodlettsville, TN 37072. *Phone:* 615-851-1088. *E-mail:* admissions@nossi.com.

PELLISSIPPI STATE TECHNICAL COMMUNITY COLLEGE
Knoxville, Tennessee

- **State-supported** 2-year, founded 1974, part of Tennessee Board of Regents
- **Calendar** semesters

- **Degree** certificates and associate
- **Suburban** 144-acre campus
- **Endowment** $2.8 million
- **Coed,** 7,833 undergraduate students

Undergraduates Students come from 23 states and territories, 41 other countries.

Freshmen *Admission:* 1,253 applied, 1,253 admitted. *Average high school GPA:* 2.5.

Faculty *Total:* 412, 41% full-time. *Student/faculty ratio:* 21:1.

Majors Accounting; accounting technician; auto mechanic/technician; business administration; business machine repair; business marketing and marketing management; chemical engineering technology; chemical technology; civil engineering technology; computer engineering technology; computer graphics; computer/information sciences; computer programming; computer science; computer science related; computer software and media applications related; computer systems networking/telecommunications; construction technology; data entry/microcomputer applications; data entry/microcomputer applications related; data processing technology; drafting; electrical/electronic engineering technology; environmental technology; film/video production; finance; geography; graphic design/commercial art/illustration; hospitality management; hotel and restaurant management; industrial arts; industrial technology; interior design; legal administrative assistant; liberal arts and sciences/liberal studies; machine technology; mechanical engineering technology; paralegal/legal assistant; secretarial science.

Academic Programs *Special study options:* academic remediation for entering students, adult/continuing education programs, advanced placement credit, cooperative education, distance learning, double majors, English as a second language, freshman honors college, honors programs, internships, part-time degree program, services for LD students, student-designed majors, summer session for credit.

Library Educational Resources Center plus 1 other with 43,000 titles, 527 serial subscriptions, an OPAC, a Web page.

Computers on Campus 1200 computers available on campus for general student use. A campuswide network can be accessed from off campus. Internet access, online (class) registration, at least one staffed computer lab available.

Student Life *Housing:* college housing not available. *Activities and Organizations:* drama/theater group, student-run newspaper, choral group, Student Government Association, Active Black Students Association, Phi Theta Kappa, Baptist Student Union, Vision. *Campus security:* 24-hour patrols. *Student Services:* personal/psychological counseling.

Athletics *Intramural sports:* basketball M/W, golf M/W, soccer M/W, softball M/W, tennis M/W, volleyball M/W.

Standardized Tests *Required for some:* ACT (for placement).

Costs (2001–02) *Tuition:* state resident $75 per credit part-time; nonresident $267 per credit part-time. *Required fees:* $829 full-time.

Applying *Options:* common application, electronic application, early admission, deferred entrance. *Application fee:* $5. *Required:* high school transcript. *Application deadline:* rolling (freshmen), rolling (transfers). *Notification:* continuous (freshmen).

Admissions Contact Admissions Coordinator, Pellissippi State Technical Community College, PO Box 22990, Knoxville, TN 37933. *Phone:* 865-694-6681. *E-mail:* latouzeau@pstcc.cc.tn.us.

ROANE STATE COMMUNITY COLLEGE

Harriman, Tennessee

- **State-supported** 2-year, founded 1971
- **Calendar** semesters
- **Degree** certificates and associate
- **Rural** 104-acre campus with easy access to Knoxville
- **Endowment** $18,123
- **Coed,** 5,233 undergraduate students, 54% full-time, 68% women, 32% men

Undergraduates 2,801 full-time, 2,432 part-time. Students come from 4 states and territories, 5 other countries, 3% are from out of state, 4% transferred in. *Retention:* 56% of 2001 full-time freshmen returned.

Freshmen *Admission:* 1,717 applied, 1,717 admitted, 966 enrolled. *Average high school GPA:* 2.87. *Test scores:* ACT scores over 18: 67%; ACT scores over 24: 12%.

Faculty *Total:* 382, 35% full-time, 9% with terminal degrees. *Student/faculty ratio:* 17:1.

Majors Accounting; art; art education; biology; business administration; business education; chemistry; computer engineering technology; computer science; corrections; criminal justice/law enforcement administration; dental hygiene; early childhood education; education; elementary education; emergency medical technology; engineering; environmental health; industrial arts education; industrial radiologic technology; laser/optical technology; law enforcement/police science; legal administrative assistant; liberal arts and sciences/liberal studies; mathematics; medical administrative assistant; medical laboratory technician; medical records administration; music teacher education; nursing; occupational therapy; physical education; physical sciences; physical therapy; pre-engineering; respiratory therapy; secretarial science; social sciences.

Academic Programs *Special study options:* academic remediation for entering students, accelerated degree program, adult/continuing education programs, advanced placement credit, cooperative education, distance learning, double majors, external degree program, freshman honors college, honors programs, independent study, internships, off-campus study, part-time degree program, services for LD students, summer session for credit. *ROTC:* Army (c).

Library Roane State Community College Library plus 1 other with 59,736 titles, 573 serial subscriptions, 8,940 audiovisual materials, an OPAC, a Web page.

Computers on Campus 750 computers available on campus for general student use. Internet access, online (class) registration, at least one staffed computer lab available.

Student Life *Housing:* college housing not available. *Activities and Organizations:* drama/theater group, student-run newspaper, choral group, Baptist Student Union, American Chemical Society, Physical Therapy Student Association, Student Artists At Roane State (S.T.A.R.S.), Phi Theta Kappa. *Campus security:* 24-hour patrols. *Student Services:* health clinic, personal/psychological counseling.

Athletics Member NJCAA. *Intercollegiate sports:* baseball M(s), basketball M(s)/W(s), softball W(s). *Intramural sports:* basketball M/W, football M, golf M, softball M/W.

Standardized Tests *Required for some:* SAT I or ACT (for placement).

Costs (2001–02) *Tuition:* state resident $1488 full-time, $64 per semester hour part-time; nonresident $5946 full-time, $224 per semester hour part-time. *Required fees:* $150 full-time, $8 per semester hour, $10 per term part-time. *Payment plan:* installment. *Waivers:* senior citizens and employees or children of employees.

Financial Aid In 2001, 97 Federal Work-Study jobs (averaging $2000).

Applying *Options:* common application, electronic application, early admission, deferred entrance. *Application fee:* $5. *Required:* high school transcript. *Application deadline:* rolling (freshmen), rolling (transfers). *Notification:* continuous (freshmen).

Admissions Contact Ms. Brenda Rector, Director of Records and Registration, Roane State Community College, 276 Patton Lane, Harriman, TN 37748. *Phone:* 865-882-4526. *Toll-free phone:* 800-343-9104. *Fax:* 865-882-4562. *E-mail:* marine_gl@a1.rscc.cc.tn.us.

SOUTH COLLEGE

Knoxville, Tennessee

- **Proprietary** 2-year, founded 1882
- **Calendar** quarters
- **Degree** certificates, diplomas, and associate
- **Urban** 2-acre campus
- **Coed, primarily women,** 411 undergraduate students

Undergraduates Students come from 2 states and territories, 16% African American, 2% Asian American or Pacific Islander, 1% Hispanic American, 0.3% Native American.

Freshmen *Admission:* 90 applied, 90 admitted.

Faculty *Total:* 38, 34% full-time. *Student/faculty ratio:* 12:1.

Majors Accounting; business administration; computer management; computer science; hotel and restaurant management; information sciences/systems; legal administrative assistant; medical administrative assistant; medical assistant; paralegal/legal assistant; physical therapy assistant; secretarial science.

Academic Programs *Special study options:* adult/continuing education programs, advanced placement credit, double majors, internships, part-time degree program, summer session for credit.

Library Knoxville Business College Library with 6,500 titles, 127 serial subscriptions, 16 audiovisual materials, a Web page.

Computers on Campus 50 computers available on campus for general student use. Internet access, at least one staffed computer lab available.

Student Life *Housing:* college housing not available. *Activities and Organizations:* Collegiate Secretaries International, Paralegal Club, Students of Medical Assisting, Empowerment. *Campus security:* evening and morning security patrols. *Student Services:* personal/psychological counseling.

Standardized Tests *Recommended:* SAT I, ACT, or CPT.

South College (continued)

Costs (2001–02) *Tuition:* $8400 full-time, $310 per credit part-time. Full-time tuition and fees vary according to program. Part-time tuition and fees vary according to course load. *Required fees:* $8400 full-time, $310 per credit. *Payment plan:* installment.

Applying *Options:* common application, early admission, deferred entrance. *Application fee:* $40. *Required:* high school transcript, interview. *Application deadline:* 10/1 (freshmen), rolling (transfers).

Admissions Contact Mr. Kevin Spath, Director of Admissions, South College, 720 North Fifth Avenue, Knoxville, TN 37917. *Phone:* 865-524-3043 Ext. 7419. *Fax:* 865-637-0127.

SOUTHWEST TENNESSEE COMMUNITY COLLEGE

Memphis, Tennessee

- **State-supported** 2-year, part of Tennessee Board of Regents
- **Calendar** semesters
- **Degree** certificates and associate
- **Urban** 100-acre campus
- **Endowment** $61,798
- **Coed,** 12,736 undergraduate students, 40% full-time, 62% women, 38% men

Undergraduates 5,109 full-time, 7,627 part-time. Students come from 10 states and territories, 3% are from out of state, 11% transferred in.

Freshmen *Admission:* 1,943 applied, 1,943 admitted, 1,933 enrolled. *Average high school GPA:* 2.25. *Test scores:* ACT scores over 18: 35%; ACT scores over 24: 3%.

Faculty *Total:* 271, 34% full-time. *Student/faculty ratio:* 18:1.

Majors Accounting; architectural engineering technology; auto mechanic/technician; biomedical engineering-related technology; business; business administration; cartography; chemical engineering technology; civil engineering technology; computer engineering technology; court reporting; criminal justice studies; dietician assistant; early childhood education; electrical/electronic engineering technology; electrical equipment installation/repair; fire science; general studies; graphic design/commercial art/illustration; health professions and related sciences; heavy equipment maintenance; horticulture services related; industrial arts; industrial technology; management information systems/business data processing; mechanical engineering technology; medical assistant; medical laboratory technician; medical radiologic technology; nursing; occupational safety/health technology; occupational therapy assistant; paralegal/legal assistant; physical therapy assistant; secretarial science.

Academic Programs *Special study options:* academic remediation for entering students, accelerated degree program, adult/continuing education programs, advanced placement credit, cooperative education, distance learning, double majors, English as a second language, internships, part-time degree program, services for LD students, student-designed majors, summer session for credit. *ROTC:* Army (c), Air Force (c).

Library Freeman Library with 40,532 titles, 210 serial subscriptions, 874 audiovisual materials, an OPAC.

Computers on Campus 800 computers available on campus for general student use. A campuswide network can be accessed from off campus. Internet access, at least one staffed computer lab available.

Student Life *Housing:* college housing not available. *Activities and Organizations:* drama/theater group, student-run newspaper, choral group, Human Key Society, NAACP, Black Student Association, Honor Society, Collegiate Secretaries. *Campus security:* 24-hour emergency response devices and patrols, late-night transport/escort service. *Student Services:* personal/psychological counseling, women's center.

Athletics Member NJCAA.

Standardized Tests *Required:* ACT (for placement).

Costs (2001–02) *Tuition:* state resident $1638 full-time, $62 per credit hour part-time; nonresident $6096 full-time, $248 per credit hour part-time. *Required fees:* $150 full-time, $10 per credit hour, $13 per term part-time.

Financial Aid In 2001, 201 Federal Work-Study jobs (averaging $2600).

Applying *Options:* common application, early admission, deferred entrance. *Application fee:* $5. *Required:* high school transcript. *Application deadlines:* 9/1 (freshmen), 9/1 (transfers). *Notification:* continuous until 9/1 (freshmen).

Admissions Contact Ms. Cindy Meziere, Assistant Director of Recruiting, Southwest Tennessee Community College, PO Box 780, Memphis, TN 38103-0780. *Phone:* 901-333-4195. *Toll-free phone:* 877-717-STCC. *Fax:* 901-333-4473.

TENNESSEE INSTITUTE OF ELECTRONICS

Knoxville, Tennessee

- **Proprietary** primarily 2-year, founded 1947
- **Calendar** quarters
- **Degrees** associate and bachelor's
- **Suburban** 1-acre campus
- **Coed**

Undergraduates Students come from 1 other state.

Faculty *Total:* 10, 90% full-time, 100% with terminal degrees.

Majors Communication equipment technology; computer engineering technology; electrical/electronic engineering technology; industrial technology; information sciences/systems.

Academic Programs *Special study options:* summer session for credit.

Library 1,200 titles, 1,000 serial subscriptions, a Web page.

Computers on Campus 15 computers available on campus for general student use. A campuswide network can be accessed from off campus. Internet access, at least one staffed computer lab available.

Student Life *Housing:* college housing not available. *Campus security:* 24-hour emergency response devices.

Applying *Application fee:* $100. *Recommended:* high school transcript. *Application deadline:* rolling (freshmen), rolling (transfers). *Notification:* continuous (freshmen).

Admissions Contact Ms. Casey Rackley, Director of Administration, Tennessee Institute of Electronics, 3203 Tazewell Pike, Knoxville, TN 37918-2530. *Phone:* 865-688-9422.

VOLUNTEER STATE COMMUNITY COLLEGE

Gallatin, Tennessee

- **State-supported** 2-year, founded 1970, part of Tennessee Board of Regents
- **Calendar** semesters
- **Degree** certificates and associate
- **Small-town** 100-acre campus with easy access to Nashville
- **Endowment** $94,515
- **Coed,** 6,822 undergraduate students, 46% full-time, 63% women, 37% men

Undergraduates 3,167 full-time, 3,655 part-time. Students come from 8 states and territories, 1% are from out of state, 10% African American, 1% Asian American or Pacific Islander, 1% Hispanic American, 0.4% Native American, 14% transferred in. *Retention:* 61% of 2001 full-time freshmen returned.

Freshmen *Admission:* 1,737 applied, 1,737 admitted, 1,181 enrolled. *Average high school GPA:* 2.6. *Test scores:* ACT scores over 18: 75%.

Faculty *Total:* 383, 36% full-time. *Student/faculty ratio:* 20:1.

Majors Business administration; fire science; health professions and related sciences; industrial arts; liberal arts and sciences/liberal studies; medical radiologic technology; medical records technology; ophthalmic medical assistant; paralegal/legal assistant; physical therapy assistant; respiratory therapy.

Academic Programs *Special study options:* academic remediation for entering students, accelerated degree program, adult/continuing education programs, advanced placement credit, distance learning, double majors, English as a second language, honors programs, part-time degree program, services for LD students, student-designed majors, summer session for credit.

Library Thigpen Learning Resource Center with 49,427 titles, 343 serial subscriptions, 2,794 audiovisual materials, an OPAC, a Web page.

Computers on Campus 400 computers available on campus for general student use. A campuswide network can be accessed from off campus. Internet access, at least one staffed computer lab available.

Student Life *Housing:* college housing not available. *Activities and Organizations:* drama/theater group, student-run newspaper, radio station, choral group, Gamma Beta Phi, Returning Women's Organization, Phi Theta Kappa, Student Government Association, The Settler. *Campus security:* 24-hour emergency response devices and patrols, late-night transport/escort service. *Student Services:* health clinic, personal/psychological counseling.

Athletics Member NJCAA. *Intercollegiate sports:* baseball M(s), basketball M(s)/W(s), softball W(s). *Intramural sports:* basketball M/W.

Standardized Tests *Required for some:* ACT (for placement).

Costs (2001–02) *Tuition:* state resident $1488 full-time, $64 per semester hour part-time; nonresident $5946 full-time, $257 per semester hour part-time. Part-time tuition and fees vary according to course load. *Required fees:* $125 full-time, $5 per semester hour. *Payment plans:* installment, deferred payment. *Waivers:* senior citizens and employees or children of employees.

Financial Aid In 2001, 40 Federal Work-Study jobs (averaging $1250). 25 State and other part-time jobs (averaging $1500).

Applying *Options:* common application, early admission, deferred entrance. *Application fee:* $10. *Required:* high school transcript. *Required for some:* essay or personal statement, minimum 2.0 GPA. *Application deadlines:* 7/31 (freshmen), 7/31 (transfers). *Notification:* continuous (freshmen).

Admissions Contact Mrs. Janice R. Roark, Director of Admission and Records, Volunteer State Community College, 1480 Nashville Pike, Gallatin, TN 37066-3188. *Phone:* 615-452-8600 Ext. 3460. *Toll-free phone:* 888-335-8722. *Fax:* 615-230-3577.

WALTERS STATE COMMUNITY COLLEGE
Morristown, Tennessee

- **State-supported** 2-year, founded 1970, part of Tennessee Board of Regents
- **Calendar** semesters
- **Degree** associate
- **Small-town** 100-acre campus
- **Endowment** $5.2 million
- **Coed,** 5,995 undergraduate students, 51% full-time, 63% women, 37% men

Undergraduates Students come from 9 states and territories, 8 other countries, 1% are from out of state.

Freshmen *Admission:* 1,600 applied, 1,600 admitted.

Faculty *Total:* 253, 44% full-time. *Student/faculty ratio:* 27:1.

Majors Agricultural mechanization; art; art education; business administration; child care/development; computer science; computer science related; criminal justice/law enforcement administration; education; industrial radiologic technology; information technology; interdisciplinary studies; liberal arts and sciences/liberal studies; medical administrative assistant; medical laboratory technician; music teacher education; nursing; physical education; pre-engineering; secretarial science.

Academic Programs *Special study options:* academic remediation for entering students, accelerated degree program, adult/continuing education programs, advanced placement credit, distance learning, part-time degree program, summer session for credit. *ROTC:* Army (c).

Library 47,857 titles, 325 serial subscriptions, 2,626 audiovisual materials.

Computers on Campus 212 computers available on campus for general student use. A campuswide network can be accessed from off campus. At least one staffed computer lab available.

Student Life *Housing:* college housing not available. *Activities and Organizations:* student-run newspaper, choral group. *Campus security:* 24-hour emergency response devices. *Student Services:* health clinic.

Athletics Member NJCAA. *Intercollegiate sports:* basketball M(s)/W(s), softball W. *Intramural sports:* baseball M, basketball M/W.

Standardized Tests *Required:* SAT I or ACT (for admission).

Costs (2001–02) *Tuition:* state resident $1488 full-time, $64 per credit hour part-time; nonresident $5946 full-time, $257 per credit hour part-time. *Required fees:* $139 full-time.

Financial Aid In 2001, 60 Federal Work-Study jobs (averaging $2400).

Applying *Options:* early admission. *Application fee:* $5. *Required:* high school transcript. *Application deadline:* rolling (freshmen), rolling (transfers). *Notification:* continuous (freshmen).

Admissions Contact Mr. James D. Wilder, Director of Student Information Systems/Admission Service, Walters State Community College, 500 South Davy Crockett Parkway, Morristown, TN 37813-6899. *Phone:* 423-585-2683. *Toll-free phone:* 800-225-4770. *Fax:* 423-585-6876. *E-mail:* pam.goodman@wscc.cc.tn.us.

TEXAS

ALVIN COMMUNITY COLLEGE
Alvin, Texas

- **State and locally supported** 2-year, founded 1949
- **Calendar** semesters
- **Degree** certificates, diplomas, and associate
- **Small-town** 113-acre campus with easy access to Houston
- **Coed,** 3,671 undergraduate students, 39% full-time, 54% women, 46% men

Undergraduates 1,425 full-time, 2,246 part-time. Students come from 10 states and territories, 48% are from out of state, 8% African American, 2% Asian American or Pacific Islander, 18% Hispanic American, 0.4% Native American, 0.2% international, 26% transferred in.

Freshmen *Admission:* 782 applied, 782 admitted, 782 enrolled.

Faculty *Total:* 240, 38% full-time. *Student/faculty ratio:* 16:1.

Majors Accounting; aerospace science; alcohol/drug abuse counseling; art; biology; business administration; business marketing and marketing management; chemical technology; child care/development; computer engineering technology; computer programming; corrections; court reporting; drafting; electrical/electronic engineering technology; emergency medical technology; law enforcement/police science; legal administrative assistant; legal studies; liberal arts and sciences/liberal studies; mathematics; medical administrative assistant; mental health/rehabilitation; music; music (voice and choral/opera performance); nursing; paralegal/legal assistant; physical education; physical sciences; radio/television broadcasting; respiratory therapy; secretarial science; theater arts/drama.

Academic Programs *Special study options:* academic remediation for entering students, accelerated degree program, adult/continuing education programs, advanced placement credit, distance learning, double majors, English as a second language, honors programs, independent study, internships, part-time degree program, services for LD students, student-designed majors, study abroad, summer session for credit.

Library Alvin Community College Library with 27,000 titles, 305 serial subscriptions, 3,799 audiovisual materials, an OPAC.

Computers on Campus 400 computers available on campus for general student use. A campuswide network can be accessed from off campus. Internet access, at least one staffed computer lab available.

Student Life *Housing:* college housing not available. *Activities and Organizations:* drama/theater group, student-run radio and television station, choral group, Student Government Association, Baptist Student Union, Pan American College Forum, Catholic Newman Association, Phi Theta Kappa. *Campus security:* 24-hour patrols, late-night transport/escort service. *Student Services:* personal/psychological counseling.

Athletics Member NJCAA. *Intercollegiate sports:* baseball M(s), softball W(s), volleyball W(s). *Intramural sports:* soccer M(c)/W(c).

Standardized Tests *Required:* TASP, Accuplacer.

Costs (2001–02) *Tuition:* state resident $384 full-time, $16 per credit part-time; nonresident $1200 full-time, $50 per credit part-time. Full-time tuition and fees vary according to course load. Part-time tuition and fees vary according to course load. *Required fees:* $272 full-time, $16 per credit, $96 per term part-time. *Payment plan:* installment. *Waivers:* senior citizens.

Financial Aid In 2001, 50 Federal Work-Study jobs (averaging $2200). 1 State and other part-time jobs (averaging $2500).

Applying *Required for some:* high school transcript. *Application deadline:* rolling (freshmen), rolling (transfers).

Admissions Contact Ms. JoAn Anderson, Director of Admissions and Advising, Alvin Community College, Alvin, TX 77511. *Phone:* 281-756-3527. *Toll-free phone:* 281-756-3531. *Fax:* 281-756-3531. *E-mail:* admiss@alvin.cc.tx.us.

AMARILLO COLLEGE
Amarillo, Texas

- **State and locally supported** 2-year, founded 1929
- **Calendar** semesters
- **Degree** certificates and associate
- **Suburban** 58-acre campus
- **Endowment** $13.6 million
- **Coed,** 8,650 undergraduate students

Undergraduates Students come from 9 states and territories, 7 other countries, 1% are from out of state.

Faculty *Total:* 280. *Student/faculty ratio:* 17:1.

Majors Accounting; aircraft mechanic/airframe; alcohol/drug abuse counseling; architectural engineering technology; art; auto mechanic/technician; behavioral sciences; biblical studies; biology; broadcast journalism; business administration; business education; chemical technology; chemistry; child care/development; computer engineering technology; computer programming; computer science; computer systems analysis; corrections; criminal justice/law enforcement administration; dental hygiene; drafting; electrical/electronic engineering technology; elementary education; emergency medical technology; engineering; English; environmental health; fine/studio arts; fire science; general studies; geology; graphic design/commercial art/illustration; heating/air conditioning/refrigeration; heavy equipment maintenance; history; industrial radiologic technology; information sciences/systems; instrumentation technology; interior design; journalism; laser/optical technology; law enforcement/police science; legal administrative assistant; liberal arts and sciences/liberal studies; machine technology; mass communications; mathematics; medical administrative assistant; medical records

Amarillo College (continued)
administration; medical technology; modern languages; mortuary science; music; music teacher education; natural sciences; nuclear medical technology; nursing; occupational therapy; photography; physical education; physical sciences; physical therapy; physics; practical nurse; pre-engineering; pre-pharmacy studies; psychology; public relations; radiological science; radio/television broadcasting; real estate; religious studies; respiratory therapy; secretarial science; social sciences; social work; speech/rhetorical studies; telecommunications; theater arts/drama; travel/tourism management; visual/performing arts.
Academic Programs *Special study options:* academic remediation for entering students, adult/continuing education programs, advanced placement credit, distance learning, English as a second language, honors programs, part-time degree program, services for LD students, summer session for credit.
Library Lynn Library Learning Center plus 1 other with 75,200 titles, 325 serial subscriptions, an OPAC.
Computers on Campus 450 computers available on campus for general student use. Internet access, at least one staffed computer lab available.
Student Life *Housing Options:* coed. *Activities and Organizations:* drama/theater group, student-run newspaper, radio station, choral group, Student Government Association, College Republicans. *Campus security:* 24-hour patrols, late-night transport/escort service. *Student Services:* personal/psychological counseling.
Athletics *Intramural sports:* basketball M/W, tennis M/W, volleyball M/W.
Standardized Tests *Required:* TASP, MAPS.
Costs (2001–02) *Tuition:* area resident $666 full-time, $21 per credit part-time; state resident $930 full-time, $21 per credit part-time; nonresident $1619 full-time, $42 per credit part-time. Full-time tuition and fees vary according to course load. Part-time tuition and fees vary according to course load. *Required fees:* $150 full-time, $7 per credit, $3 per term part-time. *Room and board:* Room and board charges vary according to housing facility. *Payment plan:* installment. *Waivers:* employees or children of employees.
Applying *Options:* early admission, deferred entrance. *Required:* high school transcript. *Notification:* continuous (freshmen).
Admissions Contact Mr. Dennis McMillan, Registrar and Director of Admissions, Amarillo College, PO Box 447, Amarillo, TX 79178-0001. *Phone:* 806-371-5024. *Fax:* 806-371-5066.

ANGELINA COLLEGE
Lufkin, Texas

- **State and locally supported** 2-year, founded 1968
- **Calendar** semesters
- **Degree** certificates, diplomas, and associate
- **Small-town** 140-acre campus
- **Endowment** $2.6 million
- **Coed,** 4,418 undergraduate students, 44% full-time, 63% women, 37% men

Undergraduates Students come from 15 states and territories, 2% are from out of state, 15% African American, 0.8% Asian American or Pacific Islander, 8% Hispanic American, 0.8% Native American, 1% live on campus. *Retention:* 44% of 2001 full-time freshmen returned.
Freshmen *Average high school GPA:* 2.75.
Faculty *Total:* 292, 30% full-time.
Majors Accounting; art; art education; auto mechanic/technician; biological/physical sciences; biology; business administration; child care/development; child care provider; child care services management; computer engineering technology; computer programming; computer science; criminal justice/law enforcement administration; data processing technology; developmental/child psychology; drafting; drafting/design technology; education (K-12); electrical/electronic engineering technology; electrical equipment installation/repair; electromechanical technology; elementary education; emergency medical technology; engineering; engineering-related technology; English; environmental technology; health education; history; humanities; human services; industrial radiologic technology; journalism; liberal arts and sciences/liberal studies; mathematics; medical laboratory technician; medical technology; music; music (piano and organ performance); music teacher education; music (voice and choral/opera performance); nursing; paralegal/legal assistant; physical education; physical sciences; physical therapy assistant; practical nurse; pre-pharmacy studies; real estate; respiratory therapy; science education; secretarial science; social sciences; social work; speech/theater education; system/networking/LAN/WAN management; teacher assistant/aide; water treatment technology; welding technology.
Academic Programs *Special study options:* academic remediation for entering students, adult/continuing education programs, advanced placement credit, cooperative education, distance learning, double majors, honors programs, internships, off-campus study, part-time degree program, services for LD students, student-designed majors, summer session for credit. *ROTC:* Army (c).
Library Angelina College Library with 37,000 titles, 270 serial subscriptions, an OPAC.
Computers on Campus 200 computers available on campus for general student use. A campuswide network can be accessed from off campus. Internet access, at least one staffed computer lab available.
Student Life *Housing Options:* coed. *Activities and Organizations:* drama/theater group, student-run newspaper, choral group, Students in Free Enterprise, Phi Theta Kappa, Student Nurses Association, Rodeo Club. *Campus security:* 24-hour patrols. *Student Services:* personal/psychological counseling.
Athletics Member NJCAA. *Intercollegiate sports:* baseball M(s), basketball M(s)/W(s). *Intramural sports:* basketball M/W, bowling M/W, golf M/W, racquetball M/W, tennis M/W, volleyball M/W, weight lifting M/W.
Standardized Tests *Required:* ACT COMPASS, TASP.
Costs (2001–02) *One-time required fee:* $180. *Tuition:* area resident $540 full-time, $18 per credit hour part-time; state resident $780 full-time, $26 per credit hour part-time; nonresident $1260 full-time, $42 per credit hour part-time. Full-time tuition and fees vary according to course load. Part-time tuition and fees vary according to course load. *Required fees:* $300 full-time, $10 per credit hour. *Room and board:* $3710. Room and board charges vary according to board plan. *Payment plan:* installment. *Waivers:* senior citizens and employees or children of employees.
Applying *Options:* common application, electronic application, early admission, deferred entrance. *Required:* high school transcript. *Application deadline:* rolling (freshmen), rolling (transfers). *Notification:* continuous (freshmen).
Admissions Contact Ms. Judith Cutting, Registrar/Enrollment Director, Angelina College, PO Box 1768, Lufkin, TX 75902-1768. *Phone:* 409-639-1301 Ext. 213. *Fax:* 409-639-4299.

THE ART INSTITUTE OF DALLAS
Dallas, Texas

Admissions Contact Mr. Donny Broughton, Director of High School and International Admissions, The Art Institute of Dallas, Two NorthPark, 8080 Park Lane, Suite 100, Dallas, TX 75231-9959. *Phone:* 214-692-8080 Ext. 620. *Toll-free phone:* 800-275-4243. *Fax:* 214-750-9460.

THE ART INSTITUTE OF HOUSTON
Houston, Texas

- **Proprietary** primarily 2-year, founded 1978, part of The Art Institutes International
- **Calendar** quarters
- **Degrees** diplomas, associate, and bachelor's
- **Urban** campus
- **Coed,** 1,679 undergraduate students, 83% full-time, 38% women, 62% men

Undergraduates 1,400 full-time, 279 part-time. Students come from 12 states and territories, 36 other countries, 15% live on campus.
Freshmen *Admission:* 317 enrolled.
Faculty *Total:* 121, 36% full-time. *Student/faculty ratio:* 18:1.
Majors Applied art; computer graphics; computer graphics; culinary arts; food products retailing; graphic design/commercial art/illustration; interior design; multimedia; Web page, digital/multimedia and information resources design.
Academic Programs *Special study options:* academic remediation for entering students, adult/continuing education programs, advanced placement credit, cooperative education, internships, off-campus study, summer session for credit.
Library Resource Center with 10,000 titles, 188 serial subscriptions, an OPAC.
Computers on Campus 194 computers available on campus for general student use. Internet access, at least one staffed computer lab available.
Student Life *Housing Options:* coed, men-only, women-only. *Activities and Organizations:* Texas Chef's Association, Association of Interior Designers, Computer Animation Society, Houston Ad Federation, International Television Association. *Campus security:* 24-hour emergency response devices. *Student Services:* personal/psychological counseling.
Athletics *Intramural sports:* basketball M, football M/W, softball M/W, volleyball M/W.
Standardized Tests *Recommended:* SAT I or ACT (for admission).
Costs (2002–03) *Tuition:* $14,625 full-time, $325 per credit part-time. Full-time tuition and fees vary according to course load. No tuition increase for student's term of enrollment. *Room only:* $4185. *Payment plans:* tuition prepayment, installment. *Waivers:* employees or children of employees.

Applying *Options:* common application, electronic application. *Application fee:* $50. *Required:* essay or personal statement, high school transcript, letters of recommendation, interview. *Required for some:* minimum 2.5 GPA, portfolio. *Recommended:* minimum 2.0 GPA. *Application deadline:* rolling (freshmen), rolling (transfers).

Admissions Contact Mr. Robert Paul Cappel, Director of Admissions, The Art Institute of Houston, 1900 Yorktown, Houston, TX 77056-4115. *Phone:* 713-623-2040 Ext. 3612. *Toll-free phone:* 800-275-4244. *Fax:* 713-966-2797. *E-mail:* aihadm@aih.aii.edu.

AUSTIN BUSINESS COLLEGE
Austin, Texas

- **Proprietary** 2-year
- **Calendar** quarters
- **Degree** certificates and associate
- **Coed,** 252 undergraduate students, 80% full-time, 79% women, 21% men

Undergraduates 201 full-time, 51 part-time. Students come from 5 states and territories, 2 other countries, 5% are from out of state.

Freshmen *Admission:* 300 applied, 275 admitted, 252 enrolled. *Average high school GPA:* 2.80.

Faculty *Total:* 35, 71% full-time. *Student/faculty ratio:* 20:1.

Majors Data entry/microcomputer applications; management information systems/business data processing.

Academic Programs *Special study options:* academic remediation for entering students, adult/continuing education programs, cooperative education, external degree program, honors programs, independent study, internships.

Library Learning Resource Center with 1,000 titles, 15 serial subscriptions, 50 audiovisual materials.

Computers on Campus 200 computers available on campus for general student use. Internet access, at least one staffed computer lab available.

Costs (2001–02) *Tuition:* Full-time tuition and fees vary according to program. Part-time tuition and fees vary according to program. No tuition increase for student's term of enrollment. Tuition varies between $7,000 and $17,000, depending on program. *Payment plans:* tuition prepayment, installment, deferred payment. *Waivers:* employees or children of employees.

Financial Aid In 2001, 10 Federal Work-Study jobs.

Applying *Required:* essay or personal statement, high school transcript, interview. *Application deadline:* rolling (freshmen), rolling (transfers).

Admissions Contact Ms. Pam Binns, Director of Admissions, Austin Business College, 2101 Interstate Highway 35, Suite 300, Austin, TX 78741. *Phone:* 512-447-9415. *Toll-free phone:* 512-447-9415. *Fax:* 512-447-0194. *E-mail:* abc@austinbusinesscollege.org.

AUSTIN COMMUNITY COLLEGE
Austin, Texas

- **District-supported** 2-year, founded 1972
- **Calendar** semesters
- **Degree** certificates and associate
- **Urban** campus
- **Coed,** 27,548 undergraduate students, 23% full-time, 55% women, 45% men

Undergraduates Students come from 93 other countries, 0.2% are from out of state, 7% African American, 6% Asian American or Pacific Islander, 21% Hispanic American, 0.9% Native American, 2% international.

Freshmen *Admission:* 27,577 applied, 27,577 admitted.

Faculty *Total:* 1,525, 25% full-time, 15% with terminal degrees.

Majors Accounting; art; astronomy; auto mechanic/technician; biology; business administration; business marketing and marketing management; chemistry; computer programming; computer programming related; computer science; computer science related; computer systems networking/telecommunications; construction technology; criminal justice/law enforcement administration; data entry/microcomputer applications; developmental/child psychology; drafting; economics; electrical/electronic engineering technology; emergency medical technology; English; fashion merchandising; finance; fire science; food sales operations; French; geology; German; graphic design/commercial art/illustration; graphic/printing equipment; heating/air conditioning/refrigeration; history; hotel and restaurant management; human services; industrial radiologic technology; industrial technology; information sciences/systems; information technology; insurance/risk management; Japanese; journalism; law enforcement/police science; legal administrative assistant; liberal arts and sciences/liberal studies; mass communications; mathematics; medical assistant; medical laboratory technician; music; nursing; occupational therapy; operating room technician; paralegal/legal assistant; photography; physical sciences; physics; political science; pre-engineering; psychology; quality control technology; radio/television broadcasting; real estate; retail management; Russian; secretarial science; sign language interpretation; social work; sociology; Spanish; speech/rhetorical studies; surveying; system/networking/LAN/WAN management; technical/business writing; welding technology.

Academic Programs *Special study options:* academic remediation for entering students, accelerated degree program, adult/continuing education programs, advanced placement credit, cooperative education, distance learning, English as a second language, external degree program, honors programs, independent study, internships, part-time degree program, services for LD students, summer session for credit. *ROTC:* Army (c), Air Force (c).

Library Main Library plus 6 others with 115,567 titles, 1,974 serial subscriptions, 14,044 audiovisual materials, an OPAC, a Web page.

Computers on Campus 225 computers available on campus for general student use. A campuswide network can be accessed from off campus. Internet access, at least one staffed computer lab available.

Student Life *Housing:* college housing not available. *Activities and Organizations:* drama/theater group, student-run newspaper. *Student Services:* personal/psychological counseling.

Athletics *Intramural sports:* basketball M/W, football M, golf M, racquetball M/W, volleyball M/W, weight lifting M/W.

Costs (2001–02) *Tuition:* area resident $960 full-time, $32 per semester hour part-time; state resident $2430 full-time, $81 per semester hour part-time; nonresident $5040 full-time, $168 per semester hour part-time. Full-time tuition and fees vary according to course load. Part-time tuition and fees vary according to course load. *Required fees:* $336 full-time, $11 per semester hour, $3 per term part-time. *Payment plan:* installment. *Waivers:* senior citizens and employees or children of employees.

Financial Aid In 2001, 200 Federal Work-Study jobs, 10 State and other part-time jobs.

Applying *Options:* electronic application. *Application deadline:* rolling (freshmen), rolling (transfers).

Admissions Contact Austin Community College, 5930 Middle Fiskville Road, Austin, TX 78752-4390. *Fax:* 512-223-7665.

BLINN COLLEGE
Brenham, Texas

- **State and locally supported** 2-year, founded 1883
- **Calendar** semesters
- **Degree** certificates, diplomas, and associate
- **Small-town** 100-acre campus with easy access to Houston
- **Endowment** $29.8 million
- **Coed,** 12,025 undergraduate students, 58% full-time, 50% women, 50% men

Undergraduates 7,006 full-time, 5,019 part-time. Students come from 36 states and territories, 57 other countries, 1% are from out of state, 7% African American, 1% Asian American or Pacific Islander, 9% Hispanic American, 0.3% Native American, 2% international, 25% transferred in, 9% live on campus.

Freshmen *Admission:* 3,348 applied, 3,348 admitted, 3,348 enrolled.

Faculty *Total:* 323. *Student/faculty ratio:* 27:1.

Majors Accounting; agricultural sciences; biology; business administration; business systems networking/ telecommunications; chemistry; child guidance; computer science; criminal justice/law enforcement administration; dental hygiene; English; fire science; French; German; history; industrial radiologic technology; legal administrative assistant; literature; mass communications; mathematics; medical records technology; mental health/rehabilitation; music; nursing; philosophy; physical education; physical therapy assistant; physics; psychology; real estate; secretarial science; Spanish; speech/rhetorical studies; theater arts/drama.

Academic Programs *Special study options:* academic remediation for entering students, adult/continuing education programs, advanced placement credit, distance learning, double majors, English as a second language, part-time degree program, services for LD students, summer session for credit.

Library W. L. Moody, Jr. Library plus 1 other with 130,000 titles, 700 serial subscriptions, an OPAC, a Web page.

Computers on Campus 1200 computers available on campus for general student use. A campuswide network can be accessed from off campus. Internet access, online (class) registration, at least one staffed computer lab available.

Student Life *Housing:* on-campus residence required through sophomore year. *Options:* men-only, women-only. *Activities and Organizations:* drama/theater group, student-run newspaper, choral group, marching band, Student Government

Blinn College (continued)
Association, Phi Theta Kappa, Baptist student ministries, Blinn Ethnic Student Organization, Circle K. *Campus security:* 24-hour emergency response devices and patrols, controlled dormitory access. *Student Services:* personal/psychological counseling.
Athletics Member NJCAA. *Intercollegiate sports:* baseball M(s), basketball M(s)/W(s), football M(s), softball W(s), volleyball W(s). *Intramural sports:* basketball M/W, football M, golf M, softball W, table tennis M/W, volleyball W.
Standardized Tests *Required:* TASP.
Costs (2001–02) *Tuition:* area resident $456 full-time, $19 per semester hour part-time; state resident $744 full-time, $32 per semester hour part-time; nonresident $2688 full-time, $113 per semester hour part-time. Full-time tuition and fees vary according to course load and location. Part-time tuition and fees vary according to course load and location. *Required fees:* $624 full-time, $26 per credit. *Room and board:* Room and board charges vary according to board plan and housing facility. *Payment plans:* installment, deferred payment.
Applying *Options:* common application, electronic application, early admission, deferred entrance. *Required:* high school transcript. *Application deadline:* rolling (freshmen), rolling (transfers).
Admissions Contact Ms. Courtney Mason, Coordinator, Recruitment and Admissions, Blinn College, 902 College Avenue, Brenham, TX 77833-4049. *Phone:* 979-830-4152. *Fax:* 979-830-4110.

BORDER INSTITUTE OF TECHNOLOGY
El Paso, Texas

- **Proprietary** 2-year
- **Calendar** quarters
- **Degree** certificates, diplomas, and associate
- 200 undergraduate students

Financial Aid In 2001, 83 Federal Work-Study jobs (averaging $410).
Admissions Contact Mr. Daniel Ujueta, Admissions Director, Border Institute of Technology, 9611 Acer Avenue, El Paso, TX 79925-6744. *Phone:* 915-593-7328 Ext. 24.

BRAZOSPORT COLLEGE
Lake Jackson, Texas

- **State and locally supported** 2-year, founded 1968
- **Calendar** semesters
- **Degree** certificates and associate
- **Small-town** 160-acre campus with easy access to Houston
- **Endowment** $3.3 million
- **Coed,** 4,022 undergraduate students, 27% full-time, 51% women, 49% men

Undergraduates 1,100 full-time, 2,922 part-time. Students come from 16 states and territories, 6 other countries, 1% are from out of state, 8% African American, 1% Asian American or Pacific Islander, 23% Hispanic American, 0.6% Native American, 0.3% international, 22% transferred in.
Freshmen *Admission:* 1,057 applied, 1,057 admitted, 648 enrolled.
Faculty *Total:* 191, 36% full-time, 5% with terminal degrees. *Student/faculty ratio:* 19:1.
Majors Agricultural business; architecture; art; auto mechanic/technician; biology; business administration; business marketing and marketing management; chemical technology; chemistry; child care/development; child care services management; computer/information sciences; computer maintenance technology; computer programming; computer programming related; computer programming (specific applications); construction technology; data processing technology; drafting; education; electrical/electronic engineering technology; elementary education; emergency medical technology; engineering; English; environmental health; foreign languages/literatures; general studies; heating/air conditioning/refrigeration; history; home economics; information technology; instrumentation technology; journalism; law enforcement/police science; liberal arts and sciences/liberal studies; mathematics; music; nursing; paralegal/legal assistant; physical education; physics; plumbing; political science; psychology; quality control technology; secondary education; secretarial science; sheet metal working; social sciences; sociology; speech/rhetorical studies; theater arts/drama; vehicle/equipment operation; welding technology.
Academic Programs *Special study options:* academic remediation for entering students, adult/continuing education programs, advanced placement credit, cooperative education, distance learning, internships, part-time degree program, summer session for credit.
Library Brazosport College Library with 58,000 titles, 350 serial subscriptions, an OPAC, a Web page.
Computers on Campus 420 computers available on campus for general student use. A campuswide network can be accessed from off campus. Internet access, online (class) registration, at least one staffed computer lab available.
Student Life *Housing:* college housing not available. *Activities and Organizations:* drama/theater group, student-run newspaper, choral group, Phi Theta Kappa, Baptist Student Ministry, Student Senate, Fencing club. *Campus security:* 24-hour patrols.
Athletics *Intramural sports:* archery M/W, basketball M/W, bowling M/W, fencing M/W, football M/W, golf M/W, soccer M/W, softball M/W, table tennis M/W, tennis M/W, volleyball M/W.
Standardized Tests *Required for some:* TASP.
Costs (2002–03) *Tuition:* area resident $770 full-time, $20 per hour part-time; state resident $1130 full-time, $32 per hour part-time; nonresident $2540 full-time, $79 per hour part-time. Full-time tuition and fees vary according to course load. Part-time tuition and fees vary according to course load. *Required fees:* $170 full-time, $4 per hour, $18 per term part-time. *Payment plan:* installment. *Waivers:* employees or children of employees.
Applying *Options:* early admission, deferred entrance. *Required for some:* high school transcript. *Application deadlines:* 8/15 (freshmen), 8/15 (transfers).
Admissions Contact Ms. Patricia S. Leyendecker, Director of Admissions/Registrar, Brazosport College, 500 College Drive, Lake Jackson, TX 77566. *Phone:* 979-230-3217. *Fax:* 979-230-3443. *E-mail:* regist@brazosport.cc.tx.us.

BROOKHAVEN COLLEGE
Farmers Branch, Texas

Admissions Contact Ms. Barbara B. Burke, Registrar, Brookhaven College, 3939 Valley View Lane, Farmers Branch, TX 75244-4997. *Phone:* 972-860-4604. *Fax:* 972-860-4897. *E-mail:* bhc2310@dcccd.edu.

CEDAR VALLEY COLLEGE
Lancaster, Texas

- **State-supported** 2-year, founded 1977, part of Dallas County Community College District System
- **Calendar** semesters
- **Degree** certificates and associate
- **Suburban** 353-acre campus with easy access to Dallas-Fort Worth
- **Coed,** 3,974 undergraduate students, 28% full-time, 59% women, 41% men

Undergraduates 1,119 full-time, 2,855 part-time. Students come from 5 other countries, 50% African American, 1% Asian American or Pacific Islander, 10% Hispanic American, 0.6% Native American, 0.4% international, 61% transferred in.
Freshmen *Admission:* 1,436 applied, 1,436 admitted, 1,436 enrolled.
Faculty *Total:* 164, 33% full-time, 13% with terminal degrees. *Student/faculty ratio:* 23:1.
Majors Accounting; auto mechanic/technician; business administration; business information/data processing related; business marketing and marketing management; computer programming; computer programming (specific applications); criminal justice/law enforcement administration; data processing technology; heating/air conditioning/refrigeration; liberal arts and sciences/liberal studies; music; radio/television broadcasting technology; real estate; secretarial science; veterinarian assistant.
Academic Programs *Special study options:* academic remediation for entering students, adult/continuing education programs, advanced placement credit, cooperative education, distance learning, English as a second language, part-time degree program, services for LD students, summer session for credit. *ROTC:* Army (c).
Library Cedar Valley College Library with 47,839 titles, 285 serial subscriptions, 15,162 audiovisual materials, an OPAC, a Web page.
Computers on Campus 457 computers available on campus for general student use. A campuswide network can be accessed from off campus. Internet access, online (class) registration, at least one staffed computer lab available.
Student Life *Housing:* college housing not available. *Activities and Organizations:* drama/theater group, choral group, African-American Student Organization, Latin-American Student Organization, Veterinary Technology Club, Phi Theta Kappa, Police Academy Club. *Campus security:* 24-hour emergency response devices and patrols. *Student Services:* health clinic, personal/psychological counseling.

Athletics Member NJCAA. *Intercollegiate sports:* baseball M, basketball M, volleyball W.
Standardized Tests *Recommended:* SAT I or ACT (for admission).
Costs (2001–02) *Tuition:* area resident $624 full-time, $26 per credit hour part-time; state resident $1104 full-time, $46 per credit hour part-time; nonresident $1824 full-time, $76 per credit hour part-time. Full-time tuition and fees vary according to course load. Part-time tuition and fees vary according to course load. *Payment plan:* installment. *Waivers:* senior citizens.
Applying *Options:* electronic application, early admission. *Required for some:* letters of recommendation, interview. *Recommended:* high school transcript. *Application deadline:* rolling (freshmen), rolling (transfers). *Notification:* continuous (freshmen).
Admissions Contact Mr. John W. Williamson, Director of Admissions/Registrar, Cedar Valley College, 3030 North Dallas Avenue, Lancaster, TX 75134-3799. *Phone:* 972-860-8201. *E-mail:* jww3310@dcccd.edu.

Center for Advanced Legal Studies
Houston, Texas

Admissions Contact 3910 Kirby Drive, Suite 200, Houston, TX 77098-4151.

Central Texas College
Killeen, Texas

- **State and locally supported** 2-year, founded 1967
- **Calendar** semesters
- **Degree** certificates and associate
- **Suburban** 500-acre campus with easy access to Austin
- **Endowment** $1.4 million
- **Coed,** 15,473 undergraduate students, 18% full-time, 42% women, 58% men

Undergraduates 2,788 full-time, 12,685 part-time. Students come from 48 states and territories, 19 other countries, 29% African American, 4% Asian American or Pacific Islander, 14% Hispanic American, 0.9% Native American, 0.4% international, 1% live on campus.
Freshmen *Admission:* 2,051 applied, 2,051 admitted.
Faculty *Total:* 675, 28% full-time, 3% with terminal degrees. *Student/faculty ratio:* 20:1.
Majors Agricultural sciences; aircraft mechanic/powerplant; aircraft pilot (professional); alcohol/drug abuse counseling; auto mechanic/technician; biology; business administration; business marketing and marketing management; chemistry; child care/guidance; computer/information sciences; computer programming; computer programming related; computer programming (specific applications); computer programming, vendor/product certification; cosmetology; criminal justice studies; data processing technology; drafting; electrical/electronic engineering technology; emergency medical technology; engineering; environmental science; equestrian studies; farm/ranch management; geology; graphic design/commercial art/illustration; graphic/printing equipment; heating/air conditioning/refrigeration; hotel and restaurant management; interdisciplinary studies; journalism; law enforcement/police science; liberal arts and sciences/liberal studies; mathematics; medical administrative assistant; medical laboratory technician; medical radiologic technology; music; nursing; office management; paralegal/legal assistant; physical education; practical nurse; radio/television broadcasting; secretarial science; social sciences; welding technology.
Academic Programs *Special study options:* academic remediation for entering students, accelerated degree program, adult/continuing education programs, advanced placement credit, English as a second language, external degree program, internships, part-time degree program, services for LD students, student-designed majors, summer session for credit.
Library Oveta Culp Hobby Memorial Library with 80,381 titles, 467 serial subscriptions, 2,590 audiovisual materials, an OPAC, a Web page.
Computers on Campus 130 computers available on campus for general student use. A campuswide network can be accessed from student residence rooms and from off campus. Internet access, at least one staffed computer lab available.
Student Life *Housing Options:* coed. *Activities and Organizations:* drama/theater group, student-run newspaper, International Student Association, We Can Do It Club, Students in Free Enterprise, Student Nurses Association, NAACP. *Campus security:* 24-hour emergency response devices and patrols.
Athletics *Intramural sports:* badminton M/W, basketball M/W, bowling M/W, football M/W, golf M/W, soccer M/W, softball M/W, table tennis M/W, tennis M/W, volleyball M/W.
Standardized Tests *Required:* TASP. *Recommended:* SAT I or ACT (for placement), SAT II: Subject Tests (for placement), SAT II: Writing Test (for placement).
Costs (2001–02) *Tuition:* area resident $480 full-time, $20 per semester hour part-time; state resident $600 full-time, $25 per semester hour part-time; nonresident $1200 full-time, $50 per semester hour part-time. Full-time tuition and fees vary according to course load. Part-time tuition and fees vary according to course load. *Required fees:* $192 full-time, $8 per semester hour. *Room and board:* $2742. *Payment plans:* installment, deferred payment. *Waivers:* senior citizens and employees or children of employees.
Financial Aid In 2001, 80 Federal Work-Study jobs.
Applying *Options:* electronic application, early admission, deferred entrance. *Required:* high school transcript, minimum 2.0 GPA. *Application deadline:* rolling (freshmen), rolling (transfers).
Admissions Contact Mr. David McClure, Dean of Guidance and Counseling, Central Texas College, PO Box 1800, Killeen, TX 76540-1800. *Phone:* 254-526-1452. *Toll-free phone:* 800-792-3348 Ext. 1132. *Fax:* 254-526-1481. *E-mail:* dmcclur@ctcd.cc.tx.us.

Cisco Junior College
Cisco, Texas

- **State and locally supported** 2-year, founded 1940
- **Calendar** semesters
- **Degree** certificates and associate
- **Rural** 40-acre campus
- **Coed,** 2,616 undergraduate students

Undergraduates Students come from 21 states and territories, 12% live on campus.
Faculty *Total:* 95. *Student/faculty ratio:* 18:1.
Majors Accounting; agricultural business; agricultural sciences; auto mechanic/technician; biology; business administration; business education; business marketing and marketing management; chemistry; child care/development; computer programming; computer science; construction technology; cosmetology; dairy science; data processing technology; developmental/child psychology; drafting; early childhood education; education; electrical/electronic engineering technology; finance; fire science; French; history; human services; law enforcement/police science; mathematics; medical technology; nursing; physical education; psychology; real estate; retail management; welding technology.
Academic Programs *Special study options:* academic remediation for entering students, advanced placement credit, part-time degree program, summer session for credit. *ROTC:* Army (c).
Library Maner Library with 34,000 titles, 173 serial subscriptions, an OPAC, a Web page.
Computers on Campus 36 computers available on campus for general student use. At least one staffed computer lab available.
Student Life *Housing:* on-campus residence required through sophomore year. *Activities and Organizations:* drama/theater group, marching band, Christian Athletes Association, Agricultural Club. *Campus security:* late-night transport/escort service.
Athletics Member NJCAA. *Intercollegiate sports:* basketball M(s)/W(s), football M(s), golf M(s), softball W, volleyball W. *Intramural sports:* badminton M/W, basketball M/W, bowling M/W, football M, golf M, volleyball M/W.
Standardized Tests *Required:* TASP. *Recommended:* SAT I and SAT II or ACT (for placement).
Costs (2001–02) *Tuition:* $291 per term part-time; nonresident $444 per term part-time. Full-time tuition and fees vary according to course load. Part-time tuition and fees vary according to course load. *Required fees:* $20 per term part-time. *Room and board:* Room and board charges vary according to gender. *Payment plan:* installment. *Waivers:* employees or children of employees.
Applying *Options:* early admission. *Application deadline:* rolling (freshmen), rolling (transfers).
Admissions Contact Mr. Olin O. Odom III, Dean of Admission/Registrar, Cisco Junior College, Box 3, Route 3, Cisco, TX 76437-9321. *Phone:* 254-442-2567 Ext. 130.

Clarendon College
Clarendon, Texas

- **State and locally supported** 2-year, founded 1898
- **Calendar** semesters
- **Degree** certificates and associate
- **Rural** 88-acre campus
- **Coed**

Clarendon College (continued)
Faculty *Student/faculty ratio:* 15:1.
Student Life *Campus security:* 8-hour patrols by trained security personnel.
Athletics Member NJCAA.
Standardized Tests *Required:* ACT (for placement), TASP.
Financial Aid In 2001, 41 Federal Work-Study jobs (averaging $985).
Applying *Options:* early admission, deferred entrance. *Required:* high school transcript. *Required for some:* letters of recommendation, interview.
Admissions Contact Ms. Markeeta Schnelle, Coordinator of Admissions and Recruiting, Clarendon College, PO Box 968, Clarendon, TX 79226-0968. *Phone:* 806-874-3571 Ext. 267. *Toll-free phone:* 800-687-9737. *Fax:* 806-874-3201.

COASTAL BEND COLLEGE
Beeville, Texas

- **County-supported** 2-year, founded 1965
- **Calendar** semesters
- **Degree** certificates and associate
- **Rural** 100-acre campus
- **Endowment** $825,011
- **Coed,** 3,259 undergraduate students, 46% full-time, 57% women, 43% men

Undergraduates 1,509 full-time, 1,750 part-time. Students come from 14 states and territories, 3 other countries, 1% are from out of state, 6% African American, 0.6% Asian American or Pacific Islander, 58% Hispanic American, 0.4% Native American, 0.1% international, 60% transferred in, 5% live on campus. *Retention:* 62% of 2001 full-time freshmen returned.
Freshmen *Admission:* 906 applied, 906 admitted, 906 enrolled.
Faculty *Total:* 179, 59% full-time, 7% with terminal degrees. *Student/faculty ratio:* 17:1.
Majors Accounting; agricultural sciences; applied art; art; art education; auto mechanic/technician; biological/physical sciences; biology; business administration; chemistry; child care/development; computer engineering technology; computer programming related; computer programming (specific applications); computer programming, vendor/product certification; computer science; computer science related; computer systems networking/telecommunications; cosmetology; criminal justice/law enforcement administration; data entry/microcomputer applications; data entry/microcomputer applications related; data processing technology; dental hygiene; developmental/child psychology; drafting; economics; education; elementary education; engineering; English; environmental technology; finance; fine/studio arts; French; geology; German; graphic design/commercial art/illustration; health education; history; information technology; journalism; law enforcement/police science; legal administrative assistant; liberal arts and sciences/liberal studies; mathematics; music; music teacher education; music (voice and choral/opera performance); nursing; petroleum technology; pharmacy; physical education; physical sciences; physics; political science; practical nurse; psychology; public relations; recreation/leisure studies; secretarial science; sociology; speech/rhetorical studies; system administration; theater arts/drama; welding technology; word processing.
Academic Programs *Special study options:* academic remediation for entering students, adult/continuing education programs, advanced placement credit, cooperative education, distance learning, internships, part-time degree program, services for LD students, summer session for credit. *ROTC:* Army (c), Air Force (c).
Library Grady C. Hogue Learning Resource Center with 37,971 titles, 268 serial subscriptions, 2,974 audiovisual materials, an OPAC.
Computers on Campus 420 computers available on campus for general student use. A campuswide network can be accessed from off campus. Internet access, at least one staffed computer lab available.
Student Life *Housing Options:* coed, men-only, women-only, disabled students. *Activities and Organizations:* drama/theater group, choral group, student government, Computer Science Club, Creative Writing Club, Drama Club, Art Club. *Campus security:* 24-hour emergency response devices. *Student Services:* personal/psychological counseling.
Athletics *Intramural sports:* archery M/W, badminton M/W, basketball M/W, bowling M/W, cross-country running M/W, golf M/W, soccer M/W, softball M/W, table tennis M/W, tennis M/W, track and field M/W, volleyball M/W, weight lifting M/W.
Standardized Tests *Required:* TASP or ACT COMPASS.
Costs (2001–02) *Tuition:* area resident $810 full-time, $27 per credit hour part-time; state resident $1410 full-time, $47 per credit hour part-time; nonresident $1530 full-time, $51 per credit hour part-time. Full-time tuition and fees vary according to course load, location, and program. Part-time tuition and fees vary according to course load, location, and program. *Required fees:* $130 full-time, $3 per credit hour, $20 per term part-time. *Room and board:* $1920; room only: $1120. Room and board charges vary according to board plan and housing facility. *Payment plan:* installment. *Waivers:* senior citizens.
Financial Aid In 2001, 55 Federal Work-Study jobs (averaging $2427). 8 State and other part-time jobs.
Applying *Options:* deferred entrance. *Required:* high school transcript. *Application deadline:* rolling (freshmen), rolling (transfers). *Notification:* continuous (freshmen).
Admissions Contact Mr. Pedro Martinez, Director of Admissions/Registrar, Coastal Bend College, 3800 Charco Road, Beeville, TX 78102-2197. *Phone:* 361-354-2245. *Fax:* 361-354-2254. *E-mail:* register@cbc.cc.tx.us.

COLLEGE OF THE MAINLAND
Texas City, Texas

- **State and locally supported** 2-year, founded 1967
- **Calendar** semesters
- **Degree** certificates, diplomas, and associate
- **Small-town** 120-acre campus with easy access to Houston
- **Coed**

Student Life *Campus security:* 24-hour emergency response devices and patrols, student patrols.
Standardized Tests *Required for some:* SAT I or ACT (for placement), TASP.
Financial Aid In 2001, 158 Federal Work-Study jobs (averaging $810). 202 State and other part-time jobs (averaging $950).
Applying *Options:* early admission, deferred entrance.
Admissions Contact Ms. Pamela Davenport, Vice President and Dean of Student Services, College of the Mainland, 1200 Amburn Road, Texas City, TX 77591-2499. *Phone:* 409-938-1211 Ext. 263. *Fax:* 409-938-1306. *E-mail:* bpeace@campus.mainland.cc.tx.us.

COLLIN COUNTY COMMUNITY COLLEGE DISTRICT
Plano, Texas

- **State and locally supported** 2-year, founded 1985
- **Calendar** semesters
- **Degree** certificates and associate
- **Suburban** campus with easy access to Dallas-Fort Worth
- **Endowment** $1.5 million
- **Coed,** 14,497 undergraduate students, 38% full-time, 56% women, 44% men

Undergraduates 5,438 full-time, 9,059 part-time. Students come from 45 states and territories, 69 other countries, 17% are from out of state, 6% African American, 4% Asian American or Pacific Islander, 7% Hispanic American, 0.5% Native American, 12% international, 12% transferred in.
Freshmen *Admission:* 2,348 applied, 2,348 admitted.
Faculty *Total:* 773, 24% full-time, 17% with terminal degrees. *Student/faculty ratio:* 22:1.
Majors Biological technology; business administration; business systems networking/ telecommunications; child care/guidance; computer engineering technology; computer/information sciences; dental hygiene; drafting; educational media technology; electrical/electronic engineering technology; electrical/electronics drafting; electrical equipment installation/repair; emergency medical technology; environmental technology; fire protection/safety technology; general studies; graphic design/commercial art/illustration; hospitality management; interior design; liberal arts and sciences/liberal studies; marketing operations; music; nursing; paralegal/legal assistant; real estate; respiratory therapy; secretarial science; sign language interpretation; water treatment technology.
Academic Programs *Special study options:* academic remediation for entering students, adult/continuing education programs, advanced placement credit, cooperative education, distance learning, English as a second language, honors programs, internships, part-time degree program, services for LD students, study abroad, summer session for credit.
Library Collin County Community College Learning Resource Center plus 2 others with 125,648 titles, 940 serial subscriptions, 15,600 audiovisual materials, an OPAC, a Web page.
Computers on Campus 3700 computers available on campus for general student use. A campuswide network can be accessed from off campus. Internet access, online (class) registration, at least one staffed computer lab available.
Student Life *Housing:* college housing not available. *Activities and Organizations:* drama/theater group, student-run radio station, choral group, Phi Theta Kappa, Collin Student Nursing Association, South Asian Student Association,

Respiratory Care Club, Dental Hygiene Student Society. *Campus security:* 24-hour emergency response devices and patrols. *Student Services:* personal/psychological counseling.
Athletics Member NJCAA. *Intercollegiate sports:* baseball M(s), basketball M(s)/W(s), softball W(s), tennis M(s)/W(s), volleyball W(s).
Costs (2001–02) *One-time required fee:* $2. *Tuition:* area resident $630 full-time, $21 per credit hour part-time; state resident $870 full-time, $29 per credit hour part-time; nonresident $1920 full-time, $64 per credit hour part-time. *Required fees:* $304 full-time, $10 per credit hour, $2 per credit hour part-time. *Payment plan:* deferred payment. *Waivers:* senior citizens and employees or children of employees.
Applying *Options:* common application, electronic application. *Required:* high school transcript. *Application deadline:* rolling (freshmen), rolling (transfers).
Admissions Contact Ms. Stephanie Meinardt, Registrar, Collin County Community College District, 2200 West University Drive, McKinney, TX 75070-8001. *Phone:* 972-881-5174. *Fax:* 972-548-6702. *E-mail:* smeinhardt@ccccd.edu.

COMMONWEALTH INSTITUTE OF FUNERAL SERVICE
Houston, Texas

- **Independent** 2-year, founded 1988
- **Calendar** quarters
- **Degree** certificates and associate
- **Urban** campus
- **Coed,** 123 undergraduate students, 100% full-time, 50% women, 50% men

Undergraduates 123 full-time. Students come from 11 states and territories, 20% are from out of state, 39% African American, 0.8% Asian American or Pacific Islander, 12% Hispanic American, 9% transferred in.
Freshmen *Admission:* 49 applied, 49 admitted, 49 enrolled.
Faculty *Total:* 8, 50% full-time. *Student/faculty ratio:* 31:1.
Majors Mortuary science.
Academic Programs *Special study options:* adult/continuing education programs, external degree program.
Library Commonwealth Institute Library and York Learning Resource Center with 1,500 titles, 12 serial subscriptions.
Computers on Campus 15 computers available on campus for general student use. At least one staffed computer lab available.
Student Life *Housing:* college housing not available. *Activities and Organizations:* student council. *Campus security:* 24-hour emergency response devices.
Standardized Tests *Recommended:* SAT I or ACT (for admission).
Costs (2002–03) *Tuition:* $8000 full-time, $13 per contact hour part-time. *Required fees:* $100 full-time.
Applying *Options:* common application. *Application fee:* $50. *Required:* high school transcript. *Application deadline:* rolling (freshmen). *Notification:* continuous (freshmen).
Admissions Contact Mrs. Patricia Moreno, Registrar, Commonwealth Institute of Funeral Service, 415 Barren Springs Drive, Houston, TX 77090. *Phone:* 281-873-0262. *Toll-free phone:* 800-628-1580. *Fax:* 281-873-5232.

COMPUTER CAREER CENTER
El Paso, Texas

- **Proprietary** 2-year
- **Calendar** 8 six-week terms
- **Degree** certificates, diplomas, and associate
- **Urban** campus
- **Coed**

Admissions Contact Ms. Sarah Hernandez, Registrar, Computer Career Center, 6101 Montana Avenue, El Paso, TX 79925. *Phone:* 915-779-8031.

COURT REPORTING INSTITUTE OF DALLAS
Dallas, Texas

- **Private** 2-year
- **Degree** associate
- **Coed, primarily women,** 600 undergraduate students
- 100% of applicants were admitted

Undergraduates Students come from 15 states and territories, 10% are from out of state.
Freshmen *Admission:* 100 applied, 100 admitted.
Faculty *Total:* 30, 50% full-time, 13% with terminal degrees. *Student/faculty ratio:* 35:1.
Majors Court reporting.
Student Life *Housing:* college housing not available. *Activities and Organizations:* student-run newspaper. *Campus security:* 24-hour patrols, late-night transport/escort service.
Costs (2001–02) *Tuition:* $5625 full-time, $1200 per quarter hour part-time. Part-time tuition and fees vary according to program. *Payment plan:* installment.
Applying *Options:* early decision. *Application fee:* $100. *Required:* high school transcript, interview.
Admissions Contact Ms. Debra Smith-Armstrong, Director of Admissions, Court Reporting Institute of Dallas, 8585 North Stemmons, #200 North, Dallas, TX 75247. *Phone:* 214-350-9722 Ext. 227. *Toll-free phone:* 800-880-9722.

CY-FAIR COLLEGE
Houston, Texas

- **State and locally supported** 2-year, founded 2002
- **Calendar** semesters
- **Degree** certificates, diplomas, and associate
- **Coed**

Costs (2002–03) *Tuition:* $28 per credit hour; $40 per credit hour fee for out-of district instate students; $55 per credit hour fee for out of state students. One time $12 registration fee. $5 per credit hour technology fee. $2 per credit hour activity fee.
Admissions Contact Dr. Earl Campa, Vice President of Student Success, Cy-Fair College, 14955 NW Freeway, Houston, TX 77040. *Phone:* 832-782-5050.

DALLAS INSTITUTE OF FUNERAL SERVICE
Dallas, Texas

Admissions Contact Mr. James Shoemake, President, Dallas Institute of Funeral Service, 3909 South Buckner Boulevard, Dallas, TX 75227. *Phone:* 214-388-5466.

DEL MAR COLLEGE
Corpus Christi, Texas

- **State and locally supported** 2-year, founded 1935
- **Calendar** semesters
- **Degree** certificates and associate
- **Urban** 159-acre campus
- **Endowment** $29.1 million
- **Coed,** 10,256 undergraduate students

Undergraduates Students come from 46 states and territories, 57 other countries, 1% are from out of state.
Faculty *Total:* 635, 48% full-time. *Student/faculty ratio:* 18:1.
Majors Accounting; applied art; architectural engineering technology; art; art education; auto mechanic/technician; biology; business administration; business machine repair; chemical technology; chemistry; child care/development; community services; computer programming; computer programming related; computer programming (specific applications); computer programming, vendor/product certification; computer science; computer science related; computer systems networking/telecommunications; computer/technical support; computer typography/composition; cosmetology; court reporting; criminal justice/law enforcement administration; culinary arts; data entry/microcomputer applications; dental hygiene; drafting; early childhood education; education; electrical/electronic engineering technology; English; finance; fine/studio arts; fire science; food products retailing; geography; geology; health education; heavy equipment maintenance; history; hotel and restaurant management; industrial radiologic technology; information sciences/systems; information technology; interdisciplinary studies; journalism; law enforcement/police science; legal administrative assistant; legal studies; liberal arts and sciences/liberal studies; machine technology; mathematics; medical laboratory technician; medical technology; mental health/rehabilitation; music; music teacher education; music (voice and choral/opera performance); nursing; physical education; physics; political science; pre-engineering; psychology; public administration; public policy analysis; radio/

Del Mar College (continued)
television broadcasting; real estate; recreation/leisure studies; respiratory therapy; retail management; secretarial science; sign language interpretation; social work; sociology; speech/rhetorical studies; system/networking/LAN/WAN management; theater arts/drama; trade/industrial education; veterinary sciences; Web/multimedia management/webmaster; Web page, digital/multimedia and information resources design; welding technology; word processing.

Academic Programs *Special study options:* academic remediation for entering students, accelerated degree program, adult/continuing education programs, advanced placement credit, cooperative education, distance learning, English as a second language, freshman honors college, honors programs, internships, part-time degree program, services for LD students, summer session for credit. *ROTC:* Army (b).

Library White Library plus 1 other with 127,717 titles, 739 serial subscriptions, an OPAC.

Computers on Campus 450 computers available on campus for general student use. Internet access, online (class) registration, at least one staffed computer lab available.

Student Life *Housing:* college housing not available. *Activities and Organizations:* drama/theater group, student-run newspaper, radio station. *Campus security:* 24-hour emergency response devices and patrols.

Athletics *Intramural sports:* archery M/W, badminton M/W, basketball M/W, bowling M/W, fencing M/W, football M/W, golf M/W, gymnastics M/W, sailing M/W, swimming M/W, tennis M/W, track and field M/W, volleyball M/W, weight lifting M/W.

Standardized Tests *Required:* TASP or ACT ASSET.

Costs (2002–03) *Tuition:* Full-time tuition and fees vary according to program. *Payment plan:* installment. *Waivers:* senior citizens and employees or children of employees.

Financial Aid In 2001, 311 Federal Work-Study jobs (averaging $2450). 408 State and other part-time jobs (averaging $2450).

Applying *Options:* early admission, deferred entrance. *Required:* high school transcript. *Application deadline:* rolling (freshmen), rolling (transfers).

Admissions Contact Ms. Frances P. Jordan, Assistant Dean of Enrollment Services and Registrar, Del Mar College, 101 Baldwin Boulevard, Corpus Christi, TX 78404-3897. *Phone:* 361-698-1248. *Toll-free phone:* 800-652-3357.

EASTFIELD COLLEGE
Mesquite, Texas

- **State and locally supported** 2-year, founded 1970, part of Dallas County Community College District System
- **Calendar** semesters
- **Degree** certificates and associate
- **Suburban** 244-acre campus with easy access to Dallas-Fort Worth
- **Coed,** 9,210 undergraduate students, 33% full-time, 57% women, 43% men

Undergraduates 3,063 full-time, 6,147 part-time. Students come from 18 states and territories, 32 other countries, 1% are from out of state, 20% African American, 5% Asian American or Pacific Islander, 18% Hispanic American, 0.3% Native American, 0.9% international, 4% transferred in. *Retention:* 62% of 2001 full-time freshmen returned.

Freshmen *Admission:* 1,393 applied, 1,393 admitted, 1,275 enrolled.

Faculty *Total:* 483, 19% full-time. *Student/faculty ratio:* 23:1.

Majors Accounting; alcohol/drug abuse counseling; auto body repair; auto mechanic/technician; business administration; business systems networking/ telecommunications; child care/guidance; computer engineering technology; computer hardware engineering; computer/information technology services administration and management related; computer programming; computer programming related; computer science related; criminal justice studies; data entry/microcomputer applications; data processing technology; drafting; electrical/electronic engineering technology; electrical/electronics drafting; executive assistant; graphic/printing equipment; heating/air conditioning/refrigeration; legal administrative assistant; liberal arts and sciences/liberal studies; psychiatric/mental health services; sign language interpretation; social work; system/networking/LAN/WAN management; word processing.

Academic Programs *Special study options:* academic remediation for entering students, adult/continuing education programs, advanced placement credit, cooperative education, distance learning, English as a second language, honors programs, part-time degree program, services for LD students, summer session for credit.

Library Eastfield College Learning Resource Center with 66,988 titles, 415 serial subscriptions, 2,620 audiovisual materials, an OPAC, a Web page.

Computers on Campus 50 computers available on campus for general student use. A campuswide network can be accessed from off campus. Internet access, at least one staffed computer lab available.

Student Life *Housing:* college housing not available. *Activities and Organizations:* drama/theater group, student-run newspaper, choral group, LULAC, Rodeo Club, PTK, Rising Star, Communications Club. *Campus security:* 24-hour emergency response devices and patrols. *Student Services:* health clinic, personal/psychological counseling, women's center.

Athletics Member NJCAA. *Intercollegiate sports:* baseball M, basketball M, golf M, tennis M/W, volleyball M/W. *Intramural sports:* basketball M, football M, softball M/W, volleyball M/W.

Costs (2001–02) *Tuition:* area resident $780 full-time, $26 per credit part-time; state resident $1380 full-time, $46 per credit part-time; nonresident $2280 full-time, $76 per credit part-time. Full-time tuition and fees vary according to course load. Part-time tuition and fees vary according to course load. *Waivers:* employees or children of employees.

Applying *Options:* early admission, deferred entrance. *Recommended:* high school transcript. *Application deadline:* rolling (freshmen), rolling (transfers). *Notification:* continuous (freshmen).

Admissions Contact Ms. Linda Richardson, Director of Admissions/Registrar, Eastfield College, 3737 Motley Drive, Mesquite, TX 75150-2099. *Phone:* 972-860-7105. *Fax:* 912-860-8306. *E-mail:* efc@dcccd.edu.

EDUCATION AMERICA, DALLAS CAMPUS
Garland, Texas

Admissions Contact 1800 East Gate Drive, Garland, TX 75041.

EDUCATION AMERICA, FORT WORTH CAMPUS
Fort Worth, Texas

Admissions Contact 300 East Loop 820, Fort Worth, TX 76112.

EDUCATION AMERICA, HOUSTON CAMPUS
Houston, Texas

Admissions Contact 9421 West Sam Houston Parkway, Houston, TX 77099.

EL CENTRO COLLEGE
Dallas, Texas

- **County-supported** 2-year, founded 1966, part of Dallas County Community College District System
- **Calendar** semesters
- **Degree** certificates and associate
- **Urban** 2-acre campus
- **Coed,** 4,923 undergraduate students, 32% full-time, 70% women, 30% men

Undergraduates 1,575 full-time, 3,348 part-time. Students come from 17 states and territories, 10 other countries, 1% are from out of state, 36% African American, 3% Asian American or Pacific Islander, 24% Hispanic American, 0.7% Native American, 3% international, 41% transferred in. *Retention:* 15% of 2001 full-time freshmen returned.

Freshmen *Admission:* 1,028 admitted, 1,028 enrolled.

Faculty *Total:* 526, 21% full-time. *Student/faculty ratio:* 18:1.

Majors Accounting; architectural engineering technology; baker/pastry chef; business administration; business computer facilities operation; cardiovascular technology; clothing/textiles; computer programming; computer science; criminal justice studies; culinary arts; data processing; data processing technology; diagnostic medical sonography; drafting; emergency medical technology; fashion design/illustration; food products retailing; food sciences; food services technology; general office/clerical; hospitality management; hotel and restaurant management; information sciences/systems; information technology; interior design; law enforcement/police science; legal administrative assistant; legal studies; liberal arts and sciences/liberal studies; medical administrative assistant; medical assistant; medical laboratory technician; medical radiologic technology; medical records administration; medical technology; medical transcription; nursing; operating room technician; paralegal/legal assistant; practical nurse; radiological science; respiratory therapy; secretarial science; Web page, digital/multimedia and information resources design.

Academic Programs *Special study options:* academic remediation for entering students, adult/continuing education programs, advanced placement credit, cooperative education, distance learning, double majors, English as a second language, freshman honors college, honors programs, internships, part-time degree program, services for LD students, summer session for credit. *ROTC:* Army (c).
Library El Centro Library with 76,814 titles, 247 serial subscriptions, 4,907 audiovisual materials, an OPAC, a Web page.
Computers on Campus 500 computers available on campus for general student use. A campuswide network can be accessed from off campus. Internet access, online (class) registration, at least one staffed computer lab available.
Student Life *Housing:* college housing not available. *Activities and Organizations:* choral group, Phi Theta Kappa, Radiology Club, SPAR (Student Programs and Resources Office), Organization of Latin American Students. *Campus security:* 24-hour emergency response devices and patrols, late-night transport/escort service. *Student Services:* health clinic, personal/psychological counseling.
Athletics Member NJCAA. *Intramural sports:* basketball M, softball M/W, volleyball M/W.
Standardized Tests *Required:* DTLS, DTMS, TASP. *Recommended:* SAT I or ACT (for placement).
Costs (2001–02) *Tuition:* area resident $700 full-time, $23 per credit part-time; state resident $1300 full-time, $43 per credit part-time; nonresident $2200 full-time, $73 per credit part-time. Full-time tuition and fees vary according to course load. Part-time tuition and fees vary according to course load. *Required fees:* $10 full-time, $5 per term part-time. *Payment plans:* tuition prepayment, installment. *Waivers:* employees or children of employees.
Applying *Options:* electronic application, early admission. *Required for some:* high school transcript. *Application deadline:* rolling (freshmen), rolling (transfers).
Admissions Contact Ms. Stevie Stewart, Director of Admissions and Registrar, El Centro College, 801 Main Street, Dallas, TX 75202. *Phone:* 214-860-2618. *E-mail:* sgs5310@dcccd.edu.

EL PASO COMMUNITY COLLEGE
El Paso, Texas

- **County-supported** 2-year, founded 1969
- **Calendar** semesters
- **Degree** certificates and associate
- **Urban** campus
- **Endowment** $24,000
- **Coed**

Student Life *Campus security:* 24-hour patrols, late-night transport/escort service.
Athletics Member NJCAA.
Standardized Tests *Required:* TASP.
Costs (2001–02) *Tuition:* state resident $1117 full-time, $339 per term part-time; nonresident $1539 full-time, $550 per term part-time. Part-time tuition and fees vary according to course load. *Required fees:* $400 full-time, $128 per term part-time.
Financial Aid In 2001, 750 Federal Work-Study jobs (averaging $1800). 50 State and other part-time jobs (averaging $1800).
Applying *Options:* early admission, deferred entrance. *Application fee:* $10.
Admissions Contact Mr. Daryle Hendry, Director of Admissions, El Paso Community College, PO Box 20500, El Paso, TX 79998-0500. *Phone:* 915-831-2580.

FRANK PHILLIPS COLLEGE
Borger, Texas

Admissions Contact Mrs. Daytha Trimble, Director of Admissions, Frank Phillips College, Borger, TX 79008-5118. *Phone:* 806-274-5311. *Toll-free phone:* 800-687-2056. *Fax:* 806-274-6835. *E-mail:* dtrimble@fpc.cc.tx.us.

GALVESTON COLLEGE
Galveston, Texas

- **State and locally supported** 2-year, founded 1967
- **Calendar** semesters
- **Degree** certificates and associate
- **Urban** 11-acre campus with easy access to Houston
- **Coed,** 2,255 undergraduate students, 30% full-time, 66% women, 34% men

Undergraduates 682 full-time, 1,573 part-time. Students come from 29 states and territories, 19 other countries, 3% are from out of state, 20% African American, 3% Asian American or Pacific Islander, 22% Hispanic American, 0.1% Native American, 2% international, 14% transferred in.
Freshmen *Admission:* 416 applied, 416 admitted, 416 enrolled.
Faculty *Total:* 101, 41% full-time, 11% with terminal degrees.
Majors Behavioral sciences; biological/physical sciences; business administration; computer science; computer science related; computer/technical support; culinary arts; data entry/microcomputer applications; education; emergency medical technology; English; history; hotel and restaurant management; humanities; information technology; law enforcement/police science; liberal arts and sciences/liberal studies; mathematics; medical radiologic technology; modern languages; music; natural sciences; nuclear medical technology; nursing; physical education; physical sciences; practical nurse; secretarial science; social sciences; social work; theater arts/drama; Web page, digital/multimedia and information resources design; word processing.
Academic Programs *Special study options:* academic remediation for entering students, adult/continuing education programs, advanced placement credit, cooperative education, distance learning, English as a second language, internships, off-campus study, part-time degree program, services for LD students, summer session for credit.
Library David Glenn Hunt Memorial Library with 43,749 titles, 1,500 audiovisual materials, an OPAC.
Computers on Campus 173 computers available on campus for general student use. Internet access, at least one staffed computer lab available.
Student Life *Housing:* college housing not available. *Activities and Organizations:* drama/theater group, choral group, student government, Phi Theta Kappa, Student Nurses Association, ATTC, Hispanic Student Organization. *Campus security:* 24-hour emergency response devices, late-night transport/escort service. *Student Services:* personal/psychological counseling.
Athletics Member NJCAA. *Intercollegiate sports:* baseball M(s), softball W(s), volleyball W(s). *Intramural sports:* basketball M/W, bowling M/W, volleyball M/W.
Costs (2001–02) *Tuition:* state resident $240 full-time, $200 per term part-time; nonresident $900 full-time, $400 per term part-time. *Required fees:* $320 full-time, $120 per term part-time.
Financial Aid In 2001, 36 Federal Work-Study jobs (averaging $2000).
Applying *Options:* common application. *Required for some:* high school transcript. *Application deadline:* rolling (freshmen), rolling (transfers). *Notification:* continuous (freshmen).
Admissions Contact Dr. Gaynelle Hayes, Vice President for Student Development Services and Enrollment Management, Galveston College, 4015 Avenue Q, Galveston, TX 77550-7496. *Phone:* 409-763-6551 Ext. 205. *Fax:* 409-762-0667. *E-mail:* lhumphries@gc.edu.

GRAYSON COUNTY COLLEGE
Denison, Texas

- **State and locally supported** 2-year, founded 1964
- **Calendar** semesters
- **Degree** certificates, diplomas, and associate
- **Rural** 500-acre campus
- **Coed,** 3,471 undergraduate students, 47% full-time, 61% women, 39% men

Undergraduates 1,623 full-time, 1,848 part-time. Students come from 3 states and territories, 2 other countries. *Retention:* 54% of 2001 full-time freshmen returned.
Freshmen *Admission:* 3,471 applied, 3,471 admitted, 1,057 enrolled.
Faculty *Total:* 219, 43% full-time. *Student/faculty ratio:* 16:1.
Majors Accounting; art; art education; auto body repair; biology; business administration; chemistry; computer engineering technology; computer science; cosmetology; criminal justice/law enforcement administration; drafting; education; electrical/electronic engineering technology; elementary education; geology; heating/air conditioning/refrigeration; landscaping management; law enforcement/police science; legal administrative assistant; liberal arts and sciences/liberal studies; machine technology; management information systems/business data processing; mathematics; medical laboratory technician; medical technology; music; nursing; physical education; physics; pre-engineering; psychology; real estate; secretarial science; sociology; speech/rhetorical studies; theater arts/drama; veterinary sciences; welding technology.

Grayson County College (continued)

Academic Programs *Special study options:* academic remediation for entering students, adult/continuing education programs, advanced placement credit, English as a second language, honors programs, part-time degree program, summer session for credit.

Library 51,500 titles, 310 serial subscriptions.

Computers on Campus 25 computers available on campus for general student use. At least one staffed computer lab available.

Student Life *Activities and Organizations:* drama/theater group.

Athletics Member NJCAA. *Intercollegiate sports:* basketball M(s)/W(s), tennis M(s)/W(s). *Intramural sports:* basketball M/W, tennis M/W.

Standardized Tests *Required:* TASP. *Recommended:* SAT I or ACT (for placement).

Costs (2002–03) *Tuition:* area resident $576 full-time, $33 per semester hour part-time; state resident $720 full-time, $39 per semester hour part-time; nonresident $1440 full-time, $75 per semester hour part-time. *Required fees:* $216 full-time, $7 per semester hour. *Room and board:* $2530.

Applying *Options:* early admission, deferred entrance. *Application deadline:* 8/31 (freshmen). *Notification:* continuous (freshmen).

Admissions Contact Dr. David Petrash, Associate Vice President for Admissions, Records and Institutional Research, Grayson County College, 6101 Grayson Drive, Denison, TX 75020-8299. *Phone:* 903-465-6030. *Fax:* 903-463-5284.

HALLMARK INSTITUTE OF AERONAUTICS
San Antonio, Texas

Admissions Contact Mr. David McSorley, Director, Hallmark Institute of Aeronautics, 8901 Wetmore Road, San Antonio, TX 78216. *Phone:* 210-690-9000. *Toll-free phone:* 800-683-3600.

HALLMARK INSTITUTE OF TECHNOLOGY
San Antonio, Texas

Admissions Contact Mr. John K. Boggs, Director of Admissions, Hallmark Institute of Technology, 10401 IH 10 West, San Antonio, TX 78230-1737. *Phone:* 210-690-9000 Ext. 212. *Toll-free phone:* 800-880-6600. *Fax:* 210-697-8225.

HILL COLLEGE OF THE HILL JUNIOR COLLEGE DISTRICT
Hillsboro, Texas

- **District-supported** 2-year, founded 1923
- **Calendar** semesters
- **Degree** certificates and associate
- **Small-town** 80-acre campus with easy access to Dallas-Fort Worth
- **Endowment** $416,886
- **Coed,** 2,421 undergraduate students, 40% full-time, 55% women, 45% men

Undergraduates 958 full-time, 1,463 part-time. Students come from 8 states and territories, 28 other countries, 6% are from out of state, 6% African American, 0.5% Asian American or Pacific Islander, 8% Hispanic American, 0.6% Native American, 3% international, 8% transferred in, 14% live on campus. *Retention:* 90% of 2001 full-time freshmen returned.

Freshmen *Admission:* 564 enrolled.

Faculty *Total:* 159, 47% full-time. *Student/faculty ratio:* 25:1.

Majors Accounting; agricultural business; agricultural economics; agricultural sciences; animal sciences; applied art; art; art education; art history; auto body repair; auto mechanic/technician; behavioral sciences; biological/physical sciences; biology; botany; business administration; business economics; ceramic arts; chemistry; child care/development; child care provider; civil engineering technology; computer programming; computer programming related; computer science; computer typography/composition; cosmetology; criminal justice/law enforcement administration; dairy science; data processing technology; developmental/child psychology; drafting; drafting/design technology; economics; education; electrical/electronic engineering technology; elementary education; engineering; engineering science; English; farm/ranch management; finance; fire science; geography; geology; graphic design/commercial art/illustration; health education; health science; heating/air conditioning/refrigeration; history; home economics; horticulture science; humanities; information sciences/systems; journalism; law enforcement/police science; liberal arts and sciences/liberal studies; machine technology; mass communications; mathematics; music; music history; music (piano and organ performance); music teacher education; music theory and composition; music (voice and choral/opera performance); photography; physical education; physical sciences; physics; political science; practical nurse; pre-engineering; psychology; public health; public policy analysis; real estate; robotics; secretarial science; social sciences; social work; sociology; Spanish; speech/rhetorical studies; theater arts/drama; welding technology; zoology.

Academic Programs *Special study options:* academic remediation for entering students, adult/continuing education programs, advanced placement credit, cooperative education, distance learning, double majors, English as a second language, honors programs, internships, part-time degree program, services for LD students, summer session for credit.

Library Hill College Library plus 1 other with 40,000 titles, 300 serial subscriptions, 500 audiovisual materials, an OPAC, a Web page.

Computers on Campus 250 computers available on campus for general student use. A campuswide network can be accessed from off campus. Internet access, at least one staffed computer lab available.

Student Life *Housing:* on-campus residence required through sophomore year. *Options:* men-only, women-only. *Activities and Organizations:* drama/theater group, choral group, International Club, Sigma Phi Omega, Phi Theta Kappa, Fellowship of Christian Athletes, Psi Beta. *Campus security:* late-night transport/escort service, controlled dormitory access, security officers.

Athletics Member NJCAA. *Intercollegiate sports:* baseball M(s), basketball M(s)/W(s), soccer W(s), softball W(s), volleyball W(s). *Intramural sports:* basketball M/W, volleyball W.

Standardized Tests *Required:* TASP. *Recommended:* SAT I or ACT (for placement).

Costs (2001–02) *Tuition:* area resident $1030 full-time, $132 per credit hour part-time; state resident $1276 full-time, $164 per credit hour part-time; nonresident $1670 full-time, $364 per credit hour part-time. Full-time tuition and fees vary according to course load. Part-time tuition and fees vary according to course load. *Required fees:* $35 full-time, $10 per term part-time. *Room and board:* $2680; room only: $700. Room and board charges vary according to board plan. *Payment plan:* installment. *Waivers:* senior citizens and employees or children of employees.

Financial Aid In 2001, 51 Federal Work-Study jobs (averaging $858). 20 State and other part-time jobs (averaging $230).

Applying *Options:* early admission, deferred entrance. *Required:* high school transcript. *Application deadline:* rolling (freshmen), rolling (transfers).

Admissions Contact Ms. Diane Harvey, Director of Admissions and Records, Hill College of the Hill Junior College District, PO Box 619, Hillsboro, TX 76645-0619. *Phone:* 254-582-2555 Ext. 315. *Fax:* 254-582-7591. *E-mail:* jcutting@hillcollege.hill-college.cc.tx.us.

HOUSTON COMMUNITY COLLEGE SYSTEM
Houston, Texas

- **State and locally supported** 2-year, founded 1971
- **Calendar** semesters
- **Degree** certificates and associate
- **Urban** campus
- **Coed,** 38,175 undergraduate students, 30% full-time, 59% women, 41% men

Undergraduates 11,602 full-time, 26,573 part-time. Students come from 134 other countries, 20% African American, 13% Asian American or Pacific Islander, 23% Hispanic American, 0.2% Native American, 11% international.

Freshmen *Admission:* 4,590 applied, 4,590 admitted, 4,590 enrolled.

Faculty *Total:* 2,019, 33% full-time, 9% with terminal degrees. *Student/faculty ratio:* 21:1.

Majors Accounting; agricultural sciences; auto mechanic/technician; business administration; business communications; business marketing and marketing management; cartography; child care/development; child care/guidance; civil engineering technology; commercial photography; computer engineering technology; computer/information sciences; computer science; construction technology; court reporting; drafting; electrical/electronic engineering technology; emergency medical technology; engineering technology; exercise sciences; fashion design/illustration; fashion merchandising; finance; fire science; graphic design/commercial art/illustration; graphic/printing equipment; health services administration; home economics; horticulture science; hotel and restaurant management; human resources management; industrial radiologic technology; industrial technology; insurance/risk management; interior design; law enforcement/police science; liberal arts and sciences/liberal studies; logistics/materials management; mass communications; medical administrative assistant; medical laboratory technician; medical radiologic technology; medical records administration; medical records technology; mental health/rehabilitation; music business management/merchandising; music theory and composition; nuclear medical technology;

nursing; occupational safety/health technology; occupational therapy assistant; paralegal/legal assistant; physical therapy assistant; psychiatric/mental health services; radio/television broadcasting technology; real estate; respiratory therapy; secretarial science; sign language interpretation; social sciences; technical/business writing; theater arts/drama; transportation technology; travel/tourism management.

Academic Programs *Special study options:* academic remediation for entering students, adult/continuing education programs, advanced placement credit, cooperative education, English as a second language, part-time degree program, services for LD students, summer session for credit. *ROTC:* Army (c).

Library Main Library plus 19 others with 125,041 titles, 1,793 serial subscriptions, 13,348 audiovisual materials, an OPAC, a Web page.

Computers on Campus 3200 computers available on campus for general student use. A campuswide network can be accessed from off campus. At least one staffed computer lab available.

Student Life *Housing:* college housing not available. *Activities and Organizations:* drama/theater group, student-run newspaper, television station, Phi Theta Kappa, Eastwood Student Association, Eagle's Club, Society of Hispanic Professional Engineers, International Student Association. *Campus security:* 24-hour emergency response devices and patrols, late-night transport/escort service. *Student Services:* personal/psychological counseling.

Standardized Tests *Required:* TASP, ACT ASSET. *Required for some:* ACT (for placement). *Recommended:* SAT I (for placement).

Costs (2001–02) *Tuition:* area resident $936 full-time, $39 per semester hour part-time; state resident $1632 full-time, $68 per semester hour part-time; nonresident $2712 full-time, $113 per semester hour part-time. *Payment plan:* installment. *Waivers:* senior citizens.

Financial Aid In 2001, 285 Federal Work-Study jobs (averaging $2000). 36 State and other part-time jobs (averaging $1600).

Applying *Options:* early admission. *Required for some:* high school transcript, interview. *Application deadline:* rolling (freshmen), rolling (transfers). *Notification:* continuous (freshmen).

Admissions Contact Ms. Mary Lemburg, Registrar, Houston Community College System, 3100 Main Street, P.O. Box 667517, Houston, TX 77266-7517. *Phone:* 713-718-8500.

HOWARD COLLEGE
Big Spring, Texas

- **State and locally supported** 2-year, founded 1945, part of Howard County Junior College District System
- **Calendar** semesters
- **Degree** certificates and associate
- **Small-town** 120-acre campus
- **Endowment** $928,972
- **Coed,** 2,135 undergraduate students, 45% full-time, 61% women, 39% men

Undergraduates 957 full-time, 1,178 part-time. Students come from 21 states and territories, 6 other countries, 9% are from out of state, 5% African American, 0.9% Asian American or Pacific Islander, 27% Hispanic American, 0.2% Native American, 0.3% international, 10% transferred in, 15% live on campus.

Freshmen *Admission:* 722 enrolled.

Faculty *Total:* 146, 66% full-time. *Student/faculty ratio:* 14:1.

Majors Accounting; agricultural sciences; alcohol/drug abuse counseling; art; auto mechanic/technician; behavioral sciences; biology; business administration; chemistry; child care/development; computer programming; computer science; computer science related; cosmetology; dental hygiene; drafting; English; finance; industrial arts; law enforcement/police science; mathematics; medical records administration; music teacher education; nursing; ornamental horticulture; physical education; practical nurse; respiratory therapy; social sciences; speech/rhetorical studies; theater arts/drama.

Academic Programs *Special study options:* academic remediation for entering students, adult/continuing education programs, advanced placement credit, cooperative education, distance learning, English as a second language, independent study, internships, part-time degree program, services for LD students, summer session for credit.

Library Howard College Library with 27,481 titles, 232 serial subscriptions.

Computers on Campus 40 computers available on campus for general student use. A campuswide network can be accessed from student residence rooms. Internet access, at least one staffed computer lab available.

Student Life *Housing:* on-campus residence required for freshman year. *Options:* men-only, women-only. *Activities and Organizations:* drama/theater group, choral group, Phi Theta Kappa, Student Government Association, Mexican American Student Association, Baptist Student Ministries. *Campus security:* 24-hour patrols. *Student Services:* health clinic, personal/psychological counseling.

Athletics Member NJCAA. *Intercollegiate sports:* baseball M(s), basketball M(s)/W(s), softball W(s). *Intramural sports:* basketball M/W, bowling M/W, football M/W, racquetball M/W, softball W, volleyball M/W.

Standardized Tests *Required:* TASP. *Required for some:* SAT I or ACT (for placement).

Costs (2001–02) *Tuition:* state resident $552 full-time, $23 per credit hour part-time; nonresident $768 full-time, $32 per credit hour part-time. Full-time tuition and fees vary according to course load, location, and program. Part-time tuition and fees vary according to course load, location, and program. *Required fees:* $578 full-time. *Payment plan:* installment. *Waivers:* senior citizens.

Applying *Options:* early admission. *Required:* high school transcript. *Application deadline:* rolling (freshmen), rolling (transfers). *Notification:* continuous until 8/31 (freshmen).

Admissions Contact Ms. Lisa Currier, Registrar, Howard College, 1001 Birdwell Lane, Big Spring, TX 79720-3702. *Phone:* 915-264-5105.

ITT TECHNICAL INSTITUTE
Austin, Texas

- **Proprietary** 2-year, founded 1985, part of ITT Educational Services, Inc
- **Calendar** quarters
- **Degree** associate
- **Urban** campus
- **Coed,** 644 undergraduate students

Majors Computer/information sciences related; computer programming; drafting; electrical/electronic engineering technologies related; information technology.

Student Life *Housing:* college housing not available.

Costs (2001–02) *Tuition:* Full-time tuition and fees vary according to program. Part-time tuition and fees vary according to program. $260—$330 per credit hour.

Financial Aid In 2001, 1 Federal Work-Study job.

Applying *Options:* deferred entrance. *Application fee:* $100. *Required:* high school transcript, interview. *Recommended:* letters of recommendation. *Application deadline:* rolling (freshmen), rolling (transfers). *Notification:* continuous (freshmen).

Admissions Contact Mr. Mark Gurganus, Director of Recruitment, ITT Technical Institute, 6330 Highway 290 East, Austin, TX 78723. *Phone:* 512-467-6800. *Toll-free phone:* 800-431-0677.

ITT TECHNICAL INSTITUTE
Houston, Texas

- **Proprietary** 2-year, founded 1985, part of ITT Educational Services, Inc
- **Calendar** quarters
- **Degree** associate
- **Suburban** 1-acre campus
- **Coed,** 567 undergraduate students

Majors Computer/information sciences related; computer programming; drafting; electrical/electronic engineering technologies related; information technology.

Student Life *Housing:* college housing not available.

Costs (2001–02) *Tuition:* Full-time tuition and fees vary according to program. Part-time tuition and fees vary according to program. $260—$330 per credit hour.

Applying *Options:* deferred entrance. *Application fee:* $100. *Required:* high school transcript, interview. *Recommended:* letters of recommendation. *Application deadline:* rolling (freshmen), rolling (transfers). *Notification:* continuous (freshmen).

Admissions Contact Mr. Robert Roloff, Director of Recruitment, ITT Technical Institute, 15621 Blue Ash Drive, Houston, TX 77090-5821. *Phone:* 281-873-0512. *Toll-free phone:* 800-879-6486. *Fax:* 281-873-0518.

ITT TECHNICAL INSTITUTE
Arlington, Texas

- **Proprietary** 2-year, founded 1982, part of ITT Educational Services, Inc
- **Calendar** quarters
- **Degree** associate

ITT Technical Institute (continued)
- **Suburban** campus with easy access to Dallas-Fort Worth
- **Coed,** 475 undergraduate students

Majors Computer/information sciences related; computer programming; drafting; electrical/electronic engineering technologies related; information technology.
Student Life *Housing:* college housing not available.
Costs (2001–02) *Tuition:* Full-time tuition and fees vary according to program. Part-time tuition and fees vary according to program. $260—$330 per credit.
Applying *Options:* deferred entrance. *Application fee:* $100. *Required:* high school transcript, interview. *Recommended:* letters of recommendation. *Application deadline:* rolling (freshmen), rolling (transfers). *Notification:* continuous (freshmen).
Admissions Contact Ms. Paulette Gallerson, Director, ITT Technical Institute, 551 Ryan Plaza Drive, Arlington, TX 76011. *Phone:* 817-794-5100.

ITT Technical Institute
Houston, Texas

- **Proprietary** 2-year, founded 1983, part of ITT Educational Services, Inc
- **Calendar** quarters
- **Degree** associate
- **Urban** 4-acre campus
- **Coed,** 569 undergraduate students

Majors Computer/information sciences related; computer programming; drafting; electrical/electronic engineering technologies related; information technology.
Student Life *Housing:* college housing not available. *Activities and Organizations:* student-run newspaper.
Costs (2001–02) *Tuition:* Full-time tuition and fees vary according to program. Part-time tuition and fees vary according to program. $260—$330 per credit hour.
Applying *Options:* deferred entrance. *Application fee:* $100. *Required:* high school transcript, interview. *Recommended:* letters of recommendation. *Application deadline:* rolling (freshmen), rolling (transfers). *Notification:* continuous (freshmen).
Admissions Contact Mr. Robert Van Elsen, Director, ITT Technical Institute, 2950 South Gessner, Houston, TX 77063-3751. *Phone:* 713-952-2294. *Toll-free phone:* 800-235-4787.

ITT Technical Institute
San Antonio, Texas

- **Proprietary** 2-year, founded 1988, part of ITT Educational Services, Inc
- **Calendar** quarters
- **Degree** associate
- **Urban** campus
- **Coed,** 699 undergraduate students

Majors Computer/information sciences related; computer programming; drafting; electrical/electronic engineering technologies related; information technology.
Student Life *Housing:* college housing not available. *Activities and Organizations:* student-run newspaper.
Costs (2001–02) *Tuition:* Full-time tuition and fees vary according to program. Part-time tuition and fees vary according to program. $260—$330 per credit hour.
Applying *Options:* deferred entrance. *Required:* high school transcript, interview. *Recommended:* letters of recommendation. *Application deadline:* rolling (freshmen), rolling (transfers). *Notification:* continuous (freshmen).
Admissions Contact Mr. Doug Howard, Director of Recruitment, ITT Technical Institute, 5700 Northwest Parkway, San Antonio, TX 78249-3303. *Phone:* 210-694-4612. *Toll-free phone:* 800-880-0570.

ITT Technical Institute
Richardson, Texas

- **Proprietary** 2-year, founded 1989
- **Calendar** quarters
- **Degree** associate
- **Suburban** campus with easy access to Dallas-Fort Worth
- **Coed,** 567 undergraduate students

Majors Computer/information sciences related; computer programming; drafting; electrical/electronic engineering technologies related; information technology.
Student Life *Housing:* college housing not available.
Costs (2001–02) *Tuition:* Full-time tuition and fees vary according to program. Part-time tuition and fees vary according to program. $260—$330 per credit hour.
Applying *Options:* deferred entrance. *Application fee:* $100. *Required:* high school transcript, interview. *Recommended:* letters of recommendation. *Application deadline:* rolling (freshmen). *Notification:* continuous (freshmen).
Admissions Contact Ms. Carrie Austin, Director, ITT Technical Institute, 2101 Waterview Parkway, Richardson, TX 75080. *Phone:* 972-279-0500. *Toll-free phone:* 888-488-5761.

ITT Technical Institute
Houston, Texas

- **Proprietary** 2-year, founded 1995, part of ITT Educational Services, Inc
- **Calendar** quarters
- **Degree** associate
- 466 undergraduate students

Majors Computer/information sciences related; computer programming; drafting; electrical/electronic engineering technologies related; information technology.
Student Life *Housing:* college housing not available.
Costs (2001–02) *Tuition:* Full-time tuition and fees vary according to program. Part-time tuition and fees vary according to program. $260—$330 per credit hour.
Applying *Options:* deferred entrance. *Application fee:* $100. *Required:* high school transcript, interview. *Recommended:* letters of recommendation. *Application deadline:* rolling (freshmen), rolling (transfers).
Admissions Contact Mr. Bob Jeffords, Director of Recruitment, ITT Technical Institute, 2222 Bay Area Boulevard, Houston, TX 77058. *Phone:* 281-486-2630. *Toll-free phone:* 888-488-9347.

Jacksonville College
Jacksonville, Texas

- **Independent Baptist** 2-year, founded 1899
- **Calendar** semesters
- **Degree** diplomas and associate
- **Small-town** 20-acre campus
- **Coed,** 259 undergraduate students, 76% full-time, 58% women, 42% men

Undergraduates 196 full-time, 63 part-time. Students come from 16 states and territories, 15 other countries, 6% are from out of state, 39% live on campus.
Freshmen *Admission:* 187 applied, 116 admitted, 89 enrolled.
Faculty *Total:* 25, 44% full-time, 8% with terminal degrees. *Student/faculty ratio:* 14:1.
Majors Biological/physical sciences; liberal arts and sciences/liberal studies.
Academic Programs *Special study options:* academic remediation for entering students, adult/continuing education programs, advanced placement credit, part-time degree program, summer session for credit.
Library Weatherby Memorial Building plus 1 other with 22,000 titles, 170 serial subscriptions.
Computers on Campus 20 computers available on campus for general student use. Internet access, at least one staffed computer lab available.
Student Life *Housing:* on-campus residence required through sophomore year. *Activities and Organizations:* drama/theater group, choral group, Drama Club, Ministerial Alliance, Mission Band. *Campus security:* 24-hour emergency response devices, evening security personnel. *Student Services:* health clinic, personal/psychological counseling.
Athletics Member NJCAA. *Intercollegiate sports:* basketball M(s)/W, volleyball W(s). *Intramural sports:* basketball M/W, table tennis M/W, tennis M/W, volleyball M/W.
Standardized Tests *Required:* TASP.
Costs (2002–03) *Comprehensive fee:* $6602 includes full-time tuition ($3600), mandatory fees ($374), and room and board ($2628). Part-time tuition: $150 per semester hour. Part-time tuition and fees vary according to course load. *Required fees:* $160 per term part-time. *Payment plan:* installment. *Waivers:* employees or children of employees.
Applying *Options:* electronic application, early admission. *Application fee:* $15. *Application deadlines:* 7/1 (freshmen), 7/1 (transfers). *Notification:* continuous until 7/1 (freshmen).

Admissions Contact Mr. Michael Fink, Director of Admissions, Jacksonville College, 105 B.J. Albritton Drive, Jacksonville, TX 75766. *Phone:* 903-586-2518 Ext. 225. *Toll-free phone:* 800-256-8522. *Fax:* 903-586-0743. *E-mail:* admissions@jacksonville-college.org.

KD STUDIO
Dallas, Texas

- **Proprietary** 2-year, founded 1979
- **Calendar** semesters
- **Degree** associate
- **Urban** campus
- **Coed,** 148 undergraduate students, 100% full-time, 50% women, 50% men

Undergraduates 148 full-time. Students come from 10 states and territories, 4% are from out of state, 24% African American, 3% Asian American or Pacific Islander, 14% Hispanic American, 0.7% Native American, 0.7% international.
Freshmen *Admission:* 29 enrolled.
Faculty *Total:* 24, 4% full-time. *Student/faculty ratio:* 15:1.
Majors Acting/directing.
Academic Programs *Special study options:* cooperative education.
Library KD Studio Library with 800 titles, 15 serial subscriptions.
Computers on Campus 1 computer available on campus for general student use. Internet access, at least one staffed computer lab available.
Student Life *Housing:* college housing not available. *Activities and Organizations:* drama/theater group, Student Council. *Campus security:* 24-hour emergency response devices and patrols.
Costs (2002–03) *Tuition:* $8050 full-time. No tuition increase for student's term of enrollment. *Required fees:* $100 full-time. *Payment plan:* installment. *Waivers:* employees or children of employees.
Applying *Options:* common application, deferred entrance. *Application fee:* $100. *Required:* essay or personal statement, high school transcript, interview, audition. *Required for some:* letters of recommendation. *Application deadline:* rolling (freshmen), rolling (transfers).
Admissions Contact Mr. T. A. Taylor, Director of Education, KD Studio, 2600 Stemmons Freeway, #117, Dallas, TX 75207. *Phone:* 214-638-0484. *Fax:* 214-630-5140. *E-mail:* information@kdstudio.com.

KILGORE COLLEGE
Kilgore, Texas

- **State and locally supported** 2-year, founded 1935
- **Calendar** semesters
- **Degree** certificates and associate
- **Small-town** 35-acre campus with easy access to Dallas-Fort Worth
- **Endowment** $4.6 million
- **Coed,** 4,194 undergraduate students, 53% full-time, 61% women, 39% men

Undergraduates 2,237 full-time, 1,957 part-time. Students come from 19 states and territories, 41 other countries, 2% are from out of state, 14% African American, 0.3% Asian American or Pacific Islander, 3% Hispanic American, 0.1% Native American, 3% international, 7% transferred in, 12% live on campus. *Retention:* 51% of 2001 full-time freshmen returned.
Freshmen *Admission:* 1,872 applied, 1,164 admitted, 1,130 enrolled. *Test scores:* SAT verbal scores over 500: 43%; SAT math scores over 500: 45%; ACT scores over 18: 70%; SAT verbal scores over 600: 8%; SAT math scores over 600: 9%; ACT scores over 24: 17%; SAT math scores over 700: 1%.
Faculty *Total:* 257, 53% full-time, 10% with terminal degrees. *Student/faculty ratio:* 18:1.
Majors Accounting; accounting technician; aerospace engineering; agricultural sciences; art; auto mechanic/technician; biological/physical sciences; business; business administration; business systems networking/ telecommunications; chemistry; child care/guidance; commercial photography; computer/information sciences; computer programming; corrections; criminal justice/law enforcement administration; criminal justice studies; dance; data processing technology; design/visual communications; diesel engine mechanic; drafting; electrical/electronic engineering technology; elementary education; emergency medical technology; English; executive assistant; fashion merchandising; finance; fire science; forestry; general studies; geology; graphic design/commercial art/illustration; graphic/printing equipment; health education; heating/air conditioning/refrigeration; industrial technology; journalism; law enforcement/police science; machine technology; management information systems/business data processing; mathematics; medical assistant; medical laboratory technician; medical radiologic technology; medical technology; metallurgical technology; music; nursing; occupational safety/health technology; operations management; paralegal/legal assistant; physical education; physical therapy assistant; physics; pre-pharmacy studies; psychology; religious studies; secretarial science; social sciences; speech/rhetorical studies; theater arts/drama; trade/industrial education.
Academic Programs *Special study options:* academic remediation for entering students, adult/continuing education programs, advanced placement credit, cooperative education, English as a second language, internships, part-time degree program, services for LD students, student-designed majors, summer session for credit. *ROTC:* Army (c).
Library Randolph C. Watson Library plus 1 other with 65,000 titles, 6,679 serial subscriptions, 13,351 audiovisual materials, an OPAC, a Web page.
Computers on Campus 302 computers available on campus for general student use. Internet access, online (class) registration, at least one staffed computer lab available.
Student Life *Housing:* on-campus residence required for freshman year. *Options:* coed, men-only, women-only. *Activities and Organizations:* drama/theater group, choral group, marching band, Phi Theta Kappa, Student Government Association, Ambucs. *Campus security:* 24-hour emergency response devices and patrols.
Athletics Member NJCAA. *Intercollegiate sports:* basketball M(s)/W(s), football M(s). *Intramural sports:* basketball M/W, football M/W, golf M/W, racquetball M/W, swimming M/W, tennis M/W, volleyball M/W.
Standardized Tests *Required:* TASP. *Recommended:* SAT I or ACT (for placement).
Costs (2001–02) *Tuition:* area resident $336 full-time, $14 per semester hour part-time; state resident $864 full-time, $36 per semester hour part-time; nonresident $1248 full-time, $52 per semester hour part-time. *Required fees:* $408 full-time, $17 per semester hour. *Room and board:* $2800. Room and board charges vary according to board plan and location. *Payment plan:* installment. *Waivers:* employees or children of employees.
Applying *Options:* early admission. *Required:* high school transcript. *Required for some:* interview. *Application deadline:* rolling (freshmen), rolling (transfers).
Admissions Contact Kilgore College, 1100 Broadway, Kilgore, TX 75662. *Phone:* 903-983-8200. *Fax:* 903-983-8607. *E-mail:* register@kilgore.cc.tx.us.

KINGWOOD COLLEGE
Kingwood, Texas

- **State and locally supported** 2-year, founded 1984, part of North Harris Montgomery Community College District
- **Calendar** semesters
- **Degree** certificates and associate
- **Suburban** 264-acre campus with easy access to Houston
- **Coed,** 5,302 undergraduate students, 34% full-time, 62% women, 38% men

Undergraduates 1,821 full-time, 3,481 part-time. Students come from 32 other countries, 0.4% are from out of state, 6% African American, 2% Asian American or Pacific Islander, 10% Hispanic American, 0.5% Native American, 1% international, 5% transferred in.
Freshmen *Admission:* 1,467 applied, 1,467 admitted, 1,687 enrolled.
Faculty *Total:* 238, 29% full-time. *Student/faculty ratio:* 16:1.
Majors Accounting; biology; business administration; computer engineering technology; computer graphics; computer/information sciences; computer typography/composition; education; English; foreign languages/literatures; information sciences/systems; mathematics; occupational therapy; practical nurse; psychology; social sciences; visual/performing arts.
Academic Programs *Special study options:* academic remediation for entering students, accelerated degree program, advanced placement credit, cooperative education, distance learning, double majors, English as a second language, external degree program, honors programs, independent study, internships, part-time degree program, services for LD students, summer session for credit.
Library Kingwood College Library with 35,000 titles, 500 serial subscriptions, an OPAC, a Web page.
Computers on Campus 540 computers available on campus for general student use. A campuswide network can be accessed from off campus. At least one staffed computer lab available.
Student Life *Housing:* college housing not available. *Activities and Organizations:* drama/theater group, student-run television station, choral group, Phi Theta Kappa, Office Administration Club, African American Student Association, Student Government Association, Delta Epsilon Chi. *Campus security:* 24-hour emergency response devices and patrols, late-night transport/escort service. *Student Services:* personal/psychological counseling.
Athletics *Intramural sports:* baseball M.

Kingwood College (continued)

Standardized Tests *Required for some:* SAT I or ACT (for placement), ACT ASSET.

Costs (2001–02) *Tuition:* area resident $744 full-time, $31 per credit part-time; state resident $1704 full-time, $71 per credit part-time; nonresident $2064 full-time, $86 per credit part-time. Full-time tuition and fees vary according to course load and program. Part-time tuition and fees vary according to course load. *Required fees:* $60 full-time, $4 per credit, $12 per term part-time. *Payment plans:* installment, deferred payment. *Waivers:* employees or children of employees.

Financial Aid In 2001, 15 Federal Work-Study jobs, 5 State and other part-time jobs. *Financial aid deadline:* 6/30.

Applying *Options:* common application, early admission. *Required:* high school transcript. *Required for some:* essay or personal statement. *Application deadline:* rolling (freshmen), rolling (transfers).

Admissions Contact Dr. Ron Shade, Dean of Student Development, Kingwood College, 2000 Kingwood Drive, Kingwood, TX 77339. *Phone:* 281-312-1444. *Fax:* 281-312-1477. *E-mail:* ronald.shade@nhmccd.edu.

LAMAR INSTITUTE OF TECHNOLOGY
Beaumont, Texas

Admissions Contact PO Box 10043, Beaumont, TX 77710. *Toll-free phone:* 800-950-8321.

LAMAR STATE COLLEGE-ORANGE
Orange, Texas

- **State-supported** 2-year, founded 1969, part of The Texas State University System
- **Calendar** semesters
- **Degree** certificates and associate
- **Small-town** 21-acre campus
- **Endowment** $5524
- **Coed,** 2,020 undergraduate students

Undergraduates Students come from 1 other state, 9% are from out of state, 15% African American, 0.7% Asian American or Pacific Islander, 2% Hispanic American, 0.5% Native American.

Freshmen *Admission:* 669 applied, 669 admitted.

Faculty *Total:* 114, 39% full-time, 14% with terminal degrees. *Student/faculty ratio:* 17:1.

Majors Accounting; architectural engineering technology; business administration; computer science; data processing technology; environmental science; information sciences/systems; liberal arts and sciences/liberal studies; literature; mass communications; mathematics; medical laboratory technician; nursing; real estate; secretarial science; social sciences.

Academic Programs *Special study options:* academic remediation for entering students, distance learning, double majors, internships, part-time degree program, summer session for credit.

Library Lamar State College-Orange Library plus 1 other with 64,328 titles, 1,290 serial subscriptions, an OPAC.

Computers on Campus 70 computers available on campus for general student use. A campuswide network can be accessed from off campus. Internet access, at least one staffed computer lab available.

Student Life *Housing:* college housing not available. *Activities and Organizations:* student-run newspaper. *Campus security:* 24-hour emergency response devices, late-night transport/escort service.

Athletics *Intramural sports:* archery M, basketball M/W, volleyball M/W, weight lifting M/W.

Standardized Tests *Required for some:* TASP.

Costs (2001–02) *Tuition:* state resident $1056 full-time, $132 per credit part-time; nonresident $6288 full-time, $262 per credit part-time. *Required fees:* $1048 full-time.

Financial Aid In 2001, 20 Federal Work-Study jobs (averaging $3000). 2 State and other part-time jobs (averaging $2000).

Applying *Options:* common application, early admission, deferred entrance. *Required:* high school transcript. *Recommended:* minimum 2.0 GPA. *Application deadline:* rolling (freshmen), rolling (transfers). *Notification:* continuous (freshmen).

Admissions Contact Kerry Olson, Director of Admissions and Financial Aid, Lamar State College-Orange, 410 Front Street, Orange, TX 77632. *Phone:* 409-882-3362. *Toll-free phone:* 800-884-7750.

LAMAR STATE COLLEGE-PORT ARTHUR
Port Arthur, Texas

- **State-supported** 2-year, founded 1909, part of The Texas State University System
- **Calendar** semesters
- **Degree** certificates and associate
- **Suburban** 34-acre campus with easy access to Houston
- **Coed,** 2,497 undergraduate students

Undergraduates 1% are from out of state, 29% African American, 6% Asian American or Pacific Islander, 9% Hispanic American, 0.4% Native American.

Freshmen *Admission:* 486 applied, 486 admitted.

Faculty *Total:* 135, 16% with terminal degrees. *Student/faculty ratio:* 30:1.

Majors Accounting; alcohol/drug abuse counseling; auto mechanic/technician; business administration; business administration/management related; child care/development; child guidance; computer/information sciences; computer maintenance technology; cosmetology; criminal justice/law enforcement administration; electrical/electronic engineering technologies related; electrical/electronic engineering technology; environmental technology; general studies; heating/air conditioning/refrigeration; heating/air conditioning/refrigeration technology; home economics; hospitality management; instrumentation technology; legal administrative assistant; management science; medical administrative assistant; medical records administration; nursing; nursing related; operating room technician; paralegal/legal assistant; practical nurse; secretarial science; welding technology.

Academic Programs *Special study options:* academic remediation for entering students, accelerated degree program, adult/continuing education programs, advanced placement credit, cooperative education, distance learning, double majors, English as a second language, honors programs, independent study, internships, off-campus study, part-time degree program, services for LD students, summer session for credit. *ROTC:* Army (c).

Library Gates Memorial Library with 43,726 titles, 3,400 serial subscriptions, 1,493 audiovisual materials, an OPAC, a Web page.

Computers on Campus A campuswide network can be accessed from off campus. Internet access, online (class) registration, at least one staffed computer lab available.

Student Life *Housing:* college housing not available. *Activities and Organizations:* drama/theater group, student-run newspaper, Historical Society, Chi Alpha, tennis, Student Government Association, Baptist Student Ministry. *Campus security:* 24-hour emergency response devices, student patrols, late-night transport/escort service. *Student Services:* personal/psychological counseling.

Standardized Tests *Required for some:* SAT I (for placement), TASP.

Costs (2002–03) *One-time required fee:* $10. *Tuition:* state resident $1980 full-time, $66 per credit part-time; nonresident $8520 full-time, $284 per credit part-time. *Required fees:* $554 full-time, $31 per term part-time. *Waivers:* senior citizens and employees or children of employees.

Applying *Options:* common application, early admission, deferred entrance. *Required:* high school transcript. *Required for some:* interview. *Application deadline:* rolling (freshmen), rolling (transfers). *Notification:* continuous (freshmen).

Admissions Contact Mr. Tom Neal, Vice President for Student Services, Lamar State College-Port Arthur, PO Box 310, Port Arthur, TX 77641-0310. *Phone:* 409-984-6156. *Toll-free phone:* 800-477-5872. *Fax:* 409-984-6025. *E-mail:* connie.nicholas@lamarpa.edu.

LAREDO COMMUNITY COLLEGE
Laredo, Texas

- **State and locally supported** 2-year, founded 1946
- **Calendar** semesters
- **Degree** certificates and associate
- **Urban** 186-acre campus
- **Endowment** $389,879
- **Coed,** 7,493 undergraduate students, 40% full-time, 59% women, 41% men

Undergraduates Students come from 4 states and territories, 5 other countries, 0.2% African American, 0.4% Asian American or Pacific Islander, 96% Hispanic American, 0.1% Native American, 1% international.

Faculty *Total:* 327, 57% full-time, 10% with terminal degrees. *Student/faculty ratio:* 20:1.

Majors Business marketing and marketing management; child care/development; computer programming; computer programming related; computer software and media applications related; computer systems networking/telecommunications; construction technology; data entry/microcomputer applications; data entry/

microcomputer applications related; data processing technology; electrical/electronic engineering technology; emergency medical technology; fashion merchandising; fire science; hotel and restaurant management; industrial radiologic technology; information sciences/systems; information technology; international business; law enforcement/police science; liberal arts and sciences/liberal studies; medical assistant; medical laboratory technician; nursing; physical therapy; radiological science; real estate; secretarial science; social sciences.

Academic Programs *Special study options:* academic remediation for entering students, adult/continuing education programs, advanced placement credit, distance learning, double majors, English as a second language, freshman honors college, honors programs, independent study, internships, part-time degree program, services for LD students, summer session for credit.

Library Yeary Library with 88,006 titles, 555 serial subscriptions, an OPAC.

Student Life *Housing Options:* coed. *Activities and Organizations:* drama/theater group, student-run newspaper, choral group. *Campus security:* 24-hour emergency response devices and patrols, student patrols. *Student Services:* personal/psychological counseling, women's center.

Athletics Member NJCAA. *Intercollegiate sports:* baseball M(s), tennis M(s)/W(s), volleyball W(s). *Intramural sports:* cross-country running M/W, gymnastics M/W, swimming M/W, tennis M/W, track and field M/W, volleyball M/W.

Standardized Tests *Recommended:* ACT (for placement).

Costs (2002–03) *Tuition:* area resident $876 full-time, $19 per credit hour part-time; state resident $1380 full-time, $42 per credit hour part-time; nonresident $2057 full-time, $70 per credit hour part-time. *Required fees:* $14 per credit hour. *Room and board:* $3641.

Financial Aid In 2001, 282 Federal Work-Study jobs (averaging $1854).

Applying *Options:* common application, early admission, deferred entrance. *Required:* high school transcript. *Application deadline:* rolling (freshmen), rolling (transfers).

Admissions Contact Ms. Josie Soliz, Admissions Records Supervisor, Laredo Community College, West End Washington Street, Laredo, TX 78040-4395. *Phone:* 956-721-5177. *Fax:* 956-721-5493.

LEE COLLEGE
Baytown, Texas

Admissions Contact Ms. Charlotte Scott, Registrar, Lee College, PO Box 818, Baytown, TX 77522-0818. *Phone:* 281-425-6399. *Toll-free phone:* 800-621-8724. *Fax:* 281-425-6831.

LON MORRIS COLLEGE
Jacksonville, Texas

- **Independent United Methodist** 2-year, founded 1854
- **Calendar** semesters
- **Degree** associate
- **Small-town** 76-acre campus
- **Endowment** $20.1 million
- **Coed,** 364 undergraduate students

Undergraduates Students come from 5 states and territories, 5% are from out of state, 16% African American, 0.5% Asian American or Pacific Islander, 11% Hispanic American, 0.8% Native American, 4% international, 90% live on campus.

Freshmen *Admission:* 317 applied, 234 admitted.

Faculty *Total:* 34, 79% full-time.

Majors Accounting; applied art; art; art education; art history; biblical studies; biology; botany; business administration; chemistry; computer science; creative writing; dance; divinity/ministry; drawing; economics; education; elementary education; engineering; English; fine/studio arts; graphic design/commercial art/illustration; history; humanities; liberal arts and sciences/liberal studies; literature; mass communications; mathematics; modern languages; music; music (piano and organ performance); music teacher education; music (voice and choral/opera performance); philosophy; physical education; physics; political science; pre-engineering; psychology; religious education; religious studies; romance languages; social sciences; sociology; Spanish; speech/rhetorical studies; theater arts/drama; theology; western civilization.

Academic Programs *Special study options:* academic remediation for entering students, advanced placement credit, English as a second language, independent study, part-time degree program.

Library Henderson Library with 26,000 titles, 265 serial subscriptions, a Web page.

Computers on Campus 28 computers available on campus for general student use. Internet access, at least one staffed computer lab available.

Student Life *Housing:* on-campus residence required through sophomore year. *Options:* men-only, women-only. *Activities and Organizations:* drama/theater group, student-run newspaper, choral group. *Campus security:* late-night transport/escort service, controlled dormitory access. *Student Services:* personal/psychological counseling.

Athletics Member NJCAA. *Intercollegiate sports:* baseball M(s), basketball M(s), golf M(s), softball W(s), volleyball W(s). *Intramural sports:* basketball M/W, cross-country running M/W, football M/W, soccer M, softball W, tennis M/W, volleyball M/W, weight lifting M/W.

Standardized Tests *Required:* SAT I or ACT (for admission).

Costs (2001–02) *Comprehensive fee:* $12,200 includes full-time tuition ($6400), mandatory fees ($1200), and room and board ($4600). Part-time tuition: $250 per credit hour. *Required fees:* $150 per credit hour. *Room and board:* College room only: $2200. *Payment plan:* installment.

Financial Aid In 2001, 63 Federal Work-Study jobs (averaging $1300). 9 State and other part-time jobs (averaging $700).

Applying *Options:* common application, deferred entrance. *Application fee:* $25. *Required:* high school transcript. *Application deadline:* rolling (freshmen), rolling (transfers).

Admissions Contact Craig Zee, Director of Admissions, Lon Morris College, 800 College Avenue, Jacksonville, TX 75766-2900. *Phone:* 903-589-4000 Ext. 4063. *Toll-free phone:* 800-259-5753. *Fax:* 903-589-4006.

MCLENNAN COMMUNITY COLLEGE
Waco, Texas

- **County-supported** 2-year, founded 1965
- **Calendar** semesters
- **Degree** certificates and associate
- **Urban** 200-acre campus
- **Coed,** 6,133 undergraduate students

Undergraduates Students come from 10 other countries, 16% African American, 1% Asian American or Pacific Islander, 12% Hispanic American, 0.3% Native American, 0.7% international.

Freshmen *Admission:* 1,904 applied, 1,904 admitted.

Faculty *Total:* 297, 53% full-time.

Majors Accounting; art education; business administration; computer engineering technology; criminal justice/law enforcement administration; developmental/child psychology; early childhood education; finance; industrial radiologic technology; information sciences/systems; law enforcement/police science; legal administrative assistant; liberal arts and sciences/liberal studies; medical administrative assistant; medical laboratory technician; medical records administration; mental health/rehabilitation; music; nursing; paralegal/legal assistant; physical education; physical therapy; real estate; respiratory therapy; secretarial science; sign language interpretation.

Academic Programs *Special study options:* academic remediation for entering students, adult/continuing education programs, advanced placement credit, cooperative education, distance learning, honors programs, internships, off-campus study, part-time degree program, services for LD students, student-designed majors, study abroad, summer session for credit. *ROTC:* Air Force (c).

Library McLennan Community College Library with 93,000 titles, 400 serial subscriptions, an OPAC, a Web page.

Computers on Campus 425 computers available on campus for general student use. A campuswide network can be accessed from off campus. Internet access, at least one staffed computer lab available.

Student Life *Housing:* college housing not available. *Activities and Organizations:* drama/theater group, student-run newspaper, choral group. *Campus security:* 24-hour emergency response devices and patrols. *Student Services:* personal/psychological counseling.

Athletics Member NJCAA. *Intercollegiate sports:* baseball M(s), basketball M(s)/W(s), golf M(s)/W(s), softball W(s). *Intramural sports:* basketball M/W, football M, gymnastics M, volleyball M/W.

Standardized Tests *Required:* TASP.

Costs (2002–03) *Tuition:* area resident $1020 full-time, $34 per credit part-time; state resident $1170 full-time, $39 per credit part-time; nonresident $2820 full-time, $94 per credit part-time. *Required fees:* $390 full-time, $13 per credit.

Financial Aid In 2001, 200 Federal Work-Study jobs (averaging $1800). 25 State and other part-time jobs (averaging $500).

Applying *Options:* early admission. *Required:* high school transcript. *Application deadline:* rolling (freshmen), rolling (transfers). *Notification:* continuous until 9/2 (freshmen).

McLennan Community College (continued)

Admissions Contact Ms. Vivian G. Jefferson, Director, Admissions and Recruitment, McLennan Community College, 1400 College Drive, Waco, TX 76708-1499. *Phone:* 254-299-8689. *Fax:* 254-299-8694. *E-mail:* ad1@mcc.cc.tx.us.

MIDLAND COLLEGE
Midland, Texas

- **State and locally supported** 2-year, founded 1969
- **Calendar** semesters
- **Degree** certificates and associate
- **Suburban** 163-acre campus
- **Endowment** $3.0 million
- **Coed,** 5,034 undergraduate students

Undergraduates Students come from 20 states and territories, 19 other countries, 1% are from out of state, 5% African American, 1% Asian American or Pacific Islander, 27% Hispanic American, 0.5% Native American, 0.8% international.

Faculty *Total:* 195, 45% full-time.

Majors Accounting; alcohol/drug abuse counseling; anthropology; art; auto mechanic/technician; aviation technology; behavioral sciences; biology; business administration; chemistry; child care/development; computer graphics; computer/information technology services administration and management related; computer programming related; computer programming (specific applications); computer programming, vendor/product certification; computer software and media applications related; computer/technical support; criminal justice/law enforcement administration; data entry/microcomputer applications related; developmental/child psychology; drawing; economics; electrical/electronic engineering technology; emergency medical technology; English; environmental technology; fine/studio arts; fire science; French; geology; German; graphic design/commercial art/illustration; heating/air conditioning/refrigeration; history; industrial radiologic technology; information sciences/systems; information technology; journalism; law enforcement/police science; legal administrative assistant; liberal arts and sciences/liberal studies; literature; mass communications; mathematics; medical records administration; modern languages; music; music teacher education; nursing; paralegal/legal assistant; petroleum technology; physical education; physics; political science; practical nurse; pre-engineering; psychology; respiratory therapy; retail management; secretarial science; sociology; Spanish; speech/rhetorical studies; system administration; veterinary technology; welding technology.

Academic Programs *Special study options:* academic remediation for entering students, adult/continuing education programs, advanced placement credit, cooperative education, English as a second language, honors programs, internships, part-time degree program, services for LD students, student-designed majors, summer session for credit.

Library Murray Fasken Learning Resource Center plus 1 other with 53,800 titles, 331 serial subscriptions, an OPAC.

Computers on Campus 250 computers available on campus for general student use. A campuswide network can be accessed from student residence rooms and from off campus. Internet access, at least one staffed computer lab available.

Student Life *Activities and Organizations:* drama/theater group, student-run newspaper, choral group, Students in Free Enterprise, Midland College Latin American Student Society, Student Government Association, Student Nurses, Baptist Student Ministries. *Campus security:* 24-hour patrols. *Student Services:* personal/psychological counseling.

Athletics Member NJCAA. *Intercollegiate sports:* basketball M(s)/W(s), golf M(s). *Intramural sports:* basketball M/W, football M/W, soccer M/W, table tennis M/W, tennis M/W, volleyball M/W.

Standardized Tests *Required:* TASP or ACT COMPASS. *Recommended:* ACT (for placement).

Costs (2001–02) *Tuition:* area resident $1066 full-time, $36 per credit hour part-time; state resident $1122 full-time, $42 per credit hour part-time; nonresident $1682 full-time, $53 per credit hour part-time. Full-time tuition and fees vary according to course load. Part-time tuition and fees vary according to course load. *Room and board:* $3120. *Payment plan:* installment. *Waivers:* employees or children of employees.

Financial Aid In 2001, 75 Federal Work-Study jobs (averaging $2000). 5 State and other part-time jobs (averaging $2000).

Applying *Options:* common application, early admission, deferred entrance. *Required:* high school transcript. *Application deadline:* rolling (freshmen), rolling (transfers). *Notification:* continuous (freshmen).

Admissions Contact Mr. Trey Whitendorph, Freshmen Admissions, Midland College, 3600 North Garfield, Midland, TX 79705-6399. *Phone:* 915-685-5502. *E-mail:* cdakil@mc.midland.cc.tx.us.

MONTGOMERY COLLEGE
Conroe, Texas

- **State and locally supported** 2-year, founded 1995, part of North Harris Montgomery Community College District
- **Calendar** semesters
- **Degree** certificates and associate
- **Suburban** campus with easy access to Houston
- **Coed**

Student Life *Campus security:* 24-hour emergency response devices and patrols, late-night transport/escort service.

Standardized Tests *Recommended:* SAT I and SAT II or ACT (for placement).

Costs (2001–02) *Tuition:* area resident $624 full-time, $26 per credit part-time; state resident $1584 full-time, $66 per credit part-time; nonresident $1944 full-time, $81 per credit part-time. Full-time tuition and fees vary according to course load. Part-time tuition and fees vary according to course load. *Required fees:* $72 full-time, $5 per credit, $12 per term part-time.

Financial Aid In 2001, 25 Federal Work-Study jobs (averaging $2500). 4 State and other part-time jobs.

Applying *Options:* common application, early admission.

Admissions Contact Ms. Suzy Englert, Admissions/Advising Coordinator, Montgomery College, 3200 College Park Drive, Conroe, TX 77384. *Phone:* 936-273-7236. *E-mail:* suzye@nhmccd.edu.

MOUNTAIN VIEW COLLEGE
Dallas, Texas

- **State and locally supported** 2-year, founded 1970, part of Dallas County Community College District System
- **Calendar** semesters
- **Degree** certificates and associate
- **Urban** 200-acre campus
- **Coed,** 6,350 undergraduate students

Undergraduates Students come from 9 states and territories, 36 other countries, 0.8% are from out of state, 29% African American, 4% Asian American or Pacific Islander, 30% Hispanic American, 0.6% Native American, 0.8% international.

Freshmen *Admission:* 565 applied, 565 admitted.

Faculty *Total:* 264, 30% full-time.

Majors Accounting; aviation management; aviation technology; computer programming; criminal justice/law enforcement administration; drafting; electrical/electronic engineering technology; electromechanical technology; engineering technology; information sciences/systems; legal administrative assistant; liberal arts and sciences/liberal studies; medical records technology; quality control technology; robotics; welding technology.

Academic Programs *Special study options:* academic remediation for entering students, adult/continuing education programs, advanced placement credit, cooperative education, distance learning, double majors, English as a second language, external degree program, freshman honors college, honors programs, independent study, internships, part-time degree program, services for LD students, summer session for credit. *ROTC:* Army (c).

Computers on Campus 200 computers available on campus for general student use. Internet access, at least one staffed computer lab available.

Student Life *Housing:* college housing not available. *Activities and Organizations:* drama/theater group, choral group. *Campus security:* 24-hour patrols, late-night transport/escort service. *Student Services:* personal/psychological counseling, women's center.

Athletics Member NJCAA. *Intercollegiate sports:* basketball M, soccer M, volleyball W. *Intramural sports:* basketball M, football M, golf M, tennis M/W.

Standardized Tests *Required:* SAT I, ACT, TASP, or MAPS.

Costs (2002–03) *Tuition:* area resident $312 full-time, $26 per credit hour part-time; state resident $552 full-time, $46 per credit hour part-time; nonresident $200 per credit hour part-time.

Financial Aid In 2001, 145 Federal Work-Study jobs (averaging $2700).

Applying *Options:* common application, electronic application, early admission, deferred entrance. *Required:* high school transcript. *Application deadline:* rolling (freshmen), rolling (transfers). *Notification:* continuous (freshmen).

Admissions Contact Glenda Hall, Registrar/Director of Enrollment Management, Mountain View College, 4849 West Illinois Avenue, Dallas, TX 75211-6599. *Phone:* 214-860-8666. *Fax:* 214-860-8570. *E-mail:* jctorres@dcccd.edu.

MTI College of Business and Technology
Houston, Texas

- **Proprietary** 2-year, founded 1984, part of MTI College of Business and Technology
- **Calendar** continuous
- **Degree** certificates, diplomas, and associate
- **Suburban** 3-acre campus
- **Coed,** 362 undergraduate students, 100% full-time, 35% women, 65% men

Undergraduates 15% African American, 4% Asian American or Pacific Islander, 38% Hispanic American, 0.6% Native American.
Freshmen *Admission:* 200 applied, 180 admitted.
Faculty *Total:* 16, 88% full-time. *Student/faculty ratio:* 18:1.
Majors Computer maintenance technology; secretarial science.
Academic Programs *Special study options:* advanced placement credit, cooperative education.
Computers on Campus 120 computers available on campus for general student use. Internet access, at least one staffed computer lab available.
Student Life *Housing:* college housing not available.
Costs (2001–02) *Tuition:* $16,500 per degree program part-time. Full-time tuition and fees vary according to program. No tuition increase for student's term of enrollment. *Payment plans:* tuition prepayment, installment. *Waivers:* employees or children of employees.
Applying *Required:* high school transcript, interview. *Application deadline:* rolling (freshmen).
Admissions Contact Mr. Derrell Beck, Admissions Manager, MTI College of Business and Technology, 1275 Space Park Drive, Houston, TX 77058. *Phone:* 281-333-3363. *Toll-free phone:* 888-532-7675. *Fax:* 281-333-4118. *E-mail:* info@mti-tex.com.

MTI College of Business and Technology
Houston, Texas

Admissions Contact 7277 Regency Square Boulevard, Houston, TX 77036-3163. *Toll-free phone:* 800-344-1990.

Navarro College
Corsicana, Texas

- **State and locally supported** 2-year, founded 1946
- **Calendar** semesters
- **Degree** certificates, diplomas, and associate
- **Small-town** 275-acre campus with easy access to Dallas-Fort Worth
- **Coed,** 4,411 undergraduate students, 57% full-time, 58% women, 42% men

Undergraduates 2,516 full-time, 1,895 part-time. Students come from 22 states and territories, 30 other countries, 25% live on campus. *Retention:* 100% of 2001 full-time freshmen returned.
Freshmen *Admission:* 4,411 applied, 4,411 admitted, 1,885 enrolled.
Faculty *Total:* 380, 26% full-time, 6% with terminal degrees.
Majors Accounting; agricultural mechanization; aircraft pilot (professional); art; aviation technology; biological/physical sciences; biology; broadcast journalism; business administration; business marketing and marketing management; chemistry; computer graphics; computer programming; computer science; corrections; criminal justice/law enforcement administration; dance; data processing technology; dental hygiene; developmental/child psychology; drafting; education; elementary education; engineering; English; fire science; graphic design/commercial art/illustration; industrial design; industrial technology; journalism; law enforcement/police science; legal administrative assistant; legal studies; mathematics; medical laboratory technician; music; music (voice and choral/opera performance); nursing; occupational therapy; paralegal/legal assistant; pharmacy; physical education; physical sciences; physics; practical nurse; pre-engineering; psychology; radio/television broadcasting; real estate; retail management; secretarial science; social sciences; sociology; speech/rhetorical studies; theater arts/drama; veterinary sciences.
Academic Programs *Special study options:* academic remediation for entering students, adult/continuing education programs, advanced placement credit, cooperative education, honors programs, part-time degree program, services for LD students, student-designed majors, summer session for credit.
Library Gaston T. Gooch Learning Resource Center with 40,000 titles, 250 serial subscriptions.
Computers on Campus 80 computers available on campus for general student use. At least one staffed computer lab available.
Student Life *Activities and Organizations:* drama/theater group, student-run television station, choral group, marching band, Student Government Association, Phi Theta Kappa, Ebony Club, Que Pasa. *Campus security:* 24-hour patrols. *Student Services:* personal/psychological counseling.
Athletics Member NJCAA. *Intercollegiate sports:* baseball M(s), basketball M(s), football M(s), golf M(s), softball W, tennis M(s)/W(s), volleyball W(s). *Intramural sports:* basketball M/W, bowling M/W, football M, soccer M, softball M/W, volleyball M/W.
Standardized Tests *Required:* TASP. *Recommended:* SAT I or ACT (for placement).
Costs (2001–02) *Tuition:* area resident $528 full-time; state resident $816 full-time; nonresident $946 full-time. Full-time tuition and fees vary according to course load. Part-time tuition and fees vary according to course load. *Required fees:* $248 full-time. *Room and board:* $3224. Room and board charges vary according to board plan. *Waivers:* employees or children of employees.
Financial Aid In 2001, 75 Federal Work-Study jobs (averaging $1877).
Applying *Options:* early admission. *Required:* high school transcript. *Application deadlines:* 9/1 (freshmen), 9/1 (transfers). *Notification:* continuous until 9/1 (freshmen).
Admissions Contact Mr. Dewayne Gragg, Registrar, Navarro College, 3200 West 7th Avenue, Corsicana, TX 75110-4899. *Phone:* 903-874-6501 Ext. 221. *Toll-free phone:* 800-NAVARRO (in-state); 800-628-2776 (out-of-state).

North Central Texas College
Gainesville, Texas

- **County-supported** 2-year, founded 1924
- **Calendar** semesters
- **Degree** certificates, diplomas, and associate
- **Rural** 132-acre campus with easy access to Dallas-Fort Worth
- **Endowment** $2.4 million
- **Coed,** 5,180 undergraduate students, 42% full-time, 59% women, 41% men

Undergraduates Students come from 14 states and territories, 21 other countries, 5% are from out of state, 2% live on campus. *Retention:* 55% of 2001 full-time freshmen returned.
Freshmen *Admission:* 1,296 applied, 1,296 admitted.
Faculty *Total:* 290, 31% full-time.
Majors Agricultural animal husbandry/production management; agricultural mechanization; auto mechanic/technician; biological/physical sciences; business administration; buying operations; computer engineering technology; computer graphics; computer/information technology services administration and management related; computer management; computer programming; computer programming related; computer programming (specific applications); computer programming, vendor/product certification; computer science; computer/technical support; criminal justice/law enforcement administration; data processing technology; drafting; drafting/design technology; electrical/electronic engineering technology; emergency medical technology; engineering-related technology; equestrian studies; farm/ranch management; industrial machinery maintenance/repair; information sciences/systems; law enforcement/police science; legal administrative assistant; liberal arts and sciences/liberal studies; machine shop assistant; machine technology; marketing operations; medical records administration; nursing; occupational therapy; paralegal/legal assistant; personal services marketing operations; pre-engineering; real estate; retailing operations; secretarial science; welding technology; word processing.
Academic Programs *Special study options:* academic remediation for entering students, adult/continuing education programs, advanced placement credit, cooperative education, distance learning, internships, part-time degree program, services for LD students, summer session for credit.
Library North Central Texas College Library plus 1 other with 44,861 titles, 273 serial subscriptions, an OPAC.
Computers on Campus 60 computers available on campus for general student use. A campuswide network can be accessed from off campus. Internet access, at least one staffed computer lab available.
Student Life *Housing Options:* coed. *Activities and Organizations:* drama/theater group, choral group, Baptist Student Ministry, Phi Theta Kappa, Nursing

North Central Texas College (continued)
Student Association, Collegiate FFA. *Campus security:* late-night transport/escort service, late night security. *Student Services:* personal/psychological counseling.
Athletics Member NJCAA. *Intercollegiate sports:* baseball M(s), equestrian sports M(s)/W(s), tennis W(s), volleyball W(s). *Intramural sports:* basketball M/W, bowling M/W, football M/W, golf M/W, tennis M/W, volleyball M/W.
Standardized Tests *Required:* TASP. *Recommended:* SAT I or ACT (for placement).
Costs (2001–02) *Tuition:* area resident $648 full-time, $27 per hour part-time; state resident $936 full-time, $39 per hour part-time; nonresident $1512 full-time, $63 per hour part-time. Full-time tuition and fees vary according to course load. Part-time tuition and fees vary according to course load. *Room and board:* $2200. Room and board charges vary according to board plan and housing facility. *Payment plan:* installment. *Waivers:* employees or children of employees.
Applying *Options:* early admission. *Required:* high school transcript. *Application deadline:* rolling (freshmen), rolling (transfers).
Admissions Contact Condoa Parrent, Director of Admissions/Registrar, North Central Texas College, 1525 West California Street, Gainesville, TX 76240-4699. *Phone:* 940-668-4222. *Fax:* 940-668-6049. *E-mail:* cparrent@nctc.cc.tx.us.

Northeast Texas Community College
Mount Pleasant, Texas

- **State and locally supported** 2-year, founded 1985
- **Calendar** semesters
- **Degree** associate
- **Rural** 175-acre campus
- **Coed,** 2,212 undergraduate students, 52% full-time, 62% women, 38% men

Undergraduates Students come from 10 states and territories, 1% are from out of state, 3% live on campus.
Faculty *Total:* 134, 38% full-time.
Majors Accounting; agricultural sciences; auto mechanic/technician; computer science; cosmetology; criminal justice/law enforcement administration; dairy science; finance; information sciences/systems; legal administrative assistant; medical administrative assistant; nursing; poultry science; range management; real estate; secretarial science.
Academic Programs *Special study options:* academic remediation for entering students, adult/continuing education programs, advanced placement credit, cooperative education, distance learning, English as a second language, independent study, part-time degree program, services for LD students, summer session for credit.
Library Learning Resource Center with 24,501 titles, 325 serial subscriptions.
Computers on Campus 126 computers available on campus for general student use. At least one staffed computer lab available.
Student Life *Activities and Organizations:* drama/theater group, student-run newspaper, choral group, Student Coordinating Board, Student Nurses Association, Criminal Justice Organization (COPSS), Baptist Student Union, Computer Club. *Campus security:* 24-hour patrols. *Student Services:* personal/psychological counseling, women's center.
Athletics Member NJCAA. *Intercollegiate sports:* baseball M(s), softball W. *Intramural sports:* tennis M/W, volleyball M/W.
Standardized Tests *Required for some:* SAT I or ACT (for placement).
Costs (2001–02) *Tuition:* state resident $432 full-time, $54 per credit hour part-time; nonresident $1032 full-time, $64 per credit hour part-time. *Required fees:* $528 full-time, $33 per credit hour. *Room and board:* $2900; room only: $1400.
Financial Aid In 2001, 70 Federal Work-Study jobs (averaging $1600). 5 State and other part-time jobs (averaging $1600).
Applying *Options:* early admission. *Application deadline:* rolling (freshmen), rolling (transfers).
Admissions Contact Ms. Sherry Keys, Director of Admissions, Northeast Texas Community College, PO Box 1307, Mount Pleasant, TX 75456-1307. *Phone:* 903-572-1911 Ext. 263. *Fax:* 903-572-6712.

North Harris College
Houston, Texas

- **State and locally supported** 2-year, founded 1972, part of North Harris Montgomery Community College District
- **Calendar** semesters
- **Degree** certificates and associate
- **Suburban** 185-acre campus
- **Coed,** 9,127 undergraduate students, 26% full-time, 61% women, 39% men

Undergraduates 2,330 full-time, 6,797 part-time. 0.5% are from out of state, 20% African American, 8% Asian American or Pacific Islander, 24% Hispanic American, 0.3% Native American, 3% international.
Freshmen *Admission:* 1,813 applied, 1,813 admitted, 1,813 enrolled.
Faculty *Total:* 497, 38% full-time.
Majors Accounting; art; art education; auto mechanic/technician; biological/physical sciences; business marketing and marketing management; child care/development; computer/information sciences; computer science; cosmetology; criminal justice/law enforcement administration; drafting; education; electrical/electronic engineering technology; emergency medical technology; finance; heating/air conditioning/refrigeration; human services; information sciences/systems; interior design; journalism; law enforcement/police science; legal administrative assistant; legal studies; liberal arts and sciences/liberal studies; management information systems/business data processing; mathematics; music; nursing; photography; physical education; political science; pre-engineering; respiratory therapy; secretarial science; sociology; speech/rhetorical studies; theater arts/drama; travel/tourism management; veterinary sciences; welding technology.
Academic Programs *Special study options:* academic remediation for entering students, adult/continuing education programs, cooperative education, distance learning, English as a second language, honors programs, independent study, internships, off-campus study, part-time degree program, services for LD students, summer session for credit. *ROTC:* Army (c).
Library Marion M. Donaldson Memorial Library with 131,851 titles, 1,203 serial subscriptions, 11,869 audiovisual materials, an OPAC, a Web page.
Computers on Campus 300 computers available on campus for general student use. A campuswide network can be accessed from off campus. At least one staffed computer lab available.
Student Life *Housing:* college housing not available. *Activities and Organizations:* drama/theater group, student-run newspaper, choral group, Phi Theta Kappa, Student Ambassadors, Hispanic Student Forum, Vietnamese Student Association, Earth Alliance. *Campus security:* 24-hour emergency response devices and patrols, late-night transport/escort service. *Student Services:* personal/psychological counseling, women's center.
Athletics *Intramural sports:* badminton M/W, baseball M/W, basketball M/W, bowling M/W, football M/W, golf M/W, gymnastics M/W, racquetball M/W, soccer M/W, softball M/W, table tennis M/W, tennis M/W, track and field M/W, volleyball M/W, weight lifting M/W.
Standardized Tests *Required for some:* SAT I or ACT (for placement), ACT ASSET.
Costs (2001–02) *Tuition:* area resident $624 full-time, $26 per credit part-time; state resident $1584 full-time, $66 per credit part-time; nonresident $1944 full-time, $81 per credit part-time. Full-time tuition and fees vary according to course load. Part-time tuition and fees vary according to course load. *Required fees:* $72 full-time, $5 per credit, $12 per term part-time. *Payment plan:* installment. *Waivers:* employees or children of employees.
Applying *Options:* early admission. *Required for some:* high school transcript, interview. *Application deadline:* rolling (freshmen), rolling (transfers).
Admissions Contact Dr. Bennie E. Lambert, Director of Admissions, North Harris College, 2700 W.W. Thorne Drive, Houston, TX 77073. *Phone:* 281-618-5410. *Fax:* 281-618-7141.

North Lake College
Irving, Texas

- **County-supported** 2-year, founded 1977, part of Dallas County Community College District System
- **Calendar** semesters
- **Degree** certificates, diplomas, and associate
- **Suburban** 250-acre campus with easy access to Dallas-Fort Worth
- **Coed**

Student Life *Campus security:* late-night transport/escort service.
Athletics Member NJCAA.
Applying *Options:* early admission. *Recommended:* high school transcript.
Admissions Contact Mr. Steve Twenge, Director of Admissions and Registration, North Lake College, 5001 North MacArthur Boulevard, Irving, TX 75038-3899. *Phone:* 972-273-3109.

Odessa College
Odessa, Texas

- **State and locally supported** 2-year, founded 1946
- **Calendar** semesters

- **Degree** certificates and associate
- **Urban** 87-acre campus
- **Endowment** $521,784
- **Coed,** 4,579 undergraduate students, 34% full-time, 60% women, 40% men

Undergraduates Students come from 32 states and territories, 1% are from out of state, 4% African American, 0.6% Asian American or Pacific Islander, 40% Hispanic American, 1% Native American, 0.1% international, 3% live on campus.
Freshmen *Admission:* 395 applied, 395 admitted.
Faculty *Total:* 291, 9% with terminal degrees. *Student/faculty ratio:* 20:1.
Majors Accounting; alcohol/drug abuse counseling; applied art; art; athletic training/sports medicine; auto mechanic/technician; biology; business administration; business systems networking/ telecommunications; chemistry; child care/ development; computer science; construction technology; cosmetology; criminal justice/law enforcement administration; culinary arts; data processing technology; drafting; early childhood education; education; electrical/electronic engineering technology; emergency medical technology; English; fashion merchandising; fire science; geology; heating/air conditioning/refrigeration; history; human services; industrial radiologic technology; information sciences/systems; law enforcement/police science; legal administrative assistant; liberal arts and sciences/ liberal studies; machine technology; mathematics; medical laboratory technician; modern languages; music; nursing; operating room technician; petroleum technology; photography; physical education; physical therapy; physics; political science; pre-engineering; psychology; radio/television broadcasting; respiratory therapy; secretarial science; social sciences; sociology; speech/rhetorical studies; teacher assistant/aide; welding technology.
Academic Programs *Special study options:* academic remediation for entering students, adult/continuing education programs, advanced placement credit, cooperative education, internships, part-time degree program, services for LD students, student-designed majors, summer session for credit.
Library Murray H. Fly Learning Resource Center with 79,882 titles, 496 serial subscriptions.
Computers on Campus 300 computers available on campus for general student use. A campuswide network can be accessed from off campus. Internet access, at least one staffed computer lab available.
Student Life *Housing Options:* coed. *Activities and Organizations:* choral group, Baptist Student Union, American Chemical Society, CAHOOTS, Physical Therapy Assistant Club, Rodeo Club. *Campus security:* 24-hour emergency response devices and patrols, late-night transport/escort service. *Student Services:* personal/psychological counseling.
Athletics Member NJCAA. *Intercollegiate sports:* baseball M(s), basketball M(s)/W(s), golf M(s), softball W(s), track and field W(s). *Intramural sports:* basketball M/W, bowling M/W, football M, racquetball M/W, softball M/W, table tennis M/W, volleyball M/W, weight lifting M/W.
Costs (2002–03) *Tuition:* state resident $264 full-time, $66 per hour part-time; nonresident $550 full-time, $325 per hour part-time. *Required fees:* $444 full-time, $19 per hour, $37 per term part-time. *Room and board:* $3100; room only: $1050.
Financial Aid In 2001, 85 Federal Work-Study jobs (averaging $1280). 7 State and other part-time jobs (averaging $882).
Applying *Options:* common application, electronic application, early admission, deferred entrance. *Application deadline:* rolling (freshmen), rolling (transfers). *Notification:* continuous (freshmen).
Admissions Contact Ms. Tanya Hughes, Director of Admissions, Odessa College, 201 West University Avenue, Odessa, TX 79764-7127. *Phone:* 915-335-6866. *E-mail:* regpe@odessa.edu.

PALO ALTO COLLEGE
San Antonio, Texas

- **State and locally supported** 2-year, founded 1987, part of Alamo Community College District System
- **Calendar** semesters
- **Degree** associate
- **Urban** campus
- **Coed**

Student Life *Campus security:* 24-hour emergency response devices and patrols.
Athletics Member NJCAA.
Standardized Tests *Required:* ACT ASSET. *Required for some:* SAT I or ACT (for placement).
Financial Aid In 2001, 272 Federal Work-Study jobs (averaging $2000).
Applying *Options:* early admission. *Required:* high school transcript.
Admissions Contact Ms. Imelda Zuniga, Director of Records and Admissions, Palo Alto College, 1400 West Villaret Boulevard, San Antonio, TX 78224. *Phone:* 210-921-5279. *Fax:* 210-921-5310. *E-mail:* pacar@accd.edu.

PANOLA COLLEGE
Carthage, Texas

- **State and locally supported** 2-year, founded 1947
- **Calendar** semesters
- **Degree** certificates, diplomas, and associate
- **Small-town** 35-acre campus
- **Endowment** $1.1 million
- **Coed**

Faculty *Student/faculty ratio:* 16:1.
Student Life *Campus security:* controlled dormitory access.
Athletics Member NJCAA.
Standardized Tests *Required:* TASP, ACT ASSET, or ACT COMPASS. *Required for some:* SAT I or ACT (for placement). *Recommended:* SAT I or ACT (for placement).
Financial Aid In 2001, 71 Federal Work-Study jobs (averaging $829).
Applying *Options:* common application, early admission. *Required for some:* high school transcript. *Recommended:* high school transcript.
Admissions Contact Ms. Barbara Simpson, Registrar/Director of Admissions, Panola College, 1109 West Panola Street, Carthage, TX 75633-2397. *Phone:* 903-693-2009. *Fax:* 903-693-2031.

PARIS JUNIOR COLLEGE
Paris, Texas

- **State and locally supported** 2-year, founded 1924
- **Calendar** semesters
- **Degree** associate
- **Rural** 54-acre campus
- **Coed**

Student Life *Campus security:* 24-hour emergency response devices and patrols, late-night transport/escort service.
Athletics Member NJCAA.
Standardized Tests *Required:* TASP.
Applying *Options:* early admission. *Required:* high school transcript.
Admissions Contact Ms. Sheila Reese, Director of Admissions, Paris Junior College, 2400 Clarksville Street, Paris, TX 75460-6298. *Phone:* 903-782-0425. *Toll-free phone:* 800-232-5804.

RANGER COLLEGE
Ranger, Texas

- **State-related** 2-year, founded 1926
- **Calendar** semesters
- **Degree** associate
- **Rural** 100-acre campus with easy access to Dallas-Fort Worth
- **Coed,** 843 undergraduate students

Undergraduates Students come from 7 states and territories, 4 other countries, 45% live on campus.
Faculty *Total:* 51, 55% full-time.
Majors Auto mechanic/technician; computer engineering technology; liberal arts and sciences/liberal studies; science education; secretarial science; welding technology.
Academic Programs *Special study options:* academic remediation for entering students, adult/continuing education programs, advanced placement credit, freshman honors college, honors programs, part-time degree program, student-designed majors, summer session for credit.
Library Golemon Library with 24,211 titles, 133 serial subscriptions.
Computers on Campus 42 computers available on campus for general student use. Internet access, at least one staffed computer lab available.
Student Life *Activities and Organizations:* choral group, marching band. *Campus security:* controlled dormitory access. *Student Services:* health clinic, personal/psychological counseling.
Athletics Member NJCAA. *Intercollegiate sports:* baseball M(s), basketball M(s)/W(s), cross-country running M(s)/W(s), football M(s), golf M(s), softball

Ranger College (continued)
W(s), track and field M(s)/W(s). *Intramural sports:* basketball M/W, football M/W, golf M/W, track and field M/W, volleyball M/W.
Standardized Tests *Recommended:* SAT I and SAT II or ACT (for placement).
Costs (2002–03) *Tuition:* state resident $672 full-time, $28 per credit part-time; nonresident $816 full-time, $34 per credit part-time. *Required fees:* $318 full-time, $12 per credit, $15 per term part-time. *Room and board:* $3016; room only: $1100.
Financial Aid In 2001, 140 Federal Work-Study jobs (averaging $800). *Financial aid deadline:* 7/15.
Applying *Options:* early admission. *Application deadline:* rolling (freshmen), rolling (transfers). *Notification:* continuous (freshmen).
Admissions Contact Dr. Jim Davis, Dean of Students, Ranger College, College Circle, Ranger, TX 76470. *Phone:* 254-647-3234 Ext. 110.

RICHLAND COLLEGE
Dallas, Texas

Admissions Contact Ms. Carol McKinney, Department Assistant, Richland College, 12800 Abrams Road, Dallas, TX 75243-2199. *Phone:* 972-238-6100.

ST. PHILIP'S COLLEGE
San Antonio, Texas

- **District-supported** 2-year, founded 1898, part of Alamo Community College District System
- **Calendar** semesters
- **Degree** certificates, diplomas, and associate
- **Urban** 16-acre campus
- **Coed,** 8,326 undergraduate students, 40% full-time, 55% women, 45% men

Undergraduates 3,315 full-time, 5,011 part-time. Students come from 50 states and territories, 8 other countries, 18% African American, 2% Asian American or Pacific Islander, 50% Hispanic American, 0.4% Native American, 0.2% international, 11% transferred in. *Retention:* 43% of 2001 full-time freshmen returned.
Freshmen *Admission:* 2,003 admitted, 2,003 enrolled.
Faculty *Total:* 510, 40% full-time, 8% with terminal degrees. *Student/faculty ratio:* 16:1.
Majors Accounting; aircraft mechanic/airframe; art; auto body repair; auto mechanic/technician; biology; biomedical technology; building maintenance/management; business administration; carpentry; chemistry; child care/guidance; child care provider; clothing/textiles; communication equipment technology; construction/building inspection; construction management; construction technology; culinary arts; data processing technology; diagnostic medical sonography; diesel engine mechanic; dietetics; dietician assistant; drafting; economics; education; electrical/electronic engineering technology; electrical equipment installation/repair; English composition; health/physical education; health unit coordination; heating/air conditioning/refrigeration; history; home furnishings; hospitality management; hotel and restaurant management; information sciences/systems; institutional food services; institutional food workers; interior architecture; interior design; leatherworking/upholstery; legal administrative assistant; liberal arts and sciences/liberal studies; machine technology; mathematics; medical administrative assistant; medical laboratory technician; medical radiologic technology; medical records administration; medical records technology; music; natural sciences; nurse assistant/aide; occupational therapy assistant; operating room technician; paralegal/legal assistant; physical therapy assistant; plumbing; political science; practical nurse; pre-dentistry; pre-engineering; pre-medicine; psychology; respiratory therapy; secretarial science; sociology; Spanish; speech/rhetorical studies; teacher assistant/aide; theater arts/drama; urban studies; welding technology.
Academic Programs *Special study options:* academic remediation for entering students, adult/continuing education programs, advanced placement credit, cooperative education, distance learning, double majors, freshman honors college, honors programs, internships, part-time degree program, services for LD students, student-designed majors, summer session for credit. *ROTC:* Army (c).
Library Main Library plus 1 other with 107,724 titles, 1,542 serial subscriptions, 10,749 audiovisual materials, an OPAC, a Web page.
Computers on Campus 885 computers available on campus for general student use. A campuswide network can be accessed from off campus that provide access to email. Internet access, online (class) registration, at least one staffed computer lab available.
Student Life *Housing:* college housing not available. *Activities and Organizations:* drama/theater group, student-run newspaper, choral group, student government, Delta Epsilon Chi, Radiography Club, Respiratory Therapy Club, Diagnostic Imaging Club. *Campus security:* 24-hour emergency response devices and patrols, late-night transport/escort service. *Student Services:* health clinic, women's center.
Athletics *Intramural sports:* basketball M/W, table tennis M/W, tennis M/W, volleyball M/W, weight lifting M/W.
Costs (2001–02) *Tuition:* area resident $900 full-time, $30 per hour part-time; state resident $1665 full-time, $56 per hour part-time; nonresident $3255 full-time, $109 per hour part-time. Full-time tuition and fees vary according to course load. Part-time tuition and fees vary according to course load. *Required fees:* $218 full-time, $109 per term part-time. *Waivers:* senior citizens and employees or children of employees.
Applying *Options:* common application, early admission. *Required:* high school transcript. *Notification:* continuous until 8/31 (freshmen).
Admissions Contact Mr. Xuri M. Allen, Director of Admissions and Enrollment Services, St. Philip's College, 1801 Martin Luther King Drive, San Antonio, TX 78203-2098. *Phone:* 210-531-4834. *Fax:* 210-531-4836. *E-mail:* xallen@accd.edu.

SAN ANTONIO COLLEGE
San Antonio, Texas

- **State and locally supported** 2-year, founded 1925, part of Alamo Community College District System
- **Calendar** semesters
- **Degree** certificates and associate
- **Urban** 45-acre campus
- **Coed,** 21,853 undergraduate students, 32% full-time, 58% women, 42% men

Undergraduates Students come from 52 states and territories, 110 other countries.
Faculty *Total:* 1,092, 28% full-time.
Majors Biological/physical sciences; business administration; business machine repair; child care/development; child care provider; child care services management; civil engineering technology; computer engineering technology; computer graphics; computer/information technology services administration and management related; computer programming; computer programming related; computer programming (specific applications); computer programming, vendor/product certification; corrections; court reporting; criminal justice/law enforcement administration; data entry/microcomputer applications; data processing technology; dental hygiene; developmental/child psychology; drafting; drafting/design technology; electrical/electronic engineering technology; engineering-related technology; engineering technology; fire science; graphic design/commercial art/illustration; industrial technology; law enforcement/police science; legal administrative assistant; liberal arts and sciences/liberal studies; mechanical engineering technology; medical assistant; metal/jewelry arts; mortuary science; nursing; postal management; psychology; public administration; radio/television broadcasting; real estate; speech/theater education; system administration; system/networking/LAN/WAN management; Web page, digital/multimedia and information resources design; word processing.
Academic Programs *Special study options:* academic remediation for entering students, adult/continuing education programs, advanced placement credit, cooperative education, English as a second language, honors programs, internships, part-time degree program, services for LD students, summer session for credit. *ROTC:* Army (c), Air Force (c).
Library 225,285 titles, 1,496 serial subscriptions.
Student Life *Housing:* college housing not available. *Activities and Organizations:* drama/theater group, student-run newspaper, radio station, choral group. *Campus security:* 24-hour patrols, late-night transport/escort service. *Student Services:* health clinic, personal/psychological counseling, women's center.
Athletics *Intramural sports:* basketball M(c)/W(c), cross-country running M/W, fencing M(c)/W(c), football M/W, golf M/W, soccer M/W, swimming M/W, tennis M/W, volleyball M/W(c), weight lifting M/W.
Standardized Tests *Required for some:* ACT ASSET, TASP, ACCUPLACER. *Recommended:* SAT I or ACT (for placement), ACT ASSET, TASP, ACCUPLACER.
Costs (2001–02) *Tuition:* area resident $636 full-time, $30 per credit part-time; state resident $1164 full-time, $35 per credit part-time; nonresident $2268 full-time, $217 per credit part-time. Full-time tuition and fees vary according to course load. Part-time tuition and fees vary according to course load. *Required fees:* $180 full-time. *Payment plan:* installment. *Waivers:* senior citizens.
Financial Aid In 2001, 500 Federal Work-Study jobs (averaging $3000).
Applying *Options:* early admission. *Required:* minimum 2.0 GPA. *Application deadline:* rolling (freshmen), rolling (transfers).

Admissions Contact Ms. Rosemarie Hoopes, Director of Admissions and Records, San Antonio College, 1300 San Pedro Avenue, San Antonio, TX 78212-4299. *Phone:* 210-733-2582.

SAN JACINTO COLLEGE CENTRAL CAMPUS
Pasadena, Texas

- **State and locally supported** 2-year, founded 1961, part of San Jacinto College District
- **Calendar** semesters
- **Degree** certificates, diplomas, and associate
- **Suburban** 141-acre campus with easy access to Houston
- **Coed,** 10,854 undergraduate students, 39% full-time, 54% women, 46% men

Undergraduates 4,248 full-time, 6,606 part-time. Students come from 4 states and territories, 78 other countries.

Freshmen *Admission:* 10,854 applied, 10,854 admitted, 2,364 enrolled.

Faculty *Total:* 387, 58% full-time, 10% with terminal degrees. *Student/faculty ratio:* 18:1.

Majors Accounting; aerospace science; aircraft pilot (professional); anatomy; anthropology; art; audio engineering; auto mechanic/technician; aviation technology; behavioral sciences; biblical studies; biological/physical sciences; biology; botany; business administration; business marketing and marketing management; chemistry; child care/development; computer programming; computer science; cosmetology; creative writing; criminal justice/law enforcement administration; data processing technology; developmental/child psychology; dietetics; drafting; drawing; early childhood education; economics; electrical/electronic engineering technology; emergency medical technology; engineering; engineering technology; English; fashion design/illustration; fashion merchandising; finance; fine/studio arts; fire science; food products retailing; geology; German; graphic design/commercial art/illustration; graphic/printing equipment; heavy equipment maintenance; history; home economics; horticulture science; hotel and restaurant management; industrial radiologic technology; interior design; journalism; law enforcement/police science; legal administrative assistant; liberal arts and sciences/liberal studies; literature; mass communications; mathematics; medical administrative assistant; medical laboratory technician; modern languages; music; music business management/merchandising; nursing; nutrition science; occupational safety/health technology; operating room technician; paralegal/legal assistant; philosophy; physical sciences; political science; pre-engineering; psychology; real estate; respiratory therapy; safety/security technology; secretarial science; sociology; Spanish; surveying; theater arts/drama; welding technology; zoology.

Academic Programs *Special study options:* academic remediation for entering students, adult/continuing education programs, English as a second language, internships, part-time degree program, services for LD students, summer session for credit.

Library Lee Davis Library with 100,000 titles, 400 serial subscriptions.

Computers on Campus 58 computers available on campus for general student use.

Student Life *Housing:* college housing not available. *Activities and Organizations:* drama/theater group, student-run newspaper. *Campus security:* 24-hour emergency response devices and patrols.

Athletics Member NJCAA. *Intercollegiate sports:* basketball M(s)/W(s), golf M(s), tennis M(s)/W(s), track and field M(s)/W(s), volleyball W(s). *Intramural sports:* basketball M/W, football M/W, racquetball M/W, volleyball W.

Standardized Tests *Required for some:* SAT I or ACT (for placement). *Recommended:* SAT I or ACT (for placement).

Costs (2001–02) *Tuition:* area resident $512 full-time, $18 per semester hour part-time; state resident $1088 full-time, $34 per semester hour part-time; nonresident $1920 full-time, $60 per semester hour part-time. Full-time tuition and fees vary according to course load. Part-time tuition and fees vary according to course load. *Required fees:* $212 full-time, $18 per semester hour, $34 per semester part-time. *Payment plan:* installment.

Applying *Options:* early admission. *Required:* high school transcript. *Application deadline:* rolling (freshmen), rolling (transfers).

Admissions Contact Dr. Fred Sallee, Registrar, San Jacinto College Central Campus, 8060 Spencer Highway, PO Box 2007, Pasadena, TX 77501-2007. *Phone:* 281-476-1501 Ext. 1843.

SAN JACINTO COLLEGE NORTH CAMPUS
Houston, Texas

- **State and locally supported** 2-year, founded 1974, part of San Jacinto College District
- **Calendar** semesters
- **Degree** certificates and associate
- **Suburban** 105-acre campus
- **Endowment** $1.4 million
- **Coed,** 5,020 undergraduate students, 39% full-time, 59% women, 41% men

Undergraduates 1,967 full-time, 3,053 part-time. Students come from 25 other countries, 1% are from out of state, 22% African American, 2% Asian American or Pacific Islander, 32% Hispanic American, 0.4% Native American, 3% international, 3% transferred in.

Freshmen *Admission:* 3,388 applied, 3,388 admitted, 3,388 enrolled.

Faculty *Total:* 298, 45% full-time, 11% with terminal degrees. *Student/faculty ratio:* 16:1.

Majors Accounting; art; auto body repair; bilingual/bicultural education; biology; business administration; chemistry; child care/development; child care/guidance; child care provider; child care services management; computer/information sciences; computer programming (specific applications); computer science; computer/technical support; construction management; construction technology; corrections; cosmetology; criminal justice/law enforcement administration; culinary arts; data processing; data processing technology; diesel engine mechanic; drafting; early childhood education; electrical and electronics equipment installation and repair related; electrical/electronic engineering technology; electrical equipment installation/repair; elementary education; emergency medical technology; English; environmental technology; general office/clerical; geology; heating/air conditioning/refrigeration; heating/air conditioning/refrigeration technology; history; information sciences/systems; institutional food workers; international business; law enforcement/police science; legal administrative assistant; management information systems/business data processing; mathematics; medical records technology; music; music (piano and organ performance); paralegal/legal assistant; pharmacy technician/assistant; physics; practical nurse; psychology; public administration; reading education; real estate; secretarial science; social sciences; sociology; Spanish; special education; speech/rhetorical studies; system/networking/LAN/WAN management; theater arts/drama; welding technology.

Academic Programs *Special study options:* academic remediation for entering students, accelerated degree program, adult/continuing education programs, advanced placement credit, distance learning, English as a second language, honors programs, internships, part-time degree program, services for LD students, summer session for credit. *ROTC:* Army (c).

Library Edwin E. Lehr Library with 53,007 titles, 420 serial subscriptions, an OPAC, a Web page.

Computers on Campus 400 computers available on campus for general student use. Internet access, at least one staffed computer lab available.

Student Life *Housing:* college housing not available. *Activities and Organizations:* drama/theater group, student-run newspaper, choral group, Phi Theta Kappa, Criminal Justice Club, Phi Beta Lambda, Hispanic Heritage Club, LVN Club. *Campus security:* 24-hour emergency response devices and patrols. *Student Services:* personal/psychological counseling.

Athletics Member NJCAA. *Intercollegiate sports:* baseball M(s), basketball W(s), golf M(s). *Intramural sports:* basketball M/W, bowling M/W, racquetball M/W, soccer M/W, softball M/W, swimming M/W, tennis M/W, volleyball M/W, weight lifting M/W.

Standardized Tests *Recommended:* SAT I or ACT (for placement).

Costs (2001–02) *Tuition:* area resident $576 full-time, $18 per credit part-time; state resident $1088 full-time, $34 per credit part-time; nonresident $1920 full-time, $60 per credit part-time. Part-time tuition and fees vary according to course load and program. *Required fees:* $270 full-time, $6 per credit, $39 per term part-time. *Payment plan:* installment. *Waivers:* senior citizens.

Applying *Options:* early admission. *Required:* high school transcript. *Required for some:* interview. *Application deadline:* rolling (freshmen), rolling (transfers). *Notification:* continuous (freshmen).

Admissions Contact Ms. Stephanie Stockstill, Coordinator, San Jacinto College North Campus, 5800 Uvalde Road, Houston, TX 77049-4599. *Phone:* 281-458-4050 Ext. 7120. *Fax:* 281-459-7125. *E-mail:* sstock@sjcd.cc.tx.us.

SAN JACINTO COLLEGE SOUTH CAMPUS
Houston, Texas

- **State and locally supported** 2-year, founded 1979, part of San Jacinto College District
- **Calendar** semesters
- **Degree** certificates, diplomas, and associate
- **Suburban** 114-acre campus
- **Coed,** 6,269 undergraduate students, 40% full-time, 56% women, 44% men

San Jacinto College South Campus (continued)

Undergraduates 2,504 full-time, 3,765 part-time. Students come from 19 states and territories, 57 other countries, 6% transferred in.

Freshmen *Admission:* 6,269 applied, 6,269 admitted, 2,628 enrolled.

Faculty *Total:* 214, 57% full-time, 22% with terminal degrees. *Student/faculty ratio:* 22:1.

Majors Accounting; art; auto mechanic/technician; behavioral sciences; biological/physical sciences; biology; business administration; chemistry; computer science; cosmetology; data processing technology; drafting; electrical/electronic engineering technology; English; environmental science; fashion design/illustration; fashion merchandising; finance; graphic design/commercial art/illustration; heating/air conditioning/refrigeration; history; information sciences/systems; legal administrative assistant; mathematics; mechanical engineering technology; music; natural sciences; nursing; occupational therapy assistant; physical education; physical therapy; practical nurse; pre-engineering; psychology; real estate; secretarial science; social sciences; sociology.

Academic Programs *Special study options:* academic remediation for entering students, adult/continuing education programs, advanced placement credit, internships, part-time degree program, services for LD students, summer session for credit.

Library San Jacinto College South Library plus 1 other with 40,000 titles, 320 serial subscriptions, an OPAC, a Web page.

Computers on Campus 370 computers available on campus for general student use. At least one staffed computer lab available.

Student Life *Housing:* college housing not available. *Activities and Organizations:* drama/theater group, choral group. *Campus security:* 24-hour patrols.

Athletics Member NJCAA. *Intercollegiate sports:* soccer M, softball W. *Intramural sports:* badminton M/W, basketball M/W, bowling M/W, football M/W, golf M/W, racquetball M/W, soccer W, softball M/W, tennis M/W, volleyball M/W.

Standardized Tests *Required:* TASP.

Costs (2001–02) *Tuition:* area resident $512 full-time, $18 per hour part-time; state resident $1088 full-time, $34 per hour part-time; nonresident $1920 full-time, $60 per hour part-time. Part-time tuition and fees vary according to course load. *Required fees:* $212 full-time, $18 per hour, $30 per hour part-time. *Payment plan:* deferred payment.

Financial Aid In 2001, 68 Federal Work-Study jobs (averaging $1352).

Applying *Options:* common application, early admission. *Application deadline:* rolling (freshmen), rolling (transfers).

Admissions Contact Ms. Susan Eason, Registrar, San Jacinto College South Campus, 13735 Beamer, Houston, TX 77089. *Phone:* 281-922-3431 Ext. 3432. *Fax:* 281-922-3485. *E-mail:* season@sjcd.cc.tx.us.

SOUTH PLAINS COLLEGE
Levelland, Texas

- **State and locally supported** 2-year, founded 1958
- **Calendar** semesters
- **Degree** associate
- **Small-town** 177-acre campus
- **Endowment** $3.0 million
- **Coed,** 8,574 undergraduate students

Undergraduates Students come from 21 states and territories, 8 other countries, 3% are from out of state, 10% live on campus.

Faculty *Total:* 375. *Student/faculty ratio:* 23:1.

Majors Accounting; advertising; agricultural economics; agricultural sciences; agronomy/crop science; art; audio engineering; auto mechanic/technician; biological/physical sciences; biology; business administration; business marketing and marketing management; carpentry; chemistry; child care/development; computer engineering technology; computer programming; computer science; cosmetology; criminal justice/law enforcement administration; data processing technology; developmental/child psychology; dietetics; drafting; education; electrical/electronic engineering technology; engineering; fashion merchandising; fire science; food products retailing; graphic design/commercial art/illustration; health services administration; heating/air conditioning/refrigeration; industrial radiologic technology; journalism; law enforcement/police science; legal administrative assistant; liberal arts and sciences/liberal studies; machine technology; mass communications; medical administrative assistant; medical records administration; mental health/rehabilitation; music; nursing; operating room technician; petroleum technology; physical education; physical therapy; postal management; practical nurse; pre-engineering; real estate; respiratory therapy; retail management; secretarial science; social work; telecommunications; welding technology.

Academic Programs *Special study options:* academic remediation for entering students, accelerated degree program, adult/continuing education programs, advanced placement credit, distance learning, part-time degree program, services for LD students, student-designed majors, summer session for credit. *ROTC:* Army (c), Air Force (c).

Library 70,000 titles, 310 serial subscriptions, an OPAC.

Computers on Campus 130 computers available on campus for general student use. Internet access, at least one staffed computer lab available.

Student Life *Housing:* on-campus residence required through sophomore year. *Options:* men-only, women-only. *Activities and Organizations:* drama/theater group, student-run newspaper, television station, choral group, student government, Phi Beta Kappa, Bleacher Bums, Law Enforcement Association. *Campus security:* 24-hour emergency response devices and patrols. *Student Services:* health clinic.

Athletics Member NJCAA. *Intercollegiate sports:* basketball M(s)/W(s), cross-country running M(s)/W(s), track and field M(s)/W(s). *Intramural sports:* basketball M/W, cross-country running M/W, football M/W, golf M/W, racquetball M/W, softball M/W, table tennis M/W, tennis M/W, volleyball M/W.

Standardized Tests *Required:* TASP. *Recommended:* SAT I and SAT II or ACT (for placement).

Costs (2001–02) *Tuition:* state resident $1022 full-time, $16 per semester hour part-time; nonresident $1802 full-time, $32 per semester hour part-time. *Room and board:* $2900.

Financial Aid In 2001, 80 Federal Work-Study jobs.

Applying *Options:* early admission. *Required:* high school transcript. *Application deadline:* rolling (freshmen), rolling (transfers).

Admissions Contact Mrs. Andrea Rangel, Dean of Admissions and Records, South Plains College, 1401 College Avenue, Levelland, TX 78336. *Phone:* 806-894-9611 Ext. 2370. *Fax:* 806-897-3167. *E-mail:* arangel@spc.cc.tx.us.

SOUTH TEXAS COMMUNITY COLLEGE
McAllen, Texas

- **District-supported** 2-year, founded 1993
- **Calendar** semesters
- **Degree** certificates and associate
- **Suburban** 20-acre campus
- **Endowment** $17,971
- **Coed,** 12,469 undergraduate students, 44% full-time, 60% women, 40% men

Undergraduates 5,438 full-time, 7,031 part-time. 0.1% African American, 0.7% Asian American or Pacific Islander, 94% Hispanic American.

Freshmen *Admission:* 922 applied, 922 admitted, 1,279 enrolled. *Test scores:* SAT verbal scores over 500: 8%; SAT math scores over 500: 9%; SAT verbal scores over 600: 1%; SAT math scores over 600: 1%.

Faculty *Total:* 592, 50% full-time, 6% with terminal degrees. *Student/faculty ratio:* 11:1.

Majors Accounting; auto mechanic/technician; behavioral sciences; business administration; computer science; computer typography/composition; developmental/child psychology; education; emergency medical technology; heating/air conditioning/refrigeration; heavy equipment maintenance; hospitality management; hotel and restaurant management; human services; industrial radiologic technology; industrial technology; information sciences/systems; interdisciplinary studies; legal administrative assistant; liberal arts and sciences/liberal studies; machine technology; medical technology; nursing; occupational therapy; paralegal/legal assistant; plastics technology.

Academic Programs *Special study options:* academic remediation for entering students, accelerated degree program, adult/continuing education programs, cooperative education, off-campus study, part-time degree program, services for LD students, summer session for credit. *ROTC:* Army (c).

Library Learning Resources Center with 12,611 titles, 177 serial subscriptions, an OPAC, a Web page.

Computers on Campus 240 computers available on campus for general student use. A campuswide network can be accessed from off campus. At least one staffed computer lab available.

Student Life *Housing:* college housing not available. *Activities and Organizations:* Beta Epsilon Mu Honor Society, Automotive Technology Club, Child Care & Development Association club, Heating, Air Conditioning, and Ventilation Club, Writing in Literary Discussion Club. *Campus security:* 24-hour emergency response devices and patrols, late-night transport/escort service. *Student Services:* personal/psychological counseling.

Athletics *Intramural sports:* badminton M/W, basketball M/W, bowling M/W, football M/W, golf M/W, racquetball M/W, soccer M/W, softball M/W, table tennis M/W, volleyball M/W.

Standardized Tests *Required for some:* TASP.
Costs (2002–03) *One-time required fee:* $65. *Tuition:* area resident $1260 full-time, $52 per credit part-time; state resident $1478 full-time, $62 per credit part-time; nonresident $2770 full-time, $115 per credit part-time. Part-time tuition and fees vary according to course load.
Financial Aid In 2001, 100 Federal Work-Study jobs (averaging $3636). 18 State and other part-time jobs (averaging $3636).
Applying *Options:* common application, early admission, deferred entrance. *Required:* high school transcript. *Application deadline:* rolling (freshmen), rolling (transfers).
Admissions Contact Mr. William Serrata, Director of Enrollment Services and Registrar, South Texas Community College, 3201 West Pecan, McAllen, TX 78501. *Phone:* 956-668-6495.

SOUTHWEST SCHOOL OF ELECTRONICS
Austin, Texas

Admissions Contact 5424 Highway 290 West, Suite 200, Austin, TX 78735-8800.

SOUTHWEST TEXAS JUNIOR COLLEGE
Uvalde, Texas

Admissions Contact Mr. Joe C. Barker, Southwest Texas Junior College, 2401 Garner Field Road, Uvalde, TX 78801. *Phone:* 830-278-4401 Ext. 7284.

TARRANT COUNTY COLLEGE DISTRICT
Fort Worth, Texas

- **County-supported** 2-year, founded 1967
- **Calendar** semesters
- **Degree** certificates and associate
- **Urban** 667-acre campus
- **Coed,** 28,751 undergraduate students

Undergraduates 12% African American, 6% Asian American or Pacific Islander, 11% Hispanic American, 0.6% Native American, 0.6% international.
Faculty *Total:* 1,245, 38% full-time. *Student/faculty ratio:* 21:1.
Majors Accounting; architectural engineering technology; auto mechanic/technician; aviation technology; business administration; business marketing and marketing management; computer programming; computer science; construction technology; criminal justice/law enforcement administration; dental hygiene; developmental/child psychology; dietetics; drafting; educational media design; electrical/electronic engineering technology; electromechanical technology; emergency medical technology; fashion merchandising; fire science; food services technology; graphic/printing equipment; heating/air conditioning/refrigeration; horticulture science; industrial radiologic technology; liberal arts and sciences/liberal studies; machine technology; mechanical engineering technology; medical laboratory technician; medical records administration; medical technology; mental health/rehabilitation; nursing; operating room technician; paralegal/legal assistant; physical therapy; postal management; quality control technology; respiratory therapy; retail management; secretarial science; sign language interpretation; welding technology.
Academic Programs *Special study options:* academic remediation for entering students, adult/continuing education programs, advanced placement credit, English as a second language, honors programs, part-time degree program, services for LD students, summer session for credit. *ROTC:* Army (c), Air Force (c).
Library 160,520 titles, 1,532 serial subscriptions, an OPAC, a Web page.
Computers on Campus 2000 computers available on campus for general student use. Internet access, online (class) registration, at least one staffed computer lab available.
Student Life *Housing:* college housing not available. *Activities and Organizations:* drama/theater group, student-run newspaper, choral group. *Campus security:* 24-hour emergency response devices and patrols. *Student Services:* health clinic, personal/psychological counseling.
Athletics *Intramural sports:* football M, golf M, sailing M/W, table tennis M, tennis M/W, volleyball M/W.
Standardized Tests *Required:* TASP.
Costs (2001–02) *Tuition:* area resident $696 full-time, $29 per semester hour part-time; state resident $960 full-time, $41 per semester hour part-time; nonresident $140 per semester hour part-time. *Required fees:* $180 full-time.
Financial Aid In 2001, 271 Federal Work-Study jobs (averaging $1349). 39 State and other part-time jobs (averaging $838).
Applying *Options:* early admission. *Application fee:* $10. *Application deadline:* rolling (freshmen), rolling (transfers).
Admissions Contact Dr. Cathie Jackson, Director of Admissions and Records, Tarrant County College District, 1500 Houston Street, Fort Worth, TX 76102-6599. *Phone:* 817-515-5291.

TEMPLE COLLEGE
Temple, Texas

- **District-supported** 2-year, founded 1926
- **Calendar** semesters
- **Degree** certificates and associate
- **Small-town** 104-acre campus
- **Coed,** 3,585 undergraduate students, 39% full-time, 61% women, 39% men

Undergraduates 1,382 full-time, 2,203 part-time. Students come from 33 states and territories, 4 other countries, 12% African American, 0.9% Asian American or Pacific Islander, 14% Hispanic American, 0.7% Native American, 0.2% international, 1% live on campus.
Freshmen *Admission:* 3,585 applied, 3,585 admitted, 939 enrolled.
Faculty *Total:* 181, 44% full-time, 15% with terminal degrees. *Student/faculty ratio:* 15:1.
Majors Art; auto mechanic/technician; business administration; computer programming; computer science; criminal justice/law enforcement administration; data processing technology; dental hygiene; drafting; electrical/electronic engineering technology; industrial technology; law enforcement/police science; liberal arts and sciences/liberal studies; medical administrative assistant; medical laboratory technician; medical technology; nursing; practical nurse; respiratory therapy; secretarial science.
Academic Programs *Special study options:* academic remediation for entering students, adult/continuing education programs, internships, part-time degree program, summer session for credit.
Library Hubert Dawson Library with 44,326 titles, 357 serial subscriptions.
Computers on Campus 100 computers available on campus for general student use. Internet access, at least one staffed computer lab available.
Student Life *Activities and Organizations:* drama/theater group. *Campus security:* 24-hour emergency response devices and patrols. *Student Services:* personal/psychological counseling.
Athletics Member NJCAA. *Intercollegiate sports:* baseball M(s), basketball M(s)/W(s), golf M(s), softball W(s), tennis M(s)/W(s). *Intramural sports:* basketball M/W, golf M/W, racquetball M/W, soccer M/W, tennis M/W, volleyball M/W.
Standardized Tests *Required for some:* TASP. *Recommended:* ACT (for placement).
Costs (2001–02) *Tuition:* area resident $1290 full-time, $43 per hour part-time; state resident $1950 full-time, $65 per hour part-time; nonresident $3720 full-time, $124 per hour part-time. Full-time tuition and fees vary according to program. Part-time tuition and fees vary according to course load and program. *Required fees:* $100 full-time. *Payment plan:* installment. *Waivers:* senior citizens and employees or children of employees.
Financial Aid In 2001, 86 Federal Work-Study jobs (averaging $826). 7 State and other part-time jobs (averaging $951).
Applying *Options:* early admission. *Required for some:* high school transcript. *Application deadlines:* 8/23 (freshmen), 8/23 (transfers).
Admissions Contact Ms. Angela Balch, Director of Admissions and Records, Temple College, 2600 South First Street, Temple, TX 76504-7435. *Phone:* 254-298-8308. *Toll-free phone:* 800-460-4636. *Fax:* 254-298-8288. *E-mail:* angela.balch@templejc.edu.

TEXARKANA COLLEGE
Texarkana, Texas

- **State and locally supported** 2-year, founded 1927
- **Calendar** semesters
- **Degree** certificates and associate
- **Urban** 88-acre campus
- **Coed,** 3,875 undergraduate students

Undergraduates Students come from 7 states and territories, 3 other countries.
Faculty *Total:* 266, 32% full-time. *Student/faculty ratio:* 15:1.
Majors Agricultural sciences; alcohol/drug abuse counseling; art; auto mechanic/technician; biology; business administration; chemistry; computer programming;

Texarkana College (continued)
computer science; cosmetology; criminal justice/law enforcement administration; data entry/microcomputer applications related; data processing technology; drafting; electrical/electronic engineering technology; emergency medical technology; engineering; finance; heating/air conditioning/refrigeration; information technology; journalism; law enforcement/police science; liberal arts and sciences/liberal studies; mathematics; music; nursing; physics; practical nurse; real estate; retail management; secretarial science; theater arts/drama; welding technology; wood science/paper technology.
Academic Programs *Special study options:* academic remediation for entering students, adult/continuing education programs, advanced placement credit, cooperative education, part-time degree program, services for LD students, summer session for credit.
Library Palmer Memorial Library with 46,700 titles, 646 serial subscriptions.
Computers on Campus 105 computers available on campus for general student use. At least one staffed computer lab available.
Student Life *Activities and Organizations:* drama/theater group, student-run newspaper, radio station, choral group, Black Student Association, Earth Club. *Campus security:* 24-hour patrols. *Student Services:* personal/psychological counseling.
Athletics Member NJCAA. *Intercollegiate sports:* baseball M(s), softball W(s). *Intramural sports:* badminton M/W, basketball M, racquetball M/W, tennis M/W, volleyball M/W.
Standardized Tests *Required:* TASP.
Costs (2001–02) *Tuition:* area resident $750 full-time, $25 per credit hour part-time; state resident $900 full-time, $38 per credit hour part-time; nonresident $1600 full-time, $58 per credit hour part-time. Part-time tuition and fees vary according to course load. *Required fees:* $34 full-time, $2 per semester hour. *Room and board:* room only: $1200. *Payment plan:* installment.
Financial Aid In 2001, 30 Federal Work-Study jobs (averaging $3090).
Applying *Options:* early admission. *Required:* high school transcript. *Application deadline:* rolling (freshmen), rolling (transfers).
Admissions Contact Mr. Van Miller, Director of Admissions, Texarkana College, 2500 North Robison Road, Texarkana, TX 75599. *Phone:* 903-838-4541 Ext. 3358. *Fax:* 903-832-5030. *E-mail:* vmiller@tc.cc.tx.us.

TEXAS CULINARY ACADEMY
Austin, Texas

- **Independent** 2-year
- **Degree** associate
- **Coed,** 200 undergraduate students, 100% full-time, 45% women, 55% men

Faculty *Total:* 18, 78% full-time.
Majors Culinary arts.
Student Life *Campus security:* 24-hour emergency response devices.
Costs (2002–03) *Tuition:* $32,000 full-time.
Applying *Required:* essay or personal statement, high school transcript.
Admissions Contact Mr. Larry Van Loon, Director of Admissions, Texas Culinary Academy, 11400 Burnet Road, Austin, TX 78758. *Phone:* 512-837-2665. *Toll-free phone:* 888-553-2433.

TEXAS SOUTHMOST COLLEGE
Brownsville, Texas

Admissions Contact Mr. Ernesto Garcia, Director of Enrollment, Texas Southmost College, 80 Fort Brown, Brownsville, TX 78520-4991. *Phone:* 956-544-8254.

TEXAS STATE TECHNICAL COLLEGE-HARLINGEN
Harlingen, Texas

- **State-supported** 2-year, founded 1967, part of Texas State Technical College System
- **Calendar** quarters
- **Degree** certificates and associate
- **Small-town** 118-acre campus
- **Coed,** 3,846 undergraduate students, 52% full-time, 50% women, 50% men

Undergraduates 2,002 full-time, 1,844 part-time. Students come from 10 states and territories, 13% transferred in, 8% live on campus.
Freshmen *Admission:* 1,980 applied, 1,980 admitted, 1,003 enrolled.
Faculty *Total:* 252, 61% full-time, 2% with terminal degrees. *Student/faculty ratio:* 16:1.
Majors Aircraft mechanic/airframe; auto body repair; biomedical engineering-related technology; chemical engineering technology; computer graphics; computer graphics; computer/information sciences; computer/information technology services administration and management related; computer maintenance technology; computer programming; computer programming related; computer programming (specific applications); computer programming, vendor/product certification; computer science; computer science related; computer software and media applications related; computer systems networking/telecommunications; computer/technical support; construction technology; data processing technology; dental assistant; dental hygiene; dental laboratory technician; drafting; electrical/electronic engineering technology; electromechanical technology; environmental technology; farm/ranch management; food services technology; graphic design/commercial art/illustration; heating/air conditioning/refrigeration; industrial technology; information technology; institutional food workers; instrumentation technology; legal administrative assistant; machine technology; medical records administration; operating room technician; secretarial science; system administration; system/networking/LAN/WAN management; Web/multimedia management/webmaster; Web page, digital/multimedia and information resources design; welding technology; word processing.
Academic Programs *Special study options:* academic remediation for entering students, adult/continuing education programs, cooperative education, distance learning, double majors, English as a second language, internships, part-time degree program, services for LD students, summer session for credit.
Library Texas State Technical College Learning Resource Center with 25,000 titles, 413 serial subscriptions, an OPAC, a Web page.
Computers on Campus 250 computers available on campus for general student use. Internet access, at least one staffed computer lab available.
Student Life *Housing Options:* men-only, women-only, disabled students. *Activities and Organizations:* student-run newspaper, Student Congress, Vocational Industrial Clubs of America, Business Professionals of America. *Campus security:* 24-hour emergency response devices and patrols, late-night transport/escort service, night watchman for housing area. *Student Services:* health clinic, personal/psychological counseling, women's center.
Athletics *Intramural sports:* badminton M/W, basketball M/W, bowling M/W, cross-country running M/W, football M/W, golf M/W, racquetball M/W, soccer M/W, softball M/W, table tennis M/W, tennis M/W, track and field M/W, volleyball M/W, weight lifting M/W.
Standardized Tests *Required:* TASP. *Recommended:* SAT I or ACT (for placement).
Costs (2001–02) *Tuition:* state resident $1332 full-time, $37 per credit hour part-time; nonresident $3420 full-time, $90 per credit hour part-time. Full-time tuition and fees vary according to course load. Part-time tuition and fees vary according to course load. *Required fees:* $936 full-time, $26 per credit hour. *Room and board:* $4407; room only: $1560. Room and board charges vary according to board plan and housing facility. *Payment plan:* installment.
Financial Aid In 2001, 200 Federal Work-Study jobs (averaging $2800). 5 State and other part-time jobs (averaging $2800).
Applying *Options:* common application, early admission, deferred entrance. *Required:* high school transcript. *Application deadline:* rolling (freshmen), rolling (transfers). *Notification:* continuous (freshmen).
Admissions Contact Mrs. Elva Short, Director of Admissions and Records, Texas State Technical College-Harlingen, 1902 North Loop 499, Harlingen, TX 78550-3697. *Phone:* 956-364-4326. *Toll-free phone:* 800-852-8784. *Fax:* 956-364-5117. *E-mail:* arangel@harlingen.tstc.edu.

TEXAS STATE TECHNICAL COLLEGE-WACO
Waco, Texas

- **State-supported** 2-year, founded 1965, part of Texas State Technical College System
- **Calendar** quarters
- **Degree** certificates and associate
- **Suburban** 200-acre campus
- **Coed,** 1,038 undergraduate students, 89% full-time, 19% women, 81% men

Undergraduates 926 full-time, 112 part-time. Students come from 32 states and territories, 47% transferred in.
Freshmen *Admission:* 1,534 applied, 1,534 admitted, 1,038 enrolled.
Faculty *Total:* 280, 89% full-time. *Student/faculty ratio:* 30:1.
Majors Agricultural/food products processing; aircraft mechanic/airframe; aircraft mechanic/powerplant; aircraft pilot (professional); audio engineering; auto

body repair; auto mechanic/technician; aviation/airway science; aviation technology; biomedical engineering-related technology; biomedical technology; chemical engineering technology; chemical technology; computer engineering technology; computer/information sciences; computer maintenance technology; computer programming; computer science; culinary arts; dental assistant; diesel engine mechanic; drafting; educational media technology; electrical/electronic engineering technology; electrical/electronics drafting; food services technology; graphic design/commercial art/illustration; graphic/printing equipment; heating/air conditioning/refrigeration; heating/air conditioning/refrigeration technology; heavy equipment maintenance; industrial technology; information sciences/systems; institutional food workers; instrumentation technology; laser/optical technology; machine technology; mechanical engineering technology; nuclear technology; occupational safety/health technology; ornamental horticulture; photographic technology; quality control technology; turf management; welding technology.

Academic Programs *Special study options:* academic remediation for entering students, adult/continuing education programs, cooperative education, distance learning, internships, part-time degree program, services for LD students, summer session for credit.

Library Texas State Technical College-Waco/Marshall Campus Library with 65,065 titles, 710 serial subscriptions, 1,904 audiovisual materials, an OPAC, a Web page.

Computers on Campus 900 computers available on campus for general student use. A campuswide network can be accessed from student residence rooms that provide access to various software packages. At least one staffed computer lab available.

Student Life *Housing:* on-campus residence required for freshman year. *Options:* coed, men-only, women-only, disabled students. *Activities and Organizations:* student-run newspaper, Automotive VICA, Society of Mexican-American Engineers and Scientists, Texas Association of Black Persons In Higher Education, Phi Theta Kappa. *Campus security:* 24-hour emergency response devices and patrols, late-night transport/escort service, controlled dormitory access. *Student Services:* health clinic, personal/psychological counseling, women's center.

Athletics *Intramural sports:* basketball M/W, football M, golf M/W, racquetball M/W, softball M/W, volleyball M/W, weight lifting M.

Standardized Tests *Required:* CPT, TASP.

Costs (2001–02) *Tuition:* state resident $1260 full-time, $42 per credit hour part-time; nonresident $4050 full-time, $135 per credit hour part-time. Full-time tuition and fees vary according to course load. Part-time tuition and fees vary according to course load. *Required fees:* $510 full-time, $15 per credit hour, $52 per year part-time. *Room and board:* room only: $2352. Room and board charges vary according to housing facility and location. *Payment plan:* installment.

Financial Aid In 2001, 125 Federal Work-Study jobs (averaging $2500). 150 State and other part-time jobs.

Applying *Options:* common application, electronic application, early admission. *Required:* high school transcript. *Required for some:* interview. *Application deadline:* rolling (freshmen), rolling (transfers). *Notification:* continuous (freshmen).

Admissions Contact Mr. Rick Gauer, Director, Recruiting and Admissions, Texas State Technical College-Waco, 3801 Campus Drive, Waco, TX 76705. *Phone:* 254-867-2026. *Toll-free phone:* 800-792-8784. *E-mail:* lrobert@tstc.edu.

Texas State Technical College-West Texas
Sweetwater, Texas

- **State-supported** 2-year, founded 1970, part of Texas State Technical College System
- **Calendar** quarters
- **Degree** certificates and associate
- **Rural** 115-acre campus
- **Endowment** $50,000
- **Coed,** 1,607 undergraduate students, 65% full-time, 42% women, 58% men

Undergraduates 1,043 full-time, 564 part-time. Students come from 3 states and territories, 1 other country, 1% are from out of state, 4% African American, 0.4% Asian American or Pacific Islander, 22% Hispanic American, 0.6% Native American, 10% transferred in, 29% live on campus.

Freshmen *Admission:* 1,192 enrolled.

Faculty *Total:* 160, 66% full-time. *Student/faculty ratio:* 10:1.

Majors Aircraft mechanic/airframe; auto mechanic/technician; business systems networking/ telecommunications; computer engineering technology; computer programming; diesel engine mechanic; drafting; electrical/electronic engineering technology; emergency medical technology; environmental technology; machine technology; medical records technology; robotics technology.

Academic Programs *Special study options:* academic remediation for entering students, adult/continuing education programs, advanced placement credit, cooperative education, distance learning, internships, part-time degree program, summer session for credit.

Library Texas State Technical College Library with 14,895 titles, 212 serial subscriptions.

Computers on Campus 25 computers available on campus for general student use. A campuswide network can be accessed from student residence rooms and from off campus. Internet access available.

Student Life *Housing Options:* coed, disabled students. *Activities and Organizations:* Student Government Association, Vocational Industrial Clubs of America, Mexican-American Student Club, Auto Tech 2000, Vocational Nursing Club. *Campus security:* 24-hour patrols. *Student Services:* health clinic, personal/psychological counseling.

Athletics *Intramural sports:* basketball M/W, bowling M/W, football M/W, golf M/W, racquetball M/W, soccer M/W, softball M/W, table tennis M/W, tennis M/W, volleyball M/W, weight lifting M/W.

Costs (2002–03) *Tuition:* area resident $2330 full-time; state resident $44 per credit part-time; nonresident $5447 full-time, $135 per credit part-time. Full-time tuition and fees vary according to course load. Part-time tuition and fees vary according to course load. *Required fees:* $16 per credit, $5 per term part-time. *Room and board:* $3550. Room and board charges vary according to board plan and housing facility. *Payment plan:* installment. *Waivers:* senior citizens.

Applying *Options:* common application, early admission, deferred entrance. *Required:* high school transcript. *Application deadline:* rolling (freshmen), rolling (transfers). *Notification:* continuous (freshmen).

Admissions Contact Ms. Maria Aguirre-Acuna, Coordinator of New Students, Texas State Technical College-West Texas, 300 College Drive, Sweetwater, TX 79556-4108. *Phone:* 915-235-7349. *Toll-free phone:* 800-592-8784. *Fax:* 915-235-7416. *E-mail:* juanita.garcia@sweetwater.tstc.edu.

Tomball College
Tomball, Texas

- **State and locally supported** 2-year, founded 1988, part of North Harris Montgomery Community College District
- **Calendar** semesters
- **Degree** certificates and associate
- **Suburban** 210-acre campus with easy access to Houston
- **Coed,** 8,357 undergraduate students, 35% full-time, 59% women, 41% men

Undergraduates 2,928 full-time, 5,429 part-time. 0.6% are from out of state, 6% African American, 5% Asian American or Pacific Islander, 12% Hispanic American, 0.4% Native American, 2% international, 6% transferred in.

Freshmen *Admission:* 2,587 enrolled.

Faculty *Total:* 359, 27% full-time.

Majors Accounting; business administration; computer programming; electrical/electronic engineering technology; human services; legal administrative assistant; medical administrative assistant; nursing; occupational therapy; veterinary technology.

Academic Programs *Special study options:* academic remediation for entering students, adult/continuing education programs, advanced placement credit, cooperative education, English as a second language, honors programs, internships, part-time degree program, services for LD students, summer session for credit.

Library Learning Resource Center with 24,063 titles, 385 serial subscriptions, an OPAC, a Web page.

Computers on Campus 92 computers available on campus for general student use. A campuswide network can be accessed from off campus. At least one staffed computer lab available.

Student Life *Housing:* college housing not available. *Activities and Organizations:* Phi Theta Kappa, Culture Club, Veterinary Technicians Student Organization, Human Services Club, Student Nurses Association, national fraternities, national sororities. *Campus security:* 24-hour emergency response devices, late-night transport/escort service, trained security personnel during open hours. *Student Services:* personal/psychological counseling.

Standardized Tests *Recommended:* SAT I or ACT (for admission).

Costs (2002–03) *Tuition:* area resident $672 full-time, $28 per credit part-time; state resident $1632 full-time, $68 per credit part-time; nonresident $2280 full-time, $95 per credit part-time. Full-time tuition and fees vary according to course load. Part-time tuition and fees vary according to course load. *Required fees:* $180 full-time, $7 per credit, $12 per term part-time. *Payment plan:* installment. *Waivers:* employees or children of employees.

Tomball College (continued)
Financial Aid In 2001, 6 Federal Work-Study jobs (averaging $3000).
Applying *Options:* common application, early admission.
Admissions Contact Mr. Larry Rideaux, Interim Dean of Enrollment Services, Tomball College, 30555 Tomball Parkway, Tomball, TX 77375-4036. *Phone:* 281-351-3334. *Fax:* 281-357-3773. *E-mail:* tc.advisors@nhmccd.edu.

TRINITY VALLEY COMMUNITY COLLEGE
Athens, Texas

- **State and locally supported** 2-year, founded 1946
- **Calendar** semesters
- **Degree** certificates, diplomas, and associate
- **Small-town** 65-acre campus with easy access to Dallas-Fort Worth
- **Coed,** 4,605 undergraduate students

Undergraduates Students come from 48 states and territories, 16% African American, 0.4% Asian American or Pacific Islander, 6% Hispanic American, 0.5% Native American, 0.7% international.
Faculty *Total:* 217, 56% full-time. *Student/faculty ratio:* 21:1.
Majors Accounting; agricultural education; animal sciences; art; auto mechanic/technician; biology; business administration; business education; business marketing and marketing management; chemistry; child care/development; computer science; corrections; cosmetology; criminal justice/law enforcement administration; dance; data processing technology; developmental/child psychology; drafting; early childhood education; earth sciences; education; elementary education; emergency medical technology; English; farm/ranch management; fashion merchandising; finance; heating/air conditioning/refrigeration; history; horticulture science; insurance/risk management; journalism; law enforcement/police science; legal administrative assistant; liberal arts and sciences/liberal studies; mathematics; music; nursing; operating room technician; physical education; physical sciences; political science; practical nurse; pre-engineering; psychology; range management; real estate; religious studies; sociology; Spanish; speech/rhetorical studies; theater arts/drama; welding technology.
Academic Programs *Special study options:* academic remediation for entering students, adult/continuing education programs, cooperative education, internships, part-time degree program, services for LD students, summer session for credit.
Library Main Library plus 1 other with 26,234 titles, 225 serial subscriptions.
Computers on Campus 66 computers available on campus for general student use. Internet access, at least one staffed computer lab available.
Student Life *Activities and Organizations:* drama/theater group, student-run newspaper, choral group, marching band, Student Senate, Phi Theta Kappa, Delta Epsilon Chi. *Campus security:* 24-hour emergency response devices and patrols, controlled dormitory access. *Student Services:* personal/psychological counseling.
Athletics Member NJCAA. *Intercollegiate sports:* basketball M(s)/W(s), football M(s), golf M(s). *Intramural sports:* basketball M/W, football M, golf M, soccer M, table tennis M/W, volleyball M/W.
Standardized Tests *Required:* TASP. *Recommended:* ACT (for placement).
Costs (2001–02) *Tuition:* area resident $180 full-time; state resident $360 full-time. *Required fees:* $120 full-time. *Room and board:* $1581; room only: $525. *Payment plan:* installment. *Waivers:* employees or children of employees.
Financial Aid In 2001, 35 Federal Work-Study jobs (averaging $1544). 5 State and other part-time jobs (averaging $1544).
Applying *Options:* common application, early admission. *Application deadline:* rolling (freshmen), rolling (transfers). *Notification:* continuous (freshmen).
Admissions Contact Dr. Collette Hilliard, Dean of Enrollment Management and Registrar, Trinity Valley Community College, 100 Cardinal Drive, Athens, TX 75751-2765. *Phone:* 903-675-6217.

TYLER JUNIOR COLLEGE
Tyler, Texas

- **State and locally supported** 2-year, founded 1926
- **Calendar** semesters
- **Degree** certificates and associate
- **Suburban** 85-acre campus
- **Coed,** 8,451 undergraduate students, 58% full-time, 58% women, 42% men

Undergraduates 4,902 full-time, 3,549 part-time. Students come from 30 states and territories, 25 other countries, 1% are from out of state, 20% African American, 1% Asian American or Pacific Islander, 6% Hispanic American, 0.4% Native American, 0.6% international, 8% live on campus.
Freshmen *Admission:* 2,754 enrolled.
Faculty *Total:* 364, 50% full-time. *Student/faculty ratio:* 28:1.
Majors Accounting; agricultural business; agricultural economics; agricultural education; agricultural sciences; art; behavioral sciences; business administration; business marketing and marketing management; computer engineering technology; computer graphics; computer programming related; computer science; computer science related; computer systems networking/telecommunications; criminal justice/law enforcement administration; data entry/microcomputer applications; dental hygiene; developmental/child psychology; drafting; electrical/electronic engineering technology; environmental technology; farm/ranch management; fashion merchandising; finance; fire science; graphic design/commercial art/illustration; graphic/printing equipment; health services administration; heating/air conditioning/refrigeration; horticulture science; human resources management; industrial radiologic technology; information technology; law enforcement/police science; legal administrative assistant; liberal arts and sciences/liberal studies; medical administrative assistant; medical laboratory technician; modern languages; music; nursing; optometric/ophthalmic laboratory technician; ornamental horticulture; petroleum technology; photography; plastics technology; postal management; practical nurse; psychology; real estate; recreation/leisure studies; respiratory therapy; secretarial science; sign language interpretation; social sciences; speech/rhetorical studies; surveying; welding technology.
Academic Programs *Special study options:* academic remediation for entering students, accelerated degree program, adult/continuing education programs, advanced placement credit, distance learning, English as a second language, freshman honors college, honors programs, part-time degree program, services for LD students, summer session for credit.
Library Vaughn Library and Learning Resource Center with 569 serial subscriptions, 64,776 audiovisual materials, an OPAC.
Computers on Campus 60 computers available on campus for general student use. Internet access, at least one staffed computer lab available.
Student Life *Housing Options:* men-only, women-only. *Activities and Organizations:* drama/theater group, student-run newspaper, choral group, marching band, student government, religious affiliation clubs, Phi Theta Kappa, national fraternities, national sororities. *Campus security:* 24-hour patrols, controlled dormitory access. *Student Services:* health clinic, personal/psychological counseling.
Athletics Member NJCAA. *Intercollegiate sports:* baseball M(s), basketball M(s)/W(s), football M(s), golf M/W, soccer M(s), tennis M(s)/W(s), volleyball W. *Intramural sports:* basketball M/W, racquetball M/W, volleyball M/W, weight lifting M/W.
Standardized Tests *Required:* TASP. *Recommended:* SAT I and SAT II or ACT (for placement).
Costs (2001–02) *Tuition:* area resident $830 full-time, $15 per semester hour part-time; state resident $1280 full-time, $30 per semester hour part-time; nonresident $1580 full-time, $40 per semester hour part-time. *Required fees:* $11 per semester hour, $10 per term part-time. *Room and board:* $2800. *Payment plan:* installment. *Waivers:* senior citizens.
Financial Aid In 2001, 37 Federal Work-Study jobs (averaging $1071). 30 State and other part-time jobs (averaging $891).
Applying *Options:* common application, early admission. *Required:* high school transcript. *Application deadline:* rolling (freshmen), rolling (transfers).
Admissions Contact Ms. Janna Chancey, Director of Enrollment Management, Tyler Junior College, PO Box 9020, Tyler, TX 75711. *Phone:* 903-510-2396. *Toll-free phone:* 800-687-5680. *Fax:* 903-510-2634. *E-mail:* klew@tjc.tyler.cc.tx.us.

UNIVERSAL TECHNICAL INSTITUTE
Houston, Texas

Admissions Contact Randy Whitman, Director of Admissions, Universal Technical Institute, 721 Lockhaven Drive, Houston, TX 77073-5598. *Phone:* 281-443-6262 Ext. 261.

VERNON COLLEGE
Vernon, Texas

- **State and locally supported** 2-year, founded 1970
- **Calendar** semesters
- **Degree** certificates and associate
- **Small-town** 100-acre campus

■ **Coed,** 2,270 undergraduate students

Undergraduates Students come from 32 states and territories, 4 other countries, 0.1% are from out of state, 7% African American, 1% Asian American or Pacific Islander, 12% Hispanic American, 1% Native American, 0.8% international.
Faculty *Total:* 128, 45% full-time. *Student/faculty ratio:* 17:1.
Majors Accounting; auto mechanic/technician; business administration; child care/guidance; cosmetology; criminal justice/law enforcement administration; data processing technology; drafting; farm/ranch management; legal studies; liberal arts and sciences/liberal studies; machine technology; medical records technology; nursing; practical nurse; secretarial science.
Academic Programs *Special study options:* academic remediation for entering students, adult/continuing education programs, advanced placement credit, cooperative education, distance learning, double majors, internships, part-time degree program, services for LD students, summer session for credit.
Library Wright Library with 29,000 titles, 200 serial subscriptions, an OPAC, a Web page.
Computers on Campus 100 computers available on campus for general student use. Internet access, online (class) registration, at least one staffed computer lab available.
Student Life *Housing Options:* men-only, women-only. *Activities and Organizations:* drama/theater group, choral group, Student Government Association, Baptist Student Union. *Campus security:* 24-hour patrols. *Student Services:* health clinic, personal/psychological counseling.
Athletics Member NJCAA. *Intercollegiate sports:* baseball M(s), equestrian sports M(s)/W(s), softball W(s), volleyball W(s). *Intramural sports:* archery M/W, basketball M/W, football M/W, golf M/W, tennis M/W, volleyball M/W.
Standardized Tests *Required:* TASP.
Costs (2001–02) *Tuition:* area resident $544 full-time, $17 per credit hour part-time; state resident $960 full-time, $30 per credit hour part-time; nonresident $2080 full-time, $65 per credit hour part-time. Full-time tuition and fees vary according to course load. Part-time tuition and fees vary according to course load. *Required fees:* $416 full-time. *Room and board:* $2243. Room and board charges vary according to board plan. *Payment plan:* installment.
Financial Aid In 2001, 50 Federal Work-Study jobs (averaging $2750). 2 State and other part-time jobs (averaging $2750).
Applying *Options:* electronic application, early admission. *Application deadline:* rolling (freshmen), rolling (transfers).
Admissions Contact Mr. Joe Hite, Dean of Admissions/Registrar, Vernon College, 4400 College Drive, Vernon, TX 76384-4092. *Phone:* 940-552-6291 Ext. 2204. *Fax:* 940-553-1753. *E-mail:* sdavenport@vrjc.cc.tx.us.

VICTORIA COLLEGE
Victoria, Texas

- **County-supported** 2-year, founded 1925
- **Calendar** semesters
- **Degree** certificates and associate
- **Urban** 80-acre campus
- **Coed,** 4,010 undergraduate students, 42% full-time, 64% women, 36% men

Undergraduates Students come from 4 states and territories, 2 other countries, 4% African American, 1% Asian American or Pacific Islander, 27% Hispanic American, 0.2% Native American, 0.3% international.
Majors Accounting; business administration; business systems networking/ telecommunications; computer programming; drafting; electrical/electronic engineering technology; emergency medical technology; industrial technology; information sciences/systems; law enforcement/police science; liberal arts and sciences/ liberal studies; medical laboratory technician; nursing; paralegal/legal assistant; respiratory therapy; secretarial science.
Academic Programs *Special study options:* academic remediation for entering students, adult/continuing education programs, advanced placement credit, part-time degree program, services for LD students, summer session for credit.
Library Victoria College Library with 150,000 titles, 1,500 serial subscriptions.
Computers on Campus 225 computers available on campus for general student use. Internet access, at least one staffed computer lab available.
Student Life *Housing:* college housing not available. *Activities and Organizations:* drama/theater group, choral group, Student Senate. *Campus security:* 24-hour emergency response devices. *Student Services:* personal/psychological counseling.
Athletics *Intramural sports:* basketball M, softball M.
Standardized Tests *Required:* TASP. *Required for some:* SAT I or ACT (for placement).
Costs (2002–03) *Tuition:* area resident $660 full-time, $22 per credit hour part-time; state resident $990 full-time, $33 per credit hour part-time; nonresident $1650 full-time, $55 per credit hour part-time. *Required fees:* $324 full-time.
Applying *Required:* high school transcript. *Application deadline:* rolling (freshmen), rolling (transfers).
Admissions Contact Mrs. Martha Watts, Registrar, Victoria College, 2200 East Red River, Victoria, TX 77901-4494. *Phone:* 361-573-3291. *Fax:* 512-582-2525.

WADE COLLEGE
Dallas, Texas

- **Proprietary** 2-year, founded 1965
- **Calendar** trimesters
- **Degree** associate
- **Urban** 175-acre campus
- **Coed, primarily women,** 87 undergraduate students, 100% full-time, 91% women, 9% men

Undergraduates 87 full-time. 40% are from out of state, 34% transferred in, 45% live on campus. *Retention:* 65% of 2001 full-time freshmen returned.
Freshmen *Admission:* 116 applied, 111 admitted, 87 enrolled.
Faculty *Total:* 12, 33% full-time. *Student/faculty ratio:* 16:1.
Majors Computer graphics; computer graphics; design/visual communications; fashion design/illustration; fashion merchandising; interior design.
Academic Programs *Special study options:* academic remediation for entering students, double majors, part-time degree program, services for LD students, summer session for credit.
Library College Library with 15,000 titles, 160 serial subscriptions, 1,500 audiovisual materials, an OPAC.
Computers on Campus 50 computers available on campus for general student use. Internet access, at least one staffed computer lab available.
Student Life *Housing Options:* coed, men-only, women-only. *Activities and Organizations:* Fashion Group, Phi Theta Kappa, Phi Beta Lambda, Interior Design Student Group. *Campus security:* 24-hour emergency response devices and patrols, late-night transport/escort service, controlled dormitory access. *Student Services:* personal/psychological counseling, women's center.
Costs (2002–03) *Tuition:* $7850 full-time, $785 per term part-time. *Required fees:* $125 full-time, $250 per term part-time. *Room only:* $3360.
Applying *Options:* common application, electronic application. *Required:* high school transcript, interview. *Application deadline:* rolling (freshmen), rolling (transfers).
Admissions Contact Ms. Suzan Wade, Admissions Director, Wade College, M5120 International Apparel Mart, PO Box 586343, Dallas, TX 75258-6343. *Phone:* 214-637-3530. *Toll-free phone:* 800-624-4850. *Fax:* 214-637-0827. *E-mail:* admissions@wadecollege.com.

WEATHERFORD COLLEGE
Weatherford, Texas

- **State and locally supported** 2-year, founded 1869
- **Calendar** semesters
- **Degree** certificates, diplomas, and associate
- **Small-town** 94-acre campus with easy access to Dallas-Fort Worth
- **Endowment** $42.5 million
- **Coed,** 3,172 undergraduate students, 53% full-time, 60% women, 40% men

Undergraduates 2% African American, 0.6% Asian American or Pacific Islander, 6% Hispanic American, 0.7% Native American, 1% international, 7% live on campus.
Freshmen *Admission:* 2,461 admitted.
Faculty *Total:* 100, 65% full-time. *Student/faculty ratio:* 31:1.
Majors Biological/physical sciences; business administration; computer graphics; computer programming; corrections; cosmetology; criminal justice/law enforcement administration; emergency medical technology; fire science; information sciences/systems; liberal arts and sciences/liberal studies; nursing; pharmacy technician/assistant; respiratory therapy; secretarial science.
Academic Programs *Special study options:* academic remediation for entering students, adult/continuing education programs, cooperative education, distance learning, freshman honors college, honors programs, internships, part-time degree program, services for LD students, student-designed majors, summer session for credit. *ROTC:* Air Force (c).
Library Weatherford College Library with 59,499 titles, 362 serial subscriptions, an OPAC, a Web page.

Weatherford College (continued)

Computers on Campus 85 computers available on campus for general student use. A campuswide network can be accessed from off campus. Internet access, at least one staffed computer lab available.

Student Life *Housing Options:* coed. *Activities and Organizations:* drama/theater group, choral group, Black Awareness Student Organization, Criminal Justice Club, Phi Theta Kappa. *Campus security:* 24-hour emergency response devices and patrols, late-night transport/escort service. *Student Services:* personal/psychological counseling.

Athletics Member NJCAA. *Intercollegiate sports:* basketball M/W, golf M, tennis M/W.

Standardized Tests *Required:* TASP. *Recommended:* SAT I or ACT (for placement).

Costs (2002–03) *Tuition:* area resident $750 full-time, $25 per semester hour part-time; state resident $990 full-time, $33 per semester hour part-time; nonresident $2400 full-time, $80 per semester hour part-time. *Required fees:* $250 full-time. *Room and board:* $2707. *Waivers:* senior citizens.

Applying *Options:* early admission. *Application deadline:* rolling (freshmen), rolling (transfers). *Notification:* continuous (freshmen).

Admissions Contact Mr. Ralph Willingham, Dean of Admissions, Weatherford College, 308 East Park Avenue, Weatherford, TX 76086-5699. *Phone:* 817-598-6248. *Toll-free phone:* 800-287-5471. *Fax:* 817-598-6205. *E-mail:* admissions@wc.edu.

WESTERN TECHNICAL INSTITUTE
El Paso, Texas

Admissions Contact Bill Terrell, Senior Vice President, Western Technical Institute, 1000 Texas Avenue, El Paso, TX 79901-1536. *Phone:* 915-532-3737.

WESTERN TECHNICAL INSTITUTE
El Paso, Texas

- **Private** 2-year

Admissions Contact 4710 Alabama Street, El Paso, TX 79930-2610.

WESTERN TEXAS COLLEGE
Snyder, Texas

- **State and locally supported** 2-year, founded 1969
- **Calendar** semesters
- **Degree** associate
- **Small-town** 165-acre campus
- **Endowment** $653,379
- **Coed,** 1,404 undergraduate students

Undergraduates Students come from 9 states and territories, 10 other countries, 20% live on campus.

Freshmen *Admission:* 1,415 applied, 1,384 admitted.

Faculty *Total:* 55, 82% full-time. *Student/faculty ratio:* 17:1.

Majors Accounting; agricultural education; agricultural sciences; art; art education; auto mechanic/technician; business administration; business marketing and marketing management; computer engineering technology; computer science; corrections; criminal justice/law enforcement administration; education; journalism; landscape architecture; law enforcement/police science; liberal arts and sciences/liberal studies; mass communications; practical nurse; recreation/leisure facilities management; secretarial science; welding technology.

Academic Programs *Special study options:* academic remediation for entering students, adult/continuing education programs, advanced placement credit, internships, part-time degree program, services for LD students, student-designed majors, summer session for credit.

Library Western Texas College Resource Center with 43,000 titles, 127 serial subscriptions, a Web page.

Computers on Campus 40 computers available on campus for general student use. At least one staffed computer lab available.

Student Life *Housing:* on-campus residence required for freshman year. *Options:* coed. *Activities and Organizations:* drama/theater group, student-run newspaper, choral group. *Campus security:* 24-hour emergency response devices and patrols. *Student Services:* personal/psychological counseling.

Athletics Member NJCAA. *Intercollegiate sports:* basketball W(s), golf M(s). *Intramural sports:* basketball M/W, bowling M/W, football M, racquetball M/W, soccer M, softball M/W, swimming M/W, tennis M/W, volleyball M/W, weight lifting M/W.

Standardized Tests *Required:* TASP. *Required for some:* ACT (for placement).

Costs (2002–03) *Tuition:* state resident $930 full-time; nonresident $1130 full-time. *Required fees:* $323 full-time. *Room and board:* $3300; room only: $1600.

Financial Aid In 2001, 30 Federal Work-Study jobs (averaging $1600).

Applying *Options:* early admission, deferred entrance. *Required:* high school transcript. *Application deadline:* rolling (freshmen), rolling (transfers). *Notification:* continuous (freshmen).

Admissions Contact Mr. Jim Clifton, Dean of Student Services, Western Texas College, 6200 College Avenue, Snyder, TX 79549-6105. *Phone:* 915-573-8511 Ext. 204. *Toll-free phone:* 888-GO-TO-WTC.

WESTWOOD COLLEGE OF AVIATION TECHNOLOGY-HOUSTON
Houston, Texas

- **Proprietary** 2-year
- **Degree** associate
- **Coed,** 380 undergraduate students

Faculty *Total:* 32, 81% full-time.

Majors Aircraft mechanic/airframe; aircraft mechanic/powerplant.

Costs (2002–03) *Tuition:* Standard program price $3,355 per term, lab fees and books additional, 5 terms/year, program length: associate degree = 7 terms.

Admissions Contact Mr. Glen E. Feist, Director of Admissions, Westwood College of Aviation Technology-Houston, 8880 Telephone Road, Houston, TX 77061. *Phone:* 713-645-4444.

WESTWOOD INSTITUTE OF TECHNOLOGY-FORT WORTH
Euless, Texas

- **Proprietary** 2-year
- **Degree** associate
- **Coed**

Majors Computer systems networking/telecommunications; graphic design/commercial art/illustration; multimedia.

Costs (2002–03) *Tuition:* $8,518 (in-district), $10,664 (out-of-district), $13,994 (out-of-state) for 16.5 month Airframe and Powerplant program. (Cost does not include books or tools which may be required).

Admissions Contact Mr. Bruce Schlee, Director of Admissions, Westwood Institute of Technology-Fort Worth, 1331 Airport Freeway, Suite 402, Euless, TX 76040. *Phone:* 817-685-9994.

WHARTON COUNTY JUNIOR COLLEGE
Wharton, Texas

- **State and locally supported** 2-year, founded 1946
- **Calendar** semesters
- **Degree** certificates and associate
- **Rural** 90-acre campus with easy access to Houston
- **Coed,** 5,281 undergraduate students

Undergraduates Students come from 8 states and territories, 5 other countries, 9% African American, 5% Asian American or Pacific Islander, 20% Hispanic American, 0.4% Native American, 0.4% international, 5% live on campus.

Faculty *Total:* 220.

Majors Agricultural sciences; art; auto mechanic/technician; behavioral sciences; biology; business administration; chemistry; computer science; criminal justice/law enforcement administration; data processing technology; dental hygiene; drafting; electrical/electronic engineering technology; English; farm/ranch management; industrial radiologic technology; mathematics; medical laboratory technician; medical records administration; music; nursing; ornamental horticulture; physical education; physical therapy; pre-engineering; secretarial science; Spanish; speech/rhetorical studies; theater arts/drama.

Academic Programs *Special study options:* academic remediation for entering students, adult/continuing education programs, advanced placement credit, part-time degree program, student-designed majors, summer session for credit.

Library J. M. Hodges Library with 51,478 titles, 536 serial subscriptions.

Computers on Campus 350 computers available on campus for general student use. At least one staffed computer lab available.
Student Life *Activities and Organizations:* drama/theater group. *Campus security:* 24-hour patrols. *Student Services:* personal/psychological counseling.
Athletics Member NJCAA. *Intercollegiate sports:* baseball M(s), volleyball W(s).
Standardized Tests *Required:* TASP. *Recommended:* SAT I or ACT (for placement).
Applying *Application fee:* $10. *Required:* high school transcript, minimum 2.0 GPA. *Application deadlines:* 8/15 (freshmen), 8/15 (transfers).
Admissions Contact Mr. Albert Barnes, Dean of Admissions and Registration, Wharton County Junior College, 911 Boling Highway, Wharton, TX 77488-3298. *Phone:* 979-532-6381 Ext. 6381.

UTAH

CERTIFIED CAREERS INSTITUTE
Salt Lake City, Utah

- **Proprietary** 2-year, founded 1983
- **Calendar** continuous
- **Degree** certificates, diplomas, and associate
- **Urban** 1-acre campus
- **Endowment** $5.0 million
- **Coed,** 300 undergraduate students

Faculty *Total:* 16, 50% full-time.
Majors Business computer facilities operation; business systems networking/telecommunications; computer/information sciences; computer programming; computer science; computer systems analysis; data processing technology; information sciences/systems.
Academic Programs *Special study options:* adult/continuing education programs, part-time degree program.
Library RCI Resource Library with a Web page.
Computers on Campus 200 computers available on campus for general student use. Internet access, at least one staffed computer lab available.
Student Life *Housing:* college housing not available.
Costs (2001–02) *Tuition:* $11 per hour part-time. 20,3000 per degree program.
Applying *Options:* common application. *Required:* interview. *Required for some:* essay or personal statement, high school transcript. *Application deadline:* rolling (freshmen), rolling (transfers). *Notification:* continuous (freshmen).
Admissions Contact Mr. Mathew Maxwell, Campus Director, Certified Careers Institute, 1455 West 2200 South, Suite 103, Salt Lake City, UT 84119. *Phone:* 801-973-7008. *Toll-free phone:* 888-316-3139. *Fax:* 801-973-6070. *E-mail:* ddelvalle@cciutah.edu.

COLLEGE OF EASTERN UTAH
Price, Utah

- **State-supported** 2-year, founded 1937, part of Utah System of Higher Education
- **Calendar** semesters
- **Degree** certificates and associate
- **Small-town** 15-acre campus
- **Coed,** 2,742 undergraduate students, 62% full-time, 54% women, 46% men

Undergraduates 1,691 full-time, 1,051 part-time. Students come from 21 states and territories, 7 other countries, 3% are from out of state, 0.7% African American, 0.8% Asian American or Pacific Islander, 3% Hispanic American, 12% Native American, 2% international, 15% live on campus. *Retention:* 40% of 2001 full-time freshmen returned.
Freshmen *Admission:* 689 enrolled. *Average high school GPA:* 3.22. *Test scores:* ACT scores over 18: 74%; ACT scores over 24: 23%; ACT scores over 30: 2%.
Faculty *Total:* 206, 40% full-time. *Student/faculty ratio:* 18:1.
Majors Auto mechanic/technician; business administration; carpentry; child care/development; computer graphics; construction technology; cosmetology; early childhood education; liberal arts and sciences/liberal studies; machine technology; mining technology; nursing; pre-engineering; secretarial science; welding technology.
Academic Programs *Special study options:* academic remediation for entering students, adult/continuing education programs, advanced placement credit, cooperative education, distance learning, English as a second language, independent study, part-time degree program, services for LD students, summer session for credit.
Library College of Eastern Utah Library with 44,490 titles, 1,464 audiovisual materials, an OPAC, a Web page.
Computers on Campus 200 computers available on campus for general student use. A campuswide network can be accessed from student residence rooms and from off campus. Internet access, online (class) registration, at least one staffed computer lab available.
Student Life *Housing Options:* coed. *Activities and Organizations:* drama/theater group, student-run newspaper, choral group. *Campus security:* 24-hour emergency response devices and patrols, late-night transport/escort service. *Student Services:* health clinic, personal/psychological counseling, women's center.
Athletics Member NJCAA. *Intercollegiate sports:* baseball M(s), basketball M(s)/W(s), golf M/W, volleyball W(s). *Intramural sports:* basketball M/W, racquetball M/W, soccer M, tennis M/W.
Standardized Tests *Required:* SAT I or ACT (for placement), ACT ASSET or ABLE.
Costs (2001–02) *Tuition:* state resident $1201 full-time, $74 per credit hour part-time; nonresident $5025 full-time, $296 per credit hour part-time. Part-time tuition and fees vary according to course load. *Required fees:* $328 full-time, $16 per credit hour. *Room and board:* $3420. Room and board charges vary according to board plan, housing facility, and location. *Waivers:* senior citizens and employees or children of employees.
Financial Aid In 2001, 52 Federal Work-Study jobs (averaging $1367). 16 State and other part-time jobs (averaging $1190).
Applying *Options:* electronic application, early admission. *Application fee:* $25. *Recommended:* high school transcript. *Application deadline:* rolling (freshmen), rolling (transfers).
Admissions Contact Mr. Todd Olsen, Director of Admissions, High School Relations, College of Eastern Utah, 451 East 400 North, Price, UT 84501. *Phone:* 435-613-5217. *Fax:* 435-613-4102. *E-mail:* janyoung@ceu.edu.

DIXIE STATE COLLEGE OF UTAH
St. George, Utah

- **State-supported** primarily 2-year, founded 1911
- **Calendar** semesters
- **Degrees** certificates, diplomas, associate, and bachelor's
- **Small-town** 60-acre campus
- **Endowment** $6.2 million
- **Coed,** 7,001 undergraduate students, 45% full-time, 51% women, 49% men

Undergraduates 3,170 full-time, 3,831 part-time. Students come from 47 states and territories, 12 other countries, 14% are from out of state, 0.6% African American, 1% Asian American or Pacific Islander, 2% Hispanic American, 1% Native American, 0.6% international, 4% transferred in, 2% live on campus. *Retention:* 41% of 2001 full-time freshmen returned.
Freshmen *Admission:* 2,473 applied, 2,292 admitted, 1,501 enrolled. *Average high school GPA:* 3.21. *Test scores:* SAT verbal scores over 500: 31%; SAT math scores over 500: 31%; ACT scores over 18: 72%; SAT verbal scores over 600: 5%; ACT scores over 24: 17%; ACT scores over 30: 1%.
Faculty *Total:* 301, 34% full-time, 44% with terminal degrees. *Student/faculty ratio:* 22:1.
Majors Accounting; agricultural sciences; aircraft pilot (professional); architectural drafting; art; art history; auto body repair; auto mechanic/technician; aviation management; biology; biotechnology research; botany; broadcast journalism; business administration; cartography; ceramic arts; chemistry; child care/guidance; communications; computer science; criminal justice studies; dance; data processing technology; dental hygiene; diesel engine mechanic; drawing; early childhood education; ecology; economics; elementary education; emergency medical technology; engineering; English; environmental science; foreign languages/literatures; forestry; general retailing/wholesaling; geology; graphic design/commercial art/illustration; health professions and related sciences; history; humanities; interior design; journalism; liberal arts and sciences/liberal studies; marine biology; mathematics; mechanical drafting; music; natural resources conservation; natural resources management; nursing; painting; philosophy; photographic technology; photography; physical education; physics; plant pathology; plant protection; political science; pre-law; printmaking; psychology; radio/television broadcasting; range management; sculpture; secondary education; secretarial science; social work; sociology; soil sciences; theater arts/drama;

Dixie State College of Utah (continued)
tourism/travel marketing related; water resources engineering; Web page, digital/multimedia and information resources design; wildlife management; zoology.

Academic Programs *Special study options:* academic remediation for entering students, adult/continuing education programs, advanced placement credit, cooperative education, distance learning, English as a second language, honors programs, part-time degree program, services for LD students, summer session for credit.

Library Val A. Browning Library with 83,160 titles, 343 serial subscriptions, 12,321 audiovisual materials, an OPAC, a Web page.

Computers on Campus A campuswide network can be accessed from student residence rooms. Internet access, online (class) registration, at least one staffed computer lab available.

Student Life *Housing Options:* coed, men-only. *Activities and Organizations:* drama/theater group, student-run newspaper, radio and television station, choral group, Dixie Spirit, Outdoor Club, Association of Women Students. *Campus security:* 24-hour emergency response devices and patrols. *Student Services:* health clinic, personal/psychological counseling.

Athletics Member NJCAA. *Intercollegiate sports:* baseball M(s), basketball M(s)/W(s), football M(s), golf M(s), soccer W(s), softball W(s), volleyball W(s). *Intramural sports:* basketball M/W, football M, golf M, soccer M/W, softball M/W, tennis M/W, volleyball M/W.

Standardized Tests *Required:* CPT or ACT COMPASS (if not submitting SAT I or ACT). *Recommended:* SAT I or ACT (for placement).

Costs (2001–02) *Tuition:* state resident $1252 full-time, $54 per credit part-time; nonresident $5476 full-time, $230 per credit part-time. Full-time tuition and fees vary according to class time. Part-time tuition and fees vary according to class time and course load. *Required fees:* $292 full-time. *Room and board:* $2850. Room and board charges vary according to board plan. *Payment plan:* installment. *Waivers:* senior citizens and employees or children of employees.

Financial Aid In 2001, 100 Federal Work-Study jobs (averaging $2200). 20 State and other part-time jobs (averaging $2200).

Applying *Options:* electronic application, early admission, deferred entrance. *Application fee:* $25. *Required:* high school transcript. *Application deadline:* rolling (freshmen), rolling (transfers).

Admissions Contact Ms. Darla Rollins, Admissions Coordinator, Dixie State College of Utah, 225 South 700 East, St. George, UT 84770-3876. *Phone:* 435-652-7702. *Toll-free phone:* 888-GO2DIXIE. *Fax:* 435-656-4005. *E-mail:* rollins@dixie.edu.

ITT TECHNICAL INSTITUTE
Murray, Utah

- **Proprietary** primarily 2-year, founded 1984, part of ITT Educational Services, Inc
- **Calendar** quarters
- **Degrees** associate and bachelor's
- **Suburban** 3-acre campus with easy access to Salt Lake City
- **Coed,** 472 undergraduate students

Majors Computer/information sciences related; computer programming; drafting; electrical/electronic engineering technologies related; industrial design; information technology.

Student Life *Housing:* college housing not available.

Costs (2001–02) *Tuition:* Full-time tuition and fees vary according to program. Part-time tuition and fees vary according to program. $260—$330 per credit hour.

Applying *Options:* deferred entrance. *Application fee:* $100. *Required:* high school transcript, interview. *Recommended:* letters of recommendation. *Application deadline:* rolling (freshmen), rolling (transfers). *Notification:* continuous (freshmen).

Admissions Contact Mr. Gary Lafe, Director of Recruitment, ITT Technical Institute, 920 West LeVoy Drive, Murray, UT 84123-2500. *Phone:* 801-263-3313. *Toll-free phone:* 800-365-2136.

LDS BUSINESS COLLEGE
Salt Lake City, Utah

- **Independent** 2-year, founded 1886, affiliated with Church of Jesus Christ of Latter-day Saints, part of Latter-day Saints Church Educational System
- **Calendar** semesters
- **Degree** certificates and associate
- **Urban** campus
- **Coed,** 422 undergraduate students, 86% full-time, 65% women, 35% men

Undergraduates 363 full-time, 59 part-time. Students come from 30 states and territories, 43 other countries, 33% are from out of state, 30% transferred in, 13% live on campus.

Freshmen *Admission:* 596 applied, 593 admitted, 422 enrolled.

Faculty *Total:* 77, 18% full-time, 4% with terminal degrees. *Student/faculty ratio:* 19:1.

Majors Accounting; business administration; information sciences/systems; information technology; interior design; legal administrative assistant; liberal arts and sciences/liberal studies; medical administrative assistant; medical assistant; medical records administration; secretarial science.

Academic Programs *Special study options:* academic remediation for entering students, adult/continuing education programs, advanced placement credit, cooperative education, internships, part-time degree program, summer session for credit.

Library LDS Business College Library with 5,000 titles, 130 serial subscriptions, an OPAC, a Web page.

Computers on Campus 350 computers available on campus for general student use. A campuswide network can be accessed from student residence rooms. Internet access, at least one staffed computer lab available.

Student Life *Housing Options:* women-only. *Activities and Organizations:* student-run newspaper, choral group, International Students Club, Latter-Day Saints Student Association. *Campus security:* 24-hour emergency response devices, controlled dormitory access.

Standardized Tests *Recommended:* ACT (for placement).

Costs (2002–03) *Comprehensive fee:* $6110 includes full-time tuition ($2260) and room and board ($3850). Full-time tuition and fees vary according to course load. Part-time tuition: $94 per credit hour. Part-time tuition and fees vary according to course load. *Payment plan:* installment. *Waivers:* employees or children of employees.

Applying *Options:* electronic application, early admission, deferred entrance. *Application fee:* $25. *Required:* high school transcript, interview. *Application deadline:* rolling (freshmen), rolling (transfers).

Admissions Contact Mr. Matt D. Tittle, Director of Regional Marketing, LDS Business College, 411 East South Temple, Salt Lake City, UT 84111-1392. *Phone:* 801-524-8146. *Toll-free phone:* 800-999-5767. *Fax:* 801-524-1900. *E-mail:* admissions@ldsbc.edu.

MOUNTAIN WEST COLLEGE
West Valley City, Utah

- **Proprietary** 2-year, founded 1982, part of Corinthian Colleges, Inc
- **Calendar** quarters
- **Degree** diplomas and associate
- **Suburban** campus
- **Coed,** 404 undergraduate students, 55% full-time, 79% women, 21% men

Undergraduates 222 full-time, 182 part-time.

Freshmen *Admission:* 356 enrolled. *Average high school GPA:* 3.00.

Faculty *Total:* 28, 25% full-time. *Student/faculty ratio:* 15:1.

Majors Accounting; business administration; business systems networking/telecommunications; information sciences/systems; medical assistant; paralegal/legal assistant; secretarial science; travel/tourism management.

Academic Programs *Special study options:* academic remediation for entering students, accelerated degree program, English as a second language, independent study, internships, part-time degree program, summer session for credit.

Library Learning Resource Center with 5,250 titles, 41 serial subscriptions.

Computers on Campus 76 computers available on campus for general student use. Internet access, at least one staffed computer lab available.

Student Life *Housing:* college housing not available. *Activities and Organizations:* Student Activity Committee.

Standardized Tests *Recommended:* SAT I or ACT (for admission).

Costs (2001–02) *Tuition:* $8460 full-time, $235 per credit hour part-time. Full-time tuition and fees vary according to course load. *Required fees:* $100 full-time, $25 per term part-time. *Payment plans:* tuition prepayment, installment. *Waivers:* employees or children of employees.

Applying *Options:* deferred entrance. *Required:* high school transcript, interview. *Application deadline:* rolling (freshmen), rolling (transfers).

Admissions Contact Mr. John Rios, Director of Admissions, Mountain West College, 3280 West 3500 South, West Valley City, UT 84119. *Phone:* 801-840-4800. *Toll-free phone:* 888-741-4271. *Fax:* 801-485-0057. *E-mail:* jrios@cci.edu.

SALT LAKE COMMUNITY COLLEGE
Salt Lake City, Utah

- **State-supported** 2-year, founded 1948, part of Utah System of Higher Education
- **Calendar** semesters
- **Degree** certificates, diplomas, and associate
- **Urban** 114-acre campus
- **Endowment** $5.1 million
- **Coed**

Faculty *Student/faculty ratio:* 19:1.
Student Life *Campus security:* 24-hour emergency response devices and patrols, late-night transport/escort service.
Athletics Member NJCAA.
Standardized Tests *Recommended:* ACT (for placement), CPT.
Applying *Options:* electronic application, early admission, deferred entrance. *Application fee:* $20.
Admissions Contact Ms. Terri Blau, Assistant Director of Admissions for School Relations, Salt Lake Community College, Salt Lake City, UT 84130. *Phone:* 801-957-4299. *Fax:* 801-957-4958.

SNOW COLLEGE
Ephraim, Utah

- **State-supported** 2-year, founded 1888, part of Utah System of Higher Education
- **Calendar** semesters
- **Degree** certificates, diplomas, and associate
- **Rural** 50-acre campus
- **Endowment** $3.8 million
- **Coed,** 2,999 undergraduate students, 82% full-time, 59% women, 41% men

Undergraduates 2,447 full-time, 552 part-time. Students come from 55 states and territories, 10 other countries, 11% are from out of state, 0.6% African American, 1% Asian American or Pacific Islander, 1% Hispanic American, 0.5% Native American, 1% transferred in, 22% live on campus.
Freshmen *Admission:* 2,422 applied, 2,422 admitted, 1,362 enrolled. *Average high school GPA:* 3.29. *Test scores:* ACT scores over 18: 72%; ACT scores over 24: 24%; ACT scores over 30: 1%.
Faculty *Total:* 148, 74% full-time, 13% with terminal degrees. *Student/faculty ratio:* 20:1.
Majors Accounting; agricultural business; agricultural economics; agricultural sciences; agronomy/crop science; animal sciences; art; auto mechanic/technician; biology; botany; business administration; business education; carpentry; chemistry; child care/development; computer science; construction management; construction technology; criminal justice/law enforcement administration; dance; early childhood education; earth sciences; economics; education; electrical/electronic engineering technology; elementary education; engineering; entomology; family/community studies; farm/ranch management; forestry; French; geography; geology; history; home economics; humanities; information sciences/systems; Japanese; liberal arts and sciences/liberal studies; mass communications; mathematics; music; music history; music teacher education; music (voice and choral/opera performance); natural resources management; natural sciences; nutrition science; philosophy; physical education; physical sciences; physics; physiology; political science; pre-engineering; range management; science education; secretarial science; sociology; soil conservation; Spanish; theater arts/drama; trade/industrial education; veterinary sciences; wildlife management; zoology.
Academic Programs *Special study options:* academic remediation for entering students, adult/continuing education programs, advanced placement credit, cooperative education, English as a second language, external degree program, honors programs, independent study, part-time degree program, services for LD students, summer session for credit.
Library Lucy Phillips Library with 31,911 titles, 1,870 audiovisual materials, an OPAC, a Web page.
Computers on Campus 220 computers available on campus for general student use. A campuswide network can be accessed from off campus. At least one staffed computer lab available.
Student Life *Housing Options:* coed. *Activities and Organizations:* drama/theater group, student-run newspaper, radio station, choral group, marching band, Drama Club, Latter-Day Saints Singers, Dead Cats Society, Associated Women Students, Associated Men Students. *Campus security:* student patrols. *Student Services:* health clinic, personal/psychological counseling.
Athletics Member NJCAA. *Intercollegiate sports:* baseball M, basketball M(s)/W(s), football M(s), golf M(s), softball W, volleyball W(s). *Intramural sports:* badminton M/W, basketball M/W, bowling M/W, football M/W, golf M/W, racquetball M/W, soccer M, softball M/W, tennis M/W, volleyball M/W, wrestling M.
Standardized Tests *Required:* ACT (for placement).
Costs (2002–03) *Tuition:* state resident $1252 full-time; nonresident $5810 full-time. Part-time tuition and fees vary according to class time, location, and program. Part-time tuition per term ranges from $122 to $570 for state residents, $529 to $2641 for nonresidents. *Required fees:* $270 full-time, $14 per credit hour. *Room and board:* $3800. Room and board charges vary according to board plan. *Waivers:* employees or children of employees.
Financial Aid In 2001, 94 Federal Work-Study jobs (averaging $1200).
Applying *Options:* early admission. *Application fee:* $20. *Required:* high school transcript. *Application deadlines:* 6/15 (freshmen), 6/1 (transfers). *Notification:* continuous (freshmen).
Admissions Contact Mr. Brach Schleuter, Coordinator of High School Relations, Snow College, 150 East College Avenue, Ephraim, UT 84627. *Phone:* 435-283-7151. *Fax:* 435-283-6879.

STEVENS-HENAGER COLLEGE
Ogden, Utah

- **Proprietary** 2-year, founded 1891, part of Bradford Schools, Inc
- **Calendar** quarters
- **Degree** associate
- **Urban** 1-acre campus with easy access to Salt Lake City
- **Coed**

Standardized Tests *Recommended:* SAT I or ACT (for admission).
Applying *Options:* early admission, deferred entrance. *Required:* high school transcript.
Admissions Contact Admissions Office, Stevens-Henager College, 2168 Washington Boulevard, Ogden, UT 84401-1420. *Phone:* 801-394-7791. *Toll-free phone:* 800-371-7791.

UTAH CAREER COLLEGE
West Jordan, Utah

Admissions Contact 1902 West 7800 South, West Jordan, UT 84088. *Toll-free phone:* 866-304-4224.

UTAH VALLEY STATE COLLEGE
Orem, Utah

- **State-supported** primarily 2-year, founded 1941, part of Utah System of Higher Education
- **Calendar** semesters
- **Degrees** diplomas, associate, and bachelor's
- **Suburban** 200-acre campus with easy access to Salt Lake City
- **Endowment** $1.7 million
- **Coed**

Faculty *Student/faculty ratio:* 20:1.
Student Life *Campus security:* 24-hour patrols.
Athletics Member NJCAA.
Standardized Tests *Required:* SAT I, ACT, or in-house tests.
Applying *Options:* electronic application, early admission, deferred entrance. *Application fee:* $30. *Recommended:* high school transcript.
Admissions Contact Mr. David Chappell, Registrar and Director of Admissions, Utah Valley State College, 800 West 1200 South Street, Orem, UT 84058-5999. *Phone:* 801-222-8460. *Fax:* 801-225-4677. *E-mail:* info@uvsc.edu.

VERMONT

COMMUNITY COLLEGE OF VERMONT
Waterbury, Vermont

- **State-supported** 2-year, founded 1970, part of Vermont State Colleges System

Community College of Vermont (continued)

- **Calendar** semesters
- **Degree** certificates, diplomas, and associate
- **Rural** campus
- **Coed,** 5,000 undergraduate students

Undergraduates Students come from 7 states and territories, 3 other countries, 3% are from out of state, 1% African American, 1% Asian American or Pacific Islander, 0.7% Hispanic American, 1% Native American, 0.1% international.
Faculty *Total:* 508.
Majors Accounting; business administration; child care/development; community services; computer science; data entry/microcomputer applications; developmental/child psychology; education; human services; industrial technology; information technology; liberal arts and sciences/liberal studies; secretarial science; social sciences; teacher assistant/aide.
Academic Programs *Special study options:* academic remediation for entering students, accelerated degree program, adult/continuing education programs, cooperative education, distance learning, double majors, English as a second language, external degree program, independent study, internships, part-time degree program, services for LD students, student-designed majors, summer session for credit.
Computers on Campus 150 computers available on campus for general student use. A campuswide network can be accessed from off campus. Internet access, at least one staffed computer lab available.
Student Life *Housing:* college housing not available.
Costs (2001–02) *Tuition:* state resident $2832 full-time, $118 per credit part-time; nonresident $5664 full-time, $236 per credit part-time. Full-time tuition and fees vary according to program and reciprocity agreements. Part-time tuition and fees vary according to program and reciprocity agreements. *Required fees:* $100 full-time, $10 per credit, $50 per term part-time. *Waivers:* senior citizens and employees or children of employees.
Financial Aid In 2001, 35 Federal Work-Study jobs (averaging $2000).
Applying *Application deadline:* rolling (freshmen), rolling (transfers).
Admissions Contact Mr. Timothy Donovan, Dean of Administration, Community College of Vermont, PO Box 120, Waterbury, VT 05676-0120. *Phone:* 802-241-3535.

LANDMARK COLLEGE
Putney, Vermont

- **Independent** 2-year, founded 1983
- **Calendar** semesters
- **Degrees** associate (offers degree program for high-potential students with dyslexia, ADHD, or specific learning disabilities)
- **Rural** 125-acre campus
- **Endowment** $293,510
- **Coed,** 367 undergraduate students, 100% full-time, 30% women, 70% men

Undergraduates 367 full-time. Students come from 41 states and territories, 9 other countries, 94% are from out of state, 5% African American, 2% Asian American or Pacific Islander, 4% Hispanic American, 0.8% Native American, 2% international, 12% transferred in, 94% live on campus.
Freshmen *Admission:* 406 applied, 306 admitted, 46 enrolled.
Faculty *Total:* 124, 100% full-time. *Student/faculty ratio:* 5:1.
Majors Liberal arts and sciences/liberal studies.
Academic Programs *Special study options:* academic remediation for entering students, adult/continuing education programs, advanced placement credit, English as a second language, honors programs, internships, services for LD students, study abroad, summer session for credit.
Library Landmark College Academic Resource Center with 32,000 titles, 202 serial subscriptions, 400 audiovisual materials.
Computers on Campus 56 computers available on campus for general student use. A campuswide network can be accessed from student residence rooms and from off campus. Internet access, at least one staffed computer lab available.
Student Life *Housing:* on-campus residence required for freshman year. *Options:* coed. *Activities and Organizations:* drama/theater group, student-run newspaper, Student Board of Representatives, Student Residence Coordinators, Student Affairs Committee, International Student Association, Multicultural Awareness Club. *Campus security:* 24-hour emergency response devices and patrols, controlled dormitory access. *Student Services:* health clinic, personal/psychological counseling, women's center.
Athletics *Intercollegiate sports:* baseball M, basketball M/W, equestrian sports M/W, soccer M/W, softball W, volleyball W. *Intramural sports:* basketball M/W, cross-country running M/W, equestrian sports M/W, skiing (cross-country) M/W, softball M/W, tennis M/W, volleyball M/W, weight lifting M/W.
Costs (2001–02) *Comprehensive fee:* $40,400 includes full-time tuition ($33,500), mandatory fees ($900), and room and board ($6000). *Room and board:* College room only: $2000.
Financial Aid *Financial aid deadline:* 3/1.
Applying *Options:* deferred entrance. *Application fee:* $50. *Required:* essay or personal statement, high school transcript, 3 letters of recommendation, interview. *Application deadline:* 5/15 (freshmen), rolling (transfers).
Admissions Contact Ms. Leatrice Johnson, Dean of Admissions and Enrollment, Landmark College, 1 River Road South, Putney, VT 05346. *Phone:* 802-387-6716. *Fax:* 802-387-6868. *E-mail:* admissions@landmark.edu.

NEW ENGLAND CULINARY INSTITUTE
Montpelier, Vermont

- **Proprietary** primarily 2-year, founded 1980
- **Calendar** quarters
- **Degrees** certificates, diplomas, associate, and bachelor's
- **Small-town** campus
- **Endowment** $50,000
- **Coed,** 639 undergraduate students, 100% full-time, 28% women, 72% men

Locations in Montpelier and Essex, Vermont. Offers Associate of Occupational Studies (AOS) degree in the culinary arts and food and beverage management, Bachelor of Arts degree in food and beverage management, and a certificate program in basic cooking. Hands-on learning in real-world food service operations. Paid internships. Contact the Institute at 877-223-6324 (toll-free) or visit the Web site http://www.ncci.edu.

Undergraduates 639 full-time. Students come from 50 states and territories, 8 other countries, 77% are from out of state, 2% African American, 0.8% Asian American or Pacific Islander, 3% Hispanic American, 0.2% Native American, 2% transferred in, 80% live on campus.
Freshmen *Admission:* 210 enrolled. *Average high school GPA:* 2.5.
Faculty *Total:* 77, 88% full-time, 4% with terminal degrees. *Student/faculty ratio:* 6:1.
Majors Culinary arts; food products retailing; hotel and restaurant management.
Academic Programs *Special study options:* internships.
Library New England Culinary Institute Library with 800 titles, 100 serial subscriptions, 100 audiovisual materials, an OPAC.
Computers on Campus 14 computers available on campus for general student use. A campuswide network can be accessed from student residence rooms. Internet access, at least one staffed computer lab available.
Student Life *Housing Options:* coed, men-only, women-only. *Activities and Organizations:* student-run newspaper, American Culinary Federation, Toastmasters, Ice Carving Club. *Campus security:* 24-hour emergency response devices. *Student Services:* personal/psychological counseling.
Standardized Tests *Recommended:* SAT I (for placement).
Costs (2001–02) *Comprehensive fee:* $23,875 includes full-time tuition ($19,660), mandatory fees ($200), and room and board ($4015). Full-time tuition and fees vary according to degree level and program. *Room and board:* College room only: $2370. *Payment plan:* installment. *Waivers:* children of alumni and employees or children of employees.
Applying *Options:* common application, electronic application, deferred entrance. *Required:* essay or personal statement, high school transcript, interview. *Application deadline:* rolling (freshmen).
Admissions Contact Ms. Linda Cooper, Director of Admissions, New England Culinary Institute, 250 Main Street, Montpelier, VT 05602. *Phone:* 802-223-9295. *Toll-free phone:* 877-223-6324. *Fax:* 802-223-0634. *E-mail:* IntInq@neci.edu.

VERMONT TECHNICAL COLLEGE
Randolph Center, Vermont

- **State-supported** primarily 2-year, founded 1866, part of Vermont State Colleges System
- **Calendar** semesters
- **Degrees** certificates, associate, and bachelor's
- **Rural** 544-acre campus
- **Endowment** $3.9 million
- **Coed,** 1,272 undergraduate students, 70% full-time, 31% women, 69% men

Vermont Tech offers education for careers in today's technology-driven workplace. Articulation agreements with other regional institutions simplify the transfer process for graduates who want to pursue higher degrees. VTC has

averaged at least 98% placement for every graduating class since 1982. Vermont Tech is a residential coeducational college offering associate and bachelor's degree programs on its 544-acre campus in central Vermont.

Undergraduates 889 full-time, 383 part-time. Students come from 10 states and territories, 19% are from out of state, 0.2% African American, 1% Asian American or Pacific Islander, 0.6% Hispanic American, 0.2% Native American, 0.1% international, 10% transferred in, 66% live on campus. *Retention:* 65% of 2001 full-time freshmen returned.

Freshmen *Admission:* 734 applied, 524 admitted, 290 enrolled. *Average high school GPA:* 3.00. *Test scores:* SAT verbal scores over 500: 41%; SAT math scores over 500: 50%; ACT scores over 18: 100%; SAT verbal scores over 600: 11%; SAT math scores over 600: 14%; SAT verbal scores over 700: 1%; SAT math scores over 700: 1%.

Faculty *Total:* 113, 62% full-time, 23% with terminal degrees. *Student/faculty ratio:* 11:1.

Majors Accounting; agribusiness; architectural engineering technology; automotive engineering technology; bioengineering; biotechnology research; business administration; business systems networking/ telecommunications; civil engineering technology; computer engineering technology; construction technology; dairy science; electrical/electronic engineering technology; electromechanical technology; engineering technology; environmental technology; horticulture science; landscaping management; mechanical engineering technology; nursing; ornamental horticulture; practical nurse; secretarial science; telecommunications; veterinary technology.

Academic Programs *Special study options:* academic remediation for entering students, accelerated degree program, advanced placement credit, cooperative education, distance learning, double majors, English as a second language, honors programs, independent study, internships, part-time degree program, services for LD students, summer session for credit. *ROTC:* Army (c).

Library Hartness Library with 57,568 titles, 1,724 serial subscriptions, 2,030 audiovisual materials, an OPAC, a Web page.

Computers on Campus 225 computers available on campus for general student use. A campuswide network can be accessed from student residence rooms and from off campus. Internet access, at least one staffed computer lab available.

Student Life *Housing Options:* coed, men-only, women-only. *Activities and Organizations:* drama/theater group, student-run radio station, ASVTC (student government), Hockey Club, student radio station, American Institute of Architecture Students, Golf Club. *Campus security:* 24-hour emergency response devices and patrols, late-night transport/escort service, controlled dormitory access. *Student Services:* health clinic, personal/psychological counseling, women's center.

Athletics Member NSCAA. *Intercollegiate sports:* baseball M, basketball M/W, ice hockey M(c)/W(c), soccer M/W, softball W, volleyball M/W. *Intramural sports:* basketball M/W, bowling M(c)/W(c), cross-country running M/W, football M/W, golf M(c)/W(c), racquetball M/W, riflery M(c)/W(c), skiing (cross-country) M(c)/W(c), soccer M/W, softball M/W, squash M/W, swimming M/W, table tennis M/W, tennis M/W, volleyball M/W, water polo M/W, weight lifting M(c)/W(c).

Standardized Tests *Required for some:* SAT I (for admission), SAT I or ACT (for admission). *Recommended:* SAT I or ACT (for admission).

Costs (2001–02) *Tuition:* state resident $5340 full-time, $223 per credit hour part-time; nonresident $10,788 full-time, $450 per credit hour part-time. Full-time tuition and fees vary according to course load, program, and reciprocity agreements. Part-time tuition and fees vary according to program and reciprocity agreements. *Required fees:* $32 per credit hour. *Room and board:* $5520; room only: $3252. Room and board charges vary according to board plan. *Payment plans:* installment, deferred payment. *Waivers:* employees or children of employees.

Financial Aid Of all full-time matriculated undergraduates who enrolled in 2001, 716 applied for aid, 604 were judged to have need. 200 Federal Work-Study jobs (averaging $1003). *Average percent of need met:* 78%. *Average need-based loan:* $2788. *Average need-based gift aid:* $3700. *Average non-need based aid:* $1000.

Applying *Options:* common application, electronic application. *Application fee:* $30. *Required:* high school transcript. *Required for some:* essay or personal statement, letters of recommendation, interview. *Recommended:* minimum 3.0 GPA, letters of recommendation, interview. *Application deadline:* rolling (freshmen), rolling (transfers). *Notification:* continuous until 9/1 (freshmen).

Admissions Contact Ms. Rosemary W. Distel, Director of Admissions, Vermont Technical College, PO Box 500, Randolph Center, VT 05061. *Phone:* 802-728-1245. *Toll-free phone:* 800-442-VTC1. *Fax:* 802-728-1390. *E-mail:* admissions@vtc.edu.

WOODBURY COLLEGE
Montpelier, Vermont

- **Independent** primarily 2-year, founded 1975
- **Calendar** trimesters
- **Degrees** certificates, associate, and bachelor's
- **Small-town** 8-acre campus
- **Endowment** $71,024
- **Coed,** 157 undergraduate students, 73% full-time, 79% women, 21% men

Undergraduates Students come from 4 states and territories, 8% are from out of state, 1% Asian American or Pacific Islander, 0.7% Native American.

Faculty *Total:* 44, 34% full-time, 50% with terminal degrees. *Student/faculty ratio:* 12:1.

Majors Community psychology; general studies; paralegal/legal assistant; peace/conflict studies.

Academic Programs *Special study options:* academic remediation for entering students, adult/continuing education programs, double majors, independent study, internships, part-time degree program, services for LD students, student-designed majors.

Library Woodbury College Library with 2,782 titles, 2 serial subscriptions.

Computers on Campus 10 computers available on campus for general student use. Internet access, at least one staffed computer lab available.

Student Life *Housing:* college housing not available. *Student Services:* personal/psychological counseling.

Costs (2002–03) *Tuition:* $12,700 full-time, $556 per credit part-time. *Required fees:* $90 full-time, $30 per term part-time. *Payment plan:* installment. *Waivers:* employees or children of employees.

Applying *Options:* electronic application. *Application fee:* $30. *Required:* essay or personal statement, interview. *Required for some:* high school transcript. *Application deadline:* rolling (freshmen), rolling (transfers).

Admissions Contact Ms. Kathleen Moore, Admissions Director, Woodbury College, 660 Elm Street, Montpelier, VT 05602. *Phone:* 802-229-0516. *Toll-free phone:* 800-639-6039. *Fax:* 802-229-2141. *E-mail:* admiss@woodbury-college.edu.

VIRGINIA

BLUE RIDGE COMMUNITY COLLEGE
Weyers Cave, Virginia

- **State-supported** 2-year, founded 1967, part of Virginia Community College System
- **Calendar** semesters
- **Degree** certificates, diplomas, and associate
- **Rural** 65-acre campus
- **Endowment** $1.2 million
- **Coed,** 1,090 undergraduate students, 44% full-time, 64% women, 36% men

Undergraduates 483 full-time, 607 part-time. Students come from 27 states and territories, 3% are from out of state, 88% transferred in. *Retention:* 42% of 2001 full-time freshmen returned.

Faculty *Total:* 166, 27% full-time. *Student/faculty ratio:* 21:1.

Majors Accounting; business administration; computer systems networking/ telecommunications; electrical/electronic engineering technology; information sciences/systems; information technology; liberal arts and sciences/liberal studies; mechanical design technology; mental health/rehabilitation; nursing; secretarial science; veterinary technology.

Academic Programs *Special study options:* academic remediation for entering students, adult/continuing education programs, advanced placement credit, cooperative education, distance learning, double majors, English as a second language, honors programs, internships, off-campus study, part-time degree program, services for LD students, study abroad, summer session for credit.

Library Houff Library with 47,044 titles, 251 serial subscriptions, an OPAC, a Web page.

Computers on Campus 191 computers available on campus for general student use. Internet access, at least one staffed computer lab available.

Student Life *Housing:* college housing not available. *Activities and Organizations:* Student Government Association, Phi Theta Kappa, Christian Fellowship, intramural athletics, special interest groups. *Campus security:* 24-hour emergency response devices and patrols, late-night transport/escort service. *Student Services:* personal/psychological counseling, women's center.

Blue Ridge Community College (continued)

Athletics *Intramural sports:* basketball M.

Standardized Tests *Recommended:* SAT I (for placement).

Costs (2002–03) *Tuition:* state resident $1355 full-time, $40 per credit hour part-time; nonresident $5733 full-time, $186 per credit hour part-time. *Required fees:* $126 full-time, $5 per credit hour. *Waivers:* senior citizens.

Financial Aid In 2001, 13 Federal Work-Study jobs (averaging $1200).

Applying *Options:* electronic application, early admission. *Required for some:* high school transcript, interview. *Application deadline:* rolling (freshmen), rolling (transfers). *Notification:* continuous (freshmen).

Admissions Contact Mr. Robert Clemmer, Coordinator of Admissions and Records, Blue Ridge Community College, PO Box 80, Weyers Cave, VA 24486-0080. *Phone:* 540-453-2251.

BRYANT AND STRATTON COLLEGE, RICHMOND

Richmond, Virginia

- **Proprietary** 2-year, founded 1952, part of Bryant and Stratton Business Institute, Inc
- **Calendar** semesters
- **Degree** diplomas and associate
- **Suburban** campus
- **Coed**

Faculty *Student/faculty ratio:* 8:1.

Student Life *Campus security:* late-night transport/escort service.

Applying *Options:* deferred entrance. *Application fee:* $25. *Required:* high school transcript, interview, entrance evaluation and placement evaluation. *Recommended:* minimum 2.0 GPA.

Admissions Contact Mr. Mark Sarver, Director of Admissions, Bryant and Stratton College, Richmond, 8141 Hull Street Road, Richmond, VA 23235-6411. *Phone:* 804-745-2444. *Fax:* 804-745-6884.

BRYANT AND STRATTON COLLEGE, VIRGINIA BEACH

Virginia Beach, Virginia

- **Proprietary** primarily 2-year, founded 1952, part of Bryant and Stratton Business Institute, Inc
- **Calendar** semesters
- **Degrees** associate and bachelor's
- **Suburban** campus
- **Coed,** 297 undergraduate students, 67% full-time, 79% women, 21% men

Undergraduates 200 full-time, 97 part-time. Students come from 1 other state, 59% African American, 2% Asian American or Pacific Islander, 8% Hispanic American, 1% Native American. *Retention:* 85% of 2001 full-time freshmen returned.

Freshmen *Admission:* 150 applied, 125 admitted, 122 enrolled.

Faculty *Total:* 36, 14% full-time, 8% with terminal degrees. *Student/faculty ratio:* 9:1.

Majors Accounting; business administration; hotel and restaurant management; information sciences/systems; legal administrative assistant; medical administrative assistant; medical assistant; paralegal/legal assistant; retail management; secretarial science; travel/tourism management.

Academic Programs *Special study options:* academic remediation for entering students, adult/continuing education programs, advanced placement credit, internships, part-time degree program, summer session for credit.

Library campus library with 9,646 titles, 131 serial subscriptions, 359 audiovisual materials.

Computers on Campus 55 computers available on campus for general student use. Internet access, at least one staffed computer lab available.

Student Life *Housing:* college housing not available. *Activities and Organizations:* student-run newspaper, Phi Beta Lambda, Alpha Beta Gamma, Student Government Association, Medical Club, Law Society. *Campus security:* late-night transport/escort service.

Costs (2002–03) *One-time required fee:* $25. *Tuition:* $9900 full-time, $330 per credit hour part-time. Full-time tuition and fees vary according to class time and course load. *Required fees:* $200 full-time, $100 per term part-time. *Payment plan:* installment. *Waivers:* employees or children of employees.

Applying *Options:* common application, electronic application, deferred entrance. *Application fee:* $25. *Required:* interview. *Required for some:* high school transcript. *Application deadline:* rolling (freshmen), rolling (transfers).

Admissions Contact Mr. Greg Smith, Director of Admissions, Bryant and Stratton College, Virginia Beach, 301 Centre Pointe Drive, Virginia Beach, VA 23462-4417. *Phone:* 757-499-7900.

CENTRAL VIRGINIA COMMUNITY COLLEGE

Lynchburg, Virginia

- **State-supported** 2-year, founded 1966, part of Virginia Community College System
- **Calendar** semesters
- **Degree** certificates, diplomas, and associate
- **Suburban** 104-acre campus
- **Endowment** $1.7 million
- **Coed,** 4,791 undergraduate students

Undergraduates Students come from 11 states and territories, 1% are from out of state.

Faculty *Total:* 173, 33% full-time.

Majors Accounting; architectural engineering technology; biological/physical sciences; business administration; business marketing and marketing management; civil engineering technology; criminal justice/law enforcement administration; drafting; education; electrical/electronic engineering technology; engineering technology; finance; general studies; graphic design/commercial art/illustration; information sciences/systems; liberal arts and sciences/liberal studies; management information systems/business data processing; mechanical engineering technology; medical laboratory technician; radiological science; respiratory therapy; retail management; secretarial science.

Academic Programs *Special study options:* academic remediation for entering students, advanced placement credit, cooperative education, distance learning, independent study, internships, part-time degree program, services for LD students, summer session for credit.

Library Bedford Learning Resources Center with 37,000 titles, 230 serial subscriptions, an OPAC, a Web page.

Computers on Campus 130 computers available on campus for general student use. Internet access, at least one staffed computer lab available.

Student Life *Housing:* college housing not available. *Activities and Organizations:* drama/theater group, student-run newspaper, Black Student Union, Data Processing Management Association, Radiology Club, Phi Theta Kappa, Respiratory Club. *Campus security:* 24-hour emergency response devices. *Student Services:* personal/psychological counseling.

Standardized Tests *Required:* ACT ASSET or ACT COMPASS.

Costs (2001–02) *Tuition:* state resident $1159 full-time, $39 per credit hour part-time; nonresident $5115 full-time, $171 per credit hour part-time. *Required fees:* $20 full-time, $10 per term.

Financial Aid In 2001, 65 Federal Work-Study jobs (averaging $2700).

Applying *Options:* early admission, deferred entrance. *Required for some:* high school transcript, interview. *Application deadline:* rolling (freshmen), rolling (transfers). *Notification:* continuous (freshmen).

Admissions Contact Judy Wilhelm, Enrollment Services Coordinator, Central Virginia Community College, 3506 Wards Road, Lynchburg, VA 24502-2498. *Phone:* 434-832-7630. *Toll-free phone:* 800-562-3060. *Fax:* 804-386-4681.

DABNEY S. LANCASTER COMMUNITY COLLEGE

Clifton Forge, Virginia

Admissions Contact Dr. Robert Goralewicz, Director of Student Services, Dabney S. Lancaster Community College, 100 Dabney Drive, PO Box 1000, Clifton Forge, VA 24422. *Phone:* 540-862-4246.

DANVILLE COMMUNITY COLLEGE

Danville, Virginia

- **State-supported** 2-year, founded 1967, part of Virginia Community College System
- **Calendar** semesters
- **Degree** certificates, diplomas, and associate
- **Urban** 65-acre campus
- **Coed,** 3,879 undergraduate students, 30% full-time, 60% women, 40% men

Undergraduates 1,168 full-time, 2,711 part-time. Students come from 9 states and territories, 3 other countries, 2% are from out of state. *Retention:* 50% of 2001 full-time freshmen returned.

Freshmen *Admission:* 307 enrolled.
Faculty *Total:* 203, 26% full-time. *Student/faculty ratio:* 19:1.
Majors Accounting; biological/physical sciences; business administration; business marketing and marketing management; computer programming; education; engineering technology; liberal arts and sciences/liberal studies; secretarial science.
Academic Programs *Special study options:* academic remediation for entering students, adult/continuing education programs, advanced placement credit, cooperative education, distance learning, honors programs, part-time degree program, summer session for credit.
Library Learning Resource Center with 41,600 titles, 345 serial subscriptions, an OPAC, a Web page.
Computers on Campus 265 computers available on campus for general student use. Internet access, at least one staffed computer lab available.
Student Life *Housing:* college housing not available. *Campus security:* 24-hour patrols.
Athletics *Intramural sports:* basketball M/W, bowling M/W, football M, golf M, softball M/W, volleyball M/W.
Standardized Tests *Required for some:* ACT ASSET.
Costs (2001–02) *Tuition:* state resident $1319 full-time, $40 per semester hour part-time; nonresident $5697 full-time, $186 per semester hour part-time. *Required fees:* $43 full-time, $4 per credit, $1 per term part-time.
Applying *Options:* early admission, deferred entrance. *Required:* high school transcript. *Application deadline:* rolling (freshmen), rolling (transfers). *Notification:* continuous (freshmen).
Admissions Contact Mr. Peter Castiglione, Director of Admissions, Danville Community College, 1008 South Main Street, Danville, VA 24541-4088. *Phone:* 434-797-8490.

DOMINION COLLEGE
Roanoke, Virginia

- **Proprietary** 2-year, founded 1963
- **Calendar** quarters
- **Degree** diplomas and associate
- **Urban** campus
- **Coed,** 197 undergraduate students, 100% full-time, 62% women, 38% men
- 79% of applicants were admitted

Undergraduates Students come from 4 states and territories, 5% are from out of state, 40% African American.
Freshmen *Admission:* 38 applied, 30 admitted.
Faculty *Total:* 31, 81% full-time. *Student/faculty ratio:* 7:1.
Majors Computer programming; information sciences/systems; medical assistant; paralegal/legal assistant.
Academic Programs *Special study options:* cooperative education, independent study, internships.
Computers on Campus 50 computers available on campus for general student use. Internet access available.
Student Life *Activities and Organizations:* student-run newspaper, Medical Club, Legal Club, Business Club.
Costs (2001–02) *Tuition:* $9630 full-time.
Applying *Options:* common application, early admission, deferred entrance. *Application fee:* $50. *Required:* high school transcript, interview.
Admissions Contact Ms. Shirley A. Long, Admissions Coordinator, Dominion College, 5372 Fallowater Lane, Roanoke, VA 24014. *Phone:* 540-776-8381. *Toll-free phone:* 800-372-7738. *Fax:* 540-776-9240.

EASTERN SHORE COMMUNITY COLLEGE
Melfa, Virginia

- **State-supported** 2-year, founded 1971, part of Virginia Community College System
- **Calendar** semesters
- **Degree** associate
- **Rural** 117-acre campus
- **Coed,** 884 undergraduate students, 21% full-time, 68% women, 32% men

Undergraduates 185 full-time, 699 part-time. 36% African American, 0.5% Asian American or Pacific Islander, 1% Hispanic American, 0.2% Native American, 1% transferred in.
Freshmen *Admission:* 168 applied, 168 admitted, 112 enrolled. *Average high school GPA:* 2.0.
Faculty *Total:* 52, 42% full-time. *Student/faculty ratio:* 13:1.
Majors Biological/physical sciences; business administration; computer/information technology services administration and management related; computer/technical support; education; electrical/electronic engineering technology; liberal arts and sciences/liberal studies; nursing; secretarial science.
Academic Programs *Special study options:* academic remediation for entering students, adult/continuing education programs, advanced placement credit, cooperative education, distance learning, English as a second language, off-campus study, part-time degree program, services for LD students, summer session for credit.
Library Learning Resources Center with 20,479 titles, 95 serial subscriptions, an OPAC, a Web page.
Computers on Campus 53 computers available on campus for general student use. At least one staffed computer lab available.
Student Life *Housing:* college housing not available. *Campus security:* night security guard. *Student Services:* personal/psychological counseling.
Athletics *Intramural sports:* basketball M/W, volleyball M/W.
Costs (2001–02) *Tuition:* state resident $891 full-time, $37 per semester hour part-time; nonresident $4104 full-time, $171 per semester hour part-time. Full-time tuition and fees vary according to course load. Part-time tuition and fees vary according to course load. *Required fees:* $72 full-time, $3 per semester hour. *Waivers:* senior citizens.
Financial Aid In 2001, 11 Federal Work-Study jobs.
Applying *Required:* high school transcript. *Application deadline:* rolling (freshmen), rolling (transfers). *Notification:* continuous (freshmen).
Admissions Contact Ms. Faye Wilson, Enrollment Services Assistant for Admissions, Eastern Shore Community College, 29300 Lankford Highway, Melfa, VA 23410. *Phone:* 757-787-5913. *Fax:* 757-787-5984. *E-mail:* eswilsf@es.cc.va.us.

ECPI COLLEGE OF TECHNOLOGY
Newport News, Virginia

- **Proprietary** 2-year, founded 1966
- **Calendar** trimesters
- **Degree** certificates, diplomas, and associate
- **Suburban** campus
- **Coed**

Undergraduates Students come from 34 states and territories, 2% are from out of state.
Freshmen *Admission:* 701 applied, 527 admitted. *Average high school GPA:* 2.5.
Faculty *Total:* 130, 51% full-time, 2% with terminal degrees. *Student/faculty ratio:* 16:1.
Majors Accounting; communication equipment technology; computer engineering technology; computer/information sciences; computer management; computer science; computer typography/composition; electrical/electronic engineering technology; electromechanical technology; engineering technology; health services administration; information sciences/systems; mechanical engineering technology; medical administrative assistant; medical records administration; telecommunications; trade/industrial education.
Academic Programs *Special study options:* adult/continuing education programs, advanced placement credit, freshman honors college, honors programs, internships, part-time degree program, summer session for credit.
Library ECPI-Virginia Beach Library with 13,014 titles, 168 serial subscriptions, an OPAC, a Web page.
Computers on Campus 100 computers available on campus for general student use. A campuswide network can be accessed from off campus. Internet access, at least one staffed computer lab available.
Student Life *Housing:* college housing not available. *Activities and Organizations:* SETA, IEEE, NVTHS, Accounting Society, CSI. *Campus security:* building and parking lot security. *Student Services:* personal/psychological counseling.
Costs (2001–02) *Tuition:* Full-time tuition and fees vary according to program.
Financial Aid In 2001, 30 Federal Work-Study jobs (averaging $2000).
Applying *Options:* common application, deferred entrance. *Application fee:* $100. *Required:* high school transcript, minimum 2.0 GPA, interview. *Notification:* continuous (freshmen).
Admissions Contact Ms. Teresa Cohn, Director of Admissions, ECPI College of Technology, 1001 Omni Boulevard, #100, Newport News, VA 23606. *Phone:* 757-838-9191.

ECPI College of Technology
Virginia Beach, Virginia

- **Proprietary** 2-year, founded 1966
- **Calendar** trimesters
- **Degree** certificates, diplomas, and associate
- **Suburban** 8-acre campus
- **Coed**

Undergraduates Students come from 34 states and territories, 40% are from out of state.
Freshmen *Admission:* 701 applied, 527 admitted. *Average high school GPA:* 2.5.
Faculty *Total:* 130, 51% full-time, 2% with terminal degrees. *Student/faculty ratio:* 16:1.
Majors Accounting; biomedical technology; business machine repair; communication equipment technology; computer engineering technology; computer/information sciences; computer management; computer programming; computer science; computer typography/composition; data processing technology; electrical/electronic engineering technology; electromechanical technology; engineering technology; health services administration; information sciences/systems; mechanical engineering technology; medical administrative assistant; medical records administration; telecommunications.
Academic Programs *Special study options:* adult/continuing education programs, advanced placement credit, freshman honors college, internships, part-time degree program, summer session for credit.
Library ECPI-Virginia Beach Library with 13,014 titles, 168 serial subscriptions, an OPAC, a Web page.
Computers on Campus 200 computers available on campus for general student use. A campuswide network can be accessed from off campus. Internet access, at least one staffed computer lab available.
Student Life *Housing:* college housing not available. *Activities and Organizations:* SETA, IEEE, NVTHS, ITE, Accounting Society. *Campus security:* building and parking lot security. *Student Services:* personal/psychological counseling.
Costs (2001–02) *Tuition:* Full-time tuition and fees vary according to program.
Financial Aid In 2001, 40 Federal Work-Study jobs (averaging $2000).
Applying *Options:* common application, deferred entrance. *Application fee:* $100. *Required:* high school transcript, minimum 2.0 GPA, interview. *Notification:* continuous (freshmen).
Admissions Contact Mr. Ronald Ballance, Vice President, ECPI College of Technology, 5555 Greenwich Road, Virginia Beach, VA 23462. *Phone:* 804-330-5533.

ECPI Technical College
Richmond, Virginia

- **Proprietary** 2-year, founded 1966
- **Calendar** trimesters
- **Degree** certificates, diplomas, and associate
- **Urban** campus
- **Coed,** 680 undergraduate students

Undergraduates Students come from 8 states and territories, 10% are from out of state.
Freshmen *Average high school GPA:* 2.5.
Faculty *Total:* 80, 51% full-time. *Student/faculty ratio:* 15:1.
Majors Accounting; business machine repair; communication equipment technology; computer/information sciences; computer management; computer programming; computer science; computer typography/composition; data processing technology; electrical/electronic engineering technology; electromechanical technology; engineering technology; health services administration; information sciences/systems; mechanical engineering technology; medical administrative assistant; medical records administration; telecommunications; trade/industrial education.
Academic Programs *Special study options:* adult/continuing education programs, advanced placement credit, freshman honors college, honors programs, internships, part-time degree program, summer session for credit.
Library ECPI-Richmond Library with 3,165 titles, 81 serial subscriptions, an OPAC, a Web page.
Computers on Campus 190 computers available on campus for general student use. A campuswide network can be accessed from off campus. Internet access, at least one staffed computer lab available.
Student Life *Housing:* college housing not available. *Activities and Organizations:* Collegiate Secretaries International, Data Processing Management Association, Student Electronics Technicians Association, Future Office Assistants, National Vocational-Technical Honor Society. *Campus security:* building and parking lot security.
Costs (2002–03) *Tuition:* Tuition varies by program. *Payment plan:* installment. *Waivers:* employees or children of employees.
Financial Aid In 2001, 30 Federal Work-Study jobs (averaging $2000).
Applying *Options:* common application, deferred entrance. *Application fee:* $100. *Required:* high school transcript, minimum 2.0 GPA, interview. *Application deadline:* rolling (freshmen), rolling (transfers). *Notification:* continuous (freshmen).
Admissions Contact Ms. Sharon Fitzgerald, Admissions Office, ECPI Technical College, 800 Moorefield Park Drive, Richmond, VA 23236. *Phone:* 804-330-5533.

ECPI Technical College
Roanoke, Virginia

- **Proprietary** 2-year, founded 1966
- **Calendar** trimesters
- **Degree** certificates, diplomas, and associate
- **Suburban** 3-acre campus
- **Coed,** 241 undergraduate students

Undergraduates Students come from 3 states and territories.
Freshmen *Admission:* 93 applied, 71 admitted. *Average high school GPA:* 2.5.
Faculty *Total:* 41, 20% full-time, 12% with terminal degrees. *Student/faculty ratio:* 15:1.
Majors Accounting; communication equipment technology; computer engineering technology; computer/information sciences; computer science; computer typography/composition; electrical/electronic engineering technology; electromechanical technology; engineering technology; health services administration; information sciences/systems; mechanical engineering technology; medical administrative assistant; medical records administration; telecommunications.
Academic Programs *Special study options:* adult/continuing education programs, advanced placement credit, freshman honors college, internships, part-time degree program, summer session for credit.
Library ECPI-Roanoke Library plus 1 other with 1,703 titles, 43 serial subscriptions, a Web page.
Computers on Campus 80 computers available on campus for general student use. A campuswide network can be accessed from off campus. Internet access, at least one staffed computer lab available.
Student Life *Housing:* college housing not available. *Activities and Organizations:* SETA, NVTHS, SAFA, FOAMA. *Campus security:* building and parking lot security.
Standardized Tests *Recommended:* SAT I and SAT II or ACT (for admission).
Costs (2002–03) *Tuition:* Tuition varies by program.
Financial Aid In 2001, 20 Federal Work-Study jobs (averaging $2000).
Applying *Options:* common application, deferred entrance. *Application fee:* $100. *Required:* minimum 2.0 GPA, interview. *Application deadline:* rolling (freshmen), rolling (transfers). *Notification:* continuous (freshmen).
Admissions Contact Heather Richards, Vice President, ECPI Technical College, 5234 Airport Road, Roanoke, VA 24012. *Phone:* 540-563-8000. *Toll-free phone:* 800-883-ECPI.

Germanna Community College
Locust Grove, Virginia

- **State-supported** 2-year, founded 1970, part of Virginia Community College System
- **Calendar** semesters
- **Degree** certificates and associate
- **Rural** 100-acre campus with easy access to Washington, DC
- **Coed,** 5,637 undergraduate students

Undergraduates Students come from 5 states and territories.
Faculty *Total:* 255, 19% full-time.
Majors Accounting; biological/physical sciences; business administration; data processing technology; education; electrical/electronic engineering technology; general studies; law enforcement/police science; liberal arts and sciences/liberal studies; nursing; secretarial science.
Academic Programs *Special study options:* academic remediation for entering students, adult/continuing education programs, off-campus study, part-time degree program, summer session for credit.

Library 22,412 titles, 160 serial subscriptions.
Computers on Campus 55 computers available on campus for general student use. At least one staffed computer lab available.
Student Life *Housing:* college housing not available. *Activities and Organizations:* student-run newspaper, Student Nurses Association, Student Government Association, Phi Theta Kappa, Students Against Substance Abuse. *Campus security:* 24-hour patrols. *Student Services:* personal/psychological counseling.
Athletics *Intramural sports:* archery M/W, basketball M/W, bowling M/W, football M/W, golf M/W, tennis M/W, volleyball M/W.
Standardized Tests *Required:* in-house placement tests.
Costs (2001–02) *Tuition:* $40 per credit part-time; state resident $1214 full-time, $40 per credit part-time; nonresident $5592 full-time, $186 per credit part-time. *Required fees:* $120 full-time, $4 per credit.
Applying *Options:* early admission. *Required for some:* high school transcript. *Application deadline:* rolling (freshmen), rolling (transfers). *Notification:* continuous (freshmen).
Admissions Contact Ms. Valerie Dent, Registrar, Germanna Community College, 2130 Germanna Highway, Locust Grove, VA 22508-2102. *Phone:* 540-727-3030.

ITT Technical Institute
Richmond, Virginia

- **Proprietary** 2-year
- **Calendar** quarters
- **Degree** associate
- **Coed,** 222 undergraduate students

Majors Computer/information sciences related; computer programming; drafting; electrical/electronic engineering technologies related; information technology.
Student Life *Housing:* college housing not available.
Costs (2001–02) *Tuition:* Full-time tuition and fees vary according to program. Part-time tuition and fees vary according to program. $260—$330 per credit hour.
Applying *Application fee:* $100. *Required:* high school transcript, interview. *Recommended:* letters of recommendation. *Application deadline:* rolling (freshmen). *Notification:* continuous (freshmen).
Admissions Contact Mr. Jeff Sikora, Director of Recruitment, ITT Technical Institute, 300 Gateway Centre Parkway, Richmond, VA 23235. *Phone:* 804-330-4992.

ITT Technical Institute
Norfolk, Virginia

- **Proprietary** primarily 2-year, founded 1988, part of ITT Educational Services, Inc
- **Calendar** quarters
- **Degrees** associate and bachelor's
- **Suburban** 2-acre campus
- **Coed,** 381 undergraduate students

Majors Computer/information sciences related; computer programming; drafting; electrical/electronic engineering technologies related; robotics technology.
Student Life *Housing:* college housing not available. *Activities and Organizations:* student-run newspaper.
Costs (2001–02) *Tuition:* Full-time tuition and fees vary according to program. Part-time tuition and fees vary according to program. $260—$330 per credit hour.
Financial Aid In 2001, 3 Federal Work-Study jobs (averaging $5000).
Applying *Options:* deferred entrance. *Application fee:* $100. *Required:* high school transcript, interview. *Recommended:* letters of recommendation. *Application deadline:* rolling (freshmen), rolling (transfers). *Notification:* continuous (freshmen).
Admissions Contact Mr. Jack Keesee, Director of Recruitment, ITT Technical Institute, 863 Glenrock Road, Suite 100, Norfolk, VA 23502-3701. *Phone:* 757-466-1260.

John Tyler Community College
Chester, Virginia

- **State-supported** 2-year, founded 1967, part of Virginia Community College System
- **Calendar** semesters
- **Degree** certificates and associate
- **Suburban** 62-acre campus with easy access to Richmond
- **Endowment** $2.0 million
- **Coed,** 5,656 undergraduate students

Undergraduates Students come from 38 states and territories, 2% are from out of state.
Faculty *Total:* 320, 22% full-time. *Student/faculty ratio:* 27:1.
Majors Architectural engineering technology; biological technology; business; electrical engineering; environmental technology; human services; liberal arts and sciences/liberal studies; management information systems/business data processing; mechanical engineering technology; mortuary science; nursing; physical therapy; safety/security technology; secretarial science.
Academic Programs *Special study options:* academic remediation for entering students, adult/continuing education programs, advanced placement credit, distance learning, external degree program, honors programs, off-campus study, part-time degree program, services for LD students, study abroad, summer session for credit. *ROTC:* Army (c).
Library John Tyler Community College Learning Resource and Technology Center with 49,393 titles, 179 serial subscriptions, 1,544 audiovisual materials, an OPAC, a Web page.
Computers on Campus 465 computers available on campus for general student use. A campuswide network can be accessed from off campus. Internet access, at least one staffed computer lab available.
Student Life *Housing:* college housing not available. *Campus security:* 24-hour patrols. *Student Services:* personal/psychological counseling.
Athletics *Intramural sports:* golf M/W, softball M/W, tennis M/W, volleyball M/W.
Costs (2001–02) *Tuition:* state resident $927 full-time, $39 per credit hour part-time; nonresident $4140 full-time, $173 per credit hour part-time. *Required fees:* $50 full-time, $3 per credit, $25 per term part-time. *Waivers:* senior citizens.
Applying *Options:* common application, early admission, deferred entrance. *Recommended:* high school transcript. *Application deadline:* rolling (freshmen). *Notification:* continuous (freshmen).
Admissions Contact Ms. Joy James, Registrar and Enrollment Services Coordinator, John Tyler Community College, 13101 Jefferson Davis Highway, Chester, VA 23831. *Phone:* 804-796-4150. *Toll-free phone:* 800-552-3490. *Fax:* 804-796-4163.

J. Sargeant Reynolds Community College
Richmond, Virginia

- **State-supported** 2-year, founded 1972, part of Virginia Community College System
- **Calendar** semesters
- **Degree** certificates and associate
- **Suburban** 207-acre campus
- **Endowment** $971,393
- **Coed,** 11,079 undergraduate students, 24% full-time, 60% women, 40% men

Undergraduates 2,647 full-time, 8,432 part-time. Students come from 33 states and territories, 53 other countries, 3% are from out of state, 38% African American, 3% Asian American or Pacific Islander, 1% Hispanic American, 0.5% Native American, 0.9% international, 13% transferred in.
Freshmen *Admission:* 2,378 applied, 2,378 admitted, 1,139 enrolled. *Average high school GPA:* 2.29.
Faculty *Total:* 583, 23% full-time. *Student/faculty ratio:* 19:1.
Majors Accounting technician; architectural engineering technology; biological/physical sciences; business administration; business marketing and marketing management; child care/guidance; civil engineering technology; community services; computer engineering technology; computer/information sciences; computer programming; computer programming related; computer science related; construction technology; criminal justice studies; culinary arts; data processing technology; dental laboratory technician; dietetics; electrical/electronic engineering technology; engineering; executive assistant; fashion merchandising; fire science; hospitality management; hotel and restaurant management; information technology; landscaping management; liberal arts and sciences/liberal studies; medical laboratory technician; music; nursing; occupational therapy assistant; opticianry; ornamental horticulture; paralegal/legal assistant; respiratory therapy; secretarial science; social sciences.
Academic Programs *Special study options:* academic remediation for entering students, adult/continuing education programs, advanced placement credit, dis-

J. Sargeant Reynolds Community College (continued)
tance learning, English as a second language, independent study, internships, off-campus study, part-time degree program, services for LD students, summer session for credit. *ROTC:* Army (c).
Library Learning Resource Center plus 2 others with 78,447 titles, 388 serial subscriptions, 1,797 audiovisual materials, an OPAC, a Web page.
Computers on Campus 983 computers available on campus for general student use. A campuswide network can be accessed from off campus that provide access to Telephone Registration for returning students. At least one staffed computer lab available.
Student Life *Housing:* college housing not available. *Activities and Organizations:* drama/theater group, choral group, Phi Theta Kappa, Student Nurses Association, SGA, Phi Beta Lambda. *Campus security:* security during open hours. *Student Services:* personal/psychological counseling.
Athletics *Intramural sports:* basketball M/W, bowling M/W, soccer M/W, softball M/W, table tennis M/W, tennis M/W, volleyball M/W.
Costs (2001–02) *Tuition:* state resident $1261 full-time, $42 per hour part-time; nonresident $5277 full-time, $176 per hour part-time. *Required fees:* $147 full-time, $5 per hour. *Waivers:* senior citizens.
Financial Aid In 2001, 115 Federal Work-Study jobs (averaging $1700).
Applying *Required:* high school transcript. *Required for some:* interview. *Application deadline:* rolling (freshmen), rolling (transfers). *Notification:* continuous (freshmen).
Admissions Contact Ms. Suzan Marshall, Director of Admissions and Records, J. Sargeant Reynolds Community College, PO Box 85622, Richmond, VA 23285-5622. *Phone:* 804-371-3029. *Fax:* 804-371-3650. *E-mail:* smarshall@jsr.vccs.edu.

LORD FAIRFAX COMMUNITY COLLEGE
Middletown, Virginia

- **State-supported** 2-year, founded 1969, part of Virginia Community College System
- **Calendar** semesters
- **Degree** certificates, diplomas, and associate
- **Rural** 100-acre campus with easy access to Washington, DC
- **Coed,** 4,587 undergraduate students, 26% full-time, 63% women, 37% men

Undergraduates 1,192 full-time, 3,395 part-time. 6% are from out of state, 5% African American, 0.9% Asian American or Pacific Islander, 2% Hispanic American, 0.4% Native American. *Retention:* 52% of 2001 full-time freshmen returned.
Freshmen *Admission:* 1,543 enrolled.
Faculty *Total:* 198, 27% full-time.
Majors Accounting; agricultural business; biological/physical sciences; business administration; civil engineering technology; communications; computer/information sciences; computer programming; dental hygiene; education; environmental technology; graphic design/commercial art/illustration; horticulture services; information sciences/systems; liberal arts and sciences/liberal studies; mechanical engineering technology; natural resources management; nursing; office management; philosophy; secretarial science.
Academic Programs *Special study options:* academic remediation for entering students, adult/continuing education programs, advanced placement credit, cooperative education, distance learning, honors programs, part-time degree program, services for LD students, summer session for credit.
Library Learning Resources Center with 41,000 titles, 300 serial subscriptions, an OPAC.
Computers on Campus 450 computers available on campus for general student use. A campuswide network can be accessed from off campus. Internet access, at least one staffed computer lab available.
Student Life *Housing:* college housing not available. *Activities and Organizations:* drama/theater group, Phi Theta Kappa, Phi Beta Lambda, Performing Arts Club, Scientific Society, Ambassadors Club. *Campus security:* late-night transport/escort service. *Student Services:* personal/psychological counseling, women's center.
Standardized Tests *Recommended:* SAT I (for placement).
Costs (2001–02) *Tuition:* state resident $891 full-time, $37 per credit part-time; nonresident $4056 full-time, $169 per credit part-time. Full-time tuition and fees vary according to course load and location. Part-time tuition and fees vary according to course load and location. *Required fees:* $52 full-time, $2 per credit, $7 per term part-time. *Payment plan:* deferred payment. *Waivers:* senior citizens.
Financial Aid In 2001, 28 Federal Work-Study jobs (averaging $1600).
Applying *Options:* early admission. *Recommended:* high school transcript. *Application deadline:* rolling (freshmen), rolling (transfers). *Notification:* continuous (freshmen).
Admissions Contact Mr. C. Todd Smith, Registrar, Lord Fairfax Community College, 173 Skirmisher Lane, Middletown, VA 22645. *Phone:* 540-868-7107. *Toll-free phone:* 800-906-5322 Ext. 7107. *Fax:* 540-868-7005. *E-mail:* lfsmitt@lf.vccs.edu.

MOUNTAIN EMPIRE COMMUNITY COLLEGE
Big Stone Gap, Virginia

- **State-supported** 2-year, founded 1972, part of Virginia Community College System
- **Calendar** semesters
- **Degree** certificates, diplomas, and associate
- **Small-town** campus with easy access to Kingsport
- **Coed,** 2,900 undergraduate students, 45% full-time, 66% women, 34% men

Undergraduates 1,300 full-time, 1,600 part-time. Students come from 3 states and territories, 1 other country, 1% are from out of state, 1% African American, 0.1% international, 3% transferred in. *Retention:* 56% of 2001 full-time freshmen returned.
Freshmen *Admission:* 800 applied, 800 admitted, 1,200 enrolled.
Faculty *Total:* 150, 47% full-time. *Student/faculty ratio:* 18:1.
Majors Accounting; biological/physical sciences; biology; business administration; business education; business marketing and marketing management; chemistry; computer systems networking/telecommunications; computer/technical support; corrections; criminal justice/law enforcement administration; data entry/microcomputer applications; drafting; education; electrical/electronic engineering technology; elementary education; engineering technology; English; environmental science; forestry; industrial technology; information sciences/systems; information technology; land use management; law enforcement/police science; legal administrative assistant; liberal arts and sciences/liberal studies; mathematics; mining technology; nursing; pre-engineering; public administration; secretarial science; water resources.
Academic Programs *Special study options:* academic remediation for entering students, adult/continuing education programs, advanced placement credit, cooperative education, distance learning, internships, part-time degree program, student-designed majors, summer session for credit.
Library Robb Hall with 21,600 titles, 105 serial subscriptions, 200 audiovisual materials, an OPAC.
Computers on Campus 400 computers available on campus for general student use. A campuswide network can be accessed from off campus. Internet access, at least one staffed computer lab available.
Student Life *Housing:* college housing not available. *Activities and Organizations:* drama/theater group, student-run television station, Phi Theta Kappa, Lambda Alpha Epsilon, MECC Group Artists, Phi Beta Lambda, Players on the Mountain. *Campus security:* 24-hour patrols. *Student Services:* personal/psychological counseling.
Athletics *Intramural sports:* basketball M/W, football M/W, golf M/W, tennis M/W, volleyball M/W.
Standardized Tests *Required:* ACT COMPASS, ACT ASSET.
Costs (2001–02) *Tuition:* state resident $1436 full-time, $42 per credit part-time; nonresident $5000 full-time, $174 per credit part-time. *Required fees:* $5 per credit.
Financial Aid In 2001, 150 Federal Work-Study jobs (averaging $1200). 30 State and other part-time jobs (averaging $650).
Applying *Options:* early admission, deferred entrance. *Required:* high school transcript. *Required for some:* minimum 2.0 GPA. *Application deadline:* rolling (freshmen), rolling (transfers). *Notification:* continuous (freshmen).
Admissions Contact Mr. Perry Carroll, Director of Admissions, Records, and Financial Aid, Mountain Empire Community College, PO Drawer 700, Big Stone Gap, VA 24219-0700. *Phone:* 276-523-2400 Ext. 219. *E-mail:* pcarroll@me.cc.va.us.

NATIONAL COLLEGE OF BUSINESS & TECHNOLOGY
Bluefield, Virginia

- **Proprietary** 2-year, founded 1886, part of National College of Business and Technology
- **Calendar** quarters
- **Degree** diplomas and associate
- **Small-town** campus
- **Coed**

Faculty *Total:* 20. *Student/faculty ratio:* 10:1.
Majors Accounting; business administration; computer science related; medical assistant; secretarial science.
Academic Programs *Special study options:* advanced placement credit, double majors, honors programs, internships, part-time degree program, services for LD students, summer session for credit.
Computers on Campus 35 computers available on campus for general student use. Internet access, at least one staffed computer lab available.
Student Life *Housing:* college housing not available.
Costs (2002–03) *Tuition:* $5013 full-time, $148 per credit hour part-time. Full-time tuition and fees vary according to course load. Part-time tuition and fees vary according to course load. *Required fees:* $45 full-time, $15 per term part-time. *Payment plans:* installment, deferred payment. *Waivers:* employees or children of employees.
Financial Aid In 2001, 5 Federal Work-Study jobs.
Applying *Options:* electronic application. *Application fee:* $30. *Recommended:* interview. *Application deadline:* rolling (freshmen), rolling (transfers).
Admissions Contact Ms. Jennifer Hooper, Admissions Representative, National College of Business & Technology, 100 Logan Street, Bluefield, VA 24605. *Phone:* 540-326-6321. *Toll-free phone:* 800-664-1886. *Fax:* 540-322-5731. *E-mail:* adm@educorp.edu.

National College of Business & Technology
Harrisonburg, Virginia

- **Proprietary** 2-year, founded 1988, part of National College of Business and Technology
- **Calendar** quarters
- **Degree** diplomas and associate
- **Small-town** campus
- **Coed**

Faculty *Total:* 20, 10% full-time. *Student/faculty ratio:* 10:1.
Majors Accounting; business administration; computer science related; medical assistant; secretarial science.
Academic Programs *Special study options:* advanced placement credit, double majors, honors programs, internships, part-time degree program, services for LD students, summer session for credit.
Computers on Campus 35 computers available on campus for general student use. Internet access, at least one staffed computer lab available.
Student Life *Housing:* college housing not available.
Costs (2002–03) *Tuition:* $5013 full-time, $148 per credit hour part-time. Full-time tuition and fees vary according to course load. Part-time tuition and fees vary according to course load. *Required fees:* $45 full-time, $15 per term part-time. *Payment plans:* installment, deferred payment. *Waivers:* employees or children of employees.
Financial Aid In 2001, 2 Federal Work-Study jobs.
Applying *Options:* electronic application. *Application fee:* $30. *Required for some:* high school transcript. *Recommended:* interview. *Application deadline:* rolling (freshmen), rolling (transfers). *Notification:* continuous (freshmen).
Admissions Contact National College of Business & Technology, 51 B Burgess Road, Harrisonburg, VA 22801. *Phone:* 540-432-0943. *Toll-free phone:* 800-664-1886. *Fax:* 540-432-1133. *E-mail:* adm@educorp.edu.

National College of Business & Technology
Danville, Virginia

- **Proprietary** 2-year, founded 1975, part of National College of Business and Technology
- **Calendar** quarters
- **Degree** diplomas and associate
- **Small-town** campus
- **Coed**

Faculty *Total:* 19, 11% full-time. *Student/faculty ratio:* 10:1.
Majors Accounting; business administration; computer science related; medical assistant; secretarial science.
Academic Programs *Special study options:* academic remediation for entering students, advanced placement credit, double majors, honors programs, internships, part-time degree program, summer session for credit.
Library 3,010 titles, 12 serial subscriptions.
Computers on Campus 35 computers available on campus for general student use. Internet access, at least one staffed computer lab available.
Costs (2002–03) *Tuition:* $5013 full-time, $148 per credit hour part-time. Full-time tuition and fees vary according to course load. Part-time tuition and fees vary according to course load. *Required fees:* $45 full-time, $15 per term part-time. *Payment plans:* installment, deferred payment. *Waivers:* employees or children of employees.
Financial Aid In 2001, 3 Federal Work-Study jobs.
Applying *Options:* electronic application. *Application fee:* $30. *Required for some:* high school transcript. *Recommended:* interview. *Application deadline:* rolling (freshmen), rolling (transfers).
Admissions Contact National College of Business & Technology, 734 Main Street, Danville, VA 24541. *Phone:* 434-793-6822. *Toll-free phone:* 800-664-1886. *Fax:* 434-793-3634. *E-mail:* adm@educorp.edu.

National College of Business & Technology
Bristol, Virginia

- **Proprietary** 2-year, founded 1992, part of National College of Business and Technology
- **Calendar** quarters
- **Degree** diplomas and associate
- **Small-town** campus
- **Coed**

Faculty *Total:* 10. *Student/faculty ratio:* 10:1.
Majors Accounting; business administration; computer science related; medical assistant; secretarial science.
Academic Programs *Special study options:* advanced placement credit, double majors, honors programs, internships, part-time degree program, services for LD students, summer session for credit.
Library National Business College-Bristol Campus Library.
Computers on Campus 35 computers available on campus for general student use. Internet access, at least one staffed computer lab available.
Student Life *Housing:* college housing not available.
Costs (2002–03) *Tuition:* $5013 full-time, $148 per credit hour part-time. Full-time tuition and fees vary according to course load. Part-time tuition and fees vary according to course load. *Required fees:* $45 full-time, $15 per term part-time. *Payment plans:* installment, deferred payment. *Waivers:* employees or children of employees.
Financial Aid In 2001, 3 Federal Work-Study jobs.
Applying *Options:* electronic application. *Application fee:* $30. *Required:* high school transcript. *Recommended:* interview. *Application deadline:* rolling (freshmen), rolling (transfers).
Admissions Contact National College of Business & Technology, 300 A Piedmont Avenue, Bristol, VA 24201. *Phone:* 540-669-5333. *Toll-free phone:* 800-664-1886. *Fax:* 540-669-4793. *E-mail:* adm@educorp.edu.

National College of Business & Technology
Lynchburg, Virginia

- **Proprietary** 2-year, founded 1979, part of National College of Business and Technology
- **Calendar** quarters
- **Degree** diplomas and associate
- **Small-town** 2-acre campus
- **Coed**

Undergraduates Students come from 15 other countries.
Faculty *Total:* 20, 10% full-time. *Student/faculty ratio:* 10:1.
Majors Accounting; business administration; computer science related; medical assistant; secretarial science.
Academic Programs *Special study options:* advanced placement credit, double majors, honors programs, internships, part-time degree program, services for LD students, summer session for credit.
Library 10 serial subscriptions.
Computers on Campus 35 computers available on campus for general student use. Internet access, at least one staffed computer lab available.
Student Life *Housing:* college housing not available.

National College of Business & Technology (continued)

Costs (2002–03) *Tuition:* $5013 full-time, $148 per credit hour part-time. Full-time tuition and fees vary according to course load. Part-time tuition and fees vary according to course load. *Required fees:* $45 full-time, $15 per term part-time. *Payment plans:* installment, deferred payment. *Waivers:* employees or children of employees.

Financial Aid In 2001, 3 Federal Work-Study jobs.

Applying *Options:* electronic application. *Application fee:* $30. *Required for some:* high school transcript. *Recommended:* interview. *Application deadline:* rolling (freshmen), rolling (transfers).

Admissions Contact Mr. George Wheelous, Admissions Representative, National College of Business & Technology, 104 Candlewood Court, Lynchburg, VA 24502. *Phone:* 804-239-3500. *Toll-free phone:* 800-664-1886. *Fax:* 434-239-3948. *E-mail:* adm@educorp.edu.

NATIONAL COLLEGE OF BUSINESS & TECHNOLOGY

Charlottesville, Virginia

- **Proprietary** 2-year, founded 1975, part of National College of Business and Technology
- **Calendar** quarters
- **Degree** certificates, diplomas, and associate
- **Small-town** campus with easy access to Richmond
- **Coed**

Faculty *Total:* 14, 14% full-time. *Student/faculty ratio:* 10:1.

Majors Accounting; business; computer science related; medical assistant; secretarial science.

Academic Programs *Special study options:* advanced placement credit, double majors, honors programs, internships, part-time degree program, services for LD students, summer session for credit.

Computers on Campus 35 computers available on campus for general student use. Internet access, at least one staffed computer lab available.

Costs (2002–03) *Tuition:* $5013 full-time, $148 per credit hour part-time. Full-time tuition and fees vary according to course load. Part-time tuition and fees vary according to course load. *Required fees:* $45 full-time, $15 per term part-time. *Payment plans:* installment, deferred payment. *Waivers:* employees or children of employees.

Financial Aid In 2001, 4 Federal Work-Study jobs.

Applying *Options:* electronic application. *Application fee:* $30. *Required for some:* high school transcript. *Recommended:* interview. *Application deadline:* rolling (freshmen), rolling (transfers).

Admissions Contact National College of Business & Technology, 1819 Emmet Street, Charlottesville, VA 22903. *Phone:* 434-295-0136. *Toll-free phone:* 800-664-1886. *Fax:* 434-979-8061. *E-mail:* mthomas@educorp.edu.

NATIONAL COLLEGE OF BUSINESS & TECHNOLOGY

Martinsville, Virginia

- **Proprietary** 2-year, founded 1975, part of National College of Business and Technology
- **Calendar** quarters
- **Degree** diplomas and associate
- **Small-town** campus
- **Coed**

Faculty *Total:* 15, 13% full-time. *Student/faculty ratio:* 10:1.

Majors Accounting; business administration; computer science related; secretarial science.

Academic Programs *Special study options:* advanced placement credit, double majors, honors programs, internships, part-time degree program, services for LD students, summer session for credit.

Computers on Campus 35 computers available on campus for general student use. Internet access, at least one staffed computer lab available.

Student Life *Housing:* college housing not available.

Costs (2002–03) *Tuition:* $5013 full-time, $148 per credit hour part-time. Full-time tuition and fees vary according to course load. Part-time tuition and fees vary according to course load. *Required fees:* $45 full-time, $15 per term part-time. *Payment plans:* installment, deferred payment. *Waivers:* employees or children of employees.

Financial Aid In 2001, 2 Federal Work-Study jobs.

Applying *Options:* electronic application. *Application fee:* $30. *Required for some:* high school transcript. *Recommended:* interview. *Application deadline:* rolling (freshmen), rolling (transfers).

Admissions Contact National College of Business & Technology, 10 Church Street, Martinsville, VA 24114. *Phone:* 276-632-5621. *Toll-free phone:* 800-664-1886 (in-state); 800-664-1866 (out-of-state). *Fax:* 276-632-7915. *E-mail:* adm@educorp.edu.

NATIONAL COLLEGE OF BUSINESS & TECHNOLOGY

Salem, Virginia

- **Proprietary** primarily 2-year, founded 1886, part of National College of Business and Technology
- **Calendar** quarters
- **Degrees** certificates, diplomas, associate, and bachelor's
- **Urban** 3-acre campus
- **Coed**

Undergraduates Students come from 15 other countries, 24% are from out of state. *Retention:* 70% of 2001 full-time freshmen returned.

Freshmen *Admission:* 346 applied, 346 admitted.

Faculty *Student/faculty ratio:* 12:1.

Majors Accounting; accounting technician; business; business marketing and marketing management; computer/information sciences; executive assistant; hospitality management; hotel and restaurant management; medical assistant; office management; secretarial science; tourism/travel marketing.

Academic Programs *Special study options:* academic remediation for entering students, advanced placement credit, double majors, internships, part-time degree program, summer session for credit.

Library Main Library plus 1 other with 25,867 titles, 40 serial subscriptions.

Computers on Campus 35 computers available on campus for general student use. Internet access, at least one staffed computer lab available.

Student Life *Housing Options:* coed.

Costs (2001–02) *Comprehensive fee:* $7308 includes full-time tuition ($5013), mandatory fees ($45), and room and board ($2250). Full-time tuition and fees vary according to course load. Part-time tuition: $148 per credit hour. Part-time tuition and fees vary according to course load. *Required fees:* $15 per term part-time. *Payment plans:* installment, deferred payment. *Waivers:* employees or children of employees.

Financial Aid In 2001, 6 Federal Work-Study jobs.

Applying *Application fee:* $30. *Required:* high school transcript. *Recommended:* interview. *Application deadline:* rolling (freshmen), rolling (transfers).

Admissions Contact Ms. Bunnie Hancock, Admissions Representative, National College of Business & Technology, PO Box 6400, Roanoke, VA 24017. *Phone:* 540-986-1800. *Toll-free phone:* 800-664-1886. *Fax:* 540-986-1344. *E-mail:* market@educorp.edu.

NEW RIVER COMMUNITY COLLEGE

Dublin, Virginia

- **State-supported** 2-year, founded 1969, part of Virginia Community College System
- **Calendar** semesters
- **Degree** certificates, diplomas, and associate
- **Rural** 100-acre campus
- **Endowment** $1.9 million
- **Coed,** 3,947 undergraduate students, 45% full-time, 51% women, 49% men

Undergraduates 1,769 full-time, 2,178 part-time. Students come from 22 states and territories, 21 other countries, 3% are from out of state, 5% African American, 0.6% Asian American or Pacific Islander, 0.5% Hispanic American, 0.3% Native American, 1% international, 5% transferred in.

Freshmen *Admission:* 503 applied, 503 admitted, 382 enrolled.

Faculty *Total:* 192, 28% full-time. *Student/faculty ratio:* 22:1.

Majors Accounting; architectural engineering technology; auto mechanic/technician; biological/physical sciences; business administration; business marketing and marketing management; child care/development; community services; computer engineering technology; computer graphics; computer typography/composition; criminal justice/law enforcement administration; drafting; education; electrical/electronic engineering technology; engineering; forensic technology;

general studies; gerontology; information sciences/systems; instrumentation technology; law enforcement/police science; liberal arts and sciences/liberal studies; machine technology; medical administrative assistant; paralegal/legal assistant; practical nurse; secretarial science; sign language interpretation; welding technology.

Academic Programs *Special study options:* academic remediation for entering students, adult/continuing education programs, advanced placement credit, cooperative education, distance learning, double majors, external degree program, internships, part-time degree program, services for LD students, summer session for credit.

Library New River Community College Library with 33,993 titles, 258 serial subscriptions, an OPAC.

Computers on Campus 120 computers available on campus for general student use. At least one staffed computer lab available.

Student Life *Housing:* college housing not available. *Activities and Organizations:* Student Government Association, Phi Beta Lambda, Instrument Society of America, Human Service Organization, Sign Language Club. *Campus security:* 24-hour patrols. *Student Services:* personal/psychological counseling.

Athletics *Intramural sports:* archery M/W, basketball M/W, bowling M/W, football M, golf M, soccer M/W, table tennis M/W, tennis M/W, volleyball M/W, weight lifting M/W.

Costs (2002–03) *Tuition:* state resident $1214 full-time, $40 per semester hour part-time; nonresident $5592 full-time, $186 per semester hour part-time. Part-time tuition and fees vary according to course load. *Required fees:* $114 full-time, $3 per semester hour, $12 per term part-time. *Waivers:* senior citizens.

Financial Aid In 2001, 150 Federal Work-Study jobs (averaging $2000).

Applying *Options:* early admission, deferred entrance. *Required for some:* high school transcript. *Application deadline:* rolling (freshmen), rolling (transfers). *Notification:* continuous (freshmen).

Admissions Contact Ms. Margaret G. Taylor, Coordinator of Admissions and Records and Student Services, New River Community College, PO Box 1127, 5251 College Drive, Dublin, VA 24084. *Phone:* 540-674-3600 Ext. 4205. *Fax:* 540-674-3644. *E-mail:* nrtaylm@nr.cc.va.us.

NORTHERN VIRGINIA COMMUNITY COLLEGE
Annandale, Virginia

- **State-supported** 2-year, founded 1965, part of Virginia Community College System
- **Calendar** semesters
- **Degree** certificates and associate
- **Suburban** 435-acre campus with easy access to Washington, DC
- **Endowment** $1.1 million
- **Coed,** 37,073 undergraduate students, 28% full-time, 56% women, 44% men

Undergraduates 2% are from out of state, 15% African American, 12% Asian American or Pacific Islander, 10% Hispanic American, 2% Native American, 4% international.

Faculty *Total:* 1,508, 33% full-time.

Majors Accounting; aircraft pilot (professional); alcohol/drug abuse counseling; applied art; architectural engineering technology; art; art history; auto mechanic/technician; aviation technology; biological/physical sciences; business administration; business marketing and marketing management; civil engineering technology; computer graphics; computer science; criminal justice/law enforcement administration; dental hygiene; dietetics; early childhood education; electrical/electronic engineering technology; emergency medical technology; engineering; fire science; food products retailing; gerontology; graphic design/commercial art/illustration; heating/air conditioning/refrigeration; horticulture science; hotel and restaurant management; human services; industrial radiologic technology; information sciences/systems; interior design; international business; law enforcement/police science; liberal arts and sciences/liberal studies; mathematics; mechanical engineering technology; medical laboratory technician; medical records administration; music; nursing; paralegal/legal assistant; photography; physical therapy; pre-engineering; psychology; purchasing/contracts management; recreation/leisure studies; religious studies; respiratory therapy; secretarial science; speech/rhetorical studies; travel/tourism management; veterinary technology.

Academic Programs *Special study options:* academic remediation for entering students, adult/continuing education programs, advanced placement credit, cooperative education, distance learning, double majors, English as a second language, external degree program, honors programs, part-time degree program, services for LD students, study abroad, summer session for credit.

Library 228,009 titles, 1,949 serial subscriptions, 12,227 audiovisual materials, an OPAC, a Web page.

Computers on Campus 2000 computers available on campus for general student use. Internet access, at least one staffed computer lab available.

Student Life *Housing:* college housing not available. *Activities and Organizations:* student-run newspaper, television station. *Campus security:* 24-hour emergency response devices, campus police.

Athletics *Intramural sports:* basketball M/W, football M/W, soccer M/W, volleyball M/W.

Costs (2001–02) *Tuition:* state resident $37 per credit hour part-time; nonresident $171 per credit hour part-time. *Required fees:* $2 per credit hour.

Applying *Options:* common application, early admission, deferred entrance. *Required for some:* high school transcript. *Application deadline:* rolling (freshmen), rolling (transfers). *Notification:* continuous (freshmen).

Admissions Contact Dr. Max L. Bassett, Dean of Academic and Student Services, Northern Virginia Community College, 4001 Wakefield Chapel Road, Annandale, VA 22003-3796. *Phone:* 703-323-3195.

PATRICK HENRY COMMUNITY COLLEGE
Martinsville, Virginia

- **State-supported** 2-year, founded 1962, part of Virginia Community College System
- **Calendar** semesters
- **Degree** associate
- **Rural** 137-acre campus
- **Coed,** 3,024 undergraduate students, 26% full-time, 63% women, 37% men

Undergraduates 785 full-time, 2,239 part-time. Students come from 3 states and territories, 24% African American, 0.5% Asian American or Pacific Islander, 0.4% Hispanic American, 0.6% Native American. *Retention:* 48% of 2001 full-time freshmen returned.

Freshmen *Admission:* 276 enrolled.

Faculty *Total:* 149, 28% full-time, 96% with terminal degrees. *Student/faculty ratio:* 39:1.

Majors Accounting; biological/physical sciences; business administration; computer programming; computer programming related; computer systems networking/telecommunications; data entry/microcomputer applications related; data processing technology; electrical/electronic engineering technology; engineering-related technology; industrial technology; information technology; liberal arts and sciences/liberal studies; nursing; secretarial science.

Academic Programs *Special study options:* academic remediation for entering students, adult/continuing education programs, advanced placement credit, cooperative education, English as a second language, internships, part-time degree program, services for LD students, summer session for credit.

Library Lester Library with 26,160 titles, 259 serial subscriptions, an OPAC, a Web page.

Computers on Campus 505 computers available on campus for general student use. A campuswide network can be accessed from off campus. At least one staffed computer lab available.

Student Life *Housing:* college housing not available. *Activities and Organizations:* drama/theater group, Student Government Association, Student Support Services, Phi Theta Kappa, Gospel Choir, Black Student Association. *Campus security:* 24-hour emergency response devices and patrols, late-night transport/escort service.

Athletics *Intramural sports:* baseball M, basketball M/W, soccer M, table tennis M/W, tennis M/W, volleyball M/W, weight lifting M/W.

Standardized Tests *Required:* ACT ASSET.

Costs (2001–02) *Tuition:* state resident $1114 full-time, $37 per semester hour part-time; nonresident $5130 full-time, $171 per semester hour part-time. Full-time tuition and fees vary according to course load. Part-time tuition and fees vary according to course load. *Required fees:* $55 full-time, $2 per semester hour, $5 per term part-time. *Waivers:* senior citizens.

Financial Aid In 2001, 41 Federal Work-Study jobs (averaging $2000).

Applying *Options:* early admission, deferred entrance. *Required:* high school transcript. *Application deadline:* rolling (freshmen), rolling (transfers). *Notification:* continuous (freshmen).

Admissions Contact Mr. Graham Valentine, Coordinator of Admissions and Records, Patrick Henry Community College, PO Box 5311, 645 Patriot Avenue, Martinsville, VA 24115. *Phone:* 276-638-8777. *Toll-free phone:* 800-232-7997. *Fax:* 276-656-0247. *E-mail:* qvalentine@ph.vccs.edu.

PAUL D. CAMP COMMUNITY COLLEGE
Franklin, Virginia

- **State-supported** 2-year, founded 1971, part of Virginia Community College System

Paul D. Camp Community College (continued)

- **Calendar** semesters
- **Degree** certificates and associate
- **Small-town** 99-acre campus
- **Endowment** $16,121
- **Coed,** 1,552 undergraduate students, 23% full-time, 67% women, 33% men

Undergraduates Students come from 2 states and territories, 2 other countries, 0.5% are from out of state.

Freshmen *Admission:* 350 applied, 350 admitted. *Average high school GPA:* 2.2.

Faculty *Total:* 74, 32% full-time. *Student/faculty ratio:* 17:1.

Majors Business administration; criminal justice/law enforcement administration; data processing technology; education; liberal arts and sciences/liberal studies; secretarial science.

Academic Programs *Special study options:* academic remediation for entering students, adult/continuing education programs, advanced placement credit, cooperative education, distance learning, honors programs, independent study, internships, off-campus study, part-time degree program, summer session for credit.

Library Paul D. Camp Community College Library with 22,000 titles, 200 serial subscriptions, an OPAC.

Computers on Campus 90 computers available on campus for general student use. At least one staffed computer lab available.

Student Life *Housing:* college housing not available. *Activities and Organizations:* student-run newspaper, African-American History Club, Phi Beta Lambda, Phi Theta Kappa, Student Government Association. *Campus security:* security staff until 7 p.m.

Standardized Tests *Required:* ACT COMPASS.

Costs (2002–03) *Tuition:* state resident $1304 full-time, $43 per semester hour part-time; nonresident $5682 full-time, $189 per semester hour part-time. Full-time tuition and fees vary according to course load. Part-time tuition and fees vary according to course load. *Required fees:* $90 full-time. *Payment plan:* tuition prepayment. *Waivers:* senior citizens.

Applying *Options:* deferred entrance. *Required:* high school transcript. *Application deadline:* rolling (freshmen), rolling (transfers). *Notification:* continuous (freshmen).

Admissions Contact Dr. Jerry J. Standahl, Director of Assessment and Student Development, Paul D. Camp Community College, PO Box 737, 100 North College Drive, Franklin, VA 23851-0737. *Phone:* 757-569-6725. *Fax:* 757-569-6795. *E-mail:* jstandahl@pc.cc.va.us.

PIEDMONT VIRGINIA COMMUNITY COLLEGE
Charlottesville, Virginia

- **State-supported** 2-year, founded 1972, part of Virginia Community College System
- **Calendar** semesters
- **Degree** certificates and associate
- **Suburban** 100-acre campus with easy access to Richmond
- **Coed,** 4,171 undergraduate students, 21% full-time, 61% women, 39% men

Undergraduates 889 full-time, 3,282 part-time. Students come from 33 states and territories, 2% are from out of state, 18% African American, 2% Asian American or Pacific Islander, 1% Hispanic American, 0.4% Native American, 0.9% international, 12% transferred in.

Freshmen *Admission:* 288 admitted, 288 enrolled.

Faculty *Total:* 232, 22% full-time. *Student/faculty ratio:* 18:1.

Majors Accounting; art; auto mechanic/technician; biological/physical sciences; business administration; business marketing and marketing management; computer programming; construction management; criminal justice/law enforcement administration; data processing technology; education; electrical/electronic engineering technology; law enforcement/police science; liberal arts and sciences/liberal studies; nursing; pre-engineering; secretarial science; theater arts/drama.

Academic Programs *Special study options:* academic remediation for entering students, adult/continuing education programs, advanced placement credit, cooperative education, distance learning, English as a second language, honors programs, independent study, part-time degree program, services for LD students, summer session for credit. *ROTC:* Army (c).

Library Jessup Library with 31,258 titles, 296 serial subscriptions, 21,448 audiovisual materials, an OPAC, a Web page.

Computers on Campus 110 computers available on campus for general student use. A campuswide network can be accessed from off campus that provide access to e-mail. Internet access, at least one staffed computer lab available.

Student Life *Housing:* college housing not available. *Activities and Organizations:* drama/theater group, student-run newspaper, choral group, Phi Theta Kappa, Black Student Alliance, Science Club, Masquers, Christian Fellowship Club. *Campus security:* 24-hour patrols.

Athletics *Intramural sports:* baseball M/W, basketball M/W, bowling M/W, football M/W, golf M/W, skiing (cross-country) M/W, soccer M/W, softball M/W, tennis M/W, volleyball M/W.

Costs (2001–02) *Tuition:* state resident $1114 full-time, $37 per credit hour part-time; nonresident $5130 full-time, $171 per credit hour part-time. Full-time tuition and fees vary according to location. Part-time tuition and fees vary according to course load and location. *Required fees:* $67 full-time, $2 per credit hour, $6 per term part-time. *Waivers:* senior citizens.

Financial Aid In 2001, 50 Federal Work-Study jobs.

Applying *Options:* common application, early admission. *Required for some:* high school transcript. *Application deadlines:* 8/26 (freshmen), 8/26 (transfers). *Notification:* continuous (freshmen).

Admissions Contact Ms. Mary Lee Walsh, Director of Student Services, Piedmont Virginia Community College, 501 College Drive, Charlottesville, VA 22902-7589. *Phone:* 434-961-5400.

RAPPAHANNOCK COMMUNITY COLLEGE
Glenns, Virginia

- **State-related** 2-year, founded 1970, part of Virginia Community College System
- **Calendar** semesters
- **Degree** certificates, diplomas, and associate
- **Rural** 217-acre campus
- **Coed,** 2,615 undergraduate students

Undergraduates Students come from 23 states and territories, 26% African American, 0.2% Asian American or Pacific Islander, 0.5% Hispanic American, 0.4% Native American.

Faculty *Total:* 79, 37% full-time.

Majors Accounting; biological/physical sciences; business administration; engineering technology; information sciences/systems; law enforcement/police science; liberal arts and sciences/liberal studies; nursing; secretarial science.

Academic Programs *Special study options:* academic remediation for entering students, adult/continuing education programs, distance learning, internships, off-campus study, part-time degree program, summer session for credit.

Library The College Library with 46,000 titles, 85 serial subscriptions, an OPAC.

Computers on Campus 195 computers available on campus for general student use. Internet access available.

Student Life *Housing:* college housing not available. *Activities and Organizations:* student-run newspaper, Phi Theta Kappa, Culture Club, Poetry Club, student government. *Campus security:* 24-hour emergency response devices. *Student Services:* personal/psychological counseling, women's center.

Athletics *Intramural sports:* baseball M, football M/W, golf M/W, softball W, tennis M/W, volleyball M/W.

Standardized Tests *Required:* CPT.

Costs (2001–02) *Tuition:* state resident $891 full-time, $37 per credit part-time; nonresident $4056 full-time, $169 per credit part-time. *Required fees:* $62 full-time, $2 per credit, $4 per term part-time.

Financial Aid In 2001, 40 Federal Work-Study jobs (averaging $1015).

Applying *Options:* common application, early admission. *Application deadline:* rolling (freshmen), rolling (transfers). *Notification:* continuous (freshmen).

Admissions Contact Ms. Wilnet Willis, Admissions and Records Officer, Rappahannock Community College, Glenns Campus, 12745 College Drive, Glenns, VA 23149-2616. *Phone:* 804-758-6742. *Fax:* 804-758-3852.

RICHARD BLAND COLLEGE OF THE COLLEGE OF WILLIAM AND MARY
Petersburg, Virginia

- **State-supported** 2-year, founded 1961, part of College of William and Mary
- **Calendar** semesters
- **Degree** associate
- **Rural** 712-acre campus with easy access to Richmond
- **Endowment** $395,891
- **Coed,** 1,304 undergraduate students, 58% full-time, 63% women, 37% men

Undergraduates 761 full-time, 543 part-time. Students come from 8 states and territories, 4 other countries, 1% are from out of state, 23% African American, 3% Asian American or Pacific Islander, 2% Hispanic American, 0.3% Native American, 0.7% international, 6% transferred in. *Retention:* 39% of 2001 full-time freshmen returned.

Freshmen *Admission:* 532 applied, 452 admitted, 389 enrolled. *Average high school GPA:* 2.70. *Test scores:* SAT verbal scores over 500: 33%; SAT math scores over 500: 26%; SAT verbal scores over 600: 6%; SAT math scores over 600: 5%.
Faculty *Total:* 65, 54% full-time, 34% with terminal degrees. *Student/faculty ratio:* 20:1.
Majors Liberal arts and sciences/liberal studies.
Academic Programs *Special study options:* academic remediation for entering students, accelerated degree program, advanced placement credit, part-time degree program, services for LD students, summer session for credit. *ROTC:* Army (c).
Library Richard Bland College Library with 65,000 titles, 9,000 serial subscriptions, 2,200 audiovisual materials, an OPAC, a Web page.
Computers on Campus 128 computers available on campus for general student use. A campuswide network can be accessed from off campus that provide access to email. Internet access, at least one staffed computer lab available.
Student Life *Housing:* college housing not available. *Activities and Organizations:* drama/theater group, student-run newspaper, choral group, RBC Newspaper, Multicultural Alliance, student government, Spanish Club, Biology Club. *Campus security:* 24-hour patrols.
Athletics *Intramural sports:* basketball M/W, golf M/W, racquetball M/W, tennis M/W, volleyball M/W.
Standardized Tests *Recommended:* SAT I or ACT (for admission).
Costs (2001–02) *Tuition:* state resident $1488 full-time, $65 per credit hour part-time; nonresident $6710 full-time, $284 per credit hour part-time. *Required fees:* $164 full-time, $4 per credit hour. *Waivers:* senior citizens.
Financial Aid In 2001, 10 Federal Work-Study jobs (averaging $2000).
Applying *Application fee:* $20. *Required:* essay or personal statement, high school transcript, minimum 2.0 GPA. *Required for some:* letters of recommendation, interview. *Application deadline:* 8/15 (freshmen), rolling (transfers). *Notification:* continuous (freshmen).
Admissions Contact Randy Dean, Director of Admissions and Student Services, Richard Bland College of The College of William and Mary, 11301 Johnson Road, Petersburg, VA 23805-7100. *Phone:* 804-862-6225. *Fax:* 804-862-6490. *E-mail:* admit@rbc.edu.

SOUTHSIDE VIRGINIA COMMUNITY COLLEGE
Alberta, Virginia

- **State-supported** 2-year, founded 1970, part of Virginia Community College System
- **Calendar** semesters
- **Degree** certificates, diplomas, and associate
- **Rural** 207-acre campus
- **Endowment** $412,823
- **Coed,** 4,313 undergraduate students, 25% full-time, 65% women, 35% men

Undergraduates 1,062 full-time, 3,251 part-time. Students come from 3 states and territories, 2 other countries, 1% are from out of state, 47% African American, 0.3% Asian American or Pacific Islander, 0.2% Hispanic American, 0.2% Native American.
Freshmen *Admission:* 270 enrolled.
Faculty *Total:* 240, 24% full-time, 7% with terminal degrees. *Student/faculty ratio:* 18:1.
Majors Biological/physical sciences; business administration; criminal justice/law enforcement administration; drafting; education; electrical/electronic engineering technology; general studies; human services; information sciences/systems; information technology; liberal arts and sciences/liberal studies; nursing; respiratory therapy; secretarial science.
Academic Programs *Special study options:* academic remediation for entering students, adult/continuing education programs, advanced placement credit, distance learning, double majors, honors programs, off-campus study, part-time degree program, services for LD students, study abroad, summer session for credit. *ROTC:* Army (c).
Library Julian M. Howell Library plus 1 other with 25,500 titles, 195 serial subscriptions, 850 audiovisual materials, an OPAC, a Web page.
Computers on Campus 200 computers available on campus for general student use. Internet access, at least one staffed computer lab available.
Student Life *Housing:* college housing not available. *Activities and Organizations:* choral group, Student Forum, Phi Theta Kappa, Phi Beta Lambda, Alpha Delta Omega.
Athletics *Intramural sports:* basketball M, softball M/W, table tennis M/W, tennis M/W, volleyball M/W.
Standardized Tests *Required:* ASSET, COMPASS.
Costs (2001–02) *Tuition:* state resident $1114 full-time, $37 per semester hour part-time; nonresident $5130 full-time, $171 per semester hour part-time. Full-time tuition and fees vary according to course load. Part-time tuition and fees vary according to course load. *Required fees:* $105 full-time, $4 per semester hour. *Waivers:* senior citizens.
Applying *Options:* common application, electronic application, early admission, deferred entrance. *Required:* high school transcript, interview. *Application deadline:* rolling (freshmen), rolling (transfers). *Notification:* continuous (freshmen).
Admissions Contact Dr. Ronald E. Mattox, Director of Admissions, Records, and Institutional Research, Southside Virginia Community College, Southside Virginia Community College, 109 Campus Drive, Alberta, VA 23821. *Phone:* 434-949-1012. *Fax:* 434-949-7863. *E-mail:* pat.watson@sv.vccs.edu.

SOUTHWEST VIRGINIA COMMUNITY COLLEGE
Richlands, Virginia

- **State-supported** 2-year, founded 1968, part of Virginia Community College System
- **Calendar** semesters
- **Degree** certificates, diplomas, and associate
- **Rural** 100-acre campus
- **Coed,** 4,621 undergraduate students

Undergraduates Students come from 6 states and territories, 6 other countries.
Faculty *Total:* 244, 43% full-time.
Majors Accounting; biological/physical sciences; business administration; drafting; education; electrical/electronic engineering technology; engineering; human services; industrial radiologic technology; information sciences/systems; land use management; law enforcement/police science; liberal arts and sciences/liberal studies; mining technology; music; nursing; respiratory therapy; secretarial science.
Academic Programs *Special study options:* academic remediation for entering students, adult/continuing education programs, advanced placement credit, distance learning, double majors, honors programs, internships, part-time degree program, summer session for credit.
Library 58,000 titles, 225 serial subscriptions, an OPAC, a Web page.
Computers on Campus 150 computers available on campus for general student use. A campuswide network can be accessed from off campus. Internet access, at least one staffed computer lab available.
Student Life *Housing:* college housing not available. *Activities and Organizations:* drama/theater group, student-run newspaper, radio and television station, PTK, PBL, Intervoice, Black Student Union, service club. *Campus security:* 24-hour emergency response devices and patrols, student patrols. *Student Services:* personal/psychological counseling, women's center.
Athletics *Intercollegiate sports:* baseball M, basketball M, golf M, rugby M. *Intramural sports:* basketball M/W, bowling M/W, football M, racquetball M/W, tennis M/W, volleyball M/W, weight lifting M/W.
Standardized Tests *Required:* SAT I or ACT (for placement), ACT ASSET.
Costs (2002–03) *Tuition:* state resident $1043 full-time, $43 per credit hour part-time; nonresident $4545 full-time, $189 per credit hour part-time. Full-time tuition and fees vary according to course load. Part-time tuition and fees vary according to course load. *Required fees:* $36 full-time, $2 per credit hour. *Payment plan:* tuition prepayment.
Financial Aid In 2001, 250 Federal Work-Study jobs (averaging $1236).
Applying *Options:* early admission, deferred entrance. *Required:* high school transcript, interview. *Application deadline:* rolling (freshmen), rolling (transfers).
Admissions Contact Mr. Roderick B. Moore, Director of Admissions, Records, and Financial Aid, Southwest Virginia Community College, Box SVCC, Richlands, VA 24641. *Phone:* 276-964-7294. *Toll-free phone:* 800-822-7822. *Fax:* 540-964-7716.

STRATFORD UNIVERSITY
Falls Church, Virginia

- **Degrees** diplomas, associate, and master's
- **Coed,** 851 undergraduate students, 100% full-time, 37% women, 63% men

Undergraduates 851 full-time. Students come from 9 states and territories, 36% are from out of state, 48% African American, 10% Asian American or Pacific Islander, 9% Hispanic American, 0.4% international, 4% transferred in.
Freshmen *Admission:* 644 enrolled. *Average high school GPA:* 2.50.
Faculty *Total:* 79, 62% full-time. *Student/faculty ratio:* 20:1.

Stratford University (continued)

Majors Business administration; business systems networking/ telecommunications; computer programming; computer programming related; computer systems networking/telecommunications; culinary arts; hotel and restaurant management.

Academic Programs *Special study options:* advanced placement credit, internships.

Library Stratford College Library with 1,500 titles, 75 serial subscriptions, 283 audiovisual materials.

Computers on Campus 7 computers available on campus for general student use. Internet access, online (class) registration available.

Student Life *Housing:* college housing not available. *Campus security:* 24-hour emergency response devices.

Costs (2002–03) *Tuition:* $14,730 full-time. Full-time tuition and fees vary according to program. No tuition increase for student's term of enrollment. *Payment plans:* tuition prepayment, installment, deferred payment.

Applying *Options:* common application, early decision. *Application fee:* $100. *Required:* high school transcript, minimum 2.0 GPA, interview. *Application deadlines:* 7/30 (freshmen), 7/30 (transfers). *Early decision:* 4/29. *Notification:* continuous until 8/6 (freshmen), 6/15 (early decision).

Admissions Contact Miss Sherrill Schwartz, Director of Admissions, Stratford University, 7777 Leesburg Pike, Falls Church, VA 22043. *Phone:* 703-821-8570 Ext. 3100. *Toll-free phone:* 800-444-0804. *Fax:* 703-734-5339.

THOMAS NELSON COMMUNITY COLLEGE

Hampton, Virginia

- **State-supported** 2-year, founded 1968, part of Virginia Community College System
- **Calendar** semesters
- **Degree** certificates, diplomas, and associate
- **Suburban** 85-acre campus with easy access to Virginia Beach
- **Coed,** 7,885 undergraduate students, 32% full-time, 60% women, 40% men

Undergraduates 2,485 full-time, 5,400 part-time. 37% African American, 4% Asian American or Pacific Islander, 4% Hispanic American, 0.7% Native American, 0.1% international.

Freshmen *Admission:* 1,233 enrolled.

Faculty *Total:* 94.

Majors Accounting; art; auto mechanic/technician; biological/physical sciences; business administration; computer science; drafting; early childhood education; electrical/electronic engineering technology; engineering; fire science; graphic design/commercial art/illustration; information sciences/systems; law enforcement/police science; liberal arts and sciences/liberal studies; mechanical engineering technology; medical laboratory technician; nursing; optometric/ophthalmic laboratory technician; photography; public administration; secretarial science; social sciences.

Academic Programs *Special study options:* academic remediation for entering students, adult/continuing education programs, advanced placement credit, cooperative education, English as a second language, external degree program, honors programs, internships, off-campus study, part-time degree program, services for LD students, summer session for credit.

Library Learning Resource Center with 66,281 titles, 467 serial subscriptions.

Computers on Campus 80 computers available on campus for general student use. At least one staffed computer lab available.

Student Life *Housing:* college housing not available. *Activities and Organizations:* student-run newspaper, choral group, Phi Theta Kappa, Future Nurses Association, Human Services Education Club, Student Government Association, Health Care Advocates. *Campus security:* 24-hour patrols. *Student Services:* personal/psychological counseling.

Athletics *Intramural sports:* basketball M/W, sailing M/W, soccer M/W, tennis M/W, volleyball M/W.

Standardized Tests *Recommended:* SAT I (for placement).

Costs (2002–03) *Tuition:* state resident $1214 full-time, $40 per credit hour part-time; nonresident $5592 full-time, $186 per credit hour part-time. *Required fees:* $111 full-time, $3 per credit hour, $11 per term part-time. *Waivers:* senior citizens.

Financial Aid In 2001, 110 Federal Work-Study jobs (averaging $3000).

Applying *Options:* early admission, deferred entrance. *Required:* high school transcript. *Application deadline:* rolling (freshmen), rolling (transfers). *Notification:* continuous (freshmen).

Admissions Contact Ms. Aileen Girard, Admissions Office Manager, Thomas Nelson Community College, PO Box 9407, 99 Thomas Nelson Drive, Hampton, VA 23670. *Phone:* 757-825-2800.

TIDEWATER COMMUNITY COLLEGE

Norfolk, Virginia

- **State-supported** 2-year, founded 1968, part of Virginia Community College System
- **Calendar** semesters
- **Degree** certificates, diplomas, and associate
- **Suburban** 520-acre campus
- **Coed,** 22,091 undergraduate students, 33% full-time, 59% women, 41% men

Undergraduates Students come from 53 states and territories, 32 other countries.

Faculty *Total:* 1,206, 22% full-time.

Majors Accounting; advertising; art; auto mechanic/technician; biological/physical sciences; business administration; business marketing and marketing management; computer programming; data processing technology; drafting; early childhood education; education; electrical/electronic engineering technology; engineering; finance; graphic design/commercial art/illustration; liberal arts and sciences/liberal studies; music; nursing; real estate; secretarial science.

Academic Programs *Special study options:* academic remediation for entering students, accelerated degree program, adult/continuing education programs, advanced placement credit, cooperative education, English as a second language, honors programs, internships, off-campus study, part-time degree program, services for LD students, summer session for credit.

Library 147,126 titles, 913 serial subscriptions.

Computers on Campus A campuswide network can be accessed from off campus. Internet access, at least one staffed computer lab available.

Student Life *Housing:* college housing not available. *Activities and Organizations:* drama/theater group, student-run newspaper. *Campus security:* 24-hour patrols. *Student Services:* personal/psychological counseling, women's center.

Athletics *Intramural sports:* basketball M/W, tennis M/W.

Standardized Tests *Required for some:* ACT COMPASS. *Recommended:* ACT COMPASS.

Costs (2002–03) *Tuition:* state resident $971 full-time, $40 per credit part-time; nonresident $4473 full-time. *Required fees:* $200 full-time, $8 per credit.

Financial Aid In 2001, 64 Federal Work-Study jobs (averaging $2000).

Applying *Options:* early admission, deferred entrance. *Application deadline:* rolling (freshmen), rolling (transfers). *Notification:* continuous (freshmen).

Admissions Contact Dr. Dick Witte, Associate Dean, Student Services, Tidewater Community College, 7000 College Drive, Portsmouth, VA 23703. *Phone:* 757-822-1068.

VIRGINIA HIGHLANDS COMMUNITY COLLEGE

Abingdon, Virginia

- **State-supported** 2-year, founded 1967, part of Virginia Community College System
- **Calendar** semesters
- **Degree** certificates, diplomas, and associate
- **Small-town** 100-acre campus
- **Coed**

Standardized Tests *Required for some:* SCAT, ACT ASSET. *Recommended:* SCAT, ACT ASSET.

Applying *Options:* early admission, deferred entrance. *Required:* high school transcript.

Admissions Contact Mr. David N. Matlock, Director of Admissions, Records, and Financial Aid, Virginia Highlands Community College, PO Box 828, Abingdon, VA 24212-0828. *Phone:* 540-676-5484 Ext. 290. *Toll-free phone:* 877-207-6115. *Fax:* 540-676-5591.

VIRGINIA WESTERN COMMUNITY COLLEGE

Roanoke, Virginia

- **State-supported** 2-year, founded 1966, part of Virginia Community College System
- **Calendar** semesters
- **Degree** certificates, diplomas, and associate
- **Urban** 70-acre campus
- **Coed,** 8,311 undergraduate students

Undergraduates Students come from 52 states and territories.

Faculty *Total:* 403, 22% full-time.

Majors Accounting; art; auto mechanic/technician; biological/physical sciences; business administration; child care/development; civil engineering technology; computer science; criminal justice/law enforcement administration; data processing technology; dental hygiene; early childhood education; education; electrical/electronic engineering technology; engineering; graphic design/commercial art/illustration; industrial radiologic technology; liberal arts and sciences/liberal studies; mechanical engineering technology; mental health/rehabilitation; nursing; pre-engineering; radiological science; radio/television broadcasting; secretarial science.

Academic Programs *Special study options:* academic remediation for entering students, adult/continuing education programs, advanced placement credit, cooperative education, distance learning, double majors, English as a second language, independent study, internships, part-time degree program, services for LD students, summer session for credit.

Library 67,129 titles, 402 serial subscriptions.

Computers on Campus 200 computers available on campus for general student use. A campuswide network can be accessed from off campus. Internet access, at least one staffed computer lab available.

Student Life *Housing:* college housing not available. *Activities and Organizations:* drama/theater group, student-run newspaper. *Student Services:* personal/psychological counseling.

Athletics *Intramural sports:* basketball M.

Standardized Tests *Recommended:* SAT I or ACT (for placement).

Costs (2001–02) *Tuition:* state resident $1300 full-time, $44 per credit part-time; nonresident $5700 full-time, $189 per credit part-time.

Applying *Options:* common application, early admission, deferred entrance. *Required:* high school transcript. *Application deadline:* rolling (freshmen), rolling (transfers). *Notification:* continuous (freshmen).

Admissions Contact Admissions Office, Virginia Western Community College, PO Box 14007, Roanoke, VA 24038. *Phone:* 540-857-7231. *Fax:* 540-857-7204.

WYTHEVILLE COMMUNITY COLLEGE
Wytheville, Virginia

- **State-supported** 2-year, founded 1967, part of Virginia Community College System
- **Calendar** semesters
- **Degree** associate
- **Rural** 141-acre campus
- **Coed**

Faculty *Student/faculty ratio:* 16:1.

Student Life *Campus security:* 24-hour emergency response devices and patrols.

Financial Aid In 2001, 125 Federal Work-Study jobs (averaging $2304).

Applying *Options:* early admission. *Required:* high school transcript. *Required for some:* interview.

Admissions Contact Ms. Sherry K. Dix, Registrar, Wytheville Community College, 1000 East Main Street, Wytheville, VA 24382-3308. *Phone:* 540-223-4755. *Toll-free phone:* 800-468-1195. *Fax:* 540-223-4860. *E-mail:* wcdixxs@wc.cc.va.us.

WASHINGTON

THE ART INSTITUTE OF SEATTLE
Seattle, Washington

- **Proprietary** 2-year, founded 1982, part of Art Institutes International
- **Calendar** quarters
- **Degree** diplomas and associate
- **Urban** campus
- **Coed,** 2,480 undergraduate students, 66% full-time, 45% women, 55% men

Undergraduates 1,629 full-time, 851 part-time. Students come from 39 states and territories, 14 other countries, 20% are from out of state, 4% African American, 8% Asian American or Pacific Islander, 3% Hispanic American, 2% Native American, 11% international, 1% transferred in.

Freshmen *Admission:* 707 applied, 615 admitted, 408 enrolled. *Average high school GPA:* 2.30.

Faculty *Total:* 195, 48% full-time, 22% with terminal degrees. *Student/faculty ratio:* 19:1.

Majors Audio engineering; computer graphics; culinary arts; fashion design/illustration; fashion merchandising; film/video production; graphic design/commercial art/illustration; industrial design; interior design; photography.

Academic Programs *Special study options:* academic remediation for entering students, adult/continuing education programs, English as a second language, honors programs, off-campus study, part-time degree program, services for LD students, summer session for credit.

Library 4,000 titles, 110 serial subscriptions.

Computers on Campus 62 computers available on campus for general student use. A campuswide network can be accessed from student residence rooms. Internet access, at least one staffed computer lab available.

Student Life *Housing Options:* coed. *Activities and Organizations:* Multicultural Affairs Organization, American Society of Interior Designers, DECA, Student Advisory Board. *Campus security:* 24-hour patrols. *Student Services:* personal/psychological counseling.

Athletics *Intramural sports:* soccer M/W, softball M/W.

Standardized Tests *Recommended:* SAT I or ACT (for admission).

Costs (2002–03) *Tuition:* $14,040 full-time, $305 per credit part-time. No tuition increase for student's term of enrollment. *Room only:* $8025. *Payment plan:* installment. *Waivers:* employees or children of employees.

Financial Aid In 2001, 36 Federal Work-Study jobs (averaging $1987).

Applying *Options:* deferred entrance. *Application fee:* $50. *Required:* essay or personal statement, high school transcript, interview. *Recommended:* 3 letters of recommendation. *Application deadline:* rolling (freshmen). *Notification:* continuous (freshmen).

Admissions Contact Ms. Laine Morgan, Director of Admissions, The Art Institute of Seattle, 2323 Elliott Avenue, Seattle, WA 98121-1642. *Phone:* 800-275-2471. *Toll-free phone:* 800-275-2471. *Fax:* 206-269-0275. *E-mail:* adm@ais.edu.

BATES TECHNICAL COLLEGE
Tacoma, Washington

- **State-supported** 2-year, part of Washington State Board for Community and Technical Colleges
- **Degree** certificates, diplomas, and associate
- **Coed,** 16,162 undergraduate students

Faculty *Total:* 290, 42% full-time, 0.3% with terminal degrees. *Student/faculty ratio:* 18:1.

Majors Accounting technician; architectural engineering technology; auto body repair; auto mechanic/technician; biomedical technology; carpentry; child care/guidance; civil engineering technology; computer maintenance technology; computer programming; court reporting; culinary arts; data processing technology; dental laboratory technician; diesel engine mechanic; electrical/electronic engineering technology; electrical/power transmission installation; fire science; heating/air conditioning/refrigeration; industrial technology; information sciences/systems; legal administrative assistant; mechanical engineering technology; radio/television broadcasting technology; secretarial science; surveying.

Student Life *Housing:* college housing not available. *Activities and Organizations:* student-run newspaper, radio and television station, Associated Student Government. *Campus security:* 24-hour emergency response devices, on-campus weekday security to 10 p.m.

Standardized Tests *Required:* ACT ASSET.

Costs (2001–02) *Tuition:* state resident $2690 full-time. Full-time tuition and fees vary according to program.

Financial Aid In 2001, 15 Federal Work-Study jobs (averaging $3500). 35 State and other part-time jobs (averaging $3500).

Applying *Application fee:* $45. *Application deadline:* rolling (freshmen). *Notification:* continuous (freshmen).

Admissions Contact Ms. Gwen Sailer, Vice President for Student Services, Bates Technical College, 1101 South Yakima Avenue, Tacoma, WA 98405. *Phone:* 253-680-7000. *Toll-free phone:* 800-562-7099. *Fax:* 253-680-7101. *E-mail:* ewebber@bates.ctc.edu.

BELLEVUE COMMUNITY COLLEGE
Bellevue, Washington

- **State-supported** 2-year, founded 1966, part of Washington State Board for Community and Technical Colleges
- **Calendar** quarters

Bellevue Community College (continued)
- **Degree** associate
- **Suburban** 96-acre campus with easy access to Seattle
- **Coed,** 21,700 undergraduate students

Faculty *Total:* 572, 23% full-time.
Majors Accounting; business administration; business marketing and marketing management; computer programming; criminal justice/law enforcement administration; data processing technology; early childhood education; educational media design; fashion merchandising; fire science; industrial radiologic technology; information sciences/systems; interior design; law enforcement/police science; liberal arts and sciences/liberal studies; nursing; real estate; recreation/leisure studies; secretarial science.
Academic Programs *Special study options:* academic remediation for entering students, adult/continuing education programs, advanced placement credit, cooperative education, English as a second language, part-time degree program, services for LD students, summer session for credit.
Library Bellevue Community College Library with 42,000 titles, 485 serial subscriptions.
Computers on Campus 600 computers available on campus for general student use. At least one staffed computer lab available.
Student Life *Housing:* college housing not available. *Activities and Organizations:* drama/theater group, student-run newspaper, radio station. *Student Services:* health clinic, personal/psychological counseling, women's center.
Athletics *Intercollegiate sports:* basketball M(s)/W(s), cross-country running M(s)/W(s), golf M(s), soccer M(s), tennis M(s)/W(s), track and field M(s)/W(s), volleyball W(s). *Intramural sports:* basketball M/W, cross-country running M/W, football M/W, skiing (cross-country) M/W, skiing (downhill) M/W, soccer W, tennis M/W, track and field M/W, volleyball M/W.
Costs (2001–02) *Tuition:* area resident $2892 full-time; nonresident $10,618 full-time. *Required fees:* $158 full-time, $4 per credit.
Financial Aid In 2001, 75 Federal Work-Study jobs (averaging $3400). 23 State and other part-time jobs (averaging $3000).
Applying *Options:* electronic application, early admission. *Application deadline:* rolling (freshmen), rolling (transfers).
Admissions Contact Ms. Tika Esler, Associate Dean of Enrollment Services, Bellevue Community College, 3000 Landerholm Circle, SE, Bellevue, WA 98007-6484. *Phone:* 425-564-2222.

BELLINGHAM TECHNICAL COLLEGE
Bellingham, Washington

- **State-supported** 2-year
- 3,791 undergraduate students, 19% full-time

Faculty *Student/faculty ratio:* 20:1.
Financial Aid In 2001, 29 State and other part-time jobs (averaging $3000).
Applying *Options:* early admission, deferred entrance. *Application fee:* $33.
Admissions Contact Bellingham Technical College, 3028 Lindbergh Avenue, Bellingham, WA 98225-1599. *Phone:* 360-738-3105 Ext. 440. *E-mail:* beltcadm@belltc.ctc.edu.

BIG BEND COMMUNITY COLLEGE
Moses Lake, Washington

- **State-supported** 2-year, founded 1962
- **Calendar** quarters
- **Degree** certificates and associate
- **Small-town** 159-acre campus
- **Endowment** $994,350
- **Coed,** 1,912 undergraduate students, 63% full-time, 58% women, 42% men

Undergraduates 1,198 full-time, 714 part-time. Students come from 6 states and territories, 3 other countries, 3% are from out of state, 1% African American, 2% Asian American or Pacific Islander, 17% Hispanic American, 1% Native American, 0.7% international, 8% transferred in, 5% live on campus.
Freshmen *Admission:* 310 applied, 310 admitted, 310 enrolled.
Faculty *Total:* 112, 42% full-time, 4% with terminal degrees. *Student/faculty ratio:* 20:1.
Majors Accounting technician; aircraft pilot (professional); auto mechanic/technician; aviation technology; civil engineering technology; industrial electronics installation/repair; industrial equipment maintenance and repair related; information sciences/systems; liberal arts and sciences/liberal studies; nursing; office management; practical nurse; teacher assistant/aide; welding technology.
Academic Programs *Special study options:* academic remediation for entering students, advanced placement credit, cooperative education, distance learning, double majors, English as a second language, off-campus study, part-time degree program, services for LD students, summer session for credit.
Library Big Bend Community College Library with 41,900 titles, 3,700 serial subscriptions, 3,150 audiovisual materials, an OPAC, a Web page.
Computers on Campus 300 computers available on campus for general student use. A campuswide network can be accessed from off campus. Internet access, online (class) registration, at least one staffed computer lab available.
Student Life *Housing Options:* coed. *Activities and Organizations:* student-run newspaper, choral group. *Campus security:* 24-hour emergency response devices, student patrols. *Student Services:* personal/psychological counseling.
Athletics *Intercollegiate sports:* baseball M(s), basketball M(s)/W(s), softball W(s), volleyball W(s).
Costs (2001–02) *Tuition:* state resident $1743 full-time, $58 per credit part-time; nonresident $6861 full-time, $229 per credit part-time. Part-time tuition and fees vary according to course load. *Room and board:* $4220. Room and board charges vary according to board plan. *Waivers:* senior citizens and employees or children of employees.
Financial Aid In 2001, 50 Federal Work-Study jobs (averaging $2700). 100 State and other part-time jobs (averaging $3240).
Applying *Options:* early admission, deferred entrance. *Application fee:* $10. *Required for some:* high school transcript. *Application deadline:* rolling (freshmen), rolling (transfers). *Notification:* continuous (freshmen).
Admissions Contact Ms. Candis Lacher, Dean of Enrollment Services, Big Bend Community College, 7662 Chanute Street, Moses Lake, WA 98837. *Phone:* 509-762-5351 Ext. 226. *Fax:* 509-762-6243. *E-mail:* candyl@bbcc.ctc.edu.

CASCADIA COMMUNITY COLLEGE
Bothell, Washington

- **State-supported** 2-year, founded 1999
- **Calendar** quarters
- **Degree** certificates and associate
- **Coed,** 2,011 undergraduate students, 68% full-time, 48% women, 52% men
- 73% of applicants were admitted

Undergraduates 1,371 full-time, 640 part-time. 0.8% African American, 7% Asian American or Pacific Islander, 5% Hispanic American, 0.4% Native American, 1% international.
Freshmen *Admission:* 880 applied, 644 admitted.
Faculty *Total:* 91, 24% full-time, 22% with terminal degrees. *Student/faculty ratio:* 20:1.
Majors Liberal arts and sciences/liberal studies; liberal arts and studies related; science technologies related.
Student Life *Housing:* college housing not available. *Campus security:* 24-hour emergency response devices, late-night transport/escort service.
Costs (2002–03) *Tuition:* state resident $1322 full-time, $63 per credit part-time; nonresident $4794 full-time, $235 per credit part-time.
Admissions Contact Mr. Jack Bautseh, Vice President for Student Success, Cascadia Community College, 18345 Campus Way NE, Bothell, WA 98011. *Phone:* 425-352-8000. *Fax:* 425-352-8137. *E-mail:* admissions@cascadia.ctc.edu.

CENTRALIA COLLEGE
Centralia, Washington

- **State-supported** 2-year, founded 1925, part of Washington State Board for Community and Technical Colleges
- **Calendar** quarters
- **Degree** certificates and associate
- **Small-town** 12-acre campus
- **Endowment** $3.8 million
- **Coed,** 3,823 undergraduate students

Undergraduates Students come from 5 states and territories, 1% are from out of state, 0.8% African American, 1% Asian American or Pacific Islander, 11% Hispanic American, 2% Native American. *Retention:* 57% of 2001 full-time freshmen returned.
Freshmen *Admission:* 1,673 applied, 1,673 admitted.
Faculty *Total:* 197, 35% full-time, 6% with terminal degrees. *Student/faculty ratio:* 22:1.
Majors Applied art; art; biological/physical sciences; biology; botany; broadcast journalism; business; business administration; business marketing and mar-

keting management; chemistry; child care/development; child care/guidance; child care services management; civil engineering technology; computer programming related; computer science related; computer systems networking/ telecommunications; corrections; criminal justice/law enforcement administration; diesel engine mechanic; early childhood education; electrical/electronic engineering technology; engineering; English; family living/parenthood; French; geology; German; graphic design/commercial art/illustration; heavy equipment maintenance; history; humanities; legal administrative assistant; liberal arts and sciences/ liberal studies; marketing operations; mass communications; mathematics; medical administrative assistant; music; natural sciences; nursing; personal services marketing operations; physical sciences; political science; practical nurse; predentistry; pre-engineering; pre-law; pre-medicine; pre-pharmacy studies; preveterinary studies; psychology; radio/television broadcasting; receptionist; recreation/leisure studies; retailing operations; retail management; secretarial science; social sciences; sociology; Spanish; surveying; system/networking/LAN/ WAN management; teacher assistant/aide; theater arts/drama; welding technology; zoology.

Academic Programs *Special study options:* academic remediation for entering students, adult/continuing education programs, advanced placement credit, cooperative education, distance learning, English as a second language, external degree program, freshman honors college, honors programs, independent study, part-time degree program, services for LD students, study abroad, summer session for credit.

Library 31,000 titles, 225 serial subscriptions, an OPAC, a Web page.

Computers on Campus 125 computers available on campus for general student use. A campuswide network can be accessed from off campus that provide access to online degree audits, transcripts. Internet access, online (class) registration, at least one staffed computer lab available.

Student Life *Housing:* college housing not available. *Activities and Organizations:* drama/theater group, student-run newspaper, radio and television station, choral group, marching band, Phi Theta Kappa, Diesel Tech Club, Business Management Association, Student Activities/Admissions Team, International Club. *Campus security:* 24-hour patrols, late-night transport/escort service. *Student Services:* personal/psychological counseling, women's center.

Athletics Member NJCAA. *Intercollegiate sports:* baseball M(s), basketball M(s)/W(s), golf W(s), softball W(s), volleyball W(s).

Standardized Tests *Required:* ACT ASSET.

Costs (2001–02) *Tuition:* state resident $1743 full-time, $58 per credit part-time; nonresident $2138 full-time, $72 per credit part-time. Full-time tuition and fees vary according to course load. Part-time tuition and fees vary according to course load. *Required fees:* $135 full-time, $4 per credit, $5 per term part-time. *Payment plan:* deferred payment. *Waivers:* senior citizens.

Applying *Options:* common application, electronic application. *Required:* high school transcript. *Application deadline:* rolling (freshmen), rolling (transfers). *Notification:* continuous until 9/15 (freshmen).

Admissions Contact Mr. Scott A. Copeland, Director of Enrollment Services, Centralia College, 600 West Locust, Centralia, WA 98531. *Phone:* 360-736-9391 Ext. 682. *Fax:* 360-330-7503. *E-mail:* admissions@centralia.ctc.edu.

CLARK COLLEGE
Vancouver, Washington

- **State-supported** 2-year, founded 1933, part of Washington State Board for Community and Technical Colleges
- **Calendar** quarters
- **Degree** certificates, diplomas, and associate
- **Urban** 80-acre campus with easy access to Portland
- **Endowment** $41.4 million
- **Coed,** 9,274 undergraduate students, 41% full-time, 60% women, 40% men

Undergraduates 3,812 full-time, 5,462 part-time. Students come from 9 states and territories, 19 other countries, 3% are from out of state, 2% African American, 5% Asian American or Pacific Islander, 4% Hispanic American, 1% Native American, 0.7% international, 3% transferred in.

Freshmen *Admission:* 2,481 applied, 2,481 admitted, 929 enrolled.

Faculty *Total:* 477, 33% full-time, 8% with terminal degrees. *Student/faculty ratio:* 23:1.

Majors Accounting; agricultural sciences; Air Force R.O.T.C./air science; alcohol/drug abuse counseling; art; auto mechanic/technician; baker/pastry chef; biological/physical sciences; business administration; business marketing and marketing management; chemistry; child care/development; communications related; computer/information sciences related; computer programming; computer programming related; construction technology; culinary arts; dental hygiene; diesel engine mechanic; early childhood education; education; electrical/electronic engineering technology; engineering; engineering technology; geology; graphic design/commercial art/illustration; graphic/printing equipment; horticulture services; industrial technology; journalism; landscaping management; legal administrative assistant; liberal arts and sciences/liberal studies; machine technology; mathematics; medical administrative assistant; medical assistant; medical technology; music; natural sciences; nursing; office management; ornamental horticulture; paralegal/legal assistant; physics; pre-engineering; retailing operations; retail management; sales operations; secretarial science; social sciences; sociology; teacher assistant/aide; technical/business writing; telecommunications; welding technology.

Academic Programs *Special study options:* academic remediation for entering students, adult/continuing education programs, advanced placement credit, cooperative education, distance learning, English as a second language, honors programs, independent study, internships, part-time degree program, services for LD students, study abroad, summer session for credit. *ROTC:* Army (b), Air Force (c).

Library Lewis D. Cannell Library with 55,091 titles, 539 serial subscriptions, 2,444 audiovisual materials, an OPAC, a Web page.

Computers on Campus 582 computers available on campus for general student use. A campuswide network can be accessed from off campus. Internet access, online (class) registration, at least one staffed computer lab available.

Student Life *Housing:* college housing not available. *Activities and Organizations:* drama/theater group, student-run newspaper, choral group, Phi Theta Kappa, Baptist Student Ministries, International Club, Justice for All, Students for Political Activism Now (SPAN). *Campus security:* late-night transport/escort service, security staff during hours of operation. *Student Services:* health clinic, personal/psychological counseling, women's center, legal services.

Athletics *Intercollegiate sports:* basketball M(s)/W(s), cross-country running M(s)/W(s), fencing M(c)/W(c), soccer M(s)/W(s), track and field M(s)/W(s), volleyball W(s). *Intramural sports:* basketball M/W, fencing M/W, football M/W, soccer M/W, softball M/W, table tennis M/W, volleyball M/W.

Standardized Tests *Recommended:* ACT ASSET.

Costs (2001–02) *Tuition:* state resident $1578 full-time, $54 per quarter hour part-time; nonresident $1973 full-time, $65 per quarter hour part-time. Full-time tuition and fees vary according to course load and reciprocity agreements. Part-time tuition and fees vary according to course load and reciprocity agreements. *Required fees:* $372 full-time. *Waivers:* senior citizens and employees or children of employees.

Financial Aid In 2001, 450 Federal Work-Study jobs (averaging $800). 350 State and other part-time jobs (averaging $1100).

Applying *Options:* common application, early admission, deferred entrance. *Required for some:* high school transcript, interview. *Application deadlines:* 8/13 (freshmen), 8/13 (transfers). *Notification:* continuous (freshmen).

Admissions Contact Ms. Lorraine Sandstrom, Registrar, Clark College, 1800 East McLoughlin Boulevard, Vancover, WA 98663. *Phone:* 360-992-2358. *Toll-free phone:* 360-992-2107. *Fax:* 360-992-2876.

CLOVER PARK TECHNICAL COLLEGE
Lakewood, Washington

- **State-supported** 2-year, founded 1942, part of Washington State Community and Technical College System
- **Degree** certificates and associate
- 7,429 undergraduate students, 23% full-time

Undergraduates 1,700 full-time, 5,729 part-time. Students come from 12 states and territories, 1% are from out of state, 10% African American, 7% Asian American or Pacific Islander, 3% Hispanic American, 1% Native American.

Freshmen *Admission:* 220 applied, 220 admitted.

Faculty *Total:* 239, 48% full-time. *Student/faculty ratio:* 25:1.

Majors Accounting technician; aircraft pilot (professional); architectural engineering technology; aviation technology; business machine repair; business marketing and marketing management; child care/guidance; communications technologies related; computer programming; computer systems networking/ telecommunications; electrical and electronics equipment installation and repair related; environmental science; graphic/printing equipment; heating/air conditioning/ refrigeration; heavy equipment maintenance; interior design; landscaping management; legal administrative assistant; mechanical engineering technology; office management; precision production trades related; quality control/safety technologies related; rehabilitation/therapeutic services related; secretarial science.

Academic Programs *Special study options:* academic remediation for entering students, accelerated degree program, cooperative education, English as a second language, internships, part-time degree program, services for LD students.

Clover Park Technical College (continued)

Library CPTC Library with 16,150 titles, 32 serial subscriptions, 2,556 audiovisual materials, an OPAC.

Computers on Campus 1063 computers available on campus for general student use. A campuswide network can be accessed from off campus. Internet access, at least one staffed computer lab available.

Student Life *Housing:* college housing not available. *Activities and Organizations:* student-run newspaper, Accounting Numbers Club, Auto Tech Club, computer users club, Social Services Club. *Campus security:* 24-hour patrols, late-night transport/escort service. *Student Services:* personal/psychological counseling.

Standardized Tests *Required:* ACT ASSET.

Costs (2001–02) *Tuition:* state resident $1871 full-time, $3 per contact hour part-time; nonresident $1871 full-time, $3 per contact hour part-time. Full-time tuition and fees vary according to course load and program. Part-time tuition and fees vary according to course load and program. *Required fees:* $475 full-time.

Applying *Options:* common application, electronic application. *Application fee:* $33. *Required for some:* high school transcript, interview. *Application deadline:* 9/23 (freshmen). *Notification:* continuous until 9/23 (freshmen).

Admissions Contact Ms. Judy Richardson, Registrar, Clover Park Technical College, 4500 Steilacoom Boulevard Southwest, Lakewood, WA 98499. *Phone:* 253-589-5570. *Fax:* 253-589-5852. *E-mail:* admissions@cptc.ctc.edu.

COLUMBIA BASIN COLLEGE
Pasco, Washington

- **State-supported** 2-year, founded 1955, part of Washington State Board for Community and Technical Colleges
- **Calendar** quarters
- **Degree** associate
- **Small-town** 156-acre campus
- **Coed**

Faculty *Student/faculty ratio:* 10:1.

Student Life *Campus security:* 24-hour patrols.

Standardized Tests *Required:* ACT ASSET.

Financial Aid In 2001, 99 Federal Work-Study jobs (averaging $1686). 183 State and other part-time jobs (averaging $2148).

Applying *Options:* common application, electronic application. *Required:* high school transcript. *Recommended:* high school transcript.

Admissions Contact Ms. Donna Korstad, Program Support Supervisor, Enrollment Management, Columbia Basin College, 2600 North 20th Avenue, Pasco, WA 99301. *Phone:* 509-547-0511 Ext. 2250. *Toll-free phone:* 509-547-0511 Ext. 2250. *Fax:* 509-546-0401.

COURT REPORTING INSTITUTE
Seattle, Washington

Admissions Contact 929 North 130th Street, Suite 2, Seattle, WA 98133.

CROWN COLLEGE
Tacoma, Washington

- **Proprietary** primarily 2-year, founded 1969
- **Calendar** continuous
- **Degrees** associate and bachelor's (bachelor's degree in public administration only)
- **Urban** campus with easy access to Seattle
- **Coed,** 199 undergraduate students
- 95% of applicants were admitted

Undergraduates Students come from 1 other country, 16% are from out of state.

Freshmen *Admission:* 21 applied, 20 admitted.

Faculty *Total:* 12, 67% full-time. *Student/faculty ratio:* 20:1.

Majors Criminal justice studies; legal administrative assistant; paralegal/legal assistant; public administration.

Academic Programs *Special study options:* academic remediation for entering students, cooperative education, distance learning, double majors, internships, off-campus study, study abroad.

Library Crown College Library plus 1 other with 9,500 titles, 37 serial subscriptions, 70 audiovisual materials, an OPAC, a Web page.

Computers on Campus 12 computers available on campus for general student use. A campuswide network can be accessed from student residence rooms and from off campus. Internet access, online (class) registration, at least one staffed computer lab available.

Student Life *Housing:* college housing not available. *Campus security:* 24-hour emergency response devices.

Standardized Tests *Required:* ABLE.

Costs (2001–02) *Tuition:* $7072 full-time. No tuition increase for student's term of enrollment. *Required fees:* $200 full-time. *Payment plan:* installment.

Applying *Options:* common application, electronic application. *Required:* essay or personal statement, high school transcript, interview. *Notification:* continuous (freshmen).

Admissions Contact Ms. Sheila Millineaux, Admissions Director, Crown College, 8739 South Hosmer, Tacoma, WA 98444. *Phone:* 253-531-3123. *Toll-free phone:* 800-755-9525. *Fax:* 253-531-3521. *E-mail:* admissions@crowncollege.edu.

EDMONDS COMMUNITY COLLEGE
Lynnwood, Washington

- **State and locally supported** 2-year, founded 1967, part of Washington State Board for Community and Technical Colleges
- **Calendar** quarters
- **Degree** certificates and associate
- **Suburban** 115-acre campus with easy access to Seattle
- **Coed,** 7,738 undergraduate students, 42% full-time, 57% women, 43% men

Undergraduates 3,280 full-time, 4,458 part-time. Students come from 52 other countries, 4% African American, 11% Asian American or Pacific Islander, 4% Hispanic American, 1% Native American, 10% international.

Freshmen *Admission:* 798 enrolled.

Faculty *Total:* 424, 34% full-time. *Student/faculty ratio:* 25:1.

Majors Accounting technician; alcohol/drug abuse counseling; business administration; business marketing and marketing management; chemical technology; child care/guidance; community health liaison; computer/information sciences related; computer maintenance technology; construction technology; culinary arts; data processing technology; electrical/electronic engineering technology; enterprise management; fire services administration; gerontology; health aide; hotel/motel services marketing operations; human resources management; international business; landscaping management; legal administrative assistant; liberal arts and sciences/liberal studies; nursery management; office management; paralegal/legal assistant; recreational therapy; retailing operations; social work; tourism/travel marketing; travel services marketing operations; vocational rehabilitation counseling.

Academic Programs *Special study options:* academic remediation for entering students, adult/continuing education programs, advanced placement credit, cooperative education, English as a second language, honors programs, off-campus study, part-time degree program, services for LD students, student-designed majors, study abroad, summer session for credit.

Library Edmonds Community College Library with 42,679 titles, 304 serial subscriptions, 6,092 audiovisual materials.

Computers on Campus 1000 computers available on campus for general student use. A campuswide network can be accessed from off campus. Internet access, online (class) registration, at least one staffed computer lab available.

Student Life *Housing:* college housing not available. *Activities and Organizations:* student-run newspaper, choral group, Phi Theta Kappa, AITP, AAWCC, International Club, Pottery/Art Club. *Campus security:* 24-hour emergency response devices and patrols, student patrols, late-night transport/escort service. *Student Services:* personal/psychological counseling, women's center.

Athletics *Intercollegiate sports:* baseball M(s), basketball M(s)/W(s), golf M(s)/W(s), soccer M(s)/W(s), softball W(s), volleyball W(s). *Intramural sports:* badminton M/W, baseball M, basketball M/W, bowling M/W, football M/W, golf M/W, soccer M, softball W, table tennis M/W, volleyball M/W.

Costs (2001–02) *Tuition:* state resident $1743 full-time, $58 per credit part-time; nonresident $6861 full-time, $229 per credit part-time. Full-time tuition and fees vary according to course load. Part-time tuition and fees vary according to course load. *Required fees:* $122 full-time, $4 per credit. *Waivers:* employees or children of employees.

Applying *Options:* common application, electronic application, early admission, deferred entrance. *Application fee:* $15. *Application deadline:* rolling (freshmen), rolling (transfers).

Admissions Contact Ms. Sharon Bench, Admissions Director, Edmonds Community College, 20000 68th Avenue West, Lynnwood, WA 98036-5999. *Phone:* 425-640-1416. *Fax:* 425-640-1159. *E-mail:* info@edcc.edu.

EVERETT COMMUNITY COLLEGE
Everett, Washington

- **State-supported** 2-year, founded 1941, part of Washington State Board for Community and Technical Colleges
- **Calendar** quarters
- **Degree** certificates, diplomas, and associate
- **Urban** 25-acre campus with easy access to Seattle
- **Endowment** $1.9 million
- **Coed,** 7,227 undergraduate students, 44% full-time, 61% women, 39% men

Undergraduates 3,152 full-time, 4,075 part-time. Students come from 11 states and territories, 17 other countries, 2% are from out of state, 2% African American, 4% Asian American or Pacific Islander, 4% Hispanic American, 2% Native American, 0.6% international, 3% transferred in. *Retention:* 52% of 2001 full-time freshmen returned.

Freshmen *Admission:* 780 admitted, 691 enrolled.

Faculty *Total:* 352, 34% full-time. *Student/faculty ratio:* 21:1.

Majors Accounting; animal sciences; anthropology; art; atmospheric sciences; aviation technology; biology; botany; business administration; business marketing and marketing management; chemistry; civil engineering technology; computer science; cosmetology; criminal justice/law enforcement administration; data processing technology; dental hygiene; drafting; drawing; early childhood education; earth sciences; ecology; economics; education; elementary education; engineering; engineering science; engineering technology; English; environmental science; film/video production; fire science; geology; German; graphic design/commercial art/illustration; history; human services; industrial arts; industrial technology; Japanese; journalism; law enforcement/police science; liberal arts and sciences/liberal studies; mathematics; medical administrative assistant; medical assistant; modern languages; mortuary science; music; nursing; occupational therapy; oceanography; optometric/ophthalmic laboratory technician; pharmacy technician/assistant; philosophy; photography; physical education; physical therapy assistant; physics; political science; practical nurse; pre-engineering; psychology; retail management; Russian; sociology; Spanish; speech/rhetorical studies; theater arts/drama; veterinarian assistant; welding technology; wildlife biology; zoology.

Academic Programs *Special study options:* academic remediation for entering students, adult/continuing education programs, advanced placement credit, cooperative education, distance learning, double majors, English as a second language, external degree program, independent study, internships, part-time degree program, services for LD students, study abroad, summer session for credit.

Library John Terrey Library/Media Center with 43,588 titles, 322 serial subscriptions, 6,775 audiovisual materials, an OPAC, a Web page.

Computers on Campus 350 computers available on campus for general student use. A campuswide network can be accessed from off campus. Internet access, online (class) registration, at least one staffed computer lab available.

Student Life *Housing:* college housing not available. *Activities and Organizations:* drama/theater group, student-run newspaper, choral group, Phi Theta Kappa, Asian Pacific Islander Student Union, Student Nurses Association, Environment Watch, Nippon Friendship Club. *Campus security:* 24-hour emergency response devices and patrols, late-night transport/escort service. *Student Services:* personal/psychological counseling, women's center.

Athletics Member NJCAA. *Intercollegiate sports:* baseball M(s), basketball M(s)/W(s), cross-country running M(s)/W(s), soccer M(s)/W(s), softball W(s), volleyball W(s). *Intramural sports:* basketball M/W, bowling M/W, crew M(c)/W(c), football M/W, golf M/W, soccer M/W, softball M/W, swimming M/W, tennis M/W, volleyball M/W, weight lifting M/W.

Standardized Tests *Recommended:* ACT ASSET, ACT COMPASS.

Costs (2001–02) *Tuition:* state resident $1738 full-time, $58 per credit part-time; nonresident $6856 full-time, $229 per credit part-time. Full-time tuition and fees vary according to course load and program. Part-time tuition and fees vary according to course load and program. *Payment plan:* deferred payment. *Waivers:* senior citizens and employees or children of employees.

Financial Aid In 2001, 152 Federal Work-Study jobs (averaging $3000). 48 State and other part-time jobs (averaging $3000).

Applying *Options:* common application, early admission, deferred entrance. *Application fee:* $20. *Recommended:* high school transcript. *Application deadline:* rolling (freshmen), rolling (transfers). *Notification:* continuous (freshmen).

Admissions Contact Ms. Linda Baca, Admissions Manager, Everett Community College, 2000 Tower Street, Everett, WA 98201-1352. *Phone:* 425-388-9219. *Fax:* 425-388-9173. *E-mail:* admissions@evcc.ctc.edu.

GRAYS HARBOR COLLEGE
Aberdeen, Washington

- **State-supported** 2-year, founded 1930, part of Washington State Board for Community and Technical Colleges
- **Calendar** quarters
- **Degree** certificates, diplomas, and associate
- **Small-town** 125-acre campus
- **Endowment** $927,238
- **Coed,** 565 undergraduate students

Undergraduates Students come from 5 other countries.

Faculty *Total:* 184, 26% full-time. *Student/faculty ratio:* 19:1.

Majors Accounting technician; agricultural business; auto mechanic/technician; business administration; carpentry; child care/guidance; corrections; diesel engine mechanic; general studies; human services; industrial technology; information sciences/systems; law enforcement/police science; liberal arts and sciences/liberal studies; machine technology; natural resources conservation; nursing; office management; welding technology.

Academic Programs *Special study options:* academic remediation for entering students, accelerated degree program, adult/continuing education programs, advanced placement credit, cooperative education, distance learning, double majors, English as a second language, external degree program, honors programs, independent study, internships, part-time degree program, services for LD students, summer session for credit.

Library Spellman Library with 39,220 titles, 2,309 audiovisual materials, an OPAC, a Web page.

Computers on Campus 145 computers available on campus for general student use. Internet access, at least one staffed computer lab available.

Student Life *Housing:* college housing not available. *Activities and Organizations:* drama/theater group, student-run newspaper, choral group, PTK, TYEE, Student Nurses Association, Human Services Student Association, student council. *Campus security:* 24-hour emergency response devices, late-night transport/escort service. *Student Services:* personal/psychological counseling, women's center.

Athletics *Intercollegiate sports:* baseball M(s), basketball M(s)/W(s), golf M(s)/W(s), soccer M(s), softball W(s), track and field M(s)/W(s), volleyball W(s).

Standardized Tests *Required:* ACT ASSET, CPT.

Costs (2001–02) *Tuition:* state resident $1743 full-time, $58 per credit part-time; nonresident $6861 full-time, $229 per credit part-time. *Required fees:* $105 full-time, $4 per credit.

Financial Aid In 2001, 97 Federal Work-Study jobs (averaging $834). 94 State and other part-time jobs (averaging $1536).

Applying *Options:* common application, electronic application, early admission. *Recommended:* high school transcript. *Application deadlines:* rolling (freshmen), 9/1 (transfers). *Notification:* continuous (freshmen).

Admissions Contact Ms. Brenda Dell, Admissions Officer, Grays Harbor College, 1620 Edward P. Smith Drive, Aberdeen, WA 98520-7599. *Phone:* 360-532-9020 Ext. 4026. *Toll-free phone:* 800-562-4830. *Fax:* 360-538-4293. *E-mail:* bdell@ghc.ctc.edu.

GREEN RIVER COMMUNITY COLLEGE
Auburn, Washington

- **State-supported** 2-year, founded 1965, part of Washington State Board for Community and Technical Colleges
- **Calendar** quarters
- **Degree** certificates, diplomas, and associate
- **Rural** 168-acre campus with easy access to Seattle
- **Coed,** 6,566 undergraduate students

Undergraduates Students come from 45 other countries, 2% are from out of state, 2% African American, 5% Asian American or Pacific Islander, 5% Hispanic American, 2% Native American, 4% international.

Faculty *Total:* 484, 25% full-time. *Student/faculty ratio:* 21:1.

Majors Accounting technician; aircraft pilot (professional); air traffic control; auto body repair; auto mechanic/technician; business marketing and marketing management; carpentry; child care/guidance; court reporting; drafting; forest harvesting production technology; information sciences/systems; law enforcement/police science; legal administrative assistant; liberal arts and sciences/liberal studies; machine technology; mechanical engineering technology; medical admin-

Green River Community College (continued)
istrative assistant; occupational therapy assistant; office management; physical therapy assistant; practical nurse; water treatment technology; welding technology.

Academic Programs *Special study options:* academic remediation for entering students, adult/continuing education programs, advanced placement credit, cooperative education, distance learning, English as a second language, internships, off-campus study, part-time degree program, services for LD students, summer session for credit.

Library Holman Library with 32,500 titles, 2,100 serial subscriptions, 4,471 audiovisual materials, an OPAC, a Web page.

Computers on Campus 104 computers available on campus for general student use. Internet access, at least one staffed computer lab available.

Student Life *Housing:* college housing not available. *Activities and Organizations:* drama/theater group, student-run newspaper, radio station, choral group, Phi Theta Kappa, Green River Christian Encounter. *Campus security:* 24-hour emergency response devices and patrols, student patrols, late-night transport/escort service. *Student Services:* health clinic, personal/psychological counseling, women's center.

Athletics Member NJCAA. *Intercollegiate sports:* baseball M(s), basketball M(s)/W(s), golf M(s)/W(s), soccer M(s)/W(s), softball W(s), tennis M(s)/W(s), volleyball W(s). *Intramural sports:* badminton M/W, basketball M/W, football M/W, tennis M/W, volleyball M/W, weight lifting M/W.

Standardized Tests *Required:* ACT ASSET or ACT COMPASS.

Costs (2001–02) *Tuition:* state resident $1743 full-time, $58 per credit part-time; nonresident $2139 full-time, $71 per credit part-time. Part-time tuition and fees vary according to course load. *Required fees:* $177 full-time. *Payment plan:* installment. *Waivers:* senior citizens.

Financial Aid In 2001, 113 Federal Work-Study jobs (averaging $2356). 174 State and other part-time jobs.

Applying *Options:* electronic application, early admission, deferred entrance. *Required for some:* high school transcript. *Application deadline:* rolling (freshmen), rolling (transfers). *Notification:* continuous (freshmen).

Admissions Contact Ms. Peggy Morgan, Program Support Supervisor, Green River Community College, 12401 Southeast 320th Street, Auburn, WA 98092-3699. *Phone:* 253-833-9111 Ext. 2513. *Fax:* 253-288-3454.

HIGHLINE COMMUNITY COLLEGE
Des Moines, Washington

- **State-supported** 2-year, founded 1961, part of Washington State Board for Community and Technical Colleges
- **Calendar** quarters
- **Degree** certificates, diplomas, and associate
- **Suburban** 81-acre campus with easy access to Seattle
- **Coed,** 6,372 undergraduate students, 51% full-time, 64% women, 36% men

Highline Community College is one of the premier community colleges in Washington State, with a safe 80-acre campus overlooking the waters of the Puget Sound. High-quality educational programs and facilities, an exceptional faculty, excellent student services, affordable cost, and convenient location combine to make Highline a great choice for a better future.

Undergraduates 3,229 full-time, 3,143 part-time. 11% African American, 17% Asian American or Pacific Islander, 5% Hispanic American, 1% Native American, 0.2% international. *Retention:* 60% of 2001 full-time freshmen returned.

Freshmen *Admission:* 3,933 applied, 3,933 admitted, 667 enrolled.

Faculty *Total:* 356, 39% full-time.

Majors Accounting; art; behavioral sciences; biological/physical sciences; business administration; computer engineering technology; computer programming; computer systems networking/telecommunications; computer typography/composition; criminal justice/law enforcement administration; cultural studies; data entry/microcomputer applications related; dental hygiene; drafting; early childhood education; education; engineering; engineering technology; English; graphic/printing equipment; health/medical laboratory technologies related; hotel and restaurant management; humanities; human services; industrial technology; interior design; international business; Internet; journalism; law enforcement/police science; legal administrative assistant; library science; marine technology; mathematics; medical assistant; music; natural sciences; nursing; paralegal/legal assistant; plastics technology; pre-engineering; psychology; respiratory therapy; romance languages; secretarial science; social sciences; transportation technology; travel/tourism management.

Academic Programs *Special study options:* academic remediation for entering students, advanced placement credit, cooperative education, English as a second language, freshman honors college, honors programs, internships, part-time degree program, services for LD students, student-designed majors, study abroad, summer session for credit. *ROTC:* Army (c), Air Force (c).

Library Highline Community College Library with 57,678 titles, 585 serial subscriptions, an OPAC.

Computers on Campus 300 computers available on campus for general student use. At least one staffed computer lab available.

Student Life *Housing:* college housing not available. *Activities and Organizations:* drama/theater group, student-run newspaper, choral group, Campus Crusade for Christ, Nursing 2002, Phi Theta Kappa, International Club, Respiratory Care. *Campus security:* 24-hour patrols. *Student Services:* health clinic, personal/psychological counseling, women's center.

Athletics Member NJCAA. *Intercollegiate sports:* basketball M(s)/W(s), cross-country running M(s)/W(s), soccer M(s)/W(s), softball W(s), track and field M(s)/W(s), volleyball W(s), wrestling M(s).

Standardized Tests *Recommended:* ACT COMPASS.

Costs (2001–02) *Tuition:* state resident $1743 full-time, $58 per quarter hour part-time; nonresident $6861 full-time, $229 per quarter hour part-time. Part-time tuition and fees vary according to course load. *Waivers:* senior citizens and employees or children of employees.

Applying *Application deadline:* rolling (freshmen), rolling (transfers).

Admissions Contact Highline Community College, PO Box 98000, 2400 South 240th Street, Des Moines, WA 98198-9800. *Phone:* 206-878-3710 Ext. 3363. *Fax:* 206-870-4855. *E-mail:* dfaison@hcc.ctc.edu.

ITT TECHNICAL INSTITUTE
Seattle, Washington

- **Proprietary** primarily 2-year, founded 1932, part of ITT Educational Services, Inc
- **Calendar** quarters
- **Degrees** associate and bachelor's
- **Urban** campus
- **Coed,** 436 undergraduate students

Majors Computer/information sciences related; computer programming; computer systems analysis; electrical/electronic engineering technologies related; information technology.

Student Life *Housing:* college housing not available.

Costs (2001–02) *Tuition:* Full-time tuition and fees vary according to program. Part-time tuition and fees vary according to program. $260—$330 per credit hour.

Applying *Options:* deferred entrance. *Application fee:* $100. *Required:* high school transcript, interview. *Recommended:* letters of recommendation. *Application deadline:* rolling (freshmen), rolling (transfers). *Notification:* continuous (freshmen).

Admissions Contact Mr. Gary Rentel, Director of Recruitment, ITT Technical Institute, 12720 Gateway Drive, Seattle, WA 98168. *Phone:* 206-244-3300. *Toll-free phone:* 800-422-2029.

ITT TECHNICAL INSTITUTE
Spokane, Washington

- **Proprietary** 2-year, founded 1985, part of ITT Educational Services, Inc
- **Calendar** quarters
- **Degree** associate
- **Suburban** 3-acre campus
- **Coed,** 422 undergraduate students

Faculty *Total:* 19, 79% full-time.

Majors Administrative/secretarial services; computer/information sciences related; computer programming; drafting; electrical/electronic engineering technologies related; information technology.

Student Life *Housing:* college housing not available.

Financial Aid In 2001, 9 Federal Work-Study jobs (averaging $4000).

Applying *Options:* deferred entrance. *Application fee:* $100. *Required:* high school transcript, interview. *Recommended:* letters of recommendation. *Application deadline:* rolling (freshmen), rolling (transfers). *Notification:* continuous (freshmen).

Admissions Contact Mr. Byron Farrelly, Assistant Director, ITT Technical Institute, North 1050 Argonne Road, Spokane, WA 99212-2682. *Phone:* 509-926-2900. *Toll-free phone:* 800-777-8324.

ITT Technical Institute
Bothell, Washington

- **Proprietary** 2-year, founded 1993, part of ITT Educational Services, Inc
- **Calendar** quarters
- **Degree** associate
- 242 undergraduate students

Majors Computer/information sciences related; computer programming; drafting; electrical/electronic engineering technologies related; information technology.

Student Life *Housing:* college housing not available.

Costs (2001–02) *Tuition:* Full-time tuition and fees vary according to program. Part-time tuition and fees vary according to program. $260—$330 per credit hour.

Applying *Options:* deferred entrance. *Application fee:* $100. *Required:* high school transcript, interview. *Recommended:* letters of recommendation. *Application deadline:* rolling (freshmen), rolling (transfers).

Admissions Contact Mr. Mike Milford, Director of Recruitment, ITT Technical Institute, 2525 223rd Street SE, Bothell, WA 98021. *Phone:* 425-485-0303. *Toll-free phone:* 800-272-3791.

Lake Washington Technical College
Kirkland, Washington

- **District-supported** 2-year, founded 1949, part of Washington State Board for Community and Technical Colleges
- **Calendar** quarters
- **Degree** certificates and associate
- **Suburban** 57-acre campus with easy access to Seattle
- **Coed,** 4,934 undergraduate students

Freshmen *Admission:* 2,298 applied, 1,162 admitted.

Faculty *Total:* 209, 25% full-time. *Student/faculty ratio:* 8:1.

Majors Accounting; auto body repair; auto mechanic/technician; child care/development; computer engineering technology; computer science; culinary arts; dental assistant; dental hygiene; diesel engine mechanic; drafting; electrical/electronic engineering technology; environmental science; horticulture science; hotel and restaurant management; legal administrative assistant; machine technology; medical assistant; secretarial science.

Academic Programs *Special study options:* academic remediation for entering students, advanced placement credit, cooperative education, English as a second language, internships, services for LD students, summer session for credit.

Library Lake Washington Technical College Library/Media Center with 18,300 titles, 770 serial subscriptions, an OPAC, a Web page.

Computers on Campus 400 computers available on campus for general student use. A campuswide network can be accessed from off campus. Internet access, at least one staffed computer lab available.

Student Life *Housing:* college housing not available. *Campus security:* 24-hour emergency response devices, late-night transport/escort service, parking lot security, security cameras. *Student Services:* personal/psychological counseling, women's center.

Standardized Tests *Required:* ACT ASSET.

Costs (2001–02) *Tuition:* area resident $2915 full-time, $51 per quarter hour part-time. Full-time tuition and fees vary according to course load and program. Part-time tuition and fees vary according to course load and program. *Payment plan:* deferred payment.

Financial Aid In 2001, 33 Federal Work-Study jobs (averaging $1990). 61 State and other part-time jobs (averaging $2705).

Applying *Options:* common application, early admission. *Required for some:* high school transcript. *Application deadline:* rolling (freshmen), rolling (transfers). *Notification:* continuous (freshmen).

Admissions Contact Mr. David Minger, Director of Admissions and Registration, Lake Washington Technical College, 11605 132nd Avenue NE, Kirkland, WA 98034-8506. *Phone:* 425-739-8233.

Lower Columbia College
Longview, Washington

- **State-supported** 2-year, founded 1934, part of Washington State Board for Community and Technical Colleges
- **Calendar** quarters
- **Degree** certificates, diplomas, and associate
- **Small-town** 30-acre campus with easy access to Portland
- **Endowment** $1.8 million
- **Coed,** 3,651 undergraduate students, 52% full-time, 59% women, 41% men

Undergraduates 1,909 full-time, 1,742 part-time. Students come from 6 states and territories, 4 other countries, 1% are from out of state, 25% transferred in. *Retention:* 36% of 2001 full-time freshmen returned.

Freshmen *Admission:* 899 applied, 899 admitted, 899 enrolled. *Average high school GPA:* 3.06.

Faculty *Total:* 215, 38% full-time. *Student/faculty ratio:* 19:1.

Majors Accounting; accounting technician; alcohol/drug abuse counseling; anthropology; art; biology; business administration; computer engineering technology; computer programming; computer science; early childhood education; earth sciences; economics; electrical/electronic engineering technology; English; fire science; geography; geology; heavy equipment maintenance; history; industrial technology; information sciences/systems; instrumentation technology; law enforcement/police science; legal administrative assistant; liberal arts and sciences/liberal studies; machine technology; mathematics; mechanical engineering technology; medical administrative assistant; music; nursing; philosophy; physical education; physics; political science; pre-engineering; psychology; secretarial science; social sciences; sociology; speech/rhetorical studies; theater arts/drama; welding technology.

Academic Programs *Special study options:* academic remediation for entering students, adult/continuing education programs, cooperative education, English as a second language, honors programs, part-time degree program, services for LD students, study abroad, summer session for credit.

Library 26,345 titles, 287 serial subscriptions.

Computers on Campus 250 computers available on campus for general student use. At least one staffed computer lab available.

Student Life *Housing:* college housing not available. *Activities and Organizations:* drama/theater group, student-run newspaper, Campus Entertainment, Phi Theta Kappa, Services and Relations Club, Multicultural Students Club, Theater Club. *Campus security:* 24-hour emergency response devices and patrols. *Student Services:* health clinic, personal/psychological counseling.

Athletics *Intercollegiate sports:* basketball M(s)/W(s), soccer M, tennis W(s), volleyball W(s). *Intramural sports:* basketball M/W, soccer M.

Standardized Tests *Required:* ACT COMPASS.

Costs (2002–03) *One-time required fee:* $12. *Tuition:* state resident $2062 full-time, $68 per credit hour part-time; nonresident $2504 full-time, $83 per credit hour part-time. *Required fees:* $36 full-time.

Financial Aid In 2001, 252 Federal Work-Study jobs (averaging $454). 447 State and other part-time jobs (averaging $2011).

Applying *Options:* early admission, deferred entrance. *Recommended:* high school transcript. *Application deadline:* rolling (freshmen), rolling (transfers). *Notification:* continuous (freshmen).

Admissions Contact Ms. Mary Harding, Vice President for Student Success, Lower Columbia College, 1600 Maple, Longview, WA 98632. *Phone:* 360-442-2301. *Toll-free phone:* 360-442-2370. *Fax:* 360-442-2379. *E-mail:* tmontoya@lcc.ctc.vdu.

North Seattle Community College
Seattle, Washington

- **State-supported** 2-year, founded 1970, part of Seattle Community College District System
- **Calendar** quarters
- **Degree** certificates, diplomas, and associate
- **Urban** 65-acre campus
- **Coed,** 6,340 undergraduate students, 39% full-time, 56% women, 44% men

Undergraduates 2,445 full-time, 3,895 part-time. Students come from 50 states and territories, 41 other countries, 1% are from out of state, 61% transferred in.

Freshmen *Admission:* 4,526 applied, 4,526 admitted, 1,796 enrolled.

Faculty *Total:* 412, 26% full-time, 10% with terminal degrees. *Student/faculty ratio:* 20:1.

Majors Accounting; applied art; art; biological/physical sciences; biomedical technology; business administration; child care/development; communication equipment technology; computer engineering technology; computer programming; computer science; construction technology; culinary arts; data processing technology; drafting; drawing; early childhood education; electrical/electronic engineering technology; electromechanical technology; emergency medical technology; food services technology; health services administration; heating/air conditioning/refrigeration; humanities; industrial arts; information sciences/systems; international business; liberal arts and sciences/liberal studies; math-

North Seattle Community College (continued)
ematics; medical administrative assistant; medical assistant; music; natural sciences; nursing; pharmacy; practical nurse; real estate; secretarial science; social sciences.

Academic Programs *Special study options:* academic remediation for entering students, accelerated degree program, adult/continuing education programs, advanced placement credit, cooperative education, distance learning, English as a second language, external degree program, honors programs, independent study, internships, off-campus study, part-time degree program, services for LD students, summer session for credit. *ROTC:* Army (c).

Library North Seattle Community College Library with 48,094 titles, 498 serial subscriptions, 2,000 audiovisual materials, an OPAC, a Web page.

Computers on Campus 200 computers available on campus for general student use. A campuswide network can be accessed from off campus. Internet access, online (class) registration, at least one staffed computer lab available.

Student Life *Housing:* college housing not available. *Activities and Organizations:* drama/theater group, student-run newspaper, television station, choral group, Black Student Union, Diversity Club, Literary Guild, Phi Theta Kappa, Vietnamese Student Association, national sororities. *Campus security:* 24-hour emergency response devices and patrols, student patrols, late-night transport/escort service, patrols by security. *Student Services:* personal/psychological counseling, women's center, legal services.

Athletics *Intercollegiate sports:* basketball M/W. *Intramural sports:* badminton M/W, basketball M/W, skiing (downhill) M/W, soccer M, tennis M/W, volleyball M/W, weight lifting M/W.

Costs (2001–02) *Tuition:* state resident $1736 full-time, $58 per credit part-time; nonresident $6854 full-time, $228 per credit part-time. Part-time tuition and fees vary according to course load. *Required fees:* $165 full-time. *Waivers:* senior citizens and employees or children of employees.

Applying *Options:* common application, electronic application, early admission, deferred entrance. *Required:* high school transcript. *Required for some:* essay or personal statement. *Application deadline:* rolling (freshmen), rolling (transfers). *Notification:* continuous until 9/24 (freshmen).

Admissions Contact Ms. Betsy Abts, Assistant Registrar, Admissions/Registration, North Seattle Community College, 9600 College Way North, Seattle, WA 98103-3599. *Phone:* 206-527-3796. *Fax:* 206-527-3671. *E-mail:* babts@sccd.ctc.edu.

NORTHWEST AVIATION COLLEGE
Auburn, Washington

Admissions Contact 506 23rd, NE, Auburn, WA 98002. *Fax:* 253-931-0768. *E-mail:* afsnac@nventure.com.

NORTHWEST INDIAN COLLEGE
Bellingham, Washington

Admissions Contact Ms. Lisa Santana, Director of Admissions, Northwest Indian College, 2522 Kwina Road, Bellingham, WA 98226. *Phone:* 360-676-2772 Ext. 271.

OLYMPIC COLLEGE
Bremerton, Washington

- **State-supported** 2-year, founded 1946, part of Washington State Board for Community and Technical Colleges
- **Calendar** quarters
- **Degree** certificates, diplomas, and associate
- **Suburban** 27-acre campus with easy access to Seattle
- **Coed,** 5,613 undergraduate students

Undergraduates Students come from 2 states and territories, 4% African American, 9% Asian American or Pacific Islander, 3% Hispanic American, 2% Native American.

Faculty *Total:* 533, 18% full-time. *Student/faculty ratio:* 25:1.

Majors Accounting; auto body repair; auto mechanic/technician; business administration; carpentry; child care/guidance; computer graphics; computer programming related; computer science related; computer software and media applications related; computer systems networking/telecommunications; corrections; cosmetology; culinary arts; drafting; electrical/electronic engineering technology; fire science; fire services administration; industrial technology; information sciences/systems; information technology; legal administrative assistant; medical assistant; nursing; office management; system/networking/LAN/WAN management; welding technology; word processing.

Academic Programs *Special study options:* academic remediation for entering students, adult/continuing education programs, advanced placement credit, cooperative education, distance learning, English as a second language, honors programs, independent study, off-campus study, part-time degree program, services for LD students, summer session for credit.

Library Haselwood Library with 51,443 titles, 541 serial subscriptions, 3,007 audiovisual materials, an OPAC, a Web page.

Computers on Campus 634 computers available on campus for general student use. A campuswide network can be accessed from off campus. Internet access, online (class) registration, at least one staffed computer lab available.

Student Life *Housing:* college housing not available. *Activities and Organizations:* drama/theater group, student-run newspaper, choral group. *Campus security:* 24-hour emergency response devices and patrols, student patrols, late-night transport/escort service. *Student Services:* personal/psychological counseling, women's center.

Athletics Member NJCAA. *Intercollegiate sports:* baseball M(s), basketball M(s)/W(s), softball W(s), volleyball W(s). *Intramural sports:* basketball M/W, volleyball M/W.

Standardized Tests *Required for some:* ACT ASSET.

Costs (2001–02) *Tuition:* state resident $1743 full-time, $58 per credit part-time; nonresident $6861 full-time, $229 per credit part-time. Full-time tuition and fees vary according to course load. Part-time tuition and fees vary according to course load. *Required fees:* $180 full-time, $5 per credit, $15 per term part-time. *Payment plan:* installment. *Waivers:* senior citizens and employees or children of employees.

Financial Aid In 2001, 110 Federal Work-Study jobs (averaging $2780). 25 State and other part-time jobs (averaging $3200).

Applying *Options:* early admission. *Required for some:* high school transcript. *Application deadline:* rolling (freshmen), rolling (transfers). *Notification:* continuous (freshmen).

Admissions Contact Mr. Nick Rengler, Interim Dean for Enrollment Services, Olympic College, Bremerton, WA 98337-1699. *Phone:* 360-475-7208. *Toll-free phone:* 800-259-6718. *Fax:* 360-475-7020. *E-mail:* gstamm@oc.ctc.edu.

PENINSULA COLLEGE
Port Angeles, Washington

- **State-supported** 2-year, founded 1961
- **Calendar** quarters
- **Degree** certificates and associate
- **Small-town** 75-acre campus
- **Coed,** 4,355 undergraduate students, 33% full-time, 55% women, 45% men

Undergraduates 1,456 full-time, 2,899 part-time. Students come from 5 other countries, 4% African American, 2% Asian American or Pacific Islander, 3% Hispanic American, 4% Native American, 2% international.

Freshmen *Admission:* 1,012 applied, 1,012 admitted, 1,024 enrolled.

Faculty *Total:* 296, 23% full-time, 3% with terminal degrees. *Student/faculty ratio:* 13:1.

Majors Accounting; alcohol/drug abuse counseling; auto mechanic/technician; biological/physical sciences; business administration; child care/development; child care services management; civil engineering technology; computer programming, vendor/product certification; criminal justice/law enforcement administration; data entry/microcomputer applications related; diesel engine mechanic; electrical/electronic engineering technology; engineering-related technology; fishing sciences; fishing technology; nursing; office management; Web page, digital/multimedia and information resources design.

Academic Programs *Special study options:* academic remediation for entering students, adult/continuing education programs, advanced placement credit, distance learning, English as a second language, honors programs, internships, part-time degree program, services for LD students, summer session for credit.

Library 33,736 titles, 383 serial subscriptions.

Computers on Campus 38 computers available on campus for general student use. A campuswide network can be accessed from student residence rooms and from off campus. At least one staffed computer lab available.

Student Life *Housing Options:* coed. *Activities and Organizations:* drama/theater group, student-run newspaper, choral group, Phi Theta Kappa, SAGE (Students Advocating Global Environmentalism). *Campus security:* 8-hour patrols by trained security personnel. *Student Services:* women's center.

Athletics *Intercollegiate sports:* baseball W, basketball M/W. *Intramural sports:* badminton M/W, basketball M/W, bowling M/W, football M, golf M, skiing (cross-country) M/W, soccer M/W, softball M/W, table tennis M/W, tennis M/W, volleyball M/W.

Standardized Tests *Required:* ACT ASSET or ACT COMPASS. *Recommended:* SAT I (for placement).
Costs (2001–02) *Tuition:* state resident $1830 full-time, $61 per credit part-time; nonresident $2225 full-time, $74 per credit part-time. *Required fees:* $127 full-time, $3 per credit, $13 per credit part-time. *Room and board:* $5403. *Payment plan:* deferred payment. *Waivers:* employees or children of employees.
Financial Aid In 2001, 25 State and other part-time jobs (averaging $2500).
Applying *Options:* common application, deferred entrance. *Required for some:* high school transcript. *Application deadline:* rolling (freshmen), rolling (transfers). *Notification:* continuous (freshmen).
Admissions Contact Mr. Thomas Woodnutt, Dean of Enrollment and Student Services, Peninsula College, 1502 East Lauridsen Boulevard, Port Angeles, WA 98362-2779. *Phone:* 360-417-6246. *Fax:* 360-457-8100. *E-mail:* admissions@pcadmin.ctc.edu.

PIERCE COLLEGE
Lakewood, Washington

- **State-supported** 2-year, founded 1967, part of Washington State Board for Community and Technical Colleges
- **Calendar** quarters
- **Degree** certificates, diplomas, and associate
- **Suburban** 140-acre campus with easy access to Seattle
- **Endowment** $4540
- **Coed,** 13,294 undergraduate students

Undergraduates Students come from 12 other countries.
Faculty *Total:* 590, 41% full-time.
Majors Accounting; alcohol/drug abuse counseling; business administration; business marketing and marketing management; computer programming; computer typography/composition; criminal justice/law enforcement administration; dental hygiene; early childhood education; electrical/electronic engineering technology; fire science; industrial technology; information sciences/systems; legal administrative assistant; liberal arts and sciences/liberal studies; medical laboratory technician; mental health/rehabilitation; paralegal/legal assistant; secretarial science; veterinary technology.
Academic Programs *Special study options:* academic remediation for entering students, adult/continuing education programs, advanced placement credit, cooperative education, English as a second language, internships, off-campus study, part-time degree program, services for LD students, summer session for credit. *ROTC:* Army (c).
Library 55,000 titles, 425 serial subscriptions.
Computers on Campus 350 computers available on campus for general student use. At least one staffed computer lab available.
Student Life *Housing:* college housing not available. *Activities and Organizations:* drama/theater group, student-run newspaper, choral group, Black Student Union, Phi Theta Kappa, Dental Hygiene Association, Veterinary Technology Association, Latino Student Union. *Campus security:* 24-hour emergency response devices and patrols, late-night transport/escort service. *Student Services:* women's center.
Athletics *Intercollegiate sports:* baseball M(s), basketball M(s)/W(s), soccer M(s), softball W(s), volleyball W(s).
Standardized Tests *Required for some:* ACT ASSET. *Recommended:* ACT ASSET.
Costs (2001–02) *Tuition:* state resident $2324 full-time, $58 per quarter hour part-time; nonresident $2850 full-time, $71 per quarter hour part-time.
Financial Aid In 2001, 242 Federal Work-Study jobs (averaging $810). 48 State and other part-time jobs (averaging $3055).
Applying *Options:* early admission. *Application deadline:* rolling (freshmen), rolling (transfers).
Admissions Contact Ms. Cindy Burbank, Director of Admissions, Pierce College, 9401 Farwest Drive, SW, Lakewood, WA 98498-1999. *Phone:* 253-964-6686. *Fax:* 253-964-6427.

PIMA MEDICAL INSTITUTE
Seattle, Washington

Admissions Contact Admissions Office, Pima Medical Institute, 1627 Eastlake Avenue East, Seattle, WA 98102. *Phone:* 206-322-6100.

RENTON TECHNICAL COLLEGE
Renton, Washington

- **State-supported** 2-year, founded 1942, part of Washington State Board for Community and Technical Colleges
- **Calendar** quarters
- **Degree** certificates, diplomas, and associate
- **Suburban** 30-acre campus with easy access to Seattle
- **Coed**

Faculty *Student/faculty ratio:* 15:1.
Student Life *Campus security:* patrols by security, security system.
Standardized Tests *Required:* ACT ASSET, SLEP.
Financial Aid In 2001, 20 Federal Work-Study jobs (averaging $1800). 100 State and other part-time jobs (averaging $2000).
Applying *Options:* early admission. *Application fee:* $25. *Recommended:* interview.
Admissions Contact Mr. Jon Pozega, Vice President for Student Services, Renton Technical College, 3000 Fourth Street, NE, Renton, WA 98056. *Phone:* 425-235-5840. *Fax:* 425-235-7832. *E-mail:* cdaniels@rtc.ctc.edu.

SEATTLE CENTRAL COMMUNITY COLLEGE
Seattle, Washington

- **State-supported** 2-year, founded 1966, part of Seattle Community College District System
- **Calendar** quarters
- **Degree** certificates and associate
- **Urban** 15-acre campus
- **Coed,** 10,500 undergraduate students

Faculty *Total:* 388, 36% full-time.
Majors Accounting; alcohol/drug abuse counseling; biological/physical sciences; biological technology; carpentry; computer typography/composition; cosmetology; culinary arts; drafting; early childhood education; fashion design/illustration; film/video production; graphic design/commercial art/illustration; graphic/printing equipment; hospitality management; hotel and restaurant management; human services; liberal arts and sciences/liberal studies; marine technology; nursing; optometric/ophthalmic laboratory technician; photography; respiratory therapy; secretarial science; sign language interpretation.
Academic Programs *Special study options:* academic remediation for entering students, adult/continuing education programs, cooperative education, English as a second language, external degree program, internships, part-time degree program, services for LD students, summer session for credit. *ROTC:* Army (c), Navy (c), Air Force (c).
Library Main Library with 56,338 titles, 425 serial subscriptions.
Computers on Campus 366 computers available on campus for general student use. At least one staffed computer lab available.
Student Life *Housing:* college housing not available. *Activities and Organizations:* drama/theater group, student-run newspaper, choral group, Triangle Club, African Brothers of Unity, MECHA, Asian/Pacific Islander Student Union, Sea-King Club for the Deaf. *Campus security:* 24-hour emergency response devices. *Student Services:* personal/psychological counseling, women's center.
Athletics *Intramural sports:* basketball M/W, softball M/W, tennis M/W, volleyball M/W, weight lifting M/W, wrestling M/W.
Standardized Tests *Required:* ACT ASSET.
Costs (2001–02) *Tuition:* state resident $1736 full-time, $88 per quarter hour part-time; nonresident $6854 full-time, $228 per quarter hour part-time. *Required fees:* $300 full-time, $100 per term part-time.
Applying *Application deadline:* rolling (freshmen), rolling (transfers).
Admissions Contact Admissions Office, Seattle Central Community College, 1701 Broadway, Seattle, WA 98122-2400. *Phone:* 206-587-5450.

SHORELINE COMMUNITY COLLEGE
Seattle, Washington

- **State-supported** 2-year, founded 1964, part of Washington State Board for Community and Technical Colleges
- **Calendar** quarters
- **Degree** certificates, diplomas, and associate
- **Suburban** 80-acre campus
- **Coed,** 7,000 undergraduate students

Shoreline Community College (continued)

Freshmen *Admission:* 1,956 applied, 1,956 admitted.

Faculty *Total:* 415, 37% full-time. *Student/faculty ratio:* 21:1.

Majors Accounting; audio engineering; auto mechanic/technician; biological technology; business administration; business marketing and marketing management; chemical engineering technology; child care/development; civil engineering technology; computer graphics; computer/information sciences; cosmetology; dental hygiene; dietetics; drafting; early childhood education; education; engineering technology; environmental technology; film/video production; graphic design/commercial art/illustration; graphic/printing equipment; individual/family development; industrial technology; international business; liberal arts and sciences/liberal studies; machine technology; marine biology; marine technology; mechanical engineering technology; medical administrative assistant; medical laboratory technician; medical laboratory technology; medical records administration; music; nursing; oceanography; photography; pre-engineering; purchasing/contracts management; retail management; teacher assistant/aide.

Academic Programs *Special study options:* academic remediation for entering students, adult/continuing education programs, advanced placement credit, cooperative education, English as a second language, internships, part-time degree program, services for LD students, study abroad, summer session for credit.

Library Ray W. Howard Library/Media Center with 79,554 titles, 1,735 serial subscriptions, an OPAC, a Web page.

Computers on Campus 385 computers available on campus for general student use. Internet access, at least one staffed computer lab available.

Student Life *Housing:* college housing not available. *Activities and Organizations:* drama/theater group, student-run newspaper, choral group, Arts and Entertainment Board, International Club, music groups. *Campus security:* 24-hour emergency response devices and patrols. *Student Services:* personal/psychological counseling, women's center.

Athletics *Intercollegiate sports:* baseball M(s), basketball M(s)/W(s), soccer M(s), softball W(s), tennis W(s), volleyball W(s). *Intramural sports:* archery M/W, badminton M/W, basketball M/W, fencing M/W, gymnastics W, racquetball M/W, skiing (cross-country) M/W, skiing (downhill) M/W, softball M/W, swimming M/W, volleyball M/W.

Standardized Tests *Required for some:* SAT I or ACT (for placement), ACT ASSET.

Costs (2001–02) *Tuition:* state resident $1743 full-time, $58 per credit part-time; nonresident $6861 full-time, $229 per credit part-time. Full-time tuition and fees vary according to course load and program. *Required fees:* $165 full-time, $6 per credit hour. *Payment plans:* installment, deferred payment. *Waivers:* senior citizens and employees or children of employees.

Applying *Options:* early admission. *Application fee:* $10. *Required:* high school transcript. *Application deadline:* rolling (freshmen), rolling (transfers).

Admissions Contact Ms. Robin Thompson, Registrar, Shoreline Community College, 16101 Greenwood Avenue North, Seattle, WA 98133. *Phone:* 206-546-4581. *Fax:* 206-546-5835.

SKAGIT VALLEY COLLEGE
Mount Vernon, Washington

- **State-supported** 2-year, founded 1926, part of Washington State Board for Community and Technical Colleges
- **Calendar** quarters
- **Degree** certificates, diplomas, and associate
- **Small-town** 85-acre campus with easy access to Seattle
- **Endowment** $3.2 million
- **Coed,** 6,174 undergraduate students

Undergraduates Students come from 4 states and territories, 23 other countries, 3% are from out of state, 1% live on campus.

Freshmen *Admission:* 1,911 applied, 1,401 admitted.

Faculty *Total:* 301. *Student/faculty ratio:* 21:1.

Majors Accounting; agricultural sciences; anthropology; art; art history; auto mechanic/technician; biological/physical sciences; biology; business administration; chemistry; child care/development; computer engineering technology; computer/information sciences; computer maintenance technology; computer science; culinary arts; cultural studies; diesel engine mechanic; early childhood education; earth sciences; economics; electrical/electronic engineering technology; English; environmental technology; family/community studies; fire science; food services technology; foreign languages/literatures; geography; graphic design/commercial art/illustration; heavy equipment maintenance; history; horticulture services; hotel and restaurant management; humanities; human services; journalism; law enforcement/police science; liberal arts and sciences/liberal studies; literature; marine technology; mathematics; medical administrative assistant; medical assistant; music; natural sciences; nursing; office management; paralegal/legal assistant; philosophy; physical education; political science; practical nurse; pre-engineering; psychology; recreation/leisure facilities management; recreation/leisure studies; secretarial science; social sciences; sociology; Spanish; speech/rhetorical studies; telecommunications; vehicle/equipment operation; welding technology.

Academic Programs *Special study options:* academic remediation for entering students, accelerated degree program, adult/continuing education programs, advanced placement credit, cooperative education, distance learning, English as a second language, external degree program, independent study, internships, part-time degree program, services for LD students, student-designed majors, study abroad, summer session for credit.

Library Norwood Cole Library with 78,631 titles, 359 serial subscriptions, 2,599 audiovisual materials, an OPAC, a Web page.

Computers on Campus 200 computers available on campus for general student use. A campuswide network can be accessed from off campus. Internet access, at least one staffed computer lab available.

Student Life *Housing Options:* men-only, women-only, disabled students. *Activities and Organizations:* drama/theater group, student-run newspaper, radio station, choral group, Phi Theta Kappa, Calling All Colors, Business Management Training, Human Services, Paralegal Club. *Campus security:* 24-hour patrols, late-night transport/escort service, telephone/pager system. *Student Services:* personal/psychological counseling, women's center.

Athletics *Intercollegiate sports:* baseball M(s), basketball M(s)/W(s), cross-country running M(s)/W(s), golf M(s)/W(s), soccer M(s)/W(s), softball W(s), tennis M(s)/W(s), volleyball W(s). *Intramural sports:* badminton M/W, basketball M/W, sailing M/W, skiing (cross-country) M/W, skiing (downhill) M/W, softball M/W, tennis M/W, volleyball M/W.

Standardized Tests *Required:* ACT ASSET.

Costs (2001–02) *Tuition:* $65 per credit part-time; state resident $2100 full-time, $75 per credit part-time; nonresident $2400 full-time. *Room and board:* room only: $3400.

Financial Aid In 2001, 100 Federal Work-Study jobs (averaging $2800).

Applying *Options:* common application, electronic application, deferred entrance. *Required for some:* high school transcript, interview. *Application deadline:* rolling (freshmen), rolling (transfers).

Admissions Contact Ms. Karen Ackelson, Admissions and Recruitment Coordinator, Skagit Valley College, 2405 College Way, Mount Vernon, WA 98273-5899. *Phone:* 360-416-7620. *Fax:* 360-416-7890. *E-mail:* ackelson@skagit.ctc.edu.

SOUTH PUGET SOUND COMMUNITY COLLEGE
Olympia, Washington

- **State-supported** 2-year, founded 1970, part of Washington State Board for Community and Technical Colleges
- **Calendar** quarters
- **Degree** certificates, diplomas, and associate
- **Suburban** 86-acre campus with easy access to Seattle
- **Coed,** 5,678 undergraduate students, 56% full-time, 61% women, 39% men

Undergraduates Students come from 19 other countries.

Faculty *Total:* 250.

Majors Accounting; auto mechanic/technician; business administration; communication equipment technology; computer/information sciences; computer programming; culinary arts; data processing technology; dental hygiene; drafting; early childhood education; electrical/electronic engineering technology; fire science; food products retailing; food services technology; horticulture science; information sciences/systems; landscaping management; legal administrative assistant; liberal arts and sciences/liberal studies; medical administrative assistant; medical assistant; nursing; paralegal/legal assistant; practical nurse; purchasing/contracts management; secretarial science; sign language interpretation; telecommunications; welding technology.

Academic Programs *Special study options:* academic remediation for entering students, adult/continuing education programs, advanced placement credit, cooperative education, English as a second language, internships, part-time degree program, services for LD students, study abroad, summer session for credit. *ROTC:* Army (c).

Library Media Center plus 1 other with 30,000 titles, 340 serial subscriptions, an OPAC.

Computers on Campus 450 computers available on campus for general student use. A campuswide network can be accessed from off campus. Internet access, at least one staffed computer lab available.

Student Life *Housing:* college housing not available. *Activities and Organizations:* student-run newspaper. *Campus security:* 24-hour emergency response devices and patrols, late-night transport/escort service. *Student Services:* personal/psychological counseling.

Athletics *Intercollegiate sports:* basketball M(s)/W(s), soccer M(s), softball W(s). *Intramural sports:* basketball M/W, softball W.

Standardized Tests *Required:* CPT. *Recommended:* SAT I or ACT (for placement).

Costs (2001–02) *Tuition:* state resident $2324 full-time, $58 per credit part-time; nonresident $2850 full-time, $71 per credit part-time.

Financial Aid In 2001, 42 Federal Work-Study jobs (averaging $3150). 14 State and other part-time jobs (averaging $4400). *Financial aid deadline:* 6/29.

Applying *Options:* early admission, deferred entrance. *Application deadline:* rolling (freshmen), rolling (transfers). *Notification:* continuous (freshmen).

Admissions Contact Mr. Jerry Haynes, Dean of Enrollment Services, South Puget Sound Community College, 2011 Mottman Road, SW, Olympia, WA 98512-6292. *Phone:* 360-754-7711 Ext. 5240. *Fax:* 360-664-4336. *E-mail:* lsmith@spscc.ctc.edu.

SOUTH SEATTLE COMMUNITY COLLEGE
Seattle, Washington

- **State-supported** 2-year, founded 1970, part of Seattle Community College District System
- **Calendar** quarters
- **Degree** certificates, diplomas, and associate
- **Urban** 65-acre campus
- **Coed**

Student Life *Campus security:* 24-hour emergency response devices and patrols.

Standardized Tests *Required for some:* ACT ASSET.

Financial Aid In 2001, 700 Federal Work-Study jobs (averaging $3000). 300 State and other part-time jobs (averaging $3500).

Applying *Options:* early admission.

Admissions Contact Ms. Kim Manderbach, Associate Dean of Enrollment Services, South Seattle Community College, 6000 16th Avenue, SW, Seattle, WA 98106-1499. *Phone:* 206-764-5378.

SPOKANE COMMUNITY COLLEGE
Spokane, Washington

- **State-supported** 2-year, founded 1963, part of Washington State Board for Community and Technical Colleges
- **Calendar** quarters
- **Degree** certificates and associate
- **Urban** 108-acre campus
- **Endowment** $33,508
- **Coed,** 7,468 undergraduate students

Undergraduates Students come from 5 states and territories, 16 other countries, 4% are from out of state.

Faculty *Total:* 456, 42% full-time.

Majors Accounting technician; agricultural business; agronomy/crop science; architectural engineering technology; auto mechanic/technician; aviation technology; biomedical technology; business administration; business marketing and marketing management; carpentry; civil engineering technology; computer programming; computer typography/composition; construction technology; corrections; cosmetology; culinary arts; data processing technology; dental hygiene; dietetics; drafting; electrical/electronic engineering technology; fire science; food services technology; forestry; heating/air conditioning/refrigeration; heavy equipment maintenance; horticulture services; hotel and restaurant management; industrial technology; landscaping management; law enforcement/police science; legal administrative assistant; liberal arts and sciences/liberal studies; machine technology; mechanical design technology; mechanical engineering technology; medical administrative assistant; medical records administration; natural resources management; nursing; operating room technician; optometric/ophthalmic laboratory technician; ornamental horticulture; paralegal/legal assistant; practical nurse; recreation/leisure facilities management; respiratory therapy; robotics; secretarial science; water resources; welding technology; wildlife management.

Academic Programs *Special study options:* academic remediation for entering students, adult/continuing education programs, advanced placement credit, cooperative education, distance learning, English as a second language, independent study, internships, part-time degree program, services for LD students, student-designed majors, summer session for credit. *ROTC:* Army (c).

Library Learning Resources Center with 38,967 titles, 466 serial subscriptions, an OPAC.

Computers on Campus 700 computers available on campus for general student use. Internet access, at least one staffed computer lab available.

Student Life *Housing:* college housing not available. *Activities and Organizations:* drama/theater group, student-run newspaper, VICA, Delta Epsilon Chi, Intercultural Student Organization, Rho Beta Psi, Student Awareness League. *Campus security:* 24-hour emergency response devices and patrols, student patrols, late-night transport/escort service.

Athletics *Intercollegiate sports:* baseball M(s), basketball M(s)/W(s), cross-country running M(s)/W(s), soccer M(s)/W(s), softball W(s), tennis M(s)/W(s), track and field M(s)/W(s), volleyball W(s). *Intramural sports:* badminton M/W, basketball M/W, bowling M/W, softball M/W, table tennis M/W, tennis M/W, volleyball M/W, water polo M/W.

Standardized Tests *Required:* ACT ASSET.

Costs (2001–02) *Tuition:* state resident $1396 full-time, $58 per quarter hour part-time; nonresident $6119 full-time, $228 per quarter hour part-time. *Required fees:* $337 full-time.

Applying *Options:* early admission, deferred entrance. *Application fee:* $10. *Recommended:* high school transcript. *Application deadline:* rolling (freshmen), rolling (transfers).

Admissions Contact Ms. Colleen Straight, Manager District Institutional Research, Spokane Community College, North 1810 Greene Street, Spokane, WA 99217-5399. *Phone:* 509-434-5240. *Toll-free phone:* 800-248-5644.

SPOKANE FALLS COMMUNITY COLLEGE
Spokane, Washington

- **State-supported** 2-year, founded 1967, part of State Board for Washington Community and Technical Colleges
- **Calendar** quarters
- **Degree** associate
- **Urban** 125-acre campus
- **Endowment** $33,407
- **Coed,** 14,974 undergraduate students

Undergraduates Students come from 6 states and territories, 14 other countries, 3% are from out of state.

Faculty *Total:* 604, 28% full-time.

Majors Accounting technician; alcohol/drug abuse counseling; art; business administration; business marketing and marketing management; child care/guidance; commercial photography; fashion merchandising; financial services marketing; general office/clerical; gerontology; graphic design/commercial art/illustration; heavy equipment maintenance; information sciences/systems; interior design; international business; leatherworking/upholstery; liberal arts and sciences/liberal studies; library assistant; mass communications; music; orthotics/prosthetics; physical therapy assistant; real estate; retail management; secretarial science; sign language interpretation; social work; sport/fitness administration; vocational rehabilitation counseling; welding technology.

Academic Programs *Special study options:* academic remediation for entering students, adult/continuing education programs, advanced placement credit, cooperative education, English as a second language, internships, part-time degree program, services for LD students, student-designed majors, summer session for credit. *ROTC:* Army (c).

Library Learning Resources Center with 58,000 titles, 705 serial subscriptions, an OPAC.

Computers on Campus 400 computers available on campus for general student use. Internet access, at least one staffed computer lab available.

Student Life *Housing:* college housing not available. *Activities and Organizations:* drama/theater group, student-run newspaper, radio station, choral group, DECA, Associated Men Students, Associated Women Students, chorale, Forensics Club. *Campus security:* late-night transport/escort service, 24-hour emergency dispatch. *Student Services:* personal/psychological counseling, women's center.

Athletics *Intercollegiate sports:* baseball M(s), basketball M(s)/W(s), cross-country running M(s)/W(s), soccer M(s)/W(s), softball W(s), tennis M(s)/W(s), track and field M(s)/W(s), volleyball W(s). *Intramural sports:* badminton M/W, basketball M/W, bowling M/W, soccer M/W, softball M/W, table tennis M/W, tennis M/W, volleyball M/W.

Standardized Tests *Required:* ACT ASSET.

Costs (2001–02) *Tuition:* state resident $1396 full-time, $58 per quarter hour part-time; nonresident $6119 full-time, $228 per quarter hour part-time. *Required fees:* $337 full-time.

Spokane Falls Community College (continued)

Applying *Options:* early admission, deferred entrance. *Application fee:* $10. *Recommended:* high school transcript. *Application deadline:* rolling (freshmen), rolling (transfers). *Notification:* continuous (freshmen).

Admissions Contact Ms. Carol Millard, Vice President of Student Services, Spokane Falls Community College, 3410 West Fort George Wright Drive, Spokane, WA 99224-5288. *Phone:* 509-533-3682. *Toll-free phone:* 888-509-7944.

TACOMA COMMUNITY COLLEGE
Tacoma, Washington

- **State-supported** 2-year, founded 1965, part of Washington State Board for Community and Technical Colleges
- **Calendar** quarters
- **Degree** certificates, diplomas, and associate
- **Urban** 150-acre campus with easy access to Seattle
- **Coed,** 7,299 undergraduate students

Undergraduates Students come from 20 other countries, 4% are from out of state, 10% African American, 8% Asian American or Pacific Islander, 5% Hispanic American, 2% Native American, 4% international.

Freshmen *Admission:* 3,864 applied, 3,864 admitted.

Faculty *Total:* 320, 34% full-time. *Student/faculty ratio:* 24:1.

Majors Accounting; alcohol/drug abuse counseling; American studies; anthropology; art; behavioral sciences; biological/physical sciences; biology; botany; business administration; business economics; chemistry; computer programming (specific applications); computer science; computer science related; computer systems networking/telecommunications; computer/technical support; criminal justice/law enforcement administration; data processing technology; earth sciences; economics; education; emergency medical technology; engineering; English; environmental science; fine/studio arts; forestry; general studies; geology; history; humanities; human services; information sciences/systems; information technology; international business; international relations; Japanese; journalism; law enforcement/police science; liberal arts and sciences/liberal studies; literature; mathematics; medical administrative assistant; medical records administration; museum studies; music; nursing; occupational therapy; oceanography; pharmacy technician/assistant; philosophy; physical education; physical sciences; physical therapy; physics; political science; pre-engineering; pre-pharmacy studies; psychology; radiological science; respiratory therapy; romance languages; Russian; secretarial science; social sciences; sociology; Spanish; speech/rhetorical studies; system/networking/LAN/WAN management; Web page, digital/multimedia and information resources design; wildlife biology; wildlife management; wood science/paper technology; word processing; zoology.

Academic Programs *Special study options:* academic remediation for entering students, accelerated degree program, adult/continuing education programs, advanced placement credit, distance learning, English as a second language, honors programs, independent study, internships, off-campus study, part-time degree program, services for LD students, student-designed majors, summer session for credit. *ROTC:* Army (c).

Library Pearl Wanamaker Library with 90,192 titles, 269 serial subscriptions, 5,281 audiovisual materials, an OPAC, a Web page.

Computers on Campus 310 computers available on campus for general student use. Internet access, online (class) registration, at least one staffed computer lab available.

Student Life *Housing:* college housing not available. *Activities and Organizations:* drama/theater group, student-run newspaper, choral group. *Campus security:* Sonitrol electronic system. *Student Services:* personal/psychological counseling, women's center.

Athletics *Intercollegiate sports:* baseball M(s), basketball M(s)/W(s), golf M(s)/W(s), soccer M(s)/W(s), volleyball W(s). *Intramural sports:* basketball M/W, bowling M/W, fencing M/W, football M/W, golf M/W, skiing (downhill) M/W, soccer M/W, softball M/W, tennis M/W, volleyball W.

Standardized Tests *Required:* ACCUPLACER.

Costs (2001–02) *Tuition:* state resident $61 per credit part-time; nonresident $231 per credit part-time.

Financial Aid In 2001, 180 Federal Work-Study jobs (averaging $3000). 600 State and other part-time jobs (averaging $3000).

Applying *Options:* early admission. *Application deadline:* rolling (freshmen), rolling (transfers).

Admissions Contact Ms. Annette Hayward, Admissions Officer, Tacoma Community College, 6501 South 19th Street, Tacoma, WA 98466. *Phone:* 253-566-5108. *Fax:* 253-566-6011. *E-mail:* ahayward@tcc.tacoma.ctc.edu.

WALLA WALLA COMMUNITY COLLEGE
Walla Walla, Washington

- **State-supported** 2-year, founded 1967, part of Washington State Board for Community and Technical Colleges
- **Calendar** quarters
- **Degree** certificates, diplomas, and associate
- **Small-town** 125-acre campus
- **Endowment** $4.0 million
- **Coed,** 6,775 undergraduate students, 45% full-time, 51% women, 49% men

Undergraduates 3,054 full-time, 3,721 part-time. Students come from 5 other countries, 12% are from out of state, 2% African American, 2% Asian American or Pacific Islander, 19% Hispanic American, 2% Native American, 0.4% international.

Freshmen *Admission:* 403 enrolled.

Faculty *Total:* 415, 27% full-time. *Student/faculty ratio:* 21:1.

Majors Accounting technician; agricultural business; agricultural mechanization; agricultural production; auto body repair; auto mechanic/technician; business administration; carpentry; child care/guidance; civil engineering technology; computer maintenance technology; corrections; cosmetology; criminal justice studies; data entry/microcomputer applications; fire services administration; general office/clerical; general retailing/wholesaling; heating/air conditioning/refrigeration; information sciences/systems; legal administrative assistant; liberal arts and sciences/liberal studies; machine technology; medical administrative assistant; nursing; office management; practical nurse; secretarial science; teacher assistant/aide; turf management; welding technology.

Academic Programs *Special study options:* academic remediation for entering students, adult/continuing education programs, advanced placement credit, cooperative education, distance learning, double majors, English as a second language, external degree program, honors programs, independent study, internships, off-campus study, part-time degree program, services for LD students, summer session for credit.

Library Walla Walla Community College Library with 45,814 titles, 428 serial subscriptions, 3,715 audiovisual materials, an OPAC.

Computers on Campus 180 computers available on campus for general student use. A campuswide network can be accessed from off campus. Internet access, online (class) registration, at least one staffed computer lab available.

Student Life *Housing:* college housing not available. *Activities and Organizations:* drama/theater group, choral group, Drama Club, Computer Club, intramurals, Nursing Club, Business Leadership Club. *Campus security:* student patrols, late-night transport/escort service. *Student Services:* personal/psychological counseling.

Athletics Member NJCAA. *Intercollegiate sports:* baseball M(s), basketball M(s)/W(s), cross-country running W(s), equestrian sports M(s)/W(s), golf M(s)/W(s), soccer M(s)/W(s), softball W(s), tennis M(s)/W(s), volleyball W(s). *Intramural sports:* basketball M/W, racquetball M/W, soccer M/W, softball M/W, table tennis M/W, tennis M/W, volleyball M/W, weight lifting M/W.

Standardized Tests *Required:* ACT ASSET and ACT COMPASS.

Costs (2002–03) *Tuition:* state resident $2103 full-time, $67 per credit part-time; nonresident $3432 full-time, $67 per credit part-time. *Payment plan:* installment. *Waivers:* senior citizens and employees or children of employees.

Financial Aid In 2001, 95 Federal Work-Study jobs (averaging $1600). 20 State and other part-time jobs (averaging $2000).

Applying *Options:* common application, electronic application. *Application fee:* $40. *Required for some:* interview. *Recommended:* high school transcript. *Application deadline:* rolling (freshmen), rolling (transfers).

Admissions Contact Ms. Sally Wagoner, Director of Admissions and Records, Walla Walla Community College, 500 Tausick Way, Walla Walla, WA 99362-9267. *Phone:* 509-527-4283. *Toll-free phone:* 877-992-9282 (in-state); 877-992-9292 (out-of-state). *Fax:* 509-527-3361. *E-mail:* admissions@mail.ww.cc.wa.us.

WENATCHEE VALLEY COLLEGE
Wenatchee, Washington

Admissions Contact Ms. Marlene Sinko, Registrar/Admissions Coordinator, Wenatchee Valley College, 1300 Fifth Street, Wenatchee, WA 98801-1799. *Phone:* 509-664-2564. *Fax:* 509-664-2511. *E-mail:* atyrrell@wvcmail.ctc.edu.

WHATCOM COMMUNITY COLLEGE
Bellingham, Washington

- **State-supported** 2-year, founded 1970, part of Washington State Board for Community and Technical Colleges

- **Calendar** quarters
- **Degree** certificates and associate
- **Small-town** 52-acre campus with easy access to Vancouver
- **Endowment** $1.5 million
- **Coed,** 3,993 undergraduate students, 56% full-time, 56% women, 44% men

Undergraduates 2,234 full-time, 1,759 part-time. 5% are from out of state, 1% African American, 4% Asian American or Pacific Islander, 4% Hispanic American, 1% Native American, 4% international.
Freshmen *Admission:* 452 enrolled.
Faculty *Total:* 212, 25% full-time.
Majors Accounting; business administration; computer engineering technology; computer science; early childhood education; graphic design/commercial art/illustration; law enforcement/police science; liberal arts and sciences/liberal studies; medical administrative assistant; medical assistant; nursing; paralegal/legal assistant; physical therapy assistant; secretarial science.
Academic Programs *Special study options:* academic remediation for entering students, accelerated degree program, adult/continuing education programs, advanced placement credit, cooperative education, distance learning, English as a second language, external degree program, honors programs, independent study, internships, part-time degree program, services for LD students, student-designed majors, study abroad, summer session for credit.
Library Whatcom Community College Library with 14,680 titles, 193 serial subscriptions, 3,653 audiovisual materials, an OPAC, a Web page.
Computers on Campus 214 computers available on campus for general student use. Internet access, at least one staffed computer lab available.
Student Life *Housing:* college housing not available. *Activities and Organizations:* drama/theater group, student-run newspaper, choral group, Anime Anonymous, Deaf Student Fellowship Club, Health and Wellness Club, Phi Theta Kappa, International Friendship Club. *Campus security:* 24-hour emergency response devices. *Student Services:* personal/psychological counseling.
Athletics *Intercollegiate sports:* basketball M(s)/W(s), volleyball W(s). *Intramural sports:* basketball M/W, soccer M/W, tennis M/W, volleyball M/W, weight lifting M/W.
Costs (2001–02) *Tuition:* state resident $1782 full-time, $59 per credit part-time; nonresident $6900 full-time, $230 per credit part-time. Part-time tuition and fees vary according to course load. *Waivers:* senior citizens and employees or children of employees.
Financial Aid In 2001, 50 Federal Work-Study jobs (averaging $3300). 80 State and other part-time jobs (averaging $3500).
Applying *Options:* common application. *Application deadline:* 6/14 (freshmen).
Admissions Contact Ms. Laine Johnston, Director, Admissions Outreach, Whatcom Community College, 237 West Kellogg Road, Bellingham, WA 98226. *Phone:* 360-676-2170 Ext. 3217. *Fax:* 360-676-2171. *E-mail:* admit@whatcom.ctc.edu.

Yakima Valley Community College
Yakima, Washington

Admissions Contact Ms. Judy Morehead, Admissions Assistant, Yakima Valley Community College, PO Box 22520, Yakima, WA 98907-2520. *Phone:* 509-574-4713. *Fax:* 509-574-6860.

WEST VIRGINIA

Fairmont State Community & Technical College
Fairmont, West Virginia

Admissions Contact 1201 Locust Avenue, Fairmont, WV 26554.

Huntington Junior College of Business
Huntington, West Virginia

- **Proprietary** 2-year, founded 1936
- **Calendar** quarters
- **Degree** associate
- **Urban** campus
- **Coed,** 600 undergraduate students

Faculty *Total:* 27, 74% full-time. *Student/faculty ratio:* 18:1.
Majors Accounting; business administration; computer programming; computer science; court reporting; dental assistant; fashion merchandising; legal administrative assistant; medical administrative assistant; medical assistant; secretarial science.
Academic Programs *Special study options:* academic remediation for entering students, part-time degree program, services for LD students, summer session for credit.
Library 1,900 titles, 35 serial subscriptions.
Computers on Campus 60 computers available on campus for general student use. At least one staffed computer lab available.
Student Life *Housing:* college housing not available.
Costs (2002–03) *Tuition:* $5550 full-time, $550 per course part-time. No tuition increase for student's term of enrollment. *Waivers:* employees or children of employees.
Applying *Required:* high school transcript. *Application deadline:* rolling (freshmen), rolling (transfers).
Admissions Contact Mr. James Garrett, Marketing Education Services Director, Huntington Junior College of Business, 900 Fifth Avenue, Huntington, WV 25701-2004. *Phone:* 304-697-7550.

Mountain State College
Parkersburg, West Virginia

- **Proprietary** 2-year, founded 1888
- **Calendar** quarters
- **Degree** diplomas and associate
- **Small-town** campus
- **Coed,** 249 undergraduate students

Undergraduates *Retention:* 70% of 2001 full-time freshmen returned.
Faculty *Total:* 10, 60% full-time, 30% with terminal degrees. *Student/faculty ratio:* 17:1.
Majors Computer/information sciences; medical assistant; medical transcription.
Costs (2001–02) *Tuition:* $7050 full-time.
Admissions Contact Ms. Linda Craig, Admissions/Retention Coordinator, Mountain State College, 1508 Spring Street, Parkersburg, WV 26101-3993. *Phone:* 304-485-5487. *Toll-free phone:* 800-841-0201. *Fax:* 304-485-3524. *E-mail:* adm@mountainstate.org.

National Institute of Technology
Cross Lanes, West Virginia

- **Proprietary** 2-year, founded 1938, part of National Education Centers, Inc
- **Calendar** quarters
- **Degree** certificates, diplomas, and associate
- **Small-town** campus
- **Coed,** 440 undergraduate students, 100% full-time, 55% women, 45% men

Undergraduates 440 full-time. Students come from 6 states and territories.
Freshmen *Admission:* 440 enrolled.
Faculty *Total:* 28, 79% full-time.
Majors Electrical/electronic engineering technology; medical assistant.
Computers on Campus 40 computers available on campus for general student use.
Student Life *Housing:* college housing not available. *Activities and Organizations:* student-run newspaper.
Financial Aid In 2001, 4 Federal Work-Study jobs (averaging $4000).
Applying *Options:* deferred entrance. *Application fee:* $50. *Required:* high school transcript. *Application deadline:* rolling (freshmen), rolling (transfers). *Notification:* continuous (freshmen).
Admissions Contact Mrs. Karen Wilkinson, Director of Admissions, National Institute of Technology, 5514 Big Tyler Road, Cross Lanes, WV 25313-1390. *Phone:* 304-776-6290 Ext. 20. *Toll-free phone:* 800-626-8379.

Potomac State College of West Virginia University
Keyser, West Virginia

- **State-supported** 2-year, founded 1901, part of West Virginia Higher Education Policy Commission

Potomac State College of West Virginia University (continued)

- **Calendar** semesters
- **Degree** certificates and associate
- **Small-town** 616-acre campus
- **Endowment** $1.8 million
- **Coed**

Faculty *Student/faculty ratio:* 16:1.
Student Life *Campus security:* 24-hour emergency response devices and patrols, controlled dormitory access.
Athletics Member NJCAA.
Standardized Tests *Required for some:* SAT I or ACT (for admission).
Costs (2001–02) *Tuition:* state resident $2278 full-time, $105 per credit hour part-time; nonresident $6966 full-time, $300 per credit hour part-time. Part-time tuition and fees vary according to course load. *Room and board:* $4196; room only: $2056. Room and board charges vary according to board plan and location.
Financial Aid In 2001, 70 Federal Work-Study jobs (averaging $1300).
Applying *Options:* electronic application, early admission, deferred entrance. *Required:* high school transcript.
Admissions Contact Ms. Beth Little, Director of Enrollment Services, Potomac State College of West Virginia University, Keyser, WV 26726. *Phone:* 304-788-6817. *Toll-free phone:* 800-262-7332 Ext. 6820. *Fax:* 304-788-6939. *E-mail:* admissions@pscvax.psc.wvnet.edu.

Southern West Virginia Community and Technical College
Mount Gay, West Virginia

- **State-supported** 2-year, founded 1971, part of State College System of West Virginia
- **Calendar** semesters
- **Degree** certificates and associate
- **Rural** 23-acre campus
- **Coed,** 2,520 undergraduate students

Undergraduates Students come from 2 states and territories, 8% are from out of state, 2% African American, 0.3% Asian American or Pacific Islander, 0.2% Hispanic American, 0.1% Native American.
Freshmen *Admission:* 960 applied, 960 admitted. *Average high school GPA:* 2.90.
Faculty *Total:* 177, 32% full-time. *Student/faculty ratio:* 30:1.
Majors Accounting; auto mechanic/technician; business administration; communication equipment technology; computer programming (specific applications); criminal justice/law enforcement administration; drafting; engineering-related technology; finance; industrial radiologic technology; information sciences/systems; liberal arts and sciences/liberal studies; medical laboratory technician; nursing; secretarial science; welding technology.
Academic Programs *Special study options:* academic remediation for entering students, adult/continuing education programs, advanced placement credit, cooperative education, external degree program, part-time degree program, services for LD students, summer session for credit.
Library 70,576 titles, 233 serial subscriptions.
Computers on Campus 92 computers available on campus for general student use. A campuswide network can be accessed from off campus. Internet access, at least one staffed computer lab available.
Student Life *Housing:* college housing not available. *Activities and Organizations:* drama/theater group, student-run television station. *Student Services:* personal/psychological counseling.
Standardized Tests *Required:* ACT (for placement).
Costs (2001–02) *Tuition:* state resident $1440 full-time, $60 per credit part-time; nonresident $5464 full-time, $228 per credit part-time. *Payment plan:* installment.
Financial Aid In 2001, 20 Federal Work-Study jobs (averaging $4200).
Applying *Options:* early admission, deferred entrance. *Application fee:* $10. *Required:* high school transcript. *Application deadline:* rolling (freshmen), rolling (transfers). *Notification:* continuous (freshmen).
Admissions Contact Mr. Roy Simmons, Registrar, Southern West Virginia Community and Technical College, PO Box 2900, Mount Gay, WV 25637-2900. *Phone:* 304-792-7160 Ext. 120. *E-mail:* admissions@southern.wvnet.edu.

West Virginia Business College
Wheeling, West Virginia

- **Private** 2-year
- **Degree** diplomas and associate
- 58 undergraduate students
- 100% of applicants were admitted

Admissions Contact Ms. Sharon Subasic, Admissions Representative, West Virginia Business College, 1052 Main Street, Wheeling, WV 26003. *Phone:* 304-232-0361. *E-mail:* wbbcwheeling@juno.com.

West Virginia Junior College
Charleston, West Virginia

- **Proprietary** 2-year, founded 1892
- **Calendar** quarters
- **Degree** associate
- **Urban** campus
- **Coed,** 230 undergraduate students

Undergraduates Students come from 6 states and territories.
Freshmen *Admission:* 130 applied, 130 admitted.
Faculty *Total:* 15.
Majors Accounting; business administration; computer typography/composition; data processing technology; legal studies; medical administrative assistant; medical assistant; secretarial science.
Academic Programs *Special study options:* adult/continuing education programs, advanced placement credit, part-time degree program, summer session for credit.
Library 1,300 titles, 40 serial subscriptions.
Computers on Campus 75 computers available on campus for general student use. Internet access, at least one staffed computer lab available.
Student Life *Housing:* college housing not available. *Student Services:* personal/psychological counseling.
Costs (2001–02) *Tuition:* $7725 full-time, $160 per quarter hour part-time. *Required fees:* $750 full-time, $250 per term part-time.
Applying *Options:* common application, early admission, deferred entrance. *Application deadline:* rolling (freshmen), rolling (transfers).
Admissions Contact Admission Department, West Virginia Junior College, 1000 Virginia Street East, Charleston, WV 25301-2817. *Phone:* 304-345-2820.

West Virginia Junior College
Morgantown, West Virginia

Admissions Contact Admissions Office, West Virginia Junior College, 148 Willey Street, Morgantown, WV 26505-5521. *Phone:* 304-296-8282.

West Virginia Northern Community College
Wheeling, West Virginia

- **State-supported** 2-year, founded 1972
- **Calendar** semesters
- **Degree** certificates and associate
- **Small-town** campus with easy access to Pittsburgh
- **Endowment** $700,706
- **Coed,** 2,994 undergraduate students

Undergraduates Students come from 5 states and territories, 17% are from out of state, 3% African American, 0.8% Asian American or Pacific Islander, 0.4% Hispanic American, 0.2% Native American.
Faculty *Total:* 131, 41% full-time. *Student/faculty ratio:* 18:1.
Majors Accounting technician; banking; business administration; computer programming; electrical/electronic engineering technology; heating/air conditioning/refrigeration; horticulture services; hospitality management; industrial technology; information technology; institutional food workers; law enforcement/police science; liberal arts and sciences/liberal studies; medical records technology; nursing; secretarial science; social work; word processing.

Academic Programs *Special study options:* academic remediation for entering students, accelerated degree program, adult/continuing education programs, advanced placement credit, distance learning, double majors, honors programs, internships, part-time degree program, student-designed majors, summer session for credit.
Library Wheeling B and O Campus Library plus 2 others with 36,650 titles, 188 serial subscriptions, 3,495 audiovisual materials, an OPAC, a Web page.
Computers on Campus 250 computers available on campus for general student use. A campuswide network can be accessed from off campus. Internet access, at least one staffed computer lab available.
Student Life *Housing:* college housing not available. *Campus security:* security personnel during evening and night classes. *Student Services:* personal/psychological counseling, women's center.
Athletics *Intramural sports:* basketball M/W, bowling M/W, softball M/W, volleyball M/W.
Standardized Tests *Required:* ACT ASSET. *Required for some:* SAT I or ACT (for placement).
Costs (2001–02) *Tuition:* state resident $1680 full-time, $70 per credit part-time; nonresident $5352 full-time, $223 per credit part-time. Full-time tuition and fees vary according to course load and reciprocity agreements. Part-time tuition and fees vary according to course load and reciprocity agreements. *Payment plan:* installment. *Waivers:* employees or children of employees.
Financial Aid In 2001, 35 Federal Work-Study jobs (averaging $1650).
Applying *Options:* common application, electronic application, early admission, deferred entrance. *Required for some:* high school transcript. *Application deadline:* rolling (freshmen), rolling (transfers).
Admissions Contact Ms. Janet M. Fike, Associate Dean of Enrollment Management, West Virginia Northern Community College, 1704 Market Street, Wheeling, WV 26003-3699. *Phone:* 304-233-5900 Ext. 4363. *Fax:* 304-233-5900 Ext. 4218.

WEST VIRGINIA UNIVERSITY AT PARKERSBURG
Parkersburg, West Virginia

- **State-supported** primarily 2-year, founded 1961, part of University System of West Virginia
- **Calendar** semesters
- **Degrees** certificates, associate, and bachelor's
- **Small-town** 140-acre campus
- **Coed,** 3,340 undergraduate students, 50% full-time, 61% women, 39% men

Undergraduates 1,668 full-time, 1,672 part-time. Students come from 3 states and territories, 4 other countries, 0.8% African American, 0.5% Asian American or Pacific Islander, 0.4% Hispanic American, 0.2% Native American, 0.1% international. *Retention:* 56% of 2001 full-time freshmen returned.
Freshmen *Admission:* 717 applied, 717 admitted, 574 enrolled. *Average high school GPA:* 3.03.
Faculty *Total:* 172, 53% full-time, 12% with terminal degrees. *Student/faculty ratio:* 18:1.
Majors Accounting; auto mechanic/technician; business administration; business marketing and marketing management; chemical engineering technology; criminal justice/law enforcement administration; data processing technology; drafting; education; electrical/electronic engineering technology; electromechanical technology; elementary education; environmental technology; finance; liberal arts and sciences/liberal studies; machine technology; mechanical engineering technology; nursing; pre-engineering; secretarial science; social work; welding technology.
Academic Programs *Special study options:* academic remediation for entering students, adult/continuing education programs, advanced placement credit, cooperative education, part-time degree program, services for LD students, study abroad, summer session for credit. *ROTC:* Army (c).
Library Main Library plus 1 other with 41,300 titles, 248 serial subscriptions, an OPAC.
Computers on Campus 100 computers available on campus for general student use. A campuswide network can be accessed from off campus. Internet access, at least one staffed computer lab available.
Student Life *Housing:* college housing not available. *Activities and Organizations:* drama/theater group, student-run newspaper. *Student Services:* health clinic, personal/psychological counseling.
Athletics *Intramural sports:* badminton M/W, basketball M/W, bowling M/W, cross-country running M/W, football M/W, golf M/W, table tennis M/W, tennis M/W, volleyball M/W, weight lifting M/W.
Standardized Tests *Required:* ACT (for placement).
Costs (2002–03) *Tuition:* state resident $1548 full-time, $65 per credit hour part-time; nonresident $4944 full-time, $206 per credit hour part-time. Full-time tuition and fees vary according to degree level. Part-time tuition and fees vary according to degree level. *Waivers:* employees or children of employees.
Applying *Options:* common application, electronic application, early admission, deferred entrance. *Required for some:* high school transcript. *Notification:* continuous (freshmen).
Admissions Contact Criss McCauley, Senior Admissions Counselor, West Virginia University at Parkersburg, 300 Campus Drive, Parkersburg, WV 26101. *Phone:* 304-424-8223. *Toll-free phone:* 800-WVA-WVUP. *Fax:* 304-424-8332.

WISCONSIN

BLACKHAWK TECHNICAL COLLEGE
Janesville, Wisconsin

- **District-supported** 2-year, founded 1968, part of Wisconsin Technical College System
- **Calendar** semesters
- **Degree** associate
- **Rural** 84-acre campus
- **Coed,** 2,300 undergraduate students

Undergraduates Students come from 4 states and territories.
Faculty *Total:* 341, 27% full-time.
Majors Accounting; aviation technology; business marketing and marketing management; computer/information sciences; culinary arts; dental hygiene; electrical/electronic engineering technology; electromechanical technology; fire science; industrial technology; law enforcement/police science; legal administrative assistant; mechanical design technology; nursing; physical therapy; radiological science; secretarial science.
Academic Programs *Special study options:* academic remediation for entering students, adult/continuing education programs, cooperative education, English as a second language, external degree program, internships, part-time degree program, services for LD students, summer session for credit.
Library Blackhawk Technical College Library with 25,000 titles, 435 serial subscriptions, an OPAC.
Computers on Campus 180 computers available on campus for general student use. Internet access, at least one staffed computer lab available.
Student Life *Housing:* college housing not available. *Activities and Organizations:* student-run newspaper. *Student Services:* personal/psychological counseling, women's center.
Costs (2001–02) *Tuition:* state resident $2010 full-time, $67 per credit hour part-time; nonresident $15,411 full-time, $514 per credit hour part-time. Full-time tuition and fees vary according to course load. Part-time tuition and fees vary according to course load. *Required fees:* $101 full-time, $3 per credit. *Payment plan:* deferred payment. *Waivers:* senior citizens.
Financial Aid In 2001, 20 Federal Work-Study jobs (averaging $2300).
Applying *Options:* common application. *Application fee:* $25. *Required:* high school transcript. *Application deadline:* rolling (freshmen), rolling (transfers). *Notification:* continuous (freshmen).
Admissions Contact Ms. Barbara Erlandson, Student Services Manager, Blackhawk Technical College, PO Box 5009, Janesville, WI 53547-5009. *Phone:* 608-757-7713. *Toll-free phone:* 800-472-0024. *Fax:* 608-757-9407.

BRYANT AND STRATTON COLLEGE
Milwaukee, Wisconsin

- **Proprietary** 2-year, founded 1863, part of Bryant and Stratton Business Institute, Inc
- **Calendar** semesters
- **Degree** associate
- **Urban** 2-acre campus
- **Coed,** 274 undergraduate students, 65% full-time, 70% women, 30% men

Undergraduates 177 full-time, 97 part-time. Students come from 1 other state, 1 other country, 71% African American, 2% Asian American or Pacific Islander, 4% Hispanic American.
Freshmen *Admission:* 224 applied, 131 admitted, 131 enrolled. *Average high school GPA:* 2.0.

Bryant and Stratton College (continued)

Faculty *Total:* 37, 16% full-time. *Student/faculty ratio:* 10:1.

Majors Accounting; business administration; information sciences/systems; information technology; legal administrative assistant; medical administrative assistant; medical assistant; secretarial science.

Academic Programs *Special study options:* academic remediation for entering students, adult/continuing education programs, advanced placement credit, cooperative education, distance learning, double majors, independent study, internships, part-time degree program, summer session for credit.

Library Bryant and Stratton College Library with 120 serial subscriptions, 100 audiovisual materials.

Computers on Campus 130 computers available on campus for general student use. Internet access, at least one staffed computer lab available.

Student Life *Housing:* college housing not available. *Activities and Organizations:* Phi Beta Lambda, Association of Information Technology Professionals, Allied Health Association, Institute of Management Accountants, Student Advisory Board. *Campus security:* 24-hour emergency response devices and patrols. *Student Services:* personal/psychological counseling.

Standardized Tests *Recommended:* SAT I or ACT (for admission).

Costs (2002–03) *One-time required fee:* $25. *Tuition:* $9900 full-time, $330 per credit hour part-time. Full-time tuition and fees vary according to class time and course load. Part-time tuition and fees vary according to class time and course load. *Required fees:* $200 full-time, $100 per term part-time. *Payment plan:* installment. *Waivers:* employees or children of employees.

Applying *Application fee:* $25. *Required:* high school transcript. *Required for some:* letters of recommendation, interview. *Recommended:* minimum 2.0 GPA. *Application deadline:* rolling (freshmen), rolling (transfers).

Admissions Contact Mr. James Palmer, Director of Admissions, Bryant and Stratton College, 310 West Wisconsin Avenue, Milwaukee, WI 53203-2214. *Phone:* 414-276-5200 Ext. 47.

CHIPPEWA VALLEY TECHNICAL COLLEGE
Eau Claire, Wisconsin

- **District-supported** 2-year, founded 1912, part of Wisconsin Technical College System
- **Calendar** semesters
- **Degree** associate
- **Urban** 160-acre campus
- **Coed,** 2,600 undergraduate students

Undergraduates Students come from 10 states and territories, 4 other countries, 5% are from out of state.

Faculty *Total:* 400, 88% full-time. *Student/faculty ratio:* 12:1.

Majors Accounting; agricultural business; alcohol/drug abuse counseling; architectural engineering technology; auto mechanic/technician; business marketing and marketing management; child care/development; civil engineering technology; computer/information sciences; construction technology; culinary arts; dairy science; data processing technology; dental hygiene; diagnostic medical sonography; drafting; electrical/electronic engineering technology; electromechanical technology; fire science; heating/air conditioning/refrigeration; hospitality management; law enforcement/police science; machine technology; mechanical design technology; medical laboratory technician; medical laboratory technology; medical radiologic technology; medical records administration; nursing; paralegal/legal assistant; quality control technology; real estate; secretarial science; welding technology.

Academic Programs *Special study options:* academic remediation for entering students, adult/continuing education programs, distance learning, double majors, English as a second language, internships, part-time degree program, services for LD students, summer session for credit.

Library Technical Resource Center with 34,000 titles, 750 serial subscriptions, an OPAC.

Computers on Campus 600 computers available on campus for general student use. Internet access, at least one staffed computer lab available.

Student Life *Housing:* college housing not available. *Activities and Organizations:* student-run newspaper. *Campus security:* 24-hour emergency response devices, late-night transport/escort service. *Student Services:* personal/psychological counseling.

Standardized Tests *Required:* ACT COMPASS. *Required for some:* ACT (for placement).

Costs (2001–02) *Tuition:* state resident $1680 full-time, $70 per credit part-time; nonresident $12,000 full-time, $500 per credit part-time. Full-time tuition and fees vary according to course load. Part-time tuition and fees vary according to course load. *Waivers:* senior citizens.

Financial Aid In 2001, 175 Federal Work-Study jobs (averaging $911).

Applying *Options:* common application, early admission, deferred entrance. *Application fee:* $30. *Required:* high school transcript. *Required for some:* interview. *Application deadline:* rolling (freshmen), rolling (transfers). *Notification:* continuous (freshmen).

Admissions Contact Mr. Timothy Shepardson, Admissions Manager, Chippewa Valley Technical College, 620 West Clairemont Avenue, Eau Claire, WI 54701-6162. *Phone:* 715-833-6245. *Toll-free phone:* 800-547-2882. *Fax:* 715-833-6470.

COLLEGE OF MENOMINEE NATION
Keshena, Wisconsin

Admissions Contact Ms. Deanna Bisley, Dean, College of Menominee Nation, PO Box 1179, Keshena, WI 54135. *Phone:* 715-799-4921. *Fax:* 715-799-1326.

FOX VALLEY TECHNICAL COLLEGE
Appleton, Wisconsin

Admissions Contact Dr. Michael Schlies, Associate Dean of Student Services, Fox Valley Technical College, 1825 North Bluemound, PO Box 2277, Appleton, WI 54912-2277. *Phone:* 920-735-5713. *Fax:* 920-735-2582.

GATEWAY TECHNICAL COLLEGE
Kenosha, Wisconsin

- **State and locally supported** 2-year, founded 1911, part of Wisconsin Technical College System
- **Calendar** semesters
- **Degree** certificates, diplomas, and associate
- **Urban** 10-acre campus with easy access to Chicago and Milwaukee
- **Coed,** 6,247 undergraduate students, 19% full-time, 60% women, 40% men

Undergraduates 1,214 full-time, 5,033 part-time. Students come from 7 states and territories.

Freshmen *Admission:* 1,078 enrolled.

Faculty *Total:* 602, 46% full-time.

Majors Accounting; aircraft pilot (professional); auto mechanic/technician; banking; business computer programming; business marketing and marketing management; business systems networking/ telecommunications; child care/development; civil engineering technology; communication equipment technology; computer graphics; corrections; court reporting; dental hygiene; electrical/electronic engineering technology; electromechanical technology; fire science; general retailing/wholesaling; heating/air conditioning/refrigeration technology; horticulture services; human services; hydraulic technology; industrial technology; interior design; law enforcement/police science; legal administrative assistant; logistics/materials management; machine technology; management information systems/business data processing; mechanical design technology; medical records administration; nursing; operating room technician; operations management; physical therapy; physical therapy assistant; quality control technology; radio/television broadcasting technology; robotics; secretarial science; technical/business writing.

Academic Programs *Special study options:* academic remediation for entering students, advanced placement credit, cooperative education, distance learning, double majors, English as a second language, independent study, internships, part-time degree program, services for LD students, student-designed majors, summer session for credit.

Library Library/Learning Resources Center with 45,433 titles, 409 serial subscriptions, 12,400 audiovisual materials, an OPAC.

Computers on Campus 840 computers available on campus for general student use. A campuswide network can be accessed from off campus. At least one staffed computer lab available.

Student Life *Housing:* college housing not available. *Activities and Organizations:* student-run newspaper, radio station. *Campus security:* 24-hour emergency response devices and patrols, late-night transport/escort service. *Student Services:* personal/psychological counseling.

Standardized Tests *Required:* ACT COMPASS or ACT ASSET. *Recommended:* ACT (for placement).

Costs (2002–03) *Tuition:* state resident $2010 full-time, $67 per credit part-time; nonresident $18,411 full-time, $514 per credit part-time. Full-time tuition and fees vary according to course load and program. Part-time tuition and

fees vary according to course load and program. *Required fees:* $235 full-time, $2 per credit. *Payment plans:* installment, deferred payment.
Applying *Options:* electronic application, early admission, deferred entrance. *Application fee:* $30. *Required for some:* high school transcript, minimum 2.0 GPA, interview. *Application deadline:* rolling (freshmen), rolling (transfers). *Notification:* continuous (freshmen).
Admissions Contact Mr. Charles Wood, Vice President of Marketing and Enrollment, Gateway Technical College, 3520 30th Avenue, Kenosha, WI 53144-1690. *Phone:* 262-564-3092. *Fax:* 262-564-2301. *E-mail:* admissions@gateway.tec.wi.us.

HERZING COLLEGE
Madison, Wisconsin

- **Proprietary** primarily 2-year, founded 1948, part of Herzing Institutes, Inc
- **Calendar** semesters
- **Degrees** diplomas, associate, and bachelor's
- **Suburban** campus with easy access to Milwaukee
- **Coed, primarily men**

Faculty *Student/faculty ratio:* 25:1.
Student Life *Campus security:* 24-hour emergency response devices.
Costs (2001–02) *One-time required fee:* $50. *Tuition:* $240 per credit part-time. Full-time tuition and fees vary according to class time and program. Part-time tuition and fees vary according to class time and program. $3,600-$4,010 per semester, including books.
Financial Aid *Financial aid deadline:* 6/30.
Applying *Options:* common application, electronic application, early admission. *Required:* high school transcript, interview.
Admissions Contact Ms. Renee Herzing, Admissions Director, Herzing College, 5218 E. Terrace Drive, Madison, WI 53718. *Phone:* 608-249-6611 Ext. 842. *Toll-free phone:* 800-582-1227. *E-mail:* mailbag@msn.herzing.edu.

ITT TECHNICAL INSTITUTE
Green Bay, Wisconsin

- **Proprietary** 2-year, founded 2000
- **Calendar** quarters
- **Coed,** 93 undergraduate students

Majors Computer/information sciences related; computer programming; drafting; electrical/electronic engineering technologies related; information technology.
Costs (2001–02) *Tuition:* Full-time tuition and fees vary according to program. Part-time tuition and fees vary according to program. $260—$330 per credit hour.
Admissions Contact Ms. Judi Hughes, ITT Technical Institute, 470 Security Boulevard, Green Bay, WI 54313. *Phone:* 920-662-9000.

ITT TECHNICAL INSTITUTE
Greenfield, Wisconsin

- **Proprietary** primarily 2-year, founded 1968, part of ITT Educational Services, Inc
- **Calendar** quarters
- **Degrees** associate and bachelor's
- **Suburban** campus with easy access to Milwaukee
- **Coed,** 421 undergraduate students

Majors Computer/information sciences related; computer programming; drafting; electrical/electronic engineering technologies related; information technology.
Student Life *Housing:* college housing not available.
Costs (2001–02) *Tuition:* Full-time tuition and fees vary according to program. Part-time tuition and fees vary according to program. $260—$330 per credit hour.
Applying *Options:* deferred entrance. *Application fee:* $100. *Required:* high school transcript, interview. *Recommended:* letters of recommendation. *Application deadline:* rolling (freshmen), rolling (transfers).
Admissions Contact Mr. Russel Gill, Director of Recruitment, ITT Technical Institute, 6300 West Layton Avenue, Greenfield, WI 53220. *Phone:* 414-282-9494.

LAC COURTE OREILLES OJIBWA COMMUNITY COLLEGE
Hayward, Wisconsin

- **Federally supported** 2-year, founded 1982
- **Calendar** semesters
- **Degree** certificates and associate
- **Rural** 2-acre campus
- **Endowment** $950,616
- **Coed,** 500 undergraduate students

Undergraduates Students come from 1 other state.
Freshmen *Admission:* 116 applied.
Faculty *Student/faculty ratio:* 20:1.
Majors Alcohol/drug abuse counseling; business administration; liberal arts and sciences/liberal studies; medical assistant; Native American studies; natural resources management; nursing; secretarial science; social work.
Academic Programs *Special study options:* academic remediation for entering students, adult/continuing education programs, distance learning, double majors, external degree program, honors programs, independent study, part-time degree program.
Library Lac Courte Oreilles Ojibwa Community College Library with 13,800 titles, 100 serial subscriptions, an OPAC.
Computers on Campus 25 computers available on campus for general student use. Internet access, at least one staffed computer lab available.
Student Life *Housing:* college housing not available. *Activities and Organizations:* student association. *Campus security:* 24-hour emergency response devices.
Athletics *Intramural sports:* basketball M, softball W, volleyball M/W, weight lifting M/W.
Standardized Tests *Required:* TABE.
Costs (2001–02) *Tuition:* $2700 full-time, $90 per semester hour part-time. *Required fees:* $50 full-time, $25 per term part-time.
Applying *Options:* common application, early admission. *Application fee:* $10. *Required:* high school transcript. *Application deadline:* rolling (freshmen), rolling (transfers).
Admissions Contact Ms. Annette Wiggins, Registrar, Lac Courte Oreilles Ojibwa Community College, 13466 West Trepania Road, Hayward, WI 54843-2181. *Phone:* 715-634-4790 Ext. 104. *Toll-free phone:* 888-526-6221.

LAKESHORE TECHNICAL COLLEGE
Cleveland, Wisconsin

- **State and locally supported** 2-year, founded 1967, part of Wisconsin Technical College System
- **Calendar** semesters
- **Degree** certificates, diplomas, and associate
- **Rural** 160-acre campus with easy access to Milwaukee
- **Coed,** 2,886 undergraduate students, 24% full-time, 61% women, 39% men

Undergraduates 687 full-time, 2,199 part-time. Students come from 3 states and territories, 2% are from out of state.
Freshmen *Admission:* 1,561 applied, 1,058 admitted, 865 enrolled.
Faculty *Total:* 514, 20% full-time. *Student/faculty ratio:* 12:1.
Majors Accounting; business marketing and marketing management; computer management; computer programming; computer programming related; computer science related; computer systems analysis; court reporting; dental hygiene; electrical/electronic engineering technology; electromechanical technology; finance; law enforcement/police science; management science; mechanical design technology; medical administrative assistant; nursing; paralegal/legal assistant; quality control technology; radiological science; secretarial science.
Academic Programs *Special study options:* academic remediation for entering students, accelerated degree program, adult/continuing education programs, advanced placement credit, cooperative education, distance learning, double majors, English as a second language, external degree program, independent study, internships, part-time degree program, services for LD students, student-designed majors, summer session for credit.
Library 15,749 titles, 350 serial subscriptions, 910 audiovisual materials, an OPAC.
Computers on Campus 625 computers available on campus for general student use. Internet access, at least one staffed computer lab available.
Student Life *Housing:* college housing not available. *Activities and Organizations:* student government, Business Professionals of America, Police Science

Lakeshore Technical College (continued)
Club, Lakeshore Student Nurse Association, Dairy Herd Club. *Campus security:* 24-hour patrols. *Student Services:* health clinic, personal/psychological counseling.

Standardized Tests *Required:* SAT I or ACT (for admission).

Costs (2002–03) *Tuition:* state resident $2090 full-time, $65 per credit part-time; nonresident $15,915 full-time, $500 per credit part-time. Full-time tuition and fees vary according to course load and program. Part-time tuition and fees vary according to course load and program. *Required fees:* $260 full-time, $6 per credit. *Payment plan:* deferred payment.

Financial Aid In 2001, 37 Federal Work-Study jobs.

Applying *Options:* common application, electronic application, early admission, deferred entrance. *Application fee:* $30. *Required for some:* high school transcript, interview. *Application deadline:* rolling (freshmen), rolling (transfers). *Notification:* continuous (freshmen).

Admissions Contact Ms. Donna Gorzelitz, Enrollment Specialist, Lakeshore Technical College, 1290 North Avenue, Cleveland, WI 53015. *Phone:* 920-693-1339. *Toll-free phone:* 888-GO TO LTC. *Fax:* 920-693-3561. *E-mail:* enroll@ltc.tec.wi.us.

MADISON AREA TECHNICAL COLLEGE
Madison, Wisconsin

Admissions Contact Ms. Maureen Menendez, Interim Admissions Administrator, Madison Area Technical College, 3550 Anderson Street, Madison, WI 53704-2599. *Phone:* 608-246-6212.

MADISON MEDIA INSTITUTE
Madison, Wisconsin

Admissions Contact 2702 Agriculture Drive, Suite 1, Madison, WI 53718. *Toll-free phone:* 800-236-4997.

MID-STATE TECHNICAL COLLEGE
Wisconsin Rapids, Wisconsin

- **State and locally supported** 2-year, founded 1917, part of Wisconsin Technical College System
- **Calendar** semesters
- **Degree** certificates, diplomas, and associate
- **Small-town** 155-acre campus
- **Endowment** $1.2 million
- **Coed,** 10,737 undergraduate students

Undergraduates Students come from 2 states and territories, 1% are from out of state.

Freshmen *Admission:* 1,100 applied, 1,045 admitted.

Faculty *Total:* 300, 67% full-time.

Majors Accounting; business administration; business marketing and marketing management; civil engineering technology; computer engineering technology; computer programming related; computer programming (specific applications); computer science related; corrections; data entry/microcomputer applications; electrical/electronic engineering technology; hotel and restaurant management; industrial technology; information sciences/systems; instrumentation technology; law enforcement/police science; mechanical design technology; nursing; quality control technology; respiratory therapy; secretarial science.

Academic Programs *Special study options:* academic remediation for entering students, adult/continuing education programs, cooperative education, distance learning, double majors, English as a second language, independent study, internships, part-time degree program, services for LD students, summer session for credit.

Library Mid-State Technical College Library with 20,148 titles, 539 serial subscriptions, 2,685 audiovisual materials, an OPAC.

Computers on Campus 120 computers available on campus for general student use. A campuswide network can be accessed from off campus. Internet access, at least one staffed computer lab available.

Student Life *Housing:* college housing not available. *Activities and Organizations:* student-run newspaper, Business Professionals of America, Civil Tech Club, Barber & Cosmetology Club, Society of Hosteurs, UICA. *Student Services:* health clinic, personal/psychological counseling, women's center.

Athletics Member NJCAA. *Intercollegiate sports:* basketball M/W, bowling M/W, golf M, volleyball W. *Intramural sports:* basketball M, bowling M/W, football M, golf M/W, volleyball M/W.

Standardized Tests *Required:* ACT ASSET. *Recommended:* SAT I or ACT (for placement).

Costs (2002–03) *Tuition:* $67 per credit part-time. *Required fees:* $27 full-time, $3 per credit.

Applying *Options:* electronic application, early admission, deferred entrance. *Application fee:* $25. *Required:* high school transcript. *Application deadline:* rolling (freshmen), rolling (transfers). *Notification:* continuous (freshmen).

Admissions Contact Ms. Carole Prochnow, Admissions Assistant, Mid-State Technical College, 500 32nd Street North, Wisconsin Rapids, WI 54494-5599. *Phone:* 715-422-5444. *Toll-free phone:* 888-575-6782. *Fax:* 715-422-5440. *E-mail:* cprochnow@midstate.tec.wi.us.

MILWAUKEE AREA TECHNICAL COLLEGE
Milwaukee, Wisconsin

- **District-supported** 2-year, founded 1912, part of Wisconsin Technical College System
- **Calendar** semesters
- **Degree** certificates, diplomas, and associate
- **Urban** campus
- **Coed,** 60,174 undergraduate students

Freshmen *Admission:* 11,000 applied, 11,000 admitted.

Faculty *Total:* 1,759, 34% full-time. *Student/faculty ratio:* 16:1.

Majors Accounting; agricultural business; alcohol/drug abuse counseling; anesthesiology; auto mechanic/technician; biomedical technology; broadcast journalism; business administration; business management/administrative services related; business marketing and marketing management; cardiovascular technology; chemical engineering technology; child care/development; civil engineering technology; communication equipment technology; computer graphics; computer/information technology services administration and management related; computer programming related; computer programming (specific applications); computer programming, vendor/product certification; computer science; computer science related; construction technology; criminal justice/law enforcement administration; culinary arts; data entry/microcomputer applications; data processing technology; dental hygiene; dietetics; drafting; ecology; educational media design; electrical/electronic engineering technology; electrical equipment installation/repair; electromechanical technology; environmental health; environmental technology; fashion merchandising; film studies; finance; fire science; food services technology; furniture design; graphic design/commercial art/illustration; graphic/printing equipment; health unit coordination; heating/air conditioning/refrigeration; hospitality/recreation marketing operations; hotel and restaurant management; hotel/motel services marketing operations; human services; industrial design; industrial radiologic technology; industrial technology; information sciences/systems; information technology; landscaping management; law enforcement/police science; legal administrative assistant; liberal arts and sciences/liberal studies; mechanical engineering technology; medical administrative assistant; medical laboratory technician; mortuary science; music; nursing; occupational therapy; opticianry; paralegal/legal assistant; photography; physical therapy; pre-engineering; publishing; radio/television broadcasting; real estate; respiratory therapy; retail management; secretarial science; surveying; system/networking/LAN/WAN management; transportation technology; travel services marketing operations; water resources; Web/multimedia management/webmaster; welding technology; word processing.

Academic Programs *Special study options:* academic remediation for entering students, adult/continuing education programs, advanced placement credit, cooperative education, distance learning, double majors, English as a second language, external degree program, freshman honors college, honors programs, independent study, internships, off-campus study, part-time degree program, services for LD students, student-designed majors, summer session for credit.

Library William F. Rasche Library plus 4 others with 60,847 titles, 856 serial subscriptions, an OPAC.

Computers on Campus 1000 computers available on campus for general student use. Internet access, online (class) registration, at least one staffed computer lab available.

Student Life *Housing:* college housing not available. *Activities and Organizations:* student-run newspaper, television station, choral group. *Campus security:* 24-hour emergency response devices and patrols, student patrols, late-night transport/escort service. *Student Services:* personal/psychological counseling, women's center, legal services.

Athletics Member NJCAA. *Intercollegiate sports:* baseball M/W, basketball M/W, bowling M/W, cross-country running M/W, soccer M, softball M/W, tennis

M/W, track and field M/W, volleyball W. *Intramural sports:* badminton M/W, baseball M/W, basketball M, bowling M/W, soccer M/W, table tennis M/W, tennis M/W, volleyball M/W.

Costs (2002–03) *Tuition:* state resident $1600 full-time, $90 per credit part-time; nonresident $9500 full-time, $481 per credit part-time. Full-time tuition and fees vary according to class time and program. Part-time tuition and fees vary according to class time and program. *Payment plan:* installment.

Applying *Options:* common application, electronic application. *Application fee:* $30. *Required:* high school transcript. *Application deadline:* rolling (freshmen), rolling (transfers). *Notification:* continuous until 8/20 (freshmen).

Admissions Contact Ms. Theresa Barry, Director of Enrollment Services, Milwaukee Area Technical College, Admissions, 700 West State Street, Milwaukee, WI 53233. *Phone:* 414-297-7227. *Toll-free phone:* 414-297-6542. *Fax:* 414-297-6371. *E-mail:* apply@matc.edu.

MORAINE PARK TECHNICAL COLLEGE

Fond du Lac, Wisconsin

- **State and locally supported** 2-year, founded 1967, part of Wisconsin Technical College System
- **Calendar** semesters
- **Degree** certificates, diplomas, and associate
- **Small-town** 40-acre campus with easy access to Milwaukee
- **Endowment** $21,500
- **Coed,** 8,943 undergraduate students

Undergraduates Students come from 18 states and territories, 4% are from out of state, 4% African American, 0.4% Asian American or Pacific Islander, 1% Hispanic American, 1% Native American.

Freshmen *Admission:* 1,606 applied, 1,606 admitted.

Faculty *Total:* 555, 28% full-time.

Majors Accounting; agricultural sciences; alcohol/drug abuse counseling; auto mechanic/technician; business marketing and marketing management; child guidance; civil engineering technology; computer engineering; computer engineering technology; computer programming; corrections; culinary arts; data processing technology; drafting; electromechanical technology; emergency medical technology; food sciences; graphic design/commercial art/illustration; hotel and restaurant management; industrial technology; machine technology; mechanical design technology; medical administrative assistant; medical records administration; nursing; secretarial science; water resources.

Academic Programs *Special study options:* academic remediation for entering students, accelerated degree program, adult/continuing education programs, advanced placement credit, distance learning, English as a second language, external degree program, independent study, internships, part-time degree program, services for LD students, summer session for credit.

Library Moraine Park Technical College Library/Learning Resource Center with 32,166 titles, 630 serial subscriptions, 13,330 audiovisual materials, an OPAC, a Web page.

Computers on Campus At least one staffed computer lab available.

Student Life *Housing:* college housing not available. *Activities and Organizations:* Student Programming Board, student government, Corrections Club, HVAC Club, Food Service Executives. *Campus security:* 24-hour emergency response devices. *Student Services:* personal/psychological counseling, women's center.

Athletics *Intramural sports:* bowling M/W, volleyball M/W.

Standardized Tests *Required for some:* ACT (for admission).

Costs (2002–03) *Tuition:* area resident $2010 full-time, $67 per credit part-time; state resident $2010 full-time, $67 per credit part-time; nonresident $581 per credit part-time. *Required fees:* $218 full-time, $67 per credit.

Financial Aid In 2001, 62 Federal Work-Study jobs (averaging $949).

Applying *Options:* electronic application, deferred entrance. *Application fee:* $30. *Required:* interview. *Recommended:* high school transcript. *Application deadline:* rolling (freshmen), rolling (transfers). *Notification:* continuous (freshmen).

Admissions Contact Ms. Susan Krueger, Student Services, Moraine Park Technical College, 235 North National Ave, PO Box 1940, Fond du Lac, WI 54936-1940. *Phone:* 920-924-3200. *Toll-free phone:* 800-472-4554. *Fax:* 920-924-3421.

NICOLET AREA TECHNICAL COLLEGE

Rhinelander, Wisconsin

- **State and locally supported** 2-year, founded 1968, part of Wisconsin Technical College System
- **Calendar** semesters
- **Degree** certificates, diplomas, and associate
- **Rural** 280-acre campus
- **Coed**

Student Life *Campus security:* 24-hour emergency response devices.

Athletics Member NJCAA.

Standardized Tests *Recommended:* ACT (for admission).

Applying *Options:* electronic application, early admission. *Application fee:* $25. *Required:* essay or personal statement, high school transcript, minimum 2.0 GPA.

Admissions Contact Ms. Susan Kordula, Director of Admissions and Marketing, Nicolet Area Technical College, Box 518, Rhinelander, WI 54501-0518. *Phone:* 715-365-4451. *Toll-free phone:* 800-544-3039 Ext. 4451. *Fax:* 715-365-4411. *E-mail:* inquire@nicolet.tec.wi.us.

NORTHCENTRAL TECHNICAL COLLEGE

Wausau, Wisconsin

- **District-supported** 2-year, founded 1912, part of Wisconsin Technical College System
- **Calendar** semesters
- **Degree** certificates, diplomas, and associate
- **Small-town** 96-acre campus
- **Endowment** $1.4 million
- **Coed,** 3,609 undergraduate students, 29% full-time, 57% women, 43% men

Undergraduates 1,057 full-time, 2,552 part-time. Students come from 3 states and territories, 2 other countries, 1% are from out of state, 4% transferred in.

Freshmen *Admission:* 1,300 applied, 800 admitted, 665 enrolled. *Average high school GPA:* 3.25.

Faculty *Total:* 226, 70% full-time, 2% with terminal degrees. *Student/faculty ratio:* 20:1.

Majors Accounting; architectural engineering technology; auto mechanic/technician; business administration; business marketing and marketing management; dental hygiene; drafting; early childhood education; electrical/electronic engineering technology; electromechanical technology; graphic/printing equipment; human services; industrial radiologic technology; industrial technology; information sciences/systems; laser/optical technology; law enforcement/police science; legal administrative assistant; machine technology; mechanical design technology; medical administrative assistant; nursing; practical nurse; radiological science; secretarial science; sign language interpretation.

Academic Programs *Special study options:* academic remediation for entering students, adult/continuing education programs, advanced placement credit, distance learning, double majors, English as a second language, independent study, internships, part-time degree program, services for LD students, student-designed majors, summer session for credit.

Library Northcentral Technical College, Wausau Campus plus 1 other with 30,000 titles, 400 serial subscriptions, an OPAC, a Web page.

Computers on Campus 1200 computers available on campus for general student use. A campuswide network can be accessed from off campus. Internet access, at least one staffed computer lab available.

Student Life *Housing:* college housing not available. *Activities and Organizations:* student-run newspaper, Student Governing Board, International Club, Habitat for Humanity, Nursing Club, Delta Epsilon Chi (Marketing Club). *Campus security:* 24-hour emergency response devices, late-night transport/escort service. *Student Services:* health clinic, personal/psychological counseling, women's center.

Athletics *Intramural sports:* badminton M/W, basketball M/W, bowling M/W, racquetball M/W, softball M/W, table tennis M/W, tennis M/W, volleyball M/W.

Standardized Tests *Required for some:* ACCUPLACER.

Financial Aid In 2001, 366 Federal Work-Study jobs (averaging $2000).

Applying *Options:* common application, electronic application, early admission, deferred entrance. *Application fee:* $25. *Required:* high school transcript. *Required for some:* interview. *Application deadline:* rolling (freshmen), rolling (transfers). *Notification:* continuous (freshmen).

Admissions Contact Carolyn Michalski, Team Leader, Student Services, Northcentral Technical College, 1000 West Campus Drive, Wausau, WI 54401-1899. *Phone:* 715-675-3331 Ext. 4285. *Fax:* 715-675-9776 Ext. 4007.

NORTHEAST WISCONSIN TECHNICAL COLLEGE

Green Bay, Wisconsin

Admissions Contact Ms. Susan Ellis, Operational Assistant, Services for Students, Northeast Wisconsin Technical College, 2740 W Mason Street, PO Box

Northeast Wisconsin Technical College (continued)
19042, Green Bay, WI 54307-9042. *Phone:* 920-498-5522 Ext. 522. *Toll-free phone:* 800-422-6982 Ext. 733. *Fax:* 920-498-6882. *E-mail:* sellis@nwtc.tec.wi.us.

SOUTHWEST WISCONSIN TECHNICAL COLLEGE
Fennimore, Wisconsin

- **State and locally supported** 2-year, founded 1967, part of Wisconsin Technical College System
- **Calendar** semesters
- **Degree** certificates, diplomas, and associate
- **Rural** 53-acre campus
- **Endowment** $935,000
- **Coed,** 2,993 undergraduate students

Undergraduates Students come from 4 states and territories, 1% are from out of state, 3% live on campus.
Faculty *Total:* 112, 73% full-time. *Student/faculty ratio:* 16:1.
Majors Accounting; agribusiness; agricultural mechanization; auto body repair; auto mechanic/technician; business marketing and marketing management; child care/development; computer management; computer programming; cosmetology; culinary arts; dairy science; data processing technology; dental assistant; drafting; electrical/electronic engineering technology; electromechanical technology; finance; food services technology; human services; legal administrative assistant; machine technology; masonry/tile setting; mechanical design technology; medical assistant; medical transcription; nurse assistant/aide; nursing; practical nurse; secretarial science; welding technology.
Academic Programs *Special study options:* academic remediation for entering students, adult/continuing education programs, advanced placement credit, distance learning, double majors, English as a second language, internships, part-time degree program, services for LD students, student-designed majors, summer session for credit.
Library Southwest Technical College Library plus 1 other with 25,000 titles, 307 serial subscriptions, 5,000 audiovisual materials, an OPAC.
Computers on Campus 250 computers available on campus for general student use. A campuswide network can be accessed from off campus. Internet access, at least one staffed computer lab available.
Student Life *Housing Options:* coed. *Activities and Organizations:* student-run newspaper, Business Professionals of America, Vocational Industrial Clubs of America, Health Occupations Students of America, Marketing and Management Association. *Student Services:* health clinic, personal/psychological counseling, women's center.
Athletics *Intramural sports:* basketball M/W, bowling M/W, softball M/W, volleyball M/W.
Standardized Tests *Required:* TABE.
Costs (2001–02) *Tuition:* $69 per credit part-time; state resident $2304 full-time, $516 per credit part-time; nonresident $17,156 full-time. Full-time tuition and fees vary according to program. Part-time tuition and fees vary according to program. *Required fees:* $5 per credit. *Room and board:* room only: $2250. *Payment plans:* installment, deferred payment. *Waivers:* senior citizens.
Applying *Options:* electronic application, early admission. *Application fee:* $30. *Required:* high school transcript, interview. *Application deadline:* rolling (freshmen).
Admissions Contact Ms. Kathy Kreul, Admissions, Southwest Wisconsin Technical College, 1800 Bronson Boulevard, Fennimore, WI 53813. *Phone:* 608-822-3262 Ext. 2355. *Toll-free phone:* 800-362-3322 Ext. 2355. *Fax:* 608-822-6019 Ext. 2355. *E-mail:* kkreul@southwest.tec.wi.us.

UNIVERSITY OF WISCONSIN-BARABOO/SAUK COUNTY
Baraboo, Wisconsin

- **State-supported** 2-year, founded 1968, part of University of Wisconsin System
- **Calendar** semesters
- **Degree** associate
- **Small-town** 68-acre campus
- **Coed,** 554 undergraduate students, 59% full-time, 59% women, 41% men

Undergraduates 326 full-time, 228 part-time. 1% are from out of state, 10% transferred in. *Retention:* 50% of 2001 full-time freshmen returned.
Freshmen *Admission:* 247 admitted, 350 enrolled.
Faculty *Total:* 42, 45% full-time, 50% with terminal degrees. *Student/faculty ratio:* 20:1.
Majors Liberal arts and sciences/liberal studies.
Academic Programs *Special study options:* academic remediation for entering students, advanced placement credit, distance learning, external degree program, independent study, off-campus study, part-time degree program, services for LD students, student-designed majors, study abroad, summer session for credit. *ROTC:* Army (c), Air Force (c).
Library T. N. Savides Library with 45,000 titles, 300 serial subscriptions, 518 audiovisual materials, an OPAC.
Computers on Campus 45 computers available on campus for general student use. A campuswide network can be accessed from off campus that provide access to financial aid application. Internet access, at least one staffed computer lab available.
Student Life *Housing:* college housing not available. *Activities and Organizations:* drama/theater group, student-run newspaper, choral group, Student Government Association, chorus and band, dance team, gaming club, business club.
Athletics Member NJCAA. *Intercollegiate sports:* basketball M(c), cross-country running M(c)/W(c), golf M/W, tennis M/W, volleyball W. *Intramural sports:* basketball W, bowling M/W, racquetball M/W, softball M/W, table tennis M/W, volleyball M/W, weight lifting M/W.
Standardized Tests *Required:* SAT I or ACT (for admission).
Costs (2001–02) *Tuition:* state resident $2635 full-time, $111 per credit part-time; nonresident $10,080 full-time, $421 per credit part-time. Full-time tuition and fees vary according to course load, program, and reciprocity agreements. Part-time tuition and fees vary according to course load, program, and reciprocity agreements. *Required fees:* $111 per credit, $1317 per term part-time. *Payment plans:* installment, deferred payment. *Waivers:* senior citizens.
Applying *Options:* electronic application, early admission, deferred entrance. *Application fee:* $35. *Required:* high school transcript. *Required for some:* interview. *Application deadline:* rolling (freshmen), rolling (transfers). *Notification:* continuous until 8/31 (freshmen).
Admissions Contact Ms. Jan Gerlach, Assistant Director of Student Services, University of Wisconsin-Baraboo/Sauk County, 1006 Connie Road, Baraboo, WI 53913-1015. *Phone:* 608-356-8724 Ext. 270. *Fax:* 608-356-4074. *E-mail:* boouinfo@uwc.edu.

UNIVERSITY OF WISCONSIN-BARRON COUNTY
Rice Lake, Wisconsin

- **State-supported** 2-year, founded 1966, part of University of Wisconsin System
- **Calendar** semesters
- **Degree** associate
- **Small-town** 142-acre campus
- **Coed,** 575 undergraduate students

Undergraduates Students come from 5 states and territories, 1 other country, 0.2% African American, 0.3% Asian American or Pacific Islander, 0.9% Hispanic American, 0.5% Native American, 0.2% international.
Faculty *Total:* 34, 53% full-time, 41% with terminal degrees.
Majors Liberal arts and sciences/liberal studies.
Academic Programs *Special study options:* academic remediation for entering students, adult/continuing education programs, advanced placement credit, distance learning, English as a second language, independent study, internships, off-campus study, part-time degree program, services for LD students, summer session for credit.
Library Main Library plus 1 other with 39,479 titles, 233 serial subscriptions, an OPAC.
Computers on Campus 50 computers available on campus for general student use. Internet access, at least one staffed computer lab available.
Student Life *Housing:* college housing not available. *Activities and Organizations:* drama/theater group, student-run newspaper, choral group, Phi Theta Kappa, student government, Encore, Delta Psi Omega, Sociology Club. *Student Services:* health clinic.
Athletics Member NJCAA. *Intercollegiate sports:* baseball M, basketball M/W, golf M/W, soccer M/W, volleyball W. *Intramural sports:* football M/W, softball M/W, table tennis M/W, volleyball M/W.
Standardized Tests *Required:* SAT I or ACT (for placement).
Costs (2001–02) *Tuition:* state resident $2422 full-time, $107 per credit part-time; nonresident $10,088 full-time, $420 per credit part-time. *Required fees:* $155 full-time, $13 per credit. *Payment plan:* installment.

Applying *Options:* electronic application, early admission, deferred entrance. *Application fee:* $35. *Required:* high school transcript. *Application deadlines:* 9/2 (freshmen), 9/2 (transfers). *Notification:* continuous (freshmen).

Admissions Contact Ms. June Brunette, Program Assistant, University of Wisconsin-Barron County, 1800 College Drive, Rice Lake, WI 54868-2497. *Phone:* 715-234-8176 Ext. 430.

UNIVERSITY OF WISCONSIN-FOND DU LAC
Fond du Lac, Wisconsin

- **State-supported** 2-year, founded 1968, part of University of Wisconsin System
- **Calendar** semesters
- **Degree** associate
- **Small-town** 182-acre campus with easy access to Milwaukee
- **Coed**

Student Life *Campus security:* 24-hour emergency response devices.

Athletics Member NJCAA.

Standardized Tests *Required:* ACT (for admission).

Applying *Options:* electronic application, deferred entrance. *Application fee:* $35. *Required:* high school transcript.

Admissions Contact Ms. Linda A. Reiss, Director of Student Services, University of Wisconsin-Fond du Lac, 400 University Drive, Fond du Lac, WI 54935-2950. *Phone:* 920-929-3606. *E-mail:* lreiss@uwc.edu.

UNIVERSITY OF WISCONSIN-FOX VALLEY
Menasha, Wisconsin

- **State-supported** 2-year, founded 1933, part of University of Wisconsin System
- **Calendar** semesters
- **Degree** associate
- **Urban** 33-acre campus
- **Coed,** 1,782 undergraduate students, 47% full-time, 54% women, 46% men

Undergraduates Students come from 3 states and territories, 4 other countries, 1% are from out of state, 0.7% African American, 2% Asian American or Pacific Islander, 1% Hispanic American, 0.5% Native American, 0.8% international.

Freshmen *Admission:* 569 applied, 458 admitted. *Average high school GPA:* 2.5.

Faculty *Total:* 57, 70% full-time.

Majors Liberal arts and sciences/liberal studies.

Academic Programs *Special study options:* academic remediation for entering students, adult/continuing education programs, advanced placement credit, cooperative education, honors programs, independent study, off-campus study, part-time degree program, services for LD students, summer session for credit.

Library 29,000 titles, 230 serial subscriptions, an OPAC, a Web page.

Computers on Campus 52 computers available on campus for general student use. A campuswide network can be accessed from off campus. Internet access, online (class) registration, at least one staffed computer lab available.

Student Life *Housing:* college housing not available. *Activities and Organizations:* drama/theater group, student-run newspaper, radio and television station, choral group, Business Club, Education Club, Earth Science Club, Computer Science Club, Political Science Club. *Student Services:* personal/psychological counseling.

Athletics Member NJCAA. *Intercollegiate sports:* basketball M/W, soccer M/W, tennis M/W, volleyball M/W. *Intramural sports:* basketball M/W, volleyball M/W.

Standardized Tests *Required:* ACT (for admission).

Costs (2002–03) *Tuition:* state resident $2624 full-time, $111 per credit part-time; nonresident $10,068 full-time, $521 per credit part-time.

Applying *Options:* common application, early admission. *Required:* high school transcript. *Notification:* continuous (freshmen).

Admissions Contact Ms. Rhonda Uschan, Director of Student Services, University of Wisconsin-Fox Valley, 1478 Midway Road, Menasha, WI 54952. *Phone:* 920-832-2620. *Toll-free phone:* 888-INFOUWC. *E-mail:* foxinfo@uwc.edu.

UNIVERSITY OF WISCONSIN-MANITOWOC
Manitowoc, Wisconsin

- **State-supported** 2-year, founded 1935, part of University of Wisconsin System
- **Calendar** semesters
- **Degree** associate
- **Small-town** 50-acre campus with easy access to Milwaukee
- **Coed,** 648 undergraduate students, 63% full-time, 58% women, 42% men

Undergraduates Students come from 3 states and territories, 4% Asian American or Pacific Islander, 0.8% Hispanic American, 0.7% Native American.

Freshmen *Admission:* 297 applied, 290 admitted. *Test scores:* ACT scores over 18: 85%; ACT scores over 24: 21%; ACT scores over 30: 1%.

Faculty *Total:* 26, 73% full-time. *Student/faculty ratio:* 21:1.

Majors Liberal arts and sciences/liberal studies.

Academic Programs *Special study options:* academic remediation for entering students, adult/continuing education programs, advanced placement credit, distance learning, off-campus study, part-time degree program, services for LD students, student-designed majors, summer session for credit.

Library 25,750 titles, 150 serial subscriptions, an OPAC.

Computers on Campus 50 computers available on campus for general student use. A campuswide network can be accessed from off campus. At least one staffed computer lab available.

Student Life *Housing:* college housing not available. *Activities and Organizations:* drama/theater group, student-run newspaper, choral group, Business Club, Drama Club, Music Club, Phi Kappa Theta, Environmental Awareness. *Student Services:* personal/psychological counseling.

Athletics *Intercollegiate sports:* basketball M/W, golf M, tennis M/W, volleyball W.

Standardized Tests *Required:* SAT I or ACT (for admission).

Costs (2001–02) *Tuition:* state resident $2596 full-time, $109 per credit part-time; nonresident $10,040 full-time, $420 per credit part-time. *Payment plan:* installment.

Applying *Options:* electronic application, early admission. *Application fee:* $35. *Required:* high school transcript. *Notification:* continuous until 7/1 (freshmen).

Admissions Contact Dr. Michael A. Herrity, Director of Student Services, University of Wisconsin-Manitowoc, 705 Viebahn Street, Manitowoc, WI 54220-6699. *Phone:* 920-683-4708. *E-mail:* mherrity@uwc.edu.

UNIVERSITY OF WISCONSIN-MARATHON COUNTY
Wausau, Wisconsin

- **State-supported** 2-year, founded 1933, part of University of Wisconsin System
- **Calendar** semesters
- **Degree** associate
- **Small-town** 7-acre campus
- **Coed**

Faculty *Student/faculty ratio:* 22:1.

Student Life *Campus security:* 24-hour emergency response devices, controlled dormitory access.

Athletics Member NJCAA.

Standardized Tests *Required:* ACT (for admission).

Applying *Options:* common application, electronic application, early admission, deferred entrance. *Application fee:* $35. *Required for some:* interview. *Recommended:* minimum 2.0 GPA.

Admissions Contact Dr. Nolan Whiz Beck, Director of Student Services, University of Wisconsin-Marathon County, 518 South Seventh Avenue, Wausau, WI 54401-5396. *Phone:* 715-261-6238. *Toll-free phone:* 888-367-8962. *Fax:* 715-848-3568.

UNIVERSITY OF WISCONSIN-MARINETTE
Marinette, Wisconsin

- **State-supported** 2-year, founded 1965, part of University of Wisconsin System
- **Calendar** semesters
- **Degree** associate
- **Small-town** 36-acre campus
- **Endowment** $200,000
- **Coed,** 535 undergraduate students

Faculty *Total:* 30, 53% full-time. *Student/faculty ratio:* 24:1.

Majors Liberal arts and sciences/liberal studies.

University of Wisconsin-Marinette (continued)

Academic Programs *Special study options:* academic remediation for entering students, adult/continuing education programs, advanced placement credit, cooperative education, distance learning, English as a second language, independent study, internships, off-campus study, part-time degree program, services for LD students, summer session for credit.

Library Main Library plus 1 other with 23,000 titles, 135 serial subscriptions.

Computers on Campus 48 computers available on campus for general student use. Internet access, at least one staffed computer lab available.

Student Life *Housing:* college housing not available. *Activities and Organizations:* drama/theater group, student-run newspaper, choral group, Student Senate, Writers Club/Literature Club, Phi Theta Kappa, Student Ambassadors. *Student Services:* personal/psychological counseling.

Athletics *Intercollegiate sports:* basketball M/W, volleyball W. *Intramural sports:* basketball M/W, football M/W, golf M/W, volleyball M/W.

Costs (2001–02) *Tuition:* state resident $1285 full-time, $107 per credit part-time; nonresident $5118 full-time, $427 per credit part-time. *Required fees:* $1 full-time, $1 per term part-time.

Applying *Options:* electronic application. *Application fee:* $35. *Required:* high school transcript. *Application deadline:* rolling (freshmen), rolling (transfers). *Notification:* continuous (freshmen).

Admissions Contact Ms. Cynthia M. Bailey, Interim Director of Student Services, University of Wisconsin-Marinette, 750 West Bay Shore, Marinette, WI 54143-4299. *Phone:* 715-735-4301. *E-mail:* ssinfo@mai.uwc.edu.

University of Wisconsin-Marshfield/Wood County

Marshfield, Wisconsin

- **State-supported** 2-year, founded 1964, part of University of Wisconsin System
- **Calendar** semesters
- **Degree** associate
- **Small-town** 71-acre campus
- **Endowment** $500,000
- **Coed,** 569 undergraduate students

Undergraduates Students come from 2 states and territories, 1% are from out of state, 0.9% African American, 0.5% Asian American or Pacific Islander, 0.2% Hispanic American, 2% Native American, 0.2% international. *Retention:* 99% of 2001 full-time freshmen returned.

Freshmen *Admission:* 322 applied, 301 admitted. *Average high school GPA:* 2.80. *Test scores:* ACT scores over 18: 95%; ACT scores over 24: 20%; ACT scores over 30: 5%.

Faculty *Total:* 36, 42% full-time. *Student/faculty ratio:* 17:1.

Majors Liberal arts and sciences/liberal studies.

Academic Programs *Special study options:* academic remediation for entering students, accelerated degree program, adult/continuing education programs, advanced placement credit, distance learning, external degree program, independent study, off-campus study, part-time degree program, services for LD students, study abroad, summer session for credit. *ROTC:* Army (c).

Library Learning Resource Center with 35,000 titles, 185 serial subscriptions, an OPAC, a Web page.

Computers on Campus 60 computers available on campus for general student use. Internet access, at least one staffed computer lab available.

Student Life *Housing:* college housing not available. *Activities and Organizations:* drama/theater group, student-run newspaper, choral group, Student Nurses Association, student newspaper, literary magazine, Student Education Association, Intervarsity Christian Fellowship. *Campus security:* 24-hour patrols, patrols by city police.

Athletics *Intercollegiate sports:* basketball M/W, golf M/W, tennis M/W, volleyball W. *Intramural sports:* basketball M/W, bowling M/W, football M/W, golf M/W, soccer M/W, table tennis M/W, tennis M/W, volleyball M/W, weight lifting M/W.

Standardized Tests *Required:* SAT I or ACT (for admission).

Costs (2001–02) *Tuition:* state resident $2422 full-time, $101 per credit part-time; nonresident $429 per credit part-time. Full-time tuition and fees vary according to course load and reciprocity agreements. Part-time tuition and fees vary according to course load and reciprocity agreements. *Required fees:* $114 full-time, $9 per credit hour, $1 per term part-time. *Payment plans:* tuition prepayment, installment, deferred payment.

Applying *Options:* common application, electronic application, early admission, deferred entrance. *Application fee:* $35. *Required:* high school transcript. *Required for some:* essay or personal statement, letters of recommendation, interview. *Application deadline:* rolling (freshmen), rolling (transfers).

Admissions Contact Mr. Jeff Meece, Director of Student Services, University of Wisconsin-Marshfield/Wood County, 2000 West Fifth Street, Marshfield, WI 54449. *Phone:* 715-389-6500. *Fax:* 715-384-1718.

University of Wisconsin-Richland

Richland Center, Wisconsin

- **State-supported** 2-year, founded 1967, part of University of Wisconsin System
- **Calendar** semesters
- **Degree** associate
- **Rural** 135-acre campus
- **Coed,** 496 undergraduate students, 64% full-time, 57% women, 43% men

Undergraduates 316 full-time, 180 part-time. Students come from 3 states and territories, 9 other countries, 2% are from out of state, 2% African American, 0.4% Asian American or Pacific Islander, 4% international, 3% transferred in, 35% live on campus. *Retention:* 48% of 2001 full-time freshmen returned.

Freshmen *Admission:* 189 applied, 302 enrolled.

Faculty *Total:* 25, 60% full-time, 56% with terminal degrees. *Student/faculty ratio:* 22:1.

Majors Biological/physical sciences; liberal arts and sciences/liberal studies.

Academic Programs *Special study options:* academic remediation for entering students, adult/continuing education programs, advanced placement credit, distance learning, external degree program, independent study, off-campus study, part-time degree program, services for LD students, study abroad, summer session for credit.

Library Miller Memorial Library with 45,000 titles, 200 serial subscriptions, an OPAC, a Web page.

Computers on Campus 45 computers available on campus for general student use. A campuswide network can be accessed from off campus. Internet access, at least one staffed computer lab available.

Student Life *Housing Options:* coed. *Activities and Organizations:* drama/theater group, student-run newspaper, choral group. *Student Services:* personal/psychological counseling.

Athletics *Intercollegiate sports:* basketball M/W, soccer M/W, volleyball W. *Intramural sports:* badminton M/W, basketball M/W, cross-country running M/W, football M/W, golf M/W, racquetball M/W, swimming M/W, table tennis M/W, tennis M/W, volleyball M/W.

Standardized Tests *Required:* SAT I or ACT (for admission). *Recommended:* ACT (for admission).

Costs (2001–02) *Tuition:* $116 per credit part-time; state resident $2422 full-time; nonresident $9866 full-time, $426 per credit part-time. Part-time tuition and fees vary according to course load. *Room and board:* room only: $2800. Room and board charges vary according to housing facility. *Payment plan:* installment.

Applying *Options:* electronic application, early admission. *Application fee:* $35. *Required:* high school transcript. *Required for some:* letters of recommendation, interview. *Application deadlines:* 8/15 (freshmen), 8/3 (transfers). *Notification:* continuous until 8/15 (freshmen).

Admissions Contact Mr. John D. Poole, Director of Student Services, University of Wisconsin-Richland, 1200 Highway 14 West, Richland Center, WI 53581. *Phone:* 608-647-8422 Ext. 223. *Fax:* 608-647-6225. *E-mail:* jpoole@uwc.edu.

University of Wisconsin-Rock County

Janesville, Wisconsin

- **State-supported** 2-year, founded 1966, part of University of Wisconsin System
- **Calendar** semesters
- **Degree** certificates and associate
- **Suburban** 50-acre campus with easy access to Milwaukee
- **Coed,** 991 undergraduate students, 53% full-time, 58% women, 42% men

Undergraduates Students come from 10 states and territories, 4 other countries, 1% are from out of state, 5% African American, 0.9% Asian American or Pacific Islander, 3% Hispanic American, 0.3% Native American, 0.4% international.

Freshmen *Admission:* 371 applied, 360 admitted.

Faculty *Total:* 44, 45% full-time, 57% with terminal degrees. *Student/faculty ratio:* 16:1.

Majors Liberal arts and sciences/liberal studies.
Academic Programs *Special study options:* academic remediation for entering students, adult/continuing education programs, advanced placement credit, distance learning, off-campus study, part-time degree program, services for LD students, summer session for credit.
Library University of Wisconsin-Rock County Library with 79,972 titles, 4,466 audiovisual materials, an OPAC, a Web page.
Computers on Campus 50 computers available on campus for general student use. At least one staffed computer lab available.
Student Life *Housing:* college housing not available. *Activities and Organizations:* drama/theater group, choral group, Student Government Association, Multicultural Student Union, U-Rock Players, Education Club, Adult Student Club.
Athletics *Intercollegiate sports:* soccer M/W, tennis M/W, volleyball W. *Intramural sports:* basketball M/W, weight lifting M/W.
Standardized Tests *Required:* ACT (for admission).
Costs (2001–02) *Tuition:* state resident $2611 full-time, $110 per credit part-time; nonresident $10,274 full-time, $428 per credit part-time. Full-time tuition and fees vary according to reciprocity agreements. Part-time tuition and fees vary according to reciprocity agreements. *Payment plans:* installment, deferred payment.
Applying *Options:* electronic application, deferred entrance. *Application fee:* $35. *Required:* high school transcript. *Application deadlines:* 7/31 (freshmen), 8/15 (transfers). *Notification:* continuous until 8/27 (freshmen).
Admissions Contact Ms. Donna Johnson, Program Manager, University of Wisconsin-Rock County, 2909 Kellogg Avenue, Janesville, WI 53456. *Phone:* 608-758-6523. *Toll-free phone:* 888-INFO-UWC. *Fax:* 608-755-2732. *E-mail:* tpickart@uwc.edu.

UNIVERSITY OF WISCONSIN-SHEBOYGAN
Sheboygan, Wisconsin

- **State-supported** 2-year, founded 1933, part of University of Wisconsin System
- **Calendar** semesters
- **Degree** associate
- **Small-town** 75-acre campus with easy access to Milwaukee
- **Coed,** 777 undergraduate students, 100% full-time, 52% women, 48% men

Undergraduates Students come from 3 states and territories, 5 other countries, 0.3% African American, 2% Asian American or Pacific Islander, 1% Hispanic American, 0.3% Native American, 0.7% international.
Freshmen *Average high school GPA:* 2.54.
Faculty *Total:* 26, 65% full-time. *Student/faculty ratio:* 17:1.
Majors Liberal arts and sciences/liberal studies.
Academic Programs *Special study options:* academic remediation for entering students, adult/continuing education programs, advanced placement credit, distance learning, independent study, off-campus study, part-time degree program, services for LD students, summer session for credit.
Library Battig Memorial Library with 40,038 titles, 154 serial subscriptions, an OPAC, a Web page.
Computers on Campus 40 computers available on campus for general student use. Internet access, at least one staffed computer lab available.
Student Life *Housing:* college housing not available. *Activities and Organizations:* drama/theater group, student-run newspaper, choral group, Student Ambassadors, Phi Theta Kappa, student government, Circle K, Zoomers (nontraditional students). *Campus security:* 24-hour patrols by city police.
Athletics Member NJCAA. *Intercollegiate sports:* basketball M/W, cross-country running M/W, golf M/W, tennis M/W, volleyball W. *Intramural sports:* archery M, basketball M/W, soccer M/W, softball M/W, volleyball M/W.
Standardized Tests *Required:* ACT (for placement).
Costs (2001–02) *Tuition:* area resident $1240 full-time.
Applying *Options:* common application, electronic application. *Application fee:* $35. *Required:* high school transcript. *Required for some:* interview. *Application deadline:* rolling (freshmen), rolling (transfers).
Admissions Contact Dr. Ronald P. Campopiano, Director of Student Services, University of Wisconsin-Sheboygan, One University Drive, Sheboygan, WI 53081-4789. *Phone:* 920-459-6633. *Fax:* 920-459-6602. *E-mail:* rcampopi@uwc.edu.

UNIVERSITY OF WISCONSIN-WASHINGTON COUNTY
West Bend, Wisconsin

- **State-supported** 2-year, founded 1968, part of University of Wisconsin System
- **Calendar** semesters
- **Degree** associate
- **Small-town** 87-acre campus with easy access to Milwaukee
- **Coed,** 941 undergraduate students

Undergraduates Students come from 2 states and territories, 2 other countries, 1% are from out of state, 0.5% Asian American or Pacific Islander, 1% Hispanic American, 0.3% Native American, 0.8% international.
Freshmen *Admission:* 431 applied, 410 admitted.
Faculty *Total:* 47, 51% full-time, 66% with terminal degrees. *Student/faculty ratio:* 20:1.
Majors Liberal arts and sciences/liberal studies.
Academic Programs *Special study options:* academic remediation for entering students, advanced placement credit, distance learning, double majors, honors programs, independent study, off-campus study, part-time degree program, services for LD students, summer session for credit.
Library University of Wisconsin-Washington County Library with 46,429 titles, 247 serial subscriptions, 4,998 audiovisual materials, an OPAC, a Web page.
Computers on Campus 78 computers available on campus for general student use. A campuswide network can be accessed from off campus. Internet access, at least one staffed computer lab available.
Student Life *Housing:* college housing not available. *Activities and Organizations:* drama/theater group, student-run newspaper, choral group, Student Government Association, Business Club, Phi Theta Kappa, Writers' Guild, Student Impact. *Student Services:* personal/psychological counseling.
Athletics Member NAIA. *Intercollegiate sports:* basketball M/W, golf M/W, soccer M/W, tennis M/W, volleyball W. *Intramural sports:* basketball M/W, football M/W, softball M/W, volleyball M/W.
Standardized Tests *Required:* ACT (for admission).
Costs (2001–02) *Tuition:* state resident $2652 full-time, $112 per credit part-time; nonresident $422 per credit part-time. Part-time tuition and fees vary according to course load and reciprocity agreements. *Payment plans:* installment, deferred payment.
Applying *Options:* electronic application, deferred entrance. *Application fee:* $35. *Required:* high school transcript. *Required for some:* essay or personal statement, interview. *Application deadline:* rolling (freshmen), rolling (transfers).
Admissions Contact Mr. Dan Cebrario, Associate Director of Student Services, University of Wisconsin-Washington County, Student Services Office, 400 University Drive, West Bend, WI 53095. *Phone:* 262-335-5201. *Fax:* 262-335-5220.

UNIVERSITY OF WISCONSIN-WAUKESHA
Waukesha, Wisconsin

- **State-supported** 2-year, founded 1966, part of University of Wisconsin System
- **Calendar** semesters
- **Degree** associate
- **Suburban** 86-acre campus with easy access to Milwaukee
- **Coed,** 2,253 undergraduate students, 53% full-time, 56% women, 44% men

Undergraduates 1,188 full-time, 1,065 part-time. Students come from 5 states and territories, 0.8% are from out of state, 2% African American, 2% Asian American or Pacific Islander, 3% Hispanic American, 0.4% Native American, 0.4% international, 7% transferred in.
Freshmen *Admission:* 2,253 enrolled.
Faculty *Total:* 79, 51% full-time, 57% with terminal degrees. *Student/faculty ratio:* 25:1.
Majors Liberal arts and sciences/liberal studies.
Academic Programs *Special study options:* academic remediation for entering students, adult/continuing education programs, advanced placement credit, honors programs, off-campus study, part-time degree program, services for LD students, student-designed majors, summer session for credit.
Library University of Wisconsin-Waukesha Library plus 1 other with 41,000 titles, 300 serial subscriptions.

University of Wisconsin-Waukesha (continued)

Computers on Campus 90 computers available on campus for general student use. Internet access, at least one staffed computer lab available.

Student Life *Housing:* college housing not available. *Activities and Organizations:* drama/theater group, student-run newspaper, radio station, choral group, student government, Student Activities Committee, Philosophy Club, Phi Theta Kappa, Ski Club. *Campus security:* late-night transport/escort service, part-time patrols by trained security personnel.

Athletics Member NJCAA. *Intercollegiate sports:* basketball M/W, golf M/W, soccer M/W, tennis M/W, volleyball W. *Intramural sports:* basketball M, bowling M/W, football M/W, skiing (downhill) M/W, table tennis M/W, volleyball M(c).

Standardized Tests *Required:* ACT (for admission). *Required for some:* SAT I (for admission).

Costs (2001–02) *Tuition:* $107 per credit part-time; state resident $2280 full-time, $107 per credit part-time; nonresident $8410 full-time, $417 per credit part-time.

Applying *Options:* early admission, deferred entrance. *Application fee:* $35. *Required:* high school transcript. *Required for some:* interview. *Application deadlines:* 8/11 (freshmen), 9/1 (transfers). *Notification:* continuous until 8/11 (freshmen).

Admissions Contact Ms. Lori Turner, Assistant Director of Student Services, University of Wisconsin-Waukesha, 1500 North University Drive. *Phone:* 262-521-5210. *Fax:* 262-521-5491. *E-mail:* lturner@uwc.edu.

WAUKESHA COUNTY TECHNICAL COLLEGE
Pewaukee, Wisconsin

- **State and locally supported** 2-year, founded 1923, part of Wisconsin Technical College System
- **Calendar** semesters
- **Degree** certificates, diplomas, and associate
- **Small-town** 137-acre campus with easy access to Milwaukee
- **Coed**

Student Life *Campus security:* patrols by police officers 8 a.m. to 10 p.m.

Athletics Member NJCAA.

Standardized Tests *Required for some:* ACT ASSET.

Financial Aid In 2001, 43 Federal Work-Study jobs (averaging $2877).

Applying *Options:* early admission. *Application fee:* $25. *Required:* high school transcript. *Required for some:* interview.

Admissions Contact Dr. Stanley P. Goran, Director of Admissions, Waukesha County Technical College, 800 Main Street, Pewaukee, WI 53072-4601. *Phone:* 262-691-5271.

WESTERN WISCONSIN TECHNICAL COLLEGE
La Crosse, Wisconsin

- **District-supported** 2-year, founded 1911, part of Wisconsin Technical College System
- **Calendar** semesters
- **Degree** certificates, diplomas, and associate
- **Urban** 10-acre campus
- **Coed,** 5,181 undergraduate students, 41% full-time, 55% women, 45% men

Undergraduates 2,132 full-time, 3,049 part-time. Students come from 3 states and territories, 7% are from out of state, 1% African American, 2% Asian American or Pacific Islander, 0.9% Hispanic American, 1% Native American, 6% transferred in, 2% live on campus.

Freshmen *Admission:* 3,675 applied, 1,975 admitted, 948 enrolled.

Faculty *Total:* 426, 44% full-time. *Student/faculty ratio:* 18:1.

Majors Accounting; agricultural mechanization; auto mechanic/technician; business administration; business administration/management related; business marketing and marketing management; child care/development; child care provider; communications technologies related; computer programming; data processing technology; dental hygiene; electrical/electronic engineering technology; electroencephalograph technology; electromechanical technology; fashion merchandising; finance; fire protection/safety technology; food services technology; graphic design/commercial art/illustration; health facilities administration; heating/air conditioning/refrigeration; human resources management; interior design; law enforcement/police science; marketing operations; mass communications; medical design technology; medical administrative assistant; medical laboratory technician; nursing; occupational therapy; office management; operating room technician; paralegal/legal assistant; physical therapy assistant; precision production trades related; public health related; radiological science; respiratory therapy; retailing operations; retail management; secretarial science; system/networking/LAN/WAN management.

Academic Programs *Special study options:* academic remediation for entering students, accelerated degree program, adult/continuing education programs, advanced placement credit, cooperative education, distance learning, English as a second language, external degree program, internships, off-campus study, part-time degree program, services for LD students, student-designed majors, summer session for credit.

Library Western Wisconsin Technical College Library plus 1 other with 31,243 titles, 313 serial subscriptions, 3,750 audiovisual materials, an OPAC.

Computers on Campus 800 computers available on campus for general student use. A campuswide network can be accessed from student residence rooms and from off campus. Internet access, online (class) registration, at least one staffed computer lab available.

Student Life *Housing Options:* coed. *Activities and Organizations:* student-run newspaper, Wisconsin Marketing Management Association (WMMA), Air Conditioning, Refrigeration Organization (ACRO), Multi Cultural Club, Business Professionals of America (BPA), Advertising Club. *Campus security:* 24-hour emergency response devices and patrols, student patrols, late-night transport/escort service, controlled dormitory access. *Student Services:* personal/psychological counseling.

Athletics Member NJCAA. *Intercollegiate sports:* baseball M, basketball M/W, volleyball W. *Intramural sports:* basketball M/W, volleyball M/W.

Standardized Tests *Recommended:* ACT (for admission).

Costs (2001–02) *Tuition:* state resident $2030 full-time, $67 per credit part-time; nonresident $14,626 full-time, $447 per credit part-time. *Required fees:* $185 full-time. *Room and board:* room only: $1900. *Payment plan:* deferred payment. *Waivers:* senior citizens.

Financial Aid In 2001, 102 Federal Work-Study jobs (averaging $1444).

Applying *Options:* common application, electronic application, early admission. *Application fee:* $30. *Required:* high school transcript. *Recommended:* interview. *Application deadline:* rolling (freshmen), rolling (transfers).

Admissions Contact Ms. Jane Wells, Manager of Admissions, Registration and Records, Western Wisconsin Technical College, PO Box 908, La Crosse, WI 54602-0908. *Phone:* 608-785-9158. *Toll-free phone:* 800-322-9982 (in-state); 800-248-9982 (out-of-state). *Fax:* 608-785-9094. *E-mail:* mildes@wwtc.edu.

WISCONSIN INDIANHEAD TECHNICAL COLLEGE
Shell Lake, Wisconsin

- **District-supported** 2-year, founded 1912, part of Wisconsin Technical College System
- **Calendar** semesters
- **Degree** certificates, diplomas, and associate
- **Endowment** $1.7 million
- **Coed,** 3,765 undergraduate students, 45% full-time, 58% women, 42% men

Undergraduates 0.3% African American, 0.3% Asian American or Pacific Islander, 0.7% Hispanic American, 3% Native American.

Faculty *Total:* 898, 17% full-time. *Student/faculty ratio:* 6:1.

Majors Accounting; administrative/secretarial services; agricultural supplies; architectural engineering technology; business computer programming; business information/data processing related; business systems networking/ telecommunications; child care/guidance; communication systems installation/repair; court reporting; criminal justice/corrections related; electromechanical technology; emergency medical technology; engineering technologies related; finance; heating/air conditioning/refrigeration technology; law enforcement/police science; marketing operations/marketing and distribution related; mechanical engineering technology; medical administrative assistant; occupational therapy; personal services marketing operations; quality control technology; retailing operations; secretarial science.

Costs (2001–02) *Tuition:* state resident $2048 full-time, $64 per credit part-time; nonresident $15,987 full-time, $500 per credit part-time.

Admissions Contact Ms. Mimi Crandall, Dean, Student Services, Wisconsin Indianhead Technical College, 505 Pine Ridge Drive, Shell Lake, WI 54871. *Phone:* 715-468-2815 Ext. 2280. *Toll-free phone:* 800-243-9482. *Fax:* 715-468-2819.

WYOMING

CASPER COLLEGE
Casper, Wyoming

- **District-supported** 2-year, founded 1945, part of Wyoming Community College Commission
- **Calendar** semesters
- **Degree** certificates, diplomas, and associate
- **Small-town** 175-acre campus
- **Endowment** $50,000
- **Coed,** 3,853 undergraduate students, 48% full-time, 60% women, 40% men

Undergraduates 1,853 full-time, 2,000 part-time. Students come from 41 states and territories, 10 other countries, 7% are from out of state, 0.7% African American, 0.2% Asian American or Pacific Islander, 2% Hispanic American, 1% Native American, 0.9% international, 38% transferred in, 16% live on campus.

Freshmen *Admission:* 1,086 applied, 816 admitted, 669 enrolled.

Faculty *Total:* 249, 57% full-time, 13% with terminal degrees. *Student/faculty ratio:* 18:1.

Majors Accounting; agricultural business; agricultural mechanization; agricultural sciences; aircraft pilot (professional); animal sciences; anthropology; applied art; art; auto mechanic/technician; behavioral sciences; biological/physical sciences; biology; botany; business administration; business education; business marketing and marketing management; carpentry; ceramic arts; chemistry; computer engineering technology; computer programming; computer science; construction technology; corrections; criminal justice/law enforcement administration; data processing technology; drafting; early childhood education; earth sciences; ecology; economics; education; electrical/electronic engineering technology; elementary education; emergency medical technology; engineering; English; fire science; French; geology; German; graphic design/commercial art/illustration; history; humanities; industrial arts; industrial radiologic technology; Italian; journalism; law enforcement/police science; legal administrative assistant; liberal arts and sciences/liberal studies; machine technology; mass communications; mathematics; medical technology; mining technology; music; music teacher education; natural sciences; nursing; occupational therapy; paralegal/legal assistant; pharmacy; pharmacy technician/assistant; photography; physical education; physical sciences; physical therapy; physics; political science; practical nurse; pre-engineering; psychology; retail management; secretarial science; social sciences; social work; sociology; Spanish; speech/rhetorical studies; theater arts/drama; veterinary sciences; welding technology; wildlife management; zoology.

Academic Programs *Special study options:* academic remediation for entering students, accelerated degree program, adult/continuing education programs, advanced placement credit, cooperative education, distance learning, English as a second language, external degree program, honors programs, internships, off-campus study, part-time degree program, services for LD students, study abroad, summer session for credit. *ROTC:* Army (c).

Library Goodstein Library with 82,336 titles, 460 serial subscriptions, an OPAC, a Web page.

Computers on Campus 130 computers available on campus for general student use. A campuswide network can be accessed from student residence rooms. At least one staffed computer lab available.

Student Life *Housing Options:* coed. *Activities and Organizations:* drama/theater group, student-run newspaper, choral group, Student Senate, Student Activities Board, Agriculture Club, Theater Club, Phi Theta Kappa. *Campus security:* 24-hour patrols, late-night transport/escort service. *Student Services:* health clinic, personal/psychological counseling, women's center.

Athletics Member NJCAA. *Intercollegiate sports:* basketball M(s)/W(s), volleyball W(s). *Intramural sports:* badminton M/W, basketball M/W, bowling M/W, field hockey M/W, football M/W, golf M/W, gymnastics M/W, racquetball M/W, skiing (cross-country) M/W, skiing (downhill) M/W, soccer M/W, softball M/W, swimming M/W, table tennis M/W, tennis M/W, volleyball M/W, water polo M/W, weight lifting M/W.

Standardized Tests *Required:* SAT I and SAT II or ACT (for placement).

Costs (2002–03) *Tuition:* state resident $1224 full-time, $51 per semester hour part-time; nonresident $3672 full-time, $153 per semester hour part-time. *Required fees:* $144 full-time, $6 per credit. *Room and board:* $2950; room only: $1500. Room and board charges vary according to board plan. *Payment plan:* installment. *Waivers:* children of alumni, senior citizens, and employees or children of employees.

Financial Aid In 2001, 78 Federal Work-Study jobs (averaging $2400).

Applying *Options:* electronic application, early admission. *Required:* high school transcript. *Required for some:* minimum 2.0 GPA. *Application deadlines:* 8/15 (freshmen), 8/15 (transfers). *Notification:* continuous until 8/15 (freshmen).

Admissions Contact Ms. Donna Hoffman, Admission Specialist, Casper College, 125 College Drive, Casper, WY 82601. *Phone:* 307-268-2458. *Toll-free phone:* 800-442-2963. *E-mail:* lking@admin.cc.whecn.edu.

CENTRAL WYOMING COLLEGE
Riverton, Wyoming

- **State and locally supported** 2-year, founded 1966, part of Wyoming Community College Commission
- **Calendar** semesters
- **Degree** certificates and associate
- **Small-town** 200-acre campus
- **Coed,** 1,544 undergraduate students, 42% full-time, 66% women, 34% men

Undergraduates 649 full-time, 895 part-time. Students come from 28 states and territories, 11 other countries, 5% are from out of state, 0.5% African American, 0.4% Asian American or Pacific Islander, 3% Hispanic American, 20% Native American, 1% international, 4% transferred in, 9% live on campus. *Retention:* 42% of 2001 full-time freshmen returned.

Freshmen *Admission:* 300 applied, 300 admitted, 300 enrolled. *Average high school GPA:* 2.95. *Test scores:* SAT verbal scores over 500: 33%; ACT scores over 18: 78%; ACT scores over 24: 30%; ACT scores over 30: 2%.

Faculty *Total:* 109, 34% full-time, 53% with terminal degrees. *Student/faculty ratio:* 14:1.

Majors Accounting; accounting technician; agricultural business; agricultural plant pathology; art; auto mechanic/technician; biology; business administration; child care/guidance; computer maintenance technology; computer science; computer systems networking/telecommunications; criminal justice/law enforcement administration; elementary education; English; environmental science; equestrian studies; general office/clerical; general studies; human services; management information systems/business data processing; music; Native American studies; nursing; operating room technician; physical sciences; pre-law; psychology; radio/television broadcasting technology; secondary education; social sciences; theater arts/drama; welding technology.

Academic Programs *Special study options:* academic remediation for entering students, adult/continuing education programs, advanced placement credit, cooperative education, distance learning, English as a second language, honors programs, independent study, off-campus study, part-time degree program, services for LD students, student-designed majors, summer session for credit.

Library Central Wyoming College Library with 53,909 titles, 233 serial subscriptions, 1,217 audiovisual materials, an OPAC, a Web page.

Computers on Campus 283 computers available on campus for general student use. A campuswide network can be accessed from off campus. Internet access, online (class) registration, at least one staffed computer lab available.

Student Life *Housing Options:* coed. *Activities and Organizations:* drama/theater group, student-run radio station, choral group, Multi-Cultural Club, Criminal Justice Club, Veterans Club, American Indian Science and Engineering Club, Science Club. *Campus security:* 24-hour patrols. *Student Services:* personal/psychological counseling.

Athletics *Intercollegiate sports:* equestrian sports M/W. *Intramural sports:* badminton M/W, basketball M/W, football M/W, skiing (downhill) M/W, soccer M/W, softball M/W, swimming M/W, table tennis M/W, tennis M/W, volleyball M/W, weight lifting M/W.

Standardized Tests *Required for some:* ACT COMPASS. *Recommended:* SAT I or ACT (for placement).

Costs (2002–03) *Tuition:* state resident $1224 full-time, $51 per credit part-time; nonresident $3672 full-time, $153 per credit part-time. Full-time tuition and fees vary according to program and reciprocity agreements. Part-time tuition and fees vary according to course load, program, and reciprocity agreements. *Required fees:* $412 full-time, $17 per credit. *Room and board:* $2750; room only: $1160. Room and board charges vary according to housing facility. *Payment plans:* installment, deferred payment. *Waivers:* employees or children of employees.

Financial Aid In 2001, 40 Federal Work-Study jobs (averaging $3000).

Applying *Options:* early admission, deferred entrance. *Recommended:* high school transcript. *Application deadline:* rolling (freshmen), rolling (transfers).

Admissions Contact Ms. Mary Gores, Admissions Officer, Central Wyoming College, 2660 Peck Avenue, Riverton, WY 82501-2273. *Phone:* 307-855-2119. *Toll-free phone:* 800-735-8418. *Fax:* 307-855-2065. *E-mail:* admit@cwc.cc.wy.us.

Eastern Wyoming College
Torrington, Wyoming

- **State and locally supported** 2-year, founded 1948, part of Wyoming Community College Commission
- **Calendar** semesters
- **Degree** certificates, diplomas, and associate
- **Rural** 40-acre campus
- **Coed,** 1,278 undergraduate students, 30% full-time, 65% women, 35% men

Eastern Wyoming College is a public 2-year community college nestled in the North Platte River Valley in Torrington, Wyoming. The academic opportunities consist of approximately 60 fields of study. There are 460 full-time students, and the student-faculty ratio is 11:1. The College encourages students to visit the campus.

Undergraduates 385 full-time, 893 part-time. Students come from 17 states and territories, 2 other countries, 27% are from out of state, 0.5% African American, 0.5% Asian American or Pacific Islander, 4% Hispanic American, 2% Native American, 0.5% international, 5% transferred in, 26% live on campus. *Retention:* 61% of 2001 full-time freshmen returned.

Freshmen *Admission:* 336 applied, 336 admitted, 176 enrolled. *Average high school GPA:* 2.87. *Test scores:* SAT verbal scores over 500: 33%; SAT math scores over 500: 33%; ACT scores over 18: 61%; SAT verbal scores over 600: 33%; ACT scores over 24: 12%.

Faculty *Total:* 137, 26% full-time. *Student/faculty ratio:* 12:1.

Majors Accounting; agribusiness; agricultural economics; agricultural education; agricultural sciences; animal sciences; art; biology; business administration; business education; business information/data processing related; child care/development; communications; cosmetology; criminal justice studies; economics; elementary education; English; farm/ranch management; foreign languages/literatures; general studies; health/medical preparatory programs related; history; law enforcement/police science; liberal arts and sciences/liberal studies; management information systems/business data processing; mathematical statistics; mathematics; mathematics education; middle school education; music; music teacher education; physical education; political science; pre-dentistry; pre-medicine; pre-pharmacy studies; pre-veterinary studies; psychology; secondary education; secretarial science; sociology; special education; veterinarian assistant; welding technology; wildlife management.

Academic Programs *Special study options:* academic remediation for entering students, accelerated degree program, adult/continuing education programs, advanced placement credit, cooperative education, distance learning, English as a second language, independent study, internships, part-time degree program, services for LD students, student-designed majors, summer session for credit.

Library Eastern Wyoming College Library plus 1 other with 30,694 titles, 105 serial subscriptions, an OPAC, a Web page.

Computers on Campus 72 computers available on campus for general student use. Internet access, at least one staffed computer lab available.

Student Life *Housing Options:* coed, men-only, women-only. *Activities and Organizations:* student-run newspaper, choral group, Criminal Justice Club, Veterinary Technology Club, Student Senate, Music Club, Rodeo Club. *Campus security:* 24-hour emergency response devices, controlled dormitory access. *Student Services:* personal/psychological counseling.

Athletics Member NJCAA. *Intercollegiate sports:* basketball M(s), equestrian sports M(s)/W(s), golf M(s), volleyball W(s). *Intramural sports:* badminton M/W, basketball M/W, bowling M/W, football M, racquetball M/W, softball M/W, table tennis M/W, tennis M/W, volleyball M/W.

Standardized Tests *Recommended:* ACT (for placement).

Costs (2002–03) *Tuition:* state resident $1224 full-time, $51 per credit hour part-time; nonresident $3672 full-time, $153 per credit hour part-time. Full-time tuition and fees vary according to reciprocity agreements. Part-time tuition and fees vary according to reciprocity agreements. *Required fees:* $512 full-time, $16 per credit hour. *Room and board:* $2866. *Payment plan:* installment. *Waivers:* children of alumni, senior citizens, and employees or children of employees.

Financial Aid In 2001, 80 Federal Work-Study jobs (averaging $1500). 60 State and other part-time jobs (averaging $1500).

Applying *Options:* early admission. *Recommended:* high school transcript, minimum 2.0 GPA. *Application deadline:* rolling (freshmen), rolling (transfers).

Admissions Contact Eastern Wyoming College, 3200 West C Street, Torrington, WY 82240. *Phone:* 307-532-8232. *Toll-free phone:* 800-658-3195. *Fax:* 307-532-8222. *E-mail:* bbates@ewc.cc.wy.us.

Laramie County Community College
Cheyenne, Wyoming

- **County-supported** 2-year, founded 1968, part of Wyoming Community College Commission
- **Calendar** semesters
- **Degree** certificates and associate
- **Small-town** 270-acre campus
- **Coed,** 3,863 undergraduate students, 35% full-time, 58% women, 42% men

Undergraduates 1,367 full-time, 2,496 part-time. Students come from 34 states and territories, 4 other countries, 13% transferred in, 2% live on campus.

Freshmen *Admission:* 618 applied, 582 admitted, 299 enrolled.

Faculty *Total:* 246, 27% full-time.

Majors Accounting; agricultural business; agricultural education; agricultural sciences; anthropology; art; auto mechanic/technician; biology; business administration; carpentry; chemistry; child care/development; civil engineering technology; computer science; construction technology; criminal justice/law enforcement administration; developmental/child psychology; early childhood education; economics; education; engineering; engineering technology; English; equestrian studies; fire science; hotel and restaurant management; industrial radiologic technology; information sciences/systems; journalism; law enforcement/police science; legal administrative assistant; liberal arts and sciences/liberal studies; mass communications; mathematics; music; nursing; paralegal/legal assistant; physical education; political science; pre-engineering; psychology; public administration; retail management; secretarial science; sociology; speech/rhetorical studies; theater arts/drama; wildlife management.

Academic Programs *Special study options:* academic remediation for entering students, adult/continuing education programs, advanced placement credit, cooperative education, distance learning, English as a second language, independent study, internships, part-time degree program, services for LD students, summer session for credit.

Library 49,000 titles, 397 serial subscriptions, 3,983 audiovisual materials, an OPAC, a Web page.

Computers on Campus 600 computers available on campus for general student use. A campuswide network can be accessed from off campus. Internet access, at least one staffed computer lab available.

Student Life *Housing Options:* coed. *Activities and Organizations:* drama/theater group, student-run newspaper, choral group. *Campus security:* 24-hour patrols, controlled dormitory access. *Student Services:* personal/psychological counseling.

Athletics *Intramural sports:* basketball M/W, racquetball M/W, soccer M/W, softball M/W, swimming M/W, tennis M/W, track and field M/W, volleyball M/W, water polo M/W.

Standardized Tests *Required:* ACT (for placement).

Costs (2001–02) *Tuition:* state resident $1224 full-time, $51 per credit hour part-time; nonresident $3672 full-time, $153 per credit hour part-time. *Required fees:* $420 full-time, $18 per credit hour. *Room and board:* $4186. *Payment plan:* installment. *Waivers:* senior citizens and employees or children of employees.

Applying *Options:* early admission. *Application fee:* $15. *Required:* high school transcript. *Required for some:* interview. *Application deadline:* rolling (freshmen), rolling (transfers). *Notification:* continuous until 8/31 (freshmen).

Admissions Contact Ms. Molly Christensen, Admissions Coordinator, Laramie County Community College, 1400 East College Drive, Cheyenne, WY 82007-3299. *Phone:* 307-778-5222 Ext. 1221. *Toll-free phone:* 800-522-2993. *Fax:* 307-778-1399.

Northwest College
Powell, Wyoming

- **State and locally supported** 2-year, founded 1946, part of Wyoming Community College Commission
- **Calendar** semesters
- **Degree** certificates and associate
- **Rural** 75-acre campus
- **Endowment** $4.6 million
- **Coed,** 1,576 undergraduate students, 68% full-time, 62% women, 38% men

Undergraduates 1,067 full-time, 509 part-time. Students come from 27 states and territories, 13 other countries, 28% are from out of state, 0.5% African

American, 0.8% Asian American or Pacific Islander, 3% Hispanic American, 1% Native American, 1% international, 9% transferred in, 46% live on campus.

Freshmen *Admission:* 1,035 applied, 855 admitted, 333 enrolled. *Average high school GPA:* 2.97. *Test scores:* ACT scores over 18: 66%; ACT scores over 24: 21%.

Faculty *Total:* 150, 56% full-time. *Student/faculty ratio:* 15:1.

Majors Accounting; agricultural business; agricultural economics; agricultural education; agricultural mechanization; agricultural sciences; agronomy/crop science; animal sciences; art; art education; biological/physical sciences; biology; botany; business administration; business education; business marketing and marketing management; chemistry; drafting; early childhood education; ecology; economics; education; elementary education; English; environmental science; equestrian studies; farm/ranch management; forestry; graphic design/commercial art/illustration; graphic/printing equipment; health education; history; humanities; information sciences/systems; journalism; liberal arts and sciences/liberal studies; mass communications; mathematics; modern languages; music; music teacher education; natural resources management; natural sciences; nursing; photography; physical education; physical sciences; physical therapy; physics; political science; practical nurse; pre-engineering; range management; recreation/leisure facilities management; recreation/leisure studies; science education; secretarial science; social sciences; sociology; speech/rhetorical studies; trade/industrial education; travel/tourism management; welding technology; wildlife management.

Academic Programs *Special study options:* academic remediation for entering students, adult/continuing education programs, advanced placement credit, cooperative education, distance learning, double majors, English as a second language, external degree program, freshman honors college, honors programs, internships, part-time degree program, services for LD students, study abroad, summer session for credit.

Library John Taggart Hinckley Library plus 1 other with 49,892 titles, 475 serial subscriptions, 4,648 audiovisual materials, an OPAC, a Web page.

Computers on Campus 300 computers available on campus for general student use. A campuswide network can be accessed from off campus. Internet access, at least one staffed computer lab available.

Student Life *Housing:* on-campus residence required for freshman year. *Options:* coed. *Activities and Organizations:* drama/theater group, student-run newspaper, choral group. *Campus security:* 24-hour emergency response devices and patrols, controlled dormitory access. *Student Services:* health clinic, personal/psychological counseling.

Athletics Member NJCAA. *Intercollegiate sports:* basketball M(s)/W(s), equestrian sports M(s)/W(s), riflery M/W, volleyball W(s), wrestling M(s). *Intramural sports:* archery M/W, badminton M/W, baseball M/W, basketball M/W, bowling M/W, cross-country running M/W, football M/W, golf M/W, gymnastics M/W, racquetball M/W, riflery M/W, sailing M/W, skiing (cross-country) M/W, skiing (downhill) M/W, soccer M/W, softball M/W, squash M/W, table tennis M/W, tennis M/W, volleyball M/W, weight lifting M/W.

Standardized Tests *Required for some:* SAT I or ACT (for admission).

Costs (2001–02) *Tuition:* state resident $1176 full-time, $49 per credit part-time; nonresident $3528 full-time, $147 per credit part-time. Full-time tuition and fees vary according to program and reciprocity agreements. Part-time tuition and fees vary according to program and reciprocity agreements. *Required fees:* $484 full-time, $18 per credit. *Room and board:* $3194. Room and board charges vary according to board plan. *Payment plan:* installment. *Waivers:* children of alumni, senior citizens, and employees or children of employees.

Financial Aid In 2001, 107 Federal Work-Study jobs (averaging $1200). 245 State and other part-time jobs (averaging $1200).

Applying *Options:* common application, electronic application, early admission, deferred entrance. *Application fee:* $10. *Required:* high school transcript. *Recommended:* minimum 2.0 GPA. *Application deadlines:* 8/15 (freshmen), 8/1 (transfers). *Notification:* continuous (freshmen).

Admissions Contact Mr. William Kuba, Director of Enrollment Services, Northwest College, 231 West Sixth Street, Powell, WY 82435. *Phone:* 307-754-6101. *Toll-free phone:* 800-442-4692. *Fax:* 307-754-6700. *E-mail:* admissions@nwc.cc.wy.us.

SHERIDAN COLLEGE

Sheridan, Wyoming

- **State and locally supported** 2-year, founded 1948, part of Wyoming Community College Commission
- **Calendar** semesters
- **Degree** certificates and associate
- **Small-town** 64-acre campus
- **Coed,** 2,730 undergraduate students, 35% full-time, 58% women, 42% men

Undergraduates 963 full-time, 1,767 part-time. Students come from 15 states and territories, 6 other countries, 6% are from out of state, 1% African American, 0.6% Asian American or Pacific Islander, 2% Hispanic American, 2% Native American, 0.9% international, 3% transferred in, 20% live on campus.

Freshmen *Admission:* 300 admitted, 300 enrolled.

Faculty *Total:* 201, 36% full-time, 5% with terminal degrees. *Student/faculty ratio:* 14:1.

Majors Agricultural business; agricultural sciences; art; biological/physical sciences; biology; business; business administration; computer programming (specific applications); computer software and media applications related; computer systems networking/telecommunications; criminal justice/law enforcement administration; data entry/microcomputer applications; dental hygiene; diesel engine mechanic; drafting; education; elementary education; engineering; engineering technology; English; foreign languages/literatures; general studies; health/physical education; heavy equipment maintenance; history; hospitality management; humanities; information sciences/systems; law enforcement/police science; liberal arts and sciences/liberal studies; machine technology; mathematics; music; nursing; respiratory therapy; secretarial science; sign language interpretation; social sciences; system/networking/LAN/WAN management; Web/multimedia management/webmaster; Web page, digital/multimedia and information resources design; welding technology.

Academic Programs *Special study options:* academic remediation for entering students, adult/continuing education programs, advanced placement credit, cooperative education, distance learning, double majors, English as a second language, independent study, internships, off-campus study, part-time degree program, services for LD students, student-designed majors, summer session for credit.

Library Griffith Memorial Library plus 1 other with 46,589 titles, 545 serial subscriptions, 17,122 audiovisual materials, an OPAC, a Web page.

Computers on Campus 200 computers available on campus for general student use. A campuswide network can be accessed from student residence rooms and from off campus. Internet access, at least one staffed computer lab available.

Student Life *Housing Options:* coed, women-only, disabled students. *Activities and Organizations:* drama/theater group, student-run newspaper, choral group, student government, Phi Theta Kappa, Art Club, Nursing Club, Police Science Club. *Campus security:* 24-hour emergency response devices, student patrols, controlled dormitory access, night patrols by certified officers. *Student Services:* personal/psychological counseling.

Athletics Member NJCAA. *Intercollegiate sports:* basketball M(s)/W(s), volleyball W(s). *Intramural sports:* basketball M/W, bowling M/W, soccer M/W, softball M/W, table tennis M/W, tennis M/W, volleyball M/W.

Costs (2002–03) *Tuition:* state resident $1224 full-time, $51 per credit hour part-time; nonresident $3672 full-time, $153 per credit hour part-time. Full-time tuition and fees vary according to course load and reciprocity agreements. Part-time tuition and fees vary according to reciprocity agreements. *Required fees:* $360 full-time, $15 per credit hour. *Room and board:* $3620. Room and board charges vary according to board plan and housing facility. *Payment plans:* installment, deferred payment. *Waivers:* senior citizens and employees or children of employees.

Financial Aid In 2001, 85 Federal Work-Study jobs (averaging $1057).

Applying *Options:* electronic application, early admission, deferred entrance. *Required for some:* high school transcript. *Recommended:* high school transcript. *Application deadline:* rolling (freshmen), rolling (transfers). *Notification:* continuous (freshmen).

Admissions Contact Mr. Zane Garstad, Admissions Counselor, Sheridan College, PO Box 1500, Sheridan, WY 82801-1500. *Phone:* 307-674-6446 Ext. 6318. *Toll-free phone:* 800-913-9139 Ext. 6138. *Fax:* 307-674-7205. *E-mail:* admissions@sc.cc.wy.us.

WESTERN WYOMING COMMUNITY COLLEGE

Rock Springs, Wyoming

- **State and locally supported** 2-year, founded 1959
- **Calendar** semesters
- **Degree** certificates, diplomas, and associate
- **Small-town** 10-acre campus
- **Coed,** 2,612 undergraduate students, 36% full-time, 64% women, 36% men

Western Wyoming Community College is a public, 2-year, comprehensive community college located in Rock Springs, Wyoming. This rural campus provides easy access to a variety of outdoor recreational opportunities, and its location on I-80 makes travel to metropolitan areas such as Denver and Salt Lake City very easy. This modern, fully enclosed campus is designed to provide comfort and safety for college students as well as up-to-date equipment and facilities. The small student-teacher ratio of 15:1 ensures that students get

Western Wyoming Community College (continued)
individualized attention in their classes. Students major in transfer programs as well as occupational programs designed to lead directly to the workforce. Western is committed to both quality and success.

Undergraduates Students come from 25 states and territories, 11 other countries, 0.5% African American, 0.9% Asian American or Pacific Islander, 5% Hispanic American, 0.6% Native American, 2% international, 12% live on campus. *Retention:* 53% of 2001 full-time freshmen returned.
Freshmen *Admission:* 866 applied, 687 admitted. *Average high school GPA:* 2.94. *Test scores:* ACT scores over 18: 90%; ACT scores over 24: 10%.
Faculty *Total:* 183, 34% full-time. *Student/faculty ratio:* 15:1.
Majors Accounting; anthropology; art; auto mechanic/technician; biological/physical sciences; biology; business administration; business marketing and marketing management; chemistry; computer programming (specific applications); computer science related; computer software and media applications related; computer typography/composition; construction technology; criminal justice/law enforcement administration; dance; data processing technology; education; electrical/electronic engineering technology; elementary education; engineering; English; French; geology; health science; history; humanities; industrial arts; industrial radiologic technology; information sciences/systems; information technology; instrumentation technology; journalism; law enforcement/police science; legal administrative assistant; liberal arts and sciences/liberal studies; machine technology; mass communications; mathematics; medical administrative assistant; medical assistant; medical laboratory technology; mining technology; music; natural sciences; nursing; physical education; physical sciences; political science; practical nurse; pre-engineering; psychology; respiratory therapy; secretarial science; social sciences; sociology; Spanish; system/networking/LAN/WAN management; theater arts/drama; welding technology.
Academic Programs *Special study options:* academic remediation for entering students, adult/continuing education programs, advanced placement credit, cooperative education, distance learning, English as a second language, freshman honors college, honors programs, independent study, internships, part-time degree program, services for LD students, summer session for credit.
Library Hay Library with 412 serial subscriptions.
Computers on Campus 120 computers available on campus for general student use. A campuswide network can be accessed from off campus. Internet access, online (class) registration, at least one staffed computer lab available.
Student Life *Housing Options:* coed. *Activities and Organizations:* drama/theater group, choral group, Phi Theta Kappa, Desert Voice, Fellowship of Christian Athletes, associated student government, LDSSA. *Campus security:* 24-hour emergency response devices, late-night transport/escort service, controlled dormitory access. *Student Services:* personal/psychological counseling, women's center.
Athletics Member NJCAA. *Intercollegiate sports:* basketball M(s)/W(s), wrestling M(s). *Intramural sports:* archery M/W, basketball M, bowling M/W, cross-country running M/W, football M, golf M, skiing (downhill) M/W, soccer M/W, softball M/W, table tennis M/W, tennis M/W, volleyball M/W, weight lifting M/W.
Standardized Tests *Required:* ACT ASSET. *Recommended:* ACT (for placement).
Costs (2002–03) *Tuition:* state resident $1474 full-time, $62 per hour part-time; nonresident $3920 full-time, $164 per hour part-time. Part-time tuition and fees vary according to course load and reciprocity agreements. *Room and board:* $2826; room only: $1330. Room and board charges vary according to board plan and housing facility. *Payment plan:* installment. *Waivers:* senior citizens and employees or children of employees.
Financial Aid In 2001, 15 Federal Work-Study jobs (averaging $1500).
Applying *Options:* common application, early admission, deferred entrance. *Required:* high school transcript. *Application deadline:* rolling (freshmen), rolling (transfers).
Admissions Contact Ms. Laurie Watkins, Assistant Director of Admissions, Western Wyoming Community College, 2500 College Drive, PO Box 428, Rock Springs, WY 82902-0428. *Phone:* 307-382-1647. *Fax:* 307-382-1636. *E-mail:* jfreeze@wwcc.cc.wy.us.

Wyoming Technical Institute
Laramie, Wyoming

- **Proprietary** 2-year, founded 1966
- **Calendar** 9-month program
- **Degree** associate
- **Rural** campus
- **Coed, primarily men,** 774 undergraduate students

Faculty *Total:* 72, 1% full-time. *Student/faculty ratio:* 11:1.
Majors Auto mechanic/technician.
Academic Programs *Special study options:* services for LD students.
Library Wyoming Technical Institute Library.
Computers on Campus 42 computers available on campus for general student use. At least one staffed computer lab available.
Student Life *Student Services:* personal/psychological counseling.
Athletics *Intercollegiate sports:* basketball W, bowling W. *Intramural sports:* softball M, volleyball M.
Costs (2001–02) *Tuition:* $16,754 full-time. *Room only:* $2475.
Financial Aid In 2001, 68 Federal Work-Study jobs (averaging $823).
Applying *Options:* common application. *Application fee:* $100. *Required:* high school transcript. *Application deadline:* rolling (freshmen).
Admissions Contact Mr. Troy Chaney, Director of Admissions, Wyoming Technical Institute, 4373 North Third Street, Laramie, WY 82072-9519. *Phone:* 307-742-3776. *Toll-free phone:* 800-521-7158.

AMERICAN SAMOA

American Samoa Community College
Pago Pago, American Samoa

Admissions Contact Mrs. Sina P. Ward, Registrar, American Samoa Community College, PO Box 2609, Pago Pago, AS 96799-2609. *Phone:* 684-699-1141.

FEDERATED STATES OF MICRONESIA

College of Micronesia-FSM
Kolonia Pohnpei, Federated States of Micronesia

Admissions Contact Mr. Wilson J. Kalio, Coordinator of Admissions and Records, College of Micronesia-FSM, PO Box 159, Kolonia Pohnpei, FM 96941-0159. *Phone:* 691-320-2480 Ext. 6200. *Fax:* 691-320-2479.

GUAM

Guam Community College
Barrigada, Guam

- **Territory-supported** 2-year, founded 1977
- **Calendar** semesters
- **Degree** certificates, diplomas, and associate
- **Suburban** 22-acre campus
- **Endowment** $6.4 million
- **Coed,** 1,754 undergraduate students, 22% full-time, 60% women, 40% men

Undergraduates 394 full-time, 1,360 part-time. Students come from 10 other countries, 0.3% African American, 91% Asian American or Pacific Islander, 0.6% Hispanic American, 0.1% Native American, 3% international.
Freshmen *Admission:* 378 applied, 375 admitted, 158 enrolled.
Faculty *Total:* 94.
Majors Accounting; architectural engineering technology; auto mechanic/technician; business administration; business marketing and marketing management; child care/development; civil engineering technology; computer programming, vendor/product certification; computer science; corrections; criminal justice/law enforcement administration; early childhood education; education; electrical/electronic engineering technology; fire science; hospitality management; hospitality/recreation marketing operations; hotel and restaurant management; hotel/motel services marketing operations; law enforcement/police science; marketing research; medical assistant; operations management; safety/security technology; secretarial science; sign language interpretation; tourism promotion operations; travel services marketing operations; travel/tourism management; vehicle parts/accessories marketing operations.
Academic Programs *Special study options:* academic remediation for entering students, adult/continuing education programs, cooperative education, double

majors, English as a second language, honors programs, independent study, internships, off-campus study, part-time degree program, services for LD students, summer session for credit. *ROTC:* Army (c).
Library 15,806 titles, 375 serial subscriptions, 1,567 audiovisual materials, an OPAC.
Computers on Campus 220 computers available on campus for general student use. Internet access, at least one staffed computer lab available.
Student Life *Housing:* college housing not available. *Activities and Organizations:* Council of Post Secondary Student Association (COPSA), Phi Theta Kappa. *Campus security:* 12-hour patrols by trained security personnel. *Student Services:* health clinic, personal/psychological counseling.
Costs (2001–02) *Tuition:* territory resident $1200 full-time, $50 per semester hour part-time; nonresident $1800 full-time, $75 per semester hour part-time. *Required fees:* $110 full-time. *Waivers:* senior citizens.
Financial Aid In 2001, 83 Federal Work-Study jobs (averaging $940).
Applying *Options:* common application, early admission. *Required:* high school transcript. *Application deadline:* rolling (freshmen). *Notification:* continuous (freshmen).
Admissions Contact Ms. Deborah D. Leon Guerrero, Registrar, Guam Community College, PO Box 23069, Sesame Street. *Phone:* 671-735-5531. *Fax:* 671-734-0540. *E-mail:* deborah@guamcc.net.

NORTHERN MARIANA ISLANDS

NORTHERN MARIANAS COLLEGE
Saipan, Northern Mariana Islands

Admissions Contact Ms. Janice Tenorio, Director of Admissions and Records, Northern Marianas College, PO Box 1250, Saipan, MP 96950-1250. *Phone:* 670-234-3690 Ext. 1400. *Fax:* 670-234-0759.

PUERTO RICO

HUERTAS JUNIOR COLLEGE
Caguas, Puerto Rico

Admissions Contact Ms. Barbara Hassim, Director of Admissions, Huertas Junior College, PO Box 8429, Caguas, PR 00726. *Phone:* 787-743-2156 Ext. 23.

HUMACAO COMMUNITY COLLEGE
Humacao, Puerto Rico

- **Private** 2-year
- **Calendar** trimesters
- **Degree** certificates, diplomas, and associate
- 403 undergraduate students, 76% full-time

Financial Aid In 2001, 64 Federal Work-Study jobs (averaging $546).
Applying *Options:* early admission. *Application fee:* $30. *Required:* high school transcript.
Admissions Contact Ms. Paula Serrano, Director of Admissions, Humacao Community College, PO Box 9139, Humacao, PR 00792. *Phone:* 787-852-2525.

INSTITUTO COMERCIAL DE PUERTO RICO JUNIOR COLLEGE
San Juan, Puerto Rico

- **Proprietary** 2-year, founded 1946
- **Calendar** trimesters
- **Degree** certificates, diplomas, and associate
- **Urban** 1-acre campus
- **Coed,** 1,562 undergraduate students, 90% full-time, 65% women, 35% men

Undergraduates 1,399 full-time, 163 part-time. 1% are from out of state.
Freshmen *Admission:* 1,637 applied, 820 admitted, 679 enrolled.
Faculty *Total:* 94, 51% full-time. *Student/faculty ratio:* 20:1.
Majors Accounting; business administration; hotel and restaurant management; information sciences/systems; secretarial science.
Academic Programs *Special study options:* adult/continuing education programs, double majors, English as a second language, independent study, part-time degree program. *ROTC:* Army (c).
Library Pedro Negron Library plus 1 other with 40,858 titles, 173 serial subscriptions, 320 audiovisual materials.
Computers on Campus 76 computers available on campus for general student use. At least one staffed computer lab available.
Student Life *Housing:* college housing not available. *Campus security:* 24-hour emergency response devices. *Student Services:* personal/psychological counseling.
Costs (2002–03) *Tuition:* $4320 full-time, $120 per credit part-time. *Required fees:* $150 full-time.
Applying *Options:* common application, early admission. *Application fee:* $25. *Required:* high school transcript, interview, proficiency in Spanish. *Recommended:* letters of recommendation. *Application deadline:* 8/15 (freshmen). *Notification:* continuous (freshmen).
Admissions Contact Admissions Office, Instituto Comercial de Puerto Rico Junior College, PO Box 190304, San Juan, PR 00919-0304. *Phone:* 787-753-6335. *Fax:* 787-763-7249. *E-mail:* la_f_mena@icpr.org.

INSTITUTO FONTECHA
San Juan, Puerto Rico

Admissions Contact PO Box 00906-6582, San Juan, PR 00906-6582.

INTERNATIONAL JUNIOR COLLEGE
San Juan, Puerto Rico

Admissions Contact PO Box 8245, San Juan, PR 00910.

NATIONAL COLLEGE OF BUSINESS & TECHNOLOGY
Bayamon, Puerto Rico

Admissions Contact PO Box 2036, Bayamon, PR 00960. *Toll-free phone:* 800-780-5188.

RAMIREZ COLLEGE OF BUSINESS AND TECHNOLOGY
San Juan, Puerto Rico

Admissions Contact Mrs. Evelyn Mercado, Director of Admissions, Ramirez College of Business and Technology, PO Box 8340, San Juan, PR 00910-0340. *Phone:* 787-763-3120.

TECHNOLOGICAL COLLEGE OF SAN JUAN
San Juan, Puerto Rico

- **City-supported** 2-year, founded 1971
- **Calendar** semesters
- **Degree** certificates, diplomas, and associate
- **Urban** 5-acre campus
- **Endowment** $14.0 million
- **Coed**

Faculty *Student/faculty ratio:* 13:1.
Student Life *Campus security:* 24-hour patrols.
Standardized Tests *Required for some:* SAT I (for admission).
Financial Aid In 2001, 127 Federal Work-Study jobs (averaging $618). 12 State and other part-time jobs (averaging $2991).
Applying *Options:* common application. *Application fee:* $15. *Required:* high school transcript, minimum 2.0 GPA, medical history. *Required for some:* letters of recommendation, interview.
Admissions Contact Mrs. Nilsa E. Rivera-Almenas, Director of Enrollment Management, Technological College of San Juan, 180 Jose R. Oliver Street, Tres Monjitas Industrial Park, San Juan, PR 00918. *Phone:* 787-250-7111 Ext. 2271. *Fax:* 787-250-7395.

UNIVERSITY OF PUERTO RICO AT CAROLINA
Carolina, Puerto Rico

Admissions Contact Mrs. Ivonne Calderon, Admissions Officer, University of Puerto Rico at Carolina, PO Box 4800, Carolina, PR 00984-4800. *Phone:* 787-257-0000 Ext. 3347.

MARSHALL ISLANDS

COLLEGE OF THE MARSHALL ISLANDS
Majuro, Marshall Islands

Admissions Contact PO Box 1258, Majuro, MH 96960, Marshall Islands.

PALAU

PALAU COMMUNITY COLLEGE
Koror, Palau

- **Territory-supported** 2-year, founded 1969
- **Calendar** semesters
- **Degree** certificates and associate
- **Small-town** 30-acre campus
- **Endowment** $297,156
- **Coed,** 582 undergraduate students, 69% full-time, 54% women, 46% men

Undergraduates 399 full-time, 183 part-time. Students come from 1 other state, 0.2% African American, 99% Asian American or Pacific Islander, 20% live on campus. *Retention:* 64% of 2001 full-time freshmen returned.

Freshmen *Admission:* 195 applied, 162 admitted. *Average high school GPA:* 2.62.

Faculty *Total:* 44, 68% full-time, 2% with terminal degrees. *Student/faculty ratio:* 12:1.

Majors Accounting; agricultural sciences; auto mechanic/technician; business education; carpentry; conservation and renewable natural resources related; construction technology; education; electrical/electronic engineering technology; hotel and restaurant management; law enforcement/police science; liberal arts and sciences/liberal studies; nursing; secretarial science.

Academic Programs *Special study options:* academic remediation for entering students, cooperative education, distance learning, double majors, English as a second language, internships, part-time degree program, summer session for credit.

Library Palau Community College Library with 15,101 titles, 666 serial subscriptions, 247 audiovisual materials, an OPAC.

Computers on Campus 52 computers available on campus for general student use.

Student Life *Housing:* on-campus residence required through sophomore year. *Options:* coed, men-only. *Activities and Organizations:* Yapese Student Organization, Chuukes Student Organization, Palauans Student Organization, Environmental Club, Writing Club. *Campus security:* late-night transport/escort service, evening patrols by trained security personnel. *Student Services:* health clinic, personal/psychological counseling, legal services.

Athletics Member NCAA. *Intramural sports:* baseball M, basketball M, softball M/W, table tennis M/W, volleyball M/W, weight lifting M, wrestling M.

Costs (2002–03) *Tuition:* area resident $1800 full-time, $60 per credit part-time. Full-time tuition and fees vary according to course load. Part-time tuition and fees vary according to course load. *Required fees:* $450 full-time, $225 per term part-time. *Room and board:* $2352; room only: $588. Room and board charges vary according to housing facility. *Payment plan:* installment. *Waivers:* employees or children of employees.

Financial Aid In 2001, 200 Federal Work-Study jobs (averaging $200).

Applying *Options:* early admission, deferred entrance. *Application fee:* $10. *Required:* high school transcript, minimum 2.00 GPA. *Application deadline:* 8/29 (freshmen), rolling (out-of-state freshmen). *Notification:* continuous (freshmen), continuous (out-of-state freshmen).

Admissions Contact Ms. Elsie Skang, Admissions Counselor, Palau Community College, PO Box 9, Koror, PW 96940-0009, Palau. *Phone:* 680-488-2470 Ext. 265. *Fax:* 680-488-4468. *E-mail:* admsfaid@belau.org.

SWITZERLAND

SCHILLER INTERNATIONAL UNIVERSITY
Engelberg, Switzerland

- **Independent** 2-year, founded 1988, part of Schiller International University
- **Calendar** semesters
- **Degree** associate
- **Urban** campus with easy access to Zurich
- **Coed,** 60 undergraduate students

Faculty *Total:* 11, 55% full-time.

Majors Hotel and restaurant management; international business; travel/tourism management.

Academic Programs *Special study options:* adult/continuing education programs, advanced placement credit, cooperative education, internships, student-designed majors, study abroad, summer session for credit.

Library 1,423 titles, 17 serial subscriptions.

Computers on Campus 7 computers available on campus for general student use.

Student Life *Housing Options:* coed. *Activities and Organizations:* student-run newspaper, student government, student newspaper. *Campus security:* 24-hour emergency response devices. *Student Services:* personal/psychological counseling.

Athletics *Intramural sports:* skiing (cross-country) M/W, skiing (downhill) M/W, swimming M/W, tennis M/W.

Standardized Tests *Required for some:* English Placement Exam.

Costs (2002–03) *Comprehensive fee:* 38,400 Swiss francs includes full-time tuition (22,000 Swiss francs) and room and board (16,400 Swiss francs).

Financial Aid *Financial aid deadline:* 6/1.

Applying *Options:* common application, deferred entrance. *Application fee:* $35. *Application deadline:* rolling (freshmen), rolling (transfers).

Admissions Contact David Edwards, Director of Studies, Schiller International University, Dorfstrasse 40, CH 6390 Engelberg, Switzerland. *Phone:* 41-(41) 639 7474. *Fax:* 41-(41) 639 7475.

Quick-Reference College Search Indexes

Associate Degree Programs at Two-Year Colleges

ACCOUNTING

Abraham Baldwin Ag Coll (GA)
Academy Coll (MN)
Adirondack Comm Coll (NY)
AIB Coll of Business (IA)
Aims Comm Coll (CO)
Albuquerque Tech Vocational Inst (NM)
Alexandria Tech Coll (MN)
Allan Hancock Coll (CA)
Allegany Coll of Maryland (MD)
Allen County Comm Coll (KS)
Allentown Business School (PA)
Alpena Comm Coll (MI)
Alvin Comm Coll (TX)
Amarillo Coll (TX)
American River Coll (CA)
Andover Coll (ME)
Angelina Coll (TX)
Anne Arundel Comm Coll (MD)
Anoka-Hennepin Tech Coll (MN)
Anoka-Ramsey Comm Coll (MN)
Arapahoe Comm Coll (CO)
Ashland Comm Coll (KY)
Asnuntuck Comm Coll (CT)
Athens Tech Coll (GA)
Atlanta Metropolitan Coll (GA)
Atlantic Cape Comm Coll (NJ)
Augusta Tech Coll (GA)
Austin Comm Coll (TX)
Bacone Coll (OK)
Bainbridge Coll (GA)
Bakersfield Coll (CA)
Baltimore City Comm Coll (MD)
Barstow Coll (CA)
Bay de Noc Comm Coll (MI)
Bay State Coll (MA)
Beaufort County Comm Coll (NC)
Bellevue Comm Coll (WA)
Belmont Tech Coll (OH)
Bergen Comm Coll (NJ)
Berkeley Coll (NJ)
Berkeley Coll (NY)
Berkeley Coll-Westchester Campus (NY)
Berkshire Comm Coll (MA)
Bessemer State Tech Coll (AL)
Black Hawk Coll, Moline (IL)
Blackhawk Tech Coll (WI)
Blair Coll (CO)
Blinn Coll (TX)
Blue Ridge Comm Coll (VA)
Borough of Manhattan Comm Coll of City U of NY (NY)
Bowling Green State U-Firelands Coll (OH)
Bradford School (OH)
Brevard Comm Coll (FL)
Briarwood Coll (CT)
Bristol Comm Coll (MA)
Bronx Comm Coll of City U of NY (NY)
Brookdale Comm Coll (NJ)
Broome Comm Coll (NY)
The Brown Mackie Coll (KS)
The Brown Mackie Coll–Olathe Campus (KS)
Bryant & Stratton Business Inst, Albany (NY)
Bryant & Stratton Business Inst, Buffalo (NY)
Bryant & Stratton Business Inst, Lackawanna (NY)
Bryant & Stratton Business Inst, Rochester (NY)
Bryant & Stratton Business Inst, Rochester (NY)
Bryant & Stratton Business Inst, Eastern Hills Cmps (NY)
Bryant & Stratton Business Inst (NY)
Bryant and Stratton Coll, Parma (OH)
Bryant and Stratton Coll, Willoughby Hills (OH)
Bryant and Stratton Coll (WI)
Bryant and Stratton Coll, Virginia Beach (VA)
Bucks County Comm Coll (PA)
Bunker Hill Comm Coll (MA)
Burlington County Coll (NJ)
Butler County Comm Coll (PA)
Butte Coll (CA)
Caldwell Comm Coll and Tech Inst (NC)
Cambria County Area Comm Coll (PA)
Cambria-Rowe Business Coll (PA)
Camden County Coll (NJ)
Cañada Coll (CA)
Cape Cod Comm Coll (MA)
Capital Comm Coll (CT)
Carl Sandburg Coll (IL)
Carroll Comm Coll (MD)
Casper Coll (WY)
Cayuga County Comm Coll (NY)
Cecil Comm Coll (MD)
Cedar Valley Coll (TX)
Central Arizona Coll (AZ)
Central Carolina Comm Coll (NC)
Central Carolina Tech Coll (SC)
Central Comm Coll–Columbus Campus (NE)
Central Comm Coll–Grand Island Campus (NE)
Central Comm Coll–Hastings Campus (NE)
Central Georgia Tech Coll (GA)
Central Lakes Coll (MN)
Central Maine Tech Coll (ME)
Central Ohio Tech Coll (OH)
Central Oregon Comm Coll (OR)
Central Pennsylvania Coll (PA)
Central Piedmont Comm Coll (NC)
Central Virginia Comm Coll (VA)
Central Wyoming Coll (WY)
Century Comm and Tech Coll (MN)
Cerritos Coll (CA)
Chabot Coll (CA)
Chaffey Coll (CA)
Chaparral Coll (AZ)
Charter Coll (AK)
Chattahoochee Tech Coll (GA)
Chattanooga State Tech Comm Coll (TN)
Chemeketa Comm Coll (OR)
Chesapeake Coll (MD)
Chipola Jr Coll (FL)
Chippewa Valley Tech Coll (WI)
Churchman Business School (PA)
Cincinnati State Tech and Comm Coll (OH)
Cisco Jr Coll (TX)
City Coll of San Francisco (CA)
City Colls of Chicago, Harry S Truman Coll (IL)
City Colls of Chicago, Malcolm X Coll (IL)
City Colls of Chicago, Richard J Daley Coll (IL)
City Colls of Chicago, Wilbur Wright Coll (IL)
Clackamas Comm Coll (OR)
Clark Coll (WA)
Cleveland Comm Coll (NC)
Clinton Comm Coll (NY)
Clovis Comm Coll (NM)
Coahoma Comm Coll (MS)
Coastal Bend Coll (TX)
Coastal Carolina Comm Coll (NC)
Coffeyville Comm Coll (KS)
Colby Comm Coll (KS)
Coll of Alameda (CA)
Coll of DuPage (IL)
Coll of Lake County (IL)
Coll of Marin (CA)
Coll of Southern Idaho (ID)
Coll of Southern Maryland (MD)
Coll of the Canyons (CA)
Coll of the Sequoias (CA)
Coll of the Siskiyous (CA)
Colorado Mountn Coll, Alpine Cmps (CO)
Colorado Mountn Coll (CO)
Colorado Mountn Coll, Timberline Cmps (CO)
Columbia-Greene Comm Coll (NY)
Columbia State Comm Coll (TN)
Columbus State Comm Coll (OH)
Columbus Tech Coll (GA)
Commonwealth Business Coll, Merrillville (IN)
Comm Coll of Aurora (CO)
The Comm Coll of Baltimore County–Catonsville Campus (MD)
Comm Coll of Beaver County (PA)
Comm Coll of Denver (CO)
Comm Coll of Rhode Island (RI)
Comm Coll of Southern Nevada (NV)
Comm Coll of Vermont (VT)
Compton Comm Coll (CA)
Connors State Coll (OK)
Consolidated School of Business, Lancaster (PA)
Consolidated School of Business, York (PA)
Corning Comm Coll (NY)
Cowley County Comm Coll and Voc-Tech School (KS)
Crafton Hills Coll (CA)
Craven Comm Coll (NC)
Cumberland County Coll (NJ)
Cuyahoga Comm Coll (OH)
Cuyamaca Coll (CA)
Cypress Coll (CA)
Danville Area Comm Coll (IL)
Danville Comm Coll (VA)
Darton Coll (GA)
Davis Coll (OH)
Daytona Beach Comm Coll (FL)
De Anza Coll (CA)
Delaware Tech & Comm Coll, Jack F Owens Cmps (DE)
Delaware Tech & Comm Coll, Stanton/ Wilmington Cmps (DE)
Delaware Tech & Comm Coll, Terry Cmps (DE)
Delgado Comm Coll (LA)
Del Mar Coll (TX)
Delta Coll (MI)
Des Moines Area Comm Coll (IA)
Dixie State Coll of Utah (UT)
Dodge City Comm Coll (KS)
Donnelly Coll (KS)
Douglas MacArthur State Tech Coll (AL)
Draughons Jr Coll (KY)
Draughons Jr Coll, Clarksville (TN)
Draughons Jr Coll, Nashville (TN)
DuBois Business Coll (PA)
Duff's Business Inst (PA)
Durham Tech Comm Coll (NC)
Dutchess Comm Coll (NY)
East Central Coll (MO)
East Central Comm Coll (MS)
Eastern Idaho Tech Coll (ID)
Eastern Oklahoma State Coll (OK)
Eastern Wyoming Coll (WY)
Eastfield Coll (TX)
East Mississippi Comm Coll (MS)
ECPI Coll of Technology, Newport News (VA)
ECPI Coll of Technology, Virginia Beach (VA)
ECPI Tech Coll, Richmond (VA)
ECPI Tech Coll, Roanoke (VA)
Edgecombe Comm Coll (NC)
Edison Comm Coll (FL)
Edison State Comm Coll (OH)
Education Direct (PA)
Elaine P. Nunez Comm Coll (LA)
El Centro Coll (TX)
Ellsworth Comm Coll (IA)
Empire Coll (CA)
Erie Business Center South (PA)
Essex County Coll (NJ)
Eugenio María de Hostos Comm Coll of City U of NY (NY)
Everest Coll (AZ)
Everett Comm Coll (WA)
Evergreen Valley Coll (CA)
Fayetteville Tech Comm Coll (NC)
Feather River Comm Coll District (CA)
Finger Lakes Comm Coll (NY)
Fiorello H LaGuardia Comm Coll of City U of NY (NY)
Fisher Coll (MA)
Flathead Valley Comm Coll (MT)
Florence-Darlington Tech Coll (SC)
Florida Comm Coll at Jacksonville (FL)
Florida National Coll (FL)
Floyd Coll (GA)
Foothill Coll (CA)
Forsyth Tech Comm Coll (NC)
Fort Berthold Comm Coll (ND)
Fort Scott Comm Coll (KS)
Frederick Comm Coll (MD)
Fullerton Coll (CA)
Fulton-Montgomery Comm Coll (NY)
Gallipolis Career Coll (OH)
Garden City Comm Coll (KS)
Gaston Coll (NC)
GateWay Comm Coll (AZ)
Gateway Comm Coll (CT)
Gateway Tech Coll (WI)
Gavilan Coll (CA)
Gem City Coll (IL)
Genesee Comm Coll (NY)
George Corley Wallace State Comm Coll (AL)
Georgia Perimeter Coll (GA)
Germanna Comm Coll (VA)
Glendale Comm Coll (CA)
Gloucester County Coll (NJ)
Gogebic Comm Coll (MI)
Golden West Coll (CA)
Grayson County Coll (TX)
Greenfield Comm Coll (MA)
Greenville Tech Coll (SC)
Griffin Tech Coll (GA)
Guam Comm Coll (GU)
Guilford Tech Comm Coll (NC)
Gulf Coast Comm Coll (FL)
Gwinnett Tech Coll (GA)
Hagerstown Business Coll (MD)
Hamilton Coll (IA)
Harford Comm Coll (MD)
Harrisburg Area Comm Coll (PA)
Harry M. Ayers State Tech Coll (AL)
Hawaii Business Coll (HI)
Hawaii Comm Coll (HI)
Hawkeye Comm Coll (IA)
Heald Coll, Schools of Business and Technology, Hayward (CA)
Heald Coll, Schools of Business and Technology, Rancho Cordova (CA)
Heald Coll, Schools of Business and Technology (HI)
Henry Ford Comm Coll (MI)
Herkimer County Comm Coll (NY)
Hesser Coll (NH)
Highland Comm Coll (IL)
Highland Comm Coll (KS)
Highline Comm Coll (WA)
Hill Coll of the Hill Jr College District (TX)
Hillsborough Comm Coll (FL)
Hinds Comm Coll (MS)
Holyoke Comm Coll (MA)
Housatonic Comm Coll (CT)
Houston Comm Coll System (TX)
Howard Coll (TX)
Howard Comm Coll (MD)
Hudson County Comm Coll (NJ)
Huntington Jr Coll of Business (WV)
Illinois Eastern Comm Colls, Olney Central Coll (IL)
Imperial Valley Coll (CA)
Independence Comm Coll (KS)
Indiana Business Coll, Anderson (IN)
Indiana Business Coll, Columbus (IN)
Indiana Business Coll, Evansville (IN)
Indiana Business Coll, Fort Wayne (IN)
Indiana Business Coll, Indianapolis (IN)
Indiana Business Coll, Lafayette (IN)
Indiana Business Coll, Marion (IN)
Indiana Business Coll, Muncie (IN)
Indiana Business Coll, Terre Haute (IN)
Indian River Comm Coll (FL)
Instituto Comercial de Puerto Rico Jr Coll (PR)
Interboro Inst (NY)
International Business Coll, Fort Wayne (IN)
Inver Hills Comm Coll (MN)
Iowa Lakes Comm Coll (IA)
Iowa Western Comm Coll (IA)
Itasca Comm Coll (MN)
Ivy Tech State Coll–Central Indiana (IN)
Ivy Tech State Coll–Columbus (IN)
Ivy Tech State Coll–Kokomo (IN)
Ivy Tech State Coll–North Central (IN)
Ivy Tech State Coll–Southeast (IN)
Jackson Comm Coll (MI)
James Sprunt Comm Coll (NC)
Jamestown Business Coll (NY)
Jamestown Comm Coll (NY)
Jefferson Coll (MO)
Jefferson Comm Coll (KY)
Jefferson Comm Coll (NY)
Jefferson Comm Coll (OH)
J. F. Drake State Tech Coll (AL)
John A. Logan Coll (IL)
Joliet Jr Coll (IL)
Jones County Jr Coll (MS)
Kankakee Comm Coll (IL)
Kansas City Kansas Comm Coll (KS)
Kaplan Coll (IA)
Kaskaskia Coll (IL)
Kauai Comm Coll (HI)
Kellogg Comm Coll (MI)
Kennebec Valley Tech Coll (ME)

Kent State U, East Liverpool Campus (OH)
Kent State U, Geauga Campus (OH)
Kent State U, Salem Campus (OH)
Kent State U, Trumbull Campus (OH)
Kent State U, Tuscarawas Campus (OH)
Keystone Coll (PA)
Kilgore Coll (TX)
Kilian Comm Coll (SD)
Kingsborough Comm Coll of City U of NY (NY)
Kingwood Coll (TX)
Kirkwood Comm Coll (IA)
Labette Comm Coll (KS)
Lake Area Tech Inst (SD)
Lakeland Comm Coll (OH)
Lake Region State Coll (ND)
Lakeshore Tech Coll (WI)
Lake Tahoe Comm Coll (CA)
Lake Washington Tech Coll (WA)
Lamar Comm Coll (CO)
Lamar State Coll–Orange (TX)
Lamar State Coll–Port Arthur (TX)
Lane Comm Coll (OR)
Lansing Comm Coll (MI)
Laramie County Comm Coll (WY)
Las Positas Coll (CA)
Laurel Business Inst (PA)
LDS Business Coll (UT)
Lenoir Comm Coll (NC)
Lewis and Clark Comm Coll (IL)
Lewis Coll of Business (MI)
Lima Tech Coll (OH)
Lincoln Coll, Lincoln (IL)
Lincoln Coll, Normal (IL)
Lincoln Land Comm Coll (IL)
Lincoln School of Commerce (NE)
Linn-Benton Comm Coll (OR)
Long Beach City Coll (CA)
Long Island Business Inst (NY)
Longview Comm Coll (MO)
Lon Morris Coll (TX)
Lorain County Comm Coll (OH)
Lord Fairfax Comm Coll (VA)
Los Angeles City Coll (CA)
Los Angeles Harbor Coll (CA)
Los Angeles Mission Coll (CA)
Los Angeles Pierce Coll (CA)
Louisiana Tech Coll–Florida Parishes Campus (LA)
Lower Columbia Coll (WA)
Luzerne County Comm Coll (PA)
Macomb Comm Coll (MI)
Madisonville Comm Coll (KY)
Manatee Comm Coll (FL)
Manchester Comm Coll (CT)
Manor Coll (PA)
Maple Woods Comm Coll (MO)
Marian Court Coll (MA)
Marion Tech Coll (OH)
Marshalltown Comm Coll (IA)
Martin Comm Coll (NC)
Massachusetts Bay Comm Coll (MA)
Massasoit Comm Coll (MA)
Mayland Comm Coll (NC)
Maysville Comm Coll (KY)
McCann School of Business (PA)
McIntosh Coll (NH)
McLennan Comm Coll (TX)
Merced Coll (CA)
Mercer County Comm Coll (NJ)
Metropolitan Comm Coll (NE)
Miami-Dade Comm Coll (FL)
Miami U–Middletown Campus (OH)
Middlesex Comm Coll (MA)
Middlesex County Coll (NJ)
Midland Coll (TX)
Midlands Tech Coll (SC)
Mid Michigan Comm Coll (MI)
Mid-Plains Comm Coll Area (NE)
Mid-State Coll (ME)
Mid-State Tech Coll (WI)
Milwaukee Area Tech Coll (WI)
Mineral Area Coll (MO)
Minnesota School of Business (MN)
Minnesota State Coll–Southeast Tech (MN)
Minnesota West Comm & Tech Coll-Pipestone Cmps (MN)
MiraCosta Coll (CA)
Mississippi Delta Comm Coll (MS)
Mississippi Gulf Coast Comm Coll (MS)
Mitchell Coll (CT)
Mitchell Comm Coll (NC)
Mitchell Tech Inst (SD)
Modesto Jr Coll (CA)
Mohave Comm Coll (AZ)
Mohawk Valley Comm Coll (NY)
Monroe Coll, Bronx (NY)
Monroe Coll, New Rochelle (NY)
Monroe Comm Coll (NY)
Monroe County Comm Coll (MI)
Montana State U Coll of Tech-Great Falls (MT)
Montcalm Comm Coll (MI)
Monterey Peninsula Coll (CA)
Montgomery Comm Coll (NC)
Montgomery County Comm Coll (PA)
Moorpark Coll (CA)
Moraine Park Tech Coll (WI)
Morgan Comm Coll (CO)
Morton Coll (IL)
Mountain Empire Comm Coll (VA)
Mountain View Coll (TX)
Mountain West Coll (UT)
Mt. Hood Comm Coll (OR)
Mount Wachusett Comm Coll (MA)
Muscatine Comm Coll (IA)
Muskingum Area Tech Coll (OH)
Nash Comm Coll (NC)
Nashville State Tech Inst (TN)
Nassau Comm Coll (NY)
National Coll of Business & Technology, Danville (KY)
National Coll of Business & Technology, Florence (KY)
National Coll of Business & Technology, Lexington (KY)
National Coll of Business & Technology, Louisville (KY)
National Coll of Business & Technology, Pikeville (KY)
National Coll of Business & Technology, Richmond (KY)
National Coll of Business & Technology, Bluefield (VA)
National Coll of Business & Technology, Bristol (VA)
National Coll of Business & Technology, Charlottesville (VA)
National Coll of Business & Technology, Danville (VA)
National Coll of Business & Technology, Harrisonburg (VA)
National Coll of Business & Technology, Lynchburg (VA)
National Coll of Business & Technology, Martinsville (VA)
National Coll of Business & Technology, Salem (VA)
Naugatuck Valley Comm Coll (CT)
Navarro Coll (TX)
Neosho County Comm Coll (KS)
Newbury Coll (MA)
New Hampshire Comm Tech Coll, Berlin/Laconia (NH)
New Hampshire Tech Inst (NH)
New Mexico Military Inst (NM)
New River Comm Coll (VA)
New York City Tech Coll of the City U of NY (NY)
Niagara County Comm Coll (NY)
North Central Michigan Coll (MI)
Northcentral Tech Coll (WI)
Northeast Comm Coll (NE)
Northeastern Tech Coll (SC)
Northeast Iowa Comm Coll (IA)
Northeast State Tech Comm Coll (TN)
Northeast Texas Comm Coll (TX)
Northern Essex Comm Coll (MA)
Northern Maine Tech Coll (ME)
Northern Oklahoma Coll (OK)
Northern Virginia Comm Coll (VA)
North Harris Coll (TX)
North Hennepin Comm Coll (MN)
North Iowa Area Comm Coll (IA)
Northland Comm and Tech Coll (MN)
North Seattle Comm Coll (WA)
North Shore Comm Coll (MA)
NorthWest Arkansas Comm Coll (AR)
Northwest Coll (WY)
Northwestern Business Coll (IL)
Northwestern Connecticut Comm-Tech Coll (CT)
Northwest Mississippi Comm Coll (MS)
Northwest-Shoals Comm Coll (AL)
Northwest State Comm Coll (OH)
Norwalk Comm Coll (CT)
Oakland Comm Coll (MI)
Oakton Comm Coll (IL)
Ocean County Coll (NJ)
Odessa Coll (TX)
Ohio Business Coll (OH)
Ohio Valley Business Coll (OH)
Okaloosa-Walton Comm Coll (FL)
Oklahoma City Comm Coll (OK)
Oklahoma State U, Oklahoma City (OK)
Oklahoma State U, Okmulgee (OK)
Olympic Coll (WA)
Onondaga Comm Coll (NY)
Orangeburg-Calhoun Tech Coll (SC)
Orange Coast Coll (CA)
Orange County Comm Coll (NY)
Ouachita Tech Coll (AR)
Oxnard Coll (CA)
Pace Inst (PA)
Paducah Comm Coll (KY)
Palau Comm CollPalau)
Palm Beach Comm Coll (FL)
Palomar Coll (CA)
Palo Verde Coll (CA)
Pamlico Comm Coll (NC)
Paradise Valley Comm Coll (AZ)
Pasadena City Coll (CA)
Patrick Henry Comm Coll (VA)
Pellissippi State Tech Comm Coll (TN)
Peninsula Coll (WA)
Penn Valley Comm Coll (MO)
Pensacola Jr Coll (FL)
Phoenix Coll (AZ)
Piedmont Comm Coll (NC)
Piedmont Tech Coll (SC)
Piedmont Virginia Comm Coll (VA)
Pierce Coll (WA)
Pima Comm Coll (AZ)
Pitt Comm Coll (NC)
Pittsburgh Tech Inst (PA)
Portland Comm Coll (OR)
Pratt Comm Coll and Area Vocational School (KS)
Prince George's Comm Coll (MD)
Queensborough Comm Coll of City U of NY (NY)
Quincy Coll (MA)
Quinsigamond Comm Coll (MA)
Rappahannock Comm Coll (VA)
Raritan Valley Comm Coll (NJ)
Rasmussen Coll Eagan (MN)
Rasmussen Coll Mankato (MN)
Rasmussen Coll Minnetonka (MN)
Rasmussen Coll St. Cloud (MN)
Reading Area Comm Coll (PA)
Red Rocks Comm Coll (CO)
Reedley Coll (CA)
Richland Comm Coll (IL)
Richmond Comm Coll (NC)
Ridgewater Coll (MN)
Riverside Comm Coll (CA)
Roane State Comm Coll (TN)
Rochester Business Inst (NY)
Rockford Business Coll (IL)
Rockingham Comm Coll (NC)
Rockland Comm Coll (NY)
Rogue Comm Coll (OR)
Rowan-Cabarrus Comm Coll (NC)
Sacramento City Coll (CA)
St. Catharine Coll (KY)
Saint Charles Comm Coll (MO)
St. Clair County Comm Coll (MI)
St. Cloud Tech Coll (MN)
St. Louis Comm Coll at Florissant Valley (MO)
St. Paul Tech Coll (MN)
St. Philip's Coll (TX)
Salem Comm Coll (NJ)
Sampson Comm Coll (NC)
San Bernardino Valley Coll (CA)
Sandhills Comm Coll (NC)
San Diego City Coll (CA)
San Diego Mesa Coll (CA)
Sanford-Brown Coll, Fenton (MO)
Sanford-Brown Coll, Hazelwood (MO)
San Jacinto Coll Central Campus (TX)
San Jacinto Coll North Campus (TX)
San Jacinto Coll South Campus (TX)
San Joaquin Delta Coll (CA)
Santa Ana Coll (CA)
Santa Barbara City Coll (CA)
Santa Fe Comm Coll (FL)
Santa Fe Comm Coll (NM)
Santa Monica Coll (CA)
Sauk Valley Comm Coll (IL)
Savannah Tech Coll (GA)
Schenectady County Comm Coll (NY)
Schoolcraft Coll (MI)
Scott Comm Coll (IA)
Scottsdale Comm Coll (AZ)
Seattle Central Comm Coll (WA)
Seminole Comm Coll (FL)
Seminole State Coll (OK)
Shasta Coll (CA)
Shoreline Comm Coll (WA)
Sierra Coll (CA)
Sinclair Comm Coll (OH)
Skagit Valley Coll (WA)
Snow Coll (UT)
Somerset Comm Coll (KY)
South Coll (NC)
South Coll (TN)
Southeast Comm Coll, Beatrice Campus (NE)
Southeast Tech Inst (SD)
Southern Ohio Coll, Cincinnati Campus (OH)
Southern West Virginia Comm and Tech Coll (WV)
South Hills School of Business & Technology, Atloona (PA)
South Hills School of Business & Technology, State College (PA)
South Plains Coll (TX)
South Puget Sound Comm Coll (WA)
South Suburban Coll (IL)
South Texas Comm Coll (TX)
South U (AL)
Southwestern Coll (CA)
Southwestern Coll of Business, Dayton (OH)
Southwestern Comm Coll (IA)
Southwestern Comm Coll (NC)
Southwest Georgia Tech Coll (GA)
Southwest Mississippi Comm Coll (MS)
Southwest Tennessee Comm Coll (TN)
Southwest Virginia Comm Coll (VA)
Southwest Wisconsin Tech Coll (WI)
Spartanburg Tech Coll (SC)
Spencerian Coll (KY)
Springfield Tech Comm Coll (MA)
Stark State Coll of Technology (OH)
State Fair Comm Coll (MO)
State U of NY Coll of A&T at Morrisville (NY)
State U of NY Coll of Technology at Alfred (NY)
State U of NY Coll of Technology at Canton (NY)
State U of NY Coll of Technology at Delhi (NY)
Suffolk County Comm Coll (NY)
Sullivan County Comm Coll (NY)
Surry Comm Coll (NC)
Sussex County Comm Coll (NJ)
Tacoma Comm Coll (WA)
Taft Coll (CA)
Tarrant County Coll District (TX)
TCI-The Coll for Technology (NY)
Terra State Comm Coll (OH)
Thomas Nelson Comm Coll (VA)
Three Rivers Comm Coll (CT)
Tidewater Comm Coll (VA)
Tomball Coll (TX)
Tompkins Cortland Comm Coll (NY)
Tri-County Comm Coll (NC)
Tri-County Tech Coll (SC)
Trident Tech Coll (SC)
Trinidad State Jr Coll (CO)
Trinity Valley Comm Coll (TX)
Triton Coll (IL)
Truckee Meadows Comm Coll (NV)
Trumbull Business Coll (OH)
Tulsa Comm Coll (OK)
Tunxis Comm Coll (CT)
Tyler Jr Coll (TX)
Ulster County Comm Coll (NY)
Umpqua Comm Coll (OR)
The U of Akron–Wayne Coll (OH)
U of Alaska Anchorage, Matanuska-Susitna Coll (AK)
U of Kentucky, Lexington Comm Coll (KY)
U of New Mexico–Gallup (NM)
U of New Mexico–Los Alamos Branch (NM)
U of Northwestern Ohio (OH)
U of Pittsburgh at Titusville (PA)
Utica School of Commerce (NY)
Vance-Granville Comm Coll (NC)
Ventura Coll (CA)
Vermilion Comm Coll (MN)
Vermont Tech Coll (VT)
Vernon Coll (TX)
Victoria Coll (TX)
Vincennes U (IN)
Vincennes U Jasper Campus (IN)
Virginia Western Comm Coll (VA)
Vista Comm Coll (CA)
Wake Tech Comm Coll (NC)
Wallace State Comm Coll (AL)
Warren County Comm Coll (NJ)
Waycross Coll (GA)
Webster Coll, Holiday (FL)
Webster Coll, Ocala (FL)
West Central Tech Coll (GA)
The Westchester Business Inst (NY)
Westchester Comm Coll (NY)
Western Nevada Comm Coll (NV)
Western Piedmont Comm Coll (NC)
Western Texas Coll (TX)
Western Wisconsin Tech Coll (WI)
Western Wyoming Comm Coll (WY)
Westmoreland County Comm Coll (PA)
West Shore Comm Coll (MI)
West Virginia Jr Coll, Charleston (WV)
West Virginia U at Parkersburg (WV)
Whatcom Comm Coll (WA)
Wilson Tech Comm Coll (NC)
Wisconsin Indianhead Tech Coll (WI)
York Tech Coll (SC)
Yorktowne Business Inst (PA)

ACCOUNTING RELATED

AIBT International Inst of the Americas (AZ)
Central Pennsylvania Coll (PA)
Virginia Coll at Jackson (MS)

ACCOUNTING TECHNICIAN

Alamance Comm Coll (NC)
Anoka-Ramsey Comm Coll, Cambridge Campus (MN)
Asheville-Buncombe Tech Comm Coll (NC)
Bates Tech Coll (WA)
Bay de Noc Comm Coll (MI)
Big Bend Comm Coll (WA)
Black Hawk Coll, Moline (IL)
Blue River Comm Coll (MO)
Cape Fear Comm Coll (NC)
Catawba Valley Comm Coll (NC)
Central Georgia Tech Coll (GA)
Central Wyoming Coll (WY)
Clover Park Tech Coll (WA)
Comm Coll of Allegheny County (PA)
Cuyamaca Coll (CA)
Delaware County Comm Coll (PA)
Edmonds Comm Coll (WA)
Front Range Comm Coll (CO)
Glendale Comm Coll (AZ)
Gloucester County Coll (NJ)
Grays Harbor Coll (WA)
Green River Comm Coll (WA)
Hagerstown Comm Coll (MD)
Helena Coll of Tech of The U of Montana (MT)
Hickey Coll (MO)
Ivy Tech State Coll–Bloomington (IN)
Ivy Tech State Coll–Central Indiana (IN)
Ivy Tech State Coll–Columbus (IN)
Ivy Tech State Coll–Eastcentral (IN)
Ivy Tech State Coll–Kokomo (IN)
Ivy Tech State Coll–Lafayette (IN)
Ivy Tech State Coll–North Central (IN)
Ivy Tech State Coll–Northeast (IN)
Ivy Tech State Coll–Northwest (IN)
Ivy Tech State Coll–Southcentral (IN)
Ivy Tech State Coll–Southeast (IN)
Ivy Tech State Coll–Southwest (IN)

Ivy Tech State Coll–Wabash Valley (IN)
Ivy Tech State Coll–Whitewater (IN)
Jefferson State Comm Coll (AL)
Johnson County Comm Coll (KS)
Johnston Comm Coll (NC)
J. Sargeant Reynolds Comm Coll (VA)
Kalamazoo Valley Comm Coll (MI)
Kellogg Comm Coll (MI)
Kilgore Coll (TX)
Lake Land Coll (IL)
Lake Michigan Coll (MI)
Lehigh Carbon Comm Coll (PA)
Louisiana Tech Coll–Delta Ouachita Campus (LA)
Louisiana Tech Coll–Natchitoches Campus (LA)
Lower Columbia Coll (WA)
Madisonville Comm Coll (KY)
McHenry County Coll (IL)
Miami U–Hamilton Campus (OH)
Minneapolis Comm and Tech Coll (MN)
Minot State U–Bottineau Campus (ND)
Moberly Area Comm Coll (MO)
Montgomery Coll (MD)
Montgomery County Comm Coll (PA)
Mott Comm Coll (MI)
Nassau Comm Coll (NY)
National Coll of Business & Technology, Salem (VA)
Northampton County Area Comm Coll (PA)
North Iowa Area Comm Coll (IA)
Northland Pioneer Coll (AZ)
Northwestern Michigan Coll (MI)
Parkland Coll (IL)
Pellissippi State Tech Comm Coll (TN)
Pennsylvania Coll of Technology (PA)
Pikes Peak Comm Coll (CO)
Polk Comm Coll (FL)
Randolph Comm Coll (NC)
St. Cloud Tech Coll (MN)
St. Petersburg Coll (FL)
San Juan Coll (NM)
Southern Ohio Coll, Northern Kentucky Campus (KY)
Southern State Comm Coll (OH)
South Piedmont Comm Coll (NC)
Southwestern Michigan Coll (MI)
Spokane Comm Coll (WA)
Spokane Falls Comm Coll (WA)
Stanly Comm Coll (NC)
Tallahassee Comm Coll (FL)
Union County Coll (NJ)
The U of Akron–Wayne Coll (OH)
U of Kentucky, Lexington Comm Coll (KY)
Walla Walla Comm Coll (WA)
Waubonsee Comm Coll (IL)
Wayne Comm Coll (NC)
Western Nevada Comm Coll (NV)
West Virginia Northern Comm Coll (WV)
Wilkes Comm Coll (NC)
Williston State Coll (ND)
Wor-Wic Comm Coll (MD)

ACTING/DIRECTING
KD Studio (TX)
Northampton County Area Comm Coll (PA)
Santa Barbara City Coll (CA)

ACTUARIAL SCIENCE
Harrisburg Area Comm Coll (PA)

ACUPUNCTURE/ORIENTAL MEDICINE
New Ctr Coll for Wholistic Health Ed & Research (NY)

ADMINISTRATIVE/SECRETARIAL SERVICES
Ancilla Coll (IN)
Bunker Hill Comm Coll (MA)
Eastern Arizona Coll (AZ)
Guilford Tech Comm Coll (NC)
Hillsborough Comm Coll (FL)
ITT Tech Inst, Spokane (WA)
Virginia Coll at Jackson (MS)
Wisconsin Indianhead Tech Coll (WI)

ADVERTISING
American River Coll (CA)
The Art Inst of Pittsburgh (PA)
Bradley Academy for the Visual Arts (PA)
Brown Coll (MN)
Central Piedmont Comm Coll (NC)
Chabot Coll (CA)
Chattanooga State Tech Comm Coll (TN)
Cypress Coll (CA)
Daytona Beach Comm Coll (FL)
Edison State Comm Coll (OH)
Erie Business Center South (PA)
Fayetteville Tech Comm Coll (NC)
Highland Comm Coll (KS)
Hussian School of Art (PA)
Long Beach City Coll (CA)
Los Angeles City Coll (CA)
Manatee Comm Coll (FL)
Middlesex County Coll (NJ)
Mississippi Delta Comm Coll (MS)
Mississippi Gulf Coast Comm Coll (MS)
Mohawk Valley Comm Coll (NY)
Northwestern Business Coll (IL)
Palomar Coll (CA)
Parkland Coll (IL)
Pasadena City Coll (CA)
Rockland Comm Coll (NY)
Sacramento City Coll (CA)
St. Clair County Comm Coll (MI)
St. Cloud Tech Coll (MN)
South Plains Coll (TX)
South Suburban Coll (IL)
Southwest Mississippi Comm Coll (MS)
Surry Comm Coll (NC)
Tidewater Comm Coll (VA)
Tulsa Comm Coll (OK)
Vincennes U (IN)

AEROSPACE ENGINEERING
Allan Hancock Coll (CA)
Kilgore Coll (TX)
Prince George's Comm Coll (MD)

AEROSPACE ENGINEERING TECHNOLOGY
Calhoun Comm Coll (AL)
Cincinnati State Tech and Comm Coll (OH)
Coll of Lake County (IL)
GateWay Comm Coll (AZ)
Pennsylvania Coll of Technology (PA)

AEROSPACE SCIENCE
Alvin Comm Coll (TX)
Comm Coll of Beaver County (PA)
Delaware Tech & Comm Coll, Terry Cmps (DE)
Miami-Dade Comm Coll (FL)
Northland Comm and Tech Coll (MN)
Orange Coast Coll (CA)
San Bernardino Valley Coll (CA)
San Jacinto Coll Central Campus (TX)
Spartan School of Aeronautics (OK)
Tulsa Comm Coll (OK)

AFRICAN-AMERICAN STUDIES
Bronx Comm Coll of City U of NY (NY)
City Coll of San Francisco (CA)
Coll of Alameda (CA)
Compton Comm Coll (CA)
Fresno City Coll (CA)
Los Angeles City Coll (CA)
Manatee Comm Coll (FL)
Nassau Comm Coll (NY)
Pasadena City Coll (CA)
San Diego City Coll (CA)
San Diego Mesa Coll (CA)
Santa Ana Coll (CA)
Santa Barbara City Coll (CA)
Southwestern Coll (CA)

AFRICAN STUDIES
MiraCosta Coll (CA)
Pasadena City Coll (CA)
Sinclair Comm Coll (OH)
Southwestern Coll (CA)

AGRIBUSINESS
Allan Hancock Coll (CA)
Crowder Coll (MO)
Eastern Arizona Coll (AZ)
Eastern Wyoming Coll (WY)
Glendale Comm Coll (AZ)
James Sprunt Comm Coll (NC)
Mineral Area Coll (MO)
Sitting Bull Coll (ND)
Southwest Wisconsin Tech Coll (WI)
Vermont Tech Coll (VT)
Wayne Comm Coll (NC)

AGRICULTURAL ANIMAL HUSBANDRY/PRODUCTION MANAGEMENT
Hopkinsville Comm Coll (KY)
Iowa Western Comm Coll (IA)
North Central Texas Coll (TX)
Pratt Comm Coll and Area Vocational School (KS)
Ridgewater Coll (MN)
Western Dakota Tech Inst (SD)

AGRICULTURAL BUSINESS
Abraham Baldwin Ag Coll (GA)
Arizona Western Coll (AZ)
Bakersfield Coll (CA)
Bismarck State Coll (ND)
Black Hawk Coll, Moline (IL)
Brazosport Coll (TX)
Butte Coll (CA)
Carl Sandburg Coll (IL)
Casper Coll (WY)
Central Comm Coll–Columbus Campus (NE)
Central Comm Coll–Hastings Campus (NE)
Central Wyoming Coll (WY)
Chippewa Valley Tech Coll (WI)
Cisco Jr Coll (TX)
City Coll of San Francisco (CA)
Coastal Georgia Comm Coll (GA)
Coffeyville Comm Coll (KS)
Colby Comm Coll (KS)
Coll of Southern Idaho (ID)
Coll of the Desert (CA)
Coll of the Redwoods (CA)
Coll of the Sequoias (CA)
Columbia State Comm Coll (TN)
County Coll of Morris (NJ)
Cumberland County Coll (NJ)
Danville Area Comm Coll (IL)
Dawson Comm Coll (MT)
Delaware Tech & Comm Coll, Jack F Owens Cmps (DE)
Delta Coll (MI)
Des Moines Area Comm Coll (IA)
Dodge City Comm Coll (KS)
Eastern Oklahoma State Coll (OK)
Ellsworth Comm Coll (IA)
Enterprise State Jr Coll (AL)
Fort Scott Comm Coll (KS)
Frederick Comm Coll (MD)
Garden City Comm Coll (KS)
Hawkeye Comm Coll (IA)
Highland Comm Coll (IL)
Highland Comm Coll (KS)
Hill Coll of the Hill Jr College District (TX)
Hinds Comm Coll (MS)
Hutchinson Comm Coll and Area Vocational School (KS)
Illinois Eastern Comm Colls, Wabash Valley Coll (IL)
Imperial Valley Coll (CA)
Indian River Comm Coll (FL)
Iowa Lakes Comm Coll (IA)
Iowa Western Comm Coll (IA)
Jefferson State Comm Coll (AL)
John Wood Comm Coll (IL)
Joliet Jr Coll (IL)
Kaskaskia Coll (IL)
Kirkwood Comm Coll (IA)
Kishwaukee Coll (IL)
Lake Area Tech Inst (SD)
Lake Land Coll (IL)
Lake Region State Coll (ND)
Lamar Comm Coll (CO)
Laramie County Comm Coll (WY)
Lenoir Comm Coll (NC)
Lewis and Clark Comm Coll (IL)
Lincoln Land Comm Coll (IL)
Linn-Benton Comm Coll (OR)
Lord Fairfax Comm Coll (VA)
Merced Coll (CA)
Milwaukee Area Tech Coll (WI)
Mississippi Delta Comm Coll (MS)
Mississippi Gulf Coast Comm Coll (MS)
Mitchell Tech Inst (SD)
Modesto Jr Coll (CA)
Northeast Comm Coll (NE)
Northeast Iowa Comm Coll (IA)
Northern Maine Tech Coll (ME)
Northern Oklahoma Coll (OK)
Northwest Coll (WY)
Northwest Mississippi Comm Coll (MS)
Otero Jr Coll (CO)
Oxnard Coll (CA)
Parkland Coll (IL)
Penn State U Beaver Campus of the Commonwealth Coll (PA)
Penn State U Delaware County Campus of the Commonwealth Coll (PA)
Penn State U DuBois Campus of the Commonwealth Coll (PA)
Penn State U Fayette Campus of the Commonwealth Coll (PA)
Penn State U Hazleton Campus of the Commonwealth Coll (PA)
Penn State U McKeesport Campus of the Commonwealth Coll (PA)
Penn State U Mont Alto Campus of the Commonwealth Coll (PA)
Penn State U New Kensington Campus of the Commonwealth Coll (PA)
Penn State U Shenango Campus of the Commonwealth Coll (PA)
Penn State U Wilkes-Barre Campus of the Commonwealth Coll (PA)
Penn State U Worthington Scranton Cmps Commonwealth Coll (PA)
Penn State U York Campus of the Commonwealth Coll (PA)
Pratt Comm Coll and Area Vocational School (KS)
Reedley Coll (CA)
Rend Lake Coll (IL)
Richland Comm Coll (IL)
Ridgewater Coll (MN)
Riverside Comm Coll (CA)
St. Catharine Coll (KY)
St. Clair County Comm Coll (MI)
San Joaquin Delta Coll (CA)
Shasta Coll (CA)
Sheridan Coll (WY)
Snow Coll (UT)
Southeast Comm Coll, Beatrice Campus (NE)
Southwestern Comm Coll (IA)
Spokane Comm Coll (WA)
State Fair Comm Coll (MO)
State U of NY Coll of A&T at Morrisville (NY)
State U of NY Coll of Technology at Alfred (NY)
Surry Comm Coll (NC)
Tyler Jr Coll (TX)
U of Northwestern Ohio (OH)
Ventura Coll (CA)
Vermilion Comm Coll (MN)
Vincennes U (IN)
Walla Walla Comm Coll (WA)
Western Dakota Tech Inst (SD)

AGRICULTURAL BUSINESS RELATED
Hiwassee Coll (TN)
North Dakota State Coll of Science (ND)

AGRICULTURAL ECONOMICS
Abraham Baldwin Ag Coll (GA)
Butte Coll (CA)
Coffeyville Comm Coll (KS)
Colby Comm Coll (KS)
Dodge City Comm Coll (KS)
Eastern Oklahoma State Coll (OK)
Eastern Wyoming Coll (WY)
Fort Scott Comm Coll (KS)
Garden City Comm Coll (KS)
Highland Comm Coll (KS)
Hill Coll of the Hill Jr College District (TX)
Hinds Comm Coll (MS)
Iowa Lakes Comm Coll (IA)
Mississippi Delta Comm Coll (MS)
North Iowa Area Comm Coll (IA)
Northwest Coll (WY)
Northwest Mississippi Comm Coll (MS)
Pratt Comm Coll and Area Vocational School (KS)
Snow Coll (UT)
South Plains Coll (TX)
Tyler Jr Coll (TX)
Vermilion Comm Coll (MN)

AGRICULTURAL EDUCATION
Chemeketa Comm Coll (OR)
Coffeyville Comm Coll (KS)
Colby Comm Coll (KS)
Coll of the Sequoias (CA)
Eastern Oklahoma State Coll (OK)
Eastern Wyoming Coll (WY)
Fort Scott Comm Coll (KS)
Highland Comm Coll (KS)
Hinds Comm Coll (MS)
Iowa Lakes Comm Coll (IA)
Kirkwood Comm Coll (IA)
Lamar Comm Coll (CO)
Laramie County Comm Coll (WY)
Linn-Benton Comm Coll (OR)
Northwest Coll (WY)
Northwest-Shoals Comm Coll (AL)
Pratt Comm Coll and Area Vocational School (KS)
Trinity Valley Comm Coll (TX)
Tyler Jr Coll (TX)
Vermilion Comm Coll (MN)
Victor Valley Coll (CA)
Western Texas Coll (TX)

AGRICULTURAL EXTENSION
Vincennes U (IN)

AGRICULTURAL/FOOD PRODUCTS PROCESSING
Texas State Tech Coll– Waco/ Marshall Campus (TX)

AGRICULTURAL MECHANIZATION
Abraham Baldwin Ag Coll (GA)
Aims Comm Coll (CO)
Beaufort County Comm Coll (NC)
Carl Sandburg Coll (IL)
Casper Coll (WY)
Coffeyville Comm Coll (KS)
Coll of the Sequoias (CA)
Cowley County Comm Coll and Voc-Tech School (KS)
Cuesta Coll (CA)
Delta Coll (MI)
Dodge City Comm Coll (KS)
Fort Scott Comm Coll (KS)
Garden City Comm Coll (KS)
Hawkeye Comm Coll (IA)
Helena Coll of Tech of The U of Montana (MT)
Highland Comm Coll (IL)
Hinds Comm Coll (MS)
Hutchinson Comm Coll and Area Vocational School (KS)
Illinois Eastern Comm Colls, Wabash Valley Coll (IL)
Imperial Valley Coll (CA)
Indian Hills Comm Coll (IA)
Iowa Lakes Comm Coll (IA)
Kishwaukee Coll (IL)
Lake Land Coll (IL)
Lane Comm Coll (OR)
Lincoln Land Comm Coll (IL)
Longview Comm Coll (MO)
Miles Comm Coll (MT)
Modesto Jr Coll (CA)
Navarro Coll (TX)
North Central Texas Coll (TX)
North Dakota State Coll of Science (ND)
Northeast Comm Coll (NE)
Northwest Coll (WY)
Northwest Mississippi Comm Coll (MS)
Oxnard Coll (CA)
Parkland Coll (IL)
Pratt Comm Coll and Area Vocational School (KS)
Rend Lake Coll (IL)
Ridgewater Coll (MN)
St. Clair County Comm Coll (MI)
San Joaquin Delta Coll (CA)
Sierra Coll (CA)
Southeast Comm Coll, Beatrice Campus (NE)
Southwest Georgia Tech Coll (GA)

Southwest Wisconsin Tech Coll (WI)
State Fair Comm Coll (MO)
State U of NY Coll of A&T at Morrisville (NY)
Vincennes U (IN)
Walla Walla Comm Coll (WA)
Walters State Comm Coll (TN)
Western Wisconsin Tech Coll (WI)

AGRICULTURAL MECHANIZATION RELATED
Garden City Comm Coll (KS)
Reedley Coll (CA)

AGRICULTURAL PLANT PATHOLOGY
Central Wyoming Coll (WY)

AGRICULTURAL PRODUCTION
Allen County Comm Coll (KS)
Black Hawk Coll, Moline (IL)
Hillsborough Comm Coll (FL)
John Wood Comm Coll (IL)
Kishwaukee Coll (IL)
Lake Land Coll (IL)
Lake Region State Coll (ND)
Mitchell Tech Inst (SD)
Modesto Jr Coll (CA)
Muscatine Comm Coll (IA)
North Dakota State Coll of Science (ND)
Northeast Comm Coll (NE)
North Iowa Area Comm Coll (IA)
Rend Lake Coll (IL)
Southern State Comm Coll (OH)
Walla Walla Comm Coll (WA)
Wayne Comm Coll (NC)

AGRICULTURAL PRODUCTION RELATED
Northwestern Michigan Coll (MI)

AGRICULTURAL SCIENCES
Abraham Baldwin Ag Coll (GA)
Andrew Coll (GA)
Arizona Western Coll (AZ)
Arkansas State U–Beebe (AR)
Bainbridge Coll (GA)
Bakersfield Coll (CA)
Barton County Comm Coll (KS)
Black Hawk Coll, Moline (IL)
Blinn Coll (TX)
Butte Coll (CA)
Casper Coll (WY)
Central Arizona Coll (AZ)
Central Texas Coll (TX)
Cerritos Coll (CA)
Chattahoochee Valley Comm Coll (AL)
Chipola Jr Coll (FL)
Cisco Jr Coll (TX)
Clark Coll (WA)
Coastal Bend Coll (TX)
Cochise Coll, Douglas (AZ)
Coffeyville Comm Coll (KS)
Colby Comm Coll (KS)
Coll of Southern Idaho (ID)
Coll of the Sequoias (CA)
Cowley County Comm Coll and Voc-Tech School (KS)
Cumberland County Coll (NJ)
Danville Area Comm Coll (IL)
Darton Coll (GA)
Daytona Beach Comm Coll (FL)
Delta Coll (MI)
Dixie State Coll of Utah (UT)
Eastern Arizona Coll (AZ)
Eastern Wyoming Coll (WY)
East Georgia Coll (GA)
Floyd Coll (GA)
Fort Scott Comm Coll (KS)
Frederick Comm Coll (MD)
Fullerton Coll (CA)
Garden City Comm Coll (KS)
Gordon Coll (GA)
Hawaii Comm Coll (HI)
Highland Comm Coll (KS)
Hill Coll of the Hill Jr College District (TX)
Holmes Comm Coll (MS)
Horry-Georgetown Tech Coll (SC)
Houston Comm Coll System (TX)
Howard Coll (TX)
Hutchinson Comm Coll and Area Vocational School (KS)
Imperial Valley Coll (CA)
Iowa Lakes Comm Coll (IA)
John A. Logan Coll (IL)
Jones County Jr Coll (MS)
Kilgore Coll (TX)
Kirkwood Comm Coll (IA)
Lamar Comm Coll (CO)
Laramie County Comm Coll (WY)
Lenoir Comm Coll (NC)
Lewis and Clark Comm Coll (IL)
Lincoln Land Comm Coll (IL)
Linn-Benton Comm Coll (OR)
Los Angeles Pierce Coll (CA)
Merced Coll (CA)
Miami-Dade Comm Coll (FL)
Mississippi County Comm Coll (AR)
Modesto Jr Coll (CA)
Moraine Park Tech Coll (WI)
New Mexico State U–Carlsbad (NM)
North Arkansas Coll (AR)
Northeast Comm Coll (NE)
Northeast Texas Comm Coll (TX)
North Idaho Coll (ID)
Northwest Coll (WY)
Northwest Mississippi Comm Coll (MS)
Owensboro Comm Coll (KY)
Palau Comm CollPalau)
Palo Verde Coll (CA)
Pensacola Jr Coll (FL)
Pratt Comm Coll and Area Vocational School (KS)
Reedley Coll (CA)
St. Catharine Coll (KY)
St. Clair County Comm Coll (MI)
San Joaquin Delta Coll (CA)
Sheridan Coll (WY)
Skagit Valley Coll (WA)
Snow Coll (UT)
Southeast Comm Coll, Beatrice Campus (NE)
South Plains Coll (TX)
State Fair Comm Coll (MO)
State U of NY Coll of A&T at Morrisville (NY)
State U of NY Coll of Technology at Alfred (NY)
Texarkana Coll (TX)
Tulsa Comm Coll (OK)
Tyler Jr Coll (TX)
Umpqua Comm Coll (OR)
Wallace State Comm Coll (AL)
Waycross Coll (GA)
Western Nebraska Comm Coll (NE)
Western Texas Coll (TX)
Wharton County Jr Coll (TX)
Williston State Coll (ND)
Young Harris Coll (GA)

AGRICULTURAL SUPPLIES
Muscatine Comm Coll (IA)
North Dakota State Coll of Science (ND)
North Iowa Area Comm Coll (IA)
Western Iowa Tech Comm Coll (IA)
Wisconsin Indianhead Tech Coll (WI)

AGRONOMY/CROP SCIENCE
Butte Coll (CA)
Chipola Jr Coll (FL)
Colby Comm Coll (KS)
Coll of the Redwoods (CA)
Cowley County Comm Coll and Voc-Tech School (KS)
Dodge City Comm Coll (KS)
Eastern Oklahoma State Coll (OK)
Fort Scott Comm Coll (KS)
Hawkeye Comm Coll (IA)
Highland Comm Coll (KS)
Hinds Comm Coll (MS)
Iowa Lakes Comm Coll (IA)
Jackson State Comm Coll (TN)
Kirkwood Comm Coll (IA)
Lamar Comm Coll (CO)
Merced Coll (CA)
Modesto Jr Coll (CA)
Northeast Comm Coll (NE)
Northwest Coll (WY)
Sierra Coll (CA)
Snow Coll (UT)
Southeast Comm Coll, Beatrice Campus (NE)
Southern Maine Tech Coll (ME)
South Plains Coll (TX)
Spokane Comm Coll (WA)
State U of NY Coll of A&T at Morrisville (NY)
Ventura Coll (CA)
Vermilion Comm Coll (MN)

AIRCRAFT MECHANIC/ AIRFRAME
Amarillo Coll (TX)
Antelope Valley Coll (CA)
City Coll of San Francisco (CA)
Cochise Coll, Douglas (AZ)
Colorado Northwestern Comm Coll (CO)
Columbus State Comm Coll (OH)
Comm Coll of the Air Force (AL)
Cowley County Comm Coll and Voc-Tech School (KS)
Enterprise State Jr Coll (AL)
Florida Comm Coll at Jacksonville (FL)
Glendale Comm Coll (CA)
Greenville Tech Coll (SC)
Hawkeye Comm Coll (IA)
Helena Coll of Tech of The U of Montana (MT)
Ivy Tech State Coll–Wabash Valley (IN)
Johnson County Comm Coll (KS)
Lincoln Land Comm Coll (IL)
Merced Coll (CA)
Mohawk Valley Comm Coll (NY)
North Central Inst (TN)
Oklahoma City Comm Coll (OK)
Pittsburgh Inst of Aeronautics (PA)
Sacramento City Coll (CA)
St. Philip's Coll (TX)
San Joaquin Valley Coll (CA)
Southwestern Michigan Coll (MI)
Texas State Tech Coll–Harlingen (TX)
Texas State Tech Coll– Waco/ Marshall Campus (TX)
Texas State Tech Coll (TX)
Trident Tech Coll (SC)
Tulsa Comm Coll (OK)
Vincennes U (IN)
Westwood Coll of Aviation Technology–Denver (CO)
Westwood Coll of Aviation Technology–Houston (TX)
Westwood Coll of Aviation Technology–Los Angeles (CA)

AIRCRAFT MECHANIC/ POWERPLANT
Antelope Valley Coll (CA)
Central Texas Coll (TX)
Colorado Northwestern Comm Coll (CO)
Florida Comm Coll at Jacksonville (FL)
Lincoln Land Comm Coll (IL)
North Central Inst (TN)
Pennsylvania Coll of Technology (PA)
Pima Comm Coll (AZ)
San Joaquin Valley Coll (CA)
Southern Arkansas U Tech (AR)
Texas State Tech Coll– Waco/ Marshall Campus (TX)
Westwood Coll of Aviation Technology–Denver (CO)
Westwood Coll of Aviation Technology–Houston (TX)
Westwood Coll of Aviation Technology–Los Angeles (CA)

AIRCRAFT PILOT (PRIVATE)
Anoka-Hennepin Tech Coll (MN)

AIRCRAFT PILOT (PROFESSIONAL)
Academy Coll (MN)
Big Bend Comm Coll (WA)
Casper Coll (WY)
Central Texas Coll (TX)
Chattanooga State Tech Comm Coll (TN)
Clover Park Tech Coll (WA)
Cochise Coll, Douglas (AZ)
Colorado Northwestern Comm Coll (CO)
Comm Coll of Allegheny County (PA)
The Comm Coll of Baltimore County–Catonsville Campus (MD)
Comm Coll of Beaver County (PA)
Compton Comm Coll (CA)
County Coll of Morris (NJ)
Cypress Coll (CA)
Dixie State Coll of Utah (UT)
Florida Comm Coll at Jacksonville (FL)
Gateway Tech Coll (WI)
Glendale Comm Coll (CA)
Green River Comm Coll (WA)
Guilford Tech Comm Coll (NC)
Indian Hills Comm Coll (IA)
Indian River Comm Coll (FL)
Inver Hills Comm Coll (MN)
Iowa Lakes Comm Coll (IA)
Jackson Comm Coll (MI)
Kaskaskia Coll (IL)
Lane Comm Coll (OR)
Lansing Comm Coll (MI)
Lehigh Carbon Comm Coll (PA)
Lenoir Comm Coll (NC)
Long Beach City Coll (CA)
Luzerne County Comm Coll (PA)
Mercer County Comm Coll (NJ)
Miami-Dade Comm Coll (FL)
Navarro Coll (TX)
Northern Virginia Comm Coll (VA)
North Shore Comm Coll (MA)
Northwestern Michigan Coll (MI)
Orange Coast Coll (CA)
Palm Beach Comm Coll (FL)
Pasadena City Coll (CA)
San Jacinto Coll Central Campus (TX)
San Juan Coll (NM)
Scott Comm Coll (IA)
Spartan School of Aeronautics (OK)
Texas State Tech Coll– Waco/ Marshall Campus (TX)
Vermilion Comm Coll (MN)
Vincennes U (IN)
Wallace State Comm Coll (AL)

AIR FORCE R.O.T.C./AIR SCIENCE
Clark Coll (WA)

AIR TRAFFIC CONTROL
Anoka-Hennepin Tech Coll (MN)
The Comm Coll of Baltimore County–Catonsville Campus (MD)
Comm Coll of Beaver County (PA)
Comm Coll of the Air Force (AL)
Green River Comm Coll (WA)
Inver Hills Comm Coll (MN)

ALCOHOL/DRUG ABUSE COUNSELING
Alvin Comm Coll (TX)
Amarillo Coll (TX)
Asnuntuck Comm Coll (CT)
Bacone Coll (OK)
Capital Comm Coll (CT)
Central Texas Coll (TX)
Century Comm and Tech Coll (MN)
Chippewa Valley Tech Coll (WI)
Clark Coll (WA)
Coll of DuPage (IL)
Coll of Lake County (IL)
Coll of the Siskiyous (CA)
Columbus State Comm Coll (OH)
Comm Coll of Allegheny County (PA)
Comm Coll of Rhode Island (RI)
Corning Comm Coll (NY)
Danville Area Comm Coll (IL)
Dawson Comm Coll (MT)
Delaware Tech & Comm Coll, Stanton/ Wilmington Cmps (DE)
Eastfield Coll (TX)
Edmonds Comm Coll (WA)
Erie Comm Coll, City Campus (NY)
Finger Lakes Comm Coll (NY)
Florida Comm Coll at Jacksonville (FL)
Fresno City Coll (CA)
Gadsden State Comm Coll (AL)
Gateway Comm Coll (CT)
Genesee Comm Coll (NY)
Housatonic Comm Coll (CT)
Howard Coll (TX)
Howard Comm Coll (MD)
Iowa Western Comm Coll (IA)
Kansas City Kansas Comm Coll (KS)
Lac Courte Oreilles Ojibwa Comm Coll (WI)
Lamar State Coll–Port Arthur (TX)
Lane Comm Coll (OR)
Lower Columbia Coll (WA)
Mesabi Range Comm and Tech Coll (MN)
Midland Coll (TX)
Milwaukee Area Tech Coll (WI)
Minneapolis Comm and Tech Coll (MN)
Mohawk Valley Comm Coll (NY)
Moraine Park Tech Coll (WI)
Mt. San Jacinto Coll (CA)
Naugatuck Valley Comm Coll (CT)
New Hampshire Tech Inst (NH)
Northern Virginia Comm Coll (VA)
North Shore Comm Coll (MA)
Northwestern Connecticut Comm-Tech Coll (CT)
Norwalk Comm Coll (CT)
Odessa Coll (TX)
Oklahoma State U, Oklahoma City (OK)
Peninsula Coll (WA)
Pierce Coll (WA)
Prairie State Coll (IL)
Ridgewater Coll (MN)
Rogue Comm Coll (OR)
St. Petersburg Coll (FL)
Sandhills Comm Coll (NC)
Seattle Central Comm Coll (WA)
Southeastern Comm Coll, South Campus (IA)
Southwestern Comm Coll (NC)
Spokane Falls Comm Coll (WA)
Suffolk County Comm Coll (NY)
Sullivan County Comm Coll (NY)
Tacoma Comm Coll (WA)
Texarkana Coll (TX)
Three Rivers Comm Coll (CT)
Tompkins Cortland Comm Coll (NY)
Triton Coll (IL)
Truckee Meadows Comm Coll (NV)
Tunxis Comm Coll (CT)
Vincennes U (IN)
Westchester Comm Coll (NY)
Wor-Wic Comm Coll (MD)

AMERICAN GOVERNMENT
Manatee Comm Coll (FL)

AMERICAN STUDIES
Anne Arundel Comm Coll (MD)
Bucks County Comm Coll (PA)
Foothill Coll (CA)
Greenfield Comm Coll (MA)
Holyoke Comm Coll (MA)
Los Angeles City Coll (CA)
Manatee Comm Coll (FL)
Miami-Dade Comm Coll (FL)
Mississippi Delta Comm Coll (MS)
Naugatuck Valley Comm Coll (CT)
Paul Smith's Coll of Arts and Sciences (NY)
Tacoma Comm Coll (WA)
Tulsa Comm Coll (OK)

ANATOMY
Cañada Coll (CA)
Riverside Comm Coll (CA)
San Jacinto Coll Central Campus (TX)

ANESTHESIOLOGY
Milwaukee Area Tech Coll (WI)

ANIMAL SCIENCES
Abraham Baldwin Ag Coll (GA)
Alamance Comm Coll (NC)
Arkansas State U–Beebe (AR)
Bakersfield Coll (CA)
Berkshire Comm Coll (MA)
Butte Coll (CA)
Camden County Coll (NJ)
Casper Coll (WY)
Coffeyville Comm Coll (KS)
Colby Comm Coll (KS)
Coll of the Sequoias (CA)
Connors State Coll (OK)
Dodge City Comm Coll (KS)
Eastern Oklahoma State Coll (OK)
Eastern Wyoming Coll (WY)
Everett Comm Coll (WA)
Fort Scott Comm Coll (KS)
Harcum Coll (PA)
Hawkeye Comm Coll (IA)
Highland Comm Coll (KS)
Hill Coll of the Hill Jr College District (TX)
James Sprunt Comm Coll (NC)
Kirkwood Comm Coll (IA)

Lamar Comm Coll (CO)
Linn-Benton Comm Coll (OR)
Los Angeles Pierce Coll (CA)
Manor Coll (PA)
Merced Coll (CA)
Mesa Tech Coll (NM)
Modesto Jr Coll (CA)
Moorpark Coll (CA)
Niagara County Comm Coll (NY)
Northwest Coll (WY)
Northwest Mississippi Comm Coll (MS)
Pratt Comm Coll and Area Vocational School (KS)
Reedley Coll (CA)
St. Catharine Coll (KY)
San Joaquin Delta Coll (CA)
Shasta Coll (CA)
Sierra Coll (CA)
Snow Coll (UT)
Southeast Comm Coll, Beatrice Campus (NE)
State U of NY Coll of A&T at Morrisville (NY)
State U of NY Coll of Technology at Alfred (NY)
Trinity Valley Comm Coll (TX)
Ventura Coll (CA)

ANIMAL SCIENCES RELATED
Front Range Comm Coll (CO)

ANTHROPOLOGY
Bakersfield Coll (CA)
Barton County Comm Coll (KS)
Cañada Coll (CA)
Casper Coll (WY)
Cerritos Coll (CA)
Chaffey Coll (CA)
Cochise Coll, Douglas (AZ)
Coll of Alameda (CA)
Coll of Southern Idaho (ID)
Coll of the Desert (CA)
Comm Coll of Southern Nevada (NV)
Crafton Hills Coll (CA)
Cypress Coll (CA)
Darton Coll (GA)
Daytona Beach Comm Coll (FL)
Delaware County Comm Coll (PA)
East Central Coll (MO)
Eastern Arizona Coll (AZ)
East Georgia Coll (GA)
Everett Comm Coll (WA)
Foothill Coll (CA)
Fresno City Coll (CA)
Fullerton Coll (CA)
Georgia Perimeter Coll (GA)
Great Basin Coll (NV)
Imperial Valley Coll (CA)
Indian River Comm Coll (FL)
Kellogg Comm Coll (MI)
Laramie County Comm Coll (WY)
Lincoln Land Comm Coll (IL)
Lower Columbia Coll (WA)
Miami-Dade Comm Coll (FL)
Miami U–Middletown Campus (OH)
Midland Coll (TX)
Monterey Peninsula Coll (CA)
Moorpark Coll (CA)
North Idaho Coll (ID)
Orange Coast Coll (CA)
Oxnard Coll (CA)
Palomar Coll (CA)
Pasadena City Coll (CA)
Pima Comm Coll (AZ)
Riverside Comm Coll (CA)
San Bernardino Valley Coll (CA)
San Diego City Coll (CA)
San Diego Mesa Coll (CA)
San Jacinto Coll Central Campus (TX)
San Joaquin Delta Coll (CA)
San Juan Coll (NM)
Santa Ana Coll (CA)
Santa Barbara City Coll (CA)
Santa Monica Coll (CA)
Sauk Valley Comm Coll (IL)
Skagit Valley Coll (WA)
Southwestern Coll (CA)
Tacoma Comm Coll (WA)
Triton Coll (IL)
Umpqua Comm Coll (OR)
Vincennes U (IN)
Western Nebraska Comm Coll (NE)
Western Wyoming Comm Coll (WY)

APPAREL MARKETING
Alexandria Tech Coll (MN)
California Design Coll (CA)
Fashion Inst of Design & Merchandising, LA Campus (CA)
Fashion Inst of Design & Merchandising, SD Campus (CA)
Fashion Inst of Design & Merchandising, SF Campus (CA)

APPLIED ART
Allan Hancock Coll (CA)
Anne Arundel Comm Coll (MD)
The Art Inst of Fort Lauderdale (FL)
The Art Inst of Houston (TX)
The Art Inst of Philadelphia (PA)
The Art Inst of Pittsburgh (PA)
Barton County Comm Coll (KS)
Bristol Comm Coll (MA)
Burlington County Coll (NJ)
Butte Coll (CA)
Camden County Coll (NJ)
Casper Coll (WY)
Centralia Coll (WA)
Central Piedmont Comm Coll (NC)
Chattanooga State Tech Comm Coll (TN)
Coastal Bend Coll (TX)
Coffeyville Comm Coll (KS)
Coll of Marin (CA)
The Comm Coll of Baltimore County–Catonsville Campus (MD)
County Coll of Morris (NJ)
Cuesta Coll (CA)
Cypress Coll (CA)
Del Mar Coll (TX)
Delta Coll (MI)
Edison Comm Coll (FL)
Evergreen Valley Coll (CA)
Georgia Perimeter Coll (GA)
Glendale Comm Coll (CA)
Henry Ford Comm Coll (MI)
Hill Coll of the Hill Jr College District (TX)
Howard Comm Coll (MD)
Iowa Lakes Comm Coll (IA)
Jefferson Davis Comm Coll (AL)
Jones County Jr Coll (MS)
Kingsborough Comm Coll of City U of NY (NY)
Kirkwood Comm Coll (IA)
Lincoln Coll, Lincoln (IL)
Lincoln Coll, Normal (IL)
Lon Morris Coll (TX)
Los Angeles City Coll (CA)
Maryland Coll of Art and Design (MD)
Merced Coll (CA)
Middlesex County Coll (NJ)
Mississippi Delta Comm Coll (MS)
Northern Virginia Comm Coll (VA)
North Seattle Comm Coll (WA)
Odessa Coll (TX)
Oklahoma City Comm Coll (OK)
Palomar Coll (CA)
Pratt Comm Coll and Area Vocational School (KS)
Ridgewater Coll (MN)
Rockland Comm Coll (NY)
San Diego Mesa Coll (CA)
Sinclair Comm Coll (OH)
Tunxis Comm Coll (CT)
U of New Mexico–Los Alamos Branch (NM)
Westchester Comm Coll (NY)

APPLIED MATHEMATICS
Chabot Coll (CA)
Jefferson Comm Coll (KY)
Lincoln Coll, Lincoln (IL)

AQUACULTURE OPERATIONS/ PRODUCTION MANAGEMENT
Brunswick Comm Coll (NC)
Hillsborough Comm Coll (FL)

ARCHAEOLOGY
East Central Coll (MO)
Palomar Coll (CA)
Pima Comm Coll (AZ)

ARCHITECTURAL DRAFTING
Albuquerque Tech Vocational Inst (NM)
Anoka-Hennepin Tech Coll (MN)
Butler County Comm Coll (PA)
Clinton Comm Coll (IA)
Coll of Lake County (IL)
Comm Coll of Allegheny County (PA)
Dixie State Coll of Utah (UT)
Dunwoody Coll of Technology (MN)
Florida Comm Coll at Jacksonville (FL)
Florida Tech Coll, Orlando (FL)
Glendale Comm Coll (AZ)
Hennepin Tech Coll (MN)
Indian River Comm Coll (FL)
Island Drafting and Tech Inst (NY)
Lincoln Land Comm Coll (IL)
Louisville Tech Inst (KY)
Montgomery Coll (MD)
New England Inst of Tech & Florida Culinary Inst (FL)
New York City Tech Coll of the City U of NY (NY)
North Hennepin Comm Coll (MN)
Northwest Tech Inst (MN)
Pima Comm Coll (AZ)
Rend Lake Coll (IL)
St. Cloud Tech Coll (MN)
Silicon Valley Coll, San Jose (CA)
Spencerian Coll–Lexington (KY)
U of Kentucky, Lexington Comm Coll (KY)
Westwood Coll of Technology–Denver North (CO)

ARCHITECTURAL ENGINEERING TECHNOLOGY
Allan Hancock Coll (CA)
Amarillo Coll (TX)
Anne Arundel Comm Coll (MD)
Arapahoe Comm Coll (CO)
Bakersfield Coll (CA)
Bates Tech Coll (WA)
Burlington County Coll (NJ)
Butler County Comm Coll (PA)
Cape Fear Comm Coll (NC)
Catawba Valley Comm Coll (NC)
Central Piedmont Comm Coll (NC)
Central Virginia Comm Coll (VA)
Cerritos Coll (CA)
Chabot Coll (CA)
Chesapeake Coll (MD)
Chippewa Valley Tech Coll (WI)
Cincinnati State Tech and Comm Coll (OH)
City Colls of Chicago, Richard J Daley Coll (IL)
City Colls of Chicago, Wilbur Wright Coll (IL)
Clover Park Tech Coll (WA)
Coastal Carolina Comm Coll (NC)
Coll of Marin (CA)
Coll of the Desert (CA)
Coll of the Redwoods (CA)
Coll of the Sequoias (CA)
Columbus State Comm Coll (OH)
The Comm Coll of Baltimore County–Catonsville Campus (MD)
Comm Coll of Beaver County (PA)
Daytona Beach Comm Coll (FL)
Delaware County Comm Coll (PA)
Delaware Tech & Comm Coll, Jack F Owens Cmps (DE)
Delaware Tech & Comm Coll, Stanton/ Wilmington Cmps (DE)
Delaware Tech & Comm Coll, Terry Cmps (DE)
Delgado Comm Coll (LA)
Del Mar Coll (TX)
Delta Coll (MI)
Doña Ana Branch Comm Coll (NM)
Durham Tech Comm Coll (NC)
Dutchess Comm Coll (NY)
El Centro Coll (TX)
Erie Comm Coll, South Campus (NY)
Essex County Coll (NJ)
Fayetteville Tech Comm Coll (NC)
Finger Lakes Comm Coll (NY)
Florida Comm Coll at Jacksonville (FL)
Forsyth Tech Comm Coll (NC)
Fort Scott Comm Coll (KS)
Front Range Comm Coll (CO)
Fullerton Coll (CA)
Gaston Coll (NC)
Golden West Coll (CA)
Grand Rapids Comm Coll (MI)
Greenville Tech Coll (SC)
Guam Comm Coll (GU)
Guilford Tech Comm Coll (NC)
Harrisburg Area Comm Coll (PA)
Hawkeye Comm Coll (IA)
Hillsborough Comm Coll (FL)
Honolulu Comm Coll (HI)
Inst of Design and Construction (NY)
Iowa Western Comm Coll (IA)
Jefferson Coll (MO)
Johnson Coll (PA)
John Tyler Comm Coll (VA)
J. Sargeant Reynolds Comm Coll (VA)
Lake Land Coll (IL)
Lamar State Coll–Orange (TX)
Lansing Comm Coll (MI)
Long Beach City Coll (CA)
Los Angeles City Coll (CA)
Los Angeles Harbor Coll (CA)
Los Angeles Pierce Coll (CA)
Louisville Tech Inst (KY)
Luzerne County Comm Coll (PA)
Macomb Comm Coll (MI)
Massasoit Comm Coll (MA)
Mayland Comm Coll (NC)
Mercer County Comm Coll (NJ)
Metropolitan Comm Coll (NE)
Miami-Dade Comm Coll (FL)
Midlands Tech Coll (SC)
MiraCosta Coll (CA)
Mississippi Delta Comm Coll (MS)
Modesto Jr Coll (CA)
Monroe County Comm Coll (MI)
Mott Comm Coll (MI)
Mt. Hood Comm Coll (OR)
Nash Comm Coll (NC)
Nashville State Tech Inst (TN)
New England Inst of Technology (RI)
New Hampshire Tech Inst (NH)
New River Comm Coll (VA)
Northampton County Area Comm Coll (PA)
Northcentral Tech Coll (WI)
North Dakota State Coll of Science (ND)
Northern Virginia Comm Coll (VA)
Northland Comm and Tech Coll (MN)
Norwalk Comm Coll (CT)
Oakton Comm Coll (IL)
Oklahoma State U, Oklahoma City (OK)
Oklahoma State U, Okmulgee (OK)
Onondaga Comm Coll (NY)
Orange Coast Coll (CA)
Orange County Comm Coll (NY)
Pasadena City Coll (CA)
Pennsylvania Coll of Technology (PA)
Pennsylvania Inst of Technology (PA)
Penn State U Fayette Campus of the Commonwealth Coll (PA)
Penn State U Worthington Scranton Cmps Commonwealth Coll (PA)
Phoenix Coll (AZ)
Pikes Peak Comm Coll (CO)
Pitt Comm Coll (NC)
Roanoke-Chowan Comm Coll (NC)
St. Clair County Comm Coll (MI)
St. Cloud Tech Coll (MN)
St. Petersburg Coll (FL)
San Bernardino Valley Coll (CA)
Sandhills Comm Coll (NC)
San Diego Mesa Coll (CA)
Santa Monica Coll (CA)
Seminole Comm Coll (FL)
Sinclair Comm Coll (OH)
Southeast Comm Coll, Milford Campus (NE)
Southeast Tech Inst (SD)
Southern Maine Tech Coll (ME)
South Suburban Coll (IL)
Southwestern Coll (CA)
Southwest Tennessee Comm Coll (TN)
Spartanburg Tech Coll (SC)
Spokane Comm Coll (WA)
Springfield Tech Comm Coll (MA)
Stark State Coll of Technology (OH)
State U of NY Coll of A&T at Morrisville (NY)
State U of NY Coll of Technology at Alfred (NY)
State U of NY Coll of Technology at Delhi (NY)
Tarrant County Coll District (TX)
Terra State Comm Coll (OH)
Thaddeus Stevens Coll of Technology (PA)
Three Rivers Comm Coll (CT)
Triangle Tech, Inc. (PA)
Triangle Tech, Inc.–Erie School (PA)
Triangle Tech, Inc.–Greensburg Center (PA)
Triton Coll (IL)
Truckee Meadows Comm Coll (NV)
U of Kentucky, Lexington Comm Coll (KY)
Ventura Coll (CA)
Vermilion Comm Coll (MN)
Vermont Tech Coll (VT)
Vincennes U (IN)
Wake Tech Comm Coll (NC)
Western Iowa Tech Comm Coll (IA)
Westmoreland County Comm Coll (PA)
Wilkes Comm Coll (NC)
Wisconsin Indianhead Tech Coll (WI)

ARCHITECTURAL ENVIRONMENTAL DESIGN
Abraham Baldwin Ag Coll (GA)
The Art Inst of Pittsburgh (PA)
Iowa Lakes Comm Coll (IA)
Queensborough Comm Coll of City U of NY (NY)
Scottsdale Comm Coll (AZ)

ARCHITECTURAL HISTORY
Belmont Tech Coll (OH)
Bucks County Comm Coll (PA)
Randolph Comm Coll (NC)

ARCHITECTURE
Allen County Comm Coll (KS)
Brazosport Coll (TX)
Brookdale Comm Coll (NJ)
Central Maine Tech Coll (ME)
Harrisburg Area Comm Coll (PA)
Howard Comm Coll (MD)
Oakland Comm Coll (MI)
Riverside Comm Coll (CA)
San Diego Mesa Coll (CA)
Tulsa Comm Coll (OK)

AREA STUDIES
Santa Fe Comm Coll (NM)

AREA STUDIES RELATED
Oklahoma City Comm Coll (OK)

ARMY R.O.T.C./MILITARY SCIENCE
Georgia Military Coll (GA)
New Mexico Military Inst (NM)
Sacramento City Coll (CA)

ART
Abraham Baldwin Ag Coll (GA)
Allan Hancock Coll (CA)
Allegany Coll of Maryland (MD)
Allen County Comm Coll (KS)
Alvin Comm Coll (TX)
Amarillo Coll (TX)
American River Coll (CA)
Andrew Coll (GA)
Angelina Coll (TX)
Anne Arundel Comm Coll (MD)
Arizona Western Coll (AZ)
The Art Inst of Philadelphia (PA)
Asnuntuck Comm Coll (CT)
Atlanta Metropolitan Coll (GA)
Austin Comm Coll (TX)
Bacone Coll (OK)
Bainbridge Coll (GA)
Bakersfield Coll (CA)
Barton County Comm Coll (KS)
Bergen Comm Coll (NJ)
Berkshire Comm Coll (MA)
Blue Ridge Comm Coll (NC)
Bradley Academy for the Visual Arts (PA)
Brazosport Coll (TX)
Bristol Comm Coll (MA)
Bronx Comm Coll of City U of NY (NY)
Brookdale Comm Coll (NJ)
Bucks County Comm Coll (PA)
Burlington County Coll (NJ)
Butte Coll (CA)
Camden County Coll (NJ)
Cañada Coll (CA)

Cape Cod Comm Coll (MA)
Casper Coll (WY)
Cecil Comm Coll (MD)
Centralia Coll (WA)
Central Oregon Comm Coll (OR)
Central Piedmont Comm Coll (NC)
Central Wyoming Coll (WY)
Cerritos Coll (CA)
Cerro Coso Comm Coll (CA)
Chabot Coll (CA)
Chaffey Coll (CA)
Chesapeake Coll (MD)
Chipola Jr Coll (FL)
Citrus Coll (CA)
City Coll of San Francisco (CA)
City Colls of Chicago, Harry S Truman Coll (IL)
City Colls of Chicago, Malcolm X Coll (IL)
City Colls of Chicago, Richard J Daley Coll (IL)
City Colls of Chicago, Wilbur Wright Coll (IL)
Clark Coll (WA)
Coahoma Comm Coll (MS)
Coastal Bend Coll (TX)
Coastal Georgia Comm Coll (GA)
Cochise Coll, Douglas (AZ)
Coffeyville Comm Coll (KS)
Coll of Alameda (CA)
Coll of Marin (CA)
Coll of Southern Idaho (ID)
Coll of the Canyons (CA)
Coll of the Desert (CA)
Coll of the Sequoias (CA)
Colorado Mountn Coll (CO)
Colorado Mountn Coll, Timberline Cmps (CO)
Columbia-Greene Comm Coll (NY)
Columbia State Comm Coll (TN)
Comm Coll of Allegheny County (PA)
The Comm Coll of Baltimore County–Catonsville Campus (MD)
Comm Coll of Rhode Island (RI)
Comm Coll of Southern Nevada (NV)
Compton Comm Coll (CA)
Cowley County Comm Coll and Voc-Tech School (KS)
Crafton Hills Coll (CA)
Crowder Coll (MO)
Cuesta Coll (CA)
Cypress Coll (CA)
Danville Area Comm Coll (IL)
Darton Coll (GA)
Daytona Beach Comm Coll (FL)
De Anza Coll (CA)
Del Mar Coll (TX)
Diné Coll (AZ)
Dixie State Coll of Utah (UT)
Dodge City Comm Coll (KS)
East Central Coll (MO)
East Central Comm Coll (MS)
Eastern Arizona Coll (AZ)
Eastern Oklahoma State Coll (OK)
Eastern Wyoming Coll (WY)
East Georgia Coll (GA)
East Mississippi Comm Coll (MS)
Edison Comm Coll (FL)
Edison State Comm Coll (OH)
Ellsworth Comm Coll (IA)
Essex County Coll (NJ)
Everett Comm Coll (WA)
Floyd Coll (GA)
Foothill Coll (CA)
Frederick Comm Coll (MD)
Fresno City Coll (CA)
Fullerton Coll (CA)
Fulton-Montgomery Comm Coll (NY)
Gaston Coll (NC)
Gavilan Coll (CA)
Georgia Perimeter Coll (GA)
Glendale Comm Coll (CA)
Golden West Coll (CA)
Gordon Coll (GA)
Grand Rapids Comm Coll (MI)
Grayson County Coll (TX)
Great Basin Coll (NV)
Greenfield Comm Coll (MA)
Harford Comm Coll (MD)
Harrisburg Area Comm Coll (PA)
Henry Ford Comm Coll (MI)
Herkimer County Comm Coll (NY)
Highland Comm Coll (IL)
Highland Comm Coll (KS)
Highline Comm Coll (WA)
Hill Coll of the Hill Jr College District (TX)
Hillsborough Comm Coll (FL)
Hinds Comm Coll (MS)
Housatonic Comm Coll (CT)
Howard Coll (TX)
Howard Comm Coll (MD)
Imperial Valley Coll (CA)
Inst of American Indian Arts (NM)
Iowa Lakes Comm Coll (IA)
Jefferson Coll (MO)
Jefferson Comm Coll (KY)
John A. Logan Coll (IL)
Joliet Jr Coll (IL)
Kellogg Comm Coll (MI)
Kent State U, Stark Campus (OH)
Keystone Coll (PA)
Kilgore Coll (TX)
Kingsborough Comm Coll of City U of NY (NY)
Kirkwood Comm Coll (IA)
Kishwaukee Coll (IL)
Labette Comm Coll (KS)
Lake Michigan Coll (MI)
Lake Tahoe Comm Coll (CA)
Lamar Comm Coll (CO)
Lansing Comm Coll (MI)
Laramie County Comm Coll (WY)
Lehigh Carbon Comm Coll (PA)
Lenoir Comm Coll (NC)
Lewis and Clark Comm Coll (IL)
Lincoln Land Comm Coll (IL)
Linn-Benton Comm Coll (OR)
Long Beach City Coll (CA)
Lon Morris Coll (TX)
Lorain County Comm Coll (OH)
Los Angeles City Coll (CA)
Los Angeles Pierce Coll (CA)
Lower Columbia Coll (WA)
Manatee Comm Coll (FL)
Maryland Coll of Art and Design (MD)
McHenry County Coll (IL)
Merced Coll (CA)
Mercer County Comm Coll (NJ)
Miami-Dade Comm Coll (FL)
Miami U–Middletown Campus (OH)
Middlesex Comm Coll (MA)
Middlesex County Coll (NJ)
Midland Coll (TX)
Mid Michigan Comm Coll (MI)
Minot State U–Bottineau Campus (ND)
MiraCosta Coll (CA)
Mississippi Gulf Coast Comm Coll (MS)
Mitchell Comm Coll (NC)
Modesto Jr Coll (CA)
Mohave Comm Coll (AZ)
Mohawk Valley Comm Coll (NY)
Monroe Comm Coll (NY)
Monroe County Comm Coll (MI)
Monterey Peninsula Coll (CA)
Montgomery County Comm Coll (PA)
Moorpark Coll (CA)
Morton Coll (IL)
Mt. San Jacinto Coll (CA)
Mount Wachusett Comm Coll (MA)
Nassau Comm Coll (NY)
Navarro Coll (TX)
New Mexico Military Inst (NM)
Northeast Comm Coll (NE)
Northern Virginia Comm Coll (VA)
North Harris Coll (TX)
North Idaho Coll (ID)
North Seattle Comm Coll (WA)
Northwest Coll (WY)
Northwestern Connecticut Comm-Tech Coll (CT)
Northwest Mississippi Comm Coll (MS)
Northwest-Shoals Comm Coll (AL)
Norwalk Comm Coll (CT)
Oakton Comm Coll (IL)
Odessa Coll (TX)
Okaloosa-Walton Comm Coll (FL)
Oklahoma City Comm Coll (OK)
Onondaga Comm Coll (NY)
Orange Coast Coll (CA)
Palm Beach Comm Coll (FL)
Palomar Coll (CA)
Parkland Coll (IL)
Pasadena City Coll (CA)
Pensacola Jr Coll (FL)
Phoenix Coll (AZ)
Piedmont Virginia Comm Coll (VA)
Pima Comm Coll (AZ)
Pratt Comm Coll and Area Vocational School (KS)
Quinsigamond Comm Coll (MA)
Red Rocks Comm Coll (CO)
Reedley Coll (CA)
Rend Lake Coll (IL)
Ridgewater Coll (MN)
Riverside Comm Coll (CA)
Roane State Comm Coll (TN)
Rockingham Comm Coll (NC)
Rockland Comm Coll (NY)
Sacramento City Coll (CA)
St. Catharine Coll (KY)
St. Clair County Comm Coll (MI)
St. Louis Comm Coll at Florissant Valley (MO)
St. Philip's Coll (TX)
San Bernardino Valley Coll (CA)
Sandhills Comm Coll (NC)
San Diego City Coll (CA)
San Diego Mesa Coll (CA)
San Jacinto Coll Central Campus (TX)
San Jacinto Coll North Campus (TX)
San Jacinto Coll South Campus (TX)
San Joaquin Delta Coll (CA)
San Juan Coll (NM)
Santa Ana Coll (CA)
Santa Fe Comm Coll (NM)
Santa Monica Coll (CA)
Sauk Valley Comm Coll (IL)
Seminole State Coll (OK)
Shasta Coll (CA)
Sheridan Coll (WY)
Sierra Coll (CA)
Sinclair Comm Coll (OH)
Skagit Valley Coll (WA)
Snow Coll (UT)
Southeast Comm Coll, Beatrice Campus (NE)
Southeastern Comm Coll (NC)
South Mountain Comm Coll (AZ)
South Plains Coll (TX)
Southwestern Coll (CA)
Spokane Falls Comm Coll (WA)
State Fair Comm Coll (MO)
Suffolk County Comm Coll (NY)
Tacoma Comm Coll (WA)
Taft Coll (CA)
Temple Coll (TX)
Texarkana Coll (TX)
Thomas Nelson Comm Coll (VA)
Tidewater Comm Coll (VA)
Trinity Valley Comm Coll (TX)
Triton Coll (IL)
Tulsa Comm Coll (OK)
Tunxis Comm Coll (CT)
Tyler Jr Coll (TX)
Umpqua Comm Coll (OR)
U of New Mexico–Gallup (NM)
Ventura Coll (CA)
Vermilion Comm Coll (MN)
Victor Valley Coll (CA)
Vincennes U (IN)
Virginia Western Comm Coll (VA)
Vista Comm Coll (CA)
Walters State Comm Coll (TN)
Waubonsee Comm Coll (IL)
Western Nebraska Comm Coll (NE)
Western Piedmont Comm Coll (NC)
Western Texas Coll (TX)
Western Wyoming Comm Coll (WY)
Wharton County Jr Coll (TX)
Young Harris Coll (GA)

ART EDUCATION
Angelina Coll (TX)
Bakersfield Coll (CA)
Chemeketa Comm Coll (OR)
Coastal Bend Coll (TX)
Coll of the Siskiyous (CA)
Compton Comm Coll (CA)
Del Mar Coll (TX)
Delta Coll (MI)
East Central Comm Coll (MS)
Eastern Arizona Coll (AZ)
Eastern Oklahoma State Coll (OK)
Ellsworth Comm Coll (IA)
Grayson County Coll (TX)
Halifax Comm Coll (NC)
Hill Coll of the Hill Jr College District (TX)
Independence Comm Coll (KS)
Indian River Comm Coll (FL)
Iowa Lakes Comm Coll (IA)
Jefferson Comm Coll (KY)
John A. Logan Coll (IL)
Jones County Jr Coll (MS)
Kellogg Comm Coll (MI)
Kirkwood Comm Coll (IA)
Kishwaukee Coll (IL)
Lincoln Coll, Lincoln (IL)
Lincoln Coll, Normal (IL)
Lon Morris Coll (TX)
Los Angeles Mission Coll (CA)
McLennan Comm Coll (TX)
Miami-Dade Comm Coll (FL)
Mississippi Delta Comm Coll (MS)
Mississippi Gulf Coast Comm Coll (MS)
Northeast Comm Coll (NE)
North Harris Coll (TX)
Northwest Coll (WY)
Oxnard Coll (CA)
Palomar Coll (CA)
Parkland Coll (IL)
Pensacola Jr Coll (FL)
Pratt Comm Coll and Area Vocational School (KS)
Roane State Comm Coll (TN)
St. Catharine Coll (KY)
Sandhills Comm Coll (NC)
Trinidad State Jr Coll (CO)
Umpqua Comm Coll (OR)
Vermilion Comm Coll (MN)
Vincennes U (IN)
Wallace State Comm Coll (AL)
Walters State Comm Coll (TN)
Waubonsee Comm Coll (IL)
Western Nebraska Comm Coll (NE)
Western Texas Coll (TX)
Young Harris Coll (GA)

ART HISTORY
Cañada Coll (CA)
De Anza Coll (CA)
Dixie State Coll of Utah (UT)
Foothill Coll (CA)
Glendale Comm Coll (CA)
Hill Coll of the Hill Jr College District (TX)
Iowa Lakes Comm Coll (IA)
Lincoln Coll, Lincoln (IL)
Lon Morris Coll (TX)
Manatee Comm Coll (FL)
Mercer County Comm Coll (NJ)
Monterey Peninsula Coll (CA)
Northern Virginia Comm Coll (VA)
Palm Beach Comm Coll (FL)
Pasadena City Coll (CA)
Rogue Comm Coll (OR)
St. Catharine Coll (KY)
Santa Barbara City Coll (CA)
Skagit Valley Coll (WA)
Umpqua Comm Coll (OR)
Vermilion Comm Coll (MN)

ARTIFICIAL INTELLIGENCE/ ROBOTICS
Arkansas State U–Beebe (AR)
Cuesta Coll (CA)
Louisville Tech Inst (KY)
Southeast Tech Inst (SD)
Vincennes U (IN)
York Tech Inst (PA)

ARTS MANAGEMENT
Cuesta Coll (CA)
Herkimer County Comm Coll (NY)
Palomar Coll (CA)

ART THERAPY
Burlington County Coll (NJ)

ASIAN-AMERICAN STUDIES
Southwestern Coll (CA)

ASIAN STUDIES
City Coll of San Francisco (CA)
Manatee Comm Coll (FL)
Miami-Dade Comm Coll (FL)
Pima Comm Coll (AZ)

ASTRONOMY
Anne Arundel Comm Coll (MD)
Austin Comm Coll (TX)
Crafton Hills Coll (CA)
Daytona Beach Comm Coll (FL)
Fullerton Coll (CA)
Iowa Lakes Comm Coll (IA)
Manatee Comm Coll (FL)
North Idaho Coll (ID)
Palomar Coll (CA)
Pasadena City Coll (CA)
Riverside Comm Coll (CA)
San Bernardino Valley Coll (CA)
Santa Monica Coll (CA)
Southwestern Coll (CA)
Tulsa Comm Coll (OK)

ATHLETIC TRAINING/SPORTS MEDICINE
Allen County Comm Coll (KS)
Barton County Comm Coll (KS)
Coffeyville Comm Coll (KS)
Coll of the Sequoias (CA)
Comm Coll of Allegheny County (PA)
Dean Coll (MA)
Dodge City Comm Coll (KS)
Foothill Coll (CA)
Fort Scott Comm Coll (KS)
Front Range Comm Coll (CO)
Garden City Comm Coll (KS)
Highland Comm Coll (KS)
Independence Comm Coll (KS)
Lorain County Comm Coll (OH)
Louisburg Coll (NC)
Meridian Comm Coll (MS)
Mitchell Coll (CT)
Neosho County Comm Coll (KS)
North Idaho Coll (ID)
Northland Comm and Tech Coll (MN)
Odessa Coll (TX)
Orange Coast Coll (CA)
Pratt Comm Coll and Area Vocational School (KS)
Santa Barbara City Coll (CA)
Santa Monica Coll (CA)
Vincennes U (IN)

ATMOSPHERIC SCIENCES
City Coll of San Francisco (CA)
Comm Coll of the Air Force (AL)
Daytona Beach Comm Coll (FL)
Everett Comm Coll (WA)
Okaloosa-Walton Comm Coll (FL)

AUDIO ENGINEERING
The Art Inst of Pittsburgh (PA)
The Art Inst of Seattle (WA)
Brookdale Comm Coll (NJ)
Full Sail Real World Education (FL)
Harford Comm Coll (MD)
International Coll of Broadcasting (OH)
Mt. San Jacinto Coll (CA)
Northeast Comm Coll (NE)
Ridgewater Coll (MN)
San Jacinto Coll Central Campus (TX)
Shoreline Comm Coll (WA)
Southern Ohio Coll, Cincinnati Campus (OH)
South Plains Coll (TX)
Texas State Tech Coll– Waco/ Marshall Campus (TX)

AUTO BODY REPAIR
Antelope Valley Coll (CA)
Bates Tech Coll (WA)
Bismarck State Coll (ND)
Black Hawk Coll, Moline (IL)
Central Comm Coll–Hastings Campus (NE)
Century Comm and Tech Coll (MN)
Clackamas Comm Coll (OR)
Coll of Southern Idaho (ID)
Cypress Coll (CA)
Dixie State Coll of Utah (UT)
Dunwoody Coll of Technology (MN)
Eastfield Coll (TX)
Erie Comm Coll, South Campus (NY)
Fayetteville Tech Comm Coll (NC)
Florida Comm Coll at Jacksonville (FL)
Fresno City Coll (CA)
Grayson County Coll (TX)
Green River Comm Coll (WA)
Hawkeye Comm Coll (IA)
Hill Coll of the Hill Jr College District (TX)
Hutchinson Comm Coll and Area Vocational School (KS)
Illinois Eastern Comm Colls, Olney Central Coll (IL)
Kaskaskia Coll (IL)

Kauai Comm Coll (HI)
Kishwaukee Coll (IL)
Lake Washington Tech Coll (WA)
Louisiana Tech Coll–Delta Ouachita Campus (LA)
Modesto Jr Coll (CA)
Montana State U Coll of Tech-Great Falls (MT)
Mott Comm Coll (MI)
Nashville Auto Diesel Coll (TN)
North Dakota State Coll of Science (ND)
Northeast Comm Coll (NE)
Olympic Coll (WA)
Parkland Coll (IL)
Pennsylvania Coll of Technology (PA)
Pikes Peak Comm Coll (CO)
Prairie State Coll (IL)
Riverland Comm Coll (MN)
St. Cloud Tech Coll (MN)
St. Philip's Coll (TX)
San Jacinto Coll North Campus (TX)
San Juan Coll (NM)
Scott Comm Coll (IA)
Southeast Tech Inst (SD)
Southwestern Comm Coll (IA)
Southwest Wisconsin Tech Coll (WI)
Stanly Comm Coll (NC)
State U of NY Coll of Technology at Alfred (NY)
Texas State Tech Coll–Harlingen (TX)
Texas State Tech Coll– Waco/Marshall Campus (TX)
Walla Walla Comm Coll (WA)
Western Iowa Tech Comm Coll (IA)

AUTO MECHANIC/TECHNICIAN

Aims Comm Coll (CO)
Alamance Comm Coll (NC)
Allan Hancock Coll (CA)
Allegany Coll of Maryland (MD)
Alpena Comm Coll (MI)
Amarillo Coll (TX)
American River Coll (CA)
Angelina Coll (TX)
Anoka-Hennepin Tech Coll (MN)
Antelope Valley Coll (CA)
Arapahoe Comm Coll (CO)
Arizona Automotive Inst (AZ)
Arizona Western Coll (AZ)
Asheville-Buncombe Tech Comm Coll (NC)
Athens Tech Coll (GA)
Austin Comm Coll (TX)
Bainbridge Coll (GA)
Bakersfield Coll (CA)
Barstow Coll (CA)
Barton County Comm Coll (KS)
Bates Tech Coll (WA)
Bay de Noc Comm Coll (MI)
Beaufort County Comm Coll (NC)
Benjamin Franklin Inst of Technology (MA)
Bergen Comm Coll (NJ)
Bessemer State Tech Coll (AL)
Big Bend Comm Coll (WA)
Bismarck State Coll (ND)
Black Hawk Coll, Moline (IL)
Brazosport Coll (TX)
Brevard Comm Coll (FL)
Brookdale Comm Coll (NJ)
Burlington County Coll (NJ)
Butte Coll (CA)
Camden County Coll (NJ)
Cape Fear Comm Coll (NC)
Carl Sandburg Coll (IL)
Casper Coll (WY)
Catawba Valley Comm Coll (NC)
Cedar Valley Coll (TX)
Central Arizona Coll (AZ)
Central Carolina Comm Coll (NC)
Central Comm Coll–Columbus Campus (NE)
Central Comm Coll–Grand Island Campus (NE)
Central Comm Coll–Hastings Campus (NE)
Central Maine Tech Coll (ME)
Central Oregon Comm Coll (OR)
Central Piedmont Comm Coll (NC)
Central Texas Coll (TX)
Central Wyoming Coll (WY)
Century Comm and Tech Coll (MN)
Cerritos Coll (CA)
Cerro Coso Comm Coll (CA)
Chabot Coll (CA)
Chaffey Coll (CA)
Chattahoochee Tech Coll (GA)
Chattanooga State Tech Comm Coll (TN)
Chemeketa Comm Coll (OR)
Chippewa Valley Tech Coll (WI)
Cisco Jr Coll (TX)
Citrus Coll (CA)
City Coll of San Francisco (CA)
Clackamas Comm Coll (OR)
Clark Coll (WA)
Clovis Comm Coll (NM)
Coastal Bend Coll (TX)
Coffeyville Comm Coll (KS)
Coll of Alameda (CA)
Coll of DuPage (IL)
Coll of Eastern Utah (UT)
Coll of Lake County (IL)
Coll of Marin (CA)
Coll of Southern Idaho (ID)
Coll of the Desert (CA)
Coll of the Redwoods (CA)
Coll of the Sequoias (CA)
Columbia-Greene Comm Coll (NY)
Columbus State Comm Coll (OH)
Comm Coll of Aurora (CO)
The Comm Coll of Baltimore County–Catonsville Campus (MD)
Comm Coll of Southern Nevada (NV)
Comm Coll of the Air Force (AL)
Compton Comm Coll (CA)
Corning Comm Coll (NY)
Cowley County Comm Coll and Voc-Tech School (KS)
Craven Comm Coll (NC)
Cuesta Coll (CA)
Cuyahoga Comm Coll (OH)
Cuyamaca Coll (CA)
Cypress Coll (CA)
Danville Area Comm Coll (IL)
Dawson Comm Coll (MT)
Daytona Beach Comm Coll (FL)
De Anza Coll (CA)
Delaware Tech & Comm Coll, Jack F Owens Cmps (DE)
Delgado Comm Coll (LA)
Del Mar Coll (TX)
Delta Coll (MI)
Denmark Tech Coll (SC)
Des Moines Area Comm Coll (IA)
Dixie State Coll of Utah (UT)
Dodge City Comm Coll (KS)
Don Bosco Coll of Science and Technology (CA)
Doña Ana Branch Comm Coll (NM)
Douglas MacArthur State Tech Coll (AL)
Dunwoody Coll of Technology (MN)
Durham Tech Comm Coll (NC)
East Central Coll (MO)
Eastern Arizona Coll (AZ)
Eastern Idaho Tech Coll (ID)
Eastern Maine Tech Coll (ME)
Eastfield Coll (TX)
East Mississippi Comm Coll (MS)
Enterprise State Jr Coll (AL)
Erie Comm Coll, South Campus (NY)
Evergreen Valley Coll (CA)
Fayetteville Tech Comm Coll (NC)
Florence-Darlington Tech Coll (SC)
Florida Comm Coll at Jacksonville (FL)
Floyd Coll (GA)
Forsyth Tech Comm Coll (NC)
Fresno City Coll (CA)
Front Range Comm Coll (CO)
Fullerton Coll (CA)
Fulton-Montgomery Comm Coll (NY)
Garden City Comm Coll (KS)
Gaston Coll (NC)
GateWay Comm Coll (AZ)
Gateway Comm Coll (CT)
Gateway Tech Coll (WI)
Gavilan Coll (CA)
Georgia Perimeter Coll (GA)
Glendale Comm Coll (AZ)
Glen Oaks Comm Coll (MI)
Gloucester County Coll (NJ)
Gogebic Comm Coll (MI)
Golden West Coll (CA)
Grand Rapids Comm Coll (MI)
Grays Harbor Coll (WA)
Green River Comm Coll (WA)
Greenville Tech Coll (SC)
Guam Comm Coll (GU)
Guilford Tech Comm Coll (NC)
Gwinnett Tech Coll (GA)
Harford Comm Coll (MD)
Harrisburg Area Comm Coll (PA)
Hawaii Comm Coll (HI)
Hawkeye Comm Coll (IA)
Helena Coll of Tech of The U of Montana (MT)
Hennepin Tech Coll (MN)
Henry Ford Comm Coll (MI)
Highland Comm Coll (IL)
Highland Comm Coll (KS)
Hill Coll of the Hill Jr College District (TX)
Honolulu Comm Coll (HI)
Houston Comm Coll System (TX)
Howard Coll (TX)
Hutchinson Comm Coll and Area Vocational School (KS)
Illinois Eastern Comm Colls, Olney Central Coll (IL)
Imperial Valley Coll (CA)
Indian Hills Comm Coll (IA)
Indian River Comm Coll (FL)
Iowa Lakes Comm Coll (IA)
Iowa Western Comm Coll (IA)
Isothermal Comm Coll (NC)
Ivy Tech State Coll–Central Indiana (IN)
Ivy Tech State Coll–Columbus (IN)
Ivy Tech State Coll–Eastcentral (IN)
Ivy Tech State Coll–Kokomo (IN)
Ivy Tech State Coll–Lafayette (IN)
Ivy Tech State Coll–North Central (IN)
Ivy Tech State Coll–Northeast (IN)
Ivy Tech State Coll–Northwest (IN)
Ivy Tech State Coll–Southcentral (IN)
Ivy Tech State Coll–Southwest (IN)
Ivy Tech State Coll–Wabash Valley (IN)
Ivy Tech State Coll–Whitewater (IN)
Jackson Comm Coll (MI)
Jefferson Coll (MO)
Jefferson Comm Coll (KY)
John A. Logan Coll (IL)
Johnson Coll (PA)
Johnson County Comm Coll (KS)
Joliet Jr Coll (IL)
Kalamazoo Valley Comm Coll (MI)
Kankakee Comm Coll (IL)
Kaskaskia Coll (IL)
Kauai Comm Coll (HI)
Kent State U, Trumbull Campus (OH)
Kilgore Coll (TX)
Kirkwood Comm Coll (IA)
Kishwaukee Coll (IL)
Lake Area Tech Inst (SD)
Lake Land Coll (IL)
Lake Region State Coll (ND)
Lake Washington Tech Coll (WA)
Lamar State Coll–Port Arthur (TX)
Lane Comm Coll (OR)
Lansing Comm Coll (MI)
Laramie County Comm Coll (WY)
Las Positas Coll (CA)
Lewis and Clark Comm Coll (IL)
Lincoln Land Comm Coll (IL)
Linn-Benton Comm Coll (OR)
Long Beach City Coll (CA)
Longview Comm Coll (MO)
Los Angeles Harbor Coll (CA)
Los Angeles Pierce Coll (CA)
Louisiana Tech Coll–Delta Ouachita Campus (LA)
Luzerne County Comm Coll (PA)
Macomb Comm Coll (MI)
Martin Comm Coll (NC)
Massasoit Comm Coll (MA)
McHenry County Coll (IL)
Merced Coll (CA)
Mesa Tech Coll (NM)
Metropolitan Comm Coll (NE)
Middlesex Comm Coll (MA)
Middlesex County Coll (NJ)
Midland Coll (TX)
Midlands Tech Coll (SC)
Mid Michigan Comm Coll (MI)
Mid-Plains Comm Coll Area (NE)
Miles Comm Coll (MT)
Milwaukee Area Tech Coll (WI)
Minnesota State Coll–Southeast Tech (MN)
MiraCosta Coll (CA)
Mississippi Gulf Coast Comm Coll (MS)
Modesto Jr Coll (CA)
Mohave Comm Coll (AZ)
Monroe Comm Coll (NY)
Monterey Peninsula Coll (CA)
Montgomery Coll (MD)
Montgomery Comm Coll (NC)
Moraine Park Tech Coll (WI)
Moraine Valley Comm Coll (IL)
Morgan Comm Coll (CO)
Morton Coll (IL)
Mott Comm Coll (MI)
Mt. Hood Comm Coll (OR)
Mt. San Jacinto Coll (CA)
Mount Wachusett Comm Coll (MA)
Nashville Auto Diesel Coll (TN)
Nashville State Tech Inst (TN)
Naugatuck Valley Comm Coll (CT)
New England Inst of Technology (RI)
New England Inst of Tech & Florida Culinary Inst (FL)
New Hampshire Comm Tech Coll, Berlin/Laconia (NH)
New River Comm Coll (VA)
Northcentral Tech Coll (WI)
North Central Texas Coll (TX)
North Dakota State Coll of Science (ND)
Northeast Comm Coll (NE)
Northeast State Tech Comm Coll (TN)
Northeast Texas Comm Coll (TX)
Northern Maine Tech Coll (ME)
Northern Virginia Comm Coll (VA)
North Harris Coll (TX)
North Hennepin Comm Coll (MN)
North Idaho Coll (ID)
North Iowa Area Comm Coll (IA)
Northland Comm and Tech Coll (MN)
Northwestern Michigan Coll (MI)
Oakland Comm Coll (MI)
Oakton Comm Coll (IL)
Odessa Coll (TX)
Okaloosa-Walton Comm Coll (FL)
Oklahoma City Comm Coll (OK)
Oklahoma State U, Okmulgee (OK)
Olympic Coll (WA)
Onondaga Comm Coll (NY)
Orangeburg-Calhoun Tech Coll (SC)
Otero Jr Coll (CO)
Ouachita Tech Coll (AR)
Oxnard Coll (CA)
Ozarka Coll (AR)
Palau Comm CollPalau)
Palomar Coll (CA)
Palo Verde Coll (CA)
Pamlico Comm Coll (NC)
Parkland Coll (IL)
Pasadena City Coll (CA)
Pellissippi State Tech Comm Coll (TN)
Peninsula Coll (WA)
Pensacola Jr Coll (FL)
Piedmont Tech Coll (SC)
Piedmont Virginia Comm Coll (VA)
Pikes Peak Comm Coll (CO)
Pima Comm Coll (AZ)
Pine Tech Coll (MN)
Portland Comm Coll (OR)
Prairie State Coll (IL)
Pratt Comm Coll and Area Vocational School (KS)
Quinsigamond Comm Coll (MA)
Randolph Comm Coll (NC)
Ranger Coll (TX)
Raritan Valley Comm Coll (NJ)
Reedley Coll (CA)
Rend Lake Coll (IL)
Richland Comm Coll (IL)
Roanoke-Chowan Comm Coll (NC)
Rockland Comm Coll (NY)
Rogue Comm Coll (OR)
Rowan-Cabarrus Comm Coll (NC)
St. Cloud Tech Coll (MN)
St. Philip's Coll (TX)
San Bernardino Valley Coll (CA)
Sandhills Comm Coll (NC)
San Diego City Coll (CA)
San Jacinto Coll Central Campus (TX)
San Jacinto Coll South Campus (TX)
San Joaquin Delta Coll (CA)
San Juan Coll (NM)
Santa Ana Coll (CA)
Santa Barbara City Coll (CA)
Santa Fe Comm Coll (FL)
Santa Monica Coll (CA)
Scott Comm Coll (IA)
Seminole Comm Coll (FL)
Sequoia Inst (CA)
Shasta Coll (CA)
Shoreline Comm Coll (WA)
Sierra Coll (CA)
Sinclair Comm Coll (OH)
Skagit Valley Coll (WA)
Snow Coll (UT)
Southeast Arkansas Coll (AR)
Southeast Comm Coll, Milford Campus (NE)
Southeast Tech Inst (SD)
Southern Maine Tech Coll (ME)
Southern West Virginia Comm and Tech Coll (WV)
South Piedmont Comm Coll (NC)
South Plains Coll (TX)
South Puget Sound Comm Coll (WA)
South Texas Comm Coll (TX)
Southwestern Coll (CA)
Southwestern Comm Coll (IA)
Southwestern Comm Coll (NC)
Southwestern Michigan Coll (MI)
Southwest Mississippi Comm Coll (MS)
Southwest Tennessee Comm Coll (TN)
Southwest Wisconsin Tech Coll (WI)
Spartanburg Tech Coll (SC)
Spokane Comm Coll (WA)
Stark State Coll of Technology (OH)
State Fair Comm Coll (MO)
State U of NY Coll of A&T at Morrisville (NY)
State U of NY Coll of Technology at Alfred (NY)
State U of NY Coll of Technology at Canton (NY)
Suffolk County Comm Coll (NY)
Surry Comm Coll (NC)
Taft Coll (CA)
Tarrant County Coll District (TX)
Temple Coll (TX)
Terra State Comm Coll (OH)
Texarkana Coll (TX)
Texas State Tech Coll– Waco/Marshall Campus (TX)
Texas State Tech Coll (TX)
Thaddeus Stevens Coll of Technology (PA)
Thomas Nelson Comm Coll (VA)
Tidewater Comm Coll (VA)
Trenholm State Tech Coll, Patterson Campus (AL)
Tri-County Comm Coll (NC)
Trident Tech Coll (SC)
Trinidad State Jr Coll (CO)
Trinity Valley Comm Coll (TX)
Triton Coll (IL)
Truckee Meadows Comm Coll (NV)
Tulsa Comm Coll (OK)
Umpqua Comm Coll (OR)
United Tribes Tech Coll (ND)
U of Arkansas at Fort Smith (AR)
U of Arkansas Comm Coll at Morrilton (AR)
U of New Mexico–Gallup (NM)
U of Northwestern Ohio (OH)
Vance-Granville Comm Coll (NC)
Ventura Coll (CA)
Vernon Coll (TX)
Victor Valley Coll (CA)
Vincennes U (IN)
Virginia Western Comm Coll (VA)
Wallace State Comm Coll (AL)
Walla Walla Comm Coll (WA)
Waubonsee Comm Coll (IL)
Waycross Coll (GA)
Wayne Comm Coll (NC)
Westchester Comm Coll (NY)
Western Dakota Tech Inst (SD)
Western Iowa Tech Comm Coll (IA)
Western Nevada Comm Coll (NV)
Western Texas Coll (TX)
Western Wisconsin Tech Coll (WI)
Western Wyoming Comm Coll (WY)
West Virginia U at Parkersburg (WV)
Westwood Coll of Technology–Denver North (CO)
Wharton County Jr Coll (TX)
Wilkes Comm Coll (NC)
Williston State Coll (ND)

Wyoming Tech Inst (WY)
York Tech Coll (SC)

AUTOMOTIVE ENGINEERING TECHNOLOGY
Arizona Automotive Inst (AZ)
Benjamin Franklin Inst of Technology (MA)
Comm Coll of Allegheny County (PA)
Corning Comm Coll (NY)
Harrisburg Area Comm Coll (PA)
Massachusetts Bay Comm Coll (MA)
Mercer County Comm Coll (NJ)
Northampton County Area Comm Coll (PA)
Pennsylvania Coll of Technology (PA)
Rend Lake Coll (IL)
Sequoia Inst (CA)
Springfield Tech Comm Coll (MA)
Sussex County Comm Coll (NJ)
Terra State Comm Coll (OH)
Vermont Tech Coll (VT)

AVIATION/AIRWAY SCIENCE
Comm Coll of the Air Force (AL)
Portland Comm Coll (OR)
Raritan Valley Comm Coll (NJ)
Texas State Tech Coll– Waco/ Marshall Campus (TX)
Tompkins Cortland Comm Coll (NY)
Tulsa Comm Coll (OK)
Vermilion Comm Coll (MN)

AVIATION MANAGEMENT
Academy Coll (MN)
Chattanooga State Tech Comm Coll (TN)
Comm Coll of Allegheny County (PA)
Cypress Coll (CA)
Delaware Tech & Comm Coll, Terry Cmps (DE)
Dixie State Coll of Utah (UT)
Florida Comm Coll at Jacksonville (FL)
Glendale Comm Coll (CA)
Guilford Tech Comm Coll (NC)
Inver Hills Comm Coll (MN)
Iowa Lakes Comm Coll (IA)
Lehigh Carbon Comm Coll (PA)
Lenoir Comm Coll (NC)
Lincoln Land Comm Coll (IL)
Long Beach City Coll (CA)
Luzerne County Comm Coll (PA)
Mercer County Comm Coll (NJ)
Miami-Dade Comm Coll (FL)
Mountain View Coll (TX)
Northland Comm and Tech Coll (MN)
Oakland Comm Coll (MI)
Palomar Coll (CA)
Pasadena City Coll (CA)
Schenectady County Comm Coll (NY)
Sinclair Comm Coll (OH)
Vermilion Comm Coll (MN)

AVIATION TECHNOLOGY
Aims Comm Coll (CO)
Antelope Valley Coll (CA)
Atlanta Metropolitan Coll (GA)
Big Bend Comm Coll (WA)
Black Hawk Coll, Moline (IL)
Blackhawk Tech Coll (WI)
Black River Tech Coll (AR)
Caldwell Comm Coll and Tech Inst (NC)
Chattanooga State Tech Comm Coll (TN)
City Coll of San Francisco (CA)
City Colls of Chicago, Richard J Daley Coll (IL)
Clover Park Tech Coll (WA)
Cochise Coll, Douglas (AZ)
Coll of Alameda (CA)
Columbus State Comm Coll (OH)
Comm Coll of Beaver County (PA)
Comm Coll of the Air Force (AL)
Cumberland County Coll (NJ)
Cuyahoga Comm Coll (OH)
Delaware Tech & Comm Coll, Terry Cmps (DE)
Delta Coll (MI)
Enterprise State Jr Coll (AL)
Everett Comm Coll (WA)
Foothill Coll (CA)
Frederick Comm Coll (MD)
Gateway Comm Coll (CT)
Gavilan Coll (CA)
Glendale Comm Coll (CA)
Greenville Tech Coll (SC)
Guilford Tech Comm Coll (NC)
Hawkeye Comm Coll (IA)
Hesston Coll (KS)
Hinds Comm Coll (MS)
Honolulu Comm Coll (HI)
Housatonic Comm Coll (CT)
Indian Hills Comm Coll (IA)
Iowa Western Comm Coll (IA)
Jackson Comm Coll (MI)
Kankakee Comm Coll (IL)
Lake Area Tech Inst (SD)
Lake Region State Coll (ND)
Lane Comm Coll (OR)
Lansing Comm Coll (MI)
Lehigh Carbon Comm Coll (PA)
Lenoir Comm Coll (NC)
Long Beach City Coll (CA)
Los Angeles Mission Coll (CA)
Macomb Comm Coll (MI)
Maple Woods Comm Coll (MO)
Miami-Dade Comm Coll (FL)
Midland Coll (TX)
Minnesota State Coll–Southeast Tech (MN)
Mountain View Coll (TX)
Mt. Hood Comm Coll (OR)
Navarro Coll (TX)
NEI Coll of Technology (MN)
Northern Virginia Comm Coll (VA)
Northland Comm and Tech Coll (MN)
Okaloosa-Walton Comm Coll (FL)
Oklahoma City Comm Coll (OK)
Oklahoma State U, Okmulgee (OK)
Orange Coast Coll (CA)
Palomar Coll (CA)
Pasadena City Coll (CA)
Pittsburgh Inst of Aeronautics (PA)
Portland Comm Coll (OR)
Reedley Coll (CA)
Sacramento City Coll (CA)
San Jacinto Coll Central Campus (TX)
Shasta Coll (CA)
Spartan School of Aeronautics (OK)
Spokane Comm Coll (WA)
Tarrant County Coll District (TX)
Texas State Tech Coll– Waco/ Marshall Campus (TX)
Three Rivers Comm Coll (CT)
Tulsa Comm Coll (OK)
Vincennes U (IN)
Wallace State Comm Coll (AL)
Wayne Comm Coll (NC)
Westwood Coll of Aviation Technology–Denver (CO)

BAKER/PASTRY CHEF
The Art Inst of New York City (NY)
Clark Coll (WA)
Coll of DuPage (IL)
El Centro Coll (TX)
Florida Culinary Inst (FL)
Luzerne County Comm Coll (PA)
Pennsylvania Coll of Technology (PA)
Sullivan County Comm Coll (NY)
Triton Coll (IL)
Vincennes U (IN)

BANKING
Adirondack Comm Coll (NY)
Alamance Comm Coll (NC)
Albuquerque Tech Vocational Inst (NM)
Alexandria Tech Coll (MN)
Allen County Comm Coll (KS)
Black Hawk Coll, Moline (IL)
Broome Comm Coll (NY)
Bucks County Comm Coll (PA)
Cambria County Area Comm Coll (PA)
Catawba Valley Comm Coll (NC)
Comm Coll of Allegheny County (PA)
Comm Coll of Rhode Island (RI)
Delaware County Comm Coll (PA)
Delaware Tech & Comm Coll, Stanton/ Wilmington Cmps (DE)
Eastern Maine Tech Coll (ME)
East Mississippi Comm Coll (MS)
Finger Lakes Comm Coll (NY)
Florida Comm Coll at Jacksonville (FL)
Gateway Tech Coll (WI)
Harrisburg Area Comm Coll (PA)
Indian River Comm Coll (FL)
Jefferson State Comm Coll (AL)
Laurel Business Inst (PA)
Luzerne County Comm Coll (PA)
Madisonville Comm Coll (KY)
Mineral Area Coll (MO)
Modesto Jr Coll (CA)
Northampton County Area Comm Coll (PA)
Ozarka Coll (AR)
Pennsylvania Coll of Technology (PA)
Pima Comm Coll (AZ)
St. Cloud Tech Coll (MN)
San Juan Coll (NM)
Seminole Comm Coll (FL)
Terra State Comm Coll (OH)
Waubonsee Comm Coll (IL)
West Virginia Northern Comm Coll (WV)
Wor-Wic Comm Coll (MD)

BEHAVIORAL SCIENCES
Adirondack Comm Coll (NY)
Amarillo Coll (TX)
Anne Arundel Comm Coll (MD)
Casper Coll (WY)
Chabot Coll (CA)
Citrus Coll (CA)
Cochise Coll, Douglas (AZ)
Coffeyville Comm Coll (KS)
Colby Comm Coll (KS)
Coll of Marin (CA)
Colorado Mountn Coll, Alpine Cmps (CO)
Colorado Mountn Coll (CO)
Colorado Mountn Coll, Timberline Cmps (CO)
Comm Coll of Southern Nevada (NV)
Compton Comm Coll (CA)
Daytona Beach Comm Coll (FL)
De Anza Coll (CA)
Dodge City Comm Coll (KS)
East Central Comm Coll (MS)
Fulton-Montgomery Comm Coll (NY)
Galveston Coll (TX)
Georgia Perimeter Coll (GA)
Gordon Coll (GA)
Greenfield Comm Coll (MA)
Harford Comm Coll (MD)
Highline Comm Coll (WA)
Hill Coll of the Hill Jr College District (TX)
Howard Coll (TX)
Imperial Valley Coll (CA)
Iowa Lakes Comm Coll (IA)
Labette Comm Coll (KS)
Lamar Comm Coll (CO)
Lincoln Coll, Lincoln (IL)
Lincoln Coll, Normal (IL)
Lincoln Land Comm Coll (IL)
Macomb Comm Coll (MI)
Miami-Dade Comm Coll (FL)
Midland Coll (TX)
MiraCosta Coll (CA)
Mississippi Delta Comm Coll (MS)
Modesto Jr Coll (CA)
Monroe Comm Coll (NY)
Moorpark Coll (CA)
Mt. San Jacinto Coll (CA)
Northwestern Connecticut Comm-Tech Coll (CT)
Orange Coast Coll (CA)
Oxnard Coll (CA)
Palo Verde Coll (CA)
Phoenix Coll (AZ)
Quincy Coll (MA)
Reading Area Comm Coll (PA)
San Diego City Coll (CA)
San Jacinto Coll Central Campus (TX)
San Jacinto Coll South Campus (TX)
San Joaquin Delta Coll (CA)
Seminole State Coll (OK)
South Texas Comm Coll (TX)
Tacoma Comm Coll (WA)
Tulsa Comm Coll (OK)
Tyler Jr Coll (TX)
Umpqua Comm Coll (OR)
Vincennes U (IN)
Vincennes U Jasper Campus (IN)
Wharton County Jr Coll (TX)

BIBLICAL STUDIES
Amarillo Coll (TX)
Baptist Bible Coll East (MA)
Crowley's Ridge Coll (AR)
Hesston Coll (KS)
Lon Morris Coll (TX)
St. Catharine Coll (KY)
San Jacinto Coll Central Campus (TX)
Somerset Christian Coll (NJ)

BILINGUAL/BICULTURAL EDUCATION
Clovis Comm Coll (NM)
San Jacinto Coll North Campus (TX)

BIOCHEMICAL TECHNOLOGY
Mid Michigan Comm Coll (MI)
Niagara County Comm Coll (NY)

BIOENGINEERING
Vermont Tech Coll (VT)

BIOLOGICAL/PHYSICAL SCIENCES
Abraham Baldwin Ag Coll (GA)
Adirondack Comm Coll (NY)
American River Coll (CA)
Andrew Coll (GA)
Angelina Coll (TX)
Anne Arundel Comm Coll (MD)
Arapahoe Comm Coll (CO)
Arizona Western Coll (AZ)
Baltimore City Comm Coll (MD)
Black Hawk Coll, Moline (IL)
Borough of Manhattan Comm Coll of City U of NY (NY)
Bowling Green State U-Firelands Coll (OH)
Brookdale Comm Coll (NJ)
Burlington County Coll (NJ)
Caldwell Comm Coll and Tech Inst (NC)
Cañada Coll (CA)
Cape Cod Comm Coll (MA)
Casper Coll (WY)
Centralia Coll (WA)
Central Oregon Comm Coll (OR)
Central Virginia Comm Coll (VA)
Cerro Coso Comm Coll (CA)
Chabot Coll (CA)
Chesapeake Coll (MD)
Chipola Jr Coll (FL)
City Colls of Chicago, Wilbur Wright Coll (IL)
Clark Coll (WA)
Cleveland Comm Coll (NC)
Clinton Comm Coll (NY)
Coastal Bend Coll (TX)
Coffeyville Comm Coll (KS)
Colby Comm Coll (KS)
Coll of Alameda (CA)
Coll of DuPage (IL)
Coll of the Canyons (CA)
Coll of the Sequoias (CA)
Colorado Mountn Coll, Alpine Cmps (CO)
Colorado Mountn Coll (CO)
Colorado Mountn Coll, Timberline Cmps (CO)
Columbia-Greene Comm Coll (NY)
Comm Coll of Aurora (CO)
The Comm Coll of Baltimore County–Catonsville Campus (MD)
Comm Coll of Rhode Island (RI)
Comm Coll of Southern Nevada (NV)
Compton Comm Coll (CA)
Corning Comm Coll (NY)
Cottey Coll (MO)
Crafton Hills Coll (CA)
Cumberland County Coll (NJ)
Cuyamaca Coll (CA)
Cypress Coll (CA)
Danville Area Comm Coll (IL)
Danville Comm Coll (VA)
Daytona Beach Comm Coll (FL)
Delaware County Comm Coll (PA)
Delgado Comm Coll (LA)
Dodge City Comm Coll (KS)
Donnelly Coll (KS)
Dutchess Comm Coll (NY)
East Central Comm Coll (MS)
Eastern Shore Comm Coll (VA)
East Mississippi Comm Coll (MS)
Edgecombe Comm Coll (NC)
Elizabethtown Comm Coll (KY)
Ellsworth Comm Coll (IA)
Enterprise State Jr Coll (AL)
Fergus Falls Comm Coll (MN)
Finger Lakes Comm Coll (NY)
Florence-Darlington Tech Coll (SC)
Floyd Coll (GA)
Fort Berthold Comm Coll (ND)
Fulton-Montgomery Comm Coll (NY)
Galveston Coll (TX)
Garden City Comm Coll (KS)
Gavilan Coll (CA)
Georgia Military Coll (GA)
Georgia Perimeter Coll (GA)
Germanna Comm Coll (VA)
Glendale Comm Coll (CA)
Glen Oaks Comm Coll (MI)
Golden West Coll (CA)
Gordon Coll (GA)
Greenfield Comm Coll (MA)
Guilford Tech Comm Coll (NC)
Harford Comm Coll (MD)
Heartland Comm Coll (IL)
Herkimer County Comm Coll (NY)
Highland Comm Coll (IL)
Highline Comm Coll (WA)
Hill Coll of the Hill Jr College District (TX)
Howard Comm Coll (MD)
Illinois Eastern Comm Colls, Frontier Comm Coll (IL)
Imperial Valley Coll (CA)
Independence Comm Coll (KS)
Iowa Lakes Comm Coll (IA)
Isothermal Comm Coll (NC)
Jacksonville Coll (TX)
Jamestown Comm Coll (NY)
Jefferson Coll (MO)
Jefferson Davis Comm Coll (AL)
John Wood Comm Coll (IL)
Jones County Jr Coll (MS)
J. Sargeant Reynolds Comm Coll (VA)
Kankakee Comm Coll (IL)
Kaskaskia Coll (IL)
Kent State U, Stark Campus (OH)
Kilgore Coll (TX)
Kirkwood Comm Coll (IA)
Lake Land Coll (IL)
Lakeland Comm Coll (OH)
Lake Tahoe Comm Coll (CA)
Lamar Comm Coll (CO)
Lansing Comm Coll (MI)
Lewis and Clark Comm Coll (IL)
Lincoln Coll, Lincoln (IL)
Lincoln Land Comm Coll (IL)
Linn-Benton Comm Coll (OR)
Longview Comm Coll (MO)
Lorain County Comm Coll (OH)
Lord Fairfax Comm Coll (VA)
Los Angeles City Coll (CA)
Louisburg Coll (NC)
Louisiana State U at Alexandria (LA)
Luzerne County Comm Coll (PA)
Manor Coll (PA)
Maple Woods Comm Coll (MO)
Marion Military Inst (AL)
Marshalltown Comm Coll (IA)
Massachusetts Bay Comm Coll (MA)
Massasoit Comm Coll (MA)
McHenry County Coll (IL)
Merced Coll (CA)
Miami U–Middletown Campus (OH)
Middlesex County Coll (NJ)
Mid Michigan Comm Coll (MI)
Minot State U–Bottineau Campus (ND)
Mississippi Gulf Coast Comm Coll (MS)
Mitchell Coll (CT)
Mitchell Comm Coll (NC)
Mohawk Valley Comm Coll (NY)
Monroe Comm Coll (NY)
Moraine Valley Comm Coll (IL)
Morgan Comm Coll (CO)
Morton Coll (IL)
Mountain Empire Comm Coll (VA)
Mt. San Jacinto Coll (CA)
Naugatuck Valley Comm Coll (CT)
Navarro Coll (TX)
Neosho County Comm Coll (KS)
New Mexico Military Inst (NM)
New River Comm Coll (VA)

Niagara County Comm Coll (NY)
North Central Texas Coll (TX)
North Country Comm Coll (NY)
Northeast Alabama Comm Coll (AL)
Northeast Comm Coll (NE)
Northern Essex Comm Coll (MA)
Northern Oklahoma Coll (OK)
Northern Virginia Comm Coll (VA)
North Harris Coll (TX)
North Idaho Coll (ID)
Northland Pioneer Coll (AZ)
North Seattle Comm Coll (WA)
Northwest Coll (WY)
Oakton Comm Coll (IL)
Okaloosa-Walton Comm Coll (FL)
Onondaga Comm Coll (NY)
Orange County Comm Coll (NY)
Otero Jr Coll (CO)
Parkland Coll (IL)
Pasadena City Coll (CA)
Patrick Henry Comm Coll (VA)
Peninsula Coll (WA)
Penn State U Beaver Campus of the Commonwealth Coll (PA)
Penn State U DuBois Campus of the Commonwealth Coll (PA)
Penn State U McKeesport Campus of the Commonwealth Coll (PA)
Penn State U New Kensington Campus of the Commonwealth Coll (PA)
Penn State U Shenango Campus of the Commonwealth Coll (PA)
Penn Valley Comm Coll (MO)
Piedmont Tech Coll (SC)
Piedmont Virginia Comm Coll (VA)
Portland Comm Coll (OR)
Pratt Comm Coll and Area Vocational School (KS)
Quincy Coll (MA)
Rainy River Comm Coll (MN)
Rappahannock Comm Coll (VA)
Red Rocks Comm Coll (CO)
Rend Lake Coll (IL)
Richland Comm Coll (IL)
Ridgewater Coll (MN)
Riverside Comm Coll (CA)
Rockingham Comm Coll (NC)
Rockland Comm Coll (NY)
Rogue Comm Coll (OR)
Sacramento City Coll (CA)
St. Catharine Coll (KY)
St. Clair County Comm Coll (MI)
Salem Comm Coll (NJ)
San Antonio Coll (TX)
Sandhills Comm Coll (NC)
San Jacinto Coll Central Campus (TX)
San Jacinto Coll South Campus (TX)
Santa Ana Coll (CA)
Schenectady County Comm Coll (NY)
Seattle Central Comm Coll (WA)
Sheridan Coll (WY)
Skagit Valley Coll (WA)
Southeast Comm Coll, Beatrice Campus (NE)
Southeastern Comm Coll (NC)
South Plains Coll (TX)
Southside Virginia Comm Coll (VA)
Southwestern Coll (CA)
Southwest Mississippi Comm Coll (MS)
Southwest Virginia Comm Coll (VA)
Spartanburg Tech Coll (SC)
State U of NY Coll of Technology at Alfred (NY)
State U of NY Coll of Technology at Canton (NY)
Suffolk County Comm Coll (NY)
Sussex County Comm Coll (NJ)
Tacoma Comm Coll (WA)
Thomas Nelson Comm Coll (VA)
Tidewater Comm Coll (VA)
Tompkins Cortland Comm Coll (NY)
Trident Tech Coll (SC)
Trinidad State Jr Coll (CO)
Triton Coll (IL)
Ulster County Comm Coll (NY)
Umpqua Comm Coll (OR)
U of New Mexico–Los Alamos Branch (NM)
U of South Carolina at Lancaster (SC)
U of South Carolina at Union (SC)
U of Wisconsin Center–Richland (WI)
Valley Forge Military Coll (PA)
Vermilion Comm Coll (MN)
Victor Valley Coll (CA)
Virginia Western Comm Coll (VA)
Waubonsee Comm Coll (IL)
Wayne Comm Coll (NC)
Weatherford Coll (TX)
Westchester Comm Coll (NY)
Western Wyoming Comm Coll (WY)
Young Harris Coll (GA)

BIOLOGICAL TECHNOLOGY

Athens Tech Coll (GA)
Bunker Hill Comm Coll (MA)
Cincinnati State Tech and Comm Coll (OH)
Collin County Comm Coll District (TX)
County Coll of Morris (NJ)
Des Moines Area Comm Coll (IA)
Ellsworth Comm Coll (IA)
Finger Lakes Comm Coll (NY)
Foothill Coll (CA)
Guilford Tech Comm Coll (NC)
Indian Hills Comm Coll (IA)
Jefferson Comm Coll (NY)
John Tyler Comm Coll (VA)
Kirkwood Comm Coll (IA)
Lake Area Tech Inst (SD)
Lansing Comm Coll (MI)
Massachusetts Bay Comm Coll (MA)
Mercer County Comm Coll (NJ)
Middlesex County Coll (NJ)
Mid Michigan Comm Coll (MI)
Monroe Comm Coll (NY)
Montana State U Coll of Tech-Great Falls (MT)
North Shore Comm Coll (MA)
Portland Comm Coll (OR)
Seattle Central Comm Coll (WA)
Shoreline Comm Coll (WA)
Southeast Arkansas Coll (AR)
Southeast Comm Coll, Beatrice Campus (NE)
State U of NY Coll of A&T at Morrisville (NY)
State U of NY Coll of Technology at Alfred (NY)
Vista Comm Coll (CA)

BIOLOGY

Abraham Baldwin Ag Coll (GA)
Adirondack Comm Coll (NY)
Allan Hancock Coll (CA)
Allegany Coll of Maryland (MD)
Allen County Comm Coll (KS)
Alpena Comm Coll (MI)
Alvin Comm Coll (TX)
Amarillo Coll (TX)
Ancilla Coll (IN)
Andrew Coll (GA)
Angelina Coll (TX)
Anne Arundel Comm Coll (MD)
Antelope Valley Coll (CA)
Arizona Western Coll (AZ)
Arkansas State U–Beebe (AR)
Atlanta Metropolitan Coll (GA)
Atlantic Cape Comm Coll (NJ)
Austin Comm Coll (TX)
Bainbridge Coll (GA)
Bakersfield Coll (CA)
Barton County Comm Coll (KS)
Bergen Comm Coll (NJ)
Berkshire Comm Coll (MA)
Blinn Coll (TX)
Brazosport Coll (TX)
Bronx Comm Coll of City U of NY (NY)
Bucks County Comm Coll (PA)
Burlington County Coll (NJ)
Butler County Comm Coll (PA)
Butte Coll (CA)
Cañada Coll (CA)
Casper Coll (WY)
Cecil Comm Coll (MD)
Centralia Coll (WA)
Central Piedmont Comm Coll (NC)
Central Texas Coll (TX)
Central Wyoming Coll (WY)
Cerritos Coll (CA)
Chabot Coll (CA)
Chaffey Coll (CA)
Chattahoochee Valley Comm Coll (AL)
Chattanooga State Tech Comm Coll (TN)
Cisco Jr Coll (TX)
Citrus Coll (CA)
Coahoma Comm Coll (MS)
Coastal Bend Coll (TX)
Coastal Georgia Comm Coll (GA)
Cochise Coll, Douglas (AZ)
Coffeyville Comm Coll (KS)
Colby Comm Coll (KS)
Coll of Alameda (CA)
Coll of Marin (CA)
Coll of Southern Idaho (ID)
Coll of the Canyons (CA)
Coll of the Desert (CA)
Coll of the Sequoias (CA)
Coll of the Siskiyous (CA)
Colorado Mountn Coll, Alpine Cmps (CO)
Colorado Mountn Coll (CO)
Colorado Mountn Coll, Timberline Cmps (CO)
Columbia State Comm Coll (TN)
Comm Coll of Allegheny County (PA)
Comm Coll of Beaver County (PA)
Comm Coll of Southern Nevada (NV)
Compton Comm Coll (CA)
Connors State Coll (OK)
Crafton Hills Coll (CA)
Crowder Coll (MO)
Cuesta Coll (CA)
Cypress Coll (CA)
Danville Area Comm Coll (IL)
Darton Coll (GA)
Daytona Beach Comm Coll (FL)
De Anza Coll (CA)
Del Mar Coll (TX)
Delta Coll (MI)
Dixie State Coll of Utah (UT)
Dodge City Comm Coll (KS)
East Central Coll (MO)
East Central Comm Coll (MS)
Eastern Arizona Coll (AZ)
Eastern Oklahoma State Coll (OK)
Eastern Wyoming Coll (WY)
East Georgia Coll (GA)
Ellsworth Comm Coll (IA)
Essex County Coll (NJ)
Everett Comm Coll (WA)
Evergreen Valley Coll (CA)
Feather River Comm Coll District (CA)
Finger Lakes Comm Coll (NY)
Foothill Coll (CA)
Frederick Comm Coll (MD)
Fullerton Coll (CA)
Fulton-Montgomery Comm Coll (NY)
Gavilan Coll (CA)
Gloucester County Coll (NJ)
Gogebic Comm Coll (MI)
Golden West Coll (CA)
Gordon Coll (GA)
Grayson County Coll (TX)
Harford Comm Coll (MD)
Harrisburg Area Comm Coll (PA)
Hawkeye Comm Coll (IA)
Herkimer County Comm Coll (NY)
Highland Comm Coll (KS)
Hill Coll of the Hill Jr College District (TX)
Hinds Comm Coll (MS)
Holmes Comm Coll (MS)
Holyoke Comm Coll (MA)
Howard Coll (TX)
Hutchinson Comm Coll and Area Vocational School (KS)
Illinois Eastern Comm Colls, Lincoln Trail Coll (IL)
Independence Comm Coll (KS)
Indian River Comm Coll (FL)
Iowa Lakes Comm Coll (IA)
Jefferson Comm Coll (KY)
Jefferson Davis Comm Coll (AL)
John A. Logan Coll (IL)
Joliet Jr Coll (IL)
Jones County Jr Coll (MS)
Kansas City Kansas Comm Coll (KS)
Kellogg Comm Coll (MI)
Kennebec Valley Tech Coll (ME)
Keystone Coll (PA)
Kingsborough Comm Coll of City U of NY (NY)
Kingwood Coll (TX)
Kirkwood Comm Coll (IA)
Labette Comm Coll (KS)
Lake Michigan Coll (MI)
Lamar Comm Coll (CO)
Lansing Comm Coll (MI)
Laramie County Comm Coll (WY)
Lewis and Clark Comm Coll (IL)
Lincoln Coll, Lincoln (IL)
Lincoln Land Comm Coll (IL)
Linn-Benton Comm Coll (OR)
Long Beach City Coll (CA)
Longview Comm Coll (MO)
Lon Morris Coll (TX)
Lorain County Comm Coll (OH)
Los Angeles City Coll (CA)
Los Angeles Harbor Coll (CA)
Los Angeles Mission Coll (CA)
Louisburg Coll (NC)
Lower Columbia Coll (WA)
Manatee Comm Coll (FL)
Maple Woods Comm Coll (MO)
Mercer County Comm Coll (NJ)
Miami-Dade Comm Coll (FL)
Middlesex County Coll (NJ)
Midland Coll (TX)
Mid Michigan Comm Coll (MI)
Minot State U–Bottineau Campus (ND)
MiraCosta Coll (CA)
Mississippi Delta Comm Coll (MS)
Modesto Jr Coll (CA)
Mohawk Valley Comm Coll (NY)
Monroe Comm Coll (NY)
Monroe County Comm Coll (MI)
Monterey Peninsula Coll (CA)
Montgomery County Comm Coll (PA)
Moorpark Coll (CA)
Mountain Empire Comm Coll (VA)
Navarro Coll (TX)
New Mexico Military Inst (NM)
Northampton County Area Comm Coll (PA)
Northeast Comm Coll (NE)
North Idaho Coll (ID)
Northwest Coll (WY)
Northwestern Connecticut Comm-Tech Coll (CT)
Odessa Coll (TX)
Okaloosa-Walton Comm Coll (FL)
Oklahoma City Comm Coll (OK)
Orange Coast Coll (CA)
Orange County Comm Coll (NY)
Otero Jr Coll (CO)
Oxnard Coll (CA)
Palm Beach Comm Coll (FL)
Palomar Coll (CA)
Palo Verde Coll (CA)
Pasadena City Coll (CA)
Pennsylvania Coll of Technology (PA)
Penn Valley Comm Coll (MO)
Pensacola Jr Coll (FL)
Pratt Comm Coll and Area Vocational School (KS)
Raritan Valley Comm Coll (NJ)
Reading Area Comm Coll (PA)
Red Rocks Comm Coll (CO)
Reedley Coll (CA)
Roane State Comm Coll (TN)
St. Catharine Coll (KY)
St. Philip's Coll (TX)
Salem Comm Coll (NJ)
San Bernardino Valley Coll (CA)
San Diego City Coll (CA)
San Diego Mesa Coll (CA)
San Jacinto Coll Central Campus (TX)
San Jacinto Coll North Campus (TX)
San Jacinto Coll South Campus (TX)
San Joaquin Delta Coll (CA)
San Juan Coll (NM)
Santa Ana Coll (CA)
Santa Barbara City Coll (CA)
Santa Fe Comm Coll (NM)
Santa Monica Coll (CA)
Sauk Valley Comm Coll (IL)
Seminole State Coll (OK)
Sheridan Coll (WY)
Sierra Coll (CA)
Skagit Valley Coll (WA)
Snow Coll (UT)
Southeast Comm Coll, Beatrice Campus (NE)
South Mountain Comm Coll (AZ)
South Plains Coll (TX)
Southwestern Coll (CA)
Southwest Mississippi Comm Coll (MS)
Springfield Tech Comm Coll (MA)
State U of NY Coll of A&T at Morrisville (NY)
Suffolk County Comm Coll (NY)
Tacoma Comm Coll (WA)
Taft Coll (CA)
Texarkana Coll (TX)
Trinidad State Jr Coll (CO)
Trinity Valley Comm Coll (TX)
Triton Coll (IL)
Tulsa Comm Coll (OK)
Umpqua Comm Coll (OR)
Union County Coll (NJ)
Ventura Coll (CA)
Vermilion Comm Coll (MN)
Victor Valley Coll (CA)
Vincennes U (IN)
Warren County Comm Coll (NJ)
Waycross Coll (GA)
Western Nebraska Comm Coll (NE)
Western Nevada Comm Coll (NV)
Western Wyoming Comm Coll (WY)
Wharton County Jr Coll (TX)
Young Harris Coll (GA)

BIOLOGY EDUCATION

Louisburg Coll (NC)
Manatee Comm Coll (FL)

BIOMEDICAL ENGINEERING-RELATED TECHNOLOGY

Cincinnati State Tech and Comm Coll (OH)
Comm Coll of the Air Force (AL)
Delaware County Comm Coll (PA)
Delgado Comm Coll (LA)
Erie Comm Coll, South Campus (NY)
Florida Comm Coll at Jacksonville (FL)
Jefferson State Comm Coll (AL)
Parkland Coll (IL)
Pennsylvania Coll of Technology (PA)
Penn State U Beaver Campus of the Commonwealth Coll (PA)
Penn State U New Kensington Campus of the Commonwealth Coll (PA)
Penn State U Wilkes-Barre Campus of the Commonwealth Coll (PA)
Schoolcraft Coll (MI)
Southeast Tech Inst (SD)
Southwest Tennessee Comm Coll (TN)
Springfield Tech Comm Coll (MA)
Stanly Comm Coll (NC)
Texas State Tech Coll–Harlingen (TX)
Texas State Tech Coll– Waco/Marshall Campus (TX)
Western Iowa Tech Comm Coll (IA)

BIOMEDICAL TECHNOLOGY

Anoka-Ramsey Comm Coll, Cambridge Campus (MN)
Bates Tech Coll (WA)
Berkshire Comm Coll (MA)
Caldwell Comm Coll and Tech Inst (NC)
Cerritos Coll (CA)
Chattahoochee Tech Coll (GA)
Delaware Tech & Comm Coll, Stanton/ Wilmington Cmps (DE)
ECPI Coll of Technology, Virginia Beach (VA)
Gateway Comm Coll (CT)
George Corley Wallace State Comm Coll (AL)
Hillsborough Comm Coll (FL)
Howard Comm Coll (MD)
Johnson Coll (PA)
Madisonville Comm Coll (KY)
Middlesex Comm Coll (MA)
Milwaukee Area Tech Coll (WI)
North Seattle Comm Coll (WA)
Oklahoma City Comm Coll (OK)
Rowan-Cabarrus Comm Coll (NC)
St. Philip's Coll (TX)
Santa Barbara City Coll (CA)
Santa Fe Comm Coll (FL)
Savannah Tech Coll (GA)
South Suburban Coll (IL)
Spokane Comm Coll (WA)

Stark State Coll of Technology (OH)
Texas State Tech Coll– Waco/ Marshall Campus (TX)
Tulsa Comm Coll (OK)

BIOTECHNOLOGY RESEARCH
Alamance Comm Coll (NC)
Briarwood Coll (CT)
Dixie State Coll of Utah (UT)
Howard Comm Coll (MD)
Lakeland Comm Coll (OH)
Northern New Mexico Comm Coll (NM)
Santa Barbara City Coll (CA)
Springfield Tech Comm Coll (MA)
Vermont Tech Coll (VT)

BOTANY
Anne Arundel Comm Coll (MD)
Casper Coll (WY)
Centralia Coll (WA)
Cerritos Coll (CA)
City Coll of San Francisco (CA)
Coffeyville Comm Coll (KS)
Coll of Southern Idaho (ID)
Coll of the Siskiyous (CA)
Dixie State Coll of Utah (UT)
East Central Coll (MO)
Everett Comm Coll (WA)
Hill Coll of the Hill Jr College District (TX)
Iowa Lakes Comm Coll (IA)
Lincoln Coll, Lincoln (IL)
Lon Morris Coll (TX)
Miami U–Middletown Campus (OH)
North Idaho Coll (ID)
Northwest Coll (WY)
Palm Beach Comm Coll (FL)
Riverside Comm Coll (CA)
San Bernardino Valley Coll (CA)
San Jacinto Coll Central Campus (TX)
San Joaquin Delta Coll (CA)
Snow Coll (UT)
Southern Maine Tech Coll (ME)
Tacoma Comm Coll (WA)
Tulsa Comm Coll (OK)

BROADCAST JOURNALISM
Adirondack Comm Coll (NY)
Amarillo Coll (TX)
Anne Arundel Comm Coll (MD)
Arizona Western Coll (AZ)
Bakersfield Coll (CA)
Bergen Comm Coll (NJ)
Black Hawk Coll, Moline (IL)
Brown Coll (MN)
Centralia Coll (WA)
Chabot Coll (CA)
Chaffey Coll (CA)
Chattanooga State Tech Comm Coll (TN)
City Coll of San Francisco (CA)
Coffeyville Comm Coll (KS)
Colby Comm Coll (KS)
Cumberland County Coll (NJ)
Delta Coll (MI)
Dixie State Coll of Utah (UT)
Dodge City Comm Coll (KS)
Draughons Jr Coll, Nashville (TN)
Finger Lakes Comm Coll (NY)
Georgia Perimeter Coll (GA)
Harford Comm Coll (MD)
Herkimer County Comm Coll (NY)
Hesser Coll (NH)
Iowa Lakes Comm Coll (IA)
Isothermal Comm Coll (NC)
Kirkwood Comm Coll (IA)
Lane Comm Coll (OR)
Lansing Comm Coll (MI)
Lincoln Coll, Lincoln (IL)
Los Angeles City Coll (CA)
Meridian Comm Coll (MS)
Miami-Dade Comm Coll (FL)
Milwaukee Area Tech Coll (WI)
Moorpark Coll (CA)
Mt. Hood Comm Coll (OR)
Mount Wachusett Comm Coll (MA)
Navarro Coll (TX)
Northeast Comm Coll (NE)
Northern Oklahoma Coll (OK)
Northland Comm and Tech Coll (MN)
Oklahoma City Comm Coll (OK)
Pasadena City Coll (CA)
Pennsylvania Coll of Technology (PA)
Pratt Comm Coll and Area Vocational School (KS)
Quincy Coll (MA)
Ridgewater Coll (MN)
St. Clair County Comm Coll (MI)
St. Louis Comm Coll at Florissant Valley (MO)
San Joaquin Delta Coll (CA)
Santa Monica Coll (CA)
Southeast Comm Coll, Beatrice Campus (NE)
Sussex County Comm Coll (NJ)
Trident Tech Coll (SC)
Vincennes U (IN)

BUILDING MAINTENANCE/ MANAGEMENT
Comm Coll of Allegheny County (PA)
Delgado Comm Coll (LA)
Erie Comm Coll, City Campus (NY)
Herkimer County Comm Coll (NY)
Ivy Tech State Coll–Bloomington (IN)
Ivy Tech State Coll–Central Indiana (IN)
Ivy Tech State Coll–Columbus (IN)
Ivy Tech State Coll–Eastcentral (IN)
Ivy Tech State Coll–Kokomo (IN)
Ivy Tech State Coll–Lafayette (IN)
Ivy Tech State Coll–Northeast (IN)
Ivy Tech State Coll–Northwest (IN)
Ivy Tech State Coll–Southcentral (IN)
Ivy Tech State Coll–Southwest (IN)
Ivy Tech State Coll–Wabash Valley (IN)
Ivy Tech State Coll–Whitewater (IN)
Luzerne County Comm Coll (PA)
Miles Comm Coll (MT)
Pima Comm Coll (AZ)
St. Philip's Coll (TX)

BUSINESS
Allen County Comm Coll (KS)
Antelope Valley Coll (CA)
Atlanta Metropolitan Coll (GA)
Bay de Noc Comm Coll (MI)
Berkeley Coll (NJ)
Bismarck State Coll (ND)
Bryant & Stratton Business Inst, Eastern Hills Cmps (NY)
Centralia Coll (WA)
Coll of Southern Idaho (ID)
Columbia State Comm Coll (TN)
Comm Coll of Rhode Island (RI)
Cuyamaca Coll (CA)
Dawson Comm Coll (MT)
Evergreen Valley Coll (CA)
Gallipolis Career Coll (OH)
GateWay Comm Coll (AZ)
Glendale Comm Coll (AZ)
Great Basin Coll (NV)
Hagerstown Comm Coll (MD)
Harrisburg Area Comm Coll (PA)
Hawkeye Comm Coll (IA)
Hutchinson Comm Coll and Area Vocational School (KS)
Jackson Comm Coll (MI)
Jefferson State Comm Coll (AL)
John Tyler Comm Coll (VA)
Kankakee Comm Coll (IL)
Kansas City Kansas Comm Coll (KS)
Keystone Coll (PA)
Kilgore Coll (TX)
Louisburg Coll (NC)
Manatee Comm Coll (FL)
Massachusetts Bay Comm Coll (MA)
Mesabi Range Comm and Tech Coll (MN)
Miami U–Middletown Campus (OH)
Minneapolis Comm and Tech Coll (MN)
Mississippi County Comm Coll (AR)
Missouri Coll (MO)
Montana State U Coll of Tech-Great Falls (MT)
Montgomery Coll (MD)
Montgomery County Comm Coll (PA)
Mott Comm Coll (MI)
National Coll of Business & Technology, Charlottesville (VA)
National Coll of Business & Technology, Salem (VA)
New Mexico State U–Alamogordo (NM)
Northampton County Area Comm Coll (PA)
North Dakota State Coll of Science (ND)
Northern New Mexico Comm Coll (NM)
Northland Pioneer Coll (AZ)
Northwest State Comm Coll (OH)
Ocean County Coll (NJ)
Orangeburg-Calhoun Tech Coll (SC)
Patricia Stevens Coll (MO)
Penn State U Wilkes-Barre Campus of the Commonwealth Coll (PA)
Pensacola Jr Coll (FL)
Piedmont Tech Coll (SC)
Reedley Coll (CA)
San Joaquin Valley Coll (CA)
Sheridan Coll (WY)
South Arkansas Comm Coll (AR)
Southeast Arkansas Coll (AR)
Southern State Comm Coll (OH)
South Hills School of Business & Technology, State College (PA)
Southwest Tennessee Comm Coll (TN)
Springfield Tech Comm Coll (MA)
Truett-McConnell Coll (GA)
Union County Coll (NJ)
U of Arkansas Comm Coll at Batesville (AR)
Victor Valley Coll (CA)
Vista Comm Coll (CA)
Western Nevada Comm Coll (NV)
Wor-Wic Comm Coll (MD)
Yorktowne Business Inst (PA)

BUSINESS ADMINISTRATION
Abraham Baldwin Ag Coll (GA)
Adirondack Comm Coll (NY)
AIB Coll of Business (IA)
Alamance Comm Coll (NC)
Albuquerque Tech Vocational Inst (NM)
Alexandria Tech Coll (MN)
Allan Hancock Coll (CA)
Allegany Coll of Maryland (MD)
Allen County Comm Coll (KS)
Allentown Business School (PA)
Alpena Comm Coll (MI)
Alvin Comm Coll (TX)
Amarillo Coll (TX)
American River Coll (CA)
Ancilla Coll (IN)
Andover Coll (ME)
Andrew Coll (GA)
Angelina Coll (TX)
Anne Arundel Comm Coll (MD)
Anoka-Ramsey Comm Coll (MN)
Anoka-Ramsey Comm Coll, Cambridge Campus (MN)
Antelope Valley Coll (CA)
Arapahoe Comm Coll (CO)
Arizona Western Coll (AZ)
Arkansas State U–Beebe (AR)
Asheville-Buncombe Tech Comm Coll (NC)
Ashland Comm Coll (KY)
Asnuntuck Comm Coll (CT)
Atlanta Metropolitan Coll (GA)
Atlantic Cape Comm Coll (NJ)
Austin Comm Coll (TX)
Bacone Coll (OK)
Bainbridge Coll (GA)
Bakersfield Coll (CA)
Baltimore City Comm Coll (MD)
Barstow Coll (CA)
Barton County Comm Coll (KS)
Bauder Coll (GA)
Bay de Noc Comm Coll (MI)
Bay State Coll (MA)
Beaufort County Comm Coll (NC)
Bellevue Comm Coll (WA)
Belmont Tech Coll (OH)
Bergen Comm Coll (NJ)
Berkeley Coll (NJ)
Berkeley Coll (NY)
Berkeley Coll-Westchester Campus (NY)
Berkshire Comm Coll (MA)
Bevill State Comm Coll (AL)
Blackfeet Comm Coll (MT)
Black Hawk Coll, Moline (IL)
Black River Tech Coll (AR)
Bladen Comm Coll (NC)
Blair Coll (CO)
Blinn Coll (TX)
Blue Ridge Comm Coll (NC)
Blue Ridge Comm Coll (VA)
Blue River Comm Coll (MO)
Borough of Manhattan Comm Coll of City U of NY (NY)
Bossier Parish Comm Coll (LA)
Bowling Green State U-Firelands Coll (OH)
Brazosport Coll (TX)
Brevard Comm Coll (FL)
Briarwood Coll (CT)
Bristol Comm Coll (MA)
Bronx Comm Coll of City U of NY (NY)
Brookdale Comm Coll (NJ)
Broome Comm Coll (NY)
The Brown Mackie Coll (KS)
The Brown Mackie Coll–Olathe Campus (KS)
Brunswick Comm Coll (NC)
Bryant & Stratton Business Inst, Albany (NY)
Bryant & Stratton Business Inst, Buffalo (NY)
Bryant & Stratton Business Inst, Lackawanna (NY)
Bryant & Stratton Business Inst, Rochester (NY)
Bryant & Stratton Business Inst, Rochester (NY)
Bryant & Stratton Business Inst (NY)
Bryant and Stratton Coll, Parma (OH)
Bryant and Stratton Coll, Willoughby Hills (OH)
Bryant and Stratton Coll (WI)
Bryant and Stratton Coll, Virginia Beach (VA)
Bucks County Comm Coll (PA)
Bunker Hill Comm Coll (MA)
Burlington County Coll (NJ)
Business Inst of Pennsylvania (PA)
Butler County Comm Coll (PA)
Caldwell Comm Coll and Tech Inst (NC)
Calhoun Comm Coll (AL)
Cambria-Rowe Business Coll (PA)
Camden County Coll (NJ)
Cañada Coll (CA)
Cape Cod Comm Coll (MA)
Cape Fear Comm Coll (NC)
Capital Comm Coll (CT)
Career Coll of Northern Nevada (NV)
Carl Sandburg Coll (IL)
Carroll Comm Coll (MD)
Carteret Comm Coll (NC)
Casper Coll (WY)
Catawba Valley Comm Coll (NC)
Cayuga County Comm Coll (NY)
Cecil Comm Coll (MD)
Cedar Valley Coll (TX)
Central Alabama Comm Coll (AL)
Central Arizona Coll (AZ)
Central Carolina Comm Coll (NC)
Central Carolina Tech Coll (SC)
Central Comm Coll–Columbus Campus (NE)
Central Comm Coll–Grand Island Campus (NE)
Central Comm Coll–Hastings Campus (NE)
Central Florida Comm Coll (FL)
Central Georgia Tech Coll (GA)
Centralia Coll (WA)
Central Lakes Coll (MN)
Central Maine Tech Coll (ME)
Central Ohio Tech Coll (OH)
Central Oregon Comm Coll (OR)
Central Pennsylvania Coll (PA)
Central Piedmont Comm Coll (NC)
Central Texas Coll (TX)
Central Virginia Comm Coll (VA)
Central Wyoming Coll (WY)
Century Comm and Tech Coll (MN)
Cerritos Coll (CA)
Cerro Coso Comm Coll (CA)
Chabot Coll (CA)
Chaffey Coll (CA)
Chaparral Coll (AZ)
Charter Coll (AK)
Chatfield Coll (OH)
Chattahoochee Tech Coll (GA)
Chattahoochee Valley Comm Coll (AL)
Chattanooga State Tech Comm Coll (TN)
Chemeketa Comm Coll (OR)
Chesapeake Coll (MD)
Chipola Jr Coll (FL)
Churchman Business School (PA)
Cincinnati State Tech and Comm Coll (OH)
Cisco Jr Coll (TX)
Citrus Coll (CA)
City Coll of San Francisco (CA)
City Colls of Chicago, Harry S Truman Coll (IL)
City Colls of Chicago, Richard J Daley Coll (IL)
City Colls of Chicago, Wilbur Wright Coll (IL)
Clark Coll (WA)
Cleveland Comm Coll (NC)
Cleveland State Comm Coll (TN)
Clinton Comm Coll (IA)
Clinton Comm Coll (NY)
Clovis Comm Coll (NM)
Coahoma Comm Coll (MS)
Coastal Bend Coll (TX)
Coastal Carolina Comm Coll (NC)
Coastal Georgia Comm Coll (GA)
Cochise Coll, Douglas (AZ)
Coffeyville Comm Coll (KS)
Colby Comm Coll (KS)
Coll of Alameda (CA)
Coll of DuPage (IL)
Coll of Eastern Utah (UT)
Coll of Lake County (IL)
Coll of Marin (CA)
Coll of Southern Idaho (ID)
Coll of Southern Maryland (MD)
Coll of the Canyons (CA)
Coll of the Desert (CA)
Coll of the Redwoods (CA)
Coll of the Sequoias (CA)
Coll of the Siskiyous (CA)
Collin County Comm Coll District (TX)
Colorado Mountn Coll, Alpine Cmps (CO)
Colorado Mountn Coll (CO)
Colorado Mountn Coll, Timberline Cmps (CO)
Columbia-Greene Comm Coll (NY)
Columbus State Comm Coll (OH)
Commonwealth Business Coll, Merrillville (IN)
Comm Coll of Allegheny County (PA)
Comm Coll of Aurora (CO)
The Comm Coll of Baltimore County–Catonsville Campus (MD)
Comm Coll of Beaver County (PA)
Comm Coll of Denver (CO)
Comm Coll of Rhode Island (RI)
Comm Coll of Southern Nevada (NV)
Comm Coll of Vermont (VT)
Compton Comm Coll (CA)
Connors State Coll (OK)
Consolidated School of Business, Lancaster (PA)
Consolidated School of Business, York (PA)
Corning Comm Coll (NY)
County Coll of Morris (NJ)
Cowley County Comm Coll and Voc-Tech School (KS)
Crafton Hills Coll (CA)
Craven Comm Coll (NC)
Crowder Coll (MO)
Cuesta Coll (CA)
Cumberland County Coll (NJ)
Cuyahoga Comm Coll (OH)
Cuyamaca Coll (CA)
Cypress Coll (CA)
Danville Area Comm Coll (IL)
Danville Comm Coll (VA)
Darton Coll (GA)
Davis Coll (OH)
Daymar Coll (KY)
Daytona Beach Comm Coll (FL)
Dean Coll (MA)
De Anza Coll (CA)
Delaware County Comm Coll (PA)
Delaware Tech & Comm Coll, Jack F Owens Cmps (DE)
Delaware Tech & Comm Coll, Stanton/ Wilmington Cmps (DE)
Delaware Tech & Comm Coll, Terry Cmps (DE)
Delgado Comm Coll (LA)
Del Mar Coll (TX)
Delta Coll (MI)

Denmark Tech Coll (SC)
Des Moines Area Comm Coll (IA)
Diné Coll (AZ)
Dixie State Coll of Utah (UT)
Dodge City Comm Coll (KS)
Doña Ana Branch Comm Coll (NM)
Donnelly Coll (KS)
Douglas Education Center (PA)
Draughons Jr Coll (KY)
Draughons Jr Coll, Clarksville (TN)
Draughons Jr Coll, Nashville (TN)
Duff's Business Inst (PA)
Durham Tech Comm Coll (NC)
Dutchess Comm Coll (NY)
Dyersburg State Comm Coll (TN)
East Arkansas Comm Coll (AR)
East Central Coll (MO)
East Central Comm Coll (MS)
Eastern Arizona Coll (AZ)
Eastern Maine Tech Coll (ME)
Eastern Oklahoma State Coll (OK)
Eastern Shore Comm Coll (VA)
Eastern Wyoming Coll (WY)
Eastfield Coll (TX)
East Georgia Coll (GA)
East Mississippi Comm Coll (MS)
Edgecombe Comm Coll (NC)
Edison Comm Coll (FL)
Edison State Comm Coll (OH)
Edmonds Comm Coll (WA)
Education America, Remington Coll, Lafayette Campus (LA)
Education Direct (PA)
El Centro Coll (TX)
Elizabethtown Comm Coll (KY)
Ellsworth Comm Coll (IA)
Enterprise State Jr Coll (AL)
Erie Business Center, Main (PA)
Erie Business Center South (PA)
Erie Comm Coll, City Campus (NY)
Erie Comm Coll, North Campus (NY)
Erie Comm Coll, South Campus (NY)
Essex County Coll (NJ)
Eugenio María de Hostos Comm Coll of City U of NY (NY)
Everett Comm Coll (WA)
Evergreen Valley Coll (CA)
Fayetteville Tech Comm Coll (NC)
Feather River Comm Coll District (CA)
Fergus Falls Comm Coll (MN)
Finger Lakes Comm Coll (NY)
Fiorello H LaGuardia Comm Coll of City U of NY (NY)
Fisher Coll (MA)
Flathead Valley Comm Coll (MT)
Florence-Darlington Tech Coll (SC)
Florida Comm Coll at Jacksonville (FL)
Florida National Coll (FL)
Floyd Coll (GA)
Foothill Coll (CA)
Forrest Jr Coll (SC)
Forsyth Tech Comm Coll (NC)
Fort Berthold Comm Coll (ND)
Fort Scott Comm Coll (KS)
Frederick Comm Coll (MD)
Fresno City Coll (CA)
Front Range Comm Coll (CO)
Fullerton Coll (CA)
Fulton-Montgomery Comm Coll (NY)
Gallipolis Career Coll (OH)
Galveston Coll (TX)
Garden City Comm Coll (KS)
Gaston Coll (NC)
Gateway Comm Coll (CT)
Gavilan Coll (CA)
Gem City Coll (IL)
Genesee Comm Coll (NY)
George Corley Wallace State Comm Coll (AL)
Georgia Military Coll (GA)
Georgia Perimeter Coll (GA)
Germanna Comm Coll (VA)
Glendale Comm Coll (AZ)
Glendale Comm Coll (CA)
Glen Oaks Comm Coll (MI)
Gloucester County Coll (NJ)
Gogebic Comm Coll (MI)
Golden West Coll (CA)
Gordon Coll (GA)
Grand Rapids Comm Coll (MI)
Grays Harbor Coll (WA)
Grayson County Coll (TX)
Great Basin Coll (NV)
Greenfield Comm Coll (MA)
Greenville Tech Coll (SC)
Guam Comm Coll (GU)
Guilford Tech Comm Coll (NC)
Gulf Coast Comm Coll (FL)
Hagerstown Business Coll (MD)
Hagerstown Comm Coll (MD)
Halifax Comm Coll (NC)
Hamilton Coll (IA)
Harcum Coll (PA)
Harford Comm Coll (MD)
Harrisburg Area Comm Coll (PA)
Hawaii Business Coll (HI)
Hawkeye Comm Coll (IA)
Haywood Comm Coll (NC)
Hazard Comm Coll (KY)
Heald Coll, Schools of Business and Technology, Rancho Cordova (CA)
Heald Coll, Schools of Business and Technology (HI)
Heartland Comm Coll (IL)
Henderson Comm Coll (KY)
Henry Ford Comm Coll (MI)
Herkimer County Comm Coll (NY)
Herzing Coll (GA)
Hesser Coll (NH)
Hesston Coll (KS)
Hibbing Comm Coll (MN)
Highland Comm Coll (IL)
Highland Comm Coll (KS)
Highline Comm Coll (WA)
Hill Coll of the Hill Jr College District (TX)
Hillsborough Comm Coll (FL)
Hinds Comm Coll (MS)
Holmes Comm Coll (MS)
Holyoke Comm Coll (MA)
Hopkinsville Comm Coll (KY)
Horry-Georgetown Tech Coll (SC)
Housatonic Comm Coll (CT)
Houston Comm Coll System (TX)
Howard Coll (TX)
Howard Comm Coll (MD)
Hudson County Comm Coll (NJ)
Huntington Jr Coll of Business (WV)
Illinois Eastern Comm Colls, Wabash Valley Coll (IL)
Imperial Valley Coll (CA)
Independence Comm Coll (KS)
Indiana Business Coll, Anderson (IN)
Indiana Business Coll, Columbus (IN)
Indiana Business Coll, Evansville (IN)
Indiana Business Coll, Fort Wayne (IN)
Indiana Business Coll, Indianapolis (IN)
Indiana Business Coll, Lafayette (IN)
Indiana Business Coll, Marion (IN)
Indiana Business Coll, Muncie (IN)
Indiana Business Coll, Terre Haute (IN)
Indian Hills Comm Coll (IA)
Indian River Comm Coll (FL)
Instituto Comercial de Puerto Rico Jr Coll (PR)
Interboro Inst (NY)
International Business Coll, Fort Wayne (IN)
Inver Hills Comm Coll (MN)
Iowa Lakes Comm Coll (IA)
Iowa Western Comm Coll (IA)
Isothermal Comm Coll (NC)
Itasca Comm Coll (MN)
Ivy Tech State Coll–Bloomington (IN)
Ivy Tech State Coll–Central Indiana (IN)
Ivy Tech State Coll–Columbus (IN)
Ivy Tech State Coll–Eastcentral (IN)
Ivy Tech State Coll–Kokomo (IN)
Ivy Tech State Coll–Lafayette (IN)
Ivy Tech State Coll–North Central (IN)
Ivy Tech State Coll–Northeast (IN)
Ivy Tech State Coll–Northwest (IN)
Ivy Tech State Coll–Southcentral (IN)
Ivy Tech State Coll–Southeast (IN)
Ivy Tech State Coll–Southwest (IN)
Ivy Tech State Coll–Wabash Valley (IN)
Ivy Tech State Coll–Whitewater (IN)
Jackson Comm Coll (MI)
Jackson State Comm Coll (TN)
James H. Faulkner State Comm Coll (AL)
James Sprunt Comm Coll (NC)
Jamestown Business Coll (NY)
Jamestown Comm Coll (NY)
Jefferson Coll (MO)
Jefferson Comm Coll (KY)
Jefferson Comm Coll (NY)
Jefferson Comm Coll (OH)
Jefferson Davis Comm Coll (AL)
John A. Logan Coll (IL)
Johnson County Comm Coll (KS)
Johnston Comm Coll (NC)
John Wood Comm Coll (IL)
Joliet Jr Coll (IL)
Jones County Jr Coll (MS)
J. Sargeant Reynolds Comm Coll (VA)
Kalamazoo Valley Comm Coll (MI)
Kansas City Kansas Comm Coll (KS)
Kaplan Coll (IA)
Kaskaskia Coll (IL)
Kellogg Comm Coll (MI)
Kennebec Valley Tech Coll (ME)
Kent State U, East Liverpool Campus (OH)
Kent State U, Geauga Campus (OH)
Kent State U, Salem Campus (OH)
Kent State U, Stark Campus (OH)
Kent State U, Trumbull Campus (OH)
Kent State U, Tuscarawas Campus (OH)
Keystone Coll (PA)
Kilgore Coll (TX)
Kilian Comm Coll (SD)
Kingsborough Comm Coll of City U of NY (NY)
Kingwood Coll (TX)
Kirkwood Comm Coll (IA)
Kishwaukee Coll (IL)
Labette Comm Coll (KS)
Lac Courte Oreilles Ojibwa Comm Coll (WI)
Lake City Comm Coll (FL)
Lake Land Coll (IL)
Lakeland Comm Coll (OH)
Lake Michigan Coll (MI)
Lake Region State Coll (ND)
Lake-Sumter Comm Coll (FL)
Lake Tahoe Comm Coll (CA)
Lamar Comm Coll (CO)
Lamar State Coll–Orange (TX)
Lamar State Coll–Port Arthur (TX)
Lane Comm Coll (OR)
Lansing Comm Coll (MI)
Laramie County Comm Coll (WY)
Las Positas Coll (CA)
Laurel Business Inst (PA)
LDS Business Coll (UT)
Lehigh Carbon Comm Coll (PA)
Lenoir Comm Coll (NC)
Lewis and Clark Comm Coll (IL)
Lewis Coll of Business (MI)
Lima Tech Coll (OH)
Lincoln Coll, Lincoln (IL)
Lincoln Coll, Normal (IL)
Lincoln Land Comm Coll (IL)
Lincoln School of Commerce (NE)
Linn-Benton Comm Coll (OR)
Long Beach City Coll (CA)
Long Island Business Inst (NY)
Longview Comm Coll (MO)
Lon Morris Coll (TX)
Lorain County Comm Coll (OH)
Lord Fairfax Comm Coll (VA)
Los Angeles City Coll (CA)
Los Angeles Harbor Coll (CA)
Los Angeles Mission Coll (CA)
Louisburg Coll (NC)
Louisiana State U at Alexandria (LA)
Louisiana State U at Eunice (LA)
Lower Columbia Coll (WA)
Luzerne County Comm Coll (PA)
Macomb Comm Coll (MI)
Madisonville Comm Coll (KY)
Manatee Comm Coll (FL)
Manchester Comm Coll (CT)
Manor Coll (PA)
Maple Woods Comm Coll (MO)
Marian Court Coll (MA)
Marion Tech Coll (OH)
Marshalltown Comm Coll (IA)
Martin Comm Coll (NC)
Massachusetts Bay Comm Coll (MA)
Massasoit Comm Coll (MA)
Mayland Comm Coll (NC)
Maysville Comm Coll (KY)
McCann School of Business (PA)
McHenry County Coll (IL)
McIntosh Coll (NH)
McLennan Comm Coll (TX)
Merced Coll (CA)
Mercer County Comm Coll (NJ)
Mesa Tech Coll (NM)
Metropolitan Comm Coll (NE)
Miami-Dade Comm Coll (FL)
Miami U–Middletown Campus (OH)
Middle Georgia Coll (GA)
Middlesex Comm Coll (MA)
Middlesex County Coll (NJ)
Midland Coll (TX)
Midlands Tech Coll (SC)
Mid Michigan Comm Coll (MI)
Mid-Plains Comm Coll Area (NE)
Mid-State Coll (ME)
Mid-State Tech Coll (WI)
Miles Comm Coll (MT)
Milwaukee Area Tech Coll (WI)
Mineral Area Coll (MO)
Minneapolis Comm and Tech Coll (MN)
Minnesota School of Business (MN)
Minot State U–Bottineau Campus (ND)
MiraCosta Coll (CA)
Mississippi Gulf Coast Comm Coll (MS)
Mitchell Coll (CT)
Mitchell Comm Coll (NC)
Modesto Jr Coll (CA)
Mohave Comm Coll (AZ)
Mohawk Valley Comm Coll (NY)
Monroe Coll, Bronx (NY)
Monroe Coll, New Rochelle (NY)
Monroe Comm Coll (NY)
Monroe County Comm Coll (MI)
Montcalm Comm Coll (MI)
Monterey Peninsula Coll (CA)
Montgomery Coll (MD)
Montgomery Comm Coll (NC)
Montgomery County Comm Coll (PA)
Moorpark Coll (CA)
Moraine Valley Comm Coll (IL)
Morgan Comm Coll (CO)
Morton Coll (IL)
Motlow State Comm Coll (TN)
Mott Comm Coll (MI)
Mountain Empire Comm Coll (VA)
Mountain West Coll (UT)
Mt. Hood Comm Coll (OR)
Mt. San Jacinto Coll (CA)
Mount Wachusett Comm Coll (MA)
Muscatine Comm Coll (IA)
Muskingum Area Tech Coll (OH)
Nash Comm Coll (NC)
Nashville State Tech Inst (TN)
Nassau Comm Coll (NY)
National Coll of Business & Technology, Danville (KY)
National Coll of Business & Technology, Florence (KY)
National Coll of Business & Technology, Lexington (KY)
National Coll of Business & Technology, Louisville (KY)
National Coll of Business & Technology, Pikeville (KY)
National Coll of Business & Technology, Richmond (KY)
National Coll of Business & Technology (TN)
National Coll of Business & Technology, Bluefield (VA)
National Coll of Business & Technology, Bristol (VA)
National Coll of Business & Technology, Danville (VA)
National Coll of Business & Technology, Harrisonburg (VA)
National Coll of Business & Technology, Lynchburg (VA)
National Coll of Business & Technology, Martinsville (VA)
Naugatuck Valley Comm Coll (CT)
Navarro Coll (TX)
Neosho County Comm Coll (KS)
Newbury Coll (MA)
New England Inst of Technology (RI)
New Hampshire Comm Tech Coll, Berlin/Laconia (NH)
New Hampshire Tech Inst (NH)
New Mexico Military Inst (NM)
New Mexico State U–Carlsbad (NM)
Newport Business Inst, Williamsport (PA)
New River Comm Coll (VA)
Niagara County Comm Coll (NY)
Northampton County Area Comm Coll (PA)
North Arkansas Coll (AR)
North Central Michigan Coll (MI)
Northcentral Tech Coll (WI)
North Central Texas Coll (TX)
North Country Comm Coll (NY)
Northeast Alabama Comm Coll (AL)
Northeast Comm Coll (NE)
Northeastern Tech Coll (SC)
Northeast State Tech Comm Coll (TN)
Northern Essex Comm Coll (MA)
Northern Maine Tech Coll (ME)
Northern Oklahoma Coll (OK)
Northern Virginia Comm Coll (VA)
North Hennepin Comm Coll (MN)
North Idaho Coll (ID)
North Iowa Area Comm Coll (IA)
Northland Comm and Tech Coll (MN)
Northland Pioneer Coll (AZ)
North Seattle Comm Coll (WA)
North Shore Comm Coll (MA)
NorthWest Arkansas Comm Coll (AR)
Northwest Coll (WY)
Northwestern Business Coll (IL)
Northwestern Connecticut Comm-Tech Coll (CT)
Northwestern Michigan Coll (MI)
Northwest Mississippi Comm Coll (MS)
Northwest-Shoals Comm Coll (AL)
Northwest State Comm Coll (OH)
Norwalk Comm Coll (CT)
Oakton Comm Coll (IL)
Ocean County Coll (NJ)
Odessa Coll (TX)
Ohio Business Coll (OH)
Okaloosa-Walton Comm Coll (FL)
Oklahoma City Comm Coll (OK)
Oklahoma State U, Oklahoma City (OK)
Oklahoma State U, Okmulgee (OK)
Olympic Coll (WA)
Onondaga Comm Coll (NY)
Orange Coast Coll (CA)
Orange County Comm Coll (NY)
Otero Jr Coll (CO)
Ouachita Tech Coll (AR)
Owensboro Comm Coll (KY)
Oxnard Coll (CA)
Ozarka Coll (AR)
Pace Inst (PA)
Paducah Comm Coll (KY)
Palm Beach Comm Coll (FL)
Palomar Coll (CA)
Palo Verde Coll (CA)
Pamlico Comm Coll (NC)
Paradise Valley Comm Coll (AZ)
Parkland Coll (IL)
Pasadena City Coll (CA)
Pasco-Hernando Comm Coll (FL)
Patrick Henry Comm Coll (VA)
Paul D. Camp Comm Coll (VA)
Paul Smith's Coll of Arts and Sciences (NY)
Pellissippi State Tech Comm Coll (TN)
Peninsula Coll (WA)
Penn Commercial Business and Tech School (PA)
Pennsylvania Coll of Technology (PA)
Pennsylvania Inst of Technology (PA)
Penn State U Beaver Campus of the Commonwealth Coll (PA)
Penn State U Delaware County Campus of the Commonwealth Coll (PA)
Penn State U DuBois Campus of the Commonwealth Coll (PA)
Penn State U Fayette Campus of the Commonwealth Coll (PA)
Penn State U Hazleton Campus of the Commonwealth Coll (PA)
Penn State U McKeesport Campus of the Commonwealth Coll (PA)

Penn State U Mont Alto Campus of the Commonwealth Coll (PA)
Penn State U New Kensington Campus of the Commonwealth Coll (PA)
Penn State U Shenango Campus of the Commonwealth Coll (PA)
Penn State U Wilkes-Barre Campus of the Commonwealth Coll (PA)
Penn State U Worthington Scranton Cmps Commonwealth Coll (PA)
Penn State U York Campus of the Commonwealth Coll (PA)
Penn Valley Comm Coll (MO)
Pensacola Jr Coll (FL)
Phoenix Coll (AZ)
Piedmont Comm Coll (NC)
Piedmont Tech Coll (SC)
Piedmont Virginia Comm Coll (VA)
Pierce Coll (WA)
Pikes Peak Comm Coll (CO)
Pima Comm Coll (AZ)
Pitt Comm Coll (NC)
Pittsburgh Tech Inst (PA)
Polk Comm Coll (FL)
Portland Comm Coll (OR)
Pratt Comm Coll and Area Vocational School (KS)
Prince George's Comm Coll (MD)
Queensborough Comm Coll of City U of NY (NY)
Quincy Coll (MA)
Quinsigamond Comm Coll (MA)
Rainy River Comm Coll (MN)
Randolph Comm Coll (NC)
Rappahannock Comm Coll (VA)
Raritan Valley Comm Coll (NJ)
Rasmussen Coll Eagan (MN)
Rasmussen Coll Mankato (MN)
Rasmussen Coll Minnetonka (MN)
Rasmussen Coll St. Cloud (MN)
Reading Area Comm Coll (PA)
Red Rocks Comm Coll (CO)
Rend Lake Coll (IL)
Richland Comm Coll (IL)
Richmond Comm Coll (NC)
Ridgewater Coll (MN)
Riverland Comm Coll (MN)
Riverside Comm Coll (CA)
Roane State Comm Coll (TN)
Roanoke-Chowan Comm Coll (NC)
Robeson Comm Coll (NC)
Rochester Business Inst (NY)
Rockford Business Coll (IL)
Rockingham Comm Coll (NC)
Rockland Comm Coll (NY)
Rogue Comm Coll (OR)
Rowan-Cabarrus Comm Coll (NC)
Sacramento City Coll (CA)
St. Catharine Coll (KY)
Saint Charles Comm Coll (MO)
St. Clair County Comm Coll (MI)
St. Cloud Tech Coll (MN)
St. Louis Comm Coll at Florissant Valley (MO)
St. Petersburg Coll (FL)
St. Philip's Coll (TX)
Salem Comm Coll (NJ)
Sampson Comm Coll (NC)
San Antonio Coll (TX)
San Bernardino Valley Coll (CA)
Sandhills Comm Coll (NC)
San Diego City Coll (CA)
San Diego Mesa Coll (CA)
Sanford-Brown Coll, Hazelwood (MO)
San Jacinto Coll Central Campus (TX)
San Jacinto Coll North Campus (TX)
San Jacinto Coll South Campus (TX)
San Joaquin Delta Coll (CA)
San Juan Coll (NM)
Santa Ana Coll (CA)
Santa Barbara City Coll (CA)
Santa Fe Comm Coll (FL)
Santa Fe Comm Coll (NM)
Santa Monica Coll (CA)
Sauk Valley Comm Coll (IL)
Schenectady County Comm Coll (NY)
Schoolcraft Coll (MI)
Scott Comm Coll (IA)
Scottsdale Comm Coll (AZ)
Seminole Comm Coll (FL)
Seminole State Coll (OK)
Shasta Coll (CA)
Sheridan Coll (WY)
Shoreline Comm Coll (WA)
Sierra Coll (CA)
Sinclair Comm Coll (OH)
Sitting Bull Coll (ND)
Skagit Valley Coll (WA)
Snead State Comm Coll (AL)
Snow Coll (UT)
Somerset Comm Coll (KY)
South Coll (NC)
South Coll (TN)
Southeast Arkansas Coll (AR)
Southeast Comm Coll (KY)
Southeast Comm Coll, Beatrice Campus (NE)
Southeastern Comm Coll (NC)
Southeastern Comm Coll, South Campus (IA)
Southeast Tech Inst (SD)
Southern Arkansas U Tech (AR)
Southern Maine Tech Coll (ME)
Southern Ohio Coll, Cincinnati Campus (OH)
Southern Ohio Coll, Northern Kentucky Campus (KY)
Southern West Virginia Comm and Tech Coll (WV)
South Mountain Comm Coll (AZ)
South Piedmont Comm Coll (NC)
South Plains Coll (TX)
South Puget Sound Comm Coll (WA)
Southside Virginia Comm Coll (VA)
South Texas Comm Coll (TX)
South U (AL)
Southwestern Coll (CA)
Southwestern Coll of Business, Dayton (OH)
Southwestern Comm Coll (IA)
Southwestern Comm Coll (NC)
Southwestern Michigan Coll (MI)
Southwestern Oklahoma State U at Sayre (OK)
Southwest Mississippi Comm Coll (MS)
Southwest Tennessee Comm Coll (TN)
Southwest Virginia Comm Coll (VA)
Spartanburg Tech Coll (SC)
Spencerian Coll (KY)
Spokane Comm Coll (WA)
Spokane Falls Comm Coll (WA)
Springfield Tech Comm Coll (MA)
Stanly Comm Coll (NC)
Stark State Coll of Technology (OH)
State Fair Comm Coll (MO)
State U of NY Coll of A&T at Morrisville (NY)
State U of NY Coll of Technology at Alfred (NY)
State U of NY Coll of Technology at Canton (NY)
State U of NY Coll of Technology at Delhi (NY)
Stone Child Coll (MT)
Stratford U (VA)
Suffolk County Comm Coll (NY)
Sullivan County Comm Coll (NY)
Surry Comm Coll (NC)
Sussex County Comm Coll (NJ)
Tacoma Comm Coll (WA)
Taft Coll (CA)
Tallahassee Comm Coll (FL)
Tarrant County Coll District (TX)
Temple Coll (TX)
Terra State Comm Coll (OH)
Texarkana Coll (TX)
Thomas Nelson Comm Coll (VA)
Three Rivers Comm Coll (CT)
Tidewater Comm Coll (VA)
Tomball Coll (TX)
Tompkins Cortland Comm Coll (NY)
Tri-County Comm Coll (NC)
Tri-County Tech Coll (SC)
Trident Tech Coll (SC)
Trinidad State Jr Coll (CO)
Trinity Valley Comm Coll (TX)
Triton Coll (IL)
Trocaire Coll (NY)
Truckee Meadows Comm Coll (NV)
Tulsa Comm Coll (OK)
Tunxis Comm Coll (CT)
Tyler Jr Coll (TX)
Ulster County Comm Coll (NY)
Umpqua Comm Coll (OR)
Union County Coll (NJ)
United Tribes Tech Coll (ND)
The U of Akron–Wayne Coll (OH)
U of Alaska Anchorage, Kenai Peninsula Coll (AK)
U of Alaska Anchorage, Kodiak Coll (AK)
U of Alaska Anchorage, Matanuska-Susitna Coll (AK)
U of Alaska Southeast, Ketchikan Campus (AK)
U of Alaska Southeast, Sitka Campus (AK)
U of Arkansas at Fort Smith (AR)
U of Arkansas Comm Coll at Hope (AR)
U of Kentucky, Lexington Comm Coll (KY)
U of New Mexico–Gallup (NM)
U of New Mexico–Los Alamos Branch (NM)
U of Northwestern Ohio (OH)
U of Pittsburgh at Titusville (PA)
U of South Carolina at Lancaster (SC)
Utica School of Commerce (NY)
Valley Forge Military Coll (PA)
Vance-Granville Comm Coll (NC)
Ventura Coll (CA)
Vermilion Comm Coll (MN)
Vermont Tech Coll (VT)
Vernon Coll (TX)
Victoria Coll (TX)
Victor Valley Coll (CA)
Villa Maria Coll of Buffalo (NY)
Vincennes U (IN)
Vincennes U Jasper Campus (IN)
Virginia Western Comm Coll (VA)
Vista Comm Coll (CA)
Volunteer State Comm Coll (TN)
Wake Tech Comm Coll (NC)
Wallace State Comm Coll (AL)
Walla Walla Comm Coll (WA)
Walters State Comm Coll (TN)
Warren County Comm Coll (NJ)
Waubonsee Comm Coll (IL)
Waycross Coll (GA)
Wayne Comm Coll (NC)
Weatherford Coll (TX)
Webster Coll, Holiday (FL)
Webster Coll, Ocala (FL)
West Central Tech Coll (GA)
The Westchester Business Inst (NY)
Westchester Comm Coll (NY)
Western Dakota Tech Inst (SD)
Western Iowa Tech Comm Coll (IA)
Western Nebraska Comm Coll (NE)
Western Nevada Comm Coll (NV)
Western Piedmont Comm Coll (NC)
Western Texas Coll (TX)
Western Wisconsin Tech Coll (WI)
Western Wyoming Comm Coll (WY)
Westmoreland County Comm Coll (PA)
West Virginia Jr Coll, Charleston (WV)
West Virginia Northern Comm Coll (WV)
West Virginia U at Parkersburg (WV)
Wharton County Jr Coll (TX)
Whatcom Comm Coll (WA)
Wilkes Comm Coll (NC)
Wilson Tech Comm Coll (NC)
Wor-Wic Comm Coll (MD)
York Tech Coll (SC)
Young Harris Coll (GA)

BUSINESS ADMINISTRATION/ MANAGEMENT RELATED

Indiana Business Coll, Columbus (IN)
Indiana Business Coll, Indianapolis (IN)
Indiana Business Coll, Lafayette (IN)
Indiana Business Coll, Muncie (IN)
Indiana Business Coll, Terre Haute (IN)
Lamar State Coll–Port Arthur (TX)
Western Wisconsin Tech Coll (WI)

BUSINESS COMMUNICATIONS

Houston Comm Coll System (TX)
Middlesex Comm Coll (MA)

BUSINESS COMPUTER FACILITIES OPERATION

Certified Careers Inst, Salt Lake City (UT)
CHI Inst (PA)
Clinton Comm Coll (IA)
Delaware County Comm Coll (PA)
El Centro Coll (TX)
Hawkeye Comm Coll (IA)
Muscatine Comm Coll (IA)
St. Cloud Tech Coll (MN)

BUSINESS COMPUTER PROGRAMMING

Alexandria Tech Coll (MN)
Black Hawk Coll, Moline (IL)
CHI Inst (PA)
Cincinnati State Tech and Comm Coll (OH)
City Colls of Chicago, Malcolm X Coll (IL)
Coastal Carolina Comm Coll (NC)
Craven Comm Coll (NC)
Delaware County Comm Coll (PA)
Dunwoody Coll of Technology (MN)
Gateway Tech Coll (WI)
Gogebic Comm Coll (MI)
Indiana Business Coll, Anderson (IN)
Indiana Business Coll, Columbus (IN)
Indiana Business Coll, Evansville (IN)
Indiana Business Coll, Indianapolis (IN)
Indiana Business Coll, Muncie (IN)
Indiana Business Coll, Terre Haute (IN)
Johnson County Comm Coll (KS)
John Wood Comm Coll (IL)
Kishwaukee Coll (IL)
Lake Land Coll (IL)
McHenry County Coll (IL)
Moraine Valley Comm Coll (IL)
North Dakota State Coll of Science (ND)
North Shore Comm Coll (MA)
Northwest Mississippi Comm Coll (MS)
Parkland Coll (IL)
Pennsylvania Coll of Technology (PA)
Pitt Comm Coll (NC)
Rend Lake Coll (IL)
St. Cloud Tech Coll (MN)
San Diego Mesa Coll (CA)
Southern State Comm Coll (OH)
South Piedmont Comm Coll (NC)
Stanly Comm Coll (NC)
Victor Valley Coll (CA)
Waubonsee Comm Coll (IL)
Western Iowa Tech Comm Coll (IA)
Wilkes Comm Coll (NC)
Wisconsin Indianhead Tech Coll (WI)

BUSINESS ECONOMICS

Anne Arundel Comm Coll (MD)
Chabot Coll (CA)
Colby Comm Coll (KS)
Coll of the Desert (CA)
Darton Coll (GA)
Georgia Perimeter Coll (GA)
Hill Coll of the Hill Jr College District (TX)
Joliet Jr Coll (IL)
Lincoln Coll, Lincoln (IL)
Manatee Comm Coll (FL)
Miami U–Middletown Campus (OH)
Morgan Comm Coll (CO)
St. Catharine Coll (KY)
San Joaquin Delta Coll (CA)
State U of NY Coll of Technology at Canton (NY)
Tacoma Comm Coll (WA)
Vermilion Comm Coll (MN)

BUSINESS EDUCATION

Allegany Coll of Maryland (MD)
Allen County Comm Coll (KS)
Amarillo Coll (TX)
Andrew Coll (GA)
Atlanta Metropolitan Coll (GA)
Bacone Coll (OK)
Bainbridge Coll (GA)
Bristol Comm Coll (MA)
Bronx Comm Coll of City U of NY (NY)
Burlington County Coll (NJ)
Butte Coll (CA)
Casper Coll (WY)
Chabot Coll (CA)
Chaffey Coll (CA)
Cisco Jr Coll (TX)
Coffeyville Comm Coll (KS)
Colby Comm Coll (KS)
Coll of Alameda (CA)
Darton Coll (GA)
Delta Coll (MI)
Eastern Arizona Coll (AZ)
Eastern Oklahoma State Coll (OK)
Eastern Wyoming Coll (WY)
East Georgia Coll (GA)
East Mississippi Comm Coll (MS)
Essex County Coll (NJ)
George Corley Wallace State Comm Coll (AL)
Georgia Perimeter Coll (GA)
Halifax Comm Coll (NC)
Harrisburg Area Comm Coll (PA)
Highland Comm Coll (KS)
Holmes Comm Coll (MS)
Holyoke Comm Coll (MA)
Independence Comm Coll (KS)
Isothermal Comm Coll (NC)
Jefferson Coll (MO)
Jefferson Comm Coll (KY)
John A. Logan Coll (IL)
Kirkwood Comm Coll (IA)
Lamar Comm Coll (CO)
Lincoln Coll, Lincoln (IL)
Lincoln Coll, Normal (IL)
Louisburg Coll (NC)
Mid-Plains Comm Coll Area (NE)
Minot State U–Bottineau Campus (ND)
Mississippi Gulf Coast Comm Coll (MS)
Morgan Comm Coll (CO)
Mountain Empire Comm Coll (VA)
Mt. Hood Comm Coll (OR)
Northeast Comm Coll (NE)
Northern Essex Comm Coll (MA)
North Idaho Coll (ID)
Northwest Coll (WY)
Palau Comm CollPalau)
Palomar Coll (CA)
Pasadena City Coll (CA)
Pine Tech Coll (MN)
Pratt Comm Coll and Area Vocational School (KS)
Prince George's Comm Coll (MD)
Reading Area Comm Coll (PA)
Roane State Comm Coll (TN)
St. Catharine Coll (KY)
Snow Coll (UT)
Southwest Mississippi Comm Coll (MS)
Trinity Valley Comm Coll (TX)
Tulsa Comm Coll (OK)
Vincennes U (IN)
Vincennes U Jasper Campus (IN)
Wallace State Comm Coll (AL)
Waycross Coll (GA)

BUSINESS INFORMATION/DATA PROCESSING RELATED

AIBT International Inst of the Americas (AZ)
Cedar Valley Coll (TX)
Eastern Wyoming Coll (WY)
Indiana Business Coll, Columbus (IN)
Indiana Business Coll, Indianapolis (IN)
Indiana Business Coll, Lafayette (IN)
Indiana Business Coll, Muncie (IN)
Indiana Business Coll, Terre Haute (IN)
Martin Comm Coll (NC)
Mid-South Comm Coll (AR)
Oakland Comm Coll (MI)
Wisconsin Indianhead Tech Coll (WI)

BUSINESS MACHINE REPAIR

Athens Tech Coll (GA)
Cañada Coll (CA)
Central Oregon Comm Coll (OR)
Central Piedmont Comm Coll (NC)
Chabot Coll (CA)
Clover Park Tech Coll (WA)
Coffeyville Comm Coll (KS)
Comm Coll of Allegheny County (PA)

De Anza Coll (CA)
Del Mar Coll (TX)
Dutchess Comm Coll (NY)
ECPI Coll of Technology, Virginia Beach (VA)
ECPI Tech Coll, Richmond (VA)
Georgia Perimeter Coll (GA)
Henry Ford Comm Coll (MI)
Herzing Coll (AL)
Iowa Lakes Comm Coll (IA)
Minnesota State Coll–Southeast Tech (MN)
Mississippi Delta Comm Coll (MS)
Moorpark Coll (CA)
Neosho County Comm Coll (KS)
Palomar Coll (CA)
Pellissippi State Tech Comm Coll (TN)
Rockingham Comm Coll (NC)
St. Catharine Coll (KY)
San Antonio Coll (TX)
Southern Maine Tech Coll (ME)

BUSINESS MANAGEMENT/ ADMINISTRATIVE SERVICES RELATED
Catawba Valley Comm Coll (NC)
Eastern Arizona Coll (AZ)
Milwaukee Area Tech Coll (WI)
Northwestern Michigan Coll (MI)
Prince Inst of Professional Studies (AL)
Queensborough Comm Coll of City U of NY (NY)
Sandhills Comm Coll (NC)
Southwestern Michigan Coll (MI)

BUSINESS MARKETING AND MARKETING MANAGEMENT
Abraham Baldwin Ag Coll (GA)
Adirondack Comm Coll (NY)
AIB Coll of Business (IA)
Aims Comm Coll (CO)
Alexandria Tech Coll (MN)
Allentown Business School (PA)
Alvin Comm Coll (TX)
American River Coll (CA)
Anne Arundel Comm Coll (MD)
Anoka-Ramsey Comm Coll (MN)
Antelope Valley Coll (CA)
Arapahoe Comm Coll (CO)
Athens Tech Coll (GA)
Augusta Tech Coll (GA)
Austin Comm Coll (TX)
Bainbridge Coll (GA)
Bakersfield Coll (CA)
Baltimore City Comm Coll (MD)
Bay de Noc Comm Coll (MI)
Bellevue Comm Coll (WA)
Berkeley Coll (NJ)
Berkeley Coll (NY)
Berkeley Coll-Westchester Campus (NY)
Berkshire Comm Coll (MA)
Black Hawk Coll, Moline (IL)
Blackhawk Tech Coll (WI)
Blue Ridge Comm Coll (NC)
Borough of Manhattan Comm Coll of City U of NY (NY)
Brazosport Coll (TX)
Brevard Comm Coll (FL)
Bristol Comm Coll (MA)
Bronx Comm Coll of City U of NY (NY)
Brookdale Comm Coll (NJ)
Broome Comm Coll (NY)
Bucks County Comm Coll (PA)
Butler County Comm Coll (PA)
Butte Coll (CA)
Camden County Coll (NJ)
Carl Sandburg Coll (IL)
Casper Coll (WY)
Catawba Valley Comm Coll (NC)
Cayuga County Comm Coll (NY)
Cecil Comm Coll (MD)
Cedar Valley Coll (TX)
Central Arizona Coll (AZ)
Central Carolina Comm Coll (NC)
Central Comm Coll–Columbus Campus (NE)
Centralia Coll (WA)
Central Lakes Coll (MN)
Central Oregon Comm Coll (OR)
Central Pennsylvania Coll (PA)
Central Piedmont Comm Coll (NC)
Central Texas Coll (TX)
Central Virginia Comm Coll (VA)
Cerritos Coll (CA)
Chaffey Coll (CA)
Chattahoochee Tech Coll (GA)
Chippewa Valley Tech Coll (WI)
Cincinnati State Tech and Comm Coll (OH)
Cisco Jr Coll (TX)
City Coll of San Francisco (CA)
City Colls of Chicago, Harry S Truman Coll (IL)
City Colls of Chicago, Richard J Daley Coll (IL)
City Colls of Chicago, Wilbur Wright Coll (IL)
Clark Coll (WA)
Clover Park Tech Coll (WA)
Coffeyville Comm Coll (KS)
Colby Comm Coll (KS)
Coll of Alameda (CA)
Coll of DuPage (IL)
Coll of Marin (CA)
Coll of Southern Idaho (ID)
Coll of the Desert (CA)
Coll of the Sequoias (CA)
Colorado Mountn Coll, Alpine Cmps (CO)
Columbus State Comm Coll (OH)
Comm Coll of Allegheny County (PA)
Comm Coll of Aurora (CO)
The Comm Coll of Baltimore County–Catonsville Campus (MD)
Comm Coll of Beaver County (PA)
Comm Coll of Rhode Island (RI)
Comm Coll of Southern Nevada (NV)
Copiah-Lincoln Comm Coll–Natchez Campus (MS)
Cowley County Comm Coll and Voc-Tech School (KS)
Crafton Hills Coll (CA)
Cuesta Coll (CA)
Cumberland County Coll (NJ)
Cuyahoga Comm Coll (OH)
Cypress Coll (CA)
Danville Area Comm Coll (IL)
Danville Comm Coll (VA)
Darton Coll (GA)
Daytona Beach Comm Coll (FL)
De Anza Coll (CA)
Delaware Tech & Comm Coll, Jack F Owens Cmps (DE)
Delaware Tech & Comm Coll, Stanton/ Wilmington Cmps (DE)
Delta Coll (MI)
Des Moines Area Comm Coll (IA)
Dodge City Comm Coll (KS)
East Central Coll (MO)
Eastern Idaho Tech Coll (ID)
Eastern Oklahoma State Coll (OK)
Edison State Comm Coll (OH)
Edmonds Comm Coll (WA)
Education Direct (PA)
Ellsworth Comm Coll (IA)
Enterprise State Jr Coll (AL)
Erie Business Center, Main (PA)
Erie Business Center South (PA)
Everett Comm Coll (WA)
Fayetteville Tech Comm Coll (NC)
Fergus Falls Comm Coll (MN)
Finger Lakes Comm Coll (NY)
Florence-Darlington Tech Coll (SC)
Florida Comm Coll at Jacksonville (FL)
Floyd Coll (GA)
Forsyth Tech Comm Coll (NC)
Fort Berthold Comm Coll (ND)
Frederick Comm Coll (MD)
Fullerton Coll (CA)
Garden City Comm Coll (KS)
Gateway Tech Coll (WI)
Genesee Comm Coll (NY)
Georgia Perimeter Coll (GA)
Gloucester County Coll (NJ)
Golden West Coll (CA)
Greenfield Comm Coll (MA)
Green River Comm Coll (WA)
Greenville Tech Coll (SC)
Guam Comm Coll (GU)
Gwinnett Tech Coll (GA)
Hagerstown Business Coll (MD)
Halifax Comm Coll (NC)
Harford Comm Coll (MD)
Harrisburg Area Comm Coll (PA)
Hawkeye Comm Coll (IA)
Henry Ford Comm Coll (MI)
Herkimer County Comm Coll (NY)
Hesser Coll (NH)
Highland Comm Coll (IL)
Hillsborough Comm Coll (FL)
Hinds Comm Coll (MS)
Houston Comm Coll System (TX)
Imperial Valley Coll (CA)
Indian River Comm Coll (FL)
Inver Hills Comm Coll (MN)
Iowa Lakes Comm Coll (IA)
Iowa Western Comm Coll (IA)
Isothermal Comm Coll (NC)
Jackson Comm Coll (MI)
Jamestown Business Coll (NY)
Jefferson Coll (MO)
Jefferson Comm Coll (NY)
Jefferson Davis Comm Coll (AL)
John A. Logan Coll (IL)
Joliet Jr Coll (IL)
J. Sargeant Reynolds Comm Coll (VA)
Kalamazoo Valley Comm Coll (MI)
Kankakee Comm Coll (IL)
Kansas City Kansas Comm Coll (KS)
Kennebec Valley Tech Coll (ME)
Kent State U, Trumbull Campus (OH)
Kingsborough Comm Coll of City U of NY (NY)
Kirkwood Comm Coll (IA)
Lake Area Tech Inst (SD)
Lake Land Coll (IL)
Lake Michigan Coll (MI)
Lakeshore Tech Coll (WI)
Lake Tahoe Comm Coll (CA)
Lamar Comm Coll (CO)
Lansing Comm Coll (MI)
Laredo Comm Coll (TX)
Las Positas Coll (CA)
Lenoir Comm Coll (NC)
Lima Tech Coll (OH)
Lincoln Coll, Lincoln (IL)
Lincoln Coll, Normal (IL)
Lincoln Land Comm Coll (IL)
Long Beach City Coll (CA)
Longview Comm Coll (MO)
Lorain County Comm Coll (OH)
Los Angeles City Coll (CA)
Macomb Comm Coll (MI)
Manchester Comm Coll (CT)
Maple Woods Comm Coll (MO)
Marion Tech Coll (OH)
Marshalltown Comm Coll (IA)
Massasoit Comm Coll (MA)
Maysville Comm Coll (KY)
McCann School of Business (PA)
Merced Coll (CA)
Meridian Comm Coll (MS)
Miami-Dade Comm Coll (FL)
Miami U–Middletown Campus (OH)
Middlesex Comm Coll (MA)
Middlesex County Coll (NJ)
Midlands Tech Coll (SC)
Mid Michigan Comm Coll (MI)
Mid-South Comm Coll (AR)
Mid-State Tech Coll (WI)
Miles Comm Coll (MT)
Milwaukee Area Tech Coll (WI)
Mineral Area Coll (MO)
Minnesota State Coll–Southeast Tech (MN)
Minot State U–Bottineau Campus (ND)
MiraCosta Coll (CA)
Mississippi Gulf Coast Comm Coll (MS)
Moberly Area Comm Coll (MO)
Modesto Jr Coll (CA)
Mohave Comm Coll (AZ)
Mohawk Valley Comm Coll (NY)
Monroe Comm Coll (NY)
Monroe County Comm Coll (MI)
Monterey Peninsula Coll (CA)
Montgomery County Comm Coll (PA)
Moorpark Coll (CA)
Moraine Park Tech Coll (WI)
Morton Coll (IL)
Mott Comm Coll (MI)
Mountain Empire Comm Coll (VA)
Mt. Hood Comm Coll (OR)
Muskingum Area Tech Coll (OH)
Nash Comm Coll (NC)
Nassau Comm Coll (NY)
National Coll of Business & Technology, Salem (VA)
Naugatuck Valley Comm Coll (CT)
Navarro Coll (TX)
Neosho County Comm Coll (KS)
Newbury Coll (MA)
New Hampshire Tech Inst (NH)
New River Comm Coll (VA)
New York City Tech Coll of the City U of NY (NY)
North Central Michigan Coll (MI)
Northcentral Tech Coll (WI)
Northeast Comm Coll (NE)
Northeastern Tech Coll (SC)
Northeast Iowa Comm Coll (IA)
Northern Essex Comm Coll (MA)
Northern Virginia Comm Coll (VA)
North Harris Coll (TX)
North Hennepin Comm Coll (MN)
North Iowa Area Comm Coll (IA)
Northland Comm and Tech Coll (MN)
North Shore Comm Coll (MA)
Northwest Coll (WY)
Northwestern Business Coll (IL)
Northwestern Michigan Coll (MI)
Northwest State Comm Coll (OH)
Norwalk Comm Coll (CT)
Oakton Comm Coll (IL)
Oklahoma State U, Okmulgee (OK)
Orange Coast Coll (CA)
Orange County Comm Coll (NY)
Ouachita Tech Coll (AR)
Oxnard Coll (CA)
Palm Beach Comm Coll (FL)
Palomar Coll (CA)
Palo Verde Coll (CA)
Pasadena City Coll (CA)
Pasco-Hernando Comm Coll (FL)
Pellissippi State Tech Comm Coll (TN)
Penn Valley Comm Coll (MO)
Phoenix Coll (AZ)
Piedmont Tech Coll (SC)
Piedmont Virginia Comm Coll (VA)
Pierce Coll (WA)
Pikes Peak Comm Coll (CO)
Polk Comm Coll (FL)
Portland Comm Coll (OR)
Pratt Comm Coll and Area Vocational School (KS)
Prince George's Comm Coll (MD)
Quincy Coll (MA)
Raritan Valley Comm Coll (NJ)
Rasmussen Coll Mankato (MN)
Rasmussen Coll Minnetonka (MN)
Rasmussen Coll St. Cloud (MN)
Reading Area Comm Coll (PA)
Red Rocks Comm Coll (CO)
Rockford Business Coll (IL)
Rockland Comm Coll (NY)
Saint Charles Comm Coll (MO)
St. Clair County Comm Coll (MI)
St. Cloud Tech Coll (MN)
St. Petersburg Coll (FL)
Salem Comm Coll (NJ)
San Bernardino Valley Coll (CA)
San Diego City Coll (CA)
San Diego Mesa Coll (CA)
San Jacinto Coll Central Campus (TX)
San Joaquin Delta Coll (CA)
Santa Ana Coll (CA)
Santa Barbara City Coll (CA)
Santa Fe Comm Coll (FL)
Sauk Valley Comm Coll (IL)
Schoolcraft Coll (MI)
Seminole Comm Coll (FL)
Shoreline Comm Coll (WA)
Sierra Coll (CA)
Sinclair Comm Coll (OH)
Sitting Bull Coll (ND)
Southeast Tech Inst (SD)
South Hills School of Business & Technology, Atloona (PA)
South Hills School of Business & Technology, State College (PA)
South Plains Coll (TX)
South Suburban Coll (IL)
Southwestern Coll (CA)
Southwestern Comm Coll (IA)
Southwestern Comm Coll (NC)
Southwest Mississippi Comm Coll (MS)
Southwest Wisconsin Tech Coll (WI)
Spartanburg Tech Coll (SC)
Spokane Comm Coll (WA)
Spokane Falls Comm Coll (WA)
Springfield Tech Comm Coll (MA)
Stark State Coll of Technology (OH)
State Fair Comm Coll (MO)
State U of NY Coll of A&T at Morrisville (NY)
State U of NY Coll of Technology at Alfred (NY)
State U of NY Coll of Technology at Delhi (NY)
Suffolk County Comm Coll (NY)
Sullivan County Comm Coll (NY)
Tallahassee Comm Coll (FL)
Tarrant County Coll District (TX)
Terra State Comm Coll (OH)
Three Rivers Comm Coll (CT)
Tidewater Comm Coll (VA)
Tompkins Cortland Comm Coll (NY)
Trident Tech Coll (SC)
Trinidad State Jr Coll (CO)
Trinity Valley Comm Coll (TX)
Triton Coll (IL)
Trocaire Coll (NY)
Truckee Meadows Comm Coll (NV)
Tulsa Comm Coll (OK)
Tunxis Comm Coll (CT)
Tyler Jr Coll (TX)
Ulster County Comm Coll (NY)
Umpqua Comm Coll (OR)
U of Arkansas Comm Coll at Morrilton (AR)
U of New Mexico–Gallup (NM)
U of Northwestern Ohio (OH)
Utica School of Commerce (NY)
Vincennes U (IN)
Wallace State Comm Coll (AL)
West Central Tech Coll (GA)
The Westchester Business Inst (NY)
Westchester Comm Coll (NY)
Western Nevada Comm Coll (NV)
Western Piedmont Comm Coll (NC)
Western Texas Coll (TX)
Western Wisconsin Tech Coll (WI)
Western Wyoming Comm Coll (WY)
Westmoreland County Comm Coll (PA)
West Shore Comm Coll (MI)
West Virginia U at Parkersburg (WV)
Williston State Coll (ND)

BUSINESS SERVICES MARKETING
Hesser Coll (NH)
Jackson Comm Coll (MI)
Lake Region State Coll (ND)
Northland Pioneer Coll (AZ)
Northwestern Michigan Coll (MI)
Union County Coll (NJ)

BUSINESS SYSTEMS ANALYSIS/ DESIGN
Cape Fear Comm Coll (NC)
Coastal Carolina Comm Coll (NC)
James Sprunt Comm Coll (NC)
Pitt Comm Coll (NC)
Randolph Comm Coll (NC)
Richmond Comm Coll (NC)
South Piedmont Comm Coll (NC)
Wayne Comm Coll (NC)
Wilkes Comm Coll (NC)

BUSINESS SYSTEMS NETWORKING/ TELECOMMUNICATIONS
Academy Coll (MN)
Adirondack Comm Coll (NY)
Alexandria Tech Coll (MN)
Allen County Comm Coll (KS)
Alpena Comm Coll (MI)
Antonelli Coll (OH)
Asheville-Buncombe Tech Comm Coll (NC)
Beckfield Coll (KY)
Bismarck State Coll (ND)
Blinn Coll (TX)
Brown Coll (MN)
Catawba Valley Comm Coll (NC)
Central Carolina Comm Coll (NC)
Certified Careers Inst, Salt Lake City (UT)
Charter Coll (AK)
Coastal Carolina Comm Coll (NC)
Collin County Comm Coll District (TX)
Comm Coll of Allegheny County (PA)
Corning Comm Coll (NY)
Craven Comm Coll (NC)
Delaware County Comm Coll (PA)

Eastern Idaho Tech Coll (ID)
Eastfield Coll (TX)
Education America, Southeast Coll of Technology, New Orleans Campus (LA)
Fayetteville Tech Comm Coll (NC)
Florida Tech Coll, Orlando (FL)
Garden City Comm Coll (KS)
Gateway Tech Coll (WI)
Glendale Comm Coll (AZ)
Harrisburg Area Comm Coll (PA)
Heartland Comm Coll (IL)
Hennepin Tech Coll (MN)
Herzing Coll, Minneapolis Drafting School Campus (MN)
Hillsborough Comm Coll (FL)
Johnson County Comm Coll (KS)
Kaplan Coll (IA)
Kilgore Coll (TX)
Louisville Tech Inst (KY)
Mercer County Comm Coll (NJ)
Mesabi Range Comm and Tech Coll (MN)
Middlesex County Coll (NJ)
Montgomery County Comm Coll (PA)
Moraine Valley Comm Coll (IL)
Mountain West Coll (UT)
Nashville State Tech Inst (TN)
Nassau Comm Coll (NY)
New England Inst of Tech & Florida Culinary Inst (FL)
North Iowa Area Comm Coll (IA)
Odessa Coll (TX)
Pace Inst (PA)
Parkland Coll (IL)
Pikes Peak Comm Coll (CO)
Pima Comm Coll (AZ)
Pitt Comm Coll (NC)
Platt Coll, Ontario (CA)
Rasmussen Coll Mankato (MN)
Rockland Comm Coll (NY)
St. Cloud Tech Coll (MN)
San Joaquin Valley Coll (CA)
Schuylkill Inst of Business and Technology (PA)
South Piedmont Comm Coll (NC)
Stanly Comm Coll (NC)
Stratford U (VA)
Tallahassee Comm Coll (FL)
Texas State Tech Coll (TX)
United Tribes Tech Coll (ND)
The U of Akron–Wayne Coll (OH)
Vermont Tech Coll (VT)
Victoria Coll (TX)
Wake Tech Comm Coll (NC)
Wisconsin Indianhead Tech Coll (WI)

BUYING OPERATIONS

Coll of DuPage (IL)
Cuyahoga Comm Coll (OH)
North Central Texas Coll (TX)

CABINET MAKING

Central Oregon Comm Coll (OR)
Coll of Southern Idaho (ID)
Fayetteville Tech Comm Coll (NC)
Ivy Tech State Coll–Central Indiana (IN)
Ivy Tech State Coll–North Central (IN)
Ivy Tech State Coll–Northwest (IN)
Ivy Tech State Coll–Southcentral (IN)
Ivy Tech State Coll–Southwest (IN)
Johnson Coll (PA)

CARDIOVASCULAR TECHNOLOGY

Albuquerque Tech Vocational Inst (NM)
Comm Coll of the Air Force (AL)
El Centro Coll (TX)
Harrisburg Area Comm Coll (PA)
Howard Comm Coll (MD)
Milwaukee Area Tech Coll (WI)
Northeast State Tech Comm Coll (TN)
North Hennepin Comm Coll (MN)
Orange Coast Coll (CA)
Southeast Tech Inst (SD)
Southern Maine Tech Coll (ME)

CARPENTRY

Alamance Comm Coll (NC)
Alexandria Tech Coll (MN)
American River Coll (CA)
Bakersfield Coll (CA)
Bates Tech Coll (WA)
Bismarck State Coll (ND)
Brevard Comm Coll (FL)
Casper Coll (WY)
Cecil Comm Coll (MD)
Clovis Comm Coll (NM)
Coffeyville Comm Coll (KS)
Coll of Eastern Utah (UT)
Coll of the Sequoias (CA)
Comm Coll of Allegheny County (PA)
Comm Coll of Aurora (CO)
Delaware Tech & Comm Coll, Jack F Owens Cmps (DE)
Delta Coll (MI)
Des Moines Area Comm Coll (IA)
Douglas MacArthur State Tech Coll (AL)
East Central Comm Coll (MS)
Eastern Maine Tech Coll (ME)
Fayetteville Tech Comm Coll (NC)
Forsyth Tech Comm Coll (NC)
Fresno City Coll (CA)
Fullerton Coll (CA)
Fulton-Montgomery Comm Coll (NY)
GateWay Comm Coll (AZ)
Gogebic Comm Coll (MI)
Grays Harbor Coll (WA)
Green River Comm Coll (WA)
Hawaii Comm Coll (HI)
Helena Coll of Tech of The U of Montana (MT)
Hennepin Tech Coll (MN)
Highland Comm Coll (KS)
Hinds Comm Coll (MS)
Honolulu Comm Coll (HI)
Hutchinson Comm Coll and Area Vocational School (KS)
Indian River Comm Coll (FL)
Iowa Lakes Comm Coll (IA)
Ivy Tech State Coll–Central Indiana (IN)
Ivy Tech State Coll–Eastcentral (IN)
Ivy Tech State Coll–Lafayette (IN)
Ivy Tech State Coll–North Central (IN)
Ivy Tech State Coll–Northwest (IN)
Ivy Tech State Coll–Southcentral (IN)
Ivy Tech State Coll–Southwest (IN)
Ivy Tech State Coll–Wabash Valley (IN)
Johnson Coll (PA)
Kauai Comm Coll (HI)
Lake Area Tech Inst (SD)
Lansing Comm Coll (MI)
Laramie County Comm Coll (WY)
Long Beach City Coll (CA)
Merced Coll (CA)
Mid-Plains Comm Coll Area (NE)
Miles Comm Coll (MT)
Minnesota State Coll–Southeast Tech (MN)
Mitchell Tech Inst (SD)
Neosho County Comm Coll (KS)
Northeast Comm Coll (NE)
Northern Maine Tech Coll (ME)
North Idaho Coll (ID)
Northland Pioneer Coll (AZ)
Olympic Coll (WA)
Palau Comm CollPalau)
Palomar Coll (CA)
Pasadena City Coll (CA)
Piedmont Tech Coll (SC)
Portland Comm Coll (OR)
Red Rocks Comm Coll (CO)
Rockingham Comm Coll (NC)
St. Cloud Tech Coll (MN)
St. Philip's Coll (TX)
Salish Kootenai Coll (MT)
San Diego City Coll (CA)
San Joaquin Delta Coll (CA)
San Juan Coll (NM)
Seattle Central Comm Coll (WA)
Sierra Coll (CA)
Sitting Bull Coll (ND)
Snow Coll (UT)
Southeast Comm Coll, Milford Campus (NE)
Southern Maine Tech Coll (ME)
South Plains Coll (TX)
Southwestern Comm Coll (IA)
Southwest Mississippi Comm Coll (MS)
Spokane Comm Coll (WA)
State U of NY Coll of Technology at Alfred (NY)
State U of NY Coll of Technology at Canton (NY)
State U of NY Coll of Technology at Delhi (NY)
Thaddeus Stevens Coll of Technology (PA)
Trenholm State Tech Coll, Patterson Campus (AL)
Triangle Tech, Inc. (PA)
Triangle Tech, Inc.–DuBois School (PA)
Trinidad State Jr Coll (CO)
Truckee Meadows Comm Coll (NV)
United Tribes Tech Coll (ND)
Vance-Granville Comm Coll (NC)
Wallace State Comm Coll (AL)
Walla Walla Comm Coll (WA)
Western Nevada Comm Coll (NV)

CARTOGRAPHY

Alexandria Tech Coll (MN)
Central Oregon Comm Coll (OR)
Dixie State Coll of Utah (UT)
Houston Comm Coll System (TX)
New Hampshire Comm Tech Coll, Berlin/Laconia (NH)
Southwest Tennessee Comm Coll (TN)
U of Arkansas at Fort Smith (AR)

CERAMIC ARTS

Casper Coll (WY)
Chaffey Coll (CA)
Coll of the Siskiyous (CA)
De Anza Coll (CA)
Dixie State Coll of Utah (UT)
Garden City Comm Coll (KS)
Glendale Comm Coll (CA)
Haywood Comm Coll (NC)
Henry Ford Comm Coll (MI)
Hill Coll of the Hill Jr College District (TX)
Inst of American Indian Arts (NM)
Iowa Lakes Comm Coll (IA)
Kirkwood Comm Coll (IA)
Lincoln Coll, Lincoln (IL)
Los Angeles City Coll (CA)
Mercer County Comm Coll (NJ)
Mohave Comm Coll (AZ)
Monterey Peninsula Coll (CA)
Montgomery Comm Coll (NC)
Oakland Comm Coll (MI)
Palm Beach Comm Coll (FL)
Palomar Coll (CA)
Pasadena City Coll (CA)
St. Catharine Coll (KY)
Ventura Coll (CA)

CERAMIC SCIENCES/ ENGINEERING

Pasadena City Coll (CA)

CHEMICAL ENGINEERING TECHNOLOGY

Alpena Comm Coll (MI)
Broome Comm Coll (NY)
Burlington County Coll (NJ)
Capital Comm Coll (CT)
Chattanooga State Tech Comm Coll (TN)
City Coll of San Francisco (CA)
City Colls of Chicago, Harry S Truman Coll (IL)
The Comm Coll of Baltimore County–Catonsville Campus (MD)
Delaware Tech & Comm Coll, Jack F Owens Cmps (DE)
Delaware Tech & Comm Coll, Stanton/ Wilmington Cmps (DE)
Delta Coll (MI)
Essex County Coll (NJ)
Florence-Darlington Tech Coll (SC)
Gloucester County Coll (NJ)
Jefferson Comm Coll (KY)
Lansing Comm Coll (MI)
Miami U–Middletown Campus (OH)
Milwaukee Area Tech Coll (WI)
Mississippi Gulf Coast Comm Coll (MS)
Mohawk Valley Comm Coll (NY)
Monroe Comm Coll (NY)
Naugatuck Valley Comm Coll (CT)
Onondaga Comm Coll (NY)
Pellissippi State Tech Comm Coll (TN)
St. Louis Comm Coll at Florissant Valley (MO)
San Bernardino Valley Coll (CA)
Schenectady County Comm Coll (NY)
Shoreline Comm Coll (WA)
Southwest Tennessee Comm Coll (TN)
Texas State Tech Coll–Harlingen (TX)
Texas State Tech Coll– Waco/ Marshall Campus (TX)
Westchester Comm Coll (NY)
West Virginia U at Parkersburg (WV)

CHEMICAL TECHNOLOGY

Alvin Comm Coll (TX)
Amarillo Coll (TX)
Brazosport Coll (TX)
Coll of Lake County (IL)
Comm Coll of Allegheny County (PA)
Comm Coll of Rhode Island (RI)
Corning Comm Coll (NY)
County Coll of Morris (NJ)
Del Mar Coll (TX)
Edmonds Comm Coll (WA)
Erie Comm Coll, North Campus (NY)
Jefferson Comm Coll (NY)
Johnson County Comm Coll (KS)
Kalamazoo Valley Comm Coll (MI)
Kellogg Comm Coll (MI)
Massachusetts Bay Comm Coll (MA)
New York City Tech Coll of the City U of NY (NY)
Northampton County Area Comm Coll (PA)
Pellissippi State Tech Comm Coll (TN)
Pensacola Jr Coll (FL)
Texas State Tech Coll– Waco/ Marshall Campus (TX)

CHEMISTRY

Abraham Baldwin Ag Coll (GA)
Allan Hancock Coll (CA)
Allegany Coll of Maryland (MD)
Allen County Comm Coll (KS)
Alpena Comm Coll (MI)
Amarillo Coll (TX)
Ancilla Coll (IN)
Andrew Coll (GA)
Anne Arundel Comm Coll (MD)
Arizona Western Coll (AZ)
Atlanta Metropolitan Coll (GA)
Atlantic Cape Comm Coll (NJ)
Austin Comm Coll (TX)
Bainbridge Coll (GA)
Bakersfield Coll (CA)
Barton County Comm Coll (KS)
Bergen Comm Coll (NJ)
Blinn Coll (TX)
Brazosport Coll (TX)
Bronx Comm Coll of City U of NY (NY)
Brookdale Comm Coll (NJ)
Bucks County Comm Coll (PA)
Burlington County Coll (NJ)
Cañada Coll (CA)
Casper Coll (WY)
Centralia Coll (WA)
Central Texas Coll (TX)
Cerritos Coll (CA)
Chabot Coll (CA)
Chaffey Coll (CA)
Chattahoochee Valley Comm Coll (AL)
Chattanooga State Tech Comm Coll (TN)
Cisco Jr Coll (TX)
City Coll of San Francisco (CA)
Clark Coll (WA)
Coahoma Comm Coll (MS)
Coastal Bend Coll (TX)
Coastal Georgia Comm Coll (GA)
Cochise Coll, Douglas (AZ)
Coffeyville Comm Coll (KS)
Colby Comm Coll (KS)
Coll of Marin (CA)
Coll of Southern Idaho (ID)
Coll of the Canyons (CA)
Coll of the Desert (CA)
Coll of the Sequoias (CA)
Coll of the Siskiyous (CA)
Columbia State Comm Coll (TN)
Comm Coll of Allegheny County (PA)
Comm Coll of Southern Nevada (NV)
Compton Comm Coll (CA)
Connors State Coll (OK)
Cowley County Comm Coll and Voc-Tech School (KS)
Crafton Hills Coll (CA)
Cuesta Coll (CA)
Cuyamaca Coll (CA)
Cypress Coll (CA)
Darton Coll (GA)
Daytona Beach Comm Coll (FL)
Del Mar Coll (TX)
Delta Coll (MI)
Dixie State Coll of Utah (UT)
Dodge City Comm Coll (KS)
East Central Coll (MO)
East Central Comm Coll (MS)
Eastern Arizona Coll (AZ)
Eastern Oklahoma State Coll (OK)
East Georgia Coll (GA)
Essex County Coll (NJ)
Everett Comm Coll (WA)
Finger Lakes Comm Coll (NY)
Foothill Coll (CA)
Frederick Comm Coll (MD)
Fullerton Coll (CA)
Gavilan Coll (CA)
Georgia Perimeter Coll (GA)
Gloucester County Coll (NJ)
Grayson County Coll (TX)
Great Basin Coll (NV)
Harford Comm Coll (MD)
Harrisburg Area Comm Coll (PA)
Herkimer County Comm Coll (NY)
Highland Comm Coll (IL)
Highland Comm Coll (KS)
Hill Coll of the Hill Jr College District (TX)
Holyoke Comm Coll (MA)
Howard Coll (TX)
Independence Comm Coll (KS)
Indian River Comm Coll (FL)
Iowa Lakes Comm Coll (IA)
Jefferson Comm Coll (KY)
John A. Logan Coll (IL)
Joliet Jr Coll (IL)
Jones County Jr Coll (MS)
Kansas City Kansas Comm Coll (KS)
Kellogg Comm Coll (MI)
Kilgore Coll (TX)
Kingsborough Comm Coll of City U of NY (NY)
Labette Comm Coll (KS)
Lake Michigan Coll (MI)
Lansing Comm Coll (MI)
Laramie County Comm Coll (WY)
Lincoln Coll, Lincoln (IL)
Lincoln Land Comm Coll (IL)
Linn-Benton Comm Coll (OR)
Longview Comm Coll (MO)
Lon Morris Coll (TX)
Lorain County Comm Coll (OH)
Los Angeles City Coll (CA)
Los Angeles Mission Coll (CA)
Louisburg Coll (NC)
Manatee Comm Coll (FL)
Maple Woods Comm Coll (MO)
Mercer County Comm Coll (NJ)
Miami-Dade Comm Coll (FL)
Miami U–Middletown Campus (OH)
Middlesex County Coll (NJ)
Midland Coll (TX)
Mid Michigan Comm Coll (MI)
Minot State U–Bottineau Campus (ND)
MiraCosta Coll (CA)
Mohawk Valley Comm Coll (NY)
Monroe Comm Coll (NY)
Monterey Peninsula Coll (CA)
Moorpark Coll (CA)
Mountain Empire Comm Coll (VA)
Navarro Coll (TX)
New Mexico Military Inst (NM)
Northampton County Area Comm Coll (PA)
Northeast Comm Coll (NE)
Northeast State Tech Comm Coll (TN)
North Idaho Coll (ID)
Northwest Coll (WY)
Odessa Coll (TX)
Okaloosa-Walton Comm Coll (FL)
Oklahoma City Comm Coll (OK)
Orange Coast Coll (CA)
Palm Beach Comm Coll (FL)
Palomar Coll (CA)
Pasadena City Coll (CA)

Penn Valley Comm Coll (MO)
Pensacola Jr Coll (FL)
Pratt Comm Coll and Area Vocational School (KS)
Raritan Valley Comm Coll (NJ)
Reading Area Comm Coll (PA)
Red Rocks Comm Coll (CO)
Riverside Comm Coll (CA)
Roane State Comm Coll (TN)
St. Catharine Coll (KY)
St. Philip's Coll (TX)
Salem Comm Coll (NJ)
San Bernardino Valley Coll (CA)
San Diego Mesa Coll (CA)
San Jacinto Coll Central Campus (TX)
San Jacinto Coll North Campus (TX)
San Jacinto Coll South Campus (TX)
San Joaquin Delta Coll (CA)
San Juan Coll (NM)
Santa Ana Coll (CA)
Santa Barbara City Coll (CA)
Santa Monica Coll (CA)
Sauk Valley Comm Coll (IL)
Sierra Coll (CA)
Skagit Valley Coll (WA)
Snow Coll (UT)
South Mountain Comm Coll (AZ)
South Plains Coll (TX)
South Suburban Coll (IL)
Southwestern Coll (CA)
Southwest Mississippi Comm Coll (MS)
Springfield Tech Comm Coll (MA)
State U of NY Coll of A&T at Morrisville (NY)
Suffolk County Comm Coll (NY)
Tacoma Comm Coll (WA)
Terra State Comm Coll (OH)
Texarkana Coll (TX)
Trinidad State Jr Coll (CO)
Trinity Valley Comm Coll (TX)
Triton Coll (IL)
Tulsa Comm Coll (OK)
Umpqua Comm Coll (OR)
Union County Coll (NJ)
Vermilion Comm Coll (MN)
Vincennes U (IN)
Waycross Coll (GA)
Western Nebraska Comm Coll (NE)
Western Wyoming Comm Coll (WY)
Wharton County Jr Coll (TX)
Young Harris Coll (GA)

CHEMISTRY EDUCATION
Louisburg Coll (NC)
Manatee Comm Coll (FL)

CHEMISTRY RELATED
Guilford Tech Comm Coll (NC)

CHILD CARE AND GUIDANCE RELATED
Comm Coll of Allegheny County (PA)
Mott Comm Coll (MI)

CHILD CARE/DEVELOPMENT
Abraham Baldwin Ag Coll (GA)
Aims Comm Coll (CO)
Allen County Comm Coll (KS)
Alvin Comm Coll (TX)
Amarillo Coll (TX)
American River Coll (CA)
Angelina Coll (TX)
Athens Tech Coll (GA)
Atlantic Cape Comm Coll (NJ)
Augusta Tech Coll (GA)
Bakersfield Coll (CA)
Barstow Coll (CA)
Barton County Comm Coll (KS)
Black Hawk Coll, Moline (IL)
Borough of Manhattan Comm Coll of City U of NY (NY)
Brazosport Coll (TX)
Brevard Comm Coll (FL)
Briarwood Coll (CT)
Bristol Comm Coll (MA)
Bronx Comm Coll of City U of NY (NY)
Central Arizona Coll (AZ)
Central Comm Coll–Grand Island Campus (NE)
Central Comm Coll–Hastings Campus (NE)
Centralia Coll (WA)
Central Pennsylvania Coll (PA)
Central Piedmont Comm Coll (NC)
Chaffey Coll (CA)
Chattahoochee Tech Coll (GA)
Chattanooga State Tech Comm Coll (TN)
Chippewa Valley Tech Coll (WI)
Cisco Jr Coll (TX)
City Colls of Chicago, Richard J Daley Coll (IL)
Clark Coll (WA)
Coastal Bend Coll (TX)
Colby Comm Coll (KS)
Coll of DuPage (IL)
Coll of Eastern Utah (UT)
Coll of Southern Idaho (ID)
Coll of the Canyons (CA)
Colorado Mountn Coll, Timberline Cmps (CO)
Columbus State Comm Coll (OH)
Comm Coll of Allegheny County (PA)
Comm Coll of Southern Nevada (NV)
Comm Coll of Vermont (VT)
Compton Comm Coll (CA)
Connors State Coll (OK)
Cowley County Comm Coll and Voc-Tech School (KS)
Crafton Hills Coll (CA)
Cuesta Coll (CA)
Danville Area Comm Coll (IL)
Daytona Beach Comm Coll (FL)
Dean Coll (MA)
De Anza Coll (CA)
Delaware Tech & Comm Coll, Jack F Owens Cmps (DE)
Del Mar Coll (TX)
Delta Coll (MI)
Des Moines Area Comm Coll (IA)
Dodge City Comm Coll (KS)
Durham Tech Comm Coll (NC)
Dutchess Comm Coll (NY)
Dyersburg State Comm Coll (TN)
Eastern Wyoming Coll (WY)
Ellsworth Comm Coll (IA)
Enterprise State Jr Coll (AL)
Feather River Comm Coll District (CA)
Foothill Coll (CA)
Forsyth Tech Comm Coll (NC)
Frederick Comm Coll (MD)
Garden City Comm Coll (KS)
Gateway Tech Coll (WI)
Gavilan Coll (CA)
Georgia Perimeter Coll (GA)
Glendale Comm Coll (CA)
Gogebic Comm Coll (MI)
Guam Comm Coll (GU)
Harcum Coll (PA)
Harford Comm Coll (MD)
Hawkeye Comm Coll (IA)
Heartland Comm Coll (IL)
Herkimer County Comm Coll (NY)
Highland Comm Coll (IL)
Hill Coll of the Hill Jr College District (TX)
Hillsborough Comm Coll (FL)
Hinds Comm Coll (MS)
Holmes Comm Coll (MS)
Housatonic Comm Coll (CT)
Houston Comm Coll System (TX)
Howard Coll (TX)
Howard Comm Coll (MD)
Hudson County Comm Coll (NJ)
Illinois Eastern Comm Colls, Wabash Valley Coll (IL)
Independence Comm Coll (KS)
Indian Hills Comm Coll (IA)
Indian River Comm Coll (FL)
Iowa Lakes Comm Coll (IA)
Iowa Western Comm Coll (IA)
Jefferson Coll (MO)
Jefferson Comm Coll (KY)
Jones County Jr Coll (MS)
Kankakee Comm Coll (IL)
Kirkwood Comm Coll (IA)
Labette Comm Coll (KS)
Lake Washington Tech Coll (WA)
Lamar State Coll–Port Arthur (TX)
Lane Comm Coll (OR)
Lansing Comm Coll (MI)
Laramie County Comm Coll (WY)
Laredo Comm Coll (TX)
Lewis and Clark Comm Coll (IL)
Lima Tech Coll (OH)
Lincoln Land Comm Coll (IL)
Linn-Benton Comm Coll (OR)
Los Angeles City Coll (CA)
Macomb Comm Coll (MI)
Manor Coll (PA)
Marshalltown Comm Coll (IA)
Massasoit Comm Coll (MA)
Metropolitan Comm Coll (NE)
Miami-Dade Comm Coll (FL)
Middlesex County Coll (NJ)
Midland Coll (TX)
Mid Michigan Comm Coll (MI)
Milwaukee Area Tech Coll (WI)
Minnesota State Coll–Southeast Tech (MN)
Mitchell Coll (CT)
Mitchell Comm Coll (NC)
Modesto Jr Coll (CA)
Mohawk Valley Comm Coll (NY)
Monroe County Comm Coll (MI)
Monterey Peninsula Coll (CA)
New River Comm Coll (VA)
Northeast Comm Coll (NE)
North Harris Coll (TX)
Northland Comm and Tech Coll (MN)
North Seattle Comm Coll (WA)
North Shore Comm Coll (MA)
Northwestern Connecticut Comm-Tech Coll (CT)
Northwest State Comm Coll (OH)
Odessa Coll (TX)
Okaloosa-Walton Comm Coll (FL)
Oklahoma City Comm Coll (OK)
Orange County Comm Coll (NY)
Otero Jr Coll (CO)
Oxnard Coll (CA)
Peninsula Coll (WA)
Pensacola Jr Coll (FL)
Piedmont Tech Coll (SC)
Polk Comm Coll (FL)
Portland Comm Coll (OR)
Pratt Comm Coll and Area Vocational School (KS)
Rasmussen Coll Eagan (MN)
Rasmussen Coll Mankato (MN)
Rasmussen Coll Minnetonka (MN)
Reading Area Comm Coll (PA)
Richland Comm Coll (IL)
Ridgewater Coll (MN)
Riverside Comm Coll (CA)
Rockingham Comm Coll (NC)
Rogue Comm Coll (OR)
Saint Charles Comm Coll (MO)
St. Clair County Comm Coll (MI)
St. Cloud Tech Coll (MN)
St. Louis Comm Coll at Florissant Valley (MO)
St. Paul Tech Coll (MN)
Salish Kootenai Coll (MT)
San Antonio Coll (TX)
Sandhills Comm Coll (NC)
San Jacinto Coll Central Campus (TX)
San Jacinto Coll North Campus (TX)
San Joaquin Delta Coll (CA)
Santa Fe Comm Coll (FL)
Sauk Valley Comm Coll (IL)
Seminole Comm Coll (FL)
Shoreline Comm Coll (WA)
Sinclair Comm Coll (OH)
Skagit Valley Coll (WA)
Snow Coll (UT)
Southern Maine Tech Coll (ME)
South Plains Coll (TX)
South Suburban Coll (IL)
Southwestern Comm Coll (NC)
Southwest Wisconsin Tech Coll (WI)
Stark State Coll of Technology (OH)
Suffolk County Comm Coll (NY)
Tompkins Cortland Comm Coll (NY)
Trinity Valley Comm Coll (TX)
Truckee Meadows Comm Coll (NV)
Tulsa Comm Coll (OK)
Umpqua Comm Coll (OR)
U of Arkansas Comm Coll at Morrilton (AR)
Vance-Granville Comm Coll (NC)
Victor Valley Coll (CA)
Vincennes U (IN)
Virginia Western Comm Coll (VA)
Wallace State Comm Coll (AL)
Walters State Comm Coll (TN)
Westchester Comm Coll (NY)
Western Wisconsin Tech Coll (WI)
Westmoreland County Comm Coll (PA)

CHILD CARE/GUIDANCE
Albuquerque Tech Vocational Inst (NM)
Alexandria Tech Coll (MN)
Anoka-Hennepin Tech Coll (MN)
Antelope Valley Coll (CA)
Asheville-Buncombe Tech Comm Coll (NC)
Bates Tech Coll (WA)
Bay de Noc Comm Coll (MI)
Calhoun Comm Coll (AL)
Central Georgia Tech Coll (GA)
Centralia Coll (WA)
Central Texas Coll (TX)
Central Wyoming Coll (WY)
Clover Park Tech Coll (WA)
Collin County Comm Coll District (TX)
Colorado Northwestern Comm Coll (CO)
Craven Comm Coll (NC)
Dawson Comm Coll (MT)
Dixie State Coll of Utah (UT)
Eastfield Coll (TX)
Edmonds Comm Coll (WA)
Erie Comm Coll, City Campus (NY)
Florida Comm Coll at Jacksonville (FL)
Gadsden State Comm Coll (AL)
Gogebic Comm Coll (MI)
Grays Harbor Coll (WA)
Green River Comm Coll (WA)
Hagerstown Comm Coll (MD)
Hesser Coll (NH)
Houston Comm Coll System (TX)
Ivy Tech State Coll–Bloomington (IN)
Ivy Tech State Coll–Columbus (IN)
Ivy Tech State Coll–Eastcentral (IN)
Ivy Tech State Coll–Kokomo (IN)
Ivy Tech State Coll–Lafayette (IN)
Ivy Tech State Coll–North Central (IN)
Ivy Tech State Coll–Northeast (IN)
Ivy Tech State Coll–Northwest (IN)
Ivy Tech State Coll–Southcentral (IN)
Ivy Tech State Coll–Southeast (IN)
Ivy Tech State Coll–Southwest (IN)
Ivy Tech State Coll–Wabash Valley (IN)
Ivy Tech State Coll–Whitewater (IN)
Jefferson State Comm Coll (AL)
Joliet Jr Coll (IL)
J. Sargeant Reynolds Comm Coll (VA)
Kansas City Kansas Comm Coll (KS)
Kilgore Coll (TX)
Kilian Comm Coll (SD)
Kishwaukee Coll (IL)
Lake Land Coll (IL)
Lake Region State Coll (ND)
Lehigh Carbon Comm Coll (PA)
Massachusetts Bay Comm Coll (MA)
McHenry County Coll (IL)
MiraCosta Coll (CA)
Mississippi County Comm Coll (AR)
Montcalm Comm Coll (MI)
Montgomery Coll (MD)
Montgomery Comm Coll (NC)
Montgomery County Comm Coll (PA)
Moraine Valley Comm Coll (IL)
Muscatine Comm Coll (IA)
Northampton County Area Comm Coll (PA)
Northland Pioneer Coll (AZ)
Northwestern Michigan Coll (MI)
Oakland Comm Coll (MI)
Ocean County Coll (NJ)
Olympic Coll (WA)
Ouachita Tech Coll (AR)
Pennsylvania Coll of Technology (PA)
Pikes Peak Comm Coll (CO)
Pima Comm Coll (AZ)
Pitt Comm Coll (NC)
Reedley Coll (CA)
Richmond Comm Coll (NC)
St. Cloud Tech Coll (MN)
St. Philip's Coll (TX)
San Jacinto Coll North Campus (TX)
Santa Barbara City Coll (CA)
Schoolcraft Coll (MI)
Scott Comm Coll (IA)
Sitting Bull Coll (ND)
Snead State Comm Coll (AL)
Southwestern Michigan Coll (MI)
Spokane Falls Comm Coll (WA)
Stanly Comm Coll (NC)
Tulsa Comm Coll (OK)
Vernon Coll (TX)
Victor Valley Coll (CA)
Walla Walla Comm Coll (WA)
Western Nevada Comm Coll (NV)
Western School of Health and Business Careers (PA)
Wilkes Comm Coll (NC)
Wisconsin Indianhead Tech Coll (WI)
Wor-Wic Comm Coll (MD)

CHILD CARE PROVIDER
Academy of Medical Arts and Business (PA)
Angelina Coll (TX)
Arapahoe Comm Coll (CO)
Brunswick Comm Coll (NC)
Cerro Coso Comm Coll (CA)
City Colls of Chicago, Malcolm X Coll (IL)
Coastal Carolina Comm Coll (NC)
Coll of DuPage (IL)
Coll of the Redwoods (CA)
Coll of the Siskiyous (CA)
Comm Coll of Allegheny County (PA)
The Comm Coll of Baltimore County–Catonsville Campus (MD)
Corning Comm Coll (NY)
Crafton Hills Coll (CA)
Dakota County Tech Coll (MN)
Eastern Arizona Coll (AZ)
Fayetteville Tech Comm Coll (NC)
Florida Comm Coll at Jacksonville (FL)
Gulf Coast Comm Coll (FL)
Harry M. Ayers State Tech Coll (AL)
Heartland Comm Coll (IL)
Herkimer County Comm Coll (NY)
Highland Comm Coll (IL)
Hill Coll of the Hill Jr College District (TX)
Iowa Western Comm Coll (IA)
Kaskaskia Coll (IL)
Kennebec Valley Tech Coll (ME)
Lehigh Carbon Comm Coll (PA)
Luzerne County Comm Coll (PA)
McHenry County Coll (IL)
Mid Michigan Comm Coll (MI)
Mineral Area Coll (MO)
Modesto Jr Coll (CA)
Montcalm Comm Coll (MI)
Moraine Valley Comm Coll (IL)
Mott Comm Coll (MI)
Muskingum Area Tech Coll (OH)
Northland Comm and Tech Coll (MN)
Orange Coast Coll (CA)
Parkland Coll (IL)
Penn Valley Comm Coll (MO)
Pima Comm Coll (AZ)
Rasmussen Coll Mankato (MN)
Rend Lake Coll (IL)
St. Philip's Coll (TX)
San Antonio Coll (TX)
San Diego Mesa Coll (CA)
San Jacinto Coll North Campus (TX)
Southern Arkansas U Tech (AR)
Surry Comm Coll (NC)
Tompkins Cortland Comm Coll (NY)
Trident Tech Coll (SC)
Triton Coll (IL)
United Tribes Tech Coll (ND)
U of Arkansas Comm Coll at Hope (AR)
Vincennes U (IN)
Waubonsee Comm Coll (IL)
Westchester Comm Coll (NY)
Western Wisconsin Tech Coll (WI)
York Tech Coll (SC)

CHILD CARE SERVICES MANAGEMENT
Academy of Medical Arts and Business (PA)
Angelina Coll (TX)
Arapahoe Comm Coll (CO)
Barton County Comm Coll (KS)
Brazosport Coll (TX)
Cape Fear Comm Coll (NC)
Central Carolina Tech Coll (SC)
Centralia Coll (WA)
Cerro Coso Comm Coll (CA)
Coll of DuPage (IL)
Dakota County Tech Coll (MN)
Fayetteville Tech Comm Coll (NC)
Florida Comm Coll at Jacksonville (FL)
Front Range Comm Coll (CO)
Highland Comm Coll (IL)
Hopkinsville Comm Coll (KY)
Iowa Western Comm Coll (IA)
Jefferson Comm Coll (OH)
Kennebec Valley Tech Coll (ME)
Kingsborough Comm Coll of City U of NY (NY)
Modesto Jr Coll (CA)
Montgomery Comm Coll (NC)
Orange Coast Coll (CA)
Peninsula Coll (WA)
Pitt Comm Coll (NC)
Rasmussen Coll Mankato (MN)
San Antonio Coll (TX)
San Jacinto Coll North Campus (TX)
Vincennes U (IN)
Western Iowa Tech Comm Coll (IA)
Wilkes Comm Coll (NC)
York Tech Coll (SC)

CHILD GUIDANCE
Antelope Valley Coll (CA)
Black Hawk Coll, Moline (IL)
Blinn Coll (TX)
Cuyamaca Coll (CA)
Dutchess Comm Coll (NY)
Elizabethtown Comm Coll (KY)
Gulf Coast Comm Coll (FL)
Hennepin Tech Coll (MN)
Ivy Tech State Coll–Central Indiana (IN)
John Wood Comm Coll (IL)
Lamar State Coll–Port Arthur (TX)
Laurel Business Inst (PA)
Lincoln Land Comm Coll (IL)
Manatee Comm Coll (FL)
Minneapolis Comm and Tech Coll (MN)
Moberly Area Comm Coll (MO)
Moraine Park Tech Coll (WI)
North Central Michigan Coll (MI)
Northland Pioneer Coll (AZ)
Palo Verde Coll (CA)
Prairie State Coll (IL)
Tulsa Comm Coll (OK)

CIVIL ENGINEERING TECHNOLOGY
Allan Hancock Coll (CA)
Alpena Comm Coll (MI)
Asheville-Buncombe Tech Comm Coll (NC)
Bates Tech Coll (WA)
Belmont Tech Coll (OH)
Big Bend Comm Coll (WA)
Black Hawk Coll, Moline (IL)
Bristol Comm Coll (MA)
Broome Comm Coll (NY)
Burlington County Coll (NJ)
Butler County Comm Coll (PA)
Butte Coll (CA)
Capital Comm Coll (CT)
Central Arizona Coll (AZ)
Central Carolina Tech Coll (SC)
Centralia Coll (WA)
Central Maine Tech Coll (ME)
Central Piedmont Comm Coll (NC)
Central Virginia Comm Coll (VA)
Chabot Coll (CA)
Chattanooga State Tech Comm Coll (TN)
Chemeketa Comm Coll (OR)
Chippewa Valley Tech Coll (WI)
Cincinnati State Tech and Comm Coll (OH)
City Coll of San Francisco (CA)
Coll of Lake County (IL)
Coll of the Siskiyous (CA)
Columbus State Comm Coll (OH)
Comm Coll of Allegheny County (PA)
The Comm Coll of Baltimore County–Catonsville Campus (MD)
Compton Comm Coll (CA)
Daytona Beach Comm Coll (FL)
Delaware Tech & Comm Coll, Jack F Owens Cmps (DE)
Delaware Tech & Comm Coll, Stanton/ Wilmington Cmps (DE)
Delaware Tech & Comm Coll, Terry Cmps (DE)
Delgado Comm Coll (LA)
Des Moines Area Comm Coll (IA)
Eastern Arizona Coll (AZ)
Education Direct (PA)
Erie Comm Coll, North Campus (NY)
Everett Comm Coll (WA)
Fayetteville Tech Comm Coll (NC)
Florence-Darlington Tech Coll (SC)
Florida Comm Coll at Jacksonville (FL)
Fullerton Coll (CA)
Gadsden State Comm Coll (AL)
Gaston Coll (NC)
Gateway Tech Coll (WI)
Gloucester County Coll (NJ)
Guam Comm Coll (GU)
Guilford Tech Comm Coll (NC)
Gulf Coast Comm Coll (FL)
Harrisburg Area Comm Coll (PA)
Hawkeye Comm Coll (IA)
Hill Coll of the Hill Jr College District (TX)
Hinds Comm Coll (MS)
Horry-Georgetown Tech Coll (SC)
Houston Comm Coll System (TX)
Independence Comm Coll (KS)
Indian River Comm Coll (FL)
Iowa Western Comm Coll (IA)
Jefferson Coll (MO)
Jefferson Comm Coll (KY)
Johnson County Comm Coll (KS)
J. Sargeant Reynolds Comm Coll (VA)
Lake Land Coll (IL)
Lakeland Comm Coll (OH)
Lansing Comm Coll (MI)
Laramie County Comm Coll (WY)
Lorain County Comm Coll (OH)
Lord Fairfax Comm Coll (VA)
Macomb Comm Coll (MI)
Manatee Comm Coll (FL)
Massasoit Comm Coll (MA)
Mercer County Comm Coll (NJ)
Metropolitan Comm Coll (NE)
Miami-Dade Comm Coll (FL)
Middlesex County Coll (NJ)
Midlands Tech Coll (SC)
Mid-State Tech Coll (WI)
Milwaukee Area Tech Coll (WI)
Mississippi Delta Comm Coll (MS)
Mohawk Valley Comm Coll (NY)
Monroe Comm Coll (NY)
Montgomery Coll (MD)
Moraine Park Tech Coll (WI)
Mt. Hood Comm Coll (OR)
Nashville State Tech Inst (TN)
Nassau Comm Coll (NY)
New Mexico Military Inst (NM)
New York City Tech Coll of the City U of NY (NY)
North Dakota State Coll of Science (ND)
Northern Essex Comm Coll (MA)
Northern Virginia Comm Coll (VA)
Northwest Mississippi Comm Coll (MS)
Ocean County Coll (NJ)
Oklahoma State U, Oklahoma City (OK)
Pasadena City Coll (CA)
Pellissippi State Tech Comm Coll (TN)
Peninsula Coll (WA)
Pennsylvania Coll of Technology (PA)
Pensacola Jr Coll (FL)
Phoenix Coll (AZ)
Portland Comm Coll (OR)
St. Cloud Tech Coll (MN)
St. Louis Comm Coll at Florissant Valley (MO)
St. Paul Tech Coll (MN)
San Antonio Coll (TX)
San Bernardino Valley Coll (CA)
Sandhills Comm Coll (NC)
San Joaquin Delta Coll (CA)
Savannah Tech Coll (GA)
Seminole Comm Coll (FL)
Shasta Coll (CA)
Shoreline Comm Coll (WA)
Sinclair Comm Coll (OH)
Southeast Comm Coll, Milford Campus (NE)
Southeast Tech Inst (SD)
Southwest Tennessee Comm Coll (TN)
Spartanburg Tech Coll (SC)
Spokane Comm Coll (WA)
Springfield Tech Comm Coll (MA)
Stark State Coll of Technology (OH)
State U of NY Coll of Technology at Alfred (NY)
State U of NY Coll of Technology at Canton (NY)
Suffolk County Comm Coll (NY)
Tallahassee Comm Coll (FL)
Three Rivers Comm Coll (CT)
Trident Tech Coll (SC)
Trinidad State Jr Coll (CO)
Tulsa Comm Coll (OK)
Umpqua Comm Coll (OR)
Union County Coll (NJ)
Vermont Tech Coll (VT)
Vincennes U (IN)
Virginia Western Comm Coll (VA)
Wake Tech Comm Coll (NC)
Walla Walla Comm Coll (WA)
Westchester Comm Coll (NY)
Western Piedmont Comm Coll (NC)

CIVIL/STRUCTURAL DRAFTING
Comm Coll of Allegheny County (PA)
Florida Tech Coll, Orlando (FL)

CLASSICS
Foothill Coll (CA)

CLINICAL/MEDICAL SOCIAL WORK
Central Comm Coll–Grand Island Campus (NE)
Central Comm Coll–Hastings Campus (NE)
Dawson Comm Coll (MT)
Wayne Comm Coll (NC)

CLOTHING/APPAREL/TEXTILE
Comm Coll of the Air Force (AL)
Delta Coll (MI)

CLOTHING/APPAREL/TEXTILE STUDIES
Fashion Inst of Design & Merchandising, LA Campus (CA)
Fashion Inst of Design & Merchandising, SF Campus (CA)
Modesto Jr Coll (CA)

CLOTHING/TEXTILES
Antelope Valley Coll (CA)
The Art Inst of Fort Lauderdale (FL)
Bradley Academy for the Visual Arts (PA)
Brooks Coll (CA)
Central Alabama Comm Coll (AL)
El Centro Coll (TX)
Hinds Comm Coll (MS)
Indian River Comm Coll (FL)
Los Angeles City Coll (CA)
Monterey Peninsula Coll (CA)
Northland Pioneer Coll (AZ)
Palm Beach Comm Coll (FL)
St. Philip's Coll (TX)
Trenholm State Tech Coll, Patterson Campus (AL)
Tri-County Tech Coll (SC)

COMMERCIAL PHOTOGRAPHY
Houston Comm Coll System (TX)
Kilgore Coll (TX)
Montgomery Coll (MD)
Oakbridge Academy of Arts (PA)
Randolph Comm Coll (NC)
Spokane Falls Comm Coll (WA)

COMMUNICATION EQUIPMENT TECHNOLOGY
Allegany Coll of Maryland (MD)
Anne Arundel Comm Coll (MD)
Arapahoe Comm Coll (CO)
The Art Inst of Pittsburgh (PA)
Athens Tech Coll (GA)
Burlington County Coll (NJ)
Cleveland Comm Coll (NC)
Coffeyville Comm Coll (KS)
Coll of DuPage (IL)
Comm Coll of Beaver County (PA)
Comm Coll of the Air Force (AL)
Dodge City Comm Coll (KS)
ECPI Coll of Technology, Newport News (VA)
ECPI Coll of Technology, Virginia Beach (VA)
ECPI Tech Coll, Richmond (VA)
ECPI Tech Coll, Roanoke (VA)
Gateway Tech Coll (WI)
Hutchinson Comm Coll and Area Vocational School (KS)
Kirkwood Comm Coll (IA)
Macomb Comm Coll (MI)
Milwaukee Area Tech Coll (WI)
Mohawk Valley Comm Coll (NY)
NEI Coll of Technology (MN)
North Seattle Comm Coll (WA)
Northwestern Connecticut Comm-Tech Coll (CT)
Ocean County Coll (NJ)
Orange Coast Coll (CA)
Paducah Tech Coll (KY)
Pasadena City Coll (CA)
Reading Area Comm Coll (PA)
St. Philip's Coll (TX)
Santa Fe Comm Coll (FL)
Southern Maine Tech Coll (ME)
Southern West Virginia Comm and Tech Coll (WV)
South Puget Sound Comm Coll (WA)
Spartan School of Aeronautics (OK)
Tennessee Inst of Electronics (TN)
Vincennes U (IN)

COMMUNICATIONS
Briarwood Coll (CT)
Coll of Southern Idaho (ID)
Dean Coll (MA)
Delaware County Comm Coll (PA)
Dixie State Coll of Utah (UT)
Dutchess Comm Coll (NY)
Eastern Wyoming Coll (WY)
Erie Comm Coll, South Campus (NY)
Foothill Coll (CA)
Gloucester County Coll (NJ)
Hutchinson Comm Coll and Area Vocational School (KS)
Kellogg Comm Coll (MI)
Keystone Coll (PA)
Lord Fairfax Comm Coll (VA)
Macomb Comm Coll (MI)
Manchester Comm Coll (CT)
Massachusetts Bay Comm Coll (MA)
Mesa Tech Coll (NM)
Miami U–Middletown Campus (OH)
Montgomery County Comm Coll (PA)
Nassau Comm Coll (NY)
New England Inst of Art & Communications (MA)
San Juan Coll (NM)
Santa Ana Coll (CA)
Santa Barbara City Coll (CA)
Union County Coll (NJ)
U of New Mexico–Gallup (NM)
Ventura Coll (CA)
Vincennes U (IN)
Waubonsee Comm Coll (IL)

COMMUNICATIONS RELATED
Calhoun Comm Coll (AL)
Clark Coll (WA)
Delgado Comm Coll (LA)
Queensborough Comm Coll of City U of NY (NY)

COMMUNICATIONS TECHNOLOGIES RELATED
Clover Park Tech Coll (WA)
Comm Coll of Allegheny County (PA)
Mott Comm Coll (MI)
Springfield Tech Comm Coll (MA)
Western Wisconsin Tech Coll (WI)

COMMUNICATION SYSTEMS INSTALLATION/REPAIR
Alexandria Tech Coll (MN)
Arapahoe Comm Coll (CO)
Coll of DuPage (IL)
Dakota County Tech Coll (MN)
Daymar Coll (KY)
Erie Comm Coll, South Campus (NY)
Fayetteville Tech Comm Coll (NC)
Herkimer County Comm Coll (NY)
Kennebec Valley Tech Coll (ME)
Modesto Jr Coll (CA)
Suffolk County Comm Coll (NY)
Wisconsin Indianhead Tech Coll (WI)

COMMUNITY HEALTH LIAISON
Bay de Noc Comm Coll (MI)
Comm Coll of Allegheny County (PA)
Edmonds Comm Coll (WA)
Erie Comm Coll, City Campus (NY)
Kingsborough Comm Coll of City U of NY (NY)
Manatee Comm Coll (FL)
Mott Comm Coll (MI)

COMMUNITY PSYCHOLOGY
Western Nebraska Comm Coll (NE)
Woodbury Coll (VT)

COMMUNITY SERVICES
Clackamas Comm Coll (OR)
Cleveland State Comm Coll (TN)
Clinton Comm Coll (NY)
Coll of the Sequoias (CA)
Comm Coll of Vermont (VT)
Crafton Hills Coll (CA)
Cumberland County Coll (NJ)
Del Mar Coll (TX)
Honolulu Comm Coll (HI)
J. Sargeant Reynolds Comm Coll (VA)
Lamar Comm Coll (CO)
Lane Comm Coll (OR)
Marshalltown Comm Coll (IA)
Mercer County Comm Coll (NJ)
Mohawk Valley Comm Coll (NY)
New River Comm Coll (VA)
Ridgewater Coll (MN)
Salem Comm Coll (NJ)
Suffolk County Comm Coll (NY)
Ulster County Comm Coll (NY)
U of New Mexico–Gallup (NM)

COMPARATIVE LITERATURE
Cerro Coso Comm Coll (CA)

COMPUTER ENGINEERING
Moraine Park Tech Coll (WI)
Santa Barbara City Coll (CA)

COMPUTER ENGINEERING RELATED
Arkansas State U–Beebe (AR)
Berkshire Comm Coll (MA)
Catawba Valley Comm Coll (NC)
Coll of the Canyons (CA)
Columbus Tech Coll (GA)
The Comm Coll of Baltimore County–Catonsville Campus (MD)
Daymar Coll (KY)
Daytona Beach Comm Coll (FL)
Electronic Insts, Middletown (PA)
Fayetteville Tech Comm Coll (NC)
Florida Computer & Business School (FL)
Gateway Comm Coll (CT)
Glendale Comm Coll (CA)
Gulf Coast Comm Coll (FL)
Itasca Comm Coll (MN)
Jefferson Comm Coll (OH)
Middle Georgia Coll (GA)
Minot State U–Bottineau Campus (ND)
Monroe Comm Coll (NY)
Okaloosa-Walton Comm Coll (FL)
Onondaga Comm Coll (NY)
Orange County Comm Coll (NY)
Sandhills Comm Coll (NC)
Sauk Valley Comm Coll (IL)
Seminole Comm Coll (FL)
Sinclair Comm Coll (OH)
Stark State Coll of Technology (OH)

Surry Comm Coll (NC)
Vincennes U (IN)
York Tech Coll (SC)

COMPUTER ENGINEERING TECHNOLOGY

Abraham Baldwin Ag Coll (GA)
Allan Hancock Coll (CA)
Allegany Coll of Maryland (MD)
Alvin Comm Coll (TX)
Amarillo Coll (TX)
American River Coll (CA)
Angelina Coll (TX)
Anne Arundel Comm Coll (MD)
Arkansas State U–Beebe (AR)
Belmont Tech Coll (OH)
Benjamin Franklin Inst of Technology (MA)
Bergen Comm Coll (NJ)
Black Hawk Coll, Moline (IL)
Bowling Green State U-Firelands Coll (OH)
Bristol Comm Coll (MA)
Brookdale Comm Coll (NJ)
Bucks County Comm Coll (PA)
Camden County Coll (NJ)
Cañada Coll (CA)
Capital Comm Coll (CT)
Carteret Comm Coll (NC)
Casper Coll (WY)
Catawba Valley Comm Coll (NC)
Cecil Comm Coll (MD)
Central Piedmont Comm Coll (NC)
Century Comm and Tech Coll (MN)
Cerro Coso Comm Coll (CA)
Chabot Coll (CA)
Chattahoochee Tech Coll (GA)
Chattanooga State Tech Comm Coll (TN)
Chemeketa Comm Coll (OR)
Chesapeake Coll (MD)
CHI Inst (PA)
Cincinnati State Tech and Comm Coll (OH)
Cleveland Comm Coll (NC)
Coastal Bend Coll (TX)
Coll of the Redwoods (CA)
Coll of the Sequoias (CA)
Collin County Comm Coll District (TX)
Colorado Mountn Coll, Alpine Cmps (CO)
Colorado Mountn Coll (CO)
Colorado Mountn Coll, Timberline Cmps (CO)
Columbus State Comm Coll (OH)
Comm Coll of Allegheny County (PA)
The Comm Coll of Baltimore County–Catonsville Campus (MD)
Comm Coll of Rhode Island (RI)
Comm Coll of Southern Nevada (NV)
Compton Comm Coll (CA)
Cuesta Coll (CA)
Cuyahoga Comm Coll (OH)
Delaware Tech & Comm Coll, Terry Cmps (DE)
Delgado Comm Coll (LA)
Des Moines Area Comm Coll (IA)
Doña Ana Branch Comm Coll (NM)
East Arkansas Comm Coll (AR)
Eastern Oklahoma State Coll (OK)
Eastfield Coll (TX)
ECPI Coll of Technology, Newport News (VA)
ECPI Coll of Technology, Virginia Beach (VA)
ECPI Tech Coll, Roanoke (VA)
Edgecombe Comm Coll (NC)
Edison State Comm Coll (OH)
Elaine P. Nunez Comm Coll (LA)
Electronic Insts, Middletown (PA)
Everest Coll (AZ)
Fiorello H LaGuardia Comm Coll of City U of NY (NY)
Flathead Valley Comm Coll (MT)
Florence-Darlington Tech Coll (SC)
Florida Comm Coll at Jacksonville (FL)
Foothill Coll (CA)
Forsyth Tech Comm Coll (NC)
Frederick Comm Coll (MD)
Fulton-Montgomery Comm Coll (NY)
Garden City Comm Coll (KS)
Gateway Comm Coll (CT)
Genesee Comm Coll (NY)
Georgia Perimeter Coll (GA)
Glendale Comm Coll (CA)
Gogebic Comm Coll (MI)
Grand Rapids Comm Coll (MI)
Grayson County Coll (TX)
Gulf Coast Comm Coll (FL)
Hawkeye Comm Coll (IA)
Heartland Comm Coll (IL)
Hesser Coll (NH)
Highline Comm Coll (WA)
Hillsborough Comm Coll (FL)
Horry-Georgetown Tech Coll (SC)
Houston Comm Coll System (TX)
Hudson County Comm Coll (NJ)
Indian Hills Comm Coll (IA)
Indian River Comm Coll (FL)
International Business Coll, Fort Wayne (IN)
Itasca Comm Coll (MN)
Jamestown Comm Coll (NY)
J. Sargeant Reynolds Comm Coll (VA)
Kellogg Comm Coll (MI)
Kent State U, East Liverpool Campus (OH)
Kent State U, Geauga Campus (OH)
Kent State U, Trumbull Campus (OH)
Kent State U, Tuscarawas Campus (OH)
Kilian Comm Coll (SD)
Kingwood Coll (TX)
Lake Washington Tech Coll (WA)
Lamar Comm Coll (CO)
Lane Comm Coll (OR)
Lansing Comm Coll (MI)
Lehigh Carbon Comm Coll (PA)
Lorain County Comm Coll (OH)
Los Angeles City Coll (CA)
Los Angeles Harbor Coll (CA)
Los Angeles Pierce Coll (CA)
Louisville Tech Inst (KY)
Lower Columbia Coll (WA)
Macomb Comm Coll (MI)
Manatee Comm Coll (FL)
Massachusetts Bay Comm Coll (MA)
McLennan Comm Coll (TX)
Merced Coll (CA)
Meridian Comm Coll (MS)
Miami U–Hamilton Campus (OH)
Miami U–Middletown Campus (OH)
Middlesex Comm Coll (MA)
Middlesex County Coll (NJ)
Mid-State Tech Coll (WI)
Miles Comm Coll (MT)
Minnesota State Coll–Southeast Tech (MN)
Minot State U–Bottineau Campus (ND)
MiraCosta Coll (CA)
Mississippi Delta Comm Coll (MS)
Mississippi Gulf Coast Comm Coll (MS)
Monroe Comm Coll (NY)
Monroe County Comm Coll (MI)
Monterey Peninsula Coll (CA)
Moraine Park Tech Coll (WI)
Mt. Hood Comm Coll (OR)
Nashville State Tech Inst (TN)
NEI Coll of Technology (MN)
New Hampshire Comm Tech Coll, Berlin/Laconia (NH)
New Hampshire Tech Inst (NH)
New River Comm Coll (VA)
North Central Texas Coll (TX)
Northeast Iowa Comm Coll (IA)
Northern Essex Comm Coll (MA)
Northern Maine Tech Coll (ME)
North Seattle Comm Coll (WA)
North Shore Comm Coll (MA)
Northwestern Connecticut Comm-Tech Coll (CT)
Northwest-Shoals Comm Coll (AL)
Oklahoma City Comm Coll (OK)
Oklahoma State U, Oklahoma City (OK)
Onondaga Comm Coll (NY)
Orange Coast Coll (CA)
Orange County Comm Coll (NY)
Paducah Tech Coll (KY)
Pamlico Comm Coll (NC)
Pasadena City Coll (CA)
Pellissippi State Tech Comm Coll (TN)
Penn State U New Kensington Campus of the Commonwealth Coll (PA)
Piedmont Comm Coll (NC)
Portland Comm Coll (OR)
Prince George's Comm Coll (MD)
Pulaski Tech Coll (AR)
Queensborough Comm Coll of City U of NY (NY)
Ranger Coll (TX)
Red Rocks Comm Coll (CO)
Rend Lake Coll (IL)
RETS Tech Center (OH)
Richmond Comm Coll (NC)
Ridgewater Coll (MN)
Roane State Comm Coll (TN)
St. Catharine Coll (KY)
St. Louis Comm Coll at Florissant Valley (MO)
St. Petersburg Coll (FL)
Salem Comm Coll (NJ)
San Antonio Coll (TX)
San Bernardino Valley Coll (CA)
Sandhills Comm Coll (NC)
San Diego City Coll (CA)
San Joaquin Delta Coll (CA)
Santa Fe Comm Coll (FL)
Seminole Comm Coll (FL)
Sierra Coll (CA)
Skagit Valley Coll (WA)
Southeast Comm Coll (KY)
Southeast Comm Coll, Milford Campus (NE)
Southeastern Comm Coll (NC)
Southern Maine Tech Coll (ME)
South Plains Coll (TX)
Southwestern Comm Coll (NC)
Southwest Tennessee Comm Coll (TN)
Springfield Tech Comm Coll (MA)
State Fair Comm Coll (MO)
State U of NY Coll of A&T at Morrisville (NY)
State U of NY Coll of Technology at Alfred (NY)
Suffolk County Comm Coll (NY)
Surry Comm Coll (NC)
TCI-The Coll for Technology (NY)
Tennessee Inst of Electronics (TN)
Texas State Tech Coll– Waco/ Marshall Campus (TX)
Texas State Tech Coll (TX)
Three Rivers Comm Coll (CT)
Trident Tech Coll (SC)
Triton Coll (IL)
Truckee Meadows Comm Coll (NV)
Tyler Jr Coll (TX)
Umpqua Comm Coll (OR)
U of Alaska Southeast, Sitka Campus (AK)
U of New Mexico–Los Alamos Branch (NM)
Vance-Granville Comm Coll (NC)
Vermilion Comm Coll (MN)
Vermont Tech Coll (VT)
Vincennes U (IN)
Wake Tech Comm Coll (NC)
Western Piedmont Comm Coll (NC)
Western Texas Coll (TX)
Westmoreland County Comm Coll (PA)
Westwood Coll of Technology–Denver North (CO)
Whatcom Comm Coll (WA)
York Tech Coll (SC)

COMPUTER GRAPHICS

Academy Coll (MN)
Adirondack Comm Coll (NY)
American River Coll (CA)
Anoka-Hennepin Tech Coll (MN)
Antelope Valley Coll (CA)
Arapahoe Comm Coll (CO)
Arkansas State U–Beebe (AR)
The Art Inst of Houston (TX)
The Art Inst of Houston (TX)
The Art Inst of Pittsburgh (PA)
The Art Inst of Seattle (WA)
Baltimore City Comm Coll (MD)
Barton County Comm Coll (KS)
Berks Tech Inst (PA)
Bradley Academy for the Visual Arts (PA)
Bradley Academy for the Visual Arts (PA)
Bristol Comm Coll (MA)
Burlington County Coll (NJ)
Camden County Coll (NJ)
Cape Cod Comm Coll (MA)
Carroll Comm Coll (MD)
Cecil Comm Coll (MD)
Cecil Comm Coll (MD)
Cerro Coso Comm Coll (CA)
CHI Inst (PA)
Coll of Eastern Utah (UT)
Coll of the Desert (CA)
Coll of the Sequoias (CA)
Coll of the Siskiyous (CA)
Columbia-Greene Comm Coll (NY)
The Comm Coll of Baltimore County–Catonsville Campus (MD)
The Comm Coll of Baltimore County–Catonsville Campus (MD)
Corning Comm Coll (NY)
Cowley County Comm Coll and Voc-Tech School (KS)
Cypress Coll (CA)
Dakota County Tech Coll (MN)
Daymar Coll (KY)
Daytona Beach Comm Coll (FL)
De Anza Coll (CA)
Delaware County Comm Coll (PA)
Delta Coll (MI)
Diablo Valley Coll (CA)
Edison State Comm Coll (OH)
Education America, Southeast Coll of Technology, New Orleans Campus (LA)
Evergreen Valley Coll (CA)
Fayetteville Tech Comm Coll (NC)
Florida Comm Coll at Jacksonville (FL)
Florida National Coll (FL)
Full Sail Real World Education (FL)
Garden City Comm Coll (KS)
Gateway Comm Coll (CT)
Gateway Tech Coll (WI)
Gavilan Coll (CA)
Genesee Comm Coll (NY)
Gloucester County Coll (NJ)
Gogebic Comm Coll (MI)
Hinds Comm Coll (MS)
Howard Comm Coll (MD)
Jackson Comm Coll (MI)
Kellogg Comm Coll (MI)
Kingwood Coll (TX)
Lakeland Comm Coll (OH)
Lansing Comm Coll (MI)
Lima Tech Coll (OH)
Lincoln Coll, Normal (IL)
Linn-Benton Comm Coll (OR)
Louisville Tech Inst (KY)
Louisville Tech Inst (KY)
Luzerne County Comm Coll (PA)
Luzerne County Comm Coll (PA)
Manatee Comm Coll (FL)
Maryland Coll of Art and Design (MD)
Mercer County Comm Coll (NJ)
Meridian Comm Coll (MS)
Mesabi Range Comm and Tech Coll (MN)
Miami-Dade Comm Coll (FL)
Middlesex County Coll (NJ)
Midland Coll (TX)
Mid Michigan Comm Coll (MI)
Miles Comm Coll (MT)
Milwaukee Area Tech Coll (WI)
Minnesota School of Business (MN)
Mississippi Gulf Coast Comm Coll (MS)
Modesto Jr Coll (CA)
Modesto Jr Coll (CA)
Mohawk Valley Comm Coll (NY)
Monroe County Comm Coll (MI)
Mount Wachusett Comm Coll (MA)
Nassau Comm Coll (NY)
Navarro Coll (TX)
New River Comm Coll (VA)
North Central Texas Coll (TX)
Northeast Alabama Comm Coll (AL)
Northern Essex Comm Coll (MA)
Northern Virginia Comm Coll (VA)
Northland Comm and Tech Coll (MN)
North Shore Comm Coll (MA)
Northwestern Connecticut Comm-Tech Coll (CT)
Oakbridge Academy of Arts (PA)
Oakton Comm Coll (IL)
Oklahoma State U, Okmulgee (OK)
Olympic Coll (WA)
Orange Coast Coll (CA)
Orange Coast Coll (CA)
Parkland Coll (IL)
Parkland Coll (IL)
Pellissippi State Tech Comm Coll (TN)
Phoenix Coll (AZ)
Pittsburgh Tech Inst (PA)
Pittsburgh Tech Inst (PA)
Platt Coll, Newport Beach (CA)
Platt Coll, Ontario (CA)
Platt Coll (CO)
Platt Coll–Los Angeles, Inc (CA)
Prairie State Coll (IL)
Quincy Coll (MA)
Rasmussen Coll Mankato (MN)
Richland Comm Coll (IL)
Ridgewater Coll (MN)
Riverside Comm Coll (CA)
Rockland Comm Coll (NY)
San Antonio Coll (TX)
San Diego Mesa Coll (CA)
Seminole Comm Coll (FL)
Shoreline Comm Coll (WA)
Silicon Valley Coll, San Jose (CA)
Sinclair Comm Coll (OH)
Southeast Tech Inst (SD)
Southern Ohio Coll, Cincinnati Campus (OH)
Southwestern Coll (CA)
Spencerian Coll–Lexington (KY)
State U of NY Coll of Technology at Alfred (NY)
State U of NY Coll of Technology at Alfred (NY)
Sullivan County Comm Coll (NY)
Tallahassee Comm Coll (FL)
Texas State Tech Coll–Harlingen (TX)
Texas State Tech Coll–Harlingen (TX)
Tompkins Cortland Comm Coll (NY)
Tompkins Cortland Comm Coll (NY)
Trident Tech Coll (SC)
Triton Coll (IL)
Triton Coll (IL)
Tulsa Comm Coll (OK)
Tyler Jr Coll (TX)
Vincennes U (IN)
Vista Comm Coll (CA)
Wade Coll (TX)
Wade Coll (TX)
Wake Tech Comm Coll (NC)
Wake Tech Comm Coll (NC)
Weatherford Coll (TX)
The Westchester Business Inst (NY)
Westmoreland County Comm Coll (PA)

COMPUTER HARDWARE ENGINEERING

The Comm Coll of Baltimore County–Catonsville Campus (MD)
Cuesta Coll (CA)
Daymar Coll (KY)
Eastfield Coll (TX)
Education America, Southeast Coll of Technology, New Orleans Campus (LA)
Electronic Insts, Middletown (PA)
Florida Comm Coll at Jacksonville (FL)
Jackson Comm Coll (MI)
Lake City Comm Coll (FL)
Louisville Tech Inst (KY)
Seminole Comm Coll (FL)
Sinclair Comm Coll (OH)
Stanly Comm Coll (NC)
Stark State Coll of Technology (OH)
Tompkins Cortland Comm Coll (NY)
Tulsa Comm Coll (OK)
Vincennes U (IN)

COMPUTER/INFORMATION SCIENCES

Academy Coll (MN)
Antelope Valley Coll (CA)
Antonelli Coll (OH)
Atlanta Metropolitan Coll (GA)
Bevill State Comm Coll (AL)
Blackhawk Tech Coll (WI)
Brazosport Coll (TX)
Bristol Comm Coll (MA)

Broome Comm Coll (NY)
The Brown Mackie Coll (KS)
Bucks County Comm Coll (PA)
Butler County Comm Coll (PA)
Calhoun Comm Coll (AL)
Cambria County Area Comm Coll (PA)
Capital Comm Coll (CT)
Career Coll of Northern Nevada (NV)
Carroll Comm Coll (MD)
Cayuga County Comm Coll (NY)
Central Arizona Coll (AZ)
Central Comm Coll–Columbus Campus (NE)
Central Comm Coll–Grand Island Campus (NE)
Central Comm Coll–Hastings Campus (NE)
Central Texas Coll (TX)
Certified Careers Inst, Salt Lake City (UT)
Chippewa Valley Tech Coll (WI)
City Colls of Chicago, Wilbur Wright Coll (IL)
Coffeyville Comm Coll (KS)
Coll of the Redwoods (CA)
Collin County Comm Coll District (TX)
Comm Coll of Beaver County (PA)
Corning Comm Coll (NY)
Darton Coll (GA)
Dawson Comm Coll (MT)
Delaware County Comm Coll (PA)
Denmark Tech Coll (SC)
Dunwoody Coll of Technology (MN)
Dutchess Comm Coll (NY)
ECPI Coll of Technology, Newport News (VA)
ECPI Coll of Technology, Virginia Beach (VA)
ECPI Tech Coll, Richmond (VA)
ECPI Tech Coll, Roanoke (VA)
Education America, Southeast Coll of Technology, New Orleans Campus (LA)
Empire Coll (CA)
Erie Comm Coll, North Campus (NY)
Evergreen Valley Coll (CA)
Fayetteville Tech Comm Coll (NC)
Finger Lakes Comm Coll (NY)
Florida Comm Coll at Jacksonville (FL)
Gadsden State Comm Coll (AL)
GateWay Comm Coll (AZ)
Hagerstown Comm Coll (MD)
Harford Comm Coll (MD)
Harrisburg Area Comm Coll (PA)
Heartland Comm Coll (IL)
Henry Ford Comm Coll (MI)
Herzing Coll (AL)
Herzing Coll, Minneapolis Drafting School Campus (MN)
Hesser Coll (NH)
Hibbing Comm Coll (MN)
Houston Comm Coll System (TX)
Hutchinson Comm Coll and Area Vocational School (KS)
Illinois Eastern Comm Colls, Frontier Comm Coll (IL)
Illinois Eastern Comm Colls, Lincoln Trail Coll (IL)
Illinois Eastern Comm Colls, Olney Central Coll (IL)
Illinois Eastern Comm Colls, Wabash Valley Coll (IL)
Indiana Business Coll, Indianapolis (IN)
Ivy Tech State Coll–Bloomington (IN)
Ivy Tech State Coll–Central Indiana (IN)
Ivy Tech State Coll–Columbus (IN)
Ivy Tech State Coll–Eastcentral (IN)
Ivy Tech State Coll–Kokomo (IN)
Ivy Tech State Coll–Lafayette (IN)
Ivy Tech State Coll–North Central (IN)
Ivy Tech State Coll–Northeast (IN)
Ivy Tech State Coll–Northwest (IN)
Ivy Tech State Coll–Southcentral (IN)
Ivy Tech State Coll–Southeast (IN)
Ivy Tech State Coll–Southwest (IN)
Ivy Tech State Coll–Wabash Valley (IN)
Ivy Tech State Coll–Whitewater (IN)
James H. Faulkner State Comm Coll (AL)
Jamestown Business Coll (NY)
Jefferson Coll (MO)
Jefferson State Comm Coll (AL)
Joliet Jr Coll (IL)
J. Sargeant Reynolds Comm Coll (VA)
Kansas City Kansas Comm Coll (KS)
Kaplan Coll (IA)
Kent State U, Salem Campus (OH)
Kilgore Coll (TX)
Kingsborough Comm Coll of City U of NY (NY)
Kingwood Coll (TX)
Lake Michigan Coll (MI)
Lake Region State Coll (ND)
Lamar State Coll–Port Arthur (TX)
Lord Fairfax Comm Coll (VA)
Louisville Tech Inst (KY)
Luzerne County Comm Coll (PA)
Manatee Comm Coll (FL)
Massachusetts Bay Comm Coll (MA)
McIntosh Coll (NH)
Miami U–Middletown Campus (OH)
Mid-South Comm Coll (AR)
Minot State U–Bottineau Campus (ND)
Mitchell Tech Inst (SD)
Moberly Area Comm Coll (MO)
Montgomery Coll (MD)
Montgomery County Comm Coll (PA)
Mott Comm Coll (MI)
Mountain State Coll (WV)
Nassau Comm Coll (NY)
National Coll of Business & Technology, Salem (VA)
NEI Coll of Technology (MN)
New England Inst of Technology (RI)
New Hampshire Comm Tech Coll, Berlin/Laconia (NH)
New Hampshire Tech Inst (NH)
Northampton County Area Comm Coll (PA)
Northern Essex Comm Coll (MA)
Northern New Mexico Comm Coll (NM)
North Harris Coll (TX)
Northland Pioneer Coll (AZ)
Northwest Mississippi Comm Coll (MS)
Oakland Comm Coll (MI)
Ocean County Coll (NJ)
Ohio Business Coll (OH)
Orange County Comm Coll (NY)
Ouachita Tech Coll (AR)
Owensboro Comm Coll (KY)
Palo Verde Coll (CA)
Parkland Coll (IL)
Pellissippi State Tech Comm Coll (TN)
Pennsylvania Coll of Technology (PA)
Phoenix Coll (AZ)
Pima Comm Coll (AZ)
Pittsburgh Tech Inst (PA)
Platt Coll–Los Angeles, Inc (CA)
Prairie State Coll (IL)
Reedley Coll (CA)
Riverside Comm Coll (CA)
Robeson Comm Coll (NC)
Rockford Business Coll (IL)
Sampson Comm Coll (NC)
San Diego Mesa Coll (CA)
San Jacinto Coll North Campus (TX)
Santa Fe Comm Coll (NM)
Schenectady County Comm Coll (NY)
Scott Comm Coll (IA)
Shoreline Comm Coll (WA)
Sinclair Comm Coll (OH)
Skagit Valley Coll (WA)
Snead State Comm Coll (AL)
South Coll (NC)
Southeast Comm Coll, Milford Campus (NE)
South Hills School of Business & Technology, State College (PA)
South Puget Sound Comm Coll (WA)
Spartanburg Tech Coll (SC)
State U of NY Coll of Technology at Alfred (NY)
Sussex County Comm Coll (NJ)
Tallahassee Comm Coll (FL)
Terra State Comm Coll (OH)
Texas State Tech Coll–Harlingen (TX)
Texas State Tech Coll– Waco/ Marshall Campus (TX)
U of Alaska Southeast, Sitka Campus (AK)
Ventura Coll (CA)
Victor Valley Coll (CA)
Vista Comm Coll (CA)
Wake Tech Comm Coll (NC)
Waubonsee Comm Coll (IL)
Waycross Coll (GA)
Westchester Comm Coll (NY)
Western Nebraska Comm Coll (NE)
Western Nevada Comm Coll (NV)
Westmoreland County Comm Coll (PA)

COMPUTER/INFORMATION SCIENCES RELATED

Bunker Hill Comm Coll (MA)
Clark Coll (WA)
Edmonds Comm Coll (WA)
Harrisburg Area Comm Coll (PA)
Herkimer County Comm Coll (NY)
Indiana Business Coll, Columbus (IN)
Indiana Business Coll, Indianapolis (IN)
Indiana Business Coll, Lafayette (IN)
Indiana Business Coll, Muncie (IN)
Indiana Business Coll, Terre Haute (IN)
ITT Tech Inst (AL)
ITT Tech Inst, Tucson (AZ)
ITT Tech Inst (AR)
ITT Tech Inst, Anaheim (CA)
ITT Tech Inst, Hayward (CA)
ITT Tech Inst, Rancho Cordova (CA)
ITT Tech Inst, San Bernardino (CA)
ITT Tech Inst, San Diego (CA)
ITT Tech Inst, Santa Clara (CA)
ITT Tech Inst, Sylmar (CA)
ITT Tech Inst, Torrance (CA)
ITT Tech Inst, West Covina (CA)
ITT Tech Inst (CO)
ITT Tech Inst, Fort Lauderdale (FL)
ITT Tech Inst, Jacksonville (FL)
ITT Tech Inst, Maitland (FL)
ITT Tech Inst, Miami (FL)
ITT Tech Inst, Tampa (FL)
ITT Tech Inst (ID)
ITT Tech Inst, Burr Ridge (IL)
ITT Tech Inst, Matteson (IL)
ITT Tech Inst, Mount Prospect (IL)
ITT Tech Inst, Fort Wayne (IN)
ITT Tech Inst, Indianapolis (IN)
ITT Tech Inst, Newburgh (IN)
ITT Tech Inst (KY)
ITT Tech Inst (LA)
ITT Tech Inst, Norwood (MA)
ITT Tech Inst, Woburn (MA)
ITT Tech Inst, Grand Rapids (MI)
ITT Tech Inst, Troy (MI)
ITT Tech Inst, Arnold (MO)
ITT Tech Inst, Earth City (MO)
ITT Tech Inst (NE)
ITT Tech Inst (NV)
ITT Tech Inst (NM)
ITT Tech Inst, Albany (NY)
ITT Tech Inst, Getzville (NY)
ITT Tech Inst, Liverpool (NY)
ITT Tech Inst, Dayton (OH)
ITT Tech Inst, Norwood (OH)
ITT Tech Inst, Strongsville (OH)
ITT Tech Inst, Youngstown (OH)
ITT Tech Inst (OR)
ITT Tech Inst, Bensalem (PA)
ITT Tech Inst, Mechanicsburg (PA)
ITT Tech Inst, Monroeville (PA)
ITT Tech Inst, Pittsburgh (PA)
ITT Tech Inst (SC)
ITT Tech Inst, Knoxville (TN)
ITT Tech Inst, Memphis (TN)
ITT Tech Inst, Nashville (TN)
ITT Tech Inst, Arlington (TX)
ITT Tech Inst, Austin (TX)
ITT Tech Inst, Houston (TX)
ITT Tech Inst, Houston (TX)
ITT Tech Inst, Houston (TX)
ITT Tech Inst, Richardson (TX)
ITT Tech Inst, San Antonio (TX)
ITT Tech Inst (UT)
ITT Tech Inst, Norfolk (VA)
ITT Tech Inst, Richmond (VA)
ITT Tech Inst, Bothell (WA)
ITT Tech Inst, Seattle (WA)
ITT Tech Inst, Spokane (WA)
ITT Tech Inst, Green Bay (WI)
ITT Tech Inst, Greenfield (WI)
Mott Comm Coll (MI)
Pennsylvania Coll of Technology (PA)
Southern Arkansas U Tech (AR)
Springfield Tech Comm Coll (MA)
Williston State Coll (ND)

COMPUTER/INFORMATION SYSTEMS SECURITY

American River Coll (CA)
Dakota County Tech Coll (MN)
Daymar Coll (KY)
Florida Comm Coll at Jacksonville (FL)
Florida National Coll (FL)
Island Drafting and Tech Inst (NY)
Laurel Business Inst (PA)
Los Angeles City Coll (CA)
Riverland Comm Coll (MN)
Seminole Comm Coll (FL)
Southwestern Coll (CA)
Tompkins Cortland Comm Coll (NY)
Triton Coll (IL)
Tulsa Comm Coll (OK)
Vista Comm Coll (CA)
York Tech Inst (PA)

COMPUTER/INFORMATION TECHNOLOGY SERVICES ADMINISTRATION AND MANAGEMENT RELATED

AIBT International Inst of the Americas (AZ)
Alpena Comm Coll (MI)
Andover Coll (ME)
Anoka-Hennepin Tech Coll (MN)
Arapahoe Comm Coll (CO)
Atlanta Metropolitan Coll (GA)
Barton County Comm Coll (KS)
Berkshire Comm Coll (MA)
Bowling Green State U-Firelands Coll (OH)
Brevard Comm Coll (FL)
Bristol Comm Coll (MA)
Brunswick Comm Coll (NC)
Bucks County Comm Coll (PA)
Cambria County Area Comm Coll (PA)
Camden County Coll (NJ)
Cayuga County Comm Coll (NY)
Central Carolina Comm Coll (NC)
Clinton Comm Coll (NY)
Coastal Carolina Comm Coll (NC)
The Comm Coll of Baltimore County–Catonsville Campus (MD)
Corning Comm Coll (NY)
Cypress Coll (CA)
Daymar Coll (KY)
Daytona Beach Comm Coll (FL)
Diablo Valley Coll (CA)
Dyersburg State Comm Coll (TN)
Eastern Shore Comm Coll (VA)
Eastfield Coll (TX)
Elaine P. Nunez Comm Coll (LA)
Flathead Valley Comm Coll (MT)
Florida Comm Coll at Jacksonville (FL)
Georgia Perimeter Coll (GA)
Gogebic Comm Coll (MI)
Guilford Tech Comm Coll (NC)
Heald Coll, Schools of Business and Technology, Hayward (CA)
Henderson Comm Coll (KY)
Hesston Coll (KS)
Horry-Georgetown Tech Coll (SC)
Howard Comm Coll (MD)
Kansas City Kansas Comm Coll (KS)
Kennebec Valley Tech Coll (ME)
Laurel Business Inst (PA)
Los Angeles City Coll (CA)
Mesabi Range Comm and Tech Coll (MN)
Middle Georgia Coll (GA)
Midland Coll (TX)
Milwaukee Area Tech Coll (WI)
Modesto Jr Coll (CA)
Naugatuck Valley Comm Coll (CT)
NEI Coll of Technology (MN)
North Central Texas Coll (TX)
Onondaga Comm Coll (NY)
Owensboro Comm Coll (KY)
Parkland Coll (IL)
Pittsburgh Tech Inst (PA)
Platt Coll (CO)
Ridgewater Coll (MN)
Rockland Comm Coll (NY)
San Antonio Coll (TX)
Sandhills Comm Coll (NC)
Schenectady County Comm Coll (NY)
Seminole Comm Coll (FL)
Sinclair Comm Coll (OH)
Southeast Comm Coll (KY)
Southeast Tech Inst (SD)
Stanly Comm Coll (NC)
Stark State Coll of Technology (OH)
Texas State Tech Coll–Harlingen (TX)
Tompkins Cortland Comm Coll (NY)
Trident Tech Coll (SC)
Trumbull Business Coll (OH)
Tulsa Comm Coll (OK)
Vincennes U (IN)
The Westchester Business Inst (NY)
York Tech Coll (SC)
York Tech Inst (PA)

COMPUTER INSTALLATION/ REPAIR

Chaparral Coll (AZ)
Coll of DuPage (IL)
Daymar Coll (KY)
Delgado Comm Coll (LA)
Harrisburg Area Comm Coll (PA)
Herkimer County Comm Coll (NY)
Hibbing Comm Coll (MN)
Kennebec Valley Tech Coll (ME)
Louisville Tech Inst (KY)
Modesto Jr Coll (CA)
Montcalm Comm Coll (MI)
Northampton County Area Comm Coll (PA)
Ridgewater Coll (MN)
Riverland Comm Coll (MN)
State U of NY Coll of Technology at Alfred (NY)
Western Dakota Tech Inst (SD)

COMPUTER MAINTENANCE TECHNOLOGY

Bates Tech Coll (WA)
Beckfield Coll (KY)
Brazosport Coll (TX)
Cape Fear Comm Coll (NC)
Central Wyoming Coll (WY)
Charter Coll (AK)
Clackamas Comm Coll (OR)
Comm Coll of Allegheny County (PA)
Corning Comm Coll (NY)
Eastern Maine Tech Coll (ME)
Edmonds Comm Coll (WA)
Electronic Computer Programming Coll (TN)
Erie Comm Coll, South Campus (NY)
Island Drafting and Tech Inst (NY)
Lamar State Coll–Port Arthur (TX)
Lorain County Comm Coll (OH)
Louisville Tech Inst (KY)
Luzerne County Comm Coll (PA)
Madisonville Comm Coll (KY)
Mitchell Tech Inst (SD)
Montgomery Coll (MD)
Montgomery County Comm Coll (PA)
Mount Wachusett Comm Coll (MA)
MTI Coll of Business and Technology, Houston (TX)
New England Inst of Technology (RI)
Pennsylvania Coll of Technology (PA)
Pima Comm Coll (AZ)
Quinsigamond Comm Coll (MA)
Schoolcraft Coll (MI)
Skagit Valley Coll (WA)
Southeast Tech Inst (SD)
Southern Arkansas U Tech (AR)
Stanly Comm Coll (NC)
Texas State Tech Coll–Harlingen (TX)

Texas State Tech Coll– Waco/ Marshall Campus (TX)
Walla Walla Comm Coll (WA)

COMPUTER MANAGEMENT
AIB Coll of Business (IA)
Andover Coll (ME)
Anne Arundel Comm Coll (MD)
Berkeley Coll (NJ)
Cayuga County Comm Coll (NY)
Central Georgia Tech Coll (GA)
The Comm Coll of Baltimore County–Catonsville Campus (MD)
Darton Coll (GA)
De Anza Coll (CA)
Delta Coll (MI)
DuBois Business Coll (PA)
ECPI Coll of Technology, Newport News (VA)
ECPI Coll of Technology, Virginia Beach (VA)
ECPI Tech Coll, Richmond (VA)
Heald Coll, Schools of Business and Technology, Hayward (CA)
Herzing Coll (GA)
Hesser Coll (NH)
Kennebec Valley Tech Coll (ME)
Lakeshore Tech Coll (WI)
Lamar Comm Coll (CO)
Lansing Comm Coll (MI)
Laurel Business Inst (PA)
Lewis Coll of Business (MI)
Lincoln Coll, Normal (IL)
McIntosh Coll (NH)
Miles Comm Coll (MT)
Mineral Area Coll (MO)
Montana State U Coll of Tech-Great Falls (MT)
North Central Texas Coll (TX)
Otero Jr Coll (CO)
Prince George's Comm Coll (MD)
Quincy Coll (MA)
Ridgewater Coll (MN)
Shasta Coll (CA)
South Coll (TN)
Southern Maine Tech Coll (ME)
Southwest Wisconsin Tech Coll (WI)
Tri-County Comm Coll (NC)
Vermilion Comm Coll (MN)
Villa Maria Coll of Buffalo (NY)

COMPUTER PROGRAMMING
Abraham Baldwin Ag Coll (GA)
Academy Coll (MN)
Alamance Comm Coll (NC)
Allegany Coll of Maryland (MD)
Alvin Comm Coll (TX)
Amarillo Coll (TX)
American River Coll (CA)
Ancilla Coll (IN)
Andover Coll (ME)
Angelina Coll (TX)
Anne Arundel Comm Coll (MD)
Antelope Valley Coll (CA)
Arapahoe Comm Coll (CO)
Asheville-Buncombe Tech Comm Coll (NC)
Athens Tech Coll (GA)
Atlanta Metropolitan Coll (GA)
Atlantic Cape Comm Coll (NJ)
Augusta Tech Coll (GA)
Austin Comm Coll (TX)
Bates Tech Coll (WA)
Beaufort County Comm Coll (NC)
Bellevue Comm Coll (WA)
Belmont Tech Coll (OH)
Bergen Comm Coll (NJ)
Berks Tech Inst (PA)
Bladen Comm Coll (NC)
Blair Coll (CO)
Blue Ridge Comm Coll (NC)
Borough of Manhattan Comm Coll of City U of NY (NY)
Bowling Green State U-Firelands Coll (OH)
Bradford School (OH)
Brazosport Coll (TX)
Brevard Comm Coll (FL)
Bristol Comm Coll (MA)
Brookdale Comm Coll (NJ)
Brown Coll (MN)
Brunswick Comm Coll (NC)
Bryant & Stratton Business Inst, Buffalo (NY)
Bryant & Stratton Business Inst, Rochester (NY)
Bryant & Stratton Business Inst, Rochester (NY)
Bucks County Comm Coll (PA)
Bunker Hill Comm Coll (MA)
Burlington County Coll (NJ)
Business Inst of Pennsylvania (PA)
Butler County Comm Coll (PA)
Cambria County Area Comm Coll (PA)
Camden County Coll (NJ)
Cañada Coll (CA)
Casper Coll (WY)
Catawba Valley Comm Coll (NC)
Cayuga County Comm Coll (NY)
Cecil Comm Coll (MD)
Cedar Valley Coll (TX)
Central Alabama Comm Coll (AL)
Central Carolina Comm Coll (NC)
Central Florida Comm Coll (FL)
Central Ohio Tech Coll (OH)
Central Piedmont Comm Coll (NC)
Central Texas Coll (TX)
Cerritos Coll (CA)
Certified Careers Inst, Salt Lake City (UT)
Chattahoochee Tech Coll (GA)
Chattanooga State Tech Comm Coll (TN)
Chemeketa Comm Coll (OR)
Chesapeake Coll (MD)
CHI Inst (PA)
Cisco Jr Coll (TX)
City Coll of San Francisco (CA)
Clark Coll (WA)
Clover Park Tech Coll (WA)
Cochise Coll, Douglas (AZ)
Coffeyville Comm Coll (KS)
Coll of Lake County (IL)
Coll of Southern Maryland (MD)
Coll of the Redwoods (CA)
Coll of the Sequoias (CA)
Coll of the Siskiyous (CA)
Columbus State Comm Coll (OH)
The Comm Coll of Baltimore County–Catonsville Campus (MD)
Comm Coll of Beaver County (PA)
Comm Coll of Denver (CO)
Comm Coll of Rhode Island (RI)
Comm Coll of Southern Nevada (NV)
Compton Comm Coll (CA)
Corning Comm Coll (NY)
Danville Area Comm Coll (IL)
Danville Comm Coll (VA)
Darton Coll (GA)
Daytona Beach Comm Coll (FL)
De Anza Coll (CA)
Delaware Tech & Comm Coll, Jack F Owens Cmps (DE)
Delaware Tech & Comm Coll, Terry Cmps (DE)
Del Mar Coll (TX)
Delta Coll (MI)
Des Moines Area Comm Coll (IA)
Dodge City Comm Coll (KS)
Dominion Coll, Roanoke (VA)
Douglas MacArthur State Tech Coll (AL)
Draughons Jr Coll, Clarksville (TN)
Draughons Jr Coll, Nashville (TN)
Duff's Business Inst (PA)
Durham Tech Comm Coll (NC)
East Central Coll (MO)
Eastfield Coll (TX)
East Mississippi Comm Coll (MS)
ECPI Coll of Technology, Virginia Beach (VA)
ECPI Tech Coll, Richmond (VA)
Edgecombe Comm Coll (NC)
Edison Comm Coll (FL)
Edison State Comm Coll (OH)
Education America, Remington Coll, Lafayette Campus (LA)
El Centro Coll (TX)
Essex County Coll (NJ)
Fayetteville Tech Comm Coll (NC)
Fiorello H LaGuardia Comm Coll of City U of NY (NY)
Florida Comm Coll at Jacksonville (FL)
Florida Computer & Business School (FL)
Florida National Coll (FL)
Florida Tech Coll, Jacksonville (FL)
Florida Tech Coll, Orlando (FL)
Floyd Coll (GA)
Garden City Comm Coll (KS)
Gaston Coll (NC)
Gavilan Coll (CA)
George Corley Wallace State Comm Coll (AL)
Georgia Perimeter Coll (GA)
Grand Rapids Comm Coll (MI)
Greenfield Comm Coll (MA)
Greenville Tech Coll (SC)
Griffin Tech Coll (GA)
Guilford Tech Comm Coll (NC)
Gulf Coast Comm Coll (FL)
Gwinnett Tech Coll (GA)
Hamilton Coll (IA)
Heartland Comm Coll (IL)
Helena Coll of Tech of The U of Montana (MT)
Hennepin Tech Coll (MN)
Herkimer County Comm Coll (NY)
Herzing Coll (AL)
Hesser Coll (NH)
Hickey Coll (MO)
Highline Comm Coll (WA)
Hill Coll of the Hill Jr College District (TX)
Hillsborough Comm Coll (FL)
Hinds Comm Coll (MS)
Howard Coll (TX)
Huntington Jr Coll of Business (WV)
Illinois Eastern Comm Colls, Lincoln Trail Coll (IL)
Indiana Business Coll, Evansville (IN)
Indiana Business Coll, Indianapolis (IN)
Indian Hills Comm Coll (IA)
Indian River Comm Coll (FL)
International Business Coll, Fort Wayne (IN)
Iowa Lakes Comm Coll (IA)
Iowa Western Comm Coll (IA)
Isothermal Comm Coll (NC)
ITT Tech Inst (AL)
ITT Tech Inst, Phoenix (AZ)
ITT Tech Inst, Tucson (AZ)
ITT Tech Inst (AR)
ITT Tech Inst, Anaheim (CA)
ITT Tech Inst, Hayward (CA)
ITT Tech Inst, Oxnard (CA)
ITT Tech Inst, Rancho Cordova (CA)
ITT Tech Inst, San Bernardino (CA)
ITT Tech Inst, San Diego (CA)
ITT Tech Inst, Santa Clara (CA)
ITT Tech Inst, Sylmar (CA)
ITT Tech Inst, Torrance (CA)
ITT Tech Inst, West Covina (CA)
ITT Tech Inst (CO)
ITT Tech Inst, Fort Lauderdale (FL)
ITT Tech Inst, Jacksonville (FL)
ITT Tech Inst, Maitland (FL)
ITT Tech Inst, Miami (FL)
ITT Tech Inst, Tampa (FL)
ITT Tech Inst (ID)
ITT Tech Inst, Burr Ridge (IL)
ITT Tech Inst, Matteson (IL)
ITT Tech Inst, Fort Wayne (IN)
ITT Tech Inst, Indianapolis (IN)
ITT Tech Inst, Newburgh (IN)
ITT Tech Inst (KY)
ITT Tech Inst (LA)
ITT Tech Inst, Norwood (MA)
ITT Tech Inst, Woburn (MA)
ITT Tech Inst, Grand Rapids (MI)
ITT Tech Inst, Troy (MI)
ITT Tech Inst, Arnold (MO)
ITT Tech Inst, Earth City (MO)
ITT Tech Inst (NE)
ITT Tech Inst (NV)
ITT Tech Inst (NM)
ITT Tech Inst, Albany (NY)
ITT Tech Inst, Getzville (NY)
ITT Tech Inst, Liverpool (NY)
ITT Tech Inst, Dayton (OH)
ITT Tech Inst, Norwood (OH)
ITT Tech Inst, Strongsville (OH)
ITT Tech Inst, Youngstown (OH)
ITT Tech Inst (OR)
ITT Tech Inst (SC)
ITT Tech Inst, Knoxville (TN)
ITT Tech Inst, Memphis (TN)
ITT Tech Inst, Nashville (TN)
ITT Tech Inst, Arlington (TX)
ITT Tech Inst, Austin (TX)
ITT Tech Inst, Houston (TX)
ITT Tech Inst, Houston (TX)
ITT Tech Inst, Houston (TX)
ITT Tech Inst, Richardson (TX)
ITT Tech Inst, San Antonio (TX)
ITT Tech Inst (UT)
ITT Tech Inst, Norfolk (VA)
ITT Tech Inst, Richmond (VA)
ITT Tech Inst, Bothell (WA)
ITT Tech Inst, Seattle (WA)
ITT Tech Inst, Spokane (WA)
ITT Tech Inst, Green Bay (WI)
ITT Tech Inst, Greenfield (WI)
Jackson Comm Coll (MI)
Jefferson Coll (MO)
Jefferson Comm Coll (KY)
Johnston Comm Coll (NC)
Joliet Jr Coll (IL)
J. Sargeant Reynolds Comm Coll (VA)
Kalamazoo Valley Comm Coll (MI)
Kaplan Coll (IA)
Kellogg Comm Coll (MI)
Kent State U, Geauga Campus (OH)
Keystone Coll (PA)
Kilgore Coll (TX)
Kirkwood Comm Coll (IA)
Lake Area Tech Inst (SD)
Lake City Comm Coll (FL)
Lakeshore Tech Coll (WI)
Lamar Comm Coll (CO)
Lane Comm Coll (OR)
Lansing Comm Coll (MI)
Laredo Comm Coll (TX)
Lenoir Comm Coll (NC)
Lewis and Clark Comm Coll (IL)
Lewis Coll of Business (MI)
Lima Tech Coll (OH)
Lincoln Coll, Lincoln (IL)
Lincoln Coll, Normal (IL)
Lincoln Land Comm Coll (IL)
Lincoln School of Commerce (NE)
Linn-Benton Comm Coll (OR)
Long Beach City Coll (CA)
Longview Comm Coll (MO)
Lorain County Comm Coll (OH)
Lord Fairfax Comm Coll (VA)
Los Angeles City Coll (CA)
Los Angeles Mission Coll (CA)
Los Angeles Pierce Coll (CA)
Louisiana State U at Eunice (LA)
Lower Columbia Coll (WA)
Manatee Comm Coll (FL)
Maple Woods Comm Coll (MO)
Mayland Comm Coll (NC)
Metropolitan Comm Coll (NE)
Miami-Dade Comm Coll (FL)
Middlesex County Coll (NJ)
Mid-Plains Comm Coll Area (NE)
Mineral Area Coll (MO)
Minneapolis Comm and Tech Coll (MN)
Minnesota State Coll–Southeast Tech (MN)
Mohawk Valley Comm Coll (NY)
Montgomery County Comm Coll (PA)
Moraine Park Tech Coll (WI)
Mountain View Coll (TX)
Naugatuck Valley Comm Coll (CT)
Navarro Coll (TX)
Newbury Coll (MA)
New Mexico Military Inst (NM)
North Central Michigan Coll (MI)
North Central Texas Coll (TX)
Northeast Comm Coll (NE)
Northeastern Tech Coll (SC)
Northeast State Tech Comm Coll (TN)
Northern Essex Comm Coll (MA)
Northern Maine Tech Coll (ME)
North Idaho Coll (ID)
North Seattle Comm Coll (WA)
North Shore Comm Coll (MA)
NorthWest Arkansas Comm Coll (AR)
Northwestern Business Coll (IL)
Northwestern Connecticut Comm-Tech Coll (CT)
Northwest Mississippi Comm Coll (MS)
Northwest-Shoals Comm Coll (AL)
Northwest State Comm Coll (OH)
Oakton Comm Coll (IL)
Ocean County Coll (NJ)
Okaloosa-Walton Comm Coll (FL)
Oklahoma State U, Oklahoma City (OK)
Orange Coast Coll (CA)
Orange County Comm Coll (NY)
Pace Inst (PA)
Palm Beach Comm Coll (FL)
Parkland Coll (IL)
Pasadena City Coll (CA)
Patrick Henry Comm Coll (VA)
Pellissippi State Tech Comm Coll (TN)
Piedmont Tech Coll (SC)
Piedmont Virginia Comm Coll (VA)
Pierce Coll (WA)
Portland Comm Coll (OR)
Prince George's Comm Coll (MD)
Quincy Coll (MA)
Quinsigamond Comm Coll (MA)
Raritan Valley Comm Coll (NJ)
Reading Area Comm Coll (PA)
Red Rocks Comm Coll (CO)
RETS Tech Center (OH)
Riverside Comm Coll (CA)
Roanoke-Chowan Comm Coll (NC)
Rochester Business Inst (NY)
Rockland Comm Coll (NY)
St. Cloud Tech Coll (MN)
St. Louis Comm Coll at Florissant Valley (MO)
St. Paul Tech Coll (MN)
St. Petersburg Coll (FL)
Sampson Comm Coll (NC)
San Antonio Coll (TX)
Sandhills Comm Coll (NC)
Sanford-Brown Coll, Hazelwood (MO)
San Jacinto Coll Central Campus (TX)
San Joaquin Delta Coll (CA)
Santa Fe Comm Coll (FL)
Santa Monica Coll (CA)
Savannah Tech Coll (GA)
Schoolcraft Coll (MI)
Schuylkill Inst of Business and Technology (PA)
Seminole Comm Coll (FL)
Southeast Comm Coll, Milford Campus (NE)
Southeast Tech Inst (SD)
Southern Arkansas U Tech (AR)
South Plains Coll (TX)
South Puget Sound Comm Coll (WA)
Southwestern Coll (CA)
Southwestern Comm Coll (IA)
Southwestern Michigan Coll (MI)
Southwest Wisconsin Tech Coll (WI)
Spokane Comm Coll (WA)
Stark State Coll of Technology (OH)
State U of NY Coll of A&T at Morrisville (NY)
Stratford U (VA)
Suffolk County Comm Coll (NY)
Surry Comm Coll (NC)
Tallahassee Comm Coll (FL)
Tarrant County Coll District (TX)
Temple Coll (TX)
Texarkana Coll (TX)
Texas State Tech Coll–Harlingen (TX)
Texas State Tech Coll– Waco/ Marshall Campus (TX)
Texas State Tech Coll (TX)
Three Rivers Comm Coll (CT)
Tidewater Comm Coll (VA)
Tomball Coll (TX)
Tri-County Tech Coll (SC)
Truckee Meadows Comm Coll (NV)
U of New Mexico–Los Alamos Branch (NM)
U of Northwestern Ohio (OH)
Vatterott Coll (MO)
Victoria Coll (TX)
Vincennes U (IN)
Vincennes U Jasper Campus (IN)
Wake Tech Comm Coll (NC)
Wallace State Comm Coll (AL)
Weatherford Coll (TX)
The Westchester Business Inst (NY)
Western Nevada Comm Coll (NV)
Western Piedmont Comm Coll (NC)
Western Wisconsin Tech Coll (WI)
West Virginia Northern Comm Coll (WV)
Westwood Coll of Technology–Chicago O'Hare (IL)
Westwood Coll of Technology–Chicago River Oaks (IL)
Westwood Coll of Technology–Denver North (CO)
Westwood Coll of Technology–Denver South (CO)

Westwood Coll of Technology–Los Angeles (CA)
Wilson Tech Comm Coll (NC)

COMPUTER PROGRAMMING RELATED

Academy of Medical Arts and Business (PA)
American River Coll (CA)
Anoka-Hennepin Tech Coll (MN)
Arapahoe Comm Coll (CO)
Austin Comm Coll (TX)
Barton County Comm Coll (KS)
Berkshire Comm Coll (MA)
Berks Tech Inst (PA)
Blue Ridge Comm Coll (NC)
Bradford School (OH)
Brazosport Coll (TX)
The Brown Mackie Coll–Olathe Campus (KS)
Brunswick Comm Coll (NC)
Bucks County Comm Coll (PA)
Cambria County Area Comm Coll (PA)
Camden County Coll (NJ)
Centralia Coll (WA)
Central Pennsylvania Coll (PA)
Central Texas Coll (TX)
Clark Coll (WA)
Coastal Bend Coll (TX)
Coll of the Desert (CA)
Coll of the Siskiyous (CA)
The Comm Coll of Baltimore County–Catonsville Campus (MD)
Corning Comm Coll (NY)
Cypress Coll (CA)
Dakota County Tech Coll (MN)
Daymar Coll (KY)
Delaware County Comm Coll (PA)
Del Mar Coll (TX)
Delta Coll (MI)
Diablo Valley Coll (CA)
Donnelly Coll (KS)
Durham Tech Comm Coll (NC)
Eastfield Coll (TX)
Education America, Remington Coll, Lafayette Campus (LA)
Education America, Southeast Coll of Technology, New Orleans Campus (LA)
Erie Business Center, Main (PA)
Fayetteville Tech Comm Coll (NC)
Fiorello H LaGuardia Comm Coll of City U of NY (NY)
Florida Comm Coll at Jacksonville (FL)
Florida National Coll (FL)
Glendale Comm Coll (CA)
Henderson Comm Coll (KY)
Herkimer County Comm Coll (NY)
Hill Coll of the Hill Jr College District (TX)
Hinds Comm Coll (MS)
Iowa Western Comm Coll (IA)
J. Sargeant Reynolds Comm Coll (VA)
Kansas City Kansas Comm Coll (KS)
Kennebec Valley Tech Coll (ME)
Kishwaukee Coll (IL)
Lake Area Tech Inst (SD)
Lakeland Comm Coll (OH)
Lakeshore Tech Coll (WI)
Laredo Comm Coll (TX)
Lincoln School of Commerce (NE)
Lorain County Comm Coll (OH)
Los Angeles City Coll (CA)
Luzerne County Comm Coll (PA)
Manatee Comm Coll (FL)
Massasoit Comm Coll (MA)
Mesabi Range Comm and Tech Coll (MN)
Midland Coll (TX)
Mid-State Tech Coll (WI)
Milwaukee Area Tech Coll (WI)
Mississippi Gulf Coast Comm Coll (MS)
North Central Texas Coll (TX)
Northeast State Tech Comm Coll (TN)
Northern Essex Comm Coll (MA)
Norwalk Comm Coll (CT)
Olympic Coll (WA)
Orangeburg-Calhoun Tech Coll (SC)
Pasco-Hernando Comm Coll (FL)
Patrick Henry Comm Coll (VA)
Pittsburgh Tech Inst (PA)
Riverside Comm Coll (CA)
Rockland Comm Coll (NY)
Saint Charles Comm Coll (MO)
St. Cloud Tech Coll (MN)
San Antonio Coll (TX)
San Diego Mesa Coll (CA)
Santa Ana Coll (CA)
Schenectady County Comm Coll (NY)
Seminole Comm Coll (FL)
Sinclair Comm Coll (OH)
Southeast Tech Inst (SD)
Southwest Mississippi Comm Coll (MS)
Stanly Comm Coll (NC)
Stark State Coll of Technology (OH)
Stratford U (VA)
Surry Comm Coll (NC)
Texas State Tech Coll–Harlingen (TX)
Tompkins Cortland Comm Coll (NY)
Triton Coll (IL)
Truckee Meadows Comm Coll (NV)
Tulsa Comm Coll (OK)
Tyler Jr Coll (TX)
U of Kentucky, Lexington Comm Coll (KY)
Vincennes U (IN)
Vincennes U Jasper Campus (IN)
The Westchester Business Inst (NY)

COMPUTER PROGRAMMING (SPECIFIC APPLICATIONS)

Academy of Medical Arts and Business (PA)
AIB Coll of Business (IA)
American River Coll (CA)
Anoka-Hennepin Tech Coll (MN)
Arapahoe Comm Coll (CO)
Berkshire Comm Coll (MA)
Bladen Comm Coll (NC)
Brazosport Coll (TX)
Brevard Comm Coll (FL)
Bristol Comm Coll (MA)
Broome Comm Coll (NY)
Bucks County Comm Coll (PA)
Caldwell Comm Coll and Tech Inst (NC)
Cambria County Area Comm Coll (PA)
Camden County Coll (NJ)
Catawba Valley Comm Coll (NC)
Cedar Valley Coll (TX)
Central Carolina Comm Coll (NC)
Central Comm Coll–Columbus Campus (NE)
Central Comm Coll–Grand Island Campus (NE)
Central Comm Coll–Hastings Campus (NE)
Central Texas Coll (TX)
Chabot Coll (CA)
Cleveland Comm Coll (NC)
Coastal Bend Coll (TX)
Coll of the Siskiyous (CA)
The Comm Coll of Baltimore County–Catonsville Campus (MD)
Cypress Coll (CA)
Dakota County Tech Coll (MN)
Daymar Coll (KY)
Daytona Beach Comm Coll (FL)
Del Mar Coll (TX)
Des Moines Area Comm Coll (IA)
Diablo Valley Coll (CA)
Edison Comm Coll (FL)
Fayetteville Tech Comm Coll (NC)
Fiorello H LaGuardia Comm Coll of City U of NY (NY)
Florida Comm Coll at Jacksonville (FL)
Florida Computer & Business School (FL)
Florida National Coll (FL)
GateWay Comm Coll (AZ)
Glendale Comm Coll (CA)
Gulf Coast Comm Coll (FL)
Heartland Comm Coll (IL)
Henderson Comm Coll (KY)
Highland Comm Coll (IL)
Horry-Georgetown Tech Coll (SC)
Inver Hills Comm Coll (MN)
Iowa Western Comm Coll (IA)
Jackson Comm Coll (MI)
Jamestown Comm Coll (NY)
Joliet Jr Coll (IL)
Kansas City Kansas Comm Coll (KS)
Kellogg Comm Coll (MI)
Lake Area Tech Inst (SD)
Lake City Comm Coll (FL)
Lake Land Coll (IL)
Lakeland Comm Coll (OH)
Lorain County Comm Coll (OH)
Los Angeles City Coll (CA)
McCann School of Business (PA)
Mesabi Range Comm and Tech Coll (MN)
Midland Coll (TX)
Mid-State Tech Coll (WI)
Milwaukee Area Tech Coll (WI)
Mohave Comm Coll (AZ)
Mohawk Valley Comm Coll (NY)
Monroe County Comm Coll (MI)
Muskingum Area Tech Coll (OH)
Naugatuck Valley Comm Coll (CT)
NEI Coll of Technology (MN)
New Hampshire Tech Inst (NH)
North Central Texas Coll (TX)
Northeast Comm Coll (NE)
Northern Essex Comm Coll (MA)
Northwestern Business Coll (IL)
Oakton Comm Coll (IL)
Okaloosa-Walton Comm Coll (FL)
Onondaga Comm Coll (NY)
Orange Coast Coll (CA)
Palm Beach Comm Coll (FL)
Parkland Coll (IL)
Pasco-Hernando Comm Coll (FL)
Pittsburgh Tech Inst (PA)
Professional Careers Inst (IN)
Richland Comm Coll (IL)
Ridgewater Coll (MN)
Riverland Comm Coll (MN)
Rockland Comm Coll (NY)
Saint Charles Comm Coll (MO)
San Antonio Coll (TX)
Sandhills Comm Coll (NC)
Sanford-Brown Coll, Fenton (MO)
San Jacinto Coll North Campus (TX)
Santa Monica Coll (CA)
Seminole Comm Coll (FL)
Sheridan Coll (WY)
Sinclair Comm Coll (OH)
Southeast Tech Inst (SD)
Southern West Virginia Comm and Tech Coll (WV)
Stanly Comm Coll (NC)
Stark State Coll of Technology (OH)
State Fair Comm Coll (MO)
Sullivan County Comm Coll (NY)
Tacoma Comm Coll (WA)
Tallahassee Comm Coll (FL)
Texas State Tech Coll–Harlingen (TX)
Trident Tech Coll (SC)
Tulsa Comm Coll (OK)
Vincennes U (IN)
Wake Tech Comm Coll (NC)
West Central Tech Coll (GA)
The Westchester Business Inst (NY)
Western Wyoming Comm Coll (WY)

COMPUTER PROGRAMMING, VENDOR/PRODUCT CERTIFICATION

Academy of Medical Arts and Business (PA)
American River Coll (CA)
Arkansas State U–Beebe (AR)
Central Texas Coll (TX)
Coastal Bend Coll (TX)
The Comm Coll of Baltimore County–Catonsville Campus (MD)
Dakota County Tech Coll (MN)
Daymar Coll (KY)
Del Mar Coll (TX)
Diablo Valley Coll (CA)
Fiorello H LaGuardia Comm Coll of City U of NY (NY)
Florida Comm Coll at Jacksonville (FL)
GateWay Comm Coll (AZ)
Guam Comm Coll (GU)
Heald Coll, Schools of Business and Technology, Hayward (CA)
Heartland Comm Coll (IL)
Henderson Comm Coll (KY)
Inver Hills Comm Coll (MN)
Lake City Comm Coll (FL)
Lorain County Comm Coll (OH)
Los Angeles City Coll (CA)
Louisville Tech Inst (KY)
Midland Coll (TX)
Milwaukee Area Tech Coll (WI)
North Central Texas Coll (TX)
Parkland Coll (IL)
Peninsula Coll (WA)
Riverland Comm Coll (MN)
San Antonio Coll (TX)
Sanford-Brown Coll, Fenton (MO)
Seminole Comm Coll (FL)
Sinclair Comm Coll (OH)
Southeast Tech Inst (SD)
Stark State Coll of Technology (OH)
Texas State Tech Coll–Harlingen (TX)
Thaddeus Stevens Coll of Technology (PA)
Tulsa Comm Coll (OK)
Vincennes U (IN)
The Westchester Business Inst (NY)

COMPUTER SCIENCE

Abraham Baldwin Ag Coll (GA)
Adirondack Comm Coll (NY)
Allan Hancock Coll (CA)
Allegany Coll of Maryland (MD)
Allen County Comm Coll (KS)
Amarillo Coll (TX)
Andover Coll (ME)
Angelina Coll (TX)
Anne Arundel Comm Coll (MD)
Arapahoe Comm Coll (CO)
Arizona Western Coll (AZ)
Asnuntuck Comm Coll (CT)
Atlanta Metropolitan Coll (GA)
Austin Comm Coll (TX)
Bacone Coll (OK)
Bakersfield Coll (CA)
Baltimore City Comm Coll (MD)
Barstow Coll (CA)
Barton County Comm Coll (KS)
Benjamin Franklin Inst of Technology (MA)
Bergen Comm Coll (NJ)
Berkshire Comm Coll (MA)
Bessemer State Tech Coll (AL)
Black Hawk Coll, Moline (IL)
Blair Coll (CO)
Blinn Coll (TX)
Blue River Comm Coll (MO)
Bronx Comm Coll of City U of NY (NY)
Broome Comm Coll (NY)
Bucks County Comm Coll (PA)
Bunker Hill Comm Coll (MA)
Burlington County Coll (NJ)
Cañada Coll (CA)
Cape Cod Comm Coll (MA)
Career Colls of Chicago (IL)
Casper Coll (WY)
Catawba Valley Comm Coll (NC)
Cayuga County Comm Coll (NY)
Central Alabama Comm Coll (AL)
Central Arizona Coll (AZ)
Central Maine Tech Coll (ME)
Central Oregon Comm Coll (OR)
Central Piedmont Comm Coll (NC)
Central Wyoming Coll (WY)
Cerritos Coll (CA)
Cerro Coso Comm Coll (CA)
Certified Careers Inst, Salt Lake City (UT)
Chabot Coll (CA)
Charter Coll (AK)
Chattanooga State Tech Comm Coll (TN)
Chemeketa Comm Coll (OR)
Chesapeake Coll (MD)
Chipola Jr Coll (FL)
Cisco Jr Coll (TX)
Citrus Coll (CA)
City Coll of San Francisco (CA)
Coahoma Comm Coll (MS)
Coastal Bend Coll (TX)
Coastal Georgia Comm Coll (GA)
Cochise Coll, Douglas (AZ)
Coffeyville Comm Coll (KS)
Colby Comm Coll (KS)
Coll of Marin (CA)
Coll of Southern Idaho (ID)
Coll of the Canyons (CA)
Coll of the Desert (CA)
Coll of the Sequoias (CA)
Coll of the Siskiyous (CA)
Columbia-Greene Comm Coll (NY)
The Comm Coll of Baltimore County–Catonsville Campus (MD)
Comm Coll of Southern Nevada (NV)
Comm Coll of Vermont (VT)
Connors State Coll (OK)
Corning Comm Coll (NY)
Crafton Hills Coll (CA)
Cuesta Coll (CA)
Cumberland County Coll (NJ)
Cypress Coll (CA)
Darton Coll (GA)
Daymar Coll (KY)
Daytona Beach Comm Coll (FL)
De Anza Coll (CA)
Del Mar Coll (TX)
Delta Coll (MI)
Diné Coll (AZ)
Dixie State Coll of Utah (UT)
Dodge City Comm Coll (KS)
Donnelly Coll (KS)
Douglas MacArthur State Tech Coll (AL)
Draughons Jr Coll, Clarksville (TN)
Draughons Jr Coll, Nashville (TN)
Dutchess Comm Coll (NY)
East Central Coll (MO)
East Central Comm Coll (MS)
Eastern Oklahoma State Coll (OK)
East Mississippi Comm Coll (MS)
ECPI Coll of Technology, Newport News (VA)
ECPI Coll of Technology, Virginia Beach (VA)
ECPI Tech Coll, Richmond (VA)
ECPI Tech Coll, Roanoke (VA)
Edison Comm Coll (FL)
Edison State Comm Coll (OH)
Education Direct (PA)
Elaine P. Nunez Comm Coll (LA)
El Centro Coll (TX)
Enterprise State Jr Coll (AL)
Erie Business Center, Main (PA)
Erie Business Center South (PA)
Essex County Coll (NJ)
Everett Comm Coll (WA)
Finger Lakes Comm Coll (NY)
Fiorello H LaGuardia Comm Coll of City U of NY (NY)
Florida Computer & Business School (FL)
Florida National Coll (FL)
Foothill Coll (CA)
Forsyth Tech Comm Coll (NC)
Fort Scott Comm Coll (KS)
Fullerton Coll (CA)
Fulton-Montgomery Comm Coll (NY)
Gallipolis Career Coll (OH)
Galveston Coll (TX)
Garden City Comm Coll (KS)
Gavilan Coll (CA)
Gem City Coll (IL)
George Corley Wallace State Comm Coll (AL)
Georgia Perimeter Coll (GA)
Glendale Comm Coll (CA)
Gloucester County Coll (NJ)
Gogebic Comm Coll (MI)
Gordon Coll (GA)
Grand Rapids Comm Coll (MI)
Grayson County Coll (TX)
Guam Comm Coll (GU)
Gwinnett Tech Coll (GA)
Harford Comm Coll (MD)
Harry M. Ayers State Tech Coll (AL)
Hawaii Business Coll (HI)
Heald Coll, Schools of Business and Technology, Hayward (CA)
Heartland Comm Coll (IL)
Henry Ford Comm Coll (MI)
Herkimer County Comm Coll (NY)
Herzing Coll (AL)
Hesser Coll (NH)
Highland Comm Coll (IL)
Highland Comm Coll (KS)
Hill Coll of the Hill Jr College District (TX)
Hinds Comm Coll (MS)
Holmes Comm Coll (MS)
Houston Comm Coll System (TX)
Howard Coll (TX)
Howard Comm Coll (MD)
Hudson County Comm Coll (NJ)

Huntington Jr Coll of Business (WV)
Indian River Comm Coll (FL)
Iowa Lakes Comm Coll (IA)
Isothermal Comm Coll (NC)
Jackson State Comm Coll (TN)
Jamestown Comm Coll (NY)
Jefferson Comm Coll (KY)
Jefferson Comm Coll (NY)
John A. Logan Coll (IL)
Kilian Comm Coll (SD)
Kingsborough Comm Coll of City U of NY (NY)
Kirkwood Comm Coll (IA)
Labette Comm Coll (KS)
Lake-Sumter Comm Coll (FL)
Lake Tahoe Comm Coll (CA)
Lake Washington Tech Coll (WA)
Lamar Comm Coll (CO)
Lamar State Coll–Orange (TX)
Laramie County Comm Coll (WY)
Las Positas Coll (CA)
Lewis Coll of Business (MI)
Lincoln Coll, Lincoln (IL)
Lincoln Coll, Normal (IL)
Lincoln Land Comm Coll (IL)
Linn-Benton Comm Coll (OR)
Longview Comm Coll (MO)
Lon Morris Coll (TX)
Lorain County Comm Coll (OH)
Los Angeles Pierce Coll (CA)
Louisburg Coll (NC)
Louisiana Tech Coll–Delta Ouachita Campus (LA)
Lower Columbia Coll (WA)
Luzerne County Comm Coll (PA)
Manor Coll (PA)
Maple Woods Comm Coll (MO)
Marshalltown Comm Coll (IA)
Massachusetts Bay Comm Coll (MA)
McCann School of Business (PA)
McIntosh Coll (NH)
Merced Coll (CA)
Mercer County Comm Coll (NJ)
Miami-Dade Comm Coll (FL)
Miami U–Middletown Campus (OH)
Middle Georgia Coll (GA)
Middlesex Comm Coll (MA)
Middlesex County Coll (NJ)
Mid Michigan Comm Coll (MI)
Milwaukee Area Tech Coll (WI)
Mississippi Gulf Coast Comm Coll (MS)
Mitchell Comm Coll (NC)
Modesto Jr Coll (CA)
Mohave Comm Coll (AZ)
Mohawk Valley Comm Coll (NY)
Monroe Coll, Bronx (NY)
Monroe Coll, New Rochelle (NY)
Monroe Comm Coll (NY)
Monterey Peninsula Coll (CA)
Moorpark Coll (CA)
Mt. San Jacinto Coll (CA)
Nassau Comm Coll (NY)
Navarro Coll (TX)
Neosho County Comm Coll (KS)
Newbury Coll (MA)
New Mexico Military Inst (NM)
New Mexico State U–Carlsbad (NM)
New York City Tech Coll of the City U of NY (NY)
Niagara County Comm Coll (NY)
North Central Texas Coll (TX)
Northeast Alabama Comm Coll (AL)
Northeastern Tech Coll (SC)
Northeast Texas Comm Coll (TX)
Northern Essex Comm Coll (MA)
Northern Oklahoma Coll (OK)
Northern Virginia Comm Coll (VA)
North Harris Coll (TX)
North Idaho Coll (ID)
Northland Comm and Tech Coll (MN)
North Seattle Comm Coll (WA)
North Shore Comm Coll (MA)
Northwestern Business Coll (IL)
Northwestern Connecticut Comm-Tech Coll (CT)
Northwest-Shoals Comm Coll (AL)
Oakton Comm Coll (IL)
Odessa Coll (TX)
Okaloosa-Walton Comm Coll (FL)
Oklahoma City Comm Coll (OK)
Oklahoma State U, Oklahoma City (OK)
Onondaga Comm Coll (NY)
Orange County Comm Coll (NY)
Palm Beach Comm Coll (FL)
Palomar Coll (CA)
Parkland Coll (IL)
Pasadena City Coll (CA)
Pellissippi State Tech Comm Coll (TN)
Penn Valley Comm Coll (MO)
Pensacola Jr Coll (FL)
Prince George's Comm Coll (MD)
Quincy Coll (MA)
Raritan Valley Comm Coll (NJ)
Reading Area Comm Coll (PA)
Red Rocks Comm Coll (CO)
RETS Tech Center (OH)
Roane State Comm Coll (TN)
Rogue Comm Coll (OR)
Sacramento City Coll (CA)
Saint Charles Comm Coll (MO)
St. Louis Comm Coll at Florissant Valley (MO)
Salish Kootenai Coll (MT)
San Bernardino Valley Coll (CA)
San Diego Mesa Coll (CA)
Sanford-Brown Coll, Fenton (MO)
San Jacinto Coll Central Campus (TX)
San Jacinto Coll North Campus (TX)
San Jacinto Coll South Campus (TX)
San Joaquin Delta Coll (CA)
San Juan Coll (NM)
Santa Ana Coll (CA)
Santa Barbara City Coll (CA)
Schenectady County Comm Coll (NY)
Seminole State Coll (OK)
Sierra Coll (CA)
Skagit Valley Coll (WA)
Snow Coll (UT)
South Coll (TN)
Southeast Comm Coll, Beatrice Campus (NE)
Southern Arkansas U Tech (AR)
Southern Ohio Coll, Cincinnati Campus (OH)
Southern Ohio Coll, Northern Kentucky Campus (KY)
South Plains Coll (TX)
South Texas Comm Coll (TX)
Southwestern Coll (CA)
Southwestern Coll of Business, Dayton (OH)
Southwestern Oklahoma State U at Sayre (OK)
Southwest Mississippi Comm Coll (MS)
Springfield Tech Comm Coll (MA)
State U of NY Coll of A&T at Morrisville (NY)
State U of NY Coll of Technology at Alfred (NY)
Stone Child Coll (MT)
Suffolk County Comm Coll (NY)
Tacoma Comm Coll (WA)
Taft Coll (CA)
Tarrant County Coll District (TX)
Temple Coll (TX)
Texarkana Coll (TX)
Texas State Tech Coll–Harlingen (TX)
Texas State Tech Coll– Waco/Marshall Campus (TX)
Thomas Nelson Comm Coll (VA)
Tompkins Cortland Comm Coll (NY)
Trinidad State Jr Coll (CO)
Trinity Valley Comm Coll (TX)
Triton Coll (IL)
Tulsa Comm Coll (OK)
Tyler Jr Coll (TX)
Ulster County Comm Coll (NY)
Umpqua Comm Coll (OR)
The U of Akron–Wayne Coll (OH)
U of New Mexico–Los Alamos Branch (NM)
Vermilion Comm Coll (MN)
Victor Valley Coll (CA)
Vincennes U (IN)
Virginia Western Comm Coll (VA)
Wallace State Comm Coll (AL)
Walters State Comm Coll (TN)
Waycross Coll (GA)
Webster Coll, Holiday (FL)
Webster Inst of Technology (FL)
Westchester Comm Coll (NY)
Western Texas Coll (TX)
Westmoreland County Comm Coll (PA)
Wharton County Jr Coll (TX)
Whatcom Comm Coll (WA)
Wor-Wic Comm Coll (MD)
Young Harris Coll (GA)

COMPUTER SCIENCE RELATED

Adirondack Comm Coll (NY)
American River Coll (CA)
Anne Arundel Comm Coll (MD)
Assumption Coll for Sisters (NJ)
Austin Comm Coll (TX)
Berks Tech Inst (PA)
Blue River Comm Coll (MO)
Broome Comm Coll (NY)
Bucks County Comm Coll (PA)
Burlington County Coll (NJ)
Camden County Coll (NJ)
Cape Cod Comm Coll (MA)
Capital Comm Coll (CT)
Cayuga County Comm Coll (NY)
Centralia Coll (WA)
Central Oregon Comm Coll (OR)
Chabot Coll (CA)
Chipola Jr Coll (FL)
Citrus Coll (CA)
Coastal Bend Coll (TX)
Colby Comm Coll (KS)
Coll of the Canyons (CA)
Coll of the Desert (CA)
Columbia-Greene Comm Coll (NY)
The Comm Coll of Baltimore County–Catonsville Campus (MD)
Corning Comm Coll (NY)
Cypress Coll (CA)
Daytona Beach Comm Coll (FL)
Delaware County Comm Coll (PA)
Del Mar Coll (TX)
Delta Coll (MI)
Diablo Valley Coll (CA)
Donnelly Coll (KS)
Eastfield Coll (TX)
Education Direct (PA)
Elaine P. Nunez Comm Coll (LA)
Ellsworth Comm Coll (IA)
Fayetteville Tech Comm Coll (NC)
Fiorello H LaGuardia Comm Coll of City U of NY (NY)
Florida Comm Coll at Jacksonville (FL)
Galveston Coll (TX)
GateWay Comm Coll (AZ)
Gateway Comm Coll (CT)
Gavilan Coll (CA)
Genesee Comm Coll (NY)
Glendale Comm Coll (CA)
Gordon Coll (GA)
Heald Coll, Schools of Business and Technology, Hayward (CA)
Heartland Comm Coll (IL)
Henderson Comm Coll (KY)
Herkimer County Comm Coll (NY)
Highland Comm Coll (IL)
Hinds Comm Coll (MS)
Holmes Comm Coll (MS)
Howard Coll (TX)
Howard Comm Coll (MD)
Iowa Lakes Comm Coll (IA)
Jamestown Comm Coll (NY)
J. Sargeant Reynolds Comm Coll (VA)
Kansas City Kansas Comm Coll (KS)
Kent State U, East Liverpool Campus (OH)
Kishwaukee Coll (IL)
Lakeshore Tech Coll (WI)
Lake-Sumter Comm Coll (FL)
Laurel Business Inst (PA)
Longview Comm Coll (MO)
Lorain County Comm Coll (OH)
Los Angeles City Coll (CA)
Luzerne County Comm Coll (PA)
Manatee Comm Coll (FL)
Manor Coll (PA)
Maple Woods Comm Coll (MO)
McCann School of Business (PA)
Middle Georgia Coll (GA)
Mid-State Tech Coll (WI)
Milwaukee Area Tech Coll (WI)
Minneapolis Comm and Tech Coll (MN)
Mississippi Gulf Coast Comm Coll (MS)
Mohave Comm Coll (AZ)
Mohawk Valley Comm Coll (NY)
Monroe Comm Coll (NY)
Monroe County Comm Coll (MI)
Nassau Comm Coll (NY)
National Coll of Business & Technology, Danville (KY)
National Coll of Business & Technology, Florence (KY)
National Coll of Business & Technology, Lexington (KY)
National Coll of Business & Technology, Louisville (KY)
National Coll of Business & Technology, Pikeville (KY)
National Coll of Business & Technology, Richmond (KY)
National Coll of Business & Technology (TN)
National Coll of Business & Technology, Bluefield (VA)
National Coll of Business & Technology, Bristol (VA)
National Coll of Business & Technology, Charlottesville (VA)
National Coll of Business & Technology, Danville (VA)
National Coll of Business & Technology, Harrisonburg (VA)
National Coll of Business & Technology, Lynchburg (VA)
National Coll of Business & Technology, Martinsville (VA)
NEI Coll of Technology (MN)
North Central Michigan Coll (MI)
North Idaho Coll (ID)
Northland Comm and Tech Coll (MN)
North Shore Comm Coll (MA)
Norwalk Comm Coll (CT)
Oakton Comm Coll (IL)
Olympic Coll (WA)
Onondaga Comm Coll (NY)
Orange County Comm Coll (NY)
Pellissippi State Tech Comm Coll (TN)
Penn Valley Comm Coll (MO)
Richland Comm Coll (IL)
Ridgewater Coll (MN)
Rockland Comm Coll (NY)
Santa Ana Coll (CA)
Santa Fe Comm Coll (NM)
Santa Monica Coll (CA)
Sauk Valley Comm Coll (IL)
Schenectady County Comm Coll (NY)
Seminole Comm Coll (FL)
Sinclair Comm Coll (OH)
Southeast Tech Inst (SD)
Southern Ohio Coll, Cincinnati Campus (OH)
Southwestern Coll (CA)
Southwestern Michigan Coll (MI)
Stark State Coll of Technology (OH)
State Fair Comm Coll (MO)
Tacoma Comm Coll (WA)
Tompkins Cortland Comm Coll (NY)
Trinidad State Jr Coll (CO)
Tulsa Comm Coll (OK)
Tyler Jr Coll (TX)
Vincennes U (IN)
Vista Comm Coll (CA)
Walters State Comm Coll (TN)
West Central Tech Coll (GA)
The Westchester Business Inst (NY)
Westchester Comm Coll (NY)
Western Wyoming Comm Coll (WY)
York Tech Inst (PA)

COMPUTER SOFTWARE AND MEDIA APPLICATIONS RELATED

AIB Coll of Business (IA)
American River Coll (CA)
Ancilla Coll (IN)
Anoka-Hennepin Tech Coll (MN)
Arapahoe Comm Coll (CO)
Barton County Comm Coll (KS)
Carteret Comm Coll (NC)
Cerro Coso Comm Coll (CA)
Coll of the Sequoias (CA)
The Comm Coll of Baltimore County–Catonsville Campus (MD)
Cypress Coll (CA)
Dakota County Tech Coll (MN)
Daymar Coll (KY)
Delta Coll (MI)
Diablo Valley Coll (CA)
Fayetteville Tech Comm Coll (NC)
Florida Comm Coll at Jacksonville (FL)
Gallipolis Career Coll (OH)
Genesee Comm Coll (NY)
Glendale Comm Coll (CA)
Kellogg Comm Coll (MI)
Kennebec Valley Tech Coll (ME)
Laredo Comm Coll (TX)
Laurel Business Inst (PA)
Los Angeles City Coll (CA)
Louisiana Tech Coll–Florida Parishes Campus (LA)
Mesabi Range Comm and Tech Coll (MN)
Midland Coll (TX)
Northland Comm and Tech Coll (MN)
Olympic Coll (WA)
Parkland Coll (IL)
Pellissippi State Tech Comm Coll (TN)
Professional Careers Inst (IN)
Rasmussen Coll Mankato (MN)
Riverland Comm Coll (MN)
San Diego Mesa Coll (CA)
Seminole Comm Coll (FL)
Sheridan Coll (WY)
Southeast Tech Inst (SD)
Stark State Coll of Technology (OH)
Texas State Tech Coll–Harlingen (TX)
Triton Coll (IL)
Tulsa Comm Coll (OK)
Vincennes U (IN)
Vista Comm Coll (CA)
The Westchester Business Inst (NY)
Western Wyoming Comm Coll (WY)

COMPUTER SOFTWARE ENGINEERING

The Comm Coll of Baltimore County–Catonsville Campus (MD)
Daymar Coll (KY)
Electronic Insts, Middletown (PA)
Florida Comm Coll at Jacksonville (FL)
Lake City Comm Coll (FL)
Mt. San Jacinto Coll (CA)
Seminole Comm Coll (FL)
Sinclair Comm Coll (OH)
Southeast Tech Inst (SD)
Stark State Coll of Technology (OH)
Tompkins Cortland Comm Coll (NY)
Tulsa Comm Coll (OK)
Vincennes U (IN)

COMPUTER SYSTEMS ANALYSIS

Albuquerque Tech Vocational Inst (NM)
Amarillo Coll (TX)
Brevard Comm Coll (FL)
Certified Careers Inst, Salt Lake City (UT)
Education America, Remington Coll, Lafayette Campus (LA)
Florida Comm Coll at Jacksonville (FL)
Hesser Coll (NH)
Illinois Eastern Comm Colls, Lincoln Trail Coll (IL)
ITT Tech Inst, Seattle (WA)
Lakeshore Tech Coll (WI)
McIntosh Coll (NH)
Mid-State Coll (ME)
Pima Comm Coll (AZ)
United Tribes Tech Coll (ND)
U of Alaska Southeast, Sitka Campus (AK)
Webster Inst of Technology (FL)

COMPUTER SYSTEMS NETWORKING/ TELECOMMUNICATIONS

Adirondack Comm Coll (NY)
AIB Coll of Business (IA)
American River Coll (CA)
Ancilla Coll (IN)
Anoka-Hennepin Tech Coll (MN)
Anoka-Ramsey Comm Coll (MN)

Anoka-Ramsey Comm Coll, Cambridge Campus (MN)
Arapahoe Comm Coll (CO)
Arkansas State U–Beebe (AR)
Austin Comm Coll (TX)
Barton County Comm Coll (KS)
Beaufort County Comm Coll (NC)
Blue Ridge Comm Coll (VA)
Bowling Green State U-Firelands Coll (OH)
Bristol Comm Coll (MA)
Broome Comm Coll (NY)
Cape Cod Comm Coll (MA)
Carteret Comm Coll (NC)
Centralia Coll (WA)
Central Wyoming Coll (WY)
Chaparral Coll (AZ)
CHI Inst (PA)
Clover Park Tech Coll (WA)
Coastal Bend Coll (TX)
Coll of Lake County (IL)
Colorado Mountn Coll (CO)
Columbia-Greene Comm Coll (NY)
The Comm Coll of Baltimore County–Catonsville Campus (MD)
Corning Comm Coll (NY)
Crowder Coll (MO)
Cuesta Coll (CA)
Cumberland County Coll (NJ)
Cypress Coll (CA)
Dakota County Tech Coll (MN)
Davis Coll (OH)
Daymar Coll (KY)
Daytona Beach Comm Coll (FL)
Delaware County Comm Coll (PA)
Del Mar Coll (TX)
Diablo Valley Coll (CA)
Education America, Remington Coll, Lafayette Campus (LA)
Electronic Insts, Middletown (PA)
Ellsworth Comm Coll (IA)
Erie Business Center, Main (PA)
Fayetteville Tech Comm Coll (NC)
Fiorello H LaGuardia Comm Coll of City U of NY (NY)
Florida Comm Coll at Jacksonville (FL)
Florida National Coll (FL)
Guilford Tech Comm Coll (NC)
Hawkeye Comm Coll (IA)
Heartland Comm Coll (IL)
Henderson Comm Coll (KY)
Herkimer County Comm Coll (NY)
Herzing Coll, Minneapolis Drafting School Campus (MN)
Hibbing Comm Coll (MN)
Highline Comm Coll (WA)
Howard Comm Coll (MD)
Island Drafting and Tech Inst (NY)
Jefferson Comm Coll (NY)
Johnson Coll (PA)
Kennebec Valley Tech Coll (ME)
Lake Area Tech Inst (SD)
Lake Land Coll (IL)
Lakeland Comm Coll (OH)
Lake-Sumter Comm Coll (FL)
Laredo Comm Coll (TX)
Laurel Business Inst (PA)
Lorain County Comm Coll (OH)
Los Angeles City Coll (CA)
Louisville Tech Inst (KY)
Luzerne County Comm Coll (PA)
Minot State U–Bottineau Campus (ND)
Mississippi Gulf Coast Comm Coll (MS)
Mitchell Tech Inst (SD)
Mohawk Valley Comm Coll (NY)
Montana State U Coll of Tech-Great Falls (MT)
Mountain Empire Comm Coll (VA)
NEI Coll of Technology (MN)
New Hampshire Tech Inst (NH)
North Central Michigan Coll (MI)
Northeast State Tech Comm Coll (TN)
Northland Comm and Tech Coll (MN)
Okaloosa-Walton Comm Coll (FL)
Olympic Coll (WA)
Onondaga Comm Coll (NY)
Parkland Coll (IL)
Pasco-Hernando Comm Coll (FL)
Patrick Henry Comm Coll (VA)
Pellissippi State Tech Comm Coll (TN)
Pioneer Pacific Coll (OR)
Pittsburgh Tech Inst (PA)
Pratt Comm Coll and Area Vocational School (KS)
Rasmussen Coll Mankato (MN)
Ridgewater Coll (MN)
Riverland Comm Coll (MN)
Riverside Comm Coll (CA)
Saint Charles Comm Coll (MO)
St. Petersburg Coll (FL)
Salem Comm Coll (NJ)
San Diego Mesa Coll (CA)
Seminole Comm Coll (FL)
Sheridan Coll (WY)
Sinclair Comm Coll (OH)
Southeast Tech Inst (SD)
Stark State Coll of Technology (OH)
State Fair Comm Coll (MO)
Stratford U (VA)
Surry Comm Coll (NC)
Tacoma Comm Coll (WA)
Texas State Tech Coll–Harlingen (TX)
Trident Tech Coll (SC)
Trinidad State Jr Coll (CO)
Triton Coll (IL)
Tulsa Comm Coll (OK)
Tyler Jr Coll (TX)
U of Arkansas Comm Coll at Batesville (AR)
U of Arkansas Comm Coll at Morrilton (AR)
U of Kentucky, Lexington Comm Coll (KY)
Vincennes U (IN)
Vincennes U Jasper Campus (IN)
Virginia Coll at Jackson (MS)
Wake Tech Comm Coll (NC)
The Westchester Business Inst (NY)
Westchester Comm Coll (NY)
Westwood Coll of Technology–Anaheim (CA)
Westwood Coll of Technology-Chicago Du Page (IL)
Westwood Coll of Technology–Chicago O'Hare (IL)
Westwood Coll of Technology–Chicago River Oaks (IL)
Westwood Coll of Technology–Denver South (CO)
Westwood Coll of Technology–Inland Empire (CA)
Westwood Coll of Technology–Los Angeles (CA)
Westwood Inst of Technology–Fort Worth (TX)
York Tech Inst (PA)

COMPUTER/TECHNICAL SUPPORT

American River Coll (CA)
Anne Arundel Comm Coll (MD)
Arapahoe Comm Coll (CO)
Baltimore City Comm Coll (MD)
Barton County Comm Coll (KS)
Bowling Green State U-Firelands Coll (OH)
Broome Comm Coll (NY)
The Brown Mackie Coll–Olathe Campus (KS)
Cambria County Area Comm Coll (PA)
Coll of the Desert (CA)
Coll of the Siskiyous (CA)
Colorado Mountn Coll (CO)
The Comm Coll of Baltimore County–Catonsville Campus (MD)
Cuesta Coll (CA)
Daymar Coll (KY)
Del Mar Coll (TX)
Diablo Valley Coll (CA)
Eastern Shore Comm Coll (VA)
Education America, Remington Coll, Lafayette Campus (LA)
Elaine P. Nunez Comm Coll (LA)
Electronic Insts, Middletown (PA)
Fayetteville Tech Comm Coll (NC)
Florida Comm Coll at Jacksonville (FL)
Florida National Coll (FL)
Gallipolis Career Coll (OH)
Galveston Coll (TX)
Glendale Comm Coll (CA)
Goodwin Coll (CT)
Hawkeye Comm Coll (IA)
Heartland Comm Coll (IL)
Highland Comm Coll (IL)
Hinds Comm Coll (MS)
Holmes Comm Coll (MS)
Inver Hills Comm Coll (MN)
Iowa Western Comm Coll (IA)
Island Drafting and Tech Inst (NY)
Itasca Comm Coll (MN)
Joliet Jr Coll (IL)
Kansas City Kansas Comm Coll (KS)
Laurel Business Inst (PA)
Linn-Benton Comm Coll (OR)
Los Angeles City Coll (CA)
Louisville Tech Inst (KY)
Manor Coll (PA)
Massasoit Comm Coll (MA)
Midland Coll (TX)
Mitchell Tech Inst (SD)
Monroe Comm Coll (NY)
Mountain Empire Comm Coll (VA)
NEI Coll of Technology (MN)
North Central Texas Coll (TX)
North Idaho Coll (ID)
Northland Comm and Tech Coll (MN)
Oakton Comm Coll (IL)
Onondaga Comm Coll (NY)
Palm Beach Comm Coll (FL)
Parkland Coll (IL)
Pittsburgh Tech Inst (PA)
Pratt Comm Coll and Area Vocational School (KS)
Rasmussen Coll Mankato (MN)
Riverland Comm Coll (MN)
Riverside Comm Coll (CA)
St. Cloud Tech Coll (MN)
San Jacinto Coll North Campus (TX)
San Joaquin Valley Coll (CA)
Seminole Comm Coll (FL)
Southeast Tech Inst (SD)
Stanly Comm Coll (NC)
Stark State Coll of Technology (OH)
Suffolk County Comm Coll (NY)
Tacoma Comm Coll (WA)
Texas State Tech Coll–Harlingen (TX)
Tompkins Cortland Comm Coll (NY)
Triton Coll (IL)
Tulsa Comm Coll (OK)
Vincennes U (IN)
Wake Tech Comm Coll (NC)
The Westchester Business Inst (NY)
Western Dakota Tech Inst (SD)
York Tech Inst (PA)

COMPUTER TYPOGRAPHY/ COMPOSITION

Abraham Baldwin Ag Coll (GA)
Bergen Comm Coll (NJ)
Bristol Comm Coll (MA)
The Brown Mackie Coll–Olathe Campus (KS)
Camden County Coll (NJ)
Chabot Coll (CA)
Chaffey Coll (CA)
Chattahoochee Tech Coll (GA)
CHI Inst (PA)
Clovis Comm Coll (NM)
Coll of DuPage (IL)
Coll of the Desert (CA)
Coll of the Redwoods (CA)
Coll of the Sequoias (CA)
Comm Coll of Beaver County (PA)
Comm Coll of Denver (CO)
Comm Coll of Southern Nevada (NV)
Cumberland County Coll (NJ)
Cuyahoga Comm Coll (OH)
Daytona Beach Comm Coll (FL)
Del Mar Coll (TX)
Doña Ana Branch Comm Coll (NM)
Durham Tech Comm Coll (NC)
ECPI Coll of Technology, Newport News (VA)
ECPI Coll of Technology, Virginia Beach (VA)
ECPI Tech Coll, Richmond (VA)
ECPI Tech Coll, Roanoke (VA)
Flathead Valley Comm Coll (MT)
Fresno City Coll (CA)
Fulton-Montgomery Comm Coll (NY)
Gateway Comm Coll (CT)
Gogebic Comm Coll (MI)
Hazard Comm Coll (KY)
Hesser Coll (NH)
Highline Comm Coll (WA)
Hill Coll of the Hill Jr College District (TX)
Holyoke Comm Coll (MA)
Housatonic Comm Coll (CT)
Indian River Comm Coll (FL)
Jefferson Comm Coll (NY)
Kilian Comm Coll (SD)
Kingwood Coll (TX)
Lamar Comm Coll (CO)
Lansing Comm Coll (MI)
Lincoln Coll, Lincoln (IL)
Lincoln Coll, Normal (IL)
Long Beach City Coll (CA)
Longview Comm Coll (MO)
Macomb Comm Coll (MI)
Minnesota State Coll–Southeast Tech (MN)
Mohawk Valley Comm Coll (NY)
Monroe Coll, Bronx (NY)
Monroe Coll, New Rochelle (NY)
Monterey Peninsula Coll (CA)
New River Comm Coll (VA)
Northeast Alabama Comm Coll (AL)
Northern Essex Comm Coll (MA)
Northwest-Shoals Comm Coll (AL)
Onondaga Comm Coll (NY)
Orange Coast Coll (CA)
Paradise Valley Comm Coll (AZ)
Pasadena City Coll (CA)
Pierce Coll (WA)
Pratt Comm Coll and Area Vocational School (KS)
Prince George's Comm Coll (MD)
Rasmussen Coll Eagan (MN)
Rasmussen Coll Mankato (MN)
St. Clair County Comm Coll (MI)
St. Cloud Tech Coll (MN)
Seattle Central Comm Coll (WA)
South Mountain Comm Coll (AZ)
South Texas Comm Coll (TX)
Spokane Comm Coll (WA)
State U of NY Coll of A&T at Morrisville (NY)
State U of NY Coll of Technology at Alfred (NY)
Three Rivers Comm Coll (CT)
Triton Coll (IL)
U of Arkansas Comm Coll at Morrilton (AR)
Utica School of Commerce (NY)
The Westchester Business Inst (NY)
Western Iowa Tech Comm Coll (IA)
Western Wyoming Comm Coll (WY)
West Virginia Jr Coll, Charleston (WV)

CONSERVATION AND RENEWABLE NATURAL RESOURCES RELATED

Palau Comm CollPalau)

CONSTRUCTION/BUILDING INSPECTION

Arapahoe Comm Coll (CO)
The Comm Coll of Baltimore County–Catonsville Campus (MD)
Iowa Western Comm Coll (IA)
Johnson Coll (PA)
Modesto Jr Coll (CA)
Orange Coast Coll (CA)
St. Philip's Coll (TX)
Vincennes U (IN)

CONSTRUCTION ENGINEERING

State U of NY Coll of Technology at Alfred (NY)

CONSTRUCTION MANAGEMENT

Arapahoe Comm Coll (CO)
City Coll of San Francisco (CA)
Coll of the Desert (CA)
Columbus State Comm Coll (OH)
The Comm Coll of Baltimore County–Catonsville Campus (MD)
Comm Coll of Southern Nevada (NV)
Delaware Tech & Comm Coll, Jack F Owens Cmps (DE)
Delaware Tech & Comm Coll, Terry Cmps (DE)
Delgado Comm Coll (LA)
Delta Coll (MI)
Frederick Comm Coll (MD)
Fresno City Coll (CA)
Gogebic Comm Coll (MI)
Gwinnett Tech Coll (GA)
Herkimer County Comm Coll (NY)
Inver Hills Comm Coll (MN)
Modesto Jr Coll (CA)
Montgomery Coll (MD)
North Hennepin Comm Coll (MN)
Oakton Comm Coll (IL)
Oklahoma State U, Oklahoma City (OK)
Palm Beach Comm Coll (FL)
Parkland Coll (IL)
Piedmont Tech Coll (SC)
Piedmont Virginia Comm Coll (VA)
Pikes Peak Comm Coll (CO)
St. Philip's Coll (TX)
San Jacinto Coll North Campus (TX)
Seminole Comm Coll (FL)
Sierra Coll (CA)
Snow Coll (UT)
State U of NY Coll of Technology at Delhi (NY)
Triton Coll (IL)
Victor Valley Coll (CA)
Western Nevada Comm Coll (NV)

CONSTRUCTION MANAGEMENT RELATED

Albuquerque Tech Vocational Inst (NM)
Guilford Tech Comm Coll (NC)
Pima Comm Coll (AZ)
Wilkes Comm Coll (NC)

CONSTRUCTION TECHNOLOGY

American River Coll (CA)
Antelope Valley Coll (CA)
Austin Comm Coll (TX)
Bessemer State Tech Coll (AL)
Brazosport Coll (TX)
Brevard Comm Coll (FL)
Butte Coll (CA)
Cambria County Area Comm Coll (PA)
Capital Comm Coll (CT)
Casper Coll (WY)
Cecil Comm Coll (MD)
Central Comm Coll–Hastings Campus (NE)
Central Maine Tech Coll (ME)
Chemeketa Comm Coll (OR)
Chippewa Valley Tech Coll (WI)
Cisco Jr Coll (TX)
Clark Coll (WA)
Coffeyville Comm Coll (KS)
Coll of Eastern Utah (UT)
Coll of Lake County (IL)
Coll of the Redwoods (CA)
Coll of the Sequoias (CA)
Comm Coll of Allegheny County (PA)
The Comm Coll of Baltimore County–Catonsville Campus (MD)
Comm Coll of Southern Nevada (NV)
Comm Coll of the Air Force (AL)
Compton Comm Coll (CA)
Crowder Coll (MO)
Cuesta Coll (CA)
Daytona Beach Comm Coll (FL)
De Anza Coll (CA)
Delaware County Comm Coll (PA)
Delaware Tech & Comm Coll, Terry Cmps (DE)
Delta Coll (MI)
Dodge City Comm Coll (KS)
Don Bosco Coll of Science and Technology (CA)
Dutchess Comm Coll (NY)
East Central Coll (MO)
Eastern Maine Tech Coll (ME)
Edmonds Comm Coll (WA)
Feather River Comm Coll District (CA)
Flathead Valley Comm Coll (MT)
Florida Comm Coll at Jacksonville (FL)
Forsyth Tech Comm Coll (NC)
Fort Berthold Comm Coll (ND)
Fresno City Coll (CA)
Fullerton Coll (CA)
Fulton-Montgomery Comm Coll (NY)

GateWay Comm Coll (AZ)
Gogebic Comm Coll (MI)
Greenville Tech Coll (SC)
Gulf Coast Comm Coll (FL)
Harrisburg Area Comm Coll (PA)
Henry Ford Comm Coll (MI)
Herkimer County Comm Coll (NY)
Highland Comm Coll (KS)
Hillsborough Comm Coll (FL)
Houston Comm Coll System (TX)
Inst of Design and Construction (NY)
Inver Hills Comm Coll (MN)
Iowa Lakes Comm Coll (IA)
Jefferson State Comm Coll (AL)
Johnson Coll (PA)
Joliet Jr Coll (IL)
J. Sargeant Reynolds Comm Coll (VA)
Kirkwood Comm Coll (IA)
Lane Comm Coll (OR)
Lansing Comm Coll (MI)
Laramie County Comm Coll (WY)
Laredo Comm Coll (TX)
Lehigh Carbon Comm Coll (PA)
Lincoln Land Comm Coll (IL)
Los Angeles Pierce Coll (CA)
Macomb Comm Coll (MI)
Manatee Comm Coll (FL)
Merced Coll (CA)
Metropolitan Comm Coll (NE)
Miami-Dade Comm Coll (FL)
Middlesex County Coll (NJ)
Mid-Plains Comm Coll Area (NE)
Miles Comm Coll (MT)
Milwaukee Area Tech Coll (WI)
Mineral Area Coll (MO)
Monroe Comm Coll (NY)
Morrison Inst of Technology (IL)
Neosho County Comm Coll (KS)
New England Inst of Technology (RI)
New York City Tech Coll of the City U of NY (NY)
North Dakota State Coll of Science (ND)
Northeast Comm Coll (NE)
Northeast Iowa Comm Coll (IA)
Northern Oklahoma Coll (OK)
Northland Pioneer Coll (AZ)
North Seattle Comm Coll (WA)
Norwalk Comm Coll (CT)
Ocean County Coll (NJ)
Odessa Coll (TX)
Okaloosa-Walton Comm Coll (FL)
Oklahoma State U, Oklahoma City (OK)
Oklahoma State U, Okmulgee (OK)
Onondaga Comm Coll (NY)
Orange Coast Coll (CA)
Orange County Comm Coll (NY)
Palau Comm CollPalau)
Palomar Coll (CA)
Pasadena City Coll (CA)
Pellissippi State Tech Comm Coll (TN)
Pennsylvania Coll of Technology (PA)
Pensacola Jr Coll (FL)
Phoenix Coll (AZ)
Piedmont Tech Coll (SC)
Pima Comm Coll (AZ)
Portland Comm Coll (OR)
Raritan Valley Comm Coll (NJ)
Richland Comm Coll (IL)
Roanoke-Chowan Comm Coll (NC)
Rockingham Comm Coll (NC)
St. Cloud Tech Coll (MN)
St. Louis Comm Coll at Florissant Valley (MO)
St. Petersburg Coll (FL)
St. Philip's Coll (TX)
San Diego Mesa Coll (CA)
San Jacinto Coll North Campus (TX)
San Joaquin Delta Coll (CA)
Santa Fe Comm Coll (FL)
Santa Fe Comm Coll (NM)
Santa Monica Coll (CA)
Seminole Comm Coll (FL)
Shasta Coll (CA)
Sierra Coll (CA)
Snow Coll (UT)
Southeast Comm Coll, Milford Campus (NE)
Southern Maine Tech Coll (ME)
South Suburban Coll (IL)
Southwestern Coll (CA)
Southwest Mississippi Comm Coll (MS)
Spokane Comm Coll (WA)
State Fair Comm Coll (MO)
State U of NY Coll of A&T at Morrisville (NY)
State U of NY Coll of Technology at Alfred (NY)
State U of NY Coll of Technology at Canton (NY)
State U of NY Coll of Technology at Delhi (NY)
Suffolk County Comm Coll (NY)
Surry Comm Coll (NC)
Tallahassee Comm Coll (FL)
Tarrant County Coll District (TX)
TCI-The Coll for Technology (NY)
Texas State Tech Coll–Harlingen (TX)
Thaddeus Stevens Coll of Technology (PA)
Tompkins Cortland Comm Coll (NY)
Trenholm State Tech Coll, Patterson Campus (AL)
Trinidad State Jr Coll (CO)
Triton Coll (IL)
Truckee Meadows Comm Coll (NV)
Tulsa Comm Coll (OK)
U of New Mexico–Gallup (NM)
Vance-Granville Comm Coll (NC)
Ventura Coll (CA)
Vermont Tech Coll (VT)
Victor Valley Coll (CA)
Vincennes U (IN)
Wallace State Comm Coll (AL)
Western Wyoming Comm Coll (WY)

CONSTRUCTION TRADES RELATED
Albuquerque Tech Vocational Inst (NM)
Comm Coll of Allegheny County (PA)
Comm Coll of Denver (CO)
Erie Comm Coll, North Campus (NY)
Palo Verde Coll (CA)
Pitt Comm Coll (NC)

CONSUMER EDUCATION
Antelope Valley Coll (CA)

CONSUMER/HOMEMAKING EDUCATION
MiraCosta Coll (CA)

CONSUMER SERVICES
City Coll of San Francisco (CA)
Los Angeles Mission Coll (CA)
Rockingham Comm Coll (NC)
San Diego City Coll (CA)

CORRECTIONS
Adirondack Comm Coll (NY)
Alpena Comm Coll (MI)
Alvin Comm Coll (TX)
Amarillo Coll (TX)
Anne Arundel Comm Coll (MD)
Antelope Valley Coll (CA)
Atlantic Cape Comm Coll (NJ)
Bakersfield Coll (CA)
Baltimore City Comm Coll (MD)
Belmont Tech Coll (OH)
Bossier Parish Comm Coll (LA)
Brevard Comm Coll (FL)
Bucks County Comm Coll (PA)
Bunker Hill Comm Coll (MA)
Casper Coll (WY)
Cayuga County Comm Coll (NY)
Central Arizona Coll (AZ)
Centralia Coll (WA)
Central Ohio Tech Coll (OH)
Chabot Coll (CA)
Chaffey Coll (CA)
Chattahoochee Tech Coll (GA)
Chesapeake Coll (MD)
Clackamas Comm Coll (OR)
Clovis Comm Coll (NM)
Coll of DuPage (IL)
Coll of Marin (CA)
Coll of the Sequoias (CA)
Columbus State Comm Coll (OH)
Comm Coll of Allegheny County (PA)
The Comm Coll of Baltimore County–Catonsville Campus (MD)
Comm Coll of Southern Nevada (NV)
Cowley County Comm Coll and Voc-Tech School (KS)
Cumberland County Coll (NJ)
Darton Coll (GA)
Daytona Beach Comm Coll (FL)
De Anza Coll (CA)
Delaware Tech & Comm Coll, Stanton/ Wilmington Cmps (DE)
Delaware Tech & Comm Coll, Terry Cmps (DE)
Delta Coll (MI)
Des Moines Area Comm Coll (IA)
Eastern Arizona Coll (AZ)
Eastern Oklahoma State Coll (OK)
Ellsworth Comm Coll (IA)
Fresno City Coll (CA)
Gateway Tech Coll (WI)
Gavilan Coll (CA)
Gogebic Comm Coll (MI)
Grand Rapids Comm Coll (MI)
Grays Harbor Coll (WA)
Guam Comm Coll (GU)
Halifax Comm Coll (NC)
Hawkeye Comm Coll (IA)
Heartland Comm Coll (IL)
Henry Ford Comm Coll (MI)
Herkimer County Comm Coll (NY)
Hesser Coll (NH)
Hillsborough Comm Coll (FL)
Indian River Comm Coll (FL)
Iowa Lakes Comm Coll (IA)
Jackson Comm Coll (MI)
Jefferson Comm Coll (OH)
Joliet Jr Coll (IL)
Kansas City Kansas Comm Coll (KS)
Kellogg Comm Coll (MI)
Kilgore Coll (TX)
Kirkwood Comm Coll (IA)
Lake Land Coll (IL)
Lakeland Comm Coll (OH)
Lake Michigan Coll (MI)
Lansing Comm Coll (MI)
Lima Tech Coll (OH)
Lincoln Coll, Lincoln (IL)
Lincoln Coll, Normal (IL)
Lincoln Land Comm Coll (IL)
Longview Comm Coll (MO)
Lorain County Comm Coll (OH)
Los Angeles City Coll (CA)
Mercer County Comm Coll (NJ)
Middlesex County Coll (NJ)
Mid Michigan Comm Coll (MI)
Mid-State Tech Coll (WI)
Mineral Area Coll (MO)
Modesto Jr Coll (CA)
Monroe Comm Coll (NY)
Montcalm Comm Coll (MI)
Moorpark Coll (CA)
Moraine Park Tech Coll (WI)
Mountain Empire Comm Coll (VA)
Navarro Coll (TX)
Northeast Comm Coll (NE)
Northland Pioneer Coll (AZ)
Northwest State Comm Coll (OH)
Olympic Coll (WA)
Penn Valley Comm Coll (MO)
Phoenix Coll (AZ)
Polk Comm Coll (FL)
Riverland Comm Coll (MN)
Roane State Comm Coll (TN)
St. Clair County Comm Coll (MI)
St. Louis Comm Coll at Florissant Valley (MO)
St. Petersburg Coll (FL)
San Antonio Coll (TX)
San Bernardino Valley Coll (CA)
San Jacinto Coll North Campus (TX)
San Joaquin Delta Coll (CA)
San Joaquin Valley Coll (CA)
Santa Fe Comm Coll (FL)
Sauk Valley Comm Coll (IL)
Schoolcraft Coll (MI)
Sierra Coll (CA)
Sinclair Comm Coll (OH)
Southwestern Coll (CA)
Southwestern Oklahoma State U at Sayre (OK)
Spokane Comm Coll (WA)
State U of NY Coll of Technology at Canton (NY)
Sullivan County Comm Coll (NY)
Three Rivers Comm Coll (CT)
Trinidad State Jr Coll (CO)
Trinity Valley Comm Coll (TX)
Truckee Meadows Comm Coll (NV)
Tulsa Comm Coll (OK)
Tunxis Comm Coll (CT)
U of New Mexico–Gallup (NM)
Vance-Granville Comm Coll (NC)
Vincennes U (IN)
Walla Walla Comm Coll (WA)
Weatherford Coll (TX)
Westchester Comm Coll (NY)
Western Nevada Comm Coll (NV)
Western Texas Coll (TX)
West Shore Comm Coll (MI)

COSMETIC SERVICES
Lorain County Comm Coll (OH)
Santa Barbara City Coll (CA)
Trinidad State Jr Coll (CO)

COSMETIC SERVICES RELATED
Comm Coll of Allegheny County (PA)
Lorain County Comm Coll (OH)

COSMETOLOGY
Albuquerque Tech Vocational Inst (NM)
Allan Hancock Coll (CA)
Athens Tech Coll (GA)
Bakersfield Coll (CA)
Barstow Coll (CA)
Black Hawk Coll, Moline (IL)
Blue Ridge Comm Coll (NC)
Brevard Comm Coll (FL)
Butte Coll (CA)
Carl Sandburg Coll (IL)
Central Texas Coll (TX)
Century Comm and Tech Coll (MN)
Cerritos Coll (CA)
Cisco Jr Coll (TX)
Citrus Coll (CA)
Clovis Comm Coll (NM)
Coastal Bend Coll (TX)
Coll of Eastern Utah (UT)
Coll of the Sequoias (CA)
Coll of the Siskiyous (CA)
Cowley County Comm Coll and Voc-Tech School (KS)
Daytona Beach Comm Coll (FL)
Del Mar Coll (TX)
Dodge City Comm Coll (KS)
Douglas MacArthur State Tech Coll (AL)
East Central Comm Coll (MS)
Eastern Wyoming Coll (WY)
East Mississippi Comm Coll (MS)
Everett Comm Coll (WA)
Fayetteville Tech Comm Coll (NC)
Fort Scott Comm Coll (KS)
Fullerton Coll (CA)
Garden City Comm Coll (KS)
Gavilan Coll (CA)
Gem City Coll (IL)
Glendale Comm Coll (CA)
Golden West Coll (CA)
Grayson County Coll (TX)
Guilford Tech Comm Coll (NC)
Haywood Comm Coll (NC)
Hill Coll of the Hill Jr College District (TX)
Honolulu Comm Coll (HI)
Howard Coll (TX)
Independence Comm Coll (KS)
Indian River Comm Coll (FL)
Isothermal Comm Coll (NC)
James Sprunt Comm Coll (NC)
John A. Logan Coll (IL)
Johnson County Comm Coll (KS)
Lake Area Tech Inst (SD)
Lamar Comm Coll (CO)
Lamar State Coll–Port Arthur (TX)
Lenoir Comm Coll (NC)
Lincoln Coll, Lincoln (IL)
Martin Comm Coll (NC)
Minnesota State Coll–Southeast Tech (MN)
MiraCosta Coll (CA)
Montcalm Comm Coll (MI)
Mt. Hood Comm Coll (OR)
Nash Comm Coll (NC)
Northeast Texas Comm Coll (TX)
North Harris Coll (TX)
Northland Comm and Tech Coll (MN)
Northland Pioneer Coll (AZ)
Oakland Comm Coll (MI)
Odessa Coll (TX)
Olympic Coll (WA)
Pasadena City Coll (CA)
Roanoke-Chowan Comm Coll (NC)
Rockingham Comm Coll (NC)
Sacramento City Coll (CA)
Sandhills Comm Coll (NC)
San Diego City Coll (CA)
San Jacinto Coll Central Campus (TX)
San Jacinto Coll North Campus (TX)
San Jacinto Coll South Campus (TX)
Santa Ana Coll (CA)
Santa Monica Coll (CA)
Seattle Central Comm Coll (WA)
Shoreline Comm Coll (WA)
Southeastern Comm Coll (NC)
Southeastern Comm Coll, South Campus (IA)
South Plains Coll (TX)
Southwestern Comm Coll (NC)
Southwest Mississippi Comm Coll (MS)
Southwest Wisconsin Tech Coll (WI)
Spokane Comm Coll (WA)
Springfield Tech Comm Coll (MA)
Stanly Comm Coll (NC)
Surry Comm Coll (NC)
Texarkana Coll (TX)
Trenholm State Tech Coll, Patterson Campus (AL)
Trinidad State Jr Coll (CO)
Trinity Valley Comm Coll (TX)
Umpqua Comm Coll (OR)
U of New Mexico–Gallup (NM)
Vance-Granville Comm Coll (NC)
Vernon Coll (TX)
Vincennes U (IN)
Wallace State Comm Coll (AL)
Walla Walla Comm Coll (WA)
Waycross Coll (GA)
Weatherford Coll (TX)

COUNSELOR EDUCATION/ GUIDANCE
Pratt Comm Coll and Area Vocational School (KS)

COURT REPORTING
AIB Coll of Business (IA)
Albuquerque Tech Vocational Inst (NM)
Alvin Comm Coll (TX)
Bates Tech Coll (WA)
Brevard Comm Coll (FL)
Butte Coll (CA)
Cambria County Area Comm Coll (PA)
Career Colls of Chicago (IL)
Cerritos Coll (CA)
Chaffey Coll (CA)
City Coll of San Francisco (CA)
Coll of Court Reporting (IN)
Coll of Marin (CA)
Comm Coll of Allegheny County (PA)
Court Reporting Inst of Dallas (TX)
Cuyahoga Comm Coll (OH)
Cypress Coll (CA)
Daytona Beach Comm Coll (FL)
Del Mar Coll (TX)
Duff's Business Inst (PA)
Gadsden State Comm Coll (AL)
GateWay Comm Coll (AZ)
Gateway Tech Coll (WI)
Green River Comm Coll (WA)
Houston Comm Coll System (TX)
Huntington Jr Coll of Business (WV)
Illinois Eastern Comm Colls, Wabash Valley Coll (IL)
James H. Faulkner State Comm Coll (AL)
Lakeshore Tech Coll (WI)
Lansing Comm Coll (MI)
Lenoir Comm Coll (NC)
Long Island Business Inst (NY)
Massachusetts Bay Comm Coll (MA)
Miami-Dade Comm Coll (FL)
Midlands Tech Coll (SC)
Mississippi Gulf Coast Comm Coll (MS)
Northland Pioneer Coll (AZ)
Northwest Mississippi Comm Coll (MS)
Oakland Comm Coll (MI)

Pensacola Jr Coll (FL)
Prince Inst of Professional Studies (AL)
Rasmussen Coll Eagan (MN)
Rasmussen Coll Minnetonka (MN)
Rasmussen Coll St. Cloud (MN)
San Antonio Coll (TX)
San Diego City Coll (CA)
South Suburban Coll (IL)
Southwest Tennessee Comm Coll (TN)
Springfield Tech Comm Coll (MA)
Stark State Coll of Technology (OH)
State Fair Comm Coll (MO)
State U of NY Coll of Technology at Alfred (NY)
Triton Coll (IL)
Wisconsin Indianhead Tech Coll (WI)

CRAFT/FOLK ART
Haywood Comm Coll (NC)

CREATIVE WRITING
Foothill Coll (CA)
Inst of American Indian Arts (NM)
Lincoln Coll, Lincoln (IL)
Lon Morris Coll (TX)
San Jacinto Coll Central Campus (TX)
Tulsa Comm Coll (OK)
Vista Comm Coll (CA)

CRIMINAL JUSTICE/ CORRECTIONS RELATED
Atlanta Metropolitan Coll (GA)
Corning Comm Coll (NY)
Oakland Comm Coll (MI)
Reedley Coll (CA)
Wisconsin Indianhead Tech Coll (WI)

CRIMINAL JUSTICE/LAW ENFORCEMENT ADMINISTRATION
Abraham Baldwin Ag Coll (GA)
Adirondack Comm Coll (NY)
AIBT International Inst of the Americas (AZ)
Aims Comm Coll (CO)
Allegany Coll of Maryland (MD)
Allen County Comm Coll (KS)
Amarillo Coll (TX)
Ancilla Coll (IN)
Andover Coll (ME)
Angelina Coll (TX)
Anne Arundel Comm Coll (MD)
Antelope Valley Coll (CA)
Arapahoe Comm Coll (CO)
Arizona Western Coll (AZ)
Arkansas State U–Mountain Home (AR)
Atlanta Metropolitan Coll (GA)
Austin Comm Coll (TX)
Bainbridge Coll (GA)
Bakersfield Coll (CA)
Barton County Comm Coll (KS)
Bay de Noc Comm Coll (MI)
Bellevue Comm Coll (WA)
Bergen Comm Coll (NJ)
Berkshire Comm Coll (MA)
Blinn Coll (TX)
Bowling Green State U-Firelands Coll (OH)
Brevard Comm Coll (FL)
Briarwood Coll (CT)
Bristol Comm Coll (MA)
Brookdale Comm Coll (NJ)
Broome Comm Coll (NY)
The Brown Mackie Coll (KS)
Bucks County Comm Coll (PA)
Bunker Hill Comm Coll (MA)
Burlington County Coll (NJ)
Butte Coll (CA)
Camden County Coll (NJ)
Cape Cod Comm Coll (MA)
Carl Sandburg Coll (IL)
Carteret Comm Coll (NC)
Casper Coll (WY)
Cayuga County Comm Coll (NY)
Cecil Comm Coll (MD)
Cedar Valley Coll (TX)
Central Arizona Coll (AZ)
Central Carolina Comm Coll (NC)
Central Florida Comm Coll (FL)
Centralia Coll (WA)
Central Ohio Tech Coll (OH)
Central Oregon Comm Coll (OR)
Central Pennsylvania Coll (PA)
Central Piedmont Comm Coll (NC)
Central Virginia Comm Coll (VA)
Central Wyoming Coll (WY)
Cerro Coso Comm Coll (CA)
Chabot Coll (CA)
Chattahoochee Valley Comm Coll (AL)
Chattanooga State Tech Comm Coll (TN)
Chemeketa Comm Coll (OR)
Chesapeake Coll (MD)
Citrus Coll (CA)
City Coll of San Francisco (CA)
Cleveland Comm Coll (NC)
Clinton Comm Coll (NY)
Coahoma Comm Coll (MS)
Coastal Bend Coll (TX)
Coastal Carolina Comm Coll (NC)
Coastal Georgia Comm Coll (GA)
Cochise Coll, Douglas (AZ)
Colby Comm Coll (KS)
Coll of DuPage (IL)
Coll of Southern Idaho (ID)
Coll of the Canyons (CA)
Coll of the Desert (CA)
Coll of the Redwoods (CA)
Coll of the Sequoias (CA)
Coll of the Siskiyous (CA)
Colorado Mountn Coll (CO)
Colorado Northwestern Comm Coll (CO)
Columbia-Greene Comm Coll (NY)
Comm Coll of Aurora (CO)
The Comm Coll of Baltimore County–Catonsville Campus (MD)
Comm Coll of Beaver County (PA)
Comm Coll of Southern Nevada (NV)
Comm Coll of the Air Force (AL)
Compton Comm Coll (CA)
Corning Comm Coll (NY)
Cowley County Comm Coll and Voc-Tech School (KS)
Crafton Hills Coll (CA)
Craven Comm Coll (NC)
Danville Area Comm Coll (IL)
Darton Coll (GA)
Daytona Beach Comm Coll (FL)
Dean Coll (MA)
De Anza Coll (CA)
Delaware Tech & Comm Coll, Jack F Owens Cmps (DE)
Delaware Tech & Comm Coll, Stanton/ Wilmington Cmps (DE)
Delaware Tech & Comm Coll, Terry Cmps (DE)
Del Mar Coll (TX)
Delta Coll (MI)
Denmark Tech Coll (SC)
Des Moines Area Comm Coll (IA)
Dodge City Comm Coll (KS)
Durham Tech Comm Coll (NC)
Dutchess Comm Coll (NY)
East Arkansas Comm Coll (AR)
East Central Coll (MO)
Eastern Arizona Coll (AZ)
Eastern Oklahoma State Coll (OK)
East Georgia Coll (GA)
East Mississippi Comm Coll (MS)
Edgecombe Comm Coll (NC)
Edison Comm Coll (FL)
Edison State Comm Coll (OH)
Ellsworth Comm Coll (IA)
Enterprise State Jr Coll (AL)
Erie Comm Coll, City Campus (NY)
Erie Comm Coll, North Campus (NY)
Essex County Coll (NJ)
Everett Comm Coll (WA)
Evergreen Valley Coll (CA)
Feather River Comm Coll District (CA)
Finger Lakes Comm Coll (NY)
Flathead Valley Comm Coll (MT)
Florence-Darlington Tech Coll (SC)
Florida Comm Coll at Jacksonville (FL)
Forsyth Tech Comm Coll (NC)
Fort Scott Comm Coll (KS)
Frederick Comm Coll (MD)
Fresno City Coll (CA)
Fulton-Montgomery Comm Coll (NY)
Garden City Comm Coll (KS)
Gaston Coll (NC)
Gavilan Coll (CA)
Genesee Comm Coll (NY)
George Corley Wallace State Comm Coll (AL)
Georgia Military Coll (GA)
Glendale Comm Coll (AZ)
Gogebic Comm Coll (MI)
Golden West Coll (CA)
Grand Rapids Comm Coll (MI)
Grayson County Coll (TX)
Greenfield Comm Coll (MA)
Greenville Tech Coll (SC)
Guam Comm Coll (GU)
Guilford Tech Comm Coll (NC)
Gulf Coast Comm Coll (FL)
Harford Comm Coll (MD)
Harrisburg Area Comm Coll (PA)
Hawaii Comm Coll (HI)
Hawkeye Comm Coll (IA)
Haywood Comm Coll (NC)
Henry Ford Comm Coll (MI)
Herkimer County Comm Coll (NY)
Hesser Coll (NH)
Highland Comm Coll (KS)
Highline Comm Coll (WA)
Hill Coll of the Hill Jr College District (TX)
Hillsborough Comm Coll (FL)
Hinds Comm Coll (MS)
Horry-Georgetown Tech Coll (SC)
Housatonic Comm Coll (CT)
Howard Comm Coll (MD)
Imperial Valley Coll (CA)
Indian Hills Comm Coll (IA)
Indian River Comm Coll (FL)
Iowa Lakes Comm Coll (IA)
Iowa Western Comm Coll (IA)
Isothermal Comm Coll (NC)
Jackson Comm Coll (MI)
Jamestown Comm Coll (NY)
Jefferson Coll (MO)
Jefferson Comm Coll (NY)
John A. Logan Coll (IL)
Kankakee Comm Coll (IL)
Kent State U, East Liverpool Campus (OH)
Kent State U, Trumbull Campus (OH)
Kilgore Coll (TX)
Kilian Comm Coll (SD)
Kirkwood Comm Coll (IA)
Labette Comm Coll (KS)
Lake City Comm Coll (FL)
Lakeland Comm Coll (OH)
Lake-Sumter Comm Coll (FL)
Lake Tahoe Comm Coll (CA)
Lamar State Coll–Port Arthur (TX)
Lane Comm Coll (OR)
Lansing Comm Coll (MI)
Laramie County Comm Coll (WY)
Lehigh Carbon Comm Coll (PA)
Lenoir Comm Coll (NC)
Lewis and Clark Comm Coll (IL)
Lincoln Coll, Lincoln (IL)
Lincoln Land Comm Coll (IL)
Linn-Benton Comm Coll (OR)
Long Beach City Coll (CA)
Longview Comm Coll (MO)
Los Angeles City Coll (CA)
Luzerne County Comm Coll (PA)
Macomb Comm Coll (MI)
Manchester Comm Coll (CT)
Maple Woods Comm Coll (MO)
Massachusetts Bay Comm Coll (MA)
Mayland Comm Coll (NC)
McIntosh Coll (NH)
McLennan Comm Coll (TX)
Miami-Dade Comm Coll (FL)
Middlesex Comm Coll (MA)
Middlesex County Coll (NJ)
Midland Coll (TX)
Midlands Tech Coll (SC)
Mid Michigan Comm Coll (MI)
Mid-Plains Comm Coll Area (NE)
Milwaukee Area Tech Coll (WI)
MiraCosta Coll (CA)
Mississippi Delta Comm Coll (MS)
Mississippi Gulf Coast Comm Coll (MS)
Mitchell Coll (CT)
Mitchell Comm Coll (NC)
Modesto Jr Coll (CA)
Mohawk Valley Comm Coll (NY)
Monroe Comm Coll (NY)
Montcalm Comm Coll (MI)
Monterey Peninsula Coll (CA)
Moorpark Coll (CA)
Mountain Empire Comm Coll (VA)
Mountain View Coll (TX)
Mount Wachusett Comm Coll (MA)
Muskingum Area Tech Coll (OH)
Nassau Comm Coll (NY)
Naugatuck Valley Comm Coll (CT)
Navarro Coll (TX)
Neosho County Comm Coll (KS)
Newbury Coll (MA)
New Hampshire Tech Inst (NH)
New Mexico Military Inst (NM)
New Mexico State U–Carlsbad (NM)
New River Comm Coll (VA)
Niagara County Comm Coll (NY)
Northampton County Area Comm Coll (PA)
North Central Michigan Coll (MI)
North Central Texas Coll (TX)
Northeast Comm Coll (NE)
Northeast Texas Comm Coll (TX)
Northern Essex Comm Coll (MA)
Northern Oklahoma Coll (OK)
Northern Virginia Comm Coll (VA)
North Harris Coll (TX)
North Idaho Coll (ID)
Northland Comm and Tech Coll (MN)
North Shore Comm Coll (MA)
NorthWest Arkansas Comm Coll (AR)
Northwestern Connecticut Comm-Tech Coll (CT)
Northwest-Shoals Comm Coll (AL)
Northwest State Comm Coll (OH)
Norwalk Comm Coll (CT)
Oakland Comm Coll (MI)
Odessa Coll (TX)
Okaloosa-Walton Comm Coll (FL)
Onondaga Comm Coll (NY)
Orange County Comm Coll (NY)
Ozarka Coll (AR)
Palm Beach Comm Coll (FL)
Palomar Coll (CA)
Palo Verde Coll (CA)
Pasadena City Coll (CA)
Pasco-Hernando Comm Coll (FL)
Paul D. Camp Comm Coll (VA)
Peninsula Coll (WA)
Penn Valley Comm Coll (MO)
Piedmont Comm Coll (NC)
Piedmont Tech Coll (SC)
Piedmont Virginia Comm Coll (VA)
Pierce Coll (WA)
Pikes Peak Comm Coll (CO)
Polk Comm Coll (FL)
Portland Comm Coll (OR)
Prairie State Coll (IL)
Prince George's Comm Coll (MD)
Quincy Coll (MA)
Quinsigamond Comm Coll (MA)
Raritan Valley Comm Coll (NJ)
Red Rocks Comm Coll (CO)
Richmond Comm Coll (NC)
Ridgewater Coll (MN)
Riverside Comm Coll (CA)
Roane State Comm Coll (TN)
Roanoke-Chowan Comm Coll (NC)
Robeson Comm Coll (NC)
Rockingham Comm Coll (NC)
Rockland Comm Coll (NY)
Rogue Comm Coll (OR)
Rowan-Cabarrus Comm Coll (NC)
Sacramento City Coll (CA)
St. Catharine Coll (KY)
Saint Charles Comm Coll (MO)
St. Clair County Comm Coll (MI)
St. Louis Comm Coll at Florissant Valley (MO)
Salem Comm Coll (NJ)
Sampson Comm Coll (NC)
San Antonio Coll (TX)
Sandhills Comm Coll (NC)
San Jacinto Coll Central Campus (TX)
San Jacinto Coll North Campus (TX)
Santa Ana Coll (CA)
Santa Barbara City Coll (CA)
Santa Fe Comm Coll (FL)
Santa Monica Coll (CA)
Sauk Valley Comm Coll (IL)
Schenectady County Comm Coll (NY)
Scottsdale Comm Coll (AZ)
Seminole Comm Coll (FL)
Shasta Coll (CA)
Sheridan Coll (WY)
Sierra Coll (CA)
Sinclair Comm Coll (OH)
Snow Coll (UT)
Southeastern Comm Coll (NC)
Southern Maine Tech Coll (ME)
Southern West Virginia Comm and Tech Coll (WV)
South Plains Coll (TX)
Southside Virginia Comm Coll (VA)
South Suburban Coll (IL)
Southwestern Coll (CA)
Spartanburg Methodist Coll (SC)
State Fair Comm Coll (MO)
State U of NY Coll of Technology at Canton (NY)
Suffolk County Comm Coll (NY)
Surry Comm Coll (NC)
Tacoma Comm Coll (WA)
Taft Coll (CA)
Tallahassee Comm Coll (FL)
Tarrant County Coll District (TX)
Temple Coll (TX)
Texarkana Coll (TX)
Three Rivers Comm Coll (CT)
Tompkins Cortland Comm Coll (NY)
Tri-County Tech Coll (SC)
Trident Tech Coll (SC)
Trinity Valley Comm Coll (TX)
Triton Coll (IL)
Truckee Meadows Comm Coll (NV)
Tulsa Comm Coll (OK)
Tunxis Comm Coll (CT)
Tyler Jr Coll (TX)
Ulster County Comm Coll (NY)
Umpqua Comm Coll (OR)
United Tribes Tech Coll (ND)
U of Arkansas Comm Coll at Hope (AR)
U of New Mexico–Gallup (NM)
U of South Carolina at Lancaster (SC)
Valley Forge Military Coll (PA)
Vance-Granville Comm Coll (NC)
Ventura Coll (CA)
Vermilion Comm Coll (MN)
Vernon Coll (TX)
Vincennes U (IN)
Virginia Western Comm Coll (VA)
Wake Tech Comm Coll (NC)
Wallace State Comm Coll (AL)
Walters State Comm Coll (TN)
Warren County Comm Coll (NJ)
Waycross Coll (GA)
Weatherford Coll (TX)
Westchester Comm Coll (NY)
Western Iowa Tech Comm Coll (IA)
Western Nevada Comm Coll (NV)
Western Piedmont Comm Coll (NC)
Western Texas Coll (TX)
Western Wyoming Comm Coll (WY)
Westmoreland County Comm Coll (PA)
West Virginia U at Parkersburg (WV)
Wharton County Jr Coll (TX)
Wilson Tech Comm Coll (NC)
Young Harris Coll (GA)

CRIMINAL JUSTICE STUDIES
Alamance Comm Coll (NC)
Albuquerque Tech Vocational Inst (NM)
Asnuntuck Comm Coll (CT)
Atlanta Metropolitan Coll (GA)
Central Carolina Tech Coll (SC)
Central Comm Coll–Grand Island Campus (NE)
Central Texas Coll (TX)
Chaparral Coll (AZ)
Crown Coll (WA)
Dixie State Coll of Utah (UT)
Draughons Jr Coll, Clarksville (TN)
Dutchess Comm Coll (NY)
Eastern Wyoming Coll (WY)
Eastfield Coll (TX)
El Centro Coll (TX)
Fayetteville Tech Comm Coll (NC)
Floyd Coll (GA)
Great Basin Coll (NV)
Hudson County Comm Coll (NJ)
Inver Hills Comm Coll (MN)
J. Sargeant Reynolds Comm Coll (VA)
Kellogg Comm Coll (MI)
Keystone Coll (PA)
Kilgore Coll (TX)
Lamar Comm Coll (CO)
Louisiana State U at Alexandria (LA)

Louisiana State U at Eunice (LA)
Manatee Comm Coll (FL)
Marian Court Coll (MA)
Mid-South Comm Coll (AR)
Minneapolis Comm and Tech Coll (MN)
Monroe County Comm Coll (MI)
Nassau Comm Coll (NY)
New Mexico State U–Alamogordo (NM)
North Country Comm Coll (NY)
Northern New Mexico Comm Coll (NM)
Northland Pioneer Coll (AZ)
Northwest State Comm Coll (OH)
Orangeburg-Calhoun Tech Coll (SC)
Parkland Coll (IL)
Pensacola Jr Coll (FL)
Phoenix Coll (AZ)
Piedmont Tech Coll (SC)
Pima Comm Coll (AZ)
San Juan Coll (NM)
Santa Fe Comm Coll (NM)
Southeastern Comm Coll, South Campus (IA)
Southwestern Oklahoma State U at Sayre (OK)
Southwest Tennessee Comm Coll (TN)
U of Arkansas Comm Coll at Batesville (AR)
Vermilion Comm Coll (MN)
Walla Walla Comm Coll (WA)
Western Nebraska Comm Coll (NE)

CRIMINOLOGY
Butler County Comm Coll (PA)
Catawba Valley Comm Coll (NC)
Daytona Beach Comm Coll (FL)
Lincoln Coll, Lincoln (IL)
Northland Comm and Tech Coll (MN)
Pensacola Jr Coll (FL)
Southeast Arkansas Coll (AR)

CULINARY ARTS
Adirondack Comm Coll (NY)
Alamance Comm Coll (NC)
Albuquerque Tech Vocational Inst (NM)
Allegany Coll of Maryland (MD)
American River Coll (CA)
The Art Inst of Atlanta (GA)
The Art Inst of Fort Lauderdale (FL)
The Art Inst of Houston (TX)
The Art Inst of Los Angeles (CA)
The Art Inst of New York City (NY)
The Art Inst of Philadelphia (PA)
The Art Inst of Seattle (WA)
The Art Insts International Minnesota (MN)
Asheville-Buncombe Tech Comm Coll (NC)
Atlantic Cape Comm Coll (NJ)
Bakersfield Coll (CA)
Baltimore International Coll (MD)
Bates Tech Coll (WA)
Berkshire Comm Coll (MA)
Black Hawk Coll, Moline (IL)
Blackhawk Tech Coll (WI)
Brevard Comm Coll (FL)
Brookdale Comm Coll (NJ)
Bucks County Comm Coll (PA)
Bunker Hill Comm Coll (MA)
California Culinary Academy (CA)
Central Oregon Comm Coll (OR)
Central Piedmont Comm Coll (NC)
Chippewa Valley Tech Coll (WI)
Cincinnati State Tech and Comm Coll (OH)
Clark Coll (WA)
Coll of DuPage (IL)
Coll of Southern Idaho (ID)
Coll of the Desert (CA)
Coll of the Sequoias (CA)
Columbus State Comm Coll (OH)
Comm Coll of Allegheny County (PA)
Comm Coll of Beaver County (PA)
Comm Coll of Southern Nevada (NV)
The Cooking and Hospitality Inst of Chicago (IL)
Culinary Arts Inst of Louisiana (LA)
Cypress Coll (CA)
Daytona Beach Comm Coll (FL)
Delaware Tech & Comm Coll, Stanton/ Wilmington Cmps (DE)
Del Mar Coll (TX)
Des Moines Area Comm Coll (IA)
Eastern Maine Tech Coll (ME)
Edmonds Comm Coll (WA)
El Centro Coll (TX)
Erie Comm Coll, City Campus (NY)
Florida Comm Coll at Jacksonville (FL)
Florida Culinary Inst (FL)
Galveston Coll (TX)
Glendale Comm Coll (CA)
Grand Rapids Comm Coll (MI)
Guilford Tech Comm Coll (NC)
Gulf Coast Comm Coll (FL)
Harrisburg Area Comm Coll (PA)
Henry Ford Comm Coll (MI)
Hibbing Comm Coll (MN)
Horry-Georgetown Tech Coll (SC)
Hudson County Comm Coll (NJ)
Indian River Comm Coll (FL)
International Academy of Design & Technology (PA)
Iowa Western Comm Coll (IA)
Jefferson Comm Coll (KY)
Joliet Jr Coll (IL)
J. Sargeant Reynolds Comm Coll (VA)
Kauai Comm Coll (HI)
Kennebec Valley Tech Coll (ME)
Keystone Coll (PA)
Kirkwood Comm Coll (IA)
Lake Washington Tech Coll (WA)
Lane Comm Coll (OR)
Lexington Coll (IL)
Linn-Benton Comm Coll (OR)
Long Beach City Coll (CA)
Los Angeles Mission Coll (CA)
Louisiana Tech Coll–Delta Ouachita Campus (LA)
Luzerne County Comm Coll (PA)
Macomb Comm Coll (MI)
Massasoit Comm Coll (MA)
McIntosh Coll (NH)
Mercer County Comm Coll (NJ)
Metropolitan Comm Coll (NE)
Middlesex County Coll (NJ)
Milwaukee Area Tech Coll (WI)
Minneapolis Comm and Tech Coll (MN)
Mitchell Tech Inst (SD)
Monroe County Comm Coll (MI)
Moraine Park Tech Coll (WI)
Moraine Valley Comm Coll (IL)
Mott Comm Coll (MI)
Muskingum Area Tech Coll (OH)
Nashville State Tech Inst (TN)
Newbury Coll (MA)
New England Culinary Inst (VT)
New Hampshire Comm Tech Coll, Berlin/Laconia (NH)
Niagara County Comm Coll (NY)
North Idaho Coll (ID)
North Seattle Comm Coll (WA)
North Shore Comm Coll (MA)
Northwestern Michigan Coll (MI)
Oakland Comm Coll (MI)
Odessa Coll (TX)
Oklahoma State U, Okmulgee (OK)
Olympic Coll (WA)
Onondaga Comm Coll (NY)
Orange Coast Coll (CA)
Oxnard Coll (CA)
Ozarka Coll (AR)
Paul Smith's Coll of Arts and Sciences (NY)
Pennsylvania Coll of Technology (PA)
Pennsylvania Inst of Culinary Arts (PA)
Penn Valley Comm Coll (MO)
Pensacola Jr Coll (FL)
Reading Area Comm Coll (PA)
Rend Lake Coll (IL)
The Restaurant School (PA)
Riverside Comm Coll (CA)
Rockland Comm Coll (NY)
St. Cloud Tech Coll (MN)
St. Philip's Coll (TX)
Sandhills Comm Coll (NC)
San Jacinto Coll North Campus (TX)
San Joaquin Delta Coll (CA)
Santa Fe Comm Coll (NM)
Schenectady County Comm Coll (NY)
Schoolcraft Coll (MI)
Scott Comm Coll (IA)
Scottsdale Comm Coll (AZ)
Seattle Central Comm Coll (WA)
Shasta Coll (CA)
Sinclair Comm Coll (OH)
Skagit Valley Coll (WA)
Southern Maine Tech Coll (ME)
South Puget Sound Comm Coll (WA)
Southwestern Comm Coll (NC)
Southwest Wisconsin Tech Coll (WI)
Spokane Comm Coll (WA)
State U of NY Coll of Technology at Alfred (NY)
State U of NY Coll of Technology at Delhi (NY)
Stratford U (VA)
Suffolk County Comm Coll (NY)
Sullivan County Comm Coll (NY)
Texas Culinary Academy (TX)
Texas State Tech Coll– Waco/ Marshall Campus (TX)
Trident Tech Coll (SC)
Triton Coll (IL)
Truckee Meadows Comm Coll (NV)
Vincennes U (IN)
Wake Tech Comm Coll (NC)
Westchester Comm Coll (NY)
Westmoreland County Comm Coll (PA)
Yorktowne Business Inst (PA)

CULINARY ARTS AND SERVICES RELATED
Fayetteville Tech Comm Coll (NC)
Linn-Benton Comm Coll (OR)
Santa Barbara City Coll (CA)

CULTURAL STUDIES
Coll of Marin (CA)
Coll of the Sequoias (CA)
Compton Comm Coll (CA)
De Anza Coll (CA)
Foothill Coll (CA)
Fresno City Coll (CA)
Fullerton Coll (CA)
Highline Comm Coll (WA)
Monterey Peninsula Coll (CA)
Orange Coast Coll (CA)
Pasadena City Coll (CA)
Riverside Comm Coll (CA)
Sacramento City Coll (CA)
Santa Ana Coll (CA)
Santa Barbara City Coll (CA)
Santa Monica Coll (CA)
Skagit Valley Coll (WA)
Ventura Coll (CA)

CUSTODIAL SERVICES RELATED
Comm Coll of Allegheny County (PA)

CYTOTECHNOLOGY
Barton County Comm Coll (KS)
Highland Comm Coll (KS)
Manor Coll (PA)

DAIRY SCIENCE
Chippewa Valley Tech Coll (WI)
Cisco Jr Coll (TX)
Coll of the Sequoias (CA)
Highland Comm Coll (KS)
Hill Coll of the Hill Jr College District (TX)
Linn-Benton Comm Coll (OR)
Modesto Jr Coll (CA)
Northeast Iowa Comm Coll (IA)
Northeast Texas Comm Coll (TX)
Northwest Mississippi Comm Coll (MS)
Southwest Wisconsin Tech Coll (WI)
State U of NY Coll of A&T at Morrisville (NY)
State U of NY Coll of Technology at Alfred (NY)
Vermont Tech Coll (VT)

DANCE
Allan Hancock Coll (CA)
Bergen Comm Coll (NJ)
Cañada Coll (CA)
Central Piedmont Comm Coll (NC)
Chaffey Coll (CA)
Citrus Coll (CA)
Coll of Marin (CA)
Compton Comm Coll (CA)
Cypress Coll (CA)
Daytona Beach Comm Coll (FL)
Dean Coll (MA)
Dixie State Coll of Utah (UT)
Fullerton Coll (CA)
Glendale Comm Coll (CA)
Henry Ford Comm Coll (MI)
Hillsborough Comm Coll (FL)
Kilgore Coll (TX)
Lake Tahoe Comm Coll (CA)
Lansing Comm Coll (MI)
Lincoln Coll, Lincoln (IL)
Long Beach City Coll (CA)
Lon Morris Coll (TX)
Louisburg Coll (NC)
Mercer County Comm Coll (NJ)
Miami-Dade Comm Coll (FL)
Middlesex County Coll (NJ)
MiraCosta Coll (CA)
Monterey Peninsula Coll (CA)
Mt. San Jacinto Coll (CA)
Nassau Comm Coll (NY)
Navarro Coll (TX)
Northern Essex Comm Coll (MA)
Orange Coast Coll (CA)
Palomar Coll (CA)
St. Catharine Coll (KY)
San Joaquin Delta Coll (CA)
Santa Ana Coll (CA)
Santa Fe Comm Coll (NM)
Santa Monica Coll (CA)
Sinclair Comm Coll (OH)
Snow Coll (UT)
Southwestern Coll (CA)
Trinity Valley Comm Coll (TX)
Westchester Comm Coll (NY)
Western Wyoming Comm Coll (WY)

DATA ENTRY/MICROCOMPUTER APPLICATIONS
Academy of Medical Arts and Business (PA)
American River Coll (CA)
Anne Arundel Comm Coll (MD)
Anoka-Hennepin Tech Coll (MN)
Anoka-Ramsey Comm Coll (MN)
Austin Business Coll (TX)
Austin Comm Coll (TX)
Barton County Comm Coll (KS)
Berkshire Comm Coll (MA)
Broome Comm Coll (NY)
The Brown Mackie Coll–Olathe Campus (KS)
Camden County Coll (NJ)
Cleveland Comm Coll (NC)
Coastal Bend Coll (TX)
Colorado Mountn Coll, Timberline Cmps (CO)
The Comm Coll of Baltimore County–Catonsville Campus (MD)
Comm Coll of Vermont (VT)
Cypress Coll (CA)
Dakota County Tech Coll (MN)
Daymar Coll (KY)
Del Mar Coll (TX)
Delta Coll (MI)
Diablo Valley Coll (CA)
Eastern Arizona Coll (AZ)
Eastfield Coll (TX)
Edgecombe Comm Coll (NC)
Ellsworth Comm Coll (IA)
Fayetteville Tech Comm Coll (NC)
Fiorello H LaGuardia Comm Coll of City U of NY (NY)
Flathead Valley Comm Coll (MT)
Florida Comm Coll at Jacksonville (FL)
Florida National Coll (FL)
Gallipolis Career Coll (OH)
Galveston Coll (TX)
Gateway Comm Coll (CT)
Glendale Comm Coll (CA)
Heartland Comm Coll (IL)
Henderson Comm Coll (KY)
Herkimer County Comm Coll (NY)
Hinds Comm Coll (MS)
Horry-Georgetown Tech Coll (SC)
Howard Comm Coll (MD)
Iowa Western Comm Coll (IA)
Itasca Comm Coll (MN)
Jackson Comm Coll (MI)
Laredo Comm Coll (TX)
Laurel Business Inst (PA)
Lorain County Comm Coll (OH)
Los Angeles City Coll (CA)
Luzerne County Comm Coll (PA)
Massasoit Comm Coll (MA)
Mid-State Tech Coll (WI)
Milwaukee Area Tech Coll (WI)
Mississippi Gulf Coast Comm Coll (MS)
Modesto Jr Coll (CA)
Mountain Empire Comm Coll (VA)
Muskingum Area Tech Coll (OH)
Northland Comm and Tech Coll (MN)
North Shore Comm Coll (MA)
Okaloosa-Walton Comm Coll (FL)
Onondaga Comm Coll (NY)
Orange County Comm Coll (NY)
Owensboro Comm Coll (KY)
Parkland Coll (IL)
Pellissippi State Tech Comm Coll (TN)
Pratt Comm Coll and Area Vocational School (KS)
Rasmussen Coll Mankato (MN)
Richland Comm Coll (IL)
Riverland Comm Coll (MN)
San Antonio Coll (TX)
Santa Ana Coll (CA)
Seminole Comm Coll (FL)
Sheridan Coll (WY)
Sinclair Comm Coll (OH)
Stark State Coll of Technology (OH)
Sullivan County Comm Coll (NY)
Thaddeus Stevens Coll of Technology (PA)
Tompkins Cortland Comm Coll (NY)
Tulsa Comm Coll (OK)
Tyler Jr Coll (TX)
U of Arkansas Comm Coll at Batesville (AR)
U of Kentucky, Lexington Comm Coll (KY)
Vincennes U (IN)
Walla Walla Comm Coll (WA)
West Central Tech Coll (GA)
The Westchester Business Inst (NY)

DATA ENTRY/MICROCOMPUTER APPLICATIONS RELATED
Academy of Medical Arts and Business (PA)
AIB Coll of Business (IA)
Anoka-Hennepin Tech Coll (MN)
Anoka-Ramsey Comm Coll (MN)
Barton County Comm Coll (KS)
The Brown Mackie Coll–Olathe Campus (KS)
Camden County Coll (NJ)
Capital Comm Coll (CT)
Coastal Bend Coll (TX)
Colorado Mountn Coll, Alpine Cmps (CO)
Colorado Mountn Coll (CO)
Colorado Mountn Coll, Timberline Cmps (CO)
The Comm Coll of Baltimore County–Catonsville Campus (MD)
Cypress Coll (CA)
Dakota County Tech Coll (MN)
Daymar Coll (KY)
Delta Coll (MI)
Diablo Valley Coll (CA)
Donnelly Coll (KS)
Edgecombe Comm Coll (NC)
Education America, Remington Coll, Lafayette Campus (LA)
Education America, Southeast Coll of Technology, New Orleans Campus (LA)
Eugenio María de Hostos Comm Coll of City U of NY (NY)
Florida Comm Coll at Jacksonville (FL)
Florida National Coll (FL)
Georgia Perimeter Coll (GA)
Glendale Comm Coll (CA)
Hawkeye Comm Coll (IA)
Heartland Comm Coll (IL)
Henderson Comm Coll (KY)
Herkimer County Comm Coll (NY)
Highline Comm Coll (WA)
Hinds Comm Coll (MS)
Itasca Comm Coll (MN)
Kellogg Comm Coll (MI)
Lake Area Tech Inst (SD)
Laredo Comm Coll (TX)
Laurel Business Inst (PA)

Lorain County Comm Coll (OH)
Los Angeles City Coll (CA)
Midland Coll (TX)
Mississippi Gulf Coast Comm Coll (MS)
Northland Comm and Tech Coll (MN)
Onondaga Comm Coll (NY)
Orange Coast Coll (CA)
Patrick Henry Comm Coll (VA)
Pellissippi State Tech Comm Coll (TN)
Peninsula Coll (WA)
Pratt Comm Coll and Area Vocational School (KS)
Rasmussen Coll Mankato (MN)
Richland Comm Coll (IL)
Riverland Comm Coll (MN)
San Diego Mesa Coll (CA)
Santa Ana Coll (CA)
Seminole Comm Coll (FL)
Sinclair Comm Coll (OH)
Southwestern Michigan Coll (MI)
Stark State Coll of Technology (OH)
Texarkana Coll (TX)
Tulsa Comm Coll (OK)
Vincennes U (IN)
Vista Comm Coll (CA)
The Westchester Business Inst (NY)
West Shore Comm Coll (MI)

DATA PROCESSING

Adirondack Comm Coll (NY)
Alexandria Tech Coll (MN)
Black Hawk Coll, Moline (IL)
Business Inst of Pennsylvania (PA)
Coll of Lake County (IL)
Comm Coll of Allegheny County (PA)
Crowder Coll (MO)
Delta Coll (MI)
DuBois Business Coll (PA)
El Centro Coll (TX)
Electronic Computer Programming Coll (TN)
Fayetteville Tech Comm Coll (NC)
Front Range Comm Coll (CO)
Gogebic Comm Coll (MI)
Helena Coll of Tech of The U of Montana (MT)
Illinois Eastern Comm Colls, Lincoln Trail Coll (IL)
Joliet Jr Coll (IL)
Kaskaskia Coll (IL)
Laurel Business Inst (PA)
Montgomery County Comm Coll (PA)
Mott Comm Coll (MI)
Northwestern Michigan Coll (MI)
Northwest State Comm Coll (OH)
Parkland Coll (IL)
Pennsylvania Coll of Technology (PA)
San Jacinto Coll North Campus (TX)
The U of Akron–Wayne Coll (OH)
Waubonsee Comm Coll (IL)
Western Nevada Comm Coll (NV)

DATA PROCESSING TECHNOLOGY

Abraham Baldwin Ag Coll (GA)
Academy of Medical Arts and Business (PA)
Adirondack Comm Coll (NY)
Albuquerque Tech Vocational Inst (NM)
Allegany Coll of Maryland (MD)
Allen County Comm Coll (KS)
Alpena Comm Coll (MI)
American River Coll (CA)
Angelina Coll (TX)
Anne Arundel Comm Coll (MD)
Antelope Valley Coll (CA)
Bainbridge Coll (GA)
Bakersfield Coll (CA)
Baltimore City Comm Coll (MD)
Bates Tech Coll (WA)
Bellevue Comm Coll (WA)
Berkshire Comm Coll (MA)
Black River Tech Coll (AR)
Borough of Manhattan Comm Coll of City U of NY (NY)
Brazosport Coll (TX)
Bronx Comm Coll of City U of NY (NY)
Broome Comm Coll (NY)
Bucks County Comm Coll (PA)
Burlington County Coll (NJ)
Butte Coll (CA)
Caldwell Comm Coll and Tech Inst (NC)
Camden County Coll (NJ)
Cañada Coll (CA)
Career Coll of Northern Nevada (NV)
Carl Sandburg Coll (IL)
Carroll Comm Coll (MD)
Casper Coll (WY)
Catawba Valley Comm Coll (NC)
Cayuga County Comm Coll (NY)
Cecil Comm Coll (MD)
Cedar Valley Coll (TX)
Central Carolina Tech Coll (SC)
Central Comm Coll–Grand Island Campus (NE)
Central Piedmont Comm Coll (NC)
Central Texas Coll (TX)
Cerritos Coll (CA)
Cerro Coso Comm Coll (CA)
Certified Careers Inst, Salt Lake City (UT)
Chabot Coll (CA)
Chattahoochee Tech Coll (GA)
Chattahoochee Valley Comm Coll (AL)
Chattanooga State Tech Comm Coll (TN)
Chesapeake Coll (MD)
Chippewa Valley Tech Coll (WI)
Cisco Jr Coll (TX)
Citrus Coll (CA)
City Colls of Chicago, Richard J Daley Coll (IL)
City Colls of Chicago, Wilbur Wright Coll (IL)
Coastal Bend Coll (TX)
Coll of Marin (CA)
Coll of the Siskiyous (CA)
Columbia-Greene Comm Coll (NY)
The Comm Coll of Baltimore County–Catonsville Campus (MD)
Comm Coll of Beaver County (PA)
Comm Coll of Southern Nevada (NV)
Compton Comm Coll (CA)
Cuesta Coll (CA)
Danville Area Comm Coll (IL)
Darton Coll (GA)
Davis Coll (OH)
Delaware Tech & Comm Coll, Jack F Owens Cmps (DE)
Delaware Tech & Comm Coll, Stanton/ Wilmington Cmps (DE)
Delaware Tech & Comm Coll, Terry Cmps (DE)
Delgado Comm Coll (LA)
Delta Coll (MI)
Des Moines Area Comm Coll (IA)
Dixie State Coll of Utah (UT)
Dodge City Comm Coll (KS)
Donnelly Coll (KS)
Durham Tech Comm Coll (NC)
East Central Coll (MO)
East Central Comm Coll (MS)
Eastfield Coll (TX)
ECPI Coll of Technology, Virginia Beach (VA)
ECPI Tech Coll, Richmond (VA)
Edgecombe Comm Coll (NC)
Edison State Comm Coll (OH)
Edmonds Comm Coll (WA)
El Centro Coll (TX)
Ellsworth Comm Coll (IA)
Essex County Coll (NJ)
Eugenio María de Hostos Comm Coll of City U of NY (NY)
Everett Comm Coll (WA)
Evergreen Valley Coll (CA)
Finger Lakes Comm Coll (NY)
Fisher Coll (MA)
Florida National Coll (FL)
Forsyth Tech Comm Coll (NC)
Frederick Comm Coll (MD)
Fullerton Coll (CA)
Fulton-Montgomery Comm Coll (NY)
Gaston Coll (NC)
Gateway Comm Coll (CT)
Georgia Perimeter Coll (GA)
Germanna Comm Coll (VA)
Glendale Comm Coll (CA)
Gloucester County Coll (NJ)
Gogebic Comm Coll (MI)
Great Basin Coll (NV)
Hagerstown Business Coll (MD)
Hamilton Coll (IA)
Hazard Comm Coll (KY)
Henderson Comm Coll (KY)
Henry Ford Comm Coll (MI)
Herzing Coll (AL)
Highland Comm Coll (IL)
Highland Comm Coll (KS)
Hill Coll of the Hill Jr College District (TX)
Hinds Comm Coll (MS)
Holmes Comm Coll (MS)
Housatonic Comm Coll (CT)
Hudson County Comm Coll (NJ)
Illinois Eastern Comm Colls, Lincoln Trail Coll (IL)
Independence Comm Coll (KS)
Iowa Lakes Comm Coll (IA)
ITT Tech Inst, Phoenix (AZ)
ITT Tech Inst, San Diego (CA)
ITT Tech Inst, Jacksonville (FL)
Jackson Comm Coll (MI)
Jefferson Coll (MO)
Jefferson Comm Coll (KY)
Jefferson Comm Coll (OH)
John A. Logan Coll (IL)
Jones County Jr Coll (MS)
J. Sargeant Reynolds Comm Coll (VA)
Kansas City Kansas Comm Coll (KS)
Keystone Coll (PA)
Kilgore Coll (TX)
Kirkwood Comm Coll (IA)
Labette Comm Coll (KS)
Lake Michigan Coll (MI)
Lamar Comm Coll (CO)
Lamar State Coll–Orange (TX)
Laredo Comm Coll (TX)
Lewis and Clark Comm Coll (IL)
Lewis Coll of Business (MI)
Lincoln Coll, Lincoln (IL)
Lincoln Coll, Normal (IL)
Lincoln Land Comm Coll (IL)
Long Beach City Coll (CA)
Longview Comm Coll (MO)
Los Angeles City Coll (CA)
Los Angeles Harbor Coll (CA)
Los Angeles Pierce Coll (CA)
Louisiana State U at Alexandria (LA)
Luzerne County Comm Coll (PA)
Maple Woods Comm Coll (MO)
Marian Court Coll (MA)
Marion Tech Coll (OH)
Merced Coll (CA)
Miami-Dade Comm Coll (FL)
Miami U–Hamilton Campus (OH)
Middle Georgia Coll (GA)
Midlands Tech Coll (SC)
Milwaukee Area Tech Coll (WI)
Mitchell Comm Coll (NC)
Mohawk Valley Comm Coll (NY)
Monroe Comm Coll (NY)
Monroe County Comm Coll (MI)
Montcalm Comm Coll (MI)
Monterey Peninsula Coll (CA)
Moorpark Coll (CA)
Moraine Park Tech Coll (WI)
Morton Coll (IL)
Nassau Comm Coll (NY)
Navarro Coll (TX)
New Mexico State U–Alamogordo (NM)
New York City Tech Coll of the City U of NY (NY)
Northampton County Area Comm Coll (PA)
North Central Michigan Coll (MI)
North Central Texas Coll (TX)
Northeast Comm Coll (NE)
Northeastern Tech Coll (SC)
Northeast State Tech Comm Coll (TN)
Northern Essex Comm Coll (MA)
Northern Maine Tech Coll (ME)
Northland Pioneer Coll (AZ)
North Seattle Comm Coll (WA)
NorthWest Arkansas Comm Coll (AR)
Northwestern Business Coll (IL)
Northwest Mississippi Comm Coll (MS)
Norwalk Comm Coll (CT)
Odessa Coll (TX)
Ohio Valley Business Coll (OH)
Oklahoma State U, Oklahoma City (OK)
Onondaga Comm Coll (NY)
Orangeburg-Calhoun Tech Coll (SC)
Orange Coast Coll (CA)
Orange County Comm Coll (NY)
Otero Jr Coll (CO)
Palm Beach Comm Coll (FL)
Pasadena City Coll (CA)
Patrick Henry Comm Coll (VA)
Paul D. Camp Comm Coll (VA)
Pellissippi State Tech Comm Coll (TN)
Penn Valley Comm Coll (MO)
Phoenix Coll (AZ)
Piedmont Tech Coll (SC)
Piedmont Virginia Comm Coll (VA)
Polk Comm Coll (FL)
Quincy Coll (MA)
Quinsigamond Comm Coll (MA)
Raritan Valley Comm Coll (NJ)
Rasmussen Coll Mankato (MN)
Reading Area Comm Coll (PA)
Ridgewater Coll (MN)
Rochester Business Inst (NY)
Rockland Comm Coll (NY)
Sacramento City Coll (CA)
St. Louis Comm Coll at Florissant Valley (MO)
St. Philip's Coll (TX)
San Antonio Coll (TX)
San Bernardino Valley Coll (CA)
San Diego City Coll (CA)
San Jacinto Coll Central Campus (TX)
San Jacinto Coll North Campus (TX)
San Jacinto Coll South Campus (TX)
Santa Fe Comm Coll (FL)
Santa Monica Coll (CA)
Sauk Valley Comm Coll (IL)
Schoolcraft Coll (MI)
Seminole Comm Coll (FL)
Snead State Comm Coll (AL)
Southeast Comm Coll (KY)
Southeast Comm Coll, Milford Campus (NE)
South Plains Coll (TX)
South Puget Sound Comm Coll (WA)
South Suburban Coll (IL)
Southwest Wisconsin Tech Coll (WI)
Spokane Comm Coll (WA)
Springfield Tech Comm Coll (MA)
State U of NY Coll of A&T at Morrisville (NY)
State U of NY Coll of Technology at Alfred (NY)
Suffolk County Comm Coll (NY)
Tacoma Comm Coll (WA)
Taft Coll (CA)
Tallahassee Comm Coll (FL)
Temple Coll (TX)
Texarkana Coll (TX)
Texas State Tech Coll–Harlingen (TX)
Three Rivers Comm Coll (CT)
Tidewater Comm Coll (VA)
Tri-County Tech Coll (SC)
Trinidad State Jr Coll (CO)
Trinity Valley Comm Coll (TX)
Triton Coll (IL)
Truckee Meadows Comm Coll (NV)
Tunxis Comm Coll (CT)
Ulster County Comm Coll (NY)
The U of Akron–Wayne Coll (OH)
Utica School of Commerce (NY)
Vance-Granville Comm Coll (NC)
Vermilion Comm Coll (MN)
Vernon Coll (TX)
Virginia Western Comm Coll (VA)
Warren County Comm Coll (NJ)
Webster Coll, Ocala (FL)
The Westchester Business Inst (NY)
Westchester Comm Coll (NY)
Western Wisconsin Tech Coll (WI)
Western Wyoming Comm Coll (WY)
Westmoreland County Comm Coll (PA)
West Shore Comm Coll (MI)
West Virginia Jr Coll, Charleston (WV)
West Virginia U at Parkersburg (WV)
Wharton County Jr Coll (TX)
Williston State Coll (ND)
York Tech Coll (SC)

DATA WAREHOUSING/MINING/ DATABASE ADMINISTRATION

Anoka-Hennepin Tech Coll (MN)
Arapahoe Comm Coll (CO)
Coll of the Sequoias (CA)
The Comm Coll of Baltimore County–Catonsville Campus (MD)
Dakota County Tech Coll (MN)
Daymar Coll (KY)
Florida Comm Coll at Jacksonville (FL)
Kansas City Kansas Comm Coll (KS)
Kennebec Valley Tech Coll (ME)
Northland Comm and Tech Coll (MN)
Seminole Comm Coll (FL)
Tulsa Comm Coll (OK)

DENTAL ASSISTANT

Academy of Medical Arts and Business (PA)
Allan Hancock Coll (CA)
Argosy U-Twin Cities (MN)
Atlanta Metropolitan Coll (GA)
Berkshire Comm Coll (MA)
Briarwood Coll (CT)
The Bryman School (AZ)
Calhoun Comm Coll (AL)
Central Comm Coll–Hastings Campus (NE)
Central Oregon Comm Coll (OR)
Century Comm and Tech Coll (MN)
Citrus Coll (CA)
Coll of Southern Idaho (ID)
Coll of the Redwoods (CA)
Comm Coll of the Air Force (AL)
Cypress Coll (CA)
Darton Coll (GA)
Delta Coll (MI)
Fayetteville Tech Comm Coll (NC)
Foothill Coll (CA)
Georgia Perimeter Coll (GA)
Harcum Coll (PA)
Hennepin Tech Coll (MN)
Hibbing Comm Coll (MN)
Huntington Jr Coll of Business (WV)
James H. Faulkner State Comm Coll (AL)
Jefferson Comm Coll (OH)
Lake Area Tech Inst (SD)
Lake Michigan Coll (MI)
Lake Washington Tech Coll (WA)
Luzerne County Comm Coll (PA)
Middlesex Comm Coll (MA)
Minnesota School of Business (MN)
Modesto Jr Coll (CA)
Montana State U Coll of Tech-Great Falls (MT)
Mott Comm Coll (MI)
New England Inst of Tech & Florida Culinary Inst (FL)
New Hampshire Tech Inst (NH)
Northwestern Michigan Coll (MI)
Ohio Valley Business Coll (OH)
Oxnard Coll (CA)
Pikes Peak Comm Coll (CO)
Reedley Coll (CA)
Sacramento City Coll (CA)
St. Cloud Tech Coll (MN)
San Diego Mesa Coll (CA)
San Joaquin Valley Coll (CA)
Southwest Wisconsin Tech Coll (WI)
Texas State Tech Coll–Harlingen (TX)
Texas State Tech Coll– Waco/ Marshall Campus (TX)
Truckee Meadows Comm Coll (NV)
Tulsa Comm Coll (OK)
Wallace State Comm Coll (AL)

DENTAL HYGIENE

Allegany Coll of Maryland (MD)
Amarillo Coll (TX)
American Inst of Health Technology, Inc. (ID)
Andrew Coll (GA)
Asheville-Buncombe Tech Comm Coll (NC)
Athens Tech Coll (GA)
Bakersfield Coll (CA)

Baltimore City Comm Coll (MD)
Bergen Comm Coll (NJ)
Black Hawk Coll, Moline (IL)
Blackhawk Tech Coll (WI)
Blinn Coll (TX)
Brevard Comm Coll (FL)
Bristol Comm Coll (MA)
Broome Comm Coll (NY)
The Brown Mackie Coll–Olathe Campus (KS)
Camden County Coll (NJ)
Cape Cod Comm Coll (MA)
Cape Fear Comm Coll (NC)
Catawba Valley Comm Coll (NC)
Central Comm Coll–Hastings Campus (NE)
Central Piedmont Comm Coll (NC)
Century Comm and Tech Coll (MN)
Cerritos Coll (CA)
Chabot Coll (CA)
Chattanooga State Tech Comm Coll (TN)
Chemeketa Comm Coll (OR)
Chippewa Valley Tech Coll (WI)
City Coll of San Francisco (CA)
City Colls of Chicago, Richard J Daley Coll (IL)
Clark Coll (WA)
Coastal Bend Coll (TX)
Coastal Carolina Comm Coll (NC)
Coastal Georgia Comm Coll (GA)
Colby Comm Coll (KS)
Coll of Alameda (CA)
Coll of Lake County (IL)
Coll of Marin (CA)
Coll of Southern Idaho (ID)
Collin County Comm Coll District (TX)
Colorado Northwestern Comm Coll (CO)
Columbia State Comm Coll (TN)
Columbus State Comm Coll (OH)
Comm Coll of Denver (CO)
Comm Coll of Rhode Island (RI)
Comm Coll of Southern Nevada (NV)
Cypress Coll (CA)
Darton Coll (GA)
Delaware Tech & Comm Coll, Stanton/ Wilmington Cmps (DE)
Delgado Comm Coll (LA)
Del Mar Coll (TX)
Delta Coll (MI)
Des Moines Area Comm Coll (IA)
Dixie State Coll of Utah (UT)
Durham Tech Comm Coll (NC)
Edison Comm Coll (FL)
Elizabethtown Comm Coll (KY)
Erie Comm Coll, North Campus (NY)
Essex County Coll (NJ)
Eugenio María de Hostos Comm Coll of City U of NY (NY)
Everett Comm Coll (WA)
Fayetteville Tech Comm Coll (NC)
Florence-Darlington Tech Coll (SC)
Florida Comm Coll at Jacksonville (FL)
Florida National Coll (FL)
Floyd Coll (GA)
Foothill Coll (CA)
Fresno City Coll (CA)
Gateway Tech Coll (WI)
Georgia Perimeter Coll (GA)
Grand Rapids Comm Coll (MI)
Greenville Tech Coll (SC)
Guilford Tech Comm Coll (NC)
Gulf Coast Comm Coll (FL)
Gwinnett Tech Coll (GA)
Harcum Coll (PA)
Harrisburg Area Comm Coll (PA)
Hawkeye Comm Coll (IA)
Highland Comm Coll (KS)
Highline Comm Coll (WA)
Hinds Comm Coll (MS)
Howard Coll (TX)
Indian River Comm Coll (FL)
Iowa Western Comm Coll (IA)
John A. Logan Coll (IL)
Johnson County Comm Coll (KS)
Kalamazoo Valley Comm Coll (MI)
Kellogg Comm Coll (MI)
Lake Land Coll (IL)
Lakeland Comm Coll (OH)
Lakeshore Tech Coll (WI)
Lake Washington Tech Coll (WA)
Lane Comm Coll (OR)
Lansing Comm Coll (MI)
Lewis and Clark Comm Coll (IL)
Lima Tech Coll (OH)
Lord Fairfax Comm Coll (VA)
Los Angeles City Coll (CA)
Luzerne County Comm Coll (PA)
Manor Coll (PA)
Marshalltown Comm Coll (IA)
Massasoit Comm Coll (MA)
Merced Coll (CA)
Meridian Comm Coll (MS)
Miami-Dade Comm Coll (FL)
Middlesex Comm Coll (MA)
Middlesex County Coll (NJ)
Midlands Tech Coll (SC)
Mid-Plains Comm Coll Area (NE)
Milwaukee Area Tech Coll (WI)
Monroe Comm Coll (NY)
Montana State U Coll of Tech-Great Falls (MT)
Monterey Peninsula Coll (CA)
Montgomery County Comm Coll (PA)
Mott Comm Coll (MI)
Mt. Hood Comm Coll (OR)
Navarro Coll (TX)
New Hampshire Tech Inst (NH)
New York City Tech Coll of the City U of NY (NY)
Northampton County Area Comm Coll (PA)
Northcentral Tech Coll (WI)
North Dakota State Coll of Science (ND)
Northern Virginia Comm Coll (VA)
Oakland Comm Coll (MI)
Onondaga Comm Coll (NY)
Orange Coast Coll (CA)
Orange County Comm Coll (NY)
Oxnard Coll (CA)
Palm Beach Comm Coll (FL)
Palomar Coll (CA)
Parkland Coll (IL)
Pasadena City Coll (CA)
Pasco-Hernando Comm Coll (FL)
Pennsylvania Coll of Technology (PA)
Pensacola Jr Coll (FL)
Phoenix Coll (AZ)
Pierce Coll (WA)
Pima Comm Coll (AZ)
Portland Comm Coll (OR)
Prairie State Coll (IL)
Quinsigamond Comm Coll (MA)
Riverside Comm Coll (CA)
Roane State Comm Coll (TN)
Sacramento City Coll (CA)
St. Cloud Tech Coll (MN)
St. Petersburg Coll (FL)
Salish Kootenai Coll (MT)
San Antonio Coll (TX)
San Bernardino Valley Coll (CA)
San Joaquin Valley Coll (CA)
Santa Fe Comm Coll (FL)
Santa Monica Coll (CA)
Shasta Coll (CA)
Sheridan Coll (WY)
Shoreline Comm Coll (WA)
Sinclair Comm Coll (OH)
South Puget Sound Comm Coll (WA)
Southwestern Coll (CA)
Spokane Comm Coll (WA)
Springfield Tech Comm Coll (MA)
Stark State Coll of Technology (OH)
Taft Coll (CA)
Tallahassee Comm Coll (FL)
Tarrant County Coll District (TX)
Temple Coll (TX)
Texas State Tech Coll–Harlingen (TX)
Trident Tech Coll (SC)
Truckee Meadows Comm Coll (NV)
Tulsa Comm Coll (OK)
Tunxis Comm Coll (CT)
Tyler Jr Coll (TX)
Union County Coll (NJ)
U of Arkansas at Fort Smith (AR)
U of Kentucky, Lexington Comm Coll (KY)
Vincennes U (IN)
Virginia Western Comm Coll (VA)
Wallace State Comm Coll (AL)
Wayne Comm Coll (NC)
West Central Tech Coll (GA)
Western Wisconsin Tech Coll (WI)
Westmoreland County Comm Coll (PA)
Wharton County Jr Coll (TX)
York Tech Coll (SC)

DENTAL LABORATORY TECHNICIAN

Atlanta Metropolitan Coll (GA)
Bates Tech Coll (WA)
Century Comm and Tech Coll (MN)
Columbus State Comm Coll (OH)
Comm Coll of the Air Force (AL)
Delgado Comm Coll (LA)
Erie Comm Coll, South Campus (NY)
J. Sargeant Reynolds Comm Coll (VA)
Middlesex Comm Coll (MA)
New York City Tech Coll of the City U of NY (NY)
Pima Comm Coll (AZ)
Texas State Tech Coll–Harlingen (TX)
U of Kentucky, Lexington Comm Coll (KY)

DESIGN/APPLIED ARTS RELATED

ITT Tech Inst, Phoenix (AZ)
ITT Tech Inst, Tampa (FL)

DESIGN/VISUAL COMMUNICATIONS

The Art Inst of New York City (NY)
Black Hawk Coll, Moline (IL)
Bradley Academy for the Visual Arts (PA)
Brookdale Comm Coll (NJ)
Bunker Hill Comm Coll (MA)
Douglas Education Center (PA)
East Central Coll (MO)
Fashion Inst of Design & Merchandising, LA Campus (CA)
Fashion Inst of Design & Merchandising, SD Campus (CA)
Fashion Inst of Design & Merchandising, SF Campus (CA)
Florida Comm Coll at Jacksonville (FL)
Fresno City Coll (CA)
Front Range Comm Coll (CO)
Harrisburg Area Comm Coll (PA)
Ivy Tech State Coll–Central Indiana (IN)
Ivy Tech State Coll–Columbus (IN)
Ivy Tech State Coll–North Central (IN)
Ivy Tech State Coll–Southcentral (IN)
Ivy Tech State Coll–Southwest (IN)
Ivy Tech State Coll–Wabash Valley (IN)
Kilgore Coll (TX)
Moraine Valley Comm Coll (IL)
Nassau Comm Coll (NY)
Northwest State Comm Coll (OH)
Parkland Coll (IL)
Pensacola Jr Coll (FL)
Pikes Peak Comm Coll (CO)
Pima Comm Coll (AZ)
Platt Coll–Los Angeles, Inc (CA)
Santa Fe Comm Coll (NM)
Shasta Coll (CA)
Trinidad State Jr Coll (CO)
Wade Coll (TX)
Waubonsee Comm Coll (IL)

DESKTOP PUBLISHING EQUIPMENT OPERATION

Brookdale Comm Coll (NJ)
Evergreen Valley Coll (CA)
Glendale Comm Coll (CA)
Hennepin Tech Coll (MN)
Lake Land Coll (IL)
Louisville Tech Inst (KY)
Parkland Coll (IL)
Springfield Tech Comm Coll (MA)
Tulsa Comm Coll (OK)
Umpqua Comm Coll (OR)

DEVELOPMENTAL/CHILD PSYCHOLOGY

Angelina Coll (TX)
Arizona Western Coll (AZ)
Austin Comm Coll (TX)
Bakersfield Coll (CA)
Brevard Comm Coll (FL)
Carl Sandburg Coll (IL)
Central Georgia Tech Coll (GA)
Central Lakes Coll (MN)
Chaffey Coll (CA)
Cisco Jr Coll (TX)
City Coll of San Francisco (CA)
City Colls of Chicago, Harry S Truman Coll (IL)
City Colls of Chicago, Richard J Daley Coll (IL)
Coastal Bend Coll (TX)
Coll of the Canyons (CA)
Coll of the Sequoias (CA)
Comm Coll of Vermont (VT)
Compton Comm Coll (CA)
Connors State Coll (OK)
De Anza Coll (CA)
Ellsworth Comm Coll (IA)
Flathead Valley Comm Coll (MT)
Fullerton Coll (CA)
Fulton-Montgomery Comm Coll (NY)
Garden City Comm Coll (KS)
Gavilan Coll (CA)
Hill Coll of the Hill Jr College District (TX)
Hinds Comm Coll (MS)
Iowa Lakes Comm Coll (IA)
Jefferson Comm Coll (OH)
Kirkwood Comm Coll (IA)
Lansing Comm Coll (MI)
Laramie County Comm Coll (WY)
Lincoln Coll, Lincoln (IL)
Long Beach City Coll (CA)
Los Angeles City Coll (CA)
Los Angeles Harbor Coll (CA)
Los Angeles Mission Coll (CA)
McLennan Comm Coll (TX)
Merced Coll (CA)
Midland Coll (TX)
MiraCosta Coll (CA)
Mississippi Delta Comm Coll (MS)
Mitchell Coll (CT)
Navarro Coll (TX)
North Idaho Coll (ID)
Palomar Coll (CA)
Palo Verde Coll (CA)
Pasadena City Coll (CA)
Ridgewater Coll (MN)
Rockland Comm Coll (NY)
San Antonio Coll (TX)
San Bernardino Valley Coll (CA)
San Diego City Coll (CA)
San Diego Mesa Coll (CA)
San Jacinto Coll Central Campus (TX)
San Joaquin Delta Coll (CA)
Santa Monica Coll (CA)
South Plains Coll (TX)
South Texas Comm Coll (TX)
Tarrant County Coll District (TX)
Trinity Valley Comm Coll (TX)
Tyler Jr Coll (TX)
United Tribes Tech Coll (ND)
Waycross Coll (GA)

DIAGNOSTIC MEDICAL SONOGRAPHY

Albuquerque Tech Vocational Inst (NM)
Argosy U-Twin Cities (MN)
Bunker Hill Comm Coll (MA)
Cape Fear Comm Coll (NC)
Central Ohio Tech Coll (OH)
Chippewa Valley Tech Coll (WI)
Coll of St. Catherine–Minneapolis (MN)
Comm Coll of Allegheny County (PA)
Delaware Tech & Comm Coll, Stanton/ Wilmington Cmps (DE)
El Centro Coll (TX)
Florida Comm Coll at Jacksonville (FL)
Florida Hospital Coll of Health Sciences (FL)
Foothill Coll (CA)
GateWay Comm Coll (AZ)
Gloucester County Coll (NJ)
Hillsborough Comm Coll (FL)
Jackson Comm Coll (MI)
Lansing Comm Coll (MI)
Lorain County Comm Coll (OH)
Montgomery Coll (MD)
New Hampshire Tech Inst (NH)
Oakland Comm Coll (MI)
Pitt Comm Coll (NC)
St. Cloud Tech Coll (MN)
St. Philip's Coll (TX)
South Hills School of Business & Technology, State College (PA)
Springfield Tech Comm Coll (MA)
Western School of Health and Business Careers (PA)

DIESEL ENGINE MECHANIC

Alexandria Tech Coll (MN)
Arizona Automotive Inst (AZ)
Bates Tech Coll (WA)
Black Hawk Coll, Moline (IL)
Central Comm Coll–Hastings Campus (NE)
Centralia Coll (WA)
Century Comm and Tech Coll (MN)
Clark Coll (WA)
Coll of Southern Idaho (ID)
Coll of the Redwoods (CA)
Dixie State Coll of Utah (UT)
Grays Harbor Coll (WA)
Great Basin Coll (NV)
Helena Coll of Tech of The U of Montana (MT)
Johnson Coll (PA)
Johnston Comm Coll (NC)
Kilgore Coll (TX)
Lake Region State Coll (ND)
Lake Washington Tech Coll (WA)
Linn-Benton Comm Coll (OR)
Louisiana Tech Coll–Delta Ouachita Campus (LA)
Massasoit Comm Coll (MA)
Mesa Tech Coll (NM)
Nashville Auto Diesel Coll (TN)
New Hampshire Comm Tech Coll, Berlin/Laconia (NH)
North Dakota State Coll of Science (ND)
Northeast Comm Coll (NE)
Peninsula Coll (WA)
Pennsylvania Coll of Technology (PA)
Raritan Valley Comm Coll (NJ)
Rend Lake Coll (IL)
Riverland Comm Coll (MN)
St. Cloud Tech Coll (MN)
St. Philip's Coll (TX)
San Jacinto Coll North Campus (TX)
San Juan Coll (NM)
Santa Ana Coll (CA)
Scott Comm Coll (IA)
Shasta Coll (CA)
Sheridan Coll (WY)
Skagit Valley Coll (WA)
Southeast Tech Inst (SD)
Texas State Tech Coll– Waco/ Marshall Campus (TX)
Texas State Tech Coll (TX)
U of Northwestern Ohio (OH)
Western Iowa Tech Comm Coll (IA)
Wilkes Comm Coll (NC)
Williston State Coll (ND)

DIETETICS

Allan Hancock Coll (CA)
Bakersfield Coll (CA)
Baltimore City Comm Coll (MD)
Black River Tech Coll (AR)
Briarwood Coll (CT)
Butler County Comm Coll (PA)
Camden County Coll (NJ)
Central Arizona Coll (AZ)
Chaffey Coll (CA)
Cincinnati State Tech and Comm Coll (OH)
City Coll of San Francisco (CA)
Coll of Southern Idaho (ID)
Columbus State Comm Coll (OH)
Delgado Comm Coll (LA)
Delta Coll (MI)
Dutchess Comm Coll (NY)
Fiorello H LaGuardia Comm Coll of City U of NY (NY)
Florida Comm Coll at Jacksonville (FL)
Fresno City Coll (CA)
Gaston Coll (NC)
Gateway Comm Coll (CT)
Harrisburg Area Comm Coll (PA)
Hinds Comm Coll (MS)
J. Sargeant Reynolds Comm Coll (VA)
Labouré Coll (MA)
Lima Tech Coll (OH)
Long Beach City Coll (CA)
Los Angeles City Coll (CA)
Manatee Comm Coll (FL)
Merced Coll (CA)
Middlesex County Coll (NJ)
Milwaukee Area Tech Coll (WI)
Mohawk Valley Comm Coll (NY)
Northern Virginia Comm Coll (VA)
Okaloosa-Walton Comm Coll (FL)

Oklahoma State U, Okmulgee (OK)
Orange Coast Coll (CA)
Pensacola Jr Coll (FL)
Portland Comm Coll (OR)
Riverside Comm Coll (CA)
Rockland Comm Coll (NY)
St. Louis Comm Coll at Florissant Valley (MO)
St. Philip's Coll (TX)
San Jacinto Coll Central Campus (TX)
Shoreline Comm Coll (WA)
Sinclair Comm Coll (OH)
Southern Maine Tech Coll (ME)
South Plains Coll (TX)
Spokane Comm Coll (WA)
State U of NY Coll of A&T at Morrisville (NY)
Suffolk County Comm Coll (NY)
Tarrant County Coll District (TX)
United Tribes Tech Coll (ND)
Vincennes U (IN)
Westchester Comm Coll (NY)
Western Nebraska Comm Coll (NE)
Westmoreland County Comm Coll (PA)

DIETICIAN ASSISTANT
Barton County Comm Coll (KS)
City Colls of Chicago, Malcolm X Coll (IL)
Comm Coll of Allegheny County (PA)
Erie Comm Coll, North Campus (NY)
Florida Comm Coll at Jacksonville (FL)
Front Range Comm Coll (CO)
Martin Comm Coll (NC)
Pennsylvania Coll of Technology (PA)
St. Philip's Coll (TX)
Southwest Tennessee Comm Coll (TN)
Truckee Meadows Comm Coll (NV)

DISTRIBUTION OPERATIONS
Coll of DuPage (IL)
The Comm Coll of Baltimore County–Catonsville Campus (MD)

DIVINITY/MINISTRY
Andrew Coll (GA)
Lon Morris Coll (TX)
Okaloosa-Walton Comm Coll (FL)

DRAFTING
Adirondack Comm Coll (NY)
Allen County Comm Coll (KS)
Alpena Comm Coll (MI)
Alvin Comm Coll (TX)
Amarillo Coll (TX)
American River Coll (CA)
Angelina Coll (TX)
Antelope Valley Coll (CA)
Arapahoe Comm Coll (CO)
Arizona Western Coll (AZ)
Arkansas State U–Beebe (AR)
The Art Inst of Pittsburgh (PA)
Athens Tech Coll (GA)
ATI Career Training Center Electronics Campus (FL)
Atlanta Metropolitan Coll (GA)
Austin Comm Coll (TX)
Bainbridge Coll (GA)
Bakersfield Coll (CA)
Baltimore City Comm Coll (MD)
Barstow Coll (CA)
Barton County Comm Coll (KS)
Bay de Noc Comm Coll (MI)
Beaufort County Comm Coll (NC)
Benjamin Franklin Inst of Technology (MA)
Bergen Comm Coll (NJ)
Berks Tech Inst (PA)
Bessemer State Tech Coll (AL)
Bevill State Comm Coll (AL)
Black Hawk Coll, Moline (IL)
Blue Ridge Comm Coll (NC)
Blue River Comm Coll (MO)
Bossier Parish Comm Coll (LA)
Brazosport Coll (TX)
Brevard Comm Coll (FL)
Brookdale Comm Coll (NJ)
Burlington County Coll (NJ)
Butler County Comm Coll (PA)
Butte Coll (CA)
Caldwell Comm Coll and Tech Inst (NC)
Calhoun Comm Coll (AL)
Carl Sandburg Coll (IL)
Casper Coll (WY)
Cayuga County Comm Coll (NY)
Central Alabama Comm Coll (AL)
Central Carolina Comm Coll (NC)
Central Comm Coll–Columbus Campus (NE)
Central Comm Coll–Grand Island Campus (NE)
Central Comm Coll–Hastings Campus (NE)
Central Ohio Tech Coll (OH)
Central Oregon Comm Coll (OR)
Central Piedmont Comm Coll (NC)
Central Texas Coll (TX)
Central Virginia Comm Coll (VA)
Cerritos Coll (CA)
Cerro Coso Comm Coll (CA)
Chaffey Coll (CA)
Chattanooga State Tech Comm Coll (TN)
Chemeketa Comm Coll (OR)
Chippewa Valley Tech Coll (WI)
Cisco Jr Coll (TX)
Citrus Coll (CA)
City Colls of Chicago, Harry S Truman Coll (IL)
City Colls of Chicago, Richard J Daley Coll (IL)
Clackamas Comm Coll (OR)
Coastal Bend Coll (TX)
Cochise Coll, Douglas (AZ)
Coffeyville Comm Coll (KS)
Coll of DuPage (IL)
Coll of Southern Idaho (ID)
Coll of the Canyons (CA)
Coll of the Desert (CA)
Coll of the Redwoods (CA)
Coll of the Sequoias (CA)
Collin County Comm Coll District (TX)
Comm Coll of Allegheny County (PA)
The Comm Coll of Baltimore County–Catonsville Campus (MD)
Comm Coll of Beaver County (PA)
Comm Coll of Denver (CO)
Comm Coll of Southern Nevada (NV)
Compton Comm Coll (CA)
Cowley County Comm Coll and Voc-Tech School (KS)
Crowder Coll (MO)
Cumberland County Coll (NJ)
Cuyamaca Coll (CA)
Danville Area Comm Coll (IL)
Daytona Beach Comm Coll (FL)
Delaware County Comm Coll (PA)
Delaware Tech & Comm Coll, Jack F Owens Cmps (DE)
Delaware Tech & Comm Coll, Stanton/ Wilmington Cmps (DE)
Delaware Tech & Comm Coll, Terry Cmps (DE)
Delgado Comm Coll (LA)
Del Mar Coll (TX)
Delta Coll (MI)
Des Moines Area Comm Coll (IA)
Don Bosco Coll of Science and Technology (CA)
Doña Ana Branch Comm Coll (NM)
Donnelly Coll (KS)
Douglas MacArthur State Tech Coll (AL)
East Arkansas Comm Coll (AR)
East Central Coll (MO)
East Central Comm Coll (MS)
Eastern Arizona Coll (AZ)
Eastfield Coll (TX)
East Mississippi Comm Coll (MS)
Edison Comm Coll (FL)
Edison State Comm Coll (OH)
Elaine P. Nunez Comm Coll (LA)
El Centro Coll (TX)
Everett Comm Coll (WA)
Evergreen Valley Coll (CA)
Finger Lakes Comm Coll (NY)
Florence-Darlington Tech Coll (SC)
Forsyth Tech Comm Coll (NC)
Fort Scott Comm Coll (KS)
Frederick Comm Coll (MD)
Fresno City Coll (CA)
Front Range Comm Coll (CO)
Fullerton Coll (CA)
Garden City Comm Coll (KS)
Gavilan Coll (CA)
Genesee Comm Coll (NY)
George Corley Wallace State Comm Coll (AL)
Glendale Comm Coll (CA)
Gloucester County Coll (NJ)
Gogebic Comm Coll (MI)
Golden West Coll (CA)
Grand Rapids Comm Coll (MI)
Grayson County Coll (TX)
Green River Comm Coll (WA)
Greenville Tech Coll (SC)
Gulf Coast Comm Coll (FL)
Gwinnett Tech Coll (GA)
Harford Comm Coll (MD)
Harry M. Ayers State Tech Coll (AL)
Hawaii Comm Coll (HI)
Hawkeye Comm Coll (IA)
Heartland Comm Coll (IL)
Henry Ford Comm Coll (MI)
Hibbing Comm Coll (MN)
Highland Comm Coll (IL)
Highland Comm Coll (KS)
Highline Comm Coll (WA)
Hill Coll of the Hill Jr College District (TX)
Hinds Comm Coll (MS)
Holmes Comm Coll (MS)
Honolulu Comm Coll (HI)
Houston Comm Coll System (TX)
Howard Coll (TX)
Hutchinson Comm Coll and Area Vocational School (KS)
Illinois Eastern Comm Colls, Lincoln Trail Coll (IL)
Independence Comm Coll (KS)
Indian Hills Comm Coll (IA)
Indian River Comm Coll (FL)
Inst of Design and Construction (NY)
Iowa Lakes Comm Coll (IA)
Isothermal Comm Coll (NC)
ITT Tech Inst (AL)
ITT Tech Inst, Phoenix (AZ)
ITT Tech Inst, Tucson (AZ)
ITT Tech Inst (AR)
ITT Tech Inst, Anaheim (CA)
ITT Tech Inst, Lathrop (CA)
ITT Tech Inst, Oxnard (CA)
ITT Tech Inst, Rancho Cordova (CA)
ITT Tech Inst, San Bernardino (CA)
ITT Tech Inst, San Diego (CA)
ITT Tech Inst, Sylmar (CA)
ITT Tech Inst, Torrance (CA)
ITT Tech Inst, West Covina (CA)
ITT Tech Inst (CO)
ITT Tech Inst, Fort Lauderdale (FL)
ITT Tech Inst, Jacksonville (FL)
ITT Tech Inst, Maitland (FL)
ITT Tech Inst, Miami (FL)
ITT Tech Inst, Tampa (FL)
ITT Tech Inst (ID)
ITT Tech Inst, Matteson (IL)
ITT Tech Inst, Mount Prospect (IL)
ITT Tech Inst, Fort Wayne (IN)
ITT Tech Inst, Indianapolis (IN)
ITT Tech Inst, Newburgh (IN)
ITT Tech Inst (KY)
ITT Tech Inst (LA)
ITT Tech Inst, Norwood (MA)
ITT Tech Inst, Woburn (MA)
ITT Tech Inst, Grand Rapids (MI)
ITT Tech Inst, Troy (MI)
ITT Tech Inst, Arnold (MO)
ITT Tech Inst, Earth City (MO)
ITT Tech Inst (NE)
ITT Tech Inst (NV)
ITT Tech Inst (NM)
ITT Tech Inst, Getzville (NY)
ITT Tech Inst, Dayton (OH)
ITT Tech Inst, Norwood (OH)
ITT Tech Inst, Strongsville (OH)
ITT Tech Inst, Youngstown (OH)
ITT Tech Inst (OR)
ITT Tech Inst, Mechanicsburg (PA)
ITT Tech Inst, Monroeville (PA)
ITT Tech Inst, Pittsburgh (PA)
ITT Tech Inst (SC)
ITT Tech Inst, Knoxville (TN)
ITT Tech Inst, Memphis (TN)
ITT Tech Inst, Nashville (TN)
ITT Tech Inst, Arlington (TX)
ITT Tech Inst, Austin (TX)
ITT Tech Inst, Houston (TX)
ITT Tech Inst, Houston (TX)
ITT Tech Inst, Houston (TX)
ITT Tech Inst, Richardson (TX)
ITT Tech Inst, San Antonio (TX)
ITT Tech Inst (UT)
ITT Tech Inst, Norfolk (VA)
ITT Tech Inst, Richmond (VA)
ITT Tech Inst, Bothell (WA)
ITT Tech Inst, Spokane (WA)
ITT Tech Inst, Green Bay (WI)
ITT Tech Inst, Greenfield (WI)
Ivy Tech State Coll–Bloomington (IN)
Ivy Tech State Coll–Central Indiana (IN)
Ivy Tech State Coll–Columbus (IN)
Ivy Tech State Coll–Eastcentral (IN)
Ivy Tech State Coll–Kokomo (IN)
Ivy Tech State Coll–Lafayette (IN)
Ivy Tech State Coll–North Central (IN)
Ivy Tech State Coll–Northeast (IN)
Ivy Tech State Coll–Northwest (IN)
Ivy Tech State Coll–Southcentral (IN)
Ivy Tech State Coll–Southwest (IN)
Ivy Tech State Coll–Wabash Valley (IN)
Jackson Comm Coll (MI)
Jefferson Coll (MO)
Jefferson Comm Coll (OH)
J. F. Drake State Tech Coll (AL)
John A. Logan Coll (IL)
Johnson Coll (PA)
Johnson County Comm Coll (KS)
Jones County Jr Coll (MS)
Kalamazoo Valley Comm Coll (MI)
Kankakee Comm Coll (IL)
Kansas City Kansas Comm Coll (KS)
Kaskaskia Coll (IL)
Kellogg Comm Coll (MI)
Kilgore Coll (TX)
Kirkwood Comm Coll (IA)
Labette Comm Coll (KS)
Lake Area Tech Inst (SD)
Lake Land Coll (IL)
Lake Michigan Coll (MI)
Lake Washington Tech Coll (WA)
Lane Comm Coll (OR)
Lansing Comm Coll (MI)
Las Positas Coll (CA)
Lehigh Carbon Comm Coll (PA)
Lenoir Comm Coll (NC)
Lewis and Clark Comm Coll (IL)
Lima Tech Coll (OH)
Linn-Benton Comm Coll (OR)
Long Beach City Coll (CA)
Longview Comm Coll (MO)
Lorain County Comm Coll (OH)
Los Angeles City Coll (CA)
Los Angeles Harbor Coll (CA)
Los Angeles Pierce Coll (CA)
Louisiana Tech Coll–Delta Ouachita Campus (LA)
Louisville Tech Inst (KY)
Luzerne County Comm Coll (PA)
Macomb Comm Coll (MI)
Manatee Comm Coll (FL)
Marion Tech Coll (OH)
Marshalltown Comm Coll (IA)
Massachusetts Bay Comm Coll (MA)
Meridian Comm Coll (MS)
Metropolitan Comm Coll (NE)
Miami-Dade Comm Coll (FL)
Middlesex Comm Coll (MA)
Middlesex County Coll (NJ)
Mid Michigan Comm Coll (MI)
Milwaukee Area Tech Coll (WI)
Minnesota State Coll–Southeast Tech (MN)
MiraCosta Coll (CA)
Mississippi Gulf Coast Comm Coll (MS)
Mitchell Comm Coll (NC)
Mitchell Tech Inst (SD)
Moberly Area Comm Coll (MO)
Mohawk Valley Comm Coll (NY)
Monroe County Comm Coll (MI)
Montcalm Comm Coll (MI)
Montgomery County Comm Coll (PA)
Moraine Park Tech Coll (WI)
Morton Coll (IL)
Mott Comm Coll (MI)
Mountain Empire Comm Coll (VA)
Mountain View Coll (TX)
Naugatuck Valley Comm Coll (CT)
Navarro Coll (TX)
New England Inst of Tech & Florida Culinary Inst (FL)
New River Comm Coll (VA)
New York City Tech Coll of the City U of NY (NY)
Niagara County Comm Coll (NY)
Northampton County Area Comm Coll (PA)
North Central Michigan Coll (MI)
Northcentral Tech Coll (WI)
North Central Texas Coll (TX)
Northeast Comm Coll (NE)
Northeast State Tech Comm Coll (TN)
Northern Maine Tech Coll (ME)
Northern Oklahoma Coll (OK)
North Harris Coll (TX)
North Idaho Coll (ID)
Northland Comm and Tech Coll (MN)
Northland Pioneer Coll (AZ)
North Seattle Comm Coll (WA)
NorthWest Arkansas Comm Coll (AR)
Northwest Coll (WY)
Northwest Mississippi Comm Coll (MS)
Northwest-Shoals Comm Coll (AL)
Odessa Coll (TX)
Okaloosa-Walton Comm Coll (FL)
Oklahoma City Comm Coll (OK)
Oklahoma State U, Oklahoma City (OK)
Oklahoma State U, Okmulgee (OK)
Olympic Coll (WA)
Onondaga Comm Coll (NY)
Orange Coast Coll (CA)
Orange County Comm Coll (NY)
Palm Beach Comm Coll (FL)
Palomar Coll (CA)
Pasadena City Coll (CA)
Pasco-Hernando Comm Coll (FL)
Pellissippi State Tech Comm Coll (TN)
Penn Commercial Business and Tech School (PA)
Pennsylvania Coll of Technology (PA)
Pensacola Jr Coll (FL)
Phoenix Coll (AZ)
Piedmont Tech Coll (SC)
Pittsburgh Tech Inst (PA)
Portland Comm Coll (OR)
Prince George's Comm Coll (MD)
Pulaski Tech Coll (AR)
Red Rocks Comm Coll (CO)
Richland Comm Coll (IL)
Ridgewater Coll (MN)
Rockland Comm Coll (NY)
Sacramento City Coll (CA)
Saint Charles Comm Coll (MO)
St. Clair County Comm Coll (MI)
St. Philip's Coll (TX)
San Antonio Coll (TX)
San Bernardino Valley Coll (CA)
San Diego City Coll (CA)
San Jacinto Coll Central Campus (TX)
San Jacinto Coll North Campus (TX)
San Jacinto Coll South Campus (TX)
San Joaquin Delta Coll (CA)
San Juan Coll (NM)
Santa Ana Coll (CA)
Santa Barbara City Coll (CA)
Santa Fe Comm Coll (FL)
Santa Fe Comm Coll (NM)
Santa Monica Coll (CA)
Sauk Valley Comm Coll (IL)
Schoolcraft Coll (MI)
Schuylkill Inst of Business and Technology (PA)
Seattle Central Comm Coll (WA)
Seminole Comm Coll (FL)
Shasta Coll (CA)
Sheridan Coll (WY)
Shoreline Comm Coll (WA)
Sierra Coll (CA)
Sinclair Comm Coll (OH)
Southeast Arkansas Coll (AR)
Southeast Comm Coll, Milford Campus (NE)
Southeast Tech Inst (SD)
Southern Arkansas U Tech (AR)
Southern Maine Tech Coll (ME)
Southern State Comm Coll (OH)
Southern West Virginia Comm and Tech Coll (WV)
South Piedmont Comm Coll (NC)
South Plains Coll (TX)

South Puget Sound Comm Coll (WA)
Southside Virginia Comm Coll (VA)
South Suburban Coll (IL)
Southwestern Comm Coll (IA)
Southwestern Michigan Coll (MI)
Southwest Virginia Comm Coll (VA)
Southwest Wisconsin Tech Coll (WI)
Spartanburg Tech Coll (SC)
Spokane Comm Coll (WA)
Stark State Coll of Technology (OH)
State U of NY Coll of A&T at Morrisville (NY)
State U of NY Coll of Technology at Alfred (NY)
State U of NY Coll of Technology at Delhi (NY)
Suffolk County Comm Coll (NY)
Surry Comm Coll (NC)
Taft Coll (CA)
Tarrant County Coll District (TX)
Temple Coll (TX)
Texarkana Coll (TX)
Texas State Tech Coll–Harlingen (TX)
Texas State Tech Coll– Waco/ Marshall Campus (TX)
Texas State Tech Coll (TX)
Thaddeus Stevens Coll of Technology (PA)
Thomas Nelson Comm Coll (VA)
Three Rivers Comm Coll (CT)
Tidewater Comm Coll (VA)
Trenholm State Tech Coll, Patterson Campus (AL)
Triangle Tech, Inc. (PA)
Triangle Tech, Inc.–DuBois School (PA)
Triangle Tech, Inc.–Erie School (PA)
Triangle Tech, Inc.–Greensburg Center (PA)
Tri-County Tech Coll (SC)
Trinidad State Jr Coll (CO)
Trinity Valley Comm Coll (TX)
Triton Coll (IL)
Truckee Meadows Comm Coll (NV)
Tulsa Comm Coll (OK)
Tyler Jr Coll (TX)
Ulster County Comm Coll (NY)
U of Arkansas at Fort Smith (AR)
U of Arkansas Comm Coll at Morrilton (AR)
Ventura Coll (CA)
Vernon Coll (TX)
Victoria Coll (TX)
Vincennes U (IN)
Wallace State Comm Coll (AL)
Waycross Coll (GA)
Western Dakota Tech Inst (SD)
Western Nevada Comm Coll (NV)
Western Piedmont Comm Coll (NC)
Westmoreland County Comm Coll (PA)
West Virginia U at Parkersburg (WV)
Wharton County Jr Coll (TX)

DRAFTING/DESIGN TECHNOLOGY

Alpena Comm Coll (MI)
Arapahoe Comm Coll (CO)
Beaufort County Comm Coll (NC)
Cape Fear Comm Coll (NC)
Central Oregon Comm Coll (OR)
The Comm Coll of Baltimore County–Catonsville Campus (MD)
Corning Comm Coll (NY)
Dakota County Tech Coll (MN)
Eastern Maine Tech Coll (ME)
Florida Comm Coll at Jacksonville (FL)
Guilford Tech Comm Coll (NC)
Gulf Coast Comm Coll (FL)
Hibbing Comm Coll (MN)
Highland Comm Coll (IL)
Hill Coll of the Hill Jr College District (TX)
Jefferson Comm Coll (OH)
Johnson Coll (PA)
Kennebec Valley Tech Coll (ME)
Louisville Tech Inst (KY)
Luzerne County Comm Coll (PA)
Mineral Area Coll (MO)
Modesto Jr Coll (CA)
Montana State U Coll of Tech–Great Falls (MT)
Muskingum Area Tech Coll (OH)
North Central Texas Coll (TX)
Northwestern Michigan Coll (MI)
Orange Coast Coll (CA)
Pittsburgh Tech Inst (PA)
Ridgewater Coll (MN)
St. Petersburg Coll (FL)
San Antonio Coll (TX)
State U of NY Coll of Technology at Alfred (NY)
State U of NY Coll of Technology at Delhi (NY)
Truckee Meadows Comm Coll (NV)
Vincennes U (IN)
Vincennes U Jasper Campus (IN)
Western Dakota Tech Inst (SD)
York Tech Coll (SC)

DRAFTING RELATED

Comm Coll of Allegheny County (PA)
Pennsylvania Coll of Technology (PA)

DRAMA/DANCE EDUCATION

Western Nebraska Comm Coll (NE)

DRAMA THERAPY

Miami-Dade Comm Coll (FL)

DRAWING

Berkshire Comm Coll (MA)
Cañada Coll (CA)
Chabot Coll (CA)
Coffeyville Comm Coll (KS)
Cuyamaca Coll (CA)
De Anza Coll (CA)
Dixie State Coll of Utah (UT)
East Central Comm Coll (MS)
Everett Comm Coll (WA)
Henry Ford Comm Coll (MI)
Inst of American Indian Arts (NM)
Iowa Lakes Comm Coll (IA)
Lincoln Coll, Lincoln (IL)
Lincoln Coll, Normal (IL)
Lon Morris Coll (TX)
Luzerne County Comm Coll (PA)
Midland Coll (TX)
Monterey Peninsula Coll (CA)
North Seattle Comm Coll (WA)
Palomar Coll (CA)
Pasadena City Coll (CA)
San Jacinto Coll Central Campus (TX)
San Joaquin Delta Coll (CA)
Vermilion Comm Coll (MN)

EARLY CHILDHOOD EDUCATION

Abraham Baldwin Ag Coll (GA)
Aims Comm Coll (CO)
Alamance Comm Coll (NC)
Allan Hancock Coll (CA)
American River Coll (CA)
Andover Coll (ME)
Anne Arundel Comm Coll (MD)
Asnuntuck Comm Coll (CT)
Atlanta Metropolitan Coll (GA)
Bainbridge Coll (GA)
Baltimore City Comm Coll (MD)
Barstow Coll (CA)
Bay State Coll (MA)
Beaufort County Comm Coll (NC)
Bellevue Comm Coll (WA)
Bergen Comm Coll (NJ)
Berkshire Comm Coll (MA)
Blackfeet Comm Coll (MT)
Blue Ridge Comm Coll (NC)
Borough of Manhattan Comm Coll of City U of NY (NY)
Brookdale Comm Coll (NJ)
Broome Comm Coll (NY)
Bucks County Comm Coll (PA)
Burlington County Coll (NJ)
Butler County Comm Coll (PA)
Butte Coll (CA)
Camden County Coll (NJ)
Cañada Coll (CA)
Cape Cod Comm Coll (MA)
Capital Comm Coll (CT)
Carroll Comm Coll (MD)
Casper Coll (WY)
Cayuga County Comm Coll (NY)
Cecil Comm Coll (MD)
Central Arizona Coll (AZ)
Central Carolina Comm Coll (NC)
Centralia Coll (WA)
Central Maine Tech Coll (ME)
Central Ohio Tech Coll (OH)
Central Piedmont Comm Coll (NC)
Cerritos Coll (CA)
Cerro Coso Comm Coll (CA)
Chabot Coll (CA)
Chaffey Coll (CA)
Chatfield Coll (OH)
Chattanooga State Tech Comm Coll (TN)
Chemeketa Comm Coll (OR)
Chesapeake Coll (MD)
Cisco Jr Coll (TX)
Clark Coll (WA)
Cleveland State Comm Coll (TN)
Coahoma Comm Coll (MS)
Colby Comm Coll (KS)
Coll of Eastern Utah (UT)
Coll of Lake County (IL)
Coll of Marin (CA)
Coll of Southern Maryland (MD)
Coll of the Canyons (CA)
Coll of the Desert (CA)
Coll of the Redwoods (CA)
Coll of the Sequoias (CA)
Coll of the Siskiyous (CA)
Colorado Mountn Coll, Timberline Cmps (CO)
Columbia State Comm Coll (TN)
Columbus State Comm Coll (OH)
Comm Coll of Aurora (CO)
The Comm Coll of Baltimore County–Catonsville Campus (MD)
Comm Coll of Denver (CO)
Comm Coll of Rhode Island (RI)
Comm Coll of Southern Nevada (NV)
Compton Comm Coll (CA)
County Coll of Morris (NJ)
Cuesta Coll (CA)
Cumberland County Coll (NJ)
Cuyahoga Comm Coll (OH)
Danville Area Comm Coll (IL)
Darton Coll (GA)
Daytona Beach Comm Coll (FL)
Delaware County Comm Coll (PA)
Delaware Tech & Comm Coll, Stanton/ Wilmington Cmps (DE)
Delaware Tech & Comm Coll, Terry Cmps (DE)
Delgado Comm Coll (LA)
Del Mar Coll (TX)
Dixie State Coll of Utah (UT)
Donnelly Coll (KS)
Durham Tech Comm Coll (NC)
Dutchess Comm Coll (NY)
East Central Comm Coll (MS)
Eastern Maine Tech Coll (ME)
Edgecombe Comm Coll (NC)
Edison State Comm Coll (OH)
Elaine P. Nunez Comm Coll (LA)
Ellsworth Comm Coll (IA)
Enterprise State Jr Coll (AL)
Essex County Coll (NJ)
Eugenio María de Hostos Comm Coll of City U of NY (NY)
Everett Comm Coll (WA)
Fayetteville Tech Comm Coll (NC)
Finger Lakes Comm Coll (NY)
Fiorello H LaGuardia Comm Coll of City U of NY (NY)
Fisher Coll (MA)
Floyd Coll (GA)
Forsyth Tech Comm Coll (NC)
Fort Berthold Comm Coll (ND)
Frederick Comm Coll (MD)
Fullerton Coll (CA)
Fulton-Montgomery Comm Coll (NY)
Gaston Coll (NC)
Gateway Comm Coll (CT)
Gavilan Coll (CA)
Genesee Comm Coll (NY)
Georgia Perimeter Coll (GA)
Glendale Comm Coll (AZ)
Gogebic Comm Coll (MI)
Great Basin Coll (NV)
Greenfield Comm Coll (MA)
Guam Comm Coll (GU)
Guilford Tech Comm Coll (NC)
Harcum Coll (PA)
Harford Comm Coll (MD)
Harrisburg Area Comm Coll (PA)
Hawaii Comm Coll (HI)
Hazard Comm Coll (KY)
Heartland Comm Coll (IL)
Herkimer County Comm Coll (NY)
Hesser Coll (NH)
Hesston Coll (KS)
Highland Comm Coll (IL)
Highline Comm Coll (WA)
Holyoke Comm Coll (MA)
Honolulu Comm Coll (HI)
Hopkinsville Comm Coll (KY)
Howard Comm Coll (MD)
Imperial Valley Coll (CA)
Independence Comm Coll (KS)
Indian River Comm Coll (FL)
Iowa Lakes Comm Coll (IA)
Isothermal Comm Coll (NC)
James Sprunt Comm Coll (NC)
Jefferson Coll (MO)
Jefferson Comm Coll (KY)
Jefferson Comm Coll (NY)
John A. Logan Coll (IL)
Johnston Comm Coll (NC)
Kauai Comm Coll (HI)
Kellogg Comm Coll (MI)
Kent State U, Salem Campus (OH)
Keystone Coll (PA)
Kingsborough Comm Coll of City U of NY (NY)
Kirkwood Comm Coll (IA)
Labette Comm Coll (KS)
Lakeland Comm Coll (OH)
Lake Tahoe Comm Coll (CA)
Lane Comm Coll (OR)
Lansing Comm Coll (MI)
Laramie County Comm Coll (WY)
Las Positas Coll (CA)
Lehigh Carbon Comm Coll (PA)
Lewis and Clark Comm Coll (IL)
Lincoln Coll, Lincoln (IL)
Long Beach City Coll (CA)
Lorain County Comm Coll (OH)
Louisiana Tech Coll–Natchitoches Campus (LA)
Lower Columbia Coll (WA)
Luzerne County Comm Coll (PA)
Macomb Comm Coll (MI)
Manatee Comm Coll (FL)
Manchester Comm Coll (CT)
Manor Coll (PA)
Mayland Comm Coll (NC)
McIntosh Coll (NH)
McLennan Comm Coll (TX)
Merced Coll (CA)
Metropolitan Comm Coll (NE)
Miami-Dade Comm Coll (FL)
Miami U–Hamilton Campus (OH)
Miami U–Middletown Campus (OH)
Middlesex Comm Coll (MA)
Middlesex County Coll (NJ)
Mid-Plains Comm Coll Area (NE)
Minnesota State Coll–Southeast Tech (MN)
MiraCosta Coll (CA)
Mississippi Gulf Coast Comm Coll (MS)
Mitchell Coll (CT)
Mitchell Comm Coll (NC)
Modesto Jr Coll (CA)
Monterey Peninsula Coll (CA)
Moorpark Coll (CA)
Mt. Hood Comm Coll (OR)
Mt. San Jacinto Coll (CA)
Nash Comm Coll (NC)
Nashville State Tech Inst (TN)
Nassau Comm Coll (NY)
Naugatuck Valley Comm Coll (CT)
New Hampshire Comm Tech Coll, Berlin/Laconia (NH)
New Hampshire Tech Inst (NH)
Northcentral Tech Coll (WI)
Northeast State Tech Comm Coll (TN)
Northern Essex Comm Coll (MA)
Northern Maine Tech Coll (ME)
Northern Virginia Comm Coll (VA)
North Seattle Comm Coll (WA)
North Shore Comm Coll (MA)
Northwest Coll (WY)
Northwestern Connecticut Comm-Tech Coll (CT)
Norwalk Comm Coll (CT)
Oakton Comm Coll (IL)
Odessa Coll (TX)
Okaloosa-Walton Comm Coll (FL)
Onondaga Comm Coll (NY)
Orangeburg-Calhoun Tech Coll (SC)
Orange Coast Coll (CA)
Otero Jr Coll (CO)
Owensboro Comm Coll (KY)
Oxnard Coll (CA)
Palm Beach Comm Coll (FL)
Palomar Coll (CA)
Palo Verde Coll (CA)
Pasadena City Coll (CA)
Penn Valley Comm Coll (MO)
Pensacola Jr Coll (FL)
Pierce Coll (WA)
Pratt Comm Coll and Area Vocational School (KS)
Prince George's Comm Coll (MD)
Quincy Coll (MA)
Quinsigamond Comm Coll (MA)
Raritan Valley Comm Coll (NJ)
Reading Area Comm Coll (PA)
Riverside Comm Coll (CA)
Roane State Comm Coll (TN)
Roanoke-Chowan Comm Coll (NC)
Robeson Comm Coll (NC)
Rowan-Cabarrus Comm Coll (NC)
Sacramento City Coll (CA)
St. Catharine Coll (KY)
St. Cloud Tech Coll (MN)
St. Petersburg Coll (FL)
Salem Comm Coll (NJ)
Salish Kootenai Coll (MT)
Sandhills Comm Coll (NC)
San Jacinto Coll Central Campus (TX)
San Jacinto Coll North Campus (TX)
San Joaquin Delta Coll (CA)
San Juan Coll (NM)
Santa Ana Coll (CA)
Santa Barbara City Coll (CA)
Santa Fe Comm Coll (FL)
Santa Fe Comm Coll (NM)
Santa Monica Coll (CA)
Scottsdale Comm Coll (AZ)
Seattle Central Comm Coll (WA)
Shasta Coll (CA)
Shoreline Comm Coll (WA)
Sierra Coll (CA)
Sinclair Comm Coll (OH)
Skagit Valley Coll (WA)
Snow Coll (UT)
Southeastern Comm Coll (NC)
Southern Maine Tech Coll (ME)
Southern State Comm Coll (OH)
South Puget Sound Comm Coll (WA)
South Suburban Coll (IL)
Southwestern Coll (CA)
Southwest Tennessee Comm Coll (TN)
Springfield Tech Comm Coll (MA)
State U of NY Coll of Technology at Canton (NY)
Suffolk County Comm Coll (NY)
Sullivan County Comm Coll (NY)
Taft Coll (CA)
Tallahassee Comm Coll (FL)
Terra State Comm Coll (OH)
Thomas Nelson Comm Coll (VA)
Three Rivers Comm Coll (CT)
Tidewater Comm Coll (VA)
Tompkins Cortland Comm Coll (NY)
Trinidad State Jr Coll (CO)
Trinity Valley Comm Coll (TX)
Triton Coll (IL)
Trocaire Coll (NY)
Truckee Meadows Comm Coll (NV)
Tulsa Comm Coll (OK)
Tunxis Comm Coll (CT)
Umpqua Comm Coll (OR)
United Tribes Tech Coll (ND)
U of Arkansas Comm Coll at Batesville (AR)
U of New Mexico–Gallup (NM)
Urban Coll of Boston (MA)
Vance-Granville Comm Coll (NC)
Ventura Coll (CA)
Vermilion Comm Coll (MN)
Victor Valley Coll (CA)
Villa Maria Coll of Buffalo (NY)
Vincennes U (IN)
Virginia Western Comm Coll (VA)
Wake Tech Comm Coll (NC)
Wallace State Comm Coll (AL)
Waubonsee Comm Coll (IL)
Western Nebraska Comm Coll (NE)
Whatcom Comm Coll (WA)
Wilson Tech Comm Coll (NC)

EARTH SCIENCES

Casper Coll (WY)
Colby Comm Coll (KS)
Diné Coll (AZ)
Everett Comm Coll (WA)

Iowa Lakes Comm Coll (IA)
Lincoln Coll, Lincoln (IL)
Lower Columbia Coll (WA)
Skagit Valley Coll (WA)
Snow Coll (UT)
Tacoma Comm Coll (WA)
Trinity Valley Comm Coll (TX)
Tulsa Comm Coll (OK)
Vermilion Comm Coll (MN)
Vincennes U (IN)

EASTERN EUROPEAN AREA STUDIES
Manatee Comm Coll (FL)

ECOLOGY
Abraham Baldwin Ag Coll (GA)
Berkshire Comm Coll (MA)
Burlington County Coll (NJ)
Casper Coll (WY)
Chabot Coll (CA)
Coll of Marin (CA)
Colorado Mountn Coll, Timberline Cmps (CO)
Dixie State Coll of Utah (UT)
East Central Coll (MO)
Everett Comm Coll (WA)
Iowa Lakes Comm Coll (IA)
Joliet Jr Coll (IL)
Milwaukee Area Tech Coll (WI)
Northwest Coll (WY)
Paul Smith's Coll of Arts and Sciences (NY)
Tulsa Comm Coll (OK)
Vermilion Comm Coll (MN)
Western Nebraska Comm Coll (NE)

ECONOMICS
Allen County Comm Coll (KS)
Anne Arundel Comm Coll (MD)
Austin Comm Coll (TX)
Bakersfield Coll (CA)
Barton County Comm Coll (KS)
Bergen Comm Coll (NJ)
Brevard Comm Coll (FL)
Cañada Coll (CA)
Casper Coll (WY)
Cerritos Coll (CA)
Cerro Coso Comm Coll (CA)
Chabot Coll (CA)
Chaffey Coll (CA)
Chemeketa Comm Coll (OR)
Coastal Bend Coll (TX)
Coffeyville Comm Coll (KS)
Coll of the Desert (CA)
Columbia State Comm Coll (TN)
Comm Coll of Southern Nevada (NV)
Compton Comm Coll (CA)
Crafton Hills Coll (CA)
Cypress Coll (CA)
Darton Coll (GA)
Daytona Beach Comm Coll (FL)
De Anza Coll (CA)
Dixie State Coll of Utah (UT)
East Central Coll (MO)
East Central Comm Coll (MS)
Eastern Oklahoma State Coll (OK)
Eastern Wyoming Coll (WY)
East Mississippi Comm Coll (MS)
Ellsworth Comm Coll (IA)
Everett Comm Coll (WA)
Floyd Coll (GA)
Foothill Coll (CA)
Fullerton Coll (CA)
GateWay Comm Coll (AZ)
Georgia Perimeter Coll (GA)
Hill Coll of the Hill Jr College District (TX)
Hinds Comm Coll (MS)
Indian River Comm Coll (FL)
Iowa Lakes Comm Coll (IA)
Jefferson Comm Coll (KY)
Jones County Jr Coll (MS)
Laramie County Comm Coll (WY)
Lincoln Coll, Lincoln (IL)
Lincoln Coll, Normal (IL)
Lincoln Land Comm Coll (IL)
Linn-Benton Comm Coll (OR)
Lon Morris Coll (TX)
Los Angeles Mission Coll (CA)
Louisburg Coll (NC)
Lower Columbia Coll (WA)
Manatee Comm Coll (FL)
Marshalltown Comm Coll (IA)
Miami-Dade Comm Coll (FL)
Miami U–Middletown Campus (OH)
Midland Coll (TX)
MiraCosta Coll (CA)
Mississippi Delta Comm Coll (MS)
Monterey Peninsula Coll (CA)
New Mexico Military Inst (NM)
Northwest Coll (WY)
Orange Coast Coll (CA)
Oxnard Coll (CA)
Palm Beach Comm Coll (FL)
Palomar Coll (CA)
Palo Verde Coll (CA)
Pasadena City Coll (CA)
Red Rocks Comm Coll (CO)
Riverside Comm Coll (CA)
St. Philip's Coll (TX)
San Bernardino Valley Coll (CA)
San Jacinto Coll Central Campus (TX)
San Joaquin Delta Coll (CA)
San Juan Coll (NM)
Santa Ana Coll (CA)
Santa Barbara City Coll (CA)
Santa Monica Coll (CA)
Sauk Valley Comm Coll (IL)
Skagit Valley Coll (WA)
Snow Coll (UT)
Southwestern Coll (CA)
Tacoma Comm Coll (WA)
Triton Coll (IL)
Tulsa Comm Coll (OK)
Umpqua Comm Coll (OR)
Vermilion Comm Coll (MN)
Western Nebraska Comm Coll (NE)

EDUCATION
Abraham Baldwin Ag Coll (GA)
Allegany Coll of Maryland (MD)
Andrew Coll (GA)
Anne Arundel Comm Coll (MD)
Arizona Western Coll (AZ)
Atlanta Metropolitan Coll (GA)
Atlantic Cape Comm Coll (NJ)
Bacone Coll (OK)
Bainbridge Coll (GA)
Barstow Coll (CA)
Barton County Comm Coll (KS)
Bergen Comm Coll (NJ)
Black Hawk Coll, Moline (IL)
Bowling Green State U-Firelands Coll (OH)
Brazosport Coll (TX)
Brookdale Comm Coll (NJ)
Bucks County Comm Coll (PA)
Bunker Hill Comm Coll (MA)
Butler County Comm Coll (PA)
Cape Cod Comm Coll (MA)
Casper Coll (WY)
Cecil Comm Coll (MD)
Central Oregon Comm Coll (OR)
Central Virginia Comm Coll (VA)
Chabot Coll (CA)
Chemeketa Comm Coll (OR)
Chipola Jr Coll (FL)
Cisco Jr Coll (TX)
City Colls of Chicago, Harry S Truman Coll (IL)
City Colls of Chicago, Richard J Daley Coll (IL)
Clark Coll (WA)
Coastal Bend Coll (TX)
Cochise Coll, Douglas (AZ)
Coffeyville Comm Coll (KS)
Colby Comm Coll (KS)
Coll of Southern Idaho (ID)
Coll of Southern Maryland (MD)
Coll of the Desert (CA)
The Comm Coll of Baltimore County–Catonsville Campus (MD)
Comm Coll of Beaver County (PA)
Comm Coll of Vermont (VT)
Connors State Coll (OK)
Cowley County Comm Coll and Voc-Tech School (KS)
Crowder Coll (MO)
Cumberland County Coll (NJ)
Danville Area Comm Coll (IL)
Danville Comm Coll (VA)
Darton Coll (GA)
Daytona Beach Comm Coll (FL)
Del Mar Coll (TX)
Des Moines Area Comm Coll (IA)
Dodge City Comm Coll (KS)
Donnelly Coll (KS)
East Central Coll (MO)
East Central Comm Coll (MS)
Eastern Oklahoma State Coll (OK)
Eastern Shore Comm Coll (VA)
East Georgia Coll (GA)
East Mississippi Comm Coll (MS)
Ellsworth Comm Coll (IA)
Enterprise State Jr Coll (AL)
Essex County Coll (NJ)
Everett Comm Coll (WA)
Fiorello H LaGuardia Comm Coll of City U of NY (NY)
Fort Scott Comm Coll (KS)
Frederick Comm Coll (MD)
Galveston Coll (TX)
Garden City Comm Coll (KS)
GateWay Comm Coll (AZ)
Genesee Comm Coll (NY)
Germanna Comm Coll (VA)
Glendale Comm Coll (CA)
Gloucester County Coll (NJ)
Gogebic Comm Coll (MI)
Gordon Coll (GA)
Grayson County Coll (TX)
Greenfield Comm Coll (MA)
Guam Comm Coll (GU)
Hagerstown Comm Coll (MD)
Halifax Comm Coll (NC)
Harford Comm Coll (MD)
Harrisburg Area Comm Coll (PA)
Hawkeye Comm Coll (IA)
Haywood Comm Coll (NC)
Highland Comm Coll (IL)
Highland Comm Coll (KS)
Highline Comm Coll (WA)
Hill Coll of the Hill Jr College District (TX)
Hutchinson Comm Coll and Area Vocational School (KS)
Illinois Eastern Comm Colls, Lincoln Trail Coll (IL)
Indian River Comm Coll (FL)
Iowa Lakes Comm Coll (IA)
Isothermal Comm Coll (NC)
Jefferson Coll (MO)
Jefferson Comm Coll (KY)
Jefferson Davis Comm Coll (AL)
John A. Logan Coll (IL)
Johnson County Comm Coll (KS)
Joliet Jr Coll (IL)
Jones County Jr Coll (MS)
Kennebec Valley Tech Coll (ME)
Kent State U, Stark Campus (OH)
Kingsborough Comm Coll of City U of NY (NY)
Kingwood Coll (TX)
Kirkwood Comm Coll (IA)
Labette Comm Coll (KS)
Lake Michigan Coll (MI)
Lansing Comm Coll (MI)
Laramie County Comm Coll (WY)
Las Positas Coll (CA)
Lehigh Carbon Comm Coll (PA)
Lincoln Coll, Lincoln (IL)
Lincoln Coll, Normal (IL)
Lincoln Land Comm Coll (IL)
Linn-Benton Comm Coll (OR)
Lon Morris Coll (TX)
Lorain County Comm Coll (OH)
Lord Fairfax Comm Coll (VA)
Luzerne County Comm Coll (PA)
Manor Coll (PA)
Miami-Dade Comm Coll (FL)
Miami U–Middletown Campus (OH)
Middlesex County Coll (NJ)
Minot State U–Bottineau Campus (ND)
Mississippi Delta Comm Coll (MS)
Mississippi Gulf Coast Comm Coll (MS)
Montgomery Coll (MD)
Mountain Empire Comm Coll (VA)
Navarro Coll (TX)
New Mexico State U–Alamogordo (NM)
New Mexico State U–Carlsbad (NM)
New River Comm Coll (VA)
Northeast Comm Coll (NE)
Northern Essex Comm Coll (MA)
North Harris Coll (TX)
North Idaho Coll (ID)
NorthWest Arkansas Comm Coll (AR)
Northwest Coll (WY)
Northwest Mississippi Comm Coll (MS)
Northwest-Shoals Comm Coll (AL)
Northwest State Comm Coll (OH)
Odessa Coll (TX)
Okaloosa-Walton Comm Coll (FL)
Otero Jr Coll (CO)
Palau Comm CollPalau)
Palm Beach Comm Coll (FL)
Palo Verde Coll (CA)
Paul D. Camp Comm Coll (VA)
Pensacola Jr Coll (FL)
Piedmont Virginia Comm Coll (VA)
Pratt Comm Coll and Area Vocational School (KS)
Prince George's Comm Coll (MD)
Raritan Valley Comm Coll (NJ)
Reading Area Comm Coll (PA)
Riverside Comm Coll (CA)
Roane State Comm Coll (TN)
Roanoke-Chowan Comm Coll (NC)
St. Catharine Coll (KY)
St. Philip's Coll (TX)
Salem Comm Coll (NJ)
San Juan Coll (NM)
Santa Fe Comm Coll (FL)
Sauk Valley Comm Coll (IL)
Schenectady County Comm Coll (NY)
Schoolcraft Coll (MI)
Sheridan Coll (WY)
Shoreline Comm Coll (WA)
Sinclair Comm Coll (OH)
Sitting Bull Coll (ND)
Snow Coll (UT)
Southeast Comm Coll, Beatrice Campus (NE)
South Plains Coll (TX)
Southside Virginia Comm Coll (VA)
South Texas Comm Coll (TX)
Southwest Mississippi Comm Coll (MS)
Southwest Virginia Comm Coll (VA)
Tacoma Comm Coll (WA)
Tidewater Comm Coll (VA)
Trinidad State Jr Coll (CO)
Trinity Valley Comm Coll (TX)
Triton Coll (IL)
Truett-McConnell Coll (GA)
Tulsa Comm Coll (OK)
Umpqua Comm Coll (OR)
U of Arkansas Comm Coll at Batesville (AR)
U of New Mexico–Gallup (NM)
Vance-Granville Comm Coll (NC)
Ventura Coll (CA)
Vermilion Comm Coll (MN)
Villa Maria Coll of Buffalo (NY)
Vincennes U (IN)
Vincennes U Jasper Campus (IN)
Virginia Western Comm Coll (VA)
Wallace State Comm Coll (AL)
Walters State Comm Coll (TN)
Warren County Comm Coll (NJ)
Waycross Coll (GA)
Western Texas Coll (TX)
Western Wyoming Comm Coll (WY)
West Virginia U at Parkersburg (WV)
Young Harris Coll (GA)

EDUCATION ADMINISTRATION
Comm Coll of the Air Force (AL)

EDUCATIONAL MEDIA DESIGN
Bellevue Comm Coll (WA)
City Coll of San Francisco (CA)
Comm Coll of the Air Force (AL)
Milwaukee Area Tech Coll (WI)
Portland Comm Coll (OR)
Southern Arkansas U Tech (AR)
Tarrant County Coll District (TX)

EDUCATIONAL MEDIA TECHNOLOGY
Brookdale Comm Coll (NJ)
Century Comm and Tech Coll (MN)
Collin County Comm Coll District (TX)
County Coll of Morris (NJ)
Hibbing Comm Coll (MN)
Hutchinson Comm Coll and Area Vocational School (KS)
Ivy Tech State Coll–North Central (IN)
Pikes Peak Comm Coll (CO)
Texas State Tech Coll– Waco/ Marshall Campus (TX)
Virginia Coll at Jackson (MS)

EDUCATION (K-12)
Angelina Coll (TX)
Cecil Comm Coll (MD)
Itasca Comm Coll (MN)
Keystone Coll (PA)
Mid Michigan Comm Coll (MI)
Pratt Comm Coll and Area Vocational School (KS)
Truckee Meadows Comm Coll (NV)
Vincennes U (IN)
Vincennes U Jasper Campus (IN)

EDUCATION (MULTIPLE LEVELS)
Carroll Comm Coll (MD)
Coastal Georgia Comm Coll (GA)
Delaware County Comm Coll (PA)
Louisburg Coll (NC)

EDUCATION RELATED
Bunker Hill Comm Coll (MA)
Corning Comm Coll (NY)
Guilford Tech Comm Coll (NC)

ELECTRICAL AND ELECTRONICS EQUIPMENT INSTALLATION AND REPAIR RELATED
Clover Park Tech Coll (WA)
San Jacinto Coll North Campus (TX)

ELECTRICAL/ELECTRONIC ENGINEERING TECHNOLOGIES RELATED
Georgia Perimeter Coll (GA)
ITT Tech Inst (AL)
ITT Tech Inst, Phoenix (AZ)
ITT Tech Inst, Tucson (AZ)
ITT Tech Inst (AR)
ITT Tech Inst, Anaheim (CA)
ITT Tech Inst, Hayward (CA)
ITT Tech Inst, Oxnard (CA)
ITT Tech Inst, Rancho Cordova (CA)
ITT Tech Inst, San Bernardino (CA)
ITT Tech Inst, San Diego (CA)
ITT Tech Inst, Santa Clara (CA)
ITT Tech Inst, Sylmar (CA)
ITT Tech Inst, Torrance (CA)
ITT Tech Inst, West Covina (CA)
ITT Tech Inst (CO)
ITT Tech Inst, Fort Lauderdale (FL)
ITT Tech Inst, Jacksonville (FL)
ITT Tech Inst, Maitland (FL)
ITT Tech Inst, Miami (FL)
ITT Tech Inst, Tampa (FL)
ITT Tech Inst (ID)
ITT Tech Inst, Burr Ridge (IL)
ITT Tech Inst, Matteson (IL)
ITT Tech Inst, Mount Prospect (IL)
ITT Tech Inst, Indianapolis (IN)
ITT Tech Inst, Newburgh (IN)
ITT Tech Inst (KY)
ITT Tech Inst (LA)
ITT Tech Inst, Norwood (MA)
ITT Tech Inst, Woburn (MA)
ITT Tech Inst, Grand Rapids (MI)
ITT Tech Inst, Troy (MI)
ITT Tech Inst, Arnold (MO)
ITT Tech Inst, Earth City (MO)
ITT Tech Inst (NE)
ITT Tech Inst (NV)
ITT Tech Inst (NM)
ITT Tech Inst, Albany (NY)
ITT Tech Inst, Getzville (NY)
ITT Tech Inst, Liverpool (NY)
ITT Tech Inst, Dayton (OH)
ITT Tech Inst, Norwood (OH)
ITT Tech Inst, Strongsville (OH)
ITT Tech Inst, Youngstown (OH)
ITT Tech Inst (OR)
ITT Tech Inst, Mechanicsburg (PA)
ITT Tech Inst, Monroeville (PA)
ITT Tech Inst, Pittsburgh (PA)
ITT Tech Inst (SC)
ITT Tech Inst, Knoxville (TN)
ITT Tech Inst, Memphis (TN)
ITT Tech Inst, Nashville (TN)
ITT Tech Inst, Arlington (TX)
ITT Tech Inst, Austin (TX)
ITT Tech Inst, Houston (TX)
ITT Tech Inst, Houston (TX)
ITT Tech Inst, Houston (TX)
ITT Tech Inst, Richardson (TX)
ITT Tech Inst, San Antonio (TX)
ITT Tech Inst (UT)
ITT Tech Inst, Norfolk (VA)
ITT Tech Inst, Richmond (VA)
ITT Tech Inst, Bothell (WA)
ITT Tech Inst, Seattle (WA)
ITT Tech Inst, Spokane (WA)
ITT Tech Inst, Green Bay (WI)

ITT Tech Inst, Greenfield (WI)
Lamar State Coll–Port Arthur (TX)
Northampton County Area Comm Coll (PA)
Southwestern Michigan Coll (MI)
Springfield Tech Comm Coll (MA)

ELECTRICAL/ELECTRONIC ENGINEERING TECHNOLOGY

Adirondack Comm Coll (NY)
Aims Comm Coll (CO)
Alamance Comm Coll (NC)
Albuquerque Tech Vocational Inst (NM)
Allan Hancock Coll (CA)
Allen County Comm Coll (KS)
Alpena Comm Coll (MI)
Alvin Comm Coll (TX)
Amarillo Coll (TX)
American River Coll (CA)
Angelina Coll (TX)
Anne Arundel Comm Coll (MD)
Anoka-Hennepin Tech Coll (MN)
Antelope Valley Coll (CA)
Arapahoe Comm Coll (CO)
Arizona Western Coll (AZ)
Arkansas State U–Beebe (AR)
Athens Tech Coll (GA)
ATI Career Training Center Electronics Campus (FL)
Augusta Tech Coll (GA)
Austin Comm Coll (TX)
Bainbridge Coll (GA)
Bakersfield Coll (CA)
Baltimore City Comm Coll (MD)
Barstow Coll (CA)
Barton County Comm Coll (KS)
Bates Tech Coll (WA)
Bay de Noc Comm Coll (MI)
Beaufort County Comm Coll (NC)
Belmont Tech Coll (OH)
Benjamin Franklin Inst of Technology (MA)
Bergen Comm Coll (NJ)
Berkshire Comm Coll (MA)
Bessemer State Tech Coll (AL)
Blackhawk Tech Coll (WI)
Bladen Comm Coll (NC)
Blue Ridge Comm Coll (NC)
Blue Ridge Comm Coll (VA)
Bossier Parish Comm Coll (LA)
Bowling Green State U-Firelands Coll (OH)
Bradley Academy for the Visual Arts (PA)
Brazosport Coll (TX)
Brevard Comm Coll (FL)
Bristol Comm Coll (MA)
Bronx Comm Coll of City U of NY (NY)
Brookdale Comm Coll (NJ)
Broome Comm Coll (NY)
Brown Coll (MN)
Brunswick Comm Coll (NC)
Bryant & Stratton Business Inst, Rochester (NY)
Bryant & Stratton Business Inst, Eastern Hills Cmps (NY)
Bryant & Stratton Business Inst (NY)
Bucks County Comm Coll (PA)
Bunker Hill Comm Coll (MA)
Burlington County Coll (NJ)
Butler County Comm Coll (PA)
Butte Coll (CA)
Caldwell Comm Coll and Tech Inst (NC)
Cambria County Area Comm Coll (PA)
Camden County Coll (NJ)
Cape Fear Comm Coll (NC)
Capital Comm Coll (CT)
Career Coll of Northern Nevada (NV)
Carl Sandburg Coll (IL)
Casper Coll (WY)
Catawba Valley Comm Coll (NC)
Cayuga County Comm Coll (NY)
Cecil Comm Coll (MD)
Central Alabama Comm Coll (AL)
Central Carolina Comm Coll (NC)
Central Comm Coll–Columbus Campus (NE)
Central Comm Coll–Grand Island Campus (NE)
Central Comm Coll–Hastings Campus (NE)
Central Florida Comm Coll (FL)
Centralia Coll (WA)
Central Ohio Tech Coll (OH)
Central Piedmont Comm Coll (NC)
Central Texas Coll (TX)
Central Virginia Comm Coll (VA)
Cerritos Coll (CA)
Cerro Coso Comm Coll (CA)
Chabot Coll (CA)
Chaffey Coll (CA)
Chattahoochee Tech Coll (GA)
Chattanooga State Tech Comm Coll (TN)
Chemeketa Comm Coll (OR)
Chesapeake Coll (MD)
CHI Inst (PA)
Chippewa Valley Tech Coll (WI)
Cincinnati State Tech and Comm Coll (OH)
Cisco Jr Coll (TX)
Citrus Coll (CA)
City Coll of San Francisco (CA)
City Colls of Chicago, Richard J Daley Coll (IL)
Clark Coll (WA)
Cleveland Comm Coll (NC)
Cleveland Inst of Electronics (OH)
Clinton Comm Coll (IA)
Clinton Comm Coll (NY)
Clovis Comm Coll (NM)
Coll of DuPage (IL)
Coll of Lake County (IL)
Coll of Marin (CA)
Coll of Southern Idaho (ID)
Coll of Southern Maryland (MD)
Coll of the Canyons (CA)
Coll of the Redwoods (CA)
Coll of the Sequoias (CA)
Collin County Comm Coll District (TX)
Columbia State Comm Coll (TN)
Columbus State Comm Coll (OH)
Comm Coll of Allegheny County (PA)
The Comm Coll of Baltimore County–Catonsville Campus (MD)
Comm Coll of Beaver County (PA)
Comm Coll of Denver (CO)
Comm Coll of Rhode Island (RI)
Comm Coll of Southern Nevada (NV)
Comm Coll of the Air Force (AL)
Compton Comm Coll (CA)
Corning Comm Coll (NY)
County Coll of Morris (NJ)
Craven Comm Coll (NC)
Crowder Coll (MO)
Cuesta Coll (CA)
Danville Area Comm Coll (IL)
Daytona Beach Comm Coll (FL)
Delaware County Comm Coll (PA)
Delaware Tech & Comm Coll, Jack F Owens Cmps (DE)
Delaware Tech & Comm Coll, Stanton/ Wilmington Cmps (DE)
Delaware Tech & Comm Coll, Terry Cmps (DE)
Delgado Comm Coll (LA)
Del Mar Coll (TX)
Des Moines Area Comm Coll (IA)
Dodge City Comm Coll (KS)
Don Bosco Coll of Science and Technology (CA)
Doña Ana Branch Comm Coll (NM)
Douglas MacArthur State Tech Coll (AL)
Dunwoody Coll of Technology (MN)
Durham Tech Comm Coll (NC)
Dutchess Comm Coll (NY)
Dyersburg State Comm Coll (TN)
East Central Coll (MO)
East Central Comm Coll (MS)
Eastern Idaho Tech Coll (ID)
Eastern Maine Tech Coll (ME)
Eastern Oklahoma State Coll (OK)
Eastern Shore Comm Coll (VA)
Eastfield Coll (TX)
East Mississippi Comm Coll (MS)
ECPI Coll of Technology, Newport News (VA)
ECPI Coll of Technology, Virginia Beach (VA)
ECPI Tech Coll, Richmond (VA)
ECPI Tech Coll, Roanoke (VA)
Edgecombe Comm Coll (NC)
Edison Comm Coll (FL)
Edison State Comm Coll (OH)
Edmonds Comm Coll (WA)
Education America, Remington Coll, Lafayette Campus (LA)
Education Direct (PA)
Elaine P. Nunez Comm Coll (LA)
Electronic Insts, Middletown (PA)
Erie Comm Coll, North Campus (NY)
Essex County Coll (NJ)
Evergreen Valley Coll (CA)
Fayetteville Tech Comm Coll (NC)
Florence-Darlington Tech Coll (SC)
Florida Comm Coll at Jacksonville (FL)
Florida Tech Coll, Jacksonville (FL)
Florida Tech Coll, Orlando (FL)
Floyd Coll (GA)
Foothill Coll (CA)
Forsyth Tech Comm Coll (NC)
Fort Scott Comm Coll (KS)
Frederick Comm Coll (MD)
Front Range Comm Coll (CO)
Fulton-Montgomery Comm Coll (NY)
Garden City Comm Coll (KS)
Gaston Coll (NC)
Gateway Comm Coll (CT)
Gateway Tech Coll (WI)
Genesee Comm Coll (NY)
George Corley Wallace State Comm Coll (AL)
Germanna Comm Coll (VA)
Glendale Comm Coll (AZ)
Golden West Coll (CA)
Grand Rapids Comm Coll (MI)
Grayson County Coll (TX)
Great Basin Coll (NV)
Greenville Tech Coll (SC)
Guam Comm Coll (GU)
Guilford Tech Comm Coll (NC)
Gulf Coast Comm Coll (FL)
Gwinnett Tech Coll (GA)
Harford Comm Coll (MD)
Harrisburg Area Comm Coll (PA)
Harry M. Ayers State Tech Coll (AL)
Hawaii Comm Coll (HI)
Heald Coll, Schools of Business and Technology (HI)
Heartland Comm Coll (IL)
Helena Coll of Tech of The U of Montana (MT)
Henderson Comm Coll (KY)
Hennepin Tech Coll (MN)
Henry Ford Comm Coll (MI)
Herzing Coll (AL)
Herzing Coll (GA)
Highland Comm Coll (IL)
Hill Coll of the Hill Jr College District (TX)
Hillsborough Comm Coll (FL)
Hinds Comm Coll (MS)
Honolulu Comm Coll (HI)
Hopkinsville Comm Coll (KY)
Horry-Georgetown Tech Coll (SC)
Houston Comm Coll System (TX)
Howard Comm Coll (MD)
Hudson County Comm Coll (NJ)
Illinois Eastern Comm Colls, Wabash Valley Coll (IL)
Independence Comm Coll (KS)
Indian Hills Comm Coll (IA)
Indian River Comm Coll (FL)
Iowa Western Comm Coll (IA)
Isothermal Comm Coll (NC)
ITT Tech Inst, Lathrop (CA)
ITT Tech Inst, Oxnard (CA)
ITT Tech Inst, Maitland (FL)
ITT Tech Inst, Mount Prospect (IL)
Ivy Tech State Coll–Bloomington (IN)
Ivy Tech State Coll–Central Indiana (IN)
Ivy Tech State Coll–Columbus (IN)
Ivy Tech State Coll–Eastcentral (IN)
Ivy Tech State Coll–Kokomo (IN)
Ivy Tech State Coll–Lafayette (IN)
Ivy Tech State Coll–North Central (IN)
Ivy Tech State Coll–Northeast (IN)
Ivy Tech State Coll–Northwest (IN)
Ivy Tech State Coll–Southcentral (IN)
Ivy Tech State Coll–Southeast (IN)
Ivy Tech State Coll–Southwest (IN)
Ivy Tech State Coll–Wabash Valley (IN)
Ivy Tech State Coll–Whitewater (IN)
Jackson Comm Coll (MI)
Jamestown Comm Coll (NY)
Jefferson Coll (MO)
Jefferson Comm Coll (KY)
Jefferson Comm Coll (OH)
J. F. Drake State Tech Coll (AL)
John A. Logan Coll (IL)
Johnson Coll (PA)
Johnston Comm Coll (NC)
John Wood Comm Coll (IL)
Joliet Jr Coll (IL)
Jones County Jr Coll (MS)
J. Sargeant Reynolds Comm Coll (VA)
Kalamazoo Valley Comm Coll (MI)
Kankakee Comm Coll (IL)
Kansas City Kansas Comm Coll (KS)
Kaskaskia Coll (IL)
Kauai Comm Coll (HI)
Kent State U, Trumbull Campus (OH)
Kent State U, Tuscarawas Campus (OH)
Kilgore Coll (TX)
Kirkwood Comm Coll (IA)
Lake Area Tech Inst (SD)
Lake City Comm Coll (FL)
Lake Land Coll (IL)
Lakeland Comm Coll (OH)
Lake Michigan Coll (MI)
Lakeshore Tech Coll (WI)
Lake Washington Tech Coll (WA)
Lamar State Coll–Port Arthur (TX)
Lane Comm Coll (OR)
Lansing Comm Coll (MI)
Laredo Comm Coll (TX)
Las Positas Coll (CA)
Lehigh Carbon Comm Coll (PA)
Lenoir Comm Coll (NC)
Lima Tech Coll (OH)
Linn-Benton Comm Coll (OR)
Long Beach City Coll (CA)
Longview Comm Coll (MO)
Lorain County Comm Coll (OH)
Los Angeles City Coll (CA)
Los Angeles Harbor Coll (CA)
Los Angeles Pierce Coll (CA)
Louisville Tech Inst (KY)
Lower Columbia Coll (WA)
Luzerne County Comm Coll (PA)
Macomb Comm Coll (MI)
Madisonville Comm Coll (KY)
Manatee Comm Coll (FL)
Maple Woods Comm Coll (MO)
Marion Tech Coll (OH)
Marshalltown Comm Coll (IA)
Massasoit Comm Coll (MA)
Mayland Comm Coll (NC)
Maysville Comm Coll (KY)
McHenry County Coll (IL)
Merced Coll (CA)
Mercer County Comm Coll (NJ)
Meridian Comm Coll (MS)
Metropolitan Comm Coll (NE)
Miami-Dade Comm Coll (FL)
Miami U–Hamilton Campus (OH)
Miami U–Middletown Campus (OH)
Middlesex Comm Coll (MA)
Middlesex County Coll (NJ)
Midland Coll (TX)
Midlands Tech Coll (SC)
Mid-Plains Comm Coll Area (NE)
Mid-State Tech Coll (WI)
Miles Comm Coll (MT)
Milwaukee Area Tech Coll (WI)
Mineral Area Coll (MO)
Minnesota State Coll–Southeast Tech (MN)
Mississippi Delta Comm Coll (MS)
Mississippi Gulf Coast Comm Coll (MS)
Mitchell Comm Coll (NC)
Mitchell Tech Inst (SD)
Moberly Area Comm Coll (MO)
Modesto Jr Coll (CA)
Mohawk Valley Comm Coll (NY)
Monroe Comm Coll (NY)
Monroe County Comm Coll (MI)
Montcalm Comm Coll (MI)
Montgomery Coll (MD)
Montgomery Comm Coll (NC)
Moorpark Coll (CA)
Mott Comm Coll (MI)
Mountain Empire Comm Coll (VA)
Mountain View Coll (TX)
Mt. Hood Comm Coll (OR)
Mount Wachusett Comm Coll (MA)
Muskingum Area Tech Coll (OH)
Nash Comm Coll (NC)
Nashville State Tech Inst (TN)
National Inst of Technology (WV)
Naugatuck Valley Comm Coll (CT)
NEI Coll of Technology (MN)
Neosho County Comm Coll (KS)
New England Inst of Technology (RI)
New England Inst of Tech & Florida Culinary Inst (FL)
New Hampshire Tech Inst (NH)
New Mexico State U–Alamogordo (NM)
New Mexico State U–Carlsbad (NM)
New River Comm Coll (VA)
New York City Tech Coll of the City U of NY (NY)
Niagara County Comm Coll (NY)
Northampton County Area Comm Coll (PA)
Northcentral Tech Coll (WI)
North Central Texas Coll (TX)
North Dakota State Coll of Science (ND)
Northeast Alabama Comm Coll (AL)
Northeast Comm Coll (NE)
Northeastern Tech Coll (SC)
Northeast Iowa Comm Coll (IA)
Northeast State Tech Comm Coll (TN)
Northern Essex Comm Coll (MA)
Northern Maine Tech Coll (ME)
Northern New Mexico Comm Coll (NM)
Northern Virginia Comm Coll (VA)
North Harris Coll (TX)
North Hennepin Comm Coll (MN)
North Idaho Coll (ID)
North Iowa Area Comm Coll (IA)
Northland Comm and Tech Coll (MN)
Northland Pioneer Coll (AZ)
North Seattle Comm Coll (WA)
NorthWest Arkansas Comm Coll (AR)
Northwestern Connecticut Comm-Tech Coll (CT)
Northwestern Michigan Coll (MI)
Northwest Mississippi Comm Coll (MS)
Northwest-Shoals Comm Coll (AL)
Northwest State Comm Coll (OH)
Norwalk Comm Coll (CT)
Oakland Comm Coll (MI)
Oakton Comm Coll (IL)
Ocean County Coll (NJ)
Odessa Coll (TX)
Okaloosa-Walton Comm Coll (FL)
Oklahoma City Comm Coll (OK)
Oklahoma State U, Oklahoma City (OK)
Oklahoma State U, Okmulgee (OK)
Olympic Coll (WA)
Onondaga Comm Coll (NY)
Orangeburg-Calhoun Tech Coll (SC)
Orange Coast Coll (CA)
Orange County Comm Coll (NY)
Owensboro Comm Coll (KY)
Oxnard Coll (CA)
Paducah Comm Coll (KY)
Paducah Tech Coll (KY)
Palau Comm CollPalau)
Palm Beach Comm Coll (FL)
Palomar Coll (CA)
Pamlico Comm Coll (NC)
Pasadena City Coll (CA)
Patrick Henry Comm Coll (VA)
Pellissippi State Tech Comm Coll (TN)
Peninsula Coll (WA)
Pennsylvania Coll of Technology (PA)
Pennsylvania Inst of Technology (PA)
Penn State U Beaver Campus of the Commonwealth Coll (PA)
Penn State U DuBois Campus of the Commonwealth Coll (PA)
Penn State U Fayette Campus of the Commonwealth Coll (PA)
Penn State U Hazleton Campus of the Commonwealth Coll (PA)
Penn State U New Kensington Campus of the Commonwealth Coll (PA)
Penn State U Wilkes-Barre Campus of the Commonwealth Coll (PA)

Penn State U York Campus of the Commonwealth Coll (PA)
Penn Valley Comm Coll (MO)
Pensacola Jr Coll (FL)
Piedmont Comm Coll (NC)
Piedmont Tech Coll (SC)
Piedmont Virginia Comm Coll (VA)
Pierce Coll (WA)
Pikes Peak Comm Coll (CO)
Pima Comm Coll (AZ)
Pitt Comm Coll (NC)
Pittsburgh Inst of Aeronautics (PA)
Pittsburgh Tech Inst (PA)
Portland Comm Coll (OR)
Prairie State Coll (IL)
Prince George's Comm Coll (MD)
Queensborough Comm Coll of City U of NY (NY)
Quinsigamond Comm Coll (MA)
Raritan Valley Comm Coll (NJ)
Reading Area Comm Coll (PA)
Red Rocks Comm Coll (CO)
Reid State Tech Coll (AL)
RETS Tech Center (OH)
Richland Comm Coll (IL)
Richmond Comm Coll (NC)
Ridgewater Coll (MN)
Roanoke-Chowan Comm Coll (NC)
Rockland Comm Coll (NY)
Rogue Comm Coll (OR)
Rowan-Cabarrus Comm Coll (NC)
Sacramento City Coll (CA)
St. Clair County Comm Coll (MI)
St. Cloud Tech Coll (MN)
St. Louis Comm Coll at Florissant Valley (MO)
St. Paul Tech Coll (MN)
St. Petersburg Coll (FL)
St. Philip's Coll (TX)
Salem Comm Coll (NJ)
San Antonio Coll (TX)
San Bernardino Valley Coll (CA)
San Diego City Coll (CA)
San Diego Mesa Coll (CA)
San Jacinto Coll Central Campus (TX)
San Jacinto Coll North Campus (TX)
San Jacinto Coll South Campus (TX)
San Joaquin Delta Coll (CA)
San Joaquin Valley Coll (CA)
Santa Ana Coll (CA)
Santa Barbara City Coll (CA)
Santa Fe Comm Coll (FL)
Santa Fe Comm Coll (NM)
Santa Monica Coll (CA)
Sauk Valley Comm Coll (IL)
Savannah Tech Coll (GA)
Schenectady County Comm Coll (NY)
Schoolcraft Coll (MI)
Scottsdale Comm Coll (AZ)
Seminole Comm Coll (FL)
Shasta Coll (CA)
Sierra Coll (CA)
Sinclair Comm Coll (OH)
Skagit Valley Coll (WA)
Snow Coll (UT)
Southeast Arkansas Coll (AR)
Southeast Comm Coll, Milford Campus (NE)
Southeastern Comm Coll (NC)
Southeast Tech Inst (SD)
Southern Maine Tech Coll (ME)
South Piedmont Comm Coll (NC)
South Plains Coll (TX)
South Puget Sound Comm Coll (WA)
Southside Virginia Comm Coll (VA)
South Suburban Coll (IL)
Southwestern Coll (CA)
Southwestern Comm Coll (NC)
Southwest Mississippi Comm Coll (MS)
Southwest Tennessee Comm Coll (TN)
Southwest Virginia Comm Coll (VA)
Southwest Wisconsin Tech Coll (WI)
Spartanburg Tech Coll (SC)
Spartan School of Aeronautics (OK)
Spencerian Coll–Lexington (KY)
Spokane Comm Coll (WA)
Springfield Tech Comm Coll (MA)
Stanly Comm Coll (NC)
State Fair Comm Coll (MO)
State U of NY Coll of A&T at Morrisville (NY)
State U of NY Coll of Technology at Alfred (NY)
State U of NY Coll of Technology at Canton (NY)
Suffolk County Comm Coll (NY)
Sullivan County Comm Coll (NY)
Surry Comm Coll (NC)
Taft Coll (CA)
Tarrant County Coll District (TX)
TCI-The Coll for Technology (NY)
Temple Coll (TX)
Tennessee Inst of Electronics (TN)
Texarkana Coll (TX)
Texas State Tech Coll–Harlingen (TX)
Texas State Tech Coll– Waco/ Marshall Campus (TX)
Texas State Tech Coll (TX)
Thaddeus Stevens Coll of Technology (PA)
Thomas Nelson Comm Coll (VA)
Three Rivers Comm Coll (CT)
Tidewater Comm Coll (VA)
Tomball Coll (TX)
Tompkins Cortland Comm Coll (NY)
Trenholm State Tech Coll, Patterson Campus (AL)
Triangle Tech, Inc. (PA)
Triangle Tech, Inc.–DuBois School (PA)
Triangle Tech, Inc.–Erie School (PA)
Tri-County Comm Coll (NC)
Tri-County Tech Coll (SC)
Trident Tech Coll (SC)
Trinidad State Jr Coll (CO)
Triton Coll (IL)
Truckee Meadows Comm Coll (NV)
Tulsa Comm Coll (OK)
Tyler Jr Coll (TX)
Umpqua Comm Coll (OR)
U of Alaska Anchorage, Kenai Peninsula Coll (AK)
U of Alaska Anchorage, Matanuska-Susitna Coll (AK)
U of Arkansas at Fort Smith (AR)
U of New Mexico–Los Alamos Branch (NM)
Vance-Granville Comm Coll (NC)
Vatterott Coll (MO)
Vermont Tech Coll (VT)
Victoria Coll (TX)
Victor Valley Coll (CA)
Vincennes U (IN)
Virginia Western Comm Coll (VA)
Wake Tech Comm Coll (NC)
Wallace State Comm Coll (AL)
Waubonsee Comm Coll (IL)
Waycross Coll (GA)
Wayne Comm Coll (NC)
West Central Tech Coll (GA)
Westchester Comm Coll (NY)
Western Dakota Tech Inst (SD)
Western Iowa Tech Comm Coll (IA)
Western Nevada Comm Coll (NV)
Western Piedmont Comm Coll (NC)
Western Wisconsin Tech Coll (WI)
Western Wyoming Comm Coll (WY)
Westmoreland County Comm Coll (PA)
West Shore Comm Coll (MI)
West Virginia Northern Comm Coll (WV)
West Virginia U at Parkersburg (WV)
Westwood Coll of Technology– Denver North (CO)
Wharton County Jr Coll (TX)
Wilkes Comm Coll (NC)
Wilson Tech Comm Coll (NC)
Wor-Wic Comm Coll (MD)
York Tech Coll (SC)

ELECTRICAL/ELECTRONICS DRAFTING
Albuquerque Tech Vocational Inst (NM)
Collin County Comm Coll District (TX)
Eastfield Coll (TX)
Florida Tech Coll, Orlando (FL)
Joliet Jr Coll (IL)
Texas State Tech Coll– Waco/ Marshall Campus (TX)

ELECTRICAL ENGINEERING
Allen County Comm Coll (KS)
Dutchess Comm Coll (NY)
Fayetteville Tech Comm Coll (NC)
John Tyler Comm Coll (VA)
Lehigh Carbon Comm Coll (PA)

ELECTRICAL EQUIPMENT INSTALLATION/REPAIR
Angelina Coll (TX)
Bismarck State Coll (ND)
Cape Fear Comm Coll (NC)
Coll of DuPage (IL)
Collin County Comm Coll District (TX)
The Comm Coll of Baltimore County–Catonsville Campus (MD)
Dakota County Tech Coll (MN)
Delgado Comm Coll (LA)
Guilford Tech Comm Coll (NC)
Harry M. Ayers State Tech Coll (AL)
Hutchinson Comm Coll and Area Vocational School (KS)
Iowa Western Comm Coll (IA)
Johnson Coll (PA)
Kennebec Valley Tech Coll (ME)
Louisville Tech Inst (KY)
Mesabi Range Comm and Tech Coll (MN)
Miles Comm Coll (MT)
Milwaukee Area Tech Coll (WI)
Modesto Jr Coll (CA)
Orange Coast Coll (CA)
Pittsburgh Tech Inst (PA)
Ridgewater Coll (MN)
Riverland Comm Coll (MN)
St. Philip's Coll (TX)
San Jacinto Coll North Campus (TX)
Santa Barbara City Coll (CA)
Southwest Tennessee Comm Coll (TN)
State U of NY Coll of Technology at Alfred (NY)
Western Dakota Tech Inst (SD)
York Tech Coll (SC)

ELECTRICAL/POWER TRANSMISSION INSTALLATION
Bates Tech Coll (WA)
Benjamin Franklin Inst of Technology (MA)
Dunwoody Coll of Technology (MN)
Johnson County Comm Coll (KS)
Luzerne County Comm Coll (PA)
Mitchell Tech Inst (SD)
Northeast Comm Coll (NE)
Orange Coast Coll (CA)
St. Cloud Tech Coll (MN)
State U of NY Coll of Technology at Delhi (NY)
Wake Tech Comm Coll (NC)
Western Nevada Comm Coll (NV)

ELECTRICAL/POWER TRANSMISSION INSTALLERS RELATED
Bismarck State Coll (ND)
Calhoun Comm Coll (AL)
Martin Comm Coll (NC)

ELECTROCARDIOGRAPH TECHNOLOGY
Southwestern Comm Coll (NC)

ELECTROENCEPHALOGRAPH TECHNOLOGY
Black Hawk Coll, Moline (IL)
Comm Coll of Allegheny County (PA)
Niagara County Comm Coll (NY)
Parkland Coll (IL)
Scott Comm Coll (IA)
Western Wisconsin Tech Coll (WI)

ELECTROMECHANICAL INSTRUMENTATION AND MAINTENANCE TECHNOLOGIES RELATED
Calhoun Comm Coll (AL)

ELECTROMECHANICAL TECHNOLOGY
Alamance Comm Coll (NC)
Angelina Coll (TX)
Athens Tech Coll (GA)
Belmont Tech Coll (OH)
Black Hawk Coll, Moline (IL)
Blackhawk Tech Coll (WI)
Bristol Comm Coll (MA)
Central Comm Coll–Columbus Campus (NE)
Central Maine Tech Coll (ME)
Central Ohio Tech Coll (OH)
Central Piedmont Comm Coll (NC)
Chabot Coll (CA)
Chattahoochee Tech Coll (GA)
Chippewa Valley Tech Coll (WI)
Cincinnati State Tech and Comm Coll (OH)
Clovis Comm Coll (NM)
Coll of DuPage (IL)
Columbus State Comm Coll (OH)
Craven Comm Coll (NC)
Delaware Tech & Comm Coll, Terry Cmps (DE)
Dutchess Comm Coll (NY)
ECPI Coll of Technology, Newport News (VA)
ECPI Coll of Technology, Virginia Beach (VA)
ECPI Tech Coll, Richmond (VA)
ECPI Tech Coll, Roanoke (VA)
Florence-Darlington Tech Coll (SC)
Forsyth Tech Comm Coll (NC)
GateWay Comm Coll (AZ)
Gateway Tech Coll (WI)
Glendale Comm Coll (CA)
Hagerstown Comm Coll (MD)
Jackson State Comm Coll (TN)
Johnson Coll (PA)
Kirkwood Comm Coll (IA)
Lake Land Coll (IL)
Lake Michigan Coll (MI)
Lakeshore Tech Coll (WI)
Lansing Comm Coll (MI)
Los Angeles Harbor Coll (CA)
Macomb Comm Coll (MI)
Martin Comm Coll (NC)
Massasoit Comm Coll (MA)
Maysville Comm Coll (KY)
Miami-Dade Comm Coll (FL)
Miami U–Middletown Campus (OH)
Milwaukee Area Tech Coll (WI)
Montgomery Coll (MD)
Montgomery County Comm Coll (PA)
Moraine Park Tech Coll (WI)
Mountain View Coll (TX)
NEI Coll of Technology (MN)
New York City Tech Coll of the City U of NY (NY)
Northampton County Area Comm Coll (PA)
North Arkansas Coll (AR)
Northcentral Tech Coll (WI)
Northeast Comm Coll (NE)
North Seattle Comm Coll (WA)
Pitt Comm Coll (NC)
Pulaski Tech Coll (AR)
Randolph Comm Coll (NC)
Raritan Valley Comm Coll (NJ)
Rockingham Comm Coll (NC)
Savannah Tech Coll (GA)
Schoolcraft Coll (MI)
Sinclair Comm Coll (OH)
Southeast Comm Coll, Milford Campus (NE)
Southeast Tech Inst (SD)
South Piedmont Comm Coll (NC)
Southwestern Comm Coll (IA)
Southwest Wisconsin Tech Coll (WI)
Springfield Tech Comm Coll (MA)
State U of NY Coll of Technology at Alfred (NY)
Tarrant County Coll District (TX)
Terra State Comm Coll (OH)
Texas State Tech Coll–Harlingen (TX)
Tri-County Tech Coll (SC)
Union County Coll (NJ)
Wake Tech Comm Coll (NC)
Wayne Comm Coll (NC)
Western Wisconsin Tech Coll (WI)
West Virginia U at Parkersburg (WV)
Wilkes Comm Coll (NC)
Wisconsin Indianhead Tech Coll (WI)

ELEMENTARY EDUCATION
Abraham Baldwin Ag Coll (GA)
Albuquerque Tech Vocational Inst (NM)
Allen County Comm Coll (KS)
Amarillo Coll (TX)
Ancilla Coll (IN)
Angelina Coll (TX)
Anne Arundel Comm Coll (MD)
Bainbridge Coll (GA)
Bowling Green State U-Firelands Coll (OH)
Brazosport Coll (TX)
Bristol Comm Coll (MA)
Burlington County Coll (NJ)
Butler County Comm Coll (PA)
Casper Coll (WY)
Cecil Comm Coll (MD)
Central Wyoming Coll (WY)
Chattahoochee Valley Comm Coll (AL)
Chesapeake Coll (MD)
City Colls of Chicago, Harry S Truman Coll (IL)
City Colls of Chicago, Malcolm X Coll (IL)
City Colls of Chicago, Richard J Daley Coll (IL)
City Colls of Chicago, Wilbur Wright Coll (IL)
Coahoma Comm Coll (MS)
Coastal Bend Coll (TX)
Coffeyville Comm Coll (KS)
Coll of Southern Idaho (ID)
Coll of Southern Maryland (MD)
Columbia State Comm Coll (TN)
The Comm Coll of Baltimore County–Catonsville Campus (MD)
Copiah-Lincoln Comm Coll–Natchez Campus (MS)
Corning Comm Coll (NY)
Cowley County Comm Coll and Voc-Tech School (KS)
Crowder Coll (MO)
Cuyamaca Coll (CA)
Danville Area Comm Coll (IL)
Darton Coll (GA)
Delta Coll (MI)
Diné Coll (AZ)
Dixie State Coll of Utah (UT)
Dodge City Comm Coll (KS)
Dutchess Comm Coll (NY)
East Central Coll (MO)
East Central Comm Coll (MS)
Eastern Arizona Coll (AZ)
Eastern Oklahoma State Coll (OK)
Eastern Wyoming Coll (WY)
East Georgia Coll (GA)
East Mississippi Comm Coll (MS)
Edison State Comm Coll (OH)
Essex County Coll (NJ)
Everett Comm Coll (WA)
Frederick Comm Coll (MD)
Fulton-Montgomery Comm Coll (NY)
Garden City Comm Coll (KS)
Genesee Comm Coll (NY)
Georgia Perimeter Coll (GA)
Grayson County Coll (TX)
Great Basin Coll (NV)
Harford Comm Coll (MD)
Harrisburg Area Comm Coll (PA)
Hill Coll of the Hill Jr College District (TX)
Hillsborough Comm Coll (FL)
Holmes Comm Coll (MS)
Holyoke Comm Coll (MA)
Howard Comm Coll (MD)
Independence Comm Coll (KS)
Iowa Lakes Comm Coll (IA)
Isothermal Comm Coll (NC)
Jefferson Coll (MO)
Jefferson Comm Coll (KY)
Jefferson Davis Comm Coll (AL)
John A. Logan Coll (IL)
Kalamazoo Valley Comm Coll (MI)
Kankakee Comm Coll (IL)
Kansas City Kansas Comm Coll (KS)
Kellogg Comm Coll (MI)
Kilgore Coll (TX)
Kingsborough Comm Coll of City U of NY (NY)
Kirkwood Comm Coll (IA)

Labette Comm Coll (KS)
Lansing Comm Coll (MI)
Lenoir Comm Coll (NC)
Lincoln Coll, Lincoln (IL)
Lincoln Land Comm Coll (IL)
Linn-Benton Comm Coll (OR)
Lon Morris Coll (TX)
Lorain County Comm Coll (OH)
Louisburg Coll (NC)
Manor Coll (PA)
Mesa Tech Coll (NM)
Miami-Dade Comm Coll (FL)
Miami U–Middletown Campus (OH)
Mid Michigan Comm Coll (MI)
Mississippi Delta Comm Coll (MS)
Mississippi Gulf Coast Comm Coll (MS)
Mitchell Comm Coll (NC)
Monroe County Comm Coll (MI)
Montgomery County Comm Coll (PA)
Mountain Empire Comm Coll (VA)
Navarro Coll (TX)
Northeast Comm Coll (NE)
Northern New Mexico Comm Coll (NM)
Northern Oklahoma Coll (OK)
North Idaho Coll (ID)
Northwest Coll (WY)
Northwest Mississippi Comm Coll (MS)
Northwest-Shoals Comm Coll (AL)
Okaloosa-Walton Comm Coll (FL)
Orange County Comm Coll (NY)
Otero Jr Coll (CO)
Palm Beach Comm Coll (FL)
Portland Comm Coll (OR)
Pratt Comm Coll and Area Vocational School (KS)
Prince George's Comm Coll (MD)
Raritan Valley Comm Coll (NJ)
Reading Area Comm Coll (PA)
Roane State Comm Coll (TN)
St. Catharine Coll (KY)
St. Louis Comm Coll at Florissant Valley (MO)
San Jacinto Coll North Campus (TX)
Sauk Valley Comm Coll (IL)
Seminole State Coll (OK)
Sheridan Coll (WY)
Snow Coll (UT)
Southeast Comm Coll, Beatrice Campus (NE)
South Suburban Coll (IL)
Southwestern Coll (CA)
Southwest Mississippi Comm Coll (MS)
Springfield Tech Comm Coll (MA)
Sullivan County Comm Coll (NY)
Trinity Valley Comm Coll (TX)
Truckee Meadows Comm Coll (NV)
Tulsa Comm Coll (OK)
Ulster County Comm Coll (NY)
Umpqua Comm Coll (OR)
U of New Mexico–Gallup (NM)
Vance-Granville Comm Coll (NC)
Vermilion Comm Coll (MN)
Vincennes U (IN)
Vincennes U Jasper Campus (IN)
Wallace State Comm Coll (AL)
Waycross Coll (GA)
Western Nebraska Comm Coll (NE)
Western Wyoming Comm Coll (WY)
Wor-Wic Comm Coll (MD)

ELEMENTARY/MIDDLE/ SECONDARY EDUCATION ADMINISTRATION
Cumberland County Coll (NJ)
Tulsa Comm Coll (OK)

EMERGENCY MEDICAL TECHNOLOGY
Allen County Comm Coll (KS)
Alvin Comm Coll (TX)
Amarillo Coll (TX)
Angelina Coll (TX)
Anne Arundel Comm Coll (MD)
Arapahoe Comm Coll (CO)
Arkansas State U–Mountain Home (AR)
Asheville-Buncombe Tech Comm Coll (NC)
Augusta Tech Coll (GA)
Austin Comm Coll (TX)
Bakersfield Coll (CA)
Baltimore City Comm Coll (MD)
Barton County Comm Coll (KS)
Belmont Tech Coll (OH)
Bevill State Comm Coll (AL)
Black River Tech Coll (AR)
Borough of Manhattan Comm Coll of City U of NY (NY)
Bossier Parish Comm Coll (LA)
Brazosport Coll (TX)
Brevard Comm Coll (FL)
Broome Comm Coll (NY)
Butler County Comm Coll (PA)
Calhoun Comm Coll (AL)
Capital Comm Coll (CT)
Casper Coll (WY)
Catawba Valley Comm Coll (NC)
Central Arizona Coll (AZ)
Central Oregon Comm Coll (OR)
Central Texas Coll (TX)
Century Comm and Tech Coll (MN)
Cerro Coso Comm Coll (CA)
Chabot Coll (CA)
Chattanooga State Tech Comm Coll (TN)
Chemeketa Comm Coll (OR)
Cincinnati State Tech and Comm Coll (OH)
City Colls of Chicago, Malcolm X Coll (IL)
Clinton Comm Coll (IA)
Coastal Carolina Comm Coll (NC)
Coffeyville Comm Coll (KS)
Coll of DuPage (IL)
Coll of the Siskiyous (CA)
Collin County Comm Coll District (TX)
Columbus State Comm Coll (OH)
Comm Coll of Southern Nevada (NV)
Compton Comm Coll (CA)
Corning Comm Coll (NY)
Cowley County Comm Coll and Voc-Tech School (KS)
Crafton Hills Coll (CA)
Darton Coll (GA)
Daytona Beach Comm Coll (FL)
Delaware Tech & Comm Coll, Jack F Owens Cmps (DE)
Delaware Tech & Comm Coll, Stanton/ Wilmington Cmps (DE)
Delgado Comm Coll (LA)
Delta Coll (MI)
Dixie State Coll of Utah (UT)
Doña Ana Branch Comm Coll (NM)
Dutchess Comm Coll (NY)
East Central Coll (MO)
Eastern Arizona Coll (AZ)
Edison Comm Coll (FL)
Elaine P. Nunez Comm Coll (LA)
El Centro Coll (TX)
Essex County Coll (NJ)
Fayetteville Tech Comm Coll (NC)
Fiorello H LaGuardia Comm Coll of City U of NY (NY)
Florida Comm Coll at Jacksonville (FL)
Floyd Coll (GA)
Foothill Coll (CA)
Fort Scott Comm Coll (KS)
Gadsden State Comm Coll (AL)
Galveston Coll (TX)
Garden City Comm Coll (KS)
Georgia Perimeter Coll (GA)
Glendale Comm Coll (AZ)
Greenville Tech Coll (SC)
Guilford Tech Comm Coll (NC)
Gulf Coast Comm Coll (FL)
Gwinnett Tech Coll (GA)
Hagerstown Comm Coll (MD)
Harrisburg Area Comm Coll (PA)
Hawkeye Comm Coll (IA)
Henry Ford Comm Coll (MI)
Highland Comm Coll (KS)
Hillsborough Comm Coll (FL)
Hinds Comm Coll (MS)
Houston Comm Coll System (TX)
Howard Comm Coll (MD)
Hutchinson Comm Coll and Area Vocational School (KS)
Independence Comm Coll (KS)
Indian River Comm Coll (FL)
Inver Hills Comm Coll (MN)
Ivy Tech State Coll–Kokomo (IN)
Ivy Tech State Coll–Southwest (IN)
Ivy Tech State Coll–Wabash Valley (IN)
Jackson Comm Coll (MI)
Jefferson Coll (MO)
Jefferson Comm Coll (OH)
John A. Logan Coll (IL)
Johnson County Comm Coll (KS)
Jones County Jr Coll (MS)
Kalamazoo Valley Comm Coll (MI)
Kankakee Comm Coll (IL)
Kansas City Kansas Comm Coll (KS)
Kellogg Comm Coll (MI)
Kennebec Valley Tech Coll (ME)
Kilgore Coll (TX)
Lake City Comm Coll (FL)
Lake-Sumter Comm Coll (FL)
Lamar Comm Coll (CO)
Lansing Comm Coll (MI)
Laredo Comm Coll (TX)
Lima Tech Coll (OH)
Lurleen B. Wallace Jr Coll (AL)
Luzerne County Comm Coll (PA)
Macomb Comm Coll (MI)
McHenry County Coll (IL)
Meridian Comm Coll (MS)
Miami-Dade Comm Coll (FL)
Midland Coll (TX)
Mid Michigan Comm Coll (MI)
Mid-Plains Comm Coll Area (NE)
Minnesota State Coll–Southeast Tech (MN)
Mississippi Gulf Coast Comm Coll (MS)
Modesto Jr Coll (CA)
Montana State U Coll of Tech-Great Falls (MT)
Montcalm Comm Coll (MI)
Montgomery Comm Coll (NC)
Moraine Park Tech Coll (WI)
Mott Comm Coll (MI)
Muscatine Comm Coll (IA)
New Hampshire Tech Inst (NH)
North Arkansas Coll (AR)
North Central Michigan Coll (MI)
North Central Texas Coll (TX)
Northeast Alabama Comm Coll (AL)
Northeast State Tech Comm Coll (TN)
Northern Maine Tech Coll (ME)
Northern Virginia Comm Coll (VA)
North Harris Coll (TX)
North Iowa Area Comm Coll (IA)
Northland Pioneer Coll (AZ)
North Seattle Comm Coll (WA)
NorthWest Arkansas Comm Coll (AR)
Oakland Comm Coll (MI)
Odessa Coll (TX)
Oklahoma City Comm Coll (OK)
Orange Coast Coll (CA)
Our Lady of the Lake Coll (LA)
Palomar Coll (CA)
Pasco-Hernando Comm Coll (FL)
Pennsylvania Coll of Technology (PA)
Penn Valley Comm Coll (MO)
Pensacola Jr Coll (FL)
Phoenix Coll (AZ)
Pikes Peak Comm Coll (CO)
Pima Comm Coll (AZ)
Polk Comm Coll (FL)
Prince George's Comm Coll (MD)
Quincy Coll (MA)
Quinsigamond Comm Coll (MA)
Roane State Comm Coll (TN)
Rockland Comm Coll (NY)
St. Cloud Tech Coll (MN)
St. Louis Comm Coll at Florissant Valley (MO)
St. Petersburg Coll (FL)
San Diego City Coll (CA)
San Jacinto Coll Central Campus (TX)
San Jacinto Coll North Campus (TX)
San Joaquin Delta Coll (CA)
Santa Fe Comm Coll (FL)
Schoolcraft Coll (MI)
Scott Comm Coll (IA)
Scottsdale Comm Coll (AZ)
Seminole Comm Coll (FL)
Sinclair Comm Coll (OH)
South Arkansas Comm Coll (AR)
Southeast Arkansas Coll (AR)
Southeastern Comm Coll, South Campus (IA)
Southern Arkansas U Tech (AR)
South Texas Comm Coll (TX)
Southwestern Coll (CA)
Southwestern Comm Coll (NC)
Southwest Mississippi Comm Coll (MS)
Tacoma Comm Coll (WA)
Tallahassee Comm Coll (FL)
Tarrant County Coll District (TX)
Texarkana Coll (TX)
Texas State Tech Coll (TX)
Trinity Valley Comm Coll (TX)
Tulsa Comm Coll (OK)
Umpqua Comm Coll (OR)
U of Arkansas at Fort Smith (AR)
U of Arkansas Comm Coll at Batesville (AR)
Victoria Coll (TX)
Wake Tech Comm Coll (NC)
Wallace State Comm Coll (AL)
Waycross Coll (GA)
Weatherford Coll (TX)
Westchester Comm Coll (NY)
Western Iowa Tech Comm Coll (IA)
West Shore Comm Coll (MI)
Wilson Tech Comm Coll (NC)
Wisconsin Indianhead Tech Coll (WI)

ENERGY MANAGEMENT TECHNOLOGY
Bismarck State Coll (ND)
Chattanooga State Tech Comm Coll (TN)
Comm Coll of Allegheny County (PA)
Henry Ford Comm Coll (MI)
Iowa Lakes Comm Coll (IA)
Lane Comm Coll (OR)
Macomb Comm Coll (MI)
Miles Comm Coll (MT)
Pikes Peak Comm Coll (CO)
Pratt Comm Coll and Area Vocational School (KS)

ENGINEERING
Adirondack Comm Coll (NY)
Albuquerque Tech Vocational Inst (NM)
Allan Hancock Coll (CA)
Allegany Coll of Maryland (MD)
Allen County Comm Coll (KS)
Amarillo Coll (TX)
Angelina Coll (TX)
Antelope Valley Coll (CA)
Arapahoe Comm Coll (CO)
Bakersfield Coll (CA)
Baltimore City Comm Coll (MD)
Berkshire Comm Coll (MA)
Brazosport Coll (TX)
Bristol Comm Coll (MA)
Brookdale Comm Coll (NJ)
Bucks County Comm Coll (PA)
Burlington County Coll (NJ)
Cañada Coll (CA)
Casper Coll (WY)
Central Arizona Coll (AZ)
Centralia Coll (WA)
Central Texas Coll (TX)
Chabot Coll (CA)
Chaffey Coll (CA)
Chemeketa Comm Coll (OR)
Cincinnati State Tech and Comm Coll (OH)
Citrus Coll (CA)
Clark Coll (WA)
Coastal Bend Coll (TX)
Coffeyville Comm Coll (KS)
Coll of DuPage (IL)
Coll of Lake County (IL)
Coll of Marin (CA)
Coll of Southern Idaho (ID)
Coll of Southern Maryland (MD)
Coll of the Sequoias (CA)
Coll of the Siskiyous (CA)
The Comm Coll of Baltimore County–Catonsville Campus (MD)
Comm Coll of Rhode Island (RI)
Compton Comm Coll (CA)
Connors State Coll (OK)
Cuesta Coll (CA)
Cumberland County Coll (NJ)
Cypress Coll (CA)
Danville Area Comm Coll (IL)
Daytona Beach Comm Coll (FL)
De Anza Coll (CA)
Delaware County Comm Coll (PA)
Delaware Tech & Comm Coll, Jack F Owens Cmps (DE)
Delaware Tech & Comm Coll, Stanton/ Wilmington Cmps (DE)
Delta Coll (MI)
Dixie State Coll of Utah (UT)
Dodge City Comm Coll (KS)
Donnelly Coll (KS)
East Central Comm Coll (MS)
Edgecombe Comm Coll (NC)
Edison Comm Coll (FL)
Edison State Comm Coll (OH)
Erie Comm Coll, North Campus (NY)
Essex County Coll (NJ)
Everett Comm Coll (WA)
Evergreen Valley Coll (CA)
Foothill Coll (CA)
Frederick Comm Coll (MD)
Fresno City Coll (CA)
Garden City Comm Coll (KS)
Georgia Military Coll (GA)
Georgia Perimeter Coll (GA)
Gogebic Comm Coll (MI)
Hagerstown Comm Coll (MD)
Harford Comm Coll (MD)
Harrisburg Area Comm Coll (PA)
Heartland Comm Coll (IL)
Highland Comm Coll (IL)
Highline Comm Coll (WA)
Hill Coll of the Hill Jr College District (TX)
Holmes Comm Coll (MS)
Howard Comm Coll (MD)
Hutchinson Comm Coll and Area Vocational School (KS)
Independence Comm Coll (KS)
Indian River Comm Coll (FL)
Itasca Comm Coll (MN)
J. Sargeant Reynolds Comm Coll (VA)
Kankakee Comm Coll (IL)
Kansas City Kansas Comm Coll (KS)
Kellogg Comm Coll (MI)
Kent State U, Trumbull Campus (OH)
Kirkwood Comm Coll (IA)
Kishwaukee Coll (IL)
Lamar Comm Coll (CO)
Lansing Comm Coll (MI)
Laramie County Comm Coll (WY)
Lehigh Carbon Comm Coll (PA)
Long Beach City Coll (CA)
Longview Comm Coll (MO)
Lon Morris Coll (TX)
Lorain County Comm Coll (OH)
Los Angeles City Coll (CA)
Manatee Comm Coll (FL)
Marion Military Inst (AL)
McHenry County Coll (IL)
Miami-Dade Comm Coll (FL)
Miami U–Middletown Campus (OH)
Middlesex County Coll (NJ)
Mitchell Coll (CT)
Mitchell Comm Coll (NC)
Modesto Jr Coll (CA)
Mohawk Valley Comm Coll (NY)
Monterey Peninsula Coll (CA)
Montgomery Coll (MD)
Moorpark Coll (CA)
Mt. San Jacinto Coll (CA)
Nassau Comm Coll (NY)
Navarro Coll (TX)
New Mexico Military Inst (NM)
New Mexico State U–Alamogordo (NM)
New River Comm Coll (VA)
Northampton County Area Comm Coll (PA)
Northeast Comm Coll (NE)
Northern Oklahoma Coll (OK)
Northern Virginia Comm Coll (VA)
North Idaho Coll (ID)
Northwestern Connecticut Comm-Tech Coll (CT)
Ocean County Coll (NJ)
Okaloosa-Walton Comm Coll (FL)
Oklahoma State U, Oklahoma City (OK)
Orange Coast Coll (CA)
Palomar Coll (CA)
Pasadena City Coll (CA)
Penn Valley Comm Coll (MO)
Piedmont Tech Coll (SC)
Portland Comm Coll (OR)
Prince George's Comm Coll (MD)
Raritan Valley Comm Coll (NJ)
Reading Area Comm Coll (PA)
Rend Lake Coll (IL)
Ridgewater Coll (MN)
Riverside Comm Coll (CA)
Roane State Comm Coll (TN)

Sacramento City Coll (CA)
St. Louis Comm Coll at Florissant Valley (MO)
San Diego Mesa Coll (CA)
San Jacinto Coll Central Campus (TX)
San Joaquin Delta Coll (CA)
San Juan Coll (NM)
Santa Ana Coll (CA)
Santa Barbara City Coll (CA)
Santa Fe Comm Coll (FL)
Santa Fe Comm Coll (NM)
Schoolcraft Coll (MI)
Sheridan Coll (WY)
Sierra Coll (CA)
Sinclair Comm Coll (OH)
Snow Coll (UT)
South Plains Coll (TX)
Southwestern Coll (CA)
Southwest Mississippi Comm Coll (MS)
Southwest Virginia Comm Coll (VA)
Springfield Tech Comm Coll (MA)
State U of NY Coll of A&T at Morrisville (NY)
Suffolk County Comm Coll (NY)
Tacoma Comm Coll (WA)
Tallahassee Comm Coll (FL)
Terra State Comm Coll (OH)
Texarkana Coll (TX)
Thomas Nelson Comm Coll (VA)
Three Rivers Comm Coll (CT)
Tidewater Comm Coll (VA)
Trinidad State Jr Coll (CO)
Tulsa Comm Coll (OK)
Tunxis Comm Coll (CT)
Ulster County Comm Coll (NY)
Umpqua Comm Coll (OR)
Union County Coll (NJ)
The U of Akron–Wayne Coll (OH)
U of New Mexico–Los Alamos Branch (NM)
Valley Forge Military Coll (PA)
Ventura Coll (CA)
Vermilion Comm Coll (MN)
Vincennes U (IN)
Virginia Western Comm Coll (VA)
Wallace State Comm Coll (AL)
Waubonsee Comm Coll (IL)
Western Nevada Comm Coll (NV)
Western Wyoming Comm Coll (WY)
Westmoreland County Comm Coll (PA)

ENGINEERING DESIGN
Chattanooga State Tech Comm Coll (TN)
The Comm Coll of Baltimore County–Catonsville Campus (MD)
Dunwoody Coll of Technology (MN)
Edison State Comm Coll (OH)
Itasca Comm Coll (MN)
Macomb Comm Coll (MI)
Miami-Dade Comm Coll (FL)
Piedmont Tech Coll (SC)
San Joaquin Delta Coll (CA)
Southern Maine Tech Coll (ME)
Triton Coll (IL)

ENGINEERING/INDUSTRIAL MANAGEMENT
Cape Fear Comm Coll (NC)
International Business Coll, Fort Wayne (IN)
Northwest State Comm Coll (OH)
Pitt Comm Coll (NC)
St. Petersburg Coll (FL)

ENGINEERING-RELATED TECHNOLOGY
Angelina Coll (TX)
Brunswick Comm Coll (NC)
The Comm Coll of Baltimore County–Catonsville Campus (MD)
Cuyahoga Comm Coll (OH)
Dakota County Tech Coll (MN)
Fayetteville Tech Comm Coll (NC)
Florida Comm Coll at Jacksonville (FL)
Gulf Coast Comm Coll (FL)
Iowa Western Comm Coll (IA)
Johnson Coll (PA)
Louisville Tech Inst (KY)
Luzerne County Comm Coll (PA)
Mid Michigan Comm Coll (MI)
North Central Texas Coll (TX)
Patrick Henry Comm Coll (VA)
Peninsula Coll (WA)
Pennsylvania Inst of Technology (PA)
San Antonio Coll (TX)
Santa Barbara City Coll (CA)
Snead State Comm Coll (AL)
Southern West Virginia Comm and Tech Coll (WV)
State U of NY Coll of Technology at Delhi (NY)
Trident Tech Coll (SC)
Triton Coll (IL)
Vincennes U (IN)
York Tech Coll (SC)

ENGINEERING SCIENCE
Adirondack Comm Coll (NY)
Asnuntuck Comm Coll (CT)
Bergen Comm Coll (NJ)
Borough of Manhattan Comm Coll of City U of NY (NY)
Broome Comm Coll (NY)
Camden County Coll (NJ)
County Coll of Morris (NJ)
Dutchess Comm Coll (NY)
Everett Comm Coll (WA)
Finger Lakes Comm Coll (NY)
Fulton-Montgomery Comm Coll (NY)
Genesee Comm Coll (NY)
Gloucester County Coll (NJ)
Greenfield Comm Coll (MA)
Highland Comm Coll (IL)
Hill Coll of the Hill Jr College District (TX)
Holyoke Comm Coll (MA)
Hudson County Comm Coll (NJ)
Itasca Comm Coll (MN)
Jamestown Comm Coll (NY)
Jefferson Comm Coll (NY)
Jones County Jr Coll (MS)
Kingsborough Comm Coll of City U of NY (NY)
Manchester Comm Coll (CT)
Mercer County Comm Coll (NJ)
Miami-Dade Comm Coll (FL)
Middlesex County Coll (NJ)
Mohawk Valley Comm Coll (NY)
Monroe Comm Coll (NY)
Montgomery County Comm Coll (PA)
Northern Essex Comm Coll (MA)
North Shore Comm Coll (MA)
Norwalk Comm Coll (CT)
Onondaga Comm Coll (NY)
Orange County Comm Coll (NY)
Parkland Coll (IL)
Pennsylvania Coll of Technology (PA)
Queensborough Comm Coll of City U of NY (NY)
Reading Area Comm Coll (PA)
St. Louis Comm Coll at Florissant Valley (MO)
State U of NY Coll of A&T at Morrisville (NY)
State U of NY Coll of Technology at Alfred (NY)
State U of NY Coll of Technology at Canton (NY)
State U of NY Coll of Technology at Delhi (NY)
Suffolk County Comm Coll (NY)
Sullivan County Comm Coll (NY)
Three Rivers Comm Coll (CT)
Tompkins Cortland Comm Coll (NY)
Westchester Comm Coll (NY)

ENGINEERING TECHNOLOGIES RELATED
Catawba Valley Comm Coll (NC)
Comm Coll of Allegheny County (PA)
Mid Michigan Comm Coll (MI)
Mott Comm Coll (MI)
Southern Arkansas U Tech (AR)
Wisconsin Indianhead Tech Coll (WI)

ENGINEERING TECHNOLOGY
Aims Comm Coll (CO)
Allan Hancock Coll (CA)
Allen County Comm Coll (KS)
American River Coll (CA)
Anne Arundel Comm Coll (MD)
Antelope Valley Coll (CA)
Arizona Western Coll (AZ)
Ashland Comm Coll (KY)
Athens Tech Coll (GA)
Atlanta Metropolitan Coll (GA)
Benjamin Franklin Inst of Technology (MA)
Berkshire Comm Coll (MA)
Black Hawk Coll, Moline (IL)
Central Piedmont Comm Coll (NC)
Central Virginia Comm Coll (VA)
Cerro Coso Comm Coll (CA)
Chabot Coll (CA)
Citrus Coll (CA)
Clark Coll (WA)
Coll of Marin (CA)
Coll of the Desert (CA)
The Comm Coll of Baltimore County–Catonsville Campus (MD)
County Coll of Morris (NJ)
Cowley County Comm Coll and Voc-Tech School (KS)
Danville Comm Coll (VA)
Darton Coll (GA)
De Anza Coll (CA)
Delaware Tech & Comm Coll, Jack F Owens Cmps (DE)
Delaware Tech & Comm Coll, Terry Cmps (DE)
Delta Coll (MI)
Denmark Tech Coll (SC)
Dodge City Comm Coll (KS)
ECPI Coll of Technology, Newport News (VA)
ECPI Coll of Technology, Virginia Beach (VA)
ECPI Tech Coll, Richmond (VA)
ECPI Tech Coll, Roanoke (VA)
Edison Comm Coll (FL)
Edison State Comm Coll (OH)
Education America, Southeast Coll of Technology, New Orleans Campus (LA)
Essex County Coll (NJ)
Everett Comm Coll (WA)
Florence-Darlington Tech Coll (SC)
Forsyth Tech Comm Coll (NC)
Garden City Comm Coll (KS)
Gateway Comm Coll (CT)
Glendale Comm Coll (AZ)
Golden West Coll (CA)
Harrisburg Area Comm Coll (PA)
Hawkeye Comm Coll (IA)
Henderson Comm Coll (KY)
Highland Comm Coll (IL)
Highline Comm Coll (WA)
Honolulu Comm Coll (HI)
Houston Comm Coll System (TX)
Independence Comm Coll (KS)
Indian River Comm Coll (FL)
Itasca Comm Coll (MN)
Kent State U, Tuscarawas Campus (OH)
Lakeland Comm Coll (OH)
Lansing Comm Coll (MI)
Laramie County Comm Coll (WY)
Lima Tech Coll (OH)
Lorain County Comm Coll (OH)
Los Angeles Harbor Coll (CA)
Louisville Tech Inst (KY)
Marion Tech Coll (OH)
Massachusetts Bay Comm Coll (MA)
Miami-Dade Comm Coll (FL)
Miami U–Hamilton Campus (OH)
Miami U–Middletown Campus (OH)
Middlesex County Coll (NJ)
Midlands Tech Coll (SC)
Montgomery County Comm Coll (PA)
Moorpark Coll (CA)
Morrison Inst of Technology (IL)
Mountain Empire Comm Coll (VA)
Mountain View Coll (TX)
Naugatuck Valley Comm Coll (CT)
New Hampshire Tech Inst (NH)
New Mexico State U–Carlsbad (NM)
North Central Michigan Coll (MI)
Northeast State Tech Comm Coll (TN)
Norwalk Comm Coll (CT)
Oklahoma State U, Oklahoma City (OK)
Pasadena City Coll (CA)
Piedmont Tech Coll (SC)
Portland Comm Coll (OR)
Rappahannock Comm Coll (VA)
Reading Area Comm Coll (PA)
St. Louis Comm Coll at Florissant Valley (MO)
San Antonio Coll (TX)
San Diego City Coll (CA)
San Jacinto Coll Central Campus (TX)
San Joaquin Delta Coll (CA)
Santa Ana Coll (CA)
Sheridan Coll (WY)
Shoreline Comm Coll (WA)
Snead State Comm Coll (AL)
Southeast Tech Inst (SD)
Southwestern Michigan Coll (MI)
Spartanburg Tech Coll (SC)
State U of NY Coll of A&T at Morrisville (NY)
State U of NY Coll of Technology at Canton (NY)
Terra State Comm Coll (OH)
Three Rivers Comm Coll (CT)
Triton Coll (IL)
Truckee Meadows Comm Coll (NV)
Tunxis Comm Coll (CT)
Ulster County Comm Coll (NY)
Vermont Tech Coll (VT)
Vincennes U (IN)
Waycross Coll (GA)
Westchester Comm Coll (NY)

ENGLISH
Abraham Baldwin Ag Coll (GA)
Allan Hancock Coll (CA)
Alpena Comm Coll (MI)
Amarillo Coll (TX)
Andrew Coll (GA)
Angelina Coll (TX)
Anne Arundel Comm Coll (MD)
Arizona Western Coll (AZ)
Atlanta Metropolitan Coll (GA)
Austin Comm Coll (TX)
Bainbridge Coll (GA)
Bakersfield Coll (CA)
Barton County Comm Coll (KS)
Black Hawk Coll, Moline (IL)
Blinn Coll (TX)
Brazosport Coll (TX)
Brookdale Comm Coll (NJ)
Burlington County Coll (NJ)
Butler County Comm Coll (PA)
Cañada Coll (CA)
Casper Coll (WY)
Centralia Coll (WA)
Central Wyoming Coll (WY)
Cerritos Coll (CA)
Cerro Coso Comm Coll (CA)
Chabot Coll (CA)
Chaffey Coll (CA)
Chemeketa Comm Coll (OR)
Citrus Coll (CA)
City Coll of San Francisco (CA)
City Colls of Chicago, Wilbur Wright Coll (IL)
Coahoma Comm Coll (MS)
Coastal Bend Coll (TX)
Coastal Georgia Comm Coll (GA)
Cochise Coll, Douglas (AZ)
Coffeyville Comm Coll (KS)
Colby Comm Coll (KS)
Coll of Alameda (CA)
Coll of Southern Idaho (ID)
Coll of the Canyons (CA)
Coll of the Desert (CA)
Coll of the Sequoias (CA)
Coll of the Siskiyous (CA)
Colorado Mountn Coll, Alpine Cmps (CO)
Colorado Mountn Coll (CO)
Colorado Mountn Coll, Timberline Cmps (CO)
Comm Coll of Allegheny County (PA)
Comm Coll of Southern Nevada (NV)
Compton Comm Coll (CA)
Crafton Hills Coll (CA)
Cuyamaca Coll (CA)
Cypress Coll (CA)
Danville Area Comm Coll (IL)
Darton Coll (GA)
Daytona Beach Comm Coll (FL)
De Anza Coll (CA)
Del Mar Coll (TX)
Delta Coll (MI)
Dixie State Coll of Utah (UT)
Dodge City Comm Coll (KS)
Donnelly Coll (KS)
East Central Coll (MO)
East Central Comm Coll (MS)
Eastern Arizona Coll (AZ)
Eastern Oklahoma State Coll (OK)
Eastern Wyoming Coll (WY)
East Georgia Coll (GA)
East Mississippi Comm Coll (MS)
Edison State Comm Coll (OH)
Everett Comm Coll (WA)
Evergreen Valley Coll (CA)
Feather River Comm Coll District (CA)
Floyd Coll (GA)
Foothill Coll (CA)
Frederick Comm Coll (MD)
Fullerton Coll (CA)
Fulton-Montgomery Comm Coll (NY)
Galveston Coll (TX)
Garden City Comm Coll (KS)
Gavilan Coll (CA)
Georgia Perimeter Coll (GA)
Glendale Comm Coll (CA)
Gloucester County Coll (NJ)
Gordon Coll (GA)
Great Basin Coll (NV)
Harford Comm Coll (MD)
Herkimer County Comm Coll (NY)
Highland Comm Coll (KS)
Highline Comm Coll (WA)
Hill Coll of the Hill Jr College District (TX)
Hinds Comm Coll (MS)
Howard Coll (TX)
Hutchinson Comm Coll and Area Vocational School (KS)
Imperial Valley Coll (CA)
Independence Comm Coll (KS)
Indian River Comm Coll (FL)
Iowa Lakes Comm Coll (IA)
Jefferson Coll (MO)
Jefferson Comm Coll (KY)
John A. Logan Coll (IL)
Joliet Jr Coll (IL)
Jones County Jr Coll (MS)
Kellogg Comm Coll (MI)
Kilgore Coll (TX)
Kingwood Coll (TX)
Kirkwood Comm Coll (IA)
Labette Comm Coll (KS)
Lake Michigan Coll (MI)
Lamar Comm Coll (CO)
Lansing Comm Coll (MI)
Laramie County Comm Coll (WY)
Lincoln Coll, Lincoln (IL)
Lincoln Land Comm Coll (IL)
Linn-Benton Comm Coll (OR)
Long Beach City Coll (CA)
Lon Morris Coll (TX)
Los Angeles City Coll (CA)
Los Angeles Mission Coll (CA)
Louisburg Coll (NC)
Lower Columbia Coll (WA)
Manatee Comm Coll (FL)
Miami-Dade Comm Coll (FL)
Miami U–Middletown Campus (OH)
Middlesex County Coll (NJ)
Midland Coll (TX)
Mid-Plains Comm Coll Area (NE)
MiraCosta Coll (CA)
Mississippi Delta Comm Coll (MS)
Modesto Jr Coll (CA)
Mohave Comm Coll (AZ)
Monroe County Comm Coll (MI)
Monterey Peninsula Coll (CA)
Mountain Empire Comm Coll (VA)
Navarro Coll (TX)
New Mexico Military Inst (NM)
Northeast Comm Coll (NE)
North Idaho Coll (ID)
Northwest Coll (WY)
Northwestern Connecticut Comm-Tech Coll (CT)
Odessa Coll (TX)
Orange Coast Coll (CA)
Oxnard Coll (CA)
Palm Beach Comm Coll (FL)
Palo Verde Coll (CA)
Pasadena City Coll (CA)
Pratt Comm Coll and Area Vocational School (KS)
Quincy Coll (MA)
Red Rocks Comm Coll (CO)
Reedley Coll (CA)
Riverside Comm Coll (CA)
Salem Comm Coll (NJ)
San Bernardino Valley Coll (CA)
San Diego City Coll (CA)
San Diego Mesa Coll (CA)
San Jacinto Coll Central Campus (TX)

San Jacinto Coll North Campus (TX)
San Jacinto Coll South Campus (TX)
San Joaquin Delta Coll (CA)
San Juan Coll (NM)
Santa Ana Coll (CA)
Santa Barbara City Coll (CA)
Santa Monica Coll (CA)
Sauk Valley Comm Coll (IL)
Seminole State Coll (OK)
Sheridan Coll (WY)
Skagit Valley Coll (WA)
Southwestern Coll (CA)
Southwest Mississippi Comm Coll (MS)
Suffolk County Comm Coll (NY)
Sussex County Comm Coll (NJ)
Tacoma Comm Coll (WA)
Taft Coll (CA)
Terra State Comm Coll (OH)
Trinidad State Jr Coll (CO)
Trinity Valley Comm Coll (TX)
Triton Coll (IL)
Tulsa Comm Coll (OK)
Umpqua Comm Coll (OR)
Vincennes U (IN)
Vista Comm Coll (CA)
Waycross Coll (GA)
Western Nebraska Comm Coll (NE)
Western Wyoming Comm Coll (WY)
Wharton County Jr Coll (TX)
Young Harris Coll (GA)

ENGLISH COMPOSITION
Allen County Comm Coll (KS)
St. Philip's Coll (TX)
Vista Comm Coll (CA)

ENGLISH EDUCATION
Louisburg Coll (NC)
Manatee Comm Coll (FL)

ENTERPRISE MANAGEMENT
Alexandria Tech Coll (MN)
Bucks County Comm Coll (PA)
Colorado Northwestern Comm Coll (CO)
Comm Coll of Allegheny County (PA)
Corning Comm Coll (NY)
Cuyamaca Coll (CA)
Delaware County Comm Coll (PA)
Eastern Arizona Coll (AZ)
Edmonds Comm Coll (WA)
Front Range Comm Coll (CO)
Mid Michigan Comm Coll (MI)
Montcalm Comm Coll (MI)
Moraine Valley Comm Coll (IL)
Mott Comm Coll (MI)
Nassau Comm Coll (NY)
Oakland Comm Coll (MI)
Palo Verde Coll (CA)
Reedley Coll (CA)
Santa Fe Comm Coll (NM)
Schoolcraft Coll (MI)
Springfield Tech Comm Coll (MA)
Terra State Comm Coll (OH)
United Tribes Tech Coll (ND)
U of New Mexico–Gallup (NM)
Waubonsee Comm Coll (IL)

ENTERPRISE MANAGEMENT RELATED
Williston State Coll (ND)

ENTOMOLOGY
Snow Coll (UT)

ENTREPRENEURSHIP
Central Pennsylvania Coll (PA)
Hesser Coll (NH)
Johnson County Comm Coll (KS)
McIntosh Coll (NH)
Santa Ana Coll (CA)
Santa Barbara City Coll (CA)
South Suburban Coll (IL)
State U of NY Coll of Technology at Alfred (NY)

ENVIRONMENTAL BIOLOGY
Truckee Meadows Comm Coll (NV)

ENVIRONMENTAL CONTROL TECHNOLOGIES RELATED
Central Carolina Tech Coll (SC)
Oakland Comm Coll (MI)
Pennsylvania Coll of Technology (PA)
Pitt Comm Coll (NC)

ENVIRONMENTAL EDUCATION
Colorado Mountn Coll, Timberline Cmps (CO)
Iowa Lakes Comm Coll (IA)
Vermilion Comm Coll (MN)

ENVIRONMENTAL ENGINEERING
Albuquerque Tech Vocational Inst (NM)
Santa Barbara City Coll (CA)

ENVIRONMENTAL HEALTH
Amarillo Coll (TX)
Brazosport Coll (TX)
Comm Coll of the Air Force (AL)
Crowder Coll (MO)
Kingsborough Comm Coll of City U of NY (NY)
Milwaukee Area Tech Coll (WI)
Mt. Hood Comm Coll (OR)
North Idaho Coll (ID)
Queensborough Comm Coll of City U of NY (NY)
Roane State Comm Coll (TN)
The U of Akron–Wayne Coll (OH)
Vincennes U (IN)

ENVIRONMENTAL SCIENCE
Anne Arundel Comm Coll (MD)
Arizona Western Coll (AZ)
Beaufort County Comm Coll (NC)
Berkshire Comm Coll (MA)
Brevard Comm Coll (FL)
Bristol Comm Coll (MA)
Bucks County Comm Coll (PA)
Burlington County Coll (NJ)
Camden County Coll (NJ)
Cañada Coll (CA)
Cape Cod Comm Coll (MA)
Cape Fear Comm Coll (NC)
Central Texas Coll (TX)
Central Wyoming Coll (WY)
Century Comm and Tech Coll (MN)
Clover Park Tech Coll (WA)
Coll of Southern Idaho (ID)
Coll of the Desert (CA)
Colorado Mountn Coll, Timberline Cmps (CO)
Colorado Northwestern Comm Coll (CO)
Comm Coll of Southern Nevada (NV)
Comm Coll of the Air Force (AL)
De Anza Coll (CA)
Delta Coll (MI)
Dixie State Coll of Utah (UT)
Eastern Oklahoma State Coll (OK)
Everett Comm Coll (WA)
Feather River Comm Coll District (CA)
Finger Lakes Comm Coll (NY)
Fort Berthold Comm Coll (ND)
Fullerton Coll (CA)
Fulton-Montgomery Comm Coll (NY)
Great Basin Coll (NV)
Harford Comm Coll (MD)
Harrisburg Area Comm Coll (PA)
Hillsborough Comm Coll (FL)
Holyoke Comm Coll (MA)
Housatonic Comm Coll (CT)
Howard Comm Coll (MD)
Iowa Lakes Comm Coll (IA)
Itasca Comm Coll (MN)
Kent State U, Salem Campus (OH)
Kent State U, Tuscarawas Campus (OH)
Keystone Coll (PA)
Lake Washington Tech Coll (WA)
Lamar State Coll–Orange (TX)
Las Positas Coll (CA)
Mid Michigan Comm Coll (MI)
Mohawk Valley Comm Coll (NY)
Monroe Comm Coll (NY)
Mountain Empire Comm Coll (VA)
Mount Wachusett Comm Coll (MA)
Muskingum Area Tech Coll (OH)
Naugatuck Valley Comm Coll (CT)
New Hampshire Comm Tech Coll, Berlin/Laconia (NH)
Northern New Mexico Comm Coll (NM)
Northwest Coll (WY)
Pamlico Comm Coll (NC)
Paul Smith's Coll of Arts and Sciences (NY)
Pensacola Jr Coll (FL)
Quincy Coll (MA)
Raritan Valley Comm Coll (NJ)
Riverside Comm Coll (CA)
St. Catharine Coll (KY)
Salish Kootenai Coll (MT)
San Bernardino Valley Coll (CA)
San Jacinto Coll South Campus (TX)
Santa Ana Coll (CA)
Santa Barbara City Coll (CA)
Santa Fe Comm Coll (FL)
Sitting Bull Coll (ND)
Southeastern Comm Coll (NC)
Southwestern Comm Coll (NC)
Stark State Coll of Technology (OH)
State U of NY Coll of A&T at Morrisville (NY)
State U of NY Coll of Technology at Alfred (NY)
State U of NY Coll of Technology at Canton (NY)
Sullivan County Comm Coll (NY)
Sussex County Comm Coll (NJ)
Tacoma Comm Coll (WA)
Tompkins Cortland Comm Coll (NY)
Trocaire Coll (NY)
Truckee Meadows Comm Coll (NV)
U of New Mexico–Los Alamos Branch (NM)
Vermilion Comm Coll (MN)
Vincennes U (IN)
Warren County Comm Coll (NJ)
Western Nevada Comm Coll (NV)

ENVIRONMENTAL TECHNOLOGY
Allan Hancock Coll (CA)
Angelina Coll (TX)
Arapahoe Comm Coll (CO)
Bakersfield Coll (CA)
Bay de Noc Comm Coll (MI)
Berkshire Comm Coll (MA)
Black Hawk Coll, Moline (IL)
Blue Ridge Comm Coll (NC)
Cambria County Area Comm Coll (PA)
Cape Cod Comm Coll (MA)
Central Alabama Comm Coll (AL)
Central Piedmont Comm Coll (NC)
Chaffey Coll (CA)
Chattanooga State Tech Comm Coll (TN)
Cincinnati State Tech and Comm Coll (OH)
City Colls of Chicago, Wilbur Wright Coll (IL)
Clinton Comm Coll (IA)
Coastal Bend Coll (TX)
Collin County Comm Coll District (TX)
Columbus State Comm Coll (OH)
Comm Coll of Allegheny County (PA)
Comm Coll of Denver (CO)
Crowder Coll (MO)
Cuyamaca Coll (CA)
Delaware Tech & Comm Coll, Jack F Owens Cmps (DE)
Elaine P. Nunez Comm Coll (LA)
Ellsworth Comm Coll (IA)
Front Range Comm Coll (CO)
Gloucester County Coll (NJ)
Harford Comm Coll (MD)
Iowa Lakes Comm Coll (IA)
Jackson Comm Coll (MI)
James H. Faulkner State Comm Coll (AL)
John Tyler Comm Coll (VA)
Kansas City Kansas Comm Coll (KS)
Kent State U, Trumbull Campus (OH)
Lamar State Coll–Port Arthur (TX)
Lord Fairfax Comm Coll (VA)
Massachusetts Bay Comm Coll (MA)
Merced Coll (CA)
Midland Coll (TX)
Milwaukee Area Tech Coll (WI)
Montgomery County Comm Coll (PA)
Muscatine Comm Coll (IA)
New Mexico State U–Carlsbad (NM)
Oklahoma State U, Oklahoma City (OK)
Pellissippi State Tech Comm Coll (TN)
Pennsylvania Coll of Technology (PA)
Pima Comm Coll (AZ)
Roanoke-Chowan Comm Coll (NC)
San Diego City Coll (CA)
San Jacinto Coll North Campus (TX)
Schoolcraft Coll (MI)
Scott Comm Coll (IA)
Shoreline Comm Coll (WA)
Skagit Valley Coll (WA)
Southern Arkansas U Tech (AR)
Southern Maine Tech Coll (ME)
Texas State Tech Coll–Harlingen (TX)
Texas State Tech Coll (TX)
Three Rivers Comm Coll (CT)
Tulsa Comm Coll (OK)
Tyler Jr Coll (TX)
Ulster County Comm Coll (NY)
U of Alaska Southeast, Sitka Campus (AK)
U of Arkansas at Fort Smith (AR)
Vermilion Comm Coll (MN)
Vermont Tech Coll (VT)
Wake Tech Comm Coll (NC)
Westchester Comm Coll (NY)
Westmoreland County Comm Coll (PA)
West Virginia U at Parkersburg (WV)

EQUESTRIAN STUDIES
Allen County Comm Coll (KS)
Black Hawk Coll, Moline (IL)
Central Texas Coll (TX)
Central Wyoming Coll (WY)
Coll of Southern Idaho (ID)
Dodge City Comm Coll (KS)
Ellsworth Comm Coll (IA)
Erie Business Center, Main (PA)
Feather River Comm Coll District (CA)
Kirkwood Comm Coll (IA)
Lamar Comm Coll (CO)
Laramie County Comm Coll (WY)
Linn-Benton Comm Coll (OR)
Los Angeles Pierce Coll (CA)
Martin Comm Coll (NC)
North Central Texas Coll (TX)
Northwest Coll (WY)
Parkland Coll (IL)
Scott Comm Coll (IA)
Scottsdale Comm Coll (AZ)
Sierra Coll (CA)
State U of NY Coll of A&T at Morrisville (NY)

EUROPEAN STUDIES
Anne Arundel Comm Coll (MD)

EXECUTIVE ASSISTANT
Adirondack Comm Coll (NY)
Alamance Comm Coll (NC)
Asheville-Buncombe Tech Comm Coll (NC)
Black Hawk Coll, Moline (IL)
Broome Comm Coll (NY)
Business Inst of Pennsylvania (PA)
Butler County Comm Coll (PA)
Cape Cod Comm Coll (MA)
Cape Fear Comm Coll (NC)
Central Pennsylvania Coll (PA)
Cincinnati State Tech and Comm Coll (OH)
Clovis Comm Coll (NM)
Coastal Carolina Comm Coll (NC)
Craven Comm Coll (NC)
Crowder Coll (MO)
Delta Coll (MI)
Eastfield Coll (TX)
Helena Coll of Tech of The U of Montana (MT)
Hickey Coll (MO)
Ivy Tech State Coll–Bloomington (IN)
Ivy Tech State Coll–Central Indiana (IN)
Ivy Tech State Coll–Columbus (IN)
Ivy Tech State Coll–Eastcentral (IN)
Ivy Tech State Coll–Kokomo (IN)
Ivy Tech State Coll–Lafayette (IN)
Ivy Tech State Coll–North Central (IN)
Ivy Tech State Coll–Northeast (IN)
Ivy Tech State Coll–Northwest (IN)
Ivy Tech State Coll–Southcentral (IN)
Ivy Tech State Coll–Southeast (IN)
Ivy Tech State Coll–Southwest (IN)
Ivy Tech State Coll–Wabash Valley (IN)
Ivy Tech State Coll–Whitewater (IN)
J. Sargeant Reynolds Comm Coll (VA)
Kalamazoo Valley Comm Coll (MI)
Kaskaskia Coll (IL)
Kellogg Comm Coll (MI)
Kennebec Valley Tech Coll (ME)
Kilgore Coll (TX)
Lake Land Coll (IL)
Laurel Business Inst (PA)
Lehigh Carbon Comm Coll (PA)
Luzerne County Comm Coll (PA)
Massasoit Comm Coll (MA)
Minot State U–Bottineau Campus (ND)
Montcalm Comm Coll (MI)
National Coll of Business & Technology, Salem (VA)
Northampton County Area Comm Coll (PA)
Northwest State Comm Coll (OH)
Ohio Valley Business Coll (OH)
Owensboro Comm Coll (KY)
Prairie State Coll (IL)
Randolph Comm Coll (NC)
Rockford Business Coll (IL)
Southern State Comm Coll (OH)
South Piedmont Comm Coll (NC)
Stanly Comm Coll (NC)
The U of Akron–Wayne Coll (OH)
U of Kentucky, Lexington Comm Coll (KY)
Waubonsee Comm Coll (IL)
Wayne Comm Coll (NC)
Western Iowa Tech Comm Coll (IA)
Wilkes Comm Coll (NC)
Yorktowne Business Inst (PA)

EXERCISE SCIENCES
Bergen Comm Coll (NJ)
Butler County Comm Coll (PA)
Camden County Coll (NJ)
Cañada Coll (CA)
Central Oregon Comm Coll (OR)
Columbia-Greene Comm Coll (NY)
County Coll of Morris (NJ)
Delaware Tech & Comm Coll, Stanton/ Wilmington Cmps (DE)
Diné Coll (AZ)
Gloucester County Coll (NJ)
Henry Ford Comm Coll (MI)
Houston Comm Coll System (TX)
Lake Michigan Coll (MI)
Minnesota School of Business (MN)
Monterey Peninsula Coll (CA)
Mount Wachusett Comm Coll (MA)
Naugatuck Valley Comm Coll (CT)
North Country Comm Coll (NY)
Oakland Comm Coll (MI)
Orange Coast Coll (CA)
Orange County Comm Coll (NY)
Santa Ana Coll (CA)
Santa Barbara City Coll (CA)
Vincennes U (IN)

FAMILY/COMMUNITY STUDIES
Garden City Comm Coll (KS)
Lincoln Land Comm Coll (IL)
Oxnard Coll (CA)
Ridgewater Coll (MN)
Skagit Valley Coll (WA)
Snow Coll (UT)

FAMILY/CONSUMER STUDIES
Allan Hancock Coll (CA)
Arizona Western Coll (AZ)
Bakersfield Coll (CA)
Butte Coll (CA)
Cowley County Comm Coll and Voc-Tech School (KS)
Cuesta Coll (CA)
Evergreen Valley Coll (CA)
Long Beach City Coll (CA)
Los Angeles City Coll (CA)
Los Angeles Mission Coll (CA)
Modesto Jr Coll (CA)
Monterey Peninsula Coll (CA)
Orange Coast Coll (CA)

Palomar Coll (CA)
Portland Comm Coll (OR)
Sacramento City Coll (CA)
San Bernardino Valley Coll (CA)
Santa Ana Coll (CA)
Vincennes U (IN)

FAMILY LIVING/PARENTHOOD
Antelope Valley Coll (CA)
Centralia Coll (WA)

FARM/RANCH MANAGEMENT
Abraham Baldwin Ag Coll (GA)
Alexandria Tech Coll (MN)
Allen County Comm Coll (KS)
Central Texas Coll (TX)
Colby Comm Coll (KS)
Colorado Northwestern Comm Coll (CO)
Cowley County Comm Coll and Voc-Tech School (KS)
Crowder Coll (MO)
Dodge City Comm Coll (KS)
Eastern Oklahoma State Coll (OK)
Eastern Wyoming Coll (WY)
Fort Berthold Comm Coll (ND)
Garden City Comm Coll (KS)
Hawkeye Comm Coll (IA)
Highland Comm Coll (KS)
Hill Coll of the Hill Jr College District (TX)
Hutchinson Comm Coll and Area Vocational School (KS)
Iowa Western Comm Coll (IA)
Kirkwood Comm Coll (IA)
Lamar Comm Coll (CO)
Mitchell Tech Inst (SD)
North Central Texas Coll (TX)
Northeast Comm Coll (NE)
Northland Comm and Tech Coll (MN)
Northwest Coll (WY)
Pratt Comm Coll and Area Vocational School (KS)
Ridgewater Coll (MN)
St. Catharine Coll (KY)
Sitting Bull Coll (ND)
Snow Coll (UT)
Texas State Tech Coll–Harlingen (TX)
Trinidad State Jr Coll (CO)
Trinity Valley Comm Coll (TX)
Tyler Jr Coll (TX)
Vernon Coll (TX)
Wallace State Comm Coll (AL)
Western Dakota Tech Inst (SD)
Wharton County Jr Coll (TX)

FASHION DESIGN/ ILLUSTRATION
Allan Hancock Coll (CA)
American River Coll (CA)
The Art Inst of Fort Lauderdale (FL)
The Art Inst of Philadelphia (PA)
The Art Inst of Seattle (WA)
Baltimore City Comm Coll (MD)
Bauder Coll (GA)
Bay State Coll (MA)
Black Hawk Coll, Moline (IL)
Brooks Coll (CA)
Burlington County Coll (NJ)
Butte Coll (CA)
California Design Coll (CA)
Cañada Coll (CA)
Cerritos Coll (CA)
Chabot Coll (CA)
Chaffey Coll (CA)
Coll of Alameda (CA)
Coll of DuPage (IL)
Coll of the Sequoias (CA)
Daytona Beach Comm Coll (FL)
El Centro Coll (TX)
Fashion Careers of California Coll (CA)
Fashion Inst of Design & Merchandising, LA Campus (CA)
Fashion Inst of Design & Merchandising, SD Campus (CA)
Fashion Inst of Design & Merchandising, SF Campus (CA)
Fisher Coll (MA)
Fullerton Coll (CA)
Garden City Comm Coll (KS)
Glendale Comm Coll (CA)
Harcum Coll (PA)
Hesser Coll (NH)
Highland Comm Coll (KS)
Hinds Comm Coll (MS)
Honolulu Comm Coll (HI)
Houston Comm Coll System (TX)
Kirkwood Comm Coll (IA)
Long Beach City Coll (CA)
Merced Coll (CA)
Miami-Dade Comm Coll (FL)
Middlesex County Coll (NJ)
Monroe Comm Coll (NY)
Moorpark Coll (CA)
Nassau Comm Coll (NY)
Palm Beach Comm Coll (FL)
Palomar Coll (CA)
Penn Valley Comm Coll (MO)
Phoenix Coll (AZ)
San Diego Mesa Coll (CA)
San Jacinto Coll Central Campus (TX)
San Jacinto Coll South Campus (TX)
Santa Ana Coll (CA)
Seattle Central Comm Coll (WA)
Tulsa Comm Coll (OK)
Ventura Coll (CA)
Vincennes U (IN)
Wade Coll (TX)
Westmoreland County Comm Coll (PA)

FASHION MERCHANDISING
Abraham Baldwin Ag Coll (GA)
American River Coll (CA)
The Art Inst of Philadelphia (PA)
The Art Inst of Seattle (WA)
Austin Comm Coll (TX)
Baltimore City Comm Coll (MD)
Barton County Comm Coll (KS)
Bauder Coll (GA)
Bay State Coll (MA)
Bellevue Comm Coll (WA)
Berkeley Coll (NJ)
Berkeley Coll (NY)
Berkeley Coll-Westchester Campus (NY)
Black Hawk Coll, Moline (IL)
Bradley Academy for the Visual Arts (PA)
Brevard Comm Coll (FL)
Briarwood Coll (CT)
Brookdale Comm Coll (NJ)
Brooks Coll (CA)
Butte Coll (CA)
California Design Coll (CA)
Carl Sandburg Coll (IL)
Central Piedmont Comm Coll (NC)
Century Comm and Tech Coll (MN)
Chabot Coll (CA)
City Coll of San Francisco (CA)
Cleveland Comm Coll (NC)
Coll of Alameda (CA)
Coll of DuPage (IL)
Coll of the Sequoias (CA)
Comm Coll of Rhode Island (RI)
Cuesta Coll (CA)
Davis Coll (OH)
Delta Coll (MI)
Des Moines Area Comm Coll (IA)
Doña Ana Branch Comm Coll (NM)
Draughons Jr Coll, Clarksville (TN)
Draughons Jr Coll, Nashville (TN)
Duff's Business Inst (PA)
Eastern Oklahoma State Coll (OK)
Ellsworth Comm Coll (IA)
Evergreen Valley Coll (CA)
Fashion Careers of California Coll (CA)
Fashion Inst of Design & Merchandising, LA Campus (CA)
Fashion Inst of Design & Merchandising, SD Campus (CA)
Fashion Inst of Design & Merchandising, SF Campus (CA)
Fisher Coll (MA)
Florida Comm Coll at Jacksonville (FL)
Fresno City Coll (CA)
Fullerton Coll (CA)
Garden City Comm Coll (KS)
Gateway Comm Coll (CT)
Genesee Comm Coll (NY)
Georgia Perimeter Coll (GA)
Grand Rapids Comm Coll (MI)
Gwinnett Tech Coll (GA)
Harcum Coll (PA)
Herkimer County Comm Coll (NY)
Hesser Coll (NH)
Houston Comm Coll System (TX)
Howard Comm Coll (MD)
Huntington Jr Coll of Business (WV)
Indiana Business Coll, Indianapolis (IN)
Indian River Comm Coll (FL)
Iowa Lakes Comm Coll (IA)
Iowa Western Comm Coll (IA)
John A. Logan Coll (IL)
Joliet Jr Coll (IL)
J. Sargeant Reynolds Comm Coll (VA)
Kilgore Coll (TX)
Kingsborough Comm Coll of City U of NY (NY)
Kirkwood Comm Coll (IA)
Laredo Comm Coll (TX)
Las Positas Coll (CA)
Lima Tech Coll (OH)
Long Beach City Coll (CA)
Merced Coll (CA)
Miami-Dade Comm Coll (FL)
Middle Georgia Coll (GA)
Middlesex Comm Coll (MA)
Middlesex County Coll (NJ)
Milwaukee Area Tech Coll (WI)
Mississippi Gulf Coast Comm Coll (MS)
Modesto Jr Coll (CA)
Monroe Comm Coll (NY)
Monterey Peninsula Coll (CA)
Nassau Comm Coll (NY)
Newbury Coll (MA)
New York City Tech Coll of the City U of NY (NY)
North Iowa Area Comm Coll (IA)
Northwestern Business Coll (IL)
Northwest Mississippi Comm Coll (MS)
Odessa Coll (TX)
Okaloosa-Walton Comm Coll (FL)
Orange Coast Coll (CA)
Oxnard Coll (CA)
Pace Inst (PA)
Palm Beach Comm Coll (FL)
Palomar Coll (CA)
Pasadena City Coll (CA)
Patricia Stevens Coll (MO)
Penn Valley Comm Coll (MO)
St. Louis Comm Coll at Florissant Valley (MO)
San Diego City Coll (CA)
San Diego Mesa Coll (CA)
San Jacinto Coll Central Campus (TX)
San Jacinto Coll South Campus (TX)
San Joaquin Delta Coll (CA)
Santa Ana Coll (CA)
Santa Fe Comm Coll (FL)
Santa Monica Coll (CA)
Scottsdale Comm Coll (AZ)
Sierra Coll (CA)
South Plains Coll (TX)
South Suburban Coll (IL)
Southwest Mississippi Comm Coll (MS)
Spokane Falls Comm Coll (WA)
Tarrant County Coll District (TX)
Trinity Valley Comm Coll (TX)
Triton Coll (IL)
Tunxis Comm Coll (CT)
Tyler Jr Coll (TX)
Vincennes U (IN)
Wade Coll (TX)
Wallace State Comm Coll (AL)
Western Wisconsin Tech Coll (WI)
Westmoreland County Comm Coll (PA)

FILM STUDIES
Allan Hancock Coll (CA)
Cochise Coll, Douglas (AZ)
De Anza Coll (CA)
Lansing Comm Coll (MI)
Long Beach City Coll (CA)
Miami-Dade Comm Coll (FL)
Milwaukee Area Tech Coll (WI)
Moorpark Coll (CA)
Orange Coast Coll (CA)
Palomar Coll (CA)
Santa Barbara City Coll (CA)
Tallahassee Comm Coll (FL)

FILM/VIDEO PRODUCTION
Anne Arundel Comm Coll (MD)
Antelope Valley Coll (CA)
The Art Inst of Atlanta (GA)
The Art Inst of Fort Lauderdale (FL)
The Art Inst of Los Angeles (CA)
The Art Inst of Philadelphia (PA)
The Art Inst of Pittsburgh (PA)
The Art Inst of Seattle (WA)
Bucks County Comm Coll (PA)
City Coll of San Francisco (CA)
Coll of DuPage (IL)
Coll of the Canyons (CA)
Cumberland County Coll (NJ)
Daytona Beach Comm Coll (FL)
Everett Comm Coll (WA)
Full Sail Real World Education (FL)
Glendale Comm Coll (AZ)
Guilford Tech Comm Coll (NC)
Holyoke Comm Coll (MA)
Lane Comm Coll (OR)
Lansing Comm Coll (MI)
Miami-Dade Comm Coll (FL)
Minneapolis Comm and Tech Coll (MN)
Orange Coast Coll (CA)
Pellissippi State Tech Comm Coll (TN)
Piedmont Comm Coll (NC)
St. Louis Comm Coll at Florissant Valley (MO)
Seattle Central Comm Coll (WA)
Shoreline Comm Coll (WA)
Southern Maine Tech Coll (ME)

FINANCE
Adirondack Comm Coll (NY)
AIB Coll of Business (IA)
American River Coll (CA)
Arapahoe Comm Coll (CO)
Arizona Western Coll (AZ)
Austin Comm Coll (TX)
Bakersfield Coll (CA)
Bergen Comm Coll (NJ)
Berkshire Comm Coll (MA)
Black Hawk Coll, Moline (IL)
Burlington County Coll (NJ)
Butte Coll (CA)
Camden County Coll (NJ)
Central Pennsylvania Coll (PA)
Central Piedmont Comm Coll (NC)
Central Virginia Comm Coll (VA)
Chabot Coll (CA)
Chattanooga State Tech Comm Coll (TN)
Chemeketa Comm Coll (OR)
Chipola Jr Coll (FL)
Cisco Jr Coll (TX)
City Coll of San Francisco (CA)
Clovis Comm Coll (NM)
Coastal Bend Coll (TX)
Coll of Southern Idaho (ID)
Columbus State Comm Coll (OH)
Comm Coll of Aurora (CO)
Comm Coll of Southern Nevada (NV)
Comm Coll of the Air Force (AL)
Cuyahoga Comm Coll (OH)
Daytona Beach Comm Coll (FL)
Del Mar Coll (TX)
Delta Coll (MI)
Dodge City Comm Coll (KS)
Doña Ana Branch Comm Coll (NM)
Edison Comm Coll (FL)
Edison State Comm Coll (OH)
Education Direct (PA)
Elizabethtown Comm Coll (KY)
Enterprise State Jr Coll (AL)
Fayetteville Tech Comm Coll (NC)
Forsyth Tech Comm Coll (NC)
Frederick Comm Coll (MD)
Fulton-Montgomery Comm Coll (NY)
GateWay Comm Coll (AZ)
Glendale Comm Coll (CA)
Gloucester County Coll (NJ)
Hill Coll of the Hill Jr College District (TX)
Hillsborough Comm Coll (FL)
Hinds Comm Coll (MS)
Holmes Comm Coll (MS)
Hopkinsville Comm Coll (KY)
Houston Comm Coll System (TX)
Howard Coll (TX)
Illinois Eastern Comm Colls, Lincoln Trail Coll (IL)
Independence Comm Coll (KS)
Indian River Comm Coll (FL)
International Business Coll, Fort Wayne (IN)
Iowa Lakes Comm Coll (IA)
Jackson Comm Coll (MI)
Jefferson Comm Coll (OH)
Jefferson Davis Comm Coll (AL)
John A. Logan Coll (IL)
Joliet Jr Coll (IL)
Kent State U, Trumbull Campus (OH)
Kilgore Coll (TX)
Kirkwood Comm Coll (IA)
Lake Area Tech Inst (SD)
Lake Michigan Coll (MI)
Lakeshore Tech Coll (WI)
Lake-Sumter Comm Coll (FL)
Lake Tahoe Comm Coll (CA)
Lansing Comm Coll (MI)
Lenoir Comm Coll (NC)
Lima Tech Coll (OH)
Lorain County Comm Coll (OH)
Los Angeles City Coll (CA)
Los Angeles Mission Coll (CA)
Macomb Comm Coll (MI)
Manatee Comm Coll (FL)
Marion Tech Coll (OH)
Mayland Comm Coll (NC)
McLennan Comm Coll (TX)
Merced Coll (CA)
Miami-Dade Comm Coll (FL)
Middlesex County Coll (NJ)
Mid Michigan Comm Coll (MI)
Milwaukee Area Tech Coll (WI)
Mississippi Gulf Coast Comm Coll (MS)
Modesto Jr Coll (CA)
Mohawk Valley Comm Coll (NY)
Monroe County Comm Coll (MI)
Morton Coll (IL)
Naugatuck Valley Comm Coll (CT)
Neosho County Comm Coll (KS)
Newbury Coll (MA)
New Mexico Military Inst (NM)
North Central Michigan Coll (MI)
Northeast Alabama Comm Coll (AL)
Northeast Texas Comm Coll (TX)
Northern Essex Comm Coll (MA)
North Harris Coll (TX)
NorthWest Arkansas Comm Coll (AR)
Norwalk Comm Coll (CT)
Oakton Comm Coll (IL)
Okaloosa-Walton Comm Coll (FL)
Oklahoma City Comm Coll (OK)
Onondaga Comm Coll (NY)
Orange County Comm Coll (NY)
Palm Beach Comm Coll (FL)
Pasadena City Coll (CA)
Pellissippi State Tech Comm Coll (TN)
Phoenix Coll (AZ)
Polk Comm Coll (FL)
Prairie State Coll (IL)
Reading Area Comm Coll (PA)
Rockland Comm Coll (NY)
St. Cloud Tech Coll (MN)
St. Louis Comm Coll at Florissant Valley (MO)
San Bernardino Valley Coll (CA)
San Diego City Coll (CA)
San Jacinto Coll Central Campus (TX)
San Jacinto Coll South Campus (TX)
Santa Barbara City Coll (CA)
Santa Fe Comm Coll (FL)
Scottsdale Comm Coll (AZ)
Seminole Comm Coll (FL)
Sinclair Comm Coll (OH)
Southeast Comm Coll, Beatrice Campus (NE)
Southeast Tech Inst (SD)
Southern West Virginia Comm and Tech Coll (WV)
South Suburban Coll (IL)
Southwestern Coll (CA)
Southwest Mississippi Comm Coll (MS)
Southwest Wisconsin Tech Coll (WI)
Springfield Tech Comm Coll (MA)
Stark State Coll of Technology (OH)
State Fair Comm Coll (MO)
State U of NY Coll of Technology at Alfred (NY)
Tallahassee Comm Coll (FL)
Terra State Comm Coll (OH)
Texarkana Coll (TX)
Tidewater Comm Coll (VA)
Trinity Valley Comm Coll (TX)
Tyler Jr Coll (TX)
Vermilion Comm Coll (MN)
Vincennes U Jasper Campus (IN)
Wallace State Comm Coll (AL)
Westchester Comm Coll (NY)

Western Piedmont Comm Coll (NC)
Western Wisconsin Tech Coll (WI)
Westmoreland County Comm Coll (PA)
West Virginia U at Parkersburg (WV)
Wisconsin Indianhead Tech Coll (WI)

FINANCIAL PLANNING
Cincinnati State Tech and Comm Coll (OH)
Howard Comm Coll (MD)

FINANCIAL SERVICES MARKETING
Hutchinson Comm Coll and Area Vocational School (KS)
Spokane Falls Comm Coll (WA)

FINE ARTS AND ART STUDIES RELATED
Ancilla Coll (IN)
Oakland Comm Coll (MI)
Reedley Coll (CA)
United Tribes Tech Coll (ND)

FINE/STUDIO ARTS
Amarillo Coll (TX)
Atlantic Cape Comm Coll (NJ)
Berkshire Comm Coll (MA)
Cerro Coso Comm Coll (CA)
Chabot Coll (CA)
Clovis Comm Coll (NM)
Coastal Bend Coll (TX)
Coll of the Siskiyous (CA)
Colorado Mountn Coll, Alpine Cmps (CO)
The Comm Coll of Baltimore County–Catonsville Campus (MD)
Cumberland County Coll (NJ)
Delgado Comm Coll (LA)
Del Mar Coll (TX)
Finger Lakes Comm Coll (NY)
Fiorello H LaGuardia Comm Coll of City U of NY (NY)
Foothill Coll (CA)
Fulton-Montgomery Comm Coll (NY)
Garden City Comm Coll (KS)
Gloucester County Coll (NJ)
Holyoke Comm Coll (MA)
Inst of American Indian Arts (NM)
Iowa Lakes Comm Coll (IA)
Jamestown Comm Coll (NY)
Kankakee Comm Coll (IL)
Lansing Comm Coll (MI)
Lincoln Coll, Lincoln (IL)
Lon Morris Coll (TX)
Manatee Comm Coll (FL)
Manchester Comm Coll (CT)
Maryland Coll of Art and Design (MD)
Middlesex County Coll (NJ)
Midland Coll (TX)
Mohawk Valley Comm Coll (NY)
Monterey Peninsula Coll (CA)
Morton Coll (IL)
Mount Wachusett Comm Coll (MA)
Niagara County Comm Coll (NY)
Northampton County Area Comm Coll (PA)
Northern New Mexico Comm Coll (NM)
Norwalk Comm Coll (CT)
Oklahoma City Comm Coll (OK)
Pratt Comm Coll and Area Vocational School (KS)
Queensborough Comm Coll of City U of NY (NY)
Randolph Comm Coll (NC)
Rockland Comm Coll (NY)
Sandhills Comm Coll (NC)
San Diego Mesa Coll (CA)
San Jacinto Coll Central Campus (TX)
Santa Barbara City Coll (CA)
Sinclair Comm Coll (OH)
South Suburban Coll (IL)
Springfield Tech Comm Coll (MA)
Sussex County Comm Coll (NJ)
Tacoma Comm Coll (WA)
U of New Mexico–Los Alamos Branch (NM)
Vista Comm Coll (CA)
Warren County Comm Coll (NJ)
Westchester Comm Coll (NY)

FIRE PROTECTION RELATED
Sussex County Comm Coll (NJ)

FIRE PROTECTION/SAFETY TECHNOLOGY
Albuquerque Tech Vocational Inst (NM)
Antelope Valley Coll (CA)
Bunker Hill Comm Coll (MA)
Capital Comm Coll (CT)
Catawba Valley Comm Coll (NC)
Central Florida Comm Coll (FL)
Coll of Lake County (IL)
Collin County Comm Coll District (TX)
Comm Coll of Allegheny County (PA)
Delaware County Comm Coll (PA)
Delgado Comm Coll (LA)
Florida Comm Coll at Jacksonville (FL)
John Wood Comm Coll (IL)
Kellogg Comm Coll (MI)
Montgomery Coll (MD)
Moraine Valley Comm Coll (IL)
Mott Comm Coll (MI)
Ocean County Coll (NJ)
Pikes Peak Comm Coll (CO)
San Juan Coll (NM)
Tulsa Comm Coll (OK)
Union County Coll (NJ)
Victor Valley Coll (CA)
Waubonsee Comm Coll (IL)
Western Nevada Comm Coll (NV)
Western Wisconsin Tech Coll (WI)

FIRE SCIENCE
Aims Comm Coll (CO)
Allan Hancock Coll (CA)
Amarillo Coll (TX)
American River Coll (CA)
Arizona Western Coll (AZ)
Austin Comm Coll (TX)
Bakersfield Coll (CA)
Barton County Comm Coll (KS)
Bates Tech Coll (WA)
Bellevue Comm Coll (WA)
Berkshire Comm Coll (MA)
Blackhawk Tech Coll (WI)
Black River Tech Coll (AR)
Blinn Coll (TX)
Brevard Comm Coll (FL)
Bristol Comm Coll (MA)
Broome Comm Coll (NY)
Bunker Hill Comm Coll (MA)
Burlington County Coll (NJ)
Butte Coll (CA)
Camden County Coll (NJ)
Cape Cod Comm Coll (MA)
Casper Coll (WY)
Central Oregon Comm Coll (OR)
Central Piedmont Comm Coll (NC)
Cerro Coso Comm Coll (CA)
Chabot Coll (CA)
Chattahoochee Valley Comm Coll (AL)
Chattanooga State Tech Comm Coll (TN)
Chemeketa Comm Coll (OR)
Chippewa Valley Tech Coll (WI)
Cincinnati State Tech and Comm Coll (OH)
Cisco Jr Coll (TX)
City Coll of San Francisco (CA)
City Colls of Chicago, Richard J Daley Coll (IL)
Coastal Carolina Comm Coll (NC)
Cochise Coll, Douglas (AZ)
Coll of DuPage (IL)
Coll of Marin (CA)
Coll of the Desert (CA)
Coll of the Sequoias (CA)
Coll of the Siskiyous (CA)
The Comm Coll of Baltimore County–Catonsville Campus (MD)
Comm Coll of Rhode Island (RI)
Comm Coll of Southern Nevada (NV)
Comm Coll of the Air Force (AL)
Compton Comm Coll (CA)
Corning Comm Coll (NY)
Crafton Hills Coll (CA)
Crowder Coll (MO)
Cuyahoga Comm Coll (OH)
Daytona Beach Comm Coll (FL)
Delaware Tech & Comm Coll, Stanton/ Wilmington Cmps (DE)
Del Mar Coll (TX)
Delta Coll (MI)
Des Moines Area Comm Coll (IA)
Dodge City Comm Coll (KS)
Doña Ana Branch Comm Coll (NM)
Durham Tech Comm Coll (NC)
East Central Coll (MO)
East Mississippi Comm Coll (MS)
Edison Comm Coll (FL)
Essex County Coll (NJ)
Everett Comm Coll (WA)
Florida Comm Coll at Jacksonville (FL)
Fresno City Coll (CA)
Gaston Coll (NC)
Gateway Comm Coll (CT)
Gateway Tech Coll (WI)
George Corley Wallace State Comm Coll (AL)
Georgia Military Coll (GA)
Georgia Perimeter Coll (GA)
Glendale Comm Coll (AZ)
Glendale Comm Coll (CA)
Greenfield Comm Coll (MA)
Greenville Tech Coll (SC)
Guam Comm Coll (GU)
Guilford Tech Comm Coll (NC)
Gulf Coast Comm Coll (FL)
Harrisburg Area Comm Coll (PA)
Hawaii Comm Coll (HI)
Hawkeye Comm Coll (IA)
Helena Coll of Tech of The U of Montana (MT)
Hennepin Tech Coll (MN)
Henry Ford Comm Coll (MI)
Hill Coll of the Hill Jr College District (TX)
Hillsborough Comm Coll (FL)
Honolulu Comm Coll (HI)
Houston Comm Coll System (TX)
Hutchinson Comm Coll and Area Vocational School (KS)
Imperial Valley Coll (CA)
Indian River Comm Coll (FL)
Iowa Western Comm Coll (IA)
Jefferson Coll (MO)
Jefferson Comm Coll (KY)
John Wood Comm Coll (IL)
Joliet Jr Coll (IL)
J. Sargeant Reynolds Comm Coll (VA)
Kalamazoo Valley Comm Coll (MI)
Kansas City Kansas Comm Coll (KS)
Kilgore Coll (TX)
Kirkwood Comm Coll (IA)
Labette Comm Coll (KS)
Lakeland Comm Coll (OH)
Lake-Sumter Comm Coll (FL)
Lake Tahoe Comm Coll (CA)
Lansing Comm Coll (MI)
Laramie County Comm Coll (WY)
Laredo Comm Coll (TX)
Las Positas Coll (CA)
Lenoir Comm Coll (NC)
Lewis and Clark Comm Coll (IL)
Lincoln Land Comm Coll (IL)
Long Beach City Coll (CA)
Lorain County Comm Coll (OH)
Los Angeles Harbor Coll (CA)
Louisiana State U at Eunice (LA)
Lower Columbia Coll (WA)
Luzerne County Comm Coll (PA)
Macomb Comm Coll (MI)
Manatee Comm Coll (FL)
Massasoit Comm Coll (MA)
McHenry County Coll (IL)
Merced Coll (CA)
Mercer County Comm Coll (NJ)
Meridian Comm Coll (MS)
Miami-Dade Comm Coll (FL)
Middlesex Comm Coll (MA)
Middlesex County Coll (NJ)
Midland Coll (TX)
Mid Michigan Comm Coll (MI)
Mid-Plains Comm Coll Area (NE)
Miles Comm Coll (MT)
Milwaukee Area Tech Coll (WI)
Mineral Area Coll (MO)
Modesto Jr Coll (CA)
Mohave Comm Coll (AZ)
Monroe Comm Coll (NY)
Montana State U Coll of Tech-Great Falls (MT)
Monterey Peninsula Coll (CA)
Mt. Hood Comm Coll (OR)
Mt. San Jacinto Coll (CA)
Mount Wachusett Comm Coll (MA)
Naugatuck Valley Comm Coll (CT)
Navarro Coll (TX)
New Mexico State U–Alamogordo (NM)
New Mexico State U–Carlsbad (NM)
Northern Virginia Comm Coll (VA)
North Hennepin Comm Coll (MN)
Northland Pioneer Coll (AZ)
North Shore Comm Coll (MA)
Northwest-Shoals Comm Coll (AL)
Norwalk Comm Coll (CT)
Oakland Comm Coll (MI)
Oakton Comm Coll (IL)
Odessa Coll (TX)
Oklahoma State U, Oklahoma City (OK)
Olympic Coll (WA)
Onondaga Comm Coll (NY)
Oxnard Coll (CA)
Palm Beach Comm Coll (FL)
Palomar Coll (CA)
Pasadena City Coll (CA)
Penn Valley Comm Coll (MO)
Pensacola Jr Coll (FL)
Phoenix Coll (AZ)
Pierce Coll (WA)
Pima Comm Coll (AZ)
Polk Comm Coll (FL)
Portland Comm Coll (OR)
Prairie State Coll (IL)
Quincy Coll (MA)
Quinsigamond Comm Coll (MA)
Red Rocks Comm Coll (CO)
Richland Comm Coll (IL)
Rockland Comm Coll (NY)
Rogue Comm Coll (OR)
St. Clair County Comm Coll (MI)
St. Louis Comm Coll at Florissant Valley (MO)
St. Petersburg Coll (FL)
San Antonio Coll (TX)
San Jacinto Coll Central Campus (TX)
San Joaquin Delta Coll (CA)
Santa Ana Coll (CA)
Santa Fe Comm Coll (FL)
Santa Monica Coll (CA)
Savannah Tech Coll (GA)
Schenectady County Comm Coll (NY)
Schoolcraft Coll (MI)
Scottsdale Comm Coll (AZ)
Seminole Comm Coll (FL)
Shasta Coll (CA)
Sierra Coll (CA)
Sinclair Comm Coll (OH)
Skagit Valley Coll (WA)
Southern Arkansas U Tech (AR)
Southern Maine Tech Coll (ME)
South Plains Coll (TX)
South Puget Sound Comm Coll (WA)
South Suburban Coll (IL)
Southwestern Coll (CA)
Southwest Tennessee Comm Coll (TN)
Spokane Comm Coll (WA)
Springfield Tech Comm Coll (MA)
Stark State Coll of Technology (OH)
Tarrant County Coll District (TX)
Thomas Nelson Comm Coll (VA)
Three Rivers Comm Coll (CT)
Triton Coll (IL)
Truckee Meadows Comm Coll (NV)
Tulsa Comm Coll (OK)
Tyler Jr Coll (TX)
Umpqua Comm Coll (OR)
U of Alaska Anchorage, Matanuska-Susitna Coll (AK)
Victor Valley Coll (CA)
Vincennes U (IN)
Volunteer State Comm Coll (TN)
Wallace State Comm Coll (AL)
Weatherford Coll (TX)
Westmoreland County Comm Coll (PA)
Wilson Tech Comm Coll (NC)

FIRE SERVICES ADMINISTRATION
Black Hawk Coll, Moline (IL)
Capital Comm Coll (CT)
Edmonds Comm Coll (WA)
Erie Comm Coll, South Campus (NY)
Jefferson State Comm Coll (AL)
Johnson County Comm Coll (KS)
Northampton County Area Comm Coll (PA)
Olympic Coll (WA)
Rend Lake Coll (IL)
Walla Walla Comm Coll (WA)

FISH/GAME MANAGEMENT
Abraham Baldwin Ag Coll (GA)
Central Oregon Comm Coll (OR)
Chattanooga State Tech Comm Coll (TN)
Coll of Southern Idaho (ID)
East Central Coll (MO)
Finger Lakes Comm Coll (NY)
Fullerton Coll (CA)
Haywood Comm Coll (NC)
Iowa Lakes Comm Coll (IA)
Itasca Comm Coll (MN)
Kirkwood Comm Coll (IA)
Mid Michigan Comm Coll (MI)
Minot State U–Bottineau Campus (ND)
Monterey Peninsula Coll (CA)
Mt. Hood Comm Coll (OR)
North Idaho Coll (ID)
Pratt Comm Coll and Area Vocational School (KS)
State U of NY Coll of A&T at Morrisville (NY)
Vermilion Comm Coll (MN)

FISHING SCIENCES
Brunswick Comm Coll (NC)
Peninsula Coll (WA)

FISHING TECHNOLOGY
Peninsula Coll (WA)

FLIGHT ATTENDANT
Cypress Coll (CA)
Mercer County Comm Coll (NJ)

FLORISTRY MARKETING
Cuyamaca Coll (CA)

FOOD/NUTRITION
Indian River Comm Coll (FL)

FOOD PRODUCTS RETAILING
Allegany Coll of Maryland (MD)
American River Coll (CA)
The Art Inst of Houston (TX)
Asnuntuck Comm Coll (CT)
Bergen Comm Coll (NJ)
Brookdale Comm Coll (NJ)
Burlington County Coll (NJ)
Camden County Coll (NJ)
Central Piedmont Comm Coll (NC)
Chaffey Coll (CA)
Comm Coll of Southern Nevada (NV)
Cypress Coll (CA)
Daytona Beach Comm Coll (FL)
Del Mar Coll (TX)
Des Moines Area Comm Coll (IA)
Dutchess Comm Coll (NY)
East Central Coll (MO)
El Centro Coll (TX)
Enterprise State Jr Coll (AL)
Fiorello H LaGuardia Comm Coll of City U of NY (NY)
Gateway Comm Coll (CT)
Greenville Tech Coll (SC)
Henry Ford Comm Coll (MI)
Hinds Comm Coll (MS)
Indian River Comm Coll (FL)
Iowa Western Comm Coll (IA)
Jefferson Comm Coll (OH)
Joliet Jr Coll (IL)
Kirkwood Comm Coll (IA)
Lane Comm Coll (OR)
Lansing Comm Coll (MI)
Lincoln Land Comm Coll (IL)
Long Beach City Coll (CA)
Los Angeles City Coll (CA)
Merced Coll (CA)
Middlesex County Coll (NJ)
Mohawk Valley Comm Coll (NY)
Monroe Comm Coll (NY)
Naugatuck Valley Comm Coll (CT)
Newbury Coll (MA)
Northern Virginia Comm Coll (VA)
Oakton Comm Coll (IL)
Oklahoma State U, Okmulgee (OK)
Onondaga Comm Coll (NY)

Orange Coast Coll (CA)
Palm Beach Comm Coll (FL)
Palomar Coll (CA)
Penn Valley Comm Coll (MO)
Phoenix Coll (AZ)
Quincy Coll (MA)
St. Louis Comm Coll at Florissant Valley (MO)
San Diego City Coll (CA)
San Diego Mesa Coll (CA)
San Jacinto Coll Central Campus (TX)
San Joaquin Delta Coll (CA)
Scottsdale Comm Coll (AZ)
Sinclair Comm Coll (OH)
Southern Maine Tech Coll (ME)
South Plains Coll (TX)
South Puget Sound Comm Coll (WA)
State Fair Comm Coll (MO)
State U of NY Coll of A&T at Morrisville (NY)
Three Rivers Comm Coll (CT)
Vermilion Comm Coll (MN)
Wallace State Comm Coll (AL)
Westchester Comm Coll (NY)
Westmoreland County Comm Coll (PA)

FOOD SALES OPERATIONS

American River Coll (CA)
Austin Comm Coll (TX)
Gloucester County Coll (NJ)
Iowa Western Comm Coll (IA)
Kirkwood Comm Coll (IA)
Raritan Valley Comm Coll (NJ)

FOOD SCIENCES

Central Piedmont Comm Coll (NC)
El Centro Coll (TX)
Greenfield Comm Coll (MA)
Hawkeye Comm Coll (IA)
Highland Comm Coll (KS)
Los Angeles City Coll (CA)
Miami-Dade Comm Coll (FL)
Modesto Jr Coll (CA)
Moraine Park Tech Coll (WI)
Mt. Hood Comm Coll (OR)
Orange Coast Coll (CA)
St. Louis Comm Coll at Florissant Valley (MO)
Vincennes U (IN)

FOOD SERVICES TECHNOLOGY

Adirondack Comm Coll (NY)
Anne Arundel Comm Coll (MD)
Arapahoe Comm Coll (CO)
Burlington County Coll (NJ)
Butler County Comm Coll (PA)
Central Piedmont Comm Coll (NC)
Cerritos Coll (CA)
Chattanooga State Tech Comm Coll (TN)
Columbus State Comm Coll (OH)
Comm Coll of Southern Nevada (NV)
Delaware Tech & Comm Coll, Stanton/ Wilmington Cmps (DE)
El Centro Coll (TX)
Fayetteville Tech Comm Coll (NC)
Fresno City Coll (CA)
Hawaii Comm Coll (HI)
Henry Ford Comm Coll (MI)
Hinds Comm Coll (MS)
Honolulu Comm Coll (HI)
Illinois Eastern Comm Colls, Lincoln Trail Coll (IL)
Indian Hills Comm Coll (IA)
Iowa Western Comm Coll (IA)
Kirkwood Comm Coll (IA)
Lane Comm Coll (OR)
Lenoir Comm Coll (NC)
Long Beach City Coll (CA)
Los Angeles City Coll (CA)
Luzerne County Comm Coll (PA)
Miami-Dade Comm Coll (FL)
Milwaukee Area Tech Coll (WI)
Modesto Jr Coll (CA)
Mohawk Valley Comm Coll (NY)
Monroe Comm Coll (NY)
North Seattle Comm Coll (WA)
Oklahoma State U, Okmulgee (OK)
Orange Coast Coll (CA)
Palomar Coll (CA)
Richland Comm Coll (IL)
Robeson Comm Coll (NC)
St. Louis Comm Coll at Florissant Valley (MO)
San Joaquin Delta Coll (CA)
Sierra Coll (CA)
Skagit Valley Coll (WA)
Southern Maine Tech Coll (ME)
South Puget Sound Comm Coll (WA)
Southwest Wisconsin Tech Coll (WI)
Spokane Comm Coll (WA)
Stark State Coll of Technology (OH)
State U of NY Coll of A&T at Morrisville (NY)
Tarrant County Coll District (TX)
Texas State Tech Coll–Harlingen (TX)
Texas State Tech Coll– Waco/ Marshall Campus (TX)
Ventura Coll (CA)
Victor Valley Coll (CA)
Westchester Comm Coll (NY)
Western Wisconsin Tech Coll (WI)

FOODS/NUTRITION STUDIES RELATED

San Diego Mesa Coll (CA)

FOOD SYSTEMS ADMINISTRATION

Coll of Lake County (IL)
Oakland Comm Coll (MI)

FOREIGN LANGUAGES EDUCATION

Manatee Comm Coll (FL)

FOREIGN LANGUAGES/ LITERATURES

Atlanta Metropolitan Coll (GA)
Brazosport Coll (TX)
Coastal Georgia Comm Coll (GA)
Coll of Southern Idaho (ID)
Comm Coll of Allegheny County (PA)
Dixie State Coll of Utah (UT)
Eastern Arizona Coll (AZ)
Eastern Wyoming Coll (WY)
Floyd Coll (GA)
Glendale Comm Coll (CA)
Hutchinson Comm Coll and Area Vocational School (KS)
Kingwood Coll (TX)
Modesto Jr Coll (CA)
Reedley Coll (CA)
San Juan Coll (NM)
Sheridan Coll (WY)
Skagit Valley Coll (WA)

FOREIGN LANGUAGES/ LITERATURES RELATED

Georgia Perimeter Coll (GA)

FOREIGN LANGUAGE TRANSLATION

Allen County Comm Coll (KS)
Indian River Comm Coll (FL)
Union County Coll (NJ)
Wilson Tech Comm Coll (NC)

FORENSIC TECHNOLOGY

Massachusetts Bay Comm Coll (MA)
New River Comm Coll (VA)
Prince George's Comm Coll (MD)
Tunxis Comm Coll (CT)

FOREST HARVESTING PRODUCTION TECHNOLOGY

Abraham Baldwin Ag Coll (GA)
Allegany Coll of Maryland (MD)
American River Coll (CA)
Chattanooga State Tech Comm Coll (TN)
Chemeketa Comm Coll (OR)
Eastern Oklahoma State Coll (OK)
East Mississippi Comm Coll (MS)
Feather River Comm Coll District (CA)
Flathead Valley Comm Coll (MT)
Green River Comm Coll (WA)
Haywood Comm Coll (NC)
Hazard Comm Coll (KY)
Horry-Georgetown Tech Coll (SC)
Itasca Comm Coll (MN)
Jefferson Comm Coll (NY)
Jones County Jr Coll (MS)
Lurleen B. Wallace Jr Coll (AL)
Montgomery Comm Coll (NC)
Mt. Hood Comm Coll (OR)
Pasadena City Coll (CA)
Paul Smith's Coll of Arts and Sciences (NY)
Pennsylvania Coll of Technology (PA)
Penn State U Mont Alto Campus of the Commonwealth Coll (PA)
Pensacola Jr Coll (FL)
Salish Kootenai Coll (MT)
Sierra Coll (CA)
Southeastern Comm Coll (NC)
State U of NY Coll of A&T at Morrisville (NY)
State U of NY Coll of Environ Sci & For Ranger Sch (NY)
State U of NY Coll of Technology at Canton (NY)
Vermilion Comm Coll (MN)
Waycross Coll (GA)
Wayne Comm Coll (NC)

FOREST MANAGEMENT

Lake City Comm Coll (FL)
Vermilion Comm Coll (MN)
Western Nebraska Comm Coll (NE)

FOREST PRODUCTS TECHNOLOGY

Central Oregon Comm Coll (OR)
Flathead Valley Comm Coll (MT)
Lake City Comm Coll (FL)
Modesto Jr Coll (CA)
Montgomery Comm Coll (NC)
York Tech Coll (SC)

FORESTRY

Abraham Baldwin Ag Coll (GA)
Allegany Coll of Maryland (MD)
Allen County Comm Coll (KS)
Andrew Coll (GA)
Bainbridge Coll (GA)
Bakersfield Coll (CA)
Barton County Comm Coll (KS)
Camden County Coll (NJ)
Central Oregon Comm Coll (OR)
Cerritos Coll (CA)
Chattahoochee Valley Comm Coll (AL)
Chattanooga State Tech Comm Coll (TN)
Chemeketa Comm Coll (OR)
City Coll of San Francisco (CA)
Coastal Georgia Comm Coll (GA)
Colby Comm Coll (KS)
Coll of Southern Idaho (ID)
Coll of the Redwoods (CA)
Coll of the Siskiyous (CA)
Copiah-Lincoln Comm Coll–Natchez Campus (MS)
Darton Coll (GA)
Daytona Beach Comm Coll (FL)
Delta Coll (MI)
Dixie State Coll of Utah (UT)
Dodge City Comm Coll (KS)
East Central Coll (MO)
Eastern Arizona Coll (AZ)
Eastern Oklahoma State Coll (OK)
Floyd Coll (GA)
Fullerton Coll (CA)
Grand Rapids Comm Coll (MI)
Highland Comm Coll (KS)
Holmes Comm Coll (MS)
Indian River Comm Coll (FL)
Itasca Comm Coll (MN)
Jefferson Coll (MO)
Jefferson Comm Coll (KY)
Joliet Jr Coll (IL)
Keystone Coll (PA)
Kilgore Coll (TX)
Kirkwood Comm Coll (IA)
Miami-Dade Comm Coll (FL)
Minot State U–Bottineau Campus (ND)
Modesto Jr Coll (CA)
Monroe Comm Coll (NY)
Mountain Empire Comm Coll (VA)
New Hampshire Comm Tech Coll, Berlin/Laconia (NH)
North Idaho Coll (ID)
North Shore Comm Coll (MA)
Northwest Coll (WY)
Northwest-Shoals Comm Coll (AL)
Palo Verde Coll (CA)
Paul Smith's Coll of Arts and Sciences (NY)
Riverside Comm Coll (CA)
Salish Kootenai Coll (MT)
Sierra Coll (CA)
Snow Coll (UT)
Spokane Comm Coll (WA)
State U of NY Coll of A&T at Morrisville (NY)
State U of NY Coll of Technology at Delhi (NY)
Tacoma Comm Coll (WA)
Trinidad State Jr Coll (CO)
Tulsa Comm Coll (OK)
Umpqua Comm Coll (OR)
Vermilion Comm Coll (MN)
Vincennes U (IN)
Waycross Coll (GA)

FORESTRY SCIENCES

Gogebic Comm Coll (MI)
Vermilion Comm Coll (MN)

FORESTRY SCIENCES RELATED

Hiwassee Coll (TN)

FRENCH

Austin Comm Coll (TX)
Bakersfield Coll (CA)
Blinn Coll (TX)
Cañada Coll (CA)
Casper Coll (WY)
Centralia Coll (WA)
Cerritos Coll (CA)
Chaffey Coll (CA)
Cisco Jr Coll (TX)
Citrus Coll (CA)
Coastal Bend Coll (TX)
Coll of Marin (CA)
Coll of the Canyons (CA)
Coll of the Desert (CA)
Coll of the Sequoias (CA)
Compton Comm Coll (CA)
Crafton Hills Coll (CA)
East Central Coll (MO)
Foothill Coll (CA)
Imperial Valley Coll (CA)
Independence Comm Coll (KS)
Indian River Comm Coll (FL)
Jefferson Comm Coll (KY)
Kirkwood Comm Coll (IA)
Lincoln Land Comm Coll (IL)
Long Beach City Coll (CA)
Los Angeles City Coll (CA)
Los Angeles Mission Coll (CA)
Manatee Comm Coll (FL)
Miami-Dade Comm Coll (FL)
Midland Coll (TX)
MiraCosta Coll (CA)
Monterey Peninsula Coll (CA)
New Mexico Military Inst (NM)
North Idaho Coll (ID)
Orange Coast Coll (CA)
Pasadena City Coll (CA)
Red Rocks Comm Coll (CO)
Riverside Comm Coll (CA)
San Bernardino Valley Coll (CA)
San Diego Mesa Coll (CA)
San Joaquin Delta Coll (CA)
Santa Barbara City Coll (CA)
Santa Monica Coll (CA)
Sauk Valley Comm Coll (IL)
Snow Coll (UT)
Southwestern Coll (CA)
Triton Coll (IL)
Tulsa Comm Coll (OK)
Vincennes U (IN)
Western Nebraska Comm Coll (NE)
Western Wyoming Comm Coll (WY)
Young Harris Coll (GA)

FURNITURE DESIGN

Catawba Valley Comm Coll (NC)
Dakota County Tech Coll (MN)
Milwaukee Area Tech Coll (WI)
Vincennes U Jasper Campus (IN)

GAMING/SPORTS OFFICIATING RELATED

Arizona Western Coll (AZ)

GENERAL OFFICE/CLERICAL

Alamance Comm Coll (NC)
Alexandria Tech Coll (MN)
Bismarck State Coll (ND)
Bunker Hill Comm Coll (MA)
Butler County Comm Coll (PA)
Central Wyoming Coll (WY)
Darton Coll (GA)
Delta Coll (MI)
East Mississippi Comm Coll (MS)
El Centro Coll (TX)
Florida Comm Coll at Jacksonville (FL)
GateWay Comm Coll (AZ)
Georgia Perimeter Coll (GA)
Helena Coll of Tech of The U of Montana (MT)
Laurel Business Inst (PA)
Minot State U–Bottineau Campus (ND)
Modesto Jr Coll (CA)
New Mexico State U–Alamogordo (NM)
North Country Comm Coll (NY)
Pennsylvania Inst of Technology (PA)
Reedley Coll (CA)
San Jacinto Coll North Campus (TX)
Sitting Bull Coll (ND)
Spokane Falls Comm Coll (WA)
Terra State Comm Coll (OH)
United Tribes Tech Coll (ND)
Walla Walla Comm Coll (WA)

GENERAL RETAILING/ WHOLESALING

Alamance Comm Coll (NC)
Asheville-Buncombe Tech Comm Coll (NC)
Century Comm and Tech Coll (MN)
Comm Coll of Rhode Island (RI)
Craven Comm Coll (NC)
Delaware County Comm Coll (PA)
Dixie State Coll of Utah (UT)
Gadsden State Comm Coll (AL)
Gateway Tech Coll (WI)
Harrisburg Area Comm Coll (PA)
Hutchinson Comm Coll and Area Vocational School (KS)
McHenry County Coll (IL)
Nassau Comm Coll (NY)
Orange Coast Coll (CA)
Pitt Comm Coll (NC)
St. Cloud Tech Coll (MN)
Walla Walla Comm Coll (WA)

GENERAL RETAILING/ WHOLESALING RELATED

Southwestern Michigan Coll (MI)

GENERAL STUDIES

Adirondack Comm Coll (NY)
Allen County Comm Coll (KS)
Amarillo Coll (TX)
Asnuntuck Comm Coll (CT)
Bacone Coll (OK)
Bevill State Comm Coll (AL)
Bladen Comm Coll (NC)
Brazosport Coll (TX)
Briarwood Coll (CT)
Bristol Comm Coll (MA)
Butler County Comm Coll (PA)
Calhoun Comm Coll (AL)
Carroll Comm Coll (MD)
Central Maine Tech Coll (ME)
Central Virginia Comm Coll (VA)
Central Wyoming Coll (WY)
Cincinnati State Tech and Comm Coll (OH)
City Colls of Chicago, Malcolm X Coll (IL)
Clackamas Comm Coll (OR)
Coll of Alameda (CA)
Collin County Comm Coll District (TX)
Colorado Northwestern Comm Coll (CO)
Comm Coll of Allegheny County (PA)
Comm Coll of Rhode Island (RI)
Connors State Coll (OK)
Copiah-Lincoln Comm Coll–Natchez Campus (MS)
Corning Comm Coll (NY)
Crowder Coll (MO)
Crowley's Ridge Coll (AR)
Cuyamaca Coll (CA)
Delaware County Comm Coll (PA)
Delgado Comm Coll (LA)
Durham Tech Comm Coll (NC)
Eastern Maine Tech Coll (ME)
Eastern Wyoming Coll (WY)
Estrella Mountain Comm Coll (AZ)
Evergreen Valley Coll (CA)
Fayetteville Tech Comm Coll (NC)
Front Range Comm Coll (CO)

Gadsden State Comm Coll (AL)
GateWay Comm Coll (AZ)
Georgia Perimeter Coll (GA)
Germanna Comm Coll (VA)
Gordon Coll (GA)
Grays Harbor Coll (WA)
Hamilton Coll (IA)
Helena Coll of Tech of The U of Montana (MT)
Howard Comm Coll (MD)
James H. Faulkner State Comm Coll (AL)
Jefferson State Comm Coll (AL)
Kellogg Comm Coll (MI)
Kennebec Valley Tech Coll (ME)
Kilgore Coll (TX)
Lake Land Coll (IL)
Lamar State Coll–Port Arthur (TX)
Louisiana State U at Eunice (LA)
Luzerne County Comm Coll (PA)
Manchester Comm Coll (CT)
Martin Comm Coll (NC)
Massachusetts Bay Comm Coll (MA)
McHenry County Coll (IL)
Miami-Dade Comm Coll (FL)
Middlesex Comm Coll (MA)
Middlesex County Coll (NJ)
Mid Michigan Comm Coll (MI)
MiraCosta Coll (CA)
Mississippi County Comm Coll (AR)
Modesto Jr Coll (CA)
Montgomery Coll (MD)
Mott Comm Coll (MI)
Mount Wachusett Comm Coll (MA)
Nassau Comm Coll (NY)
New Hampshire Comm Tech Coll, Berlin/Laconia (NH)
New Hampshire Tech Inst (NH)
New River Comm Coll (VA)
Niagara County Comm Coll (NY)
Northampton County Area Comm Coll (PA)
North Arkansas Coll (AR)
Norwalk Comm Coll (CT)
Ocean County Coll (NJ)
Our Lady of the Lake Coll (LA)
Palo Verde Coll (CA)
Parkland Coll (IL)
Pennsylvania Coll of Technology (PA)
Pensacola Jr Coll (FL)
Pikes Peak Comm Coll (CO)
Pima Comm Coll (AZ)
Quinsigamond Comm Coll (MA)
Reedley Coll (CA)
San Juan Coll (NM)
Santa Fe Comm Coll (NM)
Sheridan Coll (WY)
Snead State Comm Coll (AL)
South Arkansas Comm Coll (AR)
Southeast Arkansas Coll (AR)
Southern Arkansas U Tech (AR)
Southern Maine Tech Coll (ME)
Southside Virginia Comm Coll (VA)
Southwestern Coll (CA)
Southwestern Michigan Coll (MI)
Southwestern Oklahoma State U at Sayre (OK)
Southwest Tennessee Comm Coll (TN)
Springfield Tech Comm Coll (MA)
State U of NY Coll of Technology at Delhi (NY)
Tacoma Comm Coll (WA)
Taft Coll (CA)
Terra State Comm Coll (OH)
Truett-McConnell Coll (GA)
The U of Akron–Wayne Coll (OH)
U of Arkansas at Fort Smith (AR)
U of New Mexico–Gallup (NM)
Vista Comm Coll (CA)
Wake Tech Comm Coll (NC)
Waubonsee Comm Coll (IL)
Western Nebraska Comm Coll (NE)
Western Nevada Comm Coll (NV)
Wilson Tech Comm Coll (NC)
Woodbury Coll (VT)
Wor-Wic Comm Coll (MD)

GEOGRAPHY
Allen County Comm Coll (KS)
Bakersfield Coll (CA)
Cambria County Area Comm Coll (PA)
Cañada Coll (CA)
Cerritos Coll (CA)
Coll of Alameda (CA)
Coll of Southern Idaho (ID)
Coll of the Canyons (CA)
Coll of the Desert (CA)
Columbia State Comm Coll (TN)
Cypress Coll (CA)
Del Mar Coll (TX)
East Central Coll (MO)
Foothill Coll (CA)
Hill Coll of the Hill Jr College District (TX)
Jefferson Coll (MO)
Jefferson Comm Coll (KY)
Joliet Jr Coll (IL)
Lake Michigan Coll (MI)
Lansing Comm Coll (MI)
Lincoln Coll, Lincoln (IL)
Lincoln Land Comm Coll (IL)
Los Angeles Mission Coll (CA)
Lower Columbia Coll (WA)
Miami U–Middletown Campus (OH)
Mississippi Delta Comm Coll (MS)
Orange Coast Coll (CA)
Pasadena City Coll (CA)
Pellissippi State Tech Comm Coll (TN)
Riverside Comm Coll (CA)
San Bernardino Valley Coll (CA)
San Diego Mesa Coll (CA)
Santa Ana Coll (CA)
Santa Barbara City Coll (CA)
Santa Monica Coll (CA)
Skagit Valley Coll (WA)
Snow Coll (UT)
Southwestern Coll (CA)
Triton Coll (IL)
Tulsa Comm Coll (OK)
Vermilion Comm Coll (MN)
Vincennes U (IN)
Western Nebraska Comm Coll (NE)

GEOLOGY
Amarillo Coll (TX)
Arizona Western Coll (AZ)
Austin Comm Coll (TX)
Bakersfield Coll (CA)
Barton County Comm Coll (KS)
Cañada Coll (CA)
Casper Coll (WY)
Centralia Coll (WA)
Central Texas Coll (TX)
Cerritos Coll (CA)
Chaffey Coll (CA)
City Coll of San Francisco (CA)
Clark Coll (WA)
Coastal Bend Coll (TX)
Coastal Georgia Comm Coll (GA)
Coll of Marin (CA)
Coll of Southern Idaho (ID)
Coll of the Canyons (CA)
Coll of the Desert (CA)
Coll of the Siskiyous (CA)
Colorado Mountn Coll, Alpine Cmps (CO)
Crafton Hills Coll (CA)
Cuesta Coll (CA)
Cypress Coll (CA)
Daytona Beach Comm Coll (FL)
Del Mar Coll (TX)
Delta Coll (MI)
Dixie State Coll of Utah (UT)
East Central Coll (MO)
Eastern Arizona Coll (AZ)
East Georgia Coll (GA)
Everett Comm Coll (WA)
Floyd Coll (GA)
Foothill Coll (CA)
Fullerton Coll (CA)
Georgia Perimeter Coll (GA)
Grand Rapids Comm Coll (MI)
Grayson County Coll (TX)
Great Basin Coll (NV)
Highland Comm Coll (IL)
Highland Comm Coll (KS)
Hill Coll of the Hill Jr College District (TX)
Iowa Lakes Comm Coll (IA)
Kilgore Coll (TX)
Lake Michigan Coll (MI)
Lansing Comm Coll (MI)
Lincoln Land Comm Coll (IL)
Lower Columbia Coll (WA)
Mesa Tech Coll (NM)
Miami-Dade Comm Coll (FL)
Midland Coll (TX)
Monterey Peninsula Coll (CA)
Moorpark Coll (CA)
North Idaho Coll (ID)
Odessa Coll (TX)
Orange Coast Coll (CA)
Palomar Coll (CA)
Pasadena City Coll (CA)
Pensacola Jr Coll (FL)
Red Rocks Comm Coll (CO)
Riverside Comm Coll (CA)
San Bernardino Valley Coll (CA)
San Jacinto Coll Central Campus (TX)
San Jacinto Coll North Campus (TX)
San Joaquin Delta Coll (CA)
San Juan Coll (NM)
Santa Ana Coll (CA)
Santa Barbara City Coll (CA)
Santa Monica Coll (CA)
Sierra Coll (CA)
Snow Coll (UT)
Southwestern Coll (CA)
Tacoma Comm Coll (WA)
Triton Coll (IL)
Tulsa Comm Coll (OK)
Vincennes U (IN)
Western Wyoming Comm Coll (WY)
Young Harris Coll (GA)

GERMAN
Austin Comm Coll (TX)
Bakersfield Coll (CA)
Blinn Coll (TX)
Cañada Coll (CA)
Casper Coll (WY)
Centralia Coll (WA)
Cerritos Coll (CA)
Chaffey Coll (CA)
Citrus Coll (CA)
Coastal Bend Coll (TX)
Coll of Marin (CA)
Coll of the Canyons (CA)
Compton Comm Coll (CA)
East Central Coll (MO)
Everett Comm Coll (WA)
Foothill Coll (CA)
Long Beach City Coll (CA)
Los Angeles City Coll (CA)
Manatee Comm Coll (FL)
Miami-Dade Comm Coll (FL)
Midland Coll (TX)
Monterey Peninsula Coll (CA)
New Mexico Military Inst (NM)
North Idaho Coll (ID)
Orange Coast Coll (CA)
Pasadena City Coll (CA)
Red Rocks Comm Coll (CO)
Riverside Comm Coll (CA)
San Bernardino Valley Coll (CA)
San Diego Mesa Coll (CA)
San Jacinto Coll Central Campus (TX)
San Joaquin Delta Coll (CA)
Santa Monica Coll (CA)
Tulsa Comm Coll (OK)
Vincennes U (IN)
Western Nebraska Comm Coll (NE)

GERONTOLOGICAL SERVICES
Comm Coll of Rhode Island (RI)
Lehigh Carbon Comm Coll (PA)
Mott Comm Coll (MI)
U of Arkansas at Fort Smith (AR)

GERONTOLOGY
American River Coll (CA)
Baltimore City Comm Coll (MD)
Camden County Coll (NJ)
Chaffey Coll (CA)
City Colls of Chicago, Wilbur Wright Coll (IL)
Columbus State Comm Coll (OH)
Delaware Tech & Comm Coll, Stanton/ Wilmington Cmps (DE)
Edmonds Comm Coll (WA)
Eugenio María de Hostos Comm Coll of City U of NY (NY)
Fiorello H LaGuardia Comm Coll of City U of NY (NY)
Gateway Comm Coll (CT)
Genesee Comm Coll (NY)
Lansing Comm Coll (MI)
Mt. San Jacinto Coll (CA)
Naugatuck Valley Comm Coll (CT)
New River Comm Coll (VA)
Northern Virginia Comm Coll (VA)
North Shore Comm Coll (MA)
Oklahoma City Comm Coll (OK)
Pima Comm Coll (AZ)
Portland Comm Coll (OR)
Ridgewater Coll (MN)
Sandhills Comm Coll (NC)
Sinclair Comm Coll (OH)
Spokane Falls Comm Coll (WA)
Union County Coll (NJ)

GRAPHIC DESIGN/COMMERCIAL ART/ILLUSTRATION
Academy Coll (MN)
Aims Comm Coll (CO)
Alamance Comm Coll (NC)
Alexandria Tech Coll (MN)
Allan Hancock Coll (CA)
Allentown Business School (PA)
Alpena Comm Coll (MI)
Amarillo Coll (TX)
Antonelli Coll (OH)
Antonelli Inst (PA)
Arapahoe Comm Coll (CO)
The Art Inst of Atlanta (GA)
The Art Inst of Fort Lauderdale (FL)
The Art Inst of Houston (TX)
The Art Inst of Los Angeles (CA)
The Art Inst of Philadelphia (PA)
The Art Inst of Pittsburgh (PA)
The Art Inst of Seattle (WA)
The Art Insts International Minnesota (MN)
Asnuntuck Comm Coll (CT)
Austin Comm Coll (TX)
Baltimore City Comm Coll (MD)
Bergen Comm Coll (NJ)
Bismarck State Coll (ND)
Bradford School (OH)
Bradley Academy for the Visual Arts (PA)
Brookdale Comm Coll (NJ)
Brooks Coll (CA)
Bryant & Stratton Business Inst, Rochester (NY)
Bryant & Stratton Business Inst, Eastern Hills Cmps (NY)
Bucks County Comm Coll (PA)
Burlington County Coll (NJ)
Butler County Comm Coll (PA)
Butte Coll (CA)
Calhoun Comm Coll (AL)
Casper Coll (WY)
Catawba Valley Comm Coll (NC)
Central Comm Coll–Columbus Campus (NE)
Central Comm Coll–Hastings Campus (NE)
Centralia Coll (WA)
Central Maine Tech Coll (ME)
Central Piedmont Comm Coll (NC)
Central Texas Coll (TX)
Central Virginia Comm Coll (VA)
Chabot Coll (CA)
Chattanooga State Tech Comm Coll (TN)
CHI Inst (PA)
Cincinnati State Tech and Comm Coll (OH)
Clark Coll (WA)
Clovis Comm Coll (NM)
Coastal Bend Coll (TX)
Colby Comm Coll (KS)
Coll of DuPage (IL)
Coll of Southern Idaho (ID)
Coll of the Redwoods (CA)
Coll of the Sequoias (CA)
Collin County Comm Coll District (TX)
Colorado Mountn Coll (CO)
Columbus State Comm Coll (OH)
Comm Coll of Allegheny County (PA)
Comm Coll of Aurora (CO)
The Comm Coll of Baltimore County–Catonsville Campus (MD)
Comm Coll of Denver (CO)
Comm Coll of Southern Nevada (NV)
Comm Coll of the Air Force (AL)
Compton Comm Coll (CA)
County Coll of Morris (NJ)
Cuyahoga Comm Coll (OH)
Cuyamaca Coll (CA)
Davis Coll (OH)
Daytona Beach Comm Coll (FL)
De Anza Coll (CA)
Delaware County Comm Coll (PA)
Delgado Comm Coll (LA)
Delta Coll of Arts and Technology (LA)
Des Moines Area Comm Coll (IA)
Dixie State Coll of Utah (UT)
Don Bosco Coll of Science and Technology (CA)
Dutchess Comm Coll (NY)
East Central Coll (MO)
Eastern Arizona Coll (AZ)
Edison State Comm Coll (OH)
Everett Comm Coll (WA)
Fashion Inst of Design & Merchandising, LA Campus (CA)
Fashion Inst of Design & Merchandising, SD Campus (CA)
Fashion Inst of Design & Merchandising, SF Campus (CA)
Fayetteville Tech Comm Coll (NC)
Finger Lakes Comm Coll (NY)
Florida Comm Coll at Jacksonville (FL)
Foothill Coll (CA)
Forsyth Tech Comm Coll (NC)
Fort Scott Comm Coll (KS)
Fresno City Coll (CA)
Full Sail Real World Education (FL)
Fulton-Montgomery Comm Coll (NY)
Garden City Comm Coll (KS)
Genesee Comm Coll (NY)
Glendale Comm Coll (AZ)
Glendale Comm Coll (CA)
Gogebic Comm Coll (MI)
Golden West Coll (CA)
Greenfield Comm Coll (MA)
Guilford Tech Comm Coll (NC)
Halifax Comm Coll (NC)
Harford Comm Coll (MD)
Harrisburg Area Comm Coll (PA)
Hawkeye Comm Coll (IA)
Henry Ford Comm Coll (MI)
Hesser Coll (NH)
Highland Comm Coll (IL)
Highland Comm Coll (KS)
Hill Coll of the Hill Jr College District (TX)
Hillsborough Comm Coll (FL)
Hinds Comm Coll (MS)
Holyoke Comm Coll (MA)
Honolulu Comm Coll (HI)
Housatonic Comm Coll (CT)
Houston Comm Coll System (TX)
Hussian School of Art (PA)
International Business Coll, Fort Wayne (IN)
Iowa Lakes Comm Coll (IA)
Iowa Western Comm Coll (IA)
Isothermal Comm Coll (NC)
James H. Faulkner State Comm Coll (AL)
James Sprunt Comm Coll (NC)
Jefferson Comm Coll (KY)
J. F. Drake State Tech Coll (AL)
Johnson County Comm Coll (KS)
Johnston Comm Coll (NC)
Kalamazoo Valley Comm Coll (MI)
Kellogg Comm Coll (MI)
Kilgore Coll (TX)
Kingsborough Comm Coll of City U of NY (NY)
Labette Comm Coll (KS)
Lakeland Comm Coll (OH)
Lake-Sumter Comm Coll (FL)
Lane Comm Coll (OR)
Lansing Comm Coll (MI)
Lehigh Carbon Comm Coll (PA)
Lenoir Comm Coll (NC)
Lincoln Coll, Lincoln (IL)
Lincoln Coll, Normal (IL)
Linn-Benton Comm Coll (OR)
Lon Morris Coll (TX)
Lord Fairfax Comm Coll (VA)
Luzerne County Comm Coll (PA)
Macomb Comm Coll (MI)
Manatee Comm Coll (FL)
Manchester Comm Coll (CT)
Maryland Coll of Art and Design (MD)
Massasoit Comm Coll (MA)
Mercer County Comm Coll (NJ)
Metropolitan Comm Coll (NE)
Miami-Dade Comm Coll (FL)
Middlesex Comm Coll (MA)
Middlesex County Coll (NJ)
Midland Coll (TX)
Midlands Tech Coll (SC)
Mid Michigan Comm Coll (MI)
Miles Comm Coll (MT)
Milwaukee Area Tech Coll (WI)
Mineral Area Coll (MO)

Minneapolis Comm and Tech Coll (MN)
Mitchell Coll (CT)
Modesto Jr Coll (CA)
Mohawk Valley Comm Coll (NY)
Monroe Comm Coll (NY)
Monterey Peninsula Coll (CA)
Montgomery Coll (MD)
Montgomery County Comm Coll (PA)
Moorpark Coll (CA)
Moraine Park Tech Coll (WI)
Mott Comm Coll (MI)
Mt. Hood Comm Coll (OR)
Nashville State Tech Inst (TN)
Nassau Comm Coll (NY)
Navarro Coll (TX)
Newbury Coll (MA)
New Mexico State U–Alamogordo (NM)
New York City Tech Coll of the City U of NY (NY)
Northampton County Area Comm Coll (PA)
Northern Essex Comm Coll (MA)
Northern Oklahoma Coll (OK)
Northern Virginia Comm Coll (VA)
North Hennepin Comm Coll (MN)
North Idaho Coll (ID)
Northwest Coll (WY)
Northwestern Connecticut Comm-Tech Coll (CT)
Northwestern Michigan Coll (MI)
Northwest Mississippi Comm Coll (MS)
Norwalk Comm Coll (CT)
Nossi Coll of Art (TN)
Oakbridge Academy of Arts (PA)
Oakton Comm Coll (IL)
Ocean County Coll (NJ)
Okaloosa-Walton Comm Coll (FL)
Oklahoma City Comm Coll (OK)
Oklahoma State U, Okmulgee (OK)
Onondaga Comm Coll (NY)
Orange Coast Coll (CA)
Palm Beach Comm Coll (FL)
Palomar Coll (CA)
Pellissippi State Tech Comm Coll (TN)
Pennsylvania Coll of Technology (PA)
Penn Valley Comm Coll (MO)
Pensacola Jr Coll (FL)
Piedmont Tech Coll (SC)
Pima Comm Coll (AZ)
Pitt Comm Coll (NC)
Pittsburgh Tech Inst (PA)
Platt Coll, Newport Beach (CA)
Platt Coll, Ontario (CA)
Platt Coll (CO)
Platt Coll–Los Angeles, Inc (CA)
Platt Coll San Diego (CA)
Portland Comm Coll (OR)
Pratt Comm Coll and Area Vocational School (KS)
Quinsigamond Comm Coll (MA)
Randolph Comm Coll (NC)
Raritan Valley Comm Coll (NJ)
Reedley Coll (CA)
Rend Lake Coll (IL)
Rockland Comm Coll (NY)
Saint Charles Comm Coll (MO)
St. Clair County Comm Coll (MI)
St. Cloud Tech Coll (MN)
St. Louis Comm Coll at Florissant Valley (MO)
St. Petersburg Coll (FL)
San Antonio Coll (TX)
San Bernardino Valley Coll (CA)
San Diego City Coll (CA)
San Jacinto Coll Central Campus (TX)
San Jacinto Coll South Campus (TX)
San Joaquin Delta Coll (CA)
San Juan Coll (NM)
Santa Ana Coll (CA)
Santa Barbara City Coll (CA)
Santa Fe Comm Coll (FL)
Santa Monica Coll (CA)
Schoolcraft Coll (MI)
Schuylkill Inst of Business and Technology (PA)
Seattle Central Comm Coll (WA)
Shoreline Comm Coll (WA)
Sinclair Comm Coll (OH)
Skagit Valley Coll (WA)
Southeast Comm Coll, Milford Campus (NE)
Southeast Tech Inst (SD)
Southern Arkansas U Tech (AR)
South Piedmont Comm Coll (NC)
South Plains Coll (TX)
South Suburban Coll (IL)
Southwestern Coll (CA)
Southwestern Comm Coll (NC)
Southwest Tennessee Comm Coll (TN)
Spokane Falls Comm Coll (WA)
Springfield Tech Comm Coll (MA)
Suffolk County Comm Coll (NY)
Sullivan County Comm Coll (NY)
Surry Comm Coll (NC)
Sussex County Comm Coll (NJ)
Terra State Comm Coll (OH)
Texas State Tech Coll–Harlingen (TX)
Texas State Tech Coll– Waco/ Marshall Campus (TX)
Thomas Nelson Comm Coll (VA)
Tidewater Comm Coll (VA)
Tompkins Cortland Comm Coll (NY)
Trident Tech Coll (SC)
Trinidad State Jr Coll (CO)
Triton Coll (IL)
Truckee Meadows Comm Coll (NV)
Tunxis Comm Coll (CT)
Tyler Jr Coll (TX)
Ulster County Comm Coll (NY)
U of Arkansas at Fort Smith (AR)
U of Arkansas Comm Coll at Morrilton (AR)
Ventura Coll (CA)
Villa Maria Coll of Buffalo (NY)
Vincennes U (IN)
Virginia Western Comm Coll (VA)
Western Wisconsin Tech Coll (WI)
Westmoreland County Comm Coll (PA)
Westwood Coll of Technology–Anaheim (CA)
Westwood Coll of Technology-Chicago Du Page (IL)
Westwood Coll of Technology–Chicago O'Hare (IL)
Westwood Coll of Technology–Chicago River Oaks (IL)
Westwood Coll of Technology–Denver North (CO)
Westwood Coll of Technology–Denver South (CO)
Westwood Coll of Technology–Inland Empire (CA)
Westwood Coll of Technology–Los Angeles (CA)
Westwood Inst of Technology–Fort Worth (TX)
Whatcom Comm Coll (WA)

GRAPHIC/PRINTING EQUIPMENT

Austin Comm Coll (TX)
Central Comm Coll–Hastings Campus (NE)
Central Maine Tech Coll (ME)
Central Piedmont Comm Coll (NC)
Central Texas Coll (TX)
Chattanooga State Tech Comm Coll (TN)
Chemeketa Comm Coll (OR)
City Coll of San Francisco (CA)
Clark Coll (WA)
Clinton Comm Coll (IA)
Clover Park Tech Coll (WA)
Coll of DuPage (IL)
The Comm Coll of Baltimore County–Catonsville Campus (MD)
Comm Coll of Denver (CO)
Comm Coll of Southern Nevada (NV)
Compton Comm Coll (CA)
Delta Coll (MI)
Des Moines Area Comm Coll (IA)
Don Bosco Coll of Science and Technology (CA)
Dunwoody Coll of Technology (MN)
Eastfield Coll (TX)
Erie Comm Coll, South Campus (NY)
Forsyth Tech Comm Coll (NC)
Fresno City Coll (CA)
Fullerton Coll (CA)
Fulton-Montgomery Comm Coll (NY)
Gogebic Comm Coll (MI)
Golden West Coll (CA)
Highline Comm Coll (WA)
Hinds Comm Coll (MS)
Houston Comm Coll System (TX)
Hutchinson Comm Coll and Area Vocational School (KS)
Iowa Lakes Comm Coll (IA)
Kilgore Coll (TX)
Kirkwood Comm Coll (IA)
Lake Land Coll (IL)
Lenoir Comm Coll (NC)
Luzerne County Comm Coll (PA)
Macomb Comm Coll (MI)
Metropolitan Comm Coll (NE)
Milwaukee Area Tech Coll (WI)
Mississippi Delta Comm Coll (MS)
Moberly Area Comm Coll (MO)
Modesto Jr Coll (CA)
Mohawk Valley Comm Coll (NY)
Monroe Comm Coll (NY)
Montgomery Coll (MD)
Moorpark Coll (CA)
Northcentral Tech Coll (WI)
Northern Oklahoma Coll (OK)
Northwest Coll (WY)
Oklahoma State U, Okmulgee (OK)
Palomar Coll (CA)
Pennsylvania Coll of Technology (PA)
Randolph Comm Coll (NC)
Sacramento City Coll (CA)
St. Cloud Tech Coll (MN)
San Diego City Coll (CA)
San Jacinto Coll Central Campus (TX)
San Joaquin Delta Coll (CA)
Santa Monica Coll (CA)
Seattle Central Comm Coll (WA)
Shoreline Comm Coll (WA)
Sinclair Comm Coll (OH)
Southeast Tech Inst (SD)
South Suburban Coll (IL)
Southwestern Michigan Coll (MI)
Springfield Tech Comm Coll (MA)
Tarrant County Coll District (TX)
Texas State Tech Coll– Waco/ Marshall Campus (TX)
Thaddeus Stevens Coll of Technology (PA)
Trenholm State Tech Coll, Patterson Campus (AL)
Triton Coll (IL)
Tyler Jr Coll (TX)
U of New Mexico–Gallup (NM)
Vincennes U (IN)
Westmoreland County Comm Coll (PA)

GRAPHIC/PRINTING EQUIPMENT RELATED

The Art Inst of Atlanta (GA)
Linn-Benton Comm Coll (OR)

GREENHOUSE MANAGEMENT

Comm Coll of Allegheny County (PA)
Kishwaukee Coll (IL)
Minot State U–Bottineau Campus (ND)

HEALTH AIDE

Allen County Comm Coll (KS)
Central Arizona Coll (AZ)
Edmonds Comm Coll (WA)
Springfield Tech Comm Coll (MA)

HEALTH EDUCATION

Andrew Coll (GA)
Angelina Coll (TX)
Anne Arundel Comm Coll (MD)
Bainbridge Coll (GA)
Bucks County Comm Coll (PA)
Cañada Coll (CA)
Chabot Coll (CA)
Chemeketa Comm Coll (OR)
Chesapeake Coll (MD)
Coahoma Comm Coll (MS)
Coastal Bend Coll (TX)
Coll of the Sequoias (CA)
Darton Coll (GA)
Daytona Beach Comm Coll (FL)
Del Mar Coll (TX)
Donnelly Coll (KS)
East Central Comm Coll (MS)
East Georgia Coll (GA)
East Mississippi Comm Coll (MS)
Florida National Coll (FL)
Fulton-Montgomery Comm Coll (NY)
Harford Comm Coll (MD)
Highland Comm Coll (KS)
Hill Coll of the Hill Jr College District (TX)
Howard Comm Coll (MD)
Kilgore Coll (TX)
Los Angeles Mission Coll (CA)
Manatee Comm Coll (FL)
Mississippi Delta Comm Coll (MS)
Northwest Coll (WY)
Palm Beach Comm Coll (FL)
Pratt Comm Coll and Area Vocational School (KS)
Prince George's Comm Coll (MD)
St. Catharine Coll (KY)
Sanford-Brown Coll, Hazelwood (MO)
Tulsa Comm Coll (OK)
Umpqua Comm Coll (OR)
U of New Mexico–Gallup (NM)
Vermilion Comm Coll (MN)
Waycross Coll (GA)
Westmoreland County Comm Coll (PA)
Young Harris Coll (GA)

HEALTH FACILITIES ADMINISTRATION

Allen County Comm Coll (KS)
The Bryman School (AZ)
Central Comm Coll–Hastings Campus (NE)
City Colls of Chicago, Malcolm X Coll (IL)
Harrisburg Area Comm Coll (PA)
Manatee Comm Coll (FL)
Western Wisconsin Tech Coll (WI)

HEALTH/MEDICAL ADMINISTRATIVE SERVICES RELATED

Catawba Valley Comm Coll (NC)
Hawaii Business Coll (HI)

HEALTH/MEDICAL DIAGNOSTIC AND TREATMENT SERVICES RELATED

Bunker Hill Comm Coll (MA)
Harcum Coll (PA)
Oakland Comm Coll (MI)
Pennsylvania Coll of Technology (PA)
Union County Coll (NJ)
Western Inst of Science & Health (CA)

HEALTH/MEDICAL LABORATORY TECHNOLOGIES RELATED

Bunker Hill Comm Coll (MA)
Highline Comm Coll (WA)
Mott Comm Coll (MI)
Oakland Comm Coll (MI)

HEALTH/MEDICAL PREPARATORY PROGRAMS RELATED

Ancilla Coll (IN)
Eastern Arizona Coll (AZ)
Eastern Wyoming Coll (WY)

HEALTH/PHYSICAL EDUCATION

Allen County Comm Coll (KS)
Antelope Valley Coll (CA)
Atlanta Metropolitan Coll (GA)
Cerro Coso Comm Coll (CA)
Cincinnati State Tech and Comm Coll (OH)
Citrus Coll (CA)
Clovis Comm Coll (NM)
Coastal Georgia Comm Coll (GA)
Comm Coll of Allegheny County (PA)
Corning Comm Coll (NY)
Dean Coll (MA)
Eastern Arizona Coll (AZ)
Georgia Perimeter Coll (GA)
Gloucester County Coll (NJ)
Lake Michigan Coll (MI)
Louisburg Coll (NC)
Luzerne County Comm Coll (PA)
Northeast Comm Coll (NE)
Pensacola Jr Coll (FL)
Reedley Coll (CA)
Riverside Comm Coll (CA)
St. Philip's Coll (TX)
Salem Comm Coll (NJ)
Santa Fe Comm Coll (NM)
Sheridan Coll (WY)
State U of NY Coll of Technology at Delhi (NY)
Western Nebraska Comm Coll (NE)

HEALTH/PHYSICAL EDUCATION/ FITNESS RELATED

Garden City Comm Coll (KS)
Indiana Business Coll-Medical (IN)
Kingsborough Comm Coll of City U of NY (NY)
Oakland Comm Coll (MI)
Pennsylvania Coll of Technology (PA)

HEALTH PROFESSIONS AND RELATED SCIENCES

AIBT International Inst of the Americas (AZ)
Comm Coll of Allegheny County (PA)
Dixie State Coll of Utah (UT)
Georgia Perimeter Coll (GA)
Indiana Business Coll, Anderson (IN)
Indiana Business Coll, Columbus (IN)
Indiana Business Coll, Evansville (IN)
Indiana Business Coll, Fort Wayne (IN)
Indiana Business Coll, Terre Haute (IN)
Indiana Business Coll-Medical (IN)
Oakland Comm Coll (MI)
Pitt Comm Coll (NC)
Southwestern Michigan Coll (MI)
Southwest Tennessee Comm Coll (TN)
Volunteer State Comm Coll (TN)

HEALTH SCIENCE

Arizona Western Coll (AZ)
Barton County Comm Coll (KS)
Bergen Comm Coll (NJ)
Borough of Manhattan Comm Coll of City U of NY (NY)
Bucks County Comm Coll (PA)
Butte Coll (CA)
Cañada Coll (CA)
Carroll Comm Coll (MD)
Coll of the Canyons (CA)
Compton Comm Coll (CA)
Cypress Coll (CA)
Daytona Beach Comm Coll (FL)
Diné Coll (AZ)
Greenville Tech Coll (SC)
Harcum Coll (PA)
Hill Coll of the Hill Jr College District (TX)
Kalamazoo Valley Comm Coll (MI)
Manor Coll (PA)
Mercer County Comm Coll (NJ)
Mohave Comm Coll (AZ)
Nassau Comm Coll (NY)
North Shore Comm Coll (MA)
Northwestern Connecticut Comm-Tech Coll (CT)
Ocean County Coll (NJ)
Orange Coast Coll (CA)
Palo Verde Coll (CA)
Queensborough Comm Coll of City U of NY (NY)
Riverside Comm Coll (CA)
San Joaquin Delta Coll (CA)
South U (AL)
Southwest Mississippi Comm Coll (MS)
Sussex County Comm Coll (NJ)
Tri-County Tech Coll (SC)
Tulsa Comm Coll (OK)
Villa Maria Coll of Buffalo (NY)
Western Wyoming Comm Coll (WY)

HEALTH SERVICES ADMINISTRATION

Cabarrus Coll of Health Sciences (NC)
Cambria County Area Comm Coll (PA)
Central Piedmont Comm Coll (NC)
Chemeketa Comm Coll (OR)
Coll of DuPage (IL)
Coll of Southern Idaho (ID)
Comm Coll of the Air Force (AL)

Consolidated School of Business, Lancaster (PA)
Consolidated School of Business, York (PA)
Des Moines Area Comm Coll (IA)
ECPI Coll of Technology, Newport News (VA)
ECPI Coll of Technology, Virginia Beach (VA)
ECPI Tech Coll, Richmond (VA)
ECPI Tech Coll, Roanoke (VA)
Essex County Coll (NJ)
GateWay Comm Coll (AZ)
Herkimer County Comm Coll (NY)
Houston Comm Coll System (TX)
Indian Hills Comm Coll (IA)
Inver Hills Comm Coll (MN)
Iowa Lakes Comm Coll (IA)
Luzerne County Comm Coll (PA)
Manatee Comm Coll (FL)
Mineral Area Coll (MO)
National Coll of Business & Technology, Louisville (KY)
North Idaho Coll (ID)
North Seattle Comm Coll (WA)
Oakland Comm Coll (MI)
Pensacola Jr Coll (FL)
St. Petersburg Coll (FL)
South Plains Coll (TX)
Tyler Jr Coll (TX)
U of Alaska Southeast, Sitka Campus (AK)

HEALTH UNIT COORDINATION
The Brown Mackie Coll–Olathe Campus (KS)
Comm Coll of Allegheny County (PA)
Dakota County Tech Coll (MN)
Lehigh Carbon Comm Coll (PA)
Milwaukee Area Tech Coll (WI)
Rasmussen Coll Mankato (MN)
Riverland Comm Coll (MN)
St. Philip's Coll (TX)
Southeast Tech Inst (SD)

HEALTH UNIT MANAGEMENT
The Brown Mackie Coll–Olathe Campus (KS)
Ridgewater Coll (MN)

HEARING SCIENCES
Arkansas State U–Mountain Home (AR)

HEATING/AIR CONDITIONING/ REFRIGERATION
Amarillo Coll (TX)
Antelope Valley Coll (CA)
Arizona Western Coll (AZ)
Asheville-Buncombe Tech Comm Coll (NC)
Athens Tech Coll (GA)
Austin Comm Coll (TX)
Bates Tech Coll (WA)
Belmont Tech Coll (OH)
Bismarck State Coll (ND)
Black Hawk Coll, Moline (IL)
Brazosport Coll (TX)
Brevard Comm Coll (FL)
Cedar Valley Coll (TX)
Central Comm Coll–Grand Island Campus (NE)
Central Comm Coll–Hastings Campus (NE)
Central Texas Coll (TX)
Century Comm and Tech Coll (MN)
Chattanooga State Tech Comm Coll (TN)
CHI Inst (PA)
Chippewa Valley Tech Coll (WI)
Clover Park Tech Coll (WA)
Clovis Comm Coll (NM)
Coll of DuPage (IL)
Coll of Lake County (IL)
Coll of Southern Idaho (ID)
Coll of the Desert (CA)
Coll of the Sequoias (CA)
Columbus State Comm Coll (OH)
Comm Coll of Allegheny County (PA)
Comm Coll of Denver (CO)
Comm Coll of Southern Nevada (NV)
Craven Comm Coll (NC)
Cypress Coll (CA)
Daytona Beach Comm Coll (FL)
Delta Coll (MI)
Des Moines Area Comm Coll (IA)
Doña Ana Branch Comm Coll (NM)
Dunwoody Coll of Technology (MN)
East Central Coll (MO)
Eastern Maine Tech Coll (ME)
Eastfield Coll (TX)
Elaine P. Nunez Comm Coll (LA)
Fayetteville Tech Comm Coll (NC)
Florence-Darlington Tech Coll (SC)
Forsyth Tech Comm Coll (NC)
Fresno City Coll (CA)
GateWay Comm Coll (AZ)
Grand Rapids Comm Coll (MI)
Grayson County Coll (TX)
Greenville Tech Coll (SC)
Guilford Tech Comm Coll (NC)
Harry M. Ayers State Tech Coll (AL)
Hawkeye Comm Coll (IA)
Heartland Comm Coll (IL)
Henry Ford Comm Coll (MI)
Hill Coll of the Hill Jr College District (TX)
Honolulu Comm Coll (HI)
Horry-Georgetown Tech Coll (SC)
Illinois Eastern Comm Colls, Lincoln Trail Coll (IL)
Indian River Comm Coll (FL)
Jefferson Coll (MO)
John A. Logan Coll (IL)
Johnston Comm Coll (NC)
Kankakee Comm Coll (IL)
Kellogg Comm Coll (MI)
Kilgore Coll (TX)
Kirkwood Comm Coll (IA)
Labette Comm Coll (KS)
Lamar State Coll–Port Arthur (TX)
Lane Comm Coll (OR)
Lansing Comm Coll (MI)
Lehigh Carbon Comm Coll (PA)
Long Beach City Coll (CA)
Louisiana Tech Coll–Delta Ouachita Campus (LA)
Louisiana Tech Coll–Mansfield Campus (LA)
Luzerne County Comm Coll (PA)
Macomb Comm Coll (MI)
Maple Woods Comm Coll (MO)
Martin Comm Coll (NC)
Massasoit Comm Coll (MA)
Metropolitan Comm Coll (NE)
Miami-Dade Comm Coll (FL)
Middlesex County Coll (NJ)
Midland Coll (TX)
Midlands Tech Coll (SC)
Mid Michigan Comm Coll (MI)
Mid-Plains Comm Coll Area (NE)
Milwaukee Area Tech Coll (WI)
Minnesota State Coll–Southeast Tech (MN)
Mitchell Tech Inst (SD)
Modesto Jr Coll (CA)
Mohawk Valley Comm Coll (NY)
Monroe Comm Coll (NY)
Morton Coll (IL)
New England Inst of Technology (RI)
New England Inst of Tech & Florida Culinary Inst (FL)
New York City Tech Coll of the City U of NY (NY)
North Dakota State Coll of Science (ND)
Northeast Comm Coll (NE)
Northern Maine Tech Coll (ME)
Northern Virginia Comm Coll (VA)
North Harris Coll (TX)
North Idaho Coll (ID)
North Iowa Area Comm Coll (IA)
North Seattle Comm Coll (WA)
Northwest Mississippi Comm Coll (MS)
Odessa Coll (TX)
Okaloosa-Walton Comm Coll (FL)
Oklahoma State U, Oklahoma City (OK)
Oklahoma State U, Okmulgee (OK)
Orange Coast Coll (CA)
Oxnard Coll (CA)
Penn Valley Comm Coll (MO)
Piedmont Tech Coll (SC)
Raritan Valley Comm Coll (NJ)
Roanoke-Chowan Comm Coll (NC)
Rockingham Comm Coll (NC)
St. Cloud Tech Coll (MN)
St. Philip's Coll (TX)
Salem Comm Coll (NJ)
San Bernardino Valley Coll (CA)
San Jacinto Coll North Campus (TX)
San Jacinto Coll South Campus (TX)
San Joaquin Delta Coll (CA)
San Joaquin Valley Coll (CA)
Sauk Valley Comm Coll (IL)
Scott Comm Coll (IA)
Sequoia Inst (CA)
Southeast Comm Coll, Milford Campus (NE)
Southeast Tech Inst (SD)
Southern Maine Tech Coll (ME)
South Plains Coll (TX)
South Texas Comm Coll (TX)
Spartanburg Tech Coll (SC)
Spokane Comm Coll (WA)
Springfield Tech Comm Coll (MA)
State U of NY Coll of Technology at Alfred (NY)
State U of NY Coll of Technology at Canton (NY)
State U of NY Coll of Technology at Delhi (NY)
Surry Comm Coll (NC)
Tarrant County Coll District (TX)
Terra State Comm Coll (OH)
Texarkana Coll (TX)
Texas State Tech Coll–Harlingen (TX)
Texas State Tech Coll– Waco/ Marshall Campus (TX)
Thaddeus Stevens Coll of Technology (PA)
Trenholm State Tech Coll, Patterson Campus (AL)
Triangle Tech, Inc. (PA)
Triangle Tech, Inc.–Greensburg Center (PA)
Tri-County Tech Coll (SC)
Trinity Valley Comm Coll (TX)
Triton Coll (IL)
Truckee Meadows Comm Coll (NV)
Tulsa Comm Coll (OK)
Tyler Jr Coll (TX)
U of Alaska Anchorage, Matanuska-Susitna Coll (AK)
U of Arkansas Comm Coll at Morrilton (AR)
U of Northwestern Ohio (OH)
Vance-Granville Comm Coll (NC)
Wallace State Comm Coll (AL)
Walla Walla Comm Coll (WA)
Waubonsee Comm Coll (IL)
Western Iowa Tech Comm Coll (IA)
Western Nevada Comm Coll (NV)
Western Wisconsin Tech Coll (WI)
Westmoreland County Comm Coll (PA)
West Virginia Northern Comm Coll (WV)
Westwood Coll of Technology–Denver North (CO)
York Tech Coll (SC)

HEATING/AIR CONDITIONING/ REFRIGERATION TECHNOLOGY
Alamance Comm Coll (NC)
Bevill State Comm Coll (AL)
Cambria County Area Comm Coll (PA)
Cincinnati State Tech and Comm Coll (OH)
Delta Coll (MI)
Dunwoody Coll of Technology (MN)
Front Range Comm Coll (CO)
Gadsden State Comm Coll (AL)
GateWay Comm Coll (AZ)
Gateway Tech Coll (WI)
Johnson County Comm Coll (KS)
Kalamazoo Valley Comm Coll (MI)
Lamar State Coll–Port Arthur (TX)
Martin Comm Coll (NC)
Mercer County Comm Coll (NJ)
Mott Comm Coll (MI)
North Dakota State Coll of Science (ND)
Northwest Mississippi Comm Coll (MS)
Oakland Comm Coll (MI)
Oakton Comm Coll (IL)
Pennsylvania Coll of Technology (PA)
St. Cloud Tech Coll (MN)
San Jacinto Coll North Campus (TX)
South Piedmont Comm Coll (NC)
Springfield Tech Comm Coll (MA)
State U of NY Coll of Technology at Delhi (NY)
TCI-The Coll for Technology (NY)
Terra State Comm Coll (OH)
Texas State Tech Coll– Waco/ Marshall Campus (TX)
Vatterott Coll (MO)
Wisconsin Indianhead Tech Coll (WI)

HEAVY EQUIPMENT MAINTENANCE
Allan Hancock Coll (CA)
Amarillo Coll (TX)
Centralia Coll (WA)
Clover Park Tech Coll (WA)
Coll of Lake County (IL)
Comm Coll of Southern Nevada (NV)
Delaware Tech & Comm Coll, Jack F Owens Cmps (DE)
Del Mar Coll (TX)
Des Moines Area Comm Coll (IA)
Eastern Maine Tech Coll (ME)
Guilford Tech Comm Coll (NC)
Hawkeye Comm Coll (IA)
Illinois Eastern Comm Colls, Olney Central Coll (IL)
Indian Hills Comm Coll (IA)
Ivy Tech State Coll–North Central (IN)
Kaskaskia Coll (IL)
Lane Comm Coll (OR)
Lansing Comm Coll (MI)
Lenoir Comm Coll (NC)
Long Beach City Coll (CA)
Longview Comm Coll (MO)
Lower Columbia Coll (WA)
Marshalltown Comm Coll (IA)
Metropolitan Comm Coll (NE)
Northern Maine Tech Coll (ME)
North Idaho Coll (ID)
Oklahoma State U, Okmulgee (OK)
Pennsylvania Coll of Technology (PA)
Red Rocks Comm Coll (CO)
Rend Lake Coll (IL)
Rogue Comm Coll (OR)
San Jacinto Coll Central Campus (TX)
Sheridan Coll (WY)
Skagit Valley Coll (WA)
South Texas Comm Coll (TX)
Southwest Georgia Tech Coll (GA)
Southwest Tennessee Comm Coll (TN)
Spokane Comm Coll (WA)
Spokane Falls Comm Coll (WA)
State U of NY Coll of Technology at Alfred (NY)
Texas State Tech Coll– Waco/ Marshall Campus (TX)
Trenholm State Tech Coll, Patterson Campus (AL)
Trinidad State Jr Coll (CO)
Vincennes U (IN)
Wake Tech Comm Coll (NC)
Waycross Coll (GA)
West Central Tech Coll (GA)

HEMATOLOGY TECHNOLOGY
Comm Coll of the Air Force (AL)

HISPANIC-AMERICAN STUDIES
San Diego City Coll (CA)

HISTORY
Abraham Baldwin Ag Coll (GA)
Adirondack Comm Coll (NY)
Allen County Comm Coll (KS)
Amarillo Coll (TX)
Andrew Coll (GA)
Angelina Coll (TX)
Atlanta Metropolitan Coll (GA)
Atlantic Cape Comm Coll (NJ)
Austin Comm Coll (TX)
Bacone Coll (OK)
Bainbridge Coll (GA)
Bakersfield Coll (CA)
Barton County Comm Coll (KS)
Bergen Comm Coll (NJ)
Blinn Coll (TX)
Brazosport Coll (TX)
Bronx Comm Coll of City U of NY (NY)
Burlington County Coll (NJ)
Cañada Coll (CA)
Cape Cod Comm Coll (MA)
Casper Coll (WY)
Centralia Coll (WA)
Cerritos Coll (CA)
Cerro Coso Comm Coll (CA)
Chabot Coll (CA)
Chaffey Coll (CA)
Cisco Jr Coll (TX)
Coastal Bend Coll (TX)
Coastal Georgia Comm Coll (GA)
Cochise Coll, Douglas (AZ)
Coffeyville Comm Coll (KS)
Colby Comm Coll (KS)
Coll of Alameda (CA)
Coll of Marin (CA)
Coll of Southern Idaho (ID)
Coll of the Canyons (CA)
Coll of the Desert (CA)
Coll of the Sequoias (CA)
Coll of the Siskiyous (CA)
Columbia State Comm Coll (TN)
Comm Coll of Southern Nevada (NV)
Compton Comm Coll (CA)
Crafton Hills Coll (CA)
Cuyamaca Coll (CA)
Cypress Coll (CA)
Danville Area Comm Coll (IL)
Darton Coll (GA)
Daytona Beach Comm Coll (FL)
De Anza Coll (CA)
Del Mar Coll (TX)
Dixie State Coll of Utah (UT)
Dodge City Comm Coll (KS)
Donnelly Coll (KS)
East Central Coll (MO)
East Central Comm Coll (MS)
Eastern Arizona Coll (AZ)
Eastern Oklahoma State Coll (OK)
Eastern Wyoming Coll (WY)
East Georgia Coll (GA)
East Mississippi Comm Coll (MS)
Ellsworth Comm Coll (IA)
Everett Comm Coll (WA)
Feather River Comm Coll District (CA)
Floyd Coll (GA)
Foothill Coll (CA)
Fullerton Coll (CA)
Fulton-Montgomery Comm Coll (NY)
Galveston Coll (TX)
Gavilan Coll (CA)
Georgia Perimeter Coll (GA)
Gloucester County Coll (NJ)
Gordon Coll (GA)
Great Basin Coll (NV)
Harford Comm Coll (MD)
Highland Comm Coll (IL)
Highland Comm Coll (KS)
Hill Coll of the Hill Jr College District (TX)
Independence Comm Coll (KS)
Indian River Comm Coll (FL)
Iowa Lakes Comm Coll (IA)
Jefferson Coll (MO)
Jefferson Comm Coll (KY)
Jefferson Davis Comm Coll (AL)
John A. Logan Coll (IL)
Joliet Jr Coll (IL)
Kellogg Comm Coll (MI)
Kirkwood Comm Coll (IA)
Labette Comm Coll (KS)
Lake Michigan Coll (MI)
Lamar Comm Coll (CO)
Lincoln Coll, Lincoln (IL)
Lincoln Land Comm Coll (IL)
Lon Morris Coll (TX)
Lorain County Comm Coll (OH)
Los Angeles City Coll (CA)
Los Angeles Mission Coll (CA)
Louisburg Coll (NC)
Lower Columbia Coll (WA)
Manatee Comm Coll (FL)
Mesa Tech Coll (NM)
Miami-Dade Comm Coll (FL)
Miami U–Middletown Campus (OH)
Middlesex County Coll (NJ)
Midland Coll (TX)
Minot State U–Bottineau Campus (ND)
MiraCosta Coll (CA)
Mississippi Delta Comm Coll (MS)
Mohave Comm Coll (AZ)
Monroe Comm Coll (NY)
Monterey Peninsula Coll (CA)
Naugatuck Valley Comm Coll (CT)
New Mexico Military Inst (NM)
Northern Essex Comm Coll (MA)
North Idaho Coll (ID)

Northwest Coll (WY)
Odessa Coll (TX)
Oklahoma City Comm Coll (OK)
Orange Coast Coll (CA)
Otero Jr Coll (CO)
Oxnard Coll (CA)
Palm Beach Comm Coll (FL)
Palo Verde Coll (CA)
Pasadena City Coll (CA)
Pensacola Jr Coll (FL)
Pratt Comm Coll and Area Vocational School (KS)
Red Rocks Comm Coll (CO)
Ridgewater Coll (MN)
Riverside Comm Coll (CA)
St. Catharine Coll (KY)
St. Philip's Coll (TX)
Salem Comm Coll (NJ)
San Bernardino Valley Coll (CA)
San Jacinto Coll Central Campus (TX)
San Jacinto Coll North Campus (TX)
San Jacinto Coll South Campus (TX)
San Joaquin Delta Coll (CA)
San Juan Coll (NM)
Santa Ana Coll (CA)
Santa Barbara City Coll (CA)
Santa Monica Coll (CA)
Sauk Valley Comm Coll (IL)
Sheridan Coll (WY)
Skagit Valley Coll (WA)
Snow Coll (UT)
South Mountain Comm Coll (AZ)
Southwestern Coll (CA)
Southwest Mississippi Comm Coll (MS)
Tacoma Comm Coll (WA)
Trinity Valley Comm Coll (TX)
Triton Coll (IL)
Tulsa Comm Coll (OK)
Umpqua Comm Coll (OR)
Vermilion Comm Coll (MN)
Vincennes U (IN)
Waycross Coll (GA)
Western Nebraska Comm Coll (NE)
Western Wyoming Comm Coll (WY)
Young Harris Coll (GA)

HOME ECONOMICS
Abraham Baldwin Ag Coll (GA)
Allen County Comm Coll (KS)
Bacone Coll (OK)
Bainbridge Coll (GA)
Barton County Comm Coll (KS)
Brazosport Coll (TX)
Butte Coll (CA)
Central Comm Coll–Columbus Campus (NE)
Cerritos Coll (CA)
Chaffey Coll (CA)
Coffeyville Comm Coll (KS)
Colby Comm Coll (KS)
Coll of the Sequoias (CA)
Coll of the Siskiyous (CA)
Compton Comm Coll (CA)
Connors State Coll (OK)
Copiah-Lincoln Comm Coll–Natchez Campus (MS)
Delta Coll (MI)
East Central Coll (MO)
Fresno City Coll (CA)
Fullerton Coll (CA)
Garden City Comm Coll (KS)
Highland Comm Coll (KS)
Hill Coll of the Hill Jr College District (TX)
Hinds Comm Coll (MS)
Holyoke Comm Coll (MA)
Houston Comm Coll System (TX)
Hutchinson Comm Coll and Area Vocational School (KS)
Indian River Comm Coll (FL)
Jefferson Comm Coll (KY)
Jones County Jr Coll (MS)
Lamar State Coll–Port Arthur (TX)
Linn-Benton Comm Coll (OR)
Long Beach City Coll (CA)
Los Angeles City Coll (CA)
Merced Coll (CA)
Minot State U–Bottineau Campus (ND)
Mississippi Delta Comm Coll (MS)
Orange Coast Coll (CA)
Oxnard Coll (CA)
Palm Beach Comm Coll (FL)
Penn Valley Comm Coll (MO)
Phoenix Coll (AZ)
Portland Comm Coll (OR)
Pratt Comm Coll and Area Vocational School (KS)
Riverside Comm Coll (CA)
San Jacinto Coll Central Campus (TX)
San Joaquin Delta Coll (CA)
Santa Monica Coll (CA)
Shasta Coll (CA)
Sierra Coll (CA)
Snow Coll (UT)
South Mountain Comm Coll (AZ)
Ventura Coll (CA)
Vermilion Comm Coll (MN)
Vincennes U (IN)

HOME ECONOMICS COMMUNICATIONS
Vincennes U (IN)

HOME ECONOMICS EDUCATION
American River Coll (CA)
Coll of the Sequoias (CA)
East Georgia Coll (GA)
Jefferson Comm Coll (KY)
Jones County Jr Coll (MS)
Los Angeles Mission Coll (CA)
Manatee Comm Coll (FL)
Northwest Mississippi Comm Coll (MS)
Okaloosa-Walton Comm Coll (FL)

HOME FURNISHINGS
Jefferson State Comm Coll (AL)
St. Philip's Coll (TX)

HOME HEALTH AIDE
Allen County Comm Coll (KS)
Laurel Business Inst (PA)
Mt. San Jacinto Coll (CA)

HOME PRODUCTS MARKETING OPERATIONS
Modesto Jr Coll (CA)

HORTICULTURE SCIENCE
Abraham Baldwin Ag Coll (GA)
American River Coll (CA)
Anne Arundel Comm Coll (MD)
Bacone Coll (OK)
Bakersfield Coll (CA)
Blue Ridge Comm Coll (NC)
Butte Coll (CA)
Central Lakes Coll (MN)
Central Piedmont Comm Coll (NC)
Chabot Coll (CA)
City Coll of San Francisco (CA)
City Colls of Chicago, Richard J Daley Coll (IL)
Coffeyville Comm Coll (KS)
Coll of the Desert (CA)
Coll of the Sequoias (CA)
Comm Coll of Southern Nevada (NV)
Cumberland County Coll (NJ)
Danville Area Comm Coll (IL)
Des Moines Area Comm Coll (IA)
East Central Coll (MO)
Eastern Oklahoma State Coll (OK)
Edison Comm Coll (FL)
Fayetteville Tech Comm Coll (NC)
Floyd Coll (GA)
Forsyth Tech Comm Coll (NC)
Fullerton Coll (CA)
Gwinnett Tech Coll (GA)
Hawkeye Comm Coll (IA)
Haywood Comm Coll (NC)
Hill Coll of the Hill Jr College District (TX)
Houston Comm Coll System (TX)
Indian Hills Comm Coll (IA)
Jefferson Comm Coll (KY)
Joliet Jr Coll (IL)
Jones County Jr Coll (MS)
Kent State U, Salem Campus (OH)
Kirkwood Comm Coll (IA)
Lake Washington Tech Coll (WA)
Lansing Comm Coll (MI)
Las Positas Coll (CA)
Lenoir Comm Coll (NC)
Linn-Benton Comm Coll (OR)
Long Beach City Coll (CA)
Los Angeles Pierce Coll (CA)
Luzerne County Comm Coll (PA)
Mayland Comm Coll (NC)
Meridian Comm Coll (MS)
Miami-Dade Comm Coll (FL)
Minot State U–Bottineau Campus (ND)
MiraCosta Coll (CA)
Mississippi Delta Comm Coll (MS)
Mississippi Gulf Coast Comm Coll (MS)
Mt. Hood Comm Coll (OR)
Naugatuck Valley Comm Coll (CT)
Northeast Comm Coll (NE)
Northern Virginia Comm Coll (VA)
Oklahoma State U, Oklahoma City (OK)
Orange Coast Coll (CA)
Pensacola Jr Coll (FL)
Reedley Coll (CA)
Rockingham Comm Coll (NC)
St. Catharine Coll (KY)
St. Clair County Comm Coll (MI)
Sampson Comm Coll (NC)
San Jacinto Coll Central Campus (TX)
Shasta Coll (CA)
Sierra Coll (CA)
Southeast Tech Inst (SD)
Southern Maine Tech Coll (ME)
South Puget Sound Comm Coll (WA)
Spartanburg Tech Coll (SC)
State Fair Comm Coll (MO)
State U of NY Coll of A&T at Morrisville (NY)
State U of NY Coll of Technology at Alfred (NY)
State U of NY Coll of Technology at Delhi (NY)
Suffolk County Comm Coll (NY)
Surry Comm Coll (NC)
Tarrant County Coll District (TX)
Trident Tech Coll (SC)
Trinity Valley Comm Coll (TX)
Tulsa Comm Coll (OK)
Tyler Jr Coll (TX)
U of Arkansas Comm Coll at Morrilton (AR)
Ventura Coll (CA)
Vermont Tech Coll (VT)
Victor Valley Coll (CA)
Vincennes U (IN)
Wallace State Comm Coll (AL)
Western Piedmont Comm Coll (NC)
Westmoreland County Comm Coll (PA)

HORTICULTURE SERVICES
Alamance Comm Coll (NC)
Anoka-Hennepin Tech Coll (MN)
Black Hawk Coll, Moline (IL)
Central Comm Coll–Hastings Campus (NE)
Clark Coll (WA)
Comm Coll of Allegheny County (PA)
Delgado Comm Coll (LA)
Fayetteville Tech Comm Coll (NC)
Front Range Comm Coll (CO)
Gateway Tech Coll (WI)
Glendale Comm Coll (AZ)
John Wood Comm Coll (IL)
Kent State U, Geauga Campus (OH)
Kishwaukee Coll (IL)
Lord Fairfax Comm Coll (VA)
McHenry County Coll (IL)
Mineral Area Coll (MO)
Minot State U–Bottineau Campus (ND)
Mississippi County Comm Coll (AR)
Montgomery Coll (MD)
North Shore Comm Coll (MA)
Rend Lake Coll (IL)
Santa Barbara City Coll (CA)
Skagit Valley Coll (WA)
Spokane Comm Coll (WA)
Tulsa Comm Coll (OK)
West Virginia Northern Comm Coll (WV)
Wilkes Comm Coll (NC)

HORTICULTURE SERVICES RELATED
Central Florida Comm Coll (FL)
Southwest Tennessee Comm Coll (TN)

HOSPITALITY MANAGEMENT
Abraham Baldwin Ag Coll (GA)
Adirondack Comm Coll (NY)
Albuquerque Tech Vocational Inst (NM)
Arizona Western Coll (AZ)
Atlantic Cape Comm Coll (NJ)
Baltimore City Comm Coll (MD)
Baltimore International Coll (MD)
Bay State Coll (MA)
Berkshire Comm Coll (MA)
Bucks County Comm Coll (PA)
Butler County Comm Coll (PA)
Cambria County Area Comm Coll (PA)
Central Comm Coll–Hastings Campus (NE)
Central Maine Tech Coll (ME)
Central Oregon Comm Coll (OR)
Central Piedmont Comm Coll (NC)
Chemeketa Comm Coll (OR)
Chippewa Valley Tech Coll (WI)
Coll of DuPage (IL)
Collin County Comm Coll District (TX)
Colorado Mountn Coll, Alpine Cmps (CO)
Comm Coll of Southern Nevada (NV)
Daytona Beach Comm Coll (FL)
Delaware Tech & Comm Coll, Jack F Owens Cmps (DE)
Delgado Comm Coll (LA)
Des Moines Area Comm Coll (IA)
Doña Ana Branch Comm Coll (NM)
East Central Coll (MO)
Edison Comm Coll (FL)
Education Direct (PA)
El Centro Coll (TX)
Fisher Coll (MA)
Florida Comm Coll at Jacksonville (FL)
Florida National Coll (FL)
Greenville Tech Coll (SC)
Guam Comm Coll (GU)
Gulf Coast Comm Coll (FL)
Harford Comm Coll (MD)
Henry Ford Comm Coll (MI)
Hillsborough Comm Coll (FL)
Holyoke Comm Coll (MA)
International Business Coll, Fort Wayne (IN)
International Coll of Hospitality Management, *César Ritz* (CT)
James H. Faulkner State Comm Coll (AL)
Jefferson Comm Coll (NY)
Jefferson State Comm Coll (AL)
Johnson County Comm Coll (KS)
J. Sargeant Reynolds Comm Coll (VA)
Kauai Comm Coll (HI)
Lakeland Comm Coll (OH)
Lake Michigan Coll (MI)
Lake-Sumter Comm Coll (FL)
Lamar State Coll–Port Arthur (TX)
Lane Comm Coll (OR)
Lansing Comm Coll (MI)
Lexington Coll (IL)
Marian Court Coll (MA)
Massachusetts Bay Comm Coll (MA)
Massasoit Comm Coll (MA)
Middlesex County Coll (NJ)
Mid Michigan Comm Coll (MI)
Mid-State Coll (ME)
Mohawk Valley Comm Coll (NY)
Monroe Coll, Bronx (NY)
Monroe Coll, New Rochelle (NY)
Monterey Peninsula Coll (CA)
Mt. Hood Comm Coll (OR)
National Coll of Business & Technology, Salem (VA)
Naugatuck Valley Comm Coll (CT)
New York City Tech Coll of the City U of NY (NY)
North Idaho Coll (ID)
North Shore Comm Coll (MA)
Northwestern Business Coll (IL)
Oklahoma State U, Okmulgee (OK)
Paul Smith's Coll of Arts and Sciences (NY)
Pellissippi State Tech Comm Coll (TN)
Pima Comm Coll (AZ)
Quincy Coll (MA)
Rasmussen Coll Mankato (MN)
Reedley Coll (CA)
Rockland Comm Coll (NY)
St. Petersburg Coll (FL)
St. Philip's Coll (TX)
San Diego City Coll (CA)
Scottsdale Comm Coll (AZ)
Seattle Central Comm Coll (WA)
Sheridan Coll (WY)
Southern Maine Tech Coll (ME)
South Texas Comm Coll (TX)
State U of NY Coll of A&T at Morrisville (NY)
Sullivan County Comm Coll (NY)
Three Rivers Comm Coll (CT)
Triton Coll (IL)
Truckee Meadows Comm Coll (NV)
United Tribes Tech Coll (ND)
Westmoreland County Comm Coll (PA)
West Virginia Northern Comm Coll (WV)
Yorktowne Business Inst (PA)
Young Harris Coll (GA)

HOSPITALITY/RECREATION MARKETING
Middlesex Comm Coll (MA)

HOSPITALITY/RECREATION MARKETING OPERATIONS
Central Oregon Comm Coll (OR)
Cumberland County Coll (NJ)
Florida Comm Coll at Jacksonville (FL)
Guam Comm Coll (GU)
Mid Michigan Comm Coll (MI)
Milwaukee Area Tech Coll (WI)
Montgomery County Comm Coll (PA)
San Diego Mesa Coll (CA)
Vincennes U (IN)

HOSPITALITY SERVICES MANAGEMENT RELATED
Fayetteville Tech Comm Coll (NC)
Hiwassee Coll (TN)
Mineral Area Coll (MO)
Southwest Georgia Tech Coll (GA)

HOTEL AND RESTAURANT MANAGEMENT
Alexandria Tech Coll (MN)
Allegany Coll of Maryland (MD)
American River Coll (CA)
Anne Arundel Comm Coll (MD)
The Art Inst of New York City (NY)
Asheville-Buncombe Tech Comm Coll (NC)
Austin Comm Coll (TX)
Bakersfield Coll (CA)
Baltimore International Coll (MD)
Bay State Coll (MA)
Bergen Comm Coll (NJ)
Berkshire Comm Coll (MA)
Bismarck State Coll (ND)
Black Hawk Coll, Moline (IL)
Brevard Comm Coll (FL)
Briarwood Coll (CT)
Broome Comm Coll (NY)
Bryant & Stratton Business Inst, Lackawanna (NY)
Bryant & Stratton Business Inst, Rochester (NY)
Bryant and Stratton Coll, Virginia Beach (VA)
Bucks County Comm Coll (PA)
Bunker Hill Comm Coll (MA)
Burlington County Coll (NJ)
Cape Cod Comm Coll (MA)
Cape Fear Comm Coll (NC)
Central Arizona Coll (AZ)
Central Comm Coll–Hastings Campus (NE)
Central Oregon Comm Coll (OR)
Central Pennsylvania Coll (PA)
Central Piedmont Comm Coll (NC)
Central Texas Coll (TX)
Chaffey Coll (CA)
Chattanooga State Tech Comm Coll (TN)
Chemeketa Comm Coll (OR)
Cincinnati State Tech and Comm Coll (OH)
City Coll of San Francisco (CA)
Coll of DuPage (IL)
Coll of Southern Idaho (ID)
Coll of the Canyons (CA)
Colorado Mountn Coll, Alpine Cmps (CO)

Columbus State Comm Coll (OH)
Comm Coll of Allegheny County (PA)
Comm Coll of Southern Nevada (NV)
Comm Coll of the Air Force (AL)
Copiah-Lincoln Comm Coll–Natchez Campus (MS)
County Coll of Morris (NJ)
Cowley County Comm Coll and Voc-Tech School (KS)
Culinary Arts Inst of Louisiana (LA)
Cypress Coll (CA)
Daytona Beach Comm Coll (FL)
Delaware County Comm Coll (PA)
Delaware Tech & Comm Coll, Jack F Owens Cmps (DE)
Delaware Tech & Comm Coll, Stanton/ Wilmington Cmps (DE)
Del Mar Coll (TX)
Des Moines Area Comm Coll (IA)
East Central Coll (MO)
East Mississippi Comm Coll (MS)
El Centro Coll (TX)
Erie Comm Coll, City Campus (NY)
Essex County Coll (NJ)
Finger Lakes Comm Coll (NY)
Flathead Valley Comm Coll (MT)
Florida Comm Coll at Jacksonville (FL)
Florida National Coll (FL)
Floyd Coll (GA)
Galveston Coll (TX)
Gateway Comm Coll (CT)
Genesee Comm Coll (NY)
Georgia Perimeter Coll (GA)
Glendale Comm Coll (CA)
Guam Comm Coll (GU)
Gwinnett Tech Coll (GA)
Harrisburg Area Comm Coll (PA)
Hawaii Comm Coll (HI)
Henry Ford Comm Coll (MI)
Hesser Coll (NH)
Highline Comm Coll (WA)
Hillsborough Comm Coll (FL)
Hinds Comm Coll (MS)
Holyoke Comm Coll (MA)
Horry-Georgetown Tech Coll (SC)
Houston Comm Coll System (TX)
Indian River Comm Coll (FL)
Instituto Comercial de Puerto Rico Jr Coll (PR)
Iowa Lakes Comm Coll (IA)
Iowa Western Comm Coll (IA)
Jefferson Coll (MO)
Jefferson Comm Coll (NY)
Johnson County Comm Coll (KS)
John Wood Comm Coll (IL)
Joliet Jr Coll (IL)
J. Sargeant Reynolds Comm Coll (VA)
Keystone Coll (PA)
Kirkwood Comm Coll (IA)
Lake Tahoe Comm Coll (CA)
Lake Washington Tech Coll (WA)
Lane Comm Coll (OR)
Lansing Comm Coll (MI)
Laramie County Comm Coll (WY)
Laredo Comm Coll (TX)
Lehigh Carbon Comm Coll (PA)
Lewis and Clark Comm Coll (IL)
Lexington Coll (IL)
Long Beach City Coll (CA)
Luzerne County Comm Coll (PA)
Manchester Comm Coll (CT)
Massasoit Comm Coll (MA)
Mercer County Comm Coll (NJ)
Meridian Comm Coll (MS)
Miami-Dade Comm Coll (FL)
Middlesex Comm Coll (MA)
Middlesex County Coll (NJ)
Mid-State Tech Coll (WI)
Milwaukee Area Tech Coll (WI)
MiraCosta Coll (CA)
Mississippi Gulf Coast Comm Coll (MS)
Mohawk Valley Comm Coll (NY)
Monroe Comm Coll (NY)
Monterey Peninsula Coll (CA)
Montgomery Coll (MD)
Montgomery County Comm Coll (PA)
Moraine Park Tech Coll (WI)
Nassau Comm Coll (NY)
National Coll of Business & Technology, Salem (VA)
Naugatuck Valley Comm Coll (CT)
Newbury Coll (MA)
New Hampshire Tech Inst (NH)
Northampton County Area Comm Coll (PA)
Northern Essex Comm Coll (MA)
Northern Virginia Comm Coll (VA)
Northwest Mississippi Comm Coll (MS)
Norwalk Comm Coll (CT)
Oakland Comm Coll (MI)
Oakton Comm Coll (IL)
Okaloosa-Walton Comm Coll (FL)
Onondaga Comm Coll (NY)
Orange Coast Coll (CA)
Oxnard Coll (CA)
Palau Comm CollPalau)
Palm Beach Comm Coll (FL)
Paul Smith's Coll of Arts and Sciences (NY)
Pellissippi State Tech Comm Coll (TN)
Pennsylvania Inst of Culinary Arts (PA)
Penn State U Beaver Campus of the Commonwealth Coll (PA)
Penn Valley Comm Coll (MO)
Pensacola Jr Coll (FL)
Pima Comm Coll (AZ)
Pittsburgh Tech Inst (PA)
Quincy Coll (MA)
Quinsigamond Comm Coll (MA)
Raritan Valley Comm Coll (NJ)
Rasmussen Coll Eagan (MN)
Rasmussen Coll Mankato (MN)
The Restaurant School (PA)
St. Philip's Coll (TX)
San Bernardino Valley Coll (CA)
Sandhills Comm Coll (NC)
San Diego Mesa Coll (CA)
San Jacinto Coll Central Campus (TX)
Santa Barbara City Coll (CA)
Santa Fe Comm Coll (NM)
Schenectady County Comm Coll (NY)
Schiller International USwitzerland)
Scottsdale Comm Coll (AZ)
Seattle Central Comm Coll (WA)
Sinclair Comm Coll (OH)
Skagit Valley Coll (WA)
South Coll (TN)
Southern Maine Tech Coll (ME)
South Texas Comm Coll (TX)
Spokane Comm Coll (WA)
State U of NY Coll of A&T at Morrisville (NY)
State U of NY Coll of Technology at Delhi (NY)
Stratford U (VA)
Three Rivers Comm Coll (CT)
Tompkins Cortland Comm Coll (NY)
Trident Tech Coll (SC)
Triton Coll (IL)
Trocaire Coll (NY)
Tulsa Comm Coll (OK)
Union County Coll (NJ)
United Tribes Tech Coll (ND)
Vincennes U (IN)
Wake Tech Comm Coll (NC)
Westchester Comm Coll (NY)
Westmoreland County Comm Coll (PA)
Westwood Coll of Technology–Denver North (CO)
Wilkes Comm Coll (NC)
Wor-Wic Comm Coll (MD)

HOTEL/MOTEL SERVICES MARKETING OPERATIONS

AIB Coll of Business (IA)
Edmonds Comm Coll (WA)
Flathead Valley Comm Coll (MT)
Guam Comm Coll (GU)
Iowa Western Comm Coll (IA)
Luzerne County Comm Coll (PA)
Milwaukee Area Tech Coll (WI)
Montgomery County Comm Coll (PA)
Pittsburgh Tech Inst (PA)
Rasmussen Coll Mankato (MN)
San Diego Mesa Coll (CA)
State U of NY Coll of Technology at Delhi (NY)
Vincennes U (IN)

HUMAN ECOLOGY

Greenfield Comm Coll (MA)
Monroe Comm Coll (NY)
Vermilion Comm Coll (MN)

HUMANITIES

Abraham Baldwin Ag Coll (GA)
Adirondack Comm Coll (NY)
Allen County Comm Coll (KS)
Ancilla Coll (IN)
Andrew Coll (GA)
Angelina Coll (TX)
Anne Arundel Comm Coll (MD)
Atlantic Cape Comm Coll (NJ)
Bacone Coll (OK)
Barstow Coll (CA)
Barton County Comm Coll (KS)
Bowling Green State U-Firelands Coll (OH)
Brookdale Comm Coll (NJ)
Bucks County Comm Coll (PA)
Butler County Comm Coll (PA)
Cañada Coll (CA)
Casper Coll (WY)
Cayuga County Comm Coll (NY)
Centralia Coll (WA)
Central Oregon Comm Coll (OR)
Cerro Coso Comm Coll (CA)
Chabot Coll (CA)
Chaffey Coll (CA)
Chemeketa Comm Coll (OR)
Chesapeake Coll (MD)
City Colls of Chicago, Richard J Daley Coll (IL)
Clinton Comm Coll (NY)
Coffeyville Comm Coll (KS)
Colby Comm Coll (KS)
Coll of Alameda (CA)
Coll of Marin (CA)
Coll of the Canyons (CA)
Coll of the Sequoias (CA)
Colorado Mountn Coll, Alpine Cmps (CO)
Colorado Mountn Coll (CO)
Colorado Mountn Coll, Timberline Cmps (CO)
Columbia-Greene Comm Coll (NY)
Comm Coll of Allegheny County (PA)
Corning Comm Coll (NY)
Crafton Hills Coll (CA)
Danville Area Comm Coll (IL)
Daytona Beach Comm Coll (FL)
Dean Coll (MA)
De Anza Coll (CA)
Dixie State Coll of Utah (UT)
Dodge City Comm Coll (KS)
Dutchess Comm Coll (NY)
East Central Coll (MO)
Erie Comm Coll, City Campus (NY)
Erie Comm Coll, North Campus (NY)
Erie Comm Coll, South Campus (NY)
Finger Lakes Comm Coll (NY)
Fisher Coll (MA)
Foothill Coll (CA)
Fresno City Coll (CA)
Fulton-Montgomery Comm Coll (NY)
Galveston Coll (TX)
Garden City Comm Coll (KS)
Glendale Comm Coll (CA)
Gogebic Comm Coll (MI)
Golden West Coll (CA)
Greenfield Comm Coll (MA)
Harford Comm Coll (MD)
Herkimer County Comm Coll (NY)
Highline Comm Coll (WA)
Hill Coll of the Hill Jr College District (TX)
Hinds Comm Coll (MS)
Housatonic Comm Coll (CT)
Imperial Valley Coll (CA)
Independence Comm Coll (KS)
Indian River Comm Coll (FL)
Iowa Lakes Comm Coll (IA)
Jamestown Comm Coll (NY)
Jefferson Comm Coll (NY)
John A. Logan Coll (IL)
Kirkwood Comm Coll (IA)
Lake Tahoe Comm Coll (CA)
Lamar Comm Coll (CO)
Lehigh Carbon Comm Coll (PA)
Lincoln Coll, Lincoln (IL)
Lincoln Coll, Normal (IL)
Lincoln Land Comm Coll (IL)
Lon Morris Coll (TX)
Los Angeles Mission Coll (CA)
Luzerne County Comm Coll (PA)
Manatee Comm Coll (FL)
Merced Coll (CA)
Mercer County Comm Coll (NJ)
Miami-Dade Comm Coll (FL)
MiraCosta Coll (CA)
Modesto Jr Coll (CA)
Mohawk Valley Comm Coll (NY)
Montgomery County Comm Coll (PA)
Mt. San Jacinto Coll (CA)
Newbury Coll (MA)
New Mexico Military Inst (NM)
Niagara County Comm Coll (NY)
North Seattle Comm Coll (WA)
Northwest Coll (WY)
Okaloosa-Walton Comm Coll (FL)
Oklahoma City Comm Coll (OK)
Onondaga Comm Coll (NY)
Orange Coast Coll (CA)
Orange County Comm Coll (NY)
Otero Jr Coll (CO)
Pratt Comm Coll and Area Vocational School (KS)
Quincy Coll (MA)
Reading Area Comm Coll (PA)
Red Rocks Comm Coll (CO)
Ridgewater Coll (MN)
Riverside Comm Coll (CA)
Rogue Comm Coll (OR)
Sacramento City Coll (CA)
St. Catharine Coll (KY)
Salem Comm Coll (NJ)
San Joaquin Delta Coll (CA)
Schenectady County Comm Coll (NY)
Sheridan Coll (WY)
Skagit Valley Coll (WA)
Snow Coll (UT)
Southwest Mississippi Comm Coll (MS)
State U of NY Coll of A&T at Morrisville (NY)
State U of NY Coll of Technology at Alfred (NY)
State U of NY Coll of Technology at Canton (NY)
State U of NY Coll of Technology at Delhi (NY)
Suffolk County Comm Coll (NY)
Tacoma Comm Coll (WA)
Tompkins Cortland Comm Coll (NY)
Tulsa Comm Coll (OK)
Ulster County Comm Coll (NY)
Umpqua Comm Coll (OR)
Victor Valley Coll (CA)
Westchester Comm Coll (NY)
Western Wyoming Comm Coll (WY)

HUMAN RESOURCES MANAGEMENT

Beaufort County Comm Coll (NC)
Brevard Comm Coll (FL)
Central Georgia Tech Coll (GA)
Columbus State Comm Coll (OH)
Comm Coll of Allegheny County (PA)
Comm Coll of the Air Force (AL)
Cumberland County Coll (NJ)
Edison State Comm Coll (OH)
Edmonds Comm Coll (WA)
Herkimer County Comm Coll (NY)
Houston Comm Coll System (TX)
Keystone Coll (PA)
Lansing Comm Coll (MI)
Marian Court Coll (MA)
Mesa Tech Coll (NM)
Moraine Valley Comm Coll (IL)
Muskingum Area Tech Coll (OH)
New Hampshire Tech Inst (NH)
Okaloosa-Walton Comm Coll (FL)
Prairie State Coll (IL)
Reading Area Comm Coll (PA)
Rockingham Comm Coll (NC)
St. Paul Tech Coll (MN)
Salem Comm Coll (NJ)
Tulsa Comm Coll (OK)
Tyler Jr Coll (TX)
Umpqua Comm Coll (OR)
Virginia Coll at Jackson (MS)
Wake Tech Comm Coll (NC)
Western Wisconsin Tech Coll (WI)

HUMAN RESOURCES MANAGEMENT RELATED

Fayetteville Tech Comm Coll (NC)

HUMAN SERVICES

Allan Hancock Coll (CA)
Allegany Coll of Maryland (MD)
American River Coll (CA)
Angelina Coll (TX)
Angelina Coll (TX)
Anne Arundel Comm Coll (MD)
Arizona Western Coll (AZ)
Asnuntuck Comm Coll (CT)
Atlanta Metropolitan Coll (GA)
Austin Comm Coll (TX)
Bakersfield Coll (CA)
Baltimore City Comm Coll (MD)
Bay de Noc Comm Coll (MI)
Berkshire Comm Coll (MA)
Blackfeet Comm Coll (MT)
Borough of Manhattan Comm Coll of City U of NY (NY)
Bowling Green State U-Firelands Coll (OH)
Bristol Comm Coll (MA)
Bristol Comm Coll (MA)
Bronx Comm Coll of City U of NY (NY)
Brookdale Comm Coll (NJ)
Broome Comm Coll (NY)
Cambria County Area Comm Coll (PA)
Camden County Coll (NJ)
Carroll Comm Coll (MD)
Central Ohio Tech Coll (OH)
Central Piedmont Comm Coll (NC)
Central Wyoming Coll (WY)
Chabot Coll (CA)
Chatfield Coll (OH)
Chemeketa Comm Coll (OR)
Chesapeake Coll (MD)
Cisco Jr Coll (TX)
Coll of DuPage (IL)
Coll of Southern Idaho (ID)
Coll of Southern Maryland (MD)
Columbia-Greene Comm Coll (NY)
Comm Coll of Denver (CO)
Comm Coll of Vermont (VT)
Compton Comm Coll (CA)
Corning Comm Coll (NY)
Crafton Hills Coll (CA)
Cuesta Coll (CA)
Cypress Coll (CA)
Danville Area Comm Coll (IL)
Daytona Beach Comm Coll (FL)
Delaware Tech & Comm Coll, Jack F Owens Cmps (DE)
Delaware Tech & Comm Coll, Stanton/ Wilmington Cmps (DE)
Delaware Tech & Comm Coll, Terry Cmps (DE)
Denmark Tech Coll (SC)
Des Moines Area Comm Coll (IA)
Edison Comm Coll (FL)
Edison State Comm Coll (OH)
Ellsworth Comm Coll (IA)
Essex County Coll (NJ)
Everett Comm Coll (WA)
Finger Lakes Comm Coll (NY)
Fiorello H LaGuardia Comm Coll of City U of NY (NY)
Flathead Valley Comm Coll (MT)
Flathead Valley Comm Coll (MT)
Florence-Darlington Tech Coll (SC)
Florida Comm Coll at Jacksonville (FL)
Floyd Coll (GA)
Fort Berthold Comm Coll (ND)
Frederick Comm Coll (MD)
Fresno City Coll (CA)
Fulton-Montgomery Comm Coll (NY)
Gateway Comm Coll (CT)
Gateway Tech Coll (WI)
Genesee Comm Coll (NY)
Glendale Comm Coll (AZ)
Grays Harbor Coll (WA)
Greenfield Comm Coll (MA)
Guilford Tech Comm Coll (NC)
Gulf Coast Comm Coll (FL)
Harrisburg Area Comm Coll (PA)
Henderson Comm Coll (KY)
Herkimer County Comm Coll (NY)
Herkimer County Comm Coll (NY)
Hesser Coll (NH)
Highland Comm Coll (IL)
Highland Comm Coll (IL)
Highline Comm Coll (WA)
Hillsborough Comm Coll (FL)
Holyoke Comm Coll (MA)
Honolulu Comm Coll (HI)
Hopkinsville Comm Coll (KY)
Hopkinsville Comm Coll (KY)
Housatonic Comm Coll (CT)
Hudson County Comm Coll (NJ)
Indian River Comm Coll (FL)

Inver Hills Comm Coll (MN)
Iowa Western Comm Coll (IA)
Iowa Western Comm Coll (IA)
Itasca Comm Coll (MN)
Jamestown Comm Coll (NY)
Jefferson Comm Coll (NY)
John Tyler Comm Coll (VA)
Kellogg Comm Coll (MI)
Kent State U, Salem Campus (OH)
Keystone Coll (PA)
Kilian Comm Coll (SD)
Kingsborough Comm Coll of City U of NY (NY)
Kirkwood Comm Coll (IA)
Lake Land Coll (IL)
Lakeland Comm Coll (OH)
Lansing Comm Coll (MI)
Lima Tech Coll (OH)
Long Beach City Coll (CA)
Longview Comm Coll (MO)
Lorain County Comm Coll (OH)
Los Angeles City Coll (CA)
Luzerne County Comm Coll (PA)
Luzerne County Comm Coll (PA)
Manchester Comm Coll (CT)
Manor Coll (PA)
Marion Tech Coll (OH)
Massachusetts Bay Comm Coll (MA)
Massasoit Comm Coll (MA)
Merced Coll (CA)
Mesabi Range Comm and Tech Coll (MN)
Mesabi Range Comm and Tech Coll (MN)
Metropolitan Comm Coll (NE)
Miles Comm Coll (MT)
Milwaukee Area Tech Coll (WI)
Milwaukee Area Tech Coll (WI)
Minneapolis Comm and Tech Coll (MN)
Mississippi Gulf Coast Comm Coll (MS)
Mitchell Coll (CT)
Mitchell Coll (CT)
Mitchell Comm Coll (NC)
Modesto Jr Coll (CA)
Modesto Jr Coll (CA)
Mohawk Valley Comm Coll (NY)
Monroe Comm Coll (NY)
Mount Wachusett Comm Coll (MA)
Naugatuck Valley Comm Coll (CT)
New Hampshire Comm Tech Coll, Berlin/Laconia (NH)
New Hampshire Tech Inst (NH)
New York City Tech Coll of the City U of NY (NY)
Niagara County Comm Coll (NY)
Northcentral Tech Coll (WI)
Northern New Mexico Comm Coll (NM)
Northern Virginia Comm Coll (VA)
North Harris Coll (TX)
North Idaho Coll (ID)
Northwestern Connecticut Comm-Tech Coll (CT)
Norwalk Comm Coll (CT)
Odessa Coll (TX)
Onondaga Comm Coll (NY)
Owensboro Comm Coll (KY)
Parkland Coll (IL)
Pasadena City Coll (CA)
Pasco-Hernando Comm Coll (FL)
Piedmont Tech Coll (SC)
Pine Tech Coll (MN)
Pratt Comm Coll and Area Vocational School (KS)
Quinsigamond Comm Coll (MA)
Raritan Valley Comm Coll (NJ)
Reading Area Comm Coll (PA)
Richmond Comm Coll (NC)
Ridgewater Coll (MN)
Ridgewater Coll (MN)
Riverland Comm Coll (MN)
Riverland Comm Coll (MN)
Rockland Comm Coll (NY)
Rockland Comm Coll (NY)
Rogue Comm Coll (OR)
Sacramento City Coll (CA)
Saint Charles Comm Coll (MO)
St. Louis Comm Coll at Florissant Valley (MO)
St. Petersburg Coll (FL)
Salish Kootenai Coll (MT)
San Bernardino Valley Coll (CA)
Sandhills Comm Coll (NC)
San Juan Coll (NM)
Sauk Valley Comm Coll (IL)
Schenectady County Comm Coll (NY)
Seattle Central Comm Coll (WA)
Sinclair Comm Coll (OH)
Sitting Bull Coll (ND)
Skagit Valley Coll (WA)
Southside Virginia Comm Coll (VA)
South Suburban Coll (IL)
South Texas Comm Coll (TX)
Southwest Virginia Comm Coll (VA)
Southwest Wisconsin Tech Coll (WI)
Stanly Comm Coll (NC)
Stark State Coll of Technology (OH)
State U of NY Coll of Technology at Alfred (NY)
State U of NY Coll of Technology at Alfred (NY)
Stone Child Coll (MT)
Suffolk County Comm Coll (NY)
Sullivan County Comm Coll (NY)
Sullivan County Comm Coll (NY)
Sussex County Comm Coll (NJ)
Tacoma Comm Coll (WA)
Three Rivers Comm Coll (CT)
Tomball Coll (TX)
Tompkins Cortland Comm Coll (NY)
Trident Tech Coll (SC)
Tulsa Comm Coll (OK)
Tunxis Comm Coll (CT)
Ulster County Comm Coll (NY)
United Tribes Tech Coll (ND)
U of Alaska Anchorage, Matanuska-Susitna Coll (AK)
U of Arkansas Comm Coll at Hope (AR)
Urban Coll of Boston (MA)
Vance-Granville Comm Coll (NC)
Westchester Comm Coll (NY)
Westchester Comm Coll (NY)
Westmoreland County Comm Coll (PA)

HYDRAULIC TECHNOLOGY
Alexandria Tech Coll (MN)
Gateway Tech Coll (WI)
Hennepin Tech Coll (MN)
North Hennepin Comm Coll (MN)

INDIVIDUAL/FAMILY DEVELOPMENT
Coll of Alameda (CA)
Cuesta Coll (CA)
Gloucester County Coll (NJ)
Harford Comm Coll (MD)
Imperial Valley Coll (CA)
Lincoln Coll, Lincoln (IL)
Mitchell Coll (CT)
Orange Coast Coll (CA)
Penn State U Delaware County Campus of the Commonwealth Coll (PA)
Penn State U DuBois Campus of the Commonwealth Coll (PA)
Penn State U Fayette Campus of the Commonwealth Coll (PA)
Penn State U Mont Alto Campus of the Commonwealth Coll (PA)
Penn State U New Kensington Campus of the Commonwealth Coll (PA)
Penn State U Shenango Campus of the Commonwealth Coll (PA)
Penn State U Worthington Scranton Cmps Commonwealth Coll (PA)
Shoreline Comm Coll (WA)

INDIVIDUAL/FAMILY DEVELOPMENT RELATED
Northwest State Comm Coll (OH)

INDUSTRIAL ARTS
Allen County Comm Coll (KS)
American River Coll (CA)
The Art Inst of Pittsburgh (PA)
Bakersfield Coll (CA)
Casper Coll (WY)
Cerritos Coll (CA)
Chabot Coll (CA)
Cleveland State Comm Coll (TN)
Coll of the Sequoias (CA)
Comm Coll of Beaver County (PA)
Cowley County Comm Coll and Voc-Tech School (KS)
Delta Coll (MI)
Dodge City Comm Coll (KS)
Eastern Oklahoma State Coll (OK)
Everett Comm Coll (WA)
Fort Scott Comm Coll (KS)
Fresno City Coll (CA)
Fullerton Coll (CA)
Garden City Comm Coll (KS)
Guilford Tech Comm Coll (NC)
Haywood Comm Coll (NC)
Highland Comm Coll (KS)
Hinds Comm Coll (MS)
Honolulu Comm Coll (HI)
Howard Coll (TX)
Long Beach City Coll (CA)
Los Angeles Pierce Coll (CA)
Merced Coll (CA)
Modesto Jr Coll (CA)
Motlow State Comm Coll (TN)
Northern Maine Tech Coll (ME)
North Seattle Comm Coll (WA)
Ouachita Tech Coll (AR)
Pellissippi State Tech Comm Coll (TN)
Pratt Comm Coll and Area Vocational School (KS)
Rockingham Comm Coll (NC)
San Diego City Coll (CA)
Santa Monica Coll (CA)
Sierra Coll (CA)
Southeast Comm Coll, Milford Campus (NE)
Southwest Tennessee Comm Coll (TN)
Taft Coll (CA)
Thaddeus Stevens Coll of Technology (PA)
Vermilion Comm Coll (MN)
Volunteer State Comm Coll (TN)
Western Piedmont Comm Coll (NC)
Western Wyoming Comm Coll (WY)

INDUSTRIAL ARTS EDUCATION
Allen County Comm Coll (KS)
Atlanta Metropolitan Coll (GA)
Eastern Arizona Coll (AZ)
Kellogg Comm Coll (MI)
Manatee Comm Coll (FL)
Roane State Comm Coll (TN)

INDUSTRIAL DESIGN
The Art Inst of Philadelphia (PA)
The Art Inst of Pittsburgh (PA)
The Art Inst of Seattle (WA)
Chaffey Coll (CA)
Iowa Western Comm Coll (IA)
Kishwaukee Coll (IL)
Las Positas Coll (CA)
Milwaukee Area Tech Coll (WI)
Navarro Coll (TX)
Oklahoma State U, Oklahoma City (OK)
Orange Coast Coll (CA)
Portland Comm Coll (OR)
Southeast Comm Coll, Milford Campus (NE)
Vincennes U (IN)

INDUSTRIAL ELECTRONICS INSTALLATION/REPAIR
Big Bend Comm Coll (WA)
Central Carolina Tech Coll (SC)
Coll of DuPage (IL)
Coll of Lake County (IL)
Johnson Coll (PA)
Kennebec Valley Tech Coll (ME)
Modesto Jr Coll (CA)
North Dakota State Coll of Science (ND)
Northland Comm and Tech Coll (MN)
Pennsylvania Coll of Technology (PA)
State U of NY Coll of Technology at Alfred (NY)
Vincennes U (IN)
Western Dakota Tech Inst (SD)
York Tech Coll (SC)

INDUSTRIAL EQUIPMENT MAINTENANCE AND REPAIR RELATED
Big Bend Comm Coll (WA)
Southwestern Michigan Coll (MI)

INDUSTRIAL MACHINERY MAINTENANCE/REPAIR
Arkansas State U–Mountain Home (AR)
Coll of Lake County (IL)
The Comm Coll of Baltimore County–Catonsville Campus (MD)
Dakota County Tech Coll (MN)
Fayetteville Tech Comm Coll (NC)
Georgia Perimeter Coll (GA)
Guilford Tech Comm Coll (NC)
Harrisburg Area Comm Coll (PA)
Heartland Comm Coll (IL)
Ivy Tech State Coll–Bloomington (IN)
Ivy Tech State Coll–Central Indiana (IN)
Ivy Tech State Coll–Columbus (IN)
Ivy Tech State Coll–Eastcentral (IN)
Ivy Tech State Coll–Kokomo (IN)
Ivy Tech State Coll–Lafayette (IN)
Ivy Tech State Coll–North Central (IN)
Ivy Tech State Coll–Northeast (IN)
Ivy Tech State Coll–Southcentral (IN)
Ivy Tech State Coll–Southeast (IN)
Ivy Tech State Coll–Southwest (IN)
Ivy Tech State Coll–Wabash Valley (IN)
Ivy Tech State Coll–Whitewater (IN)
Johnson Coll (PA)
Kaskaskia Coll (IL)
Kennebec Valley Tech Coll (ME)
Louisville Tech Inst (KY)
Mississippi County Comm Coll (AR)
Moraine Valley Comm Coll (IL)
North Central Texas Coll (TX)
Pennsylvania Coll of Technology (PA)
Rend Lake Coll (IL)
Riverland Comm Coll (MN)
Southern Arkansas U Tech (AR)
Southwestern Michigan Coll (MI)
U of Arkansas Comm Coll at Hope (AR)
Vincennes U (IN)
Waubonsee Comm Coll (IL)
York Tech Coll (SC)

INDUSTRIAL/MANUFACTURING ENGINEERING
Manchester Comm Coll (CT)
Mount Wachusett Comm Coll (MA)
Nashville State Tech Inst (TN)
Northern New Mexico Comm Coll (NM)
Pima Comm Coll (AZ)
Santa Barbara City Coll (CA)

INDUSTRIAL PRODUCTION TECHNOLOGIES RELATED
Cape Fear Comm Coll (NC)
Erie Comm Coll, City Campus (NY)
Pennsylvania Coll of Technology (PA)
Richmond Comm Coll (NC)

INDUSTRIAL RADIOLOGIC TECHNOLOGY
Aims Comm Coll (CO)
Allegany Coll of Maryland (MD)
Amarillo Coll (TX)
Angelina Coll (TX)
Anne Arundel Comm Coll (MD)
Athens Tech Coll (GA)
Austin Comm Coll (TX)
Bakersfield Coll (CA)
Bellevue Comm Coll (WA)
Bergen Comm Coll (NJ)
Blinn Coll (TX)
Brevard Comm Coll (FL)
Burlington County Coll (NJ)
Cañada Coll (CA)
Carl Sandburg Coll (IL)
Carteret Comm Coll (NC)
Casper Coll (WY)
Central Florida Comm Coll (FL)
Central Maine Tech Coll (ME)
Chattahoochee Valley Comm Coll (AL)
Chattanooga State Tech Comm Coll (TN)
City Coll of San Francisco (CA)
Cleveland Comm Coll (NC)
Columbia State Comm Coll (TN)
Columbus State Comm Coll (OH)
Comm Coll of Denver (CO)
Comm Coll of Southern Nevada (NV)
Compton Comm Coll (CA)
Cowley County Comm Coll and Voc-Tech School (KS)
Crafton Hills Coll (CA)
Cumberland County Coll (NJ)
Cuyahoga Comm Coll (OH)
Cypress Coll (CA)
Danville Area Comm Coll (IL)
Daytona Beach Comm Coll (FL)
Delaware Tech & Comm Coll, Stanton/ Wilmington Cmps (DE)
Del Mar Coll (TX)
Delta Coll (MI)
Doña Ana Branch Comm Coll (NM)
Essex County Coll (NJ)
Florence-Darlington Tech Coll (SC)
Forsyth Tech Comm Coll (NC)
Fresno City Coll (CA)
Gateway Comm Coll (CT)
George Corley Wallace State Comm Coll (AL)
Greenville Tech Coll (SC)
Griffin Tech Coll (GA)
Gulf Coast Comm Coll (FL)
Gwinnett Tech Coll (GA)
Henry Ford Comm Coll (MI)
Highland Comm Coll (KS)
Hillsborough Comm Coll (FL)
Hinds Comm Coll (MS)
Horry-Georgetown Tech Coll (SC)
Houston Comm Coll System (TX)
Illinois Eastern Comm Colls, Olney Central Coll (IL)
Indian Hills Comm Coll (IA)
Indian River Comm Coll (FL)
Jackson Comm Coll (MI)
Jefferson Comm Coll (OH)
Kankakee Comm Coll (IL)
Labette Comm Coll (KS)
Labouré Coll (MA)
Laramie County Comm Coll (WY)
Laredo Comm Coll (TX)
Las Positas Coll (CA)
Lima Tech Coll (OH)
Lincoln Land Comm Coll (IL)
Long Beach City Coll (CA)
Lorain County Comm Coll (OH)
Los Angeles City Coll (CA)
Marion Tech Coll (OH)
Marshalltown Comm Coll (IA)
McLennan Comm Coll (TX)
Merced Coll (CA)
Midland Coll (TX)
Mid Michigan Comm Coll (MI)
Mid-Plains Comm Coll Area (NE)
Milwaukee Area Tech Coll (WI)
Mississippi Gulf Coast Comm Coll (MS)
Mohawk Valley Comm Coll (NY)
Monroe Comm Coll (NY)
Montcalm Comm Coll (MI)
Muskingum Area Tech Coll (OH)
Naugatuck Valley Comm Coll (CT)
Northcentral Tech Coll (WI)
Northern Essex Comm Coll (MA)
Northern New Mexico Comm Coll (NM)
Northern Virginia Comm Coll (VA)
NorthWest Arkansas Comm Coll (AR)
Odessa Coll (TX)
Orange Coast Coll (CA)
Orange County Comm Coll (NY)
Our Lady of the Lake Coll (LA)
Paducah Comm Coll (KY)
Palm Beach Comm Coll (FL)
Pasadena City Coll (CA)
Penn Valley Comm Coll (MO)
Portland Comm Coll (OR)
Reading Area Comm Coll (PA)
Ridgewater Coll (MN)
Roane State Comm Coll (TN)
St. Petersburg Coll (FL)
San Diego Mesa Coll (CA)
San Jacinto Coll Central Campus (TX)
San Joaquin Delta Coll (CA)
Santa Fe Comm Coll (FL)
Sauk Valley Comm Coll (IL)
Sinclair Comm Coll (OH)
Southern Maine Tech Coll (ME)
Southern West Virginia Comm and Tech Coll (WV)
South Plains Coll (TX)
South Suburban Coll (IL)

South Texas Comm Coll (TX)
Southwest Virginia Comm Coll (VA)
Tarrant County Coll District (TX)
Trocaire Coll (NY)
Truckee Meadows Comm Coll (NV)
Tulsa Comm Coll (OK)
Tyler Jr Coll (TX)
U of Kentucky, Lexington Comm Coll (KY)
Vance-Granville Comm Coll (NC)
Virginia Western Comm Coll (VA)
Wallace State Comm Coll (AL)
Walters State Comm Coll (TN)
West Central Tech Coll (GA)
Westchester Comm Coll (NY)
Western Wyoming Comm Coll (WY)
Wharton County Jr Coll (TX)

INDUSTRIAL TECHNOLOGY

Albuquerque Tech Vocational Inst (NM)
Alexandria Tech Coll (MN)
Allen County Comm Coll (KS)
Anne Arundel Comm Coll (MD)
Arkansas State U–Mountain Home (AR)
Austin Comm Coll (TX)
Bakersfield Coll (CA)
Bates Tech Coll (WA)
Bergen Comm Coll (NJ)
Bismarck State Coll (ND)
Black Hawk Coll, Moline (IL)
Blackhawk Tech Coll (WI)
Black River Tech Coll (AR)
Blue Ridge Comm Coll (NC)
Bowling Green State U-Firelands Coll (OH)
Brunswick Comm Coll (NC)
Caldwell Comm Coll and Tech Inst (NC)
Cambria County Area Comm Coll (PA)
Catawba Valley Comm Coll (NC)
Central Arizona Coll (AZ)
Central Comm Coll–Columbus Campus (NE)
Central Comm Coll–Grand Island Campus (NE)
Central Comm Coll–Hastings Campus (NE)
Central Georgia Tech Coll (GA)
Central Ohio Tech Coll (OH)
Central Oregon Comm Coll (OR)
Central Piedmont Comm Coll (NC)
Century Comm and Tech Coll (MN)
Cerritos Coll (CA)
Chabot Coll (CA)
Chemeketa Comm Coll (OR)
Cincinnati State Tech and Comm Coll (OH)
City Coll of San Francisco (CA)
Clark Coll (WA)
Cleveland State Comm Coll (TN)
Clinton Comm Coll (NY)
Coffeyville Comm Coll (KS)
Coll of DuPage (IL)
Comm Coll of Allegheny County (PA)
The Comm Coll of Baltimore County–Catonsville Campus (MD)
Comm Coll of the Air Force (AL)
Comm Coll of Vermont (VT)
Corning Comm Coll (NY)
Crowder Coll (MO)
Cuesta Coll (CA)
Cumberland County Coll (NJ)
Danville Area Comm Coll (IL)
De Anza Coll (CA)
Delaware Tech & Comm Coll, Stanton/ Wilmington Cmps (DE)
Delaware Tech & Comm Coll, Terry Cmps (DE)
Dodge City Comm Coll (KS)
Don Bosco Coll of Science and Technology (CA)
Dunwoody Coll of Technology (MN)
East Central Coll (MO)
Edison State Comm Coll (OH)
Education Direct (PA)
Everett Comm Coll (WA)
Evergreen Valley Coll (CA)
Fayetteville Tech Comm Coll (NC)
Forsyth Tech Comm Coll (NC)
Fresno City Coll (CA)
Front Range Comm Coll (CO)
Fullerton Coll (CA)
Garden City Comm Coll (KS)
GateWay Comm Coll (AZ)
Gateway Comm Coll (CT)
Gateway Tech Coll (WI)
Glendale Comm Coll (AZ)
Glendale Comm Coll (CA)
Grand Rapids Comm Coll (MI)
Grays Harbor Coll (WA)
Great Basin Coll (NV)
Greenfield Comm Coll (MA)
Greenville Tech Coll (SC)
Griffin Tech Coll (GA)
Guilford Tech Comm Coll (NC)
Halifax Comm Coll (NC)
Haywood Comm Coll (NC)
Heartland Comm Coll (IL)
Henry Ford Comm Coll (MI)
Highline Comm Coll (WA)
Hopkinsville Comm Coll (KY)
Houston Comm Coll System (TX)
Hutchinson Comm Coll and Area Vocational School (KS)
Illinois Eastern Comm Colls, Lincoln Trail Coll (IL)
Illinois Eastern Comm Colls, Wabash Valley Coll (IL)
Ivy Tech State Coll–Lafayette (IN)
Ivy Tech State Coll–Wabash Valley (IN)
Jackson Comm Coll (MI)
Jackson State Comm Coll (TN)
Jefferson Comm Coll (OH)
Joliet Jr Coll (IL)
Kellogg Comm Coll (MI)
Kent State U, Geauga Campus (OH)
Kent State U, Salem Campus (OH)
Kent State U, Trumbull Campus (OH)
Kent State U, Tuscarawas Campus (OH)
Kilgore Coll (TX)
Kirkwood Comm Coll (IA)
Labette Comm Coll (KS)
Lake Land Coll (IL)
Lakeland Comm Coll (OH)
Lake Michigan Coll (MI)
Lane Comm Coll (OR)
Lansing Comm Coll (MI)
Lehigh Carbon Comm Coll (PA)
Lenoir Comm Coll (NC)
Lima Tech Coll (OH)
Linn-Benton Comm Coll (OR)
Long Beach City Coll (CA)
Lorain County Comm Coll (OH)
Los Angeles Pierce Coll (CA)
Lower Columbia Coll (WA)
Manchester Comm Coll (CT)
Marion Tech Coll (OH)
Miami-Dade Comm Coll (FL)
Miami U–Middletown Campus (OH)
Middlesex County Coll (NJ)
Mid-State Tech Coll (WI)
Milwaukee Area Tech Coll (WI)
Mineral Area Coll (MO)
Minnesota State Coll–Southeast Tech (MN)
MiraCosta Coll (CA)
Mitchell Comm Coll (NC)
Moberly Area Comm Coll (MO)
Mohawk Valley Comm Coll (NY)
Monroe Comm Coll (NY)
Monroe County Comm Coll (MI)
Montcalm Comm Coll (MI)
Moraine Park Tech Coll (WI)
Mountain Empire Comm Coll (VA)
Mt. Hood Comm Coll (OR)
Mount Wachusett Comm Coll (MA)
Muskingum Area Tech Coll (OH)
Nashville State Tech Inst (TN)
Naugatuck Valley Comm Coll (CT)
Navarro Coll (TX)
NEI Coll of Technology (MN)
New England Inst of Technology (RI)
New Hampshire Comm Tech Coll, Berlin/Laconia (NH)
New Mexico State U–Carlsbad (NM)
Northcentral Tech Coll (WI)
North Dakota State Coll of Science (ND)
Northeast State Tech Comm Coll (TN)
North Hennepin Comm Coll (MN)
Northland Pioneer Coll (AZ)
Northwestern Michigan Coll (MI)
Northwest State Comm Coll (OH)
Oakland Comm Coll (MI)
Oklahoma State U, Oklahoma City (OK)
Oklahoma State U, Okmulgee (OK)
Olympic Coll (WA)
Ouachita Tech Coll (AR)
Paducah Tech Coll (KY)
Parkland Coll (IL)
Patrick Henry Comm Coll (VA)
Pellissippi State Tech Comm Coll (TN)
Pennsylvania Coll of Technology (PA)
Penn State U DuBois Campus of the Commonwealth Coll (PA)
Penn State U Hazleton Campus of the Commonwealth Coll (PA)
Penn State U York Campus of the Commonwealth Coll (PA)
Pensacola Jr Coll (FL)
Pierce Coll (WA)
Pitt Comm Coll (NC)
Prairie State Coll (IL)
Pulaski Tech Coll (AR)
Raritan Valley Comm Coll (NJ)
Reading Area Comm Coll (PA)
Rend Lake Coll (IL)
Richland Comm Coll (IL)
Rogue Comm Coll (OR)
Rowan-Cabarrus Comm Coll (NC)
St. Clair County Comm Coll (MI)
St. Paul Tech Coll (MN)
St. Petersburg Coll (FL)
Salem Comm Coll (NJ)
Sampson Comm Coll (NC)
San Antonio Coll (TX)
San Diego City Coll (CA)
Santa Ana Coll (CA)
Santa Barbara City Coll (CA)
Schenectady County Comm Coll (NY)
Schoolcraft Coll (MI)
Seminole Comm Coll (FL)
Shoreline Comm Coll (WA)
Sierra Coll (CA)
Sinclair Comm Coll (OH)
South Arkansas Comm Coll (AR)
Southeast Arkansas Coll (AR)
Southeast Comm Coll, Milford Campus (NE)
Southeastern Comm Coll (NC)
Southeast Tech Inst (SD)
Southern Arkansas U Tech (AR)
South Hills School of Business & Technology, State College (PA)
South Suburban Coll (IL)
South Texas Comm Coll (TX)
Southwest Tennessee Comm Coll (TN)
Spokane Comm Coll (WA)
Stanly Comm Coll (NC)
Stark State Coll of Technology (OH)
State Fair Comm Coll (MO)
State U of NY Coll of Technology at Canton (NY)
Suffolk County Comm Coll (NY)
Temple Coll (TX)
Tennessee Inst of Electronics (TN)
Terra State Comm Coll (OH)
Texas State Tech Coll–Harlingen (TX)
Texas State Tech Coll– Waco/ Marshall Campus (TX)
Three Rivers Comm Coll (CT)
Trident Tech Coll (SC)
Trinidad State Jr Coll (CO)
Triton Coll (IL)
Tulsa Comm Coll (OK)
Ulster County Comm Coll (NY)
Union County Coll (NJ)
U of Arkansas Comm Coll at Batesville (AR)
Vance-Granville Comm Coll (NC)
Vermilion Comm Coll (MN)
Victoria Coll (TX)
Vincennes U Jasper Campus (IN)
Wake Tech Comm Coll (NC)
Waubonsee Comm Coll (IL)
Western Nevada Comm Coll (NV)
Western Piedmont Comm Coll (NC)
West Virginia Northern Comm Coll (WV)
Wilson Tech Comm Coll (NC)
Wor-Wic Comm Coll (MD)

INFORMATION SCIENCES/ SYSTEMS

Adirondack Comm Coll (NY)
Aims Comm Coll (CO)
Alamance Comm Coll (NC)
Albuquerque Tech Vocational Inst (NM)
Allan Hancock Coll (CA)
Allen County Comm Coll (KS)
Allentown Business School (PA)
Amarillo Coll (TX)
Anne Arundel Comm Coll (MD)
Anoka-Ramsey Comm Coll (MN)
Arapahoe Comm Coll (CO)
Arizona Western Coll (AZ)
Arkansas State U–Beebe (AR)
Arkansas State U–Mountain Home (AR)
Ashland Comm Coll (KY)
Augusta Tech Coll (GA)
Austin Comm Coll (TX)
Bainbridge Coll (GA)
Bakersfield Coll (CA)
Baltimore City Comm Coll (MD)
Barton County Comm Coll (KS)
Bates Tech Coll (WA)
Bay de Noc Comm Coll (MI)
Beaufort County Comm Coll (NC)
Bellevue Comm Coll (WA)
Berkshire Comm Coll (MA)
Big Bend Comm Coll (WA)
Black River Tech Coll (AR)
Blue Ridge Comm Coll (NC)
Blue Ridge Comm Coll (VA)
Blue River Comm Coll (MO)
Bossier Parish Comm Coll (LA)
Brown Coll (MN)
Bryant & Stratton Business Inst, Albany (NY)
Bryant & Stratton Business Inst, Buffalo (NY)
Bryant & Stratton Business Inst, Lackawanna (NY)
Bryant & Stratton Business Inst, Rochester (NY)
Bryant & Stratton Business Inst, Rochester (NY)
Bryant & Stratton Business Inst, Eastern Hills Cmps (NY)
Bryant & Stratton Business Inst (NY)
Bryant and Stratton Coll (WI)
Bryant and Stratton Coll, Virginia Beach (VA)
Bucks County Comm Coll (PA)
Cañada Coll (CA)
Cape Cod Comm Coll (MA)
Cayuga County Comm Coll (NY)
Cecil Comm Coll (MD)
Central Alabama Comm Coll (AL)
Central Carolina Comm Coll (NC)
Central Georgia Tech Coll (GA)
Central Pennsylvania Coll (PA)
Central Virginia Comm Coll (VA)
Certified Careers Inst, Salt Lake City (UT)
Chabot Coll (CA)
Chaffey Coll (CA)
Chattahoochee Valley Comm Coll (AL)
Chattanooga State Tech Comm Coll (TN)
Cincinnati State Tech and Comm Coll (OH)
City Colls of Chicago, Harry S Truman Coll (IL)
Cochise Coll, Douglas (AZ)
Coffeyville Comm Coll (KS)
Coll of Alameda (CA)
Coll of Marin (CA)
Coll of Southern Maryland (MD)
Coll of the Canyons (CA)
Coll of the Sequoias (CA)
Columbia-Greene Comm Coll (NY)
Columbia State Comm Coll (TN)
Commonwealth Business Coll, Merrillville (IN)
Comm Coll of Aurora (CO)
The Comm Coll of Baltimore County–Catonsville Campus (MD)
Comm Coll of Beaver County (PA)
Comm Coll of Denver (CO)
Comm Coll of Southern Nevada (NV)
Compton Comm Coll (CA)
Cumberland County Coll (NJ)
Cuyamaca Coll (CA)
Cypress Coll (CA)
Danville Area Comm Coll (IL)
Daytona Beach Comm Coll (FL)
De Anza Coll (CA)
Delaware County Comm Coll (PA)
Delaware Tech & Comm Coll, Stanton/ Wilmington Cmps (DE)
Del Mar Coll (TX)
Delta Coll (MI)
Diné Coll (AZ)
Dodge City Comm Coll (KS)
Dominion Coll, Roanoke (VA)
Draughons Jr Coll (KY)
Draughons Jr Coll, Clarksville (TN)
Draughons Jr Coll, Nashville (TN)
Durham Tech Comm Coll (NC)
Dutchess Comm Coll (NY)
East Central Coll (MO)
Eastern Arizona Coll (AZ)
ECPI Coll of Technology, Newport News (VA)
ECPI Coll of Technology, Virginia Beach (VA)
ECPI Tech Coll, Richmond (VA)
ECPI Tech Coll, Roanoke (VA)
Elaine P. Nunez Comm Coll (LA)
El Centro Coll (TX)
Elizabethtown Comm Coll (KY)
Erie Business Center, Main (PA)
Erie Comm Coll, City Campus (NY)
Erie Comm Coll, North Campus (NY)
Erie Comm Coll, South Campus (NY)
Essex County Coll (NJ)
Evergreen Valley Coll (CA)
Fayetteville Tech Comm Coll (NC)
Fiorello H LaGuardia Comm Coll of City U of NY (NY)
Florida Comm Coll at Jacksonville (FL)
Floyd Coll (GA)
Fort Berthold Comm Coll (ND)
Fullerton Coll (CA)
Fulton-Montgomery Comm Coll (NY)
Garden City Comm Coll (KS)
Gaston Coll (NC)
Gavilan Coll (CA)
Gem City Coll (IL)
Genesee Comm Coll (NY)
Gloucester County Coll (NJ)
Grays Harbor Coll (WA)
Greenfield Comm Coll (MA)
Green River Comm Coll (WA)
Guilford Tech Comm Coll (NC)
Hagerstown Business Coll (MD)
Hamilton Coll (IA)
Harcum Coll (PA)
Harford Comm Coll (MD)
Haywood Comm Coll (NC)
Hazard Comm Coll (KY)
Heald Coll, Schools of Business and Technology (HI)
Heartland Comm Coll (IL)
Henry Ford Comm Coll (MI)
Herkimer County Comm Coll (NY)
Herzing Coll (AL)
Herzing Coll (GA)
Hesser Coll (NH)
Highland Comm Coll (KS)
Hill Coll of the Hill Jr College District (TX)
Hillsborough Comm Coll (FL)
Holyoke Comm Coll (MA)
Howard Comm Coll (MD)
Illinois Eastern Comm Colls, Frontier Comm Coll (IL)
Imperial Valley Coll (CA)
Indian River Comm Coll (FL)
Instituto Comercial de Puerto Rico Jr Coll (PR)
Itasca Comm Coll (MN)
ITT Tech Inst, Lathrop (CA)
ITT Tech Inst, Earth City (MO)
Jamestown Comm Coll (NY)
Jefferson Coll (MO)
Jefferson Comm Coll (NY)
J. F. Drake State Tech Coll (AL)
John A. Logan Coll (IL)
Kankakee Comm Coll (IL)
Kingwood Coll (TX)
Lakeland Comm Coll (OH)
Lamar Comm Coll (CO)
Lamar State Coll–Orange (TX)
Lansing Comm Coll (MI)
Laramie County Comm Coll (WY)
Laredo Comm Coll (TX)
Las Positas Coll (CA)

LDS Business Coll (UT)
Lehigh Carbon Comm Coll (PA)
Lewis Coll of Business (MI)
Lima Tech Coll (OH)
Lincoln Coll, Normal (IL)
Lorain County Comm Coll (OH)
Lord Fairfax Comm Coll (VA)
Los Angeles Harbor Coll (CA)
Louisburg Coll (NC)
Louisiana Tech Coll–Florida Parishes Campus (LA)
Lower Columbia Coll (WA)
Macomb Comm Coll (MI)
Madisonville Comm Coll (KY)
Manatee Comm Coll (FL)
Manchester Comm Coll (CT)
Martin Comm Coll (NC)
Massachusetts Bay Comm Coll (MA)
Massasoit Comm Coll (MA)
McIntosh Coll (NH)
McLennan Comm Coll (TX)
Mesa Tech Coll (NM)
Miami-Dade Comm Coll (FL)
Miami U–Middletown Campus (OH)
Middle Georgia Coll (GA)
Middlesex County Coll (NJ)
Midland Coll (TX)
Mid Michigan Comm Coll (MI)
Mid-State Coll (ME)
Mid-State Tech Coll (WI)
Milwaukee Area Tech Coll (WI)
Minnesota School of Business (MN)
Minot State U–Bottineau Campus (ND)
MiraCosta Coll (CA)
Mitchell Tech Inst (SD)
Mohawk Valley Comm Coll (NY)
Monroe Coll, Bronx (NY)
Monroe Coll, New Rochelle (NY)
Monroe Comm Coll (NY)
Monterey Peninsula Coll (CA)
Montgomery County Comm Coll (PA)
Moorpark Coll (CA)
Mountain Empire Comm Coll (VA)
Mountain View Coll (TX)
Mountain West Coll (UT)
Mount Wachusett Comm Coll (MA)
Nashville State Tech Inst (TN)
Naugatuck Valley Comm Coll (CT)
NEI Coll of Technology (MN)
Neosho County Comm Coll (KS)
New Mexico State U–Carlsbad (NM)
New River Comm Coll (VA)
New York City Tech Coll of the City U of NY (NY)
Niagara County Comm Coll (NY)
Northcentral Tech Coll (WI)
North Central Texas Coll (TX)
Northeast Alabama Comm Coll (AL)
Northeast Texas Comm Coll (TX)
Northern Oklahoma Coll (OK)
Northern Virginia Comm Coll (VA)
North Harris Coll (TX)
North Seattle Comm Coll (WA)
North Shore Comm Coll (MA)
Northwest Coll (WY)
Northwestern Connecticut Comm-Tech Coll (CT)
Northwest-Shoals Comm Coll (AL)
Norwalk Comm Coll (CT)
Oakton Comm Coll (IL)
Ocean County Coll (NJ)
Odessa Coll (TX)
Oklahoma State U, Okmulgee (OK)
Olympic Coll (WA)
Onondaga Comm Coll (NY)
Orange Coast Coll (CA)
Orange County Comm Coll (NY)
Oxnard Coll (CA)
Ozarka Coll (AR)
Paducah Comm Coll (KY)
Palomar Coll (CA)
Parkland Coll (IL)
Pasadena City Coll (CA)
Penn State U DuBois Campus of the Commonwealth Coll (PA)
Penn State U Fayette Campus of the Commonwealth Coll (PA)
Penn State U Hazleton Campus of the Commonwealth Coll (PA)
Penn State U Mont Alto Campus of the Commonwealth Coll (PA)
Penn State U New Kensington Campus of the Commonwealth Coll (PA)
Penn State U Shenango Campus of the Commonwealth Coll (PA)
Penn State U Wilkes-Barre Campus of the Commonwealth Coll (PA)
Penn State U Worthington Scranton Cmps Commonwealth Coll (PA)
Penn State U York Campus of the Commonwealth Coll (PA)
Pensacola Jr Coll (FL)
Phoenix Coll (AZ)
Pierce Coll (WA)
Pioneer Pacific Coll (OR)
Platt Coll, Newport Beach (CA)
Platt Coll–Los Angeles, Inc (CA)
Polk Comm Coll (FL)
Portland Comm Coll (OR)
Prince George's Comm Coll (MD)
Pulaski Tech Coll (AR)
Queensborough Comm Coll of City U of NY (NY)
Quincy Coll (MA)
Quinsigamond Comm Coll (MA)
Rappahannock Comm Coll (VA)
Raritan Valley Comm Coll (NJ)
Reading Area Comm Coll (PA)
Reedley Coll (CA)
Richland Comm Coll (IL)
Ridgewater Coll (MN)
Rockingham Comm Coll (NC)
Rowan-Cabarrus Comm Coll (NC)
St. Catharine Coll (KY)
St. Clair County Comm Coll (MI)
St. Louis Comm Coll at Florissant Valley (MO)
St. Petersburg Coll (FL)
St. Philip's Coll (TX)
Salem Comm Coll (NJ)
Sandhills Comm Coll (NC)
San Jacinto Coll North Campus (TX)
San Jacinto Coll South Campus (TX)
San Juan Coll (NM)
Santa Ana Coll (CA)
Santa Barbara City Coll (CA)
Santa Fe Comm Coll (FL)
Santa Monica Coll (CA)
Scottsdale Comm Coll (AZ)
Seminole Comm Coll (FL)
Sheridan Coll (WY)
Sierra Coll (CA)
Sinclair Comm Coll (OH)
Snow Coll (UT)
Somerset Comm Coll (KY)
South Coll (TN)
Southeastern Comm Coll, South Campus (IA)
Southeast Tech Inst (SD)
Southern Maine Tech Coll (ME)
Southern Ohio Coll, Northern Kentucky Campus (KY)
Southern West Virginia Comm and Tech Coll (WV)
South Mountain Comm Coll (AZ)
South Puget Sound Comm Coll (WA)
Southside Virginia Comm Coll (VA)
South Suburban Coll (IL)
South Texas Comm Coll (TX)
South U (AL)
Southwestern Coll (CA)
Southwestern Comm Coll (NC)
Southwest Georgia Tech Coll (GA)
Southwest Virginia Comm Coll (VA)
Spokane Falls Comm Coll (WA)
Stanly Comm Coll (NC)
State Fair Comm Coll (MO)
State U of NY Coll of A&T at Morrisville (NY)
State U of NY Coll of Technology at Canton (NY)
State U of NY Coll of Technology at Delhi (NY)
Suffolk County Comm Coll (NY)
Sullivan County Comm Coll (NY)
Surry Comm Coll (NC)
Tacoma Comm Coll (WA)
Terra State Comm Coll (OH)
Texas State Tech Coll– Waco/ Marshall Campus (TX)
Thaddeus Stevens Coll of Technology (PA)
Thomas Nelson Comm Coll (VA)
Tompkins Cortland Comm Coll (NY)
Trenholm State Tech Coll, Patterson Campus (AL)
Trinidad State Jr Coll (CO)
Triton Coll (IL)
Truckee Meadows Comm Coll (NV)
Tulsa Comm Coll (OK)
Tunxis Comm Coll (CT)
Ulster County Comm Coll (NY)
Union County Coll (NJ)
U of Arkansas Comm Coll at Morrilton (AR)
U of Kentucky, Lexington Comm Coll (KY)
Utica School of Commerce (NY)
Ventura Coll (CA)
Victoria Coll (TX)
Victor Valley Coll (CA)
Vincennes U (IN)
Walla Walla Comm Coll (WA)
Warren County Comm Coll (NJ)
Weatherford Coll (TX)
West Central Tech Coll (GA)
The Westchester Business Inst (NY)
Westchester Comm Coll (NY)
Western Wyoming Comm Coll (WY)
Westmoreland County Comm Coll (PA)
Wilson Tech Comm Coll (NC)

INFORMATION TECHNOLOGY

Adirondack Comm Coll (NY)
AIBT International Inst of the Americas (AZ)
Anoka-Hennepin Tech Coll (MN)
Arkansas State U–Beebe (AR)
Austin Comm Coll (TX)
Barton County Comm Coll (KS)
Bauder Coll (GA)
Berks Tech Inst (PA)
Bladen Comm Coll (NC)
Blue Ridge Comm Coll (VA)
Bowling Green State U-Firelands Coll (OH)
Brazosport Coll (TX)
Bristol Comm Coll (MA)
Broome Comm Coll (NY)
The Brown Mackie Coll–Olathe Campus (KS)
Bryant & Stratton Business Inst, Albany (NY)
Bryant & Stratton Business Inst, Rochester (NY)
Bryant & Stratton Business Inst, Rochester (NY)
Bryant & Stratton Business Inst (NY)
Bryant and Stratton Coll, Parma (OH)
Bryant and Stratton Coll, Willoughby Hills (OH)
Bryant and Stratton Coll (WI)
Bucks County Comm Coll (PA)
Burlington County Coll (NJ)
Caldwell Comm Coll and Tech Inst (NC)
Camden County Coll (NJ)
Cape Cod Comm Coll (MA)
Capital Comm Coll (CT)
Carteret Comm Coll (NC)
Catawba Valley Comm Coll (NC)
Cecil Comm Coll (MD)
Central Carolina Comm Coll (NC)
Central Comm Coll–Columbus Campus (NE)
Central Comm Coll–Grand Island Campus (NE)
Central Comm Coll–Hastings Campus (NE)
Cleveland Comm Coll (NC)
Coastal Bend Coll (TX)
Colorado Northwestern Comm Coll (CO)
The Comm Coll of Baltimore County–Catonsville Campus (MD)
Comm Coll of Vermont (VT)
Corning Comm Coll (NY)
Cuesta Coll (CA)
Davis Coll (OH)
Daytona Beach Comm Coll (FL)
Del Mar Coll (TX)
Delta Coll (MI)
Diablo Valley Coll (CA)
Draughons Jr Coll (KY)
Durham Tech Comm Coll (NC)
Edgecombe Comm Coll (NC)
Edison Comm Coll (FL)
El Centro Coll (TX)
Fayetteville Tech Comm Coll (NC)
Florida Comm Coll at Jacksonville (FL)
Galveston Coll (TX)
GateWay Comm Coll (AZ)
Gavilan Coll (CA)
Gogebic Comm Coll (MI)
Gordon Coll (GA)
Hawkeye Comm Coll (IA)
Heartland Comm Coll (IL)
Henderson Comm Coll (KY)
Hinds Comm Coll (MS)
Howard Comm Coll (MD)
Indiana Business Coll, Columbus (IN)
Indiana Business Coll, Evansville (IN)
Indiana Business Coll, Indianapolis (IN)
Indiana Business Coll, Lafayette (IN)
Indiana Business Coll, Muncie (IN)
Indiana Business Coll, Terre Haute (IN)
Iowa Lakes Comm Coll (IA)
Itasca Comm Coll (MN)
ITT Tech Inst (AL)
ITT Tech Inst, Tucson (AZ)
ITT Tech Inst (AR)
ITT Tech Inst, Anaheim (CA)
ITT Tech Inst, Hayward (CA)
ITT Tech Inst, Oxnard (CA)
ITT Tech Inst, Rancho Cordova (CA)
ITT Tech Inst, San Bernardino (CA)
ITT Tech Inst, Santa Clara (CA)
ITT Tech Inst, Sylmar (CA)
ITT Tech Inst, Torrance (CA)
ITT Tech Inst, West Covina (CA)
ITT Tech Inst (CO)
ITT Tech Inst, Fort Lauderdale (FL)
ITT Tech Inst, Maitland (FL)
ITT Tech Inst, Miami (FL)
ITT Tech Inst, Tampa (FL)
ITT Tech Inst (ID)
ITT Tech Inst, Burr Ridge (IL)
ITT Tech Inst, Matteson (IL)
ITT Tech Inst, Mount Prospect (IL)
ITT Tech Inst, Fort Wayne (IN)
ITT Tech Inst, Indianapolis (IN)
ITT Tech Inst, Newburgh (IN)
ITT Tech Inst (KY)
ITT Tech Inst (LA)
ITT Tech Inst, Norwood (MA)
ITT Tech Inst, Woburn (MA)
ITT Tech Inst, Grand Rapids (MI)
ITT Tech Inst, Troy (MI)
ITT Tech Inst, Arnold (MO)
ITT Tech Inst, Earth City (MO)
ITT Tech Inst (NE)
ITT Tech Inst (NV)
ITT Tech Inst (NM)
ITT Tech Inst, Albany (NY)
ITT Tech Inst, Getzville (NY)
ITT Tech Inst, Liverpool (NY)
ITT Tech Inst, Dayton (OH)
ITT Tech Inst, Norwood (OH)
ITT Tech Inst, Strongsville (OH)
ITT Tech Inst, Youngstown (OH)
ITT Tech Inst (OR)
ITT Tech Inst, Bensalem (PA)
ITT Tech Inst, Mechanicsburg (PA)
ITT Tech Inst, Monroeville (PA)
ITT Tech Inst, Pittsburgh (PA)
ITT Tech Inst (SC)
ITT Tech Inst, Knoxville (TN)
ITT Tech Inst, Memphis (TN)
ITT Tech Inst, Nashville (TN)
ITT Tech Inst, Arlington (TX)
ITT Tech Inst, Austin (TX)
ITT Tech Inst, Houston (TX)
ITT Tech Inst, Houston (TX)
ITT Tech Inst, Houston (TX)
ITT Tech Inst, Richardson (TX)
ITT Tech Inst, San Antonio (TX)
ITT Tech Inst (UT)
ITT Tech Inst, Richmond (VA)
ITT Tech Inst, Bothell (WA)
ITT Tech Inst, Seattle (WA)
ITT Tech Inst, Spokane (WA)
ITT Tech Inst, Green Bay (WI)
ITT Tech Inst, Greenfield (WI)
Jamestown Comm Coll (NY)
Johnson Coll (PA)
J. Sargeant Reynolds Comm Coll (VA)
Lake Area Tech Inst (SD)
Lake Land Coll (IL)
Lake Region State Coll (ND)
Laredo Comm Coll (TX)
Laurel Business Inst (PA)
LDS Business Coll (UT)
Lincoln School of Commerce (NE)
Lorain County Comm Coll (OH)
Los Angeles City Coll (CA)
Louisville Tech Inst (KY)
Mayland Comm Coll (NC)
Mesabi Range Comm and Tech Coll (MN)
Midland Coll (TX)
Miles Comm Coll (MT)
Milwaukee Area Tech Coll (WI)
Minot State U–Bottineau Campus (ND)
Mississippi Gulf Coast Comm Coll (MS)
Mohave Comm Coll (AZ)
Monroe Comm Coll (NY)
Monroe County Comm Coll (MI)
Mountain Empire Comm Coll (VA)
Nash Comm Coll (NC)
Naugatuck Valley Comm Coll (CT)
NEI Coll of Technology (MN)
North Central Michigan Coll (MI)
North Iowa Area Comm Coll (IA)
Northland Comm and Tech Coll (MN)
Ohio Valley Business Coll (OH)
Okaloosa-Walton Comm Coll (FL)
Olympic Coll (WA)
Onondaga Comm Coll (NY)
Orange County Comm Coll (NY)
Owensboro Comm Coll (KY)
Pasco-Hernando Comm Coll (FL)
Patrick Henry Comm Coll (VA)
Platt Coll, Newport Beach (CA)
Platt Coll, Ontario (CA)
Platt Coll–Los Angeles, Inc (CA)
Queensborough Comm Coll of City U of NY (NY)
Randolph Comm Coll (NC)
St. Cloud Tech Coll (MN)
Sampson Comm Coll (NC)
Santa Ana Coll (CA)
Santa Barbara City Coll (CA)
Sauk Valley Comm Coll (IL)
Savannah Tech Coll (GA)
Schenectady County Comm Coll (NY)
Seminole Comm Coll (FL)
Sinclair Comm Coll (OH)
Southeast Comm Coll (KY)
Southeast Tech Inst (SD)
Southside Virginia Comm Coll (VA)
Southwestern Coll (CA)
Southwest Mississippi Comm Coll (MS)
Spartanburg Methodist Coll (SC)
Stark State Coll of Technology (OH)
Suffolk County Comm Coll (NY)
Surry Comm Coll (NC)
Tacoma Comm Coll (WA)
Texarkana Coll (TX)
Texas State Tech Coll–Harlingen (TX)
Trinidad State Jr Coll (CO)
Tulsa Comm Coll (OK)
Tyler Jr Coll (TX)
U of Arkansas Comm Coll at Batesville (AR)
Vincennes U (IN)
Walters State Comm Coll (TN)
Webster Inst of Technology (FL)
The Westchester Business Inst (NY)
Western Nebraska Comm Coll (NE)
Western Wyoming Comm Coll (WY)
West Shore Comm Coll (MI)
West Virginia Northern Comm Coll (WV)
York Tech Inst (PA)

INSTITUTIONAL FOOD SERVICES

Comm Coll of Allegheny County (PA)
Florida Comm Coll at Jacksonville (FL)
Hibbing Comm Coll (MN)
Mott Comm Coll (MI)

North Dakota State Coll of Science (ND)
St. Philip's Coll (TX)
Santa Barbara City Coll (CA)

INSTITUTIONAL FOOD WORKERS
Asheville-Buncombe Tech Comm Coll (NC)
Cape Fear Comm Coll (NC)
Delgado Comm Coll (LA)
Elaine P. Nunez Comm Coll (LA)
Harrisburg Area Comm Coll (PA)
MiraCosta Coll (CA)
Pennsylvania Coll of Technology (PA)
Pikes Peak Comm Coll (CO)
St. Philip's Coll (TX)
San Jacinto Coll North Campus (TX)
Santa Barbara City Coll (CA)
Texas State Tech Coll–Harlingen (TX)
Texas State Tech Coll– Waco/ Marshall Campus (TX)
West Virginia Northern Comm Coll (WV)
Wilkes Comm Coll (NC)

INSTITUTIONAL FOOD WORKERS RELATED
Front Range Comm Coll (CO)

INSTRUMENTATION TECHNOLOGY
Amarillo Coll (TX)
Black Hawk Coll, Moline (IL)
Brazosport Coll (TX)
Brevard Comm Coll (FL)
Butler County Comm Coll (PA)
Cape Fear Comm Coll (NC)
Central Carolina Comm Coll (NC)
Chabot Coll (CA)
Chattanooga State Tech Comm Coll (TN)
Colorado Northwestern Comm Coll (CO)
Comm Coll of Rhode Island (RI)
Copiah-Lincoln Comm Coll– Natchez Campus (MS)
Delaware Tech & Comm Coll, Stanton/ Wilmington Cmps (DE)
East Mississippi Comm Coll (MS)
Henry Ford Comm Coll (MI)
Lamar State Coll–Port Arthur (TX)
Lenoir Comm Coll (NC)
Lower Columbia Coll (WA)
Mesabi Range Comm and Tech Coll (MN)
Miami-Dade Comm Coll (FL)
Mid-State Tech Coll (WI)
Monroe Comm Coll (NY)
Moraine Valley Comm Coll (IL)
Mott Comm Coll (MI)
Nassau Comm Coll (NY)
New River Comm Coll (VA)
Northeast State Tech Comm Coll (TN)
Northern Maine Tech Coll (ME)
Oklahoma State U, Oklahoma City (OK)
Orangeburg-Calhoun Tech Coll (SC)
Pennsylvania Coll of Technology (PA)
St. Cloud Tech Coll (MN)
Salem Comm Coll (NJ)
San Juan Coll (NM)
Savannah Tech Coll (GA)
Spartan School of Aeronautics (OK)
Texas State Tech Coll–Harlingen (TX)
Texas State Tech Coll– Waco/ Marshall Campus (TX)
Trenholm State Tech Coll, Patterson Campus (AL)
U of Alaska Anchorage, Kenai Peninsula Coll (AK)
Wake Tech Comm Coll (NC)
Western Wyoming Comm Coll (WY)

INSTRUMENT CALIBRATION/ REPAIR
Florida Comm Coll at Jacksonville (FL)
Ridgewater Coll (MN)

INSURANCE MARKETING
Heartland Comm Coll (IL)
Tulsa Comm Coll (OK)

INSURANCE/RISK MANAGEMENT
Austin Comm Coll (TX)
Central Piedmont Comm Coll (NC)
City Coll of San Francisco (CA)
Comm Coll of Allegheny County (PA)
Daytona Beach Comm Coll (FL)
Enterprise State Jr Coll (AL)
Florida Comm Coll at Jacksonville (FL)
Houston Comm Coll System (TX)
Isothermal Comm Coll (NC)
Laurel Business Inst (PA)
Lenoir Comm Coll (NC)
Merced Coll (CA)
Mohawk Valley Comm Coll (NY)
Nassau Comm Coll (NY)
Oklahoma City Comm Coll (OK)
Onondaga Comm Coll (NY)
Richland Comm Coll (IL)
St. Catharine Coll (KY)
San Diego City Coll (CA)
Suffolk County Comm Coll (NY)
Trinity Valley Comm Coll (TX)
Tulsa Comm Coll (OK)

INTERDISCIPLINARY STUDIES
Bowling Green State U-Firelands Coll (OH)
Central Texas Coll (TX)
Chabot Coll (CA)
Columbia-Greene Comm Coll (NY)
County Coll of Morris (NJ)
Del Mar Coll (TX)
Evergreen Valley Coll (CA)
Great Basin Coll (NV)
Harcum Coll (PA)
Hawkeye Comm Coll (IA)
Jefferson Coll (MO)
Jefferson Comm Coll (NY)
Kilian Comm Coll (SD)
Miami U–Middletown Campus (OH)
Mt. San Jacinto Coll (CA)
North Country Comm Coll (NY)
North Shore Comm Coll (MA)
Pasadena City Coll (CA)
Ridgewater Coll (MN)
South Texas Comm Coll (TX)
State U of NY Coll of Technology at Canton (NY)
Triton Coll (IL)
The U of Akron–Wayne Coll (OH)
U of South Carolina at Sumter (SC)
Vermilion Comm Coll (MN)
Walters State Comm Coll (TN)
Western Nebraska Comm Coll (NE)

INTERIOR ARCHITECTURE
Delgado Comm Coll (LA)
Inst of Design and Construction (NY)
Northampton County Area Comm Coll (PA)
St. Philip's Coll (TX)

INTERIOR DESIGN
Alexandria Tech Coll (MN)
Allan Hancock Coll (CA)
Amarillo Coll (TX)
American River Coll (CA)
Antelope Valley Coll (CA)
Antonelli Coll (OH)
The Art Inst of Houston (TX)
The Art Inst of Philadelphia (PA)
The Art Inst of Pittsburgh (PA)
The Art Inst of Seattle (WA)
The Art Insts International Minnesota (MN)
Bakersfield Coll (CA)
Barton County Comm Coll (KS)
Bauder Coll (GA)
Bellevue Comm Coll (WA)
Berkeley Coll (NJ)
Black Hawk Coll, Moline (IL)
Bradley Academy for the Visual Arts (PA)
Brookdale Comm Coll (NJ)
Brooks Coll (CA)
Cañada Coll (CA)
Cape Fear Comm Coll (NC)
Carteret Comm Coll (NC)
Central Piedmont Comm Coll (NC)
Century Comm and Tech Coll (MN)
Chaffey Coll (CA)
City Coll of San Francisco (CA)
Clover Park Tech Coll (WA)
Coll of DuPage (IL)
Coll of Marin (CA)
Coll of the Canyons (CA)
Coll of the Desert (CA)
Coll of the Sequoias (CA)
Collin County Comm Coll District (TX)
The Comm Coll of Baltimore County–Catonsville Campus (MD)
Cuesta Coll (CA)
Davis Coll (OH)
Daytona Beach Comm Coll (FL)
Delta Coll (MI)
Dixie State Coll of Utah (UT)
East Central Coll (MO)
El Centro Coll (TX)
Ellsworth Comm Coll (IA)
Fashion Inst of Design & Merchandising, LA Campus (CA)
Fashion Inst of Design & Merchandising, SD Campus (CA)
Fashion Inst of Design & Merchandising, SF Campus (CA)
Florida Comm Coll at Jacksonville (FL)
Fullerton Coll (CA)
Garden City Comm Coll (KS)
Gateway Tech Coll (WI)
Gwinnett Tech Coll (GA)
Halifax Comm Coll (NC)
Harcum Coll (PA)
Harford Comm Coll (MD)
Hawkeye Comm Coll (IA)
Henry Ford Comm Coll (MI)
Hesser Coll (NH)
Highline Comm Coll (WA)
Hillsborough Comm Coll (FL)
Houston Comm Coll System (TX)
Indian River Comm Coll (FL)
Ivy Tech State Coll–North Central (IN)
Ivy Tech State Coll–Southwest (IN)
Joliet Jr Coll (IL)
Kirkwood Comm Coll (IA)
Las Positas Coll (CA)
LDS Business Coll (UT)
Long Beach City Coll (CA)
Louisville Tech Inst (KY)
Metropolitan Comm Coll (NE)
Miami-Dade Comm Coll (FL)
Modesto Jr Coll (CA)
Monroe Comm Coll (NY)
Montana State U Coll of Tech-Great Falls (MT)
Monterey Peninsula Coll (CA)
Nassau Comm Coll (NY)
Newbury Coll (MA)
New England Inst of Technology (RI)
Northern Virginia Comm Coll (VA)
North Harris Coll (TX)
Oakland Comm Coll (MI)
Okaloosa-Walton Comm Coll (FL)
Onondaga Comm Coll (NY)
Orange Coast Coll (CA)
Palm Beach Comm Coll (FL)
Palomar Coll (CA)
Palo Verde Coll (CA)
Pasadena City Coll (CA)
Patricia Stevens Coll (MO)
Pellissippi State Tech Comm Coll (TN)
Phoenix Coll (AZ)
Pikes Peak Comm Coll (CO)
Prairie State Coll (IL)
Randolph Comm Coll (NC)
St. Philip's Coll (TX)
San Bernardino Valley Coll (CA)
San Diego City Coll (CA)
San Diego Mesa Coll (CA)
San Jacinto Coll Central Campus (TX)
San Joaquin Delta Coll (CA)
Santa Barbara City Coll (CA)
Santa Fe Comm Coll (NM)
Santa Monica Coll (CA)
Scott Comm Coll (IA)
Scottsdale Comm Coll (AZ)
Seminole Comm Coll (FL)
Sierra Coll (CA)
Sinclair Comm Coll (OH)
Spokane Falls Comm Coll (WA)
Suffolk County Comm Coll (NY)
Triton Coll (IL)
Tulsa Comm Coll (OK)
Villa Maria Coll of Buffalo (NY)
Vincennes U (IN)
Wade Coll (TX)
Wallace State Comm Coll (AL)
Western Piedmont Comm Coll (NC)
Western Wisconsin Tech Coll (WI)

INTERIOR ENVIRONMENTS
Bradley Academy for the Visual Arts (PA)
Dakota County Tech Coll (MN)
Louisville Tech Inst (KY)
Modesto Jr Coll (CA)
Orange Coast Coll (CA)
Vincennes U (IN)

INTERNATIONAL BUSINESS
Albuquerque Tech Vocational Inst (NM)
Berkeley Coll (NJ)
Berkeley Coll (NY)
Berkeley Coll-Westchester Campus (NY)
Brevard Comm Coll (FL)
Broome Comm Coll (NY)
Cincinnati State Tech and Comm Coll (OH)
The Comm Coll of Baltimore County–Catonsville Campus (MD)
Edmonds Comm Coll (WA)
Foothill Coll (CA)
Frederick Comm Coll (MD)
Fullerton Coll (CA)
GateWay Comm Coll (AZ)
Highline Comm Coll (WA)
Iowa Western Comm Coll (IA)
Kirkwood Comm Coll (IA)
Lansing Comm Coll (MI)
Laredo Comm Coll (TX)
Long Beach City Coll (CA)
Luzerne County Comm Coll (PA)
Manor Coll (PA)
Mohawk Valley Comm Coll (NY)
Monroe Comm Coll (NY)
Monterey Peninsula Coll (CA)
Mott Comm Coll (MI)
Northern Virginia Comm Coll (VA)
Northland Comm and Tech Coll (MN)
North Seattle Comm Coll (WA)
Oakland Comm Coll (MI)
Oakton Comm Coll (IL)
Oklahoma State U, Oklahoma City (OK)
Palomar Coll (CA)
Paradise Valley Comm Coll (AZ)
Pima Comm Coll (AZ)
Raritan Valley Comm Coll (NJ)
St. Paul Tech Coll (MN)
San Jacinto Coll North Campus (TX)
Schiller International USwitzerland)
Shoreline Comm Coll (WA)
Spokane Falls Comm Coll (WA)
Stark State Coll of Technology (OH)
Tacoma Comm Coll (WA)
Tompkins Cortland Comm Coll (NY)
Triton Coll (IL)
Tulsa Comm Coll (OK)
Vincennes U (IN)
Westchester Comm Coll (NY)
Young Harris Coll (GA)

INTERNATIONAL RELATIONS
Allan Hancock Coll (CA)
Bronx Comm Coll of City U of NY (NY)
Brookdale Comm Coll (NJ)
Cochise Coll, Douglas (AZ)
De Anza Coll (CA)
Harrisburg Area Comm Coll (PA)
Kellogg Comm Coll (MI)
Macomb Comm Coll (MI)
Massachusetts Bay Comm Coll (MA)
Miami-Dade Comm Coll (FL)
Mohawk Valley Comm Coll (NY)
Naugatuck Valley Comm Coll (CT)
Northern Essex Comm Coll (MA)
Santa Barbara City Coll (CA)
Tacoma Comm Coll (WA)
Tulsa Comm Coll (OK)

INTERNET
Guilford Tech Comm Coll (NC)
Highline Comm Coll (WA)
Lake-Sumter Comm Coll (FL)
Pasco-Hernando Comm Coll (FL)
Richmond Comm Coll (NC)
U of Arkansas Comm Coll at Batesville (AR)

ITALIAN
Casper Coll (WY)
Chabot Coll (CA)
Coll of the Desert (CA)
Lincoln Land Comm Coll (IL)
Los Angeles Mission Coll (CA)
Miami-Dade Comm Coll (FL)
San Diego Mesa Coll (CA)
San Joaquin Delta Coll (CA)
Triton Coll (IL)
Tulsa Comm Coll (OK)

ITALIAN STUDIES
San Diego Mesa Coll (CA)

JAPANESE
Austin Comm Coll (TX)
Citrus Coll (CA)
Everett Comm Coll (WA)
Foothill Coll (CA)
MiraCosta Coll (CA)
St. Catharine Coll (KY)
San Joaquin Delta Coll (CA)
Snow Coll (UT)
Tacoma Comm Coll (WA)
Tulsa Comm Coll (OK)

JAZZ
Compton Comm Coll (CA)
Iowa Lakes Comm Coll (IA)
Kirkwood Comm Coll (IA)
Lincoln Coll, Lincoln (IL)
Manatee Comm Coll (FL)
Miami-Dade Comm Coll (FL)

JOURNALISM
Abraham Baldwin Ag Coll (GA)
Allen County Comm Coll (KS)
Amarillo Coll (TX)
American River Coll (CA)
Andrew Coll (GA)
Angelina Coll (TX)
Austin Comm Coll (TX)
Bacone Coll (OK)
Bainbridge Coll (GA)
Bakersfield Coll (CA)
Barton County Comm Coll (KS)
Black Hawk Coll, Moline (IL)
Brazosport Coll (TX)
Brookdale Comm Coll (NJ)
Bucks County Comm Coll (PA)
Burlington County Coll (NJ)
Cañada Coll (CA)
Casper Coll (WY)
Central Texas Coll (TX)
Cerritos Coll (CA)
Chabot Coll (CA)
Chaffey Coll (CA)
Citrus Coll (CA)
City Coll of San Francisco (CA)
City Colls of Chicago, Harry S Truman Coll (IL)
City Colls of Chicago, Richard J Daley Coll (IL)
City Colls of Chicago, Wilbur Wright Coll (IL)
Clark Coll (WA)
Coastal Bend Coll (TX)
Cochise Coll, Douglas (AZ)
Coffeyville Comm Coll (KS)
Colby Comm Coll (KS)
Coll of Marin (CA)
Coll of the Canyons (CA)
Coll of the Desert (CA)
Coll of the Sequoias (CA)
Comm Coll of Allegheny County (PA)
Compton Comm Coll (CA)
Connors State Coll (OK)
Cowley County Comm Coll and Voc-Tech School (KS)
Cuesta Coll (CA)
Danville Area Comm Coll (IL)
Darton Coll (GA)
Daytona Beach Comm Coll (FL)
De Anza Coll (CA)
Delaware County Comm Coll (PA)
Delaware Tech & Comm Coll, Jack F Owens Cmps (DE)

Del Mar Coll (TX)
Delta Coll (MI)
Dixie State Coll of Utah (UT)
Dodge City Comm Coll (KS)
East Central Coll (MO)
East Central Comm Coll (MS)
Eastern Oklahoma State Coll (OK)
Enterprise State Jr Coll (AL)
Everett Comm Coll (WA)
Floyd Coll (GA)
Fresno City Coll (CA)
Fullerton Coll (CA)
Garden City Comm Coll (KS)
Gavilan Coll (CA)
Georgia Perimeter Coll (GA)
Glendale Comm Coll (CA)
Golden West Coll (CA)
Gordon Coll (GA)
Harrisburg Area Comm Coll (PA)
Highland Comm Coll (KS)
Highline Comm Coll (WA)
Hill Coll of the Hill Jr College District (TX)
Hinds Comm Coll (MS)
Housatonic Comm Coll (CT)
Imperial Valley Coll (CA)
Indian River Comm Coll (FL)
Iowa Lakes Comm Coll (IA)
Iowa Western Comm Coll (IA)
Jefferson Coll (MO)
John A. Logan Coll (IL)
Kansas City Kansas Comm Coll (KS)
Kellogg Comm Coll (MI)
Kilgore Coll (TX)
Kingsborough Comm Coll of City U of NY (NY)
Kirkwood Comm Coll (IA)
Lansing Comm Coll (MI)
Laramie County Comm Coll (WY)
Lincoln Coll, Lincoln (IL)
Lincoln Land Comm Coll (IL)
Linn-Benton Comm Coll (OR)
Long Beach City Coll (CA)
Lorain County Comm Coll (OH)
Los Angeles City Coll (CA)
Los Angeles Mission Coll (CA)
Los Angeles Pierce Coll (CA)
Luzerne County Comm Coll (PA)
Manatee Comm Coll (FL)
Manchester Comm Coll (CT)
Miami-Dade Comm Coll (FL)
Middlesex County Coll (NJ)
Midland Coll (TX)
MiraCosta Coll (CA)
Monroe County Comm Coll (MI)
Moorpark Coll (CA)
Mt. Hood Comm Coll (OR)
Navarro Coll (TX)
Northampton County Area Comm Coll (PA)
Northeast Comm Coll (NE)
Northern Essex Comm Coll (MA)
North Harris Coll (TX)
North Idaho Coll (ID)
Northwest Coll (WY)
Northwest Mississippi Comm Coll (MS)
Ocean County Coll (NJ)
Orange Coast Coll (CA)
Oxnard Coll (CA)
Palm Beach Comm Coll (FL)
Palomar Coll (CA)
Pasadena City Coll (CA)
Pensacola Jr Coll (FL)
Pima Comm Coll (AZ)
Ridgewater Coll (MN)
Riverside Comm Coll (CA)
St. Catharine Coll (KY)
St. Clair County Comm Coll (MI)
St. Louis Comm Coll at Florissant Valley (MO)
Salem Comm Coll (NJ)
San Bernardino Valley Coll (CA)
San Diego City Coll (CA)
San Jacinto Coll Central Campus (TX)
San Joaquin Delta Coll (CA)
Santa Ana Coll (CA)
Santa Monica Coll (CA)
Shasta Coll (CA)
Sierra Coll (CA)
Skagit Valley Coll (WA)
Southeast Comm Coll, Beatrice Campus (NE)
South Plains Coll (TX)
Southwestern Coll (CA)
State U of NY Coll of A&T at Morrisville (NY)
Suffolk County Comm Coll (NY)
Sussex County Comm Coll (NJ)
Tacoma Comm Coll (WA)
Taft Coll (CA)
Texarkana Coll (TX)
Trinidad State Jr Coll (CO)
Trinity Valley Comm Coll (TX)
Triton Coll (IL)
Tulsa Comm Coll (OK)
Ulster County Comm Coll (NY)
Umpqua Comm Coll (OR)
Ventura Coll (CA)
Vincennes U (IN)
Western Nebraska Comm Coll (NE)
Western Texas Coll (TX)
Western Wyoming Comm Coll (WY)
Young Harris Coll (GA)

JUDAIC STUDIES
Manatee Comm Coll (FL)

LABORATORY ANIMAL MEDICINE
Manor Coll (PA)
State U of NY Coll of Technology at Delhi (NY)

LABOR/PERSONNEL RELATIONS
City Coll of San Francisco (CA)
Comm Coll of Rhode Island (RI)
Kingsborough Comm Coll of City U of NY (NY)
Lansing Comm Coll (MI)
Macomb Comm Coll (MI)
Oklahoma State U, Oklahoma City (OK)
Onondaga Comm Coll (NY)
Quincy Coll (MA)
Rockingham Comm Coll (NC)
San Diego City Coll (CA)
Sinclair Comm Coll (OH)
Tulsa Comm Coll (OK)
Wallace State Comm Coll (AL)

LANDSCAPE ARCHITECTURE
American River Coll (CA)
Anne Arundel Comm Coll (MD)
Butte Coll (CA)
City Coll of San Francisco (CA)
Coll of Marin (CA)
Columbus State Comm Coll (OH)
The Comm Coll of Baltimore County–Catonsville Campus (MD)
Foothill Coll (CA)
Keystone Coll (PA)
Kirkwood Comm Coll (IA)
Lansing Comm Coll (MI)
Lenoir Comm Coll (NC)
Los Angeles Pierce Coll (CA)
Merced Coll (CA)
Miami-Dade Comm Coll (FL)
Minot State U–Bottineau Campus (ND)
Modesto Jr Coll (CA)
Monroe Comm Coll (NY)
Oakland Comm Coll (MI)
Oklahoma State U, Oklahoma City (OK)
Onondaga Comm Coll (NY)
Pasadena City Coll (CA)
Portland Comm Coll (OR)
Riverside Comm Coll (CA)
St. Catharine Coll (KY)
San Diego Mesa Coll (CA)
Southwestern Coll (CA)
State U of NY Coll of A&T at Morrisville (NY)
State U of NY Coll of Technology at Canton (NY)
State U of NY Coll of Technology at Delhi (NY)
Trinidad State Jr Coll (CO)
Triton Coll (IL)
Truckee Meadows Comm Coll (NV)
Tulsa Comm Coll (OK)
Ventura Coll (CA)
Vincennes U (IN)
Wake Tech Comm Coll (NC)
Western Texas Coll (TX)

LANDSCAPING MANAGEMENT
Abraham Baldwin Ag Coll (GA)
Cape Fear Comm Coll (NC)
Central Oregon Comm Coll (OR)
Chabot Coll (CA)
Cincinnati State Tech and Comm Coll (OH)
Clark Coll (WA)
Clover Park Tech Coll (WA)
Coll of DuPage (IL)
Coll of Lake County (IL)
Coll of Marin (CA)
Comm Coll of Allegheny County (PA)
Comm Coll of Southern Nevada (NV)
Cuyamaca Coll (CA)
Danville Area Comm Coll (IL)
Edmonds Comm Coll (WA)
Georgia Perimeter Coll (GA)
Glendale Comm Coll (AZ)
Grayson County Coll (TX)
Hinds Comm Coll (MS)
Horry-Georgetown Tech Coll (SC)
James H. Faulkner State Comm Coll (AL)
Joliet Jr Coll (IL)
J. Sargeant Reynolds Comm Coll (VA)
Kishwaukee Coll (IL)
Lake City Comm Coll (FL)
Los Angeles Pierce Coll (CA)
Milwaukee Area Tech Coll (WI)
MiraCosta Coll (CA)
Northeast Comm Coll (NE)
North Shore Comm Coll (MA)
Northwestern Michigan Coll (MI)
Parkland Coll (IL)
Pensacola Jr Coll (FL)
St. Catharine Coll (KY)
St. Petersburg Coll (FL)
Sandhills Comm Coll (NC)
Santa Barbara City Coll (CA)
Southern Maine Tech Coll (ME)
South Puget Sound Comm Coll (WA)
Southwestern Coll (CA)
Spokane Comm Coll (WA)
Springfield Tech Comm Coll (MA)
State U of NY Coll of A&T at Morrisville (NY)
State U of NY Coll of Technology at Alfred (NY)
State U of NY Coll of Technology at Delhi (NY)
Triton Coll (IL)
Tulsa Comm Coll (OK)
Vermont Tech Coll (VT)

LAND USE MANAGEMENT
Colorado Mountn Coll, Timberline Cmps (CO)
Fullerton Coll (CA)
Mountain Empire Comm Coll (VA)
St. Catharine Coll (KY)
Southwest Virginia Comm Coll (VA)
Vermilion Comm Coll (MN)

LASER/OPTICAL TECHNOLOGY
Albuquerque Tech Vocational Inst (NM)
Amarillo Coll (TX)
Camden County Coll (NJ)
Central Carolina Comm Coll (NC)
Cincinnati State Tech and Comm Coll (OH)
Durham Tech Comm Coll (NC)
Elaine P. Nunez Comm Coll (LA)
Essex County Coll (NJ)
Front Range Comm Coll (CO)
Indian Hills Comm Coll (IA)
Massachusetts Bay Comm Coll (MA)
Miami-Dade Comm Coll (FL)
Monroe Comm Coll (NY)
Moorpark Coll (CA)
Northcentral Tech Coll (WI)
Pennsylvania Coll of Technology (PA)
Portland Comm Coll (OR)
Queensborough Comm Coll of City U of NY (NY)
Roane State Comm Coll (TN)
Schoolcraft Coll (MI)
Southeast Tech Inst (SD)
Southern Ohio Coll, Cincinnati Campus (OH)
Springfield Tech Comm Coll (MA)
Texas State Tech Coll– Waco/ Marshall Campus (TX)
Three Rivers Comm Coll (CT)
Vincennes U (IN)

LATIN AMERICAN STUDIES
City Coll of San Francisco (CA)
Fullerton Coll (CA)
Manatee Comm Coll (FL)
Miami-Dade Comm Coll (FL)
Pasadena City Coll (CA)
San Diego City Coll (CA)

LATIN (ANCIENT AND MEDIEVAL)
Tulsa Comm Coll (OK)

LAW AND LEGAL STUDIES RELATED
United Tribes Tech Coll (ND)

LAW ENFORCEMENT/POLICE SCIENCE
Abraham Baldwin Ag Coll (GA)
Adirondack Comm Coll (NY)
Aims Comm Coll (CO)
Alexandria Tech Coll (MN)
Allan Hancock Coll (CA)
Alpena Comm Coll (MI)
Alvin Comm Coll (TX)
Amarillo Coll (TX)
Anne Arundel Comm Coll (MD)
Antelope Valley Coll (CA)
Arapahoe Comm Coll (CO)
Arizona Western Coll (AZ)
Asheville-Buncombe Tech Comm Coll (NC)
Ashland Comm Coll (KY)
Atlantic Cape Comm Coll (NJ)
Austin Comm Coll (TX)
Bakersfield Coll (CA)
Baltimore City Comm Coll (MD)
Barton County Comm Coll (KS)
Bay de Noc Comm Coll (MI)
Beaufort County Comm Coll (NC)
Bellevue Comm Coll (WA)
Berkshire Comm Coll (MA)
Black Hawk Coll, Moline (IL)
Blackhawk Tech Coll (WI)
Bladen Comm Coll (NC)
Blue River Comm Coll (MO)
Bossier Parish Comm Coll (LA)
Brazosport Coll (TX)
Brevard Comm Coll (FL)
Bucks County Comm Coll (PA)
Bunker Hill Comm Coll (MA)
Burlington County Coll (NJ)
Butler County Comm Coll (PA)
Butte Coll (CA)
Cape Fear Comm Coll (NC)
Carl Sandburg Coll (IL)
Casper Coll (WY)
Catawba Valley Comm Coll (NC)
Cayuga County Comm Coll (NY)
Cecil Comm Coll (MD)
Central Ohio Tech Coll (OH)
Central Piedmont Comm Coll (NC)
Central Texas Coll (TX)
Century Comm and Tech Coll (MN)
Cerritos Coll (CA)
Chabot Coll (CA)
Chattahoochee Tech Coll (GA)
Chippewa Valley Tech Coll (WI)
Cisco Jr Coll (TX)
Citrus Coll (CA)
City Coll of San Francisco (CA)
City Colls of Chicago, Harry S Truman Coll (IL)
City Colls of Chicago, Richard J Daley Coll (IL)
City Colls of Chicago, Wilbur Wright Coll (IL)
Clackamas Comm Coll (OR)
Clinton Comm Coll (NY)
Clovis Comm Coll (NM)
Coastal Bend Coll (TX)
Cochise Coll, Douglas (AZ)
Coll of DuPage (IL)
Coll of Lake County (IL)
Coll of Marin (CA)
Coll of Southern Idaho (ID)
Coll of the Canyons (CA)
Coll of the Desert (CA)
Coll of the Sequoias (CA)
Coll of the Siskiyous (CA)
Columbus State Comm Coll (OH)
Comm Coll of Allegheny County (PA)
The Comm Coll of Baltimore County–Catonsville Campus (MD)
Comm Coll of Beaver County (PA)
Comm Coll of Rhode Island (RI)
Comm Coll of Southern Nevada (NV)
Compton Comm Coll (CA)
Connors State Coll (OK)
County Coll of Morris (NJ)
Cowley County Comm Coll and Voc-Tech School (KS)
Cumberland County Coll (NJ)
Cuyahoga Comm Coll (OH)
Danville Area Comm Coll (IL)
Dawson Comm Coll (MT)
Daytona Beach Comm Coll (FL)
Dean Coll (MA)
De Anza Coll (CA)
Delaware County Comm Coll (PA)
Delaware Tech & Comm Coll, Stanton/ Wilmington Cmps (DE)
Delgado Comm Coll (LA)
Del Mar Coll (TX)
Delta Coll (MI)
Des Moines Area Comm Coll (IA)
Durham Tech Comm Coll (NC)
Dyersburg State Comm Coll (TN)
East Arkansas Comm Coll (AR)
East Central Coll (MO)
Eastern Arizona Coll (AZ)
Eastern Wyoming Coll (WY)
Edison State Comm Coll (OH)
El Centro Coll (TX)
Elizabethtown Comm Coll (KY)
Enterprise State Jr Coll (AL)
Erie Comm Coll, North Campus (NY)
Essex County Coll (NJ)
Everett Comm Coll (WA)
Feather River Comm Coll District (CA)
Fergus Falls Comm Coll (MN)
Finger Lakes Comm Coll (NY)
Florida Comm Coll at Jacksonville (FL)
Floyd Coll (GA)
Forsyth Tech Comm Coll (NC)
Fresno City Coll (CA)
Fullerton Coll (CA)
Gadsden State Comm Coll (AL)
Galveston Coll (TX)
Garden City Comm Coll (KS)
Gateway Tech Coll (WI)
Gavilan Coll (CA)
George Corley Wallace State Comm Coll (AL)
Germanna Comm Coll (VA)
Glendale Comm Coll (AZ)
Glendale Comm Coll (CA)
Gloucester County Coll (NJ)
Golden West Coll (CA)
Grand Rapids Comm Coll (MI)
Grays Harbor Coll (WA)
Grayson County Coll (TX)
Green River Comm Coll (WA)
Greenville Tech Coll (SC)
Griffin Tech Coll (GA)
Guam Comm Coll (GU)
Guilford Tech Comm Coll (NC)
Hagerstown Comm Coll (MD)
Halifax Comm Coll (NC)
Harrisburg Area Comm Coll (PA)
Hawkeye Comm Coll (IA)
Henry Ford Comm Coll (MI)
Herkimer County Comm Coll (NY)
Hesser Coll (NH)
Hibbing Comm Coll (MN)
Highland Comm Coll (KS)
Highline Comm Coll (WA)
Hill Coll of the Hill Jr College District (TX)
Hillsborough Comm Coll (FL)
Hinds Comm Coll (MS)
Holyoke Comm Coll (MA)
Honolulu Comm Coll (HI)
Hopkinsville Comm Coll (KY)
Houston Comm Coll System (TX)
Howard Coll (TX)
Hutchinson Comm Coll and Area Vocational School (KS)
Illinois Eastern Comm Colls, Olney Central Coll (IL)
Indian River Comm Coll (FL)
Inver Hills Comm Coll (MN)
Iowa Lakes Comm Coll (IA)
Iowa Western Comm Coll (IA)
Isothermal Comm Coll (NC)
Jackson Comm Coll (MI)
James Sprunt Comm Coll (NC)
Jamestown Comm Coll (NY)
Jefferson Comm Coll (OH)
Jefferson Davis Comm Coll (AL)
Jefferson State Comm Coll (AL)

Johnson County Comm Coll (KS)
Johnston Comm Coll (NC)
John Wood Comm Coll (IL)
Joliet Jr Coll (IL)
Jones County Jr Coll (MS)
Kalamazoo Valley Comm Coll (MI)
Kankakee Comm Coll (IL)
Kansas City Kansas Comm Coll (KS)
Kaskaskia Coll (IL)
Kellogg Comm Coll (MI)
Kent State U, Tuscarawas Campus (OH)
Kilgore Coll (TX)
Kirkwood Comm Coll (IA)
Kishwaukee Coll (IL)
Labette Comm Coll (KS)
Lake Land Coll (IL)
Lakeland Comm Coll (OH)
Lake Michigan Coll (MI)
Lake Region State Coll (ND)
Lakeshore Tech Coll (WI)
Lake Tahoe Comm Coll (CA)
Lansing Comm Coll (MI)
Laramie County Comm Coll (WY)
Laredo Comm Coll (TX)
Las Positas Coll (CA)
Lehigh Carbon Comm Coll (PA)
Lenoir Comm Coll (NC)
Lima Tech Coll (OH)
Lincoln Coll, Lincoln (IL)
Lincoln Land Comm Coll (IL)
Longview Comm Coll (MO)
Lorain County Comm Coll (OH)
Los Angeles City Coll (CA)
Los Angeles Harbor Coll (CA)
Los Angeles Mission Coll (CA)
Louisiana State U at Eunice (LA)
Lower Columbia Coll (WA)
Macomb Comm Coll (MI)
Madisonville Comm Coll (KY)
Maple Woods Comm Coll (MO)
Massasoit Comm Coll (MA)
Mayland Comm Coll (NC)
McHenry County Coll (IL)
McLennan Comm Coll (TX)
Merced Coll (CA)
Mercer County Comm Coll (NJ)
Metropolitan Comm Coll (NE)
Miami-Dade Comm Coll (FL)
Middle Georgia Coll (GA)
Middlesex County Coll (NJ)
Midland Coll (TX)
Mid-State Tech Coll (WI)
Milwaukee Area Tech Coll (WI)
Mineral Area Coll (MO)
Minneapolis Comm and Tech Coll (MN)
MiraCosta Coll (CA)
Mississippi County Comm Coll (AR)
Mississippi Gulf Coast Comm Coll (MS)
Moberly Area Comm Coll (MO)
Modesto Jr Coll (CA)
Mohave Comm Coll (AZ)
Monroe Comm Coll (NY)
Monroe County Comm Coll (MI)
Monterey Peninsula Coll (CA)
Montgomery Coll (MD)
Montgomery Comm Coll (NC)
Montgomery County Comm Coll (PA)
Moorpark Coll (CA)
Moraine Valley Comm Coll (IL)
Morton Coll (IL)
Mott Comm Coll (MI)
Mountain Empire Comm Coll (VA)
Mt. San Jacinto Coll (CA)
Nash Comm Coll (NC)
Nashville State Tech Inst (TN)
Navarro Coll (TX)
Neosho County Comm Coll (KS)
New Mexico Military Inst (NM)
New River Comm Coll (VA)
North Central Michigan Coll (MI)
Northcentral Tech Coll (WI)
North Central Texas Coll (TX)
Northeast Comm Coll (NE)
Northern Virginia Comm Coll (VA)
North Harris Coll (TX)
North Hennepin Comm Coll (MN)
North Idaho Coll (ID)
North Iowa Area Comm Coll (IA)
Northland Comm and Tech Coll (MN)
Northwestern Connecticut Comm-Tech Coll (CT)
Northwestern Michigan Coll (MI)
Northwest-Shoals Comm Coll (AL)
Northwest State Comm Coll (OH)
Oakton Comm Coll (IL)
Ocean County Coll (NJ)
Odessa Coll (TX)
Okaloosa-Walton Comm Coll (FL)
Oklahoma State U, Oklahoma City (OK)
Orange County Comm Coll (NY)
Owensboro Comm Coll (KY)
Palau Comm CollPalau)
Palm Beach Comm Coll (FL)
Palomar Coll (CA)
Palo Verde Coll (CA)
Penn Valley Comm Coll (MO)
Phoenix Coll (AZ)
Piedmont Virginia Comm Coll (VA)
Pima Comm Coll (AZ)
Pioneer Pacific Coll (OR)
Pitt Comm Coll (NC)
Polk Comm Coll (FL)
Quincy Coll (MA)
Randolph Comm Coll (NC)
Rappahannock Comm Coll (VA)
Reedley Coll (CA)
Rend Lake Coll (IL)
Richland Comm Coll (IL)
Ridgewater Coll (MN)
Riverland Comm Coll (MN)
Roane State Comm Coll (TN)
Rockingham Comm Coll (NC)
Saint Charles Comm Coll (MO)
St. Louis Comm Coll at Florissant Valley (MO)
St. Petersburg Coll (FL)
San Antonio Coll (TX)
San Bernardino Valley Coll (CA)
Sandhills Comm Coll (NC)
San Jacinto Coll Central Campus (TX)
San Jacinto Coll North Campus (TX)
San Joaquin Delta Coll (CA)
San Juan Coll (NM)
Santa Ana Coll (CA)
Santa Fe Comm Coll (FL)
Santa Monica Coll (CA)
Sauk Valley Comm Coll (IL)
Schoolcraft Coll (MI)
Scott Comm Coll (IA)
Seminole State Coll (OK)
Sheridan Coll (WY)
Sierra Coll (CA)
Sinclair Comm Coll (OH)
Skagit Valley Coll (WA)
South Arkansas Comm Coll (AR)
Southeast Comm Coll (KY)
Southern Maine Tech Coll (ME)
South Piedmont Comm Coll (NC)
South Plains Coll (TX)
South Suburban Coll (IL)
Southwestern Comm Coll (NC)
Southwest Virginia Comm Coll (VA)
Spokane Comm Coll (WA)
Springfield Tech Comm Coll (MA)
Stanly Comm Coll (NC)
State U of NY Coll of Technology at Canton (NY)
Suffolk County Comm Coll (NY)
Tacoma Comm Coll (WA)
Temple Coll (TX)
Terra State Comm Coll (OH)
Texarkana Coll (TX)
Thomas Nelson Comm Coll (VA)
Trinidad State Jr Coll (CO)
Trinity Valley Comm Coll (TX)
Triton Coll (IL)
Truckee Meadows Comm Coll (NV)
Tulsa Comm Coll (OK)
Tyler Jr Coll (TX)
Union County Coll (NJ)
United Tribes Tech Coll (ND)
Vance-Granville Comm Coll (NC)
Vermilion Comm Coll (MN)
Victoria Coll (TX)
Victor Valley Coll (CA)
Vincennes U (IN)
Vincennes U Jasper Campus (IN)
Wake Tech Comm Coll (NC)
Wallace State Comm Coll (AL)
Waubonsee Comm Coll (IL)
Wayne Comm Coll (NC)
Westchester Comm Coll (NY)
Western Dakota Tech Inst (SD)
Western Nevada Comm Coll (NV)
Western Piedmont Comm Coll (NC)
Western Texas Coll (TX)
Western Wisconsin Tech Coll (WI)
Western Wyoming Comm Coll (WY)
Westmoreland County Comm Coll (PA)
West Shore Comm Coll (MI)
West Virginia Northern Comm Coll (WV)
Whatcom Comm Coll (WA)
Wilkes Comm Coll (NC)
Wisconsin Indianhead Tech Coll (WI)
Wor-Wic Comm Coll (MD)

LEATHERWORKING/ UPHOLSTERY

St. Philip's Coll (TX)
Spokane Falls Comm Coll (WA)

LEGAL ADMINISTRATIVE ASSISTANT

AIB Coll of Business (IA)
Alamance Comm Coll (NC)
Alexandria Tech Coll (MN)
Allan Hancock Coll (CA)
Allegany Coll of Maryland (MD)
Allentown Business School (PA)
Alvin Comm Coll (TX)
Amarillo Coll (TX)
American River Coll (CA)
Andover Coll (ME)
Anoka-Ramsey Comm Coll (MN)
Arapahoe Comm Coll (CO)
Atlanta Metropolitan Coll (GA)
Austin Comm Coll (TX)
Bakersfield Coll (CA)
Baltimore City Comm Coll (MD)
Bates Tech Coll (WA)
Bay State Coll (MA)
Bergen Comm Coll (NJ)
Bismarck State Coll (ND)
Black Hawk Coll, Moline (IL)
Blackhawk Tech Coll (WI)
Blinn Coll (TX)
Bradford School (OH)
Briarwood Coll (CT)
Bristol Comm Coll (MA)
Bryant & Stratton Business Inst, Buffalo (NY)
Bryant & Stratton Business Inst, Lackawanna (NY)
Bryant & Stratton Business Inst, Rochester (NY)
Bryant & Stratton Business Inst (NY)
Bryant and Stratton Coll (WI)
Bryant and Stratton Coll, Virginia Beach (VA)
Burlington County Coll (NJ)
Business Inst of Pennsylvania (PA)
Butler County Comm Coll (PA)
Butte Coll (CA)
Cambria-Rowe Business Coll (PA)
Cape Cod Comm Coll (MA)
Career Colls of Chicago (IL)
Carteret Comm Coll (NC)
Casper Coll (WY)
Central Arizona Coll (AZ)
Central Carolina Comm Coll (NC)
Central Florida Comm Coll (FL)
Centralia Coll (WA)
Central Lakes Coll (MN)
Central Pennsylvania Coll (PA)
Central Piedmont Comm Coll (NC)
Century Comm and Tech Coll (MN)
Cerritos Coll (CA)
Chabot Coll (CA)
Chaffey Coll (CA)
Chaparral Coll (AZ)
Chattahoochee Valley Comm Coll (AL)
Chattanooga State Tech Comm Coll (TN)
Chesapeake Coll (MD)
Churchman Business School (PA)
City Coll of San Francisco (CA)
Clark Coll (WA)
Clover Park Tech Coll (WA)
Clovis Comm Coll (NM)
Coastal Bend Coll (TX)
Cochise Coll, Douglas (AZ)
Coffeyville Comm Coll (KS)
Coll of DuPage (IL)
Coll of the Redwoods (CA)
Columbus State Comm Coll (OH)
Comm Coll of Allegheny County (PA)
The Comm Coll of Baltimore County–Catonsville Campus (MD)
Comm Coll of Denver (CO)
Comm Coll of Rhode Island (RI)
Comm Coll of Southern Nevada (NV)
Consolidated School of Business, Lancaster (PA)
Consolidated School of Business, York (PA)
Craven Comm Coll (NC)
Crowder Coll (MO)
Crown Coll (WA)
Cumberland County Coll (NJ)
Cypress Coll (CA)
Danville Area Comm Coll (IL)
Darton Coll (GA)
Davis Coll (OH)
Daytona Beach Comm Coll (FL)
Delaware Tech & Comm Coll, Jack F Owens Cmps (DE)
Del Mar Coll (TX)
Delta Coll (MI)
Des Moines Area Comm Coll (IA)
Dodge City Comm Coll (KS)
Draughons Jr Coll (KY)
Draughons Jr Coll, Clarksville (TN)
DuBois Business Coll (PA)
Duff's Business Inst (PA)
East Central Coll (MO)
Eastern Oklahoma State Coll (OK)
Eastfield Coll (TX)
Edmonds Comm Coll (WA)
El Centro Coll (TX)
Ellsworth Comm Coll (IA)
Empire Coll (CA)
Enterprise State Jr Coll (AL)
Erie Business Center, Main (PA)
Erie Business Center South (PA)
Fergus Falls Comm Coll (MN)
Fiorello H LaGuardia Comm Coll of City U of NY (NY)
Florida National Coll (FL)
Fort Scott Comm Coll (KS)
Frederick Comm Coll (MD)
Fresno City Coll (CA)
Fullerton Coll (CA)
Fulton-Montgomery Comm Coll (NY)
Garden City Comm Coll (KS)
Gateway Comm Coll (CT)
Gateway Tech Coll (WI)
Gavilan Coll (CA)
Gem City Coll (IL)
Glendale Comm Coll (CA)
Gloucester County Coll (NJ)
Gogebic Comm Coll (MI)
Golden West Coll (CA)
Grand Rapids Comm Coll (MI)
Grayson County Coll (TX)
Green River Comm Coll (WA)
Hagerstown Business Coll (MD)
Hamilton Coll (IA)
Harrisburg Area Comm Coll (PA)
Heald Coll, Schools of Business and Technology, Hayward (CA)
Heald Coll, Schools of Business and Technology, Rancho Cordova (CA)
Heald Coll, Schools of Business and Technology (HI)
Helena Coll of Tech of The U of Montana (MT)
Hennepin Tech Coll (MN)
Henry Ford Comm Coll (MI)
Hibbing Comm Coll (MN)
Hickey Coll (MO)
Highland Comm Coll (KS)
Highline Comm Coll (WA)
Hillsborough Comm Coll (FL)
Holyoke Comm Coll (MA)
Howard Comm Coll (MD)
Huntington Jr Coll of Business (WV)
Indiana Business Coll, Indianapolis (IN)
Interboro Inst (NY)
International Business Coll, Fort Wayne (IN)
Inver Hills Comm Coll (MN)
Iowa Lakes Comm Coll (IA)
Iowa Western Comm Coll (IA)
Jamestown Business Coll (NY)
Jefferson Coll (MO)
Jefferson Comm Coll (OH)
John A. Logan Coll (IL)
John Wood Comm Coll (IL)
Kalamazoo Valley Comm Coll (MI)
Kellogg Comm Coll (MI)
Kennebec Valley Tech Coll (ME)
Kent State U, East Liverpool Campus (OH)
Kilian Comm Coll (SD)
Kirkwood Comm Coll (IA)
Labette Comm Coll (KS)
Lake Land Coll (IL)
Lake Michigan Coll (MI)
Lake Washington Tech Coll (WA)
Lamar Comm Coll (CO)
Lamar State Coll–Port Arthur (TX)
Lansing Comm Coll (MI)
Laramie County Comm Coll (WY)
Laurel Business Inst (PA)
LDS Business Coll (UT)
Lehigh Carbon Comm Coll (PA)
Lenoir Comm Coll (NC)
Lewis and Clark Comm Coll (IL)
Lewis Coll of Business (MI)
Lima Tech Coll (OH)
Lincoln Coll, Normal (IL)
Lincoln School of Commerce (NE)
Linn-Benton Comm Coll (OR)
Long Beach City Coll (CA)
Longview Comm Coll (MO)
Los Angeles City Coll (CA)
Los Angeles Harbor Coll (CA)
Lower Columbia Coll (WA)
Macomb Comm Coll (MI)
Manchester Comm Coll (CT)
Manor Coll (PA)
Maple Woods Comm Coll (MO)
Marian Court Coll (MA)
Massasoit Comm Coll (MA)
McIntosh Coll (NH)
McLennan Comm Coll (TX)
Merced Coll (CA)
Metropolitan Comm Coll (NE)
Miami-Dade Comm Coll (FL)
Miami U–Middletown Campus (OH)
Middlesex County Coll (NJ)
Midland Coll (TX)
Mid Michigan Comm Coll (MI)
Mid-State Coll (ME)
Milwaukee Area Tech Coll (WI)
Minneapolis Comm and Tech Coll (MN)
Minnesota State Coll–Southeast Tech (MN)
Mohawk Valley Comm Coll (NY)
Monroe Comm Coll (NY)
Monroe County Comm Coll (MI)
Montana State U Coll of Tech-Great Falls (MT)
Monterey Peninsula Coll (CA)
Morton Coll (IL)
Mott Comm Coll (MI)
Mountain Empire Comm Coll (VA)
Mountain View Coll (TX)
Mt. Hood Comm Coll (OR)
Nash Comm Coll (NC)
Nassau Comm Coll (NY)
Naugatuck Valley Comm Coll (CT)
Navarro Coll (TX)
Newport Business Inst, Williamsport (PA)
Northampton County Area Comm Coll (PA)
North Central Michigan Coll (MI)
Northcentral Tech Coll (WI)
North Central Texas Coll (TX)
Northeast Alabama Comm Coll (AL)
Northeast Comm Coll (NE)
Northeast Texas Comm Coll (TX)
Northern Maine Tech Coll (ME)
North Harris Coll (TX)
North Idaho Coll (ID)
North Iowa Area Comm Coll (IA)
Northland Comm and Tech Coll (MN)
Northland Pioneer Coll (AZ)
North Shore Comm Coll (MA)
Northwestern Business Coll (IL)
Northwestern Michigan Coll (MI)
Northwest State Comm Coll (OH)
Odessa Coll (TX)
Ohio Business Coll (OH)
Oklahoma State U, Okmulgee (OK)
Olympic Coll (WA)
Orange Coast Coll (CA)
Otero Jr Coll (CO)
Ouachita Tech Coll (AR)
Palm Beach Comm Coll (FL)
Palomar Coll (CA)
Pasadena City Coll (CA)
Pellissippi State Tech Comm Coll (TN)

Penn Commercial Business and Tech School (PA)
Penn Valley Comm Coll (MO)
Phoenix Coll (AZ)
Piedmont Tech Coll (SC)
Pierce Coll (WA)
Polk Comm Coll (FL)
Portland Comm Coll (OR)
Quincy Coll (MA)
Rasmussen Coll Mankato (MN)
Rasmussen Coll Minnetonka (MN)
Rasmussen Coll St. Cloud (MN)
Reading Area Comm Coll (PA)
Richland Comm Coll (IL)
Ridgewater Coll (MN)
Riverland Comm Coll (MN)
Roane State Comm Coll (TN)
Rockford Business Coll (IL)
Rockingham Comm Coll (NC)
Sacramento City Coll (CA)
St. Catharine Coll (KY)
St. Clair County Comm Coll (MI)
St. Cloud Tech Coll (MN)
St. Petersburg Coll (FL)
St. Philip's Coll (TX)
Salem Comm Coll (NJ)
San Antonio Coll (TX)
San Diego City Coll (CA)
San Diego Mesa Coll (CA)
San Jacinto Coll Central Campus (TX)
San Jacinto Coll North Campus (TX)
San Jacinto Coll South Campus (TX)
Santa Fe Comm Coll (FL)
Shasta Coll (CA)
Sierra Coll (CA)
Sinclair Comm Coll (OH)
South Coll (TN)
Southeast Comm Coll, Beatrice Campus (NE)
South Hills School of Business & Technology, Altoona (PA)
South Hills School of Business & Technology, State College (PA)
South Piedmont Comm Coll (NC)
South Plains Coll (TX)
South Puget Sound Comm Coll (WA)
South Texas Comm Coll (TX)
Southwestern Coll (CA)
Southwest Mississippi Comm Coll (MS)
Southwest Wisconsin Tech Coll (WI)
Spokane Comm Coll (WA)
Springfield Tech Comm Coll (MA)
Stanly Comm Coll (NC)
Stark State Coll of Technology (OH)
State Fair Comm Coll (MO)
State U of NY Coll of A&T at Morrisville (NY)
Tallahassee Comm Coll (FL)
Texas State Tech Coll–Harlingen (TX)
Thaddeus Stevens Coll of Technology (PA)
Three Rivers Comm Coll (CT)
Tomball Coll (TX)
Trinity Valley Comm Coll (TX)
Triton Coll (IL)
Trocaire Coll (NY)
Truckee Meadows Comm Coll (NV)
Trumbull Business Coll (OH)
Tulsa Comm Coll (OK)
Tunxis Comm Coll (CT)
Tyler Jr Coll (TX)
Umpqua Comm Coll (OR)
The U of Akron–Wayne Coll (OH)
U of Northwestern Ohio (OH)
Vance-Granville Comm Coll (NC)
Vincennes U (IN)
Vincennes U Jasper Campus (IN)
Wake Tech Comm Coll (NC)
Wallace State Comm Coll (AL)
Walla Walla Comm Coll (WA)
Wayne Comm Coll (NC)
Webster Coll, Ocala (FL)
Westchester Comm Coll (NY)
Western Iowa Tech Comm Coll (IA)
Western Piedmont Comm Coll (NC)
Western Wyoming Comm Coll (WY)
Westmoreland County Comm Coll (PA)

LEGAL STUDIES

Alvin Comm Coll (TX)
Bay State Coll (MA)
City Colls of Chicago, Harry S Truman Coll (IL)
City Colls of Chicago, Richard J Daley Coll (IL)
Coll of the Siskiyous (CA)
The Comm Coll of Baltimore County–Catonsville Campus (MD)
Del Mar Coll (TX)
Delta Coll (MI)
Draughons Jr Coll, Nashville (TN)
Edison Comm Coll (FL)
Edison State Comm Coll (OH)
El Centro Coll (TX)
Florida National Coll (FL)
Foothill Coll (CA)
Gloucester County Coll (NJ)
Hillsborough Comm Coll (FL)
Iowa Lakes Comm Coll (IA)
Kirkwood Comm Coll (IA)
Macomb Comm Coll (MI)
Metropolitan Comm Coll (NE)
Miami-Dade Comm Coll (FL)
Midlands Tech Coll (SC)
Navarro Coll (TX)
North Harris Coll (TX)
Northland Comm and Tech Coll (MN)
Okaloosa-Walton Comm Coll (FL)
Oxnard Coll (CA)
Pasadena City Coll (CA)
Rasmussen Coll Mankato (MN)
Reading Area Comm Coll (PA)
St. Louis Comm Coll at Florissant Valley (MO)
Santa Ana Coll (CA)
Santa Barbara City Coll (CA)
Santa Fe Comm Coll (FL)
Trident Tech Coll (SC)
Tulsa Comm Coll (OK)
Vernon Coll (TX)
Webster Coll, Holiday (FL)
West Virginia Jr Coll, Charleston (WV)

LIBERAL ARTS AND SCIENCES/ LIBERAL STUDIES

Abraham Baldwin Ag Coll (GA)
Adirondack Comm Coll (NY)
Aims Comm Coll (CO)
Alamance Comm Coll (NC)
Albuquerque Tech Vocational Inst (NM)
Allan Hancock Coll (CA)
Allegany Coll of Maryland (MD)
Alpena Comm Coll (MI)
Alvin Comm Coll (TX)
Amarillo Coll (TX)
American River Coll (CA)
Ancilla Coll (IN)
Angelina Coll (TX)
Anne Arundel Comm Coll (MD)
Anoka-Ramsey Comm Coll (MN)
Antelope Valley Coll (CA)
Arapahoe Comm Coll (CO)
Arizona Western Coll (AZ)
Arkansas State U–Beebe (AR)
Arkansas State U–Mountain Home (AR)
Asheville-Buncombe Tech Comm Coll (NC)
Ashland Comm Coll (KY)
Asnuntuck Comm Coll (CT)
Assumption Coll for Sisters (NJ)
Atlantic Cape Comm Coll (NJ)
Austin Comm Coll (TX)
Bacone Coll (OK)
Bainbridge Coll (GA)
Bakersfield Coll (CA)
Baltimore City Comm Coll (MD)
Barstow Coll (CA)
Barton County Comm Coll (KS)
Bay de Noc Comm Coll (MI)
Bay State Coll (MA)
Beaufort County Comm Coll (NC)
Bellevue Comm Coll (WA)
Bergen Comm Coll (NJ)
Berkshire Comm Coll (MA)
Bethany Lutheran Coll (MN)
Bevill State Comm Coll (AL)
Big Bend Comm Coll (WA)
Bismarck State Coll (ND)
Blackfeet Comm Coll (MT)
Black Hawk Coll, Moline (IL)
Black River Tech Coll (AR)
Bladen Comm Coll (NC)
Blue Ridge Comm Coll (NC)
Blue Ridge Comm Coll (VA)
Blue River Comm Coll (MO)
Borough of Manhattan Comm Coll of City U of NY (NY)
Bossier Parish Comm Coll (LA)
Bowling Green State U-Firelands Coll (OH)
Brazosport Coll (TX)
Brevard Comm Coll (FL)
Bristol Comm Coll (MA)
Bronx Comm Coll of City U of NY (NY)
Brookdale Comm Coll (NJ)
Broome Comm Coll (NY)
Brunswick Comm Coll (NC)
Bucks County Comm Coll (PA)
Bunker Hill Comm Coll (MA)
Burlington County Coll (NJ)
Butler County Comm Coll (PA)
Butte Coll (CA)
Caldwell Comm Coll and Tech Inst (NC)
Calhoun Comm Coll (AL)
Cambria County Area Comm Coll (PA)
Camden County Coll (NJ)
Cañada Coll (CA)
Cape Cod Comm Coll (MA)
Cape Fear Comm Coll (NC)
Capital Comm Coll (CT)
Carl Sandburg Coll (IL)
Carroll Comm Coll (MD)
Carteret Comm Coll (NC)
Cascadia Comm Coll (WA)
Casper Coll (WY)
Catawba Valley Comm Coll (NC)
Cayuga County Comm Coll (NY)
Cecil Comm Coll (MD)
Cedar Valley Coll (TX)
Central Alabama Comm Coll (AL)
Central Arizona Coll (AZ)
Central Carolina Comm Coll (NC)
Central Carolina Tech Coll (SC)
Central Comm Coll–Columbus Campus (NE)
Central Comm Coll–Grand Island Campus (NE)
Central Comm Coll–Hastings Campus (NE)
Centralia Coll (WA)
Central Lakes Coll (MN)
Central Oregon Comm Coll (OR)
Central Piedmont Comm Coll (NC)
Central Texas Coll (TX)
Central Virginia Comm Coll (VA)
Century Comm and Tech Coll (MN)
Cerritos Coll (CA)
Cerro Coso Comm Coll (CA)
Chabot Coll (CA)
Chaffey Coll (CA)
Chatfield Coll (OH)
Chattahoochee Valley Comm Coll (AL)
Chattanooga State Tech Comm Coll (TN)
Chemeketa Comm Coll (OR)
Chesapeake Coll (MD)
Chipola Jr Coll (FL)
Cincinnati State Tech and Comm Coll (OH)
Citrus Coll (CA)
City Colls of Chicago, Harry S Truman Coll (IL)
City Colls of Chicago, Malcolm X Coll (IL)
City Colls of Chicago, Richard J Daley Coll (IL)
City Colls of Chicago, Wilbur Wright Coll (IL)
Clackamas Comm Coll (OR)
Clark Coll (WA)
Cleveland Comm Coll (NC)
Cleveland State Comm Coll (TN)
Clinton Comm Coll (IA)
Clinton Comm Coll (NY)
Clovis Comm Coll (NM)
Coahoma Comm Coll (MS)
Coastal Bend Coll (TX)
Coastal Carolina Comm Coll (NC)
Coastal Georgia Comm Coll (GA)
Coastline Comm Coll (CA)
Cochise Coll, Douglas (AZ)
Coffeyville Comm Coll (KS)
Colby Comm Coll (KS)
Coll of Alameda (CA)
Coll of DuPage (IL)
Coll of Eastern Utah (UT)
Coll of Marin (CA)
Coll of St. Catherine–Minneapolis (MN)
Coll of Southern Idaho (ID)
Coll of Southern Maryland (MD)
Coll of the Canyons (CA)
Coll of the Desert (CA)
Coll of the Sequoias (CA)
Collin County Comm Coll District (TX)
Colorado Mountn Coll, Alpine Cmps (CO)
Colorado Mountn Coll (CO)
Colorado Mountn Coll, Timberline Cmps (CO)
Colorado Northwestern Comm Coll (CO)
Columbia-Greene Comm Coll (NY)
Columbia State Comm Coll (TN)
Columbus State Comm Coll (OH)
Comm Coll of Allegheny County (PA)
Comm Coll of Aurora (CO)
The Comm Coll of Baltimore County–Catonsville Campus (MD)
Comm Coll of Beaver County (PA)
Comm Coll of Denver (CO)
Comm Coll of Rhode Island (RI)
Comm Coll of Southern Nevada (NV)
Comm Coll of Vermont (VT)
Compton Comm Coll (CA)
Copiah-Lincoln Comm Coll–Natchez Campus (MS)
Corning Comm Coll (NY)
Cottey Coll (MO)
County Coll of Morris (NJ)
Cowley County Comm Coll and Voc-Tech School (KS)
Crafton Hills Coll (CA)
Craven Comm Coll (NC)
Crowder Coll (MO)
Cuesta Coll (CA)
Cumberland County Coll (NJ)
Cuyahoga Comm Coll (OH)
Cuyamaca Coll (CA)
Cypress Coll (CA)
Danville Area Comm Coll (IL)
Danville Comm Coll (VA)
Darton Coll (GA)
Dawson Comm Coll (MT)
Daytona Beach Comm Coll (FL)
Dean Coll (MA)
De Anza Coll (CA)
Deep Springs Coll (CA)
Delaware County Comm Coll (PA)
Del Mar Coll (TX)
Delta Coll (MI)
Des Moines Area Comm Coll (IA)
Diablo Valley Coll (CA)
Diné Coll (AZ)
Dixie State Coll of Utah (UT)
Dodge City Comm Coll (KS)
Donnelly Coll (KS)
Durham Tech Comm Coll (NC)
Dutchess Comm Coll (NY)
Dyersburg State Comm Coll (TN)
East Arkansas Comm Coll (AR)
East Central Coll (MO)
East Central Comm Coll (MS)
Eastern Arizona Coll (AZ)
Eastern Shore Comm Coll (VA)
Eastern Wyoming Coll (WY)
Eastfield Coll (TX)
East Georgia Coll (GA)
East Mississippi Comm Coll (MS)
Edgecombe Comm Coll (NC)
Edison Comm Coll (FL)
Edison State Comm Coll (OH)
Edmonds Comm Coll (WA)
Elaine P. Nunez Comm Coll (LA)
El Centro Coll (TX)
Elizabethtown Comm Coll (KY)
Ellsworth Comm Coll (IA)
Emory U, Oxford Coll (GA)
Enterprise State Jr Coll (AL)
Erie Comm Coll, City Campus (NY)
Erie Comm Coll, North Campus (NY)
Erie Comm Coll, South Campus (NY)
Essex County Coll (NJ)
Estrella Mountain Comm Coll (AZ)
Eugenio María de Hostos Comm Coll of City U of NY (NY)
Everett Comm Coll (WA)
Evergreen Valley Coll (CA)
Fayetteville Tech Comm Coll (NC)
Feather River Comm Coll District (CA)
Fergus Falls Comm Coll (MN)
Finger Lakes Comm Coll (NY)
Fiorello H LaGuardia Comm Coll of City U of NY (NY)
Fisher Coll (MA)
Flathead Valley Comm Coll (MT)
Florence-Darlington Tech Coll (SC)
Florida Comm Coll at Jacksonville (FL)
Florida National Coll (FL)
Floyd Coll (GA)
Foothill Coll (CA)
Fort Berthold Comm Coll (ND)
Fort Scott Comm Coll (KS)
Frederick Comm Coll (MD)
Fresno City Coll (CA)
Front Range Comm Coll (CO)
Fullerton Coll (CA)
Fulton-Montgomery Comm Coll (NY)
Gadsden State Comm Coll (AL)
Galveston Coll (TX)
Garden City Comm Coll (KS)
GateWay Comm Coll (AZ)
Gateway Comm Coll (CT)
Gavilan Coll (CA)
Genesee Comm Coll (NY)
Georgia Military Coll (GA)
Germanna Comm Coll (VA)
Glendale Comm Coll (AZ)
Glendale Comm Coll (CA)
Glen Oaks Comm Coll (MI)
Gloucester County Coll (NJ)
Gogebic Comm Coll (MI)
Golden West Coll (CA)
Grand Rapids Comm Coll (MI)
Grays Harbor Coll (WA)
Grayson County Coll (TX)
Greenfield Comm Coll (MA)
Green River Comm Coll (WA)
Greenville Tech Coll (SC)
Guilford Tech Comm Coll (NC)
Gulf Coast Comm Coll (FL)
Hagerstown Comm Coll (MD)
Halifax Comm Coll (NC)
Harcum Coll (PA)
Harford Comm Coll (MD)
Harrisburg Area Comm Coll (PA)
Hawaii Comm Coll (HI)
Hawaii Tokai International Coll (HI)
Hawkeye Comm Coll (IA)
Haywood Comm Coll (NC)
Hazard Comm Coll (KY)
Heartland Comm Coll (IL)
Henry Ford Comm Coll (MI)
Herkimer County Comm Coll (NY)
Hesser Coll (NH)
Hesston Coll (KS)
Hibbing Comm Coll (MN)
Highland Comm Coll (IL)
Highland Comm Coll (KS)
Hill Coll of the Hill Jr College District (TX)
Hillsborough Comm Coll (FL)
Hinds Comm Coll (MS)
Hiwassee Coll (TN)
Holmes Comm Coll (MS)
Holy Cross Coll (IN)
Holyoke Comm Coll (MA)
Honolulu Comm Coll (HI)
Hopkinsville Comm Coll (KY)
Housatonic Comm Coll (CT)
Houston Comm Coll System (TX)
Howard Comm Coll (MD)
Hudson County Comm Coll (NJ)
Hutchinson Comm Coll and Area Vocational School (KS)
Illinois Eastern Comm Colls, Frontier Comm Coll (IL)
Illinois Eastern Comm Colls, Lincoln Trail Coll (IL)
Illinois Eastern Comm Colls, Olney Central Coll (IL)
Illinois Eastern Comm Colls, Wabash Valley Coll (IL)
Imperial Valley Coll (CA)
Independence Comm Coll (KS)
Indian Hills Comm Coll (IA)
Indian River Comm Coll (FL)
Inver Hills Comm Coll (MN)
Iowa Lakes Comm Coll (IA)
Iowa Western Comm Coll (IA)
Isothermal Comm Coll (NC)
Itasca Comm Coll (MN)
Jackson Comm Coll (MI)
Jackson State Comm Coll (TN)
Jacksonville Coll (TX)

James H. Faulkner State Comm Coll (AL)
James Sprunt Comm Coll (NC)
Jamestown Comm Coll (NY)
Jefferson Coll (MO)
Jefferson Comm Coll (KY)
Jefferson Comm Coll (NY)
Jefferson Davis Comm Coll (AL)
Jefferson State Comm Coll (AL)
John A. Logan Coll (IL)
Johnson County Comm Coll (KS)
Johnston Comm Coll (NC)
John Tyler Comm Coll (VA)
John Wood Comm Coll (IL)
Joliet Jr Coll (IL)
J. Sargeant Reynolds Comm Coll (VA)
Kalamazoo Valley Comm Coll (MI)
Kankakee Comm Coll (IL)
Kansas City Kansas Comm Coll (KS)
Kaskaskia Coll (IL)
Kauai Comm Coll (HI)
Kellogg Comm Coll (MI)
Kennebec Valley Tech Coll (ME)
Kent State U, East Liverpool Campus (OH)
Kent State U, Geauga Campus (OH)
Kent State U, Salem Campus (OH)
Kent State U, Stark Campus (OH)
Kent State U, Trumbull Campus (OH)
Kent State U, Tuscarawas Campus (OH)
Keystone Coll (PA)
Kingsborough Comm Coll of City U of NY (NY)
Kirkwood Comm Coll (IA)
Kishwaukee Coll (IL)
Labette Comm Coll (KS)
Lac Courte Oreilles Ojibwa Comm Coll (WI)
Lake City Comm Coll (FL)
Lake Land Coll (IL)
Lakeland Comm Coll (OH)
Lake Michigan Coll (MI)
Lake Region State Coll (ND)
Lake-Sumter Comm Coll (FL)
Lake Tahoe Comm Coll (CA)
Lamar Comm Coll (CO)
Lamar State Coll–Orange (TX)
Landmark Coll (VT)
Lane Comm Coll (OR)
Lansing Comm Coll (MI)
Laramie County Comm Coll (WY)
Laredo Comm Coll (TX)
Las Positas Coll (CA)
LDS Business Coll (UT)
Lehigh Carbon Comm Coll (PA)
Lenoir Comm Coll (NC)
Lewis and Clark Comm Coll (IL)
Lewis Coll of Business (MI)
Lincoln Coll, Lincoln (IL)
Lincoln Coll, Normal (IL)
Lincoln Land Comm Coll (IL)
Linn-Benton Comm Coll (OR)
Long Beach City Coll (CA)
Longview Comm Coll (MO)
Lon Morris Coll (TX)
Lorain County Comm Coll (OH)
Lord Fairfax Comm Coll (VA)
Los Angeles City Coll (CA)
Los Angeles Harbor Coll (CA)
Los Angeles Mission Coll (CA)
Los Angeles Pierce Coll (CA)
Louisburg Coll (NC)
Louisiana State U at Alexandria (LA)
Lower Columbia Coll (WA)
Lurleen B. Wallace Jr Coll (AL)
Luzerne County Comm Coll (PA)
Macomb Comm Coll (MI)
Manatee Comm Coll (FL)
Manchester Comm Coll (CT)
Manor Coll (PA)
Maple Woods Comm Coll (MO)
Marian Court Coll (MA)
Marion Military Inst (AL)
Marshalltown Comm Coll (IA)
Martin Comm Coll (NC)
Marymount Coll, Palos Verdes, California (CA)
Massachusetts Bay Comm Coll (MA)
Massasoit Comm Coll (MA)
Mayland Comm Coll (NC)
Maysville Comm Coll (KY)
McHenry County Coll (IL)
McLennan Comm Coll (TX)
Merced Coll (CA)
Mercer County Comm Coll (NJ)
Mesabi Range Comm and Tech Coll (MN)
Metropolitan Comm Coll (NE)
Miami U–Hamilton Campus (OH)
Miami U–Middletown Campus (OH)
Middle Georgia Coll (GA)
Middlesex Comm Coll (MA)
Midland Coll (TX)
Midlands Tech Coll (SC)
Mid Michigan Comm Coll (MI)
Mid-Plains Comm Coll Area (NE)
Mid-South Comm Coll (AR)
Miles Comm Coll (MT)
Milwaukee Area Tech Coll (WI)
Mineral Area Coll (MO)
Minneapolis Comm and Tech Coll (MN)
Minot State U–Bottineau Campus (ND)
MiraCosta Coll (CA)
Mississippi Delta Comm Coll (MS)
Mississippi Gulf Coast Comm Coll (MS)
Mitchell Coll (CT)
Mitchell Comm Coll (NC)
Moberly Area Comm Coll (MO)
Mohave Comm Coll (AZ)
Mohawk Valley Comm Coll (NY)
Monroe Comm Coll (NY)
Monroe County Comm Coll (MI)
Montcalm Comm Coll (MI)
Monterey Peninsula Coll (CA)
Montgomery Coll (MD)
Montgomery Comm Coll (NC)
Montgomery County Comm Coll (PA)
Moorpark Coll (CA)
Moraine Valley Comm Coll (IL)
Morgan Comm Coll (CO)
Morton Coll (IL)
Motlow State Comm Coll (TN)
Mott Comm Coll (MI)
Mountain Empire Comm Coll (VA)
Mountain View Coll (TX)
Mt. Hood Comm Coll (OR)
Mount Wachusett Comm Coll (MA)
Muscatine Comm Coll (IA)
Nash Comm Coll (NC)
Nassau Comm Coll (NY)
Naugatuck Valley Comm Coll (CT)
NEI Coll of Technology (MN)
Neosho County Comm Coll (KS)
New Hampshire Comm Tech Coll, Berlin/Laconia (NH)
New Hampshire Tech Inst (NH)
New Mexico Military Inst (NM)
New Mexico State U–Alamogordo (NM)
New Mexico State U–Carlsbad (NM)
New River Comm Coll (VA)
New York City Tech Coll of the City U of NY (NY)
Niagara County Comm Coll (NY)
Northampton County Area Comm Coll (PA)
North Arkansas Coll (AR)
North Central Michigan Coll (MI)
North Central Texas Coll (TX)
North Country Comm Coll (NY)
North Dakota State Coll of Science (ND)
Northeast Alabama Comm Coll (AL)
Northeast Comm Coll (NE)
Northeastern Tech Coll (SC)
Northeast Iowa Comm Coll (IA)
Northeast State Tech Comm Coll (TN)
Northern Essex Comm Coll (MA)
Northern Oklahoma Coll (OK)
Northern Virginia Comm Coll (VA)
North Harris Coll (TX)
North Hennepin Comm Coll (MN)
North Idaho Coll (ID)
North Iowa Area Comm Coll (IA)
Northland Comm and Tech Coll (MN)
Northland Pioneer Coll (AZ)
North Seattle Comm Coll (WA)
North Shore Comm Coll (MA)
NorthWest Arkansas Comm Coll (AR)
Northwest Coll (WY)
Northwestern Connecticut Comm-Tech Coll (CT)
Northwestern Michigan Coll (MI)
Northwest Mississippi Comm Coll (MS)
Northwest-Shoals Comm Coll (AL)
Norwalk Comm Coll (CT)
Oakton Comm Coll (IL)
Ocean County Coll (NJ)
Odessa Coll (TX)
Okaloosa-Walton Comm Coll (FL)
Oklahoma City Comm Coll (OK)
Onondaga Comm Coll (NY)
Orangeburg-Calhoun Tech Coll (SC)
Orange Coast Coll (CA)
Orange County Comm Coll (NY)
Otero Jr Coll (CO)
Ouachita Tech Coll (AR)
Owensboro Comm Coll (KY)
Oxnard Coll (CA)
Ozarka Coll (AR)
Palau Comm CollPalau)
Palm Beach Comm Coll (FL)
Palomar Coll (CA)
Palo Verde Coll (CA)
Pamlico Comm Coll (NC)
Paradise Valley Comm Coll (AZ)
Parkland Coll (IL)
Pasadena City Coll (CA)
Pasco-Hernando Comm Coll (FL)
Patrick Henry Comm Coll (VA)
Paul D. Camp Comm Coll (VA)
Paul Smith's Coll of Arts and Sciences (NY)
Pellissippi State Tech Comm Coll (TN)
Pennsylvania Coll of Technology (PA)
Penn State U Beaver Campus of the Commonwealth Coll (PA)
Penn State U Delaware County Campus of the Commonwealth Coll (PA)
Penn State U DuBois Campus of the Commonwealth Coll (PA)
Penn State U Fayette Campus of the Commonwealth Coll (PA)
Penn State U Hazleton Campus of the Commonwealth Coll (PA)
Penn State U McKeesport Campus of the Commonwealth Coll (PA)
Penn State U Mont Alto Campus of the Commonwealth Coll (PA)
Penn State U New Kensington Campus of the Commonwealth Coll (PA)
Penn State U Shenango Campus of the Commonwealth Coll (PA)
Penn State U Wilkes-Barre Campus of the Commonwealth Coll (PA)
Penn State U Worthington Scranton Cmps Commonwealth Coll (PA)
Penn State U York Campus of the Commonwealth Coll (PA)
Penn Valley Comm Coll (MO)
Pensacola Jr Coll (FL)
Phoenix Coll (AZ)
Piedmont Comm Coll (NC)
Piedmont Tech Coll (SC)
Piedmont Virginia Comm Coll (VA)
Pierce Coll (WA)
Pikes Peak Comm Coll (CO)
Pima Comm Coll (AZ)
Pitt Comm Coll (NC)
Polk Comm Coll (FL)
Portland Comm Coll (OR)
Prairie State Coll (IL)
Pratt Comm Coll and Area Vocational School (KS)
Prince George's Comm Coll (MD)
Queensborough Comm Coll of City U of NY (NY)
Quincy Coll (MA)
Quinsigamond Comm Coll (MA)
Rainy River Comm Coll (MN)
Randolph Comm Coll (NC)
Ranger Coll (TX)
Rappahannock Comm Coll (VA)
Raritan Valley Comm Coll (NJ)
Reading Area Comm Coll (PA)
Red Rocks Comm Coll (CO)
Reedley Coll (CA)
Rend Lake Coll (IL)
Richard Bland Coll of the Coll of William and Mary (VA)
Richland Comm Coll (IL)
Richmond Comm Coll (NC)
Rich Mountain Comm Coll (AR)
Ridgewater Coll (MN)
Riverland Comm Coll (MN)
Riverside Comm Coll (CA)
Roane State Comm Coll (TN)
Roanoke-Chowan Comm Coll (NC)
Rockingham Comm Coll (NC)
Rockland Comm Coll (NY)
Rogue Comm Coll (OR)
Rowan-Cabarrus Comm Coll (NC)
Sacramento City Coll (CA)
St. Catharine Coll (KY)
Saint Charles Comm Coll (MO)
St. Clair County Comm Coll (MI)
St. Louis Comm Coll at Florissant Valley (MO)
St. Petersburg Coll (FL)
St. Philip's Coll (TX)
Salem Comm Coll (NJ)
Salish Kootenai Coll (MT)
Sampson Comm Coll (NC)
San Antonio Coll (TX)
San Bernardino Valley Coll (CA)
Sandhills Comm Coll (NC)
San Diego City Coll (CA)
San Diego Mesa Coll (CA)
San Jacinto Coll Central Campus (TX)
San Joaquin Delta Coll (CA)
Santa Ana Coll (CA)
Santa Barbara City Coll (CA)
Santa Fe Comm Coll (FL)
Santa Monica Coll (CA)
Sauk Valley Comm Coll (IL)
Schenectady County Comm Coll (NY)
Schoolcraft Coll (MI)
Scott Comm Coll (IA)
Seattle Central Comm Coll (WA)
Seminole Comm Coll (FL)
Seminole State Coll (OK)
Sheridan Coll (WY)
Shoreline Comm Coll (WA)
Sierra Coll (CA)
Sinclair Comm Coll (OH)
Sitting Bull Coll (ND)
Skagit Valley Coll (WA)
Snead State Comm Coll (AL)
Snow Coll (UT)
Southeast Comm Coll (KY)
Southeast Comm Coll, Beatrice Campus (NE)
Southeastern Comm Coll (NC)
Southeastern Comm Coll, South Campus (IA)
Southern Maine Tech Coll (ME)
Southern State Comm Coll (OH)
Southern West Virginia Comm and Tech Coll (WV)
South Mountain Comm Coll (AZ)
South Piedmont Comm Coll (NC)
South Plains Coll (TX)
South Puget Sound Comm Coll (WA)
Southside Virginia Comm Coll (VA)
South Suburban Coll (IL)
South Texas Comm Coll (TX)
Southwestern Coll (CA)
Southwestern Comm Coll (IA)
Southwestern Comm Coll (NC)
Southwestern Michigan Coll (MI)
Southwest Mississippi Comm Coll (MS)
Southwest Virginia Comm Coll (VA)
Spartanburg Methodist Coll (SC)
Spartanburg Tech Coll (SC)
Spokane Comm Coll (WA)
Spokane Falls Comm Coll (WA)
Springfield Tech Comm Coll (MA)
State Fair Comm Coll (MO)
State U of NY Coll of A&T at Morrisville (NY)
State U of NY Coll of Technology at Alfred (NY)
State U of NY Coll of Technology at Canton (NY)
Stone Child Coll (MT)
Suffolk County Comm Coll (NY)
Sullivan County Comm Coll (NY)
Surry Comm Coll (NC)
Sussex County Comm Coll (NJ)
Tacoma Comm Coll (WA)
Taft Coll (CA)
Tallahassee Comm Coll (FL)
Tarrant County Coll District (TX)
Temple Coll (TX)
Texarkana Coll (TX)
Thomas Nelson Comm Coll (VA)
Three Rivers Comm Coll (CT)
Tidewater Comm Coll (VA)
Tompkins Cortland Comm Coll (NY)
Tri-County Comm Coll (NC)
Tri-County Tech Coll (SC)
Trident Tech Coll (SC)
Trinidad State Jr Coll (CO)
Trinity Valley Comm Coll (TX)
Triton Coll (IL)
Trocaire Coll (NY)
Truckee Meadows Comm Coll (NV)
Truett-McConnell Coll (GA)
Tulsa Comm Coll (OK)
Tunxis Comm Coll (CT)
Tyler Jr Coll (TX)
Ulster County Comm Coll (NY)
Umpqua Comm Coll (OR)
Union County Coll (NJ)
The U of Akron–Wayne Coll (OH)
U of Alaska Anchorage, Kenai Peninsula Coll (AK)
U of Alaska Anchorage, Kodiak Coll (AK)
U of Alaska Anchorage, Matanuska-Susitna Coll (AK)
U of Alaska Southeast, Ketchikan Campus (AK)
U of Alaska Southeast, Sitka Campus (AK)
U of Arkansas at Fort Smith (AR)
U of Arkansas Comm Coll at Hope (AR)
U of Arkansas Comm Coll at Morrilton (AR)
U of Kentucky, Lexington Comm Coll (KY)
U of New Mexico–Gallup (NM)
U of New Mexico–Los Alamos Branch (NM)
U of Pittsburgh at Titusville (PA)
U of South Carolina at Beaufort (SC)
U of South Carolina at Lancaster (SC)
U of South Carolina at Sumter (SC)
U of South Carolina at Union (SC)
U of Wisconsin Center–Baraboo/Sauk County (WI)
U of Wisconsin Center–Barron County (WI)
U of Wisconsin Center–Fox Valley (WI)
U of Wisconsin Center–Manitowoc County (WI)
U of Wisconsin Center–Marinette County (WI)
U of Wisconsin Center–Marshfield/Wood County (WI)
U of Wisconsin Center–Richland (WI)
U of Wisconsin Center–Rock County (WI)
U of Wisconsin Center–Sheboygan County (WI)
U of Wisconsin Center–Washington County (WI)
U of Wisconsin Center–Waukesha County (WI)
Urban Coll of Boston (MA)
Valley Forge Military Coll (PA)
Vance-Granville Comm Coll (NC)
Ventura Coll (CA)
Vermilion Comm Coll (MN)
Vernon Coll (TX)
Victoria Coll (TX)
Victor Valley Coll (CA)
Villa Maria Coll of Buffalo (NY)
Vincennes U (IN)
Vincennes U Jasper Campus (IN)
Virginia Western Comm Coll (VA)
Vista Comm Coll (CA)
Volunteer State Comm Coll (TN)
Wake Tech Comm Coll (NC)
Wallace State Comm Coll (AL)
Walla Walla Comm Coll (WA)
Walters State Comm Coll (TN)
Warren County Comm Coll (NJ)
Waubonsee Comm Coll (IL)
Waycross Coll (GA)
Wayne Comm Coll (NC)
Weatherford Coll (TX)
Wentworth Military Academy and Jr Coll (MO)
Westchester Comm Coll (NY)
Western Iowa Tech Comm Coll (IA)
Western Nebraska Comm Coll (NE)
Western Nevada Comm Coll (NV)
Western Piedmont Comm Coll (NC)

Western Texas Coll (TX)
Western Wyoming Comm Coll (WY)
Westmoreland County Comm Coll (PA)
West Shore Comm Coll (MI)
West Virginia Northern Comm Coll (WV)
West Virginia U at Parkersburg (WV)
Whatcom Comm Coll (WA)
Wilkes Comm Coll (NC)
Williston State Coll (ND)
Wilson Tech Comm Coll (NC)
York Tech Coll (SC)
Young Harris Coll (GA)

LIBERAL ARTS AND STUDIES RELATED
Cascadia Comm Coll (WA)
Hagerstown Comm Coll (MD)
Martin Comm Coll (NC)
Northampton County Area Comm Coll (PA)
Southwestern Michigan Coll (MI)

LIBRARY ASSISTANT
Citrus Coll (CA)
Clovis Comm Coll (NM)
Coll of Lake County (IL)
Northern New Mexico Comm Coll (NM)
Northland Pioneer Coll (AZ)
Oakland Comm Coll (MI)
Spokane Falls Comm Coll (WA)

LIBRARY SCIENCE
Allen County Comm Coll (KS)
Brookdale Comm Coll (NJ)
Citrus Coll (CA)
City Coll of San Francisco (CA)
City Colls of Chicago, Wilbur Wright Coll (IL)
Colby Comm Coll (KS)
Coll of DuPage (IL)
Coll of Southern Idaho (ID)
Cuesta Coll (CA)
Doña Ana Branch Comm Coll (NM)
East Central Coll (MO)
East Central Comm Coll (MS)
Foothill Coll (CA)
Fresno City Coll (CA)
Fullerton Coll (CA)
Highland Comm Coll (KS)
Highline Comm Coll (WA)
Indian River Comm Coll (FL)
Lenoir Comm Coll (NC)
Lewis and Clark Comm Coll (IL)
Merced Coll (CA)
Oxnard Coll (CA)
Palomar Coll (CA)
Pasadena City Coll (CA)
Portland Comm Coll (OR)
Riverside Comm Coll (CA)
Sacramento City Coll (CA)
Santa Ana Coll (CA)
Tulsa Comm Coll (OK)
Wallace State Comm Coll (AL)

LINGUISTICS
Foothill Coll (CA)

LITERATURE
Andrew Coll (GA)
Atlantic Cape Comm Coll (NJ)
Bergen Comm Coll (NJ)
Blinn Coll (TX)
Chabot Coll (CA)
Comm Coll of Southern Nevada (NV)
Compton Comm Coll (CA)
East Central Comm Coll (MS)
Foothill Coll (CA)
Iowa Lakes Comm Coll (IA)
Lamar Comm Coll (CO)
Lamar State Coll–Orange (TX)
Lincoln Land Comm Coll (IL)
Lon Morris Coll (TX)
Miami-Dade Comm Coll (FL)
Midland Coll (TX)
Oklahoma City Comm Coll (OK)
Otero Jr Coll (CO)
Palm Beach Comm Coll (FL)
Pratt Comm Coll and Area Vocational School (KS)
Sacramento City Coll (CA)
San Jacinto Coll Central Campus (TX)
San Joaquin Delta Coll (CA)
Skagit Valley Coll (WA)
Southwestern Coll (CA)
Tacoma Comm Coll (WA)

LITHOGRAPHY
Pennsylvania Coll of Technology (PA)

LOGISTICS/MATERIALS MANAGEMENT
Brevard Comm Coll (FL)
Columbus State Comm Coll (OH)
Comm Coll of the Air Force (AL)
Gateway Tech Coll (WI)
Houston Comm Coll System (TX)
Prairie State Coll (IL)
Sinclair Comm Coll (OH)
Springfield Tech Comm Coll (MA)
Waubonsee Comm Coll (IL)

MACHINE SHOP ASSISTANT
Cape Fear Comm Coll (NC)
Coll of Lake County (IL)
Comm Coll of Allegheny County (PA)
Corning Comm Coll (NY)
Dakota County Tech Coll (MN)
Delgado Comm Coll (LA)
Eastern Arizona Coll (AZ)
Erie Comm Coll, North Campus (NY)
Florida Comm Coll at Jacksonville (FL)
Front Range Comm Coll (CO)
Harry M. Ayers State Tech Coll (AL)
Ivy Tech State Coll–Central Indiana (IN)
Johnson Coll (PA)
Lehigh Carbon Comm Coll (PA)
Maple Woods Comm Coll (MO)
Modesto Jr Coll (CA)
North Central Texas Coll (TX)
North Dakota State Coll of Science (ND)
Northwestern Michigan Coll (MI)
Orange Coast Coll (CA)
Pima Comm Coll (AZ)
Pitt Comm Coll (NC)
Ridgewater Coll (MN)
Riverland Comm Coll (MN)
Southwestern Michigan Coll (MI)
U of Arkansas Comm Coll at Hope (AR)
Vincennes U (IN)
Western Dakota Tech Inst (SD)

MACHINE TECHNOLOGY
Alamance Comm Coll (NC)
Alexandria Tech Coll (MN)
Allan Hancock Coll (CA)
Alpena Comm Coll (MI)
Amarillo Coll (TX)
Asheville-Buncombe Tech Comm Coll (NC)
Athens Tech Coll (GA)
Bakersfield Coll (CA)
Bay de Noc Comm Coll (MI)
Black Hawk Coll, Moline (IL)
Blue Ridge Comm Coll (NC)
Butler County Comm Coll (PA)
Casper Coll (WY)
Central Comm Coll–Columbus Campus (NE)
Central Comm Coll–Hastings Campus (NE)
Central Maine Tech Coll (ME)
Central Piedmont Comm Coll (NC)
Century Comm and Tech Coll (MN)
Cerritos Coll (CA)
Cerro Coso Comm Coll (CA)
Chattanooga State Tech Comm Coll (TN)
Chippewa Valley Tech Coll (WI)
City Colls of Chicago, Richard J Daley Coll (IL)
City Colls of Chicago, Wilbur Wright Coll (IL)
Clackamas Comm Coll (OR)
Clark Coll (WA)
Clinton Comm Coll (IA)
Coffeyville Comm Coll (KS)
Coll of DuPage (IL)
Coll of Eastern Utah (UT)
Coll of Marin (CA)
Coll of the Redwoods (CA)
The Comm Coll of Baltimore County–Catonsville Campus (MD)
Compton Comm Coll (CA)
Corning Comm Coll (NY)
Cowley County Comm Coll and Voc-Tech School (KS)
De Anza Coll (CA)
Delgado Comm Coll (LA)
Del Mar Coll (TX)
Delta Coll (MI)
Des Moines Area Comm Coll (IA)
Durham Tech Comm Coll (NC)
East Central Coll (MO)
Eastern Maine Tech Coll (ME)
Fayetteville Tech Comm Coll (NC)
Florence-Darlington Tech Coll (SC)
Forsyth Tech Comm Coll (NC)
Fresno City Coll (CA)
Gateway Tech Coll (WI)
George Corley Wallace State Comm Coll (AL)
Glendale Comm Coll (CA)
Grays Harbor Coll (WA)
Grayson County Coll (TX)
Green River Comm Coll (WA)
Greenville Tech Coll (SC)
Guilford Tech Comm Coll (NC)
Gwinnett Tech Coll (GA)
Harry M. Ayers State Tech Coll (AL)
Hawkeye Comm Coll (IA)
Haywood Comm Coll (NC)
Heartland Comm Coll (IL)
Helena Coll of Tech of The U of Montana (MT)
Hennepin Tech Coll (MN)
Hill Coll of the Hill Jr College District (TX)
Hinds Comm Coll (MS)
Horry-Georgetown Tech Coll (SC)
Hutchinson Comm Coll and Area Vocational School (KS)
Illinois Eastern Comm Colls, Wabash Valley Coll (IL)
Indian Hills Comm Coll (IA)
Iowa Western Comm Coll (IA)
Isothermal Comm Coll (NC)
Ivy Tech State Coll–Bloomington (IN)
Ivy Tech State Coll–Central Indiana (IN)
Ivy Tech State Coll–Columbus (IN)
Ivy Tech State Coll–Eastcentral (IN)
Ivy Tech State Coll–Kokomo (IN)
Ivy Tech State Coll–Lafayette (IN)
Ivy Tech State Coll–North Central (IN)
Ivy Tech State Coll–Northeast (IN)
Ivy Tech State Coll–Northwest (IN)
Ivy Tech State Coll–Southcentral (IN)
Ivy Tech State Coll–Southwest (IN)
Ivy Tech State Coll–Wabash Valley (IN)
Ivy Tech State Coll–Whitewater (IN)
Jackson Comm Coll (MI)
Jefferson Coll (MO)
J. F. Drake State Tech Coll (AL)
John A. Logan Coll (IL)
Johnson Coll (PA)
Johnson County Comm Coll (KS)
Johnston Comm Coll (NC)
Kalamazoo Valley Comm Coll (MI)
Kankakee Comm Coll (IL)
Kellogg Comm Coll (MI)
Kennebec Valley Tech Coll (ME)
Kilgore Coll (TX)
Lake Area Tech Inst (SD)
Lakeland Comm Coll (OH)
Lake Michigan Coll (MI)
Lake Washington Tech Coll (WA)
Lansing Comm Coll (MI)
Lewis and Clark Comm Coll (IL)
Linn-Benton Comm Coll (OR)
Long Beach City Coll (CA)
Lorain County Comm Coll (OH)
Los Angeles Pierce Coll (CA)
Louisiana Tech Coll–Delta Ouachita Campus (LA)
Lower Columbia Coll (WA)
Macomb Comm Coll (MI)
Maple Woods Comm Coll (MO)
Marshalltown Comm Coll (IA)
Meridian Comm Coll (MS)
Midlands Tech Coll (SC)
Mid Michigan Comm Coll (MI)
Mid-Plains Comm Coll Area (NE)
Minnesota State Coll–Southeast Tech (MN)
MiraCosta Coll (CA)
Mitchell Comm Coll (NC)
Modesto Jr Coll (CA)
Mohawk Valley Comm Coll (NY)
Moraine Park Tech Coll (WI)
Muscatine Comm Coll (IA)
New River Comm Coll (VA)
Northcentral Tech Coll (WI)
North Central Texas Coll (TX)
Northeastern Tech Coll (SC)
Northeast State Tech Comm Coll (TN)
Northern Essex Comm Coll (MA)
North Idaho Coll (ID)
Northwest Mississippi Comm Coll (MS)
Northwest State Comm Coll (OH)
Oakland Comm Coll (MI)
Oakton Comm Coll (IL)
Odessa Coll (TX)
Oklahoma State U, Okmulgee (OK)
Onondaga Comm Coll (NY)
Orangeburg-Calhoun Tech Coll (SC)
Orange Coast Coll (CA)
Ouachita Tech Coll (AR)
Oxnard Coll (CA)
Pasadena City Coll (CA)
Pellissippi State Tech Comm Coll (TN)
Piedmont Tech Coll (SC)
Pikes Peak Comm Coll (CO)
Pine Tech Coll (MN)
Pitt Comm Coll (NC)
Portland Comm Coll (OR)
Randolph Comm Coll (NC)
Reading Area Comm Coll (PA)
Reedley Coll (CA)
Richmond Comm Coll (NC)
St. Clair County Comm Coll (MI)
St. Cloud Tech Coll (MN)
St. Philip's Coll (TX)
San Bernardino Valley Coll (CA)
San Diego City Coll (CA)
San Joaquin Delta Coll (CA)
Scott Comm Coll (IA)
Sheridan Coll (WY)
Shoreline Comm Coll (WA)
Sinclair Comm Coll (OH)
Southeast Comm Coll, Milford Campus (NE)
Southeast Tech Inst (SD)
Southern Maine Tech Coll (ME)
South Piedmont Comm Coll (NC)
South Plains Coll (TX)
South Suburban Coll (IL)
South Texas Comm Coll (TX)
Southwest Mississippi Comm Coll (MS)
Southwest Wisconsin Tech Coll (WI)
Spartanburg Tech Coll (SC)
Spokane Comm Coll (WA)
State Fair Comm Coll (MO)
State U of NY Coll of Technology at Alfred (NY)
Surry Comm Coll (NC)
Tarrant County Coll District (TX)
Texas State Tech Coll–Harlingen (TX)
Texas State Tech Coll– Waco/ Marshall Campus (TX)
Texas State Tech Coll (TX)
Thaddeus Stevens Coll of Technology (PA)
Trenholm State Tech Coll, Patterson Campus (AL)
Tri-County Tech Coll (SC)
Trident Tech Coll (SC)
Triton Coll (IL)
U of Alaska Anchorage, Kenai Peninsula Coll (AK)
U of Arkansas at Fort Smith (AR)
U of Arkansas Comm Coll at Morrilton (AR)
Ventura Coll (CA)
Vernon Coll (TX)
Vincennes U (IN)
Wake Tech Comm Coll (NC)
Wallace State Comm Coll (AL)
Walla Walla Comm Coll (WA)
Waycross Coll (GA)
Wayne Comm Coll (NC)
Western Iowa Tech Comm Coll (IA)
Western Nevada Comm Coll (NV)
Western Wyoming Comm Coll (WY)
West Shore Comm Coll (MI)
West Virginia U at Parkersburg (WV)
York Tech Coll (SC)

MAJOR APPLIANCE INSTALLATION/REPAIR
Dunwoody Coll of Technology (MN)

MANAGEMENT INFORMATION SYSTEMS/BUSINESS DATA PROCESSING
Alexandria Tech Coll (MN)
Arapahoe Comm Coll (CO)
Ashland Comm Coll (KY)
Austin Business Coll (TX)
Career Coll of Northern Nevada (NV)
Central Virginia Comm Coll (VA)
Central Wyoming Coll (WY)
Century Comm and Tech Coll (MN)
Cincinnati State Tech and Comm Coll (OH)
Clovis Comm Coll (NM)
Commonwealth Business Coll, Merrillville (IN)
Comm Coll of Allegheny County (PA)
Comm Coll of the Air Force (AL)
County Coll of Morris (NJ)
Craven Comm Coll (NC)
Delaware County Comm Coll (PA)
Delaware Tech & Comm Coll, Stanton/ Wilmington Cmps (DE)
Delta Coll of Arts and Technology (LA)
East Central Coll (MO)
Eastern Wyoming Coll (WY)
Evergreen Valley Coll (CA)
Fayetteville Tech Comm Coll (NC)
Florida Tech Coll, Orlando (FL)
Front Range Comm Coll (CO)
Gateway Tech Coll (WI)
Glendale Comm Coll (AZ)
Grayson County Coll (TX)
Gwinnett Tech Coll (GA)
Hagerstown Comm Coll (MD)
Harrisburg Area Comm Coll (PA)
Haywood Comm Coll (NC)
Heartland Comm Coll (IL)
Hesser Coll (NH)
Hopkinsville Comm Coll (KY)
Hutchinson Comm Coll and Area Vocational School (KS)
International Academy of Design & Technology (PA)
John Tyler Comm Coll (VA)
Kalamazoo Valley Comm Coll (MI)
Kaskaskia Coll (IL)
Kilgore Coll (TX)
Kirkwood Comm Coll (IA)
Lake Region State Coll (ND)
Lamar Comm Coll (CO)
Lansing Comm Coll (MI)
Louisiana Tech Coll–Natchitoches Campus (LA)
Manchester Comm Coll (CT)
Martin Comm Coll (NC)
Merced Coll (CA)
Mercer County Comm Coll (NJ)
Miami-Dade Comm Coll (FL)
Miami U–Middletown Campus (OH)
Mississippi Delta Comm Coll (MS)
Modesto Jr Coll (CA)
Montcalm Comm Coll (MI)
Montgomery Coll (MD)
Montgomery Comm Coll (NC)
Montgomery County Comm Coll (PA)
Mott Comm Coll (MI)
Mount Wachusett Comm Coll (MA)
Nassau Comm Coll (NY)
NEI Coll of Technology (MN)
North Harris Coll (TX)
North Hennepin Comm Coll (MN)
Northwestern Michigan Coll (MI)
Ouachita Tech Coll (AR)
Pikes Peak Comm Coll (CO)
Raritan Valley Comm Coll (NJ)
Rochester Business Inst (NY)
Salem Comm Coll (NJ)
San Jacinto Coll North Campus (TX)
Shasta Coll (CA)
South Arkansas Comm Coll (AR)
Southeast Comm Coll (KY)
Southern Maine Tech Coll (ME)
South Suburban Coll (IL)

Southwest Tennessee Comm Coll (TN)
Tallahassee Comm Coll (FL)
Trinidad State Jr Coll (CO)
Triton Coll (IL)
Trumbull Business Coll (OH)
Union County Coll (NJ)
The U of Akron–Wayne Coll (OH)
U of Arkansas at Fort Smith (AR)
Victor Valley Coll (CA)
Vincennes U (IN)
Vincennes U Jasper Campus (IN)
The Westchester Business Inst (NY)
Western Nevada Comm Coll (NV)
Wor-Wic Comm Coll (MD)
Yorktowne Business Inst (PA)

MANAGEMENT SCIENCE
Cape Cod Comm Coll (MA)
Fayetteville Tech Comm Coll (NC)
GateWay Comm Coll (AZ)
Hamilton Coll (IA)
Harrisburg Area Comm Coll (PA)
Hazard Comm Coll (KY)
Lakeshore Tech Coll (WI)
Lamar State Coll–Port Arthur (TX)
Louisburg Coll (NC)
Oakland Comm Coll (MI)
Oakton Comm Coll (IL)
Phoenix Coll (AZ)
Prairie State Coll (IL)
Reedley Coll (CA)
Santa Ana Coll (CA)
Tulsa Comm Coll (OK)
Western Nevada Comm Coll (NV)

MARINE BIOLOGY
Daytona Beach Comm Coll (FL)
Dixie State Coll of Utah (UT)
Lincoln Coll, Lincoln (IL)
Massachusetts Bay Comm Coll (MA)
Mitchell Coll (CT)
Shoreline Comm Coll (WA)
Southern Maine Tech Coll (ME)

MARINE MAINTENANCE
Cape Fear Comm Coll (NC)
New England Inst of Technology (RI)

MARINE SCIENCE
Anne Arundel Comm Coll (MD)
Atlantic Cape Comm Coll (NJ)
Coll of the Redwoods (CA)
Indian River Comm Coll (FL)
Northwestern Michigan Coll (MI)

MARINE TECHNOLOGY
Cape Fear Comm Coll (NC)
Coll of Marin (CA)
Highline Comm Coll (WA)
Honolulu Comm Coll (HI)
Kingsborough Comm Coll of City U of NY (NY)
Louisville Tech Inst (KY)
North Idaho Coll (ID)
Orange Coast Coll (CA)
Santa Barbara City Coll (CA)
Seattle Central Comm Coll (WA)
Shoreline Comm Coll (WA)
Skagit Valley Coll (WA)

MARITIME SCIENCE
Northwestern Michigan Coll (MI)

MARKETING/DISTRIBUTION EDUCATION
Louisburg Coll (NC)
Northwest Mississippi Comm Coll (MS)
Parkland Coll (IL)

MARKETING MANAGEMENT AND RESEARCH RELATED
Oakland Comm Coll (MI)

MARKETING OPERATIONS
Broome Comm Coll (NY)
Central Carolina Tech Coll (SC)
Centralia Coll (WA)
Coll of DuPage (IL)
Collin County Comm Coll District (TX)
The Comm Coll of Baltimore County–Catonsville Campus (MD)
Cuyahoga Comm Coll (OH)
Dakota County Tech Coll (MN)
Fayetteville Tech Comm Coll (NC)
Iowa Western Comm Coll (IA)
Kennebec Valley Tech Coll (ME)
Montgomery County Comm Coll (PA)
North Central Texas Coll (TX)
Norwalk Comm Coll (CT)
Pittsburgh Tech Inst (PA)
Ridgewater Coll (MN)
San Diego Mesa Coll (CA)
Vincennes U (IN)
Western Dakota Tech Inst (SD)
Western Wisconsin Tech Coll (WI)

MARKETING OPERATIONS/ MARKETING AND DISTRIBUTION RELATED
Wisconsin Indianhead Tech Coll (WI)

MARKETING RESEARCH
Guam Comm Coll (GU)
Riverside Comm Coll (CA)
San Diego Mesa Coll (CA)

MASONRY/TILE SETTING
Fayetteville Tech Comm Coll (NC)
Florida Comm Coll at Jacksonville (FL)
Ivy Tech State Coll–Central Indiana (IN)
Ivy Tech State Coll–Columbus (IN)
Ivy Tech State Coll–Eastcentral (IN)
Ivy Tech State Coll–Lafayette (IN)
Ivy Tech State Coll–North Central (IN)
Ivy Tech State Coll–Northeast (IN)
Ivy Tech State Coll–Northwest (IN)
Ivy Tech State Coll–Southcentral (IN)
Ivy Tech State Coll–Southwest (IN)
Ivy Tech State Coll–Wabash Valley (IN)
Mississippi Delta Comm Coll (MS)
Pennsylvania Coll of Technology (PA)
Southwest Wisconsin Tech Coll (WI)
State U of NY Coll of Technology at Alfred (NY)
State U of NY Coll of Technology at Delhi (NY)
Western Nevada Comm Coll (NV)

MASS COMMUNICATIONS
Adirondack Comm Coll (NY)
Allegany Coll of Maryland (MD)
Amarillo Coll (TX)
Andrew Coll (GA)
Anne Arundel Comm Coll (MD)
Asnuntuck Comm Coll (CT)
Austin Comm Coll (TX)
Bacone Coll (OK)
Bergen Comm Coll (NJ)
Blinn Coll (TX)
Bristol Comm Coll (MA)
Brookdale Comm Coll (NJ)
Bucks County Comm Coll (PA)
Butler County Comm Coll (PA)
Camden County Coll (NJ)
Cape Cod Comm Coll (MA)
Casper Coll (WY)
Central Comm Coll–Hastings Campus (NE)
Centralia Coll (WA)
Central Pennsylvania Coll (PA)
Chabot Coll (CA)
Chattanooga State Tech Comm Coll (TN)
Chipola Jr Coll (FL)
City Colls of Chicago, Richard J Daley Coll (IL)
Cochise Coll, Douglas (AZ)
Coffeyville Comm Coll (KS)
Colby Comm Coll (KS)
Coll of Marin (CA)
Coll of the Desert (CA)
Coll of the Sequoias (CA)
Columbia State Comm Coll (TN)
The Comm Coll of Baltimore County–Catonsville Campus (MD)
Comm Coll of Southern Nevada (NV)
Crowder Coll (MO)
Cuesta Coll (CA)
Daytona Beach Comm Coll (FL)
De Anza Coll (CA)
Dodge City Comm Coll (KS)
Dutchess Comm Coll (NY)
East Central Coll (MO)
Enterprise State Jr Coll (AL)
Finger Lakes Comm Coll (NY)
Frederick Comm Coll (MD)
Fullerton Coll (CA)
Fulton-Montgomery Comm Coll (NY)
Genesee Comm Coll (NY)
Georgia Military Coll (GA)
Glendale Comm Coll (CA)
Grand Rapids Comm Coll (MI)
Greenfield Comm Coll (MA)
Harford Comm Coll (MD)
Harrisburg Area Comm Coll (PA)
Henderson Comm Coll (KY)
Henry Ford Comm Coll (MI)
Hesser Coll (NH)
Hill Coll of the Hill Jr College District (TX)
Hillsborough Comm Coll (FL)
Hinds Comm Coll (MS)
Holyoke Comm Coll (MA)
Houston Comm Coll System (TX)
Iowa Lakes Comm Coll (IA)
Jamestown Comm Coll (NY)
Jefferson Comm Coll (KY)
Kirkwood Comm Coll (IA)
Lamar Comm Coll (CO)
Lamar State Coll–Orange (TX)
Lansing Comm Coll (MI)
Laramie County Comm Coll (WY)
Lincoln Coll, Lincoln (IL)
Lon Morris Coll (TX)
Lorain County Comm Coll (OH)
Los Angeles City Coll (CA)
Manatee Comm Coll (FL)
Mercer County Comm Coll (NJ)
Miami-Dade Comm Coll (FL)
Miami U–Middletown Campus (OH)
Middlesex Comm Coll (MA)
Midland Coll (TX)
Mineral Area Coll (MO)
Modesto Jr Coll (CA)
Monroe Comm Coll (NY)
Monroe County Comm Coll (MI)
Monterey Peninsula Coll (CA)
Nassau Comm Coll (NY)
Newbury Coll (MA)
Niagara County Comm Coll (NY)
Northeast Comm Coll (NE)
North Idaho Coll (ID)
Northland Comm and Tech Coll (MN)
Northwest Coll (WY)
Norwalk Comm Coll (CT)
Oklahoma City Comm Coll (OK)
Orange Coast Coll (CA)
Paducah Comm Coll (KY)
Palm Beach Comm Coll (FL)
Pasadena City Coll (CA)
Pennsylvania Coll of Technology (PA)
Phoenix Coll (AZ)
Pratt Comm Coll and Area Vocational School (KS)
Quincy Coll (MA)
Red Rocks Comm Coll (CO)
Ridgewater Coll (MN)
Rockland Comm Coll (NY)
Sacramento City Coll (CA)
St. Clair County Comm Coll (MI)
St. Louis Comm Coll at Florissant Valley (MO)
Salem Comm Coll (NJ)
San Jacinto Coll Central Campus (TX)
Santa Monica Coll (CA)
Sierra Coll (CA)
Sinclair Comm Coll (OH)
Snow Coll (UT)
South Mountain Comm Coll (AZ)
South Plains Coll (TX)
Spokane Falls Comm Coll (WA)
State Fair Comm Coll (MO)
Tompkins Cortland Comm Coll (NY)
Triton Coll (IL)
Tulsa Comm Coll (OK)
Ulster County Comm Coll (NY)
Vermilion Comm Coll (MN)
Vincennes U (IN)
Waubonsee Comm Coll (IL)
Westchester Comm Coll (NY)
Western Texas Coll (TX)
Western Wisconsin Tech Coll (WI)
Western Wyoming Comm Coll (WY)

MATERIALS SCIENCE
Central Arizona Coll (AZ)
GateWay Comm Coll (AZ)
Greenville Tech Coll (SC)
Henry Ford Comm Coll (MI)
Macomb Comm Coll (MI)
Neosho County Comm Coll (KS)
Northern Essex Comm Coll (MA)
North Hennepin Comm Coll (MN)
Schenectady County Comm Coll (NY)
Tulsa Comm Coll (OK)

MATHEMATICAL STATISTICS
Chabot Coll (CA)
Daytona Beach Comm Coll (FL)
Eastern Wyoming Coll (WY)
Jefferson Comm Coll (KY)
Lincoln Coll, Lincoln (IL)
Manatee Comm Coll (FL)
Pasadena City Coll (CA)

MATHEMATICS
Abraham Baldwin Ag Coll (GA)
Adirondack Comm Coll (NY)
Allen County Comm Coll (KS)
Alpena Comm Coll (MI)
Alvin Comm Coll (TX)
Amarillo Coll (TX)
American River Coll (CA)
Ancilla Coll (IN)
Andrew Coll (GA)
Angelina Coll (TX)
Anne Arundel Comm Coll (MD)
Antelope Valley Coll (CA)
Arizona Western Coll (AZ)
Arkansas State U–Beebe (AR)
Atlanta Metropolitan Coll (GA)
Atlantic Cape Comm Coll (NJ)
Austin Comm Coll (TX)
Bacone Coll (OK)
Bainbridge Coll (GA)
Bakersfield Coll (CA)
Barstow Coll (CA)
Barton County Comm Coll (KS)
Bergen Comm Coll (NJ)
Blinn Coll (TX)
Borough of Manhattan Comm Coll of City U of NY (NY)
Brazosport Coll (TX)
Bristol Comm Coll (MA)
Bronx Comm Coll of City U of NY (NY)
Brookdale Comm Coll (NJ)
Bucks County Comm Coll (PA)
Butler County Comm Coll (PA)
Butte Coll (CA)
Cañada Coll (CA)
Cape Cod Comm Coll (MA)
Casper Coll (WY)
Cayuga County Comm Coll (NY)
Cecil Comm Coll (MD)
Centralia Coll (WA)
Central Oregon Comm Coll (OR)
Central Texas Coll (TX)
Cerritos Coll (CA)
Cerro Coso Comm Coll (CA)
Chabot Coll (CA)
Chaffey Coll (CA)
Chattahoochee Valley Comm Coll (AL)
Chemeketa Comm Coll (OR)
Chesapeake Coll (MD)
Cisco Jr Coll (TX)
Citrus Coll (CA)
City Coll of San Francisco (CA)
Clark Coll (WA)
Clovis Comm Coll (NM)
Coastal Bend Coll (TX)
Coastal Georgia Comm Coll (GA)
Coffeyville Comm Coll (KS)
Colby Comm Coll (KS)
Coll of Alameda (CA)
Coll of Marin (CA)
Coll of Southern Idaho (ID)
Coll of the Canyons (CA)
Coll of the Desert (CA)
Coll of the Sequoias (CA)
Coll of the Siskiyous (CA)
Colorado Mountn Coll, Alpine Cmps (CO)
Colorado Mountn Coll (CO)
Colorado Mountn Coll, Timberline Cmps (CO)
Columbia-Greene Comm Coll (NY)
Columbia State Comm Coll (TN)
Comm Coll of Allegheny County (PA)
Comm Coll of Southern Nevada (NV)
Compton Comm Coll (CA)
Connors State Coll (OK)
Corning Comm Coll (NY)
Crafton Hills Coll (CA)
Crowder Coll (MO)
Cuesta Coll (CA)
Cumberland County Coll (NJ)
Cypress Coll (CA)
Danville Area Comm Coll (IL)
Darton Coll (GA)
Daytona Beach Comm Coll (FL)
De Anza Coll (CA)
Del Mar Coll (TX)
Dixie State Coll of Utah (UT)
Dodge City Comm Coll (KS)
Donnelly Coll (KS)
Dutchess Comm Coll (NY)
East Central Coll (MO)
East Central Comm Coll (MS)
Eastern Arizona Coll (AZ)
Eastern Oklahoma State Coll (OK)
Eastern Wyoming Coll (WY)
East Georgia Coll (GA)
East Mississippi Comm Coll (MS)
Edison State Comm Coll (OH)
Ellsworth Comm Coll (IA)
Essex County Coll (NJ)
Everett Comm Coll (WA)
Feather River Comm Coll District (CA)
Finger Lakes Comm Coll (NY)
Foothill Coll (CA)
Fort Berthold Comm Coll (ND)
Frederick Comm Coll (MD)
Fullerton Coll (CA)
Fulton-Montgomery Comm Coll (NY)
Galveston Coll (TX)
Garden City Comm Coll (KS)
Gavilan Coll (CA)
Genesee Comm Coll (NY)
Georgia Perimeter Coll (GA)
Glendale Comm Coll (CA)
Gloucester County Coll (NJ)
Gogebic Comm Coll (MI)
Golden West Coll (CA)
Gordon Coll (GA)
Grayson County Coll (TX)
Great Basin Coll (NV)
Greenfield Comm Coll (MA)
Harford Comm Coll (MD)
Harrisburg Area Comm Coll (PA)
Herkimer County Comm Coll (NY)
Highland Comm Coll (IL)
Highland Comm Coll (KS)
Highline Comm Coll (WA)
Hill Coll of the Hill Jr College District (TX)
Hinds Comm Coll (MS)
Housatonic Comm Coll (CT)
Howard Coll (TX)
Hutchinson Comm Coll and Area Vocational School (KS)
Imperial Valley Coll (CA)
Independence Comm Coll (KS)
Indian River Comm Coll (FL)
Iowa Lakes Comm Coll (IA)
Jamestown Comm Coll (NY)
Jefferson Coll (MO)
Jefferson Comm Coll (KY)
Jefferson Comm Coll (NY)
John A. Logan Coll (IL)
Joliet Jr Coll (IL)
Jones County Jr Coll (MS)
Kansas City Kansas Comm Coll (KS)
Kellogg Comm Coll (MI)
Kilgore Coll (TX)
Kingsborough Comm Coll of City U of NY (NY)
Kingwood Coll (TX)
Kirkwood Comm Coll (IA)
Labette Comm Coll (KS)
Lake Michigan Coll (MI)
Lake Tahoe Comm Coll (CA)
Lamar Comm Coll (CO)
Lamar State Coll–Orange (TX)
Lansing Comm Coll (MI)
Laramie County Comm Coll (WY)
Lehigh Carbon Comm Coll (PA)
Lincoln Coll, Lincoln (IL)
Lincoln Land Comm Coll (IL)
Linn-Benton Comm Coll (OR)
Long Beach City Coll (CA)

Lon Morris Coll (TX)
Lorain County Comm Coll (OH)
Los Angeles City Coll (CA)
Los Angeles Mission Coll (CA)
Louisburg Coll (NC)
Lower Columbia Coll (WA)
Luzerne County Comm Coll (PA)
Merced Coll (CA)
Mercer County Comm Coll (NJ)
Miami-Dade Comm Coll (FL)
Miami U–Middletown Campus (OH)
Middlesex County Coll (NJ)
Midland Coll (TX)
Mid Michigan Comm Coll (MI)
Minot State U–Bottineau Campus (ND)
MiraCosta Coll (CA)
Mississippi Delta Comm Coll (MS)
Mitchell Comm Coll (NC)
Modesto Jr Coll (CA)
Mohave Comm Coll (AZ)
Mohawk Valley Comm Coll (NY)
Monroe Comm Coll (NY)
Monroe County Comm Coll (MI)
Monterey Peninsula Coll (CA)
Montgomery County Comm Coll (PA)
Moorpark Coll (CA)
Mountain Empire Comm Coll (VA)
Mt. San Jacinto Coll (CA)
Nassau Comm Coll (NY)
Naugatuck Valley Comm Coll (CT)
Navarro Coll (TX)
New Mexico Military Inst (NM)
Niagara County Comm Coll (NY)
Northampton County Area Comm Coll (PA)
North Country Comm Coll (NY)
Northeast Comm Coll (NE)
Northern Virginia Comm Coll (VA)
North Harris Coll (TX)
North Idaho Coll (ID)
North Seattle Comm Coll (WA)
Northwest Coll (WY)
Northwestern Connecticut Comm-Tech Coll (CT)
Odessa Coll (TX)
Okaloosa-Walton Comm Coll (FL)
Oklahoma City Comm Coll (OK)
Onondaga Comm Coll (NY)
Orange Coast Coll (CA)
Otero Jr Coll (CO)
Oxnard Coll (CA)
Palm Beach Comm Coll (FL)
Palomar Coll (CA)
Pasadena City Coll (CA)
Pensacola Jr Coll (FL)
Pratt Comm Coll and Area Vocational School (KS)
Quincy Coll (MA)
Raritan Valley Comm Coll (NJ)
Red Rocks Comm Coll (CO)
Reedley Coll (CA)
Ridgewater Coll (MN)
Riverside Comm Coll (CA)
Roane State Comm Coll (TN)
Rockland Comm Coll (NY)
Rogue Comm Coll (OR)
Sacramento City Coll (CA)
St. Catharine Coll (KY)
St. Louis Comm Coll at Florissant Valley (MO)
St. Philip's Coll (TX)
Salem Comm Coll (NJ)
San Bernardino Valley Coll (CA)
Sandhills Comm Coll (NC)
San Diego City Coll (CA)
San Diego Mesa Coll (CA)
San Jacinto Coll Central Campus (TX)
San Jacinto Coll North Campus (TX)
San Jacinto Coll South Campus (TX)
San Joaquin Delta Coll (CA)
San Juan Coll (NM)
Santa Ana Coll (CA)
Santa Barbara City Coll (CA)
Santa Monica Coll (CA)
Sauk Valley Comm Coll (IL)
Schenectady County Comm Coll (NY)
Scottsdale Comm Coll (AZ)
Seminole State Coll (OK)
Sheridan Coll (WY)
Skagit Valley Coll (WA)
Snow Coll (UT)
South Mountain Comm Coll (AZ)
South Suburban Coll (IL)
Southwestern Coll (CA)
Springfield Tech Comm Coll (MA)
State U of NY Coll of A&T at Morrisville (NY)
State U of NY Coll of Technology at Alfred (NY)
State U of NY Coll of Technology at Delhi (NY)
Suffolk County Comm Coll (NY)
Sullivan County Comm Coll (NY)
Tacoma Comm Coll (WA)
Taft Coll (CA)
Terra State Comm Coll (OH)
Texarkana Coll (TX)
Tompkins Cortland Comm Coll (NY)
Trinity Valley Comm Coll (TX)
Triton Coll (IL)
Tulsa Comm Coll (OK)
Ulster County Comm Coll (NY)
Umpqua Comm Coll (OR)
Vermilion Comm Coll (MN)
Victor Valley Coll (CA)
Vincennes U (IN)
Waycross Coll (GA)
Western Nebraska Comm Coll (NE)
Western Nevada Comm Coll (NV)
Western Wyoming Comm Coll (WY)
Wharton County Jr Coll (TX)
Young Harris Coll (GA)

MATHEMATICS/COMPUTER SCIENCE
Adirondack Comm Coll (NY)
Crowder Coll (MO)
Dean Coll (MA)
Fresno City Coll (CA)

MATHEMATICS EDUCATION
Eastern Wyoming Coll (WY)
Louisburg Coll (NC)
Manatee Comm Coll (FL)
Northwest Mississippi Comm Coll (MS)

MECHANICAL DESIGN TECHNOLOGY
Adirondack Comm Coll (NY)
Arapahoe Comm Coll (CO)
Asheville-Buncombe Tech Comm Coll (NC)
Black Hawk Coll, Moline (IL)
Blackhawk Tech Coll (WI)
Blue Ridge Comm Coll (VA)
Bowling Green State U-Firelands Coll (OH)
Butler County Comm Coll (PA)
Carroll Comm Coll (MD)
Cayuga County Comm Coll (NY)
Central Maine Tech Coll (ME)
Chattanooga State Tech Comm Coll (TN)
Chemeketa Comm Coll (OR)
Chippewa Valley Tech Coll (WI)
Coll of DuPage (IL)
Comm Coll of Allegheny County (PA)
Comm Coll of Southern Nevada (NV)
Cuyamaca Coll (CA)
De Anza Coll (CA)
Delta Coll (MI)
Edgecombe Comm Coll (NC)
Edison State Comm Coll (OH)
Forsyth Tech Comm Coll (NC)
Garden City Comm Coll (KS)
Gateway Tech Coll (WI)
Hawkeye Comm Coll (IA)
Heartland Comm Coll (IL)
Hennepin Tech Coll (MN)
Iowa Western Comm Coll (IA)
Isothermal Comm Coll (NC)
Jefferson Coll (MO)
Joliet Jr Coll (IL)
Kirkwood Comm Coll (IA)
Lakeshore Tech Coll (WI)
Lansing Comm Coll (MI)
Lenoir Comm Coll (NC)
Lima Tech Coll (OH)
Lorain County Comm Coll (OH)
Louisville Tech Inst (KY)
Luzerne County Comm Coll (PA)
Macomb Comm Coll (MI)
Mid-State Tech Coll (WI)
Minnesota State Coll–Southeast Tech (MN)
Mohawk Valley Comm Coll (NY)
Moraine Park Tech Coll (WI)
Niagara County Comm Coll (NY)
Northcentral Tech Coll (WI)
Northeastern Tech Coll (SC)
Northeast Iowa Comm Coll (IA)
North Iowa Area Comm Coll (IA)
Oakton Comm Coll (IL)
Phoenix Coll (AZ)
Prairie State Coll (IL)
Raritan Valley Comm Coll (NJ)
St. Cloud Tech Coll (MN)
Sauk Valley Comm Coll (IL)
Southeast Comm Coll, Milford Campus (NE)
South Suburban Coll (IL)
Southwest Wisconsin Tech Coll (WI)
Spokane Comm Coll (WA)
State U of NY Coll of Technology at Alfred (NY)
Thaddeus Stevens Coll of Technology (PA)
Triangle Tech, Inc. (PA)
Triangle Tech, Inc.–Erie School (PA)
Triangle Tech, Inc.–Greensburg Center (PA)
Western Wisconsin Tech Coll (WI)
Westmoreland County Comm Coll (PA)

MECHANICAL DRAFTING
Adirondack Comm Coll (NY)
Alexandria Tech Coll (MN)
Anoka-Hennepin Tech Coll (MN)
Black Hawk Coll, Moline (IL)
Brookdale Comm Coll (NJ)
Butler County Comm Coll (PA)
Central Carolina Tech Coll (SC)
Comm Coll of Allegheny County (PA)
Dixie State Coll of Utah (UT)
Erie Comm Coll, South Campus (NY)
Florida Tech Coll, Orlando (FL)
Gaston Coll (NC)
Island Drafting and Tech Inst (NY)
Louisville Tech Inst (KY)
Midlands Tech Coll (SC)
Morrison Inst of Technology (IL)
Mott Comm Coll (MI)
North Hennepin Comm Coll (MN)
Northwest Tech Inst (MN)
Orangeburg-Calhoun Tech Coll (SC)
Piedmont Tech Coll (SC)
Rowan-Cabarrus Comm Coll (NC)
St. Cloud Tech Coll (MN)
Silicon Valley Coll, San Jose (CA)
Spencerian Coll–Lexington (KY)
Springfield Tech Comm Coll (MA)
Stanly Comm Coll (NC)
Wake Tech Comm Coll (NC)
Westwood Coll of Technology–Denver North (CO)
York Tech Coll (SC)

MECHANICAL ENGINEERING
Northwest State Comm Coll (OH)

MECHANICAL ENGINEERING TECHNOLOGIES RELATED
Pennsylvania Inst of Technology (PA)
Penn State U McKeesport Campus of the Commonwealth Coll (PA)
Penn State U Wilkes-Barre Campus of the Commonwealth Coll (PA)

MECHANICAL ENGINEERING TECHNOLOGY
Adirondack Comm Coll (NY)
Alamance Comm Coll (NC)
Anne Arundel Comm Coll (MD)
Asheville-Buncombe Tech Comm Coll (NC)
Augusta Tech Coll (GA)
Bates Tech Coll (WA)
Benjamin Franklin Inst of Technology (MA)
Black Hawk Coll, Moline (IL)
Blue Ridge Comm Coll (NC)
Bristol Comm Coll (MA)
Broome Comm Coll (NY)
Camden County Coll (NJ)
Cape Fear Comm Coll (NC)
Capital Comm Coll (CT)
Catawba Valley Comm Coll (NC)
Central Ohio Tech Coll (OH)
Central Piedmont Comm Coll (NC)
Central Virginia Comm Coll (VA)
Chattanooga State Tech Comm Coll (TN)
Cincinnati State Tech and Comm Coll (OH)
Citrus Coll (CA)
City Coll of San Francisco (CA)
Clover Park Tech Coll (WA)
Coffeyville Comm Coll (KS)
Coll of Lake County (IL)
Columbus State Comm Coll (OH)
Columbus Tech Coll (GA)
Comm Coll of Southern Nevada (NV)
Compton Comm Coll (CA)
Corning Comm Coll (NY)
County Coll of Morris (NJ)
Craven Comm Coll (NC)
Danville Area Comm Coll (IL)
Delaware County Comm Coll (PA)
Delaware Tech & Comm Coll, Stanton/ Wilmington Cmps (DE)
Delta Coll (MI)
ECPI Coll of Technology, Newport News (VA)
ECPI Coll of Technology, Virginia Beach (VA)
ECPI Tech Coll, Richmond (VA)
ECPI Tech Coll, Roanoke (VA)
Edgecombe Comm Coll (NC)
Education Direct (PA)
Erie Comm Coll, North Campus (NY)
Finger Lakes Comm Coll (NY)
Gadsden State Comm Coll (AL)
Garden City Comm Coll (KS)
Gaston Coll (NC)
Gateway Comm Coll (CT)
Georgia Perimeter Coll (GA)
Green River Comm Coll (WA)
Greenville Tech Coll (SC)
Hagerstown Comm Coll (MD)
Harrisburg Area Comm Coll (PA)
Hawaii Comm Coll (HI)
Hawkeye Comm Coll (IA)
Highland Comm Coll (IL)
Iowa Western Comm Coll (IA)
Isothermal Comm Coll (NC)
Jamestown Comm Coll (NY)
Jefferson Comm Coll (KY)
Jefferson Comm Coll (OH)
John Tyler Comm Coll (VA)
Kalamazoo Valley Comm Coll (MI)
Kent State U, Trumbull Campus (OH)
Kent State U, Tuscarawas Campus (OH)
Kirkwood Comm Coll (IA)
Lakeland Comm Coll (OH)
Lansing Comm Coll (MI)
Lehigh Carbon Comm Coll (PA)
Lima Tech Coll (OH)
Lord Fairfax Comm Coll (VA)
Louisville Tech Inst (KY)
Lower Columbia Coll (WA)
Madisonville Comm Coll (KY)
Marion Tech Coll (OH)
Massachusetts Bay Comm Coll (MA)
McHenry County Coll (IL)
Miami U–Hamilton Campus (OH)
Miami U–Middletown Campus (OH)
Middlesex County Coll (NJ)
Midlands Tech Coll (SC)
Milwaukee Area Tech Coll (WI)
Mohawk Valley Comm Coll (NY)
Monroe Comm Coll (NY)
Montgomery County Comm Coll (PA)
Moraine Valley Comm Coll (IL)
Mott Comm Coll (MI)
Mt. Hood Comm Coll (OR)
Naugatuck Valley Comm Coll (CT)
New Hampshire Tech Inst (NH)
New York City Tech Coll of the City U of NY (NY)
Northern Virginia Comm Coll (VA)
Northwest State Comm Coll (OH)
Onondaga Comm Coll (NY)
Orangeburg-Calhoun Tech Coll (SC)
Pasadena City Coll (CA)
Pellissippi State Tech Comm Coll (TN)
Pennsylvania Inst of Technology (PA)
Penn State U Beaver Campus of the Commonwealth Coll (PA)
Penn State U DuBois Campus of the Commonwealth Coll (PA)
Penn State U Hazleton Campus of the Commonwealth Coll (PA)
Penn State U McKeesport Campus of the Commonwealth Coll (PA)
Penn State U New Kensington Campus of the Commonwealth Coll (PA)
Penn State U Shenango Campus of the Commonwealth Coll (PA)
Penn State U York Campus of the Commonwealth Coll (PA)
Piedmont Tech Coll (SC)
Portland Comm Coll (OR)
Queensborough Comm Coll of City U of NY (NY)
Reading Area Comm Coll (PA)
Red Rocks Comm Coll (CO)
The Refrigeration School (AZ)
Richmond Comm Coll (NC)
St. Louis Comm Coll at Florissant Valley (MO)
San Antonio Coll (TX)
San Jacinto Coll South Campus (TX)
San Joaquin Delta Coll (CA)
Schoolcraft Coll (MI)
Shoreline Comm Coll (WA)
Sinclair Comm Coll (OH)
Southeast Comm Coll, Milford Campus (NE)
Southeast Tech Inst (SD)
South Piedmont Comm Coll (NC)
Southwest Tennessee Comm Coll (TN)
Spartanburg Tech Coll (SC)
Spokane Comm Coll (WA)
Springfield Tech Comm Coll (MA)
Stark State Coll of Technology (OH)
State U of NY Coll of A&T at Morrisville (NY)
State U of NY Coll of Technology at Alfred (NY)
State U of NY Coll of Technology at Canton (NY)
Suffolk County Comm Coll (NY)
Tarrant County Coll District (TX)
Terra State Comm Coll (OH)
Texas State Tech Coll– Waco/ Marshall Campus (TX)
Thomas Nelson Comm Coll (VA)
Three Rivers Comm Coll (CT)
Trident Tech Coll (SC)
Tulsa Comm Coll (OK)
Union County Coll (NJ)
U of Kentucky, Lexington Comm Coll (KY)
Vermont Tech Coll (VT)
Vincennes U (IN)
Virginia Western Comm Coll (VA)
Wake Tech Comm Coll (NC)
Wayne Comm Coll (NC)
Westchester Comm Coll (NY)
Westmoreland County Comm Coll (PA)
West Virginia U at Parkersburg (WV)
Wilson Tech Comm Coll (NC)
Wisconsin Indianhead Tech Coll (WI)
York Tech Coll (SC)

MECHANICS AND REPAIR RELATED
Southwestern Michigan Coll (MI)

MEDICAL ADMINISTRATIVE ASSISTANT
Academy of Medical Arts and Business (PA)
Adirondack Comm Coll (NY)
AIB Coll of Business (IA)
Alamance Comm Coll (NC)
Alexandria Tech Coll (MN)
Allegany Coll of Maryland (MD)
Allentown Business School (PA)
Alvin Comm Coll (TX)
Amarillo Coll (TX)
American River Coll (CA)
Andover Coll (ME)
Anoka-Hennepin Tech Coll (MN)
Anoka-Ramsey Comm Coll (MN)

Antelope Valley Coll (CA)
Athens Tech Coll (GA)
ATI Career Training Center Electronics Campus (FL)
Baltimore City Comm Coll (MD)
Barton County Comm Coll (KS)
Bay de Noc Comm Coll (MI)
Bay State Coll (MA)
Beaufort County Comm Coll (NC)
Bergen Comm Coll (NJ)
Bismarck State Coll (ND)
Black Hawk Coll, Moline (IL)
Blair Coll (CO)
Brevard Comm Coll (FL)
Briarwood Coll (CT)
Bristol Comm Coll (MA)
Bronx Comm Coll of City U of NY (NY)
The Brown Mackie Coll–Olathe Campus (KS)
Bryant & Stratton Business Inst, Buffalo (NY)
Bryant & Stratton Business Inst, Lackawanna (NY)
Bryant & Stratton Business Inst, Rochester (NY)
Bryant & Stratton Business Inst, Rochester (NY)
Bryant and Stratton Coll (WI)
Bryant and Stratton Coll, Virginia Beach (VA)
Business Inst of Pennsylvania (PA)
Butler County Comm Coll (PA)
Butte Coll (CA)
Caldwell Comm Coll and Tech Inst (NC)
Cambria-Rowe Business Coll (PA)
Cape Cod Comm Coll (MA)
Career Colls of Chicago (IL)
Central Arizona Coll (AZ)
Central Carolina Comm Coll (NC)
Central Comm Coll–Hastings Campus (NE)
Centralia Coll (WA)
Central Lakes Coll (MN)
Central Maine Tech Coll (ME)
Central Pennsylvania Coll (PA)
Central Piedmont Comm Coll (NC)
Central Texas Coll (TX)
Century Comm and Tech Coll (MN)
Cerritos Coll (CA)
Chaffey Coll (CA)
Chattanooga State Tech Comm Coll (TN)
Chemeketa Comm Coll (OR)
Chesapeake Coll (MD)
CHI Inst (PA)
Churchman Business School (PA)
City Colls of Chicago, Harry S Truman Coll (IL)
City Colls of Chicago, Richard J Daley Coll (IL)
Clark Coll (WA)
Cleveland Comm Coll (NC)
Clovis Comm Coll (NM)
Coastal Carolina Comm Coll (NC)
Cochise Coll, Douglas (AZ)
Coffeyville Comm Coll (KS)
Coll of Marin (CA)
Colorado Northwestern Comm Coll (CO)
Columbus State Comm Coll (OH)
Comm Coll of Allegheny County (PA)
Comm Coll of Aurora (CO)
The Comm Coll of Baltimore County–Catonsville Campus (MD)
Comm Coll of Beaver County (PA)
Comm Coll of Denver (CO)
Comm Coll of Rhode Island (RI)
Comm Coll of Southern Nevada (NV)
Consolidated School of Business, Lancaster (PA)
Consolidated School of Business, York (PA)
Crafton Hills Coll (CA)
Craven Comm Coll (NC)
Crowder Coll (MO)
Cypress Coll (CA)
Danville Area Comm Coll (IL)
Darton Coll (GA)
Davis Coll (OH)
Daytona Beach Comm Coll (FL)
Delaware Tech & Comm Coll, Jack F Owens Cmps (DE)
Delaware Tech & Comm Coll, Stanton/ Wilmington Cmps (DE)
Delta Coll (MI)
Des Moines Area Comm Coll (IA)
Dodge City Comm Coll (KS)
Douglas Education Center (PA)
DuBois Business Coll (PA)
Duff's Business Inst (PA)
Durham Tech Comm Coll (NC)
East Central Coll (MO)
ECPI Coll of Technology, Newport News (VA)
ECPI Coll of Technology, Virginia Beach (VA)
ECPI Tech Coll, Richmond (VA)
ECPI Tech Coll, Roanoke (VA)
Edison State Comm Coll (OH)
El Centro Coll (TX)
Ellsworth Comm Coll (IA)
Enterprise State Jr Coll (AL)
Erie Business Center, Main (PA)
Erie Business Center South (PA)
Essex County Coll (NJ)
Eugenio María de Hostos Comm Coll of City U of NY (NY)
Everett Comm Coll (WA)
Fergus Falls Comm Coll (MN)
Flathead Valley Comm Coll (MT)
Florida National Coll (FL)
Florida Tech Coll, Orlando (FL)
Fort Scott Comm Coll (KS)
Frederick Comm Coll (MD)
Fresno City Coll (CA)
Fulton-Montgomery Comm Coll (NY)
Gallipolis Career Coll (OH)
Gateway Comm Coll (CT)
Gem City Coll (IL)
Glendale Comm Coll (CA)
Gloucester County Coll (NJ)
Gogebic Comm Coll (MI)
Grand Rapids Comm Coll (MI)
Green River Comm Coll (WA)
Hagerstown Business Coll (MD)
Halifax Comm Coll (NC)
Hamilton Coll (IA)
Hawkeye Comm Coll (IA)
Heald Coll, Schools of Business and Technology, Hayward (CA)
Heald Coll, Schools of Business and Technology, Rancho Cordova (CA)
Heald Coll, Schools of Business and Technology (HI)
Helena Coll of Tech of The U of Montana (MT)
Hennepin Tech Coll (MN)
Henry Ford Comm Coll (MI)
Herkimer County Comm Coll (NY)
Hesser Coll (NH)
Hibbing Comm Coll (MN)
Highland Comm Coll (KS)
Hillsborough Comm Coll (FL)
Houston Comm Coll System (TX)
Howard Comm Coll (MD)
Huntington Jr Coll of Business (WV)
Illinois Eastern Comm Colls, Olney Central Coll (IL)
Indiana Business Coll, Indianapolis (IN)
Indian River Comm Coll (FL)
IntelliTec Medical Inst (CO)
Interboro Inst (NY)
Inver Hills Comm Coll (MN)
Iowa Lakes Comm Coll (IA)
Iowa Western Comm Coll (IA)
Itasca Comm Coll (MN)
Jackson Comm Coll (MI)
Jamestown Business Coll (NY)
Jefferson Coll (MO)
Jefferson Comm Coll (NY)
Jefferson Comm Coll (OH)
Johnston Comm Coll (NC)
John Wood Comm Coll (IL)
Kalamazoo Valley Comm Coll (MI)
Kellogg Comm Coll (MI)
Kilian Comm Coll (SD)
Kirkwood Comm Coll (IA)
Labette Comm Coll (KS)
Lake Land Coll (IL)
Lake Michigan Coll (MI)
Lakeshore Tech Coll (WI)
Lake Tahoe Comm Coll (CA)
Lamar Comm Coll (CO)
Lamar State Coll–Port Arthur (TX)
Laurel Business Inst (PA)
LDS Business Coll (UT)
Lenoir Comm Coll (NC)
Lewis and Clark Comm Coll (IL)
Lewis Coll of Business (MI)
Lima Tech Coll (OH)
Lincoln Coll, Normal (IL)
Lincoln School of Commerce (NE)
Linn-Benton Comm Coll (OR)
Long Beach City Coll (CA)
Longview Comm Coll (MO)
Los Angeles City Coll (CA)
Los Angeles Harbor Coll (CA)
Lower Columbia Coll (WA)
Luzerne County Comm Coll (PA)
Macomb Comm Coll (MI)
Manchester Comm Coll (CT)
Manor Coll (PA)
Maple Woods Comm Coll (MO)
Marian Court Coll (MA)
Marion Tech Coll (OH)
Martin Comm Coll (NC)
Mayland Comm Coll (NC)
McIntosh Coll (NH)
McLennan Comm Coll (TX)
Merced Coll (CA)
Miami-Dade Comm Coll (FL)
Miami U–Middletown Campus (OH)
Midlands Tech Coll (SC)
Mid Michigan Comm Coll (MI)
Mid-Plains Comm Coll Area (NE)
Mid-State Coll (ME)
Miles Comm Coll (MT)
Milwaukee Area Tech Coll (WI)
Minnesota State Coll–Southeast Tech (MN)
Minnesota West Comm & Tech Coll-Pipestone Cmps (MN)
Minot State U–Bottineau Campus (ND)
Mitchell Tech Inst (SD)
Mohawk Valley Comm Coll (NY)
Monroe County Comm Coll (MI)
Montana State U Coll of Tech-Great Falls (MT)
Montcalm Comm Coll (MI)
Monterey Peninsula Coll (CA)
Moraine Park Tech Coll (WI)
Morton Coll (IL)
Mott Comm Coll (MI)
Mt. Hood Comm Coll (OR)
Nash Comm Coll (NC)
Nassau Comm Coll (NY)
Naugatuck Valley Comm Coll (CT)
Newport Business Inst, Williamsport (PA)
New River Comm Coll (VA)
Northampton County Area Comm Coll (PA)
Northcentral Tech Coll (WI)
Northeast Alabama Comm Coll (AL)
Northeast Comm Coll (NE)
Northeast Texas Comm Coll (TX)
Northern Essex Comm Coll (MA)
Northern Maine Tech Coll (ME)
North Idaho Coll (ID)
North Iowa Area Comm Coll (IA)
North Seattle Comm Coll (WA)
North Shore Comm Coll (MA)
Northwestern Business Coll (IL)
Northwest Mississippi Comm Coll (MS)
Northwest State Comm Coll (OH)
Ohio Business Coll (OH)
Ohio Valley Business Coll (OH)
Oklahoma State U, Okmulgee (OK)
Orange Coast Coll (CA)
Otero Jr Coll (CO)
Ouachita Tech Coll (AR)
Palomar Coll (CA)
Penn Commercial Business and Tech School (PA)
Pennsylvania Coll of Technology (PA)
Penn Valley Comm Coll (MO)
Pensacola Jr Coll (FL)
Phoenix Coll (AZ)
Piedmont Comm Coll (NC)
Piedmont Tech Coll (SC)
Pima Comm Coll (AZ)
Pitt Comm Coll (NC)
Polk Comm Coll (FL)
Portland Comm Coll (OR)
Quincy Coll (MA)
Rasmussen Coll Eagan (MN)
Rasmussen Coll Mankato (MN)
Rasmussen Coll Minnetonka (MN)
Rasmussen Coll St. Cloud (MN)
Reading Area Comm Coll (PA)
Rend Lake Coll (IL)
Richland Comm Coll (IL)
Ridgewater Coll (MN)
Riverland Comm Coll (MN)
Roane State Comm Coll (TN)
Rockingham Comm Coll (NC)
Sacramento City Coll (CA)
St. Catharine Coll (KY)
St. Clair County Comm Coll (MI)
St. Cloud Tech Coll (MN)
St. Paul Tech Coll (MN)
St. Philip's Coll (TX)
Salem Comm Coll (NJ)
Sandhills Comm Coll (NC)
San Jacinto Coll Central Campus (TX)
San Joaquin Valley Coll (CA)
Santa Fe Comm Coll (FL)
Scottsdale Comm Coll (AZ)
Shasta Coll (CA)
Shoreline Comm Coll (WA)
Sierra Coll (CA)
Sinclair Comm Coll (OH)
Skagit Valley Coll (WA)
South Coll (TN)
Southeast Comm Coll, Beatrice Campus (NE)
Southeastern Comm Coll, South Campus (IA)
Southern Ohio Coll, Cincinnati Campus (OH)
South Hills School of Business & Technology, Atloona (PA)
South Hills School of Business & Technology, State College (PA)
South Piedmont Comm Coll (NC)
South Plains Coll (TX)
South Puget Sound Comm Coll (WA)
Spartanburg Tech Coll (SC)
Spokane Comm Coll (WA)
Springfield Tech Comm Coll (MA)
Stanly Comm Coll (NC)
State Fair Comm Coll (MO)
State U of NY Coll of A&T at Morrisville (NY)
Surry Comm Coll (NC)
Tacoma Comm Coll (WA)
Temple Coll (TX)
Terra State Comm Coll (OH)
Three Rivers Comm Coll (CT)
Tomball Coll (TX)
Trident Tech Coll (SC)
Trocaire Coll (NY)
Truckee Meadows Comm Coll (NV)
Trumbull Business Coll (OH)
Tulsa Comm Coll (OK)
Tunxis Comm Coll (CT)
Tyler Jr Coll (TX)
Umpqua Comm Coll (OR)
The U of Akron–Wayne Coll (OH)
U of Northwestern Ohio (OH)
Vance-Granville Comm Coll (NC)
Vermilion Comm Coll (MN)
Vincennes U (IN)
Vincennes U Jasper Campus (IN)
Vista Comm Coll (CA)
Wake Tech Comm Coll (NC)
Wallace State Comm Coll (AL)
Walla Walla Comm Coll (WA)
Walters State Comm Coll (TN)
Wayne Comm Coll (NC)
Webster Coll, Ocala (FL)
The Westchester Business Inst (NY)
Western Iowa Tech Comm Coll (IA)
Western Piedmont Comm Coll (NC)
Western Wisconsin Tech Coll (WI)
Western Wyoming Comm Coll (WY)
Westmoreland County Comm Coll (PA)
West Virginia Jr Coll, Charleston (WV)
Whatcom Comm Coll (WA)
Wisconsin Indianhead Tech Coll (WI)
Yorktowne Business Inst (PA)

MEDICAL ANATOMY

Fayetteville Tech Comm Coll (NC)

MEDICAL ASSISTANT

Academy of Medical Arts and Business (PA)
AIBT International Inst of the Americas (AZ)
Alamance Comm Coll (NC)
Allan Hancock Coll (CA)
Andover Coll (ME)
Anne Arundel Comm Coll (MD)
Arapahoe Comm Coll (CO)
Argosy U-Twin Cities (MN)
Athens Tech Coll (GA)
Atlanta Metropolitan Coll (GA)
Austin Comm Coll (TX)
Barstow Coll (CA)
Bay State Coll (MA)
Belmont Tech Coll (OH)
Bergen Comm Coll (NJ)
Berkshire Comm Coll (MA)
Berks Tech Inst (PA)
Blair Coll (CO)
Bossier Parish Comm Coll (LA)
Bradford School (OH)
Brevard Comm Coll (FL)
Briarwood Coll (CT)
Broome Comm Coll (NY)
The Brown Mackie Coll–Olathe Campus (KS)
Bryant & Stratton Business Inst, Albany (NY)
Bryant & Stratton Business Inst, Buffalo (NY)
Bryant & Stratton Business Inst, Rochester (NY)
Bryant & Stratton Business Inst, Rochester (NY)
Bryant and Stratton Coll, Parma (OH)
Bryant and Stratton Coll (WI)
Bryant and Stratton Coll, Virginia Beach (VA)
The Bryman School (AZ)
Bucks County Comm Coll (PA)
Burlington County Coll (NJ)
Business Inst of Pennsylvania (PA)
Butler County Comm Coll (PA)
Cabarrus Coll of Health Sciences (NC)
Capital Comm Coll (CT)
Career Coll of Northern Nevada (NV)
Carteret Comm Coll (NC)
Central Carolina Comm Coll (NC)
Central Comm Coll–Hastings Campus (NE)
Central Oregon Comm Coll (OR)
Central Pennsylvania Coll (PA)
Central Piedmont Comm Coll (NC)
Century Comm and Tech Coll (MN)
Cerritos Coll (CA)
Chabot Coll (CA)
Charter Coll (AK)
Chemeketa Comm Coll (OR)
CHI Inst (PA)
Cincinnati State Tech and Comm Coll (OH)
City Colls of Chicago, Malcolm X Coll (IL)
Clark Coll (WA)
Coll of Marin (CA)
Coll of the Desert (CA)
Coll of the Redwoods (CA)
Commonwealth Business Coll, Merrillville (IN)
Comm Coll of Allegheny County (PA)
Comm Coll of Aurora (CO)
Comm Coll of Southern Nevada (NV)
Cuesta Coll (CA)
Darton Coll (GA)
Davis Coll (OH)
De Anza Coll (CA)
Delaware County Comm Coll (PA)
Delaware Tech & Comm Coll, Jack F Owens Cmps (DE)
Delta Coll (MI)
Delta Coll of Arts and Technology (LA)
Des Moines Area Comm Coll (IA)
Dominion Coll, Roanoke (VA)
Douglas Education Center (PA)
Draughons Jr Coll (KY)
Draughons Jr Coll, Clarksville (TN)
Draughons Jr Coll, Nashville (TN)
Duff's Business Inst (PA)
Dutchess Comm Coll (NY)
Eastern Idaho Tech Coll (ID)
Eastern Oklahoma State Coll (OK)
Edgecombe Comm Coll (NC)
Education America, Remington Coll, Lafayette Campus (LA)
El Centro Coll (TX)
Empire Coll (CA)
Erie Business Center, Main (PA)
Everett Comm Coll (WA)
Flathead Valley Comm Coll (MT)
Florida National Coll (FL)
Forsyth Tech Comm Coll (NC)

Fresno City Coll (CA)
Gaston Coll (NC)
Gem City Coll (IL)
George Corley Wallace State Comm Coll (AL)
Georgia Perimeter Coll (GA)
Glendale Comm Coll (CA)
Guam Comm Coll (GU)
Guilford Tech Comm Coll (NC)
Gwinnett Tech Coll (GA)
Hagerstown Business Coll (MD)
Hamilton Coll (IA)
Harford Comm Coll (MD)
Haywood Comm Coll (NC)
Henry Ford Comm Coll (MI)
Hesser Coll (NH)
Highline Comm Coll (WA)
Hudson County Comm Coll (NJ)
Huntington Jr Coll of Business (WV)
Indiana Business Coll, Columbus (IN)
Indiana Business Coll, Evansville (IN)
Indiana Business Coll, Fort Wayne (IN)
Indiana Business Coll, Indianapolis (IN)
Indiana Business Coll, Terre Haute (IN)
Indiana Business Coll-Medical (IN)
IntelliTec Medical Inst (CO)
International Business Coll, Fort Wayne (IN)
Iowa Lakes Comm Coll (IA)
Iowa Western Comm Coll (IA)
Ivy Tech State Coll–Central Indiana (IN)
Ivy Tech State Coll–Columbus (IN)
Ivy Tech State Coll–Eastcentral (IN)
Ivy Tech State Coll–Kokomo (IN)
Ivy Tech State Coll–Lafayette (IN)
Ivy Tech State Coll–North Central (IN)
Ivy Tech State Coll–Northeast (IN)
Ivy Tech State Coll–Northwest (IN)
Ivy Tech State Coll–Southcentral (IN)
Ivy Tech State Coll–Southeast (IN)
Ivy Tech State Coll–Southwest (IN)
Ivy Tech State Coll–Wabash Valley (IN)
Ivy Tech State Coll–Whitewater (IN)
Jackson Comm Coll (MI)
James Sprunt Comm Coll (NC)
Jefferson Comm Coll (OH)
Jefferson Davis Comm Coll (AL)
Johnston Comm Coll (NC)
Kalamazoo Valley Comm Coll (MI)
Kaplan Coll (IA)
Kennebec Valley Tech Coll (ME)
Kilgore Coll (TX)
Kirkwood Comm Coll (IA)
Lac Courte Oreilles Ojibwa Comm Coll (WI)
Lake Area Tech Inst (SD)
Lake Tahoe Comm Coll (CA)
Lake Washington Tech Coll (WA)
Lansing Comm Coll (MI)
Laredo Comm Coll (TX)
Laurel Business Inst (PA)
LDS Business Coll (UT)
Lehigh Carbon Comm Coll (PA)
Lenoir Comm Coll (NC)
Lincoln School of Commerce (NE)
Linn-Benton Comm Coll (OR)
Long Beach City Coll (CA)
Martin Comm Coll (NC)
Massasoit Comm Coll (MA)
McIntosh Coll (NH)
Merced Coll (CA)
Miami-Dade Comm Coll (FL)
Middlesex Comm Coll (MA)
Mid Michigan Comm Coll (MI)
Mid-State Coll (ME)
Minnesota School of Business (MN)
Minnesota West Comm & Tech Coll-Pipestone Cmps (MN)
Minot State U–Bottineau Campus (ND)
Mitchell Comm Coll (NC)
Mitchell Tech Inst (SD)
Modesto Jr Coll (CA)
Montana State U Coll of Tech-Great Falls (MT)
Monterey Peninsula Coll (CA)
Montgomery Comm Coll (NC)
Mountain State Coll (WV)
Mountain West Coll (UT)
Mt. Hood Comm Coll (OR)
Mount Wachusett Comm Coll (MA)
Muskingum Area Tech Coll (OH)
National Coll of Business & Technology, Danville (KY)
National Coll of Business & Technology, Florence (KY)
National Coll of Business & Technology, Louisville (KY)
National Coll of Business & Technology, Pikeville (KY)
National Coll of Business & Technology, Richmond (KY)
National Coll of Business & Technology (TN)
National Coll of Business & Technology, Bluefield (VA)
National Coll of Business & Technology, Bristol (VA)
National Coll of Business & Technology, Charlottesville (VA)
National Coll of Business & Technology, Danville (VA)
National Coll of Business & Technology, Harrisonburg (VA)
National Coll of Business & Technology, Lynchburg (VA)
National Coll of Business & Technology, Salem (VA)
National Inst of Technology (WV)
New England Inst of Technology (RI)
New England Inst of Tech & Florida Culinary Inst (FL)
Niagara County Comm Coll (NY)
Northeast State Tech Comm Coll (TN)
North Iowa Area Comm Coll (IA)
Northland Pioneer Coll (AZ)
North Seattle Comm Coll (WA)
Northwestern Business Coll (IL)
Northwestern Connecticut Comm-Tech Coll (CT)
Oakland Comm Coll (MI)
Ocean County Coll (NJ)
Ohio Valley Business Coll (OH)
Olympic Coll (WA)
Orange Coast Coll (CA)
Pace Inst (PA)
Palomar Coll (CA)
Pamlico Comm Coll (NC)
Pasadena City Coll (CA)
Penn Commercial Business and Tech School (PA)
Phoenix Coll (AZ)
Pioneer Pacific Coll (OR)
Pitt Comm Coll (NC)
Portland Comm Coll (OR)
Rasmussen Coll Mankato (MN)
RETS Tech Center (OH)
Richmond Comm Coll (NC)
Rockford Business Coll (IL)
Rockingham Comm Coll (NC)
Salem Comm Coll (NJ)
San Antonio Coll (TX)
San Diego Mesa Coll (CA)
San Joaquin Valley Coll (CA)
Santa Ana Coll (CA)
Shasta Coll (CA)
Silicon Valley Coll, San Jose (CA)
Sinclair Comm Coll (OH)
Skagit Valley Coll (WA)
South Coll (NC)
South Coll (TN)
Southern Maine Tech Coll (ME)
Southern Ohio Coll, Cincinnati Campus (OH)
Southern Ohio Coll, Northern Kentucky Campus (KY)
Southern State Comm Coll (OH)
South Piedmont Comm Coll (NC)
South Puget Sound Comm Coll (WA)
South U (AL)
Southwestern Coll of Business, Dayton (OH)
Southwest Tennessee Comm Coll (TN)
Southwest Wisconsin Tech Coll (WI)
Springfield Tech Comm Coll (MA)
Stanly Comm Coll (NC)
Stark State Coll of Technology (OH)
State U of NY Coll of Technology at Alfred (NY)
Suffolk County Comm Coll (NY)
Tri-County Comm Coll (NC)
Tri-County Tech Coll (SC)
Trocaire Coll (NY)
Tulsa Comm Coll (OK)
Union County Coll (NJ)
U of Alaska Southeast, Sitka Campus (AK)
U of Northwestern Ohio (OH)
Vance-Granville Comm Coll (NC)
Ventura Coll (CA)
Vincennes U (IN)
Virginia Coll at Jackson (MS)
Wallace State Comm Coll (AL)
Wayne Comm Coll (NC)
Webster Coll, Holiday (FL)
Webster Coll, Ocala (FL)
Webster Inst of Technology (FL)
Western Piedmont Comm Coll (NC)
Western School of Health and Business Careers (PA)
Western Wyoming Comm Coll (WY)
West Virginia Jr Coll, Charleston (WV)
Westwood Coll of Technology–Denver North (CO)
Whatcom Comm Coll (WA)
Wilkes Comm Coll (NC)
Yorktowne Business Inst (PA)

MEDICAL DIETICIAN

Comm Coll of the Air Force (AL)

MEDICAL LABORATORY ASSISTANT

Bunker Hill Comm Coll (MA)
Muskingum Area Tech Coll (OH)
Orangeburg-Calhoun Tech Coll (SC)
Riverside Comm Coll (CA)

MEDICAL LABORATORY TECHNICIAN

Alamance Comm Coll (NC)
Albuquerque Tech Vocational Inst (NM)
Alexandria Tech Coll (MN)
Allegany Coll of Maryland (MD)
Angelina Coll (TX)
Arapahoe Comm Coll (CO)
Argosy U-Twin Cities (MN)
Arkansas State U–Beebe (AR)
Asheville-Buncombe Tech Comm Coll (NC)
Atlanta Metropolitan Coll (GA)
Austin Comm Coll (TX)
Barton County Comm Coll (KS)
Beaufort County Comm Coll (NC)
Bergen Comm Coll (NJ)
Bevill State Comm Coll (AL)
Bismarck State Coll (ND)
Black Hawk Coll, Moline (IL)
Brevard Comm Coll (FL)
Bristol Comm Coll (MA)
Bronx Comm Coll of City U of NY (NY)
Brookdale Comm Coll (NJ)
Broome Comm Coll (NY)
Camden County Coll (NJ)
Central Georgia Tech Coll (GA)
Central Maine Tech Coll (ME)
Central Piedmont Comm Coll (NC)
Central Texas Coll (TX)
Central Virginia Comm Coll (VA)
Chippewa Valley Tech Coll (WI)
Cincinnati State Tech and Comm Coll (OH)
City Colls of Chicago, Malcolm X Coll (IL)
Clinton Comm Coll (NY)
Coastal Carolina Comm Coll (NC)
Coastal Georgia Comm Coll (GA)
Coll of Lake County (IL)
Columbia State Comm Coll (TN)
Columbus State Comm Coll (OH)
Comm Coll of Allegheny County (PA)
The Comm Coll of Baltimore County–Catonsville Campus (MD)
Comm Coll of Beaver County (PA)
Comm Coll of Rhode Island (RI)
Comm Coll of Southern Nevada (NV)
Comm Coll of the Air Force (AL)
County Coll of Morris (NJ)
Darton Coll (GA)
Delaware Tech & Comm Coll, Jack F Owens Cmps (DE)
Delgado Comm Coll (LA)
Del Mar Coll (TX)
Des Moines Area Comm Coll (IA)
Dutchess Comm Coll (NY)
Eastern Maine Tech Coll (ME)
Eastern Oklahoma State Coll (OK)
El Centro Coll (TX)
Erie Comm Coll, North Campus (NY)
Eugenio María de Hostos Comm Coll of City U of NY (NY)
Fergus Falls Comm Coll (MN)
Florence-Darlington Tech Coll (SC)
Gadsden State Comm Coll (AL)
Genesee Comm Coll (NY)
George Corley Wallace State Comm Coll (AL)
Georgia Perimeter Coll (GA)
Grayson County Coll (TX)
Greenville Tech Coll (SC)
Guilford Tech Comm Coll (NC)
Halifax Comm Coll (NC)
Harcum Coll (PA)
Harford Comm Coll (MD)
Harrisburg Area Comm Coll (PA)
Hawkeye Comm Coll (IA)
Hazard Comm Coll (KY)
Hibbing Comm Coll (MN)
Hinds Comm Coll (MS)
Housatonic Comm Coll (CT)
Houston Comm Coll System (TX)
Indian River Comm Coll (FL)
IntelliTec Medical Inst (CO)
Ivy Tech State Coll–North Central (IN)
Ivy Tech State Coll–Wabash Valley (IN)
Jefferson State Comm Coll (AL)
John A. Logan Coll (IL)
John Wood Comm Coll (IL)
J. Sargeant Reynolds Comm Coll (VA)
Kankakee Comm Coll (IL)
Kellogg Comm Coll (MI)
Kilgore Coll (TX)
Lake Area Tech Inst (SD)
Lake City Comm Coll (FL)
Lakeland Comm Coll (OH)
Lamar State Coll–Orange (TX)
Laredo Comm Coll (TX)
Lehigh Carbon Comm Coll (PA)
Lewis and Clark Comm Coll (IL)
Lorain County Comm Coll (OH)
Louisiana State U at Alexandria (LA)
Manchester Comm Coll (CT)
Manor Coll (PA)
Marion Tech Coll (OH)
McLennan Comm Coll (TX)
MedVance Inst (LA)
MedVance Inst (TN)
Mercer County Comm Coll (NJ)
Meridian Comm Coll (MS)
Miami-Dade Comm Coll (FL)
Middlesex Comm Coll (MA)
Middlesex County Coll (NJ)
Midlands Tech Coll (SC)
Mid-Plains Comm Coll Area (NE)
Milwaukee Area Tech Coll (WI)
Mineral Area Coll (MO)
Minnesota West Comm & Tech Coll-Pipestone Cmps (MN)
Mississippi Delta Comm Coll (MS)
Mississippi Gulf Coast Comm Coll (MS)
Mitchell Tech Inst (SD)
Montgomery County Comm Coll (PA)
Moraine Valley Comm Coll (IL)
Nassau Comm Coll (NY)
Navarro Coll (TX)
New Mexico State U–Alamogordo (NM)
North Arkansas Coll (AR)
Northeast Iowa Comm Coll (IA)
Northern Virginia Comm Coll (VA)
North Hennepin Comm Coll (MN)
North Iowa Area Comm Coll (IA)
Oakton Comm Coll (IL)
Ocean County Coll (NJ)
Odessa Coll (TX)
Orangeburg-Calhoun Tech Coll (SC)
Orange County Comm Coll (NY)
Our Lady of the Lake Coll (LA)
Pamlico Comm Coll (NC)
Penn State U Hazleton Campus of the Commonwealth Coll (PA)
Penn State U New Kensington Campus of the Commonwealth Coll (PA)
Phoenix Coll (AZ)
Pierce Coll (WA)
Portland Comm Coll (OR)
Queensborough Comm Coll of City U of NY (NY)
Reading Area Comm Coll (PA)
Rend Lake Coll (IL)
Roane State Comm Coll (TN)
St. Paul Tech Coll (MN)
St. Petersburg Coll (FL)
St. Philip's Coll (TX)
San Bernardino Valley Coll (CA)
Sandhills Comm Coll (NC)
San Diego Mesa Coll (CA)
San Jacinto Coll Central Campus (TX)
Sauk Valley Comm Coll (IL)
Scott Comm Coll (IA)
Seminole State Coll (OK)
Shoreline Comm Coll (WA)
Somerset Comm Coll (KY)
South Arkansas Comm Coll (AR)
Southeast Comm Coll (KY)
Southeastern Comm Coll (NC)
Southeast Tech Inst (SD)
Southern West Virginia Comm and Tech Coll (WV)
Southwestern Comm Coll (NC)
Southwestern Oklahoma State U at Sayre (OK)
Southwest Georgia Tech Coll (GA)
Southwest Tennessee Comm Coll (TN)
Spartanburg Tech Coll (SC)
Springfield Tech Comm Coll (MA)
Stark State Coll of Technology (OH)
State U of NY Coll of A&T at Morrisville (NY)
State U of NY Coll of Technology at Canton (NY)
Tarrant County Coll District (TX)
Temple Coll (TX)
Thomas Nelson Comm Coll (VA)
Tri-County Tech Coll (SC)
Trident Tech Coll (SC)
Tulsa Comm Coll (OK)
Tyler Jr Coll (TX)
Union County Coll (NJ)
U of New Mexico–Gallup (NM)
Victoria Coll (TX)
Vincennes U (IN)
Wake Tech Comm Coll (NC)
Wallace State Comm Coll (AL)
Walters State Comm Coll (TN)
Waycross Coll (GA)
Westchester Comm Coll (NY)
Western Iowa Tech Comm Coll (IA)
Western Nevada Comm Coll (NV)
Western Piedmont Comm Coll (NC)
Western School of Health and Business Careers (PA)
Western Wisconsin Tech Coll (WI)
Wharton County Jr Coll (TX)
York Tech Coll (SC)

MEDICAL LABORATORY TECHNOLOGY

Argosy U-Twin Cities (MN)
Athens Tech Coll (GA)
Burlington County Coll (NJ)
Camden County Coll (NJ)
Cecil Comm Coll (MD)
Central Maine Tech Coll (ME)
Chippewa Valley Tech Coll (WI)
Darton Coll (GA)
Delaware Tech & Comm Coll, Jack F Owens Cmps (DE)
Ellsworth Comm Coll (IA)
Fayetteville Tech Comm Coll (NC)
Fergus Falls Comm Coll (MN)
Florida Comm Coll at Jacksonville (FL)
Frederick Comm Coll (MD)
Harford Comm Coll (MD)
Iowa Lakes Comm Coll (IA)
Jefferson Comm Coll (NY)
Mohawk Valley Comm Coll (NY)
Northwest-Shoals Comm Coll (AL)
Phoenix Coll (AZ)
Portland Comm Coll (OR)
Reading Area Comm Coll (PA)

Rowan-Cabarrus Comm Coll (NC)
Schoolcraft Coll (MI)
Shoreline Comm Coll (WA)
Vincennes U (IN)
Western Wyoming Comm Coll (WY)

MEDICAL OFFICE MANAGEMENT
Academy of Medical Arts and Business (PA)
American Inst of Health Technology, Inc. (ID)
Beaufort County Comm Coll (NC)
Briarwood Coll (CT)
The Brown Mackie Coll (KS)
Daymar Coll (KY)
Douglas Education Center (PA)
Erie Comm Coll, North Campus (NY)
Fayetteville Tech Comm Coll (NC)
Florida Comm Coll at Jacksonville (FL)
Gaston Coll (NC)
Lamar Comm Coll (CO)
McCann School of Business (PA)
Minnesota School of Business (MN)
Minot State U–Bottineau Campus (ND)
Patricia Stevens Coll (MO)
Pennsylvania Inst of Technology (PA)
Pikes Peak Comm Coll (CO)
Prince George's Comm Coll (MD)
St. Cloud Tech Coll (MN)
Spencerian Coll (KY)
The U of Akron–Wayne Coll (OH)
U of Arkansas Comm Coll at Batesville (AR)
Virginia Coll at Jackson (MS)
Wayne Comm Coll (NC)

MEDICAL PHYSIOLOGY
Comm Coll of the Air Force (AL)

MEDICAL RADIOLOGIC TECHNOLOGY
Argosy U-Twin Cities (MN)
Asheville-Buncombe Tech Comm Coll (NC)
Bacone Coll (OK)
Black Hawk Coll, Moline (IL)
Broome Comm Coll (NY)
The Bryman School (AZ)
Bunker Hill Comm Coll (MA)
Caldwell Comm Coll and Tech Inst (NC)
Camden County Coll (NJ)
Cape Fear Comm Coll (NC)
Capital Comm Coll (CT)
Carolinas Coll of Health Sciences (NC)
Catawba Valley Comm Coll (NC)
Central Ohio Tech Coll (OH)
Central Texas Coll (TX)
Century Comm and Tech Coll (MN)
Chaffey Coll (CA)
Chesapeake Coll (MD)
Chippewa Valley Tech Coll (WI)
City Colls of Chicago, Malcolm X Coll (IL)
City Colls of Chicago, Wilbur Wright Coll (IL)
Clovis Comm Coll (NM)
Coastal Georgia Comm Coll (GA)
Coll of Lake County (IL)
Coll of St. Catherine–Minneapolis (MN)
Coll of Southern Idaho (ID)
Comm Coll of Allegheny County (PA)
Comm Coll of Rhode Island (RI)
Comm Coll of the Air Force (AL)
Darton Coll (GA)
Delgado Comm Coll (LA)
El Centro Coll (TX)
Erie Comm Coll, City Campus (NY)
Eugenio María de Hostos Comm Coll of City U of NY (NY)
Florida Comm Coll at Jacksonville (FL)
Florida Hospital Coll of Health Sciences (FL)
Foothill Coll (CA)
Gadsden State Comm Coll (AL)
Galveston Coll (TX)
GateWay Comm Coll (AZ)
Hagerstown Comm Coll (MD)
Harrisburg Area Comm Coll (PA)
Hazard Comm Coll (KY)
Houston Comm Coll System (TX)
Hutchinson Comm Coll and Area Vocational School (KS)
Indiana Business Coll, Anderson (IN)
Indiana Business Coll, Columbus (IN)
Indiana Business Coll, Evansville (IN)
Indiana Business Coll, Fort Wayne (IN)
Indiana Business Coll, Marion (IN)
Indiana Business Coll, Terre Haute (IN)
Indiana Business Coll-Medical (IN)
Ivy Tech State Coll–Central Indiana (IN)
Ivy Tech State Coll–Eastcentral (IN)
Ivy Tech State Coll–Wabash Valley (IN)
Jefferson State Comm Coll (AL)
Johnston Comm Coll (NC)
John Wood Comm Coll (IL)
Kaskaskia Coll (IL)
Kellogg Comm Coll (MI)
Kent State U, Salem Campus (OH)
Keystone Coll (PA)
Kilgore Coll (TX)
Kishwaukee Coll (IL)
Lake Michigan Coll (MI)
Lansing Comm Coll (MI)
Manatee Comm Coll (FL)
Massachusetts Bay Comm Coll (MA)
Massasoit Comm Coll (MA)
Mercer County Comm Coll (NJ)
Meridian Comm Coll (MS)
Midlands Tech Coll (SC)
Mineral Area Coll (MO)
Mississippi Delta Comm Coll (MS)
Montcalm Comm Coll (MI)
Montgomery Coll (MD)
Moraine Valley Comm Coll (IL)
Mott Comm Coll (MI)
Nassau Comm Coll (NY)
New York City Tech Coll of the City U of NY (NY)
Northampton County Area Comm Coll (PA)
North Arkansas Coll (AR)
North Country Comm Coll (NY)
Northern New Mexico Comm Coll (NM)
North Hennepin Comm Coll (MN)
North Shore Comm Coll (MA)
Oakland Comm Coll (MI)
Orangeburg-Calhoun Tech Coll (SC)
Owensboro Comm Coll (KY)
Parkland Coll (IL)
Pennsylvania Coll of Technology (PA)
Piedmont Tech Coll (SC)
Pima Comm Coll (AZ)
Pitt Comm Coll (NC)
Quinsigamond Comm Coll (MA)
Riverland Comm Coll (MN)
St. Philip's Coll (TX)
Santa Barbara City Coll (CA)
Scott Comm Coll (IA)
South Arkansas Comm Coll (AR)
Southeast Comm Coll (KY)
Southwestern Comm Coll (NC)
Southwestern Oklahoma State U at Sayre (OK)
Southwest Georgia Tech Coll (GA)
Southwest Tennessee Comm Coll (TN)
Spartanburg Tech Coll (SC)
Springfield Tech Comm Coll (MA)
Union County Coll (NJ)
U of Arkansas at Fort Smith (AR)
U of Kentucky, Lexington Comm Coll (KY)
Volunteer State Comm Coll (TN)
Wake Tech Comm Coll (NC)
Waycross Coll (GA)
Western School of Health and Business Careers (PA)
Wor-Wic Comm Coll (MD)
York Tech Coll (SC)

MEDICAL RECORDS ADMINISTRATION
Adirondack Comm Coll (NY)
Albuquerque Tech Vocational Inst (NM)
Amarillo Coll (TX)
Andover Coll (ME)
Arapahoe Comm Coll (CO)
Baltimore City Comm Coll (MD)
Barton County Comm Coll (KS)
Black Hawk Coll, Moline (IL)
Bowling Green State U-Firelands Coll (OH)
Briarwood Coll (CT)
Bristol Comm Coll (MA)
Broome Comm Coll (NY)
The Brown Mackie Coll–Olathe Campus (KS)
Brunswick Comm Coll (NC)
Business Inst of Pennsylvania (PA)
Central Piedmont Comm Coll (NC)
Chabot Coll (CA)
Chattanooga State Tech Comm Coll (TN)
Chemeketa Comm Coll (OR)
CHI Inst (PA)
Chippewa Valley Tech Coll (WI)
Cincinnati State Tech and Comm Coll (OH)
City Coll of San Francisco (CA)
City Colls of Chicago, Harry S Truman Coll (IL)
Coll of DuPage (IL)
Coll of St. Catherine–Minneapolis (MN)
Columbus State Comm Coll (OH)
Comm Coll of Southern Nevada (NV)
Cypress Coll (CA)
Darton Coll (GA)
Daytona Beach Comm Coll (FL)
Dodge City Comm Coll (KS)
Draughons Jr Coll (KY)
Draughons Jr Coll, Clarksville (TN)
Draughons Jr Coll, Nashville (TN)
Durham Tech Comm Coll (NC)
East Central Comm Coll (MS)
ECPI Coll of Technology, Newport News (VA)
ECPI Coll of Technology, Virginia Beach (VA)
ECPI Tech Coll, Richmond (VA)
ECPI Tech Coll, Roanoke (VA)
Edgecombe Comm Coll (NC)
Edison State Comm Coll (OH)
Elaine P. Nunez Comm Coll (LA)
El Centro Coll (TX)
Enterprise State Jr Coll (AL)
Erie Business Center South (PA)
Florence-Darlington Tech Coll (SC)
Florida Comm Coll at Jacksonville (FL)
Fort Berthold Comm Coll (ND)
Fresno City Coll (CA)
Gateway Tech Coll (WI)
George Corley Wallace State Comm Coll (AL)
Glendale Comm Coll (CA)
Gogebic Comm Coll (MI)
Hagerstown Business Coll (MD)
Harrisburg Area Comm Coll (PA)
Henry Ford Comm Coll (MI)
Highland Comm Coll (KS)
Hinds Comm Coll (MS)
Holmes Comm Coll (MS)
Holyoke Comm Coll (MA)
Houston Comm Coll System (TX)
Howard Coll (TX)
Indian Hills Comm Coll (IA)
Indian River Comm Coll (FL)
John A. Logan Coll (IL)
Kennebec Valley Tech Coll (ME)
Kirkwood Comm Coll (IA)
Labouré Coll (MA)
Lake-Sumter Comm Coll (FL)
Lamar State Coll–Port Arthur (TX)
LDS Business Coll (UT)
McLennan Comm Coll (TX)
Meridian Comm Coll (MS)
Miami-Dade Comm Coll (FL)
Midland Coll (TX)
Midlands Tech Coll (SC)
Mississippi Delta Comm Coll (MS)
Mohawk Valley Comm Coll (NY)
Monroe Coll, Bronx (NY)
Monroe Comm Coll (NY)
Montana State U Coll of Tech-Great Falls (MT)
Moraine Park Tech Coll (WI)
North Central Texas Coll (TX)
Northeast Iowa Comm Coll (IA)
Northern Essex Comm Coll (MA)
Northern Virginia Comm Coll (VA)
Oakton Comm Coll (IL)
Oklahoma City Comm Coll (OK)
Onondaga Comm Coll (NY)
Penn Valley Comm Coll (MO)
Pensacola Jr Coll (FL)
Phoenix Coll (AZ)
Polk Comm Coll (FL)
Portland Comm Coll (OR)
Prince George's Comm Coll (MD)
Rasmussen Coll Eagan (MN)
Rasmussen Coll Mankato (MN)
Rasmussen Coll St. Cloud (MN)
Reading Area Comm Coll (PA)
Ridgewater Coll (MN)
Roane State Comm Coll (TN)
Rockland Comm Coll (NY)
Saint Charles Comm Coll (MO)
St. Petersburg Coll (FL)
St. Philip's Coll (TX)
San Diego Mesa Coll (CA)
Santa Fe Comm Coll (FL)
Shoreline Comm Coll (WA)
Sinclair Comm Coll (OH)
South Plains Coll (TX)
Southwestern Comm Coll (NC)
Spokane Comm Coll (WA)
Stark State Coll of Technology (OH)
State Fair Comm Coll (MO)
State U of NY Coll of Technology at Alfred (NY)
Tacoma Comm Coll (WA)
Tarrant County Coll District (TX)
Texas State Tech Coll–Harlingen (TX)
Trocaire Coll (NY)
Tulsa Comm Coll (OK)
United Tribes Tech Coll (ND)
Vermilion Comm Coll (MN)
Vincennes U (IN)
Virginia Coll at Jackson (MS)
Wallace State Comm Coll (AL)
Westmoreland County Comm Coll (PA)
Wharton County Jr Coll (TX)

MEDICAL RECORDS TECHNOLOGY
Blinn Coll (TX)
Catawba Valley Comm Coll (NC)
Central Comm Coll–Hastings Campus (NE)
Central Oregon Comm Coll (OR)
Coll of Lake County (IL)
Comm Coll of Allegheny County (PA)
Darton Coll (GA)
Delgado Comm Coll (LA)
Dyersburg State Comm Coll (TN)
Electronic Computer Programming Coll (TN)
Erie Comm Coll, North Campus (NY)
Fayetteville Tech Comm Coll (NC)
Houston Comm Coll System (TX)
Hudson County Comm Coll (NJ)
Hutchinson Comm Coll and Area Vocational School (KS)
Indiana Business Coll, Indianapolis (IN)
Indiana Business Coll, Muncie (IN)
James Sprunt Comm Coll (NC)
Johnson County Comm Coll (KS)
Lehigh Carbon Comm Coll (PA)
Monroe Coll, Bronx (NY)
Monroe Coll, New Rochelle (NY)
Montana State U Coll of Tech-Great Falls (MT)
Montgomery Coll (MD)
Moraine Valley Comm Coll (IL)
Mountain View Coll (TX)
North Dakota State Coll of Science (ND)
North Hennepin Comm Coll (MN)
Ozarka Coll (AR)
Pitt Comm Coll (NC)
Rend Lake Coll (IL)
Rowan-Cabarrus Comm Coll (NC)
St. Philip's Coll (TX)
San Jacinto Coll North Campus (TX)
San Juan Coll (NM)
Santa Barbara City Coll (CA)
Schoolcraft Coll (MI)
South Hills School of Business & Technology, State College (PA)
South Piedmont Comm Coll (NC)
Tallahassee Comm Coll (FL)
Texas State Tech Coll (TX)
United Tribes Tech Coll (ND)
Vernon Coll (TX)
Volunteer State Comm Coll (TN)
West Virginia Northern Comm Coll (WV)
Williston State Coll (ND)

MEDICAL TECHNOLOGY
Amarillo Coll (TX)
Andrew Coll (GA)
Angelina Coll (TX)
Anne Arundel Comm Coll (MD)
Arapahoe Comm Coll (CO)
Athens Tech Coll (GA)
Butte Coll (CA)
Casper Coll (WY)
Central Piedmont Comm Coll (NC)
Chattahoochee Valley Comm Coll (AL)
CHI Inst (PA)
Chipola Jr Coll (FL)
Cisco Jr Coll (TX)
City Colls of Chicago, Harry S Truman Coll (IL)
City Colls of Chicago, Richard J Daley Coll (IL)
Clark Coll (WA)
Coahoma Comm Coll (MS)
Coll of St. Catherine–Minneapolis (MN)
Coll of Southern Idaho (ID)
Columbus State Comm Coll (OH)
Comm Coll of Southern Nevada (NV)
Cuyahoga Comm Coll (OH)
Del Mar Coll (TX)
Dodge City Comm Coll (KS)
Eastern Oklahoma State Coll (OK)
Edison Comm Coll (FL)
El Centro Coll (TX)
Ellsworth Comm Coll (IA)
Floyd Coll (GA)
Fort Scott Comm Coll (KS)
Grayson County Coll (TX)
Henderson Comm Coll (KY)
Highland Comm Coll (KS)
Holmes Comm Coll (MS)
Holyoke Comm Coll (MA)
Howard Comm Coll (MD)
Jackson Comm Coll (MI)
Jackson State Comm Coll (TN)
Joliet Jr Coll (IL)
Kilgore Coll (TX)
Labouré Coll (MA)
Lansing Comm Coll (MI)
Louisburg Coll (NC)
Marian Court Coll (MA)
Miami-Dade Comm Coll (FL)
Mineral Area Coll (MO)
Monroe County Comm Coll (MI)
North Idaho Coll (ID)
Northwest-Shoals Comm Coll (AL)
Okaloosa-Walton Comm Coll (FL)
Orange Coast Coll (CA)
Pensacola Jr Coll (FL)
Phoenix Coll (AZ)
Reading Area Comm Coll (PA)
South Texas Comm Coll (TX)
Suffolk County Comm Coll (NY)
Tarrant County Coll District (TX)
Temple Coll (TX)
Vincennes U (IN)
Waycross Coll (GA)
Westchester Comm Coll (NY)
Western Nebraska Comm Coll (NE)
Young Harris Coll (GA)

MEDICAL TRANSCRIPTION
AIBT International Inst of the Americas (AZ)
The Brown Mackie Coll (KS)
Central Arizona Coll (AZ)
El Centro Coll (TX)
Erie Business Center, Main (PA)
Kaplan Coll (IA)
Laurel Business Inst (PA)
Mid Michigan Comm Coll (MI)
Montana State U Coll of Tech-Great Falls (MT)
Mountain State Coll (WV)
Northland Pioneer Coll (AZ)
Oakland Comm Coll (MI)
Prince Inst of Professional Studies (AL)
Rockford Business Coll (IL)
Saint Charles Comm Coll (MO)

Southeast Tech Inst (SD)
Southwest Wisconsin Tech Coll (WI)
Western Dakota Tech Inst (SD)
Westwood Coll of Technology–Denver North (CO)
Williston State Coll (ND)

MENTAL HEALTH/ REHABILITATION
Alvin Comm Coll (TX)
Anne Arundel Comm Coll (MD)
Belmont Tech Coll (OH)
Blinn Coll (TX)
Blue Ridge Comm Coll (VA)
Columbus State Comm Coll (OH)
The Comm Coll of Baltimore County–Catonsville Campus (MD)
Comm Coll of the Air Force (AL)
Del Mar Coll (TX)
Dutchess Comm Coll (NY)
Evergreen Valley Coll (CA)
Fiorello H LaGuardia Comm Coll of City U of NY (NY)
Gateway Comm Coll (CT)
Glendale Comm Coll (CA)
Hopkinsville Comm Coll (KY)
Housatonic Comm Coll (CT)
Houston Comm Coll System (TX)
Jefferson Comm Coll (KY)
Kingsborough Comm Coll of City U of NY (NY)
Lenoir Comm Coll (NC)
Los Angeles City Coll (CA)
Macomb Comm Coll (MI)
Marshalltown Comm Coll (IA)
McLennan Comm Coll (TX)
Metropolitan Comm Coll (NE)
Middlesex Comm Coll (MA)
Mohawk Valley Comm Coll (NY)
Mt. Hood Comm Coll (OR)
Muskingum Area Tech Coll (OH)
Naugatuck Valley Comm Coll (CT)
New Hampshire Tech Inst (NH)
North Country Comm Coll (NY)
Northern Essex Comm Coll (MA)
North Shore Comm Coll (MA)
Orange County Comm Coll (NY)
Oxnard Coll (CA)
Pierce Coll (WA)
Prairie State Coll (IL)
Reading Area Comm Coll (PA)
Ridgewater Coll (MN)
St. Clair County Comm Coll (MI)
San Bernardino Valley Coll (CA)
Sandhills Comm Coll (NC)
Sauk Valley Comm Coll (IL)
Sinclair Comm Coll (OH)
South Plains Coll (TX)
South Suburban Coll (IL)
Southwestern Comm Coll (NC)
Tarrant County Coll District (TX)
Truckee Meadows Comm Coll (NV)
Virginia Western Comm Coll (VA)
Wallace State Comm Coll (AL)

MENTAL HEALTH SERVICES RELATED
Oakland Comm Coll (MI)
Pitt Comm Coll (NC)

METAL/JEWELRY ARTS
The Art Inst of Pittsburgh (PA)
Flathead Valley Comm Coll (MT)
Garden City Comm Coll (KS)
Gem City Coll (IL)
Haywood Comm Coll (NC)
Inst of American Indian Arts (NM)
Mesa Tech Coll (NM)
Mohave Comm Coll (AZ)
Monterey Peninsula Coll (CA)
Oklahoma State U, Okmulgee (OK)
Palomar Coll (CA)
Pasadena City Coll (CA)
San Antonio Coll (TX)

METALLURGICAL TECHNOLOGY
Comm Coll of the Air Force (AL)
Don Bosco Coll of Science and Technology (CA)
Illinois Eastern Comm Colls, Olney Central Coll (IL)
Kilgore Coll (TX)
Linn-Benton Comm Coll (OR)
Macomb Comm Coll (MI)
Mississippi County Comm Coll (AR)

Mohawk Valley Comm Coll (NY)
Ridgewater Coll (MN)
Schoolcraft Coll (MI)
Sierra Coll (CA)
Southeast Comm Coll, Milford Campus (NE)

METALLURGY
Cerritos Coll (CA)
Schoolcraft Coll (MI)
Southeast Comm Coll, Milford Campus (NE)

MEXICAN-AMERICAN STUDIES
Cerritos Coll (CA)
Coll of Alameda (CA)
Compton Comm Coll (CA)
Fresno City Coll (CA)
Los Angeles City Coll (CA)
Pasadena City Coll (CA)
San Diego City Coll (CA)
San Diego Mesa Coll (CA)
Santa Ana Coll (CA)
Santa Barbara City Coll (CA)
Southwestern Coll (CA)

MICROBIOLOGY/ BACTERIOLOGY
Riverside Comm Coll (CA)

MIDDLE SCHOOL EDUCATION
Eastern Wyoming Coll (WY)
Lincoln Coll, Lincoln (IL)
Lincoln Land Comm Coll (IL)
Miami-Dade Comm Coll (FL)
Ozarka Coll (AR)
Vincennes U (IN)

MILITARY STUDIES
Truckee Meadows Comm Coll (NV)

MILITARY TECHNOLOGY
Calhoun Comm Coll (AL)
Comm Coll of the Air Force (AL)

MINING TECHNOLOGY
Casper Coll (WY)
Coll of Eastern Utah (UT)
Eastern Arizona Coll (AZ)
Illinois Eastern Comm Colls, Wabash Valley Coll (IL)
Mountain Empire Comm Coll (VA)
Rend Lake Coll (IL)
Sierra Coll (CA)
Southwest Virginia Comm Coll (VA)
Trinidad State Jr Coll (CO)
Western Wyoming Comm Coll (WY)

MODERN LANGUAGES
Amarillo Coll (TX)
Brookdale Comm Coll (NJ)
Cape Cod Comm Coll (MA)
Citrus Coll (CA)
City Colls of Chicago, Harry S Truman Coll (IL)
City Colls of Chicago, Richard J Daley Coll (IL)
City Colls of Chicago, Wilbur Wright Coll (IL)
Coll of the Sequoias (CA)
East Central Coll (MO)
Everett Comm Coll (WA)
Galveston Coll (TX)
Imperial Valley Coll (CA)
Independence Comm Coll (KS)
Lon Morris Coll (TX)
Middlesex County Coll (NJ)
Midland Coll (TX)
Northwest Coll (WY)
Odessa Coll (TX)
Okaloosa-Walton Comm Coll (FL)
Oklahoma City Comm Coll (OK)
Otero Jr Coll (CO)
Pasadena City Coll (CA)
San Diego City Coll (CA)
San Jacinto Coll Central Campus (TX)
Santa Ana Coll (CA)
Tyler Jr Coll (TX)

MORTUARY SCIENCE
Allen County Comm Coll (KS)
Amarillo Coll (TX)
American Acad McAllister Inst of Funeral Service (NY)
Arapahoe Comm Coll (CO)

Arkansas State U–Mountain Home (AR)
Briarwood Coll (CT)
Carl Sandburg Coll (IL)
Catawba Valley Comm Coll (NC)
Cincinnati Coll of Mortuary Science (OH)
City Colls of Chicago, Malcolm X Coll (IL)
Commonwealth Inst of Funeral Service (TX)
The Comm Coll of Baltimore County–Catonsville Campus (MD)
Cypress Coll (CA)
Delgado Comm Coll (LA)
Delta Coll (MI)
East Mississippi Comm Coll (MS)
Everett Comm Coll (WA)
Fayetteville Tech Comm Coll (NC)
Fiorello H LaGuardia Comm Coll of City U of NY (NY)
Florence-Darlington Tech Coll (SC)
Forsyth Tech Comm Coll (NC)
Gupton-Jones Coll of Funeral Service (GA)
Highland Comm Coll (KS)
Jefferson State Comm Coll (AL)
John A. Gupton Coll (TN)
John Tyler Comm Coll (VA)
Kansas City Kansas Comm Coll (KS)
Luzerne County Comm Coll (PA)
Mercer County Comm Coll (NJ)
Miami-Dade Comm Coll (FL)
Mid-America Coll of Funeral Service (IN)
Milwaukee Area Tech Coll (WI)
Monroe County Comm Coll (MI)
Mt. Hood Comm Coll (OR)
Nassau Comm Coll (NY)
Northampton County Area Comm Coll (PA)
Piedmont Tech Coll (SC)
Pittsburgh Inst of Mortuary Science, Inc (PA)
St. Petersburg Coll (FL)
San Antonio Coll (TX)
Simmons Inst of Funeral Service (NY)
State U of NY Coll of Technology at Canton (NY)
U of Arkansas Comm Coll at Hope (AR)
Vincennes U (IN)
Worsham Coll of Mortuary Science (IL)

MULTI/INTERDISCIPLINARY STUDIES RELATED
Brookdale Comm Coll (NJ)
Central Carolina Tech Coll (SC)
Mid-South Comm Coll (AR)
Snead State Comm Coll (AL)
U of Arkansas at Fort Smith (AR)
Williston State Coll (ND)

MULTIMEDIA
The Art Inst of Atlanta (GA)
The Art Inst of Houston (TX)
The Art Inst of Los Angeles (CA)
The Art Inst of Philadelphia (PA)
The Art Insts International Minnesota (MN)
Comm Coll of Denver (CO)
Full Sail Real World Education (FL)
Hillsborough Comm Coll (FL)
Platt Coll (CO)
Platt Coll San Diego (CA)
Raritan Valley Comm Coll (NJ)
San Diego Mesa Coll (CA)
Westwood Coll of Technology–Anaheim (CA)
Westwood Coll of Technology–Chicago Du Page (IL)
Westwood Coll of Technology–Chicago O'Hare (IL)
Westwood Coll of Technology–Chicago River Oaks (IL)
Westwood Coll of Technology–Denver South (CO)
Westwood Coll of Technology–Inland Empire (CA)
Westwood Coll of Technology–Los Angeles (CA)
Westwood Inst of Technology–Fort Worth (TX)

MUSEUM STUDIES
Inst of American Indian Arts (NM)
Tacoma Comm Coll (WA)

MUSIC
Abraham Baldwin Ag Coll (GA)
Adirondack Comm Coll (NY)
Allan Hancock Coll (CA)
Allen County Comm Coll (KS)
Alvin Comm Coll (TX)
Amarillo Coll (TX)
American River Coll (CA)
Andrew Coll (GA)
Angelina Coll (TX)
Anne Arundel Comm Coll (MD)
Antelope Valley Coll (CA)
Arizona Western Coll (AZ)
Atlanta Metropolitan Coll (GA)
Austin Comm Coll (TX)
Bakersfield Coll (CA)
Barton County Comm Coll (KS)
Bergen Comm Coll (NJ)
Blinn Coll (TX)
Brazosport Coll (TX)
Bronx Comm Coll of City U of NY (NY)
Brookdale Comm Coll (NJ)
Bucks County Comm Coll (PA)
Burlington County Coll (NJ)
Butte Coll (CA)
Caldwell Comm Coll and Tech Inst (NC)
Calhoun Comm Coll (AL)
Cañada Coll (CA)
Cape Cod Comm Coll (MA)
Carroll Comm Coll (MD)
Casper Coll (WY)
Cedar Valley Coll (TX)
Centralia Coll (WA)
Central Piedmont Comm Coll (NC)
Central Texas Coll (TX)
Central Wyoming Coll (WY)
Cerritos Coll (CA)
Cerro Coso Comm Coll (CA)
Chabot Coll (CA)
Chaffey Coll (CA)
Chattahoochee Valley Comm Coll (AL)
Chesapeake Coll (MD)
Citrus Coll (CA)
City Coll of San Francisco (CA)
City Colls of Chicago, Malcolm X Coll (IL)
City Colls of Chicago, Richard J Daley Coll (IL)
City Colls of Chicago, Wilbur Wright Coll (IL)
Clark Coll (WA)
Coastal Bend Coll (TX)
Coffeyville Comm Coll (KS)
Colby Comm Coll (KS)
Coll of Marin (CA)
Coll of Southern Idaho (ID)
Coll of the Desert (CA)
Coll of the Sequoias (CA)
Coll of the Siskiyous (CA)
Collin County Comm Coll District (TX)
Columbia State Comm Coll (TN)
Comm Coll of Allegheny County (PA)
The Comm Coll of Baltimore County–Catonsville Campus (MD)
Comm Coll of Rhode Island (RI)
Comm Coll of Southern Nevada (NV)
Compton Comm Coll (CA)
Cowley County Comm Coll and Voc-Tech School (KS)
Crafton Hills Coll (CA)
Crowder Coll (MO)
Cypress Coll (CA)
Darton Coll (GA)
Daytona Beach Comm Coll (FL)
De Anza Coll (CA)
Delgado Comm Coll (LA)
Del Mar Coll (TX)
Delta Coll (MI)
Dixie State Coll of Utah (UT)
Dodge City Comm Coll (KS)
East Central Coll (MO)
East Central Comm Coll (MS)
Eastern Arizona Coll (AZ)
Eastern Oklahoma State Coll (OK)
Eastern Wyoming Coll (WY)
East Mississippi Comm Coll (MS)
Edison Comm Coll (FL)

Essex County Coll (NJ)
Everett Comm Coll (WA)
Finger Lakes Comm Coll (NY)
Foothill Coll (CA)
Fort Scott Comm Coll (KS)
Fullerton Coll (CA)
Galveston Coll (TX)
Garden City Comm Coll (KS)
Gavilan Coll (CA)
Georgia Perimeter Coll (GA)
Glendale Comm Coll (CA)
Golden West Coll (CA)
Grand Rapids Comm Coll (MI)
Grayson County Coll (TX)
Harford Comm Coll (MD)
Harrisburg Area Comm Coll (PA)
Highland Comm Coll (KS)
Highline Comm Coll (WA)
Hill Coll of the Hill Jr College District (TX)
Hillsborough Comm Coll (FL)
Hinds Comm Coll (MS)
Holyoke Comm Coll (MA)
Howard Comm Coll (MD)
Imperial Valley Coll (CA)
Independence Comm Coll (KS)
Indian River Comm Coll (FL)
Iowa Lakes Comm Coll (IA)
Isothermal Comm Coll (NC)
Jamestown Comm Coll (NY)
Jefferson Coll (MO)
Jefferson Davis Comm Coll (AL)
Joliet Jr Coll (IL)
Jones County Jr Coll (MS)
J. Sargeant Reynolds Comm Coll (VA)
Kellogg Comm Coll (MI)
Kilgore Coll (TX)
Kingsborough Comm Coll of City U of NY (NY)
Kirkwood Comm Coll (IA)
Labette Comm Coll (KS)
Lake Michigan Coll (MI)
Lake Tahoe Comm Coll (CA)
Lansing Comm Coll (MI)
Laramie County Comm Coll (WY)
Lewis and Clark Comm Coll (IL)
Lincoln Coll, Lincoln (IL)
Lincoln Land Comm Coll (IL)
Long Beach City Coll (CA)
Lon Morris Coll (TX)
Lorain County Comm Coll (OH)
Los Angeles City Coll (CA)
Los Angeles Mission Coll (CA)
Los Angeles Pierce Coll (CA)
Lower Columbia Coll (WA)
Manatee Comm Coll (FL)
Manchester Comm Coll (CT)
McHenry County Coll (IL)
McLennan Comm Coll (TX)
Merced Coll (CA)
Mercer County Comm Coll (NJ)
Miami-Dade Comm Coll (FL)
Middlesex County Coll (NJ)
Midland Coll (TX)
Milwaukee Area Tech Coll (WI)
Minot State U–Bottineau Campus (ND)
MiraCosta Coll (CA)
Mississippi Delta Comm Coll (MS)
Modesto Jr Coll (CA)
Mohave Comm Coll (AZ)
Monroe Comm Coll (NY)
Monterey Peninsula Coll (CA)
Moorpark Coll (CA)
Morton Coll (IL)
Mt. San Jacinto Coll (CA)
Naugatuck Valley Comm Coll (CT)
Navarro Coll (TX)
Niagara County Comm Coll (NY)
Northeast Comm Coll (NE)
Northern Essex Comm Coll (MA)
Northern Virginia Comm Coll (VA)
North Harris Coll (TX)
North Idaho Coll (ID)
North Seattle Comm Coll (WA)
Northwest Coll (WY)
Northwest-Shoals Comm Coll (AL)
Oakton Comm Coll (IL)
Odessa Coll (TX)
Okaloosa-Walton Comm Coll (FL)
Oklahoma City Comm Coll (OK)
Onondaga Comm Coll (NY)
Orange Coast Coll (CA)
Palm Beach Comm Coll (FL)
Palomar Coll (CA)
Pasadena City Coll (CA)
Pensacola Jr Coll (FL)
Pima Comm Coll (AZ)

Pratt Comm Coll and Area Vocational School (KS)
Raritan Valley Comm Coll (NJ)
Ridgewater Coll (MN)
Riverside Comm Coll (CA)
Sacramento City Coll (CA)
St. Catharine Coll (KY)
St. Louis Comm Coll at Florissant Valley (MO)
St. Philip's Coll (TX)
San Bernardino Valley Coll (CA)
Sandhills Comm Coll (NC)
San Diego City Coll (CA)
San Diego Mesa Coll (CA)
San Jacinto Coll Central Campus (TX)
San Jacinto Coll North Campus (TX)
San Jacinto Coll South Campus (TX)
San Joaquin Delta Coll (CA)
San Juan Coll (NM)
Santa Ana Coll (CA)
Santa Barbara City Coll (CA)
Santa Monica Coll (CA)
Sauk Valley Comm Coll (IL)
Schenectady County Comm Coll (NY)
Shasta Coll (CA)
Sheridan Coll (WY)
Shoreline Comm Coll (WA)
Sinclair Comm Coll (OH)
Skagit Valley Coll (WA)
Snow Coll (UT)
Southeastern Comm Coll (NC)
South Mountain Comm Coll (AZ)
South Plains Coll (TX)
Southwestern Coll (CA)
Southwestern Comm Coll (IA)
Southwest Mississippi Comm Coll (MS)
Southwest Virginia Comm Coll (VA)
Spokane Falls Comm Coll (WA)
Suffolk County Comm Coll (NY)
Tacoma Comm Coll (WA)
Texarkana Coll (TX)
Tidewater Comm Coll (VA)
Trinidad State Jr Coll (CO)
Trinity Valley Comm Coll (TX)
Triton Coll (IL)
Truett-McConnell Coll (GA)
Tulsa Comm Coll (OK)
Tyler Jr Coll (TX)
Umpqua Comm Coll (OR)
Ventura Coll (CA)
Vermilion Comm Coll (MN)
Victor Valley Coll (CA)
Villa Maria Coll of Buffalo (NY)
Vincennes U (IN)
Wallace State Comm Coll (AL)
Waubonsee Comm Coll (IL)
Western Wyoming Comm Coll (WY)
Wharton County Jr Coll (TX)
Young Harris Coll (GA)

MUSICAL INSTRUMENT TECHNOLOGY
Minnesota State Coll–Southeast Tech (MN)
Orange Coast Coll (CA)
Queensborough Comm Coll of City U of NY (NY)

MUSIC BUSINESS MANAGEMENT/ MERCHANDISING
American River Coll (CA)
Century Comm and Tech Coll (MN)
Full Sail Real World Education (FL)
Houston Comm Coll System (TX)
Independence Comm Coll (KS)
Lincoln Coll, Lincoln (IL)
New England Inst of Art & Communications (MA)
Northeast Comm Coll (NE)
Orange Coast Coll (CA)
San Jacinto Coll Central Campus (TX)
Schenectady County Comm Coll (NY)
Villa Maria Coll of Buffalo (NY)

MUSIC (GENERAL PERFORMANCE)
Berkshire Comm Coll (MA)
Comm Coll of the Air Force (AL)
Fresno City Coll (CA)
Manatee Comm Coll (FL)
Nassau Comm Coll (NY)
Northeast Comm Coll (NE)
Parkland Coll (IL)
Reedley Coll (CA)

MUSIC HISTORY
Hill Coll of the Hill Jr College District (TX)
Lincoln Coll, Lincoln (IL)
Snow Coll (UT)

MUSIC (PIANO AND ORGAN PERFORMANCE)
Angelina Coll (TX)
Fresno City Coll (CA)
Hill Coll of the Hill Jr College District (TX)
Iowa Lakes Comm Coll (IA)
Lincoln Coll, Lincoln (IL)
Lon Morris Coll (TX)
Miami-Dade Comm Coll (FL)
St. Catharine Coll (KY)
San Jacinto Coll North Campus (TX)

MUSIC RELATED
Young Harris Coll (GA)

MUSIC TEACHER EDUCATION
Amarillo Coll (TX)
Angelina Coll (TX)
Casper Coll (WY)
Chattahoochee Valley Comm Coll (AL)
Coastal Bend Coll (TX)
Coffeyville Comm Coll (KS)
Colby Comm Coll (KS)
Coll of Lake County (IL)
Del Mar Coll (TX)
Delta Coll (MI)
Dodge City Comm Coll (KS)
East Central Comm Coll (MS)
Eastern Wyoming Coll (WY)
Essex County Coll (NJ)
Frederick Comm Coll (MD)
Highland Comm Coll (IL)
Hill Coll of the Hill Jr College District (TX)
Holmes Comm Coll (MS)
Howard Coll (TX)
Independence Comm Coll (KS)
Iowa Lakes Comm Coll (IA)
Jefferson Comm Coll (KY)
Jones County Jr Coll (MS)
Lon Morris Coll (TX)
Manatee Comm Coll (FL)
Miami-Dade Comm Coll (FL)
Midland Coll (TX)
Mississippi Delta Comm Coll (MS)
Northeast Comm Coll (NE)
North Idaho Coll (ID)
Northwest Coll (WY)
Northwest Mississippi Comm Coll (MS)
Parkland Coll (IL)
Pensacola Jr Coll (FL)
Roane State Comm Coll (TN)
Sandhills Comm Coll (NC)
Schoolcraft Coll (MI)
Snow Coll (UT)
Southwest Mississippi Comm Coll (MS)
Tulsa Comm Coll (OK)
Umpqua Comm Coll (OR)
Vincennes U (IN)
Walters State Comm Coll (TN)
Waubonsee Comm Coll (IL)
Western Nebraska Comm Coll (NE)
Young Harris Coll (GA)

MUSIC THEORY AND COMPOSITION
Hill Coll of the Hill Jr College District (TX)
Houston Comm Coll System (TX)
Manatee Comm Coll (FL)

MUSIC THERAPY
Pasadena City Coll (CA)

MUSIC (VOICE AND CHORAL/ OPERA PERFORMANCE)
Alvin Comm Coll (TX)
Angelina Coll (TX)
Coastal Bend Coll (TX)
Coffeyville Comm Coll (KS)
Del Mar Coll (TX)
Fresno City Coll (CA)
Hill Coll of the Hill Jr College District (TX)
Iowa Lakes Comm Coll (IA)
Jones County Jr Coll (MS)
Kirkwood Comm Coll (IA)
Lansing Comm Coll (MI)
Lincoln Coll, Lincoln (IL)
Lon Morris Coll (TX)
Navarro Coll (TX)
Reedley Coll (CA)
Snow Coll (UT)

NATIVE AMERICAN STUDIES
Bacone Coll (OK)
Blackfeet Comm Coll (MT)
Central Wyoming Coll (WY)
Diné Coll (AZ)
Fresno City Coll (CA)
Itasca Comm Coll (MN)
Lac Courte Oreilles Ojibwa Comm Coll (WI)
North Idaho Coll (ID)
Pima Comm Coll (AZ)
Salish Kootenai Coll (MT)
Santa Barbara City Coll (CA)
Sitting Bull Coll (ND)

NATURAL RESOURCES CONSERVATION
Berkshire Comm Coll (MA)
Dixie State Coll of Utah (UT)
Ellsworth Comm Coll (IA)
Finger Lakes Comm Coll (NY)
Fulton-Montgomery Comm Coll (NY)
Grays Harbor Coll (WA)
Highland Comm Coll (KS)
Iowa Lakes Comm Coll (IA)
Joliet Jr Coll (IL)
Kirkwood Comm Coll (IA)
Muscatine Comm Coll (IA)
Pensacola Jr Coll (FL)
State U of NY Coll of A&T at Morrisville (NY)
Vermilion Comm Coll (MN)
Vincennes U (IN)

NATURAL RESOURCES MANAGEMENT
American River Coll (CA)
Bacone Coll (OK)
Butte Coll (CA)
Central Carolina Tech Coll (SC)
Cerro Coso Comm Coll (CA)
Coll of the Desert (CA)
Coll of the Siskiyous (CA)
Delta Coll (MI)
Dixie State Coll of Utah (UT)
Finger Lakes Comm Coll (NY)
Greenfield Comm Coll (MA)
Hawkeye Comm Coll (IA)
Itasca Comm Coll (MN)
Lac Courte Oreilles Ojibwa Comm Coll (WI)
Lord Fairfax Comm Coll (VA)
Muskingum Area Tech Coll (OH)
Northwest Coll (WY)
Pikes Peak Comm Coll (CO)
Sacramento City Coll (CA)
Salish Kootenai Coll (MT)
San Joaquin Delta Coll (CA)
Shasta Coll (CA)
Snow Coll (UT)
Spokane Comm Coll (WA)
State U of NY Coll of A&T at Morrisville (NY)
Trinidad State Jr Coll (CO)
Ventura Coll (CA)
Vermilion Comm Coll (MN)
Vincennes U (IN)

NATURAL RESOURCES MANAGEMENT/PROTECTIVE SERVICES RELATED
Reedley Coll (CA)
St. Petersburg Coll (FL)
Santa Fe Comm Coll (NM)

NATURAL RESOURCES PROTECTIVE SERVICES
Finger Lakes Comm Coll (NY)

NATURAL SCIENCES
Amarillo Coll (TX)
Andrew Coll (GA)
Black Hawk Coll, Moline (IL)
Casper Coll (WY)
Centralia Coll (WA)
Chabot Coll (CA)
Citrus Coll (CA)
Clark Coll (WA)
Coll of Marin (CA)
Coll of Southern Idaho (ID)
Coll of the Canyons (CA)
Colorado Mountn Coll (CO)
Cypress Coll (CA)
Feather River Comm Coll District (CA)
Galveston Coll (TX)
Gavilan Coll (CA)
Golden West Coll (CA)
Highline Comm Coll (WA)
Independence Comm Coll (KS)
Iowa Lakes Comm Coll (IA)
Jefferson Comm Coll (NY)
Lake Tahoe Comm Coll (CA)
Merced Coll (CA)
Miami-Dade Comm Coll (FL)
Minot State U–Bottineau Campus (ND)
Moorpark Coll (CA)
Naugatuck Valley Comm Coll (CT)
North Seattle Comm Coll (WA)
Northwest Coll (WY)
Orange Coast Coll (CA)
Sacramento City Coll (CA)
St. Philip's Coll (TX)
Salish Kootenai Coll (MT)
San Jacinto Coll South Campus (TX)
San Joaquin Delta Coll (CA)
Skagit Valley Coll (WA)
Snow Coll (UT)
Umpqua Comm Coll (OR)
U of Pittsburgh at Titusville (PA)
Victor Valley Coll (CA)
Western Wyoming Comm Coll (WY)
Young Harris Coll (GA)

NEUROSCIENCE
Pamlico Comm Coll (NC)

NUCLEAR MEDICAL TECHNOLOGY
Amarillo Coll (TX)
Bronx Comm Coll of City U of NY (NY)
Caldwell Comm Coll and Tech Inst (NC)
Chattanooga State Tech Comm Coll (TN)
Coll of DuPage (IL)
Comm Coll of Allegheny County (PA)
Comm Coll of the Air Force (AL)
Compton Comm Coll (CA)
Delaware Tech & Comm Coll, Stanton/ Wilmington Cmps (DE)
Florida Hospital Coll of Health Sciences (FL)
Forsyth Tech Comm Coll (NC)
Galveston Coll (TX)
GateWay Comm Coll (AZ)
Gateway Comm Coll (CT)
Gloucester County Coll (NJ)
Harrisburg Area Comm Coll (PA)
Hillsborough Comm Coll (FL)
Houston Comm Coll System (TX)
Howard Comm Coll (MD)
Lorain County Comm Coll (OH)
Los Angeles City Coll (CA)
Oakland Comm Coll (MI)
Orange Coast Coll (CA)
Pitt Comm Coll (NC)
Prince George's Comm Coll (MD)
Santa Fe Comm Coll (FL)
Southeast Tech Inst (SD)
Springfield Tech Comm Coll (MA)
Triton Coll (IL)
Union County Coll (NJ)
U of Kentucky, Lexington Comm Coll (KY)
Vincennes U (IN)

NUCLEAR TECHNOLOGY
Allen County Comm Coll (KS)
Chattanooga State Tech Comm Coll (TN)
Florida Comm Coll at Jacksonville (FL)
Georgia Military Coll (GA)
Joliet Jr Coll (IL)
Lake Michigan Coll (MI)
Salem Comm Coll (NJ)
Texas State Tech Coll– Waco/ Marshall Campus (TX)
Three Rivers Comm Coll (CT)
Westmoreland County Comm Coll (PA)

NURSE ASSISTANT/AIDE
Allen County Comm Coll (KS)
Cabarrus Coll of Health Sciences (NC)
Comm Coll of Allegheny County (PA)
Glendale Comm Coll (AZ)
Johnson County Comm Coll (KS)
Lake Region State Coll (ND)
Louisiana Tech Coll–Mansfield Campus (LA)
Mineral Area Coll (MO)
Modesto Jr Coll (CA)
St. Philip's Coll (TX)
Sandhills Comm Coll (NC)
Southwest Wisconsin Tech Coll (WI)
Trinidad State Jr Coll (CO)
Western Iowa Tech Comm Coll (IA)

NURSERY MANAGEMENT
Comm Coll of Allegheny County (PA)
Cuyamaca Coll (CA)
Edmonds Comm Coll (WA)
Foothill Coll (CA)
Modesto Jr Coll (CA)
Northeast Comm Coll (NE)
Pennsylvania Coll of Technology (PA)

NURSING
Abraham Baldwin Ag Coll (GA)
Adirondack Comm Coll (NY)
Alamance Comm Coll (NC)
Albuquerque Tech Vocational Inst (NM)
Allan Hancock Coll (CA)
Allegany Coll of Maryland (MD)
Alpena Comm Coll (MI)
Alvin Comm Coll (TX)
Amarillo Coll (TX)
American River Coll (CA)
Andrew Coll (GA)
Angelina Coll (TX)
Anne Arundel Comm Coll (MD)
Anoka-Ramsey Comm Coll (MN)
Anoka-Ramsey Comm Coll, Cambridge Campus (MN)
Antelope Valley Coll (CA)
Arapahoe Comm Coll (CO)
Arizona Western Coll (AZ)
Arkansas State U–Beebe (AR)
Asheville-Buncombe Tech Comm Coll (NC)
Ashland Comm Coll (KY)
Athens Tech Coll (GA)
Atlantic Cape Comm Coll (NJ)
Austin Comm Coll (TX)
Bacone Coll (OK)
Bainbridge Coll (GA)
Bakersfield Coll (CA)
Baltimore City Comm Coll (MD)
Barton County Comm Coll (KS)
Bay de Noc Comm Coll (MI)
Beaufort County Comm Coll (NC)
Bellevue Comm Coll (WA)
Belmont Tech Coll (OH)
Bergen Comm Coll (NJ)
Berkshire Comm Coll (MA)
Bevill State Comm Coll (AL)
Big Bend Comm Coll (WA)
Black Hawk Coll, Moline (IL)
Blackhawk Tech Coll (WI)
Black River Tech Coll (AR)
Blinn Coll (TX)
Blue Ridge Comm Coll (NC)
Blue Ridge Comm Coll (VA)
Borough of Manhattan Comm Coll of City U of NY (NY)
Bowling Green State U-Firelands Coll (OH)
Brazosport Coll (TX)
Brevard Comm Coll (FL)
Bristol Comm Coll (MA)
Bronx Comm Coll of City U of NY (NY)
Brookdale Comm Coll (NJ)
Broome Comm Coll (NY)
Bucks County Comm Coll (PA)
Bunker Hill Comm Coll (MA)
Burlington County Coll (NJ)

Butler County Comm Coll (PA)
Butte Coll (CA)
Cabarrus Coll of Health Sciences (NC)
Caldwell Comm Coll and Tech Inst (NC)
Calhoun Comm Coll (AL)
Camden County Coll (NJ)
Cape Cod Comm Coll (MA)
Cape Fear Comm Coll (NC)
Capital Comm Coll (CT)
Carl Sandburg Coll (IL)
Carolinas Coll of Health Sciences (NC)
Carroll Comm Coll (MD)
Casper Coll (WY)
Catawba Valley Comm Coll (NC)
Cayuga County Comm Coll (NY)
Cecil Comm Coll (MD)
Central Alabama Comm Coll (AL)
Central Arizona Coll (AZ)
Central Carolina Comm Coll (NC)
Central Carolina Tech Coll (SC)
Central Comm Coll–Grand Island Campus (NE)
Central Florida Comm Coll (FL)
Centralia Coll (WA)
Central Lakes Coll (MN)
Central Maine Medical Center School of Nursing (ME)
Central Maine Tech Coll (ME)
Central Ohio Tech Coll (OH)
Central Oregon Comm Coll (OR)
Central Piedmont Comm Coll (NC)
Central Texas Coll (TX)
Central Wyoming Coll (WY)
Century Comm and Tech Coll (MN)
Cerritos Coll (CA)
Chabot Coll (CA)
Chaffey Coll (CA)
Chattahoochee Valley Comm Coll (AL)
Chattanooga State Tech Comm Coll (TN)
Chemeketa Comm Coll (OR)
Chipola Jr Coll (FL)
Chippewa Valley Tech Coll (WI)
Cincinnati State Tech and Comm Coll (OH)
Cisco Jr Coll (TX)
City Coll of San Francisco (CA)
City Colls of Chicago, Harry S Truman Coll (IL)
City Colls of Chicago, Malcolm X Coll (IL)
City Colls of Chicago, Richard J Daley Coll (IL)
Clackamas Comm Coll (OR)
Clark Coll (WA)
Cleveland State Comm Coll (TN)
Clinton Comm Coll (IA)
Clinton Comm Coll (NY)
Clovis Comm Coll (NM)
Coastal Bend Coll (TX)
Coastal Carolina Comm Coll (NC)
Coastal Georgia Comm Coll (GA)
Cochise Coll, Douglas (AZ)
Cochran School of Nursing (NY)
Coffeyville Comm Coll (KS)
Colby Comm Coll (KS)
Coll of DuPage (IL)
Coll of Eastern Utah (UT)
Coll of Lake County (IL)
Coll of Marin (CA)
Coll of St. Catherine–Minneapolis (MN)
Coll of Southern Idaho (ID)
Coll of Southern Maryland (MD)
Coll of the Canyons (CA)
Coll of the Desert (CA)
Coll of the Redwoods (CA)
Coll of the Sequoias (CA)
Collin County Comm Coll District (TX)
Colorado Mountn Coll (CO)
Columbia-Greene Comm Coll (NY)
Columbia State Comm Coll (TN)
Columbus State Comm Coll (OH)
Comm Coll of Allegheny County (PA)
The Comm Coll of Baltimore County–Catonsville Campus (MD)
Comm Coll of Beaver County (PA)
Comm Coll of Denver (CO)
Comm Coll of Rhode Island (RI)
Comm Coll of Southern Nevada (NV)
Compton Comm Coll (CA)
Connors State Coll (OK)
Corning Comm Coll (NY)
County Coll of Morris (NJ)
Craven Comm Coll (NC)
Crowder Coll (MO)
Cuesta Coll (CA)
Cumberland County Coll (NJ)
Cuyahoga Comm Coll (OH)
Cypress Coll (CA)
Danville Area Comm Coll (IL)
Darton Coll (GA)
Daytona Beach Comm Coll (FL)
De Anza Coll (CA)
Delaware County Comm Coll (PA)
Delaware Tech & Comm Coll, Jack F Owens Cmps (DE)
Delaware Tech & Comm Coll, Stanton/ Wilmington Cmps (DE)
Delaware Tech & Comm Coll, Terry Cmps (DE)
Delgado Comm Coll (LA)
Del Mar Coll (TX)
Delta Coll (MI)
Des Moines Area Comm Coll (IA)
Dixie State Coll of Utah (UT)
Dodge City Comm Coll (KS)
Doña Ana Branch Comm Coll (NM)
Donnelly Coll (KS)
Durham Tech Comm Coll (NC)
Dutchess Comm Coll (NY)
Dyersburg State Comm Coll (TN)
East Central Coll (MO)
East Central Comm Coll (MS)
Eastern Arizona Coll (AZ)
Eastern Maine Tech Coll (ME)
Eastern Oklahoma State Coll (OK)
Eastern Shore Comm Coll (VA)
East Georgia Coll (GA)
Edgecombe Comm Coll (NC)
Edison Comm Coll (FL)
Edison State Comm Coll (OH)
El Centro Coll (TX)
Elizabethtown Comm Coll (KY)
Ellis Hospital School of Nursing (NY)
Ellsworth Comm Coll (IA)
Erie Comm Coll, City Campus (NY)
Erie Comm Coll, North Campus (NY)
Essex County Coll (NJ)
Eugenio María de Hostos Comm Coll of City U of NY (NY)
Everett Comm Coll (WA)
Evergreen Valley Coll (CA)
Fayetteville Tech Comm Coll (NC)
Fergus Falls Comm Coll (MN)
Finger Lakes Comm Coll (NY)
Fiorello H LaGuardia Comm Coll of City U of NY (NY)
Florence-Darlington Tech Coll (SC)
Florida Comm Coll at Jacksonville (FL)
Florida Hospital Coll of Health Sciences (FL)
Floyd Coll (GA)
Forsyth Tech Comm Coll (NC)
Fort Scott Comm Coll (KS)
Frederick Comm Coll (MD)
Fresno City Coll (CA)
Front Range Comm Coll (CO)
Fulton-Montgomery Comm Coll (NY)
Gadsden State Comm Coll (AL)
Galveston Coll (TX)
Garden City Comm Coll (KS)
Gaston Coll (NC)
GateWay Comm Coll (AZ)
Gateway Tech Coll (WI)
Gavilan Coll (CA)
Genesee Comm Coll (NY)
George Corley Wallace State Comm Coll (AL)
Georgia Perimeter Coll (GA)
Germanna Comm Coll (VA)
Glendale Comm Coll (AZ)
Glendale Comm Coll (CA)
Glen Oaks Comm Coll (MI)
Gloucester County Coll (NJ)
Gogebic Comm Coll (MI)
Golden West Coll (CA)
Gordon Coll (GA)
Grand Rapids Comm Coll (MI)
Grays Harbor Coll (WA)
Grayson County Coll (TX)
Great Basin Coll (NV)
Greenfield Comm Coll (MA)
Greenville Tech Coll (SC)
Guilford Tech Comm Coll (NC)
Gulf Coast Comm Coll (FL)
Hagerstown Comm Coll (MD)
Halifax Comm Coll (NC)
Harford Comm Coll (MD)
Harrisburg Area Comm Coll (PA)
Hawaii Comm Coll (HI)
Hawkeye Comm Coll (IA)
Haywood Comm Coll (NC)
Hazard Comm Coll (KY)
Heartland Comm Coll (IL)
Helene Fuld Coll of Nursing of North General Hosp (NY)
Henderson Comm Coll (KY)
Henry Ford Comm Coll (MI)
Hesston Coll (KS)
Hibbing Comm Coll (MN)
Highland Comm Coll (IL)
Highland Comm Coll (KS)
Highline Comm Coll (WA)
Hillsborough Comm Coll (FL)
Hinds Comm Coll (MS)
Holmes Comm Coll (MS)
Holyoke Comm Coll (MA)
Hopkinsville Comm Coll (KY)
Horry-Georgetown Tech Coll (SC)
Housatonic Comm Coll (CT)
Houston Comm Coll System (TX)
Howard Coll (TX)
Howard Comm Coll (MD)
Hudson County Comm Coll (NJ)
Hutchinson Comm Coll and Area Vocational School (KS)
Illinois Eastern Comm Colls, Frontier Comm Coll (IL)
Illinois Eastern Comm Colls, Olney Central Coll (IL)
Imperial Valley Coll (CA)
Indian Hills Comm Coll (IA)
Indian River Comm Coll (FL)
Inver Hills Comm Coll (MN)
Iowa Lakes Comm Coll (IA)
Iowa Western Comm Coll (IA)
Ivy Tech State Coll–Bloomington (IN)
Ivy Tech State Coll–Central Indiana (IN)
Ivy Tech State Coll–Eastcentral (IN)
Ivy Tech State Coll–Lafayette (IN)
Ivy Tech State Coll–North Central (IN)
Ivy Tech State Coll–Northwest (IN)
Ivy Tech State Coll–Southcentral (IN)
Ivy Tech State Coll–Southeast (IN)
Ivy Tech State Coll–Southwest (IN)
Ivy Tech State Coll–Whitewater (IN)
Jackson Comm Coll (MI)
Jackson State Comm Coll (TN)
James Sprunt Comm Coll (NC)
Jamestown Comm Coll (NY)
Jefferson Coll (MO)
Jefferson Comm Coll (KY)
Jefferson Comm Coll (NY)
Jefferson Davis Comm Coll (AL)
Jefferson State Comm Coll (AL)
John A. Logan Coll (IL)
Johnson County Comm Coll (KS)
Johnston Comm Coll (NC)
John Tyler Comm Coll (VA)
John Wood Comm Coll (IL)
Joliet Jr Coll (IL)
Jones County Jr Coll (MS)
J. Sargeant Reynolds Comm Coll (VA)
Kalamazoo Valley Comm Coll (MI)
Kankakee Comm Coll (IL)
Kansas City Kansas Comm Coll (KS)
Kaskaskia Coll (IL)
Kauai Comm Coll (HI)
Kellogg Comm Coll (MI)
Kennebec Valley Tech Coll (ME)
Kent State U, East Liverpool Campus (OH)
Kent State U, Tuscarawas Campus (OH)
Kilgore Coll (TX)
Kingsborough Comm Coll of City U of NY (NY)
Kirkwood Comm Coll (IA)
Kishwaukee Coll (IL)
Labette Comm Coll (KS)
Labouré Coll (MA)
Lac Courte Oreilles Ojibwa Comm Coll (WI)
Lake City Comm Coll (FL)
Lake Land Coll (IL)
Lakeland Comm Coll (OH)
Lake Michigan Coll (MI)
Lakeshore Tech Coll (WI)
Lake-Sumter Comm Coll (FL)
Lamar Comm Coll (CO)
Lamar State Coll–Orange (TX)
Lamar State Coll–Port Arthur (TX)
Lane Comm Coll (OR)
Lansing Comm Coll (MI)
Laramie County Comm Coll (WY)
Laredo Comm Coll (TX)
Lehigh Carbon Comm Coll (PA)
Lenoir Comm Coll (NC)
Lewis and Clark Comm Coll (IL)
Lima Tech Coll (OH)
Lincoln Coll, Lincoln (IL)
Lincoln Coll, Normal (IL)
Lincoln Land Comm Coll (IL)
Linn-Benton Comm Coll (OR)
Long Beach City Coll (CA)
Lorain County Comm Coll (OH)
Lord Fairfax Comm Coll (VA)
Los Angeles Harbor Coll (CA)
Los Angeles Pierce Coll (CA)
Louisburg Coll (NC)
Louisiana State U at Alexandria (LA)
Louisiana State U at Eunice (LA)
Lower Columbia Coll (WA)
Luzerne County Comm Coll (PA)
Macomb Comm Coll (MI)
Madisonville Comm Coll (KY)
Manatee Comm Coll (FL)
Maric Coll (CA)
Marion Tech Coll (OH)
Marshalltown Comm Coll (IA)
Massachusetts Bay Comm Coll (MA)
Massasoit Comm Coll (MA)
Mayland Comm Coll (NC)
Maysville Comm Coll (KY)
McLennan Comm Coll (TX)
Merced Coll (CA)
Mercer County Comm Coll (NJ)
Meridian Comm Coll (MS)
Metropolitan Comm Coll (NE)
Miami-Dade Comm Coll (FL)
Miami U–Hamilton Campus (OH)
Miami U–Middletown Campus (OH)
Middle Georgia Coll (GA)
Middlesex Comm Coll (MA)
Middlesex County Coll (NJ)
Midland Coll (TX)
Midlands Tech Coll (SC)
Mid Michigan Comm Coll (MI)
Mid-Plains Comm Coll Area (NE)
Mid-State Tech Coll (WI)
Miles Comm Coll (MT)
Milwaukee Area Tech Coll (WI)
Mineral Area Coll (MO)
Minneapolis Comm and Tech Coll (MN)
Minnesota State Coll–Southeast Tech (MN)
Mississippi County Comm Coll (AR)
Mississippi Delta Comm Coll (MS)
Mississippi Gulf Coast Comm Coll (MS)
Mitchell Comm Coll (NC)
Moberly Area Comm Coll (MO)
Modesto Jr Coll (CA)
Mohave Comm Coll (AZ)
Mohawk Valley Comm Coll (NY)
Monroe Comm Coll (NY)
Monroe County Comm Coll (MI)
Montcalm Comm Coll (MI)
Monterey Peninsula Coll (CA)
Montgomery Coll (MD)
Montgomery County Comm Coll (PA)
Moorpark Coll (CA)
Moraine Park Tech Coll (WI)
Moraine Valley Comm Coll (IL)
Morton Coll (IL)
Motlow State Comm Coll (TN)
Mott Comm Coll (MI)
Mountain Empire Comm Coll (VA)
Mt. Hood Comm Coll (OR)
Mt. San Jacinto Coll (CA)
Mount Wachusett Comm Coll (MA)
Nash Comm Coll (NC)
Nassau Comm Coll (NY)
Naugatuck Valley Comm Coll (CT)
Navarro Coll (TX)
Neosho County Comm Coll (KS)
New Hampshire Comm Tech Coll, Berlin/Laconia (NH)
New Hampshire Tech Inst (NH)
New Mexico State U–Alamogordo (NM)
New Mexico State U–Carlsbad (NM)
New York City Tech Coll of the City U of NY (NY)
Niagara County Comm Coll (NY)
Northampton County Area Comm Coll (PA)
North Arkansas Coll (AR)
North Central Michigan Coll (MI)
Northcentral Tech Coll (WI)
North Central Texas Coll (TX)
North Country Comm Coll (NY)
Northeast Alabama Comm Coll (AL)
Northeast Comm Coll (NE)
Northeast Iowa Comm Coll (IA)
Northeast Texas Comm Coll (TX)
Northern Essex Comm Coll (MA)
Northern Maine Tech Coll (ME)
Northern Oklahoma Coll (OK)
Northern Virginia Comm Coll (VA)
North Harris Coll (TX)
North Hennepin Comm Coll (MN)
North Idaho Coll (ID)
North Iowa Area Comm Coll (IA)
Northland Comm and Tech Coll (MN)
Northland Pioneer Coll (AZ)
North Seattle Comm Coll (WA)
North Shore Comm Coll (MA)
NorthWest Arkansas Comm Coll (AR)
Northwest Coll (WY)
Northwestern Michigan Coll (MI)
Northwest Mississippi Comm Coll (MS)
Northwest-Shoals Comm Coll (AL)
Northwest State Comm Coll (OH)
Norwalk Comm Coll (CT)
Oakland Comm Coll (MI)
Oakton Comm Coll (IL)
Ocean County Coll (NJ)
Odessa Coll (TX)
Okaloosa-Walton Comm Coll (FL)
Oklahoma City Comm Coll (OK)
Oklahoma State U, Oklahoma City (OK)
Olympic Coll (WA)
Onondaga Comm Coll (NY)
Orangeburg-Calhoun Tech Coll (SC)
Orange County Comm Coll (NY)
Otero Jr Coll (CO)
Our Lady of the Lake Coll (LA)
Owensboro Comm Coll (KY)
Paducah Comm Coll (KY)
Palau Comm CollPalau)
Palm Beach Comm Coll (FL)
Palomar Coll (CA)
Parkland Coll (IL)
Pasadena City Coll (CA)
Pasco-Hernando Comm Coll (FL)
Patrick Henry Comm Coll (VA)
Peninsula Coll (WA)
Pennsylvania Coll of Technology (PA)
Penn State U Fayette Campus of the Commonwealth Coll (PA)
Penn State U Mont Alto Campus of the Commonwealth Coll (PA)
Penn State U Worthington Scranton Cmps Commonwealth Coll (PA)
Penn Valley Comm Coll (MO)
Pensacola Jr Coll (FL)
Phillips Beth Israel School of Nursing (NY)
Phoenix Coll (AZ)
Piedmont Comm Coll (NC)
Piedmont Tech Coll (SC)
Piedmont Virginia Comm Coll (VA)
Pikes Peak Comm Coll (CO)
Pima Comm Coll (AZ)
Pitt Comm Coll (NC)
Polk Comm Coll (FL)
Portland Comm Coll (OR)
Prairie State Coll (IL)
Pratt Comm Coll and Area Vocational School (KS)
Prince George's Comm Coll (MD)
Queensborough Comm Coll of City U of NY (NY)
Quincy Coll (MA)
Quinsigamond Comm Coll (MA)
Randolph Comm Coll (NC)
Rappahannock Comm Coll (VA)
Raritan Valley Comm Coll (NJ)
Reading Area Comm Coll (PA)
Rend Lake Coll (IL)

Richland Comm Coll (IL)
Richmond Comm Coll (NC)
Ridgewater Coll (MN)
Riverland Comm Coll (MN)
Riverside Comm Coll (CA)
Roane State Comm Coll (TN)
Roanoke-Chowan Comm Coll (NC)
Robeson Comm Coll (NC)
Rockingham Comm Coll (NC)
Rockland Comm Coll (NY)
Rogue Comm Coll (OR)
Rowan-Cabarrus Comm Coll (NC)
Sacramento City Coll (CA)
St. Catharine Coll (KY)
Saint Charles Comm Coll (MO)
St. Clair County Comm Coll (MI)
Saint Joseph's Hospital Health Center School of Nursing (NY)
St. Louis Comm Coll at Florissant Valley (MO)
St. Luke's Coll of Nursing and Health Sciences (IA)
St. Petersburg Coll (FL)
Salem Comm Coll (NJ)
Salish Kootenai Coll (MT)
Sampson Comm Coll (NC)
San Antonio Coll (TX)
San Bernardino Valley Coll (CA)
Sandhills Comm Coll (NC)
San Diego City Coll (CA)
San Jacinto Coll Central Campus (TX)
San Jacinto Coll South Campus (TX)
San Joaquin Delta Coll (CA)
San Juan Coll (NM)
Santa Ana Coll (CA)
Santa Barbara City Coll (CA)
Santa Fe Comm Coll (FL)
Santa Fe Comm Coll (NM)
Santa Monica Coll (CA)
Sauk Valley Comm Coll (IL)
Schoolcraft Coll (MI)
Scott Comm Coll (IA)
Scottsdale Comm Coll (AZ)
Seattle Central Comm Coll (WA)
Seminole Comm Coll (FL)
Seminole State Coll (OK)
Shasta Coll (CA)
Sheridan Coll (WY)
Shoreline Comm Coll (WA)
Sierra Coll (CA)
Sinclair Comm Coll (OH)
Skagit Valley Coll (WA)
Somerset Comm Coll (KY)
Southeast Comm Coll (KY)
Southeastern Comm Coll (NC)
Southeastern Comm Coll, South Campus (IA)
Southern Maine Tech Coll (ME)
Southern State Comm Coll (OH)
Southern West Virginia Comm and Tech Coll (WV)
South Plains Coll (TX)
South Puget Sound Comm Coll (WA)
Southside Virginia Comm Coll (VA)
South Suburban Coll (IL)
South Texas Comm Coll (TX)
Southwestern Coll (CA)
Southwestern Comm Coll (IA)
Southwestern Comm Coll (NC)
Southwestern Michigan Coll (MI)
Southwestern Oklahoma State U at Sayre (OK)
Southwest Mississippi Comm Coll (MS)
Southwest Tennessee Comm Coll (TN)
Southwest Virginia Comm Coll (VA)
Southwest Wisconsin Tech Coll (WI)
Spokane Comm Coll (WA)
Springfield Tech Comm Coll (MA)
Stanly Comm Coll (NC)
Stark State Coll of Technology (OH)
State Fair Comm Coll (MO)
State U of NY Coll of A&T at Morrisville (NY)
State U of NY Coll of Technology at Alfred (NY)
State U of NY Coll of Technology at Canton (NY)
State U of NY Coll of Technology at Delhi (NY)
Suffolk County Comm Coll (NY)
Sullivan County Comm Coll (NY)
Surry Comm Coll (NC)
Tacoma Comm Coll (WA)
Tallahassee Comm Coll (FL)
Tarrant County Coll District (TX)
Temple Coll (TX)
Texarkana Coll (TX)
Thomas Nelson Comm Coll (VA)
Three Rivers Comm Coll (CT)
Tidewater Comm Coll (VA)
Tomball Coll (TX)
Tompkins Cortland Comm Coll (NY)
Tri-County Comm Coll (NC)
Tri-County Tech Coll (SC)
Trident Tech Coll (SC)
Trinidad State Jr Coll (CO)
Trinity Valley Comm Coll (TX)
Triton Coll (IL)
Trocaire Coll (NY)
Truckee Meadows Comm Coll (NV)
Tulsa Comm Coll (OK)
Tyler Jr Coll (TX)
Ulster County Comm Coll (NY)
Umpqua Comm Coll (OR)
Union County Coll (NJ)
United Tribes Tech Coll (ND)
U of Arkansas at Fort Smith (AR)
U of Arkansas Comm Coll at Batesville (AR)
U of Kentucky, Lexington Comm Coll (KY)
U of New Mexico–Gallup (NM)
U of South Carolina at Lancaster (SC)
Vance-Granville Comm Coll (NC)
Ventura Coll (CA)
Vermont Tech Coll (VT)
Vernon Coll (TX)
Victoria Coll (TX)
Victor Valley Coll (CA)
Vincennes U (IN)
Virginia Western Comm Coll (VA)
Wake Tech Comm Coll (NC)
Wallace State Comm Coll (AL)
Walla Walla Comm Coll (WA)
Walters State Comm Coll (TN)
Waubonsee Comm Coll (IL)
Waycross Coll (GA)
Wayne Comm Coll (NC)
Weatherford Coll (TX)
Westchester Comm Coll (NY)
Western Iowa Tech Comm Coll (IA)
Western Nebraska Comm Coll (NE)
Western Nevada Comm Coll (NV)
Western Piedmont Comm Coll (NC)
Western Wisconsin Tech Coll (WI)
Western Wyoming Comm Coll (WY)
Westmoreland County Comm Coll (PA)
West Shore Comm Coll (MI)
West Virginia Northern Comm Coll (WV)
West Virginia U at Parkersburg (WV)
Wharton County Jr Coll (TX)
Whatcom Comm Coll (WA)
Wilkes Comm Coll (NC)
Wilson Tech Comm Coll (NC)
Wor-Wic Comm Coll (MD)
York Tech Coll (SC)
Young Harris Coll (GA)

NURSING RELATED
Lamar State Coll–Port Arthur (TX)
Southeast Tech Inst (SD)

NURSING (SURGICAL)
Comm Coll of Allegheny County (PA)

NUTRITION SCIENCE
American Academy of Nutrition, Coll of Nutrition (TN)
Bakersfield Coll (CA)
Camden County Coll (NJ)
Colby Comm Coll (KS)
Compton Comm Coll (CA)
Cuesta Coll (CA)
Daytona Beach Comm Coll (FL)
Dutchess Comm Coll (NY)
Holyoke Comm Coll (MA)
Lincoln Coll, Lincoln (IL)
Mohawk Valley Comm Coll (NY)
North Shore Comm Coll (MA)
Northwest Mississippi Comm Coll (MS)
Okaloosa-Walton Comm Coll (FL)
Orange Coast Coll (CA)
Palm Beach Comm Coll (FL)
San Diego Mesa Coll (CA)
San Jacinto Coll Central Campus (TX)
Santa Ana Coll (CA)
Sinclair Comm Coll (OH)
Snow Coll (UT)
State U of NY Coll of A&T at Morrisville (NY)

NUTRITION STUDIES
Antelope Valley Coll (CA)
Harrisburg Area Comm Coll (PA)

OCCUPATIONAL HEALTH/ INDUSTRIAL HYGIENE
Niagara County Comm Coll (NY)
Northampton County Area Comm Coll (PA)

OCCUPATIONAL SAFETY/ HEALTH TECHNOLOGY
Broome Comm Coll (NY)
Camden County Coll (NJ)
Central Maine Tech Coll (ME)
Clinton Comm Coll (IA)
The Comm Coll of Baltimore County–Catonsville Campus (MD)
Comm Coll of the Air Force (AL)
Cuyamaca Coll (CA)
Delaware Tech & Comm Coll, Stanton/ Wilmington Cmps (DE)
Delgado Comm Coll (LA)
Durham Tech Comm Coll (NC)
GateWay Comm Coll (AZ)
Honolulu Comm Coll (HI)
Houston Comm Coll System (TX)
Ivy Tech State Coll–Central Indiana (IN)
Ivy Tech State Coll–Northeast (IN)
Ivy Tech State Coll–Northwest (IN)
Ivy Tech State Coll–Wabash Valley (IN)
Kilgore Coll (TX)
Las Positas Coll (CA)
Mineral Area Coll (MO)
Muscatine Comm Coll (IA)
NorthWest Arkansas Comm Coll (AR)
Paradise Valley Comm Coll (AZ)
Pikes Peak Comm Coll (CO)
Salem Comm Coll (NJ)
San Diego City Coll (CA)
San Jacinto Coll Central Campus (TX)
Scott Comm Coll (IA)
Southwest Tennessee Comm Coll (TN)
Texas State Tech Coll– Waco/ Marshall Campus (TX)
Trinidad State Jr Coll (CO)
Tulsa Comm Coll (OK)
The U of Akron–Wayne Coll (OH)
Wallace State Comm Coll (AL)

OCCUPATIONAL THERAPY
Allegany Coll of Maryland (MD)
Amarillo Coll (TX)
Andrew Coll (GA)
Austin Comm Coll (TX)
Bay State Coll (MA)
Bristol Comm Coll (MA)
Caldwell Comm Coll and Tech Inst (NC)
Casper Coll (WY)
Chattanooga State Tech Comm Coll (TN)
City Colls of Chicago, Wilbur Wright Coll (IL)
Coastal Georgia Comm Coll (GA)
Coffeyville Comm Coll (KS)
Coll of DuPage (IL)
Coll of Southern Idaho (ID)
The Comm Coll of Baltimore County–Catonsville Campus (MD)
Comm Coll of Southern Nevada (NV)
Danville Area Comm Coll (IL)
Daytona Beach Comm Coll (FL)
Durham Tech Comm Coll (NC)
East Central Comm Coll (MS)
Everett Comm Coll (WA)
Fiorello H LaGuardia Comm Coll of City U of NY (NY)
Florence-Darlington Tech Coll (SC)
Floyd Coll (GA)
Genesee Comm Coll (NY)
George Corley Wallace State Comm Coll (AL)
Herkimer County Comm Coll (NY)
Highland Comm Coll (KS)
Hillsborough Comm Coll (FL)
John A. Logan Coll (IL)
Kent State U, East Liverpool Campus (OH)
Keystone Coll (PA)
Kingwood Coll (TX)
Kirkwood Comm Coll (IA)
Louisburg Coll (NC)
Manatee Comm Coll (FL)
Manor Coll (PA)
Milwaukee Area Tech Coll (WI)
Monterey Peninsula Coll (CA)
Morgan Comm Coll (CO)
Mt. Hood Comm Coll (OR)
Muskingum Area Tech Coll (OH)
Nashville State Tech Inst (TN)
Navarro Coll (TX)
North Central Texas Coll (TX)
North Shore Comm Coll (MA)
Oklahoma City Comm Coll (OK)
Orange County Comm Coll (NY)
Palm Beach Comm Coll (FL)
Pasadena City Coll (CA)
Penn State U Mont Alto Campus of the Commonwealth Coll (PA)
Penn State U Shenango Campus of the Commonwealth Coll (PA)
Penn State U Worthington Scranton Cmps Commonwealth Coll (PA)
Penn Valley Comm Coll (MO)
Quinsigamond Comm Coll (MA)
Roane State Comm Coll (TN)
Rockland Comm Coll (NY)
Sacramento City Coll (CA)
Saint Charles Comm Coll (MO)
Santa Ana Coll (CA)
Sinclair Comm Coll (OH)
South Texas Comm Coll (TX)
Southwestern Comm Coll (NC)
Stark State Coll of Technology (OH)
Tacoma Comm Coll (WA)
Tomball Coll (TX)
Trident Tech Coll (SC)
Tulsa Comm Coll (OK)
Vincennes U (IN)
Wallace State Comm Coll (AL)
Western Wisconsin Tech Coll (WI)
Wisconsin Indianhead Tech Coll (WI)

OCCUPATIONAL THERAPY ASSISTANT
Adirondack Comm Coll (NY)
American Inst of Health Technology, Inc. (ID)
Anoka-Hennepin Tech Coll (MN)
Atlantic Cape Comm Coll (NJ)
Briarwood Coll (CT)
Cabarrus Coll of Health Sciences (NC)
Cape Fear Comm Coll (NC)
Cincinnati State Tech and Comm Coll (OH)
Cleveland State Comm Coll (TN)
Coll of DuPage (IL)
Coll of St. Catherine–Minneapolis (MN)
Comm Coll of Allegheny County (PA)
Comm Coll of Rhode Island (RI)
Darton Coll (GA)
Delaware Tech & Comm Coll, Stanton/ Wilmington Cmps (DE)
Delgado Comm Coll (LA)
Erie Comm Coll, North Campus (NY)
Florida Hospital Coll of Health Sciences (FL)
Green River Comm Coll (WA)
Guilford Tech Comm Coll (NC)
Harcum Coll (PA)
Houston Comm Coll System (TX)
Ivy Tech State Coll–Central Indiana (IN)
Jamestown Comm Coll (NY)
Jefferson State Comm Coll (AL)
Johnson County Comm Coll (KS)
J. Sargeant Reynolds Comm Coll (VA)
Kansas City Kansas Comm Coll (KS)
Kennebec Valley Tech Coll (ME)
Lake Area Tech Inst (SD)
Lake Michigan Coll (MI)
Lehigh Carbon Comm Coll (PA)
Lewis and Clark Comm Coll (IL)
Lincoln Land Comm Coll (IL)
Madisonville Comm Coll (KY)
Manatee Comm Coll (FL)
Manchester Comm Coll (CT)
Massachusetts Bay Comm Coll (MA)
Middle Georgia Coll (GA)
Mott Comm Coll (MI)
New England Inst of Technology (RI)
North Dakota State Coll of Science (ND)
Parkland Coll (IL)
Pennsylvania Coll of Technology (PA)
Penn State U DuBois Campus of the Commonwealth Coll (PA)
Pitt Comm Coll (NC)
Polk Comm Coll (FL)
Quinsigamond Comm Coll (MA)
Rend Lake Coll (IL)
Riverland Comm Coll (MN)
Rockingham Comm Coll (NC)
St. Philip's Coll (TX)
San Jacinto Coll South Campus (TX)
Schoolcraft Coll (MI)
Scott Comm Coll (IA)
South Suburban Coll (IL)
Southwestern Oklahoma State U at Sayre (OK)
Southwest Georgia Tech Coll (GA)
Southwest Tennessee Comm Coll (TN)
Springfield Tech Comm Coll (MA)
Stanly Comm Coll (NC)
State U of NY Coll of Technology at Canton (NY)
Tulsa Comm Coll (OK)
Union County Coll (NJ)
Western Inst of Science & Health (CA)
Western Iowa Tech Comm Coll (IA)

OCEANOGRAPHY
Arizona Western Coll (AZ)
Everett Comm Coll (WA)
Fullerton Coll (CA)
Miami-Dade Comm Coll (FL)
Riverside Comm Coll (CA)
Shoreline Comm Coll (WA)
Southern Maine Tech Coll (ME)
Tacoma Comm Coll (WA)
Tulsa Comm Coll (OK)

OFFICE MANAGEMENT
Alexandria Tech Coll (MN)
Alpena Comm Coll (MI)
Berkeley Coll (NY)
Berkeley Coll-Westchester Campus (NY)
Big Bend Comm Coll (WA)
Central Texas Coll (TX)
Cincinnati State Tech and Comm Coll (OH)
Clackamas Comm Coll (OR)
Clark Coll (WA)
Clover Park Tech Coll (WA)
Comm Coll of Allegheny County (PA)
Comm Coll of the Air Force (AL)
Consolidated School of Business, Lancaster (PA)
Consolidated School of Business, York (PA)
Cuyamaca Coll (CA)
Delaware County Comm Coll (PA)
Delta Coll (MI)
Edmonds Comm Coll (WA)
Erie Comm Coll, City Campus (NY)
Erie Comm Coll, North Campus (NY)
Erie Comm Coll, South Campus (NY)
Fisher Coll (MA)
Florida Comm Coll at Jacksonville (FL)
Gogebic Comm Coll (MI)
Grays Harbor Coll (WA)
Great Basin Coll (NV)
Green River Comm Coll (WA)

Harry M. Ayers State Tech Coll (AL)
Howard Comm Coll (MD)
Lake Land Coll (IL)
Lake Region State Coll (ND)
Lord Fairfax Comm Coll (VA)
McIntosh Coll (NH)
Miami U–Middletown Campus (OH)
Middlesex Comm Coll (MA)
Mid-South Comm Coll (AR)
Mid-State Coll (ME)
Minnesota School of Business (MN)
Modesto Jr Coll (CA)
Mott Comm Coll (MI)
National Coll of Business & Technology, Salem (VA)
New England Inst of Tech & Florida Culinary Inst (FL)
Northwest Mississippi Comm Coll (MS)
Oakland Comm Coll (MI)
Olympic Coll (WA)
Peninsula Coll (WA)
Piedmont Tech Coll (SC)
Saint Charles Comm Coll (MO)
St. Cloud Tech Coll (MN)
Skagit Valley Coll (WA)
South Coll (NC)
Southern Arkansas U Tech (AR)
State U of NY Coll of Technology at Canton (NY)
The U of Akron–Wayne Coll (OH)
Vista Comm Coll (CA)
Walla Walla Comm Coll (WA)
Western Wisconsin Tech Coll (WI)

OPERATING ROOM TECHNICIAN
Austin Comm Coll (TX)
Baltimore City Comm Coll (MD)
Berkshire Comm Coll (MA)
Bismarck State Coll (ND)
Blue Ridge Comm Coll (NC)
Brevard Comm Coll (FL)
The Bryman School (AZ)
Bunker Hill Comm Coll (MA)
Cabarrus Coll of Health Sciences (NC)
Central Wyoming Coll (WY)
Cincinnati State Tech and Comm Coll (OH)
City Colls of Chicago, Malcolm X Coll (IL)
Coastal Carolina Comm Coll (NC)
Coll of DuPage (IL)
Coll of Southern Idaho (ID)
Columbus State Comm Coll (OH)
Comm Coll of Allegheny County (PA)
Comm Coll of the Air Force (AL)
Cuyahoga Comm Coll (OH)
Darton Coll (GA)
Delaware County Comm Coll (PA)
Delta Coll (MI)
Durham Tech Comm Coll (NC)
Edgecombe Comm Coll (NC)
El Centro Coll (TX)
Fayetteville Tech Comm Coll (NC)
GateWay Comm Coll (AZ)
Gateway Tech Coll (WI)
Guilford Tech Comm Coll (NC)
Hinds Comm Coll (MS)
Ivy Tech State Coll–Central Indiana (IN)
Ivy Tech State Coll–Eastcentral (IN)
Ivy Tech State Coll–Lafayette (IN)
Ivy Tech State Coll–Northwest (IN)
Ivy Tech State Coll–Southwest (IN)
Ivy Tech State Coll–Wabash Valley (IN)
Lamar State Coll–Port Arthur (TX)
Lansing Comm Coll (MI)
Lorain County Comm Coll (OH)
Luzerne County Comm Coll (PA)
Manchester Comm Coll (CT)
Marshalltown Comm Coll (IA)
Metropolitan Comm Coll (NE)
Mt. Hood Comm Coll (OR)
Nassau Comm Coll (NY)
New England Inst of Technology (RI)
Niagara County Comm Coll (NY)
North Arkansas Coll (AR)
Northeast Comm Coll (NE)
Northeast State Tech Comm Coll (TN)
Oakland Comm Coll (MI)
Odessa Coll (TX)
Oklahoma City Comm Coll (OK)
Our Lady of the Lake Coll (LA)
Polk Comm Coll (FL)
Quincy Coll (MA)
St. Cloud Tech Coll (MN)
St. Philip's Coll (TX)
Sandhills Comm Coll (NC)
San Jacinto Coll Central Campus (TX)
San Joaquin Valley Coll (CA)
Savannah Tech Coll (GA)
Sinclair Comm Coll (OH)
Southeast Arkansas Coll (AR)
Southeast Tech Inst (SD)
Southern Maine Tech Coll (ME)
South Plains Coll (TX)
Southwestern Coll (CA)
Spokane Comm Coll (WA)
Springfield Tech Comm Coll (MA)
Tarrant County Coll District (TX)
Texas State Tech Coll–Harlingen (TX)
Trinity Valley Comm Coll (TX)
Trocaire Coll (NY)
Tulsa Comm Coll (OK)
U of Arkansas at Fort Smith (AR)
Waycross Coll (GA)
Western School of Health and Business Careers (PA)
Western Wisconsin Tech Coll (WI)

OPERATIONS MANAGEMENT
Alamance Comm Coll (NC)
Alexandria Tech Coll (MN)
Asheville-Buncombe Tech Comm Coll (NC)
Catawba Valley Comm Coll (NC)
Central Carolina Comm Coll (NC)
Durham Tech Comm Coll (NC)
Gaston Coll (NC)
Gateway Tech Coll (WI)
Great Basin Coll (NV)
Guam Comm Coll (GU)
Johnston Comm Coll (NC)
Kilgore Coll (TX)
Kishwaukee Coll (IL)
Lehigh Carbon Comm Coll (PA)
Massasoit Comm Coll (MA)
McHenry County Coll (IL)
Mineral Area Coll (MO)
Pitt Comm Coll (NC)
South Piedmont Comm Coll (NC)
Stark State Coll of Technology (OH)
Waubonsee Comm Coll (IL)

OPHTHALMIC MEDICAL ASSISTANT
Volunteer State Comm Coll (TN)

OPHTHALMIC MEDICAL TECHNOLOGY
Penn Valley Comm Coll (MO)
Triton Coll (IL)

OPHTHALMIC/OPTOMETRIC SERVICES
Howard Comm Coll (MD)
Luzerne County Comm Coll (PA)

OPHTHALMIC/OPTOMETRIC SERVICES RELATED
Mid Michigan Comm Coll (MI)

OPTICIANRY
Cuyahoga Comm Coll (OH)
Erie Comm Coll, North Campus (NY)
Harrisburg Area Comm Coll (PA)
J. Sargeant Reynolds Comm Coll (VA)
Milwaukee Area Tech Coll (WI)
Suffolk County Comm Coll (NY)
Triton Coll (IL)

OPTICS
Corning Comm Coll (NY)

OPTOMETRIC/OPHTHALMIC LABORATORY TECHNICIAN
Central Pennsylvania Coll (PA)
Comm Coll of Aurora (CO)
Comm Coll of the Air Force (AL)
Durham Tech Comm Coll (NC)
East Mississippi Comm Coll (MS)
Everett Comm Coll (WA)
Georgia Perimeter Coll (GA)
Hillsborough Comm Coll (FL)
Interboro Inst (NY)
Lakeland Comm Coll (OH)
Los Angeles City Coll (CA)
Miami-Dade Comm Coll (FL)
New York City Tech Coll of the City U of NY (NY)
Portland Comm Coll (OR)
Raritan Valley Comm Coll (NJ)
St. Cloud Tech Coll (MN)
Seattle Central Comm Coll (WA)
Spokane Comm Coll (WA)
Thomas Nelson Comm Coll (VA)
Triton Coll (IL)
Tyler Jr Coll (TX)
Westmoreland County Comm Coll (PA)

ORNAMENTAL HORTICULTURE
Abraham Baldwin Ag Coll (GA)
Antelope Valley Coll (CA)
Bakersfield Coll (CA)
Bergen Comm Coll (NJ)
Bessemer State Tech Coll (AL)
Bronx Comm Coll of City U of NY (NY)
Butte Coll (CA)
Cerritos Coll (CA)
Chabot Coll (CA)
City Coll of San Francisco (CA)
Clackamas Comm Coll (OR)
Clark Coll (WA)
Coll of DuPage (IL)
Coll of Lake County (IL)
Coll of the Desert (CA)
Coll of the Sequoias (CA)
Comm Coll of Allegheny County (PA)
Comm Coll of Southern Nevada (NV)
Cumberland County Coll (NJ)
Cuyamaca Coll (CA)
Danville Area Comm Coll (IL)
Finger Lakes Comm Coll (NY)
Foothill Coll (CA)
Forsyth Tech Comm Coll (NC)
Fullerton Coll (CA)
Golden West Coll (CA)
Gwinnett Tech Coll (GA)
Hawkeye Comm Coll (IA)
Hillsborough Comm Coll (FL)
Howard Coll (TX)
J. Sargeant Reynolds Comm Coll (VA)
Kirkwood Comm Coll (IA)
Kishwaukee Coll (IL)
Lenoir Comm Coll (NC)
Long Beach City Coll (CA)
Los Angeles Pierce Coll (CA)
Merced Coll (CA)
Mercer County Comm Coll (NJ)
Metropolitan Comm Coll (NE)
Miami-Dade Comm Coll (FL)
Minot State U–Bottineau Campus (ND)
MiraCosta Coll (CA)
Mississippi Gulf Coast Comm Coll (MS)
Modesto Jr Coll (CA)
Monterey Peninsula Coll (CA)
Mt. Hood Comm Coll (OR)
Oakland Comm Coll (MI)
Orange Coast Coll (CA)
Pennsylvania Coll of Technology (PA)
Pensacola Jr Coll (FL)
San Joaquin Delta Coll (CA)
Santa Barbara City Coll (CA)
Santa Fe Comm Coll (FL)
Shasta Coll (CA)
Sierra Coll (CA)
Spokane Comm Coll (WA)
State U of NY Coll of Technology at Alfred (NY)
Texas State Tech Coll– Waco/ Marshall Campus (TX)
Triton Coll (IL)
Tulsa Comm Coll (OK)
Tyler Jr Coll (TX)
U of Arkansas Comm Coll at Morrilton (AR)
Ventura Coll (CA)
Vermont Tech Coll (VT)
Victor Valley Coll (CA)
Wharton County Jr Coll (TX)

ORTHOPTICS
Oklahoma City Comm Coll (OK)

ORTHOTICS/PROSTHETICS
Century Comm and Tech Coll (MN)
Spokane Falls Comm Coll (WA)

PAINTING
Cuyamaca Coll (CA)
Dixie State Coll of Utah (UT)
Lincoln Coll, Lincoln (IL)
Luzerne County Comm Coll (PA)

PALEONTOLOGY
Mesa Tech Coll (NM)

PARALEGAL/LEGAL ASSISTANT
Academy of Medical Arts and Business (PA)
Albuquerque Tech Vocational Inst (NM)
Allegany Coll of Maryland (MD)
Alvin Comm Coll (TX)
American River Coll (CA)
Andover Coll (ME)
Angelina Coll (TX)
Anne Arundel Comm Coll (MD)
Arapahoe Comm Coll (CO)
Athens Tech Coll (GA)
Atlantic Cape Comm Coll (NJ)
Austin Comm Coll (TX)
Baltimore City Comm Coll (MD)
Beckfield Coll (KY)
Bergen Comm Coll (NJ)
Berkeley Coll (NJ)
Berkeley Coll (NY)
Berkeley Coll-Westchester Campus (NY)
Black Hawk Coll, Moline (IL)
Blair Coll (CO)
Bradford School (OH)
Brazosport Coll (TX)
Brevard Comm Coll (FL)
Briarwood Coll (CT)
Bronx Comm Coll of City U of NY (NY)
Brookdale Comm Coll (NJ)
Broome Comm Coll (NY)
The Brown Mackie Coll (KS)
The Brown Mackie Coll–Olathe Campus (KS)
Bryant & Stratton Business Inst, Albany (NY)
Bryant & Stratton Business Inst, Rochester (NY)
Bryant & Stratton Business Inst, Eastern Hills Cmps (NY)
Bryant & Stratton Business Inst (NY)
Bryant and Stratton Coll, Virginia Beach (VA)
Bucks County Comm Coll (PA)
Caldwell Comm Coll and Tech Inst (NC)
Calhoun Comm Coll (AL)
Cañada Coll (CA)
Cape Cod Comm Coll (MA)
Cape Fear Comm Coll (NC)
Carteret Comm Coll (NC)
Casper Coll (WY)
Catawba Valley Comm Coll (NC)
Central Carolina Comm Coll (NC)
Central Carolina Tech Coll (SC)
Central Comm Coll–Grand Island Campus (NE)
Central Pennsylvania Coll (PA)
Central Piedmont Comm Coll (NC)
Central Texas Coll (TX)
Chippewa Valley Tech Coll (WI)
Clark Coll (WA)
Cleveland State Comm Coll (TN)
Clovis Comm Coll (NM)
Coastal Carolina Comm Coll (NC)
Coll of Southern Maryland (MD)
Coll of the Redwoods (CA)
Coll of the Sequoias (CA)
Collin County Comm Coll District (TX)
Colorado Northwestern Comm Coll (CO)
Columbus State Comm Coll (OH)
Commonwealth Business Coll, Merrillville (IN)
Comm Coll of Allegheny County (PA)
Comm Coll of Aurora (CO)
Comm Coll of Denver (CO)
Comm Coll of Rhode Island (RI)
Comm Coll of Southern Nevada (NV)
Comm Coll of the Air Force (AL)
Compton Comm Coll (CA)
Corning Comm Coll (NY)
Crown Coll (WA)
Cuyahoga Comm Coll (OH)
Cuyamaca Coll (CA)
Daymar Coll (KY)
Daytona Beach Comm Coll (FL)
De Anza Coll (CA)
Delaware County Comm Coll (PA)
Delta Coll (MI)
Des Moines Area Comm Coll (IA)
Dominion Coll, Roanoke (VA)
Doña Ana Branch Comm Coll (NM)
Duff's Business Inst (PA)
Durham Tech Comm Coll (NC)
Dutchess Comm Coll (NY)
Eastern Idaho Tech Coll (ID)
Edison State Comm Coll (OH)
Edmonds Comm Coll (WA)
Education America, Remington Coll, Lafayette Campus (LA)
Elaine P. Nunez Comm Coll (LA)
El Centro Coll (TX)
Erie Business Center, Main (PA)
Erie Comm Coll, City Campus (NY)
Eugenio María de Hostos Comm Coll of City U of NY (NY)
Everest Coll (AZ)
Evergreen Valley Coll (CA)
Fayetteville Tech Comm Coll (NC)
Finger Lakes Comm Coll (NY)
Fiorello H LaGuardia Comm Coll of City U of NY (NY)
Fisher Coll (MA)
Florence-Darlington Tech Coll (SC)
Florida Comm Coll at Jacksonville (FL)
Florida National Coll (FL)
Florida Tech Coll, Orlando (FL)
Floyd Coll (GA)
Forsyth Tech Comm Coll (NC)
Frederick Comm Coll (MD)
Fresno City Coll (CA)
Fullerton Coll (CA)
Gadsden State Comm Coll (AL)
Gaston Coll (NC)
Gem City Coll (IL)
Genesee Comm Coll (NY)
Gloucester County Coll (NJ)
Greenville Tech Coll (SC)
Guilford Tech Comm Coll (NC)
Gulf Coast Comm Coll (FL)
Hagerstown Business Coll (MD)
Harford Comm Coll (MD)
Harrisburg Area Comm Coll (PA)
Henry Ford Comm Coll (MI)
Herkimer County Comm Coll (NY)
Hesser Coll (NH)
Hickey Coll (MO)
Highline Comm Coll (WA)
Hinds Comm Coll (MS)
Horry-Georgetown Tech Coll (SC)
Houston Comm Coll System (TX)
Hudson County Comm Coll (NJ)
Hutchinson Comm Coll and Area Vocational School (KS)
Indian River Comm Coll (FL)
Interboro Inst (NY)
International Business Coll, Fort Wayne (IN)
Inver Hills Comm Coll (MN)
Iowa Lakes Comm Coll (IA)
Iowa Western Comm Coll (IA)
Ivy Tech State Coll–Central Indiana (IN)
Ivy Tech State Coll–Eastcentral (IN)
Ivy Tech State Coll–Northeast (IN)
Ivy Tech State Coll–Northwest (IN)
James H. Faulkner State Comm Coll (AL)
Jefferson Comm Coll (NY)
Johnson County Comm Coll (KS)
Johnston Comm Coll (NC)
J. Sargeant Reynolds Comm Coll (VA)
Kansas City Kansas Comm Coll (KS)
Kellogg Comm Coll (MI)
Kilgore Coll (TX)
Kirkwood Comm Coll (IA)
Lakeland Comm Coll (OH)
Lake Region State Coll (ND)
Lakeshore Tech Coll (WI)
Lake-Sumter Comm Coll (FL)
Lamar State Coll–Port Arthur (TX)
Lansing Comm Coll (MI)
Laramie County Comm Coll (WY)
Lehigh Carbon Comm Coll (PA)
Lima Tech Coll (OH)

Lincoln Coll, Normal (IL)
Lincoln School of Commerce (NE)
Louisiana State U at Alexandria (LA)
Louisiana State U at Eunice (LA)
Luzerne County Comm Coll (PA)
Macomb Comm Coll (MI)
Manatee Comm Coll (FL)
Manchester Comm Coll (CT)
Manor Coll (PA)
Marion Tech Coll (OH)
Massachusetts Bay Comm Coll (MA)
McCann School of Business (PA)
McIntosh Coll (NH)
McLennan Comm Coll (TX)
Mercer County Comm Coll (NJ)
Metropolitan Comm Coll (NE)
Miami-Dade Comm Coll (FL)
Middlesex Comm Coll (MA)
Middlesex County Coll (NJ)
Midland Coll (TX)
Milwaukee Area Tech Coll (WI)
Minnesota School of Business (MN)
Mississippi Gulf Coast Comm Coll (MS)
Montgomery Coll (MD)
Mountain West Coll (UT)
Mt. San Jacinto Coll (CA)
Mount Wachusett Comm Coll (MA)
Muskingum Area Tech Coll (OH)
Nassau Comm Coll (NY)
Naugatuck Valley Comm Coll (CT)
Navarro Coll (TX)
Newbury Coll (MA)
New Hampshire Tech Inst (NH)
New Mexico State U–Alamogordo (NM)
New Mexico State U–Carlsbad (NM)
New River Comm Coll (VA)
New York City Tech Coll of the City U of NY (NY)
Northampton County Area Comm Coll (PA)
North Central Michigan Coll (MI)
North Central Texas Coll (TX)
Northeast Alabama Comm Coll (AL)
Northeast Comm Coll (NE)
Northern Essex Comm Coll (MA)
Northern Virginia Comm Coll (VA)
North Hennepin Comm Coll (MN)
North Idaho Coll (ID)
Northland Comm and Tech Coll (MN)
Northland Pioneer Coll (AZ)
North Shore Comm Coll (MA)
Northwestern Business Coll (IL)
Northwestern Connecticut Comm-Tech Coll (CT)
Northwestern Michigan Coll (MI)
Northwest Mississippi Comm Coll (MS)
Northwest State Comm Coll (OH)
Norwalk Comm Coll (CT)
Oakland Comm Coll (MI)
Ocean County Coll (NJ)
Okaloosa-Walton Comm Coll (FL)
Orangeburg-Calhoun Tech Coll (SC)
Ouachita Tech Coll (AR)
Pace Inst (PA)
Palomar Coll (CA)
The Paralegal Inst, Inc. (AZ)
Pasco-Hernando Comm Coll (FL)
Patricia Stevens Coll (MO)
Pellissippi State Tech Comm Coll (TN)
Penn Commercial Business and Tech School (PA)
Pennsylvania Coll of Technology (PA)
Penn Valley Comm Coll (MO)
Pensacola Jr Coll (FL)
Phoenix Coll (AZ)
Pierce Coll (WA)
Pikes Peak Comm Coll (CO)
Pima Comm Coll (AZ)
Pioneer Pacific Coll (OR)
Pitt Comm Coll (NC)
Platt Coll, Ontario (CA)
Platt Coll–Los Angeles, Inc (CA)
Portland Comm Coll (OR)
Prince George's Comm Coll (MD)
Quincy Coll (MA)
Raritan Valley Comm Coll (NJ)
Rasmussen Coll Mankato (MN)
RETS Tech Center (OH)
Rockford Business Coll (IL)
Rockingham Comm Coll (NC)
Rowan-Cabarrus Comm Coll (NC)
St. Petersburg Coll (FL)
St. Philip's Coll (TX)
San Diego City Coll (CA)
Sanford-Brown Coll, Fenton (MO)
Sanford-Brown Coll, Hazelwood (MO)
San Jacinto Coll Central Campus (TX)
San Jacinto Coll North Campus (TX)
San Juan Coll (NM)
Santa Fe Comm Coll (NM)
Schenectady County Comm Coll (NY)
Seminole Comm Coll (FL)
Shasta Coll (CA)
Sinclair Comm Coll (OH)
Skagit Valley Coll (WA)
South Coll (NC)
South Coll (TN)
Southeast Arkansas Coll (AR)
South Puget Sound Comm Coll (WA)
South Suburban Coll (IL)
South Texas Comm Coll (TX)
South U (AL)
Southwestern Comm Coll (NC)
Southwestern Michigan Coll (MI)
Southwest Tennessee Comm Coll (TN)
Spokane Comm Coll (WA)
Suffolk County Comm Coll (NY)
Sullivan County Comm Coll (NY)
Surry Comm Coll (NC)
Sussex County Comm Coll (NJ)
Tallahassee Comm Coll (FL)
Tarrant County Coll District (TX)
Tompkins Cortland Comm Coll (NY)
Trident Tech Coll (SC)
Tulsa Comm Coll (OK)
U of Arkansas at Fort Smith (AR)
U of New Mexico–Gallup (NM)
U of Northwestern Ohio (OH)
Victoria Coll (TX)
Vincennes U (IN)
Volunteer State Comm Coll (TN)
Wallace State Comm Coll (AL)
Warren County Comm Coll (NJ)
Westchester Comm Coll (NY)
Western Dakota Tech Inst (SD)
Western Nevada Comm Coll (NV)
Western Piedmont Comm Coll (NC)
Western School of Health and Business Careers (PA)
Western Wisconsin Tech Coll (WI)
Westmoreland County Comm Coll (PA)
Whatcom Comm Coll (WA)
Wilson Tech Comm Coll (NC)
Woodbury Coll (VT)

PARKS, RECREATION, LEISURE AND FITNESS STUDIES RELATED

Atlanta Metropolitan Coll (GA)

PASTORAL COUNSELING

Hesston Coll (KS)

PEACE/CONFLICT STUDIES

Berkshire Comm Coll (MA)
Woodbury Coll (VT)

PERSONAL/MISCELLANEOUS SERVICES

Allegany Coll of Maryland (MD)
Lorain County Comm Coll (OH)

PERSONAL SERVICES MARKETING OPERATIONS

Centralia Coll (WA)
North Central Texas Coll (TX)
Wisconsin Indianhead Tech Coll (WI)

PETROLEUM TECHNOLOGY

Bakersfield Coll (CA)
Barton County Comm Coll (KS)
Coastal Bend Coll (TX)
Midland Coll (TX)
Odessa Coll (TX)
South Plains Coll (TX)
Tulsa Comm Coll (OK)
Tyler Jr Coll (TX)
U of Alaska Anchorage, Kenai Peninsula Coll (AK)

PHARMACY

Abraham Baldwin Ag Coll (GA)
Arapahoe Comm Coll (CO)
Barton County Comm Coll (KS)
Casper Coll (WY)
Cerritos Coll (CA)
City Colls of Chicago, Richard J Daley Coll (IL)
Coastal Bend Coll (TX)
Colby Comm Coll (KS)
Columbia State Comm Coll (TN)
Comm Coll of Southern Nevada (NV)
Durham Tech Comm Coll (NC)
East Central Coll (MO)
East Central Comm Coll (MS)
Gateway Comm Coll (CT)
Highland Comm Coll (KS)
Holmes Comm Coll (MS)
Indian River Comm Coll (FL)
Iowa Lakes Comm Coll (IA)
Isothermal Comm Coll (NC)
Lorain County Comm Coll (OH)
Miami-Dade Comm Coll (FL)
Mid Michigan Comm Coll (MI)
Navarro Coll (TX)
North Seattle Comm Coll (WA)
Northwest-Shoals Comm Coll (AL)
Pasadena City Coll (CA)
Riverside Comm Coll (CA)
St. Clair County Comm Coll (MI)
Vincennes U (IN)

PHARMACY TECHNICIAN/ ASSISTANT

Bunker Hill Comm Coll (MA)
Casper Coll (WY)
Century Comm and Tech Coll (MN)
Clinton Comm Coll (IA)
Comm Coll of Allegheny County (PA)
Comm Coll of the Air Force (AL)
Darton Coll (GA)
Draughons Jr Coll, Clarksville (TN)
Everett Comm Coll (WA)
Fayetteville Tech Comm Coll (NC)
Harrisburg Area Comm Coll (PA)
Hillsborough Comm Coll (FL)
Midlands Tech Coll (SC)
Muscatine Comm Coll (IA)
North Dakota State Coll of Science (ND)
Oakland Comm Coll (MI)
Pima Comm Coll (AZ)
San Jacinto Coll North Campus (TX)
San Joaquin Valley Coll (CA)
Santa Ana Coll (CA)
Scott Comm Coll (IA)
Silicon Valley Coll, San Jose (CA)
Tacoma Comm Coll (WA)
U of Northwestern Ohio (OH)
Wake Tech Comm Coll (NC)
Weatherford Coll (TX)
Western School of Health and Business Careers (PA)

PHILOSOPHY

Allen County Comm Coll (KS)
Andrew Coll (GA)
Bakersfield Coll (CA)
Barton County Comm Coll (KS)
Bergen Comm Coll (NJ)
Blinn Coll (TX)
Burlington County Coll (NJ)
Cañada Coll (CA)
Cape Cod Comm Coll (MA)
Cerritos Coll (CA)
Chaffey Coll (CA)
Coastal Georgia Comm Coll (GA)
Coll of Alameda (CA)
Coll of Marin (CA)
Coll of the Desert (CA)
Compton Comm Coll (CA)
Crafton Hills Coll (CA)
Cypress Coll (CA)
Danville Area Comm Coll (IL)
Darton Coll (GA)
Daytona Beach Comm Coll (FL)
De Anza Coll (CA)
Dixie State Coll of Utah (UT)
Donnelly Coll (KS)
East Central Coll (MO)
Everett Comm Coll (WA)
Floyd Coll (GA)
Foothill Coll (CA)
Fullerton Coll (CA)
Georgia Perimeter Coll (GA)
Harford Comm Coll (MD)
Indian River Comm Coll (FL)
Iowa Lakes Comm Coll (IA)
Jefferson Comm Coll (KY)
Kellogg Comm Coll (MI)
Lake Michigan Coll (MI)
Lansing Comm Coll (MI)
Lincoln Coll, Lincoln (IL)
Lincoln Coll, Normal (IL)
Lincoln Land Comm Coll (IL)
Lon Morris Coll (TX)
Lord Fairfax Comm Coll (VA)
Los Angeles Mission Coll (CA)
Lower Columbia Coll (WA)
Manatee Comm Coll (FL)
Miami-Dade Comm Coll (FL)
Miami U–Middletown Campus (OH)
MiraCosta Coll (CA)
Monterey Peninsula Coll (CA)
Orange Coast Coll (CA)
Oxnard Coll (CA)
Palm Beach Comm Coll (FL)
Pasadena City Coll (CA)
Pensacola Jr Coll (FL)
Riverside Comm Coll (CA)
San Bernardino Valley Coll (CA)
San Jacinto Coll Central Campus (TX)
San Joaquin Delta Coll (CA)
San Juan Coll (NM)
Santa Ana Coll (CA)
Santa Barbara City Coll (CA)
Santa Monica Coll (CA)
Sauk Valley Comm Coll (IL)
Skagit Valley Coll (WA)
Snow Coll (UT)
Southwestern Coll (CA)
Tacoma Comm Coll (WA)
Triton Coll (IL)
Tulsa Comm Coll (OK)

PHOTOGRAPHIC TECHNOLOGY

Catawba Valley Comm Coll (NC)
County Coll of Morris (NJ)
Dixie State Coll of Utah (UT)
Northland Pioneer Coll (AZ)
Randolph Comm Coll (NC)
Suffolk County Comm Coll (NY)
Texas State Tech Coll– Waco/ Marshall Campus (TX)

PHOTOGRAPHY

Adirondack Comm Coll (NY)
Allan Hancock Coll (CA)
Amarillo Coll (TX)
Andrew Coll (GA)
Anne Arundel Comm Coll (MD)
Antelope Valley Coll (CA)
Antonelli Coll (OH)
Antonelli Inst (PA)
The Art Inst of Atlanta (GA)
The Art Inst of Fort Lauderdale (FL)
The Art Inst of Philadelphia (PA)
The Art Inst of Pittsburgh (PA)
The Art Inst of Seattle (WA)
Austin Comm Coll (TX)
Bakersfield Coll (CA)
Bergen Comm Coll (NJ)
Brevard Comm Coll (FL)
Brookdale Comm Coll (NJ)
Butte Coll (CA)
Carteret Comm Coll (NC)
Casper Coll (WY)
Catawba Valley Comm Coll (NC)
Cecil Comm Coll (MD)
Cerritos Coll (CA)
Chabot Coll (CA)
Chaffey Coll (CA)
Citrus Coll (CA)
City Coll of San Francisco (CA)
City Colls of Chicago, Richard J Daley Coll (IL)
Coll of DuPage (IL)
Coll of Southern Idaho (ID)
Colorado Mountn Coll (CO)
The Comm Coll of Baltimore County–Catonsville Campus (MD)
Comm Coll of Denver (CO)
Comm Coll of Southern Nevada (NV)
Compton Comm Coll (CA)
Cuyahoga Comm Coll (OH)
Cypress Coll (CA)
Daytona Beach Comm Coll (FL)
De Anza Coll (CA)
Dixie State Coll of Utah (UT)
Everett Comm Coll (WA)
Fiorello H LaGuardia Comm Coll of City U of NY (NY)
Foothill Coll (CA)
Fort Scott Comm Coll (KS)
Fresno City Coll (CA)
Glendale Comm Coll (CA)
Greenfield Comm Coll (MA)
Gwinnett Tech Coll (GA)
Harford Comm Coll (MD)
Harrisburg Area Comm Coll (PA)
Hawkeye Comm Coll (IA)
Hennepin Tech Coll (MN)
Herkimer County Comm Coll (NY)
Hill Coll of the Hill Jr College District (TX)
Holyoke Comm Coll (MA)
Howard Comm Coll (MD)
Inst of American Indian Arts (NM)
Iowa Lakes Comm Coll (IA)
Lansing Comm Coll (MI)
Lincoln Coll, Lincoln (IL)
Linn-Benton Comm Coll (OR)
Long Beach City Coll (CA)
Los Angeles City Coll (CA)
Los Angeles Pierce Coll (CA)
Luzerne County Comm Coll (PA)
Macomb Comm Coll (MI)
Mercer County Comm Coll (NJ)
Metropolitan Comm Coll (NE)
Miami-Dade Comm Coll (FL)
Middlesex County Coll (NJ)
Milwaukee Area Tech Coll (WI)
Modesto Jr Coll (CA)
Monterey Peninsula Coll (CA)
Moorpark Coll (CA)
Mott Comm Coll (MI)
Mt. San Jacinto Coll (CA)
Nashville State Tech Inst (TN)
Nassau Comm Coll (NY)
Northern Virginia Comm Coll (VA)
North Harris Coll (TX)
Northwest Coll (WY)
Nossi Coll of Art (TN)
Oakland Comm Coll (MI)
Odessa Coll (TX)
Oklahoma State U, Okmulgee (OK)
Onondaga Comm Coll (NY)
Orange Coast Coll (CA)
Palm Beach Comm Coll (FL)
Palomar Coll (CA)
Pasadena City Coll (CA)
Prairie State Coll (IL)
Randolph Comm Coll (NC)
Ridgewater Coll (MN)
Rockland Comm Coll (NY)
St. Louis Comm Coll at Florissant Valley (MO)
San Bernardino Valley Coll (CA)
San Diego City Coll (CA)
San Joaquin Delta Coll (CA)
Santa Ana Coll (CA)
Santa Monica Coll (CA)
Scottsdale Comm Coll (AZ)
Seattle Central Comm Coll (WA)
Shoreline Comm Coll (WA)
Sierra Coll (CA)
Southwestern Coll (CA)
Sullivan County Comm Coll (NY)
Thomas Nelson Comm Coll (VA)
Tyler Jr Coll (TX)
Ventura Coll (CA)
Villa Maria Coll of Buffalo (NY)
Westmoreland County Comm Coll (PA)

PHYSICAL EDUCATION

Abraham Baldwin Ag Coll (GA)
Allan Hancock Coll (CA)
Alvin Comm Coll (TX)
Amarillo Coll (TX)
Andrew Coll (GA)
Angelina Coll (TX)
Anne Arundel Comm Coll (MD)
Arizona Western Coll (AZ)
Bakersfield Coll (CA)
Barstow Coll (CA)
Barton County Comm Coll (KS)
Berkshire Comm Coll (MA)
Black Hawk Coll, Moline (IL)
Blinn Coll (TX)
Brazosport Coll (TX)
Bucks County Comm Coll (PA)
Butler County Comm Coll (PA)
Butte Coll (CA)
Cañada Coll (CA)

Cape Cod Comm Coll (MA)
Casper Coll (WY)
Central Texas Coll (TX)
Cerritos Coll (CA)
Chabot Coll (CA)
Chaffey Coll (CA)
Chattahoochee Valley Comm Coll (AL)
Chemeketa Comm Coll (OR)
Chesapeake Coll (MD)
Cisco Jr Coll (TX)
Citrus Coll (CA)
City Colls of Chicago, Harry S Truman Coll (IL)
City Colls of Chicago, Malcolm X Coll (IL)
Clinton Comm Coll (NY)
Coastal Bend Coll (TX)
Cochise Coll, Douglas (AZ)
Coffeyville Comm Coll (KS)
Colby Comm Coll (KS)
Coll of Marin (CA)
Coll of Southern Idaho (ID)
Coll of the Canyons (CA)
Coll of the Desert (CA)
Coll of the Sequoias (CA)
Coll of the Siskiyous (CA)
Columbia State Comm Coll (TN)
Compton Comm Coll (CA)
Cowley County Comm Coll and Voc-Tech School (KS)
Crafton Hills Coll (CA)
Crowder Coll (MO)
Cuesta Coll (CA)
Cypress Coll (CA)
Danville Area Comm Coll (IL)
Darton Coll (GA)
Daytona Beach Comm Coll (FL)
Dean Coll (MA)
De Anza Coll (CA)
Del Mar Coll (TX)
Dixie State Coll of Utah (UT)
Dodge City Comm Coll (KS)
East Central Coll (MO)
Eastern Oklahoma State Coll (OK)
Eastern Wyoming Coll (WY)
East Georgia Coll (GA)
Ellsworth Comm Coll (IA)
Essex County Coll (NJ)
Everett Comm Coll (WA)
Finger Lakes Comm Coll (NY)
Foothill Coll (CA)
Frederick Comm Coll (MD)
Fullerton Coll (CA)
Fulton-Montgomery Comm Coll (NY)
Gadsden State Comm Coll (AL)
Galveston Coll (TX)
Garden City Comm Coll (KS)
Gavilan Coll (CA)
Genesee Comm Coll (NY)
Georgia Perimeter Coll (GA)
Grayson County Coll (TX)
Harrisburg Area Comm Coll (PA)
Herkimer County Comm Coll (NY)
Highland Comm Coll (KS)
Hill Coll of the Hill Jr College District (TX)
Hillsborough Comm Coll (FL)
Howard Coll (TX)
Imperial Valley Coll (CA)
Independence Comm Coll (KS)
Indian River Comm Coll (FL)
Iowa Lakes Comm Coll (IA)
Jefferson Coll (MO)
Jefferson Davis Comm Coll (AL)
John A. Logan Coll (IL)
Joliet Jr Coll (IL)
Jones County Jr Coll (MS)
Kansas City Kansas Comm Coll (KS)
Kellogg Comm Coll (MI)
Kilgore Coll (TX)
Kirkwood Comm Coll (IA)
Labette Comm Coll (KS)
Lake Tahoe Comm Coll (CA)
Lansing Comm Coll (MI)
Laramie County Comm Coll (WY)
Lincoln Coll, Lincoln (IL)
Lincoln Coll, Normal (IL)
Lincoln Land Comm Coll (IL)
Long Beach City Coll (CA)
Lon Morris Coll (TX)
Lorain County Comm Coll (OH)
Los Angeles Mission Coll (CA)
Lower Columbia Coll (WA)
Manatee Comm Coll (FL)
McLennan Comm Coll (TX)
Merced Coll (CA)
Miami-Dade Comm Coll (FL)
Middlesex County Coll (NJ)
Midland Coll (TX)
Minot State U–Bottineau Campus (ND)
Mississippi Delta Comm Coll (MS)
Mitchell Coll (CT)
Mitchell Comm Coll (NC)
Modesto Jr Coll (CA)
Mohawk Valley Comm Coll (NY)
Monroe Comm Coll (NY)
Monterey Peninsula Coll (CA)
Montgomery County Comm Coll (PA)
Mt. San Jacinto Coll (CA)
Navarro Coll (TX)
New Mexico Military Inst (NM)
Niagara County Comm Coll (NY)
Northeast Comm Coll (NE)
Northern Essex Comm Coll (MA)
North Harris Coll (TX)
Northwest Coll (WY)
Northwest Mississippi Comm Coll (MS)
Odessa Coll (TX)
Okaloosa-Walton Comm Coll (FL)
Orange Coast Coll (CA)
Oxnard Coll (CA)
Palm Beach Comm Coll (FL)
Palomar Coll (CA)
Pasadena City Coll (CA)
Pratt Comm Coll and Area Vocational School (KS)
Prince George's Comm Coll (MD)
Ridgewater Coll (MN)
Roane State Comm Coll (TN)
Sacramento City Coll (CA)
St. Catharine Coll (KY)
San Bernardino Valley Coll (CA)
San Diego City Coll (CA)
San Diego Mesa Coll (CA)
San Jacinto Coll South Campus (TX)
San Joaquin Delta Coll (CA)
Santa Barbara City Coll (CA)
Santa Monica Coll (CA)
Sauk Valley Comm Coll (IL)
Seminole State Coll (OK)
Sinclair Comm Coll (OH)
Skagit Valley Coll (WA)
Snow Coll (UT)
South Mountain Comm Coll (AZ)
South Plains Coll (TX)
Southwest Mississippi Comm Coll (MS)
State U of NY Coll of Technology at Delhi (NY)
Tacoma Comm Coll (WA)
Taft Coll (CA)
Trinidad State Jr Coll (CO)
Trinity Valley Comm Coll (TX)
Tulsa Comm Coll (OK)
Umpqua Comm Coll (OR)
U of New Mexico–Gallup (NM)
Vermilion Comm Coll (MN)
Vincennes U (IN)
Walters State Comm Coll (TN)
Waycross Coll (GA)
Western Wyoming Comm Coll (WY)
Wharton County Jr Coll (TX)

PHYSICAL SCIENCES

Abraham Baldwin Ag Coll (GA)
Alvin Comm Coll (TX)
Amarillo Coll (TX)
American River Coll (CA)
Angelina Coll (TX)
Antelope Valley Coll (CA)
Arkansas State U–Beebe (AR)
Austin Comm Coll (TX)
Barton County Comm Coll (KS)
Black Hawk Coll, Moline (IL)
Butler County Comm Coll (PA)
Butte Coll (CA)
Casper Coll (WY)
Cecil Comm Coll (MD)
Centralia Coll (WA)
Central Oregon Comm Coll (OR)
Central Wyoming Coll (WY)
Cerro Coso Comm Coll (CA)
Chaffey Coll (CA)
Chesapeake Coll (MD)
Citrus Coll (CA)
City Colls of Chicago, Wilbur Wright Coll (IL)
Clovis Comm Coll (NM)
Coastal Bend Coll (TX)
Coll of the Canyons (CA)
Coll of the Siskiyous (CA)
Colorado Mountn Coll, Alpine Cmps (CO)
Compton Comm Coll (CA)
Crowder Coll (MO)
Dodge City Comm Coll (KS)
East Central Comm Coll (MS)
Eastern Oklahoma State Coll (OK)
Ellsworth Comm Coll (IA)
Fort Scott Comm Coll (KS)
Frederick Comm Coll (MD)
Fresno City Coll (CA)
Fulton-Montgomery Comm Coll (NY)
Galveston Coll (TX)
Golden West Coll (CA)
Gordon Coll (GA)
Harrisburg Area Comm Coll (PA)
Highland Comm Coll (IL)
Highland Comm Coll (KS)
Hill Coll of the Hill Jr College District (TX)
Howard Comm Coll (MD)
Hutchinson Comm Coll and Area Vocational School (KS)
Imperial Valley Coll (CA)
Independence Comm Coll (KS)
Iowa Lakes Comm Coll (IA)
Jefferson Coll (MO)
Jones County Jr Coll (MS)
Lamar Comm Coll (CO)
Lincoln Coll, Lincoln (IL)
Long Beach City Coll (CA)
Los Angeles Mission Coll (CA)
Merced Coll (CA)
Miami-Dade Comm Coll (FL)
Middlesex County Coll (NJ)
MiraCosta Coll (CA)
Mitchell Coll (CT)
Montgomery County Comm Coll (PA)
Naugatuck Valley Comm Coll (CT)
Navarro Coll (TX)
Neosho County Comm Coll (KS)
North Idaho Coll (ID)
Northwest Coll (WY)
Northwestern Connecticut Comm-Tech Coll (CT)
Orange County Comm Coll (NY)
Otero Jr Coll (CO)
Palm Beach Comm Coll (FL)
Pasadena City Coll (CA)
Pennsylvania Coll of Technology (PA)
Portland Comm Coll (OR)
Pratt Comm Coll and Area Vocational School (KS)
Quincy Coll (MA)
Reedley Coll (CA)
Ridgewater Coll (MN)
Riverside Comm Coll (CA)
Roane State Comm Coll (TN)
Sacramento City Coll (CA)
San Bernardino Valley Coll (CA)
San Diego City Coll (CA)
San Diego Mesa Coll (CA)
San Jacinto Coll Central Campus (TX)
San Joaquin Delta Coll (CA)
San Juan Coll (NM)
Santa Fe Comm Coll (NM)
Seminole State Coll (OK)
Snow Coll (UT)
Southeast Comm Coll, Beatrice Campus (NE)
Southwestern Coll (CA)
Southwest Mississippi Comm Coll (MS)
Tacoma Comm Coll (WA)
Taft Coll (CA)
Trinity Valley Comm Coll (TX)
Tulsa Comm Coll (OK)
Ulster County Comm Coll (NY)
Umpqua Comm Coll (OR)
Union County Coll (NJ)
U of New Mexico–Gallup (NM)
Ventura Coll (CA)
Vermilion Comm Coll (MN)
Victor Valley Coll (CA)
Western Nevada Comm Coll (NV)
Western Wyoming Comm Coll (WY)

PHYSICAL THERAPY

Allan Hancock Coll (CA)
Allen County Comm Coll (KS)
Amarillo Coll (TX)
Andrew Coll (GA)
Arapahoe Comm Coll (CO)
Athens Tech Coll (GA)
Baltimore City Comm Coll (MD)
Barton County Comm Coll (KS)
Bay State Coll (MA)
Berkshire Comm Coll (MA)
Blackhawk Tech Coll (WI)
Bossier Parish Comm Coll (LA)
Caldwell Comm Coll and Tech Inst (NC)
Casper Coll (WY)
Central Piedmont Comm Coll (NC)
Cerritos Coll (CA)
Chattanooga State Tech Comm Coll (TN)
City Coll of San Francisco (CA)
Coastal Georgia Comm Coll (GA)
Colby Comm Coll (KS)
Coll of Southern Idaho (ID)
Columbia State Comm Coll (TN)
Cowley County Comm Coll and Voc-Tech School (KS)
Danville Area Comm Coll (IL)
Daytona Beach Comm Coll (FL)
De Anza Coll (CA)
Delta Coll (MI)
Dodge City Comm Coll (KS)
Donnelly Coll (KS)
East Central Comm Coll (MS)
Essex County Coll (NJ)
Fiorello H LaGuardia Comm Coll of City U of NY (NY)
Florence-Darlington Tech Coll (SC)
Floyd Coll (GA)
Gateway Tech Coll (WI)
Genesee Comm Coll (NY)
George Corley Wallace State Comm Coll (AL)
Georgia Perimeter Coll (GA)
Greenville Tech Coll (SC)
Gwinnett Tech Coll (GA)
Herkimer County Comm Coll (NY)
Highland Comm Coll (KS)
Hillsborough Comm Coll (FL)
Holmes Comm Coll (MS)
Housatonic Comm Coll (CT)
Indian Hills Comm Coll (IA)
Indian River Comm Coll (FL)
Jackson State Comm Coll (TN)
Jefferson Comm Coll (KY)
John Tyler Comm Coll (VA)
Kent State U, East Liverpool Campus (OH)
Keystone Coll (PA)
Kingsborough Comm Coll of City U of NY (NY)
Laredo Comm Coll (TX)
Lima Tech Coll (OH)
Louisburg Coll (NC)
Macomb Comm Coll (MI)
Manatee Comm Coll (FL)
Manor Coll (PA)
McLennan Comm Coll (TX)
Meridian Comm Coll (MS)
Miami-Dade Comm Coll (FL)
Mid Michigan Comm Coll (MI)
Milwaukee Area Tech Coll (WI)
Monroe County Comm Coll (MI)
Monterey Peninsula Coll (CA)
Morgan Comm Coll (CO)
Morton Coll (IL)
Mt. Hood Comm Coll (OR)
Mount Wachusett Comm Coll (MA)
Nash Comm Coll (NC)
Northeast Comm Coll (NE)
Northern Virginia Comm Coll (VA)
NorthWest Arkansas Comm Coll (AR)
Northwest Coll (WY)
Oakton Comm Coll (IL)
Odessa Coll (TX)
Oklahoma City Comm Coll (OK)
Onondaga Comm Coll (NY)
Orange County Comm Coll (NY)
Paducah Comm Coll (KY)
Palm Beach Comm Coll (FL)
Penn Valley Comm Coll (MO)
Pensacola Jr Coll (FL)
Riverside Comm Coll (CA)
Roane State Comm Coll (TN)
Sanford-Brown Coll, Hazelwood (MO)
San Jacinto Coll South Campus (TX)
Scott Comm Coll (IA)
Seminole Comm Coll (FL)
Sinclair Comm Coll (OH)
South Plains Coll (TX)
Southwestern Comm Coll (NC)
Southwest Georgia Tech Coll (GA)
Stark State Coll of Technology (OH)
Suffolk County Comm Coll (NY)
Tacoma Comm Coll (WA)
Tarrant County Coll District (TX)
Trident Tech Coll (SC)
Tulsa Comm Coll (OK)
Tunxis Comm Coll (CT)
Vincennes U (IN)
Wallace State Comm Coll (AL)
Waycross Coll (GA)
Western Nebraska Comm Coll (NE)
Wharton County Jr Coll (TX)
Young Harris Coll (GA)

PHYSICAL THERAPY ASSISTANT

Adirondack Comm Coll (NY)
Allegany Coll of Maryland (MD)
Angelina Coll (TX)
Anoka-Hennepin Tech Coll (MN)
Anoka-Ramsey Comm Coll (MN)
Anoka-Ramsey Comm Coll, Cambridge Campus (MN)
Ashland Comm Coll (KY)
Atlantic Cape Comm Coll (NJ)
Berkshire Comm Coll (MA)
Black Hawk Coll, Moline (IL)
Blinn Coll (TX)
Broome Comm Coll (NY)
Butler County Comm Coll (PA)
Cape Cod Comm Coll (MA)
Capital Comm Coll (CT)
Carroll Comm Coll (MD)
Central Ohio Tech Coll (OH)
Central Pennsylvania Coll (PA)
Colby Comm Coll (KS)
Coll of DuPage (IL)
Coll of St. Catherine–Minneapolis (MN)
Comm Coll of Allegheny County (PA)
Comm Coll of Rhode Island (RI)
Comm Coll of the Air Force (AL)
Darton Coll (GA)
Delaware Tech & Comm Coll, Stanton/ Wilmington Cmps (DE)
Delgado Comm Coll (LA)
Delta Coll (MI)
Dutchess Comm Coll (NY)
Everett Comm Coll (WA)
Fayetteville Tech Comm Coll (NC)
Florida Comm Coll at Jacksonville (FL)
Floyd Coll (GA)
GateWay Comm Coll (AZ)
Gateway Tech Coll (WI)
Green River Comm Coll (WA)
Guilford Tech Comm Coll (NC)
Gulf Coast Comm Coll (FL)
Harcum Coll (PA)
Hazard Comm Coll (KY)
Hesser Coll (NH)
Houston Comm Coll System (TX)
Indian River Comm Coll (FL)
Ivy Tech State Coll–Eastcentral (IN)
Ivy Tech State Coll–Northwest (IN)
Jefferson State Comm Coll (AL)
Johnson County Comm Coll (KS)
Kankakee Comm Coll (IL)
Kansas City Kansas Comm Coll (KS)
Kaskaskia Coll (IL)
Kellogg Comm Coll (MI)
Kennebec Valley Tech Coll (ME)
Keystone Coll (PA)
Kilgore Coll (TX)
Kingsborough Comm Coll of City U of NY (NY)
Lake Area Tech Inst (SD)
Lake City Comm Coll (FL)
Lake Land Coll (IL)
Lehigh Carbon Comm Coll (PA)
Lincoln Land Comm Coll (IL)
Lorain County Comm Coll (OH)
Madisonville Comm Coll (KY)
Manatee Comm Coll (FL)
Manchester Comm Coll (CT)
Marion Tech Coll (OH)
Martin Comm Coll (NC)
Massachusetts Bay Comm Coll (MA)
Massasoit Comm Coll (MA)
Mercer County Comm Coll (NJ)
Middle Georgia Coll (GA)
Midlands Tech Coll (SC)
Montana State U Coll of Tech-Great Falls (MT)
Montgomery Coll (MD)

Mott Comm Coll (MI)
Muskingum Area Tech Coll (OH)
Nassau Comm Coll (NY)
Naugatuck Valley Comm Coll (CT)
Niagara County Comm Coll (NY)
North Iowa Area Comm Coll (IA)
North Shore Comm Coll (MA)
Our Lady of the Lake Coll (LA)
Pasco-Hernando Comm Coll (FL)
Penn State U DuBois Campus of the Commonwealth Coll (PA)
Penn State U Hazleton Campus of the Commonwealth Coll (PA)
Penn State U Mont Alto Campus of the Commonwealth Coll (PA)
Penn State U Shenango Campus of the Commonwealth Coll (PA)
Pensacola Jr Coll (FL)
Polk Comm Coll (FL)
Professional Skills Inst (OH)
Riverland Comm Coll (MN)
Rockingham Comm Coll (NC)
Sacramento City Coll (CA)
St. Petersburg Coll (FL)
St. Philip's Coll (TX)
San Diego Mesa Coll (CA)
San Juan Coll (NM)
Somerset Comm Coll (KY)
South Arkansas Comm Coll (AR)
South Coll (TN)
Southeast Comm Coll (KY)
Southwestern Oklahoma State U at Sayre (OK)
Southwest Tennessee Comm Coll (TN)
Spokane Falls Comm Coll (WA)
Springfield Tech Comm Coll (MA)
Stanly Comm Coll (NC)
State U of NY Coll of Technology at Canton (NY)
Union County Coll (NJ)
U of Pittsburgh at Titusville (PA)
Villa Maria Coll of Buffalo (NY)
Volunteer State Comm Coll (TN)
Western Inst of Science & Health (CA)
Western Iowa Tech Comm Coll (IA)
Western Nebraska Comm Coll (NE)
Western Wisconsin Tech Coll (WI)
Whatcom Comm Coll (WA)
Williston State Coll (ND)

PHYSICIAN ASSISTANT
Barton County Comm Coll (KS)
City Colls of Chicago, Malcolm X Coll (IL)
Coastal Georgia Comm Coll (GA)
Coll of Southern Idaho (ID)
Cuyahoga Comm Coll (OH)
Delta Coll (MI)
Floyd Coll (GA)
Foothill Coll (CA)
Manatee Comm Coll (FL)
Tulsa Comm Coll (OK)

PHYSICS
Allan Hancock Coll (CA)
Allen County Comm Coll (KS)
Amarillo Coll (TX)
Andrew Coll (GA)
Arizona Western Coll (AZ)
Atlanta Metropolitan Coll (GA)
Austin Comm Coll (TX)
Bakersfield Coll (CA)
Barton County Comm Coll (KS)
Bergen Comm Coll (NJ)
Blinn Coll (TX)
Brazosport Coll (TX)
Brookdale Comm Coll (NJ)
Burlington County Coll (NJ)
Casper Coll (WY)
Cecil Comm Coll (MD)
Cerritos Coll (CA)
Chabot Coll (CA)
Chaffey Coll (CA)
Chattahoochee Valley Comm Coll (AL)
Clark Coll (WA)
Coastal Bend Coll (TX)
Coastal Georgia Comm Coll (GA)
Coll of Marin (CA)
Coll of Southern Idaho (ID)
Coll of the Desert (CA)
Coll of the Siskiyous (CA)
Columbia State Comm Coll (TN)
Comm Coll of Allegheny County (PA)
Compton Comm Coll (CA)
Crafton Hills Coll (CA)
Cuesta Coll (CA)
Cuyamaca Coll (CA)
Cypress Coll (CA)
Darton Coll (GA)
Daytona Beach Comm Coll (FL)
De Anza Coll (CA)
Del Mar Coll (TX)
Dixie State Coll of Utah (UT)
Dodge City Comm Coll (KS)
East Central Coll (MO)
Eastern Arizona Coll (AZ)
Everett Comm Coll (WA)
Finger Lakes Comm Coll (NY)
Foothill Coll (CA)
Fullerton Coll (CA)
Georgia Perimeter Coll (GA)
Grayson County Coll (TX)
Great Basin Coll (NV)
Harford Comm Coll (MD)
Highland Comm Coll (IL)
Hill Coll of the Hill Jr College District (TX)
Holyoke Comm Coll (MA)
Indian River Comm Coll (FL)
John A. Logan Coll (IL)
Joliet Jr Coll (IL)
Kansas City Kansas Comm Coll (KS)
Kellogg Comm Coll (MI)
Kilgore Coll (TX)
Kingsborough Comm Coll of City U of NY (NY)
Lamar Comm Coll (CO)
Lincoln Land Comm Coll (IL)
Linn-Benton Comm Coll (OR)
Lon Morris Coll (TX)
Lorain County Comm Coll (OH)
Los Angeles City Coll (CA)
Los Angeles Harbor Coll (CA)
Louisburg Coll (NC)
Lower Columbia Coll (WA)
Manatee Comm Coll (FL)
Mercer County Comm Coll (NJ)
Miami-Dade Comm Coll (FL)
Miami U–Middletown Campus (OH)
Middlesex County Coll (NJ)
Midland Coll (TX)
MiraCosta Coll (CA)
Mohawk Valley Comm Coll (NY)
Monroe Comm Coll (NY)
Monterey Peninsula Coll (CA)
Navarro Coll (TX)
New Mexico Military Inst (NM)
Northampton County Area Comm Coll (PA)
Northeast Comm Coll (NE)
North Idaho Coll (ID)
Northwest Coll (WY)
Odessa Coll (TX)
Okaloosa-Walton Comm Coll (FL)
Oklahoma City Comm Coll (OK)
Orange Coast Coll (CA)
Pasadena City Coll (CA)
Pensacola Jr Coll (FL)
Red Rocks Comm Coll (CO)
Salem Comm Coll (NJ)
San Bernardino Valley Coll (CA)
San Diego Mesa Coll (CA)
San Jacinto Coll North Campus (TX)
San Juan Coll (NM)
Santa Ana Coll (CA)
Santa Barbara City Coll (CA)
Santa Monica Coll (CA)
Sauk Valley Comm Coll (IL)
Snow Coll (UT)
South Mountain Comm Coll (AZ)
Southwestern Coll (CA)
State U of NY Coll of A&T at Morrisville (NY)
Tacoma Comm Coll (WA)
Texarkana Coll (TX)
Triton Coll (IL)
Tulsa Comm Coll (OK)
Vermilion Comm Coll (MN)
Vincennes U (IN)
Western Nebraska Comm Coll (NE)
Young Harris Coll (GA)

PHYSICS EDUCATION
Manatee Comm Coll (FL)

PHYSIOLOGY
Chabot Coll (CA)
Joliet Jr Coll (IL)
Snow Coll (UT)

PLANT PATHOLOGY
Dixie State Coll of Utah (UT)

PLANT PROTECTION
Dixie State Coll of Utah (UT)
Los Angeles Pierce Coll (CA)
Tulsa Comm Coll (OK)

PLANT SCIENCES
Mercer County Comm Coll (NJ)
Northwest Mississippi Comm Coll (MS)
Reedley Coll (CA)

PLASTICS TECHNOLOGY
Cerritos Coll (CA)
Cincinnati State Tech and Comm Coll (OH)
Coll of DuPage (IL)
Cumberland County Coll (NJ)
Elaine P. Nunez Comm Coll (LA)
Grand Rapids Comm Coll (MI)
Hennepin Tech Coll (MN)
Highline Comm Coll (WA)
Isothermal Comm Coll (NC)
Kalamazoo Valley Comm Coll (MI)
Kellogg Comm Coll (MI)
Lorain County Comm Coll (OH)
Macomb Comm Coll (MI)
Montcalm Comm Coll (MI)
Mount Wachusett Comm Coll (MA)
Northwest State Comm Coll (OH)
Pennsylvania Coll of Technology (PA)
Randolph Comm Coll (NC)
St. Clair County Comm Coll (MI)
St. Petersburg Coll (FL)
Schenectady County Comm Coll (NY)
Sinclair Comm Coll (OH)
Southeast Comm Coll, Milford Campus (NE)
South Texas Comm Coll (TX)
State U of NY Coll of A&T at Morrisville (NY)
Terra State Comm Coll (OH)
Tyler Jr Coll (TX)
Wake Tech Comm Coll (NC)

PLUMBING
Bakersfield Coll (CA)
Brazosport Coll (TX)
Brevard Comm Coll (FL)
Cecil Comm Coll (MD)
Delta Coll (MI)
Fayetteville Tech Comm Coll (NC)
Forsyth Tech Comm Coll (NC)
GateWay Comm Coll (AZ)
Ivy Tech State Coll–Central Indiana (IN)
Ivy Tech State Coll–Eastcentral (IN)
Ivy Tech State Coll–North Central (IN)
Ivy Tech State Coll–Northeast (IN)
Ivy Tech State Coll–Northwest (IN)
Ivy Tech State Coll–Southcentral (IN)
Ivy Tech State Coll–Southwest (IN)
Ivy Tech State Coll–Wabash Valley (IN)
Kellogg Comm Coll (MI)
Luzerne County Comm Coll (PA)
Macomb Comm Coll (MI)
New England Inst of Technology (RI)
Northern Maine Tech Coll (ME)
Oklahoma State U, Okmulgee (OK)
Palomar Coll (CA)
St. Cloud Tech Coll (MN)
St. Philip's Coll (TX)
Southeast Comm Coll, Milford Campus (NE)
Southern Maine Tech Coll (ME)
State U of NY Coll of Technology at Alfred (NY)
State U of NY Coll of Technology at Canton (NY)
State U of NY Coll of Technology at Delhi (NY)
Thaddeus Stevens Coll of Technology (PA)
Trenholm State Tech Coll, Patterson Campus (AL)
Truckee Meadows Comm Coll (NV)
Western Nevada Comm Coll (NV)

POLITICAL SCIENCE
Abraham Baldwin Ag Coll (GA)
Allen County Comm Coll (KS)
Atlanta Metropolitan Coll (GA)
Austin Comm Coll (TX)
Bacone Coll (OK)
Bainbridge Coll (GA)
Bakersfield Coll (CA)
Barton County Comm Coll (KS)
Bergen Comm Coll (NJ)
Brazosport Coll (TX)
Brookdale Comm Coll (NJ)
Burlington County Coll (NJ)
Butte Coll (CA)
Cañada Coll (CA)
Casper Coll (WY)
Centralia Coll (WA)
Cerritos Coll (CA)
Chabot Coll (CA)
Chaffey Coll (CA)
Chemeketa Comm Coll (OR)
Coastal Bend Coll (TX)
Coastal Georgia Comm Coll (GA)
Cochise Coll, Douglas (AZ)
Coffeyville Comm Coll (KS)
Colby Comm Coll (KS)
Coll of Alameda (CA)
Coll of Marin (CA)
Coll of Southern Idaho (ID)
Coll of the Canyons (CA)
Coll of the Desert (CA)
Columbia State Comm Coll (TN)
Copiah-Lincoln Comm Coll–Natchez Campus (MS)
Crafton Hills Coll (CA)
Cypress Coll (CA)
Darton Coll (GA)
De Anza Coll (CA)
Del Mar Coll (TX)
Dixie State Coll of Utah (UT)
Dodge City Comm Coll (KS)
Donnelly Coll (KS)
East Central Coll (MO)
East Central Comm Coll (MS)
Eastern Arizona Coll (AZ)
Eastern Oklahoma State Coll (OK)
Eastern Wyoming Coll (WY)
East Georgia Coll (GA)
Ellsworth Comm Coll (IA)
Everett Comm Coll (WA)
Finger Lakes Comm Coll (NY)
Floyd Coll (GA)
Foothill Coll (CA)
Fullerton Coll (CA)
Gavilan Coll (CA)
Gloucester County Coll (NJ)
Gordon Coll (GA)
Harford Comm Coll (MD)
Highland Comm Coll (IL)
Highland Comm Coll (KS)
Hill Coll of the Hill Jr College District (TX)
Hinds Comm Coll (MS)
Independence Comm Coll (KS)
Indian River Comm Coll (FL)
Iowa Lakes Comm Coll (IA)
Jefferson Coll (MO)
Jefferson Comm Coll (KY)
Jefferson Davis Comm Coll (AL)
John A. Logan Coll (IL)
Joliet Jr Coll (IL)
Kellogg Comm Coll (MI)
Kirkwood Comm Coll (IA)
Lake Michigan Coll (MI)
Laramie County Comm Coll (WY)
Lincoln Coll, Lincoln (IL)
Lincoln Land Comm Coll (IL)
Lon Morris Coll (TX)
Lorain County Comm Coll (OH)
Louisburg Coll (NC)
Lower Columbia Coll (WA)
Marshalltown Comm Coll (IA)
Merced Coll (CA)
Miami-Dade Comm Coll (FL)
Miami U–Middletown Campus (OH)
Middlesex County Coll (NJ)
Midland Coll (TX)
MiraCosta Coll (CA)
Mississippi Delta Comm Coll (MS)
Monroe Comm Coll (NY)
Monterey Peninsula Coll (CA)
Northern Essex Comm Coll (MA)
North Harris Coll (TX)
North Idaho Coll (ID)
Northwest Coll (WY)
Odessa Coll (TX)
Oklahoma City Comm Coll (OK)
Orange Coast Coll (CA)
Otero Jr Coll (CO)
Palm Beach Comm Coll (FL)
Palo Verde Coll (CA)
Pasadena City Coll (CA)
Pima Comm Coll (AZ)
Quincy Coll (MA)
Reading Area Comm Coll (PA)
Red Rocks Comm Coll (CO)
Riverside Comm Coll (CA)
St. Philip's Coll (TX)
Salem Comm Coll (NJ)
San Bernardino Valley Coll (CA)
San Diego City Coll (CA)
San Jacinto Coll Central Campus (TX)
San Joaquin Delta Coll (CA)
San Juan Coll (NM)
Santa Ana Coll (CA)
Santa Barbara City Coll (CA)
Santa Monica Coll (CA)
Sauk Valley Comm Coll (IL)
Skagit Valley Coll (WA)
Snow Coll (UT)
South Mountain Comm Coll (AZ)
Southwestern Coll (CA)
Tacoma Comm Coll (WA)
Trinity Valley Comm Coll (TX)
Triton Coll (IL)
Tulsa Comm Coll (OK)
Umpqua Comm Coll (OR)
Vermilion Comm Coll (MN)
Vincennes U (IN)
Waycross Coll (GA)
Western Nebraska Comm Coll (NE)
Western Wyoming Comm Coll (WY)
Young Harris Coll (GA)

POLITICAL SCIENCE/ GOVERNMENT RELATED
Georgia Perimeter Coll (GA)

PORTUGUESE
Miami-Dade Comm Coll (FL)

POSTAL MANAGEMENT
Allen County Comm Coll (KS)
Central Piedmont Comm Coll (NC)
Comm Coll of Denver (CO)
Daytona Beach Comm Coll (FL)
Fayetteville Tech Comm Coll (NC)
Hinds Comm Coll (MS)
Lenoir Comm Coll (NC)
Longview Comm Coll (MO)
Mayland Comm Coll (NC)
Miami-Dade Comm Coll (FL)
Mississippi Gulf Coast Comm Coll (MS)
San Antonio Coll (TX)
San Diego City Coll (CA)
South Plains Coll (TX)
Tarrant County Coll District (TX)
Tyler Jr Coll (TX)
Wallace State Comm Coll (AL)

POULTRY SCIENCE
Abraham Baldwin Ag Coll (GA)
Crowder Coll (MO)
Modesto Jr Coll (CA)
Northeast Texas Comm Coll (TX)
Northwest Mississippi Comm Coll (MS)
Sampson Comm Coll (NC)
Surry Comm Coll (NC)
Wallace State Comm Coll (AL)
Wayne Comm Coll (NC)

PRACTICAL NURSE
Alexandria Tech Coll (MN)
Allan Hancock Coll (CA)
Alpena Comm Coll (MI)
Amarillo Coll (TX)
Angelina Coll (TX)
Arizona Western Coll (AZ)
Athens Tech Coll (GA)
Atlanta Metropolitan Coll (GA)
Bainbridge Coll (GA)
Bay de Noc Comm Coll (MI)
Belmont Tech Coll (OH)
Berkshire Comm Coll (MA)
Bessemer State Tech Coll (AL)
Big Bend Comm Coll (WA)
Black Hawk Coll, Moline (IL)
Brevard Comm Coll (FL)
Butte Coll (CA)
Carl Sandburg Coll (IL)
Carteret Comm Coll (NC)

Casper Coll (WY)
Central Arizona Coll (AZ)
Central Comm Coll–Columbus Campus (NE)
Central Comm Coll–Grand Island Campus (NE)
Centralia Coll (WA)
Central Oregon Comm Coll (OR)
Central Piedmont Comm Coll (NC)
Central Texas Coll (TX)
Cerro Coso Comm Coll (CA)
Chattahoochee Valley Comm Coll (AL)
Chemeketa Comm Coll (OR)
Citrus Coll (CA)
City Coll of San Francisco (CA)
Clinton Comm Coll (IA)
Coastal Bend Coll (TX)
Coffeyville Comm Coll (KS)
Colby Comm Coll (KS)
Coll of Southern Maryland (MD)
Coll of the Canyons (CA)
Colorado Mountn Coll (CO)
Comm Coll of Allegheny County (PA)
Comm Coll of Beaver County (PA)
Comm Coll of Southern Nevada (NV)
Danville Area Comm Coll (IL)
Darton Coll (GA)
Daytona Beach Comm Coll (FL)
De Anza Coll (CA)
Delaware Tech & Comm Coll, Jack F Owens Cmps (DE)
Delaware Tech & Comm Coll, Terry Cmps (DE)
Delta Coll (MI)
Des Moines Area Comm Coll (IA)
Dodge City Comm Coll (KS)
Douglas MacArthur State Tech Coll (AL)
Durham Tech Comm Coll (NC)
East Arkansas Comm Coll (AR)
Eastern Maine Tech Coll (ME)
Elaine P. Nunez Comm Coll (LA)
El Centro Coll (TX)
Everett Comm Coll (WA)
Fayetteville Tech Comm Coll (NC)
Feather River Comm Coll District (CA)
Fergus Falls Comm Coll (MN)
Fort Berthold Comm Coll (ND)
Fresno City Coll (CA)
Galveston Coll (TX)
Gavilan Coll (CA)
George Corley Wallace State Comm Coll (AL)
Glendale Comm Coll (CA)
Gogebic Comm Coll (MI)
Gordon Coll (GA)
Grand Rapids Comm Coll (MI)
Green River Comm Coll (WA)
Hawaii Comm Coll (HI)
Hawkeye Comm Coll (IA)
Heartland Comm Coll (IL)
Helena Coll of Tech of The U of Montana (MT)
Hill Coll of the Hill Jr College District (TX)
Hinds Comm Coll (MS)
Horry-Georgetown Tech Coll (SC)
Howard Coll (TX)
Howard Comm Coll (MD)
Illinois Eastern Comm Colls, Olney Central Coll (IL)
Imperial Valley Coll (CA)
Indian Hills Comm Coll (IA)
Indian River Comm Coll (FL)
Iowa Western Comm Coll (IA)
Isothermal Comm Coll (NC)
Itasca Comm Coll (MN)
Jackson Comm Coll (MI)
Jefferson Coll (MO)
Jefferson Comm Coll (OH)
John A. Logan Coll (IL)
Johnson County Comm Coll (KS)
Jones County Jr Coll (MS)
Kellogg Comm Coll (MI)
Kingwood Coll (TX)
Kirkwood Comm Coll (IA)
Lake Area Tech Inst (SD)
Lake Michigan Coll (MI)
Lamar Comm Coll (CO)
Lamar State Coll–Port Arthur (TX)
Lansing Comm Coll (MI)
Lehigh Carbon Comm Coll (PA)
Lincoln Coll, Lincoln (IL)
Lincoln Coll, Normal (IL)
Louisiana Tech Coll–Mansfield Campus (LA)
Marshalltown Comm Coll (IA)
Merced Coll (CA)
Metropolitan Comm Coll (NE)
Midland Coll (TX)
Mid Michigan Comm Coll (MI)
Mid-Plains Comm Coll Area (NE)
Mineral Area Coll (MO)
Minnesota State Coll–Southeast Tech (MN)
MiraCosta Coll (CA)
Montana State U Coll of Tech-Great Falls (MT)
Mott Comm Coll (MI)
Muscatine Comm Coll (IA)
Navarro Coll (TX)
Neosho County Comm Coll (KS)
New River Comm Coll (VA)
Northcentral Tech Coll (WI)
North Dakota State Coll of Science (ND)
Northeast Comm Coll (NE)
Northern Maine Tech Coll (ME)
North Idaho Coll (ID)
North Iowa Area Comm Coll (IA)
Northland Comm and Tech Coll (MN)
North Seattle Comm Coll (WA)
Northwest Coll (WY)
Northwest Mississippi Comm Coll (MS)
Northwest-Shoals Comm Coll (AL)
Oakland Comm Coll (MI)
Ouachita Tech Coll (AR)
Pasadena City Coll (CA)
Pennsylvania Coll of Technology (PA)
Quincy Coll (MA)
Reading Area Comm Coll (PA)
Ridgewater Coll (MN)
Rockingham Comm Coll (NC)
Sacramento City Coll (CA)
St. Cloud Tech Coll (MN)
St. Philip's Coll (TX)
Sampson Comm Coll (NC)
Sandhills Comm Coll (NC)
San Diego City Coll (CA)
San Jacinto Coll North Campus (TX)
San Jacinto Coll South Campus (TX)
San Joaquin Delta Coll (CA)
San Joaquin Valley Coll (CA)
Santa Barbara City Coll (CA)
Scott Comm Coll (IA)
Sierra Coll (CA)
Skagit Valley Coll (WA)
Southeast Comm Coll, Beatrice Campus (NE)
Southeastern Comm Coll, South Campus (IA)
Southern Maine Tech Coll (ME)
South Plains Coll (TX)
South Puget Sound Comm Coll (WA)
Southwestern Comm Coll (IA)
Southwest Wisconsin Tech Coll (WI)
Spokane Comm Coll (WA)
State Fair Comm Coll (MO)
Surry Comm Coll (NC)
Temple Coll (TX)
Texarkana Coll (TX)
Trinidad State Jr Coll (CO)
Trinity Valley Comm Coll (TX)
Triton Coll (IL)
Tyler Jr Coll (TX)
Union County Coll (NJ)
United Tribes Tech Coll (ND)
U of Arkansas Comm Coll at Morrilton (AR)
Vance-Granville Comm Coll (NC)
Vermont Tech Coll (VT)
Vernon Coll (TX)
Vincennes U (IN)
Wallace State Comm Coll (AL)
Walla Walla Comm Coll (WA)
Western Texas Coll (TX)
Western Wyoming Comm Coll (WY)
Westmoreland County Comm Coll (PA)
West Shore Comm Coll (MI)
Williston State Coll (ND)

PRECISION METAL WORKING RELATED

Lehigh Carbon Comm Coll (PA)
Northwest State Comm Coll (OH)
Reedley Coll (CA)

PRECISION PRODUCTION TRADES RELATED

Clover Park Tech Coll (WA)
Mott Comm Coll (MI)
Southwestern Michigan Coll (MI)
Western Wisconsin Tech Coll (WI)

PRE-DENTISTRY

Allen County Comm Coll (KS)
Centralia Coll (WA)
Coastal Georgia Comm Coll (GA)
Eastern Wyoming Coll (WY)
Georgia Perimeter Coll (GA)
Howard Comm Coll (MD)
Lincoln Land Comm Coll (IL)
St. Philip's Coll (TX)
Tulsa Comm Coll (OK)
Western Nebraska Comm Coll (NE)

PRE-ENGINEERING

Abraham Baldwin Ag Coll (GA)
Adirondack Comm Coll (NY)
Alpena Comm Coll (MI)
Amarillo Coll (TX)
American River Coll (CA)
Andrew Coll (GA)
Anoka-Ramsey Comm Coll (MN)
Anoka-Ramsey Comm Coll, Cambridge Campus (MN)
Arizona Western Coll (AZ)
Atlanta Metropolitan Coll (GA)
Austin Comm Coll (TX)
Barton County Comm Coll (KS)
Bay de Noc Comm Coll (MI)
Berkshire Comm Coll (MA)
Black Hawk Coll, Moline (IL)
Bowling Green State U-Firelands Coll (OH)
Bronx Comm Coll of City U of NY (NY)
Burlington County Coll (NJ)
Butler County Comm Coll (PA)
Caldwell Comm Coll and Tech Inst (NC)
Cape Cod Comm Coll (MA)
Casper Coll (WY)
Centralia Coll (WA)
Central Oregon Comm Coll (OR)
Cerritos Coll (CA)
Cerro Coso Comm Coll (CA)
Chabot Coll (CA)
Chattahoochee Valley Comm Coll (AL)
Chipola Jr Coll (FL)
City Coll of San Francisco (CA)
City Colls of Chicago, Harry S Truman Coll (IL)
City Colls of Chicago, Richard J Daley Coll (IL)
City Colls of Chicago, Wilbur Wright Coll (IL)
Clark Coll (WA)
Coastal Georgia Comm Coll (GA)
Cochise Coll, Douglas (AZ)
Coffeyville Comm Coll (KS)
Colby Comm Coll (KS)
Coll of Eastern Utah (UT)
Coll of the Canyons (CA)
Coll of the Desert (CA)
Coll of the Sequoias (CA)
Columbia State Comm Coll (TN)
The Comm Coll of Baltimore County–Catonsville Campus (MD)
Compton Comm Coll (CA)
Corning Comm Coll (NY)
Cowley County Comm Coll and Voc-Tech School (KS)
Crafton Hills Coll (CA)
Crowder Coll (MO)
Cuesta Coll (CA)
Cumberland County Coll (NJ)
Danville Area Comm Coll (IL)
Darton Coll (GA)
De Anza Coll (CA)
Del Mar Coll (TX)
Delta Coll (MI)
Diné Coll (AZ)
Dodge City Comm Coll (KS)
East Central Coll (MO)
East Central Comm Coll (MS)
Eastern Oklahoma State Coll (OK)
East Mississippi Comm Coll (MS)
Edison State Comm Coll (OH)
Ellsworth Comm Coll (IA)
Enterprise State Jr Coll (AL)
Essex County Coll (NJ)
Everett Comm Coll (WA)
Evergreen Valley Coll (CA)
Fergus Falls Comm Coll (MN)
Finger Lakes Comm Coll (NY)
Garden City Comm Coll (KS)
Gavilan Coll (CA)
Georgia Military Coll (GA)
Georgia Perimeter Coll (GA)
Golden West Coll (CA)
Grayson County Coll (TX)
Greenfield Comm Coll (MA)
Greenville Tech Coll (SC)
Henry Ford Comm Coll (MI)
Hibbing Comm Coll (MN)
Highland Comm Coll (IL)
Highland Comm Coll (KS)
Highline Comm Coll (WA)
Hill Coll of the Hill Jr College District (TX)
Hinds Comm Coll (MS)
Holyoke Comm Coll (MA)
Horry-Georgetown Tech Coll (SC)
Housatonic Comm Coll (CT)
Imperial Valley Coll (CA)
Independence Comm Coll (KS)
Indian River Comm Coll (FL)
Iowa Lakes Comm Coll (IA)
Isothermal Comm Coll (NC)
Itasca Comm Coll (MN)
Jamestown Comm Coll (NY)
Jefferson Coll (MO)
Jefferson Comm Coll (NY)
John A. Logan Coll (IL)
Joliet Jr Coll (IL)
Kalamazoo Valley Comm Coll (MI)
Kirkwood Comm Coll (IA)
Labette Comm Coll (KS)
Lake Michigan Coll (MI)
Lamar Comm Coll (CO)
Lansing Comm Coll (MI)
Laramie County Comm Coll (WY)
Lenoir Comm Coll (NC)
Lewis and Clark Comm Coll (IL)
Lincoln Land Comm Coll (IL)
Linn-Benton Comm Coll (OR)
Long Beach City Coll (CA)
Longview Comm Coll (MO)
Lon Morris Coll (TX)
Lorain County Comm Coll (OH)
Los Angeles Harbor Coll (CA)
Los Angeles Pierce Coll (CA)
Louisburg Coll (NC)
Lower Columbia Coll (WA)
Macomb Comm Coll (MI)
Maple Woods Comm Coll (MO)
Marshalltown Comm Coll (IA)
Merced Coll (CA)
Mesabi Range Comm and Tech Coll (MN)
Metropolitan Comm Coll (NE)
Miami-Dade Comm Coll (FL)
Miami U–Middletown Campus (OH)
Middlesex Comm Coll (MA)
Midland Coll (TX)
Mid Michigan Comm Coll (MI)
Milwaukee Area Tech Coll (WI)
Mississippi Gulf Coast Comm Coll (MS)
Moberly Area Comm Coll (MO)
Mohawk Valley Comm Coll (NY)
Monroe County Comm Coll (MI)
Mountain Empire Comm Coll (VA)
Naugatuck Valley Comm Coll (CT)
Navarro Coll (TX)
Neosho County Comm Coll (KS)
New Mexico Military Inst (NM)
North Central Michigan Coll (MI)
North Central Texas Coll (TX)
Northeast Alabama Comm Coll (AL)
Northern Virginia Comm Coll (VA)
North Harris Coll (TX)
North Hennepin Comm Coll (MN)
North Shore Comm Coll (MA)
Northwest Coll (WY)
Northwestern Connecticut Comm-Tech Coll (CT)
Northwest-Shoals Comm Coll (AL)
Oakland Comm Coll (MI)
Oakton Comm Coll (IL)
Odessa Coll (TX)
Oklahoma City Comm Coll (OK)
Otero Jr Coll (CO)
Palm Beach Comm Coll (FL)
Palo Verde Coll (CA)
Pensacola Jr Coll (FL)
Piedmont Virginia Comm Coll (VA)
Polk Comm Coll (FL)
Portland Comm Coll (OR)
Pratt Comm Coll and Area Vocational School (KS)
Quinsigamond Comm Coll (MA)
Rainy River Comm Coll (MN)
Reading Area Comm Coll (PA)
Richland Comm Coll (IL)
Ridgewater Coll (MN)
Roane State Comm Coll (TN)
Saint Charles Comm Coll (MO)
St. Louis Comm Coll at Florissant Valley (MO)
St. Philip's Coll (TX)
San Bernardino Valley Coll (CA)
Sandhills Comm Coll (NC)
San Diego City Coll (CA)
San Jacinto Coll Central Campus (TX)
San Jacinto Coll South Campus (TX)
Santa Monica Coll (CA)
Sauk Valley Comm Coll (IL)
Seminole State Coll (OK)
Shoreline Comm Coll (WA)
Skagit Valley Coll (WA)
Snow Coll (UT)
South Mountain Comm Coll (AZ)
South Plains Coll (TX)
South Suburban Coll (IL)
Southwestern Coll (CA)
State U of NY Coll of A&T at Morrisville (NY)
Tacoma Comm Coll (WA)
Taft Coll (CA)
Three Rivers Comm Coll (CT)
Trinidad State Jr Coll (CO)
Trinity Valley Comm Coll (TX)
Tulsa Comm Coll (OK)
Umpqua Comm Coll (OR)
U of New Mexico–Los Alamos Branch (NM)
Vermilion Comm Coll (MN)
Vincennes U (IN)
Virginia Western Comm Coll (VA)
Wake Tech Comm Coll (NC)
Walters State Comm Coll (TN)
Western Nebraska Comm Coll (NE)
Western Piedmont Comm Coll (NC)
Western Wyoming Comm Coll (WY)
West Virginia U at Parkersburg (WV)
Wharton County Jr Coll (TX)
Young Harris Coll (GA)

PRE-LAW

Allen County Comm Coll (KS)
Centralia Coll (WA)
Central Wyoming Coll (WY)
Dixie State Coll of Utah (UT)
Eastern Arizona Coll (AZ)
Kellogg Comm Coll (MI)
Lincoln Land Comm Coll (IL)
Louisburg Coll (NC)
Riverside Comm Coll (CA)
Western Nebraska Comm Coll (NE)

PRE-MEDICINE

Allen County Comm Coll (KS)
Centralia Coll (WA)
City Colls of Chicago, Malcolm X Coll (IL)
Coastal Georgia Comm Coll (GA)
Eastern Arizona Coll (AZ)
Eastern Wyoming Coll (WY)
Georgia Perimeter Coll (GA)
Howard Comm Coll (MD)
Kellogg Comm Coll (MI)
Lincoln Land Comm Coll (IL)
Louisburg Coll (NC)
St. Philip's Coll (TX)
San Juan Coll (NM)
Tulsa Comm Coll (OK)
Western Nebraska Comm Coll (NE)

PRE-PHARMACY STUDIES

Allen County Comm Coll (KS)
Amarillo Coll (TX)
Andrew Coll (GA)
Angelina Coll (TX)

Centralia Coll (WA)
City Colls of Chicago, Malcolm X Coll (IL)
Coastal Georgia Comm Coll (GA)
Coll of Southern Idaho (ID)
Delta Coll (MI)
Dodge City Comm Coll (KS)
Eastern Arizona Coll (AZ)
Eastern Wyoming Coll (WY)
Georgia Perimeter Coll (GA)
Howard Comm Coll (MD)
Kellogg Comm Coll (MI)
Kilgore Coll (TX)
Lincoln Land Comm Coll (IL)
Louisburg Coll (NC)
Luzerne County Comm Coll (PA)
Manatee Comm Coll (FL)
Monroe Comm Coll (NY)
Reading Area Comm Coll (PA)
Tacoma Comm Coll (WA)
Tulsa Comm Coll (OK)
Western Nebraska Comm Coll (NE)

PRE-THEOLOGY
Bacone Coll (OK)
Kellogg Comm Coll (MI)

PRE-VETERINARY STUDIES
Allen County Comm Coll (KS)
Centralia Coll (WA)
Coastal Georgia Comm Coll (GA)
Eastern Wyoming Coll (WY)
Howard Comm Coll (MD)
Kellogg Comm Coll (MI)
Lincoln Land Comm Coll (IL)
Louisburg Coll (NC)
Tulsa Comm Coll (OK)
Western Nebraska Comm Coll (NE)

PRINTING PRESS OPERATION
Lake Land Coll (IL)

PRINTMAKING
De Anza Coll (CA)
Dixie State Coll of Utah (UT)
Florida Comm Coll at Jacksonville (FL)
Inst of American Indian Arts (NM)

PROFESSIONAL STUDIES
Pratt Comm Coll and Area Vocational School (KS)

PROTECTIVE SERVICES RELATED
Pima Comm Coll (AZ)

PSYCHIATRIC/MENTAL HEALTH SERVICES
Bunker Hill Comm Coll (MA)
Comm Coll of Allegheny County (PA)
Comm Coll of Rhode Island (RI)
Cypress Coll (CA)
Dutchess Comm Coll (NY)
Eastfield Coll (TX)
Hagerstown Comm Coll (MD)
Houston Comm Coll System (TX)
Ivy Tech State Coll–Central Indiana (IN)
Ivy Tech State Coll–Eastcentral (IN)
Ivy Tech State Coll–Northeast (IN)
Ivy Tech State Coll–Southcentral (IN)
Ivy Tech State Coll–Wabash Valley (IN)
Montgomery Coll (MD)
Montgomery County Comm Coll (PA)
North Dakota State Coll of Science (ND)
Pennsylvania Coll of Technology (PA)
Pikes Peak Comm Coll (CO)
Pitt Comm Coll (NC)
San Joaquin Delta Coll (CA)
South Piedmont Comm Coll (NC)
Wayne Comm Coll (NC)

PSYCHOLOGY
Abraham Baldwin Ag Coll (GA)
Allegany Coll of Maryland (MD)
Allen County Comm Coll (KS)
Amarillo Coll (TX)
Andrew Coll (GA)
Atlanta Metropolitan Coll (GA)
Atlantic Cape Comm Coll (NJ)
Austin Comm Coll (TX)
Bainbridge Coll (GA)
Bakersfield Coll (CA)
Barton County Comm Coll (KS)
Bergen Comm Coll (NJ)
Blinn Coll (TX)
Brazosport Coll (TX)
Bronx Comm Coll of City U of NY (NY)
Brookdale Comm Coll (NJ)
Bucks County Comm Coll (PA)
Burlington County Coll (NJ)
Butler County Comm Coll (PA)
Butte Coll (CA)
Cañada Coll (CA)
Cape Cod Comm Coll (MA)
Casper Coll (WY)
Centralia Coll (WA)
Central Wyoming Coll (WY)
Cerritos Coll (CA)
Cerro Coso Comm Coll (CA)
Chabot Coll (CA)
Chaffey Coll (CA)
Cisco Jr Coll (TX)
City Coll of San Francisco (CA)
Clovis Comm Coll (NM)
Coastal Bend Coll (TX)
Coastal Georgia Comm Coll (GA)
Cochise Coll, Douglas (AZ)
Coffeyville Comm Coll (KS)
Colby Comm Coll (KS)
Coll of Alameda (CA)
Coll of Marin (CA)
Coll of Southern Idaho (ID)
Coll of the Canyons (CA)
Coll of the Desert (CA)
Coll of the Siskiyous (CA)
Colorado Mountn Coll (CO)
Colorado Mountn Coll, Timberline Cmps (CO)
Columbia State Comm Coll (TN)
Comm Coll of Allegheny County (PA)
Compton Comm Coll (CA)
Connors State Coll (OK)
Crafton Hills Coll (CA)
Crowder Coll (MO)
Cuesta Coll (CA)
Cypress Coll (CA)
Danville Area Comm Coll (IL)
Darton Coll (GA)
Daytona Beach Comm Coll (FL)
De Anza Coll (CA)
Delaware County Comm Coll (PA)
Del Mar Coll (TX)
Delta Coll (MI)
Dixie State Coll of Utah (UT)
Dodge City Comm Coll (KS)
Donnelly Coll (KS)
East Central Coll (MO)
East Central Comm Coll (MS)
Eastern Arizona Coll (AZ)
Eastern Oklahoma State Coll (OK)
Eastern Wyoming Coll (WY)
East Georgia Coll (GA)
East Mississippi Comm Coll (MS)
Ellsworth Comm Coll (IA)
Everett Comm Coll (WA)
Finger Lakes Comm Coll (NY)
Fisher Coll (MA)
Floyd Coll (GA)
Foothill Coll (CA)
Frederick Comm Coll (MD)
Fullerton Coll (CA)
Fulton-Montgomery Comm Coll (NY)
GateWay Comm Coll (AZ)
Gavilan Coll (CA)
Genesee Comm Coll (NY)
Georgia Perimeter Coll (GA)
Gloucester County Coll (NJ)
Gogebic Comm Coll (MI)
Gordon Coll (GA)
Grayson County Coll (TX)
Great Basin Coll (NV)
Harcum Coll (PA)
Harford Comm Coll (MD)
Harrisburg Area Comm Coll (PA)
Hesser Coll (NH)
Highland Comm Coll (IL)
Highland Comm Coll (KS)
Highline Comm Coll (WA)
Hill Coll of the Hill Jr College District (TX)
Hinds Comm Coll (MS)
Howard Comm Coll (MD)
Hutchinson Comm Coll and Area Vocational School (KS)
Imperial Valley Coll (CA)
Independence Comm Coll (KS)
Indian River Comm Coll (FL)
Iowa Lakes Comm Coll (IA)
Jefferson Coll (MO)
John A. Logan Coll (IL)
Joliet Jr Coll (IL)
Kankakee Comm Coll (IL)
Kellogg Comm Coll (MI)
Kilgore Coll (TX)
Kingwood Coll (TX)
Kirkwood Comm Coll (IA)
Lake Michigan Coll (MI)
Lake Tahoe Comm Coll (CA)
Laramie County Comm Coll (WY)
Lincoln Coll, Lincoln (IL)
Lincoln Coll, Normal (IL)
Lincoln Land Comm Coll (IL)
Lon Morris Coll (TX)
Lorain County Comm Coll (OH)
Los Angeles City Coll (CA)
Los Angeles Mission Coll (CA)
Louisburg Coll (NC)
Lower Columbia Coll (WA)
Manatee Comm Coll (FL)
Manor Coll (PA)
Miami-Dade Comm Coll (FL)
Miami U–Middletown Campus (OH)
Middlesex County Coll (NJ)
Midland Coll (TX)
Mid Michigan Comm Coll (MI)
MiraCosta Coll (CA)
Mitchell Coll (CT)
Mitchell Comm Coll (NC)
Mohave Comm Coll (AZ)
Monroe County Comm Coll (MI)
Monterey Peninsula Coll (CA)
Navarro Coll (TX)
Newbury Coll (MA)
Northern Virginia Comm Coll (VA)
North Idaho Coll (ID)
Odessa Coll (TX)
Oklahoma City Comm Coll (OK)
Otero Jr Coll (CO)
Palm Beach Comm Coll (FL)
Palo Verde Coll (CA)
Pasadena City Coll (CA)
Pensacola Jr Coll (FL)
Pratt Comm Coll and Area Vocational School (KS)
Quincy Coll (MA)
Reading Area Comm Coll (PA)
Red Rocks Comm Coll (CO)
Ridgewater Coll (MN)
Riverside Comm Coll (CA)
Sacramento City Coll (CA)
St. Philip's Coll (TX)
San Antonio Coll (TX)
San Bernardino Valley Coll (CA)
San Diego City Coll (CA)
San Diego Mesa Coll (CA)
San Jacinto Coll Central Campus (TX)
San Jacinto Coll North Campus (TX)
San Jacinto Coll South Campus (TX)
San Joaquin Delta Coll (CA)
San Juan Coll (NM)
Santa Ana Coll (CA)
Santa Barbara City Coll (CA)
Santa Monica Coll (CA)
Sauk Valley Comm Coll (IL)
Skagit Valley Coll (WA)
South Mountain Comm Coll (AZ)
Southwestern Coll (CA)
Tacoma Comm Coll (WA)
Terra State Comm Coll (OH)
Trinidad State Jr Coll (CO)
Trinity Valley Comm Coll (TX)
Triton Coll (IL)
Tulsa Comm Coll (OK)
Tyler Jr Coll (TX)
Umpqua Comm Coll (OR)
Vermilion Comm Coll (MN)
Vincennes U (IN)
Vincennes U Jasper Campus (IN)
Waycross Coll (GA)
Western Nebraska Comm Coll (NE)
Western Wyoming Comm Coll (WY)
Young Harris Coll (GA)

PUBLIC ADMINISTRATION
Anne Arundel Comm Coll (MD)
Barton County Comm Coll (KS)
Citrus Coll (CA)
City Coll of San Francisco (CA)
County Coll of Morris (NJ)
Del Mar Coll (TX)
East Central Coll (MO)
Eugenio María de Hostos Comm Coll of City U of NY (NY)
Fayetteville Tech Comm Coll (NC)
Fort Berthold Comm Coll (ND)
Hinds Comm Coll (MS)
Housatonic Comm Coll (CT)
Jefferson Coll (MO)
Lansing Comm Coll (MI)
Laramie County Comm Coll (WY)
Los Angeles City Coll (CA)
Manatee Comm Coll (FL)
Mesa Tech Coll (NM)
Miami-Dade Comm Coll (FL)
Middle Georgia Coll (GA)
Mountain Empire Comm Coll (VA)
Mt. San Jacinto Coll (CA)
Northeast Comm Coll (NE)
Palomar Coll (CA)
Pikes Peak Comm Coll (CO)
Reading Area Comm Coll (PA)
Red Rocks Comm Coll (CO)
Salem Comm Coll (NJ)
San Antonio Coll (TX)
San Jacinto Coll North Campus (TX)
San Joaquin Delta Coll (CA)
San Juan Coll (NM)
Scottsdale Comm Coll (AZ)
Sinclair Comm Coll (OH)
Southwestern Coll (CA)
Tallahassee Comm Coll (FL)
Thomas Nelson Comm Coll (VA)
Three Rivers Comm Coll (CT)
Vincennes U (IN)
Westchester Comm Coll (NY)
Westmoreland County Comm Coll (PA)

PUBLIC HEALTH
City Coll of San Francisco (CA)
Hill Coll of the Hill Jr College District (TX)

PUBLIC HEALTH EDUCATION/ PROMOTION
Coll of Southern Idaho (ID)

PUBLIC HEALTH RELATED
Western Wisconsin Tech Coll (WI)

PUBLIC POLICY ANALYSIS
Anne Arundel Comm Coll (MD)
Del Mar Coll (TX)
Fort Scott Comm Coll (KS)
Hill Coll of the Hill Jr College District (TX)

PUBLIC RELATIONS
Amarillo Coll (TX)
Black Hawk Coll, Moline (IL)
Brookdale Comm Coll (NJ)
Coastal Bend Coll (TX)
Comm Coll of Beaver County (PA)
Comm Coll of the Air Force (AL)
Crowder Coll (MO)
Glendale Comm Coll (AZ)
Golden West Coll (CA)
Harford Comm Coll (MD)
Kellogg Comm Coll (MI)
Kirkwood Comm Coll (IA)
Lansing Comm Coll (MI)
Los Angeles City Coll (CA)
Northwestern Business Coll (IL)
Vincennes U (IN)

PUBLISHING
Hennepin Tech Coll (MN)
Milwaukee Area Tech Coll (WI)
Westmoreland County Comm Coll (PA)

PURCHASING/CONTRACTS MANAGEMENT
Cincinnati State Tech and Comm Coll (OH)
Columbus State Comm Coll (OH)
Comm Coll of the Air Force (AL)
De Anza Coll (CA)
Fullerton Coll (CA)
Herkimer County Comm Coll (NY)
Northern Virginia Comm Coll (VA)
Shoreline Comm Coll (WA)
South Puget Sound Comm Coll (WA)
Tulsa Comm Coll (OK)

QUALITY CONTROL/SAFETY TECHNOLOGIES RELATED
Clover Park Tech Coll (WA)

QUALITY CONTROL TECHNOLOGY
Arkansas State U–Beebe (AR)
Austin Comm Coll (TX)
Bowling Green State U-Firelands Coll (OH)
Brazosport Coll (TX)
Brevard Comm Coll (FL)
Butler County Comm Coll (PA)
Central Carolina Comm Coll (NC)
Central Comm Coll–Columbus Campus (NE)
Century Comm and Tech Coll (MN)
Chaffey Coll (CA)
Chippewa Valley Tech Coll (WI)
Coll of the Canyons (CA)
Columbus State Comm Coll (OH)
Comm Coll of Allegheny County (PA)
The Comm Coll of Baltimore County–Catonsville Campus (MD)
Delta Coll (MI)
Des Moines Area Comm Coll (IA)
Edison State Comm Coll (OH)
Elizabethtown Comm Coll (KY)
Fort Scott Comm Coll (KS)
Gateway Tech Coll (WI)
Grand Rapids Comm Coll (MI)
Heartland Comm Coll (IL)
Henry Ford Comm Coll (MI)
Illinois Eastern Comm Colls, Frontier Comm Coll (IL)
Illinois Eastern Comm Colls, Lincoln Trail Coll (IL)
Kishwaukee Coll (IL)
Lakeshore Tech Coll (WI)
Lamar Comm Coll (CO)
Lansing Comm Coll (MI)
Lima Tech Coll (OH)
Longview Comm Coll (MO)
Lorain County Comm Coll (OH)
Los Angeles Pierce Coll (CA)
Macomb Comm Coll (MI)
Mid-State Tech Coll (WI)
Monroe Comm Coll (NY)
Moraine Valley Comm Coll (IL)
Mott Comm Coll (MI)
Mountain View Coll (TX)
Naugatuck Valley Comm Coll (CT)
Northampton County Area Comm Coll (PA)
Oklahoma State U, Oklahoma City (OK)
Onondaga Comm Coll (NY)
Pennsylvania Coll of Technology (PA)
Ridgewater Coll (MN)
St. Clair County Comm Coll (MI)
St. Petersburg Coll (FL)
Santa Ana Coll (CA)
Schenectady County Comm Coll (NY)
Sinclair Comm Coll (OH)
Southeast Comm Coll, Milford Campus (NE)
Spartan School of Aeronautics (OK)
Springfield Tech Comm Coll (MA)
Tarrant County Coll District (TX)
Terra State Comm Coll (OH)
Texas State Tech Coll– Waco/ Marshall Campus (TX)
Tri-County Tech Coll (SC)
Tulsa Comm Coll (OK)
Waubonsee Comm Coll (IL)
Wisconsin Indianhead Tech Coll (WI)

RADIOLOGICAL SCIENCE
Amarillo Coll (TX)
Blackhawk Tech Coll (WI)
Brookdale Comm Coll (NJ)
Carolinas Coll of Health Sciences (NC)
Central Virginia Comm Coll (VA)
Comm Coll of Denver (CO)
Comm Coll of Southern Nevada (NV)
Delta Coll (MI)
Eastern Maine Tech Coll (ME)
Edgecombe Comm Coll (NC)
Edison Comm Coll (FL)
El Centro Coll (TX)

Fayetteville Tech Comm Coll (NC)
Florida Hospital Coll of Health Sciences (FL)
Floyd Coll (GA)
Foothill Coll (CA)
Georgia Perimeter Coll (GA)
Hillsborough Comm Coll (FL)
Holyoke Comm Coll (MA)
Jackson State Comm Coll (TN)
Lakeland Comm Coll (OH)
Lakeshore Tech Coll (WI)
Laredo Comm Coll (TX)
Los Angeles City Coll (CA)
Louisiana State U at Eunice (LA)
Madisonville Comm Coll (KY)
Manatee Comm Coll (FL)
Miami-Dade Comm Coll (FL)
Middlesex Comm Coll (MA)
Middlesex County Coll (NJ)
Mitchell Tech Inst (SD)
Niagara County Comm Coll (NY)
Northcentral Tech Coll (WI)
Pasco-Hernando Comm Coll (FL)
Pensacola Jr Coll (FL)
Polk Comm Coll (FL)
Prince George's Comm Coll (MD)
Rowan-Cabarrus Comm Coll (NC)
St. Petersburg Coll (FL)
Sandhills Comm Coll (NC)
Sanford-Brown Coll, Fenton (MO)
Sinclair Comm Coll (OH)
Southeast Arkansas Coll (AR)
Southern Maine Tech Coll (ME)
Tacoma Comm Coll (WA)
Triton Coll (IL)
Trocaire Coll (NY)
Truckee Meadows Comm Coll (NV)
Tulsa Comm Coll (OK)
Virginia Western Comm Coll (VA)
Waycross Coll (GA)
Western Nebraska Comm Coll (NE)
Western Wisconsin Tech Coll (WI)

RADIO/TELEVISION BROADCASTING
Adirondack Comm Coll (NY)
Allegany Coll of Maryland (MD)
Alvin Comm Coll (TX)
Amarillo Coll (TX)
The Art Inst of Fort Lauderdale (FL)
The Art Inst of Pittsburgh (PA)
Austin Comm Coll (TX)
Black Hawk Coll, Moline (IL)
Brevard Comm Coll (FL)
Bucks County Comm Coll (PA)
Cayuga County Comm Coll (NY)
Central Carolina Comm Coll (NC)
Centralia Coll (WA)
Central Texas Coll (TX)
Chabot Coll (CA)
Chattanooga State Tech Comm Coll (TN)
Coahoma Comm Coll (MS)
Coffeyville Comm Coll (KS)
Colby Comm Coll (KS)
The Comm Coll of Baltimore County–Catonsville Campus (MD)
Comm Coll of Southern Nevada (NV)
Cuesta Coll (CA)
Daytona Beach Comm Coll (FL)
De Anza Coll (CA)
Del Mar Coll (TX)
Delta Coll (MI)
Dixie State Coll of Utah (UT)
Dodge City Comm Coll (KS)
Douglas MacArthur State Tech Coll (AL)
Draughons Jr Coll, Clarksville (TN)
Draughons Jr Coll, Nashville (TN)
Foothill Coll (CA)
Fullerton Coll (CA)
Golden West Coll (CA)
Gulf Coast Comm Coll (FL)
Herkimer County Comm Coll (NY)
Hesser Coll (NH)
Holmes Comm Coll (MS)
Hutchinson Comm Coll and Area Vocational School (KS)
Illinois Eastern Comm Colls, Wabash Valley Coll (IL)
International Coll of Broadcasting (OH)
Iowa Lakes Comm Coll (IA)
Isothermal Comm Coll (NC)
Kirkwood Comm Coll (IA)
Lake Land Coll (IL)
Lane Comm Coll (OR)
Lansing Comm Coll (MI)
Lewis and Clark Comm Coll (IL)
Lincoln Coll, Lincoln (IL)
Long Beach City Coll (CA)
Los Angeles City Coll (CA)
Manatee Comm Coll (FL)
Miami-Dade Comm Coll (FL)
Milwaukee Area Tech Coll (WI)
Modesto Jr Coll (CA)
Mt. Hood Comm Coll (OR)
National Coll of Business & Technology, Lexington (KY)
Navarro Coll (TX)
NEI Coll of Technology (MN)
Newbury Coll (MA)
Northeast Comm Coll (NE)
Northland Comm and Tech Coll (MN)
Northwest Mississippi Comm Coll (MS)
Odessa Coll (TX)
Onondaga Comm Coll (NY)
Oxnard Coll (CA)
Palomar Coll (CA)
Parkland Coll (IL)
Pasadena City Coll (CA)
Pima Comm Coll (AZ)
St. Louis Comm Coll at Florissant Valley (MO)
San Antonio Coll (TX)
San Bernardino Valley Coll (CA)
San Diego City Coll (CA)
Santa Monica Coll (CA)
Sullivan County Comm Coll (NY)
Tompkins Cortland Comm Coll (NY)
Tri-County Tech Coll (SC)
Tulsa Comm Coll (OK)
Vincennes U (IN)
Virginia Western Comm Coll (VA)

RADIO/TELEVISION BROADCASTING TECHNOLOGY
Bates Tech Coll (WA)
Black Hawk Coll, Moline (IL)
Briarwood Coll (CT)
Brookdale Comm Coll (NJ)
Bunker Hill Comm Coll (MA)
Cayuga County Comm Coll (NY)
Cedar Valley Coll (TX)
Central Comm Coll–Hastings Campus (NE)
Central Wyoming Coll (WY)
Cincinnati State Tech and Comm Coll (OH)
County Coll of Morris (NJ)
Gadsden State Comm Coll (AL)
Gateway Tech Coll (WI)
Hillsborough Comm Coll (FL)
Houston Comm Coll System (TX)
Jefferson State Comm Coll (AL)
John Wood Comm Coll (IL)
Kellogg Comm Coll (MI)
Luzerne County Comm Coll (PA)
Manatee Comm Coll (FL)
Mercer County Comm Coll (NJ)
Mineral Area Coll (MO)
New England Inst of Art & Communications (MA)
New England Inst of Technology (RI)
Northampton County Area Comm Coll (PA)
Northwest Mississippi Comm Coll (MS)
Parkland Coll (IL)
Santa Fe Comm Coll (NM)
Schoolcraft Coll (MI)
Scott Comm Coll (IA)
Wilkes Comm Coll (NC)

RANGE MANAGEMENT
Colby Comm Coll (KS)
Coll of Southern Idaho (ID)
Dixie State Coll of Utah (UT)
Eastern Oklahoma State Coll (OK)
Lamar Comm Coll (CO)
Northeast Texas Comm Coll (TX)
Northwest Coll (WY)
St. Catharine Coll (KY)
Snow Coll (UT)
Trinity Valley Comm Coll (TX)
Vermilion Comm Coll (MN)

READING EDUCATION
East Mississippi Comm Coll (MS)
San Jacinto Coll North Campus (TX)

REAL ESTATE
Alamance Comm Coll (NC)
Amarillo Coll (TX)
American River Coll (CA)
Angelina Coll (TX)
Anne Arundel Comm Coll (MD)
Antelope Valley Coll (CA)
Ashland Comm Coll (KY)
Austin Comm Coll (TX)
Bakersfield Coll (CA)
Bellevue Comm Coll (WA)
Bergen Comm Coll (NJ)
Black Hawk Coll, Moline (IL)
Blinn Coll (TX)
Brevard Comm Coll (FL)
Butte Coll (CA)
Camden County Coll (NJ)
Carl Sandburg Coll (IL)
Catawba Valley Comm Coll (NC)
Cedar Valley Coll (TX)
Central Piedmont Comm Coll (NC)
Cerritos Coll (CA)
Chabot Coll (CA)
Chaffey Coll (CA)
Chemeketa Comm Coll (OR)
Chippewa Valley Tech Coll (WI)
Cincinnati State Tech and Comm Coll (OH)
Cisco Jr Coll (TX)
Citrus Coll (CA)
City Coll of San Francisco (CA)
Coll of DuPage (IL)
Coll of Marin (CA)
Coll of Southern Idaho (ID)
Coll of the Canyons (CA)
Coll of the Desert (CA)
Coll of the Redwoods (CA)
Coll of the Sequoias (CA)
Collin County Comm Coll District (TX)
Columbia-Greene Comm Coll (NY)
Columbus State Comm Coll (OH)
Comm Coll of Allegheny County (PA)
The Comm Coll of Baltimore County–Catonsville Campus (MD)
Comm Coll of Southern Nevada (NV)
Compton Comm Coll (CA)
Cuesta Coll (CA)
Cuyahoga Comm Coll (OH)
Cuyamaca Coll (CA)
Danville Area Comm Coll (IL)
De Anza Coll (CA)
Del Mar Coll (TX)
Delta Coll (MI)
Dodge City Comm Coll (KS)
Durham Tech Comm Coll (NC)
East Mississippi Comm Coll (MS)
Edgecombe Comm Coll (NC)
Edison State Comm Coll (OH)
Elizabethtown Comm Coll (KY)
Enterprise State Jr Coll (AL)
Florida Comm Coll at Jacksonville (FL)
Foothill Coll (CA)
Forsyth Tech Comm Coll (NC)
Fresno City Coll (CA)
Fullerton Coll (CA)
GateWay Comm Coll (AZ)
Glendale Comm Coll (AZ)
Glendale Comm Coll (CA)
Golden West Coll (CA)
Grayson County Coll (TX)
Harrisburg Area Comm Coll (PA)
Henry Ford Comm Coll (MI)
Hill Coll of the Hill Jr College District (TX)
Hinds Comm Coll (MS)
Houston Comm Coll System (TX)
Iowa Lakes Comm Coll (IA)
Isothermal Comm Coll (NC)
Jefferson Comm Coll (KY)
Jefferson Comm Coll (OH)
Joliet Jr Coll (IL)
Kankakee Comm Coll (IL)
Kent State U, Trumbull Campus (OH)
Lake Tahoe Comm Coll (CA)
Lamar State Coll–Orange (TX)
Lane Comm Coll (OR)
Lansing Comm Coll (MI)
Laredo Comm Coll (TX)
Las Positas Coll (CA)
Lehigh Carbon Comm Coll (PA)
Lincoln Land Comm Coll (IL)
Long Beach City Coll (CA)
Lorain County Comm Coll (OH)
Los Angeles City Coll (CA)
Los Angeles Harbor Coll (CA)
Los Angeles Mission Coll (CA)
Los Angeles Pierce Coll (CA)
Luzerne County Comm Coll (PA)
Madisonville Comm Coll (KY)
Mayland Comm Coll (NC)
McHenry County Coll (IL)
McLennan Comm Coll (TX)
Merced Coll (CA)
Miami U–Middletown Campus (OH)
Milwaukee Area Tech Coll (WI)
MiraCosta Coll (CA)
Modesto Jr Coll (CA)
Monterey Peninsula Coll (CA)
Montgomery County Comm Coll (PA)
Morton Coll (IL)
Mt. San Jacinto Coll (CA)
Nassau Comm Coll (NY)
Navarro Coll (TX)
New Hampshire Tech Inst (NH)
North Central Texas Coll (TX)
Northeast Alabama Comm Coll (AL)
Northeast Comm Coll (NE)
Northeast Texas Comm Coll (TX)
Northern Essex Comm Coll (MA)
North Seattle Comm Coll (WA)
Oakton Comm Coll (IL)
Ocean County Coll (NJ)
Okaloosa-Walton Comm Coll (FL)
Orange County Comm Coll (NY)
Oxnard Coll (CA)
Palomar Coll (CA)
Pasadena City Coll (CA)
Phoenix Coll (AZ)
Pima Comm Coll (AZ)
Portland Comm Coll (OR)
Rainy River Comm Coll (MN)
Raritan Valley Comm Coll (NJ)
Red Rocks Comm Coll (CO)
Ridgewater Coll (MN)
Sacramento City Coll (CA)
St. Louis Comm Coll at Florissant Valley (MO)
San Antonio Coll (TX)
San Bernardino Valley Coll (CA)
San Diego City Coll (CA)
San Diego Mesa Coll (CA)
San Jacinto Coll Central Campus (TX)
San Jacinto Coll North Campus (TX)
San Jacinto Coll South Campus (TX)
San Juan Coll (NM)
Santa Ana Coll (CA)
Santa Barbara City Coll (CA)
Santa Monica Coll (CA)
Scottsdale Comm Coll (AZ)
Shasta Coll (CA)
Sierra Coll (CA)
Sinclair Comm Coll (OH)
Southern State Comm Coll (OH)
South Plains Coll (TX)
Southwestern Coll (CA)
Spokane Falls Comm Coll (WA)
Suffolk County Comm Coll (NY)
Texarkana Coll (TX)
Tidewater Comm Coll (VA)
Trinity Valley Comm Coll (TX)
Triton Coll (IL)
Truckee Meadows Comm Coll (NV)
Tyler Jr Coll (TX)
U of Kentucky, Lexington Comm Coll (KY)
Ventura Coll (CA)
Victor Valley Coll (CA)
Wallace State Comm Coll (AL)
Western Nevada Comm Coll (NV)
Westmoreland County Comm Coll (PA)

RECEPTIONIST
Adirondack Comm Coll (NY)
Alexandria Tech Coll (MN)
Centralia Coll (WA)
Minot State U–Bottineau Campus (ND)

RECREATIONAL THERAPY
Butler County Comm Coll (PA)
Carteret Comm Coll (NC)
Colorado Mountn Coll (CO)
Comm Coll of Allegheny County (PA)
The Comm Coll of Baltimore County–Catonsville Campus (MD)
Cuesta Coll (CA)
Edmonds Comm Coll (WA)
Mitchell Coll (CT)
Moraine Valley Comm Coll (IL)
Northwestern Connecticut Comm-Tech Coll (CT)
Norwalk Comm Coll (CT)
Santa Barbara City Coll (CA)
State U of NY Coll of Technology at Canton (NY)
Suffolk County Comm Coll (NY)
Tulsa Comm Coll (OK)
Vincennes U (IN)
Western Piedmont Comm Coll (NC)

RECREATION/LEISURE FACILITIES MANAGEMENT
Abraham Baldwin Ag Coll (GA)
Allen County Comm Coll (KS)
Butler County Comm Coll (PA)
Butte Coll (CA)
Cerro Coso Comm Coll (CA)
Coastal Georgia Comm Coll (GA)
Coll of the Desert (CA)
Colorado Mountn Coll, Alpine Cmps (CO)
Colorado Mountn Coll, Timberline Cmps (CO)
Compton Comm Coll (CA)
County Coll of Morris (NJ)
Cuesta Coll (CA)
Erie Comm Coll, South Campus (NY)
Finger Lakes Comm Coll (NY)
Frederick Comm Coll (MD)
Hawkeye Comm Coll (IA)
Horry-Georgetown Tech Coll (SC)
James H. Faulkner State Comm Coll (AL)
Keystone Coll (PA)
Kirkwood Comm Coll (IA)
Minot State U–Bottineau Campus (ND)
Modesto Jr Coll (CA)
Mohawk Valley Comm Coll (NY)
Monterey Peninsula Coll (CA)
Moraine Valley Comm Coll (IL)
Muskingum Area Tech Coll (OH)
North Country Comm Coll (NY)
Northwest Coll (WY)
Northwestern Connecticut Comm-Tech Coll (CT)
Palomar Coll (CA)
Paul Smith's Coll of Arts and Sciences (NY)
Santa Fe Comm Coll (FL)
Skagit Valley Coll (WA)
Southeastern Comm Coll (NC)
Southwestern Coll (CA)
Spokane Comm Coll (WA)
State U of NY Coll of A&T at Morrisville (NY)
State U of NY Coll of Technology at Delhi (NY)
Vermilion Comm Coll (MN)
Wayne Comm Coll (NC)
Western Nevada Comm Coll (NV)
Western Texas Coll (TX)

RECREATION/LEISURE STUDIES
Allan Hancock Coll (CA)
Allegany Coll of Maryland (MD)
American River Coll (CA)
Atlanta Metropolitan Coll (GA)
Bakersfield Coll (CA)
Bellevue Comm Coll (WA)
Bergen Comm Coll (NJ)
Camden County Coll (NJ)
Cape Cod Comm Coll (MA)
Centralia Coll (WA)
Cerritos Coll (CA)
Chabot Coll (CA)
Chesapeake Coll (MD)
City Coll of San Francisco (CA)
Coastal Bend Coll (TX)
Coll of the Desert (CA)
Colorado Mountn Coll, Timberline Cmps (CO)

The Comm Coll of Baltimore County–Catonsville Campus (MD)
Comm Coll of Denver (CO)
Comm Coll of Southern Nevada (NV)
Comm Coll of the Air Force (AL)
Compton Comm Coll (CA)
Cowley County Comm Coll and Voc-Tech School (KS)
Del Mar Coll (TX)
Dutchess Comm Coll (NY)
East Central Coll (MO)
East Georgia Coll (GA)
Enterprise State Jr Coll (AL)
Fayetteville Tech Comm Coll (NC)
Feather River Comm Coll District (CA)
Frederick Comm Coll (MD)
Fresno City Coll (CA)
Fullerton Coll (CA)
Glendale Comm Coll (CA)
Gordon Coll (GA)
Greenfield Comm Coll (MA)
Iowa Lakes Comm Coll (IA)
Jefferson Davis Comm Coll (AL)
Kingsborough Comm Coll of City U of NY (NY)
Kirkwood Comm Coll (IA)
Miami-Dade Comm Coll (FL)
Mineral Area Coll (MO)
Mitchell Coll (CT)
Mohawk Valley Comm Coll (NY)
Monroe Comm Coll (NY)
Muskingum Area Tech Coll (OH)
Northern Essex Comm Coll (MA)
Northern Virginia Comm Coll (VA)
Northwest Coll (WY)
Northwestern Connecticut Comm-Tech Coll (CT)
Norwalk Comm Coll (CT)
Onondaga Comm Coll (NY)
Orange County Comm Coll (NY)
Palomar Coll (CA)
Pasadena City Coll (CA)
San Bernardino Valley Coll (CA)
San Diego City Coll (CA)
San Diego Mesa Coll (CA)
San Juan Coll (NM)
Santa Barbara City Coll (CA)
Santa Fe Comm Coll (NM)
Santa Monica Coll (CA)
Skagit Valley Coll (WA)
Southeastern Comm Coll (NC)
State U of NY Coll of Technology at Delhi (NY)
Suffolk County Comm Coll (NY)
Taft Coll (CA)
Tallahassee Comm Coll (FL)
Tompkins Cortland Comm Coll (NY)
Tyler Jr Coll (TX)
Ulster County Comm Coll (NY)
Vance-Granville Comm Coll (NC)
Ventura Coll (CA)
Vermilion Comm Coll (MN)
Vincennes U (IN)
Young Harris Coll (GA)

RECREATION PRODUCTS/ SERVICES MARKETING OPERATIONS
Cerro Coso Comm Coll (CA)
Vincennes U (IN)

REHABILITATION/THERAPEUTIC SERVICES RELATED
Clover Park Tech Coll (WA)
Comm Coll of Rhode Island (RI)
Springfield Tech Comm Coll (MA)
Union County Coll (NJ)

REHABILITATION THERAPY
Iowa Lakes Comm Coll (IA)
Nassau Comm Coll (NY)
Wayne Comm Coll (NC)

RELIGIOUS EDUCATION
Lincoln Coll, Lincoln (IL)
Lon Morris Coll (TX)

RELIGIOUS STUDIES
Allen County Comm Coll (KS)
Amarillo Coll (TX)
Andrew Coll (GA)
Chaffey Coll (CA)
Cowley County Comm Coll and Voc-Tech School (KS)
Crafton Hills Coll (CA)
East Central Coll (MO)
Fullerton Coll (CA)
Kilgore Coll (TX)
Lansing Comm Coll (MI)
Lon Morris Coll (TX)
Manatee Comm Coll (FL)
Northern Virginia Comm Coll (VA)
Orange Coast Coll (CA)
Palm Beach Comm Coll (FL)
Pasadena City Coll (CA)
Pensacola Jr Coll (FL)
Queen of the Holy Rosary Coll (CA)
San Bernardino Valley Coll (CA)
San Joaquin Delta Coll (CA)
Trinity Valley Comm Coll (TX)
Tulsa Comm Coll (OK)
Wallace State Comm Coll (AL)
Young Harris Coll (GA)

RESPIRATORY THERAPY
Albuquerque Tech Vocational Inst (NM)
Allegany Coll of Maryland (MD)
Alvin Comm Coll (TX)
Amarillo Coll (TX)
American River Coll (CA)
Andrew Coll (GA)
Angelina Coll (TX)
Ashland Comm Coll (KY)
Athens Tech Coll (GA)
Atlantic Cape Comm Coll (NJ)
Augusta Tech Coll (GA)
Baltimore City Comm Coll (MD)
Barton County Comm Coll (KS)
Bergen Comm Coll (NJ)
Berkshire Comm Coll (MA)
Borough of Manhattan Comm Coll of City U of NY (NY)
Bossier Parish Comm Coll (LA)
Bowling Green State U-Firelands Coll (OH)
Brevard Comm Coll (FL)
Brookdale Comm Coll (NJ)
Butte Coll (CA)
Camden County Coll (NJ)
Carteret Comm Coll (NC)
Catawba Valley Comm Coll (NC)
Central Piedmont Comm Coll (NC)
Central Virginia Comm Coll (VA)
Chattanooga State Tech Comm Coll (TN)
Cincinnati State Tech and Comm Coll (OH)
City Coll of San Francisco (CA)
City Colls of Chicago, Malcolm X Coll (IL)
Coastal Georgia Comm Coll (GA)
Coll of DuPage (IL)
Coll of St. Catherine–Minneapolis (MN)
Coll of Southern Idaho (ID)
Coll of the Desert (CA)
Collin County Comm Coll District (TX)
Columbia State Comm Coll (TN)
Columbus State Comm Coll (OH)
Comm Coll of Allegheny County (PA)
Comm Coll of Rhode Island (RI)
Comm Coll of Southern Nevada (NV)
Compton Comm Coll (CA)
Copiah-Lincoln Comm Coll–Natchez Campus (MS)
County Coll of Morris (NJ)
Crafton Hills Coll (CA)
Cuyahoga Comm Coll (OH)
Danville Area Comm Coll (IL)
Darton Coll (GA)
Daytona Beach Comm Coll (FL)
Delaware County Comm Coll (PA)
Delaware Tech & Comm Coll, Stanton/ Wilmington Cmps (DE)
Delgado Comm Coll (LA)
Del Mar Coll (TX)
Delta Coll (MI)
Des Moines Area Comm Coll (IA)
Dodge City Comm Coll (KS)
Doña Ana Branch Comm Coll (NM)
Durham Tech Comm Coll (NC)
Edgecombe Comm Coll (NC)
Edison Comm Coll (FL)
El Centro Coll (TX)
Erie Comm Coll, North Campus (NY)
Fayetteville Tech Comm Coll (NC)
Florence-Darlington Tech Coll (SC)
Florida Comm Coll at Jacksonville (FL)
Floyd Coll (GA)
Foothill Coll (CA)
Forsyth Tech Comm Coll (NC)
Frederick Comm Coll (MD)
Fresno City Coll (CA)
Front Range Comm Coll (CO)
GateWay Comm Coll (AZ)
Genesee Comm Coll (NY)
George Corley Wallace State Comm Coll (AL)
Gloucester County Coll (NJ)
Greenville Tech Coll (SC)
Guilford Tech Comm Coll (NC)
Gulf Coast Comm Coll (FL)
Gwinnett Tech Coll (GA)
Harrisburg Area Comm Coll (PA)
Hawkeye Comm Coll (IA)
Henry Ford Comm Coll (MI)
Highland Comm Coll (KS)
Highline Comm Coll (WA)
Hillsborough Comm Coll (FL)
Hinds Comm Coll (MS)
Holmes Comm Coll (MS)
Houston Comm Coll System (TX)
Howard Coll (TX)
Indian River Comm Coll (FL)
Ivy Tech State Coll–Central Indiana (IN)
Ivy Tech State Coll–Northeast (IN)
Ivy Tech State Coll–Northwest (IN)
Jackson State Comm Coll (TN)
Jefferson Comm Coll (KY)
Jefferson Comm Coll (OH)
Johnson County Comm Coll (KS)
J. Sargeant Reynolds Comm Coll (VA)
Kalamazoo Valley Comm Coll (MI)
Kankakee Comm Coll (IL)
Kansas City Kansas Comm Coll (KS)
Kaskaskia Coll (IL)
Kennebec Valley Tech Coll (ME)
Kirkwood Comm Coll (IA)
Labette Comm Coll (KS)
Lakeland Comm Coll (OH)
Lane Comm Coll (OR)
Lansing Comm Coll (MI)
Lehigh Carbon Comm Coll (PA)
Lima Tech Coll (OH)
Lincoln Land Comm Coll (IL)
Louisiana State U at Eunice (LA)
Luzerne County Comm Coll (PA)
Macomb Comm Coll (MI)
Madisonville Comm Coll (KY)
Manatee Comm Coll (FL)
Manchester Comm Coll (CT)
Massachusetts Bay Comm Coll (MA)
Massasoit Comm Coll (MA)
Maysville Comm Coll (KY)
McLennan Comm Coll (TX)
Mercer County Comm Coll (NJ)
Meridian Comm Coll (MS)
Metropolitan Comm Coll (NE)
Miami-Dade Comm Coll (FL)
Middlesex County Coll (NJ)
Midland Coll (TX)
Midlands Tech Coll (SC)
Mid-Plains Comm Coll Area (NE)
Mid-State Tech Coll (WI)
Milwaukee Area Tech Coll (WI)
Mississippi Gulf Coast Comm Coll (MS)
Modesto Jr Coll (CA)
Mohawk Valley Comm Coll (NY)
Monroe County Comm Coll (MI)
Montana State U Coll of Tech-Great Falls (MT)
Moraine Valley Comm Coll (IL)
Mott Comm Coll (MI)
Mt. Hood Comm Coll (OR)
Nassau Comm Coll (NY)
Northern Essex Comm Coll (MA)
Northern Virginia Comm Coll (VA)
North Harris Coll (TX)
North Shore Comm Coll (MA)
NorthWest Arkansas Comm Coll (AR)
Northwest Mississippi Comm Coll (MS)
Norwalk Comm Coll (CT)
Oakland Comm Coll (MI)
Odessa Coll (TX)
Oklahoma City Comm Coll (OK)
Onondaga Comm Coll (NY)
Orangeburg-Calhoun Tech Coll (SC)
Orange Coast Coll (CA)
Parkland Coll (IL)
Penn Valley Comm Coll (MO)
Pensacola Jr Coll (FL)
Piedmont Tech Coll (SC)
Pima Comm Coll (AZ)
Pitt Comm Coll (NC)
Prince George's Comm Coll (MD)
Quinsigamond Comm Coll (MA)
Raritan Valley Comm Coll (NJ)
Reading Area Comm Coll (PA)
Roane State Comm Coll (TN)
Robeson Comm Coll (NC)
Rockingham Comm Coll (NC)
Rockland Comm Coll (NY)
Rogue Comm Coll (OR)
St. Paul Tech Coll (MN)
St. Petersburg Coll (FL)
St. Philip's Coll (TX)
Sandhills Comm Coll (NC)
Sanford-Brown Coll, Fenton (MO)
San Jacinto Coll Central Campus (TX)
San Joaquin Valley Coll (CA)
Santa Fe Comm Coll (FL)
Santa Monica Coll (CA)
Scott Comm Coll (IA)
Seattle Central Comm Coll (WA)
Seminole Comm Coll (FL)
Sheridan Coll (WY)
Sinclair Comm Coll (OH)
Southeast Comm Coll (KY)
Southern Maine Tech Coll (ME)
South Plains Coll (TX)
Southside Virginia Comm Coll (VA)
Southwestern Comm Coll (NC)
Southwest Georgia Tech Coll (GA)
Southwest Virginia Comm Coll (VA)
Spartanburg Tech Coll (SC)
Spokane Comm Coll (WA)
Springfield Tech Comm Coll (MA)
Stanly Comm Coll (NC)
Stark State Coll of Technology (OH)
Sussex County Comm Coll (NJ)
Tacoma Comm Coll (WA)
Tallahassee Comm Coll (FL)
Tarrant County Coll District (TX)
Temple Coll (TX)
Trident Tech Coll (SC)
Triton Coll (IL)
Tulsa Comm Coll (OK)
Tyler Jr Coll (TX)
Union County Coll (NJ)
U of Arkansas at Fort Smith (AR)
U of Arkansas Comm Coll at Hope (AR)
U of Kentucky, Lexington Comm Coll (KY)
Victoria Coll (TX)
Victor Valley Coll (CA)
Vincennes U (IN)
Volunteer State Comm Coll (TN)
Wallace State Comm Coll (AL)
Waycross Coll (GA)
Weatherford Coll (TX)
Westchester Comm Coll (NY)
Western School of Health and Business Careers (PA)
Western Wisconsin Tech Coll (WI)
Western Wyoming Comm Coll (WY)

RESTAURANT OPERATIONS
City Colls of Chicago, Malcolm X Coll (IL)
Coll of DuPage (IL)
Comm Coll of Allegheny County (PA)
Cuyahoga Comm Coll (OH)
Erie Comm Coll, North Campus (NY)
Kaskaskia Coll (IL)
Keystone Coll (PA)
Linn-Benton Comm Coll (OR)
Moraine Valley Comm Coll (IL)
Orange Coast Coll (CA)
Pima Comm Coll (AZ)
Rasmussen Coll Mankato (MN)
State U of NY Coll of Technology at Alfred (NY)
State U of NY Coll of Technology at Delhi (NY)
Vincennes U (IN)

RETAILING OPERATIONS
Alexandria Tech Coll (MN)
Catawba Valley Comm Coll (NC)
Centralia Coll (WA)
Clark Coll (WA)
Coll of DuPage (IL)
Comm Coll of Allegheny County (PA)
Comm Coll of Rhode Island (RI)
Draughons Jr Coll, Clarksville (TN)
Edmonds Comm Coll (WA)
Ellsworth Comm Coll (IA)
Florida Comm Coll at Jacksonville (FL)
Garden City Comm Coll (KS)
Jefferson State Comm Coll (AL)
Johnson County Comm Coll (KS)
Montgomery County Comm Coll (PA)
Moraine Valley Comm Coll (IL)
North Central Texas Coll (TX)
Orange Coast Coll (CA)
Patricia Stevens Coll (MO)
Pitt Comm Coll (NC)
Waubonsee Comm Coll (IL)
Wayne Comm Coll (NC)
Western Wisconsin Tech Coll (WI)
Wisconsin Indianhead Tech Coll (WI)

RETAIL MANAGEMENT
American River Coll (CA)
Anne Arundel Comm Coll (MD)
Arapahoe Comm Coll (CO)
Austin Comm Coll (TX)
Bay State Coll (MA)
Bergen Comm Coll (NJ)
Bessemer State Tech Coll (AL)
Black Hawk Coll, Moline (IL)
Bowling Green State U-Firelands Coll (OH)
Bristol Comm Coll (MA)
Bryant and Stratton Coll, Virginia Beach (VA)
Bucks County Comm Coll (PA)
Cambria County Area Comm Coll (PA)
Casper Coll (WY)
Cayuga County Comm Coll (NY)
Centralia Coll (WA)
Central Pennsylvania Coll (PA)
Central Piedmont Comm Coll (NC)
Central Virginia Comm Coll (VA)
Chabot Coll (CA)
Chattanooga State Tech Comm Coll (TN)
Cisco Jr Coll (TX)
Clark Coll (WA)
Clinton Comm Coll (NY)
Coffeyville Comm Coll (KS)
Coll of Marin (CA)
Colorado Mountn Coll, Alpine Cmps (CO)
Columbus State Comm Coll (OH)
Comm Coll of Southern Nevada (NV)
Cowley County Comm Coll and Voc-Tech School (KS)
Delaware Tech & Comm Coll, Jack F Owens Cmps (DE)
Del Mar Coll (TX)
Delta Coll (MI)
Des Moines Area Comm Coll (IA)
Doña Ana Branch Comm Coll (NM)
Dutchess Comm Coll (NY)
Edison State Comm Coll (OH)
Ellsworth Comm Coll (IA)
Enterprise State Jr Coll (AL)
Everett Comm Coll (WA)
Fashion Inst of Design & Merchandising, LA Campus (CA)
Fashion Inst of Design & Merchandising, SD Campus (CA)
Fashion Inst of Design & Merchandising, SF Campus (CA)
Finger Lakes Comm Coll (NY)
Fort Scott Comm Coll (KS)
Garden City Comm Coll (KS)
Gateway Comm Coll (CT)
Genesee Comm Coll (NY)
Georgia Perimeter Coll (GA)
Glendale Comm Coll (AZ)
Gloucester County Coll (NJ)
Golden West Coll (CA)
Harcum Coll (PA)
Harford Comm Coll (MD)
Harrisburg Area Comm Coll (PA)
Hesser Coll (NH)
Holyoke Comm Coll (MA)
Howard Comm Coll (MD)
Indian River Comm Coll (FL)
International Business Coll, Fort Wayne (IN)

Iowa Lakes Comm Coll (IA)
Iowa Western Comm Coll (IA)
Jefferson Coll (MO)
Jefferson Comm Coll (NY)
Jefferson Comm Coll (OH)
John A. Logan Coll (IL)
Kirkwood Comm Coll (IA)
Lansing Comm Coll (MI)
Laramie County Comm Coll (WY)
Laurel Business Inst (PA)
Lenoir Comm Coll (NC)
Lima Tech Coll (OH)
Long Beach City Coll (CA)
Lorain County Comm Coll (OH)
Los Angeles City Coll (CA)
Madisonville Comm Coll (KY)
Merced Coll (CA)
Middlesex Comm Coll (MA)
Middlesex County Coll (NJ)
Midland Coll (TX)
Miles Comm Coll (MT)
Milwaukee Area Tech Coll (WI)
Minnesota State Coll–Southeast Tech (MN)
Mohawk Valley Comm Coll (NY)
Monroe Comm Coll (NY)
Navarro Coll (TX)
Newbury Coll (MA)
Niagara County Comm Coll (NY)
North Country Comm Coll (NY)
North Hennepin Comm Coll (MN)
North Iowa Area Comm Coll (IA)
Northland Comm and Tech Coll (MN)
Oakland Comm Coll (MI)
Orange County Comm Coll (NY)
Paducah Comm Coll (KY)
Parkland Coll (IL)
Quincy Coll (MA)
Quinsigamond Comm Coll (MA)
Raritan Valley Comm Coll (NJ)
Reading Area Comm Coll (PA)
Ridgewater Coll (MN)
St. Cloud Tech Coll (MN)
Salem Comm Coll (NJ)
Shoreline Comm Coll (WA)
Sinclair Comm Coll (OH)
South Plains Coll (TX)
South Suburban Coll (IL)
Southwestern Comm Coll (IA)
Spokane Falls Comm Coll (WA)
Stark State Coll of Technology (OH)
Suffolk County Comm Coll (NY)
Sullivan County Comm Coll (NY)
Sussex County Comm Coll (NJ)
Tarrant County Coll District (TX)
Texarkana Coll (TX)
Three Rivers Comm Coll (CT)
Triton Coll (IL)
Ulster County Comm Coll (NY)
Westchester Comm Coll (NY)
Western Wisconsin Tech Coll (WI)
Westmoreland County Comm Coll (PA)

ROBOTICS
Black Hawk Coll, Moline (IL)
Camden County Coll (NJ)
Cecil Comm Coll (MD)
Chattanooga State Tech Comm Coll (TN)
Cumberland County Coll (NJ)
Des Moines Area Comm Coll (IA)
Dutchess Comm Coll (NY)
Gateway Tech Coll (WI)
Henry Ford Comm Coll (MI)
Hill Coll of the Hill Jr College District (TX)
Indian Hills Comm Coll (IA)
Jackson Comm Coll (MI)
Jefferson Coll (MO)
Kansas City Kansas Comm Coll (KS)
Kirkwood Comm Coll (IA)
Lima Tech Coll (OH)
Lorain County Comm Coll (OH)
Louisville Tech Inst (KY)
Macomb Comm Coll (MI)
Mountain View Coll (TX)
North Iowa Area Comm Coll (IA)
Oklahoma State U, Okmulgee (OK)
Raritan Valley Comm Coll (NJ)
St. Clair County Comm Coll (MI)
San Diego City Coll (CA)
Sinclair Comm Coll (OH)
Spokane Comm Coll (WA)
Tulsa Comm Coll (OK)
Vincennes U (IN)
Wake Tech Comm Coll (NC)
Westmoreland County Comm Coll (PA)

ROBOTICS TECHNOLOGY
Comm Coll of Allegheny County (PA)
ITT Tech Inst, Newburgh (IN)
Ivy Tech State Coll–Columbus (IN)
Ivy Tech State Coll–Eastcentral (IN)
Ivy Tech State Coll–Lafayette (IN)
Ivy Tech State Coll–North Central (IN)
Ivy Tech State Coll–Northeast (IN)
Ivy Tech State Coll–Southcentral (IN)
Ivy Tech State Coll–Southeast (IN)
Ivy Tech State Coll–Southwest (IN)
Ivy Tech State Coll–Wabash Valley (IN)
Ivy Tech State Coll–Whitewater (IN)
Jefferson State Comm Coll (AL)
Kellogg Comm Coll (MI)
Louisville Tech Inst (KY)
Mott Comm Coll (MI)
Oakland Comm Coll (MI)
Pikes Peak Comm Coll (CO)
Schoolcraft Coll (MI)
Spartanburg Tech Coll (SC)
Terra State Comm Coll (OH)
Texas State Tech Coll (TX)
Waubonsee Comm Coll (IL)

ROMANCE LANGUAGES
Coll of the Desert (CA)
Highline Comm Coll (WA)
Lon Morris Coll (TX)
Tacoma Comm Coll (WA)

RUSSIAN
Austin Comm Coll (TX)
Everett Comm Coll (WA)
San Diego Mesa Coll (CA)
Tacoma Comm Coll (WA)
Tulsa Comm Coll (OK)

RUSSIAN/SLAVIC STUDIES
Manatee Comm Coll (FL)

SAFETY/SECURITY TECHNOLOGY
Cuyahoga Comm Coll (OH)
Des Moines Area Comm Coll (IA)
Guam Comm Coll (GU)
Interboro Inst (NY)
John Tyler Comm Coll (VA)
Lakeland Comm Coll (OH)
Macomb Comm Coll (MI)
Pine Tech Coll (MN)
San Jacinto Coll Central Campus (TX)
Truckee Meadows Comm Coll (NV)
Tulsa Comm Coll (OK)

SALES OPERATIONS
Century Comm and Tech Coll (MN)
Clark Coll (WA)
Coll of DuPage (IL)
Cuyahoga Comm Coll (OH)
Hibbing Comm Coll (MN)
Iowa Western Comm Coll (IA)
McHenry County Coll (IL)
Moraine Valley Comm Coll (IL)
Orange Coast Coll (CA)
Pittsburgh Tech Inst (PA)
Santa Barbara City Coll (CA)

SANITATION TECHNOLOGY
Bay de Noc Comm Coll (MI)
Kirkwood Comm Coll (IA)
Palomar Coll (CA)
Red Rocks Comm Coll (CO)

SCIENCE EDUCATION
Angelina Coll (TX)
Chemeketa Comm Coll (OR)
Colby Comm Coll (KS)
Comm Coll of Southern Nevada (NV)
Dutchess Comm Coll (NY)
East Central Comm Coll (MS)
Eastern Oklahoma State Coll (OK)
Harrisburg Area Comm Coll (PA)
Holmes Comm Coll (MS)
Independence Comm Coll (KS)
Iowa Lakes Comm Coll (IA)
Jones County Jr Coll (MS)
Manatee Comm Coll (FL)
Miami-Dade Comm Coll (FL)
Mississippi Delta Comm Coll (MS)
Northwest Coll (WY)
Northwest Mississippi Comm Coll (MS)
Ranger Coll (TX)
Sandhills Comm Coll (NC)
Snow Coll (UT)
Vermilion Comm Coll (MN)
Vincennes U (IN)

SCIENCE TECHNOLOGIES RELATED
Cascadia Comm Coll (WA)
Comm Coll of Allegheny County (PA)
Front Range Comm Coll (CO)
Victor Valley Coll (CA)

SCIENCE/TECHNOLOGY AND SOCIETY
Southeast Arkansas Coll (AR)

SCULPTURE
De Anza Coll (CA)
Dixie State Coll of Utah (UT)
Inst of American Indian Arts (NM)
Mercer County Comm Coll (NJ)
Monterey Peninsula Coll (CA)

SECONDARY EDUCATION
Allen County Comm Coll (KS)
Brazosport Coll (TX)
Central Wyoming Coll (WY)
City Colls of Chicago, Malcolm X Coll (IL)
Dixie State Coll of Utah (UT)
Eastern Arizona Coll (AZ)
Eastern Wyoming Coll (WY)
Floyd Coll (GA)
Howard Comm Coll (MD)
Kellogg Comm Coll (MI)
Mid Michigan Comm Coll (MI)
Truckee Meadows Comm Coll (NV)
Western Nebraska Comm Coll (NE)
Wor-Wic Comm Coll (MD)

SECRETARIAL SCIENCE
Abraham Baldwin Ag Coll (GA)
Adirondack Comm Coll (NY)
AIB Coll of Business (IA)
Aims Comm Coll (CO)
Albuquerque Tech Vocational Inst (NM)
Alexandria Tech Coll (MN)
Allan Hancock Coll (CA)
Allegany Coll of Maryland (MD)
Allen County Comm Coll (KS)
Allentown Business School (PA)
Alpena Comm Coll (MI)
Alvin Comm Coll (TX)
Amarillo Coll (TX)
American River Coll (CA)
Andover Coll (ME)
Angelina Coll (TX)
Anne Arundel Comm Coll (MD)
Anoka-Ramsey Comm Coll (MN)
Antelope Valley Coll (CA)
Arapahoe Comm Coll (CO)
Arizona Western Coll (AZ)
Arkansas State U–Mountain Home (AR)
Ashland Comm Coll (KY)
Asnuntuck Comm Coll (CT)
Athens Tech Coll (GA)
Atlanta Metropolitan Coll (GA)
Augusta Tech Coll (GA)
Austin Comm Coll (TX)
Bacone Coll (OK)
Bainbridge Coll (GA)
Bakersfield Coll (CA)
Baltimore City Comm Coll (MD)
Barstow Coll (CA)
Barton County Comm Coll (KS)
Bates Tech Coll (WA)
Bay de Noc Comm Coll (MI)
Bay State Coll (MA)
Beaufort County Comm Coll (NC)
Bellevue Comm Coll (WA)
Belmont Tech Coll (OH)
Bergen Comm Coll (NJ)
Berkshire Comm Coll (MA)
Bessemer State Tech Coll (AL)
Bevill State Comm Coll (AL)
Bismarck State Coll (ND)
Blackfeet Comm Coll (MT)
Black Hawk Coll, Moline (IL)
Blackhawk Tech Coll (WI)
Bladen Comm Coll (NC)
Blair Coll (CO)
Blinn Coll (TX)
Blue Ridge Comm Coll (NC)
Blue Ridge Comm Coll (VA)
Blue River Comm Coll (MO)
Borough of Manhattan Comm Coll of City U of NY (NY)
Bowling Green State U-Firelands Coll (OH)
Bradford School (OH)
Brazosport Coll (TX)
Brevard Comm Coll (FL)
Briarwood Coll (CT)
Bristol Comm Coll (MA)
Bronx Comm Coll of City U of NY (NY)
Brookdale Comm Coll (NJ)
Broome Comm Coll (NY)
Brunswick Comm Coll (NC)
Bryant & Stratton Business Inst, Albany (NY)
Bryant & Stratton Business Inst, Buffalo (NY)
Bryant & Stratton Business Inst, Lackawanna (NY)
Bryant & Stratton Business Inst, Rochester (NY)
Bryant & Stratton Business Inst, Rochester (NY)
Bryant & Stratton Business Inst, Eastern Hills Cmps (NY)
Bryant & Stratton Business Inst (NY)
Bryant and Stratton Coll, Parma (OH)
Bryant and Stratton Coll, Willoughby Hills (OH)
Bryant and Stratton Coll (WI)
Bryant and Stratton Coll, Virginia Beach (VA)
Bucks County Comm Coll (PA)
Bunker Hill Comm Coll (MA)
Burlington County Coll (NJ)
Business Inst of Pennsylvania (PA)
Butler County Comm Coll (PA)
Butte Coll (CA)
Caldwell Comm Coll and Tech Inst (NC)
Cambria-Rowe Business Coll (PA)
Camden County Coll (NJ)
Cañada Coll (CA)
Cape Cod Comm Coll (MA)
Capital Comm Coll (CT)
Carl Sandburg Coll (IL)
Carteret Comm Coll (NC)
Casper Coll (WY)
Catawba Valley Comm Coll (NC)
Cecil Comm Coll (MD)
Cedar Valley Coll (TX)
Central Alabama Comm Coll (AL)
Central Arizona Coll (AZ)
Central Carolina Comm Coll (NC)
Central Carolina Tech Coll (SC)
Central Comm Coll–Columbus Campus (NE)
Central Comm Coll–Grand Island Campus (NE)
Central Comm Coll–Hastings Campus (NE)
Centralia Coll (WA)
Central Lakes Coll (MN)
Central Maine Tech Coll (ME)
Central Ohio Tech Coll (OH)
Central Oregon Comm Coll (OR)
Central Piedmont Comm Coll (NC)
Central Texas Coll (TX)
Central Virginia Comm Coll (VA)
Century Comm and Tech Coll (MN)
Cerritos Coll (CA)
Chabot Coll (CA)
Chaffey Coll (CA)
Chaparral Coll (AZ)
Chattahoochee Valley Comm Coll (AL)
Chattanooga State Tech Comm Coll (TN)
Chemeketa Comm Coll (OR)
Chesapeake Coll (MD)
Chippewa Valley Tech Coll (WI)
Churchman Business School (PA)
Citrus Coll (CA)
City Colls of Chicago, Malcolm X Coll (IL)
City Colls of Chicago, Richard J Daley Coll (IL)
Clark Coll (WA)
Cleveland Comm Coll (NC)
Cleveland State Comm Coll (TN)
Clinton Comm Coll (IA)
Clinton Comm Coll (NY)
Clover Park Tech Coll (WA)
Clovis Comm Coll (NM)
Coahoma Comm Coll (MS)
Coastal Bend Coll (TX)
Cochise Coll, Douglas (AZ)
Coffeyville Comm Coll (KS)
Coll of Alameda (CA)
Coll of DuPage (IL)
Coll of Eastern Utah (UT)
Coll of Lake County (IL)
Coll of Marin (CA)
Coll of the Canyons (CA)
Coll of the Desert (CA)
Coll of the Redwoods (CA)
Coll of the Sequoias (CA)
Coll of the Siskiyous (CA)
Collin County Comm Coll District (TX)
Colorado Northwestern Comm Coll (CO)
Columbia-Greene Comm Coll (NY)
Columbia State Comm Coll (TN)
Columbus State Comm Coll (OH)
Columbus Tech Coll (GA)
Comm Coll of Allegheny County (PA)
Comm Coll of Aurora (CO)
The Comm Coll of Baltimore County–Catonsville Campus (MD)
Comm Coll of Beaver County (PA)
Comm Coll of Denver (CO)
Comm Coll of Rhode Island (RI)
Comm Coll of Southern Nevada (NV)
Comm Coll of Vermont (VT)
Compton Comm Coll (CA)
Copiah-Lincoln Comm Coll–Natchez Campus (MS)
Corning Comm Coll (NY)
County Coll of Morris (NJ)
Cowley County Comm Coll and Voc-Tech School (KS)
Crafton Hills Coll (CA)
Crowder Coll (MO)
Cuesta Coll (CA)
Cumberland County Coll (NJ)
Cuyahoga Comm Coll (OH)
Cypress Coll (CA)
Danville Comm Coll (VA)
Darton Coll (GA)
Davis Coll (OH)
Dawson Comm Coll (MT)
Daymar Coll (KY)
Daytona Beach Comm Coll (FL)
De Anza Coll (CA)
Delaware Tech & Comm Coll, Jack F Owens Cmps (DE)
Delaware Tech & Comm Coll, Stanton/ Wilmington Cmps (DE)
Delaware Tech & Comm Coll, Terry Cmps (DE)
Delgado Comm Coll (LA)
Del Mar Coll (TX)
Delta Coll (MI)
Denmark Tech Coll (SC)
Des Moines Area Comm Coll (IA)
Diné Coll (AZ)
Dixie State Coll of Utah (UT)
Dodge City Comm Coll (KS)
Doña Ana Branch Comm Coll (NM)
Douglas Education Center (PA)
Douglas MacArthur State Tech Coll (AL)
Draughons Jr Coll (KY)
Draughons Jr Coll, Clarksville (TN)
Draughons Jr Coll, Nashville (TN)
DuBois Business Coll (PA)
Duff's Business Inst (PA)
Durham Tech Comm Coll (NC)
Dutchess Comm Coll (NY)
East Central Coll (MO)
Eastern Idaho Tech Coll (ID)
Eastern Maine Tech Coll (ME)
Eastern Oklahoma State Coll (OK)
Eastern Shore Comm Coll (VA)
Eastern Wyoming Coll (WY)
East Mississippi Comm Coll (MS)
Edgecombe Comm Coll (NC)
Edison State Comm Coll (OH)
Elaine P. Nunez Comm Coll (LA)
El Centro Coll (TX)
Elizabethtown Comm Coll (KY)
Ellsworth Comm Coll (IA)
Empire Coll (CA)
Enterprise State Jr Coll (AL)

Erie Business Center, Main (PA)
Erie Business Center South (PA)
Erie Comm Coll, City Campus (NY)
Erie Comm Coll, North Campus (NY)
Erie Comm Coll, South Campus (NY)
Essex County Coll (NJ)
Eugenio María de Hostos Comm Coll of City U of NY (NY)
Everest Coll (AZ)
Feather River Comm Coll District (CA)
Fergus Falls Comm Coll (MN)
Finger Lakes Comm Coll (NY)
Fiorello H LaGuardia Comm Coll of City U of NY (NY)
Flathead Valley Comm Coll (MT)
Florence-Darlington Tech Coll (SC)
Florida Comm Coll at Jacksonville (FL)
Florida National Coll (FL)
Forsyth Tech Comm Coll (NC)
Fort Berthold Comm Coll (ND)
Fort Scott Comm Coll (KS)
Frederick Comm Coll (MD)
Fresno City Coll (CA)
Front Range Comm Coll (CO)
Fulton-Montgomery Comm Coll (NY)
Gadsden State Comm Coll (AL)
Gallipolis Career Coll (OH)
Galveston Coll (TX)
Garden City Comm Coll (KS)
Gateway Tech Coll (WI)
Gavilan Coll (CA)
Gem City Coll (IL)
Genesee Comm Coll (NY)
Germanna Comm Coll (VA)
Glendale Comm Coll (AZ)
Glendale Comm Coll (CA)
Gogebic Comm Coll (MI)
Golden West Coll (CA)
Gordon Coll (GA)
Grand Rapids Comm Coll (MI)
Grayson County Coll (TX)
Greenfield Comm Coll (MA)
Greenville Tech Coll (SC)
Griffin Tech Coll (GA)
Guam Comm Coll (GU)
Gulf Coast Comm Coll (FL)
Gwinnett Tech Coll (GA)
Hagerstown Business Coll (MD)
Halifax Comm Coll (NC)
Hamilton Coll (IA)
Harford Comm Coll (MD)
Harrisburg Area Comm Coll (PA)
Hawaii Comm Coll (HI)
Hawkeye Comm Coll (IA)
Hazard Comm Coll (KY)
Heald Coll, Schools of Business and Technology, Hayward (CA)
Heald Coll, Schools of Business and Technology, Rancho Cordova (CA)
Heald Coll, Schools of Business and Technology (HI)
Heartland Comm Coll (IL)
Henderson Comm Coll (KY)
Henry Ford Comm Coll (MI)
Herzing Coll (AL)
Hesser Coll (NH)
Hibbing Comm Coll (MN)
Highland Comm Coll (IL)
Highland Comm Coll (KS)
Highline Comm Coll (WA)
Hill Coll of the Hill Jr College District (TX)
Hillsborough Comm Coll (FL)
Hinds Comm Coll (MS)
Holmes Comm Coll (MS)
Holyoke Comm Coll (MA)
Hopkinsville Comm Coll (KY)
Horry-Georgetown Tech Coll (SC)
Housatonic Comm Coll (CT)
Houston Comm Coll System (TX)
Howard Comm Coll (MD)
Huntington Jr Coll of Business (WV)
Hutchinson Comm Coll and Area Vocational School (KS)
Illinois Eastern Comm Colls, Frontier Comm Coll (IL)
Illinois Eastern Comm Colls, Lincoln Trail Coll (IL)
Illinois Eastern Comm Colls, Olney Central Coll (IL)
Illinois Eastern Comm Colls, Wabash Valley Coll (IL)
Imperial Valley Coll (CA)
Independence Comm Coll (KS)
Indiana Business Coll, Anderson (IN)
Indiana Business Coll, Columbus (IN)
Indiana Business Coll, Evansville (IN)
Indiana Business Coll, Fort Wayne (IN)
Indiana Business Coll, Indianapolis (IN)
Indiana Business Coll, Lafayette (IN)
Indiana Business Coll, Marion (IN)
Indiana Business Coll, Muncie (IN)
Indiana Business Coll, Terre Haute (IN)
Indian River Comm Coll (FL)
Instituto Comercial de Puerto Rico Jr Coll (PR)
Interboro Inst (NY)
International Business Coll, Fort Wayne (IN)
Inver Hills Comm Coll (MN)
Iowa Lakes Comm Coll (IA)
Iowa Western Comm Coll (IA)
Isothermal Comm Coll (NC)
Itasca Comm Coll (MN)
Jackson Comm Coll (MI)
James H. Faulkner State Comm Coll (AL)
James Sprunt Comm Coll (NC)
Jamestown Business Coll (NY)
Jefferson Coll (MO)
Jefferson Comm Coll (NY)
Jefferson Comm Coll (OH)
Jefferson Davis Comm Coll (AL)
Jefferson State Comm Coll (AL)
J. F. Drake State Tech Coll (AL)
Johnson County Comm Coll (KS)
Johnston Comm Coll (NC)
John Tyler Comm Coll (VA)
John Wood Comm Coll (IL)
Joliet Jr Coll (IL)
J. Sargeant Reynolds Comm Coll (VA)
Kankakee Comm Coll (IL)
Kansas City Kansas Comm Coll (KS)
Kauai Comm Coll (HI)
Kellogg Comm Coll (MI)
Kennebec Valley Tech Coll (ME)
Kent State U, Salem Campus (OH)
Kent State U, Trumbull Campus (OH)
Kent State U, Tuscarawas Campus (OH)
Kilgore Coll (TX)
Kilian Comm Coll (SD)
Kingsborough Comm Coll of City U of NY (NY)
Kirkwood Comm Coll (IA)
Kishwaukee Coll (IL)
Labette Comm Coll (KS)
Lac Courte Oreilles Ojibwa Comm Coll (WI)
Lake City Comm Coll (FL)
Lake Land Coll (IL)
Lakeland Comm Coll (OH)
Lake Region State Coll (ND)
Lakeshore Tech Coll (WI)
Lake Tahoe Comm Coll (CA)
Lake Washington Tech Coll (WA)
Lamar Comm Coll (CO)
Lamar State Coll–Orange (TX)
Lamar State Coll–Port Arthur (TX)
Lane Comm Coll (OR)
Lansing Comm Coll (MI)
Laramie County Comm Coll (WY)
Laredo Comm Coll (TX)
Las Positas Coll (CA)
Laurel Business Inst (PA)
LDS Business Coll (UT)
Lehigh Carbon Comm Coll (PA)
Lenoir Comm Coll (NC)
Lewis and Clark Comm Coll (IL)
Lewis Coll of Business (MI)
Lima Tech Coll (OH)
Lincoln Land Comm Coll (IL)
Lincoln School of Commerce (NE)
Linn-Benton Comm Coll (OR)
Long Beach City Coll (CA)
Long Island Business Inst (NY)
Longview Comm Coll (MO)
Lorain County Comm Coll (OH)
Lord Fairfax Comm Coll (VA)
Los Angeles City Coll (CA)
Los Angeles Harbor Coll (CA)
Los Angeles Mission Coll (CA)
Louisiana State U at Eunice (LA)
Lower Columbia Coll (WA)
Luzerne County Comm Coll (PA)
Macomb Comm Coll (MI)
Madisonville Comm Coll (KY)
Manatee Comm Coll (FL)
Manchester Comm Coll (CT)
Manor Coll (PA)
Maple Woods Comm Coll (MO)
Marian Court Coll (MA)
Marion Tech Coll (OH)
Marshalltown Comm Coll (IA)
Martin Comm Coll (NC)
Massasoit Comm Coll (MA)
Mayland Comm Coll (NC)
Maysville Comm Coll (KY)
McCann School of Business (PA)
McHenry County Coll (IL)
McIntosh Coll (NH)
McLennan Comm Coll (TX)
MedVance Inst (TN)
Merced Coll (CA)
Mercer County Comm Coll (NJ)
Meridian Comm Coll (MS)
Mesabi Range Comm and Tech Coll (MN)
Metropolitan Comm Coll (NE)
Miami-Dade Comm Coll (FL)
Miami U–Middletown Campus (OH)
Middlesex County Coll (NJ)
Midland Coll (TX)
Midlands Tech Coll (SC)
Mid Michigan Comm Coll (MI)
Mid-Plains Comm Coll Area (NE)
Mid-State Coll (ME)
Mid-State Tech Coll (WI)
Miles Comm Coll (MT)
Milwaukee Area Tech Coll (WI)
Mineral Area Coll (MO)
Minneapolis Comm and Tech Coll (MN)
Minnesota State Coll–Southeast Tech (MN)
Minnesota West Comm & Tech Coll-Pipestone Cmps (MN)
Minot State U–Bottineau Campus (ND)
MiraCosta Coll (CA)
Mississippi Delta Comm Coll (MS)
Mississippi Gulf Coast Comm Coll (MS)
Mitchell Comm Coll (NC)
Mitchell Tech Inst (SD)
Moberly Area Comm Coll (MO)
Modesto Jr Coll (CA)
Mohawk Valley Comm Coll (NY)
Monroe Coll, Bronx (NY)
Monroe Coll, New Rochelle (NY)
Monroe Comm Coll (NY)
Monroe County Comm Coll (MI)
Montana State U Coll of Tech-Great Falls (MT)
Montcalm Comm Coll (MI)
Monterey Peninsula Coll (CA)
Montgomery Comm Coll (NC)
Montgomery County Comm Coll (PA)
Moraine Park Tech Coll (WI)
Moraine Valley Comm Coll (IL)
Morgan Comm Coll (CO)
Morton Coll (IL)
Mott Comm Coll (MI)
Mountain Empire Comm Coll (VA)
Mountain West Coll (UT)
Mt. Hood Comm Coll (OR)
Mt. San Jacinto Coll (CA)
MTI Coll of Business and Technology, Houston (TX)
Muscatine Comm Coll (IA)
Muskingum Area Tech Coll (OH)
Nash Comm Coll (NC)
Nashville State Tech Inst (TN)
Nassau Comm Coll (NY)
National Coll of Business & Technology, Danville (KY)
National Coll of Business & Technology, Florence (KY)
National Coll of Business & Technology, Lexington (KY)
National Coll of Business & Technology, Louisville (KY)
National Coll of Business & Technology, Pikeville (KY)
National Coll of Business & Technology, Richmond (KY)
National Coll of Business & Technology (TN)
National Coll of Business & Technology, Bluefield (VA)
National Coll of Business & Technology, Bristol (VA)
National Coll of Business & Technology, Charlottesville (VA)
National Coll of Business & Technology, Danville (VA)
National Coll of Business & Technology, Harrisonburg (VA)
National Coll of Business & Technology, Lynchburg (VA)
National Coll of Business & Technology, Martinsville (VA)
National Coll of Business & Technology, Salem (VA)
Naugatuck Valley Comm Coll (CT)
Navarro Coll (TX)
Neosho County Comm Coll (KS)
New Hampshire Comm Tech Coll, Berlin/Laconia (NH)
New Mexico State U–Alamogordo (NM)
New Mexico State U–Carlsbad (NM)
Newport Business Inst, Williamsport (PA)
New River Comm Coll (VA)
Niagara County Comm Coll (NY)
North Arkansas Coll (AR)
North Central Michigan Coll (MI)
Northcentral Tech Coll (WI)
North Central Texas Coll (TX)
North Dakota State Coll of Science (ND)
Northeast Alabama Comm Coll (AL)
Northeast Comm Coll (NE)
Northeastern Tech Coll (SC)
Northeast State Tech Comm Coll (TN)
Northeast Texas Comm Coll (TX)
Northern Essex Comm Coll (MA)
Northern Maine Tech Coll (ME)
Northern Oklahoma Coll (OK)
Northern Virginia Comm Coll (VA)
North Harris Coll (TX)
North Hennepin Comm Coll (MN)
North Idaho Coll (ID)
North Iowa Area Comm Coll (IA)
Northland Comm and Tech Coll (MN)
Northland Pioneer Coll (AZ)
North Seattle Comm Coll (WA)
North Shore Comm Coll (MA)
NorthWest Arkansas Comm Coll (AR)
Northwest Coll (WY)
Northwestern Business Coll (IL)
Northwestern Connecticut Comm-Tech Coll (CT)
Northwest-Shoals Comm Coll (AL)
Norwalk Comm Coll (CT)
Oakton Comm Coll (IL)
Ocean County Coll (NJ)
Odessa Coll (TX)
Ohio Business Coll (OH)
Okaloosa-Walton Comm Coll (FL)
Oklahoma State U, Okmulgee (OK)
Onondaga Comm Coll (NY)
Orangeburg-Calhoun Tech Coll (SC)
Orange Coast Coll (CA)
Orange County Comm Coll (NY)
Otero Jr Coll (CO)
Ouachita Tech Coll (AR)
Oxnard Coll (CA)
Ozarka Coll (AR)
Pace Inst (PA)
Paducah Comm Coll (KY)
Palau Comm CollPalau)
Palm Beach Comm Coll (FL)
Palomar Coll (CA)
Palo Verde Coll (CA)
Pamlico Comm Coll (NC)
Paradise Valley Comm Coll (AZ)
Parkland Coll (IL)
Pasadena City Coll (CA)
Patrick Henry Comm Coll (VA)
Paul D. Camp Comm Coll (VA)
Pellissippi State Tech Comm Coll (TN)
Penn Commercial Business and Tech School (PA)
Pennsylvania Coll of Technology (PA)
Penn Valley Comm Coll (MO)
Pensacola Jr Coll (FL)
Phoenix Coll (AZ)
Piedmont Tech Coll (SC)
Piedmont Virginia Comm Coll (VA)
Pierce Coll (WA)
Pima Comm Coll (AZ)
Pine Tech Coll (MN)
Pitt Comm Coll (NC)
Portland Comm Coll (OR)
Pratt Comm Coll and Area Vocational School (KS)
Pulaski Tech Coll (AR)
Quincy Coll (MA)
Quinsigamond Comm Coll (MA)
Rainy River Comm Coll (MN)
Ranger Coll (TX)
Rappahannock Comm Coll (VA)
Raritan Valley Comm Coll (NJ)
Rasmussen Coll Mankato (MN)
Rasmussen Coll Minnetonka (MN)
Rasmussen Coll St. Cloud (MN)
Reading Area Comm Coll (PA)
Red Rocks Comm Coll (CO)
Reedley Coll (CA)
Reid State Tech Coll (AL)
Rend Lake Coll (IL)
Richland Comm Coll (IL)
Richmond Comm Coll (NC)
Rich Mountain Comm Coll (AR)
Ridgewater Coll (MN)
Riverland Comm Coll (MN)
Roane State Comm Coll (TN)
Roanoke-Chowan Comm Coll (NC)
Robeson Comm Coll (NC)
Rockingham Comm Coll (NC)
Rockland Comm Coll (NY)
Rogue Comm Coll (OR)
Sacramento City Coll (CA)
St. Catharine Coll (KY)
Saint Charles Comm Coll (MO)
St. Clair County Comm Coll (MI)
St. Cloud Tech Coll (MN)
St. Louis Comm Coll at Florissant Valley (MO)
St. Paul Tech Coll (MN)
St. Philip's Coll (TX)
Salem Comm Coll (NJ)
Salish Kootenai Coll (MT)
Sampson Comm Coll (NC)
San Bernardino Valley Coll (CA)
Sandhills Comm Coll (NC)
San Diego City Coll (CA)
San Diego Mesa Coll (CA)
Sanford-Brown Coll, Hazelwood (MO)
San Jacinto Coll Central Campus (TX)
San Jacinto Coll North Campus (TX)
San Jacinto Coll South Campus (TX)
San Juan Coll (NM)
Santa Ana Coll (CA)
Santa Barbara City Coll (CA)
Santa Fe Comm Coll (NM)
Santa Monica Coll (CA)
Sauk Valley Comm Coll (IL)
Savannah Tech Coll (GA)
Schenectady County Comm Coll (NY)
Schoolcraft Coll (MI)
Scott Comm Coll (IA)
Scottsdale Comm Coll (AZ)
Seattle Central Comm Coll (WA)
Seminole Comm Coll (FL)
Seminole State Coll (OK)
Shasta Coll (CA)
Sheridan Coll (WY)
Sierra Coll (CA)
Sinclair Comm Coll (OH)
Sitting Bull Coll (ND)
Skagit Valley Coll (WA)
Snow Coll (UT)
Somerset Comm Coll (KY)
South Arkansas Comm Coll (AR)
South Coll (TN)
Southeast Comm Coll (KY)
Southeast Comm Coll, Beatrice Campus (NE)
Southeastern Comm Coll (NC)
Southeastern Comm Coll, South Campus (IA)
Southern Ohio Coll, Cincinnati Campus (OH)
Southern West Virginia Comm and Tech Coll (WV)
South Hills School of Business & Technology, State College (PA)
South Mountain Comm Coll (AZ)
South Plains Coll (TX)

South Puget Sound Comm Coll (WA)
Southside Virginia Comm Coll (VA)
South Suburban Coll (IL)
Southwestern Coll (CA)
Southwestern Coll of Business, Dayton (OH)
Southwestern Comm Coll (IA)
Southwestern Comm Coll (NC)
Southwestern Michigan Coll (MI)
Southwest Georgia Tech Coll (GA)
Southwest Mississippi Comm Coll (MS)
Southwest Tennessee Comm Coll (TN)
Southwest Virginia Comm Coll (VA)
Southwest Wisconsin Tech Coll (WI)
Spartanburg Methodist Coll (SC)
Spartanburg Tech Coll (SC)
Spokane Comm Coll (WA)
Spokane Falls Comm Coll (WA)
Springfield Tech Comm Coll (MA)
Stark State Coll of Technology (OH)
State Fair Comm Coll (MO)
State U of NY Coll of A&T at Morrisville (NY)
Stone Child Coll (MT)
Sullivan County Comm Coll (NY)
Surry Comm Coll (NC)
Sussex County Comm Coll (NJ)
Tacoma Comm Coll (WA)
Taft Coll (CA)
Tallahassee Comm Coll (FL)
Tarrant County Coll District (TX)
TCI-The Coll for Technology (NY)
Temple Coll (TX)
Terra State Comm Coll (OH)
Texarkana Coll (TX)
Texas State Tech Coll–Harlingen (TX)
Thomas Nelson Comm Coll (VA)
Three Rivers Comm Coll (CT)
Tidewater Comm Coll (VA)
Tompkins Cortland Comm Coll (NY)
Tri-County Comm Coll (NC)
Tri-County Tech Coll (SC)
Trident Tech Coll (SC)
Trinidad State Jr Coll (CO)
Triton Coll (IL)
Trocaire Coll (NY)
Truckee Meadows Comm Coll (NV)
Trumbull Business Coll (OH)
Tulsa Comm Coll (OK)
Tunxis Comm Coll (CT)
Tyler Jr Coll (TX)
Ulster County Comm Coll (NY)
Umpqua Comm Coll (OR)
Union County Coll (NJ)
The U of Akron–Wayne Coll (OH)
U of Alaska Anchorage, Kenai Peninsula Coll (AK)
U of Alaska Anchorage, Kodiak Coll (AK)
U of Alaska Anchorage, Matanuska-Susitna Coll (AK)
U of Alaska Southeast, Ketchikan Campus (AK)
U of Arkansas at Fort Smith (AR)
U of Arkansas Comm Coll at Morrilton (AR)
U of Kentucky, Lexington Comm Coll (KY)
U of New Mexico–Gallup (NM)
U of New Mexico–Los Alamos Branch (NM)
U of Northwestern Ohio (OH)
U of South Carolina at Lancaster (SC)
Utica School of Commerce (NY)
Vance-Granville Comm Coll (NC)
Ventura Coll (CA)
Vermont Tech Coll (VT)
Vernon Coll (TX)
Victoria Coll (TX)
Victor Valley Coll (CA)
Villa Maria Coll of Buffalo (NY)
Vincennes U (IN)
Vincennes U Jasper Campus (IN)
Virginia Coll at Jackson (MS)
Virginia Western Comm Coll (VA)
Wallace State Comm Coll (AL)
Walla Walla Comm Coll (WA)
Walters State Comm Coll (TN)
Warren County Comm Coll (NJ)
Waubonsee Comm Coll (IL)
Waycross Coll (GA)
Weatherford Coll (TX)
Webster Coll, Ocala (FL)
West Central Tech Coll (GA)
The Westchester Business Inst (NY)
Westchester Comm Coll (NY)
Western Nevada Comm Coll (NV)
Western Piedmont Comm Coll (NC)
Western Texas Coll (TX)
Western Wisconsin Tech Coll (WI)
Western Wyoming Comm Coll (WY)
Westmoreland County Comm Coll (PA)
West Virginia Jr Coll, Charleston (WV)
West Virginia Northern Comm Coll (WV)
West Virginia U at Parkersburg (WV)
Wharton County Jr Coll (TX)
Whatcom Comm Coll (WA)
Williston State Coll (ND)
Wilson Tech Comm Coll (NC)
Wisconsin Indianhead Tech Coll (WI)
Wor-Wic Comm Coll (MD)
York Tech Coll (SC)
Yorktowne Business Inst (PA)

SECURITY

Brevard Comm Coll (FL)
Comm Coll of the Air Force (AL)
Hesser Coll (NH)
Nassau Comm Coll (NY)
San Joaquin Valley Coll (CA)

SHEET METAL WORKING

Brazosport Coll (TX)
Comm Coll of Allegheny County (PA)
Ivy Tech State Coll–Central Indiana (IN)
Ivy Tech State Coll–Lafayette (IN)
Ivy Tech State Coll–North Central (IN)
Ivy Tech State Coll–Northeast (IN)
Ivy Tech State Coll–Northwest (IN)
Ivy Tech State Coll–Southcentral (IN)
Ivy Tech State Coll–Southwest (IN)
Ivy Tech State Coll–Wabash Valley (IN)
Kellogg Comm Coll (MI)
Northwest State Comm Coll (OH)
Western Nevada Comm Coll (NV)

SIGN LANGUAGE INTERPRETATION

American River Coll (CA)
Austin Comm Coll (TX)
Black Hawk Coll, Moline (IL)
Blue Ridge Comm Coll (NC)
Central Piedmont Comm Coll (NC)
Chattanooga State Tech Comm Coll (TN)
Cincinnati State Tech and Comm Coll (OH)
Coll of the Sequoias (CA)
Collin County Comm Coll District (TX)
Columbus State Comm Coll (OH)
Comm Coll of Allegheny County (PA)
The Comm Coll of Baltimore County–Catonsville Campus (MD)
Comm Coll of Southern Nevada (NV)
Cowley County Comm Coll and Voc-Tech School (KS)
Delaware Tech & Comm Coll, Stanton/ Wilmington Cmps (DE)
Delgado Comm Coll (LA)
Del Mar Coll (TX)
Eastfield Coll (TX)
Florida Comm Coll at Jacksonville (FL)
Floyd Coll (GA)
Front Range Comm Coll (CO)
Georgia Perimeter Coll (GA)
Golden West Coll (CA)
Guam Comm Coll (GU)
Hillsborough Comm Coll (FL)
Houston Comm Coll System (TX)
Iowa Western Comm Coll (IA)
John A. Logan Coll (IL)
Johnson County Comm Coll (KS)
Lansing Comm Coll (MI)
Los Angeles Pierce Coll (CA)
McLennan Comm Coll (TX)
Miami-Dade Comm Coll (FL)
Mott Comm Coll (MI)
Mount Wachusett Comm Coll (MA)
Nashville State Tech Inst (TN)
New River Comm Coll (VA)
Northcentral Tech Coll (WI)
Northern Essex Comm Coll (MA)
Northwestern Connecticut Comm-Tech Coll (CT)
Oklahoma State U, Oklahoma City (OK)
Palomar Coll (CA)
Pasadena City Coll (CA)
Pikes Peak Comm Coll (CO)
Pima Comm Coll (AZ)
Portland Comm Coll (OR)
Riverside Comm Coll (CA)
St. Louis Comm Coll at Florissant Valley (MO)
St. Paul Tech Coll (MN)
St. Petersburg Coll (FL)
Santa Fe Comm Coll (NM)
Scott Comm Coll (IA)
Seattle Central Comm Coll (WA)
Sheridan Coll (WY)
Sinclair Comm Coll (OH)
Southeast Tech Inst (SD)
South Puget Sound Comm Coll (WA)
Spartanburg Tech Coll (SC)
Spokane Falls Comm Coll (WA)
Suffolk County Comm Coll (NY)
Tarrant County Coll District (TX)
Terra State Comm Coll (OH)
Tulsa Comm Coll (OK)
Tyler Jr Coll (TX)
Union County Coll (NJ)
Vincennes U (IN)
Waubonsee Comm Coll (IL)
Wilson Tech Comm Coll (NC)

SMALL ENGINE MECHANIC

Century Comm and Tech Coll (MN)
North Dakota State Coll of Science (ND)
Southwestern Coll (CA)

SOCIAL PSYCHOLOGY

Manatee Comm Coll (FL)

SOCIAL SCIENCE EDUCATION

Louisburg Coll (NC)
Northwest Mississippi Comm Coll (MS)

SOCIAL SCIENCES

Abraham Baldwin Ag Coll (GA)
Adirondack Comm Coll (NY)
Allan Hancock Coll (CA)
Allegany Coll of Maryland (MD)
Amarillo Coll (TX)
American River Coll (CA)
Ancilla Coll (IN)
Andrew Coll (GA)
Angelina Coll (TX)
Anne Arundel Comm Coll (MD)
Arizona Western Coll (AZ)
Arkansas State U–Beebe (AR)
Atlantic Cape Comm Coll (NJ)
Barstow Coll (CA)
Bowling Green State U-Firelands Coll (OH)
Brazosport Coll (TX)
Brookdale Comm Coll (NJ)
Bucks County Comm Coll (PA)
Butte Coll (CA)
Casper Coll (WY)
Centralia Coll (WA)
Central Oregon Comm Coll (OR)
Central Texas Coll (TX)
Central Wyoming Coll (WY)
Cerro Coso Comm Coll (CA)
Chabot Coll (CA)
Chaffey Coll (CA)
Chemeketa Comm Coll (OR)
Chesapeake Coll (MD)
Citrus Coll (CA)
City Coll of San Francisco (CA)
Clark Coll (WA)
Clinton Comm Coll (NY)
Cochise Coll, Douglas (AZ)
Coffeyville Comm Coll (KS)
Coll of Alameda (CA)
Coll of the Canyons (CA)
Coll of the Desert (CA)
Coll of the Sequoias (CA)
Coll of the Siskiyous (CA)
Colorado Mountn Coll, Alpine Cmps (CO)
Colorado Mountn Coll (CO)
Colorado Mountn Coll, Timberline Cmps (CO)
Columbia-Greene Comm Coll (NY)
Comm Coll of Allegheny County (PA)
The Comm Coll of Baltimore County–Catonsville Campus (MD)
Comm Coll of Southern Nevada (NV)
Comm Coll of Vermont (VT)
Compton Comm Coll (CA)
Corning Comm Coll (NY)
Cypress Coll (CA)
Danville Area Comm Coll (IL)
Daytona Beach Comm Coll (FL)
Dean Coll (MA)
De Anza Coll (CA)
Diné Coll (AZ)
Dodge City Comm Coll (KS)
Dutchess Comm Coll (NY)
East Central Comm Coll (MS)
East Mississippi Comm Coll (MS)
Edison Comm Coll (FL)
Enterprise State Jr Coll (AL)
Essex County Coll (NJ)
Feather River Comm Coll District (CA)
Finger Lakes Comm Coll (NY)
Foothill Coll (CA)
Fresno City Coll (CA)
Fulton-Montgomery Comm Coll (NY)
Galveston Coll (TX)
Garden City Comm Coll (KS)
Gavilan Coll (CA)
Glendale Comm Coll (CA)
Gloucester County Coll (NJ)
Gogebic Comm Coll (MI)
Harford Comm Coll (MD)
Harrisburg Area Comm Coll (PA)
Highline Comm Coll (WA)
Hill Coll of the Hill Jr College District (TX)
Hinds Comm Coll (MS)
Housatonic Comm Coll (CT)
Houston Comm Coll System (TX)
Howard Coll (TX)
Howard Comm Coll (MD)
Hutchinson Comm Coll and Area Vocational School (KS)
Imperial Valley Coll (CA)
Indian River Comm Coll (FL)
Iowa Lakes Comm Coll (IA)
Jamestown Comm Coll (NY)
J. Sargeant Reynolds Comm Coll (VA)
Kilgore Coll (TX)
Kingwood Coll (TX)
Kirkwood Comm Coll (IA)
Labette Comm Coll (KS)
Lake Tahoe Comm Coll (CA)
Lamar Comm Coll (CO)
Lamar State Coll–Orange (TX)
Laredo Comm Coll (TX)
Lehigh Carbon Comm Coll (PA)
Lincoln Coll, Normal (IL)
Long Beach City Coll (CA)
Lon Morris Coll (TX)
Lorain County Comm Coll (OH)
Los Angeles Mission Coll (CA)
Lower Columbia Coll (WA)
Luzerne County Comm Coll (PA)
Manatee Comm Coll (FL)
Massachusetts Bay Comm Coll (MA)
Merced Coll (CA)
Miami-Dade Comm Coll (FL)
Miami U–Middletown Campus (OH)
Middlesex County Coll (NJ)
MiraCosta Coll (CA)
Modesto Jr Coll (CA)
Mohawk Valley Comm Coll (NY)
Monroe Comm Coll (NY)
Montgomery County Comm Coll (PA)
Mt. San Jacinto Coll (CA)
Navarro Coll (TX)
Newbury Coll (MA)
New Mexico Military Inst (NM)
Niagara County Comm Coll (NY)
Northeast Comm Coll (NE)
North Idaho Coll (ID)
North Seattle Comm Coll (WA)
Northwest Coll (WY)
Northwestern Connecticut Comm-Tech Coll (CT)
Odessa Coll (TX)
Okaloosa-Walton Comm Coll (FL)
Orange Coast Coll (CA)
Otero Jr Coll (CO)
Palm Beach Comm Coll (FL)
Pasadena City Coll (CA)
Piedmont Comm Coll (NC)
Pratt Comm Coll and Area Vocational School (KS)
Quincy Coll (MA)
Raritan Valley Comm Coll (NJ)
Reading Area Comm Coll (PA)
Reedley Coll (CA)
Riverside Comm Coll (CA)
Roane State Comm Coll (TN)
Rogue Comm Coll (OR)
Sacramento City Coll (CA)
St. Catharine Coll (KY)
Salem Comm Coll (NJ)
San Diego City Coll (CA)
San Diego Mesa Coll (CA)
San Jacinto Coll North Campus (TX)
San Jacinto Coll South Campus (TX)
San Joaquin Delta Coll (CA)
Santa Ana Coll (CA)
Schenectady County Comm Coll (NY)
Seminole State Coll (OK)
Sheridan Coll (WY)
Skagit Valley Coll (WA)
Southwest Mississippi Comm Coll (MS)
State U of NY Coll of A&T at Morrisville (NY)
State U of NY Coll of Technology at Alfred (NY)
State U of NY Coll of Technology at Canton (NY)
State U of NY Coll of Technology at Delhi (NY)
Suffolk County Comm Coll (NY)
Tacoma Comm Coll (WA)
Taft Coll (CA)
Thomas Nelson Comm Coll (VA)
Tompkins Cortland Comm Coll (NY)
Triton Coll (IL)
Tulsa Comm Coll (OK)
Tyler Jr Coll (TX)
Ulster County Comm Coll (NY)
Umpqua Comm Coll (OR)
Victor Valley Coll (CA)
Vincennes U (IN)
Vincennes U Jasper Campus (IN)
Warren County Comm Coll (NJ)
Westchester Comm Coll (NY)
Western Wyoming Comm Coll (WY)

SOCIAL STUDIES EDUCATION

Manatee Comm Coll (FL)
Northwest Mississippi Comm Coll (MS)

SOCIAL WORK

Abraham Baldwin Ag Coll (GA)
Alamance Comm Coll (NC)
Alexandria Tech Coll (MN)
Allegany Coll of Maryland (MD)
Allen County Comm Coll (KS)
Amarillo Coll (TX)
Andrew Coll (GA)
Angelina Coll (TX)
Asheville-Buncombe Tech Comm Coll (NC)
Atlanta Metropolitan Coll (GA)
Atlantic Cape Comm Coll (NJ)
Austin Comm Coll (TX)
Barton County Comm Coll (KS)
Bay de Noc Comm Coll (MI)
Beaufort County Comm Coll (NC)
Brookdale Comm Coll (NJ)
Bucks County Comm Coll (PA)
Capital Comm Coll (CT)
Casper Coll (WY)
Central Carolina Comm Coll (NC)
Central Piedmont Comm Coll (NC)
Century Comm and Tech Coll (MN)
Chipola Jr Coll (FL)
City Coll of San Francisco (CA)
City Colls of Chicago, Richard J Daley Coll (IL)
Coahoma Comm Coll (MS)
Cochise Coll, Douglas (AZ)

Coffeyville Comm Coll (KS)
Colby Comm Coll (KS)
Coll of Lake County (IL)
Comm Coll of Allegheny County (PA)
Comm Coll of Rhode Island (RI)
Comm Coll of the Air Force (AL)
Compton Comm Coll (CA)
Connors State Coll (OK)
Cowley County Comm Coll and Voc-Tech School (KS)
Cumberland County Coll (NJ)
Danville Area Comm Coll (IL)
Darton Coll (GA)
Dean Coll (MA)
Del Mar Coll (TX)
Delta Coll (MI)
Des Moines Area Comm Coll (IA)
Diné Coll (AZ)
Dixie State Coll of Utah (UT)
Dodge City Comm Coll (KS)
East Central Coll (MO)
Eastfield Coll (TX)
Edgecombe Comm Coll (NC)
Edmonds Comm Coll (WA)
Ellsworth Comm Coll (IA)
Galveston Coll (TX)
GateWay Comm Coll (AZ)
Gogebic Comm Coll (MI)
Halifax Comm Coll (NC)
Harrisburg Area Comm Coll (PA)
Hesser Coll (NH)
Highland Comm Coll (KS)
Hill Coll of the Hill Jr College District (TX)
Holmes Comm Coll (MS)
Illinois Eastern Comm Colls, Wabash Valley Coll (IL)
Indian River Comm Coll (FL)
Iowa Lakes Comm Coll (IA)
Jefferson Coll (MO)
Jefferson Comm Coll (KY)
John A. Logan Coll (IL)
Kellogg Comm Coll (MI)
Kirkwood Comm Coll (IA)
Lac Courte Oreilles Ojibwa Comm Coll (WI)
Lake Land Coll (IL)
Lamar Comm Coll (CO)
Lansing Comm Coll (MI)
Lincoln Land Comm Coll (IL)
Lorain County Comm Coll (OH)
Louisburg Coll (NC)
Manatee Comm Coll (FL)
Manchester Comm Coll (CT)
Mesa Tech Coll (NM)
Miami-Dade Comm Coll (FL)
Miami U–Middletown Campus (OH)
Midlands Tech Coll (SC)
Mississippi Delta Comm Coll (MS)
Mitchell Comm Coll (NC)
Monroe County Comm Coll (MI)
Muskingum Area Tech Coll (OH)
Naugatuck Valley Comm Coll (CT)
New Mexico State U–Alamogordo (NM)
New Mexico State U–Carlsbad (NM)
Northampton County Area Comm Coll (PA)
Northwest State Comm Coll (OH)
Ocean County Coll (NJ)
Okaloosa-Walton Comm Coll (FL)
Owensboro Comm Coll (KY)
Palm Beach Comm Coll (FL)
Piedmont Tech Coll (SC)
Pratt Comm Coll and Area Vocational School (KS)
Reading Area Comm Coll (PA)
Ridgewater Coll (MN)
Sacramento City Coll (CA)
St. Catharine Coll (KY)
San Diego City Coll (CA)
San Juan Coll (NM)
Santa Fe Comm Coll (NM)
Sitting Bull Coll (ND)
South Piedmont Comm Coll (NC)
South Plains Coll (TX)
Southwestern Coll (CA)
Spokane Falls Comm Coll (WA)
Terra State Comm Coll (OH)
Tulsa Comm Coll (OK)
Umpqua Comm Coll (OR)
The U of Akron–Wayne Coll (OH)
Vincennes U (IN)
Vincennes U Jasper Campus (IN)
Waubonsee Comm Coll (IL)
Western Nebraska Comm Coll (NE)
West Virginia Northern Comm Coll (WV)
West Virginia U at Parkersburg (WV)

SOCIOLOGY

Abraham Baldwin Ag Coll (GA)
Allegany Coll of Maryland (MD)
Allen County Comm Coll (KS)
Andrew Coll (GA)
Atlanta Metropolitan Coll (GA)
Atlantic Cape Comm Coll (NJ)
Austin Comm Coll (TX)
Bacone Coll (OK)
Bainbridge Coll (GA)
Bakersfield Coll (CA)
Barton County Comm Coll (KS)
Bergen Comm Coll (NJ)
Brazosport Coll (TX)
Brookdale Comm Coll (NJ)
Burlington County Coll (NJ)
Cañada Coll (CA)
Casper Coll (WY)
Centralia Coll (WA)
Cerritos Coll (CA)
Chabot Coll (CA)
Chaffey Coll (CA)
Chesapeake Coll (MD)
Clark Coll (WA)
Coastal Bend Coll (TX)
Coastal Georgia Comm Coll (GA)
Coffeyville Comm Coll (KS)
Colby Comm Coll (KS)
Coll of Alameda (CA)
Coll of Marin (CA)
Coll of Southern Idaho (ID)
Coll of the Desert (CA)
Coll of the Sequoias (CA)
Columbia State Comm Coll (TN)
Comm Coll of Allegheny County (PA)
Comm Coll of Southern Nevada (NV)
Compton Comm Coll (CA)
Connors State Coll (OK)
Crafton Hills Coll (CA)
Cypress Coll (CA)
Darton Coll (GA)
Daytona Beach Comm Coll (FL)
De Anza Coll (CA)
Delaware County Comm Coll (PA)
Del Mar Coll (TX)
Dixie State Coll of Utah (UT)
East Central Coll (MO)
Eastern Arizona Coll (AZ)
Eastern Oklahoma State Coll (OK)
Eastern Wyoming Coll (WY)
East Georgia Coll (GA)
East Mississippi Comm Coll (MS)
Ellsworth Comm Coll (IA)
Everett Comm Coll (WA)
Finger Lakes Comm Coll (NY)
Floyd Coll (GA)
Foothill Coll (CA)
Fullerton Coll (CA)
Garden City Comm Coll (KS)
Gavilan Coll (CA)
Gloucester County Coll (NJ)
Gogebic Comm Coll (MI)
Gordon Coll (GA)
Grayson County Coll (TX)
Great Basin Coll (NV)
Harford Comm Coll (MD)
Highland Comm Coll (IL)
Highland Comm Coll (KS)
Hill Coll of the Hill Jr College District (TX)
Hinds Comm Coll (MS)
Independence Comm Coll (KS)
Indian River Comm Coll (FL)
Iowa Lakes Comm Coll (IA)
Jefferson Coll (MO)
Jefferson Comm Coll (KY)
Joliet Jr Coll (IL)
Kellogg Comm Coll (MI)
Kirkwood Comm Coll (IA)
Lake Michigan Coll (MI)
Laramie County Comm Coll (WY)
Lincoln Coll, Lincoln (IL)
Lincoln Land Comm Coll (IL)
Lon Morris Coll (TX)
Lorain County Comm Coll (OH)
Los Angeles City Coll (CA)
Los Angeles Mission Coll (CA)
Louisburg Coll (NC)
Lower Columbia Coll (WA)
Miami-Dade Comm Coll (FL)
Miami U–Middletown Campus (OH)
Middlesex County Coll (NJ)
Midland Coll (TX)
Mid Michigan Comm Coll (MI)
MiraCosta Coll (CA)
Mohave Comm Coll (AZ)
Monterey Peninsula Coll (CA)
Navarro Coll (TX)
Newbury Coll (MA)
North Harris Coll (TX)
North Idaho Coll (ID)
Northwest Coll (WY)
Odessa Coll (TX)
Oklahoma City Comm Coll (OK)
Orange Coast Coll (CA)
Oxnard Coll (CA)
Palo Verde Coll (CA)
Pasadena City Coll (CA)
Pima Comm Coll (AZ)
Pratt Comm Coll and Area Vocational School (KS)
Quincy Coll (MA)
Red Rocks Comm Coll (CO)
Ridgewater Coll (MN)
St. Catharine Coll (KY)
St. Philip's Coll (TX)
Salem Comm Coll (NJ)
San Bernardino Valley Coll (CA)
San Diego City Coll (CA)
San Diego Mesa Coll (CA)
San Jacinto Coll Central Campus (TX)
San Jacinto Coll North Campus (TX)
San Jacinto Coll South Campus (TX)
San Joaquin Delta Coll (CA)
San Juan Coll (NM)
Santa Ana Coll (CA)
Santa Barbara City Coll (CA)
Santa Monica Coll (CA)
Sauk Valley Comm Coll (IL)
Skagit Valley Coll (WA)
Snow Coll (UT)
South Mountain Comm Coll (AZ)
Southwestern Coll (CA)
Tacoma Comm Coll (WA)
Trinity Valley Comm Coll (TX)
Tulsa Comm Coll (OK)
Umpqua Comm Coll (OR)
Vermilion Comm Coll (MN)
Vincennes U (IN)
Vincennes U Jasper Campus (IN)
Waycross Coll (GA)
Western Nebraska Comm Coll (NE)
Western Wyoming Comm Coll (WY)
Young Harris Coll (GA)

SOIL CONSERVATION

Snow Coll (UT)
Southeast Comm Coll, Beatrice Campus (NE)
Trinidad State Jr Coll (CO)
Vermilion Comm Coll (MN)

SOIL SCIENCES

Dixie State Coll of Utah (UT)

SOLAR TECHNOLOGY

Chabot Coll (CA)
Comm Coll of Allegheny County (PA)
Red Rocks Comm Coll (CO)
Southeast Comm Coll, Milford Campus (NE)
Truckee Meadows Comm Coll (NV)

SPANISH

Allan Hancock Coll (CA)
Arizona Western Coll (AZ)
Austin Comm Coll (TX)
Bakersfield Coll (CA)
Blinn Coll (TX)
Cañada Coll (CA)
Casper Coll (WY)
Centralia Coll (WA)
Cerritos Coll (CA)
Cerro Coso Comm Coll (CA)
Chabot Coll (CA)
Chaffey Coll (CA)
Citrus Coll (CA)
Cochise Coll, Douglas (AZ)
Coll of Alameda (CA)
Coll of Marin (CA)
Coll of the Canyons (CA)
Coll of the Sequoias (CA)
Compton Comm Coll (CA)
Crafton Hills Coll (CA)
De Anza Coll (CA)
East Central Coll (MO)
Everett Comm Coll (WA)
Florida National Coll (FL)
Foothill Coll (CA)
Fresno City Coll (CA)
Gavilan Coll (CA)
Gordon Coll (GA)
Hill Coll of the Hill Jr College District (TX)
Imperial Valley Coll (CA)
Independence Comm Coll (KS)
Indian River Comm Coll (FL)
Jefferson Coll (MO)
Jefferson Comm Coll (KY)
Kirkwood Comm Coll (IA)
Lake Tahoe Comm Coll (CA)
Lincoln Coll, Lincoln (IL)
Long Beach City Coll (CA)
Lon Morris Coll (TX)
Los Angeles City Coll (CA)
Los Angeles Mission Coll (CA)
Manatee Comm Coll (FL)
Miami-Dade Comm Coll (FL)
Miami U–Middletown Campus (OH)
Midland Coll (TX)
MiraCosta Coll (CA)
Monterey Peninsula Coll (CA)
New Mexico Military Inst (NM)
North Idaho Coll (ID)
Orange Coast Coll (CA)
Oxnard Coll (CA)
Pasadena City Coll (CA)
Red Rocks Comm Coll (CO)
Riverside Comm Coll (CA)
St. Catharine Coll (KY)
St. Philip's Coll (TX)
San Bernardino Valley Coll (CA)
San Diego Mesa Coll (CA)
San Jacinto Coll Central Campus (TX)
San Jacinto Coll North Campus (TX)
San Joaquin Delta Coll (CA)
Santa Barbara City Coll (CA)
Santa Fe Comm Coll (NM)
Sauk Valley Comm Coll (IL)
Skagit Valley Coll (WA)
Snow Coll (UT)
Southwestern Coll (CA)
Tacoma Comm Coll (WA)
Trinity Valley Comm Coll (TX)
Triton Coll (IL)
Tulsa Comm Coll (OK)
Vincennes U (IN)
Vista Comm Coll (CA)
Western Nebraska Comm Coll (NE)
Western Wyoming Comm Coll (WY)
Wharton County Jr Coll (TX)
Young Harris Coll (GA)

SPECIAL EDUCATION

Comm Coll of Rhode Island (RI)
Eastern Wyoming Coll (WY)
Kellogg Comm Coll (MI)
Lehigh Carbon Comm Coll (PA)
Louisburg Coll (NC)
Northampton County Area Comm Coll (PA)
San Jacinto Coll North Campus (TX)

SPEECH EDUCATION

Northwest Mississippi Comm Coll (MS)

SPEECH-LANGUAGE PATHOLOGY

Cape Fear Comm Coll (NC)
Catawba Valley Comm Coll (NC)
Coll of DuPage (IL)
Crafton Hills Coll (CA)
Fayetteville Tech Comm Coll (NC)
Guilford Tech Comm Coll (NC)
Parkland Coll (IL)
Randolph Comm Coll (NC)
Southwestern Comm Coll (NC)
Wilkes Comm Coll (NC)

SPEECH/RHETORICAL STUDIES

Abraham Baldwin Ag Coll (GA)
Allen County Comm Coll (KS)
Amarillo Coll (TX)
Andrew Coll (GA)
Arkansas State U–Beebe (AR)
Atlanta Metropolitan Coll (GA)
Austin Comm Coll (TX)
Bainbridge Coll (GA)
Bakersfield Coll (CA)
Black Hawk Coll, Moline (IL)
Blinn Coll (TX)
Brazosport Coll (TX)
Brookdale Comm Coll (NJ)
Cañada Coll (CA)
Casper Coll (WY)
Cerritos Coll (CA)
Chaffey Coll (CA)
City Colls of Chicago, Harry S Truman Coll (IL)
City Colls of Chicago, Richard J Daley Coll (IL)
City Colls of Chicago, Wilbur Wright Coll (IL)
Coastal Bend Coll (TX)
Coll of Marin (CA)
Coll of the Desert (CA)
Coll of the Sequoias (CA)
Columbia State Comm Coll (TN)
Compton Comm Coll (CA)
Crafton Hills Coll (CA)
Cuyamaca Coll (CA)
Cypress Coll (CA)
Darton Coll (GA)
De Anza Coll (CA)
Del Mar Coll (TX)
Dodge City Comm Coll (KS)
East Central Coll (MO)
Eastern Oklahoma State Coll (OK)
Everett Comm Coll (WA)
Foothill Coll (CA)
Fresno City Coll (CA)
Fullerton Coll (CA)
Garden City Comm Coll (KS)
Glendale Comm Coll (CA)
Grayson County Coll (TX)
Hill Coll of the Hill Jr College District (TX)
Howard Coll (TX)
Indian River Comm Coll (FL)
Iowa Lakes Comm Coll (IA)
Jefferson Coll (MO)
Kilgore Coll (TX)
Lansing Comm Coll (MI)
Laramie County Comm Coll (WY)
Lincoln Land Comm Coll (IL)
Long Beach City Coll (CA)
Lon Morris Coll (TX)
Los Angeles City Coll (CA)
Los Angeles Mission Coll (CA)
Louisburg Coll (NC)
Lower Columbia Coll (WA)
Manatee Comm Coll (FL)
Miami-Dade Comm Coll (FL)
Midland Coll (TX)
Mid Michigan Comm Coll (MI)
MiraCosta Coll (CA)
Modesto Jr Coll (CA)
Monroe County Comm Coll (MI)
Navarro Coll (TX)
Northeast Comm Coll (NE)
Northern Virginia Comm Coll (VA)
North Harris Coll (TX)
Northwest Coll (WY)
Odessa Coll (TX)
Palomar Coll (CA)
Pasadena City Coll (CA)
Pima Comm Coll (AZ)
Pratt Comm Coll and Area Vocational School (KS)
Ridgewater Coll (MN)
Riverside Comm Coll (CA)
Sacramento City Coll (CA)
St. Philip's Coll (TX)
San Diego City Coll (CA)
San Diego Mesa Coll (CA)
San Jacinto Coll North Campus (TX)
San Joaquin Delta Coll (CA)
Sauk Valley Comm Coll (IL)
Shasta Coll (CA)
Skagit Valley Coll (WA)
Tacoma Comm Coll (WA)
Trinity Valley Comm Coll (TX)
Triton Coll (IL)
Tulsa Comm Coll (OK)
Tyler Jr Coll (TX)
Vermilion Comm Coll (MN)
Wharton County Jr Coll (TX)

SPEECH/THEATER EDUCATION

Angelina Coll (TX)
Coll of the Siskiyous (CA)
Highland Comm Coll (IL)
Iowa Western Comm Coll (IA)
Mid Michigan Comm Coll (MI)

Pratt Comm Coll and Area Vocational School (KS)
San Antonio Coll (TX)
Vincennes U (IN)

SPEECH THERAPY
Mount Wachusett Comm Coll (MA)

SPORT/FITNESS ADMINISTRATION
Barton County Comm Coll (KS)
Bucks County Comm Coll (PA)
Butler County Comm Coll (PA)
Central Oregon Comm Coll (OR)
Coahoma Comm Coll (MS)
Columbus State Comm Coll (OH)
Dean Coll (MA)
Herkimer County Comm Coll (NY)
Hesser Coll (NH)
Holyoke Comm Coll (MA)
Howard Comm Coll (MD)
Keystone Coll (PA)
Kingsborough Comm Coll of City U of NY (NY)
Lorain County Comm Coll (OH)
Louisburg Coll (NC)
Mitchell Coll (CT)
New Hampshire Tech Inst (NH)
New Mexico Military Inst (NM)
Northampton County Area Comm Coll (PA)
North Iowa Area Comm Coll (IA)
Oakland Comm Coll (MI)
Spokane Falls Comm Coll (WA)
State U of NY Coll of Technology at Alfred (NY)
Sullivan County Comm Coll (NY)
Tompkins Cortland Comm Coll (NY)
Vincennes U (IN)

STATIONARY ENERGY SOURCES INSTALLATION
Alexandria Tech Coll (MN)
Ivy Tech State Coll–Bloomington (IN)
Ivy Tech State Coll–Central Indiana (IN)
Ivy Tech State Coll–Columbus (IN)
Ivy Tech State Coll–Eastcentral (IN)
Ivy Tech State Coll–Kokomo (IN)
Ivy Tech State Coll–Lafayette (IN)
Ivy Tech State Coll–North Central (IN)
Ivy Tech State Coll–Northeast (IN)
Ivy Tech State Coll–Southcentral (IN)
Ivy Tech State Coll–Southwest (IN)
Ivy Tech State Coll–Wabash Valley (IN)
Ivy Tech State Coll–Whitewater (IN)

STRINGED INSTRUMENTS
Miami-Dade Comm Coll (FL)
Minnesota State Coll–Southeast Tech (MN)

SURVEYING
Asheville-Buncombe Tech Comm Coll (NC)
Austin Comm Coll (TX)
Bakersfield Coll (CA)
Bates Tech Coll (WA)
Burlington County Coll (NJ)
Centralia Coll (WA)
Central Piedmont Comm Coll (NC)
Chabot Coll (CA)
Chattanooga State Tech Comm Coll (TN)
The Comm Coll of Baltimore County–Catonsville Campus (MD)
Comm Coll of Southern Nevada (NV)
Cuyamaca Coll (CA)
Delaware Tech & Comm Coll, Terry Cmps (DE)
Eastern Oklahoma State Coll (OK)
Fayetteville Tech Comm Coll (NC)
Flathead Valley Comm Coll (MT)
Guilford Tech Comm Coll (NC)
Hawkeye Comm Coll (IA)
Indian River Comm Coll (FL)
Lansing Comm Coll (MI)
Macomb Comm Coll (MI)
Miami-Dade Comm Coll (FL)
Middle Georgia Coll (GA)
Middlesex County Coll (NJ)
Milwaukee Area Tech Coll (WI)
Mohawk Valley Comm Coll (NY)
New Hampshire Comm Tech Coll, Berlin/Laconia (NH)
Oklahoma State U, Oklahoma City (OK)
Palm Beach Comm Coll (FL)
Palomar Coll (CA)
Paul Smith's Coll of Arts and Sciences (NY)
Pennsylvania Coll of Technology (PA)
Penn State U Wilkes-Barre Campus of the Commonwealth Coll (PA)
Red Rocks Comm Coll (CO)
Sacramento City Coll (CA)
Sandhills Comm Coll (NC)
San Jacinto Coll Central Campus (TX)
Santa Fe Comm Coll (NM)
Sierra Coll (CA)
Sinclair Comm Coll (OH)
Southeast Comm Coll, Milford Campus (NE)
Southeast Tech Inst (SD)
Stark State Coll of Technology (OH)
State U of NY Coll of Environ Sci & For Ranger Sch (NY)
State U of NY Coll of Technology at Alfred (NY)
Sullivan County Comm Coll (NY)
Tulsa Comm Coll (OK)
Tyler Jr Coll (TX)
U of Arkansas Comm Coll at Morrilton (AR)
Vincennes U (IN)
Wake Tech Comm Coll (NC)
Westwood Coll of Technology–Denver North (CO)

SYSTEM ADMINISTRATION
American River Coll (CA)
Andover Coll (ME)
Anne Arundel Comm Coll (MD)
Anoka-Hennepin Tech Coll (MN)
Barton County Comm Coll (KS)
Berkeley Coll (NJ)
Cambria County Area Comm Coll (PA)
Camden County Coll (NJ)
Cape Cod Comm Coll (MA)
CHI Inst (PA)
Coastal Bend Coll (TX)
Cumberland County Coll (NJ)
Cypress Coll (CA)
Dakota County Tech Coll (MN)
Daymar Coll (KY)
Electronic Insts, Middletown (PA)
Florida National Coll (FL)
GateWay Comm Coll (AZ)
Harry M. Ayers State Tech Coll (AL)
Hinds Comm Coll (MS)
Lake Area Tech Inst (SD)
Lakeland Comm Coll (OH)
Laurel Business Inst (PA)
Los Angeles City Coll (CA)
Louisville Tech Inst (KY)
Midland Coll (TX)
Minot State U–Bottineau Campus (ND)
Parkland Coll (IL)
Randolph Comm Coll (NC)
Rasmussen Coll Mankato (MN)
Ridgewater Coll (MN)
San Antonio Coll (TX)
Seminole Comm Coll (FL)
Sinclair Comm Coll (OH)
Southeast Tech Inst (SD)
Stanly Comm Coll (NC)
Texas State Tech Coll–Harlingen (TX)
Thaddeus Stevens Coll of Technology (PA)
Tompkins Cortland Comm Coll (NY)
Tulsa Comm Coll (OK)
Vincennes U (IN)
Wake Tech Comm Coll (NC)
The Westchester Business Inst (NY)
York Tech Inst (PA)

SYSTEM/NETWORKING/LAN/WAN MANAGEMENT
Adirondack Comm Coll (NY)
AIB Coll of Business (IA)
American River Coll (CA)
Angelina Coll (TX)
Anoka-Hennepin Tech Coll (MN)
Anoka-Ramsey Comm Coll (MN)
Austin Comm Coll (TX)
Berks Tech Inst (PA)
Blue Ridge Comm Coll (NC)
The Brown Mackie Coll–Olathe Campus (KS)
Cambria County Area Comm Coll (PA)
Camden County Coll (NJ)
Central Comm Coll–Columbus Campus (NE)
Central Comm Coll–Grand Island Campus (NE)
Central Comm Coll–Hastings Campus (NE)
Centralia Coll (WA)
Cleveland Comm Coll (NC)
The Comm Coll of Baltimore County–Catonsville Campus (MD)
Cuesta Coll (CA)
Cypress Coll (CA)
Davis Coll (OH)
Daymar Coll (KY)
Del Mar Coll (TX)
Durham Tech Comm Coll (NC)
Eastfield Coll (TX)
Edgecombe Comm Coll (NC)
Edison Comm Coll (FL)
Education America, Southeast Coll of Technology, New Orleans Campus (LA)
Electronic Insts, Middletown (PA)
Fayetteville Tech Comm Coll (NC)
Fiorello H LaGuardia Comm Coll of City U of NY (NY)
Florida Comm Coll at Jacksonville (FL)
Florida National Coll (FL)
Genesee Comm Coll (NY)
Georgia Perimeter Coll (GA)
Gogebic Comm Coll (MI)
Hawkeye Comm Coll (IA)
Heartland Comm Coll (IL)
Herkimer County Comm Coll (NY)
Hinds Comm Coll (MS)
Holmes Comm Coll (MS)
Inver Hills Comm Coll (MN)
Island Drafting and Tech Inst (NY)
Itasca Comm Coll (MN)
Jackson Comm Coll (MI)
Johnson Coll (PA)
Lakeland Comm Coll (OH)
Laurel Business Inst (PA)
Los Angeles City Coll (CA)
McCann School of Business (PA)
Milwaukee Area Tech Coll (WI)
Mineral Area Coll (MO)
Minot State U–Bottineau Campus (ND)
Naugatuck Valley Comm Coll (CT)
NEI Coll of Technology (MN)
Northland Comm and Tech Coll (MN)
Olympic Coll (WA)
Onondaga Comm Coll (NY)
Owensboro Comm Coll (KY)
Palm Beach Comm Coll (FL)
Parkland Coll (IL)
Pittsburgh Tech Inst (PA)
Rasmussen Coll Mankato (MN)
Ridgewater Coll (MN)
Rockland Comm Coll (NY)
Sampson Comm Coll (NC)
San Antonio Coll (TX)
Sandhills Comm Coll (NC)
San Jacinto Coll North Campus (TX)
Santa Barbara City Coll (CA)
Seminole Comm Coll (FL)
Sheridan Coll (WY)
Silicon Valley Coll, San Jose (CA)
Sinclair Comm Coll (OH)
Southeast Tech Inst (SD)
Southwest Mississippi Comm Coll (MS)
Stanly Comm Coll (NC)
Tacoma Comm Coll (WA)
Tallahassee Comm Coll (FL)
Texas State Tech Coll–Harlingen (TX)
Thaddeus Stevens Coll of Technology (PA)
Triton Coll (IL)
Tulsa Comm Coll (OK)
U of Arkansas Comm Coll at Batesville (AR)
U of Kentucky, Lexington Comm Coll (KY)
Vincennes U (IN)
Webster Inst of Technology (FL)
The Westchester Business Inst (NY)
Western Wisconsin Tech Coll (WI)
Western Wyoming Comm Coll (WY)
York Tech Inst (PA)

SYSTEMS ENGINEERING
Minnesota School of Business (MN)

SYSTEMS SCIENCE/THEORY
Miami U–Middletown Campus (OH)

TEACHER ASSISTANT/AIDE
Alamance Comm Coll (NC)
Angelina Coll (TX)
Antelope Valley Coll (CA)
Athens Tech Coll (GA)
Big Bend Comm Coll (WA)
Blackfeet Comm Coll (MT)
Brunswick Comm Coll (NC)
Bucks County Comm Coll (PA)
Carteret Comm Coll (NC)
Catawba Valley Comm Coll (NC)
Centralia Coll (WA)
Chabot Coll (CA)
Chemeketa Comm Coll (OR)
City Colls of Chicago, Harry S Truman Coll (IL)
City Colls of Chicago, Malcolm X Coll (IL)
City Colls of Chicago, Richard J Daley Coll (IL)
Clark Coll (WA)
Clovis Comm Coll (NM)
Cochise Coll, Douglas (AZ)
Coll of the Desert (CA)
Comm Coll of Southern Nevada (NV)
Comm Coll of Vermont (VT)
Compton Comm Coll (CA)
Danville Area Comm Coll (IL)
Delaware County Comm Coll (PA)
Delta Coll (MI)
Des Moines Area Comm Coll (IA)
Durham Tech Comm Coll (NC)
Ellsworth Comm Coll (IA)
Fort Scott Comm Coll (KS)
Fresno City Coll (CA)
Fulton-Montgomery Comm Coll (NY)
Garden City Comm Coll (KS)
Illinois Eastern Comm Colls, Frontier Comm Coll (IL)
Indian River Comm Coll (FL)
Isothermal Comm Coll (NC)
John A. Logan Coll (IL)
Joliet Jr Coll (IL)
Kirkwood Comm Coll (IA)
Lake Michigan Coll (MI)
Lamar Comm Coll (CO)
Lansing Comm Coll (MI)
Lewis and Clark Comm Coll (IL)
Lincoln Land Comm Coll (IL)
Linn-Benton Comm Coll (OR)
Los Angeles City Coll (CA)
Los Angeles Mission Coll (CA)
Manchester Comm Coll (CT)
Merced Coll (CA)
Mercer County Comm Coll (NJ)
Miami-Dade Comm Coll (FL)
Middlesex County Coll (NJ)
MiraCosta Coll (CA)
Moorpark Coll (CA)
Nash Comm Coll (NC)
Neosho County Comm Coll (KS)
New Hampshire Tech Inst (NH)
New Mexico State U–Alamogordo (NM)
Northland Pioneer Coll (AZ)
Ocean County Coll (NJ)
Odessa Coll (TX)
Pasadena City Coll (CA)
Prairie State Coll (IL)
Ridgewater Coll (MN)
Rockingham Comm Coll (NC)
St. Cloud Tech Coll (MN)
St. Philip's Coll (TX)
Sandhills Comm Coll (NC)
San Diego City Coll (CA)
Shoreline Comm Coll (WA)
Sierra Coll (CA)
Sitting Bull Coll (ND)
Southeastern Comm Coll (NC)
South Suburban Coll (IL)
Vance-Granville Comm Coll (NC)
Victor Valley Coll (CA)
Walla Walla Comm Coll (WA)

TEACHER EDUCATION RELATED
Comm Coll of Allegheny County (PA)
Northampton County Area Comm Coll (PA)

TEACHER EDUCATION, SPECIFIC PROGRAMS RELATED
Comm Coll of Allegheny County (PA)
Pennsylvania Coll of Technology (PA)

TECHNICAL/BUSINESS WRITING
Austin Comm Coll (TX)
Black Hawk Coll, Moline (IL)
Cincinnati State Tech and Comm Coll (OH)
Clark Coll (WA)
Clovis Comm Coll (NM)
Coll of Lake County (IL)
Columbus State Comm Coll (OH)
De Anza Coll (CA)
Florida National Coll (FL)
Gateway Tech Coll (WI)
Golden West Coll (CA)
Herkimer County Comm Coll (NY)
Houston Comm Coll System (TX)
Linn-Benton Comm Coll (OR)
Oklahoma State U, Oklahoma City (OK)
Paul Smith's Coll of Arts and Sciences (NY)
San Diego Mesa Coll (CA)
State U of NY Coll of A&T at Morrisville (NY)
Terra State Comm Coll (OH)
Three Rivers Comm Coll (CT)

TECHNICAL EDUCATION
North Dakota State Coll of Science (ND)

TELECOMMUNICATIONS
Amarillo Coll (TX)
Anne Arundel Comm Coll (MD)
Bossier Parish Comm Coll (LA)
Brookdale Comm Coll (NJ)
Broome Comm Coll (NY)
Butte Coll (CA)
Cayuga County Comm Coll (NY)
Central Carolina Comm Coll (NC)
Central Maine Tech Coll (ME)
Chaffey Coll (CA)
CHI Inst (PA)
Cincinnati State Tech and Comm Coll (OH)
City Colls of Chicago, Richard J Daley Coll (IL)
Clark Coll (WA)
Coffeyville Comm Coll (KS)
Comm Coll of Beaver County (PA)
Compton Comm Coll (CA)
Cuesta Coll (CA)
Daytona Beach Comm Coll (FL)
Des Moines Area Comm Coll (IA)
Dutchess Comm Coll (NY)
ECPI Coll of Technology, Newport News (VA)
ECPI Coll of Technology, Virginia Beach (VA)
ECPI Tech Coll, Richmond (VA)
ECPI Tech Coll, Roanoke (VA)
Gadsden State Comm Coll (AL)
Golden West Coll (CA)
Gwinnett Tech Coll (GA)
Herkimer County Comm Coll (NY)
Highland Comm Coll (KS)
Hinds Comm Coll (MS)
Howard Comm Coll (MD)
Illinois Eastern Comm Colls, Lincoln Trail Coll (IL)
Jefferson Coll (MO)
Kansas City Kansas Comm Coll (KS)
Kirkwood Comm Coll (IA)
Lake Land Coll (IL)

Lansing Comm Coll (MI)
Los Angeles City Coll (CA)
Massachusetts Bay Comm Coll (MA)
McIntosh Coll (NH)
Meridian Comm Coll (MS)
Middlesex Comm Coll (MA)
Midlands Tech Coll (SC)
Miles Comm Coll (MT)
Mitchell Tech Inst (SD)
Mohawk Valley Comm Coll (NY)
Monroe Comm Coll (NY)
Moorpark Coll (CA)
Mount Wachusett Comm Coll (MA)
NEI Coll of Technology (MN)
New York City Tech Coll of the City U of NY (NY)
Niagara County Comm Coll (NY)
Northwest Mississippi Comm Coll (MS)
Onondaga Comm Coll (NY)
Oxnard Coll (CA)
Palomar Coll (CA)
Pasadena City Coll (CA)
Queensborough Comm Coll of City U of NY (NY)
Reading Area Comm Coll (PA)
St. Louis Comm Coll at Florissant Valley (MO)
St. Petersburg Coll (FL)
San Bernardino Valley Coll (CA)
San Diego City Coll (CA)
Santa Ana Coll (CA)
Schenectady County Comm Coll (NY)
Seminole Comm Coll (FL)
Skagit Valley Coll (WA)
South Plains Coll (TX)
South Puget Sound Comm Coll (WA)
Southwestern Coll (CA)
Suffolk County Comm Coll (NY)
Trident Tech Coll (SC)
Tulsa Comm Coll (OK)
Vermont Tech Coll (VT)
Wake Tech Comm Coll (NC)

TEXTILE ARTS
Antelope Valley Coll (CA)
Compton Comm Coll (CA)
Haywood Comm Coll (NC)
Highland Comm Coll (KS)
Inst of American Indian Arts (NM)
Monterey Peninsula Coll (CA)
Pasadena City Coll (CA)

THEATER ARTS/DRAMA
Allen County Comm Coll (KS)
Alvin Comm Coll (TX)
Amarillo Coll (TX)
American Academy of Dramatic Arts (NY)
American Academy of Dramatic Arts/Hollywood (CA)
American River Coll (CA)
Andrew Coll (GA)
Arizona Western Coll (AZ)
Bacone Coll (OK)
Bainbridge Coll (GA)
Bakersfield Coll (CA)
Barton County Comm Coll (KS)
Bergen Comm Coll (NJ)
Berkshire Comm Coll (MA)
Black Hawk Coll, Moline (IL)
Blinn Coll (TX)
Brazosport Coll (TX)
Brookdale Comm Coll (NJ)
Bucks County Comm Coll (PA)
Burlington County Coll (NJ)
Camden County Coll (NJ)
Cañada Coll (CA)
Cape Cod Comm Coll (MA)
Casper Coll (WY)
Centralia Coll (WA)
Central Wyoming Coll (WY)
Cerritos Coll (CA)
Chaffey Coll (CA)
Chattahoochee Valley Comm Coll (AL)
Citrus Coll (CA)
City Colls of Chicago, Richard J Daley Coll (IL)
Coastal Bend Coll (TX)
Coffeyville Comm Coll (KS)
Colby Comm Coll (KS)
Coll of Marin (CA)
Coll of Southern Idaho (ID)
Coll of the Desert (CA)
Coll of the Sequoias (CA)
Coll of the Siskiyous (CA)
Colorado Mountn Coll (CO)
Comm Coll of Allegheny County (PA)
The Comm Coll of Baltimore County–Catonsville Campus (MD)
Comm Coll of Rhode Island (RI)
Comm Coll of Southern Nevada (NV)
Compton Comm Coll (CA)
Cowley County Comm Coll and Voc-Tech School (KS)
Crafton Hills Coll (CA)
Crowder Coll (MO)
Cumberland County Coll (NJ)
Cypress Coll (CA)
Darton Coll (GA)
Daytona Beach Comm Coll (FL)
Dean Coll (MA)
De Anza Coll (CA)
Del Mar Coll (TX)
Delta Coll (MI)
Dixie State Coll of Utah (UT)
Dodge City Comm Coll (KS)
East Central Coll (MO)
Eastern Arizona Coll (AZ)
Eastern Oklahoma State Coll (OK)
Everett Comm Coll (WA)
Finger Lakes Comm Coll (NY)
Foothill Coll (CA)
Fresno City Coll (CA)
Fullerton Coll (CA)
Fulton-Montgomery Comm Coll (NY)
Galveston Coll (TX)
Garden City Comm Coll (KS)
Genesee Comm Coll (NY)
Georgia Perimeter Coll (GA)
Glendale Comm Coll (CA)
Gloucester County Coll (NJ)
Gordon Coll (GA)
Grayson County Coll (TX)
Guilford Tech Comm Coll (NC)
Harrisburg Area Comm Coll (PA)
Henry Ford Comm Coll (MI)
Highland Comm Coll (IL)
Highland Comm Coll (KS)
Hill Coll of the Hill Jr College District (TX)
Hillsborough Comm Coll (FL)
Hinds Comm Coll (MS)
Holyoke Comm Coll (MA)
Houston Comm Coll System (TX)
Howard Coll (TX)
Howard Comm Coll (MD)
Indian River Comm Coll (FL)
Jefferson Coll (MO)
Jefferson Davis Comm Coll (AL)
Joliet Jr Coll (IL)
Kansas City Kansas Comm Coll (KS)
Kellogg Comm Coll (MI)
Kilgore Coll (TX)
Kingsborough Comm Coll of City U of NY (NY)
Kirkwood Comm Coll (IA)
Lake Michigan Coll (MI)
Lake Tahoe Comm Coll (CA)
Lansing Comm Coll (MI)
Laramie County Comm Coll (WY)
Lincoln Coll, Lincoln (IL)
Lincoln Land Comm Coll (IL)
Linn-Benton Comm Coll (OR)
Long Beach City Coll (CA)
Lon Morris Coll (TX)
Lorain County Comm Coll (OH)
Los Angeles City Coll (CA)
Los Angeles Mission Coll (CA)
Los Angeles Pierce Coll (CA)
Lower Columbia Coll (WA)
Manatee Comm Coll (FL)
Manchester Comm Coll (CT)
Massachusetts Bay Comm Coll (MA)
Merced Coll (CA)
Mercer County Comm Coll (NJ)
Miami-Dade Comm Coll (FL)
Middlesex Comm Coll (MA)
Middlesex County Coll (NJ)
Mid Michigan Comm Coll (MI)
MiraCosta Coll (CA)
Mississippi Delta Comm Coll (MS)
Modesto Jr Coll (CA)
Monterey Peninsula Coll (CA)
Moorpark Coll (CA)
Nassau Comm Coll (NY)
Navarro Coll (TX)
Niagara County Comm Coll (NY)
Northeast Comm Coll (NE)
Northern Essex Comm Coll (MA)
North Harris Coll (TX)
North Idaho Coll (ID)
Oklahoma City Comm Coll (OK)
Orange Coast Coll (CA)
Otero Jr Coll (CO)
Oxnard Coll (CA)
Palm Beach Comm Coll (FL)
Palomar Coll (CA)
Pasadena City Coll (CA)
Pensacola Jr Coll (FL)
Piedmont Virginia Comm Coll (VA)
Pikes Peak Comm Coll (CO)
Pima Comm Coll (AZ)
Raritan Valley Comm Coll (NJ)
Ridgewater Coll (MN)
Riverside Comm Coll (CA)
Rockland Comm Coll (NY)
Sacramento City Coll (CA)
St. Louis Comm Coll at Florissant Valley (MO)
St. Philip's Coll (TX)
San Diego City Coll (CA)
San Jacinto Coll Central Campus (TX)
San Jacinto Coll North Campus (TX)
San Joaquin Delta Coll (CA)
San Juan Coll (NM)
Santa Ana Coll (CA)
Santa Barbara City Coll (CA)
Santa Monica Coll (CA)
Sauk Valley Comm Coll (IL)
Schenectady County Comm Coll (NY)
Scottsdale Comm Coll (AZ)
Shasta Coll (CA)
Sinclair Comm Coll (OH)
Snow Coll (UT)
Southwestern Coll (CA)
Suffolk County Comm Coll (NY)
Texarkana Coll (TX)
Three Rivers Comm Coll (CT)
Trinidad State Jr Coll (CO)
Trinity Valley Comm Coll (TX)
Triton Coll (IL)
Tulsa Comm Coll (OK)
Umpqua Comm Coll (OR)
Ventura Coll (CA)
Vermilion Comm Coll (MN)
Victor Valley Coll (CA)
Vincennes U (IN)
Western Wyoming Comm Coll (WY)
Wharton County Jr Coll (TX)
Young Harris Coll (GA)

THEATER DESIGN
Comm Coll of Rhode Island (RI)
Florida Comm Coll at Jacksonville (FL)
Fresno City Coll (CA)
Howard Comm Coll (MD)
Nassau Comm Coll (NY)
Santa Barbara City Coll (CA)

THEOLOGY
Assumption Coll for Sisters (NJ)
Highland Comm Coll (KS)
Lon Morris Coll (TX)
Mid-America Baptist Theological Seminary (TN)
Riverside Comm Coll (CA)

TOOL/DIE MAKING
Alexandria Tech Coll (MN)
Asheville-Buncombe Tech Comm Coll (NC)
Bevill State Comm Coll (AL)
Calhoun Comm Coll (AL)
Craven Comm Coll (NC)
Dunwoody Coll of Technology (MN)
Fayetteville Tech Comm Coll (NC)
Gadsden State Comm Coll (AL)
Hawkeye Comm Coll (IA)
Ivy Tech State Coll–Bloomington (IN)
Ivy Tech State Coll–Central Indiana (IN)
Ivy Tech State Coll–Columbus (IN)
Ivy Tech State Coll–Eastcentral (IN)
Ivy Tech State Coll–Kokomo (IN)
Ivy Tech State Coll–Lafayette (IN)
Ivy Tech State Coll–North Central (IN)
Ivy Tech State Coll–Northeast (IN)
Ivy Tech State Coll–Northwest (IN)
Ivy Tech State Coll–Southcentral (IN)
Ivy Tech State Coll–Southwest (IN)
Ivy Tech State Coll–Wabash Valley (IN)
Ivy Tech State Coll–Whitewater (IN)
Kishwaukee Coll (IL)
North Iowa Area Comm Coll (IA)
Northwest State Comm Coll (OH)
Pennsylvania Coll of Technology (PA)
Prairie State Coll (IL)
Terra State Comm Coll (OH)
Wake Tech Comm Coll (NC)
Western Iowa Tech Comm Coll (IA)
Wilson Tech Comm Coll (NC)

TOURISM PROMOTION OPERATIONS
AIB Coll of Business (IA)
Central Oregon Comm Coll (OR)
Coll of DuPage (IL)
Comm Coll of Allegheny County (PA)
Florida National Coll (FL)
Guam Comm Coll (GU)
Herkimer County Comm Coll (NY)
Lehigh Carbon Comm Coll (PA)
Rasmussen Coll Mankato (MN)
Westchester Comm Coll (NY)

TOURISM/TRAVEL MARKETING
Edmonds Comm Coll (WA)
Harrisburg Area Comm Coll (PA)
Lehigh Carbon Comm Coll (PA)
Moraine Valley Comm Coll (IL)
National Coll of Business & Technology, Salem (VA)
Pittsburgh Tech Inst (PA)

TOURISM/TRAVEL MARKETING RELATED
Dixie State Coll of Utah (UT)

TRADE/INDUSTRIAL EDUCATION
Compton Comm Coll (CA)
Del Mar Coll (TX)
ECPI Coll of Technology, Newport News (VA)
ECPI Tech Coll, Richmond (VA)
Ellsworth Comm Coll (IA)
Florence-Darlington Tech Coll (SC)
Florida National Coll (FL)
Garden City Comm Coll (KS)
Isothermal Comm Coll (NC)
Kilgore Coll (TX)
Lenoir Comm Coll (NC)
Manatee Comm Coll (FL)
Neosho County Comm Coll (KS)
Northeast Iowa Comm Coll (IA)
Northwest Coll (WY)
Portland Comm Coll (OR)
Pratt Comm Coll and Area Vocational School (KS)
Snow Coll (UT)
Southwestern Comm Coll (NC)
Spartanburg Tech Coll (SC)
U of Arkansas Comm Coll at Hope (AR)
Victor Valley Coll (CA)

TRANSPORTATION AND MATERIALS MOVING RELATED
Palo Verde Coll (CA)

TRANSPORTATION TECHNOLOGY
Central Piedmont Comm Coll (NC)
Chattanooga State Tech Comm Coll (TN)
City Coll of San Francisco (CA)
City Colls of Chicago, Richard J Daley Coll (IL)
Coll of DuPage (IL)
The Comm Coll of Baltimore County–Catonsville Campus (MD)
Delaware Tech & Comm Coll, Stanton/ Wilmington Cmps (DE)
Fort Scott Comm Coll (KS)
Henry Ford Comm Coll (MI)
Highline Comm Coll (WA)
Houston Comm Coll System (TX)
Illinois Eastern Comm Colls, Wabash Valley Coll (IL)
Middlesex County Coll (NJ)
Milwaukee Area Tech Coll (WI)
Nassau Comm Coll (NY)
North Hennepin Comm Coll (MN)
Oxnard Coll (CA)
Sacramento City Coll (CA)
San Diego City Coll (CA)
Sinclair Comm Coll (OH)
Southeast Comm Coll, Milford Campus (NE)
Triton Coll (IL)

TRAVEL SERVICES MARKETING OPERATIONS
AIB Coll of Business (IA)
Coll of DuPage (IL)
Dakota County Tech Coll (MN)
Edmonds Comm Coll (WA)
Florida Comm Coll at Jacksonville (FL)
Guam Comm Coll (GU)
Herkimer County Comm Coll (NY)
Luzerne County Comm Coll (PA)
Milwaukee Area Tech Coll (WI)
Moraine Valley Comm Coll (IL)
Northampton County Area Comm Coll (PA)
Pittsburgh Tech Inst (PA)
Rasmussen Coll Mankato (MN)
San Diego Mesa Coll (CA)
Tompkins Cortland Comm Coll (NY)
Waubonsee Comm Coll (IL)

TRAVEL/TOURISM MANAGEMENT
Adirondack Comm Coll (NY)
AIB Coll of Business (IA)
Allentown Business School (PA)
Amarillo Coll (TX)
Arapahoe Comm Coll (CO)
Atlantic Cape Comm Coll (NJ)
Bay State Coll (MA)
Bergen Comm Coll (NJ)
Berkshire Comm Coll (MA)
Blair Coll (CO)
Blue Ridge Comm Coll (NC)
Bradford School (OH)
Briarwood Coll (CT)
Bryant & Stratton Business Inst, Rochester (NY)
Bryant and Stratton Coll, Virginia Beach (VA)
Butler County Comm Coll (PA)
Butte Coll (CA)
Cañada Coll (CA)
Central Pennsylvania Coll (PA)
Central Piedmont Comm Coll (NC)
Chabot Coll (CA)
Coll of DuPage (IL)
Comm Coll of Denver (CO)
Consolidated School of Business, Lancaster (PA)
Consolidated School of Business, York (PA)
Corning Comm Coll (NY)
Cypress Coll (CA)
Danville Area Comm Coll (IL)
Davis Coll (OH)
Daytona Beach Comm Coll (FL)
Dutchess Comm Coll (NY)
East Central Coll (MO)
Erie Business Center, Main (PA)
Erie Business Center South (PA)
Finger Lakes Comm Coll (NY)
Fiorello H LaGuardia Comm Coll of City U of NY (NY)
Fisher Coll (MA)
Florida National Coll (FL)
Foothill Coll (CA)
Fullerton Coll (CA)
Genesee Comm Coll (NY)
Guam Comm Coll (GU)
Gwinnett Tech Coll (GA)
Hamilton Coll (IA)
Harrisburg Area Comm Coll (PA)
Hawaii Business Coll (HI)
Heald Coll, Schools of Business and Technology (HI)
Herkimer County Comm Coll (NY)
Hesser Coll (NH)
Highline Comm Coll (WA)
Holyoke Comm Coll (MA)
Houston Comm Coll System (TX)
Indiana Business Coll, Indianapolis (IN)
Indiana Business Coll, Muncie (IN)
International Business Coll, Fort Wayne (IN)
Iowa Lakes Comm Coll (IA)
Jefferson Comm Coll (NY)

John A. Logan Coll (IL)
Johnson County Comm Coll (KS)
Kaplan Coll (IA)
Kent State U, Trumbull Campus (OH)
Kingsborough Comm Coll of City U of NY (NY)
Lakeland Comm Coll (OH)
Lansing Comm Coll (MI)
Lincoln Coll, Lincoln (IL)
Lincoln Coll, Normal (IL)
Lincoln School of Commerce (NE)
Long Beach City Coll (CA)
Lorain County Comm Coll (OH)
Los Angeles City Coll (CA)
Luzerne County Comm Coll (PA)
Maple Woods Comm Coll (MO)
Marian Court Coll (MA)
Massasoit Comm Coll (MA)
Mayland Comm Coll (NC)
McIntosh Coll (NH)
Miami-Dade Comm Coll (FL)
Mid-State Coll (ME)
Mineral Area Coll (MO)
MiraCosta Coll (CA)
Monroe Comm Coll (NY)
Mountain West Coll (UT)
Mt. Hood Comm Coll (OR)
Muskingum Area Tech Coll (OH)
Newbury Coll (MA)
New Hampshire Tech Inst (NH)
Northern Essex Comm Coll (MA)
Northern Virginia Comm Coll (VA)
North Harris Coll (TX)
North Shore Comm Coll (MA)
Northwest Coll (WY)
Northwestern Business Coll (IL)
Pace Inst (PA)
Palomar Coll (CA)
Pasadena City Coll (CA)
Patricia Stevens Coll (MO)
Paul Smith's Coll of Arts and Sciences (NY)
Pennsylvania Coll of Technology (PA)
Phoenix Coll (AZ)
Pima Comm Coll (AZ)
Quincy Coll (MA)
Quinsigamond Comm Coll (MA)
Raritan Valley Comm Coll (NJ)
Rasmussen Coll Eagan (MN)
Rasmussen Coll Mankato (MN)
Rasmussen Coll St. Cloud (MN)
Reading Area Comm Coll (PA)
Ridgewater Coll (MN)
Rockingham Comm Coll (NC)
Rockland Comm Coll (NY)
St. Petersburg Coll (FL)
San Diego City Coll (CA)
San Diego Mesa Coll (CA)
San Joaquin Valley Coll (CA)
Santa Ana Coll (CA)
Schenectady County Comm Coll (NY)
Schiller International USwitzerland)
Sinclair Comm Coll (OH)
Southwestern Coll (CA)
State U of NY Coll of A&T at Morrisville (NY)
State U of NY Coll of Technology at Delhi (NY)
Sullivan County Comm Coll (NY)
Three Rivers Comm Coll (CT)
Tompkins Cortland Comm Coll (NY)
Tulsa Comm Coll (OK)
U of Alaska Southeast, Ketchikan Campus (AK)
U of Northwestern Ohio (OH)
Webster Coll, Holiday (FL)
Webster Inst of Technology (FL)
Westchester Comm Coll (NY)
Westmoreland County Comm Coll (PA)

TURF MANAGEMENT
Brunswick Comm Coll (NC)
Central Oregon Comm Coll (OR)
Cincinnati State Tech and Comm Coll (OH)
Comm Coll of Allegheny County (PA)
Cuyamaca Coll (CA)
Guilford Tech Comm Coll (NC)
Kishwaukee Coll (IL)
Lake City Comm Coll (FL)
Minot State U–Bottineau Campus (ND)
Northeast Comm Coll (NE)
Northland Pioneer Coll (AZ)
Northwestern Michigan Coll (MI)
Sandhills Comm Coll (NC)
Southeast Tech Inst (SD)
State U of NY Coll of Technology at Delhi (NY)
Texas State Tech Coll– Waco/ Marshall Campus (TX)
Walla Walla Comm Coll (WA)
Wayne Comm Coll (NC)
Western Iowa Tech Comm Coll (IA)

URBAN STUDIES
Comm Coll of Rhode Island (RI)
Lorain County Comm Coll (OH)
Riverside Comm Coll (CA)
St. Philip's Coll (TX)

VEHICLE/EQUIPMENT OPERATION
Brazosport Coll (TX)
Comm Coll of the Air Force (AL)
Skagit Valley Coll (WA)
Western Nevada Comm Coll (NV)

VEHICLE/MOBILE EQUIPMENT MECHANICS AND REPAIR RELATED
Albuquerque Tech Vocational Inst (NM)
North Dakota State Coll of Science (ND)
Pennsylvania Coll of Technology (PA)
Victor Valley Coll (CA)

VEHICLE PARTS/ACCESSORIES MARKETING OPERATIONS
Dakota County Tech Coll (MN)
Guam Comm Coll (GU)

VEHICLE/PETROLEUM PRODUCTS MARKETING
Central Comm Coll–Hastings Campus (NE)

VETERINARIAN ASSISTANT
Berkshire Comm Coll (MA)
Cedar Valley Coll (TX)
County Coll of Morris (NJ)
Eastern Wyoming Coll (WY)
Everett Comm Coll (WA)
Johnson Coll (PA)
Joliet Jr Coll (IL)
Lehigh Carbon Comm Coll (PA)
Minnesota School of Business (MN)
Northampton County Area Comm Coll (PA)
Parkland Coll (IL)
Pima Comm Coll (AZ)
Snead State Comm Coll (AL)
Sussex County Comm Coll (NJ)

VETERINARY SCIENCES
Black Hawk Coll, Moline (IL)
Casper Coll (WY)
Colby Comm Coll (KS)
Del Mar Coll (TX)
Eastern Oklahoma State Coll (OK)
Grayson County Coll (TX)
Highland Comm Coll (KS)
Hinds Comm Coll (MS)
Holmes Comm Coll (MS)
Holyoke Comm Coll (MA)
Isothermal Comm Coll (NC)
Kirkwood Comm Coll (IA)
Lorain County Comm Coll (OH)
Macomb Comm Coll (MI)
Manor Coll (PA)
Miami-Dade Comm Coll (FL)
Monroe County Comm Coll (MI)
Navarro Coll (TX)
North Harris Coll (TX)
Northwest-Shoals Comm Coll (AL)
Pasadena City Coll (CA)
Reading Area Comm Coll (PA)
Snow Coll (UT)
State U of NY Coll of Technology at Alfred (NY)
Suffolk County Comm Coll (NY)
Vincennes U (IN)

VETERINARY TECHNOLOGY
Argosy U-Twin Cities (MN)
Bel-Rea Inst of Animal Technology (CO)
Bergen Comm Coll (NJ)
Blue Ridge Comm Coll (VA)
Brevard Comm Coll (FL)
Central Carolina Comm Coll (NC)
Colby Comm Coll (KS)
Coll of Southern Idaho (ID)
Colorado Mountn Coll (CO)
Columbia State Comm Coll (TN)
Columbus State Comm Coll (OH)
Comm Coll of Denver (CO)
Comm Coll of Southern Nevada (NV)
Cuyahoga Comm Coll (OH)
Delaware Tech & Comm Coll, Jack F Owens Cmps (DE)
Fiorello H LaGuardia Comm Coll of City U of NY (NY)
Foothill Coll (CA)
Gaston Coll (NC)
Harcum Coll (PA)
Hinds Comm Coll (MS)
Holyoke Comm Coll (MA)
Jefferson Coll (MO)
Johnson County Comm Coll (KS)
Kirkwood Comm Coll (IA)
Lansing Comm Coll (MI)
Los Angeles Pierce Coll (CA)
Manor Coll (PA)
Maple Woods Comm Coll (MO)
Midland Coll (TX)
Northeast Comm Coll (NE)
Northern Virginia Comm Coll (VA)
North Shore Comm Coll (MA)
Northwestern Connecticut Comm-Tech Coll (CT)
Pierce Coll (WA)
Ridgewater Coll (MN)
St. Petersburg Coll (FL)
San Diego Mesa Coll (CA)
San Joaquin Valley Coll (CA)
State U of NY Coll of Technology at Canton (NY)
State U of NY Coll of Technology at Delhi (NY)
Tomball Coll (TX)
Tri-County Tech Coll (SC)
Trident Tech Coll (SC)
Tulsa Comm Coll (OK)
Vermont Tech Coll (VT)
Western School of Health and Business Careers (PA)

VISUAL AND PERFORMING ARTS RELATED
The Art Inst of Philadelphia (PA)
Comm Coll of Allegheny County (PA)
Florida Comm Coll at Jacksonville (FL)
Santa Fe Comm Coll (NM)

VISUAL/PERFORMING ARTS
Amarillo Coll (TX)
Brookdale Comm Coll (NJ)
Bucks County Comm Coll (PA)
Citrus Coll (CA)
Holyoke Comm Coll (MA)
Hutchinson Comm Coll and Area Vocational School (KS)
Kansas City Kansas Comm Coll (KS)
Kingwood Coll (TX)
Mt. San Jacinto Coll (CA)
Nassau Comm Coll (NY)
Queensborough Comm Coll of City U of NY (NY)
Raritan Valley Comm Coll (NJ)

VOCATIONAL REHABILITATION COUNSELING
Edmonds Comm Coll (WA)
Manatee Comm Coll (FL)
Spokane Falls Comm Coll (WA)

WATER RESOURCES
Bay de Noc Comm Coll (MI)
Cecil Comm Coll (MD)
Citrus Coll (CA)
Coll of Southern Idaho (ID)
Coll of the Canyons (CA)
Colorado Mountn Coll, Timberline Cmps (CO)
Delta Coll (MI)
Dodge City Comm Coll (KS)
Doña Ana Branch Comm Coll (NM)
Feather River Comm Coll District (CA)
Fort Scott Comm Coll (KS)
Imperial Valley Coll (CA)
Indian River Comm Coll (FL)
Iowa Lakes Comm Coll (IA)
Kirkwood Comm Coll (IA)
Lenoir Comm Coll (NC)
Milwaukee Area Tech Coll (WI)
Minot State U–Bottineau Campus (ND)
Moraine Park Tech Coll (WI)
Mountain Empire Comm Coll (VA)
Northeast Alabama Comm Coll (AL)
Palomar Coll (CA)
Red Rocks Comm Coll (CO)
St. Petersburg Coll (FL)
San Diego Mesa Coll (CA)
Spokane Comm Coll (WA)
Three Rivers Comm Coll (CT)
Ventura Coll (CA)
Vermilion Comm Coll (MN)

WATER RESOURCES ENGINEERING
Dixie State Coll of Utah (UT)
Santa Ana Coll (CA)

WATER TRANSPORTATION RELATED
Northwestern Michigan Coll (MI)

WATER TREATMENT TECHNOLOGY
Angelina Coll (TX)
Bay de Noc Comm Coll (MI)
Brevard Comm Coll (FL)
Clackamas Comm Coll (OR)
Collin County Comm Coll District (TX)
Delta Coll (MI)
Florida Comm Coll at Jacksonville (FL)
Green River Comm Coll (WA)
Linn-Benton Comm Coll (OR)
New Hampshire Comm Tech Coll, Berlin/Laconia (NH)
Northwest-Shoals Comm Coll (AL)
St. Cloud Tech Coll (MN)
San Juan Coll (NM)
Springfield Tech Comm Coll (MA)
Trinidad State Jr Coll (CO)
U of Alaska Southeast, Sitka Campus (AK)
Vermilion Comm Coll (MN)

WEB/MULTIMEDIA MANAGEMENT/WEBMASTER
American River Coll (CA)
Andover Coll (ME)
Anoka-Hennepin Tech Coll (MN)
Antonelli Coll (OH)
Bradley Academy for the Visual Arts (PA)
Bristol Comm Coll (MA)
Cambria County Area Comm Coll (PA)
Camden County Coll (NJ)
Cape Cod Comm Coll (MA)
Central Comm Coll–Columbus Campus (NE)
Central Comm Coll–Grand Island Campus (NE)
Central Comm Coll–Hastings Campus (NE)
Central Pennsylvania Coll (PA)
Cerro Coso Comm Coll (CA)
Columbia-Greene Comm Coll (NY)
The Comm Coll of Baltimore County–Catonsville Campus (MD)
Dakota County Tech Coll (MN)
Daymar Coll (KY)
Del Mar Coll (TX)
Delta Coll (MI)
Fayetteville Tech Comm Coll (NC)
Flathead Valley Comm Coll (MT)
Florida Comm Coll at Jacksonville (FL)
Florida Computer & Business School (FL)
Hawkeye Comm Coll (IA)
Horry-Georgetown Tech Coll (SC)
Itasca Comm Coll (MN)
Kansas City Kansas Comm Coll (KS)
Kennebec Valley Tech Coll (ME)
Lake Area Tech Inst (SD)
Lakeland Comm Coll (OH)
Los Angeles City Coll (CA)
Mid-South Comm Coll (AR)
Milwaukee Area Tech Coll (WI)
Minneapolis Comm and Tech Coll (MN)
Minot State U–Bottineau Campus (ND)
Monroe County Comm Coll (MI)
Northern Essex Comm Coll (MA)
Northland Comm and Tech Coll (MN)
Onondaga Comm Coll (NY)
Pioneer Pacific Coll (OR)
Pittsburgh Tech Inst (PA)
Ridgewater Coll (MN)
Riverland Comm Coll (MN)
Saint Charles Comm Coll (MO)
St. Petersburg Coll (FL)
Salem Comm Coll (NJ)
Sandhills Comm Coll (NC)
Seminole Comm Coll (FL)
Sheridan Coll (WY)
Sinclair Comm Coll (OH)
Southeast Tech Inst (SD)
Southwestern Coll (CA)
Stanly Comm Coll (NC)
Stark State Coll of Technology (OH)
Sullivan County Comm Coll (NY)
Texas State Tech Coll–Harlingen (TX)
Trident Tech Coll (SC)
Triton Coll (IL)
Tulsa Comm Coll (OK)
Vincennes U (IN)
Wake Tech Comm Coll (NC)
The Westchester Business Inst (NY)

WEB PAGE DESIGN
Academy Coll (MN)
Berkeley Coll (NJ)

WEB PAGE, DIGITAL/ MULTIMEDIA AND INFORMATION RESOURCES DESIGN
Adirondack Comm Coll (NY)
American River Coll (CA)
Anoka-Hennepin Tech Coll (MN)
Arapahoe Comm Coll (CO)
The Art Inst of Houston (TX)
Barton County Comm Coll (KS)
Bradley Academy for the Visual Arts (PA)
Broome Comm Coll (NY)
Camden County Coll (NJ)
Cape Cod Comm Coll (MA)
Capital Comm Coll (CT)
Cerro Coso Comm Coll (CA)
Coll of the Redwoods (CA)
Coll of the Sequoias (CA)
Coll of the Siskiyous (CA)
The Comm Coll of Baltimore County–Catonsville Campus (MD)
Cuesta Coll (CA)
Cypress Coll (CA)
Dakota County Tech Coll (MN)
Davis Coll (OH)
Daymar Coll (KY)
Delaware County Comm Coll (PA)
Del Mar Coll (TX)
Delta Coll (MI)
Diablo Valley Coll (CA)
Dixie State Coll of Utah (UT)
Education America, Remington Coll, Lafayette Campus (LA)
El Centro Coll (TX)
Erie Business Center, Main (PA)
Fayetteville Tech Comm Coll (NC)
Florida Comm Coll at Jacksonville (FL)
Florida National Coll (FL)
Galveston Coll (TX)
Georgia Perimeter Coll (GA)
Hawaii Business Coll (HI)
Hawkeye Comm Coll (IA)
Heartland Comm Coll (IL)
Hibbing Comm Coll (MN)
Horry-Georgetown Tech Coll (SC)
Itasca Comm Coll (MN)
Jackson Comm Coll (MI)
Joliet Jr Coll (IL)
Kansas City Kansas Comm Coll (KS)
Kennebec Valley Tech Coll (ME)
Lake City Comm Coll (FL)
Lakeland Comm Coll (OH)
Laurel Business Inst (PA)

Los Angeles City Coll (CA)
Louisville Tech Inst (KY)
Mesabi Range Comm and Tech Coll (MN)
Minneapolis Comm and Tech Coll (MN)
Minot State U–Bottineau Campus (ND)
Monroe County Comm Coll (MI)
Montana State U Coll of Tech-Great Falls (MT)
Muskingum Area Tech Coll (OH)
Northern Essex Comm Coll (MA)
Northland Comm and Tech Coll (MN)
Northwestern Business Coll (IL)
Onondaga Comm Coll (NY)
Palm Beach Comm Coll (FL)
Parkland Coll (IL)
Peninsula Coll (WA)
Pennsylvania Inst of Technology (PA)
Pittsburgh Tech Inst (PA)
Platt Coll (CO)
Rasmussen Coll Mankato (MN)
Ridgewater Coll (MN)
Riverland Comm Coll (MN)
San Antonio Coll (TX)
Seminole Comm Coll (FL)
Sheridan Coll (WY)
Southeast Tech Inst (SD)
Southwestern Coll (CA)
Stanly Comm Coll (NC)
Stark State Coll of Technology (OH)
Tacoma Comm Coll (WA)
Texas State Tech Coll–Harlingen (TX)
Thaddeus Stevens Coll of Technology (PA)
Tompkins Cortland Comm Coll (NY)
Trident Tech Coll (SC)
Triton Coll (IL)
Tulsa Comm Coll (OK)
Vincennes U (IN)
Vista Comm Coll (CA)
Wake Tech Comm Coll (NC)
The Westchester Business Inst (NY)
York Tech Inst (PA)

WELDING TECHNOLOGY
Aims Comm Coll (CO)
Alamance Comm Coll (NC)
Alexandria Tech Coll (MN)
Allan Hancock Coll (CA)
American River Coll (CA)
Angelina Coll (TX)
Antelope Valley Coll (CA)
Arizona Western Coll (AZ)
Austin Comm Coll (TX)
Bainbridge Coll (GA)
Bakersfield Coll (CA)
Barton County Comm Coll (KS)
Beaufort County Comm Coll (NC)
Belmont Tech Coll (OH)
Bevill State Comm Coll (AL)
Big Bend Comm Coll (WA)
Bismarck State Coll (ND)
Brazosport Coll (TX)
Brevard Comm Coll (FL)
Butte Coll (CA)
Cape Fear Comm Coll (NC)
Casper Coll (WY)
Cecil Comm Coll (MD)
Central Comm Coll–Columbus Campus (NE)
Central Comm Coll–Grand Island Campus (NE)
Central Comm Coll–Hastings Campus (NE)
Centralia Coll (WA)
Central Oregon Comm Coll (OR)
Central Piedmont Comm Coll (NC)
Central Texas Coll (TX)
Central Wyoming Coll (WY)
Cerritos Coll (CA)
Cerro Coso Comm Coll (CA)
Chabot Coll (CA)
Chattanooga State Tech Comm Coll (TN)
Chemeketa Comm Coll (OR)
Chippewa Valley Tech Coll (WI)
Cisco Jr Coll (TX)
Clark Coll (WA)
Coastal Bend Coll (TX)
Coffeyville Comm Coll (KS)
Coll of DuPage (IL)
Coll of Eastern Utah (UT)
Coll of Southern Idaho (ID)
Coll of the Canyons (CA)
Coll of the Desert (CA)
Coll of the Redwoods (CA)
Coll of the Sequoias (CA)
Coll of the Siskiyous (CA)
Comm Coll of Allegheny County (PA)
Comm Coll of Southern Nevada (NV)
Compton Comm Coll (CA)
Cowley County Comm Coll and Voc-Tech School (KS)
Cuesta Coll (CA)
Danville Area Comm Coll (IL)
Delaware Tech & Comm Coll, Jack F Owens Cmps (DE)
Del Mar Coll (TX)
Delta Coll (MI)
Des Moines Area Comm Coll (IA)
Dodge City Comm Coll (KS)
Doña Ana Branch Comm Coll (NM)
Douglas MacArthur State Tech Coll (AL)
Dunwoody Coll of Technology (MN)
East Central Coll (MO)
Eastern Arizona Coll (AZ)
Eastern Idaho Tech Coll (ID)
Eastern Maine Tech Coll (ME)
Eastern Wyoming Coll (WY)
Everett Comm Coll (WA)
Fayetteville Tech Comm Coll (NC)
Forsyth Tech Comm Coll (NC)
Fort Scott Comm Coll (KS)
Front Range Comm Coll (CO)
Garden City Comm Coll (KS)
George Corley Wallace State Comm Coll (AL)
Glendale Comm Coll (CA)
Grand Rapids Comm Coll (MI)
Grays Harbor Coll (WA)
Grayson County Coll (TX)
Great Basin Coll (NV)
Green River Comm Coll (WA)
Hawaii Comm Coll (HI)
Hawkeye Comm Coll (IA)
Heartland Comm Coll (IL)
Helena Coll of Tech of The U of Montana (MT)
Hill Coll of the Hill Jr College District (TX)
Hinds Comm Coll (MS)
Honolulu Comm Coll (HI)
Hutchinson Comm Coll and Area Vocational School (KS)
Imperial Valley Coll (CA)
Iowa Lakes Comm Coll (IA)
Isothermal Comm Coll (NC)
Jefferson Coll (MO)
John A. Logan Coll (IL)
Kalamazoo Valley Comm Coll (MI)
Kankakee Comm Coll (IL)
Kaskaskia Coll (IL)
Kellogg Comm Coll (MI)
Kirkwood Comm Coll (IA)
Lake Area Tech Inst (SD)
Lamar State Coll–Port Arthur (TX)
Lane Comm Coll (OR)
Lansing Comm Coll (MI)
Las Positas Coll (CA)
Lenoir Comm Coll (NC)
Lincoln Land Comm Coll (IL)
Linn-Benton Comm Coll (OR)
Long Beach City Coll (CA)
Los Angeles Pierce Coll (CA)
Louisiana Tech Coll–Delta Ouachita Campus (LA)
Louisiana Tech Coll–Mansfield Campus (LA)
Lower Columbia Coll (WA)
Macomb Comm Coll (MI)
Metropolitan Comm Coll (NE)
Midland Coll (TX)
Mid Michigan Comm Coll (MI)
Mid-Plains Comm Coll Area (NE)
Milwaukee Area Tech Coll (WI)
Minnesota State Coll–Southeast Tech (MN)
Mississippi Gulf Coast Comm Coll (MS)
Moberly Area Comm Coll (MO)
Modesto Jr Coll (CA)
Mohawk Valley Comm Coll (NY)
Monroe County Comm Coll (MI)
Mountain View Coll (TX)
Neosho County Comm Coll (KS)
New Mexico State U–Carlsbad (NM)
New River Comm Coll (VA)
North Central Texas Coll (TX)
North Dakota State Coll of Science (ND)
Northeast Comm Coll (NE)
Northeast State Tech Comm Coll (TN)
North Harris Coll (TX)
North Idaho Coll (ID)
North Iowa Area Comm Coll (IA)
Northland Comm and Tech Coll (MN)
Northwest Coll (WY)
Oakland Comm Coll (MI)
Odessa Coll (TX)
Okaloosa-Walton Comm Coll (FL)
Olympic Coll (WA)
Orange Coast Coll (CA)
Oxnard Coll (CA)
Palomar Coll (CA)
Pasadena City Coll (CA)
Pikes Peak Comm Coll (CO)
Pima Comm Coll (AZ)
Portland Comm Coll (OR)
Pratt Comm Coll and Area Vocational School (KS)
Randolph Comm Coll (NC)
Ranger Coll (TX)
Red Rocks Comm Coll (CO)
Reedley Coll (CA)
Roanoke-Chowan Comm Coll (NC)
St. Clair County Comm Coll (MI)
St. Cloud Tech Coll (MN)
St. Philip's Coll (TX)
San Bernardino Valley Coll (CA)
San Diego City Coll (CA)
San Jacinto Coll Central Campus (TX)
San Jacinto Coll North Campus (TX)
San Juan Coll (NM)
Santa Ana Coll (CA)
Santa Monica Coll (CA)
Schoolcraft Coll (MI)
Shasta Coll (CA)
Sheridan Coll (WY)
Sierra Coll (CA)
Skagit Valley Coll (WA)
Southeast Comm Coll, Milford Campus (NE)
Southeastern Comm Coll (NC)
Southern West Virginia Comm and Tech Coll (WV)
South Plains Coll (TX)
South Puget Sound Comm Coll (WA)
Southwestern Michigan Coll (MI)
Southwest Mississippi Comm Coll (MS)
Southwest Wisconsin Tech Coll (WI)
Spokane Comm Coll (WA)
Spokane Falls Comm Coll (WA)
State Fair Comm Coll (MO)
State U of NY Coll of Technology at Alfred (NY)
State U of NY Coll of Technology at Delhi (NY)
Tarrant County Coll District (TX)
Terra State Comm Coll (OH)
Texarkana Coll (TX)
Texas State Tech Coll–Harlingen (TX)
Texas State Tech Coll– Waco/ Marshall Campus (TX)
Trenholm State Tech Coll, Patterson Campus (AL)
Triangle Tech, Inc.–DuBois School (PA)
Trinity Valley Comm Coll (TX)
Triton Coll (IL)
Truckee Meadows Comm Coll (NV)
Tyler Jr Coll (TX)
United Tribes Tech Coll (ND)
U of Arkansas at Fort Smith (AR)
U of Arkansas Comm Coll at Morrilton (AR)
U of New Mexico–Gallup (NM)
Vance-Granville Comm Coll (NC)
Ventura Coll (CA)
Victor Valley Coll (CA)
Vincennes U (IN)
Wallace State Comm Coll (AL)
Walla Walla Comm Coll (WA)
Waycross Coll (GA)
Western Nevada Comm Coll (NV)
Western Texas Coll (TX)
Western Wyoming Comm Coll (WY)
Westmoreland County Comm Coll (PA)
West Shore Comm Coll (MI)
West Virginia U at Parkersburg (WV)
York Tech Coll (SC)

WESTERN CIVILIZATION
Lamar Comm Coll (CO)
Lincoln Coll, Lincoln (IL)
Lon Morris Coll (TX)

WILDLIFE BIOLOGY
Colby Comm Coll (KS)
Dodge City Comm Coll (KS)
Eastern Arizona Coll (AZ)
Ellsworth Comm Coll (IA)
Everett Comm Coll (WA)
Feather River Comm Coll District (CA)
Holmes Comm Coll (MS)
Iowa Lakes Comm Coll (IA)
Keystone Coll (PA)
Kirkwood Comm Coll (IA)
Minot State U–Bottineau Campus (ND)
North Idaho Coll (ID)
Pratt Comm Coll and Area Vocational School (KS)
Tacoma Comm Coll (WA)
Vermilion Comm Coll (MN)

WILDLIFE MANAGEMENT
Abraham Baldwin Ag Coll (GA)
Casper Coll (WY)
Cerritos Coll (CA)
Chattanooga State Tech Comm Coll (TN)
City Coll of San Francisco (CA)
Coll of the Siskiyous (CA)
Comm Coll of Southern Nevada (NV)
Dixie State Coll of Utah (UT)
East Central Coll (MO)
Eastern Oklahoma State Coll (OK)
Eastern Wyoming Coll (WY)
Flathead Valley Comm Coll (MT)
Frederick Comm Coll (MD)
Front Range Comm Coll (CO)
Fullerton Coll (CA)
Haywood Comm Coll (NC)
Iowa Lakes Comm Coll (IA)
Itasca Comm Coll (MN)
Keystone Coll (PA)
Kirkwood Comm Coll (IA)
Laramie County Comm Coll (WY)
Minot State U–Bottineau Campus (ND)
Monterey Peninsula Coll (CA)
Moorpark Coll (CA)
North Idaho Coll (ID)
Northwest Coll (WY)
Penn State U DuBois Campus of the Commonwealth Coll (PA)
Pratt Comm Coll and Area Vocational School (KS)
Snow Coll (UT)
Spokane Comm Coll (WA)
State U of NY Coll of A&T at Morrisville (NY)
Tacoma Comm Coll (WA)
Vermilion Comm Coll (MN)

WIND/PERCUSSION INSTRUMENTS
Coffeyville Comm Coll (KS)
Iowa Lakes Comm Coll (IA)
Kirkwood Comm Coll (IA)
Miami-Dade Comm Coll (FL)

WOMEN'S STUDIES
Bergen Comm Coll (NJ)
Chabot Coll (CA)
City Coll of San Francisco (CA)
Foothill Coll (CA)
Fresno City Coll (CA)
Kansas City Kansas Comm Coll (KS)
Lincoln Land Comm Coll (IL)
Manatee Comm Coll (FL)
Monterey Peninsula Coll (CA)
Northern Essex Comm Coll (MA)
Palomar Coll (CA)
Sacramento City Coll (CA)
Santa Ana Coll (CA)
Southwestern Coll (CA)
Suffolk County Comm Coll (NY)
Tompkins Cortland Comm Coll (NY)

WOOD SCIENCE/PAPER TECHNOLOGY
Allen County Comm Coll (KS)
Bakersfield Coll (CA)
Bay de Noc Comm Coll (MI)
Haywood Comm Coll (NC)
Kennebec Valley Tech Coll (ME)
State U of NY Coll of A&T at Morrisville (NY)
State U of NY Coll of Technology at Canton (NY)
Tacoma Comm Coll (WA)
Texarkana Coll (TX)

WOODWORKING
Bucks County Comm Coll (PA)
Coll of Southern Idaho (ID)
State U of NY Coll of Technology at Delhi (NY)

WORD PROCESSING
Academy of Medical Arts and Business (PA)
Adirondack Comm Coll (NY)
Anoka-Ramsey Comm Coll (MN)
Assumption Coll for Sisters (NJ)
Baltimore City Comm Coll (MD)
Barton County Comm Coll (KS)
Broome Comm Coll (NY)
Camden County Coll (NJ)
Coastal Bend Coll (TX)
Coll of the Desert (CA)
Coll of the Sequoias (CA)
Columbus Tech Coll (GA)
The Comm Coll of Baltimore County–Catonsville Campus (MD)
Corning Comm Coll (NY)
Cypress Coll (CA)
Dakota County Tech Coll (MN)
Daymar Coll (KY)
Del Mar Coll (TX)
Delta Coll (MI)
Diablo Valley Coll (CA)
Eastfield Coll (TX)
Edgecombe Comm Coll (NC)
Fayetteville Tech Comm Coll (NC)
Flathead Valley Comm Coll (MT)
Florida Comm Coll at Jacksonville (FL)
Florida National Coll (FL)
Galveston Coll (TX)
Gateway Comm Coll (CT)
Gogebic Comm Coll (MI)
Goodwin Coll (CT)
Hawkeye Comm Coll (IA)
Henderson Comm Coll (KY)
Horry-Georgetown Tech Coll (SC)
Iowa Western Comm Coll (IA)
Itasca Comm Coll (MN)
Kellogg Comm Coll (MI)
Kishwaukee Coll (IL)
Laurel Business Inst (PA)
Lincoln School of Commerce (NE)
Lorain County Comm Coll (OH)
Los Angeles City Coll (CA)
Massasoit Comm Coll (MA)
Milwaukee Area Tech Coll (WI)
Mississippi Gulf Coast Comm Coll (MS)
Modesto Jr Coll (CA)
Mohave Comm Coll (AZ)
Mohawk Valley Comm Coll (NY)
Monroe County Comm Coll (MI)
Naugatuck Valley Comm Coll (CT)
North Central Texas Coll (TX)
Northern Essex Comm Coll (MA)
Northland Comm and Tech Coll (MN)
Okaloosa-Walton Comm Coll (FL)
Olympic Coll (WA)
Orange Coast Coll (CA)
Orange County Comm Coll (NY)
Owensboro Comm Coll (KY)
Palm Beach Comm Coll (FL)
Pratt Comm Coll and Area Vocational School (KS)
Rasmussen Coll Mankato (MN)
Richland Comm Coll (IL)
Riverland Comm Coll (MN)
Riverside Comm Coll (CA)
St. Cloud Tech Coll (MN)
Sampson Comm Coll (NC)
San Antonio Coll (TX)

Santa Ana Coll (CA)
Schenectady County Comm Coll (NY)
Seminole Comm Coll (FL)
Sinclair Comm Coll (OH)
Stanly Comm Coll (NC)
Stark State Coll of Technology (OH)
Tacoma Comm Coll (WA)
Tallahassee Comm Coll (FL)
Texas State Tech Coll–Harlingen (TX)
Thaddeus Stevens Coll of Technology (PA)
Trumbull Business Coll (OH)
Tulsa Comm Coll (OK)
U of Kentucky, Lexington Comm Coll (KY)
Vincennes U (IN)
Vincennes U Jasper Campus (IN)
Wake Tech Comm Coll (NC)
West Central Tech Coll (GA)
The Westchester Business Inst (NY)
West Virginia Northern Comm Coll (WV)

ZOOLOGY
Casper Coll (WY)
Centralia Coll (WA)
Cerritos Coll (CA)
Chabot Coll (CA)
Colby Comm Coll (KS)
Coll of Southern Idaho (ID)
Coll of the Siskiyous (CA)
The Comm Coll of Baltimore County–Catonsville Campus (MD)
Connors State Coll (OK)
Daytona Beach Comm Coll (FL)
Dixie State Coll of Utah (UT)
East Central Coll (MO)
Everett Comm Coll (WA)
Fullerton Coll (CA)
Hill Coll of the Hill Jr College District (TX)
Jefferson Comm Coll (KY)
Joliet Jr Coll (IL)
Lincoln Coll, Lincoln (IL)
Miami U–Middletown Campus (OH)
North Idaho Coll (ID)
Palm Beach Comm Coll (FL)
Palomar Coll (CA)
Pensacola Jr Coll (FL)
San Bernardino Valley Coll (CA)
San Jacinto Coll Central Campus (TX)
Snow Coll (UT)
Tacoma Comm Coll (WA)
Tulsa Comm Coll (OK)

Associate Degree Programs at Four-Year Colleges

ACCOUNTING
Alvernia Coll (PA)
American U of Puerto Rico (PR)
Baker Coll of Auburn Hills (MI)
Baker Coll of Cadillac (MI)
Baker Coll of Clinton Township (MI)
Baker Coll of Flint (MI)
Baker Coll of Jackson (MI)
Baker Coll of Muskegon (MI)
Baker Coll of Owosso (MI)
Baker Coll of Port Huron (MI)
Becker Coll (MA)
Benedictine Coll (KS)
Bluefield State Coll (WV)
Brewton-Parker Coll (GA)
Brigham Young U–Hawaii (HI)
British Columbia Inst of Technology (BC, Canada)
California Coll for Health Sciences (CA)
California U of Pennsylvania (PA)
Caribbean U (PR)
Central Christian Coll of Kansas (KS)
Champlain Coll (VT)
Chestnut Hill Coll (PA)
Clayton Coll & State U (GA)
Cleary U (MI)
Coll of Mount St. Joseph (OH)
Coll of St. Joseph (VT)
Colorado Tech U Sioux Falls Campus (SD)
Columbia Union Coll (MD)
Davenport U, Dearborn (MI)
Davenport U, Grand Rapids (MI)
Davenport U, Kalamazoo (MI)
Davenport U, Lansing (MI)
Davenport U, Warren (MI)
David N. Myers U (OH)
Davis & Elkins Coll (WV)
Evangel U (MO)
Fairmont State Coll (WV)
Faulkner U (AL)
Ferris State U (MI)
Florida Metropolitan U-Fort Lauderdale Coll (FL)
Florida Metropolitan U-Tampa Coll, Lakeland (FL)
Florida Metropolitan U-Orlando Coll, North (FL)
Florida Metropolitan U-Orlando Coll, South (FL)
Florida Metropolitan U-Tampa Coll (FL)
Franciscan U of Steubenville (OH)
Franklin U (OH)
Friends U (KS)
Glenville State Coll (WV)
Goldey-Beacom Coll (DE)
Gwynedd-Mercy Coll (PA)
Hannibal-LaGrange Coll (MO)
Haskell Indian Nations U (KS)
Husson Coll (ME)
Immaculata Coll (PA)
Indiana Inst of Technology (IN)
Indiana Wesleyan U (IN)
Inter American U of PR, Aguadilla Campus (PR)
Inter Amer U of PR, Barranquitas Campus (PR)
Inter American U of PR, San Germán Campus (PR)
International Coll (FL)
Johnson & Wales U (RI)
Johnson State Coll (VT)
Jones Coll (FL)
Kansas State U (KS)
King's Coll (PA)
Lake Superior State U (MI)
Lewis-Clark State Coll (ID)
Macon State Coll (GA)
Manchester Coll (IN)
Mansfield U of Pennsylvania (PA)
Marian Coll (IN)
Marygrove Coll (MI)
Merrimack Coll (MA)
Methodist Coll (NC)
Midland Lutheran Coll (NE)
Missouri Southern State Coll (MO)
Montana State U–Billings (MT)
Mount Aloysius Coll (PA)
Mount Ida Coll (MA)
Mount Marty Coll (SD)
Mount Olive Coll (NC)
National American U, Colorado Springs (CO)
National American U (NM)
National American U (SD)
National American U–Sioux Falls Branch (SD)
Northeastern U (MA)
Northwood U (MI)
Northwood U, Florida Campus (FL)
Northwood U, Texas Campus (TX)
Oakland City U (IN)
Oakwood Coll (AL)
Ohio U–Lancaster (OH)
Oklahoma Wesleyan U (OK)
Pace U (NY)
Point Park Coll (PA)
Presentation Coll (SD)
Purdue U North Central (IN)
Rogers State U (OK)
Sacred Heart U (CT)
St. Augustine Coll (IL)
Saint Francis U (PA)
St. John's U (NY)
Saint Joseph's U (PA)
Shawnee State U (OH)
Siena Heights U (MI)
Sinte Gleska U (SD)
Si Tanka Huron U (SD)
Southeastern U (DC)
Southern Adventist U (TN)
Southern New Hampshire U (NH)
Southern Vermont Coll (VT)
Southwest Baptist U (MO)
Southwest State U (MN)
State U of NY Coll of A&T at Cobleskill (NY)
Strayer U (DC)
Sullivan U (KY)
Teikyo Post U (CT)
Thiel Coll (PA)
Thomas Coll (ME)
Thomas Edison State Coll (NJ)
Thomas More Coll (KY)
Tiffin U (OH)
Tri-State U (IN)
U of Alaska Anchorage (AK)
U of Charleston (WV)
U of Cincinnati (OH)
U of Dubuque (IA)
The U of Findlay (OH)
U of Great Falls (MT)
The U of Maine at Augusta (ME)
U of Maine at Machias (ME)
U of Mary (ND)
U of Minnesota, Crookston (MN)
U of Puerto Rico, Humacao U Coll (PR)
U of Puerto Rico at Ponce (PR)
U of Rio Grande (OH)
U of Saint Francis (IN)
U of the District of Columbia (DC)
U of the Virgin Islands (VI)
U of Toledo (OH)
The U of West Alabama (AL)
Urbana U (OH)
Villa Julie Coll (MD)
Waldorf Coll (IA)
Walsh U (OH)
Washington & Jefferson Coll (PA)
Webber International U (FL)
West Virginia State Coll (WV)
West Virginia U Inst of Technology (WV)
Wilson Coll (PA)
Youngstown State U (OH)

ACCOUNTING RELATED
Chestnut Hill Coll (PA)
Park U (MO)

ACCOUNTING TECHNICIAN
Baker Coll of Flint (MI)
British Columbia Inst of Technology (BC, Canada)
Gannon U (PA)
Kent State U (OH)
Lake Superior State U (MI)
New York Inst of Technology (NY)
Ohio U (OH)
Pace U (NY)
Peirce Coll (PA)
Robert Morris Coll (IL)
The U of Akron (OH)
U of Alaska Fairbanks (AK)
The U of Montana–Missoula (MT)
U of Rio Grande (OH)
Youngstown State U (OH)

ACTING/DIRECTING
Central Christian Coll of Kansas (KS)

ADMINISTRATION OF SPECIAL EDUCATION
Becker Coll (MA)

ADMINISTRATIVE/ SECRETARIAL SERVICES
The U of Akron (OH)

ADVERTISING
Academy of Art Coll (CA)
The Art Inst of California (CA)
Fashion Inst of Technology (NY)
Johnson & Wales U (RI)
Martin Methodist Coll (TN)
New England School of Communications (ME)
Northwood U (MI)
Northwood U, Florida Campus (FL)
Northwood U, Texas Campus (TX)
Pacific Union Coll (CA)
U of the District of Columbia (DC)
West Virginia State Coll (WV)
Xavier U (OH)

AEROSPACE ENGINEERING TECHNOLOGY
British Columbia Inst of Technology (BC, Canada)
Central Missouri State U (MO)
Purdue U (IN)
Saint Louis U (MO)
U of New Haven (CT)

AEROSPACE SCIENCE
Coll of Aeronautics (NY)
Daniel Webster Coll (NH)

AGRIBUSINESS
Morehead State U (KY)
Penn State U at Erie, The Behrend Coll (PA)
Penn State U Lehigh Valley Cmps of Berks-Lehigh Valley Coll (PA)

AGRICULTURAL ANIMAL HUSBANDRY/PRODUCTION MANAGEMENT
Saint Mary-of-the-Woods Coll (IN)
U Coll of the Cariboo (BC, Canada)
U of Connecticut (CT)
U of New Hampshire (NH)

AGRICULTURAL BUSINESS
Andrews U (MI)
Central Christian Coll of Kansas (KS)
Clayton Coll & State U (GA)
Dickinson State U (ND)
Dordt Coll (IA)
Lindsey Wilson Coll (KY)
Martin Methodist Coll (TN)
MidAmerica Nazarene U (KS)
Montana State U–Northern (MT)
North Carolina State U (NC)
Penn State U Altoona Coll (PA)
Penn State U Berks Cmps of Berks-Lehigh Valley Coll (PA)
Rogers State U (OK)
Southwest State U (MN)
State U of NY Coll of A&T at Cobleskill (NY)
U of Minnesota, Crookston (MN)
U of New Hampshire (NH)

AGRICULTURAL BUSINESS RELATED
Penn State U Abington Coll (PA)
Penn State U Schuylkill Campus of the Capital Coll (PA)
Penn State U Univ Park Campus (PA)

AGRICULTURAL ECONOMICS
The U of British Columbia (BC, Canada)

AGRICULTURAL EDUCATION
U of New Hampshire (NH)

AGRICULTURAL ENGINEERING
State U of NY Coll of A&T at Cobleskill (NY)

AGRICULTURAL/FOOD PRODUCTS PROCESSING
North Carolina State U (NC)

AGRICULTURAL MECHANIZATION
Andrews U (MI)
Clayton Coll & State U (GA)
Eastern Kentucky U (KY)
Montana State U–Northern (MT)
State U of NY Coll of A&T at Cobleskill (NY)
Virginia Polytechnic Inst and State U (VA)

AGRICULTURAL PRODUCTION
Western Kentucky U (KY)

AGRICULTURAL SCIENCES
Andrews U (MI)
Clayton Coll & State U (GA)
Dalton State Coll (GA)
Lincoln U (MO)
Macon State Coll (GA)
North Carolina State U (NC)
Oklahoma Panhandle State U (OK)
South Dakota State U (SD)
Southern Utah U (UT)
State U of NY Coll of A&T at Cobleskill (NY)
Sterling Coll (VT)
U of Delaware (DE)
U of Minnesota, Crookston (MN)

AGRONOMY/CROP SCIENCE
Andrews U (MI)
State U of NY Coll of A&T at Cobleskill (NY)
U of Minnesota, Crookston (MN)

AIRCRAFT MECHANIC/ AIRFRAME
British Columbia Inst of Technology (BC, Canada)
Clayton Coll & State U (GA)
Coll of Aeronautics (NY)
Kansas State U (KS)
Lewis U (IL)
Southern Illinois U Carbondale (IL)
State U of NY at Farmingdale (NY)
U of Alaska Anchorage (AK)
U of Alaska Fairbanks (AK)
Utah State U (UT)
Wentworth Inst of Technology (MA)

AIRCRAFT MECHANIC/ POWERPLANT
British Columbia Inst of Technology (BC, Canada)
Embry-Riddle Aeronautical U (FL)
Embry-Riddle Aeronautical U, Extended Campus (FL)
Idaho State U (ID)
Kansas State U (KS)
State U of NY at Farmingdale (NY)
Thomas Edison State Coll (NJ)

AIRCRAFT PILOT (PRIVATE)
Central Christian Coll of Kansas (KS)

AIRCRAFT PILOT (PROFESSIONAL)
Andrews U (MI)
Baker Coll of Flint (MI)
Baker Coll of Muskegon (MI)
Central Christian Coll of Kansas (KS)
Coll of Aeronautics (NY)
Daniel Webster Coll (NH)
Embry-Riddle Aeronautical U (FL)
Florida Inst of Technology (FL)
Kansas State U (KS)
Southern Illinois U Carbondale (IL)
Thomas Edison State Coll (NJ)
U of Alaska Anchorage (AK)
U of Alaska Fairbanks (AK)
U of Dubuque (IA)
U of Minnesota, Crookston (MN)
Winona State U (MN)

AIR TRAFFIC CONTROL
Thomas Edison State Coll (NJ)
U of Alaska Anchorage (AK)

ALCOHOL/DRUG ABUSE COUNSELING
Indiana Wesleyan U (IN)
Keene State Coll (NH)
Newman U (KS)
Rogers State U (OK)
The U of Akron (OH)
U of Great Falls (MT)
U of Toledo (OH)

AMERICAN HISTORY
Central Christian Coll of Kansas (KS)

AMERICAN STUDIES
Martin Methodist Coll (TN)

ANIMAL SCIENCES
Andrews U (MI)
Becker Coll (MA)
Mount Ida Coll (MA)
State U of NY Coll of A&T at Cobleskill (NY)
Sul Ross State U (TX)
U of Connecticut (CT)
U of Minnesota, Crookston (MN)
U of New Hampshire (NH)

ANTHROPOLOGY
Richmond, The American International U in LondonUnited Kingdom)
Université Laval (QC, Canada)

APPAREL MARKETING
The U of Montana–Missoula (MT)

APPLIED ART
Academy of Art Coll (CA)
Friends U (KS)
National American U (NM)
Newschool of Architecture & Design (CA)
New World School of the Arts (FL)
Rochester Inst of Technology (NY)
The U of Maine at Augusta (ME)
U of Maine at Presque Isle (ME)
The U of Montana–Western (MT)
Valdosta State U (GA)
Villa Julie Coll (MD)

APPLIED MATHEMATICS
Central Methodist Coll (MO)
Hawai'i Pacific U (HI)
State U of NY at Farmingdale (NY)

AQUACULTURE OPERATIONS/ PRODUCTION MANAGEMENT
Purdue U (IN)
The U of British Columbia (BC, Canada)

ARCHAEOLOGY
Baltimore Hebrew U (MD)
Université Laval (QC, Canada)
Weber State U (UT)

ARCHITECTURAL DRAFTING
Baker Coll of Flint (MI)
Baker Coll of Muskegon (MI)
British Columbia Inst of Technology (BC, Canada)
Indiana State U (IN)
Indiana U–Purdue U Indianapolis (IN)
Montana Tech of The U of Montana (MT)
U of Toledo (OH)
Western Kentucky U (KY)

ARCHITECTURAL ENGINEERING TECHNOLOGY
Baker Coll of Cadillac (MI)
Baker Coll of Clinton Township (MI)
Baker Coll of Owosso (MI)
Baker Coll of Port Huron (MI)
Bluefield State Coll (WV)
British Columbia Inst of Technology (BC, Canada)
Central Christian Coll of Kansas (KS)
Clayton Coll & State U (GA)
Ferris State U (MI)
Indiana U–Purdue U Fort Wayne (IN)
Newschool of Architecture & Design (CA)
Norfolk State U (VA)
Northern Kentucky U (KY)
Northern Michigan U (MI)
Purdue U (IN)
Purdue U Calumet (IN)
Purdue U North Central (IN)
Southern Illinois U Carbondale (IL)
State U of NY at Farmingdale (NY)
Thomas Edison State Coll (NJ)
U of Alaska Anchorage (AK)
U of Cincinnati (OH)
The U of Maine at Augusta (ME)
U of the District of Columbia (DC)
Wentworth Inst of Technology (MA)
West Virginia State Coll (WV)

ARCHITECTURAL ENVIRONMENTAL DESIGN
Northern Michigan U (MI)

ARCHITECTURE
Central Christian Coll of Kansas (KS)
Coll of Staten Island of the City U of NY (NY)
New York Inst of Technology (NY)

ARMY R.O.T.C./MILITARY SCIENCE
Methodist Coll (NC)

ART
Academy of Art Coll (CA)
Adrian Coll (MI)
Armstrong Atlantic State U (GA)
The Art Inst of Colorado (CO)
Ashland U (OH)
Brevard Coll (NC)
Brewton-Parker Coll (GA)
Burlington Coll (VT)
Carroll Coll (MT)
Central Christian Coll of Kansas (KS)
Clayton Coll & State U (GA)
Coll of Mount St. Joseph (OH)
Defiance Coll (OH)
Eastern New Mexico U (NM)
Fashion Inst of Technology (NY)
Felician Coll (NJ)
Friends U (KS)
Huron U USA in LondonUnited Kingdom)
Immaculata Coll (PA)
Indiana Wesleyan U (IN)
John Brown U (AR)
Lourdes Coll (OH)
Macon State Coll (GA)
Maharishi U of Management (IA)
Manchester Coll (IN)
Mansfield U of Pennsylvania (PA)
Marian Coll (IN)
Martin Methodist Coll (TN)
Mesa State Coll (CO)
Methodist Coll (NC)
Montreat Coll (NC)
Mount Olive Coll (NC)
Newschool of Architecture & Design (CA)
New World School of the Arts (FL)
North Greenville Coll (SC)
Ohio U–Lancaster (OH)
Open Learning Agency (BC, Canada)
Parsons School of Design, New School U (NY)
Pontifical Catholic U of Puerto Rico (PR)
Reinhardt Coll (GA)
Richmond, The American International U in LondonUnited Kingdom)
Rivier Coll (NH)
Rochester Inst of Technology (NY)
Rogers State U (OK)
Sacred Heart U (CT)
Shawnee State U (OH)
Siena Heights U (MI)
Sinte Gleska U (SD)
State U of NY Empire State Coll (NY)
Suffolk U (MA)
U of Rio Grande (OH)
U of Toledo (OH)
U of Wisconsin–Green Bay (WI)
Villa Julie Coll (MD)
Waldorf Coll (IA)
West Virginia State Coll (WV)
York Coll of Pennsylvania (PA)

ART EDUCATION
Central Christian Coll of Kansas (KS)
Clayton Coll & State U (GA)
Immaculata Coll (PA)
Martin Methodist Coll (TN)
Waldorf Coll (IA)

ART HISTORY
Chestnut Hill Coll (PA)
Lourdes Coll (OH)
Richmond, The American International U in LondonUnited Kingdom)
Thomas More Coll (KY)

ATHLETIC TRAINING/SPORTS MEDICINE
Central Christian Coll of Kansas (KS)

AUDIO ENGINEERING
Five Towns Coll (NY)
New England School of Communications (ME)

AUTO BODY REPAIR
British Columbia Inst of Technology (BC, Canada)
Georgia Southwestern State U (GA)
Idaho State U (ID)
Montana Tech of The U of Montana (MT)
Southern Adventist U (TN)
Weber State U (UT)

AUTO MECHANIC/TECHNICIAN
Andrews U (MI)
Arkansas State U (AR)
Baker Coll of Flint (MI)
Boise State U (ID)
British Columbia Inst of Technology (BC, Canada)
Central Missouri State U (MO)
Ferris State U (MI)
Lamar U (TX)
McPherson Coll (KS)
Mesa State Coll (CO)
Montana State U–Billings (MT)
Montana State U–Northern (MT)
Montana Tech of The U of Montana (MT)
Northern Michigan U (MI)
Oakland City U (IN)
Pittsburg State U (KS)
Southern Adventist U (TN)
Southern Illinois U Carbondale (IL)
Southern Utah U (UT)
U of Alaska Anchorage (AK)
U of Alaska Southeast (AK)
Walla Walla Coll (WA)
Weber State U (UT)
West Virginia U Inst of Technology (WV)

AUTOMOTIVE ENGINEERING TECHNOLOGY
West Virginia U Inst of Technology (WV)

AVIATION/AIRWAY SCIENCE
Embry-Riddle Aeronautical U (FL)
Embry-Riddle Aeronautical U, Extended Campus (FL)
Indiana State U (IN)

AVIATION MANAGEMENT
Clayton Coll & State U (GA)
Daniel Webster Coll (NH)
Embry-Riddle Aeronautical U (FL)
Everglades Coll (FL)
Fairmont State Coll (WV)
Florida Inst of Technology (FL)
Northern Kentucky U (KY)
Park U (MO)
U of Alaska Anchorage (AK)
U of Dubuque (IA)
U of the District of Columbia (DC)

AVIATION TECHNOLOGY
Andrews U (MI)
Baker Coll of Flint (MI)
British Columbia Inst of Technology (BC, Canada)
Clayton Coll & State U (GA)
Coll of Aeronautics (NY)
Fairmont State Coll (WV)
Georgia Southwestern State U (GA)
Hampton U (VA)
Lewis U (IL)
Mountain State U (WV)
Northern Michigan U (MI)
U of Alaska Anchorage (AK)
U of Alaska Fairbanks (AK)
U of Minnesota, Crookston (MN)
U of the District of Columbia (DC)
Walla Walla Coll (WA)
Wentworth Inst of Technology (MA)

BAKER/PASTRY CHEF
Johnson & Wales U (RI)
Southern New Hampshire U (NH)

BANKING
Kent State U (OH)
Mountain State U (WV)
Pace U (NY)
Touro Coll (NY)
The U of Akron (OH)
U of Indianapolis (IN)

BEHAVIORAL SCIENCES
Central Christian Coll of Kansas (KS)
Circleville Bible Coll (OH)
Felician Coll (NJ)
Lewis-Clark State Coll (ID)
Martin Methodist Coll (TN)
Methodist Coll (NC)
Mount Aloysius Coll (PA)
Oklahoma Wesleyan U (OK)
U System Coll for Lifelong Learning (NH)
Waldorf Coll (IA)

BIBLICAL LANGUAGES/ LITERATURES
Baltimore Hebrew U (MD)
Bethel Coll (IN)
Indiana Wesleyan U (IN)

BIBLICAL STUDIES
Alaska Bible Coll (AK)
American Baptist Coll of American Baptist Theol Sem (TN)
Appalachian Bible Coll (WV)
Baltimore Hebrew U (MD)
Barclay Coll (KS)
Beacon Coll and Graduate School (GA)
Bethel Coll (IN)
Beulah Heights Bible Coll (GA)
Boise Bible Coll (ID)
California Christian Coll (CA)
Calvary Bible Coll and Theological Seminary (MO)
Central Bible Coll (MO)
Central Christian Coll of Kansas (KS)
Central Christian Coll of the Bible (MO)
Cincinnati Bible Coll and Seminary (OH)
Circleville Bible Coll (OH)
Clear Creek Baptist Bible Coll (KY)
Columbia International U (SC)
Covenant Coll (GA)
Crown Coll (MN)
Dallas Baptist U (TX)
Eastern Mennonite U (VA)
Emmaus Bible Coll (IA)
Faith Baptist Bible Coll and Theological Seminary (IA)
Faulkner U (AL)
Florida Christian Coll (FL)
Fresno Pacific U (CA)
Geneva Coll (PA)
God's Bible School and Coll (OH)
Grace Coll (IN)
Grace U (NE)
Heritage Christian U (AL)
Hillsdale Free Will Baptist Coll (OK)
Hobe Sound Bible Coll (FL)
Houghton Coll (NY)
John Brown U (AR)
Lancaster Bible Coll (PA)
LIFE Bible Coll (CA)
Lincoln Christian Coll (IL)
Manhattan Christian Coll (KS)
Montreat Coll (NC)
Nazarene Bible Coll (CO)
Northwest Christian Coll (OR)
Oak Hills Christian Coll (MN)
Oakwood Coll (AL)
Ohio Valley Coll (WV)
Pacific Union Coll (CA)
Patten Coll (CA)
Philadelphia Biblical U (PA)
Practical Bible Coll (NY)
Reformed Bible Coll (MI)
Roanoke Bible Coll (NC)
Samford U (AL)
Shasta Bible Coll (CA)
Simpson Coll and Graduate School (CA)
Southeastern Bible Coll (AL)
Southern Methodist Coll (SC)
Southwestern Assemblies of God U (TX)
Southwestern Coll (AZ)
Tabor Coll (KS)
Trinity Bible Coll (ND)
Trinity Coll of Florida (FL)
Universidad Adventista de las Antillas (PR)
Valley Forge Christian Coll (PA)
Waldorf Coll (IA)
Warner Pacific Coll (OR)
Washington Bible Coll (MD)
Western Baptist Coll (OR)
William Tyndale Coll (MI)

BIOLOGICAL/PHYSICAL SCIENCES
Aquinas Coll (MI)
Bluefield State Coll (WV)
Bryn Athyn Coll of the New Church (PA)
Central Christian Coll of Kansas (KS)
Clayton Coll & State U (GA)
Crown Coll (MN)
Dalton State Coll (GA)
Indiana U East (IN)
Martin Methodist Coll (TN)
Medgar Evers Coll of the City U of NY (NY)
Montana Tech of The U of Montana (MT)
Mount Ida Coll (MA)
Mount Olive Coll (NC)
Ohio U (OH)
Ohio U–Chillicothe (OH)
Ohio U–Lancaster (OH)
Ohio U–Southern Campus (OH)
Ohio U–Zanesville (OH)
Penn State U Altoona Coll (PA)
Penn State U Schuylkill Campus of the Capital Coll (PA)
Rochester Coll (MI)
Sacred Heart U (CT)
Shawnee State U (OH)
State U of NY Coll of A&T at Cobleskill (NY)
State U of NY Empire State Coll (NY)
Tri-State U (IN)
U of Cincinnati (OH)
Valparaiso U (IN)
Villa Julie Coll (MD)
Waldorf Coll (IA)
Washburn U of Topeka (KS)

BIOLOGICAL SPECIALIZATIONS RELATED
Kent State U (OH)

BIOLOGICAL TECHNOLOGY
British Columbia Inst of Technology (BC, Canada)
Ferris State U (MI)
Northeastern U (MA)
State U of NY Coll of A&T at Cobleskill (NY)
U of the District of Columbia (DC)
Villa Julie Coll (MD)
Weber State U (UT)

BIOLOGY
Adrian Coll (MI)
Brewton-Parker Coll (GA)
Central Christian Coll of Kansas (KS)
Chestnut Hill Coll (PA)
Clayton Coll & State U (GA)
Crown Coll (MN)
Cumberland U (TN)
Felician Coll (NJ)
Fresno Pacific U (CA)
Indiana U–Purdue U Fort Wayne (IN)
Indiana U South Bend (IN)
Indiana Wesleyan U (IN)
Lindsey Wilson Coll (KY)
Lourdes Coll (OH)
Macon State Coll (GA)
Maharishi U of Management (IA)
Martin Methodist Coll (TN)
Mesa State Coll (CO)
Methodist Coll (NC)

Montana Tech of The U of Montana (MT)
Mount Olive Coll (NC)
Oklahoma Wesleyan U (OK)
Pine Manor Coll (MA)
Presentation Coll (SD)
Reinhardt Coll (GA)
Rochester Inst of Technology (NY)
Rogers State U (OK)
Sacred Heart U (CT)
Shawnee State U (OH)
Thomas Edison State Coll (NJ)
Thomas More Coll (KY)
U of Dubuque (IA)
U of Rio Grande (OH)
The U of Tampa (FL)
U of Toledo (OH)
U of Wisconsin–Green Bay (WI)
Villa Julie Coll (MD)
Waldorf Coll (IA)
Wright State U (OH)
York Coll of Pennsylvania (PA)

BIOMEDICAL ENGINEERING-RELATED TECHNOLOGY
Edinboro U of Pennsylvania (PA)
Indiana U–Purdue U Indianapolis (IN)
Penn State U Berks Cmps of Berks-Lehigh Valley Coll (PA)
State U of NY at Farmingdale (NY)
Thomas Edison State Coll (NJ)

BIOMEDICAL TECHNOLOGY
Baker Coll of Flint (MI)
Faulkner U (AL)
U of Arkansas for Medical Sciences (AR)
Wentworth Inst of Technology (MA)

BIOTECHNOLOGY RESEARCH
British Columbia Inst of Technology (BC, Canada)

BRITISH LITERATURE
Maharishi U of Management (IA)

BROADCAST JOURNALISM
Calvary Bible Coll and Theological Seminary (MO)
Cornerstone U (MI)
Evangel U (MO)
Five Towns Coll (NY)
John Brown U (AR)
Manchester Coll (IN)
Martin Methodist Coll (TN)
New England School of Communications (ME)
Ohio U–Zanesville (OH)
Rogers State U (OK)
Trevecca Nazarene U (TN)
Waldorf Coll (IA)

BUILDING MAINTENANCE/ MANAGEMENT
Park U (MO)

BUSINESS
Anderson U (IN)
Atlanta Christian Coll (GA)
Baker Coll of Flint (MI)
Bayamón Central U (PR)
Bluefield State Coll (WV)
Brescia U (KY)
California Coll for Health Sciences (CA)
California U of Pennsylvania (PA)
Cameron U (OK)
Castleton State Coll (VT)
Champlain Coll (VT)
Coll of Staten Island of the City U of NY (NY)
Crown Coll (MN)
Cumberland U (TN)
Dalton State Coll (GA)
Eastern Nazarene Coll (MA)
Gannon U (PA)
Hillsdale Free Will Baptist Coll (OK)
Idaho State U (ID)
Indiana U East (IN)
Indiana U Kokomo (IN)
Indiana U South Bend (IN)
Indiana U Southeast (IN)
Kent State U (OH)
Limestone Coll (SC)
Macon State Coll (GA)
Marygrove Coll (MI)
Marymount Coll of Fordham U (NY)
Montana State U–Billings (MT)
New Mexico State U (NM)
Nicholls State U (LA)
Northeastern U (MA)
Northern Kentucky U (KY)
Peirce Coll (PA)
Penn State U Abington Coll (PA)
Penn State U Altoona Coll (PA)
Penn State U at Erie, The Behrend Coll (PA)
Penn State U Harrisburg Campus of the Capital Coll (PA)
Penn State U Lehigh Valley Cmps of Berks-Lehigh Valley Coll (PA)
Penn State U Schuylkill Campus of the Capital Coll (PA)
Penn State U Univ Park Campus (PA)
Southern Nazarene U (OK)
Southwest Baptist U (MO)
Southwestern Assemblies of God U (TX)
Thomas More Coll (KY)
Thomas U (GA)
Troy State U Montgomery (AL)
U of Massachusetts Lowell (MA)
The U of Montana–Western (MT)
U of Southern Indiana (IN)
Webber International U (FL)
Western Governors U (UT)
Xavier U (OH)

BUSINESS ADMINISTRATION
Adrian Coll (MI)
Alabama State U (AL)
Alaska Pacific U (AK)
Alderson-Broaddus Coll (WV)
Alvernia Coll (PA)
American Indian Coll of the Assemblies of God, Inc (AZ)
American InterContinental U (CA)
American InterContinental U, Atlanta (GA)
American International Coll (MA)
American U of Puerto Rico (PR)
American U of RomeItaly)
Andrews U (MI)
Anna Maria Coll (MA)
Austin Peay State U (TN)
Averett U (VA)
Baker Coll of Auburn Hills (MI)
Baker Coll of Cadillac (MI)
Baker Coll of Clinton Township (MI)
Baker Coll of Flint (MI)
Baker Coll of Jackson (MI)
Baker Coll of Muskegon (MI)
Baker Coll of Owosso (MI)
Baker Coll of Port Huron (MI)
Ball State U (IN)
Baptist Bible Coll (MO)
Bay Path Coll (MA)
Becker Coll (MA)
Benedictine Coll (KS)
Benedictine U (IL)
Bentley Coll (MA)
Bethel Coll (IN)
Brewton-Parker Coll (GA)
Briarcliffe Coll (NY)
British Columbia Inst of Technology (BC, Canada)
Bryan Coll (TN)
California U of Pennsylvania (PA)
Campbellsville U (KY)
Cardinal Stritch U (WI)
Caribbean U (PR)
Carroll Coll (MT)
Central Baptist Coll (AR)
Central Christian Coll of Kansas (KS)
Chaminade U of Honolulu (HI)
Champlain Coll (VT)
Charleston Southern U (SC)
Chestnut Hill Coll (PA)
Clarion U of Pennsylvania (PA)
Clayton Coll & State U (GA)
Cleary U (MI)
Coll of Mount St. Joseph (OH)
Coll of Mount Saint Vincent (NY)
Coll of St. Joseph (VT)
Coll of Saint Mary (NE)
Coll of Santa Fe (NM)
Colorado Tech U Sioux Falls Campus (SD)
Columbia Coll (MO)
Columbia Coll (PR)
Concordia Coll (NY)
Concordia U (OR)
Covenant Coll (GA)
Crown Coll (MN)
Dakota State U (SD)
Dakota Wesleyan U (SD)
Dallas Baptist U (TX)
Dalton State Coll (GA)
Daniel Webster Coll (NH)
Davenport U, Dearborn (MI)
Davenport U, Grand Rapids (MI)
Davenport U, Kalamazoo (MI)
Davenport U, Lansing (MI)
Davenport U, Warren (MI)
David N. Myers U (OH)
Davis & Elkins Coll (WV)
Defiance Coll (OH)
East-West U (IL)
Edinboro U of Pennsylvania (PA)
Embry-Riddle Aeronautical U (FL)
Embry-Riddle Aeronautical U, Extended Campus (FL)
Emmanuel Coll (GA)
Excelsior Coll (NY)
Fairmont State Coll (WV)
Faulkner U (AL)
Fayetteville State U (NC)
Felician Coll (NJ)
Five Towns Coll (NY)
Florida Metropolitan U-Fort Lauderdale Coll (FL)
Florida Metropolitan U-Tampa Coll, Lakeland (FL)
Florida Metropolitan U-Orlando Coll, North (FL)
Florida Metropolitan U-Orlando Coll, South (FL)
Florida Metropolitan U-Tampa Coll (FL)
Franciscan U of Steubenville (OH)
Fresno Pacific U (CA)
Friends U (KS)
Gannon U (PA)
Geneva Coll (PA)
Goldey-Beacom Coll (DE)
Grace Bible Coll (MI)
Grand View Coll (IA)
Gwynedd-Mercy Coll (PA)
Haskell Indian Nations U (KS)
Hawai'i Pacific U (HI)
Hilbert Coll (NY)
Huron U USA in LondonUnited Kingdom)
Husson Coll (ME)
Immaculata Coll (PA)
Indiana Inst of Technology (IN)
Indiana State U (IN)
Indiana U Northwest (IN)
Indiana U of Pennsylvania (PA)
Indiana U–Purdue U Fort Wayne (IN)
Indiana Wesleyan U (IN)
Inst of Computer Technology (CA)
Inter American U of PR, Aguadilla Campus (PR)
Inter Amer U of PR, Barranquitas Campus (PR)
Inter American U of PR, San Germán Campus (PR)
International Coll (FL)
Johnson & Wales U (CO)
Johnson & Wales U (RI)
Johnson State Coll (VT)
Jones Coll (FL)
Kansas Wesleyan U (KS)
Kent State U (OH)
King's Coll (PA)
LaGrange Coll (GA)
Lake Superior State U (MI)
Lincoln Memorial U (TN)
Lindsey Wilson Coll (KY)
Long Island U, Brooklyn Campus (NY)
Lourdes Coll (OH)
Lyndon State Coll (VT)
MacMurray Coll (IL)
Macon State Coll (GA)
Maharishi U of Management (IA)
Maine Maritime Academy (ME)
Manchester Coll (IN)
Mansfield U of Pennsylvania (PA)
Marian Coll (IN)
Marietta Coll (OH)
Martin Methodist Coll (TN)
Mayville State U (ND)
Medaille Coll (NY)
Medgar Evers Coll of the City U of NY (NY)
Mercyhurst Coll (PA)
Merrimack Coll (MA)
Mesa State Coll (CO)
Methodist Coll (NC)
MidAmerica Nazarene U (KS)
Midway Coll (KY)
Missouri Baptist Coll (MO)
Missouri Southern State Coll (MO)
Missouri Valley Coll (MO)
Missouri Western State Coll (MO)
Montana State U–Billings (MT)
Montana State U–Northern (MT)
Montreat Coll (NC)
Mountain State U (WV)
Mount Aloysius Coll (PA)
Mount Ida Coll (MA)
Mount Marty Coll (SD)
Mount Olive Coll (NC)
Mount St. Mary's Coll (CA)
Mount Vernon Nazarene U (OH)
Murray State U (KY)
National American U, Colorado Springs (CO)
National American U (NM)
National American U (SD)
National American U–St. Paul Campus (MN)
National American U–Sioux Falls Branch (SD)
The National Hispanic U (CA)
New Mexico Inst of Mining and Technology (NM)
New York Inst of Technology (NY)
Niagara U (NY)
Northeastern U (MA)
Northern Kentucky U (KY)
Northern Michigan U (MI)
Northern State U (SD)
Northwest Coll (WA)
Northwestern State U of Louisiana (LA)
Northwood U (MI)
Northwood U, Florida Campus (FL)
Northwood U, Texas Campus (TX)
Notre Dame Coll (OH)
Nyack Coll (NY)
Oakland City U (IN)
Ohio U (OH)
Ohio U–Chillicothe (OH)
Ohio U–Lancaster (OH)
Oklahoma Panhandle State U (OK)
Oklahoma Wesleyan U (OK)
Peirce Coll (PA)
Penn State U Berks Cmps of Berks-Lehigh Valley Coll (PA)
Pikeville Coll (KY)
Pine Manor Coll (MA)
Point Park Coll (PA)
Pontifical Catholic U of Puerto Rico (PR)
Presentation Coll (SD)
Providence Coll (RI)
Purdue U North Central (IN)
Reinhardt Coll (GA)
Richmond, The American International U in LondonUnited Kingdom)
Rider U (NJ)
Rivier Coll (NH)
Robert Morris Coll (IL)
Robert Morris U (PA)
Rochester Inst of Technology (NY)
Rogers State U (OK)
Roger Williams U (RI)
Rust Coll (MS)
Sacred Heart U (CT)
Sage Coll of Albany (NY)
St. Augustine Coll (IL)
St. Francis Coll (NY)
Saint Francis U (PA)
St. Gregory's U (OK)
Saint Joseph's Coll (IN)
Saint Joseph's U (PA)
Saint Peter's Coll (NJ)
Salem International U (WV)
Salve Regina U (RI)
Schiller International UFrance)
Schiller International USpain)
Shawnee State U (OH)
Shaw U (NC)
Shepherd Coll (WV)
Siena Heights U (MI)
Sinte Gleska U (SD)
Si Tanka Huron U (SD)
Southeastern U (DC)
Southern New Hampshire U (NH)
Southern Vermont Coll (VT)
Southern Wesleyan U (SC)
Southwest Baptist U (MO)
Southwestern Assemblies of God U (TX)
Southwest State U (MN)
Spring Hill Coll (AL)
State U of NY at Farmingdale (NY)
State U of NY Coll of A&T at Cobleskill (NY)
State U of NY Empire State Coll (NY)
Strayer U (DC)
Sullivan U (KY)
Taylor U (IN)
Taylor U, Fort Wayne Campus (IN)
Teikyo Post U (CT)
Thomas Coll (ME)
Thomas Edison State Coll (NJ)
Tiffin U (OH)
Trinity Bible Coll (ND)
Tri-State U (IN)
Troy State U Dothan (AL)
Tulane U (LA)
Union Coll (NE)
Universidad Adventista de las Antillas (PR)
Université Laval (QC, Canada)
The U of Akron (OH)
U of Alaska Anchorage (AK)
U of Alaska Fairbanks (AK)
U of Alaska Southeast (AK)
U of Bridgeport (CT)
U of Charleston (WV)
U of Cincinnati (OH)
U of Dubuque (IA)
The U of Findlay (OH)
U of Great Falls (MT)
U of Indianapolis (IN)
The U of Maine at Augusta (ME)
U of Maine at Fort Kent (ME)
U of Maine at Machias (ME)
U of Mary (ND)
U of Minnesota, Crookston (MN)
The U of Montana–Western (MT)
U of New Hampshire (NH)
U of New Haven (CT)
U of Phoenix–Phoenix Campus (AZ)
U of Puerto Rico, Humacao U Coll (PR)
U of Puerto Rico at Ponce (PR)
U of Rio Grande (OH)
U of Saint Francis (IN)
The U of Scranton (PA)
U of Sioux Falls (SD)
U of Southern Maine (ME)
U of the Virgin Islands (VI)
U of Toledo (OH)
U of Wisconsin–Green Bay (WI)
U System Coll for Lifelong Learning (NH)
Upper Iowa U (IA)
Urbana U (OH)
Villa Julie Coll (MD)
Waldorf Coll (IA)
Walla Walla Coll (WA)
Walsh U (OH)
Washington & Jefferson Coll (PA)
Wayland Baptist U (TX)
Waynesburg Coll (PA)
Webber International U (FL)
Wentworth Inst of Technology (MA)
Wesley Coll (DE)
Western Baptist Coll (OR)
Western Kentucky U (KY)
West Virginia State Coll (WV)
West Virginia U Inst of Technology (WV)
Williams Baptist Coll (AR)
Wilson Coll (PA)
York Coll of Pennsylvania (PA)
Youngstown State U (OH)

BUSINESS ADMINISTRATION/ MANAGEMENT RELATED
American InterContinental U Online (IL)
Chestnut Hill Coll (PA)
DeVry Coll of Technology (NJ)

BUSINESS COMMUNICATIONS
Central Christian Coll of Kansas (KS)
Chestnut Hill Coll (PA)

BUSINESS COMPUTER FACILITIES OPERATION
Dalton State Coll (GA)
Medgar Evers Coll of the City U of NY (NY)

BUSINESS COMPUTER PROGRAMMING
Idaho State U (ID)
Kent State U (OH)

Macon State Coll (GA)
Robert Morris Coll (IL)
Southern Illinois U Carbondale (IL)
U of Toledo (OH)

BUSINESS ECONOMICS
Central Christian Coll of Kansas (KS)
Northwood U (MI)
Saint Peter's Coll (NJ)
Urbana U (OH)

BUSINESS EDUCATION
Central Christian Coll of Kansas (KS)
Clayton Coll & State U (GA)
Faulkner U (AL)
Lindsey Wilson Coll (KY)
Macon State Coll (GA)
Martin Methodist Coll (TN)
Sinte Gleska U (SD)
U of the District of Columbia (DC)

BUSINESS MACHINE REPAIR
Boise State U (ID)
Faulkner U (AL)
Lamar U (TX)
U of Alaska Anchorage (AK)

BUSINESS MANAGEMENT/ ADMINISTRATIVE SERVICES RELATED
The U of Akron (OH)

BUSINESS MARKETING AND MARKETING MANAGEMENT
American InterContinental U, Atlanta (GA)
Baker Coll of Auburn Hills (MI)
Baker Coll of Cadillac (MI)
Baker Coll of Clinton Township (MI)
Baker Coll of Flint (MI)
Baker Coll of Jackson (MI)
Baker Coll of Muskegon (MI)
Baker Coll of Owosso (MI)
Baker Coll of Port Huron (MI)
Ball State U (IN)
Bluefield State Coll (WV)
Boise State U (ID)
British Columbia Inst of Technology (BC, Canada)
Central Christian Coll of Kansas (KS)
Champlain Coll (VT)
Chestnut Hill Coll (PA)
Clayton Coll & State U (GA)
Cleary U (MI)
Dalton State Coll (GA)
Daniel Webster Coll (NH)
Davenport U, Dearborn (MI)
Davenport U, Grand Rapids (MI)
Davenport U, Kalamazoo (MI)
Davenport U, Warren (MI)
David N. Myers U (OH)
Five Towns Coll (NY)
Florida Metropolitan U-Fort Lauderdale Coll (FL)
Florida Metropolitan U-Tampa Coll, Lakeland (FL)
Florida Metropolitan U-Orlando Coll, North (FL)
Florida Metropolitan U-Tampa Coll (FL)
Hawai'i Pacific U (HI)
Idaho State U (ID)
Inter American U of PR, Aguadilla Campus (PR)
Johnson & Wales U (CO)
Johnson & Wales U (RI)
King's Coll (PA)
Lewis-Clark State Coll (ID)
Martin Methodist Coll (TN)
Mount Ida Coll (MA)
New England School of Communications (ME)
Northeastern U (MA)
Northwood U (MI)
Northwood U, Florida Campus (FL)
Northwood U, Texas Campus (TX)
Purdue U North Central (IN)
Rochester Inst of Technology (NY)
Sage Coll of Albany (NY)
Saint Joseph's U (PA)
Saint Peter's Coll (NJ)
Siena Heights U (MI)
Southeastern U (DC)
Southern New Hampshire U (NH)
Southwest State U (MN)
Strayer U (DC)
Sullivan U (KY)
Teikyo Post U (CT)
Thomas Edison State Coll (NJ)
Touro Coll (NY)
U of Bridgeport (CT)
U of Cincinnati (OH)
U of Sioux Falls (SD)
U of the District of Columbia (DC)
U of Toledo (OH)
Urbana U (OH)
Walsh U (OH)
Webber International U (FL)
Weber State U (UT)
West Virginia State Coll (WV)
Wilson Coll (PA)
Wright State U (OH)
Youngstown State U (OH)

BUSINESS SERVICES MARKETING
Southern New Hampshire U (NH)

BUSINESS SYSTEMS ANALYSIS/ DESIGN
U of Toledo (OH)

BUSINESS SYSTEMS NETWORKING/ TELECOMMUNICATIONS
Baker Coll of Flint (MI)
Champlain Coll (VT)
Crown Coll (MN)
Davenport U, Dearborn (MI)
Davenport U, Warren (MI)
DeVry Coll of Technology (NJ)
Peirce Coll (PA)
Robert Morris Coll (IL)

BUYING OPERATIONS
The U of Akron (OH)

CABINET MAKING
British Columbia Inst of Technology (BC, Canada)

CARDIOVASCULAR TECHNOLOGY
British Columbia Inst of Technology (BC, Canada)
Molloy Coll (NY)
Nebraska Methodist Coll of Nursing & Allied Health (NE)
U of Toledo (OH)

CARPENTRY
British Columbia Inst of Technology (BC, Canada)
Central Christian Coll of Kansas (KS)
Southern Utah U (UT)

CARTOGRAPHY
Mansfield U of Pennsylvania (PA)

CERAMIC ARTS
Friends U (KS)
Rochester Inst of Technology (NY)

CHEMICAL ENGINEERING
U of New Haven (CT)

CHEMICAL ENGINEERING TECHNOLOGY
Ball State U (IN)
Excelsior Coll (NY)
Ferris State U (MI)
Kansas State U (KS)
Lawrence Technological U (MI)
Michigan Technological U (MI)
U of Cincinnati (OH)
U of the District of Columbia (DC)
U of Toledo (OH)
West Virginia State Coll (WV)

CHEMICAL TECHNOLOGY
British Columbia Inst of Technology (BC, Canada)
Indiana U–Purdue U Fort Wayne (IN)
State U of NY Coll of A&T at Cobleskill (NY)
U of Massachusetts Lowell (MA)
U of Puerto Rico, Humacao U Coll (PR)
U of Toledo (OH)
Weber State U (UT)

CHEMISTRY
Adrian Coll (MI)
Bethel Coll (IN)
Castleton State Coll (VT)
Central Christian Coll of Kansas (KS)
Central Methodist Coll (MO)
Chestnut Hill Coll (PA)
Clayton Coll & State U (GA)
Dalton State Coll (GA)
Fayetteville State U (NC)
Indiana U–Purdue U Fort Wayne (IN)
Indiana U South Bend (IN)
Indiana Wesleyan U (IN)
Keene State Coll (NH)
Lake Superior State U (MI)
Lindsey Wilson Coll (KY)
Lourdes Coll (OH)
Macon State Coll (GA)
Maharishi U of Management (IA)
Martin Methodist Coll (TN)
Methodist Coll (NC)
Millersville U of Pennsylvania (PA)
Ohio Dominican Coll (OH)
Oklahoma Wesleyan U (OK)
Rochester Inst of Technology (NY)
Rogers State U (OK)
Sacred Heart U (CT)
Saint Joseph's U (PA)
Siena Heights U (MI)
Thomas Edison State Coll (NJ)
Thomas More Coll (KY)
U of Indianapolis (IN)
U of New Haven (CT)
U of Rio Grande (OH)
The U of Tampa (FL)
U of Wisconsin–Green Bay (WI)
Villa Julie Coll (MD)
Waldorf Coll (IA)
Wright State U (OH)
York Coll of Pennsylvania (PA)

CHILD CARE/DEVELOPMENT
Abilene Christian U (TX)
Alabama State U (AL)
Boise State U (ID)
Eastern Kentucky U (KY)
Evangel U (MO)
Fairmont State Coll (WV)
Ferris State U (MI)
Franciscan U of Steubenville (OH)
Friends U (KS)
Grambling State U (LA)
Lamar U (TX)
Midway Coll (KY)
Mount Ida Coll (MA)
Northern Michigan U (MI)
Ohio U (OH)
Ohio U–Lancaster (OH)
Purdue U Calumet (IN)
Reformed Bible Coll (MI)
Southeast Missouri State U (MO)
Southern Utah U (UT)
Trevecca Nazarene U (TN)
U of Cincinnati (OH)
U of Minnesota, Crookston (MN)
U of the District of Columbia (DC)
Villa Julie Coll (MD)
Waldorf Coll (IA)
Washburn U of Topeka (KS)
Weber State U (UT)
Youngstown State U (OH)

CHILD CARE/GUIDANCE
The Baptist Coll of Florida (FL)
Central Missouri State U (MO)
Eastern New Mexico U (NM)
Henderson State U (AR)
Southeast Missouri State U (MO)
U of Central Arkansas (AR)
Weber State U (UT)
Youngstown State U (OH)

CHILD CARE PROVIDER
Idaho State U (ID)
Lewis-Clark State Coll (ID)
Mayville State U (ND)
Mercy Coll (NY)
Pacific Union Coll (CA)
Southeastern U (DC)
U of Alaska Fairbanks (AK)

CHILD CARE SERVICES MANAGEMENT
Chestnut Hill Coll (PA)
Lewis-Clark State Coll (ID)
Mount Aloysius Coll (PA)
Mount Vernon Nazarene U (OH)
U Coll of the Cariboo (BC, Canada)

CHILD GUIDANCE
Siena Heights U (MI)
Thomas Edison State Coll (NJ)
Tougaloo Coll (MS)

CITY/COMMUNITY/REGIONAL PLANNING
U of the District of Columbia (DC)

CIVIL ENGINEERING
U of New Haven (CT)

CIVIL ENGINEERING TECHNOLOGY
Bluefield State Coll (WV)
British Columbia Inst of Technology (BC, Canada)
Caribbean U (PR)
Coll of Staten Island of the City U of NY (NY)
Fairmont State Coll (WV)
Ferris State U (MI)
Idaho State U (ID)
Indiana U–Purdue U Fort Wayne (IN)
Indiana U–Purdue U Indianapolis (IN)
Kansas State U (KS)
Lawrence Technological U (MI)
Michigan Technological U (MI)
Missouri Western State Coll (MO)
Montana State U–Northern (MT)
Murray State U (KY)
Point Park Coll (PA)
Purdue U Calumet (IN)
Purdue U North Central (IN)
Thomas Edison State Coll (NJ)
U of Cincinnati (OH)
U of Massachusetts Lowell (MA)
U of New Hampshire (NH)
U of Puerto Rico at Ponce (PR)
U of Southern Indiana (IN)
U of the District of Columbia (DC)
U of Toledo (OH)
Wentworth Inst of Technology (MA)
West Virginia U Inst of Technology (WV)
Youngstown State U (OH)

CIVIL/STRUCTURAL DRAFTING
British Columbia Inst of Technology (BC, Canada)
Montana Tech of The U of Montana (MT)

CLOTHING/TEXTILES
Indiana U Bloomington (IN)

COMMERCIAL PHOTOGRAPHY
Paier Coll of Art, Inc. (CT)

COMMUNICATION EQUIPMENT TECHNOLOGY
Bluefield State Coll (WV)
Ferris State U (MI)
Wilmington Coll (DE)

COMMUNICATIONS
Baker Coll of Jackson (MI)
Brigham Young U–Hawaii (HI)
Castleton State Coll (VT)
Clearwater Christian Coll (FL)
Coll of Mount St. Joseph (OH)
Indiana Wesleyan U (IN)
Lyndon State Coll (VT)
New England School of Communications (ME)
Sage Coll of Albany (NY)
Southeastern Louisiana U (LA)
Southern Nazarene U (OK)
Southwestern Assemblies of God U (TX)
Thomas More Coll (KY)
Tri-State U (IN)
The U of Montana–Missoula (MT)
U of New Haven (CT)
U of Rio Grande (OH)
U of Southern Indiana (IN)

COMMUNICATIONS RELATED
New England School of Communications (ME)

COMMUNICATIONS TECHNOLOGIES RELATED
New England School of Communications (ME)

COMMUNICATION SYSTEMS INSTALLATION/REPAIR
Idaho State U (ID)
U Coll of the Cariboo (BC, Canada)

COMMUNITY SERVICES
Alabama State U (AL)
Cazenovia Coll (NY)
Fairmont State Coll (WV)
Martin Methodist Coll (TN)
Midland Lutheran Coll (NE)
Montana State U–Northern (MT)
Samford U (AL)
State U of NY Empire State Coll (NY)
Thomas Edison State Coll (NJ)
Touro Coll (NY)
The U of Findlay (OH)
U of New Hampshire (NH)
U of New Mexico (NM)
Waldorf Coll (IA)

COMPUTER EDUCATION
Baker Coll of Flint (MI)

COMPUTER ENGINEERING
The U of Scranton (PA)

COMPUTER ENGINEERING RELATED
Western Governors U (UT)

COMPUTER ENGINEERING TECHNOLOGY
Andrews U (MI)
Baker Coll of Owosso (MI)
Capitol Coll (MD)
Clayton Coll & State U (GA)
Coleman Coll (CA)
Dalton State Coll (GA)
Eastern Kentucky U (KY)
Education America, Southeast Coll of Technology, Mobile Campus (AL)
Excelsior Coll (NY)
Glenville State Coll (WV)
Haskell Indian Nations U (KS)
Johnson & Wales U (RI)
Kansas State U (KS)
Lake Superior State U (MI)
Lewis-Clark State Coll (ID)
Missouri Tech (MO)
National American U (SD)
Northeastern U (MA)
Oakland City U (IN)
Ohio U–Lancaster (OH)
Oregon Inst of Technology (OR)
Peirce Coll (PA)
Purdue U Calumet (IN)
Purdue U North Central (IN)
Rochester Inst of Technology (NY)
Rogers State U (OK)
U of Cincinnati (OH)
U of Hartford (CT)
U of the District of Columbia (DC)
Weber State U (UT)
Wentworth Inst of Technology (MA)

COMPUTER GRAPHICS
Academy of Art Coll (CA)
The Art Inst of California-San Francisco (CA)
The Art Inst of Colorado (CO)
The Art Inst of Portland (OR)
The Art Inst of Washington (VA)
Baker Coll of Cadillac (MI)
Coll of Aeronautics (NY)
The Illinois Inst of Art (IL)
International Academy of Design & Technology (FL)
International Acad of Merchandising & Design, Ltd (IL)
New England School of Communications (ME)
Newschool of Architecture & Design (CA)
U of Advancing Computer Technology (AZ)
Villa Julie Coll (MD)

COMPUTER/INFORMATION SCIENCES
Alderson-Broaddus Coll (WV)
Bluefield State Coll (WV)
Chaminade U of Honolulu (HI)
Coleman Coll (CA)
Colorado Tech U Denver Campus (CO)
Dalton State Coll (GA)
Edinboro U of Pennsylvania (PA)
Education America, Southeast Coll of Technology, Mobile Campus (AL)
Florida Metropolitan U-Orlando Coll, South (FL)
Indiana Wesleyan U (IN)
International Coll (FL)
Kentucky State U (KY)
King's Coll (PA)
Lyndon State Coll (VT)
Oklahoma Panhandle State U (OK)
Pacific Union Coll (CA)
Penn State U Schuylkill Campus of the Capital Coll (PA)
Rocky Mountain Coll (MT)
Sacred Heart U (CT)
Sage Coll of Albany (NY)
Southern New Hampshire U (NH)
Thomas Coll (ME)
Thomas Edison State Coll (NJ)
Thomas More Coll (KY)
Tri-State U (IN)
Troy State U Montgomery (AL)
Tulane U (LA)
U of Alaska Anchorage (AK)
U of Charleston (WV)
U of Cincinnati (OH)
The U of Montana–Western (MT)
U of New Haven (CT)
U of Southern Indiana (IN)
Villa Julie Coll (MD)
Virginia Coll at Birmingham (AL)
Weber State U (UT)
Wiley Coll (TX)
Youngstown State U (OH)

COMPUTER/INFORMATION SCIENCES RELATED
Strayer U (DC)

COMPUTER INSTALLATION/ REPAIR
Dalton State Coll (GA)
U Coll of the Cariboo (BC, Canada)
U of Alaska Fairbanks (AK)

COMPUTER MAINTENANCE TECHNOLOGY
Collins Coll: A School of Design and Technology (AZ)
Dalton State Coll (GA)
Peirce Coll (PA)
State U of NY Coll of A&T at Cobleskill (NY)

COMPUTER MANAGEMENT
Champlain Coll (VT)
Daniel Webster Coll (NH)
Davenport U, Lansing (MI)
Faulkner U (AL)
Five Towns Coll (NY)
Mount Ida Coll (MA)
Northwood U (MI)
Northwood U, Florida Campus (FL)
Oakland City U (IN)
Thomas Coll (ME)
U of Great Falls (MT)
U System Coll for Lifelong Learning (NH)

COMPUTER PROGRAMMING
Atlantic Union Coll (MA)
Baker Coll of Flint (MI)
Baker Coll of Muskegon (MI)
Baker Coll of Owosso (MI)
Baker Coll of Port Huron (MI)
Briarcliffe Coll (NY)
California U of Pennsylvania (PA)
Caribbean U (PR)
Castleton State Coll (VT)
Charleston Southern U (SC)
Cleary U (MI)
Coll of Staten Island of the City U of NY (NY)
Columbus State U (GA)
Dakota State U (SD)
Daniel Webster Coll (NH)
Davenport U, Grand Rapids (MI)
Davenport U, Kalamazoo (MI)
Florida Metropolitan U-Fort Lauderdale Coll (FL)
Florida Metropolitan U-Tampa Coll, Lakeland (FL)
Florida Metropolitan U-Orlando Coll, North (FL)
Florida Metropolitan U-Tampa Coll (FL)
Friends U (KS)
Globe Inst of Technology (NY)
Gwynedd-Mercy Coll (PA)
Indiana U East (IN)
Johnson & Wales U (RI)
Kansas State U (KS)
Limestone Coll (SC)
Lindsey Wilson Coll (KY)
Macon State Coll (GA)
Martin Methodist Coll (TN)
Midland Lutheran Coll (NE)
National American U (SD)
National American U–Sioux Falls Branch (SD)
The National Hispanic U (CA)
New York U (NY)
Oakland City U (IN)
Oregon Inst of Technology (OR)
Pontifical Catholic U of Puerto Rico (PR)
Purdue U Calumet (IN)
Purdue U North Central (IN)
Richmond, The American International U in LondonUnited Kingdom)
Rogers State U (OK)
Saint Francis U (PA)
Saint Joseph's Coll (IN)
Saint Joseph's U (PA)
State U of NY at Farmingdale (NY)
State U of NY Coll of A&T at Cobleskill (NY)
Tiffin U (OH)
U of Advancing Computer Technology (AZ)
U of Arkansas at Little Rock (AR)
U of Cincinnati (OH)
U of Indianapolis (IN)
U of Toledo (OH)
Villa Julie Coll (MD)
Waldorf Coll (IA)
Walla Walla Coll (WA)
West Virginia State Coll (WV)
York Coll of Pennsylvania (PA)
Youngstown State U (OH)

COMPUTER SCIENCE
Arkansas Baptist Coll (AR)
Arkansas Tech U (AR)
Baker Coll of Owosso (MI)
Bayamón Central U (PR)
Bethel Coll (IN)
Black Hills State U (SD)
Brigham Young U–Hawaii (HI)
British Columbia Inst of Technology (BC, Canada)
Carroll Coll (MT)
Central Christian Coll of Kansas (KS)
Central Methodist Coll (MO)
Chestnut Hill Coll (PA)
Clayton Coll & State U (GA)
Columbia Union Coll (MD)
Columbus State U (GA)
Creighton U (NE)
Dalton State Coll (GA)
Davis & Elkins Coll (WV)
Defiance Coll (OH)
East-West U (IL)
Excelsior Coll (NY)
Felician Coll (NJ)
Florida Metropolitan U-Tampa Coll, Lakeland (FL)
Florida Metropolitan U-Tampa Coll (FL)
Friends U (KS)
Glenville State Coll (WV)
Indiana U–Purdue U Fort Wayne (IN)
Indiana U South Bend (IN)
Indiana U Southeast (IN)
Inst of Computer Technology (CA)
Inter American U of PR, Aguadilla Campus (PR)
Inter Amer U of PR, Barranquitas Campus (PR)
Johnson & Wales U (RI)
Kansas Wesleyan U (KS)
Keene State Coll (NH)
Limestone Coll (SC)
Lincoln U (MO)
Lyndon State Coll (VT)
Macon State Coll (GA)
Maharishi U of Management (IA)
Manchester Coll (IN)
Martin Methodist Coll (TN)
McNeese State U (LA)
Medgar Evers Coll of the City U of NY (NY)
Merrimack Coll (MA)
Mesa State Coll (CO)
Methodist Coll (NC)
Millersville U of Pennsylvania (PA)
Missouri Southern State Coll (MO)
Montana Tech of The U of Montana (MT)
Mountain State U (WV)
Mount Aloysius Coll (PA)
Oakland City U (IN)
Ohio U–Lancaster (OH)
Ohio U–Southern Campus (OH)
Point Park Coll (PA)
Richmond, The American International U in LondonUnited Kingdom)
Rivier Coll (NH)
Rochester Inst of Technology (NY)
Rogers State U (OK)
Sacred Heart U (CT)
St. Francis Coll (NY)
Saint Joseph's Coll (IN)
Saint Joseph's U (PA)
Southeastern U (DC)
Southern Adventist U (TN)
Southwest Baptist U (MO)
State U of NY at Farmingdale (NY)
State U of NY Coll of A&T at Cobleskill (NY)
Sullivan U (KY)
Tabor Coll (KS)
Thomas Edison State Coll (NJ)
Universidad Adventista de las Antillas (PR)
U of Dubuque (IA)
The U of Findlay (OH)
U of Maine at Fort Kent (ME)
U of Puerto Rico at Ponce (PR)
U of Rio Grande (OH)
U of the Virgin Islands (VI)
Waldorf Coll (IA)
Weber State U (UT)
Wentworth Inst of Technology (MA)
West Virginia State Coll (WV)
Wiley Coll (TX)

COMPUTER SOFTWARE AND MEDIA APPLICATIONS RELATED
New England School of Communications (ME)

COMPUTER SYSTEMS ANALYSIS
Baker Coll of Flint (MI)
Becker Coll (MA)
British Columbia Inst of Technology (BC, Canada)
Kansas State U (KS)

COMPUTER SYSTEMS NETWORKING/ TELECOMMUNICATIONS
Education America, Southeast Coll of Technology, Mobile Campus (AL)
Sage Coll of Albany (NY)
Strayer U (DC)

COMPUTER TYPOGRAPHY/ COMPOSITION
Baker Coll of Auburn Hills (MI)
Baker Coll of Cadillac (MI)
Baker Coll of Clinton Township (MI)
Baker Coll of Flint (MI)
Baker Coll of Jackson (MI)
Baltimore Hebrew U (MD)
Davis & Elkins Coll (WV)
Faulkner U (AL)
McNeese State U (LA)
Northern Michigan U (MI)
U of Toledo (OH)

CONSTRUCTION MANAGEMENT
Baker Coll of Flint (MI)
British Columbia Inst of Technology (BC, Canada)
John Brown U (AR)
Pratt Inst (NY)
U of New Hampshire (NH)
Wentworth Inst of Technology (MA)

CONSTRUCTION TECHNOLOGY
Abilene Christian U (TX)
Andrews U (MI)
Baker Coll of Owosso (MI)
British Columbia Inst of Technology (BC, Canada)
Central Christian Coll of Kansas (KS)
Central Missouri State U (MO)
Coll of Staten Island of the City U of NY (NY)
Fairmont State Coll (WV)
Ferris State U (MI)
Lake Superior State U (MI)
Lawrence Technological U (MI)
Northern Michigan U (MI)
Purdue U Calumet (IN)
Purdue U North Central (IN)
State U of NY at Farmingdale (NY)
Tri-State U (IN)
The U of Akron (OH)
U of Alaska Southeast (AK)
U of Cincinnati (OH)
U of New Hampshire (NH)
U of Toledo (OH)
Wentworth Inst of Technology (MA)

CONSTRUCTION TRADES RELATED
British Columbia Inst of Technology (BC, Canada)

CORRECTIONS
Armstrong Atlantic State U (GA)
Baker Coll of Muskegon (MI)
Bluefield State Coll (WV)
Eastern Kentucky U (KY)
John Jay Coll of Criminal Justice, the City U of NY (NY)
Lake Superior State U (MI)
Lamar U (TX)
Macon State Coll (GA)
Marygrove Coll (MI)
Murray State U (KY)
Northeastern U (MA)
U of Indianapolis (IN)
U of the District of Columbia (DC)
U of Toledo (OH)
Washburn U of Topeka (KS)
Weber State U (UT)
West Virginia U Inst of Technology (WV)
Xavier U (OH)
York Coll of Pennsylvania (PA)
Youngstown State U (OH)

COSMETOLOGY
Lamar U (TX)

COUNSELING PSYCHOLOGY
Central Christian Coll of Kansas (KS)

COUNSELOR EDUCATION/ GUIDANCE
Central Christian Coll of Kansas (KS)
Martin Methodist Coll (TN)
Our Lady of Holy Cross Coll (LA)

COURT REPORTING
Florida Metropolitan U-Orlando Coll, North (FL)
Johnson & Wales U (RI)
Metropolitan Coll, Tulsa (OK)
Northwood U, Texas Campus (TX)
U of Cincinnati (OH)
Villa Julie Coll (MD)
Washburn U of Topeka (KS)

CREATIVE WRITING
Maharishi U of Management (IA)
Manchester Coll (IN)
U of Maine at Presque Isle (ME)
The U of Tampa (FL)

CRIMINAL JUSTICE/LAW ENFORCEMENT ADMINISTRATION
Adrian Coll (MI)
Anderson U (IN)
Armstrong Atlantic State U (GA)
Ashland U (OH)
Ball State U (IN)
Bay Path Coll (MA)
Becker Coll (MA)
Bemidji State U (MN)
Boise State U (ID)
Cameron U (OK)
Campbellsville U (KY)
Castleton State Coll (VT)
Chaminade U of Honolulu (HI)
Champlain Coll (VT)
Chestnut Hill Coll (PA)
Clayton Coll & State U (GA)
Columbia Coll (MO)
Columbus State U (GA)
Dakota Wesleyan U (SD)
Dalton State Coll (GA)
Defiance Coll (OH)
Eastern Kentucky U (KY)
Faulkner U (AL)
Finlandia U (MI)
Florida Metropolitan U-Tampa Coll (FL)
Fort Valley State U (GA)
Glenville State Coll (WV)
Grambling State U (LA)
Hannibal-LaGrange Coll (MO)
Hilbert Coll (NY)
Indiana U Northwest (IN)
Indiana U South Bend (IN)
Johnson & Wales U (RI)
Kansas Wesleyan U (KS)
LaGrange Coll (GA)
Lake Superior State U (MI)
Lewis-Clark State Coll (ID)
Lincoln U (MO)
Louisiana Coll (LA)
Lourdes Coll (OH)
MacMurray Coll (IL)
Macon State Coll (GA)
Mansfield U of Pennsylvania (PA)
Martin Methodist Coll (TN)
Mercyhurst Coll (PA)
Mesa State Coll (CO)
Methodist Coll (NC)
Mount Ida Coll (MA)
New Mexico State U (NM)
Northern Michigan U (MI)
Ohio U–Southern Campus (OH)
Rogers State U (OK)
St. Francis Coll (NY)
St. John's U (NY)
Saint Joseph's U (PA)
Salve Regina U (RI)
Siena Heights U (MI)
Si Tanka Huron U (SD)
Southern Utah U (UT)
Southern Vermont Coll (VT)
State U of NY at Farmingdale (NY)
Suffolk U (MA)
Thomas Edison State Coll (NJ)
Thomas More Coll (KY)
Thomas U (GA)
Tri-State U (IN)
U of Cincinnati (OH)
The U of Findlay (OH)
U of Indianapolis (IN)
The U of Maine at Augusta (ME)
U of Maine at Fort Kent (ME)
U of Maine at Presque Isle (ME)
U of New Haven (CT)
The U of South Dakota (SD)
U of the District of Columbia (DC)
Urbana U (OH)
Washburn U of Topeka (KS)
West Virginia State Coll (WV)
York Coll of Pennsylvania (PA)
Youngstown State U (OH)

CRIMINAL JUSTICE STUDIES
Augusta State U (GA)
Bethel Coll (IN)
Cazenovia Coll (NY)
Central Christian Coll of Kansas (KS)
Champlain Coll (VT)
Colorado Tech U Sioux Falls Campus (SD)
Florida Metropolitan U-Orlando Coll, South (FL)
Idaho State U (ID)
Indiana U East (IN)
Indiana U Kokomo (IN)
Indiana U–Purdue U Fort Wayne (IN)
Indiana U–Purdue U Indianapolis (IN)
Indiana Wesleyan U (IN)
Kent State U (OH)
King's Coll (PA)
Manchester Coll (IN)
Missouri Western State Coll (MO)

Mountain State U (WV)
Mount Aloysius Coll (PA)
Penn State U Altoona Coll (PA)
Pikeville Coll (KY)
St. Gregory's U (OK)
Shaw U (NC)
Shepherd Coll (WV)
The U of Scranton (PA)
Weber State U (UT)

CRIMINOLOGY
Ball State U (IN)
Faulkner U (AL)
Indiana State U (IN)
Indiana U of Pennsylvania (PA)
Marquette U (WI)
U of the District of Columbia (DC)

CROP PRODUCTION MANAGEMENT
U of Massachusetts Amherst (MA)

CULINARY ARTS
The Art Inst of Colorado (CO)
The Art Inst of Phoenix (AZ)
Baker Coll of Muskegon (MI)
Boise State U (ID)
The Culinary Inst of America (NY)
Johnson & Wales U (CO)
Johnson & Wales U (RI)
Johnson & Wales U (VA)
Kendall Coll (IL)
Mercyhurst Coll (PA)
Mesa State Coll (CO)
Oakland City U (IN)
Purdue U Calumet (IN)
Saint Francis U (PA)
Southern New Hampshire U (NH)
State U of NY Coll of A&T at Cobleskill (NY)
Sullivan U (KY)
The U of Akron (OH)
U of Alaska Anchorage (AK)
U of Alaska Fairbanks (AK)
The U of Montana–Missoula (MT)
U of New Hampshire (NH)
West Virginia U Inst of Technology (WV)

CULINARY ARTS AND SERVICES RELATED
New York Inst of Technology (NY)
Shepherd Coll (WV)

CULTURAL STUDIES
Baltimore Hebrew U (MD)
Indiana Wesleyan U (IN)

CYTOTECHNOLOGY
Indiana U–Purdue U Indianapolis (IN)
Indiana U Southeast (IN)

DAIRY SCIENCE
Eastern Kentucky U (KY)
State U of NY Coll of A&T at Cobleskill (NY)
U of New Hampshire (NH)

DANCE
New World School of the Arts (FL)

DATA PROCESSING
Austin Peay State U (TN)
Baker Coll of Clinton Township (MI)
Central Christian Coll of Kansas (KS)
Montana State U–Billings (MT)
Montana Tech of The U of Montana (MT)
Pace U (NY)
Peirce Coll (PA)
The U of Akron (OH)
The U of Montana–Western (MT)
U of Rio Grande (OH)
Youngstown State U (OH)

DATA PROCESSING TECHNOLOGY
American InterContinental U Online (IL)
Baker Coll of Auburn Hills (MI)
Baker Coll of Cadillac (MI)
Baker Coll of Clinton Township (MI)
Baker Coll of Flint (MI)
Baker Coll of Jackson (MI)
Baker Coll of Muskegon (MI)
Baker Coll of Owosso (MI)
Baker Coll of Port Huron (MI)
British Columbia Inst of Technology (BC, Canada)
Cameron U (OK)
Campbellsville U (KY)
Clayton Coll & State U (GA)
Davenport U, Kalamazoo (MI)
Dordt Coll (IA)
Five Towns Coll (NY)
Florida Metropolitan U-Tampa Coll, Lakeland (FL)
Florida Metropolitan U-Orlando Coll, North (FL)
Florida Metropolitan U-Tampa Coll (FL)
Hawai'i Pacific U (HI)
Idaho State U (ID)
Lake Superior State U (MI)
Lamar U (TX)
Lincoln U (MO)
Macon State Coll (GA)
Missouri Southern State Coll (MO)
Montana State U–Billings (MT)
Montana Tech of The U of Montana (MT)
Murray State U (KY)
New York Inst of Technology (NY)
Northern Michigan U (MI)
Northern State U (SD)
Peirce Coll (PA)
Sacred Heart U (CT)
Saint Francis U (PA)
St. John's U (NY)
Saint Peter's Coll (NJ)
Shawnee State U (OH)
Sinte Gleska U (SD)
State U of NY at Farmingdale (NY)
State U of NY Coll of A&T at Cobleskill (NY)
Thomas More Coll (KY)
U of Cincinnati (OH)
The U of Montana–Western (MT)
U of the Virgin Islands (VI)
U of Toledo (OH)
Valdosta State U (GA)
Waldorf Coll (IA)
Western Kentucky U (KY)
West Virginia U Inst of Technology (WV)
Wright State U (OH)
Youngstown State U (OH)

DENTAL ASSISTANT
U of Alaska Anchorage (AK)
U of Puerto Rico Medical Sciences Campus (PR)
U of Southern Indiana (IN)

DENTAL HYGIENE
Armstrong Atlantic State U (GA)
Baker Coll of Port Huron (MI)
Clayton Coll & State U (GA)
Dalton State Coll (GA)
East Tennessee State U (TN)
Ferris State U (MI)
Indiana U Northwest (IN)
Indiana U–Purdue U Fort Wayne (IN)
Indiana U–Purdue U Indianapolis (IN)
Indiana U South Bend (IN)
Lamar U (TX)
Macon State Coll (GA)
Minnesota State U, Mankato (MN)
Missouri Southern State Coll (MO)
Mount Ida Coll (MA)
New York U (NY)
Northeastern U (MA)
Oregon Inst of Technology (OR)
Shawnee State U (OH)
Southern Adventist U (TN)
State U of NY at Farmingdale (NY)
Tennessee State U (TN)
U of Alaska Anchorage (AK)
U of Arkansas for Medical Sciences (AR)
U of Bridgeport (CT)
U of Louisiana at Monroe (LA)
U of Louisville (KY)
U of New England (ME)
U of New Haven (CT)
U of New Mexico (NM)
U of Puerto Rico Medical Sciences Campus (PR)
The U of South Dakota (SD)
U of Southern Indiana (IN)
Weber State U (UT)
Western Kentucky U (KY)
West Liberty State Coll (WV)
West Virginia U Inst of Technology (WV)
Wichita State U (KS)
Youngstown State U (OH)

DENTAL LABORATORY TECHNICIAN
Idaho State U (ID)
Indiana U–Purdue U Fort Wayne (IN)
Louisiana State U Health Sciences Center (LA)
Southern Illinois U Carbondale (IL)

DESIGN/VISUAL COMMUNICATIONS
American InterContinental U, Atlanta (GA)
The Art Inst of Phoenix (AZ)
Collins Coll: A School of Design and Technology (AZ)
International Academy of Design & Technology (FL)
Pace U (NY)
Robert Morris Coll (IL)
Shepherd Coll (WV)

DESKTOP PUBLISHING EQUIPMENT OPERATION
Touro Coll (NY)

DEVELOPMENTAL/CHILD PSYCHOLOGY
Central Christian Coll of Kansas (KS)
Fresno Pacific U (CA)
Mount Ida Coll (MA)
Southern Vermont Coll (VT)
U of Sioux Falls (SD)
Villa Julie Coll (MD)
Waldorf Coll (IA)

DIAGNOSTIC MEDICAL SONOGRAPHY
Baker Coll of Owosso (MI)
Coll of St. Catherine (MN)
Mercy Coll of Health Sciences (IA)
Mountain State U (WV)
Nebraska Methodist Coll of Nursing & Allied Health (NE)
New York U (NY)
U of Toledo (OH)

DIESEL ENGINE MECHANIC
British Columbia Inst of Technology (BC, Canada)
Georgia Southwestern State U (GA)
Idaho State U (ID)
Montana State U–Billings (MT)
U of Alaska Anchorage (AK)
Weber State U (UT)

DIETETICS
Ball State U (IN)
Faulkner U (AL)
Loma Linda U (CA)
Oakwood Coll (AL)
Pacific Union Coll (CA)
Purdue U Calumet (IN)
Rochester Inst of Technology (NY)
U of Minnesota, Crookston (MN)
U of New Hampshire (NH)
Youngstown State U (OH)

DIETICIAN ASSISTANT
Pacific Union Coll (CA)
Youngstown State U (OH)

DIVINITY/MINISTRY
Atlantic Union Coll (MA)
Bethany Coll of the Assemblies of God (CA)
Boise Bible Coll (ID)
Calvary Bible Coll and Theological Seminary (MO)
Carson-Newman Coll (TN)
Central Christian Coll of Kansas (KS)
Clear Creek Baptist Bible Coll (KY)
Faith Baptist Bible Coll and Theological Seminary (IA)
Faulkner U (AL)
Florida Christian Coll (FL)
Manhattan Christian Coll (KS)
MidAmerica Nazarene U (KS)
Mount Olive Coll (NC)
Nebraska Christian Coll (NE)
Pacific Union Coll (CA)
Sacred Heart Major Seminary (MI)
St. Louis Christian Coll (MO)
Waldorf Coll (IA)
Warner Pacific Coll (OR)

DRAFTING
Abilene Christian U (TX)
Andrews U (MI)
Baker Coll of Auburn Hills (MI)
Baker Coll of Cadillac (MI)
Baker Coll of Clinton Township (MI)
Baker Coll of Flint (MI)
Baker Coll of Muskegon (MI)
Baker Coll of Owosso (MI)
Baker Coll of Port Huron (MI)
Black Hills State U (SD)
Boise State U (ID)
British Columbia Inst of Technology (BC, Canada)
California U of Pennsylvania (PA)
Cameron U (OK)
Central Christian Coll of Kansas (KS)
Central Missouri State U (MO)
Clayton Coll & State U (GA)
Dalton State Coll (GA)
Eastern Kentucky U (KY)
Education America, Southeast Coll of Technology, Mobile Campus (AL)
Fairmont State Coll (WV)
Ferris State U (MI)
Georgia Southwestern State U (GA)
Hamilton Tech Coll (IA)
Idaho State U (ID)
Keene State Coll (NH)
Lake Superior State U (MI)
Lamar U (TX)
Lewis-Clark State Coll (ID)
Lincoln U (MO)
Missouri Southern State Coll (MO)
Montana State U–Billings (MT)
Montana State U–Northern (MT)
Montana Tech of The U of Montana (MT)
Murray State U (KY)
Northern Michigan U (MI)
Northern State U (SD)
Ohio U–Lancaster (OH)
Robert Morris Coll (IL)
Saint Francis U (PA)
Shawnee State U (OH)
Southern Utah U (UT)
Thomas Edison State Coll (NJ)
Tri-State U (IN)
The U of Akron (OH)
U of Alaska Anchorage (AK)
U of Alaska Fairbanks (AK)
U of Cincinnati (OH)
U of Puerto Rico at Ponce (PR)
U of Rio Grande (OH)
U of Toledo (OH)
Utah State U (UT)
Virginia Coll at Birmingham (AL)
Weber State U (UT)
West Virginia State Coll (WV)
West Virginia U Inst of Technology (WV)
Wright State U (OH)
Youngstown State U (OH)

DRAFTING/DESIGN TECHNOLOGY
Dalton State Coll (GA)
Idaho State U (ID)
Kentucky State U (KY)
LeTourneau U (TX)
Lewis-Clark State Coll (ID)
Tri-State U (IN)
U Coll of the Cariboo (BC, Canada)
Youngstown State U (OH)

DRAWING
Academy of Art Coll (CA)
Central Christian Coll of Kansas (KS)
Northern Michigan U (MI)
Parsons School of Design, New School U (NY)
Sacred Heart U (CT)

EARLY CHILDHOOD EDUCATION
Arkansas Tech U (AR)
Atlantic Union Coll (MA)
Baker Coll of Clinton Township (MI)
Baker Coll of Muskegon (MI)
Baker Coll of Owosso (MI)
Bay Path Coll (MA)
Becker Coll (MA)
Bethany Coll of the Assemblies of God (CA)
Bethel Coll (IN)
Brewton-Parker Coll (GA)
California Coll for Health Sciences (CA)
California U of Pennsylvania (PA)
Caribbean U (PR)
Cazenovia Coll (NY)
Central Christian Coll of Kansas (KS)
Champlain Coll (VT)
Clayton Coll & State U (GA)
Coll of Saint Mary (NE)
Columbia Union Coll (MD)
Crown Coll (MN)
Eastern Nazarene Coll (MA)
Edinboro U of Pennsylvania (PA)
Friends U (KS)
Gannon U (PA)
Hofstra U (NY)
Hope International U (CA)
Indiana State U (IN)
Indiana U–Purdue U Fort Wayne (IN)
Indiana U–Purdue U Indianapolis (IN)
Indiana U South Bend (IN)
Johnson Bible Coll (TN)
Kansas Wesleyan U (KS)
Keene State Coll (NH)
Kendall Coll (IL)
Lake Superior State U (MI)
Lourdes Coll (OH)
Lynn U (FL)
Manchester Coll (IN)
Maranatha Baptist Bible Coll (WI)
Marian Coll (IN)
Martin Methodist Coll (TN)
Marygrove Coll (MI)
Mercyhurst Coll (PA)
Mesa State Coll (CO)
Midland Lutheran Coll (NE)
Midway Coll (KY)
Montana State U–Billings (MT)
Mount Aloysius Coll (PA)
Mount Ida Coll (MA)
Mount St. Mary's Coll (CA)
New York U (NY)
Ohio U–Southern Campus (OH)
Pacific Union Coll (CA)
Point Park Coll (PA)
Purdue U Calumet (IN)
Rivier Coll (NH)
Rust Coll (MS)
St. Augustine Coll (IL)
Saint Joseph's Coll (IN)
State U of NY Coll of A&T at Cobleskill (NY)
Taylor U (IN)
Taylor U, Fort Wayne Campus (IN)
Teikyo Post U (CT)
Tennessee State U (TN)
Tougaloo Coll (MS)
U of Alaska Fairbanks (AK)
U of Alaska Southeast (AK)
U of Arkansas at Pine Bluff (AR)
U of Great Falls (MT)
U of Minnesota, Crookston (MN)
The U of Montana–Western (MT)
U of Rio Grande (OH)
U of Sioux Falls (SD)
U System Coll for Lifelong Learning (NH)
Valley Forge Christian Coll (PA)
Villa Julie Coll (MD)
Waldorf Coll (IA)
Washburn U of Topeka (KS)
Western Kentucky U (KY)
William Tyndale Coll (MI)
Wilmington Coll (DE)
Xavier U (OH)

EARTH SCIENCES
Adrian Coll (MI)
Indiana U East (IN)
U of Wisconsin–Green Bay (WI)

EASTERN EUROPEAN AREA STUDIES
Baltimore Hebrew U (MD)

ECOLOGY
Sterling Coll (VT)

ECONOMICS
Adrian Coll (MI)
Central Christian Coll of Kansas (KS)
Clayton Coll & State U (GA)
Dalton State Coll (GA)
Macon State Coll (GA)
Martin Methodist Coll (TN)
Methodist Coll (NC)
Northwood U (MI)
Richmond, The American International U in LondonUnited Kingdom)
Sacred Heart U (CT)
State U of NY Empire State Coll (NY)
Strayer U (DC)
Thomas More Coll (KY)
Université Laval (QC, Canada)
U of Sioux Falls (SD)
The U of Tampa (FL)
U of Wisconsin–Green Bay (WI)
Washington & Jefferson Coll (PA)

EDUCATION
Alabama State U (AL)
Baltimore Hebrew U (MD)
Brewton-Parker Coll (GA)
Calvary Bible Coll and Theological Seminary (MO)
Caribbean U (PR)
Central Baptist Coll (AR)
Central Christian Coll of Kansas (KS)
Cincinnati Bible Coll and Seminary (OH)
Circleville Bible Coll (OH)
Clayton Coll & State U (GA)
Cumberland U (TN)
Dalton State Coll (GA)
Evangel U (MO)
Fayetteville State U (NC)
Friends U (KS)
Lamar U (TX)
Macon State Coll (GA)
Maharishi U of Management (IA)
Martin Methodist Coll (TN)
Medgar Evers Coll of the City U of NY (NY)
Mountain State U (WV)
The National Hispanic U (CA)
Pontifical Catholic U of Puerto Rico (PR)
Puget Sound Christian Coll (WA)
Reinhardt Coll (GA)
Sinte Gleska U (SD)
Southwestern Assemblies of God U (TX)
State U of NY Empire State Coll (NY)
North American Baptist Coll & Edmonton Baptist Sem (AB, Canada)
Tennessee Temple U (TN)
U of Southern Indiana (IN)
Waldorf Coll (IA)
Wayland Baptist U (TX)

EDUCATION ADMINISTRATION
Shasta Bible Coll (CA)

EDUCATIONAL MEDIA DESIGN
Bayamón Central U (PR)
Ferris State U (MI)

EDUCATIONAL MEDIA TECHNOLOGY
U of Wisconsin–Superior (WI)

EDUCATION OF THE HEARING IMPAIRED
Ohio U–Chillicothe (OH)

EDUCATION RELATED
Kent State U (OH)

ELECTRICAL/ELECTRONIC ENGINEERING TECHNOLOGIES RELATED
Boise State U (ID)
New York Inst of Technology (NY)
U of Southern Indiana (IN)

ELECTRICAL/ELECTRONIC ENGINEERING TECHNOLOGY
Andrews U (MI)
Arkansas State U (AR)
Arkansas Tech U (AR)
Baker Coll of Cadillac (MI)
Baker Coll of Muskegon (MI)
Baker Coll of Owosso (MI)
Bluefield State Coll (WV)
Boise State U (ID)
Briarcliffe Coll (NY)
British Columbia Inst of Technology (BC, Canada)
Capitol Coll (MD)
Clayton Coll & State U (GA)
Colorado Tech U (CO)
Columbia Coll (PR)
Columbus State U (GA)
Dalton State Coll (GA)
DeVry Coll of Technology (NJ)
DeVry Inst of Technology (NY)
DeVry U (AZ)
DeVry U, Fremont (CA)
DeVry U, Long Beach (CA)
DeVry U, Pomona (CA)
DeVry U, West Hills (CA)
DeVry U, Colorado Springs (CO)
DeVry U (FL)
DeVry U, Alpharetta (GA)
DeVry U, Decatur (GA)
DeVry U, Addison (IL)
DeVry U, Chicago (IL)
DeVry U, Tinley Park (IL)
DeVry U (MO)
DeVry U (OH)
DeVry U (TX)
DeVry U (VA)
DeVry U (WA)
Eastern Kentucky U (KY)
Embry-Riddle Aeronautical U (FL)
Excelsior Coll (NY)
Fairmont State Coll (WV)
Fort Valley State U (GA)
Georgia Southwestern State U (GA)
Hamilton Tech Coll (IA)
Idaho State U (ID)
Indiana State U (IN)
Indiana U–Purdue U Fort Wayne (IN)
Indiana U–Purdue U Indianapolis (IN)
Johnson & Wales U (RI)
Kansas State U (KS)
Keene State Coll (NH)
Kentucky State U (KY)
Lake Superior State U (MI)
Lamar U (TX)
Lawrence Technological U (MI)
Lewis-Clark State Coll (ID)
Lincoln U (MO)
McNeese State U (LA)
Merrimack Coll (MA)
Mesa State Coll (CO)
Michigan Technological U (MI)
Missouri Tech (MO)
Missouri Western State Coll (MO)
Montana State U–Northern (MT)
Murray State U (KY)
Northeastern U (MA)
Northern Michigan U (MI)
Northern State U (SD)
Northwestern State U of Louisiana (LA)
Ohio U–Lancaster (OH)
Oregon Inst of Technology (OR)
Pittsburg State U (KS)
Point Park Coll (PA)
Purdue U (IN)
Purdue U Calumet (IN)
Purdue U North Central (IN)
Shepherd Coll (WV)
Southern Illinois U Carbondale (IL)
Southern U and A&M Coll (LA)
Southern Utah U (UT)
State U of NY at Farmingdale (NY)
Thomas Edison State Coll (NJ)
U of Alaska Anchorage (AK)
U of Arkansas at Little Rock (AR)
U of Cincinnati (OH)
U of Massachusetts Lowell (MA)
The U of Montana–Missoula (MT)
U of Puerto Rico, Humacao U Coll (PR)
U of Southern Indiana (IN)
U of the District of Columbia (DC)
U of Toledo (OH)
Virginia Coll at Birmingham (AL)
Washburn U of Topeka (KS)
Weber State U (UT)
Wentworth Inst of Technology (MA)
West Virginia State Coll (WV)
West Virginia U Inst of Technology (WV)
Wichita State U (KS)
Youngstown State U (OH)

ELECTRICAL/ELECTRONICS DRAFTING
Johnson & Wales U (RI)

ELECTRICAL ENGINEERING
Fairfield U (CT)
Missouri Tech (MO)
U of New Haven (CT)

ELECTRICAL EQUIPMENT INSTALLATION/REPAIR
Idaho State U (ID)
U Coll of the Cariboo (BC, Canada)

ELECTRICAL/POWER TRANSMISSION INSTALLATION
British Columbia Inst of Technology (BC, Canada)

ELECTROMECHANICAL INSTRUMENTATION AND MAINTENANCE TECHNOLOGIES RELATED
Southeast Missouri State U (MO)

ELECTROMECHANICAL TECHNOLOGY
Clayton Coll & State U (GA)
Excelsior Coll (NY)
Idaho State U (ID)
Michigan Technological U (MI)
Northern Michigan U (MI)
Rochester Inst of Technology (NY)
Shawnee State U (OH)
Shepherd Coll (WV)
U of the District of Columbia (DC)
Walla Walla Coll (WA)

ELEMENTARY EDUCATION
Alaska Pacific U (AK)
Central Christian Coll of Kansas (KS)
Champlain Coll (VT)
Clayton Coll & State U (GA)
Hillsdale Free Will Baptist Coll (OK)
Inter Amer U of PR, Barranquitas Campus (PR)
Macon State Coll (GA)
New Mexico Highlands U (NM)
Ozark Christian Coll (MO)
Rogers State U (OK)
Sage Coll of Albany (NY)
Southeastern Bible Coll (AL)
Villa Julie Coll (MD)

EMERGENCY MEDICAL TECHNOLOGY
American Coll of Prehospital Medicine (FL)
Arkansas State U (AR)
Baker Coll of Cadillac (MI)
Baker Coll of Clinton Township (MI)
Baker Coll of Muskegon (MI)
Ball State U (IN)
Clayton Coll & State U (GA)
Comm Hospital Roanoke Valley–Coll of Health Scis (VA)
Creighton U (NE)
Davenport U, Grand Rapids (MI)
Eastern Kentucky U (KY)
Faulkner U (AL)
Hannibal-LaGrange Coll (MO)
Indiana U–Purdue U Indianapolis (IN)
Montana State U–Billings (MT)
Nebraska Methodist Coll of Nursing & Allied Health (NE)
Nicholls State U (LA)
Rogers State U (OK)
Saint Francis U (PA)
Shawnee State U (OH)
Shepherd Coll (WV)
Southern Illinois U Carbondale (IL)
Southwest Baptist U (MO)
U of Alaska Anchorage (AK)
U of Arkansas for Medical Sciences (AR)
U of Pittsburgh at Johnstown (PA)
U of the District of Columbia (DC)
U of Toledo (OH)
Valdosta State U (GA)
Weber State U (UT)
Western Kentucky U (KY)
Youngstown State U (OH)

ENERGY MANAGEMENT TECHNOLOGY
Baker Coll of Flint (MI)
Northeastern U (MA)
U of Cincinnati (OH)

ENGINEERING
Brescia U (KY)
Central Christian Coll of Kansas (KS)
Clayton Coll & State U (GA)
Coll of Staten Island of the City U of NY (NY)
Columbia Union Coll (MD)
Daniel Webster Coll (NH)
Faulkner U (AL)
Geneva Coll (PA)
Lake Superior State U (MI)
Mesa State Coll (CO)
Montana Tech of The U of Montana (MT)
Mountain State U (WV)
Northeastern U (MA)
Robert Morris U (PA)
Roger Williams U (RI)
Southern Adventist U (TN)
Union Coll (NE)
U of New Haven (CT)
Waldorf Coll (IA)
Youngstown State U (OH)

ENGINEERING RELATED
British Columbia Inst of Technology (BC, Canada)

ENGINEERING-RELATED TECHNOLOGY
Arkansas State U (AR)
Idaho State U (ID)
Lewis-Clark State Coll (ID)
Missouri Tech (MO)
New Mexico State U (NM)
Rochester Inst of Technology (NY)
Tri-State U (IN)

ENGINEERING SCIENCE
Daniel Webster Coll (NH)
Merrimack Coll (MA)
Rochester Inst of Technology (NY)
U of Cincinnati (OH)

ENGINEERING TECHNOLOGIES RELATED
Kent State U (OH)
Point Park Coll (PA)
Rogers State U (OK)
Shepherd Coll (WV)
Western Kentucky U (KY)

ENGINEERING TECHNOLOGY
Andrews U (MI)
Clayton Coll & State U (GA)
Coll of Aeronautics (NY)
Embry-Riddle Aeronautical U (FL)
Fairmont State Coll (WV)
John Brown U (AR)
Lake Superior State U (MI)
Macon State Coll (GA)
Montana Tech of The U of Montana (MT)
New Mexico State U (NM)
Northeastern U (MA)
Pacific Union Coll (CA)
Purdue U North Central (IN)
Rochester Inst of Technology (NY)
State U of NY Coll of A&T at Cobleskill (NY)
U of Alaska Anchorage (AK)
U of the District of Columbia (DC)
Wentworth Inst of Technology (MA)
Youngstown State U (OH)

ENGLISH
Adrian Coll (MI)
Brewton-Parker Coll (GA)
Carroll Coll (MT)
Central Christian Coll of Kansas (KS)
Central Methodist Coll (MO)
Clayton Coll & State U (GA)
Clearwater Christian Coll (FL)
Coll of Santa Fe (NM)
Dalton State Coll (GA)
Felician Coll (NJ)
Fresno Pacific U (CA)
Hannibal-LaGrange Coll (MO)
Hillsdale Free Will Baptist Coll (OK)
Indiana U–Purdue U Fort Wayne (IN)
Indiana Wesleyan U (IN)
Lindsey Wilson Coll (KY)
Lourdes Coll (OH)
Macon State Coll (GA)
Maharishi U of Management (IA)
Manchester Coll (IN)
Martin Methodist Coll (TN)
Mesa State Coll (CO)
Methodist Coll (NC)
Montreat Coll (NC)
Pine Manor Coll (MA)
Presentation Coll (SD)
Richmond, The American International U in LondonUnited Kingdom)
Sacred Heart U (CT)
Siena Heights U (MI)
Thomas More Coll (KY)
Université Laval (QC, Canada)
U of Dubuque (IA)
U of Rio Grande (OH)
The U of Tampa (FL)
U of the District of Columbia (DC)
U of Wisconsin–Green Bay (WI)
Waldorf Coll (IA)
Xavier U (OH)

ENGLISH COMPOSITION
Central Christian Coll of Kansas (KS)
Penn State U Berks Cmps of Berks-Lehigh Valley Coll (PA)

ENGLISH EDUCATION
Lyndon State Coll (VT)

ENTERPRISE MANAGEMENT
Baker Coll of Flint (MI)
British Columbia Inst of Technology (BC, Canada)
Davenport U, Dearborn (MI)
Davenport U, Warren (MI)
Lyndon State Coll (VT)
Morehead State U (KY)
Northwood U (MI)
Northwood U, Texas Campus (TX)
The U of Akron (OH)

ENTREPRENEURSHIP
Baker Coll of Flint (MI)
Baker Coll of Jackson (MI)
Johnson & Wales U (RI)
Thomas Edison State Coll (NJ)
The U of Findlay (OH)

ENVIRONMENTAL ENGINEERING
British Columbia Inst of Technology (BC, Canada)
Ohio U (OH)
Ohio U–Chillicothe (OH)

ENVIRONMENTAL HEALTH
British Columbia Inst of Technology (BC, Canada)
Missouri Southern State Coll (MO)
The U of Akron (OH)

ENVIRONMENTAL SCIENCE
Defiance Coll (OH)
Dickinson State U (ND)
Macon State Coll (GA)
Maharishi U of Management (IA)
Montreat Coll (NC)
Mountain State U (WV)
Northeastern U (MA)
Ohio U–Chillicothe (OH)
Richmond, The American International U in LondonUnited Kingdom)
Southeast Missouri State U (MO)
Southern Vermont Coll (VT)
State U of NY Coll of A&T at Cobleskill (NY)
Sterling Coll (VT)
Thomas Edison State Coll (NJ)
U of Cincinnati (OH)
U of Dubuque (IA)
The U of Findlay (OH)
U of Saint Francis (IN)
U of Toledo (OH)
U of Wisconsin–Green Bay (WI)

ENVIRONMENTAL TECHNOLOGY
Baker Coll of Flint (MI)
Baker Coll of Owosso (MI)
Baker Coll of Port Huron (MI)
Glenville State Coll (WV)

Kansas State U (KS)
Mesa State Coll (CO)
New York Inst of Technology (NY)
Northeastern U (MA)
U of Cincinnati (OH)
U of the District of Columbia (DC)
U of Toledo (OH)
Wentworth Inst of Technology (MA)

EQUESTRIAN STUDIES
Centenary Coll (NJ)
Delaware Valley Coll (PA)
Johnson & Wales U (RI)
Midway Coll (KY)
Mount Ida Coll (MA)
Murray State U (KY)
Ohio U (OH)
Rogers State U (OK)
Saint Mary-of-the-Woods Coll (IN)
State U of NY Coll of A&T at Cobleskill (NY)
Teikyo Post U (CT)
The U of Findlay (OH)
U of Massachusetts Amherst (MA)
U of Minnesota, Crookston (MN)
U of New Hampshire (NH)

EUROPEAN STUDIES
Richmond, The American International U in LondonUnited Kingdom)

EXECUTIVE ASSISTANT
Baker Coll of Flint (MI)
Kentucky State U (KY)
Montana Tech of The U of Montana (MT)
The U of Akron (OH)
The U of Montana–Missoula (MT)
Western Kentucky U (KY)
Youngstown State U (OH)

EXERCISE SCIENCES
Atlantic Union Coll (MA)
Maharishi U of Management (IA)
Manchester Coll (IN)
Thomas More Coll (KY)

FAMILY/COMMUNITY STUDIES
Baker Coll of Flint (MI)
Central Christian Coll of Kansas (KS)
Southern Nazarene U (OK)
State U of NY Coll of A&T at Cobleskill (NY)

FAMILY/CONSUMER STUDIES
Dalton State Coll (GA)
Fairmont State Coll (WV)

FAMILY STUDIES
Southern Nazarene U (OK)

FARM/RANCH MANAGEMENT
Johnson & Wales U (RI)
Midway Coll (KY)
Oklahoma Panhandle State U (OK)
Rogers State U (OK)

FASHION DESIGN/ ILLUSTRATION
Academy of Art Coll (CA)
American InterContinental U (CA)
American InterContinental U, Atlanta (GA)
The Art Inst of California-San Francisco (CA)
The Art Inst of Portland (OR)
Cazenovia Coll (NY)
Fashion Inst of Technology (NY)
The Illinois Inst of Art (IL)
Indiana U Bloomington (IN)
International Academy of Design & Technology (FL)
International Acad of Merchandising & Design, Ltd (IL)
Mount Ida Coll (MA)
Parsons School of Design, New School U (NY)

FASHION MERCHANDISING
Academy of Art Coll (CA)
American InterContinental U (CA)
American InterContinental U, Atlanta (GA)
Central Missouri State U (MO)
Fairmont State Coll (WV)
International Acad of Merchandising & Design, Ltd (IL)
Johnson & Wales U (RI)
Laboratory Inst of Merchandising (NY)
Lynn U (FL)
Marygrove Coll (MI)
Mount Ida Coll (MA)
Northwood U (MI)
Northwood U, Texas Campus (TX)
Parsons School of Design, New School U (NY)
Shepherd Coll (WV)
Southern New Hampshire U (NH)
Thomas Coll (ME)
The U of Akron (OH)
U of Bridgeport (CT)
U of the District of Columbia (DC)
Weber State U (UT)
West Virginia State Coll (WV)

FILM STUDIES
Academy of Art Coll (CA)
Burlington Coll (VT)
Florida Metropolitan U-Fort Lauderdale Coll (FL)
Indiana U South Bend (IN)

FILM/VIDEO AND PHOTOGRAPHIC ARTS RELATED
New England School of Communications (ME)
Robert Morris Coll (IL)

FILM/VIDEO PRODUCTION
Academy of Art Coll (CA)
American InterContinental U (CA)
American InterContinental U, Atlanta (GA)
The Art Inst of Colorado (CO)
The Art Inst of Phoenix (AZ)
Burlington Coll (VT)
Collins Coll: A School of Design and Technology (AZ)
Five Towns Coll (NY)
Florida Metropolitan U-Orlando Coll, North (FL)
New England School of Communications (ME)
Rochester Inst of Technology (NY)
Southern Adventist U (TN)
Waldorf Coll (IA)

FINANCE
British Columbia Inst of Technology (BC, Canada)
California Coll for Health Sciences (CA)
Caribbean U (PR)
Central Christian Coll of Kansas (KS)
Clayton Coll & State U (GA)
Davenport U, Dearborn (MI)
Davenport U, Warren (MI)
Fairmont State Coll (WV)
Hilbert Coll (NY)
Indiana U South Bend (IN)
Indiana Wesleyan U (IN)
Johnson & Wales U (RI)
Marian Coll (IN)
Methodist Coll (NC)
Northeastern U (MA)
Northwood U (MI)
Northwood U, Florida Campus (FL)
Northwood U, Texas Campus (TX)
Pace U (NY)
Sacred Heart U (CT)
Saint Joseph's U (PA)
Saint Peter's Coll (NJ)
Southeastern U (DC)
Thomas Edison State Coll (NJ)
U of Cincinnati (OH)
Waldorf Coll (IA)
Walsh U (OH)
Washburn U of Topeka (KS)
Webber International U (FL)
West Virginia State Coll (WV)
Youngstown State U (OH)

FINANCIAL MANAGEMENT AND SERVICES RELATED
British Columbia Inst of Technology (BC, Canada)

FINANCIAL PLANNING
British Columbia Inst of Technology (BC, Canada)

FINE/STUDIO ARTS
Academy of Art Coll (CA)
Cazenovia Coll (NY)
Chestnut Hill Coll (PA)
Manchester Coll (IN)
New World School of the Arts (FL)
Pace U (NY)
Pine Manor Coll (MA)
Richmond, The American International U in LondonUnited Kingdom)
Rochester Inst of Technology (NY)
Sage Coll of Albany (NY)
Université Laval (QC, Canada)

FIRE PROTECTION/SAFETY TECHNOLOGY
British Columbia Inst of Technology (BC, Canada)
Comm Hospital Roanoke Valley–Coll of Health Scis (VA)
Montana State U–Billings (MT)
Thomas Edison State Coll (NJ)
The U of Akron (OH)
U of Nebraska–Lincoln (NE)
U of New Haven (CT)
U of Toledo (OH)

FIRE SCIENCE
Eastern Kentucky U (KY)
Lake Superior State U (MI)
Lamar U (TX)
Providence Coll (RI)
U of Alaska Anchorage (AK)
U of Alaska Fairbanks (AK)
U of Cincinnati (OH)
U of the District of Columbia (DC)

FISH/GAME MANAGEMENT
State U of NY Coll of A&T at Cobleskill (NY)
Winona State U (MN)

FLIGHT ATTENDANT
U of Louisiana at Monroe (LA)

FOLKLORE
Université Laval (QC, Canada)

FOOD PRODUCTS RETAILING
Ball State U (IN)
Ferris State U (MI)
Johnson & Wales U (RI)
Lamar U (TX)
Northern Michigan U (MI)
Purdue U Calumet (IN)
Rochester Inst of Technology (NY)
U of Minnesota, Crookston (MN)
U of New Hampshire (NH)
Washburn U of Topeka (KS)

FOOD SALES OPERATIONS
Saint Joseph's U (PA)

FOOD SCIENCES
Lamar U (TX)
Macon State Coll (GA)

FOOD SERVICES TECHNOLOGY
Purdue U Calumet (IN)
State U of NY Coll of A&T at Cobleskill (NY)
U of the District of Columbia (DC)

FOREIGN LANGUAGES/ LITERATURES
Dalton State Coll (GA)

FOREIGN LANGUAGES/ LITERATURES RELATED
U of Alaska Fairbanks (AK)

FORENSIC TECHNOLOGY
British Columbia Inst of Technology (BC, Canada)

FOREST HARVESTING PRODUCTION TECHNOLOGY
Glenville State Coll (WV)
Michigan Technological U (MI)
U of New Hampshire (NH)

FOREST MANAGEMENT
British Columbia Inst of Technology (BC, Canada)
U of Maine at Presque Isle (ME)

FOREST PRODUCTS TECHNOLOGY
British Columbia Inst of Technology (BC, Canada)
The U of British Columbia (BC, Canada)
U of Maine at Fort Kent (ME)
U of New Hampshire (NH)

FORESTRY
Clayton Coll & State U (GA)
Columbus State U (GA)
Dalton State Coll (GA)
Sterling Coll (VT)
Thomas Edison State Coll (NJ)
U of Maine at Fort Kent (ME)
Winona State U (MN)

FRENCH
Adrian Coll (MI)
Chestnut Hill Coll (PA)
Clayton Coll & State U (GA)
Indiana U–Purdue U Fort Wayne (IN)
Methodist Coll (NC)
Université Laval (QC, Canada)
U of Wisconsin–Green Bay (WI)
Xavier U (OH)

FURNITURE DESIGN
Rochester Inst of Technology (NY)

GENERAL OFFICE/CLERICAL
Youngstown State U (OH)

GENERAL RETAILING/ WHOLESALING
U of New Haven (CT)

GENERAL STUDIES
American Military U (VA)
Anderson U (IN)
Arkansas State U (AR)
Arkansas Tech U (AR)
Austin Peay State U (TN)
Avila Coll (MO)
Black Hills State U (SD)
Castleton State Coll (VT)
Central Baptist Coll (AR)
City U (WA)
Clearwater Christian Coll (FL)
Coll of Mount St. Joseph (OH)
Crown Coll (MN)
Dalton State Coll (GA)
Eastern Connecticut State U (CT)
Eastern Mennonite U (VA)
Eastern Nazarene Coll (MA)
Eastern New Mexico U (NM)
Endicott Coll (MA)
Finlandia U (MI)
Franciscan U of Steubenville (OH)
Hillsdale Free Will Baptist Coll (OK)
Hope International U (CA)
Idaho State U (ID)
Indiana U Bloomington (IN)
Indiana U East (IN)
Indiana U Kokomo (IN)
Indiana U Northwest (IN)
Indiana U of Pennsylvania (PA)
Indiana U–Purdue U Fort Wayne (IN)
Indiana U–Purdue U Indianapolis (IN)
Indiana U South Bend (IN)
Indiana U Southeast (IN)
Indiana Wesleyan U (IN)
Johnson State Coll (VT)
Louisiana Tech U (LA)
Macon State Coll (GA)
Monmouth U (NJ)
Morehead State U (KY)
Mount Aloysius Coll (PA)
Mount Marty Coll (SD)
Nicholls State U (LA)
Northwest Christian Coll (OR)
Northwestern State U of Louisiana (LA)
Nyack Coll (NY)
Okanagan U Coll (BC, Canada)
Oklahoma Panhandle State U (OK)
Palm Beach Atlantic Coll (FL)
Peirce Coll (PA)
Rider U (NJ)
Rochester Inst of Technology (NY)
Shepherd Coll (WV)
Siena Heights U (MI)
Silver Lake Coll (WI)
Simpson Coll and Graduate School (CA)
Si Tanka Huron U (SD)
South Dakota School of Mines and Technology (SD)
Southeastern Louisiana U (LA)
Southern Adventist U (TN)
Southern Arkansas U–Magnolia (AR)
Southwest Baptist U (MO)
Southwestern Assemblies of God U (TX)
Trevecca Nazarene U (TN)
U of Arkansas at Little Rock (AR)
U of Central Arkansas (AR)
U of Louisiana at Monroe (LA)
U of Mobile (AL)
U of New Haven (CT)
U of North Florida (FL)
U of Rio Grande (OH)
U System Coll for Lifelong Learning (NH)
Utah State U (UT)
Warner Southern Coll (FL)
Western Kentucky U (KY)

GEOGRAPHY
Fayetteville State U (NC)
Université Laval (QC, Canada)
The U of Tampa (FL)
Wright State U (OH)

GEOLOGY
Clayton Coll & State U (GA)
Dalton State Coll (GA)
Mesa State Coll (CO)

GERMAN
Adrian Coll (MI)
Fayetteville State U (NC)
Indiana U–Purdue U Fort Wayne (IN)
Methodist Coll (NC)
U of Wisconsin–Green Bay (WI)
Waldorf Coll (IA)
Xavier U (OH)

GERONTOLOGICAL SERVICES
U of Toledo (OH)

GERONTOLOGY
Chestnut Hill Coll (PA)
Coll of Mount St. Joseph (OH)
King's Coll (PA)
Lourdes Coll (OH)
Manchester Coll (IN)
Millersville U of Pennsylvania (PA)
Ohio Dominican Coll (OH)
Pontifical Catholic U of Puerto Rico (PR)
Siena Heights U (MI)
Thomas More Coll (KY)
U of Toledo (OH)
West Virginia State Coll (WV)
Winona State U (MN)

GRAPHIC DESIGN/COMMERCIAL ART/ILLUSTRATION
Academy of Art Coll (CA)
American InterContinental U (CA)
American InterContinental U, Atlanta (GA)
Andrews U (MI)
Art Academy of Cincinnati (OH)
The Art Inst of California (CA)
The Art Inst of California-San Francisco (CA)
The Art Inst of Colorado (CO)
The Art Inst of Phoenix (AZ)
The Art Inst of Portland (OR)
The Art Inst of Washington (VA)
Baker Coll of Auburn Hills (MI)
Baker Coll of Clinton Township (MI)
Baker Coll of Flint (MI)
Baker Coll of Muskegon (MI)
Baker Coll of Owosso (MI)
Baker Coll of Port Huron (MI)
Becker Coll (MA)
Briarcliffe Coll (NY)
British Columbia Inst of Technology (BC, Canada)
Champlain Coll (VT)
Coll of Mount St. Joseph (OH)
Collins Coll: A School of Design and Technology (AZ)
Fairmont State Coll (WV)
Fashion Inst of Technology (NY)
Felician Coll (NJ)

Ferris State U (MI)
Florida Metropolitan U-Orlando Coll, North (FL)
Florida Metropolitan U-Tampa Coll (FL)
Friends U (KS)
The Illinois Inst of Art (IL)
Indiana U–Purdue U Fort Wayne (IN)
International Academy of Design & Technology (FL)
Lewis-Clark State Coll (ID)
Mesa State Coll (CO)
Montana State U–Northern (MT)
Mount Ida Coll (MA)
Newschool of Architecture & Design (CA)
New World School of the Arts (FL)
Northeastern U (MA)
Northern Michigan U (MI)
Northern State U (SD)
Oakwood Coll (AL)
Pace U (NY)
Parsons School of Design, New School U (NY)
Pratt Inst (NY)
Robert Morris Coll (IL)
Rochester Inst of Technology (NY)
Rogers State U (OK)
Sacred Heart U (CT)
Sage Coll of Albany (NY)
Silver Lake Coll (WI)
Southern Illinois U Carbondale (IL)
State U of NY at Farmingdale (NY)
Suffolk U (MA)
The U of Maine at Augusta (ME)
U of New Haven (CT)
U of Saint Francis (IN)
U of the District of Columbia (DC)
Villa Julie Coll (MD)
Virginia Intermont Coll (VA)
Waldorf Coll (IA)
Walla Walla Coll (WA)
Watkins Coll of Art and Design (TN)

GRAPHIC/PRINTING EQUIPMENT
Andrews U (MI)
Ball State U (IN)
Central Missouri State U (MO)
Chowan Coll (NC)
Fairmont State Coll (WV)
Ferris State U (MI)
Idaho State U (ID)
Lewis-Clark State Coll (ID)
Murray State U (KY)
Pacific Union Coll (CA)
Rochester Inst of Technology (NY)
U of the District of Columbia (DC)
West Virginia U Inst of Technology (WV)

HEALTH AIDE
Gannon U (PA)

HEALTH EDUCATION
Central Christian Coll of Kansas (KS)
Clayton Coll & State U (GA)
Dalton State Coll (GA)
Martin Methodist Coll (TN)
Waldorf Coll (IA)

HEALTH/MEDICAL ADMINISTRATIVE SERVICES RELATED
British Columbia Inst of Technology (BC, Canada)
Kent State U (OH)

HEALTH/MEDICAL DIAGNOSTIC AND TREATMENT SERVICES RELATED
British Columbia Inst of Technology (BC, Canada)
Kent State U (OH)

HEALTH/MEDICAL LABORATORY TECHNOLOGIES RELATED
The U of Akron (OH)

HEALTH/PHYSICAL EDUCATION
Central Christian Coll of Kansas (KS)

HEALTH/PHYSICAL EDUCATION/ FITNESS RELATED
Robert Morris Coll (IL)

HEALTH PROFESSIONS AND RELATED SCIENCES
British Columbia Inst of Technology (BC, Canada)
East Tennessee State U (TN)
Lock Haven U of Pennsylvania (PA)

HEALTH SCIENCE
Bloomsburg U of Pennsylvania (PA)
California Coll for Health Sciences (CA)
Comm Hospital Roanoke Valley–Coll of Health Scis (VA)
Covenant Coll (GA)
Howard Payne U (TX)
Macon State Coll (GA)
Martin Methodist Coll (TN)
Newman U (KS)
Northwest Coll (WA)
Union Coll (NE)
Waldorf Coll (IA)

HEALTH SERVICES ADMINISTRATION
Baker Coll of Auburn Hills (MI)
Baker Coll of Flint (MI)
Baker Coll of Muskegon (MI)
Bay Path Coll (MA)
British Columbia Inst of Technology (BC, Canada)
Chestnut Hill Coll (PA)
Davenport U, Kalamazoo (MI)
Davis & Elkins Coll (WV)
Martin Methodist Coll (TN)
Methodist Coll (NC)
New York U (NY)
Peirce Coll (PA)
Providence Coll (RI)
Purdue U North Central (IN)
Saint Joseph's U (PA)
Southeastern U (DC)
The U of Scranton (PA)
Virginia Coll at Birmingham (AL)
West Virginia U Inst of Technology (WV)

HEARING SCIENCES
Ohio U (OH)

HEATING/AIR CONDITIONING/ REFRIGERATION
Boise State U (ID)
British Columbia Inst of Technology (BC, Canada)
Ferris State U (MI)
Lamar U (TX)
Lewis-Clark State Coll (ID)
Montana State U–Billings (MT)
Northern Michigan U (MI)
Oakland City U (IN)
U of Alaska Anchorage (AK)
U of Cincinnati (OH)

HEATING/AIR CONDITIONING/ REFRIGERATION TECHNOLOGY
Central Missouri State U (MO)

HEAVY EQUIPMENT MAINTENANCE
British Columbia Inst of Technology (BC, Canada)
Ferris State U (MI)
Georgia Southwestern State U (GA)
Lewis-Clark State Coll (ID)
Mesa State Coll (CO)
Montana State U–Northern (MT)
U of Alaska Anchorage (AK)
The U of Montana–Missoula (MT)

HEBREW
Baltimore Hebrew U (MD)

HISTORY
Adrian Coll (MI)
Brewton-Parker Coll (GA)
Central Christian Coll of Kansas (KS)
Chaminade U of Honolulu (HI)
Chestnut Hill Coll (PA)
Clayton Coll & State U (GA)
Dalton State Coll (GA)
Fayetteville State U (NC)
Felician Coll (NJ)
Fresno Pacific U (CA)
Indiana U East (IN)
Indiana U–Purdue U Fort Wayne (IN)
Indiana Wesleyan U (IN)
Lindsey Wilson Coll (KY)
Lourdes Coll (OH)
Macon State Coll (GA)
Marian Coll (IN)
Martin Methodist Coll (TN)
Methodist Coll (NC)
Millersville U of Pennsylvania (PA)
Pine Manor Coll (MA)
Richmond, The American International U in LondonUnited Kingdom)
Rogers State U (OK)
Sacred Heart U (CT)
State U of NY Empire State Coll (NY)
Thomas More Coll (KY)
Université Laval (QC, Canada)
U of Rio Grande (OH)
The U of Tampa (FL)
U of the District of Columbia (DC)
U of Wisconsin–Green Bay (WI)
Villa Julie Coll (MD)
Waldorf Coll (IA)
Wright State U (OH)
Xavier U (OH)

HISTORY OF PHILOSOPHY
Martin Methodist Coll (TN)

HOME ECONOMICS
Clayton Coll & State U (GA)
Mount Vernon Nazarene U (OH)
U of Alaska Anchorage (AK)
Waldorf Coll (IA)

HORTICULTURE SCIENCE
Andrews U (MI)
Boise State U (ID)
Eastern Kentucky U (KY)
Murray State U (KY)
State U of NY Coll of A&T at Cobleskill (NY)
Thomas Edison State Coll (NJ)
U of Connecticut (CT)
U of Minnesota, Crookston (MN)
U of New Hampshire (NH)

HORTICULTURE SERVICES
Kent State U (OH)
U of Connecticut (CT)
U of Massachusetts Amherst (MA)

HORTICULTURE SERVICES RELATED
U of Massachusetts Amherst (MA)

HOSPITALITY MANAGEMENT
Baker Coll of Flint (MI)
Baker Coll of Owosso (MI)
Champlain Coll (VT)
Kendall Coll (IL)
Lewis-Clark State Coll (ID)
National American U (NM)
Siena Heights U (MI)
The U of Akron (OH)
U of Alaska Southeast (AK)
U of Minnesota, Crookston (MN)
U of the District of Columbia (DC)
Washburn U of Topeka (KS)
Youngstown State U (OH)

HOSPITALITY/RECREATION MARKETING OPERATIONS
Champlain Coll (VT)
U Coll of the Cariboo (BC, Canada)
The U of Akron (OH)

HOTEL AND RESTAURANT MANAGEMENT
Baker Coll of Muskegon (MI)
Baker Coll of Owosso (MI)
Baker Coll of Port Huron (MI)
Bluefield State Coll (WV)
Champlain Coll (VT)
Davenport U, Grand Rapids (MI)
Florida Metropolitan U-Fort Lauderdale Coll (FL)
Indiana U–Purdue U Fort Wayne (IN)
Indiana U–Purdue U Indianapolis (IN)
Johnson & Wales U (RI)
Kendall Coll (IL)
Mercyhurst Coll (PA)
Mesa State Coll (CO)
Mount Ida Coll (MA)
National American U, Colorado Springs (CO)
National American U (NM)
National American U–Sioux Falls Branch (SD)
Northeastern U (MA)
Northwood U (MI)
Northwood U, Florida Campus (FL)
Northwood U, Texas Campus (TX)
Peirce Coll (PA)
Penn State U Berks Cmps of Berks-Lehigh Valley Coll (PA)
Presentation Coll (SD)
Purdue U Calumet (IN)
Purdue U North Central (IN)
Rochester Inst of Technology (NY)
State U of NY Coll of A&T at Cobleskill (NY)
Sullivan U (KY)
Thomas Edison State Coll (NJ)
The U of Akron (OH)
U of Minnesota, Crookston (MN)
U of New Haven (CT)
U of the Virgin Islands (VI)
Webber International U (FL)
West Virginia State Coll (WV)
Youngstown State U (OH)

HOTEL/MOTEL SERVICES MARKETING OPERATIONS
Champlain Coll (VT)
Lewis-Clark State Coll (ID)
U Coll of the Cariboo (BC, Canada)

HUMAN ECOLOGY
Sterling Coll (VT)

HUMANITIES
Bryn Athyn Coll of the New Church (PA)
Burlington Coll (VT)
Canisius Coll (NY)
Central Christian Coll of Kansas (KS)
Faulkner U (AL)
Felician Coll (NJ)
Huron U USA in LondonUnited Kingdom)
Immaculata Coll (PA)
Macon State Coll (GA)
Martin Methodist Coll (TN)
Mesa State Coll (CO)
Michigan Technological U (MI)
Montana State U–Northern (MT)
Ohio U (OH)
Sage Coll of Albany (NY)
St. Gregory's U (OK)
Saint Joseph's Coll (IN)
Saint Peter's Coll (NJ)
Samford U (AL)
Shawnee State U (OH)
State U of NY Empire State Coll (NY)
U of Cincinnati (OH)
The U of Findlay (OH)
U of Sioux Falls (SD)
U of Wisconsin–Green Bay (WI)
Villa Julie Coll (MD)
Waldorf Coll (IA)
Washburn U of Topeka (KS)
Wichita State U (KS)

HUMAN RESOURCES MANAGEMENT
Baker Coll of Owosso (MI)
British Columbia Inst of Technology (BC, Canada)
Central Christian Coll of Kansas (KS)
Chestnut Hill Coll (PA)
King's Coll (PA)
Montana Tech of The U of Montana (MT)
Northeastern U (MA)
Thomas Edison State Coll (NJ)
The U of Findlay (OH)
The U of Montana–Western (MT)
U of Richmond (VA)
U System Coll for Lifelong Learning (NH)
Urbana U (OH)

HUMAN RESOURCES MANAGEMENT RELATED
King's Coll (PA)
Park U (MO)

HUMAN SERVICES
Adrian Coll (MI)
Audrey Cohen Coll (NY)
Baker Coll of Clinton Township (MI)
Baker Coll of Flint (MI)
Baker Coll of Muskegon (MI)
Becker Coll (MA)
Burlington Coll (VT)
Champlain Coll (VT)
Grace Bible Coll (MI)
Hilbert Coll (NY)
Indiana U East (IN)
Kendall Coll (IL)
Kent State U (OH)
Martin Methodist Coll (TN)
Mercy Coll (NY)
Merrimack Coll (MA)
Montreat Coll (NC)
Mount Aloysius Coll (PA)
Mount Ida Coll (MA)
Mount Vernon Nazarene U (OH)
New York U (NY)
Northern Kentucky U (KY)
Ohio U (OH)
Ohio U–Chillicothe (OH)
Saint Joseph's U (PA)
Sinte Gleska U (SD)
Southern Vermont Coll (VT)
State U of NY Empire State Coll (NY)
U of Alaska Anchorage (AK)
U of Cincinnati (OH)
U of Great Falls (MT)
The U of Maine at Augusta (ME)
U of Maine at Fort Kent (ME)
U of Maine at Fort Kent (ME)
U of Saint Francis (IN)
The U of Scranton (PA)
Waldorf Coll (IA)
Walsh U (OH)

INDIVIDUAL/FAMILY DEVELOPMENT
Penn State U Altoona Coll (PA)
Penn State U Schuylkill Campus of the Capital Coll (PA)
Penn State U Univ Park Campus (PA)
State U of NY Empire State Coll (NY)

INDIVIDUAL/FAMILY DEVELOPMENT RELATED
U of Toledo (OH)
Utah State U (UT)

INDUSTRIAL ARTS
Austin Peay State U (TN)
Central Christian Coll of Kansas (KS)
Dalton State Coll (GA)
Eastern Kentucky U (KY)
U of Cincinnati (OH)
The U of Montana–Missoula (MT)
Weber State U (UT)

INDUSTRIAL ARTS EDUCATION
Arkansas State U (AR)

INDUSTRIAL DESIGN
Academy of Art Coll (CA)
Ferris State U (MI)
Northern Michigan U (MI)
Oakland City U (IN)
Ohio U–Lancaster (OH)
Rochester Inst of Technology (NY)
Wentworth Inst of Technology (MA)

INDUSTRIAL ELECTRONICS INSTALLATION/REPAIR
Dalton State Coll (GA)
Lewis-Clark State Coll (ID)
U Coll of the Cariboo (BC, Canada)

INDUSTRIAL MACHINERY MAINTENANCE/REPAIR
British Columbia Inst of Technology (BC, Canada)
Dalton State Coll (GA)

INDUSTRIAL/MANUFACTURING ENGINEERING
U of New Haven (CT)
U of Toledo (OH)

INDUSTRIAL PRODUCTION TECHNOLOGIES RELATED
Kent State U (OH)
U of Nebraska–Lincoln (NE)

INDUSTRIAL RADIOLOGIC TECHNOLOGY
Armstrong Atlantic State U (GA)
Baker Coll of Owosso (MI)
Ball State U (IN)
Boise State U (ID)
Faulkner U (AL)
Ferris State U (MI)
Fort Hays State U (KS)
The George Washington U (DC)
Gwynedd-Mercy Coll (PA)
Inter American U of PR, San Germán Campus (PR)
Lamar U (TX)
Mesa State Coll (CO)
Newman U (KS)
Northern Kentucky U (KY)
Shawnee State U (OH)
U of Arkansas for Medical Sciences (AR)
U of Cincinnati (OH)
U of the District of Columbia (DC)
Washburn U of Topeka (KS)
Widener U (PA)
Xavier U (OH)

INDUSTRIAL TECHNOLOGY
Andrews U (MI)
Baker Coll of Muskegon (MI)
Ball State U (IN)
British Columbia Inst of Technology (BC, Canada)
Central Missouri State U (MO)
Coleman Coll (CA)
Dalton State Coll (GA)
Eastern Kentucky U (KY)
Edinboro U of Pennsylvania (PA)
Excelsior Coll (NY)
Fairmont State Coll (WV)
Ferris State U (MI)
Georgia Southwestern State U (GA)
Indiana U–Purdue U Fort Wayne (IN)
Kansas State U (KS)
Keene State Coll (NH)
Kent State U (OH)
Lawrence Technological U (MI)
Mesa State Coll (CO)
Missouri Western State Coll (MO)
Montana State U–Northern (MT)
Morehead State U (KY)
Murray State U (KY)
Northern Michigan U (MI)
Ohio U–Lancaster (OH)
Oklahoma Panhandle State U (OK)
Penn State U at Erie, The Behrend Coll (PA)
Purdue U Calumet (IN)
Purdue U North Central (IN)
Roger Williams U (RI)
Southeastern Louisiana U (LA)
Southern Arkansas U–Magnolia (AR)
Thomas Edison State Coll (NJ)
Tri-State U (IN)
The U of Akron (OH)
U of Alaska Fairbanks (AK)
U of Arkansas at Pine Bluff (AR)
U of Cincinnati (OH)
U of New Haven (CT)
U of Puerto Rico at Ponce (PR)
U of Rio Grande (OH)
U of Toledo (OH)
Weber State U (UT)
Wentworth Inst of Technology (MA)
Wright State U (OH)

INFORMATION SCIENCES/ SYSTEMS
Albertus Magnus Coll (CT)
Alvernia Coll (PA)
Baker Coll of Cadillac (MI)
Baker Coll of Clinton Township (MI)
Baker Coll of Flint (MI)
Baker Coll of Jackson (MI)
Baker Coll of Muskegon (MI)
Baker Coll of Owosso (MI)
Baker Coll of Port Huron (MI)
Ball State U (IN)
Briarcliffe Coll (NY)
British Columbia Inst of Technology (BC, Canada)
Campbellsville U (KY)
Champlain Coll (VT)
Clayton Coll & State U (GA)
Coll of Mount St. Joseph (OH)
Coll of St. Joseph (VT)
Coll of Saint Mary (NE)
Colorado Tech U Denver Campus (CO)
Colorado Tech U Sioux Falls Campus (SD)
Columbia Coll (MO)
Dakota State U (SD)
Dalton State Coll (GA)
Daniel Webster Coll (NH)
Davenport U, Grand Rapids (MI)
Davenport U, Kalamazoo (MI)
Davenport U, Lansing (MI)
Denver Tech Coll (CO)
DeVry Coll of Technology (NJ)
DeVry U, Colorado Springs (CO)
Education America, Southeast Coll of Technology, Mobile Campus (AL)
Fairmont State Coll (WV)
Faulkner U (AL)
Georgia Southwestern State U (GA)
Goldey-Beacom Coll (DE)
Husson Coll (ME)
Indiana Inst of Technology (IN)
Indiana U–Purdue U Fort Wayne (IN)
Johnson State Coll (VT)
Jones Coll (FL)
Kendall Coll (IL)
Limestone Coll (SC)
Macon State Coll (GA)
Mansfield U of Pennsylvania (PA)
Midway Coll (KY)
Missouri Southern State Coll (MO)
Montana State U–Northern (MT)
Mountain State U (WV)
Mount Olive Coll (NC)
Murray State U (KY)
National American U, Colorado Springs (CO)
National American U (NM)
National American U (SD)
National American U–St. Paul Campus (MN)
National American U–Sioux Falls Branch (SD)
The National Hispanic U (CA)
Newman U (KS)
Oakland City U (IN)
Oakwood Coll (AL)
Oklahoma Panhandle State U (OK)
Oklahoma Wesleyan U (OK)
Pacific Union Coll (CA)
Peirce Coll (PA)
Penn State U Altoona Coll (PA)
Penn State U Berks Cmps of Berks-Lehigh Valley Coll (PA)
Penn State U Lehigh Valley Cmps of Berks-Lehigh Valley Coll (PA)
Penn State U Schuylkill Campus of the Capital Coll (PA)
Penn State U Univ Park Campus (PA)
Purdue U North Central (IN)
Richmond, The American International U in LondonUnited Kingdom)
Rivier Coll (NH)
Rogers State U (OK)
Roger Williams U (RI)
St. Francis Coll (NY)
Saint Peter's Coll (NJ)
Shawnee State U (OH)
Shepherd Coll (WV)
Siena Heights U (MI)
Si Tanka Huron U (SD)
Southeastern U (DC)
Southern New Hampshire U (NH)
Southern Utah U (UT)
Southwestern Adventist U (TX)
State U of NY at Farmingdale (NY)
State U of NY Coll of A&T at Cobleskill (NY)
Strayer U (DC)
Touro Coll (NY)
Trevecca Nazarene U (TN)
Tulane U (LA)
Union Coll (NE)
U of Alaska Anchorage (AK)
U of Charleston (WV)
U of Cincinnati (OH)
U of Indianapolis (IN)
The U of Maine at Augusta (ME)
U of Massachusetts Lowell (MA)
U of Minnesota, Crookston (MN)
The U of Montana–Western (MT)
U of Pittsburgh at Bradford (PA)
The U of Scranton (PA)
The U of Tampa (FL)
U of Wisconsin–Green Bay (WI)
Villa Julie Coll (MD)
Waldorf Coll (IA)
Washburn U of Topeka (KS)
Weber State U (UT)
Western Governors U (UT)
Youngstown State U (OH)

INFORMATION TECHNOLOGY
Arkansas Tech U (AR)
Western Governors U (UT)

INSTITUTIONAL FOOD WORKERS
Fairmont State Coll (WV)
State U of NY Coll of A&T at Cobleskill (NY)

INSTRUMENTATION TECHNOLOGY
Clayton Coll & State U (GA)
Idaho State U (ID)
McNeese State U (LA)
Shawnee State U (OH)

INSTRUMENT CALIBRATION/ REPAIR
Idaho State U (ID)

INSURANCE/RISK MANAGEMENT
Mercyhurst Coll (PA)
Thomas Edison State Coll (NJ)
Université Laval (QC, Canada)
U of Cincinnati (OH)

INTERDISCIPLINARY STUDIES
Bluefield State Coll (WV)
Burlington Coll (VT)
Cameron U (OK)
Cardinal Stritch U (WI)
Central Methodist Coll (MO)
Coll of Mount Saint Vincent (NY)
Friends U (KS)
Hillsdale Free Will Baptist Coll (OK)
Kansas State U (KS)
Maharishi U of Management (IA)
Montana State U–Northern (MT)
Mountain State U (WV)
Northwest Coll (WA)
Ohio Dominican Coll (OH)
Ohio U–Southern Campus (OH)
State U of NY Empire State Coll (NY)
Suffolk U (MA)
Tabor Coll (KS)
Unity Coll (ME)
The U of Akron (OH)
U of Sioux Falls (SD)
U of Wisconsin–Green Bay (WI)
Villa Julie Coll (MD)

INTERIOR ARCHITECTURE
Kent State U (OH)
U of New Haven (CT)

INTERIOR DESIGN
Academy of Art Coll (CA)
American InterContinental U (CA)
American InterContinental U, Atlanta (GA)
The Art Inst of Portland (OR)
Baker Coll of Auburn Hills (MI)
Baker Coll of Clinton Township (MI)
Baker Coll of Flint (MI)
Baker Coll of Muskegon (MI)
Baker Coll of Owosso (MI)
Baker Coll of Port Huron (MI)
Becker Coll (MA)
British Columbia Inst of Technology (BC, Canada)
Coll of Mount St. Joseph (OH)
Eastern Kentucky U (KY)
Fairmont State Coll (WV)
Harrington Inst of Interior Design (IL)
The Illinois Inst of Art (IL)
Indiana U–Purdue U Fort Wayne (IN)
International Academy of Design & Technology (FL)
International Acad of Merchandising & Design, Ltd (IL)
Marian Coll (IN)
Martin Methodist Coll (TN)
Mount Ida Coll (MA)
New York School of Interior Design (NY)
Pacific Union Coll (CA)
Parsons School of Design, New School U (NY)
Robert Morris Coll (IL)
Rochester Inst of Technology (NY)
Sage Coll of Albany (NY)
Southern Utah U (UT)
Watkins Coll of Art and Design (TN)
Weber State U (UT)
Wentworth Inst of Technology (MA)

INTERNATIONAL BUSINESS
British Columbia Inst of Technology (BC, Canada)
Florida Metropolitan U-Fort Lauderdale Coll (FL)
Northwood U (MI)
Northwood U, Florida Campus (FL)
Northwood U, Texas Campus (TX)
Richmond, The American International U in LondonUnited Kingdom)
Saint Peter's Coll (NJ)
Schiller International U (FL)
Schiller International UFrance)
Schiller International UGermany)
Schiller International USpain)
Schiller International UUnited Kingdom)
Southern New Hampshire U (NH)
State U of NY Coll of A&T at Cobleskill (NY)
Thomas Edison State Coll (NJ)
Webber International U (FL)

INTERNATIONAL RELATIONS
Richmond, The American International U in LondonUnited Kingdom)
Thomas More Coll (KY)

INTERNET
Strayer U (DC)

ITALIAN
Immaculata Coll (PA)

JAPANESE
Winona State U (MN)

JAZZ
Five Towns Coll (NY)
Indiana U South Bend (IN)
Southern U and A&M Coll (LA)
Université Laval (QC, Canada)
The U of Maine at Augusta (ME)

JOURNALISM
Ball State U (IN)
Bethel Coll (IN)
Central Christian Coll of Kansas (KS)
Clayton Coll & State U (GA)
Creighton U (NE)
Dalton State Coll (GA)
Davis & Elkins Coll (WV)
Evangel U (MO)
Indiana U Southeast (IN)
John Brown U (AR)
Macon State Coll (GA)
Manchester Coll (IN)
Point Park Coll (PA)
Villa Julie Coll (MD)
Waldorf Coll (IA)

JUDAIC STUDIES
Baltimore Hebrew U (MD)

LABORATORY ANIMAL MEDICINE
Thomas Edison State Coll (NJ)

LABOR/PERSONNEL RELATIONS
Indiana U Bloomington (IN)
Indiana U Kokomo (IN)
Indiana U Northwest (IN)
Indiana U–Purdue U Fort Wayne (IN)
Indiana U–Purdue U Indianapolis (IN)
Indiana U South Bend (IN)
Indiana U Southeast (IN)
Providence Coll (RI)
State U of NY Empire State Coll (NY)
Université Laval (QC, Canada)
Youngstown State U (OH)

LANDSCAPE ARCHITECTURE
Eastern Kentucky U (KY)
Kent State U (OH)
State U of NY at Farmingdale (NY)
State U of NY Coll of A&T at Cobleskill (NY)
Temple U (PA)
U of Arkansas at Little Rock (AR)
U of New Hampshire (NH)

LANDSCAPING MANAGEMENT
Eastern Kentucky U (KY)
North Carolina State U (NC)
State U of NY Coll of A&T at Cobleskill (NY)
U of Massachusetts Amherst (MA)
U of New Hampshire (NH)

LAND USE MANAGEMENT
Pacific Union Coll (CA)

LASER/OPTICAL TECHNOLOGY
Capitol Coll (MD)
Excelsior Coll (NY)
Idaho State U (ID)
Indiana U Bloomington (IN)
Pacific Union Coll (CA)

LATIN AMERICAN STUDIES
U Coll of the Fraser Valley (BC, Canada)

LAW AND LEGAL STUDIES RELATED
Wilson Coll (PA)

LAW ENFORCEMENT/POLICE SCIENCE
Arkansas State U (AR)
Armstrong Atlantic State U (GA)
Becker Coll (MA)
Bluefield State Coll (WV)
Caribbean U (PR)
Dalton State Coll (GA)
Defiance Coll (OH)
Eastern Kentucky U (KY)
Edinboro U of Pennsylvania (PA)
Fairmont State Coll (WV)
Fayetteville State U (NC)
John Jay Coll of Criminal Justice, the City U of NY (NY)
Lake Superior State U (MI)
Lewis-Clark State Coll (ID)
MacMurray Coll (IL)
Macon State Coll (GA)
Martin Methodist Coll (TN)
Mercyhurst Coll (PA)
Middle Tennessee State U (TN)
Missouri Southern State Coll (MO)
Nicholls State U (LA)
Northeastern U (MA)
Northern Kentucky U (KY)
Northern Michigan U (MI)
Northwestern State U of Louisiana (LA)
Ohio U (OH)
Ohio U–Chillicothe (OH)
Ohio U–Lancaster (OH)
Rogers State U (OK)
Southeastern Louisiana U (LA)
Southern Illinois U Carbondale (IL)
Southern U and A&M Coll (LA)
Tiffin U (OH)
The U of Akron (OH)
U of Arkansas at Little Rock (AR)
U of Arkansas at Pine Bluff (AR)
U of Cincinnati (OH)
U of Louisiana at Monroe (LA)
U of the District of Columbia (DC)
U of the Virgin Islands (VI)
U of Toledo (OH)
U of Wisconsin–Superior (WI)
Waldorf Coll (IA)
Washburn U of Topeka (KS)
Weber State U (UT)

York Coll of Pennsylvania (PA)
Youngstown State U (OH)

LEGAL ADMINISTRATIVE ASSISTANT
Baker Coll of Auburn Hills (MI)
Baker Coll of Clinton Township (MI)
Baker Coll of Flint (MI)
Baker Coll of Jackson (MI)
Baker Coll of Muskegon (MI)
Baker Coll of Owosso (MI)
Baker Coll of Port Huron (MI)
Ball State U (IN)
Caribbean U (PR)
Central Missouri State U (MO)
Clarion U of Pennsylvania (PA)
Clayton Coll & State U (GA)
Davenport U, Dearborn (MI)
Davenport U, Grand Rapids (MI)
Davenport U, Kalamazoo (MI)
Davenport U, Warren (MI)
David N. Myers U (OH)
Ferris State U (MI)
Hannibal-LaGrange Coll (MO)
Husson Coll (ME)
Johnson & Wales U (RI)
Lamar U (TX)
Lewis-Clark State Coll (ID)
Martin Methodist Coll (TN)
Mesa State Coll (CO)
Midland Lutheran Coll (NE)
Montana State U–Billings (MT)
Montana Tech of The U of Montana (MT)
Mountain State U (WV)
Northern Michigan U (MI)
Ohio U–Lancaster (OH)
Oregon Inst of Technology (OR)
Pacific Union Coll (CA)
Peirce Coll (PA)
Presentation Coll (SD)
Robert Morris Coll (IL)
Rogers State U (OK)
Sacred Heart U (CT)
Shawnee State U (OH)
Sullivan U (KY)
Thomas Coll (ME)
U of Cincinnati (OH)
The U of Montana–Missoula (MT)
U of Richmond (VA)
U of Rio Grande (OH)
U of the District of Columbia (DC)
U of Toledo (OH)
Washburn U of Topeka (KS)
West Virginia U Inst of Technology (WV)
Wright State U (OH)
Youngstown State U (OH)

LEGAL STUDIES
Becker Coll (MA)
Central Christian Coll of Kansas (KS)
Clayton Coll & State U (GA)
Hartford Coll for Women (CT)
Hilbert Coll (NY)
Lake Superior State U (MI)
Mount Ida Coll (MA)
Ohio Dominican Coll (OH)
Sage Coll of Albany (NY)
Southeastern U (DC)
The U of Montana–Missoula (MT)

LIBERAL ARTS AND SCIENCES/ LIBERAL STUDIES
Adams State Coll (CO)
Adelphi U (NY)
Alabama State U (AL)
Albertus Magnus Coll (CT)
Alderson-Broaddus Coll (WV)
Alvernia Coll (PA)
Alverno Coll (WI)
American International Coll (MA)
American U (DC)
American U of Puerto Rico (PR)
American U of RomeItaly)
Anderson Coll (SC)
Andrews U (MI)
Aquinas Coll (MI)
Aquinas Coll (TN)
Armstrong Atlantic State U (GA)
Ashland U (OH)
Augusta State U (GA)
Averett U (VA)
Ball State U (IN)
Bay Path Coll (MA)
Becker Coll (MA)
Bemidji State U (MN)
Bethany Coll of the Assemblies of God (CA)
Bethel Coll (IN)
Bethel Coll (MN)
Bluefield State Coll (WV)
Brescia U (KY)
Brevard Coll (NC)
Brewton-Parker Coll (GA)
Briar Cliff U (IA)
Bryan Coll (TN)
Burlington Coll (VT)
Butler U (IN)
Campbell U (NC)
Canisius Coll (NY)
Cardinal Stritch U (WI)
Cazenovia Coll (NY)
Centenary Coll (NJ)
Champlain Coll (VT)
Charleston Southern U (SC)
Charter Oak State Coll (CT)
Christendom Coll (VA)
Clarion U of Pennsylvania (PA)
Clarke Coll (IA)
Colby-Sawyer Coll (NH)
Coll of St. Catherine (MN)
Coll of St. Joseph (VT)
Coll of Saint Mary (NE)
The Coll of Saint Thomas More (TX)
Coll of Staten Island of the City U of NY (NY)
Colorado Christian U (CO)
Columbia Coll (MO)
Columbia Union Coll (MD)
Columbus State U (GA)
Concordia Coll (NY)
Concordia U (MI)
Concordia U (MN)
Concordia U (OR)
Crown Coll (MN)
Cumberland U (TN)
Dakota State U (SD)
Dakota Wesleyan U (SD)
Dallas Baptist U (TX)
Daniel Webster Coll (NH)
Dickinson State U (ND)
Dominican Coll (NY)
Eastern Connecticut State U (CT)
Eastern U (PA)
East Texas Baptist U (TX)
East-West U (IL)
Edgewood Coll (WI)
Edinboro U of Pennsylvania (PA)
Emmanuel Coll (GA)
Endicott Coll (MA)
Excelsior Coll (NY)
Fairleigh Dickinson U, Teaneck-Hackensack Campus (NJ)
Fairmont State Coll (WV)
Faulkner U (AL)
Fayetteville State U (NC)
Felician Coll (NJ)
Ferris State U (MI)
Five Towns Coll (NY)
Florida A&M U (FL)
Florida Atlantic U (FL)
Florida Coll (FL)
Florida State U (FL)
Franklin Coll SwitzerlandSwitzerland)
Fresno Pacific U (CA)
Gannon U (PA)
Grace Bible Coll (MI)
Grace U (NE)
Grand View Coll (IA)
Gwynedd-Mercy Coll (PA)
Hannibal-LaGrange Coll (MO)
Hartford Coll for Women (CT)
Haskell Indian Nations U (KS)
Hilbert Coll (NY)
Hillsdale Free Will Baptist Coll (OK)
Immaculata Coll (PA)
Indiana State U (IN)
John Brown U (AR)
Johnson State Coll (VT)
John Wesley Coll (NC)
Keene State Coll (NH)
Kent State U (OH)
Kentucky State U (KY)
LaGrange Coll (GA)
Lake Superior State U (MI)
La Salle U (PA)
Lebanon Valley Coll (PA)
Lewis-Clark State Coll (ID)
Limestone Coll (SC)
Long Island U, C.W. Post Campus (NY)
Loras Coll (IA)
Lourdes Coll (OH)
Lyndon State Coll (VT)
Macon State Coll (GA)
Mansfield U of Pennsylvania (PA)
Marian Coll (IN)
Marietta Coll (OH)
Martin Methodist Coll (TN)
Marygrove Coll (MI)
Marymount Coll of Fordham U (NY)
Marymount U (VA)
McNeese State U (LA)
Medaille Coll (NY)
Medgar Evers Coll of the City U of NY (NY)
Mercy Coll (NY)
Mercyhurst Coll (PA)
Merrimack Coll (MA)
Mesa State Coll (CO)
Methodist Coll (NC)
MidAmerica Nazarene U (KS)
Minnesota Bible Coll (MN)
Minnesota State U, Mankato (MN)
Minnesota State U Moorhead (MN)
Missouri Valley Coll (MO)
Molloy Coll (NY)
Montana Tech of The U of Montana (MT)
Montreat Coll (NC)
Mount Aloysius Coll (PA)
Mount Ida Coll (MA)
Mount Marty Coll (SD)
Mount Olive Coll (NC)
Mount St. Clare Coll (IA)
Mount St. Mary's Coll (CA)
Mount Vernon Nazarene U (OH)
Murray State U (KY)
National American U (SD)
The National Hispanic U (CA)
National U (CA)
Neumann Coll (PA)
Newman U (KS)
New Mexico Inst of Mining and Technology (NM)
New Mexico State U (NM)
New York U (NY)
Niagara U (NY)
Northeastern U (MA)
Northern Michigan U (MI)
Northern State U (SD)
North Greenville Coll (SC)
Northwest Coll (WA)
Northwestern Coll (MN)
Nyack Coll (NY)
Oak Hills Christian Coll (MN)
Oakland City U (IN)
The Ohio State U at Lima (OH)
The Ohio State U at Marion (OH)
The Ohio State U–Mansfield Campus (OH)
The Ohio State U–Newark Campus (OH)
Ohio U (OH)
Ohio U–Chillicothe (OH)
Ohio U–Lancaster (OH)
Ohio U–Southern Campus (OH)
Ohio U–Zanesville (OH)
Ohio Valley Coll (WV)
Okanagan U Coll (BC, Canada)
Oklahoma Wesleyan U (OK)
Oregon Inst of Technology (OR)
Pace U (NY)
Pacific Union Coll (CA)
Patten Coll (CA)
Peace Coll (NC)
Penn State U Abington Coll (PA)
Penn State U Altoona Coll (PA)
Penn State U at Erie, The Behrend Coll (PA)
Penn State U Harrisburg Campus of the Capital Coll (PA)
Penn State U Lehigh Valley Cmps of Berks-Lehigh Valley Coll (PA)
Penn State U Schuylkill Campus of the Capital Coll (PA)
Penn State U Univ Park Campus (PA)
Pine Manor Coll (MA)
Point Park Coll (PA)
Presentation Coll (SD)
Providence Coll (RI)
Reformed Bible Coll (MI)
Reinhardt Coll (GA)
Richmond, The American International U in LondonUnited Kingdom)
Rivier Coll (NH)
Robert Morris U (PA)
Rochester Coll (MI)
Rogers State U (OK)
Roger Williams U (RI)
Sacred Heart U (CT)
Sage Coll of Albany (NY)
St. Augustine Coll (IL)
St. Cloud State U (MN)
St. Francis Coll (NY)
St. Gregory's U (OK)
St. John's U (NY)
Saint Joseph's U (PA)
Saint Leo U (FL)
St. Louis Christian Coll (MO)
Saint Martin's Coll (WA)
Saint Mary Coll (KS)
Saint Mary-of-the-Woods Coll (IN)
Salem International U (WV)
Salve Regina U (RI)
Schiller International U (FL)
Schiller International UFrance)
Schiller International UGermany)
Schiller International USpain)
Schiller International UUnited Kingdom)
Schiller International U, American Coll of SwitzerlandSwitzerland)
Schreiner U (TX)
Simon's Rock Coll of Bard (MA)
Sinte Gleska U (SD)
Southeastern Bible Coll (AL)
Southern Connecticut State U (CT)
Southern New Hampshire U (NH)
Southern Polytechnic State U (GA)
Southern Vermont Coll (VT)
Spring Arbor U (MI)
State U of NY at Farmingdale (NY)
State U of NY Coll of A&T at Cobleskill (NY)
Stephens Coll (MO)
Strayer U (DC)
Taylor U, Fort Wayne Campus (IN)
Teikyo Post U (CT)
Tennessee Temple U (TN)
Thiel Coll (PA)
Thomas Edison State Coll (NJ)
Thomas More Coll (KY)
Thomas U (GA)
Toccoa Falls Coll (GA)
Touro Coll (NY)
Trinity Bible Coll (ND)
Tri-State U (IN)
The U of Akron (OH)
U of Alaska Fairbanks (AK)
U of Alaska Southeast (AK)
U of Bridgeport (CT)
U of Central Florida (FL)
U of Cincinnati (OH)
U of Delaware (DE)
U of Florida (FL)
U of Hartford (CT)
U of Indianapolis (IN)
U of La Verne (CA)
The U of Maine at Augusta (ME)
U of Maine at Fort Kent (ME)
U of Maine at Machias (ME)
U of Maine at Presque Isle (ME)
U of Minnesota, Crookston (MN)
U of New Hampshire (NH)
U of Pennsylvania (PA)
U of Puerto Rico at Ponce (PR)
U of South Florida (FL)
U of Toledo (OH)
U of Wisconsin–Eau Claire (WI)
U of Wisconsin–La Crosse (WI)
U of Wisconsin–Oshkosh (WI)
U of Wisconsin–Platteville (WI)
U of Wisconsin–Stevens Point (WI)
U of Wisconsin–Superior (WI)
U of Wisconsin–Whitewater (WI)
U System Coll for Lifelong Learning (NH)
Upper Iowa U (IA)
Urbana U (OH)
Villa Julie Coll (MD)
Villanova U (PA)
Virginia Intermont Coll (VA)
Waldorf Coll (IA)
Walsh U (OH)
Washburn U of Topeka (KS)
Waynesburg Coll (PA)
Weber State U (UT)
Wesley Coll (DE)
Western Connecticut State U (CT)
Western International U (AZ)
Western New England Coll (MA)
Western Oregon U (OR)
West Virginia State Coll (WV)
West Virginia U Inst of Technology (WV)
White Pines Coll (NH)
Wichita State U (KS)
Williams Baptist Coll (AR)
William Tyndale Coll (MI)
Wilmington Coll (DE)
Wilson Coll (PA)
Winona State U (MN)
Xavier U (OH)
York Coll (NE)
York Coll of Pennsylvania (PA)

LIBERAL ARTS AND STUDIES RELATED
Penn State U Berks Cmps of Berks-Lehigh Valley Coll (PA)
Troy State U Dothan (AL)
Troy State U Montgomery (AL)
The U of Akron (OH)

LIBRARY SCIENCE
Ohio Dominican Coll (OH)
The U of Maine at Augusta (ME)
The U of Montana–Western (MT)
U of the District of Columbia (DC)

LINGUISTICS
Oklahoma Wesleyan U (OK)
Université Laval (QC, Canada)

LITERATURE
Fayetteville State U (NC)
Friends U (KS)
Maharishi U of Management (IA)
Manchester Coll (IN)
Montreat Coll (NC)
Richmond, The American International U in LondonUnited Kingdom)
Sacred Heart U (CT)
Université Laval (QC, Canada)

LOGISTICS/MATERIALS MANAGEMENT
Northeastern U (MA)
Park U (MO)
The U of Akron (OH)

MACHINE SHOP ASSISTANT
Dalton State Coll (GA)
Idaho State U (ID)

MACHINE TECHNOLOGY
Boise State U (ID)
British Columbia Inst of Technology (BC, Canada)
Coll of Aeronautics (NY)
Ferris State U (MI)
Georgia Southwestern State U (GA)
Idaho State U (ID)
Lake Superior State U (MI)
Lamar U (TX)
Mesa State Coll (CO)
Missouri Southern State Coll (MO)
Montana State U–Northern (MT)
Weber State U (UT)

MAJOR APPLIANCE INSTALLATION/REPAIR
Lewis-Clark State Coll (ID)

MANAGEMENT INFORMATION SYSTEMS/BUSINESS DATA PROCESSING
Arkansas State U (AR)
Bayamón Central U (PR)
Colorado Tech U Sioux Falls Campus (SD)
Columbia Coll (PR)
Daniel Webster Coll (NH)
Davenport U, Dearborn (MI)
Davenport U, Warren (MI)
Florida Metropolitan U-Fort Lauderdale Coll (FL)
Globe Inst of Technology (NY)
Husson Coll (ME)
Johnson State Coll (VT)
Lake Superior State U (MI)
Lindsey Wilson Coll (KY)
Lock Haven U of Pennsylvania (PA)
National American U (NM)
National American U–St. Paul Campus (MN)
National American U–Sioux Falls Branch (SD)
Northeastern U (MA)
Northern Michigan U (MI)
Northwood U, Texas Campus (TX)
Robert Morris Coll (IL)
St. Augustine Coll (IL)

Southeastern U (DC)
Taylor U (IN)
Thiel Coll (PA)
The U of Akron (OH)
Weber State U (UT)
Wilson Coll (PA)
Wright State U (OH)

MANAGEMENT SCIENCE
British Columbia Inst of Technology (BC, Canada)
Northeastern U (MA)

MARINE SCIENCE
State U of NY Maritime Coll (NY)
U of the District of Columbia (DC)

MARINE TECHNOLOGY
Thomas Edison State Coll (NJ)
U of Alaska Southeast (AK)

MARITIME SCIENCE
Maine Maritime Academy (ME)
Martin Methodist Coll (TN)

MARKETING OPERATIONS
Champlain Coll (VT)
Dalton State Coll (GA)
New England School of Communications (ME)
Purdue U North Central (IN)
Robert Morris Coll (IL)
U Coll of the Cariboo (BC, Canada)

MARRIAGE/FAMILY COUNSELING
Central Christian Coll of Kansas (KS)
Martin Methodist Coll (TN)

MASS COMMUNICATIONS
Adrian Coll (MI)
Becker Coll (MA)
Black Hills State U (SD)
Central Christian Coll of Kansas (KS)
Champlain Coll (VT)
Clayton Coll & State U (GA)
Cornerstone U (MI)
Creighton U (NE)
Evangel U (MO)
Five Towns Coll (NY)
Fresno Pacific U (CA)
Lewis-Clark State Coll (ID)
Macon State Coll (GA)
Martin Methodist Coll (TN)
Methodist Coll (NC)
Montreat Coll (NC)
Mount Ida Coll (MA)
Point Park Coll (PA)
Reinhardt Coll (GA)
Richmond, The American International U in LondonUnited Kingdom)
Sacred Heart U (CT)
Salem International U (WV)
Université Laval (QC, Canada)
U Coll of the Fraser Valley (BC, Canada)
U of Dubuque (IA)
U of Rio Grande (OH)
Villa Julie Coll (MD)
Waldorf Coll (IA)
West Virginia State Coll (WV)

MATERIALS SCIENCE
U of New Hampshire (NH)

MATHEMATICS
Brewton-Parker Coll (GA)
Central Baptist Coll (AR)
Central Christian Coll of Kansas (KS)
Clayton Coll & State U (GA)
Creighton U (NE)
Dalton State Coll (GA)
Fayetteville State U (NC)
Felician Coll (NJ)
Fresno Pacific U (CA)
Hillsdale Free Will Baptist Coll (OK)
Indiana U East (IN)
Indiana U–Purdue U Fort Wayne (IN)
Indiana Wesleyan U (IN)
Lindsey Wilson Coll (KY)
Macon State Coll (GA)
Maharishi U of Management (IA)
Martin Methodist Coll (TN)
Mesa State Coll (CO)
Methodist Coll (NC)
Richmond, The American International U in LondonUnited Kingdom)
Rochester Inst of Technology (NY)
Rogers State U (OK)
Sacred Heart U (CT)
State U of NY Empire State Coll (NY)
Thomas Edison State Coll (NJ)
Thomas More Coll (KY)
Thomas U (GA)
Tri-State U (IN)
U of Great Falls (MT)
U of Rio Grande (OH)
The U of Tampa (FL)
U of Wisconsin–Green Bay (WI)
Waldorf Coll (IA)
Warner Pacific Coll (OR)
York Coll of Pennsylvania (PA)

MECHANICAL DESIGN TECHNOLOGY
Clayton Coll & State U (GA)
Ferris State U (MI)
Lincoln U (MO)

MECHANICAL DRAFTING
Baker Coll of Flint (MI)
British Columbia Inst of Technology (BC, Canada)
Indiana U–Purdue U Indianapolis (IN)
Montana Tech of The U of Montana (MT)
Purdue U (IN)

MECHANICAL ENGINEERING
Fairfield U (CT)
U of New Haven (CT)

MECHANICAL ENGINEERING TECHNOLOGIES RELATED
U of Southern Indiana (IN)

MECHANICAL ENGINEERING TECHNOLOGY
Andrews U (MI)
Baker Coll of Flint (MI)
Bluefield State Coll (WV)
British Columbia Inst of Technology (BC, Canada)
Excelsior Coll (NY)
Fairmont State Coll (WV)
Ferris State U (MI)
Indiana U–Purdue U Fort Wayne (IN)
Indiana U–Purdue U Indianapolis (IN)
Johnson & Wales U (RI)
Kansas State U (KS)
Kent State U (OH)
Lake Superior State U (MI)
Lawrence Technological U (MI)
Michigan Technological U (MI)
Murray State U (KY)
New York Inst of Technology (NY)
Northeastern U (MA)
Point Park Coll (PA)
Purdue U Calumet (IN)
Purdue U North Central (IN)
State U of NY at Farmingdale (NY)
Thomas Edison State Coll (NJ)
The U of Akron (OH)
U of Arkansas at Little Rock (AR)
U of Cincinnati (OH)
U of New Haven (CT)
U of Rio Grande (OH)
U of Southern Indiana (IN)
U of the District of Columbia (DC)
U of Toledo (OH)
Weber State U (UT)
Wentworth Inst of Technology (MA)
West Virginia U Inst of Technology (WV)
Youngstown State U (OH)

MECHANICS AND REPAIR RELATED
British Columbia Inst of Technology (BC, Canada)

MEDICAL ADMINISTRATIVE ASSISTANT
Baker Coll of Auburn Hills (MI)
Baker Coll of Cadillac (MI)
Baker Coll of Clinton Township (MI)
Baker Coll of Flint (MI)
Baker Coll of Jackson (MI)
Baker Coll of Muskegon (MI)
Baker Coll of Owosso (MI)
Baker Coll of Port Huron (MI)
Boise State U (ID)
British Columbia Inst of Technology (BC, Canada)
Caribbean U (PR)
Davenport U, Dearborn (MI)
Davenport U, Grand Rapids (MI)
Davenport U, Kalamazoo (MI)
Davenport U, Lansing (MI)
Dickinson State U (ND)
Hannibal-LaGrange Coll (MO)
Husson Coll (ME)
Lamar U (TX)
Lewis-Clark State Coll (ID)
Martin Methodist Coll (TN)
Mesa State Coll (CO)
Midland Lutheran Coll (NE)
Montana State U–Billings (MT)
Montana Tech of The U of Montana (MT)
Northern Michigan U (MI)
Ohio U–Lancaster (OH)
Oregon Inst of Technology (OR)
Pacific Union Coll (CA)
Peirce Coll (PA)
Presentation Coll (SD)
Sullivan U (KY)
Thomas Coll (ME)
Universidad Adventista de las Antillas (PR)
The U of Akron (OH)
U of Cincinnati (OH)
The U of Montana–Missoula (MT)
U of Rio Grande (OH)
Washburn U of Topeka (KS)
West Virginia U Inst of Technology (WV)
Wright State U (OH)
Youngstown State U (OH)

MEDICAL ASSISTANT
Arkansas Tech U (AR)
Baker Coll of Auburn Hills (MI)
Baker Coll of Cadillac (MI)
Baker Coll of Clinton Township (MI)
Baker Coll of Flint (MI)
Baker Coll of Jackson (MI)
Baker Coll of Muskegon (MI)
Baker Coll of Owosso (MI)
Baker Coll of Port Huron (MI)
Bluefield State Coll (WV)
Clayton Coll & State U (GA)
Colorado Tech U Sioux Falls Campus (SD)
Davenport U, Grand Rapids (MI)
Davenport U, Kalamazoo (MI)
Davenport U, Lansing (MI)
Eastern Kentucky U (KY)
Faulkner U (AL)
Florida Metropolitan U-Orlando Coll, North (FL)
Florida Metropolitan U-Orlando Coll, South (FL)
Florida Metropolitan U-Tampa Coll (FL)
Georgia Southwestern State U (GA)
Husson Coll (ME)
Idaho State U (ID)
International Coll (FL)
Jones Coll (FL)
Mountain State U (WV)
Mount Aloysius Coll (PA)
National American U–Sioux Falls Branch (SD)
Ohio U (OH)
Palmer Coll of Chiropractic (IA)
Presentation Coll (SD)
Robert Morris Coll (IL)
The U of Akron (OH)
U of Alaska Anchorage (AK)
U of Alaska Fairbanks (AK)
U of Toledo (OH)
Virginia Coll at Birmingham (AL)
Waldorf Coll (IA)
West Virginia State Coll (WV)
Youngstown State U (OH)

MEDICAL ILLUSTRATING
Clayton Coll & State U (GA)

MEDICAL LABORATORY ASSISTANT
Youngstown State U (OH)

MEDICAL LABORATORY TECHNICIAN
Baker Coll of Owosso (MI)
Bluefield Coll (VA)
British Columbia Inst of Technology (BC, Canada)
City U (WA)
Clayton Coll & State U (GA)
Coll of Staten Island of the City U of NY (NY)
Dakota State U (SD)
Dalton State Coll (GA)
Eastern Kentucky U (KY)
Fairmont State Coll (WV)
Faulkner U (AL)
Felician Coll (NJ)
Ferris State U (MI)
Friends U (KS)
The George Washington U (DC)
Indiana U Northwest (IN)
Macon State Coll (GA)
Marshall U (WV)
Martin Methodist Coll (TN)
Northeastern U (MA)
Northern Michigan U (MI)
Presentation Coll (SD)
Shawnee State U (OH)
State U of NY at Farmingdale (NY)
State U of NY Coll of A&T at Cobleskill (NY)
U of Alaska Anchorage (AK)
U of Cincinnati (OH)
The U of Maine at Augusta (ME)
U of Maine at Presque Isle (ME)
U of Rio Grande (OH)
U of the District of Columbia (DC)
Villa Julie Coll (MD)
Weber State U (UT)
Youngstown State U (OH)

MEDICAL LABORATORY TECHNOLOGY
British Columbia Inst of Technology (BC, Canada)
Evangel U (MO)
Ferris State U (MI)
Lewis-Clark State Coll (ID)
Purdue U North Central (IN)
Villa Julie Coll (MD)

MEDICAL OFFICE MANAGEMENT
Dalton State Coll (GA)
The U of Akron (OH)
Youngstown State U (OH)

MEDICAL RADIOLOGIC TECHNOLOGY
Arkansas State U (AR)
Bluefield State Coll (WV)
British Columbia Inst of Technology (BC, Canada)
Coll of St. Catherine (MN)
Fairleigh Dickinson U, Florham-Madison Campus (NJ)
Fairleigh Dickinson U, Teaneck-Hackensack Campus (NJ)
Gannon U (PA)
Holy Family Coll (PA)
Idaho State U (ID)
Indiana U Northwest (IN)
Indiana U–Purdue U Indianapolis (IN)
Indiana U South Bend (IN)
Kent State U (OH)
Loma Linda U (CA)
Marygrove Coll (MI)
MCP Hahnemann U (PA)
Mercy Coll of Health Sciences (IA)
Missouri Southern State Coll (MO)
Morehead State U (KY)
New York U (NY)
Northern Kentucky U (KY)
Robert Morris U (PA)
Saint Joseph's Coll (ME)
Shawnee State U (OH)
Southern Adventist U (TN)
Thomas Edison State Coll (NJ)
The U of Akron (OH)
U of Louisville (KY)
U of New Mexico (NM)
U of Puerto Rico Medical Sciences Campus (PR)
U of Southern Indiana (IN)
Weber State U (UT)

MEDICAL RECORDS ADMINISTRATION
Baker Coll of Auburn Hills (MI)
Baker Coll of Cadillac (MI)
Baker Coll of Clinton Township (MI)
Baker Coll of Flint (MI)
Baker Coll of Jackson (MI)
Baker Coll of Port Huron (MI)
Boise State U (ID)
California Coll for Health Sciences (CA)
Clayton Coll & State U (GA)
Coll of Saint Mary (NE)
Dakota State U (SD)
Dalton State Coll (GA)
Davenport U, Kalamazoo (MI)
Eastern Kentucky U (KY)
Fairmont State Coll (WV)
Faulkner U (AL)
Ferris State U (MI)
Gwynedd-Mercy Coll (PA)
Indiana U Northwest (IN)
Inter American U of PR, San Germán Campus (PR)
International Coll (FL)
Montana State U–Billings (MT)
Park U (MO)
Presentation Coll (SD)
Universidad Adventista de las Antillas (PR)
Washburn U of Topeka (KS)

MEDICAL RECORDS TECHNOLOGY
Baker Coll of Flint (MI)
Baker Coll of Jackson (MI)
Coll of St. Catherine (MN)
Idaho State U (ID)
Louisiana Tech U (LA)
Macon State Coll (GA)
Missouri Western State Coll (MO)
Molloy Coll (NY)
New York U (NY)
Robert Morris Coll (IL)
Weber State U (UT)
Western Kentucky U (KY)

MEDICAL TECHNOLOGY
Arkansas State U (AR)
Clayton Coll & State U (GA)
Dalton State Coll (GA)
Faulkner U (AL)
Gwynedd-Mercy Coll (PA)
Indiana U East (IN)
Mayo School of Health Sciences (MN)
Northern Michigan U (MI)
Purdue U North Central (IN)
Rochester Inst of Technology (NY)
Valdosta State U (GA)
Villa Julie Coll (MD)
Weber State U (UT)

MEDICAL TRANSCRIPTION
Baker Coll of Flint (MI)
Baker Coll of Jackson (MI)
Dalton State Coll (GA)

MENTAL HEALTH/ REHABILITATION
Evangel U (MO)
Felician Coll (NJ)
Lake Superior State U (MI)
St. Augustine Coll (IL)
U of Toledo (OH)
Washburn U of Topeka (KS)

MENTAL HEALTH SERVICES RELATED
U of Alaska Fairbanks (AK)

METAL/JEWELRY ARTS
Rochester Inst of Technology (NY)

METALLURGICAL TECHNOLOGY
Montana State U–Northern (MT)
Purdue U Calumet (IN)

MIDDLE EASTERN STUDIES
Baltimore Hebrew U (MD)

MILITARY STUDIES
Hawai'i Pacific U (HI)

MINING TECHNOLOGY
British Columbia Inst of Technology (BC, Canada)

MISSIONARY STUDIES
Central Christian Coll of Kansas (KS)
Circleville Bible Coll (OH)
Faith Baptist Bible Coll and Theological Seminary (IA)
Hillsdale Free Will Baptist Coll (OK)
Hobe Sound Bible Coll (FL)
Hope International U (CA)
Manhattan Christian Coll (KS)
Southern Methodist Coll (SC)

MODERN LANGUAGES
Macon State Coll (GA)
Sacred Heart U (CT)
York Coll of Pennsylvania (PA)

MORTUARY SCIENCE
Lynn U (FL)
Mount Ida Coll (MA)
Point Park Coll (PA)

MULTI/INTERDISCIPLINARY STUDIES RELATED
Ohio U (OH)
Shepherd Coll (WV)
The U of Akron (OH)
U of Alaska Fairbanks (AK)
U of Toledo (OH)

MULTIMEDIA
The Art Inst of Colorado (CO)
The Art Inst of Portland (OR)
International Academy of Design & Technology (FL)
International Acad of Merchandising & Design, Ltd (IL)
New England School of Communications (ME)

MUSIC
Bethel Coll (IN)
Brevard Coll (NC)
Brewton-Parker Coll (GA)
Brigham Young U–Hawaii (HI)
Calvary Bible Coll and Theological Seminary (MO)
Central Baptist Coll (AR)
Central Christian Coll of Kansas (KS)
Chestnut Hill Coll (PA)
Chowan Coll (NC)
Clayton Coll & State U (GA)
Crown Coll (MN)
Dallas Baptist U (TX)
Emmanuel Coll (GA)
Five Towns Coll (NY)
Fresno Pacific U (CA)
Grace Bible Coll (MI)
Grace U (NE)
Grand View Coll (IA)
Hillsdale Free Will Baptist Coll (OK)
Indiana Wesleyan U (IN)
John Brown U (AR)
Lourdes Coll (OH)
Macon State Coll (GA)
Marian Coll (IN)
Martin Methodist Coll (TN)
Mesa State Coll (CO)
Methodist Coll (NC)
Montreat Coll (NC)
Mount Olive Coll (NC)
New World School of the Arts (FL)
Peace Coll (NC)
Reinhardt Coll (GA)
Sacred Heart U (CT)
Saint Joseph's Coll (IN)
Southwestern Assemblies of God U (TX)
Thomas More Coll (KY)
Trinity Bible Coll (ND)
U of Rio Grande (OH)
The U of Tampa (FL)
U of the District of Columbia (DC)
Waldorf Coll (IA)
Williams Baptist Coll (AR)
York Coll of Pennsylvania (PA)

MUSICAL INSTRUMENT TECHNOLOGY
Central Christian Coll of Kansas (KS)
Indiana U Bloomington (IN)

MUSIC BUSINESS MANAGEMENT/ MERCHANDISING
Central Christian Coll of Kansas (KS)
Chowan Coll (NC)
Five Towns Coll (NY)
Friends U (KS)
Glenville State Coll (WV)

MUSIC CONDUCTING
Central Christian Coll of Kansas (KS)

MUSIC (GENERAL PERFORMANCE)
Central Christian Coll of Kansas (KS)

MUSIC HISTORY
Central Christian Coll of Kansas (KS)

MUSIC (PIANO AND ORGAN PERFORMANCE)
Bethel Coll (IN)
Brewton-Parker Coll (GA)
Central Christian Coll of Kansas (KS)
Five Towns Coll (NY)
John Brown U (AR)
New World School of the Arts (FL)
Pacific Union Coll (CA)
Waldorf Coll (IA)

MUSIC TEACHER EDUCATION
Calvary Bible Coll and Theological Seminary (MO)
Central Christian Coll of Kansas (KS)
Chestnut Hill Coll (PA)
Martin Methodist Coll (TN)
Montreat Coll (NC)
Union Coll (NE)
Waldorf Coll (IA)

MUSIC THEORY AND COMPOSITION
Central Christian Coll of Kansas (KS)

MUSIC (VOICE AND CHORAL/ OPERA PERFORMANCE)
Brewton-Parker Coll (GA)
Calvary Bible Coll and Theological Seminary (MO)
Central Christian Coll of Kansas (KS)
Five Towns Coll (NY)
New World School of the Arts (FL)
Waldorf Coll (IA)

NATIVE AMERICAN LANGUAGES
Idaho State U (ID)

NATIVE AMERICAN STUDIES
Rogers State U (OK)
Sinte Gleska U (SD)

NATURAL RESOURCES CONSERVATION
Sterling Coll (VT)
U of Minnesota, Crookston (MN)

NATURAL RESOURCES MANAGEMENT
Haskell Indian Nations U (KS)
Lake Superior State U (MI)
Sinte Gleska U (SD)
Sterling Coll (VT)
U of Alaska Fairbanks (AK)
U of Minnesota, Crookston (MN)

NATURAL SCIENCES
Alderson-Broaddus Coll (WV)
Central Christian Coll of Kansas (KS)
Charleston Southern U (SC)
Felician Coll (NJ)
Fresno Pacific U (CA)
Gwynedd-Mercy Coll (PA)
Lourdes Coll (OH)
Medgar Evers Coll of the City U of NY (NY)
Roberts Wesleyan Coll (NY)
Thomas Edison State Coll (NJ)
U of Cincinnati (OH)
U of Puerto Rico at Ponce (PR)
U of Toledo (OH)
Villanova U (PA)
Waldorf Coll (IA)

NAVAL ARCHITECTURE/MARINE ENGINEERING
British Columbia Inst of Technology (BC, Canada)

NONPROFIT/PUBLIC MANAGEMENT
Davenport U, Dearborn (MI)
Davenport U, Warren (MI)

NUCLEAR ENGINEERING
Arkansas Tech U (AR)

NUCLEAR MEDICAL TECHNOLOGY
Ball State U (IN)
British Columbia Inst of Technology (BC, Canada)
Dalton State Coll (GA)
Ferris State U (MI)
The George Washington U (DC)
Kent State U (OH)
Molloy Coll (NY)
Thomas Edison State Coll (NJ)
The U of Findlay (OH)
West Virginia State Coll (WV)

NUCLEAR TECHNOLOGY
Excelsior Coll (NY)
Thomas Edison State Coll (NJ)

NURSE ASSISTANT/AIDE
Central Christian Coll of Kansas (KS)
Montana Tech of The U of Montana (MT)

NURSERY MANAGEMENT
State U of NY Coll of A&T at Cobleskill (NY)

NURSING
Alcorn State U (MS)
Alvernia Coll (PA)
Angelo State U (TX)
Aquinas Coll (TN)
Arkansas State U (AR)
Armstrong Atlantic State U (GA)
Atlantic Union Coll (MA)
Augusta State U (GA)
Ball State U (IN)
Bayamón Central U (PR)
Becker Coll (MA)
Bethel Coll (IN)
Bluefield State Coll (WV)
Boise State U (ID)
British Columbia Inst of Technology (BC, Canada)
Cardinal Stritch U (WI)
Castleton State Coll (VT)
Central Christian Coll of Kansas (KS)
Clarion U of Pennsylvania (PA)
Coll of Saint Mary (NE)
Coll of Staten Island of the City U of NY (NY)
Columbia Coll (MO)
Columbia Coll (PR)
Comm Hospital Roanoke Valley–Coll of Health Scis (VA)
Covenant Coll (GA)
Dakota Wesleyan U (SD)
Dalton State Coll (GA)
Davis & Elkins Coll (WV)
Deaconess Coll of Nursing (MO)
Eastern Kentucky U (KY)
Excelsior Coll (NY)
Fairmont State Coll (WV)
Felician Coll (NJ)
Ferris State U (MI)
Finlandia U (MI)
Gardner-Webb U (NC)
Gwynedd-Mercy Coll (PA)
Hannibal-LaGrange Coll (MO)
Hillsdale Free Will Baptist Coll (OK)
Houston Baptist U (TX)
Indiana State U (IN)
Indiana U East (IN)
Indiana U Kokomo (IN)
Indiana U Northwest (IN)
Indiana U–Purdue U Fort Wayne (IN)
Indiana U–Purdue U Indianapolis (IN)
Indiana U South Bend (IN)
Inter Amer U of PR, Barranquitas Campus (PR)
Jewish Hospital Coll of Nursing and Allied Health (MO)
Kansas Wesleyan U (KS)
Kent State U (OH)
Kentucky State U (KY)
Lamar U (TX)
Lester L. Cox Coll of Nursing and Health Sciences (MO)
Lincoln Memorial U (TN)
Lincoln U (MO)
Lock Haven U of Pennsylvania (PA)
Loma Linda U (CA)
Louisiana Tech U (LA)
Macon State Coll (GA)
Marshall U (WV)
Marymount U (VA)
McNeese State U (LA)
Mercy Coll of Health Sciences (IA)
Mesa State Coll (CO)
Midway Coll (KY)
Mississippi U for Women (MS)
Montana State U–Northern (MT)
Montana Tech of The U of Montana (MT)
Morehead State U (KY)
Mount Aloysius Coll (PA)
Mount St. Mary's Coll (CA)
Nebraska Methodist Coll of Nursing & Allied Health (NE)
Newman U (KS)
Nicholls State U (LA)
Norfolk State U (VA)
Northern Kentucky U (KY)
North Georgia Coll & State U (GA)
Northwestern State U of Louisiana (LA)
Oakwood Coll (AL)
Ohio U (OH)
Ohio U–Chillicothe (OH)
Ohio U–Zanesville (OH)
Oklahoma Panhandle State U (OK)
Pace U (NY)
Pacific Union Coll (CA)
Park U (MO)
Penn State U Altoona Coll (PA)
Pikeville Coll (KY)
Presentation Coll (SD)
Purdue U (IN)
Purdue U Calumet (IN)
Purdue U North Central (IN)
Regis Coll (MA)
Reinhardt Coll (GA)
Rivier Coll (NH)
Rogers State U (OK)
Shawnee State U (OH)
Shepherd Coll (WV)
Si Tanka Huron U (SD)
Southern Adventist U (TN)
Southern Arkansas U–Magnolia (AR)
Southern Vermont Coll (VT)
Southwest Baptist U (MO)
Southwestern Adventist U (TX)
State U of NY at Farmingdale (NY)
Sul Ross State U (TX)
Tennessee State U (TN)
Thomas U (GA)
Trinity Coll of Nursing and Health Sciences Schools (IL)
Troy State U (AL)
Universidad Adventista de las Antillas (PR)
U of Alaska Anchorage (AK)
U of Arkansas at Little Rock (AR)
U of Charleston (WV)
U of Cincinnati (OH)
U of Indianapolis (IN)
The U of Maine at Augusta (ME)
U of Maine at Presque Isle (ME)
U of Mobile (AL)
U of New England (ME)
U of Pittsburgh at Bradford (PA)
U of Puerto Rico, Humacao U Coll (PR)
U of Rio Grande (OH)
U of South Carolina Aiken (SC)
U of South Carolina Spartanburg (SC)
The U of South Dakota (SD)
U of Southern Indiana (IN)
U of the District of Columbia (DC)
U of the Virgin Islands (VI)
U of Toledo (OH)
The U of West Alabama (AL)
Waldorf Coll (IA)
Walsh U (OH)
Warner Pacific Coll (OR)
Weber State U (UT)
Wesley Coll (DE)
Western Kentucky U (KY)

NURSING ADMINISTRATION
British Columbia Inst of Technology (BC, Canada)

NURSING (PEDIATRIC)
British Columbia Inst of Technology (BC, Canada)

NURSING RELATED
British Columbia Inst of Technology (BC, Canada)
Coll of Staten Island of the City U of NY (NY)
Rogers State U (OK)

NURSING SCIENCE
Inter American U of PR, Aguadilla Campus (PR)
Trinity Coll of Nursing and Health Sciences Schools (IL)

NURSING (SURGICAL)
British Columbia Inst of Technology (BC, Canada)

NUTRITION SCIENCE
Cedar Crest Coll (PA)
Eastern Kentucky U (KY)
Pacific Union Coll (CA)
State U of NY at Farmingdale (NY)
U of New Hampshire (NH)

NUTRITION STUDIES
Southern Adventist U (TN)
U of Maine at Presque Isle (ME)

OCCUPATIONAL HEALTH/ INDUSTRIAL HYGIENE
British Columbia Inst of Technology (BC, Canada)

OCCUPATIONAL SAFETY/ HEALTH TECHNOLOGY
Ferris State U (MI)
Indiana U Bloomington (IN)
Lamar U (TX)
Montana Tech of The U of Montana (MT)
Murray State U (KY)
Shepherd Coll (WV)
Southwest Baptist U (MO)
U of Cincinnati (OH)
U of New Haven (CT)
Washburn U of Topeka (KS)

OCCUPATIONAL THERAPY
Clarkson Coll (NE)
Clayton Coll & State U (GA)
Dalton State Coll (GA)
Faulkner U (AL)
Lourdes Coll (OH)
Oakwood Coll (AL)
Penn State U Berks Cmps of Berks-Lehigh Valley Coll (PA)
Shawnee State U (OH)
Southern Adventist U (TN)
Touro Coll (NY)
U of Puerto Rico at Ponce (PR)

OCCUPATIONAL THERAPY ASSISTANT
Baker Coll of Muskegon (MI)
Bay Path Coll (MA)
Becker Coll (MA)
California U of Pennsylvania (PA)
Clarion U of Pennsylvania (PA)
Coll of St. Catherine (MN)
Comm Hospital Roanoke Valley–Coll of Health Scis (VA)
Kent State U (OH)
Loma Linda U (CA)
Mountain State U (WV)
Mount Aloysius Coll (PA)
Mount St. Mary's Coll (CA)
U of Louisiana at Monroe (LA)
U of Puerto Rico, Humacao U Coll (PR)
U of Southern Indiana (IN)
Wichita State U (KS)

OFFICE MANAGEMENT
Baker Coll of Flint (MI)
Baker Coll of Jackson (MI)
Dalton State Coll (GA)
Emmanuel Coll (GA)
Georgia Southwestern State U (GA)
Lake Superior State U (MI)
Park U (MO)
Peirce Coll (PA)
Union Coll (NE)
Youngstown State U (OH)

OPERATING ROOM TECHNICIAN
Baker Coll of Clinton Township (MI)
Baker Coll of Flint (MI)
Baker Coll of Jackson (MI)
Baker Coll of Muskegon (MI)
Boise State U (ID)
Loma Linda U (CA)
Mercy Coll of Health Sciences (IA)
Mount Aloysius Coll (PA)
Presentation Coll (SD)
The U of Akron (OH)
U of Arkansas for Medical Sciences (AR)
The U of Montana–Missoula (MT)
U of Pittsburgh at Johnstown (PA)
West Virginia U Inst of Technology (WV)

OPERATIONS MANAGEMENT
Baker Coll of Flint (MI)
British Columbia Inst of Technology (BC, Canada)
Education America, Southeast Coll of Technology, Mobile Campus (AL)
Indiana State U (IN)
Indiana U–Purdue U Fort Wayne (IN)
Indiana U–Purdue U Indianapolis (IN)
Northern Kentucky U (KY)
Purdue U (IN)
Thomas Edison State Coll (NJ)

OPTICAL TECHNICIAN
Indiana U Bloomington (IN)

OPTICIANRY
The U of Akron (OH)

OPTOMETRIC/OPHTHALMIC LABORATORY TECHNICIAN
Indiana U Bloomington (IN)
Rochester Inst of Technology (NY)
U of Puerto Rico Medical Sciences Campus (PR)

ORNAMENTAL HORTICULTURE
Eastern Kentucky U (KY)
Ferris State U (MI)
State U of NY at Farmingdale (NY)
State U of NY Coll of A&T at Cobleskill (NY)
U of Massachusetts Amherst (MA)
U of New Hampshire (NH)
Utah State U (UT)

PAINTING
Central Christian Coll of Kansas (KS)

PARALEGAL/LEGAL ASSISTANT
Anna Maria Coll (MA)
Atlantic Union Coll (MA)
Ball State U (IN)
Bay Path Coll (MA)
Becker Coll (MA)
Bluefield State Coll (WV)
Boise State U (ID)
Briarcliffe Coll (NY)
Champlain Coll (VT)
Clayton Coll & State U (GA)
Coll of Mount St. Joseph (OH)
Coll of Saint Mary (NE)
Davenport U, Grand Rapids (MI)
Davenport U, Kalamazoo (MI)
David N. Myers U (OH)
Eastern Kentucky U (KY)
Faulkner U (AL)
Ferris State U (MI)
Florida Metropolitan U-Fort Lauderdale Coll (FL)
Florida Metropolitan U-Tampa Coll, Lakeland (FL)
Florida Metropolitan U-Orlando Coll, North (FL)
Florida Metropolitan U-Orlando Coll, South (FL)
Florida Metropolitan U-Tampa Coll (FL)
Gannon U (PA)
Glenville State Coll (WV)
Grambling State U (LA)
Hartford Coll for Women (CT)
Hilbert Coll (NY)
Huntingdon Coll (AL)
Husson Coll (ME)
Indiana U South Bend (IN)
International Coll (FL)
Johnson & Wales U (RI)
Jones Coll (FL)
Kansas City Coll of Legal Studies (MO)
Kent State U (OH)
Lake Superior State U (MI)
Lewis-Clark State Coll (ID)
Long Island U, Brooklyn Campus (NY)
Marywood U (PA)
McNeese State U (LA)
Merrimack Coll (MA)
Metropolitan Coll, Tulsa (OK)
Midway Coll (KY)
Missouri Western State Coll (MO)
Mountain State U (WV)
Mount Aloysius Coll (PA)
National American U (SD)
National American U–Sioux Falls Branch (SD)
Nicholls State U (LA)
Ohio U–Chillicothe (OH)
Peirce Coll (PA)
Providence Coll (RI)
Robert Morris Coll (IL)
Rogers State U (OK)
Sacred Heart U (CT)
Sage Coll of Albany (NY)
St. John's U (NY)
Saint Mary-of-the-Woods Coll (IN)
Shawnee State U (OH)
Shepherd Coll (WV)
Suffolk U (MA)
Sullivan U (KY)
Teikyo Post U (CT)
Thomas Coll (ME)
Thomas Edison State Coll (NJ)
Tulane U (LA)
The U of Akron (OH)
U of Alaska Anchorage (AK)
U of Alaska Fairbanks (AK)
U of Alaska Southeast (AK)
U of Cincinnati (OH)
U of Great Falls (MT)
U of Hartford (CT)
U of Indianapolis (IN)
U of Louisville (KY)
The U of Montana–Missoula (MT)
U of Toledo (OH)
Villa Julie Coll (MD)
Virginia Coll at Birmingham (AL)
Washburn U of Topeka (KS)
Wesley Coll (DE)
Western Kentucky U (KY)
Wichita State U (KS)
Widener U (PA)
William Woods U (MO)

PASTORAL COUNSELING
Boise Bible Coll (ID)
Calvary Bible Coll and Theological Seminary (MO)
Central Christian Coll of Kansas (KS)
Indiana Wesleyan U (IN)
Mercyhurst Coll (PA)
Nebraska Christian Coll (NE)
Notre Dame Coll (OH)
Oakwood Coll (AL)

PERFUSION TECHNOLOGY
Boise State U (ID)

PETROLEUM TECHNOLOGY
British Columbia Inst of Technology (BC, Canada)
McNeese State U (LA)
Montana Tech of The U of Montana (MT)
Nicholls State U (LA)
U of Alaska Anchorage (AK)

PHARMACY
Clayton Coll & State U (GA)
Martin Methodist Coll (TN)

PHARMACY TECHNICIAN/ ASSISTANT
Baker Coll of Flint (MI)
Baker Coll of Jackson (MI)
Baker Coll of Muskegon (MI)
Mount Aloysius Coll (PA)

PHILOSOPHY
Baltimore Hebrew U (MD)
Clayton Coll & State U (GA)
Dalton State Coll (GA)
Felician Coll (NJ)
Martin Methodist Coll (TN)
Methodist Coll (NC)
Sacred Heart U (CT)
Saint John's Seminary Coll of Liberal Arts (MA)
Thomas More Coll (KY)
Université Laval (QC, Canada)
The U of Tampa (FL)
U of the District of Columbia (DC)
U of Wisconsin–Green Bay (WI)
York Coll of Pennsylvania (PA)

PHOTOGRAPHIC TECHNOLOGY
Southern Illinois U Carbondale (IL)

PHOTOGRAPHY
Academy of Art Coll (CA)
Andrews U (MI)
The Art Inst of Colorado (CO)
Central Christian Coll of Kansas (KS)
New World School of the Arts (FL)
Pacific Union Coll (CA)
Paier Coll of Art, Inc. (CT)
Rochester Inst of Technology (NY)
Sage Coll of Albany (NY)
The U of Maine at Augusta (ME)
Villa Julie Coll (MD)
Watkins Coll of Art and Design (TN)

PHYSICAL EDUCATION
Adrian Coll (MI)
Brewton-Parker Coll (GA)
Central Christian Coll of Kansas (KS)
Clayton Coll & State U (GA)
Fresno Pacific U (CA)
Haskell Indian Nations U (KS)
Hillsdale Free Will Baptist Coll (OK)
Macon State Coll (GA)
Martin Methodist Coll (TN)
Methodist Coll (NC)
Montreat Coll (NC)
Université Laval (QC, Canada)
U of Rio Grande (OH)
Waldorf Coll (IA)

PHYSICAL SCIENCES
Central Christian Coll of Kansas (KS)
Faulkner U (AL)
Martin Methodist Coll (TN)
Purdue U (IN)
Roberts Wesleyan Coll (NY)
Rogers State U (OK)
U of the District of Columbia (DC)
Villa Julie Coll (MD)
Waldorf Coll (IA)

PHYSICAL SCIENCE TECHNOLOGIES RELATED
The U of Akron (OH)
Western Kentucky U (KY)

PHYSICAL THERAPY
Alvernia Coll (PA)
Central Christian Coll of Kansas (KS)
Clarkson Coll (NE)
Clayton Coll & State U (GA)
Dalton State Coll (GA)
Davenport U, Lansing (MI)
Fairmont State Coll (WV)
Faulkner U (AL)
Lasell Coll (MA)
Lynn U (FL)
Macon State Coll (GA)
Martin Methodist Coll (TN)
Mercyhurst Coll (PA)
Midway Coll (KY)
Oakwood Coll (AL)
Shawnee State U (OH)
Southern Adventist U (TN)
Touro Coll (NY)
U of Central Arkansas (AR)
U of Cincinnati (OH)
U of Evansville (IN)
U of Puerto Rico at Ponce (PR)
Washburn U of Topeka (KS)

PHYSICAL THERAPY ASSISTANT
Arkansas State U (AR)
Baker Coll of Flint (MI)
Baker Coll of Muskegon (MI)
Becker Coll (MA)
Central Christian Coll of Kansas (KS)
Coll of St. Catherine (MN)
Comm Hospital Roanoke Valley–Coll of Health Scis (VA)
Endicott Coll (MA)
Fairleigh Dickinson U, Florham-Madison Campus (NJ)
Finlandia U (MI)
Idaho State U (ID)
Kent State U (OH)
Loma Linda U (CA)
Missouri Western State Coll (MO)
Mountain State U (WV)
Mount Aloysius Coll (PA)
Mount St. Mary's Coll (CA)
New York U (NY)
Southern Illinois U Carbondale (IL)
U of Central Arkansas (AR)
U of Evansville (IN)
U of Indianapolis (IN)
U of Puerto Rico, Humacao U Coll (PR)
Wichita State U (KS)

PHYSICIAN ASSISTANT
Central Christian Coll of Kansas (KS)
Dalton State Coll (GA)
Northeastern U (MA)
Southern Adventist U (TN)

PHYSICS
Adrian Coll (MI)
Clayton Coll & State U (GA)
Dalton State Coll (GA)
Macon State Coll (GA)
Mesa State Coll (CO)
Thomas Edison State Coll (NJ)
Thomas More Coll (KY)
U of the Virgin Islands (VI)
Waldorf Coll (IA)
York Coll of Pennsylvania (PA)

PHYSIOLOGY
Martin Methodist Coll (TN)

PLANT PROTECTION
North Carolina State U (NC)

PLANT SCIENCES
State U of NY Coll of A&T at Cobleskill (NY)

PLASTICS ENGINEERING
Kent State U (OH)

PLASTICS TECHNOLOGY
British Columbia Inst of Technology (BC, Canada)
Ferris State U (MI)
Kent State U (OH)
Shawnee State U (OH)

PLUMBING
British Columbia Inst of Technology (BC, Canada)

POLITICAL SCIENCE
Adrian Coll (MI)
Brewton-Parker Coll (GA)
Clayton Coll & State U (GA)
Dalton State Coll (GA)
Fayetteville State U (NC)
Fresno Pacific U (CA)
Indiana U–Purdue U Fort Wayne (IN)
Indiana Wesleyan U (IN)
Macon State Coll (GA)
Medaille Coll (NY)
Methodist Coll (NC)
Richmond, The American International U in LondonUnited Kingdom)
Rogers State U (OK)
Sacred Heart U (CT)
Thomas More Coll (KY)
Université Laval (QC, Canada)
The U of Scranton (PA)
The U of Tampa (FL)
U of Toledo (OH)
U of Wisconsin–Green Bay (WI)
Villa Julie Coll (MD)
Xavier U (OH)
York Coll of Pennsylvania (PA)

POSTAL MANAGEMENT
Macon State Coll (GA)
Washburn U of Topeka (KS)

PRACTICAL NURSE
Central Christian Coll of Kansas (KS)
Dickinson State U (ND)
Lamar U (TX)
Medgar Evers Coll of the City U of NY (NY)
Montana State U–Billings (MT)
The U of Montana–Missoula (MT)
U of the District of Columbia (DC)

PRE-DENTISTRY
Central Christian Coll of Kansas (KS)

PRE-ENGINEERING
Anderson U (IN)
Atlantic Union Coll (MA)
Boise State U (ID)
Brescia U (KY)
Briar Cliff U (IA)
Campbell U (NC)
Charleston Southern U (SC)
Clayton Coll & State U (GA)
Coll of Aeronautics (NY)
Columbus State U (GA)
Covenant Coll (GA)
Eastern Kentucky U (KY)
Edgewood Coll (WI)
Faulkner U (AL)
Ferris State U (MI)
Fort Valley State U (GA)
Friends U (KS)
Hannibal-LaGrange Coll (MO)
Keene State Coll (NH)
LaGrange Coll (GA)
Lewis-Clark State Coll (ID)
Lindsey Wilson Coll (KY)
Macon State Coll (GA)
Marian Coll (IN)
Medgar Evers Coll of the City U of NY (NY)
Mesa State Coll (CO)
Methodist Coll (NC)
Minnesota State U, Mankato (MN)
Missouri Southern State Coll (MO)
Montana State U–Billings (MT)
Montreat Coll (NC)
Newman U (KS)
Niagara U (NY)
Northern State U (SD)
Pacific Union Coll (CA)
Purdue U North Central (IN)
Richmond, The American International U in LondonUnited Kingdom)
Roberts Wesleyan Coll (NY)
St. Gregory's U (OK)
Schreiner U (TX)
Shawnee State U (OH)
Siena Heights U (MI)
Southern Utah U (UT)
U of New Hampshire (NH)
U of Sioux Falls (SD)
The U of South Dakota (SD)
Valdosta State U (GA)
Waldorf Coll (IA)
Washburn U of Topeka (KS)
West Virginia State Coll (WV)
Winona State U (MN)

PRE-MEDICINE
Central Christian Coll of Kansas (KS)
Schiller International USpain)
Schiller International UUnited Kingdom)
State U of NY Coll of A&T at Cobleskill (NY)

PRE-PHARMACY STUDIES
Brevard Coll (NC)
Central Christian Coll of Kansas (KS)

Dalton State Coll (GA)
Emmanuel Coll (GA)
Macon State Coll (GA)

PRE-THEOLOGY
Manchester Coll (IN)
Nazarene Bible Coll (CO)

PRE-VETERINARY STUDIES
Central Christian Coll of Kansas (KS)
Schiller International USpain)
Schiller International UUnited Kingdom)

PRINTMAKING
Academy of Art Coll (CA)
New World School of the Arts (FL)

PROFESSIONAL STUDIES
Champlain Coll (VT)
Ohio Valley Coll (WV)
Thomas Coll (ME)

PSYCHIATRIC/MENTAL HEALTH SERVICES
Lake Superior State U (MI)
Northern Kentucky U (KY)
U of Toledo (OH)

PSYCHOLOGY
Adrian Coll (MI)
Bay Path Coll (MA)
Bluefield State Coll (WV)
Brewton-Parker Coll (GA)
Central Christian Coll of Kansas (KS)
Central Methodist Coll (MO)
Chestnut Hill Coll (PA)
Clayton Coll & State U (GA)
Crown Coll (MN)
Dalton State Coll (GA)
Davis & Elkins Coll (WV)
Eastern New Mexico U (NM)
Felician Coll (NJ)
Fresno Pacific U (CA)
Hillsdale Free Will Baptist Coll (OK)
Indiana U–Purdue U Fort Wayne (IN)
Lourdes Coll (OH)
Macon State Coll (GA)
Maharishi U of Management (IA)
Marian Coll (IN)
Martin Methodist Coll (TN)
Methodist Coll (NC)
Montana State U–Billings (MT)
Mount Olive Coll (NC)
Richmond, The American International U in LondonUnited Kingdom)
Sacred Heart U (CT)
Salem International U (WV)
Siena Heights U (MI)
Southwestern Assemblies of God U (TX)
Thomas More Coll (KY)
U of Rio Grande (OH)
The U of Tampa (FL)
U of Wisconsin–Green Bay (WI)
Villa Julie Coll (MD)
Waldorf Coll (IA)
Wright State U (OH)
Xavier U (OH)

PUBLIC ADMINISTRATION
Central Methodist Coll (MO)
David N. Myers U (OH)
Indiana U Bloomington (IN)
Indiana U Northwest (IN)
Indiana U–Purdue U Fort Wayne (IN)
Indiana U–Purdue U Indianapolis (IN)
Indiana U South Bend (IN)
Macon State Coll (GA)
Medgar Evers Coll of the City U of NY (NY)
Plymouth State Coll (NH)
Point Park Coll (PA)
Southeastern U (DC)
Thomas Edison State Coll (NJ)
U of the District of Columbia (DC)
U of Wisconsin–Green Bay (WI)

PUBLIC ADMINISTRATION AND SERVICES RELATED
The U of Akron (OH)

PUBLIC HEALTH
Martin Methodist Coll (TN)
U of Alaska Fairbanks (AK)

PUBLIC POLICY ANALYSIS
Indiana U Bloomington (IN)
Saint Peter's Coll (NJ)

PUBLIC RELATIONS
Champlain Coll (VT)
John Brown U (AR)
Johnson & Wales U (RI)
New England School of Communications (ME)
Xavier U (OH)

PURCHASING/CONTRACTS MANAGEMENT
Mercyhurst Coll (PA)
Northeastern U (MA)
Saint Joseph's U (PA)
Strayer U (DC)
Thomas Edison State Coll (NJ)

QUALITY CONTROL TECHNOLOGY
Baker Coll of Cadillac (MI)
Baker Coll of Flint (MI)
Baker Coll of Muskegon (MI)
Eastern Kentucky U (KY)
U of Cincinnati (OH)

RABBINICAL/TALMUDIC STUDIES
Baltimore Hebrew U (MD)
Université Laval (QC, Canada)

RADIOLOGICAL SCIENCE
Allen Coll (IA)
Boise State U (ID)
Champlain Coll (VT)
Clarkson Coll (NE)
Clayton Coll & State U (GA)
Dalton State Coll (GA)
Indiana U Northwest (IN)
Mansfield U of Pennsylvania (PA)
Mayo School of Health Sciences (MN)
Mesa State Coll (CO)
Midwestern State U (TX)
Mount Aloysius Coll (PA)
Washburn U of Topeka (KS)

RADIO/TELEVISION BROADCASTING
Ashland U (OH)
Lewis-Clark State Coll (ID)
New England School of Communications (ME)
Northwestern Coll (MN)
Ohio U (OH)
Ohio U–Zanesville (OH)
Rogers State U (OK)
Salem International U (WV)
Xavier U (OH)
York Coll of Pennsylvania (PA)

RADIO/TELEVISION BROADCASTING TECHNOLOGY
British Columbia Inst of Technology (BC, Canada)
East Stroudsburg U of Pennsylvania (PA)
Lyndon State Coll (VT)
Mountain State U (WV)
New England School of Communications (ME)
New York Inst of Technology (NY)
Southern Adventist U (TN)

REAL ESTATE
British Columbia Inst of Technology (BC, Canada)
Caribbean U (PR)
Fairmont State Coll (WV)
Ferris State U (MI)
Kent State U (OH)
Lamar U (TX)
Saint Francis U (PA)
Thomas Edison State Coll (NJ)
U of Cincinnati (OH)
U of Toledo (OH)

RECEPTIONIST
The U of Montana–Missoula (MT)

RECREATIONAL THERAPY
Indiana Inst of Technology (IN)
Johnson & Wales U (RI)
Northeastern U (MA)
U of Southern Maine (ME)

RECREATION/LEISURE FACILITIES MANAGEMENT
Eastern Kentucky U (KY)
Indiana Inst of Technology (IN)
Johnson & Wales U (RI)
Martin Methodist Coll (TN)
State U of NY Coll of A&T at Cobleskill (NY)
U of Maine at Machias (ME)
Webber International U (FL)

RECREATION/LEISURE STUDIES
Brevard Coll (NC)
Brewton-Parker Coll (GA)
Central Christian Coll of Kansas (KS)
Clayton Coll & State U (GA)
Eastern Kentucky U (KY)
Johnson & Wales U (RI)
Mount Olive Coll (NC)
Oklahoma Panhandle State U (OK)
Thomas Edison State Coll (NJ)
U of Maine at Machias (ME)
U of Maine at Presque Isle (ME)
U of the District of Columbia (DC)

RECREATION PRODUCTS/ SERVICES MARKETING OPERATIONS
U Coll of the Cariboo (BC, Canada)

RELIGIOUS EDUCATION
Baltimore Hebrew U (MD)
The Baptist Coll of Florida (FL)
Boise Bible Coll (ID)
Calvary Bible Coll and Theological Seminary (MO)
Central Baptist Coll (AR)
Central Bible Coll (MO)
Cincinnati Bible Coll and Seminary (OH)
Circleville Bible Coll (OH)
Cornerstone U (MI)
Dallas Baptist U (TX)
Eastern Nazarene Coll (MA)
Grace Bible Coll (MI)
Great Lakes Christian Coll (MI)
Hillsdale Free Will Baptist Coll (OK)
Houghton Coll (NY)
Indiana Wesleyan U (IN)
Manhattan Christian Coll (KS)
Mercyhurst Coll (PA)
Methodist Coll (NC)
MidAmerica Nazarene U (KS)
Nazarene Bible Coll (CO)
Nebraska Christian Coll (NE)
Reformed Bible Coll (MI)
Waldorf Coll (IA)
Warner Pacific Coll (OR)
Washington Bible Coll (MD)

RELIGIOUS MUSIC
Aquinas Coll (MI)
The Baptist Coll of Florida (FL)
Boise Bible Coll (ID)
Calvary Bible Coll and Theological Seminary (MO)
Central Bible Coll (MO)
Cincinnati Bible Coll and Seminary (OH)
Circleville Bible Coll (OH)
Clearwater Christian Coll (FL)
Gwynedd-Mercy Coll (PA)
Hillsdale Free Will Baptist Coll (OK)
Immaculata Coll (PA)
Indiana Wesleyan U (IN)
Manhattan Christian Coll (KS)
MidAmerica Nazarene U (KS)
Mount Vernon Nazarene U (OH)
Nazarene Bible Coll (CO)
Nebraska Christian Coll (NE)
Saint Joseph's Coll (IN)

RELIGIOUS STUDIES
Adrian Coll (MI)
Aquinas Coll (MI)
Atlantic Union Coll (MA)
Baltimore Hebrew U (MD)
Boise Bible Coll (ID)
Brescia U (KY)
Brewton-Parker Coll (GA)
Central Christian Coll of Kansas (KS)
Circleville Bible Coll (OH)
Felician Coll (NJ)
Global U of the Assemblies of God (MO)
Grace Bible Coll (MI)
Griggs U (MD)
Holy Apostles Coll and Seminary (CT)
Howard Payne U (TX)
Kentucky Mountain Bible Coll (KY)
Liberty U (VA)
Lourdes Coll (OH)
Manchester Coll (IN)
Maranatha Baptist Bible Coll (WI)
Martin Methodist Coll (TN)
MidAmerica Nazarene U (KS)
Missouri Baptist Coll (MO)
Montreat Coll (NC)
Mount Marty Coll (SD)
Mount Olive Coll (NC)
New Orleans Baptist Theological Seminary (LA)
Oakwood Coll (AL)
Ouachita Baptist U (AR)
Presentation Coll (SD)
Sacred Heart U (CT)
Southwestern Coll (AZ)
Tabor Coll (KS)
Thomas More Coll (KY)
The U of Findlay (OH)
U of Great Falls (MT)
U of Sioux Falls (SD)
Waldorf Coll (IA)
Washington Bible Coll (MD)
Wayland Baptist U (TX)

RESPIRATORY THERAPY
Armstrong Atlantic State U (GA)
Ball State U (IN)
California Coll for Health Sciences (CA)
Champlain Coll (VT)
Coll of St. Catherine (MN)
Columbia Union Coll (MD)
Comm Hospital Roanoke Valley–Coll of Health Scis (VA)
Dakota State U (SD)
Dalton State Coll (GA)
Faulkner U (AL)
Ferris State U (MI)
Gannon U (PA)
Gwynedd-Mercy Coll (PA)
Indiana U Northwest (IN)
Indiana U–Purdue U Indianapolis (IN)
Lamar U (TX)
Loma Linda U (CA)
Macon State Coll (GA)
Mansfield U of Pennsylvania (PA)
Marygrove Coll (MI)
Mayo School of Health Sciences (MN)
Midland Lutheran Coll (NE)
Missouri Southern State Coll (MO)
Molloy Coll (NY)
Mountain State U (WV)
Nebraska Methodist Coll of Nursing & Allied Health (NE)
Newman U (KS)
New York U (NY)
Nicholls State U (LA)
Northern Kentucky U (KY)
Our Lady of Holy Cross Coll (LA)
Point Park Coll (PA)
St. Augustine Coll (IL)
Shawnee State U (OH)
Shenandoah U (VA)
Southern Adventist U (TN)
Southern Illinois U Carbondale (IL)
Thomas Edison State Coll (NJ)
Universidad Adventista de las Antillas (PR)
The U of Akron (OH)
U of Arkansas for Medical Sciences (AR)
The U of Montana–Missoula (MT)
U of Pittsburgh at Johnstown (PA)
U of Southern Indiana (IN)
U of the District of Columbia (DC)
U of Toledo (OH)
Weber State U (UT)
Western Kentucky U (KY)
West Virginia U Inst of Technology (WV)
York Coll of Pennsylvania (PA)
Youngstown State U (OH)

RESTAURANT OPERATIONS
Johnson & Wales U (RI)
Lewis-Clark State Coll (ID)
U of New Hampshire (NH)

RETAILING OPERATIONS
Johnson & Wales U (RI)
Robert Morris Coll (IL)

RETAIL MANAGEMENT
Baker Coll of Owosso (MI)
Fairmont State Coll (WV)
Johnson & Wales U (RI)
Lewis-Clark State Coll (ID)
Mount Ida Coll (MA)
Sullivan U (KY)
Thomas Edison State Coll (NJ)
U of Minnesota, Crookston (MN)
U of Toledo (OH)
York Coll of Pennsylvania (PA)

ROBOTICS
Clayton Coll & State U (GA)
Lamar U (TX)
Pacific Union Coll (CA)
U of Cincinnati (OH)

ROBOTICS TECHNOLOGY
British Columbia Inst of Technology (BC, Canada)
Indiana U–Purdue U Indianapolis (IN)
Purdue U (IN)
U of Rio Grande (OH)

SAFETY/SECURITY TECHNOLOGY
Eastern Kentucky U (KY)
John Jay Coll of Criminal Justice, the City U of NY (NY)
Keene State Coll (NH)
Lamar U (TX)
Ohio U (OH)
Ohio U–Chillicothe (OH)
U of Cincinnati (OH)

SALES OPERATIONS
The U of Akron (OH)
U of Toledo (OH)

SCIENCE EDUCATION
Central Christian Coll of Kansas (KS)
Martin Methodist Coll (TN)
U of Cincinnati (OH)

SCIENCE TECHNOLOGIES RELATED
British Columbia Inst of Technology (BC, Canada)
Ohio Valley Coll (WV)

SCIENCE/TECHNOLOGY AND SOCIETY
Samford U (AL)

SCULPTURE
Academy of Art Coll (CA)
New World School of the Arts (FL)

SECONDARY EDUCATION
Rogers State U (OK)

SECRETARIAL SCIENCE
Alabama State U (AL)
American U of Puerto Rico (PR)
Arkansas State U (AR)
Atlantic Union Coll (MA)
Baker Coll of Auburn Hills (MI)
Baker Coll of Cadillac (MI)
Baker Coll of Clinton Township (MI)
Baker Coll of Flint (MI)
Baker Coll of Jackson (MI)
Baker Coll of Muskegon (MI)
Baker Coll of Owosso (MI)
Baker Coll of Port Huron (MI)
Ball State U (IN)
Baptist Bible Coll (MO)
Baptist Bible Coll of Pennsylvania (PA)
Bayamón Central U (PR)
Black Hills State U (SD)
Bluefield State Coll (WV)
Briarcliffe Coll (NY)
British Columbia Inst of Technology (BC, Canada)
Campbellsville U (KY)
Caribbean U (PR)

Cedarville U (OH)
Central Missouri State U (MO)
Clayton Coll & State U (GA)
Clearwater Christian Coll (FL)
Coleman Coll (CA)
Columbia Coll (PR)
Concordia Coll (NY)
Dakota State U (SD)
Davenport U, Dearborn (MI)
Davenport U, Grand Rapids (MI)
Davenport U, Kalamazoo (MI)
Davenport U, Lansing (MI)
David N. Myers U (OH)
Davis & Elkins Coll (WV)
Dickinson State U (ND)
Dordt Coll (IA)
Eastern Kentucky U (KY)
Eastern Oregon U (OR)
Evangel U (MO)
Fairmont State Coll (WV)
Faith Baptist Bible Coll and Theological Seminary (IA)
Faulkner U (AL)
Fayetteville State U (NC)
Florida Metropolitan U-Tampa Coll, Lakeland (FL)
Fort Hays State U (KS)
Fort Valley State U (GA)
Glenville State Coll (WV)
God's Bible School and Coll (OH)
Grace Coll (IN)
Hannibal-LaGrange Coll (MO)
Haskell Indian Nations U (KS)
Henderson State U (AR)
Hobe Sound Bible Coll (FL)
Husson Coll (ME)
Idaho State U (ID)
Indiana State U (IN)
Inter American U of PR, Aguadilla Campus (PR)
Inter Amer U of PR, Barranquitas Campus (PR)
Inter American U of PR, San Germán Campus (PR)
Johnson & Wales U (RI)
Jones Coll (FL)
Kent State U (OH)
Kentucky Christian Coll (KY)
Lake Superior State U (MI)
Lamar U (TX)
Lancaster Bible Coll (PA)
Lewis-Clark State Coll (ID)
Lincoln Christian Coll (IL)
Lincoln U (MO)
Macon State Coll (GA)
Maranatha Baptist Bible Coll (WI)
Martin Methodist Coll (TN)
Mayville State U (ND)
McNeese State U (LA)
Mercyhurst Coll (PA)
Mesa State Coll (CO)
Montana State U–Billings (MT)
Montana Tech of The U of Montana (MT)
Morehead State U (KY)
Mountain State U (WV)
Mount Vernon Nazarene U (OH)
Murray State U (KY)
Nebraska Christian Coll (NE)
New York Inst of Technology (NY)
Nicholls State U (LA)
Northern State U (SD)
Northwestern Coll (IA)
Northwestern State U of Louisiana (LA)
Oakland City U (IN)
Oakwood Coll (AL)
Ohio U (OH)
Ohio U–Chillicothe (OH)
Ohio U–Lancaster (OH)
Oklahoma Wesleyan U (OK)
Oregon Inst of Technology (OR)
Pacific Union Coll (CA)
Peirce Coll (PA)
Pillsbury Baptist Bible Coll (MN)
Pontifical Catholic U of Puerto Rico (PR)
Presentation Coll (SD)
Reformed Bible Coll (MI)
Robert Morris Coll (IL)
Robert Morris U (PA)
Rogers State U (OK)
St. Augustine Coll (IL)
Shawnee State U (OH)
Southeastern Louisiana U (LA)
Southern Adventist U (TN)
Southern Arkansas U–Magnolia (AR)
Southwest Baptist U (MO)
Southwestern Adventist U (TX)
Sullivan U (KY)
Sul Ross State U (TX)
Tabor Coll (KS)
Tennessee State U (TN)
Thomas Coll (ME)
Trinity Baptist Coll (FL)
Trinity Bible Coll (ND)
Universidad Adventista de las Antillas (PR)
U of Alaska Fairbanks (AK)
U of Alaska Southeast (AK)
U of Cincinnati (OH)
The U of Findlay (OH)
U of Maine at Machias (ME)
The U of Montana–Western (MT)
U of Puerto Rico, Humacao U Coll (PR)
U of Puerto Rico at Ponce (PR)
U of Puerto Rico, Cayey U Coll (PR)
U of Rio Grande (OH)
U of Sioux Falls (SD)
U of Southern Indiana (IN)
U of the District of Columbia (DC)
U of the Virgin Islands (VI)
U of Toledo (OH)
Utah State U (UT)
Virginia Coll at Birmingham (AL)
Washburn U of Topeka (KS)
Weber State U (UT)
West Virginia State Coll (WV)
West Virginia U Inst of Technology (WV)
Wiley Coll (TX)
Williams Baptist Coll (AR)
Winona State U (MN)
Wright State U (OH)
Youngstown State U (OH)

SECURITY
Youngstown State U (OH)

SHEET METAL WORKING
British Columbia Inst of Technology (BC, Canada)

SIGN LANGUAGE INTERPRETATION
Bethel Coll (IN)
Cincinnati Bible Coll and Seminary (OH)
Coll of St. Catherine (MN)
Eastern Kentucky U (KY)
Fairmont State Coll (WV)
Gardner-Webb U (NC)
Mount Aloysius Coll (PA)
Nebraska Christian Coll (NE)
Roanoke Bible Coll (NC)
Rochester Inst of Technology (NY)
Tennessee Temple U (TN)
U of Arkansas at Little Rock (AR)
U of Louisville (KY)

SMALL ENGINE MECHANIC
British Columbia Inst of Technology (BC, Canada)
The U of Montana–Missoula (MT)

SOCIAL PSYCHOLOGY
Central Christian Coll of Kansas (KS)
Park U (MO)

SOCIAL SCIENCES
Adrian Coll (MI)
Brewton-Parker Coll (GA)
Bryn Athyn Coll of the New Church (PA)
Campbellsville U (KY)
Canisius Coll (NY)
Central Christian Coll of Kansas (KS)
Chaminade U of Honolulu (HI)
Chestnut Hill Coll (PA)
Clayton Coll & State U (GA)
Crown Coll (MN)
Evangel U (MO)
Faulkner U (AL)
Felician Coll (NJ)
Indiana Wesleyan U (IN)
Lindsey Wilson Coll (KY)
Mesa State Coll (CO)
Montana State U–Northern (MT)
Montreat Coll (NC)
Ohio U (OH)
Ohio U–Zanesville (OH)
Richmond, The American International U in LondonUnited Kingdom)
Rogers State U (OK)
Sage Coll of Albany (NY)
Saint Peter's Coll (NJ)
Samford U (AL)
Shawnee State U (OH)
Southwestern Assemblies of God U (TX)
State U of NY Empire State Coll (NY)
Touro Coll (NY)
Tri-State U (IN)
U of Cincinnati (OH)
The U of Findlay (OH)
U of Sioux Falls (SD)
U of Southern Indiana (IN)
U of Toledo (OH)
Valparaiso U (IN)
Villa Julie Coll (MD)
Waldorf Coll (IA)
Warner Pacific Coll (OR)

SOCIAL WORK
Central Christian Coll of Kansas (KS)
Champlain Coll (VT)
Dalton State Coll (GA)
Edinboro U of Pennsylvania (PA)
Indiana U East (IN)
Mansfield U of Pennsylvania (PA)
Martin Methodist Coll (TN)
Methodist Coll (NC)
Mount Ida Coll (MA)
Mount Vernon Nazarene U (OH)
New York U (NY)
Northern State U (SD)
Siena Heights U (MI)
Suffolk U (MA)
U of Cincinnati (OH)
U of Rio Grande (OH)
U of Toledo (OH)
U of Wisconsin–Green Bay (WI)
Waldorf Coll (IA)
Wright State U (OH)
Youngstown State U (OH)

SOCIOLOGY
Adrian Coll (MI)
Brewton-Parker Coll (GA)
Central Christian Coll of Kansas (KS)
Chestnut Hill Coll (PA)
Clayton Coll & State U (GA)
Dalton State Coll (GA)
Fayetteville State U (NC)
Felician Coll (NJ)
Fresno Pacific U (CA)
Friends U (KS)
Grand View Coll (IA)
Lourdes Coll (OH)
Macon State Coll (GA)
Martin Methodist Coll (TN)
Methodist Coll (NC)
Montana State U–Billings (MT)
Penn State U Univ Park Campus (PA)
Richmond, The American International U in LondonUnited Kingdom)
Sacred Heart U (CT)
Thomas More Coll (KY)
Université Laval (QC, Canada)
U of Dubuque (IA)
U of Rio Grande (OH)
The U of Scranton (PA)
The U of Tampa (FL)
Villa Julie Coll (MD)
Waldorf Coll (IA)
Wright State U (OH)
Xavier U (OH)

SOIL CONSERVATION
U of Minnesota, Crookston (MN)

SPANISH
Adrian Coll (MI)
Central Christian Coll of Kansas (KS)
Chestnut Hill Coll (PA)
Clayton Coll & State U (GA)
Fayetteville State U (NC)
Fresno Pacific U (CA)
Friends U (KS)
Indiana U–Purdue U Fort Wayne (IN)
Methodist Coll (NC)
Montreat Coll (NC)
Sacred Heart U (CT)
Thomas More Coll (KY)
Université Laval (QC, Canada)
The U of Tampa (FL)
U of Wisconsin–Green Bay (WI)
Waldorf Coll (IA)
Xavier U (OH)

SPECIAL EDUCATION
Edinboro U of Pennsylvania (PA)
Montana State U–Billings (MT)

SPECIAL EDUCATION RELATED
Minot State U (ND)

SPEECH-LANGUAGE PATHOLOGY
Baker Coll of Muskegon (MI)
Indiana State U (IN)
Southern Adventist U (TN)

SPEECH/RHETORICAL STUDIES
Clayton Coll & State U (GA)
Dalton State Coll (GA)
Ferris State U (MI)
Macon State Coll (GA)
New England School of Communications (ME)
Waldorf Coll (IA)

SPEECH/THEATER EDUCATION
Idaho State U (ID)

SPORT/FITNESS ADMINISTRATION
Central Christian Coll of Kansas (KS)
Champlain Coll (VT)
Lake Superior State U (MI)
Webber International U (FL)

STRINGED INSTRUMENTS
Five Towns Coll (NY)
New World School of the Arts (FL)

SURVEYING
British Columbia Inst of Technology (BC, Canada)
Caribbean U (PR)
Ferris State U (MI)
Glenville State Coll (WV)
Kansas State U (KS)
Northeastern U (MA)
Thomas Edison State Coll (NJ)
The U of Akron (OH)
U of Alaska Anchorage (AK)
U of New Hampshire (NH)

SYSTEM ADMINISTRATION
Denver Tech Coll (CO)
DeVry U, Colorado Springs (CO)
Western Governors U (UT)

SYSTEMS ENGINEERING
Missouri Tech (MO)

TAXATION
British Columbia Inst of Technology (BC, Canada)

TEACHER ASSISTANT/AIDE
Alabama State U (AL)
Alverno Coll (WI)
Boise State U (ID)
Concordia U (MN)
Dordt Coll (IA)
Johnson Bible Coll (TN)
Lamar U (TX)
Martin Methodist Coll (TN)
Mount Ida Coll (MA)
New Mexico Highlands U (NM)
New Mexico State U (NM)
Our Lady of Holy Cross Coll (LA)
St. John's U (NY)
U of New Mexico (NM)

TECHNICAL/BUSINESS WRITING
Ferris State U (MI)
Mansfield U of Pennsylvania (PA)

TECHNICAL EDUCATION
New York Inst of Technology (NY)
Northern Kentucky U (KY)
Western Kentucky U (KY)

TELECOMMUNICATIONS
Briarcliffe Coll (NY)
Cameron U (OK)
Capitol Coll (MD)
Champlain Coll (VT)
Clayton Coll & State U (GA)
Coll of Saint Mary (NE)
Columbia Coll–Hollywood (CA)
Ferris State U (MI)
Five Towns Coll (NY)
Murray State U (KY)
Northeastern U (MA)
Salem International U (WV)
State U of NY Coll of A&T at Cobleskill (NY)
Waldorf Coll (IA)

TEXTILE ARTS
Academy of Art Coll (CA)

THEATER ARTS/DRAMA
Adrian Coll (MI)
Brigham Young U–Hawaii (HI)
Central Christian Coll of Kansas (KS)
Clayton Coll & State U (GA)
Five Towns Coll (NY)
Indiana U Bloomington (IN)
Macon State Coll (GA)
Martin Methodist Coll (TN)
Mesa State Coll (CO)
Methodist Coll (NC)
New World School of the Arts (FL)
North Greenville Coll (SC)
Richmond, The American International U in LondonUnited Kingdom)
Thomas More Coll (KY)
Université Laval (QC, Canada)
U Coll of the Fraser Valley (BC, Canada)
U of Sioux Falls (SD)
U of Wisconsin–Green Bay (WI)
Villa Julie Coll (MD)
Waldorf Coll (IA)

THEATER DESIGN
Indiana U Bloomington (IN)
Johnson State Coll (VT)
U of Rio Grande (OH)

THEOLOGY
Appalachian Bible Coll (WV)
The Baptist Coll of Florida (FL)
Briar Cliff U (IA)
Calvary Bible Coll and Theological Seminary (MO)
Central Christian Coll of Kansas (KS)
Circleville Bible Coll (OH)
Creighton U (NE)
Franciscan U of Steubenville (OH)
Griggs U (MD)
Heritage Bible Coll (NC)
Marian Coll (IN)
Martin Methodist Coll (TN)
Notre Dame Coll (OH)
Ohio Dominican Coll (OH)
Ozark Christian Coll (MO)
San Jose Christian Coll (CA)
Southwestern Coll (AZ)
Université Laval (QC, Canada)
Waldorf Coll (IA)
Washington Bible Coll (MD)
Williams Baptist Coll (AR)
William Tyndale Coll (MI)
Xavier U (OH)

THEOLOGY/MINISTRY RELATED
Brescia U (KY)
Central Baptist Coll (AR)

TOOL/DIE MAKING
Southern Illinois U Carbondale (IL)

TOURISM PROMOTION OPERATIONS
Champlain Coll (VT)
U Coll of the Cariboo (BC, Canada)

TOURISM/TRAVEL MARKETING
Johnson & Wales U (RI)
Pontifical Catholic U of Puerto Rico (PR)
State U of NY Coll of A&T at Cobleskill (NY)
The U of Montana–Western (MT)

TRADE/INDUSTRIAL EDUCATION
British Columbia Inst of Technology (BC, Canada)

Cincinnati Bible Coll and Seminary (OH)
Eastern Kentucky U (KY)
Murray State U (KY)
Purdue U (IN)
Sinte Gleska U (SD)
Valdosta State U (GA)

TRANSPORTATION ENGINEERING
British Columbia Inst of Technology (BC, Canada)

TRANSPORTATION TECHNOLOGY
Baker Coll of Flint (MI)
Maine Maritime Academy (ME)
U of Cincinnati (OH)
U of Toledo (OH)

TRAVEL SERVICES MARKETING OPERATIONS
Champlain Coll (VT)

TRAVEL/TOURISM MANAGEMENT
American InterContinental U (CA)
American InterContinental U, Atlanta (GA)
Baker Coll of Flint (MI)
Baker Coll of Muskegon (MI)
Black Hills State U (SD)
Brigham Young U–Hawaii (HI)
British Columbia Inst of Technology (BC, Canada)
Champlain Coll (VT)
Johnson & Wales U (RI)
Mansfield U of Pennsylvania (PA)
Mesa State Coll (CO)
Midland Lutheran Coll (NE)
Mountain State U (WV)
Mount Ida Coll (MA)
National American U, Colorado Springs (CO)
National American U–Sioux Falls Branch (SD)
Ohio U (OH)
Robert Morris Coll (IL)
Rochester Inst of Technology (NY)
Schiller International U (FL)
Sullivan U (KY)
U of Alaska Southeast (AK)
The U of Montana–Western (MT)
U of New Haven (CT)
Webber International U (FL)

TURF MANAGEMENT
North Carolina State U (NC)
State U of NY Coll of A&T at Cobleskill (NY)
U of Massachusetts Amherst (MA)

URBAN STUDIES
Beulah Heights Bible Coll (GA)
Clayton Coll & State U (GA)
Mount St. Mary's Coll (CA)
Saint Peter's Coll (NJ)
U of the District of Columbia (DC)
U of Wisconsin–Green Bay (WI)

VEHICLE/EQUIPMENT OPERATION
Baker Coll of Flint (MI)
The U of Montana–Missoula (MT)

VEHICLE MARKETING OPERATIONS
Northwood U, Florida Campus (FL)
Northwood U, Texas Campus (TX)

VEHICLE/MOBILE EQUIPMENT MECHANICS AND REPAIR RELATED
British Columbia Inst of Technology (BC, Canada)
U of Alaska Fairbanks (AK)

VEHICLE PARTS/ACCESSORIES MARKETING OPERATIONS
Northwood U, Florida Campus (FL)
Northwood U, Texas Campus (TX)

VETERINARIAN ASSISTANT
Purdue U (IN)
Wilson Coll (PA)

VETERINARY SCIENCES
Clayton Coll & State U (GA)
Fort Valley State U (GA)
Martin Methodist Coll (TN)
Waldorf Coll (IA)

VETERINARY TECHNOLOGY
Becker Coll (MA)
Fairmont State Coll (WV)
Fort Valley State U (GA)
Lincoln Memorial U (TN)
Medaille Coll (NY)
Mount Ida Coll (MA)
National American U (SD)
Northwestern State U of Louisiana (LA)
Sul Ross State U (TX)

VISUAL/PERFORMING ARTS
Indiana U East (IN)
Maharishi U of Management (IA)

WATER RESOURCES
Lake Superior State U (MI)
Montana State U–Northern (MT)
U of the District of Columbia (DC)

WATER TREATMENT TECHNOLOGY
Lake Superior State U (MI)
U of the District of Columbia (DC)

WEB/MULTIMEDIA MANAGEMENT/WEBMASTER
Education America, Southeast Coll of Technology, Mobile Campus (AL)
New England School of Communications (ME)

WEB PAGE, DIGITAL/ MULTIMEDIA AND INFORMATION RESOURCES DESIGN
New England School of Communications (ME)

WELDING TECHNOLOGY
Boise State U (ID)
British Columbia Inst of Technology (BC, Canada)
Excelsior Coll (NY)
Ferris State U (MI)
Idaho State U (ID)
Lamar U (TX)
Lewis-Clark State Coll (ID)
Mesa State Coll (CO)
Montana State U–Northern (MT)
Oakland City U (IN)
U of Alaska Anchorage (AK)
The U of Montana–Missoula (MT)
U of Toledo (OH)

WESTERN CIVILIZATION
Central Christian Coll of Kansas (KS)

WILDLIFE BIOLOGY
Central Christian Coll of Kansas (KS)
Martin Methodist Coll (TN)
Waldorf Coll (IA)

WILDLIFE MANAGEMENT
British Columbia Inst of Technology (BC, Canada)
Martin Methodist Coll (TN)
State U of NY Coll of A&T at Cobleskill (NY)
Sterling Coll (VT)
U of Minnesota, Crookston (MN)
Waldorf Coll (IA)
Winona State U (MN)

WIND/PERCUSSION INSTRUMENTS
Five Towns Coll (NY)
New World School of the Arts (FL)

WOMEN'S STUDIES
Indiana U–Purdue U Fort Wayne (IN)
Nazarene Bible Coll (CO)

WOOD SCIENCE/PAPER TECHNOLOGY
U of Louisiana at Monroe (LA)

ZOOLOGY
Central Christian Coll of Kansas (KS)
Martin Methodist Coll (TN)

2001–02 Changes in Two-Year Institutions

Following is an alphabetical listing of institutions that have recently closed, merged with other institutions, or changed their name or status. In the case of a name change, the former name appears first, followed by the new name.

ACA College of Design (Cincinnati, OH): name changed to The Art Institute of Cincinnati.

Academy of Business College (Phoenix, AZ): name changed to Rhodes College.

Altoona School of Commerce (Atloona, PA): name changed to South Hills School of Business & Technology.

American Academy of Dramatic Arts/West (Hollywood, CA): name changed to American Academy of Dramatic Arts/Hollywood.

American Institute of Business (Des Moines, IA): name changed to AIB College of Business.

American Institute of Commerce (Davenport, IA): name changed to Kaplan College.

American School of Business (Shreveport, LA): not eligible for inclusion.

Augusta Technical Institute (Augusta, GA): name changed to Augusta Technical College.

Belleville Area College (Belleville, IL): name changed to Southwestern Illinois College.

Bryant and Stratton Business Institute (Liverpool, NY): name changed to Bryant and Stratton Business Institute, North Campus.

Bryant and Stratton Business Institute, Eastern Hills Campus (Amherst, NY): name changed to Bryant and Stratton Business Institute, Amherst Campus.

Carroll Technical Institute (Carrollton, GA): name changed to West Central Technical College.

Cecils Junior College of Business (Asheville, NC): name changed to Cecils College.

Central Community College–Platte Campus (Columbus, NE): name changed to Central Community College–Columbus Campus.

Charles County Community College (La Plata, MD): name changed to College of Southern Maryland.

Charles Stewart Mott Community College (Flint, MI): name changed to Mott Community College.

Chattahoochee Technical Institute (Marietta, GA): name changed to Chattahoochee Technical College.

Chesterfield-Marlboro Technical College (Cheraw, SC): name changed to Northeastern Technical College.

Colorado Aero Tech (Broomfield, CO): name changed to Westwood College of Aviation Technology&-Denver.

Computer Learning Centers, Inc. (Alexandria, VA):closed.

Computer Learning Centers, Inc. (Anaheim, CA):closed.

Computer Learning Centers, Inc. (Los Angeles, CA): closed.

Computer Learning Centers, Inc. (Philadelphia, PA): closed.

Computer Learning Centers, Inc. (San Francisco, CA): closed.

Computer Learning Centers, Inc. (San Jose, CA):closed.

Computer Tech (Pittsburgh, PA): name changed to International Academy of Design & Technology.

Cumberland School of Technology (Baton Rouge, LA): name changed to MedVance Institute.

Cumberland School of Technology (Cookeville, TN): name changed to MedVance Institute.

DeKalb Technical Institute (Clarkston, GA): name changed to DeKalb Technical College.

Dixie College (St. George, UT): name changed to Dixie State College of Utah.

ECPI Computer Institute (Richmond, VA): name changed to ECPI Technical College.

Franklin Institute of Boston (Boston, MA): name changed to Benjamin Franklin Institute of Technology.

Fugazzi College (Nashville, TN): name changed to National College of Business & Technology.

Great Lakes College (Midland, MI): name changed to Davenport University.

Griffin Technical Institute (Griffin, GA): name changed to Griffin Technical College.

Gwinnett Technical Institute (Lawrenceville, GA): name changed to Gwinnett Technical College.

Hiram G. Andrews Center (Johnstown, PA): name changed to Commonwealth Technical Institute.

Katharine Gibbs School (Providence, RI): not eligible for inclusion.

Kemper Military School and College (Boonville, MO): closed.

Lamson Junior College (Tempe, AZ): name changed to Lamson College.

Le Chef College of Hospitality Careers (Austin, TX): name changed to Texas Culinary Academy.

Luna Vocational Technical Institute (Las Vegas, NM): name changed to Luna Community College.

Macon Technical Institute (Macon, GA): name changed to Central Georgia Technical College.

Manor Junior College (Jenkintown, PA): name changed to Manor College.

Maric College of Medical Careers (San Diego, CA): name changed to Maric College.

Minnesota West Community and Technical College–Canby Campus (Canby, MN): closed.

Minnesota West Community and Technical College–Granite Falls Campus (Granite Falls, MN):closed.

Minnesota West Community and Technical College–Jackson Campus (Jackson, MN): closed.

Minnesota West Community and Technical College–Worthington Campus (Worthington, MN):closed.

National Business College (Bluefield, VA): name changed to National College of Business & Technology.

National Business College (Bristol, VA): name changed to National College of Business & Technology.

National Business College (Charlottesville, VA): name changed to National College of Business & Technology.

National Business College (Danville, KY): name changed to National College of Business & Technology.

National Business College (Danville, VA): name changed to National College of Business & Technology.

National Business College (Florence, KY): name changed to National College of Business & Technology.

National Business College (Harrisonburg, VA): name changed to National College of Business & Technology.

National Business College (Lexington, KY): name changed to National College of Business & Technology.

National Business College (Louisville, KY): name changed to National College of Business & Technology.

National Business College (Lynchburg, VA): name changed to National College of Business & Technology.

National Business College (Martinsville, VA): name changed to National College of Business & Technology.

National Business College (Pikeville, KY): name changed to National College of Business & Technology.

National Business College (Richmond, KY): name changed to National College of Business & Technology.

National Business College (Salem, VA): name changed to National College of Business & Technology.

National Institute for Paralegal Arts and Sciences (Boca Raton, FL): name changed to College for Professional Studies.

Nielsen Electronics Institute (North Charleston, SC): closed.

Northeast Iowa Community College, Peosta Campus (Peosta, IA): closed.

Northwestern College (Lima, OH): name changed to University of Northwestern Ohio.

Northwestern Technical Institute (Rock Springs, GA): name changed to Northwestern Technical College.

PPI Health Careers School (Colorado Springs, CO): name changed to IntelliTec Medical Institute.

Remington College–Education America, Inc. (Lafayette, LA): name changed to Education America, Remington College, Lafayette Campus.

Savannah Technical Institute (Savannah, GA): name changed to Savannah Technical College.

Southeast College of Technology (Memphis, TN): name changed to Education America, Southeast College of Technology, Memphis Campus.

Southeast College of Technology (Metairie, LA): name changed to Education America, Southeast College of Technology, New Orleans Campus.

Southwest Florida College of Business (Fort Myers, FL): name changed to Southwest Florida College.

Southwest Institute (El Paso, TX): name changed to Border Institute of Technology.

Springfield College (Springfield, MO): name changed to Rhodes College.

State Technical Institute at Memphis (Memphis, TN): name changed to Southwest Tennessee Community College.

Stautzenberger College (Findlay, OH): name changed to Southern Ohio College, Findlay Campus.

Technical Trades Institute (Colorado Springs, CO): name changed to IntelliTec College.

Technical Trades Institute (Grand Junction, CO): name changed to IntelliTec College.

Technological College of the Municipality of San Juan (San Juan, PR): name changed to Technological College of San Juan.

Thomas Technical Institute (Thomasville, GA): name changed to Southwest Georgia Technical College.

University of Puerto Rico, Carolina Regional College (Carolina, PR): name changed to University of Puerto Rico at Carolina.

Webster College (Fairmont, WV): closed.

West Georgia Technical Institute (LaGrange, GA): name changed to West Georgia Technical College.

Alphabetical Listing of Colleges and Universities

This index gives the page locations of various entries for all the colleges and universities in this section. The page numbers for the college profiles with *Special Announcements* are in italic type.

NOTES

Notes

Notes

Notes

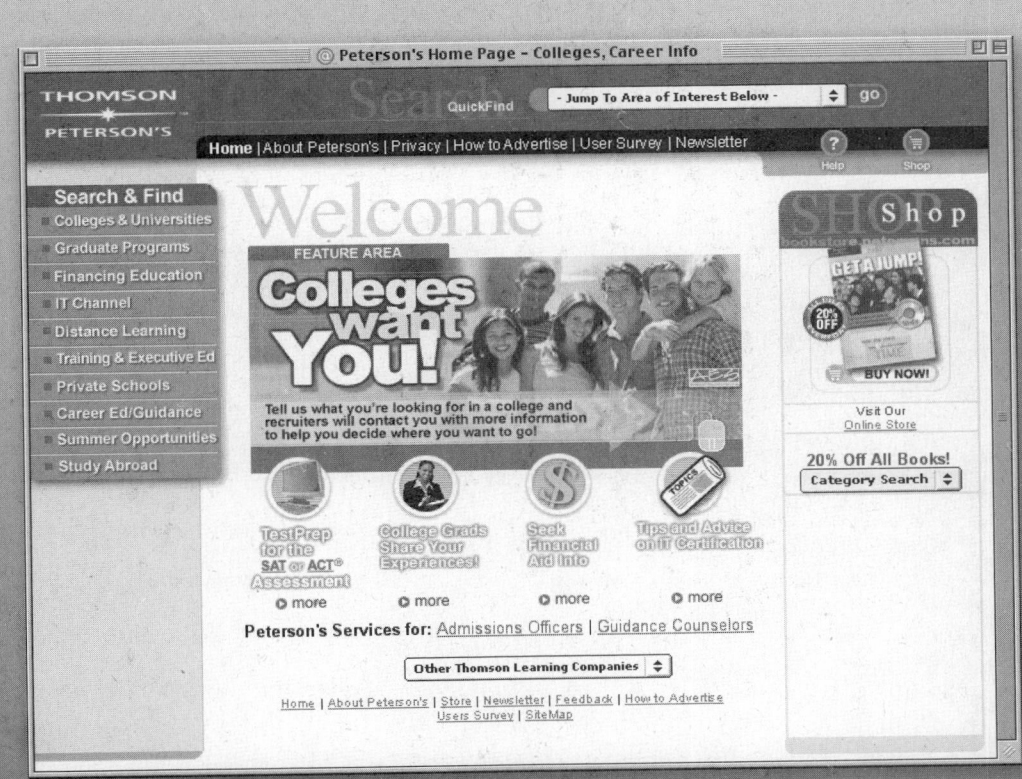

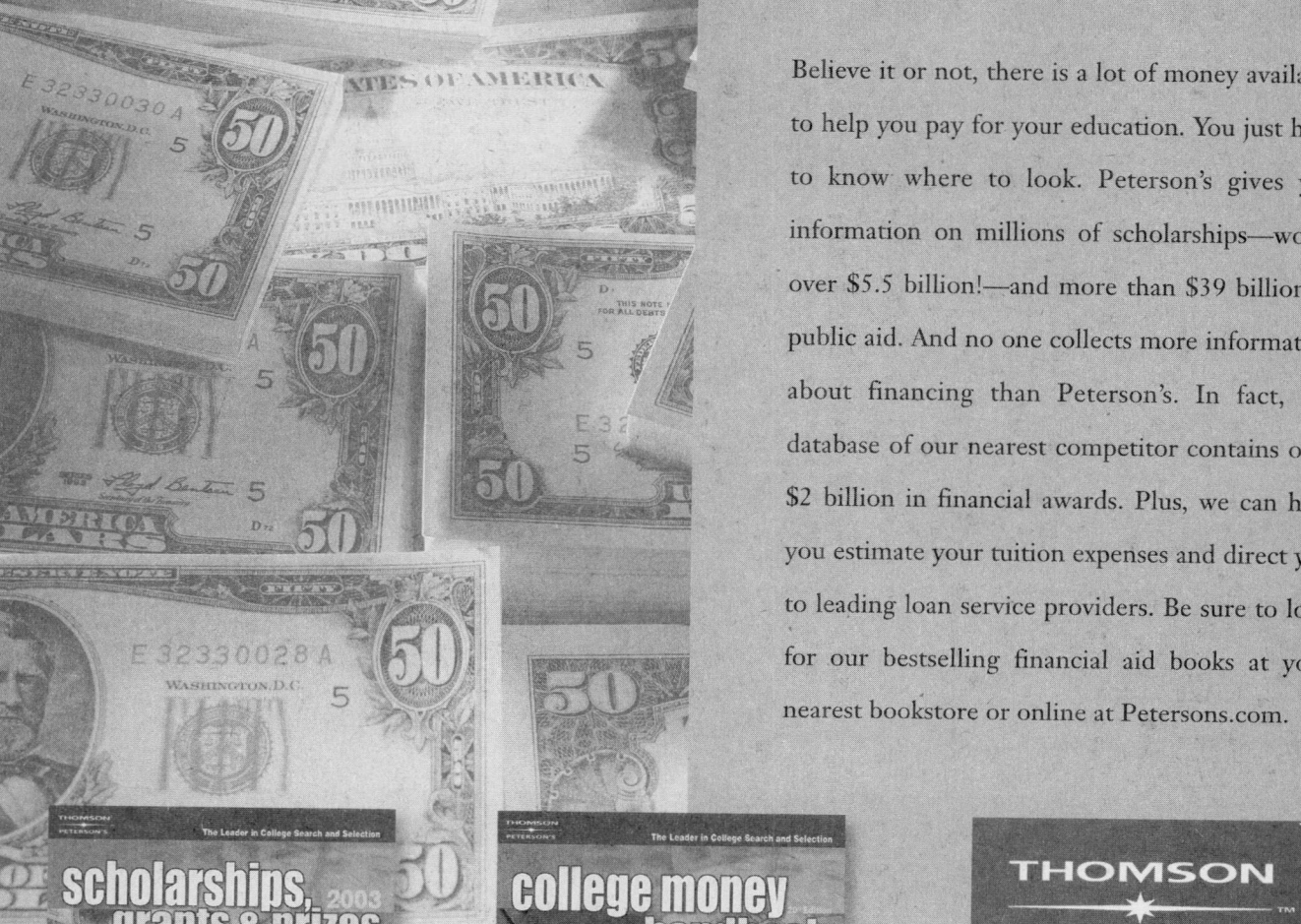